California's Geographic Names

California's Geographic Names

A Gazetteer of Historic and Modern Names of the State

David L. Durham

Clovis, California

Quill Driver Books/Word Dancer Press, Inc.
8386 N. Madsen Avenue
Clovis, CA 93611
(209) 322-5917

Printed in the United States of America
on acid-free paper

Quill Driver Books/Word Dancer Press, Inc.
Project Cadre
Doris Hall
Stephen Blake Mettee
Cindy Wathen

ISBN 1-884995-14-4

Library of Congress Cataloging-in-Publication Data

Durham, David L., 1925 -
California's geographic names : a gazetteer of historic and modern names of the state / David L. Durham.
p. cm.
Includes bibliographical references and index.
ISBN 1-884995-14-4
1. Names, Geographical--California. 2. California--History, Local. I. Title.
F859.D87 1998
917.94'003--dc21 98-2858
CIP

To my wife Nancy, whose patience and understanding contributed so much to this book.

Contents

Gazetteer

Illustrations

Acknowledgments

I wish to thank Beverly Cola of the museum at Placerville for sharing with me some of her wonderful store of local history and Forest M. Clingan of Dunlap and Charles W. Clough of Fresno for volunteering information on names in their part of the world.

Introduction

Purpose, organization and scope

This gazetteer gives the location of geographic features of the State of California. For convienence the State has been divided into eleven multiple-county regions. The counties and the region to which each has been assigned are listed under the heading "Counties of California and Corresponding Region" begining on page *xiii*. The index lists place names in the gazetteer and gives the region or regions in which each name appears.

United States government quadrangle maps, which are detailed, somewhat authoritative, and generally available, are the primary source of information. The gazetteer includes only features that are named on quadrangle maps, or that can be related to features named on the maps. It lists relief features, water features, and most kinds of cultural features, but omits names of streets, parks, schools, churches, cemeteries, dams and the like. Some names simply identify a person or family living at a site because such places are landmarks in sparsely settled parts of the state.

The listing of names in the gazetteer is alphabetical, and multiword names are alphabetized as one word. Terms abbreviated on maps are given in full in the alphabetical list, and numerals in names are listed in alphabetical order rather than in numerical order. In addition to the principal entries, the list includes cross references to variant names, obsolete names and key words in multiword English-language names. For each principal entry, the name is followed by the name of the county or counties in which the feature lies, a classifying term, general and specific locations, identification of one or more quadrangle maps that show the name and other information. All features named in an entry generally belong to the same county. The classifying terms are defined under the heading "Geographic Terms" beginning on page 1493.

Locations and measurements are from quadrangle maps, distances and directions are approximate, and latitude and longitude generally are to the nearest five seconds. Distances between post offices are measured by road, as the mail would be carried. Other distances are measured in a straight line unless the measurement is given with a qualifying expression such as "downstream" or "by road." Townships (T) and Ranges (R) in the northwest part of the state refer to Humboldt Base and Meridian, those in the south part of the state refer to San Bernardino Base and Meridian, and the others refer to Mount Diablo Base and Meridian. For streams, the location given generally is the place that the stream joins another stream, enters the sea or a lake, or debouches into a canyon or valley. For features of considerable areal extent, the location given ordinarily is near the center, except for cities and towns, for which the location given is near the center of the downtown part, or at the city hall or civic center. Measurements to or from areal features usually are to or from the center. Specific locations are omitted for some very large or poorly defined places. Quadrangle maps are listed under "References Cited" for each region, along with books, articles and other maps. The references identify sources of data and provide leads to additional information. If a name applies to more than one feature in a county, the features are numbered and identified elsewhere in the list by that number in parentheses following the name.

Counties of California
Del Norte
Siskiyou
Modoc
Humboldt
Trinity
Shasta
Lassen
Tehama
Plumas
Butte
Glenn
Sierra
Mendocino
Colusa
Sutter
Yuba
Nevada
Placer
Lake
Yolo
El Dorado
Sonoma
Napa
Alpine
Sacramento
Amador
Solano
Marin
Calaveras
Tuolumne
Mono
Contra Costa
San Joaquin
San Francisco
Alameda
Stanislaus
Mariposa
San Mateo
Santa Clara
Merced
Santa Cruz
Madera
San Benito
Fresno
Inyo
Tulare
Monterey
Kings
San Luis Obispo
Kern
San Bernardino
Santa Barbara
Ventura
Los Angeles
Riverside
Orange
San Diego
Imperial

Counties of California and Corresponding Region

County	Region
Alameda	San Francisco Bay (Part 5)
Alpine	East Sierra (Part 9)
Amador	South Sacramento Valley (Part 4)
Butte	North Sacramento Valley (Part 2)
Calaveras	North San Joaquin Valley (Part 6)
Colusa	South Sacramento Valley (Part 4)
Contra Costa	San Francisco Bay (Part 5)
Del Norte	North Coast (Part 1)
El Dorado	South Sacramento Valley (Part 4)
Fresno	South San Joaquin Valley (Part 8)
Glenn	North Sacramento Valley (Part 2)
Humboldt	North Coast (Part 1)
Imperial	Southeast (Part 11)
Inyo	East Sierra (Part 9)
Kern	South San Joaquin Valley (Part 8)
Kings	South San Joaquin Valley (Part 8)
Lake	North Coast (Part 1)
Lassen	Northeast (Part 3)
Los Angeles	South Coast (Part 10)
Madera	North San Joaquin Valley (Part 6)
Marin	San Francisco Bay (Part 5)
Mariposa	North San Joaquin Valley (Part 6)
Mendocino	North Coast (Part 1)
Merced	North San Joaquin Valley (Part 6)
Modoc	Northeast (Part 3)
Mono	East Sierra (Part 9)
Monterey	Central Coast (Part 7)
Napa	San Francisco Bay (Part 5)
Nevada	South Sacramento Valley (Part 4)
Orange	South Coast (Part 10)
Placer	South Sacramento Valley (Part 4)
Plumas	Northeast (Part 3)
Riverside	Southeast (Part 11)
Sacramento	South Sacramento Valley (Part 4)
San Benito	Central Coast (Part 7)
San Bernardino	Southeast (Part 11)
San Diego	South Coast (Part 10)
San Francisco	San Francisco Bay (Part 5)
San Joaquin	North San Joaquin Valley (Part 6)
San Luis Obispo	Central Coast (Part 7)
San Mateo	San Francisco Bay (Part 5)
Santa Barbara	Central Coast (Part 7)
Santa Clara	San Francisco Bay (Part 5)
Santa Cruz	Central Coast (Part 7)

County	Region
Shasta	North Sacramento Valley (Part 2)
Sierra	South Sacramento Valley (Part 4)
Siskiyou	North Sacramento Valley (Part 2)
Solano	San Francisco Bay (Part 5)
Sonoma	San Francisco Bay (Part 5)
Stanislaus	North San Joaquin Valley (Part 6)
Sutter	South Sacramento Valley (Part 4)
Tehama	North Sacramento Valley (Part 2)
Trinity	North Coast (Part 1)
Tulare	South San Joaquin Valley (Part 8)
Tuolumne	North San Joaquin Valley (Part 6)
Ventura	South Coast (Part 10)
Yolo	South Sacramento Valley (Part 4)
Yuba	South Sacramento Valley (Part 4)

California's Geographic Names

Part One
North Coast Region

Del Norte, Humboldt, Lake, Mendocino and Trinity Counties

Part One-
North Coast Region

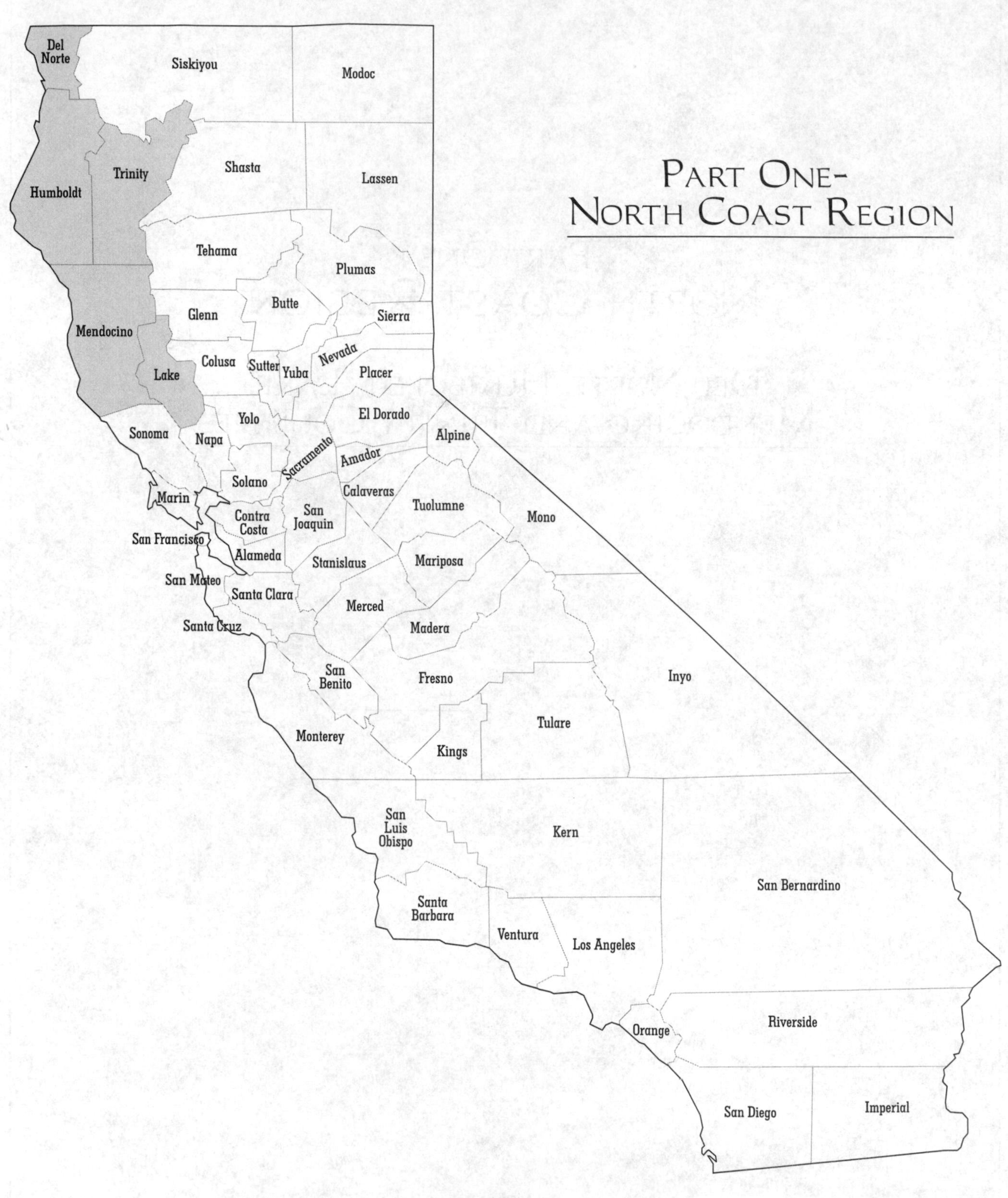

Del Norte
Siskiyou
Modoc
Humboldt
Trinity
Shasta
Lassen
Tehama
Plumas
Butte
Glenn
Sierra
Mendocino
Colusa
Sutter
Yuba
Nevada
Placer
Lake
Yolo
El Dorado
Sonoma
Napa
Alpine
Sacramento
Amador
Solano
Calaveras
Marin
Contra Costa
San Joaquin
Tuolumne
Mono
San Francisco
Alameda
Stanislaus
Mariposa
San Mateo
Santa Clara
Merced
Santa Cruz
Madera
San Benito
Fresno
Inyo
Tulare
Monterey
Kings
San Luis Obispo
Kern
San Bernardino
Santa Barbara
Ventura
Los Angeles
Orange
Riverside
San Diego
Imperial

North Coast Region Del Norte, Humboldt, Lake, Mendocino and Trinity Counties

Regional Setting

General.—This section concerns geographic features in five counties—Del Norte, Humboldt, Lake, Mendocino, and Trinity—that lie in the sparsely settled northwest part of the State of California. All Townships (T) South refer to Humboldt Base; Townships North with Ranges (R) East refer to Humboldt Base and Meridian; Townships North with Ranges West refer to Mount Diablo Base and Meridian, except in coastal Del Norte and Humboldt Counties, where they refer to Humboldt Base and Meridian. The early presence in the region of American explorers and gold seekers is recorded in geographic names still in use. Lumbering, mining, fishing, recreation, and ranching support the present-day population. The map on the facing page shows the location of the North Coast Region and the counties in it.

Del Norte County.—Del Norte County is at the extreme northwest corner of California. It is mainly mountainous; the principal lowlands are near the coast, and it is there that most of the inhabitants live. The state legislature created Del Norte County in 1857 from part of Klamath County, an early county that has disappeared; Del Norte County lost considerable territory along its east boundary in 1858, 1872, and 1887, and the south boundary was adjusted in 1874 (Coy, 1923, p. 94-95). Crescent City is and always has been the county seat; the name "Del Norte" reflects the location of the county at the northwest corner of the state—*del norte* means "of the north" in Spanish (Hoover, Rensch, and Rensch, p. 67).

Humboldt County.—Humboldt County lies along the coast between Del Norte County to the north and Mendocino County to the south. The residents live mainly at places near the coast and along major rivers. The state legislature created Humboldt County in 1853 from territory of previously formed Trinity County; most of present Humboldt County that lies north of the mouth of Mad River was added in 1875 after neighboring Klamath County was dissolved (Coy, 1923, p. 110-111). Union (present Arcata) was the county seat until 1856, when Eureka received the honor; the county and its great bay preserve the name of Baron Alexander von Humboldt (Hoover, Rensch, and Rensch, p. 99).

Lake County.—Lake County lies inland from Humboldt County. Residents of Lake County live mainly around Clear Lake and in lowlands near the lake. The county was organized in 1861 from that part of Napa County near Clear Lake, and in 1864 the boundary of the county was redefined; another major change in the boundary came in 1868, when Long Valley was annexed from Colusa County—subsequent boundary changes have been minor (Coy, 1923, p. 127-132). The county name is from Clear Lake; Lakeport has always been the county seat, except for a few years after a fire destroyed the courthouse in 1867 and the county government moved temporarily to Lower Lake (Hoover, Rensch, and Rensch, p. 138).

Mendocino County.—Mendocino County is along the coast south of Humboldt County, and extends inland to Trinity County and Lake County. The inhabitants of Mendocino County are concentrated near the coast, and along the valley of Eel River and the valley of Russian River. Mendocino County was one of the original counties that the state legislature created in 1850, but the county government was not organized until 1859; the first county boundaries were somewhat uncertain, and numerous boundary adjustments have been made over the years (Coy, 1923, p. 166-177). The name "Mendocino" first was applied to the cape in Humboldt County, and only later to Mendocino County; Ukiah has been the county seat from the beginning (Hoover, Rensch, and Rensch, p. 195).

Trinity County.—Trinity County lies east of Humboldt County and includes upper reaches of Klamath River, Trinity River, and Eel River. The sparse population of the county is concentrated at early mining sites. Trinity County was one of the original counties that the state legislature created in 1850, and it was organized in 1851 when more than half of its original territory was detached to form now-defunct Klamath County—Trinity County lost territory again in 1853 when Humboldt County was organized, but it regained area in 1855 and again in 1872 (Coy, 1923, p. 278-281). Weaverville always has been the county seat; the county name is from Trinity Bay, which was in the original territory of Trinity County (Hoover, Rensch, and Rensch, p. 552).

North Coast Region
Del Norte, Humboldt, Lake, Mendocino and Trinity Counties

— A —

Abalobadiah Creek [MENDOCINO]: *stream,* flows nearly 3 miles to the sea 5 miles south of Westport (lat. 39°33'55" N, long. 123°46' W; at W line sec. 28, T 20 N, R 17 W). Named on Inglenook (1966) 7.5' quadrangle. The canyon of the stream is called Lobadlah Gulch on Cape Vizcaino (1950) 15' quadrangle.

Abalone Point [HUMBOLDT]: *promontory,* 5.25 miles north of Trinidad (lat. 41°08'05" N, long. 124°09'40" W; sec. 27, T 9 N, R 1 W); the promontory is part of a larger feature called Patricks Point. Named on Trinidad (1966) 7.5' quadrangle.

Abalone Point [MENDOCINO]: *promontory,* 2 miles north of Westport along the coast (lat. 39°40'05" N, long. 123°47'30" W; on N line sec. 19, T 21 N, R 17 W). Named on Westport (1966) 7.5' quadrangle.

Able Spring [LAKE]: *spring,* 9 miles north-northeast of Clearlake Oaks (lat. 39°08'50" N, long. 122°37'50" W; sec. 16, T 15 N, R 7 W). Named on Clearlake Oaks (1960) 15' quadrangle. Called Ables Spring on Bartlett Springs (1944) 15' quadrangle.

Abrams: see **Goldfield Campground** [TRINITY].

Achelth Creek [HUMBOLDT]: *stream,* flows nearly 2 miles to Klamath River 0.25 mile northwest of Johnsons (lat. 41°21'15" N, long. 123°52'35" W; sec. 7, T 11 N, R 3 E). Named on Holter Ridge (1983) and Johnsons (1982) 7.5' quadrangles.

Ackerman Creek [MENDOCINO]: *stream,* flows 11 miles to Russian River 2 miles north-northeast of Ukiah (lat. 39°10'45" N, long. 123°11'40" W). Named on Boonville (1959) 15' quadrangle, and on Ukiah (1958) 7.5' quadrangle.

Acorn: see **Korbel** [HUMBOLDT].

Adams [LAKE]: *settlement,* 3 miles north of Whispering Pines (lat. 38°51'25" N, long. 122°43'05" W; sec. 26, T 12 N, R 8 W). Named on Whispering Pines (1958) 7.5' quadrangle. Postal authorities established Adams post office in 1908 and discontinued it in 1960; the place also was known as Adams Springs (Salley, p. 1). The name commemorates Charles Adams, who acquired the property in 1869 (Hanna, p. 2). The resort at the site had accommodations for about 400 people in 1910 (Waring, p. 189). A new hotel was built there in 1927 (Averill, 1929, p. 344).

Adams Creek [HUMBOLDT]: *stream,* flows 0.5 mile to Klamath River 4 miles southwest of Orleans (lat. 41°15'35" N, long. 123°35'10" W). Named on Orleans (1978) 7.5' quadrangle.

Adams Creek [MENDOCINO]: *stream,* flows 1.5 miles to Yale Creek 2.25 miles southeast of Ornbaun Valley (lat. 38°53'15" N, long. 123°16'40" W; sec. 14, T 12 N, R 13 W). Named on Ornbaun Valley (1960) 15' quadrangle.

Adams Creek [TRINITY]: *stream,* flows 2.5 miles to Coffee Creek 8.5 miles west of Billys Peak (1) (lat. 41°07'20" N, long. 122°55'20" W; sec. 29, T 38 N, R 9 W); the stream heads at Adams Lake. Named on Coffee Creek (1955) 15' quadrangle. North Fork enters from the north 0.5 mile upstream from the mouth of the main creek; it is nearly 2 miles long and is named on Coffee Creek (1955) 15' quadrangle.

Adams Lake [TRINITY]: *lake,* 600 feet long, 10 miles west of Billys Peak (1) (lat. 41°06'45" N, long. 122°57'45" W); the lake is at the head of Adams Creek. Named on Coffee Creek (1955) 15' quadrangle.

Adams Ridge [MENDOCINO]: *ridge,* southeast- to east-trending, 5 miles long, 7 miles northeast of the village of Point Arena (lat. 38°58'30" N, long. 123°35'30" W). Named on Point Arena (1960) 15' quadrangle.

Adams Springs: see **Adams** [LAKE].

Adams Station [DEL NORTE]: *locality,* at the west end of Gasquet along Smith River (lat. 41°50'35" N, long. 123°59'30" W; sec. 19, T 17 N, R 2 E). Named on Gasquet (1981) 7.5' quadrangle. The name is for Mary Adams Peacock, who had a tavern at the place during the days of stage travel (Hanna, p. 2).

Addington Springs [LAKE]: *springs,* 16 miles north of Clearlake Oaks (lat. 39°14'55" N, long. 122°42'35" W; near W line sec. 12, T 16 N, R 8 W). Named on Clearlake Oaks (1960) 15' quadrangle.

Adele: see **Fields Landing** [HUMBOLDT].

Adobe Creek [LAKE]: *stream,* flows 11 miles to Clear Lake 2.25 miles east-southeast of Lakeport (lat. 39°01'45" N, long. 122°52'35" W). Named on Highland Springs (1959), Kelseyville (1959), Lakeport (1958), and Lucerne (1958) 7.5' quadrangles. Called Doba Cr. on Chandler's (1901) map.

Adobe Creek [MENDOCINO]: *stream,* flows 2.25 miles to East Fork Russian River 1.5 miles north-northwest of the town of Potter Valley (lat. 39°20'45" N, long. 123°07' W; sec. 7, T 17 N, R 11 W). Named on Potter Valley (1960) 7.5' quadrangle.

Agate Beach [HUMBOLDT]: *beach,* 6 miles north of Trinidad along the coast (lat. 41°08'40" N, long. 124°08'30" W; on S line sec. 23, T 9 N, R 1 W). Named on Trinidad (1966) 7.5' quadrangle. According to Turner (p.1), the beach is a popular place to gather agates.

Agate Beach [MENDOCINO]: *beach,* 0.5 mile north of downtown Mendocino along the coast (lat. 39°18'55" N, long. 123°47'55" W; near S line sec. 19, T 17 N, R 17 W). Named on Mendocino (1960) 7.5' quadrangle.

Ah Pah Creek [HUMBOLDT]: *stream,* flows 5.25 miles to Klamath River 6 miles northwest of Johnsons (lat. 41°25'15" N, long. 123°56'20" W; sec. 22, T 12 N, R 2 E). Named on Ah Pah Ridge (1983) and Fern Canyon (1966) 7.5' quadrangles. The name "Ah Pah" is of Indian origin (Kroeber, p. 34). North Fork enters from the northwest near the mouth of the main stream; it is 5.25 miles long and is named on Ah Pah Ridge (1983) and Fern Canyon (1966) 7.5' quadrangles. South Fork enters from the south nearly 1 mile upstream from the mouth of the main stream; it is 3.25 miles long and is named on Ah Pah Ridge (1983) 7.5' quadrangle.

Ah Pah Ridge [HUMBOLDT]: *ridge,* east- to north-trending, 3.5 miles long, 5 miles northwest of Johnsons (lat. 41°23' N, long. 123°56'35" W). Named on Ah Pah Ridge (1983) 7.5' quadrangle.

Aikens Creek [HUMBOLDT]: *stream,* flows 3.25 miles to Klamath River 4 miles northeast of Weitchpec (lat. 41°13'45" N, long. 123°39'05" W). Named on Weitchpec (1979) 7.5' quadrangle.

Airplane Meadow [MENDOCINO]: *area,* 16 miles northeast of Covelo (lat. 39°56'55" N, long. 123°02' W; sec. 12, T 24 N, R 11 W). Named on Leech Lake Mountain (1966) 7.5' quadrangle.

Alaska Ridge [MENDOCINO]: *ridge,* generally west-trending, 2 miles long, 8 miles north of Boonville (lat. 39°07'30" N, long. 123°22' W). Named on Boonville (1959) 15' quadrangle.

Albee: see **Eureka** [HUMBOLDT].

Albee Creek [HUMBOLDT]: *stream,* flows nearly 2 miles to Bull Creek (1) 10 miles south-southeast of Scotia (lat. 40°21'10" N, long. 124°00'20" W; near W line sec. 30, T 1 S, R 2 E). Named on Bull Creek (1969) 7.5' quadrangle.

Albee Creek Campground [HUMBOLDT]: *locality,* 10 miles south-southeast of Scotia (lat. 40°21'10" N, long. 124°00'30" W; near E line sec. 25, T 1 S, R 1 E); the place is near the mouth of Albee Creek. Named on Bull Creek (1969) 7.5' quadrangle.

Albee-John [HUMBOLDT]: *area,* nearly 6 miles south of Coyote Peak (lat. 41°02'50" N, long. 123°51'15" W; on S line sec. 29, T 8 N, R 3 E). Named on Hupa Mountain (1982) 7.5' quadrangle.

Albeeville: see **Eureka** [HUMBOLDT].

Albion [MENDOCINO]: *village,* 15 miles south of Fort Bragg (lat. 39°13'25" N, long. 123°46' W; near NW cor. sec. 28, T 16 N, R 17 W). Named on Albion (1960) 7.5' quadrangle. Postal authorities established Albion post office in 1859 (Frickstad, p. 93). The community began with construction of Albion steam mill at the site in 1853 (Hanna, p. 5).

Albion Cove [MENDOCINO]: *embayment,* 0.5 mile northwest of Albion along the coast at the mouth of Albion River (lat. 39°13'40" N, long. 123°46'20" W). Named on Albion (1960) 7.5' quadrangle. A pyramidal feature 30 feet high that is situated about in the middle of the embayment is called Mooring Rock (United States Coast and Geodetic Survey, p. 141).

Albion Flat [MENDOCINO]: *area,* at Albion (lat. 39°13'35" N, long. 123°46' W; at NW cor. sec. 28, T 16 N, R 17 W); the place is near the mouth of Albion River. Named on Albion (1960) 7.5' quadrangle.

Albion Head [MENDOCINO]: *promontory,* less than 1 mile northwest of

Albion along the coast (lat. 39°14' N, long. 123°46'45" W; sec. 20, T 16 N, R 17 W). Named on Albion (1960) 7.5' quadrangle.

Albion Ridge [MENDOCINO]: *ridge*, generally west-trending, 11 miles long, south of Albion River and South Fork Albion River; Albion is near the west end. Named on Navarro (1961) 15' quadrangle.

Albion River [MENDOCINO]: *stream*, flows 17 miles to the sea near Albion (lat. 39°13'35" N, long. 123°46'10" W; near NW cor. sec. 28, T 16 N, R 17 W). Named on Comptche (1960) 15' quadrangle, and on Albion (1960) and Elk (1960) 7.5' quadrangles. Called Rio Albion on a diseño made in 1844 (Becker, R.H., 1969). William A. Richardson, a native of Britain, gave the name "Albion" to a land grant that he applied for in 1844, and to the river (Gudde, 1949, p. 6). North Fork enters from the north nearly 1 mile west of Comptche; it is 4.5 miles long and is named on Comptche (1960) 15' quadrangle. South Fork enters from the south 4.5 miles west of Comptche; it is 6.25 miles long and is named on Comptche (1960) and Navarro (1961) 15' quadrangles. Little North Fork enters South Fork 2.25 miles upstream from the mouth of South Fork; it is 1.25 miles long and is named on Elk (1960) 7.5' quadrangle.

Alder Basin [TRINITY]: *relief feature*, 8 miles south of Black Rock Mountain (lat. 40°05'20" N, long. 123°00' W). Named on Black Rock Mountain (1954) and Yolla Bolly (1954) 15 quadrangles.

Alder Basin Creek [TRINITY]: *stream*, flows 2.25 miles to Middle Fork Eel River 8 miles south of Black Rock Mountain (lat. 40°05'20" N, long. 123°02'20" W; sec. 19, T 26 N, R 10 W); the stream heads at Alder Basin. Named on Black Rock Mountain (1954) 15' quadrangle.

Alder Butte: see **Split Rock** [DEL NORTE].

Alder Canyon [LAKE]: *canyon*, drained by a stream that flows 2 miles to Willow Creek (2) 6.5 miles west of Lakeport (lat. 39°04'10" N, long. 123°02' W; sec. 14, T 14 N, R 11 W). Named on Purdys Gardens (1958) 7.5' quadrangle.

Alder Creek [LAKE]:

(1) *stream*, flows nearly 2 miles to Eel River 6 miles north-northeast of the town of Potter Valley [MENDOCINO] (lat. 39°23'15" N, long. 123°02'30" W; sec. 26, T 18 N, R 11 W). Named on Potter Valley (1960) 15' quadrangle.

(2) *stream*, flows 2 miles to North Fork Cache Creek 8 miles northeast of the town of Upper Lake (lat. 39°14'35" N, long. 122°48'05" W). Named on Bartlett Mountain (1958) 7.5' quadrangle.

(3) *stream*, flows nearly 4 miles to Kelsey Creek 10 miles south-southeast of Kelseyville (lat. 38°51'05" N, long. 122°45'20" W; sec. 33, T 12 N, R 8 W). Named on The Geysers (1959) 7.5' quadrangle.

Alder Creek [MENDOCINO]:

(1) *stream*, flows 4 miles to join Cold Creek (4) and form Mill Creek (1) 4.25 miles north-northwest of Covelo (lat. 39°50'50" N, long. 123°17'20" W; near SE cor. sec. 15, T 23 N, R 13 W). Named on Covelo West (1967) 7.5' quadrangle.

(2) *stream*, flows 3.5 miles to Cherry Creek (2) 4.25 miles north-northeast of Longvale (lat. 39°36'40" N, long. 123°23'45" W; sec. 3, T 20 N, R 14 W). Named on Laytonville (1967) and Longvale (1966) 7.5' quadrangles.

(3) *stream*, flows 1.5 miles to Berry Canyon 3.5 miles east-northeast of Willits (lat. 39°25'40" N, long. 123°17'20" W; sec. 10, T 18 N, R 13 W). Named on Willits (1961) 15' quadrangle.

(4) *stream*, flows 14 miles to the sea 9 miles south of Elk (lat. 39°00'15" N, long. 123°41'45" W; sec. 12, T 13 N, R 17 W). Named on Navarro (1961), Ornbaun Valley (1960), and Point Arena (1960) 15' quadrangles. North Fork enters from the northeast 10 miles northeast of the village of Point Arena; it is 4 miles long and is named on Ornbaun Valley (1960) and Point Arena (1960) 15' quadrangles.

(5) *stream*, flows 2.25 miles to Rancheria Creek (2) 8 miles northwest of Ornbaun Valley (lat. 38°59'10" N, long. 123°25'15" W; near E line sec. 17, T 13 N, R 14 W). Named on Ornbaun Valley (1960) 15' quadrangle.

(6) *stream*, flows 1.5 miles to Sonoma County 5.25 miles southeast of Monument Peak (lat. 38°50'05" N, long. 123°53'40" W; at SE cor. sec. 30, T 12 N, R 9 W). Named on Asti (1959) 7.5' quadrangle.

(7) *stream*, flows 2.25 miles to Eel River 7.25 miles northeast of Longvale (lat. 39°37'15" N, long. 123°19'25" W; sec. 5, T 20 N, R 13 W). Named on Dos Rios (1967) and Willis Ridge (1966) 7.5' quadrangles. Called Indian Creek on Laytonville (1951) 15' quadrangle.

Alder Creek [MENDOCINO-TRINITY]: *stream*, heads in Trinity County and flows 3 miles to Middle Fork Eel River 16 miles northeast of Covelo in Mendocino County (lat. 39°57'30" N, long. 123°01'50" W; sec. 1, T 24 N, R 11 W). Named on Leech Lake Mountain (1966) 7.5' quadrangle.

Alder Flat [HUMBOLDT]: *area*, 6.5 miles east of Dinsmore (lat. 40°29'40" N, long. 123°43'35" W; sec. 4, T 1 N, R 4 E). Named on Larabee Valley (1977) 7.5' quadrangle.

Alder Gulch [TRINITY]:

(1) *canyon*, drained by a stream that flows 1.5 miles to Trinity River 6.5 miles north of Trinity Center (lat. 41°05'55" N, long. 122°42'30" W; near W line sec. 32, T 38 N, R 7 W). Named on Bonanza King (1955) 15' quadrangle.

(2) *canyon*, drained by a stream that flows 1.5 miles to Trinity River 7 miles east-southeast of Weaverville (lat. 40°42'20" N, long. 122°48'50" W; sec. 19, T 33 N, R 8 W). Named on Weaverville (1950) 15' quadrangle.

(3) *canyon*, drained by a stream that flows 3 miles to Carr Creek (2) 7 miles east-northeast of Hayfork (lat. 40°35'25" N, long. 123°03'55" W; at SW cor. sec. 25, T 32 N, R 11 W). Named on Hayfork (1951) 15' quadrangle.

Alderpoint [HUMBOLDT]: *village*, 11 miles east-northeast of Garberville (lat. 40°10'35" N, long. 123°36'40" W; sec. 27, 28, T 3 S, R 5 E). Named on Alderpoint (1969) 7.5' quadrangle. California Mining Bureau's (1917b) map has the form "Alder Point" for the name. Postal authorities established Alderpoint post office in 1911 (Frickstad, p. 41). The community began in 1910 as a center for railroad construction; the name is from the alder trees at the place (Hanna, p. 6).

Alder Spring [HUMBOLDT]:

(1) *spring*, 5.25 miles east-southeast of Honeydew (lat. 40°12'40" N, long. 124°01'45" W). Named on Honeydew (1970) 7.5' quadrangle.

(2) *spring*, 4.25 miles east-northeast of Blocksburg (lat. 40°17'45" N, long. 123°33'45" W). Named on Black Lassic (1979) 7.5' quadrangle.

Alder Spring [MENDOCINO]: *spring*, 3 miles south-southwest of Ukiah (lat. 39°06'50" N, long. 123°14'10" W; sec. 36, T 15 N, R 13 W). Named on Elledge Peak (1958) 7.5' quadrangle.

Alder Spring Ridge [LAKE]: *ridge*, northeast-trending, 2 miles long, 7 miles northeast of the town of Upper Lake (lat. 39°14' N, long. 122°49'05" W); the ridge is northwest of Alder Creek (2). Named on Bartlett Mountain (1958) 7.5' quadrangle.

Al Hazen Ridge [HUMBOLDT]: *ridge*, northeast-trending, 1.5 miles long, 5 miles east-northeast of Showers Mountain (lat. 40°36'15" N, long. 123°36'15" W). Named on Blake Mountain (1979) 7.5' quadrangle.

Alkali Lake: see **Borax Lake** [LAKE].

Allen Creek [HUMBOLDT]:

(1) *stream*, flows nearly 2 miles to Klamath River 4.5 miles southwest of Orleans (lat. 41°15'30" N, long. 123°36'15" W). Named on Hopkins Butte (1979) and Orleans (1978) 7.5' quadrangles.

(2) *stream*, flows 2.25 miles to Yager Creek 6.25 miles east-southeast of Fortuna (lat. 40°34'25" N, long. 124°02'10" W; near W line sec. 11, T 2 N, R 1 E). Named on Hydesville (1979) 7.5' quadrangle.

(3) *stream*, flows 1.25 miles to the flood plain of Eel River 1.5 miles east-southeast of Redcrest (lat. 40°23'15" N, long. 123°55'20" W; near S line sec. 11, T 1 S, R 2 E). Named on Redcrest (1969) 7.5' quadrangle.

Allen Creek [TRINITY]: *stream*, flows nearly 3 miles to Eltapom Creek 6 miles north of Hyampom (lat. 40°41'55" N, long. 123°27'15" W). Named on Hyampom (1951) 15' quadrangle.

Allen Creek: see **Bartlett Creek** [LAKE].

Allens Gulch [DEL NORTE]: *canyon*, drained by a stream that flows 2.5 miles to Craigs Creek 10.5 miles east-northeast of Crescent City (lat. 41°48' N, long. 123°00'20" W). Named on Gasquet (1981) and Hiouchi (1966) 7.5' quadrangles.

Allen Spring [TRINITY]: *spring*, 6.5 miles south-southwest of Forest Glen (lat. 40°17'15" N, long. 123°22'50" W; near SE cor. sec. 16, T 2 S, R 7 E). Named on Ruth Reservoir (1978) 7.5' quadrangle.

Allen Springs [LAKE]: *spring*, 9.5 miles north of Clearlake Oaks (lat. 39°09'35" N, long. 122°39'50" W; at W line sec. 8, T 15 N, R 7 W). Named on Clearlake Oaks (1960) 15' quadrangle. Postal authorities established Allen Springs post office in 1874, discontinued it for a time in 1885, discontinued it again in 1894, reestablished it in 1896, and discontinued it finally in 1906 (Salley, p. 5). The name commemorates George Allen, who located the spring in 1871 (Palmer, p. 208). The spring was the basis of a resort (Anderson, p. 76-77; Bradley, p. 211).

Alley: see **Charlie Alley Peak** [LAKE]; **John Alley Ridge** [LAKE]; **Sam Alley Ridge** [LAKE].

Alley Camp [LAKE]: *locality*, 4.25 miles north-northeast of the town of Upper Lake (lat. 39°13'05" N, long. 122°52' W; sec. 28, T 16 N, R 9 W). Named on Bartlett Mountain (1958) 7.5' quadrangle.

Alley Creek [LAKE]: *stream*, flows 6.25 miles to Clover Creek 1 mile northeast of the town of Upper Lake (lat. 39°10'40" N, long. 122°53'45" W; sec. 6, T 15 N, R 9 W). Named on Bartlett Mountain (1958) and Upper Lake (1958) 7.5' quadrangles.

Alliance [HUMBOLDT]: *settlement*, 1 mile north-northwest of downtown Arcata (lat. 40°53'15" N, long. 124°05'15" W; sec. 20, T 6 N, R 1 E). Named on Arcata North (1959) 7.5' quadrangle. Postal authorities established Alliance post office in 1892 and discontinued it in 1920; the name is from an organization of farmers in the neighborhood (Salley, p. 5). The place also was known as McGilvary Corners and as Alliance Corners (Turner, p. 5).

Alliance Corners: see **Alliance** [HUMBOLDT].

Alpine [MENDOCINO]: *locality*, 12 miles north of Comptche along California Western Railroad (lat. 39°26'05" N, long. 123°35'10" W; at NW cor. sec. 7, T 18 N, R 15 W). Named on Comptche (1960) 15' quadrangle. Called Alpine Junction on O'Brien's (1953) map.

Alpine Gulch [MENDOCINO]: *canyon*, drained by a stream that flows 1 mile to Noyo River 12 miles north of Comptche at Alpine (lat. 39°26'10" N, long. 123°35' W; at S line sec. 6, T 18 N, R 15 W). Named on Comptche

(1960) 15' quadrangle.

Alpine Junction: see **Alpine** [MENDOCINO].

Alpine Lake [TRINITY]: *lake*, 1600 feet long, 15 miles north of Weaverville (lat. 40°56'30" N, long. 122°59'30" W; at NW cor. sec. 35, T 36 N, R 10 W). Named on Trinity Dam (1950) 15' quadrangle.

Al Slides [LAKE]: *relief feature*, 7 miles northeast of the town of Lower Lake along North Fork Cache Creek (lat. 38°59'20" N, long. 122°31'40" W). Named on Lower Lake (1958) 7.5' quadrangle.

Altaville: see **Low Divide** [DEL NORTE].

Alton [HUMBOLDT]: *village*, 3.5 miles south-southeast of Fortuna (lat. 40°32'50" N, long. 124°08'25" W; at NE cor. sec. 23, T 2 N, R 1 E). Named on Fortuna (1959) 7.5' quadrangle. Postal authorities established Hansen post office in 1888, changed the name to Alton in 1889, and discontinued it in 1965; the name "Hansen" was for Mads P. Hansen, first postmaster (Salley, p. 6, 93). According to Gudde (1949, p. 9), S.R. Perry named the place in 1862 for his home town, Alton, Illinois. According to Hanna (p. 9), the name "Alton" is a corruption of the name of the founder of the community, Alta Oliver, who laid out the townsite about 1887.

Altoona: see **Trinity Center** [TRINITY]:

Alum Spring: see **Chalk Mountain** [LAKE].

Alviso Ridge [MENDOCINO]: *ridge*, generally west-trending, 3.5 miles long, 4 miles north-northeast of Westport (lat. 39°41'40" N, long. 123°45'35" W). Named on Lincoln Ridge (1966) and Westport (1966) 7.5' quadrangles.

Amelia Butte [HUMBOLDT]: *peak*, 4.5 miles south-southeast of Showers Mountain (lat. 40°31'25" N, long. 123°39'20" W; sec. 30, T 2 N, R 5 E). Altitude 3964 feet. Named on Showers Mountain (1978) 7.5' quadrangle.

Amel Lake [LAKE]: *intermittent lake*, 4100 feet long, 4 miles south-southwest of Jericho Valley (lat. 38°46'55" N, long. 122°28'25" W; on N line sec. 25, T 11 N, R 6 W). Named on Jericho Valley (1958) 7.5' quadrangle.

Ames Opening [MENDOCINO]: *area*, 7.25 miles south-southeast of Branscomb (lat. 39°33'30" N, long. 123°34'30" W; sec. 30, T 20 N, R 15 W). Named on Sherwood Peak (1967) 7.5' quadrangle.

Ammon Creek [HUMBOLDT]: *stream*, flows 2 miles to South Fork Trinity River 8 miles south-southeast of the settlement of Willow Creek (lat. 40°50'05" N, long. 123°34' W). Named on Hennessy Peak (1979) 7.5' quadrangle.

Ammon Ridge [HUMBOLDT]: *ridge*, generally northeast-trending, 2.5 miles long, 10 miles south of Willow Creek (3) (lat. 40°47'50" N, long. 123°39'30" W). Named on Grouse Mountain (1979) 7.5' quadrangle.

Anada: see **Anada Creek** [TRINITY]; **Ruth** [TRINITY].

Anada Creek [TRINITY]: *stream*, flows 1.5 miles to Mad River 6 miles south of Forest Glen (lat. 40°17'20" N, long. 123°20'10" W; sec. 13, T 2 S, R 7 E). Named on Forest Glen (1979) 7.5' quadrangle. The name recalls Anada post office, which was situated near the mouth of the creek (Jones, p. 336).

Anchor Bay [MENDOCINO]: *settlement*, 3.5 miles northwest of Gualala (lat. 38°48'10" N, long. 123°34'35" W; sec. 18, T 11 N, R 15 W). Named on Gualala (1960) 7.5' quadrangle.

Anchor Creek [MENDOCINO]: *stream*, flows less than 0.25 mile to Sonoma County 9.5 miles south of Hopland (lat. 38°50'20" N, long. 123°05'25" W; at S line sec. 33, T 12 N, R 11 W). Named on Cloverdale (1960) 7.5' quadrangle.

Anderson: see **Boonville** [MENDOCINO]; **Camp Anderson** [HUMBOLDT].

Anderson Cliff [MENDOCINO]: *escarpment*, north-northwest-trending, 1.5 miles long, 9.5 miles southwest of Piercy along the coast (lat. 39°52'10" N, long. 123°54'35" W; sec. 6, 7, T 23 N, R 18 W). Named on Bear Harbor (1969) and Mistake Point (1969) 7.5' quadrangles.

Anderson Creek [HUMBOLDT]:

(1) *stream*, flows nearly 2 miles to South Fork Eel River 0.5 mile south east of Phillipsville (lat. 40°12'10" N, long. 123°46'35" W; near W line sec. 18, T 3 S, R 4 E). Named on Miranda (1970) 7.5' quadrangle.

(2) *stream*, flows 1.25 miles to Mattole River 10 miles west-southwest of Garberville (lat. 40°01'50" N, long. 123°57'20" W). Named on Briceland (1969) 7.5' quadrangle.

Anderson Creek [LAKE]:

(1) *stream*, heads in Glenn County and flows nearly 7 miles in Lake County to Eel River 5 miles east of Hull Mountain (lat. 39°30'35" N, long. 122°50'40" W; near N line sec. 14, T 19 N, R 9 W). Named on Crockett Peak (1967), Felkner Hill (1968), and Kneecap Ridge (1967) 7.5' quadrangles.

(2) *stream*, flows 4.5 miles to Putah Creek 3 miles southeast of Whispering Pines (lat. 38°46'40" N, long. 122°40'45" W; sec. 30, T 11 N, R 7 W). Named on Whispering Pines (1958) 7.5' quadrangle.

Anderson Creek [MENDOCINO]:

(1) *stream*, flows 5.25 miles to Indian Creek (2) 5.5 miles west-southwest of Piercy (lat. 39°56'50" N, long. 123°53'50" W; near S line sec. 7, T 24 N, R 18 W). Named on Bear Harbor (1969) 7.5' quadrangle.

(2) *stream*, flows 14 miles to join Rancheria Creek (2) and form Navarro River 5 miles west-northwest of Boonville (lat. 39°03'10" N, long. 123°26'25" W; near SE cor. sec. 19, T 14 N, R 14 W). Named on Boonville (1959) and Ornbaun Valley (1960) 15' quadrangles. Present Jimmy Creek is called North Fork Anderson Creek (2) on Boonville (1943) 15' quadrangle.

Anderson Flat [LAKE]: *area*, less than 1 mile northwest of the town of Lower Lake, where Cache Creek leaves Clear Lake (lat. 38°55'20" N, long. 122°37'05" W; in and near sec. 3, T 12 N, R. 7 W). Named on Lower Lake (1958) 7.5' quadrangle.

Anderson Ford [HUMBOLDT]: *locality*, 5.5 miles southeast of Showers Mountain (lat. 40°31'25" N, long. 123°37'20" W; sec. 28, T 2 N, R 5 E). Named on Blake Mountain (1979) 7.5' quadrangle.

Anderson Gulch [MENDOCINO]:

(1) *canyon*, drained by a stream that flows 1.5 miles to the sea 10 miles south-southwest of Piercy (lat. 39°51'10" N, long. 123°53'15" W; sec. 17, T 23 N, R 18 W). Named on Mistake Point (1969) 7.5' quadrangle.

(2) *canyon*, drained by a stream that flows 0.5 mile to South Fork Albion River 8 miles north-northeast of Elk (lat. 39°14'40" N, long. 123°40'05" W; sec. 17, T 16 N, R 16 W). Named on Elk (1960) 7.5' quadrangle.

(3) *canyon*, drained by a stream that flows 1.5 miles to South Fork Big River 4.5 miles east of Comptche (lat. 39°15'15" N, long. 123°30'35" W; sec. 11, T 16 N, R 15 W). Named on Comptche (1960) 15' quadrangle.

Anderson Gulch [TRINITY]: *canyon*, drained by a stream that flows 1.5 miles to Indian Creek (2) 7 miles south-southeast of Weaverville (lat. 40°38'10" N, long. 122°54'15" W; at S line sec. 8, T 32 N, R 9 W). Named on Weaverville (1950) 15' quadrangle.

Andersonia [MENDOCINO]: *locality*, 1 mile north-northwest of Piercy along South Fork Eel River (lat. 39°58'40" N, long. 123°48'15" W; sec. 35, T 5 S, R 3 E). Named on Piercy (1969) 7.5' quadrangle. Postal authorities established Andersonia post office in 1904 and discontinued it in 1906 (Salley, p. 7). The name commemorates Jeff Anderson, who built a saw-mill at the place in 1903 (Gudde, 1969, p. 10).

Anderson Island [LAKE]: *island*, 0.25 mile long, 3.5 miles west of Clearlake Oaks in Clear Lake (lat. 39°00'55" N, long. 122°44'35" W). Named on Clearlake Oaks (1958) 7.5' quadrangle.

Anderson Ridge [LAKE]: *ridge*, generally west-trending, 5 miles long, 4 miles north of Crockett Peak (lat. 39°29'05" N, long. 122°46'45" W); the ridge is south of Anderson Creek (1). Named on Stonyford (1951) 15' quadrangle, and on Crockett Peak (1967) 7.5' quadrangle. The name commemorates Bob Anderson, a stockman in the neighborhood in the late nineteenth century (Gudde, 1969, p. 10).

Anderson Springs [LAKE]: *settlement*, 3 miles south-southeast of Whispering Pines (lat. 38°46'30" N, long. 122°41'30" W; sec. 25, T 11 N, R 8 W); the place is along Anderson Creek (2). Named on Whispering Pines (1958) 7.5' quadrangle. Dr. A. Anderson and L.S. Patriquin located the springs at the place in 1873 and opened them to the public in 1874 (Palmer, p. 151). Irelan (p. 327) noted that the springs are situated at the head of a feature called Lacoma Valley.

Anderson Valley [MENDOCINO]: *valley*, 10 miles long, center about 4 miles northwest of Boonville (lat. 39°02'45" N, long. 123°25' W); the valley is along Anderson Creek (2) and the upper reaches of Navarro River. Named on Boonville (1959) and Ornbaun Valley (1960) 15' quadrangles. The name commemorates Walter Anderson, who settled in the valley in 1851 (Gudde, 1949, p. 11).

Andy: see **Mount Andy** [HUMBOLDT].

Anna Lake: see **Lake Anna** [TRINITY].

Antenna Ridge [HUMBOLDT]: *ridge*, west- to southwest-trending, 3 miles long, center 2 miles west-northwest of Orleans Mountain (lat. 41°17'15" N, long. 123°29'15" W). Named on Orleans (1978) and Orleans Mountain (1974) 7.5' quadrangles.

Anthony Peak [MENDOCINO]: *peak*, 15 miles east-northeast of Covelo near Mendocino-Tehama County line (lat. 39°50'45" N, long. 122°57'50" W; near W line sec. 15, T 23 N, R 10 W). Altitude 6954 feet. Named on Mendocino Pass (1967) 7.5' quadrangle.

Anthony Ridge [MENDOCINO]: *ridge*, southwest- to west-trending, 6.5 miles long, 13 miles east-northeast of Covelo (lat. 39°49'45" N, long. 123°00'30" W); Anthony Peak is at the east end of the ridge. Named on Mendocino Pass (1967) and Newhouse Ridge (1967) 7.5' quadrangles.

Antone Basin [TRINITY]: *relief feature*, 16 miles southwest of Black Rock Mountain (lat. 40°02'05" N, long. 123°11'30" W; sec. 8, 9, T 25 N, R 12 W); the feature is along Antone Creek. Named on Black Rock Mountain (1954) 15' quadrangle.

Antone Creek [HUMBOLDT]: *stream*, flows nearly 2 miles to Bear River 6.25 miles west-southwest of Scotia (lat. 40°26'10" N, long. 124°12'15" W; sec. 29, T 1 N, R 1 W). Named on Taylor Peak (1969) 7.5' quadrangle.

Antone Creek [TRINITY]: *stream*, flows 3.5 miles to Casoose Creek 17 miles southwest of Black Rock Mountain (lat. 40°00'50" N, long. 123°12'40" W; near S line sec. 16, T 25 N, R 12 W). Named on Black Rock Mountain (1954) 15' quadrangle.

Antone Lake [TRINITY]: *lake*, 300 feet long, 16 miles southwest of Black Rock Mountain (lat. 40°02'20" N, long. 123°12'50" W; sec. 9, T 25 N, R 12 W). Named on Black Rock Mountain (1954) 15' quadrangle.

Ant Point [TRINITY]: *peak*, 13 miles southwest of Black Rock Mountain (lat. 40°04' N, long. 123°11' W; sec. 35, T 26 N, R 12 W). Altitude 5058 feet. Named on Black Rock Mountain (1954) 15' quadrangle.

Ant Ridge [MENDOCINO-TRINITY]: *ridge,* south- to west-trending, 2.5 miles long, 9 miles north of Anthony Peak on Mendocino-Trinity County line (lat. 39°58'30" N, long. 122°59'30" W). Named on Buck Rock (1967) and Leech Lake Mountain (1966) 7.5' quadrangles.

Appletree Creek [LAKE]: *stream,* flows 1.25 miles to Dry Creek (3) 4 miles west-southwest of Middletown (lat. 38°44'10" N, long. 122°41' W; near S line sec. 6, T 10 N, R 7 W). Named on Mount Saint Helena (1959) 7.5' quadrangle.

Apple Tree Ridge [HUMBOLDT]: *ridge,* generally west-trending, 2.5 miles long, center 2 miles northeast of Petrolia (lat. 40°20'35" N, long. 124°16' W). Named on Buckeye Mountain (1970) and Petrolia (1969) 7.5' quadrangles.

Appletree Spring [LAKE]: *spring,* 4 miles northeast of Hull Mountain (lat. 39°33'45" N, long. 122°52'45" W; sec. 28, T 20 N, R 9 W). Named on Hull Mountain (1967) 7.5' quadrangle.

Arabella: see **Long Valley** [LAKE] (2).

Arbor Camp Ridge [HUMBOLDT]: *ridge,* west-southwest- to south-trending, 2.25 miles long, nearly 2 miles south-southwest of Coyote Peak (lat. 41°06'15" N, long. 123°52'30" W). Named on Hupa Mountain (1982) and Panther Creek (1982) 7.5' quadrangles.

Arcata [HUMBOLDT]: *town,* 6 miles northeast of Eureka (lat. 40°52'15" N, long. 124°05' W). Named on Arcata North (1959) and Arcata South (1959) 7.5' quadrangles. Postal authorities established Union Town post office in 1852 and changed the name to Arcata in 1860 (Frickstad, p. 47). A group called Union Company founded the place in 1850 and called it Union Town, although the name generally was shortened to Union; residents gave the name "Arcata" to the community in 1860 (Coy, 1929, p. 56, 199). Camp Curtis, located 1.5 miles north of Arcata, was the headquarters of the Mountain Battalion, a group of soldiers under the command of Captain Owsley from 1862 until 1864 (Hoover, Rensch, and Rensch, p. 100; Palais, p. 48). S. Daby established Daby's Ferry 5 miles north of Union (present Arcata) where the main road crossed Mad River; Indian trouble shut down the ferry in 1862 (Bledsoe, p. 212). Postal authorities established Mower post office 28 miles northeast of Arcata in 1884 and discontinued it in 1888; the name was for Lloyd W. Mower, first postmaster (Salley, p. 148).

Arcata Bay [HUMBOLDT]: *bay,* the northeast extension of Humboldt Bay; between Eureka and Arcata (lat. 40°50' N, long. 124°07'30" W). Named on Arcata South (1959) and Eureka (1958) 7.5' quadrangles. United States Board on Geographic Names (1960b, p. 5) approved the name "Arcata Bay" for the north part of Humboldt Bay, and rejected the name "North Bay" for that part.

Arcata Bottoms [HUMBOLDT]: *area,* lowlands at and west of Arcata between Arcata Bay and Mad River (lat. 40°53'15" N, long. 124°06'30" W). Named on Arcata North (1959), Arcata South (1959), Eureka (1958), and Tyee City (1959) 7.5' quadrangles.

Arcata Channel [HUMBOLDT]: *channel,* extends into Arcata Bay from the north end of Humboldt Bay; the southeast end is about 1.25 miles northwest of downtown Eureka (lat. 40°49'15" N, long. 124°10'15" W). Named on Eureka (1958) 7.5' quadrangle.

Arch of the Navarro [MENDOCINO]: *rock,* 2.25 miles south of Albion, and 400 feet offshore (lat. 39°11'25" N, long. 123°45'50" W); the feature is 1200 feet west of the mouth of Navarro River. Named on Albion (1960) 7.5' quadrangle.

Arena: see **Point Arena** [MENDOCINO].

Arena Cove [MENDOCINO]: *embayment,* 1 mile east-northeast of the village of Point Arena along the coast (lat. 38°54'50" N, long. 123°42'40" W; sec. 11, T 12 N, R 17 W). Named on Point Arena (1960) 7.5' quadrangle. Vander Leck's (1920a) map has the name "Port of Pt. Arena" at the place.

Arena Point: see **Point Arena** [MENDOCINO] (1).

Arena Rock [MENDOCINO]: *rock,* 5.5 miles north-northwest of the village of Point Arena, and 1.5 miles north of Point Arena (1) (lat. 38°58'35" N, long. 123°44'50" W). Named on Point Arena (1960) 7.5' quadrangle.

Arkansas Bar: see **Weaverville** [TRINITY].

Arlynda Corners [HUMBOLDT]: *locality,* 1.25 miles north-northeast of Ferndale (lat. 40°35'40" N, long. 124°15'15" W; near SE cor. sec. 35, T 2 N, R 2 W). Named on Ferndale (1959) 7.5' quadrangle. John Gardner Kenyon proposed the name "Arlynda" in 1882 from an Indian word with the meaning "merchandise" or "property"—some people wanted to call the place Washington Corners (Turner, p. 9).

Armstrong Creek [TRINITY]: *stream,* flows 3 miles to Mad River 9.5 miles east-northeast of Kettenpom (lat. 40°13'20" N, long. 123°18'10" W; near N line sec. 8, T 3 S, R 8 E). Named on Shannon Butte (1967) 7.5' quadrangle.

Arnold [MENDOCINO]: *locality,* 3 miles southeast of Longvale along Northwestern Pacific Railroad (lat. 39°31'10" N, long. 123°23'30" W; near NE cor. sec. 10, T 19 N, R 14 W). Named on Longvale (1966) 7.5' quadrangle.

Arnold Creek [HUMBOLDT]: *stream,* flows nearly 2 miles to Larabee Creek 5.5 miles southwest of Bridgeville (lat. 40°24'20" N, long. 123°51'40" W; sec. 5, T 1 S, R 3 E). Named on Bridgeville (1969) 7.5' quadrangle.

Arthur: see **Ukiah** [MENDOCINO].

Arts Peak [TRINITY]: *peak,* 12.5 miles southeast of Weaverville (lat. 40°36'10" N, long. 122°47'10" W; on W line sec. 28, T 32 N, R 8 W). Altitude 4302 feet. Named on Weaverville (1950) 15' quadrangle.

Arvola Gulch [MENDOCINO]: *canyon,* drained by a stream that flows 1.5 miles to Chamberlain Creek 8.5 miles north-northeast of Comptche (lat. 39°22'50" N, long. 123°32'45" W; near SW cor. sec. 28, T 18 N, R 15 W). Named on Comptche (1960) 15' quadrangle.

Asa Bean Crossing [TRINITY]: *locality,* 16 miles south-southwest of Black Rock Mountain along Middle Fork Eel River (lat. 39°59' N, long. 123°05'20" W; near SE cor. sec. 28, T 25 N, R 11 W). Named on Leech Lake Mountain (1966) 7.5' quadrangle.

Asa Bean Flat [TRINITY]: *area,* 16 miles south-southwest of Black Rock Mountain (lat. 39°58'50" N, long. 123°06'10" W; near NW cor. sec. 33, T 25 N, R 11 W). Named on Leech Lake Mountain (1966) 7.5' quadrangle.

Asa Bean Ridge [MENDOCINO]: *ridge,* south-trending, 3.5 miles long, 9 miles northeast of Covelo (lat. 39°53' N, long. 123°08'10" W). Named on Bluenose Ridge (1967) and Covelo East (1967) 7.5' quadrangles.

Asbestos Gulch [TRINITY]: *canyon,* drained by a stream that flows 1.5 miles to East Fork Trinity River 14 miles northeast of Trinity Center (lat. 41°08'05" N, long. 122°29' W; sec. 19, T 38 N, R 5 W). Named on Dunsmuir (1954) 15' quadrangle.

Asbill Creek [LAKE]: *stream,* flows 4.5 miles to Soda Creek (2) 9 miles northeast of Middletown (lat. 38°51'55" N, long. 122°31'05" W; near NW cor. sec. 27, T 12 N, R 6 W). Named on Middletown (1958) 7.5' quadrangle. The stream also was known as Conns Creek for a pioneer family of the region (Gudde, 1969, p. 15), but United States Board on Geographic Names (1962b, p. 14) rejected this name for the feature.

Asbill Creek [MENDOCINO]: *stream,* formed by the confluence of East Fork and West Fork, flows 0.5 mile to North Fork Eel River 5.5 miles northeast of Spyrock (2) (lat. 39°55'55" N, long. 123°21'50" W). Named on Mina (1967) 7.5' quadrangle. East Fork and West Fork each are 4 miles long; both forks are named on Mina (1967) 7.5' quadrangle.

Ash Creek [MENDOCINO]: *stream,* flows 4.5 miles to Russian River 9.5 miles south-southeast of Hopland just inside Sonoma County (lat. 38°51'10" N, long. 123°01'40" W; near N line sec. 36, T 12 N, R 11 W). Named on Asti (1959) and Cloverdale (1960) 7.5' quadrangles.

Ashfield Butte [HUMBOLDT]: *peak,* 5.5 miles north-northwest of Lone Star Junction (lat. 40°42'35" N, long. 123°55' W; near S line sec. 23, T 4 N, R 2 E); the peak is 0.25 mile south of Ashfield Ridge. Named on Iaqua Buttes (1979) 7.5' quadrangle. The name "Ashfield Buttes" is for William Ashfield, a farmer; the feature also was called Flagstaff Butte (Turner, p. 9).

Ashfield Ridge [HUMBOLDT]: *ridge,* generally east-trending, 2 miles long, 6 miles north-northwest of Lone Star Junction (lat. 40°42'45" N, long. 123°54'45" W; mainly in sec. 23, 24, T 4 N, R 2 E). Named on Iaqua Buttes (1979) 7.5' quadrangle.

Ash Hollow [MENDOCINO]: *canyon,* drained by a stream that flows 1.5 miles to Hulls Creek 9 miles north-northeast of Covelo (lat. 39°54'55" N, long. 123°12'55" W; near NE cor. sec. 29, T 24 N, R 12 W). Named on Covelo (1926) 15' quadrangle.

Ash Hollow [TRINITY]: *canyon,* 0.5 mile long, just north-northwest of Weaverville (lat. 40°44'25" N, long. 122°36'35" W; near SE cor. sec. 1, T 33 N, R 10 W). Named on Weaverville (1950) 15' quadrangle.

Ashmore Ridge [MENDOCINO]: *ridge,* southwest-trending, less than 0.5 mile long, 10 miles southwest of Ukiah (lat. 39°03'35" N, long. 123°04'10" W; sec. 21, T 14 N, R 11 W). Named on Purdys Gardens (1958) 7.5' quadrangle.

Astorg Spring: see **Glenbrook** [LAKE].

Asylum [MENDOCINO]: *locality,* at the south edge of Ukiah along Northwestern Pacific Railroad (lat. 39°08' N, long. 123°11'55" W). Named on Ukiah (1958) 7.5' quadrangle, which shows Mendocino state hospital situated 2 miles east of.the place.

Atchison Creek [MENDOCINO]: *stream,* heads in Glenn County and flows 1.5 miles in Mendocino County to Black Butte River 15 miles north of Hull Mountain (lat. 39°43'55" N, long. 122°56'35" W; sec. 26, T 22 N, R 10 W). Named on Plaskett Ridge (1967) 7.5' quadrangle.

Atkinson Flat [MENDOCINO]: *area,* 4.5 miles east of Covelo (lat. 39°47'25" N, long. 123°09'50" W; near S line sec. 2, T 22 N, R 12 W). Named on Covelo East (1967) 7.5' quadrangle. Covelo (1952) 15' quadrangle shows the place as part of Etsel Flat.

Atwell Creek [HUMBOLDT]: *stream,* flows 4 miles to Howe Creek 3.5 miles west-northwest of Scotia (lat. 40°29'40" N, long. 124°10'05" W; sec. 3, T 1 N, R 1 W). Named on Taylor Peak (1969) 7.5' quadrangle.

Austin Creek: see **Gibson Creek** [MENDOCINO] (2).

Austrian Gulch: see **West Weaver Creek** [TRINITY].

Auto Rest: see **Forest Glen** [TRINITY].

Azbil Flat [HUMBOLDT]: *area,* 8.5 miles southwest of Dinsmore (lat. 40°25'20" N, long. 123°43'45" W; sec. 33, T 1 N, R 4 E). Named on Larabee Valley (1977) 7.5' quadrangle.

– B –

Bachelor: see **Saratoga Springs** [LAKE].

Bachelor's Peak: see **Hells Peak** [LAKE].

Bachelor Valley [LAKE]: *valley*, 3.5 miles west-northwest of the town of Upper Lake (lat. 39°11'30" N, long. 122°58' W). Named on Upper Lake (1958) 7.5' quadrangle. Goodyear (1890a, p. 248) used the form "Bachelor's Valley" for the name, which commemorates four bachelors who were early settlers at the place (Gudde, 1969, p. 18).

Backbone Creek [TRINITY]: *stream*, flows 4.5 miles to North Fork Trinity River 11.5 miles north of Helena (lat. 40°56'10" N, long. 123°09'20" W). Named on Helena (1951) 15' quadrangle.

Backbone Ridge [TRINITY]: *ridge*, west-southwest- to south-trending, 14 miles long, center 7.5 miles north of Helena (lat. 40°53' N, long. 123°08'30" W). Named on Helena (1951) 15' quadrangle.

Bacon Flat [HUMBOLDT]: *area*, 1 mile north-northeast of Orleans (lat. 41°18'50" N, long. 123°32' W; sec. 30, T 11 N, R 6 E). Named on Orleans (1978) 7.5' quadrangle.

Bad Creek [LAKE]: *stream*, flows 1 mile to Big Canyon Creek about 3.5 miles northeast of Whispering Pines (lat. 38°50'55" N, long. 122°39'55" W; sec. 32, T 12 N, R 7 W). Named on Whispering Pines (1958) 7.5' quadrangle.

Baechtel Creek [MENDOCINO]: *stream*, flows 6 miles to Little Lake Valley 1.5 miles south of downtown Willits (lat. 39°23' N, long. 123°21'05" W; near W line sec. 30, T 18 N, R 13 W). Named on Willits (1961) 15' quadrangle.

Bagdad: see **Helena** [TRINITY].

Bahia del Cabo: see **Humboldt Bay** [HUMBOLDT].

Bahia Grande Cerca del Cabo: see **Humboldt Bay** [HUMBOLDT].

Bailey Canyon Campground [TRINITY]: *locality*, 4.5 miles southwest of Forest Glen along Ruth Reservoir (lat. 40°20'25" N, long. 123°23'55" W; near NW cor. sec. 33, T 1 S, R 7 E). Named on Ruth Reservoir (1978) 7.5' quadrangle.

Bailey Creek [MENDOCINO]: *stream*, flows 2 miles to South Branch of North Fork Navarro River 11.5 miles north-northwest of Boonville (lat. 39°09'25" N, long. 123°28' W; sec. 13, T 15 N, R 15 W). Named on Boonville (1959) 15' quadrangle, which shows Old Bailey place near the stream.

Bailey Gulch [MENDOCINO]: *canyon*, drained by a stream that flows less than 1 mile to South Branch of North Fork Navarro River 2.25 miles north-northeast of Navarro (lat. 39°10'05" N, long. 123°31'30" W; near SE cor. sec. 8, T 15 N, R 15 W). Named on Navarro (1961) 15' quadrangle.

Bailey Ridge [HUMBOLDT]: *ridge*, east-northeast-trending, 1 mile long, 5.5 miles east of Showers Mountain (lat. 35°20' N, long. 123°35'40" W; on N line sec. 3, T 2 N, R 5 E). Named on Blake Mountain (1979) 7.5' quadrangle.

Bailey Ridge [MENDOCINO]: *ridge*, generally east-trending, 4 miles long, 12.5 miles north-northwest of Boonville (lat. 39°10'55" N, long. 123°27' W). Named on Boonville (1959) 15' quadrangle.

Bailey Summit [MENDOCINO]: *pass*, 14 miles north-northwest of Boonville at the west end of Bailey Ridge (lat. 39°10'55" N, long. 123°29'15" W; near SE cor. sec. 3, T 15 N, R 15 W); the pass is at the head of Bailey Creek. Named on Boonville (1959) 15' quadrangle.

Bairs: see **Green Point** [HUMBOLDT].

Bake Oven Ridge [TRINITY]: *ridge*, southwest- to south-trending, 6 miles long, 12 miles south-southeast of Salmon Mountain (lat. 41°01'30" N, long. 123°18'40" W). Named on Ironside Mountain (1951) 15' quadrangle, and on Dees Peak (1978) 7.5' quadrangle.

Baker: see **Fort Baker** [HUMBOLDT].

Baker Creek [HUMBOLDT]:

(1) *stream*, flows 3.5 miles to Van Duzen River 4 miles south-southwest of Showers Mountain (lat. 40°31'35" N, long. 123°43'45" W; near E line sec. 28, T 2 N, R 4 E). Named on Showers Mountain (1978) 7.5' quadrangle.

(2) *stream*, flows 2.25 miles to Mattole River 9.5 miles southwest of Garberville (lat. 40°00'30" N, long. 123°55'45" W). Named on Briceland (1969) 7.5' quadrangle.

Baker Creek [MENDOCINO]: *stream*, flows 3.5 miles to Forsythe Creek 8 miles west-southwest of the town of Potter Valley (lat. 39°15'55" N, long. 123°14' W; at S line sec. 6, T 16 N, R 12 W). Named on Potter Valley (1960) 15' quadrangle. The stream drains McGee Canyon.

Baker Creek [TRINITY]: *stream*, flows 2 miles to East Fork Trinity River 13 miles northeast of Trinity Center (lat. 41°07'40" N, long. 122°30'15" W; sec. 25, T 38 N, R 6 W). Named on Dunsmuir (1954) 15' quadrangle. United States Board on Geographic Names (1968a, p. 4) approved the name "Baker Hollow" for a ravine at the head of Baker Creek (lat. 41°05'40" N, long. 122°28'50" W), and rejected the name "Jose's Hollow" for the feature.

Baker Flat [DEL NORTE]: *area*, 12 miles northeast of Gasquet along Shelly Creek (lat. 41°58' N, long. 123°48'20" W; sec. 11, T 18 N, R 3 E). Named on Shelly Creek Ridge (1982) 7.5' quadrangle.

Baker 40 Creek [MENDOCINO]: *stream*, flows 1 mile to Tomki Creek 8 miles east-southeast of Longvale (lat. 39°30'35" N, long. 123°17'40" W; near SW cor. sec. 10, T 19 N, R 13 W). Named on Willis Ridge (1966) 7.5' quadrangle.

Baker Gulch [TRINITY]: *canyon*, drained by a stream that flows 3 miles to Trinity River 7 miles east of Weaverville (lat. 40°44'40" N, long. 122°48'20" W; near E line sec. 6, T 33 N, R 8 W). Named on Trinity Dam (1950) and Weaverville (1950) 15' quadrangles.

Baker Hollow: see **Baker Creek** [TRINITY].

Baker Soda Spring: see **Lower Lake** [LAKE].

Balcom Creek [HUMBOLDT]: *stream*, flows 1.25 miles to Larabee Creek 2.5 miles east-northeast of Redcrest (lat. 40°24'30" N, long. 123°54' W; sec. 1, T 1 S, R 2 E). Named on Redcrest (1969) 7.5' quadrangle. Called Fish Creek on Dyerville (1921) 15' quadrangle.

Bald Hill [DEL NORTE]: *ridge*, northwest-trending, 1.5 miles long, 9 miles east of Crescent City (lat. 41°45'15" N, long. 124°01'15" W). Named on Childs Hill (1966) and Hiouchi (1966) 7.5' quadrangles.

Bald Hill [HUMBOLDT]: *ridge*, generally southeast-trending, 1 mile long, 5.5 miles north-northwest of Hoopa (lat. 41°07'25" N, long. 123°42'55" W; sec. 33, 34, T 9 N, R 4 E). Named on Hoopa (1979) and Weitchpec (1979) 7.5' quadrangles.

Bald Hill [MENDOCINO]:

(1) *ridge*, north-northwest-trending, less than 1 mile long, nearly 3 miles east-northeast of Fort Bragg (lat. 39°28' N, long. 123°45'25" W; sec. 33, T 19 N, R 17 W). Named on Fort Bragg (1960) 7.5' quadrangle.

(2) *ridge*, northwest-trending, 3 miles long, 3.5 miles north-northwest of Navarro (lat. 39°11'30" N, long. 123°34'30" W). Named on Navarro (1961) 15' quadrangle.

(3) *ridge*, south-southwest-trending, 1 mile long, 9 miles south-southeast of Elk (lat. 39°01' N, long. 123°41'30" W; in and near sec. 4, T 13 N, R 16 W). Named on Mallo Pass Creek (1960) 7.5' quadrangle.

Bald Hill: see **Little Bald Hill** [HUMBOLDT].

Bald Hill Canyon [LAKE]: *canyon*, drained by a stream that flows 1.5 miles to Wolf Creek 6 miles north-northeast of Clearlake Oaks (lat. 39°05'35" N, long. 122°36'35" W). Named on Clearlake Oaks (1960) 15' quadrangle.

Bald Hill Creek [MENDOCINO]: *stream*, flows 1.5 miles to North Fork Ten Mile River nearly 4 miles west-southwest of Branscomb (lat. 39°36'10" N, long. 123°38'25" W; near S line sec. 9, T 20 N, R 16 W). Named on Dutchmans Knoll (1966) and Lincoln Ridge (1966) 7.5' quadrangles.

Bald Hills [HUMBOLDT]: *ridge*, northwest-trending, 7.5 miles long, 6 miles northwest of Coyote Peak (lat. 41°11'25" N, long. 123°56' W). Named on Bald Hills (1982) and French Camp Ridge (1983) 7.5' quadrangles. According to Gibbs (p. 133-134), the name is from the open areas of rich grass on south slopes of the feature.

Bald Hills: see **Orick** [HUMBOLDT].

Bald Jesse [HUMBOLDT]: *ridge*, northwest-trending, 1 mile long, 6 miles south of Lone Star Junction (lat. 40°32'35" N, long. 123°52'40" W; sec. 19, T 2 N, R 3 E). Named on Owl Creek (1979) and Yager Junction (1979) 7.5' quadrangles.

Bald Mill Creek [MENDOCINO]: *stream*, flows 1 mile to Anderson Creek (2) 4 miles north-northeast of Ornbaun Valley (lat. 38°57'50" N, long. 123°16'15" W; at S line sec. 22, T 13 N, R 13 W). Named on Ornbaun Valley (1960) 15' quadrangle.

Bald Mountain [HUMBOLDT]: *peak*, 6.5 miles east of the town of Blue Lake (lat. 40°52'55" N, long. 123°51'55" W; at N line sec. 29, T 6 N, R 3 E). Altitude 3176 feet. Named on Lord-Ellis Summit (1973) 7.5' quadrangle.

Bald Mountain [LAKE]: *peak*, 5 miles north-northwest of the town of Lower Lake (lat. 38°58'45" N, long. 122°38'35" W; sec. 16, T 13 N, R 7 W). Altitude 2197 feet. Named on Clearlake Highlands (1958) 7.5' quadrangle.

Bald Mountain [MENDOCINO]:

(1) *ridge*, north-northwest-trending, 0.5 mile long, 6.5 miles southwest of Leggett (lat. 39°48'20" N, long. 123°37'10" W; at NE cor. sec. 33, T 23 N, R 16 W). Named on Tan Oak Park (1969) 7.5' quadrangle. Present Bald Mountain (1) is shown as the northwest part of Brush Mountain (1) on Leggett (1952) 15' quadrangle.

(2) *peak*, 6 miles north of Eden Valley (lat. 39°42'50" N, long. 123°10'35" W; near NE cor. sec. 3, T 21 N, R 12 W). Named on Jamison Ridge (1967) 7.5' quadrangle.

(3) *relief feature*, 4 miles east-northeast of Longvale (lat. 39°34'20" N, long. 123°21'15" W; at E line sec. 24, T 20 N, R 14 W). Named on Willis Ridge (1966) 7.5' quadrangle.

(4) *ridge*, north-northwest-trending, 1.5 miles long, 4 miles south of Eden Valley (lat. 39°34' N, long. 123°11'05" W). Named on Brushy Mountain (1966) 7.5' quadrangle. On Eden Valley (1952) 15' quadrangle, the name applies to a peak at the north end of the ridge.

(5) *peak*, 7 miles northwest of Hull Mountain (lat. 39°37'15" N, long. 122°58'20" W; sec. 4, T 20 N, R 10 W). Altitude 6740 feet. Named on Hull Mountain (1967) 7.5' quadrangle.

(6) *peak*, 10.5 miles northeast of Spyrock (2) (lat. 39°58'05" N, long. 123°17' W). Altitude 3938 feet. Named on Mina (1967) 7.5' quadrangle.

Bald Mountain Canyon [MENDOCINO]: *canyon,* drained by a stream that flows nearly 3 miles to Middle Fork Eel River 5.5 miles north of Eden Valley (lat. 39°42'40" N, long. 123°11'45" W; sec. 4, T 21 N, R 12 W); the canyon is 1 mile west of Bald Mountain (2). Named on Jamison Ridge (1967) 7.5' quadrangle.

Bald Mountain Creek [HUMBOLDT]: *stream,* flows 2.5 miles to North Fork Mad River 4 miles east-northeast of the town of Blue Lake (lat. 40°53'55" N, long. 123°54'55" W; near S line sec. 14, T 6 N, R 2 E). Named on Blue Lake (1979) 7.5' quadrangle. Called Pollock Creek on Blue Lake (1951) 15' quadrangle.

Bald Mountain Creek: see **Jiggs Creek** [HUMBOLDT].

Bald Peaks of Plummer [TRINITY]: *peaks,* 8.5 miles north of Forest Glen (lat. 40°29'35" N, long. 123°17'55" W; sec. 5, T 1 N, R 8 E); the peaks are at the head of Plummer Creek. Named on Naufus Creek (1979) 7.5' quadrangle.

Baldwin Ridge [HUMBOLDT]: *ridge,* north-northwest-trending, less than 1 mile long, 1.5 miles east of the settlement of Willow Creek (lat. 40°56'10" N, long. 123°36'05" W). Named on Salyer (1979) 7.5' quadrangle.

Baldy: see **Little Baldy** [MENDOCINO]; **Mount Baldy**, under **Weaver Bally Mountain** [TRINITY].

Baldy Creek [MENDOCINO]: *stream,* flows 5 miles to Black Butte River 10.5 miles north of Hull Mountain (lat. 39°40'05" N, long. 123°55' W; near N line sec. 24, T 21 N, R 10 W). Named on Plaskett Ridge (1967) 7.5' quadrangle.

Baldy Mountain [LAKE]:

(1) *peak,* 3 miles north of Cold Spring Mountain (lat. 39°08'30" N, long. 122°29'50" W; near S line sec. 14, T 15 N, R 6 W). Altitude 3404 feet. Named on Wilbur Springs (1961) 15' quadrangle.

(2) *peak,* 5 miles southeast of Wilson Valley (2) (lat. 38°55'45" N, long. 122°24' W). Altitude 2220 feet. Named on Wilson Valley (1958) 7.5' quadrangle.

Baldy Peak [DEL NORTE]: *peak,* 1.5 miles west of Harrington Peak (lat. 41°40'25" N, long. 123°43'10" W). Altitude 5775 feet. Named on Prescott Mountain (1981) 7.5' quadrangle.

Baldy Ridge: see **Little Baldy Ridge** [MENDOCINO].

Bally [HUMBOLDT]: *area,* 8 miles southwest of Dinsmore (lat. 40°25'35" N, long. 123°43'35" W; near N line sec. 33, T 1 N, R 4 E). Named on Larabee Valley (1977) 7.5' quadrangle.

Bally: see **Little Bally** [TRINITY]; **Mount Bally**, under **Weaver Bally Mountain** [TRINITY].

Bally Peak [LAKE]: *peak,* 5.5 miles north-northeast of the town of Lower Lake (lat. 38°58'40" N, long. 122°33'25" W). Altitude 2288 feet. Named on Lower Lake (1958) 7.5' quadrangle.

Balm of Gilead Creek [TRINITY]: *stream,* flows 8.5 miles to Middle Fork Eel River 13 miles south-southwest of Black Rock Mountain (lat. 40°01'50" N, long. 123°05'25" W; sec. 9, T 25 N, R 11 W). Named on Black Rock Mountain (1954) and Yolla Bolly (1954) 15' quadrangles.

Baptiste Orchard [MENDOCINO]: *area,* 1.25 miles west-southwest of Branscomb (lat. 39°38'55" N, long. 123°38'50" W; sec. 28, T 21 N, R 16 W). Named on Lincoln Ridge (1966) 7.5' quadrangle.

Barber Creek [HUMBOLDT]:

(1) *stream,* flows 3.25 miles to Eel River 3.5 miles south of Fortuna (lat. 40°32'50" N, long. 124°09'40" W; sec. 22, T 2 N, R 1 W). Named on Fortuna (1959) 7.5' quadrangle. The name commemorates Joseph Tillinghast Barber, who had a patent for land in the neighborhood (Turner, p. 13).

(2) *stream,* flows 4.5 miles to Van Duzen River 1.25 miles south-southwest of Hydesville (lat. 40°32'05" N, long. 124°06'50" W; near S line sec. 19, T 2 N, R 1 E). Named on Hydesville (1979) 7.5' quadrangle.

Barber Prairie [HUMBOLDT]: *area,* nearly 2 miles southwest of Coyote Peak (lat. 41°06'50" N, long. 123°52'50" W; sec. 6, T 8 N, R 3 E). Named on Hupa Mountain (1982) and Panther Creek (1982) 7.5' quadrangles.

Bar Creek [MENDOCINO]: *stream,* flows 4.25 miles to Middle Fork Eel River 10.5 miles east-northeast of Covelo (lat. 39°50'50" N, long. 123°03'35" W; near W line sec. 14, T 23 N, R 11 W). Named on Mendocino Pass (1967) and Newhouse Ridge (1967) 7.5' quadrangles.

Bar Creek [TRINITY]: *stream,* flows 3.25 miles to join Panther Creek (4) and form West Fork of North Fork Eel River 6.25 miles north-northeast of Kettenpom (lat. 40°14'40" N, long. 123°25'55" W; sec. 31, T 2 S, R 7 E). Named on Ruth Reservoir (1978) and Zenia (1967) 7.5' quadrangles. On Kettenpom (1955) and Pickett Peak (1954) 15' quadrangles, most of present Bar Creek is called West Fork of North Fork Eel River; on Pickett Peak (1954) 15' quadrangle, the uppermost part of present Bar Creek is shown as a tributary of West Fork of North Fork Eel River. United States Board on Geographic Names (1969a, p. 2) rejected the names "North Fork of Eel River" and "West Fork of North Fork Eel River" for present Bar Creek.

Bar Gulch [TRINITY]: *canyon,* drained by a stream that flows 2 miles to Hayfork Creek 2.25 miles west of Hayfork (lat. 40°33'20" N, long. 123°13'30" W; sec. 9, T 31 N, R 12 W). Named on Hayfork (1951) and Hyampom (1951) 15' quadrangles.

Bark Camp [MENDOCINO]: *locality,* 7 miles east-southeast of Branscomb (lat. 39°37'05" N, long. 123°30'35" W). Named on Branscomb (1921) 15' quadrangle.

Barkdull: see **Pepperwood** [HUMBOLDT].

Barkdull Prairie [HUMBOLDT]: *area,* 4.25 miles south-southeast of Scotia (lat. 40°25'40" N, long. 124°03'25" W; sec. 34, T 1 N, R 1 E). Named on Scotia (1970) 7.5' quadrangle.

Barker Creek [LAKE]: *stream,* flows nearly 2 miles to Rice Creek 1 mile north-northwest of Potato Hill (lat. 39°22' N, long. 122°48'55" W). Named on Potato Hill (1967) 7.5' quadrangle.

Barker Creek [TRINITY]: *stream,* flows 7 miles to Hayfork Creek 3.5 miles east of Hayfork (lat. 40°03'30" N, long. 123°06'45" W; sec. 9, T 31 N, R 11 W); the stream heads near Barker Mountain. Named on Hayfork (1951) 15' quadrangle.

Barker Creek: see **Little Barker Creek** [TRINITY].

Barker Mountain [TRINITY]: *peak,* 8 miles north-northeast of Hayfork (lat. 40°39' N, long. 123°06'25" W; on W line sec. 3, T 32 N, R 11 W); the peak is near the head of Barker Creek. Altitude 5818 feet. Named on Hayfork (1951) 15' quadrangle.

Barkerville [LAKE]: *locality,* 11 miles north-northeast of Clearlake Oaks along North Fork Cache Creek (lat. 39°09'20" N, long. 122°33'45" W; near SE cor. sec. 7, T 15 N, R 6 W). Named on Clearlake Oaks (1960) 15' quadrangle.

Bark Shanty Creek: see **Little Bark Shanty Creek** [TRINITY].

Barkshed Opening [MENDOCINO]: *area,* 4.5 miles north of Boonville (lat. 39°04'30" N, long. 123°21' W; sec. 13, T 14 N, R 14 W). Named on Boonville (1959) 15' quadrangle.

Barleyfield Creek [TRINITY]: *stream,* flows 2.5 miles to Reading Creek 11 miles south-southeast of Weaverville (lat. 40°34'45" N, long. 122°53'10" W; near S line sec. 33, T 32 N, R 9 W). Named on Weaverville (1950) 15' quadrangle.

Barleyfield Peak [TRINITY]: *peak,* 12.5 miles south-southeast of Weaverville (lat. 40°34'20" N, long. 122°50' W; sec. 1, T 31 N, R 9 W); the peak is near the head of Barleyfield Creek. Altitude 5267 feet. Named on Weaverville (1950) 15' quadrangle.

Barley Lake [MENDOCINO]: *lake,* 500 feet long, 5.25 miles north-northwest of Hull Mountain (lat. 39°35'25" N, long. 122°58'40" W; at E line sec. 17, T 20 N, R 10 W). Named on Hull Mountain (1967) 7.5' quadrangle.

Barlow Gulch [MENDOCINO]: *canyon,* drained by a stream that flows 1 mile to Little North Fork Ten Mile River nearly 7 miles west-southwest of Branscomb (lat. 39°36'10" N, long. 123°43'55" W; near SE cor. sec. 10, T 20 N, R 17 W). Named on Dutchmans Knoll (1966) 7.5' quadrangle.

Barn Creek [HUMBOLDT]: *stream,* flows 2.5 miles to Thurman Creek 5.25 miles north-northwest of Blocksburg (lat. 40°21' N, long. 123°39'30" W; at W line sec. 30, T 1 S, R 5 E). Named on Blocksburg (1969) and Larabee Valley (1977) 7.5' quadrangles.

Barnes Creek [TRINITY]: *stream,* flows 1 mile to Mad River 7 miles south of Forest Glen (lat. 40°16'10" N, long. 123°19'40" W; near NE cor. sec. 25, T 2 S, R 7 E). Named on Forest Glen (1979) 7.5' quadrangle.

Barney Creek [HUMBOLDT]: *stream,* flows nearly 4 miles to Mosquito Creek 11.5 miles south of the settlement of Willow Creek (lat. 40°46'30" N, long. 123°37'30" W). Named on Grouse Mountain (1979) 7.5' quadrangle. Called Dirty Camp Creek on China Flat (1922) 15' quadrangle.

Barney Gulch [TRINITY]: *canyon,* drained by a stream that flows nearly 3 miles to East Fork of North Fork Trinity River 3.25 miles north of Helena (lat. 40°49'15" N, long. 123°07'25" W; at SW cor. sec. 4, T 34 N, R 11 W). Named on Helena (1951) 15' quadrangle. Called Noonan Gl. on United States Geological Survey's (1915) map.

Barney Meadow [MENDOCINO]: *area,* 17 miles northeast of Covelo (lat. 39°56'55" N, long. 123°00'45" W; sec. 7, T 24 N, R 10 W). Named on Covelo (1926) 15' quadrangle.

Barn Opening [MENDOCINO]: *area,* 8 miles west of Ornbaun Valley (lat. 38°55'50" N, long. 123°26'55" W; near N line sec. 5, T 12 N, R 14 W). Named on Ornbaun Valley (1960) 15' quadrangle.

Barnum Ridge [TRINITY]: *ridge,* south-trending, 4 miles long, 8 miles east of Burnt Ranch (lat. 40°48'45" N, long. 123°19'25" W). Named on Ironside Mountain (1951) 15' quadrangle.

Barrel Spring [LAKE]: *spring,* 3 miles north of Cold Spring Mountain (lat. 39°08'30" N, long. 122°28'45" W; near SW cor. sec. 13, T 15 N, R 6 W). Named on Wilbur Springs (1961) 15' quadrangle.

Barren Butte [DEL NORTE-HUMBOLDT]: *peak,* 13 miles east-southeast of Klamath Glen on Del Norte-Humboldt County line (lat. 41°25'05" N, long. 123°46'05" W). Altitude 4371 feet. Named on Blue Creek Mountain (1982) 7.5' quadrangle.

Barron Creek [TRINITY]: *stream,* flows 2.5 miles to New River 13 miles south-southeast of Salmon Mountain (lat. 41°00'20" N, long. 123°20'45" W). Named on Dees Peak (1978) and Trinity Mountain (1979) 7.5' quadrangles.

Barry Creek [TRINITY]: *stream,* flows 4.25 miles to Mad River 10.5 miles east of Kettenpom (lat. 40°11'30" N, long. 123°16'15" W; sec. 21, T 3 S, R 8 E). Named on Black Rock Mountain (1954) 15' quadrangle, and on

Shannon Butte (1967) 7.5' quadrangle.

Barry Ridge [HUMBOLDT]: *ridge,* generally east-trending, 1.25 miles long, 8 miles northwest of Lone Star Junction (lat. 40°43'20" N, long. 123°58' W). Named on Iagua Buttes (1979) 7.5' quadrangle. The name is for Ed Barry and Mary Barry, early settlers in the neighborhood (Turner, p. 13).

Bartlett Creek [LAKE]: *stream,* formed by the confluence of North Fork and South Fork, flows 6.5 miles to North Fork Cache Creek 10 miles north of Clearlake Oaks (lat. 39°10' N, long. 122°38'25" W; sec. 9, T 15 N, R 7 W). Named on Clearlake Oaks (1960) 15' quadrangle. Waring (p. 198) called the feature Allen Creek—Allen Springs settlement is along it. The stream also was called Middle Fork Cache Creek (Hoover, Rensch, and Rensch, p. 140). North Fork, which heads on Bartlett Mountain, is 3 miles long, and South Fork is 2.5 miles long; both forks are named on Clearlake Oaks (1960) 15' quadrangle, and on Bartlett Mountain (1958) 7.5' quadrangle.

Bartlett Flat [LAKE]: *area,* 11 miles north-northwest of Clearlake Oaks (lat. 39°10'45" N, long. 122°43'30" W); the place is along Bartlett Creek. Named on Clearlake Oaks (1960) 15' quadrangle.

Bartlett Mountain [LAKE]: *ridge,* generally south- to south-southeast-trending, 4 miles long, 7 miles east of the town of Upper Lake (lat. 39°09'45" N, long. 122°46'55" W). Named on Bartlett Mountain (1958) 7.5' quadrangle. Goodyear (1890a, p. 255) called the feature Bartlett's Ridge.

Bartlett Mountain Summit [LAKE]: *pass,* 7.5 miles east-southeast of the town of Upper Lake (lat. 39°08'05" N, long. 122°46'30" W; sec. 20, T 15 N, R 8 W). Named on Bartlett Mountain (1958) 7.5' quadrangle.

Bartlett Springs [LAKE]: *locality,* 11 miles north of Clearlake Oaks (lat. 39°11' N, long. 122°42'10" W; sec. 2, T 15 N, R 8 W); the place is along Bartlett Creek. Named on Clearlake Oaks (1960) 15' quadrangle. Postal authorities established Bartlett Springs post office in 1873 and discontinued it in 1935 (Frickstad, p. 63). Green Bartlett discovered springs at the place in 1869 and found that use of the water gave him relief from his rheumatism; he started a resort at the site and eventually had accommodations for more than 500 people (Bradley, p. 212-213). A small resort called Hoppins Springs was situated at the east boundary of the Bartlett Springs property; it consisted of two small springs and several cottages (Waring, p. 201). Postal authorities established Pences post office 12.5 miles east of Bartlett Springs in 1895 and discontinued it the same year; the name was for the operator of a resort (Salley, p. 169).

Bartlett's Ridge: see **Bartlett Mountain** [LAKE].

Barton Gulch [MENDOCINO]: *canyon,* drained by a stream that flows 2.25 miles to Navarro River nearly 4 miles north-northeast of Elk (lat. 39°10'45" N, long. 123°40'50" W; sec. 7, T 15 N, R 16 W). Named on Elk (1960) 7.5' quadrangle.

Basil: see **Redwood Valley** [MENDOCINO] (2).

Basin: see **The Basin** [HUMBOLDT].

Basin Creek [HUMBOLDT]: *stream,* flows nearly 4 miles to Eel River 4 miles west-southwest of Blocksburg (lat. 40°15'05" N, long. 123°42'05" W; near W line sec. 35, T 2 S, R 4 E). Named on Blocksburg (1969) 7.5' quadrangle.

Basin Gulch [TRINITY]: *canyon,* drained by a stream that flows nearly 2 miles to Rattlesnake Creek (2) 4.25 miles east-northeast of Forest Glen (lat. 40°24'25" N, long. 123°15'25" W; sec. 31, T 30 N, R 12 W). Named on Naufus Creek (1979) 7.5' quadrangle.

Basin Gulch Creek: see **Glade Creek** [TRINITY].

Basin Ridge [LAKE]: *ridge,* south- to southeast-trending, 0.5 mile long, 9 miles west of Lakeport (lat. 39°04' N, long. 123°04'40" W); the ridge is southwest of Red Mountain Basin. Named on Purdys Gardens (1958) 7.5' quadrangle.

Baton Flat [LAKE]: *area,* 7 miles northeast of the town of Lower Lake along Cache Creek (lat. 38°58'40" N, long. 122°31' W). Named on Lower Lake (1958) 7.5' quadrangle.

Battery Point [DEL NORTE]: *promontory,* along the coast at Crescent City (lat. 41°44'50" N, long. 124°12'05" W). Named on Sister Rocks (1966) 7.5' quadrangle. Three brass cannons salvaged from the steamer *America* were placed at the point in 1855 (Hoover, Rensch, and Rensch, p. 71).

Battle Creek [TRINITY]:

(1) *stream,* flows nearly 4 miles to Eagle Creek (1) 8 miles southeast of Salmon Mountain (lat. 41°05'05" N, long. 123°19'15" W). Named on Dees Peak (1978) 7.5' quadrangle.

(2) *stream,* flows 3.5 miles to Coffee Creek 5 miles west-southwest of Billys Peak (1) (lat. 41°06'45" N, long. 122°51'45" W; sec. 35, T 38 N, R 9 W); the stream heads near Battle Mountain. Named on Coffee Creek (1955) 15' quadrangle.

Battle Island: see **Bloody Island** [LAKE].

Battle Mountain [TRINITY]: *peak,* about 7 miles southwest of Billys Peak (1) (lat. 41°04'20" N, long. 122°52'20" W; near NE cor. sec. 15, T 37 N, R 9 W). Altitude 7919 feet. Named on Coffee Creek (1955) 15' quadrangle.

Bauer: see **Camp Bauer** [HUMBOLDT].

Baxter Gulch [TRINITY]:

(1) *canyon,* drained by a stream that flows 2.5 miles to North Fork Trinity River 4.5 miles north-northwest of Helena (lat. 40°50' N, long. 123°09'30" W; sec. 6, T 34 N, R 11 W). Named on Helena (1951) 15' quadrangle.

(2) *canyon,* drained by a stream that flows 2.25 miles to Rush Creek 5.5 miles northeast of Weaverville (lat. 40°46'45" N, long. 122°51'15" W; near N line sec. 26, T 34 N, R 9 W). Named on Trinity Dam (1950) 15' quadrangle.

Baxter Ridge [TRINITY]: *ridge,* south-southeast-trending, 2 miles long, 6 miles northeast of Weaverville (lat. 40°47'45" N, long. 122°52' W); the ridge is west of Baxter Gulch (2). Named on Trinity Dam (1950) 15' quadrangle.

Baylis Point [LAKE]: *promontory,* 5 miles northwest of the town of Lower Lake along Clear Lake (lat. 38°57'05" N, long. 122°41'15" W; on E line sec. 25, T 13 N, R 8 W). Named on Clearlake Highlands (1958) 7.5' quadrangle.

Bay of the Indians: see **Humboldt Bay** [HUMBOLDT].

Bayside [HUMBOLDT]: *village,* 2.25 miles south-southeast of Arcata (lat. 40°50'35" N, long. 124°03'45" W; sec. 3, 4, T 5 N, R 21 E). Named on Arcata South (1959) 7.5' quadrangle. Postal authorities established Bayside post office in 1886 (Frickstad, p. 41).

Bay View [HUMBOLDT]: *district,* 2.5 miles south-southwest of downtown Eureka (lat. 40°46'20" N, long. 124°10'55" W; sec. 33, T 5 N, R 1 W). Named on Eureka (1958) 7.5' quadrangle. Postal authorities established Bayview post office in 1925 and discontinued it in 1935 (Frickstad, p. 41).

Beach Creek [HUMBOLDT]:

(1) *stream,* flows 1.25 miles to the sea 5 miles north of Trinidad (lat. 41°08' N, long. 124°09'35" W; sec. 27, T 9 N, R 1 W). Named on Trinidad (1966) 7.5' quadrangle.

(2) *stream,* flows 4.25 miles to Maple Creek (1) 5.5 miles east-northeast of Trinidad (lat. 41°05'15" N, long. 124°02'45" W; near S line sec. 10, T 8 N, R 1 E). Named on Crannell (1966) 7.5' quadrangle.

Beach Rock [HUMBOLDT]: *rock,* 0.5 mile southeast of Cape Mendocino, and 350 feet offshore (lat. 40°25'55" N, long. 124°24'10" W; sec. 34, T 1 N, R 3 W). Named on Cape Mendocino (1969) 7.5' quadrangle.

Beadstead: see **The Bedstead** [TRINITY].

Beakban Island [LAKE]: *island,* 450 feet long, 3.25 miles north-northwest of the town of Lower Lake, and 250 feet offshore in Clear Lake (lat. 38°57'05" N, long. 122°38'35" W). Named on Clearlake Highlands (1958) 7.5' quadrangle.

Beal Creek [MENDOCINO]: *stream,* flows 1 mile to Little River 2.25 miles south-southeast of Mendocino (lat. 39°16'35" N, long. 123°47'15" W; near W line sec. 5, T 16 N, R 17 W). Named on Mendocino (1960) 7.5' quadrangle.

Beal's Landing: see **Westport** [MENDOCINO].

Bean: see **Asa Bean Crossing** [TRINITY]; **Asa Bean Flat** [TRINITY]; **Asa Bean Ridge** [MENDOCINO].

Bean Canyon [LAKE]: *canyon,* drained by a stream that flows 3 miles to Stanton Creek 11 miles northeast of Clearlake Oaks (lat. 39°08'20" N, long. 122°32'10" W; near SW cor. sec. 16, T 15 N, R 6 W). Named on Clearlake Oaks (1960) 15' quadrangle.

Bean Creek [MENDOCINO]: *stream,* flows 2 miles to Tomki Creek 6 miles east-southeast of Longvale (lat. 39°31'40" N, long. 123°19'20" W; sec. 5, T 19 N, R 13 W). Named on Willis Ridge (1966) 7.5' quadrangle.

Bean Glade [LAKE]: *area,* 12 miles northeast of Clearlake Oaks (lat. 39°07'50" N, long. 122°30'20" W; sec. 22, T 15 N, R 6 W); the place is near the head of Bean Canyon. Named on Clearlake Oaks (1960) 15' quadrangle.

Bean Gulch [TRINITY]: *canyon,* drained by a stream that flows 1.5 miles to Hayfork Creek 1 mile west-southwest of Hayfork (lat. 40°33' N, long. 123°12' W; sec. 10, T 31 N, R 12 W). Named on Hayfork (1951) 15' quadrangle.

Bean Rock [MENDOCINO]: *relief feature,* 6 miles north of Hull Rock (lat. 39°36'25" N, long. 122°55'40" W; sec. 11, T 20 N, R 10 W). Named on Hull Mountain (1967) 7.5' quadrangle.

Bear Basin [DEL NORTE]: *relief feature,* 6.25 miles south-southwest of Broken Rib Mountain (lat. 41°48'10" N, long. 123°44'05" W). Named on Devils Punchbowl (1981) 7.5' quadrangle.

Bear Basin [TRINITY]: *relief feature,* 17 miles north of Weaverville (lat. 40°58'15" N, long. 122°52'15" W); the feature is along upper reaches of Bear Creek (3). Named on Trinity Dam (1950) 15' quadrangle.

Bear Basin: see **Little Bear Basin** [DEL NORTE].

Bear Basin Butte [DEL NORTE]: *peak,* 6 miles south-southwest of Broken Rib Mountain (lat. 41°48'35" N, long. 123°44'25" W); the peak is 0.5 mile northwest of Bear Basin. Altitude 5292 feet. Named on Devils Punchbowl (1981) 7.5' quadrangle.

Bear Buttes [HUMBOLDT]: *ridge,* east-trending, less than 1 mile long, 3.25 miles west-south west of Phillipsville (lat. 40°10'55" N, long. 123°50'05" W). Named on Miranda (1970) 7.5' quadrangle.

Bear Canyon [HUMBOLDT]: *canyon,* drained by a stream that flows 2.5 miles to South Fork Eel River 0.5 mile north of Garberville (lat. 40°06'25" N, long. 123°47'45" W; at S line sec. 13, T 4 S, R 3 E). Named on Garberville (1970) 7.5' quadrangle.

Bear Canyon [MENDOCINO]: *canyon,* drained by a stream that flows 3.5 miles to North Fork Eel River 8 miles northeast of Spyrock (2) (lat. 39°57'30" N, long. 123°20'05" W). Named on Mina (1967) 7.5' quadrangle.

Bear Canyon [TRINITY]: *canyon,* drained by a stream that flows nearly 3 miles to Kekawaka Creek 8 miles south-southeast of Kettenpom (lat. 40°02'50" N, long. 123°24'15" W; at NE cor. sec. 8, T 5 S, R 7 E). Named on Lake Mountain (1967) 7.5' quadrangle.

Bear Canyon Creek [LAKE]: *stream,* flows nearly 2 miles to Anderson Creek 3 miles south-southeast of Whispering Pines (lat. 38°46'30" N, long. 122°41'15" W; sec. 25, T 11 N, R 8 W). Named on Whispering Pines (1958) 7.5' quadrangle.

Bear Creek [DEL NORTE]: *stream,* flows 2.5 miles to Diamond Creek 8.5 miles north-northeast of Gasquet (lat. 41°57'35" N, long. 123°55'20" W; at SE cor. sec. 10, T 18 N, R 2 E). Named on Gasquet (1951) 15' quadrangle.

Bear Creek [HUMBOLDT]:

(1) *stream,* flows 5 miles to Klamath River nearly 5 miles northwest of Johnsons (lat. 41°24'10" N, long. 123°55'45" W; sec. 27, T 12 N, R 2 E). Named on Ah Pah Ridge (1983) and Blue Creek Mountain (1982) 7.5' quadrangles.

(2) *stream,* flows 1 mile to Maple Creek (2) 8.5 miles southeast of the town of Blue Lake (lat. 40°47'55" N, long. 123°52'05" W; sec. 20, T 5 N, R 3 E). Named on Korbel (1979) and Maple Creek (1977) 7.5' quadrangles.

(3) *stream,* flows 3.5 miles to Mad River 4.5 miles southeast of Showers Mountain (lat. 40°32'10" N, long. 123°38' W; sec. 20, T 2 N, R 5 E). Named on Showers Mountain (1978) 7.5' quadrangle.

(4) *stream,* flows 5.25 miles to Eel River 2.5 miles northwest of Redcrest (lat. 40°25'50" N, long. 123°58'50" W; at N line sec. 32, T 1 N, R 2 E). Named on Redcrest (1969) and Scotia (1970) 7.5' quadrangles. South Fork enters from the south 7.5 miles southeast of Scotia and is nearly 1 mile long. West Fork enters from the west 7.5 miles southeast of Scotia and is 1 mile long. Both forks are named on Scotia (1970) 7.5' quadrangle.

(5) *stream,* flows 2.5 miles to Little Van Duzen River 6 miles northeast of Blocksburg (lat. 40°21'05" N, long. 123°35'20" W; sec. 27, T 1 S, R 5 E). Named on Black Lassic (1979) 7.5' quadrangle.

(6) *stream,* flows 1 mile to Mattole River 3.5 miles southwest of Petrolia (lat. 40°17'20" N, long. 124°20'05" W; near S line sec. 18, T 2 S, R 2 W). Named on Petrolia (1969) 7.5' quadrangle.

(7) *stream,* formed by the confluence of North Fork and South Fork, flows 6.5 miles to Mattole River 11 miles west of Garberville (lat. 40°08'05" N, long. 123°59'45" W; at S line sec. 6, T 4 S, R 2 E). Named on Ettersburg (1969), Honeydew (1970), and Shelter Cove (1969) 7.5' quadrangles. North Fork is 4.25 miles long and is named on Honeydew (1970) 7.5' quadrangle. South Fork is 10 miles long and is named on Briceland (1969), Honeydew (1970), and Shelter Cove (1969) 7.5' quadrangles.

(8) *stream,* flows 4 miles to Grouse Creek (2) 7.25 miles east of Board Camp Mountain (lat. 40°42'20" N, long. 123°35'20" W). Named on Sims Mountain (1979) 7.5' quadrangle.

Bear Creek [LAKE]:

(1) *stream,* flows 7.5 miles to Rice Fork 4 miles west-southwest of Potato Hill (lat. 39°19'30" N, long. 122°52'10" W; sec. 16, T 17 N, R 9 W). Named on Potato Hill (1967) 7.5' quadrangle.

(2) *stream,* flows 2.5 miles to West Fork Middle Creek 4.25 miles southwest of Three Crossings (lat. 39°16'15" N, long. 122°58'30" W; sec. 4, T 16 N, R 10 W). Named on Elk Mountain (1967) and Upper Lake (1958) 7.5' quadrangles.

Bear Creek [MENDOCINO]:

(1) *stream,* flows 3 miles to Middle Fork Eel River 15 miles east-northeast of Covelo (lat. 39°54'35" N, long. 123°00'35" W; sec. 30, T 24 N, R 10 W). Named on Buck Rock (1967) and Leech Lake Mountain (1966) 7.5' quadrangles.

(2) *stream,* flows 2.5 miles to Usal Creek 8 miles south-southwest of Piercy (lat. 39°51'45" N, long. 123°50'30" W). Named on Hales Grove (1970) and Piercy (1969) 7.5' quadrangles.

(3) *stream,* flows nearly 2 miles to Hollow Tree Creek 13 miles south of Piercy (lat. 39°47'10" N, long. 123°45' W; sec. 4, T 22 N, R 17 W). Named on Hales Grove (1970) 7.5' quadrangle.

(4) *stream,* flows nearly 5 miles to Elk Creek 8 miles east-southeast of Eden Valley (lat. 39°34'45" N, long. 123°02'45" W). Named on Hull Mountain (1967) and Sanhedrin Mountain (1966) 7.5' quadrangles.

(5) *stream,* flows nearly 2 miles to South Fork Eel River 2 miles southeast of Branscomb (lat. 39°38'10" N, long. 123°35'40" W; near N line sec. 36, T 21 N, R 16 W). Named on Cahto Peak (1967) 7.5' quadrangle. Called Taylor Creek on Branscomb (1951) 15' quadrangle, where present Taylor Creek is called Bear Creek.

(6) *stream,* flows 2.5 miles to South Branch of North Fork Navarro River 10.5 miles north-northwest of Boonville (lat. 39°08'55" N, long. 123°26'25" W; sec. 19, T 15 N, R 14 W). Named on Boonville (1959) 15' quadrangle.

(7) *stream,* flows 2 miles to Robinson Creek (2) 7 miles southwest of Ornbaun Valley (lat. 38°50'50" N, long. 123°24'05" W; near NW cor. sec. 35, T 12 N, R 14 W). Named on Ornbaun Valley (1960) 15' quadrangle. Present Robinson Creek (2) is called Bear Creek on Ornbaun (1944) 15' quadrangle.

Bear Creek [TRINITY]:

(1) *stream,* flows 4 miles to join High Camp Creek and form Trinity River 4 miles south-southeast of China Mountain, which is in Siskiyou County (lat. 41°19'30" N, long. 122°33'10" W; sec. 16, T 40 N, R 6 W). Named on China Mountain (1955) 15' quadrangle.

(2) *stream,* flows 4 miles to Trinity River 13 miles north of Trinity Center (lat. 41°11'40" N, long. 122°39' W; sec. 34, T 39 N, R 7 W); the stream heads at Big Bear Lake. Named on Bonanza King (1955) 15' quadrangle.

(3) *stream,* flows 4 miles to Swift Creek (1) 10 miles south-southwest of Billys Peak (1) (lat. 41°00'15" N, long. 122°50'25" W; sec. 1, T 36 N, R 9 W). Named on Trinity Dam (1950) 15' quadrangle.

(4) *stream,* flows 2.5 miles to Canyon Creek (1) 9.5 miles northeast of Helena (lat. 40°53'20" N, long. 123°01'25" W). Named on Helena (1951) 15' quadrangle.

(5) *stream,* flows 2 miles to Hayfork Creek 3.25 miles east-northeast of Hyampom (lat. 40°37'45" N, long. 123°23'15" W; near NE cor. sec. 21, T 3 N, R 7 E). Named on Hyampom (1951) 15' quadrangle.

(6) *stream,* flows 5.5 miles to Hayfork Creek 8.5 miles east of Hyampom (lat. 40°36'15" N, long. 123°17' W; at S line sec. 28, T 3 N, R 8 E). Named on Hayfork (1951) and Hyampom (1951) 15' quadrangles. Called Little Cr. on United States Geological Survey's (1915) map.

Bear Creek: see **Bear Gulch** [TRINITY] (2); **Grapevine Creek** [HUMBOLDT-TRINITY]; **Hardy Creek** [MENDOCINO]; **Little Bear Creek** [MENDOCINO]; **Robinson Creek** [MENDOCINO] (2).

Bear Creek Cabin [TRINITY]: *locality,* 5 miles southeast of China Mountain, which is in Siskiyou County (lat. 41°19'05" N, long. 122°31'30" W; sec. 23, T 40 N, R 6 W); the place is along Bear Creek (1). Named on China Mountain (1955) 15' quadrangle.

Bear Creek Campground [LAKE]: *locality,* 2.5 miles southwest of Potato Hill (lat. 39°19'20" N, long. 122°50'10" W; near S line sec. 14, T 17 N, R 9 W); the place is along Bear Creek (1). Named on Potato Hill (1967) 7.5' quadrangle.

Bear Cub [DEL NORTE]: *peak,* 2.5 miles east of Broken Rib Mountain (lat. 41°53'30" N, long. 123°36'35" W); the peak is less than 1 mile southwest of Polar Bear Mountain. Altitude 6028 feet. Named on Polar Bear Mountain (1982) 7.5' quadrangle.

Bear Flat [TRINITY]: *area,* 9.5 miles northeast of Trinity Center along East Fork Trinity River (lat. 40°07' N, long. 122°34'15" W; at NW cor. sec. 33, T 38 N, R 6 W). Named on Bonanza King (1955) 15' quadrangle.

Bear Gulch [HUMBOLDT]: *canyon,* drained by a stream that flows nearly 2 miles to the sea 6.25 miles west-southwest of Ferndale (lat. 40°32'15" N, long. 124°22'05" W; sec. 23, T 2 N, R 3 W). Named on Ferndale (1959) 7.5' quadrangle.

Bear Gulch [LAKE]: *canyon,* drained by a stream that flows 2 miles to Lake Pillsbury 0.5 mile west-northwest of Bear Mountain (lat. 39°24'35" N, long. 122°54'45" W). Named on Lake Pillsbury (1967) 7.5' quadrangle.

Bear Gulch [MENDOCINO]: *canyon,* drained by a stream that flows 1 mile to South Fork Noyo River 9.5 miles north-northwest of Comptche (lat. 39°23'05" N, long. 123°40'20" W; at N line sec. 32, T 18 N, R 16 W). Named on Comptche (1960) 15' quadrangle.

Bear Gulch [TRINITY]:

(1) *canyon,* drained by a stream that flows 2 miles to Stuart Fork 17 miles north of Weaverville (lat. 40°58'25" N, long. 122°57'25" W; near SE cor. sec. 13, T 36 N, R 10 W). Named on Trinity Dam (1950) 15' quadrangle.

(2) *canyon,* drained by a stream that flows 2.25 miles to Clair Engle Lake 9 miles north-northeast of Weaverville (lat. 40°51'05" N, long. 122°52'15" W; sec. 34, T 35 N, R 9 W). Named on Trinity Dam (1950) 15' quadrangle. United States Board on Geographic Names (1983d, p. 5) approved the name "Cummings Creek" for the stream in the canyon, and rejected the names "Bear Creek" and "Bear Gulch." At the same time, the Board (p. 4) approved the name "Bear Gulch" for a nearby ravine, 1 mile long, that trends northeast to Clair Engle Lake (lat. 40°51'16" N, long. 122°52'31" W; sec. 34, T 35 N, R 9 W).

(3) *canyon,* drained by a stream that flows 3.5 miles to Trinity River 12.5 miles northeast of Weaverville (lat. 40°50'50" N, long. 122°44'35" W; sec. 35, T 35 N, R 8 W). Named on Schell Mountain (1950) 15' quadrangle.

(4) *canyon,* drained by a stream that flows 1.5 miles to West Weaver Creek 4 miles northwest of Weaverville (lat. 40°46'20" N, long. 122°58'45" W; sec. 27, T 34 N, R 10 W). Named on Trinity Dam (1950) 15' quadrangle.

(5) *canyon,* drained by a stream that flows less than 1 mile to Trinity River 10 miles east-northeast of Weaverville (lat. 40°47'15" N, long. 122°45'45" W; sec. 22, T 34 N, R 8 W). Named on Schell Mountain (1950) and Trinity Dam (1950) 15' quadrangles.

(6) *canyon,* drained by a stream that flows 2.25 miles to Big East Fork Canyon Creek (1) 8 miles northeast of Helena (lat. 40°51' N, long. 123°00'55" W). Named on Helena (1951) and Trinity Dam (1950) 15' quadrangles.

Bear Gulch: see **Big Bear Gulch** [TRINITY]; **Little Bear Gulch** [TRINITY].

Bear Harbor [MENDOCINO]: *embayment,* 8.5 mile southwest of Piercy (lat. 39°54'45" N, long. 123°56'25" W; sec. 26, T 24 N, R 19 W). Named on Bear Harbor (1969) 7.5' quadrangle. Piercy (1950) 15' quadrangle has the name for a locality at the place.

Bear Haven Creek [MENDOCINO]: *stream,* flows 5.25 miles to Middle Fork Ten Mile River 7.5 miles south-southwest of Branscomb (lat. 39°33'20" N, long. 123°40'45" W; sec. 31, T 20 N, R 16 W). Named on Dutchmans Knoll (1966) 7.5' quadrangle. South Fork enters 0.5 mile upstream from the mouth of the main creek; it is nearly 2 miles long and is named on Dutchmans Knoll (1966) 7.5' quadrangle.

Bear Haven Creek: see **Little Bear Haven Creek** [MENDOCINO].

Bear Lake [TRINITY]: *intermittent lake,* 600 feet long, 5.5 miles north of Kettenpom (lat. 40°14'20" N, long. 123°28'15" W; at N line sec. 2, T 3 S, R 6 E). Named on Kettenpom (1955) 15' quadrangle.

Bear Lake: see **Big Bear Lake** [TRINITY]; **Foster Lake** [TRINITY]; **Little Bear Lake** [TRINITY].

Bear Lake Camp [TRINITY]: *locality,* 5 miles north of Kettenpom (lat. 40°13'55" N, long. 123°27'55" W; sec. 2, T 3 S, R 6 E); the place is 0.5 mile southeast of Bear Lake. Named on Zenia (1967) 7.5' quadrangle, which does not show Bear Lake.

Bear Mountain [DEL NORTE]: *peak,* 4.25 miles southwest of Preston Peak on Del Norte-Siskiyou County line (lat. 41°47'45" N, long. 123°40'15" W). Altitude 6411 feet. Named on Devils Punchbowl (1981) 7.5' quadrangle.

Bear Mountain [LAKE]: *peak,* 25 miles north of Lakeport (lat. 39°24'25" N, long. 122°54' W). Altitude 2705 feet. Named on Lake Pillsbury (1967) 7.5' quadrangle.

Bear Paw [DEL NORTE]: *ridge,* 2 miles long, 7.25 miles south of Broken Rib Mountain (lat. 41°47'10" N, long. 123°40'15" W); the ridge is less than 1 mile south of Bear Mountain. Named on Devils Punchbowl (1981) 7.5' quadrangle. United States Board on Geographic Names (1965d, p. 7) noted that the ridge is linked to Bear Mountain as a paw is linked to a bear.

Bear Peak [LAKE]: *peak,* 3.25 miles southwest of Three Crossings along Blue Creek (lat. 39°15'25" N, long. 122°58'50" W; sec. 9, T 16 N, R 10 W). Altitude 3242 feet. Named on Elk Mountain (1967) 7.5' quadrangle.

Bear Pen Canyon [MENDOCINO]: *canyon,* drained by a stream that flows nearly 3 miles to Burger Creek 3.5 miles east of Laytonville (lat. 39°41'40" N, long. 123°24'45" W). Named on Laytonville (1967) 7.5' quadrangle.

Bear Pen Creek [MENDOCINO]:

(1) *stream,* flows nearly 4 miles to South Fork Eel River 2.25 miles south-southeast of Piercy (lat. 39°56'10" N, long. 123°46'35" W; near SE cor. sec. 7, T 24 N, R 17 W). Named on Piercy (1969) and Sanhedrin Mountain (1966) 7.5' quadrangles.

(2) *stream,* flows less than 1 mile to Hollow Tree Creek 8.5 miles northwest of Branscomb (lat. 39°44'50" N, long. 123°43'20" W; sec. 23, T 22 N, R 17 W). Named on Lincoln Ridge (1966) 7.5' quadrangle.

(3) *stream,* flows nearly 4 miles to Garcia Creek 8.5 miles south of Eden Valley (lat. 39°30'10" N, long. 123°09'45" W; sec. 14, T 19 N, R 12 W). Named on Brushy Mountain (1966) and Sanhedrin Mountain (1966) 7.5' quadrangles.

Bear Pen Flat [HUMBOLDT]: *area,* 8 miles north-northeast of Johnsons (lat. 41°27'35" N, long. 123°49'10" W). Named on Blue Creek Mountain (1982) 7.5' quadrangle.

Bear Pen Ridge [MENDOCINO]: *ridge,* generally north-northwest-trending, 2.5 miles long, 3.5 miles east-northeast of Elk (lat. 39°09'15" N, long. 123°39'30" W). Named on Elk (1960) 7.5' quadrangle.

Bear Prairie [HUMBOLDT]: *area,* 6.5 miles north-northwest of Coyote Peak (lat. 41°13'10" N, long. 123°55'15" W; around SW cor. sec. 26, T 10 N, R 2 E). Named on Bald Hills (1982) 7.5' quadrangle.

Bear Prairie: see **Little Bear Prairie** [HUMBOLDT].

Bear Ridge: see **Bunker Hill** [HUMBOLDT].

Bear River [HUMBOLDT]: *stream,* flows 26 miles to the sea 2.5 miles north-northeast of Cape Mendocino (lat. 40°28'35" N, long. 124°23'20" W; at S line sec. 10, T 1 N, R 3 W). Named on Bull Creek (1969), Cape Mendocino (1969), Capetown (1969), Scotia (1970), and Taylor Peak (1969) 7.5' quadrangles. The name was given after a grizzly bear mangled Lewis K. Wood of the Gregg party near the stream in 1850 (Gudde, 1949, p. 26). South Fork enters from the south 6.5 miles east-southeast of Cape Mendocino; it is 8 miles long and is named on Capetown (1969) and Taylor Peak (1969) 7.5' quadrangles.

Bear River Range: see **Bear River Ridge** [HUMBOLDT].

Bear River Ridge [HUMBOLDT]: *ridge,* extends for 16 miles on the north side of Bear River from the coast to near Scotia. Named on Capetown (1969), Ferndale (1959), and Taylor Peak (1969) 7.5' quadrangles. Chase (p. 292) referred to Bear River Range.

Bear Rock: see **Little Bear Rock** [MENDOCINO].

Bearskin Canyon [MENDOCINO]: *canyon,* drained by a stream that flows 1.5 miles to Tomki Creek 7.25 miles north-northwest of the town of Potter Valley (lat. 39°24'55" N, long. 123°10' W; at E line sec. 15, T 18 N, R 12 W). Named on Potter Valley (1960) 15' quadrangle.

Bear Spring [LAKE]: *spring,* 5 miles south-southeast of Wilson Valley (2) (lat. 38°54'30" N, long. 122°25'50" W). Named on Wilson Valley (1958) 7.5' quadrangle.

Beartooth Mountain [TRINITY]: *peak,* 9.5 miles northeast of Burnt Ranch (lat. 40°55'15" N, long. 123°21'50" W). Altitude 4645 feet. Named on Ironside Mountain (1951) 15' quadrangle.

Bear Trap Creek [HUMBOLDT]: *stream,* flows 3 miles to Honeydew Creek 1 mile south-southeast of Honeydew (lat. 40°13'55" N, long. 124°06'55" W; near SW cor. sec. 6, T 3 S, R 1 E); the stream is northwest of Bear Trap Ridge. Named on Honeydew (1970) and Shubrick Peak (1969) 7.5' quadrangles.

Beartrap Creek [MENDOCINO]: *stream,* flows 1.5 miles to Rancheria Creek (2) 10 miles northwest of Ornbaun Valley (lat. 39°00' N, long. 123°26'50" W; sec. 7, T 13 N, R 14 W). Named on Ornbaun Valley (1960) 15' quadrangle.

Bear Trap Gulch [TRINITY]: *canyon,* drained by a stream that flows 1.5 miles to Reading Creek 13 miles south-southeast of Weaverville (lat. 40°33'10" N, long. 122°51'15" W; sec. 11, T 31 N, R 9 W). Named on Weaverville (1950) 15' quadrangle.

Bear Trap Ridge [HUMBOLDT]: *ridge,* east-northeast- to north-northeast-trending, 4.25 miles long, center 2.5 miles south-southwest of Honeydew (lat. 40°12'40" N, long. 124°08'20" W). Named on Honeydew (1970) and Shubrick Peak (1969) 7.5' quadrangles.

Bear Trap Spring [MENDOCINO]: *spring,* 11.5 miles northeast of Covelo (lat. 39°54'05" N, long. 123°05' W; near SE cor. sec. 28, T 24 N, R 11 W). Named on Leech Lake Mountain (1966) 7.5' quadrangle.

Bear Valley Meadows Camp [TRINITY]: *locality,* 15 miles north of Helena (lat. 40°59'05" N, long. 123°04'25" W). Named on Helena (1951) 15' quadrangle.

Bear Wallow [DEL NORTE]: *water feature,* 4.5 miles north-northeast of Broken Rib Mountain (lat. 41°57'05" N, long. 123°39'10" W). Named on Broken Rib Mountain (1982) 7.5' quadrangle.

Bear Wallow [MENDOCINO]: *relief feature,* 12 miles northeast of Covelo (lat. 39°55'40" N, long. 123°06'30" W; at S line sec. 17, T 24 N, R 11 W). Named on Leech Lake Mountain (1966) 7.5' quadrangle.

Bear Wallow Camp [TRINITY]:

(1) *locality,* 13 miles north-northwest of Helena (lat. 40°57'30" N, long. 123°10'50" W); the place is at Bear Wallow Meadows. Named on Helena (1951) 15' quadrangle.

(2) *locality,* 6 miles north-northwest of Kettenpom (lat. 40°14'40" N, long. 123°29'05" W; sec. 34, T 2 S, R 6 E). Named on Zenia (1967) 7.5' quadrangle.

Bearwallow Camp [TRINITY]: *locality,* 4.5 miles south of Black Rock Mountain (lat. 40°08'30" N, long. 123°00'50" W; sec. 32, T 27 N, R 10 W). Named on Black Rock Mountain (1954) 15' quadrangle.

Bear Wallow Creek [MENDOCINO]:

(1) *stream,* flows 2.25 miles to Huckleberry Creek 7.5 miles northwest of Branscomb (lat. 39°43'55" N, long. 123°43'25" W; near W line sec. 26, T 22 N, R 17 W). Named on Lincoln Ridge (1966) 7.5' quadrangle.

(2) *stream,* flows 2.5 miles to Rancheria Creek (2) 9 miles northwest of Ornbaun Valley (lat. 38°59'40" N, long. 123°26' W; near SW cor. sec. 8, T 13 N, R 14 W). Named on Boonville (1959) and Ornbaun Valley (1960) 15' quadrangles.

Bear Wallow Creek [TRINITY]: *stream,* flows 3.5 miles to Plummer Creek 8 miles north-northwest of Forest Glen (lat. 40°28'40" N, long. 123°23'20" W; sec. 9, T 1 N, R 7 E). Named on Naufus Creek (1979) and Sportshaven (1973) 7.5' quadrangles.

Bear Wallow Creek: see **Little Bear Wallow Creek** [MENDOCINO]; **Little Bear Wallow Creek** [TRINITY].

Bear Wallow Gulch [HUMBOLDT]: *canyon,* drained by a stream that flows nearly 1 mile to Red Cap Creek 9.5 miles east-northeast of Weitchpec (lat. 41°14'30" N, long. 123°32'30" W). Named on Hopkins Butte (1979) 7.5' quadrangle.

Bear Wallow Meadow [TRINITY]: *area,* partly marsh, 5.5 miles north-northwest of Forest Glen (lat. 40°27'05" N, long. 123°21' W; sec. 23, T 1 N, R 7 E); the place is at the head of a branch of Bear Wallow Creek. Named on Naufus Creek (1979) 7.5' quadrangle.

Bear Wallow Meadow: see **Little Bear Wallow Meadow** [TRINITY].

Bear Wallow Meadows [TRINITY]: *area,* 13 miles north-northwest of Helena (lat. 40°57'35" N, long. 123°11' W). Named on Helena (1951) 15' quadrangle.

Bear Wallow Mountain [TRINITY]: *ridge,* north-northwest-trending, 1 mile long, 6 miles north-northwest of Forest Glen (lat. 40°26'40" N, long. 123°23'20" W; on S line sec. 21, T 1 N, R 7 E). Named on Sportshaven (1973) 7.5' quadrangle.

Bearwallow Ridge [HUMBOLDT]: *ridge,* north-northwest- to northwest-trending, 2 miles long, 4 miles south of Honeydew (lat. 40°11'15" N, long. 124°07' W). Named on Honeydew (1970) and Shubrick Peak (1969) 7.5' quadrangles.

Bear Wallows [DEL NORTE]: *lakes,* largest 250 feet long, 1.5 miles west-northwest of Harrington Mountain (lat. 41°40'55" N, long. 123°42'55" W). Named on Prescott Mountain (1981) 7.5' quadrangle.

Beasley Creek [MENDOCINO]: *stream,* flows 1 mile to Rancheria Creek (2) 2.25 miles north-northwest of Ornbaun Valley (lat. 38°56'40" N, long. 123°19'15" W; near W line sec. 32, T 13 N, R 13 W). Named on Ornbaun Valley (1960) 15' quadrangle.

Beatrice [HUMBOLDT]: *locality,* 4 miles south of Fields Landing along Salmon Creek (1) (lat. 40°40'10" N, long. 124°12'05" W; sec. 5, T 3 N, R 1 W). Named on Fields Landing (1959) 7.5' quadrangle. Postal authorities established Beatrice post office in 1884 and discontinued it in 1955 (Frickstad, p. 41). The place was called Salmon Creek before the post office opened and the name was changed to Beatrice for Mrs. Beatrice White, first postmaster (Gudde, 1949, p. 26).

Beatty Creek [HUMBOLDT]: *stream,* flows 3 miles to Eel River 8.5 miles east of Weott (lat. 40°18'50" N, long. 123°45'45" W; near S line sec. 6, T 2 S, R 4 E). Named on Blocksburg (1969) and Myers Flat (1969) 7.5' quadrangles.

Beaver Butte [HUMBOLDT]: *peak,* 8 miles south of Coyote Peak (lat. 41°00'55" N, long. 123°50'55" W; at NW cor. sec. 9, T 7 N, R 3 E). Altitude 2614 feet. Named on Hupa Mountain (1982) 7.5' quadrangle.

Beaver Creek [HUMBOLDT]:

(1) *stream,* flows 1.5 miles to Redwood Creek (1) 8 miles south of Coyote Peak (lat. 41°01'10" N, long. 123°52'10" W; near SE cor. sec. 6, T 7 N, R 3 E); the stream heads on Beaver Ridge. Named on Hupa Mountain (1982) 7.5' quadrangle.

(2) *stream,* flows 1.5 miles to Trinity River 4 miles north-northwest of Hoopa (lat. 41°06'05" N, long. 123°42'35" W; sec. 3, T 8 N, R 4 E). Named on Hoopa (1979) 7.5' quadrangle.

Beaver Creek [MENDOCINO]: *stream,* flows nearly 7 miles to Middle Fork Eel River 16 miles northeast of Covelo (lat. 39°56' N, long. 123°00'05" W; near W line sec. 17, T 24 N, R 10 W). Named on Buck Rock (1967) and Leech Lake Mountain (1966) 7.5' quadrangles.

Beaver Flat [HUMBOLDT]: *area,* 8 miles south of Coyote Peak (lat. 41°01'50" N, long. 123°52'10" W); the place is north of the mouth of Beaver Creek (1). Named on Hupa Mountain (1982) 7.5' quadrangle.

Beaver Ridge [HUMBOLDT]: *ridge,* generally north-trending, 4 miles long, 9 miles south of Coyote Peak (lat. 41°00'40" N, long. 123°49'25" W). Named on Hupa Mountain (1982) and Lord-Ellis Summit (1973) 7.5' quadrangles.

Beaver Slide [TRINITY]: *relief feature,* 8 miles east-northeast of Kettenpom (lat. 40°12' N, long. 123°19' W; sec. 18, T 3 S, R 8 E). Named on Shannon Butte (1967) 7.5' quadrangle.

Becker Racetrack [HUMBOLDT]: *area,* 8 miles east of Showers Mountain on Henry Ridge (lat. 40°34'15" N, long. 123°33'05" W; sec. 12, T 2 N, R 5 E). Named on Blake Mountain (1979) 7.5' quadrangle.

Becker Ridge [HUMBOLDT]: *ridge,* generally east-trending, 1.25 miles long, 5.5 miles east of Showers Mountain (lat. 40°34'15" N, long. 123°35'30" W). Named on Blake Mountain (1979) 7.5' quadrangle.

Bedford Rock [MENDOCINO]: *relief feature,* 12.5 miles southeast of Ukiah (lat. 39°01'50" N, long. 123°03'20" W; sec. 3, T 13 N, R 11 W). Named on Purdys Gardens (1958) 7.5' quadrangle.

Bed Rock Creek: see **Haynes Creek** [MENDOCINO]; **Skunk Lake Creek** [MENDOCINO].

Beebe Creek [MENDOCINO]: *stream,* flows 4 miles to Rancheria Creek (2) 1.5 miles east of Ornbaun Valley (lat. 38°54'45" N, long. 123°15'35" W; near SW cor. sec. 1, T 12 N, R 13 W). Named on Hopland (1960) and Ornbaun Valley (1960) 15' quadrangles.

Beebe Opening [MENDOCINO]: *area,* 9 miles west of Ornbaun Valley (lat. 38°55'25" N, long. 123°27'50" W; at SE cor. sec. 36, T 13 N, R 15 W). Named on Ornbaun Valley (1960) 15' quadrangle.

Bee Branch Creek [MENDOCINO]: *stream,* flows 1 mile to Alder Creek (4) 4 miles east-northeast of Willits (lat. 39°26' N, long. 123°17'10" W; near N line sec. 10, T 18 N, R 13 W). Named on Willits (1961) 15' quadrangle.

Bee Creek [HUMBOLDT]: *stream,* flows 2 miles to Bluff Creek [DEL NORTE-HUMBOLDT] 8 miles west of Orleans (lat. 41°17'35" N, long. 123°41'35" W). Named on Fish Lake (1974) 7.5' quadrangle.

Bee Lake [HUMBOLDT]: *lake,* 500 feet long, 10 miles west of Orleans (lat. 41°17'15" N, long. 123°43'40" W); the lake is on the northeast side of Bee Mountain at the head of Bee Creek. Named on Fish Lake (1974) 7.5' quadrangle.

Bee Mountain [HUMBOLDT]: *ridge,* southeast-trending, 5 miles long, 10 miles west of Orleans (lat. 41°17'10" N, long. 123°44' W). Named on Fish Lake (1974) 7.5' quadrangle.

Beer Bottle Creek [HUMBOLDT]: *stream,* flows 1.5 miles to Bear River 6 miles south-southwest of Scotia (lat. 40°23'55" N, long. 124°08'15" W; near W line sec. 12, T 1 S, R 1 W). Named on Taylor Peak (1969) 7.5' quadrangle.

Bee Tree Creek [HUMBOLDT]: *stream,* flows 1 mile to Mosquito Creek 10 miles south of the settlement of Willow Creek (lat. 40°42'35" N, long. 123°37'45" W). Named on Grouse Mountain (1979) 7.5' quadrangle.

Bee Tree Creek [MENDOCINO]: *stream,* flows 1.5 miles to Alder Creek (5) 10.5 miles south-southwest of Navarro (lat. 39°00'15" N, long. 123°35'45" W; sec. 11, T 13 N, R 16 W). Named on Navarro (1961) 15' quadrangle.

Bee Tree Flat [TRINITY]: *area,* 5 miles southeast of Forest Glen along South Fork Trinity River (lat. 40°19'20" N, long. 123°15'40" W; sec. 31, T 29 N, R 12 W). Named on Forest Glen (1979) 7.5' quadrangle.

Bee Tree Gap [TRINITY]: *pass,* 15 miles north of Weaverville (lat. 40°56'25" N, long. 122°52'45" W; near N line sec. 34, T 36 N, R 9 W). Named on Trinity Dam (1950) 15' quadrangle. United States Board on Geographic Names (1984a, p. 3) gave a slightly different location for the feature (lat. 40°56'22" N, long. 122°48'15" W; sec. 32, T 36 N, R 8 W).

Behr Soda Spring: see **Fraser Point** [LAKE].

Bell: see **Tom Bell Creek** [MENDOCINO]; **Tom Bell Flat** [MENDOCINO].

Bell Creek [HUMBOLDT]:

(1) *stream,* flows 4 miles to Lawrence Creek 5 miles west-northwest of Lone Star Junction (lat. 40°40'25" N, long. 123°57'25" W; sec. 4, T 3 N, R 2 E). Named on Iaqua Buttes (1979) 7.5' quadrangle.

(2) *stream,* flows 1.5 miles to Eel River 4.25 miles east of Weott (lat. 40°20' N, long. 123°50'45" W; sec. 33, T 1 S, R 3 E). Named on Myers Flat (1969) 7.5' quadrangle.

Bell Creek [TRINITY]: *stream,* flows 5 miles to New River 4.5 miles north-northeast of Burnt Ranch (lat. 40°52'10" N, long. 123°26'35" W). Named on Ironside Mountain (1951) 15' quadrangle.

Belleview [HUMBOLDT]: *locality,* 6.5 miles south-southeast of Fortuna (lat. 40°30'25" N, long. 124°07'10" W; on W line sec. 31, T 2 N, R 1 E). Named on Hydesville (1979) 7.5' quadrangle.

Bell Gulch [TRINITY]: *canyon,* drained by a stream that flows 1.5 miles to Trinity River 12.5 miles northeast of Hayfork (lat. 40°41'15" N, long. 123°01'45" W; sec. 29, T 33 N, R 10 W). Named on Hayfork (1951) 15' quadrangle.

Bell Mountain [MENDOCINO]: *peak,* 1 mile southeast of Westport (lat. 39°37'25" N, long. 123°46'20" W; near S line sec. 32, T 21 N, R 17 W). Named on Inglenook (1966) and Westport (1966) 7.5' quadrangles. United States Coast and Geodetic Survey (p. 142) referred to Bells Mountain, but United States Board on Geographic Names (1968a, p. 4) rejected this form of the name.

Bell Point [MENDOCINO]: *promontory,* less than 1 mile south of Westport along the coast (lat. 39°37'40" N, long. 123°47'10" W; sec. 31, T 21 N, R 17 W). Named on Westport (1966) 7.5' quadrangle. United States Board on Geographic Names (1968a, p. 4) rejected the form "Bells Point" for the name.

Bells Harbor: see **Little River** [MENDOCINO] (2).

Bells Mountain: see **Bell Mountain** [MENDOCINO].

Bells Point: see **Bell Point** [MENDOCINO].

Bell Spring [MENDOCINO]: *spring,* 16 miles northeast of Covelo (lat. 39°58' N, long. 123°03'55" W; near NE cor. sec. 3, T 24 N, R 11 W). Named on Leech Lake Mountain (1966) 7.5' quadrangle. On Covelo (1952) 15' quadrangle, the name applies to a spring located nearly 1 mile farther southeast (sec. 2, T 24 N, R 11 W).

Bell Springs [MENDOCINO]:

(1) *locality,* 3.5 miles north-northwest of Spyrock along Northwestern Pacific Railroad (lat. 39°55'25" N, long. 123°28'20" W; sec. 18, T 24 N, R 14 W). Named on Updegraff Ridge (1967) 7.5' quadrangle. Called Bell Springs Sta. on O'Brien's (1953) map.

(2) *locality,* 9 miles northeast of Leggett (lat. 39°57'05" N, long. 123°35' W; near SW cor. sec. 6, T 24 N, R 15 W). Named on Bell Springs (1969) 7.5' quadrangle. Postal authorities established Bell Springs post office in 1920 and discontinued it in 1961 (Salley, p. 18). Jim Graham named the place in 1861 when he found two small cowbells there (Carranco and Beard, p. 180).

Bell Springs Creek [MENDOCINO]: *stream,* flows 7 miles to Eel River 4 miles north-northwest of Spyrock (lat. 39°56' N, long. 123°28'20" W; sec. 18, T 24 N, R 14 W); the stream heads at Bell Springs Mountain. Named on Bell Springs (1969) and Updegraff Ridge (1967) 7.5' quadrangles.

Bell Springs Mountain [MENDOCINO]: *peak,* 9 miles northeast of Leggett (lat. 39°57'20" N, long. 123°35'25" W; sec. 2, T 24 N, R 16 W); the peak is 0.5 mile northwest of Bell Springs (2). Named on Bell Springs (1969) 7.5' quadrangle.

Bell Springs Station: see **Bell Springs** [MENDOCINO] (1).

Bells Valley: see **Feliz Creek** [MENDOCINO].

Bell Swamps [HUMBOLDT]: *marshes,* 3.25 miles west-southwest of Trinity Mountain (lat. 41°01'05" N, long. 123°28'15" W). Named on Trinity Mountain (1979) 7.5' quadrangle.

Bell Valley [MENDOCINO]: *canyon,* 4.5 miles east-northeast of Boonville along Soda Creek (5) (lat. 39°01'30" N, long. 123°17'30" W). Named on Boonville (1959) 15' quadrangle.

Bemis: see **Camp Bemis** [HUMBOLDT].

Benbow [HUMBOLDT]: *settlement,* 2 miles south-southeast of Garberville (lat. 40°04'10" N, long. 123°47' W; in and near sec. 31, T 4 S, R 4 E). Named on Garberville (1970) 7.5' quadrangle. Postal authorities established Benbow post office in 1929 and discontinued it in 1953 (Frickstad, p. 41). The name, given in 1926, is for the Benbow family, who had a summer resort at the place (Gudde, 1949, p. 28).

Benbow Lake [HUMBOLDT]: *lake,* behind a dam on South Fork Eel River 2.5 miles south of Garberville (lat. 40°03'55" N, long. 123°48' W; sec. 36, T 4 S, R 3 E). Named on Garberville (1970) 7.5' quadrangle. Called Lake Benbow on Garberville (1949) 15' quadrangle. United States Board on Geographic Names (1973b, p. 2) gave the names "Lake Benbow" and "Benbow Reservoir" as variants.

Benbow Reservoir: see **Benbow Lake** [HUMBOLDT].

Bendmore Creek: see **Benmore Creek** [LAKE] (2).

Bendmore Valley: see **Benmore Valley** [LAKE].

Benjamin Flat [TRINITY]: *area,* 14 miles north-northeast of Hayfork along Trinity River (lat. 40°44' N, long. 123°03'45" W). Named on Hayfork (1951) 15' quadrangle. The name commemorates E.M. Benjamin, an engineer for development of the water system from Canyon Creek (1) (Jones, p. 184).

Ben Moore Creek: see **Benmore Creek** [LAKE] (2).

Ben Moore Valley: see **Benmore Valley** [LAKE].

Benmore Canyon [LAKE]: *canyon,* drained by a stream that flows 6 miles to North Fork Cache Creek 5.5 miles east of Clearlake Oaks (lat. 39°01'20" N, long. 122°34'20" W). Named on Clearlake Oaks (1960) and Wilbur Springs (1961) 15' quadrangles. The name commemorates Ben Moore, a stock rustler of the 1850's (Gudde, 1969, p. 27).

Benmore Creek [LAKE]:

(1) *stream,* flows 3 miles to Eel River 5 miles west of Bear Mountain (lat. 39°24'15" N, long. 122°59'35" W; sec. 21, T 18 N, R 10 W). Named on Elk Mountain (1967) and Lake Pillsbury (1967) 7.5' quadrangles.

(2) *stream,* flows 6.25 miles to Scotts Creek 4 miles west-southwest of Lakeport (lat. 39°01'05" N, long. 122°58'50" W; sec. 33, T 14 N, R 10 W). Named on Lakeport (1958) and Purdys Gardens (1958) 7.5' quadrangles. United States Board on Geographic Names (1961a, p. 17) rejected the names "Bendmore Creek," "Ben Moore Creek," and "Ben More Creek" for the feature.

Benmore Ridge Camp [LAKE]: *locality,* 5 miles west-southwest of Lakeport (lat. 39°01'40" N, long. 123°00'15" W; near SE cor. sec. 30, T 14 N, R 10 W); the place is near a branch of Benmore Creek (2). Named on Purdys Gardens (1958) 7.5' quadrangle.

Benmore Valley [LAKE]: *valley,* 6.25 miles west-southwest of Lakeport (lat. 39°00'50" N, long. 123°01'15" W; mainly in sec. 1, 2, T 13 N, R 11 W); the valley is along Benmore Creek (2). Named on Hopland (1960) and Purdys Gardens (1958) 7.5' quadrangles. Called Bendmore Valley on Ukiah (1920) 15' quadrangle, but United States Board on Geographic Names (1961a, p. 17) rejected the names "Bendmore Valley" and "Ben Moore Valley" for the feature.

Bennett Creek [MENDOCINO]: *stream,* flows 2 miles to Sanhedrin Creek 5.25 miles south-southeast of Eden Valley (lat. 39°36'10" N, long. 123°05'25" W); the stream goes through Bennett Valley. Named on Sanhedrin Mountain (1966) 7.5' quadrangle.

Bennett Peak [HUMBOLDT]: *peak,* 9 miles east-southeast of Board Camp Mountain (lat. 40°40' N, long. 123°33'10" W; sec. 1, T 3 N, R 5 E). Named on Sims Mountain (1979) 7.5' quadrangle.

Bennett Valley [MENDOCINO]: *valley,* 5 miles east-southeast of Eden Valley (lat. 39°35'55" N, long. 123°06'15" W). Named on Sanhedrin Mountain (1966) 7.5' quadrangle.

Bens Creek [HUMBOLDT]: *stream,* flows 2.25 miles to Klamath River 0.5 mile west-northwest of Weitchpec (lat. 41°11'35" N, long. 123°42'30" W; at S line sec. 4, T 9 N, R 4 E). Named on Weitchpec (1979) 7.5' quadrangle.

Benson Gulch [TRINITY]: *canyon,* drained by a stream that flows 1 mile to Coffee Creek 2.25 miles southwest of Billys Peak (1) (lat. 41°06'50" N, long. 122°48'20" W; near N line sec. 32, T 38 N, R 8 W). Named on Coffee Creek (1955) 15' quadrangle.

Benson Ridge [LAKE]: *ridge,* southwest-trending, 1.5 miles long, 2.25 miles east-southeast of Kelseyville (lat. 38°57'30" N, long. 122°48' W). Named on Kelseyville (1959) 7.5' quadrangle.

Bentley: see **Spyrock** [MENDOCINO] (2).

Bentley Basin [MENDOCINO]: *relief feature,* 8 miles east-southeast of Covelo (lat. 39°45'45" N, long. 123°05'45" W; sec. 16, 17, T 22 N, R 11 W). Named on Newhouse Ridge (1967) 7.5' quadrangle.

Bentley Ridge [MENDOCINO]: *ridge,* south-southwest-trending, 2.5 miles long, 9 miles north-northeast of Eden Valley (lat. 39°44'30" N, long. 123°05'30" W). Named on Newhouse Ridge (1967) and Thatcher Ridge (1967) 7.5' quadrangles.

Berger Bay [LAKE]: *embayment,* 2 miles north of Lakeport along Clear Lake (lat. 39°04'20" N, long. 122°54'40" W; near SE cor. sec. 12, T 14 N, R 10 W). Named on Lakeport (1958) 7.5' quadrangle.

Berry Canyon [MENDOCINO]: *canyon,* drained by Berry Creek, which flows 1.5 miles to Little Lake Valley 3 miles east-northeast of Willits (lat. 39°20'30" N, long. 123°18' W; near E line sec. 9, T 18 N, R 13 W). Named on Willits (1961) 15' quadrangle.

Berry Creek [LAKE]: *stream,* flows 1.5 miles to Eel River 4.25 miles west of Crockett Peak (lat. 39°25'30" N, long. 122°51'20" W). Named on Crockett Peak (1967) 7.5' quadrangle.

Berry Creek [MENDOCINO]: *stream,* flows 1.5 miles to Little Lake Valley 3 miles east-northeast of Willits (lat. 39°20'30" N, long. 123°18' W; near E line sec. 9, T 18 N, R 13 W); the stream drains Berry Canyon. Named on Willits (1961) 15' quadrangle.

Berry Glenn [HUMBOLDT]: *locality,* 2.25 miles north-northeast of Orick along Prairie Creek (lat. 41°19' N, long. 124°02'25" W; near N line sec. 27, T 11 N, R 1 E). Named on Orick (1966) 7.5' quadrangle. Jean Battrel, who helped her husband run a store at the site, named the place; she sold pies, jellies, and jams made from berries that grew there (Turner, p. 19).

Berry Gulch [MENDOCINO]: *canyon,* drained by a stream that flows 2.5 miles to Little North Fork Big River 7.25 miles northeast of Comptche (lat. 39°20'50" N, long. 123°40'20" W; sec. 8, T 17 N, R 16 W). Named on Comptche (1960) 15' quadrangle.

Berry Patch Ridge [MENDOCINO]: *ridge,* north-trending, 1 mile long, 10.5 miles east of Covelo (lat. 39°45'45" N, long. 123°03'25" W; near W line sec. 14, T 22 N, R 11 W). Named on Newhouse Ridge (1967) 7.5' quadrangle.

Berry Summit [HUMBOLDT]: *pass,* 11.5 miles east of the town of Blue Lake (lat. 40°53'45" N, long. 123°46'10" W; at N line sec. 19, T 6 N, R 4 E). Named on Lord-Ellis Summit (1973) 7.5' quadrangle. Blue Lake (1951) 15' quadrangle shows the feature situated 0.5 mile farther south along an earlier roadway.

Berteleda: see **Fort Dick** [DEL NORTE].

Bertha: see **Saratoga Springs** [LAKE].

Betty Gulch [TRINITY]: *canyon,* drained by a stream that flows 2 miles to Browns Creek 13 miles south of Weaverville (lat. 40°33' N, long. 122°55'30" W; sec. 7, T 31 N, R 9 W). Named on Weaverville (1950) 15' quadrangle.

Bevans Creek [LAKE]: *stream,* flows 3.5 miles to Rice Fork 2.5 miles northeast of Three Crossings (lat. 39°20'35" N, long. 122°53' W; sec. 9, T 17 N, R 9 W); the stream is south of Bevans Ridge. Named on Elk Mountain (1967) 7.5' quadrangle.

Bevans Creek [MENDOCINO]: *stream,* flows 5 miles to East Fork Russian River 0.5 mile south-southeast of the town of Potter Valley (lat. 39°18'45" N, long. 123°06'15" W; sec. 20, T 17 N, R 11 W). Named on Potter Valley (1960) 15' quadrangle.

Bevans Flat [LAKE]: *area,* 1.5 miles north-northeast of Three Crossings (lat. 39°20'20" N, long. 122°54'25" W; on E line sec. 7, T 17 N, R 9 W); the place is along Bevans Creek. Named on Elk Mountain (1967) 7.5' quadrangle.

Bevans Ridge [LAKE]: *ridge,* south-southeast- to east-southeast-trending, 2 miles long, 3 miles north-northeast of Three Crossings (lat. 39°21'30" N, long. 122°54'20" W). Named on Elk Mountain (1967) 7.5' quadrangle.

Bidden Creek [TRINITY]:

(1) *stream,* flows 2 miles to Trinity River 2 miles southeast of Burnt Ranch (lat. 40°47'25" N, long. 123°27' W; near SE cor. sec. 24, T 5 N, R 8 E). Named on Ironside Mountain (1951) 15' quadrangle.

(2) *stream,* flows 1.5 miles to Corral Creek (1) 9 miles northeast of Hyampom (lat. 40°42'05" N, long. 123°18'45" W; near S line sec. 19, T 4 N, R 8 E). Named on Hyampom (1951) 15' quadrangle.

Bidden Creek: see **Little Bidden Creek** [TRINITY].

Bierce Creek [TRINITY]: *stream,* flows 4.25 miles to South Fork Trinity River 9 miles south of Dubakella Mountain (lat. 40°15'30" N, long. 123°09'40" W; sec. 24, T 28 N, R 12 W). Named on Black Rock Mountain (1954) and Dubakella Mountain (1954) 15' quadrangles.

Bierce Ridge [TRINITY]: *ridge,* north-northeast- to northwest-trending, 3.5 miles long, 7.5 miles west-northwest of Black Rock Mountain (lat. 40°14' N, long. 123°08'10" W); the ridge is east of Bierce Creek. Named on Black Rock Mountain (1954) and Dubakella Mountain (1954) 15' quadrangles.

Big Bar [TRINITY]: *village,* 14 miles northeast of Hyampom along Trinity River (lat. 40°44'20" N, long. 123°15' W). Named on Hayfork (1951) and Hyampom (1951) 15' quadrangles. Postal authorities established Big Bar post office in 1851, discontinued it in 1872, reestablished it in 1874, moved it 1 mile east in 1908, discontinued it in 1942, and reestablished it in 1948 (Salley, p. 21). The original community of Big Bar was situated at the mouth of Big Bar Creek, but after the gold there was mined out, the post office was moved down the river to Cox's Bar, but kept the name "Big Bar" (Jones, p. 229). The name "Cox" recalls Isaac Cox, who had a store at Cox Bar from 1853 until 1857 (Gudde, 1975, p. 85). A mining place called Vance's Bar, located on the north bank of Trinity River opposite Cox Bar, was settled in 1850 (Gudde, 1975, p. 359).

Big Bar Creek [TRINITY]: *stream,* flows 5.5 miles to Trinity River 13 miles north of Hayfork (lat. 40°44'20" N, long. 123°11'10" W); the creek enters the river nearly 4 miles upstream from present Big Bar. Named on Hayfork (1951) 15' quadrangle. The stream formerly was called Little Weaver Creek (Jones, p. 229). A mining place called Big Flat was situated along Trinity River above the mouth of present Big Bar Creek (Gudde, 1975, p. 36).

Big Bear Gulch [TRINITY]: *canyon,* drained by a stream that flows 1.5

miles to Mumbo Creek 14 miles north-northeast of Trinity Center (lat. 41°12' N, long. 122°34'25" W; near E line sec. 32, T 39 N, R 6 W); the mouth of the canyon is located nearly 1 mile down Mumbo Creek from the mouth of Little Bear Gulch. Named on Bonanza King (1955) 15' quadrangle.

Big Bear Lake [TRINITY]: *lake*, 1600 feet long, 13 miles north of Trinity Center (lat. 41°11'40" N, long. 122°42'50" W; sec. 31, T 39 N, R 7 W); the lake is 0.5 mile west-northwest of Little Bear Lake at the head of Bear Creek (2). Named on Bonanza King (1955) 15' quadrangle. Called Log Lake on Etna (1934) 30' quadrangle.

Big Bend [HUMBOLDT]: *bend*, 3.25 miles east-northeast of Lone Star Junction along Mad River (lat. 40°38'50" N, long. 123°49'05" W; on S line sec. 10, T 3 N, R 3 E). Named on Mad River Buttes (1977) 7.5' quadrangle.

Big Bend [MENDOCINO]: *bend*, 3.25 miles south-southeast of Leggett along South Fork Eel River (lat. 39°49'30" N, long. 123°40'55" W; at NE cor. sec. 26, T 23 N, R 17 W). Named on Leggett (1969) 7.5' quadrangle.

Big Bend: see **The Big Bend** [MENDOCINO].

Big Bend Creek [MENDOCINO]: *stream*, flows 3.5 miles to Eel River 1 mile north-northwest of Spyrock (2) (lat. 39°53'35" N, long. 123°27' W). Named on Updegraff Ridge (1967) 7.5' quadrangle.

Big Borax Lake: see **Borax Lake** [LAKE].

Big Boulder Lake: see **Boulder Lake** [TRINITY].

Big Butte [TRINITY]: *peak*, 14 miles south-southwest of Black Rock Mountain (lat. 40°02'15" N, long. 123°09'45" W; near E line sec. 11, T 25 N, R 12 W); the feature is 1.5 miles south-southeast of Little Butte. Altitude 5922 feet. Named on Black Rock Mountain (1954) 15' quadrangle.

Big Canyon [MENDOCINO]:

(1) *canyon*, drained by a stream that flows less than 1 mile to Little Creek 5.5 miles east-northeast of Willits (lat. 39°26'15" N, long. 123°15'25" W; sec. 1, T 18 N, R 13 W). Named on Willits (1961) 15' quadrangle.

(2) *canyon*, 7 miles west-northwest of Boonville along Rancheria Creek (2) (lat. 39°02'20" N, long. 123°28'15" W). Named on Boonville (1959) 15' quadrangle.

Big Canyon [TRINITY]: *canyon*, drained by a stream that flows 2 miles to Hayfork Creek 6 miles east of Hyampom (lat. 40°37'15" N, long. 123°20'20" W; near S line sec. 24, T 3 N, R 7 E). Named on Hyampom (1951) 15' quadrangle.

Big Canyon Creek [LAKE]: *stream*, flows 8 miles to Putah Creek 3.5 miles north of Middletown (lat. 38°48'20" N, long. 122°36'50" W). Named on Middletown (1958) and Whispering Pines (1958) 7.5' quadrangles.

Big Chemise Knob [MENDOCINO]: *peak*, 2.5 miles east-southeast of Dos Rios (lat. 39°42'30" N, long. 123°18'15" W); the feature is less than 1 mile east-southeast of Little Chemise Knob. Altitude 2244 feet. Named on Dos Rios (1967) 7.5' quadrangle.

Big Creek [HUMBOLDT]:

(1) *stream*, flows 2.5 miles to Trinity River 4 miles south-southeast of Weitchpec (lat. 41°07'55" N, long. 123°41'20" W; sec. 26, T 9 N, R 4 E). Named on Weitchpec (1979) 7.5' quadrangle.

(2) *stream*, flows 2.5 miles to the sea 7.5 miles southwest of Honeydew (lat. 40°09'25" N, long. 124°12'35" W; sec. 32, T 3 S, R 1 W); the stream is southeast of Hadley Peak. Named on Shubrick Peak (1969) 7.5' quadrangle. Called Hadley Creek on Point Delgada (1949) 15' quadrangle, and United States Board on Geographic Names (1974a, p. 2) gave this name as a variant. The name "Hadley Creek" was for Alfred Augustus Hadley, who settled in the neighborhood in 1857 (Turner, p. 100, 103).

Big Creek [HUMBOLDT-TRINITY]: *stream*, heads in Humboldt County and flows 5 miles to South Fork Trinity River 3 miles northwest of Hyampom in Trinity County (lat. 40°38'45" N, long. 123°29'35" W; near SW cor. sec. 10, T 3 N, R 6 E). Named on Hyampom (1951) 15' quadrangle, and on Sims Mountain (1979) 7.5' quadrangle.

Big Creek [TRINITY]:

(1) *stream*, flows 12.5 miles to Hayfork Creek 2 miles east of Hayfork (lat. 40°33'05" N, long. 123°08'30" W; at W line sec. 8, T 31 N, R 11 W). Named on Hayfork (1951) 15' quadrangle. East Fork enters from the east 9 miles north-northeast of Hayfork; it is 1.5 miles long and is named on Hayfork (1951) 15' quadrangle.

(2) *stream*, flows 8 miles to New River 4.5 miles north-northeast of Burnt Ranch (lat. 40°52'05" N, long. 123°25'45" W); the stream is south of Big Mountain. Named on Ironside Mountain (1951) 15' quadrangle.

Big Creek: see **Big Flat Creek** [HUMBOLDT]; **Hells Half Acre Creek** [TRINITY].

Big Dann Creek [MENDOCINO]: *stream*, flows 4 miles to South Fork Eel River 2 miles south-southeast of Leggett (lat. 39°50'15" N, long. 123°42' W; near NE cor. sec. 23, T 23 N, R 17 W). Named on Leggett (1969) 7.5' quadrangle. Called Big Dan Creek on Leggett (1952) 15' quadrangle.

Big Darby Peak [MENDOCINO]: *peak*, 4 miles northeast of Willits (lat. 39°26'50" N, long. 123°17'55" W; near NW cor. sec. 3, T 18 N, R 13 W); the peak is 1.25 miles west of Little Darby Peak. Altitude 2833 feet. Named on Willits (1961) 15' quadrangle.

Big Finley Creek [HUMBOLDT]: *stream*, flows 3 miles to Mattole River 11 miles west of Garberville (lat. 40°05'15" N, long. 123°59'55" W; sec. 30, T 4 S, R 2 E); the stream is south of Little Finley Creek. Named on Shelter Cove (1969) 7.5' quadrangle.

Big Flat [DEL NORTE]: *area*, 5.25 miles north-northwest of Buck Mountain (lat. 41°41'30" N, long. 123°53'30" W). Named on Cant Hook Mountain (1982) 7.5' quadrangle.

Big Flat [HUMBOLDT]: *area*, 8 miles south-southwest of Honeydew along the coast (lat. 40°07'55" N, long. 124°10'55" W; mainly in sec. 9, T 4 S, R 1 W). Named on Shubrick Peak (1969) 7.5' quadrangle. On Point Delgada (1949) 15' quadrangle, the name applies also to present Miller Flat.

Big Flat [MENDOCINO]:

(1) *area*, nearly 2 miles south-southwest of Leggett (lat. 39°50'30" N, long. 123°43'35" W; sec. 15, T 23 N, R 17 W). Named on Leggett (1969) 7.5' quadrangle.

(2) *area*, 8.5 miles north-northeast of Covelo (lat. 39°54'45" N, long. 123°12'15" W). Named on Bluenose Ridge (1967) 7.5' quadrangle.

Big Flat [TRINITY]:

(1) *area*, 10 miles west-southwest of Billys Peak (1) (lat. 41°04'30" N, long. 122°56'15" W; sec. 7, T 37 N, R 9 W). Named on Coffee Creek (1955) 15' quadrangle.

(2) *area*, 15 miles south-southeast of Weaverville (lat. 40°31'35" N, long. 122°51'05" W; sec. 23, T 31 N, R 9 W). Named on Weaverville (1950) 15' quadrangle.

Big Flat: see **Big Bar Creek** [TRINITY].

Big Flat Campground [DEL NORTE]: *locality*, 5.25 miles north-northwest of Buck Mountain (lat. 41°41'15" N, long. 123°54'30" W; near NE cor. sec. 23, T 15 N, R 2 E). Named on Cant Hook Mountain (1982) 7.5' quadrangle.

Big Flat Campground [TRINITY]: *locality*, 13 miles north of Hayfork along Trinity River (lat. 40°44'20" N, long. 123°12'15" W). Named on Hayfork (1951) 15' quadrangle.

Big Flat Creek [HUMBOLDT]: *stream*, flows 3.5 miles to the sea 8.5 miles south-southwest of Honeydew (lat. 40°07'40" N, long. 124°10'30" W; sec. 10, T 4 S, R 1 W); the mouth of the stream is at the southeast end of Big Flat. Named on Shubrick Peak (1969) 7.5' quadrangle. Called Big Creek on Point Delgada (1920) 15' quadrangle. North Fork enters from the north 1.25 miles upstream from the mouth of the main creek; it is 2.5 miles long and is named on Shubrick Peak (1969) 7.5' quadrangle.

Big Flat of Naufus [TRINITY]: *area*, 6 miles north of Forest Glen (lat. 40°27'35" N, long. 123°19'20" W; near SW cor. sec. 18, T 1 N, R 8 E); the place is along Naufus Creek. Named on Naufus Creek (1979) 7.5' quadrangle.

Big Foot Canyon [MENDOCINO]: *canyon*, drained by a stream that flows 1.5 miles to Dry Creek (2) 9 miles south-southwest of Hopland (lat. 38°51'20" N, long. 123°10'20" W; near SE cor. sec. 27, T 12 N, R 12 W); the canyon heads near Big Foot Mountain. Named on Hopland (1960) 15' quadrangle.

Big Foot Creek [HUMBOLDT]: *stream*, flows 1.5 miles to Bluff Creek [DEL NORTE-HUMBOLDT] 8.5 miles west of Orleans (lat. 41°18'50" N, long. 123°42'05" W). Named on Fish Lake (1974) 7.5' quadrangle.

Big Foot Mountain [MENDOCINO]: *peak*, 8 miles south-southwest of Hopland (lat. 38°52'20" N, long. 123°11'45" W; sec. 21, T 12 N, R 12 W). Altitude 2090 feet. Named on Hopland (1960) 15' quadrangle.

Big French Creek [TRINITY]: *stream*, flows 11 miles to Trinity River 9 miles east-southeast of Burnt Ranch (lat. 40°46'45" N, long. 123°18'30" W; sec. 29, T 5 N, R 8 E). Named on Helena (1951) and Ironside Mountain (1951) 15' quadrangles. Called French Cr. on Miller's (1890) map. East Fork enters from the southeast 7.5 miles upstream from the mouth of the main creek; it is nearly 4 miles long and is named on Helena (1951) and Ironside Mountain (1951) 15' quadrangles.

Biggar Rock [MENDOCINO]: *rock*, 1.5 miles south-southwest of Albion, and 450 feet offshore (lat. 39°12'20" N, long. 123°46'25" W). Named on Albion (1960) 7.5' quadrangle.

Biggs Gulch [MENDOCINO]: *canyon*, drained by a stream that flows 1.25 miles to South Fork Big River 4.5 miles east-northeast of Comptche (lat. 39°17'15" N, long. 123°30'55" W; near E line sec. 34, T 17 N, R 15 W). Named on Comptche (1960) and Willits (1961) 15' quadrangles. Cecil Mallory had a logging camp called Slide Camp in the 1920's on the steep hillside opposite Biggs Gulch (Jackson, Francis, p. 24, 33).

Big Gulch [MENDOCINO]:

(1) *canyon*, drained by a stream that flows 1.25 miles to Little North Fork Navarro River 4.25 miles north-northeast of Navarro (lat. 39°12'10" N, long. 123°30'15" W; sec. 35, T 16 N, R 15 W). Named on Navarro (1961) 15' quadrangle.

(2) *canyon*, drained by a stream that flows 1.5 miles to the sea 1 mile northwest of Gualala (lat. 38°46'35" N, long. 123°32'25" W; sec. 28, T 11 N, R 15 W). Named on Gualala (1960) 7.5' quadrangle.

Big Hill [HUMBOLDT]:

(1) *peak*, 9 miles south of Scotia (lat. 40°20'50" N, long. 124°04'50" W). Altitude 3042 feet. Named on Bull Creek (1969) 7.5' quadrangle.

(2) *peak*, 4 miles north-northeast of Hoopa (lat. 41°05'55" N, long.

123°38'05" W; at N line sec. 8, T 8 N, R 5 E). Altitude 3578 feet. Named on Hoopa (1979) 7.5' quadrangle.

Big Horse Opening [MENDOCINO]: *area,* 9 miles west-northwest of Ornbaun Valley (lat. 38°56'55" N, long. 123°27'45" W; near E line sec. 36, T 13 N, R 15 W). Named on Ornbaun Valley (1960) 15' quadrangle.

Big Hunter [TRINITY]: *peak,* 7 miles west-southwest of Black Rock Mountain (lat. 40°10'20" N, long. 123°08' W; sec. 20, T 27 N, R 11 W). Altitude 5248 feet. Named on Black Rock Mountain (1954) 15' quadrangle.

Big Lagoon [HUMBOLDT]:

(1) *lake,* 3.5 miles long, 9 miles north of Trinidad (lat. 41°11' N, long. 124°07' W). Named on Rodgers Peak (1966) and Trinidad (1966) 7.5' quadrangles. The feature is separated from the sea by a sandy beach. Captain Jonathan Winship, commander of the *O'Cain,* led a party ashore in 1805 and explored the lake, which they called Washington Inlet (Coy, 1929, p. 28).

(2) *settlement,* 7 miles north of Trinidad (lat. 41°09'40" N, long. 124°07'55" W; near SW cor. sec. 13, T T 9 N, R 1 W); the place is near the southwest corner of Big Lagoon (1). Named on Trinidad (1966) 7.5' quadrangle.

Big Lake [HUMBOLDT]: *lake,* 750 feet long, 11 miles south of the settlement of Willow Creek (lat. 40°46'55" N, long. 123°36'05" W). Named on Hennessy Peak (1979) 7.5' quadrangle

Big Lake [TRINITY]: *lake,* 1100 feet long, 2.25 miles south of Burnt Ranch (lat. 40°46'45" N, long. 123°28'35" W; sec. 26, T 5 N, R 6 E). Named on Ironside Mountain (1951) 15' quadrangle.

Big Marshy Lake [TRINITY]: *lake,* 800 feet long, 6 miles north of Billys Peak (1) (lat. 41°13'20" N, long. 122°45'50" W); the feature is 700 feet west-northwest of Little Marshy Lake. Named on Coffee Creek (1955) 15' quadrangle.

Big Meadow [TRINITY]: *area,* 5.5 miles south-southeast of Black Lassic (lat. 40°15'45" N, long. 123°30'15" W; sec. 28, T 2 S, R 6 E). Named on Black Lassic (1979) and Ruth Reservoir (1978) 7.5' quadrangles. Called Big Meadows on Hoaglin (1935) 30' quadrangle. United States Board on Geographic Names (1978a, p. 5) approved the name "Big Meadow Springs" for springs located in Big Meadow.

Big Meadow Camp [TRINITY]: *locality,* 5.5 miles south-southeast of Black Lassic at present Big Meadow (lat. 40°15'50" N, long. 123°30'15" W). Named on Blocksburg (1949) 15' quadrangle.

Big Meadow Creek [TRINITY]: *stream,* flows nearly 3 miles to West Fork Van Duzen River 10 miles southwest of Forest Glen (lat. 40°17'25" N, long. 123°29' W); the stream heads east of Big Meadow. Named on Ruth Reservoir (1978) 7.5' quadrangle.

Big Meadow Springs: see **Big Meadow** [TRINITY].

Big Mountain [HUMBOLDT]: *ridge,* south-trending, 1 mile long, 6.25 miles southwest of Honeydew (lat. 40°10'40" N, long. 124°12' W; sec. 29, T 3 S, R 1 W). Named on Shubrick Peak (1969) 7.5' quadrangle.

Big Mountain [TRINITY]: *peak,* 6.5 miles northeast of Burnt Ranch (lat. 40°52'40" N, long. 123°23'30" W). Named on Ironside Mountain (1951) 15' quadrangle.

Big Opening [HUMBOLDT]: *area,* 4 miles east-northeast of Board Camp Mountain along Grouse Creek (2) (lat. 40°43'15" N, long. 123°37'45" W). Named on Board Camp Mountain (1977) 7.5' quadrangle.

Big Opening [MENDOCINO]: *area,* nearly 5 miles north-northeast of Boonville (lat. 39°04'30" N, long. 123°20'10" W; sec. 18, T 14 N, R 13 W). Named on Boonville (1959) 15' quadrangle.

Big Openings [LAKE]: *areas,* 8.5 miles north-northeast of the town of Potter Valley [MENDOCINO] (lat. 39°26' N, long. 123°03'30" W; sec. 3, 10, 11, T 18 N, R 11 W). Named on Potter Valley (1960) 15' quadrangle.

Big Pepperwood Creek [MENDOCINO]: *stream,* flows nearly 2 miles to Sonoma County 12.5 miles southwest of Ornbaun Valley (lat. 38°46'40" N, long. 123°27'30" W; at SW cor. sec. 20, T 11 N, R 14 W). Named on Ornbaun Valley (1960) 15' quadrangle.

Big Prairie [HUMBOLDT]: *area,* 7 miles north-northeast of Coyote Peak (lat. 41°13'55" N, long. 123°49' W; in and near sec. 27, T 10 N, R 3 E). Named on French Camp Ridge (1983) 7.5' quadrangle.

Big Rainbow [HUMBOLDT]: *peak,* 9 miles south of Scotia (lat. 40°21'20" N, long. 124°08' W). Named on Glynn (1919) 15' quadrangle.

Big Ridge [LAKE]: *ridge,* north-northeast-trending, 1 mile long, 6.5 miles south-southwest of Potato Hill (lat. 39°16' N, long. 122°51'15" W). Named on Potato Hill (1967) 7.5' quadrangle.

Big River [MENDOCINO]: *stream,* flows 40 miles to the sea 0.25 mile south-southeast of downtown Mendocino at Mendocino Bay (lat. 39°18'10" N, long. 123°47'35" W; sec. 30, T 17 N, R 17 W). Named on Comptche (1960) and Willits (1961) 15' quadrangles, and on Mendocino (1960) 7.5' quadrangle. Called Rio Grande on a diseño made in 1844 (Becker, R.H., 1969). Bancroft's (1864) map has the designation "Rio Grande or Big R." for the stream. North Fork enters Big River from the north 3 miles north-east of Comptche; it is 14 miles long and is named on Comptche (1960) and Willits (1961) 15' quadrangles. East Branch of North Fork enters North Fork from the east 4.25 miles north-northeast of Comptche; it is 7.5 miles long and is named on Comptche (1960) and Willits (1961) 15' quadrangles. Little North Fork enters Big River from the north 7 miles west-northwest of Comptche; it is 6.25 miles long and is named on Comptche (1960) 15' quadrangle. East Branch of Little North Fork enters Little North Fork from the east 7 miles northwest of Comptche; it is 2.5 miles long and is named on Comptche (1960) 15' quadrangle. South Fork enters Big River from the south 4 miles east-northeast of Comptche; it is 20 miles long and in named on Boonvlle (1959) and Comptche (1960) 15' quadrangles.

Big River: see **Mendocino** [MENDOCINO].

Big River Lagoon: see **Big River Laguna** [MENDOCINO].

Big River Laguna [MENDOCINO]: *marsh,* 5.25 miles west-northwest of Comptche along the course of Laguna Creek (lat. 39°17'35" N, long. 123°40'50" W; sec. 31, 32, T 17 N, R 16 W). Named on Comptche (1960) 15' quadrangle. Called Big River Lagoon on Glenblair (1943) 15' quadrangle.

Big Rock [HUMBOLDT]: *relief feature,* 0.5 mile southeast of Orleans (lat. 41°17'55" N, long. 123°31'50" W). Named on Orleans (1978) 7.5' quadrangle.

Big Rock [LAKE]: *relief feature,* 2.5 miles southeast of Three Crossings (lat. 39°17'20" N, long. 122°53'10" W; near NE cor. sec. 32, T 17 N, R 9 W). Named on Elk Mountain (1967) 7.5' quadrangle.

Big Rock [MENDOCINO]:

(1) *peak,* 5.5 miles northeast of Branscomb (lat. 39°42'20" N, long. 123°33'05" W; near SE cor. sec. 32, T 22 N, R 15 W). Altitude 2726 feet. Named on Cahto Peak (1967) 7.5' quadrangle.

(2) *relief feature,* 2 miles west of Covelo (lat. 39°47'15" N, long. 123°17'05" W; at SW cor. sec. 2, T 22 N, R 13 W). Named on Covelo West (1967) 7.5' quadrangle.

Big Rock Creek [MENDOCINO]:

(1) *stream,* flows 4.5 miles to Tenmile Creek 8 miles northeast of Branscomb (lat. 39°44'10" N, long. 123°30'50" W; near E line sec. 27, T 22 N, R 15 W); the stream goes past Big Rock (1). Named on Cahto Peak (1967) 7.5' quadrangle.

(2) *stream,* flows 2 miles to Town Creek 1.5 miles west of Covelo (lat. 39°47'40" N, long. 123°16'30" W; sec. 2, T 22 N, R 13 W); the stream goes past Big Rock (2). Named on Covelo West (1967) 7.5' quadrangle.

Big Rock Gulch [HUMBOLDT]: *canyon,* drained by a stream that flows 1 mile to Klamath River opposite Orleans (lat. 41°18'05" N, long. 123°32'15" W); the canyon is southwest of Big Rock. Named on Orleans (1978) 7.5' quadrangle.

Big Rough Canyon [MENDOCINO]: *canyon,* drained by a stream that flows 1 milc to Camp Creek 7 miles west-northwest of Ornbaun Valley (lat. 38°58' N, long. 123°25'05" W; at W line sec. 21, T 13 N, R 14 W). Named on Ornbaun Valley (1960) 15' quadrangle.

Big Salmon Creek [MENDOCINO]: *stream,* flows 7.5 miles to the sea 0.5 mile south of Albion (lat. 39°12'55" N, long. 123°46'05" W; near W line sec. 28, T 16 N, R 17 W). Named on Albion (1960) and Elk (1960) 7.5' quadrangles.

Big Signal: see **Big Signal Peak** [MENDOCINO].

Big Signal Peak [MENDOCINO]: *peak,* 9 miles south-southeast of Eden Valley (lat. 39°30'55" N, long. 123°05'45" W; sec. 8, T 19 N, R 11 W); the peak is 1.5 miles west-northwest of Little Signal Peak at the northwest end of Sanhedrin Mountain. Altitude 6175 feet. Named on Sanhedrin Mountain (1966) 7.5' quadrangle. Called Mount Sanhedrin on Eden Valley (1952) 15' quadrangle, but United States Board on Geographic Names (1969a, p. 2) rejected the names "Mount Sanhedrin" and "Big Signal" for the feature.

Big Slide [HUMBOLDT]: *relief feature,* 8 miles east of Board Camp Mountain (lat. 40°43'30" N, long. 123°34'15" W). Named on Sims Mountain (1979) 7.5' quadrangle.

Big Slide Campground [TRINITY]: *locality,* 4 miles northwest of Hyampom along South Fork Trinity River (lat. 40°39'50" N, long. 123°29'40" W; at W line sec. 3, T 3 N, R 6 E). Named on Hyampom (1951) 15' quadrangle.

Big Slide Creek [TRINITY]: *stream,* flows less than 1 mile to South Fork Trinity River 4.5 miles north-northwest of Hyampom (lat. 40°40'10" N, long. 123°30'10" W; sec. 4, T 3 N, R 6 E). Named on Sims Mountain (1979) 7.5' quadrangle.

Big Slough: see **Hookton Slough** [HUMBOLDT].

Big Soda Spring [LAKE]: *spring,* 7.5 miles east-southeast of Lakeport (lat. 39°00'30" N, long. 122°47'15" W; sec. 6, T 13 N, R 8 W); the spring is at the east end of Soda Bay (1). Named on Lucerne (1958) 7.5' quadrangle.

Big Spring [HUMBOLDT]:

(1) *spring,* nearly 6 miles south of Garberville (lat. 40°01' N, long. 123°47' W; sec. 13, T 5 S, R 3 E). Named on Garberville (1970) 7.5' quadrangle.

(2) *spring,* 6.25 miles west of Alderpoint (lat. 40°10'30" N, long. 123°43'50" W). Named on Fort Seward (1969) 7.5' quadrangle.

Big Spring [LAKE]: *spring,* less than 1 mile west-southwest of Potato Hill (lat. 39°21' N, long. 122°49' W; near SE cor. sec. 1, T 17 N, R 9 W). Named on Potato Hill (1967) 7.5' quadrangle.

Big Spring [TRINITY]: *spring,* 19 miles north-northeast of Weaverville (lat. 40°58' N, long. 122°45'10" W; near E line sec. 22, T 36 N, R 8 W). Named on Trinity Dam (1950) 15' quadrangle.

Big Squaw Valley [LAKE]: *valley,* 3 miles north of Bear Mountain (lat. 39°27'

N, long. 122°54'20" W; on S line sec. 36, T 19 N, R 10 W); the valley is along Squaw Valley Creek. Named on Lake Pillsbury (1967) 7.5' quadrangle.

Bigtree Gulch [HUMBOLDT]: *canyon*, drained by a stream that flows less than 0.5 mile to Trinity River 2.5 miles south-southeast of Weitchpec (lat. 41°09'20" N, long. 123°41'05" W; near N line sec. 23, T 9 N, R 4 E). Named on Weitchpec (1979) 7.5' quadrangle.

Big Valley [LAKE]: *valley*, south of Clear Lake, between Lakeport and Kelseyville (center near lat. 39°00' N, long. 122°52' W). Named on Highland Springs (1959), Kelseyville (1959), Lakeport (1958), and Lucerne (1958) 7.5' quadrangles.

Big Valley: see **Lakeport** [LAKE].

Big Water Canyon [MENDOCINO]: *canyon*, drained by a stream that flows 1.25 miles to Middle Fork Eel River 3.5 miles east-southeast of Dos Rios (lat. 39°42'05" N, long. 123°17'35" W); the mouth of the canyon is 0.5 mile upstream from the mouth of Little Water Canyon. Named on Dos Rios (1967) 7.5' quadrangle.

Big White Rock [MENDOCINO]: *rock*, 10 miles south-southwest of Piercy, and 400 feet offshore (lat. 39°50'45" N, long. 123°53'05" W). Named on Mistake Point (1969) 7.5' quadrangle.

Billie Gulch [TRINITY]: *canyon*, drained by a stream that flows 1.5 miles to East Fork Trinity River 23 miles northeast of Weaverville (lat. 40°59'10" N, long. 122°38'15" W; at N line sec. 14, T 36 N, R 7 W). Named on Schell Mountain (1950) 15' quadrangle.

Billings Creek [MENDOCINO]: *stream*, flows 7.5 miles to North Fork Gualala River 7 miles southwest of Ornbaun Valley (lat. 38°51'10" N, long. 123°24'30" W; sec. 27, T 12 N, R 14 W). Named on Ornbaun Valley (1960) 15' quadrangle.

Billy Goat Peak [HUMBOLDT]: *peak*, 5.25 miles northwest of Blocksburg (lat. 40°19'20" N, long. 123°43'10" W; near W line sec. 3, T 2 S, R 4 E). Named on Blocksburg (1969) 7.5' quadrangle.

Billy Gulch [TRINITY]: *canyon*, drained by a stream that flows 1 mile to East Fork Hayfork Creek 9 miles east-southeast of Hayfork (lat. 40°30'10" N, long. 123°02' W; near N line sec. 31, T 31 N, R 10 W). Named on Hayfork (1951) 15' quadrangle.

Billy Pike Creek [MENDOCINO]: *stream*, flows 2 miles to Black Butte River 15 miles north of Hull Mountain (lat. 39°43'45" N, long. 123°56'30" W; near S line sec. 26, T 22 N, R 10 W). Named on Plaskett Ridge (1967) 7.5' quadrangle.

Billy Pike Ridge [MENDOCINO]: *ridge*, northeast-trending, 2 miles long, 14 miles north of Hull Mountain (lat. 39°43'15" N, long. 122°57'30" W); the ridge is northwest of Billy Pike Creek. Named on Plaskett Ridge (1967) 7.5' quadrangle.

Billy Prairie [HUMBOLDT]: *area*, 8 miles south of Coyote Peak (lat. 41°01'05" N, long. 123°50'45" W; near SW cor. sec. 4, T 7 N, R 3 E). Named on Hupa Mountain (1982) 7.5' quadrangle.

Billys Gulch [TRINITY]: *canyon*, drained by a stream that flows 1.5 miles to Davis Creek (2) 16 miles northeast of Weaverville (lat. 40°55'15" N, long. 122°46' W; sec. 3, T 35 N, R 8 W). Named on Schell Mountain (1950) and Trinity Dam (1950) 15' quadrangles.

Billys Peak [TRINITY]:

(1) *peak*, 29 miles north-northeast of Weaverville (lat. 41°08' N, long. 122°46'10" W; sec. 22, T 38 N, R 8 W). Altitude 7343 feet. Named on Coffee Creek (1955) 15' quadrangle.

(2) *peak*, 16 miles northeast of Weaverville (lat. 40°54'55" N, long. 122°44'20" W; sec. 2, T 35 N, R 8 W). Named on Schell Mountain (1950) 15' quadrangle.

Billy Williams Creek [MENDOCINO]: *stream*, flows 2.5 miles to Black Butte Creek 11.5 miles east of Covelo (lat. 39°47'25" N, long. 123°01'55" W; sec. 1, T 22 N, R 11 W); the stream is southeast of Billy Williams Ridge, and northwest of Newhouse Ridge. Named on Newhouse Ridge (1967) 7.5' quadrangle. Present Shields Creek is called Billy Williams Creek on Covelo (1952) 15' quadrangle, and present Billy Williams Creek is called Newhouse Creek on the same quadrangle—United States Board on Geographic Names (1969a, p. 2) rejected the name "Newhouse Creek" for present Billy Williams Creek.

Billy Williams Ridge [MENDOCINO]: *ridge*, north-northeast- to east-trending, 2.5 miles long, 10 miles east of Covelo (lat. 39°47'10" N, long. 123°03'40" W). Named on Newhouse Ridge (1967) 7.5' quadrangle.

Birdie M Gulch [TRINITY]: *canyon*, drained by a stream that flows 1.5 miles to New River 10.5 miles north-northeast of Burnt Ranch (lat. 40°56'30" N, long. 123°23' W). Named on Ironside Mountain (1951) 15' quadrangle.

Bird Island [HUMBOLDT]: *island*, 350 feet long, 1.5 miles north of downtown Eureka in Arcata Bay (lat. 40°49'35" N, long. 124°09'15" W). Named on Eureka (1958) 7.5' quadrangle.

Bishop Mountain [LAKE]: *ridge*, southeast-trending, 1.25 miles long, 1.5 miles southwest of Jericho Valley (lat. 38°49'10" N, long. 122°27'35" W). Named on Jericho Valley (1958) 7.5' quadrangle.

Black Basin [TRINITY]: *relief feature*, 17 miles north of Weaverville (lat. 40°58'15" N, long. 122°53'20" W; around NE cor. sec. 21, T 36 N, R 9 W). Named on Trinity Dam (1950) 15' quadrangle. The name is for an early sheepman in the neighborhood (Jones, p. 12).

Black Butte [DEL NORTE]: *peak*, 5 miles east-northeast of Broken Rib Mountain (lat. 41°55'10" N, long. 123°36'10" W). Altitude 6020 feet. Named on Polar Bear Mountain (1982) 7.5' quadrangle.

Black Butte [HUMBOLDT]:

(1) *peak*, 2 miles northwest of Showers Mountain (lat. 40°36'05" N, long. 123°43'15" W; near N line sec. 34, T 3 N, R 4 E). Altitude 4132 feet. Named on Showers Mountain (1978) 7.5' quadrangle.

(2) *peak*, 5 miles south-southwest of Lone Star Junction (lat. 40°33'45" N, long. 123°54'35" W; near SE cor. sec. 11, T 2 N, R 2 E). Altitude 3167 feet. Named on Owl Creek (1979) 7.5' quadrangle.

Black Butte Creek: see **Butte Creek** [HUMBOLDT] (2).

Black Butte River [MENDOCINO]: *stream*, heads in Glenn County and flows 16 miles in Mendocino County to Middle Fork Eel River 9 miles east-northeast of Covelo (lat. 39°49'25" N, long. 123°05'10" W; sec. 28, T 23 N, R 11 W). Named on Mendocino Pass (1967), Newhouse Ridge (1967), and Plaskett Ridge (1967) 7.5' quadrangles. United States Board on Geographic Names (1933, p. 148) rejected the names "Poopoteyuk River" and "South Fork of Middle Fork Eel River" for the stream.

Black Creek [DEL NORTE]: *stream*, flows 2.5 miles to Dunn Creek 7 miles northeast of Broken Rib Mountain (lat. 41°56'45" N, long. 123°35'05" W); the stream heads east of Black Butte. Named on Polar Bear Mountain (1982) 7.5' quadrangle.

Black Creek [HUMBOLDT]: *stream*, flows nearly 6 miles to Mad River 8 miles south-southeast of Korbel (lat. 40°45'45" N, long. 123°53'15" W; near NW cor. sec. 6, T 4 N, R 3 E). Named on Iagua Buttes (1979) and Korbel (1979) 7.5' quadrangles. Called Black Dog Creek on Manning and Ogle's (1950) map.

Black Dog Creek [HUMBOLDT]: *stream*, flows 1.5 miles to Mad River 2.5 miles south-southwest of Korbel (lat. 40°50'05" N, long. 123°58'35" W; sec. 8, T 5 N, R 2 E). Named on Korbel (1979) 7.5' quadrangle.

Black Dog Creek: see **Black Creek** [HUMBOLDT].

Blackeye Canyon [LAKE]: *canyon*, drained by a stream that flows 2.25 miles to the northeast end of Burns Valley 5 miles north of the town of Lower Lake (lat. 38°59' N, long. 122°36' W; near S line sec. 11, T 13 N, R 7 W). Named on Lower Lake (1958) 7.5' quadrangle.

Black Fox Rock [HUMBOLDT]: *relief feature*, 8 miles east-southeast of Board Camp Mountain (lat. 40°39'20" N, long. 123°34'50" W; sec. 11, T 3 N, R 5 E). Named on Sims Mountain (1979) 7.5' quadrangle.

Blackhawk Bar [DEL NORTE]: *locality*, 3.25 miles north of Buck Mountain along South Fork Smith River (lat. 41°40'45" N, long. 123°52'25" W); the place is near the mouth of Blackhawk Creek. Named on Cant Hook Mountain (1982) and Ship Mountain (1982) 7.5' quadrangles. United States Board on Geographic Names (1942, p. 5-6) rejected the name "Indian Bar" for the place.

Blackhawk Creek [DEL NORTE]: *stream*, flows 2 miles to South Fork Smith River 3.5 miles north of Buck Mountain near Blackhawk Bar (lat. 41°41' N, long. 123°52'25" W). Named on Ship Mountain (1982) 7.5' quadrangle.

Black Lassic [TRINITY]: *peak*, 19 miles south-southwest of Hyampom (lat. 40°19'40" N, long. 123°32'25" W); the peak is less than 1 mile east-northeast of Mount Lassic [HUMBOLDT]. Altitude 5898 feet. Named on Black Lassic (1979) 7.5' quadrangle. The term "Lassic" is from a group of Indians known by the name of their last chief, Lassik (Gudde, 1949, p. 183).

Black Lassic Creek [TRINITY]: *stream*, flows 3.5 miles to Van Duzen River 8.5 miles west of Forest Glen (lat. 40°21'05" N, long. 123°28'55" W; sec. 27, T 1 S, R 6 E); the stream heads near Black Lassic. Named on Black Lassic (1979) and Ruth Reservoir (1978) 7.5' quadrangles.

Black Mountain [HUMBOLDT]:

(1) *peak*, 10 miles east of Weitchpec (lat. 41°12'05" N, long. 123°30'55" W). Altitude 3627 feet. Named on Hopkins Butte (1979) 7.5' quadrangle.

(2) *peak*, 3 miles north of Orleans (lat. 41°20'40" N, long. 123°32'55" W). Altitude 3223 feet. Named on Orleans (1978) 7.5' quadrangle.

Black Mountain [TRINITY]: *peak*, 31 miles south of Etna on Trinity-Siskiyou County line (lat. 41°00'30" N, long. 122°54'45" W; near E line sec. 5, T 36 N, R 9 W). Altitude 8019 feet. Named on Coffee Creek (1955) 15' quadrangle.

Black Oak Creek [MENDOCINO]: *stream*, flows 1.5 miles to Eel River nearly 5 miles south-southeast of Spyrock (2) (lat. 39°48'45" N, long. 123°24'50" W; near W line sec. 34, T 23 N, R 14 W). Named on Iron Peak (1967) 7.5' quadrangle.

Black Oak Mountain [MENDOCINO]: *peak*, 5.5 miles north-northeast of Branscomb (lat. 39°43'55" N, long. 123°36' W; near NW cor. sec. 26, T 22 N, R 16 W). Altitude 3708 feet. Named on Cahto Peak (1967) 7.5' quadrangle.

Black Oak Ridge [MENDOCINO]: *ridge*, northwest-trending, 1 mile long, 4 miles north-northeast of Boonville (lat. 39°04' N, long. 123°20'50" W). Named on Boonville (1959) 15' quadrangle.

Black Oak Springs [LAKE]: *springs*, 7 miles west of the town of Upper Lake (lat. 39°09'40" N, long. 123°02'15" W; sec. 14, T 15 N, R 11 W). Named on Cow Mountain (1958) 7.5' quadrangle.

Black Oak Springs Creek [LAKE]: *stream,* flows 2.5 miles to Scotts Creek 7.5 miles west-southwest of the town of Upper Lake (lat. 39°08'05" N, long. 123°02'20" W; sec. 26, T 15 N, R 11 W); the stream heads at Black Oak Springs. Named on Cow Mountain (1958) 7.5' quadrangle.

Black Oak Villa [LAKE]: *locality,* 7 miles east-southeast of Middletown (lat. 38°42'55" N, long. 122°29'10" W; sec. 14, T 10 N, R 6 W). Named on Aetna Springs (1958) 7.5' quadrangle.

Black Rock [HUMBOLDT]:

(1) *relief feature,* 10 miles south-southwest of the settlement of Willow Creek (lat. 40°48'35" N, long. 123°41'55" W; near SW cor. sec. 14, T 5 N, R 4 E). Named on Grouse Mountain (1979) 7.5' quadrangle.

(2) *rock,* 8.5 miles south-southwest of Honeydew, and just offshore (lat. 40°07'45" N, long. 124°11' W). Named on Shubrick Peak (1969) 7.5' quadrangle.

Black Rock [MENDOCINO]: *peak,* 4 miles northeast of Laytonville (lat. 39°43'55" N, long. 123°25'30" W; near E line sec. 28, T 22 N, R 14 W). Altitude 4005 feet. Named on Laytonville (1967) 7.5' quadrangle.

Black Rock: see **Black Rock Mountain** [TRINITY]; **Little Black Rock** [MENDOCINO]; **Little Black Rock** [TRINITY].

Black Rock Creek [LAKE]: *stream,* flows about 1.5 miles to Dry Creek (3) nearly 3 miles southwest of Middletown (lat. 38°43'50" N, long. 122°39'25" W; sec. 8, T 10 N, R 7 W). Named on Mount Saint Helena (1959) 7.5' quadrangle.

Black Rock Lake [TRINITY]: *lake,* 600 feet long, 0.5 mile north-northeast of Black Rock Mountain (lat. 40°12'50" N, long. 123°00'10" W; near SW cor. sec. 4, T 27 N, R 10 W). Named on Black Rock Mountain (1954) 15' quadrangle.

Black Rock Mountain [TRINITY]: *peak,* 37 miles south of Weaverville (lat. 40°12'15" N, long. 123°00'30" W; sec. 8, T 27 N, R 10 W). Altitude 7755 feet. Named on Black Rock Mountain (1954) 15' quadrangle. Called Black Rock on Hoaglin (1935) 30' quadrangle. United States Board on Geographic Names (1982a, p. 3) approved the name "Blue Slide" for a peak, altitude 5588 feet, located 6.5 miles southwest of Black Rock Mountain (lat. 40°08'16" N, long. 123°05'53" W; sec. 34, T 27 N, R 11 W), and rejected the name "Blue Point" for the feature—the name "Blue Slide" is for steep slopes of blue rock on the peak.

Blacks Camp [TRINITY]: *locality,* 12 miles west-southwest of Black Rock Mountain (lat. 40°07' N, long. 123°12'50" W; sec. 10, T 26 N, R 12 W). Named on Black Rock Mountain (1954) 15' quadrangle. A man named Black built a cabin at the place (Jones, p. 364).

Black's Camp Ridge: see **Jones Ridge** [TRINITY].

Blacks Flat [TRINITY]: *area,* 4 miles north-northwest of Helena along North Fork Trinity River (lat. 40°49'40" N, long. 123°08'45" W; sec. 6, T 34 N, R 11 W). Named on Helena (1951) 15' quadrangle.

Blacks Lake: see **Salmon Mountain** [HUMBOLDT-TRINITY].

Blacksmith Creek [MENDOCINO]: *stream,* flows 3.25 miles to Eden Creek in Eden Valley (lat. 39°37'25" N, long. 123°11'15" W; sec. 4, T 20 N, R 12 W). Named on Brushy Mountain (1966) 7.5' quadrangle.

Blaine: see **Mary Blaine Meadow** [TRINITY]; **Mary Blaine Mountain** [TRINITY]; **Orick** [HUMBOLDT].

Blair Creek [TRINITY]: *stream,* flows 1.25 miles to Mad River 10 miles east-northeast of Kettenpom (lat. 40°14' N, long. 123°18'20" W; at W line sec. 5, T 3 S, R 8 E). Named on Shannon Butte (1967) 7.5' quadrangle.

Blair Gulch [MENDOCINO]: *canyon,* drained by a stream that flows less than 1 mile to Little North Fork Ten Mile River 6.5 miles west-southwest of Branscomb (lat. 39°36'25" N, long. 123°43'50" W; at E line sec. 10, T 20 N, R 17 W). Named on Dutchmans Knoll (1966) 7.5' quadrangle.

Blake Mountain [HUMBOLDT]: *peak,* 7.5 miles east-northeast of Showers Mountain (lat. 40°36'50" N, long. 123°33'35" W; sec. 25, T 3 N, R 5 E). Altitude 5905 feet. Named on Blake Mountain (1979) 7.5' quadrangle.

Blake Spring Campground [HUMBOLDT]: *locality,* 7.5 miles east-northeast of Showers Mountain (lat. 40°36'40" N, long. 123°33'30" W; sec. 25, T 3 N, R 5 E); the place is on Blake Mountain. Named on Blake Mountain (1979) 7.5' quadrangle.

Bland Mountain: see **Leech Lake Mountain** [MENDOCINO].

Blands Cove [MENDOCINO]: *marsh,* 13 miles northeast of Covelo (lat. 39°54'35" N, long. 123°03'20" W; sec. 26, T 24 N, R 11 W). Named on Leech Lake Mountain (1966) 7.5' quadrangle. Covelo (1952) 15' quadrangle shows a lake at the place, and Covelo (1926) 15' quadrangle shows an intermittent lake there.

Blanket Creek [HUMBOLDT]: *stream,* flows 2.5 miles to Little Van Duzen River 6.5 miles north-northeast of Blocksburg (lat. 40°21'50" N, long. 123°35'25" W; sec. 22, T 1 S, R 5 E). Named on Black Lassic (1979) 7.5' quadrangle.

Blank Rock [HUMBOLDT]: *rock,* 1 mile west-southwest of Trinidad, and 1700 feet west of Trinidad Head (lat. 41°03'20" N, long. 124°09'30" W). Named on Trinidad (1966) 7.5' quadrangle.

Blanton Creek [HUMBOLDT]: *stream,* flows 2.5 miles to Yager Creek 8 miles east-southeast of Fortuna (lat. 40°34'35" N, long. 124°00'35" W; near N line sec. 12, T 2 N, R 1 E); the stream heads near Blanton Prairie. Named on Hydesville (1979) 7.5' quadrangle.

Blanton Prairie [HUMBOLDT]: *area,* 6.5 miles east of Fortuna (lat. 40°36'25" N, long. 124°01'55" W; on S line sec. 26, T 3 N, R 1 E). Named on Hydesville (1979) 7.5' quadrangle. The name is for John and Elizabeth Blanton, who settled at the place in 1871 (Turner, p. 23).

Blocksburg [HUMBOLDT]: *village,* 15 miles east-southeast of Weott (lat. 40°16'35" N, long. 123°38'15" W; sec. 20, T 2 S, R 5 E). Named on Blocksburg (1969) 7.5' quadrangle. Postal authorities established Blocksburgh post office in 1877 and changed the name to Blocksburg (without the final "h") in 1893 (Frickstad, p. 41). The name is for Benjamin Blockburger, who started a store at the place in 1872 (Gudde, 1949, p. 33). Coy (1929, p. 247) referred to "Powellville, or Blockburger's." The community initially was called Powellville for Joseph James Powell, the first settler and store operator there (Turner, p. 172).

Blodgett Canyon [LAKE]: *canyon,* drained by a stream that flows 2.25 miles to Wolf Creek 6 miles north-northeast of Clearlake Oaks (lat. 39°05'55" N, long. 122°36'35" W). Named on Clearlake Oaks (1960) 15' quadrangle. On Bartlett Springs (1944) 15' quadrangle, the name applies to a shorter canyon that opens into the canyon of Wolf Creek 0.5 mile farther upstream.

Bloody Camp [HUMBOLDT]: *locality,* 2 miles west-southwest of Weitchpec (lat. 41°10'35" N, long. 123°44'35" W). Named on Weitchpec (1979) 7.5' quadrangle. This appears to be the place that Gibbs (p. 135) referred to when he noted that the name recalls that Indians murdered two white people there.

Bloody Island [LAKE]: *hill,* 1.5 miles south-southeast of the town of Upper Lake (lat. 39°08'55" N, long. 122°53'40" W; sec. 18, T 15 N, R 9 W). Named on Upper Lake (1958) 7.5' quadrangle. Soldiers led by Captain Nathaniel Lyon practically annihilated hundreds of Indians at the site in 1850 after Indians murdered two Americans near present Kelseyville (Hoover, Rensch, and Rensch, p. 139). Gudde (1949, p. 25) referred to the place as Battle Island.

Bloody Nose Creek [HUMBOLDT]: *stream,* flows nearly 2 miles to Trinity River at the settlement of Willow Creek (lat. 40°56'20" N, long. 123°37'05" W; sec. 33, T 7 N, R 5 E). Named on Salyer (1979) and Willow Creek (1979) 7.5' quadrangles.

Bloody Rock [LAKE]: *peak,* 5 miles northwest of Crockett Peak (lat. 39°28'25" N, long. 122°51'05" W; on W line sec. 26, T 19 N, R 9 W). Named on Crockett Peak (1967) 7.5' quadrangle.

Bloody Run [HUMBOLDT]: *stream,* flows nearly 3 miles to Van Duzen River 3.5 miles east-southeast of Yager Junction (lat. 40°31'35" N, long. 123°45'50" W; near NW cor. sec. 29, T 2 N, R 4 E). Named on Showers Mountain (1978) and Yager Junction (1979) 7.5' quadrangles.

Bloody Run: see **Bloody Run Creek** [MENDOCINO].

Bloody Run Creek [MENDOCINO]: *stream,* flows 4.5 miles to Outlet Creek 5.5 miles northeast of Longvale (lat. 39°36'55" N, long. 123°21'30" W; sec. 1, T 20 N, R 14 W). Named on Willis Ridge (1966) 7.5' quadrangle. Called Bloody Run on Laytonville (1919) 15' quadrangle.

Bloody Run Creek [TRINITY]: *stream,* flows 2 miles to Eagle Creek (3) 4 miles north of Billys Peak (1) (lat. 41°11'30" N, long. 122°45'30" W; near SE cor. sec. 34, T 39 N, R 8 W). Named on Coffee Creek (1955) 15' quadrangle.

Bloody Run Ridge [HUMBOLDT]: *ridge,* north-northwest-trending, 2 miles long, 5 miles south-southwest of Showers Mountain (lat. 40°30'50" N, long. 123°44'15" W; sec. 28, 33, T 2 N, R 4 E); the ridge is northeast of Bloody Run. Named on Showers Mountain (1978) 7.5' quadrangle.

Bloyd Creek [HUMBOLDT]: *stream,* flows nearly 1 mile to lowlands along Eel River 3.5 miles east of Weott (lat. 40°20'10" N, long. 123°51'20" W; sec. 32, T 1 S, R 3 E). Named on Myers Flat (1969) 7.5' quadrangle.

Blue Banks [MENDOCINO]: *relief feature,* 10.5 miles north-northwest of Hull Mountain (lat. 39°40'10" N, long. 122°58'55" W; near NW cor. sec. 21, T 21 N, R 10 W). Named on Plaskett Ridge (1967) 7.5' quadrangle.

Blue Creek [DEL NORTE]: *stream,* flows 0.25 mile to the State of Oregon 15 miles northeast of Gasquet (lat. 41°59'50" N, long. 123°45'10" W; sec. 33, T 19 N, R 4 E). Named on Shelly Creek Ridge (1982) 7.5' quadrangle.

Blue Creek [DEL NORTE-HUMBOLDT]: *stream,* heads in Del Norte County and flows 23 miles to Klamath River 6 miles north-northwest of Johnsons in Humboldt County (lat. 41°25'35" N, long. 123°55'45" W; sec. 15, T 12 N, R 2 E). Named on Ah Pah Ridge (1983), Blue Creek Mountain (1982), Chimney Rock (1981). and Summit Valley (1981) 7.5' quadrangles. East Fork enters nearly 6 miles upstream from the entrance of the main creek into Humboldt County; it is 10 miles long and is named on Blue Creek Mountain (1982), Chimney Rock (1981), Lonesome Ridge (1974), and Summit Valley (1981) 7.5' quadrangles. West Fork enters 3.25 miles upstream from the mouth of the main creek; it is 6 miles long and is named on Ah Pah Ridge (1983) and Klamath Glen (1982) 7.5' quadrangles. Crescent City Fork enters 10 miles upstream from the mouth of the main creek; it is 8.5 miles long and is named on Blue Creek Mountain (1982) and Summit Valley (1981) 7.5' quadrangles. Crescent City Fork is called West Fork Blue Creek on Preston Peak (1922) 30' quadrangle. United States Board on Geographic Names (1978b, p. 4) approved the name "Flatiron Lake" for a lake, 250 feet long, near the head of Blue Creek (lat.

41°35'40" N, long. 123°42'31" W; sec. 22, T 14 N, R 4 E).

Blue Creek Campground [HUMBOLDT]: *locality,* 7 miles north-northwest of Johnsons along Blue Creek [DEL NORTE-HUMBOLDT] (lat. 41°26'45" N, long. 123°54'15" W; near E line sec. 11, T 12 N, R 2 E). Named on Ah Pah Ridge (1983) 7.5' quadrangle.

Blue Creek Lodge [HUMBOLDT]: *locality,* 6.5 miles north-northwest of Johnsons along Klamath River (lat. 41°26' N, long. 123°55'45" W; sec. 15, T 12 N, R 2 E); the place is 0.5 mile north of the mouth of Blue Creek [DEL NORTE-HUMBOLDT]. Site named on Ah Pah Ridge (1983) 7.5' quadrangle.

Blue Creek Mountain [DEL NORTE]: *ridge,* west-northwest-trending, 1 mile long, 14 miles east-southeast of Klamath Glen (lat. 41°23'35" N, long. 123°45'30" W). Named on Blue Creek Mountain (1982) 7.5' quadrangle.

Blue Creek Mountain Ridge [HUMBOLDT]: *ridge,* generally east-trending, 6 miles long, center 5.5 miles northeast of Johnsons (lat. 41°24'55" N, long. 123°48'45" W); the ridge is west of Blue Creek Mountain [DEL NORTE]. Named on Blue Creek Mountain (1982) 7.5' quadrangle.

Blue Divide [TRINITY]: *pass,* 17 miles north-northeast of Trinity Center (lat. 41°13'45" N, long. 122°33'15" W; near N line sec. 21, T 39 N, R 6 W). Named on Bonanza King (1955) 15' quadrangle.

Blue Gulch [TRINITY]: *canyon,* drained by a stream that flows 3 miles to Ditch Gulch 1.25 miles north-northwest of Dubakella Mountain (lat. 40°25'45" N, long. 123°09'40" W; at N line sec. 25, T 30 N, R 12 W). Named on Dubakella Mountain (1954) 15' quadrangle.

Blue Jacket Butte [HUMBOLDT]: *peak,* 3.25 miles west of Blocksburg (lat. 40°16'15" N, long. 123°42' W; sec. 23, T 2 S, R 4 E). Altitude 2314 feet. Named on Blocksburg (1969) 7.5' quadrangle.

Blue Lake [HUMBOLDT]:
(1) *lake,* 650 feet long, 9 miles west-southwest of Orleans (lat. 41°15'05" N, long. 123°41'50" W). Named on Fish Lake (1974) 7.5' quadrangle.
(2) *town,* 10 miles northeast of Eureka along Mad River (lat. 40°52'50" N, long. 123°59'15" W; around NE cor. sec. 30, T 6 N, R 2 E). Named on Blue Lake (1979) 7.5' quadrangle. Postal authorities established Blue Lake post office in 1878 (Frickstad, p. 41). The community first was called Scottsville for a man named Scott who kept a hotel at the place (Hanna, p. 35). Postal authorities established Three Cabins post office 15 miles southeast of Blue Lake post office in 1884 and discontinued it in 1886 (Salley, p. 221). Manning and Ogle's (1950) map shows a place called Northern Redwood Camp located 5.25 miles northeast of the town of Blue Lake (lat. 40°56'35" N, long. 123°55'35" W).

Blue Lake: see **Blue Lakes** [LAKE]; **Butler Valley** [HUMBOLDT]; **Lower Blue Lake** [LAKE].

Blue Lakes [LAKE]: *lakes,* two, largest 3800 feet long, 6 miles west of the town of Upper Lake (lat. 39°10'35" N, long. 123°00'55" W; sec. 6, 7, T 15 N, R 10 W). Named on Cow Mountain (1958) 7.5' quadrangle. The two lakes are connected by a waterway called The Narrows (1). A post office called Blue Lake operated for a time in 1871 at a vacation camp at the lakes (Salley, p. 23). Bradley (p. 215) referred to a place called Blue Lakes, which also was the site of Midlake post office, located "between the upper and lower lakes"—that is, between present Blue Lakes and present Lower Lake. The water of the lakes has a beautiful blue color (Menefee, p. 225). According to Palmer (p. 209), Blue Lakes resort is in what is known as Blue Lakes Cañon.

Blue Lakes: see **Midlake**, under **Saratoga Springs** [LAKE].

Blue Lakes Cañon: see **Blue Lakes** [LAKE].

Blue Mountain [TRINITY]: *peak,* 21 miles northeast of Weaverville on Trinity-Shasta County line (lat. 40°54' N, long. 122°36' W). Altitude 5336 feet. Named on Schell Mountain (1950) 15' quadrangle.

Bluenose Peak [TRINITY]: *peak,* 17 miles south-southeast of Weaverville on Trinity-Shasta County line (lat. 40°30'05" N, long. 122°50' W; near N line sec. 35, T 31 N, R 9 W). Altitude 5555 feet. Named on Weaverville (1950) 15' quadrangle.

Bluenose Ridge [MENDOCINO]: *ridge,* southwest-trending, 5 miles long, 8 miles north-northeast of Covelo (lat. 39°54' N, long. 123°11' W); Bluenose Rock is at the southwest end of the ridge. Named on Bluenose Ridge (1967) 7.5' quadrangle.

Bluenose Rock [MENDOCINO]: *peak,* 6.5 miles north of Covelo (lat. 39°53'05" N, long. 123°13'40" W; on E line sec. 6, T 23 N, R 12 W). Named on Bluenose Ridge (1967) 7.5' quadrangle.

Blue Point [TRINITY]: *peak,* 7 miles southwest of Black Rock Mountain (lat. 40°08'15" N, long. 123°05'50" W; near SW cor. sec. 34, T 27 N, R 11 W). Altitude 5622 feet. Named on Black Rock Mountain (1954) 15' quadrangle.

Blue Point: see **Blue Slide**, under **Black Rock Mountain** [TRINITY].

Blue Point Ridge [TRINITY]: *ridge,* northwest-trending, 2 miles long, center 1 mile west of Dubakella Mountain (lat. 40°23'05" N, long. 123°09'45" W; sec. 1, 12, T 29 N, R 12 W). Named on Dubakella Mountain (1954) 15' quadrangle.

Blue Ridge [DEL NORTE]: *ridge,* 6.25 miles long, 8 miles northeast of Buck Mountain (lat. 41°43' N, long. 123°45'45" W). Named on Hurdygurdy Butte (1982) and Ship Mountain (1982) 7.5' quadrangles.

Blue Ridge [TRINITY]:
(1) *ridge,* northwest-trending, 3 miles long, 9.5 miles northeast of Trinity Center (lat. 41°05'40" N, long. 122°33'15" W). Named on Bonanza King (1955) 15' quadrangle.
(2) *ridge,* west-trending, 1 mile long, 9 miles north of Helena (lat. 40°54'15" N, long. 123°09'30" W; mainly in sec. 7, T 35 N, R 11 W). Named on Helena (1951) 15' quadrangle. United States Geological Survey's (1915) map shows a place called Blue Ridge Camp located near the north end of Blue Ridge (2).
(3) *ridge,* generally west-southwest-trending, 2.5 miles long, 9.5 miles south-southwest of Cecilville, which is in Siskiyou County (lat. 41°01'30" N, long. 123°13' W). Named on Cecil Lake (1979) 7.5' quadrangle.
(4) *ridge,* generally west-southwest-trending, 2 miles long, 16 miles southeast of Weaverville on Trinity-Shasta County line (lat. 40°34'10" N, long. 122°44' W). Named on Shasta Bally (1978) 7.5' quadrangle.

Blue Ridge Camp: see **Blue Ridge** [TRINITY] (2).

Blue Rock [MENDOCINO]: *relief feature,* 7.25 miles east of Leggett (lat. 39°53'10" N, long. 123°35'25" W; sec. 35, T 24 N, R 16 W). Named on Bell Springs (1969) 7.5' quadrangle.

Blue Rock: see **Cummings Creek** [MENDOCINO].

Blue Rock Creek [MENDOCINO]: *stream,* flows 8 miles to Eel River 2.5 miles northwest of Spyrock (2) (lat. 39°54'20" N, long. 123°28'20" W; at S line sec. 19, T 24 N, R 15 W). Named on Bell Springs (1969) and Updegraff Ridge (1967) 7.5' quadrangles.

Blueschist Narrows [MENDOCINO]: *narrows,* 7.5 miles northeast of Covelo along Williams Creek (1) (lat. 39°51'55" N, long. 123°51'40" W; at SW cor. sec. 7, T 23 N, R 11 W). Named on Covelo East (1967) 7.5' quadrangle. The name is from outcrops at the place of rock called blueschist (United States Board on Geographic Names, 1969a, p. 2).

Blue Slide [HUMBOLDT]:
(1) *relief feature,* nearly 4 miles west of Bridgeville on the north side of Van Duzen River (lat. 40°28'45" N, long. 123°52'05" W; sec. 8, T 1 N, R 3 E). Named on Bridgeville (1969) 7.5' quadrangle.
(2) *relief feature,* 4 miles northwest of Weott on the north side of Bull Creek (2) (lat. 40°21'15" N, long. 123°59'05" W; sec. 29, T 1 S, R 2 E). Named on Weott (1969) 7.5' quadrangle.

Blue Slide: see **Black Rock Mountain** [TRINITY].

Blue Slide Creek [HUMBOLDT]:
(1) *stream,* flows 3.5 miles to Mad River 7.25 miles north of Lone Star Junction (lat. 40°44'20" N, long. 123°53' W; near S line sec. 7, T 4 N, R 3 E). Named on Iaqua Buttes (1979) 7.5' quadrangle.
(2) *stream,* flows 1.5 miles to Van Duzen River 6 miles north of Redcrest (lat. 40°29'10" N, long. 123°57'35" W; sec. 9, T 1 N, R 2 E). Named on Redcrest (1969) 7.5' quadrangle.
(3) *stream,* flows 7.25 miles to Mattole River 12 miles west-southwest of Phillipsville (lat. 40°08'35" N, long. 123°59'25" W; sec. 6, T 4 S, R 2 E). Named on Ettersburg (1969) 7.5' quadrangle.

Blue Slide Creek [MENDOCINO]: *stream,* heads in Glenn County and flows 3 miles to Black Butte River 6.25 miles south of Anthony Peak (lat. 39°45'20" N, long. 123°57'35" W; near S line sec. 15, T 22 N, R 10 W). Named on Mendocino Pass (1967) 7.5' quadrangle.

Blue Slide Creek [TRINITY]: *stream,* flows nearly 2 miles to Mad River 5 miles south-southwest of Forest Glen (lat. 40°18'05" N, long. 123°20'45" W; near SE cor. sec. 11, T 2 S, R 7 E). Named on Forest Glen (1979) 7.5' quadrangle.

Blue Slides Creek [LAKE]: *stream,* flows 4 miles to Bear Creek (1) 2.25 miles southwest of Potato Hill (lat. 39°19'15" N, long. 122°50'45" W; near SW cor. sec. 14, T 17 N, R 9 W); the stream is south of Blue Slides Ridge. Named on Potato Hill (1967) 7.5' quadrangle. Called Blue Slide Creek on Lake Pillsbury (1951) 15' quadrangle, but United States Board on Geographic Names (1969b, p. 4) rejected this form for the name.

Blue Slides Lake [LAKE]: *lake,* 450 feet long, 2.5 miles south-southeast of Potato Hill (lat. 39°19'20" N, long. 122°46'50" W; sec. 17, T 17 N, R 8 W); the lake is near the east end of Blue Slides Ridge. Named on Potato Hill (1967) 7.5' quadrangle. United States Board on Geographic Names (1969b, p. 4) rejected the form "Blue Slide Lake" for the name.

Blue Slides Ridge [LAKE]: *ridge,* generally west-trending, 2.5 miles long, nearly 2 miles south of Potato Hill (lat. 39°19'30" N, long. 122°48' W). Named on Potato Hill (1967) 7.5' quadrangle. Called Blue Slide Ridge on Lake Pillsbury (1951) 15' quadrangle, but United States Board on Geographic Names (1969b, p. 4) rejected this form of the name.

Bluff Creek [DEL NORTE-HUMBOLDT]: *stream,* heads in Del Norte County and flows 25 miles to Klamath River 4.5 miles northeast of Weitchpec in Humboldt County (lat. 41°14'25" N, long. 123°39'05" W). Named on Fish Lake (1974), Lonesome Ridge (1974), and Weitchpec (1979) 7.5' quadrangles. Gibbs noted in 1851 that a high point that forms a landmark gives the name "Bluff Creek" to the stream (Gudde, 1949, p. 34-35). East Fork enters from the northeast 1 mile upstream from the entrance of the main creek into Humboldt County, and is 5 miles long. North Fork enters from the north 7.25 miles upstream from the entrance of the main creek into Humboldt County, and is 3.5 miles long. Both forks are named on Lonesome Ridge (1974) 7.5' quadrangle.

Bluff Creek [HUMBOLDT]:

(1) *stream,* flows 1 mile to Eel River 3.25 miles east-northeast of Weott, and just east of Thompson Bluff (lat. 40°20'20" N, long. 123°51'55" W; sec. 32, T 1 S, R 3 E). Named on Myers Flat (1969) 7.5' quadrangle.

(2) *stream,* flows nearly 1 mile to South Fork Eel River 1.25 miles north-northwest of Garberville (lat. 40°06'55" N, long. 123°48'05" W; sec. 13, T 4 S, R 3 E). Named on Garberville (1970) 7.5' quadrangle.

Bluff Creek [TRINITY]: *stream,* flows nearly 7 miles to Kettenpom Creek 4.25 miles east of Kettenpom (lat. 40°09'50" N, long. 123°22'40" W; sec. 34, T 3 S, R 7 E). Named on Zenia (1967) 7.5' quadrangle.

Bluff Lake [TRINITY]: *lake,* 650 feet long, 2.25 miles south-southeast of China Mountain, which is in Siskiyou County (lat. 41°20'50" N, long. 122°33'30" W; near N line sec. 9, T 40 N, R 6 W). Named on China Mountain (1955) 15' quadrangle.

Bluff Prairie: see **Shively** [HUMBOLDT].

Bluford Creek [TRINITY]: *stream,* flows 4 miles to Mud Creek (2) 5 miles east-northeast of Alderpoint [HUMBOLDT] (lat. 40°12'05" N, long. 123°31'15" W; sec. 17, T 3 S, R 6 E). Named on Alderpoint (1969) 7.5' quadrangle.

Blunts Reef [HUMBOLDT]: *rocks,* 3.25 miles west-northwest of Cape Mendocino (lat. 40°26'55" N, long. 124°28'05" W). Named on Cape Mendocino (1969) 7.5' quadrangle. Vancouver discovered the feature, but it remained nameless until 1841, when Wilkes named it for Simon F. Blunt, a midshipman on the *Porpoise* (Gudde, 1949, p. 35). United States Board on Geographic Names (1933, p. 153) rejected the form "Blunt's Reef" for the name.

Board Camp Butte [HUMBOLDT]: *peak,* nearly 1 mile southeast of Board Camp Mountain (lat. 40°41'25" N, long. 123°42'20" W; near NE cor. sec. 34, T 4 N, R 4 E). Altitude 5045 feet. Named on Board Camp Mountain (1977) 7.5' quadrangle.

Board Camp Mountain [HUMBOLDT]: *peak,* 19 miles southeast of the settlement of Willow Creek (lat. 40°41'25" N, long. 123°42'20" W; near NE cor. sec. 34, T 4 N, R 4 E). Altitude 5187 feet. Named on Board Camp Mountain (1977) 7.5' quadrangle.

Boardman Camp [LAKE]: *locality,* 5 miles north-northwest of Bear Mountain (lat. 39°28'40" N, long. 122°55'45" W; sec. 26, T 19 N, R 10 W); the place is southwest of the crest of Boardman Ridge. Named on Lake Pillsbury (1967) 7.5' quadrangle.

Boardman Creek [LAKE]: *stream,* heads just inside Mendocino County and flows 2.5 miles to Smokehouse Creek 7 miles north-northwest of Bear Mountain (lat. 39°29'35" N, long. 122°38'15" W; sec. 21, T 19 N, R 10 W); the stream is west of Boardman Ridge. Named on Hull Mountain (1967) and Lake Pillsbury (1967) 7.5' quadrangles.

Boardman Gulch [MENDOCINO]: *canyon,* drained by a stream that flows 2 miles to South Fork Big River 13 miles southwest of Willits (lat. 39°15'05" N, long. 123°29'45" W; sec. 14, T 16 N, R 15 W). Named on Willits (1961) 15' quadrangle.

Boardman Ridge [LAKE-MENDOCINO]: *ridge,* extends for 4.25 miles south and southeast from Hull Mountain; center 6 miles north-northwest of Bear Mountain (lat. 39°29'30" N, long. 122°55'30" W). Named on Hull Mountain (1967) and Lake Pillsbury (1967) 7.5' quadrangles. The name, given in the 1880's, commemorates Oscar Boardman and his brother, who ran stock on the ridge (Gudde, 1969, p. 32-33).

Boardman Ridge [MENDOCINO]: *ridge,* west-northwest-trending, 1.5 miles long, 13 miles east-northeast of Covelo (lat. 39°50'50" N, long. 123°00'55" W). Named on Newhouse Ridge (1967) 7.5' quadrangle.

Board Tree Canyon [MENDOCINO]: *canyon,* drained by a stream that flows nearly 2 miles to White Rock Creek 12 miles west of Covelo (lat. 39°45'50" N, long. 123°28'05" W; near N line sec. 18, T 22 N, R 14 W). Named on Iron Peak (1967) 7.5' quadrangle.

Boat Creek [HUMBOLDT]: *stream,* flows 1.5 miles to the sea 8.5 miles north of Orick (lat. 41°24'20" N, long. 124°04' W; near N line sec. 28, T 12 N, R 1 E). Named on Fern Canyon (1966) 7.5' quadrangle.

Bobcat Canyon [MENDOCINO]: *canyon,* drained by a stream that flows 1 mile to Camp Creek 7 miles west-northwest of Ornbaun Valley (lat. 38°57'45" N, long. 123°25' W; near NW cor. sec. 28, T 13 N, R 14 W). Named on Ornbaun Valley (1960) 15' quadrangle.

Bob Hill Gulch [HUMBOLDT]: *canyon,* drained by a stream that flows less than 1 mile to Henderson Gulch 3.5 miles south-southeast of downtown Eureka (lat. 40°45'15" N, long. 124°08' W; sec. 1, T 4 N, R 1 W). Named on Eureka (1958) 7.5' quadrangle.

Boehne Butte [HUMBOLDT]: *hill,* 4.25 miles north-northwest of Alderpoint along Eel River (lat. 40°13'50" N, long. 123°39'05" W; near E line sec. 6, T 3 S, R 5 E). Named on Fort Seward (1969) 7.5' quadrangle. The name commemorates Mae Boehne and Frank Boehne, who homesteaded near the feature (Turner, p. 24).

Boggs Lake [LAKE]: *lake,* 2250 feet long, 7 miles south-southeast of Kelseyville (lat. 38°53'10" N, long. 122°46'30" W; sec. 17, 18, T 12 N, R 8 W). Named on Kelseyville (1959) 7.5' quadrangle. Bogg's sawmill was located by the lake (Palmer, p. 8).

Boggs Mountain [LAKE]: *ridge,* northwest-trending, 4 miles long, center 1.5 miles northeast of Whispering Pines (lat. 38°49'45" N, long. 122°41'45" W). Named on Whispering Pines (1958) 7.5' quadrangle.

Bogus Creek [HUMBOLDT]: *stream,* flows 1.25 miles to South Fork Salmon Creek (3) 5.25 miles west of Phillipsville (lat. 40°11'45" N, long. 123°52'50" W; at S line sec. 18, T 3 S, R 3 E). Named on Ettersburg (1969) and Miranda (1970) 7.5' quadrangles.

Bohana Ridge [HUMBOLDT]: *ridge,* generally west-trending, 2.5 miles long, center 2.25 miles south of Lone Star Junction (lat. 40°36' N, long. 123°52'45" W). Named on Owl Creek (1979) and Yager Junction (1979) 7.5' quadrangles.

Bohn Lake: see **Lower Bohn Lake** [LAKE]; **Upper Bohn Lake** [LAKE].

Bohn Valley [LAKE]: *valley,* 7.5 miles east of Middletown (lat. 38°44'10" N, long. 122°28'15" W; on S line sec. 1, T 10 N, R 6 W). Named on Aetna Springs (1958) 7.5' quadrangle. Called Round Valley on Pope Valley (1921) 15' quadrangle, which shows Round Valley Peak situated just south of the valley.

Boise Creek [HUMBOLDT]:

(1) *stream,* flows 8.5 miles to Klamath River 2.25 miles southwest of Orleans (lat. 41°16'55" N, long. 123°34'30" W; sec. 2, T 10 N, R 5 E). Named on Orleans (1978) and Orleans Mountain (1974) 7.5' quadrangles. North Fork enters from the north 2.5 miles west-southwest of Orleans Mountain; it is 2.5 miles long and is named on Orleans Mountain (1974) 7.5' quadrangle. Little South Fork enters from the south 3.5 miles south-southeast of Orleans; it is 2 miles long and is named on Hopkins Butte (1979), Orleans (1978), and Salmon Mountain (1978) 7.5' quadrangles.

(2) *stream,* flows 1.5 miles to Willow Creek (1) 1.5 miles west-northwest of the settlement of Willow Creek (lat. 40°56'50" N, long. 123°39'15" N; sec. 30, T 7 N, R 5 E). Named on Willow Creek (1979) 7.5' quadrangle.

Boise Creek Campground [HUMBOLDT]: *locality,* 1.5 miles north-northwest of the settlement of Willow Creek (lat. 40°56'40" N, long. 123°39'25" W; near S line sec. 30, T 7 N, R 5 E); the place is along Boise Creek (2). Named on Willow Creek (1979) 7.5' quadrangle.

Boles Opening [TRINITY]: *area,* 9 miles west-southwest of Forest Glen (lat. 40°18' N, long. 123°27'55" W; sec. 11, T 2 S, R 6 E). Named on Ruth Reservoir (1978) 7.5' quadrangle.

Bolt Diggings: see **Eastman Gulch** [TRINITY].

Bonanza Creek: see **Deer Creek** [MENDOCINO] (2).

Bonanza Gulch [HUMBOLDT]: *canyon,* drained by a stream that flows 1.5 miles to Bear River 6 miles east-northeast of Cape Mendocino (lat. 40°27'45" N, long. 124°18' W; at S line sec. 16, T 1 N, R 2 W). Named on Capetown (1969) 7.5' quadrangle.

Bonanza King [TRINITY]: *ridge,* north-trending, 4 miles long, 7.5 miles north-northeast of Trinity Center (lat. 41°06' N, long. 122°37'20" W). Named on Bonanza King (1955) 15' quadrangle, which shows Bonanza King mine near the south end of the feature. Etna (1934) 30' quadrangle has the name "Bonanza King" for a peak situated near the south end of the ridge.

Bonanza Springs [LAKE]: *locality,* nearly 4 miles north-northeast of Whispering Pines (lat. 38°51'35" N, long. 122°41'05" W; sec. 30, T 12 N, R 7 W). Named on Whispering Pines (1958) 7.5' quadrangle. The place was a camping resort after fire destroyed the hotel there (Bradley, p. 215). Waring (p. 190-191) used the name "Spiers Springs" for two springs located about 3 miles southeast of Bonanza Springs. Bradley (p. 223) noted that Spiers Spring, or Red Wing Spring, (sec. 5, T 11 N, R 7 W) originally was known as Copsey's Spring for the first owner; the place had a hotel and spring water there was bottled for sale.

Bonanzo Creek: see **Deer Creek** [MENDOCINO] (2).

Bond Creek [HUMBOLDT]: *stream,* flows 1.5 miles to Redwood Creek (1) 14 miles north-northeast of Trinidad (lat. 41°14' N, long. 124°01'10" W; at W line sec. 24, T 10 N, R 1 E). Named on Rodgers Peak (1966) 7.5' quadrangle.

Bond Creek [MENDOCINO]: *stream,* flows 4.5 miles to Hollow Tree Creek 7 miles south of Leggett (lat. 39°46' N, long. 123°44'15" W; near N line sec. 15, T 22 N, R 17 W). Named on Leggett (1969) 7.5' quadrangle.

Bonee Gulch [MENDOCINO]: *canyon,* drained by a stream that flows 1 mile to Greenwood Creek 0.25 mile south-southeast of Elk (lat. 39°07'35" N, long. 123°42'50" W; sec. 35, T 15 N, R 17 W). Named on Elk (1960) and Mallo Pass (1960) 7.5' quadrangles.

Bone Flat [HUMBOLDT]: *area,* 1.5 miles northeast of Yager Junction (lat. 40°33'50" N, long. 123°48' W; near SE cor. sec. 11, T 2 N, R 3 E). Named on Yager Junction (1979) 7.5' quadrangle. According to Turner (p. 25), the name is from bones left from carcasses used to bait coyote traps at the place.

Bone Gulch [TRINITY]: *canyon,* drained by a stream that flows 1.25 miles to a branch of Rattlesnake Creek (2) 3 miles west-northwest of Dubakella Mountain (lat. 40°24' N, long. 123°11'50" W; at N line sec. 3, T 29 N, R 12 W). Named on Dubakella Mountain (1954) 15' quadrangle.

Bonfield Flat: see **Thurston Creek** [LAKE].

Boonville [MENDOCINO]: *town,* 12.5 miles southwest of Ukiah in Anderson Valley (lat. 39°00'35" N, long. 123°22'10" W; around SE cor. sec. 2, T 13 N, R 14 W). Named on Boonville (1959) 15' quadrangle. Postal authorities established Anderson post office in 1858 and moved it 2 miles south in 1875, when they changed the name to Boonville (Salley, p. 7)—Walter Anderson settled about 1 mile northwest of present Boonville in 1851 at a place that had a hotel, blacksmith shop, and store (Carpenter, p. 49). John Burgots founded present Boonville in 1862 when he built a hotel there; the site first was called The Corners (Hanna, p. 38). Alonzo Kendall built another hotel at present Boonville in 1864 and called the village Kendall's City, but when W.W. Boone bought a store there he managed to give his name to the place (Carpenter, p. 49-50). California Mining Bureau's (1909c) map shows a place called Fairbanks located 4 miles by stage line east of Boonville. Postal authorities established Fairbanks post office in 1893 and discontinued it in 1910; the name was for Isabel G. Fairbanks, first postmaster (Salley, p. 72). The same map shows a place called Comfort located 11.5 miles west of Boonville at the end of a stage line. Postal authorities established Comfort post office in 1902, moved it 1.5 miles northwest in 1905, and discontinued it in 1911 (Salley, p. 49).

Booth Crossing [LAKE]: *locality,* 3.25 miles west-southwest of Hull Mountain along Smokehouse Creek (lat. 39°30'10" N, long. 122°59'45" W; sec. 17, T 19 N, R 10 W). Named on Hull Mountain (1967) 7.5' quadrangle.

Booth Gulch [MENDOCINO]: *canyon,* drained by a stream that flows 2 miles to Middle Fork Ten Mile Creek 8 miles south of Branscomb (lat. 39°32'20" N, long. 123°35'55" W; sec. 1, T 19 N, R 16 W). Named on Sherwood Peak (1967) 7.5' quadrangle.

Booth Knoll [TRINITY]: *peak,* 10 miles south-southeast of Alderpoint [HUMBOLDT] (lat. 40°02'50" N, long. 123°31'55" W; at N line sec. 8, T 5 S, R 6 E). Altitude 2427 feet. Named on Jewett Rock (1969) 7.5' quadrangle.

Booths Run [HUMBOLDT]: *stream,* flows nearly 5 miles to Lawrence Creek 5 miles west-northwest of Lone Star Junction (lat. 40°39'45" N, long. 123°58' W; near NE cor. sec. 8, T 3 N, R 2 E). Named on Iaqua Buttes (1979) 7.5' quadrangle. According to Turner (p. 25), the name recalls a Mr. Booth who ran up the stream to escape from Indians who were chasing him.

Bootjack Prairie [HUMBOLDT]: *area,* 5.25 miles south-southwest of Lone Star Junction (lat. 40°33'45" N, long. 123°55'05" W; on S line sec. 11, T 2 N, R 2 E). Named on Owl Creek (1979) 7.5' quadrangle.

Borax Lake [LAKE]: *lake,* 4400 feet long, 6.5 miles north-northwest of the town of Lower Lake (lat. 38°59'20" N, long. 122°40'35" W; sec. 7, T 13 N, R 7 W). Named on Clearlake Highlands (1958) 7.5' quadrangle. Dr. John A. Veatch discovered borax in 1856 at what then was called Big Borax Lake, and later simply Borax Lake; recovery of borax began there in 1864, but the operation moved to Little Borax Lake in 1868 (Hoover, Rensch, and Rensch, p. 141). Dr. Veatch originally referred to the feature as Alkali lake, or as Lake Káysa from the Indian name (Browne and Taylor, p. 184). Anderson (p. 101) called the feature Borax Pond.

Borax Lake: see **Little Borax Lake** [LAKE].

Borax Pond: see **Borax Lake** [LAKE].

Borax Springs: see **Sulphur Bank** [LAKE].

Bordy Creek [TRINITY]: *stream,* flows 1 mile to Trinity River 13 miles north of Hayfork (lat. 40°44'05" N, long. 123°13'55" W). Named on Hayfork (1951) 15' quadrangle.

Bosch Canyon [LAKE]: *canyon,* drained by a stream that flows 1 mile to Morgan Valley 5.5 miles south-southeast of Wilson Valley (2) (lat. 38°52'55" N, long. 122°25'05" W; near S line sec. 16, T 12 N, R 5 W). Named on Wilson Valley (1958) 7.5' quadrangle.

Bosworth Creek [HUMBOLDT]: *stream,* flows 2.5 miles to Larabee Creek nearly 7 miles northwest of Blocksburg (lat. 40°21'10" N, long. 123°43'10" W; near NW cor. sec. 27, T 1 S, R 4 E). Named on Blocksburg (1969) 7.5' quadrangle.

Bottleneck Spring [HUMBOLDT]: *spring,* 11.5 miles south-southwest of the settlement of Willow Creek (lat. 40°46'40" N, long. 123°40'55" W; near NW cor. sec. 36, T 5 N, R 4 E). Named on Grouse Mountain (1979) 7.5' quadrangle.

Bottle Rock: see **Glenbrook** [LAKE].

Bottom Creek [MENDOCINO]: *stream,* flows 2 miles to Little North Fork Navarro River 14 miles north-northwest of Boonville (lat. 39°11'50" N, long. 123°28'40" W; sec. 36, T 16 N, R 15 W). Named on Boonville (1959) 15' quadrangle.

Boulder Creek [DEL NORTE]:

(1) *stream,* flows less than 1 mile to Elevenmile Creek 6.5 miles northeast of Gasquet (lat. 41°54' N, long. 123°51'50" W; sec. 5, T 17 N, R 3 E). Named on Shelly Creek Ridge (1982) 7.5' quadrangle.

(2) *stream,* flows 2 miles to South Fork Smith River 9 miles northwest of Buck Mountain (lat. 41°43'30" N, long. 123°58'20" W; sec. 5, T 15 N, R 2 E). Named on Cant Hook Mountain (1982) 7.5' quadrangle.

Boulder Creek [HUMBOLDT]: *stream,* flows 11 miles to Mad River 9 miles south-southeast of Korbel (lat. 40°45'15" N, long. 123°52'30" W; sec. 6, T 4 N, R 3 E). Named on Board Camp Mountain (1977), Mad River Buttes (1977), and Maple Creek (1977) 7.5' quadrangles.

Boulder Creek [TRINITY]:

(1) *stream,* flows 6.25 miles to Coffee Creek 2.25 miles south of Billys Peak (1) (lat. 41°06'05" N, long. 122°46'30" W; near NE cor. sec. 4, T 37 N, R 8 W). Named on Coffee Creek (1955) 15' quadrangle.

(2) *stream,* flows 2 miles to Stuart Fork 14 miles north of Weaverville (lat. 40°55'30" N, long. 122°57'30" W). Named on Trinity Dam (1950) 15' quadrangle.

(3) *stream,* flows 3.25 miles to Eel River 7 miles south-southwest of Kettenpom (lat. 40°03'40" N, long. 123°29'50" W; at N line sec. 3, T 5 S, R 6 E). Named on Lake Mountain (1967) 7.5' quadrangle.

(4) *stream,* flows 1.5 miles to Canyon Creek (1) 14 miles north-northeast of Helena (lat. 40°57'15" N, long. 123°01'10" W). Named on Helena (1951) 15' quadrangle.

Boulder Creek: see **Little Boulder Creek** [HUMBOLDT]; **Little Boulder Creek** [TRINITY].

Boulder Creek Lake: see **Boulder Lake** [TRINITY].

Boulder Creek Lakes [TRINITY]: *lakes,* three, largest 1200 feet long, 13 miles north-northeast of Helena (lat. 40°56'45" N, long. 123°02'15" W); the lakes are along Boulder Creek (4). Named on Helena (1951) 15' quadrangle.

Boulder Flat [HUMBOLDT]: *area,* 5.5 miles north of Blocksburg (lat. 40°21'20" N, long. 123°38'15" W; near N line sec. 29, T 1 S, R 5 E). Named on Blocksburg (1969) 7.5' quadrangle.

Boulder Flat Creek [HUMBOLDT]: *stream,* flows 3.25 miles to Larabee Creek 4 miles north-northwest of Blocksburg (lat. 40°20'05" N, long. 123°39'45" W; near W line sec. 31, T 1 S, R 5 E); the stream goes past Boulder Flat. Named on Black Lassic (1979) and Blocksburg (1969) 7.5' quadrangles.

Boulder Lake [TRINITY]: *lake,* 900 feet long, 6.25 miles south-southwest of Billys Peak (1) (lat. 41°03' N, long. 122°48'25" W; sec. 20, T 37 N, R 8 W); the lake is along a branch of Boulder Creek (1). Named on Coffee Creek (1955) 15' quadrangle. United States Board on Geographic Names (1978b, p. 3) rejected the names "Big Boulder Lake" and "Boulder Creek Lake" for the feature.

Boulder Lake: see **Little Boulder Lake** [TRINITY].

Boulder Peak [TRINITY]: *peak,* 16 miles northeast of Trinity Center on Trinity-Shasta County line (lat. 41°10'40" N, long. 122°28'35" W; near SE cor. sec. 6, T 38 N, R 5 W). Altitude 6968 feet. Named on Dunsmuir (1954) 15' quadrangle.

Boulder Ridge [DEL NORTE]: *ridge,* north-trending, 1 mile long, 8 miles northwest of Buck Mountain (lat. 41°42'20" N, long. 123°57'45" W); the ridge is east of Boulder Creek. Named on Cant Hook Mountain (1982) 7.5' quadrangle.

Boundary Basin [LAKE]: *area,* 5.25 miles west of Lakeport (lat. 39°02'15" N, long. 123°00'35" W; near SE cor. sec. 25, T 14 N, R 11 W). Named on Purdys Gardens (1958) 7.5' quadrangle.

Boundary Creek [HUMBOLDT]: *stream,* flows 1.25 miles to Mad River 2.25 miles southwest of Korbel (lat. 40°50'45" N, long. 123°59'15" W; at E line sec. 6, T 5 N, R 2 E). Named on Korbel (1979) 7.5' quadrangle.

Boundary Ridge [LAKE]: *ridge,* south-southeast-trending, 1.5 miles long, 4.5 miles west-southwest of Lakeport (lat. 39°01'55" N, long. 122°59'50" W; in and near sec. 29, T 14 N, R 10 W). Named on Lakeport (1958) 7.5' quadrangle.

Bourns Gulch [MENDOCINO]: *canyon,* 1 mile long, 2 miles northwest of Gualala (lat. 38°47'30" N, long. 123°33' W; sec. 21, T 11 N, R 15 W). Named on Gualala (1960) 7.5' quadrangle. United States Board on Geographic Names (1962c, p. 17) rejected the names "Bournes Gulch," "Bourn Gulch," and "Bowen Gulch" for the feature, and pointed out that the name is for the Bourn family, early settlers in the neighborhood.

Bourns Landing [MENDOCINO]: *locality,* 2.25 miles northwest of Gualala along the coast (lat. 38°47'05" N, long. 123°33'40" W; sec. 20, T 11 N, R 15 W). Named on Gualala (1960) 7.5' quadrangle. Carpenter (p. 54) referred to Bourne's Landing. United States Board on Geographic Names (1962c, p. 17) rejected the names "Bournes Landing," "Bourn Landing," and "Bowen Landing" for the place.

Bourns Rock [MENDOCINO]: *rock,* 1.5 miles west-northwest of Gualala, and 2000 feet offshore (lat. 38°46'45" N, long. 123°33'20" W); the rock is 0.5 mile southeast of Bourns Landing. Named on Gualala (1960) 7.5' quadrangle. United States Board on Geographic Names (1962c, p. 18) rejected the names "Bournes Rock," "Bourn Rock," and "Bowen Rock" for the feature.

Bowen Gulch: see **Bourns Gulch** [MENDOCINO].

Bowen Landing: see **Bourns Landing** [MENDOCINO].

Bowen Rock: see **Bourns Rock** [MENDOCINO].

Bowerman Gulch [TRINITY]: *canyon,* drained by a stream that flows 2 miles to East Fork Stuart Fork 15 miles northeast of Weaverville (lat. 40°54'10" N, long. 122°46' W; at W line sec. 10, T 35 N, R 8 W); the canyon heads at Bowerman Peak. Named on Schell Mountain (1950) and Trinity Dam (1950) 15' quadrangles.

Bowerman Meadows [TRINITY]: *area,* 14 miles north-northeast of Weaverville (lat. 40°55'30" N, long. 122°51' W). Named on Trinity Dam

(1950) 15' quadrangle. The name commemorates Jake Bowerman, a Minersville cattleman (Jones, p. 12).

Bowerman Peak [TRINITY]:

(1) *peak,* 15 miles northwest of Weaverville (lat. 40°53'40" N, long. 122°43'50" W; near E line sec. 14, T 35 N, R 8 W); on Bowerman Ridge at the head of Bowerman Gulch. Altitude 4216 feet. Named on Schell Mountain (1950) 15' quadrangle.

(2) *peak,* 4 miles east of Salmon Mountain (lat. 41°11'05" N, long. 123°20'05" W). Altitude 5029 feet. Named on Youngs Peak (1979) 7.5' quadrangle.

Bowerman Ridge [TRINITY]: *ridge,* generally south-trending, 6.5 miles long, 14 miles northeast of Weaverville (lat. 40°52'30" N, long. 122°44'45" W). Named on Schell Mountain (1950) and Trinity Dam (1950) 15' quadrangles.

Bowery Flat [LAKE]: *area,* 1.5 miles east-northeast of Crockett Peak (lat. 39°26'30" N, long. 122°44'50" W). Named on Saint John Mountain (1968) 7.5' quadrangle.

Bowman Gulch [MENDOCINO]: *canyon,* drained by a stream that flows nearly 1 mile to South Fork Big River 4.5 miles east of Comptche (lat. 39°15'35" N, long. 123°30'20" W; sec. 11, T 16 N, R 15 W); the canyon is north of Bowman Ridge. Named on Willits (1961) 15' quadrangle.

Bowman Ridge [MENDOCINO]: *ridge,* generally west-trending, 2 miles long, 13 miles southwest of Willits (lat. 39°15'35" N, long. 123°29'30" W). Named on Comptche (1960) and Willits (1961) 15' quadrangles.

Bowman Spring [HUMBOLDT]: *spring,* 6.25 miles east-northeast of Hoopa (lat. 41°05'05" N, long. 123°34'10" W; near SE cor. sec. 11, T 8 N, R 5 E). Named on Tish Tang Point (1978) 7.5' quadrangle.

Box Camp [HUMBOLDT]: *locality,* 7.5 miles east-northeast of Hoopa (lat. 41°05'10" N, long. 123°32'25" W). Named on Hoopa (1952) 15' quadrangle.

Box Canyon [LAKE]: *canyon,* drained by a stream that flows 2 miles to Benmore Canyon 8.5 miles east-northeast of Clearlake Oaks (lat. 39°03'20" N, long. 122°31'30" W). Named on Clearlake Oaks (1960) and Wilbur Springs (1961) 15' quadrangles.

Box Canyon [TRINITY]:

(1) *narrows,* 0.5 mile southeast of Burnt Ranch along Trinity River (lat. 40°48'15" N, long. 123°27'50" W; on W line sec. 13, T 5 N, R 6 E). Named on Ironside Mountain (1951) 15' quadrangle.

(2) *canyon,* 3.5 miles long, along Browns Creek above a point 15 miles south of Weaverville (lat. 40°30'50" N, long. 122°56'40" W; sec. 25, T 31 N, R 10 W). Named on Chanchelulla Peak (1951) and Weaverville (1950) 15' quadrangles.

Box Spring [MENDOCINO]: *spring,* 7 miles south of Eden Valley (lat. 39°31'30" N, long. 123°11'15" W; near NE cor. sec. 9, T 19 N, R 12 W). Named on Brushy Mountain (1966) 7.5' quadrangle.

Box Spring Ridge [MENDOCINO]: *ridge,* west-trending, 2 miles long, 7 miles south of Eden Valley (lat. 39°31'40" N, long. 123°12'10" W); Box Spring is near the east end of the ridge. Named on Brushy Mountain (1966) 7.5' quadrangle.

Boyes Creek [HUMBOLDT]: *stream,* flows 2.25 miles to Prairie Creek 6 miles north-northeast of Orick (lat. 41°21'55" N, long. 124°01'15" W; sec. 2, T 11 N, R 1 E). Named on Holter Ridge (1983) and Orick (1966) 7.5' quadrangles. Turner (p. 26) associated the name with William Boyes, who owned land in the neighborhood.

Boyes Creek [MENDOCINO]: *stream,* flows 3.25 miles to Busch Creek nearly 3 miles northwest of the town of Potter Valley (lat. 39°20'45" N, long. 123°08'45" W; sec. 12, T 17 N, R 12 W). Named on Redwood Valley (1960) 7.5' quadrangle.

Boyle Creek: see **Doyle Creek** [MENDOCINO].

Boynton Prairie [HUMBOLDT]: *area,* 3.5 miles south of Korbel (lat. 40°47'30" N, long. 123°58'05" W; sec. 28, 29, T 5 N, R 2 E). Named on Korbel (1979) 7.5' quadrangle. The name commemorates Paul Boynton, who moved to the place in 1853; Indians killed him within 200 yards of his house in 1858 (Turner, p. 26).

Bracut [HUMBOLDT]: *locality,* 3 miles south of Arcata along Northwestern Pacific Railroad (lat. 40°49'35" N, long. 124°05' W). Named on Arcata South (1959) 7.5' quadrangle. Called Brainard on Eureka (1942) 15' quadrangle.

Bradburn Creek [TRINITY]: *stream,* flows 4.5 miles to West Fork of North Fork Eel River 5 miles northeast of Kettenpom (lat. 40°12'40" N, long. 123°23'40" W; near S line sec. 9, T 3 S, R 7 E). Named on Zenia (1967) 7.5' quadrangle.

Bradford Creek [HUMBOLDT]: *stream,* flows 3.5 miles to Redwood Creek (1) 12 miles south-southwest of the settlement of Willow Creek (lat. 40°47'20" N, long. 123°44'20" W; at E line sec. 29, T 5 N, R 4 E). Named on Grouse Mountain (1979) 7.5' quadrangle.

Bradford Creek [LAKE]: *stream,* flows 2 miles to Saint Helena Creek 3.5 south-southeast of Middletown (lat. 38°42'05" N, long. 122°36' W; sec. 23, T 10 N, R 7 W). Named on Detert Reservoir (1958) 7.5' quadrangle.

Brad Turner Creek [MENDOCINO]: *stream,* flows nearly 2 miles to Eel River 2.25 miles south of Dos Rios (lat. 39°41'05" N, long. 123°21'25" W; at N line sec. 18, T 21 N, R 13 W). Named on Dos Rios (1967) and Laytonville (1967) 7.5' quadrangles.

Bragdon [TRINITY]: *locality,* 16 miles northeast of Weaverville (lat. 40°53'30" N, long. 122°41'50" W; sec. 18, T 35 N, R 7 W); the place is at the mouth of Bragdon Gulch. Named on Weaverville (1913) 30' quadrangle. Postal authorities established Bragdon post office in 1898 and discontinued it in 1903; the name was for Edwin H. Bragdon, first postmaster (Salley, p. 26). They established Five Pines post office at the place in 1914 and discontinued it in 1924—this post office name was for nearby Five Pines mine (Jones, p. 39; Salley, p. 75).

Bragdon Gulch [TRINITY]: *canyon,* drained by a stream that flows 6 miles to Trinity River 16 miles northeast of Weaverville (lat. 40°53'30" N, long. 122°42'10" W; sec. 18, T 35 N, R 7 W). Named on Schell Mountain (1950) 15' quadrangle.

Bragg: see **Fort Bragg** [MENDOCINO].

Brainard [HUMBOLDT]: *locality,* 4 miles south-southwest of Arcata along Northwestern Pacific Railroad (lat. 40°48'45" N, long. 124°06'30" W). Named on Arcata South (1959) 7.5' quadrangle. Present Bracut is called Brainard on Eureka (1942) 15' quadrangle.

Brandon Gulch [MENDOCINO]: *canyon,* drained by a stream that flows nearly 2 miles to North Fork of South Fork Noyo River 11 miles north-northwest of Comptche (lat. 39°24'15" N, long. 123°40'50" W; sec. 19, T 18 N, R 16 W). Named on Comptche (1960) 15' quadrangle. Called Camp 6 Gulch on O'Brien's (1953) map.

Brandt Ridge [MENDOCINO]: *ridge,* southeast-trending, 3 miles long, 11.5 miles west-southwest of Ornbaun Valley (lat. 38°50'20" N, long. 123°29'35" W). Named on Ornbaun Valley (1960) and Point Arena (1960) 15' quadrangles.

Brannan Bluff: see **Table Bluff** [HUMBOLDT] (1).

Brannan Creek [HUMBOLDT]: *stream,* flows 2.25 miles to Willow Creek (1) 1.5 miles west-northwest of the settlement of Willow Creek (lat. 40°56'50" N, long. 123°39'40" W; near SW cor. sec. 30, T 7 N, R 5 E); the stream heads near Brannan Mountain. Named on Willow Creek (1979) 7.5' quadrangle

Brannan Creek: see **Little Brannan Creek** [HUMBOLDT].

Brannan Mountain [HUMBOLDT]: *peak,* 3.5 miles northwest of the settlement of Willow Creek (lat. 40°58'05" N, long. 123°41'15" W; at N line sec. 26, T 7 N, R 4 E). Altitude 4001 feet. Named on Willow Creek (1979) 7.5' quadrangle.

Brannon River: see **Eel River** [HUMBOLDT-LAKE-MENDOCINO-TRINITY].

Branscomb [MENDOCINO]: *village,* 8 miles west-southwest of Laytonville (lat. 39°39'15" N, long. 123°37'30" W; near SW cor. sec. 23, T 21 N, R 16 W). Named on Cahto Peak (1967) and Lincoln Ridge (1966) 7.5' quadrangles. Postal authorities established Branscomb post office in 1894 and named it for Benjamin F. Branscomb, a pioneer settler at the place (Salley, p. 26). Waring (p. 177) described Cantwell Soda Spring, a small spring of carbonated water situated in a ravine about 0.25 mile north of Branscomb and named for an owner of the property there.

Branstetter Ridge [HUMBOLDT]: *ridge,* generally west-trending, 5.5 miles long, 5 miles east-southeast of Cape Mendocino (lat. 40°24'40" N, long. 124°19'15" W). Named on Capetown (1969) 7.5' quadrangle.

Brays Opening [HUMBOLDT]: *area,* 1 mile east-northeast of Board Camp Mountain (lat. 40°42'15" N, long. 123°42'10" W; near NW cor. sec. 26, T 4 N, R 4 E). Named on Board Camp Mountain (1977) 7.5' quadrangle.

Brays Opening Creek [HUMBOLDT]: *stream,* flows 1 mile to Grouse Creek (2) 3 miles east of Board Camp Mountain (lat. 41°41'40" N, long. 123°39'35" W). Named on Board Camp Mountain (1977) 7.5' quadrangle.

Breckeen Creek [HUMBOLDT]: *stream,* flows 1 mile to South Fork Trinity River 9 miles east-northeast of Board Camp Mountain (lat. 40°44'20" N, long. 123°32'45" W). Named on Sims Mountain (1979) 7.5' quadrangle.

Bremer Creek [HUMBOLDT]: *stream,* flows 2.25 miles to Trinity River 1 mile west-northwest of the settlement of Willow Creek (lat. 40°56'50" N, long. 123°36'35" W). Named on Salyer (1979) 7.5' quadrangle.

Bret Creek [HUMBOLDT]: *stream,* flows 1.5 miles to Tish Tang a Tang Creek 5.5 miles northwest of Trinity Mountain (lat. 41°04'35" N, long. 123°29'55" W); the stream heads at Bret Hole. Named on Trinity Mountain (1979) 7.5' quadrangle.

Bret Hole [HUMBOLDT]: *relief feature,* 4 miles northwest of Trinity Mountain (lat. 41°04'05" N, long. 123°28'15" W). Named on Trinity Mountain (1979) 7.5' quadrangle.

Brewery Hill [LAKE]: *peak,* 1.5 miles west-northwest of Lakeport (lat. 39°03'35" N, long. 122°56'20" W; sec. 23, T 14 N, R 10 W). Named on Lakeport (1958) 7.5' quadrangle.

Briceland [HUMBOLDT]: *village,* nearly 6 miles west of Garberville (lat. 40°06'30" N, long. 123°54' W; at SW cor. sec. 18, T 4 S, R 3 E). Named on Briceland (1969) 7.5' quadrangle. Postal authorities established Briceland post office in 1889 and discontinued it in 1968 (Salley, p. 26). The name commemorates John C. Briceland, who bought the land at the place about 1889 (Gudde, 1949, p. 40).

Bridge Camp [TRINITY]: *locality,* 10 miles north of Weaverville along Stuart

Fork (lat. 40°52'25" N, long. 122°55' W; sec. 20, T 35 N, R 9 W). Named on Trinity Dam (1950) 15' quadrangle.

Bridge Creek [HUMBOLDT]:
(1) *stream*, flows 7.5 miles to Redwood Creek (1) 7.5' miles west-northwest of Coyote Peak (lat. 41°11'35" N, long. 123°58'55" W). Named on Bald Hills (1982), Panther Creek (1982), and Rodgers Peak (1966) 7.5' quadrangles.
(2) *stream*, flows 8.5 miles to North Fork Elk River (1) 7.5 miles east-southeast of Fields Landing (lat. 40°41'35" N, long. 124°04'55" W; near NW cor. sec. 33, T 4 N, R 1 E). Named on McWhinney Creek (1979) 7.5' quadrangle. West Fork enters from the north 0.25 mile upstream from the mouth of the main creek; it is 1.25 miles long and is named on McWhinney Creek (1979) 7.5' quadrangle.
(3) *stream*, flows 1.5 miles to Eel River 2 miles north-northeast of Redcrest (lat. 40°25'30" N, long. 123°56'05" W; sec. 34, T 1 N, R 2 E). Named on Redcrest (1969) 7.5' quadrangle.
(4) *stream*, flows 2 miles to South Fork Eel River nearly 5 miles southeast of Weott (lat. 40°16'55" N, long. 123°51'20" W; near E line sec. 20, T 2 S, R 3 E). Named on Myers Flat (1969) 7.5' quadrangle.
(5) *stream*, flows 3.5 miles to Mattole River 10 miles west-southwest of Garberville (lat. 40°03'30" N, long. 123°58'20" W). Named on Briceland (1969) and Shelter Cover (1969) 7.5' quadrangles.

Bridge Creek [MENDOCINO]: *stream*, flows nearly 3 miles to South Branch of North Fork Navarro River 10.5 miles north-northwest of Boonville (lat. 39°09' N, long. 123°26'10" W; near NW cor. sec. 20, T 15 N, R 14 W). Named on Boonville (1959) 15' quadrangle.

Bridge Creek Ridge [HUMBOLDT]: *ridge*, north-northwest-trending, 3 miles long, 6 miles west-northwest of Coyote Peak (lat. 41°09'30" N, long. 123°58' W); the ridge is east of Bridge Creek (1). Named on Bald Hills (1982) 7.5' quadrangle.

Bridge Gulch [TRINITY]:
(1) *canyon*, drained by a stream that flows 2 miles to Trinity River 17 miles northeast of Weaverville (lat. 40°54'15" N, long. 122°41'45" W; sec. 18, T 35 N, R 7 W). Named on Schell Mountain (1950) 15' quadrangle.
(2) *canyon*, drained by a stream that flows nearly 4 miles to Hayfork Creek 6.5 miles east-southeast of Hayfork (lat. 40°30'20" N, long. 123°04'50" W). Named on Dubakella Mountain (1954) and Hayfork (1951) 15' quadrangles. Dubakella Mountain (1954) 15' quadrangle shows a natural bridge located along the stream.

Bridgeport: see **Bridgeport Landing** [MENDOCINO]; **Bridgeville** [HUMBOLDT].

Bridgeport Landing [MENDOCINO]: *locality*, 5 miles south-southeast of Elk along the coast (lat. 39°03'45" N, long. 123°41'40" W; sec. 24, T 14 N, R 17 W). Site named on Mallo Pass Creek (1960) 7.5' quadrangle. Walter Jackson (p. 1) noted that the shipping point for Bridgeport was just west of the hamlet of Bridgeport, where Miller post office was located. Postal authorities established Miller post office in 1873, discontinued it in 1880, reestablished it in 1883, and discontinued it in 1908 (Frickstad, p. 96). Walter Jackson (p. 3) mentioned that Bridgeport shipping point was at what was called Irish Bay, for A.J. Irish, who leased the shipping site in 1862 and built a slide chute. A safer anchorage situated 2 miles to the south at a place called New Haven eventually superceded the Bridgeport shipping point (Jackson, Walter, p. 1).

Bridges Creek [MENDOCINO]: *stream*, flows nearly 4 miles to South Fork Eel River 4.5 miles south-southeast of Piercy (lat. 39°54'25" N, long. 123°45'05" W; near SW cor. sec. 21, T 24 N, R 17 W). Named on Noble Butte (1969) and Piercy (1969) 7.5' quadrangles.

Bridges Creek: see **Twin Bridges Creek** [MENDOCINO].

Bridgeville [HUMBOLDT]: *village*, 12 miles north-northeast of Weott (lat. 40°28'10" N, long. 123°47'50" W; near NE cor. sec. 14, T 1 N, R 3 E). Named on Bridgeville (1969) 7.5' quadrangle. Postal authorities established Bridgeville post office in 1877 (Frickstad, p. 42). The name was given to the place when a bridge was built across Van Duzen River there about 1875; previously it was called Robinsons Ferry (Hanna, p. 41). The name "Robinson's Ferry" was for William Slaughter Robinson, a local rancher; after the bridge was built, the place became known as Bridgeport, but postal authorities changed the name to Bridgeville to avoid confusion with Bridgeport in Mono County (Turner, p. 29).

Bright Ridge [MENDOCINO]: *ridge*, northeast-trending, 2 miles long, center less than 2 miles southwest of Eden Valley (lat. 39°36'20" N, long. 123°12'15" W). Named on Brushy Mountain (1966) 7.5' quadrangle.

Brin Canyon [MENDOCINO]: *canyon*, drained by a stream that flows 3.5 miles to Horse Canyon 12.5 miles north of Covelo (lat. 39°58'25" N, long. 123°14'30" W; sec. 31, T 25 N, R 12 W). Named on Bluenose Ridge (1967) 7.5' quadrangle.

Brinkman Butte [HUMBOLDT]: *peak*, 2 miles south-southeast of Showers Mountain (lat. 40°32'05" N, long. 123°40'40" W; sec. 24, T 2 N, R 4 E). Altitude 3932 feet. Named on Showers Mountain (1978) 7.5' quadrangle.

Broaddus Creek [MENDOCINO]: *stream*, flows 5 miles to Little Lake Valley at Willits (lat. 39°24'15" N, long. 123°21'30" W; near N line sec. 24, T 18 N, R 14 W). Named on Willits (1961) 15' quadrangle. Called Brouddus Creek on O'Brien's (1953) map.

Brock Creek [HUMBOLDT]:
(1) *stream*, flows 3.5 miles to Eel River 7.5 miles northwest of Alderpoint (lat. 40°14'55" N, long. 123°43'05" W; sec. 34, T 2 S, R 4 E). Named on Fort Seward (1969) 7.5' quadrangle.
(2) *locality*, 7.5 miles northwest of Alderpoint along Northwestern Pacific Railroad (lat. 40°14'55" N, long. 123°42'50" W; sec. 34, T 2 S, R 4 E); the place is near the mouth of Brock Creek (1). Named on Alderpoint (1949) 15' quadrangle.

Brock Gulch [TRINITY]:
(1) *canyon*, drained by a stream that flows 3 miles to East Fork of North Fork Trinity River 1 mile north of Helena (lat. 40°47'15" N, long. 123°07'30" W). Named on Helena (1951) 15' quadrangle.
(2) *canyon*, drained by a stream that flows 2 miles to Salt Creek (4) 2 miles south of Hayfork (lat. 40°31'40" N, long. 123°11'15" W; sec. 23, T 31 N, R 12 W). Named on Hayfork (1951) 15' quadrangle.

Broken Kettle Creek [DEL NORTE]: *stream*, flows 3.5 miles to Elk Creek (2) 7 miles north of Broken Rib Mountain (lat. 41°59'20" N, long. 123°42'55" W; near NW cor. sec. 2, T 18 N, R 4 E). Named on Broken Rib Mountain (1982) and Shelly Creek Ridge (1982) 7.5' quadrangles.

Broken Rib Mountain [DEL NORTE]: *peak*, 15 miles east of Gasquet (lat. 41°53'20" N, long. 123°41'25" W). Altitude 5812 feet. Named on Broken Rib Mountain (1982) 7.5' quadrangle. The name is from an incident in 1915 involving United States Geological Survey personnel (Gudde, 1949, p. 41).

Broken Rib Peak: see **Youngs Peak** [DEL NORTE].

Broken Rock Spring [DEL NORTE]: *spring*, 6 miles northeast of Klamath Glen (lat. 41°34'55" N, long. 123°55'10" W). Named on Klamath Glen (1982) 7.5' quadrangle.

Brooks Creek: see **Hennessy Creek** [TRINITY].

Brooks Ridge [TRINITY]: *ridge*, generally west-trending, 2 miles long, 2.5 miles south of Black Rock Mountain (lat. 41°10'05" N, long. 123°00'10" W). Named on Black Rock Mountain (1954) and Yolla Bolly (1954) 15' quadrangles.

Brother Jonathan Rock: see **Star Rock** [DEL NORTE].

Brothers: see **The Brothers** [HUMBOLDT].

Brouddus Creek: see **Broaddus Creek** [MENDOCINO].

Brown Camp [TRINITY]: *locality*, 12.5 miles south-southwest of Black Rock Mountain (lat. 40°03' N, long. 123°07'15" W; sec. 6, T 25 N, R 11 W). Named on Black Rock Mountain (1954) 15' quadrangle.

Brown Creek [HUMBOLDT]:
(1) *stream*, flows 2.25 miles to Prairie Creek 7.25 miles north-northeast of Orick (lat. 41°23'10" N, long. 124°01' W; near NE cor. sec. 35, T 12 N, R 1 E). Named on Ah Pah Ridge (1983) and Fern Canyon (1966) 7.5' quadrangles.
(2) *stream*, flows 1 mile to Hoopa Valley 1.5 miles northwest of Hoopa (lat. 41°03'45" N, long. 123°41'40" W; sec. 23, T 8 N, R 4 E). Named on Hoopa (1979) 7.5' quadrangle.
(3) *stream*, flows 3.5 miles to Van Duzen River 0.25 mile east-northeast of Bridgeville (lat. 40°28'20" N, long. 123°47'40" W; near SW cor. sec. 12, T 1 N, R 3 E). Named on Bridgeville (1969) and Yager Junction (1979) 7.5' quadrangles.

Brown Creek [HUMBOLDT]: *stream*, heads in Siskiyou County and flows 3 miles to Wilder Creek nearly 4 miles north-northwest of Orleans (lat. 41°21'10" N, long. 123°34' W). Named on Bark Shanty Gulch (1974) and Orleans (1978) 7.5' quadrangles.

Brown Rock [DEL NORTE]: *rock*, 4 miles northwest of Crescent City, and 3000 feet offshore (lat. 41°47'20" N, long. 124°15'45" W). Named on Crescent City (1966) 7.5' quadrangle.

Brown's Camp: see **Stafford** [HUMBOLDT].

Browns Camp [TRINITY]: *locality*, 10 miles northeast of Kettenpom along Mad River (lat. 40°14'30" N, long. 123°18'35" W; near SE cor. sec. 31, T 2 S, R 8 E). Named on Shannon Butte (1967) 7.5' quadrangle.

Browns Canyon [HUMBOLDT-TRINITY]: *canyon*, drained by a stream that heads in Humboldt County and flows 3 miles to Van Duzen River 7 miles southeast of Dinsmore [HUMBOLDT] in Trinity County (lat. 40°24'40" N, long. 123°31'20" W; near N line sec. 5, T 1 S, R 6 E). Named on Dinsmore (1977) 7.5' quadrangle.

Browns Creek [TRINITY]: *stream*, flows 22 miles to Trinity River 5.25 miles south-southwest of Weaverville (lat. 40°40'05" N, long. 122°59'20" W; sec. 34, T 33 N, R 10 W). Named on Chanchelulla Peak (1951) and Weaverville (1950) 15' quadrangles. East Fork enters from the southeast 14 miles south of Weaverville; it is 6.25 miles long and is named on Chanchelulla Peak (1951) and Weaverville (1950) 15' quadrangles. Gudde (1975, p. 265) listed a mining place called Pike County Bar that was situated along Trinity River opposite the mouth of Browns Creek.

Browns Creek: see **Little Browns Creek** [TRINITY]; **Little Browns Creek**, under **Little Creek** [TRINITY].

Browns Gulch [HUMBOLDT]: *canyon*, drained by a stream that flows 1.25 miles to North Fork Elk River (1) 6 miles east-southeast of Fields Landing (lat. 40°42' N, long. 124°06'40" W; sec. 30, T 4 N, R 1 E). Named on

McWhinney Creek (1979) 7.5' quadrangle.

Browns Lake: see **Fish Lake** [HUMBOLDT].

Browns Landing [LAKE]: *locality*, 3 miles northwest of the town of Lower Lake along Clear Lake (lat. 38°56'25" N, long. 122°39'05" W; sec. 29, T 13 N, R 7 W). Named on Clearlake Highlands (1958) 7.5' quadrangle.

Brown's Mill: see **Stafford** [HUMBOLDT].

Browns Mountain [TRINITY]:

(1) *ridge*, south- to southwest-trending, 8 miles long, center 3 miles southeast of Weaverville (lat. 40°42' N, long. 122°54' W). Named on Trinity Dam (1950) and Weaverville (1950) 15' quadrangles. Brown (p. 920) used the form "Brown's Mountain" for the name.

(2) *ridge*, south- to southeast-trending, 3.5 miles long, 6.5 miles south-southwest of Weaverville (lat. 40°38'40" N, long. 122°58' W). Named on Weaverville (1950) 15' quadrangle.

Browns Rock [HUMBOLDT]: *relief feature*, 5.25 miles south-southeast of Dinsmore (lat. 40°25'25" N, long. 123°33'35" W; sec. 36, T 1 N, R 5 E). Named on Dinsmore (1977) 7.5' quadrangle.

Brownsville: see **Samoa** [HUMBOLDT].

Bruhel Point [MENDOCINO]: *promontory*, 2 miles south of Westport along the coast (lat. 39°36'30" N, long. 123°47'10" W; sec. 7, T 20 N, R 17 W). Named on Inglenook (1966) 7.5' quadrangle.

Brush Creek [MENDOCINO]: *stream*, flows 12 miles to the sea 4.5 miles north of the village of Point Arena (lat. 38°53'35" N, long. 123°42'40" W; sec. 23, T 13 N, R 17 W). Named on Point Arena (1960) 15' quadrangle. South Fork enters from the south 9 miles upstream from the mouth of the main creek; it is 2 miles long and is named on Point Arena (1960) 15' quadrangle.

Brush Creek [TRINITY]: *stream*, flows 2.25 miles to lowlands 22 miles northeast of Weaverville (lat. 40°59'55" N, long. 122°41'30" W; sec. 8, T 36 N, R 7 W). Named on Bonanza King (1955) and Schell Mountain (1950) 15' quadrangles.

Brush Mountain [HUMBOLDT]: *peak*, 2.5 miles southwest of the settlement of Willow Creek (lat. 40°54'55" N, long. 123°40'05" W; sec. 12, T 6 N, R 4 E). Altitude 3988 feet. Named on Willow Creek (1979) 7.5' quadrangle.

Brush Mountain [MENDOCINO]:

(1) *ridge*, south-southeast- to south-trending, 1.5 miles long, 7.5 miles southeast of Leggett (lat. 39°47'25" N, long. 123°36'50" W). Named on Tan Oak Park (1969) 7.5' quadrangle. On Leggett (1952) 15' quadrangle, the name "Brush Mountain" applies to present Brush Mountain (1) and present Bald Mountain (1) together.

(2) *peak*, 8.5 miles southeast of Branscomb (lat. 39°34'50" N, long. 123°30'15" W; at SE cor. sec. 15, T 20 N, R 15 W). Altitude 3104 feet. Named on Sherwood Peak (1967) 7.5' quadrangle.

Brush Mountain [TRINITY]: *ridge*, generally southeast-trending, 2 miles long, 17 miles southwest of Black Rock Mountain (lat. 40°01'50" N, long. 123°13'45" W). Named on Black Rock Mountain (1954) 15' quadrangle.

Brushy Camp Ridge [LAKE]: *ridge*, generally west-trending, 7 miles long, center 7 miles east of Hull Mountain (lat. 39°31'20" N, long. 122°48'15" W). Named on Felkner Hill (1968) and Kneecap Ridge (1967) 7.5' quadrangles. The east end of the ridge is in Glenn County.

Brushy Creek [DEL NORTE]: *stream*, flows nearly 3 miles to Elk Creek (2) 6 miles north of Broken Rib Mountain (lat. 41°58'30" N, long. 123°41'55" W; at NW cor. sec. 12, T 18 N, R 4 E). Named on Broken Rib Mountain (1982) 7.5' quadrangle.

Brushy Creek [HUMBOLDT]: *stream*, flows 2.25 miles to Bear River 6 miles south of Scotia (lat. 40°23'30" N, long. 124°06' W). Named on Scotia (1970) 7.5' quadrangle.

Brushy Creek [LAKE]: *stream*, flows 3 miles to Cache Creek 1 mile southeast of Wilson Valley (2) (lat. 38°57'40" N, long. 122°27'20" W; sec. 19, T 13 N, R 5 W). Named on Wilson Valley (1958) 7.5' quadrangle.

Brushy Creek [MENDOCINO]: *stream*, flows 2.5 miles to Eel River 10.5 miles east-southeast of Laytonville (lat. 39°37'05" N, long. 123°18'50" W; near W line sec. 4, T 20 N, R 13 W). Named on Dos Rio (1967) and Willis Ridge (1966) 7.5' quadrangles. Called Indian Creek on Laytonville (1951) 15' quadrangle, where present Indian Creek (3) is called Brushy Creek.

Brushy Creek [TRINITY]: *stream*, flows 2 miles to Slide Creek 10 miles south-southeast of Salmon Mountain (lat. 41°03'20" N, long. 123°19'05" W). Named on Dees Peak (1978) 7.5' quadrangle.

Brushy Creek: see **Indian Creek** [MENDOCINO] (3).

Brushy Lake [MENDOCINO]: *lake*, 625 feet long, 3 miles southwest of Eden Valley (lat. 39°56'10" N, long. 123°13'55" W; sec. 7, T 20 N, R 12 W); the lake is less than 1 mile northeast of Brushy Mountain. Named on Brushy Mountain (1966) 7.5' quadrangle.

Brushy Gulch [DEL NORTE]: *canyon*, drained by a stream that flows 1.25 miles to East Fork Bluff Creek 18 miles east-southeast of Klamath Glen (lat. 41°24'50" N, long. 123°40'55" W). Named on Lonesome Ridge (1974) 7.5' quadrangle.

Brushy Mountain [HUMBOLDT]:

(1) *ridge*, north-to northwest-trending, 2 miles long, 7 miles east-northeast of Weott (lat. 40°21'15" N, long. 123°48'05" W; mainly in sec. 23, 26, T 1 S, R 3 E). Named on Myers Flat (1969) 7.5' quadrangle.

(2) *ridge*, north-northeast-trending, 1 mile long, 4.5 miles southwest of Honeydew (lat. 40°11'15" N, long. 124°10'25" W). Named on Shubrick Peak (1969) 7.5' quadrangle.

Brushy Mountain [MENDOCINO]: *peak*, 3.5 miles southwest of Eden Valley (lat. 39°35'40" N, long. 123°14'20" W; on W line sec. 18, T 20 N, R 12 W). Altitude 4864 feet. Named on Brushy Mountain (1966) 7.5' quadrangle.

Brushy Mountain [TRINITY]:

(1) *peak*, 11 miles east-northeast of Burnt Ranch (lat. 40°53'10" N, long. 123°17'50" W). Altitude 6179 feet. Named on Ironside Mountain (1951) 15' quadrangle.

(2) *ridge*, north-trending, 2.25 miles long, 7.5 miles southeast of Dubakalla Mountain on Trinity-Shasta County line (lat. 40°18' N, long. 123°03'55" W; sec. 2, 11, T 28 N, R 11 W). Named on Dubakella Mountain (1954) 15' quadrangle.

Brushy Opening [MENDOCINO]: *area*, 10 miles south-southwest of Navarro (lat. 39°00'50" N, long. 123°37' W; around SE cor. sec. 3, T 13 N, R 16 W). Named on Navarro (1961) 15' quadrangle.

Brushy Ridge [HUMBOLDT]: *ridge*, south-southwest- to west-trending, 3.25 miles long, 9 miles south-southwest of Scotia (lat. 40°21'35" N, long. 124°10'20" W). Named on Buckeye Mountain (1970) and Taylor Peak (1969) 7.5' quadrangles.

Brushy Ridge [LAKE]: *ridge*, generally north-northwest-trending, less than 1 mile long, 8 miles west of Lakeport (lat. 39°03'25" N, long. 123°03'15" W; sec. 22, T 14 N, R 11 W). Named on Purdys Gardens (1958) 7.5' quadrangle.

Brushy Sky High [LAKE]: *peak*, 5.5 miles east of the town of Lower Lake (lat. 38°55'05" N, long. 122°30'20" W; sec. 3, T 12 N, R 6 W); the peak is less than 1 mile northeast of the peak called Sky High. Altitude 3196 feet. Named on Lower Lake (1958) 7.5' quadrangle.

Bryan: see **Larabee** [HUMBOLDT].

Bryant: see **Larabee** [HUMBOLDT].

Bryant Ridge [HUMBOLDT]: *ridge*, east-northeast-trending, 1 mile long, 5.5 miles east of Showers Mountain (lat. 40°35' N, long. 123°35'30" W; mainly in sec. 3, T 2 N, R 5 E). Named on Blake Mountain (1979) 7.5' quadrangle.

Bryon Gulch [TRINITY]: *canyon*, drained by a stream that flows 1.25 miles to Reading Creek 14 miles south-southeast of Weaverville (lat. 40°32'20" N, long. 122°51' W; sec. 14, T 31 N, R 9 W). Named on Weaverville (1950) 15' quadrangle.

Bucha Ridge [MENDOCINO]: *ridge*, generally west-trending, 11 miles long, 5 miles south of Branscomb (lat. 39°35'10" N, long. 123°37'10" W). Named on Dutchmans Knoll (1966) and Sherwood Peak (1967) 7.5' quadrangles.

Buck Buttes [HUMBOLDT]: *ridge*, east-southeast-trending, 1 mile long, 5.5 miles west-northwest of the settlement of Willow Creek (lat. 40°58'30" N, .long. 123°43'40" W; sec. 21, T 7 N, R 4 E). Named on Willow Creek (1979) 7.5' quadrangle.

Buck Camp Ridge [DEL NORTE]: *ridge*, north-northwest-trending, 1 mile long, less than 1 mile west of Sawtooth Mountain (lat. 41°36'35" N, long. 123°43'25" W). Named on Chimney Rock (1981) 7.5' quadrangle.

Buck Canyon [LAKE]: *canyon*, 6 miles west-southwest of Lakeport along Benmore Creek (lat. 39°01'50" N, long. 123°01'10" W; in and near sec. 36, T 14 N, R 11 W); the canyon is south of Buck Ridge (2). Named on Purdys Gardens (1958) 7.5' quadrangle.

Buck Creek [DEL NORTE]: *stream*, flows 7 miles to South Fork Smith River 1.5 miles northeast of Buck Mountain (lat. 41°39'05" N, long. 123°50'40" W). Named on Ship Mountain (1982) and Summit Valley (1981) 7.5' quadrangles.

Buck Creek [HUMBOLDT]: *stream*, flows 1.5 miles to the sea 6.5 miles north-northwest of Point Delgada (lat. 40°06'30" N, long. 124°07'15" W). Named on Honeydew (1970) and Shelter Cove (1969) 7.5' quadrangles.

Buck Creek [MENDOCINO]:

(1) *stream*, flows nearly 1 mile to Eel River 5 miles north of Spyrock (2) (lat. 39°57'05" N, long. 123°26'35" W; near S line sec. 5, T 24 N, R 14 W). Named on Updegraph Ridge (1967) 7.5' quadrangle. On Spyrock (1952) 15' quadrangle, the name applies to a creek that enters Eel River 0.5 mile farther upstream (sec. 8, T 24 N, R 14 E).

(2) *stream*, flows 4 miles to Middle Fork Eel River 11 miles east-northeast of Covelo (lat. 39°51'35" N, long. 123°03'30" W; near SW cor. sec. 11, T 23 N, R 11 W). Named on Mendocino Pass (1967) and Newhouse Ridge (1967) 7.5' quadrangles.

(3) *stream*, flows less than 1 mile to a pond just northwest of Branscomb (lat. 39°39'20" N, long. 123°37'35" W; sec. 22, T 21 N, R 16 W). Named on Cahto Peak (1967) 7.5' quadrangle.

Buck Creek: see **Little Buck Creek**, under **Buck Mountain Creek** [HUMBOLDT].

Buck Creek Campsite [DEL NORTE]: *locality*, 1.5 miles northeast of Buck Mountain along South Fork Smith River (lat. 41°39'05" N, long. 123°50'40" W); the place is at the mouth of Buck Creek. Named on Ship Mountain

(1982) 7.5' quadrangle.

Buck-Eye Bar: see **Reading Creek** [TRINITY].

Buckeye Canyon [LAKE]: *canyon*, drained by a stream that flows 2.25 miles to the northeast end of Burns Valley 5 miles north of the town of Lower Lake (lat. 38°59' N, long. 122°36' W; near S line sec. 11, T 13 N, R 7 W). Named on Lower Lake (1958) 7.5' quadrangle.

Buckeye Creek [MENDOCINO]: *stream*, flows 1.25 miles to Sonoma County 12.5 miles south-southwest of Hopland (lat. 38°48'35" N, long. 123°12'05" W; at S line sec. 9, T 11 N, R 12 W). Named on Hopland (1960) 15' quadrangle.

Buckeye Creek [TRINITY]:

(1) *stream*, flows 5 miles to the canyon of Trinity River 2.25 miles north of Trinity Center (lat. 41°02'25" N, long. 122°41'50" W; sec. 29, T 37 N, R 7 W). Named on Bonanza King (1955) and Coffee Creek (1955) 15' quadrangles.

(2) *stream*, flows 3.5 miles to Clair Engle Lake 8 miles northeast of Weaverville (lat. 40°48'30" N, long. 122°49'05" W; sec. 18, T 34 N, R 8 W); the stream is north of Buckeye Ridge. Named on Trinity Dam (1950) 15' quadrangle.

(3) *stream*, flows nearly 2 miles to South Fork Trinity River 6 miles north-northwest of Hyampom (lat. 40°41'40" N, long. 123°30'20" W). Named on Hyampom (1951) 15' quadrangle, and on Sims Mountain (1979) 7.5' quadrangle.

Buckeye Mountain [HUMBOLDT]: *ridge*, southeast-trending, 1.25 miles long, 11 miles south-southwest of Scotia (lat. 40°20'10" N, long. 124°11'35" W). Named on Buckeye Mountain (1970) 7.5' quadrangle.

Buckeye Ridge [HUMBOLDT]: *ridge*, south-southwest-trending, 0.25 mile long, 6 miles east-southeast of Honeydew (lat. 40°12'05" N, long. 124°01'40" W). Named on Honeydew (1970) 7.5' quadrangle.

Buckeye Ridge [TRINITY]: *ridge*, southeast- to north-northeast-trending, 6 miles long, 7 miles northeast of Weaverville (lat. 40°47' N, long. 122°49'30" W); the ridge is south of Buckeye Creek (2). Named on Trinity Dam (1950) 15' quadrangle.

Buck Flat [HUMBOLDT]: *area*, 11 miles south-southwest of the settlement of Willow Creek (lat. 40°47'25" N, long. 123°41'10" W; near NE cor. sec. 26, T 5 N, R 4 E). Named on Grouse Mountain (1979) 7.5' quadrangle.

Buck Flats [LAKE]: *area*, about 6 miles east-southeast of Wilson Valley (2) along Cache Creek (lat. 38°56' N, long. 122°22'20" W; sec. 35, T 13 N, R 5 W); the place is just north of Buck Island. Named on Glascock Mountain (1958) 7.5' quadrangle.

Buck Gulch [HUMBOLDT]: *canyon*, drained by a stream that flows 1.25 miles to Miller Creek (2) 6.5 miles west of Garberville (lat. 40°07'15" N, long. 123°54'55" W; near SW cor. sec. 12, T 4 S, R 2 E). Named on Briceland (1969) and Ettersburg (1969) 7.5' quadrangles.

Buck Gulch [TRINITY]:

(1) *canyon*, drained by a stream that flows 1.5 miles to Clair Engle Lake 11.5 miles north-northeast of Weaverville (lat. 40°51'55" N, long. 122°48'45" W; sec. 30, T 35 N, R 8 W); the canyon is south of Buck Ridge (1). Named on Trinity Dam (1950) 15' quadrangle.

(2) *canyon*, drained by a stream that flows 1 mile to Indian Valley Creek 10 miles southeast of Hyampom (lat. 40°30'50" N, long. 123°18'45" W; sec. 31, T 2 N, R 8 E). Named on Hyampom (1951) 15' quadrangle.

Buckhorn: see **Buckhorn Station** [TRINITY].

Buckhorn Bally [TRINITY]: *peak*, 14 miles east-southeast of Weaverville on Trinity-Shasta County line (lat. 40°37'05" N, long. 122°42'35" W; near E line sec. 24, T 32 N, R 8 W). Named on Shasta Bally (1978) 7.5' quadrangle.

Buckhorn Camp [TRINITY]: *locality*, 9 miles east-northeast of Burnt Ranch (lat. 40°51'35" N, long. 123°19'15" W). Named on Ironside Mountain (1951) 15' quadrangle.

Buckhorn Cove [MENDOCINO]: *embayment*, 3.25 miles south of Mendocino along the coast (lat. 39°15'30" N, long. 123°47' W; sec. 8, T 16 N, R 17 W); the feature is at the mouth of Buckhorn Creek (3). Named on Mendocino (1960) 7.5' quadrangle.

Buckhorn Creek [MENDOCINO]:

(1) *stream*, flows 4.25 miles to Black Butte River 10 miles north of Hull Mountain (lat. 39°39'45" N, long. 122°54'50" W; sec. 24, T 21 N, R 10 W); the stream is southeast of Buckhorn Ridge (1). Named on Hull Mountain (1967) and Plaskett Ridge (1967) 7.5' quadrangles.

(2) *stream*, flows 2 miles to Little North Fork Ten Mile River 6.25 miles southwest of Branscomb (lat. 39°35'40" N, long. 123°42'45" W; near W line sec. 13, T 20 N, R 17 W); the stream is southeast of Buckhorn Ridge (2). Named on Dutchmans Knoll (1966) 7.5' quadrangle.

(3) *stream*, flows 1.5 miles to the sea 3.25 miles south of Mendocino at Buckhorn Cove (lat. 39°15'35" N, long. 123°47' W; sec. 8, T 16 N, R 17 W). Named on Mendocino (1960) 7.5' quadrangle.

Buckhorn Creek [TRINITY]: *stream*, flows nearly 5 miles to Eltapom Creek 5.5 miles north of Hyampom (lat. 40°41'10" N, long. 123°27'45" W). Named on Hyampom (1951) 15' quadrangle.

Buckhorn Ridge [MENDOCINO]:

(1) *ridge*, northeast-trending, nearly 3 miles long, 9 miles north of Hull Mountain (lat. 39°39' N, long. 122°56'10" W); the ridge is northwest of Buckhorn Creek (1). Named on Plaskett Ridge (1967) 7.5' quadrangle.

(2) *ridge*, west- to southwest-trending, nearly 2 miles long, 5.25 miles southwest of Branscomb (lat. 39°36'50" N, long. 123°42'35" W); the ridge is northwest of Buckhorn Creek (2). Named on Dutchmans Knoll (1966) 7.5' quadrangle.

Buckhorn Spring [MENDOCINO]: *spring*, 4 miles southwest of Eden Valley (lat. 39°34'50" N, long. 123°13'30" W; sec. 19, T 20 N, R 12 W). Named on Brushy Mountain (1966) 7.5' quadrangle.

Buckhorn Station [TRINITY]: *locality*, 9.5 miles east-southeast of Weaverville (lat. 40°40' N, long. 122°47' W; at S line sec. 33, T 33 N, R 8 W); the place is 4 miles by road west of Buckhorn Summit. Named on Weaverville (1950) 15' quadrangle. Called Buckhorn on Weaverville (1913) 30' quadrangle. Called Buck Horn Station on Red Bluff (1894) 1° quadrangle.

Buckhorn Summit [TRINITY]: *pass*, 12.5 miles east-southeast of Weaverville on Trinity-Shasta County line (lat. 40°38'05" N, long. 122°44' W; sec. 14, T 32 N, R 8 W). Named on French Gulch (1979) 7.5' quadrangle.

Buckingham Bluffs [LAKE]: *relief feature*, 4 miles east-northeast of Kelseyville (lat. 38°59'35" N, long. 122°45'45" W; sec. 8, T 13 N, R 8 W); the feature is on the northeast side of Buckingham Peak. Named on Kelseyville (1959) 7.5' quadrangle.

Buckingham Park [LAKE]: *settlement*, 9 miles east-southeast of Lakeport along Clear Lake (lat. 39°00'55" N, long. 122°45'20" W; sec. 33, T 14 N, R 8 W, and sec. 4, T 13 N, R 8 W). Named on Lucerne (1958) 7.5' quadrangle. United States Board on Geographic Names (1962c, p. 14) rejected the name "Buckingham Peninsula" for the place. The name is from the family that lived at the site in the 1880's and 1890's (Gudde, 1969, p. 40).

Buckingham Peak [LAKE]: *peak*, 11 miles east of Kelseyville (lat. 38°59'20" N, long. 122°46'05" W; sec. 8, T 13 N, R 8 W). Altitude 3967 feet. Named on Kelseyville (1959) 7.5' quadrangle. United States Board on Geographic Names (1962b, p. 14) rejected the name "North Peak" for the feature, which is at the north end of Mount Konocti.

Buckingham Peninsula: see **Buckingham Park** [LAKE].

Buckingham Point [LAKE]: *promontory*, 4 miles west of Clearlake Oaks near the east end of The Narrows (2) (lat. 39°01'35" N, long. 122°44'50" W). Named on Clearlake Oaks (1958) 7.5' quadrangle.

Buck Island [LAKE]: *hill*, about 6 miles east-southeast of Wilson Valley (2) (lat. 38°55'50" N, long. 122°22'25" W; sec. 35, T 13 N, R 5 W). Named on Glascock Mountain (1958) and Wilson Valley (1958) 7.5' quadrangles.

Buck Lake [TRINITY]: *lake*, 300 feet long, 8.5 miles west-northwest of Billys Peak (1) (lat. 41°11'30" N, long. 122°54'10" W). Named on Coffee Creek (1955) 15' quadrangle.

Buckman's Prairie: see **Fieldbrook** [HUMBOLDT].

Buck Mountain [DEL NORTE]: *peak*, 16 miles south-southeast of Gasquet at the north end of Lems Ridge (lat. 41°38' N, long. 123°52' W). Altitude 3827 feet. Named on Ship Mountain (1982) 7.5' quadrangle.

Buck Mountain [HUMBOLDT]: *ridge*, east-southeast-trending, 2 miles long, 4 miles south-southeast of Dinsmore (lat. 40°26'20" N, long. 123°34'40" W). Named on Dinsmore (1977) 7.5' quadrangle.

Buck Mountain [LAKE]: *peak*, 3.5 miles south-southeast of Wilson Valley (2) (lat. 38°55'35" N, long. 122°26'20" W). Named on Wilson Valley (1958) 7.5' quadrangle.

Buck Mountain [MENDOCINO]: *ridge*, northwest-trending, 2.5 miles long, 9.5 miles north of Covelo (lat. 39°56' N, long. 123°14'15" W). Named on Bluenose Ridge (1967) and Mina (1967) 7.5' quadrangles.

Buck Mountain: see **Little Buck Mountain** [HUMBOLDT].

Buck Mountain Creek [HUMBOLDT]: *stream*, flows nearly 5 miles to East Branch of South Fork Eel River 3 miles southeast of Garberville (lat. 40°04'05" N, long. 123°50'05" W; sec. 32, T 4 S, R 4 E). Named on Garberville (1970) and Harris (1969) 7.5' quadrangles. Called Little Buck Cr. on Briceland (1921) 15' quadrangle.

Buck Mountain Lake [MENDOCINO]: *lake*, about 500 feet long, 11 miles east-northeast of Spyrock (2) (lat. 39°56'40" N, long. 123°15'25" W); the lake is near the northwest end of Buck Mountain. Named on Mina (1967) 7.5' quadrangle.

Bucknell: see **Covelo** [MENDOCINO].

Bucknell Creek [LAKE-MENDOCINO]: *stream*, heads in Lake County and flows 8.5 miles to Eel River 5 miles northeast of the town of Potter Valley in Mendocino County (lat. 39°22'40" N, long. 123°03' W). Named on Potter Valley (1960) 15' quadrangle, and on Elk Mountain (1967) 7.5' quadrangle. Called Bushnell Creek on Pomo (1943) 15' quadrangle, and called Buckner Creek on Hullville (1922) 15' quadrangle.

Bucknell Spring [MENDOCINO]: *spring*, 8 miles east-southeast of Covelo (lat. 39°45'20" N, long. 123°06'10" W). Named on Newhouse Ridge (1967) 7.5' quadrangle.

Buckner Creek [MENDOCINO]: *stream*, flows 1.25 miles to Sonoma County 12.5 miles south-southwest of Hopland (lat. 38°48'35" N, long. 123°12'05" W; at S line sec. 9, T 11 N, R 12 W). Named on Hopland (1960) 15' quadrangle.

Buckner Creek: see **Bucknell Creek** [LAKE-MENDOCINO].

Buck Pasture [HUMBOLDT]: *area,* 5.5 miles north-northeast of Blocksburg (lat. 40°20'45" N, long. 123°35' W; near SW cor. sec. 26, T 1 S, R 5 E). Named on Black Lassic (1979) 7.5' quadrangle.

Buck Peak [MENDOCINO]: *peak,* 9 miles west-northwest of Ornbaun Valley (lat. 38°57'20" N, long. 123°27'50" W; sec. 25, T 13 N, R 15 W). Altitude 2692 feet. Named on Ornbaun Valley (1960) 15' quadrangle.

Buck Ridge [LAKE]:

(1) *ridge,* southwest- to west-trending, 2 miles long, 6 miles east of the town of Upper Lake (lat. 39°09'35" N, long. 122°47'50" W; on E line sec. 12, T 15 N, R 9 W). Named on Bartlett Mountain (1958) 7.5' quadrangle.

(2) *ridge,* south-southwest-trending, 0.5 mile long, nearly 6 miles west of Lakeport (lat. 39°02'15" N, long. 123°01'15" W; on S line sec. 25, T 14 N, R 11 W). Named on Purdys Gardens (1958) 7.5' quadrangle.

Buck Ridge [TRINITY]:

(1) *ridge,* southeast-trending, 1 mile long, 11.5 miles north-northeast of Weaverville (lat. 40°52'35" N, long. 122°49'45" W; mainly in sec. 24, T 35 N, R 9 W); the ridge is north of Buck Creek (1). Named on Trinity Dam (1950) 15' quadrangle.

(2) *ridge,* northwest-trending, 3 miles long, 4.5 miles west-northwest of Black Rock Mountain (lat. 40°13'20" N, long. 123°05'15" W). Named on Black Rock Mountain (1954) 15' quadrangle.

(3) *ridge,* generally south-southwest-trending, 4 miles long, 10 miles south-southwest of Black Rock Mountain (lat. 40°04'30" N, long. 123°05'30" W). Named on Black Rock Mountain (1954) 15' quadrangle.

Buck Rock [HUMBOLDT]:

(1) *relief feature,* 4.5 miles south-southeast of Dinsmore (lat. 40°25'55" N, long. 123°33'55" W; sec. 25, T 1 N, R 5 E); the feature is on Buck Mountain. Named on Dinsmore (1977) 7.5' quadrangle.

(2) *peak,* 8 miles south-southwest of Dinsmore (lat. 40°23' N, long. 123°39'45" W; near NW cor. sec. 18, T 1 S, R 5 E). Named on Larabee Valley (1977) 7.5' quadrangle.

Buck Rock [LAKE]: *peak,* 4 miles west of Middletown (lat. 38°44'35" N, long. 122°41' W; near SW cor. sec. 6, T 10 N, R 7 W). Altitude 2834 feet. Named on Mount Saint Helena (1959) 7.5' quadrangle.

Buck Rock [MENDOCINO]:

(1) *relief feature,* 10.5 miles west-southwest of Covelo (lat. 39°45'30" N, long. 123°25'45" W; sec. 16, T 22 N, R 14 W). Named on Iron Peak (1967) 7.5' quadrangle.

(2) *peak,* 4.25 miles north of Anthony Peak on Mendocino-Tehama County line (lat. 39°54'30" N, long. 122°56'50" W; near E line sec. 27, T 24 N, R 10 W). Altitude 6658 feet. Named on Buck Rock (1967) 7.5' quadrangle.

Buck Rock: see **Eagle Rock** [HUMBOLDT]; **Little Buck Rock** [MENDOCINO].

Buck Rock Creek [MENDOCINO]: *stream,* flows 3.5 miles to Beaver Creek 7 miles north-northwest of Anthony Peak (lat. 39°56'05" N, long. 122°59'50" W; sec. 17, T 24 N, R 10 W); the stream heads near Buck Rock (2). Named on Buck Rock (1967) 7.5' quadrangle.

Bucksnort Creek [LAKE]: *stream,* flows 13 miles to Putah Creek nearly 4 miles south-southwest of Jericho Valley (lat. 38°46'50" N, long. 122°27'15" W; sec. 30, T 11 N, R 5 W). Named on Detert Reservoir (1958), Jericho Valley (1958), and Middletown (1958) 7.5' quadrangles. United States Board on Geographic Names (1962b, p. 14) rejected the form "Bucksnorter Creek" for the name.

Bucksnorter Creek: see **Bucksnort Creek** [LAKE].

Bucksport [HUMBOLDT]: *locality,* 2.5 miles southwest of downtown Eureka along Northwestern Pacific Railroad (lat. 40°46'30" N, long. 124°11'35" W; sec. 33, T 5 N, R 1 W). Named on Eureka (1958) 7.5' quadrangle. The name recalls the community of Buck's Port, or Bucksport, that David A. Buck laid out in 1850 on the east side of Humboldt Bay about 5 miles northeast of the bay entrance; Buck was a member of the Gregg party, which explored the place in 1849 (Coy, 1929, p. 57). Postal authorities established Bucksport post office in 1855 and discontinued it in 1863 (Frickstad, p. 42). In 1850 members of the Laura Virginia Company laid out a community called Humboldt City along the bay just south of the later site of Bucksport, but in 1851 the place was nearly deserted (Hoover, Rensch, and Rensch, p. 102). Colonel Francis J. Lippitt, 2nd California Infantry, occupied a military post called Lippitt that functioned at Bucksport for a few months in 1862 (Frazer, p. 25).

Buck Spring [TRINITY]:

(1) *spring,* 10.5 miles northwest of Forest Glen (lat. 40°28'40" N, long. 123°28'05" W; sec. 11, T 1 N, R 6 E). Named on Sportshaven (1973) 7.5' quadrangle.

(2) *spring,* 5.25 miles northeast of Forest Glen (lat. 40°25'55" N, long. 123°15'30" W; near S line sec. 19, T 30 N, R 12 W). Named on Naufus Creek (1979) 7.5' quadrangle.

(3) *spring,* 6.25 miles northwest of Helena (lat. 40°49'55" N, long. 123°13' W). Named on Helena (1951) 15' quadrangle.

Bud Creek [MENDOCINO]: *stream,* flows 2.5 miles to Tomki Creek nearly 6 miles east-southeast of Longvale (lat. 39°32'05" N, long. 123°19'30" W; sec. 5, T 19 N, R 13 W). Named on Willis Ridge (1966) 7.5' quadrangle.

Bug Creek [HUMBOLDT]: *stream,* flows 4.5 miles to Mad River 3.25 miles south-southwest of Board Camp Mountain (lat. 40°39'10" N, long. 123°44'15" W). Named on Board Camp Mountain (1977) and Mad River Buttes (1977) 7.5' quadrangles. West Fork enters 0.5 mile upstream from the mouth of the main creek; it is 2.5 miles long and is named on Board Camp Mountain (1977) 7.5' quadrangle.

Bug Creek Butte [HUMBOLDT]: *peak,* 8 miles northeast of Lone Star Junction (lat. 40°41'45" N, long. 123°45'10" W; sec. 29, T 4 N, R 4 E). Altitude 5259 feet. Named on Mad River Buttes (1977) 7.5' quadrangle.

Buhne Point [HUMBOLDT]: *promontory,* 1 mile north of Fields Landing along the east side of Humboldt Bay (lat. 40°44'30" N, long. 124°12'50" W; near W line sec. 8, T 4 N, R 1 W). Named on Fields Landing (1959) 7.5' quadrangle. United States Board on Geographic Names (1943, p. 10) rejected the name "Humboldt Point" for the feature. The name "Buhne" commemorates Second Officer Buhne of the *Laura Virginia,* who led a party in the ship's boats across the bar into Humboldt Bay in 1850 (Bledsoe, p. 55-56).

Buhne Spit Shoal [HUMBOLDT]: *shoal,* 1.25 miles north of Fields Landing in Humboldt Bay (lat. 40°44'40" N, long. 124°12'50" W); the feature is north of Buhne Point. Named on Fields Landing (1959) 7.5' quadrangle.

Bukers Prairie [HUMBOLDT]: *area,* 5 miles south-southwest of Johnsons (lat. 41°17'35" N, long. 123°55'40" W; sec. 34, T 11 N, R 2 E). Named on Holter Ridge (1983) 7.5' quadrangle.

Bullards Basin [TRINITY]: *relief feature,* 9 miles southwest of Billys Peak (1) (lat. 41°02'55" N, long. 122°54' W; sec. 21, T 37 N, R 9 W). Named on Coffee Creek (1955) 15' quadrangle.

Bull Creek [HUMBOLDT]:

(1) *stream,* flows 14 miles to South Fork Eel River 1.5 miles northeast of Weott (lat. 40°20'20" N, long. 123°56'15" W). Named on Bull Creek (1969) and Weott (1969) 7.5' quadrangles. The name is from an incident of the early 1850's, when Indians stole a bull from a white settler and killed the animal by the stream; settlers eventually killed the Indians in retaliation (Turner, p. 33).

(2) *stream,* flows 5 miles to Trinity River 2 miles south-southeast of Weitchpec (lat. 41°09'45" N, long. 123°41'35" W; sec. 14, T 9 N, R 4 E). Named on Hopkins Butte (1979) and Weitchpec (1979) 7.5' quadrangles.

(3) *locality,* 11 miles south-southeast of Scotia along Bull Creek (1) (lat. 40°20'10" N, long. 124°01'30" W; at W line sec. 30, T 1 S, R 1 E). Named on Bull Creek (1969) 7.5' quadrangle. Called Bull Creek Settlement on Glynn (1919) 15' quadrangle. On Scotia (1950) 15' quadrangle, the name applies to buildings along the creek 0.5 to 1 mile farther downstream.

Bull Creek [MENDOCINO]: *stream,* flows 1 mile to Outlet Creek 4.5 miles north-northwest of Willits (lat. 39°28'30" N, long. 123°22'30" W; at E line sec. 26, T 19 N, R 14 W). Named on Willits (1961) 15' quadrangle.

Bull Creek [TRINITY]: *stream,* flows 1.5 miles to Trinity River 4.25 miles south-southeast of China Mountain, which is in Siskiyou County (lat. 41°19'10" N, long. 122°33'15" W; near N line sec. 21, T 40 N, R 6 W); the stream heads near Bull Lake. Named on China Mountain (1955) 15' quadrangle.

Bull Creek Flat: see **Lower Bull Creek Flat** [HUMBOLDT]; **Upper Bull Creek Flat** [HUMBOLDT].

Bull Creek Settlement: see **Bull Creek** [HUMBOLDT] (3).

Bull Lake [TRINITY]: *lake,* 650 feet long, 4.25 miles south-southwest of China Mountain, which is in Siskiyou County (lat. 41°19'10" N, long. 122°35'35" W; near N line sec. 19, T 40 N, R 6 W); the lake is near the head of Bull Creek. Named on China Mountain (1955) 15' quadrangle.

Bullock Creek [MENDOCINO]: *stream,* flows 2 miles to West Branch Indian Creek (1) 7 miles north-northwest of Boonville (lat. 39°06' N, long. 123°26'05" W; near W line sec. 5, T 14 N, R 14 W). Named on Boonville (1959) 15' quadrangle.

Bull Ridge [TRINITY]: *ridge,* generally north-trending, 1.5 miles long, 14 miles southwest of Black Rock Mountain (lat. 40°02'50" N, long. 123°10'10" W; mainly in sec. 2, T 25 N, R 12 W). Named on Black Rock Mountain (1954) 15' quadrangle.

Bull Rock [MENDOCINO]: *shoal,* 1 mile west-southwest of Albion, and 0.5 mile offshore (lat. 39°12'55" N, long. 123°47'05" W). Named on Albion (1960) 7.5' quadrangle.

Bull Team Gulch [MENDOCINO]: *canyon,* drained by a stream that flows 1 mile to South Fork Albion River 7.25 miles north-northwest of Navarro (lat. 39°14'20" N, long. 123°36'55" W; near N line sec. 23, T 16 N, R 16 W). Named on Navarro (1961) 15' quadrangle.

Bully Choop Mountain [TRINITY]: *peak,* 15 miles southeast of Weaverville on Trinity-Shasta County line (lat. 40°33'20" N, long. 122°46' W; near E line sec. 9, T 31 N, R 8 W). Altitude 6974 feet. Named on Weaverville (1950) 15' quadrangle. According to Goodyear (1890a, p. 255), the name has the meaning "needle peak" in an Indian dialect.

Bully Choop Mountains: see **Trinity Mountains** [TRINITY].

Bulwinkle: see **Crannell** [HUMBOLDT].

Bulwinkle Creek [HUMBOLDT]: *stream,* flows 2 miles to Little River 4.5 miles southeast of Trinidad (lat. 41°00'35" N, long. 124°05'25" W; sec. 8, T 7 N, R 1 E). Named on Arcata North (1959) and Crannell (1966)

7.5' quadrangles.

Bummer Lake [DEL NORTE]: *lake,* 400 feet long, 10 miles east of Crescent City (lat. 41°44'25" N, long. 124°00'20" W; sec. 36, T 16 N, R 1 E). Named on Childs Hill (1966) 7.5' quadrangle. Shown as an intermittent lake on Klamath (1952) 15' quadrangle.

Bummer Lake Creek [DEL NORTE]: *stream,* flows 4 miles to East Fork Mill Creek 7.25 miles east-southeast of Crescent City (lat. 41°43'40" N, long. 124°04' W; sec. 4, T 15 N, R 1 E); the stream heads near Bummer Lake. Named on Childs Hill (1966) 7.5' quadrangle.

Bumphead Glade [LAKE]: *area,* 1 mile east of Bear Mountain (lat. 39°24'20" N, long. 122°52'50" W). Named on Lake Pillsbury (1967) 7.5' quadrangle.

Bunchgrass Creek [HUMBOLDT]: *stream,* flows 2.5 miles to Mill Creek (2) 6.5 miles north-northeast of Hoopa (lat. 41°07'30" N, long. 123°36'20" W; near E line sec. 33, T 9 N, R 5 E). Named on Tish Tang Point (1978) 7.5' quadrangle.

Bunch Grass Ridge [HUMBOLDT]: *ridge,* west-trending, 2 miles long, 4 miles east of Weitchpec (lat. 41°10'30" N, long. 123°38' W). Named on Hopkins Butte (1979) 7.5' quadrangle.

Buncker Gulch [MENDOCINO]: *canyon,* drained by a stream that flows nearly 3 miles to Hare Creek 11.5 miles northwest of Comptche (lat. 39°23'15" N, long. 123°43'55" W; near SE cor. sec. 26, T 18 N, R 17 W). Named on Comptche (1960) 15' quadrangle.

Bundle Prairie Creek [HUMBOLDT]: *stream,* flows 0.5 mile to Mattole River 1.5 miles southwest of Honeydew (lat. 40°13'50" N, long. 124°08'30" W; at S line sec. 2, T 3 S, R 1 W). Named on Shubrick Peak (1969) 7.5' quadrangle.

Bunker Hill [HUMBOLDT]: *peak,* 7.5 miles northeast of Cape Mendocino on Bear River Ridge (lat. 40°29'50" N, long. 124°17'35" W; sec. 4, T 1 N, R 2 W). Altitude 2464 feet. Named on Capetown (1969) 7.5' quadrangle. United States Board on Geographic Names (1962b, p. 14) rejected the name "Bear Ridge" for the feature.

Burbeck [MENDOCINO]: *locality,* 5 miles west-northwest of Willits along California Western Railroad (lat. 39°25'45" N, long. 123°26'25" W; sec. 8, T 18 N, R 14 W); the place is near the mouth of Burbeck Creek. Named on Willits (1961) 15' quadrangle.

Burbeck Creek [MENDOCINO]: *stream,* flows 2 miles to Noyo River 5 miles west-northwest of Willits (lat. 39°25'45" N, long. 123°25'20" W; sec. 8, T 18 N, R 14 W). Named on Willits (1961) 15' quadrangle.

Burger Bay [LAKE]: *embayment,* 2 miles north of Lakeport along Clear Lake (lat. 39°04'20" N, long. 122°54'40" W; on E line sec. 12, T 14 N, R 10 W). Named on Lakeport (1958) 7.5' quadrangle.

Burger Creek [MENDOCINO]: *stream,* flows 8 miles to Eel River less than 1 mile north-northwest of Dos Rios (lat. 39°43'25" N, long. 123°21'55" W; at NE cor. sec. 36, T 22 N, R 14 W). Named on Dos Rios (1967) and Laytonville (1967) 7.5' quadrangles.

Burger Lake [LAKE]: *lake,* 1350 feet long, 2.5 miles north-northwest of Lakeport (lat. 39°04'50" N, long. 122°56'10" W; sec. 11, T 14 N, R 10 W). Named on Lakeport (1958) 7.5' quadrangle.

Burgess Creek [TRINITY]: *stream,* flows 2.5 miles to Hembrey Creek 5.5 miles east of Alderpoint [HUMBOLDT] (lat. 40°11'05" N, long. 123°30'20" W; sec. 21, T 3 S, R 6 E). Named on Alderpoint (1969) and Zenia (1967) 7.5' quadrangles. United States Board on Geographic Names (1969a, p. 2) rejected the names "Hembrey Creek" and "South Fork Dobbins Creek" for the stream.

Burgess Creek: see **Hembrey Creek** [TRINITY].

Burgess Ridge [HUMBOLDT]: *ridge,* northwest-to west-trending, 1 mile long, 13 miles south-southwest of Scotia (lat. 40°18'50" N, long. 124°12'25" W). Named on Buckeye Mountain (1970) 7.5' quadrangle.

Burlington [HUMBOLDT]: *locality,* 1 mile southeast of Weott (lat. 40°18'35" N, long. 123°54'25" W; near NW cor. sec. 12, T 2 S, R 2 E). Named on Weott (1969) 7.5' quadrangle. A CCC camp was at the site in in the 1930's; the place also had the names "Tighe" and "Green's Camp" (Turner, p. 34).

Burns Camp [MENDOCINO]: *locality,* 4 miles north-northwest of Comptche (lat. 39°19'10" N, long. 123°36'50" W; sec. 23, T 17 N, R 16 W). Named on Comptche (1960) 15' quadrangle.

Burns Creek [HUMBOLDT]: *stream,* flows about 1.5 miles to Bull Creek (1) 11.5 miles south-southeast of Scotia (lat. 40°19'20" N, long. 124°02'05" W; near S line sec. 2, T 2 S, R 1 E). Named on Bull Creek (1969) 7.5' quadrangle.

Burns Creek [MENDOCINO]: *stream,* flows 5 miles to Blue Rock Creek 2.25 miles northwest of Spyrock (2) (lat. 39°53'50" N, long. 123°28'45" W; near E line sec. 25, T 24 N, R 15 W). Named on Iron Peak (1967), Tan Oak Park (1969), and Updegraff Ridge (1967) 7.5' quadrangles.

Burns Flat [MENDOCINO]: *area,* 12 miles west-southwest of Leggett (lat. 39°46'35" N, long. 123°31'15" W; sec. 10, T 22 N, R 15 W). Named on Tan Oak Park (1969) 7.5' quadrangle.

Burns Valley [LAKE]: *valley,* 4 miles north of the town of Lower Lake (lat. 38°58'15" N, long. 122°37'30" W). Named on Clearlake Highlands (1958) and Lower Lake (1958) 7.5' quadrangles. G.F. Becker (p. 240) referred to Burns's Valley, and Goodyear (1890a, p. 234) mentioned Burns' Valley. The name "Burns" commemorates an early settler in the Lower Lake neighborhood (Gudde, 1949, p. 45).

Burnt Ranch [TRINITY]: *village,* 29 miles west of Weaverville along Trinity River (lat. 40°48'35" N, long. 123°28'30" W; sec. 14, T 5 N, R 6 E). Named on Ironside Mountain (1951) 15' quadrangle. Postal authorities established Burntranch post office in 1858, discontinued it in 1863, reestablished it in 1870 with the name "Burnt Ranch," moved it 1 mile northwest in 1898, and moved it 1.5 miles south in 1938 (Salley, p. 30). Indians burned a ranch at the site in the early 1850's, giving the village its name (Jones, p. 247). The place also was called McWhorter's (Hoover, Rensch, and Rensch, p. 557).

Burnt Ranch Creek [HUMBOLDT]: *stream,* flows 1.5 miles to Pine Creek (1) 5 miles east of Coyote Peak (lat. 41°08'25" N, long. 123°45'55" W; sec. 30, T 9 N, R 4 E). Named on French Camp Ridge (1983) and Weitchpec (1979) 7.5' quadrangles. The name recalls a destroyed Indian village that Gibbs (p. 135) mentioned.

Burnt Ranch Falls [TRINITY]: *waterfall,* 1.25 miles north of Burnt Ranch along Trinity River (lat. 40°49'40" N, long. 123°28'35" W; sec. 11, T 5 N, R 6 E). Named on Ironside Mountain (1951) 15' quadrangle.

Burnt Ranch Prairie [HUMBOLDT]: *area,* 4.5 miles east of Coyote Peak (lat. 41°08'45" N, long. 123°46'10" W; mainly in sec. 19, T 9 N, R 4 E); the place is north-northeast of the mouth of Burnt Ranch Creek. Named on French Camp Ridge (1983) 7.5' quadrangle.

Burr Creek [HUMBOLDT]:

(1) *stream,* flows nearly 3 miles to Little Van Duzen River 3.25 miles west-southwest of Dinsmore (lat. 40°28'10" N, long. 123°39'35" W; sec. 18, T 1 N, R 5 E); the stream goes through Burr Valley. Named on Larabee Valley (1977) 7.5' quadrangle.

(2) *stream,* flows 4.5 miles to Larabee Creek 4.5 miles south of Bridgeville (lat. 40°24'15" N, long. 123°47'10" W; sec. 1, T 1 S, R 3 E). Named on Bridgeville (1969) and Larabee Valley (1977) 7.5' quadrangles.

Burr Creek: see **Little Burr Creek** [HUMBOLDT].

Burright Creek [MENDOCINO]: *stream,* flows 4 miles to East Fork Russian River 1.5 miles south-southeast of the town of Potter Valley (lat. 39°17'15" N, long. 123°05' W; sec. 33, T 17 N, R 11 W). Named on Potter Valley (1960) 15' quadrangle.

Burrill Creek [HUMBOLDT]: *stream,* flows 1.5 miles to Klamath River 7.5 miles northeast of Coyote Peak (lat. 41°13' N, long. 123°45'45" W; sec. 31, T 10 N, R 4 E). Named on French Camp Ridge (1983) and Weitchpec (1979) 7.5' quadrangles.

Burrill Peak [HUMBOLDT]: *peak,* 3.5 miles north of Weitchpec (lat. 41°14'10" N, long. 123°42'45" W. Altitude 4349 feet. Named on Weitchpec (1979) 7.5' quadrangle.

Burris: see **Denny** [TRINITY].

Burris Creek [HUMBOLDT]: *stream,* flows nearly 2 miles to the sea 3.25 miles north-northwest of Trinidad (lat. 41°06'05" N, long. 124°09'35" W; sec. 3, T 8 N, R 1 W). Named on Trinidad (1966) 7.5' quadrangle.

Burr Valley [HUMBOLDT]: *valley,* 2.5 miles south-southwest of Dinsmore (lat. 40°27'40" N, long. 123°37'40" W; on E line sec. 17, T 1 N, R 5 E). Named on Larabee Valley (1977) 7.5' quadrangle.

Busch Creek [MENDOCINO]: *stream,* flows nearly 7 miles to East Fork Russian River 1 mile north of the town of Potter Valley (lat. 39°20'25" N, long. 123°06'45" W; near E line sec. 7, T 17 N, R 11 W). Named on Potter Valley (1960) and Redwood Valley (1960) 7.5' quadrangles. Called Bush Creek on Pomo (1943) 15' quadrangle.

Bush Creek: see **Busch Creek** [MENDOCINO].

Bushnell Creek: see **Bucknell Creek** [LAKE-MENDOCINO].

Bushy Camp [LAKE]: *locality,* 7 miles west of Lakeport (lat. 39°03'30" N, long. 123°02'40" W; near W line sec. 23, T 14 N, R 11 W). Named on Purdys Gardens (1958) 7.5' quadrangle.

Bus McGall Peak [MENDOCINO]: *peak,* 9 miles south of Ukiah (lat. 39°00'45" N, long. 123°11'35" W; near W line sec. 4, T 13 N, R 12 W). Altitude 2206 feet. Named on Ukiah (1958) 7.5' quadrangle.

Butcherknife Creek [LAKE]: *stream,* flows nearly 2 miles to Putah Creek 4.25 miles south of Jericho Valley (lat. 38°46'10" N, long. 122°25'45" W; sec. 29, T 11 N, R 5 W). Named on Jericho Valley (1958) 7.5' quadrangle.

Butler Creek [HUMBOLDT]: *stream,* flows 1.25 miles to the sea 10.5 miles north of Orick (lat. 41°26'20" N, long. 124°03'40" W; sec. 9, T 12 N, R 1 E). Named on Fern Canyon (1966) 7.5' quadrangle.

Butler Creek [MENDOCINO]: *stream,* flows nearly 3 miles to Hollow Tree Creek 7.25 miles northwest of Branscomb (lat. 39°44'15" N, long. 123°42'20" W; near NW cor. sec. 25, T 22 N, R 17 W). Named on Leggett (1969) and Lincoln Ridge (1966) 7.5' quadrangles.

Butler Valley [HUMBOLDT]: *valley,* 8 miles south-southeast of Korbel along Mad River (lat. 40°45'55" N, long. 123°54' W; on S line sec. 36, T 5 N, R 2 E). Named on Korbel (1979) 7.5' quadrangle. The name commemorates Jed Butler, who came to the place in the 1850's (Turner, p. 35). United States Board on Geographic Names (1971b, p. 2) approved the name "Blue Lake" for a lake behind a dam on Mad River 8.5 miles southeast of the town of Blue Lake (sec. 36, T 5 N, R 2 E), and gave the name "Butler Valley Reservoir" as a variant.

Butler Valley Reservoir: see **Blue Lake**, under **Butler Valley** [HUMBOLDT].

Butt Camp [HUMBOLDT]: *locality,* 4.5 miles south of Fortuna (lat. 40°31'55" N, long. 124°08'40" W). Named on Rohnerville (1920) 15' quadrangle.

Butte Camp [HUMBOLDT]: *locality,* 2 miles west-northwest of Weitchpec (lat. 41°12'05" N, long. 123°44'25" W; sec. 5, T 9 N, R 4 E). Named on Weitchpec (1979) 7.5' quadrangle.

Butte Camp [TRINITY]: *locality,* 13 miles southwest of Black Rock Mountain (lat. 40°03'45" N, long. 123°10'40" W; sec. 35, T 26 N, R 12 W); the place is 0.5 mile west-northwest of Little Butte. Named on Black Rock Mountain (1954) 15' quadrangle.

Butte Creek [HUMBOLDT]:

(1) *stream,* flows 1.25 miles to North Fork Yager Creek 3 miles east-southeast of Lone Star Junction (lat. 40°36'55" N, long. 123°49'20" W; sec. 27, T 3 N, R 3 E). Named on Mad River Buttes (1977) and Yager Junction (1979) 7.5' quadrangles.

(2) *stream,* flows 5.5 miles to Little Van Duzen River 4.25 miles southwest of Dinsmore (lat. 40°26'50" N, long. 123°39'15" W; near NE cor. sec. 25, T 1 N, R 4 E); the stream heads at the southeast end of Larabee Buttes. Named on Larabee Valley (1977) 7.5' quadrangle. Called Black Butte Creek on South Fork Peak (1929) 15' quadrangle.

(3) *stream,* flows 3 miles to South Fork Eel River 2 miles west-northwest of Phillipsville (lat. 40°13'15" N, long. 123°49'20" W; sec. 10, T 3 S, R 3 E); the stream heads at Bear Buttes. Named on Miranda (1970) 7.5' quadrangle.

Butte Creek [MENDOCINO]: *stream,* heads in Glenn County and flows 1.5 miles in Mendocino County to Black Butte Creek 14 miles north of Hull Mountain (lat. 39°43'25" N, long. 122°56'05" W; sec. 35, T 22 N, R 10 W). Named on Plaskett Ridge (1967) 7.5' quadrangle.

Butte Creek: see **Little Butte Creek** [HUMBOLDT].

Butter Creek [TRINITY]: *stream,* flows 8.5 miles to South Fork Trinity River 3.25 miles south of Hyampom (lat. 40°34'15" N, long. 123°26'35" W; sec. 12, T 2 N, R 6 E). Named on Hyampom (1951) 15' quadrangle.

Butter Creek Caves [TRINITY]: *cave,* 4 miles southeast of Hyampom (lat. 40°35' N, long. 123°23'30" W; sec. 4, T 2 N, R 7 E); near Butter Creek. Named on Hyampom (1951) 15' quadrangle.

Butter Creek Meadows [TRINITY]: *area,* 7.5 miles west-southwest of Hyampom (lat. 40°33'50" N, long. 123°19'30" W; on E line sec. 2, T 2 N, R 7 E); the area is near the head of Butter Creek. Named on Hyampom (1951) 15' quadrangle.

Butterfly Creek [HUMBOLDT]: *stream,* flows 1 mile to Trinity River 0.5 mile south-southeast of the settlement of Willow Creek (lat. 40°55'50" N, long. 123°37'20" W; near S line sec. 33, T 7 N, R 5 E). Named on Willow Creek (1979) 7.5' quadrangle.

Butterfly Flat [TRINITY]: *area,* 10 miles southeast of Salmon Mountain along Slide Creek (lat. 41°04'25" N, long. 123°16'15" W). Named on Dees Peak (1978) 7.5' quadrangle.

Buttermilk Creek [MENDOCINO]: *stream,* flows 2.5 miles to Williams Creek (1) 10.5 miles northeast of Covelo (lat. 39°54' N, long. 123°07'10" W). Named on Leech Lake Mountain (1966) 7.5' quadrangle.

Butte Rock [LAKE]: *relief feature,* 5.5 miles south-southeast of Wilson Valley (2) (lat. 38°54' N, long. 122°25'25" W). Named on Wilson Valley (1958) 7.5' quadrangle.

Butts Canyon [LAKE]: *canyon,* 4.5 miles long, along Butts Creek 8.5 miles east-southeast of Middletown on Lake-Napa County line (lat. 38°42'20" N, long. 122°27'45" W). Named on Aetna Springs (1958) and Detert Reservoir (1958) 7.5' quadrangles.

Butts Creek [LAKE]: *stream,* flows 2.5 miles to Napa County 8.5 miles east-southeast of Middletown (lat. 38°42'20" N, long. 122°27'45" W). Named on Aetna Springs (1958) 7.5' quadrangle.

Buzzard Creek [HUMBOLDT]: *stream,* flows 1.5 miles to Pecwan Creek 4 miles northeast of Johnsons (lat. 41°23'15" N, long. 123°48'40" W). Named on Blue Creek Mountain (1982) 7.5' quadrangle.

Buzzard Rock [HUMBOLDT]: *relief feature,* 3.5 miles west-northwest of Weott (lat. 40°20'30" N, long. 123°59'05" W; at N line sec. 32, T 1 S, R 2 E). Named on Weott (1969) 7.5' quadrangle.

Buzzard Rock [LAKE]: *relief feature,* 4 miles west of Lakeport (lat. 39°02'55" N, long. 122°59'25" W; sec. 20, T 14 N, R 10 W). Named on Lakeport (1958) 7.5' quadrangle.

Buzzard Roost [MENDOCINO]: *relief feature,* 11.5 miles north of Hull Mountain (lat. 39°40'55" N, long. 122°58'30" W; near N line sec. 16, T 21 N, R 10 W). Named on Plaskett Ridge (1967) 7.5' quadrangle.

Buzzards Peak [HUMBOLDT]: *peak,* 6 miles southwest of Fortuna (lat. 40°31'45" N, long. 124°13'05" W; near E line sec. 30, T 2 N, R 1 W). Altitude 1455 feet. Named on Fortuna (1959) 7.5' quadrangle.

Bybee Gulch [DEL NORTE]: *canyon,* drained by a stream that flows 1 mile to East Fork Illinois River 7.5 miles north-northeast of Broken Rib Mountain (lat. 41°59'25" N, long. 123°37'40" W; sec. 33, T 19 N, R 5 E). Named on Broken Rib Mountain (1982) 7.5' quadrangle

Byrons Creek [TRINITY]: *stream,* flows nearly 3 miles to East Fork Hayfork Creek 16 miles south of Weaverville (lat. 40°30'30" N, long. 122°59'15" W; near W line sec. 27, T 31 N, R 10 W). Named on Chanchelulla Peak (1951) and Weaverville (1950) 15' quadrangles.

— C —

Cabbage Patch [LAKE]: *area,* 4 miles north of Bear Mountain (lat. 39°27'50" N, long. 122°53'50" W; near N line sec. 32, T 19 N, R 9 W). Named on Lake Pillsbury (1967) 7.5' quadrangle.

Cabin Creek [HUMBOLDT]: *stream,* flows 1.5 miles to Eel River 2 miles north of Weott (lat. 40°21' N, long. 123°55'45" W; near E line sec. 27, T 1 S, R 2 E). Named on Weott (1969) 7.5' quadrangle.

Cabin Creek [MENDOCINO]: *stream,* flows about 0.5 mile to Mill Creek (12) nearly 2 miles west-southwest of Ornbaun Valley (lat. 38°54'15" N, long. 123°20'05" W; sec. 8, T 12 N, R 13 W). Named on Ornbaun Valley (1960) 15' quadrangle.

Cabin Creek [TRINITY]: *stream,* flows nearly 3 miles to East Fork New River 11 miles southwest of Cecilville, which is in Siskiyou County (lat. 41°00'50" N, long. 123°14'40" W). Named on Cecil Lake (1979) 7.5' quadrangle.

Cabin Gulch [TRINITY]: *canyon,* drained by a stream that flows 1.5 miles to Cedar Creek (2) 4 miles east-northeast of Trinity Center (lat. 41°02'05" N, long. 122°37'40" W; sec. 25, T 37 N, R 7 W). Named on Bonanza King (1955) 15' quadrangle.

Cabin Peak [TRINITY]: *peak,* 10.5 miles south-southwest of Cecilville, which is in Siskiyou County (lat. 41°00'05" N, long. 123°12'05" W); the peak is near the head of a branch of Cabin Creek. Altitude 6866 feet. Named on Helena (1951) 15' quadrangle, and on Cecil Lake (1979) 7.5' quadrangle.

Cable Creek [MENDOCINO]: *stream,* flows 1.25 miles to Middle Fork Eel River 1.25 miles east-southeast of Dos Rios (lat. 39°42'30" N, long. 123°20'05" W; sec. 5, T 21 N, R 13 W). Named on Dos Rios (1967) 7.5' quadrangle.

Cable Creek [TRINITY]: *stream,* flows 3.5 miles to South Fork Trinity River 4.5 miles southeast of Forest Glen (lat. 40°19'20" N, long. 123°16' W; near W line sec. 31, T 29 N, R 12 W). Named on Forest Glen (1979) 7.5' quadrangle.

Cabo Blanco de San Sebastian: see **Point Saint George** [DEL NORTE].

Cabo de Fortunas: see **Point Arena** [MENDOCINO] (1).

Cabrillo Point: see **Point Cabrillo** [MENDOCINO].

Cache Camp: see **Cache Saddle** [DEL NORTE].

Cache Creek [LAKE]: *stream,* heads at Clear Lake and flows 25 miles in Lake County to Yolo County 6.25 miles southeast of Wilson Valley (2) (lat. 38°55'30" N, long. 122°22'25" W; at S line sec. 35, T 13 N, R 5 W). Named on Glascock Mountain (1958), Lower Lake (1958), and Wilson Valley (1958) 7.5' quadrangles. Trappers of Hudson's Bay Company called the stream *Rivière la Cache* before 1832 because they had a cache or hiding place there (Gudde, 1949, p. 47-48). Tyson (p. 21) called the stream Cash creek. Chandler (p. 11) noted that the stream flows though open country for 5 miles below Clear Lake, and then follows Cache Creek Canyon for 25 miles. North Fork enters 7.5 miles northeast of the town of Lower Lake; it is 36 miles long and is named on Clearlake Oaks (1960) 15' quadrangle, and on Bartlett Mountain (1958), Lower Lake (1958), and Potato Hill (1967) 7.5' quadrangles. North Fork is called North Cache Cr. on Chandler's (1901) map. Present Bartlett Creek was called Middle Fork Cache Creek at one time (Hoover, Rensch, and Rensch, p. 140).

Cache Creek Canyon: see **Cache Creek** [LAKE].

Cache Creek Ridge [LAKE]: *ridge,* south- to southeast-trending, 8 miles long, center 3.5 miles east-southeast of Wilson Valley (2) (lat. 38°57'30" N, long. 122°24'15" W); the ridge is north of Cache Creek. Named on Wilbur Springs (1961) 15' quadrangle, and on Wilson Valley (1958) 7.5' quadrangle.

Cache Saddle [DEL NORTE]: *pass,* 5.5 miles northeast of Klamath Glen (lat. 41°34'40" N, long. 123°55'40" W). Named on Klamath Glen (1982) 7.5' quadrangle. Preston Peak (1922) 30' quadrangle shows a place called Cache Camp at the site.

Caesar Peak [TRINITY]: *peak,* 11 miles south-southeast of Cecilville, which is in Siskiyou County, on Siskiyou-Trinity County line (lat. 41°00'15" N, long. 123°02'10" W). Altitude 8920 feet. Named on Thompson Peak (1979) 7.5' quadrangle.

Cagle Ridge [HUMBOLDT]: *ridge,* east-northeast-trending, 2.25 miles long, 5 miles north-northwest of Coyote Peak (lat. 41°11'35" N, long. 123°54'20" W). Named on Bald Hills (1982) 7.5' quadrangle. The name commemorates Henry Cagle, a farmer (Turner, p. 35).

Cagle Ridge Prairie [HUMBOLDT]: *area,* 4.5 miles north-northwest of Coyote Peak (lat. 41°11'25" N, long. 123°54' W); the place is on the south side of Cagle Ridge. Named on Bald Hills (1982) 7.5' quadrangle.

Cahto: see **Laytonville** [MENDOCINO].

Cahto Creek [MENDOCINO]: *stream,* flows 5.5 miles to Tenmile Creek just west of Laytonville (lat. 39°40'50" N, long. 123°29'10" W; at N line sec. 13, T 21 N, R 15 W). Named on Cahto Peak (1967) and Laytonville (1967) 7.5' quadrangles.

Cahto Peak [MENDOCINO]: *peak*, 3.5 miles northeast of Branscomb (lat. 39°41'10" N, long. 123°34'45" W; sec. 7, T 21 N, R 15 W). Altitude 4233 feet. Named on Cahto Peak (1967) 7.5' quadrangle. The name "Cahto" is of Indian origin (Kroeber, p. 36).

Cain Rock [HUMBOLDT]:
(1) *relief feature*, 2.5 miles south-southeast of Alderpoint (lat. 40°08'25" N, long. 123°36' W; sec. 3, T 4 S, R 5 E). Named on Alderpoint (1969) 7.5' quadrangle. The name commemorates Frank L. Cain, the first settler in the Alderpoint neighborhood (Turner, p. 35).
(2) *locality*, 3 miles south-southeast of Alderpoint along Northwestern Pacific Railroad (lat. 40°08'15" N, long. 123°35'30" W; at SW cor. sec. 2, T 4 S, R 5 E). Named on Alderpoint (1969) 7.5' quadrangle. On Harris (1920) 15' quadrangle, the name applies to a place located along the railroad about 1 mile north-northwest of present Cain Rock (2).

Calamese Rock [MENDOCINO]: *relief feature*, 6 miles north of Hull Mountain (lat. 39°36'55" N, long. 122°55'50" W; on S line sec. 2, T 20 N, R 10 W). Named on Hull Mountain (1967) 7.5' quadrangle.

Caldwell Pines [LAKE]: *locality*, 9.5 miles south of Kelseyville (lat. 38°50'45" N, long. 122°48'45" W; sec. 36, T 12 N, R 9 W). Named on The Geysers (1959) 7.5' quadrangle.

Calf Creek [HUMBOLDT]: *stream*, flows about 1.25 miles to Bull Creek (2) 3.5 miles northwest of Weott (lat. 40°20'55" N, long. 123°58'30" W; sec. 29, T 1 S, R 2 E); the stream is about 1 mile west of Cow Creek (1). Named on Weott (1969) 7.5' quadrangle.

Callayomi: see **Collayomi** [LAKE].

Calmia Lake: see **Kalmia Lake**, under **Mirror Lake** [TRINITY].

Calpella [MENDOCINO]: *town*, 6 miles north of Ukiah along Russian River (lat. 39°14'10" N, long. 123°12'05" W). Named on Ukiah (1958) 7.5' quadrangle. Postal authorities established Calpella post office in 1860, discontinued it in 1868, reestablished it in 1872, discontinued it in 1920, and reestablished it 2 miles north of the previous site the same year (Salley, p. 32). Colonel C.H. Veeder and his son-in-law, James Pettus, laid out the community in 1858—the town was a rival of Ukiah for a time (Gudde, 1949, p. 52; Landsman, 1977a, p. 23). The name is of Indian origin (Kroeber, p. 37).

Calville [HUMBOLDT]: *settlement*, 4.5 miles north of Arcata (lat. 40°56'10" N, long. 124°05'20" W; sec. 5, T 6 N, R 1 E). Named on Arcata North (1959) 7.5' quadrangle.

Camel Back Ridge [LAKE]: *ridge*, northwest-trending, 1.5 miles long, 5.25 miles south-southeast of Kelseyville (lat. 38°54'25" N, long. 122°48'45" W). Named on Kelseyville (1959) 7.5' quadrangle.

Camel Rock [HUMBOLDT]: *rock*, less than 1 mile south-southeast of Trinidad, and 1100 feet offshore (lat. 41°03' N, long. 124°08' W). Named on Trinidad (1966) 7.5' quadrangle. Called Double Rock on Trinidad (1952) 15' quadrangle, but United States Board on Geographic Names (1968a, p. 4) rejected this name for the feature.

Camel Rock [MENDOCINO]: *relief feature*, 9 miles northeast of Leggett (lat. 39°56'30" N, long. 123°34'20" W; sec. 7, T 24 N, R 15 W). Named on Bell Springs (1969) 7.5' quadrangle. The feature had the early name "Saddle Rock" (Carranco and Beard, p. 347).

Cameron [MENDOCINO]: *locality*, 2 miles east-northeast of Comptche (lat. 39°16'50" N, long. 123°33'10" W; sec. 5, T 16 N, R 15 W). Named on Comptche (1960) 15' quadrangle.

Cameron Creek [HUMBOLDT]: *stream*, flows 3.5 miles to Eel River 8 miles east of Weott (lat 40°19'10" N, long. 123°46'10" W; sec. 6, T 2 S, R 4 E). Named on Myers Flat (1969) 7.5' quadrangle.

Cameron Ridge [HUMBOLDT]: *ridge*, south-trending, 2.5 miles long, 4 miles south-southeast of Board Camp Mountain (lat. 40°38'45" N, long. 123°41'25" W). Named on Board Camp Mountain (1977) 7.5' quadrangle.

Camp Anderson [HUMBOLDT]: *locality*, 10 miles northeast of the town of Blue Lake (lat. 40°58'15" N, long. 123°50'20" W; near SE cor. sec. 28, T 7 N, R 3 E). Site named on Lord-Ellis Summit (1973) 7.5' quadrangle. Captain Charles D. Douglas established the military post in 1862 as a protection against hostile Indians—the name was for Colonel Allen L. Anderson, 8th California Infantry; the place was abandoned in 1862, used again in 1864, and abandoned permanently in 1866 (Frazer, p. 19).

Camp Bauer [HUMBOLDT]: *locality*, 2 miles east of the town of Blue Lake along North Fork Mad River (lat. 40°52'45" N, long. 123°57' W; near E line sec. 28, T 6 N, R 2 E). Named on Blue Lake (1979) 7.5' quadrangle.

Campbell Creek [HUMBOLDT]: *stream*, flows 7.25 miles to Trinity River 2.25 miles southeast of Hoopa (lat. 41°01'25" N, long. 123°38'45" W; sec. 6, T 7 N, R 5 E). Named on Hoopa (1979) and Willow Creek (1979) 7.5' quadrangles. The name is for T.J. Campbell, who with a partner had a gristmill at the mouth of the stream in the late 1860's (Turner, p. 40).

Campbell Creek [MENDOCINO]: *stream*, flows 5 miles to South Fork Ten Mile River 11 miles south-southwest of Branscomb (lat. 39°30'45" N, long. 123°42'50" W; near E line sec. 14, T 19 N, R 17 W). Named on Dutchmans Knoll (1966) 7.5' quadrangle.

Campbell Ridge [MENDOCINO]: *ridge*, generally southeast-trending, 1.5 miles long, 6.5 miles west of Ornbaun Valley (lat. 38°56'05" N, long. 123°25'30" W). Named on Ornbaun Valley (1960) 15' quadrangle.

Campbell Ridge [TRINITY]: *ridge*, south-trending, 2.25 miles long, 1.5 miles north-northwest of Salyer (lat. 40°54'50" N, long. 123°35'45" W). Named on Salyer (1979) 7.5' quadrangle. The name commemorates Thomas Campbell, a settler in the region in the 1860's (Jones, p. 251).

Camp Bemis [HUMBOLDT]: *locality*, 6.5 miles north-northeast of Redcrest (lat. 40°29'30" N, long. 123°54'20" W; near SW cor. sec. 1, T 1 N, R 2 E). Named on Redcrest (1969) 7.5' quadrangle. The place was a lumber camp; Bemis Land Company purchased the land there originally (Turner, p. 36).

Camp Carter [TRINITY]: *locality*, 8.5 miles southeast of Hyampom (lat. 40°32'05" N, long. 123°19'35" W; near E line sec. 24, T 2 N, R 7 E). Named on Hyampom (1951) 15' quadrangle.

Camp Cheerio [MENDOCINO]: *locality*, 4 miles south-southeast of Willits (lat. 39°21'35" N, long. 123°19'05" W; near NW cor. sec. 5, T 17 N, R 13 W). Named on Willits (1942) 15' quadrangle.

Camp Chicago [DEL NORTE]: *locality*, 3.5 miles northeast of Broken Rib Mountain (lat. 41°55'35" N, long. 123°38'40" W); the place is near the head of Chicago Creek. Site named on Broken Rib Mountain (1982) 7.5' quadrangle.

Camp Creek [HUMBOLDT]: *stream*, heads in Siskiyou County and flows 15 miles to Klamath River 1.25 miles west-southwest of Orleans in Humboldt County (lat. 41°17'35" N, long. 123°33'40" W). Named on Bark Shanty Gulch (1974) and Orleans (1978) 7.5' quadrangles.

Camp Creek [MENDOCINO]: *stream*, flows 7 miles to Rancheria Creek (2) 7.25 miles northwest of Ornbaun Valley (lat. 38°59'10" N, long. 123°25'15" W; near W line sec. 21, T 13 N, R 14 W). Named on Ornbaun Valley (1960) 15' quadrangle.

Camp Curtis: see **Arcata** [HUMBOLDT].

Camp 8 Gulch: see **Noyo River** [MENDOCINO].

Camp Five: see **Elinor** [HUMBOLDT].

Camp 4 Flat: see **Korbel** [HUMBOLDT].

Camp Gaston: see **Fort Gaston**, under **Hoopa Valley** [HUMBOLDT].

Camp Grant [HUMBOLDT]:
(1) *locality*, nearly 2 miles northeast of Weott on the south side of Eel River (lat. 40°20'25" N, long. 123°53'45" W; sec. 36, T 1 S, R 2 E). Site named on Weott (1969) 7.5' quadrangle. Postal authorities established Camp Grant post office in 1868 and discontinued it in 1895 (Frickstad, p. 42). Fort Grant, established along Eel River in 1863, usually was referred to as Camp Grant (Whiting and Whiting, p. 30).
(2) *locality*, 2.5 miles east-northeast of Weott along Northwestern Pacific Railroad (lat. 40°20'30" N, long. 123°52'40" W; at S line sec. 30, T 1 S, R 3 E); the place is about 1 mile east of the site of Camp Grant (1). Named on Weott (1949) 15' quadrangle.

Camp Grant [MENDOCINO]: *locality*, 9 miles south of Eden Valley along Eel River (lat. 39°30'05" N, long. 123°12'35" W; sec. 17, T 19 N, R 12 W). Named on Eden Valley (1929) 15' quadrangle.

Camp Grant Flat [HUMBOLDT]: *area*, 2.25 miles northeast of Weott along the south side of Eel River (lat. 40°20'35" N, long. 123°53'15" W); the site of Camp Grant (1) is at the place. Named on Weott (1969) 7.5' quadrangle.

Camp Gulch [TRINITY]: *canyon*, drained by a stream that flows 1.25 miles to Reading Creek 8 miles south of Weaverville (lat. 40°37'20" N, long. 122°56'10" W; near SW cor. sec. 18, T 32 N, R 9 W). Named on Weaverville (1950) 15' quadrangle.

Camp Inis [LAKE]: *locality*, 5.25 miles west of the town of Upper Lake (lat. 39°10'05" N, long. 123°00'15" W). Named on Ukiah (1920) 15' quadrangle. The name was coined in the 1890's from the term "Campini's Campgrounds" (Gudde, 1969, p. 50).

Camp Klamath [DEL NORTE]: *locality*, 1.5 miles east of the mouth of Klamath River (lat. 41°32'25" N, long. 124°02'55" W; around SW cor. sec. 3, T 13 N, R 1 E); the place is on the east side of Klamath River. Named on Klamath (1952) 15' quadrangle.

Camp Lincoln: see **Elk Valley** [DEL NORTE] (1).

Camp Long: see **Elk Valley** [DEL NORTE] (1).

Camp Marwedel [MENDOCINO]: *locality*, 11 miles north of Comptche along California Western Railroad (lat. 39°25'30" N, long. 123°34'30" W; sec. 7, T 18 N, R 15 W). Named on Comptche (1960) 15' quadrangle.

Camp Mattole [HUMBOLDT]: *locality*, 16 miles south-southwest of Scotia (lat. 40°16'30" N, long. 124°13'15" W; at S line sec. 19, T 2 S, R 1 W); the place is along Mattole River. Named on Buckeye Mountain (1970) 7.5' quadrangle.

Camp Meeting Ridge [MENDOCINO]: *ridge*, generally north-trending, 2 miles long, 8 miles east of Eden Valley (lat. 39°39'10" N, long. 123°02'35" W). Named on Thatcher Ridge (1967) 7.5' quadrangle. Eden Valley (1929) 15' quadrangle has the form "Campmeeting Ridge" for the name.

Camp Navarro [MENDOCINO]: *locality*, nearly 2 miles northwest of Navarro (lat. 39°10'10" N, long. 123°33'25" W; near SW cor. sec. 7, T 15 N, R 15 W). Named on Navarro (1961) 15' quadrangle.

Camp Nine [HUMBOLDT]: *locality*, 4.5 miles north-northwest of present Redcrest along a rail line (lat. 40°27'15" N, long. 123°59'30" W). Named on Dyerville (1921) 15' quadrangle. Officials of Pacific Lumber Company opened the logging camp in 1902 (Turner, p. 39).

Camp 19: see **Old Camp 19** [MENDOCINO]; **Trinidad** [HUMBOLDT].
Camp Noyo [MENDOCINO]: *locality,* 11.5 miles north of Comptche along California Western Railroad (lat. 35°26' N, long. 123°35'40" W; sec. 12, T 18 N, R 16 W); the place is along Noyo River. Named on Comptche (1960) 15' quadrangle.
Camp Rest [MENDOCINO]: *locality,* 5 miles south-southwest of Spyrock (2) along Northwestern Pacific Railroad (lat. 39°48'40" N, long. 123°24'20" W; sec. 34, T 23 N, R 14 W). Named on Iron Peak (1967) 7.5' quadrangle.
Camp Saint Albert [MENDOCINO]: *locality,* 11 miles north of Comptche along Noyo River (lat. 39°25'20" N, long. 123°33' W; near SE cor. sec. 8, T 18 N, R 15 W). Named on Comptche (1960) 15' quadrangle
Camp Saint Michael [MENDOCINO]: *locality,* 4.5 miles southeast of Leggett along South Fork Eel River (lat. 39°49'10" N, long. 123°39' W; near N line sec. 29, T 23 N, R 16 W). Named on Leggett (1969) 7.5' quadrangle.
Camp Seabow [MENDOCINO]: *locality,* 10 miles southeast of Leggett along Tenmile Creek (lat. 39°45'20" N, long. 123°35'35" W; sec. 14, T 22 N, R 16 W). Named on Tan Oak Park (1969) 7.5' quadrangle. Leggett (1952) 15' quadrangle has the form "Camp Sebow" for the name.
Camp Sebow: see **Camp Seabow** [MENDOCINO].
Camp Seven: see **Old Camp Seven** [MENDOCINO].
Camp Siverado [MENDOCINO]: *locality,* 12 miles north of Comptche along Noyo River (lat. 39°25'25" N, long. 123°36'30" W; near NE cor. sec. 14, T 18 N, R 16 W). Named on Comptche (1960) 7.5' quadrangle.
Camp 6 Gulch: see **Brandon Gulch** [MENDOCINO].
Camp 16 Gulch [MENDOCINO]: *canyon,* drained by a stream that flows 2 miles to Flynn Creek 4.25 miles northwest of Navarro (lat. 39°11'30" N, long. 123°36'10" W; near NW cor. sec. 2, T 15 N, R 16 W). Named on Navarro (1961) 15' quadrangle.
Camp 10 Gulch: see **Noyo River** [MENDOCINO].
Camp Three Spur [MENDOCINO]: *locality,* 11.5 miles north of Comptche along California Western Railroad (lat. 39°20'20" N, long. 123°36'30" W; sec. 14, T 18 N, R 16 W). Named on Comptche (1960) 15' quadrangle.
Camp Trinity [TRINITY]: *locality,* 4 miles east of Hyampom (lat. 40°37'15" N, long. 123°22'30" W; sec. 22, T 3 N, R 7 E). Named on Hyampom (1951) 15' quadrangle.
Camp Weott [HUMBOLDT]: *locality,* 4 miles north-northwest of Ferndale (lat. 40°37'15" N, long. 124°18' W). Named on Ferndale (1943) 15' quadrangle. Residents of the place built cabins on property rented from the county; a flood in 1955 destroyed the cabins, and they were not rebuilt—the place also had the name "Fish Camp" (Edeline, p. 76).
Camp Wright: see **Round Valley** [MENDOCINO].
Canadian Bar [TRINITY]: *locality,* 7.5 miles east-southeast of Burnt Ranch along Trinity River (lat. 40°47' N, long. 123°20'10" W). Named on Ironside Mountain (1951) 15' quadrangle.
Canadian Creek [TRINITY]: *stream,* flows 5 miles to Trinity River 7.5 miles east-southeast of Burnt Ranch (lat. 40°46'40" N, long. 123°20'15" W); the mouth of the creek is just upstream from Canadian Bar. Named on Ironside Mountain (1951) 15' quadrangle.
Candy Mountain [HUMBOLDT]: *peak,* 4 miles north of Trinidad (lat. 41°07' N, long. 124°08'30" W; at S line sec. 35, T 9 N, R 1 W). Altitude 883 feet. Named on Trinidad (1966) 7.5' quadrangle.
Cannibal Island [HUMBOLDT]: *island,* nearly 2 miles long, 5 miles north-northwest of Ferndale between North Bay, Sevenmile Slough, Eel River, and Mosley Slough (lat. 40°39' N, long. 124°17'15" W). Named on Cannibal Island (1959) 7.5' quadrangle. According to Turner (p. 40), the name is from a comparison made between the residents of the island, who were constantly fighting, and a bunch of cannibals.
Cannonball Beach [HUMBOLDT]: *beach,* 5 miles north-northwest of Trinidad along the coast between Abalone Point and Palmers Point (lat. 41°07'55" N, long. 124°09'40" W; at S line sec. 27, T 9 N, R 1 W). Named on Trinidad (1966) 7.5' quadrangle.
Cannon Ball Creek [TRINITY]: *stream,* flows 2.5 miles to Indian Creek (2) 12.5 miles southeast of Weaverville (lat. 40°35'30" N, long. 122°47'30" W; near N line sec. 32, T 32 N, R 8 W). Named on Weaverville (1950) 15' quadrangle. United States Board on Geographic Names (1978a, p. 5) rejected the form "Cannonball Creek" for the name.
Cannon Ball Flat [TRINITY]: *area,* 12.5 miles southeast of Weaverville (lat. 40°35'30" N, long. 122°47'30" W; near N line sec. 32, T 32 N, R 8 W); the place is at the mouth of Cannon Ball Creek. Named on Weaverville (1950) 15' quadrangle. United States Board on Geographic Names (1978a, p. 5) rejected the form "Cannonball Flat" for the name.
Cannon City: see **Canyon City** [TRINITY].
Canoe Creek [HUMBOLDT]: *stream,* flows nearly 4 miles to South Fork Eel River 2 miles south-southeast of Weott (lat. 40°17'40" N, long. 123°54' W; sec. 13, T 2 S, R 2 E). Named on Weott (1969) 7.5' quadrangle. North Fork enters from the north-northwest 2 miles upstream from the mouth of the main creek; it is 2.5 miles long and is named on Weott (1969) 7.5' quadrangle.
Canon City: see **Canyon City** [TRINITY].
Canon Creek [HUMBOLDT]: *stream,* flows 6.5 miles to Mad River 2.5 miles south-southeast of Korbel (lat. 40°50'05" N, long. 123°56'20" W; sec. 10, T 5 N, R 2 E). Named on Korbel (1979) and Maple Creek (1977) 7.5' quadrangles.
Canterbury Lodge [MENDOCINO]: *locality,* 3.5 miles east-northeast of the village of Point Arena (lat. 38°55'20" N, long. 123°37'40" W). Named on Point Arena (1943) 15' quadrangle.
Cant Hook Creek [DEL NORTE]: *stream,* flows nearly 3 miles to South Fork Smith River 8 miles north-northwest of Buck Mountain (lat. 41°43'05" N, long. 123°56'35" W; near SW cor. sec. 3, T 15 N, R 2 E). Named on Cant Hook Mountain (1982) 7.5' quadrangle. Called Canthook Creek on Ship Mountain (1952) 15' quadrangle, and United States Board on Geographic Names (1983b, p. 1) approved this form of the name, which Gudde (1949, p. 55) pointed out is from a tool used to turn logs.
Cant Hook Mountain [DEL NORTE]: *peak,* 8 miles north-northwest of Buck Mountain (lat. 41°43'35" N, long. 123°55'35" W; near E line sec. 3, T 15 N, R 2 E). Altitude 2719 feet. Named on Cant Hook Mountain (1982) 7.5' quadrangle. Called Canthook Mountain on Ship Mountain (1952) 15' quadrangle, and United States Board on Geographic Names (1983b, p. 1) approved this form of the name.
Cant Hook Prairie [DEL NORTE]: *area,* 7.5 miles north-northwest of Buck Mountain (lat. 41°43'30" N, long. 123°54'20" W; sec. 1, T 15 N, R 2 E); the place is 1 mile east of Cant Hook Mountain. Named on Cant Hook Mountain (1982) 7.5' quadrangle. Called Canthook Prairie on Ship Mountain (1952) 15' quadrangle, and United States Board on Geographic Names (1983b, p. 1) approved this form of the name.
Cantwell Soda Spring: see **Branscomb** [MENDOCINO].
Canyon City [TRINITY]: *locality,* 5.5 miles northeast of Helena (lat. 40°49'55" N, long. 123°03' W; near E line sec. 1, T 34 N, R 11 W); the place is along Canyon Creek (1). Site named on Helena (1951) 15' quadrangle. The place is called Cannon City on Miller's (1890) map, and Bancroft (p. 370) called it Cañon City. Postal authorities established Canon City post office in 1856 and discontinued it in 1857 (Frickstad, p. 206). The mining camp at the site began in 1851 and first was known as Jackass Gulch from the death there of an animal that fell over a precipice (Gudde, 1975 p. 60, 172).
Canyon Creek [HUMBOLDT]: *stream,* flows 3 miles to North Fork Mad River 6 miles north-northeast of the town of Blue Lake (lat. 40°57'45" N, long. 123°56'50" W; sec. 28, T 7 N, R 2 E). Named on Blue Lake (1979) 7.5' quadrangle.
Canyon Creek [TRINITY]:
(1) *stream,* flows 20 miles to Trinity River 14 miles north-northeast of Hayfork at Junction City (lat. 40°43'50" N, long. 123°03'15" W). Named on Hayfork (1951) and Helena (1951) 15' quadrangles. Big East Fork enters from the east 7.25 miles northeast of Helena; it is 5.25 miles long and is named on Helena (1951) and Trinity Dam (1950) 15' quadrangles—it is called East Fork on United States Geological Survey's (1915) map. Little East Fork enters from the east 8 miles northeast of Helena, and 1 mile upstream from the mouth of Big East Fork; it is 2.5 miles long and is named on Helena (1951) 15' quadrangle—it is called North Fork on United States Geological Survey's (1915) map, and is called East Fork on Averill's (1940) map.
(2) *stream,* flows 1.5 miles to South Fork Trinity River 5.5 miles north-northwest of Hyampom (lat. 40°41'10" N, long. 123°30'30" W). Named on Sims Mountain (1979) 7.5' quadrangle.
Canyon Creek: see **Big Canyon Creek** [LAKE].
Canyon Creek Falls [TRINITY]: *waterfall,* 13 miles north-northeast of Helena (lat. 40°55'55" N, long. 123°01'20" W); the feature is along Canyon Creek (1). Named on Helena (1951) 15' quadrangle.
Canyon Creek Lakes [TRINITY]: *lakes,* three, largest 1700 feet long, 15 miles north-northeast of Helena (lat. 40°58'30" N, long. 123°01'30" W); the lakes are near the head of Canyon Creek (1). Named on Helena (1951) 15' quadrangle.
Canyon Creek Meadows: see **Lower Canyon Creek Meadows** [TRINITY]; **Upper Canyon Creek Meadows** [TRINITY].
Cape Fortunas: see **False Cape** [HUMBOLDT].
Cape Horn [HUMBOLDT]:
(1) *locality,* 6 miles south of Arcata (lat. 40°47'05" N, long. 124°03'25" W; sec. 27, T 5 N, R 1 E). Named on Arcata South (1959) 7.5' quadrangle.
(2) *relief feature,* 2 miles northwest of Orleans along Camp Creek (lat. 41°19'15" N, long. 123°34'15" W). Named on Orleans (1978) 7.5' quadrangle.
Cape Horn [MENDOCINO]:
(1) *bend,* nearly 3 miles southwest of Navarro along Navarro River (lat. 39°07'20" N, long. 123°34'40" W; near N line sec. 36, T 15 N, R 16 W). Named on Navarro (1961) 15' quadrangle.
(2) *locality,* 4.5 miles east of Elk (lat. 39°08'10" N, long. 123°38' W). Named on Navarro (1943) 15' quadrangle.
Capehorn: see **Van Arsdale Reservoir** [MENDOCINO].
Cape Horn Bar: see **Reading Creek** [TRINITY].
Capell: see **Fort Capell**, under **Pecwan Creek** [HUMBOLDT].
Cape Mendocino [HUMBOLDT]: *promontory,* 28 miles south-southwest

of Eureka along the coast (lat. 40°26'20" N, long. 124°24'30" W; sec. 28, T 1 N, R 3 W). Named on Cape Mendocino (1969) 7.5' quadrangle. Circumstances surrounding discovery and naming of the feature are obscure; the earliest certain use of the name is on maps of 1587, but Malaspina was the first to give the cape its approximately correct location (Wagner, p. 396-397). According to Coy (1929, p. 19-20), there is little doubt that the name honors Antonio de Mendoza, viceroy of New Spain at the time of the Cabrillo expedition, but Gudde (1949, p. 210) pointed out that this origin for the name has never been substantiated.

Cape Ridge [HUMBOLDT]: *ridge,* generally west-trending, 6.5 miles long, center 3 miles east of Cape Mendocino (lat. 40°26'35" N, long. 124°20'30" W); Cape Mendocino is at the west end of the ridge. Named on Cape Mendocino (1969) and Capetown (1969) 7.5' quadrangles.

Cape Saint George: see **Point Saint George** [DEL NORTE].

Capetown [HUMBOLDT]: *locality,* 3 miles northeast of Cape Mendocino along Bear River (lat. 40°28' N, long. 124°22' W; on E line sec. 14, T 1 N, R 3 W). Named on Capetown (1969) 7.5' quadrangle. Postal authorities established Gas Jet post office at the site of present Capetown in 1868 and discontinued it in 1876; the name was from gas escaping from a well drilled for oil (Salley, p. 83). They established False Cape post office in 1870, changed the name to Capetown in 1879, and discontinued it in 1937 (Salley, p. 37, 73).

Cape Vizcaino [MENDOCINO]: *promontory,* 6.5 miles north-northwest of Westport (lat. 39°43'40" N, long. 123°49'45" W; sec. 26, T 22 N, R 18 W). Named on Westport (1966) 7.5' quadrangle. United States Coast and Geodetic Survey applied the name to honor the explorer, Vizcaino (Wagner, p. 421). A rocky lime-covered islet that lies close to, and almost is connected with Cape Vizcaino, is called Island Knob (United States Coast and Geodetic Survey, p. 142).

Cappell Creek [HUMBOLDT]: *stream,* flows 5 miles to Klamath River 5.5 miles south-southwest of Johnsons (lat. 41°16'55" N, long. 123°49'20" W). Named on Johnsons (1982) 7.5' quadrangle. The name is from an Indian village (Gudde, 1949, p. 55).

Cappell Flat [HUMBOLDT]: *area,* 5.5 miles south-southeast of Johnsons (lat. 41°16'40" N, long. 123°49'20" W; at N line sec. 10, T 10 N, R 3 E); the place is across Klamath River from the mouth of Cappell Creek. Named on Johnsons (1982) 7.5' quadrangle.

Cap Rock [HUMBOLDT]: *rock,* 1.25 miles southeast of Trinidad, and 1200 feet offshore (lat. 41°02'35" N, long. 124°07'35" W). Named on Trinidad (1966) 7.5' quadrangle.

Captain Creek [HUMBOLDT]: *stream,* flows 2 miles to Redwood Creek (1) 8.5 miles east-northeast of the town of Blue Lake (lat. 40°54'50" N, long. 123°48'45" W; near SW cor. sec. 11, T 6 N, R 3 E). Named on Lord-Ellis Summit (1973) 7.5' quadrangle. United States Board on Geographic Names (1978b, p. 3) approved the form "Captains Creek" for the name.

Captain Haun Creek [HUMBOLDT]: *stream,* flows 1.25 miles to Klamath River 3.5 miles south-southwest of Orleans (lat. 41°15'40" N, long. 123°34'35" W). Named on Hopkins Butte (1979) and Orleans (1978) 7.5' quadrangles.

Captain John Gulch [HUMBOLDT]: *canyon,* drained by a stream that flows 1.5 miles to Trinity River 1.25 miles east-southeast of Hoopa (lat. 41°02'20" N, long. 123°39'20" W; near N line sec. 31, T 8 N, R 5 E); the canyon heads at Captain John Mountain. Named on Hoopa (1979) 7.5' quadrangle.

Captain John Mountain [HUMBOLDT]: *ridge,* south-southwest-trending, 0.5 mile long, 2.5 miles east-northeast of Hoopa (lat. 41°03'50" N, long. 123°37'45" W; sec. 20, T 8 N, R 5 E). Named on Hoopa (1979) 7.5' quadrangle.

Captains Creek: see **Captain Creek** [HUMBOLDT].

Caraway Creek [TRINITY]: *stream,* flows 1.5 miles to New River 14 miles north-northeast of Burnt Ranch (lat. 41°58'45" N, long. 123°20'50" W). Named on Ironside Mountain (1951) 15' quadrangle.

Carbon: see **Covelo** [MENDOCINO].

Cardenas Creek [MENDOCINO]: *stream,* flows 2.25 miles to Hulls Creek 12 miles north-northeast of Covelo (lat. 39°57' N, long. 123°09'25" W; sec. 11, T 24 N, R 12 W). Named on Bluenose Ridge (1967) 7.5' quadrangle.

Carey: see **Covelo** [MENDOCINO].

Carey Ridge [TRINITY]: *ridge,* generally west-southwest-trending, 1.5 miles long, 10.5 miles south-southeast of Salmon Mountain (lat. 41°04'30" N, long. 123°18'15" W). Named on Dees Peak (1978) 7.5' quadrangle.

Carlin Creek: see **Kerlin Creek** [TRINITY].

Carlotta [HUMBOLDT]: *village,* 6.5 miles southeast of Fortuna (lat. 40°32'15" N, long. 124°03'35" W; near SW cor. sec. 22, T 2 N, R 1 E). Named on Hydesville (1979) 7.5' quadrangle. Postal authorities established Carlotta post office in 1903 (Frickstad, p. 42). When the railroad reached the place in 1903, John M. Vance laid out the community and named it for his daughter (Gudde, 1949, p. 56).

Carlsbad Spring [LAKE]: *spring,* 4.5 miles south-southeast of Kelseyville along Cole Creek (lat. 38°55'05" N, long. 122°47'55" W; near E line sec. 1, T 12 N, R 9 W). Named on Kelseyville (1959) 7.5' quadrangle. A small resort was at the site before 1905 (Waring, p. 187).

Carr Creek [TRINITY]:

(1) *stream,* flows 2 miles to Trinity River 12 miles northeast of Hayfork (lat. 40°40'20" N, long. 123°01'40" W; sec. 32, T 33 N, R 10 W). Named on Hayfork (1951) 15' quadrangle.

(2) *stream,* formed by the confluence of East Fork and West Fork, flows 4.5 miles to Hayfork Creek 4.25 miles east of Hayfork (lat. 40°33'35" N, long. 123°06'15" W; sec. 10, T 31 N, R 11 W). Named on Hayfork (1951) 15' quadrangle. East Fork and West Fork each are 2 miles long; both forks are named on Hayfork (1951) 15' quadrangle.

Carr Gulch [TRINITY]: *canyon,* drained by a stream that flows 1.25 miles to Trinity River 4 miles north of Trinity Center (lat. 41°03'45" N, long. 122°42' W; sec. 17, T 37 N, R 7 W). Named on Bonanza King (1955) 15' quadrangle.

Carrier Gulch [TRINITY]: *canyon,* 2 miles long, opens into the canyon of Hayfork Creek 6 miles east-southeast of Hayfork (lat. 40°31' N, long. 123°05' W). Named on Dubakella Mountain (1954) and Hayfork (1951) 15' quadrangles.

Carrville [TRINITY]: *locality,* 4.25 miles north of Trinity Center along Trinity River (lat. 41°03'55" N, long. 122°42'15" W; near W line sec. 17, T 37 N, R 7 W); the place is at the mouth of Carr Gulch. Named on Bonanza King (1955) 15' quadrangle. Postal authorities established Carrville post office in 1882, moved it 1.5 miles north in 1940, and discontinued it in 1943; the name was for James E. Carr, first postmaster (Salley, p. 38). California Mining Bureau's (1909b) map shows a place called Dodge located 13 miles north of Carrville by stage. Postal authorities established Dodge post office in 1895 and discontinued it in 1908; the name was for Wilbur S. Dodge, landowner at the place (Salley, p. 60).

Carson Creek [HUMBOLDT]:

(1) *stream,* flows 1 mile to Grouse Creek (2) 3 miles east-southeast of Board Camp Mountain (lat. 40°41'05" N, long. 123°39'45" W). Named on Board Camp Mountain (1977) 7.5' quadrangle.

(2) *stream,* flows 2.25 miles to Larabee Creek 3 miles east of Redcrest (lat. 40°24'30" N, long. 123°53'30" W; near E line sec. 1, T 1 S, R 2 E). Named on Redcrest (1969) 7.5' quadrangle.

Carson Opening [HUMBOLDT]: *area,* 7.25 miles east-northeast of Showers Mountain (lat. 40°37'25" N, long. 123°34'10" W; sec. 23, T 3 N, R 5 E). Named on Blake Mountain (1979) 7.5' quadrangle.

Carter: see **Camp Carter** [TRINITY].

Carter Creek [HUMBOLDT]: *stream,* flows 3 miles to Eel River just east of Alderpoint (lat. 40°10'30" N, long. 123°36'10" W; sec. 27, T 3 S, R 5 E). Named on Alderpoint (1969) 7.5' quadrangle.

Carter Glades [LAKE]: *area,* 3.5 miles east of the town of Upper Lake (lat. 39°09'50" N, long. 122°50'35" W; sec. 10, T 15 N, R 9 W). Named on Bartlett Mountain (1958) 7.5' quadrangle.

Carter Gulch [TRINITY]: *canyon,* drained by a stream that flows 4 miles to Hayfork Creek at Hayfork (lat. 40°33'10" N, long. 123°10'55" W; at E line sec. 11, T 31 N, R 12 W). Named on Hayfork (1951) 15' quadrangle.

Casabonne Peak [MENDOCINO]: *peak,* 6.5 miles northeast of Boonville (lat. 39°04'45" N, long. 123°17'20" W; near NE cor. sec. 16, T 14 N, R 13 W). Named on Boonville (1959) 15' quadrangle.

Case Creek: see **Little Case Creek** [MENDOCINO].

Case Opening [MENDOCINO]: *area,* 5.5 miles south-southeast of Branscomb (lat. 39°35'20" N, long. 123°34'25" W; sec. 18, T 20 N, R 15 W). Named on Sherwood Peak (1967) 7.5' quadrangle.

Cash Creek: see **Cache Creek** [LAKE].

Cashlapooda Creek [HUMBOLDT]: *stream,* flows 2.5 miles to Van Duzen River 2.5 miles southeast of Yager Junction (lat. 40°31'35" N, long. 123°47'10" W; sec. 25, T 2 N, R 3 E). Named on Yager Junction (1979) 7.5' quadrangle.

Casket Rock [MENDOCINO]: *rock,* 0.5 mile west of Elk, and 1500 feet offshore (lat. 39°07'50" N, long. 123°43'35" W). Named on Elk (1960) 7.5' quadrangle.

Casoose Creek [TRINITY]: *stream,* flows 7.5 miles to Hulls Creek 13 miles north of Covelo [MENDOCINO] (lat. 39°58'45" N, long. 123°14'45" W; at W line sec. 31, T 25 N, R 12 W). Named on Black Rock Mountain (1954) 15' quadrangle, and on Bluenose Ridge (1967) 7.5' quadrangle.

Caspar [MENDOCINO]: *town,* 4 miles north of Mendocino (lat. 39°21'50" N, long. 123°48'50" W; sec. 1, T 17 N, R 18 W); the town is 0.5 mile southeast of Caspar Point near the mouth of Caspar Creek. Named on Mendocino (1960) 7.5' quadrangle. Postal authorities established Caspar post office in 1874 (Frickstad, p. 94). Jacob Green purchased the sawmill at the place in 1864 and gave the name "Caspar" to the community there to honor Siegfried Caspar, who settled at the site before 1860 (Gudde, 1969, p. 56).

Caspar Anchorage [MENDOCINO]: *anchorage,* 4 miles north-northwest of Mendocino along the coast (lat. 39°21'50" N, long. 123°49'15" W; sec. 1, T 17 N, R 18 W); the anchorage is off the mouth of Caspar Creek. Named on Mendocino (1960) 7.5' quadrangle.

Caspar Creek [MENDOCINO]: *stream,* flows 8 miles to the sea 4 miles north-northwest of Mendocino (lat. 39°21'40" N, long. 123°49' W; sec. 1, T 17 N, R 18 W); the mouth of the stream is 0.5 mile southeast of Caspar

Point. Named on Comptche (1960) 15' quadrangle, and on Mendocino (1960) 7.5' quadrangle.

Caspar Point [MENDOCINO]: *promontory,* 4.5 miles north-northwest of Mendocino (lat. 39°22'05" N, long. 123°49'30" W; sec. 1, T 17 N, R 18 W). Named on Mendocino (1960) 7.5' quadrangle.

Cassidy Creek [LAKE]: *stream,* flows 2.5 miles to Bucksnort Creek 4.5 miles east-southeast of Middletown (lat. 38°43'10" N, long. 122°32'20" W). Named on Detert Reservoir (1958) 7.5' quadrangle.

Castle Garden [MENDOCINO]: *relief feature,* 11 miles north-northwest of Boonville (lat. 39°09'25" N, long. 123°25'45" W; sec. 17, T 15 N, R 14 W). Named on Boonville (1959) 15' quadrangle.

Castle Hot Springs: see **Castle Rock Springs** [LAKE].

Castle Peak [MENDOCINO]: *peak,* 13 miles north-northeast of Covelo (lat. 39°57'05" N, long. 123°07'20" W; on W line sec. 8, T 24 N, R 11 W). Altitude 6216 feet. Named on Bluenose Ridge (1967) and Leech Lake Mountain (1966) 7.5' quadrangles.

Castle Rock [DEL NORTE]: *island,* 2.5 miles west of Crescent City, and 0.5 mile offshore (lat. 41°45'40" N, long. 124°14'55" W). Named on Crescent City (1966) 7.5' quadrangle.

Castle Rock [TRINITY]: *peak,* 9.5 miles north-northwest of Hyampom (lat. 40°45' N, long. 123°31' W). Named on Sims Mountain (1979) 7.5' quadrangle. Willow Creek (1952) 15' quadrangle shows the feature situated nearly 1 mile farther northeast, but United States Board on Geographic Names (1977c, p. 4) approved the present location.

Castle Rock Springs [LAKE]: *locality,* 3 miles south of Whispering Pines (lat. 38°46'15" N, long. 122°42'55" W; near N line sec. 35, T 11 N, R 8 W). Named on Whispering Pines (1958) 7.5' quadrangle. Called Houdd Gibson Camp on Lower Lake (1945) 15' quadrangle. Postal authorities established Castle Springs post office 6 miles northwest of Middleton—presumably at present Castle Rock Springs—in 1911 and discontinued it in 1917 (Salley, p. 40). The place also was called Castle Hot Springs, Mills Hot Spring, Mills' Mineral Springs, and Noble's Springs (Anderson, p. 194; Bradley, p. 216; Waring, p. 91-92).

Castle Springs: see **Castle Rock Springs** [LAKE].

Catenberg Canyon: see **Kattenburg Canyon** [LAKE].

Catfish Lake [HUMBOLDT]: *lake,* 750 feet long, 3.5 miles south-southeast of Fields Landing (lat. 40°40'50" N, long. 124°10'55" W; at S line sec. 33, T 4 N, R 1 W). Named on Fields Landing (1959) 7.5' quadrangle.

Catfish Pond [LAKE]: *lake,* 350 feet long, 1 mile east of Potato Hill (lat. 39°21'05" N, long. 122°46'55" W; sec. 5, T 17 N, R 8 W). Named on Potato Hill (1967) 7.5' quadrangle.

Catheys Peak [HUMBOLDT]: *peak,* 15 miles south of Scotia (lat. 40°16'30" N, long. 124°04'50" W; near W line sec. 28, T 2 S, R 1 E). Named on Bull Creek (1969) 7.5' quadrangle. California Mining Bureau's (1917b) map has the form "Cathys Pk." for the name, which commemorates George Cathey, who settled in the neighborhood about 1871 (Turner, p. 45).

Caution [TRINITY]: *locality,* 10.5 miles east-southeast of present Kettenpom (lat. 40°06'20" N, long. 123°17'10" W; sec. 21, T 26 N, R 8 E). Named on Island Mountain (1922) 15' quadrangle. Postal authorities established Caution post office in 1901, moved it 2.5 miles northwest in 1903, discontinued it in 1913, reestablished it in 1915, and discontinued it in 1938 (Salley, p. 40).

Cavanaugh Creek [HUMBOLDT]: *stream,* flows 1.5 miles to Klamath River 2.5 miles east-northeast of Weitchpec (lat. 41°12'05" N, long. 123°39'45" W; sec. 1, T 9 N, R 4 E). Named on Weitchpec (1979) 7.5' quadrangle.

Cavanaugh Gulch [MENDOCINO]: *canyon,* drained by a stream that flows 1.25 miles to the sea 2 miles north-northwest of Elk (lat. 39°09'10" N, long. 123°44'05" W; sec. 22, T 15 N, R 17 W). Named on Elk (1960) 7.5' quadrangle.

Cavanough Gulch [MENDOCINO]: *canyon,* drained by a stream that flows 1.25 miles to North Fork Ten Mile Creek 4.5 miles south-southwest of Branscomb (lat. 39°35'55" N, long. 123°40'25" W; near E line sec. 18, T 20 N, R 16 W). Named on Dutchmans Knoll (1966) 7.5' quadrangle.

Cave Creek [MENDOCINO]: *stream,* flows 4.5 miles to Tomki Creek 10 miles northwest of the town of Potter Valley (lat. 39°25'20" N, long. 123°14'15" W). Named on Potter Valley (1960) 15' quadrangle.

Cave Creek [TRINITY]: *stream,* flows nearly 3 miles to South Fork Trinity River less than 1 mile northwest of Forest Glen (lat. 40°22'50" N, long. 123°20'05" W; sec. 13, T 1 S, R 7 E); the stream goes past Marble Caves. Named on Naufus Creek (1979) 7.5' quadrangle.

Cave Creek: see **Little Cave Creek** [MENDOCINO].

Cedar Basin [TRINITY]: *relief feature,* 2 miles southeast of Black Rock Mountain (lat. 40°11' N, long. 122°58'50" W; sec. 15, T 27 N, R 10 W). Named on Yolla Bolly (1954) 15' quadrangle.

Cedar Camp [HUMBOLDT]: *locality,* 7.5 miles northwest of Orleans (lat. 41°22'15" N, long. 123°40'55" W). Named on Fish Lake (1974) 7.5' quadrangle.

Cedar Camp Spring [DEL NORTE]: *spring,* 4 miles south-southeast of Buck Mountain (lat. 41°35' N, long. 123°49'45" W). Named on Summit Valley (1981) 7.5' quadrangle.

Cedar Canyon [TRINITY]: *canyon,* drained by a stream that flows 1.5 miles to Hulls Creek 15 miles southeast of Kettenpom (lat. 39°59'45" N, long. 123°15'50" W). Named in Mina (1967) 7.5' quadrangle.

Cedar Creek [DEL NORTE]: *stream,* flows 2.25 miles to Smith River 7.25 miles east-northeast of Crescent City (lat. 41°47'25" N, long. 124°04'35" W; near SW cor. sec. 9, T 16 N, R 1 E). Named on Hiouchi (1966) 7.5' quadrangle.

Cedar Creek [HUMBOLDT]:

(1) *stream,* flows 2 miles to Camp Creek 5.5 miles northwest of Orleans (lat. 41°21'20" N, long. 123°37'25" W). Named on Fish Lake (1974) 7.5' quadrangle.

(2) *stream,* flows 9 miles to Horse Linto Creek 5 miles southeast of Hoopa (lat. 41°00'20" N, long. 123°36'10" W). Named on Ironside Mountain (1951) 15' quadrangle, and on Salyer (1979) and Tish Tang Point (1978) 7.5' quadrangles.

(3) *stream,* flows 2.25 miles to Willow Creek (1) 6.5 miles west-southwest of the settlement of Willow Creek (lat. 40°54'15" N, long. 123°44'35" W; sec. 17, T 6 N, R 4 E). Named on Willow Creek (1979) 7.5' quadrangle.

Cedar Creek [LAKE]: *stream,* flows 1.5 miles to Panther Creek (1) 9 miles north-northeast of the town of Potter Valley [MENDOCINO] (lat. 39°26'30" N, long. 123°02'50" W; sec. 2, T 18 N, R 11 W). Named on Potter Valley (1960) 15' quadrangle.

Cedar Creek [MENDOCINO]: *stream,* flows 7 miles to South Fork Eel River 2 miles south-southeast of Leggett (lat. 39°50'20" N, long. 123°42'25" W; at S line sec. 14, T 23 N, R 17 W). Named on Bell Springs (1969) and Noble Butte (1969) 7.5' quadrangles. North Fork enters from the north 3.25 miles upstream from the mouth of the main creek; it is 1.5 miles long and is named on Noble Butte (1969) 7.5' quadrangle.

Cedar Creek [TRINITY]:

(1) *stream,* flows nearly 4 miles to Trinity River 5 miles south of China Mountain, which is in Siskiyou County (lat. 41°18'20" N, long. 122°34' W; at N line sec. 28, T 40 N, R 6 W). Named on China Mountain (1955) 15' quadrangle.

(2) *stream,* flows 6 miles to East Fork Trinity River 3.5 miles east of Trinity Center (lat. 41°00'35" N, long. 122°37'10" W; sec. 1, T 36 N, R 7 W). Named on Bonanza King (1955) 15' quadrangle.

Cedar Creek: see **Cedar Flat Creek** [TRINITY]; **Little Cedar Creek** [MENDOCINO]; **Panther Creek** [LAKE] (1).

Cedar Flat [MENDOCINO]: *area,* 1.5 miles south-southeast of Leggett (lat. 39°50'35" N, long. 123°42' W; at E line sec. 14, T 23 N, R 17 W). Named on Leggett (1969) 7.5' quadrangle.

Cedar Flat [TRINITY]: *locality,* 2.25 miles southeast of Burnt Ranch along Trinity River (lat. 40°47'20" N, long. 123°26'30" W). Named on Ironside Mountain (1951) 15' quadrangle. Postal authorities established Cedar Flat post office in 1879 and discontinued it in 1883 (Frickstad, p. 206).

Cedar Flat Creek [TRINITY]: *stream,* flows 4 miles to Trinity River 2.25 miles southeast of Burnt Ranch (lat. 40°47'20" N, long. 123°26'20" W); the mouth of the stream is at Cedar Flat. Named on Ironside Mountain (1951) 15' quadrangle. Called Cedar Creek on United States Geological Survey's (1915) map.

Cedar Forest Camp Ground [DEL NORTE]: *locality,* 4.25 miles east-northeast of Gasquet along Middle Fork Smith River (lat. 41°51'20" N, long. 123°53'05" W; near W line sec. 19, T 17 N, R 3 E). Named on Gasquet (1951) 15' quadrangle.

Cedar Gap [TRINITY]: *pass,* 12 miles west of Black Rock Mountain (lat. 40°14'20" N, long. 123°13'30" W; sec. 33, T 28 N, R 12 W). Named on Black Rock Mountain (1954) 15' quadrangle.

Cedar Gulch [HUMBOLDT]: *canyon,* drained by a stream that flows 1.25 miles to Camp Creek 2.25 miles northwest of Orleans (lat. 41°19'25" N, long. 123°34'10" W). Named on Orleans (1978) 7.5' quadrangle.

Cedar Gulch [TRINITY]: *canyon,* drained by a stream that flows 4 miles to Hayfork Creek 1.25 miles west-southwest of Hayfork (lat. 40°33' N, long. 123°12'20" W; sec. 10, T 31 N, R 12 W). Named on Hayfork (1951) 15' quadrangle.

Cedar Rustic Campground [DEL NORTE]: *locality,* 10 miles east-northeast of Gasquet along Middle Fork Smith River (lat. 41°52'35" N, long. 123°49'50" W; near SE cor. sec. 9, T 17 N, R 3 E). Named on Shelly Creek Ridge (1982) 7.5' quadrangle.

Cedars: see **The Cedars** [LAKE]; **The Cedars** [TRINITY].

Cedar Spring [DEL NORTE]: *spring,* 4.5 miles east-southeast of Gasquet (lat. 41°49'55" N, long. 123°52'55" W; near S line sec. 30, T 17 N, R 3 E). Named on Gasquet (1981) 7.5' quadrangle.

Cedar Spring [HUMBOLDT]: *spring,* 6.5 miles west-northwest of Orleans (lat. 41°20'20" N, long. 123°39'05" W). Named on Fish Lake (1974) 7.5' quadrangle.

Cedar Spring [MENDOCINO]: *spring,* 6 miles north-northeast of Leggett on Red Mountain (1) (lat. 39°56'30" N, long. 123°40'10" W; sec. 7, T 24 N, R 16 W). Named on Noble Butte (1969) 7.5' quadrangle.

Cedar Spring [TRINITY]: *spring,* 4.25 miles north-northeast of Forest Glen (lat. 40°26'10" N, long. 123°18'20" W; near W line sec. 29, T 1 N, R 8 E). Named on Naufus Creek (1979) 7.5' quadrangle.

Cedar Springs [MENDOCINO]: *spring,* 13 miles northeast of Covelo (lat.

39°56'50" N, long. 123°04'30" W; sec. 10, T 24 N, R 11 W). Named on Leech Lake Mountain (1966) 7.5' quadrangle.

Cedar Springs Ridge [MENDOCINO]: *ridge*, generally east-northeast-trending, 2.5 miles long, 14 miles northeast of Covelo (lat. 39°56'50" N, long. 123°04' W); the feature called Cedar Springs is on the ridge. Named on Leech Lake Mountain (1966) 7.5' quadrangle.

Cedar Trough [DEL NORTE]: *water feature*, 11 miles north-northeast of Gasquet (lat. 41°58'10" N, long. 123°50'05" W; sec. 9, T 18 N, R 3 E). Named on Shelly Creek Ridge (1982) 7.5' quadrangle. Gasquet (1951) 15' quadrangle shows Cedar Trough Camp Ground near the site.

Cedar Trough Camp Ground: see **Cedar Trough** [DEL NORTE].

Cement Bluff [TRINITY]: *relief feature*, 2.5 miles south-southeast of China Mountain, which is in Siskiyou County, along High Camp Creek (lat. 41°20'45" N, long. 122°33'10" W; sec. 9, T 40 N, R 6 W). Named on China Mountain (1955) 15' quadrangle.

Cement Creek [TRINITY]: *stream*, flows 2.5 miles to Swift Creek (1) 19 miles north-northeast of Weaverville (lat. 40°57'40" N, long. 122°45'05" W; near W line sec. 23, T 36 N, R 8 W). Named on Trinity Dam (1950) 15' quadrangle.

Center Ridge [MENDOCINO]: *ridge*, south-southeast-trending, about 2 miles long, 8 miles north of Comptche (lat. 39°22'45" N, long. 123°33'40" W). Named on Comptche (1960) 15' quadrangle.

Centerville: see **Centerville City** [HUMBOLDT].

Centerville Beach [HUMBOLDT]: *beach*, nearly 5 miles west of Ferndale (lat. 40°34'25" N, long. 124°21' W; sec. 12, T 2 N, R 3 W); the beach is at the site of Centerville City. Named on Ferndale (1943) 15' quadrangle.

Centerville Beach: see **Centerville City** [HUMBOLDT].

Centerville City [HUMBOLDT]: *locality*, 4.5 miles west of Ferndale (lat. 40°34'25" N, long. 124°20'55" W). Named on Cape Fortunas (1920) 15' quadrangle. Postal authorities established Pacific post office at the site in 1861 and discontinued it in 1864 (Salley, p. 164). United States Board on Geographic Names (1962b, p. 15) approved the name "Centerville Beach" for the place, and rejected the name "Centerville." Oil from Petrolia was shipped to Eureka from Centerville City, which was founded in 1852; the community was at the height of its prosperity from the 1850's until the 1870's (Carlson, p. 21).

Centerville Slough [HUMBOLDT]: *water feature*, 4 miles west-northwest of Ferndale near the coast (lat. 40°35'30" N, long. 124°20'10" W; on S line sec. 31, T 3 N, R 2 W). Named on Ferndale (1959) 7.5' quadrangle.

Ceremonial Rock [HUMBOLDT]: *relief feature*, 5.5 miles north of Trinidad on Patricks Point (lat. 41°08'20" N, long. 124°09'15" W; on W line sec. 26, T 9 N, R 1 W). Named on Trinidad (1966) 7.5' quadrangle.

Chadbourne Gulch [MENDOCINO]: *canyon*, drained by a stream that flows 2 miles to the sea 2.5 miles south of Westport (lat. 39°36'50" N, long. 123°46'55" W; sec. 8, T 20 N, R 17 W). Named on Inglenook (1966) 7.5' quadrangle.

Chadd Creek [HUMBOLDT]: *stream*, flows 4.25 miles to Eel River 2 miles northwest of Redcrest (lat. 40°25'15" N, long. 123°58'30" W; sec. 32, T 1 N, R 2 E). Named on Redcrest (1969) 7.5' quadrangle.

Chadd Prairie [HUMBOLDT]: *area*, 1 mile west-northwest of Redcrest (lat. 40°24'20" N, long. 123°57'50" W; at W line sec. 4, T 1 S, R 2 E). Named on Redcrest (1969) 7.5' quadrangle.

Chair Creek [LAKE]: *stream*, flows 2 miles to Middle Creek (2) 5.25 miles north-northwest of the town of Upper Lake (lat. 39°14'15" N, long. 122°56'40" W; near SW cor. sec. 14, T 16 N, R 10 W). Named on Upper Lake (1958) 7.5' quadrangle.

Chalk Mountain [LAKE]: *relief feature*, 6.5 miles northeast of Clearlake Oaks (lat. 39°04'15" N, long. 122°04'45" W; near SE cor. sec. 12, T 14 N, R 7 W). Named on Clearlake Oaks (1960) 15' quadrangle, which shows a quarry at the site. Waring (p. 197) noted that a feature called Alum Spring is situated on the side of a ravine at the southwest base of Chalk Mountain.

Chalk Mountains [HUMBOLDT]: *ridge*, west-northwest-trending, 7 miles long, center 4 miles west-southwest of Bridgeville (lat. 40°26'45" N, long. 123°52'15" W). Named on Bridgeville (1969) and Redcrest (1969) 7.5' quadrangles.

Chalk Rock [HUMBOLDT]: *relief feature*, 3 miles south-southwest of Bridgeville (lat. 40°25'45" N, long. 123°48'45" W; at SE cor. sec. 27, T 1 N, R 3 E). Named on Bridgeville (1969) 7.5' quadrangle.

Chamberlain Creek [MENDOCINO]: *stream*, flows nearly 4 miles to North Fork Big River 6.5 miles north-northeast of Comptche (lat. 39°21'10" N, long. 123°33'20" W; near S line sec. 5, T 17 N, R 15 W). Named on Comptche (1960) 15' quadrangle.

Chamberlain Ridge [MENDOCINO]: *ridge*, south- to west-southwest-trending, 4 miles long, 8.5 miles north-northeast of Comptche (lat. 39°22'30" N, long. 123°31' W); the ridge is east of Chamberlain Creek. Named on Comptche (1960) 15' quadrangle.

Chamisa Gap [LAKE]: *pass*, 6 miles northwest of the town of Lower Lake (lat. 38°58'45" N, long. 122°40'40" W; sec. 13, T 13 N, R 7 W). Named on Clearlake Highlands (1958) 7.5' quadrangle.

Chamisal Mountain [HUMBOLDT-MENDOCINO]: *ridge*, north-north-west-trending, 4 miles long, 10 miles west of Piercy on Humboldt-Mendocino County line (lat. 39°59'45" N, long. 123°59'50" W). Named on Bear Harbor (1969), Briceland (1969) and Shelter Cove (1969) 7.5' quadrangles. Called Chemese Mt. on Vander Leck's (1920b) map.

Chamise Creek [HUMBOLDT-MENDOCINO-TRINITY]: *stream*, heads in Mendocino County and flows 12 miles to Eel River in Trinity County 9 miles southeast of Alderpoint [HUMBOLDT] (lat. 40°04'20" N, long. 123°30'55" W; at E line sec. 32, T 4 S, R 6 E). Named on Bell Springs (1969) and Jewett Rock (1969) 7.5' quadrangles. Called Chemise Creek on Harris (1920) 15' quadrangle.

Chanchelulla Creek [TRINITY]: *stream*, flows 3 miles to Browns Creek 3 miles east-southeast of Chanchelulla Peak (lat. 40°27'45" N, long. 122°56'20" W; sec. 12, T 30 N, R 10 W). Named on Chanchelulla Peak (1951) 15' quadrangle.

Chanchelulla Gulch [TRINITY]: *canyon*, drained by a stream that flows nearly 3 miles to Hayfork Creek 6 miles east-northeast of Dubakella Mountain (lat. 40°25'45" N, long. 123°03' W; sec. 25, T 30 N, R 11 W). Named on Dubakella Mountain (1954) 15' quadrangle.

Chanchelulla Mountain: see **Chanchelulla Peak** [TRINITY].

Chanchelulla Peak [TRINITY]: *peak*, 11.5 miles east-southeast of Hayfork (lat. 40°28'25" N, long. 122°59'25" W; at NE cor. sec. 9, T 30 N, R 10 W). Altitude 6399 feet. Named on Chanchelulla Peak (1951) 15' quadrangle. Called Chanchelulla Mountain on Red Bluff (1894) 1° quadrangle, and called Chance Lulo Mt. on California Mining Bureau's (1917b) map. The name appears to be of Indian origin (Kroeber, p. 38).

Chandans Creek [LAKE]: *stream*, flows nearly 3 miles to Rocky Creek 5.5 miles south of Wilson Valley (2) (lat. 38°53'35" N, long. 122°28'20" W; near N line sec. 13, T 12 N, R 5 W). Named on Wilson Valley (1958) 7.5' quadrangle.

Chaparral Creek [HUMBOLDT]: *stream*, flows 2 miles to Cooskie Creek 6.5 miles south of Petrolia (lat. 40°13'40" N, long. 124°17'50" W; near N line sec. 9, T 3 S, R 2 W). Named on Cooskie Creek (1969) 7.5' quadrangle.

Chaparral Mountain [TRINITY]: *ridge*, east-southeast- to east-trending, 2.5 miles long, 8.5 miles north of Hyampom (lat. 40°44'05" N, long. 123°25'30" W). Named on Hyampom (1951) 15' quadrangle.

Chaparral Mountain: see **Chapparral Mountain** [HUMBOLDT]; **Little Chaparral Mountain** [HUMBOLDT].

Chaplton Creek [TRINITY]: *stream*, flows 1.5 miles to South Fork Trinity River 4 miles southeast of Forest Glen (lat. 40°19'40" N, long. 123°16'50" W; near N line sec. 4, T 2 S, R 8 E). Named on Forest Glen (1979) 7.5' quadrangle.

Chapparral Mountain [HUMBOLDT]: *peak*, 7 miles northeast of Lone Star Junction on Mad River Buttes (lat. 40°42'10" N, long. 123°46'30" W; near NW cor. sec. 30, T 4 N, R 4 E). Altitude 5115 feet. Named on Mad River Buttes (1977) 7.5' quadrangle. Called Chaparral Mountain on Iaqua Buttes (1950) 15' quadrangle.

Charcoal Ridge [MENDOCINO]: *ridge*, north-trending, 1 mile long, 8 miles north-northwest of Hull Mountain (lat. 39°37'55" N, long. 122°58'40" W; in and near sec. 33, T 21 N, R 10 W). Named on Plaskett Ridge (1967) 7.5' quadrangle.

Charles Mountain [HUMBOLDT]: *ridge*, east-southeast- to south-south-east-trending, 7.5 miles long, center 7 miles north of Blocksburg (lat. 40°22'45" N, long. 123°38'30" W). Named on Black Lassic (1979), Blocksburg (1969), and Larabee Valley (1977) 7.5' quadrangles. The name is for brothers Leon Charles and George Charles, local ranchers (Turner, p. 46).

Charlie Alley Peak [LAKE]: *peak*, nearly 4 miles north-northeast of the town of Upper Lake (lat. 39°13' N, long. 122°52'35" W). Named on Upper Lake (1958) 7.5' quadrangle.

Charlie Creek: see **Little Charlie Creek** [MENDOCINO].

Charlton Creek [MENDOCINO]: *stream*, flows 4 miles to Chamise Creek 11.5 miles northeast of Leggett (lat. 39°59'25" N, long. 123°34'35" W; sec. 26, T 5 S, R 5 E). Named on Bell Springs (1969) 7.5' quadrangle.

Chase Ledge [DEL NORTE]: *shoal*, 2.5 miles south-southeast of Crescent City, and 2 miles offshore (lat. 41°43'05" N, long. 124°11'15" W). Named on Sister Rocks (1966) 7.5' quadrangle.

Cheenitch Creek [HUMBOLDT]: *stream*, flows 2.5 miles to Klamath River opposite the north end of Orleans (lat. 41°18'20" N, long. 123°31'55" W). Named on Orleans (1978) 7.5' quadrangle.

Cheerio: see **Camp Cheerio** [MENDOCINO].

Chemese Mountain: see **Chamisal Mountain** [HUMBOLDT-MENDOCINO].

Chemise Creek [HUMBOLDT]: *stream*, flows 1.25 miles to the sea 2.5 miles east-southeast of Point Delgada (lat. 40°00'15" N, long. 124°01'30" W). Named on Shelter Cove (1969) 7.5' quadrangle.

Chemise Creek: see **Chamise Creek** [HUMBOLDT-MENDOCINO-TRINITY].

Chemise Knob: see **Big Chemise Knob** [MENDOCINO]; **Little Chemise Knob** [MENDOCINO].

Cherry Camp [TRINITY]: *locality*, 8 miles south-southwest of Black Rock

Mountain (lat. 40°06'20" N, long. 123°04'20" W; sec. 14, T 26 N, R 11 W). Named on Black Rock Mountain (1954) 15' quadrangle.

Cherry Creek [MENDOCINO]:

(1) *stream,* flows 4.25 miles to Eel River nearly 6 miles south-southeast of Spyrock (2) (lat. 39°48'05" N, long. 123°24' W; near NW cor. sec. 2, T 22 N, R 14 W). Named on Covelo West (1967) and Iron Peak (1967) 7.5' quadrangles.

(2) *stream,* flows 3.5 miles to Outlet Creek 4.5 miles north-northeast of Longvale (lat. 39°36'40" N, long. 123°22'55" W; sec. 2, T 20 N, R 14 W). Named on Longvale (1966) 7.5' quadrangle.

(3) *stream,* flows 1 mile to Sonoma County 9.5 miles south of Hopland (lat. 38°50'20" N, long. 123°06'45" W; at S line sec. 32, T 12 N, R 11 W). Named on Hopland (1960) 15' quadrangle.

Cherry Flat [TRINITY]:

(1) *area,* 11 miles north of Weaverville along Stuart Fork (lat. 40°53'05" N, long. 122°55'45" W; near S line sec. 18, T 35 N, R 9 W). Named on Trinity Dam (1950) 15' quadrangle.

(2) *area,* 10.5 miles east of Burnt Ranch along Big French Creek (lat. 40°50'25" N, long. 123°16'50" W; at N line sec. 4, T 5 N, R 8 E). Named on Ironside Mountain (1951) 15' quadrangle.

Cherry Glade Creek [TRINITY]: *stream,* flows 1.5 miles to Mad River 8.5 miles west-northwest of Forest Glen (lat. 40°24'55" N, long. 123°28'20" W; near SW cor. sec. 35, T 1 N, R 6 E). Named on Sportshaven (1973) 7.5' quadrangle.

Cherry Hill [MENDOCINO]: *relief feature,* 5.25 miles north of Hull Mountain (lat. 39°36' N, long. 122°55'55" W; sec. 11, T 20 N, R 10 W). Named on Hull Mountain (1967) 7.5' quadrangle.

Cherry Lake [MENDOCINO]: *intermittent lake,* 250 feet long, 2.5 miles north-northeast of Anthony Peak (lat. 39°52'40" N, long. 122°57'05" W; sec. 3, T 23 N, R 10 W). Named on Buck Rock (1967) 7.5' quadrangle.

Cherry Spring [MENDOCINO]: *spring,* 10 miles north of Covelo (lat. 39°56'05" N, long. 123°13'35" W; near W line sec. 17, T 24 N, R 12 W). Named on Bluenose Ridge (1967) 7.5' quadrangle.

Chervimov Opening [HUMBOLDT]: *area,* 12.5 miles south-southwest of Alderpoint (lat. 40°00'25" N, long. 123°40'55" W; near W line sec. 24, T 5 S, R 4 E). Named on Harris (1969) 7.5' quadrangle.

Chicago: see **Camp Chicago** [DEL NORTE].

Chicago Camp [TRINITY]: *locality,* 3.5 miles south-southeast of Black Rock Mountain (lat. 40°09'20" N, long. 122°59'15" W; at E line sec. 28, T 27 N, R 10 W); the place is 0.5 mile southeast of Chicago Rock. Named on Black Rock Mountain (1954) 15' quadrangle.

Chicago Creek [DEL NORTE]: *stream,* flows 1.5 miles to East Fork Illinois Creek 8.5 miles north-northeast of Broken Rib Mountain (lat. 41°57'30" N, long. 123°37'50" W); the stream is west of Chicago Peak. Named on Broken Rib Mountain (1982) 7.5' quadrangle.

Chicago Peak [DEL NORTE]: *peak,* 4.25 miles northeast of Broken Rib Mountain (lat. 41°56'10" N, long. 123°38' W). Altitude 5484 feet. Named on Broken Rib Mountain (1982) 7.5' quadrangle.

Chicago Rock [TRINITY]: *peak,* 2 miles south-southeast of Black Rock Mountain (lat. 40°09'40" N, long. 122°59'35" W; sec. 28, T 27 N, R 10 W). Named on Yolla Bolly (1954) 15' quadrangle.

Chicken Flat [TRINITY]: *area,* 12 miles northeast of Weaverville (lat. 40°51'15" N, long. 122°47' W; around SW cor. sec. 28, T 35 N, R 8 W). Named on Trinity Lake (1950) 15' quadrangle. Water of Clair Engle Lake now covers the place.

Chicken Springs Reservoir [LAKE]: *lake,* 150 feet long, 2.5 miles southwest of Highland Springs (lat. 38°54'45" N, long. 122°56'30" W; sec. 2, T 12 N, R 10 W). Named on Highland Springs (1959) 7.5' quadrangle.

Chief Spring [MENDOCINO]: *spring,* 13 miles north-northwest of Hull Mountain (lat. 39°42'05" N, long. 122°59'30" W; sec. 5, T 21 N, R 10 W). Named on Plaskett Ridge (1967) 7.5' quadrangle.

Chilcoot Creek [TRINITY]: *stream,* flows 1.5 miles to High Camp Creek 3.5 miles south-southeast of China Mountain, which is in Siskiyou County (lat. 41°19'55" N, long. 122°33'05" W; near NE cor. sec. 16, T 40 N, R 6 W). Named on China Mountain (1955) 15' quadrangle. United States Board on Geographic Names (1979, p. 3) approved the name "Chilcoot Pass" for a pass at the head of Chilcoot Creek on Trinity-Siskiyou County line (lat. 41°19'50" N, long. 122°35'12" W; sec. 17, T 40 N, R 6 W).

Chilcoot Pass: see **Chilcoot Creek** [TRINITY].

Childers Peak [LAKE]: *peak,* nearly 4 miles east-northeast of Whispering Pines (lat. 38°50'35" N, long. 122°37'45" W; near SW cor. sec. 34, T 12 N, R 7 W). Altitude 2188 feet. Named on Whispering Pines (1958) 7.5' quadrangle.

Childs Hill [DEL NORTE]: *ridge,* northeast-trending, 1.5 miles long, 9.5 miles east-southeast of Crescent City (lat. 41°42'05" N, long. 124°01'45" W; mainly in sec. 11, 14, T 15 N, R 1 E). Named on Childs Hill (1966) 7.5' quadrangle.

Childs Hill Prairie [HUMBOLDT]: *area,* 4 miles northwest of Coyote Peak on Bald Hills (lat. 41°10'15" N, long. 123°55'10" W). Named on Bald Hills (1982) 7.5' quadrangle. William Childs and Barney Childs purchased the ranch at the place in 1885 (Turner, p. 49).

Chilkoot Pass [TRINITY]: *pass,* nearly 5 miles south-southwest of Cecilville, which is in Siskiyou County, on Siskiyou-Trinity County line (lat. 41°04'55" N, long. 123°09'55" W). Named on Cecil Lake (1979) 7.5' quadrangle.

Chimmekanee Creek [HUMBOLDT]: *stream,* flows 1 mile to Klamath River 2 miles southwest of Orleans (lat. 41°17'05" N, long. 123°34'05" W; sec. 2, T 10 N, R 5 E). Named on Orleans (1978) 7.5' quadrangle.

Chimney Peak: see **Chimney Rock** [MENDOCINO] (1).

Chimney Rock [DEL NORTE]: *relief feature,* nearly 2 miles south of Sawtooth Mountain (lat. 41°35'10" N, long. 123°42'40" W). Named on Chimney Rock (1981) 7.5' quadrangle.

Chimney Rock [HUMBOLDT]: *relief feature,* 3.25 miles east-southeast of Yager Junction (lat. 40°31'55" N, long. 123°45'45" W; near SW cor. sec. 20, T 2 N, R 4 E). Named on Yager Junction (1979) 7.5' quadrangle.

Chimney Rock [MENDOCINO]:

(1) *relief feature,* 6.5 miles south-southeast of Piercy (lat. 39°52'35" N, long. 123°50'55" W). Altitude 1404 feet. Named on Piercy (1969) 7.5' quadrangle. Called Chimney Pk. on O'Brien's (1953) map.

(2) *relief feature,* 5.25 miles east of Leggett (lat. 39°52'25" N, long. 123°37' W; near N line sec. 3, T 23 N, R 16 W). Named on Tan Oak Park (1969) 7.5' quadrangle.

(3) *relief feature,* 9.5 miles east-northeast of Eden Valley (lat. 39°40'45" N, long. 123°01'25" W). Named on Thatcher Ridge (1967) 7.5' quadrangle.

Chimney Rock Creek [MENDOCINO]: *stream,* flows 2.5 miles to Usal Creek nearly 7 miles south-southwest of Piercy, and 0.5 mile west-northwest of Chimney Rock (1) (lat. 39°52'45" N, long. 123°51'25" W). Named on Piercy (1969) 7.5' quadrangle.

China Creek [HUMBOLDT]:

(1) *stream,* flows less than 1 mile to Klamath River nearly 7 miles south-southeast of Johnsons (lat. 41°16'15" N, long. 123°47'45" W; sec. 11, T 10 N, R 3 E). Named on Johnsons (1982) 7.5' quadrangle.

(2) *stream,* flows 2.25 miles to Trinity River 1 mile south-southeast of the settlement of Willow Creek at China Flat (lat. 40°55'30" N, long. 123°37'05" W; sec. 4, T 6 N, R 5 E). Named on Salyer (1979) and Willow Creek (1979) 7.5' quadrangles.

(3) *stream,* flows 2.5 miles to Redwood Creek (2) 6.25 miles west of Garberville (lat. 40°05'50" N, long. 123°54'35" W; sec. 24, T 4 S, R 2 E). Named on Briceland (1969) 7.5' quadrangle.

China Creek [HUMBOLDT]: *stream,* heads in Siskiyou County and flows 3 miles to Camp Creek nearly 6 miles northwest of Orleans in Humboldt County (lat. 41°21'30" N, long. 123°37'15" W). Named on Fish Lake (1974), Lonesome Ridge (1974), and Orleans (1978) 7.5' quadrangles.

China Creek [TRINITY]:

(1) *stream,* flows 5 miles to New River 6.5 miles north-northeast of Burnt Ranch (lat. 40°53'40" N, long. 123°25'20" W); the stream heads near China Peak. Named on Ironside Mountain (1951) 15' quadrangle. Called Indian Creek on United States Geological Survey's (1915) map.

(2) *stream,* flows 3.25 miles to North Fork Trinity River 13 miles north of Helena (lat. 40°57'30" N, long. 123°09'15" W). Named on Helena (1951) 15' quadrangle.

(3) *stream,* flows 1 mile to East Fork Trinity River 5.5 miles east-northeast of Trinity Center (lat. 41°02'15" N, long. 122°35'45" W; sec. 30, T 37 N, R 6 W). Named on Bonanza King (1955) 15' quadrangle.

China Flat [HUMBOLDT]: *area,* 1.25 miles south-southeast of the settlement of Willow Creek along Trinity River (lat. 40°55'20" N, long. 123°37' W; sec. 4, T 6 N, R 5 E). Named on Salyer (1979) 7.5' quadrangle.

China Flat: see **Willow Creek** [HUMBOLDT] (3).

China Gardens Camp [TRINITY]: *locality,* 7.5 miles south of Cecilville, which is in Siskiyou County (lat. 41°02'10" N, long. 123°08'05" W). Site named on Cecil Lake (1979) 7.5' quadrangle.

China Gate [MENDOCINO]: *pass,* 6.5 miles north-northeast of Boonville (lat. 39°06' N, long. 123°19'40" W; sec. 6, T 14 N, R 13 W). Named on Boonville (1959) 15' quadrangle.

China Gulch [HUMBOLDT]: *canyon,* drained by a stream that flows 0.5 mile to Wilder Creek 3.25 miles northwest of Orleans (lat. 41°20'45" N, long. 123°34'10" W). Named on Orleans (1978) 7.5' quadrangle.

China Gulch [MENDOCINO]:

(1) *canyon,* 2 miles long, opens into the head of Schooner Gulch 8.5 miles north-northwest of Gualala (lat. 38°52'05" N, long. 123°37'10" W; near N line sec. 34, T 12 N, R 16 W). Named on Gualala (1960) 7.5' quadrangle.

(2) *canyon,* drained by a stream that flows 1.5 miles to Gualala River at Gualala (lat. 38°45'55" N, long. 123°31'35" W; near S line sec. 27, T 11 N, R 15 W). Named on Gualala (1960) 7.5' quadrangle.

China Gulch [TRINITY]:

(1) *canyon,* drained by a stream that flows 1 mile to Little Browns Creek 3.5 miles northeast of Weaverville (lat. 40°45'35" N, long. 122°53'05" W; sec. 33, T 34 N, R 9 W). Named on Trinity Dam (1950) 15' quadrangle.

(2) *canyon,* drained by a stream that flows 0.5 mile to Sidney Gulch 0.5 mile west-northwest of the center of Weaverville (lat. 40°44'15" N, long. 122°57' W; near N line sec. 12, T 33 N, R 10 W). Named on Weaverville (1950) 15' quadrangle.

(3) *canyon*, drained by a stream that flows 0.5 mile to Trinity River 4 miles southeast of Weaverville (lat. 40°41'30" N, long. 122°53'05" W; near NE cor. sec. 28, T 33 N, R 9 W). Named on Weaverville (1950) 15' quadrangle.

(4) *canyon*, drained by a stream that flows 1 mile to South Fork Indian Creek (2) 12.5 miles south-southeast of Weaverville (lat. 40°34'45" N, long. 122°48'45" W; near S line sec. 31, T 32 N, R 8 W). Named on Weaverville (1950) 15' quadrangle.

(5) *canyon*, drained by a stream that flows 5 miles to Hayfork Creek 8.5 miles north-northeast of Dubakella Mountain (lat. 40°29'45" N, long. 123°04'40" W). Named on Dubakella Mountain (1954) and Hayfork (1951) 15' quadrangles.

China Peak [TRINITY]: *peak*, 9 miles east-northeast of Burnt Ranch (lat. 40°53'15" N, long. 123°20' W); the peak is near the head of China Creek (1). Altitude 5403 feet. Named on Ironside Mountain (1951) 15' quadrangle.

China Slide [TRINITY]: *relief feature*, 1.5 miles southeast of Burnt Ranch on the southwest side of Trinity River (lat. 40°47'30" N, long. 123°27'30" W; sec. 24, T 5 N, R 6 E); the feature is 0.5 mile upstream from the mouth of Dixon Bar Creek. Named on Ironside Mountain (1951) 15' quadrangle. A mining place called Dixons Bar was located at China Slide; the name was for "Old Joe" Dixon (Jones, p. 247).

China Spring [TRINITY]: *spring*, 6.5 miles south-southeast of Cecilville, which is in Siskiyou County (lat. 41°03'20" N, long. 123°04'50" W). Named on Thompson Peak (1979) 7.5' quadrangle.

China Springs [TRINITY]: *spring*, 7.5 miles north of Helena (lat. 40°52'50" N, long. 123°08'30" W; at SW cor. sec. 17, T 35 N, R 11 W). Named on Helena (1951) 15' quadrangle.

China Springs Gulch [TRINITY]: *canyon*, drained by a stream that flows 1 mile to East Fork of North Fork Trinity River 7 miles north of Helena (lat. 41°52'35" N, long. 123°07'45" W; sec. 20, T 35 N, R 11 W); the canyon heads at China Springs. Named on Helena (1951) 15' quadrangle.

Chinkhollow Creek [TRINITY]: *stream*, flows 1.5 miles to Coffee Creek 4 miles west-southwest of Billys Peak (1) (lat. 41°07'15" N, long. 122°50'40" W; sec. 25, T 38 N, R 9 W). Named on Coffee Creek (1955) 15' quadrangle.

Chinquapin Butte [TRINITY]: *peak*, 7.5 miles south-southeast of Forest Glen (lat. 40°16'20" N, long. 123°15'40" W; near S line sec. 18, T 28 N, R 12 W). Altitude 5870 feet. Named on Forest Glen (1979) 7.5' quadrangle.

Chinquapin Gulch [TRINITY]: *canyon*, drained by a stream that flows 0.5 mile to Trinity River 7.25 miles north of Trinity Center (lat. 41°06'30" N, long. 122°42'20" W; at E line sec. 31, T 38 N, R 7 W). Named on Bonanza King (1955) 15' quadrangle.

Chipmunk Meadow [TRINITY]: *area*, 6.25 miles west-northwest of Billys Peak (1) (lat. 41°09'15" N, long. 122°52'30" W; sec. 15, T 38 N, R 9 W). Named on Coffee Creek (1955) 15' quadrangle.

Chipmunk Spring [MENDOCINO]: *spring*, 0.5 mile northwest of Hull Mountain (lat. 39°31'40" N, long. 122°56'40" W; sec. 3, T 19 N, R 10 W). Named on Hull Mountain (1952) 15' quadrangle.

Chocolate Peak [LAKE]: *peak*, 9 miles north of Clearlake Oaks (lat. 39°08'40" N, long. 122°38' W; sec. 16, T 15 N, R 7 W). Altitude 3620 feet. Named on Clearlake Oaks (1960) 15' quadrangle.

Choptoy Creek [TRINITY]: *stream*, flows nearly 2 miles to Ruth Reservoir 4.5 miles south-southwest of Forest Glen (lat. 40°19'05" N, long. 123°22'25" W; sec. 3, T 2 S, R 7 E). Named on Forest Glen (1979) 7.5' quadrangle.

Chqui Creek [HUMBOLDT]: *stream*, flows 1 mile to Klamath River 7.5 miles southeast of Johnsons (lat. 41°15'55" N, long. 123°46'55" W; near S line sec. 12, T 10 N, R 3 E). Named on Johnsons (1982) 7.5' quadrangle.

Chris Creek [HUMBOLDT]: *stream*, flows 2.5 miles to Larabee Creek 1.5 miles northeast of Redcrest (lat. 40°24'45" N, long. 123°55'25" W; sec. 2, T 1 S, R 2 E). Named on Redcrest (1969) 7.5' quadrangle. Called Criss Creek on Dyerville (1921) 15' quadrangle.

Chris Gap [TRINITY]: *pass*, 6 miles north-northwest of Forest Glen (lat. 40°26'35" N, long. 123°22'45" W; near NW cor. sec. 27, T 1 N, R 7 E). Named on Sportshaven (1973) 7.5' quadrangle.

Chris Rock [MENDOCINO]: *rock*, 5.5 miles north-northwest of Westport, and 350 feet offshore (lat. 39°42'50" N, long. 123°49'05" W). Named on Westport (1966) 7.5' quadrangle.

Christie Gulch [HUMBOLDT]: *canyon*, drained by a stream that flows 0.5 mile to Camp Creek 3.25 miles northwest of Orleans (lat. 41°20'25" N, long. 123°34'45" W). Named on Orleans (1978) 7.5' quadrangle.

Christine: see **Philo** [MENDOCINO].

Christine Junction: see **Philo** [MENDOCINO].

Christmas Prairie [HUMBOLDT]: *area*, 9 miles east of the town of Blue Lake (lat. 40°52'25" N, long. 123°49'15" W; sec. 27, T 6 N, R 3 E). Named on Lord-Ellis Summit (1973) and Maple Creek (1977) 7.5' quadrangles. The name is from a fight between soldiers and Indians at the place on Christmas day of 1854 (Turner, p. 49).

Christmas Rock [HUMBOLDT]: *shoal*, nearly 6 miles southwest of Petrolia, and 0.5 mile offshore (lat. 40°16'25" N, long. 124°22'25" W). Named on Petrolia (1969) 7.5' quadrangle.

Chrome Gulch [TRINITY]: *canyon*, drained by a stream that flows 1.5 miles to Mumbo Creek 12 miles north-northeast of Trinity Center (lat. 41°09'20" N, long. 122°34'45" W; sec. 17, T 38 N, R 6 W). Named on Bonanza King (1955) 15' quadrangle.

Church Gulch [TRINITY]: *canyon*, drained by a stream that flows 1 mile to Deadwood Creek 11 miles east of Weaverville (lat. 40°43' N, long. 122°44'45" W; near W line sec. 14, T 33 N, R 8 W). Named on French Gulch (1979) 7.5' quadrangle.

Churchman Creek [MENDOCINO]: *stream*, flows 4 miles to South Fork Tenmile River 16 miles north-northwest of Comptche (lat. 39°29' N, long. 123°40'10" W; near S line sec. 20, T 19 N, R 16 W). Named on Comptche (1960) 15' quadrangle.

Cinch Creek [MENDOCINO]: *stream*, flows 2 miles to Bell Springs Creek 4.25 miles north-northwest of Spyrock (2) (lat. 39°56'05" N, long. 123°28'25" W; near SW cor. sec. 7, T 24 N, R 14 W). Named on Updegraff Ridge (1967) 7.5' quadrangle.

Cinnabar: see **Cinnabar Gulch** [TRINITY].

Cinnabar Gulch [TRINITY]: *canyon*, drained by a stream that flows 1 mile to Crow Creek 13 miles northeast of Trinity Center (lat. 41°09'05" N, long. 122°31'10" W; sec. 14, T 38 N, R 6 W). Named on Bonanza King (1955) 15' quadrangle, which shows Integral mine situated 1 mile west-southwest of the mouth of Cinnabar Gulch (sec. 15, T 38 N, R 6 W). Postal authorities established Integral post office in 1893, discontinued it in 1895, reestablished it 1901, and discontinued it in 1903 (Salley, p. 104). They established Cinnabar post office in 1895 and discontinued it in 1901, when they moved it 1 mile northeast and changed the name to Itegral, presumably for Integral mine—the site also was called Garretson Soda Springs (Salley, p. 44).

Circle Point [HUMBOLDT]: *peak*, 10 miles east-northeast of the town of Blue Lake (lat. 40°55'25" N, long. 123°48'30" W; near NW cor. sec. 11, T 6 N, R 3 E). Altitude 2136 feet. Named on Lord-Ellis Summit (1973) 7.5' quadrangle, which shows a highway that makes an almost complete circle around the peak.

City of Eureka Reservoir [HUMBOLDT]: *lake*, behind a dam on Mad River 3.5 miles south of Korbel (lat. 40°49'15" N, long. 123°57'15" W; sec. 16, T 5 N, R 2 E). Named on Blue Lake (1951) 15' quadrangle.

Clair Engle Lake [TRINITY]: *lake*, behind a dam on Trinity River 10.5 miles east-northeast of Weaverville (lat. 40°48' N, long. 122°45'45" W; sec. 15, T 34 N, R 8 W). Named on Trinity Dam (1950) 15' quadrangle. Called Trinity Lake on Trinity Lake (1950) 15' quadrangle. United States Board on Geographic Names (1965a, p. 9) approved the name "Clair Engle Lake," given in 1964 by congressional action, and rejected the names "Trinity Lake" and "Trinity Reservoir" for the feature. The name honors Clair Engle, senator from California.

Clam Beach [HUMBOLDT]: *locality*, 8.5 miles north of Arcata (lat. 40°59'40" N, long. 124°06'40" W; sec. 18, T 7 N, R 1 E). Named on Arcata North (1959) 7.5' quadrangle.

Clamitte River: see **Klamath River** [DEL NORTE-HUMBOLDT].

Clapboard Gulch [TRINITY]: *canyon*, drained by a stream that flows 1 mile to Dobbins Gulch 5 miles north of Dubakella Mountain (lat. 40°28'20" N, long. 123°09'15" W; at W line sec. 7, T 30 N, R 11 W). Named on Dubakella Mountain (1954) 15' quadrangle.

Clapp Gulch [HUMBOLDT]: *canyon*, drained by a stream that flows 2 miles to Elk River (1) 3.5 miles east-southeast of Fields Landing (lat. 40°42'05" N, long. 124°09'15" W; sec. 26, T 4 N, R 1 W). Named on Fields Landing (1959) 7.5' quadrangle.

Clare Mill [MENDOCINO]: *locality*, 4 miles west of Willits along California Western Railroad (lat. 39°25' N, long. 123°25'30" W; near W line sec. 16, T 18 N, R 14 W). Named on Willits (1961) 15' quadrangle.

Clark Creek [TRINITY]: *stream*, flows 3.5 miles to Eltapom Creek nearly 6 miles north of Hyampom (lat. 40°41'50" N, long. 123°25'45" W; near N line sec. 30, T 4 N, R 7 E). Named on Hyampom (1951) 15' quadrangle.

Clark Mountain [HUMBOLDT]: *peak*, 3.5 miles northeast of Redcrest (lat. 40°25'55" N, long. 123°53'35" W; at S line sec. 25, T 1 N, R 2 E). Named on Redcrest (1969) 7.5' quadrangle.

Clark Opening [MENDOCINO]: *area*, 4.5 miles east of Comptche along South Fork Big River (lat. 39°16'20" N, long. 123°30'20" W; sec. 2, T 16 N, R 15 W); the place is just downstream from the mouth of Ramon Creek. Named on Comptche (1960) 15' quadrangle. The area also had the names "John Clark Opening" and "Ramon Opening" (Jackson, Francis, p. 32).

Clark Peak [LAKE]: *peak*, 2.25 miles east of Kelseyville (lat. 38°59'05" N, long. 122°47'35" W; on S line sec. 7, T 13 N, R 8 W). Named on Kelseyville (1959) 7.5' quadrangle. United States Board on Geographic Names (1962b, p. 15) rejected the form "Clarks Peak" for the name, which is for Peter Clark, an early homesteader in Big Valley (Gudde, 1969, p. 66).

Clarks Basin [TRINITY]: *relief feature*, 15 miles southwest of Black Rock Mountain (lat. 40°03'10" N, long. 123°11'45" W; at NW cor. sec. 3, T 25 N, R 12 W). Named on Black Rock Mountain (1954) 15' quadrangle.

Clarks Butte [HUMBOLDT]: *peak*, 8 miles west of Phillipsville (lat. 40°11'20" N, long. 123°56' W; sec. 22, T 3 S, R 2 E). Altitude 2788 feet.

Named on Ettersburg (1969) 7.5' quadrangle.

Clarks Creek [DEL NORTE]: *stream*, formed by the confluence of East Fork and West Fork, flows 1 mile to Smith River 7 miles northeast of Crescent City (lat. 41°49'05" N, long. 124°06'20" W; sec. 31, T 17 N, R 1 W). Named on Hiouchi (1966) 7.5' quadrangle. East Fork and West Fork each are about 1 mile long; both forks are named on Hiouchi (1966) 7.5' quadrangle.

Clarks Peak: see **Clark Peak** [LAKE].

Clawton Gulch [TRINITY]: *canyon*, drained by a stream that flows 2 miles to Trinity River 18 miles northeast of Weaverville (lat. 40°55' N, long. 122°41'50" W; sec. 6, T 35 N, R 7 W). Named on Schell Mountain (1950) 15' quadrangle.

Clayton Creek [LAKE]: *stream*, flows 1.5 miles to Copsey Creek 1 mile southeast of the town of Lower Lake (lat. 38°54' N, long. 122°35'50" W; sec. 11, T 12 N, R 7 W). Named on Lower Lake (1958) 7.5' quadrangle.

Clearbrook: see **Melbourne** [MENDOCINO].

Clear Creek [HUMBOLDT]:

(1) *stream*, flows 2 miles to Maple Creek (1) 7 miles east-northeast of Trinidad (lat. 41°05'30" N, long. 124°01' W; sec. 12, T 8 N, R 1 E). Named on Crannell (1966) and Panther Creek (1982) 7.5' quadrangles.

(2) *stream*, flows 2 miles to Mattole River nearly 1.5 miles southeast of Petrolia (lat. 40°18'40" N, long. 124°16' W; sec. 11, T 2 S, R 2 W). Named on Petrolia (1969) 7.5 quadrangle.

Clear Creek [TRINITY]: *stream*, flows 1.5 miles to South Fork Trinity River 2 miles west of Forest Glen (lat. 40°22'45" N, long. 123°21'45" W; sec. 14, T 1 S, R 7 E). Named on Forest Glen (1979) and Naufus Creek (1979) 7.5' quadrangles.

Clear Creek: see **Clear Gulch** [TRINITY].

Clear Gulch [TRINITY]: *canyon*, drained by a stream that flows 4 miles to Canyon Creek (1) 15 miles north-northeast of Hayfork (lat. 40°44'45" N, long. 123°03'05" W). Named on Hayfork (1951) and Helena (1951) 15' quadrangles. United States Geological Survey's (1915) map has the name "Clear Cr." for the stream in the canyon. East Fork opens into the main gulch from the east 6.25 miles east of Helena; it is 1 mile long and is named on Helena (1951) 15' quadrangle. West Branch opens into the main gulch nearly 6 miles east of Helena; it is 2.5 miles long and is named on Helena {1951) 15' quadrangle.

Clear Lake [HUMBOLDT]: *lake*, 250 feet long, 9.5 miles south-southwest of the settlement of Willow Creek (lat. 40°48'55" N, long. 123°41'45" W; sec. 14, T 5 N, R 4 E). Named on Grouse Mountain (1979) 7.5' quadrangle.

Clear Lake [LAKE]: *lake*, 20 miles long, southwest of the center of Lake County (lat. 39°02' N, long. 122°45' W). Named on Clearlake Highlands (1958), Clearlake Oaks (1958), and Lakeport (1958) 7.5' quadrangles. On Bancroft's (1864) map, the northwest part of present Clear Lake is called Upper Lake, and the southeast part is called Lower Lake. The name "Clear Lake" is from the clearness of the water (Menefee, p. 224). Spaniards used the names "Laguna" and "Laguna Grande" for the feature (Gudde, 1949, p. 70). It was called Laguna Grande de Napa in 1852 (Landsman, 1977a, p. 5). The two parts of the lake are connected by a water passage called The Narrows (2); the northwest part is Clear Lake proper, and the southeast part has two divisions, called East Lake and Lower Lake (Hoover, Rensch, and Rensch, p. 139).

Clear Lake: see **Clearlake Park** [LAKE].

Clearlake: see **Clearlake Highlands** [LAKE]; **Clearlake Park** [LAKE].

Clearlake Highlands [LAKE]: *town*, 3.5 miles north-northwest of the town of Lower Lake (lat. 38°57'30" N, long. 122°38'45" W; in and near sec. 21, T 13 N, R 7 W) Named on Clearlake Highlands (1958) 7.5' quadrangle. The place now is part of the community of Clearlake, which incorporated in 1980. Postal authorities established Clearlake Highlands post office in 1925 (Frickstad, p. 63). United States Board on Geographic Names (1962b, p. 15) rejected the form "Clear Lake Highlands" for the name. Chandler's (1901) map shows a place called Floyds Landing located along Clear Lake at present Clearlake Highlands (in present sec. 28, T 13 N, R 7 W).

Clearlake Oaks [LAKE]: *town*, 13 miles east of Lakeport along Clear Lake (lat. 39°01'25" N, long. 122°40'45" W; in and near sec. 31, T 14 N, R 7 W). Named on Clearlake Oaks (1958) 7.5' quadrangle. United States Board on Geographic Names (1962b, p. 15) rejected the name "Stubbs" for the place, and rejected the form "Clear Lake Oaks" for the name. Postal authorities established Stubbs post office in 1926 and changed the name to Clearlake Oaks in 1935; the name "Stubbs" was for Charles Stubbs, a landowner (Salley, p. 214).

Clearlake Park [LAKE]: *town*, 4.5 miles north-northwest of the town of Lower Lake (lat. 38°58' N, long. 122°39' W; in and near sec. 20, T 13 N, R 7 W). Named on Clearlake Highlands (1958) 7.5' quadrangle. The place now is part of the community of Clearlake, which incorporated in 1980. Postal authorities established Clearlake post office in 1923 and changed the name to Clearlake Park in 1937 (Frickstad, p. 63). United States Board on Geographic Names (1962b, p. 15) rejected the form "Clear Lake Park" for the name, and rejected the name "Clear Lake" for the town.

Clear Lake Villas: see **Nice** [LAKE].

Clearwater Gulch [HUMBOLDT]: *canyon*, drained by a stream that flows 1.5 miles to Klamath River nearly 4 miles northeast of Weitchpec (lat. 41°13'10" N, long. 123°38'45" W). Named on Weitchpec (1979) 7.5' quadrangle.

Cleland Mountain [MENDOCINO]: *ridge*, south-southeast-trending, 1 mile long, 3 miles south-southwest of Ukiah (lat. 39°00'45" N, long. 123°13'50" W). Named on Elledge Peak (1958) 7.5' quadrangle.

Clemhurst Spur [MENDOCINO]: *locality*, 5.5 miles south-southeast of Ukiah along Northwestern Pacific Railroad (lat. 39°04'45" N. long. 123°10'15" W). Named on Ukiah (1920) 15' quadrangle.

Clems Flat [TRINITY]: *area*, 9 miles east-northeast of Hayfork (lat. 40°37'35" N, long. 123°02'15" W; sec. 18, T 32 N, R 10 W). Named on Hayfork (1951) 15' quadrangle.

Cleone [MENDOCINO]: *town*, 3.25 miles north-northeast of Fort Bragg (lat. 39°29'25" N, long. 123°47'05" W; near SW cor. sec. 20, T 19 N, R 17 W). Named on Fort Bragg (1960) 7.5' quadrangle. Postal authorities established Kanuck post office 3.5 miles north of Fort Bragg in 1883, changed the name to Cleone the same year, and discontinued it in 1908 (Salley, p. 46, 109). The name "Cleone" is of Indian origin (Kroeber, p. 39). Ties, piles, and bark were shipped from a chute and wharf at the place (Carpenter, p. 78).

Cleone: see **Lake Cleone** [MENDOCINO].

Cleveland: see **Ferndale** [HUMBOLDT].

Cleveland Meadow [TRINITY]: *area*, 8 miles west-northwest of Black Rock Mountain (lat. 40°14'10" N, long. 123°09'15" W; at W line sec. 31, T 28 N, R 11 W). Named on Black Rock Mountain (1954) 15' quadrangle.

Cliff Ridge [MENDOCINO]: *ridge*, generally north-northwest-trending, 12 miles long, between Greenwood Creek and Elk Creek (4). Named on Navarro (1961) 15' quadrangle. The name recalls Osro Clift, who bought land on the ridge in 1882 (Jackson, Walter, p. 9), but United States Board on Geographic Names (1963, p. 6) rejected the form "Clift Ridge" for the name.

Clifton Ridge [MENDOCINO]: *ridge*, southwest- to south-southwest-trending, 2.5 miles long, 16 miles north of Hull Mountain on Mendocino-Glenn County line (lat. 39°44'45" N, long. 122°56'15" W). Named on Mendocino Pass (1967) and Plaskett Ridge (1967) 7.5' quadrangles.

Clift Ridge: see **Cliff Ridge** [MENDOCINO].

Climbing Spring [TRINITY]: *spring*, 10.5 miles east-southeast of Kettenpom (lat. 40°05'35" N, long. 123°16'50" W; at S line sec. 21, T 4 S, R 8 E). Named on Long Ridge (1967) 7.5' quadrangle.

Clirliah Creek [HUMBOLDT]: *stream*, flows 2 miles to Klamath River 3.5 miles south of Johnsons (lat. 41°18' N, long. 123°52'20" W; sec. 31, T 10 N, R 3 E). Named on Holter Ridge (1983) 7.5' quadrangle.

Cloney Gulch [HUMBOLDT]: *canyon*, drained by a stream that flows 4 miles to Freshwater Creek 8 miles south-southeast of Arcata (lat. 40°45'30" N, long. 124°02'55" W; sec. 3, T 4 N, R 1 E). Named on Arcata South (1959) 7.5' quadrangle. The name is for Mike Cloney and his brother Tom, who logged in the neighborhood in the 1880's (Turner, p. 50).

Clover Creek [LAKE]: *stream*, flows 8 miles to Middle Creek (2) 0.5 mile south-southwest of the town of Upper Lake (lat. 39°09'35" N, long. 122°54'45" W; near E line sec. 12, T 15 N, R 10 W). Named on Bartlett Mountain (1958) and Upper Lake (1958) 7.5' quadrangles.

Cloverdale Peak [MENDOCINO]: *peak*, nearly 3 miles southwest of Monument Peak (lat. 38°53' N, long. 123°59'35" W; sec. 17, T 12 N, R 10 W). Altitude 2924 feet. Named on Highland Springs (1959) 7.5' quadrangle.

Clover Gulch [TRINITY]:

(1) *canyon*, drained by a stream that flows 1 mile to Salt Creek (4) 7 miles north of Dubakella Mountain (lat. 40°29' N, long. 123°10' W; sec. 1, T 30 N, R 12 W). Named on Dubakella Mountain (1954) 15' quadrangle.

(2) *canyon*, drained by a stream that flows 2.5 miles to Mad River 11.5 miles west-southwest of Black Rock Mountain (lat. 40°09'35" N, long. 123°13'15" W; sec. 28, T 27 N, R 12 W). Named on Black Rock Mountain (1954) 15' quadrangle.

(3) *canyon*, 1 mile long, nearly 6 miles south of Forest Glen (lat. 40°17'30" N, long. 123°20'45" W; on E line sec. 14, T 2 S, R 7 E). Named on Forest Glen (1979) 7.5' quadrangle.

Clover Gulch: see **Little Clover Gulch** [TRINITY].

Clover Valley [LAKE]: *valley*, center 1.5 miles east-northeast of the town of Upper Lake (lat. 39°10'30" N, long. 122°52'45" W); the valley is along Clover Creek. Named on Bartlett Mountain (1958) and Upper Lake (1958) 7.5' quadrangles.

Clow Canyon [MENDOCINO]: *canyon*, drained by a stream that flows 1.25 miles to Navarro River 4 miles northwest of Boonville (lat. 39°02'50" N, long. 123°25'10" W; sec. 29, T 14 N, R 14 W). Named on Boonville (1959) 15' quadrangle.

Clow Mountain [MENDOCINO]: *ridge*, generally west-northwest-trending, 3 miles long, 6.5 miles north-northwest of Boonville (lat. 39°06'10" N, long. 123°24'20" W). Named on Boonville (1959) 15' quadrangle.

Clow Ridge [MENDOCINO]: *ridge*, generally north-northeast-trending, 1.25 miles long, 6.5 miles north-northwest of Boonville (lat. 39°06'20" N, long. 123°24'15" W); Clow Mountain is at the south end of the ridge. Named on

Boonville (1959) 15' quadrangle.

Cluster Cone Rocks [MENDOCINO]: *rocks*, 9 miles southwest of Piercy near the coast (lat. 39°54'40" N, long. 123°56'25" W). Named on Bear Harbor (1969) 7.5' quadrangle. United States Coast and Geodetic Survey (p. 143) described Cluster Cone Rock as a prominent 68-foot pinnacle, the largest and whitest of a small cluster of 6 rocks, 200 yards offshore.

Coal Creek [MENDOCINO]: *stream*, flows about 1.25 miles to Salt Creek (1) 4.5 miles east-southeast of Dos Rios (lat. 39°41'05" N, long. 123°16'30" W; near N line sec. 14, T 21 N, R 13 W). Named on Dos Rios (1967) 7.5' quadrangle.

Cobb [LAKE]: *village*, 1 mile northwest of Whispering Pines (lat. 38°49'25" N, long. 122°43'15" W; near SW cor. sec. 11, T 11 N, R 8 W); the village is near the southeast end of Cobb Valley. Named on Whispering Pines (1958) 7.5' quadrangle. Postal authorities established Cobb post office in 1911 (Salley, p. 47).

Cobb Creek: see **Kelsey Creek** [LAKE].

Cobb Mountain [LAKE]: *peak*, 1.5 miles west-southwest of Whispering Pines (lat. 38°48'25" N, long. 122°44'20" W; on E line sec. 16, T 11 N, R 8 W). Named on Whispering Pines (1958) 7.5' quadrangle.

Cobb Mountain Range: see **Mayacmas Mountains** [LAKE-MENDOCINO].

Cobb Ridge [TRINITY]: *ridge*, west-trending, 1.5 miles long, 10.5 miles west-southwest of Black Rock Mountain (lat. 40°09' N, long. 123°11'30" W; sec. 34, 35, T 27 N, R 12 W). Named on Black Rock Mountain (1954) 15' quadrangle.

Cobb Valley [LAKE]: *valley*, 2 miles northwest of Whispering Pines along Kelsey Creek (lat. 38°50'05" N, long. 122°44'10" W; in and near sec. 3, T 11 N, R 8 W). Named on Whispering Pines (1958) 7.5' quadrangle. The name commemorates John Cobb, first settler in the neighborhood, who farmed in the valley (Hanna, p. 67). Anderson (p. 163) called the place Cobb's Valley, and noted that a resort called Gordon's Mineral Springs was located there. Waring (p. 93) used the name "Gordon Hot Spring."

Coby [HUMBOLDT]: *locality*, 3 miles west of the present settlement of Willow Creek (lat. 40°57'10" N, long. 123°41'30" W). Named on China Flat (1922) 15' quadrangle.

Cockerell Canyon [LAKE]: *canyon*, drained by a stream that flows 1.5 miles to Putah Creek 3.5 miles north of Middletown (lat. 38°48'10" N, long. 122°36'45" W). Named on Middletown (1958) and Whispering Pines (1958) 7.5' quadrangles.

Cock Robin Island [HUMBOLDT]: *island*, nearly 1.5 miles long, 3.5 miles north-northwest of Ferndale between Eel River and an arm of that river (lat. 40°37'45" N, long. 124°17' W). Named on Cannibal Island (1959) and Ferndale (1959) 7.5' quadrangles.

Coeur: see **White Rock City** [TRINITY].

Coffee: see **Goldfield Campground** [TRINITY].

Coffee Creek [HUMBOLDT]: *stream*, flows nearly 1 mile to Salt River 4 miles west-southwest of Fortuna (lat. 40°34'50" N, long. 124°13'25" W). Named on Fortuna (1959) 7.5' quadrangle. The name is from the color of the water in the creek in the summer (Turner, p. 51).

Coffee Creek [TRINITY]: *stream*, flows 17 miles to Trinity River 5.5 miles north of Trinity Center (lat. 41°05'10" N, long. 122°42'05" W). Named on Bonanza King (1955) and Coffee Creek (1955) 15' quadrangles. The name reportedly came after high water in the stream swept away a pack mule loaded with coffee (Gudde, 1969, p. 69). East Fork enters from the northeast 3 miles west-southwest of Billys Peak (1) and is 5.25 miles long. North Fork enters from the northwest 4 miles west-southwest of Billys Peak (1) and is 7.5 miles long. South Fork enters 8 miles west of Billys Peak (1) and is 5 miles long. All three forks are named on Coffee Creek (1955) 15' quadrangle.

Coffee Mill Flat [MENDOCINO]: *area*, 11 miles north of Hull Mountain (lat. 39°40'35" N, long. 122°58'35" W; sec. 16, T 21 N, R 10 W). Named on Plaskett Ridge (1967) 7.5' quadrangle.

Coffee Pot [TRINITY]: *peak*, 4.25 miles south-southeast of Black Lassic (lat. 40°16'50" N, long. 123°30'45" W). Named on Black Lassic (1979) 7.5' quadrangle.

Colby Reef [MENDOCINO]: *shoal*, 4 miles south of Mendocino (lat. 39°15' N, long. 123°47'45" W). Named on Albion (1960) and Mendocino (1960) 7.5' quadrangles. United States Coast and Geodetic Survey (p. 141) described the feature as a rocky patch covered by 1.5 fathoms.

Cold Camp Creek [TRINITY]: *stream*, flows 2.5 miles to Indian Valley Creek 5.25 miles south-southeast of Hyampom (lat. 40°33'20" N, long. 123°24'30" W; sec. 17, T 2 N, R 7 E); the stream heads at Cold Spring (1). Named on Hyampom (1951) 15' quadrangle. Called Cold Creek on United States Geological Survey's (1915) map.

Cold Canyon [LAKE]: *canyon*, drained by a stream that flows nearly 2 miles to Wolf Creek 6 miles northeast of Clearlake Oaks (lat. 39°05'20" N, long. 122°36'20" W; sec. 2, T 14 N, R 7 W). Named on Clearlake Oaks (1960) 15' quadrangle.

Cold Creek [HUMBOLDT]: *stream*, flows nearly 1 mile to Burr Creek (2) 3.5 miles south-southeast of Bridgeville (lat. 40°25'15" N, long. 123°46'45" W). Named on Bridgeville (1969) 7.5' quadrangle.

Cold Creek [LAKE]: *stream*, flows nearly 6 miles to Eel River 4.25 miles northwest of Crockett Peak (lat. 39°28'15" N, long. 122°49'55" W; at W line sec. 25, T 19 N, R 9 W). Named on Crockett Peak (1967) and Saint John Mountain (1968) 7.5' quadrangles.

Cold Creek [MENDOCINO]:

(1) *stream*, flows 2.25 miles to Grub Creek 9.5 miles southeast of Leggett (lat. 39°46'40" N, long. 123°34'45" W; sec. 7, T 22 N, R 15 W). Named on Tan Oak Park (1969) 7.5' quadrangle.

(2) *stream*, heads in Glenn County and flows 1.5 miles in Mendocino County to Black Butte River 12 miles north of Hull Mountain (lat. 39°41'45" N, long. 122°55'10" W; near N line sec. 12, T 21 N, R 10 W). Named on Plaskett Ridge (1967) 7.5' quadrangle.

(3) *stream*, flows 8.5 miles to East Fork Russian River 8 miles north-northeast of Ukiah (lat. 39°14'45" N, long. 123°07'40" W; sec. 18, T 16 N, R 11 W). Named on Cow Mountain (1958) and Ukiah (1958) 7.5' quadrangles.

(4) *stream*, flows 5.25 miles to join Alder Creek (2) and form Mill Creek (1) 4.25 miles north-northwest of Covelo (lat. 39°50'50" N, long. 123°17'20" W; near SE cor. sec. 15, T 23 N, R 13 W). Named on Covelo West (1967) and Mina (1967) 7.5' quadrangles. Called Cole Creek on Spyrock (1952) 15' quadrangle.

Cold Creek [TRINITY]:

(1) *stream*, flows 1 mile to South Fork Trinity River 4 miles south of Hyampom (lat. 40°33'45" N, long. 123°27'25" W; near SW cor. sec. 12, T 2 N, R 6 E). Named on Hyampom (1951) 15' quadrangle.

(2) *stream*, flows 2 miles to Salt Creek (4) 3.5 miles north-northeast of Dubakella Mountain (lat. 40°26'15" N, long. 123°07'45" W; sec. 20, T 30 N, R 11 W). Named on Dubakella Mountain (1954) 15' quadrangle.

Cold Creek: see **Cold Camp Creek** [TRINITY]; **Cole Creek** [LAKE]; **Cole Creek** [TRINITY].

Cold Gulch [TRINITY]: *canyon*, drained by a stream that flows 1.5 miles to Trinity River 9.5 miles north of Trinity Center (lat. 41°08'35" N, long. 122°40'45" W; sec. 21, T 38 N, R 7 W). Named on Bonanza King (1955) 15' quadrangle.

Cold Spring Canyon [LAKE]: *canyon*, drained by a stream that flows 3.25 miles to Wolf Creek 9 miles northeast of Clearlake Oaks (lat. 39°05'05" N, long. 122°32'10" W; sec. 4, T 14 N, R 6 W). Named on Clearlake Oaks (1960) and Wilbur Springs (1961) 15' quadrangles.

Cold Spring Mountain [DEL NORTE]: *peak*, 5 miles northeast of Gasquet (lat. 41°53'40" N, long. 123°53'40" W). Altitude 3722 feet. Named on Gasquet (1951) 15' quadrangle.

Cold Spring Mountain [LAKE]: *peak*, 11.5 miles east-northeast of Clearlake Oaks on Lake-Colusa County line (lat. 39°05'50" N, long. 122°29'15" W; sec. 35, T 15 N, R 6 W). Named on Wilbur Springs (1961) 15' quadrangle.

Cold Spring Mountain [MENDOCINO]: *peak*, 9 miles south of Navarro (lat. 39°01'20" N, long. 123°31'20" W; on S line sec. 33, T 14 N, R 15 W); the peak is 0.5 mile south of Cold Spring (2). Altitude 2736 feet. Named on Navarro (1961) 15' quadrangle.

Cold Springs Campground [TRINITY]: *locality*, nearly 6 miles northwest of Dubakella Mountain (lat. 40°26'55" N, long. 123°12'50" W; near E line sec. 16, T 30 N, R 12 W). Named on Dubakella Mountain (1954) 15' quadrangle.

Cold Springs Creek [MENDOCINO]: *stream*, flows 2 miles to Rancheria Creek (2) 6.5 miles west-northwest of Boonville (lat. 39°01'50" N, long. 123°29'15" W; sec. 35, T 14 N, R 15 W). Named on Boonville (1959) and Navarro (1961) 15' quadrangles.

Cold Springs Creek [TRINITY]: *stream*, flows 3 miles to South Fork Trinity River 4.25 miles south of Hyampom (lat. 40°33'15" N, long. 123°27'25" W; near W line sec. 13, T 2 N, R 6 E). Named on Hyampom (1951) 15' quadrangle, and on Blake Mountain (1979) 7.5' quadrangle.

Coldwater Creek [DEL NORTE]: *stream*, flows 1.5 miles to Hardscrabble Creek 11 miles northeast of Crescent City (lat. 41°50'45" N, long. 124°01'35" W). Named on Hiouchi (1966) 7.5' quadrangle.

Cole Creek [LAKE]: *stream*, flows 15 miles to Kelsey Creek 6 miles east-southeast of Lakeport (lat. 39°01'05" N, long. 122°48'50" W; sec. 36, T 14 N, R 9 W). Named on Clearlake Highlands (1958), Kelseyville (1959), and Lucerne (1958) 7.5' quadrangles. Called Cold Creek on Lakeport (1938) and Lower Lake (1945) 15' quadrangles, but United States Board on Geographic Names (1962b, p. 15) rejected this name for the feature. The name "Cole Creek" is from the Indian pronunciation of the American name "Cold Creek" (Gudde, 1969, p. 70).

Cole Creek [TRINITY]: *stream*, flows 1 mile to Rush Creek 7 miles north of Weaverville (lat. 40°49'45" N, long. 122°54'30" W; near S line sec. 5, T 34 N, R 9 W). Named on Trinity Dam (1950) 15' quadrangle. United States Board on Geographic Names (1983d, p. 4) approved the name "Cold Creek" for the stream.

Cole Creek: see **Cold Creek** [MENDOCINO] (4); **Rumsey Slough** [LAKE]; **Thompson Creek** [LAKE] (2).

Coleman Creek [HUMBOLDT]: *stream*, flows 3.5 miles to Eel River 5 miles west-northwest of Blocksburg (lat. 40°17'40" N, long. 123°43'45" W; sec. 16, T 2 S, R 4 E). Named on Blocksburg (1969) 7.5' quadrangle.

Coleman Creek [MENDOCINO]: *stream*, flows 8 miles to Pieta Creek 5.25

miles southeast of Hopland (lat. 38°55'25" N, long. 123°03'25" W; sec. 2, T 12 N, R 11 W). Named on Highland Springs (1959) and Hopland (1960) 7.5' quadrangles.

Coleridge [TRINITY]: *locality*, 5.25 miles north of Helena along East Fork of North Fork Trinity River (lat. 40°51' N, long. 123°08' W; at N line sec. 32, T 35 N, R 11 W). Site named on Helena (1951) 15' quadrangle. Postal authorities established Coleridge post office in 1889 and discontinued it in 1907 (Frickstad, p. 206). California Mining Bureau's (1917b) map has the alternate name "Enterprise" for the place.

Colgrove Branch [HUMBOLDT]: *stream*, flows 2.25 miles to Mill Creek (2) 8.5 miles east-southeast of Weitchpec (lat. 41°08'10" N, long. 123°33'50" W). Named on Hopkins Butte (1979) 7.5' quadrangle.

Collayomi [LAKE]: *land grant*, at and near Middletown and Long Valley (1). Named on Detert Reservoir (1958), Middletown (1958), Mount Saint Helena (1959), and Whispering Pines (1958) 7.5' quadrangles. Robert T. Ridley received 3 leagues in 1844 or 1845; Archibald A. Ritchie and Paul S. Forbes claimed 8242 acres patented in 1863 (Cowan, p. 29—Cowan gave the form "Callayomi" as an alternate; Perez, p. 63). The name is of Indian origin (Kroeber, p. 39).

Collayomi Valley [LAKE]: *valley*, at and near Middletown along Putah Creek and Saint Helena Creek on Collayomi grant. Named on Detert Reservoir (1958), Middletown (1958), Mount Saint Helena (1959), and Whispering Pines (1958) 7.5' quadrangles.

College Cove [HUMBOLDT]: *embayment*, less than 1 mile northwest of Trinidad along the coast (lat. 41°04' N, long. 124°09' W; sec. 23, T 8 N, R 1 W). Named on Trinidad (1966) 7.5' quadrangle.

Collins Bar Creek [TRINITY]: *stream*, flows less than 1 mile to Trinity River nearly 1 mile southeast of Burnt Ranch (lat. 40°48'10" N, long. 123°27'45" W; near SW cor. sec. 13, T 5 N, R 6 E). Named on Ironside Mountain (1951) 15' quadrangle.

Collins Creek [TRINITY]: *stream*, flows 2 miles to South Fork Trinity River 1.5 miles southeast of Forest Glen (lat. 40°21'30" N, long. 123°18'10" W; at N line sec. 29, T 1 S, R 8 E). Named on Forest Glen (1979) 7.5' quadrangle.

Collins Gulch [HUMBOLDT]: *canyon*, drained by a stream that flows less than 1 mile to Mattole River 4 miles west-southwest of Petrolia (lat. 40°17'40" N, long. 124°21'05" W; sec. 13, T 2 S, R 3 W); the canyon heads at Collins Point. Named on Petrolia (1969) 7.5' quadrangle.

Collins Landing [MENDOCINO]: *locality*, 3 miles northwest of Gualala along the coast (lat. 38°47'40" N, long. 123°34'05" W; near N line sec. 20, T 11 N, R 15 W). Named on Gualala (1960) 7.5' quadrangle.

Collins Point [HUMBOLDT]: *relief feature*, 3.5 miles west-southwest of Petrolia (lat. 40°18'20" N, long. 124°20'50" W; at W line sec. 7, T 2 S, R 2 W); the feature is at the head of Collins Gulch. Named on Petrolia (1969) 7.5' quadrangle.

Collins Ridge [TRINITY]: *ridge*, northwest-trending, 2 miles long, 8.5 miles west-southwest of Black Rock Mountain (lat. 40°09'30" N, long. 123°09' W). Named on Black Rock Mountain (1954) 15' quadrangle.

Collins Spring [HUMBOLDT]: *spring*, 3 miles west-southwest of Petrolia (lat. 40°18'15" N, long. 124°20'20" W; near S line sec. 7, T 2 S, R 2 W); the spring is 0.5 mile east-southeast of Collins Point. Named on Petrolia (1969) 7.5' quadrangle.

Colson Gulch [MENDOCINO]: *canyon*, drained by a stream that flows less than 1 mile to Floodgate Creek 2 miles south of Navarro (lat. 39°07'20" N, long. 123°32'50" W; near NE cor. sec. 31, T 15 N, R 15 W). Named on Navarro (1961) 15' quadrangle.

Comfort: see **Boonville** [MENDOCINO].

Complexion Canyon [LAKE]: *canyon*, drained by a stream that flows 2 miles to Kilpepper Creek 13 miles northeast of Clearlake Oaks (lat. 39°10'05" N, long. 122°30'45" W; near N line sec. 10, T 15 N, R 6 W); Complexion Spring is in the canyon. Named on Clearlake Oaks (1960) 15' quadrangle.

Complexion Spring [LAKE]: *spring*, 13 miles northeast of Clearlake Oaks (lat. 39°10'10" N, long. 122°30'45" W; near S line sec. 3, T 15 N, R 6 W). Named on Clearlake Oaks (1960) 15' quadrangle. The claim was made that water from the spring improved a person's complexion (Bradley, p. 217).

Comptche [MENDOCINO]: *village*, 17 miles southeast of Fort Bragg (lat. 39°15'55" N, long. 123°35'10" W; in and near sec. 12, T 16 N, R 16 W). Named on Comptche (1960) 15' quadrangle. Postal authorities established Comptche post office in 1877, discontinued it the same year, and reestablished it in 1879 (Frickstad, p. 94). California Mining Bureau's (1917c) map shows a place called Half Way located 4 miles east-southeast of Comptche.

Comstock Slide [TRINITY]: *relief feature*, 16 miles east-northeast of Weaverville (lat. 40°50'25" N, long. 122°39'45" W). Named on Schell Mountain (1950) 15' quadrangle.

Con Creek [MENDOCINO]: *stream*, flows 3.5 miles to Anderson Creek (2) 1.5 miles northwest of Boonville (lat. 39°01'45" N, long. 123°23'25" W; sec. 34, T 14 N, R 14 W). Named on Boonville (1959) 15' quadrangle.

Cone Rock [DEL NORTE]: *rock*, 4.5 miles northwest of the town of Smith River, and 3600 feet offshore (lat. 41°58'25" N, long. 124°13' W). Named on Smith River (1966) 7.5' quadrangle.

Cone Rock [HUMBOLDT]: *rock*, 4 miles northwest of Trinidad, and 1.25 miles offshore (lat. 41°06'35" N, long. 124°11'05" W). Named on Trinidad (1966) 7.5' quadrangle. The feature has a conical shape (United States Coast and Geodetic Survey, p. 148).

Conical Rock [HUMBOLDT]: *rock*, 6 miles southwest of Petrolia, and 450 feet off Point Gorda (lat. 40°15'40" N, long. 124°21'50" W). Named on Petrolia (1969) 7.5' quadrangle.

Conical Rock: see **Sharp Point** [HUMBOLDT].

Conklin Creek [HUMBOLDT]: *stream*, flows 2.5 miles to Mattole River 14 miles south-southwest of Scotia (lat. 40°18'30" N, long. 124°14'10" W; sec. 12, T 2 S, R 2 W). Named on Buckeye Mountain (1970) 7.5' quadrangle.

Conley Creek [HUMBOLDT]: *stream*, formed by the confluence of North Fork and South Fork, flows 3.5 miles to Dobbyn Creek 4.25 miles north-northwest of Alderpoint (lat. 40°14'15" N, long. 123°38'20" W; sec. 5, T 3 S, R 5 E). Named on Black Lassic (1979), Blocksburg (1969), and Fort Seward (1969) 7.5' quadrangles. North Fork is 2.5 miles long and South Fork is 3.5 miles long. Both forks are named on Black Lassic (1979) 7.5' quadrangle.

Conner Cabin Spring [MENDOCINO]: *spring*, 7 miles north-northwest of Eden Valley (lat. 39°43'15" N, long. 123°14'30" W; sec. 31, T 22 N, R 12 W). Named on Jamison Ridge (1967) 7.5' quadrangle.

Conner Creek: see **Connor Creek** [TRINITY].

Connick Creek [HUMBOLDT]:

(1) *stream*, flows 2 miles to Bull Creek (2) 3.25 miles northwest of Weott (lat. 40°21' N, long. 123°58'10" W; sec. 29, T 1 S, R 2 E). Named on Weott (1969) 7.5' quadrangle.

(2) *stream*, flows nearly 3 miles to South Fork Eel River about 0.5 mile west-southwest of Garberville (lat. 40°05'45" N, long. 123°48'15" W; at W line sec. 24, T 4 S, R 3 E). Named on Garberville (1970) 7.5' quadrangle.

Connor Creek [TRINITY]: *stream*, flows 4.5 miles to Trinity River 2.5 miles east-southeast of Helena (lat. 40°45'15" N, long. 123°04'05" W). Named on Hayfork (1951) 15' quadrangle. Called Conner Cr. on United States Geological Survey's (1915) map, and United States Board on Geographic Names (1983d, p. 4) approved this name for the stream.

Connors Resort [MENDOCINO]: *locality*, 3.5 miles east-northeast of the village of Point Arena (lat. 38°55'40" N, long. 123°37'15" W). Named on Point Arena (1943) 15' quadrangle.

Conns Creek: see **Asbill Creek** [LAKE].

Conrad Gulch [TRINITY]: *canyon*, drained by a stream that flows 2 miles to Canyon Creek (1) 4 miles east-northeast of Helena (lat. 40°47'40" N, long. 123°03'25" W; sec. 24, T 34 N, R 11 W). Named on Helena (1951) 15' quadrangle.

Conway Lake [TRINITY]: *lake*, 400 feet long, 7 miles southwest of Billys Peak (1) (lat. 41°02'55" N, long. 122°50'45" W; sec. 24, T 37 N, R 9 W). Named on Coffee Creek (1955) 15' quadrangle. The name commemorates Frederick Edmond Conway, an early settler in the neighborhood (United States Board on Geographic Names, 1954, p. 3).

Conways Landing: see **Fish Rock** [MENDOCINO].

Cook Creek [MENDOCINO]: *stream*, flows 3 miles to North Branch of North Fork Navarro River 2.5 miles north of Navarro (lat. 39°11'10" N, long. 123°33' W; sec. 6, T 15 N, R 15 W). Named on Navarro (1961) 15' quadrangle.

Cook Gulch [HUMBOLDT]: *canyon*, drained by a stream that flows 1 mile to Mattole River 16 miles south-southwest of Scotia (lat. 40°15'15" N, long. 124°11'15" W; sec. 33, T 2 S, R 1 W); the canyon is west of Cook Ridge. Named on Buckeye Mountain (1970) and Shubrick Peak (1969) 7.5' quadrangles.

Cookhouse Gulch [MENDOCINO]: *canyon*, drained by a stream that flows 0.5 mile to South Branch of North Fork Navarro River 1.5 miles northeast of Navarro (lat. 39°09'50" N, long. 123°31'10" W; sec. 16, T 15 N, R 15 W). Named on Navarro (1961) 15' quadrangle.

Cook Ridge [HUMBOLDT]: *ridge*, north-northeast-trending, 1.25 miles long, 4.5 miles west of Honeydew (lat. 40°14'45" N, long. 124°11'20" W). Named on Buckeye Mountain (1970) and Shubrick Peak (1969) 7.5' quadrangles. The Cook family had a ranch in the neighborhood (Turner, p. 52).

Cooks Beach [MENDOCINO]: *beach*, 2.25 miles northwest of Gualala along the coast (lat. 38°47'20" N, long. 123°33'35" W; sec. 20, T 11 N, R 15 W). Named on Gualala (1960) 7.5' quadrangle.

Cook Spring: see **Yager Creek** [HUMBOLDT].

Cook Spring Creek [HUMBOLDT]: *stream*, flows 1.25 miles to Redwood Creek (1) 9.5 miles east of Korbel (lat. 40°50'55" N, long. 123°46'45" W; near E line sec. 1, T 5 N, R 3 E). Named on Maple Creek (1977) 7.5' quadrangle.

Coon Creek [DEL NORTE]: *stream*, flows 10.5 miles to South Fork Smith River 5.5 miles south-southwest of Gasquet (lat. 41°46'05" N, long. 123°59'50" W). Named on Gasquet (1981) 7.5' quadrangle.

Coon Creek [HUMBOLDT]:

(1) *stream,* flows less than 1 mile to Little River 4.5 miles southeast of Trinidad (lat. 41°00'35" N, long. 124°05'15" W; sec. 8, T 7 N, R 1 E). Named on Crannell (1966) 7.5' quadrangle.

(2) *stream,* flows 1.5 miles to Klamath River 8 miles southeast of Johnsons (lat. 41°15'40" N, long. 123°46'45" W; sec. 13, T 10 N, R 3 E). Named on Johnsons (1982) 7.5' quadrangle.

(3) *stream,* flows 2 miles to South Fork Eel River 3.5 miles south-southeast of Weott (lat. 40°16'40" N, long. 123°53'15" W; sec. 19, T 2 S, R 3 E). Named on Weott (1969) 7.5' quadrangle.

(4) *stream,* flows 2 miles to Butte Creek (3) 2 miles west of Phillipsville (lat. 40°12'50" N, long. 123°49'20" W; near S line sec. 10, T 3 S, R 3 E). Named on Miranda (1970) 7.5' quadrangle.

(5) *stream,* flows 5 miles to Trinity River 3.25 miles north of the settlement of Willow Creek (lat. 40°59'15" N, long. 123°37'55" W; near S line sec. 8, T 7 N, R 5 E). Named on Salyer (1979) and Willow Creek (1979) 7.5' quadrangles. The canyon of the stream is called Racoon Gulch on China Flat (1922) 15' quadrangle.

Coon Creek [MENDOCINO]: *stream,* flows 1.5 miles to North Fork Navarro River 3.25 miles west of Navarro (lat. 39°09'30" N, long. 123°36' W; sec. 14, T 15 N, R 16 W). Named on Navarro (1961) 15' quadrangle.

Coon Creek [TRINITY]: *stream,* flows 2.5 miles to South Fork Trinity River 7.5 miles south of Salyer (lat. 40°47'05" N, long. 123°33'30" W). Named on Hennessy Peak (1979) 7.5' quadrangle.

Coon Gulch [TRINITY]: *canyon,* drained by a stream that flows 1 mile to Van Duzen River 8.5 miles west of Forest Glen (lat. 40°20'55" N, long. 123°28'40" W; sec. 27, T 1 S, R 6 E). Named on Ruth Reservoir (1978) 7.5' quadrangle.

Coon Lake [MENDOCINO]: *lake,* 200 feet long, 12 miles southeast of Ukiah (lat. 39°01'05" N, long. 123°04'25" W; sec. 4, T 13 N, R 11 W). Named on Purdys Gardens (1958) 7.5' quadrangle.

Coon Mountain: see **Lower Coon Mountain** [DEL NORTE]; **Upper Coon Mountain** [DEL NORTE].

Coon Ridge [HUMBOLDT]: *ridge,* southwest-trending, 1 mile long, 16 miles south of Scotia (lat. 40°15'30" N, long. 124°09'10" W). Named on Buckeye Mountain (1970) 7.5' quadrangle. According to Turner (p. 52), John Coon named the feature because he shot a racoon there.

Coonrod Gulch [TRINITY]: *canyon,* drained by a stream that flows 1 mile to Hayfork Creek 2.25 miles east of Hayfork (lat. 40°32'45" N, long. 123°08'30" W; at SE cor. sec. 7, T 31 N, R 11 W). Named on Hayfork (1951) 15' quadrangle.

Cooper [LAKE]: *locality,* 6.5 miles northwest of the town of Upper Lake (lat. 39°13'10" N, long. 123°00'10" W; near NE cor. sec. 30, T 16 N, R 10 W). Named on Cow Mountain (1958) 7.5' quadrangle.

Cooper Canyon [HUMBOLDT]: *canyon,* drained by a stream that flows 1.25 miles to Eureka Slough 1 mile east of downtown Eureka (lat. 40°48'20" N, long. 124°08'25" W; sec. 23, T 5 N, R 1 W). Named on Eureka (1958) 7.5' quadrangle.

Cooper Creek [HUMBOLDT]: *stream,* flows 3.25 miles to Larabee Creek 2.5 miles north-northwest of Blocksburg (lat. 40°18'30" N, long. 123°39'25" W; sec. 7, T 2 S, R 5 E). Named on Black Lassic (1979) and Blocksburg (1969) 7.5' quadrangles.

Cooper Creek [LAKE]: *stream,* flows 6 miles to Tule Lake (2) nearly 3 miles west of the town of Upper Lake (lat. 39°10'05" N, long. 122°57'30" W; sec. 10, T 15 N, R 10 W). Named on Cow Mountain (1958) and Upper Lake (1958) 7.5' quadrangles.

Cooper Gulch [TRINITY]: *canyon,* drained by a stream that flows 1 mile to the canyon of Trinity River 7.25 miles east of Weaverville (lat. 40°44'50" N, long. 122°48'10" W; near W line sec. 5, T 33 N, R 8 W). Named on Trinity Dam (1950) and Weaverville (1950) 15' quadrangles.

Cooper Mill Creek [HUMBOLDT]: *stream,* flows 4 miles to Yager Creek 6 miles east-southeast of Fortuna (lat. 40°33'35" N, long. 124°30'55" W; sec. 15, T 2 N, R 1 E). Named on Hydesville (1979) 7.5' quadrangle. The name is from the grist mill that the five Cooper brothers built on their ranch; the stream sometimes is called Indian Creek (Turner, p. 52).

Coopers Bar [TRINITY]: *locality,* 2 miles east-southeast of Helena (lat. 40°45'50" N, long. 123°05'30" W; around NE cor. sec. 34, T 34 N, R 11 W). Named on Helena (1951) 15' quadrangle. The place also was known as McGillivrays Bar (Gudde, 1975, p. 82). Joseph McGillivray came to present Cooper's Bar in 1851 (Jones, p. 186).

Cooskie Creek [HUMBOLDT]: *stream,* flows 4 miles to the sea 7 miles south of Petrolia (lat. 40°13'10" N, long. 124°18'35" W; near E line sec. 8, T 3 S, R 2 W); the stream heads at Cooskie Ridge. Named on Cooskie Creek (1969) 7.5' quadrangle.

Cooskie Mountain [HUMBOLDT]: *peak,* 5 miles south of Petrolia (lat. 40°15'20" N, long. 124°15'55" W; near NW cor. sec. 35, T 2 S, R 2 W). Named on Petrolia (1969) 7.5' quadrangle. The name is of Indian origin (Turner, p. 52).

Cooskie Ridge [HUMBOLDT]: *ridge,* generally north-trending, 3.5 miles long, nearly 6 miles west of Honeydew (lat. 40°13' N, long. 124°14'55" W); Cooskie Mountain is at the north end. Named on Cooskie Creek (1969), Petrolia (1969), and Shubrick Peak (1969) 7.5' quadrangles.

Copper Butte [LAKE]: *peak,* 3 miles west of Crockett Peak (lat. 39°25'55" N, long. 122°49'50" W). Altitude 4114 feet. Named on Crockett Peak (1967) 7.5' quadrangle.

Copper Butte Creek [LAKE]: *stream,* flows 3.25 miles to Eel River 4.25 miles west of Crockett Peak (lat. 39°25'50" N, long. 122°51'10" W); the stream is south of Copper Butte. Named on Crockett Peak (1967) 7.5' quadrangle.

Copper Creek [DEL NORTE]: *stream,* flows 4 miles to Rowdy Creek 5.5 miles east-northeast of the town of Smith River (lat. 41°57'20" N, long. 124°03'35" W; sec. 16, T 18 N, R 15 E). Named on High Divide (1966) 7.5' quadrangle.

Copper Creek [HUMBOLDT]: *stream,* flows 2.25 miles to Redwood Creek (1) 4 miles west-northwest of Coyote Peak (lat. 41°08'55" N, long. 123°56' W; at S line sec. 22, T 9 N, R 2 E). Named on Bald Hills (1982) 7.5' quadrangle.

Copper Creek [TRINITY]: *stream,* flows 3.5 miles to Trinity River 4 miles north of Trinity Center (lat. 41°03'35" N, long. 122°42' W; at S line sec. 17, T 37 N, R 7 W). Named on Bonanza King (1955) 15' quadrangle.

Copper Hill [TRINITY]: *peak,* 3.5 miles north-northwest of Forest Glen (lat. 40°25'20" N, long. 123°20'25" W; sec. 36, T 1 N, R 7 E). Altitude 4885 feet. Named on Naufus Creek (1979) 7.5' quadrangle.

Copper Mine Creek: see **Tunnel Creek** [TRINITY].

Copsy Creek [LAKE]: *stream,* flows 8 miles to Cache Creek 1.25 miles northeast of the town of Lower Lake (lat. 38°55'20" N, long. 122°35'35" W; near W line sec. 1, T 12 N, R 7 W). Named on Lower Lake (1958) and Whispering Pines (1958) 7.5' quadrangles. United States Board on Geographic Names (1962b, p. 15) rejected the name "Herndon Creek" for the feature.

Copsey's Spring: see **Spiers Springs**, under **Bonanza Springs** [LAKE].

Corbet Creek [MENDOCINO]: *stream,* flows 3.25 miles to Eel River 4.5 miles south-southeast of Spyrock (2) (lat. 39°49'05" N, long. 123°24'55" W; near W line sec. 34, T 23 N, R 14 W). Named on Iron Peak (1967) 7.5' quadrangle.

Corbin Creek [LAKE]: *stream,* heads in Glenn County and flows 7.5 miles in Lake County to Eel River 4.5 miles east of Hull Mountain (lat. 39°31'40" N, long. 122°51' W; at W line sec. 2, T 19 N, R 9 W). Named on Felkner Hill (1968) and Kneecap Ridge (1967) 7.5' quadrangles.

Corey Peak [TRINITY]: *peak,* 17 miles east-southeast of Etna, which is in Siskiyou County, on Trinity-Siskiyou County line (lat. 41°19'45" N, long. 122°36'10" W; sec. 18, T 40 N, R 6 W). Altitude 7737 feet. Named on China Mountain (1955) 15' quadrangle.

Corner Creek [HUMBOLDT]:

(1) *stream,* flows 3.25 miles to Lawrence Creek 6 miles west of Lone Star Junction (lat. 40°37'05" N, long. 123°59'20" W; near N line sec. 30, T 3 N, R 2 E). Named on Hydesville (1979) and Owl Creek (1979) 7.5' quadrangles.

(2) *stream,* flows 1.25 miles to South Fork Eel River 0.5 mile northwest of Weott (lat. 40°19'40" N, long. 123°55'40" W; near SW cor. sec. 35, T 1 S, R 2 E). Named on Weott (1969) 7.5' quadrangle.

Corners: see **The Corners**, under **Boonville** [MENDOCINO].

Corral Bottom [TRINITY]: *valley,* 9 miles northeast of Hyampom (lat. 40°42'10" N, long. 123°19'45" W); the valley is along Corral Creek (1). Named on Hyampom (1951) 15' quadrangle.

Corral Creek [HUMBOLDT]: *stream,* flows 2.5 miles to Tish Tang a Tang Creek 9 miles east of Hoopa (lat. 41°04'30" N, long. 123°30'35" W). Named on Tish Tang Point (1978) and Trinity Mountain (1979) 7.5' quadrangles.

Corral Creek [MENDOCINO]:

(1) *stream,* flows 1.5 miles to Outlet Creek 2 miles east-northeast of Longvale (lat. 39°34'05" N, long. 123°23'45" W; sec. 22, T 20 N, R 14 W). Named on Longvale (1966) 7.5' quadrangle.

(2) *stream,* flows 3 miles to Russian River 6 miles west of the town of Potter Valley (lat. 39°20'05" N, long. 123°13'20" W; near NW cor. sec. 17, T 17 N, R 12 W). Named on Redwood Valley (1960) 7.5' quadrangle.

(3) *stream,* flows less than 1 mile to Redwood Creek (6) nearly 2 miles west-northwest of Ornbaun Valley (lat. 38°55'30" N, long. 123°20' W; sec. 5, T 12 N, R 13 W). Named on Ornbaun Valley (1960) 15' quadrangle.

Corral Creek [TRINITY]:

(1) *stream,* flows 12.5 miles to Hayfork Creek 4.5 miles east of Hyampom (lat. 40°37'45" N, long. 123°21'45" W; sec. 23, T 3 N, R 7 E). Named on Hyampom (1951) 15' quadrangle.

(2) *stream,* flows 1.5 miles to Indian Creek (2) 13 miles southeast of Weaverville (lat. 40°35'25" N, long. 122°46'35" W; sec. 33, T 32 N, R 8 W). Named on Weaverville (1950) 15' quadrangle.

Corral Gulch [TRINITY]:

(1) *canyon,* drained by a stream that flows 2.5 miles to Indian Valley Creek 8 miles south-southeast of Hyampom (lat. 40°31'30" N, long. 123°21'40" W; sec. 26, T 2 N, R 7 E). Named on Hyampom (1951) 15' quadrangle.

(2) *canyon,* drained by a stream that flows 1.5 miles to Browns Creek 3.5 miles east of Chanchelulla Peak (lat. 40°28'15" N, long. 122°55'35" W;

sec. 7, T 30 N, R 9 W). Named on Chanchelulla Peak (1951) 15' quadrangle.

Cotineva: see **Rockport** [MENDOCINO].

Cotineva Creek: see **Cottaneva Creek** [MENDOCINO].

Cotineva Ridge: see **Cottaneva Ridge** [MENDOCINO].

Cottaneva Creek [MENDOCINO]: *stream,* formed by the confluence of North Fork and Middle Fork, flows 4.5 miles to the sea 7.25 miles north-northwest of Westport (lat. 39°44'10" N, long. 123°49'40" W; at N line sec. 26, T 22 N, R 18 W). Named on Hales Grove (1970) and Westport (1966) 7.5' quadrangles. Called Cottoneva Creek on Cape Vizcaino (1950) and Piercy (1950) 15' quadrangles. United States Board on Geographic Names (1968b, p. 5) rejected the names "Cotineva Creek," "Cottoneva Creek," "Cottonwood Creek," and "Rockport Creek" for the feature. Middle Fork is nearly 2 miles long and North Fork is 7 miles long; both forks are named on Hales Grove (1970) 7.5' quadrangle. South Fork enters from the southeast at Rockport, less than 1 mile upstream from the mouth of the main creek; it is 3.5 miles long and is named on Westport (1966) 7.5' quadrangle. United States Board on Geographic Names (1968b, p. 6) rejected the name "Rockport Creek" for South Fork.

Cottaneva Needle [MENDOCINO]: *rock,* 8 miles north-northwest of Westport, and 700 feet offshore (lat. 39°44'55" N, long. 123°50'10" W); the feature is 1 mile north-northwest of the mouth of Cottaneva Creek. Named on Westport (1966) 7.5' quadrangle.

Cottaneva Ridge [MENDOCINO]: *ridge,* generally west-trending, 2.5 miles long, 7 miles north of Westport (lat. 39°44'20" N, long. 123°47' W); the ridge is south of South Fork Cottaneva Creek. Named on Westport (1966) 7.5' quadrangle. Called Cottoneva Ridge on Cape Vizcaino (1950) 15' quadrangle, but United States Board on Geographic Names (1968a, p. 4) rejected the names "Cotineva Ridge," "Cotteneva Ridge," and "Cottoneva Ridge" for the feature.

Cottaneva Valley [MENDOCINO]: *canyon,* 15 miles south of Piercy (lat. 39°45'55" N, long. 123°49'35" W); the canyon is along Cottaneva Creek. Named on Hales Grove (1970) 7.5' quadrangle.

Cotteneva Ridge: see **Cottaneva Ridge** [MENDOCINO].

Cottoneva Creek: see **Cottaneva Creek** [MENDOCINO].

Cottoneva Ridge: see **Cottaneva Ridge** [MENDOCINO].

Cottonwood Creek [TRINITY]: *stream,* flows 2.25 miles to Salt Creek (2) 9 miles southeast of Kettenpom (lat. 41°03'30" N, long. 123°21'20" W). Named on Lake Mountain (1967) and Long Ridge (1967) 7.5' quadrangles.

Cottonwood Creek: see **Cottaneva Creek** [MENDOCINO].

Coulborn Creek [MENDOCINO]: *stream,* flows 2.5 miles to Indian Creek (2) 5 miles west-southwest of Piercy (lat. 39°57'50" N, long. 123°53'25" W; at E line sec. 6, T 24 N, R 18 W). Named on Bear Harbor (1969) 7.5' quadrangle.

Coumbs Springs: see **Deer Lick Springs** [TRINITY].

Counterfeit Hill [LAKE]: *peak,* 7.25 miles west-northwest of the town of Lower Lake (lat. 38°56'35" N, long. 122°44'25" W; on E line sec. 28, T 13 N, R 8 W). Named on Clearlake Highlands (1958) 7.5' quadrangle.

Counts Hill Prairie [HUMBOLDT]: *area,* 5.5 miles northwest of Coyote Peak (lat. 41°11'25" N, long. 123°56' W). Named on Bald Hills (1982) 7.5' quadrangle.

County Line Creek [TRINITY]: *stream,* flows 1.5 miles to Mad River 9.5 miles southwest of Hyampom just inside Humboldt County (lat. 40°29'55" N, long. 123°32'35" W; sec. 6, T 1 N, R 6 E). Named on Blake Mountain (1979) 7.5' quadrangle.

County Line Ridge [LAKE]: *ridge,* generally east-southeast-trending, 3 miles long, 6 miles south-southeast of Cold Spring Mountain on Lake-Colusa County line (lat. 39°01'20" N, long. 122°25'40" W). Named on Wilbur Springs (1961) 15' quadrangle.

Cove: see **The Cove,** under **Helena** [TRINITY].

Covelo [MENDOCINO]: *town,* about 14 miles east-northeast of Laytonville (lat. 39°42'35" N, long. 123°14'50" W; at E line sec. 1, T 22 N, R 13 W). Named on Covelo East (1967) and Covelo West (1967) 7.5' quadrangles. Postal authorities established Covelo post office in 1870 (Frickstad, p. 94). C.H. Eberle named the town for a Swiss village; the first store at the site opened in 1860 (Carpenter, p. 107). Postal authorities established Carey post office 16 miles south of Covelo in 1891, changed the name to Jeram in 1896, and discontinued it in 1897; the name "Carey" was for George R. Carey, first postmaster, and the name "Jeram" was for Father Jeram, who started a settlement of Slavonian followers in Eden Valley (Salley, p. 37, 107). Postal authorities established Poonkiny post office 12 miles southwest of Covelo in 1896 and discontinued it in 1900; the name is of Indian origin (Salley, p. 176). They established Bucknell post office north of Covelo (SW quarter sec. 12, T 24 N, R 13 W) in 1922 and discontinued it in 1923; the name was for Charles M. Bucknell, a settler of 1893 (Salley, p. 28). A coal-mining camp called Carbon was situated 6 miles from Covelo in the 1890's along Middle Fork Eel River (Mosier, p. 4).

Cove Rock [MENDOCINO]: *rock,* 1.5 miles west-northwest of Elk, and 1200 feet offshore (lat. 39°08'25" N, long. 123°44'25" W). Named on Elk (1960) 7.5' quadrangle.

Covington Gulch [MENDOCINO]: *canyon,* drained by a stream that flows 1.5 miles to Hare Creek 3 miles southeast of Fort Bragg (lat. 39°24'30" N, long. 123°46'15" W; near E line sec. 20, T 18 N, R 17 W). Named on Fort Bragg (1960) 7.5' quadrangle.

Covington Mill [TRINITY]: *locality,* 15 miles north-northeast of Weaverville along East Fork Stuart Fork (lat. 40°54'35" N, long. 122°46'10" W). Named on Trinity Dam (1950) 15' quadrangle.

Cowan Creek [HUMBOLDT]: *stream,* flows 2.25 miles to Mad River 3.25 miles east-northeast of Lone Star Junction (lat. 40°39'15" N, long. 123°49'10" W; sec. 10, T 3 N, R 3 E). Named on Mad River Buttes (1977) 7.5' quadrangle.

Cow Creek [HUMBOLDT]:

(1) *stream,* flows 2 miles to Bull Creek (2) 3 miles northwest of Weott (lat. 40°20'55" N, long. 123°57'45" W; sec. 28, T 1 S, R 2 E). Named on Weott (1969) 7.5' quadrangle.

(2) *stream,* flows 4.5 miles to Grouse Creek (2) 4.5 miles east-northeast of Board Camp Mountain (lat. 40°43'20" N, long. 123°38'20" W). Named on Board Camp Mountain (1977) and Grouse Mountain (1979) 7.5' quadrangles. Called Happy Camp Creek on China Flat (1922) 15' quadrangle.

Cow Creek [TRINITY]: *stream,* flows 1.5 miles to Trinity River 4.25 miles north-northwest of Burnt Ranch (lat. 40°52' N, long. 123°29'55" W). Named on Ironside Mountain (1951) 15' quadrangle.

Cow Creek Ridge [HUMBOLDT]: *ridge,* generally southeast-trending, 2 miles long, 3.25 miles northeast of Board Camp Mountain (lat. 40°43'55" N, long. 123°40'30" W); the ridge is southwest of Cow Creek (2). Named on Board Camp Mountain (1977) 7.5' quadrangle.

Cow Flat [MENDOCINO]: *area,* 11 miles southeast of Eden Valley (lat. 39°30'45" N, long. 123°03'45" W; at S line sec. 11, T 19 N, R 11 W). Named on Sanhedrin Mountain (1966) 7.5' quadrangle.

Cow Glade [LAKE]: *area,* 2.5 miles south-southwest of Highland Springs (lat. 38°54'20" N, long. 122°55'30" W; near N line sec. 12, T 12 N, R 10 W). Named on Highland Springs (1959) 7.5' quadrangle.

Cow Gulch [TRINITY]:

(1) *canyon,* drained by a stream that flows 1 mile to Indian Valley Creek 10.5 miles southeast of Hyampom (lat. 40°30'45" N, long. 123°18'30" W; near E line sec. 31, T 2 N, R 8 E). Named on Hyampom (1951) 15' quadrangle.

(2) *canyon,* drained by a stream that flows 1.5 miles to Salt Gulch 5 miles north-northeast of Dubakella Mountain (lat. 40°27'15" N, long. 123°07'05" W; at E line sec. 17, T 30 N, R 11 W). Named on Dubakella Mountain (1954) 15' quadrangle.

Cow Gulch: see **Little Cow Gulch** [TRINITY].

Cow Mountain [LAKE-MENDOCINO]: *ridge,* northwest-trending, 7.5 miles long, 7 miles east-northeast of Ukiah on Lake-Mendocino County line (lat. 39°11'40" N, long. 123°04'45" W). Named on Cow Mountain (1958) and Purdys Gardens (1958) 7.5' quadrangles.

Cow Mountain [MENDOCINO]:

(1) *peak,* 8.5 miles east of Leggett (lat. 39°51'05" N, long. 123°33'20" W; sec. 8, T 23 N, R 15 W). Altitude 3753 feet. Named on Tan Oak Park (1969) 7.5' quadrangle.

(2) *peak,* nearly 6 miles north of Boonville (lat. 39°05'30" N, long. 123°21'15" W; near N line sec. 12, T 14 N, R 14 W). Named on Boonville (1959) 15' quadrangle.

Cow Mountain: see **Cow Mountain Ridge** [LAKE]; **Little Cow Mountain** [LAKE].

Cow Mountain Ridge [LAKE-MENDOCINO]: *ridge,* generally south-trending, 11 miles long, center about 7 miles east of Ukiah (lat. 39°08' N, long. 123°04'30" W); the ridge extends south from Cow Mountain [LAKE-MENDOCINO] along Lake-Mendocino County line. Named on Cow Mountain (1958) and Purdys Gardens (1958) 7.5' quadrangles. United States Board on Geographic Names (1961a, p. 18) rejected the name "Cow Mountain" for the ridge.

Cow Pasture Spring [HUMBOLDT]: *area,* 12 miles south-southwest of Scotia (lat. 40°19'50" N, long. 124°12'40" W). Named on Buckeye Mountain (1970) 7.5' quadrangle.

Cow Prairie [HUMBOLDT]: *area,* 4.5 miles south of Coyote Peak (lat. 41°04'10" N, long. 123°52'05" W; on W line sec. 20, T 8 N, R 3 E). Named on Hupa Mountain (1982) 7.5' quadrangle. Called Monroe Flat on Coyote Peak (1952) 15' quadrangle, but United States Board on Geographic Names (1983d, p. 4) rejected this name for the feature.

Cowshed Gulch [MENDOCINO]: *canyon,* drained by a stream that flows 0.5 mile to Mallo Paso Creek 8.5 miles south-southeast of Elk (lat. 39°01'35" N, long. 123°37'45" W; near NW cor. sec. 3, T 13 N, R 16 W). Named on Navarro (1961) 15' quadrangle.

Cow Springs [MENDOCINO]: *spring,* 5.5 miles north of Boonville (lat. 39°05'20" N, long. 123°21'05" W; sec. 12, T 14 N, R 14 W); the spring is on the south side of Cow Mountain (1). Named on Boonville (1959) 15' quadrangle.

Cox Creek [HUMBOLDT]: *stream,* flows 2 miles to Sproul Creek 6.5 miles southwest of Garberville (lat. 40°01'20" N, long. 123°51'45" W). Named on Garberville (1970) 7.5' quadrangle.

Cox Creek [TRINITY]: *stream,* flows nearly 4 miles to North Fork Eel River

5.5 miles east of Kettenpom (lat. 40°09'25" N, long. 123°21'35" W; sec. 35, T 3 S, R 7 E). Named on Shannon Butte (1967) 7.5' quadrangle.

Cox Opening [MENDOCINO]: *area,* 12 miles southwest of Ornbaun Valley (lat. 38°46'45" N, long. 123°26'20" W; at SW cor. sec. 21, T 11 N, R 14 W). Named on Ornbaun Valley (1960) 15' quadrangle.

Cox's Bar: see **Big Bar** [TRINITY].

Coy Bar Creek: see **Price Creek** [TRINITY].

Coyote Creek [HUMBOLDT]:

(1) *stream,* flows 1.5 miles to Blue Creek 6.5 miles north of Johnsons (lat. 41°26'30" N, long. 123°51' W). Named on Blue Creek Mountain (1982) 7.5' quadrangle.

(2) *stream,* flows nearly 1 mile to Trinity River 3 miles south-southeast of Weitchpec (lat. 41°08'50" N, long. 123°40'55" W; near E line sec. 23, T 9 N, R 4 E). Named on Weitchpec (1979) 7.5' quadrangle.

(3) *stream,* flows 3.25 miles to Van Duzen River 2.5 miles southeast of Yager Junction (lat. 40°31'25" N, long. 123°47'25" W; sec. 25, T 2 N, R 3 E). Named on Yager Junction (1979) 7.5' quadrangle.

(4) *stream,* flows 2.5 miles to Mad River 2.25 miles northeast of Showers Mountain (lat. 40°36'10" N, long. 123°40'05" W; near N line sec. 36, T 3 N, R 4 E). Named on Showers Mountain (1978) 7.5' quadrangle.

(5) *stream,* flows 3.5 miles to Redwood Creek (1) 3.25 miles west-southwest of Coyote Peak (lat. 41°07' N, long. 123°55' W; sec. 2, T 8 N, R 2 E). Named on Bald Hills (1982), Hupa Mountain (1982), and Panther Creek (1982) 7.5' quadrangles.

Coyote Creek [LAKE]: *stream,* flows nearly 6 miles to Putah Creek 4.5 miles east-northeast of Middletown (lat. 38°47'05" N, long. 122°32'25" W); the stream goes through Coyote Valley. Named on Middletown (1958) 7.5' quadrangle.

Coyote Flat [HUMBOLDT]: *area,* 2 miles west of Showers Mountain (lat. 40°35' N, long. 123°44' W; mainly in sec. 4, T 2 N, R 4 E). Named on Showers Mountain (1978) 7.5' quadrangle.

Coyote Peak [HUMBOLDT]: *peak,* 8.5 miles west-southwest of Weitchpec (lat. 41°08' N, long. 123°51'30" W; near N line sec. 32, T 9 N, R 3 E). Altitude 3170 feet. Named on French Camp Ridge (1983) 7.5' quadrangle.

Coyote Peak [TRINITY]: *peak,* 25 miles south of Etna, which is in Siskiyou County, on Trinity-Siskiyou County line (lat. 41°05'45" N, long. 122°58'10" W). Named on Coffee Creek (1955) 15' quadrangle.

Coyote Rock [HUMBOLDT]: *relief feature,* 4000 feet west-southwest of Coyote Peak (lat. 41°07'40" N, long. 123°52'20" W; sec. 31, T 9 N, R 3 E). Named on French Camp Ridge (1983) 7.5' quadrangle.

Coyote Rock [MENDOCINO]:

(1) *relief feature,* 5.5 miles north-northeast of Covelo (lat. 39°52' N, long. 123°12'20" W; sec. 9, T 23 N, R 12 W). Named on Covelo East (1967) 7.5' quadrangle.

(2) *relief feature,* 8 miles north-northwest of Hull Mountain (lat. 39°37'35" N, long. 122°59'05" W; near N line sec. 5, T 20 N, R 10 W). Named on Plaskett Ridge (1967) 7.5' quadrangle.

(3) *relief feature,* 2 miles north-northeast of Spyrock (2) (lat. 39°54'20" N, long. 123°25'15" W). Named on Updegraff Ridge (1967) 7.5' quadrangle.

Coyote Rocks [LAKE]: *relief feature,* 4.5 miles northwest of Bear Mountain (lat. 39°27'15" N, long. 122°57'35" W; near SE cor. sec. 33, T 19 N, R 10 W). Named on Lake Pillsbury (1967) 7.5' quadrangle.

Coyote Valley [HUMBOLDT]: *canyon,* drained by a stream that flows 2.25 miles to an unnamed stream 3.5 miles east-northeast of Yager Junction (lat. 40°34'25" N, long. 123°45'50" W; near NE cor. sec. 7, T 2 N, R 4 E). Named on Showers Mountain (1978) and Yager Junction (1979) 7.5' quadrangles.

Coyote Valley [LAKE]: *valley,* 4 miles northeast of Middletown along Putah Creek (lat. 38°47'30" N, long. 122°33'30" W). Named on Middletown (1958) 7.5' quadrangle. Postal authorities established Kayote post office about 4 miles northeast of present Middletown in Coyote Valley in 1859 and discontinued in 1862 (Salley, p. 109). Goodyear (1890a, p. 229) mentioned a place called Guenoc that was situated in Coyote Valley. Postal authorities established Guenoc post office in 1867 and discontinued it in 1880 (Frickstad, p. 63). The community called Guenoc began when the first store opened at the site in 1866, but after Middletown started, the inhabitants of Guenoc moved there (Palmer, p. 147).

Coyote Valley Reservoir: see **Lake Mendocino** [MENDOCINO].

Crab Park [HUMBOLDT]: *locality,* 5.25 miles north-northwest of Ferndale on Mosley Island (lat. 40°08'35" N, long. 124°18'10" W). Named on Ferndale (1943) 15' quadrangle.

Crabtree Hot Springs [LAKE]: *springs,* 4.5 miles south of Potato Hill along Rice Fork (lat. 39°17'25" N, long. 122°49'20" W; on N line sec. 36, T 17 N, R 9 W). Named on Potato Hill (1967) 7.5' quadrangle. Mr. Crabtree filed on the springs about 1875 (Waring, p. 106).

Crabtree Lodge [LAKE]: *locality,* 8 miles northeast of the town of Upper Lake along North Fork Cache Creek (lat. 39°14'35" N, long. 122°48'10" W). Named on Bartlett Mountain (1958) 7.5' quadrangle.

Crack Canyon [LAKE]: *canyon,* drained by a stream that flows 3 miles to Cache Creek 4 miles east-southeast of Wilson Valley (2) (lat. 38°56'35" N, long. 122°24'35" W; near E line sec. 28, T 13 N, R 5 W). Named on Wilson Valley (1958) 7.5' quadrangle.

Craigs Creek [DEL NORTE]: *stream,* flows 9.5 miles to Smith River 9.5 miles east-northeast of Crescent City (lat. 41°47'25" N, long. 124°01'25" W). Named on Gasquet (1981) and Hiouchi (1966) 7.5' quadrangles.

Craigs Creek Mountain [DEL NORTE]: *peak,* 4.5 miles south-southwest of Gasquet (lat. 41°47' N, long. 123°59'45" W); the peak is south of Craigs Creek. Altitude 2222 feet. Named on Gasquet (1981) 7.5' quadrangle.

Crannell [HUMBOLDT]: *town,* 4.5 miles southeast of Trinidad along Little River (lat. 41°00'40" N, long. 124°04'45" W). Named on Crannell (1966) 7.5' quadrangle. Postal authorities established Bulwinkle post office on a site owned by Conrad Bulwinkle in 1909, changed the name to Crannell in 1922, and discontinued it in 1969 (Salley, p. 29, 52). The name "Crannell" honored Levi Crannell, president of Little River Redwood Company; the town was abandoned in 1969 (Carranco and Sorensen, p. 58, 69).

Crater [MENDOCINO]: *locality,* nearly 4 miles west of Willits along California Western Railroad (lat. 39°25'20" N, long. 123°25'15" W; near S line sec. 9, T 18 N, R 14 W). Named on Willits (1961) 15' quadrangle.

Crawford Creek [HUMBOLDT]: *stream,* flows 3 miles to Klamath River 1.25 miles west-southwest of Orleans (lat. 41°17'45" N, long. 123°33'50" W). Named on Orleans (1978) 7.5' quadrangle.

Crawford Creek [MENDOCINO]: *stream,* flows 2.25 miles to Russian River 10 miles south-southeast of Ukiah (lat. 39°01'05" N, long. 123°07'35" W). Named on Elledge Peak (1958) 7.5' quadrangle, which shows P.C. Crawford ranch near the stream.

Crazy Bear Pass [MENDOCINO]: *pass,* 12.5 miles north-northeast of Covelo (lat. 39°57'15" N, long. 123°09' W; sec. 12, T 24 N, R 12 W). Named on Bluenose Ridge(1967) 7.5' quadrangle.

Crazy Creek [LAKE]: *stream,* flows 6.25 miles to Putah Creek 5.25 miles east-northeast of Middletown (lat. 38°46'35" N, long. 122°31 20" W). Named on Middletown (1958) 7.5' quadrangle.

Crazy Peak [DEL NORTE]: *peak,* 6.25 miles northeast of Broken Rib Mountain (lat. 41°57'05" N, long. 123°36'05" W). Altitude 5185 feet. Named on Polar Bear Mountain (1982) 7.5' quadrangle.

Crazy Spring [HUMBOLDT]: *spring,* 7.5 miles southwest of Dinsmore (lat. 40°25'30" N, long. 123°42'45" W; sec. 34, T 1 N, R 4 E). Named on Larabee Valley (1977) 7.5' quadrangle.

Crescent City [DEL NORTE]: *town,* about 17 miles south of California-Oregon State line along the coast (lat. 41°45'15" N, long. 124°12' W). Named on Crescent City (1966) and Sister Rocks (1966) 7.5' quadrangles. Postal authorities established Crescent City post office in 1853 (Frickstad, p. 24), and the town incorporated in 1854. A.M. Rosborough purchased 320 acres of land and laid out town lots at the place in 1853; he is believed to have named the community for the semi-circular shape of the bay or roadstead there (Bledsoe, p. 70; McBeth, p. 37). A party that camped at the site in 1852 gave the name "Paragon Bay" to the roadstead at present Crescent City to commemorate the ship *Paragon,* which met with disaster there in 1850 (Bancroft, p. 504; Bledsoe, p. 69-70). Crawford (1894, p. 100) noted that a man named Yates was washing sand to recover gold at Yates' Beach, situated 1 mile south of Crescent City. California Mining Bureau's (1909a) map shows a place called Wakefield located along the railroad just north of Crescent City. Postal authorities established Wakefield post office 3 miles northeast of Crescent City in 1905 and discontinued it in 1918; the name was for William Wakefield, first postmaster (Salley, p. 233). Gold mines were found in 1856 six miles east of Crescent City, where a place called Villardville for a Frenchman, A. Villard, was laid out (Hoover, Rensch, and Rensch, p. 71).

Crescent City Fork: see **Blue Creek** [DEL NORTE-HUMBOLDT].

Criss Creek: see **Chris Creek** [HUMBOLDT].

Crittendon [MENDOCINO]: *locality,* 3.5 miles west-northwest of Hopland (lat. 38°55'45" N, long. 123°10'40" W). Named on Hopland (1944) 15' quadrangle.

Crocker Creek [MENDOCINO]: *stream,* flows 5.5 miles to Elk Creek 9 miles east-southeast of Eden Valley (lat. 39°33'35" N, long. 123°02'05" W). Named on Sanhedrin Mountain (1966) 7.5' quadrangle.

Crockett Camp: see **West Crockett Camp** [LAKE].

Crockett Peak [LAKE]: *peak,* 7 miles east-northeast of Bear Mountain (lat. 39°25'50" N, long. 122°46'30" W). Altitude 6172 feet. Named on Crockett Peak (1967) 7.5' quadrangle.

Crogan Creek: see **Oregon Creek** [HUMBOLDT].

Crogan Hole: see **Grogan Hole** [HUMBOLDT].

Crooked Gulch [MENDOCINO]: *canyon,* drained by a stream that flows about 3 miles to Hulls Creek 10.5 miles east-northeast of Spyrock (2) (lat. 39°57' N, long. 123°16'10" W). Named on Mina (1967) 7.5' quadrangle.

Crooked Prairie [HUMBOLDT]: *area,* 10 miles west-southwest of Phillipsville (lat. 40°09'55" N, long. 123°58' W; around NE cor. sec. 32, T 3 S, R 2 E). Named on Ettersburg (1969) 7.5' quadrangle.

Crooks Creek [HUMBOLDT-TRINITY]: *stream,* heads in Humboldt County and flows 2 miles to Van Duzen River 8 miles southeast of Dinsmore [HUMBOLDT] in Trinity County (lat. 40°23'40" N, long. 123°31'05" W; sec. 8, T 1 S, R 8 E); the stream is south of Crooks Ridge. Named on

Dinsmore(1977) 7.5' quadrangle.

Crooks Ridge [HUMBOLDT-TRINITY]: *ridge*, east-northeast-trending, 1.5 miles long, 7.5 miles south-southeast of Dinsmore [HUMBOLDT] on Humboldt-Trinity County line (lat. 40°23'40" N, long. 123°32'30" W; sec. 7, T 1 S, R 6 E). Named on Dinsmore (1977) 7.5' quadrangle.

Crosby Gulch [TRINITY]: *canyon*, drained by a stream that flows 2 miles to Coffee Creek 9 miles west of Billys Peak (1) (lat. 41°06'20" N, long. 122°56' W; sec. 31, T 38 N, R 9 W). Named on Coffee Creek (1955) 15' quadrangle. Called Crosbys Gl. on Averill's (1940) map.

Cross Spring [LAKE]: *spring*, nearly 5 miles east-northeast of Clearlake Oaks (lat. 39°02'40" N, long. 122°35'35" W; near E line sec. 23, T 14 N, R 7 W). Named on Clearlake Oaks (1960) 15' quadrangle.

Crow Creek [TRINITY]: *stream*, flows 4 miles to East Fork Trinity River 12 miles northeast of Trinity Center (lat. 41°07'40" N, long. 122°32' W; sec. 27, T 38 N, R 6 E). Named on Bonanza King (1955) 15' quadrangle. West Branch enters from the northwest 2.5 miles upstream from the mouth of the main creek; it is 1.5 miles long and is named on Bonanza King (1955) 15' quadrangle.

Crowley [MENDOCINO]: *locality*, nearly 4 miles west of Willits (lat. 39°24'05" N, long. 123°25'20" W; sec. 16, T 18 N, R 14 W). Named on Willits (1961) 15' quadrangle.

Crows Bar: see **Rush Creek** [TRINITY].

Crumpy Gulch [TRINITY]: *canyon*, drained by a stream that flows less than 1 mile to East Branch of East Fork of North Fork Trinity River 9 miles north of Helena (lat. 40°54'20" N, long. 123°06'45" W; sec. 9, T 35 N, R 11 W). Named on Helena (1951) 15' quadrangle.

Cruso Cabin Creek [MENDOCINO]: *stream*, flows 3 miles to join Elkhorn Creek (1) and form East Branch of South Fork Eel River 7 miles northeast of Leggett (lat. 39°56'10" N, long. 123°37'10" W; near SW cor. sec. 10, T 24 N, R 16 W). Named on Bell Springs (1969) 7.5' quadrangle.

Crystal Creek [TRINITY]: *stream*, flows 1.5 miles to Coffee Creek 2.25 miles south-southwest of Billys Peak (1) (lat. 41°06'10" N, long. 122°46'50" W; near S line sec. 33, T 38 N, R 8 W). Named on Coffee Creek (1955) 15' quadrangle.

Crystal Peak [MENDOCINO]: *peak*, 10 miles south-southwest of Hopland (lat. 38°50'40" N, long. 123°11'45" W; sec. 33, T 12 N, R 12 W). Named on Hopland (1960) 15' quadrangle.

Crystal Spring [TRINITY]: *spring*, 16 miles east-northeast of Weaverville (lat. 40°50'35" N, long. 122°39'55" W). Named on Schell Mountain (1950) 15' quadrangle.

Cub Creek [MENDOCINO]: *stream*, flows 0.5 mile to Bear Pen Creek 3 miles South of Piercy (lat. 39°55'15" N, long. 123°47'40" W; near SW cor. sec. 18, T 24 N, R 17 W). Named on Piercy (1969) 7.5' quadrangle.

Cub Wallow [TRINITY]: *relief feature*, 7.5 miles south-southwest of Billys Peak (1) at the head of Boulder Creek (1) (lat. 41°02'05" N, long. 122°49'45" W; sec. 30, T 37 N, R 8 W). Named on Coffee Creek (1955) 15' quadrangle.

Cuddeback: see **Cuddeback Creek** [HUMBOLDT].

Cuddeback Creek [HUMBOLDT]: *stream*, flows 2.25 miles to Van Duzen River 7 miles southeast of Fortuna (lat. 40°31'50" N, long. 124°02'35" W; near NE cor. sec. 27, T 2 N, R 1 E). Named on Hydesville (1979) 7.5' quadrangle. California Mining Bureau's (1909b) map shows a place called Guddeback (an obvious misspelling of the name "Cuddeback") located 1 mile southeast of Carlotta—a site near the mouth of present Cuddeback Creek. Postal authorities established Cuddeback post office 4 miles southeast of Hydesville in 1895 and discontinued it in 1914 (Salley, p 53). Henry Brown Cuddeback and his wife homesteaded at the site of Cuddeback in 1853 (Turner, p. 54).

Cuddy Prairie [HUMBOLDT]: *area*, 5.25 miles north of Coyote Peak (lat. 41°12'40" N, long. 123°52'35" W; sec. 31, T 10 N, R 3 E). Named on Bald Hills (1982) and French Camp Ridge (1983) 7.5' quadrangles. Coyote Peak (1952) 15' quadrangle shows Cuddy cabin at the place, and Coyote Peak (1945) 15' quadrangle has the name "Cuddy" there.

Cuffeys Cove [MENDOCINO]: *embayment*, 1 mile northwest of Elk along the coast (lat. 39°08'25" N, long. 123°43'45" W; at N line sec. 27, T 15 N, R 17 W). Named on Elk (1960) 7.5' quadrangle. Postal authorities established Cuffey's Cove post office in 1870 and discontinued it in 1888 (Frickstad, p. 94). The name was given in jest for the first inhabitant of the place, Nigger Nat (Landsman, 1977b, p. 29). The term "Cuffey," or "Cuffy," meant either "bear" or "negro" in early American slang (Hanna, p. 79). United States Board on Geographic Names (1968a, p. 4) rejected the forms "Cufee's Cove," "Cuffey Cove," and "Cuffy Cove." for the name.

Cuffeys Inlet [MENDOCINO]: *embayment*, 1.25 miles northwest of Elk along the coast (lat. 39°08'30" N, long. 123°44'05" W; on S line sec. 22, T 15 N, R 17 W); the embayment is just west of Cuffeys Cove. Named on Elk (1960) 7.5' quadrangle. United States Coast and Geodetic Survey (p. 140) used the form "Cuffey Inlet" for the name.

Cuffeys Point [MENDOCINO]: *promontory*, 1.25 miles west-northwest of Elk along the coast (lat. 39°08'25" N, long. 123°44'05" W); the feature is west of Cuffeys Cove and Cuffeys Inlet. Named on Elk (1960) 7.5' quadrangle.

Cuffy Cove: see **Cuffeys Cove** [MENDOCINO]; **Greenwood Cove** [MENDOCINO].

Cummings [MENDOCINO]: *village*, about 5 miles east-southeast of Leggett along Rattlesnake Creek (2) (lat. 39°50' N, long. 123°37'50" W; at N line sec. 21, T 23 N, R 16 W). Named on Leggett (1969) 7.5' quadrangle. Postal authorities established Cummings post office in 1888, discontinued it in 1899, and reestablished it in 1900 (Frickstad, p. 94). The name commemorates Jonathan Cummings, who preempted a homestead along Eel River in the early 1870's (Gudde, 1949, p. 86). California Mining Bureau's (1909c) map shows a place called Redwine located 5 miles by stage line northeast of Cummings. Postal authorities established Redwine post office in 1904, moved it 6 miles west in 1905, and discontinued it in 1915; the name was for Ida Redwine, first postmaster (Salley, p. 183).

Cummings Creek [HUMBOLDT]: *stream*, flows 5.5 miles to Van Duzen River 8.5 miles southeast of Fortuna (lat. 40°31'15" N, long. 124°01'50" W; sec. 26, T 2 N, R 1 E). Named on Hydesville (1979) and Owl Creek (1979) 7.5' quadrangles.

Cummings Creek [MENDOCINO]: *stream*, flows 2.25 miles to Rattlesnake Creek (2) 8 miles east-southeast of Leggett (lat. 39°49'40" N, long. 123°34'15" W; near E line sec. 19, T 23 N, R 15 W). Named on Tan Oak Park (1969) 7.5' quadrangle. California Mining Bureau's (1917c) map shows a locality called Blue Rock situated about 5 miles north of Cummings.

Cummings Creek: see **Bear Gulch** [TRINITY] (2).

Cummings Creek Camp [HUMBOLDT]: *locality*, 9.5 miles southeast of Fortuna (lat. 40°30'40" N, long. 124°00'50" W; sec. 36, T 2 N, R 1 E); the place is near the mouth of Cummings Creek. Named on Fortuna (1959) 7.5' quadrangle.

Cummiskey: see **Cummiskey Creek** [MENDOCINO].

Cummiskey Creek [MENDOCINO]: *stream*, flows 11 miles to Russian River 7 miles south-southeast of Hopland (lat. 38°58' N, long. 123°03'15" W; near S line sec. 14, T 12 N, R 11 W). Named on Hopland (1960) 15' quadrangle. California Mining Bureau's (1917c) map shows a place called Cummiskey located about 7 miles south-southeast of Hopland along the railroad.

Cuneo Campground [HUMBOLDT]: *locality*, 11 miles south-southeast of Scotia (lat. 40°20'05" N, long. 124°02'05" W; sec. 35, T 1 S, R 1 E); the place is along Cuneo Creek. Named on Bull Creek (1969) 7.5' quadrangle.

Cuneo Creek [HUMBOLDT]: *stream*, flows nearly 3 miles to Bull Creek (1) 11 miles south-southeast of Scotia (lat. 40°20' N, long. 124°01'30" W; near W line sec. 36, T 1 S, R 1 E). Named on Bull Creek (1969) 7.5' quadrangle. North Fork enters from the northwest less than 1 mile upstream from the mouth of the main creek and is 2 miles long. South Fork enters from the southwest nearly 1 mile upstream from the mouth of the main creek and is 1.5 miles long. Both forks are named on Bull Creek (1969) 7.5' quadrangle.

Cuneo Ridge [HUMBOLDT]: *ridge*, east- to southeast-trending, 1 mile long, 10 miles south-southeast of Scotia between (lat. 40°20'30" N, long. 124°02'45" W; at NE cor. sec. 34, T 1 S, R 1 E); the ridge is between Cuneo Creek and North Fork Cuneo Creek. Named on Bull Creek (1969) 7.5' quadrangle.

Curless Prairie [HUMBOLDT]: *area*, 12.5 miles south of Scotia (lat. 40°17'55" N, long. 124°06'25" W; sec 17, 18, T 2 S, R 1 E). Named on Bull Creek (1969) 7.5' quadrangle.

Curley Cow Creek [MENDOCINO]: *stream*, flows 3.5 miles to Sherwood Creek nearly 3 miles south of Longvale (lat. 39°30'50" N, long. 123°26' W; sec. 8, T 19 N, R 14 W). Named on Longvale (1966) 7.5' quadrangle.

Curtis: see **Camp Curtis**, under **Arcata** [HUMBOLDT].

Cushing Creek [DEL NORTE]: *stream*, flows 1 mile to the sea 4 miles southeast of Crescent City (lat. 41°42'50" N, long. 124°08'40" W; near N line sec. 11, T 15 N, R 1 W). Named on Sister Rocks (1966) 7.5' quadrangle.

Cushman Camp [MENDOCINO]: *locality*, 7.5 miles north-northwest of Hull Mountain (lat. 39°37'25" N, long. 122°58'55" W; sec. 5, T 20 N, R 10 W). Named on Hull Mountain (1967) 7.5' quadrangle.

Cushman Lake [MENDOCINO]: *intermittent lake*, 100 feet long, 6.5 miles north of Hull Mountain (lat. 39°37' N, long. 122°57'25" W; near W line sec. 3, T 20 N, R 10 W). Named on Hull Mountain (1967) 7.5' quadrangle.

Cutfinger Creek [TRINITY]: *stream*, flows 2.5 miles to Middle Fork Eel River 7 miles south of Black Rock Mountain (lat. 40°06'25" N, long. 123°01'40" W; near N line sec. 18, T 26 N, R 10 W). Named on Black Rock Mountain (1954) 15' quadrangle.

Cutler Thicket [TRINITY]: *area*, 7.5 miles south-southeast of Forest Glen (lat. 40°16'10" N, long. 123°16'55" W; on S line sec. 21, T 2 S, R 8 E). Named on Forest Glen (1979) 7.5' quadrangle.

Cutoff Slough [HUMBOLDT]: *water feature*, joins Salt River 4 miles northwest of Ferndale (lat. 40°37'05" N, long. 124°18'55" W). Named on Ferndale(1959) 7.5' quadrangle.

Cutten [HUMBOLDT]: *district*, 2.5 miles south-southeast of downtown Eureka (lat. 40°46'10" N, long. 124°08'30" W; near SE cor. sec. 35, T 5 N, R 1 W). Named on Eureka (1958) 7.5' quadrangle. Postal authorities established Cutten post office, named for the Cutten family, 3.5 miles south of Eureka post office in 1929 (Salley, p. 54).

Cutthroat Gulch [TRINITY]: *canyon,* drained by a stream that flows 0.5 mile to Trinity River 2.5 miles southwest of Helena (lat. 40°45'05" N, long. 123°09'50" W; at W line sec. 31, T 34 N, R 11 W). Named on Helena (1951) 15' quadrangle. The name came after discovery at the place of a Chinese prospector whose throat had been cut (Gudde, 1949, p. 87).

– D –

Daby Island [HUMBOLDT]: *island,* a marshy place, 2200 feet long, just north of downtown Eureka in Humboldt Bay (lat. 40°48'40" N, long. 124°09' W). Named on Eureka (1958) 7.5' quadrangle. Captain Stillman Burnap Daby owned the place (Turner, p. 57).

Daby's Ferry: see **Arcata** [HUMBOLDT].

Dago Creek [MENDOCINO]: *stream,* flows nearly 3 miles to Rancheria Creek (2) 6.5 miles west-northwest of Boonville (lat. 39°02'50" N, long. 123°28'55" W; sec. 26, T 14 N, R 15 W). Named on Boonville (1959) and Navarro (1961) 15' quadrangles.

Dairy Creek [HUMBOLDT]:

(1) *stream,* flows 6 miles to North Fork Yager Creek 2 miles southeast of Lone Star Junction (lat. 40°36'45" N, long. 123°50'45" W; sec. 28, T 3 N, R 3 E). Named on Yager Junction (1979) 7.5' quadrangle.

(2) *stream,* flows 3 miles to Little Van Duzen River 6 miles south of Dinsmore (lat. 40°24'20" N, long. 123°36'45" W; sec. 4, T 1 S, R 5 E). Named on Dinsmore (1977) 7.5' quadrangle.

Dairy Ridge [HUMBOLDT]: *ridge,* generally northwest-trending, 4 miles long, center 3 miles north-northeast of Yager Junction (lat. 40°35'10" N, long. 123°48'30" W); the feature is east of Dairy Creek (1). Named on Yager Junction (1979) 7.5' quadrangle.

Daley Gulch [TRINITY]: *canyon,* drained by a stream that flows 1 mile to North Fork Coffee Creek 7 miles west-northwest of Billys Peak (1) (lat. 41°10'20" N, long. 122°53'05" W; near N line sec. 10, T 38 N, R 9 W). Named on Coffee Creek (1955) 15' quadrangle.

Dali-Dona [LAKE]: *peak,* 6.5 miles east-southeast of Lakeport (lat. 39°00'10" N, long. 122°48'50" W; sec. 1, T 13 N, R 9 W). Altitude 1916 feet. Named on Lucerne (1958) 7.5' quadrangle.

Damnation Creek [DEL NORTE]: *stream,* flows 2 miles to the sea 8 miles south-southeast of Crescent City (lat. 41°39'10" N, long. 124°07'40" W; sec. 36, T 15 N, R 1 W). Named on Childs Hill (1966) and Sister Rocks (1966) 7.5' quadrangles.

Damon Ridge [HUMBOLDT]: *ridge,* generally south-trending, nearly 2 miles long, 17 miles south-southwest of Scotia (lat. 40°15'10" N, long. 124°12'30" W). Named on Buckeye Mountain (1970) and Shubrick Peak (1969) 7.5' quadrangles.

Dan East Creek [HUMBOLDT]: *stream,* flows 1.25 miles to Pilot Creek nearly 7 miles southeast of Board Camp Mountain (lat. 40°38'25" N, long. 123°36'55" W; sec. 16, T 3 N, R 5 E). Named on Sims Mountain (1979) 7.5' quadrangle.

Danger Creek [HUMBOLDT]: *stream,* flows 2.5 miles to Van Duzen River 3 miles east-southeast of Yager Junction (lat. 40°31'45" N, long. 123°46'10" W; near N line sec. 30, T 2 N, R 4 E). Named on Yager Junction (1979) 7.5' quadrangle.

Danger Point [DEL NORTE]: *ridge,* southwest-trending, 0.5 mile long, 3 miles east of Gasquet (lat. 41°51'05" N, long. 123°54'55" W). Named on Gasquet (1981) 7.5' quadrangle.

Dann Creek: see **Big Dann Creek** [MENDOCINO]; **Little Dann Creek** [MENDOCINO].

Dann Valley [MENDOCINO]: *area,* 2 miles south-southeast of Leggett (lat. 39°50'30" N, long. 123°41'40" W; sec. 13, T 23 N, R 17 W); the place is east of the confluence of Big Dann Creek and Little Dann Creek. Named on Leggett (1969) 7.5' quadrangle. Called Dan Valley on Leggett (1952) 15' quadrangle.

Dan Rice Creek [TRINITY]: *stream,* flows 1.5 miles to Scott Mountain Creek 10 miles south-southwest of China Mountain, which is in Siskiyou County (lat. 41°15'15" N, long. 122°40'15" W; sec. 9, T 39 N, R 7 W). Named on China Mountain (1955) 15' quadrangle.

Dans Creek [DEL NORTE-HUMBOLDT]: *stream,* heads in Humboldt County and flows 2.5 miles to Bluff Creek 16 miles east-southeast of Klamath Glen in Del Norte County (lat. 41°23'40" N, long. 123°42'50" W). Named on Lonesome Ridge (1974) 7.5' quadrangle.

Dan Valley: see **Dann Valley** [MENDOCINO].

Darby Peak: see **Big Darby Peak** [MENDOCINO]; **Little Darby Peak** [MENDOCINO];

Dark Canyon [MENDOCINO]: *canyon,* drained by a stream that flows 1 mile to Jack of Hearts Creek 5.5 miles north-northwest of Branscomb (lat. 39°43'40" N, long. 123°39'40" W; near E line sec. 30, T 22 N, R 16 W). Named on Lincoln Ridge (1966) 7.5' quadrangle.

Dark Canyon: see **Harris** [HUMBOLDT].

Dark Canyon Creek [TRINITY]: *stream,* flows 3.25 miles to East Fork of South Fork Trinity River 4.5 miles west-northwest of Black Rock Mountain (lat. 40°14'30" N, long. 123°05'20" W; at SW cor. sec. 26, T 28 N, R 11 W). Named on Black Rock Mountain (1954) and Dubakella Mountain (1954) 15' quadrangles.

Dark Gulch [MENDOCINO]:

(1) *canyon,* drained by a stream that flows 1.5 miles to the sea 10 miles south-southwest of Piercy (lat. 39°50'50" N, long. 123°53' W; sec. 17, T 23 N, R 18 W). Named on Hales Grove (1970) and Mistake Point (1969) 7.5' quadrangles.

(2) *canyon,* drained by a stream that flows 2.25 miles to South Fork Big River 17 miles north of Boonville (lat. 39°14'50" N, long. 123°24'50" W; sec. 16, T 16 N, R 14 W). Named on Boonville (1959) and Willits (1961) 15' quadrangles.

Dark Gulch [TRINITY]: *canyon,* drained by a stream that flows 0.5 mile to Trinity River 6 miles east-southeast of Weaverville (lat. 40°42'15" N, long. 122°50'15" W; sec. 24, T 33 N, R 9 W). Named on Weaverville (1950) 15' quadrangle.

Darlingtonia [DEL NORTE]: *locality,* 1.5 miles east-southeast of Gasquet on the south side of Middle Fork Smith River (lat. 41°50'15" N, long. 123°56'30" W; at W line sec. 27, T 17 N, R 2 E). Named on Gasquet (1951) 15' quadrangle.

Darnell Creek [HUMBOLDT]: *stream,* flows nearly 1 mile to Eel River 4 miles north-northwest of Redcrest (lat. 40°27'10" N, long. 123°59'15" W; near E line sec. 19, T 1 N, R 2 E). Named on Redcrest (1969) 7.5' quadrangle.

Dashields Creek [TRINITY]: *stream,* flows 1.5 miles to Mad River nearly 7 miles south of Forest Glen (lat. 40°16'35" N, long. 123°19'40" W; near E line sec. 24, T 2 S, R 7 E). Named on Forest Glen (1979) 7.5' quadrangle.

Dashiell Creek [LAKE]: *stream,* flows 2 miles to Eel River 6.5 miles north-northeast of the town of Potter Valley [MENDOCINO] (lat. 39°23'50" N, long. 123°02'05" W; sec. 24, T 18 N, R 11 W). Named on Potter Valley (1960) 15' quadrangle.

Creek [MENDOCINO]: *stream,* flows 8 miles to South Fork Big Creek 16 miles north-northwest of Boonville (lat. 39°13'45" N, long. 123°27'45" W; sec. 19, T 16 N, R 14 W). Named on Boonville (1959) 15' quadrangle.

Dauphiny Creek [HUMBOLDT]: *stream,* flows 1.5 miles to Larabee Creek 3 miles east of Redcrest (lat. 40°24'30" N, long. 123°53'30" W; sec. 1, T 1 S, R 2 E). Named on Redcrest (1969) 7.5' quadrangle.

Dave Phelps Ridge [LAKE]: *ridge,* generally southwest-trending, 1.25 miles long, 3.5 miles north of the town of Upper Lake (lat. 39°13' N, long. 122°54'10" W; in and near sec. 30, T 16 N, R 9 W). Named on Upper Lake (1958) 7.5' quadrangle.

Davies Creek: see **Davis Creek** [HUMBOLDT] (1).

Davis: see **Judge Davis Canyon** [LAKE].

Davis Creek [HUMBOLDT]:

(1) *stream,* flows 4.5 miles to the sea 4.25 miles south-southeast of Cape Mendocino (lat. 40°23'05" N, long. 124°22'05" W; sec. 14, T 1 S, R 3 W). Named on Capetown (1969) 7.5' quadrangle. United States Board on Geographic Names (1939, p. 12) rejected the name "Davies Creek" for the feature.

(2) *stream,* flows 10 miles to Mill Creek (7) 10 miles southwest of Dinsmore (lat. 40°23'30" N, long. 123°44'05" W; sec. 9, T 1 S, R 4 E). Named on Larabee Valley (1977) 7.5' quadrangle.

(3) *stream,* flows 4 miles to Maple Creek (2) 8 miles southeast of Korbel (lat. 40°46'30" N, long. 123°32'35" W; sec. 31, T 5 N, R 3 E). Named on Maple Creek (1977) 7.5' quadrangle.

Davis Creek [MENDOCINO]: *stream,* flows 7 miles to Little Lake Valley 2.5 miles east-southeast of Willits (lat. 39°23'45" N, long. 123°18'45" W; sec. 21, T 18 N, R 13 W). Named on Willits (1961) 15' quadrangle.

Davis Creek [TRINITY]:

(1) *stream,* flows 1 mile to Trinity River 9.5 miles north of Trinity Center (lat. 41°08'25" N, long. 122°41'10" W; at W line sec. 21, T 38 N, R 7 W). Named on Bonanza King (1955) 15' quadrangle.

(2) *stream,* flows 4.5 miles to East Fork Stuart Fork 16 miles north-northeast of Weaverville (lat. 40°54'55" N, long. 122°46'10" W; near SE cor. sec. 4, T 35 N, R 8 W). Named on Trinity Dam (1950) 15' quadrangle.

Davis Salt Ground [MENDOCINO]: *area,* 6.5 miles northwest of Covelo (lat. 39°51'45" N, long. 123°19'45" W; on S line sec. 8, T 23 N, R 13 W). Named on Covelo West (1967) 7.5' quadrangle.

Dawes [MENDOCINO]: *locality,* 2.5 miles southeast of Hopland (lat. 38°57' N, long. 123°05' W). Named on Hopland (1944) 15' quadrangle.

Dayle Creek [LAKE]: *stream,* flows 4 miles to Cooper Creek 3 miles west-northwest of the town of Upper Lake in Bachelor Valley (lat. 39°10'15" N, long. 122°57'50" W; near W line sec. 3, T 15 N, R 10 W). Named on Cow Mountain (1958) and Upper Lake (1958) 7.5' quadrangles.

Day Opening [HUMBOLDT]: *area,* 6 miles east-northeast of Showers Mountain (lat. 40°36'55" N, long. 123°35'40" W; sec. 27, T 3 N, R 5 E). Named on Blake Mountain (1979) 7.5' quadrangle.

Deacon Creek [TRINITY]: *stream,* flows 1.5 miles to Coffee Creek 5.5 miles west-southwest of Billys Peak (1) (lat. 41°06'50" N, long. 122°52'20" W; near N line sec. 34, T 38 N, R 9 W). Named on Coffee Creek (1955) 15' quadrangle.

Dead Cow Lake [MENDOCINO]: *lake*, 300 feet long, 5.5 miles south-southeast of Dos Rios (lat. 39°38'40" N, long. 123°18'30" W; near SE cor. sec. 28, T 21 N, R 13 W). Named on Dos Rios (1967) 7.5' quadrangle.

Dead Cow Spring [LAKE]: *spring*, 2.25 miles north-northeast of Bear Mountain (lat. 39°26'05" N, long. 122°52'35" W). Named on Lake Pillsbury (1967) 7.5' quadrangle.

Deadfall Creek [TRINITY]: *stream*, flows about 2.5 miles to Bear Creek (1) 4 miles south-southeast of China Mountain, which is in Siskiyou County (lat. 41°19'40" N, long. 122°32'25" W; sec. 15, T 40 N, R 6 W); the stream heads near Deadfall Lakes. Named on China Mountain (1955) 15' quadrangle.

Deadfall Lakes [TRINITY]: *lakes*, largest 1700 feet long, 6 miles southeast of China Mountain, which is in Siskiyou County (lat. 41°19' N, long. 122°30' W; in and near sec. 24, T 40 N, R 6 W). Named on China Mountain (1955) and Weed (1954) 15' quadrangles.

Dead Horse Canyon [MENDOCINO]: *canyon*, drained by a stream that flows 1 mile to Russian River 8 miles west-northwest of the town of Potter Valley (lat. 39°22'40" N, long. 123°14'05" W; near N line sec. 31, T 18 N, R 12 W). Named on Potter Valley (1960) 15' quadrangle.

Dead Horse Canyon: see **Sportsman Creek** [MENDOCINO].

Deadhorse Creek [TRINITY]: *stream*, flows 1 mile to North Fork Swift Creek (1) nearly 7 miles south of Billys Peak (1) (lat. 41°01'45" N, long. 122°44'55" W; at S line sec. 26, T 37 N, R 8 W). Named on Coffee Creek (1955) 15' quadrangle.

Dead Horse Flat [LAKE]: *area*, less than 0.5 mile southeast of Middletown (lat. 38°49'50" N, long. 122°36'35" W). Named on Detert Reservoir (1958) 7.5' quadrangle.

Dead Horse Gulch [DEL NORTE]: *canyon*, drained by a stream that flows 0.5 mile to Middle Fork Smith River 7.5 miles east-northeast of Gasquet (lat. 41°52'55" N, long. 123°49'35" W; sec. 10, T 17 N, R 3 E). Named on Shelly Creek Ridge (1982) 7.5' quadrangle.

Dead Horse Gulch [MENDOCINO]: *canyon*, drained by a stream that flows 1.5 miles to North Fork Navarro River 3.5 miles west of Navarro (lat. 39°09'15" N, long. 123°36'35" W; near SE cor. sec. 15, T 15 N, R 16 W). Named on Navarro (1961) 15' quadrangle.

Dead Lake [DEL NORTE]: *lake*, 3100 feet long, 2.25 miles north-northwest of Crescent City (lat. 41°47' N, long. 124°13'30" W; mainly in sec. 18, T 16 N, R 1 W). Named on Crescent City (1966) 7.5' quadrangle.

Deadman Canyon [LAKE]: *canyon*, drained by a stream that flows nearly 3 miles to Cache Creek 6.5 miles northeast of the town of Lower Lake (lat. 38°58'20" N, long. 122°31'15" W). Named on Lower Lake (1958) 7.5' quadrangle.

Deadman Gulch [MENDOCINO]: *canyon*, drained by a stream that flows nearly 1 mile to Albion River 8 miles north of Elk (lat. 39°14'40" N, long. 123°43'25" W; sec. 14, T 16 N, R 17 W). Named on Comptche (1960) 15' quadrangle, and on Elk (1960) 7.5' quadrangle.

Deadman Gulch [TRINITY]: *canyon*, drained by a stream that flows 1.5 miles to South Fork Coffee Creek 8.5 miles west of Billys Peak (1) (lat. 41°09'15" N, long. 122°55'15" W; sec. 17, T 38 N, R 9 W); the canyon heads near Deadman Peak. Named on Coffee Creek (1955) 15' quadrangle.

Deadman Peak [TRINITY]: *peak*, 20 miles south of Etna, which is in Siskiyou County, on Trinity-Siskiyou County line (lat. 41°10'40" N, long. 122°56' W; sec. 6, T 38 N, R 9 W). Named on Coffee Creek (1955) 15' quadrangle. On Etna (1934) 30' quadrangle, the name applies to a peak located about 2 miles farther west.

Deadman Ridge [HUMBOLDT]: *ridge*, north-northwest-trending, 2 miles long, 4.25 miles east of Board Camp Mountain (lat. 40°41'55" N, long. 123°38'05" W). Named on Board Camp Mountain (1977) 7.5' quadrangle.

Deadmans Flat [MENDOCINO]: *area*, 11.5 miles north of the town of Potter Valley (lat. 35°28'55" N, long. 123°04'25" W; at SE cor. sec. 21, T 19 N, R 11 W). Named on Potter Valley (1960) 15' quadrangle.

Dead Mans Gulch [HUMBOLDT]: *canyon*, drained by a stream that flows nearly 1 mile to the sea 0.5 mile east-northeast of Point Delgada (lat. 40°01'30" N, long. 124°03'20" W; sec. 15, T 5 S, R 1 E). Named on Shelter Cove (1969) 7.5' quadrangle.

Deadman Spring [TRINITY]: *spring*, 7 miles south of Salmon Mountain (lat. 41°05'10" N, long. 123°23'10" W). Named on Trinity Mountain (1979) 7.5' quadrangle.

Dead Puppy Ridge [TRINITY]: *ridge*, north-northeast- to north-northwest-trending, 2 miles long, 6.5 miles south-southwest of Black Rock Mountain (lat. 40°07'15" N, long. 123°03'30" W). Named on Black Rock Mountain (1954) 15' quadrangle.

Deadshot Gulch [TRINITY]: *canyon*, drained by a stream that flows 1 mile to Browns Creek 3.25 miles east of Chanchelulla Peak (lat. 40°28'50" N, long. 122°55'50" W; at E line sec. 1, T 30 N, R 10 W). Named on Chanchelulla Peak (1951) 15' quadrangle.

Deadwood [TRINITY]: *locality*, 11 miles east of Weaverville (lat. 40°43'10" N, long. 122°43'50" W; near NE cor. sec. 14, T 33 N, R 8 W). Named on French Gulch (1979) 7.5' quadrangle. Postal authorities established Deadwood post office in 1886 and discontinued it in 1915; the name was from dead trees at the place (Salley, p. 56).

Deadwood Creek [TRINITY]: *stream*, flows 5.5 miles to Trinity River 7.25 miles east of Weaverville (lat. 40°43' N, long. 122°48' W; sec. 17, T 33 N, R 8 W). Named on Weaverville (1950) 15' quadrangle, and on French Gulch (1979) 7.5' quadrangle. South Fork enters from the south-southeast 11 miles east of Weaverville; it is 1.5 miles long and is named on French Gulch (1979) 7.5' quadrangle.

Deafy Ridge [LAKE]: *ridge*, south-southwest- to south-trending, less than 1 mile long, 8 miles east of Hull Mountain (lat. 39°30'20" N, long. 122°47'10" W). Named on Kneecap Ridge (1967) 7.5' quadrangle.

Dean Canyon Creek: see **Dean Creek** [HUMBOLDT] (2).

Dean Creek [HUMBOLDT]:

(1) *stream*, flows nearly 3 miles to Eel River 0.5 mile north of Scotia (lat. 40°29'30" N, long. 124°06' W; near SW cor. sec. 5, T 1 N, R 1 E). Named on Scotia (1970) and Taylor Peak (1969) 7.5' quadrangles. The name commemorates Hiram W. Dean (Turner, p. 58).

(2) *stream*, flows 5.25 miles to South Fork Eel River 4.5 miles south-southwest of Phillipsburg (lat. 40°08'35" N, long. 123°48'30" W; sec. 2, T 4 S, R 3 E). Named on Fort Seward (1969), Harris (1969), and Miranda (1970) 7.5' quadrangles. Called Dean Canyon Creek on Briceland (1921) 15' quadrangle. The name commemorates Samuel R. Dean, who came to Humboldt County in 1878 (Turner, p. 58).

Dean Creek [MENDOCINO]: *stream*, flows 2 miles to Eel River 1.5 miles south of Dos Rios (lat. 39°41'40" N, long. 123°21'30" W; sec. 7, T 21 N, R 13 W). Named on Dos Rios (1967) and Laytonville (1967) 7.5' quadrangles.

Dean's Corner: see **Grizzly Bluff** [HUMBOLDT].

De Camp [MENDOCINO]: *locality*, 2 miles north of Willits along Northwestern Pacific Railroad (lat. 39°26'20" N, long. 123°21'15" W; near E line sec. 1, T 18 N, R 14 W). Named on Willits (1942) 15' quadrangle.

Decker Creek [HUMBOLDT]: *stream*, flows 3 miles to South Fork Eel River 1 mile northwest of Weott (lat. 40°20'05" N, long. 123°56' W; sec. 34, T 1 S, R 2 E). Named on Weott (1969) 7.5 quadrangle. United States Board on Geographic Names (1973b, p. 3) gave the names "Sit-se-tal-ko" and "Sitsetalko Creek" as variants.

Decy Canyon [LAKE]: *canyon*, drained by a stream that flows 1.5 miles to Middle Creek (2) 3 miles north of the town of Upper Lake (lat. 39°12'35" N, long. 122°54'55" W; sec. 25, T 16 N, R 10 W). Named on Upper Lake (1958) 7.5' quadrangle.

Dedrick [TRINITY]: *locality*, 8 miles northeast of Helena along Canyon Creek (1) (lat. 40°51'50" N, long. 123°02'10" W). Named on Helena (1951) 15' quadrangle. Postal authorities established Dedrick post office in 1891 and discontinued it in 1941 (Frickstad, p. 206). The name was for D.C. Dedrick, who was the original locator of Chloride mine (Jones, p. 194).

Deep Creek [TRINITY]: *stream*, flows 4.5 miles to Stuart Fork 13 miles north of Weaverville (lat. 40°54'35" N, long. 122°56'50" W). Named on Trinity Dam (1950) 15' quadrangle.

Deep Creek: see **Little Deep Creek** [TRINITY].

Deep Gulch [TRINITY]:

(1) *canyon*, drained by a stream that flows 2.5 miles to South Fork Trinity River less than 1 mile south of Hyampom (lat. 40°36'15" N, long. 123°26'50" W; sec. 25, T 3 N, R 6 E). Named on Hyampom (1951) 15' quadrangle.

(2) *canyon*, drained by a stream that flows less than 1 mile to Hayfork Creek 4.5 miles east of Hayfork (lat. 40°32'45" N, long. 123°05'45" W). Named on Hayfork (1951) 15' quadrangle.

(3) *canyon*, drained by a stream that flows 1 mile to Trinity River 13 miles north-northeast of Hayfork (lat. 40°42'50" N, long. 123°02'50" W; sec. 19, T 33 N, R 10 W). Named on Hayfork (1951) 15' quadrangle.

(4) *canyon*, drained by a stream that flows about 1.25 miles to Dry Gulch (3) nearly 4 miles south-southeast of Salyer (lat. 40°50'15" N, long. 123°33'45" W). Named on Hennessy Peak (1979) 7.5' quadrangle.

Deep Gulch: see **Trinity Alps Creek** [TRINITY].

Deep Hole Creek [MENDOCINO]: *stream*, flows 6.5 miles to Elk Creek (2) 4 miles east of Eden Valley (lat. 39°37'15" N, long. 123°06'25" W); the stream goes through Deep Hole Valley. Named on Brushy Mountain (1966) and Sanhedrin Mountain (1966) 7.5' quadrangles.

Deep Hole Valley [MENDOCINO]: *valley*, 3.25 miles southeast of Eden Valley (lat. 39°35'35" N, long. 123°08'25" W; sec. 13, T 20 N, R 12 W). Named on Brushy Mountain (1966) 7.5' quadrangle.

Deep Hollow Creek [TRINITY]: *stream*, flows 2.5 miles to Mad River 8 miles south of Forest Glen (lat. 40°15'15" N, long. 123°19'15" W; sec. 31, T 2 S, R 8 E). Named on Forest Glen (1979) and Shannon Butte (1967) 7.5' quadrangles.

Deep Hollow Creek: see **Lynch Creek** [TRINITY] (1).

Deer Creek [DEL NORTE]: *stream*, flows 2.5 miles to South Fork Smith River 9.5 miles northwest of Buck Mountain (lat. 41°44'20" N, long. 123°58'45" W). Named on Cant Hook Mountain (1982) 7.5' quadrangle.

Deer Creek [HUMBOLDT]:

(1) *stream*, flows 3.5 miles to Mad River 3 miles north of Showers Mountain (lat. 40°37'20" N, long. 123°42'15" W; sec. 22, T 3 N, R 4 E). Named on Board Camp Mountain (1977) and Showers Mountain (1978) 7.5'

quadrangles.

(2) *stream,* flows 1.5 miles to Little Van Duzen River 7.25 miles south of Dinsmore (lat. 40°23'10" N, long. 123°36'40" W; near SE cor. sec. 9, T 1 S, R 5 E). Named on Dinsmore (1977) and Larabee Valley (1977) 7.5' quadrangles.

Deer Creek [LAKE]: *stream,* flows 7 miles to Rice Fork 2 miles south-southwest of Bear Mountain (lat. 39°22'40" N, long. 122°54'35" W). Named on Crockett Peak (1967), Elk Mountain (1967), Lake Pillsbury (1967), and Potato Hill (1967) 7.5' quadrangles.

Deer Creek [MENDOCINO]:

(1) *stream,* flows 1.25 miles to South Fork Eel River 4 miles north-northwest of Branscomb (lat. 39°42'35" N, long. 123°39'05" W; near N line sec. 4, T 21 N, R 16 W). Named on Lincoln Ridge (1966) 7.5' quadrangle.

(2) *stream,* flows 1 mile to North Branch of North Fork Navarro River 2 miles north of Navarro (lat. 39°10'50" N, long. 123°32'05" W; at NE cor. sec. 7, T 15 N, R 15 W). Named on Navarro (1961) 15' quadrangle. Called Bonanzo Cr. on Navarro (1943) 15' quadrangle, and called Bonanza Cr. on Saddle Point (1944) 15' quadrangle.

Deer Creek [TRINITY]:

(1) *stream,* flows 6 miles to Stuart Fork 15 miles north of Weaverville (lat. 40°57'05" N, long. 122°56'50" W; sec. 30, T 36 N, R 9 W); the stream heads at Deer Lake. Named on Trinity Dam (1950) 15' quadrangle.

(2) *stream,* flows 3 miles to Trinity River 13 miles northeast of Hyampom (lat. 40°44'40" N, long. 123°16'10" W). Named on Hyampom (1951) 15' quadrangle.

Deer Creek: see **Little Deer Creek** [HUMBOLDT]; **Little Deer Creek** [TRINITY].

Deer Creek Camp [LAKE]: *locality,* 4 miles west-northwest of Potato Hill (lat. 39°22'35" N, long. 122°52' W; near NW cor. sec. 34, T 18 N, R 9 W). Named on Lake Pillsbury (1951) 15' quadrangle.

Deer Creek Camp [TRINITY]: *locality,* 17 miles north of Weaverville (lat. 40°58' N, long. 122°53'55" W; sec. 21, T 36 N, R 9 W); the place is along Deer Creek (1). Named on Trinity Dam (1950) 15' quadrangle.

Deer Creek Pass [TRINITY]: *pass,* 15 miles north of Weaverville (lat. 40°56'25" N, long. 122°53'20" W; at NW cor. sec. 34, T 36 N, R 9 W); the pass is at the head of Deer Creek (1). Named on Trinity Dam (1950) 15' quadrangle.

Deer Flat [TRINITY]: *area,* about 9 miles south-southwest of Billys Peak (1) (lat. 41°00'35" N, long. 122°48'40" W; sec. 5, T 36 N, R 8 W). Named on Coffee Creek (1955) 15' quadrangle.

Deer Gulch [TRINITY]:

(1) *canyon,* drained by a stream that flows 1.5 miles to Rush Creek 5.5 miles northeast of Weaverville (lat. 40°46'15" N, long. 122°50'45" W; near E line sec. 26, T 34 N, R 9 W). Named on Trinity Dam (1950) 15' quadrangle.

(2) *canyon,* drained by a stream that flows 2 miles to Salt Creek (4) 3.5 miles northeast of Dubakella Mountain (lat. 40°25'25" N, long. 123°06'15" W; sec. 28, T 30 N, R 11 W). Named on Dubakella Mountain (1954) 15' quadrangle.

Deerhorn Camp [HUMBOLDT]: *locality,* 3.25 miles east of Weitchpec (lat. 41°10'55" N, long. 123°38'40" W; near NE cor. sec. 7, T 9 N, R 5 E). Named on Weitchpec (1979) 7.5' quadrangle. United States Board on Geographic Names (1978b, p. 4) rejected the form "Deer Horn Camp" for the name.

Deerhorn Creek [HUMBOLDT]: *stream,* flows 2 miles to Bull Creek (3) 2.5 miles east-southeast of Weitchpec (lat. 41°10'10" N, long. 123°39'55" W; sec. 13, T 9 N, R 4 E). Named on Weitchpec (1979) 7.5' quadrangle.

Deering Gulch [HUMBOLDT]: *canyon,* 1.25 miles long, 5.5 miles south of Fields Landing (lat. 40°38'45" N, long. 124°12' W; sec. 8, 17, T 3 N, R 1 W). Named on Fields Landing (1959) 7.5 quadrangle.

Deer Lake [TRINITY]: *lake,* 500 feet long, 15 miles north of Weaverville (lat. 40°56'40" N, long. 122°53'30" W; near SE cor. sec. 28, T 36 N, R 9 W); the lake is at the head of Deer Creek (1). Named on Trinity Dam (1950) 15' quadrangle.

Deer Lick Creek [DEL NORTE]: *stream,* flows 3 miles to East Fork Bluff Creek 16 miles east-southeast of Klamath Glen (lat. 41°24' N, long. 123°42'35" W). Named on Lonesome Ridge (1974) 7.5' quadrangle.

Deer Lick Creek [MENDOCINO-TRINITY]: *stream,* heads in Trinity County and flows 2.25 miles to Middle Fork Eel River 17 miles northeast of Covelo in Mendocino County (lat. 39°58'15" N, long. 123°02'40" W; near SE cor. sec. 35, T 25 N, R 11 W). Named on Leech Lake Mountain (1966) 7.5' quadrangle.

Deer Lick Lake [DEL NORTE]: *lake,* 650 feet long, 17 miles east-southeast of Klamath Glen (lat. 41°24'10" N, long. 123°41'40" W); the lake is north of Deer Lick Creek. Named on Lonesome Ridge (1974) 7.5' quadrangle.

Deer Lick Saddle [HUMBOLDT]: *pass,* 2 miles south-southeast of Orleans (lat. 41°16'25" N, long. 123°31'25" W). Named on Orleans (1978) 7.5' quadrangle.

Deer Lick Springs [TRINITY]: *locality,* 3.25 miles east of Chanchelulla Peak (lat. 40°28'40" N, long. 122°55'50" W; at W line sec. 6, T 30 N, R 9 W). Named on Chanchelulla Peak (1951) 15' quadrangle. John Coumbs homesteaded at the place in 1882; the springs there first were called Coumbs Springs, and then Mystic Springs, before they received the present name (Jones, p. 327, 329).

Deer Lodge [MENDOCINO]: *locality,* 2 miles north-northwest of Dos Rios along Northwestern Pacific Railroad (lat. 39°44'35" N, long. 123°22'25" W; sec. 24, T 22 N, R 14 W). Named on Dos Rios (1967) 7.5' quadrangle.

Deer Rock [MENDOCINO]: *relief feature,* 15 miles west-northwest of Covelo (lat. 39°54'05" N, long. 123°29' W; sec. 25, T 24 N, R 15 W). Named on Updegraff Ridge (1967) 7.5' quadrangle.

Deer Valley [LAKE]: *area,* nearly 4 miles south-southeast of Three Crossings (lat. 39°16'15" N, long. 122°53' W). Named on Elk Mountain (1967) 7.5' quadrangle.

Deer Valley Campground [LAKE]: *locality,* 4 miles south-southeast of Three Crossings (lat. 39°15'55" N, long. 122°53' W); the place is 0.25 mile south of Deer Valley. Named on Elk Mountain (1967) 7.5' quadrangle.

Dees Peak [TRINITY]: *peak,* 9.5 miles southeast of Salmon Mountain on Trinity-Siskiyou County line (lat. 41°06'15" N, long. 123°15'40" W). Altitude 6904 feet. Named on Dees Peak (1978) 7.5' quadrangle.

De Haven [MENDOCINO]: *locality,* 1.5 miles north of Westport (lat. 39°39'35" N, long. 123°46'55" W; at W line sec. 20, T 21 N, R 17 W); the place is near the mouth of De Haven Creek. Named on Westport (1966) 7.5' quadrangle. The name commemorates John J. De Haven, who was a district attorney, assemblyman, and state senator (Gudde, 1969, p. 86).

De Haven Creek [MENDOCINO]: *stream,* flows 5.5 miles to the sea 1.5 miles north of Westport (lat. 39°39'35" N, long. 123°47'05" W; sec. 19, T 21 N, R 17 W). Named on Lincoln Ridge (1966) and Westport (1966) 7.5' quadrangles. Called Gordons Creek on Cape Vizcaino (1921) 15' quadrangle. United States Coast Survey named the feature for Alexander Gordon, who purchased land by the stream in 1875 (Gudde, 1949, p. 132). North Fork enters from the north 2.5 miles upstream from the mouth of the creek; it is 1.25 miles long and is named on Lincoln Ridge (1966) 7.5' quadrangle.

Delgada: see **Point Arena** [MENDOCINO] (1); **Point Delgada** [HUMBOLDT].

Delilah Creek [DEL NORTE]: *stream,* flows 2.25 miles to Ritmer Creek 2 miles west of the town of Smith River (lat. 41°55'55" N, long. 124°11' W; sec. 21, T 18 N, R 1 W). Named on Smith River (1966) 7.5' quadrangle. Called Mitchell Creek on Point Saint George (1945) 15' quadrangle.

Dell: see **The Dell** [LAKE].

Dellavan: see **Hardy** [MENDOCINO].

Del Loma [TRINITY]: *village,* 8 miles east-southeast of Burnt Ranch along Trinity River (lat. 40°46'45" N, long. 123°19'50" W). Named on Ironside Mountain (1951) 15' quadrangle. Called Taylor Flat on United States Geological Survey's (1915) map. Postal authorities established Del Loma post office in 1928 and discontinued it in 1953 (Frickstad, p. 206). A man named. Taylor settled at Taylor's Flat in 1853; after James King and his wife moved to the community about 1926, Mrs. King changed the name of the place to Del Loma (Jones, p. 241, 243). Gudde (1975, p. 209, 273, 365) listed three mining places along Trinity River near present Del Loma: Martins Bar, located 1 mile above Taylor Flat; Pony Point, located 1 mile below Taylor Flat; and Watson Bar, located below Taylor Flat. Crawford (1896, p. 466) noted that Watson's Bar mine was situated along Trinity River 2 miles below Taylor Flat.

Del Loma Cave [TRINITY]: *cave,* 8 miles east-southeast of Burnt Ranch (lat. 40°46'40" N, long. 123°19'15" W); the feature is just east of Del Loma. Named on Ironside Mountain (1951) 15' quadrangle.

Delmont Ridge [HUMBOLDT]: *ridge,* southeast-trending, 0.5 mile long, 5.5 miles east-southeast of Board Camp Mountain (lat. 40°39'15" N, long. 123°37'45" W; sec. 8, T 3 N, R 5 E). Named on Board Camp Mountain (1977) 7.5' quadrangle.

Del Ponte Ridge [DEL NORTE]: *ridge,* west-southwest-trending, 2.25 miles long, 4 miles east-southeast of the mouth of Klamath River (lat. 41°31'40" N, long. 124°00'30" W). Named on Klamath Glen (1982) and Requa (1966) 7.5' quadrangles.

Democrat Gulch [TRINITY]: *canyon,* drained by a stream that flows 3.5 miles to Weaver Creek 3.5 miles south of Weaverville (lat. 40°41'10" N, long. 122°56' W; sec. 30, T 33 N, R 9 W). Named on Weaverville (1950) 15' quadrangle.

Denman Creek [HUMBOLDT]: *stream,* flows 1.25 miles to North Fork Mad River 4.5 miles northeast of the town of Blue Lake (lat. 40°55'45" N, long. 123°56' W; sec. 3, T 6 N, R 2 E). Named on Blue Lake (1979) 7.5' quadrangle.

Denney Creek: see **Denny Creek** [TRINITY].

Dennison Springs: see **Hazel Spring** [LAKE].

Denny [TRINITY]: *village,* 10.5 miles north-northeast of Burnt Ranch along New River (lat. 40°56'40" N, long. 123°23'10" W). Named on Ironside Mountain (1951) 15' quadrangle. Postal authorities established Denny post office at the site in 1920, when they moved the former Denny post office from present Old Denny (Salley, p. 58). The Frank J. Ladd family, who had mined at present Old Denny, started building a new town of Denny, sometimes called New Denny, in 1920 near an early mining settlement called Quinby (Jones, p. 255). Postal authorities established Burris post office in 1904, moved it less than 1 mile north in 1906, changed the name to Quinby in 1907, moved it less than 1 mile west in 1907, and discontinued it in 1915; the name "Burris" was for Frank P. Burris, first postmaster, and the misspelled name "Quinby" was for a prospector named Quimby (Salley, p. 30, 180).

Denny: see **Old Denny** [TRINITY].

Denny Creek [TRINITY]: *stream*, flows 2.25 miles to Trinity River 13 miles northeast of Hyampom near Big Bar (lat. 40°44'30" N, long. 123°15'50" W; near N line sec. 6, T 33 N, R 12 W). Named on Ironside Mountain (1951) 15' quadrangle. Called Denney Creek on Hyampom (1951) 15' quadrangle, but United States Board on Geographic Names (1983c, p. 5) rejected this form for the name.

Desert [HUMBOLDT]: *area*, 7 miles northeast of Blocksburg (lat. 40°20'45" N, long. 123°32'45" W). Named on Black Lassic (1979) 7.5' quadrangle.

Detert Reservoir [LAKE]: *lake*, nearly 1 mile long, behind a dam on Bucksnort Creek 5.25 miles east-southeast of Middletown (lat. 38°43'35" N, long. 122°31'20" W). Named on Detert Reservoir (1958) 7.5' quadrangle. United States Board on Geographic Names (1991, p. 4) rejected the name "Guenoc Lake" for the feature.

Devil Camp [TRINITY]: *locality*, 9.5 miles south-southeast of Dubakella Mountain (lat. 40°15'15" N, long. 123°05'30" W; at S line sec. 22, T 28 N, R 11 W). Named on Dubakella Mountain (1954) 15' quadrangle.

Devil Creek [HUMBOLDT]:

(1) *stream*, flows 3 miles to Mad River 4 miles south-southeast of Korbel (lat. 40°28'25" N, long. 123°54'50" W; sec. 23, T 5 N, R 2 E). Named on Korbel (1979) 7.5' quadrangle.

(2) *stream*, flows 1.5 miles to Klamath River 6.5 miles south-southeast of Johnsons (lat. 47°16'30" N, long. 123°48'05" W; sec. 11, T 10 N, R 3 E). Named on Johnsons (1982) 7.5' quadrangle.

Devils Backbone [HUMBOLDT-TRINITY]: *ridge*, south-trending, 5 miles long, center 4 miles south-southwest of Salmon Mountain on Humboldt-Trinity County line (lat. 41°07'40" N, long. 123°25'40" W). Named on Salmon Mountain (1978) and Trinity Mountain (1979) 7.5' quadrangles.

Devils Backbone [TRINITY]: *ridge*, east-trending, nearly 1 mile long, 7 miles west-southwest of Forest Glen (lat. 40°20'55" N, long. 123°27'10" W; on W line sec. 25, T 1 S, R 6 E). Named on Ruth Reservoir (1978) 7.5' quadrangle.

Devils Basin [MENDOCINO]: *relief feature*, 3 miles north-northwest of Elk along the coast (lat. 39°10'10" N, long. 123°44'40" W; on N line sec. 16, T 15 N, R 17 W). Named on Elk (1960) 7.5' quadrangle.

Devils Canyon [HUMBOLDT]: *canyon*, drained by a stream that flows 2 miles to Grouse Creek (2) 6.5 miles east of Board Camp Mountain (lat. 40°42'25" N, long. 123°35'35" W). Named on Sims Mountain (1979) 7.5' quadrangle.

Devils Canyon [TRINITY]:

(1) *canyon*, drained by a stream that flows 10 miles to New River 12.5 miles north-northeast of Burnt Ranch (lat. 40°57'40" N, long. 123°20'50" W). Named on Helena (1951) and Ironside Mountain (1951) 15' quadrangles. Averill's (1940) map has the name "Devils Canyon Cr." for the stream in the canyon.

(2) *canyon*, drained by a stream that flows 2 miles to Stuart Fork 18 miles north of Weaverville (lat. 40°59' N, long. 122°57'30" W; sec. 13, T 36 N, R 10 W). Named on Trinity Dam (1950) 15' quadrangle.

Devils Canyon Creek: see **Devils Canyon** [TRINITY] (1).

Devils Creek [HUMBOLDT]:

(1) *stream*, flows 2 miles to Oil Creek (3) 11 miles south-southwest of Scotia (lat. 40°19'30" N, long. 124°08'40" W; sec. 2, T 2 S, R 1 W). Named on Buckeye Mountain (1970) 7.5' quadrangle.

(2) *stream*, flows 3.5 miles to Redwood Creek (1) 3.5 miles west of Coyote Peak (lat. 41°07'35" N, long. 123°55'50" W). Named on Panther Creek (1982) 7.5' quadrangle.

Devils Creek [TRINITY]: *stream*, flows 2 miles to East Fork Trinity River 6.5 miles northeast of Trinity Center (lat. 41°04' N, long. 122°35'20" W; at E line sec. 18, T 37 N, R 6 W); the stream heads at Devils Lake. Named on Bonanza King (1955) 15' quadrangle.

Devils Den [MENDOCINO]: *area*, 13 miles east-northeast of Covelo (lat. 39°53'55" N, long. 123°01'45" W; on N line sec. 36, T 24 N, R 11 W). Named on Leech Lake Mountain (1966) 7.5' quadrangle.

Devils Elbow [HUMBOLDT]:

(1) *bend*, 6 miles north-northeast of Redcrest along Van Duzen River (lat. 40°28'45" N, long. 123°54'40" W; sec. 11, T 1 N, R 2 E). Named on Redcrest (1969) 7.5' quadrangle.

(2) *locality*, 5 miles east of Weott at a sharp bend in a road (lat. 40°19'15" N, long. 123°50' W; on W line sec. 3, T 2 S, R 3 E). Named on Myers Flat (1969) 7.5' quadrangle.

Devils Elbow [TRINITY]: *relief feature*, nearly 5 miles southeast of Forest Glen along South Fork Trinity River (lat. 40°19'20" N, long. 123°45'50" W; sec. 31, T 29 N, R 12 W). Named on Forest Glen (1979) 7.5' quadrangle.

Devils Elbow Creek [HUMBOLDT]: *stream*, flows less than 0.5 mile to Eel River 5 miles east of Weott (lat. 40°19'20" N, long. 123°50' W; at W line sec. 3, T 2 S, R 3 E); the mouth of the stream is near Devils Elbow (2). Named on Myers Flat (1969) 7.5' quadrangle.

Devils Gap [DEL NORTE]: *narrows*, 7.5 miles southeast of Gasquet along Hurdygurdy Creek (lat. 41°46'30" N, long. 123°51'15" W). Named on Hurdygurdy Butte (1982) 7.5' quadrangle.

Devils Gate [HUMBOLDT]: *relief feature*, nearly 2.5 miles south-southeast of Cape Mendocino along the coast (lat. 40°24'25" N, long. 124°23'25" W; sec. 3, T 1 S, R 3 W). Named on Cape Mendocino (1969) 7.5' quadrangle. The feature is an opening between rocks that is so narrow that wagons could not pass through it; drivers either had to wait for low tide or had to take an overland detour to get by the spot (Turner, p. 59).

Devils Gate Rock [HUMBOLDT]: *rock*, 3 miles south-southeast of Cape Mendocino, and 3500 feet offshore (lat. 40°23'50" N, long. 124°23'35" W). Named on Cape Mendocino (1969) 7.5' quadrangle.

Devils Gulch [TRINITY]: *canyon*, drained by a stream that flows 3.5 miles to Summit Creek 7 miles east of Hayfork (lat. 40°34'45" N, long. 123°03'15" W; sec. 36, T 32 N, R 11 W). Named on Hayfork (1951) 15' quadrangle.

Devils Hole [HUMBOLDT]:

(1) *relief feature*, 3 miles northwest of Trinity Mountain (lat. 41°03'55" N, long. 123°27'15" W). Named on Trinity Mountain (1979) 7.5' quadrangle.

(2) *canyon*, 0.5 mile long, along upper reaches of Devils Creek (1) above a point 9.5 miles south of Scotia (lat. 40°20'45" N, long. 124°07'50" W; at S line sec. 25, T 1 S, R 1 W). Named on Scotia (1970) 7.5' quadrangle.

Devils Hole Prairie [HUMBOLDT]: *area*, 10 miles south of Scotia (lat. 40°20'55" N, long. 124°07'50" W; sec. 36, T 1 S, R 1 W); the place is south of Devils Hole (2). Named on Buckeye Mountain (1970) and Bull Creek (1969) 7.5' quadrangles.

Devils Hole Ridge [TRINITY]: *ridge*, south-southwest-trending, 3.5 miles long, 6 miles south-southeast of Black Rock Mountain on Trinity-Tehama County line (lat. 40°07' N, long. 122°58'05" W). Named on Yolla Bolly (1954) 15' quadrangle.

Devils Kitchen [TRINITY]: *relief feature*, 1.5 miles north-northwest of Forest Glen (lat. 40°23'45" N, long. 123°20' W; sec. 12, T 1 S, R 7 E). Named on Naufus Creek (1979) 7.5' quadrangle.

Devils Lake [TRINITY]: *lake*, 650 feet long, 8 miles east-northeast of Trinity Center (lat. 41°03'30" N, long. 122°33'25" W; on N line sec. 21, T 37 N, R 6 W). Named on Bonanza King (1955) 15' quadrangle.

Devils Nest [MENDOCINO]: *relief feature*, 6 miles north of Navarro (lat. 39°14'15" N, long. 123°33'15" W; near NE cor. sec. 20, T 16 N, R 15 W). Named on Navarro (1961) 15' quadrangle.

Devils Pass [HUMBOLDT]: *pass*, 6.5 miles west of Coyote Peak (lat. 41°06'45" N, long. 123°58'55" W); the pass is near the head of Devils Creek (2). Named on Panther Creek (1982) 7.5' quadrangle.

Devils Rock Garden [MENDOCINO]: *relief feature*, 5 miles north-northwest of Hull Mountain (lat. 39°35'15" N, long. 122°58'05" W; sec. 16, T 20 N, R 10 W). Named on Hull Mountain (1967) 7.5' quadrangle.

Devils Slide [MENDOCINO]: *relief feature*, 10.5 miles west-northwest of Ornbaun Valley (lat. 38°59' N, long. 123°28'15" W; near S line sec. 13, T 13 N, R 15 W). Named on Ornbaun Valley (1960) 15' quadrangle.

Dewaren Creek [MENDOCINO]: *stream*, flows 2 miles to North Fork Noyo River 15 miles north of Comptche (lat. 39°28'35" N, long. 123°33'10" W; sec. 29, T 19 N, R 15 W). Named on Comptche (1960) 15' quadrangle.

Dewarren Creek: see **Middle Fork of North Fork**, under **Noyo River** [MENDOCINO].

Dewell Garden [MENDOCINO]: *area*, 15 miles northeast of Covelo (lat. 39°56'25" N, long. 123°02'35" W; on N line sec. 13, T 24 N, R 11 W). Named on Leech Lake Mountain (1966) 7.5' quadrangle. On Covelo (1952) 15' quadrangle, the name applies to a nearby area.

Dewell Lake [MENDOCINO]: *intermittent lake*, 400 feet long, 16 miles northeast of Covelo (lat. 39°57'40" N, long. 123°02'50" W; sec. 2, T 24 N, R 11 W). Named on Leech Lake Mountain (1966) 7.5' quadrangle.

Diamond Creek [DEL NORTE]: *stream*, heads in the State of Oregon and flows 8.5 miles in Del Norte County to North Fork Smith River 8 miles north of Gasquet (lat. 41°57'50" N, long. 123°57'20" W; sec. 9, T 18 N, R 2 E). Named on Gasquet (1951) 15' quadrangle. North Fork enters 3.5 miles upstream from the mouth of the main creek; it heads in the State of Oregon, is 2 miles long in Del Norte County, and is named on Gasquet (1951) 15' quadrangle.

Diamond Creek [HUMBOLDT]: *stream*, flows 2 miles to Maple Creek (1) 7 miles north-northeast of Trinidad (lat. 41°09'15" N, long. 124°05'50" W; at E line sec. 19, T 9 N, R 1 E). Named on Rodgers Peak (1966) 7.5' quadrangle.

Diamond Lake [TRINITY]:

(1) *lake*, 700 feet long, 8 miles east-northeast of Trinity Center (lat. 41°03'35" N, long. 122°33'25" W; on S line sec. 16, T 37 N, R 6 W). Named on Bonanza King (1955) 15' quadrangle.

(2) *lake*, 450 feet long, 15 miles north of Weaverville (lat. 40°56'35" N, long. 122°54'15" W; at S line sec. 28, T 36 N, R 9 W). Named on Trinity Dam (1950) 15' quadrangle.

Diamond Prairie [HUMBOLDT]: *area*, 7.5 miles south of Korbel (lat. 40°45'25" N, long. 123°57'45" W; sec. 4, T 4 N, R 2 E). Named on Korbel (1979) 7.5' quadrangle. The name is from the shape of the feature (Turner, p. 59).
Dick: see **Fort Dick** [DEL NORTE].
Dicks Butte [MENDOCINO]: *peak*, 7.25 miles north of Hull Mountain (lat. 39°37'35" N, long. 122°56'45" W; at N line sec. 3, T 20 N, R 10 W). Altitude 6301 feet. Named on Plaskett Ridge (1967) 7.5' quadrangle. On Hull (1952) 15' quadrangle, the name applies to a feature located nearly 1 mile farther southeast (near W line sec. 2, T 20 N, R 10 W). United States Board on Geographic Names (1969b, p. 4) rejected the name "Umbrella Butte" for the feature.
Dickson Butte [HUMBOLDT]: *peak*, 8 miles west of Phillipsville (lat. 40°12'55" N, long. 123°56'30" W; sec. 10, T 3 S, R 2 E). Named on Ettersburg (1969) 7.5' quadrangle. The name commemorates David Dickson and William Dickson, who bought land at the place in 1877 (Turner, p. 59).
Dietz Gulch [MENDOCINO]: *canyon*, drained by a stream that flows 1.5 miles Big River nearly 4 miles northeast of Monache (lat. 39°17'55" N, long. 123°32'15" W; sec. 28, T 17 N, R 15 W). Named on Comptche (1960) 15' quadrangle.
Digger Creek [HUMBOLDT]: *stream*, flows nearly 2 miles to Yager Creek 1 mile southwest of Lone Star Junction (lat. 40°37'25" N, long. 123°53'40" W; sec. 24, T 3 N, R 2 E). Named on Iaqua Buttes (1979) 7.5' quadrangle.
Digger Creek [MENDOCINO]:
(1) *stream*, flows 1.5 miles to Rocktree Creek 6 miles northeast of Willits (lat. 35°27'35" N, long. 123°16' W; sec. 35, T 19 N, R 13 W). Named on Willits (1961) 15' quadrangle.
(2) *stream*, flows nearly 3 miles to the sea 2.5 miles south of Fort Bragg (lat. 39°24'30" N, long. 123°48'55" W; sec. 24, T 18 N, R 18 W). Named on Fort Bragg (1960) 7.5' quadrangle.
Digger Creek [TRINITY]: *stream*, flows 1 mile to Clair Engle Lake 12 miles northeast of Weaverville (lat. 40°52' N, long. 122°48' W; sec. 29, T 35 N, R 8 W). Named on Trinity Dam (1950) 15' quadrangle.
Digger Gulch [TRINITY]:
(1) *canyon*, drained by a stream that flows 3.5 miles to Trinity River 11.5 miles northeast of Weaverville (lat. 40°49'40" N, long. 122°45'45" W; sec. 3, T 34 N, R 8 W). Named on Schell Mountain (1950) and Trinity Lake (1950) 15' quadrangles.
(2) *canyon*, drained by a stream that flows 2.25 miles to Hayfork Creek 2.25 miles west of Hayfork (lat. 40°33'20" N, long. 123°13'30" W; sec. 9, T 31 N, R 12 W). Named on Hayfork (1951) 15' quadrangle.
Digger Pine Flat [TRINITY]: *area*, nearly 5 miles north-northwest of Helena along North Fork Trinity River (lat. 40°50'15" N, long. 123°09'45" W; near SW cor. sec. 31, T 35 N, R 11 W). Named on Helena (1951) 15' quadrangle.
Diggersville: see **Minersville** [TRINITY].
Diggins Creek [MENDOCINO]: *stream*, flows 2.25 miles to North Fork Eel River 8.5 miles northeast of Spyrock (2) (lat. 39°57'20" N, long. 123°20'10" W; sec. 5, T 24 N, R 13 W). Named on Mina (1967) 7.5' quadrangle.
Dillon Cove [TRINITY]: *embayment*, 5.5 miles west-southwest of Forest Glen along Ruth Reservoir (lat. 40°20'15" N, long. 123°24'55" W; on and near W line sec. 32, T 1 S, R 7 E). Named on Ruth Reservoir (1978) 7.5' quadrangle.
Dingman Creek [MENDOCINO]: *stream*, flows nearly 3 miles to Black Butte River 13 miles north of Hull Mountain (lat. 39°42'50" N, long. 122°55'50" W; near SE cor. sec. 35, T 22 N, R 10 W). Named on Plaskett Ridge (1967) 7.5' quadrangle.
Dingman Ridge [MENDOCINO]:
(1) *ridge*, south- to south-southeast-trending, 3 miles long, 4 miles east-southeast of Covelo on the east side of Round Valley (lat. 39°46'15" N, long. 123°10'45" W). Named on Covelo East (1967) 7.5' quadrangle.
(2) *ridge*, northeast-trending, 2 miles long, 13 miles north of Hull Mountain (lat. 39°42'50" N, long. 122°57'30" W); the ridge is northwest of Dingman Creek. Named on Plaskett Ridge (1967) 7.5' quadrangle.
Dinner Creek [HUMBOLDT]:
(1) *stream*, flows nearly 3 miles to Eel River 2.25 miles southeast of Scotia (lat. 40°27'20" N, long. 124°04'40" W; sec. 21, T 1 N, R 1 E); the stream is west of Twin Creek. Named on Scotia (1970) 7.5' quadrangle. Glynn (1919) 15' quadrangle shows present Dinner Creek (1) joining Twin Creek, and has the name "Twin Creeks" for both streams.
(2) *stream*, flows nearly 2 miles to China Creek (3) 7 miles west of Garberville (lat. 40°06'15" N, long. 123°55'35" W). Named on Briceland (1969) 7.5' quadrangle.
Dinner Gulch [TRINITY]: *canyon*, drained by a stream that flows 1.25 miles to Hayfork Creek 7.5 miles east of Hyampom (lat. 40°37'25" N, long. 123°18'15" W; sec. 20, T 3 N, R 8 E). Named on Hyampom (1951) 15' quadrangle.
Dinsmore [HUMBOLDT]: *village*, 20 miles northeast of Weott along Van Duzen River (lat. 40°29'30" N, long. 123°36'20" W; on W line sec. 3, T 1 N, R 5 E). Named on Dinsmore (1977) 7.5' quadrangle. Called Dinsmores on Blocksburg (1949) 15' quadrangle; United States Board on Geographic Names (1976b, p. 4) gave the name "Dinsmores" as a variant.
Dinsmores [HUMBOLDT]: *locality*, 2.5 miles northwest of Board Camp Mountain (lat. 40°43'10" N, long. 123°44'15" W; near NW cor. sec. 21, T 4 N, R 4 E). Named on Board Camp Mountain (1977) 7.5' quadrangle.
Dinsmores: see **Dinsmore** [HUMBOLDT].
Dinsmore Soda Spring: see **Wolf Creek** [LAKE].
Dinty: see **Larabee** [HUMBOLDT].
Dirty Camp Creek: see **Barney Creek** [HUMBOLDT].
Ditch Creek: see **Ditch Gulch** [TRINITY].
Ditch Gulch [TRINITY]: *canyon*, drained by a stream that flows 6.5 miles to Salt Creek (4) nearly 5 miles north of Dubakella Mountain (lat. 40°27'10" N, long. 123°09'30" W; near E line sec. 13, T 30 N, R 12 W). Named on Dubakella Mountain (1954) 15' quadrangle. Hoaglin (1935) 30' quadrangle has the name "Ditch Creek" for the stream in the canyon.
Division Creek [MENDOCINO]: *stream*, flows 2.5 miles to Middle Fork Eel River 3.25 miles south of Dos Rios (lat. 39°40'15" N, long. 123°20'35" W; near NE cor. sec. 19, T 21 N, R 13 W). Named on Dos Rios (1967) 7.5' quadrangle.
Divide Lake [HUMBOLDT]: *lake*, 950 feet long, 9.5 miles west-southwest of Orleans (lat. 41°15'30" N, long. 123°42'50" W). Named on Fish Lake (1974) 7.5' quadrangle.
Dixon Bar Creek [TRINITY]: *stream*, flows 1.5 miles to Trinity River 1 mile southeast of Burnt Ranch (lat. 40°48' N, long. 123°27'30" W; sec. 24, T 5 N, R 6 E). Named on Ironside Mountain (1951) 15' quadrangle.
Dixons Bar: see **China Slide** [TRINITY].
Doan Creek [MENDOCINO]: *stream*, flows nearly 3 miles to Town Creek 2.25 miles west of Covelo (lat. 39°47'55" N, long. 123°17'15" W; sec. 3, T 22 N, R 13 W). Named on Covelo West (1967) 7.5' quadrangle.
Doan Ridge [MENDOCINO]: *ridge*, northeast-trending, 2 miles long, 15 miles north of Hull Mountain (lat. 39°44' N, long. 122°59'20" W). Named on Plaskett Ridge (1967) and Thatcher Ridge (1967) 7.5' quadrangles.
Doba Creek: see **Adobe Creek** [LAKE].
Dobbin Creek: see **Dobbyn Creek** [HUMBOLDT].
Dobbins Creek, South Fork: see **Burgess Creek** [TRINITY].
Dobbins Gulch [TRINITY]: *canyon*, drained by a stream that flows 3 miles to Salt Creek (4) 6.25 miles north of Dubakella Mountain (lat. 40°28'25" N, long. 123°10' W; at S line sec. 1, T 30 N, R 12 W). Named on Dubakella Mountain (1954) 15' quadrangle.
Dobbyn Creek [HUMBOLDT]: *stream*, formed by the confluence of North Dobbyn Creek and South Dobbyn Creek, flows 3.5 miles to Eel River 4.5 miles north-northwest of Alderpoint (lat. 40°13'50" N, long. 123°39'25" W; sec. 6, T 3 S, R 5 E). Named on Alderpoint (1969) and Fort Seward (1969) 7.5' quadrangles. Called Dobbin Creek on Harris (1920) 15' quadrangle. On South Fork Peak (1929) 15' quadrangle, present North Dobbyn Creek is called Dobbyn Creek.
Dobbyn Creek: see **North Dobbyn Creek** [HUMBOLDT-TRINITY]; **South Dobbyn Creek** [HUMBOLDT-TRINITY].
Docker Hill [MENDOCINO]: *ridge*, northwest-trending, 1.5 miles long, 2 miles north-northeast of Comptche (lat. 39°17'40" N, long. 123°34'35" W; on N line sec. 31, T 17 N, R 15 W). Named on Comptche (1960) 15' quadrangle.
Doctor Rock [DEL NORTE]: *peak*, 11.5 miles east of Klamath Glen (lat. 41°32'20" N, long. 123°46'45" W). Named on Summit Valley (1981) 7.5' quadrangle. The name is a rough translation of an Indian term that is the equivalent of the word "medicine" (Stewart, G.R., p. 139).
Doctors Creek [MENDOCINO]: *stream*, flows 1 mile to Lynch Creek 7 miles south of Leggett (lat. 39°45'45" N, long. 123°42'45" W; sec. 14, T 22 N, R 17 W). Named on Leggett (1969) 7.5' quadrangle.
Dodge: see **Carrville** [TRINITY]:
Dodge Gulch [MENDOCINO]: *canyon*, drained by a stream that flows 0.5 mile to Cottaneva Creek 7 miles north-northwest of Westport (lat. 39°44'10" N, long. 123°49'10" W; near SE cor. sec. 23, T 22 N, R 18 W). Named on Westport (1966) 7.5' quadrangle.
Doe Campground: see **Little Doe Campground** [MENDOCINO].
Doe Canyon [LAKE]: *canyon*, drained by a stream that flows 2 miles to the canyon of Wolf Creek 6 miles northeast of Clearlake Oaks (lat. 39°35'10" N, long. 122°36'20" W; near SW cor. sec. 2, T 14 N, R 7 W). Named on Clearlake Oaks (1960) 15' quadrangle.
Doe Canyon [MENDOCINO]: *canyon*, drained by a stream that flows 2.25 miles to Middle Fork Eel River 7.5 miles north-northeast of Eden Valley (lat. 39°43'55" N, long. 123°07'50" W). Named on Jamison Ridge (1967) and Thatcher Ridge (1967) 7.5' quadrangles.
Doe Creek [HUMBOLDT]: *stream*, flows 1.5 miles to North Branch of North Fork Elk River (1) 10.5 miles east-southeast of Fields Landing (lat. 40°41'20" N, long. 124°01'20" W; sec. 36, T 4 N, R 1 E). Named on McWhinney Creek (1979) 7.5' quadrangle.
Doe Flat [TRINITY]: *area*, about 3 miles north-northwest of Billys Peak (1) (lat. 41°10'15" N, long. 122°47' W; sec. 9, T 38 N, R 8 W); the place is less than 1 mile east of Doe Lake. Named on Coffee Creek (1955) 15' quadrangle.

Doe Gulch [TRINITY]: *canyon*, drained by a stream that flows 1.5 miles to Mumbo Creek 11 miles north-northeast of Trinity Center (lat. 41°08'10" N, long. 122°34' W; sec. 21, T 38 N, R 6 W). Named on Bonanza King (1955) 15' quadrangle.

Doe Lake [TRINITY]: *lake*, 600 feet long, 3 miles northwest of Billys Peak (1) (lat. 41°10'05" N, long. 122°48' W; sec. 8, T 38 N, R 8 W); the lake is less than 1 mile west of Doe Flat. Named on Coffee Creek (1955) 15' quadrangle.

Doe Ridge [TRINITY]: *ridge*, generally southwest-trending, 2 miles long, 8.5 miles southwest of Black Rock Mountain (lat. 40°06'45" N, long. 123°06'20" W). Named on Black Rock Mountain (1954) 15' quadrangle.

Doe Ridge: see **Little Doe Ridge** [MENDOCINO].

Doe Rock [MENDOCINO]: *relief feature*, 1.5 miles south-southwest of Monument Peak (lat. 38°53'30" N, long. 123°58'05" W; near NW cor. sec. 15, T 12 N, R 10 W). Named on Highland Springs (1959) 7.5' quadrangle.

Doe Rock [TRINITY]: *relief feature*, 6.25 miles south-southwest of Hyampom (lat. 40°32'55" N, long. 123°30'55" W; at E line sec. 17, T 2 N, R 6 E). Named on Blake Mountain (1979) 7.5' quadrangle.

Dog Gulch [TRINITY]: *canyon*, drained by a stream that flows 1.25 miles to South Fork Trinity Creek 8.5 miles south of Dubakella Mountain (lat. 40°15'50" N, long. 123°09'45" W; sec. 24, T 28 N, R 12 W). Named on Dubakella Mountain (1954) 15' quadrangle.

Doghouse Creek [MENDOCINO]: *stream*, flows 2.25 miles to Middle Fork Eel River 1.5 miles east-southeast of Dos Rios (lat. 39°42'20" N, long. 123°19'45" W; sec. 5, T 21 N, R 13 W). Named on Dos Rios (1967) 7.5' quadrangle.

Dog Rock [LAKE]: *relief feature*, 3 miles west-southwest of Middletown near Dry Creek (3) (lat. 38°43'55" N, long. 122°40' W; at W line sec. 8, T 10 N, R 7 W). Named on Mount Saint Helena (1959) 7.5' quadrangle.

Dog Run Spring [TRINITY]: *spring*, 7.5 miles north-northeast of Hayfork (lat. 40°39'10" N, long. 123°07'20" W; sec. 4, T 32 N, R 11 W). Named on Hayfork (1951) 15' quadrangle.

Dogtown: see **Harris** [HUMBOLDT].

Dogwood Gulch [DEL NORTE]: *canyon*, drained by a stream that flows 1 mile to East Fork Bluff Creek 18 miles east-southeast of Klamath Glen (lat. 41°24'46" N, long. 123°40'05" W). Named on Lonesome Ridge (1974) 7.5' quadrangle.

Dolason Hill Prairie [HUMBOLDT]: *area*, 7.25 miles northwest of Coyote Peak on Bald Hills (lat. 41°12'25" N, long. 123°57'20" W). Named on Bald Hills (1982) 7.5' quadrangle.

Dolf Creek [HUMBOLDT]: *stream*, flows 1.25 miles to North Fork Mad River 6 miles north-northeast of the town of Blue Lake (lat. 40°57'55" N, long. 123°57'25" W; sec. 28, T 7 N, R 2 E). Named on Blue Lake (1979) 7.5' quadrangle.

Dollar: see **Jim Dollar Mountain** [LAKE].

Dollar Bend [DEL NORTE]: *bend*, 8 miles east-northeast of Gasquet along Middle Fork Smith River (lat. 41°53'05" N, long. 123°49'30" W; sec. 10, T 17 N, R 3 E). Named on Shelly Creek Ridge (1982) 7.5' quadrangle.

Dolores Creek [HUMBOLDT]: *stream*, flows 0.5 mile to Little Van Duzen River 7 miles north-northeast of Blocksburg (lat. 40°22'10" N, long. 123°35'40" W; near N line sec. 22, T 1 S, R 5 E). Named on Black Lassic (1979) and Dinsmore (1977) 7.5' quadrangles.

Domingo Creek [HUMBOLDT]: *stream*, flows nearly 2 miles to the sea 5 miles northwest of Petrolia (lat. 40°22'05" N, long. 124°21'45" W; sec. 24, T 1 S, R 3 W). Named on Capetown (1969) and Petrolia (1969) 7.5' quadrangles.

Domingo Creek: see **Mill Creek** [HUMBOLDT] (2), **Middle Fork**.

Dominie Creek [DEL NORTE]: *stream*, flows 4.25 miles to Rowdy Creek at the town of Smith River (lat. 41°55'40" N, long. 124°08'35" W; sec. 26, T 18 N, R 1 W). Named on High Divide (1966) and Smith River (1966) 7.5' quadrangles.

Donahue Flat [HUMBOLDT]: *area*, 5.5 miles north of Orleans at or on Humboldt-Siskiyou County line (lat. 41°22'55" N, long. 123°31'10" W). Named on Bark Shanty Gulch (1974) 7.5' quadrangle.

Donaldson Creek [TRINITY]: *stream*, flows about 2.5 miles to Big Creek (1) 5.5 miles north of Hayfork (lat. 40°38' N, long. 123°09'45" W; near SW cor. sec. 7, T 32 N, R 11 W). Named on Hayfork (1951) 15' quadrangle.

Donelly Creek [MENDOCINO]: *stream*, flows 2.5 miles to Anderson Creek (2) at Boonville (lat. 39°00'50" N, long. 123°22'20" W; sec. 2, T 13 N, R 14 W). Named on Boonville (1959) 15' quadrangle.

Don Juan Creek [TRINITY]: *stream*, flows 3.5 miles to Trinity River 3 miles southeast of Burnt Ranch (lat. 40°47'10" N, long. 123°25'30" W). Named on Ironside Mountain (1951) 15' quadrangle.

Don Juan Point [TRINITY]: *relief feature*, 3.25 miles southeast of Burnt Ranch along Trinity River (lat. 40°47'10" N, long. 123°25'15" W); the feature is just upstream from the mouth of Don Juan Creek. Named on Ironside Mountain (1951) 15' quadrangle.

Donkey Point [HUMBOLDT]: *relief feature*, 2.5 miles south-southeast of Yager Junction (lat. 40°31'05" N, long. 123°48' W; on N line sec. 35, T 2 N, R 3 E). Named on Yager Junction (1979) 7.5' quadrangle.

Donnelly Gulch [MENDOCINO]: *canyon*, drained by a stream that flows 1.5 miles to Big Salmon Creek 5.5 miles north-northeast of Elk (lat. 39°12'10" N, long. 123°39'50" W; sec. 32, T 16 N, R 16 W). Named on Elk (1960) 7.5' quadrangle.

Donnelly Gulch [TRINITY]: *canyon*, drained by a stream that flows 1.25 miles to Deadwood Creek 11 miles east of Weaverville (lat. 40°42'55" N, long. 122°44'10" W; sec. 14, T 33 N, R 8 W). Named on French Gulch (1979) 7.5' quadrangle.

Donohue Flat Creek [HUMBOLDT]: *stream*, flows 2.5 miles to Klamath River 6.5 miles north-northwest of Orleans Mountain (lat. 41°22' N, long. 123°29'35" W). Named on Bark Shanty Gulch (1974), Orleans (1978), and Orleans Mountain (1974) 7.5' quadrangles.

Donovan Valley [LAKE]: *valley*, 2.5 miles northwest of Highland Springs (lat. 38°57'40" N, long. 122°56'45" W; sec. 22, 23, T 13 N, R 10 W). Named on Highland Springs (1959) 7.5' quadrangle.

Doolan's Ukiah Vichy Springs: see **Vichy Springs** [MENDOCINO].

Dooley Creek [MENDOCINO]: *stream*, flows 4.5 miles to Russian River 0.5 mile east of Hopland (lat. 38°58'25" N, long. 123°06'25" W). Named on Hopland (1960) 7.5' quadrangle.

Doolin Creek [MENDOCINO]: *stream*, flows 4 miles to Russian River 1.5 miles southeast of Ukiah (lat. 39°08'05" N, long. 123°11'05" W). Named on Ukiah (1958) 7.5' quadrangle.

Dora Creek [MENDOCINO]: *stream*, flows 1.25 miles to South Fork Eel River 5 miles south-southeast of Piercy (lat. 39°53'55" N, long. 123°45'05" W; near W line sec. 28, T 24 N, R 17 W). Named on Noble Butte (1969) 7.5' quadrangle.

Dorleska: see **Goldfield Campground** [TRINITY].

Dorn Bay [LAKE]: *embayment*, 6.5 miles south-southeast of Lakeport along Clear Lake (lat. 39°00'45" N, long. 122°48'15" W; on S line sec. 36, T 14 N, R 9 W). Named on Lucerne (1958) 7.5' quadrangle. United States Board on Geographic Names (1962b, p. 16) ruled that Dorn Bay is not part of Soda Bay.

Dorr Creek [LAKE]: *stream*, flows 2.25 miles to Scotts Creek 5.5 miles northwest of Lakeport (lat. 39°06'40" N, long. 122°58'35" W; sec. 33, T 15 N, R 10 W). Named on Lakeport (1958) and Upper Lake (1958) 7.5' quadrangles.

Dorr Ridge [HUMBOLDT]: *ridge*, east-northeast-trending, 1 mile long, 5 miles east-northeast of Showers Mountain (lat. 40°35'25" N, long. 123°36'10" W; on W line sec. 34, T 3 N, R 5 E). Named on Blake Mountain (1979) 7.5' quadrangle.

Dos Rios [MENDOCINO]: *village*, 7 miles east-northeast of Laytonville (lat. 39°43' N, long. 123°21'10" W; near S line sec. 31, T 22 N, R 13 W); the village is near the confluence of Eel River and Middle Fork Eel River. Named on Dos Rios (1967) 7.5' quadrangle. Postal authorities established Two Rivers post office in 1912 and translated the name to Dos Rios in 1915; the name "Two Rivers" was from the proximity of the place to the confluence of Eel River and Middle Fork Eel River (Salley, p. 226).

Dot Creek [HUMBOLDT]: *stream*, flows 1.25 miles to Red Cap Creek 6 miles north-northwest of Trinity Mountain (lat. 41°07'15" N, long. 123°26'55" W). Named on Trinity Mountain (1979) 7.5' quadrangle.

Doty Creek [MENDOCINO]: *stream*, flows 2.5 miles to Little North Fork Gualala River 4 miles north of Gualala (lat. 38°49'15" N, long. 123°31'55" W; near NW cor. sec. 10, T 11 N, R 15 W). Named on Gualala (1960) 7.5' quadrangle.

Double Cabin Flat [TRINITY]: *area*, 2 miles southeast of Forest Glen along South Fork Trinity River (lat. 40°21' N, long. 123°18'10" W; sec. 29, T 1 S, R 8 E). Named on Forest Glen (1979) 7.5' quadrangle.

Double Cabins [TRINITY]: *locality*, nearly 7 miles west-northwest of Black Rock Mountain (lat. 40°14'50" N, long. 123°07'20" W; near E line sec. 29, T 28 N, R 11 W). Named on Black Rock Mountain (1954) 15' quadrangle, which shows a ruin at the site.

Double Cone Rock [MENDOCINO]: *rock*, 14 miles south of Piercy, and 800 feet offshore (lat. 39°46'30" N, long. 123°50'20" W). Named on Hales Grove (1970) 7.5' quadrangle.

Double Gate Ridge [TRINITY]: *ridge*, generally northeast-trending, 2.25 miles long, 3 miles northeast of Kettenpom (lat. 40°11'05" N, long. 123°25'10" W). Named on Zenia (1967) 7.5' quadrangle. The name is from a fence that separates a sheep range from a cattle range (Gudde, 1949, p. 98).

Double Rock [MENDOCINO]: *rock*, 9 miles west-southwest of Piercy, and 650 feet offshore (lat. 39°56'30" N, long. 123°58'05" W). Named on Bear Harbor (1969) 7.5' quadrangle.

Double Rock: see **Camel Rock** [HUMBOLDT].

Douglas City [TRINITY]: *village*, 5.5 miles south of Weaverville along Trinity River (lat. 40°39'10" N, long. 122°50'30" W; near SE cor. sec. 1, T 32 N, R 10 W). Named on Weaverville (1950) 15' quadrangle. Postal authorities established Douglas City post office in 1859 (Frickstad, p. 207). The original settlement was called Kanaka Bar; it was moved about 0.25 mile up the slope in 1859 and renamed for Stephen A. Douglas, who debated Lincoln that year (Jones, p. 269). California Mining Bureau's (1917b) map shows a place called Oriole located southeast of Douglas City. Postal authorities established Oriole post office 7 miles southeast of Douglas City in 1905 and discontinued it in 1907 (Salley, p. 162). Gudde (1975, p. 324, 347) listed a mining place called Smith Flat located along Trinity River opposite Douglas City, and a mining place called Texas Bar located along the river east of Douglas City.

Douglas Park [DEL NORTE]: *locality,* 7.5 miles east-northeast of Crescent City on the south side of Smith River (lat. 41°47'15" N, long. 124°03'45" W; near NE cor. sec. 16, T 16 N, R 1 E). Named on Hiouchi (1966) 7.5' quadrangle.

Dows Prairie [HUMBOLDT]: *area,* 7 miles north of Arcata (lat. 40°58'30" N, long. 124°06' W). Named on Arcata North (1959) 7.5' quadrangle. Bledsoe (p. 226) referred to Dow's Prairie. The name commemorates Joseph Dow, who came to the place in the middle 1860's (Turner, p. 63). Postal authorities established Dow's Prairie post office 7 miles north of Arcata in 1877, discontinued it for a time in 1891, and changed the name to McKinleyville in 1903 (Salley, p. 61).

Doyle Creek [MENDOCINO]: *stream,* flows 3 miles to the sea 4 miles north-northwest of Mendocino at Caspar Anchorage (lat. 39°21'35" N, long. 123°49'05" W; sec. 1, T 17 N, R 18 W). Named on Mendocino (1960) 7.5' quadrangle. Called Boyle Creek on Fort Bragg (1943) 15' quadrangle. United States Board on Geographic Names (1943, p. 11) rejected the names "Boyles Creek" and "Young's Creek" for the stream.

Dragon Channel: see **Point Saint George** [DEL NORTE].

Dragon Rocks: see **Point Saint George** [DEL NORTE].

Dragsaw Spring [HUMBOLDT]: *spring,* 4 miles north of Weitchpec (lat. 41°14'40" N, long. 123°41'35" W). Named on Weitchpec (1979) 7.5' quadrangle.

Drewry Creek [MENDOCINO]: *stream,* flows 2.5 miles to Chamise Creek 11 miles northeast of Leggett (lat. 39°59'35" N, long. 123°35'25" W; near W line sec. 26, T 5 S, R 5 E). Named on Bell Springs (1969) 7.5' quadrangle. Leggett (1952) 15' quadrangle shows Drewry ranch near the stream.

Drinkwater Gulch [TRINITY]: *stream,* flows 2 miles to Hayfork Creek 3 miles west of Hayfork (lat. 40°33'45" N, long. 123°14'15" W; at W line sec. 4, T 31 N, R 12 W). Named on Hayfork (1951) and Hyampom (1951) 15' quadrangles.

Dry Bridge Mountain [MENDOCINO]: *peak,* 9.5 miles west-northwest of Ornbaun Valley (lat. 38°59' N, long. 123°27'25" W; near SE cor. sec. 13, T 13 N, R 15 W). Named on Ornbaun Valley (1960) 15' quadrangle.

Dry Creek [HUMBOLDT]:

(1) *stream,* flows 2.5 miles to Mad River 3 miles south of Korbel (lat. 40°49'45" N, long. 123°58'10" W; at E line sec. 8, T 5 N, R 2 E). Named on Korbel (1979) 7.5' quadrangle.

(2) *stream,* flows 1 mile to South Fork Eel River 7.5 miles southeast of Weott (lat. 40°15'10" N, long. 123°49'20" W; near N line sec. 34, T 2 S, R 3 E). Named on Myers Flat (1969) 7.5' quadrangle.

(3) *stream,* flows 2.25 miles to Chamise Creek 10 miles south-southeast of Alderpoint (lat. 40°02'15" N, long. 123°33'10" W; sec. 7, T 5 S, R 6 E). Named on Jewett Rock (1969) 7.5' quadrangle.

(4) *stream,* flows nearly 4 miles to Mattole River 3.25 miles east-southeast of Honeydew (lat. 40°13'45" N, long. 124°03'45" W). Named on Bull Creek (1969) and Honeydew (1970) 7.5' quadrangles.

Dry Creek [LAKE]:

(1) *stream,* flows 2.25 miles to Rice Creek 3 miles west of Potato Hill (lat. 39°20'40" N, long. 122°51'40" W; sec. 10, T 17 N, R 9 W). Named on Potato Hill (1967) 7.5' quadrangle.

(2) *stream,* flows 3.5 miles to Cache Creek 3.35 miles northeast of the town of Lower Lake (lat. 38°56'20" N, long. 122°33'40" W). Named on Lower Lake (1958) 7.5' quadrangle.

(3) *stream,* flows 6 miles to Putah Creek 0.5 mile north of Middletown (lat. 38°45'35" N, long. 122°36'50" W). Named on Middletown (1958), Mount Saint Helena (1959), and Whispering Pines (1958) 7.5' quadrangles. South Fork enters from the southwest 3 miles west-southwest of Middletown; it is nearly 2 miles long and is named on Mount Saint Helena (1959) 7.5' quadrangle.

Dry Creek [MENDOCINO]:

(1) *stream,* flows 2 miles to an unnamed stream 10.5 miles west-southwest of Ornbaun Valley (lat. 38°49'55" N, long. 123°28'15" W; sec. 6, T 11 N, R 14 W). Named on Ornbaun Valley (1960) 15' quadrangle.

(2) *stream,* flows 14 miles to Sonoma County 11.5 miles south of Hopland (lat. 38°48'35" N, long. 123°09'40" W; at S line sec. 11, T 11 N, R 12 W). Named on Hopland (1960) 15' quadrangle.

Dry Dock Gulch [MENDOCINO]: *canyon,* drained by a stream that flows less than 1 mile to Big River 8 miles west-northwest of Comptche (lat. 39°18' N, long. 123°43'35" W; at S line sec. 26, T 17 N, R 17 W). Named on Comptche (1960) 15' quadrangle.

Dry Gulch [HUMBOLDT]: *canyon,* drained by a stream that flows 0.5 mile to Klamath River 8.5 miles southeast of Johnsons (lat. 41°15'10" N, long. 123°46'25" W). Named on Johnsons (1982) 7.5' quadrangle.

Dry Gulch [TRINITY]:

(1) *canyon,* 1 mile long, 3 miles northwest of Dubakella Mountain (lat. 40°25' N long. 123°11' W; on N line sec. 35, T 30 N, R 12 W). Named on Dubakella Mountain (1954) 15' quadrangle.

(2) *canyon,* drained by a stream that flows 1 mile to New River 9.5 miles north-northeast of Burnt Ranch (lat. 40°55'50" N, long. 123°23'40" W). Named on Ironside Mountain (1951) 15' quadrangle.

(3) *canyon,* drained by a stream that flows 2.25 miles to South Fork Trinity River nearly 4 miles south-southeast of Salyer (lat. 40°50'20" N, long. 123°33'50" W). Named on Hennessy Peak (1979) 7.5' quadrangle.

Dry Lagoon [HUMBOLDT]: *marsh,* 11.5 miles north of Trinidad near the coast (lat. 41°13'30" N, long. 124°06'10" W). Named on Rodgers Peak (1966) 7.5' quadrangle. A sandy beach separates the feature from the sea.

Dry Lake [DEL NORTE]: *lake,* 600 feet long, 9 miles north of Buck Mountain (lat. 41°44'35" N, long. 123°52'35" W). Named on Cant Hook Mountain (1982) 7.5' quadrangle.

Dry Lake [HUMBOLDT]:

(1) *intermittent lake,* 3.5 miles north of Weitchpec (lat. 41°14'30" N, long. 123°41'55" W). Named on Weitchpec (1979) 7.5' quadrangle.

(2) *intermittent lake,* 250 feet long, 10 miles south of the settlement of Willow Creek (lat. 40°48'05" N, long. 123°36'15" W). Named on Hennessy Peak (1979) 7.5' quadrangle.

(3) *intermittent lake,* 5.5 miles west of Dinsmore (lat. 40°29'25" N, long. 123°42'25" W; sec. 3, T 1 N, R 4 E). Named on Larabee Valley (1977) 7.5' quadrangle.

(4) *intermittent lake,* 300 feet long, 4.25 miles east-northeast of Blocksburg (lat. 40°17'10" N, long. 123°33'05" W). Named on Black Lassic (1979) 7.5' quadrangle.

Dry Lake [LAKE]: *intermittent lake,* 700 feet long, 1.5 miles west of the town of Lower Lake (lat. 38°54'40" N, long. 122°38'20" W; on S line sec. 4, T 12 N, R 7 W). Named on Clearlake Highlands (1958) 7.5' quadrangle.

Dry Lake [TRINITY]: *intermittent lake,* 1150 feet long, 10.5 miles south of Kettenpom (lat. 40°00'45" N, long. 123°25'10" W; near W line sec. 20, T 5 S, R 7 E). Named on Lake Mountain (1967) 7.5' quadrangle.

Dubakella Creek [TRINITY]: *stream,* flows 4 miles to Hayfork Creek 3.5 miles east-southeast of Dubakella Mountain (lat. 40°21'40" N, long. 123°05'10" W; at S line sec. 15, T 29 N, R 11 W); the stream heads near South Dubakella Mountain. Named on Dubakella Mountain (1954) 15' quadrangle.

Dubakella Mountain [TRINITY]: *peak,* 12 miles south of Hayfork (lat. 40°23' N, long. 123°08'45" W; near N line sec. 7, T 29 N, R 11 W). Altitude 5881 feet. Named on Dubakella Mountain (1954) 15' quadrangle. United States Board on Geographic Names (1979, p. 5) approved the name "Seven Up Cedars Spring" for a spring situated 3 miles southwest of Dubakella Mountain (lat. 40°21'40" N, long. 123°11'40" W; sec. 15, T 29 N, R 12 W), and rejected the form "Seven up Cedars Spring" for the name, which reportedly is from the game of seven-up poker that a group of cowboys played when they took refuge in a burned-out cedar tree at the place during a storm.

Duckett Bluff [HUMBOLDT]: *relief feature,* 1.5 miles north of Weott (lat. 40°20'40" N, long. 123°55'45" W; near SE cor. sec. 27, T 1 S, R 2 E). Named on Weott (1969) 7.5' quadrangle.

Duck Pond Gulch [MENDOCINO]: *canyon,* drained by a stream that flows 1.5 miles to Albion River 8 miles north of Elk (lat. 39°14'45" N, long. 123°22'50" W; at W line sec. 13, T 16 N, R 17 W). Named on Elk (1960) 7.5' quadrangle

Duffey: see **Fort Bragg** [MENDOCINO].

Duffy Gulch [MENDOCINO]: *canyon,* drained by a stream that flows 2.5 miles to Noyo River 12 miles north of Comptche (lat. 39°26'05" N, long. 123°35'15" W; sec. 12, T 18 N, R 16 W). Named on Comptche (1960) 15' quadrangle.

Duffys Reef [MENDOCINO]: *rocks,* 8.5 miles southwest of Piercy, and 500 feet offshore (lat. 39°54'15" N, long. 123°55'45" W). Named on Bear Harbor (1969) 7.5' quadrangle.

Dugan's Ferry: see **Ferndale** [HUMBOLDT].

Dugans Opening [MENDOCINO]: *area,* 6 miles south of Piercy (lat. 39°52'50" N, long. 123°48'45" W). Named on Piercy (1969) 7.5' quadrangle.

Duke Creek [HUMBOLDT]: *stream,* flows 1.5 miles to Strawberry Creek 7.5 miles north of Arcata (lat. 40°59' N, long. 124°05'35" W; sec. 20, T 7 N, R 1 E). Named on Arcata North (1959) 7.5' quadrangle.

Duncan Creek [HUMBOLDT]: *stream,* flows 1 mile to Mattole River 4.5 miles east-southeast of Honeydew (lat. 40°12'35" N, long. 124°02'55" W). Named on Honeydew (1970) 7.5' quadrangle.

Duncan Creek [MENDOCINO]: *stream,* flows 3 miles to Feliz Creek 1.25 miles west of Hopland (lat. 38°58'15" N, long. 123°08'25" W). Named on Hopland (1960) 15' quadrangle.

Duncan Creek [TRINITY]: *stream,* flows 4.5 miles to Carr Creek (2) 5.5 miles east-northeast of Hayfork (lat. 40°34'45" N, long. 123°05' W; near SW cor. sec. 35, T 32 N, R 11 W). Named on Hayfork (1951) 15' quadrangle. South Fork enters from the south 2.25 miles upstream from the mouth of the main creek; it is 2 miles long and is named on Hayfork (1951) 15' quadrangle.

Duncan Flat [HUMBOLDT]: *area,* 5.5 miles southeast of Honeydew (lat. 40°11'40" N, long. 124°02'25" W). Named on Honeydew (1970) 7.5' quadrangle.

Duncan Gulch [TRINITY]: *canyon,* drained by a stream that flows 5 miles to Hayfork Creek 2.5 miles east of Hayfork (lat. 40°33'10" N, long. 123°08'15" W; sec. 8, T 31 N, R 11 W). Named on Hayfork (1951) 15' quadrangle.

Duncan Hill [TRINITY]: *peak,* 3.5 miles east-northeast of Hayfork (lat. 40°34'25" N, long. 123°07'30" W; near NW cor. sec. 4, T 31 N, R 11 W); the peak is west of Duncan Gulch. Named on Hayfork (1951) 15' quadrangle.

Duncan Mineral Springs: see **Duncan Springs** [MENDOCINO].

Duncan Peak [MENDOCINO]: *peak,* 2.25 miles southwest of Hopland (lat. 38°56'50" N, long. 123°08'10" W; sec. 35, T 13 N, R 12 W); the peak is 1 mile west-southwest of Duncan Springs. Altitude 2638 feet. Named on Hopland (1960) 15' quadrangle. Called Duncans Pk. on Hopland (1944) 15' quadrangle.

Duncan Springs [MENDOCINO]: *locality,* 1.5 miles south-southwest of Hopland (lat. 38°57'10" N, long. 123°07'30" W). Named on Hopland (1960) 7.5' quadrangle. O'Brien (1953, p. 365) listed Duncan Mineral Springs. The place was a resort as early as the 1880's (Waring, p. 167).

Dunfield Flats [LAKE]: *area,* 3 miles east of Wilson Valley (2) (lat. 38°30'20" N, long. 122°24'45" W; near SE cor. sec. 16, T 13 N, R 5 W). Named on Wilson Valley (1958) 7.5' quadrangle.

Dunlap [MENDOCINO]: *locality,* 6.25 miles north-northeast of Comptche (lat. 39°21'10" N, long. 123°33'20" W). Named on Glenblair (1943) 15' quadrangle.

Dunlap Gulch [HUMBOLDT]: *canyon,* drained by a stream that flows 1.25 miles to North Fork Elk River (1) 5.5 miles east-southeast of Fields Landing (lat. 40°42'05" N, long. 124°07'05" W; sec. 30, T 4 N, R 1 E). Named on McWhinney Creek (1979) 7.5' quadrangle.

Dunlap Pass [MENDOCINO]: *pass,* 6 miles north of Comptche (lat. 39°20'55" N, long. 123°34'15" W; sec. 7, T 17 N, R 15 W). Named on Comptche (1960) 15' quadrangle.

Dunn Creek [DEL NORTE]: *stream,* flows 9 miles to the State of Oregon 8.5 miles north-northeast of Broken Rib Mountain (lat. 42°00' N, long. 123°37'20" W; sec. 34, T 19 N, R 5 E). Named on Polar Bear Mountain (1982) 7.5' quadrangle. North Fork enters from the northeast 1.5 miles upstream from the entrance of the main creek into Oregon; North Fork heads in Oregon, is 1.5 miles long, and is named on Polar Bear Mountain (1982) 7.5' quadrangle.

Dunn Creek [MENDOCINO]: *stream,* flows nearly 2 miles to North Fork Cottaneva Creek 13 miles south of Piercy (lat. 39°47'35" N, long. 123°48'55" W; near N line sec. 1, T 22 N, R 18 W). Named on Hales Grove (1970) 7.5' quadrangle.

Dunnigan Hill [LAKE]: *peak,* 3.5 miles east-southeast of Jericho Valley (lat. 38°48'40" N, long. 122°22'40" W; on S line sec. 11, T 11 N, R 5 W). Named on Jericho Valley (1958) 7.5' quadrangle.

Dunn Prairie [HUMBOLDT]: *area,* 2 miles northeast of Weitchpec (lat. 41°12'10" N, long. 123°40'35" W; sec. 1, T 9 N, R 4 E). Named on Weitchpec (1979) 7.5' quadrangle.

Dunn Ridge [HUMBOLDT]: *ridge,* west-trending, 1 mile long, 12 miles northeast of the town of Blue Lake (lat. 40°59'15" N, long. 123°48'30" W). Named on Lord-Ellis Summit (1973) 7.5' quadrangle.

Durington Creek: see **Perington Creek** [HUMBOLDT].

Durkee's Ferry: see **Weitchpec** [HUMBOLDT].

Durphy Creek [HUMBOLDT]: *stream,* flows 2.5 miles to South Fork Eel River 5.25 miles south of Garberville (lat. 40°01'20" N, long. 123°47'25" W; near W line sec. 13, T 5 S, R 3 E). Named on Garberville (1970) 7.5' quadrangle.

Durr Creek [HUMBOLDT]: *stream,* flows 1.5 miles to the sea 2.5 miles south-southeast of Cape Mendocino (lat. 40°24'35" N, long. 124°23'30" W; sec. 3, T 1 S, R 3 W). Named on Cape Mendocino (1969) and Capetown (1969) 7.5' quadrangles.

Dutch Charlie Creek [MENDOCINO]: *stream,* flows 4.25 miles to South Fork Eel River 3 miles northwest of Branscomb (lat. 39°41'25" N, long. 123°39'30" W; sec. 9, T 21 N, R 16 W). Named on Lincoln Ridge (1966) 7.5' quadrangle.

Dutch Creek [TRINITY]: *stream,* flows 4.5 miles to Trinity River 12 miles northeast of Hayfork (lat. 40°39'50" N, long. 123°01' W; near NE cor. sec. 5, T 32 N, R 10 W). Named on Hayfork (1951) 15' quadrangle.

Dutch Gulch [TRINITY]: *canyon,* drained by a stream that flows 1 mile to Clair Engle Lake 9.5 miles northeast of Weaverville (lat. 40°48'55" N, long. 122°48' W; near W line sec. 8, T 34 N, R 8 W). Named on Trinity Dam (1950) 15' quadrangle.

Dutch Henry Creek [MENDOCINO]:

(1) *stream,* flows 6 miles to Long Valley Creek 0.5 mile north-northwest of Longvale (lat. 39°33'50" N, long. 123°26' W; at S line sec. 20, T 20 N, R 14 W). Named on Longvale (1966) and Sherwood Peak (1967) 7.5' quadrangles.

(2) *stream,* flows 1.5 miles to Willits Creek 3.25 miles northwest of Willits (lat. 39°20'45" N, long. 123°23'25" W; near NW cor. sec. 2, T 18 N, R 14 W). Named on Willits (1961) 15' quadrangle.

(3) *stream,* flows 3.5 miles to North Branch of North Fork Navarro River 3 miles north-northwest of Navarro (lat. 39°11'45" N, long. 123°33'20" W; near S line sec. 32, T 16 N, R 15 W). Named on Navarro (1961) 15' quadrangle.

Dutchman Camp [TRINITY]: *locality,* nearly 2 miles north of Black Lassic (lat. 40°22' N, long. 123°32'30" W; sec. 17, T 1 S, R 6 E). Named on Black Lassic (1979) 7.5' quadrangle.

Dutchman Creek [TRINITY]: *stream,* flows 2.5 miles to North Fork Eel River 5 miles east-northeast of Kettenpom (lat. 40°10'35" N, long. 123°22'20" W; sec. 27, T 3 S, R 7 E). Named on Shannon Butte (1967) 7.5' quadrangle.

Dutchmans Flat [MENDOCINO]: *area,* 11 miles south of Piercy along South Fork Mule Creek (lat. 39°48'55" N, long. 123°47'05" W; sec. 30, T 23 N, R 17 W). Named on Hales Grove (1970) 7.5' quadrangle.

Dutchmans Knoll [MENDOCINO]: *peak,* 9.5 miles south of Branscomb (lat. 39°30'55" N, long. 123°38'10" W; sec. 10, T 19 N, R 16 W). Named on Dutchmans Knoll (1966) 7.5' quadrangle.

Dutch Oven Creek [LAKE]:

(1) *stream,* flows 2.25 miles to Corbin Creek 7.5 miles east of Hull Mountain (lat. 39°32'35" N, long. 122°47'45" W; near E line sec. 31, T 20 N, R 8 W). Named on Kneecap Ridge (1967) 7.5' quadrangle.

(2) *stream,* heads in Glenn County and flows 2.5 miles in Lake County to Corbin Creek 10.5 miles east of Hull Mountain (lat. 39°32'50" N, long. 122°44'30" W; sec. 34, T 20 N, R 8 W). Named on Felkner Hill (1968) 7.5' quadrangle.

Dutton Creek [TRINITY]: *stream,* flows 3.5 miles to Trinity River 4.5 miles south-southwest of Weaverville (lat. 40°40'30" N, long. 122°58'10" W; sec. 35, T 33 N, R 10 W). Named on Weaverville (1950) 15' quadrangle. Called Dutton's Creek on Miller's (1890) map.

Dwight Creek [DEL NORTE]: *stream,* flows 1 mile to the State of Oregon 8 miles north-northwest of Broken Rib Mountain (lat. 41°59'50" N, long. 123°43'55" W; sec. 34, T 19 N, R 4 E). Named on Broken Rib Mountain (1982) 7.5' quadrangle.

Dye: see **Tom Dye Rock** [LAKE].

Dyer Creek [TRINITY]: *stream,* flows 2.25 miles to New River 4.5 miles north-northeast of Burnt Ranch (lat. 40°51'50" N, long. 123°27'10" W). Named on Ironside Mountain (1951) 15' quadrangle.

Dyer Gulch [HUMBOLDT]: *canyon,* drained by a stream that flows 2.25 miles to Slate Creek 5 miles west of Orleans (lat. 41°18'35" N, long. 123°38'05" W). Named on Fish Lake (1974) and Orleans (1978) 7.5' quadrangles.

Dyerville [HUMBOLDT]: *locality,* 2 miles north of Weott along South Fork Eel River (lat. 40°21'20" N, long. 123°55'25" W; near N line sec. 26, T 1 S, R 2 E). Site named on Weott (1969) 7.5' quadrangle. Postal authorities established Dyerville post office in 1890 and discontinued it in 1933, when the site was flooded; they reestablished the post office 1 mile farther south with the name "South Fork" (Salley, p. 63). They established Helper post office 9.5 miles west of Dyerville in 1902 and discontinued it in 1904; the name was for the locomotives called helpers that were used to help pull trains up the grade (Salley, p. 95). They established Youngs post office 7 miles south of Dyerville in 1912 and discontinued in 1914; the name was George B. Young, first postmaster (Salley, p. 245).

— E —

Eachus Lake [LAKE]: *lake,* 1100 feet long, 3 miles north-northwest of Lakeport (lat. 39°05'05" N, long. 122°55'55" W; near SE cor. sec. 2, T 14 N, R 10 W). Named on Lakeport (1958) 7.5' quadrangle.

Eades Field [TRINITY]: *area,* 21 miles northeast of Weaverville (lat. 40°58'20" N, long. 122°41'15" W; at and near NE cor. sec. 20, T 36 N, R 7 W). Named on Schell Mountain (1950) 15' quadrangle.

Eagle Creek [MENDOCINO]: *stream,* flows 1 mile to Dutch Charlie Creek 4 miles west-northwest of Branscomb (lat. 39°41'15" N, long. 123°41'20" W; at E line sec. 12, T 21 N, R 17 W). Named on Lincoln Ridge (1966) 7.5' quadrangle.

Eagle Creek [TRINITY]:

(1) *stream,* flows 7.5 miles to Slide Creek 10 miles south-southeast of Salmon Mountain (lat. 41°03'20" N, long. 123°19'55" W). Named on Dees Peak (1978) and Youngs Peak (1979) 7.5' quadrangles. North Fork enters from the northwest 1.5 miles upstream from the mouth of the main creek; it is 7 miles long and is named on Dees Peak (1978) and Youngs Peak (1979) 7.5' quadrangles. United States Board on Geographic Names (1977b, p. 5) gave the name "North Fork New River" as a variant name for present North Fork Eagle Creek.

(2) *stream,* flows 2.5 miles to Trinity River 2.5 miles southwest of Helena (lat. 40°45'05" N, long. 123°09'50" W; at W line sec. 31, T 34 N, R 11 W). Named on Hayfork (1951) 15' quadrangle.

(3) *stream,* flows 9 miles to Trinity River 10 miles north of Trinity Center

(lat. 41°09' N, long. 122°40'05" W; near E line sec. 16, T 38 N, R 7 W); the stream heads near Eagle Peak. Named on Bonanza King (1955) and Coffee Creek (1955) 15' quadrangles.

Eagle Creek Benches [TRINITY]: *relief feature,* 4.5 miles north of Billys Peak (1) (lat. 41°12'10" N, long. 122°46'30" W; sec. 33, 34, T 39 N, R 8 W); the feature is on the south side of Eagle Creek (3). Named on Coffee Creek (1955) 15' quadrangle.

Eagle Creek Campground [TRINITY]: *locality,* 10 miles north of Trinity Center along Trinity River (lat. 41°09'05" N, long. 122°40'05" W; at E line sec. 16, T 38 N, R 7 W); the place is at the mouth of Eagle Creek (3). Named on Bonanza King (1955) 15' quadrangle.

Eagle Peak [MENDOCINO]: *peak,* 9 miles south of Willits (lat. 39°16'45" N, long. 123°19'50" W; near SW cor. sec. 32, T 17 N, R 13 W). Altitude 2699 feet. Named on Willits (1961) 15' quadrangle.

Eagle Peak [TRINITY]: *peak,* 18 miles south-southeast of Etna, which is in Siskiyou County, on Trinity-Siskiyou County line (lat. 41°12'15" N, long. 122°48' W; at N line sec. 32, T 39 N, R 8 W). Altitude 7789 feet. Named on Coffee Creek (1955) 15' quadrangle.

Eagle Point [HUMBOLDT]: *peak,* 5 miles southeast of Weott (lat. 40°16'35" N, long. 123°51'20" W; near E line sec. 20, T 2 S, R 3 E). Named on Myers Flat (1969) 7.5' quadrangle.

Eagle Prairie: see **Rio Dell** [HUMBOLDT].

Eagle Rock [HUMBOLDT]: *relief feature,* 3.5 miles south of Coyote Peak (lat. 41°04'25" N, long. 123°57'10" W; sec. 17, T 8 N, R 3 E). Named on Hupa Mountain (1982) 7.5' quadrangle. Called Buck Rock on Coyote Peak (1945) 15' quadrangle.

Eagle Rock [MENDOCINO]: *peak,* 11 miles north-northeast of Boonville (lat. 39°09'40" N, long. 123°17'50" W; sec. 16, T 15 N, R 13 W). Named on Boonville (1959) 15' quadrangle.

Eagle Rock [TRINITY]: *relief feature,* 11.5 miles northeast of Hyampom (lat. 40°45' N, long. 123°19'25" W; near W line sec. 6, T 4 N, R 8 E). Named on Hyampom (1951) 15' quadrangle.

Eaglewood: see **Englewood** [HUMBOLDT].

Earl: see **Lake Earl** [DEL NORTE].

East: see **Dan East Creek** [HUMBOLDT].

East Creek [HUMBOLDT-TRINITY]: *stream,* heads in Trinity County and flows 3.5 miles to Pilot Creek 7 miles east-southeast of Showers Mountain in Humboldt County (lat. 40°32'35" N, long. 123°34'15" W; near NE cor. sec. 23, T 2 N, R 5 E). Named on Blake Mountain (1979) 7.5' quadrangle.

East End [MENDOCINO]: *relief feature,* 6 miles west of Ornbaun Valley (lat. 38°55'30" N, long. 123°24'40" W; sec. 3, T 12 N, R 14 W). Named on Ornbaun Valley (1960) 15' quadrangle.

East End Creek [MENDOCINO]: *stream,* flows 1 mile to Garcia River 7.5 miles west of Ornbaun Valley (lat. 38°54'40" N, long. 123°24'35" W; sec. 3, T 12 N, R 14 W). Named on Ornbaun Valley (1960) 15' quadrangle.

East Fork Campground [HUMBOLDT]: *locality,* 4.5 miles west-southwest of the settlement of Willow Creek (lat. 40°54'25" N, long. 123°42'20" W; sec. 15, T 6 N, R 4 E); the place is at the mouth of East Fork Willow Creek (1). Named on Willow Creek (1952) 15' quadrangle.

East Fork Lakes [TRINITY]: *lakes,* largest 400 feet long, 8.5 miles north-northwest of Weaverville (lat. 40°51' N, long. 122°58'20" W); the lakes are near the head of Big East Fork Canyon Creek (1). Named on Trinity Dam (1950) 15' quadrangle.

East Glade [LAKE]: *area,* 13 miles north-northeast of Clearlake Oaks (lat. 39°12'05" N, long. 122°35'30" W). Named on Clearlake Oaks (1960) 15' quadrangle.

East Hayshed Creek [TRINITY]: *stream,* flows 3 miles to Hayshed Creek 7.5 miles northeast of Hyampom (lat. 40°42'10" N, long. 123°21'35" W; near SW cor. sec. 23, T 4 N, R 7 E). Named on Hyampom (1951) 15' quadrangle.

East Hopland: see **Old Hopland**, under **Hopland** [MENDOCINO].

East Lake: see **Clear Lake** [LAKE].

Eastlake: see **Sulphur Bank** [LAKE].

East Lake Slough: see **Eel River** [HUMBOLDT].

Eastman Creek [MENDOCINO]: *stream,* flows 3 miles to Middle Fork Eel River 1.5 miles east-southeast of Dos Rios (lat. 39°42'30" N, long. 123°19'55" W; sec. 5, T 21 N, R 13 W). Named on Dos Rios (1967) 7.5' quadrangle.

Eastman Gulch [TRINITY]: *canyon,* drained by a stream that flows 4.25 miles to Trinity River 8.5 miles east of Weaverville (lat. 40°45'15" N, long. 122°46'45" W; at S line sec. 33, T 34 N, R 8 W). Named on Schell Mountain (1950) and Trinity Dam (1950) 15' quadrangles. The name recalls Charles Eastman, who acquired land in the neighborhood (Jones, p. 272). South Fork branches south 2.25 miles upstream from the mouth of the main canyon; it is 1.5 miles long and is named on Schell Mountain (1950) 15' quadrangle, and on French Gulch (1979) 7.5' quadrangle. Gudde (1975, p. 42-43) listed a mining place called Bolt Diggings that was situated along Trinity River opposite the mouth of Eastman Gulch.

East Peak: see **Wright Peak** [LAKE].

East Point [HUMBOLDT]: *peak,* 7 miles southwest of Scotia (lat. 40°24'55" N, long. 124°12'25" W; sec. 5, T 1 S, R 1 W). Altitude 2660 feet. Named on Taylor Peak (1969) 7.5' quadrangle.

East Ridge [TRINITY]: *ridge,* southeast-trending, 1.5 miles long, 9 miles south-southwest of Black Rock Mountain (lat. 40°05' N, long. 123°03'45" W). Named on Black Rock Mountain (1954) 15' quadrangle.

East Rock [DEL NORTE]: *rock,* 6 miles northwest of Crescent City, and 3 miles off Point Saint George (lat. 41°48'40" N, long. 124°18' W). Named on Eureka (1958) 1° x 2° quadrangle.

East Sunnyside: see **Pine Hill** [HUMBOLDT].

East Tule Creek [TRINITY]: *stream,* flows 4 miles to Tule Creek 3.25 miles southwest of Hayfork (lat. 40°31'10" N, long. 123°13'40" W; sec. 21, T 31 N, R 12 W). Named on Dubakella Mountain (1954) and Hayfork (1951) 15' quadrangles.

East Valdor Gulch [TRINITY]: *canyon,* 1.5 miles long, joins West Valdor Gulch 2.25 miles east of Helena (lat. 40°46'10" N, long. 123°05' W; near SW cor. sec. 26, T 34 N, R 11 W). Named on Helena (1951) 15' quadrangle.

East Weaver Balley: see **Monument Peak** [TRINITY] (1).

East Weaver Creek [TRINITY]: *stream,* flows 9.5 miles to join West Weaver Creek and form Weaver Creek less than 1 mile south of the center of Weaverville (lat. 40°43'20" N, long. 122°56'20" W; near NW cor. sec. 18, T 33 N, R 9 W). Named on Trinity Dam (1950) and Weaverville (1950) 15' quadrangles. Called East Fork Weaver Creek on Weaverville (1913) 30' quadrangle. East Branch of East Weaver Creek enters 3 miles north-northeast of Weaverville; it is 4 miles long and is named on Trinity Dam (1950) 15' quadrangle.

East Weaver Lake [TRINITY]: *lake,* 350 feet long, 6.5 miles north-northwest of Weaverville (lat. 40°48'50" N, long. 122°59'05" W); the lake is at the head of a branch of East Weaver Creek. Named on Trinity Dam (1950) 15' quadrangle.

Eaton H. Magoon Lake: see **Upper Bohn Lake** [LAKE].

Eaton Prairie [HUMBOLDT]: *area,* 5 miles south-southeast of Showers Mountain (lat. 40°30'45" N, long. 123°39'50" W; on E line sec. 36, T 2 N, R 4 E). Named on Showers Mountain (1978) 7.5' quadrangle.

Eaton Roughs [HUMBOLDT]: *relief feature,* 3.25 miles south-southeast of Showers Mountain (lat. 40°32' N, long. 123°40'30" W; sec. 24, 25, T 2 N, R 4 E). Named on Showers Mountain (1978) 7.5' quadrangle. The name commemorates George Eaton, a homesteader of the 1860's who ran cattle at the place (Turner, p. 68).

Eberle Flat: see **Eberly Flat** [MENDOCINO].

Eberle Ridge: see **Eberly Ridge** [MENDOCINO].

Eberly Flat [MENDOCINO]: *area,* 5 miles north-northwest of Covelo (lat. 39°51'55" N, long. 123°16'15" W; sec. 11, T 23 N, R 13 W). Named on Covelo West (1967) 7.5' quadrangle. United States Board on Geographic Names (1991, p. 4) approved the form "Eberle Flat" for the name, which commemorates Charles Eberle, who arrived in the neighborhood in 1857.

Eberly Ridge [MENDOCINO]: *ridge,* generally west-trending, 2.5 miles long, 6.25 miles west of Covelo (lat. 39°46'35" N, long. 123°21'40" W). Named on Covelo West (1967) and Iron Peak (1967) 7.5' quadrangles. United States Board on Geographic Names (1991, p. 4) approved the form "Eberle Ridge" for the name.

Echo: see **Hopland** [MENDOCINO].

Echo Flat [TRINITY]: *area,* 12.5 miles north-northeast of Weaverville (lat. 40°53'15" N, long. 122°49'30" W; on E line sec. 13, T 35 N, R 9 W). Named on Trinity Dam (1950) 15' quadrangle.

Echo Lake [TRINITY]: *lake,* 650 feet long, 14 miles north of Weaverville (lat. 40°55'10" N, long. 122°52'55" W). Named on Trinity Dam (1950) 15' quadrangle.

Eddy Mountain: see **Mount Eddy** [TRINITY].

Eddys: see **The Eddys** [TRINITY].

Eddyville [HUMBOLDT]: *locality,* 6.5 miles south of Arcata (lat. 40°46'45" N, long. 124°04'30" W; at N line sec. 33, T 5 N, R 1 E). Named on Eureka (1942) 15' quadrangle. The place was the original lumber camp of Pacific Lumber Company when the company began logging in 1916 (Carranco and Sorensen, p. 147).

Eden: see **Eden Valley** [MENDOCINO].

Eden Creek [MENDOCINO]: *stream,* flows about 11.5 miles to Elk Creek (2) 4 miles east-northeast of Eden Valley (lat. 39°39'25" N, long. 123°07'25" W; near S line sec. 19, T 21 N, R 11 W); the stream goes through Eden Valley. Named on Brushy Mountain (1966) and Jamison Ridge (1967) 7.5' quadrangles.

Eden Valley [MENDOCINO]: *valley,* 17 miles north-northeast of Willits (lat. 39°37'35" N, long. 123°11' W). Named on Brushy Mountain (1966) and Jamison Ridge (1967) 7.5' quadrangles. Pierce Asbill named the place in 1854 for its fancied resemblance to the biblical Eden (Keller, p. 2). Postal authorities established Eden post office 26 miles north of Willits in 1880 and discontinued it in 1881 (Salley, p. 65).

Edgar Spring [HUMBOLDT]: *spring,* 5.25 miles east-southeast of Showers Mountain (lat. 40°33'45" N, long. 123°36' W; near SW cor. sec. 10, T 2 N, R 5 E). Named on Blake Mountain (1979) 7.5' quadrangle.

Edwards Creek [MENDOCINO]: *stream,* flows 4 miles to Russian River

8.5 miles south-southeast of Hopland (lat. 38°51'55" N, long. 123°02'30" W; near NE cor. sec. 25, T 12 N, R 11 W). Named on Cloverdale (1960) 7.5' quadrangle.

Eel River [HUMBOLDT-LAKE-MENDOCINO-TRINITY]: *stream,* heads in Mendocino County and flows about 175 miles in Humboldt, Lake, Mendocino, and Trinity Counties to the sea 4.5 miles northwest of Ferndale (lat. 49°37'35" N, long. 124°19'05" W). Named on Eureka (1958), Redding (1958), and Ukiah (1957) 1° x 2° quadrangles. The part of the river upstream from the mouth of Middle Fork is called South Eel River on Hullville (1922), Laytonville (1919), and Pomo (1943) 15' quadrangles. According to United States Board on Geographic Names (1933, p. 283), extending the name "Eel River" to the source of the longest branch eliminates the name "South Eel River," and also removes the confusion arising from the proximity of South Fork Eel River to a stream called South Eel River. Rogers and Johnston's (1857) map has the designation "Mendocino or Eel R." for the stream. On Ferndale (1943) 15' quadrangle, Eel River is shown passing north of Cock Robin Island, and present Eel River, which is situated south of the island, is called East Lake Slough—Cape Fortunas (1920) 15' quadrangle has the form "Eastlake Slough" for the name. Members of the Gregg party named Eel River in 1849 after they had lived for several days on eels obtained from Indians there (Bledsoe, p. 42). When the *General Morgan* anchored off the mouth of Eel River in 1850, Samuel Brannan and his brother John were in charge of two boats that entered present Eel River, which the brothers named Brannan River (Coy, 1929, p. 47). Middle Fork Eel River heads in Trinity County and flows about 60 miles to join the main stream from the east near Dos Rios; it is named on Redding (1958) and Ukiah (1957) 1° x 2° quadrangles. North Fork of Middle Fork enters Middle Fork from the northwest 13 miles south-southwest of Black Rock Mountain; it is 11.5 miles long and is named on Black Rock Mountain (1954) 15' quadrangle. United States Board on Geographic Names (1933, p. 517) rejected the name "North Fork of Middle Fork Eel River" for present Middle Fork Eel River. North Fork Eel River is formed by the confluence of its East Fork and West Fork in Trinity County, and flows 33 miles to join the main stream near Ramsey; it is named on Redding (1958) and Ukiah (1957) 1° x 2° quadrangles. United States Board on Geographic Names (1933, p. 559) rejected the name "South Fork of Middle Fork Eel River" for present North Fork Eel River, and (p. 148) for present Black Butte River; later the Board (1969a, p. 4) rejected the name "East Branch of North Fork of Eel River" for present North Fork. East Fork of North Fork is 3 miles long and is named on Zenia (1967) 7.5' quadrangle. Present East Fork of North Fork is called East Branch on Island Mountain (1922) 15' quadrangle, but United States Board on Geographic Names (1969a, p. 2) rejected the names "East Branch of North Fork of Eel River" and "North Fork Eel River" for present East Fork of North Fork Eel River. West Fork of North Fork Eel River is formed by the confluence of Bar Creek and Panther Creek (4); it is 4 miles long and is named on Zenia (1967) 7.5' quadrangle. Present West Fork of North Fork Eel River is called West Branch on Island Mountain (1922) 15' quadrangle, but United States Board on Geographic Names (1969a, p. 4-5) rejected the names "North Fork Eel River," "West Branch of North Fork of Eel River," and "West Fork of North Fork Eel River" for the stream. South Fork Eel River heads in Mendocino County and joins the main stream from the south near the community of South Fork [HUMBOLDT]; it is 85 miles long and is named on Redding (1958) and Ukiah (1957) 1° x 2° quadrangles. Present South Fork is called Kelsey's R. on Eddy's (1854) map. East Branch of South Fork Eel River, which is formed by the confluence of Cruso Cabin Creek and Elkhorn Creek (1) in Mendocino County, joins South Fork from the east near Benbow; it is 20 miles long and is named on Ukiah (1957) 1° x 2° quadrangle.

Eel River: see **Rohnerville** [HUMBOLDT].

Eel Rock [HUMBOLDT]: *village,* 5 miles west of Blocksburg (lat. 40°17'15" N, long. 123°43'50" W; sec. 16, T 2 S, R 4 E); the place is along Eel River. Named on Blocksburg (1969) 7.5' quadrangle. Postal authorities established Eel Rock post office in 1915 and discontinued it in 1960; the name was for a landmark in Eel River (Salley, p. 66).

Eighteen Creek [HUMBOLDT]: *stream,* flows 1 mile to Luffenholtz Creek 3 miles east of Trinidad (lat. 41°02'55" N, long. 124°05'10" W; sec. 29, T 8 N, R 1 E). Named on Crannell (1966) 7.5' quadrangle.

Eighteenmile Creek [DEL NORTE]: *stream,* flows 3.25 miles to Middle Fork Smith River 3.5 miles east of Gasquet (lat. 41°50'45" N, long. 123°55'15" W; sec. 23, T 17 N, R 2 E). Named on Gasquet (1951) 15' quadrangle.

Eightmile Camp [TRINITY]: *locality,* 1.5 miles south-southwest of Salmon Mountain (lat. 41°09'45" N, long. 123°25'30" W); the place is near the head of a branch of Eightmile Creek. Named on Salmon Mountain (1955) 15' quadrangle.

Eightmile Creek [DEL NORTE]: *stream,* flows 7.5 miles to South Fork Smith River 3 miles east-northeast of Buck Mountain (lat. 41°38'35" N, long. 123°48'30" W). Named on Chimney Rock (1981), Ship Mountain (1982), and Summit Valley (1981) 7.5' quadrangles.

Eightmile Creek [TRINITY]: *stream,* flows 6.5 miles to Virgin Creek 6 miles south of Salmon Mountain (lat. 41°05'50" N, long. 123°23'35" W). Named on Salmon Mountain (1978) and Trinity Mountain (1979) 7.5' quadrangles.

Eightmile Glade [LAKE]: *area,* 6.5 miles west-northwest of Lakeport (lat. 39°04'45" N, long. 123°01'55" W; on S line sec. 11, T 14 N, R 11 W). Named on Purdys Gardens (1958) 7.5' quadrangle.

Eightmile Ridge [HUMBOLDT-TRINITY]: *ridge,* generally west-trending, 6 miles long, center 8 miles east-southeast of Showers Mountain on Humboldt-Trinity County line (lat. 40°31'30" N, long. 123°34' W). Named on Blake Mountain (1979) 7.5' quadrangle.

Eightmile Ridge [LAKE]: *ridge,* generally east-trending, 1.5 miles long, 9 miles west-northwest of Lakeport (lat. 39°04'40" N, long. 123°04'45" W; sec. 16, 17, T 14 N, R 11 W). Named on Purdys Gardens (1958) 7.5' quadrangle.

Eightmile Valley [LAKE]: *valley,* 9 miles west-northwest of Lake port (lat. 39°05'20" N, long. 123°04'25" W; sec. 9, T 14 N, R 11 W); the valley is north of Eightmile Ridge. Named on Purdys Gardens (1958) 7.5' quadrangle.

Elam Creek [HUMBOLDT]: *stream,* flows 2.5 miles to Redwood Creek (1) 2.5 miles southwest of Orick (lat. 41°15'50" N, long. 124°01'30" W; sec. 11, T 10 N, R 1 E). Named on Orick (1966) and Rodgers Peak (1966) 7.5' quadrangles.

Elder [HUMBOLDT]: *locality,* 11 miles west-southwest of Weitchpec (lat. 41°08'10" N, long. 123°44'55" W). Named on Hoopa (1935) 30' quadrangle. Postal authorities established Elder post office in 1893, moved it 2.5 miles north in 1909, and discontinued it in 1913; the name was for elder trees at the site (Salley, p. 66).

Elderberry Duff [TRINITY]: *relief feature,* 18 miles north of Weaverville (lat. 40°59'05" N, long. 122°52' W; near N line sec. 14, T 36 N, R 9 W). Named on Trinity Dam (1950) 15' quadrangle.

Elder Creek [MENDOCINO]: *stream,* flows 4.5 miles to South Fork Eel River 5.25 miles north-northwest of Branscomb (lat. 39°43'45" N, long. 123°38'50" W; sec. 29, T 22 N, R 16 W). Named on Cahto Peak (1967) and Lincoln Ridge (1966) 7.5' quadrangles.

Eldridge Creek [MENDOCINO]: *stream,* flows 5.25 miles to join Jack Smith Creek and form Seward Creek 11.5 miles south-southeast of Willits (lat. 39°15'40" N, long. 127°15'50" W; sec. 11, T 16 N, R 13 W). Named on Boonville (1959) and Willits (1961) 15' quadrangles. On Willits (1942) 15' quadrangle, present Jack Smith Creek is called Seward Creek.

Eleanor Lake: see **Lake Eleanor** [TRINITY].

Election Camp [TRINITY]: *locality,* 7.5 miles southwest of Cecilville, which is in Siskiyou County (lat. 41°04'15" N, long. 123°14'15" W). Site named on Cecil Lake (1979) 7.5' quadrangle.

Election Gap [TRINITY]: *pass,* 7.25 miles southwest of Cecilville, which is in Siskiyou County, on Trinity-Siskiyou County line (lat. 41°04'35" N, long. 123°14'15" W); the pass is near the site of Election Camp. Named on Cecil Lake (1979) 7.5' quadrangle.

Elevenmile Creek [DEL NORTE]: *stream,* flows 1.25 miles to Patrick Creek 7 miles northeast of Gasquet (lat. 41°54'05" N, long. 123°51'15" W; sec. 5, T 17 N, R 3 E). Named on Shelly Creek Ridge (1982) 7.5' quadrangle.

Elinor [HUMBOLDT]: *locality,* 5 miles east-southeast of Scotia on the south side of Eel River (lat. 40°27' N, long. 124°01' W; sec. 24, T 1 N, R 1 E). Named on Scotia (1950) 15' quadrangle. Called Camp Five on Eureka (1949) 1° x 2° quadrangle. Glynn (1919) 15' quadrangle shows Elinor situated across the river to the west of Camp Five at present Elinor Flat. Postal authorities established Elinor post office in 1906 and discontinued it in 1914 (Frickstad, p. 42).

Elinor Flat [HUMBOLDT]: *area,* 4 miles east-southeast of Scotia on the north side of Eel River (lat. 40°27'10" N, long. 124°02'05" W; sec. 23, T 1 N, R 1 E). Named on Scotia (1970) 7.5' quadrangle.

Elinor Junction [HUMBOLDT]: *locality,* 4.25 miles east-southeast of Scotia along Northwestern Pacific Railroad (lat. 40°27'10" N, long. 124°02' W; sec. 23, T 1 N, R 1 E); the place is at present Elinor Flat, where a rail line branches to Elinor. Named on Scotia (1950) 15' quadrangle.

Elk [MENDOCINO]: *village,* 22 miles south of Fort Bragg (lat. 39°07'50" N, long. 123°43' W; sec. 26, T 15 N, R 17 W). Named on Elk (1960) 7.5' quadrangle. Postal authorities established Elk post office in 1887 (Frickstad, p. 94) at a community called Greenwood (Hoover, Rensch, and Rensch, p. 198). The name "Greenwood" was for five Greenwood brothers who came to the site in 1851 (Landsman, 1977b, p. 74). California Mining Bureau's (1909c) map shows a place called Salsig located southeast of Elk at the end of a stage line, and California Mining Bureau's (1917c) map shows a place called Manzanita situated along a railroad about 10 miles southeast of Elk. Postal authorities established Salsig post office in 1904, changed the name to Manzanita in 1912, and discontinued it in 1915; the name "Salsig" was for Edgar Budd Salsig and Company—the firm had lumber mills in the neighborhood (Salley, p. 132, 192.)

Elk Camp [DEL NORTE]: *locality,* 9 miles north-northeast of Gasquet (lat. 41°57'10" N, long. 123°52'30" W; sec. 18, T 18 N, R 3 E). Named on Gasquet (1951) 15' quadrangle.

Elk Camp [HUMBOLDT]: *locality,* 8 miles northwest of Coyote Peak (lat. 41°13'20" N, long. 123°57'30" W; at S line sec. 28, T 10 N, R 2 E). Named on Bald Hills (1982) 7.5' quadrangle. The name is from a natural salt lick used by elk (Turner, p. 72).

Elk Camp Ridge [DEL NORTE]: *ridge,* south- to west-trending, 9.5 miles long, center 5 miles northeast of Gasquet (lat. 41°53'30" N, long. 123°53'30" W); Elk Camp is at the north end of the ridge. Named on Gasquet (1951) 15' quadrangle.

Elk Canyon [LAKE]: *canyon,* 2 miles long, along Cooper Creek above a point 5.25 miles northwest of the town of Upper Lake (lat. 39°12'25" N, long. 122°59'15" W; sec. 29, T 16 N, R 10 W). Named on Upper Lake (1958) 7.5' quadrangle.

Elk Creek [DEL NORTE]:

(1) *stream,* flows nearly 4 miles to the sea at Crescent City (lat. 41°45'10" N, long. 124°11'25" W; sec. 28, T 16 N, R 1 W); the stream drains Elk Valley (1). Named on Crescent City (1966) 7.5' quadrangle.

(2) *stream,* flows 5.5 miles to the State of Oregon 7.5 miles north of Broken Rib Mountain (lat. 41°59'20" N, long. 123°43'05" W; near W line sec. 35, T 19 N, R 4 E). Named on Broken Rib Mountain (1982) 7.5' quadrangle.

Elk Creek [HUMBOLDT]: *stream,* flows 5.25 miles to South Fork Eel River 5 miles southeast of Weott (lat. 40°16'40" N, long. 123°51'10" W; near W line sec. 21, T 2 S, R 3 E). Named on Myers Flat (1969) 7.5' quadrangle.

Elk Creek [MENDOCINO]:

(1) *stream,* flows 3.5 miles to Redwood Creek (2) 7 miles east-southeast of Leggett (lat. 39°49'35" N, long. 123°35'30" W; sec. 23, T 23 N, R 16 W). Named on Tan Oak Park (1969) 7.5' quadrangle.

(2) *stream,* flows 16 miles to Middle Fork Eel River 4.25 miles northeast of Eden Valley (lat. 39°40'35" N, long. 123°08' W; near W line sec. 18, T 21 N, R 11 W). Named on Hull Mountain (1967), Jamison Ridge (1967), Sanhedrin Mountain (1966), and Thatcher Ridge (1967) 7.5' quadrangles.

(3) *stream,* flows 1.5 miles to String Creek 5.5 miles north-northeast of Willits (lat. 39°28'45" N, long. 123°18' W; near SE cor. sec. 21, T 19 N, R 13 W). Named on Willits (1961) 15' quadrangle. North Fork enters from the north nearly 1 mile upstream from the mouth of the main creek; it is 0.5 mile long and is named on Willits (1961) 15' quadrangle.

(4) *stream,* flows 12.5 miles to the sea 2 miles south-southeast of Elk (lat. 39°06'10" N, long. 123°42'25" W; sec. 2, T 14 N, R 17 W). Named on Navarro (1961) 15' quadrangle. Present Three Springs Creek is called North Fork [Elk Creek] on Navarro (1943) 15' quadrangle.

Elk Grove [HUMBOLDT]: *locality,* 6 miles north-northeast of Orick (lat. 41°21'55" N, long. 124°01'10" W; sec. 2, T 11 N, R 1 E); the place is at present Elk Prairie (1). Named on Orick (1952) 15' quadrangle.

Elk Gulch [TRINITY]: *canyon,* drained by a stream that flows 2.5 miles to Stuart Fork 9.5 miles north of Weaverville (lat. 40°51'45" N, long. 122°54'10" W; at W line sec. 28, T 35 N, R 9 W). Named on Trinity Dam (1950) 15' quadrangle.

Elk Head [HUMBOLDT]: *promontory,* 1 mile northwest of Trinidad along the coast (lat. 41°04'05" N, long. 124°09'25" W; sec. 22, T 8 N, R 1 W). Named on Trinidad (1966) 7.5' quadrangle.

Elkhorn Bar [DEL NORTE]: *locality,* 2.5 miles east-northeast of Buck Mountain along South Fork Smith River (lat. 41°39' N, long. 123°49' W). Named on Ship Mountain (1982) 7.5' quadrangle.

Elkhorn Creek [MENDOCINO]:

(1) *stream,* flows 3 miles to join Cruso Cabin Creek and form East Branch of South Fork Eel River 7 miles northeast of Leggett (lat. 39°56'10" N, long. 123°37'10" W; near SW cor. sec. 10, T 24 N, R 16 W). Named on Bell Springs (1969) and Noble Butte (1969) 7.5' quadrangles.

(2) *stream,* flows 1.5 miles to Dry Creek (2) 7.25 miles southwest of Hopland (lat. 38°53'35" N, long. 123°12'05" W). Named on Hopland (1960) 15' quadrangle.

Elkhorn Gulch [MENDOCINO]: *canyon,* drained by a stream that flows nearly 1 mile to South Branch of North Fork Navarro River 1.5 miles northeast of Navarro (lat. 39°09'50" N, long. 123°31'10" W; sec. 16, T 15 N, R 15 W). Named on Navarro (1961) 15' quadrangle.

Elkhorn Ridge [MENDOCINO]: *ridge,* generally north-trending, 6.5 miles long, center about 7 miles south-southeast of Leggett (lat. 39°46'15" N, long. 123°40'35" W). Named on Leggett (1969) and Lincoln Ridge (1966) 7.5' quadrangles.

Elkins Creek [MENDOCINO]: *stream,* flows 1.25 miles to Rancheria Creek (2) 1 mile north of Ornbaun Valley (lat. 38°55'45" N, long. 123°18'10" W; sec. 4, T 12 N, R 13 W). Named on Ornbaun Valley (1960) 15' quadrangle.

Elk Knob [LAKE]: *peak,* 5.25 miles north-northeast of the town of Upper Lake (lat. 39°14' N, long. 122°51'35" W); the peak is south of Elk Valley. Named on Bartlett Mountain (1958) 7.5' quadrangle.

Elk Lake [DEL NORTE]: *lake,* 300 feet long, 9 miles south-southwest of Broken Rib Mountain (lat. 41°46' N, long. 123°44'55" W). Named on Devils Punchbowl (1981) 7.5' quadrangle.

Elk Mountain [HUMBOLDT]: *peak,* 9 miles east-southeast of Weott (lat. 40°15'40" N, long. 123°46'20" W; sec. 30, T 2 S, R 4 E). Altitude 2600 feet. Named on Myers Flat (1969) 7.5' quadrangle.

Elk Mountain [LAKE]: *ridge,* southwest-trending, 1 mile long, 2.5 miles south-southwest of Three Crossings (lat. 39°16'55" N, long. 122°56'10" W; mainly in sec. 36, T 17 N, R 10 W). Named on Elk Mountain (1967) 7.5' quadrangle.

Elk Prairie [HUMBOLDT]:

(1) *area,* 5.5 miles north-northeast of Orick along Prairie Creek (lat. 41°21'35" N, long. 124°01'25" W; sec. 2, 11, T 11 N, R 1 E). Named on Orick (1966) 7.5' quadrangle.

(2) *area,* 8 miles north-northeast of the town of Blue Lake (lat. 40°58'50" N, long. 123°54'10" W; near NW cor. sec. 24, T 7 N, R 2 E). Named on Blue Lake (1979) 7.5' quadrangle.

(3) *area,* 6.5 miles east-southeast of Weott (lat. 40°17'20" N, long. 123°48'35" W; mainly in sec. 14, T 2 S, R 3 E). Named on Myers Flat (1969) 7.5' quadrangle.

Elk Prairie [MENDOCINO]: *area,* 2.25 miles northeast of Gualala along North Fork Gualala River (lat. 38°47'35" N, long. 123°30'10" W; on N line sec. 23, T 11 N, R 15 W). Named on Gualala (1960) 7.5' quadrangle.

Elk Prairie: see **Fruitland** [HUMBOLDT].

Elk Range [MENDOCINO]: *ridge,* south-southwest-trending, 1.5 miles long, 9.5 miles south-southwest of Hopland (lat. 38°50'45" N, long. 123°09'50" W; mainly in sec. 35, T 12 N, R 12 W). Named on Hopland (1960) 15' quadrangle.

Elk Ridge [HUMBOLDT]: *ridge,* north-northwest- to west-trending, 2.5 miles long, 8.5 miles west of Phillipsville (lat. 40°13' N, long. 123°56'30" W). Named on Ettersburg (1969) 7.5' quadrangle.

Elk River [HUMBOLDT]:

(1) *stream,* formed by the confluence of North Fork and South Fork, flows 9.5 miles to Humboldt Bay 3 miles southwest of downtown Eureka (lat. 40°46'15" N, long. 124°11'45" W). Named on Eureka (1958) and Fields Landing (1959) 7.5' quadrangles. The Gregg party camped at the site of Arcata in 1849 and named Elk River after they had a Christmas diner of elk meat (Bancroft, p. 502). North Fork is 15 miles long and is named on Fields Landing (1959), Iaqua Buttes (1979), and McWhinney Creek (1979) 7.5' quadrangles. South Fork is 10 miles long and is named on Fields Landing (1959) and McWhinney Creek (1979) 7.5' quadrangles. North Branch of North Fork enters North Fork 10 miles east-southeast of Fields Landing; it is nearly 3 miles long and is named on Iaqua Buttes (1979) and McWhinney Creek (1979) 7.5' quadrangles. United States Board on Geographic Names (1962b, p. 19) rejected the name "North Fork Elk River" for present North Branch of North Fork Elk River. South Branch of North Fork Elk River enters North Fork from the southeast 10 miles east-southeast of Fields Landing; it is 1.5 miles long and is named on McWhinney Creek (1979) 7.5' quadrangle. Little North Fork enters North Branch of North Fork Elk River from the north-northeast 1 mile upstream from the mouth of North Branch; it is less than 1 mile long and is named on McWhinney Creek (1979) 7.5' quadrangle. Little South Fork Elk River enters South Fork Elk River from the southeast 7.25 miles east-southeast of Fields Landing; it is 3.5 miles long and is named on McWhinney Creek (1979) 7.5' quadrangle.

(2) *settlement,* 2.25 miles east-northeast of Fields Landing (lat. 40°44'10" N, long. 124°10' W; near NW cor. sec. 15, T 4 N, R 1 W); the place is near Elk River (1). Named on Fields Landing (1959) 7.5' quadrangle.

Elk River Corners [HUMBOLDT]: *locality,* 3.5 miles south-southwest of downtown Eureka (lat. 40°45'10" N, long. 124°11'05" W; near S line sec. 4, T 4 N, R 1 W); the place is near Elk River (1). Named on Eureka (1958) 7.5' quadrangle.

Elk Valley [DEL NORTE]:

(1) *valley,* extends for about 4 miles northeast from Crescent City (center near lat. 41°46'30" N, long. 124°10' W); Elk Creek (1) drains the valley. Named on Crescent City (1966) 7.5' quadrangle. A group of travelers passed through the valley in 1852 and named it for large herds of elk seen there (Bledsoe, p. 69). A military post called Camp Lincoln was established 5 miles northeast of Crescent City in Elk Valley in 1862 and abandoned in 1870 (Hoover, Rensch, and Rensch, p. 72). The post also was referred to as Fort Lincoln, Lincoln's Fort, Camp Long, and Long's Fort (Whiting and Whiting, p. 40). The post was intended to protect settlers from marauding Indians (Palais, p. 52).

(2) *valley,* 7.25 miles north of Broken Rib Mountain (lat. 41°59'35" N, long. 123°42'55" W); the place is along Elk Creek (2) at California-Oregon State line. Named on Broken Rib Mountain (1982) 7.5' quadrangle.

(3) *valley,* 2 miles south-southeast of Sawtooth Mountain near the head of Blue Creek (lat. 41°35'15" N, long. 123°41'30" W). Named on Chimney Rock (1981) 7.5' quadrangle.

Elk Valley [LAKE]: *valley,* 5.5 miles north-northeast of the town of Upper Lake (lat. 39°14'10" N, long. 122°51'40" W); the valley is north of Elk Knob. Named on Bartlett Mountain (1958) 7.5' quadrangle.

Elledge Peak [MENDOCINO]: *peak,* 7.5 miles south of Ukiah (lat. 39°02'30" N, long. 123°13'45" W; near W line sec. 30, T 14 N, R 12 W). Altitude 2765 feet. Named on Elledge Peak (1958) 7.5' quadrangle.

Ellington Gulch [HUMBOLDT]: *canyon,* drained by a stream that flows 1 mile to Van Duzen River 4 miles south-southwest of Showers Mountain (lat. 40°31'45" N, long. 123°44' W; at N line sec. 28, T 2 N, R 4 E). Named on Showers Mountain (1978) 7.5' quadrangle.

Elliott Springs: see **Highland Springs** [LAKE].

Ellis Creek [MENDOCINO]: *stream,* flows 3.5 miles to Elk Creek (2) 4 miles east of Eden Valley (lat. 39°37'15" N, long. 123°06'25" W). Named on Brushy Mountain (1966) and Sanhedrin Mountain (1966) 7.5' quadrangles.

Ellis Flat [LAKE]: *area,* 4.25 miles east-northeast of the town of Upper Lake (lat. 39°11'10" N, long. 122°50'05" W; near W line sec. 2, T 15 N, R 9 W). Named on Bartlett Mountain (1958) 7.5' quadrangle.

Ellison Creek [HUMBOLDT]: *stream,* flows 3 miles to North Fork Yager Creek 2.5 miles east-southeast of Lone Star Junction (lat. 40°36'50" N, long. 123°50'10" W; near E line sec. 28, T 3 N, R 3 E). Named on Mad River Buttes (1977) and Yager Junction (1979) 7.5' quadrangles.

El Roble [MENDOCINO]: *locality,* 4.5 miles south-southeast of Ukiah along Northwestern Pacific Railroad (lat. 39°05'20" N, long. 123°10'50" W). Named on Elledge Peak (1958) 7.5' quadrangle. Called El Roble Siding on Ukiah (1920) 15' quadrangle.

Eltapom Creek [TRINITY]: *stream,* flows 7 miles to South Fork Trinity River 4 miles northwest of Hyampom (lat. 40°39'45" N, long. 123°29'35" W; sec. 3, T 3 N, R 6 E). Named on Hyampom (1951) 15' quadrangle. The name is of Indian origin (Gudde, 1949, p. 107).

Ely Flat [LAKE]: *area,* 7.5 miles west-northwest of the town of Lower Lake (lat. 38°56'55" N, long. 122°44'35" W; mainly in sec. 28, T 13 N, R 8 W). Named on Clearlake Highlands (1958) 7.5' quadrangle.

Ely's: see **Kelseyville** [LAKE].

Emandal Resort [MENDOCINO]: *locality,* 12.5 miles north-northwest of the town of Potter Valley along Eel River (lat. 39°29'30" N, long. 123°10'45" W; sec. 22, T 19 N, R 12 W). Named on Potter Valley (1960) 15' quadrangle.

Emerald Lake [TRINITY]: *lake,* 1900 feet long, 20 miles north of Weaverville (lat. 41°00'20" N, long. 122°59'50" W). Named on Coffee Creek (1955) 15' quadrangle.

Emigrant Creek [TRINITY]: *stream,* flows 2.25 miles to Slide Creek 10 miles southeast of Salmon Mountain (lat. 41°03'55" N, long. 123°18' W). Named on Dees Peak (1978) 7.5' quadrangle.

Empire [MENDOCINO]: *locality,* 7 miles east-southeast of Leggett along South Fork Eel River (lat. 39°49'35" N, long. 123°35'30" W; sec. 23, T 23 N, R 16 W). Named on Leggett (1952) 15' quadrangle.

En Cimo: see **Sylvandale** [MENDOCINO].

Enderts Beach [DEL NORTE]: *beach,* 4.5 miles southeast of Crescent City along the coast (lat. 41°42'05" N, long. 124°08'30" W; sec. 11, 14, T 15 N, R 1 W). Named on Sister Rocks (1966) 7.5' quadrangle. The name commemorates Fred W. Endert of Crescent City (Gudde, 1949, p. 108).

England Springs: see **Highland Springs** [LAKE].

Engle: see **Clair Engle Lake** [TRINITY].

Englevale: see **Englewood** [HUMBOLDT].

Englewood [HUMBOLDT]: *settlement,* 0.5 mile east-southeast of Redcrest (lat. 40°23'50" N, long. 123°56'20" W; sec. 10, T 1 S, R 2 E). Named on Redcrest (1969) 7.5' quadrangle. Called Eaglewood on Vander Leck's (1920b) map. Postal authorities established Englewood post office in 1880, discontinued it in 1891, reestablished it with the name "Englevale" in 1893, and discontinued it in 1894 (Salley, p. 70).

Englewood: see **Holmes Flat** [HUMBOLDT].

English Ridge [MENDOCINO]: *ridge,* south-trending, 1.5 miles long, 6.25 miles south-southwest of Eden Valley (lat. 39°32'45" N, long. 123°14' W). Named on Brushy Mountain (1966) 7.5' quadrangle.

Enni Camp [TRINITY]: *locality,* 15 miles north of Helena along Rattlesnake Creek (1) (lat. 40°59'05" N, long. 123°05' W). Named on Helena (1951) 15' quadrangle. United States Board on Geographic Names (1984a, p. 3) approved the name "Enos Camp" for the place, and noted that the name reportedly is for Marvin Enos, a former resident and packer in the region.

Enos Camp: see **Enni Camp** [TRINITY].

Enquist Creek [HUMBOLDT]: *stream,* flows 2 miles to Horse Mountain Creek 7 miles south-southwest of the settlement of Willow Creek (lat. 40°51'05" N, long. 123°41'35" W; near N line sec. 2, T 5 N, R 4 E). Named on Grouse Mountain (1979) 7.5' quadrangle.

Enright Gulch [TRINITY]: *canyon,* drained by a stream that flows 0.5 mile to the canyon of Trinity River 3 miles north of Trinity Center (lat. 41°02'50" N, long. 122°42' W; sec. 20, T 37 N, R 7 W). Named on Bonanza King (1955) 15' quadrangle.

Enterprise [LAKE]: *locality,* 3.5 miles north-northwest of Three Crossings (lat. 39°21'50" N, long. 122°57' W; at S line sec. 35, T 18 N, R 10 W). Named on Elk Mountain (1967) 7.5' quadrangle.

Enterprise: see **Coleridge** [TRINITY].

Ericson Ridge [LAKE]: *ridge,* east-southeast-trending, 4 miles long, 11.5 miles north-northeast of the town of Potter Valley [MENDOCINO] (lat. 39°27'50" N, long. 123°00' W). Named on Lake Pillsbury (1951) and Potter Valley (1960) 15' quadrangles.

Er-Wern Ridge [DEL NORTE]: *ridge,* south- to south-southwest-trending, 3.25 miles long, 3.5 miles north-northeast of the mouth of Klamath River (lat. 41°35'45" N, long. 124°03'05" W). Named on Requa (1966) 7.5' quadrangle.

Espee Ridge [MENDOCINO]: *ridge,* west-trending, 2 miles long, 1.5 miles north of Anthony Peak (lat. 39°52'10" N, long. 122°58'15" W). Named on Mendocino Pass (1967) 7.5' quadrangle.

Essenpries Mill [HUMBOLDT]: *locality,* 2.25 miles northwest of Weitchpec (lat. 41°12'35" N, long. 123°44'20" W). Site named on Weitchpec (1979) 7.5' quadrangle.

Essex [HUMBOLDT]: *locality,* 3.5 miles northeast of Arcata along Mad River (lat. 40°54'25" N, long. 124°02'05" W; sec. 14, T 6 N, R 1 E). Named on Arcata North (1959) 7.5' quadrangle. The place also was known as Glen Essex (Turner, p. 75).

Essex Gulch [HUMBOLDT]: *canyon,* drained by a stream that flows 2 miles to Mad River 3.25 miles northeast of Arcata (lat. 40°54'20" N, long. 124°02'10" W; sec. 14, T 6 N, R 1 E); the mouth of the canyon is at Essex. Named on Arcata North (1959) 7.5' quadrangle.

Essex Pond [HUMBOLDT]: *lake,* 1500 feet long, 4 miles northeast of Arcata (lat. 40°54'40" N, long. 124°01'40" W; on N line sec. 14, T 6 N, R 1 E); the lake is 0.5 mile northeast of Essex. Named on Arcata North (1959) 7.5' quadrangle.

Esther: see **Mount Esther**, under **Harbin Mountain** [LAKE].

Etsel Flat [MENDOCINO]: *area,* 5 miles east of Covelo along Middle Fork Eel River (lat. 39°47' N, long. 123°09'20" W; near sec. 2, 11, T 22 N, R 12 W). Named on Covelo East (1967) 7.5' quadrangle. On Covelo (1952) 15' quadrangle, the name applies to present Etsel Flat and present Atkinson Flat together.

Etsel Crossing [MENDOCINO]: *locality,* nearly 5 miles east of Covelo along Middle Fork Eel River (lat. 39°47'10" N, long. 123°09'30" W; near N line sec. 11, T 22 N, R 12 W); the place is at present Etsel Flat. Named on Covelo (1926) 15' quadrangle.

Etsel Ridge [MENDOCINO]: *ridge,* northwest-trending, 8 miles long, center 11 miles northeast of Eden Valley (lat. 39°43'45" N, long. 123°01'45" W). Named on Newhouse Ridge (1967), Plaskett Ridge (1967), and Thatcher Ridge (1967) 7.5' quadrangles.

Ettawa Springs [LAKE]: *locality,* 2.5 miles north-northeast of Whispering Pines (lat. 38°51'05" N, long. 122°41'40" W; near N line sec. 36, T 12 N, R 8 W). Named on Whispering Pines (1958) 7.5' quadrangle.

Ettersburg [HUMBOLDT]: *locality,* 12.5 miles west-southwest of Phillipsville (lat. 40°08'20" N, long. 123°59'45" W; sec. 6, T 4 S, R 2 E). Named on Ettersburg (1969) 7.5' quadrangle. Postal authorities established Ettersburg post office in 1902, discontinued it in 1906, reestablished it in 1915, and discontinued it in 1965 (Salley, p. 71). Albert F. Etter homesteaded at the place in 1894; the name "Ettersburg" is from the ancestral Etter family castle on the Rhine (Gudde, 1949, p. 111). Vander Leck's (1920b) map shows a place called Wilder located about 3 miles south-southeast of a place called Etter. Postal authorities established Wilder post office in 1896 and discontinued it in 1902 (Salley, p. 240).

Eubank Creek [HUMBOLDT]: *stream,* flows 3.5 miles to Mattole River 11 miles west of Garberville (lat. 40°05'15" N, long. 123°59'55" W; sec. 30, T 4 S, R 2 E). Named on Briceland (1969) 7.5' quadrangle.

Eureka [HUMBOLDT]: *city,* at about the center of the Humboldt County coast at Humboldt Bay (lat. 40°48'10" N, long. 124°09'40" W). Named on Arcata South (1959) and Eureka (1958) 7.5' quadrangles. Members of Mendocino Exploring Company arrived at Humboldt Bay in 1850 and laid out the city of Eureka (Coy, 1929, p. 57-58). Postal authorities established Eureka post office in 1853 (Frickstad, p. 43), and the city incorporated in 1856. Captain Robert C. Buchanan established Fort Humboldt in 1853 on a bluff at Bucksport in the present city of Eureka; the post was abandoned in 1867 (Frazer, p. 24). Eureka (1958) 7.5' quadrangle shows Fort Humboldt State Historical Monument just east of present Bucksport (lat. 40°46'40" N, long. 124°11'10" W; sec. 33, T 5 N, R 71 W). Iaqua Mineral Water Spring, also called Iaqua Medicinal Spring, was situated on the waterfront at Eureka; the spring water was shipped to San Francisco, where it was bottled (Lowell, p. 409; Laizure, p. 320). Postal authorities established Myrtle Grove post office in present Eureka in 1877, discontinued it in 1879, and reestablished it with the name "Myrtletowne" in 1952; the name was from myrtle trees at the site (Salley, p. 149). They established Scribner post office 12 miles south of Eureka in 1889 and discontinued it in 1894; the name was for Mrs. Leila M. Scribner, first postmaster (Salley, p. 200). They established Albeeville post office, named for J.P. Albee, first postmaster, 1.5 miles south of Eureka in 1862 and discontinued it in 1863; they reestablished it with the name "Albee" as a station of Eureka post office in 1952 and discontinued it in 1962 (Salley, p. 3).

Eureka Hill [MENDOCINO]: *ridge,* generally southeast-trending, 2.5 miles long, 8 miles east of the village of Point Arena (lat. 38°54'20" N, long. 123°32'45" W). Named on Point Arena (1960) 15' quadrangle.

Eureka Slough [HUMBOLDT]: *water feature,* opens into Humboldt Bay just north of downtown Eureka (lat. 40°48'40" N, long. 124°08'45" W). Named on Arcata South (1959) and Eureka (1958) 7.5' quadrangles.

Evans Bar [TRINITY]: *locality,* 12 miles northeast of Hayfork along Trinity River (lat. 40°40'30" N, long. 123°01'35" W; mainly in sec. 32, T 33 N, R

10 W). Named on Hayfork (1951) 15' quadrangle.

Evans Glade [LAKE]: *area,* 7.5 miles north of Clearlake Oaks (lat. 39°07'50" N, long. 122°39'50" W; near SW cor. sec. 20, T 15 N, R 7 W). Named on Clearlake Oaks (1960) 15' quadrangle.

Evans Peak [LAKE]: *peak,* nearly 7 miles north of Clearlake Oaks (lat. 39°07'25" N, long. 122°40'30" W; sec. 30, T 15 N, R 7 W). Altitude 4005 feet. Named on Clearlake Oaks (1958) 7.5' quadrangle.

Everts Ridge [HUMBOLDT]: *ridge,* generally west-trending, 2 miles long, 15 miles south-southwest of Scotia (lat. 40°17'25" N, long. 124°13' W). Named on Buckeye Mountain (1970) 7.5' quadrangle. John Everts arrived in the neighborhood of Petrolia in 1869 (Turner, p. 76).

Ewing Gulch [TRINITY]: *canyon,* drained by a stream that flows 1.5 miles to Hayfork Creek at Hayfork (lat. 40°33'10" N, long. 123°10'50" W; at W line sec. 12, T 31 N, R 12 W). Named on Hayfork (1951) 15' quadrangle.

Excelssior Valley [LAKE]: *valley,* 2 miles south-southeast of the town of Lower Lake (lat. 38°53' N, long. 122°36' W). Named on Lower Lake (1958) and Middletown (1958) 7.5' quadrangles.

— F —

Fagg Town: see **Weaverville** [TRINITY].

Fairbanks: see **Boonville** [MENDOCINO].

Fairhaven [HUMBOLDT]: *village,* 2.25 miles west-southwest of downtown Eureka on Samoa Peninsula (lat. 40°47'10" N, long. 124°12' W; sec. 20, T 5 N, R 1 W). Named on Eureka (1958) 7.5' quadrangle. The Fay brothers, who had a shingle mill there, named the place for their former home town of Fairhaven, Connecticut (Turner, p. 76). The community has the name "Rolph" on Eureka (1942) 15' quadrangle. Postal authorities established Rolph post office in 1918 and discontinued it in 1921 (Frickstad, p. 46)—the name was for James Rolph, who was governor of California from 1931 until 1934 (Gudde, 1949, p. 290).

Fairoaks [MENDOCINO]: *locality,* 2 miles south-southeast of downtown Willits (lat. 39°22'40" N, long. 123°20'20" W; at S line sec. 30, T 18 N, R 13 W). Named on Willits (1942) 15' quadrangle. O'Brien's (1953) map has the form "Fair Oaks" for the name.

Fairview: see **Fairview Camp** [TRINITY].

Fairview Camp [TRINITY]: *locality,* 11 miles east-northeast of Weaverville along Trinity River (lat. 40°48'35" N, long. 122°45'45" W; on N line sec. sec. 15, T 34 N, R 8 W). Named on Trinity Lake (1950) 15' quadrangle. Weaverville (1913) 30' quadrangle has the name "Fairview" at the place. Water of Clair Engle Lake now covers the site.

Fairy Gulch: see **Ferry Gulch** [TRINITY].

Falk [HUMBOLDT]: *locality,* 5.5 miles west-southwest of Fields Landing along South Fork Elk River (1) (lat. 40°41'05" N, long. 124°07'25" W; near E line sec. 36, T 4 N, R 1 W). Ruins named on McWhinney Creek (1979) 7.5' quadrangle. Postal authorities established Falk post office in 1899 and discontinued it in 1935 (Frickstad, p. 43). The name was for Noah H. Falk and his brother Elijah H. Falk, who were prominent lumbermen (Gudde, 1949, p. 112).

Fall Canyon [LAKE]: *canyon,* drained by a stream that flows 1 mile to the canyon of Scotts Creek 4.25 miles west of the town of Upper Lake (lat. 39°09'20" N, long. 122°59'05" W; near NW cor. sec. 16, T 15 N, R 10 W). Named on Upper Lake (1958) 7.5' quadrangle.

Fall Creek [DEL NORTE]: *stream,* flows nearly 5 miles to Siskiyou Fork Smith River 10.5 miles east of Gasquet (lat. 41°51'55" N, long. 123°46'10" W). Named on Broken Rib Mountain (1982), Devils Punchbowl (1981), and Hurdygurdy Butte (1982) 7.5' quadrangles.

Fall Creek [TRINITY]:

(1) *stream,* flows less than 1 mile to East Fork New River 15 miles north-northeast of Burnt Ranch (lat. 40°59' N, long. 123°19'15" W). Named on Ironside Mountain (1951) 15' quadrangle.

(2) *stream,* flows 1.5 miles to New River 11.5 miles north-northeast of Burnt Ranch (lat. 40°57'15" N, long. 123°22'30" W). Named on Ironside Mountain (1951) 15' quadrangle.

Fall Gulch [TRINITY]: *canyon,* drained by a stream that flows 1.5 miles to Salt Creek (4) 3.5 miles north-northeast of Dubakella Mountain (lat. 40°25'35" N, long. 123°06'45" W; sec. 28, T 30 N, R 11 W). Named on Dubakella Mountain (1954) 15' quadrangle.

Falls Gulch [HUMBOLDT]: *canyon,* drained by a stream that flows nearly 2 miles to Cloney Gulch 7.5 miles south-southeast of Arcata (lat. 40°45'50" N, long. 124°02'20" W; sec. 2, T 4 N, R 1 E). Named on Arcata South (1959) 7.5' quadrangle.

False Cape [HUMBOLDT]: *promontory,* 7 miles southwest of Ferndale along the coast (lat. 40°30'35" N, long. 124°23'10" W; sec. 35, T 7 N, R 3 W). Named on Ferndale (1959) 7.5' quadrangle. Called Cape Fortunas on Cape Fortunas (1920) 15' quadrangle, but United States Board on Geographic Names (1940, p. 16) rejected this name for the feature. Gibbs (p. 129) called the promontory False Cape Mendocino in 1851, and Davidson gave it the name "Cape Fortunas" in 1854 (Gudde, 1949, p. 113).

False Cape: see **Capetown** [HUMBOLDT].

False Cape Mendocino: see **False Cape** [HUMBOLDT].

False Cape Rock [HUMBOLDT]: *rock,* 8.5 miles southwest of Ferndale, and 0.5 mile west of False Cape (lat. 40°30'35" N, long. 124°23'40" W). Named on Ferndale (1959) 7.5' quadrangle.

False Klamath Cove [DEL NORTE]: *embayment,* 4 miles north-northwest of the mouth of Klamath River along the coast (lat. 41°36' N, long. 124°06' W; sec. 18, 19, T 14 N, R 1 E). Named on Requa (1966) 7.5' quadrangle. Called False Klamath on United States Coast Survey's (1854) map. Early-day sailors sometimes mistook this embayment for the cove at the mouth of Klamath River, and named it to reflect this mistake (Waterman, p. 230).

False Klamath Rock [DEL NORTE]: *island,* 600 feet long, 3.5 miles north-northwest of the mouth of Klamath River, and 1650 feet offshore (lat. 41°35'40" N, long. 124°06'40" W); the feature is less than 1 mile south-west of False Klamath Cove. Named on Requa (1966) 7.5' quadrangle. The name is from False Klamath Cove (Gudde, 1949, p. 113).

Farley [MENDOCINO]: *locality,* 5.25 miles northeast of Longvale along Northwestern Pacific Railroad (lat. 39°36'55" N, long. 123°22' W; sec. 1, T 20 N, R 14 W). Named on Willis Ridge (1966) 7.5' quadrangle. Postal authorities established Farley post office in 1915 and discontinued it in 1942 (Frickstad, p. 94). Jackson Farley settled on a ranch at the site in 1857 (Hanna, p. 103).

Farley Creek [TRINITY]: *stream,* flows nearly 2 miles to South Fork Trinity River 2 miles southeast of Forest Glen (lat. 40°21'05" N, long. 123°18'10" W; sec. 29, T 1 S, R 8 E). Named on Forest Glen (1979) 7.5' quadrangle.

Farley Gulch [TRINITY]: *canyon,* drained by a stream that flows less than 1 mile to Clair Engle Lake 13 miles northeast of Weaverville (lat. 40°52' N, long. 122°46'40" W; near N line sec. 28, T 35 N, R 8 W). Named on Trinity Dam (1950) 15' quadrangle.

Farley Lake [MENDOCINO]: *lake,* 225 feet long, 4.5 miles southeast of Laytonville (lat. 39°38'50" N, long. 123°24'40" W; sec. 27, T 21 N, R 14 W); the lake is 0.5 mile southeast of Farley Peak. Named on Laytonville (1967) 7.5' quadrangle.

Farley Peak [MENDOCINO]: *peak,* 4 miles southeast of Laytonville (lat. 39°39'10" N, long. 123°24'55" W; near SW cor. sec. 22, T 21 N, R 14 W). Altitude 3500 feet. Named on Laytonville (1967) 7.5' quadrangle.

Faulkner Prairie [HUMBOLDT]: *area,* 9 miles south-southeast of Coyote Peak (lat. 41°00'40" N, long. 123°48'35" W; on W line sec. 11, T 7 N, R 3 E). Named on Hupa Mountain (1982) 7.5' quadrangle.

Faun Prairie: see **Fawn Prairie** [HUMBOLDT].

Fauntleroy Rock [DEL NORTE]: *rock,* less than 1 mile offshore at Crescent City (lat. 41°44'20" N, long. 124°11'20" W). Named on Sister Rocks (1966) 7.5' quadrangle.

Fauntleroy Rock [HUMBOLDT]: *rock,* nearly 2 miles west-southwest of Cape Mendocino (lat. 40°25'50" N, long. 124°26'25" W). Named on Cape Mendocino (1969) 7.5' quadrangle. The name commemorates the brig *R.H. Fauntleroy,* the survey vessel that George Davidson used between 1854 and 1858; the brig was named for Robert H. Fauntleroy of United States Coast Survey, who was Davidson's father-in-law (Gudde, 1949, p. 114).

Fawn Butte [TRINITY]: *peak,* 10.5 miles south of Salmon Mountain (lat. 41°02'05" N, long. 123°23'55" W); the peak is near the head of a branch of Fawn Creek. Named on Trinity Mountain (1979) 7.5' quadrangle.

Fawn Creek [TRINITY]: *stream,* flows 3.25 miles to Virgin Creek 11 miles south-southeast of Salmon Mountain (lat. 41°01'45" N, long. 123°21'05" W); the stream is north of Fawn Ridge. Named on Dees Peak (1978) and Trinity Mountain (1979) 7.5' quadrangles.

Fawn Lodge [TRINITY]: *locality,* 7 miles southeast of Weaverville along Grass Valley Creek (lat. 40°40'35" N, long. 122°49'45" W; sec. 36, T 33 N, R 9 W). Named on Weaverville (1950) 15' quadrangle. Postal authorities established Fawn Lodge post office in 1931 and discontinued it in 1937 (Frickstad, p. 207).

Fawn Prairie [HUMBOLDT]: *area,* 7 miles northeast of the town of Blue Lake (lat. 40°57'30" N, long. 123°53'55" W; near S line sec. 25, T 7 N, R 2 E). Named on Blue Lake (1979) 7.5' quadrangle. A military post was at the site in 1863 (Hoover, Rensch, and Rensch, p. 100). Turner (p. 79) used the form "Faun Prairie" for the name.

Fawn Ridge [TRINITY]: *ridge,* east-trending, 2.5 miles long, 12 miles south of Salmon Mountain (lat. 41°00'45" N, long. 123°22'15" W); the feature is south of Fawn Creek. Named on Dees Peak (1978) and Trinity Mountain (1979) 7.5' quadrangles.

Fay Slough [HUMBOLDT]: *water feature,* 4.5 miles south of Arcata in lowlands near Arcata Bay (lat. 40°48'05" N, long. 124°06'10" W). Named on Arcata South (1959) 7.5' quadrangle. The name commemorates George M. Fay and his brother Nathan M. Fay, who had a shingle mill near the feature (Turner, p. 79).

Feeney's Crossing: see **Feeny Gulch** [TRINITY].

Feeny Gulch [TRINITY]: *canyon,* drained by a stream that flows 4.5 miles to Trinity River 15 miles northeast of Weaverville (lat. 40°52'45" N, long. 122°42'40" W; at W line sec. 19, T 35 N, R 7 W); the feature opens into the canyon of Trinity River 7 miles downstream from the mouth of East

Fork Trinity River. Named on Schell Mountain (1950) 15' quadrangle. Red Bluff (1894) 1° quadrangle has the name "Feeny" at the mouth of present Feeny Gulch. The name commemorates Richard H. Feeney, who lived in the neighborhood (Jones, p. 41). Hoover, Rensch, and Rensch (p. 557) noted that Fitch's Ferry, or Feeney's Crossing, was situated 7 miles below the mouth of East Fork Trinity River.

Feeny Ridge [TRINITY]: *ridge*, west-northwest-trending, 3.5 miles long, 18 miles northeast of Weaverville (lat. 40°53' N, long. 122°40' W); the feature is north of Feeny Gulch. Named on Schell Mountain (1950) 15' quadrangle.

Feese Creek [HUMBOLDT]: *stream*, flows less than 1 mile to South Fork Eel River 2 miles southeast of Weott (lat. 40°18'10" N, long. 123°53'40" W; near E line sec. 12, T 2 S, R 2 E). Named on Weott (1969) 7.5' quadrangle.

Feliz Creek [MENDOCINO]: *stream*, flows 8 miles to lowlands near Russian River 0.5 mile west of Hopland (lat. 38°58'20" N, long. 123°07'45" W). Named on Hopland (1960) and Ukiah (1958) 7.5' quadrangles. The name commemorates Fernando Feliz, who received Sanel grant in 1844 (Gudde, 1949, p. 114). Middle Fork enters 6.5 miles upstream from the mouth of the main creek; it is 3.5 miles long and is named on Hopland (1960) and Ounbaun Valley (1960) 15' quadrangles. North Fork enters from the northwest 10.5 miles upstream from the mouth of the main creek; it is 1 mile long and is named on Boonville (1959) 15' quadrangle. O'Brien's (1953) map shows a feature called Bells Valley located 2.25 miles west-northwest of Hopland along Feliz Creek.

Felter Gulch [TRINITY]: *canyon*, drained by a stream that flows 1.25 miles to Oregon Gulch 15 miles north-northeast of Hayfork (lat. 40°43'45" N, long. 123°02' W; at W line sec. 8, T 33 N, R 10 W). Named on Hayfork (1951) 15' quadrangle.

Felt Springs [HUMBOLDT]: *springs*, 3.25 miles east-northeast of Fortuna (lat. 40°37'10" N, long. 124°05'50" W; near NW cor. sec. 29, T 3 N, R 1 E). Named on Hydesville (1979) 7.5' quadrangle. The name is for Dr. Theodore Dwight Felt, who built a resort at the place (Turner, p. 79). A hotel there burned in 1878, and another hotel there burned in 1894, after which the place was abandoned as a resort (Waring, p. 300).

Fenton Ridge [TRINITY]: *ridge*, generally west-southwest-trending, 2 miles long, 10 miles south of Kettenpom (lat. 40°01'05" N, long. 123°27'45" W). Named on Lake Mountain (1967) 7.5' quadrangle.

Ferguson Gulch [MENDOCINO]: *canyon*, drained by a stream that flows 1.5 miles to the sea nearly 4 miles northwest of Gualala (lat. 38°48'10" N, long. 123°34'55" W; sec. 18, T 11 N, R 15 W). Named on Gualala (1960) 7.5' quadrangle.

Fernbridge [HUMBOLDT]: *locality*, 3 miles west-northwest of Fortuna (lat. 40°36'55" N, long. 124°12' W; sec. 29, T 3 N, R 1 W). Named on Fortuna (1959) 7.5' quadrangle. Postal authorities established Fernbridge post office in 1924 (Frickstad, p. 43). The place is at the approach to Fern bridge, which spans Eel River (Hanna, p. 105).

Fern Campground [TRINITY]: *locality*, 2.5 miles south-southwest of Forest Glen (lat. 40°20'25" N, long. 123°20'30" W; sec. 36, T 1 S, R 7 E). Named on Forest Glen (1979) 7.5' quadrangle.

Fern Canyon [HUMBOLDT]: *canyon*, drained by Home Creek, which flows 2.5 miles to the sea 8 miles north of Orick (lat. 41°24'10" N, long. 124°04' W; sec. 28, T 12 N, R 1 E). Named on Fern Canyon (1966) 7.5' quadrangle. A lush growth of ferns covers the walls of the canyon (Trexler, p. 154).

Fern Canyon [MENDOCINO]: *canyon*, nearly 3 miles southeast of Mendocino along Little River (1) (lat. 39°16'35" N, long. 123°45'20" W; sec. 4, 5, T 16 N, R 17 W). Named on Mendocino (1960) 7.5' quadrangle.

Fern Cottage [HUMBOLDT]: *locality*, 2.5 miles west of Ferndale (lat. 40°34'55" N, long. 124°18'35" W; near W line sec. 4, T 2 N, R 2 W). Named on Ferndale (1959) 7.5' quadrangle.

Fern Creek [HUMBOLDT]: *stream*, flows 1 mile to Cedar Creek (2) 9 miles east of the settlement of Willow Creek (lat. 40°55'55" N, long. 123°29'45" W). Named on Ironside Mountain (1951) 15' quadrangle.

Fern Creek: see **Horse Creek** [TRINITY].

Ferndale [HUMBOLDT]: *town*, 16 miles south-southwest of Eureka (lat. 40°34'40" N, long. 124°15'40" W; sec. 2, 11, T 2 N, R 2 W). Named on Ferndale (1959) 7.5' quadrangle. Postal authorities established Ferndale post office in 1860 (Frickstad, p. 43), and the town incorporated in 1893. The community began when S.L. Shaw started a hotel on his property there in 1860 (Coy, 1929, p. 102). The name is from the luxuriant growth of ferns in the neighborhood (Gudde, 1949, p. 115). Jacob Gyer laid out a town called Meridian in 1878 at a site 1 mile west of Ferndale (Edeline, p. 95). R.M. Dugan was granted a license in 1861 for Dugan's Ferry, located on Eel River along the road from Ferndale to Eureka; he moved the ferry 0.75 mile upstream from its original location in 1873 (to center of sec. 24, T T 3 N, R 2 W), and the ferry was discontinued in 1913 (Edeline, p. 109-110). Settlers started a port on Eel River near Dugan's Ferry and named it Cleveland for the schooner *Mary Cleveland*, which entered Eel River in 1866; the settlement there was short-lived (Edeline, p. 62). Postal authorities established Cleveland post office 3 miles north of Ferndale (SW quarter sec. 25, T 3 N, R 2 W) in 1866 and discontinued it in 1868 (Salley, p. 46).

Fern Glade [TRINITY]: *area*, 4.25 miles west-northwest of Black Rock Mountain (lat. 40°13'30" N, long. 123°05' W; at SW cor. sec. 35, T 28 N, R 11 W). Named on Black Rock Mountain (1954) 15' quadrangle.

Fern Patch [HUMBOLDT]: *area*, 9 miles southwest of Dinsmore (lat. 40°25'05" N, long. 123°44'20" W; on W line sec. 33, T 1 N, R 4 E). Named on Larabee Valley (1977) 7.5' quadrangle.

Fern Point [TRINITY]: *relief feature*, 13 miles south-southwest of Black Rock Mountain (lat. 40°02'05" N, long. 123°06'05" W; near W line sec. 9, T 25 N, R 11 W). Named on Black Rock Mountain (1954) 15' quadrangle.

Fern Prairie [HUMBOLDT]:

(1) *area*, nearly 2 miles north-northeast of Weitchpec (lat. 41°12'40" N, long. 123°41'15" W). Named on Weitchpec (1979) 7.5' quadrangle.

(2) *area*, 9 miles east of the town of Blue Lake (lat. 40°53'40" N, long. 123°49'10" W; near NE cor. sec. 22, T 6 N, R 3 E). Named on Lord-Ellis Summit (1973) 7.5' quadrangle.

Fern Ridge [HUMBOLDT]: *ridge*, northwest- to west-trending, nearly 1 mile long, 3 miles northwest of Yager Junction (lat. 40°34'35" N, long. 123°51'55" W; on S line sec. 5, T 2 N, R 3 E). Named on Yager Junction (1979) 7.5' quadrangle.

Fernwood [HUMBOLDT]: *locality*, 6 miles east of Korbel (lat. 40°52'10" N, long. 123°51' W; near SW cor. sec. 28, T 6 N, R 3 E). Named on Maple Creek (1977) 7.5' quadrangle.

Ferris Camp [DEL NORTE]: *locality*, 15 miles east-southeast of Klamath Glen along Bluff Creek (lat. 41°26'30" N, long. 123°42' W. Named on Orleans (1952) 15' quadrangle.

Ferris Canyon [LAKE]: *canyon*, drained by a stream that flows 2 miles to Cache Creek 2.5 miles east-northeast of the town of Lower Lake (lat. 38°55'20" N, long. 122°33'55" W; sec. 6, T 12 N, R 6 W). Named on Lower Lake (1958) 7.5' quadrangle.

Ferry Gulch [HUMBOLDT]: *canyon*, drained by a stream that flows 1.25 miles to Hoopa Valley 0.5 mile north-northeast of Hoopa (lat. 41°03'30" N, long. 123°40'20" W; sec. 24, T 8 N, R 4 E). Named on Hoopa (1979) 7.5' quadrangle.

Ferry Gulch [TRINITY]: *canyon*, drained by a stream that flows 1.5 miles to Trinity River 9 miles east-northeast of Weaverville (lat. 40°41'20" N, long. 122°46'45" W; sec. 28, T 34 N, R 8 W). Named on Trinity Dam (1950) 15' quadrangle. Called Fairy Gl. on Weaverville (1913) 30' quadrangle. A ferry on Trinity River was near the canyon (Jones, p. 275).

Ferry Point [HUMBOLDT]: *relief feature*, 1.5 miles north-northeast of Hoopa (lat. 41°04'10" N, long. 123°39'40" W; at SW cor. sec. 18, T 8 N, R 5 E); the feature is north of Ferry Gulch. Named on Hoopa (1979) 7.5' quadrangle.

Fickle Hill [HUMBOLDT]: *ridge*, generally southeast-trending, 10 miles long, center 4 miles east-southeast of Arcata (lat. 40°50'15" N, long. 124°00'55" W). Named on Arcata North (1959), Arcata South (1959), and Korbel (1979) 7.5' quadrangles.

Fiddle Prairie [HUMBOLDT]: *area*, 4 miles southwest of Honeydew (lat. 40°12'05" N, long. 124°10'30" W; at SW cor. sec. 15, T 3 S, R 1 W). Named on Shubrick Peak (1969) 7.5' quadrangle. The name is from the fiddlelike shape of the area in plan view (Turner, p. 80).

Fieldbrook [HUMBOLDT]: *settlement*, 7 miles north-northeast of Arcata (lat. 40°57'30" N, long. 124°02'05" W; sec. 26, T 7 N, R 1 E). Named on Arcada North (1959) 7.5' quadrangle. Postal authorities established Fieldbrook post office in 1902 and discontinued it in 1932 (Frickstad, p. 43). The settlement is at a place that was called Buckman's Prairie, for the first white resident, before the community was laid out (Cargill, p. 16). The name "Fieldbrook" was given for brooks located east and west of the place (Gudde, 1949, p. 115).

Fielder Creek [HUMBOLDT]: *stream*, flows 2 miles to lowlands along Van Duzen River 8.5 miles southeast of Fortuna (lat. 40°31'30" N, long. 124°01'25" W; at W line sec. 25, T 2 N, R 1 E). Named on Hydesville (1979) 7.5' quadrangle.

Fields Landing [HUMBOLDT]: *village*, 6 miles south-southwest of Eureka along Humboldt Bay (lat. 40°43'30" N, long. 124°12'55" W; sec. 17, 18, T 4 N, R 1 W). Named on Fields Landing (1959) 7.5' quadrangle. Fortuna (1944) 15' quadrangle has the name "South Bay Sta." at the place. The name "Fields Landing" commemorates Waterman Field, who came to Humboldt County in the 1860's (Gudde, 1949, p. 115). Postal authorities established Adele post office 7 miles south of Eureka in 1889, and changed the name to Fields Landing the same year; the name "Adele" was for Adele Haughwout, first white child born at the site (Salley, p. 1).

Fields Landing Channel: see **Hookton Channel** [HUMBOLDT].

Filaree Flat [HUMBOLDT]: *area*, 4 miles northeast of Showers Mountain (lat. 40°36'30" N, long. 123°38'05" W; sec. 29, T 3 N, R 5 E). Named on Showers Mountain (1978) 7.5' quadrangle.

Finch Creek [HUMBOLDT]: *stream*, flows 1.5 miles to Eel River 2 miles west-northwest of Fortuna (lat. 40°36'40" N, long. 124°11'30" W; sec. 28, T 3 N, R 1 W). Named on Fields Landing (1959) and Fortuna (1959)

7.5' quadrangles.

Finley [LAKE]: *village,* 3.5 miles southeast of Lakeport (lat. 39°00'10" N, long. 122°52'30" W; on W line sec. 4, T 13 N, R 9 W). Named on Lakeport (1958) and Lucerne (1958) 7.5' quadrangles. Postal authorities established Finley post office in 1907 (Frickstad, p. 63). The name is from Samuel Finley Sylar, an early settler (Hanna, p. 106).

Finley Creek: see **Big Finley Creek** [HUMBOLDT]; **Little Finley Creek** [HUMBOLDT].

Finley Gulch [TRINITY]: *canyon,* drained by a stream that flows 0.5 mile to Little Browns Creek 7 miles north-northeast of Weaverville (lat. 40°46'40" N, long. 122°53'30" W; sec. 28, T 34 N, R 9 W). Named on Trinity Dam (1950) 15' quadrangle.

Finners Gulch: see **Fleener Creek** [HUMBOLDT].

Finney Valley [MENDOCINO]: *valley,* 4.25 miles east of Willits (lat. 39°25' N, long. 123°16'30" W; at NW cor. sec. 14, T 18 N, R 13 W). Named on Willits (1961) 15' quadrangle.

Fir Cove Campground [TRINITY]: *locality,* 4.5 miles west-southwest of Forest Glen along Ruth Reservoir (lat. 40°20'40" N, long. 123°24'15" W; near SE cor. sec. 29, T 1 S, R 7 E). Named on Ruth Reservoir (1978) 7.5' quadrangle.

Fire Hill [HUMBOLDT]: *peak,* 8 miles south of Honeydew (lat. 40°07'40" N, long. 124°07'05" W; near W line sec. 7, T 4 S, R 1 E). Altitude 2938 feet. Named on Honeydew (1970) 7.5' quadrangle.

Fir Root Spring [LAKE]: *spring,* nearly 4 miles south-southeast of Potato Hill (lat. 39°18'15" N, long. 122°46'10" W; at N line sec. 28, T 17 N, R 8 W). Named on Potato Hill (1967) 7.5' quadrangle.

Fir Root Spring: see **Grassy Flats** [TRINITY].

First Creek [HUMBOLDT]: *stream,* flows 0.5 mile to Camp Creek nearly 5 miles northwest of Orleans (lat. 41°21'05" N, long. 123°36'20" W); the mouth of the stream is 2000 feet from the mouth of Second Creek. Named on Orleans (1952) 15' quadrangle.

Fish Camp: see **Camp Weott** [HUMBOLDT].

Fish Creek [HUMBOLDT]:

(1) *stream,* flows 2.5 miles to Van Duzen River 2.5 miles west-southwest of Bridgeville (lat. 40°27'35" N, long. 123°50'35" W; sec. 16, T 1 N, R 3 E). Named on Bridgeville (1969) 7.5' quadrangle.

(2) *stream,* flows 3.25 miles to South Fork Eel River 1 mile northwest of Phillipsville (lat. 40°13'15" N, long. 123°48' W; sec. 11, T 3 S, R 3 E). Named on Miranda (1970) and Myers Flat (1969) 7.5' quadrangles.

(3) *stream,* flows 2 miles to South Fork Eel River 3 miles south-southeast of Garberville (lat. 40°03'35" N, long. 123°46'55" W; near NE cor. sec. 1, T 5 S, R 3 E). Named on Garberville (1970) 7.5' quadrangle.

(4) *stream,* flows 3.25 miles to Bluff Creek [DEL NORTE-HUMBOLDT] 10.5 miles west-northwest of Orleans (lat. 41°21'55" N, long. 123°43'20" W). Named on Fish Lake (1974) 7.5' quadrangle.

(5) *stream,* flows 1.5 miles to Lawrence Creek 6 miles west of Lone Star Junction (lat. 40°37'55" N, long. 123°59'30" W; sec. 19, T 3 N, R 2 E). Named on Iaqua Buttes (1979) and McWhinney Creek (1979) 7.5' quadrangles.

Fish Creek [MENDOCINO]: *stream,* flows 7 miles to Eel River 8 miles east of Longvale (lat. 39°33'25" N, long. 123°17'05" W; near N line sec. 34, T 20 N, R 13 W). Named on Brushy Mountain (1966) and Willis Ridge (1966) 7.5' quadrangles.

Fish Creek: see **Balcom Creek** [HUMBOLDT].

Fish Creek Butte: see **Slate Creek Butte** [HUMBOLDT].

Fisher [HUMBOLDT]: *locality,* 5.25 miles north-northwest of Arcata (lat. 40°56'30" N, long. 124°07'05" W; at SW cor. sec. 31, T 7 N, R 1 E). Named on Arcata North (1959) 7.5' quadrangle.

Fisher Creek [MENDOCINO]: *stream,* flows 2 miles to Russian River 6 miles west of the town of Potter Valley (lat. 39°19'40" N, long. 123°13'15" W; near W line sec. 15, T 17 N, R 12 W). Named on Redwood Valley (1960) 7.5' quadrangle.

Fisher Gulch [TRINITY]: *canyon,* drained by a stream that flows 2.5 miles to Canyon Creek (1) 6 miles northeast of Helena (lat. 40°50'10" N, long. 123°02'55" W). Named on Helena (1951) 15' quadrangle.

Fisher Ridge [MENDOCINO]: *ridge,* west- to southwest-trending, 2 miles long, 9.5 miles west-southwest of Ornbaun Valley (lat. 38°50'35" N, long. 123°27'35" W). Named on Ornbaun Valley (1960) 15' quadrangle.

Fisher Ridge [TRINITY]:

(1) *ridge,* north-trending, 1.25 miles long, 6.5 miles northwest of Forest Glen (lat. 40°27'30" N, long. 123°23'50" W). Named on Sportshaven (1973) 7.5' quadrangle.

(2) *ridge,* generally west-southwest-trending, 2 miles long, 2 miles south-southeast of Black Rock Mountain (lat. 40°10'10" N, long. 122°59'45" W). Named on Black Rock Mountain (1954) and Yolla Bolly (1954) 15' quadrangles.

Fish Lake [HUMBOLDT]: *lake,* 1600 feet long, 8 miles west-southwest of Orleans (lat. 41°15'50" N, long. 123°40'55" W). Named on Fish Lake (1974) 7.5' quadrangle. Called Browns Lake on Hoopa (1935) 30' quadrangle.

Fish Rock [MENDOCINO]: *village,* 4 miles northwest of Gualala (lat. 38°48'15" N, long. 123°35' W; sec. 18, T 11 N, R 15 W); the village is 0.5 mile northeast of Fish Rocks. Named on Gualala (1960) 7.5' quadrangle. California Mining Bureau's (1909c) map has the form "Fishrock" for the name. Postal authorities established Conways Landing post office in 1870, changed the name to Fish Rock in 1871, discontinued it in 1873, reestablished it in 1885, moved it 2 miles north in 1908, and discontinued it in 1910; the name "Conways Landing" was for the developer at the site of an open-sea loading point for small coastal lumber boats (Salley, p. 49, 75).

Fish Rock Beach [MENDOCINO]: *beach,* 3.5 miles northwest of Gualala along the coast (lat. 38°48'10" N, long. 123°34'50" W; sec. 18, T 11 N, R 15 W). Named on Gualala (1960) 7.5' quadrangle.

Fish Rock Gulch [MENDOCINO]: *canyon,* drained by a stream that flows 2 miles to the sea 3.5 miles northwest of Gualala (lat. 38°48'10" N, long. 123°34'45" W; sec. 18, T 11 N, R 15 W); the mouth of the canyon is at Fish Rock Beach. Named on Gualala (1960) 7.5' quadrangle.

Fish Rocks [MENDOCINO]: *islands,* two, largest 950 feet long, 4 miles west-northwest of Gualala, and 650 feet offshore (lat. 38°48' N, long. 123°35'30" W). Named on Gualala (1960) 7.5' quadrangle.

Fishtown Creek [MENDOCINO]: *stream,* flows 1.5 miles to Middle Fork Eel River 16 miles northeast of Covelo (lat. 39°55'10" N, long. 123°00'30" W; sec. 19, T 24 N, R 10 W). Named on Buck Rock (1967) and Leech Lake Mountain (1966) 7.5' quadrangles.

Fitch's Ferry: see **Feeny Gulch** [TRINITY].

Five Cent Gulch [TRINITY]: *canyon,* drained by a stream that flows 2 miles to the canyon of East Weaver Creek less than 1 mile east-northeast of Weaverville (lat. 40°44'20" N, long. 122°55'30" W; near S line sec. 6, T 33 N, R 9 W); the canyon is east of Ten Cent Gulch. Named on Trinity Dam (1950) and Weaverville (1950) 15' quadrangles.

Fivemile Creek [HUMBOLDT]: *stream,* flows less than 0.5 mile to Klamath River 3.5 miles north-northeast of Orleans (lat. 41°20'40" N, long. 123°30'10" W). Named on Orleans Mountain (1974) 7.5' quadrangle.

Five Pines: see **Bragdon** [TRINITY].

Five Spring Creek [LAKE]: *stream,* flows less than 1 mile to Corbin Creek 8.5 miles east-northeast of Hull Mountain (lat. 39°33' N, long. 122°46'40" W; near NE cor. sec. 32, T 20 N, R 8 W). Named on Kneecap Ridge (1967) 7.5' quadrangle.

Five Spring Ridge [LAKE]: *ridge,* generally west-trending, 1.5 miles long, 9 miles east of Hull Mountain (lat. 39°32'25" N, long. 122°46'15" W); the ridge is south of Five Spring Creek. Named on Kneecap Ridge (1967) 7.5' quadrangle.

Flag Peak [LAKE]: *peak,* 4 miles south of Middletown (lat. 38°41'50" N, long. 122°37'40" W; near W line sec. 22, T 10 N, R 7 W). Named on Mount Saint Helena (1959) 7.5' quadrangle.

Flagstaff Butte: see **Ashfield Buttes** [HUMBOLDT].

Flanigan Creek [HUMBOLDT]: *stream,* flows 1 mile to Van Duzen River 9 miles south-southwest of Lone Star Junction (lat. 40°30'35" N, long. 123°59'15" W; sec. 31, T 2 N, R 2 E). Named on Owl Creek (1979) 7.5' quadrangle.

Flatiron Lake: see **Blue Creek** [DEL NORTE-HUMBOLDT].

Flatiron Rock [HUMBOLDT]: *island,* 775 feet long, 1 mile west of Trinidad (lat. 41°03'35" N, long. 124°09'45" W); the island is 0.5 mile west-northwest of Trinidad Head. Named on Trinidad (1966) 7.5' quadrangle. Trinidad (1952) 15' quadrangle has the name "Off Trinidad Rock" for the feature. United States Board on Geographic Names (1968a, p. 5) rejected the names "Off Trinidad Head" and "Off-Trinidad Head" for the feature.

Flat Rock [DEL NORTE]: *rock,* 750 feet offshore at Crescent City (lat. 41°44'40" N, long. 124°11'45" W). Named on Sister Rocks (1966) 7.5' quadrangle.

Flat Rock [HUMBOLDT]: *rock,* less than 0.5 mile south-southeast of Trinidad in Trinidad Bay (lat. 41°03'10" N, long. 124°08'20" W). Named on Trinidad (1966) 7.5' quadrangle.

Flat Rock Creek [MENDOCINO]: *stream,* flows 1 mile to the sea 9 miles west-southwest of Piercy (lat. 39°55'40" N, long. 123°57'25" W; sec. 22, T 24 N, R 19 W). Named on Bear Harbor (1969) 7.5' quadrangle.

Fleener Creek [HUMBOLDT]: *stream,* flows 3 miles to the sea 5 miles west-southwest of Ferndale (lat. 40°33'30" N, long. 124°21'25" W; sec. 13, T 2 N, R 3 W). Named on Ferndale (1959) 7.5' quadrangle. The name commemorates Simon Peter Cartwright Fleener, a rancher (Turner, p. 83). The canyon of the stream is called Finners Gulch on Cape Fortunas (1920) 15' quadrangle.

Fleming Creek [MENDOCINO]: *stream,* flows 2 miles to South Fork Garcia River 5 miles north-northwest of Gualala (lat. 38°50'20" N, long. 123°32'45" W; sec. 4, T 11 N, R 15 W); the stream is south of Fleming Ridge. Named on Gualala (1960) 7.5' quadrangle.

Fleming Ridge [MENDOCINO]: *ridge,* southwest-trending, 1.5 miles long, 5.5 miles north of Gualala (lat. 38°50'50" N, long. 123°31'40" W); the ridge is north of Fleming Creek. Named on Gualala (1960) 7.5' quadrangle.

Flint Ridge [DEL NORTE]: *ridge,* west-trending, 1.5 miles long, 1.5 miles south-southeast of the mouth of Klamath River (lat. 41°31'30" N, long. 124°04' W). Named on Requa (1966) 7.5' quadrangle.

Flint Rock Head [DEL NORTE]: *promontory,* 1.5 miles south of the mouth of Klamath River along the coast (lat. 41°31'30" N, long. 124°05' W; on S line sec. 8, T 13 N, R 1 E); the feature is at the west end of Flint Ridge. Named on Requa (1966) 7.5' quadrangle. According to an Indian legend, a supernatural being tried to turn rock at the place into obsidian so that Indians could get material for arrowheads, but produced flint instead (Waterman, p. 233).

Floodgate: see **Floodgate Creek** [MENDOCINO].

Floodgate Creek [MENDOCINO]: *stream,* flows 2.25 miles to Navarro River 2.25 miles south of Navarro (lat. 39°07'15" N, long. 123°32'45" W; near W line sec. 32, T 15 N, R 15 W). Named on Navarro (1961) 15' quadrangle. California Mining Bureau's (1917c) map shows a place called Floodgate located 2 miles southeast of Navarro at the end of a rail line.

Floyds Landing: see **Clearlake Highlands** [LAKE].

Flume Creek [TRINITY]: *stream,* flows 0.5 mile to a pipeline just west of Trinity Center (lat. 41°00'15" N, long. 122°42' W; sec. 5, T 36 N, R 7 W). Named on Bonanza King (1955) 15' quadrangle.

Flume Gulch [MENDOCINO]: *canyon,* drained by a stream that flows 3.5 miles to Navarro River 3.5 miles north-northeast of Elk (lat. 39°10'25" N, long. 123°40'35" W; sec. 7, T 15 N, R 16 W). Named on Elk (1960) 7.5' quadrangle.

Flume Gulch [TRINITY]: *canyon,* drained by a stream that flows 2.5 miles to Rattlesnake Creek (2) 1 mile east of Forest Glen (lat. 40°22'25" N, long. 123°18'10" W; sec. 17, T 1 S, R 8 E). Named on Naufus Creek (1979) 7.5' quadrangle.

Flumeville [MENDOCINO]: *locality,* 1.5 miles north-northwest of the village of Point Arena (lat. 38°55'45" N, long. 123°42'30" W; sec. 2, T 12 N, R 17 W). Named on Point Arena (1960) 7.5' quadrangle.

Flyblow Camp [TRINITY]: *locality,* 8.5 miles south-southeast of Dubakella Mountain (lat. 40°16'10" N, long. 123°06' W; near NW cor. sec. 22, T 28 N, R 11 W). Named on Dubakella Mountain (1954) 15' quadrangle.

Flyblow Gulch [HUMBOLDT]: *canyon,* drained by a stream that flows 2.5 miles to the sea 8 miles southwest of Ferndale (lat. 40°30'05" N, long. 124°22'55" W; sec. 2, T 1 N, R 3 W). Named on Capetown (1969) and Ferndale (1959) 7.5' quadrangles.

Fly Creek [MENDOCINO]: *stream,* flows 4.5 miles to Middle Fork Eel River 14 miles east-northeast of Covelo (lat. 39°53'50" N, long. 123°01'05" W; sec. 31, T 24 N, R 10 W). Named on Buck Rock (1967), Leech Lake Mountain (1966), and Mendocino Pass (1967) 7.5' quadrangles.

Flyette Prairie [HUMBOLDT]: *area,* 6.25 miles south-southeast of Coyote Peak (lat. 41°02'50" N, long. 123°49'35" W). Named on Hupa Mountain (1982) 7.5' quadrangle.

Flynn Creek [MENDOCINO]: *stream,* flows nearly 5 miles to North Fork Navarro River 1.5 miles west-northwest of Navarro (lat. 39°09'40" N, long. 123°35' W; sec. 13, T 15 N, R 16 W). Named on Navarro (1961) 15' quadrangle.

Flynn Hills [MENDOCINO]: *ridge,* west-northwest-trending, 3 miles long, 2 miles north-northeast of Navarro (lat. 39°10'30" N, long. 123°31'45" W). Named on Navarro (1961) 15' quadrangle.

Flynn Hills Opening [MENDOCINO]: *area,* 1.25 miles north of Navarro (lat. 39°10'10" N, long. 123°32'45" W; near SE cor. sec. 7, T 15 N, R 15 W); the place is at the west end of Flynn Hills. Named on Navarro (1961) 15' quadrangle.

Fool Gulch [TRINITY]: *canyon,* drained by a stream that flows 3 miles to Halls Gulch 5 miles east of Trinity Center (lat. 41°00'50" N, long. 122°35'40" W; sec. 6, T 36 N, R 6 W). Named on Bonanza King (1955) and Schell Mountain (1950) 15' quadrangles.

Fool Gulch Camp [TRINITY]: *locality,* 27 miles northeast of Weaverville (lat. 40°59'55" N, long. 122°33'25" W; sec. 9, T 36 N, R 6 W); the place is at the head of Fool Gulch. Named on Schell Mountain (1950) 15' quadrangle.

Foot of Bull Ridge [TRINITY]: *ridge,* south-southwest- to west-southwest-trending, 1.5 miles long, 16 miles south-southwest of Black Rock Mountain (lat. 40°00'45" N, long. 123°10'30" W). Named on Black Rock Mountain (1954) 15' quadrangle.

Footsteps Rocks [DEL NORTE]: *relief feature,* 5 miles north-northwest of the mouth of Klamath River along the coast (lat. 41°37' N, long. 124°06'50" W; sec. 7, T 14 N, R 1 E). Named on Requa (1966) 7.5' quadrangle.

Forbes Creek [LAKE]: *stream,* flows 4.25 miles to Clear Lake at Lakeport, which first was called Forbestown (lat. 39°02'25" N, long. 122°54'40" W; at SE cor. sec. 24, T 14 N, R 10 W). Named on Lakeport (1958) 7.5' quadrangle.

Forbestown: see **Lakeport** [LAKE].

Ford Flat [LAKE]: *area,* 1.25 miles south-southwest of Whispering Pines (lat. 38°47'45" N, long. 122°43' W; sec. 23, T 11 N, R 8 W). Named on Whispering Pines (1958) 7.5' quadrangle. Called Fords Flat on Lower Lake (1945) 15' quadrangle.

Ford Prairie [HUMBOLDT]: *area,* 5 miles north of Coyote Peak (lat. 41°12'20" N, long. 123°52'25" W; on N line sec. 6, T 9 N, R 3 E). Named on Bald Hills (1982) and French Camp Ridge (1983) 7.5' quadrangles.

Forest Glen [TRINITY]: *village,* 15 miles south-southwest of Hayfork (lat. 40°22'25" N, long. 123°19'30" W; around SW cor. sec. 18, T 1 S, R 18 E). Named on Forest Glen (1979) 7.5' quadrangle. Postal authorities established Auto Rest post office in 1917 and changed the name to Forest Glen in 1920 (Salley, p. 12). Charles Brewer started a travelers stop that was called Auto Rest before new owners expanded the place and changed the name to Forest Glen; in the past, the site of present Forest Glen post office was known as Taylors Flat, and the name "Forest Glen" applied only to a resort located across the river from the present post office (Jones 326, 366).

Forest Glen Campground [TRINITY]: *locality,* 0.25 mile northwest of Forest Glen (lat. 40°22'35" N, long. 123°19'35" W; at E line sec. 13, T 1 S, R 7 E). Named on Naufus Creek (1979) 7.5' quadrangle.

Forest Glen Creek: see **Glen Creek** [TRINITY].

Forest Home [HUMBOLDT]: *locality,* 2.25 miles southwest of Scotia (lat. 40°27'20" N, long. 124°08' W; sec. 24, T 1 N, R 1 W). Named on Taylor Peak (1969) 7.5' quadrangle.

Forest Lake [LAKE]: *locality,* 0.25 mile northwest of Whispering Pines (lat. 38°49'05" N, long. 122°42'55" W; near SW cor. sec. 11, T 11 N, R 8 W). Named on Whispering Pines (1958) 7.5' quadrangle.

Forestville: see **Scotia** [HUMBOLDT].

Fork Camp [HUMBOLDT]: *locality,* less than 0.5 mile southeast of Board Camp Mountain (lat. 40°41'40" N, long. 123°42'45" W; near S line sec. 27, T 4 N, R 4 E). Named on Board Camp Mountain (1977) 7.5' quadrangle.

Forks: see **The Forks** [MENDOCINO].

Forks Camp [MENDOCINO]: *locality,* 9 miles southeast of Eden Valley (lat. 39°32'10" N, long. 123°04'20" W; near NW cor. sec. 3, T 19 N, R 11 W). Named on Eden Valley (1929) 15' quadrangle.

Forks Creek [MENDOCINO]: *stream,* flows about 1.5 miles to Elk Creek (2) 8.5 miles east-southeast of Eden Valley (lat. 39°34'25" N, long. 123°02'45" W). Named on Sanhedrin Mountain (1966) 7.5' quadrangle.

Forsythe Creek [MENDOCINO]: *stream,* flows 13 miles to Russian River 7.25 miles southwest of the town of Potter Valley (lat. 39°15' N, long. 123°12'10" W). Named on Potter Valley (1960) and Willits (1961) 15' quadrangles. The name is for Benjamin Franklin Forsythe, who settled in the neighborhood in 1857 (Gudde, 1949, p. 119).

Fort Baker [HUMBOLDT]: *locality,* 4 miles south-southwest of Showers Mountain (lat. 40°31'20" N, long. 123°43'10" W; sec. 27, T 2 N, R 4 E). Site named on Showers Mountain (1978) 7.5' quadrangle. Captain Thomas E. Ketcham, 3rd California Infantry, established the military post at the place in 1862, and the facility was abandoned in 1863; the name honored Colonel Edward D. Baker, 71st Pennsylvania Infantry, who was killed at the Battle of Ball's Bluff, Virginia, in 1861—Baker had been a senator from California (Frazer, p. 19-20).

Fort Bragg [MENDOCINO]: *town,* 24 miles west of Willits (lat. 39°26'40" N, long. 123°48'15" W; in and near sec. 7, T 18 N, R 17 W). Named on Fort Bragg (1960) 7.5' quadrangle. Postal authorities established Fort Bragg post office in 1858, discontinued it the same year, reestablished it in 1861, discontinued it in 1862, and reestablished it in 1885 (Frickstad, p. 94). The town incorporated in 1889. Lieutenant Horatio Gates Gibson, 3rd United States Artillery, established a military post on an Indian reservation at the site in 1857 and named the post Fort Bragg for Captain Braxton Bragg, also of the 3rd Artillery; the military facility was abandoned in 1864 (Frazer, p. 22). The town began in 1885, when a mill was moved to the place from Ten Mile River (Carpenter, p. 75). California Mining Bureau's (1909c) map shows a place called Gracy located about 16 miles by railroad east of Fort Bragg. Postal authorities established Gracy post office in 1896, moved it 1 mile south in 1899, moved it 2 miles northeast in 1902, moved it 2.25 miles southeast in 1905, and discontinued it in 1908 (Salley, p. 87). California Mining Bureau's (1909c) map also shows a place called Duffey situated 2.25 miles east of Gracy. Postal authorities established Duffey post office in 1904 and discontinued it in 1912; the name was for a pioneer family (Salley, p. 62). They established Ulco post office 17 miles east of Fort Bragg in 1931 and discontinued it in 1932; the name was from Union Lumber Company, which operated in the neighborhood (Salley, p. 227). According to Gudde (1949, p. 389), the flat-lying terrain between Fort Bragg and Mendocino was called White Plains because alkaline soil there appears white in places.

Fort Capell: see **Pecwan Creek** [HUMBOLDT].

Fort Dick [DEL NORTE]: *village,* 8 miles north-northeast of Crescent City (lat. 41°52' N, long. 124°08'55" W; sec. 14, T 17 N, R 1 W). Named on Crescent City (1966) 7.5' quadrangle. Postal authorities established Fort Dick post office in 1917 (Frickstad, p. 24). The name is from a log house built for defense against Indians; the place was called Newburg when a shake-and-shingle mill was moved there in 1888, but later the old name was revived (Gudde, 1949, p. 119). Wells' (1946) map shows a place called Berteleda located just south of Fort Dick.

Fort Gaston: see **Hoopa Valley** [HUMBOLDT].

Fort Grant: see **Camp Grant** [HUMBOLDT] (1).

Fort Humboldt: see **Eureka** [HUMBOLDT].

Fort Iaqua: see **Kneeland** [HUMBOLDT].

Fort Lincoln: see **Elk Valley** [DEL NORTE] (1).

Fort Lyons: see **Mad River** [HUMBOLDT-TRINITY].

Fort Seward [HUMBOLDT]: *village,* 3.5 miles north-northwest of Alderpoint along Eel River (lat. 40°13'20" N, long. 123°38'30" W; sec. 8, T 3 S, R 5 E). Named on Fort Seward (1969) 7.5' quadrangle. Postal authorities established Fort Seward post office in 1912 and discontinued it in 1972 (Salley, p. 78). The village began when Major Charles S. Lovell, 10th United States Infantry, established a military post called Fort Seward at the site in 1861; the military facility was abandoned in 1862—the name was for Secretary of State William H. Seward of Lincoln's cabinet (Frazer, p. 31).

Fort Seward Creek: see **Powers Creek** [HUMBOLDT] (2).

Fort Turwar: see **Turwar Valley** [DEL NORTE].

Fortuna [HUMBOLDT]: *town,* 14 miles south of Eureka along Eel River (lat. 40°35'50" N, long. 124°09'15" W; in and near sec. 35, T 3 N, R 1 W). Named on Fortuna (1959) 7.5' quadrangle. Postal authorities established Slide post office in 1876 and changed the name to Fortuna in 1888 (Frickstad, p. 46). The town incorporated in 1906. A minister named Gardner opened the place for settlement in the late 1870's and called it Fortune because he thought it was an ideal place to live, but later he gave the town the more euphonious name "Fortuna"—the community also had the early name "Springville" for the many springs nearby; the name "Slide" for the post office was from a landslide northwest of the town (Gudde, 1949, p. 120).

Fortunas: see **Cape Fortunas**, under **False Cape** [HUMBOLDT].

Fortune: see **Fortuna** [HUMBOLDT].

Fort Weller: see **Redwood Valley** [MENDOCINO] (1).

Fort Wool: see **Weitchpec** [HUMBOLDT].

Fort Wright: see **Round Valley** [MENDOCINO].

Forty-acre Opening [MENDOCINO]: *area,* 7 miles east-northeast of Ukiah (lat. 39°11'10" N, long. 123°05'10" W; on W line sec. 4, T 15 N, R 11 W). Named on Cow Mountain (1958) 7.5' quadrangle.

Fortyfour Creek [HUMBOLDT]: *stream,* flows 3 miles to Redwood Creek (1) 13 miles north-northeast of Trinidad (lat. 41°13'15" N, long. 124°00'40" W; sec. 25, T 10 N, R 1 E). Named on Rodgers Peak (1966) 7.5' quadrangle.

Forty Springs Valley [LAKE]: *valley,* 6 miles east-southeast of the town of Upper Lake along Gilbert Creek (lat. 39°07'45" N, long. 122°48'50" W; near SW cor. sec. 24, T 15 N, R 9 W). Named on Bartlett Mountain (1958) 7.5' quadrangle.

Foss Camp [TRINITY]: *locality,* nearly 6 miles south of Dubakella Mountain (lat. 40°18'05" N, long. 123°08'25" W; sec. 6, T 28 N, R 11 W). Named on Dubakella Mountain (1954) 15' quadrangle.

Fossil Creek [MENDOCINO]: *stream,* flows 2.5 miles to Middle Fork Eel River 16 miles northeast of Covelo (lat. 39°57'10" N, long. 123°01'50" W; sec. 12, T 24 N, R 11 W). Named on Leech Lake Mountain (1966) 7.5' quadrangle.

Foster Creek [MENDOCINO]:

(1) *stream,* flows nearly 1 mile to Elkhorn Creek (1) 6.25 miles northeast of Leggett (lat. 39°55' N, long. 123°37'35" W; sec. 16, T 24 N, R 16 W). Named on Noble Butte (1969) 7.5' quadrangle.

(2) *stream,* flows 4.5 miles to Rattlesnake Creek (2) 6 miles east-southeast of Leggett (lat. 39°49'50" N, long. 123°36'45" W; sec. 22, T 23 N, R 16 W). Named on Tan Oak Park (1969) 7.5' quadrangle.

Foster Creek [TRINITY]: *stream,* flows nearly 2 miles to Swift Creek (1) 20 miles northeast of Weaverville (lat. 40°58'55" N, long. 122°43' W; sec. 18, T 36 N, R 7 W). Named on Schell Mountain (1950) 15' quadrangle.

Foster Glades [TRINITY]: *area,* 16 miles north-northeast of Covelo [MENDOCINO] (lat. 39°59'25" N, long. 123°05'10" W; near W line sec. 27, T 25 N, R 11 W). Named on Leech Lake Mountain (1966) 7.5' quadrangle.

Foster Lake [TRINITY]: *lake,* 900 feet long, 7.5 miles southwest of Billys Peak (1) (lat. 41°02'50" N, long. 122°51'20" W; sec. 23, T 37 N, R 9 W). Named on Coffee Creek (1955) 15' quadrangle. Called Bear Lake on Etna (1934) 30' quadrangle, but United States Board on Geographic Names (1954, p. 3) rejected this designation for the feature, and noted that the name "Foster" commemorates William Foster, an early settler who helped maintain sport fishing in the region.

Foster Mountain [MENDOCINO]: *peak,* 9 miles north-northwest of the town of Potter Valley (lat. 39°26'20" N, long. 123°10'20" W; near SE cor. sec. 3, T 18 N, R 12 W). Altitude 3104 feet. Named on Potter Valley (1960) 15' quadrangle.

Found Lake [TRINITY]: *lake,* 400 feet long, 6.5 miles south-southwest of Billys Peak (1) (lat. 41°02'40" N, long. 122°48'50" W; at NE cor. sec. 30, T 37 N, R 8 W). Named on Coffee Creek (1955) 15' quadrangle.

Fountain: see **Hopland** [MENDOCINO].

Fountain of Youth Camp [LAKE]: *locality,* 8 miles west-northwest of Lakeport (lat. 39°05'05" N, long. 123°03'15" W; sec. 10, T 14 N, R 11 W). Named on Purdys Gardens (1958) 7.5' quadrangle.

Fourbit Gulch [TRINITY]: *canyon,* drained by a stream that flows nearly 0.5 mile to East Fork Hayfork Creek 9 miles north-northeast of Dubakella Mountain (lat. 40°29'35" N, long. 123°03'25" W); the mouth of the canyon is 800 feet up East Fork Hayfork Creek from the mouth of Twobit Gulch. Named on Dubakella Mountain (1954) 15' quadrangle.

Four Brothers [DEL NORTE]: *peaks,* four, 7.5 to 9 miles north-northeast of Buck Mountain (north peak at lat. 41°44'55" N, long. 122°47'05" W; south peak at lat. 41°43'40" N, long. 123°47'40" W). Named on Ship Mountain (1982) 7.5' quadrangle. United States Board on Geographic Names (1943, p. 13) approved the name "Ship Mountain" for the ridge that has the four peaks, and rejected the name "Four Brothers" for the ridge. Later the Board (1983a, p. 3) approved the name "Four Brothers" for the peaks, and reported that William Lewis, the first forest ranger in the Gasquet district, named the peaks before 1914 for the four Kelsey brothers, who built the Kelsey trail.

Four Corners [MENDOCINO]: *locality,* 9 miles west of Piercy (lat. 39°58'25" N, long. 123°57'55" W; sec. 32, T 5 S, R 21 E). Named on Bear Harbor (1969) 7.5' quadrangle. Called French on Kenny (1920) 15' quadrangle. Postal authorities established French post office in 1897 and discontinued it in 1901; the name was for David S. French, first postmaster (Salley, p. 80). They established Scottsville post office 4 miles east of French post office in 1899 and discontinued it in 1903 (Salley, p. 199).

Four Corners Rock [TRINITY]: *peak,* 11 miles southwest of Black Rock Mountain (lat. 40°05'30" N, long. 123°09'15" W; on W line sec. 19, T 26 N, R 11 W). Altitude 5406 feet. Named on Black Rock Mountain (1954) 15' quadrangle.

Fourmile Creek [HUMBOLDT]:

(1) *stream,* flows nearly 2 miles to Madden Creek 4.25 miles south of the settlement of Willow Creek (lat. 40°52'40" N, long. 123°37'55" W; near E line sec. 20, T 6 N, R 5 E). Named on Willow Creek (1979) 7.5' quadrangle.

(2) *stream,* flows 5.5 miles to the sea 6 miles southwest of Petrolia (lat. 40°15'20" N, long. 124°21'25" W; sec. 36, T 2 S, R 3 W). Named on Petrolia (1969) 7.5' quadrangle.

(3) *stream,* flows 3 miles to Mattole River 4.5 miles southeast of Honeydew (lat. 40°11'50" N, long. 124°03'20" W). Named on Honeydew (1970) 7.5' quadrangle.

Fourmile Creek [TRINITY]: *stream,* flows 1 mile to Virgin Creek 9 miles south-southeast of Salmon Mountain (lat. 41°03'10" N, long. 123°22' W). Named on Dees Peak (1978) 7.5' quadrangle.

Fourmile Glade [LAKE]: *area,* 6.5 miles west of Lakeport (lat. 39°02'45" N, long. 123°02'05" W; sec. 26, T 14 N, R 11 W). Named on Purdys Gardens (1958) 7.5' quadrangle.

Fourmile Ridge [LAKE]: *ridge,* north-trending, 1 mile long, 7 miles west of Lakeport (lat. 39°02'15" N, long. 123°02'35" W; sec. 26, 35, T 14 N, R 11 W). Named on Purdys Gardens (1958) 7.5' quadrangle.

Four Pines [MENDOCINO]: *locality,* 9 miles east of Eden Valley (lat. 39°36'40" N, long. 123°00'50" W; near NW cor. sec. 7, T 20 N, R 10 W). Site named on Sanhedrin Mountain (1966) 7.5' quadrangle.

Fourpoint Canyon [LAKE]: *canyon,* drained by a stream that flows 1.5 miles to Panther Creek (2) 8 miles west-northwest of Lakeport (lat. 39°04'30" N, long. 123°03'35" W; sec. 15, T 14 N, R 11 W). Named on Purdys Gardens (1958) 7.5' quadrangle.

Fox Camp Creek [HUMBOLDT]: *stream,* flows 1.5 miles to Rattlesnake Creek (2) 11.5 miles south of Scotia (lat. 40°19'05" N, long. 124°05'05" W; near NE cor. sec. 8, T 2 S, R 1 E). Named on Bull Creek (1969) 7.5' quadrangle.

Fox Camp Spring [HUMBOLDT]: *spring,* 10.5 miles south of Scotia (lat. 40°19'55" N, long. 124°03'55" W; near SE cor. sec. 33, T 1 S, R 1 E). Named on Bull Creek (1969) 7.5' quadrangle.

Fox Creek [HUMBOLDT]: *stream,* flows 2.5 miles to Van Duzen River 10.5 miles southwest of Lone Star Junction (lat. 40°30'40" N, long. 123°59'55" W; sec. 31, T 2 N, R 2 E). Named on Hydesville (1979) and Owl Creek (1979) 7.5' quadrangles.

Fox Creek [MENDOCINO]: *stream,* flows 1.5 miles to South Fork Eel River 6 miles north of Branscomb (lat. 39°44'25" N, long. 123°37'55" W; sec. 21, T 22 N, R 16 W). Named on Cahto Peak (1967) and Lincoln Ridge (1966) 7.5' quadrangles.

Fox Gulch [MENDOCINO]: *canyon,* drained by a stream that flows 0.5 mile to Signal Port Creek 6.25 miles northwest of Gualala (lat. 38°49'50" N, long. 123°36'50" W; sec. 2, T 11 N, R 16 W). Named on Gualala (1960) 7.5' quadrangle.

Fox Gulch [TRINITY]:

(1) *canyon,* drained by a stream that flows 1.5 miles to East Fork of North Fork Trinity River 2 miles north of Helena (lat. 40°48'15" N, long. 123°07'15" W; sec. 16, T 34 N, R 11 W). Named on Helena (1951) 15' quadrangle.

(2) *canyon,* drained by a stream that flows 2 miles to Browns Creek 3.25 miles east of Chanchelulla Peak (lat. 40°28'10" N, long. 122°55'40" W; sec. 7, T 30 N, R 9 W). Named on Chanchelulla Peak (1951) 15' quadrangle.

Fox Peak [MENDOCINO]: *peak,* 10 miles east-southeast of Longvale (lat. 39°30'15" N, long. 123°15'40" W; near W line sec. 13, T 19 N, R 13 W). Altitude 2939 feet. Named on Laytonville (1951) 15' quadrangle.

Fox Ridge [DEL NORTE]: *ridge*, north- to northeast-trending, 7 miles long, 7 miles north of Buck Mountain between Hurdygurdy Creek and Jones Creek (lat. 41°44' N, long. 123°52' W). Named on Cant Hook Mountain (1982), Hurdygurdy Butte (1982), and Ship Mountain (1982) 7.5' quadrangles.

Fox Spring [HUMBOLDT]: *spring*, 6 miles south-southeast of Honeydew (lat. 40°09'55" N, long. 124°04'40" W; at NW cor. sec. 33, T 3 S, R 1 E). Named on Honeydew (1970) 7.5' quadrangle.

Francis: see **White Rock City** [TRINITY].

Francis Creek [HUMBOLDT]: *stream*, flows 5 miles to Salt River 1.25 miles north of Ferndale (lat. 40°35'40" N, long. 124°15'45" W; sec. 35, T 3 N, R 2 W). Named on Ferndale (1959) 7.5' quadrangle. The name commemorates Francis Francis, an early settler (Carlson, p. 13).

Frank: see **Shelter Cove** [HUMBOLDT] (2)

Franklin Canyon [LAKE]: *canyon*, drained by a stream that flows nearly 2 miles to Bartlett Creek 11 miles north-northwest of Clearlake Oaks (lat. 39°10'35" N, long. 122°43'40" W; sec. 3, T 15 N, R 8 W). Named on Clearlake Oaks (1960) 15' quadrangle.

Franks Canyon [MENDOCINO]: *canyon*, drained by a stream that flows 3 miles to Dry Creek (2) 11 miles south-southwest of Hopland (lat. 38°49'20" N, long. 123°10'10" W; near NW cor. sec. 11, T 11 N, R 12 W). Named on Hopland (1960) 15' quadrangle.

Fraser Creek: see **Kinsey Creek** [HUMBOLDT] (1).

Fraser Point [LAKE]: *promontory*, 8 miles northwest of the town of Lower Lake along Clear Lake (lat. 38°58'55" N, long. 122°43'55" W; sec. 15, T 13 N, R 8 W). Named on Clearlake Highlands (1958) 7.5' quadrangle. Bradley (p. 215) noted that a feature called Behr Soda Spring, owned by John Behr, was located 5 miles east of Kelseyville at the edge of Clear Lake (sec. 10, T 13 N, R 8 W)—a site just northwest of present Fraser Point.

Fraser Ridge: see **Kinsey Ridge** [HUMBOLDT] (1).

Frazer Creek [MENDOCINO]: *stream*, flows 1.5 miles to Seaside Creek 5.5 miles south of Westport (lat. 39°33'30" N, long. 123°45'45" W; sec. 33, T 20 N, R 17 W). Named on Inglenook (1966) 7.5' quadrangle.

Frazier Gardens [TRINITY]: *area*, 7 miles south of Kettenpom (lat. 40°02'55" N, long. 123°26'40" W; near SE cor. sec. 1, T 5 S, R 6 E). Named on Lake Mountain (1967) 7.5' quadrangle.

Freathy Creek: see **Water Gulch** [MENDOCINO].

Freeman Creek [HUMBOLDT]: *stream*, flows 1.5 miles to Little River 5.25 miles east-southeast of Trinidad (lat. 41°01'20" N, long. 124°03'15" W; sec. 3, T 7 N, R 1 E). Named on Crannell (1966) 7.5' quadrangle.

Freese Creek [HUMBOLDT]: *stream*, flows 3.5 miles to join Indian Creek (3) and form North Fork Yager Creek 4 miles north-northeast of Yager Junction (lat. 40°36'10" N, long. 123°47'40" W; near NW cor. sec. 36, T 3 N, R 3 E). Named on Showers Mountain (1978) and Yager Junction (1979) 7.5' quadrangles. The name commemorates Johathon Freese and Elizabeth Freese, who settled in the neighborhood before 1878 (Turner, p. 88).

Freethy Gulch: see **Frethy Gulch** [TRINITY].

Freezeout [TRINITY]: *locality*, 2.25 miles south-southeast of Black Lassic (lat. 40°18'45" N, long. 123°30'45" W). Named on Black Lassic (1979) 7.5' quadrangle.

Freezeout Spring [LAKE]: *spring*, 7.5 miles south-southeast of Potato Hill (lat. 39°15'45" N, long. 122°43'15" W; sec. 2, T 16 N, R 8 W). Named on Fouts Springs (1968) 7.5' quadrangle.

French: see **Four Corners** [MENDOCINO].

French Bar [TRINITY]: *locality*, 9 miles east-southeast of Burnt Ranch along Trinity River (lat. 40°46'45" N, long. 123°18'20" W; sec. 29, T 5 N, R 8 E); the place is at the mouth of Big French Creek. Named on Ironside Mountain (1951) 15' quadrangle.

French Camp [HUMBOLDT]: *locality*, 2.5 miles east-northeast of Coyote Peak (lat. 41°09'05" N, long. 123°49'10" W; sec. 22, T 9 N, R 3 E). Named on French Camp Ridge (1983) 7.5' quadrangle.

French Camp Ridge [HUMBOLDT]: *ridge*, north-trending, 5 miles long, center 3.5 miles northeast of Coyote Peak (lat. 41°10'30" N, long. 123°49' W); French Camp is near the south end of the feature. Named on French Camp Ridge (1983) 7.5' quadrangle.

French Cove [TRINITY]:

(1) *relief feature*, 10.5 miles southwest of Billys Peak (1) (lat. 41°01' N, long. 122°53'35" W; near S line sec. 33, T 37 N, R 9 W). Named on Coffee Creek (1955) 15' quadrangle.

(2) *relief feature*, 14 miles south of Black Rock Mountain (lat. 40°00'20" N, long. 122°57'40" W; sec. 22, T 25 N, R 10 W). Named on Yolla Bolly (1954) 15' quadrangle.

French Creek [HUMBOLDT]: *stream*, flows nearly 2 miles to Mattole River 11 miles west-northwest of Garberville (lat. 40°08'15" N, long. 123°59'25" W; sec. 6, T 4 S, R 2 E). Named on Honeydew (1970) 7.5' quadrangle.

French Creek [LAKE]: *stream*, flows 4 miles to Rice Fork 4.5 miles south-southwest of Potato Hill (lat. 39°17'25" N, long. 122°50' W; near SE cor. sec. 26, T 17 N, R 9 W); the stream heads at French Ridge. Named on Bartlett Mountain (1958) and Potato Hill (1967) 7.5' quadrangles.

French Creek: see **Big French Creek** [TRINITY]; **Little French Creek** [TRINITY].

French Flat [DEL NORTE]: *area*, 1.5 miles south of Gasquet (lat. 41°49'30" N, long. 123°58'15" W; sec. 32, T 17 N, R 2 E). Named on Gasquet (1981) 7.5' quadrangle. Preston Peak (1922) 30' quadrangle shows a locality called French Hill at present French Flat.

French Gulch [DEL NORTE]: *canyon*, 0.5 mile long, 1.5 miles south of Gasquet at the head of Redwood Creek (lat. 41°49'25" N, long. 123°58'10" W; sec. 32, T 16 N, R 2 E); the canyon is southeast of French Flat. Named on Gasquet (1981) 7.5' quadrangle.

French Gulch [HUMBOLDT]: *canyon*, drained by a stream that flows 0.5 mile to Eel River 7.5 miles south-southeast of Fortuna (lat. 40°30'20" N, long. 124°05'20" W; at S line sec. 32, T 2 N, R 1 E). Named on Hydesville (1979) 7.5' quadrangle. Turner (p. 91) used the form "French's Gulch" for the name, which he noted commemorates John French, who had a shingle bolt operation at the place in the late 1880's.

French Gulch [TRINITY]: *canyon*, drained by a stream that flows 1 mile to Rattlesnake Creek (1) 15 miles north of Helena (lat. 40°59'10" N, long. 123°09'15" W). Named on Helena (1951) 15' quadrangle.

French Hill [DEL NORTE]: *ridge*, southwest-trending, 0.5 mile long, 2 miles south-southwest of Gasquet (lat. 41°49'10" N, long. 123°58'45" W; sec. 31, 32, T 17 N, R 2 E); the ridge is southwest of French Flat. Named on Gasquet (1981) 7.5' quadrangle.

French Hill: see **French Flat** [DEL NORTE].

Frenchman Creek [HUMBOLDT]: *stream*, flows 3.5 miles to Jewett Creek (2) 4.5 miles south of Alderpoint (lat. 40°06'30" N, long. 123°37'25" W; near S line sec. 16, T 4 S, R 5 E). Named on Harris (1969) 7.5' quadrangle.

French Ridge [LAKE]: *ridge*, generally east-northeast-trending, 2.25 miles long, 7 miles northeast of the town of Upper Lake (lat. 39°14'45" N, long. 122°49'30" W). Named on Bartlett Mountain (1958) and Potato Hill (1967) 7.5' quadrangles.

French Town: see **Weaverville** [TRINITY].

Freshwater [HUMBOLDT]: *village*, 7.5 miles south of Arcata (lat. 40°45'40" N, long. 124°03'35" W; near W line sec. 3, T 4 N, R 1 E); the place is along Freshwater Creek. Named on Arcata South (1959) 7.5' quadrangle. Turner (p. 91) gave the alternate names "Wrangletown," "Garfield," "Hardscrabble," and "Lambertville" for the place.

Freshwater Corners [HUMBOLDT]: *locality*, 6 miles south of Arcata (lat. 40°47'05" N, long. 124°05'05" W; near E line sec. 29, T 5 N, R 1 E); the place is 2 miles northwest of Freshwater. Named on Arcata South (1959) 7.5' quadrangle.

Freshwater Creek [HUMBOLDT]: *stream*, flows 14 miles to Freshwater Slough about 6 miles south of Arcata (lat. 40°47'15" N, long. 124°05'45" W; sec. 29, T 5 N, R 1 E). Named on Arcata South (1959), Iaqua Buttes (1979), and McWhinney Creek (1979) 7.5' quadrangles. South Fork enters from the south 6.5 miles upstream from the mouth of the main creek; it is 4.5 miles long and is named on Iaqua Buttes (1979) and McWhinney Creek (1979) 7.5' quadrangles.

Freshwater Creek: see **Little Freshwater Creek** [HUMBOLDT].

Freshwater Junction [HUMBOLDT]: *locality*, 2 miles east of downtown Eureka along Northwestern Pacific Railroad (lat. 40°48'20" N, long. 124°07'15" W; sec. 24, T 5 N, R 1 W). Named on Eureka (1942) 15' quadrangle, which shows the junction of Pacific Lumber Company Railroad and Northwestern Pacific Railroad at the place.

Freshwater Lagoon [HUMBOLDT]: *lake*, 7100 feet long, 2 miles southwest of Orick near the coast (lat. 41°16'05" N, long. 124°05'30" W; on W line sec. 8, T 10 N, R 1 E). Named on Orick (1966) 7.5' quadrangle. The water in the lake is fresh (Waterman, p. 264).

Freshwater Rocks [HUMBOLDT]: *rocks*, 2.5 miles southwest of Orick, and 350 feet offshore (lat. 41°15'55" N, long. 124°06' W); the rocks are west of Freshwater Lagoon. Named on Orick (1966) 7.5' quadrangle. United States Board on Geographic Names (1957, p. 1) rejected the name "Sharp Point" for the feature.

Freshwater Slough [HUMBOLDT]: *water feature*, joins Eureka Slough 5 miles south-southwest of Arcata (lat. 40°48'05" N, long. 124°07' W); the feature is the extension of Freshwater Creek. Named on Arcata South (1959) 7.5' quadrangle. Frethy Gulch [TRINITY]: canyon, drained by a stream that flows 1.5 miles to Trinity River 20 miles northeast of Weaverville (lat. 40°56'50" N, long. 122°41'05" W; near W line sec. 28, T 36 N, R 7 W). Named on Schell Mountain (1950) 15' quadrangle. United States Board on Geographic Names (1983d, p. 5) approved the form "Freethy Gulch" for the name, which reportedly is for Richard Freethy, who came to the neighborhood in the late nineteenth century.

Friday Camp [HUMBOLDT]: *locality*, 8 miles south-southwest of the settlement of Willow Creek (lat. 40°49'50" N, long. 123°41'15" W; sec. 11, T 5 N, R 4 E). Named on Grouse Mountain (1979) 7.5' quadrangle.

Friday Ridge [HUMBOLDT]: *ridge*, north-trending, 4 miles long, 6.5 miles south-southwest of the settlement of Willow Creek (lat. 40°51'15" N, long. 123°40'35" W). Named on Grouse Mountain (1979) and Willow Creek (1979) 7.5' quadrangles.

Friend Lake [TRINITY]: *lake*, 450 feet long, 8 miles north-northwest of

Forest Glen (lat. 40°29' N, long. 123°22'10" W; sec. 10, T 1 N, R 7 E). Named on Naufus Creek (1979) 7.5' quadrangle, which shows Friend place near the lake.

Friend Mountain [TRINITY]: *peak,* 10 miles south-southeast of Hyampom (lat. 40°30'10" N, long. 123°20'20" W; on N line sec. 1, T 1 N, R 7 E); the peak is 2.5 miles northeast of Friend Lake. Altitude 4505 feet. Named on Hyampom (1951) 15' quadrangle, and on Naufus Creek (1979) 7.5' quadrangle.

Frietas Gulch [TRINITY]: *canyon,* drained by a stream that flows 1.25 miles to Indian Creek (2) 10.5 miles south-southeast of Weaverville (lat. 40°36' N, long. 122°50'40" W; at E line sec. 26, T 32 N, R 9 W). Named on Weaverville (1950) 15' quadrangle. The misspelled name is for Joseph Freitas, a Portuguese immigrant who lived in the neighborhood (Jones, p. 302).

Frost Creek [HUMBOLDT]:
(1) *stream,* flows nearly 2 miles to Larabee Creek 8.5 miles northwest of Blocksburg (lat. 40°22'20" N, long. 123°44'30" W; sec. 17, T 1 S, R 4 E). Named on Blocksburg (1969) and Larabee Valley (1977) 7.5' quadrangles.
(2) *stream,* flows 1.25 miles to Redwood Creek (2) 5 miles west of Garberville (lat. 40°06'50" N, long. 123°53'05" W; near E line sec. 18, T 4 S, R 3 E). Named on Briceland (1969) and Garberville (1970) 7.5' quadrangles.

Fruit Island [LAKE]: *island,* 750 feet long, 3.25 miles west-southwest of Clearlake Oaks in Clear Lake (lat. 39°00'35" N, long. 122°43'55" W). Named on Clearlake Oaks (1958) 7.5' quadrangle.

Fruit Lake [MENDOCINO]: *intermittent lake,* 175 feet long, 2.5 miles north-northeast of Ornbaun Valley (lat. 38°56'55" N, long. 123°16'55" W; near N line sec. 34, T 13 N, R 13 W). Named on Ornbaun Valley (1960) 15' quadrangle.

Fruitland [HUMBOLDT]: *settlement,* 6 miles east-southeast of Weott (lat. 40°17'45" N, long. 123°49'10" W; sec. 15, T 2 S, R 3 E); the place is 0.5 mile northwest of Elk Prairie (2). Named on Myers Flat (1969) 7.5' quadrangle. Postal authorities established Fruitland post office in 1890 and discontinued it in 1934 (Frickstad, p. 43). A colony of Dutch people planted fruit orchards at the place, but the venture failed (Turner, p. 91-92). According to Hanna (p. 114), the place also was known as Elk Prairie. Postal authorities established an Elk Prairie post office 8 miles northwest of Camp Grant post office in 1886 and discontinued it in 1887 (Salley, p. 67).

Frying Pan [TRINITY]: *locality,* 8.5 miles south of Black Rock Mountain (lat. 40°05'05" N, long. 122°58'40" W; near S line sec. 22, T 26 N, R 10 W). Named on Yolla Bolly (1954) 15' quadrangle.

Fuller Canyon [LAKE]: *canyon,* drained by stream that flows 2 miles to South Fork Long Valley Creek 6 miles north-northwest of Clearlake Oaks (lat. 39°06'20" N, long. 122°43'10" W; near W line sec. 35, T 15 N, R 8 W). Named on Clearlake Oaks (1958) 7.5' quadrangle. The name is for the Fuller family, settlers of 1905 (Gudde, 1969, p. 115).

Fuller Creek [LAKE]: *stream,* flows 3 miles to join Mill Creek (1) and form Salmon Creek 6.25 miles northwest of Bear Mountain (lat. 39°28'35" N, long. 122°58'35" W; near E line sec. 29, T 19 N, R 10 W). Named on Potter Valley (1960) 15' quadrangle, and on Lake Pillsbury (1967) 7.5' quadrangle. On Lake Pillsbury (1951) 15' quadrangle, present Salmon Creek is considered part of Fuller Creek.

Fulton Gulch [TRINITY]: *canyon,* drained by a stream that flows 2.25 miles to East Fork Hayfork Creek 8.5 miles east-southeast of Hayfork (lat. 40°30'15" N, long. 123°02'15" W; at S line sec. 30, T 31 N, R 10 W). Named on Hayfork (1951) 15' quadrangle.

Fulweiter Creek [MENDOCINO]: *stream,* flows 1.25 miles to Little Lake Valley 3 miles east-southeast of Willits (lat. 39°23'50" N, long. 123°18' W; sec. 21, T 18 N, R 13 W). Named on Willits (1961) 15' quadrangle.

– G –

Gainor Peak: see **Gaynor Peak** [HUMBOLDT].

Gallagher Creek [LAKE]: *stream,* flows 2 miles to Putah Creek 4.25 miles northeast of Middletown (lat. 38°47'40" N, long. 122°33'15" W). Named on Middletown (1958) 7.5' quadrangle.

Gans: see **Orick** [HUMBOLDT].

Gans Prairie [HUMBOLDT]: *area,* 3 miles east-southeast of Orick (lat. 41°16'35" N, long. 124°00'15" W; near S line sec. 1, T 10 N, R 1 E). Named on Orick (1966) 7.5' quadrangle.

Gant Gulch [TRINITY]: *canyon,* drained by a stream that flows 2.5 miles to East Fork Hayfork Creek 10 miles north-northeast of Dubakella Mountain (lat. 40°29'50" N, long. 123°02'55" W). Named on Dubakella Mountain (1954) and Hayfork (1951) 15' quadrangles. Called Grant Gulch on Averill's (1940) map.

Gap: see **The Gap** [HUMBOLDT].

Garberville [HUMBOLDT]: *town,* 52 miles south-southeast of Eureka along South Fork Eel River (lat. 40°06' N, long. 123°47'40" W; sec. 24, T 4 S, R 3 E). Named on Garberville (1970) 7.5' quadrangle. Postal authorities established Garberville post office in 1874 (Frickstad, p. 43). J.E. Wood founded the community in 1862 (Turner, p. 92). The name is for Jacob C. Garber, who settled at the site in the 1870's (Gudde, 1949, p. 124). Postal authorities established Hartsook post office 6.5 miles south of Garberville in 1926 and moved it 0.5 mile north in 1938, when they changed the name to Richardson Grove; the name "Hartsook" was for a resort operator, and Richardson Grove post office is at a state park named for Friend W. Richardson, governor of California from 1923 until 1927 (Salley, p. 94, 184).

Garby's Spring: see **Ukiah** [MENDOCINO].

Garcia Creek [MENDOCINO]: *stream,* flows 8 miles to Eel River 12.5 miles north-northwest of the town of Potter Valley (lat. 39°29'35" N, long. 123°10'05" W; near E line sec. 22, T 19 N, R 12 W). Named on Potter Valley (1960) 15' quadrangle, and on Brushy Mountain (1966) 7.5' quadrangle. Called Garsey Creek on Eden Valley (1952) 15' quadrangle.

Garcia River [MENDOCINO]: *stream,* flows 37 miles to the sea nearly 4 miles northwest of the village of Point Arena (lat. 38°57'15" N, long. 123°43'55" W; at N line sec. 34, T 13 N, R 17 W). Named on Ornbaun Valley (1960) and Point Arena (1960) 15' quadrangles. The name commemorates Rafael Garcia, who had an unconfirmed land grant near Point Arena (Hoover, Rensch, and Rensch, p. 195). North Fork enters 8 miles upstream from the mouth of the main river and is 7 miles long. South Fork enters from the south-southeast 15 miles upstream from the mouth of the main river and is 3.5 miles long. Both forks are named on Point Arena (1960) 15' quadrangle. A resort called Point Arena Hot Springs was situated close to the north bank of Garcia River (W half of NE quarter sec. 27, T 12 N, R 15 W) (Jennings, p. 61).

Garden Gulch [TRINITY]:
(1) *canyon,* drained by a stream that flows nearly 4 miles to Sidney Gulch in Weaverville (lat. 40°44'05" N, long. 122°36'25" W; near E line sec. 12, T 33 N, R 10 W). Named on Trinity Dam (1950) and Weaverville (1950) 15' quadrangles.
(2) *canyon,* drained by a stream that flows 3 miles to Carr Creek (2) 5.5 miles east-northeast of Hayfork (lat. 40°34'40" N, long. 123°05'10" W; near SE cor. sec. 34, T 32 N, R 11 W). Named on Hayfork (1951) 15' quadrangle.
(3) *canyon,* drained by a stream that flows about 1.25 miles to Salt Creek (4) 4.5 miles north of Dubakella Mountain (lat. 40°26'45" N, long. 123°08'30" W; near S line sec. 18, T 30 N, R 11 W). Named on Dubakella Mountain (1954) 15' quadrangle.

Gardner Gulch [TRINITY]:
(1) *canyon,* drained by a stream that flows 2 miles to Shock Creek 8 miles east of Hayfork (lat. 40°34'30" N, long. 123°02'20" W; at N line sec. 6, T 31 N, R 10 W). Named on Hayfork (1951) 15' quadrangle.
(2) *canyon,* drained by a stream that flows 1 mile to Philpot Creek 6 miles north-northwest of Dubakella Mountain (lat. 40°28'10" N, long. 123°10'15" W; near W line sec. 12, T 30 N, R 12 W). Named on Dubakella Mountain (1954) 15' quadrangle.

Garfield: see **Freshwater** [HUMBOLDT].

Garner Island [LAKE]: *island,* 350 feet long, 2.25 miles northwest of the town of Lower Lake in Clear Lake (lat. 38°56' N, long. 122°38'30" W; sec. 33, T 13 N, R 7 W). Named on Clearlake Highlands (1958) 7.5' quadrangle.

Garner Prairie [HUMBOLDT]: *area,* 3.5 miles southeast of Korbel (lat. 40°49'40" N, long. 123°55'15" W; sec. 11, T 5 N, R 2 E). Named on Korbel (1979) 7.5' quadrangle.

Garretson Soda Springs: see **Cinnabar Gulch** [TRINITY].

Garrett Creek [HUMBOLDT]: *stream,* flows 2.5 miles to Redwood Creek (1) nearly 4 miles south-southwest of Coyote Peak (lat. 41°04'55" N, long. 123°52'45" W; sec. 18, T 8 N, R 3 E). Named on Hupa Mountain (1982) and Panther Creek (1982) 7.5' quadrangles.

Garrett Mountain [LAKE]: *peak,* 5.25 miles east of the town of Potter Valley [MENDOCINO] (lat. 39°19'20" N, long. 123°00'35" W; at N line sec. 20, T 17 N, R 10 W). Altitude 3961 feet. Named on Potter Valley (1960) 7.5' quadrangle.

Garsey Creek: see **Garcia Creek** [MENDOCINO].

Gary Creek [HUMBOLDT]: *stream,* flows nearly 2 miles to South Fork Trinity River 13 miles south-southeast of the settlement of Willow Creek (lat. 40°45'30" N, long. 123°33'10" W). Named on Hennessy Peak (1979) and Sims Mountain (1979) 7.5' quadrangles.

Gas Camp: see **Wheel Gulch** [MENDOCINO].

Gas Creek [TRINITY]: *stream,* flows 3 miles to North Fork Trinity River 15 miles north of Helena (lat. 40°59'05" N, long. 123°09'45" W). Named on Helena (1951) 15' quadrangle.

Gas Jet: see **Capetown** [HUMBOLDT].

Gas Mine Ridge [MENDOCINO]: *ridge,* southwest- to west-trending, 2.5 miles long, 7 miles west-northwest of Covelo (lat. 39°50'05" N, long. 123°22'10" W). Named on Covelo West (1967) and Iron Peak (1967) 7.5' quadrangles.

Gasquet [DEL NORTE]: *village,* 13 miles east-northeast of Crescent City (lat. 41°50'50" N, long. 123°58' W; sec. 19, 20, T 17 N, R 2 E). Named on Gasquet (1981) 7.5' quadrangle. Postal authorities established Gasquet post office in 1879, discontinued it in 1902, and reestablished it in 1949;

the name is for Horace Gasquet, first postmaster, who settled at the site in the 1850's and operated a stage stop (Salley, p. 83).

Gasquet Mountain [DEL NORTE]: *peak,* 2.25 miles north-northwest of Gasquet (lat. 41°52'45" N, long. 123°59' W; at E line sec. 7, T 17 N, R 2 E). Altitude 2620 feet. Named on Gasquet (1951) 15' quadrangle.

Gas Spring [LAKE]: *spring,* 12 miles north of Clearlake Oaks (lat. 39°11'15" N, long. 122°41'50" W; near NW cor. sec. 1, T 15 N, R 8 W). Named on Clearlake Oaks (1960) 15' quadrangle.

Gaston: see **Fort Gaston**, under **Hoopa Valley** [HUMBOLDT].

Gates Creek [MENDOCINO]: *stream,* flows 4 miles to Daugherty Creek 14 miles north-northwest of Boonville (lat. 35°12'20" N, long. 123°26' W; near N line sec. 32, T 16 N, R 14 W). Named on Boonville (1959) 15' quadrangle.

Gates Creek [TRINITY]: *stream,* flows 3 miles to Corral Creek (1) 4.5 miles east-northeast of Hyampom (lat. 40°38'05" N, long. 123°21'45" W; near SW cor. sec. 14, T 3 N, R 7 E). Named on Hyampom (1951) 15' quadrangle.

Gaus: see **Orick** [HUMBOLDT].

Gaynor Peak [HUMBOLDT]: *peak,* 12 miles south-southeast of the settlement of Willow Creek (lat. 40°46'05" N, long. 123°34'20" W). Altitude 3442 feet. Named on Hennessy Peak (1979) 7.5' quadrangle. United States Board on Geographic Names (1982c, p. 2) approved the designation "Gainor Peak" for the feature, and noted that the name reportedly commemorates George Gainor, who homesteaded in the neighborhood in 1916.

Gebhardt Lake: see **McCreary Lake** [LAKE].

Gemmill Gulch [TRINITY]: *canyon,* drained by a stream that flows 0.5 mile to Hayfork Creek nearly 6 miles northeast of Dubakella Mountain (lat. 40°25'50" N, long. 123°03'20" W; at N line sec. 25, T 30 N, R 11 W). Named on Dubakella Mountain (1954) 15' quadrangle.

George Lambert Canyon [MENDOCINO]: *canyon,* drained by a stream that flows 3.5 miles to Middle Fork Eel River 6 miles east-southeast of Covelo (lat. 39°45'40" N, long. 123°08'35" W; sec. 13, T 22 N, R 12 W); the canyon is northwest of George Lambert Ridge. Named on Covelo East (1967) and Newhouse Ridge (1967) 7.5' quadrangles.

George Lambert Ridge [MENDOCINO]: *ridge,* generally west-southwest-trending, 2.5 miles long, 7.5 miles east of Covelo (lat. 39°46'30" N, long. 123°06'45" W). Named on Covelo East (1967) and Newhouse Ridge (1967) 7.5' quadrangles.

Georges Valley [TRINITY]: *relief feature,* 13 miles south-southwest of Black Rock Mountain (lat. 40°01'20" N, long. 123°04'20" W; sec. 15, T 25 N, R 11 W). Named on Black Rock Mountain (1954) 15' quadrangle.

German Creek [MENDOCINO]: *stream,* flows 3 miles to Camp Creek 6 miles east-northeast of Ornbaun Valley (lat. 38°56'20" N, long. 123°24'25" W; sec. 33, T 13 N, R 14 W). Named on Ornbaun Valley (1960) 15' quadrangle.

German Gap [MENDOCINO]: *pass,* 8 miles west-northwest of Ornbaun Valley (lat. 38°57'40" N, long. 123°26'40" W; sec. 30, T 13 N, R 14 W); the pass is at the head of German Creek. Named on Ornbaun Valley (1960) 15' quadrangle.

German Opening [MENDOCINO]: *area,* 6.25 miles west-northwest of Ornbaun Valley (lat. 38°56'30" N, long. 123°20'50" W; sec. 33, T 13 N, R 14 W). Named on Ornbaun Valley (1960) 15' quadrangle.

German Ridge [MENDOCINO]: *ridge,* southeast-trending, 2 miles long, 7.5 miles west-northwest of Ornbaun Valley (lat. 38°57'15" N, long. 123°25'45" W); the ridge is northeast of German Creek. Named on Ornbaun Valley (1960) 15' quadrangle.

Getchell Gulch [MENDOCINO]: *canyon,* drained by a stream that flows 1.5 miles to the sea 3 miles northwest of Gualala (lat. 38°47'50" N, long. 123°34'15" W; near SW cor. sec. 17, T 11 N, R 15 W). Named on Gualala (1960) 7.5' quadrangle. Point Arena (1943) 15' quadrangle has the form "Getchel" for the name, but United States Board on Geographic Names (1962c, p. 18) rejected the names "Getchel Gulch" and "Steep Gulch" for the canyon, and noted that the name "Getchell" is for an early settler.

Geyser Rock [LAKE]: *relief feature,* 12 miles south-southeast of Kelseyville on Lake-Sonoma County line (lat. 38°48'50" N, long. 122°45'55" W; at S line sec. 8, T 11 N, R 8 W). Named on The Geysers (1959) 7.5' quadrangle.

Giacomini Prairie [HUMBOLDT]: *area,* 2.25 miles south of Scotia (lat. 40°26'50" N, long. 124°06'15" W; on S line sec. 19, T 1 N, R 1 E). Named on Scotia (1970) 7.5' quadrangle.

Gibson: see **Houdd Gibson Camp**, under **Castle Rock Springs** [LAKE].

Gibson Creek [HUMBOLDT]: *stream,* flows 1.5 miles to Mattole River 9.5 miles southwest of Garberville (lat. 40°01'20" N, long. 123°56'15" W). Named on Briceland (1969) 7.5' quadrangle.

Gibson Creek [MENDOCINO]:

(1) *stream,* flows 1.5 miles to Cold Creek (4) 7.5 miles east of Spyrock (2) (lat. 39°52'40" N, long. 123°17'55" W; sec. 3, T 23 N, R 13 W). Named on Mina (1967) 7.5' quadrangle.

(2) *stream,* flows 3 miles to lowlands along Russian River at Ukiah (lat. 39°09' N, long. 123°13'05" W). Named on Boonville (1959) 15' quadrangle, and on Ukiah (1958) 7.5' quadrangle. Called Austin Creek on Ukiah (1944) 15' quadrangle, but United States Board on Geographic Names (1962a, p. 12) rejected this name for the stream.

Gibson Gulch [TRINITY]: *canyon,* 0.25 mile long, opens into the canyon of East Fork Trinity River 24 miles northeast of Weaverville (lat. 40°59'15" N, long. 122°38' W; near SE cor. sec. 11, T 36 N, R 7 W). Named on Schell Mountain (1950) 15' quadrangle.

Gibson Hill [LAKE]: *peak,* 6 miles south-southeast of Cold Spring Mountain (lat. 39°00'55" N, long. 122°27'25" W; sec. 31, T 14 N, R 5 W). Named on Wilbur Springs (1961) 15' quadrangle.

Gibson Meadow [TRINITY]: *area,* 16 miles north-northeast of Weaverville (lat. 40°57'15" N, long. 122°51' W; sec. 25, T 36 N, R 9 W); the place is 1.5 miles northeast of Gibson Peak. Named on Trinity Dam (1950) 15' quadrangle.

Gibson Peak [TRINITY]: *peak,* 15 miles north-northeast of Weaverville (lat. 40°56'35" N, long. 122°52'20" W; on S line sec. 26, T 36 N, R 9 W). Altitude 8400 feet. Named on Trinity Dam (1950) 15' quadrangle. Called Granite Pk. on Weaverville (1913) 30' quadrangle, but United States Board on Geographic Names (1949, p. 3) rejected the names "Granite Peak" and "Thompson Peak" for the feature.

Gibson Ridge [HUMBOLDT]: *ridge,* north-northwest-trending, 4.25 miles long, 8 miles southwest of Garberville (lat. 40°02'30" N, long. 123°55'10" W). Named on Briceland (1969) 7.5' quadrangle.

Gibson Ridge [LAKE]: *ridge,* south- to south-southwest-trending, 2 miles long, 6 miles east-northeast of Hull Mountain (lat. 39°33'15" N, long. 122°50' W). Named on Kneecap Ridge (1967) 7.5' quadrangle.

Giddings Bar [TRINITY]: *locality,* 16 miles northeast of Weaverville along Trinity River (lat. 40°53' N, long. 122°42'20" W; on N line sec. 19, T 35 N, 7 W). Named on Schell Mountain (1950) 15' quadrangle.

Gifford Springs: see **Middletown** [LAKE].

Gilbert Creek [DEL NORTE]: *stream,* flows 4.25 miles to the sea 4.5 miles northwest of the town of Smith River (lat. 41°58'50" N, long. 124°12'15" W; sec. 5, T 18 N, R 1 W). Named on Smith River (1966) 7.5' quadrangle.

Gilbert Creek [LAKE]: *stream,* flows 5.25 miles to Clover Creek 3 miles east-southeast of the town of Upper Lake (lat. 39°09'20" N, long. 122°51'25" W; near NE cor. sec. 16, T 15 N, R 9 W). Named on Bartlett Mountain (1958) 7.5' quadrangle.

Gilham Butte [HUMBOLDT]: *peak,* 11 miles west of Phillipsville (lat. 40°13'25" N, long. 123°59'30" W; sec. 7, T 3 S, R 2 E). Named on Ettersburg (1969) 7.5' quadrangle.

Gilham Creek [HUMBOLDT]: *stream,* flows nearly 3 miles to Mattole River 5 miles east-southeast of Honeydew (lat. 40°12'45" N, long. 124°02'25" W). Named on Honeydew (1970) 7.5' quadrangle.

Gill Creek [MENDOCINO]: *stream,* flows 4.5 miles to Eel River 7.5 miles west of Covelo (lat. 39°47'30" N, long. 123°33'20" W; sec. 2, T 22 N, R 14 W). Named on Covelo West (1967) and Iron Peak (1967) 7.5' quadrangles.

Gilliam Rock [LAKE]: *relief feature,* 2.25 miles west-southwest of Highland Springs (lat. 38°55'25" N, long. 122°56'35" W; near NW cor. sec. 2, T 12 N, R 10 W). Named on Highland Springs (1959) 7.5' quadrangle.

Gilman Creek [TRINITY]: *stream,* flows nearly 2 miles to North Fork Eel River 5.5 miles east-northeast of Kettenpom (lat. 41°11'45" N, long. 123°22'10" W; at S line sec. 15, T 3 S, R 7 E). Named on Shannon Butte (1967) 7.5' quadrangle.

Gist Creek [HUMBOLDT]: *stream,* flows 2.5 miles to Klamath River 0.5 mile west-northwest of Weitchpec (lat. 41°11'25" N, long. 123°42'50" W; near W line sec. 10, T 9 N, R 4 E). Named on Weitchpec (1979) 7.5' quadrangle.

Gitchell Creek [HUMBOLDT]: *stream,* flows nearly 3 miles to the sea 5.25 miles north-northwest of the village of Shelter Cove (lat. 40°05'35" N, long. 124°06'05" W; at N line sec. 20, T 4 S, R 1 E). Named on Shelter Cove (1969) 7.5' quadrangle.

Glade Camp: see **Lower Glade Camp** [TRINITY]; **Upper Glade Camp** [TRINITY].

Glade Campground [TRINITY]: *locality,* 5.25 miles northeast of Forest Glen (lat. 40°25'45" N, long. 123°15'25" W; at N line sec. 30, T 30 N, R 12 W). Named on Pickett Peak (1954) 15' quadrangle.

Glade Camp Spring [TRINITY]: *spring,* 4.5 miles northeast of Forest Glen (lat. 40°25'35" N, long. 123°16'05" W; at W line sec. 30, T 30 N, R 12 W). Named on Naufus Creek (1979) 7.5' quadrangle.

Glade Creek [TRINITY]: *stream,* flows 2.5 miles to Post Creek 4.25 miles east-northeast of Forest Glen (lat. 40°24'25" N, long. 123°15'30" W; sec. 31, T 30 N, R 12 W). Named on Dubakella Mountain (1954) and Pickett Peak (1954) 15' quadrangles. United States Board on Geographic Names (1978a, p. 5) rejected the name "Basin Gulch Creek" for the stream.

Glenblair [MENDOCINO]: *locality,* 15 miles north-northwest of Comptche (lat. 39°27'25" N, long. 123°43'20" W; near N line sec. 2, T 18 N, R 17 W). Named on Comptche (1960) 15' quadrangle. Postal authorities established Glenblair post office in 1903 and discontinued it in 1928 (Frickstad, p. 94). The name recalls Glen Blair Lumber Company, which shipped redwood to Fort Bragg by rail from the site (Crump, p. 27). California Mining Bureau's (1909c) map shows a place called Junction located 3.25 miles southwest of Glenblair, where the rail line to Glenblair leaves the main line; the same place is called Glenblair Junction on California Division of Highways (1934) map.

Glenblair Junction: see **Glenblair** [MENDOCINO].

Glenbrook [LAKE]: *locality,* 10 miles south-southeast of Kelseyville (lat. 38°51'05" N, long. 122°45'25" W; near NW cor. sec. 33, T 12 N, R 8 W). Named on The Geysers (1959) 7.5' quadrangle. Called Glenbrook Resort on Kelseyville (1944) 15' quadrangle. Postal authorities established Glenbrook post office in 1871 and discontinued it in 1911 (Frickstad, p. 63). They established Bottle Rock post office 7.5 miles north of Glenbrook post office (NE quarter sec. 34, T 13 N, R 8 W) in 1876 and discontinued it in 1877; the name was for the glasslike obsidian found in the neighborhood (Salley, p. 25). A short tunnel dug at a mining prospect less than 1 mile southeast of Glenbrook post office produced water that was shipped to San Francisco in tanks, carbonated there, and bottled for table use; the feature was called Astorg Spring, and was known locally as Tunnel Spring (Waring, p. 188-189).

Glenbrook Resort: see **Glenbrook** [LAKE].

Glen Creek [TRINITY]: *stream,* flows nearly 3 miles to South Fork Trinity River at Forest Glen (lat. 40°22'30" N, long. 123°19'40" W; near SE cor. sec. 13, T 1 S, R 7 E). Named on Forest Glen (1979) 7.5' quadrangle. Called Forest Glen Creek on Anada (1918) 15' quadrangle.

Glendale [HUMBOLDT]: *settlement,* 4 miles east-northeast of Arcata along Mad River (lat. 40°54' N, long. 124°01' W; sec. 13, T 6 N, R 1 E). Named on Arcata North (1959) 7.5' quadrangle.

Glen Essex: see **Essex** [HUMBOLDT].

Glenhaven [LAKE]: *village,* 3 miles west of Clearlake Oaks along Clear Lake (lat. 39°01'35" N, long. 122°43'55" W; sec. 27, 34, T 14 N, R 8 W). Named on Clearlake Oaks (1958) 7.5' quadrangle.

Glenmark: see **Willits** [MENDOCINO].

Glennan Gulch: see **Glennen Gulch** [MENDOCINO].

Glennen Gulch [MENDOCINO]: *canyon,* drained by a stream that flows 1.5 miles to the sea 2.5 miles northwest of Gualala (lat. 38°47'25" N, long. 123°33'35" W; sec. 20, T 11 N, R 15 W). Named on Gualala (1960) 7.5' quadrangle. Called Glennan Gulch on Point Arena (1943) 15' quadrangle, but United States Board on Geographic Names (1962c, p. 19) rejected this form of the name.

Glennison Gap [TRINITY]: *pass,* 4 miles northwest of Weaverville (lat. 40°46'20" N, long. 122°59'25" W; sec. 27, T 34 N, R 10 W). Named on Trinity Dam (1950) 15' quadrangle.

Glenview [LAKE]: *settlement,* nearly 7 miles southeast of Kelseyville (lat. 38°54' N, long. 122°45'30" W; near W line sec. 9, T 12 N, R 8 W). Named on Kelseyville (1959) 7.5' quadrangle.

Globe Mill [TRINITY]: *locality,* 9.5 miles northeast of Helena along Canyon Creek (1) (lat. 40°53'05" N, long. 123°01'20" W). Named on Helena (1951) 15' quadrangle.

Glory Hole Gulch [LAKE]: *canyon,* 0.5 mile long, 6 miles south-southeast of Cold Spring Mountain (lat. 39°01'15" N, long. 122°26'25" W; sec. 32, T 14 N, R 5 W). Named on Wilbur Springs (1961) 15' quadrangle.

Goat Camp [MENDOCINO]: *locality,* 5.5 miles north-northeast of Hull Mountain (lat. 39°36'10" N, long. 122°54'25" W; sec. 12, T 20 N, R 10 W); the place is about 0.5 mile east-northeast of Goat Rock (1). Named on Hull Mountain (1967) 7.5' quadrangle.

Goat Camp [TRINITY]: *locality,* 2 miles south of Black Lassic (lat. 40°18'35" N, long. 123°32'30" W); the place is 1 mile north-northeast of Goat Hill [HUMBOLDT]. Named on Blocksburg (1949) 15' quadrangle.

Goat Hill [HUMBOLDT]: *ridge,* north-trending, 0.5 mile long, 5 miles east-northeast of Blocksburg near Humboldt-Trinity County line (lat. 40°17'55" N, long. 123°32'45" W). Named on Black Lassic (1979) 7.5' quadrangle.

Goat Hill [LAKE]: *peak,* 7 miles east of Middletown (lat. 38°44'20" N, long. 122°29' W). Altitude 1751 feet. Named on Aetna Springs (1958) 7.5' quadrangle.

Goat Island [MENDOCINO]: *island,* 950 feet long, 0.5 mile west of Mendocino, and 200 feet offshore (lat. 39°18'25" N, long. 123°48'40" W; sec. 25, T 17 N, R 18 W). Named on Mendocino (1960) 7.5' quadrangle.

Goat Mountain [LAKE]: *peak,* 7.25 miles southeast of Potato Hill on Lake-Colusa County line (lat. 39°15'35" N, long. 122°42'50" W; near SE cor. sec. 2, T 16 N, R 8 W). Altitude 6121 feet. Named on Fouts Springs (1968) 7.5' quadrangle.

Goat Ridge [MENDOCINO]: *ridge,* west-trending, 1.5 miles long, 7 miles north-northeast of Boonville (lat. 39°06' N, long. 123°18'45" W). Named on Boonville (1959) 15' quadrangle.

Goat Rock [HUMBOLDT]:

(1) *relief feature,* 1.25 miles west of Bridgeville (lat. 40°28' N, long. 123°49'20" W; sec. 15, T 1 N, R 3 E). Bridgeville (1969) 7.5' quadrangle.

(2) *peak,* 7.5 miles west-southwest of Phillipsville (lat. 40°10'25" N, long. 123°55'15" W; sec. 26, T 3 S, R 2 E). Named on Ettersburg (1969) 7.5' quadrangle.

(3) *relief feature,* 4 miles northeast of Blocksburg (lat. 40°18'15" N, long. 123°34'30" W). Named on Black Lassic (1979) 7.5' quadrangle.

Goat Rock [MENDOCINO]:

(1) *relief feature,* 5.5 miles north of Hull Mountain (lat. 39°36' N, long. 122°54'50" W; near W line sec. 12, T 20 N, R 10 W). Named on Hull Mountain (1967) 7.5' quadrangle.

(2) *relief feature,* 9 miles south of Ukiah (lat. 39°01' N, long. 123°11'55" W; sec. 5, T 13 N, R 12 W). Named on Elledge Peak (1958) 7.5' quadrangle.

Goat Rock: see **Sharp Point** [HUMBOLDT].

Goat Spring [HUMBOLDT]: *spring,* 5.25 miles east-northeast of Blocksburg (lat. 40°18'45" N, long. 123°32'45" W). Named on Black Lassic (1979) 7.5' quadrangle.

Gobbis Soda Spring: see **Ukiah** [MENDOCINO].

Godwood Creek [HUMBOLDT]: *stream,* flows 2.25 miles to Prairie Creek 6 miles north-northeast of Orick (lat. 41°21'55" N, long. 124°01'20" W; sec. 2, T 11 N, R 1 E). Named on Fern Canyon (1966) and Orick (1966) 7.5' quadrangles. John Godwood homesteaded near the stream about 1882 (Turner, p. 96).

Goff: see **Jim Goff Gulch** [HUMBOLDT].

Goforth Creek [MENDOCINO]: *stream,* flows 3.5 miles to Middle Fork Eel River less than 1 mile southeast of Dos Rios (lat. 39°42'40" N, long. 123°20'30" W; near E line sec. 6, T 21 N, R 13 W). Named on Covelo West (1967) and Dos Rios (1967) 7.5' quadrangles.

Gold Bar [TRINITY]: *locality,* 6 miles east-southeast of Weaverville along Trinity River (lat. 40°42'20" N, long. 122°50' W; sec. 24, T 33 N, R 9 W). Named on Weaverville (1950) 15' quadrangle.

Gold Bluffs [HUMBOLDT]: *escarpment,* extends along the coast for 11 miles north from the mouth of Redwood Creek (1); the center is 6 miles north of Orick (lat. 41°22'30" N, long. 124°04'15" W). Named on Fern Canyon (1966) and Orick (1966) 7.5' quadrangles. Hermann Ehrenberg discovered the feature in 1850 and named it for the gold-bearing sand there (Gudde, 1949, p. 130).

Golden City: see **Ridgeville** [TRINITY].

Goldfield Campground [TRINITY]: *locality,* 2 miles south of Billys Peak (1) along Coffee Creek (lat. 41°06'10" N, long. 122°46'40" W; near SE cor. sec. 33, T 38 N, R 8 W). Named on Coffee Creek (1955) 15' quadrangle, which shows Dorleska mine situated 7.5 miles west-southwest of the campground (near NE cor. sec. 20, T 37 N, R 9 W). Etna (1934) 30' quadrangle shows a place called Coffee located at or near present Goldfield Campground. Postal authorities established Coffee post office in 1882, discontinued it in 1887, reestablished it in 1891, discontinued it in 1895, reestablished it in 1901, moved it 1 mile east in 1906, and discontinued it in 1937 (Salley, p. 47). They established Abrams post office in 1895, discontinued it the same year, reestablished it in 1896, moved it 6 miles south in 1901, changed the name to Dorleska in 1902, and discontinued it in 1916; the name "Abrams" was for James Abrams, who owned a trading post at the place (Salley, p. 1, 60). According to Lanphere and Irwin (p. 101-102), postal authorities established Abrams post office in 1895 at Upper Nash mine (SE quarter sec. 30, T 38 N, R 9 W), and moved it in 1901 from Lower Nash mine to the village of Dorleska (SE quarter sec. 17, T 37 N, R 9 W) near Dorleska mine (SW quarter sec. 27, T 38 N, R 9 W); they changed the post office name to Dorleska in 1902 and moved it back to Upper Nash mine in 1912. California Mining Bureau's (1917b) map shows a place called Nash located about 5 miles west of Coffee along present Coffee Creek.

Gold Point [LAKE]: *relief feature,* 10 miles north of Clearlake Oaks along Bartlett Creek (lat. 39°10'05" N, long. 122°41'30" W; sec. 12, T 15 N, R 8 W). Named on Clearlake Oaks (1960) 15' quadrangle.

Goodman Prairie Creek [HUMBOLDT]: *stream,* flows 4.5 miles to Mad River 4.5 miles north of Lone Star Junction (lat. 40°42' N, long. 123°51'35" W; near E line sec. 29, T 4 N, R 3 E). Named on Mad River Buttes (1977) 7.5' quadrangle. Turner (p. 96) associated the name with William Goodman and Richard Goodman, who owned land near the stream before 1874.

Goods Creek [TRINITY]: *stream,* flows 2.5 miles to Hayfork Creek 4.5 miles east of Dubakella Mountain (lat. 40°23'30" N, long. 123°03'30" W; sec. 1, T 29 N, R 11 W); the stream heads near Goods Mountain. Named on Dubakella Mountain (1954) 15' quadrangle. South Fork enters from the south less than 1 mile upstream from the mouth of the main creek; it is 2.5 miles long and is named on Dubakella Mountain (1954) 15' quadrangle.

Goods Gulch [TRINITY]:

(1) *canyon,* drained by a stream that flows about 1 mile to Indian Creek (2) 8 miles south-southeast of Weaverville (lat. 40°37'30" N, long. 122°54' W; near SW cor. sec. 18, T 32 N, R 9 W). Named on Weaverville (1950) 15' quadrangle.

(2) *canyon,* drained by a stream that flows 2 miles to Dobbins Gulch 6.25 miles north of Dubakella Mountain (lat. 40°28'30" N, long. 123°09' W; near S line sec. 6, T 30 N, R 11 W). Named on Dubakella Mountain (1954) 15' quadrangle.

Goods Mountain [TRINITY]: *peak,* 7.5 miles east of Dubakella Mountain on Trinity-Shasta County line (lat. 40°23'25" N, long. 123°00'15" W; near SW cor. sec. 4, T 29 N, R 10 W). Named on Dubakella Mountain (1954) 15' quadrangle. United States Board on Geographic Names (1983b, p. 1) located the peak nearly 1 mile farther southwest (lat. 40°22'55" N, long.

123°00'55" W; sec. 8, T 29 N, R 10 W).

Goose Creek [DEL NORTE]: *stream*, flows 17 miles to South Fork Smith River 5.5 miles north-northwest of Buck Mountain (lat. 41°41'10" N, long. 123°55'25" W; near W line sec. 23, T 15 N, R 2 E). Named on Cant Hook Mountain (1982) and Klamath Glen (1982) 7.5' quadrangles. East Fork enters from the east 10 miles upstream from the mouth of the main creek; it is 7.5 miles long and is named on Klamath Glen (1982) and Summit Valley (1981) 7.5' quadrangles.

Gooseneck Point [LAKE]: *promontory*, 6 miles northwest of the town of Lower Lake along Clear Lake (lat. 38°58'35" N, long. 122°41'05" W; sec. 13, T 13 N, R 7 W). Named on Clearlake Highlands (1958) 7.5' quadrangle.

Gopher Creek [HUMBOLDT]: *stream*, flows less than 1 mile to Bull Creek (2) 4.5 miles west-northwest of Weott (lat. 40°20'55" N, long. 123°59'50" W; sec. 30, T 1 S, R 2 E). Named on Weott (1969) 7.5' quadrangle.

Gorda Rock [HUMBOLDT]: *rock*, 6.5 miles southwest of Petrolia, and 4500 feet south-southwest of Punta Gorda.(lat. 40°15' N, long. 124°22' W). Named on Cooskie Creek (1969) 7.5' quadrangle.

Gordon Creek [DEL NORTE]: *stream*, flows 6.25 miles to South Fork Smith River 8.5 miles north-northwest of Buck Mountain (lat. 41°43'25" N, long. 123°56'55" W; sec. 4, T 15 N, R 2 E). Named on Cant Hook Mountain (1982) and Gasquet (1981) 7.5' quadrangles.

Gordon Hill [MENDOCINO]: *peak*, 2.25 miles north of Westport (lat. 39°40'10" N, long. 123°46'45" W; near SW cor. sec. 17, T 21 N, R 17 W). Altitude 773 feet. Named on Westport (1966) 7.5' quadrangle. Officials of United States Coast Survey named the feature for Alexander Gordon, who in 1875 purchased the tract of land that includes the peak (Gudde, 1949, p. 132).

Gordon Hot Spring: see **Cobb Valley** [LAKE].

Gordon Mountain [DEL NORTE]: *ridge*, south-trending, less than 2 miles long, 6 miles east-southeast of Gasquet (lat. 41°48' N, long. 123°52' W). Named on Hurdygurdy Butte (1982) 7.5' quadrangle.

Gordon Ridge [HUMBOLDT]: *ridge*, northwest-trending, 2 miles long, 3 miles northwest of Lone Star Junction (lat. 40°40'05" N, long. 123°54'45" W; mainly in sec. 1, 2, T 3 N, R 2 E). Named on Iaqua Buttes (1979) 7.5' quadrangle. Shown as part of Iaqua Buttes on Iaqua Buttes (1950) 15' quadrangle, but United States Board on Geographic Names (1978a, p. 5) rejected the name "Iaqua Buttes" for the feature.

Gordons Creek: see **De Haven Creek** [MENDOCINO].

Gordon's Mineral Springs: see **Cobb Valley** [LAKE].

Gosinta Creek [HUMBOLDT]: *stream*, flows 1.5 miles to North Fork Mad River 4.25 miles northeast of the town of Blue Lake (lat. 40°55'25" N, long. 123°55'30" W; near W line sec. 11, T 6 N, R 2 E). Named on Blue Lake (1979) 7.5' quadrangle.

Gould Bar [HUMBOLDT]: *locality*, less than 0.5 mile south of Weott along South Fork Eel River (lat. 40°18'55" N, long. 123°55'15" W; sec. 2, T 2 S, R 2 E). Named on Weott (1969) 7.5' quadrangle.

Government Spring [HUMBOLDT]: *spring*, 0.25 mile west of Showers Mountain (lat. 40°34'45" N, long. 123°42' W; sec. 2, T 2 N, R 4 E). Named on Showers Mountain (1978) 7.5' quadrangle. The name is from the location of the spring at the lower end of a forty-acre tract of government-owned land (Turner, p. 97).

Gowan Creek [MENDOCINO]: *stream*, flows 0.5 mile to Navarro River 7 miles northwest of Boonville (lat. 39°04'30" N, long. 123°27'45" W; sec. 13, T 14 N, R 15 W). Named on Boonville (1959) 15' quadrangle.

Gozem Peak [TRINITY]: *peak*, 9.5 miles east-northeast of Trinity Center (lat. 41°04'45" N, long. 122°32'15" W; sec. 10, T 37 N, R 6 W). Named on Bonanza King (1955) 15' quadrangle.

Grace Creek [TRINITY]: *stream*, flows 1.25 miles to Mad River 7.5 miles west-northwest of Forest Glen (lat. 40°24'05" N, long. 123°27'55" W; sec. 2, T 1 S, R 6 E). Named on Sportshaven (1973) 7.5' quadrangle.

Gracy: see **Fort Bragg** [MENDOCINO].

Grader Gulch [TRINITY]: *canyon*, drained by a stream that flows 1.25 miles to East Fork Trinity River 15 miles northeast of Trinity Center (lat. 41°08'50" N, long. 122°28'15" W; sec. 17, T 38 N, R 5 W). Named on Dunsmuir (1954) 15' quadrangle.

Graham Creek [HUMBOLDT]: *stream*, flows nearly 4 miles to Mad River 4.25 miles north-northeast of Lone Star Junction (lat. 40°41'35" N, long. 123°51'05" W; near S line sec. 28, T 4 N, R 3 E). Named on Mad River Buttes (1977) 7.5' quadrangle. John R. Graham and Sarah Preston Graham homesteaded in the neighborhood in the early 1870's; the name of the creek commemorates the Graham family (Turner, p. 97).

Graham Gulch [HUMBOLDT]: *canyon*, drained by a stream that flows 2.5 miles to Freshwater Creek 8 miles south of Arcata (lat. 40°45'15" N, long. 124°02'20" W; sec. 3, T 4 N, R 1 E). Named on Arcata South (1959) 7.5' quadrangle. Frank Graham and Alexander Graham owned land at the place before 1875 (Turner, p. 97).

Graham Lake [TRINITY]: *lake*, 300 feet long, 5.5 miles east-northeast of Alderpoint [HUMBOLDT] (lat. 40°13'25" N, long. 123°31'30" W; near N line sec. 8, T 3 S, R 6 E). Named on Alderpoint (1969) 7.5' quadrangle.

Graham Ridge [HUMBOLDT]: *ridge*, generally north-northeast-trending, 1.5 miles long, 7 miles north-northeast of Lone Star Junction (lat. 40°43'30" N, long. 123°49'05" W). Named on Mad River Buttes (1977) 7.5' quadrangle.

Grand Slide: see **Hoboken** [TRINITY].

Granite Butte [HUMBOLDT]: *relief feature*, 4 miles east-southeast of Arcata (lat. 40°51'20" N, long. 124°00'45" W; near S line sec. 36, T 6 N, R 1 E). Named on Arcata South (1959) 7.5' quadrangle.

Granite Canyon [TRINITY]: *canyon*, drained by a stream that flows 2 miles to South Fork Trinity River 1.5 miles west of Forest Glen (lat. 40°22'40" N, long. 123°21'15" W; sec. 14, T 1 S, R 7 E). Named on Forest Glen (1979) and Naufus Creek (1979) 7.5' quadrangles.

Granite Canyon: see **Granite Creek** [TRINITY] (2).

Granite Creek [TRINITY]:

(1) *stream*, flows 4 miles to North Fork Coffee Creek 5.5 miles west-northwest of Billys Peak (1) (lat. 41°10' N, long. 122°51'30" W; sec. 11, T 38 N, R 9 W); one branch of the stream heads at Granite Lake (1). Named on Coffee Creek (1955) 15' quadrangle.

(2) *stream*, flows 3 miles to Swift Creek (1) 19 miles north-northeast of Weaverville (lat. 40°53'55" N, long. 122°48'50" W; near W line sec. 17, T 36 N, R 8 W); the stream heads at Granite Lake (2). Named on Trinity Dam (1950) 15' quadrangle. On Weaverville (1913) 30' quadrangle, the canyon of the stream has the name "Granite Canyon."

Granite Lake [TRINITY]:

(1) *lake*, 800 feet long, 4.25 miles northwest of Billy Peak (1) (lat. 41°10'45" N, long. 122°49'15" W; sec. 6, T 38 N, R 8 W); the lake is at the head of a branch of Granite Creek (1). Named on Coffee Creek (1955) 15' quadrangle.

(2) *lake*, 1400 feet long, 16 miles north-northeast of Weaverville (lat. 40°57'10" N, long. 122°51'20" W; on W line sec. 25, T 36 N, R 9 W); the lake is at the head of Granite Creek (2). Named on Trinity Dam (1950) 15' quadrangle.

Granite Peak [TRINITY]: *peak*, 13 miles north-northeast of Weaverville (lat. 40°54'35" N, long. 122°52'20" W); the peak is 1.25 miles east of Red Mountain (3). Altitude 8091 feet. Named on Trinity Dam (1950) 15' quadrangle. United States Board on Geographic Names (1949, p. 3) rejected the designation "Red Mountain" for the peak.

Granite Peak: see **Gibson Peak** [TRINITY]; **Little Granite Peak** [TRINITY].

Granny Creek [HUMBOLDT]: *stream*, flows 1.5 miles to Mattole River 16 miles south-southwest of Scotia (lat. 40°15'40" N, long. 124°11'30" W; near SW cor. sec. 28, T 2 S, R 1 W). Named on Buckeye Mountain (1970) and Shubrick Peak (1969) 7.5' quadrangles. The name was for Granny Wilkinson (Turner, p. 97).

Grant: see **Camp Grant** [HUMBOLDT]; **Camp Grant** [MENDOCINO].

Grant Gulch [TRINITY]: *canyon*, drained by a stream that flows 1 mile to Indian Creek (2) 6 miles south of Weaverville (lat. 40°38'55" N, long. 122°54'50" W; near N line sec. 8, T 32 N, R 9 W). Named on Weaverville (1950) 15' quadrangle.

Grant Gulch: see **Gant Gulch** [TRINITY].

Grantville: see **Lower Lake** [LAKE].

Grapevine Creek [HUMBOLDT-TRINITY]: *stream*, heads in Humboldt County and flows 2.25 miles to South Fork Trinity River 7 miles north-northwest of Hyampom in Trinity County (lat. 40°42'25" N, long. 123°31'10" W). Named on Sims Mountain (1979) 7.5' quadrangle. Called Bear Creek on Pilot Creek (1922) 15' quadrangle.

Grapevine Creek [LAKE]:

(1) *stream*, flows less than 1 mile to Eel River 4 miles west-southwest of Crockett Peak (lat. 39°24'45" N, long. 122°51'50" W). Named on Crockett Peak (1967) 7.5' quadrangle.

(2) *stream*, flows 2 miles to North Fork Cache Creek 11 miles north of Clearlake Oaks (lat. 39°11' N, long. 122°40'25" W; sec. 6, T 15 N, R 7 W). Named on Clearlake Oaks (1960) 15' quadrangle.

Grapevine Creek [MENDOCINO]: *stream*, flows 1.25 miles to Mud Creek (3) nearly 2 miles east of Branscomb (lat. 39°39'20" N, long. 123°35'25" W; sec. 24, T 21 N, R 16 E). Named on Cahto Peak (1967) 7.5' quadrangle.

Grapevine Flat [MENDOCINO]: *area*, 5.25 miles west-northwest of Covelo (lat. 39°51'40" N, long. 123°17'25" W; near S line sec. 10, T 23 N, R 13 W). Named on Covelo West (1967) 7.5' quadrangle.

Grapevine Gulch [TRINITY]:

(1) *canyon*, drained by a stream that flows 1 mile to Hayfork Creek 3.25 miles east of Hayfork (lat. 40°33'25" N, long. 123°07'20" W; at W line sec. 9, T 31 N, R 11 W). Named on Hayfork (1951) 15' quadrangle.

(2) *canyon*, drained by a stream that flows 1 mile to Salt Gulch 5.25 miles north-northeast of Dubakella Mountain (lat. 40°27'20" N, long. 123°06'45" W; sec. 16, T 30 N, R 11 W). Named on Dubakella Mountain (1954) 15' quadrangle.

Grapevine Spring [MENDOCINO]: *spring*, 10 miles west-southwest of Covelo (lat. 39°45'20" N, long. 123°25'45" W; sec. 16, T 22 N, R 14 W). Named on Iron Peak (1967) 7.5' quadrangle.

Grapewine Creek [MENDOCINO]: *stream*, flows 2 miles to Redwood Creek

(2) 10 miles east-southeast of Leggett (lat. 39°48'30" N, long. 123°32'50" W; near W line sec. 28, T 23 N, R 15 W). Named on Tan Oak Park (1969) 7.5' quadrangle.

Grasshopper Camp [TRINITY]: *locality,* 2.25 miles north-northeast of Black Rock Mountain (lat. 40°14'20" N, long. 122°59'20" W; near SE cor. sec. 28, T 28 N, R 10 W). Named on Yolla Bolly (1954) 15' quadrangle.

Grasshopper Flat [TRINITY]: *area,* 7 miles northeast of Helena near Canyon Creek (1) (lat. 40°51'20" N, long. 123°02'50" W). Named on Helena (1951) 15' quadrangle. Fishermen named the area after they found that it was a good place to catch grasshoppers for bait (Jones, p. 193).

Grasshopper Hill [HUMBOLDT]: *peak,* 7.25 miles north-northeast of Point Delgada (lat. 40°07'05" N, long. 124°00'45" W; sec. 13, T 4 S, R 1 E). Named on Shelter Cove (1969) 7.5' quadrangle.

Grasshopper Mountain [HUMBOLDT]: *peak,* 3 miles east-southeast of Weott (lat. 40°18'25" N, long. 123°58'35" W; sec. 8, T 2 S, R 2 E). Altitude 3379 feet. Named on Weott (1969) 7.5' quadrangle. The ridge on which the peak lies is called Grass Hopper Ridge on Vander Leck's (1920b) map.

Grasshopper Prairie [HUMBOLDT]: *area,* 2.25 miles south-southwest of Weitchpec (lat. 41°09'25" N, long. 123°43'10" W; around NE cor. sec. 21, T 9 N, R 4 E). Named on Weitchpec (1979) 7.5' quadrangle.

Grass Hopper Ridge: see **Grasshopper Mountain** [HUMBOLDT].

Grass Valley Creek [TRINITY]: *stream,* flows 14 miles to Trinity River 5.25 miles east-southeast of Weaverville (lat. 40°41'30" N, long. 122°51'25" W; near N line sec. 26, T 33 N, R 9 W). Named on Weaverville (1950) 15' quadrangle, and on Shasta Bally (1978) 7.5' quadrangle.

Grass Valley Creek: see **Little Grass Valley Creek** [TRINITY].

Grassy Creek [HUMBOLDT]:

(1) *stream,* flows 1 mile to Luffenholtz Creek 3 miles east of Trinidad (lat. 41°03'05" N, long. 124°05'05" W; sec. 29, T 8 N, R 1 E). Named on Crannell (1966) 7.5' quadrangle.

(2) *stream,* flows 3 miles to marsh along Lindsay Creek 4.25 miles northeast of Arcata (lat. 40°55'10" N, long. 124°01'45" W; sec. 11, T 6 N, R 1 E). Named on Arcata North (1959) and Blue Lake (1979) 7.5' quadrangles.

Grassy Flat Campground [DEL NORTE]: *locality,* 4.25 miles east of Gasquet along Middle Fork Smith River (lat. 41°51'25" N, long. 123°53'15" W). Named on Gasquet (1981) 7.5' quadrangle.

Grassy Flat Creek [TRINITY]: *stream,* flows 2.5 miles to Hayfork Creek 5 miles east of Hyampom (lat. 40°37'45" N, long. 123°22'30" W; sec. 22, T 3 N, R 7 E); the stream heads at Grassy Flats. Named on Hyampom (1951) 15' quadrangle.

Grassy Flats [TRINITY]: *area,* 5 miles east-southeast of Hyampom (lat. 40°35'45" N, long. 123°21'45" W; sec. 34, 35, T 3 N, R 7 E); the place is at the head of Grassy Flat Creek. Named on Hyampom (1951) 15' quadrangle. United States Board on Geographic Names (1984b, p. 4) approved the name "Fir Root Spring" for a spring in Grassy Flats (lat. 40°35'38" N, long. 123°21'37" W; sec. 35, T 3 N, R 7 E).

Grassy Lake [MENDOCINO]:

(1) *lake,* 425 feet long, 6.5 miles northeast of Spyrock (2) (lat. 39°57' N, long. 123°21'50" W; near SW cor. sec. 6, T 24 N, R 13 W). Named on Mina (1967) 7.5' quadrangle.

(2) *lake,* 800 feet long, 4 miles southeast of Dos Rios (lat. 39°40'25" N, long. 123°18'05" W; near SW cor. sec. 15, T 21 N, R 13 W). Named on Dos Rios (1967) 7.5' quadrangle.

Grassy Mountain [TRINITY]: *peak,* 6 miles east-southeast of Hyampom (lat. 40°35'45" N, long. 123°20'30" W; sec. 36, T 3 N, R 7 E); the peak is 1 mile east of Grassy Flats. Named on Hyampom (1951) 15' quadrangle.

Grassy Point Creek: see **Lupton Creek** [HUMBOLDT].

Gratten Creek [TRINITY]: *stream,* flows 2 miles to North Fork Swift Creek (1) 20 miles north-northeast of Weaverville (lat. 40°59'10" N, long. 122°43'35" W; at NE cor. sec. 13, T 36 N, R 8 W). Named on Schell Mountain (1950) 15' quadrangle.

Gratten Flat [TRINITY]: *area,* 20 miles north-northeast of Weaverville (lat. 40°58'45" N, long. 122°44'15" W; sec. 14, T 36 N, R 8 W); the place is along Gratten Creek. Named on Schell Mountain (1950) 15' quadrangle.

Gravel Creek: see **Graves Creek** [TRINITY].

Gravelly Bar Creek [HUMBOLDT]: *stream,* flows nearly 2 miles to Mad River 4 miles south of Board Camp Mountain (lat. 40°38'15" N, long. 123°42'55" W; sec. 15, T 3 N, R 4 E). Named on Board Camp Mountain (1977) 7.5' quadrangle.

Gravelly Valley [LAKE]: *valley,* 4 miles northwest of Bear Mountain (lat. 39°27' N, long. 122°57'15" W). Named on Lake Pillsbury (1967) 7.5' quadrangle. The name is from gravel left in the valley by winter floods (Gudde, 1949, p. 134). Water of Lake Pillsbury now covers part of the valley.

Gravelly Valley: see **Hullville** [LAKE].

Graves Creek [TRINITY]: *stream,* flows 3 miles to Trinity River 14 miles north of Trinity Center (lat. 41°12'05" N, long. 122°38'45" W; near NW cor. sec. 35, T 39 N, R 7 W). Named on Bonanza King (1955) 15' quadrangle. Called Gravel Creek on Etna (1934) 30' quadrangle.

Graveyard Creek [MENDOCINO]: *stream,* flows 2 miles to Anderson Creek (2) 1.25 miles northwest of Boonville (lat. 39°01'30" N, long. 123°23'05" W; sec. 34, T 14 N, R 14 W). Named on Boonville (1959) 15' quadrangle, which shows Evergreen cemetery near the mouth of the stream.

Graveyard Point [LAKE]: *promontory,* 2.5 miles west-northwest of Bear Mountain (lat. 39°25'10" N, long. 122°56'45" W; near NE cor. sec. 14, T 18 N, R 10 W). Named on Lake Pillsbury (1967) 7.5' quadrangle.

Graveyard Prairie: see **Tish Tang a Tang Ridge** [HUMBOLDT].

Grayback: see **Little Grayback** [DEL NORTE].

Gray Creek [HUMBOLDT]: *stream,* flows 3.5 miles to marsh along Big Lagoon 7 miles north-northeast of Trinidad (lat. 41°09'20" N, long. 124°06'15" W; sec. 19, T 9 N, R 1 E). Named on Crannell (1966) and Rodgers Peak (1966) 7.5' quadrangles.

Gray Creek [TRINITY]: *stream,* flows 1.5 miles to Trinity River 4.5 miles east-southeast of Salyer (lat. 40°51'40" N, long. 123°30'35" W). Named on Hennessy Peak (1979) 7.5' quadrangle.

Great Break: see **The Great Break** [HUMBOLDT].

Great Butte [HUMBOLDT]: *peak,* nearly 5 miles west-northwest of Blocksburg (lat. 40°18'35" N, long. 123°43' W; sec. 10, T 2 S, R 4 E). Named on Blocksburg (1969) 7.5' quadrangle.

Green Gulch [TRINITY]: *canyon,* drained by a stream that flows 1 mile to Indian Valley Creek 9.5 miles southeast of Hyampom (lat. 40°31' N, long. 123°19'30" W; at SE cor. sec. 25, T 2 N, R 7 E). Named on Hyampom (1951) 15' quadrangle.

Greenhorn Gulch [TRINITY]: *canyon,* drained by a stream that flows 2.25 miles to East Fork Stuart Fork 15 miles north-northeast of Weaverville (lat. 40°54'20" N, long. 122°46'10" W; at W line sec. 10, T 35 N, R 8 W). Named on Trinity Dam (1950) 15' quadrangle.

Green Lambert Canyon [MENDOCINO]: *canyon,* drained by a stream that flows 4 miles to Middle Fork Eel River 6 miles east-southeast of Covelo (lat. 39°45'35" N, long. 123°08'30" W; sec. 13, T 22 N, R 12 W). Named on Covelo East (1967) and Newhouse Ridge (1967) 7.5' quadrangles.

Greenlow Creek [HUMBOLDT]: *stream,* flows nearly 3 miles to Eel River 4.5 miles southeast of Scotia (lat. 40°26'40" N, long. 124°01'45" W; near N line sec. 26, T 1 N, R 1 E). Named on Scotia (1970) 7.5' quadrangle.

Green Mountain [TRINITY]:

(1) *peak,* 12.5 miles east-northeast of Burnt Ranch (lat. 40°54'10" N, long. 123°16'30" W). Altitude 6374 feet. Named on Ironside Mountain (1951) 15' quadrangle.

(2) *peak,* 10 miles west-southwest of Forest Glen (lat. 40°19'20" N, long. 123°29'35" W). Altitude 5305 feet. Named on Ruth Reservoir (1978) 7.5' quadrangle.

Greenough Ridge [MENDOCINO]: *ridge,* east-southeast-trending, 4.25 miles long, 10.5 miles south-southwest of Willits (lat. 39°16'10" N, long. 123°25' W). Named on Willits (1961) 15' quadrangle.

Greenough Roughs [MENDOCINO]: *relief feature,* 10.5 miles south-southwest of Willits (lat. 39°16'10" N, long. 123°25'25" W; sec. 4, 5, T 16 N, R 14 W); the feature is on Greenough Ridge. Named on Willits (1961) 15' quadrangle.

Green Point [HUMBOLDT]: *relief feature,* 8.5 miles east-northeast of the town of Blue Lake (lat. 40°54'50" N, long. 123°32'15" W). Named on Lord-Ellis Summit (1973) 7.5' quadrangle. California Mining Bureau's (1917b) map shows a locality called Green Point situated along Redwood Creek (1) east of the present relief feature called Green Point. Blue Lake (1951) 15" quadrangle shows Green Point Sch. at about this same site. California Mining Bureau's (1917b) map also shows a place called Bairs located along Redwood Creek (1) about 4 miles north of the relief feature called Green Point; Tom Bairs had a hotel at the site (Turner, p. 10).

Green Point Ridge [HUMBOLDT]: *ridge,* generally southeast-trending, 2 miles long, 8 miles east-northeast of the town of Blue Lake (lat. 40°55'15" N, long. 123°50'30" W); Green Point is at the southeast end of the ridge. Named on Lord-Ellis Summit (1973) 7.5' quadrangle.

Green Ridge [HUMBOLDT]: *ridge,* southwest- to south-southwest-trending, 2 miles long, 10.5 miles south of Scotia (lat. 40°19'55" N, long. 124°07'15" W). Named on Buckeye Mountain (1970) and Bull Creek (1969) 7.5' quadrangles.

Green Rock [HUMBOLDT]: *rock,* 1.5 miles northwest of Trinidad, and 1700 feet offshore (lat. 41°04'35" N, long. 124°09'55" W). Named on Trinidad (1966) 7.5' quadrangle

Green's Camp: see **Burlington** [HUMBOLDT].

Green Springs [MENDOCINO]: *springs,* 9 miles north of Anthony Peak (lat. 39°58'20" N, long. 122°56' W; sec. 35, T 25 N, R 10 W). Named on Buck Rock (1967) 7.5' quadrangle.

Green Trees [MENDOCINO]: *locality,* 4 miles north-northeast of Boonville (lat. 39°03'20" N, long. 123°19'45" W; sec. 19, T 14 N, R 13 W). Named on Boonville (1959) 15' quadrangle.

Greenwood: see **Elk** [MENDOCINO]; **Greenwood Creek** [MENDOCINO].

Greenwood Cove [MENDOCINO]: *embayment,* along the coast at Elk (lat. 39°07'55" N, long. 123°43'25" W); the embayment is north of the mouth of Greenwood Creek. Named on Elk (1960) 7.5' quadrangle. Called Cuffy Cove on Navarro (1943) 15' quadrangle.

Greenwood Creek [HUMBOLDT]: *stream,* flows 1.25 miles to White Oak Creek 2.5 miles east-northeast of Board Camp Mountain (lat. 40°43' N, long. 123°40'15" W; sec. 24, T 4 N, R 4 E). Named of Board Camp Mountain (1977) 7.5' quadrangle.

Greenwood Creek [MENDOCINO]: *stream,* flows 16 miles to the sea 0.25 mile south of Elk (lat. 39°07'35" N, long. 123°43' W). Named on Navarro (1961) 15' quadrangle. The name is from a community called Greenwood that Britton Greenwood founded at the mouth of the stream in 1862 (Gudde, 1949, p. 135). South Fork enters from the southeast 6 miles south of Navarro; it is 2.25 miles long and is named on Navarro (1961) 15' quadrangle.

Greenwood Ridge [MENDOCINO]: *ridge,* generally west-northwest-trending, 13 miles long, between Greenwood Creek and Navarro River. Named on Navarro (1961) 15' quadrangle.

Gregg Creek [HUMBOLDT]: *stream,* flows 1.5 miles to Willow Creek (1) 3.5 miles west-southwest of the settlement of Willow Creek (lat. 40°55'20" N, long. 123°41'40" W; sec. 11, T 6 N, R 4 E). Named on Willow Creek (1979) 7.5' quadrangle. The name is for Dr. Josiah Gregg (Turner, p. 98).

Greggs Peak [HUMBOLDT]: *peak,* 12 miles south-southeast of Scotia (lat. 40°18'35" N, long. 124°02'45" W; near SE cor. sec. 10, T 2 S, R 1 E). Named on Bull Creek (1969) 7.5' quadrangle.

Gregg's Point: see **Trinidad Head** [HUMBOLDT].

Grey Rocks [TRINITY]: *relief feature,* north-trending, 2 miles long, 16 miles northeast of Trinity Center on Trinity-Shasta County line (lat. 41°07'45" N, long. 122°26'45" W). Named on Dunsmuir (1954) 15' quadrangle.

Griffin Creek [DEL NORTE]: *stream,* flows 4 miles to Middle Fork Smith River 12 miles east-northeast of Gasquet (lat. 41°55'10" N, long. 123°45'45" W). Named on Broken Rib Mountain (1982) and Shelly Creek Ridge (1982) 7.5' quadrangles.

Griffith Hill: see **Pig Toe** [HUMBOLDT].

Grigsby Canyon [LAKE]: *canyon,* drained by a stream that flows 1 mile to Grizzly Creek (1) 4 miles south of Cold Spring Mountain (lat. 39°02'20" N, long. 122°28'50" W; near SW cor. sec. 24, T 14 N, R 6 W). Named on Wilbur Springs (1961) 15' quadrangle.

Grigsby Draw [LAKE]: *canyon,* 0.5 mile long, 3 miles northwest of the town of Lower Lake (lat. 38°56'10" N, long. 122°39'15" W; sec. 32, T 13 N, R 7 W). Named on Clearlake Highlands (1958) 7.5' quadrangle.

Grindstone Creek [HUMBOLDT]: *stream,* flows 3.5 miles to Mattole River 7.5 miles southeast of Honeydew (lat. 40°10'30" N, long. 124°00'45" W; sec. 25, T 3 S, R 1 E). Named on Ettersburg (1969) and Honeydew (1970) 7.5' quadrangles. The canyon of the stream is called Grizzly Gulch on Kneeland (1922) 15' quadrangle.

Grindstone Openings [HUMBOLDT]: *areas,* 7.5 miles southeast of Honeydew (lat. 40°10'45" N, long. 124°00'10" W; near NW cor. sec. 30, T 3 S, R 1 E); the openings are east of Grindstone Creek. Named on Honeydew (1970) 7.5' quadrangle.

Griner Peak [LAKE]: *peak,* 3.25 miles southwest of the town of Upper Lake (lat. 39°07'50" N, long. 122°57'05" W; sec. 22, T 15 N, R 10 W). Altitude 2350 feet. Named on Upper Lake (1958) 7.5' quadrangle.

Grist Creek [MENDOCINO]: *stream,* flows 7 miles to Mill Creek (1) 2.25 miles east-southeast of Covelo in Round Valley (lat. 39°47'05" N, long. 123°12'25" W; near NW cor. sec. 9, T 22 N, R 12 W). Named on Covelo East (1967) and Covelo West (1967) 7.5' quadrangles.

Grizzly Bluff [HUMBOLDT]: *locality,* 2.5 miles south-southwest of Fortuna (lat. 40°33'45" N, long. 124°10'15" W). Named on Rohnerville (1920) 15' quadrangle. Postal authorities established Grizzly Bluff post office in 1890 and discontinued it in 1933 (Frickstad, p. 43). The name, given soon after settlement of the site, was for grizzly bears and scenic bluffs there (Carlson, p. 31). Henry Dean, Nehemiah Patrick, and Lemuel Church first called the place Dean's Corner (Turner, p. 99).

Grizzly Butte [TRINITY]: *peak,* 8 miles south-southeast of Cecilville, which is in Siskiyou County, on Siskiyou-Trinity County line (lat. 41°02'45" N, long. 123°03'15" W); the peak is above Grizzly Creek [TRINITY]. Altitude 6990 feet. Named on Thompson Peak (1979) 7.5' quadrangle.

Grizzly Camp [HUMBOLDT]: *locality,* 1.5 miles south-southwest of Trinity Mountain along East Fork Horse Linto Creek (lat. 41°00'50" N, long. 123°25'35" W). Named on Trinity Mountain (1979) 7.5' quadrangle.

Grizzly Canyon [LAKE]:

(1) *canyon,* drained by a stream that flows nearly 4 miles to West Fork Middle Creek (2) 4.25 miles southwest of Three Crossings (lat. 39°16'20" N, long. 122°58'30" W; sec. 4, T 16 N, R 10 W). Named on Elk Mountain (1967) 7.5' quadrangle.

(2) *canyon,* drained by a stream that flows 6.5 miles to North Fork Cache Creek 7 miles northeast of the town of Lower Lake (lat. 38°59'20" N, long. 122°32'15" W). Named on Clearlake Oaks (1960) and Wilbur Springs (1961) 15' quadrangles, and on Lower Lake (1958) 7.5' quadrangle.

Grizzly Creek [HUMBOLDT]: *stream,* flows 6 miles to Van Duzen River 6.25 miles north-northeast of Redcrest (lat. 40°29'10" N, long. 123°54'20" W; near W line sec. 12, T 1 N, R 2 E). Named on Owl Creek (1979), Redcrest (1969), and Yager Junction (1979) 7.5' quadrangles.

Grizzly Creek [LAKE]:

(1) *stream,* flows 1.5 miles to Grizzly Canyon (2) 6.25 miles south of Cold Spring Mountain (lat. 39°01'30" N, long. 122°28'10" W; near SE cor. sec. 25, T 14 N, R 6 W). Named on Wilbur Springs (1961) 15' quadrangle.

(2) *stream,* flows 1.5 miles to Saint Helena Creek 4.25 miles south of Middletown (lat. 38°41'35" N, long. 122°35'50" W; at S line sec. 23, T 10 N, R 7 W). Named on Detert Reservoir (1958) 7.5' quadrangle.

Grizzly Creek [MENDOCINO]: *stream,* flows less than 1 mile to South Fork Eel River nearly 3 miles southeast of Leggett (lat. 39°50' N, long. 123°40'55" W; near E line sec. 24, T 23 N, R 17 W). Named on Leggett (1969) 7.5' quadrangle.

Grizzly Creek [TRINITY]: *stream,* flows 7.5 miles to North Fork Trinity River 7.25 miles south of Cecilville, which is in Siskiyou County (lat. 41°01'45" N, long. 123°09'25" W); the stream heads at Grizzly Lake. Named on Cecil Lake (1979) and Thompson Peak (1979) 7.5' quadrangles.

Grizzly Gulch [MENDOCINO]: *canyon,* drained by a stream that flows 1.25 miles to Middle Fork Eel River 6.5 miles north-northeast of Eden Valley (lat. 39°42'20" N, long. 123°06'55" W; at E line sec. 6, T 21 N, R 11 W). Named on Jamison Ridge (1967) and Thatcher Ridge (1967) 7.5' quadrangles.

Grizzly Gulch: see **Grindstone Creek** [HUMBOLDT].

Grizzly Lake [TRINITY]: *lake,* 2100 feet long, 10 miles south-southeast of Cecilville, which is in Siskiyou County (lat. 41°00'35" N, long. 123°02'55" W); the lake is at the head of Grizzly Creek. Named on Thompson Peak (1979) 7.5' quadrangle.

Grizzly Meadows [TRINITY]: *area,* 9.5 miles south-southeast of Cecilville, which is in Siskiyou County (lat. 41°01' N, long. 123°03' W); the place is near the head of Grizzly Creek. Named on Thompson Peak (1979) 7.5' quadrangle. On Cecilville (1955) 15' quadrangle, the name "Grizzly Meadows" applies to an area that is situated 1 mile farther north along Grizzly Creek.

Grizzly Medical Springs: see **Grizzly Spring** [LAKE].

Grizzly Mountain [TRINITY]: *peak,* 11.5 miles southwest of Forest Glen (lat. 40°15'10" N, long. 123°28'35" W; near E line sec. 34, T 2 S, R 6 E). Altitude 5458 feet. Named on Ruth Reservoir (1978) and Zenia (1967) 7.5' quadrangles. The name is from an encounter between Tim Willburn and a grizzly bear at the place about 1857 (Jones, p. 356).

Grizzly Peak [LAKE]: *peak,* 6.5 miles south of Wilson Valley (2) (lat. 38°52'45" N, long. 122°27'15" W; sec. 19, T 12 N, R 5 W). Named on Wilson Valley (1958) 7.5' quadrangle.

Grizzly Peak [MENDOCINO]: *peak,* 4.25 miles north-northeast of Ornbaun Valley (lat. 38°58'15" N, long. 123°16'45" W; sec. 22, T 13 N, R 13 W). Named on Ornbaun Valley (1960) 15' quadrangle.

Grizzly Point [MENDOCINO]: *relief feature,* 7 miles northeast of Willits (lat. 39°28'50" N, long. 123°15'50" W; near NE cor. sec. 26, T 19 N, R 13 W). Named on Willits (1961) 15' quadrangle.

Grizzly Spring [LAKE]: *spring,* nearly 7 miles south of Cold Spring Mountain (lat. 39°00'10" N, long. 122°29'50" W); the spring is in Grizzly Canyon (2). Named on Wilbur Springs (1961) 15' quadrangle. Water from two springs was used by campers for bathing; the spring water also was bottled and sold locally (Waring, p. 193-194). Bradley (p. 217) called the feature Grizzly Medical Springs, and noted that the place also was called Richardson's Springs, for the owner, Samuel Richardson.

Grogan Hole [HUMBOLDT]: *relief feature,* 5.25 miles northwest of Trinity Mountain at the confluence of Oregon Creek and Tish Tang a Tang Creek (lat. 41°05'05" N, long. 123°29'15" W). Named on Salmon Mountain (1955) 15' quadrangle. United States Board on Geographic Names (1981c, p. 3) approved the name Crogan Hole for the feature—this name commemorates Barney Crogan, who grazed cattle at the place in the nineteenth century.

Grooms Hill [LAKE]: *peak,* 2 miles southwest of Middletown (lat. 38°44' N, long. 122°38'15" W; sec. 9, T 10 N, R 7 W). Named on Mount Saint Helena (1959) 7.5' quadrangle.

Groshong Gulch [MENDOCINO]: *canyon,* drained by a stream that flows 1.5 miles to South Fork Gualala River 14 miles southwest of Ornbaun Valley in Sonoma County (lat. 38°46'40" N, long. 123°29'40" W; sec. 25, T 11 N, R 15 W). Named on Ornbaun Valley (1960) 15' quadrangle.

Grotzman Creek [HUMBOLDT]: *stream,* flows less than 1 mile to lowlands 1 mile southeast of Arcata at Sunny Brae (lat. 40°51'40" N, long. 124°04' W; sec. 33, T 6 N, R 1 E). Named on Arcata South (1959) 7.5' quadrangle.

Grouse: see **Zenia** [TRINITY].

Grouse Creek [HUMBOLDT]:

(1) *stream,* flows 2.25 miles to North Fork Yager Creek 1.25 miles southwest of Lone Star Junction (lat. 40°37'15" N, long. 123°53'50" W; near S line sec. 24, T 3 N, R 2 E). Named on Iaqua Buttes (1979) and Owl Creek (1979) 7.5' quadrangles.

(2) *stream,* flows 15 miles to South Fork Trinity River 9.5 miles east-northeast of Board Camp Mountain (lat. 40°44' N, long. 123°32'35" W). Named on Board Camp Mountain (1977) and Sims Mountain (1979) 7.5' quadrangles.

Grouse Creek [TRINITY]: *stream,* flows 3 miles to East Fork Trinity River 7.5 miles northeast of Trinity Center (lat. 41°05'05" N, long. 122°35'10" W; sec. 8, T 37 N, R 6 W); the stream heads at Grouse Lake. Named on

Bonanza King (1955) 15' quadrangle.

Grouse Lake [TRINITY]: *lake,* 1400 feet long, 8.5 miles east-northeast of Trinity Center (lat. 41°04' N, long. 122°32'45" W; sec. 15, T 37 N, R 6 W); the lake is at the head of Grouse Creek. Named on Bonanza King (1955) 15' quadrangle.

Grouse Mountain [HUMBOLDT]: *peak,* 13 miles south of the settlement of Willow Creek (lat. 40°45'35" N, long. 123°40'45" W; sec. 1, T 4 N, R 4 E). Altitude 5410 feet. Named on Grouse Mountain (1979) 7.5' quadrangle.

Grouse Prairie [TRINITY]: *area,* 3 miles northwest of Forest Glen (lat. 40°24'20" N, long. 123°22' W; at E line sec. 2, T 1 S, R 7 E). Named on Naufus Creek (1979) 7.5' quadrangle.

Grouse Ridge [TRINITY]:

(1) *ridge,* generally north-trending, 3 miles long, 9 miles west-southwest of Billys Peak (1) on Trinity-Siskiyou County line (lat. 41°04'15" N, long. 122°55'20" W). Named on Coffee Creek (1955) 15' quadrangle.

(2) *ridge,* west-southwest-trending, 1 mile long, 6 miles south-southeast of Black Rock Mountain (lat. 40°07'15" N, long. 122°58'45" W; mainly in sec. 10, T 26 N, R 10 W). Named on Yolla Bolly (1954) 15' quadrangle.

(3) *ridge,* west-trending, 2 miles long, 8.5 miles west-southwest of Black Rock Mountain (lat. 40°08'20" N, long. 123°08'40" W; on and near N line sec. 6, T 26 N, R 11 W). Named on Black Rock Mountain (1954) 15' quadrangle.

Grouse Spring [LAKE]: *spring,* 2.25 miles north of Whispering Pines (lat. 38°50'50" N, long. 122°42'35" W; sec. 35, T 12 N, R 8 W). Named on Whispering Pines (1958) 7.5' quadrangle.

Grove [MENDOCINO]: *locality,* 12.5 miles north-northwest of Comptche along California Western Railroad (lat. 39°26'15" N, long. 123°39'50" W; near NW cor. sec. 9, T 18 N, R 16 W). Named on Comptche (1960) 15' quadrangle. Called Grove Junction on O'Brien's (1953) map.

Grove Junction: see **Grove** [MENDOCINO].

Groves Prairie [HUMBOLDT]: *area,* 8 miles east of the settlement of Willow Creek (lat. 40°57'20" N, long. 123°29'10" W). Named on Ironside Mountain (1951) 15' quadrangle. The name is for Dave Groves, who came to the place in the late 1860's (Gudde, 1949, p. 136).

Groves Prairie Creek [HUMBOLDT]: *stream,* flows 3 miles to Cedar Creek (2) 6 miles east of the settlement of Willow Creek (lat. 40°56'05" N, long. 123°30'50" W); the stream heads at Groves Prairie. Named on Ironside Mountain (1951) 15' quadrangle, and on Salyer (1979) 7.5' quadrangle.

Grub Creek [MENDOCINO]: *stream,* flows 2.5 miles to Tenmile Creek 10 miles southeast of Leggett (lat. 39°46'05" N, long. 123°34'30" W; near N line sec. 18, T 22 N, R 15 W). Named on Tan Oak Park (1969) 7.5' quadrangle.

Grub Gulch [TRINITY]: *canyon,* less than 1 mile long, opens into the canyon of West Weaver Creek 1.5 miles west of Weaverville (lat. 40°44'15" N, long. 122°58' W; sec. 11, T 33 N, R 10 W). Named on Weaverville (1950) 15' quadrangle.

Gschwend Creek [MENDOCINO]: *stream,* flows 1.5 miles to Bullock Creek 7.5 miles north-northwest of Boonville (lat. 39°06'10" N, long. 123°25'40" W; near S line sec. 32, T 15 N, R 14 W). Named on Boonville (1959) 15' quadrangle.

Gualala [MENDOCINO]: *village,* 26 miles southwest of Hopland along the coast (lat. 38°46' N, long. 123°31'40" W; sec. 27, T 11 N, R 15 W). Named on Gualala (1960) 7.5' quadrangle. Postal authorities established Gualala post office in 1862 (Frickstad, p. 95). The name also had the forms "Guadala," "Walhalla," and "Wallala" (Becker, G.F., p. 213.) United States Board on Geographic Names (1933, p. 342) rejected the form "Wallholla" for the name.

Gualala Mountain [MENDOCINO]: *peak,* 11 miles west-southwest of Ornbaun Valley (lat. 38°51'20" N, long. 123°29'45" W; sec. 35, T 12 N, R 15 W). Named on Ornbaun Valley (1960) 15' quadrangle, and on Gualala (1960) 7.5' quadrangle.

Gualala River [MENDOCINO]: *stream,* formed by the confluence of North Fork and South Fork 1.5 miles east-northeast of Gualala (South Fork is in Sonoma County), flows 3.5 miles to the sea at Gualala (lat. 38°46'10" N, long. 123°32' W; at W line sec. 29, T 11 N, R 15 W). Named on Ornbaun Valley (1960) and Point Arena (1960) 15' quadrangles. The stream forms part of Mendocino-Sonoma County line. United States Board on Geographic Names (1933, p. 342) rejected the form "Wallholla River" for the name. North Fork is 14 miles long and is named on Ornbaun Valley (1960) and Point Arena (1960) 15' quadrangles. Little North Fork enters North Fork 2 miles north-northeast of Gualala; it is 4.25 miles long and is named on Point Arena (1960) 15' quadrangle.

Gube Mountain [MENDOCINO]: *peak,* 4.5 miles south of Ornbaun Valley (lat. 38°51' N, long. 123°19' W; near NW cor. sec. 33, T 12 N, R 13 W). Altitude 2602 feet. Named on Ornbaun Valley (1960) 15' quadrangle.

Guenoc [LAKE]: *land grant,* east and northeast of Middletown; includes Coyote Valley and Long Valley (1). Named on Aetna Springs (1958), Detert Reservoir (1958), Jericho Valley (1958), and Middletown (1958) 7.5' quadrangles. George Rock received 6 leagues in 1845; Archibald A. Ritchie and Paul S. Forbes claimed 21,220 acres patented in 1865 (Cowan, p. 39; Perez, p. 68).

Guenoc: see **Coyote Valley** [LAKE].

Guenoc Lake: see **Detert Reservoir** [LAKE].

Gulch C [MENDOCINO]: *canyon,* drained by a stream that flows 1.5 miles to Noyo River nearly 7 miles west-northwest of Willits (lat. 39°25'50" N, long. 123°28'20" W; sec. 12, T 18 N, R 15 W). Named on Willits (1961) 15' quadrangle.

Gulch 8 [MENDOCINO]: *canyon,* drained by a stream that flows 0.25 mile to Perry Gulch 1.25 miles southwest of Navarro (lat. 39°07'55" N, long. 123°34'25" W; sec. 25, T 15 N, R 16 W); the mouth of the canyon is nearly opposite the mouth of Gulch 7. Named on Navarro (1961) 15' quadrangle.

Gulch Eleven [MENDOCINO]: *canyon,* drained by a stream that flows nearly 2 miles to South Fork Tenmile River 15 miles north of Comptche (lat. 39°28'45" N, long. 123°35'30" W; sec. 25, T 19 N, R 16 W). Named on Comptche (1960) 7.5' quadrangle.

Gulch 15 [MENDOCINO]: *canyon,* drained by a stream that flows 1 mile to John Smith Creek 5 miles north of Navarro (lat. 39°13'20" N, long. 123°31'50" W; near NE cor. sec. 28, T 16 N, R 15 W). Named on Navarro (1961) 15' quadrangle.

Gulch 5 [MENDOCINO]: *canyon,* drained by a stream that flows less than 1 mile to Perry Gulch 1.25 miles west-southwest of Navarro (lat. 39°08'30" N, long. 123°33'50" W; sec. 19, T 15 N, R 15 W); the canyon is between Gulch 4 and Gulch 6. Named on Navarro (1961) 15' quadrangle.

Gulch Five [MENDOCINO]: *canyon,* drained by a stream that flows 0.5 mile to Noyo River 12 miles north-northeast of Comptche (lat. 39°26' N, long. 123°31'50" W; near NE cor. sec. 9, T 18 N, R 15 W). Named on Comptche (1960) 15' quadrangle.

Gulch 4 [MENDOCINO]: *canyon,* drained by a stream that flows less than 0.5 mile to Perry Gulch 1.25 miles west-southwest of Navarro (lat. 39°08'35" N, long. 123°33'45" W; sec. 19, T 15 N, R 15 W); the canyon is between Gulch 3 and Gulch 5. Named on Navarro (1961) 15' quadrangle.

Gulch 9 [MENDOCINO]: *canyon,* drained by a stream that flows 0.5 mile to Perry Gulch 1.5 miles southwest of Navarro (lat. 39°08'15" N, long. 123°24' W; near NW cor. sec. 30, T 15 N, R 15 W); the mouth of the canyon is 0.5 mile upstream from the mouth of Gulch 8. Named on Navarro (1961) 15' quadrangle.

Gulch 1 [MENDOCINO]: *canyon,* drained by a stream that flows 0.5 mile to Perry Gulch less than 0.5 mile southwest of Navarro (lat. 39°08'35" N, long. 123°33'10" W; sec. 19, T 15 N, R 15 W); the mouth of the canyon is 900 feet northeast of the mouth of Gulch 2. Named on Navarro (1961) 15' quadrangle.

Gulch One [MENDOCINO]:

(1) *canyon,* drained by a stream that flows less than 1 mile to the canyon of Ten Mile River 9 miles southwest of Branscomb (lat. 39°33'10" N, long. 123°43'50" W; at E line sec. 34, T 20 N, R 17 W). Named on Dutchmans Knoll (1966) 7.5' quadrangle.

(2) *canyon,* drained by a stream that flows 1 mile to Redwood Creek (3) 16 miles north of Comptche (lat. 39°29'35" N, long. 123°36'20" W; near E line sec. 23, T 19 N, R 16 W). Named on Comptche (1960) 15' quadrangle.

Gulch 7 [MENDOCINO]: *canyon,* drained by a stream that flows 1 mile to Perry Gulch 1.25 miles southwest of Navarro (lat. 39°07'55" N, long. 123°34'30" W; sec. 25, T 15 N, R 16 W); the mouth of the canyon is 160 feet west-southwest of the mouth of Gulch 6. Named on Navarro (1961) 15' quadrangle.

Gulch Seven [MENDOCINO]: *canyon,* drained by a stream that flows nearly 3 miles to North Fork Noyo River 13 miles north-northeast of Comptche (lat. 39°26'50" N, long. 123°31'15" W; sec. 3, T 18 N, R 15 W). Named on Comptche (1960) and Willits (1961) 15' quadrangles. Willits (1942) 15' quadrangle has the form "Gulch No. 7" for the name.

Gulch 6 [MENDOCINO]: *canyon,* drained by a stream that flows 1 mile to Perry Gulch 2 miles southwest of Navarro (lat. 39°08'05" N, long. 123°34'10" W; near E line sec. 25, T 15 N, R 16 W); the canyon is between Gulch 5 and Gulch 7. Named on Navarro (1961) 15' quadrangle.

Gulch Sixteen [MENDOCINO]: *canyon,* drained by a stream that flows 1 mile to an unnamed branch of Chamberlain Creek 8 miles north of Comptche (lat. 39°22'45" N, long. 123°34'40" W; sec. 31, T 18 N, R 15 W). Named on Comptche (1960) 15' quadrangle.

Gulch Thirtyone [MENDOCINO]: *canyon,* drained by a stream that flows 1.5 miles to Noyo River 12 miles north of Comptche (lat. 39°26'10" N, long. 123°34'40" W; at N line sec. 7, T 18 N, R 15 W). Named on Comptche (1960) 15' quadrangle.

Gulch 3 [MENDOCINO]: *canyon,* drained by a stream that flows 0.25 mile to Perry Creek 1 mile south-southwest of Navarro (lat. 39°08'30" N, long. 123°33'30" W; sec. 19, T 15 N, R 15 W). Named on Navarro (1961) 15' quadrangle.

Gulch Three [MENDOCINO]: *canyon,* drained by a stream that flows 1.25 miles to Ten Mile River 8 miles southwest of Branscomb (lat. 39°34' N, long. 123°43'20" W; sec. 26, T 20 N, R 17 W); the mouth of the canyon is less than 0.5 mile upstream from the mouth of Gulch Two. Named on

Dutchmans Knoll (1966) 7.5' quadrangle.

Gulch 2 [MENDOCINO]: *canyon,* drained by a stream that flows 0.5 mile to Perry Gulch 1 mile southwest of Navarro (lat. 39°08'30" N, long. 123°33'20" W; sec. 19, T 15 N, R 15 W); the canyon is between Gulch 1 and Gulch 3. Named on Navarro (1961) 15' quadrangle.

Gulch Two [MENDOCINO]: *canyon,* drained by a stream that flows nearly 1 mile to Ten Mile River 8 miles southwest of Branscomb (lat. 39°33'45" N, long. 123°43'15" W; sec. 26, T 20 N, R 17 W); the mouth of the canyon is 2 miles upstream from the mouth of Gulch One (1). Named on Dutchmans Knoll (1966) 7.5' quadrangle.

Gunari Gulch [MENDOCINO]: *canyon,* drained by a stream that flows 0.5 mile to South Fork Albion River 8 miles north-northeast of Elk (lat. 39°14'35" N, long. 123°39'55" W; sec. 17, T 16 N, R 16 W). Named on Elk (1960) 7.5' quadrangle.

Gunbarrel Campsite [DEL NORTE]: *locality,* 5 miles east-northeast of Buck Mountain along South Fork Smith River (lat. 41°39'40" N, long. 123°46'45" W); the place is near Gunbarrel Slide. Named on Ship Mountain (1982) 7.5' quadrangle.

Gunbarrel Slide [DEL NORTE]: *relief feature,* 5.25 miles west-northwest of Buck Mountain (lat. 41°39'45" N, long. 123°46'20" W). Named on Ship Mountain (1982) 7.5' quadrangle.

Gunderson Rock [MENDOCINO]: *rock,* less than 0.5 mile south-southwest of Elk, and 500 feet offshore (lat. 39°07'35" N, long. 123°43'10" W). Named on Elk (1960) 7.5' quadrangle.

Gunning Creek [LAKE]: *stream,* flows about 2 miles to Anderson Creek (2) 2.25 miles south of Whispering Pines (lat. 38°46'50" N, long. 122°42'30" W; sec. 26, T 11 N, R 8 W). Named on Whispering Pines (1958) 7.5' quadrangle.

Gunrack Ridge [HUMBOLDT]: *ridge,* west-southwest-trending, 1 mile long, 11.5 miles east-southeast of Korbel (lat. 40°49'55" N, long. 123°45'10" W; mainly in sec. 8, T 5 N, R 4 E). Named on Grouse Mountain (1979) and Maple Creek (1977) 7.5' quadrangles.

Gunsight Peak [TRINITY]: *peak,* 15 miles south-southeast of Weaverville (lat. 40°32'30" N, long. 122°48'35" W; sec. 18, T 31 N, R 8 W). Altitude 5733 feet. Named on Weaverville (1950) 15' quadrangle.

Gunther Creek [LAKE]: *stream,* flows 2 miles to Soda Creek (2) 3.5 miles southwest of Jericho Valley (lat. 38°48'15" N, long. 122°29'25" W; sec. 14, T 11 N, R 6 W). Named on Jericho Valley (1958) 7.5' quadrangle.

Gunther Island [HUMBOLDT]: *island,* 1.25 miles long, largely marsh, 1 mile north-northwest of downtown Eureka in Humboldt Bay (lat. 40°48'55" N, long. 124°10'05" W). Named on Eureka (1958) 7.5' quadrangle. United States Board on Geographic Names (1943, p. 11) approved the name "Gunther Island" for the feature, and rejected the name "Indian Island," but later (1971b, p. 3) the Board reversed this decision. The name "Indian Island" is from the massacre of Indians who gathered on the island in 1860 for an annual festival (Hoover, Rensch, and Rensch, p. 100). The name "Gunther Island" is from the owner of the island at the time of the massacre (Palais, p. 47).

Guntleys: see **Philo** [MENDOCINO].

Guptil Gulch [HUMBOLDT]: *canyon,* 1.5 miles long, 7.5 miles south of Arcata (lat. 40°45'35" N, long. 124°06'30" W; mainly in sec. 6, T 4 N, R 1 E). Named on Arcata South (1959) and McWhinney Creek (1979) 7.5' quadrangles.

Gurley Gulch [TRINITY]: *canyon,* drained by a stream that flows 1.5 miles to Hayfork Creek 7.5 miles north-northeast of Dubakella Mountain (lat. 40°29'30" N, long. 123°04'25" W). Named on Dubakella Mountain (1954) 15' quadrangle.

Gut Creek [MENDOCINO]: *stream,* flows 2 miles to an unnamed branch of Indian Creek (1) 5.5 miles north-northeast of Boonville (lat. 39°04'55" N, long. 123°19'45" W; sec. 7, T 14 N, R 13 W). Named on Boonville (1959) 15' quadrangle.

Guthrie Creek [HUMBOLDT]: *stream,* flows 6.5 miles to the sea 6 miles west-southwest of Ferndale (lat. 40°32'35" N, long. 124°21'50" W; sec. 24, T 2 N, R 3 W). Named on Ferndale (1959) 7.5' quadrangle. On Cape Fortunas (1920) 15' quadrangle, the canyon of the stream is called Guthries Gulch.

Guthries Gulch: see **Guthrie Creek** [HUMBOLDT].

Guy Creek [HUMBOLDT]: *stream,* flows nearly 1 mile to Holm Creek 3 miles east-northeast of Showers Mountain (lat. 40°34'55" N, long. 123°38'20" W; near W line sec. 5, T 2 N, R 5 E); the stream heads at Guy Lake. Named on Showers Mountain (1978) 7.5' quadrangle.

Guy Lake [HUMBOLDT]: *lake,* 150 feet long, 4 miles east of Showers Mountain (lat. 40°34'55" N, long. 123°37'25" W; at E line sec. 5, T 2 N, R 5 E). Named on Blake Mountain (1979) 7.5' quadrangle.

Gwin Gulch [TRINITY]: *canyon,* drained by a stream that flows 3.5 miles to Canyon Creek (1) 4.5 miles northeast of Helena (lat. 40°44'10" N, long. 123°03'45" W; sec. 12, T 34 N, R 11 W). Named on Helena (1951) 15' quadrangle.

Gyon Bluffs [HUMBOLDT]: *escarpment,* 2.5 miles southwest of Orick along the coast (lat. 41°15'45" N, long. 124°05'50" W; sec. 7, T 10 N, R 1 E). Named on Orick (1966) 7.5' quadrangle.

Gypsy Creek [TRINITY]: *stream,* flows 2 miles to Salt Creek (2) 7.25 miles southeast of Kettenpom (lat. 40°04'25" N, long. 123°21'55" W; sec. 34, T 4 S, R 7 E). Named on Long Ridge (1967) 7.5' quadrangle.

— H —

Ha Amar Creek [HUMBOLDT]: *stream,* flows nearly 1 mile to Klamath River 2.5 miles south-southeast of Johnsons (lat. 41°19' N, long. 123°50'55" W; near NE cor. sec. 29, T 11 N, R 3 E). Named on Johnsons (1982) 7.5' quadrangle..

Hachinhama: see **Lake Hachinhama**, under **Little Borax Lake** [LAKE].

Hacker Creek [HUMBOLDT]: *stream,* flows 1.25 miles to South Fork Salmon Creek 6 miles west-southwest of Phillipsville (lat. 40°10'30" N, long. 123°53'30" W; near E line sec. 25, T 3 S, R 2 E). Named on Ettersburg (1969) 7.5' quadrangle.

Hacketsville [HUMBOLDT]: *locality,* 3.5 miles west of Scotia along Howe Creek (lat. 40°29'15" N, long. 124°10'10" W; sec. 10, T 1 N, R 1 W). Named on Taylor Peak (1969) 7.5' quadrangle. A logging camp was started at the place in the 1920's (Carranco and Sorensen, p. 154). The name is for Walter Hackett, a local landowner (Turner, p. 100).

Hackney Spring: see **Wildwood** [TRINITY].

Hadley: see **Trinidad** [HUMBOLDT].

Hadley Creek: see **Big Creek** [HUMBOLDT] (2).

Hadley Peak [HUMBOLDT]: *peak,* 6.25 miles southwest of Honeydew (lat. 40°10'35" N, long. 124°12'05" W; sec. 29, T 3 S, R 1 W). Altitude 3010 feet. Named on Shubrick Peak (1969) 7.5' quadrangle.

Haehl Creek [MENDOCINO]: *stream,* flows 2 miles to Little Lake Valley 2 miles south-southeast of downtown Willits (lat. 39°23' N, long. 123°20'25" W; sec. 30, T 18 N, R 13 W). Named on Willits (1961) 15' quadrangle.

Hagen Lake [MENDOCINO]: *lake,* 1000 feet long, 11.5 miles southeast of Ukiah (lat. 39°01'05" N, long. 123°05' W; on W line sec. 4, T 13 N, R 11 W). Named on Purdys Gardens (1958) 7.5' quadrangle.

Hail Creek [LAKE-MENDOCINO]: *stream,* mainly in Mendocino County, flows 3.25 miles to Tyler Creek 2.25 miles east-southeast of Monument Peak (lat. 38°52'55" N, long. 122°54'25" W; sec. 18, T 12 N, R 9 W). Named on Asti (1959), Highland Springs (1959), and The Geysers (1959) 7.5' quadrangles.

Hailstone Camp [TRINITY]: *locality,* 12.5 miles east-northeast of Burnt Ranch (lat. 40°54'20" N, long. 123°16'40" W). Named on Ironside Mountain (1951) 15' quadrangle.

Haines Flat [DEL NORTE]: *area,* 9.5 miles north-northwest of Buck Mountain (lat. 41°44'50" N, long. 123°56'10" W). Named on Cant Hook Mountain (1982) 7.5' quadrangle. Bancroft (p. 370) referred to Hayne Flat.

Hair Seal Rock [HUMBOLDT]: *rock,* 3.5 miles west of Petrolia, and 500 feet offshore (lat. 40°19'35" N, long. 124°21'10" W; sec. 1, T 2 S, R 2 W). Named on Petrolia (1969) 7.5' quadrangle.

Halagow Creek [HUMBOLDT]: *stream,* flows 1.5 miles to Klamath River less than 1 mile northwest of Johnsons (lat. 41°21'35" N, long. 123°53'05" W; at W line sec. 7, T 11 N, R 3 E). Named on Holter Ridge (1983) and Johnsons (1982) 7.5' quadrangles. The name is of Indian origin (Gudde, 1949, p. 140).

Hale Creek [MENDOCINO]: *stream,* flows 1.5 miles to Eel River 6 miles north of the town of Potter Valley (lat. 39°24'30" N, long. 123°07'30" W; near N line sec. 19, T 18 N, R 11 W). Named on Potter Valley (1960) 15' quadrangle.

Hale Creek [TRINITY]: *stream,* flows 2 miles to Mad River 6 miles west of Forest Glen (lat. 40°22'25" N, long. 123°26'15" W; sec. 13, T 1 S, R 6 E). Named on Ruth Reservoir (1978) 7.5' quadrangle.

Hale Ridge [LAKE]: *ridge,* generally west-trending, 3 miles long, 5 miles south of Potato Hill (lat. 39°16'45" N, long. 122°47'15" W). Named on Potato Hill (1967) 7.5' quadrangle.

Hales Grove [MENDOCINO]: *settlement,* 11 miles south of Piercy along South Fork Mule Creek (lat. 39°49'05" N, long. 123°46'55" W; sec. 30, T 23 N, R 17 W). Named on Hales Grove (1970) 7.5' quadrangle. Called Monroe on Kenny (1920) 15' quadrangle. Postal authorities established Monroe post office in 1897, moved it 0.5 mile west in 1898, moved it 1 mile east in 1900, moved it 1 mile east again in 1905, and discontinued it in 1912; the place also was known as Monroeville (Salley, p. 144). California Mining Bureau's (1917c) map shows a place called Tolson located about 5 miles north-northeast of Monroe along South Fork Eel River. Postal authorities established Tolson post office in 1906 and discontinued it in 1907 (Salley, p. 223).

Half Lake [HUMBOLDT]: *lake,* 150 feet long, 2.5 miles north-northwest of Weitchpec (lat. 41°13'25" N, long. 123°43'30" W). Named on Weitchpec (1979) 7.5' quadrangle.

Half Way: see **Comptche** [MENDOCINO].

Halfway Gulch [TRINITY]: *canyon,* drained by a stream that flows 0.5 mile to Van Ness Creek 16 miles east-northeast of Weaverville (lat. 40°50'55" N, long. 122°40'40" W). Named on Schell Mountain (1950) 15' quadrangle.

Halfway House Gulch [MENDOCINO]: *canyon,* 1.5 miles long, 6.5 miles north-northeast of Navarro (lat. 39°14'15" N, long. 123°30'15" W; sec. 14, 23, T 16 N, R 15 W). Named on Navarro (1961) 15' quadrangle.

Halfway Ridge [TRINITY]: *ridge,* east-northeast- to north-trending, 2.5 miles long, 7 miles east-southeast of Hyampom (lat. 40°36' N, long. 123°19' W). Named on Hyampom (1951) 15' quadrangle.

Hall Bluff [DEL NORTE]: *relief feature,* along the coast at Crescent City (lat. 41°45'05" N, long. 124°12'40" W; sec. 29, T 16 N, R 1 W). Named on Crescent City (1966) 7.5' quadrangle.

Hall City: see **Hall City Creek** [TRINITY].

Hall City Caves [TRINITY]: *cave,* 7.5 miles east of Dubakella Mountain (lat. 40°24'25" N, long. 123°00'30" W; at E line sec. 32, T 30 N, R 10 W). Named on Dubakella Mountain (1954) 15' quadrangle. United States Board on Geographic Names (1983c, p. 5) approved the singular form "Hall City Cave" for the name.

Hall City Creek [TRINITY]: *stream,* flows 3.5 miles to Hayfork Creek 5 miles east of Dubakella Mountain (lat. 40°24' N, long. 123°03'30" W; near N line sec. 1, T 29 N, R 11 W). Named on Dubakella Mountain (1954) 15' quadrangle. The name recalls the mining camp of Hall City that W.R. Hall and Edgar Landis started in 1896; the camp was abandoned by 1915 (Jones, p. 329).

Hall Creek [HUMBOLDT]: *stream,* flows 1.5 miles to Mill Creek (4) 4.5 miles east-northeast of Arcata (lat. 40°54'05" N, long. 124°00'25" W; near SE cor. sec. 13, T 6 N, R 1 E). Named on Arcata North (1959) 7.5' quadrangle.

Hall Creek [MENDOCINO]: *stream,* flows 1.5 miles to Ram Spring Creek 6.5 miles east-northeast of Spyrock (2) (lat. 39°56' N, long. 123°20'40" W). Named on Mina (1967) 7.5' quadrangle.

Hall Gulch [MENDOCINO]: *canyon,* 2.25 miles long, opens into the head of Schooner Gulch 8.5 miles north-northwest of Gualala (lat. 38°52'05" N, long. 123°37'10" W; near N line sec. 34, T 12 N, R 16 W). Named on Gualala (1960) 7.5' quadrangle.

Halls Gulch [TRINITY]: *canyon,* drained by a stream that flows 6.5 miles to East Fork Trinity River 4.25 miles east of Trinity Center (lat. 41°00'50" N, long. 122°36'30" W; near NW cor. sec. 6, T 36 N, R 6 W). Named on Bonanza King (1955) 15' quadrangle.

Halsey Ridge [TRINITY]: *ridge,* south-southwest-trending, 2.5 miles long, 2 miles east of Burnt Ranch (lat. 40°48'45" N, long. 123°26'15" W). Named on Ironside Mountain (1951) 15' quadrangle.

Haman Creek [HUMBOLDT-TRINITY]: *stream,* heads in Trinity County and flows 2.5 miles to Eel River 4 miles south-southeast of Alderpoint in Humboldt County (lat. 40°07'30" N, long. 123°34'30" W). Named on Alderpoint (1969) 7.5' quadrangle. Called Hamann Creek on Alderpoint (1949) 15' quadrangle, and United States Board on Geographic Names (1973a, p. 3) gave the names "Hamann Creek" and "Hammon Creek" as variants.

Haman Ridge [TRINITY]: *ridge,* generally south-trending, 6.5 miles long, 8 miles south-southeast of Kettenpom (lat. 40°03'15" N, long. 123°23'15" W). Named on Lake Mountain (1967) and Long Ridge (1967) 7.5' quadrangles.

Ham Canyon [MENDOCINO]: *canyon,* drained by a stream that flows 2.25 miles to Rancheria Creek (2) 4.25 miles west-northwest of Boonville (lat. 39°02'15" N, long. 123°26'30" W; at N line sec. 31, T 14 N, R 14 W). Named on Boonville (1959) 15' quadrangle.

Hamilton Opening [MENDOCINO]: *area,* 8 miles south of Navarro (lat. 39°02'20" N, long. 123°33' W; near S line sec. 29, T 14 N, R 15 W). Named on Navarro (1961) 15' quadrangle.

Hammerhorn Campground [MENDOCINO]: *locality,* 7.5 miles north of Anthony Peak (lat. 39°56'55" N, long. 122°59'25" W; sec. 8, T 24 N, R 10 W); the place is by Hammerhorn Lake. Named on Buck Rock (1967) 7.5' quadrangle.

Hammerhorn Creek [MENDOCINO-TRINITY]: *stream,* heads in Trinity County and flows 4 miles to Middle Fork Eel River 16 miles northeast of Covelo in Mendocino County (lat. 39°56'25" N, long. 123°00'30" W; sec. 18, T 24 N, R 10 W); the stream heads at Hammerhorn Ridge. Named on Buck Rock (1967) and Leech Lake Mountain (1966) 7.5' quadrangles.

Hammerhorn Lake [MENDOCINO]: *lake,* 650 feet long, 7.5 miles north of Anthony Peak (lat. 39°56'55" N, long. 122°59'20" W; sec. 8, T 24 N, R 10 W). Named on Buck Rock (1967) 7.5' quadrangle.

Hammerhorn Mountain [TRINITY]: *peak,* 15 miles south of Black Rock Mountain on Trinity-Tehama County line (lat. 40°00'10" N, long. 122°57' W; near E line sec. 22, T 25 N, R 10 W). Altitude 7567 feet. Named on Yolla Bolly (1954) 15' quadrangle.

Hammerhorn Ridge [TRINITY]: *ridge,* west-trending, 5.5 miles long, 19 miles northeast of Covelo [MENDOCINO] (lat. 39°59'30" N, long. 122°59'45" W). Named on Buck Rock (1967) and Leech Lake Mountain (1966) 7.5' quadrangles.

Hammon Creek: see **Haman Creek** [HUMBOLDT].

Hamner Flat [HUMBOLDT]: *area,* 2.5 miles northwest of Alderpoint near Eel River (lat. 40°11'50" N, long. 123°38'55" W; near SW cor. sec. 17, T 3 S, R 5 E). Named on Fort Seward (1969) 7.5' quadrangle.

Ham Pass [MENDOCINO]: *pass,* 10.5 miles northeast of Covelo on Pine Ridge (1) (lat. 39°53'15" N, long. 123°05'15" W; at N line sec. 4, T 23 N, R 11 W). Named on Leech Lake Mountain (1966) 7.5' quadrangle.

Hancorne Prairie [HUMBOLDT]: *area,* 6.5 miles south of Johnsons (lat. 41°15'25" N, long. 123°52'55" W; sec. 18, T 10 N, R 3 E). Named on Bald Hills (1982) and Holter Ridge (1983) 7.5' quadrangles. Called Hancorn Prairie on Coyote Peak (1945) and Tectah Creek (1945) 15' quadrangles. Thomas Walter Hancorne built a cabin at the place (Turner, p. 103).

Hand Flat [MENDOCINO]: *area,* 9.5 miles north-northeast of Eden Valley (lat. 39°44'20" N, long. 123°05' W). Named on Thatcher Ridge (1967) 7.5' quadrangle.

Hanes Ridge [MENDOCINO]: *ridge,* southeast-trending, 1.5 miles long, 9.5 miles west-northwest of Ornbaun Valley (lat. 38°57'15" N, long. 123°28' W). Named on Ornbaun Valley (1960) 15' quadrangle.

Hanks Camp [LAKE]: *locality,* 10 miles north of Clearlake Oaks along Bartlett Creek (lat. 39°10' N, long. 122°40'45" W; near W line sec. 7, T 15 N, R 7 W). Named on Clearlake Oaks (1960) 15' quadrangle.

Hannah: see **Mount Hannah** [LAKE].

Hansen: see **Alton** [HUMBOLDT].

Hansen Hill [HUMBOLDT]: *peak,* 1 mile north-northeast of Yager Junction (lat. 40°33'40" N, long. 123°48'55" W; near NE cor. sec. 15, T 2 N, R 3 E). Altitude 3588 feet. Named on Yager Junction (1979) 7.5' quadrangle. The name commemorates H. Chris Hansen, a sheep rancher who owned property at the place (Turner, p. 103).

Hansen Ridge [HUMBOLDT]: *ridge,* northwest-trending, 1.25 miles long, 12.5 miles south-southeast of Scotia (lat. 40°18'45" N, long. 124°00'45" W; mainly in sec. 12, T 2 S, R 1 E). Named on Bull Creek (1969) 7.5' quadrangle.

Hansens Curve [MENDOCINO]: *bend,* 6.5 miles west-northwest of Comptche along Big River (lat. 39°17'10" N, long. 123°42'20" W; near S line sec. 36, T 17 N, R 17 W). Named on Comptche (1960) 15' quadrangle.

Hanson Creek [MENDOCINO]: *stream,* flows 3.5 miles to Haynes Creek 8.5 miles east-northeast of Eden Valley (lat. 39°41'20" N, long. 123°02'45" W). Named on Thatcher Ridge (1967) 7.5' quadrangle.

Hans Ottoson Opening [MENDOCINO]: *area,* 10.5 miles south-southwest of Willits on Greenough Ridge (lat. 39°16'40" N, long. 123°26'45" W; near NW cor. sec. 5, T 16 N, R 14 E). Named on Willits (1961) 15' quadrangle.

Happy Camp [HUMBOLDT]: *locality,* 8 miles east of the settlement of Willow Creek (lat. 40°55'20" N, long. 123°29'10" W). Named on Ironside Mountain (1951) 15' quadrangle.

Happy Camp Creek [TRINITY]: *stream,* flows nearly 5 miles to South Fork Trinity River 8 miles south-southwest of Dubakella Mountain (lat. 40°16'35" N, long. 123°11'40" W; at E line sec. 15, T 28 N, R 12 W). Named on Black Rock Mountain (1954) and Dubakella Mountain (1954) 15' quadrangles.

Happy Camp Creek: see **Cow Creek** [HUMBOLDT] (2).

Happy Camp Mountain [TRINITY]: *peak,* 6.25 miles north of Burnt Ranch (lat. 40°53'55" N, long. 123°28'45" W). Named on Ironside Mountain (1951) 15' quadrangle.

Happy Camp Spring [TRINITY]: *spring,* 11.5 miles west-northwest of Black Rock Mountain (lat. 40°14'50" N, long. 123°12'45" W; near E line sec. 28, T 28 N, R 12 W). Named on Black Rock Mountain (1954) 15' quadrangle.

Happy Hollow [MENDOCINO]: *relief feature,* 7.25 miles east of Covelo (lat. 39°47' N, long. 123°06'45" W; near NW cor. sec. 8, T 22 N, R 11 W). Named on Covelo (1952) 15' quadrangle.

Happy Jack Spring [HUMBOLDT]: *spring,* 7.5 miles east-southeast of Showers Mountain (lat. 40°32'15" N, long. 123°34'05" W; at E line sec. 23, T 2 N, R 5 E). Named on Blake Mountain (1979) 7.5' quadrangle.

Happy Valley [HUMBOLDT]: *area,* 7 miles south-southeast of Scotia (lat. 40°27'50" N, long. 124°03'50" W). Named on Scotia (1970) 7.5' quadrangle.

Harbin Creek [LAKE]: *stream,* flows nearly 5 miles to Putah Creek 2.25 miles north of Middletown (lat. 38°47'10" N, long. 122°36'20" W); the stream goes past Harbin Springs. Named on Middletown (1958) and Whispering Pines (1958) 7.5' quadrangles.

Harbin Mountain [LAKE]: *peak,* 4 miles east-southeast of Whispering Pines (lat. 38°47'30" N, long. 122°38'40" W; sec. 21, T 11 N, R 7 W); the peak is 0.5 mile east-northeast of Harbin Springs. Altitude 2585 feet. Named on Whispering Pines (1958) 7.5' quadrangle. A peak on a ridge that extends southeast from Harbin Mountain to Puta Creek is called Mount Esther (Goodyear, 1890a, p. 229).

Harbin Springs [LAKE]: *locality,* 3.5 miles east-southeast of Whispering Pines (lat. 38°47'15" N, long. 122°39'15" W; sec. 20, T 11 N, R 7 W). Named on Whispering Pines (1958) 7.5' quadrangle, which shows Harbin Springs Annex located less than 0.5 mile farther northwest. The name commemorates James M. Harbin, who came to California in 1846 and later settled at the springs (Hanna, p. 133). Harbin and Ritchie discovered springs at the site in 1852; Harbin bought out Ritchie and in 1860 he built a house with five rooms for bathing over the springs (Menefee, p. 242). By 1909 the place had accommodations for about 200 people (Waring, p. 94). Goodyear (1890a, p. 230) called the place Harbin's Springs.

Hardin [MENDOCINO]: *locality,* 4.25 miles southeast of Monument Peak (lat. 38°52'20" N, long. 123°53'30" W). Named on Kelseyville (1944) 15' quadrangle.

Hardin Mountain [DEL NORTE]: *ridge,* south-trending, less than 1 mile long, 6.25 miles north-northwest of Buck Mountain (lat. 41°42' N, long. 123°54'55" W; sec. 11, 14, T 15 N, R 2 E). Named on Cant Hook Mountain (1982) 7.5' quadrangle.

Hardscrabble: see **Freshwater** [HUMBOLDT].

Hardscrabble Creek [DEL NORTE]: *stream,* flows 6.25 miles to Smith River 11 miles northeast of Crescent City (lat. 41°50'20" N, long. 124°01'30" W). Named on High Divide (1966) and Hiouchi (1966) 7.5' quadrangles.

Hardscrabble Creek [TRINITY]: *stream,* flows 2 miles to Coffee Creek nearly 7 miles west of Billys Peak (1) (lat. 41°07'10" N, long. 122°53'45" W; sec. 28, T 38 N, R 9 W). Named on Coffee Creek (1955) 15' quadrangle.

Hardy [MENDOCINO]: *locality,* 5.25 miles north of Westport (lat. 39°42'45" N, long. 123°48'10" W; near SE cor.sec. 36, T 22 N, R 18 W); the place is near the mouth of Hardy Creek. Named on Westport (1966) 7.5' quadrangle. Postal authorities established Hardy post office in 1902 and discontinued it in 1915—the original application for a post office was made under the name "Hardyville" (Salley, p. 93). The name "Hardy" commemorates R.A. Hardy, who received a franchise in 1892 for a wharf and chute located 6 miles north of Westport (Carpenter, p. 130). Chase (p. 280) referred to the place as the little town of Hardy Creek. California Mining Bureau's (1917c) map shows a place called Dellavan situated near the coast between Hardy.and Westport.

Hardy Creek [MENDOCINO]: *stream,* formed by the confluence of Middle Fork and North Fork, flows 2 miles to the sea 5.25 miles north-northwest of Westport (lat. 39°42'40" N, long. 123°48'25" W; at N line sec. 1, T 21 N, R 18 W). Named on Westport (1966) 7.5' quadrangle. Middle Fork and North Fork each are 2 miles long. South Fork, which enters less than 0.25 mile downstream from the confluence of Middle Fork and North Fork, is nearly 2 miles long. All three forks are named on Westport (1966) 7.5' quadrangle. South Fork is called Bear Creek on Cape Vizcaino (1950) 15' quadrangle.

Hardy Creek: see **Hardy** [MENDOCINO].

Hardy Ridge [MENDOCINO]: *ridge,* west-southwest-trending, nearly 3 miles long, 5.25 miles north of Westport (lat. 39°42'55" N, long. 123°46'45" W); the ridge is south of Hardy Creek. Named on Westport (1966) 7.5' quadrangle.

Hardy Rock [MENDOCINO]: *rock,* 5 miles north-northwest of Westport near the coast (lat. 39°42'25" N, long. 123°48'25" W); the feature is 0.25 mile south of the mouth of Hardy Creek. Named on Westport (1966) 7.5' quadrangle.

Hardyville: see **Hardy** [MENDOCINO].

Hare Creek [MENDOCINO]: *stream,* flows 8 miles to the sea 2 miles south of Fort Bragg (lat. 39°25' N, long. 123°48'40" W; near S line sec. sec. 13, T 18 N, R 18 W). Named on Comptche (1960) 15' quadrangle, and on Fort Bragg (1960) 7.5' quadrangle. South Fork enters from the south 5.5 miles upstream from the mouth of the main creek; it is 1.25 miles long and is named on Comptche (1960) 15' quadrangle.

Harley Gulch [LAKE]: *canyon,* drained by a stream that flows nearly 6 miles to Cache Creek 1 mile north-northwest of Wilson Valley (2) (lat. 38°59'15" N, long. 122°28'40" W). Named on Wilbur Springs (1961) 15' quadrangle, and on Wilson Valley (1958) 7.5' quadrangle.

Harmonica Creek [HUMBOLDT]: *stream,* flows 4.25 miles to Bear River nearly 7 miles south-southeast of Scotia (lat. 40°23'05" N, long. 124°04'30" W). Named on Bull Creek (1969) and Scotia (1970) 7.5' quadrangles

Harper Creek [HUMBOLDT]: *stream,* flows nearly 2 miles to Bull Creek (2) 4 miles west-northwest of Weott (lat. 40°21' N, long. 123°59'10" W; near W line sec. 29, T 1 S, R 2 E). Named on Weott (1969) 7.5' quadrangle..

Harrington Creek [DEL NORTE]: *stream,* flows 7 miles to South Fork Smith River 5 miles east-northeast of Buck Mountain (lat. 41°39'45" N, long. 123°46'45" W); the stream heads at Harrington Lake. Named on Prescott Mountain (1981) and Ship Mountain (1982) 7.5' quadrangles. Called Herrington Creek on Preston Peak (1922) 30' quadrangle, which shows Herrington ranch near the head of the stream.

Harrington Flat [LAKE]: *area,* 4 miles north-northwest of Whispering Pines (lat. 38°52'05" N, long. 122°44'30" W; at NE cor. sec. 28, T 12 N, R 8 W). Named on Whispering Pines (1958) 7.5' quadrangle.

Harrington Lake [DEL NORTE]: *lake,* 19 miles northeast of Klamath Glen (lat. 41°40'25" N, long. 123°41'20" W); the lake is 1000 feet west of Harrington Mountain. Named on Prescott Mountain (1981) 7.5' quadrangle. Preston Peak (1922) 30' quadrangle shows Herrington ranch at the site.

Harrington Mountain [DEL NORTE]: *peak,* 6 miles west-southwest of Bear Peak, which is in Siskiyou County (lat. 41°40'25" N, long. 123°41'05" W). Altitude 5891 feet. Named on Prescott Mountain (1981) 7.5' quadrangle.

Harris [HUMBOLDT]: *locality,* 7 miles west-southwest of Alderpoint (lat. 40°05' N, long. 123°39'30" W; sec. 30, T 4 S, R 5 E). Named on Harris (1969) 7.5' quadrangle, which shows Harris P.O. located 2.5 miles farther south-southeast (lat. 40°02'55" N, long. 123°38'30" W; near S line sec. 5, T 5 S, R 5 E). Postal authorities established Dark Canyon post office in 1878 and discontinued it in 1882, when they moved it 5 miles north and changed the name to Harris for William C. Harris, first postmaster; they moved Harris post office 3.5 miles south in 1946 and discontinued it in 1974 (Salley, p. 55, 93). The place also was called Dogtown (Carranco and Beard, p. 197) and Spruce Grove (Salley, p. 93).

Harris Creek [HUMBOLDT]: *stream,* flows nearly 2 miles to Mattole River 9.5 miles south-southwest of Garberville at Whitethorn (lat. 40°01'20" N, long. 123°56'30" W). Named on Briceland (1969) 7.5' quadrangle.

Harris Creek [LAKE]: *stream,* flows nearly 3 miles to Copsey Creek 5.5 miles northeast of Whispering Pines (lat. 38°51'30" N, long. 122°37'35" W; sec. 27, T 12 N, R 7 W). Named on Middletown (1958) and Whispering Pines (1958) 7.5' quadrangles.

Harris Ridge [HUMBOLDT]: *ridge,* northeast-trending, 1 mile long, 4 miles west of Honeydew (lat. 40°14'55" N, long. 124°11'55" W). Named on Buckeye Mountain (1970) and Shubrick Peak (1969) 7.5' quadrangles.

Harrow Creek [HUMBOLDT]: *stream,* flows 2 miles to Mattole River 7 miles southeast of Honeydew (lat. 40°10'35" N, long. 124°01'15" W; sec. 25, T 3 S, R 1 E). Named on Honeydew (1970) 7.5' quadrangle.

Harrow Prairie [HUMBOLDT]: *area,* 6.5 miles southeast of Scotia (lat. 40°24'15" N, long. 124°01'30" W; around SW cor. sec. 1, T 1 S, R 1 E). Named on Scotia (1970) 7.5' quadrangle.

Harry Weir Creek [HUMBOLDT]: *stream,* flows 2.5 miles to Redwood Creek (1) 8 miles west-northwest of Coyote Peak (lat. 41°11'50" N, long. 123°59'35" W). Named on Bald Hills (1982) 7.5' quadrangle. Turner (p. 104) used the form "Wier" for the name, and noted that Harry Wier was a logger and woods foreman for Arcata Redwood Company.

Hartsook: see **Garberville** [HUMBOLDT].

Hartsook Creek [HUMBOLDT]: *stream,* flows 1.25 miles to South Fork Eel River 6 miles south of Garberville (lat. 40°00'45" N, long. 123°47'10" W; at N line sec. 24, T 5 S, R 3 E). Named on Garberville (1970) 7.5' quadrangle.

Harts Valley [HUMBOLDT]: *area,* 5.25 miles northeast of Yager Junction (lat. 40°36'20" N, long. 123°45'20" W). Named on Yager Junction (1979) 7.5' quadrangle.

Hastings Creek [TRINITY]: *stream,* flows 2 miles to Mad River 4 miles east of Dinsmore [HUMBOLDT] (lat. 40°29'10" N, long. 123°31'55" W; at SE cor. sec. 6, T 1 N, R 6 E). Named on Blake Mountain (1979) and Dinsmore (1977) 7.5' quadrangles.

Hatchery Creek [HUMBOLDT]: *stream,* flows 2 miles to North Fork Mad River 0.5 mile northeast of Korbel (lat. 40°52'30" N, long. 123°57'05" W; sec. 28, T 6 N, R 2 E). Named on Korbel (1979) 7.5' quadrangle.

Hatchet Creek [TRINITY]: *stream,* flows 3.5 miles to Trinity River 1 mile north-northwest of Trinity Center (lat. 41°01'10" N, long. 122°40'55" W; sec. 33, T 37 N, R 7 W). Named on Bonanza King (1955) 15' quadrangle.

Hatchet Flat [MENDOCINO]: *area,* 5 miles north-northeast of the town of Potter Valley (lat. 39°23'35" N, long. 123°05' W; at N line sec. 28, T 18 N, R 11 W). Named on Potter Valley (1960) 15' quadrangle.

Hatfield Prairie [HUMBOLDT]: *area,* 5 miles south-southeast of Korbel (lat. 40°48'35" N, long. 123°54'25" W; at NW cor. sec. 24, T 5 N, R 2 E). Named on Korbel (1979) 7.5' quadrangle.

Hathaway Creek [MENDOCINO]: *stream,* flows 4.5 miles to Garcia River 2.5 miles north-northwest of the village of Point Arena (lat. 38°56'35" N, long. 123°43'05" W; sec. 35, T 13 N, R 17 W). Named on Point Arena (1960) 7.5' quadrangle.

Hatzis Flat [DEL NORTE]: *area,* 2.5 miles east-southeast of the mouth of Klamath River (lat. 41°32'10" N, long. 124°02' W; near NE cor. sec. 10, T 13 N, R 1 E). Named on Requa (1966) 7.5' quadrangle.

Haun: see **Captain Haun Creek** [HUMBOLDT].

Haun Creek [MENDOCINO]: *stream,* flows 1 mile to South Fork Eel River 0.5 mile south-southeast of Branscomb (lat. 39°38'50" N, long. 123°37'20" W; near W line sec. 26, T 21 N, R 16 W). Named on Cahto Peak (1967) and Lincoln Ridge (1966) 7.5' quadrangles.

Havens Anchorage [MENDOCINO]: *anchorage,* 3.5 miles northwest of Gualala (lat. 38°48' N, long. 123°35' W). Named on Gualala (1960) 7.5' quadrangle. Officials of United States Coast Survey named the place before 1855 (Gudde, 1949, p. 144).

Havens Neck [MENDOCINO]: *peninsula,* 5 miles northwest of Gualala along the coast (lat. 38°48'30" N, long. 123°36' W; at N line sec. 13, T 11 N, R 16 W). Named on Gualala (1960) 7.5' quadrangle.

Hawk Butte [MENDOCINO]: *peak,* 3 miles north-northeast of Ornbaun Valley (lat. 38°57' N, long. 123°17'10" W; near SW cor. sec. 27, T 13 N, R 13 W). Altitude 2493 feet. Named on Ornbaun Valley (1960) 15' quadrangle.

Hawk Creek [TRINITY]: *stream,* flows 1 mile to Corral Creek (1) 10 miles northeast of Hyampom (lat. 40°42'20" N, long. 123°17'50" W; sec. 20, T

4 N, R 8 E). Named on Hyampom (1951) 15' quadrangle.

Hawkins Bar [TRINITY]: *locality,* 3.5 miles east-southeast of Salyer along Trinity River (lat. 40°52'15" N, long. 123°31'15" W). Named on Hennessy Peak (1979) 7.5' quadrangle. Postal authorities established Hawkinsbar post office in 1899 and discontinued it in 1902; the name commemorates the prospector who discovered gold at the place in 1850 (Salley, p. 94).

Hawkins Creek [TRINITY]: *stream,* flows nearly 4 miles to Trinity River 3.25 miles east of Salyer (lat. 40°52'55" N, long. 123°31'25" W). Named on Salyer (1979) 7.5' quadrangle.

Hawk Slough [HUMBOLDT]: *water feature,* enters North Bay 6.25 miles north of Ferndale (lat. 40°39'50" N, long. 124°17'05" W). Named on Cannibal Island (1959) and Fields Landing (1959) 7.5' quadrangles.

Hayden Roughs [TRINITY]: *area,* 14 miles west-southwest of Black Rock Mountain (lat. 40°07' N, long. 123°15' W). Named on Black Rock Mountain (1954) 15' quadrangle, and on Long Ridge (1967) 7.5' quadrangle. The name commemorates Tom Hayden, who was a cattleman in the neighborhood (Jones, p. 364).

Haydens Gulch [DEL NORTE]: *canyon,* drained by a stream that flows 1 mile to Hurdygurdy Creek 7 miles north-northwest of Buck Mountain (lat. 41°42'50" N, long. 123°53'55" W; sec. 12, T 15 N, R 2 E). Named on Cant Hook Mountain (1982) 7.5' quadrangle.

Haydon Rock [MENDOCINO]: *relief feature,* 10 miles north-northwest of Hull Mountain (lat. 39°39'50" N, long. 122°59'20" W; sec. 20, T 21 N, R 10 W). Named on Plaskett Ridge (1967) 7.5' quadrangle.

Hayfield Creek [HUMBOLDT]: *stream,* flows nearly 3 miles to Larabee Creek 4 miles north-northwest of Blocksburg (lat. 40°19'55" N, long. 123°39'40" W; sec. 31, T 1 S, R 5 E). Named on Black Lassic (1979) and Blocksburg (1969) 7.5' quadrangles.

Hayfield Creek [MENDOCINO]: *stream,* flows 1 mile to North Fork Gualala River 8 miles southwest of Ornbaun Valley (lat. 38°50'40" N, long. 123°25'05" W; sec. 34, T 12 N, R 14 W). Named on Ornbaun Valley (1960) 15' quadrangle.

Hayfork [TRINITY]: *town,* 18 miles southwest of Weaverville (lat. 40°33'15" N, long. 123°11' W; in and near sec. 11, T 31 N, R 12 W); the town is along Hayfork Creek. Named on Hayfork (1951) 15' quadrangle. Postal authorities established Hay Fork post office in 1861, discontinued it in 1863, reestablished it in 1878, and changed the name to Hayfork in 1895—the place also was called Kingsberry and Hay Town (Salley, p. 95).

Hay Fork Baldy: see **Hayfork Bally** [TRINITY].

Hayfork Bally [TRINITY]: *peak,* 7.5 miles north-northwest of Hayfork (lat. 40°39'30" N, long. 123°13' W). Altitude 6273 feet. Named on Hayfork (1951) 15' quadrangle. Called Hay Fork Baldy on United States Geological Survey's (1915) map. United States Board on Geographic Names (1967, p. 5) approved the name "Love Letter Spring" for a feature located on the east side of Hayfork Bally (lat. 40'39'10" N, long. 123°11'55" W).

Hayfork Creek [TRINITY]: *stream,* flows 50 miles to South Fork Trinity River at Hyampom (lat. 40°36'50" N, long. 123°27' W; sec. 25, T 3 N, R 6 E). Named on Dubakella Mountain (1954), Hayfork (1951), and Hyampom (1951) 15' quadrangles. The stream is called both Hay Fork and Hay Fork River on Miller's (1890) map. East Fork enters from the northeast 8.5 miles north-northeast of Dubakella Mountain; it is 6.5 miles long and is named on Dubakella Mountain (1954), Hayfork (1951), and Weaverville (1950) 15' quadrangles. North Fork of East Fork enters East Fork from the north 16 miles south of Weaverville; it is 3.5 miles long and is named on Weaverville (1950) 15' quadrangle. Present North Fork of East Fork Hayfork Creek is called N. Fk. Hay Fork on Weaverville (1913) 30' quadrangle.

Hayfork Divide [TRINITY]: *ridge,* generally east-southeast-trending, 15 miles long, center 10 miles east-northeast of Hayfork (lat. 40°35'45" N, long. 123°00'15" W); the ridge separates Hayfork Creek drainage from Trinity River drainage. Named on Hayfork (1951) and Weaverville (1950) 15' quadrangles. Called Hay Fork Mountain on Weaverville (1913) 30' quadrangle, and called Hayfork Mountains on Miller's (1890) map.

Hay Fork Mountain: see **Hayfork Divide** [TRINITY].

Hay Fork River: see **Hayfork Creek** [TRINITY].

Hayfork Summit [TRINITY]: *pass,* 10 miles east-northeast of Hayfork (lat. 40°35'45" N, long. 123°00'15" W; near SW cor. sec. 28, T 32 N, R 10 W). Named on Hayfork (1951) 15' quadrangle.

Hayfork Valley [TRINITY]: *valley,* along Hayfork Creek at Hayfork (lat. 40°33'15" N, long. 123°11' W). Named on Hayfork (1951) 15' quadrangle. Brown (p. 920) used the form "Hay Fork Valley" for the name.

Hay Gulch [TRINITY]: *canyon,* drained by a stream that flows 4.5 miles to Trinity River 18 miles northeast of Weaverville (lat. 40°55'20" N, long. 122°41'10" W; sec. 5, T 35 N, R 7 W). Named on Schell Mountain (1950) 15' quadrangle.

Haylock Gulch [TRINITY]: *canyon,* drained by a stream that flows 3 miles to Clair Engle Lake 8 miles northeast of Weaverville (lat. 40°48'50" N, long. 122°49'15" W; sec. 7, T 34 N, R 8 W). Named on Trinity Dam (1950) 15' quadrangle.

Hayne Flat: see **Haines Flat** [DEL NORTE].

Haynes Creek [MENDOCINO]: *stream,* flows 4.5 miles to Thatchers Creek 8 miles east-northeast of Eden Valley (lat. 39°40'15" N, long. 123°03' W). Named on Thatcher Ridge (1967) 7.5' quadrangle. Called Redrock Creek on Eden Valley (1929) 15' quadrangle, and on Eden Valley (1952) 15' quadrangle, present Red Rock Creek is shown as part of Haynes Creek. United States Board on Geographic Names (1969a, p. 3) rejected the name "Bed Rock Creek" for present Haynes Creek

Haynes Creek: see **Skunk Lake Creek** [MENDOCINO].

Haynes Delight [TRINITY]: *area,* 10 miles south-southwest of Black Rock Mountain (lat. 40°04'05" N, long. 123°04'15" W; sec. 35, T 26 N, R 11 W). Named on Black Rock Mountain (1954) 15' quadrangle.

Haynes Flat [MENDOCINO]: *area,* 9 miles east-northeast of Eden Valley (lat. 39°41'40" N, long. 123°02'15" W); the place is along Haynes Creek. Named on Thatcher Ridge (1967) 7.5' quadrangle.

Haynes Hill [MENDOCINO]: *peak,* 9 miles east-northeast of Eden Valley (lat. 39°40'55" N, long. 123°01'55" W); the peak is east of Haynes Creek. Altitude 3999 feet. Named on Thatcher Ridge (1967) 7.5' quadrangle.

Haypress Meadow [TRINITY]: *area,* 10.5 miles east-northeast of Hyampom along Corral Creek (1) (lat. 40°41'35" N, long. 123°16'45" W; on E line sec. 28, T 4 N, R 8 E). Named on Hyampom (1951) 15' quadrangle.

Hay Shed Basin [MENDOCINO]: *relief feature,* 10 miles east-southeast of Covelo (lat. 39°45'15" N, long. 123°04' W; sec. 22, T 22 N, R 11 W). Named on Covelo (1952) 15' quadrangle.

Hayshed Basin [MENDOCINO]: *relief feature,* 10 miles northeast of Eden Valley (lat. 39°44'15" N, long. 123°03'45" W). Named on Newhouse Ridge (1967) and Thatcher Ridge (1967) 7.5' quadrangles.

Hayshed Creek [MENDOCINO]: *stream,* flows 6.25 miles to Middle Fork Eel River 6 miles northeast of Eden Valley (lat. 39°41'35" N, long. 123°06'40" W); the stream heads at Hayshed Basin. Named on Thatcher Ridge (1967) 7.5' quadrangle.

Hayshed Creek [TRINITY]: *stream,* flows about 3 miles to Corral Creek (1) 7.5 miles northeast of Hyampom (lat. 40°42'10" N, long. 123°21'35" W; near SW cor. sec. 23, T 4 N, R 7 E). Named on Hyampom (1951) 15' quadrangle.

Hayshed Creek: see **East Hayshed Creek** [TRINITY]; **West Hayshed Creek** [TRINITY].

Hayshed Gulch [MENDOCINO]: *canyon,* drained by a stream that flows 1.5 miles to Noyo River 14 miles northwest of Comptche (lat. 39°25'40" N, long. 123°44'35" W; at N line sec. 15, T 18 N, R 17 W). Named on Comptche (1960) 15' quadrangle.

Hayshed Siding [MENDOCINO]: *locality,* 14 miles northwest of Comptche along California Western Railroad (lat. 39°25'40" N, long. 123°44'35" W; at N line sec. 15, T 18 N, R 17 W); the place is at the mouth of Hayshed Gulch. Named on Comptche (1960) 15' quadrangle.

Haystack [DEL NORTE]: *peak,* 2.5 miles north-northeast of Broken Rib Mountain (lat. 41°55'20" N, long. 123°40'05" W). Altitude 5474 feet. Named on Broken Rib Mountain (1982) 7.5' quadrangle.

Haystack: see **Laurel Butte** [DEL NORTE].

Hay Town: see **Hayfork** [TRINITY].

Hayville Sulphur Spring: see **Upper Lake** [LAKE].

Hayward Flat [TRINITY]: *area,* 13 miles northeast of Weaverville along East Fork Stuart Fork (lat. 40°52' N, long. 122°45'50" W; on N line sec. 27, T 35 N, R 8 W). Named on Trinity Lake (1950) 15' quadrangle. Water of Clair Engle Lake now covers the place.

Hayward Gulch [TRINITY]: *canyon,* drained by a stream that flows 0.5 mile to Clair Engle Lake 14 miles northeast of Weaverville (lat. 40°52'40" N, long. 122°46'20" W; sec. 21, T 35 N, R 8 W). Named on Trinity Dam (1950) 15' quadrangle.

Hayward Spring [LAKE]: *spring,* 10.5 miles east of Hull Mountain (lat. 39°30'55" N, long. 122°44'25" W). Named on Felkner Hill (1968) 7.5' quadrangle.

Hayworth Creek [MENDOCINO]: *stream,* flows 5.5 miles to North Fork Noyo River 13 miles north-northeast of Comptche (lat. 39°27'15" N, long. 123°32' W; sec. 33, T 19 N, R 15 W). Named on Comptche (1960) and Willits (1961) 15' quadrangles. North Fork enters from the north 2.5 miles upstream from the mouth of the main creek; it is 3 miles long and is named on Comptche (1960) and Willits (1961) 15' quadrangles, and on Longvale (1966) 7.5' quadrangle.

Hazel Gulch [MENDOCINO]: *canyon,* drained by a stream that flows 4 miles to Big Salmon Creek 5.5 miles north-northeast of Elk (lat. 39°12'10" N, long. 123°40' W; sec. 32, T 16 N, R 16 W). Named on Elk (1960) 7.5' quadrangle.

Hazel Gulch [TRINITY]: *canyon,* drained by a stream that flows nearly 2 miles to Browns Creek 11.5 miles south of Weaverville (lat. 40°34'15" N, long. 122°55'30" W; sec. 6, T 31 N, R 9 W). Named on Weaverville (1950) 15' quadrangle.

Hazel Spring [LAKE]: *spring,* 5.25 miles northeast of the town of Upper Lake (lat. 39°12'40" N, long. 122°49'50" W; sec. 26, T 16 N, R 9 W). Named on Bartlett Mountain (1958) 7.5' quadrangle. The feature also was known as Dennison Springs (Waring, p. 202).

Hazel View Summit [DEL NORTE]: *pass,* 6.5 miles north-northwest of Broken Rib Mountain (lat. 41°58'20" N, long. 123°44'45" W; sec. 9, T 18

N, R 4 E). Named on Broken Rib Mountain (1982) 7.5' quadrangle.

Hazen: see **Al Hazen Ridge** [HUMBOLDT].

Head Camp [HUMBOLDT]: *locality,* nearly 6 miles northwest of Orleans (lat. 41°21'20" N, long. 123°37'20" W). Named on Orleans (1978) 7.5' quadrangle.

Head Nigger: see **Negro Head** [MENDOCINO].

Hearn Gulch [MENDOCINO]: *canyon,* drained by a stream that flows less than 1 mile to the sea 4.5 miles south-southeast of the village of Point Arena at Saunders Landing (lat. 38°51'05" N, long. 123°38'55" W; sec. 4, T 11 N, R 16 W). Named on Saunders Reef (1960) 7.5' quadrangle. United States Board on Geographic Names (1962c, p. 19) rejected the name "Rocky Gulch" for the feature.

Hearst [MENDOCINO]: *locality,* 13 miles north-northwest of the town of Potter Valley along Eel River (lat. 39°29'30" N, long. 123°17'40" W; sec. 20, T 19 N, R 12 W). Named on Potter Valley (1960) 15' quadrangle. Postal authorities established Hearst post office in 1891, moved it 2.5 miles north in 1898, and discontinued it in 1953; the name was for George Hearst, senator from California from 1887 until 1891 (Salley, p. 95). According to Waring (p. 174-175), Hearst post office was at a small mountain resort called Travelers Home, and 1 mile west of Travelers Home was Kinsner Soda Spring, which produced water sold in Willits for table use. Postal authorities established Sawyers post office 2.5 miles west of Hearst in 1898 and discontinued in 1903; the name was for Marvin L. Sawyer, first postmaster (Salley, p. 199).

Heck Creek [HUMBOLDT]: *stream,* flows nearly 2 miles to Trinity River 2 miles southeast of Hoopa (lat. 41°01'35" N, long. 123°38'50" W; near S line sec. 31, T 8 N, R 5 E). Named on Hoopa (1979) 7.5' quadrangle.

Heckman Island [HUMBOLDT]: *island,* 1500 feet long, 4.5 miles north-northwest of Ferndale near the mouth of Eel River (lat. 40°38' N, long. 124°18'15" W). Named on Cannibal Island (1959) 7.5' quadrangle.

Height Gulch: see **Hight Gulch** [HUMBOLDT].

Helena [TRINITY]: *village,* 10 miles west-northwest of Weaverville along North Fork Trinity River just north of the mouth of that fork (lat. 40°46'25" N, long. 123°07'40" W). Named on Helena (1951) 15' quadrangle. The community began in 1851 as a mining camp known at various times as North Fork, Bagdad, and The Cove (Hanna, p. 136). When postal authorities established Helena post office in 1891, they rejected the name "North Fork" for it, and named it instead for the postmaster's wife (Salley, p. 95). Present Helena post office is situated at the community of North Fork about 1.5 miles up Trinity River from the first site of the post office (Gudde, 1975, p. 245-246).

Hell Gate [HUMBOLDT]: *rock,* 2.5 miles south-southeast of Cape Mendocino, and about 450 feet offshore (lat. 40°24'15" N, long. 124°23'20" W). Named on Cape Mendocino (1969) 7.5' quadrangle.

Hell Gate [TRINITY]: *narrows,* 0.5 mile southeast of the center of Forest Glen along South Fork Trinity River (lat. 40°22'10" N, long. 123°19' W; near N line sec. 19, T 1 S, R 8 E). Named on Forest Glen (1979) 7.5' quadrangle.

Hellhole Canyon [MENDOCINO]: *canyon,* drained by a stream that flows 1.5 miles to Middle Fork Eel River 13 miles east-northeast of Covelo (lat. 39°52'45" N, long. 123°02'10" W; sec. 1, T 23 N, R 11 W). Named on Leech Lake Mountain (1966) 7.5' quadrangle. Covelo (1926) 15' quadrangle has the form "Hell Hole Canyon" for the name.

Hells Canyon [LAKE]: *canyon,* drained by a stream that flows 3 miles to Long Canyon 10 miles northeast of Clearlake Oaks (lat. 39°07'50" N, long. 122°33'30" W; at E line sec. 19, T 15 N, R 6 W). Named on Clearlake Oaks (1960) 15' quadrangle.

Hell's Delight: see **Hells Peak** [LAKE].

Hells Delight Canyon [MENDOCINO]: *canyon,* 1.25 miles long, 4.5 miles south-southwest of the town of Potter Valley on the uppermost reaches of White Creek (lat. 39°15'45" N, long. 123°09' W). Named on Redwood Valley (1960) 7.5' quadrangle.

Hells Half Acre [LAKE]: *area,* 6.5 miles north-northeast of Middletown (lat. 38°47'35" N, long. 122°30' W; sec. 22, 23, T 11 N, R 6 W). Named on Jericho Valley (1958) and Middletown (1958) 7.5' quadrangles.

Hells Half Acre [MENDOCINO]: *area,* 6.25 miles north of Hull Mountain (lat. 39°36'45" N, long. 122°56'50" W; on S line sec. 3, T 20 N, R 10 W). Named on Hull Mountain (1967) 7.5' quadrangle.

Hells Half Acre Creek [TRINITY]: *stream,* flows 2.5 miles to South Fork Trinity River 9 miles south of Salyer (lat. 40°46'05" N, long. 123°33'15" W; sec. 31, T 5 N, R 6 E). Named on Hennessy Peak (1979) 7.5' quadrangle. Called Big Creek on China Flat (1922) 15' quadrangle.

Hells Peak [LAKE]: *peak,* 6 miles northwest of the town of Upper Lake (lat. 39°12'50" N, long. 122°59'50" W; sec. 29, T 16 N, R 10 W). Altitude 2325 feet. Named on Upper Lake (1958) 7.5' quadrangle. This seems to be the feature that Goodyear (1890a, p. 248-249) climbed when he described going to the head of Bachelor's Valley and ascending Bachelor's Peak, called also Hell's Delight

Hells Rock [LAKE]: *relief feature,* 6.5 miles west of the town of Upper Lake (lat. 39°13' N, long. 123°00'05" W). Named on Ukiah (1920) 15' quadrangle.

Hell to Find Lake: see **Wildwood** [TRINITY].

Helmke Spring [HUMBOLDT]: *spring,* 4.5 miles west of Alderpoint (lat. 40°10'55" N, long. 123°41'35" W). Named on Fort Seward (1969) 7.5' quadrangle.

Helper: see **Dyerville** [HUMBOLDT].

Hely Creek [HUMBOLDT]: *stream,* flows 4 miles to Van Duzen River 7 miles north-northwest of Redcrest (lat. 40°29'55" N, long. 123°58'35" W; sec. 5, T 1 N, R 2 E). Named on Owl Creek (1979) 7.5' quadrangle.

Hembrey Creek [TRINITY]: *stream,* flows 3 miles to South Dobbyn Creek 5 miles east of Alderpoint [HUMBOLDT] (lat. 40°10'55" N, long. 123°30'55" W; at SE cor. sec. 20, T 3 S, R 6 E). Named on Alderpoint (1969) and Zenia (1967) 7.5' quadrangles. United States Board on Geographic Names (1969a, p. 3) rejected the name "Burgess Creek" for the feature.

Hembrey Creek: see **Burgess Creek** [TRINITY].

Hemlock [MENDOCINO]: *locality,* 8 miles northeast of Ukiah (lat. 39°13' N, long. 123°04'55" W). Named on Ukiah (1920) 15' quadrangle. Cow Mountain (1958) 7.5' quadrangle shows Hemlock ranch near the site. Postal authorities established Hemlock post office in 1890 and discontinued it in 1916 (Frickstad, p. 95).

Henderson Gulch [HUMBOLDT]: *canyon,* drained by a stream that flows 1.5 miles to Ryan Creek 3.5 miles south-southeast of downtown Eureka (lat. 40°45'20" N, long. 124°07'55" W; sec. 1, T 4 N, R 1 W). Named on Eureka (1958) and Fields Landing (1959) 7.5' quadrangles. The name commemorates James W. Henderson, who was a promoter of the first railroad in Humboldt County (Turner, p. 106).

Henderson Point [LAKE]: *promontory,* 8 miles east-southeast of Lakeport along Clear Lake (lat. 39°00'40" N, long. 122°46'35" W; on W line sec. 5, T 13 N, R 8 W). Named on Lucerne (1958) 7.5' quadrangle.

Hendricks Creek [LAKE]: *stream,* flows 5.25 miles to Scotts Creek 4.5 miles northwest of Lakeport (lat. 39°06'05" N, long. 122°57'40" W; sec. 34, T 15 N, R 10 W). Named on Lakeport (1958) and Purdys Gardens (1958) 7.5' quadrangles.

Henly Creek [MENDOCINO]: *stream,* flows 2.25 miles to Bell Springs Creek 12 miles east-northeast of Leggett (lat. 39°56'25" N, long. 123°30'45" W; near E line sec. 10, T 24 N, R 15 W). Named on Bell Springs (1969) 7.5' quadrangle.

Hennessy Creek [TRINITY]: *stream,* flows 3.25 miles to Trinity River 1.5 miles north of Burnt Ranch (lat. 40°49'45" N, long. 123°28'45" W; at N line sec. 11, T 5 N, R 6 E); the stream heads near the south end of Hennessy Ridge. Named on Ironside Mountain (1951) 15' quadrangle, and on Hennessy Peak (1979) 7.5' quadrangle. The stream was called Brooks Creek before the P.O.M. Hennessey family acquired large water rights from it (Jones, p. 249).

Hennessy Peak [TRINITY]: *peak,* 6.5 miles south-southeast of Salyer (lat. 40°48'25" N, long. 123°31'50" W; sec. 17, T 5 N, R 6 E). Altitude 3714 feet. Named on Hennessy Peak (1979) 7.5' quadrangle.

Hennessy Ridge [TRINITY]: *ridge,* generally south-southeast-trending, 4 miles long, 3 miles southeast of Salyer (lat. 40°51'30" N, long. 123°32'30" W). Named on Hennessy Peak (1979) and Salyer (1979) 7.5' quadrangles.

Henry Ridge [HUMBOLDT-TRINITY]: *ridge,* southwest- to south-trending, 2.5 miles long, 7.5 miles east of Showers Mountain on Humboldt-Trinity County line (lat. 40°34'05" N, long. 123°33'15" W). Named on Blake Mountain (1979) 7.5' quadrangle.

Henry Siding [MENDOCINO]: *locality,* 8 miles south-southeast of Ukiah along Northwestern Pacific Railroad (lat. 39°02'50" N, long. 123°08'55" W). Named on Ukiah (1920) 15' quadrangle. Ukiah (1944) 15' quadrangle shows Henry ranch near the site.

Henrys Landing: see **Southport Landing** [HUMBOLDT].

Hensley Creek [MENDOCINO]: *stream,* flows nearly 7 miles to Russian River 2.5 miles north of Ukiah (lat. 39°11'05" N, long. 123°12' W). Named on Boonville (1959) 15' quadrangle, and on Ukiah (1958) 7.5' quadrangle.

Henthorne Lakes [TRINITY]: *lakes,* two, largest 750 feet long, 15 miles southwest of Black Rock Mountain (lat. 40°00'50" N, long. 123°07' W; at S line sec. 17, T 25 N, R 11 W). Named on Black Rock Mountain (1954) 15' quadrangle. United States Board on Geographic Names (1982b, p. 3) approved the name "Henthorne Lake" for the largest of the two Lakes.

Herman Creek [LAKE]: *stream,* flows nearly 2 miles to Dry Creek (3) 3 miles west-southwest of Middletown (lat. 38°43'50" N, long. 122°39'30" W; sec. 8, T 10 N, R 7 W). Named on Mount Saint Helena (1959) 7.5' quadrangle.

Hermitage: see **The Hermitage** [MENDOCINO]; **Yorkville** [MENDOCINO].

Hermit Rock [TRINITY]: *relief feature,* 3 miles west-southwest of Black Rock Mountain (lat. 40°11'25" N, long. 123°03'30" W; sec. 13, T 27 N, R 11 W). Named on Black Rock Mountain (1954) 15' quadrangle.

Herndon Creek [LAKE]: *stream,* flows 3.5 miles to Cache Creek 1.5 miles northeast of the town of Lower Lake (lat. 38°55'25" N, long. 122°35'25" W; sec. 1, T 12 N, R 7 W). Named on Lower Lake (1958) 7.5' quadrangle.

Herndon Creek: see **Copsey Creek** [LAKE].

Herrington Creek: see **Harrington Creek** [DEL NORTE].

Hesse Flat [LAKE]: *area,* 6.5 miles west of the town of Upper Lake (lat. 38°55'50" N, long. 122°44'05" W; sec. 34, T 13 N, R 8 W). Named on Clearlake Highlands (1958) 7.5' quadrangle.

Hetten: see **Ruth** [TRINITY].

Hetten Cove [TRINITY]: *embayment,* 5.25 miles southwest of Forest Glen along Ruth Reservoir (lat. 40°19' N, long. 123°23'30" W; near S line sec. 4, T 2 S, R 7 E); the embayment is at the mouth of Hetten Creek. Named on Ruth Reservoir (1978) 7.5' quadrangle.

Hetten Creek [TRINITY]: *stream,* flows 2 miles to Ruth Reservoir 5.25 miles southwest of Forest Glen (lat. 40°18'50" N, long. 123°23'40" W; at S line sec. 4, T 2 S, R 7 E). Named on Ruth Reservoir (1978) 7.5' quadrangle.

Hetten Ridge [TRINITY]: *ridge,* north-northwest-trending, 2.5 miles long, 9.5 miles south-southwest of Forest Glen (lat. 40°16' N, long. 123°25'25" W); the ridge is southwest of Hettenshaw Valley. Named on Ruth Reservoir (1978) 7.5' quadrangle.

Hetten Rock [TRINITY]: *peak,* 8.5 miles southwest of Forest Glen (lat. 40°17'30" N, long. 123°26'35" W; sec. 13, T 2 S, R 6 E). Altitude 4045 feet. Named on Ruth Reservoir (1978) 7.5' quadrangle.

Hettenshaw Peak [TRINITY]: *peak,* 8.5 miles south-southwest of Forest Glen (lat. 40°15'30" N, long. 123°23'05" W; near SE cor. sec. 28, T 2 S, R 7 E); the peak is 2 miles southeast of Hettenshaw Valley. Altitude 4660 feet. Named on Ruth Reservoir (1978) 7.5' quadrangle.

Hettenshaw Valley [TRINITY]: *valley,* 8 miles south-southwest of Forest Glen at the head of Van Duzen River (lat. 40°17' N, long. 123°25' W). Named on Ruth Reservoir (1978) 7.5' quadrangle. The name is of Indian origin (Kroeber, p. 42).

Heustis Prairie [HUMBOLDT]: *area,* 12 miles east-southeast of Korbel (lat. 40°46'50" N, long. 123°45'25" W; on S line sec. 29, T 5 N, R 4 E). Named on Maple Creek (1977) 7.5' quadrangle.

Hi Chute Ridge [MENDOCINO]: *ridge,* south-southeast-trending, 2.5 miles long, 7 miles west-northwest of Comptche (lat. 39°18' N, long. 123°42'30" W). Named on Comptche (1960) 15' quadrangle.

Hickory Creek [TRINITY]: *stream,* flows 2.5 miles to Coffee Creek nearly 7 miles west of Billy Peak (1) (lat. 41°07'10" N, long. 122°53'45" W; sec. 28, T 38 N, R 9 W). Named on Coffee Creek (1955) 15' quadrangle.

Hidden Lake [LAKE]: *lake,* 1300 feet long, 4.25 miles north-northwest of Lakeport (lat. 39°05'50" N, long. 122°57'50" W; near N line sec. 3, T 14 N, R 10 W). Named on Lakeport (1958) 7.5' quadrangle.

Hidden Lake [TRINITY]: *lake,* 300 feet long, 3 miles south of Burnt Ranch (lat. 40°46'05" N, long. 123°28'45" W; sec. 35, T 5 N, R 6 E). Named on Ironside Mountain (1951) 15' quadrangle.

Hidden Springs Campground [HUMBOLDT]: *locality,* 4.5 miles southeast of Weott (lat. 40°16'35" N, long. 123°51'50" W; sec. 20, T 2 S, R 3 E). Named on Myers Flat (1969) 7.5' quadrangle.

High Bluff [DEL NORTE]: *relief feature,* 2.5 miles south of the mouth of Klamath River along the coast (lat. 41°30'45" N, long. 124°04'50" W; near S line sec. 17, T 13 N, R 1 E). Named on Requa (1966) 7.5' quadrangle.

High Camp Creek [TRINITY]: *stream,* flows 3.5 miles to join Bear Creek (1) and form Trinity River 4 miles south-southeast of China Mountain, which is in Siskiyou County (lat. 41°19'30" N, long. 122°33'10" W; sec. 16, T 40 N, R 6 W). Named on China Mountain (1955) 15' quadrangle. United States Board on Geographic Names (1979, p. 3-4) approved the name "High Camp Pass" for a pass at the head of High Camp Creek on Trinity-Siskiyou County line (lat. 41°21'10" N, long. 122°35'05" W; sec. 31, T 41 N, R 6 W).

High Camp Pass: see **High Camp Creek** [TRINITY].

High Divide [DEL NORTE]: *ridge,* south-southeast-trending, 2 miles long, 5 miles east-southeast of the town of Smith River (lat. 41°54'30" N, long. 124°03' W; in and near sec. 34, T 18 N, R 1 E); the ridge is west of Low Divide. Named on High Divide (1966) 7.5' quadrangle.

High Dome [DEL NORTE]: *peak,* 9 miles northeast of Gasquet (lat. 41°56'40" N, long. 123°51' W; near NE cor. sec. 20, T 18 N, R 3 E). Named on Shelly Creek Ridge (1982) 7.5' quadrangle.

High Glade Spring [LAKE]: *spring,* 6 miles northeast of the town of Upper Lake (lat. 39°12'40" N, long. 122°48'45" W; sec. 25, T 16 N, R 9 W). Named on Bartlett Mountain (1958) 7.5' quadrangle.

Highland: see **Highland Springs** [LAKE].

Highland Creek [LAKE]: *stream,* flows 7 miles to Adobe Creek 1.25 miles north-northeast of Highland Springs (lat. 39°57'05" N, long. 122°53'35" W; near NW cor. sec. 29, T 13 N, R 9 W). Named on Highland Springs (1959) 7.5' quadrangle.

Highland Lakes [TRINITY]: *lakes,* four, largest 900 feet long, 11 miles east-northeast of Trinity Center (lat. 41°05'20" N, long. 122°30'20" W; sec. 1, T 37 N, R 6 W). Named on Bonanza King (1955) 15' quadrangle.

Highland Springs [LAKE]: *locality,* 5 miles southwest of Kelseyville (lat. 38°56'15" N, long. 122°54'25" W; sec. 31, T 13 N, R 9 W). Named on Highland Springs (1959) 7.5' quadrangle. Postal authorities established Highland Springs post office in 1875 and discontinued it in 1880; they established Highland post office in 1880, changed the name to Highland Springs in 1884, and discontinued it in 1921 (Frickstad, p. 64). Development of the property as a resort began in the 1870's (Palmer, p. 186). The place eventually had accommodations for 315 guests (Bradley, p. 218). California Mining Bureau's (1917c) map shows a place called Elliott Springs located about 4 miles south-southeast of Highland Springs. Waring (p. 186) noted that England Springs is another name for Elliott Springs—the name "England" is from the first owner of the place.

High Peak [MENDOCINO]: *peak,* nearly 6 miles north-northeast of the town of Potter Valley (lat. 39°24'15" N, long. 123°04'50" W; sec. 21, T 16 N, R 11 W). Altitude 3830 feet. Named on Potter Valley (1960) 15' quadrangle.

High Plateau Creek [DEL NORTE]: *stream,* flows 2.5 miles to Diamond Creek 8 miles north of Gasquet (lat. 41°57'20" N, long. 123°55'50" W; sec. 15, T 18 N, R 2 E); the stream heads at High Plateau Mountain. Named on Gasquet (1951) 15' quadrangle.

High Plateau Mountain [DEL NORTE]: *ridge,* west- to southwest-trending, 3 miles long, 5 miles north-northeast of Gasquet (lat. 41°54'45" N, long. 123°56' W). Named on Gasquet (1951) 15' quadrangle.

High Point [LAKE]: *peak,* 9.5 miles east of Hull Mountain on Brushy Camp Ridge (lat. 39°30'55" N, long. 122°45'40" W). Altitude 5847 feet. Named on Kneecap Ridge (1967) 7.5' quadrangle.

High Prairie [TRINITY]: *area,* 6.5 miles southwest of Cecilville, which is in Siskiyou County, on Trinity-Siskiyou County line (lat. 41°04'25" N, long. 123°12'45" W). Named on Cecil Lake (1979) 7.5' quadrangle.

High Prairie [HUMBOLDT]:

(1) *area,* 9 miles east-southeast of Korbel (lat. 40°49'05" N, long. 123°48'10" W; sec. 14, T 5 N, R 3 E). Named on Maple Creek (1977) 7.5' quadrangle.

(2) *area,* 9 miles south-southeast of Scotia (lat. 40°21'25" N, long. 124°02'55" W). Named on Bull Creek (1969) 7.5' quadrangle.

High Prairie Creek [DEL NORTE]: *stream,* flows 4.5 miles to Salt Creek 1.5 miles north-northeast of the mouth of Klamath River (lat. 41°34'05" N, long. 124°04'15" W; at N line sec. 33, T 14 N, R 1 E). Named on Requa (1966) 7.5' quadrangle. On Klamath (1952) 15' quadrangle, the name "High Prairie Creek" applies to present Salt Creek below the junction of High Prairie Creek and present Salt Creek.

High Prairie Creek [HUMBOLDT]: *stream,* flows 4.25 miles to Redwood Creek (1) 11 miles east-southeast of Korbel (lat. 40°49'15" N, long. 123°45'50" W; sec. 18, T 5 N, R 4 E); the stream goes past High Prairie (1). Named on Maple Creek (1977) 7.5' quadrangle.

High Rock [HUMBOLDT]: *relief feature,* 3.5 miles north of Weott along Eel River (lat. 40°22'25" N, long. 123°55'20" W). Named on Weott (1969) 7.5' quadrangle.

High Rock [LAKE]: *peak,* 4 miles east-northeast of Hull Mountain (lat. 39°33'10" N, long. 122°52'20" W; at S line sec. 28, T 20 N, R 9 W). Altitude 4027 feet. Named on Kneecap Ridge (1967) 7.5' quadrangle.

High Salt Ground [HUMBOLDT]: *area,* 6.5 miles southeast of Board Camp Mountain (lat. 40°37'30" N, long. 123°38'20" W; sec. 20, T 3 N, R 5 E). Named on Board Camp Mountain (1977) and Showers Mountain (1978) 7.5' quadrangles.

High Salt Ground [MENDOCINO]: *ridge,* south-trending, 1.5 miles long, 7.5 miles northeast of Willits (lat. 39°29'30" N, long. 123°15'30" W). Named on Willits (1961) 15' quadrangle.

High Spring [HUMBOLDT]: *spring,* 0.25 mile south of Salmon Mountain (lat. 41°10'40" N, long. 123°24'30" W). Named on Salmon Mountain (1978) 7.5' quadrangle.

Hight Gulch [HUMBOLDT]: *canyon,* drained by a stream that flows 2.5 miles to Eel River 1.5 miles south-southeast of Alderpoint (lat. 40°09'25" N, long. 123°35'50" W; sec. 34, T 3 S, R 5 E). Named on Alderpoint (1969) 7.5' quadrangle. Called Hite Gulch on Alderpoint (1949) 15' quadrangle, but United States Board on Geographic Names (1973a, p. 3) rejected the names "Hite Gulch" and "Height Gulch" for the feature.

High Tip [MENDOCINO]: *peak,* 9 miles west-southwest of Piercy near the coast (lat. 39°55'25" N, long. 123°57'10" W; sec. 22, T 24 N, R 19 W). Altitude 372 feet. Named on Bear Harbor (1969) 7.5' quadrangle.

High Valley [LAKE]: *valley,* nearly 2 miles north of Clearlake Oaks (lat. 39°03' N, long. 122°41'15" W). Named on Clearlake Oaks (1958) 7.5' quadrangle. Postal authorities established High Valley post office in High Valley [HUMBOLDT-LAKE] 2 miles east of the east shore of Clear Lake in 1872 and discontinued in 1875 (Salley, p. 97).

High Valley [HUMBOLDT-LAKE]: *area,* 3 miles east-southeast of Highland Springs on Humboldt-Lake County line (lat. 38°55'40" N, long. 122°57'35" W; sec. 34, T 13 N, R 10 W). Named on Highland Springs (1959) 7.5' quadrangle. The name is from the 400-foot height of the central part of the valley above the level of Clear Lake (Upson and Kunkel, p. 65).

High Valley: see **Little High Valley** [LAKE].

High Valley Creek [LAKE]: *stream,* flows 4.5 miles to Kelsey Creek 8 miles south-southeast of Kelseyville (lat. 38°52'10" N, long. 122°47'35" W; at N line sec. 30, T 12 N, R 8 W). Named on The Geysers (1959) 7.5' quadrangle.

High Valley Ridge [LAKE]: *ridge,* southeast- to east-trending, 11 miles long, center 3.5 miles north-northwest of Clearlake Oaks (lat. 39°04' N, long.

122°42' W); the ridge is north of High Valley. Named on Clearlake Oaks (1960) 15' quadrangle, and on Lucerne (1958) 7.5' quadrangle.

Hill: see **Bob Hill Gulch** [HUMBOLDT].

Hill Creek [LAKE]: *stream*, flows 3.5 miles to McGaugh Creek 2 miles northwest of Kelseyville (lat. 38°59'35" N, long. 122°51'40" W; sec. 9, T 13 N, R 9 W). Named on Kelseyville (1959) 7.5' quadrangle.

Hilltop Spring [MENDOCINO]: *spring*, 3.5 miles southwest of Hopland (lat. 38°56'10" N, long. 123°09'30" W; at S line sec. 34, T 13 N, R 12 W). Named on Hopland (1960) 15' quadrangle.

Hiltabidels Opening [MENDOCINO]: *area*, 4.5 miles north-northeast of Leggett (lat. 39°55'25" N, long. 123°40'50" W; on E line sec. 13, T 24 N, R 17 W). Named on Noble Butte (1969) 7.5' quadrangle.

Hilton: see **Mount Hilton**, under **Thompson Peak** [TRINITY] (2).

Hiouchi [DEL NORTE]: *settlement*, 7.5 miles east-northeast of Crescent City along Smith River (lat. 41°47'30" N, long. 124°04'15" W; sec. 9, T 16 N, R 1 E). Named on Hiouchi (1966) 7.5' quadrangle.

Hitchcock Creek [TRINITY]: *stream*, flows 2.5 miles to South Fork Trinity River 5 miles south of Hyampom (lat. 40°32'40" N, long. 123°27'20" W; near NW cor. sec. 24, T 2 N, R 6 E). Named on Hyampom (1951) 15' quadrangle.

Hite Gulch: see **Hight Gulch** [HUMBOLDT].

H.J: see **The H.J.** [HUMBOLDT].

Hoadley Gulch [TRINITY]: *canyon*, drained by a stream that flows 3.5 miles to Trinity River 7.25 miles east-southeast of Weaverville at Lewiston (lat. 40°42'25" N, long. 122°48'25" W; near E line sec. 19, T 33 N, R 8 W). Named on Weaverville (1950) 15' quadrangle. Jones (p. 292) associated the name with J.F. Hoadley, who came to Lewiston in 1853 and was justice of the peace and postmaster.

Hoadley Peaks [TRINITY]: *peaks*, 10.5 miles east-southeast of Weaverville on Trinity-Shasta County line (lat. 40°41'20" N, long. 122°45' W; sec. 27, T 33 N, R 8 W); the peaks are at the head of Hoadley Gulch. Named on Weaverville (1950) 15' quadrangle, and on French Gulch (1979) 7.5' quadrangle. Called Trinity Mountain on Red Bluff (1894) 1° quadrangle, and called Hoadley Pk. on Weaverville (1913) 30' quadrangle.

Hoagland Creek [HUMBOLDT]: *stream*, flows 3.5 miles to Van Duzen River 0.5 mile southwest of Bridgeville (lat. 40°28' N, long. 123°48'15" W; sec. 14, T 1 N, R 3 E). Named on Bridgeville (1969) 7.5' quadrangle.

Hoaglin: see **Hoaglin Valley** [TRINITY].

Hoaglin Creek [TRINITY]: *stream*, flows 3.5 miles to Salt Creek (2) 7 miles southeast of Kettenpom (lat. 40°05'55" N, long. 123°21'25" W; sec. 23, T 4 S, R 7 E). Named on Lake Mountain (1967) and Long Ridge (1967) 7.5' quadrangles.

Hoaglin Valley [TRINITY]: *valley*, 4.5 miles southeast of Kettenpom (lat. 40°06'45" N, long. 123°23'45" W); the valley is along upper reaches of Hoaglin Creek. Named on Lake Mountain (1967) 7.5' quadrangle. Hoaglin (1935) 30' quadrangle shows a place called Hoaglin in Hoaglin Valley (sec. 16, T 4 S, R 7 E). Postal authorities established Hoaglin post office in 1893 and discontinued it in 1936—the name was for the pioneer Hoaglin family (Salley, p. 98). California Mining Bureau (1917b) map shows a place called Seven Cedars located about half way between Hoaglin and Zenia. Postal authorities established Seven Cedars post office in 1912 at a resort 6.5 miles northwest of Hoaglin and discontinued it in 1916 (Salley, p. 202).

Hobart Creek [TRINITY]: *stream*, flows 2 miles to Ruth Reservoir 4.5 miles south-southwest of Forest Glen (lat. 40°18'45" N, long. 123°21'25" W; sec. 11, T 2 S, R 7 E). Named on Forest Glen (1979) 7.5' quadrangle.

Hobel Creek [TRINITY]: *stream*, flows 4 miles to Davis Creek (2) 16 miles north-northeast of Weaverville (lat. 40°55'15" N, long. 122°46' W; sec. 3, T 35 N, R 8 W). Named on Schell Mountain (1950) and Trinity Dam (1950) 15' quadrangles.

Hobergs [LAKE]: *locality*, 2.25 miles north-northwest of Whispering Pines (lat. 38°50'40" N, long. 122°43'25" W; on N line sec. 3, T 11 N, R 8 W). Named on Whispering Pines (1958) 7.5' quadrangle. Postal authorities established Hobergs post office in 1929 and discontinued it in 1970 (Salley, p. 98). Gustave Hoberg opened a summer resort at the place in 1885 (Hanna, p. 139).

Hobo Gulch Camp [TRINITY]: *locality*, 10.5 miles north of Helena along North Fork Trinity River (lat. 40°55'30" N, long. 123°09'10" W; near NW cor. sec. 6, T 35 N, R 11 W). Named on Helena (1951) 15' quadrangle.

Hoboken [TRINITY]: *locality*, 5.5 miles north-northeast of Burnt Ranch along New River (lat. 40°53' N, long. 123°26' W). Named on Ironside Mountain (1951) 15' quadrangle. Postal authorities established Hoboken post office, named for Hoboken Hydraulic Mining Company, in 1892 and discontinued it in 1893; the place also was called Hoboken Bar and Grand Slide (Salley, p. 98).

Hoboken Bar: see **Hoboken** [TRINITY].

Hocker Flat [TRINITY]: *area*, 15 miles north-northeast of Hayfork along Trinity River (lat. 40°44'40" N, long. 123°04' W). Named on Hayfork (1951) 15' quadrangle.

Hocker Meadow [TRINITY]: *area*, 13 miles north-northeast of Hayfork (lat. 40°44'05" N, long. 123°07'10" W). Named on Hayfork (1951) 15' quadrangle.

Hoffman Creek [LAKE]: *stream*, flows 1.5 miles to Saint Helena Creek 4 miles south-southeast of Middletown (lat. 38°41'50" N, long. 122°35'50" W; sec. 23, T 10 N, R 7 W). Named on Detert Reservoir (1958) 7.5' quadrangle.

Hoffman Flat [TRINITY]: *area*, 4.5 miles southeast of Forest Glen along South Fork Trinity River (lat. 40°19'30" N, long. 123°16'05" W; on W line sec. 31, T 29 N, R 12 W). Named on Forest Glen (1979) 7.5' quadrangle. United States Board on Geographic Names (1978a, p. 6) rejected the name "Stockton Flat" for the place, and noted that the name "Hoffman" commemorates Jack Hoffman, who homesteaded at the site and is buried there.

Hogback Creek [HUMBOLDT]: *stream*, flows 1.5 miles to Van Duzen River nearly 5 miles south of Showers Mountain (lat. 40°30'30" N, long. 123°41'40" W; sec. 35, T 2 N, R 4 E). Named on Showers Mountain (1978) 7.5' quadrangle.

Hogback Ridge [HUMBOLDT]: *ridge*, generally north-trending, 1.5 miles long, 8.5 miles south of the settlement of Willow Creek (lat. 40°49'20" N, long. 123°36'55" W). Named on Hennessy Peak (1979) 7.5' quadrangle.

Hogback Ridge [LAKE]: *ridge*, northwest-trending, 4.5 miles long, 3 miles east-southeast of the town of Upper Lake (lat. 39°08'40" N, long. 122°51'05" W). Named on Bartlett Mountain (1958) and Upper Lake (1958) 7.5' quadrangles.

Hog Hole [MENDOCINO]: *relief feature*, 3.25 miles east-southeast of Dos Rios on the north side of Middle Fork Eel River (lat. 39°42'10" N, long. 123°17'40" W). Named on Dos Rios (1967) 7.5' quadrangle.

Hog Hole Ridge [MENDOCINO]: *ridge*, generally east-southeast-trending, 1.5 miles long, 3.25 miles east of Dos Rios (lat. 39°42'30" N, long. 123°17'45" W); the ridge is north of Hog Hole. Named on Dos Rios (1967) 7.5' quadrangle.

Hog Hollow Creek [LAKE]: *stream*, flows 2.25 miles to North Fork Cache Creek 5.5 miles east of Clearlake Oaks (lat. 39°01'35" N, long. 122°34'25" W). Named on Clearlake Oaks (1960) 15' quadrangle.

Hog Lake [MENDOCINO]: *intermittent lake*, 200 feet long, 11 miles southeast of Ukiah (lat. 39°01'55" N, long. 123°04'40" W; sec. 33, T 14 N, R 11 W). Named on Purdys Gardens (1958) 7.5' quadrangle.

Hogpen Slough [HUMBOLDT]: *water feature*, joins Quill Slough 5.5 miles north of Ferndale (lat. 40°39'10" N, long. 124°15'35" W). Named on Cannibal Island (1959) and Fields Landing (1959) 7.5' quadrangles.

Hog Point [LAKE]: *peak*, 5 miles north-northwest of the town of Upper Lake (lat. 39°13'45" N, long. 122°57'20" W; sec. 22, T 16 N, R 10 W). Altitude 3049 feet. Named on Upper Lake (1958) 7.5' quadrangle.

Hog Prairie [HUMBOLDT]: *area*, 5 miles west-northwest of Coyote Peak along Redwood Creek (1) (lat. 41°10'10" N, long. 123°56'40" W; at E line sec. 16, T 9 N, R 2 E). Named on Bald Hills (1982) 7.5' quadrangle.

Hog Ranch Creek [HUMBOLDT]: *stream*, flows 1.25 miles to Pine Creek (1) 5 miles east of Coyote Peak (lat. 41°07'40" N, long. 123°45'40" W; at N line sec. 31, T 9 N, R 4 E). Named on French Camp Ridge (1983) and Weitchpec (1979) 7.5' quadrangles.

Hog Ranch Prairie [HUMBOLDT]: *area*, 4.25 miles south-southwest of Weitchpec (lat. 41°07'55" N, long. 123°44'50" W; sec. 29, T 9 N, R 4 E). Named on French Camp Ridge (1983) and Weitchpec (1979) 7.5' quadrangles.

Hog Ranch Ridge [HUMBOLDT]: *ridge*, generally northeast-trending, 1 mile long, 5 miles east-southeast of Coyote Peak (lat. 41°06'35" N, long. 123°45'50" W; in and near sec. 6, T 8 N, R 4 E). Named on Hupa Mountain (1982) 7.5' quadrangle.

Hog Ranch Ridge [MENDOCINO]: *ridge*, generally north-trending, 1.5 miles long, 8.5 miles west-northwest of Ornbaun Valley (lat. 38°58'15" N, long. 123°26'15" W). Named on Ornbaun Valley (1960) 15' quadrangle.

Hogshed Creek [MENDOCINO]: *stream*, flows 1.5 miles to South Fork Eel River 6.5 miles south-southeast of Leggett (lat. 39°47'15" N, long. 123°38'40" W; sec. 5, T 22 N, R 16 W). Named on Leggett (1969) and Tan Oak Park (1969) 7.5' quadrangles.

Hoil Creek [MENDOCINO]: *stream*, flows 2 miles to Tyler Creek 3 miles southeast of Monument Peak (lat. 38°53' N, long. 122°54'25" W; sec. 18, T 12 N, R 9 W). Named on Asti (1959), Highland Springs (1959), and The Geysers (1959) 7.5' quadrangles.

Hole Creek [LAKE]: *stream*, flows 3.5 miles to Jericho Creek 0.5 mile north-northeast of Jericho Valley (lat. 38°50'20" N, long. 120°25'45" W; near NE cor. sec. 5, T 11 N, R 5 W). Named on Jericho Valley (1958) 7.5' quadrangle.

Hole-in-the-Ground [DEL NORTE]: *relief feature*, 7.5 miles east-northeast of the town of Smith River (lat. 41°58'30" N, long. 124°01' W; at SW cor. sec. 1, T 18 N, R 1 E). Named on High Divide (1966) 7.5' quadrangle. Called Hole in the Ground (without the hyphens) on Crescent City (1952) 15' quadrangle.

Hole in the Ground [HUMBOLDT]: *area*, 3 miles west of Alderpoint (lat. 40°10'30" N, long. 123°40'15" W). Named on Fort Seward (1969) 7.5' quadrangle.

Hole in the Ground [TRINITY]: *relief feature*, 11.5 miles south of Black

Rock Mountain along Minnie Creek (lat. 40°02'30" N, long. 123°00' W; at NE cor. sec. 3, 8, T 25 N, R 10 W). Named on Black Rock Mountain (1954) and Yolla Bolly (1954) 15' quadrangles.

Hollister Creek [HUMBOLDT]: *stream*, flows 2.5 miles to South Fork Bear River 6.5 miles east of Cape Mendocino (lat. 40°25'40" N, long. 124°17'10" W; sec. 34, T 1 N, R 2 W). Named on Capetown (1969) 7.5' quadrangle.

Hollister Ridge [HUMBOLDT]: *ridge*, generally northeast-trending, 1.5 miles long, 8 miles east-southeast of Cape Mendocino (lat. 40°25'10" N, long. 124°15'30" W); the ridge is east of Hollister Creek. Named on Capetown (1969) and Taylor Peak (1969) 7.5' quadrangles.

Hollow Tree Creek [MENDOCINO]: *stream*, flows 15 miles to South Fork Eel River 1 mile southwest of Leggett (lat. 39°51'25" N, long. 123°43'35" W; sec. 10, T 23 N, R 17 W). Named on Hales Grove (1970), Leggett (1969), and Lincoln Ridge (1966) 7.5' quadrangles. On Kenny (1920) 15' quadrangle, the name applied also to present Mule Creek and South Fork Mule Creek.

Holly Creek [TRINITY]: *stream*, flows 1.5 miles to Ruth Reservoir 5.25 miles south-southwest of Forest Glen (lat. 40°18' N, long. 123°21' W; sec. 14, T 2 S, R 7 E). Named on Forest Glen (1979) 7.5' quadrangle.

Holm Buttes [HUMBOLDT]: *relief feature*, 4.5 miles east of Showers Mountain (lat. 40°35'25" N, long. 123°36'35" W; at S line sec. 33, T 3 N, R 5 E); the feature is at the northeast end of Holm Ridge. Named on Blake Mountain (1979) 7.5' quadrangle.

Holm Creek [HUMBOLDT]: *stream*, flows nearly 2 miles to Mad River 2.5 miles east of Showers Mountain (lat. 40°34'40" N, long. 123°38'45" W; sec. 6, T 2 N, R 5 E); the stream is north of Holm Ridge. Named on Blake Mountain (1979) and Showers Mountain (1978) 7.5' quadrangles.

Holmen Ridge [MENDOCINO]: *ridge*, generally north-trending, 2.5 miles long, 5 miles east of Laytonville (lat. 39°40'45" N, long. 123°23'10" W. Named on Laytonville (1967) 7.5' quadrangle.

Holmes [HUMBOLDT]: *village*, 2.25 miles north of Redcrest (lat. 40°25'05" N, long. 123°56'30" W; sec. 33, 34, T 1 N, R 2 E); the village is at Holmes Flat. Named on Redcrest (1969) 7.5' quadrangle. Postal authorities established Holmes post office in 1910 and discontinued it in 1965 (Salley, p. 99). The place first was called Holmes Camp for the head of the logging company that operated there (Gudde, 1949, p. 151). Postal authorities established Skelly post office 3.5 miles south of Holmes in 1916, moved it 1.5 miles south in 1938, and discontinued it in 1943 (Salley, p. 205).

Holmes Camp: see **Holmes** [HUMBOLDT].

Holmes Flat [HUMBOLDT]: *area*, 1.25 miles north of Redcrest along Eel River (lat. 40°25'10" N, long. 123°56'50" W; sec. 33, 34, T 1 N, R 2 E). Named on Redcrest (1969) 7.5' quadrangle. Joe Holmes owned the place, which first was called Englewood (Eich, p. 99).

Holm Ridge [HUMBOLDT]: *ridge*, southeast-trending, 1.5 miles long, 3.5 miles east of Showers Mountain (lat. 40°34'45" N, long. 123°37'30" W). Named on Blake Mountain (1979) and Showers Mountain (1978) 7.5' quadrangles. The name commemorates Hans Peter Holm, a prominent stockman of Humboldt County (Turner, p. 107).

Holohan Gulch [MENDOCINO]: *canyon*, drained by a stream that flows 1.25 miles to Red Mountain Creek 5 miles north of Leggett (lat. 39°56' N, long. 123°44'10" W; near NE cor. sec. 16, T 24 N, R 17 W). Named on Noble Butte (1969) 7.5' quadrangle.

Holter Ridge [HUMBOLDT]: *ridge*, generally north-northeast-trending, 5 miles long, 6 miles southwest of Johnsons (lat. 41°17'45" N, long. 123°57'50" W). Named Holter Ridge (1983) 7.5' quadrangle.

Home Creek [HUMBOLDT]: *stream*, flows 2.5 miles to the sea 8 miles north of Orick (lat. 41°24'10" N, long. 124°04' W; sec. 28, T 12 N, R 1 E). Named on Fern Canyon (1966) 7.5' quadrangle, which shows the stream in Fern Canyon.

Homers Spring [HUMBOLDT]: *spring*, 3.5 miles northeast of Board Camp Mountain (lat. 40°43'50" N, long. 123°39'40" W). Named on Board Camp Mountain (1977) 7.5' quadrangle.

Homestead Opening [HUMBOLDT]: *area*, 12 miles south-southwest of Scotia (lat. 40°19'25" N, long. 124°11'35" W; on W line sec. 4, T 2 S, R 1 W). Named on Buckeye Mountain (1970) 7.5' quadrangle.

Honda Cove [HUMBOLDT]: *embayment*, 2 miles southeast of Trinidad along the coast (lat. 41°02'05" N, long. 124°07' W; sec. 31, T 8 N, R 1 E). Named on Crannell (1966) 7.5' quadrangle.

Honey Creek [MENDOCINO]: *stream*, flows 1.5 miles to Bear Wallow Creek (2) 3 miles west-southwest of Boonville (lat. 39°00'10" N, long. 123°25'20" W; sec. 8, T 13 N, R 14 W). Named on Boonville (1959) and Ornbaun Valley (1960) 15' quadrangles.

Honeydew [HUMBOLDT]: *locality*, 17 miles south of Scotia (lat. 40°14'35" N, long. 124°07'20" W; near NE cor. sec. 1, T 3 S, R 1 W); the place is along Mattole River 0.5 mile northwest of the mouth of Honeydew Creek. Named on Honeydew (1970) 7.5' quadrangle. Called Honey Dew on Point Delgada (1920) 15' quadrangle. Postal authorities established Honeydew post office in 1926 (Frickstad, p. 44).

Honeydew Creek [HUMBOLDT]: *stream*, flows 6.5 miles to Mattole River 0.5 mile southeast of Honeydew (lat. 40°14'10" N, long. 124°06'55" W). Named on Honeydew (1970) and Shubrick Peak (1969) 7.5' quadrangles. Called Honey Dew Creek on Point Delgada (1920) 15' quadrangle. The name "Honeydew" supposedly originated when a group of pioneers camped under cottonwood trees by the stream and in the morning found that their bedding was covered with a sweet sticky substance that had dripped from the blossoms of the trees (Quimby, p. 162). East Fork enters 2.5 miles south of Honeydew; it is 5 miles long and is named on Honeydew (1970) 7.5' quadrangle. Upper East Fork enters from the east 3.5 miles south-southwest of Honeydew; it is 2.5 miles long and is named on Shubrick Peak (1969) 7.5' quadrangle—this same fork is called Upper North Fork on Honeydew (1970) 7.5' quadrangle. West Fork enters from the west-southwest 3.25 miles south of Honeydew; it is 1.5 miles long and is named on Shubrick Peak (1969) 7.5' quadrangle.

Honeymoon Cove [LAKE]: *embayment*, 2.5 miles southwest of Clearlake Oaks along Clear Lake (lat. 39°00'10" N, long. 122°43'05" W; sec. 2, T 13 N, R 8 W). Named on Clearlake Oaks (1958) 7.5' quadrangle.

Hoodoo Creek [LAKE]: *stream*, flows 2.5 miles to Dry Creek (3) 1 mile west-southwest of Middletown (lat. 38°44'50" N, long. 122°37'50" W). Named on Mount Saint Helena (1959) 7.5' quadrangle.

Hoodoo Gulch [MENDOCINO]: *canyon*, drained by a stream that flows 1 mile to North Fork Gualala River 11.5 miles southwest of Ornbaun Valley (lat. 38°48'35" N, long. 123°28'30" W; sec. 7, T 11 N, R 14 W). Named on Ornbaun Valley (1960) 15' quadrangle.

Hooker Creek [HUMBOLDT]: *stream*, flows nearly 2 miles to South Fork Eel River 2 miles south of Phillipsville (lat. 40°10'40" N, long. 123°46'50" W). Named on Miranda (1970) 7.5' quadrangle.

Hooker Mountain [HUMBOLDT]: *peak*, nearly 2 miles south-southwest of Coyote Peak (lat. 41°06'35" N, long. 123°52'15" W; near SE cor. sec. 6, T 8 N, R 3 E). Altitude 3141 feet. Named on Hupa Mountain (1982) 7.5' quadrangle.

Hookton [HUMBOLDT]: *locality*, 3.5 miles south of Fields Landing (lat. 40°40'25" N, long. 124°13' W; near E line sec. 6, T 3 N, R 1 W). Named on Fields Landing (1959) 7.5' quadrangle. John Hookton founded the place (Johnson, p. 24).

Hookton Channel [HUMBOLDT]: *channel*, extends for 4.25 miles from the mouth of Hookton Slough through Humboldt Bay to the entrance of the bay. Named on Eureka (1958) and Fields Landing (1959) 7.5' quadrangles. United States Board on Geographic Names (1940, p. 21) rejected the name "Fields Landing Channel" for the feature.

Hookton Slough [HUMBOLDT]: *water feature*, enters Humboldt Bay 2 miles south of Fields Landing (lat. 40°41'50" N, long. 124°13'20" W). Named on Fields Landing (1959) 7.5' quadrangle. Johnson (p. 24) gave the alternate name "Big Slough" for the feature.

Hoopa [HUMBOLDT]: *town*, 10 miles south of Weitchpec along Trinity River (lat. 41°02'55" N, long. 123°40'35" W; sec. 25, T 8 N, R 4 E); the town is in Hoopa Valley. Named on Hoopa (1979) 7.5' quadrangle. Postal authorities established Hoopa Valley post office in 1861, changed the name to Hoopa in 1895, changed it to Hupa in 1900, and changed it back to Hoopa in 1902 (Salley, p. 100). United States Board on Geographic Names (1933, p. 373) rejected the form "Hupa" for the name.

Hoopa Campground [HUMBOLDT]: *locality*, 2.5 miles southeast of Hoopa along Trinity River (lat. 41°01'30" N, long. 123°38'35" W; near NE cor. sec. 6, T 7 N, R 5 E). Named on Hoopa (1979) 7.5' quadrangle.

Hoopa Mountain: see **Hupa Mountain** [HUMBOLDT].

Hoopa Valley [HUMBOLDT]: *valley*, 6.5 miles long, at and near Hoopa along Trinity River (center near lat. 41°03'45" N, long. 123°41' W). Named on Hoopa (1979) 7.5' quadrangle. United States Board on Geographic Names (1933, p. 373) rejected the form "Hupa" for the name, which is from the Indian designation for the place (Kroeber, p. 42). Captain Edmund Underwood established a military post called Fort Gaston in Hoopa Valley on the west side of Trinity River about 14 miles above its confluence with Klamath River; the name commemorated Lieutenant William Gaston, killed in 1858 during an expedition against the Spokane Indians—the post, which also was called Camp Gaston, was abandoned in 1892 (Frazer, p. 23).

Hoopa Valley: see **Hoopa** [HUMBOLDT].

Hoosimbim Mountain [TRINITY]: *peak*, 12 miles south-southwest of Weaverville (lat. 40°33'40" N, long. 122°59'45" W; sec. 4, T 31 N, R 10 W). Altitude 5403 feet. Named on Weaverville (1950) 15' quadrangle.

Hoover Creek [HUMBOLDT]: *stream*, flows 2.5 miles to North Dobbyn Creek 4 miles north-northeast of Alderpoint (lat. 40°13'45" N, long. 123°34'40" W; sec. 2, T 3 S, R 5 E). Named on Alderpoint (1969) and Black Lassic (1979) 7.5' quadrangles.

Hopah Mountain: see **Hupa Mountain** [HUMBOLDT].

Hope Creek [HUMBOLDT]: *stream*, flows less than 0.5 mile to Prairie Creek 11 miles north of Orick (lat. 41°26'20" N, long. 124°02'25" W; sec. 10, T 12 N, R 1 E). Named on Fern Canyon (1966) 7.5' quadrangle.

Hop Flat [MENDOCINO]: *area*, 4 miles northeast of Elk along Navarro River (lat. 39°10'20" N, long. 123°40'05" W; sec. 7, T 15 N, R 16 W). Named on Elk (1960) 7.5' quadrangle.

Hopkins Butte [HUMBOLDT]: *peak*, 5 miles east-northeast of Weitchpec (lat. 41°12'50" N, long. 123°37' W); the peak is north of Hopkins Creek.

Altitude 4026 feet. Named on Hopkins Butte (1979) 7.5' quadrangle.

Hopkins Camp [TRINITY]: *locality,* 5.5 miles south-southwest of Black Rock Mountain (lat. 40°08'10" N, long. 123°04' W; near SW cor. sec. 36, T 27 N, R 11 W). Named on Black Rock Mountain (1954) 15' quadrangle.

Hopkins Creek [HUMBOLDT]: *stream,* flows 5.5 miles to Klamath River 2.5 miles north-northeast of Weitchpec (lat. 41°12'10" N, long. 123°39'35" W; near E line sec. 1, T 9 N, R 4 E). Named on Hopkins Butte (1979) and Weitchpec (1979) 7.5' quadrangles.

Hopkins Hollow [TRINITY]: *relief feature,* 11 miles south-southeast of Black Rock Mountain (lat. 40°03'15" N, long. 122°57'10" W; near N line sec. 3, T 25 N, R 10 W); the feature is 1.5 miles east of Hopkins Peak. Named on Yolla Bolly (1954) 15' quadrangle.

Hopkins Peak [TRINITY]: *peak,* 11 miles south of Black Rock Mountain (lat. 40°03'05" N, long. 122°58'50" W; sec. 4, T 25 N, R 10 W). Altitude 6749 feet. Named on Yolla Bolly (1954) 15' quadrangle.

Hopland [MENDOCINO]: *town,* 13 miles south-southeast of Ukiah on the west side of Russian River (lat. 38°58'25" N, long. 123°06'55" W); the place is on Sanel grant. Named on Hopland (1960) 7.5' quadrangle, which shows a place called Old Hopland situated 1 mile to the east across Russian River (lat. 38°59'05" N, long. 123°05'55" W). Present Old Hopland is called East Hopland on Hopland (1944) 15' quadrangle, but United States Board on Geographic Names (1962b, p. 20) rejected the names "Hopland" and "East Hopland" for the place. Postal authorities established Sanel post office in 1860, discontinued it for a time in 1869, and discontinued it again in 1879, when they moved the post office 1 mile east and changed the name to Hopland; they moved Hopland post office 1 mile west and changed the name to Sanel in 1890, and changed the name back to Hopland in 1891 (Salley, p. 100, 193). Fernando Feliz, who received Sanel grant in 1844, built an adobe house just south of present Hopland, and the community that grew up there was called Sanel (Hoover, Rensch, and Rensch, p. 196). Sanel began in 1859 on the west side of Russian River with a saloon and store, but in 1874 the town moved to the east side of the river to be by a toll road there; when the railroad was built on the west side of the river, the town moved back to the original site (Carpenter, p. 101). Eventually the name "Sanel" was dropped, the name "Hopland" was adopted for the community on the west side of the river, and the place on the east side became Old Hopland—the name "Hopland" is from the success that Stephen Warren Knowles had in introducing hop culture to the neighborhood (Hoover, Rensch, and Rensch, p. 196). California Mining Bureau's (1917c) map shows a place called Echo located about 8 miles south-southeast of Hopland near where Hopland (1944) 15' quadrangle shows Echo ranch. California Mining Bureau's (1917c) map also shows a place called Fountain situated 2.5 miles south of Hopland along the railroad near where Hopland (1944) 15' quadrangle shows Fountain ranch.

Hoppaw [DEL NORTE]: *village,* 3 miles east-southeast of the mouth of Klamath River (lat. 41°31'30" N, long. 124°01'40" W; near SW cor. sec. 11, T 13 N, R 1 E); the village is along Hoppaw Creek. Named on Requa (1966) 7.5' quadrangle.

Hoppaw Creek [DEL NORTE]: *stream,* flows 5 miles to Klamath River 2.5 miles southeast of the mouth of that river (lat. 41°31'25" N, long. 124°02'30" W; at N line sec. 15, T 13 N, R 1 E). Named on Klamath Glen (1982) and Requa (1966) 7.5' quadrangles. Called Wacket Creek on Bancroft's (1864) map. According to Kroeber (p. 42), who used the form "Hoppow" for the name, the stream is named for an Indian village.

Hoppaw Ridge [DEL NORTE]: *ridge,* south-southwest-trending, 1.5 miles long, 3.5 miles east of the mouth of Klamath River (lat. 41°32'20" N, long. 124°02'25" W); the ridge is north of Hoppaw Creek. Named on Requa (1966) 7.5' quadrangle.

Hoppaw Saddle [DEL NORTE]: *pass,* 3 miles east of the mouth of Klamath River (lat. 41°32'50" N, long. 124°01'30" W; sec. 2, T 13 N, R 1 E); the pass is 0.5 mile west-northwest of Hoppaw Ridge. Named on Requa (1966) 7.5' quadrangle.

Hopper Flat [MENDOCINO]: *area,* 5 miles east-southeast of Willits (lat. 39°22'15" N, long. 123°16'30" W; sec. 35, T 18 N, R 13 W). Named on Willits (1961) 15' quadrangle. Called Hoppers Flat on O'Brien's (1953) map.

Hoppins Springs: see **Bartlett Springs** [LAKE].

Horse Camp [DEL NORTE]: *locality,* 1 mile south-southwest of Sawtooth Mountain (lat. 41°36'05" N, long. 123°43'10" W). Site named on Chimney Rock (1981) 7.5' quadrangle.

Horse Camp [MENDOCINO]: *locality,* 9.5 miles east of Covelo (lat. 39°46'15" N, long. 123°04'20" W; at N line sec. 15, T 22 N, R 11 W). Named on Newhouse Ridge (1967) 7.5' quadrangle.

Horse Canyon [MENDOCINO]: *canyon,* drained by a stream that flows 4 miles to Hulls Creek 12.5 miles north of Covelo (lat. 39°58'35" N, long. 123°14'45" W). Named on Bluenose Ridge (1967) 7.5' quadrangle.

Horse Canyon: see **Little Horse Canyon** [MENDOCINO].

Horse Creek [DEL NORTE]: *stream,* flows 1 mile to South Fork Smith River 1.5 miles north of Buck Mountain (lat. 41°39'30" N, long. 123°51'50" W). Named on Cant Hook Mountain (1982) and Ship Mountain (1982) 7.5' quadrangles.

Horse Creek [HUMBOLDT]: *stream,* flows 5 miles to Butte Creek (2) 5.5 miles southwest of Dinsmore (lat. 40°26' N, long. 123°40'10" W; near SE cor. sec. 25, T 1 N, R 4 E). Named on Larabee Valley (1977) 7.5' quadrangle.

Horse Creek [LAKE]: *stream,* flows 3.25 miles to Eel River 4.5 miles east of Hull Mountain (lat. 39°31'30" N, long. 122°51' W; near SE cor. sec. 3, T 19 N, R 9 W); the stream is south of Horse Ridge. Named on Hull Mountain (1967) and Kneecap Ridge (1967) 7.5' quadrangles.

Horse Creek [MENDOCINO]:

(1) *stream,* flows 2.5 miles to North Fork Eel River 5.5 miles northeast of Spyrock (2) (lat. 39°56' N, long. 123°22'10" W). Named on Mina (1967) and Updegraff Ridge (1967) 7.5' quadrangles.

(2) *stream,* flows 4 miles to Rancheria Creek (2) nearly 5 miles west of Boonville (lat. 39°00'35" N, long. 123°27'30" W; near SE cor. sec. 1, T 13 N, R 15 W). Named on Boonville (1959) and Navarro (1961) 15' quadrangles.

Horse Creek [TRINITY]: *stream,* flows 2.5 miles to Tangle Blue Creek 15 miles north of Trinity Center (lat. 41°13'35" N, long. 122°42'25" W; near E line sec. 19, T 39 N, R 7 W). Named on Bonanza King (1955) 15' quadrangle. Called Fern Cr. on Etna (1934) 30' quadrangle.

Horse Flat [DEL NORTE]: *area,* 8 miles north of Buck Mountain along Hurdygurdy Creek (lat. 41°43'55" N, long. 123°53' W). Named on Cant Hook Mountain (1982) 7.5' quadrangle.

Horse Flat: see **Idlewild** [DEL NORTE].

Horse Glade: see **Horse Glade Camp** [LAKE].

Horse Glade Camp [LAKE]: *locality,* 7.25 miles southwest of Potato Hill (lat. 39°15'55" N, long. 122°43'35" W; sec. 2, T 16 N, R 8 W). Named on Fouts Springs (1968) 7.5' quadrangle. Stonyford (1951) 15' quadrangle shows Horse Glade at the site.

Horse Gulch [HUMBOLDT]: *canyon,* drained by a stream that flows less than 1 mile to McCready Gulch 6.5 miles south-southeast of Arcata (lat. 40°46'35" N, long. 124°03' W; sec. 34, T 5 N, R 1 E). Named on Arcata South (1959) 7.5' quadrangle.

Horsehead Mountain [TRINITY]: *peak,* 8 miles southwest of Black Rock Peak (lat. 40°08'10" N, long. 123°07'30" W; at S line sec. 37, T 27 N, R 11 W). Altitude 5864 feet. Named on Black Rock Mountain (1954) 15' quadrangle. The name is from a horse skull that lay by the trail near the peak (Gudde, 1949, p. 154).

Horsehead Ridge [TRINITY]: *ridge,* north-northwest-trending, 5 miles long, 7 miles west-southwest of Black Rock Mountain (lat. 40°10'15" N, long. 123°08' W); Horsehead Mountain is at the south end of the ridge. Named on Black Rock Mountain (1954) 15' quadrangle.

Horse Heaven Meadows [TRINITY]: *area,* 16 miles northeast of Trinity Center at the head of East Fork Trinity River (lat. 41°09'30" N, long. 122°27'15" W; on W line sec. 16, T 38 N, R 5 W). Named on Dunsmuir (1954) 15' quadrangle.

Horse Linto Creek [HUMBOLDT]: *stream,* flows 17 miles to Trinity River 4.5 miles southeast of Hoopa (lat. 41°00'05" N, long. 123°37'10" W). Named on Ironside Mountain (1951) 15' quadrangle, and on Tish Tang Point (1978) and Trinity Mountain (1979) 7.5' quadrangles. East Fork enters from the southeast 8 miles east-northeast of the settlement of Willow Creek; it is 6.5 miles long and is named on Ironside Mountain (1951) 15' quadrangle, and on Trinity Mountain (1979) 7.5' quadrangle. The name is the Americanized version of the Indian designation of a village located at the mouth of the stream (Kroeber, p. 43).

Horse Mane Creek [TRINITY]: *stream,* flows 3 miles to Browns Creek 13 miles south of Weaverville (lat. 40°32'30" N, long. 122°56' W; at E line sec. 13, T 31 N, R 10 W); the stream heads at Horse Mane Ridge. Named on Weaverville (1950) 15' quadrangle.

Horse Mane Ridge [TRINITY]: *ridge,* north-trending, 2 miles long, 14 miles south of Weaverville (lat. 40°32' N, long. 122°52'45" W). Named on Weaverville (1950) 15' quadrangle.

Horse Mountain [HUMBOLDT]:

(1) *peak,* 7 miles southwest of the settlement of Willow Creek (lat. 40°52'30" N, long. 123°43'55" W; sec. 28, T 6 N, R 4 E). Altitude 4952 feet. Named on Grouse Mountain (1979) 7.5' quadrangle.

(2) *peak,* 4.5 miles north of Point Delgada (lat. 40°05'15" N, long. 124°04'45" W; sec. 24, T 4 S, R 1 E). Named on Shelter Cove (1969) 7.5' quadrangle.

Horse Mountain [LAKE]: *ridge,* west-trending, 1 mile long, 2.5 miles west-southwest of Three Crossings (lat. 39°18'20" N, long. 122°58'10" W; at N line sec. 27, T 17 N, R 10 W). Named on Elk Mountain (1967) 7.5' quadrangle.

Horse Mountain: see **Little Horse Mountain** [LAKE].

Horse Mountain Campground [HUMBOLDT]: *locality,* nearly 6 miles north of Point Delgada (lat. 40°06'20" N, long. 124°03'50" W; near NE cor. sec. 21, T 4 S, R 1 E); the place is west of Horse Mountain Ridge. Named on Shelter Cove (1969) 7.5' quadrangle.

Horse Mountain Creek [HUMBOLDT]:

(1) *stream,* flows 3 miles to East Fork Willow Creek (1) 7 miles south-southwest of the settlement of Willow Creek (lat. 40°50'55" N, long.

123°41'05" W; sec. 2, T 5 N, R 4 E). Named on Grouse Mountain (1979) 7.5' quadrangle.

(2) *stream,* flows 2.5 miles to the sea 3.25 miles north-northwest of Point Delgada (lat. 40°04'05" N, long. 124°04'50" W; sec. 33, T 4 S, R 1 E); the stream heads on Horse Mountain Ridge east of Horse Mountain (2). Named on Shelter Cove (1969) 7.5' quadrangle.

Horse Mountain Ridge [HUMBOLDT]: *ridge,* south-southeast-trending, 4 miles long, 6.5 miles north of Point Delgada (lat. 40°06'45" N, long. 124°04'45" W); Horse Mountain (2) is near the south end of the ridge. Named on Honeydew (1970) and Shelter Cove (1969) 7.5' quadrangles.

Horse Opening: see **Big Horse Opening** [MENDOCINO]; **Little Horse Opening** [MENDOCINO].

Horse Pasture [TRINITY]: *area,* 7.5 miles south-southeast of Forest Glen (lat. 40°16'15" N, long. 123°16' W; at NW cor. sec. 19, T 28 N, R 12 W). Named on Forest Glen (1979) 7.5' quadrangle.

Horse Pasture Creek [HUMBOLDT]: *stream,* flows 2.25 miles to East Branch of South Fork Eel River 10.5 miles southwest of Alderpoint (lat. 40°03'35" N, long. 123°44'05" W; sec. 4, T 5 S, R 4 E). Named on Harris (1969) 7.5' quadrangle.

Horse Pasture Gulch [LAKE]: *canyon,* drained by a stream that flows 1.5 miles to Lake Pillsbury 2 miles northwest of Bear Mountain (lat. 39°25'45" N, long. 122°55'40" W; sec. 12, T 18 N, R 10 W). Named on Lake Pillsbury (1967) 7.5' quadrangle.

Horse Pasture Ridge [MENDOCINO]: *ridge,* generally west-northwest-trending, 4.5 miles long, 6 miles east of Eden Valley (lat. 39°38'30" N, long. 123°04'45" W). Named on Thatcher Ridge (1967) 7.5' quadrangle.

Horse Prairie [HUMBOLDT]: *area,* 1.5 miles south of Redcrest (lat. 40°22'35" N, long. 123°57'15" W; sec. 16, T 1 S, R 2 E). Named on Redcrest (1969) and Weott (1969) 7.5' quadrangles.

Horse Ranch Lake [TRINITY]: *lake,* 850 feet long, 11.5 miles south of Kettenpom (lat. 39°59'50" N, long. 123°25'15" W; near W line sec. 29, T 5 S, R 7 E). Named on Updegraff Ridge (1967) 7.5' quadrangle.

Horse Ranch Peak [TRINITY]: *peak,* 11 miles south-southeast of Kettenpom (lat. 40°00'10" N, long. 123°25'05" W; on S line sec. 20, T 5 S, R 7 E). Altitude 4156 feet. Named on Lake Mountain (1967) 7.5' quadrangle.

Horse Range Creek [HUMBOLDT]: *stream,* flows 4 miles to Cedar Creek (2) 5 miles northeast of the settlement of Willow Creek (lat. 40°59'35" N, long. 123°33'40" W). Named on Salyer (1979) 7.5' quadrangle.

Horse Ridge [HUMBOLDT]: *ridge,* southwest-trending, less than 1 mile long, 15 miles south-southwest of Scotia (lat. 40°16'15" N, long. 124°10" W; sec. 27, T 2 S, R 1 W). Named on Buckeye Mountain (1970) 7.5' quadrangle.

Horse Ridge [LAKE]: *ridge,* east-northeast-trending, 2.5 miles long, 2.5 miles east of Hull Mountain (lat. 39°31'25" N, long. 122°53'10" W). Named on Hull Mountain (1967) and Kneecap Ridge (1967) 7.5' quadrangles.

Horse Ridge [TRINITY]:

(1) *ridge,* south-southwest-trending, 2 miles long, 16 miles south-southwest of Black Rock Mountain (lat. 40°01'15" N, long. 123°10'45" W). Named on Black Rock Mountain (1954) 15' quadrangle.

(2) *ridge,* generally south-trending, 3.5 miles long, 10 miles east-northeast of Kettenpom (lat. 40°14' N, long. 123°16'30" W). Named on Forest Glen (1979) and Shannon Butte (1967) 7.5' quadrangles.

Horse Rock [LAKE]: *peak,* 14 miles north of Clearlake Oaks on Lake-Colusa County line (lat. 39°13'25" N, long. 122°40'15" W). Named on Clearlake Oaks (1960) 15' quadrangle.

Horseshoe Bend [LAKE]: *embayment,* 8.5 miles east-southeast of Lakeport along Clear Lake (lat. 39°00'20" N, long. 122°45'45" W; sec. 4, 5, T 13 N, R 8 W). Named on Lucerne (1958) 7.5' quadrangle.

Horseshoe Bend [MENDOCINO]: *bend,* 6.5 miles north of Branscomb along South Fork Eel River (lat. 39°45' N, long. 123°38'15" W; at SW cor. sec. 16, T 22 N, R 16 W). Named on Leggett (1969) and Lincoln Ridge (1966) 7.5' quadrangles. Branscomb (1921) 15' quadrangle has the form "Horse Shoe Bend" for the name.

Horseshoe Lake [TRINITY]: *lake,* 800 feet long, 18 miles north of Weaverville (lat. 40°59'35" N, long. 122°54'35" W; sec. 9 T 36 N, R 9 W). Named on Trinity Dam (1950) 15' quadrangle.

Horsetail Gulch [MENDOCINO]: *canyon,* drained by a stream that flows 1.5 miles to Middle Fork Ten Mile River 8 miles south of Branscomb (lat. 39°32'40" N, long. 123°39'10" W). Named on Dutchmans Knoll (1966) 7.5' quadrangle.

Horsethief Canyon [MENDOCINO]: *canyon,* drained by a stream that heads in Sonoma County and flows 1.5 miles to Rockpile Creek 10 miles south-southwest of Ornbaun Valley in Mendocino County (lat. 38°47'05" N, long. 123°22'45" W; sec. 24, T 11 N, R 14 W). Named on Ornbaun Valley (1960) 15' quadrangle.

Horsethief Creek [MENDOCINO]: *stream,* flows less than 1 mile to Daugherty Creek 12.5 miles north of Boonville (lat. 39°11'20" N, long. 123°25'10" W; near E line sec. 5, T 15 N, R 14 W); the stream heads near Horsethief Opening. Named on Boonville (1959) 15' quadrangle.

Horsethief Opening [MENDOCINO]: *area,* 13 miles north of Boonville (lat. 39°11'35" N, long. 123°24'35" W; near SE cor. sec. 33, T 16 N, R 14 W). Named on Boonville (1959) 15' quadrangle.

Horse Trail Ridge [HUMBOLDT]: *ridge,* northwest- to west-northwest-trending, 6 miles long, 11 miles east-southeast of Weitchpec (lat. 41°08'40" N, long. 123°30'15" W). Named on Hopkins Butte (1979), Salmon Mountain (1978), and Trinity Mountain (1979) 7.5' quadrangles.

Hosea Creek [MENDOCINO]: *stream,* flows nearly 3 miles to Middle Fork Eel River 2 miles east-southeast of Dos Rios (lat. 39°42'20" N, long. 123°19'05" W). Named on Dos Rios (1967) 7.5' quadrangle.

Hosea Ridge [MENDOCINO]: *ridge,* 2.5 miles east of Dos Rios (lat. 39°43'25" N, long. 123°18'20" W); the ridge is east of Hosea Creek. Named on Dos Rios (1967) 7.5' quadrangle.

Hospital Creek [HUMBOLDT]: *stream,* flows 4 miles to Trinity River at Hoopa (lat. 41°02'45" N, long. 123°40'15" W; sec. 25, T 8 N, R 4 E). Named on Hoopa (1979) 7.5' quadrangle.

Hospital Creek [LAKE]: *stream,* flows 2.25 miles to North Fork Cache Creek 12 miles north of Clearlake Oaks (lat. 39°11'30" N, long. 122°41'10" W). Named on Clearlake Oaks (1960) 15' quadrangle.

Hospital Mountain [HUMBOLDT]: *peak,* 2.5 miles south-southwest of Hoopa (lat. 41°01' N, long. 123°42'05" W; sec. 3, T 7 N, R 4 E); the peak is west of the upper reaches of Hospital Creek. Altitude 3478 feet. Named on Hoopa (1979) 7.5' quadrangle.

Hospital Ridge [HUMBOLDT]: *ridge,* north- to northeast-trending, 2 miles long, 1.25 miles southwest of Hoopa (lat. 41°02' N, long. 123°41'30" W; sec. 26, 35, T 8 N, R 4 E); the ridge is west of Hospital Creek. Named on Hoopa (1979) 7.5' quadrangle.

Hostler Creek [HUMBOLDT]: *stream,* flows 7.5 miles to Trinity River 2 miles north-northwest of Hoopa (lat. 41°04'30" N, long. 123°41'15" W; sec. 14, T 8 N, R 4 E). Named on Hoopa (1979) and Tish Tang Point (1978) 7.5' quadrangles.

Hostler Point [HUMBOLDT]: *relief feature,* 3 miles north of Hoopa (lat. 41°05'30" N, long. 123°39'50" W; sec. 12, T 8 N, R 4 E); the feature is north of Hostler Creek. Named on Hoopa (1979) 7.5' quadrangle.

Hostler Ridge [HUMBOLDT]: *ridge,* generally west-trending, 4 miles long, 4.5 miles east-northeast of Hoopa (lat. 41°04' N, long. 123°35'45" W); the ridge is south of Hostler Creek. Named on Tish Tang Point (1978) 7.5' quadrangle.

Hotchkiss Bar [TRINITY]: *locality,* 15 miles northeast of Weaverville along Trinity River (lat. 40°51'55" N, long. 122°43'15" W; near N line sec. 25, T 35 N, R 8 W). Named on Schell Mountain (1950) 15' quadrangle.

Hotel Gulch [MENDOCINO]: *canyon,* drained by a stream that flows 2 miles to Usal Creek 10 miles south of Piercy (lat. 39°50'05" N, long. 123°50'30" W; sec. 22, T 23 N, R 18 W). Named on Hales Grove (1970) 7.5' quadrangle.

Hot Sigler Springs: see **Seigler Springs** [LAKE].

Houdd Gibson Camp: see **Castle Rock Springs** [LAKE].

Hough Ridge [LAKE]: *ridge,* generally east-trending, 4 miles long, 10 miles north-northeast of Clearlake Oaks (lat. 39°09'05" N, long. 122°35'35" W); the ridge is south of Hough Springs. Named on Clearlake Oaks (1960) 15' quadrangle.

Hough's Mineral Springs: see **Hough Springs** [LAKE].

Hough Springs [LAKE]: *locality,* 10 miles north-northeast of Clearlake Oaks along North Fork Cache Creek (lat. 39°09'40" N, long. 122°36'45" W; sec. 10, T 15 N, R 7 W). Named on Clearlake Oaks (1960) 15' quadrangle. Postal authorities established Hough Springs post office in 1882, discontinued it in 1886, reestablished it in 1887, and discontinued it in 1892 (Frickstad, p. 64). A hotel and cottages at the site furnished accommodations for 100 people in 1910 (Waring, p. 197). Anderson (p. 180) called the place Hough's Mineral Springs.

Houghton Creek [LAKE]: *stream,* flows 1.5 miles to Kelsey Creek less than 1 mile north-northwest of Whispering Pines (lat. 38°49'25" N, long. 122°43'10" W; at W line sec. 11, T 11 N, R 8 W). Named on Whispering Pines (1958) 7.5' quadrangle.

Howard Creek [MENDOCINO]:

(1) *stream,* flows 5 miles to Middle Fork Eel River 15 miles east-northeast of Covelo (lat. 39°54'25" N, long. 123°00'50" W; sec. 30, T 24 N, R 10 W). Named on Buck Rock (1967) and Leech Lake Mountain (1966) 7.5' quadrangles.

(2) *stream,* flows 3.5 miles to the sea 3 miles north of Westport (lat. 39°40'40" N, long. 123°47'25" W; sec. 18, T 21 N, R 17 W). Named on Lincoln Ridge (1966) and Westport (1966) 7.5' quadrangles.

(3) *stream,* flows 5.25 miles to Russian River 3 miles north-northeast of Ukiah (lat. 39°10'45" N, long. 123°11'50" W). Named on Cow Mountain (1958) and Ukiah (1958) 7.5' quadrangles.

Howard Creek: see **Little Howard Creek** [MENDOCINO].

Howard Lake [MENDOCINO]:

(1) *lake,* 1450 feet long, 3 miles north-northwest of Anthony Peak (lat. 39°52'50" N, long. 122°31'50" W; sec. 5, T 23 N, R 10 W); the lake is along a branch of Howard Creek (1). Named on Buck Rock (1967) 7.5' quadrangle.

(2) *lake,* 200 feet long, 4 miles southeast of Dos Rios (lat. 39°40'50" N, long. 123°17'40" W; sec. 15, T 21 N, R 13 W). Named on Dos Rios (1967)

7.5' quadrangle.

Howard Mill [LAKE]: *locality,* 1.25 miles southwest of present Three Crossings (lat. 39°18'15" N, long. 122°56'20" W; near NW cor. sec. 25, T 17 N, R 10 W). Named on Lake Pillsbury (1951) 15' quadrangle. Elk Mountain (1967) 7.5' quadrangle shows Howard Mill Station near the site.

Howard Peak [LAKE]: *peak,* 3.5 miles east of Kelseyville on Mount Konocti (lat. 38°58'25" N, long. 122°46'10" W; sec. 17, T 13 N, R 8 W). Altitude 4286 feet. Named on Kelseyville (1959) 7.5' quadrangle. United States Board on Geographic Names (1962b, p . 18) rejected the name "Middle Peak" for the feature.

Howard's Bluff: see **Red Bluff** [HUMBOLDT].

Howard Springs [LAKE]: *locality,* 3.5 miles north-northeast of Whispering Pines (lat. 38°51'30" N, long. 122°40'25" W; sec. 30, T 12 N, R 7 W). Named on Whispering Pines (1958) 7.5' quadrangle. The name commemorates C.W. Howard, who opened the springs to the public in 1877 (Palmer, p. 153).

Howe Creek [HUMBOLDT]: *stream,* flows 5 miles to Eel River about 6 miles south of Fortuna (lat. 40°30'50" N, long. 124°09'25" W; near W line sec. 35, T 2 N, R 1 W). Named on Fortuna (1959) and Taylor Peak (1969) 7.5' quadrangles.

Howell Creek [MENDOCINO]: *stream,* flows 5.5 miles to Russian River 4 miles south-southeast of Ukiah (lat. 39°05'50" N, long. 123°10'30" W). Named on Elledge Peak (1958) 7.5' quadrangle.

Hower [HUMBOLDT]: *locality,* 10 miles west of Hoopa (present Hupa) (lat. 41°01'55" N, long. 123°52' W). Named on Hoopa (1935) 30' quadrangle.

Howes Camp [LAKE]: *locality,* 9 miles east-southeast of the town of Upper Lake (lat. 39°07'40" N, long. 122°45'15" W; near S line sec. 21, T 15 N, R 8 W). Named on Bartlett Mountain (1958) 7.5' quadrangle.

Howland Hill [DEL NORTE]: *peak,* 3.5 miles east of Crescent City (lat. 41°45'20" N, long. 124°07'50" W; sec. 25, T 16 N, R 1 W). Altitude 690 feet. Named on Crescent City (1966) 7.5' quadrangle.

Howland Summit [DEL NORTE]: *pass,* 3.25 miles east of Crescent City (lat. 41°45'40" N, long. 124°08'20" W; near SE cor. sec. 23, T 16 N, R 1 W); the pass is 0.5 mile northwest of Howland Hill. Named on Crescent City (1966) 7.5' quadrangle.

Hoxie Crossing [TRINITY]: *locality,* 14 miles south-southwest of Black Rock Mountain (lat. 40°01' N, long. 123°06'45" W; sec. 17, T 25 N, R 11 W). Named on Black Rock Mountain (1954) 15' quadrangle.

Hubbard Prairie [HUMBOLDT]: *area,* 6.25 miles south-southeast of Scotia (lat. 40°23'50" N, long. 124°02'55" W). Named on Scotia (1970) 7.5' quadrangle.

Huckleberry Campground [HUMBOLDT]: *locality,* 5.25 miles south of Garberville (lat. 40°01'20" N, long. 123°47'40" W; on E line sec. 14, T 5 S, R 3 E). Named on Garberville (1970) 7.5' quadrangle.

Huckleberry Creek [MENDOCINO]: *stream,* flows 1.5 miles to Hollow Tree Creek 8 miles northwest of Branscomb (lat. 39°44'20" N, long. 123°43'05" W; near S line sec. 23, T 22 N, R 17 W). Named on Lincoln Ridge (1966) 7.5' quadrangle.

Huckleberry Pass [MENDOCINO]: *pass,* 8.5 miles northwest of Branscomb (lat. 39°43'55" N, long. 123°44'35" W; near W line sec. 27, T 22 N, R 17 W); the pass is near the head of Huckleberry Creek. Named on Lincoln Ridge (1966) 7.5' quadrangle.

Hudson Creek [TRINITY]: *stream,* flows 1 mile to Trinity River 2.5 miles northwest of Salyer (lat. 40°55'05" N, long. 123°36'45" W; at E line sec. 4, T 6 N, R 5 E). Named on Salyer (1979) 7.5' quadrangle.

Huestis Rock [HUMBOLDT]: *peak,* 6 miles west-northwest of Alderpoint (lat. 40°12'20" N, long. 123°43' W; sec. 15, T 3 S, R 4 E). Named on Fort Seward (1969) 7.5' quadrangle. The name commemorates Joel Huestis, who in 1850 brought the first wagon overland into Humboldt County (Turner, p. 112).

Hull Creek [MENDOCINO]: *stream,* flows 3.5 miles to Eel River 3.5 miles north-northeast of Hull Mountain (lat. 39°03'50" N, long. 122°54'05" W; near NE cor. sec. 25, T 20 N, R 10 W). Named on Hull Mountain (1967) 7.5' quadrangle.

Hull Mountain [LAKE-MENDOCINO]: *peak,* 32 miles north of Lakeport on Lake-Mendocino County line (lat. 39°31'20" N, long. 122°56'10" W; near NW cor. sec. 11, T 19 N, R 10 W). Altitude 6873 feet. Named on Hull Mountain (1967) 7.5' quadrangle, which shows Hull's grave situated 0.5 mile northwest of the peak. James Hull built a hunting cabin near the peak in 1856 and died there of wounds inflicted by a grizzly bear (Carranco and Beard, p. 161).

Hulls Creek [MENDOCINO-TRINITY]: *stream,* heads in Mendocino County and flows 16 miles to North Fork Eel River 15 miles southeast of Kettenpom in Trinity County (lat. 40°00'15" N, long. 123°16'20" W). Named on Bluenose Ridge (1967), Long Ridge (1967), and Mina (1967) 7.5' quadrangles.

Hulls Valley [MENDOCINO]: *valley,* 10 miles east of Spyrock (2) along a south branch of Hulls Creek (lat. 39°53'20" N, long. 123°15'20" W). Named on Bluenose Ridge (1967) and Mina (1967) 7.5' quadrangles.

Hullville [LAKE]: *village,* 3 miles east-southeast of Bear Mountain near the confluence of Eel River and Salmon Creek in Gravelly Valley (lat. 39°25' N, long. 122°57' W). Named on Hullville (1922) 15' quadrangle. Water of Lake Pillsbury now covers the site. Postal authorities established Gravelly Valley post office in 1874, changed the name to Hullville in 1889, and discontinued it in 1935 (Frickstad, p. 63, 64). California Mining Bureau's (1909c) map shows a place called Sanhedrin located west of Hullville near Lake-Mendocino County line. Postal authorities established Sanhedrin post office 16 miles northeast of Potter Valley post office in 1896 and discontinued it in 1907, when they moved the service to Hullville (Salley, p. 194).

Humboldt: see **Fort Humboldt**, under **Eureka** [HUMBOLDT].

Humboldt Bay [HUMBOLDT]: *bay,* 10 miles long, the entrance is 4.5 miles southwest of downtown Eureka (lat. 40°45'30" N, long. 124°13'45" W). Named on Cannibal Island (1959), Eureka (1958), and Fields Landing (1959) 7.5' quadrangles. Wagner (p. 459) believed that present Humboldt Bay probably is the Bahia Grande Cerca del Cabo, or Baia del Cabo of early Spanish maps. In 1806 Captain Johathan Winship, an American employee of Russian-American Fur Company, brought his ship, the *O'Cain,* into the bay, which he called Bay of the Indians for numerous Indian villages along the shore; Winship gave the name "Rezanov" to the entrance of the bay to honor Count Rezanov (Hoover, Rensch, and Rensch, p. 101). Josiah Gregg and his companions found the bay in 1849 and called it Trinity Bay, confusing it with present Trinidad Bay; then in 1850 Douglass Ottinger, commander of the trading ship *Laura Virginia,* named the feature for Alexander von Humboldt (Hanna, p. 143). Members of the expedition under Samuel Brannan in the ship *General Morgan* called the feature Mendocino Bay in 1850 (Coy, 1929, p. 48).

Humboldt Bluff: see **Red Bluff** [HUMBOLDT].

Humboldt City: see **Bucksport** [HUMBOLDT].

Humboldt Creek [HUMBOLDT]: *stream,* flows 1 mile to the sea nearly 2 miles north-northwest of Point Delgada (lat. 40°02'45" N, long. 124°04'45" W; near N line sec. 9, T 5 S, R 1 E). Named on Shelter Cove (1969) 7.5' quadrangle.

Humboldt Flat [DEL NORTE]: *area,* 2 miles southwest of Gasquet (lat. 41°49'30" N, long. 123°59'35" W; sec. 31, T 17 N, R 2 E). Named on Gasquet (1981) 7.5' quadrangle.

Humboldt Hill [HUMBOLDT]: *ridge,* northwest-tending, 1.5 miles long, 1.5 miles southeast of Fields Landing (lat. 40°42'35" N, long. 124°11'45" W). Named on Fields Landing (1959) 7.5' quadrangle.

Humboldt Point: see **Buhne Point** [HUMBOLDT].

Humbug Creek [HUMBOLDT]: *stream,* flows 1.5 miles to Mad River 6.5 miles east-northeast of Lone Star Junction (lat. 40°39'10" N, long. 123°45'10" W). Named on Mad River Buttes (1977) 7.5' quadrangle.

Hummingbird Creek [LAKE]: *stream,* flows 3.25 miles to Eel River 5 miles west-southwest of Crockett Peak (lat. 39°24'35" N, long. 122°52' W). Named on Crockett Peak (1967) 7.5' quadrangle.

Hummingbird Creek [MENDOCINO]: *stream,* flows 1 mile to Sonoma County nearly 7 miles southeast of Monument Peak (lat. 38°51' N, long. 122°51'30" W; at S line sec. 27, T 12 N, R 9 W). Named on The Geysers (1959) 7.5' quadrangle.

Humphrey Creek [HUMBOLDT]: *stream,* flows 2 miles to Middle Fork Yager Creek 3.25 miles south of Lone Star Junction (lat. 40°34'50" N, long. 123°53'05" W; sec. 6, T 2 N, R 3 E). Named on Owl Creek (1979) and Yager Junction (1979) 7.5' quadrangles.

Hump Rock [DEL NORTE]: *rock,* 5.25 miles west-northwest of Crescent City, and 1.25 miles off Point Saint George (lat. 41°46'55" N, long. 124°18' W). Named on Eureka (1958) 7.5' quadrangle.

Humstead Ridge [HUMBOLDT]: *ridge,* generally west-trending, 1.25 miles long, 2 miles west-northwest of Yager Junction (lat. 40°33'25" N, long. 123°51'20" W; sec. 16, 17, T 2 N, R 3 E). Named on Yager Junction (1979) 7.5' quadrangle.

Hundred Acre Field [HUMBOLDT]: *area,* 9 miles south of Coyote Peak (lat. 41°00'30" N, long. 123°49'25" W; sec. 10, T 7 N, R 3 E). Named on Hupa Mountain (1982) 7.5' quadrangle.

Hungry Hollow [HUMBOLDT]: *canyon,* less than 1 mile long, 4 miles east of Korbel (lat. 40°52' N, long. 123°53' W; sec. 31, T 6 N, R 3 E). Named on Korbel (1979) 7.5' quadrangle.

Hungry Hollow Creek [MENDOCINO]: *stream,* flows 1.5 miles to Mill Creek (9) 9 miles north-northwest of Boonville (lat. 39°07'35" N, long. 123°26'55" W; sec. 30, T 15 N, R 14 W). Named on Boonville (1959) 15' quadrangle.

Hunter: see **Big Hunter** [TRINITY].

Hunter Camp [TRINITY]: *locality,* 11 miles south of Black Rock Mountain (lat. 40°02'45" N, long. 123°00'35" W; sec. 6, T 25 N, R 10 W). Named on Black Rock Mountain (1954) 15' quadrangle.

Hunter Creek [DEL NORTE]: *stream,* flows 7 miles to Klamath River 1 mile east of the mouth of that river (lat. 41°32'50" N, long. 124°03'40" W). Named on Requa (1966) 7.5' quadrangle. Called Hunters C. on Goddard's (1857) map. West Fork enters 4 miles upstream from the mouth of the main creek; it is nearly 7 miles long and is named on Childs Hill (1966) and Requa (1966) 7.5' quadrangles. West Fork is called Hunter

Creek on Klamath (1952) 15' quadrangle.

Hunter Point [LAKE]: *peak,* 4 miles northwest of the town of Upper Lake (lat. 39°12'45" N, long. 122°57'10" W; sec. 27, T 16 N, R 10 W). Altitude 2964 feet. Named on Upper Lake (1958) 7.5' quadrangle.

Hunter Rock [DEL NORTE]: *island,* 500 feet long, nearly 4 miles northwest of the town of Smith River (lat. 41°57'55" N, long. 124°12'40" W). Named on Smith River (1966) 7.5' quadrangle.

Hunters Camp [MENDOCINO]: *locality,* 2.5 miles south-southwest of Dos Rios (lat. 39°41'05" N, long. 123°22'15" W; sec. 12, T 21 N, R 14 W). Named on Dos Rios (1967) 7.5' quadrangle.

Hunters Camp [TRINITY]:
(1) *locality,* 6.5 miles south-southeast of Cecilville, which is in Siskiyou County (lat. 41°03'25" N, long. 123°04'50" W). Named on Thompson Peak (1979) 7.5' quadrangle.
(2) *locality,* 14 miles north-northwest of Helena (lat. 40°58'10" N, long. 123°12'20" W). Named on Helena (1951) 15' quadrangle.

Hunting Creek [LAKE]: *stream,* heads in Morgan Valley and flows 12.5 miles to Putah Creek 4.5 miles south of Jericho Valley (lat. 38°46'05" N, long. 122°24'55" W; near S line sec. 28, T 11 N, R 5 W). Named on Jericho Valley (1958) and Knoxville (1958) 7.5' quadrangles. The stream forms part of Lake-Yolo County line.

Hupa: see **Hoopa** [HUMBOLDT].

Hupa Mountain [HUMBOLDT]: *peak,* 5.25 miles south-southeast of Coyote Peak on Pine Ridge (lat. 41°04'15" N, long. 123°48'15" W). Altitude 4092 feet. Named on Hupa Mountain (1982) 7.5' quadrangle. Called Hoopa Mountain on Hoopa (1935) 15' quadrangle. United States Board on Geographic Names (1933, p. 380) rejected the forms "Hoopa," "Hoopah," "Hopah," "Hupâ," "Hupô," "Noh-tin-oah," and "Up-pa" for the name.

Hupa Valley: see **Hoopa Valley** [HUMBOLDT].

Hurdygurdy Butte [DEL NORTE]: *peak,* 15 miles east-southeast of Gasquet (lat. 41°46'45" N, long. 123°45'45" W); the peak is south of the head of Hurdygurdy Creek. Named on Hurdygurdy Butte (1982) 7.5' quadrangle.

Hurdygurdy Creek [DEL NORTE]: *stream,* flows 15 miles to South Fork Smith River 5.25 miles north-northwest of Buck Mountain (lat. 41°41'05" N, long. 123°54'50" W). Named on Cant Hook Mountain (1982), Hurdygurdy Butte (1982), and Ship Mountain (1982) 7.5' quadrangles. Wells' (1946) map shows a place called Vans Camp located near the head of an unnamed branch of Hurdygurdy Creek (near NW cor. sec. 30, T 16 N, R 3 E).

Hutsinpillar Creek [DEL NORTE]: *stream,* flows 1 mile to Smith River 3.5 miles south-southeast of the town of Smith River (lat. 41°52'45" N, long. 124°07'55" W; sec. 12, T 17 N, R 1 W). Named on High Divide (1966) and Smith River (1966) 7.5' quadrangles.

Hyampom [TRINITY]: *village,* 28 miles west-southwest of Weaverville along South Fork Trinity River (lat. 40°37' N, long. 123°26'55" W; at and near N line sec. 25, T 3 N, R 6 E); the village is near the southeast end of Hyampom Valley. Named on Hyampom (1951) 15' quadrangle. Postal authorities established Hyampom post office in 1890 and moved it 1 mile east in 1906 (Salley, p. 102). The name is of Indian origin (Kroeber, p. 43).

Hyampom Creek [TRINITY]: *stream,* flows about 3 miles to Corral Creek (1) 6.5 miles northeast of Hyampom (lat. 40°41'30" N, long. 123°22'15" W; sec. 27, T 4 N, R 7 E). Named on Hyampom (1951) 15' quadrangle.

Hyampom Mountain [TRINITY]: *ridge,* southeast-trending, 2 miles long, 6.5 miles north-northeast of Hyampom (lat. 40°42'05" N, long. 123°24' W); the ridge is southwest of Hyampom Creek. Named on Hyampom (1951) 15' quadrangle.

Hyampom Valley [TRINITY]: *valley,* along South Fork Trinity River at and northwest of Hyampom (lat. 40°37'30" N, long. 123°28'15" W). Named on Hyampom (1951) 15' quadrangle.

Hydesville [HUMBOLDT]: *town,* 4.5 miles southeast of Fortuna (lat. 40°32'50" N, long. 124°05'50" W; around NW cor. sec. 20, T 2 N, R 1 E). Named on Hydesville (1979) 7.5' quadrangle. Postal authorities established Hydesville post office in 1861 (Frickstad, p. 44). The name commemorates John Hyde, who donated the land for the community (Bledsoe, p. 102).

— I —

Iaqua: see **Kneeland** [HUMBOLDT].

Iaqua Buttes [HUMBOLDT]: *ridge,* northwest-trending, 1.5 miles long, 2.5 miles north of Lone Star Junction (lat. 40°41'10" N, long. 123°52'55" W; mainly in sec. 31, T 4 N, R 3 E). Named on Iaqua Buttes (1979) and Mad River Buttes (1977) 7.5' quadrangles. On Iaqua Buttes (1950) 15' quadrangle, the name apples to both present Iaqua Buttes and present Gordon Ridge, as well as to the ridge connecting these two features. The name seem to be from a word used by Indians of the region as a greeting and as a farewell (Kroeber, p. 43).

Iaqua Creek [HUMBOLDT]: *stream,* flows 0.5 mile to North Fork Yager Creek 1.5 miles south-southeast of Lone Star Junction (lat. 40°36'55" N, long. 123°51'50" W; sec. 29, T 3 N, R 3 E). Named on Yager Junction (1979) 7.5' quadrangle.

Iaqua Medicinal Spring: see **Eureka** [HUMBOLDT].

Iaqua Mineral Water Spring: see **Eureka** [HUMBOLDT].

Icebox Creek [TRINITY]: *stream,* flows 1 mile to Trinity River 3 miles east-southeast of Salyer (lat. 40°52'55" N, long. 123°31'45" W). Named on Hennessy Peak (1979) 7.5' quadrangle.

Idaho Bar [TRINITY]: *locality,* 1 mile southeast of Helena along Trinity River (lat. 40°45'55" N, long. 123°06'45" W; near NE cor. sec. 33, T 34 N, R 11 W). Named on Helena (1951) 15' quadrangle.

Idlewild [DEL NORTE]: *locality,* 11 miles east-northeast of Gasquet along Middle Fork Smith River (lat. 41°53'55" N, long. 123°46'10" W). Named on Shelly Creek Ridge (1982) 7.5' quadrangle. Called Horse Flat on Gasquet (1951) 15' quadrangle, but United States Board on Geographic Names (1979, p. 4) rejected this name for the place. Gasquet (1945) 15' quadrangle shows Idlewild Resort at the site. United States Board on Geographic Names (1983a, p. 4) approved the name "Idlewild Creek" for a stream that heads at Wounded Knee Mountain and flows 2.2 miles to Middle Fork Smith River just south of Idlewild (lat. 41°53'52" N, long. 123°46'17" W); the name, given in the 1920's, is from Idlewild Resort, which was located at the mouth of the stream. The Board at the same time (p. 5) approved the name "Stephens Creek" for another stream that heads at Wounded Knee Mountain and flows 2.2 miles to Idlewild Creek 0.6 mile southeast of Idlewild (lat. 41°53'50" N, long. 123°45'53" W); the name honors Garee Stephens, who founded the conservation group called Friends of Del Norte County, and who was involved in the protection of the Smith River watershed.

Idlewild Creek: see **Idlewild** [DEL NORTE].

Idlewild Resort: see **Idlewild** [DEL NORTE].

Ikes Creek [HUMBOLDT]: *stream,* flows 2.5 miles to Klamath River 6 miles north-northwest of Orleans Mountain (lat. 41°21'45" N, long. 123°29'30" W). Named on Orleans Mountain (1974) 7.5' quadrangle. The name is for an Indian called Little Ike (Gudde, 1949, p. 159).

Illinois River, East Fork [DEL NORTE]: *stream,* flows 8.5 miles to the State of Oregon 8.5 miles north-northeast of Broken Rib Mountain (lat. 42°00' N, long. 123°37'20" W; sec. 34, T 19 N, R 5 E). Named on Broken Rib Mountain (1982) and Polar Bear Mountain (1982) 7.5' quadrangles. Illinois River in the State of Oregon got its name after the Althouse brothers from Peoria, Illinois, discovered gold along the stream (McArthur, p. 378-379).

Illinois River, West Fork [DEL NORTE]: *stream,* flows 1.5 miles to the State of Oregon 14 miles northeast of Gasquet (lat. 41°59'50" N, long. 123°46'25" W). Named on Shelly Creek Ridge (1982) 7.5' quadrangle.

Impassable Rock [MENDOCINO]: *relief feature,* 7.25 miles south-southeast of Eden Valley (lat. 39°32'10" N, long. 123°07'15" W; near N line sec. 6, T 19 N, R 11 W). Named on Sanhedrin Mountain (1966) 7.5' quadrangle.

Impassable Rocks [MENDOCINO]: *relief feature,* 6.25 miles south of Willits (lat. 39°19'10" N, long. 123°22'05" W; near NE cor. sec. 23, T 17 N, R 14 W). Named on Willits (1961) 15' quadrangle.

Indeek: see **Indian Creek** [TRINITY] (3).

Indian Bar [DEL NORTE]: *locality,* 4.5 miles north of Buck Mountain along South Fork Smith River (lat. 41°41' N, long. 123°53' W). Named on Cant Hook Mountain (1982) 7.5' quadrangle.

Indian Bar: see **Blackhawk Bar** [DEL NORTE].

Indian Beach [LAKE]: *beach,* 2.5 miles west of Clearlake Oaks along Clear Lake (lat. 39°01'25" N, long. 122°43'25" W; near E line sec. 34, T 14 N, R 8 W). Named on Clearlake Oaks (1958) 7.5' quadrangle.

Indian Butte [HUMBOLDT]: *peak,* 6.5 miles southwest of the settlement of Willow Creek (lat. 40°53'15" N, long. 123°43'55" W; sec. 21, T 6 N, R 4 E). Altitude 4510 feet. Named on Willow Creek (1979) 7.5' quadrangle.

Indian Creek [HUMBOLDT]:
(1) *stream,* flows 2.5 miles to Blue Creek 7.25 miles north-northeast of Johnsons (lat. 41°27'05" N, long. 123°49'50" W). Named on Blue Creek Mountain (1982) 7.5' quadrangle.
(2) *stream,* flows 1.5 miles to Klamath River 4 miles northeast of Weitchpec (lat. 41°13'30" N, long. 123°38'45" W). Named on Hopkins Butte (1979) and Weitchpec (1979) 7.5' quadrangles.
(3) *stream,* flows nearly 3 miles to join Freese Creek and form North Fork Yager Creek 4 miles north-northeast of Yager Junction (lat. 40°36'10" N, long. 123°47'40" W; near NW cor. sec. 36, T 3 N, R 3 E). Named on Yager Junction (1979) 7.5' quadrangle.
(4) *stream,* flows 2.25 miles to Mattole River 3.5 miles southeast of Petrolia (lat. 40°17'10" N, long. 124°14'50" W; sec. 24, T 2 S, R 2 W). Named on Petrolia (1969) 7.5' quadrangle.

Indian Creek [LAKE]: *stream,* flows 5.5 miles to North Fork Cache Creek 7 miles north-northeast of the town of Lower Lake (lat. 38°59'50" N, long. 122°33' W). Named on Clearlake Oaks (1960) 15' quadrangle, and on Lower Lake (1958) 7.5' quadrangle.

Indian Creek [MENDOCINO]:
(1) *stream,* flows 12.5 miles to Navarro River 5 miles northeast of Boonville in Anderson Valley (lat. 39°03'30" N, long. 123°26'30" W; sec. 19, T 14

N, R 14 W). Named on Boonville (1959) 15' quadrangle. North Fork enters the main stream from the north 4.5 miles north of Boonville and is 6.5 miles long. West Branch enters the main stream from the northwest 6 miles north-northwest of Boonville and is 2.25 miles long. West Branch of North Fork enters North Fork from the north 7 miles north of Boonville and is 1.5 miles long. The fork and branches are named on Boonville (1959) 15' quadrangle.

(2) *stream*, flows 13 miles to South Fork Eel River 1 mile north-northwest of Piercy (lat. 39°58'35" N, long. 123°48'15" W; sec. 35, T 5 S, R 3 E). Named on Bear Harbor (1969) and Piercy (1969) 7.5' quadrangles. On Kenny (1920) 15' quadrangle, the name Indian Creek applies to present Moody Creek above the present confluence of Indian Creek and Moody Creek.

(3) *stream*, flows nearly 4 miles to Eel River 7.25 miles east-northeast of Longvale (lat. 39°36'05" N, long. 123°18'20" W; sec. 9, T 20 N, R 13 W). Named on Brushy Mountain (1966) and Willis Ridge (1966) 7.5' quadrangles. Called Brushy Creek on Laytonville (1951) 15' quadrangle, where present Brushy Creek is called Indian Creek.

Indian Creek [TRINITY]:

(1) *stream*, flows 3 miles to East Fork of North Fork Trinity River 6.5 miles north of Helena (lat. 40°52' N, long. 123°07'45" W; sec. 20, T 35 N, R 11 W). Named on Helena (1951) 15' quadrangle.

(2) *stream*, flows 13 miles to Trinity River 5.5 miles south-southeast of Weaverville (lat. 40°39'30" N, long. 122°54'45" W; sec. 5, T 32 N, R 9 W). Named on Weaverville (1950) 15' quadrangle, and on Shasta Bally (1978) 7.5' quadrangle. South Fork enters from the southeast 11 miles south-southeast of Weaverville; it is 4 miles long and is named on Weaverville (1950) 15' quadrangle.

(3) *locality*, about 10 miles southeast of Weaverville along Indian Creek (2) (lat. 40°36' N, long. 122°51' W; sec. 26, T 32 N, R 9 W). Named on Weaverville (1913) 30' quadrangle. Called Indian Creek Town on Red Bluff (1894) 1° quadrangle. The post office at the place was called Indeek—a contraction of the name "Indian Creek" (Jones, p. 302). Postal authorities established Indeek post office in 1882 and discontinued it in 1883 (Frickstad, p. 207).

Indian Creek: see **Alder Creek** [MENDOCINO] (7); **China Creek** [TRINITY] (1); **Cooper Mill Creek** [HUMBOLDT]; **Indian Valley Creek** [TRINITY]; **Inman Creek** [MENDOCINO].

Indian Creek Town: see **Indian Creek** [TRINITY] (3).

Indian Field Ridge [HUMBOLDT]: *ridge*, generally north-trending, nearly 6 miles long, center 13 miles east-northeast of the town of Blue Lake (lat. 40°57'15" N, long. 123°45'20" W). Named on Lord-Ellis Summit (1973) and Willow Creek (1979) 7.5' quadrangles.

Indian Island [LAKE]: *island*, 1050 feet long, 2.5 miles northwest of the town of Lower Lake in Clear Lake (lat. 38°56'25" N, long. 122°38'35" W). Named on Clearlake Highlands (1958) 7.5' quadrangle.

Indian Island: see **Gunther Island** [HUMBOLDT].

Indianola [HUMBOLDT]:

(1) *settlement*, 4 miles south of Arcata (lat. 40°48'50" N, long. 124°04'55" W; sec. 16, 17, T 5 N, R 1 E). Named on Arcata South (1959) 7.5' quadrangle. Postal authorities established Indianola post office in 1900 and discontinued it in 1915 (Frickstad, p. 44).

(2) *locality*, 3 miles south-southwest of Fields Landing (lat. 40°41'10" N, long. 124°13'55" W; near W line sec. 31, T 3 N, R 1 W). Named on Fields Landing (1959) 7.5' quadrangle.

Indian Prairie [HUMBOLDT]:

(1) *area*, 6 miles east-southeast of Cape Mendocino (lat. 40°25'15" N, long. 124°17'50" W; near S line sec. 33, T 1 N, R 2 W). Named on Capetown (1969) 7.5' quadrangle.

(2) *area*, 4.5 miles south-southwest of Coyote Peak (lat. 41°05'10" N, long. 123°52'45" W; sec. 18, T 8 N, R 3 E). Named on Panther Creek (1982) 7.5' quadrangle.

Indian Ridge [LAKE]: *ridge*, south-southwest- to west-southwest-trending, 12.5 miles north-northeast of Clearlake Oaks (lat. 39°11' N, long. 122°35' W). Named on Clearlake Oaks (1960) 15' quadrangle.

Indian Rocks [HUMBOLDT]: *relief feature*, 1.25 miles north-northwest of Salmon Mountain on Humboldt-Siskiyou County line (lat. 41°12' N, long. 123°25'15" W). Named on Salmon Mountain (1978) 7.5' quadrangle.

Indian Scalp River: see **Klamath River** [DEL NORTE-HUMBOLDT].

Indian Spring [HUMBOLDT]: *spring*, less than 1 mile south-southeast of Showers Mountain (lat. 40°34' N, long. 123°41'30" W; sec. 11, T 2 N, R 4 E). Named on Showers Mountain (1978) 7.5' quadrangle.

Indian Springs [TRINITY]: *spring*, 10 miles south of Kettenpom (lat. 40°01'15" N, long. 123°25'50" W; near S line sec. 18, T 5 S, R 7 E). Named on Lake Mountain (1967) 7.5' quadrangle.

Indian Valley [TRINITY]: *valley*, 9.5 miles southeast of Hyampom (lat. 40°31' N, long. 123°19'30" W). Named on Hyampom (1951) 15' quadrangle.

Indian Valley: see **Little Indian Valley** [LAKE].

Indian Valley Creek [TRINITY]: *stream*, flows 10 miles to Butter Creek 4 miles south-southeast of Hyampom (lat. 40°34'05" N, long. 123°25'10" W; near W line sec. 8, T 2 N, R 7 E); the stream heads at Indian Valley. Named on Hyampom (1951) 15' quadrangle. Called Indian Creek on United States Geological Survey's (1915) map.

Inglenook [MENDOCINO]: *settlement*, 8 miles south of Westport (lat. 39°31'50" N, long. 123°45'30" W; mainly in sec. 9, T 19 N, R 17 W); the place is along Inglenook Creek. Named on Inglenook (1966) 7.5' quadrangle. Postal authorities established Inglenook post office in 1880 and discontinued it in 1919; Major Henry Lockhart, who built a lumber mill at the site, named the place (Salley, p. 104).

Inglenook Creek [MENDOCINO]: *stream*, flows nearly 2 miles to the sea 7.5 miles south of Westport (lat. 39°31'50" N, long. 123°46'25" W; near N line sec. 8, T 19 N, R 17 W). Named on Dutchmans Knoll (1966) and Inglenook (1966) 7.5' quadrangles.

Ingram [MENDOCINO]: *locality*, 6.5 miles south-southwest of Hopland (lat. 38°53'25" N, long. 123°10'35" W). Named on Hopland (1944) 15' quadrangle.

Ingram Creek [MENDOCINO]: *stream*, flows 2 miles to Dry Creek (2) 6.5 miles south-southwest of Hopland (lat. 38°53'15" N, long. 123°10'10" W; sec. 14, T 12 N, R 12 W). Named on Hopland (1960) 15' quadrangle.

Inis: see **Camp Inis** [LAKE].

Inman Creek [MENDOCINO]: *stream*, flows 5.25 miles to Garcia River 10 miles west of Ornbaun Valley (lat. 38°54'25" N, long. 123°29'30" W; near N line sec. 14, T 12 N, R 15 W). Named on Ornbaun Valley (1960) 15' quadrangle. Called Indian Creek on Ornbaun (1944) 15' quadrangle.

Inspiration Point [MENDOCINO]: *locality*, 3.5 miles east of Dos Rios (lat. 39°43'45" N, long. 123°15'05" W; on S line sec. 25, T 22 N, R 13 W). Named on Dos Rios (1967) 7.5' quadrangle.

Integral: see **Cinnabar Gulch** [TRINITY].

Irene Peak [MENDOCINO]: *peak*, 5.25 miles south-southwest of Willits (lat. 39°20'20" N, long. 123°23' W; sec. 11, T 17 N, R 14 W). Altitude 2836 feet. Named on Willits (1961) 15' quadrangle.

Irish Bay: see **Bridgeport Landing** [MENDOCINO].

Irish Creek: see **Irish Gulch** [MENDOCINO].

Irish Gulch [MENDOCINO]: *canyon*, drained by a stream that flows 3 miles to the sea 8 miles south of Elk (lat. 39°01'10" N, long. 123°41'25" W; sec. 1, T 13 N, R 17 W). Named on Mallo Pass Creek (1960) 7.5' quadrangle. The stream in the canyon is called Irish Creek on Navarro (1943) 15' quadrangle. The first settlers near the canyon were Irish (Carpenter, p. 53).

Irishmans Flat [MENDOCINO]: *area*, 3.25 miles northeast of the town of Potter Valley (lat. 39°20'50" N, long.123°03'20" W; near NE cor. sec. 10, T 17 N, R 11 W). Named on Potter Valley (1960) 7.5' quadrangle.

Irish Mountain [TRINITY]: *peak*, 5 miles north-northwest of Forest Glen (lat. 40°26'20" N, long. 123°22' W; sec. 27, T 1 N, R 7 E). Named on Naufus Creek (1979) 7.5' quadrangle.

Irma: see **Island Mountain** [TRINITY].

Irmulco [MENDOCINO]: *locality*, 12 miles north-northeast of Comptche along California Western Railroad (lat. 39°25'15" N, long. 123°30'15" W; at N line sec. 14, T 18 N, R 15 W). Named on Comptche (1960) 15' quadrangle. Postal authorities established Irmulco post office in 1911 and discontinued it in 1927 (Frickstad, p. 95). The name is from the Irvine and Muir Lumber Company (Crump, p. 118).

Iron Creek [MENDOCINO]: *stream*, flows 5.25 miles to Woodman Creek 7 miles south of Spyrock (2) (lat. 39°46'20" N, long. 123°26'15" W; sec. 9, T 22 N, R 14 W); the stream heads near Iron Peak. Named on Iron Peak (1967) 7.5' quadrangle. Called North Fork [of Woodman Creek] on Spyrock (1952) 15' quadrangle.

Iron Peak [MENDOCINO]: *peak*, 5.25 miles south-southwest of Spyrock (2) (lat. 39°48'30" N, long. 123°28'50" W; sec. 25, T 23 N, R 15 W). Altitude 4485 feet. Named on Iron Peak (1967) 7.5' quadrangle.

Ironside Mountain [TRINITY]: *ridge*, west-northwest-trending, 1.5 miles long, 2.25 miles northeast of Burnt Ranch (lat. 40°49'50" N, long. 123°26'30" W). Named on Ironside Mountain (1951) 15' quadrangle. Called Ironsides Mtn. on Averill's (1940) map.

Iron Spring [MENDOCINO]: *spring*, 7 miles north of Eden Valley (lat. 39°43'45" N, long. 123°11'45" W; near S line sec. 28, T 22 N, R 12 W). Named on Jamison Ridge (1967) 7.5' quadrangle.

Islam John Creek [MENDOCINO]: *stream*, flows 2 miles to Hollow Tree Creek nearly 5 miles south-southwest of Leggett (lat. 39°47'40" N, long. 123°44'35" W; sec. 33, T 23 N, R 17 W). Named on Leggett (1969) 7.5' quadrangle.

Island: see **Island Mountain** [TRINITY]; **The Island** [HUMBOLDT]; **The Island** [LAKE]; **The Island** [MENDOCINO].

Island Knob: see **Cape Vizcaino** [MENDOCINO].

Island Lake [DEL NORTE]: *lake*, 700 feet long, 9 miles south of Broken Rib Mountain (lat. 41°45'35" N, long. 123°41'45" W). Named on Devils Punchbowl (1981) 7.5' quadrangle.

Island Mountain [HUMBOLDT-MENDOCINO-TRINITY]: *ridge*, generally north-northeast-trending, 4 miles long, 11 miles south-southeast of Alderpoint [HUMBOLDT] in Humboldt, Mendocino, and Trinity Counties (lat. 40°02' N, long. 123°32'20" W). Named on Alderpoint (1949), Leggett (1952), and Spyrock (1952) 15' quadrangles. The first settlers in the region gave the name to the feature in the 1850's because streams nearly encircled it (Gudde, 1969, p. 153).

Island Mountain [TRINITY]: *locality*, 9 miles south of Kettenpom along Northwestern Pacific Railroad (lat. 40°01'40" N, long. 123°29'25" W; sec. 15, T 5 S, R 6 E). Named on Lake Mountain (1967) 7.5' quadrangle. Postal authorities established Island post office, named for nearby Island Mountain, in Humboldt County in 1905 and discontinued it in 1907, when they moved it and changed the name to Irma—the name "Irma" was for Irma Morrison, first postmaster; they moved Irma post office 0.5 mile east into Trinity County in 1910 and discontinued it in 1915, when they changed the name to Island Mountain; they discontinued Island Mountain post office in 1973 (Salley, p. 105).

Italian Creek [TRINITY]: *stream*, flows 3 miles to Trinity River 6 miles east of Burnt Ranch (lat. 40°47'45" N, long. 123°21'45" W). Named on Ironside Mountain (1951) 15' quadrangle.

Italian Gulch [TRINITY]: *canyon*, drained by a stream that flows less than 1 mile to East Fork Stuart Fork 6.25 miles northeast of Weaverville (lat. 40°51'45" N, long. 122°46'15" W; sec. 28, T 35 N, R 8 W). Named on Trinity Lake (1950) 15' quadrangle.

Iversen: see **Iversen Landing** [MENDOCINO].

Iversen Landing [MENDOCINO]: *locality*, 8 miles south-southeast of the village of Point Arena along the coast (lat. 38°50'45" N, long. 123°38'35" W; at W line sec. 3, T 11 N, R 16 W). Named on Saunders Reef (1960) 7.5' quadrangle. Called Iverson Landing on Point Arena (1943) 15' quadrangle, but United States Board on Geographic Names (1962c, p. 19) rejected this form for the name. California Mining Bureau's (1909c) map shows a place called Iversen located 5.75 miles by road southeast of the village of Point Arena. Postal authorities established Iverson post office, named for Charles Iverson, 5 miles south of Point Arena post office in 1890 and discontinued it in 1910 (Salley, p. 106).

Iversen Point [MENDOCINO]: *promontory*, 5 miles south-southeast of the village of Point Arena along the coast (lat. 38°50'45" N, long. 123°38'45" W; sec. 4, T 11 N, R 16 W). Named on Saunders Reef (1960) 7.5' quadrangle. Called Iverson Point on Point Arena (1943) 15' quadrangle, but United States Board on Geographic Names (1962c, p. 20) rejected this form for the name, which reportedly is for Niels Iversen, a Danish sea captain who settled in the neighborhood in the early 1870's.

Iverson: see **Iversen Landing** [MENDOCINO].

—J—

Jackass Cone [MENDOCINO]: *rock*, 10 miles south-southwest of Piercy, and 550 feet offshore (lat. 39°51'40" N, long. 123°54'20" W). Named on Mistake Point (1969) 7.5' quadrangle.

Jackass Creek [HUMBOLDT]: *stream*, flows 3 miles to Eel River 2.5 miles northwest of Alderpoint (lat. 40°12'05" N, long. 123°38'55" W; at W line sec. 17, T 3 S, R 5 E). Named on Fort Seward (1969) 7.5' quadrangle. Called Soda Creek on Alderpoint (1949) 15' quadrangle. On Fort Seward (1969) 7.5' quadrangle, the name "Soda Creek" applies to a stream located about 0.5 mile south of present Jackass Creek.

Jackass Creek [MENDOCINO]: *stream*, flows 2.25 miles to the sea 9 miles southwest of Piercy (lat. 39°52'50" N, long. 123°54'45" W; sec. 1, T 23 N, R 19 W); the stream heads on Jackass Ridge. Named on Bear Harbor (1969) 7.5' quadrangle. North Fork enters from the north 2000 feet upstream from the mouth of the main creek and is nearly 3 miles long. East Branch of North Fork enters North Fork from the northeast less than 1 mile upstream from the mouth of North Fork and is 1.25 miles long. North Fork and its branch are named on Bear Harbor (1969) 7.5' quadrangle.

Jackass Creek: see **Little Jackass Creek** [MENDOCINO].

Jackass Gulch: see **Canyon City** [TRINITY].

Jackass Peak [TRINITY]: *peak*, 22 miles northeast of Weaverville (lat. 40°57'40" N, long. 122°37'150" W; sec. 23, T 36 N, R 7 W); the peak is 1.5 miles east of Jackass Spring. Altitude 4487 feet. Named on Schell Mountain (1950) 15' quadrangle.

Jackass Ridge [MENDOCINO]: *ridge*, north-northwest-to northwest-trending, 3 miles long, 7 miles southwest of Piercy (lat. 39°54' N, long. 123°53' W). Named on Bear Harbor (1969) and Piercy (1969) 7.5' quadrangles.

Jackass Spring [TRINITY]: *spring*, 21 miles northeast of Weaverville (lat. 40°57'45" N, long. 122°39'30" W; sec. 22, T 36 N, R 7 W); the spring is 1.5 miles west of Jackass Peak. Named on Schell Mountain (1950) 15' quadrangle.

Jack Canyon [LAKE]: *canyon*, drained by a stream that flows 3 miles to Cache Creek at Wilson Valley (2) (lat. 38°58'20" N, long. 122°28' W). Named on Wilson Valley (1958) 7.5' quadrangle.

Jack Hollow [MENDOCINO]: *area*, 10.5 miles east-northeast of Eden Valley (lat. 39°41'10" N, long. 123°00'15" W; on E line sec. 7, T 21 N, R 10 W). Named on Thatcher Ridge (1967) 7.5' quadrangle.

Jack Hollow Creek [MENDOCINO]: *stream*, flows 4 miles to Thatcher Creek 8 miles east-northeast of Eden Valley (lat. 39°40'10" N, long. 123°02'50" W); one branch of the stream heads at Jack Hollow. Named on Plaskett Ridge (1967) and Thatcher Ridge (1967) 7.5' quadrangles.

Jack of Hearts Creek [MENDOCINO]: *stream*, flows 3.5 miles to South Fork Eel River 5 miles north-northwest of Branscomb (lat. 39°43'25" N, long. 123°39' W; sec. 29, T 22 N, R 16 W). Named on Lincoln Ridge (1966) 7.5' quadrangle.

Jack Peters Gulch [MENDOCINO]: *canyon*, drained by a stream that flows 2 miles to the sea less than 1 mile north of downtown Mendocino (lat. 39°19'10" N, long. 123°48' W; sec. 19, T 17 N, R 17 W). Named on Mendocino (1960) 7.5' quadrangle.

Jack Rabbit Valley [HUMBOLDT]: *area*, 3.5 miles south-southeast of Dinsmore on Buck Mountain (lat. 40°26'30" N, long. 123°34'55" W; near N line sec. 26, T 1 N, R 5 E). Named on Dinsmore (1977) 7.5' quadrangle.

Jack Smith Creek [MENDOCINO]: *stream*, flows nearly 6 miles to join Eldridge Creek and form Seward Creek 11.5 miles south-southeast of Willits (lat. 39°15'40" N, long. 123°15'50" W; sec. 11, T 16 N, R 13 W). Named on Willits (1961) 15' quadrangle. Called Seward Creek on Willits (1942) 15' quadrangle.

Jackson Creek [HUMBOLDT]: *stream*, flows 1.25 miles to North Fork Mad River 5 miles north-northeast of the town of Blue Lake (lat. 40°56'30" N, long. 123°56'20" W; at N line sec. 3, T 6 N, R 2 E). Named on Blue Lake (1979) 7.5' quadrangle.

Jackson Pinnacle [MENDOCINO]: *relief feature*, 9 miles southwest of Piercy along the coast (lat. 39°53'35" N, long. 123°55'20" W; sec. 36, T 24 N, R 19 W). Named on Bear Harbor (1969) 7.5' quadrangle. According to United States Coast and Geodetic Survey (p. 142-143), the feature is a black rock, 45 feet high, that lies so close to the rocky beach that from the sea it is difficult to distinguish from the bluff behind it.

Jackson Valley: see **Mud Springs** [MENDOCINO].

Jackson Valley Mineral Springs: see **Mud Springs** [MENDOCINO].

Jackson Valley Mud Springs: see **Mud Springs** [MENDOCINO].

Jacks Opening [MENDOCINO]: *area*, 8 miles east of the village of Point Arena (lat. 38°55'35" N, long. 123°32'45" W; sec. 5, T 12 N, R 15 W). Named on Point Arena (1960) 15' quadrangle.

Jacobsen's Valley: see **Miranda** [HUMBOLDT].

Jacoby Creek [HUMBOLDT]: *stream*, flows 10 miles to Arcata Bay 2 miles south of Arcata (lat. 40°50'35" N, long. 124°05' W). Named on Arcata South (1959) and Korbel (1979) 7.5' quadrangles. The name commemorates Agustus Jacoby, an early settler (Turner, p. 120).

Jago Bay [LAKE]: *embayment*, 4 miles northwest of the town of Lower Lake along Clear Lake (lat. 38°56'45" N, long. 122°40'15" W; sec. 30, T 13 N, R 7 W). Named on Clearlake Highlands (1958) 7.5' quadrangle.

Jakes Creek [MENDOCINO]: *stream*, flows 3.25 miles to Vasser Creek 6.5 miles east-southeast of Hopland (lat. 38°55'50" N, long. 123°00'15" W; sec. 32, T 13 N, R 10 W). Named on Highland Springs (1959) and Hopland (1960) 7.5' quadrangles.

Jakes Hunting Ground [TRINITY]: *area*, 16 miles northeast of Burnt Ranch (lat. 40°58' N, long. 123°15'25" W). Named on Ironside Mountain (1951) 15' quadrangle.

Jakes Lower Camp [TRINITY]: *locality*, 15 miles northeast of Burnt Ranch (lat. 40°58'05" N, long. 123°16'15" W). Named on Ironside Mountain (1951) 15' quadrangle.

Jakes Opening [MENDOCINO]: *area*, 5 miles northeast of Boonville (lat. 39°03' N, long. 123°17'30" W; on N line sec. 28, T 14 N, R 13 W). Named on Boonville (1959) 15' quadrangle.

Jakes Upper Camp [TRINITY]: *locality*, 15 miles north-northwest of Helena (lat. 40°57'55" N, long. 123°14'45" W). Named on Helena (1951) 15' quadrangle.

James Creek [MENDOCINO]: *stream*, flows 4.5 miles to North Fork Big River 7.25 miles northeast of Comptche (lat. 39°20'50" N, long. 123°30'45" W; at W line sec. 11, T 17 N, R 15 W). Named on Comptche (1960) and Willits (1961) 15' quadrangles. North Fork enters from the northwest 2.5 miles upstream from the mouth of the main creek; it is nearly 3 miles long and is named on Comptche (1960) and Willits (1961) 15' quadrangles.

James Creek [TRINITY]: *stream*, flows 1 mile to Hayfork Creek 10 miles east of Hyampom (lat. 40°35'50" N, long. 123°15'55" W). Named on Hyampom (1951) 15' quadrangle.

Jameson Creek [HUMBOLDT]: *stream*, flows 2.5 miles to Strongs Creek 1.25 miles southeast of Fortuna (lat. 40°34'55" N, long. 124°08'05" W; at W line sec. 1, T 2 N, R 1 W). Named on Fortuna (1959) and Hydesville (1979) 7.5' quadrangles.

Jamison Ridge [MENDOCINO]: *ridge*, generally east-southeast-trending, 2.5 miles long, 4.5 miles northwest of Eden Valley (lat. 39°40'50" N, long. 123°13'50" W). Named on Jamison Ridge (1967) 7.5' quadrangle.

Janes Creek [HUMBOLDT]: *stream*, flows 2.5 miles to McDaniel Slough less than 1.5 miles north of downtown Arcata (lat. 40°53'30" N, long. 124°04'45" E; near W line sec. 21, T 6 N, R 1 E). Named on Arcata North (1959) and Arcata South (1959) 7.5' quadrangles. The name commemorates Henry Fletcher Janes, the first Justice of the Peace in

Humboldt County (Turner, p. 120).

Jaqua: see **Kneeland** [HUMBOLDT].

Jarbow Ridge [MENDOCINO]: *ridge*, generally northeast-trending, 1.5 miles long, 4.5 miles north-northwest of Eden Valley (lat. 39°41'35" N, long. 123°12'15" W; mainly in sec. 9, T 21 N, R 12 W). Named on Jamison Ridge (1967) 7.5' quadrangle.

Jarbow Spring [MENDOCINO]: *spring*, 5 miles north of Eden Valley (lat. 39°41'40" N, long. 123°12'05" W; sec. 9, T 21 N, R 12 W); the spring is on Jarbow Ridge. Named on Jamison Ridge (1967) 7.5' quadrangle.

Jarnigan Pond [HUMBOLDT]: *lake*, 450 feet long, 4 miles north of Lone Star Junction (lat. 40°41'20" N, long. 123°51'50" W; sec. 32, T 4 N, R 3 E). Named on Mad River Buttes (1977) 7.5' quadrangle.

Jedediah Mountain [DEL NORTE]: *peak*, 4 miles south of Broken Rib Mountain (lat. 41°45'20" N, long. 123°41'35" W). Named on Devils Punchbowl (1981) 7.5' quadrangle. United States Board on Geographic Names (1965d, p. 9-10) noted that the name is for Jedediah Smith, who was in the region in 1828, but the Board rejected the name "Jedediah Smith Mountain" for the feature.

Jedediah Smith Mountain: see **Jedediah Mountain** [DEL NORTE].

Jeep Peak [MENDOCINO]: *peak*, nearly 4 miles south-southwest of Hopland (lat. 38°55'45" N, long. 123°09'20" W; sec. 1, T 12 N, R 12 W). Named on Hopland (1960) 15' quadrangle.

Jeffry Gulch [HUMBOLDT]: *canyon*, drained by a stream that flows 2 miles to Mattole River 0.5 mile southwest of Petrolia (lat. 40°19'10" N, long. 124°17'45" W; sec. 4, T 2 S, R 2 W). Named on Petrolia (1969) 7.5' quadrangle.

Jennings Gulch [TRINITY]: *canyon*, drained by a stream that flows 1.5 miles to Trinity River 8.5 miles east of Weaverville (lat. 40°44'45" N, long. 122°46'55" W; sec. 4, T 33 N, R 8 W). Named on Weaverville (1950) 15' quadrangle.

Jeram: see **Covelo** [MENDOCINO].

Jericho Creek [LAKE]: *stream*, flows nearly 7 miles to Hunting Creek 3 miles southeast of Jericho Valley (lat. 38°30'25" N, long. 122°24'10" W; near S line sec. 15, T 11 N, R 5 W). Named on Jericho Valley (1958) 7.5' quadrangle.

Jericho Valley [LAKE]: *valley*, 11 miles southeast of the town of Lower Lake (lat. 38°50' N, long. 122°26' W; sec. 5, T 11 N, R 5 W); the valley is along Jericho Creek. Named on Jericho Valley (1958) 7.5' quadrangle.

Jerkey Camp [LAKE]: *locality*, 7 miles west of Lakeport (lat. 39°02'25" N, long. 123°02'25" W; sec. 26, T 14 N, R 11 W). Named on Purdys Gardens (1958) 7.5' quadrangle.

Jerry Gulch [TRINITY]: *canyon*, drained by a stream that flows 3.25 miles to North Fork Eel River 14 miles south-southeast of Kettenpom (lat. 39°59' N, long. 123°20'30" W). Named on Lake Mountain (1967), Long Ridge (1967), and Mina (1967) 7.5' quadrangles.

Jerusalem: see **New Jerusalem**, under **Petrolia** [HUMBOLDT].

Jerusalem Valley [LAKE]: *valley*, 3.5 miles west-southwest of Jericho Valley along Soda Creek (2) (lat. 38°49'10" N, long. 122°29'40" W; sec. 11, T 11 N, R 6 W). Named on Jericho Valley (1958) 7.5' quadrangle. Charles Copsey's daughter Saphonia named the place (Gudde,. 1969, p. 157).

Jerusalem Valley Creek: see **Soda Creek** [LAKE] (2).

Jesse Gulch [TRINITY]: *canyon*, drained by a stream that flows 1 mile to Reading Creek 6.5 miles south of Weaverville (lat. 40°38'10" N, long. 122°56'30" W; at N line sec. 13, T 32 N, R 10 W). Named on Weaverville (1950) 15' quadrangle.

Jesse Spring [LAKE]: *spring*, 14 miles north of Clearlake Oaks (lat. 39°13'20" N, long. 122°40'30" W). Named on Clearlake Oaks (1960) 15' quadrangle.

Jessup Gulch [TRINITY]: *canyon*, drained by a stream that flows 1.25 miles to Deadwood Creek 8 miles east of Weaverville (lat. 40°43' N, long. 122°47'15" W; at E line sec. 17, T 33 N, R 8 W). Named on Weaverville (1950) 15' quadrangle.

Jewett [HUMBOLDT]: *locality*, 4.25 miles south-southeast of Alderpoint along Northwestern Pacific Railroad (lat. 40°07'15" N, long. 123°34'25" W). Named on Harris (1920) 15' quadrangle.

Jewett Creek [HUMBOLDT]:

(1) *stream*, flows 3 miles to Bear Creek (7) 9.5 miles southeast of Honeydew (lat. 40°07'45" N, long. 124°00'30" W). Named on Honeydew (1970) 7.5' quadrangle.

(2) *stream*, flows 6 miles to Eel River 3 miles south-southeast of Alderpoint (lat. 40°08'05" N, long. 123°35'30" W; near NW cor. sec. 11, T 4 S, R 5 E); the stream is in Jewett Valley. Named on Alderpoint (1969), Harris (1969), and Jewett Rock (1969) 7.5' quadrangles.

Jewett Ridge [HUMBOLDT]: *ridge*, east-southeast-trending, 3 miles long, 8 miles south-southeast of Honeydew (lat. 40°08'10" N, long. 124°02'45" W); the ridge is southwest of Jewett Creek (1). Named on Honeydew (1970) and Shelter Cove (1969) 7.5' quadrangles.

Jewett Rock [HUMBOLDT]: *peak*, 6.25 miles south of Alderpoint (lat. 40°05'10" N, long. 123°36'20" W; sec. 27, T 4 S, R 5 E); the peak is east of Jewett Valley. Altitude 2796 feet. Named on Jewett Rock (1969) 7.5' quadrangle.

Jewett Valley [HUMBOLDT]: *valley*, 6.5 miles south of Alderpoint (lat. 40°04'50" N, long. 123°37'15" W; sec. 28, T 4 S, R 5 E). Named on Jewett Rock (1969) 7.5' quadrangle. The name is for Enoch Phillips Jewett, who came in 1863 to what then was known as Little Valley and bought a squatter's claim on ten thousand acres before the valley was renamed for him (Turner, p. 121).

Jiggs Creek [HUMBOLDT]: *stream*, flows nearly 2 miles to North Fork Mad River 3 miles east of the town of Blue Lake (lat. 40°53'30" N, long. 123°55'55" W; sec. 22, T 6 N, R 2 E). Named on Blue Lake (1979) and Korbel (1979) 7.5' quadrangles. Called Bald Mountain Creek on Blue Lake (1951) 15' quadrangle, but United States Board on Geographic Names (1978a, p. 6) rejected this name for the stream.

Jim Dollar Mountain [LAKE]: *peak*, 2.5 miles west-northwest of Jericho Valley (lat. 38°50'40" N, long. 122°28'35" W; sec. 36, T 12 N, R 6 W). Altitude 2394 feet. Named on Jericho Valley (1958) 7.5' quadrangle.

Jim Goff Gulch [HUMBOLDT]: *canyon*, drained by a stream that flows 1.5 miles to lowlands along Mattole River 2.25 miles southwest of Petrolia (lat. 40°18'20" N, long. 124°19'10" W; sec. 8, T 2 S, R 2 W). Named on Petrolia (1969) 7.5' quadrangle. The name commemorates a rancher in the canyon (United States Board on Geographic Names, 1973b, p. 3).

Jim Jam Ridge [TRINITY]: *ridge*, generally west-trending, 4.5 miles long, 14 miles northeast of Burnt Ranch (lat. 40°57'10" N, long. 123°18' W). Named on Ironside Mountain (1951) 15' quadrangle. According to Gudde (1949, p. 166), the term "jim jams" refers to the condition brought on by an over-indulgence in alcohol, and was applied to the ridge in the 1890's by some miners after one of their drunken companions—with a pocket full of rifle shells—rolled into a campfire there.

Jimmy Creek [MENDOCINO]: *stream*, flows nearly 4 miles to Anderson Creek (2) 5.5 miles north of Ornbaun Valley (lat. 38°55'25" N, long. 123°18'20" W; near N line sec. 17, T 13 N, R 13 W). Named on Boonville (1959) and Ornbaun Valley (1960) 15' quadrangles. Called North Fork Anderson Creek (2) on Boonville (1943) 15' quadrangle.

Jims Creek [TRINITY]: *stream*, flows 3 miles to Plummer Creek 8 miles north-northwest of Forest Glen (lat. 40°28'45" N, long. 123°23' W; sec. 9, T 1 N, R 7 E). Named on Hyampom (1951) 15' quadrangle, and on Sportshaven (1973) 7.5' quadrangle. Called Nafus Cr. on Anada (1918) 15' quadrangle.

Jims Ridge [TRINITY]: *ridge*, generally south-trending, 1 mile long, 9.5 miles north-northwest of Forest Glen (lat. 40°29'50" N, long. 123°23'45" W; sec. 4, T 1 N, R 7 E); the ridge is east of Jims Creek. Named on Sportshaven (1973) 7.5' quadrangle.

Jim Wilson Flat [TRINITY]: *area*, 14 miles northeast of Weaverville along Trinity River (lat. 40°51'10" N, long. 122°44'10" W; at N line sec. 35, T 35 N, R 8 W). Named on Schell Mountain (1950) 15' quadrangle.

Joe Basin [TRINITY]: *area*, 9 miles south-southeast of Forest Glen (lat. 40°15'20" N, long. 123°15'30" W; near N line sec. 30, T 28 N, R 12 W). Named on Forest Glen (1979) 7.5' quadrangle.

Joel Flat [HUMBOLDT]: *area*, 3.25 miles north of Petrolia (lat. 40°22'20" N, long. 124°17'15" W; near NE cor. sec. 21, T 1 S, R 2 W). Named on Capetown (1969) and Petrolia (1969) 7.5' quadrangles.

Joe Marine Creek [HUMBOLDT]: *stream*, flows less than 1 mile to Klamath River 3 miles east-northeast of Weitchpec (lat. 41°12' 35" N, long. 123°39'20" W). Named on Weitchpec (1979) 7.5' quadrangle.

Joes Peak [TRINITY]: *peak*, 11 miles southeast of Weaverville (lat. 40°37' N, long. 122°47'40" W; sec. 20, T 32 N, R 8 W). Altitude 4556 feet. Named on Weaverville (1950) 15' quadrangle.

John: see **Captain John Gulch** [HUMBOLDT]; **Captain John Mountain** [HUMBOLDT]; **Mount John**, under **Signal Peak** [LAKE].

John Alley Ridge [LAKE]: *ridge*, generally south-southwest-trending, 2 miles long, 3 miles north-northeast of the town of Upper Lake (lat. 39°12'15" N, long. 122°53'05" W; sec. 29, 32, T 16 N, R 9 W). Named on Upper Lake (1958) 7.5' quadrangle.

John Clark Opening: see **Clark Opening** [MENDOCINO].

John Creek [MENDOCINO]: *stream*, flows nearly 3 miles to Alder Creek (5) 10.5 miles south-southwest of Navarro (lat. 39°00'20" N, long. 123°36' W; sec. 11, T 13 N, R 16 W). Named on Navarro (1961) and Point Arena (1960) 15' quadrangles.

Johnny Jack Ridge [HUMBOLDT]: *ridge*, southwest-trending, 1.25 miles long, 5.25 miles south of Petrolia (lat. 40°15' N, long. 124°18' W; sec. 32, 33, T 2 S, R 2 W). Named on Cooskie Creek (1969) and Petrolia (1969) 7.5' quadrangles.

Johnny Woodin Ridge [MENDOCINO]: *ridge*, southeast-trending, 1.25 miles long, 10.5 miles west-southwest of Ornbaun Valley (lat. 38°50'50" N, long. 123°28'45" W). Named on Ornbaun Valley (1960) 15' quadrangle.

John Smith Creek [MENDOCINO]: *stream*, flows 3.25 miles to join Little North Fork Navarro River and form North Branch of North Fork Navarro River 4 miles north of Navarro (lat. 39°12'25" N, long. 123°32'10" W; sec. 33, T 16 N, R 15 W). Named on Navarro (1961) 15' quadrangle.

Johnson Camp [HUMBOLDT]: *locality*, 3 miles west of Weott (lat. 40°19'40" N, long. 123°58'30" W; at N line sec. 5, T 2 S, R 2 E). Named on Weott (1969) 7.5' quadrangle.

Johnson Creek [HUMBOLDT]:
(1) *stream*, flows less than 1 mile to the sea 15 miles north of Orick (lat. 41°27'50" N, long. 124°03'50" W; near N line sec. 4, T 12 N, R 1 E). Named on Fern Canyon (1966) 7.5' quadrangle.
(2) *stream*, flows 1 mile to Skunk Cabbage Creek 1.5 miles north of Orick (lat. 41°18'35" N, long. 124°03'10" W; near W line sec. 27, T 11 N, R 1 E). Named on Orick (1966) 7.5' quadrangle.
(3) *stream*, flows nearly 4 miles to Klamath River 0.25 mile south-southeast of Johnsons (lat. 41°20'50" N, long. 123°52'10" W; sec. 18, T 11 N, R 3 E). Named on Holter Ridge (1983) and Johnsons (1982) 7.5' quadrangles.

Johnson Creek [MENDOCINO]:
(1) *stream*, flows 2 miles to South Fork Big River 16 miles north-northwest of Boonville (lat. 39°14'10" N, long. 123°26'30" W; near NW cor. sec. 20, T 16 N, R 14 W). Named on Boonville (1959) and Willits (1961) 15' quadrangles.
(2) *stream*, flows 4 miles to Gates Creek 14 miles north of Boonville (lat. 39°12'25" N, long. 123°24'40" W; near NE cor. sec. 33, T 16 N, R 14 W). Named on Boonville (1959) 15' quadrangle.
(3) *stream*, flows 3.5 miles to Duncan Creek nearly 2 miles west-southwest of Hopland (lat. 38°57'50" N, long. 123°08'45" W; at N line sec. 26, T 13 N, R 12 W). Named on Hopland (1960) 15' quadrangle.
(4) *stream*, flows nearly 3 miles to John Smith Creek 5.5 miles north of Navarro (lat. 39°13'40" N, long. 123°32'10" W; near S line sec. 21, T 16 N, R 15 W). Named on Navarro (1961) 15' quadrangle.

Johnson Creek [TRINITY]:
(1) *stream*, flows 1.5 miles to South Fork Trinity River 4 miles south of Hyampom (lat. 40°33'30" N, long. 123°27'30" W; near NE cor. sec. 14, T 2 N, R 6 E). Named on Hyampom (1951) 15' quadrangle.
(2) *stream*, flows 2 miles to Mad River 7.25 miles south of Forest Glen (lat. 40°16'05" N, long. 123°19'30" W; at W line sec. 30, T 2 S, R 8 E). Named on Forest Glen (1979) 7.5' quadrangle.

Johnson Flat [HUMBOLDT]: *area*, 6.25 miles west of Garberville (lat. 40°07'10" N, long. 123°54'40" W; at N line sec. 13, T 4 S, R 2 E). Named on Briceland (1969) 7.5' quadrangle.

Johnson Flats: see **Johnson Glades** [LAKE].

Johnson Glades [LAKE]: *areas*, 8 miles north-northwest of Clearlake Oaks (lat. 39°08'15" N, long. 122°42'55" W; sec. 23, T 15 N, R 8 W). Named on Clearlake Oaks (1960) 15' quadrangle. Called Johnson Flats on Bartlett Springs (1944) 15' quadrangle.

Johnson Glades [TRINITY]: *area*, 7.5 miles south of Forest Glen (lat. 40°16' N, long. 123°18' W; sec. 20, 29, T 2 S, R 8 E); the place is south of Johnson Creek (2). Named on Forest Glen (1979) 7.5' quadrangle.

Johnson Gulch [HUMBOLDT]: *canyon*, drained by a stream that flows 2 miles to Bear River 4.25 miles east-northeast of Cape Mendocino (lat. 40°27'35" N, long. 124°20'10" W; sec. 19, T 1 N, R 2 W). Named on Capetown (1969) 7.5' quadrangle.

Johnson Gulch [TRINITY]:
(1) *canyon*, drained by a stream that flows about 1.5 miles to Indian Creek (2) 10 miles south-southeast of Weaverville (lat. 40°36'15" N, long. 122°51'45" W; near W line sec. 20, T 32 N, R 9 W). Named on Weaverville (1950) 15' quadrangle.
(2) *canyon*, drained by a stream that flows 2 miles to Browns Creek 14 miles south of Weaverville (lat. 40°31'35" N, long. 122°56'20" W; sec. 24, T 31 N, R 10 W). Named on Weaverville (1950) 15' quadrangle.

Johnson Point [TRINITY]: *relief feature*, 12 miles northeast of Hayfork along Trinity River (lat. 40°40' N, long. 123°00'45" W; at SW cor. sec. 33, T 33 N, R 10 W). Named on Hayfork (1951) 15' quadrangle.

Johnson Prairie [HUMBOLDT]:
(1) *area*, 4.5 miles west-northwest of the settlement of Willow Creek (lat. 40°57'40" N, long. 123°42'30" W; sec. 27, T 7 N, R 4 E). Named on Willow Creek (1979) 7.5' quadrangle.
(2) *area*, 5 miles west-northwest of Weott (lat. 40°21'30" N, long. 124°00' W; on S line sec. 19, T 1 S, R 2 E). Named on Bull Creek (1969) and Weott (1969) 7.5' quadrangles.
(3) *area*, 2.5 miles south-southwest of Coyote Peak (lat. 41°06'05" N, long. 123°53'20" W; on E line sec. 12, T 8 N, R 2 E). Named on Panther Creek (1982) 7.5' quadrangle.

Johnson Ridge [HUMBOLDT]: *ridge*, east-trending, 1.25 miles long, 5 miles south of Lone Star Junction (lat. 40°33'40" N, long. 123°53'45" W). Named on Owl Creek (1979) 7.5' quadrangle.

Johnsons [HUMBOLDT]: *village*, 14 miles northwest of Weitchpec along Klamath River (lat. 41°21'05" N, long. 123°52'20" W; sec. 7, T 11 N, R 3 E). Named on Johnsons (1982) 7.5' quadrangle. Called Klamath on Hoopa (1935) 30' quadrangle.

John Thomas Creek [LAKE]: *stream*, flows 2.5 miles to Hunting Creek 3.25 miles south-southeast of Jericho Valley (lat. 38°47' 25" N, long. 122°24'25" W; at W line sec. 22, T 11 N, R 5 W). Named on Jericho Valley (1958) 7.5' quadrangle.

John Wilson Creek: see **Wilson Creek** [MENDOCINO] (2).

Jolly Giant Creek [HUMBOLDT]: *stream*, flows 1.5 miles to lowlands in Arcata (lat. 40°52'50" N, long. 124°04'45" W; near W line sec. 28, T 6 N, R 1 E). Named on Arcata North (1959) and Arcata South (1959) 7.5' quadrangles.

Jonathan Creek [TRINITY]: *stream*, flows 1 mile to the canyon of Mad River 8 miles south of Forest Glen (lat. 40°15'25" N, long. 123°19' W; at S line sec. 30, T 2 S, R 8 E). Named on Forest Glen (1979) 7.5' quadrangle.

Jonathan Rock: see **Star Rock** [DEL NORTE].

Jones Bay [LAKE]: *embayment*, 3.5 miles northwest of the town of Lower Lake along Clear Lake (lat. 38°56'55" N, long. 122°39'35" W; sec. 29, T 13 N, R 7 W). Named on Clearlake Highlands (1958) 7.5' quadrangle.

Jones Creek [DEL NORTE]: *stream*, flows 13 miles to South Fork Smith River nearly 5 miles north-northwest of Buck Mountain (lat. 41°41' N, long. 123°53'30" W; sec. 24, T 15 N, R 2 E). Named on Cant Hook Mountain (1982), Hurdygurdy Butte (1982), and Ship Mountain (1982) 7.5' quadrangles.

Jones Creek [HUMBOLDT-MENDOCINO]: *stream*, heads in Humboldt County and flows 2.5 miles to Indian Creek (2) 2.25 miles northwest of Piercy in Mendocino County (lat. 39°59'10" N, long. 123°49'45" W; near SW cor. sec. 27, T 5 S, R 3 E). Named on Garberville (1970) and Piercy (1969) 7.5' quadrangles.

Jones Creek [LAKE]: *stream*, flows 1.5 miles to Kelsey Creek 0.5 mile north-northwest of Whispering Pines (lat. 38°49'15" N, long. 122°42'55" W; sec. 11, T 11 N, R 8 W). Named on Whispering Pines (1958) 7.5' quadrangle.

Jones Creek: see **Little Jones Creek** [DEL NORTE].

Jones Gulch [TRINITY]: *canyon*, drained by a stream that flows 1 mile to Canyon Creek (1) 8 miles northeast of Helena (lat. 40°52' N, long. 123°02'05" W). Named on Helena (1951) 15' quadrangle.

Jones Point [HUMBOLDT]: *relief feature*, nearly 2 miles east-southeast of Hoopa (lat. 41°02'30" N, long. 123°38'25" W; near SW cor. sec. 29, T 8 N, R 5 E). Named on Hoopa (1979) 7.5' quadrangle.

Jones Prairie [HUMBOLDT]: *area*, 3.5 miles west-southwest of Fields Landing along Elk Creek (1) (lat. 40°42'05" N, long. 124°09'05" W; sec. 26, T 4 N, R 1 W). Named on Fields Landing (1959) 7.5' quadrangle. The name is for D.R. Jones (Turner, p. 122).

Jones Ridge [DEL NORTE]: *ridge*, 2 miles long, 4.25 miles north of Buck Mountain (lat. 47°41'30" N, long. 123°52'30" W). Named on Cant Hook Mountain (1982) and Ship Mountain 1982) 7.5' quadrangles.

Jones Ridge [TRINITY]: *ridge*, generally northwest-trending, 5 miles long, 12.5 miles west-southwest of Black Rock Mountain (lat. 40°06'15" N, long. 123°12'15" W). Named on Black Rock Mountain (1954) 15' quadrangle. The feature first was called Black's Camp Ridge—Blacks Camp is on the north side of it (Jones, p. 364).

Jordan Creek [DEL NORTE]: *stream*, flows 5 miles to Lake Earl 4.5 miles north-northeast of Crescent City (lat. 41°48'55" N, long. 124°10'30" W). Named on Crescent City (1966) 7.5' quadrangle.

Jordan Creek [HUMBOLDT]: *stream*, flows 3.25 miles to Eel River 4.25 miles southeast of Scotia (lat. 40°26'40" N, long. 124°02'05" W; near N line sec. 26, T 1 N, R 1 E). Named on Scotia (1970) 7.5' quadrangle.

Jordan Flat [MENDOCINO]: *area*, 8 miles north of the town of Potter Valley (lat. 39°26' N, long. 123°05' W; near N line sec. 9, T 18 N, R 11 W). Named on Potter Valley (1960) 15' quadrangle.

Jose Opening [MENDOCINO]: *area*, 10.5 miles north-northeast of Covelo (lat. 39°56' N, long. 123°11'20" W; around SE cor. sec. 16, T 24 N, R 12 W). Named on Bluenose Ridge (1967) 7.5' quadrangle.

Joseph Creek [TRINITY]: *stream*, flows about 1.5 miles to Indian Creek (2) 11 miles southeast of Weaverville (lat. 40°36' N, long. 122°48'45" W; sec. 30, T 32 N, R 8 W). Named on Weaverville (1950) 15' quadrangle.

Jose's Hollow: see **Baker Hollow**, under **Baker Creek** [TRINITY].

Juan Creek [MENDOCINO]: *stream*, formed by the confluence of North Fork and South Fork, flows 3.5 miles to the sea 4.5 miles north-northwest of Westport (lat. 39°42'10" N, long. 123°48'10" W; near E line sec. 1, T 21 N, R 18 W). Named on Lincoln Ridge (1966) and Westport (1966) 7.5' quadrangles. North Fork is 1 mile long, and South Fork is 2 miles long; both forks are named on Lincoln Ridge (1966) 7.5' quadrangle.

Juan Creek: see **Little Juan Creek** [MENDOCINO].

Jud Creek [TRINITY]: *stream*, flows 3 miles to Hayfork Creek 9 miles east of Hyampom (lat. 40°35'45" N, long. 123°16'45" W; sec. 33, T 3 N, R 8 E). Named on Hyampom (1951) 15' quadrangle.

Judge Davis Canyon [LAKE]: *canyon*, drained by a stream that flows about 3.25 miles to Cache Creek 1 mile southeast of Wilson Valley (2) (lat. 38°57'40" N, long. 122°27'30" W; near NW cor. sec. 19, T 13 N, R 5 W). Named on Wilson Valley (1958) 7.5' quadrangle.

Jug Handle Creek [MENDOCINO]: *stream*, flows 4.25 miles to the sea 4.5 miles south of Fort Bragg (lat. 39°22'35" N, long. 123°49' W; sec. 36, T 18 N, R 18 W). Named on Fort Bragg (1960) and Mendocino (1960) 7.5' quadrangles. The name is from the jug-handle shape of the turn made by an old road where it crossed the stream (Gudde, 1969, p. 159).

Juhaze Prairie [HUMBOLDT]: *area,* 1.5 miles south-southwest of Scotia (lat. 40°27'45" N, long. 124°06'25" W; on S line sec. 18, T 1 N, R 1 E). Named on Scotia (1970) 7.5' quadrangle.

Julias Creek [MENDOCINO]: *stream,* flows 2.25 miles to South Fork Usal Creek 10 miles south of Piercy (lat. 39°50'10" N, long. 123°48'20" W). Named on Hales Grove (1970) 7.5' quadrangle.

Julias Opening [MENDOCINO]: *area,* 7.5 miles south of Piercy (lat. 39°52'10" N, long. 123°47'55" W; near SW cor. sec. 6, T 23 N, R 17 W); the place is near the head of Julias Creek. Named on Hales Grove (1970) 7.5' quadrangle.

Jumpoff Creek [MENDOCINO]: *stream,* flows 11 miles to Black Butte River 11.5 miles east of Covelo (lat. 39°47'55" N, long. 123°01'50" W; at S line sec. 36, T 23 N, R 11 W). Named on Mendocino Pass (1967) and Newhouse Ridge (1967) 7.5' quadrangles.

Junction: see **Glenblair** [MENDOCINO].

Junction City [TRINITY]: *village,* 14 miles north-northeast of Hayfork (lat. 40°43'55" N, long. 123°03'05" W); the village is at the confluence of Trinity River and Canyon Creek (1). Named on Hayfork (1951) 15' quadrangle. Postal authorities established Messerville post office in 1860 and changed the name to Junction City in 1861 (Salley, p. 139). The place first known as Milltown for the sawmill that Seeley and Dowles built there in 1852 (Hanna, p. 157). It also was called Oregon Gulch (Gudde, 1975, p. 214). Postal authorities established Trinity post office 5 miles northwest of Junction City along Trinity River in 1854 and discontinued it in 1878 (Salley, p. 224).

– K –

Kalmia Lake: see **Mirror Lake** [TRINITY].

Kaluna Cliff [HUMBOLDT]: *relief feature,* 2.5 miles north of Point Delgada (lat. 40°03'20" N, long. 124°04'10" W; sec. 4, T 5 S, R 1 E). Named on Shelter Cove (1969) 7.5' quadrangle. The name is for the brig *Kaluna,* wrecked at the base of the cliff in 1867 (Turner, p. 123).

Kanaka Bar: see **Douglas City** [TRINITY].

Kanaka Glade [LAKE]: *area,* 14 miles north-northeast of Clearlake Oaks (lat. 39°12'20" N, long. 122°35'05" W). Named on Clearlake Oaks (1960) 15' quadrangle.

Kanakti Mountain: see **Mount Konocti** [LAKE].

Kane Opening [MENDOCINO]: *area,* 2 miles south-southwest of Navarro (lat. 39°07'20" N, long. 123°33'15" W; sec. 31, T 15 N, R 15 W). Named on Navarro (1961) 15' quadrangle.

Kanick Rapids [HUMBOLDT]: *water feature,* 8.5 miles north-northeast of Coyote Peak along Klamath River (lat. 41°14'25" N, long. 123°46'10" W; at E line sec. 24, T 10 N, R 3 E). Named on French Camp Ridge (1983) 7.5' quadrangle.

Kanuck: see **Cleone** [MENDOCINO].

Kapple Creek [HUMBOLDT]: *stream,* flows 2 miles to Eel River 3.5 miles east-northeast of Weott (lat. 40°20'35" N, long. 123°51'35" W; near S line sec. 29, T 1 S, R 3 E). Named on Myers Flat (1969) 7.5' quadrangle.

Kass Creek [MENDOCINO]: *stream,* flows 3.5 miles to South Fork Noyo River 13 miles north-northwest of Comptche (lat. 39°25' N, long. 123°43'10" W; sec. 14, T 18 N, R 17 W). Named on Comptche (1960) 15' quadrangle.

Kattenburg Canyon [LAKE]: *canyon,* drained by a stream that flows 4 miles to North Fork Cache Creek 9 miles northeast of Clearlake Oaks in Little Indian Valley (lat. 39°05'45" N, long. 122°32'15" W; near SW cor. sec. 33, T 15 N, R 6 W). Named on Clearlake Oaks (1960) 15' quadrangle. Called Catenberg Canyon on Bartlett Springs (1944) 15' quadrangle, but United States Board on Geographic Names (1968a, p. 5) rejected this form for the name.

Kauffman Spring [HUMBOLDT]: *spring,* 5 miles south of Garberville (lat. 40°01'25" N, long. 123°47'15" W; sec. 13, T 5 S, R 3 E). Named on Garberville (1970) 7.5' quadrangle.

Kayote: see **Coyote Valley** [LAKE].

Káysa: see **Lake Káysa**, under **Borax Lake** [LAKE].

Keene Summit [MENDOCINO]: *pass,* 6 miles north-northwest of Navarro (lat. 39°13'30" N, long. 123°35'45" W; near S line sec. 24, T 16 N, R 16 W). Named on Navarro (1961) 15' quadrangle.

Kekawaka [TRINITY]: *locality,* 7.5 miles southeast of Alderpoint [HUMBOLDT] (lat. 40°05'45" N, long. 122°31'05" W; near SE cor. sec. 20, T 4 S, R 6 E); the place is near the mouth of Kekawaka Creek. Named on Jewett Rock (1969) 7.5' quadrangle.

Kekawaka Creek [TRINITY]: *stream,* flows 12.5 miles to Eel River 7.5 miles southeast of Alderpoint [HUMBOLDT] (lat. 40°05'35" N, long. 123°31' W; at S line sec. 20, T 4 S, R 6 E). Named on Jewett Rock (1969) and Lake Mountain (1967) 7.5' quadrangles. The name presumably is of Indian origin (Kroeber, p. 44).

Kellogg Gulch [TRINITY]: *canyon,* drained by a stream that flows 3.5 miles to Hayfork Creek at Hayfork (lat. 40°33'10" N, long. 123°11' W; near E line sec. 11, T 31 N, R 12 W). Named on Hayfork (1951) 15' quadrangle.

Kelly Canyon [MENDOCINO]: *canyon,* drained by a stream that flows 3 miles to Middle Fork Eel River 6.25 miles north-northwest of Eden Valley (lat. 39°42'20" N, long. 123°14'50" W; at E line sec. 1, T 21 N, R 13 W). Named on Dos Rios (1967) and Jamison Ridge (1967) 7.5' quadrangles.

Kelly Creek [DEL NORTE]: *stream,* flows 3.5 miles to Middle Fork Smith River 6 miles east-northeast of Gasquet (lat. 41°51'50" N, long. 123°51'20" W; sec. 17, T 17 N, R 3 E); the mouth of the stream is 1 mile west-northwest of Kelly Peak. Named on Hurdygurdy Butte (1982) 7.5' quadrangle.

Kelly Creek [HUMBOLDT]: *stream,* flows 2.5 miles to Mad River nearly 4 miles east of Arcata (lat. 40°53' N, long. 124°00'40" W; at N line sec. 25, T 6 N, R 1 E). Named on Arcata North (1959) and Arcata South (1959) 7.5' quadrangles.

Kelly Gulch [MENDOCINO]: *canyon,* drained by a stream that flows 1 mile to South Fork Big River 4 miles east-northeast of Comptche (lat. 39°17'45" N, long. 123°31'30" W; near N line sec. 34, T 17 N, R 15 W). Named on Comptche (1960) 15' quadrangle.

Kelly Peak [DEL NORTE]: *peak,* 6.5 miles east of Gasquet (lat. 41°51'30" N, long. 123°50'25" W; sec. 21, T 17 N, R 3 E). Altitude 2862 feet. Named on Hurdygurdy Butte (1982) 7.5' quadrangle.

Kelsey Creek [LAKE]: *stream,* flows 22 miles to Clear Lake 6 miles east-southeast of Lakeport (lat. 39°01'10" N, long. 122°48'45" W; sec. 36, T 14 N, R 9 W). Named on Kelseyville (1959), Lucerne (1958), The Geysers (1959), and Whispering Pines (1958) 7.5' quadrangles. According to Palmer (p. 7), the stream is called Cobb Creek where it flows in Cobb Valley.

Kelsey Creek: see **Kelseyville** [LAKE].

Kelsey Peak: see **North Kelsey Peak** [TRINITY]; **South Kelsey Peak** [TRINITY].

Kelsey's River: see **South Fork**, under **Eel River** [LAKE-HUMBOLDT-MENDOCINO-TRINITY].

Kelsey Town: see **Kelseyville** [LAKE].

Kelseyville [LAKE]: *town,* 6 miles southeast of Lakeport (lat. 38°58'40" N, long. 122°50'15" W; sec. 14, 15, T 13 N, R 9 W). Named on Kelseyville (1959) 7.5' quadrangle. Postal authorities established Uncle Sam post office, named for nearby Uncle Sam Mountain (present Mount Konocti), in 1858 and changed the name to Kelseyville in 1882 (Salley, p. 227). The place first was called Kelsey Town in memory of Andrew Kelsey, the first settler in Lake County (Gudde, 1949, p. 172). The first business was a blacksmith shop that opened in 1857, but the second business did not open until 1864; the community also was called Kelsey Creek in the early days (Palmer, p. 113, 183). Postal authorities established Ely's post office 7 miles east of Kelseyville in 1887 and discontinued it in 1890; the name was for Benjamin Ely, Sr., first postmaster (Salley, p. 69). Anderson (p. 266-268) described Young's Natural Gas Well and Mineral Springs, located on the east edge of Kelseyville, where gas and mineral water shot 40 feet into the air from a well drilled by W.G. Young in 1888; the water was used locally for medicinal purposes.

Kendall Gulch [HUMBOLDT]: *canyon,* drained by a stream that flows 1 mile to Mattole River 2 miles west of Honeydew (lat. 40°14'25" N, long. 124°09'45" W; sec. 3, T 3 S, R 1 W). Named on Shubrick Peak (1969) 7.5' quadrangle.

Kendall's City: see **Boonville** [MENDOCINO].

Kennedy Flats [LAKE]: *area,* about 2.25 miles southeast of Wilson Valley (2) along Cache Creek (lat. 38°56'45" N, long. 122°25'15" W; sec. 28, 29, T 13 N, R 5 W). Named on Wilson Valley (1958) 7.5' quadrangle.

Kenny [MENDOCINO]: *locality,* 6.5 miles southwest of Piercy (lat. 39°55'15" N, long. 123°53'55" W; sec. 19, T 24 N, R 18 W). Site named on Bear Harbor (1969) 7.5' quadrangle. Postal authorities established Kenny post office in 1888, discontinued it in 1903, reestablished it in 1907, and discontinued it in 1924; the name was for the Kenny family, pioneers in the neighborhood (Salley, p. 110).

Kenny Creek [MENDOCINO]: *stream,* flows 4 miles to South Fork Eel River 1 mile west-northwest of Branscomb (lat. 39°39'35" N, long. 123°38'25" W; near W line sec. 22, T 21 N, R 16 W). Named on Cahto Peak (1967) and Lincoln Ridge (1966) 7.5' quadrangles.

Keno: see **Keno Camp** [TRINITY].

Keno Camp [TRINITY]: *locality,* 12 miles east of Weaverville (lat. 40°45'25" N, long. 122°42'15" W). Named on Schell Mountain (1950) 15' quadrangle. Weaverville (1913) 30' quadrangle shows a place called Keno located about 0.5 mile west of the site of present Keno Camp (sec. 36, T 34 N, R 8 W).

Kents Landing: see **Little River** [MENDOCINO] (2).

Kenyon: see **Port Kenyon** [HUMBOLDT].

Kergerson Lake [HUMBOLDT]: *lake,* 400 feet long, 7.5 miles west-southwest of Dinsmore (lat. 40°26'30" N, long. 123°43'25" W; near N line sec. 28, T 1 N, R 4 E). Named on Larabee Valley (1977) 7.5' quadrangle.

Kerlin Creek [TRINITY]: *stream,* flows 4.5 miles to South Fork Trinity River 2.25 miles northwest of Hyampom (lat. 40°38'10" N, long. 123°28'55" W; sec. 15, T 3 N, R 6 E). Named on Hyampom (1951) 15' quadrangle, and on Blake Mountain (1979) 7.5' quadrangle. Called Carlin Cr. on United States Geological Survey's (1915) map.

Kerr Creek [HUMBOLDT]: *stream,* flows 1.5 miles to South Fork Eel River 4.5 miles south-southeast of Weott (lat. 40°16'05" N, long. 123°52'40" W; near N line sec. 30, T 2 S, R 3 E); the stream heads at Kerr Peak. Named on Weott (1969) 7.5' quadrangle.

Kerr Peak [HUMBOLDT]: *peak,* 4.5 miles south-southeast of Weott (lat. 40°15'15" N, long. 123°54' W; at S line sec. 25, T 2 S, R 2 E). Named on Weott (1969) 7.5' quadrangle.

Kettenpom [TRINITY]: *locality,* 17 miles south-southwest of Forest Glen (lat. 40°09'25" N, long. 123°27'35" W; near E line sec. 35, T 3 S, R 6 E). Named on Zenia (1967) 7.5' quadrangle.

Kettenpom Creek [TRINITY]: *stream,* flows 5.5 miles to North Fork Eel River 5 miles east of Kettenpom (lat. 40°10'25" N, long. 123°22'10" W; sec. 27, T 3 S, R 7 E). Named on Lake Mountain (1967), Shannon Butte (1967), and Zenia (1967) 7.5' quadrangles.

Kettenpom Peak [TRINITY]: *peak,* 1 mile south-southwest of Kettenpom (lat. 40°08'45" N, long. 123°28'05" W; sec. 2, T 4 S, R 6 E). Altitude 4089 feet. Named on Zenia (1967) 7.5' quadrangle. The name is of Indian origin (Jones, p. 353).

Kettenpom Valley [TRINITY]: *valley,* 4 miles east-southeast of Kettenpom (lat. 40°07'45" N, long. 123°23'50" W); the valley is along Kettenpom Creek. Named on Lake Mountain (1967) and Zenia (1967) 7.5' quadrangles.

Kettinelbe: see **Phillipsville** [HUMBOLDT].

Ketty Gulch [MENDOCINO]: *canyon,* drained by a stream that flows 1.5 miles to Big Salmon Creek 5 miles north-northeast of Elk (lat. 39°12' N, long. 123°41'10" W; near S line sec. 31, T 16 N, R 16 W). Named on Elk (1960) 7.5' quadrangle.

Keystone Flat [TRINITY]: *area,* 11.5 miles north of Helena along North Fork Trinity River (lat. 40°56'10" N, long. 123°09'20" W); the place is 0.5 mile east-northeast of Keystone Meadows. Named on Helena (1951) 15' quadrangle.

Keystone Meadows [TRINITY]: *area,* 11 miles north of Helena (lat. 40°55'55" N, long. 123°09'50" W). Named on Helena (1951) 15' quadrangle.

Kibbey Peak [MENDOCINO]: *peak,* 4 miles east of the town of Potter Valley (lat. 39°19'50" N, long. 123°02'10" W; near W line sec. 13, T 17 N, R 11 W). Altitude 3380 feet. Named on Potter Valley (1960) 7.5' quadrangle.

Kibesillah [MENDOCINO]: *locality,* 3.25 miles south of Westport (lat. 39°35'25" N, long. 123°45'40" W; at N line sec. 20, T 20 N, R 17 W); the place is 0.25 mile east of the mouth of Kibesillah Creek. Named on Inglenook (1966) 7.5' quadrangle. Postal authorities established Kibesillah post office in 1874 and discontinued it in 1889 (Frickstad, p. 95). Kroeber (p. 45) suggested an Indian origin for the name.

Kibesillah Creek [MENDOCINO]: *stream,* flows 1.25 miles to the sea 2.25 miles south of Westport (lat. 39°35'30" N, long. 123°46'55" W; near S line sec. 17, T 20 N, R 17 W). Named on Inglenook (1966) 7.5' quadrangle.

Kibesillah Hill [MENDOCINO]: *peak,* 2.5 miles south of Westport (lat. 39°36'10" N, long. 123°46'50" W; sec. 17, T 20 N, R 17 W); the peak is west of Kibesillah Creek. Named on Inglenook (1966) 7.5' quadrangle.

Kibesillah Rock [MENDOCINO]: *rock,* 4 miles south of Westport, and 850 feet offshore (lat. 39°34'50" N, long. 123°46'45" W); the rock is less than 1 mile south of the mouth of Kibesillah Creek. Named on Inglenook (1966) 7.5' quadrangle. On Cape Vizcaino (1950) 15' quadrangle, the name applies to a feature located 1 mile farther south.

Kidwell Gulch [MENDOCINO]: *canyon,* drained by a stream that flows 1.5 miles to Big River 4.5 miles northwest of Comptche (lat. 39°18'55" N, long. 123°38'25" W; near SW cor. sec. 22, T 17 N, R 16 W). Named on Comptche (1960) 15' quadrangle.

Kiler Creek [HUMBOLDT]: *stream,* flows 2.5 miles to Eel River 1.5 miles south-southeast of Scotia (lat. 40°27'35" N, long. 124°05'20" W; near N line sec. 20, T 1 N, R 1 E). Named on Scotia (1970) 7.5' quadrangle.

Kilgore Ridge [MENDOCINO]: *ridge,* northeast-trending, 2 miles long, 14 miles north of Hull Mountain (lat. 39°44' N, long. 122°59'25" W). Named on Plaskett Ridge (1967) 7.5' quadrangle.

Kilpatrick Creek [LAKE]: *stream,* flows about 0.5 mile to Middle Creek (2) 4 miles north-northwest of the town of Upper Lake (lat. 39°13'10" N, long. 122°56'05" W; sec. 26, T 16 N, R 10 W). Named on Upper Lake (1958) 7.5' quadrangle.

Kilpepper Creek [LAKE]: *stream,* flows 3.5 miles to Stanton Creek 12 miles northeast of Clearlake Oaks (lat. 39°09'35" N, long. 122°32'05" W; sec. 9, T 15 N, R 6 W). Named on Clearlake Oaks (1960) and Wilbur Springs (1961) 15' quadrangles.

Kimball Gulch [MENDOCINO]: *canyon,* drained by a stream that flows 1.5 miles to South Fork Cottaneva Creek 7.5 miles north of Westport (lat. 39°44'45" N, long. 123°47'15" W; sec. 19, T 22 N, R 17 W). Named on Hales Grove (1970) and Westport (1966) 7.5' quadrangles.

Kimtu Meadows [HUMBOLDT]: *locality,* 2.25 miles southwest of Garberville along South Fork Eel River (lat. 40°04'30" N, long. 123°49'15" W; near NW cor. sec. 35, T 4 S, R 3 E). Named on Garberville (1970) 7.5' quadrangle.

Kingfisher Point [TRINITY]: *relief feature,* 2 miles west-northwest of Forest Glen (lat. 40°23'20" N, long. 123°21'25" W; near S line sec. 11, T 1 S, R 7 E). Named on Naufus Creek (1979) 7.5' quadrangle.

King Peak [HUMBOLDT]: *peak,* 6 miles south of Honeydew (lat. 40°09'25" N, long. 124°07'20" W); the feature is in King Range. Altitude 4088 feet. Named on Honeydew (1970) 7.5' quadrangle. Called Kings Peak on Eureka (1958) 1° x 2° quadrangle. The feature is the highest point on a well-known landfall generally called Three Peaks; in clear weather the landfall is visible seaward for about 75 miles (United States Coast and Geodetic Survey, p. 143). According to Gannett (p. 175), the name "King" is for an army captain.

King Range [HUMBOLDT]: *range,* between Honeydew and the coast; King Peak is a high point of the range. Named on Point Delgada (1949) 15' quadrangle. Chase (p. 287) called the feature King's Peak Range.

King Salmon [HUMBOLDT]: *locality,* 1 mile north of Fields Landing along Humboldt Bay (lat. 40°44'35" N, long. 124°13' W). Named on Fields Landing (1959) 7.5' quadrangle. United States Board on Geographic Names (1977a, p. 4) approved the name "King Salmon Slough" for a canal, 0.5 mile long, that extends southwest to Hookton Channel in Humboldt Bay 0.8 mile north of Fields Landing (lat. 40°44'11" N, long. 124°13'08" W).

King Salmon Slough: see **King Salmon** [HUMBOLDT].

Kingsberry: see **Hayfork** [TRINITY].

Kingsbury Gulch [TRINITY]: *canyon,* drained by a stream that flows 4.5 miles to Hayfork Creek at Hayfork (lat. 40°32'55" N, long. 123°11' W; sec. 11, T 31 N, R 12 W). Named on Hayfork (1951) 15' quadrangle. The canyon divides at the head into Middle Fork and North Fork, each of which is 1 mile long. East Fork opens into the main canyon from the east nearly 3 miles south-southeast of Hayfork and is 1.5 miles long. All three forks are named on Hayfork (1951) 15' quadrangle.

Kings Crossing [HUMBOLDT]: *locality,* 5.5 miles south-southeast of Coyote Peak along Lacks Creek (lat. 41°03'20" N, long. 123°49'40" W). Named on Hupa Mountain (1982) 7.5' quadrangle.

Kings Peak: see **King Peak** [HUMBOLDT].

King's Peak Range: see **King Range** [HUMBOLDT].

Kings Valley [DEL NORTE]: *area,* 6 miles north-northeast of Crescent City (lat. 41°50'15" N, long. 124°09'10" W). Named on Crescent City (1966) 7.5' quadrangle.

Kinman Pond [HUMBOLDT]: *lake,* 300 feet long, 5.5 miles west-southwest of Scotia on Bear River Ridge (lat. 40°27'40" N, long. 124°12'20" W; at N line sec. 20, T 1 N, R 1 W). Named on Taylor Peak (1969) 7.5' quadrangle. According to Gannett (p. 176), the name commemorates Seth Kinman, an early settler.

Kinney Public Camp [TRINITY]: *locality,* 8 miles north-northeast of Weaverville (lat. 40°50'10" N, long. 122°53'30" W; sec. 4, T 34 N, R 9 W). Named on Trinity Dam (1950) 15' quadrangle.

Kinsey Creek [HUMBOLDT]:

(1) *stream,* flows 1.5 miles to the sea 7.5 miles southwest of Honeydew (lat. 40°10'20" N, long. 124°13'45" W; sec. 30, T 3 S, R 1 W). Named on Shubrick Peak (1969) 7.5' quadrangle. Called Fraser Creek on Point Delgada (1949) 15' quadrangle, and United States Board on Geographic Names (1974a, p. 3) gave this name as a variant.

(2) *stream,* flows 2.25 miles to South Fork Salmon Creek 6 miles west-southwest of Phillipsville (lat. 40°10'50" N, long. 123°53'20" W; near SW cor. sec. 19, T 3 S, R 3 E). Named on Ettersburg (1969) 7.5' quadrangle.

Kinsey Creek: see **Oat Creek** [HUMBOLDT].

Kinsey Ridge [HUMBOLDT]:

(1) *ridge,* southwest-trending, 1.5 miles long, 6.5 miles southwest of Honeydew (lat. 40°11'10" N, long. 124°13'05" W); the ridge is on the northwest side of Kinsey Creek (1). Named on Shubrick Peak (1969) 7.5' quadrangle. Called Fraser Ridge on Point Delgada (1949) 15' quadrangle, and United States Board on Geographic Names (1974a, p. 3) gave this name as a variant.

(2) *ridge,* generally north-trending, 5 miles long, center 2.25 miles north-northeast of Board Camp Mountain (lat. 40°43'35" N, long. 123°41'50" W). Named on Board Camp Mountain (1977) and Grouse Mountain (1979) 7.5' quadrangles.

Kinsner Soda Spring: see **Hearst** [MENDOCINO].

Kirkham Creek [HUMBOLDT]: *stream,* flows 2.5 miles to Trinity River 3 miles north of the settlement of Willow Creek (lat. 40°58'50" N, long. 123°38'15" W; sec. 17, T 7 N, R 5 E). Named on Willow Creek (1979) 7.5' quadrangle.

Kit Prairie [HUMBOLDT]: *area,* nearly 5 miles south-southeast of Coyote Peak (lat. 41°03'10" N, long. 123°49'45" W; at SE cor. sec. 21, T 8

N, R 3 E). Named on Hupa Mountain (1982) 7.5' quadrangle.

Kittinelbe: see **Phillipsville** [HUMBOLDT].

Klamath [DEL NORTE]: *village*, 2.5 miles east-southeast of the mouth of Klamath River on the right bank of the stream (lat. 41°31'35" N, long. 124°02'15" W; sec. 10, T 13 N, R 1 E). Named on Requa (1966) 7.5' quadrangle. Klamath (1952) 15' quadrangle shows a much larger community. Postal authorities established Klamath post office in 1887, discontinued it in 1915, and reestablished it in 1927 (Salley, p. 112). About 1850 Herman Ehernberg and his party laid out Klamath City 3 miles from the mouth of Klamath River on the left bank; eventually the present village developed on the opposite side of the stream (McBeth, p. 66).

Klamath: see **Camp Klamath** [DEL NORTE]; **Johnsons** [HUMBOLDT].

Klamath City: see **Klamath** [DEL NORTE].

Klamath Cove: see **False Klamath Cove** [DEL NORTE].

Klamath Glen [DEL NORTE]: *village*, 5 miles east-southeast of the mouth of Klamath River (lat. 41°30'45" N, long. 123°59'30" W; sec. 18, T 13 N, R 2 E, and sec. 13, T 13 N, R 1 E); the village is along Klamath River. Named on Klamath Glen (1982) 7.5' quadrangle.

Klamath River [DEL NORTE-HUMBOLDT]: *stream*, heads in the State of Oregon and flows about 190 miles in Del Norte, Humboldt, and Siskiyou Counties to the sea 16 miles south-southeast of Crescent City (lat. 41°32'50" N, long. 124°04'50" W; sec. 5, T 13 N, R 1 E). Named on Eureka (1958) and Weed (1963) 1° x 2° quadrangles. Called Smiths R. on Burr's (1839) map, called Too too tut na or Klamet R. on Wilkes' (1841) map, called Smith's R. on Frémont's (1845) map, called Tlamath R. on Tanner's (1849) map, and called R. del Tlamachi on Ferry's (1851) map. The feature also was known as Clamitte River and Indian Scalp River (Hoover, Rensch, and Rensch, p. 504). Most early maps showed Klamath River reaching the sea in the present State of Oregon; the lower part of present Klamath River was represented as a continuation of present Trinity River, and was called Smith's River for Jedediah Smith, who explored the region in 1828—by 1851 the name "Smith's River" no longer was applied to present Klamath River, and later the name "Smith" was given to present Smith River (Hoover, Rensch, and Rensch, p. 68). A feature called Tucker Rock is situated at the mouth of Klamath River—the name is for M.G. Tucker, an early settler (McBeth (p. 47).

Klamath Rock: see **False Klamath Rock** [DEL NORTE].

Knack Creek [HUMBOLDT]: *stream*, flows 3 miles to Larabee Creek 11 miles southwest of Dinsmore (lat. 40°22'45" N, long. 123°44'50" W; sec. 17, T 1 S, R 4 E). Named on Larabee Valley (1977) 7.5' quadrangle.

Kneecap [LAKE]: *peak*, 8 miles east-northeast of Hull Mountain (lat. 39°34'20" N, long. 122°48'15" W; sec. 19, T 20 N, R 8 W). Named on Kneecap Ridge (1967) 7.5' quadrangle.

Kneecap Ridge [LAKE]: *ridge*, south-southwest- to west-trending, 4.5 miles long, 8 miles east-northeast of Hull Mountain on Lake-Glenn County line (lat. 39°34'20" N, long. 122°48'15" W); the peak called Kneecap is on the ridge. Named on Kneecap Ridge (1967) 7.5' quadrangle.

Kneeland [HUMBOLDT]: *village*, 7.5 miles south-southwest of Korbel (lat. 40°45'40" N, long. 123°59'35" W; sec. 6, T 4 N, R 2 E). Named on Korbel (1979) 7.5' quadrangle. On Kneeland (1922) 15' quadrangle, the village is shown situated about 3 miles farther southeast (sec. 15, T 4 N, R 2 E). Postal authorities established Kneeland post office in 1880, discontinued it in 1891, and reestablished it in 1892; the name commemorates John A. Kneeland and Tom Kneeland, the first men to settle at the place, which also was known as Kneeland Prairie (Salley, p. 113). Kneeland (1922) 15' quadrangle shows a place called Iaqua located 5.5 miles south of Kneeland (near SE cor. sec. 10, T 3 N, R 2 E), and also shows Fort Iaqua situated 4 miles east-southeast of Iaqua near present Iaqua Creek (sec. 29, T 3 N, R 3 E). Fort Iaqua was a military post started in 1863 and abandoned in 1866 (Hoover, Rensch, and Rensch, p. 100). Postal authorities established Jaqua post office in 1880, changed the name to Iaqua the same year, discontinued it in 1903, reestablished it in 1909, and discontinued it in 1920 (Salley, p. 102). Kneeland (1922) 15' quadrangle shows a place called Mountain View located about 5 miles east-southeast of Kneeland; Mad River Buttes (1977) 7.5' quadrangle shows Mountain View ranch at the same place. Postal authorities established Mandala post office 13.5 miles east of Kneeland in 1884, discontinued it for a time in 1887, and discontinued it finally in 1888; the name was for Mandala Kneeland—she and her brothers were the first white settlers at present Kneeland (Salley, p. 131).

Kneeland Prairie: see **Kneeland** [HUMBOLDT].

Knight Hill [MENDOCINO]: *peak*, 9.5 miles south-southeast of Ukiah (lat. 39°01'45" N, long. 123°08'10" W). Named on Elledge Peak (1958) 7.5' quadrangle.

Knob: see **The Knob** [TRINITY].

Knobcone Camp [LAKE]: *locality*, 6.5 miles west of Lakeport (lat. 39°02'40" N, long. 123°02' W; sec. 26, T 14 N, R 11 W). Named on Purdys Gardens (1958) 7.5' quadrangle.

Knobcone Spring [LAKE]: *spring*, 6.25 miles south of Potato Hill (lat. 39°16'40" N, long. 122°48'55" W). Named on Potato Hill (1967) 7.5' quadrangle.

Knocti: see **Lower Lake** [LAKE].

Knopti Creek [DEL NORTE]: *stream*, flows 5.25 miles to Middle Fork Smith River 3.5 miles northwest of Broken Rib Mountain (lat. 41°55'55" N, long. 123°44'10" W). Named on Broken Rib Mountain (1982) 7.5' quadrangle.

Knowles Gulch [TRINITY]: *canyon*, drained by a stream that flows 1.5 miles to Miners Creek 9.5 miles east-northeast of Hyampom (lat. 40°39'10" N, long. 123°16'35" W; near E line sec. 9, T 3 N, R 8 E). Named on Hyampom (1951) 15' quadrangle.

Knulthkarn Creek [HUMBOLDT]: *stream*, flows 1 mile to Klamath River 1.25 miles southeast of Johnsons (lat. 41°20'20" N, long. 123°51'15" W; sec. 17, T 11 N, R 3 E). Named on Johnsons (1982) 7.5' quadrangle. The name is the American version of an Indian term (Gudde, 1949, p. 177).

Knutz Creek [HUMBOLDT]: *stream*, flows 1.25 miles to Canon Creek 4 miles east-southeast of Korbel (lat. 40°51'10" N, long. 123°53'10" W; at N line sec. 6, T 5 N, R 3 E). Named on Korbel (1979) 7.5' quadrangle.

Konocti: see **Mount Konocti** [LAKE].

Konocti Bay [LAKE]: *embayment*, 7.5 miles northwest of the town of Lower Lake along Clear Lake (lat. 38°58'15" N, long. 122°43'45" W); the feature is 5 miles east-southeast of Mount Konocti. Named on Clearlake Highlands (1958) 7.5' quadrangle. United States Board on Geographic Names (1962a, p. 12) rejected the form "Konokti Bay" for the name.

Konokti Mountain: see **Pine Mountain** [LAKE] (3).

Kono Tayee Point [LAKE]: *promontory*, 8 miles east of Lakeport on the north side of the west end of The Narrows (2) (lat. 39°02'10" N, long. 122°45'45" W; sec. 29, T 14 N, R 8 W). Named on Lucerne (1958) 7.5' quadrangle.

Korbel [HUMBOLDT]: *village*, 1.5 miles east-southeast of the town of Blue Lake (lat. 40°52'10" N, long. 123°57'30" W; sec. 28, T 6 N, R 2 E). Named on Korbel (1979) 7.5' quadrangle. Postal authorities established Korbel post office in 1891 (Frickstad, p. 44). The place first was called North Fork, but the name was changed to Korbel in 1891 for the Korbel brothers, founders of Humboldt Lumber Mill Company in 1883 (Carranco and Sorensen, p. 8, 11, 13). Postal authorities established Acorn post office 8 miles northeast of Korbel in 1891, moved it 4 miles south in 1892, and discontinued it in 1904 (Salley, p. 1). The name "Acorn" was for Alonzo Acorn and Elizabeth Acorn (Turner, p. 1). California Mining Bureau's (1917b) map shows a place called Riverside located about 4 miles south-southeast of Korbel along a railroad that follows Mad River. Manning and Ogle's (1950) map shows a place called Camp 4 Flat situated 3 miles south-southeast of Korbel along Mad River (sec. 10, T 5 N, R 2 E).

Korblex [HUMBOLDT]: *locality*, 2.25 miles north-northeast of Arcata along Arcata and Mad River Railroad (lat. 40°54'15" N, long. 124°04'15" W; sec. 16, T 6 N, R 1 E). Named on Arcata North (1959) 7.5' quadrangle.

Kroll Creek [LAKE]: *stream*, flows 1.5 miles to Dry Creek (3) 2.5 miles southwest of Middletown (lat. 38°44' N, long. 122°39'05" W; sec. 8, T 10 N, R 7 W). Named on Mount Saint Helena (1959) 7.5' quadrangle.

Krueger Creek [HUMBOLDT]: *stream*, flows 1.5 miles to North Fork Mad River 5 miles north-northeast of the town of Blue Lake (lat. 40°56'45" N, long. 123°56'15" W; near W line sec. 34, T 7 N, R 2 E). Named on Blue Lake (1979) 7.5' quadrangle.

Kuntz: see **Ruth** [TRINITY].

Kuntz Canyon [HUMBOLDT-TRINITY]: *canyon*, drained by a stream that heads in Humboldt County and flows 2 miles to Van Duzen River 4 miles east-southeast of Dinsmore [HUMBOLDT] just inside Trinity County (lat. 40°27'40" N, long. 123°32'25" W; sec. 18, T 1 N, R 6 E). Named on Dinsmore (1977) 7.5' quadrangle.

— L —

Lacks Creek [HUMBOLDT]: *stream*, flows 8 miles to Redwood Creek (1) 5 miles south of Coyote Peak (lat. 41°03'40" N, long. 123°52'20" W; near SE cor. sec. 19, T 8 N, R 3 E). Named on Hupa Mountain (1982) and Lord-Ellis Summit (1973) 7.5' quadrangles. Called Luck Creek on Hoopa (1935) 30' quadrangle.

Lacoma Valley: see **Anderson Springs** [LAKE].

Ladder Ridge [LAKE]: *ridge*, generally west-southwest-trending, 3 miles long, 4.5 miles east of the town of Upper Lake (lat. 39°10'15" N, long. 122°49'45" W). Named on Bartlett Mountain (1958) 7.5' quadrangle.

Ladder Rock [HUMBOLDT]: *relief feature*, 3.5 miles west of Trinity Mountain (lat. 41°02'15" N, long. 123°28'45" W). Named on Trinity Mountain (1979) 7.5' quadrangle.

La Doo Creek [HUMBOLDT]: *stream*, flows 2.5 miles to West Fork Sproul Creek 7 miles southwest of Garberville (lat. 40°02'20" N, long. 123°53'45" W). Named on Briceland (1969) 7.5' quadrangle.

Ladybug Creek [LAKE]: *stream*, flows 2.5 miles to North Fork Cache Creek 15 miles north of Clearlake Oaks (lat. 39°12' N, long. 122°42'30"

W). Named on Clearlake Oaks (1960) 15' quadrangle.

Lady Gulch [TRINITY]: *canyon,* drained by a stream that flows 1 mile to Coffee Creek 8.5 miles west of Billys Peak (1) (lat. 41°07'20" N, long. 122°55'15" W; sec. 29, T 38 N, R 9 W). Named on Coffee Creek (1955) 15' quadrangle.

La Fume Basin [TRINITY]: *area,* 8 miles south-southeast of Forest Glen (lat. 40°15'45" N, long. 123°16'10" W; near E line sec. 28, T 2 S, R 8 E). Named on Forest Glen (1979) 7.5' quadrangle.

Lagoon: see **The Lagoon** [MENDOCINO].

Lagoon Creek [MENDOCINO]: *stream,* flows 2 miles to an unnamed lake near the coast 4 miles north of the village of Point Arena (lat. 38°57'50" N, long. 123°41'50" W; sec. 25, T 13 N, R 17 W). Named on Point Arena (1960) 7.5' quadrangle.

Lagoon Creek Pond: see **Mill Pond** [DEL NORTE].

Lagoon Pond: see **Mill Pond** [DEL NORTE].

Laguna: see **Clear Lake** [LAKE].

Laguna Creek [MENDOCINO]: *stream,* flows 5 miles to Big River 5.5 miles west-northwest of Comptche (lat. 39°17'15" N, long. 123°41'20" W; sec. 31, T 17 N, R 16 W); the stream goes through Big River Laguna. Named on Comptche (1960) 15' quadrangle.

Laguna de Guenoc: see **McCreary Lake** [LAKE].

Laguna Grande: see **Clear Lake** [LAKE].

Laguna Grande de Napa: see **Clear Lake** [LAKE].

Laguna Point [MENDOCINO]: *promontory,* 3 miles north of Fort Bragg along the coast (lat. 39°29'20" N, long. 123°48'15" W; sec. 19, T 19 N, R 17 W). Named on Fort Bragg (1960) 7.5' quadrangle.

Laird Meadow [DEL NORTE]: *area,* 16 miles east-southeast of Klamath Glen near Del Norte-Humboldt County line (lat. 41°23' N, long. 123°44'10" W). Named on Lonesome Ridge (1974) 7.5' quadrangle.

Lake Anna [TRINITY]: *lake,* 650 feet long, 14 miles north-northeast of Weaverville (lat. 40°55'50" N, long. 123°52'30" W; at SW cor. sec. 35, T 36 N, R 9 W). Named on Trinity Dam (1950) 15' quadrangle. United States Board on Geographic Names (1965b, p. 13) rejected the form "Anna Lake" for the name.

Lake Benbow: see **Benbow Lake** [HUMBOLDT].

Lake City [TRINITY]: *locality,* 13 miles south-southeast of Salmon Mountain (lat. 41°01'05" N, long. 123°16'40" W). Site named on Dees Peak (1978) 7.5' quadrangle. The place was an early mining camp that Indians reportedly burned in 1864 (United States Board on Geographic Names, 1977b, p. 4).

Lake Cleone [MENDOCINO]: *lake,* 1700 feet long, 3 miles north of Fort Bragg (lat. 39°29'20" N, long. 123°47'35" W; at S line sec. 19, T 19 N, R 17 W); the lake is 0.5 mile west-southwest of Cleone. Named on Fort Bragg (1960) 7.5' quadrangle.

Lake Creek [HUMBOLDT]: *stream,* flows 3.25 miles to North Fork Elk River (1) 7 miles east-southeast of Fields Landing (lat. 40°41'30" N, long. 124°05'25" W; near N line sec. 32, T 4 N, R 1 E). Named on McWhinney Creek (1979) 7.5' quadrangle.

Lake Earl [DEL NORTE]: *lake,* 3.5 miles long, 5 miles north of Crescent City (lat. 41°49' N, long. 124°11'10" W). Named on Crescent City (1966) 7.5' quadrangle. Called Talawa Lake on Goddard's (1857) map; the word "Talawa" is from the Indian name for a native village near the lake (Kroeber, p. 61).

Lake Eleanor [TRINITY]: *lake,* 450 feet long, 20 miles north-northeast of Weaverville (lat. 40°59'20" N, long. 122°46'25" W; near E line sec. 9, T 36 N, R 8 W). Named on Trinity Dam (1950) 15' quadrangle. Called Eleanor Lake on Averill's (1940) map. Fred Conway, of Conway Lake, discovered the feature and named it for his wife (Jones, p. 10).

Lake Gulch [MENDOCINO]: *canyon,* drained by a stream that flows 0.5 mile to Churchman Creek 15 miles north of Comptche (lat. 39°28'55" N, long. 123°37'40" W; at N line sec. 27, T 19 N, R 16 W). Named on Comptche (1960) 15' quadrangle.

Lake Gulch [TRINITY]: *canyon,* drained by a stream that flows 1 mile to Reading Creek 13 miles south-southeast of Weaverville (lat. 40°33'05" N, long. 122°51'15" W; sec. 11, T 31 N, R 9 W). Named on Weaverville (1950) 15' quadrangle.

Lake Hachinhama: see **Little Borax Lake** [LAKE].

Lake Hill: see **Lake Ridge** [HUMBOLDT].

Lake Káysa: see **Borax Lake** [LAKE].

Lake Lee [MENDOCINO]: *lake,* 100 feet long, 6.25 miles northwest of the town of Potter Valley (lat. 39°23' N, long. 123°11'30" W; sec. 28, T 18 N, R 12 W). Named on Potter Valley (1960) 15' quadrangle.

Lake Mendocino [MENDOCINO]: *lake,* behind a dam on East Fork Russian River 3.5 miles north-northeast of Ukiah (lat. 39°11'50" N, long. 123°11' W). Named on Ukiah (1958) 7.5' quadrangle. United States Board on Geographic Names (1960b, p. 9) rejected the name "Coyote Valley Reservoir" for the feature.

Lake Mountain [HUMBOLDT]: *peak,* 9 miles east of Board Camp Mountain (lat. 40°40'55" N, long. 123°33' W). Altitude 3932 feet. Named on Sims Mountain (1979) 7.5' quadrangle.

Lake Mountain [TRINITY]: *ridge,* north-trending, 2.5 miles long, 10 miles south-southeast of Kettenpom (lat. 40°01' N, long. 123°25' W; sec. 17, 20, T 5 S, R 7 E). Named on Lake Mountain (1967) 7.5' quadrangle, which shows Lake Mountain ranch situated 1.25 miles east of the ridge (near N line sec. 21, T 5 S, R 7 E). Postal authorities established Lake Mountain post office, named for the ranch, in 1878, discontinued it the same year, reestablished it in 1909, discontinued it in 1917, reestablished it in 1920, discontinued it in 1923, reestablished it in 1936, and discontinued it in 1953 (Salley, p. 116).

Lake Pillsbury [LAKE]: *lake,* behind a dam on Eel River 3 miles west of Bear Mountain (lat. 39°24'25" N, long. 122°57'30" W; on S line sec. 14, T 18 N, R 10 W). Named on Lake Pillsbury (1967) 7.5' quadrangle. The name commemorates E.S. Pillsbury, an organizer of Snow Mountain Water and Power Company in 1906; the reservoir filled for the first time in 1922 (Gudde, 1949, p. 262).

Lakeport [LAKE]: *town,* west of the center of Lake County on the west side of Clear Lake (lat. 39°02'45" N, long. 122°54'50" W; in and near sec. 24, T 14 N, R 10 W). Named on Lakeport (1958) 7.5' quadrangle. Postal authorities established Big Valley post office on the west side of Clear Lake in 1858 and changed the name to Lakeport in 1861 (Salley, p. 21). The place first was called Forbestown for William Forbes, owner of the land there; the name was changed to Lakeport when the community became the county seat (Gudde, 1949, p. 180).

Lakeport Lake: see **Scotts Creek** [LAKE].

Lakeport Peak [LAKE]: *peak,* 2.5 miles southwest of Lakeport (lat. 39°01'05" N, long. 122°56'30" W; sec. 35, T 14 N, R 10 W). Altitude 2180 feet. Named on Lakeport (1958) 7.5' quadrangle.

Lakeport Reservoir: see **Scotts Creek** [LAKE].

Lake Prairie [HUMBOLDT]:

(1) *lake,* 1550 feet long, 10.5 miles east-southeast of Korbel (lat. 40°47'15" N, long. 123°47'35" W; sec. 25, T 5 N, R 3 E). Named on Maple Creek (1977) 7.5' quadrangle.

(2) *area,* 1.25 miles north-northeast of Weitchpec (lat. 41°12'25" N, long. 123°41'50" W; around NE cor. sec. 3, T 9 N, R 4 E). Named on Weitchpec (1979) 7.5' quadrangle.

Lake Prairie Creek [HUMBOLDT]: *stream,* flows 2.5 miles to Redwood Creek (1) 12.5 miles east-southeast of Korbel (lat. 40°48' 05" N, long. 123°44'55" W; sec. 20, T 5 N, R 4 E); the stream heads at Lake Prairie (1). Named on Maple Creek (1977) 7.5' quadrangle.

Lake Ridge [HUMBOLDT]: *ridge,* west-trending, 2 miles long, 7.5 miles south of Petrolia (lat. 40°13'05" N, long. 124°16' W). Named on Cooskie Creek (1969) 7.5' quadrangle. United States Board on Geographic Names (1974b, p. 2) gave the name "Lake Hill" as a variant.

Lake Ridge [MENDOCINO]:

(1) *ridge,* west-southwest-trending, 3 miles long, 11 miles south-southeast of Branscomb (lat. 39°30'30" N, long. 123°34' W). Named on Sherwood Peak (1967) 7.5' quadrangle.

(2) *ridge,* west-trending, 3 miles long, 3.5 miles north-northeast of Navarro (lat. 39°12' N, long. 123°31'30" W). Named on Navarro (1961) 15' quadrangle.

Lake Talawa [DEL NORTE]: *lake,* nearly 1.5 miles long, 5.5 miles north of Crescent City (lat. 41°50' N, long. 124°12'55" W). Named on Crescent City (1966) 7.5' quadrangle. The feature is connected to Lake Earl, which is called Talawa Lake on Goddard's (1857) map. The word "Talawa" is from the Indian name for a native village near the lake (Kroeber, p. 61).

Lakeview: see **Point Lakeview** [LAKE].

Lamb Creek [TRINITY]: *stream,* flows 2.5 mile to Mad River 6 miles east-southeast of Dinsmore [HUMBOLDT] (lat. 40°27' N, long. 123°30'10" W; sec. 21, T 1 N, R 6 E). Named on Dinsmore (1977) and Sportshaven (1973) 7.5' quadrangles.

Lambert: see **George Lambert Canyon** [MENDOCINO]; **George Lambert Ridge** [MENDOCINO]; **Green Lambert Canyon** [MENDOCINO].

Lambert Ridge [MENDOCINO]: *ridge,* northwest-trending, 3.5 miles long, 4.5 miles west of Boonville (lat. 39°01'15" N, long. 123°27'15" W). Named on Boonville (1959) 15' quadrangle.

Lambertville: see **Freshwater** [HUMBOLDT].

Lamb Gap [TRINITY]: *pass,* 8 miles northwest of Forest Glen (lat. 40°26'15" N, long. 123°27' W; sec. 25, T 1 N, R 6 E). Named on Sportshaven (1973) 7.5' quadrangle.

Lance Gulch [TRINITY]: *canyon,* drained by a stream that flows 1 mile to the canyon of East Weaver Creek less than 1 mile east of the center of Weaverville (lat. 40°44' N, long. 122°55'30" W; sec. 7, T 33 N, R 9 W). Named on Weaverville (1950) 15' quadrangle.

Landers Creek [TRINITY]: *stream,* flows nearly 2 miles to Swift Creek (1) 10 miles south-southwest of Billys Peak (1) (lat. 41°00'45" N, long. 122°52' W; near NW cor. sec. 2, T 36 N, R 9 W); the stream heads near Landers Lake. Named on Coffee Creek (1955) 15' quadrangle.

Landers Lake [TRINITY]: *lake,* 650 feet long, 9.5 miles southwest of Billys Peak (1) (lat. 41°01'55" N, long. 122°53'15" W; near SW cor. sec. 27, T 37 N, R 9 W). Named on Coffee Creek (1955) 15' quadrangle.

Landis Gulch [TRINITY]: *canyon,* drained by a stream that flows 1 mile to Hayfork Creek 5 miles east of Dubakella Mountain (lat. 40°24' N, long. 123°03'30" W; near N line sec. 1, T 29 N, R 11 W). Named on Dubakella Mountain (1954) 15' quadrangle.

Lane Redwood Flat [MENDOCINO]: *locality*, 6 miles south-southeast of Piercy along South Fork Eel River (lat. 39°53'50" N, long. 123°45'10" W; near W line sec. 28, T 24 N, R 17 W). Named on Piercy (1950) 15' quadrangle.

Lang: see **Tom Lang Gulch** [TRINITY].

Langdon Flat [TRINITY]: *area*, 12.5 miles northeast of Weaverville along Trinity River (lat. 40°50'30" N, long. 122°45' W). Named on Schell Mountain (1950) and Trinity Lake (1950) 15' quadrangles. Water of Clair Engle Lake now covers the place.

Langdon Gulch [TRINITY]: *canyon*, drained by a stream that flows 2.25 miles to Langdon Flat 12.5 miles northeast of Weaverville (lat. 40°50'15" N, long. 122°45'15" W; sec. 3, T 34 N, R 8 W). Named on Schell Mountain (1950) 15' quadrangle.

Langtry Lake: see **McCreary Lake** [LAKE].

Larabee [HUMBOLDT]: *locality*, 1 mile east-northeast of Redcrest along Northwestern Pacific Railroad (lat. 40°24'20" N, long. 123°55'40" W; on W line sec. 2, T 1 S, R 2 E); the place is near the mouth of Larabee Creek. Named on Redcrest (1969) 7.5' quadrangle. Called Larrabee on California Mining Bureau's (1917b) map. Postal authorities established Laribee post office in 1888, discontinued it in 1891, reestablished it in 1892, discontinued it in 1899, reestablished it with the name "Larabee" in 1921, and discontinued it in 1925 (Salley, p. 118). They established Dinty post office 10 miles north of Blocksburg in 1921 and discontinued it the same year, when they moved the service to Larabee (Salley, p. 59). California Mining Bureau's (1917b) map shows a place called Bryan situated along the railroad between Shively and Larrabee (present Larabee). Vander Leck's (1920b) map shows a place called Bryant located on the east side of Eel River about 1 mile north of present Larabee.

Larabee Buttes [HUMBOLDT]: *ridge*, northwest-trending, 1.5 miles long, 7.5 miles southwest of Dinsmore (lat. 40°25'45" N, long. 123°43'15" W); the ridge is 2.25 miles southwest of Larabee Valley. Named on Larabee Valley (1977) 7.5' quadrangle.

Larabee Creek [HUMBOLDT]: *stream*, flows 25 miles to Eel River 1 mile northeast of Redcrest (lat. 40°24'35" N, long. 123°55'55" W; sec. 3, T 1 S, R 2 E). Named on Blocksburg (1969), Bridgeville (1969), Larabee Valley (1977), and Redcrest (1969) 7.5' quadrangles. Hank Larabee had a cattle ranch along the stream (Carranco and Beard, p. 63).

Larabee Creek: see **Little Larabee Creek** [HUMBOLDT].

Larabee Valley [HUMBOLDT]: *valley*, 5.25 miles southwest of Dinsmore (lat. 40°26'40" N, long. 123°40'45" W). Named on Larabee Valley (1977) 7.5' quadrangle.

Largo [MENDOCINO]: *locality*, 10 miles south-southeast of Ukiah along Northwestern Pacific Railroad (lat. 39°01'20" N, long. 123°07'45" W). Named on Elledge Peak (1958) 7.5' quadrangle. Postal authorities established Largo post office in 1889, moved it 0.75 mile northwest in 1897, and discontinued it in 1905; the name recalls Lemuel F. Long, who settled at the place in 1858—*largo* has the meaning "long" in Spanish (Salley, p. 118).

Laribee: see **Larabee** [HUMBOLDT].

Larmer Gulch [MENDOCINO]: *canyon*, drained by a stream that flows 0.5 mile to South Fork Albion River 6.5 miles northwest of Navarro (lat. 39°13'30" N, long. 123°37'10" W; near S line sec. 23, T 16 N, R 16 W). Named on Navarro (1961) 15' quadrangle.

Larmour Creek [MENDOCINO]: *stream*, flows 4 miles to Garcia River 7.5 miles west of Ornbaun Valley (lat. 38°55'30" N, long. 123°26'40" W; sec. 5, T 12 N, R 14 W). Named on Ornbaun Valley (1960) 15' quadrangle.

La Rue Gulch [HUMBOLDT]: *canyon*, drained by a stream that flows 1.25 miles to the sea 3.25 miles west of Petrolia (lat. 40°19'10" N, long. 124°20'50" W; sec. 1, T 2 S, R 3 W). Named on Petrolia (1969) 7.5' quadrangle.

Lassecks Peak: see **Mount Lassic** [HUMBOLDT].

Lassic Peak: see **Mount Lassic** [HUMBOLDT].

Last Chance Camp [TRINITY]: *locality*, 7 miles south-southwest of Cecilville, which is in Siskiyou County (lat. 41°03'15" N, long. 123°11'40" W). Site named on Cecil Lake (1979) 7.5' quadrangle.

Last Chance Creek [HUMBOLDT]: *stream*, flows 2.25 miles to Grouse Creek (2) 5 miles east northeast of Board Camp Mountain (lat. 40°43' N, long. 123°37'25" W); the stream heads at Last Chance Ridge. Named on Sims Mountain (1979) 7.5' quadrangle.

Last Chance Gulch [TRINITY]: *canyon*, drained by a stream that flows 1 mile to Little Browns Creek 3 miles east-northeast of Weaverville (lat. 40°44'55" N, long. 122°53'10" W; sec. 4, T 33 N, R 9 W). Named on Trinity Dam (1950) and Weaverville (1950) 15' quadrangles.

Last Chance Ridge [HUMBOLDT]: *ridge*, 2 miles long, 5.25 miles east of Board Camp Mountain (lat. 40°41' N, long. 123°37'30" W). Named on Board Camp Mountain (1977) and Sims Mountain (1979) 7.5' quadrangles.

Last Prairie [HUMBOLDT]: *area*, 8 miles south-southeast of Coyote Peak (lat. 41°02'10" N, long. 123°47'25" W; on W line sec. 36, T 8 N, R 3 E). Named on Hupa Mountain (1982) 7.5' quadrangle.

Lauder Flat [LAKE-MENDOCINO]: *area*, 5.25 miles northeast of the town of Potter Valley [MENDOCINO] along Eel River on Lake-Mendocino County line (lat. 39°22'45" N, long. 123°02'50" N; on S line sec. 26, T 18 N, R 11 W). Named on Potter Valley (1960) 15' quadrangle.

Laughlin [MENDOCINO]: *locality*, 7.5 miles west-southwest of the town of Potter Valley along Northwestern Pacific Railroad (lat. 39°16'45" N, long. 123°14' W; near S line sec. 31, T 17 N, R 12 W). Named on Redwood Valley (1960) 7.5' quadrangle. Postal authorities established Laughlin post office for a time in 1902, established it again in 1903, and discontinued it 1911; the name was for James H. Laughlin, Jr., a pioneer landowner in the vicinity (Salley, p. 119).

Laughlin Range [MENDOCINO]: *ridge*, west-trending, less than 1 mile long, 7.5 miles southeast of Willits (lat. 39°19'25" N, long. 123°16'15" W; in and near sec. 14, T 17 N, R 13 W). Named on Willits (1961) 15' quadrangle.

Laurel Beach [LAKE]: *beach*, 4.25 miles southeast of the town of Upper Lake along Clear Lake (lat. 39°07'20" N, long. 122°51'05" W; sec. 27, T 15 N, R 9 W). Named on Lucerne (1958) 7.5' quadrangle.

Laurel Butte [DEL NORTE]: *peak*, 3.25 miles north-northwest of Broken Rib Mountain (lat. 41°55'55" N, long. 123°43' W). Named on Broken Rib Mountain (1982) 7.5' quadrangle. Called Haystack on Preston Peak (1922) 30' quadrangle.

Laurel Creek [HUMBOLDT]: *stream*, flows less than 1 mile to South Fork Eel River 5 miles south of Garberville (lat. 40°01'40" N, long. 123°47'30" W; near NW cor. sec. 13, T 5 S, R 3 E). Named on Garberville (1970) 7.5' quadrangle.

Laurel Creek [MENDOCINO]: *stream*, flows nearly 2 miles to Tomki Creek 3.5 miles east of Longvale (lat. 39°32'55" N, long. 123°21'40" W; sec. 36, T 20 N, R 14 W). Named on Willis Ridge (1966) 7.5' quadrangle.

Laurel Dell: see **Saratoga Springs** [LAKE].

Laurel Gulch [MENDOCINO]: *canyon*, drained by a stream that flows 2 miles to the sea less than 1 mile northwest of Elk (lat. 39°08'20" N, long. 123°43'35" W; sec. 27, T 15 N, R 17 W). Named on Elk (1960) 7.5' quadrangle.

Lawrence Creek [HUMBOLDT]: *stream*, flows 14 miles to Yager Creek 7 miles west-southwest of Lone Star Junction (lat. 40°34'50" N, long. 123°59'30" W; sec. 6, T 2 N, R 2 E). Named on Iaqua Buttes (1979) and Owl Creek (1979) 7.5' quadrangles.

Lawyers Bar: see **Sawyers Bar Camp Ground** [DEL NORTE].

Laytonville [MENDOCINO]: *town*, 20 miles north-northwest of Willits (lat. 39°41'10" N, long. 123°28'45" W; sec. 12, T 21 N, R 15 W). Named on Laytonville (1967) 7.5' quadrangle. Postal authorities established Laytonville post office in 1879 (Frickstad, p. 95). F.B. Layton founded the town when he built a blacksmith shop and dwelling place at the site in 1874 (Carpenter, p. 113). Postal authorities established Cahto post office 3 miles southwest of Laytonville in 1863 and discontinued it in 1901 (Salley, p. 31). Robert White and John P. Simpson started the community of Cahto in 1856, opened a hotel there in 1861, and opened a store in 1865 (Carpenter, p. 114). California Mining Bureau's (1917c) map shows the place with the misspelled name "Canto." Postal authorities established Tilly post office 9 miles west of Cahto post office in 1883 and discontinued it in 1887 (Salley, p. 222).

Lazy Creek [MENDOCINO]: *stream*, flows 2 miles to Navarro River 9.5 miles northwest of Boonville (lat. 39°06' N, long. 123°30' W; sec. 3, T 14 N, R 15 W). Named on Boonville (1959) 15' quadrangle.

Lazyman Flat [TRINITY]: *area*, 13 miles south of Black Rock Mountain (lat. 40°00'35" N, long. 123°01'25" W; near NW cor. sec. 19, T 25 N, R 10 W). Named on Black Rock Mountain (1954) 15' quadrangle.

Leary Creek [HUMBOLDT]: *stream*, flows 3.5 miles to Red Cap Creek 9 miles east-northeast of Weitchpec (lat. 41°14'05" N, long. 123°32'40" W). Named on Hopkins Butte (1979) 7.5' quadrangle. Middle Fork enters 0.5 mile upstream from the mouth of the main creek; it is 2.5 miles long and is named on Hopkins Butte (1979) 7.5' quadrangle. South Fork enters Middle Fork from the south 0.5 mile upstream from the mouth of Middle Fork; it is 1 mile long and is named on Hopkins Butte (1979) 7.5' quadrangle.

Lee: see **Lake Lee** [MENDOCINO].

Leech Lake [MENDOCINO]: *lake*, 350 feet long, 12 miles northeast of Covelo (lat. 39°55'05" N, long. 123°05'10" W; near E line sec. 21, T 24 N, R 11 W). Named on Leech Lake Mountain (1966) 7.5' quadrangle.

Leech Lake Mountain [MENDOCINO]: *peak*, 12.5 miles northeast of Covelo (lat. 39°55'25" N, long. 123°05' W); the peak is 0.5 mile north-northeast of Leech Lake. Altitude 6637 feet. Named on Leech Lake Mountain (1966) 7.5' quadrangle. Lieutenant Augustus G. Tassen, a topographical officer at Camp Wright in Round Valley, gave the name "Bland Mountain" to present Leech Lake Mountain in the 1870's (Carranco and Beard, p. 5).

Lee Creek [LAKE]: *stream*, flows nearly 2 miles to Alder Creek (3) 11 miles south-southeast of Kelseyville (lat. 38°49'50" N, long. 122°45'30" W; near SE cor. sec. 5, T 11 N, R 8 W). Named on The Geysers (1959) and Whispering Pines (1958) 7.5' quadrangles.

Lee Creek [MENDOCINO]: *stream,* flows 2 miles to Garcia River 5.25 miles east of the village of Point Arena (lat. 38°53'40" N, long. 123°35'40" W; near NE cor. sec. 23, T 12 N, R 16 W). Named on Point Arena (1960) 15' quadrangle.

Leggett [MENDOCINO]: *village,* 17 miles northwest of Laytonville along South Fork Eel River (lat. 39°51'55" N, long. 123°42'50" W); the village is in Leggett Valley. Named on Leggett (1969) 7.5' quadrangle. Postal authorities established Leggett post office in 1949 (Frickstad, p. 95). The community was known as Leggett Valley before postal authorities shortened the name (Gudde, 1969, p. 175).

Leggett: see **South Leggett** [MENDOCINO].

Leggett Creek [HUMBOLDT]: *stream,* flows 4.25 miles to South Fork Eel River nearly 6 miles south-southwest of Phillipsville (lat. 40°07'50" N, long. 123°49'15" W; sec. 11, T 4 S, R 3 E). Named on Miranda (1970) 7.5' quadrangle.

Leggett Valley [MENDOCINO]: *valley,* 17 miles northwest of Laytonville along South Fork Eel River (lat. 39°51'15" N, long. 123°43' W). Named on Leggett (1969) 7.5' quadrangle. The name commemorates an early pioneer (Gudde, 1969, p. 175).

Leggett Valley: see **Leggett** [MENDOCINO].

Leggit Creek [HUMBOLDT]: *stream,* flows 2 miles to Mad River 3.5 miles east-northeast of Arcata (lat. 40°53'25" N, long. 124°00'55" W; sec. 24, T 6 N, R 1 E). Named on Arcata North (1959) 7.5' quadrangle.

Lemonade Spring [TRINITY]: *spring,* 7 miles west-northwest of Forest Glen (lat. 40°25'35" N, long. 123°26'30" W; sec. 36, T 1 N, R 6 E). Named on Sportshaven (1973) 7.5' quadrangle.

Lems Ridge [DEL NORTE]: *ridge,* generally south-trending, 3.25 miles long (lat. 41°36'45" N, long. 123°52'15" W). Named on Klamath Glen (1982), Ship Mountain (1982), and Summit Valley (1981) 7.5' quadrangles.

Leonard Lake [MENDOCINO]: *lake,* 0.5 mile long, 10 miles south of Willits (lat. 39°16'05" N, long. 123°27' W; sec. 1, T 16 N, R 14 W). Named on Willits (1961) 15' quadrangle. The name commemorates John Leonard, who owned the lake (Gudde, 1949, p. 186).

Le Perron Flat [HUMBOLDT]: *area,* 10.5 miles east-northeast of Weitchpec (lat. 41°14'35" N, long. 123°31'10" W); the place is 0.5 mile north-northwest of Le Perron Peak. Named on Hopkins Butte (1979) 7.5' quadrangle.

Le Perron Peak [HUMBOLDT]: *peak,* 10.5 miles east-northeast of Weitchpec (lat. 41°14'05" N, long. 123°30'45" W). Named on Hopkins Butte (1979) 7.5' quadrangle. The name is for Yves Le Perron, a miner (Turner, p. 130).

Le Perron Peak Spring [HUMBOLDT]: *spring,* 10.5 miles east-northeast of Weitchpec (lat. 41°14'15" N, long. 123°31' W); the spring is 0.25 mile northwest of Le Perron Peak. Named on Hopkins Butte (1979) 7.5' quadrangle.

Lepoil Rock [HUMBOLDT]: *rock,* 1 mile northwest of Trinidad, and 750 feet offshore (lat. 41°04' N, long. 124°09'35" W). Named on Trinidad (1966) 7.5' quadrangle.

Lewis Creek [MENDOCINO]: *stream,* flows nearly 2 miles to Tenmile Creek 8.5 miles northeast of Branscomb (lat. 39°44'20" N, long. 123°30'50" W; at N line sec. 27, T 22 N, R 15 W). Named on Cahto Peak (1967), Iron Peak (1967), and Tan Oak Park (1969) 7.5' quadrangles.

Lewis Gulch [HUMBOLDT]: *canyon,* drained by a stream that flows nearly 1.5 miles to Klamath River 8 miles southeast of Johnsons (lat. 41°15'30" N, long. 123°46'35" W; sec. 13, T 10 N, R 3 E). Named on Johnsons (1982) 7.5' quadrangle.

Lewis Opening [HUMBOLDT]: *area,* 12 miles south-southwest of Alderpoint (lat. 40°00'45" N, long. 123°40'30" W; near N line sec. 24, T 5 S, R 4 E). Named on Harris (1969) 7.5' quadrangle.

Lewiston [TRINITY]: *town,* 7.5 miles east-southeast of Weaverville along Trinity River (lat. 40°42'25" N, long. 122°48'20" W; around NW cor. sec. 20, T 33 N, R 8 W). Named on Weaverville (1950) 15' quadrangle. Called Lewistown on Red Bluff (1894) 1° quadrangle, and called Leviston on Miller's (1890) map. The place also was known as Louiston (Hanna, p. 171). Postal authorities established Lewiston post office in 1854, discontinued it the same year, and reestablished it in 1855 (Frickstad, p. 208). B.F. Lewis had a trading post and ferry at the site (Jones, p. 271).

Lewiston Lake [TRINITY]: *lake,* behind a dam on Trinity River 7.5 miles east of Weaverville (lat. 40°43'30" N, long. 122°47'40" W; sec. 8, T 33 N, R 8 W). Named on Trinity Dam (1950) 15' quadrangle. Called Lewiston Reservoir on Trinity Lake (1950) 15' quadrangle, but United States Board on Geographic Names (1965c, p. 11) rejected this name for the feature.

Lewiston Reservoir: see **Lewiston Lake** [TRINITY].

Lewistown: see **Lewiston** [TRINITY].

Lick Creek [TRINITY]:

(1) *stream,* flows 1.5 miles to North Fork Coffee Creek 4.5 miles west-northwest of Billys Peak (1) (lat. 41°09'20" N, long. 122°50'40" W; sec. 13, T 38 N, R 9 W). Named on Coffee Creek (1955) 15' quadrangle.

(2) *stream,* flows 3.25 miles to North Fork Swift Creek (1) 3 miles west-northwest of Trinity Center (lat. 41°01' N, long. 122°44'45" W; sec. 35, T 37 N, R 8 W). Named on Bonanza King (1955) and Coffee Creek (1955) 15' quadrangles.

Lick Creek: see **Little Lick Creek** [TRINITY].

Lightfoot Creek [TRINITY]: *stream,* flows 2 miles to North Fork Eel River 9 miles east-southeast of Kettenpom (lat. 40°05'35" N, long. 123°19' W; near N line sec. 30, T 4 S, R 8 E). Named on Long Ridge (1967) 7.5' quadrangle.

Lightning Camp [MENDOCINO]: *locality,* 13 miles north-northeast of Covelo (lat. 39°58'30" N, long. 123°11'25" W; sec. 34, T 25 N, R 12 W). Named on Bluenose Ridge (1967) 7.5' quadrangle. The place received its name after lightning killed 400 sheep there (Jones, p. 362).

Lightning Camp Ridge [TRINITY]:

(1) *ridge,* west- to southwest-trending, 2.5 miles long, 10 miles south-southwest of Black Rock Mountain (lat. 40°05' N, long. 123°06'30" W). Named on Black Rock Mountain (1954) 15' quadrangle.

(2) *ridge,* generally northwest-trending, 2 miles long, 14 miles north of Covelo [MENDOCINO] near Mendocino-Trinity County line (lat. 39°59'15" N, long. 123°11'50" W); Lightning Camp [MENDOCINO] is near the south end of the ridge. Named on Bluenose Ridge (1967) 7.5' quadrangle.

Lily Lake [TRINITY]:

(1) *intermittent lake,* 4.25 miles south-southeast of Hyampom (lat. 40°33'30" N, long. 123°25'10" W; on E line sec. 18, T 2 N, R 7 E). Named on Hyampom (1951) 15' quadrangle.

(2) *lake,* 200 feet long, 17 miles northeast of Covelo [MENDOCINO] (lat. 39°58'55" N, long. 123°03' W; near N line sec. 35, T 25 N, R 11 W). Named on Leech Lake Mountain (1966) 7.5' quadrangle.

Lily Lake: see **Lily Pad Lake** [MENDOCINO].

Lily Pad Lake [MENDOCINO]: *lake,* 250 feet long, 10 miles south-southeast of Eden Valley (lat. 39°30'45" N, long. 123°04'45" W; near S line sec. 9, T 19 N, R 11 W). Named on Sanhedrin Mountain (1966) 7.5' quadrangle. Called Lily Lake on Eden Valley (1929) 15' quadrangle.

Lilypad Lake [TRINITY]: *lake,* 500 feet long, 7.5 miles south-southwest of Billys Peak (1) (lat. 41°01'45" N, long. 122°48'25" W; near N line sec. 32, T 37 N, R 8 W). Named on Coffee Creek (1955) 15' quadrangle.

Limb Camp Creek [HUMBOLDT]: *stream,* flows 1.5 miles to Trinity River nearly 4 miles south-southeast of Weitchpec (lat. 41°08' N, long. 123°41'15" W; sec. 26, T 9 N, R 4 E). Named on Weitchpec (1979) 7.5' quadrangle.

Limedyke Mountain [TRINITY]: *peak,* 6.5 miles south-southeast of Hyampom (lat. 40°31'35" N, long. 123°25' W; sec. 29, T 2 N, R 7 E). Altitude 4694 feet. Named on Hyampom (1951) 15' quadrangle.

Limekiln Gulch [TRINITY]: *canyon,* drained by a stream that flows 1 mile to Trinity River 4 miles southeast of Weaverville (lat. 40°41'30" N, long. 122°53'15" W; near N line sec. 28, T 33 N, R 9 W). Named on Weaverville (1950) 15' quadrangle. Gudde (1975, p. 194) used the form "Lime Kiln Gulch" for the name, and noted that a place called Point Bar is opposite the mouth of the canyon. Postal authorities established Limestairs post office in Lime Kiln Gulch (SW quarter sec. 19, T 5 N, R 6 E) in 1916 and discontinued it in 1928 (Salley, p. 122).

Limestairs: see **Limekiln Gulch** [TRINITY].

Limestone Creek [TRINITY]: *stream,* flows 2 miles to Big Creek (1) 8 miles north-northeast of Hayfork (lat. 40°40' N, long. 123°08'45" W); the stream is west of Limestone Ridge (2). Named on Hayfork (1951) 15' quadrangle.

Limestone Gulch [TRINITY]: *canyon,* drained by a stream that flows 1 mile to Hayfork Creek 3.5 miles east of Hayfork (lat. 40°33'20" N, long. 123°07'10" W; sec. 9, T 31 N, R 11 W). Named on Hayfork (1951) 15' quadrangle.

Limestone Ridge [TRINITY]:

(1) *ridge,* south-trending, 16 miles long, center about 13 miles north-northwest of Helena (lat. 40°57' N, long. 123°14' W). Named on Helena (1951) 15' quadrangle, and on Cecil Lake (1979) 7.5' quadrangle.

(2) *ridge,* south-trending, 1.5 miles long, 9.5 miles north of Hayfork (lat. 40°41'15" N, long. 123°08'40" W). Named on Hayfork (1951) 15' quadrangle.

Lincoln: see **Camp Lincoln** and **Fort Lincoln**, under **Elk Valley** [DEL NORTE] (1).

Lincoln Bluff [LAKE]: *relief feature,* 4 miles east-southeast of the town of Upper Lake (lat. 39°09'15" N, long. 122°50' W; near NW cor. sec. 14, T 15 N, R 9 W). Named on Bartlett Mountain (1958) 7.5' quadrangle.

Lincoln Ridge [MENDOCINO]: *ridge,* irregular, but generally southwest-trending, 8.5 miles long, center about 5.5 miles west-northwest of Branscomb (lat. 39°42' N, long. 123°43' W). Named on Lincoln Ridge (1966) and Westport (1966) 7.5' quadrangles.

Lincoln Rock [LAKE]: *relief feature,* 2.25 miles south of Whispering Pines (lat. 38°46'50" N, long. 122°43'10" W; near W line sec. 26, T 11 N, R 8

W). Named on Whispering Pines (1958) 7.5' quadrangle.

Lincoln's Fort: see **Elk Valley** [DEL NORTE] (1).

Lindquist Ridge [LAKE]: *ridge*, north-trending, 1 mile long, 2.5 miles south-southwest of Middletown (lat. 38°43'10" N, long. 122°38'30" W; sec. 9, 16, T 10 N, R 7 W). Named on Mount Saint Helena (1959) 7.5' quadrangle.

Lindsay Creek [HUMBOLDT]: *stream*, flows 7 miles to Mad River 3.25 miles northeast of Arcata (lat. 40°54'20" N, long. 124°02'10" W; sec. 14, T 6 N, R 1 E). Named on Arcata North (1959) 7.5' quadrangle. The name is for William Robert Lindsay, an early settler along the creek (Turner, p. 131).

Line Gulch [HUMBOLDT]: *canyon*, drained by a stream that flows 3.5 miles to Dobbyn Creek 4 miles north of Alderpoint (lat. 40°14' N, long. 123°37'30" W; sec. 4, T 3 S, R 5 E). Named on Alderpoint (1969) and Black Lassic (1979) 7.5' quadrangles.

Line Gulch [MENDOCINO-TRINITY]: *canyon*, drained by a stream that heads in Mendocino County and flows 3.5 miles to Middle Fork Eel River 16 miles northeast of Covelo [MENDOCINO] just inside Trinity County (lat. 39°58'50" N, long. 123°05'15" W; near NW cor. sec. 34, T 25 N, R 11 W). Named on Leech Lake Mountain (1966) 7.5' quadrangle.

Line Gulch [TRINITY]: *canyon*, drained by a stream that flows 3.25 miles to South Dobbyn Creek 5.25 miles east of Alderpoint [HUMBOLDT] (lat. 40°10'20" N, long. 123°30'35" W; sec. 28, T 3 S, R 6 E). Named on Alderpoint (1969) and Zenia (1967) 7.5' quadrangles. The stream in the canyon is called Yew Wood Cr. on Alderpoint (1949) 15' quadrangle.

Linton Ridge [TRINITY]: *ridge*, generally west-trending, 4.5 miles long, 19 miles northeast of Weaverville (lat. 40°54'35" N, long. 122°38'30" W). Named on Schell Mountain (1950) 15' quadrangle.

Lion Lake [TRINITY]: *lake*, 500 feet long, 7.25 miles southwest of Billys Peak (1) (lat. 41°02'50" N, long. 122°50'55" W; on W line sec. 24, T 37 N, R 9 W). Named on Coffee Creek (1955) 15' quadrangle.

Lippitt: see **Bucksport** [HUMBOLDT].

Lipps Camp [TRINITY]: *locality*, 8.5 miles south of Salmon Mountain (lat. 41°03'45" N, long. 123°26'15" W). Named on Trinity Mountain (1979) 7.5' quadrangle.

Liscom Hill [HUMBOLDT]: *relief feature*, 3 miles north-northeast of the town of Blue Lake (lat. 40°55'10" N, long. 123°57'35" W; sec. 9, T 6 N, R 2 E). Named on Blue Lake (1979) 7.5' quadrangle. The name commemorates Charles Henry Liscom, who had a claim on the feature (Turner, p. 131).

Liscom Slough [HUMBOLDT]: *stream*, flows 3 miles to Mad River Slough 3 miles west of Arcata (lat. 40°52'35" N, long. 124°08'10" W). Named on Arcata North (1959), Arcata South (1959), Eureka (1958), and Tyee City (1959) 7.5' quadrangles.

Little Bald Hill [HUMBOLDT]: *peak*, 6.25 miles southwest of Ferndale on Oil Creek Ridge (lat. 40°31'10" N, long. 124°21'20" W; at S line sec. 25, T 2 N, R 3 W). Named on Ferndale (1959) 7.5' quadrangle.

Little Baldy [MENDOCINO]:

(1) *peak*, 9.5 miles north-northeast of Covelo (lat. 39°55'35" N, long. 123°12'15" W; sec. 21, T 24 N, R 12 W). Altitude 3646 feet. Named on Bluenose Ridge (1967) 7.5' quadrangle.

(2) *peak*, 1.25 miles west of Anthony Peak (lat. 39°51' N, long. 122°59'15" W; near E line sec. 17, T 23 N, R 10 W). Altitude 5932 feet. Named on Mendocino Pass (1967) 7.5' quadrangle.

(3) *peak*, 8 miles north of Hull Mountain (lat. 39°37'55" N, long. 122°57'35" W; sec. 34, T 21 N, R 10 W); the feature is 1 mile northeast of Bald Mountain (5). Altitude 6212 feet. Named on Plaskett Ridge (1967) 7.5' quadrangle.

(4) *peak*, 6 miles east-northeast of Spyrock (2) (lat. 39°54'50" N, long. 123°20'40" W). Altitude 3021 feet. Named on Mina (1967) 7.5' quadrangle.

Little Baldy Ridge [MENDOCINO]: *ridge*, generally northwest trending, 2 miles long, 14 miles east-northeast of Covelo (lat. 39°51'30" N, long. 123°00' W); little Baldy (2) is at the southeast end of the ridge. Named on Mendocino Pass (1967) and Newhouse Ridge (1967) 7.5' quadrangles.

Little Bally [TRINITY]: *peak*, 5 miles east of Helena (lat. 40°46' N, long. 123°02' W). Altitude 4210 feet. Named on Helena (1951) 15' quadrangle.

Little Barker Creek [TRINITY]: *stream*, flows 3 miles to Barker Creek 4.5 miles northeast of Hayfork (lat. 40°35'30" N, long. 123°06'55" W; sec. 28, T 32 N, R 11 W). Named on Hayfork (1951) 15' quadrangle.

Little Bark Shanty Creek [TRINITY]: *stream*, flows 2 miles to East Fork Browns Creek 16 miles south of Weaverville (lat. 40°29'50" N, long. 122°53'20" W; sec. 33, T 31 N, R 9 W). Named on Weaverville (1950) 15' quadrangle.

Little Bear Basin [DEL NORTE]: *area*, 8 miles south-southwest of Broken Rib Mountain (lat. 41°46'30" N, long. 123°44'15" W); the place is 2 miles south of Bear Basin. Named on Preston Peak (1956) 15' quadrangle.

Little Bear Creek [MENDOCINO]: *stream*, flows nearly 2 miles to Usal Creek 8 miles south-southwest of Piercy (lat. 39°51'45" N, long. 123°50'30" W); the mouth of the creek is 250 feet downstream from the mouth of Bear Creek (2). Named on Hales Grove (1970) and Piercy (1969) 7.5' quadrangles.

Little Bear Gulch [TRINITY]:

(1) *canyon*, drained by a stream that flows 1.5 miles to Mumbo Creek 15 miles north-northeast of Trinity Center (lat. 41°12'15" N, long. 122°33'40" W; near N line sec. 33, T 39 N, R 6 W); the mouth of the canyon is nearly 1 mile upstream along Mumbo Creek from the mouth of Big Bear Gulch. Named on Bonanza King (1955) 15' quadrangle.

(2) *canyon*, drained by a stream that flows 1 mile to Trinity River 14 miles northeast of Weaverville (lat. 40°51'25" N, long. 122°43'10" W; sec. 25, T 35 N, R 8 W); the mouth of the canyon is 2 miles upstream along Trinity River from the mouth of Bear Gulch (3). Named on Schell Mountain (1950) 15' quadrangle.

Little Bear Haven Creek [MENDOCINO]: *stream*, flows 2.5 miles to Middle Fork Ten Mile River 7.5 miles south of Branscomb (lat. 39°32'50" N, long. 123°38'15" W; near SE cor. sec. 33, T 20 N, R 16 W). Named on Dutchmans Knoll (1966) and Sherwood Peak (1967) 7.5' quadrangles.

Little Bear Lake [TRINITY]: *lake*, 900 feet long, 12.5 miles north of Trinity Center (lat. 41°11'25" N, long. 122°42'10" W; on N line sec. 5, T 38 N, R 7 W); the lake is 0.5 mile east-southeast of Big Bear Lake. Named on Bonanza King (1955) 15' quadrangle. Called Bear Lake on Etna (1934) 30' quadrangle.

Little Bear Prairie [HUMBOLDT]: *area*, 6 miles north-northwest of Coyote Peak (lat. 41°13' N, long. 123°54' W; near W line sec. 36, T 10 N, R 2 E); the place is less than 1 mile east of Bear Prairie. Named on Bald Hills (1982) 7.5' quadrangle.

Little Bear Rock [MENDOCINO]: *relief feature*, 5 miles north-northeast of Hull Mountain (39°35' N, long. 122°53'30" W; near S line sec. 17, T 20 N, R 9 W). Named on Hull Mountain (1967) 7.5' quadrangle.

Little Bear Wallow Creek [MENDOCINO]: *stream*, flows nearly 1 mile to Huckleberry Creek 7.5 miles northwest of Branscomb (lat. 39°43'50" N, long. 123°43'30" W; near W line sec. 26, T 22 N, R 17 W); the mouth of the creek is 600 feet upstream along Huckleberry Creek from the mouth of Bear Wallow Creek (1). Named on Lincoln Ridge (1966) 7.5' quadrangle.

Little Bear Wallow Creek [TRINITY]: *stream*, flows 4.25 miles to South Fork Trinity River 6 miles northwest of Forest Glen (lat. 40°25'35" N, long. 123°24'30" W; sec. 32, T 1 N, R 7 E). Named on Naufus Creek (1979) and Sportshaven (1973) 7.5' quadrangles. Called Bearwallow Cr. on Hoaglin (1935) 30' quadrangle, and called Bear Wallow Creek on Anada (1918) 15' quadrangle.

Little Bear Wallow Meadow [TRINITY]: *area*, 4.5 miles north-northwest of Forest Glen (lat. 40°26'10" N, long. 123°20'55" W; sec. 25, 26, T 1 N, R 7 E); the place is at the head of Little Bear Wallow Creek. Named on Naufus Creek (1979) 7.5' quadrangle.

Little Bidden Creek [TRINITY]: *stream*, flows 1 mile to Trinity River 2 miles southeast of Burnt Ranch (lat. 40°47'25" N, long. 123°27'05" W; near SE cor. sec. 24, T 5 N, R 6 E); the mouth of the creek is 400 feet downstream along Trinity River from the mouth of Bidden Creek (1). Named on Ironside Mountain (1951) 15' quadrangle.

Little Black Rock [MENDOCINO]: *peak*, 5 miles northeast of Laytonville (lat. 39°44'35" N, long. 123°25'10" W; sec. 22, T 22 N, R 14 W); the peak is 1 mile north-northeast of Black Rock. Altitude 3855 feet. Named on Laytonville (1967) 7.5' quadrangle.

Little Black Rock [TRINITY]: *peak*, 5.25 miles east-southeast of Dubakella Mountain on Trinity-Shasta County line (lat. 40°20'55" N, long. 123°03'25" W; sec. 24, T 29 N, R 11 W). Named on Dubakella Mountain (1954) 15' quadrangle.

Little Borax Lake [LAKE]: *lake*, 1450 feet long, 9 miles east-southeast of Lakeport (lat. 39°00'10" N, long. 122°45'20" W; sec. 4, T 13 N, R 8 W). Named on Lucerne (1958) 7.5' quadrangle. Commercial extraction of borax from the lake began in 1869; the feature first was called Lake Hachinhama (Simoons, p. 301).

Little Boulder Creek [HUMBOLDT]: *stream*, flows 3.5 miles to Boulder Creek 8 miles north-northeast of Lone Star Junction (lat. 40°44'10" N, long. 123°48'35" W; near S line sec. 11, T 4 N, R 3 E). Named on Mad River Buttes (1977) and Maple Creek (1977) 7.5' quadrangles.

Little Boulder Creek [TRINITY]: *stream*, flows 4 miles to Coffee Creek 6.25 miles north-northwest of Trinity Center (lat. 41°05'10" N, long. 122°44'40" W; near N line sec. 11, T 37 N, R 8 W); the stream heads at Little Boulder Lake and joins Coffee Creek 2.25 miles downstream from the mouth of Boulder Creek (1). Named on Bonanza King (1955) and Coffee Creek (1955) 15' quadrangles.

Little Boulder Lake [TRINITY]: *lake*, 700 feet long, 6 miles south-southwest of Billys Peak (1) (lat. 41°02'50" N, long. 122°47'45" W; near SE cor. sec. 20, T 37 N, R 8 W); the lake is at the head of Little Boulder Creek. Named on Coffee Creek (1955) 15' quadrangle.

Little Brannan Creek [HUMBOLDT]: *stream*, flows 1.25 miles to Brannan Creek 2 miles west-northwest of the settlement of Willow Creek (lat. 40°57' N, long. 123°40'05" W; sec. 25, T 7 N, R 4 E). Named on Willow Creek (1979) 7.5' quadrangle.

Little Browns Creek [TRINITY]: *stream*, flows 10 miles to Weaver Creek 2.5 miles south of Weaverville (lat. 40°41'45" N, long. 122°55'40" W; at S line sec. 19, T 33 N, R 9 W). Named on Trinity Dam (1950) and Weaverville (1950) 15' quadrangles. Called Browns Creek on Weaverville (1913) 30' quadrangle.

Little Browns Creek: see **Little Creek** [TRINITY] (1).

Little Buck Creek: see **Buck Mountain Creek** [HUMBOLDT].

Little Buck Mountain [HUMBOLDT]: *peak*, 9 miles southwest of Alderpoint (lat. 40°06'10" N, long. 123°44'55" W; at E line sec. 20, T 4 S, R 4 E). Altitude 2338 feet. Named on Garberville (1970) and Harris (1969) 7.5' quadrangles.

Little Buck Rock [MENDOCINO]: *relief feature*, 5.5 miles north-northeast of Anthony Peak (lat. 39°55'20" N, long. 122°56'05" W; sec. 23, T 24 N, R 10 W); the feature is 1.25 miles northeast of Buck Rock. Named on Buck Rock (1967) 7.5' quadrangle.

Little Burr Creek [HUMBOLDT]: *stream*, flows 2.25 miles to Burr Creek 3 miles south-southeast of Bridgeville (lat. 40°25'55" N, long. 123°46'15" W; sec. 30, T 1 N, R 4 E). Named on Bridgeville (1969) and Larabee Valley (1977) 7.5' quadrangles.

Little Butte [MENDOCINO]: *relief feature*, 8 miles north-northeast of Leggett (lat. 39°58'10" N, long. 123°39'35" W; near NE cor. sec. 6, T 24 N, R 16 W). Named on Noble Butte (1969) 7.5' quadrangle. Called Noble Butte on Leggett (1952) 15' quadrangle.

Little Butte [TRINITY]: *peak*, 13 miles southwest of Black Rock Mountain (lat. 40°03'30" N, long. 123°10' W; sec. 36, T 26 N, R 12 W); the peak is 1.5 miles north-northwest of Big Butte. Altitude 5632 feet. Named on Black Rock Mountain (1954) 15' quadrangle.

Little Butte Creek [HUMBOLDT]: *stream*, flows 1.5 miles to Ellison Creek 2 miles east-southeast of Lone Star Junction (lat. 40°37'15" N, long. 123°50'30" W; near S line sec. 21, T 3 N, R 3 E). Named on Mad River Buttes (1977) and Yager Junction (1979) 7.5' quadrangles.

Little Case Creek [MENDOCINO]: *stream*, flows 3.25 miles to Tenmile Creek 7 miles east-northeast of Branscomb (lat. 39°41'30" N, long. 123°30'05" W; sec. 11, T 21 N, R 15 W). Named on Cahto Peak (1967) 7.5' quadrangle.

Little Cave Creek [MENDOCINO]: *stream*, flows nearly 2 miles to Cave Creek 8 miles northwest of the town of Potter Valley (lat. 39°23'35" N, long. 123°13'45" W; at S line sec. 19, T 18 N, R 12 W). Named on Potter Valley (1960) and Willits (1961) 15' quadrangles.

Little Cedar Creek [MENDOCINO]: *stream*, flows 1.5 miles to Cedar Creek 4.5 miles east of Leggett (lat. 39°52'35" N, long. 123°37'40" W; at N line sec. 4, T 23 N, R 16 W). Named on Leggett (1969) 7.5' quadrangle.

Little Chaparral Mountain [HUMBOLDT]: *peak*, 5 miles south of Petrolia (lat. 40°15'10" N, long. 124°16'40" W; sec. 34, T 2 S, R 2 W). Altitude 2653 feet. Named on Petrolia (1969) 7.5' quadrangle.

Little Charlie Creek [MENDOCINO]: *stream*, flows 1.5 miles to South Fork Eel River 3.25 miles north-northwest of Branscomb (lat. 39°41'45" N, long. 123°39'05" W; near N line sec. 9, T 21 N, R 16 W); the stream enters South Fork Eel River 0.5 mile downstream from the mouth of Dutch Charlie Creek. Named on Lincoln Ridge (1966) 7.5' quadrangle.

Little Chemise Knob [MENDOCINO]: *peak*, 2 miles east of Dos Rios (lat. 39°42'50" N, long. 123°19' W); the peak is less than 1 mile north-northwest of Big Chemise Knob. Altitude 1999 feet. Named on Dos Rios (1967) 7.5' quadrangle.

Little Clover Gulch [TRINITY]: *canyon*, drained by a stream that flows 1 mile to North Fork Mad River 11.5 miles west-southwest of Black Rock Mountain (lat. 40°10'05" N, long. 123°13'20" W; near N line sec. 26, T 27 N, R 12 W); the canyon is north of Clover Gulch (2). Named on Black Rock Mountain (1954) 15' quadrangle.

Little Cow Gulch [TRINITY]: *canyon*, drained by a stream that flows 1.5 miles to Salt Gulch 4.5 miles north-northeast of Dubakella Mountain (lat. 40°27' N, long. 123°07'30" W; sec. 17, T 30 N, R 11 W); the mouth of the canyon is 0.5 mile below the mouth of Cow Gulch (2). Named on Dubakella Mountain (1954) 15' quadrangle.

Little Cow Mountain [LAKE]: *ridge*, south- to southeast-trending, 3 miles long, 6.5 miles west-southwest of the town of Upper Lake (lat. 39°07'55" N, long. 123°01'05" W). Named on Cow Mountain (1958) and Purdys Gardens (1958) 7.5' quadrangles.

Little Creek [HUMBOLDT]: *stream*, flows 0.5 mile to Prairie Creek 10 miles north of Orick (lat. 41°25'35" N, long. 124°02'10" W; sec. 15, T 12 N, R 1 E). Named on Fern Canyon (1966) 7.5' quadrangle.

Little Creek [MENDOCINO]: *stream*, flows about 2 miles to Tomki Creek 11 miles northwest of the town of Potter Valley (lat. 39°26' N, long. 123°14'40" W; near SE cor. sec. 1, T 18 N, R 13 W). Named on Willits (1961) 15' quadrangle.

Little Creek [TRINITY]:

(1) *stream*, flows 6 miles to Browns Creek 7.5 miles south of Weaverville (lat. 40°37'35" N, long. 122°57'30" W; at E line sec. 14, T 32 N, R 10 W). Named on Weaverville (1950) 15' quadrangle. Called Little Browns Cr. on Averill's (1940) map.

(2) *stream*, flows 7 miles to Hayfork Creek 10 miles east of Hyampom (lat. 40°35'10" N, long. 123°15'30" W). Named on Hayfork (1951) and Hyampom (1951) 15' quadrangles. Called Middle Creek on United States Geological Survey's (1915) map.

Little Creek: see **Bear Creek** [TRINITY] (6).

Little Dann Creek [MENDOCINO]: *stream*, flows nearly 2 miles to Big Dann Creek 1.5 miles south-southeast of Leggett (lat. 39°50'35" N, long. 123°41'55" W; at W line sec. 13, T 23 N, R 17 W). Named on Leggett (1969) 7.5' quadrangle. Called Little Dan Creek on Leggett (1952) 15' quadrangle.

Little Darby Peak [MENDOCINO]: *peak*, 5.25 miles east-northeast of Willits (lat. 39°26'50" N, long. 123°16'15" W; sec. 2, T 18 N, R 13 W); the peak is 1.25 miles east of Big Darby Peak. Altitude 2828 feet. Named on Willits (1961) 15' quadrangle.

Little Deep Creek [TRINITY]: *stream*, flows 2.5 miles to Stuart Fork 12 miles north of Weaverville (lat. 40°54'15" N, long. 122°56'40" W); the mouth of the stream is 0.5 mile downstream along Stuart Fork from the mouth of Deep Creek. Named on Trinity Dam (1950) 15' quadrangle.

Little Deer Creek [HUMBOLDT]: *stream*, flows 2.5 miles to Deer Creek (1) 5 miles south-southeast of Board Camp Mountain (lat. 40°37'50" N, long. 123°41'15" W; sec. 23, T 3 N, R 4 E). Named on Board Camp Mountain (1977) 7.5' quadrangle.

Little Deer Creek [TRINITY]: *stream*, flows 1.25 miles to Deer Creek (1) 16 miles north of Weaverville (lat. 40°57'45" N, long. 122°56'15" W; near E line sec. 19, T 36 N, R 9 W). Named on Trinity Dam (1950) 15' quadrangle.

Little Doe Campground [MENDOCINO]: *locality*, nearly 4 miles north-northwest of Anthony Peak (lat. 39°53'40" N, long. 122°59'15" W; sec. 32, T 24 N, R 10 W). Named on Buck Rock (1967) 7.5' quadrangle.

Little Doe Ridge [MENDOCINO]: *ridge*, west-trending, 2 miles long, 5 miles north-northwest of Anthony Peak (lat. 39°02'10" N, long. 122°59'15" W). Named on Buck Rock (1967) and Leech Lake Mountain (1966) 7.5' quadrangles.

Littlefield Creek [TRINITY]:

(1) *stream*, flows 2 miles to Mad River 8.5 miles south of Forest Glen (lat. 40°14'55" N, long. 123°19'05" W; sec. 31, T 2 S, R 8 E). Named on Forest Glen (1979) and Shannon Butte (1967) 7.5' quadrangles.

(2) *stream*, flows 2 miles to Red Mountain Creek (2) 12 miles east-southeast of Kettenpom (lat. 40°04'30" N, long. 123°15'45" W; sec. 30, T 26 N, R 12 W). Named on Black Rock Mountain (1954) 15' quadrangle, and on Long Ridge (1967) 7.5' quadrangle.

Little Finley Creek [HUMBOLDT]: *stream*, flows 3.5 miles to Mattole River 6.5 miles northeast of Point Delgada (lat. 40°06' N, long. 124°00'05" W; near W line sec. 19, T 4 S, R 2 E); the stream is north of Big Finley Creek. Named on Shelter Cove (1969) 7.5' quadrangle.

Little French Creek [TRINITY]: *stream*, flows 6 miles to Trinity River 9.5 miles east-southeast of Burnt Ranch (lat. 40°46'15" N, long. 123°18'15" W; at S line sec. 29, T 5 N, R 8 E); the stream enters Trinity River 1 mile upstream from the mouth of Big French Creek. Named on Helena (1951) and Ironside Mountain (1951) 15' quadrangles.

Little Freshwater Creek [HUMBOLDT]: *stream*, flows 3.5 miles to Freshwater Creek 8 miles south of Arcata near Freshwater (lat. 40°45'25" N, long. 124°03'45" W; at W line sec. 3, T 4 N, R 1 E). Named on Arcata South (1959) and McWhinney Creek (1979) 7.5' quadrangles.

Little Granite Peak [TRINITY]: *peak*, 14 miles north of Weaverville (lat. 40°56' N, long. 122°59'50" W). Altitude 8043 feet. Named on Helena (1951) and Trinity Dam (1950) 15' quadrangles.

Little Grass Valley Creek [TRINITY]: *stream*, flows 7 miles to Grass Valley Creek 8.5 miles southeast of Weaverville (lat. 40°39'45" N, long. 122°48'10" W; near W line sec. 5, T 32 N, R 8 W). Named on Weaverville (1950) 15' quadrangle, and on French Gulch (1979) and Shasta Bally (1978) 7.5' quadrangles.

Little Grayback [DEL NORTE]: *peak*, 10 miles northeast of Broken Rib Mountain on Del Norte-Siskiyou County line (lat. 41°58'40" N, long. 123°32'05" W). Altitude 6161 feet. Named on Polar Bear Mountain (1982) 7.5' quadrangle.

Little Head [HUMBOLDT]: *promontory*, along the coast at Trinidad (lat. 41°03'25" N, long. 124°08'45" W; sec. 26, T 8 N, R 1 W); the feature is just east of Trinidad Head. Named on Trinidad (1966) 7.5' quadrangle. Called Little Trinidad Head on Trinidad (1952) 15' quadrangle.

Little High Valley [LAKE]: *valley*, 7.5 miles north-northeast of Middletown (lat. 38°51'30" N, long. 122°34'45" W; sec. 25, T 12 N, R 7 W, and sec. 30, T 12 N, R 6 W). Named on Middletown (1958) 7.5' quadrangle.

Little Horse Canyon [MENDOCINO]: *canyon*, drained by a stream that flows 1.5 miles to Horse Canyon 11.5 miles north of Covelo (lat. 39°57'30" N, long. 123°13'40" W; near NE cor. sec. 7, T 24 N, R 12 W). Named on Bluenose Ridge (1967) 7.5' quadrangle.

Little Horse Mountain [LAKE]: *ridge*, generally west-northwest-tending, 1.5 miles long, 6.5 miles south of Potato Hill (lat. 39°15'15" N, long. 122°48'15" W). Named on Bartlett Mountain (1958) and Potato Hill (1967) 7.5' quadrangles.

Little Horse Opening [MENDOCINO]: *area,* 10 miles west-northwest of Ornbaun Valley (lat. 38°57'05" N, long. 123°28'45" W; on W line sec. 36, T 13 N, R 15 W); the place is 1 mile west of Big Horse Opening. Named on Ornbaun Valley (1960) 15' quadrangle.

Little Howard Creek [MENDOCINO]: *stream,* flows 1 mile to the sea 3.25 miles north of Westport (lat. 39°41'05" N, long. 123°47'30" W; sec. 7, T 21 N, R 17 W); the mouth of the stream is 0.5 mile north of the mouth of Howard Creek (2). Named on Westport (1966) 7.5' quadrangle.

Little Indian Valley [LAKE]: *valley,* 5.5 miles long, along North Fork Cache Creek above a point 9 miles northeast of Clearlake Oaks (lat. 39°05' N, long. 122°32'10" W). Named on Clearlake Oaks (1960) 15' quadrangle. Called Upper Indian Valley on Chandler's (1901) map. United States Board on Geographic Names (1968a, p. 5) rejected the designation "Indian Valley" for the feature.

Little Jackass Creek [MENDOCINO]: *stream,* flows 1 mile to the sea 10 miles south-southwest of Piercy (lat. 39°51'35" N, long. 123°54'05" W). Named on Mistake Point (1969) 7.5' quadrangle.

Little Jones Creek [DEL NORTE]: *stream,* flows nearly 4 miles to Middle Fork Smith River 7.25 miles east-northeast of Gasquet (lat. 41°52'05" N, long. 123°49'55" W; near E line sec. 16, T 17 N, R 3 E). Named on Hurdygurdy Butte (1982) 7.5' quadrangle. Called Jones Creek on Gasquet (1951) 15' quadrangle, but United States Board on Geographic Names (1979, p. 4) rejected this name for the feature.

Little Juan Creek [MENDOCINO]: *stream,* flows nearly 3 miles to Juan Creek 4.5 miles north of Westport (lat. 39°42'10" N, long. 123°47'50" W; sec. 6, T 21 N, R 17 W). Named on Westport (1966) 7.5' quadrangle.

Little Lake: see **Willits** [MENDOCINO].

Little Lake Valley [MENDOCINO]: *valley,* about 6 miles long, at and near Willits (lat. 39°25'30" N, long. 123°20' W). Named on Willits (1961) 15' quadrangle. The name is from a small lake located near the south end of the valley (Gudde, 1949, p. 189).

Little Larabee Creek [HUMBOLDT]: *stream,* flows 6.25 miles to Van Duzen River 1 mile northeast of Bridgeville (lat. 40°28'40" N, long. 123°46'50" W; sec. 12, T 1 N, R 3 E). Named on Bridgeville (1969) and Larabee Valley (1977) 7.5' quadrangles.

Little Lick Creek [TRINITY]: *stream,* flows 1.5 miles to North Fork Coffee Creek 4.5 miles west-northwest of Billys Peak (1) (lat. 41°08'50" N, long. 122°50'30" W; sec. 13, T 38 N, R 9 W); the mouth of the creek is 0.5 mile downstream from the mouth of Lick Creek. Named on Coffee Creek (1955) 15' quadrangle. South Fork enters 0.5 mile upstream from the mouth of the main creek; it is 1 mile long and is named on Coffee Creek (1955) 15' quadrangle.

Little Lost Man Creek [HUMBOLDT]: *stream,* flows nearly 5 miles to Prairie Creek 3.25 miles north-northeast of Orick (lat. 41°19' 45" N, long. 124°01'50" W; sec. 23, T 11 N, R 1 E). Named on Holter Ridge (1983) and Orick (1966) 7.5' quadrangles.

Little Low Gap Creek [MENDOCINO]: *stream,* flows 1 mile to Low Gap Creek (4) 3.5 miles south-southeast of Leggett (lat. 39°49'05" N, long. 123°40'55" W; near E line sec. 25, T 23 N, R 17 E). Named on Leggett (1969) 7.5' quadrangle.

Little Mahalock Creek: see **Mahala Creek** [HUMBOLDT].

Little Marshy Lake [TRINITY]: *lake,* 400 feet long, 6 miles north of Billys Peak (1) (lat. 41°13'15" N, long. 122°45'30" W; near SE cor. sec. 22, T 39 N, R 8 W); the lake is 700 feet east-southeast of Big Marshy Lake. Named on Coffee Creek (1955) 15' quadrangle.

Little McDonald Gulch [MENDOCINO]: *canyon,* drained by a stream that flows nearly 1 mile to Albion River less than 1 mile southeast of Comptche (lat. 39°15'20" N, long. 123°34'50" W; sec. 7, T 16 N, R 15 W); the mouth of the creek is 150 feet downstream along Albion River from the mouth of McDonald Gulch. Named on Comptche (1960) 15' quadrangle.

Little Mill Creek [DEL NORTE]: *stream,* flows 3 miles to Smith River 9 miles north-northeast of Crescent City (lat. 41°52'55" N, long. 124°07'25" W; near S line sec. 12, T 17 N, R 1 W). Named on High Divide (1966) and Hiouchi (1966) 7.5' quadrangles.

Little Mingo Creek [HUMBOLDT]: *stream,* flows 1 mile to South Fork Trinity River 11 miles south-southeast of the settlement of Willow Creek (lat. 40°47'15" N, long. 123°33'50" W); the mouth of the creek is less than 0.5 mile upstream from the mouth of Mingo Creek. Named on Hennessy Peak (1979) 7.5' quadrangle.

Little Moorehead Ridge [HUMBOLDT]: *ridge,* northeast-trending, 1.5 miles long, 5 miles west-southwest of Honeydew (lat. 40°13'05" N, long. 124°12'30" W); the ridge is north of Moorhead Ridge. Named on Shubrick Peak (1969) 7.5' quadrangle.

Little Mule Creek [TRINITY]: *stream,* flows 2.5 miles to Mule Creek 12 miles north-northeast of Weaverville (lat. 40°52'15" N, long. 122°48'45" W; sec. 19, T 35 N, R 8 W). Named on Trinity Dam (1950) 15' quadrangle.

Little Palmer Creek [HUMBOLDT]: *stream,* flows 1.5 miles to lowlands along Eel River 1.5 miles west-northwest of Fortuna (lat. 40°36'15" N, long. 124°10'45" W; near NE cor. sec. 33, T 3 N, R 1 W). Named on Fortuna (1959) 7.5' quadrangle.

Little Papoose Creek [TRINITY]: *stream,* flows 2.5 miles to Papoose Creek 11.5 miles east-northeast of Weaverville (lat. 40°48'10" N, long. 122°44' W; near E line sec. 14, T 34 N, R 8 W). Named on Schell Mountain (1950) 15' quadrangle.

Little Penny [MENDOCINO]: *relief feature,* 8.5 miles west of Ornbaun Valley (lat. 38°55'25" N, long. 123°27'35" W; near E line sec. 6, T 12 N, R 14 W). Named on Ornbaun Valley (1960) 15' quadrangle.

Little Picayune Creek [TRINITY]: *stream,* flows 3.25 miles to Picayune Creek 8 miles south of China Mountain, which is in Siskiyou County (lat. 41°16' N, long. 122°33'15" W; sec. 4, T 39 N, R 6 W). Named on Bonanza King (1955) and China Mountain (1955) 15' quadrangles.

Little Pilot Rock [HUMBOLDT]: *relief feature,* 3.5 miles north-northeast of Showers Mountain (lat. 40°37'25" N, long. 123°39'35" W; near W line sec. 19, T 3 N, R 5 E); the feature is less than 1 mile west of Pilot Rock (2). Named on Showers Mountain (1978) 7.5' quadrangle.

Little Pine Creek [HUMBOLDT]: *stream,* flows 5 miles to Pine Creek (1) 4 miles east-northeast of Coyote Peak (lat. 41°08'50" N, long. 123°02'05" W; sec. 24, T 9 N, R 3 E). Named on French Camp Ridge (1983) and Hupa Mountain (1982) 7.5' quadrangles.

Little Pine Flat [MENDOCINO]: *area,* 9.5 miles east-northeast of Spyrock (2) (lat. 39°56'15" N, long. 123°17' W); the place is 0.5 mile south of Pine Flat. Named on Mina (1967) 7.5' quadrangle.

Little Pinnacle [LAKE]: *relief feature,* 7.25 miles east of the town of Upper Lake (lat. 39°09'30" N, long. 122°46'25" W; near N line sec. 17, T 15 N, R 8 W). Altitude 4524 feet. Named on Bartlett Mountain (1958) 7.5' quadrangle.

Little Prairie [TRINITY]: *locality,* 10.5 miles east-southeast of Burnt Ranch along Trinity River (lat. 40°45'40" N, long. 123°17' W; sec. 33, T 5 N, R 8 E); the place is opposite the mouth of Prairie Creek. Named on Ironside Mountain (1951) 15' quadrangle.

Little Rainbow Ridge [HUMBOLDT]: *ridge,* generally southwest-trending, 2 miles long, 10 miles south-southwest of Scotia (lat. 40°20'45" N, long. 124°08'45" W); the ridge extends southwest from Rainbow Ridge. Named on Buckeye Mountain (1970) 7.5' quadrangle.

Little Rattlesnake Creek [TRINITY]: *stream,* flows 3 miles to Rattlesnake Creek (2) 1 mile east of Forest Glen (lat. 40°22'25" N, long. 123°18'10" W; near S line sec. 17, T 1 S, R 8 E). Named on Forest Glen (1979) 7.5' quadrangle.

Little Rattlesnake Mountain [DEL NORTE}: *ridge,* generally northwest-trending, 3.5 miles long, 7 miles northwest of Buck Mountain (lat. 41°41'15" N, long. 123°57'30" W); the ridge is north of Rattlesnake Mountain. Named on Cant Hook Mountain (1982) 7.5' quadrangle.

Little Red Cap Gulch [HUMBOLDT]: *canyon,* drained by a stream that flows less than 1 mile to Klamath River 3.5 miles west-southwest of Orleans (lat. 41°16'30" N, long. 123°36'05" W); the mouth of the canyon is 750 feet upstream from the mouth of Red Cap Gulch. Named on Orleans (1978) 7.5' quadrangle.

Little Red Mountain [MENDOCINO]: *ridge,* generally west-trending, 1.5 miles long, 3 miles east of Leggett (lat. 39°52'15" N, long. 123°39'30" W). Named on Leggett (1969) 7.5' quadrangle.

Little Red Mountain Creek [TRINITY]: *stream,* flows 3 miles to Red Mountain Creek 16 miles southwest of Black Rock Mountain (lat. 40°04'45" N, long. 123°15' W; near E line sec. 31, T 26 N, R 12 W). Named on Black Rock Mountain (1954) 15' quadrangle, and on Long Ridge (1967) 7.5' quadrangle. Called North Fk. [of Red Mountain Creek] on Hoaglin (1935) 30' quadrangle.

Little Red Rock Mountain [MENDOCINO]: *peak,* 12.5 miles southwest of Ornbaun Valley (lat. 38°47'15" N, long. 123°28'30" W; near W line sec. 19, T 11 N, R 14 W). Altitude 1385 feet. Named on Ornbaun Valley (1960) 15' quadrangle.

Little Ripstein Gulch [TRINITY]: *canyon,* drained by a stream that flows 2.5 miles to Canyon Creek (1) 8.5 miles northeast of Helena (lat. 40°52'30" N, long. 123°01'55" W); the mouth of the canyon is 0.5 mile downstream from the mouth of Ripstein Gulch. Named on Helena (1951) 15' quadrangle.

Little River [HUMBOLDT]: *stream,* flows 18 miles to the sea 2.5 miles southeast of Trinidad (lat. 41°01'40" N, long. 124°06'35" W; near N line sec. 6, T 7 N, R 1 E). Named on Blue Lake (1979), Crannell (1966), and Panther Creek (1982) 7.5' quadrangles. South Fork enters from the southeast 4.25 miles upstream from the mouth of the main river; it is 3.25 miles long and is named on Arcata North (1959) and Crannell (1966) 7.5' quadrangles. Lower South Fork enters from the south 7.5 miles upstream from the mouth of the main river; it is 5 miles long, and is named on Arcata North (1959), Blue Lake (1979), and Crannell (1966) 7.5' quadrangles. Upper South Fork enters from the south 10.5 miles southwest of Coyote Peak; it is 4 miles long and is named on Panther Creek (1982) 7.5' quadrangle. Wagner (p. 394-395) thought that present Little River probably is the stream that Hezeta called Rio de los Tortolas in 1775.

Little River [MENDOCINO]:

(1) *stream,* flows 5.5 miles to the sea 2.25 miles south of Mendocino (lat. 39°16'25" N, long. 123°47'25" W; sec. 6, T 16 N, R 17 W). Named on Comptche (1960) 15' quadrangle, and on Mendocino (1960) 7.5' quadrangle. The name was given to distinguish the stream from nearby Big River (Hanna, p. 172).

(2) *settlement,* 2.5 miles south-southeast of Mendocino along the coast (lat. 39°16'15" N, long. 123°47'15" W; around SW cor. sec. 5, T 16 N, R 17 W); the place is just south of the mouth of Little River (1). Named on Mendocino (1960) 7.5' quadrangle. Postal authorities established Little River post office in 1865, changed the name to Littleriver in 1894; discontinued it in 1929, and reestablished it 1930 (Salley, p. 123). Lloyd Bell and Samuel Bell came to the place before 1856, and for a time the community there was called Bells Harbor; after W.H. Kent bought the Bell property in 1856, the place was referred to as Kents Landing before it received the present name about 1864 (Hanna, p. 172).

Little River Rock [HUMBOLDT]: *island,* 500 feet long, 2 miles south-southeast of Trinidad, and 1000 feet offshore (lat. 41°02'10" N, long. 124°07'20" W). Named on Crannell (1966) 7.5' quadrangle.

Little Rock Creek [MENDOCINO]: *stream,* flows 1.5 miles to South Fork Eel River nearly 4 miles southeast of Branscomb (lat. 39°37'25" N, long. 123°33'55" W). Named on Cahto Peak (1967) 7.5' quadrangle.

Little Round Mountain [LAKE]:

(1) *peak,* nearly 4 miles east of Hull Mountain (lat. 39°30'40" N, long. 122°52' W; near SW cor. sec. 10, T 19 N, R 9 W); the lake is 4.5 miles south of Round Mountain (1). Named on Kneecap Ridge (1967) 7.5' quadrangle.

(2) *peak,* 4 miles west-northwest of Three Crossings (lat. 39°20'20" N, long. 122°59'20" W; sec. 9, T 17 N, R 10 W). Altitude 3403 feet. Named on Elk Mountain (1967) 7.5' quadrangle.

Little Round Mountain [TRINITY]: *peak,* 3.5 miles north-northeast of Kettenpom (lat. 40°12'10" N, long. 123°25'40" W; sec. 18, T 3 S, R 7 E); the peak is 2 miles southeast of Round Mountain (1). Altitude 4137 feet. Named on Zenia (1967) 7.5' quadrangle.

Little Round Mountain Creek [LAKE]: *stream,* flows nearly 2 miles to Rattlesnake Creek (1) 6.5 miles northwest of Crockett Peak (lat. 39°29'40" N, long. 122°51'50" W; near N line sec. 22, T 19 N, R 9 W). Named on Crockett Peak (1967), Hull Mountain (1967), and Kneecap Ridge (1967) 7.5' quadrangles.

Little Roycroft Gulch [TRINITY]: *canyon,* drained by a stream that flows 1 mile to Trinity River 10 miles east-northeast of Weaverville (lat. 40°47'15" N, long. 122°46'10" W; near E line sec. 21, T 34 N, R 8 W); the mouth of the canyon is 0.25 mile downstream along Trinity River from the mouth of Roycroft Gulch. Named on Trinity Dam (1950) 15' quadrangle.

Little Salmon Creek [HUMBOLDT]: *stream,* flows 3 miles to Salmon Creek (1) 4.5 miles south-southeast of Fields Landing (lat. 40°39'35" N, long. 124°11'30" W; sec. 9, T 3 N, R 1 W). Named on Fields Landing (1959) 7.5' quadrangle.

Little Salmon Creek [MENDOCINO]: *stream,* flows 3 miles to Big Salmon Creek 1.5 miles south of Albion (lat. 39°12'55" N, long. 123°45'50" W; sec. 28, T 16 N, R 17 W). Named on Albion (1960) and Elk (1960) 7.5' quadrangles.

Little Salt Creek [MENDOCINO]: *stream,* flows 1.5 miles to Short Creek 5 miles north-northeast of Covelo (lat. 39°51'50" N, long. 123°13'25" W; sec. 8, T 23 N, R 12 W). Named on Covelo East (1967) 7.5' quadrangle.

Little Salt Creek [TRINITY]: *stream,* flows nearly 1 mile to Salt Creek (3) 15 miles north of Weaverville (lat. 40°56'50" N, long. 122°56'10" W; near E line sec. 30, T 36 N, R 9 W). Named on Trinity Dam (1950) 15' quadrangle.

Little Sandy Bar Creek [TRINITY]: *stream,* flows 1.25 miles to Trinity River 4.5 miles east of Burnt Ranch (lat. 40°48' N, long. 123°23'15" W); the mouth of the stream is 0.25 mile upstream from the mouth of Sandy Bar Creek. Named on Ironside Mountain (1951) 15' quadrangle.

Little Sanger Peak [DEL NORTE]: *peak,* 4 miles north-northeast of Broken Rib Mountain (lat. 41°56'20" N, long. 123°39'05" W); the peak is 1.25 miles north of Sanger Peak. Named on Broken Rib Mountain (1982) 7.5' quadrangle.

Little Signal [LAKE]: *peak,* 12.5 miles north of the town of Potter Valley [MENDOCINO] (lat. 39°29'50" N, long. 123°03'40" W; on S line sec. 15, T 19 N, R 11 W). Altitude 5841 feet. Named on Potter Valley (1960) 15' quadrangle. The feature is located nearly 1 mile southeast of Little Signal Peak [MENDOCINO].

Little Signal: see **Little Signal Peak** [MENDOCINO].

Little Signal Peak [MENDOCINO]: *peak,* 10.5 miles south-southeast of Eden Valley (lat. 39°30'25" N, long. 123°04'15" W; near W line sec. 15, T 19 N, R 11 W); the peak is 1.5 miles east-southeast of Big Signal Peak. Altitude 5622 feet. Named on Sanhedrin Mountain (1966) 7.5' quadrangle. United States Board on Geographic Names (1969a, p. 3) rejected the name "Little Signal" for the feature.

Little Soda Creek [LAKE]: *stream,* flows nearly 4 miles to Rice Fork 4.25 miles southwest of Potato Hill (lat. 39°18'45" N, long. 122°51'50" W; sec. 22, T 17 N, R 9 W). Named on Elk Mountain (1967) and Potato Hill (1967) 7.5' quadrangles.

Little Sproul Creek [HUMBOLDT]: *stream,* flows 2.5 miles to Sproul Creek 3 miles southwest of Garberville (lat. 40°04'05" N, long. 123°50'05" W; sec. 34, T 4 S, R 3 E). Named on Garberville (1970) 7.5' quadrangle. Called Little Sproule Creek on Briceland (1921) 15' quadrangle, and called Little Sprowl Creek on Garberville (1949) 15' quadrangle. United States Board on Geographic Names (1973b, p. 3) gave the name "Little Sprowl Creek" as a variant.

Little Squaw Valley [LAKE]: *valley,* 4 miles west-southwest of Bear Mountain (lat. 39°23'45" N, long. 122°58'20" W; sec. 22, T 18 N, R 10 W). Named on Lake Pillsbury (1967) 7.5' quadrangle.

Little Stonewall Pass [TRINITY]: *pass,* 14 miles north of Weaverville (lat. 40°55'35" N, long. 122°53' W); the pass is 1 mile south-southwest of Stonewall Pass. Named on Trinity Dam (1950) 15' quadrangle.

Little Sulphur Bank: see **Sulphur Bank** [LAKE].

Little Swede Creek [TRINITY]: *stream,* flows 1.25 miles to Trinity River 6.5 miles east of Burnt Ranch (lat. 40°47'30" N, long. 123°21' W); the mouth of the creek is 0.5 mile upstream from the mouth of Swede Creek. Named on Ironside Mountain (1951) 15' quadrangle. Called Little Sweede Cr. on Miller's (1890) map.

Little Thatcher Creek [MENDOCINO]: *stream,* flows 3.5 miles to Elk Creek 5 miles east of Eden Valley (lat. 39°36'45" N, long. 123°05'30" W); the stream heads near Thatcher Butte. Named on Sanhedrin (1966) 7.5' quadrangle.

Little Trinidad Head: see **Little Head** [HUMBOLDT].

Little Trinity River [TRINITY]: *stream,* flows 5.25 miles to Trinity River 9 miles south-southwest of China Mountain, which is in Siskiyou County (lat. 41°15'20" N, long. 122°37'40" W; near W line sec. 12, T 39 N, R 7 W). Named on China Mountain (1955) 15' quadrangle.

Little Valley [MENDOCINO]:

(1) *valley,* 2 miles west-northwest of Covelo (lat. 39°48'20" N, long. 123°16'50" W; near SW cor. sec. 35, T 23 N, R 13 E). Named on Covelo West (1967) 7.5' quadrangle.

(2) *valley,* 18 miles north-northwest of Comptche (lat. 39°29'40" N, long. 123°43'30" W; mainly in sec. 23, 26, T 19 N, R 17 W). Named on Comptche (1960) 15' quadrangle, and on Dutchmans Knoll (1966) 7.5' quadrangle.

Little Valley: see **Jewett Valley** [HUMBOLDT].

Little Valley Creek [MENDOCINO]:

(1) *stream,* flows 2.5 miles to Town Creek nearly 2 miles west-northwest of Covelo (lat. 39°48' N, long. 123°16'50" W; near NW cor. sec. 2, T 22 N, R 13 W); the stream goes through Little Valley (1). Named on Covelo West (1967) 7.5' quadrangle.

(2) *stream,* flows 4 miles to Pudding Creek 16 miles north-northwest of Comptche (lat. 39°28' N, long. 123°43'30" W); the stream goes through Little Valley (2). Named on Comptche (1960) 15' quadrangle, and on Dutchmans Knoll (1966) 7.5' quadrangle.

Little Van Duzen River [HUMBOLDT]: *stream,* flows 16 miles to Van Duzen River 3 miles west-southwest of Dinsmore (lat. 40°28'55" N, long. 123°39'45" W; sec. 7, T 1 N, R 5 E). Named on Black Lassic (1979), Dinsmore (1977), and Larabee Valley (1977) 7.5' quadrangles. Called South Fork Van Duzen River on Blocksburg (1949) 15' quadrangle. United States Board on Geographic Names (1977a, p. 6) approved the name "Little Van Duzen River" for the stream, and gave the name "South Fork Van Duzen River" as a variant.

Little Water Canyon [MENDOCINO]: *canyon,* drained by a stream that flows nearly 1 mile to Middle Fork Eel River 3 miles east-southeast of Dos Rios (lat. 39°42'10" N, long. 123°18'10" W); the mouth of the canyon is 0.5 mile downstream from the mouth of Big Water Canyon. Named on Dos Rios (1967) 7.5' quadrangle.

Little Weaver Creek: see **Big Bar Creek** [TRINITY].

Little Windy Ridge [HUMBOLDT]: *ridge,* south-southwest-trending, 1 mile long, 3 miles north-northeast of Showers Mountain (lat. 40°37'05" N, long. 123°40' W; sec. 24, 25, T 3 N, R 4 E); the ridge extends south-southwest from Windy Ridge. Named on Showers Mountain (1978) 7.5' quadrangle.

Live Oak Hollow [LAKE]: *canyon,* drained by a stream that flows 1 mile to North Fork Cache Creek 8 miles northeast of the town of Upper Lake (lat. 39°14'35" N, long. 122°47'40" W). Named on Bartlett Mountain (1958) 7.5' quadrangle.

"L" Lake [TRINITY]: *lake,* 1200 feet long, 16 miles north-northeast of Helena (lat. 40°58'55" N, long. 123°00'45" W). Named on Helena (1951) 15' quadrangle.

Lobadlah Gulch: see **Abalobadiah Creek** [MENDOCINO].

Loch Lomond [LAKE]: *settlement,* 3.5 miles north of Whispering Pines (lat. 38°51'50" N, long. 122°43'05" W; sec. 26, T 12 N, R 8 W). Named on Whispering Pines (1958) 7.5' quadrangle.

Lockharts [HUMBOLDT]: *locality,* 10 miles east of Weitchpec (lat. 41°12'40" N, long. 123°31'05" W). Site named on Hopkins Butte (1979) 7.5' quadrangle.

Loconoma Valley: see **Middletown** [LAKE].

Logan Basin [MENDOCINO]: *relief feature*, 11.5 miles north-northwest of Hull Mountain (lat. 39°40'50" N, long. 122°59' W; at W line sec. 16, T 21 N, R 10 W). Named on Plaskett Ridge (1967) 7.5' quadrangle.

Logan Gulch [TRINITY]: *canyon*, drained by a stream that flows 2.5 miles to Trinity River 1.5 miles southwest of Helena (lat. 40°45'30" N, long. 123°09' W; sec. 31, T 34 N, R 11 W). Named on Helena (1951) 15' quadrangle. Jones (p. 226) noted that J. Logan and Boone Logan had a trading post and mine at the canyon.

Logan Spring [LAKE]: *spring*, 4 miles west of Bear Mountain (lat. 39°24'25" N, long. 122°58'20" W; near N line sec. 22, T 18 N, R 10 W). Named on Lake Pillsbury (1967) 7.5' quadrangle.

Log Cabin Creek [MENDOCINO]: *stream*, flows 1 mile to Little North Fork Gualala River 3.25 miles north of Gualala (lat. 38°48'50" N, long. 123°31'25" W; sec. 10, T 11 N, R 15 W). Named on Gualala (1960) 7.5' quadrangle.

Logging Gulch [HUMBOLDT]: *canyon*, drained by a stream that flows less than 1 mile to Wilder Creek 3.5 miles north-northwest of Orleans (lat. 41°21'10" N, long. 123°34' W). Named on Orleans (1978) 7.5' quadrangle.

Log Lake [TRINITY]: *lake*, 650 feet long, 14 miles north of Trinity Center (lat. 41°12'25" N, long. 122°42'40" W; sec. 30, T 39 N, R 7 W). Named on Bonanza King (1955) 15' quadrangle. Called Moss Lake on Etna (1934) 30' quadrangle.

Log Lake: see **Big Bear Lake** [TRINITY].

Log Ridge [LAKE]: *ridge*, north- to northeast-trending, 2 miles long, 5 miles west-southwest of Bear Mountain (lat. 39°22'30" N, long. 122°59' W). Named on Elk Mountain (1967) and Lake Pillsbury (1967) 7.5' quadrangles.

Lois Lake [TRINITY]: *lake*, 400 feet long, 10 miles south-southeast of Cecilville, which is in Siskiyou County (lat. 41°00'40" N, long. 123°03'45" W). Named on Thompson Peak (1979) 7.5' quadrangle.

Loleta [HUMBOLDT]: *town*, 5.5 miles south of Fields Landing (lat. 40°38'30" N, long. 124°13'20" W; sec. 18, T 3 N, R 1 W). Named on Fields Landing (1959) 7.5' quadrangle. Postal authorities established Swauger post office in 1888 and changed the name to Loleta in 1898 (Frickstad, p. 46). When the railroad reached the place in 1883, the station there was called Swauger for Samuel A. Swauger, owner of the property; residents changed the name in 1893 to Loleta, which according to local tradition is an Indian word (Gudde, 1949, p. 191), but Kroeber (p. 46) thought that the name most likely is from the Spanish woman's name "Lolita."

Lone Pine Corrals [TRINITY]: *locality*, 7.25 miles south of Kettenpom (lat. 40°03'15" N, long. 123°26'15" W; sec. 6, T 5 S, R 7 E). Named on Lake Mountain (1967) 7.5' quadrangle.

Lone Pine Mountain [HUMBOLDT]: *peak*, 4.25 miles northwest of Hoopa (lat. 41°05'45" N, long. 123°43'45" W; sec. 9, T 8 N, R 4 E). Altitude 1526 feet. Named on Hoopa (1979) 7.5' quadrangle.

Lone Pine Ridge [HUMBOLDT]: *ridge*, generally northwest-trending, 7.5 miles long, nearly 7 miles northeast of the settlement of Willow Creek (lat. 40°59'15" N, long. 124°25' W). Named on Ironside Mountain (1951) 15' quadrangle, and on Salyer (1979) and Tish Tang Point (1978) 7.5' quadrangles.

Lone Pine Ridge [LAKE]: *ridge*, south-southwest-trending, 1.5 miles long, 13 miles north-northeast of Clearlake Oaks (lat. 39°12' N, long. 122°36'15" W). Named on Clearlake Oaks (1960) 15' quadrangle.

Lonesome Ridge [DEL NORTE]: *ridge*, southwest-trending, 4.5 miles long, 16 miles east-southeast of Klamath Glen (lat. 41°28'15" N, long. 123°41' W). Named on Lonesome Ridge (1974) 7.5' quadrangle.

Lone Star: see **Lone Star Junction** [HUMBOLDT].

Lone Star Creek [HUMBOLDT]: *stream*, flows 2.25 miles to Grouse Creek (1) 1.25 miles west-southwest of Lone Star Junction (lat. 40°37'20" N, long. 123°53'45" W; near S line sec. 24, T 3 N, R 2 E). Named on Iaqua Buttes (1979) and Mad River Buttes (1977) 7.5' quadrangles. The name is from Lone Star ranch; the ranch name is from a wild steer that had a lone star on its head (Turner, p. 135).

Lone Star Junction [HUMBOLDT]: *locality*, 18 miles south-southeast of the town of Blue Lake (lat. 40°38' N, long. 123°52'35" W; near N line sec. 19, T 3 N, R 3 E). Named on Iaqua Buttes (1979) 7.5' quadrangle. Kneeland (1922) 15' quadrangle shows a place called Lone Star located about 1.5 miles north-northeast of present Lone Star Junction.

Lone Tree Ridge [MENDOCINO]: *ridge*, west- to northwest-trending, 3 miles long, 3.25 miles north of Boonville (lat. 39°03'15" N, long. 123°21' W). Named on Boonville (1959) 15' quadrangle.

Long: see **Camp Long**, under **Elk Valley** [DEL NORTE] (1); **Tom Long Creek** [HUMBOLDT-MENDOCINO]; **Tom Long Gulch**, under **Tom Lang Gulch** [TRINITY].

Long Branch: see **Long Branch Creek** [MENDOCINO].

Long Branch Creek [MENDOCINO]: *stream*, flows 4 miles to Tomki Creek 8.5 miles northwest of the town of Potter Valley (lat. 39°25'25" N, long. 123°11'50" W; at S line sec. 9, T 18 N, R 12 W). Named on Potter Valley (1960) 15' quadrangle. Called Long Branch on Pomo (1943) 15' quadrangle.

Long Cabin [TRINITY]: *locality*, 17 miles north of Weaverville (lat. 40°58' N, long. 122°53' W; sec. 22, T 36 N, R 9 W). Named on Trinity Dam (1950) 15' quadrangle. United States Board on Geographic Names (1983d, p. 5) approved the form "Longs Cabin" for the name, and noted that Harlan Long, a sheepman, reportedly built a cabin at the place.

Long Canyon [LAKE]: *canyon*, drained by a stream that flows nearly 5 miles to Little Indian Valley 10 miles northeast of Clearlake Oaks (lat. 39°07'45" N, long. 122°33' W; sec. 20, T 15 N, R 6 W). Named on Clearlake Oaks (1960) 15' quadrangle.

Long Canyon [TRINITY]: *canyon*, drained by a stream that flows 2 miles to East Fork Stuart Fork 15 miles north-northeast of Weaverville (lat. 40°55'40" N, long. 122°50'15" W). Named on Trinity Dam (1950) 15' quadrangle.

Long Doe Ridge [MENDOCINO]: *ridge*, east-trending, 5.5 miles long, 8 miles east of Eden Valley (lat. 39°36'50" N, long. 123°02' W). Named on Hull Mountain (1967) and Sanhedrin Mountain (1966) 7.5' quadrangles.

Long Glade [TRINITY]: *area*, 8.5 miles south-southeast of Forest Glen (lat. 40°15'10" N, long. 123°17' W; near NW cor. sec. 33, T 2 S, R 8 E). Named on Forest Glen (1979) 7.5' quadrangle.

Long Gulch [TRINITY]:

(1) *canyon*, drained by a stream that flows 1.25 miles to Last Chance Gulch 2.5 miles northeast of Weaverville (lat. 40°45'05" N, long. 122°53'40" W; near N line sec. 4, T 34 N, R 9 W). Named on Trinity Dam (1950) 15' quadrangle.

(2) *canyon*, drained by a stream that flows nearly 3 miles to North Rattlesnake Creek 2.5 miles north-northeast of Forest Glen (lat. 40°24'10" N, long. 123°17'55" W; sec. 5, T 1 S, R 8 E). Named on Naufus Creek (1979) 7.5' quadrangle.

Long Opening Creek [MENDOCINO]: *stream*, flows 2.5 miles to Garcia Creek 9 miles south of Eden Valley (lat. 39°30' N, long. 123°09'45" W; sec. 14, T 19 N, R 12 W). Named on Brushy Mountain (1966) and Sanhedrin Mountain (1966) 7.5' quadrangles.

Long Point [MENDOCINO]: *ridge*, south-trending, 1.5 miles long, 11.5 miles south-southwest of Willits (lat. 39°15'30" N, long. 123°25'55" W; mainly in sec. 8, T 16 N, R 14 W). Named on Willits (1961) 15' quadrangle.

Long Prairie [HUMBOLDT]:

(1) *area*, 7 miles northeast of the town of Blue Lake (lat. 40°56' 15" N, long. 123°52'40" W; mainly in sec. 6, T 6 N, R 3 E). Named on Blue Lake (1979) and Lord-Ellis Summit (1973) 7.5' quadrangles.

(2) *area*, 2.25 miles south of Coyote Peak (lat. 41°06' N, long. 123°51'25" W; sec. 8, T 8 N, R 3 E). Named on Hupa Mountain (1982) 7.5' quadrangle.

Long Prairie Creek [HUMBOLDT]: *stream*, flows 2.5 miles to North Fork Mad River 4.25 miles east-northeast of the town of Blue Lake (lat. 40°54'50" N, long. 123°54'55" W; sec. 11, T 6 N, R 2 E); the stream heads near Long Prairie (1). Named on Blue Lake (1979) and Lord-Ellis Summit (1973) 7.5' quadrangles.

Long Ridge [HUMBOLDT]:

(1) *ridge*, north-northeast-trending, 2.5 miles long, 7.25 miles northeast of Hoopa (lat. 41°07'05" N, long. 123°34'30" W). Named on Tish Tang Point (1978) 7.5' quadrangle.

(2) *ridge*, generally west-trending, 2.5 miles long, 8.5 miles south-southwest of Scotia (lat. 40°22'35" N, long. 124°11' W). Named on Bull Creek (1969) and Taylor Peak (1969) 7.5' quadrangles.

(3) *ridge*, east- to south-trending, 2 miles long, 13 miles south of Scotia (lat. 40°17'10" N, long. 124°07'45" W). Named on Buckeye Mountain (1970) and Bull Creek (1969) 7.5' quadrangles.

Long Ridge [LAKE]:

(1) *ridge*, generally west-trending, 4.5 miles long, 3 miles south of Potato Hill (lat. 39°18'30" N, long. 122°48'45" W). Named on Potato Hill (1967) 7.5' quadrangle.

(2) *ridge*, east-southeast- to southeast-trending, 1.5 miles long, 2.5 miles west of Middletown (lat. 38°44'45" N, long. 122°39'45" W). Named on Mount Saint Helena (1959) and Whispering Pines (1958) 7.5' quadrangles.

Long Ridge [TRINITY]:

(1) *ridge*, generally south-trending, 8 miles long, 9 miles southeast of Kettenpom (lat. 40°04'15" N, long. 123°20' W). Named on Long Ridge (1967) 7.5' quadrangle.

(2) *ridge*, west-trending, 2 miles long, 7 miles south of Black Rock Mountain (lat. 40°05'55" N, long. 123°01' W). Named on Black Rock Mountain (1954) 15' quadrangle.

Long Ridge Creek [HUMBOLDT]: *stream*, flows nearly 2 miles to Upper North Fork Mattole River 14 miles south of Scotia (lat. 40°16'30" N, long. 124°07'40" W; near S line sec. 24, T 2 S, R 1 W); the stream heads on Long Ridge (3). Named on Buckeye Mountain (1970) 7.5' quadrangle.

Long Rock [DEL NORTE]: *rock*, 6 miles northwest of Crescent City, and 2.5 miles off Point Saint George (lat. 41°48' N, long. 124°17'45" W).

Named on Eureka (1958) 1° x 2° quadrangle.

Longs Cabin: see **Long Cabin** [TRINITY].

Long's Fort: see **Elk Valley** [DEL NORTE] (1).

Long Tule Point [LAKE]: *promontory,* 3 miles east-southeast of Lakeport along Clear Lake (lat. 39°02'05" N, long. 122°51'35" W; sec. 28, T 14 N, R 9 W). Named on Lucerne (1958) 7.5' quadrangle.

Longvale [MENDOCINO]: *village,* 9.5 miles south-southeast of Laytonville (lat. 39°33'20" N, long. 123°25'40" W; near W line sec. 28, T 20 N, R 14 W). Named on Longvale (1966) 7.5' quadrangle. Postal authorities established Longvale post office in 1911 and discontinued it in 1958 (Salley, p. 126).

Longvale Creek: see **Long Valley Creek** [MENDOCINO].

Long Valley [LAKE]:

(1) *valley,* center about 2.5 miles east-southeast of Middletown (lat. 38°44'30" N, long. 122°34' W). Named on Detert Reservoir (1958) and Middletown (1958) 7.5' quadrangles.

(2) *valley,* 6 miles long, along Long Valley Creek above a point 3.5 miles northeast of Clearlake Oaks (lat. 39°03'50" N, long. 122°38' W). Named on Clearlake Oaks (1958) 7.5' quadrangle. California Mining Bureau's (1909c) map shows a place called Arabella located 20 miles by stage line north of the town of Lower Lake. Postal authorities established Arabella post office in the valley in 1888, moved it 6 miles northwest in 1903, and discontinued it in 1920; the name was for the wife of the first postmaster (Salley, p. 9). Bradley (p. 224) noted that Quigley Soda Springs were located on Quigley ranch at Arabella.

Long Valley Creek [LAKE]: *stream,* flows 14 miles to North Fork Cache Creek 5.5 miles east-northeast of Clearlake Oaks (lat. 39°02'50" N, long. 122°34'40" W; sec. 24, T 14 N, R 7 W); the stream goes through Long Valley (2). Named on Clearlake Oaks (1960) 15' quadrangle, and on Bartlett Mountain (1958) 7.5' quadrangle. South Fork enters in Long Valley (2); it is 5 miles long and is named on Clearlake Oaks (1958) and Lucerne (1958) 7.5' quadrangles.

Long Valley Creek [MENDOCINO]: *stream,* flows 9 miles to Outlet Creek just southeast of Longvale (lat. 39°33'05" N, long. 123°25'25" W; near S line sec. 28, T 20 N, R 14 W). Named on Laytonville (1967) and Longvale (1966) 7.5' quadrangles. Called Longvale Creek on Laytonville (1919) 15' quadrangle.

Long Valley Ridge [LAKE]: *ridge,* generally east-southeast-trending, 4 miles long, 8 miles north-northwest of Clearlake Oaks (lat. 39°07'25" N, long. 122°44'25" W); the ridge is south of Long Valley (2). Named on Clearlake Oaks (1960) 15' quadrangle, and on Bartlett Mountain (1958) 7.5' quadrangle.

Lookout Creek [MENDOCINO]: *stream,* flows about 3 miles to Elk Creek (2) 4 miles west of Hull Mountain (lat. 39°31'35" N, long. 122°00'10" W; near S line sec. 6, T 19 N, R 10 W). Named on Hull Mountain (1967) 7.5' quadrangle.

Lookout Mountain [DEL NORTE]: *peak,* 5.25 miles east-northeast of Broken Rib Mountain on Del Norte-Siskiyou County line (lat. 41°54'25" N, long. 123°35'30" W). Altitude 6372 feet. Named on Polar Bear Mountain (1982) 7.5' quadrangle.

Lookout Mountain [MENDOCINO]: *peak,* 3.5 miles southwest of Hopland (lat. 38°56' N, long. 123°09'30" W; near N line sec. 2, T 12 N, R 12 W). Named on Hopland (1960) 15' quadrangle.

Lookout Peak [MENDOCINO]: *peak,* 2.25 miles west-southwest of Ukiah (lat. 39°08'10" N, long. 123°14'40" W; near NW cor. sec. 25, T 15 N, R 13 W). Named on Ukiah (1958) 7.5' quadrangle.

Lookout Point [HUMBOLDT]:

(1) *promontory,* 1.5 miles west-southwest of Orick along the coast south of the mouth of Redwood Creek (1) (lat. 41°16'50" N, long. 124°05'30" W; sec. 5, T 10 N, R 1 E). Named on Orick (1966) 7.5' quadrangle.

(2) *peak,* 5.5 miles northeast of Johnsons (lat. 41°24'55" N, long. 123°48'35" W). Named on Blue Creek Mountain (1982) 7.5' quadrangle.

Lookout Ridge [TRINITY]: *ridge,* west-northwest-trending, 2 miles long, 11 miles east-northeast of Weaverville (lat. 40°46'30" N, long. 122°43'30" W). Named on Schell Mountain (1950) 15' quadrangle.

Lookout Rock [HUMBOLDT]:

(1) *relief feature,* 5.5 miles north of Trinidad on Patrick Point (lat. 41°08'25" N, long. 124°09'35" W; sec. 27, T 9 N, R 1 W). Named on Trinidad (1966) 7.5' quadrangle.

(2) *relief feature,* 5.5 miles south-southeast of Showers Mountain (lat. 40°30'40" N, long. 123°38'35" W; near W line sec. 32, T 2 N, R 5 E). Named on Showers Mountain (1978) 7.5' quadrangle.

Lopez Creek [DEL NORTE]: *stream,* flows 2.5 miles to the sea 3.5 miles northwest of the town of Smith River (lat. 41°57'35" N, long. 124°12'20" W; near S line sec. 8, T 18 N, R 1 W). Named on Smith River (1966) 7.5' quadrangle.

Lord-Ellis Summit [HUMBOLDT]: *pass,* 7.5 miles east-northeast of the town of Blue Lake (lat. 40°55'45" N, long. 123°51'35" W; sec. 5, T 6 N, R 3 E). Named on Lord-Ellis Summit (1973) 7.5' quadrangle. Called Lord Ellis Summit (without the hyphen) on Blue Lake (1951) 15' quadrangle, and United States Board on Geographic Names (1975, p. 5) gave this as a variant form of the name—the Board noted that the name commemorates William Lord and a Mr. Ellis, the first two signers of the petition for a road over the pass.

Lorenz Gulch: see **Steiner Flat** [TRINITY].

Loretta Falls [DEL NORTE]: *waterfall,* 11 miles northeast of Broken Rib Mountain (lat. 41°59'40" N, long. 123°32'05" W; sec. 32, T 19 N, R 6 E). Named on Polar Bear Mountain (1982) 7.5' quadrangle.

Lost Cabin Creek [MENDOCINO]: *stream,* flows 2 miles to Hulls Creek 10 miles north of Covelo (lat. 39°56'20" N, long. 123°16'15" W). Named on Mina (1967) 7.5' quadrangle.

Lost Canyon [HUMBOLDT]: *canyon,* drained by a stream that flows 1.5 miles to Little Van Duzen River 4.5 miles northeast of Blocksburg (lat. 40°19'45" N, long. 123°35'05" W; near SW cor. sec. 35, T 1 S, R 5 E); the canyon is west of Lost Ridge. Named on Black Lassic (1979) 7.5' quadrangle.

Lost Creek [MENDOCINO]:

(1) *stream,* flows 2 miles to Rancheria Creek (2) 1 mile east-northeast of Ornbaun Valley (lat. 38°55'10" N, long. 123°17'25" W; sec. 3, T 12 N, R 13 W). Named on Ornbaun Valley (1960) 15' quadrangle.

(2) *stream,* flows 1 mile to North Fork Gualala River 10.5 miles southwest of Ornbaun Valley (lat. 38°49'10" N, long. 123°27'15" W; sec. 8, T 11 N, R 14 W). Named on Ornbaun Valley (1960) 15' quadrangle.

Lost Creek [TRINITY]: *stream,* flows 2.25 miles to Mad River 11 miles west-southwest of Black Rock Mountain (lat. 40°07'25" N, long. 123°10'50" W; sec. 11, T 26 N, R 12 W). Named on Black Rock Mountain (1954) 15' quadrangle.

Lost Lake [HUMBOLDT]: *lake,* 225 miles long, 4.5 miles east of Blocksburg (lat. 40°17'10" N, long. 123°33'05" W). Named on Black Lassic (1979) 7.5' quadrangle.

Lost Lake [TRINITY]:

(1) *lake,* 300 feet long, 7.5 miles south-southwest of China Mountain, which is in Siskiyou County (lat. 41°16'50" N, long. 122°38'40" W; sec. 35, T 40 N, R 7 W). Named on China Mountain (1955) 15' quadrangle.

(2) *lake,* 350 feet long, 8 miles south of Kettenpom (lat. 40°02'45" N, long. 123°26'10" W; near N line sec. 7, T 5 S, R 7 E). Named on Lake Mountain (1967) 7.5' quadrangle.

Lost Man Creek [HUMBOLDT]: *stream,* flows 6.25 miles to Prairie Creek 3.5 miles north-northeast of Orick (lat. 41°19'55" N, long. 124°01'40" W; near N line sec. 23, T 11 N, R 1 E). Named on Holter Ridge (1983) and Orick (1966) 7.5' quadrangles. A timber locator out to stake a claim in the early days lost his way near the head of the stream and was never heard from again (Turner, p. 136).

Lost Man Creek [MENDOCINO]: *stream,* flows 2 miles to Hollow Tree Creek 5 miles south-southwest of Leggett (lat. 39°47'50" N, long. 123°44'35" W; near S line sec. 33, T 23 N, R 17 W). Named on Leggett (1969) 7.5' quadrangle.

Lost Man Creek: see **Little Lost Man Creek** [HUMBOLDT].

Lost Meadow [HUMBOLDT]: *area,* 7 miles south-southeast of Korbel along Mad River (lat. 40°46'40" N, long. 123°54'15" W; sec. 36, T 5 N, R 2 E). Named on Korbel (1979) 7.5' quadrangle.

Lost Pipe Creek [MENDOCINO]: *stream,* flows 1.25 miles to Wallers Creek 5.25 miles south of Leggett (lat. 39°47'20" N, long. 123°43'40" W; near E line sec. 3, T 22 N, R 17 W). Named on Leggett (1969) 7.5' quadrangle.

Lost Ridge [HUMBOLDT]: *ridge,* north-northwest-trending, 1.25 miles long, 4 miles northeast of Blocksburg (lat. 40°18'45" N, long. 123°34'45" W); the ridge is east of Lost Canyon. Named on Black Lassic (1979) 7.5' quadrangle.

Lost Valley [MENDOCINO]: *valley,* 8 miles southeast of Ukiah (lat. 39°04'15" N, long. 123°05'45" W; on N line sec. 17, T 14 N, R 11 W). Named on Purdys Gardens (1958) 7.5' quadrangle.

Louiston: see **Lewiston** [TRINITY].

Louse Camp [DEL NORTE]: *locality,* 16 miles east-southeast of Klamath Glen along Bluff Creek at the mouth of Notice Creek (lat. 41°24'10" N, long. 123°42'55" W). Named on Lonesome Ridge (1974) 7.5' quadrangle.

Lousy Creek [TRINITY]: *stream,* flows 2.5 miles to North Fork Eel River 13 miles southeast of Kettenpom (lat. 39°59'55" N, long. 123°19'15" W; sec. 30, T 5 S, R 8 E). Named on Long Ridge (1967) 7.5' quadrangle. Postal authorities established Wilson post office 30 miles northwest of Covelo [MENDOCINO] at the head of a branch of Lousy Creek (SE quarter sec. 18, T 5 S, R 7 E) in 1880 and discontinued in 1881 (Salley, p. 241).

Love Letter Spring: see **Hayfork Bally** [TRINITY].

Lover's Leap: see **Squaw Rock** [MENDOCINO] (2).

Lowden [TRINITY]: *locality,* 5.5 miles east-southeast of Weaverville along Trinity River (lat. 40°41'30" N, long. 122°51'30" W); the place is at the mouth of Grass Valley Creek, where Weaverville (1950) 15' quadrangle shows Lowden ranch (sec. 26, T 33 N, R 9 W). Named on Weaverville (1913) 30' quadrangle. Postal authorities established Lowden's Ranch post office in 1874 and discontinued it in 1908; the name was from the property of Olsen E. Lowden, first postmaster (Salley, p. 128).

Lowden's Ranch: see **Lowden** [TRINITY].

Low Divide [DEL NORTE]: *pass*, 6 miles east-southeast of the town of Smith River, between the heads of Copper Creek and Hardscrabble Creek (lat. 41°54'35" N, long. 124°01'55" W; sec. 35, T 18 N, R 1 E). Named on High Divide (1966) 7.5' quadrangle. Brewer (p. 486) mentioned a little mining town of the 1860's located at the site; this community was called Low Divide, or Altaville, and had cabins, stores, saloons, and a "hotel." Whitney (p. 363) noted that a place called Meyer's was situated about 3 miles west of Altaville.

Lower Blue Lake [LAKE]: *lake*, 0.5 mile long, nearly 5 miles west of the town of Upper Lake (lat. 39°09'45" N, long. 122°59'50" W; sec. 8, T 15 N, R 10 W). Named on Cow Mountain (1958) and Upper Lake (1958) 7.5' quadrangles.

Lower Bohn Lake [LAKE]: *lake*, 900 feet long, 8 miles east of Middletown (lat. 38°44'20" N, long. 122°27'55" W; sec. 1, T 10 N, R 6 W); the lake is in Bohn Valley 1 mile west-northwest of Upper Bohn Lake. Named on Aetna Springs (1958) 7.5' quadrangle.

Lower Bull Creek Flat [HUMBOLDT]: *area*, nearly 2 miles northwest of Weott (lat. 40°20'30" N, long. 123°56'30" W; near N line sec. 34, T 1 S, R 2 E); the place is on the north side of Bull Creek (1). Named on Weott (1969) 7.5' quadrangle. Present Lower Bull Creek Flat and present Upper Bull Creek Flat together have the name "Bull Creek Flat" on Weott (1949) 15' quadrangle.

Lower Canyon Creek Meadows [TRINITY]: *area*, 8.5 miles northeast of Helena (lat. 40°52'25" N, long. 123°01'45" W); the place is along Canyon Creek (1). Named on Helena (1951) 15' quadrangle.

Lower Coon Mountain [DEL NORTE]: *ridge*, south- to west-trending, 5.5 miles long, 4.5 miles south-southeast of Gasquet (lat. 41°47'30" N, long. 123°55'15" W); the ridge is west of Upper Coon Mountain across Coon Creek. Named on Gasquet (1981) 7.5' quadrangle.

Lower Glade Camp [TRINITY]: *locality*, 12.5 miles south of Black Rock Mountain (lat. 40°01'45" N, long. 123°03'10" W; at S line sec. 11, T 25 N, R 11 W); the place is about 1 mile southeast of Upper Glade Camp. Named on Black Rock Mountain (1954) 15' quadrangle.

Lower Lake [LAKE]: *town*, 13 miles east-southeast of Kelseyville (lat. 38°54'35" N, long. 122°36'40" W; around SW cor. sec. 2, T 12 N, R 7 W). Named on Lower Lake (1958) 7.5' quadrangle. Postal authorities established Lower Lake post office in 1858 (Frickstad, p. 64). Mr. E. Mitchell built the first house at the site in 1858; the name is from the nearby part of Clear Lake that generally was called Lower Lake (Gudde, 1949, p. 196; Hoover, Rensch, and Rensch, p. 142). Palmer (p. 113) gave the name "Grantville" as an early designation for the community. California Mining Bureau's (1909c) map shows a place called Reiff located 11 miles by stage line east of Lower Lake. Postal authorities established Reiff post office 11 miles southeast of Lower Lake in 1881, moved it 2 miles southeast in 1891, moved it 2 miles west in 1899, discontinued it in 1918, reestablished it in 1923, and discontinued it in 1941; the name was for John Reiff, first postmaster (Salley, p. 183). A small spring of carbonated water known as Baker Soda Spring was situated about halfway between Lower Lake and Reiff post office (Waring, p. 193). Postal authorities established Morgan post office 9 miles east of Lower Lake in 1868 and discontinued it in 1872; the name was for Charles Morgan, a settler of 1854 (Salley, p. 146). They established Putah post office 8 miles south of Lower Lake in 1892 and discontinued it in 1900; the name was for the location of the post office along Putah Creek (Salley, p. 179). They established Nita post office 11 miles northeast of Lower Lake in 1893 and discontinued it in 1898; the name was for a daughter of the first postmaster (Salley, p. 154). They established Knocti post office 5 miles northwest of Lower Lake in 1925 and discontinued it the same year (Salley, p. 113).

Lower Lake [TRINITY]: *lake*, 300 feet long, 10 miles south of Kettenpom (lat. 40°01' N, long. 123°29'30" W; near N line sec. 22, T 5 S, R 6 E); the lake is 1 mile west-northwest of Upper Lake. Named on Lake Mountain (1967) 7.5' quadrangle.

Lower Lake: see **Clear Lake** [LAKE].

Lower Nye Camp: see **Lower Nye Campground** [LAKE].

Lower Nye Campground [LAKE]: *locality*, nearly 3 miles west-northwest of Crockett Peak along Skeleton Creek (lat. 39°26'35" N, long. 122°49'30" W). Named on Crockett Peak (1967) 7.5' quadrangle. Called Lower Nye Camp on Lake Pillsbury (1951) 15' quadrangle.

Lowery Creek [MENDOCINO]: *stream*, flows less than 1 mile to Rancheria Creek (2) 1.5 miles east of Ornbaun Valley (lat. 38°54'45" N, long. 123°16'35" W; near S line sec. 2, T 12 N, R 13 W). Named on Ornbaun Valley (1960) 15' quadrangle.

Lowery Lake [MENDOCINO]: *lake*, 1150 feet long, 6.5 miles east-northeast of Spyrock (2) (lat. 39°53'50" N, long. 123°18'55" W). Named on Mina (1967) 7.5' quadrangle.

Lowery Ridge: see **Lowrey Ridge** [TRINITY].

Low Gap [HUMBOLDT]:

(1) *pass*, 4.5 miles south-southeast of Coyote Peak (lat. 41°04'30" N, long. 123°49'40" W). Named on Hupa Mountain (1982) 7.5' quadrangle.

(2) *pass*, 6 miles west-northwest of Lone Star Junction (lat. 40°39'45" N, long. 123°59'05" W; near NE cor. sec. 7, T 3 N, R 2 E). Named on Iaqua Buttes (1979) 7.5' quadrangle.

Low Gap [LAKE]:

(1) *pass*, 5.5 miles northeast of Hull Mountain (lat. 39°34'40" N, long. 122°51'55" W; near NW cor. sec. 22, T 20 N, R 9 W). Kneecap Ridge (1967) 7.5' quadrangle.

(2) *pass*, 3 miles northeast of Crockett Peak (lat. 39°27'45" N, long. 122°44'20" W). Named on Saint John Mountain (1968) 7.5' quadrangle.

(3) *pass*, 5.5 miles east-northeast of the town of Upper Lake (lat. 39°11'45" N, long. 122°48'40" W; sec. 36, T 16 N, R 9 W). Named on Bartlett Mountain (1958) 7.5' quadrangle.

Low Gap [MENDOCINO]:

(1) *pass*, 5.5 miles south-southeast of Leggett (lat. 39°47'20" N, long. 123°41'05" W; near NW cor. sec. 6, T 22 N, R 16 W). Named on Leggett (1969) 7.5' quadrangle.

(2) *pass*, 3.5 miles south-southwest of Eden Valley (lat. 39°34'35" N, long. 123°12'15" W; at W line sec. 21, T 20 N, R 12 W). Named on Brushy Mountain (1966) 7.5' quadrangle.

(3) *pass*, 6.5 miles north-northeast of Willits (lat. 39°29'45" N, long. 123°17'40" W; sec. 15, T 19 N, R 13 W). Named on Willits (1961) 15' quadrangle.

(4) *pass*, 12 miles north-northwest of Comptche (lat. 39°25'50" N, long. 123°40'10" W; sec. 8, T 18 N, R 16 W). Named on Comptche (1960) 15' quadrangle.

(5) *locality*, 10.5 miles north of Boonville (lat. 39°09'50" N, long. 123°22'45" W; near NW cor. sec. 14, T 15 N, R 14 W); the place is at the head of Low Gap Creek (3). Named on Boonville (1959) 15' quadrangle. Postal authorities established Low Gap post office in 1877, discontinued it in 1878, reestablished it in 1881, and discontinued it in 1893 (Frickstad, p. 96).

Low Gap [TRINITY]:

(1) *pass*, 5 miles north-northwest of Weaverville (lat. 40°47'45" N, long. 122°58'15" W; on N line sec. 23, T 34 N, R 10 W). Named on Trinity Dam (1950) 15' quadrangle.

(2) *pass*, 5 miles east-southeast of Dinsmore [HUMBOLDT] (lat. 40°27'40" N, long. 123°31'20" W; sec. 17, T 1 N, R 6 E). Named on Dinsmore (1977) 7.5' quadrangle.

Low Gap: see **West Low Gap**, under **Martin Gap** [TRINITY].

Low Gap Campsite [TRINITY]: *locality*, 7 miles south-southeast of Cecilville, which is in Siskiyou County (lat. 41°02'55" N, long. 123°04'45" W). Named on Thompson Peak (1979) 7.5' quadrangle.

Low Gap Creek [HUMBOLDT]: *stream*, flows nearly 2 miles to Willow Creek (1) 12.5 miles east of the town of Blue Lake (lat. 40°54'25" N, long. 123°45'10" W; near NW cor. sec. 17, T 6 N, R 4 E). Named on Lord-Ellis Summit (1973) 7.5' quadrangle.

Low Gap Creek [MENDOCINO]:

(1) *stream*, flows nearly 3 miles to South Fork Eel River 2.5 miles north-northeast of Piercy (lat. 39°59'55" N, long. 123°46'45" W; near S line sec. 24, T 5 S, R 3 E). Named on Noble Butte (1969) and Piercy (1969) 7.5' quadrangles.

(2) *stream*, flows 3.25 miles to Eden Creek at the south end of Eden Valley (lat. 39°36'30" N, long. 123°11'05" W; at E line sec. 9, T 20 N, R 12 W); the stream heads at Low Gap (2). Named on Brushy Mountain (1966) 7.5' quadrangle.

(3) *stream*, flows 1.5 miles to South Branch of North Fork Navarro River 9 miles north of Boonville (lat. 39°08'20" N, long. 123°22'30" W; sec. 23, T 15 N, R 14 W); the stream heads at Low Gap (5). Named on Boonville (1959) 15' quadrangle.

(4) *stream*, flows 2.5 miles to South Fork Eel River 3.5 miles southeast of Leggett (lat. 39°49'25" N, long. 123°40'40" W; near SW cor. sec. 19, T 23 N, R 16 W); the stream heads near Low Gap (1). Named on Leggett (1969) 7.5' quadrangle.

(5) *stream*, flows nearly 2 miles to the sea 9 miles north of Piercy (lat. 39°57' N, long. 123°58'15" W; sec. 9, T 24 N, R 19 W). Named on Bear Harbor (1969) 7.5' quadrangle.

Low Gap Creek: see **Little Low Gap Creek** [MENDOCINO].

Low Mountain [TRINITY]: *peak*, 10 miles west of Black Rock Mountain (lat. 40°10'50" N, long. 123°11'45" W; sec. 22, T 27 N, R 12 W). Altitude 4354 feet. Named on Black Rock Mountain (1954) 15' quadrangle

Low Mountain Gulch [TRINITY]: *canyon*, drained by a stream that flows 2.5 miles to North Fork Mad River 11 miles west-southwest of Black Rock Mountain (lat. 40°10'15" N, long. 123°13' W; near S line sec. 21, T 27 N, R 12 W); the canyon is south of Low Mountain. Named on Black Rock Mountain (1954) 15' quadrangle.

Lowrey Ridge [TRINITY]: *ridge*, west-northwest-trending, 1.5 miles long, 8.5 miles south of Black Rock Mountain (lat. 40°05' N, long. 123°01' W). Named on Black Rock Mountain (1954) 15' quadrangle. United States Board on Geographic Names (1982b, p. 3) approved the name "Lowery Ridge" for the feature, and rejected the names "Lowrey Ridge" and "Lowry Ridge."

Low Rock [DEL NORTE]: *rock*, 4 miles west of the town of Smith River, and 1 mile offshore (lat. 41°55'55" N, long. 124°13'20" W). Named on Smith River (1966) 7.5' quadrangle.

Lowry Ridge: see **Lowrey Ridge** [TRINITY].

Luccock Bar [TRINITY]: *locality*, 4.25 miles east of Burnt Ranch (lat. 40°48'10" N, long. 123°23'15" W). Named on Ironside Mountain (1951) 15' quadrangle.

Lucerne [LAKE]: *town*, 7.25 miles east-northeast of Lakeport (lat. 39°05'30" N, long. 122°47'30" W; mainly in sec. 6, T 14 N, R 8 W). Named on Lucerne (1958) 7.5' quadrangle.

Luck Creek: see **Lacks Creek** [HUMBOLDT].

Lucky Canyon [LAKE]: *canyon*, drained by a stream that flows 0.5 mile to Grizzly Canyon (2) 5.25 miles south of Cold Spring Mountain (lat. 39°01'20" N, long. 122°29'05" W). Named on Wilbur Springs (1961) 15' quadrangle.

Lucky Lake [TRINITY]: *lake*, 300 feet long, 14 miles south-southwest of Black Rock Mountain (lat. 40°00'50" N, long. 123°05'10" W; near SW cor. sec. 15, T 25 N, R 11 W). Named on Black Rock Mountain (1954) 15' quadrangle.

Lucy Gulch [HUMBOLDT-TRINITY]: *canyon*, drained by a stream that heads in Humboldt County and flows 2.5 miles to Big Creek [HUMBOLDT-TRINITY] 4.5 miles west-northwest of Hyampom in Trinity County (lat. 40°38'55" N, long. 123°31'40" W; near S line sec. 8, T 3 N, R 6 E). Named on Sims Mountain (1979) 7.5' quadrangle.

Luebow Point [LAKE]: *promontory*, 3.5 miles northwest of the town of Lower Lake along Clear Lake (lat. 38°57'05" N, long. 122°39'15" W; sec. 29, T 13 N, R 7 W). Named on Clearlake Highlands (1958) 7.5' quadrangle.

Luella Lake [TRINITY]: *lake*, 400 feet long, 16 miles north of Weaverville (lat. 40°57'10" N, long. 122°54'05" W; sec. 28, T 36 N, R 9 W). Named on Trinity Dam (1950) 15' quadrangle.

Luffenholtz: see **Trinidad** [HUMBOLDT].

Luffenholtz Creek [HUMBOLDT]: *stream*, flows 4 miles to the sea nearly 2 miles southeast of Trinidad (lat. 41°02'30" N, long. 124°07'10" W; near NE cor. sec. 36, T 8 N, R 1 W). Named on Crannell (1966) 7.5' quadrangle. United States Board on Geographic Names (1968a, p. 5) rejected the names "Lutfenholts Creek" and "South Fork Luffenholtz Creek" for the stream. The name "Luffenholtz" commemorates a mill owner who settled in the vicinity in 1851 (Gudde, 1949, p. 197). North Fork enters from the north about 1 mile upstream from the mouth of the main creek; it is nearly 2 miles long and is named on Crannell (1966) 7.5' quadrangle. On Trinidad (1952) 15' quadrangle, present North Fork is considered to be the main creek, and the present main creek above the confluence with North Fork is called South Fork.

Luke Prairie [HUMBOLDT]: *area*, 4 miles northwest of Weott (lat. 40°21' 20" N, long. 123°59' W; near NW cor. sec. 29, T 1 S, R 2 E). Named on Weott (1969) 7.5' quadrangle. The name is for Bill Luke, a teamster in the tanbark industry, and his wife (Turner, p. 136).

Lupton Creek [HUMBOLDT]: *stream*, flows 4 miles to Redwood Creek (1) 9 miles east of the town of Blue Lake (lat. 40°54' 25" N, long. 123°48' 55" W; near E line sec. 15, T 6 N, R 3 E). Named on Lord-Ellis Summit (1973) 7.5' quadrangle. Called Grassy Point Creek on Manning and Ogle's (1950) map.

Lutfenholts Creek: see **Luffenholtz Creek** [HUMBOLDT].

Lynch Creek [MENDOCINO]: *stream*, flows 1 mile to Michaels Creek 7 miles south of Leggett (lat. 39°45'50" N, long. 123°43' W; sec. 14, T 22 N, R 17 W). Named on Leggett (1969) 7.5' quadrangle.

Lynch Creek [TRINITY]:

(1) *stream*, flows nearly 2 miles to Deep Hollow Creek 8.5 miles northeast of Kettenpom (lat. 40°14' 40" N, long. 123°20' 40" W; at W line sec. 36, T 2 S, R 7 E). Named on Shannon Butte (1967) 7.5' quadrangle. Called Deep Hollow Creek on Kettenpom (1955) 15' quadrangle, but United States Board on Geographic Names (1969a, p. 3) rejected this name.

(2) *stream*, flows 2.5 miles to Casoose Creek 17 miles southwest of Black Rock Mountain (lat. 40°00'50" N, long. 123°12'15" W; near S line sec. 16, T 25 N, R 12 W). Named on Black Rock Mountain (1954) 15' quadrangle.

Lynch Gap [MENDOCINO]: *pass*, 7.25 miles northwest of Branscomb (lat. 39°43'20" N, long. 123°43'45" W; near NE cor. sec. 34, T 22 N, R 17 W). Named on Lincoln Ridge (1966) 7.5' quadrangle.

Lyons: see **Fort Lyons**, under **Mad River** [HUMBOLDT-TRINITY].

Lyons Creek [LAKE]: *stream*, flows 3.5 miles to Clear Lake 4.25 miles north-northeast of Lakeport (lat. 39°06'20" N, long. 122°53'35" W; near E line sec. 31, T 15 N, R 9 W). Named on Lakeport (1958) 7.5' quadrangle.

Lyons Valley [LAKE]: *valley*, 10 miles west-northwest of Lakeport (lat. 39°07'N, long. 123°05' W; sec. 33, T 15 N, R 11 W). Named on Purdys Gardens (1958) 7.5' quadrangle.

Lyons Valley Creek [LAKE]: *stream*, flows 1.5 miles to Scotts Creek 9 miles northwest of Lakeport (lat. 39°07'25" N, long. 123°03'15" W; sec. 34, T 15 N, R 11 W); the stream heads at Lyons Valley. Named on Purdys Gardens (1958) 7.5' quadrangle.

—M—

Mack Gulch [MENDOCINO]: *canyon*, drained by a stream that flows nearly 0.5 mile to South Fork Albion River 8 miles north-northeast of Elk (lat. 39°14'30" N, long. 123°39'50" W; sec. 17, T 16 N, R 16 W). Named on Elk (1960) 7.5' quadrangle.

Mad Creek [MENDOCINO]: *stream*, flows 1.5 miles to Redwood Creek (2) 6 miles east-southeast of Leggett (lat. 39°49'45" N, long. 123°36'20" W; sec. 22, T 23 N, R 16 W). Named on Tan Oak Park (1969) 7.5' quadrangle.

Madden Creek [HUMBOLDT]: *stream*, flows 10 miles to South Fork Trinity River 4 miles south of the settlement of Willow Creek (lat. 40°52'50" N, long. 123°36'40" W; at W line sec. 22, T 6 N, R 5 E). Named on Grouse Mountain (1979), Salyer (1979), and Willow Creek (1979) 7.5' quadrangles.

Maddox Lake [TRINITY]: *intermittent lake*, nearly 5 miles south-southeast of Hyampom (lat. 40°33'15" N, long. 123°25'15" W; on E line sec. 18, T 2 N, R 7 E). Named on Hyampom (1951) 15' quadrangle.

Mad River [HUMBOLDT-TRINITY]: *stream*, heads in Trinity County and flows about 100 miles to the sea 5 miles north-northwest of Arcata in Humboldt County (lat. 40°56'N, long. 124°08'W; sec. 1, T 6 N, R 1 W). Named on Eureka (1958), Redding (1958), and Weed (1963) 1° x 2° quadrangles. Members of the Gregg exploring party named the river in 1849 for Gregg's reaction when the party would not wait for him to make observations on the latitude of the mouth of the stream (Bledsoe, p. 39-40). North Fork (1) enters nearly 4 miles east-northeast of Arcata; it is 16 miles long and is named on Arcata North (1959), Arcata South (1959), Blue Lake (1979), and Korbel (1979) 7.5' quadrangles. East Fork of North Fork (1) enters North Fork (1) 6 miles north-northeast of the town of Blue Lake; it is 2.5 miles long and is named on Blue Lake (1979) 7.5' quadrangle. North Fork (2) enters from the north 12 miles west-southwest of Black Rock Mountain; it is 5.5 miles long and is named on Black Rock Mountain (1954) 15' quadrangle. South Fork enters from the south-southwest 12 miles west-southwest of Black Rock Mountain; it is 4 miles long and is named on Black Rock Mountain (1954) 15' quadrangle, and on Shannon Butte (1967) 7.5' quadrangle. In 1862 Captain Charles Heffernan established a short-lived military post called Fort Lyons on the right side of Mad River about 20 miles east of Arcata—the name was for Brigadier General Nathaniel Lyon, who was killed in 1861 at the Battle Wilson's Creek in Missouri (Frazer, p. 25).

Mad River [TRINITY]: *village*, 6 miles east-southeast of Dinsmore [HUMBOLDT] along Mad River [HUMBOLDT-TRINITY] (lat. 40°27'10" N, long. 123°30'25" W; sec. 21, T 1 N, R 6 E). Named on Dinsmore (1977) 7.5' quadrangle. Called Mad River Camp on Blocksburg (1949) 15' quadrangle. Postal authorities established Mad River post office in 1872, discontinued it in 1877, reestablished it in 1932, discontinued it in 1943, and reestablished it in 1952; in the 1970's the post office was located 4.5 miles southeast of Cobb [LAKE] and 14 miles northwest of Forest Glen (Salley, p. 130).

Mad River Butte [HUMBOLDT]: *ridge*, north- to northeast-trending, 2 miles long, 7 miles northeast of Lone Star Junction (lat. 40°42'10" N, long. 123°46'35" W). Named on Mad River Buttes (1977) 7.5' quadrangle.

Mad River Camp: see **Mad River** [TRINITY].

Mad River Campground [TRINITY]: *locality*, 8 miles west-northwest of Forest Glen along Mad River (lat. 40°24'10" N, long. 123°27'55" W; sec. 2, T 1 S, R 6 E). Named on Sportshaven (1973) 7.5' quadrangle.

Mad River Ridge [HUMBOLDT-TRINITY]: *ridge*, generally southeast-trending, 23 miles long, southwest of Eel River on Humboldt-Trinity County line, mainly in Trinity County. Named on Dinsmore (1977), Forest Glen (1979), Ruth Reservoir (1978), and Sportshaven (1973) 7.5' quadrangles.

Mad River Rock [TRINITY]: *peak*, 8 miles west of Forest Glen (lat. 40°22'25" N, long. 123°28'35" W; sec. 15, T 1 S, R 6 E). Altitude 4603 feet. Named on Ruth Reservoir (1978) 7.5' quadrangle.

Mad River Slough [HUMBOLDT]: *water feature*, opens into Arcata Bay 4.25 miles north of Eureka (lat. 40°51'55" N, long. 124°08'55" W; sec. 35, T 6 N, R 1 W). Named on Arcata North (1959), Eureka (1958), and Tyee City (1959) 7.5' quadrangles. The feature is an abandoned mouth of Mad River (Evanson, p. 6).

Mad River Slough Channel [HUMBOLDT]: *channel*, extends for nearly 4 miles from the mouth of Mad River Slough through Arcata Bay to Arcata Channel 1.5 miles north of downtown Eureka (lat. 40°49'30" N, long. 124°09'55" W). Named on Eureka (1958) 7.5' quadrangle.

Madrona Camp [DEL NORTE]: *locality*, 8 miles southeast of Gasquet (lat. 41°45'15" N, long. 123°52'45" W). Named on Preston Peak (1922) 30'quadrangle.

Madrone Campground [HUMBOLDT]: *locality*, 5.5 miles south of Garberville (lat. 40°01'10" N, long. 123°47'35" W; near W line sec. 13, T 5 S., R 3 E). Named on Garberville (1970) 7.5' quadrangle.

Madrone Creek [HUMBOLDT]: *stream*, flows 2 miles to Mad River 4 miles north-northeast of Lone Star Junction (lat. 40°41'30" N, long. 123°51'10" W; near NW cor. sec. 33, T 4 N, R 3 E). Named on Mad River Buttes (1977) 7.5' quadrangle.

Madrone Spring [LAKE]:

(1) *spring*, 5 miles south of Potato Hill (lat. 39°16'40" N, long. 122°48'55" W; near SE cor. sec. 36, T 17 N, R 9 W). Named on Potato Hill (1967) 7.5' quadrangle.

(2) *spring*, 4.5 miles north of the town of Upper Lake (lat. 39°13'55" N, long. 122°54'40" W). Named on Upper Lake (1958) 7.5' quadrangle.

Mae Creek: see **May Creek** [HUMBOLDT].

Magoon: see **Eaton H. Magoon Lake**, under **Upper Bohn Lake** [LAKE].

Mahala Creek [HUMBOLDT]: *stream*, flows 1.5 miles to South Fork Trinity River 6.5 miles south-southeast of the settlement of Willow Creek (lat. 40°51'25" N, long. 123°34'55" W; sec. 35, T 6 N, R 5 E). Named on Hennessy Peak (1979) 7.5' quadrangle. Called Little Mahalock Creek on China Flat (1922) 15' quadrangle.

Mahalock Creek: see **Little Mahalock Creek,** under **Mahala Creek** [HUMBOLDT].

Mahnke Peak: see **Mayacmas Mountains** [LAKE-MENDOCINO].

Mail Ridge [HUMBOLDT]: *ridge*, 1 mile long, 15 miles south-southwest of Scotia (lat. 40°16'50" N, long. 124°11'05" W; sec. 21, T 2 S, R 1 W). Named on Buckeye Mountain (1970) 7.5' quadrangle.

Mail Ridge [HUMBOLDT-MENDOCINO]: *ridge*, generally north-northwest-trending, 30 miles long, between Eel River and South Fork Eel River; center about 10 miles north-northeast of Leggett. Named on Alderpoint (1949) and Leggett (1952) 15' quadrangles, and on Fort Seward (1969), Harris (1969), Jewett Rock (1969), Miranda (1970), Myers Flat (1969), and Weott (1969) 7.5' quadrangles. The old mail-stage route ran along the ridge (Hoover, Rensch, and Rensch, p. 103).

Major Creek [HUMBOLDT]: *stream*, flows 1 mile to the sea 4.25 miles north-northwest of Orick (lat. 41°20'50" N, long. 124°04'40" W; near N line sec. 17, T 11 N, R 1 E). Named on Orick (1966) 7.5' quadrangle.

Malacomas Range: see **Mayacmas Mountains** [LAKE].

Mallo Pass Creek [MENDOCINO]: *stream*, flows 4.5 miles to the sea 7 miles south of Elk (lat. 39°02'05" N, long. 123°41'20" W; sec. 36, T 14 N, R 17 W). Named on Navarro (1961) 15' quadrangle.

Mallory Spring [MENDOCINO]: *spring*, 13 miles north of Comptche (lat. 39°26'50" N, long. 123°38'30" W; at W line sec. 3, T 18 N, R 16 W). Named on Comptche (1960) 15' quadrangle.

Malo Creek [LAKE]: *stream*, flows 2 miles to Big Canyon Creek 4 miles east-northeast of Whispering Pines (lat. 38°49'55" N, long. 122°38'35" W; sec. 4, T 11 N, R 7 W). Named on Whispering Pines (1958) 7.5' quadrangle.

Mal Pass [MENDOCINO]: *pass*, 7.25 miles west-northwest of Ornbaun Valley (lat. 38°56'30" N, long. 123°26'W; sec. 32, T 13 N, R 14 W). Named on Ornbaun Valley (1960) 15' quadrangle.

Mal Pass: see **Point Mal Pass** [HUMBOLDT].

Manchester [MENDOCINO]: *village*, 4 miles north of the village of Point Arena (lat. 38°58'05" N, long. 123°41'10" W; around NE cor. sec. 25, T 13 N, R 17 W). Named on Point Arena (1960) 7.5' quadrangle. Postal authorities established Manchester post office in 1871, discontinued it in 1876, and reestablished it in 1877; the name was from the hometown of an early settler (Salley, p. 131).

Mandala: see **Kneeland** [HUMBOLDT].

Manila [HUMBOLDT]: *town*, 3.25 miles north of downtown Eureka on Samoa Peninsula (lat. 40°51'N, long. 124°09'45" W). Named on Eureka (1958) 7.5' quadrangle. The town was started at the close of World War II and was named in keeping with a Pacific theme (Turner, p. 140).

Manly Gulch [MENDOCINO]: *canyon*, drained by a stream that flows 1 mile to Little North Fork Big River 8 miles northwest of Comptche (lat. 39°20'05" N, long. 123°42'W; near E line sec. 13, T 17 N, R 17 W). Named on Comptche (1960) 15' quadrangle.

Manning Creek [LAKE]: *stream*, flows 6.25 miles to Clear Lake 1.25 miles south-southeast of Lakeport (lat. 39°01'40" N, long. 122°54'35" W). Named on Highland Springs (1959) and Lakeport (1958) 7.5' quadrangles.

Manning Flat [LAKE]: *area*, 4.5 miles west of the town of Lower Lake (lat. 38°55'10" N, long. 122°41'50" W; sec. 1, T 12 N, R 8 W). Named on Clearlake Highlands (1958) 7.5' quadrangle.

Mansfield Break: see **Star Rock** [DEL NORTE].

Manzanita: see **Elk** [MENDOCINO].

Manzanita Butte [TRINITY]: *peak*, 24 miles northeast of Weaverville (lat. 40°59'30" N, long. 122°38'40" W; sec. 11, T 36 N, R 7 W). Named on Schell Mountain (1950) 15' quadrangle.

Manzanita Creek [TRINITY]: *stream*, flows 7 miles to Trinity River 13 miles north-northwest of Hayfork (lat. 40°44'20" N, long. 123°14'35" W); the stream is west of Manzanita Ridge. Named on Hayfork (1951) and Helena (1951) 15' quadrangles.

Manzanita Flat [MENDOCINO]: *area*, 5 miles east-southeast of Willits (lat. 39°23'20" N, long. 123°15'50" W; at E line sec. 26, T 18 N, R 13 W). Named on Willits (1961) 15' quadrangle.

Manzanita Flat [TRINITY]: *area*, 10.5 miles north of Helena along East Fork of North Fork Trinity River (lat. 40°55'25" N, long. 123°07'45" W; sec. 5, T 35 N, R 11 W). Named on Helena (1951) 15' quadrangle.

Manzanita Ridge [TRINITY]: *ridge*, south- to southwest-trending, 7 miles long, center 4 miles west of Helena (lat. 40°46'N, long. 123°12'W). Named on Hayfork (1951) and Helena (1951) 15' quadrangles.

Mapel Creek [DEL NORTE]: *stream*, flows about 1.25 miles to Elk Creek (2) 6.25 miles north of Broken Rib Mountain (lat. 41°58'55" N, long. 123°42'20" W; sec. 2, T 18 N, R 4 E). Named on Broken Rib Mountain (1982) 7.5' quadrangle.

Maple Creek [HUMBOLDT]:

(1) *stream*, flows 16 miles to marsh along Big Lagoon (1) 7.25 miles north of Trinidad (lat. 41°09'35" N, long. 124°06'05" W; sec. 18, T 9 N, R 1 E). Named on Crannell (1966), Panther Creek (1982), and Rodgers Peak (1966) 7.5' quadrangles. North Fork enters 1.5 miles upstream from the mouth of the main creek; it is 7.25 miles long and is named on Crannell (1966) and Rodgers Peak (1966) 7.5' quadrangles.

(2) *stream*, flows 9.5 miles to Mad River 8 miles south-southeast of Korbel (lat. 40°45'50" N, long. 123°53'15" W; near NW cor. sec. 6, T 4 N, R 3 E). Named on Korbel (1979) and Maple Creek (1977) 7.5' quadrangles.

(3) *settlement*, 9 miles south-southeast of Korbel (lat. 40°45'45" N, long. 123°52'10" W; near NW cor. sec. 5, T 4 N, R 3 E). Named on Maple Creek (1977) 7.5' quadrangle. Postal authorities established Maple Creek post office in 1886 and discontinued it in 1923 (Frickstad, p. 45). California Mining Bureau's (1909b) map has the form "Maplecreek" for the name. California Mining Bureau's (1917b) map shows a place called McDuff located 11 miles southeast of the settlement of Maple Creek. Postal authorities established McDuff post office in 1909 and discontinued it in 1910 (Frickstad, p. 45). California Mining Bureau's (1917b) map also shows a place called Showers Pass situated about 5 miles east of McDuff. Postal authorities established Showers Pass post office in 1915 and discontinued it in 1937 (Frickstad, p. 46).

Maple Creek [MENDOCINO]: *stream*, flows 1.5 miles to Rancheria Creek (2) 1 mile north-northeast of Ornbaun Valley (lat. 38°55'35" N, long. 123°17'45" W). Named on Ornbaun Valley (1960) 15' quadrangle.

Maple Creek [MENDOCINO-TRINITY]: *stream*, heads in Trinity County and flows 2.5 miles to Middle Fork Eel River 16 miles northeast of Covelo in Mendocino County (lat. 39°57'40" N, long. 123°01'55" W; sec. 1, T 24 N, R 11 W). Named on Leech Lake Mountain (1966) 7.5' quadrangle.

Maple Creek [TRINITY]: *stream*, flows 2.5 miles to Dutch Creek 11 miles northeast of Hayfork (lat. 40°39'35" N, long. 123°01'45" W; sec. 5, T 32 N, R 10 W). Named on Hayfork (1951) 15' quadrangle.

Maple Creek: see **M Line Creek** [HUMBOLDT].

Maple Flat [TRINITY]: *area*, 12.5 miles east-northeast of Kettenpom (lat. 40°14'40" N, long. 123°15'10" W; near S line sec. 30, T 28 N, R 12 W). Named on Shannon Butte (1967) 7.5' quadrangle.

Maple Grove [HUMBOLDT]: *locality*, nearly 2 miles west of Bridgeville (lat. 40°28'10" N, long. 123°49'55" W; near NW cor. sec. 15, T 1 N, R 3 E). Named on Bridgeville (1969) 7.5' quadrangle.

Maple Spring [HUMBOLDT]:

(1) *spring*, 4.25 miles north-northeast of the settlement of Willow Creek (lat. 40°59'25" N, long. 123°34'45" W). Named on Salyer (1979) 7.5' quadrangle.

(2) *spring*, 5 miles east-southeast of Showers Mountain (lat. 40°32'55" N, long. 123°36'25" W; near SE cor. sec. 16, T 2 N, R 5 E). Named on Blake Mountain (1979) 7.5' quadrangle.

Marble Caves [TRINITY]: *caves*, nearly 2 miles north-northwest of Forest Glen near Cave Creek (lat. 40°23'55" N, long. 123°20'W; sec. 12, T 1 S, R 7 E). Named on Naufus Creek (1979) 7.5' quadrangle.

Marble Gulch [MENDOCINO]: *canyon*, drained by a stream that flows nearly 3 miles to North Fork Noyo River 12 miles north-northeast of Comptche (lat. 39°25'45" N, long. 123°32'30" W; sec. 9, T 18 N, R 15 W). Named on Comptche (1960) 15' quadrangle, which shows Marble place situated near the head of the canyon.

Marble Springs [TRINITY]: *springs*, 16 miles north-northwest of Helena (lat. 40°59'45" N, long. 123°13'W). Named on Helena (1951) 15' quadrangle.

Mare Basin [MENDOCINO]: *relief feature*, 0.5 mile southwest of Anthony Peak (lat. 39°50'25" N, long. 122°58'15" W; on N line sec. 21, T 23 N, R 10 W). Named on Mendocino Pass (1967) 7.5' quadrangle.

Mareep Creek [HUMBOLDT]: *stream*, flows 2 miles to Klamath River 7 miles southeast of Johnsons (lat. 41°16'10" N, long. 123°47'20" W; near W line sec. 12, T 10 N, R 3 E). Named on Johnsons (1982) 7.5' quadrangle. The name is from an Indian village that was situated near the mouth of the stream (Gudde, 1949, p. 204).

Marie Creek [TRINITY]: *stream*, flows 2.25 miles to South Fork Trinity River 3.25 miles southeast of Forest Glen (lat. 40°20'10" N, long. 123°17'10" W; near W line sec. 33, T 1 S, R 8 E). Named on Forest Glen (1979) 7.5' quadrangle.

Marine: see **Joe Marine Creek** [HUMBOLDT].

Mariposa Creek [MENDOCINO]: *stream*, flows 3 miles to Russian River 6 miles west of the town of Potter Valley (lat. 39°19'30" N, long. 123°13'15"

W). Named on Redwood Valley (1960) 7.5' quadrangle.

Marlow Campsite [DEL NORTE]: *locality,* 8 miles northeast of Klamath Glen on Lems Ridge (lat. 41°35'25" N, long. 123°52'35" W). Named on Klamath Glen (1982) 7.5' quadrangle. Called Marlow Camp on Ship Mountain (1952) 15' quadrangle.

Marshall Creek [TRINITY]: *stream,* flows 1.25 miles to Ruth Reservoir nearly 5 mile south-southwest of Forest Glen (lat. 40°18'35" N, long. 123°21'35" W; sec. 11, T 2 S, R 7 E). Named on Forest Glen (1979) 7.5' quadrangle.

Marshall Crossing Creek [HUMBOLDT]: *stream,* flows nearly 2 miles to Mill Creek (2) 5.5 miles north-northeast of Hoopa (lat. 41°07' N, long. 123°36'50" W; sec. 33, T 9 N, R 5 E). Named on Tish Tang Point (1978) 7.5' quadrangle.

Marshall Opening [HUMBOLDT]: *area,* 2.5 miles north of Phillipsville (lat. 40°14'45" N, long. 123°46'45" W; on E line sec. 36, T 2 S, R 3 E). Named on Miranda (1970) and Myers Flat (1969) 7.5' quadrangles.

Marshall Rock [TRINITY]: *peak,* 5.25 miles south-southwest of Forest Glen (lat. 40°18'20" N, long. 123°22'15" W; sec. 10, T 2 S, R 7 E); the peak is west of Marshall Creek. Altitude 3598 feet. Named on Forest Glen (1979) 7.5' quadrangle.

Marsh Creek [MENDOCINO]: *stream,* flows 3 miles to Albion River 0.5 mile south of Comptche (lat. 39°15'15" N, long. 123°35'30" W; near S line sec. 12, T 16 N, R 16 W). Named on Navarro (1961) 15' quadrangle.

Marsh Gulch [MENDOCINO]: *canyon,* drained by a stream that flows 2.5 miles to Navarro River 3.25 miles north of Elk (lat. 39°10'40" N, long. 123°42'30" W; sec. 11, T 15 N, R 17 W). Named on Elk (1960) 7.5' quadrangle.

Marshy Lake: see **Big Marshy Lake** [TRINITY]; **Little Marshy Lake** [TRINITY].

Martin Creek [HUMBOLDT]: *stream,* flows 3 miles to Larabee Creek 8 miles northwest of Blocksburg (lat. 40°21'55" N, long. 123°44'05" W). Named on Blocksburg (1969) and Larabee Valley (1977) 7.5' quadrangles.

Martin Creek [MENDOCINO]:

(1) *stream,* flows nearly 1 mile to De Haven Creek 2 miles north-northeast of Westport (lat. 39°39'45" N, long. 123°46'W; near E line sec. 20, T 21 N, R 17 W). Named on Westport (1966) 7.5' quadrangle.

(2) *stream,* flows 4.5 miles to Big River 8.5 miles south-southwest of Willits (lat. 39°18'35" N, long. 123°26'40" W; sec. 20, T 17 N, R 14 W). Named on Willits (1961) 15' quadrangle.

Martin Gap [TRINITY]: *pass,* 3.5 miles west of Black Rock Mountain (lat. 40°12'35" N, long. 123°04'20" W; near S line sec. 2, T 27 N, R 11 W). Named on Black Rock Mountain (1954) 15' quadrangle, which shows Martin cabin located 1800 feet north-northeast of the feature. United States Board on Geographic Names (1969a, p. 5) approved the name "West Low Gap" for the pass.

Martin Gulch [TRINITY]: *canyon,* drained by a stream that flows nearly 2 miles to Rattlesnake Creek (1) 16 miles north of Helena (lat. 40°59'50" N, long. 123°08'30" W). Named on Helena (1951) 15' quadrangle.

Martini Spring [MENDOCINO]: *spring,* 6.5 miles north-northeast of Eden Valley (lat. 39°43'05" N, long. 123°58'55" W; sec. 36, T 22 N, R 12 W). Named on Jamison Ridge (1967) 7.5' quadrangle.

Martins Bar: see **Del Loma** [TRINITY].

Martins Ferry [HUMBOLDT]: *locality,* 7.5 miles northeast of Coyote Peak along Klamath River (lat. 41°12'30" N, long. 123°45'15" W; near SE cor. sec. 31, T 10 N, R 4 E). Site named on French Camp Ridge (1983) 7.5' quadrangle. Postal authorities established Martins Ferry post office in 1861, discontinued it in 1862, reestablished it in 1865, and discontinued it in 1891; the name was for John F. Martin, first postmaster, who operated a ferry (Salley, p. 134). A military post was at the site in the 1860's (Hoover, Rensch, and Rensch, p. 100).

Martin Slough [HUMBOLDT]: *stream,* flows 3 miles to Swain Slough 3.5 miles south-southwest of downtown Eureka (lat. 40°45'10" N, long. 124°10'50" W; near S line sec. 4, T 4 N, R 1 W). Named on Eureka (1958) 7.5' quadrangle.

Marwedel: see **Camp Marwedel** [MENDOCINO].

Mary Ann Ridge [LAKE]: *ridge,* generally east-trending, 4 miles long, 12.5 miles north-northwest of Clearlake Oaks (lat. 39°11'10" N, long. 122°45'W). Named on Clearlake Oaks (1960) 15' quadrangle, and on Bartlett Mountain (1958) 7.5' quadrangle.

Mary Blaine Meadow [TRINITY]: *area,* 10 miles southeast of Salmon Mountain (lat. 41°05'20" N, long. 123°15'25" W). Named on Dees Peak (1978) 7.5' quadrangle. Mary Blaine operated a saloon and travelers stop located about 100 yards below the meadow (Jones, p. 265).

Mary Blaine Mountain [TRINITY]: *peak,* 10 miles southeast of Salmon Mountain on Trinity-Siskiyou County line (lat. 41°05'35" N, long. 123°15'25" W); the peak is 0.25 mile north of Mary Blaine Meadow. Altitude 6747 feet. Named on Dees Peak (1978) 7.5' quadrangle.

Marysville [TRINITY]: *locality,* 10 miles southeast of Salmon Mountain (lat. 41°05'N, long. 123°16'35" W). Site named on Dees Peak (1978) 7.5' quadrangle. Peter Larcine started the place about 1883 and named it for his daughter, Mary, who died there (Jones, p. 264).

Mason Gulch [HUMBOLDT]: *canyon,* drained by a stream that flows 1.5 miles to the settlement of Willow Creek 11.5 miles east of the town of Blue Lake (lat. 40°54'10" N, long. 123°45'55" W; sec. 18, T 6 N, R 4 E). Named on Lord-Ellis Summit (1973) 7.5' quadrangle.

Masterson Meadow [TRINITY]: *area,* 8 miles south-southwest of China Mountain, which is in Siskiyou County (lat. 41°16'40" N, long. 122°39'35" W; on N line sec. 3, T 39 N, R 7 W). Named on China Mountain (1955) 15' quadrangle.

Masterson Meadow Creek [TRINITY]: *stream,* flows 3 miles to Little Trinity River 8 miles south-southwest of China Mountain, which is in Siskiyou County (lat. 41°16'N, long. 122°37'40" W; at E line sec. 2, T 39 N, R 7 W); the stream goes through Masterson Meadow. Named on China Mountain (1955) 15' quadrangle.

Masterson Meadow Lake [TRINITY]: *lake,* 300 feet long, 8.5 miles south-west of China Mountain, which is in Siskiyou County (lat. 41°16'50" N, long. 122°40'10" W; sec. 33, T 40 N, R 7 W); the lake is 0.5 mile west-northwest of Masterson Meadow. Named on China Mountain (1955) 15' quadrangle.

Mate Creek: see **Moat Creek** [MENDOCINO].

Mather Creek [HUMBOLDT]: *stream,* flows 2.5 miles to Lindsay Creek 7 miles north-northeast of Arcata (lat. 40°58'05" N, long. 124°02'35" W; near NE cor. sec. 27, T 7 N, R 1 E). Named on Arcata North (1959) 7.5' quadrangle.

Mathews Peak: see **Wright Peak** [LAKE].

Mathison Peak [MENDOCINO]: *peak,* 5.5 miles west of Comptche (lat. 39°16'20" N, long. 123°41'30" W; near S line sec. 6, T 16 N, R 16 W). Altitude 1030 feet. Named on Comptche (1960) 15' quadrangle.

Matilla Gulch [MENDOCINO]: *canyon,* 1 mile long, 6.5 miles north of Navarro (lat. 39°14'35" N, long. 123°31'45" W; sec. 15, 16, T 16 N, R 15 W). Named on Navarro (1961) 15' quadrangle.

Matthews Creek [HUMBOLDT]: *stream,* flows 1 mile to Eel River 3.5 miles north of Weott (lat. 40°22'20" N, long. 123°55'20" W; near S line sec. 14, T 1 S, R 2 E). Named on Weott (1969) 7.5' quadrangle.

Mattole: see **Camp Mattole** [HUMBOLDT]; **Petrolia** [HUMBOLDT]; **Upper Mattole** [HUMBOLDT].

Mattole Beach [HUMBOLDT]: *beach,* 4.5 miles west-southwest of Petrolia along the coast (lat. 40°17'20" N, long. 124°21'25" W; sec. 13, 24, T 2 S, R 3 W); the beach is south of the mouth of Mattole River. Named on Petrolia (1969) 7.5' quadrangle. Cape Mendocino (1950) 15' quadrangle has the name on the beach situated north of the mouth of Mattole River.

Mattole Canyon [HUMBOLDT]: *canyon,* drained by a stream that flows 6.25 miles to Mattole River 12 miles west-southwest of Phillipsburg (lat. 40°09'05" N, long. 124°00'W; near S line sec. 31, T 3 S, R 2 E). Named on Ettersburg (1969) 7.5' quadrangle.

Mattole Point [HUMBOLDT]: *promontory,* nearly 4 miles west-southwest of Petrolia (lat. 40°18'20" N, long. 124°21'10" W; sec. 12, T 2 S, R 3 W); the feature is just north of the mouth of Mattole River. Named on Petrolia (1969) 7.5' quadrangle.

Mattole River [HUMBOLDT-MENDOCINO]: *stream,* heads in Mendocino County and flows 50 miles to the sea 4 miles west-southwest of Petrolia in Humboldt County (lat. 40°18'10" N, long. 124°21'10" W; at S line sec. 12, T 2 S, R 3 W). Named on Bear Harbor (1969), Briceland (1969), Ettersburg (1969), Honeydew (1970), Shelter Cove (1969), and Shubrick Peak (1969) 7.5' quadrangles. The name "Mattole" is of Indian origin (Kroeber, p. 47). North Fork enters from the north 0.5 mile southwest of Petrolia; it is 12.5 miles long and is named on Buckeye Mountain (1970), Petrolia (1969), and Taylor Peak (1969) 7.5' quadrangles. East Branch of North Fork enters North Fork 5 miles upstream from the mouth of that fork; it is 7.25 miles long and is named on Buckeye Mountain (1970) and Petrolia (1969) 7.5' quadrangles. Present East Branch of North Fork is called North Fork on Glynn (1919) 15' quadrangle. Upper North Fork is formed by the confluence of Oil Creek (3) and Rattlesnake Creek (2); it flows nearly 4 miles to Mattole River 0.5 mile west of Honeydew, and is named on Buckeye Mountain (1970) and Bull Creek (1969) 7.5' quadrangles.

Maupin Gulch [TRINITY]: *canyon,* drained by a stream that flows 1.5 miles to Browns Creek 15 miles south of Weaverville (lat. 40°31'10" N, long. 122°56'35" W; sec. 24, T 31 N, R 10 W). Named on Weaverville (1950) 15' quadrangle.

Mauser Glade [LAKE]: *area,* 1.5 miles northwest of Potato Hill (lat. 39°21'50" N, long. 122°49'40" W). Named on Potato Hill (1967) 7.5' quadrangle.

Mawah Creek [HUMBOLDT]: *stream,* flows 3.25 miles to Klamath River 7.25 miles southwest of Johnsons (lat. 41°16'05" N, long. 123°47'10" W; sec. 12, T 10 N, R 3 E). Named on Fish Lake (1974) and Johnsons (1982) 7.5' quadrangles. The name is of Indian origin (Gudde, 1949, p. 208).

Maxwell Creek [HUMBOLDT]: *stream,* flows 2.25 miles to Larabee Creek 5.25 miles south of Bridgeville (lat. 40°23'35" N, long. 123°48'W; sec. 11, T 1 S, R 3 E). Named on Bridgeville (1969) 7.5' quadrangle.

Maxwell Creek [TRINITY]: *stream,* flows 4 miles to Trinity River 12 miles northeast of Hayfork (lat. 40°40'N, long. 123°00'30" W; at S line sec. 33,

T 33 N, R 10 W). Named on Hayfork (1951) 15' quadrangle.

Mayacmas Mountains [LAKE-MENDOCINO]: *range*, between Russian River and Clear Lake in Lake, Mendocino, and Sonoma Counties. Named on Santa Rosa (1958) and Ukiah (1957) 1° x 2° quadrangles. United States Board on Geographic Names (1933, p. 525) approved the name "Miyakma Range" for the feature, and rejected the names "Cobb Mountain Range," "Malacomas Range," "Mayacmis Range," and "St. Helena Range." Later, the Board (1942, p. 35) approved the name "Mayacmas Mountains" for the feature, and rejected the names "Miyakma Range" and "Mayacamas Mountains." According to Gudde (1949, p. 208), the name is for Indians who lived on the west side of the range. United States Board on Geographic Names (1970, p. 2) approved the name "Mahnke Peak" for a feature in Mayacmas Mountains near the southeasternmost corner of Mendocino County (lat. 38°51'46" N, long. 122°51'13" W)—the name is for John Christian Christof Mahnke and his family, who had a ranch near the peak for 70 years

May Creek [HUMBOLDT]: *stream*, flows 2.5 miles to Prairie Creek 4.5 miles north-northeast of Orick (lat. 41°20'50" N, long. 124°01'40" W; at N line sec. 14, T 11 N, R 1 E). Named on Holter Ridge (1983) and Orick (1966) 7.5' quadrangles. Turner (p. 144) gave the alternate form "Mae Creek" for the name.

Maynard Creek [TRINITY]: *stream*, flows 1.25 miles to Mad River 10 miles west-northwest of Forest Glen (lat. 40°26'10" N, long. 123°29'20" W; sec. 27, T 1 N, R 6 E). Named on Sportshaven (1973) 7.5' quadrangle.

McAlister Creek [HUMBOLDT]: *stream*, flows 1.5 miles to South Fork Trinity River 14 miles south-southeast of the settlement of Willow Creek (lat. 40°45'10" N, long. 123°33'40" W). Named on Hennessy Peak (1979) and Sims Mountain (1979) 7.5' quadrangles.

McAllister Ridge [MENDOCINO]: *ridge*, generally southeast-trending, 2 miles long, 10 miles south of Navarro (lat. 39°00'45" N, long. 123°30'15" W). Named on Navarro (1961) 15' quadrangle.

McAlvey Ridge [HUMBOLDT]: *ridge*, west-trending, 2 miles long, 4.5 miles east of Lone Star Junction (lat. 40°37'20" N, long. 123°47'20" W). Named on Yager Junction (1979) 7.5' quadrangle.

McArthur Creek [HUMBOLDT]: *stream*, flows nearly 5 miles to Redwood Creek (1) 2 miles east-southeast of Orick (lat. 41°16'35" N, long. 124°01'40" W; near S line sec. 2, T 10 N, R 1 E). Named on Orick (1966) and Rodgers Peak (1966) 7.5' quadrangles.

McAtee Bar [TRINITY]: *locality*, 11 miles north-northeast of Burnt Ranch along New River (lat. 40°57'N, long. 123°23'W). Named on Ironside Mountain (1951) 15' quadrangle.

McCabe Point [LAKE]: *peak*, 4.5 miles north of the town of Upper Lake on Pitney Ridge (lat. 39°13'55" N, long. 122°54'20" W). Named on Upper Lake (1958) 7.5' quadrangle.

McCabe Ridge [LAKE]: *ridge*, south-southwest-trending, 1.5 miles long, nearly 4 miles north of the town of Upper Lake (lat. 39°13'15" N, long. 122°55'W); McCabe Point is at the north end of the ridge. Named on Upper Lake (1958) 7.5' quadrangle.

McCann [HUMBOLDT]: *locality*, 4.5 miles east of Weott along Northwestern Pacific Railroad (lat. 40°19'25" N, long. 123°50'05" W; at E line sec. 4, T 2 S, R 3 E); the place is 0.5 mile southeast of the mouth of McCann Creek. Named on Myers Flat (1969) 7.5' quadrangle. Postal authorities established McCann post office in 1919 and discontinued it in 1959 (Salley, p. 136). The name, applied in 1881 to a stage station, was for Willard O. McCann, who had a lumber mill at the place between 1869 and 1888 (Turner, p. 145).).

McCann Creek [HUMBOLDT]: *stream*, flows 1.5 miles to Eel River 4.25 miles east of Weott (lat. 40°19'45" N, long. 123°50'30" W; near S line sec. 33, T 1 S, R 3 E). Named on Myers Flat (1969) 7.5' quadrangle.

McCarvey Creek [MENDOCINO]: *stream*, flows 1.5 miles to South Branch of North Fork Navarro River 10 miles north-northeast of Boonville (lat. 39°09'10" N, long. 123°25'W; near SW cor. sec. 16, T 15 N, R 14 W). Named on Boonville (1959) 15' quadrangle.

McChristian Creek [MENDOCINO]: *stream*, heads in Sonoma County and flows 3 miles to Dry Creek (2) 11 miles south-southwest of Hopland in Mendocino County (lat. 38°49'05" N, long. 123°10'W; sec. 11, T 11 N, R 12 W). Named on Hopland (1960) 15' quadrangle.

McClellan Mountain [HUMBOLDT]: *ridge*, southeast-trending, 1 mile long, 5.5 miles west of Dinsmore (lat. 40°29'25" N, long. 123°42'50" W; mainly in sec. 3, T 1 N, R 4 E). Named on Larabee Valley (1977) 7.5' quadrangle. The name commemorates Hugh Webster McClellan, a sheep rancher at the place (Turner, p. 145).

McClellan Rock [HUMBOLDT]: *relief feature*, 5.5 miles west-southwest of Dinsmore (lat. 40°28'30" N, long. 123°42'25" W; near SE cor. sec. sec. 10, T 1 N, R 4 E); the feature is 1 mile south of the southeast end of McClellan Mountain. Named on Larabee Valley (1977) 7.5' quadrangle.

McCloud Creek [HUMBOLDT]: *stream*, flows 2 miles to South Fork Elk River (1) 6 miles southeast of Fields Landing (lat. 40°40'55" N, long. 124°07'20" W; near SE cor. sec. 36, T 4 N, R 1 W). Named on McWhinney Creek (1979) 7.5' quadrangle.

McClure Creek [LAKE-MENDOCINO]: *stream*, heads just inside Lake County and flows 7 miles to Mill Creek (13) 2 miles southeast of Ukiah in Mendocino County (lat. 39°08'N, long. 123°10'40" W). Named on Cow Mountain (1958) and Ukiah (1958) 7.5' quadrangles.

McCombs Camp [MENDOCINO]: *locality*, 12.5 miles north of Hull Mountain (lat. 39°41'50" N, long. 122°58'30" W; near N line sec. 9, T 21 N, R 10 W). Named on Plaskett Ridge (1967) 7.5' quadrangle.

McConnahas Creek: see **McConnahas Mill Creek** [HUMBOLDT].

McConnahas Mill Creek [HUMBOLDT]: *stream*, flows 2.25 miles to the sea 0.5 mile southeast of Trinidad (lat. 41°03'20" N, long. 124°08'05" W; sec. 25, T 8 N, R 1 W). Named on Crannell (1966) and Trinidad (1966) 7.5' quadrangles. United States Board on Geographic Names (1968a, p. 5) rejected the name "McConnahas Creek" for the stream. The name is from the mill that Burr McConnaha had along the creek in the 1920's (Turner, p. 145).

McCord Prairie [HUMBOLDT]: *area*, 3.5 miles south-southwest of Lone Star Junction (lat. 40°34'45" N; sec. 123°54'30" W; near NE cor. sec. 2, T 2 N, R 2 E). Named on Owl Creek (1979) 7.5' quadrangle.

McCovey Gulch [TRINITY]: *canyon*, drained by a stream that flows 1.5 miles to Hayfork Creek 2.5 miles east of Hayfork (lat. 40°33'10" N, long. 123°08'15" W; sec. 8, T 31 N, R 11 W). Named on Hayfork (1951) 15' quadrangle.

McCoy Creek [MENDOCINO]: *stream*, flows nearly 5 miles to South Fork Eel River 1 mile east-southeast of Piercy (lat. 39°57'25" N, long. 123°46'40" W; sec. 6, T 24 N, R 17 W). Named on Noble Butte (1969) and Piercy (1969) 7.5' quadrangles. North Fork enters from the north-northeast nearly 2 miles upstream from the mouth of the main creek; it is 2.5 miles long and is named on Noble Butte (1969) and Piercy (1969) 7.5' quadrangles.

McCoy Ridge [MENDOCINO]: *ridge*, east-trending, 2.5 miles long, 10.5 miles north of Hull Mountain (lat. 39°40'35" N, long. 122°56'45" W). Named on Plaskett Ridge (1967) 7.5' quadrangle.

McCoy Spring [MENDOCINO]: *spring*, 11 miles north of Hull Mountain (lat. 39°40'50" N, long. 123°56'35" W; sec. 14, T 21 N, R 10 W); the spring is on the north side of McCoy Ridge. Named on Plaskett Ridge (1967) 7.5' quadrangle.

McCready Gulch [HUMBOLDT]: *canyon*, drained by a stream that flows nearly 3 miles to Freshwater Creek 7.25 miles south of Arcata (lat. 40°45'50" N, long. 124°03'50" W; near NE cor. sec. 4, T 4 N, R 1 E). Named on Arcata South (1959) 7.5' quadrangle.

McCreary Glade [LAKE]: *area*, 5 miles east of the town of Potter Valley [MENDOCINO] (lat. 39°18'50" N, long. 123°00'50" W; sec. 20, T 17 N, R 10 W). Named on Potter Valley (1960) 7.5' quadrangle. Pomo (1943) 15' quadrangle shows McCreary place at the site.

McCreary Lake [LAKE]: *lake*, 4800 feet long, behind a dam on Bucksnort Creek 6 miles east of Middletown (lat. 38°45'25" N, long. 122°30'15" W). Named on Jericho Valley (1958) and Middletown (1958) 7.5' quadrangles. A diseño of Guenoc grant made in 1845 has the name "Laguna de Guenoc" at the site (Becker, R.H., 1964). United States Board on Geographic Names (1962b, p. 18) rejected the name "Gebhardt Lake" for the feature, and noted (1991, p. 5) that it also was known as Langtry Lake, for Lily Langtry, a British actress who owned land at the site from 1888 until 1908.

McCullah Spring [TRINITY]: *spring*, 10 miles south-southeast of Dubakella Mountain (lat. 40°15'35" N, long. 123°02'30" W; sec. 19, T 28 N, R 10 W). Named on Dubakella Mountain (1954) 15' quadrangle.

McDaniel Slough [HUMBOLDT]: *stream*, flows 3.5 miles to marsh along Arcata Bay 1 mile southwest of downtown Arcata (lat. 40°51'35" N, long. 124°05'55" W; near E line sec. 31, T 6 N, R 1 E). Named on Arcata North (1959) and Arcata South (1959) 7.5' quadrangles.

McDirrmid's Prairie: see **Metropolitan** [HUMBOLDT].

McDonald: see **Tom McDonald Creek** [HUMBOLDT].

McDonald Creek [HUMBOLDT]: *stream*, flows nearly 4 miles to Stone Lagoon 12 miles north-northeast of Trinidad (lat. 41°13'45" N, long. 124°05'30" W); the stream heads opposite the head of Tom McDonald Creek. Named on Rodgers Peak (1966) 7.5' quadrangle.

McDonald Creek [MENDOCINO]: *stream*, flows nearly 2 miles to Cummiskey Creek 5.25 miles south-southeast of Hopland (lat. 38°54'05" N, long. 123°05'15" W; sec. 9, T 12 N, R 11 W). Named on Hopland (1960) 7.5' quadrangle.

McDonald Creek [TRINITY]: *stream*, flows 3.5 miles to Trinity River 0.25 mile north of Burnt Ranch (lat. 40°48'55" N, long. 123°28'20" W; at N line sec. 14, T 5 N, R 6 E). Named on Ironside Mountain (1951) 15' quadrangle, and on Hennessy Peak (1979) 7.5' quadrangle.

McDonald Gulch [MENDOCINO]: *canyon*, drained by a stream that flows 2.5 miles to Albion River less than 1 mile southeast of Comptche (lat. 39°15'15" N, long. 123°34'50" W; near S line sec. 7, T 16 N, R 15 W). Named on Comptche (1960) and Navarro (1961) 15' quadrangles.

McDonald Gulch: see **Little McDonald Gulch** [MENDOCINO].

McDonald Lake [TRINITY]: *lake*, 900 feet long, 1 mile north-northeast of Billys Peak (1) (lat. 41°08'55" N, long. 122°45'15" W; near SW cor. sec. 14, T 38 N, R 8 W). Named on Coffee Creek (1955) 15' quadrangle. United States Board on Geographic Names (1954, p. 3) rejected the name "Middle Stoddard Lake" for the feature, and noted that the name "McDonald" honors Warren Peter McDonald, who aided conservation of wildlife in the region.

McDonald Mountain House [MENDOCINO]: *locality*, 7 miles south of Hopland (lat. 38°52'30" N, long. 123°06'15" W). Named on Hopland (1944) 15' quadrangle.

McDowell Creek [MENDOCINO]: *stream*, flows 7 miles to Dooley Creek 2 miles east of Hopland (lat. 38°58'15" N, long. 123°04'40" W); the stream goes through McDowell Valley. Named on Highland Springs (1959) and Hopland (1960) 7.5' quadrangles.

McDowell Springs: see **McDowell Valley** [MENDOCINO].

McDowell Valley [MENDOCINO]: *valley*, 4 miles east of Hopland (lat. 38°58'15" N, long. 123°02'30" W). Named on Hopland (1960) 7.5' quadrangle. Waring (p. 168-169) noted that McDowell Springs, which issue at the south edge of McDowell Valley, are the basis of a resort that opened around 1902 or 1903 and that had accommodations for about 50 guests in 1909.

McDuff: see **Maple Creek** [HUMBOLDT] (3).

McDuff Camp [DEL NORTE]: *locality*, 16 miles east-southeast of Klamath Glen along Bluff Creek (lat. 41°25'05" N, long. 123°43'15" W). Named on Orleans (1952) 15' quadrangle.

McDuffy Opening [MENDOCINO]: *area*, 5 miles east-northeast of Comptche (lat. 39°18'N, long. 123°30'45" W; on E line sec. 27, T 17 N, R 15 W). Named on Comptche (1960) 15' quadrangle.

McFarland Gulch [HUMBOLDT]: *canyon*, drained by a stream that flows 0.5 mile to Aikens Creek 3.5 miles northeast of Weitchpec (lat. 41°13'15" N, long. 123°39'40" W). Named on Weitchpec (1979) 7.5' quadrangle.

McFarland Ridge: see **Wildwood** [TRINITY].

McGall: see **Bus McGall Peak** [MENDOCINO].

McGann Gulch [MENDOCINO]: *canyon*, drained by a stream that flows 2.25 miles to North Fork Gulalala River 11.5 miles southwest of Ornbaun Valley (lat. 38°48'40" N, long. 123°28'25" W; sec. 7, T 11 N, R 14 W). Named on Ornbaun Valley (1960) 15' quadrangle.

McGarvey Creek [DEL NORTE-HUMBOLDT]: *stream*, heads in Humboldt County and flows 5 miles to Klamath River less than 1 mile south of Klamath Glen in Del Norte County (lat. 41°30'10" N, long. 123°59'40" W; sec. 24, T 13 N, R 1 E). Named on Fern Canyon (1966) and Klamath Glen (1982) 7.5' quadrangles.

McGaugh Slough [LAKE]: *stream*, flows 4.25 miles to marsh along Clear Lake 3.25 miles east-southeast of Lakeport (lat. 39°01'25" N, long. 122°51'45" W; sec. 33, T 14 N, R 9 W). Named on Kelseyville (1959) and Lucerne (1958) 7.5' quadrangles.

McGee Canyon [MENDOCINO]: *canyon*, drained by Bates Creek, which flows 3.5 miles to Forsythe Creek 8 miles west-southwest of the town of Potter Valley (lat. 39°15'55" N, long. 123°14'W; at S line sec. 6, T 16 N, R 12 W). Named on Potter Valley (1960) and Willits (1961) 15' quadrangles.

McGillivrays Bar: see **Coopers Bar** [TRINITY].

McGilvary Corners: see **Alliance** [HUMBOLDT].

McGinnis Creek [HUMBOLDT]: *stream*, flows 4.5 miles to Mattole River 14 miles south-southwest of Scotia (lat. 40°18'20" N, long. 124°14'15" W; sec. 12, T 2 S, R 2 W). Named on Buckeye Mountain (1970) 7.5' quadrangle.

McGregor Canyon [LAKE]: *canyon*, drained by a stream that flows 0.5 mile to Scotts Creek 4 miles west of Lakeport (lat. 39°03'15" N, long. 122°59'10" W; near NE cor. sec. 20, T 14 N, R 10 W); the canyon is west of McGregor Ridge. Named on Lakeport (1958) 7.5' quadrangle.

McGregor Ridge [LAKE]: *ridge*, south-southeast-trending, 1.5 long, 3.5 miles west of Lakeport (lat. 39°03'20" N, long. 122°58'55" W; on S line sec. 16, T 14 N, R 10 W). Named on Lakeport (1958) 7.5' quadrangle.

McGuire Gulch [TRINITY]: *canyon*, drained by a stream that flows 1.25 miles to Coffee Creek nearly 2.5 miles southwest of Billy Peak (1) (lat. 41°06'30" N, long. 122°48'W; sec. 32, T 32 N, R 8 W). Named on Coffee Creek (1955) 15' quadrangle.

McGuire Hill [MENDOCINO]: *peak*, 6.5 miles north-northwest of Comptche (lat. 39°21'20" N, long. 123°37'15" W; near NW cor. sec. 11, T 17 N, R 16 W). Altitude 742 feet. Named on Comptche (1960) 15' quadrangle.

McGuire Ridge [MENDOCINO]: *ridge*, east- to north-trending, 3 miles long, 9.5 miles southwest of Ornbaun Valley (lat. 38°48'N, long. 123°24'10" W). Named on Ornbaun Valley (1960) 15' quadrangle.

McGuire Peak [LAKE]: *peak*, 3.5 miles southeast of Middletown (lat. 38°42'25" N, long. 122°34'30" W; near SW cor. sec. 18, T 10 N, R 6 W). Altitude 2758 feet. Named on Detert Reservoir (1958) 7.5' quadrangle.

McIntire Creek [LAKE]: *stream*, flows 4 miles to Cole Creek (2) 2.5 miles south-southeast of Kelseyville (lat. 38°56'35" N, long. 122°48'50" W; sec. 25, T 13 N, R 9 W). Named on Kelseyville (1959) 7.5' quadrangle.

McIntyre Gulch [TRINITY]: *canyon*, drained by a stream that flows 1.25 miles to Trinity River 5.25 miles south-southeast of Weaverville (lat. 40°39'45" N, long. 122°54'W; near NW cor. sec. 4, T 32 N, R 9 W). Named on Weaverville (1950) 15' quadrangle.

McKay Camp [TRINITY]: *locality*, 11 miles north-northeast of Helena along Canyon Creek (1) (lat. 40°54'30" N, long. 123°01'15" W). Named on Helena (1951) 15' quadrangle.

McKay Gulch [MENDOCINO]: *canyon*, drained by a stream that flows 0.25 mile to Albion River 6.25 miles west of Comptche (lat. 39°15'15" N, long. 123°42'20" W; sec. 13, T 16 N, R 17 W). Named on Comptche (1960) 15' quadrangle.

McKee: see **Mount M' Kee**, under **Mount Konocti** [LAKE].

McKee Creek [HUMBOLDT]:

(1) *stream*, flows 2.5 miles to Mattole River 9.5 miles west-southwest of Garberville (lat. 40°03'45" N, long. 123°57'50" W; near SW cor. sec. 33, T 4 S, R 2 E). Named on Briceland (1969) 7.5' quadrangle.

(2) *stream*, flows 1.25 miles to the sea 2 miles east-southeast of Shelter Cove (2) (lat. 40°00'50" N, long. 124°02'05" W; sec. 23, T 5 S, R 1 E). Named on Shelter Cove (1969) 7.5' quadrangle.

McKinley Creek [MENDOCINO]: *stream*, flows 0.5 mile to South Fork Eel River 5.5 miles north of Branscomb (lat. 39°44'05" N, long. 123°37'45" W; at S line sec. 21, T 22 N, R 16 W). Named on Cahto Peak (1967) and Lincoln Ridge (1966) 7.5' quadrangles.

McKinleyville [HUMBOLDT]: *town*, 5.25 miles north of Arcata (lat. 40°56'45" N, long. 124°06'W; sec. 31, 32, T 7 N, R 1 E). Named on Arcata North (1959) 7.5' quadrangle. Postal authorities established McKinleyville post office in 1903, discontinued it in 1921, and reestablished it in 1955 (Salley, p. 136). Isaac Minor started a community called Minorsville at the site in 1897; the residents changed the name to McKinleyville following the assassination of President McKinley (Turner, p. 146).

McKinney Gulch [TRINITY]: *canyon*, drained by a stream that flows 2 miles to Trinity River 14 miles north-northeast of Hayfork (lat. 40°43'45" N, long. 123°03'40" W). Named on Hayfork (1951) 15' quadrangle.

McKinzey Gulch [TRINITY]: *canyon*, drained by a stream that flows 1.5 miles to Sidney Gulch 1 mile northwest of Weaverville (lat. 40°44'20" N, long. 122°57'W; at S line sec. 1, T 33 N, R 10 W). Named on Trinity Dam (1950) and Weaverville (1950) 15' quadrangles.

McLeod Creek [LAKE]: *stream*, flows 1.5 miles to Rice Creek 3.5 miles west of Potato Hill (lat. 39°20'55" N, long. 122°52'10" W; near SE cor. sec. 4, T 17 N, R 9 W). Named on Potato Hill (1967) 7.5' quadrangle.

McLeod Ridge [LAKE]: *ridge*, generally northwest-trending, 2.25 miles long, 1.5 miles west-southwest of Bear Mountain (lat. 39°24'N, long. 122°55'30" W). Named on Lake Pillsbury (1967) 7.5' quadrangle.

McMahon Creek [HUMBOLDT]: *stream*, flows 3 miles to Larabee Creek 3.25 miles north-northwest of Blocksburg (lat. 40°19'15" N, long. 123°39'45" W; sec. 6, T 2 S, R 5 E). Named on Black Lassic (1979) and Blocksburg (1969) 7.5' quadrangles.

McMullen Creek [MENDOCINO]: *stream*, flows 2.5 miles to Noyo River 6 miles west-northwest of Willits (lat. 39°25'50" N, long. 123°27'30" W; sec. 7, T 18 N, R 14 W). Named on Willits (1961) 15' quadrangle. Called McMullan Creek on Willits (1942) 15' quadrangle, and called McMillan Cr. on O' Brien's (1953) map.

McNab Creek [MENDOCINO]: *stream*, flows 5.5 miles to Russian River 9 miles south-southeast of Ukiah (lat. 39°01'50" N, long. 123°07'55" W). Named on Elledge Peak (1958) 7.5' quadrangle, which shows McNab ranch near the stream.

McNeil Creek [HUMBOLDT]: *stream*, flows 0.5 mile to the sea 2 miles north-northwest of Trinidad (lat. 41°05'20" N, long. 124°09'10" W; near S line sec. 11, T 8 N, R 1 W). Named on Trinidad (1966) 7.5' quadrangle.

McNulty Slough [HUMBOLDT]: *water feature*, joins North Bay 6.25 miles north of Ferndale (lat. 40°39'55" N, long. 124°17'15" W). Named on Cannibal Island (1959) 7.5' quadrangle. Present North Bay is called McNulty Slough on Cape Fortunas (1920) 15' quadrangle. The feature first was called Waite's Slough for Ethan Waite (Turner, p. 146, 223).

McNutt Gulch [HUMBOLDT]: *canyon*, drained by a stream that flows 4.25 miles to the sea 4.5 miles west-northwest of Petrolia (lat. 40°21'20" N, long. 124°21'40" W; sec. 25, T 1 S, R 3 W). Named on Petrolia (1969) 7.5' quadrangle. The name commemorates John McNutt, who had a claim along the stream in 1863 (Turner, p. 146).

McWhinney Creek [HUMBOLDT]: *stream*, flows 1.5 miles to North Fork Elk River (1) 8 miles east-southeast of Fields Landing (lat. 40°41'35" N, long. 124°03'50" W; near NE cor. sec. 33, T 4 N, R 1 E). Named on McWhinney Creek (1979) 7.5' quadrangle.

McWhorter's : see **Burnt Ranch** [TRINITY].

Measly Creek [MENDOCINO]: *stream*, flows 1 mile to Rattlesnake Creek (2) 4.5 miles east-southeast of Leggett (lat. 39°49'55" N, long. 123°38'20" W; near E line sec. 20, T 23 N, R 16 W). Named on Leggett (1969) 7.5' quadrangle.

Medicine Hill [MENDOCINO]: *hill*, 2.25 miles north-northwest of Covelo (lat. 39°49'25" N, long. 123°16'10" W; sec. 26, T 23 N, R 13 W). Named on Covelo West (1967) 7.5' quadrangle.

Megram Ridge [TRINITY]: *ridge*, north-trending, 4.5 miles long, center 5.5 miles south-southeast of Salmon Mountain (lat. 41°06'30" N, long. 123°22'25" W). Named on Youngs Peak (1979) 7.5' quadrangle.

Megwil Point [HUMBOLDT]: *promontory*, 1 mile northwest of Trinidad along the coast (lat. 41°04'10" N, long. 124°09'30" W; sec. 22, T 8 N, R 1 W). Named on Trinidad (1966) 7.5' quadrangle.

Melbourne [MENDOCINO]: *locality*, 3.5 miles west-northwest of Comptche (lat. 39°17'N, long. 123°39'W; near S line sec. 33, T 17 N, R 16 W). Named on Comptche (1960) 15' quadrangle. Called Melburne on California Mining Bureau's (1909c) map. Postal authorities established Melburne post office in 1901 and discontinued it in 1918; the post office name also had the form "Melbourne" (Salley, p. 137). Francis Jackson (p. 102) noted that Melborne Camp was referred to as Ross's Camp, for William Ross, who operated it. California Mining Bureau's (1917c) map shows a place called Clearbrook located 2 miles west-northwest of Melbourne at the end of a rail line.

Melburne: see **Melbourne** [MENDOCINO].

Mendenhall Camp [MENDOCINO]: *locality,* 4 miles northwest of Hull Mountain (lat. 39°34'10" N, long. 122°58'45" W; near SE cor. sec. 20, T 20 N, R 10 W); the place is near Mendenhall Creek. Named on Hull Mountain (1967) 7.5' quadrangle.

Mendenhall Creek [MENDOCINO]: *stream,* flows 5 miles to Elk Creek (2) 11 miles east-southeast of Eden Valley (lat. 39°32'50" N, long. 123°00'55" W; at W line sec. 31, T 20 N, R 10 W). Named on Hull Mountain (1967) and Sanhedrin Mountain (1966) 7.5' quadrangles.

Mendenhall Creek: see **Sportsman Creek** [MENDOCINO].

Mendocino [MENDOCINO]: *town,* 9.5 miles south of Fort Bragg (lat. 39°18'20" N, long. 123°47'50" W; sec. 30, T 17 N, R 17 W). Named on Mendocino (1960) 7.5' quadrangle. Called Mendocino City on Bancroft's (1864) map. Postal authorities established Mendocino post office in 1858 (Frickstad, p. 96). William Kasten, the first settler at the site, arrived about 1850 and was followed in 1852 by Harry Meiggs, who started lumbering operations in the neighborhood; the town was laid out in 1869 and named for Cape Mendocino—the place first was known as Big River for the nearby stream (Hanna, p. 189).

Mendocino: see **Cape Mendocino** [HUMBOLDT]; **Lake Mendocino** [MENDOCINO].

Mendocino Bay [MENDOCINO]: *embayment,* just south of Mendocino along the coast at the mouth of Big River (lat. 39°17'50" N, long. 123°48'W). Named on Mendocino (1960) 7.5' quadrangle.

Mendocino Bay: see **Humboldt Bay** [HUMBOLDT].

Mendocino City: see **Mendocino** [MENDOCINO].

Mendocino River: see **Eel River** [HUMBOLDT-LAKE-MENDOCINO-TRINITY].

Mendocino Woodlands [MENDOCINO]: *locality,* 7 miles west-northwest of Comptche (lat. 39°19'10" N, long. 123°42'05" W; sec. 24, T 17 N, R 17 W). Named on Comptche (1960) 15' quadrangle.

Menzel Gulch [TRINITY]: *canyon,* drained by a stream that flows 2 miles to Cedar Creek 4 miles northeast of Trinity Center (lat. 41°02'25" N, long. 122°38'W; sec. 26, T 37 N, R 7 W). Named on Bonanza King (1955) 15' quadrangle.

Meridian: see **Ferndale** [HUMBOLDT].

Messerville: see **Junction City** [TRINITY].

Meter Meadow [TRINITY]: *area,* 13 miles north of Trinity Center (lat. 41°11'25" N, long. 122°38'45" W; at NW cor. sec. 2, T 38 N, R 7 W). Named on Bonanza King (1955) 15' quadrangle.

Metropolitan [HUMBOLDT]: *locality,* nearly 6 miles south of Fortuna along Eel River (lat. 40°30'55" N, long. 124°08'35" W; sec. 35, T 2 N, R 1 W). Named on Fortuna (1959) 7.5' quadrangle. Postal authorities established Metropolitan post office in 1905 and discontinued it in 1933 (Frickstad, p. 45). In 1904 Metropolitan Redwood Lumber Company built a mill at the site, which previously was known as McDiarmid's Prairie for Finley McDiarmid; Indians killed McDiarmid in his cabin at the place in 1851 (Turner, p. 145, 149).

Metropolitan Creek: see **Slater Creek** [HUMBOLDT].

Mettah [HUMBOLDT]: *locality,* nearly 3 miles south of Johnsons along Klamath River (lat. 41°18'35" N, long. 123°52'15" W; sec. 30, T 11 N, R 3 E); the place is near the mouth of Mettah Creek. Named on Johnsons (1982) 7.5' quadrangle. Postal authorities established Mettah post office in 1924 and discontinued it in 1925 (Salley, p. 139).

Mettah Creek [HUMBOLDT]: *stream,* flows 7.25 miles to Klamath River 3 miles south of Johnsons (lat. 41°18'30" N, long. 123°52'15" W; sec. 30, T 11 N, R 3 E). Named on Bald Hills (1982), Holter Ridge (1983), and Johnsons (1982) 7.5' quadrangles. The name is from an Indian village that was located along Klamath River (Kroeber, p. 47).

Mettick Creek [MENDOCINO]: *stream,* flows 2.25 miles to South Fork Big River 4.5 miles east of Comptche (lat. 39°15'30" N, long. 123°30'20" W; sec. 11, T 16 N, R 15 W). Named on Comptche (1960) 15' quadrangle. Called Mettrick Creek on O' Brien's (1953) map.

Mewhinny Creek [MENDOCINO]: *stream,* flows 6.5 miles to East Fork Russian River 3.5 miles south of the town of Potter Valley (lat. 39°16'10" N, long. 123°06'W; sec. 5, T 16 N, R 11 W). Named on Cow Mountain (1958) and Potter Valley (1960) 7.5' quadrangles. Pomo (1943) 15' quadrangle shows Mewhinney ranch near the stream.

Mexico Ridge [MENDOCINO]: *ridge,* north-northeast-trending, 1 mile long, 8.5 miles east of Covelo (lat. 39°47'30" N, long. 123°05'15" W; mainly in sec. 4, T 22 N, R 11 W). Named on Newhouse Ridge (1967) 7.5' quadrangle.

Meyer Gulch [MENDOCINO]: *canyon,* drained by a stream that flows 2 miles to Mill Creek (9) 2.5 miles southeast of Navarro (lat. 39°07'30" N, long. 123°30'25" W; at S line sec. 27, T 15 N, R 15 W). Named on Navarro (1961) 15' quadrangle.

Meyer's : see **Low Divide** [DEL NORTE].

Meyers Creek [LAKE]: *stream,* flows less than 1 mile to lowlands near Dry Creek (2) 2 miles west-southwest of Middletown (lat. 38°44'35" N, long. 122°39'W; sec. 5, T 10 N, R 7 W). Named on Mount Saint Helena (1959) 7.5' quadrangle.

Meyers Landing: see **Southport Landing** [HUMBOLDT].

Meyers Spring [MENDOCINO]: *spring,* 5 miles northeast of Laytonville (lat. 39°44'15" N, long. 123°24'40" W; at S line sec. 22, T 22 N, R 14 W). Named on Laytonville (1967) 7.5' quadrangle.

Michaels Creek [MENDOCINO]: *stream,* flows 2.5 miles to Hollow Tree Creek 7 miles south of Leggett (lat. 39°45'45" N, long. 123°43'15" W; sec. 14, T 22 N, R 17 W). Named on Leggett (1969) 7.5' quadrangle.

Mickey Ridge: see **North Mickey Ridge** [TRINITY]; **South Mickey Ridge** [TRINITY].

Midas Gulch [TRINITY]: *canyon,* drained by a stream that flows 2 miles to Browns Creek 3.5 miles south-southeast of Chanchelulla Peak (lat. 40°25'30" N, long. 122°58'10" W; near E line sec. 27, T 30 N, R 10 W). Named on Chanchelulla Peak (1951) 15' quadrangle.

Middle Creek [HUMBOLDT]: *stream,* flows 3 miles to Mattole River 4 miles east-southeast of Honeydew (lat. 40°13'45" N, long. 124°02'45" W). Named on Bull Creek (1969) and Honeydew (1970) 7.5' quadrangles.

Middle Creek [LAKE]:

(1) *stream,* flows nearly 2 miles to Glenn County 6.5 miles northeast of Hull Mountain (lat. 39°34'50" N, long. 122°50'25" W; at N line sec. 23, T 20 N, R 9 W); the stream is on the southwest side of Middle Ridge. Named on Kneecap Ridge (1967) 7.5' quadrangle.

(2) *stream,* formed by the confluence of East Fork and West Fork, flows 8.5 miles to join Scotts Creek and form Rodman Slough 1.25 miles south of the town of Upper Lake (lat. 39°08'55" N, long. 122°54'40" W; at E line sec. 13, T 15 N, R 10 W). Named on Upper Lake (1958) 7.5' quadrangle. East Fork in 9 miles long and is named on Bartlett Mountain (1958), Elk Mountain (1967), and Upper Lake (1958) 7.5' quadrangles. West Fork, which is 6.5 miles long, is east of Middle Mountain and is named on Elk Mountain (1967) and Potter Valley (1960) 7.5' quadrangles.

(3) *stream,* flows 3.25 miles to North Fork Cache Creek nearly 7 miles northeast of the town of Lower Lake (lat. 38°59'20" N, long. 122°32'15" W). Named on Clearlake Oaks (1960) 15' quadrangle, and on Lower Lake (1958) 7.5' quadrangle.

Middle Creek [MENDOCINO]: *stream,* flows 2.25 miles to Hollow Tree Creek 11.5 miles south of Piercy (lat. 39°48'55" N, long. 123°45'45" W; sec. 29, T 23 N, R 17 W). Named on Hales Grove (1970) 7.5' quadrangle.

Middle Creek [TRINITY]:

(1) *stream,* flows 1 mile to Stuart Fork 11 miles north of Trinity Dam (lat. 40°53'N, long. 122°55'50" W). Named on Trinity Dam (1950) 15' quadrangle.

(2) *stream,* flows 2 miles to South Fork Trinity River 3 miles northwest of Hyampom (lat. 41°38'40" N, long. 123°29'30" W; near NW cor. sec. 15, T 3 N, R 6 E). Named on Hyampom (1951) 15' quadrangle, and on Sims Mountain (1979) 7.5' quadrangle.

Middle Creek: see **Little Creek** [TRINITY] (2); **Mill Creek** [MENDOCINO] (13).

Middle Creek Campground [LAKE]: *locality,* 4.5 miles south-southwest of Three Crossings (lat. 39°15'10" N, long. 122°57'W; sec. 10, T 16 N, R 10 W); the place is near the confluence of East Fork and West Fork Middle Creek (2). Named on Elk Mountain (1967) 7.5' quadrangle

Middle Creek Flat [LAKE]: *area,* 4.5 miles northeast of the town of Upper Lake (lat. 39°12'40" N, long. 122°51'W; sec. 27, T 16 N, R 9 W); the place is along Middle Creek (2). Named on Bartlett Mountain (1958) 7.5' quadrangle.

Middle Creek Valley [LAKE]: *valley,* 2.25 miles north of the town of Upper Lake (lat. 39°11'50" N, long. 122°54'15" W); the valley is along Middle Creek (2). Named on Upper Lake (1958) 7.5' quadrangle.

Middle Mountain [LAKE-MENDOCINO]: *ridge,* generally southeast-trending, 10 miles long, center 6 miles northwest of the town of Upper Lake on Lake-Mendocino County line (lat. 39°14'N, long. 122°58'30" W); the ridge is southwest of Middle Creek (2). Named on Elk Mountain (1967), Potter Valley (1960), and Upper Lake (1958) 7.5' quadrangles.

Middle Peak [TRINITY]: *peak,* 13 miles north-northeast of Weaverville (lat. 40°55'N, long. 122°52'40" W). Altitude 8095 feet. Named on Trinity Dam (1950) 15' quadrangle.

Middle Peak: see **Howard Peak** [LAKE].

Middle Ridge [HUMBOLDT]:

(1) *ridge,* southwest-trending, 0.5 mile long, 6 miles east-southeast of Honeydew (lat. 40°11'55" N, long. 124°01'25" W; near NW cor. sec. 24, T 3 S, R 1 E). Named on Honeydew (1970) 7.5' quadrangle.

(2) *ridge,* east-trending, 2.5 miles long, 4 miles west-northwest of Alderpoint (lat. 40°12'20" N, long. 123°40'50" W). Named on Fort Seward (1969)

7.5' quadrangle.

Middle Ridge [LAKE]: *ridge,* northwest-trending, 1.5 miles long, 7 miles northeast of Hull Mountain on Lake-Glenn County line (lat. 39°34'50" N, long. 122°49'45" W); the ridge is northeast of Middle Creek (1). Named on Kneecap Ridge (1967) 7.5' quadrangle.

Middle Ridge [MENDOCINO]: *ridge,* west-northwest-trending, 1 mile long, 6 miles north of Boonville (lat. 39°05'45" N, long. 123°22'W). Named on Boonville (1959) 15' quadrangle.

Middle Rock [MENDOCINO]: *rock,* 14 miles south of Piercy, and 550 feet offshore (lat. 39°46'40" N, long. 123°50'20" W). Named on Hales Grove (1970) 7.5' quadrangle.

Middle Stoddard Lake: see **McDonald Lake** [TRINITY].

Middleton: see **Middletown** [LAKE].

Middleton Creek [MENDOCINO]: *stream,* flows 1 miles to South Fork Eel River 5.25 miles east-southeast of Cahto Peak (lat. 39°37'40" N, long. 123°32'05" W; sec. 33, T 21 N, R 15 W). Named on Cahto Peak (1967) and Sherwood Peak (1967) 7.5' quadrangles.

Middleton Gulch [TRINITY]: *canyon,* drained by a stream that flows 3.25 miles to Browns Creek 13 miles south of Weaverville (lat. 40°32'50" N, long. 122°55'30" W; sec. 7, T 31 N, R 9 W). Named on Weaverville (1950) 15' quadrangle.

Middletown [LAKE]: *town,* 11 miles south of the town of Lower Lake (lat. 38°45'10" N, long. 122°37'05" W). Named on Detert Reservoir (1958) and Middletown (1958) 7.5' quadrangles. Postal authorities established Middleton post office in 1871 and changed the name to Middletown in 1875 (Frickstad, p. 64). J.H. Berry built the first house at the site in 1870 (Palmer, p. 147). The town was started in 1871 and named for its location halfway between the towns of Lower Lake in Lake County and Calistoga in Napa County (Hanna, p. 192). Kroeber (p. 46) stated that Middletown is situated in Loconoma Valley, which was named for an Indian village that was near the site of the present town. Postal authorities established Mirabel post office 4 miles south of Middletown in 1892 and discontinued it in 1893; the name was from Mirabel mine (Salley, p. 142)—Detert Reservoir (1958) 7.5' quadrangle shows the mine situated 3.5 miles south of Middletown (sec. 23, T 10 N, R 7 W). Waring (p. 357-358) noted that Gifford Springs, located about 10 miles by road northwest of Middletown, consists of two small springs that were improved and opened to the public as a mountain resort before 1910. California Mining Bureau's (1909c) map shows a place called Quicksilver located just south of Middletown near Lake-Sonoma County line.

Midlake: see **Blue Lakes** [LAKE]; **Saratoga Springs** [LAKE].

Midway Point [DEL NORTE]: *promontory,* 7.5 miles south-southeast of Crescent City along the coast (lat. 41°39'30" N, long. 124°08'05" W; sec. 25, T 15 N, R 1 W). Named on Sister Rocks (1966) 7.5' quadrangle.

Mikes Peak [TRINITY]: *peak,* 10 miles southeast of Weaverville (lat. 40°37'40" N, long. 122°48'35" W; sec. 18, T 32 N, R 8 W). Altitude 4776 feet. Named on Weaverville (1950) 15' quadrangle.

Mikes Ridge [MENDOCINO]: *ridge,* southwest-trending, 1 mile long, 7 miles west of Ornbaun Valley (lat. 38°55'45" N, long. 123°26'10" W; near N line sec. 4, T 12 N, R 14 W). Named on Ornbaun Valley (1960) 15' quadrangle.

Mikes Rock [TRINITY]: *peak,* 12 miles southwest of Black Rock Mountain (lat. 40°05'20" N, long. 123°10'15" W; near W line sec. 24, T 26 N, R 12 W). Named on Black Rock Mountain (1954) 15' quadrangle. The name is for Mike Flournoy, who loved to sit on the peak when he was young—Mike's father ran sheep in the neighborhood (Jones, p. 363).

Milk Camp [TRINITY]: *locality,* 11.5 miles southeast of Salmon Mountain (lat. 41°02'25" N, long. 123°16'40" W); the place is at the head of Milk Creek. Named on Dees Peak (1978) 7.5' quadrangle.

Milk Creek [TRINITY]: *stream,* flows 2.5 miles to Pony Creek (1) 13 miles south-southeast of Salmon Mountain (lat. 41°00'50" N, long. 123°17'W). Named on Dees Peak (1978) 7.5' quadrangle.

Milk Gulch [TRINITY]: *canyon,* drained by a stream that flows 1.5 miles to Grizzly Creek 7.25 miles south of Cecilville, which is in Siskiyou County (lat. 41°02'20" N, long. 123°06'30" W). Named on Cecilville (1955) 15' quadrangle.

Milk Ranch Creek [HUMBOLDT]: *stream,* flows 2.25 miles to South Fork Eel River 6.5 miles south of Garberville (lat. 40°00'15" N, long. 123°46'35" W; sec. 24, T 5 S, R 3 E). Named on Garberville (1970) and Harris (1969) 7.5' quadrangles.

Milk Ranch Creek [TRINITY]: *stream,* flows 2 miles to North Fork Coffee Creek 6.25 miles west-northwest of Billys Peak (1) (lat. 41°10'20" N, long. 122°52'10" W; sec. 11, T 38 N, R 9 W). Named on Coffee Creek (1955) 15' quadrangle. Called Mill Ranch Cr. on Etna (1934) 30'quadrangle.

Mill Creek [DEL NORTE]: *stream,* formed by the confluence of East Fork and West Branch, flows 5.5 miles to Smith River 6.5 miles east-northeast of Crescent City (lat. 41°47'30" N, long. 124°05'W). Named on Childs Hill (1966) and Hiouchi (1966) 7.5' quadrangles. East Fork is 6 miles long, and West Branch is 7.5 miles long; both are named on Childs Hill (1966) 7.5' quadrangle. West Branch is called Mill Creek on Klamath (1952) 15' quadrangle, but United States Board on Geographic Names (1968a, p. 8) rejected this name for the feature.

Mill Creek [HUMBOLDT]:

(1) *stream,* flows 3 miles to the sea near Trinidad (lat. 41°03'40" N, long. 124°08'55" W; sec. 23, T 8 N, R 1 W). Named on Crannell (1966) and Trinidad (1966) 7.5' quadrangles. The name is from Luffenholtz Lumber mill, which Byron Deming and William March moved to the stream in 1853 (Turner, p. 150).

(2) *stream,* flows 15 miles to Trinity River 3 miles north-northwest of Hoopa (lat. 41°05'25" N, long. 123°42'10" W). Named on Hoopa (1979), Hopkins Butte (1979), and Tish Tang Point (1978) 7.5' quadrangles. Middle Fork enters 8 miles northeast of Hoopa; it is 4.25 miles long and is named on Hopkins Butte (1979), Salmon Mountain (1978), and Tish Tang Point (1978) 7.5' quadrangles; United States Board on Geographic Names (1981c, p. 3) rejected the name "Middle Fork Mill Creek" for this stream, and approved the name "Domingo Creek" for it—the name "Domingo" commemorates Domingo Balbobonos, a Peruvian who packed supplies to the mines, and who had a stopping place for his mules by the creek. North Fork enters from the northeast 7.5 miles east-southeast of Weitchpec; it is 4 miles long and is named on Hopkins Butte (1979) 7.5' quadrangle. South Fork enters Middle Fork from the southeast 8.5 miles northeast of Hoopa; it is 2.25 miles long and is named on Tish Tang Point (1978) 7.5' quadrangle; United States Board on Geographic Names (1981c, p. 4) rejected the name "South Fork Mill Creek" for this stream, and approved the name "South Fork Domingo Creek."

(3) *stream,* flows 3.5 miles to Mad River 4 miles north-northwest of Arcata (lat. 40°55'30" N, long. 124°06'45" W; sec. 7, T 6 N, R 1 E). Named on Arcata North (1959) 7.5' quadrangle.

(4) *stream,* flows 2 miles to Noisy Creek (1) 4.25 miles east-northeast of Arcata (lat. 40°54'05" N, long. 124°00'30" W; near SE cor. sec. 13, T 6 N, R 1 E). Named on Blue Lake (1979) and Arcata North (1959) 7.5' quadrangles.

(5) *stream,* flows 3.25 miles to Sulphur Creek (1) 0.5 mile south of Dinsmore (lat. 40°28'55" N, long. 123°36'25" W; at W line sec. 10, T 1 N, R 5 E). Named on Dinsmore (1977) 7.5' quadrangle.

(6) *stream,* flows 2.5 miles to Bull Creek (1) 10 miles south-southeast of Scotia (lat. 40°21'N, long. 124°01'10" W; sec. 25, T 1 S, R 1 E). Named on Bull Creek (1969) 7.5' quadrangle.

(7) *stream,* flows 3.5 miles to Larabee Creek 6.5 miles south-southeast of Bridgeville (lat. 40°23'N, long. 123°45'W; at N line sec. 17, T 1 S, R 4 E). Named on Larabee Valley (1977) 7.5' quadrangle. Middle Branch enters 1 mile upstream from the mouth of the main creek; it is 1.5 miles long and is named on Larabee Valley (1977) 7.5' quadrangle.

(8) *stream,* flows 2 miles to Mattole River 2 miles south-southwest of Petrolia (lat. 40°17'50" N, long. 124°18'20" W; sec. 16, T 2 S, R 2 W). Named on Petrolia (1969) 7.5' quadrangle.

(9) *stream,* flows 2.5 miles to Mattole River 1 mile south-southeast of Petrolia (lat. 40°18'50" N, long. 124°16'45" W; sec. 10, T 2 S, R 2 W). Named on Buckeye Mountain (1970) and Petrolia (1969) 7.5' quadrangles.

(10) *stream,* flows 1.5 miles to South Fork Eel River 0.25 mile south of Weott (lat. 40°19'N, long. 123°55'20" W; sec. 2, T 2 S, R 2 E). Named on Weott (1969) 7.5' quadrangle.

(11) *stream,* flows 1.5 miles to Eel River 4.5 miles west of Blocksburg (lat. 40°16'05" N, long. 123°43'30" W; near NE cor. sec. 28, T 2 S, R 4 E). Named on Blocksburg (1969) 7.5' quadrangle.

(12) *stream,* flows 2.5 miles to Salmon Creek (3) 4.25 miles west-northwest of Phillipsville (lat. 40°13'45" N, long. 123°51'40" W; sec. 5, T 3 S, R 3 E). Named on Ettersburg (1969) and Miranda (1970) 7.5' quadrangles.

(13) *stream,* flows 1.5 miles to Eel River (lat. 40°09'10" N, long. 123°36'W; near S line sec. 34, T 3 S, R 5 E). Named on Alderpoint (1969) and Fort Seward (1969) 7.5' quadrangles.

(14) *stream,* flows 2.5 miles to Mattole River 10 miles west-southwest of Garberville (lat. 40°01'30" N, long. 123°56'50" W). Named on Briceland (1969) 7.5' quadrangle.

(15) *stream,* flows 1.5 miles to Redwood Creek (1) 9 miles south of Coyote Peak (lat. 41°00'05" N, long. 123°51'30" W; at S line sec. 8, T 7 N, R 3 E). Named on Hupa Mountain (1982) 7.5' quadrangle.

(16) *stream,* flows 1 mile to North Fork Mad River less than 1 mile south-southwest of Korbel (lat. 40°51'50" N, long. 123°58'15" W; sec. 37, T 6 N, R 2 E). Named on Korbel (1979) 7.5' quadrangle.

Mill Creek [HUMBOLDT-TRINITY]: *stream,* heads just inside Humboldt County and flows 4.5 miles to South Fork Trinity River 3 miles northwest of Hyampom in Trinity County (lat. 40°38'45" N, long. 123°29'30" W; at S line sec. 10, T 3 N, R 6 E). Named on Hyampom (1951) 15' quadrangle, and on Blake Mountain (1979) and Sims Mountain (1979) 7.5' quadrangles.

Mill Creek [LAKE]:

(1) *stream,* flows 6.25 miles to join Fuller Creek and form Salmon Creek 6.25 miles northwest of Bear Mountain (lat. 39°28'35" N, long. 122°58'35" W; near E line sec. 29, T 19 N, R 10 W). Named on Potter Valley (1960) 15' quadrangle, and on Lake Pillsbury (1967) and Sanhedrin Mountain (1966) 7.5' quadrangles.

(2) *stream,* flows 1.5 miles to Big Canyon Creek 2.5 miles northeast of

Whispering Pines (lat. 38°51'N, long. 122°41'55" W; sec. 36, T 12 N, R 8 W). Named on Whispering Pines (1958) 7.5' quadrangle.

Mill Creek [MENDOCINO]:

(1) *stream,* formed by the confluence of Cold Creek (4) and Alder Creek (2), flows 12.5 miles to Middle Fork Eel River 8 miles north-northeast of Eden Valley (lat. 39°44'20" N, long. 123°08'30" W; sec. 25, T 22 N, R 12 W). Named on Covelo East (1967), Covelo West (1967), and Jamison Ridge (1967) 7.5' quadrangles.

(2) *stream,* flows 3 miles to South Fork Eel River 2 miles northwest of Leggett (lat. 39°53'10" N, long. 123°44'35" W; at N line sec. 4, T 23 N, R 17 W). Named on Hales Grove (1970), Leggett (1969), and Noble Butte (1969) 7.5' quadrangles.

(3) *stream,* flows 3.5 miles to Little Case Creek 6.25 miles east-northeast of Branscomb (lat. 39°41'N, long. 123°30'55" W; near SE cor. sec. 10, T 21 N, R 15 W). Named on Cahto Peak (1967) 7.5' quadrangle.

(4) *stream,* flows 3.25 miles to Ten Mile River 9 miles southwest of Branscomb (lat. 39°32'55" N, long. 123°44'05" W; near SE cor. sec. 34, T 20 N, R 17 W). Named on Dutchmans Knoll (1966) 7.5' quadrangle.

(5) *stream,* flows 2.5 miles to Lake Cleone 3 miles north-northeast of Fort Bragg (lat. 39°29'15" N, long. 123°47'25" W; at S line sec. 19, T 19 N, R 17 W). Named on Fort Bragg (1960) 7.5' quadrangle.

(6) *stream,* enters Little Lake Valley at Willits (lat. 39°24'50" N, long. 123°21'15" W; at W line sec. 18, T 18 N, R 13 W). Named on Willits (1961) 15' quadrangle.

(7) *stream,* flows 4 miles to Eel River 4.25 miles north of the town of Potter Valley (lat. 39°23'05" N, long. 123°06'45" W; near E line sec. 30, T 18 N, R 11 W). Named on Potter Valley (1960) 15' quadrangle.

(8) *stream,* flows 8 miles to Forsythe Creek 10.5 miles south-southeast of Willits (lat. 39°16'45" N, long. 123°15'35" W; near SW cor. sec. 36, T 17 N, R 13 W). Named on Willits (1961) 15' quadrangle.

(9) *stream,* flows 8.5 miles to Navarro River 4 miles south-southeast of Navarro (lat. 39°07'30" N, long. 123°30'25" W; at S line sec. 27, T 15 N, R 15 W). Named on Boonville (1959) and Navarro (1961) 15' quadrangles.

(10) *stream,* flows 2.5 miles to Brush Creek about 4 miles north-northeast of the village of Point Arena (lat. 38°57'50" N, long. 123°39'35" W; sec. 29, T 13 N, R 16 W). Named on Point Arena (1960) 7.5' quadrangle.

(11) *stream,* flows 2.5 miles to Robinson Creek (1) at Boonville (lat. 39°00'35" N, long. 123°22'15" W; sec. 2, T 13 N, R 14 W). Named on Boonville (1959) and Ornbaun Valley (1960) 15' quadrangles.

(12) *stream,* flows 6.5 miles to Garcia River 3.5 miles west-southwest of Ornbaun Valley (lat. 38°53'45" N, long. 123°22'W; at SW cor. sec. 7, T 12 N, R 13 W). Named on Ornbaun Valley (1960) 15' quadrangle.

(13) *stream,* flows 5 miles to Russian River 1.5 mile southeast of Ukiah (lat. 39°08'05" N, long. 123°11'05" W). Named on Purdys Gardens (1958) and Ukiah (1958) 7.5' quadrangles. Called Middle Creek on Ukiah (1944) 15' quadrangle, but United States Board on Geographic Names (1961a, p. 18) rejected this name for the stream. North Fork enters from the northeast 1.5 miles upstream from the mouth of the main creek; it is nearly 5 miles long and is named on Cow Mountain (1958) and Ukiah (1958) 7.5' quadrangles. United States Board on Geographic Names (1961a, p. 18) rejected the names "Middle Creek" and "North Fork Middle Creek" for present North Fork Mill Creek (13).

Mill Creek [TRINITY]:

(1) *stream,* flows 2.5 miles to Rattlesnake Creek (1) 9 miles south of Cecilville, which is in Siskiyou County (lat. 41°00'35" N, long. 123°06'25" W). Named on Thompson Peak (1979) 7.5' quadrangle.

(2) *stream,* flows 1.5 miles to Trinity River 22 miles northeast of Weaverville (lat. 40°59'35" N, long. 122°40'20" W; sec. 9, T 36 N, R 7 W). Named on Schell Mountain (1950) 15' quadrangle.

(3) *stream,* flows 3 miles to Trinity River 14 miles north-northeast of Hayfork (lat. 40°43'45" N, long. 123°02'50" W; near NW cor. sec. 18, T 33 N, R 10 W). Named on Hayfork (1951) 15' quadrangle.

(4) *stream,* flows 3.5 miles to Trinity River 2 miles southeast of Burnt Ranch (lat. 40°47'20" N, long. 123°26'40" W). Named on Ironside Mountain (1951) 15' quadrangle.

Mill Creek: see **Little Mill Creek** [DEL NORTE]; **North Mill Creek** [MENDOCINO].

Mill Creek Falls [MENDOCINO]: *waterfall,* 2 miles northwest of Leggett along Mill Creek (2) (lat. 39°52'25" N, long. 123°44'40" W; sec. 4, T 23 N, R 17 W). Named on Noble Butte (1969) 7.5' quadrangle.

Mill Creek Gap [HUMBOLDT]: *pass,* 7.25 miles east of Weitchpec (lat. 41°10'55" N, long. 123°34'05" W); the pass is near the head of a tributary to Mill Creek (2). Named on Hopkins Butte (1979) 7.5' quadrangle.

Mill Creek Lakes [HUMBOLDT]: *lakes,* two, largest 600 feet long, 7 miles northwest of Trinity Mountain (lat. 41°06'50" N, long. 123°29'30" W); the lakes are at the head of a branch of Mill Creek (2). Named on Trinity Mountain (1979) 7.5' quadrangle.

Mill Creek Ridge [HUMBOLDT]: *ridge,* generally northeast-trending, 6 miles long, 5 miles southeast of Weitchpec (lat. 41°08'30" N, long. 123°38'W); the ridge is northwest of Mill Creek (2). Named on Hopkins Butte (1979) and Weitchpec (1979) 7.5' quadrangles.

Miller: see **Bridgeport Landing** [MENDOCINO].

Miller Creek [HUMBOLDT]:

(1) *stream,* flows 1.25 miles to Bull Creek (2) 2.5 miles northwest of Weott (lat. 40°21'N, long. 123°58'40" W; sec. 29, T 1 S, R 2 E). Named on Weott (1969) 7.5' quadrangle.

(2) *stream,* flows nearly 4 miles to Redwood Creek (2) 6 miles west of Garberville (lat. 40°06'15" N, long. 123°54'05" W; near NW cor. sec. 19, T 4 S, R 2 E). Named on Briceland (1969) and Ettersburg (1969) 7.5' quadrangles.

Miller Creek [TRINITY]:

(1) *stream,* flows 1.5 miles to Scott Mountain Creek about 10 miles southwest of China Mountain, which is in Siskiyou County (lat. 41°15'45" N, long. 122°41'25" W; at S line sec. 5, T 39 N, R 7 W); the stream joins Scott Mountain Creek at the mouth of Miller Gulch, but otherwise is unrelated to Miller Gulch. Named on China Mountain (1955) 15' quadrangle.

(2) *stream,* flows 1.5 miles to Trinity River 1 mile southwest of Helena (lat. 40°45'45" N, long. 123°08'15" W; at N line sec. 32, T 34 N, R 11 W). Named on Hayfork (1951) and Helena (1951) 15' quadrangles.

Miller Flat [HUMBOLDT]: *area,* 8.5 miles south-southwest of Honeydew (lat. 40°07'40" N, long. 124°10'20" W; sec. 10, T 4 S, R 1 W). Named on Shubrick Peak (1969) 7.5' quadrangle. Shown as part of Big Flat on Point Delgada (1949) 15' quadrangle. United States Board on Geographic Names (1974a, p. 3) gave the name "Big Flat" as a variant—the Board noted that the name "Miller" commemorates the operators of a hotel at the site in the 1850's.

Miller Gulch [TRINITY]: *canyon,* drained by a stream that flows 1.5 miles to Scott Mountain Creek 10 miles southwest of China Mountain, which is in Siskiyou County (lat. 41°15'45" N, long. 122°41'25" W; at S line sec. 5, T 39 N, R 7 W). Named on China Mountain (1955) 15' quadrangle.

Miller Peak: see **Miller Ridge** [HUMBOLDT].

Miller Prairie [HUMBOLDT]: *area,* 6.5 miles northeast of the town of Blue Lake (lat. 40°56'30" N, long. 123°53'30" W; near NE cor. sec. 1, T 6 N, R 2 E). Named on Blue Lake (1979) 7.5' quadrangle.

Miller Ridge [HUMBOLDT]: *ridge,* southwest-trending, 2.5 miles long, 7.25 miles south of Honeydew (lat. 40°08'25" N, long. 124°08'25" W). Named on Shubrick Peak (1969) 7.5' quadrangle. Vander Leck's (1920b) map has the name "Miller Pk." at or near present Miller Ridge.

Miller Spring [TRINITY]: *spring,* 9 miles northwest of Forest Glen (lat. 40°27'15" N, long. 123°27'30" W; near E line sec. 23, T 1 N, R 6 E). Named on Sportshaven (1973) 7.5' quadrangle.

Mill Gulch [TRINITY]:

(1) *canyon,* drained by a stream that flows less than 1 mile to Deadwood Creek 11 miles east of Weaverville (lat. 40°43'15" N, long. 122°43'45" W; at NW cor. sec. 13, T 33 N, R 8 W). Named on French Gulch (1979) 7.5' quadrangle.

(2) *canyon,* drained by a stream that flows about 1.5 miles to Salt Creek (4) 7.5 miles north of Dubakella Mountain (lat. 40°29'30" N, long. 123°10'05" W; sec. 36, T 31 N, R 12 W). Named on Dubakella Mountain (1954) 15' quadrangle.

(3) *canyon,* drained by a stream that flows 1.5 miles to Grizzly Creek 7.25 miles south of Cecilville, which is in Siskiyou County (lat. 41°02'20" N, long. 123°06'30" W). Named on Thompson Peak (1979) 7.5' quadrangle.

Mill Pond [DEL NORTE]: *lake,* 900 feet long, 3.25 miles north-northwest of the mouth of Klamath River (lat. 41°35'30" N, long. 124°05'45" W; sec. 19, 20, T 14 N, R 1 E). Named on Klamath (1952) 15' quadrangle. United States Board on Geographic Names (1978b, p. 4) approved the name "Lagoon Pond" for the feature, and rejected the names "Mill Pond" and "Lagoon Creek Pond" for it.

Mill Ranch Creek: see **Milk Ranch Creek** [TRINITY].

Mills Creek [MENDOCINO]: *stream,* flows 4 miles to the sea 5.5 miles south-southeast of Elk (lat. 39°03'20" N, long. 123°41'35" W; at S line sec. 24, T 14 N, R 17 W). Named on Mallo Pass Creek (1960) 7.5' quadrangle. United States Board on Geographic Names (1963, p. 6) rejected the name "Stewart Creek" for the stream.

Mills Creek [TRINITY]: *stream,* flows 1 mile to New River 11.5 miles north-northeast of Burnt Ranch (lat. 40°57'15" N, long. 123°22'25" W); the stream is west of Mills Hill. Named on Ironside Mountain (1951) 15' quadrangle.

Mills Hill [TRINITY]: *relief feature,* 12 miles north-northeast of Burnt Ranch (lat. 40°57'30" N, long. 123°22'W); the feature is east of Mills Creek. Named on Ironside Mountain (1951) 15' quadrangle.

Mills Hot Spring: see **Castle Rock Springs** [LAKE].

Mills' Mineral Springs: see **Castle Rock Springs** [LAKE].

Milltown: see **Junction City** [TRINITY].

Mina [MENDOCINO]: *locality,* 7.5 miles northeast of Spyrock (2) (lat. 39°57'55" N, long. 123°21'25" W; sec. 6, T 24 N, R 13 W). Named on Mina (1967) 7.5' quadrangle. Postal authorities established Mina post office in 1914 and discontinued it in 1938 (Frickstad, p. 96).

Miner Creek: see **Miners Creek** [TRINITY].

Miner Ridge [MENDOCINO]: *ridge,* west-trending, less than 0.5 mile long, 8 miles southeast of Ukiah (lat. 39°04'35" N, long. 123°05'45" W; sec. 17, T 14 N, R 11 W). Named on Purdys Gardens (1958) 7.5' quadrangle.

Miners Creek [HUMBOLDT]: *stream,* flows 3 miles to Klamath River 9 miles north-northeast of Coyote Peak (lat. 41°14'55" N, long. 123°46'30" W; near NE cor. sec. 24, T 10 N, R 3 E). Named on Fish Lake (1974), French Camp Ridge (1983), and Johnsons (1982) 7.5' quadrangles.

Miners Creek [TRINITY]: *stream,* flows 6.5 miles to Hayfork Creek 7 miles east of Hyampom (lat. 40°38'10" N, long. 123°19'15" W; sec. 18, T 3 N, R 8 E). Named on Hyampom (1951) 15' quadrangle. Called Miner Creek on United States Geological Survey's (1915) map. West Fork enters from the north-northwest nearly 0.5 mile upstream from the mouth of the main creek; it is 3.25 miles long and is named on Hyampom (1951) 15' quadrangle.

Minersville [TRINITY]: *locality,* 11 miles northeast of Weaverville near the confluence of Stuart Fork and East Fork Stuart Fork (lat. 40°50'N, long. 122°46'45" W; sec. 4, T 34 N, R 8 W). Named on Trinity Lake (1950) 15' quadrangle. Called Minersville P.O. on Weaverville (1913) 30'quadrangle. Water of Clair Engle Lake now covers the site. Postal authorities established Minersville post office in 1856, discontinued it in 1864, reestablished it in 1874, moved it 2 miles northeast in 1901, and discontinued it in 1954 (Salley, p. 141). Bancroft (p. 370) used the designation "Miners, or Diggers, ville" for a place along Stewart Fork."

Minersville: see **Old Minersville** [TRINITY].

Mingo Creek [HUMBOLDT]: *stream,* flows nearly 2 miles to South Fork Trinity River 11 miles south-southeast of the settlement of Willow Creek (lat. 40°47'25" N, long. 123°33'55" W). Named on Hennessy Peak (1979) 7.5' quadrangle. The name reportedly is from a dog lost at the place about 1910 (United States Board on Geographic Names, 1978a, p. 6). North Fork enters less than 0.5 mile upstream from the mouth of the main creek; it is 1.5 miles long and is named on Hennessy Peak (1979) 7.5' quadrangle—United States Board on Geographic Names (1978a, p. 7) rejected the name "Mingo Creek" for North Fork.

Mingo Creek: see **Little Mingo Creek** [HUMBOLDT].

Minnehaha Creek [TRINITY]: *stream,* flows 3.5 miles to Trinity River 8 miles north of Trinity Center (lat. 41°07'25" N, long. 122°41'55" W; sec. 29, T 38 N, R 7 W). Named on Bonanza King (1955) 15' quadrangle.

Minnie Creek [MENDOCINO]: *stream,* flows 3 miles to Rancheria Creek (2) 9 miles northwest of Ornbaun Valley (lat. 38°59'40" N, long. 123°26'W; at N line sec. 17, T 13 N, R 14 W). Named on Ornbaun Valley (1960) 15' quadrangle. South Fork enters from the south 1.5 miles upstream from the mouth of the main stream; it is 1 mile long and is named on Ornbaun Valley (1960) 15' quadrangle.

Minnie Creek [TRINITY]: *stream,* flows 3 miles to Balm of Gilead Creek 11.5 miles south of Black Rock Mountain (lat. 40°02'30" N, long. 123°00'15" W; at NE cor. sec. 7, T 25 N, R 10 W). Named on Black Rock Mountain (1954) and Yolla Bolly (1954) 15' quadrangles.

Minnie Lake [TRINITY]: *lake,* 150 feet long, 12.5 miles south-southeast of Black Rock Mountain (lat. 40°01'50" N, long. 122°57'30" W; sec. 10, T 25 N, R 10 W); the lake is at the head of Minnie Creek. Named on Yolla Bolly (1954) 15' quadrangle.

Minon Creek [HUMBOLDT]: *stream,* flows 3 miles to Redwood Creek (1) 11 miles south-southwest of the settlement of Willow Creek (lat. 40°48'25" N, long. 123°44'50" W; sec. 20, T 5 N, R 4 E). Named on Grouse Mountain (1979) 7.5' quadrangle.

Minor Creek [HUMBOLDT]: *stream,* flows 6 miles to Redwood Creek (1) 9.5 miles northeast of the town of Blue Lake (lat. 40°57'35" N, long. 123°50'10" W; sec. 28, T 7 N, R 3 E). Named on Lord-Ellis Summit (1973) 7.5' quadrangle. The name commemorates Isaac Minor, who settled in Humboldt County in 1853 (Turner, p. 150).

Minorsville: see **McKinleyville** [HUMBOLDT].

Mirabel: see **Middletown** [LAKE].

Miranda [HUMBOLDT]: *village,* 2.5 miles northwest of Phillipsville (lat. 40°14'05" N, long. 123°49'20" W; sec. 3, T 3 S, R 3 E). Named on Miranda (1970) 7.5' quadrangle. Postal authorities established Miranda post office in 1905 (Frickstad, p. 45). The place was known as Jacobsen's Valley before the post office came (Turner, p. 151).

Mirror Lake [TRINITY]: *lake,* 1300 feet long, 16 miles north-northeast of Helena (lat. 41°59'45" N, long. 123°01'35" W). Named on Helena (1951) 15' quadrangle. United States Board on Geographic Names (1984c, p. 2) approved the name "Kalmia Lake" for a feature, 0.1 mile long, located 0.5 mile south of Mirror Lake (lat. 40°59'20" N, long. 123°01'50" W; sec. 8, T 36 N, R 10 W), and rejected the form "Calmia Lake" for the name.

Misery Creek [MENDOCINO]: *stream,* flows 1 mile to Elder Creek 4.5 miles north of Branscomb (lat. 39°43'10" N, long. 123°36'40" W; at N line sec. 34, T 22 N, R 16 W). Named on Cahto Peak (1967) 7.5' quadrangle.

Mississippi Creek [MENDOCINO]: *stream,* flows 3.5 miles to Black Butte River 6 miles south of Anthony Peak (lat. 39°45'45" N, long. 122°59'W; at W line sec. 16, T 22 N, R 10 W). Named on Mendocino Pass (1967), Plaskett Ridge (1967), and Thatcher Ridge (1967) 7.5' quadrangles.

Mistake Point [MENDOCINO]: *promontory,* 10 miles south-southwest of Piercy along the coast (lat. 39°51'35" N, long. 123°54'10" W; sec. 7, T 23 N, R 18 W). Named on Mistake Point (1969) 7.5' quadrangle.

Mitchell Creek [MENDOCINO]:

(1) *stream,* flows nearly 1 mile to Hollow Tree Creek 6.5 miles northwest of Branscomb (lat. 39°43'55" N, long. 123°41'30" W; near E line sec. 25, T 22 N, R 17 W). Named on Lincoln Ridge (1966) 7.5' quadrangle.

(2) *stream,* flows nearly 4 miles to the sea 3.5 miles south of Fort Bragg (lat. 39°23'35" N, long. 123°48'55" W; sec. 25, T 18 N, R 18 W). Named on Fort Bragg (1960) 7.5' quadrangle.

Mitchell Creek: see **Delilah Creek** [DEL NORTE].

Mitzie Creek [HUMBOLDT]: *stream,* flows less than 1 mile to South Fork Eel River 6.5 miles south of Garberville (lat. 40°00'30" N, long. 123°46'35" W; near W line sec. 24, T 5 S, R 3 E). Named on Garberville (1970) 7.5' quadrangle.

Miyakma Range: see **Mayacmas Mountains** [LAKE].

M Line Creek [HUMBOLDT]: *stream,* flows 3.25 miles to Maple Creek (1) 3.5 miles northeast of Trinidad (lat. 41°04'40" N, long. 124°05'W; sec. 17, T 8 N, R 1 E). Named on Crannell (1966) 7.5' quadrangle. United States Board on Geographic Names (1968a, p. 6) rejected the name "Maple Creek" for the stream.

Moat Creek [MENDOCINO]: *stream,* flows 3.5 miles to the sea 2.25 miles south-southeast of the village of Point Arena (lat. 38°52'55" N, long. 123°40'25" W; sec. 30, T 12 N, R 16 W). Named on Point Arena (1960) 7.5' quadrangle. Called Mate Creek on Point Arena (1943) 15' quadrangle, but United States Board on Geographic Names (1963, p. 7) rejected this name for the stream.

Modesto Camp [MENDOCINO]: *locality,* 4.5 miles east of Covelo near Middle Fork Eel River (lat. 39°46'55" N, long. 123°09'40" W; sec. 11, T 22 N, R 12 W). Named on Covelo East (1967) 7.5' quadrangle.

Molaine Corrals: see **Mullane Corral** [TRINITY].

Molassas Creek [HUMBOLDT]: *stream,* flows nearly 2 miles to Redwood Creek (1) 10.5 miles northeast of the town of Blue Lake (lat. 40°59'45" N, long. 123°51'20" W; sec. 17, T 7 N, R 3 E). Named on Lord-Ellis Summit (1973) 7.5' quadrangle.

Molesworth Creek [LAKE]: *stream,* flows 2.5 miles to Clearlake 2 miles northwest of the town of Lower Lake (lat. 38°56'05" N, long. 122°38'W; sec. 33, T 13 N, R 7 W). Named on Clearlake Highlands (1958) and Lower Lake (1958) 7.5' quadrangles.

Moline Corral: see **Mullane Corral** [TRINITY].

Monahan Creek [MENDOCINO]: *stream,* flows 2 miles to Pardaloe Creek 2.5 miles south-southwest of Ornbaun Valley (lat. 38°52'40" N, long. 123°19'15" W; near E line sec. 20, T 12 N, R 13 W). Named on Ornbaun Valley (1960) 15' quadrangle.

Monitor Island [LAKE]: *island,* 200 feet long, 6.5 miles northwest of the town of Lower Lake in Clear Lake (lat. 38°58'35" N, long. 122°42'W); the feature is 750 feet off Monitor Point. Named on Clearlake Highlands (1958) 7.5' quadrangle.

Monitor Point [LAKE]: *promontory,* 6.5 miles northwest of the town of Lower Lake along Clear Lake (lat. 38°58'45" N, long. 122°41'50" W; sec. 13, T 13 N, R 8 W). Named on Clearlake Highlands (1958) 7.5' quadrangle.

Monkey Creek [DEL NORTE]: *stream,* flows 7.5 miles to Middle Fork Smith River 8 miles east-northeast of Gasquet (lat. 41°53'N, long. 123°49'05" W; sec. 10, T 17 N, R 3 E). Named on Shelly Creek Ridge (1982) 7.5' quadrangle.

Monkey Creek [TRINITY]: *stream,* flows 2.5 miles to Trinity River 13 miles northeast of Hyampom (lat. 40°45'N, long. 123°16'30" W). Named on Hyampom (1951) 15' quadrangle.

Monkey Creek Ridge [DEL NORTE]: *ridge,* generally south-trending, 7.5 miles long, center 11.5 miles northeast of Gasquet (lat. 41°56'30" N, long. 123°46'50" W); the ridge is mainly east of Monkey Creek. Named on Shelly Creek Ridge (1982) 7.5' quadrangle.

Monkey Gulch [HUMBOLDT]: *canyon,* drained by a stream that flows less than 0.5 mile to Trinity River 2.5 miles south-southeast of Weitchpec (lat. 41°09'05" N, long. 123°40'55" W; near E line sec. 23, T 9 N, R 4 E). Named on Weitchpec (1979) 7.5' quadrangle.

Monkey Rock [MENDOCINO]: *peak,* 2.25 miles northwest of Hull Mountain (lat. 39°32'55" N, long. 122°57'30" W; near E line sec. 33, T 20 N, R 10 W). Named on Hull Mountain (1967) 7.5' quadrangle.

Monroe: see **Hales Grove** [MENDOCINO].

Monroe Creek [HUMBOLDT-TRINITY]: *stream,* heads just inside Humboldt County and flows 2.5 miles to South Fork Trinity River 5.5 miles north-northwest of Hyampom in Trinity County (lat. 40°40'25" N, long. 123°30'10" W). Named on Sims Mountain (1979) 7.5' quadrangle.

Monroe Flat [HUMBOLDT]: *area,* 4.5 miles south of Coyote Peak (lat. 41°04'30" N, long. 123°51'30" W; at N line sec. 20, T 8 N, R 3 E). Named on Hupa Mountain (1982) 7.5' quadrangle.

Monroe Flat: see **Cow Prairie** [HUMBOLDT].

Monroeville: see **Hales Grove** [MENDOCINO].

Montgomery Basin [TRINITY]: *area,* 7.5 miles south-southeast of Forest Glen (lat. 40°16'N, long. 123°16'30" W; sec. 28, T 2 S, R 8 E). Named on Forest Glen (1979) 7.5' quadrangle.

Montgomery Creek [MENDOCINO]: *stream,* flows 2.25 miles to South

Fork Big River 16 miles north of Boonville (lat. 39°14'05" N, long. 123°23'45" W; near NE cor. sec. 22, T 16 N, R 14 W). Named on Boonville (1959) 15' quadrangle.

Montgomery Flat [MENDOCINO]: *area*, 15 miles north of Boonville (lat. 39°13'50" N, long. 123°23'30" W; at E line sec. 22, T 16 N, R 14 W); the place is along Montgomery Creek. Named on Boonville (1959) 15' quadrangle.

Montgomery Glade [LAKE]: *area*, 5.5 miles west-southwest of Bear Mountain (lat. 39°22'45" N, long. 122°59'55" W; on S line sec. 28, T 18 N, R 10 W). Named on Lake Pillsbury (1967) 7.5' quadrangle.

Montgomery Ridge [TRINITY]: *ridge*, east-southeast-trending, 2.5 miles long, 7.25 miles northeast of Weaverville (lat. 40°48'40" N, long. 122°51'15" W). Named on Trinity Dam (1950) 15' quadrangle.

Monumental [DEL NORTE]: *locality*, 12 miles northeast of Gasquet (lat. 41°58'25" N, long. 123°48'10" W; sec. 11, T 18 N, R 3 E). Site named on Shelly Creek Ridge (1982) 7.5' quadrangle. Postal authorities established Monumental post office in 1904 and discontinued it in 1911 (Frickstad, p. 24). The place was a mining camp for Monumental Consolidated quartz mine; it had a store, bunkhouse, cookhouse, office, laboratory, and barn (Lowell, p. 389).

Monument Creek [HUMBOLDT]: *stream*, flows 9 miles to Eel River 0.5 mile southwest of Scotia (lat. 40°28'25" N, long. 124°06'15" W; near N line sec. 18, T 1 N, R 1 E); the stream heads at Monument Ridge. Named on Scotia (1970) 7.5' quadrangle.

Monument Peak [MENDOCINO]: *peak*, 9.5 miles east-southeast of Hopland (lat. 38°54'40" N, long. 122°57'15" W; near S line sec. 3, T 12 N, R 10 W). Altitude 3320 feet. Named on Highland Springs (1959) 7.5' quadrangle.

Monument Peak [TRINITY]:

(1) *peak*, 7.5 miles north-northwest of Weaverville on Weaver Valley Mountain (present Weaver Bally) (lat. 40°49'55" N, long. 122°58'35" W). Altitude 7771 feet. Named on Trinity Dam (1950) 15' quadrangle. Called Weaver Bally on Weaverville (1913) 30'quadrangle, but United States Board on Geographic Names (1983d, p. 6) rejected the names "Weaver Bally," "East Weaver Bally," and "Weaver Bally Mountain" for the peak.

(2) *peak*, 10.5 miles northeast of Hyampom (lat. 40°43'45" N, long. 123°19'W; at S line sec. 7, T 4 N, R 8 E). Altitude 5216 feet. Named on Hyampom (1951) 15' quadrangle.

Monument Peak: see **Mount Pierce** [HUMBOLDT].

Monument Ridge [HUMBOLDT]: *ridge*, generally west-trending, 4.25 miles long, 4.25 miles south of Scotia (lat. 40°25'15" N, long. 124°05'30" W); Mount Pierce, which has the alternate name "Monument Peak," is on the ridge. Named on Scotia (1970) and Taylor Peak (1969) 7.5' quadrangles.

Moody [MENDOCINO]: *locality*, 4 miles west of Piercy along Indian Creek (2) (lat. 39°58'10" N, long. 123°52'W; at N line sec. 4, T 24 N, R 18 W). Site named on Piercy (1969) 7.5' quadrangle. Postal authorities established Moody post office in 1900 and discontinued it in 1912; the name commemorates Louis A. Moody, first postmaster (Salley, p. 146).

Moody Creek [MENDOCINO]: *stream*, flows 2.5 miles to Indian Creek (2) 4 miles west-southwest of Piercy (lat. 39°57'40" N, long. 123°52'30" W; sec. 5, T 24 N, R 18 W); the stream is 0.5 mile southwest of the site of Moody. Named on Bear Harbor (1969) 7.5' quadrangle. On Kenny (1920) 15' quadrangle, present Moody Creek is shown as part of Indian Creek (2).

Moody Ridge [HUMBOLDT]: *ridge*, generally west-northwest-trending, 3 miles long, 4 miles west of Honeydew (lat. 40°14'15" N, long. 124°12'W). Named on Shubrick Peak (1969) 7.5' quadrangle.

Moon Creek [HUMBOLDT]: *stream*, flows 1.5 miles to Redwood Creek (1) 10 miles northeast of the town of Blue Lake (lat. 40°58'35" N, long. 123°50'40" W; sec. 21, T 7 N, R 3 E). Named on Lord-Ellis Summit (1973) 7.5' quadrangle.

Mooney Gulch [TRINITY]: *canyon*, drained by a stream that flows nearly 4 miles to Trinity River 9 miles east-northeast of Weaverville (lat. 40°46'40" N, long. 122°46'20" W; sec. 28, T 34 N, R 8 W). Named on Schell Mountain (1950) and Trinity Dam (1950) 15' quadrangles. Mr. Mooney operated a ferry at the mouth of Mooney Gulch (Jones, p. 275).

Moonstone [HUMBOLDT]: *locality*, 2.5 miles southeast of Trinidad (lat. 41°01'50" N, long. 124°06'35" W; near S line sec. 31, T 8 N, R 1 E); the place is near Moonstone Beach. Named on Crannell (1966) 7.5' quadrangle.

Moonstone Beach [HUMBOLDT]: *beach*, 2.5 miles southeast of Trinidad along the coast (lat. 41°01'45" N, long. 124°06'45" W; near S line sec. 31, T 8 N, R 1 E). Named on Trinidad (1952) 15' quadrangle.

Moore Creek [MENDOCINO]: *stream*, flows 2.5 miles to Davis Creek 3 miles east-southeast of Willits (lat. 39°23'10" N, long. 123°18'10" W; sec. 28, T 18 N, R 13 W). Named on Willits (1961) 15' quadrangle.

Moore Creek [TRINITY]: *stream*, flows 2 miles to Trinity River 16 miles northeast of Weaverville (lat. 40°52'55" N, long. 122°42'30" W; near NW cor. sec. 19, T 35 N, R 7 W). Named on Schell Mountain (1950) 15' quadrangle.

Moorehead Ridge [HUMBOLDT]: *ridge*, generally east-trending, 1.25 miles long, 5 miles west-southwest of Honeydew (lat. 40°12'40" N, long. 124°12'W; mainly in sec. 17, T 3 S, R 1 W). Named on Shubrick Peak (1969) 7.5' quadrangles.

Moorehead Ridge: see **Little Moorehead Ridge** [HUMBOLDT].

Moore Hill [HUMBOLDT]: *peak*, 3 miles west-southwest of Petrolia (lat. 40°18'20" N, long. 124°20'10" W; near S line sec. 7, T 2 S, R 2 W). Named on Petrolia (1969) 7.5' quadrangle.

Moores Prairie [HUMBOLDT]: *area*, 1.5 miles west-southwest of Scotia (lat. 40°28'10" N, long. 124°07'35" W; sec. 13, T 1 N, R 1 W). Named on Scotia (1970) and Taylor Peak (1969) 7.5' quadrangles.

Mooring Rock: see **Albion Cove** [MENDOCINO].

Moose Peak [TRINITY]: *peak*, 10 miles south of Kettenpom (lat. 40°00'55" N, long. 123°28'55" W; near NE cor. sec. 22, T 5 S, R 6 E). Altitude 1787 feet. Named on Lake Mountain (1967) 7.5' quadrangle.

Morek Creek [HUMBOLDT]: *stream*, flows 3.25 miles to Klamath River 8.5 miles south-southeast of Johnsons (lat. 41°16'35" N, long. 123°49'55" W; at E line sec. 9, T 10 N, R 3 E). Named on Johnsons (1982) 7.5' quadrangle. Called Morley Creek on French Camp Ridge (1983) 7.5' quadrangle.

Morgan: see **Lower Lake** [LAKE].

Morgan Creek [HUMBOLDT]: *stream*, flows 2.25 miles to Mad River 3.5 miles south-southwest of Board Camp Mountain (lat. 40°39'05" N, long. 123°45'W). Named on Board Camp Mountain (1977) 7.5' quadrangle.

Morgan Gulch [TRINITY]: *canyon*, drained by a stream that flows 1.5 miles to Hayfork Creek nearly 2 miles east-southeast of Hayfork (lat. 40°32'45" N, long. 123°09'W; sec. 18, T 31 N, R 11 W); the canyon is west of Morgan Hill. Named on Hayfork (1951) 15' quadrangle.

Morgan Hill [TRINITY]: *peak*, 2.25 miles east-southeast of Hayfork (lat. 40°32'25" N, long. 123°08'30" W; at E line sec. 18, T 31 N, R 11 W). Named on Hayfork (1951) 15' quadrangle.

Morgan Rock [MENDOCINO]: *rock*, 9 miles west-southwest of Piercy, and 450 feet offshore (lat. 39°55'05" N, long. 123°56'45" W). Named on Bear Harbor (1969) 7.5' quadrangle.

Morgan Slough [HUMBOLDT]: *water feature*, joins Eel River 3.5 miles north-northwest of Ferndale (lat. 40°37'15" N, long. 124°18'05" W). Named on Ferndale (1959) 7.5' quadrangle.

Morgan Valley [LAKE]: *valley*, 7 miles south-southeast of Wilson Valley (2) (lat. 38°52'45" N, long. 122°26'W). Named on Jericho Valley (1958) and Wilson Valley (1958) 7.5' quadrangles.

Morley Creek: see **Morek Creek** [HUMBOLDT].

Morris Meadows [TRINITY]: *area*, 16 miles north of Weaverville along Stuart Fork (lat. 40°58'N, long. 123°57'W). Named on Trinity Dam (1950) 15' quadrangle. The name commemorates James Morris, a Weaverville cattleman (Jones, p. 10).

Morris Meadows Camp [TRINITY]: *locality*, 17 miles north of Weaverville along Stuart Fork (lat. 40°58'15" N, long. 122°57'15" W; at NW cor. sec. 19, T 36 N, R 9 W); the place is near the north end of Morris Meadows. Named on Trinity Dam (1950) 15' quadrangle.

Morrison Camp [TRINITY]: *locality*, 12.5 miles south-southwest of Black Rock Mountain (lat. 40°03'N, long. 123°08'10" W; near E line sec. 1, T 25 N, R 12 W). Named on Black Rock Mountain (1954) 15' quadrangle. The name is for a rancher who camped at the place all one summer with his son, who had tuberculosis—high altitude was believed to benefit tubercular patients (Jones, p. 362-363).

Morrison Creek [DEL NORTE]: *stream*, flows nearly 4 miles to Smith River 2.5 miles south-southwest of the town of Smith River (lat. 41°54'15" N, long. 124°09'25" W; near E line sec. 34, T 18 N, R 1 W). Named on High Divide (1966) and Smith River (1966) 7.5' quadrangles.

Morrison Creek [LAKE]: *stream*, flows 2.25 miles to Clear Lake 7 miles east-northeast of Lakeport (lat. 39°05'45" N, long. 122°48'10" W; sec. 1, T 14 N, R 9 W). Named on Lucerne (1958) 7.5' quadrangle.

Morrison Creek [MENDOCINO]: *stream*, flows 7.25 miles to Russian River 5.5 miles south-southeast of Ukiah (lat. 39°04'40" N, long. 123°09'45" W); the stream heads near Morrison Ridge. Named on Elledge Peak (1958) and Purdys Gardens (1958) 7.5' quadrangles.

Morrison Gulch [HUMBOLDT]: *canyon*, drained by a stream that flows nearly 2 miles to Jacoby Creek 4 miles southeast of Arcata (lat. 40°49'30" N, long. 124°02'10" W; at S line sec. 11, T 5 N, R 1 E). Named on Arcata South (1959) 7.5' quadrangle.

Morrison Gulch [MENDOCINO]:

(1) *canyon*, drained by a stream that flows 1 mile to Albion River 1 mile west-southwest of Comptche (lat. 39°15'35" N, long. 123°35'35" W; sec. 11, T 16 N, R 16 W). Named on Comptche (1960) 15' quadrangle.

(2) *canyon*, drained by a stream that flows 2 miles to the sea 6 miles south-southeast of the village of Point Arena (lat. 38°50'20" N, long. 123°37'55" W). Named on Point Arena (1960) 15' quadrangle. United States Board on Geographic Names (1962c, p. 21) rejected the name "Pound Gulch" for the feature

Morrison Gulch [TRINITY]:

(1) *canyon*, drained by a stream that flows nearly 2 miles to North Fork Trinity River 10 miles south of Cecilville, which is in Siskiyou County (lat. 41°00'10" N, long. 123°09'25" W). Named on Cecil Lake (1979) 7.5'

quadrangle, which shows Morrison cabin situated near the mouth of the canyon.

(2) *canyon,* drained by a stream that flows 1 mile to Coffee Creek 5.5 miles north-northwest of Trinity Center (lat. 41°04'50" N, long. 122°43'55" W; sec. 12, T 37 N, R 8 W). Named on Bonanza King (1955) 15' quadrangle.

Morrison Ridge [MENDOCINO]: *ridge,* generally southwest-trending, less than 1 mile long, 10 miles southeast of Ukiah (lat. 39°03'15" N, long. 123°04'15" W; sec. 21, T 14 N, R 11 W). Named on Purdys Gardens (1958) 7.5' quadrangle.

Morton Soda Spring: see **Soda Creek** [LAKE] (1).

Mosley Island [HUMBOLDT]: *island,* 1.25 miles long, 5 miles north-northwest of Ferndale between North Bay, Mosley Slough, and Eel River (lat. 40°38'35" N, long. 124°17'55" W). Named on Cannibal Island (1959) 7.5' quadrangle.

Mosley Slough [HUMBOLDT]: *water feature,* 5 miles north-northwest of Ferndale along the northeast side of Mosley Island (lat. 40°38'45" N, long. 124°17'50" W). Named on Cannibal Island (1959) 7.5' quadrangle.

Mosquito Creek [HUMBOLDT]: *stream,* flows 7 miles to Grouse Creek (2) 5.5 miles east-northeast of Board Camp Mountain (lat. 40°43'10" N, long. 123°37'05" W). Named on Board Camp Mountain (1977), Grouse Mountain (1979), Hennessy Peak (1979), and Sims Mountain (1979) 7.5' quadrangles.

Mosquito Gulch [TRINITY]: *canyon,* drained by a stream that flows 1 mile to Strope Creek 14 miles north-northeast of Weaverville (lat. 40°53'20" N, long. 122°47'30" W; at E line sec. 17, T 35 N, R 8 W). Named on Trinity Dam (1950) 15' quadrangle.

Mosquito Hollow [TRINITY]: *area,* 5 miles northwest of Helena (lat. 40°49'45" N, long. 123°11'30" W). Named on Helena (1951) 15' quadrangle.

Mosquito Lake [HUMBOLDT]: *lake,* 600 feet long, 9 miles northwest of Orleans (lat. 41°22'25" N, long. 123°40'55" W). Named on Fish Lake (1974) 7.5' quadrangle.

Mosquito Lake [TRINITY]: *lake,* 600 feet long, nearly 7 miles north of Billys Peak (1) (lat. 41°14'N, long. 122°45'05" W; near N line sec. 23, T 39 N, R 8 W). Named on Coffee Creek (1955) 15' quadrangle.

Moss Gulch [TRINITY]: *canyon,* drained by a stream that flows less than 1 mile to Trinity River 20 miles northeast of Weaverville (lat. 40°56'20" N, long. 122°41'25" W; sec. 32, T 36 N, R 7 W). Named on Schell Mountain (1950) 15' quadrangle.

Moss Lake: see **Log Lake** [TRINITY].

Mountain Creek [HUMBOLDT]: *stream,* flows 3 miles to Larabee Creek 1.25 miles north-northwest of Blocksburg (lat. 40°17'40" N, long. 123°39'W; near E line sec. sec. 18, T 2 S, R 5 E). Named on Black Lassic (1979) and Blocksburg (1969) 7.5' quadrangles.

Mountain View: see **Kneeland** [HUMBOLDT].

Mount Andy [HUMBOLDT]: *peak,* 8.5 miles north-northeast of Lone Star Junction (lat. 40°44'15" N, long. 123°47'30" W; sec. 12, T 4 N, R 3 E). Altitude 3946 feet. Named on Mad River Buttes (1977) 7.5' quadrangle.

Mount Baldy [HUMBOLDT]: *ridge,* northwest-trending, less than 1 mile long, 7 miles southwest of Bridgeville (lat. 40°23'N, long. 123°52'15" W). Named on Bridgeville (1969) 7.5' quadrangle.

Mount Baldy: see **Weaver Bally Mountain** [TRINITY].

Mount Bally: see **Weaver Bally Mountain** [TRINITY].

Mount Eddy [TRINITY]: *peak,* 9 miles west of the town of Mount Shasta, which is in Siskiyou County, on Trinity-Siskiyou County line (lat. 41°19'10" N, long. 122°28'40" W; at N line sec. 18, T 40 N, R 5 W). Altitude 9025 feet. Named on Weed (1954) 15' quadrangle. Called Eddy Mt. on Shasta (1894) 1° quadrangle. The name commemorates Nelson Harvey Eddy, a pioneer of Shasta Valley (Stewart, C.L., p. 65).

Mount Esther: see **Harbin Mountain** [LAKE].

Mount Hannah [LAKE]: *peak,* 7.5 miles west-southwest of the town of Lower Lake (lat. 38°53'15" N, long. 122°44'45" W; sec. 16, T 12 N, R 8 W). Altitude 3978 feet. Named on Clearlake Highlands (1958) 7.5' quadrangle.

Mount Hannah Lodge [LAKE]: *locality,* 6.5 miles west-southwest of the town of Lower Lake (lat. 38°53'15" N, long. 122°43'45" W; sec. 15, T 12 N, R 8 W); the place is less than 1 mile east of Mount Hannah. Named on Clearlake Highlands (1958) 7.5' quadrangle.

Mount Hilton: see **Thompson Peak** [TRINITY] (2).

Mount John: see **Signal Peak** [LAKE].

Mount Konocti [LAKE]: *ridge,* south-southwest-trending, 2 miles long, 2.25 miles east of Kelseyville (lat. 38°58'50" N, long. 122°46'30" W). Named on Kelseyville (1959) 7.5' quadrangle. George Gibbs gave the name "Mount M' Kee" to the ridge to honor Colonel Redick McKee, who explored the region in 1851 (Gudde, 1949, p. 177). G.F. Becker (p. 233) noted the alternate name "Uncle Sam Mountain" for the feature. United States Board on Geographic Names (1933, p. 435) approved the name "Konokti Mountain" for the ridge, and rejected the names "Kanakti Mountain," "Kanokti Mountain," "Konochti Mountain," and "Uncle Sam Mountain." Later the Board (1962a, p. 12) approved the name "Mount Konocti," and rejected the names "Konokti Mountain," "Konockti Mountain," "Mount Konochti," "Mount Konokti," and "Mount M' Kee." The name "Konocti" is of Indian origin (Kroeber, p. 44).

Mount Lassic [HUMBOLDT]; *peak,* 6 miles northeast of Blocksburg (lat. 40°20'05" N, long. 123°33'15" W; sec. 36, T 1 S, R 5 E); the peak is less than 1 mile west-southwest of Black Lassic [TRINITY], and less than 1 mile west-northwest of Red Lassic [TRINITY]. Altitude 5876 feet. Named on Black Lassic (1979) 7.5' quadrangle. Called Lassek Peak on California Mining Bureau's (1917b) map. Blocksburg (1949) 15' quadrangle has the alternate name "Signal Peak" for the feature; United States Board on Geographic Names (1981b, p. 4) approved this name and rejected the names "Mount Lassic," "Lassic Peak," "Lassecks Peak," "Red Lassic," and "Red Peak." The name "Lasseck" is said to be from an Indian chief (Kroeber, p. 46). The name "Signal Peak" is from a heliograph station located on the peak about 1900 (United States Board on Geographic Names, 1981a, p.4).

Mount Olive [LAKE]: *peak,* 4 miles southeast of Kelseyville (lat. 38°55'55" N, long. 122°47'25" W; sec. 31, T 13 N, R 8 W). Altitude 2485 feet. Named on Kelseyville (1959) 7.5' quadrangle.

Mount Pierce [HUMBOLDT]: *peak,* 4.5 miles south-southwest of Scotia (lat. 40°25'05" N, long. 124°07'10" W; at NE cor. sec. 1, T 1 S, R 1 W.). Altitude 3185 feet. Named on Scotia (1970) 7.5' quadrangle, which gives the name "Monument Peak" as an alternate. Henry Washington established the initial point for Humboldt Base and Meridian on the peak in 1853 and named the feature for President Pierce (Gudde, 1969, p. 245).

Mount Sanhedrin: see **Big Signal Peak** [MENDOCINO].

Mount Toorup: see **Red Mountain** [DEL NORTE].

Mount Turep: see **Red Mountain** [DEL NORTE].

Mouse Pass [MENDOCINO]: *pass,* 3 miles west of Navarro (lat. 39°08'45" N, long. 123°35'53" W; sec. 23, T 15 N, R 16 W). Named on Navarro (1961) 15' quadrangle.

Mower: see **Arcata** [HUMBOLDT].

Mowry Creek [HUMBOLDT]: *stream,* flows 1.25 miles to South Fork Eel River 2.25 miles southeast of Weott (lat. 40°17'50" N, long. 123°53'45" W; sec. 13, T 2 S, R 2 E). Named on Weott (1969) 7.5' quadrangle.

Muckawee Gulch [TRINITY]: *canyon,* drained by a stream that flows nearly 2 miles to Rush Creek 5.25 miles east of Weaverville (lat. 40°44'20" N, long. 122°50'15" W; at S line sec. 1, T 33 N, R 9 W). Named on Trinity Dam (1950) and Weaverville (1950) 15' quadrangles.

Mud Creek [HUMBOLDT]: *stream,* flows 1.25 miles to Donahue Flat Creek 5.25 miles north-northeast of Orleans (lat. 41°22'55" N, long. 123°30'20" W). Named on Orleans (1978) 7.5' quadrangle.

Mud Creek [MENDOCINO]:

(1) *stream,* flows 1.5 miles to Red Mountain Creek 5 miles north of Leggett (lat. 39°56'N, long. 123°43'50" W; near N line sec. 15, T 24 N, R 17 W). Named on Noble Butte (1969) 7.5' quadrangle.

(2) *stream,* flows nearly 4 miles to Cold Creek (4) 5.25 miles north-northwest of Covelo (lat. 39°51'35" N, long. 123°17'40" W; at N line sec. 15, T 23 N, R 13 W). Named on Covelo West (1967) 7.5' quadrangle.

(3) *stream,* flows 4.5 miles to South Fork Eel River less than 1 mile southeast of Branscomb (lat. 39°38'40" N, long. 123°36'55" W; sec. 26, T 21 N, R 16 W). Named on Cahto Peak (1967) 7.5' quadrangle. The stream goes past Mud Springs, and Waring (p. 176) called it Mud Springs Creek.

Mud Creek [TRINITY]:

(1) *stream,* flows nearly 1 mile to South Fork Trinity River less than 0.5 mile south-southeast of the center of Forest Glen (lat. 40°22'05" N, long. 123°19'15" W; sec. 19, T 1 S, R 8 E). Named on Forest Glen (1979) 7.5' quadrangle.

(2) *stream,* flows 5 miles to South Dobbyn Creek 4.5 miles east of Alderpoint [HUMBOLDT] (lat. 40°11'15" N, long. 123°31'40" W; sec. 20, T 3 S, R 6 E). Named on Alderpoint (1969) and Zenia (1967) 7.5' quadrangles.

Mud Lake [TRINITY]: *lake,* 100 feet long, 9 miles southwest of Black Rock Mountain (lat. 40°06'10" N, long. 123°07'W; near W line sec. 16, T 26 N, R 11 W). Named on Black Rock Mountain (1954) 15' quadrangle.

Muddy Creek [HUMBOLDT]:

(1) *stream,* flows 1 mile to Klamath River less than 0.5 mile east of Weitchpec (lat. 41°11'15" N, long. 123°41'50" W; near E line sec. 10, T 9 N, R 4 E). Named on Weitchpec (1979) 7.5' quadrangle.

(2) *stream,* flows nearly 1 mile to Little Larabee Creek 6.5 miles west-southwest of Dinsmore (lat. 40°28'25" N, long. 123°43'30" W; near SE cor. sec. 9, T 1 N, R 4 E). Named on Larabee Valley (1977) 7.5' quadrangle.

Muddy Gulch Creek [MENDOCINO]: *stream,* flows 1 mile to South Fork Eel River 1.5 miles northwest of Branscomb (lat. 39°40'20" N, long. 123°38'45" W; sec. 16, T 21 N, R 16 W). Named on Lincoln Ridge (1966) 7.5' quadrangle.

Mud Gulch [MENDOCINO]: *canyon,* drained by a stream that flows 1 mile to Dutch Henry Creek (3) 4.5 miles north-northwest of Navarro (lat. 39°12'40" N, long. 123°34'45" W; near S line sec. 30, T 16 N, R 15 W). Named on Navarro (1961) 15' quadrangle.

Mud Lake [DEL NORTE]: *lake,* 550 feet long, 7 miles east-northeast of Broken Rib Mountain (lat. 41°54'35" N, long. 123°33'45" W). Named on Polar Bear Mountain (1982) 7.5' quadrangle.

Mud Lake [HUMBOLDT]: *intermittent lake,* 200 feet long, 10.5 miles south-southwest of the settlement of Willow Creek (lat. 40°47'50" N, long. 123°41'20" W; sec. 23, T 5 N, R 4 E). Named on Grouse Mountain (1979) 7.5' quadrangle.

Mud Lake [MENDOCINO]: *lake,* 1000 feet long, 9.5 miles south of Willits (lat. 39°16'30" N, long. 123°22'05" W; near NW cor. sec. 1, T 16 N, R 14 W). Named on Willits (1961) 15' quadrangle.

Mud Spring [DEL NORTE]: *spring,* 5.5 miles west-northwest of Buck Mountain on Rattlesnake Mountain (lat. 41°39'05" N, long. 123°57'35" W). Named on Cant Hook Mountain (1982) 7.5' quadrangle.

Mud Spring [HUMBOLDT]:

(1) *spring,* 7.25 miles west-northwest of Orleans (lat. 41°20'50" N, long. 123°39'50" W). Named on Fish Lake (1974) 7.5' quadrangle.

(2) *spring,* 7 miles east-southeast of Honeydew (lat. 40°11'30" N, long. 124°00'40" W; sec. 24, T 3 S, R 1 E). Named on Honeydew (1970) 7.5' quadrangle.

(3) *spring,* 5 miles east of Showers Mountain (lat. 40°34'30" N, long. 123°36'W; near SW cor. sec. 3, T 2 N, R 5 E). Named on Blake Mountain (1979) 7.5' quadrangle.

Mud Spring [MENDOCINO]: *spring,* 7.5 miles north of Eden Valley (lat. 39°44'05" N, long. 123°12'25" W; sec. 28, T 22 N, R 12 W). Named on Jamison Ridge (1967) 7.5' quadrangle.

Mud Spring [TRINITY]:

(1) *spring,* 11 miles northeast of Hyampom (lat. 40°42'50" N, long. 123°17'20" W; near N line sec. 21, T 4 N, R 8 E). Named on Hyampom (1951) 15' quadrangle.

(2) *spring,* 5.5 miles north-northeast of Forest Glen (lat. 40°26'25" N, long. 123°15'40" W; sec. 19, T 30 N, R 12 W). Named on Naufus Creek (1979) 7.5' quadrangle.

(3) *spring,* 2 miles south-southwest of Dubakella Mountain (lat. 40°21'20" N, long. 123°09'35" W; near NE cor. sec. 24, T 29 N, R 12 W). Named on Dubakella Mountain (1954) 15' quadrangle.

Mud Springs [HUMBOLDT]: *spring,* 6 miles east-northeast of Hoopa (lat. 41°05'05" N, long. 123°34'30" W; near S line sec. 11, T 8 N, R 5 E). Named on Tish Tang Point (1978) 7.5' quadrangle.

Mud Springs [MENDOCINO]: *springs,* 2 miles east of Branscomb (lat. 39°39'25" N, long. 123°35'10" W; at W line sec. 19, T 21 N, R 15 W); the springs are near Mud Creek (3). Named on Cahto Peak (1967) 7.5' quadrangle. Waring (p. 176) called the feature Jackson Valley Mud Springs, and described it as a group of mud springs that have built up small, well-formed craters in which the mud is kept in constant motion by bubbles of gas. Waring (p. 176) also listed Jackson Valley Mineral Springs, three springs that rise close together on the south bank of Mud Springs Creek 0.75 mile southwest of Jackson Valley Mud Springs; these springs are the basis of a small camping resort and are named for their location in Jackson Valley.

Mud Springs [TRINITY]: *spring,* 17 miles south-southeast of Weaverville (lat. 40°30'55" N, long. 122°47'45" W; near N line sec. 29, T 31 N, R 8 W). Named on Weaverville (1950) 15' quadrangle.

Mud Springs Creek [MENDOCINO]: *stream,* flows 3.5 miles to Tenmile Creek 7 miles east-northeast of Branscomb (lat. 39°41'40" N, long. 123°30'10" W; sec. 11, T 21 N, R 15 W). Named on Cahto Peak (1967) 7.5' quadrangle.

Mud Springs Creek [MENDOCINO]: see **Mud Creek** [MENDOCINO] (3).

Muir [MENDOCINO]: *locality,* less than 1 mile southeast of downtown Willits along Northwestern Pacific Railroad (lat. 39°23'50" N, long. 123°20'30" W; sec. 19, T 18 N, R 13 W). Named on Willits (1961) 15' quadrangle.

Muir Canyon [MENDOCINO]: *canyon,* about 2 miles long, along Baechtel Creek 3 miles south-southwest of Willits (lat. 39°27'05" N, long. 123°22'W; sec. 35, 36, T 18 N, R 14 W). Named on Willits (1961) 15' quadrangle.

Muir Springs: see **Willits** [MENDOCINO].

Muldoon Gulch [TRINITY]: *canyon,* drained by a stream that flows 2 miles to Salt Creek (4) 2 miles northeast of Dubakella Mountain (lat. 40°24'45" N, long. 123°06'15" W; sec. 33, T 30 N, R 11 W). Named on Dubakella Mountain (1954) 15' quadrangle.

Mule Basin [HUMBOLDT]: *relief feature,* 4 miles south-southeast of Showers Mountain (lat. 40°31'45" N, long. 123°39'50" W; near NE cor. sec. 25, T 2 N, R 4 E). Named on Showers Mountain (1978) 7.5' quadrangle.

Mule Basin Creek [HUMBOLDT]: *stream,* flows nearly 3 miles to Baker Creek (1) 3 miles south-southwest of Showers Mountain (lat. 40°32'20" N, long. 123°42'40" W; sec. 22, T 2 N, R 4 E); the stream heads southwest of Mule Basin. Named on Showers Mountain (1978) 7.5' quadrangle.

Mule Creek [HUMBOLDT]:

(1) *stream,* flows 1 mile to North Fork Mad River 4.5 miles northeast of the town of Blue Lake (lat. 40°56'10" N, long. 123°56'05" W; sec. 3, T 6 N, R 2 E). Named on Blue Lake (1979) 7.5' quadrangle.

(2) *stream,* flows 2 miles to Butte Creek (2) 6 miles southwest of Dinsmore (lat. 40°25'45" N, long. 123°40'20" W; at S line sec. 25, T 1 N, R 4 E). Named on Larabee Valley (1977) 7.5' quadrangle.

Mule Creek [MENDOCINO]: *stream,* flows 3.5 miles to Hollow Tree Creek 9 miles south of Piercy (lat. 39°49'N, long. 123°45'50" W; sec. 29, T 23 N, R 17 W). Named on Hales Grove (1970) 7.5' quadrangle. South Fork enters 0.5 mile upstream from the mouth of the main creek; it is 1.5 miles long and is named on Hales Grove (1970) 7.5' quadrangle. On Kenny (1920) 15' quadrangle, present South Fork and present Mule Creek below the entrance of South Fork are called Hollow Tree Creek.

Mule Creek [TRINITY]: *stream,* flows 4 miles to Clair Engle Lake 12 miles north-northeast of Weaverville (lat. 40°52'10" N, long. 122°48'40" W; at S line sec. 19, T 35 N, R 8 W). Named on Trinity Dam (1950) 15' quadrangle.

Mule Creek: see **Little Mule Creek** [TRINITY].

Mule Gulch [TRINITY]:

(1) *canyon,* drained by a stream that flows about 2 miles to Indian Creek (2) 11 miles south-southeast of Weaverville (lat. 40°35'55" N, long. 122°49'40" W; near E line sec. 25, T 32 N, R 9 W). Named on Weaverville (1950) 15' quadrangle.

(2) *canyon,* drained by a stream that flows 3 miles to South Fork Trinity River 3 miles southwest of Black Rock Mountain (lat. 40°10'30" N, long. 123°02'45" W; near W line sec. 19, T 27 N, R 10 W); the feature is east of Mule Ridge (2). Named on Black Rock Mountain (1954) 15' quadrangle.

Mule Opening [MENDOCINO]: *area,* 8.5 miles west-northwest of Ornbaun Valley (lat. 38°57'N, long. 123°27'05" W; near N line sec. 31, T 13 N, R 14 W). Named on Ornbaun Valley (1960) 15' quadrangle.

Mule Ridge [TRINITY]:

(1) *ridge,* southeast-trending, 1.5 miles long, 2 miles south-southeast of Black Lassic (lat. 40°18'40" N, long. 123°31'35" W). Named on Black Lassic (1979) 7.5' quadrangle. On Blocksburg (1949) and Pickett Peak (1954) 15' quadrangles, the name applies to a much larger ridge situated between Van Duzen River and West Fork Van Duzen River, but United States Board on Geographic Names (1978a, p. 7) restricted use of the name to present Mule Ridge (1), and noted that sheepmen put their mules to pasture at the place.

(2) *ridge,* north-northeast-trending, 2 miles long, 4.25 miles southwest of Black Rock Mountain (lat. 40°09'25" N, long. 123°03'35" W; mainly in sec. 25, T 27 N, R 11 W); the ridge is west of Mule Gulch (2). Named on Black Rock Mountain (1954) 15' quadrangle.

Mule Slide [TRINITY]: *relief feature,* less than 1 mile southeast of Black Lassic (lat. 40°19'20" N, long. 123°31'40" W). Named on Black Lassic (1979) 7.5' quadrangle.

Mule Spring [HUMBOLDT]: *spring,* 5.5 miles east of Board Camp Mountain (lat. 40°40'50" N, long. 123°36'20" W). Named on Sims Mountain (1979) 7.5' quadrangle.

Mullane Corral [TRINITY]: *relief feature,* 7.5 miles southwest of Cecilville, which is in Siskiyou County (lat. 41°03'45" N, long. 123°13'55" W); the feature is near Mullane Lake. Named on Cecil Lake (1979) 7.5' quadrangle. Called Moline Corral on Cecilville (1955) 15' quadrangle, but United States Board on Geographic Names (1978a, p. 7) rejected this name for the feature. Gudde (1949, p. 220) used the form "Molaine Corrals" for the name, and noted that Jim Molaine had a holding pasture for cattle at the site in 1887.

Mullane Lake [TRINITY]: *lake,* 150 feet long, 7.5 miles southwest of Cecilville, which is in Siskiyou County (lat. 41°03'55" N, long. 123°14'W); the lake is near Mullane Corral. Named on Cecil Lake (1979) 7.5' quadrangle.

Mumbo Basin [TRINITY]: *relief feature,* 16 miles northeast of Trinity Center (lat. 41°11'45" N, long. 122°31'W; sec. 35, T 39 N, R 6 W); the feature is near the head of Mumbo Creek. Named on Bonanza King (1955) 15' quadrangle.

Mumbo Creek [TRINITY]: *stream,* flows 10 miles to East Fork Trinity River 10.5 miles northeast of Trinity Center (lat. 41°07'20" N, long. 122°33'30" W; sec. 28, T 38 N, R 6 W); the stream heads at Upper Mumbo Lake. Named on Bonanza King (1955) 15' quadrangle. Called N. Fk. [of E. Fk. Trinity River] on Miller's (1890) map.

Mumbo Lake [TRINITY]: *lake,* 700 feet long, 16 miles northeast of Trinity Center (lat. 41°11'30" N, long. 122°30'30" W; on E line sec. 35, T 39 N, R 6 W); the lake is near the head of Mumbo Creek. Named on Bonanza King (1955) 15' quadrangle.

Mumbo Lake: see **Upper Mumbo Lake** [TRINITY].

Mumford Basin [TRINITY]: *relief feature,* 18 miles north of Weaverville (lat. 40°59'15" N, long. 122°53'15" W; near SW cor. sec. 10, T 36 N, R 9 W). Named on Trinity Dam (1950) 15' quadrangle.

Mumford Meadow [TRINITY]: *area,* 10 miles south-southwest of Billys Peak (1) (lat. 41°00'45" N long. 122°52'25" W; near N line sec. 3, T 36 N, R 9 W). Named on Coffee Creek (1955) 15' quadrangle.

Mumford Peak [TRINITY]: *peak,* 18 miles north of Weaverville (lat. 40°59'20" N, long. 122°53'45" W; near S line sec. 9, T 36 N, R 9 W); the peak is just west of Mumford Basin. Altitude 7346 feet. Named on Trinity Dam (1950) 15' quadrangle.

Munger Gulch [TRINITY]: *canyon,* drained by a stream that flows 2 miles to Sidney Gulch 2 miles north-northwest of Weaverville (lat. 40°45'05"

N, long. 122°57'10" W; sec. 1, T 33 N, R 10 W). Named on Trinity Dam (1950) 15' quadrangle.

Murphy Creek [MENDOCINO]: *stream,* flows 5 miles to Williams Creek (1) 7 miles northeast of Covelo (lat. 39°51'15" N, long. 123°08'35" W; sec. 13, T 23 N, R 12 W). Named on Bluenose Ridge (1967) and Covelo East (1967) 7.5' quadrangles.

Murphy Glades [TRINITY]: *area,* 9.5 miles southwest of Forest Glen (lat. 40°17'50" N, long. 123°28'10" W; at N line sec. 14, T 2 S, R 6 E). Named on Ruth Reservoir (1978) 7.5' quadrangle.

Murphy Meadow [HUMBOLDT]: *valley,* 8 miles east-southeast of Korbel (lat. 40°49'N, long. 123°49'15" W). Named on Maple Creek (1977) 7.5' quadrangle.

Murray Gulch [MENDOCINO]: *canyon,* drained by a stream that flows 2 miles to Navarro River 3.5 miles north-northeast of Elk (lat. 39°10'45" N, long. 123°42'05" W; sec. 12, T 15 N, R 17 W). Named on Elk (1960) 7.5' quadrangle.

Murray Opening [MENDOCINO]: *area,* 5.5 miles west of Boonville (lat. 39°01'45" N, long. 123°28'10" W; sec. 1, T 13 N, R 15 W). Named on Boonville (1959) 15' quadrangle.

Muslatt Lake [DEL NORTE]: *lake,* 400 feet long, 3 miles north-northeast of Buck Mountain (lat. 41°40'30" N, long. 123°50'55" W); the lake is west of Muslatt Mountain. Named on Ship Mountain (1982) 7.5' quadrangle.

Muslatt Mountain [DEL NORTE]: *ridge,* generally north-trending, 1 mile long, 3 miles north-northeast of Buck Mountain (lat. 41°40'30" N, long. 123°50'40" W). Named on Ship Mountain (1982) 7.5' quadrangle. The name has an Indian origin (Gudde, 1949, p. 229).

Mussell Point [HUMBOLDT]: *promontory,* nearly 3 miles north-northwest of Orick along the coast (lat. 41°19'20" N, long. 124°05'05" W; sec. 20, T 11 N, R 1 E). Named on Orick (1966) 7.5' quadrangle.

Mussel Rock [DEL NORTE]: *rock,* 2 miles south-southeast of Crescent City, and 1 mile offshore (lat. 41°43'40" N, long. 124°10'40" W). Named on Sister Rocks (1966) 7.5' quadrangle.

Mussel Rock [HUMBOLDT]:

(1) *rock,* 7.5 miles west-southwest of Ferndale, and 0.5 mile offshore (lat. 40°31'20" N, long. 124°23'20" W). Named on Ferndale (1959) 7.5' quadrangle.

(2) *rock,* 4.5 miles west-northwest of Petrolia, and 1000 feet offshore (lat. 40°20'50" N, long. 124°22'W. Named on Petrolia (1969) 7.5' quadrangle.

Mussel Rocks [HUMBOLDT]: *rocks,* nearly 6 miles north of Trinidad along the coast (lat. 41°08'35" N, long. 124°09'25" W; sec. 27, T 9 N, R 1 W). Named on Trinidad (1966) 7.5' quadrangle.

Musser Hill [TRINITY]: *ridge,* generally south-southeast-trending, 4.5 miles long, center 3 miles north-northeast of Weaverville (lat. 40°46'N, long. 122°54'W). Named on Trinity Dam (1950) and Weaverville (1950) 15' quadrangles.

Mustard Gulch [MENDOCINO]:

(1) *canyon,* drained by a stream that flows 1 mile to North Fork Navarro River 2 miles northwest of Navarro (lat. 39°10'10" N, long. 123°34'10" W; at E line sec. 12, T 15 N, R 15 W). Named on Navarro (1961) 15' quadrangle.

(2) *canyon,* drained by a stream that flows 1.5 miles to Navarro River 4.5 miles east-northeast of Elk (lat. 39°09'55" N, long. 123°38'30" W; near NW cor. sec. 16, T 15 N, R 16 W). Named on Navarro (1961) 15' quadrangle.

Muzzleloader Creek [DEL NORTE]: *stream,* flows 3.25 miles to Jones Creek 5.5 miles north of Buck Mountain (lat. 41°42'55" N, long. 123°51'05" W). Named on Ship Mountain (1982) 7.5' quadrangle.

Myers: see **Myers Flat** [HUMBOLDT].

Myers Flat [HUMBOLDT]: *village,* 4.5 miles south-southeast of Weott (lat. 40°16'N, long. 123°52'15" W; on W line sec. 29, T 2 S, R 3 E). Named on Myers Flat (1969) and Weott (1969) 7.5' quadrangles. Called Myers on Dyerville (1921) 15' quadrangle. Postal authorities established Myers Flat post office in 1949; the word "Flat" was added to the name "Myers" because of Myers post office in El Dorado County (Salley, p. 149). The name "Myers" here is from Grant Myers ranch (Gudde, 1969, p. 216).

Myers Landing: see **Southport Landing** [HUMBOLDT].

Mynot Creek [DEL NORTE]: *stream,* flows 3.25 miles to Spruce Creek 1.25 miles east of the mouth of Klamath River (lat. 41°32'55" N, long. 124°03'25" W; sec. 4, T 13 N, R 1 E). Named on Requa (1966) 7.5' quadrangle.

Mynot Ridge [DEL NORTE]: *ridge,* generally west-trending, 3 miles long, 3.25 miles east of the mouth of Klamath River (lat. 41°33'N, long. 124°01'W). Named on Requa (1966) 7.5' quadrangle.

Myrick Prairie [HUMBOLDT]: *area,* 7.5 miles east of Fortuna (lat. 40°36'15" N, long. 124°00'35" W; near NE cor. sec. 36, T 3 N, R 1 E). Named on Hydesville (1979) 7.5' quadrangle.

Myrtle Creek [DEL NORTE]: *stream,* flows 6.5 miles to Smith River 8.5 miles east-northeast of Crescent City (lat. 41°48'05" N, long. 124°03'10" W). Named on High Divide (1966) and Hiouchi (1966) 7.5' quadrangles.

Myrtle Grove: see **Eureka** [HUMBOLDT].

Myrtletowne: see **Eureka** [HUMBOLDT].

Mystic Springs: see **Deer Lick Springs** [TRINITY].

—N—

Nacko Creek: see **Notchko Creek** [HUMBOLDT].

Nadelos Campground [HUMBOLDT]: *locality,* 3.25 miles east of Point Delgada along South Fork Bear Creek (7) (lat. 40°01'15" N, long. 124°00'15" W). Named on Shelter Cove (1969) 7.5' quadrangle.

Nafus Creek: see **Jims Creek** [TRINITY].

Nancy Creek [TRINITY]: *stream,* flows 1.5 miles to Stuart Fork 14 miles north of Weaverville (lat. 40°56'15" N, long. 122°57'15" W; at E line sec. 36, T 36 N, R 10 W). Named on Trinity Dam (1950) 15' quadrangle.

Nanning Creek [HUMBOLDT]: *stream,* flows nearly 3 miles to Eel River 1.5 miles north-northeast of Scotia (lat. 40°30'05" N, long. 124°05'15" W; sec. 5, T 1 N, R 1 E). Named on Scotia (1970) 7.5' quadrangle.

Napho Peak: see **Neafus Peak** [TRINITY].

Narrows: see **The Narrows** [HUMBOLDT]; **The Narrows** [LAKE].

Nash: see **Goldfield Campground** [TRINITY]; **Nashmead** [MENDOCINO].

Nashmead [MENDOCINO]: *locality,* 4 miles south-southeast of Spyrock (2) along Northwestern Pacific Railroad (lat 39°49'20" N, long. 123°24'50" W; near E line sec. 28, T 23 N, R 14 W). Named on Iron Peak (1967) 7.5' quadrangle. Called Nash on Spyrock (1920) 15' quadrangle. Postal authorities established Nashmead post office in 1915 and discontinued it in 1960; J. Nash was the first postmaster—the place itself first was called Nash (Salley, p. 150). The name "Nashmead" is a contraction of the term "Nash's Meadows" (Hanna, p. 207).

Natchko Creek: see **Notchko Creek** [HUMBOLDT].

Naufus Creek [TRINITY]: *stream,* flows 5.25 miles to Plummer Creek 7.25 miles north-northwest of Forest Glen (lat. 40°28'30" N, long. 123°21'45" W; near E line sec. 10, T 1 N, R 7 E). Named on Naufus Creek (1979) 7.5' quadrangle. On Hoaglin (1935) 30'quadrangle, present Naufus Creek is shown as the upper part of Plummer Creek, and the upper part of present Plummer Creek is called Naufus Creek.

Naufus Spike Camp [TRINITY]: *locality,* 6 miles north-northeast of Forest Glen (lat. 40°27'25" N, long. 123°16'55" W; near N line sec. 21, T 1 N, R 8 E); the place is near the head of Naufus Creek. Named on Naufus Creek (1979) 7.5' quadrangle.

Navarro [MENDOCINO]: *village,* 18 miles west of Ukiah (lat. 39°09'N, long. 123°32'30" W; in and near sec. 20, T 15 N, R 15 W). Named on Navarro (1961) 15' quadrangle. Called Novarro on Bancroft's (1864) map. Postal authorities established Navarro Ridge post office in 1867, changed the name to Navarro in 1888, and discontinued it in 1902; they reestablished Navarro post office in 1914 at a location 14 miles to the east at present Navarro, where the post office had been called Wendling (Salley, p. 152). Postal authorities established Wendling post office in 1902; the name was for the builder of a shingle mill at the place (Salley, p. 236). An overnight stage stop called North Fork House was located about 1 mile west of present Navarro in 1878 (Brereton, introduction).

Navarro: see **Camp Navarro** [MENDOCINO].

Navarro Head [MENDOCINO]: *relief feature,* 2 miles north of Albion (lat. 39°11'50" N, long. 123°45'45" W; sec. 5, T 15 N, R 17 W); the feature is near the mouth of Navarro River. Named on Albion (1960) 7.5' quadrangle.

Navarro Point [MENDOCINO]: *promontory,* 2 miles south of Albion (lat. 39°11'45" N, long. 123°46'15" W). Named on Albion (1960) 7.5' quadrangle.

Navarro Ridge [MENDOCINO]: *ridge,* west- to west-northwest-trending, 7 miles long, center about 4 miles north of Elk (lat. 39°11'15" N, long. 123°42'15" W). Named on Albion (1960) and Elk (1960) 7.5' quadrangles.

Navarro Ridge: see **Navarro** [MENDOCINO].

Navarro River [MENDOCINO]: *stream,* formed by the confluence of Anderson Creek (2) and Rancheria Creek (2) in Anderson Valley, flows 27 miles to the sea 2.25 miles south of Albion (lat. 39°11'30" N, long. 123°45'35" W; near E line sec. 5, T 15 N, R 17 W). Named on Boonville (1959) and Navarro (1961) 15' quadrangles. Called Novarro Riv. on Bancroft's (1864) map. North Fork is formed by the confluence of its North Branch and its South Branch nearly 2 miles north-northwest of Navarro; North Fork flows 6 miles to the main river 9 miles upstream from the mouth of that river, and is named on Navarro (1961) 15' quadrangle. North Branch of North Fork is formed by the confluence of Jack Smith Creek and Little North Fork Navarro River; it is 4 miles long and is named on Navarro (1961) 15' quadrangle. South Branch of North Fork is 17 miles long and is named on Boonville (1959) and Navarro (1961) 15' quadrangles—it is called South Branch Navarro River on Boonville (1943) 15' quadrangle. Little North Fork Navarro River joins North Branch of North Fork Navarro River 4 miles north of Navarro; it is 6.25 miles long and is named on Boonville (1959) and Navarro (1961) 15' quadrangles—it is called Little Fork Navarro River on Boonville (1943) 15' quadrangle.

Neafus Peak [TRINITY]: *peak,* nearly 5 miles east-southeast of Alderpoint (lat. 40°08'25" N, long. 123°32'W; near W line sec. 5, T 4 S, R 6 E). Altitude 3980 feet. Named on Alderpoint (1969) 7.5' quadrangle. Called Napho Peak on California Mining Bureau's (1917b) map. The name "Neafus" commemorates Jim Neafus, a pioneer in the neighborhood (Jones, p. 346).

Neaman Gulch [TRINITY]: *canyon,* 0.5 mile long, opens into the canyon of Trinity River 5.5 miles south of Weaverville (lat. 40°39'20" N, long. 122°55'15" W; near E line sec. 6, T 32 N, R 9 W). Named on Weaverville (1950) 15' quadrangle.

Nebo Rock [MENDOCINO]: *relief feature,* 12 miles east of Covelo (lat. 39°48'35" N, long. 123°01'35" W; near NE cor. sec. 36, T 23 N, R 11 W). Named on Newhouse Ridge (1967) 7.5' quadrangle.

Needle Rock [MENDOCINO]:
(1) *rock,* 9 miles west-southwest of Piercy, and 50 feet offshore (lat. 39°56'40" N, long. 123°58'05" W). Named on Bear Harbor (1969) 7.5' quadrangle.
(2) *locality,* 9 miles west-southwest of present Piercy (lat. 39°56'30" N, long. 123°57'45" W); the place is near present Needle Rock (1). Named on Kenny (1920) 15' quadrangle. Captain Morgan and his son settled at the place in 1868 and started a shipping point (Carpenter, p. 131).

Neefus Gulch [MENDOCINO]: *canyon,* drained by a stream that flows 2 miles to North Fork Navarro River 2 miles northwest of Navarro (lat. 39°10'10" N, long. 123°34'W; near SW cor. sec. 7, T 15 N, R 15 W). Named on Navarro (1961) 15' quadrangle.

Negro Head [MENDOCINO]: *relief feature,* less than 2 miles north-northwest of Eden Valley (lat. 39°39'05" N, long. 123°11'45" W; sec. 28, T 21 N, R 12 W). Named on Jamison Ridge (1967) 7.5' quadrangle. Called Nigger Head on Eden Valley (1929) 15' quadrangle, but United States Board on Geographic Names (1964, p. 12) rejected the names "Nigger Head" and "Head Nigger" for the feature.

Negro Joe Ridge [HUMBOLDT]: *ridge,* northeast-trending, 1.25 miles long, 10.5 miles east of the town of Blue Lake (lat. 40°53'50" N, long. 123°47'30" W). Named on Lord-Ellis Summit (1973) 7.5' quadrangle. Called Negro Ridge on Blue Lake (1951) 15' quadrangle. United States Board on Geographic Names (1976a, p. 2) gave the names "Negro Ridge" and "Nigger Joe Ridge" as variants.

Negro Ridge: see **Negro Joe Ridge** [HUMBOLDT].

Nelson Creek [HUMBOLDT]: *stream,* flows 3.5 miles to Bear River 6.5 miles south Scotia (lat. 40°23'05" N, long. 124°04'50" W). Named on Bull Creek (1969) and Scotia (1970) 7.5' quadrangles.

Nelson Creek [TRINITY]: *stream,* flows 3 miles to East Fork Trinity River 24 miles northeast of Weaverville (lat. 40°59'45" N, long. 122°37'20" W; sec. 12, T 36 N, R 7 W). Named on Schell Mountain (1950) 15' quadrangle.

Nelson Creek Gap [TRINITY]: *pass,* 23 miles northeast of Weaverville (lat. 40°57'40" N, long. 122°37'15" W; sec. 24, T 36 N, R 7 W); the pass is near the head of Nelson Creek. Named on Schell Mountain (1950) 15' quadrangle.

Newberg: see **Newburg** [HUMBOLDT].

Newburg [HUMBOLDT]: *locality,* 1.5 miles east of Fortuna (lat. 40°36'N, long. 124°07'30" W; sec. 36, T 3 N, R 1 W). Named on Fortuna (1959) and Hydesville (1979) 7.5' quadrangles. Called Newberg on Rohnerville (1920) 15' quadrangle, but United States Board on Geographic Names (1961b, p. 11) rejected this form for of the name. Eel River Valley Lumber Company built the town of Newberg, later called Newburg, in 1884 (Carranco and Sorensen, p. 151).

Newburg: see **Fort Dick** [DEL NORTE].

New Denny: see **Denny** [TRINITY].

Newgard Bluff [MENDOCINO]: *relief feature,* 4.5 miles northeast of Elk along Navarro River (lat. 39°10'N, long. 123°38'50" W; at N line sec. 17, T 15 N, R 16 W). Named on Elk (1960) 7.5' quadrangle.

New Haven: see **Bridgeport Landing** [MENDOCINO].

Newhouse Creek [MENDOCINO]: *stream,* flows 1.5 miles to Billy Williams Creek 10.5 miles east of Covelo (lat. 39°46'50" N, long. 123°03'05" W; sec. 11, T 22 N, R 11 W); the stream is west of Newhouse Ridge. Named on Newhouse Ridge (1967) 7.5' quadrangle. On Covelo (1952) 15' quadrangle, present Newhouse Creek and present Billy Williams Creek below their confluence are called Newhouse Creek.

Newhouse Ridge [MENDOCINO]: *ridge,* north-northeast- to northeast-trending, 2 miles long, 11 miles east of Covelo (lat. 39°46'15" N, long. 123°02'20" W). Named on Newhouse Ridge (1967) 7.5' quadrangle.

New Jerusalem: see **Petrolia** [HUMBOLDT].

Newman Creek [HUMBOLDT]: *stream,* flows 4 miles to Eel River 2 miles northeast of Weott (lat. 40°20'40" N, long. 123°54'W; near S line sec. 25, T 1 S, R 2 E). Named on Myers Flat (1969) and Weott (1969) 7.5' quadrangles.

Newman Gulch [MENDOCINO]: *canyon,* drained by a stream that flows nearly 1 mile to Noyo River 1.5 miles east-southeast of Fort Bragg (lat. 39°26'05" N, long. 123°46'40" W; sec. 8, T 18 N, R 17 W). Named on Fort Bragg (1960) 7.5' quadrangle.

Newman Springs [LAKE]: *locality,* 15 miles north of Clearlake Oaks (lat. 39°11'45" N, long. 122°42'50" W); the place is along Soup Creek. Named on Clearlake Oaks (1960) 15' quadrangle. The place also was called Soap Creek Springs—the term "soap" in the name was from borax in the spring water; a resort used the water (Waring, p. 202; Bradley, p. 221).

New Orleans Bar: see **Orleans** [HUMBOLDT].

Newport [MENDOCINO]: *locality,* 4.25 miles south of Westport along the coast (lat. 39°34'35" N, long. 123°46'30" W; near S line sec. 20, T 20 N, R 17 W). Named on Inglenook (1966) 7.5' quadrangle. The place was a shipping point for lumber (Carpenter, p. 79).

New River [TRINITY]: *stream,* formed by the confluence of Slide Creek and Virgin Creek, flows 20 miles to Trinity River 2.5 miles north of Burnt Ranch (lat. 40°50'45" N, long. 123°28'45" W). Named on Ironside Mountain (1951) 15' quadrangle, and on Dees Peak (1978) 7.5' quadrangle. East Fork enters from the east-northeast 15 miles upstream from the mouth of the main river and is 12 miles long; it is named on Ironside Mountain (1951) 15' quadrangle, and on Cecil Lake (1979) and Dees Peak (1978) 7.5' quadrangles. South Fork of East Fork enters East Fork from the south 15 miles southeast of Salmon Mountain; it is nearly 4 miles long and is named on Helena (1951) and Ironside Mountain (1951) 15' quadrangles, and on Dees Peak (1978) 7.5' quadrangle.

New River: see **Slide Creek** [TRINITY].

New River, North Fork: see **Eagle Creek** [TRINITY] (1), **North Fork**.

New River City: see **Old Denny** [TRINITY].

New River Lake: see **Rattlesnake Lake** [TRINITY].

New Ruth Reservoir: see **Ruth Reservoir** [TRINITY].

Newton Creek [MENDOCINO]: *stream,* flows 1 mile to Pardaloe Creek 2.5 miles south of Ornbaun Valley (lat. 38°52'30" N, long. 123°18'30" W; sec. 21, T 12 N, R 13 W). Named on Ornbaun Valley (1960) 15' quadrangle.

New York Bar [TRINITY]: *locality,* 3 miles southeast of Burnt Ranch along Trinity River (lat. 41°47'10" N, long. 123°25'35" W). Named on Ironside Mountain (1951) 15' quadrangle.

Nice [LAKE]: *town,* 4.5 miles southeast of the town of Upper Lake (lat. 39°07'25" N, long. 122°50'45" W; sec. 27, T 15 N, R 9 W). Named on Bartlett Mountain (1958) and Lucerne (1958) 7.5' quadrangles. Postal authorities established Nice post office in 1930 (Frickstad, p. 64). The place first was called Clear Lake Villas, but Charles William Bayne, a former resident of Nice, France, changed the name about 1930 (Gudde, 1949, p. 236; Hanna, p. 211).

Nicholas Creek [TRINITY]: *stream,* flows less than 1 mile to Coffee Creek 4.5 miles west-southwest of Billys Peak (1) (lat. 41°07'05" N, long. 122°51'10" W; near SE cor. sec. 26, T 38 N, R 9 W). Named on Coffee Creek (1955) 15' quadrangle.

Nickel Creek [DEL NORTE]: *stream,* flows nearly 2 miles to the sea 5 miles southeast of Crescent City (lat. 41°42'N, long. 124°08'29" W; at S line sec. 11, T 15 N, R 1 W). Named on Childs Hill (1966) and Sister Rocks (1966) 7.5' quadrangles.

Nickowitz Creek [DEL NORTE-HUMBOLDT]: *stream,* heads in Del Norte County and flows 7.5 miles to Blue Creek 9.5 miles east-southeast of Klamath Glen in Humboldt County (lat. 41°27'25" N, long. 123°49'10" W). Named on Blue Creek Mountain (1982) and Lonesome Ridge (1974) 7.5' quadrangles.

Nickowitz Peak [DEL NORTE]: *peak,* 12.5 miles east of Klamath Glen (lat. 41°28'25" N, long. 123°45'30" W). Altitude 4003 feet. Named on Blue Creek Mountain (1982) 7.5' quadrangle.

Niemela Gulch [MENDOCINO]: *canyon,* drained by a stream that flows 1 mile to John Smith Creek 4.5 miles north of Navarro (lat. 39°12'55" N, long. 123°32'15" W; sec. 28, T 16 N, R 15 W). Named on Navarro (1961) 15' quadrangle.

Nigger Gulch [TRINITY]: *canyon,* drained by a stream that flows 1.5 miles to Hayfork Creek 5 miles east of Hayfork (lat. 40°32'20" N, long. 123°05'20" W). Named on Hayfork (1951) 15' quadrangle.

Nigger Head [HUMBOLDT]: *peak,* nearly 6 miles southwest of Weott (lat. 40°15'20" N, long. 123°59'05" W; near SW cor. sec. 29, T 2 S, R 2 E). Named on Weott (1949) 15' quadrangle.

Nigger Head: see **Negro Head** [MENDOCINO].

Nigger Joe Ridge: see **Negro Joe Ridge** [HUMBOLDT].

Nita: see **Lower Lake** [LAKE].

Nixon Creek [HUMBOLDT]: *stream,* flows 1.5 miles to Trinity River 4 miles south-southeast of Weitchpec (lat. 41°07'55" N, long. 123°41'20" W; sec. 26, T 9 N, R 4 E). Named on Weitchpec (1979) 7.5' quadrangle. United States Board on Geographic Names (1978b, p. 5) rejected the form "Nixons Creek" for the name.

Nixon Ridge [HUMBOLDT]: *ridge,* generally northwest-trending, 2.25 miles long, 11 miles east-northeast of the town of Blue Lake (lat. 40°56'45" N, long. 123°48'W). Named on Lord-Ellis Summit (1973) 7.5' quadrangle.

Noble Butte [MENDOCINO]: *peak,* 8 miles north-northeast of Leggett (lat. 39°58'35" N, long. 123°40'45" W; sec. 36, T 5 S, R 4 E). Altitude 2435 feet. Named on Noble Butte (1969) 7.5' quadrangle. Present Little Butte is called Noble Butte on Leggett (1952) 15' quadrangle.

Noble's Springs: see **Castle Rock Springs** [LAKE].

Noh-tin-oah Mountain: see **Hupa Mountain** [HUMBOLDT].

Noisy Creek [HUMBOLDT]:

(1) *stream,* flows 2.5 miles to Mad River 3.5 miles northeast of Arcata (lat. 40°54'N, long. 124°01'30" W; near SE cor. sec. 14, T 6 N, R 1 E). Named on Arcata North (1959) and Blue Lake (1979) 7.5' quadrangles.

(2) *stream,* flows 7.5 miles to Redwood Creek (1) 8.5 miles east of Korbel (lat. 40°52'N, long. 123°47'35" W; at N line sec. 36, T 6 N, R 3 E). Named on Lord-Ellis Summit (1973) and Maple Creek (1977) 7.5' quadrangles.

Nome Cult Valley: see **Round Valley** [MENDOCINO].

Noonan Gulch [TRINITY]:

(1) *canyon,* drained by a stream that flows 0.5 mile to East Fork of North Fork Trinity River 10 miles north of Helena (lat. 40°55'10" N, long. 123°07'50" W; sec. 5, T 35 N, R 11 W). Named on Helena (1951) 15' quadrangle.

(2) *canyon,* drained by a stream that flows 0.5 mile to East Fork of North Fork Trinity River 5 miles north of Helena (lat. 40°50'45" N, long. 123°07'30" W; at W line sec. 33, T 35 N, R 11 W). Named on Helena (1951) 15' quadrangle.

Noonan Gulch: see **Barney Gulch** [TRINITY].

Nooning Creek [HUMBOLDT]: *stream,* flows 1.5 miles to Mattole River 11 miles west-southwest of Garberville (lat. 40°03'55" N, long. 123°59'40" W; sec. 31, T 4 S, R 2 E). Named on Briceland (1969) and Shelter Cove (1969) 7.5' quadrangles.

Nooning Ground [HUMBOLDT]: *area,* 3.5 miles east-northeast of Point Delgada (lat. 40°02'55" N, long. 124°00'40" W; near SE cor. sec. 1, T 5 S, R 1 E); the place is near the head of Nooning Creek. Named on Shelter Cove (1969) 7.5' quadrangle.

No Pass: see **Point No Pass** [MENDOCINO].

Norden Gulch [MENDOCINO]: *canyon,* drained by a stream that flows less than 1 mile to South Fork Albion River 8 miles north-northeast of Elk (lat. 39°14'25" N, long. 123°39'15" W; sec. 16, T 16 N, R 16 W). Named on Elk (1960) 7.5' quadrangle.

Norman Springs [LAKE]: *spring,* 2.25 miles west of Jericho Valley (lat. 38°50'05" N, long. 122°28'30" W; sec. 1, T 11 N, R 6 W). Named on Jericho Valley (1958) 7.5' quadrangle. On Morgan Valley (1944) 15' quadrangle, the name applies to a locality at the site.

Norse Butte [TRINITY]: *peak,* 6.25 miles west-northwest of Forest Glen (lat. 40°24'N, long. 123°26'15" W; near SE cor. sec. 1, T 1 N, R 6 E). Named on Sportshaven (1973) 7.5' quadrangle. The misspelled name commemorates a settler named Norris who lived at the foot of the peak (Gudde, 1949, p. 238).

North Bay [HUMBOLDT]: *bay,* 5 miles north-northwest of Ferndale (lat. 40°39'30" N, long. 124°17'50" W). Named on Cannibal Island (1959) 7.5' quadrangle. The bay extends north-northeast from the mouth of Eel River. Called McNulty Slough on Cape Fortunas (1920) 15' quadrangle.

North Bay: see **Arcata Bay** [HUMBOLDT].

North Cache Creek: see **North Fork**, under **Cache Creek** [LAKE].

North Creek [HUMBOLDT]: *stream,* flows less than 1 mile to South Fork Eel River 5.25 miles south of Garberville (lat. 40°01'25" N, long. 123°47'30" W; near W line sec. 13, T 5 S, R 3 E). Named on Garberville (1970) 7.5' quadrangle.

North Dobbyn Creek [HUMBOLDT-TRINITY]: *stream,* heads in Trinity County and flows 6.5 miles to join South Dobbyn Creek and form Dobbyn Creek 3 miles north of Alderpoint in Humboldt County (lat. 40°13'20" N, long. 123°36'05" W; sec. 10, T 3 S, R 5 E). Named on Alderpoint (1969) and Black Lassic (1979) 7.5' quadrangles. Called Dobbyn Creek on South Fork Peak (1929) 15' quadrangle.

Northern Redwood Camp: see **Blue Lake** [HUMBOLDT] (2).

North Fork: see: **Helena** [TRINITY]; **Korbel** [HUMBOLDT].

North Fork Camp [MENDOCINO]: *locality,* 4.25 miles north-northeast of Comptche (lat. 39°19'01" N, long. 123°33'20" W; sec. 20, T 17 N, R 15 W); the place is along North Fork Big River at the mouth of East Branch of North Fork. Named on Comptche (1960) 15' quadrangle.

North Fork Gulch [TRINITY]: *canyon,* drained by a stream that flows 2.5 miles to North Fork Trinity River less than 2 miles northwest of Helena (lat. 40°47'45" N, long. 123°08'45" W; sec. 18, T 34 N, R 11 W). Named on Helena (1951) 15 quadrangle.

North Fork House: see **Navarro** [MENDOCINO].

North Fork Pasture [HUMBOLDT]: *area,* nearly 5 miles south-southeast of Coyote Peak (lat. 41°04'N, long. 123°50'15" W; mainly in sec. 21, T 8 N, R 3 E). Named on Hupa Mountain (1982) 7.5' quadrangle.

North Glade [LAKE]: *area,* 2 miles west-northwest of Potato Hill (lat. 39°21'50" N, long. 122°50'15" W). Named on Potato Hill (1967) 7.5' quadrangle.

North Kelsey Peak [TRINITY]: *peak,* 8.5 miles west of Black Rock Mountain (lat. 40°12'30" N, long. 123°10'W; sec. 12, T 27 N, R 12 W); the peak is 1 mile west-northwest of South Kelsey Peak. Named on Black Rock Mountain (1954) 15' quadrangle. The name commemorates Samuel Kelsey, an early explorer who led pack parties in the region (Jones, p. 366).

North Mickey Ridge [TRINITY]: *ridge,* east- to southeast-trending, 1.5 miles long, 6.5 miles south-southeast of Black Rock Mountain (lat. 40°06'55" N, long. 123°02'30" W; on E line sec. 12, T 26 N, R 11 W); the ridge is 1 mile north of South Mickey Ridge. Named on Black Rock Mountain (1954) 15' quadrangle.

North Mill Creek [MENDOCINO]: *stream,* flows 1 mile to Mill Creek (12) 1 mile west-southwest of Ornbaun Valley (lat. 38°54'20" N, long. 123°19'20" W; near E line sec. 8, T 12 N, R 13 W). Named on Ornbaun Valley (1960) 15' quadrangle.

North Peak: see **Buckingham Peak** [LAKE].

North Philpot Creek: see **North Fork**, under **Philpot Creek** [TRINITY].

Northport Gulch [MENDOCINO]: *canyon,* drained by a stream that flows less than 0.5 mile to the sea 10 miles south-southwest of Piercy (lat. 39°51'20" N, long. 123°53'35" W; sec. 17, T 23 N, R 18 W). Named on Mistake Point (1969) 7.5' quadrangle.

North Post Creek [TRINITY]: *stream,* flows nearly 4 miles to Post Creek 3.5 miles northeast of Forest Glen (lat. 40°24'15" N, long. 123°16'05" W; at W line sec. 31, T 30 N, R 12 W). Named on Naufus Creek (1979) 7.5' quadrangle.

North Rattlesnake Creek [TRINITY]: *stream,* flows 4.5 miles to Rattlesnake Creek (2) 1.5 miles east-northeast of Forest Glen (lat. 40°23'N, long. 123°17'50" W; sec. 17, T 1 S, R 8 E). Named on Naufus Creek (1979) 7.5' quadrangle.

North Ridge [LAKE]:

(1) *ridge,* east-trending, 1 mile long, 5.25 miles west-northwest of Bear Mountain (lat. 39°25'55" N, long. 122°59'45" W; sec. 9, T 18 N, R 10 W); the ridge is 1 mile north of South Ridge. Named on Lake Pillsbury (1967) 7.5' quadrangle.

(2) *ridge,* north-northwest-trending, less than 1 mile long, 2 miles south of Crockett Peak (lat. 39°23'55" N, long. 122°46'50" W; mainly in sec. 20, T 18 N, R 8 W). Named on Crockett Peak (1967) 7.5' quadrangle.

North Ridge [MENDOCINO]: *ridge,* north- to northwest-trending, less than 1 mile long, 7 miles north of Boonville (lat. 39°06'30" N, long. 123°20'40" W); the ridge is north of South Ridge. Named on Boonville (1959) 15' quadrangle.

North Rock [HUMBOLDT]: *rock,* 7.5 miles west-southwest of Ferndale, and 1800 feet offshore (lat. 40°31'20" N, long. 124°23'10" W). Named on Ferndale (1943) 15' quadrangle.

North Rock [MENDOCINO]: *rock,* 9 miles west-southwest of Piercy, and 500 feet offshore (lat. 39°55'10" N, long. 123°57'05" W). Named on Bear Harbor (1969) 7.5' quadrangle.

North Slide Peak [HUMBOLDT]: *peak,* 5 miles southwest of Honeydew (lat. 40°11'N, long. 124°10'45" W). Named on Shubrick Peak (1969) 7.5' quadrangle.

North Spit [HUMBOLDT]: *peninsula,* the southwest end of Somoa Peninsula that separates the north part of Humboldt Bay from the sea (lat. 40°47'15" N, long. 124°12'15" W). Named on Eureka (1958) 7.5' quadrangle.

Northspur [MENDOCINO]: *locality,* 11 miles north of Comptche along California Western Railroad (lat. 39°25'20" N, long. 123°33'W; near SE cor. sec. 8, T 18 N, R 15 W). Named on Comptche (1960) 15' quadrangle. Postal authorities established Northspur post office in 1910 and discontinued it in 1922 (Frickstad, p. 96). The railroad had a station called Noyo Lodge located 0.8 mile west of Northspur (Crump, p. 56).

North Trinity Mountain [HUMBOLDT]: *peak,* 6.25 miles northwest of Trinity Mountain (lat. 41°06'20" N, long. 123°29'05" W. Altitude 6342 feet. Named on Trinity Mountain (1979) 7.5' quadrangle.

North Twin Gulch [TRINITY]: *canyon,* drained by a stream that flows 1 mile to the canyon of Trinity River 20 miles northeast of Weaverville (lat. 40°56'45" N, long. 122°41'15" W; sec. 29, T 36 N, R 7 W); the mouth of the canyon is 600 feet north of the mouth of South Twin Gulch. Named on Schell Mountain (1950) 15' quadrangle.

Northwestern: see **Willits** [MENDOCINO].

North Yolla Bolly Mountains [TRINITY]: *range,* 2 miles east-southeast of Black Rock Mountain on Trinity-Tehama County line (lat. 40°11'45" N, long. 122°58'20" W). Named on Yolla Bolly (1954) 15' quadrangle. Called North Yallo Bally Mt. on Red Bluff (1894) 1° quadrangle. United States Board on Geographic Names (1982c, p. 2) rejected the names "North Yallo Bally," "North Yolla Bolly," "North Yolla Bolly Mountain," "Yalla Balla," "Yalla Balley," "Yalla Bally," "Yallo Bally," "Yola Bola," "Yola Buli," "Yolla Balley," "Yolla Bally," "Yolla Bolly," and "Yollo Bolly Mountains" for the feature. The name "Yolla Bolly" is of Indian origin (Kroeber, p. 67).

Norton Creek [HUMBOLDT]:

(1) *stream,* flows nearly 2 miles to Trinity River 2.5 miles south-southeast of Weitchpec (lat. 41°08'20" N, long. 123°41'05" W; sec. 26, T 9 N, R 4 E). Named on Weitchpec (1979) 7.5' quadrangle.

(2) *stream,* flows 3.25 miles to Widow White Creek 6.25 miles north-northwest of Arcata (lat. 40°57'35" N, long. 124°06'45" W; sec. 30, T 7 N, R 1 E). Named on Arcata North (1959) 7.5' quadrangle.

Norton Diggings: see **Strope Creek** [TRINITY].

Norway Gulch [TRINITY]: *canyon,* drained by a stream that flows 2 miles to North Fork Trinity River 8.5 miles north-northwest of Helena (lat.

40°53'30" N, long. 123°09'50" W). Named on Helena (1951) 15' quadrangle.

Nose Rock [MENDOCINO]: *rock*, 1 mile west-southwest of Elk, and 3500 feet offshore (lat. 39°07'35" N, long. 123°43'50" W). Named on Elk (1960) 7.5' quadrangle. Officials of United States Coast Survey named the feature (Gudde, 1949, p. 239).

Notchko [HUMBOLDT]: *locality*, nearly 4 miles south of Johnsons along Klamath River (lat. 41°17'45" N, long. 123°52'05" W); the place is 0.5 mile northwest of the mouth of Notchko Creek. Named on Johnsons (1982) 7.5' quadrangle.

Notchko Creek [HUMBOLDT]: *stream*, flows 1.5 miles to Klamath River 4.25 miles south of Johnsons (lat. 41°17'20" N, long. 123°51'50" W; near SW cor. sec. 32, T 11 N, R 3 E). Named on Holter Ridge (1983) and Johnsons (1982) 7.5' quadrangles. Called Notchkoo Creek on Tectah Creek (1952) 15' quadrangle. United States Board on Geographic Names (1984b, p. 4) approved the name "Nacko Creek" for the stream, and rejected the names "Notchko Creek," "Notchkoo Creek," and "Natchko Creek." The name is of Indian origin (Gudde, 1949, p. 231).

Notice Creek [DEL NORTE]: *stream*, flows 3.5 miles to Bluff Creek 16 miles east-southeast of Klamath Glen (lat. 41°24'10" N, long. 123°42'50" W). Named on Blue Creek Mountain (1982) and Lonesome Ridge (1974) 7.5' quadrangles.

Novarro: see **Navarro** [MENDOCINO].

Novarro River: see **Navarro River** [MENDOCINO].

Noyo [MENDOCINO]: *village*, 1 mile south of downtown Fort Bragg (lat. 39°25'45" N, long. 123°48'10" W; sec. 18, T 18 N, R 17 W); the place is along Noyo River. Named on Fort Bragg (1960) 7.5' quadrangle. Postal authorities established Noyo River post office at the site in 1859 and discontinued it in 1860; they reestablished the post office with the name "Noyo" in 1872 and discontinued it in 1918 (Salley, p. 157).

Noyo: see **Camp Noyo** [MENDOCINO].

Noyo Anchorage: see **Noyo River** [MENDOCINO].

Noyo Bay [MENDOCINO]: *embayment*, 1.25 miles south-southwest of downtown Fort Bragg along the coast (lat. 39°25'45" N, long. 123°48'45" W; sec. 13, T 18 N, R 18 W); the feature is at the mouth of Noyo River. Named on Fort Bragg (1960) 7.5' quadrangle.

Noyo Hill [MENDOCINO]: *peak*, 12.5 miles northwest of Comptche (lat. 39°24'25" N, long. 123°44'10" W; sec. 22, T 18 N, R 17 W). Named on Comptche (1960) 15' quadrangle.

Noyo Lodge: see **Northspur** [MENDOCINO].

Noyo River [MENDOCINO]: *stream*, flows 30 miles to the sea 1 mile south of downtown Fort Bragg (lat. 39°25'35" N, long. 123°48'30" W; sec. 13, T 18 N, R 18 W). Named on Comptche (1960) and Willits (1961) 15' quadrangles, and on Fort Bragg (1960) 7.5' quadrangle. The named is from an Indian village that was located at the mouth of Pudding Creek (Kroeber, p. 51). The stream also had the designation "Rio Grande River" (Landsman, 1977b, p. 8). South Fork enters from the southeast 6.25 miles upstream from the mouth of the main river; it is 9.5 miles long and is named on Comptche (1960) 15' quadrangle. North Fork of South Fork enters South Fork from the north nearly 4 miles upstream from the mouth of South Fork; it is 7.5 miles long and is named on Comptche (1960) 15' quadrangle. North Fork Noyo River enters from the north 15 miles upstream from the mouth of South Fork Noyo River; it is 6.25 miles long and is named on Comptche (1960) 15' quadrangle. Little North Fork enters North Fork Noyo River from the north 3.5 miles upstream from the mouth of South Fork Noyo River; it is 4.5 miles long and is named on Comptche (1960) 15' quadrangle. Middle Fork of North Fork enters North Fork from the northeast 5 miles upstream from the mouth of North Fork; it is 3 miles long and is named on Comptche (1960) 15' quadrangle. Present Middle Fork of North Fork Noyo River is called North Fork Noyo River on Glenblair (1943) 15' quadrangle, where present North Fork Noyo River above the confluence with present Middle Fork of North Fork is called Dewarren Creek. O' Brien's (1953) map has the name "Camp 8 Gulch" for a canyon that is drained by a stream that enters North Fork of South Fork Noyo River from the north (NW quarter sec. 22, T 18 N, R 16 W), and has the name "Camp 10 Gulch" for a canyon that is drained by a stream that enters North Fork of South Fork Noyo River from the southeast (near S line sec. 23, T 18 N, R 16 W). United States Coast and Geodetic Survey (p. 141) applied the name "Noyo Anchorage" to the sheltered place at the mouth of Noyo River.

Noyo River: see **Noyo** [MENDOCINO].

Nursey Gulch [MENDOCINO]: *canyon*, drained by a stream that flows less than 1 mile to Albion River 8 miles north-northeast of Elk (lat. 39°13'30" N, long. 123°37'55" W; at S line sec. 22, T 16 N, R 16 W). Named on Elk (1960) 7.5' quadrangle.

Nutmeg Spring [LAKE]: *spring*, 2 miles west-northwest of Whispering Pines (lat. 38°49'40" N, long. 122°44'30" W; near NE cor. sec. 9, T 11 N, R 8 W). Named on Whispering Pines (1958) 7.5' quadrangle.

Nye Camp: see **Lower Nye Campground** [LAKE]; **Upper Nye Camp** [LAKE].

Nye Campground: see **Lower Nye Campground** [LAKE].

Nye Creek [MENDOCINO]: *stream*, flows 2 miles to Alder Creek (5) 7.5 miles north-northeast of the village of Point Arena (lat. 39°00'N, long. 123°37'W; sec. 10, T 13 N, R 16 W). Named on Point Arena (1960) 15' quadrangle.

— O —

Oak Cove [LAKE]: *embayment*, 5 miles northwest of the town of Lower Lake along Clear Lake (lat. 38°58'15" N, long. 122°40'W; at SW cor. sec. 17, T 13 N, R 7 W). Named on Clearlake Highlands (1958) 7.5' quadrangle.

Oak Flat [TRINITY]:

(1) *area*, 10 miles east of Burnt Ranch (lat. 40°49'45" N, long. 123°17'W; sec. 4, T 5 N, R 8 E). Named on Ironside Mountain (1951) 15' quadrangle.

(2) *area*, 2.5 miles south of Hyampom along South Fork Trinity River (lat. 40°34'N, long. 123°26'35" W; sec. 12, T 2 N, R 6 E). Named on Hyampom (1951) 15' quadrangle.

(3) *area*, 13 miles north of Weaverville along Stuart Fork (lat. 40°55'25" N, long. 122°37'20" W). Named on Trinity Dam (1950) 15' quadrangle.

Oak Flat Campground [HUMBOLDT]: *locality*, 5.5 miles south of Garberville (lat. 40°01'N, long. 123°47'15" W; sec. 13, T 5 S, R 3 E). Named on Garberville (1970) 7.5' quadrangle.

Oak Flat Campground [LAKE]: *locality*, nearly 4 miles northwest of Bear Mountain at the north side of Lake Pillsbury (lat. 39°26'35" N, long. 122°57'10" W; sec. 2, T 18 N, R 10 W). Named on Lake Pillsbury (1967) 7.5' quadrangle.

Oak Glen [HUMBOLDT]: *locality*, 5.25 miles west of Blocksburg (lat. 40°16'55" N, long. 123°44'25" W; near NW cor. sec. 21, T 2 S, R 4 E). Named on Blocksburg (1969) 7.5' quadrangle.

Oak Knob [HUMBOLDT]: *peak*, 6.5 miles south of the settlement of Willow Creek (lat. 40°50'55" N, long. 123°36'50" W). Named on Hennessy Peak (1979) 7.5' quadrangle.

Oak Ridge [HUMBOLDT]: *ridge*, generally west-northwest-trending, 1.5 miles long, 4 miles southwest of Bridgeville (lat. 40°26'20" N, long. 123°51'30" W). Named on Bridgeville (1969) 7.5' quadrangle.

Oak Ridge [TRINITY]: *ridge*, south-southeast- to east-trending, about 4 miles long, 6.5 miles southeast of Hyampom (lat. 40°33'15" N, long. 123°22'W). Named on Hyampom (1951) 15' quadrangle.

Oaks: see **The Oaks** [MENDOCINO].

Oasis [MENDOCINO]: *locality*, 6 miles east of Hopland (lat. 38°58'50" N, long. 123°00'10" W). Named on Hopland (1944) 15' quadrangle.

Oat Creek [HUMBOLDT]: *stream*, flows 2 miles to the sea 8 miles southwest of Honeydew (lat. 40°10'45" N, long. 124°14'35" W; sec. 25, T 3 S, R 2 W); the stream is southeast of Oat Ridge and northwest of Kinsey Ridge. Named on Shubrick Peak (1969) 7.5' quadrangle. Called Kinsey Creek on Point Delgada (1949) 15' quadrangle. United States Board on Geographic Names (1974a, p. 3) approved the name "Oat Creek" for the stream, and gave the name "Kinsey Creek" as a variant.

Oat Gap [MENDOCINO]: *pass*, 6 miles north-northeast of the town of Potter Valley (lat. 39°23'50" N, long. 123°03'30" W; near W line sec. 22, T 18 N, R 11 W). Named on Potter Valley (1960) 15' quadrangle.

Oat Hill [HUMBOLDT]: *peak*, 6 miles west-southwest of Honeydew (lat. 40°12'N, long. 124°13'30" W; on S line sec. 18, T 3 S, R 1 W); the peak is near the northeast end of Oat Ridge. Altitude 2392 feet. Named on Shubrick Peak (1969) 7.5' quadrangle.

Oat Hill [LAKE]: *peak*, 1.5 miles east of Jericho Valley (lat. 38°50'10" N, long. 122°24'25" W; near W line sec. 3, T 11 N, R 5 W). Named on Jericho Valley (1958) 7.5' quadrangle.

Oat Ridge [HUMBOLDT]: *ridge*, southwest-trending, 2 miles long, 7 miles west-southwest of Honeydew (lat. 40°11'40" N, long. 124°14'W); Oat Hill is near the northeast end of the ridge. Named on Shubrick Peak (1969) 7.5' quadrangle.

Oat Ridge [MENDOCINO]: *ridge*, south-southeast-trending, 4 miles long, 7 miles northeast of Willits (lat. 39°29'N, long. 123°16'20" W). Named on Willits (1961) 15' quadrangle, and on Willis Ridge (1966) 7.5' quadrangle.

Observatory Hill [MENDOCINO]: *peak*, 9 miles northwest of Comptche (lat. 39°20'15" N, long. 123°43'15" W; near N line sec. 14, T 17 N, R 17 W). Altitude 953 feet. Named on Comptche (1960) 15' quadrangle.

Ocean House [HUMBOLDT]: *locality*, 0.5 mile southeast of Cape Mendocino (lat. 40°25'50" N, long. 124°23'55" W; sec. 34, T 1 N, R 3 W). Named on Cape Mendocino (1969) 7.5' quadrangle.

O' Connell Gulch [TRINITY]: *canyon*, drained by a stream that flows 2 miles to Reading Creek 11.5 miles south-southeast of Weaverville (lat. 40°34'35" N, long. 122°53'W; at S line sec. 33, T 32 N, R 9 W). Named on Weaverville (1950) 15' quadrangle.

O' Conner Gulch [MENDOCINO]: *canyon*, drained by a stream that flows 1.25 miles to North Fork Ten Mile River 4 miles south-southwest of Branscomb (lat. 39°36'15" N, long. 123°39'45" W; near S line sec. 8, T 20 N, R 16 W); the canyon heads at O' Conner Orchard. Named on Dutchmans Knoll (1966) 7.5' quadrangle.

O' Conner Orchard [MENDOCINO]: *area,* 3.25 miles southeast of Branscomb (lat. 39°37'15" N, long. 123°40'05" W; sec. 5, T 20 N, R 16 W). Named on Dutchmans Knoll (1966) 7.5' quadrangle.

Off Rock [HUMBOLDT]: *rock,* 3750 feet west-northwest of Cape Mendocino (lat. 40°26'35" N, long. 124°25'15" W). Named on Cape Mendocino (1969) 7.5' quadrangle.

Off Trinidad Head: see **Flatiron Rock** [HUMBOLDT].

Off Trinidad Rock: see **Flatiron Rock** [HUMBOLDT].

Ogelene Canyon [LAKE]: *canyon,* drained by a stream that flows 1.5 miles to the northeasternmost end of Burns Valley 5 miles north of the town of Lower Lake (lat. 38°59'N, long. 122°36'W; near S line sec. 11, T 13 N, R 7 W). Named on Lower Lake (1958) 7.5' quadrangle. United States Board on Geographic Names (1977c, p. 5) approved the name "Ogulin Canyon" for the feature, and gave the name "Ogelene Canyon" as a variant.

Ogulin Canyon: see **Ogelene Canyon** [LAKE].

Ohman Creek [HUMBOLDT]: *stream,* flows nearly 4 miles to South Fork Eel River 1.5 miles southeast of Phillipsville (lat. 40°11'35" N, long. 123°46'05" W; sec. 19, T 3 S, R 4 E). Named on Fort Seward (1969) and Miranda (1970) 7.5' quadrangles.

Oil Creek [HUMBOLDT]:

(1) *stream,* flows 6.5 miles to the sea 7 miles west-southwest of Ferndale (lat. 40°31'20" N, long. 124°22'45" W). Named on Ferndale (1959) 7.5' quadrangle.

(2) *stream,* flows 3.5 miles to Eel River nearly 5 miles south of Fortuna (lat. 40°31'40" N, long. 124°09'40" W; sec. 27, T 2 N, R 1 W). Named on Fortuna (1959) and Taylor Peak (1969) 7.5' quadrangles.

(3) *stream,* flows 4 miles to join Rattlesnake Creek (2) and form Upper North Fork Mattole River 13 miles south of Scotia (lat. 40°17'25" N, long. 124°06'35" W; near N line sec. 19, T 2 S, R 1 E). Named on Buckeye Mountain (1970) and Bull Creek (1969) 7.5 quadrangles.

Oil Creek Ridge [HUMBOLDT]: *ridge,* west-southwest- to west-trending, 3 miles long, 6 miles southwest of Ferndale (lat. 40°30'50" N, long. 124°20'30" W); the feature is north of Oil Creek (1). Named on Ferndale (1959) 7.5' quadrangle.

Old Camp 19 [MENDOCINO]: *locality,* 6.25 miles north of Comptche along Caspar Lumber Company's railroad (lat. 39°21'15" N, long. 123°36'30" W). Named on Glenblair (1943) 15' quadrangle.

Old Camp Seven [MENDOCINO]: *locality,* 11.5 miles north of Comptche along California Western Railroad (lat. 39°25'35" N, long. 123°34'05" W; near E line sec. 7, T 18 N, R 15 W). Named on Comptche (1960) 15' quadrangle.

Old Denny [TRINITY]: *locality,* 10 miles southeast of Salmon Mountain (lat. 41°04'35" N, long. 123°16'15" W). Named on Dees Peak (1978) 7.5' quadrangle. Called New River City on Miller's (1890) map, and called Denny on Sawyers Bar (1923) 30'quadrangle. Postal authorities established Denny post office in 1890 and moved it 20 miles south to the former site of Quimby post office in 1920 (Salley, p. 58). Settlers gave the name "New River City" to present Old Denny in 1882, but when postal officials rejected this name, the residents chose the name "Denny" for the owner of the store at the place (Gudde, 1949, p. 93).

Old Hopland: see **Hopland** [MENDOCINO].

Old Man Gulch [TRINITY]: *canyon,* drained by a stream that flows 1.5 miles to Indian Creek (2) 9 miles south-southeast of Weaverville (lat. 40°36'45" N, long. 122°52'30" W; sec. 22, T 32 N, R 9 W). Named on Weaverville (1950) 15' quadrangle.

Old Man Ridge [MENDOCINO]: *ridge,* generally north-northeast-trending, 2 miles long, 6.5 miles east-northeast of Eden Valley (lat. 39°39'15" N, long. 123°04'15" W). Named on Thatcher Ridge (1967) 7.5' quadrangle.

Old Minersville [TRINITY]: *locality,* 12 miles northeast of Weaverville (lat. 40°51'N, long. 122°47'W; sec. 33, T 35 N, R 8 W); the place is 1.25 miles north of Minersville, and is called Minersville on Weaverville (1913) 30'quadrangle. Named on Trinity Lake (1950) 15' quadrangle. Water of Clair Engle Lake now covers the site.

Old Ornbaun Hot Springs [MENDOCINO]: *locality,* in Ornbaun Valley (lat. 38°54'45" N, long. 123°18'35" W); the place is near the site of present Ornbaun Springs. Named on Ornbaun (1944) 15' quadrangle.

Old Red Rock Place [MENDOCINO]: *locality,* 11 miles southwest of Ornbaun Valley (lat. 38°47'35" N, long. 123°26'20" W). Named on Ornbaun Valley (1960) 15' quadrangle.

Olds Creek [MENDOCINO]: *stream,* flows 4 miles to Noyo River 12 miles north-northeast of Comptche (lat. 39°25'15" N, long. 123°30'10" W; near N line sec. 14, T 18 N, R 15 W). Named on Willits (1961) 15' quadrangle.

Old Woman Canyon [MENDOCINO]: *canyon,* drained by a stream that flows nearly 4 miles to Twin Bridges Creek 7 miles south-southwest of Eden Valley (lat. 39°32'N, long. 123°13'40" W). Named on Brushy Mountain (1966) 7.5' quadrangle. Called Old Womans Canyon on Eden Valley (1929) 15' quadrangle.

Old Womans Home [TRINITY]: *area,* 11 miles southwest of Forest Glen (lat. 40°16'35" N, long. 123°29'20" W). Named on Ruth Reservoir (1978) 7.5' quadrangle.

Olive: see **Mount Olive** [LAKE].

Olmstead Creek [HUMBOLDT]: *stream,* flows 1 mile to Mad River 2 miles east of Showers Mountain (lat. 40°34'50" N, long. 123°39'55" W; near W line sec. 6, T 2 N, R 5 E). Named on Showers Mountain (1978) 7.5' quadrangle.

Olsen Creek [HUMBOLDT]: *stream,* flows about 2.5 miles to Indian Creek (3) 3.5 miles northeast of Yager Junction (lat. 40°35'10" N, long. 123°46'45" W; near E line sec. 1, T 2 N, R 3 E). Named on Showers Mountain (1978) and Yager Junction (1979) 7.5' quadrangles.

Olsen Creek [TRINITY]:

(1) *stream,* flows 4.25 miles to Hayfork Creek at Hyampom (lat. 40°37'05" N, long. 123°26'35" W; at S line sec. 24, T 3 N, R 6 E). Named on Hyampom (1951) 15' quadrangle.

(2) *stream,* flows 1.5 miles to Mad River 9 miles west-northwest of Forest Glen (lat. 40°25'30" N, long. 123°28'45" W; sec. 34, T 1 N, R 6 E). Named on Sportshaven (1973) 7.5' quadrangle.

Olsen Crossing [HUMBOLDT]: *locality,* nearly 2 miles east of Showers Mountain along Mad River (lat. 40°34'55" N, long. 123°39'45" W; at E line sec. 1, T 2 N, R 4 E). Named on Showers Mountain (1978) 7.5' quadrangle. The name is for Frank Olsen (Turner, p. 163).

Omagaar Creek [DEL NORTE-HUMBOLDT]: *stream,* heads in Humboldt County and flows 3.25 miles to Klamath River 2.5 miles southeast of Klamath Glen in Del Norte County (lat. 41°29'15" N, long. 123°57'45" W; sec. 29, T 13 N, R 2 E). Named on Ah Pah Ridge (1983) 7.5' quadrangle. Called Omager Creek on Tectah Creek (1952) 15' quadrangle. United States Board on Geographic Names (1984b, p. 4) approved the name "Omogar Creek" for the feature, and rejected the names "Omagaar Creek," "Omagar Creek," and "Omager Creek" for it. The name is of Indian origin (Kroeber, p. 52).

Omager Creek: see **Omagaar Creek** [DEL NORTE-HUMBOLDT].

Omenoku Point [HUMBOLDT]: *promontory,* less than 1 mile northwest of Trinidad along the coast (lat. 41°04'N, long. 124°09'20" W; sec. 23, T 8 N, R 1 W). Named on Trinidad (1966) 7.5' quadrangle. The name is of Indian origin (Gudde, 1949, p. 243).

Omogar Creek: see **Omagaar Creek** [DEL NORTE-HUMBOLDT].

One Eyed Creek [MENDOCINO]: *stream,* flows 1.5 miles to Burger Creek 4.5 miles east-northeast of Laytonville (lat. 39°42'35" N, long. 123°24'05" W; near SW cor. sec. 35, T 22 N, R 14 W). Named on Laytonville (1967) 7.5' quadrangle. On Laytonville (1951) 15' quadrangle, the name has the form "One-eyed Creek."

Oneeyed Flat [TRINITY]: *area,* 6 miles north of Trinity Center along Trinity River (lat. 41°05'30" N, long. 122°42'20" W; on W line sec. 5, T 37 N, R 7 W). Named on Bonanza King (1955) 15' quadrangle.

100 Acre Prairie [HUMBOLDT]: *area,* 5 miles east-southeast of Coyote Peak (lat. 41°06'10" N, long. 123°46'20" W; sec. 6, T 8 N, R 4 E). Named on Hupa Mountain (1982) 7.5' quadrangle.

O' Neil Ridge [MENDOCINO]: *ridge,* generally east-trending, 2 miles long, 12.5 miles north of Hull Mountain (lat. 39°42'05" N, long. 122°57'15" W). Named on Plaskett Ridge (1967) 7.5' quadrangle, which shows O' Neil place on the ridge.

Onemile Camp [TRINITY]: *locality,* 6.25 miles south-southwest of Salmon Mountain (lat. 41°06'N, long. 123°26'05" W). Named on Trinity Mountain (1979) 7.5' quadrangle.

Onion Camp [TRINITY]: *locality,* 10.5 miles north of Burnt Ranch (lat. 40°57'40" N, long. 123°27'W). Named on Ironside Mountain (1951) 15' quadrangle.

Onion Lake [HUMBOLDT]: *lake,* 350 feet long, 12 miles west-northwest of Orleans (lat. 41°22'45" N, long. 123°44'55" W). Lonesome Ridge (1974) 7.5' quadrangle.

Onion Mountain [HUMBOLDT]: *peak,* 12 miles west-northwest of Orleans (lat. 41°22'25" N, long. 123°44'55" W). Altitude 4776 feet. Named on Fish Lake (1974) 7.5' quadrangle.

Onion Patch Gulch [MENDOCINO]: *canyon,* drained by a stream that flows 1 mile to Flynn Creek 4.25 miles northwest of Navarro (lat. 39°11'20" N, long. 123°36'05" W; sec. 2, T 15 N, R 16 W). Named on Navarro (1961) 15' quadrangle.

Ora Lake [LAKE]: *lake,* 1100 feet long, 4 miles west-northwest of Lakeport (lat. 39°03'55" N, long. 122°58'45" W; sec. 16, T 14 N, R 10 W). Named on Lakeport (1958) 7.5' quadrangle.

Oregon Creek [HUMBOLDT]: *stream,* flows 1 mile to Tish Tang a Tang Creek 5.25 miles northwest of Trinity Mountain (lat. 41°05'05" N, long. 123°29'15" W). Named on Trinity Mountain (1979) 7.5' quadrangle. United States Board on Geographic Names (1981c, p. 3) rejected the name "Oregon Creek" for the stream, and approved the name "Crogan Creek," which commemorates Barney Crogan, who grazed cattle in the neighborhood in the 1880's .

Oregon Gulch [TRINITY]: *canyon,* drained by a stream that flows 3 miles to Trinity River 14 miles north-northeast of Hayfork (lat. 40°43'15" N, long. 123°02'30" W; sec. 18, T 33 N, R 10 W). Named on Hayfork (1951) and Weaverville (1950) 15' quadrangles.

Oregon Gulch: see **Junction City** [TRINITY].

Oregon Mountain [TRINITY]: *peak,* 2.5 miles west-southwest of Weaverville (lat. 40°43'10" N, long. 122°58'45" W; near E line sec. 15, T 33 N, R 10 W). Altitude 3942 feet. Named on Weaverville (1950) 15' quadrangle.

Orick [HUMBOLDT]: *town,* 34 miles north of Eureka (lat. 41°17'10" N, long. 124°03'35" W; near NE cor. sec. 4, T 10 N, R 1 E). Named on Orick (1966) 7.5' quadrangle. Postal authorities established Orick post office in 1887 (Frickstad, p. 45). The name is from an Indian village that was situated on the south side of the mouth of Redwood Creek (1) 1.5 miles below present Orick (Kroeber, p. 53). Postal authorities established Bald Hills post office 10 miles southeast of Orick in 1867 and discontinued it in 1878; the name was from bare hills left by lumbering operations (Salley, p. 13). They established Blaine post office 8 miles south of Orick in 1893 and discontinued it in 1895; the name was for Secretary of State James G. Blaine (Salley, p. 22). They established Gaus post office 13 miles southeast of Orick in 1887, changed the name to Gans in 1888, moved it 2.5 miles south in 1898, moved it 3 miles north in 1900, and discontinued it in 1904 (Salley, p. 82). The name "Gans" was for George W. Gans, who claimed land in Bald Hills in 1864 (Turner, p. 92).

Orick Hill [HUMBOLDT]: *peak,* 1 mile north of Orick (lat. 41°18'05" N, long. 124°03'50" W; near N line sec. 13, T 11 N, R 1 E). Altitude 872 feet. Named on Orick (1966) 7.5' quadrangle.

Oriole: see **Douglas City** [TRINITY].

Orleans [HUMBOLDT]: *town,* 12 miles northeast of Weitchpec (lat. 41°18'10" N, long. 123°32'20" W). Named on Orleans (1978) 7.5' quadrangle. Postal authorities established Orleans post office in 1857 (Frickstad, p. 45). The place first was called New Orleans Bar; the name was shortened to Orleans Bar in 1855, when the place became the seat of short-lived Klamath County (Gudde, 1949, p. 245).

Orleans Bar: see **Orleans** [HUMBOLDT].

Orleans Mountain [HUMBOLDT]: *peak,* nearly 5 miles east-southeast of Orleans on Humboldt-Siskiyou County line (lat. 41°16'45" N, long. 123°27'10" W). Altitude 6188 feet. Named on Orleans Mountain (1974) 7.5' quadrangle.

Ornbaun: see **Ornbaun Valley** [MENDOCINO].

Ornbaun Creek [MENDOCINO]:

(1) *stream,* flows 1.5 miles to Anderson Creek (2) 1.25 miles northwest of Boonville (lat. 39°01'20" N, long. 123°23'W; at S line sec. 34, T 14 N, R 14 W). Named on Boonville (1959) 15' quadrangle.

(2) *stream,* flows 1.5 miles to Rancheria Creek (2) 2.5 miles north-northwest of Ornbaun Valley (lat. 38°56'50" N, long. 123°19'50" W; near NW cor. sec. 32, T 13 N, R 13 W). Named on Ornbaun Valley (1960) 15' quadrangle.

Ornbaun Hot Springs: see **Old Ornbaun Hot Springs** [MENDOCINO].

Ornbaun Springs [MENDOCINO]: *spring,* in Ornbaun Valley (lat. 38°54'40" N, long. 123°18'20" W; at S line sec. 4, T 12 N, R 13 W). Named on Ornbaun Valley (1960) 15' quadrangle.

Ornbaun Valley [MENDOCINO]: *valley,* 11 miles west-southwest of Hopland (lat. 38°54'45" N, long. 123°18'15" W; around SE cor. sec. 4, T 12 N, R 13 W). Named on Ornbaun Valley (1960) 15' quadrangle. The name commemorates John S. Ornbaun, who came to Mendocino County in 1854 and had a stock ranch in the valley (Gudde, 1949, p. 245). O' Brien's (1953) map shows a place called Ornbaun located just east of present Ornbaun Valley along Rancheria Creek (2) (near center sec. 3, T 12 N, R 13 W). Ornbaun (1944) 15' quadrangle shows Ornbaun ranch at or near the site. Postal authorities established Ornbaun post office in 1897, moved it 1.25 miles northeast in 1907, moved it 3 miles west in 1908, and discontinued it in 1926; the name was for John S. Ornbaun (Salley, p. 163).

Orr Peak [LAKE]: *peak,* 2.5 miles west-northwest of Lakeport (lat. 39°03'40" N, long. 122°57'25" W; sec. 15, T 14 N, R 10 W). Altitude 1824 feet. Named on Lakeport (1958) 7.5' quadrangle.

Orrs: see **Orrs Springs** [MENDOCINO].

Orrs Creek [MENDOCINO]: *stream,* flows 8 miles to Russian River 1.25 miles east-northeast of Ukiah (lat. 39°09'35" N, long. 123°11'15" W). Named on Boonville (1959) 15' quadrangle, and on Ukiah (1958) 7.5' quadrangle.

Orrs Springs [MENDOCINO]: *locality,* 15 miles north of Boonville (lat. 39°13'45" N, long. 123°21'55" W; sec. 24, T 16 N, R 14 W). Named on Boonville (1959) 15' quadrangle. Postal authorities established Orrs post office in 1889, discontinued it in 1911, reestablished it in 1915, and discontinued it in 1933; the name was for Samuel Orr (Salley, p. 163). Samuel Orr's son, John L. Orr, developed a hot-springs resort and stage station at the place (Hanna, p. 221).

Ort Creek [HUMBOLDT]: *stream,* flows 1.25 miles to Eel River 6.5 miles northwest of Alderpoint (lat. 40°14'20" N, long. 123°41'55" W; sec. 2, T 3 S, R 4 E). Named on Fort Seward (1969) 7.5' quadrangle.

Orton Creek [HUMBOLDT]: *stream,* flows 1 mile to lowlands along Elk River (2) 2.5 miles east-northeast of Fields Landing (lat. 40°44'10" N, long. 124°10'15" W; near N line sec. 15, T 4 N, R 1 W). Named on Fields Landing (1959) 7.5' quadrangle.

Ossagon Creek [HUMBOLDT]: *stream,* flows 1.5 miles to the sea 11 miles north of Orick (lat. 41°26'35" N, long. 124°03'45" W; sec. 9, T 12 N, R 1 E). Named on Fern Canyon (1966) 7.5' quadrangle. The name is the American version of an Indian word (Turner, p. 165).

Ottoson: see **Hans Ottoson Opening** [MENDOCINO].

Outer Break [HUMBOLDT]: *rock,* 2 miles south of Cape Mendocino (lat. 40°24'55" N, long. 124°24'40" W). Named on Cape Mendocino (1969) 7.5' quadrangle.

Outlet [MENDOCINO]: *locality,* 4 miles north of Willits along Northwestern Pacific Railroad (lat. 39°28'N, long. 123°21'30" W; sec. 25, T 19 N, R 14 W); the place is along Outlet Creek. Named on Willits (1961) 15' quadrangle. Postal authorities established Outlet post office in 1917 and discontinued it in 1933 (Frickstad, p. 97).

Outlet: see **The Outlet** [MENDOCINO].

Outlet Creek [MENDOCINO]: *stream,* flows 18 miles from Little Lake Valley to Eel River 6.25 miles south of Dos Rios (lat. 39°37'35" N, long. 123°20'40" W; near SE cor.sec. 31, T 21 N, R 13 W). Named on Willits (1961) 15' quadrangle, and on Longvale (1966) and Willis Ridge (1966) 7.5' quadrangles.

Owens Creek [TRINITY]: *stream,* formed by the confluence of Middle Fork and South Fork, flows 0.5 mile to Stuart Fork 12 miles north of Weaverville (lat. 40°53'45" N, long. 122°56'15" W). Named on Trinity Dam (1950) 15' quadrangle. Middle Fork is 3 miles long and South Fork is 2.5 miles long. North Fork enters from the northwest just below the confluence of Middle Fork and South Fork, and is 2.5 miles long. All three forks are named on Trinity Dam (1950) 15' quadrangle.

Owl Creek [HUMBOLDT]:

(1) *stream,* flows 1.25 miles to South Fork Yager Creek 6 miles south-southwest of Lone Star Junction (lat. 40°33'20" N, long. 123°56'05" W; sec. 15, T 2 N, R 2 E). Named on Owl Creek (1979) 7.5' quadrangle.

(2) *stream,* flows 2.5 miles to Pilot Creek 5.5 miles east-northeast of Showers Mountain (lat. 40°36'55" N, long. 123°36'W; sec. 27, T 3 N, R 5 E). Named on Blake Mountain (1979) and Showers Mountain (1978) 7.5' quadrangles.

Owl Gulch [HUMBOLDT]: *canyon,* drained by a stream that flows 0.5 mile to Klamath River 1.5 miles west-southwest of Orleans (lat. 41°17'45" N, long. 123°34'W). Named on Orleans (1978) 7.5' quadrangle.

— P —

Pacific: see **Centerville City** [HUMBOLDT].

Pacific Point [LAKE]: *peak,* 14 miles north-northeast of Clearlake Oaks on Lake-Colusa County line (lat. 39°12'50" N, long. 122°35'45" W); the peak is on Pacific Ridge. Named on Clearlake Oaks (1960) 15' quadrangle.

Pacific Ridge [LAKE]: *ridge,* generally east-trending, 11 miles long, center 14 miles north-northeast of Clearlake Oaks on Lake-Colusa County line (lat. 39°13'15" N, long. 122°37'W). Named on Clearlake Oaks (1960) 15' quadrangle. The name is from Pacific City, a temporary community during the copper boom of the 1860's (Gudde, 1969, p. 233).

Packard Ridge [MENDOCINO]: *ridge,* generally west-trending, 6 miles long, center about 5.25 miles west of Branscomb (lat. 39°39'N, long. 123°43'15" W). Named on Lincoln Ridge (1966) and Westport (1966) 7.5' quadrangles.

Packeka Creek [HUMBOLDT]: *stream,* flows 2.25 miles to Mosquito Creek 13 miles south of the settlement of Willow Creek (lat. 40°45'15" N, long. 123°37'35" W). Named on Grouse Mountain (1979) 7.5' quadrangle.

Packer Gulch [TRINITY]: *canyon,* drained by a stream that flows 2 miles to Trinity River 19 miles northeast of Weaverville (lat. 40°55'45" N, long. 122°41'25" W; at S line sec. 32, T 36 N, R 7 W). Named on Schell Mountain (1950) 15' quadrangle.

Packers Creek [TRINITY]: *stream,* flows 3 miles to Big Creek (1) 7 miles north of Hayfork (lat. 40°39'15" N, long. 123°09'20" W; sec. 6, T 32 N, R 11 W). Named on Hayfork (1951) 15' quadrangle.

Packers Peak [TRINITY]: *peak,* 26 miles south of Etna, which is in Siskiyou County, on Trinity-Siskiyou County line (lat. 41°05'30" N, long. 122°58'10" W). Altitude 7828 feet. Named on Coffee Creek (1955) 15' quadrangle.

Packsaddle Creek [DEL NORTE]: *stream,* flows 4.5 miles to Middle Fork Smith River 11.5 miles east-northeast of Gasquet (lat. 41°54'40" N, long. 123°50'W). Named on Broken Rib Mountain (1982) and Shelly Creek Ridge (1982) 7.5' quadrangles.

Packsaddle Creek [LAKE]: *stream,* flows 4 miles to Rice Fork 2.5 miles southwest of Bear Mountain (lat. 39°23'05" N, long. 122°56'05" W; sec. 25, T 18 N, R 10 W). Named on Elk Mountain (1967) and Lake Pillsbury (1967) 7.5' quadrangles.

Packsaddle Ridge [HUMBOLDT]: *ridge,* north-northwest- to northwest-trending, 3.5 miles long, 10 miles east of Weitchpec (lat. 41°10'05" N, long. 123°30'55" W). Named on Hopkins Butte (1979) and Salmon Mountain (1978) 7.5' quadrangles.

Packwood Flat [TRINITY]: *area,* 7 miles east of Kettenpom (lat. 40°08'25" N, long. 123°20'W; near S line sec. 1, T 4 S, R 7 E). Named on Shannon Butte (1967) 7.5' quadrangle.

Packy Spring [HUMBOLDT]: *spring,* 5 miles east-southeast of Showers

Mountain (lat. 40°33'45" N, long. 123°36'45" W; sec. 9, T 2 N, R 5 E). Named on Blake Mountain (1979) 7.5' quadrangle.

Page Gulch [TRINITY]: *canyon,* drained by a stream that flows 1.5 miles to Dutton Creek 2.25 miles south-southwest of Weaverville (lat. 40°41'45" N, long. 122°58'20" W; at S line sec. 23, T 33 N, R 10 W). Named on Weaverville (1950) 15' quadrangle.

Painter Creek [HUMBOLDT]: *stream,* flows 1.5 miles to McKee Creek (1) 9 miles west-southwest of Garberville (lat. 40°04'05" N, long. 123°57'35" W; sec. 33, T 4 S, R 2 E). Named on Briceland (1969) 7.5' quadrangle.

Painter Gulch [HUMBOLDT]: *canyon,* 1.25 miles long, 6.5 miles north-northwest of Lone Star Junction (lat. 40°42'40" N, long. 123°56'30" W; mainly in sec. 22, T 4 N, R 2 E). Named on Iaqua Buttes (1979) 7.5' quadrangle.

Palace of the Oaks [TRINITY]: *locality,* 11 miles east-northeast of Weaverville (lat. 40°46'50" N, long. 122°44'50" W; near NW cor. sec. 26, T 34 N, R 8 W). Named on Schell Mountain (1950) 15' quadrangle.

Palace Rock [HUMBOLDT]: *relief feature,* 1.5 miles southeast of Yager Junction (lat. 40°32'N, long. 123°47'50" W; near SE cor. sec. 23, T 2 N, R 3 E). Named on Yager Junction (1979) 7.5' quadrangle. According to Turner (p. 165), the name is from a brothel that was in a tent near the feature—the word "palace" commonly was used for such an establishment.

Palmer Creek [HUMBOLDT]:

(1) *stream,* flows 2.25 miles to Mad River 2 miles west of Korbel (lat. 40°52'20" N, long. 123°59'55" W; sec. 30, T 6 N, R 2 E). Named on Arcata South (1959) 7.5' quadrangle.

(2) *stream,* flows 2.25 miles to lowlands along Eel River 1.25 miles west-northwest of Fortuna (lat. 40°36'20" N, long. 124°10'30" W; near NW cor. sec. 34, T 3 N, R 1 W). Named on Fields Landing (1959) and Fortuna (1959) 7.5' quadrangles.

Palmer Creek [LAKE]: *stream,* flows 3 miles to Soda Creek (2) 9 miles northeast of Middletown (lat. 38°51'35" N, long. 122°30'45" W; sec. 27, T 12 N, R 6 W). Named on Jericho Valley (1958), Middletown (1958), and Wilson Valley (1958) 7.5' quadrangles.

Palmer Creek [MENDOCINO]: *stream,* flows 1 mile to Billings Creek nearly 6 miles west-southwest of Ornbaun Valley (lat. 38°52'10" N, long. 123°23'40" W; sec. 23, T 12 N, R 14 W). Named on Ornbaun Valley (1960) 15' quadrangle.

Palmer Creek: see **Little Palmer Creek** [HUMBOLDT].

Palmers Point [HUMBOLDT]: *promontory,* 5 miles north-northwest of Trinidad (lat. 41°07'50" N, long. 124°09'50" W; near N line sec. 34, T 9 N, R 1 W); the promontory is part of the larger feature called Patricks Point (1). Named on Trinidad (1966) 7.5' quadrangle. Called Patricks Point on Trinidad (1952) 15' quadrangle, but United States Board on Geographic Names (1968a, p. 6) rejected this name for present Palmers Point.

Pamore Creek: see **Parramore Creek** [LAKE].

Pansy Gulch [TRINITY]: *canyon,* 1 mile long, on upper reaches of Gratten Creek 20 miles north-northeast of Weaverville (lat. 40°58'35" N, long. 122°45'W). Named on Schell Mountain (1950) and Trinity Dam (1950) 15' quadrangles.

Panther Basin [TRINITY]: *relief feature,* 13 miles south-southeast of Kettenpom (lat. 39°59'30" N, long. 123°18'55" W). Named on Mina (1967) 7.5' quadrangle.

Panther Camp [TRINITY]: *locality,* 11 miles east-northeast of Burnt Ranch (lat. 40°52'55" N, long. 123°17'25" W). Named on Ironside Mountain (1951) 15' quadrangle.

Panther Canyon [HUMBOLDT]: *canyon,* drained by a stream that flows 1.25 miles to East Branch of South Fork Eel River 2 miles southeast of Garberville (lat. 40°04'30" N, long. 123°46'10" W; near E line sec. 31, T 4 S, R 4 E). Named on Garberville (1970) 7.5' quadrangle.

Panther Canyon [LAKE]:

(1) *canyon,* drained by a stream that flows 2 miles to West Fork Middle Creek (2) 4.25 miles southwest of Three Crossings (lat. 39°17'N, long. 122°59'10" W; sec. 33, T 17 N, R 10 W). Named on Elk Mountain (1967) 7.5' quadrangle.

(2) *canyon,* drained by a stream that flows 2.5 miles to Wolf Creek nearly 6 miles northeast of Clearlake Oaks (lat. 39°05'N, long. 122°36'10" W; at N line sec. 11, T 14 N, R 7 W). Named on Clearlake Oaks (1960) 15' quadrangle.

Panther Creek [HUMBOLDT]:

(1) *stream,* flows 2.5 miles to Bradford Creek 12 miles south-southwest of the settlement of Willow Creek (lat. 40°47'15" N, long. 123°43'55" W; sec. 28, T 5 N, R 4 E). Named on Grouse Mountain (1979) 7.5' quadrangle.

(2) *stream,* flows nearly 2 miles to Shively Creek 3.25 miles north-northwest of Redcrest (lat. 40°26'30" N, long. 123°58'35" W; sec. 29, T 1 N, R 2 E). Named on Redcrest (1969) 7.5' quadrangle.

(3) *stream,* flows 2 miles to Little Van Duzen River 6.5 miles south of Dinsmore (lat. 40°23'45" N, long. 123°36'30" W; near E line sec. 9, T 1 S, R 5 E). Named on Dinsmore (1977) 7.5' quadrangle.

(4) *stream,* flows 3.25 miles to Redwood Creek (1) 4 miles southwest of Coyote Peak (lat. 41°05'20" N, long. 123°54'25" W; near NE cor. sec. 14, T 8 N, R 2 E). Named on Panther Creek (1982) 7.5' quadrangle.

(5) *stream,* flows 1 mile to Grouse Creek (2) 5 miles east-northeast of Board Camp Mountain (lat. 40°43'05" N, long. 123°37'40" W). Named on Board Camp Mountain (1977) 7.5' quadrangle.

(6) *stream,* flows 1.5 miles to Bull Creek (1) 14 miles south-southeast of Scotia (lat. 40°17'25" N, long. 124°00'35" W; at NE cor. sec. 24, T 2 S, R 2 E). Named on Bull Creek (1969) 7.5' quadrangle.

Panther Creek [LAKE]:

(1) *stream,* flows 5.25 miles to join Welch Creek and form Soda Creek (1) 5 miles west-northwest of Bear Mountain (lat. 39°26'20" N, long. 122°59'05" W; near SE cor. sec. 4, T 18 N, R 10 W). Named on Lake Pillsbury (1951) and Potter Valley (1960) 15' quadrangles. Called Cedar Creek on Pomo (1943) 15' quadrangle.

(2) *stream,* flows 2.5 miles to Willow Creek (2) 8 miles west-northwest of Lakeport (lat. 39°05'25" N, long. 123°03'15" W; sec. 10, T 14 N, R 11 W); the stream is west of Panther Ridge. Named on Purdys Gardens (1958) 7.5' quadrangle.

Panther Creek [TRINITY]:

(1) *stream,* flows 5.5 miles to New River 7.25 miles north-northeast of Burnt Ranch (lat. 40°54'20" N, long. 123°25'30" W). Named on Ironside Mountain (1951) 15' quadrangle.

(2) *stream,* flows 2.25 miles to Trinity River 7.25 miles east-southeast of Burnt Ranch (lat. 40°46'20" N, long. 123°20'50" W). Named on Ironside Mountain (1951) and Hyampom (1951) 15' quadrangles.

(3) *stream,* flows 1 mile to South Fork Trinity River 7.25 miles north-northwest of Hyampom (lat. 40°42'35" N, long. 123°31'05" W). Named on Sims Mountain (1979) 7.5' quadrangle.

(4) *stream,* flows 2.5 miles to join Bar Creek and form West Fork of North Fork Eel River 6.25 miles north-northeast of Kettenpom (lat. 40°14'40" N, long. 123°25'55" W; sec. 31, T 2 S, R 7 E); the stream is south of Panther Rock (2). Named on Zenia (1967) 7.5' quadrangle.

Panther Creek Camp [TRINITY]: *locality,* 7.25 miles north-northeast of Burnt Ranch along New River (lat. 40°54'30" N, long. 123°25'30" W); the place is near the mouth of Panther Creek (1). Named on Ironside Mountain (1951) 15' quadrangle.

Panther Flat Campground [DEL NORTE]: *locality,* 2 miles east of Gasquet along Middle Fork Smith River (lat. 41°50'35" N, long. 123°55'45" W). Named on Gasquet (1981) 7.5' quadrangle.

Panther Gap [HUMBOLDT]: *pass,* 14 miles south of Scotia (lat. 40°17'10" N, long. 124°07'55" W; sec. 22, T 2 S, R 1 E); the pass is near the head of a branch of Panther Creek (6). Named on Bull Creek (1969) 7.5' quadrangle.

Panther Gulch [TRINITY]: *canyon,* drained by a stream that flows nearly 2 miles to Salt Creek (4) 3.25 miles northeast of Dubakella Mountain (lat. 40°25'15" N, long. 123°06'15" W; sec. 28, T 30 N, R 11 W). Named on Dubakella Mountain (1954) 15' quadrangle.

Panther Peak [HUMBOLDT]: *peak,* 9.5 miles south-southwest of Alderpoint (lat. 40°03'40" N, long. 123°42'W; near N line sec. 2, T 5 S, R 4 E). Altitude 1862 feet. Named on Harris (1969) 7.5' quadrangle.

Panther Ridge [HUMBOLDT]: *ridge,* northeast- to east-northeast-trending, 2 miles long, center 1.25 miles southwest of the settlement of Willow Creek (lat. 40°55'45" N, long. 123°38'45" W). Named on Willow Creek (1979) 7.5' quadrangle.

Panther Ridge [LAKE]: *ridge,* north-northwest- to north-trending, 1 mile long, 8 miles west of Lakeport (lat. 39°03'50" N, long. 123°03'45" W; sec. 15, 22, T 14 N, R 11 W); the ridge is east of Panther Creek (2). Named on Purdys Gardens (1958) 7.5' quadrangle.

Panther Ridge [MENDOCINO]: *ridge,* northeast-trending, 2 miles long, 2.5 miles northeast of Hull Mountain (lat. 39°33'N, long. 122°54'W). Named on Hull Mountain (1967) 7.5' quadrangle.

Panther Rock [MENDOCINO]:

(1) *relief feature,* 5 miles northeast of Covelo (lat. 39°51'05" N, long. 123°11'35" W; near E line sec. 16, T 23 N, R 12 W). Named on Covelo East (1967) 7.5' quadrangle.

(2) *relief feature,* 3.5 miles northeast of Hull Mountain (lat. 39°33'45" N, long. 122°53'30" W; sec. 29, T 20 N, R 9 W). Named on Hull Mountain (1967) 7.5' quadrangle.

Panther Rock [TRINITY]:

(1) *relief feature,* 15 miles northeast of Trinity Center (lat. 41°10'05" N, long. 122°29'20" W; at W line sec. 7, T 38 N, R 5 W). Named on Dunsmuir (1954) 15' quadrangle.

(2) *relief feature,* 6.25 miles north of Kettenpom (lat. 40°14'50" N, long. 123°26'25" W; sec. 36, T 2 S, R 6 E); the feature is north of Panther Creek (4). Named on Zenia (1967) 7.5' quadrangle.

(3) *peak,* 3.25 miles north of Kettenpom (lat. 40°12'20" N, long. 123°27'35" W; near E line sec. 14, T 3 S, R 6 E). Named on Kettenpom (1955) 15' quadrangle.

Panwauket Gulch [TRINITY]: *canyon,* drained by a stream that flows 3 miles to Reading Creek 10 miles south-southeast of Weaverville (lat. 40°35'40" N, long. 122°53'55" W; near SW cor. sec. 28, T 32 N, R 9 W). Named on Weaverville (1950) 15' quadrangle. Called Panweckett Cr. on

Averill's (1940) map.

Papoose: see **Papoose Creek** [TRINITY].

Papoose Creek [TRINITY]: *stream*, formed by the confluence of East Fork and South Fork, flows 4.25 miles to Trinity River 10.5 miles north-northeast of Weaverville (lat. 40°48'20" N, long. 122°45'45" W; sec. 15, T 34 N, R 8 W). Named on Schell Mountain (1950) and Trinity Lake (1950) 15' quadrangles. East Fork is 1.5 miles long and South Fork is 2.25 miles long; both forks are named on Schell Mountain (1950) 15' quadrangle. North Fork enters from the northeast less than 1 mile downstream from the confluence of East Fork and South Fork; it is 2.5 miles long and is named on Schell Mountain (1950) 15' quadrangle. The mouth of Papoose Creek is about 4 miles by road south-southeast of Old Minersville; according to Salley (p. 166), postal authorities established Papoose post office 4 miles south-southeast of Minersville in 1904 and discontinued it in 1909.

Papoose Creek: see **Little Papoose Creek** [TRINITY].

Papoose Lake [TRINITY]: *lake*, 1700 feet long, 14 miles north of Helena (lat. 40°57'20" N, long. 123°27'W). Named on Helena (1951) 15' quadrangle.

Pappas Flat [DEL NORTE]: *area*, just west of Gasquet along Smith River (lat. 41°50'45" N, long. 123°59'45" W; sec. 19, T 17 N, R 2 E). Named on Gasquet (1981) 7.5' quadrangle.

Paradise: see **Shively** [HUMBOLDT].

Paradise Canyon [LAKE]:

(1) *canyon*, drained by a stream that flows nearly 1 mile to North Fork Cache Creek 7 miles east-northeast of Clearlake Oaks (lat. 39°04'15" N, long. 122°33'35" W); the canyon heads opposite the head of Paradise Canyon (2). Named on Clearlake Oaks (1960) 15' quadrangle.

(2) *canyon*, drained by a stream that flows less than 1 mile to Benmore Canyon 8 miles east-northeast of Clearlake Oaks (lat. 39°02'45" N, long. 122°31'55" W; sec. 21, T 14 N, R 6 W); the canyon heads opposite the head of Paradise Canyon (1). Named on Clearlake Oaks (1960) 15' quadrangle.

Paradise Cove [LAKE]: *embayment*, 2.5 miles west-southwest of Clearlake Oaks along Clear Lake just east of Sulphur Bank Point (lat. 39°00'25" N, long. 122°43'10" W; sec. 2, T 13 N, R 8 W). Named on Clearlake Oaks (1958) 7.5' quadrangle.

Paradise Flat [DEL NORTE]: *area*, 10 miles northwest of Buck Mountain along South Fork Smith River (lat. 41°44'45" N, long. 123°59'05" W). Named on Cant Hook Mountain (1982) 7.5' quadrangle.

Paradise Peak [TRINITY]: *peak*, 16 miles southeast of Weaverville on Trinity-Shasta County line (lat. 40°33'15" N, long. 122°44'35" W; sec. 11, T 31 N, R 8 W). Named on Shasta Bally (1978) 7.5' quadrangle.

Paradise Ridge [HUMBOLDT]: *ridge*, southeast- to south-trending, 4 miles long, 5.5 miles north-northeast of Point Delgado (lat. 40°06'N, long. 124°02'20" W). Named on Shelter Cove (1969) 7.5' quadrangle.

Paradise Valley [LAKE]:

(1) *valley*, 9 miles east of Lakeport on the north side of The Narrows (2) (lat. 39°02'45" N, long. 122°45'15" W; sec. 21, 28, T 14 N, R 8 W). Named on Clearlake Oaks (1958) and Lucerne (1958) 7.5' quadrangles.

(2) *valley*, 2.5 miles southeast of Jericho Valley along Jericho Creek at its confluence with Hunting Creek (lat. 38°48'20" N, long. 122°24'W; mainly in sec. 15, T 11 N, R 5 W). Named on Jericho Valley (1958) 7.5' quadrangle.

Paradise Valley [MENDOCINO]: *valley*, 3.25 miles north of Eden Valley (lat. 39°40'30" N, long. 123°11'45" W). Named on Jamison Ridge (1967) 7.5' quadrangle.

Paragon Bay: see **Crescent City** [DEL NORTE].

Paralyze Canyon [MENDOCINO]: *canyon*, drained by a stream that flows 2.5 miles to Elder Creek 4.5 miles north-northeast of Branscomb (lat. 39°43'05" N, long. 123°36'10" W; near NE cor. sec. 34, T 22 N, R 16 W). Named on Cahto Peak (1967) 7.5' quadrangle.

Paramore Spring: see **Parramore Springs** [LAKE].

Pardaloe Creek [MENDOCINO]: *stream*, flows 4 miles to Garcia River 2.5 miles southwest of Ornbaun Valley (lat. 38°53'15" N, long. 123°20'30" W; sec. 18, T 12 N, R 13 W); the stream heads at Pardaloe Peak. Named on Ornbaun Valley (1960) 15' quadrangle.

Pardaloe Peak [MENDOCINO]: *peak*, 3.5 miles south-southeast of Ornbaun Valley (lat. 38°51'50" N, long. 123°16'40" W; near N line sec. 26, T 12 N, R 13 W). Named on Ornbaun Valley (1960) 15' quadrangle.

Pardee Creek [HUMBOLDT]: *stream*, flows 2.5 miles to Redwood Creek (1) 12.5 miles south-southwest of the settlement of Willow Creek (lat. 40°46'45" N, long. 123°44'10" W; near NW cor. sec. 33, T 5 N, R 4 E). Named on Grouse Mountain (1979) and Maple Creek (1977) 7.5' quadrangles.

Parington Creek: see **Perington Creek** [HUMBOLDT].

Parker Creek [MENDOCINO]: *stream*, flows 1.5 miles to Indian Creek (2) 2.5 miles west-northwest of Piercy (lat. 39°59'05" N, long. 123°50'30" W; near S line sec. 28, T 5 S, R 3 E). Named on Piercy (1969) 7.5' quadrangle.

Parker Creek [TRINITY]: *stream*, flows 2.5 miles to Swift Creek (1) 9.5 miles south-southwest of Billys Peak (1) (lat. 41°00'15" N, long. 122°50'10" W; at E line sec. 1, T 36 N, R 9 W). Named on Coffee Creek (1955) 15' quadrangle.

Parker Meadow [TRINITY]: *area*, 9.5 miles south-southwest of Billys Peak (1) along Swift Creek (1) (lat. 41°00'35" N, long. 122°51'W; on W line sec. 1, T 36 N, R 9 W). Named on Coffee Creek (1955) 15' quadrangle.

Park Gulch [MENDOCINO]: *canyon*, drained by a stream that flows 1.25 miles to Chamberlain Creek 7 miles north-northeast of Comptche (lat. 39°21'40" N, long. 123°33'15" W; sec. 5, T 17 N, R 15 W). Named on Comptche (1960) 15' quadrangle.

Parkhurst Ridge [HUMBOLDT]: *ridge*, generally south-trending, 3 miles long, 14 miles south of Scotia (lat. 40°17'N, long. 124°09'W). Named on Buckeye Mountain (1970) 7.5' quadrangle. The name commemorates William Jefferson Parkhurst (Turner, p. 166).

Parkinson Gulch [MENDOCINO]: *canyon*, drained by a stream that flows 2.25 miles to Indian Creek (1) 6 miles north-northwest of Boonville (lat. 39°05'10" N, long. 123°24'40" W; sec. 9, T 14 N, R 14 W). Named on Boonville (1959) 15' quadrangle.

Parlin Creek [MENDOCINO]: *stream*, flows 4.5 miles to South Fork Noyo River 8 miles north-northwest of Comptche (lat. 39°22'10" N, long. 123°39'30" W; at N line sec. 4, T 17 N, R 16 W). Named on Comptche (1960) 15' quadrangle.

Parramore Creek [LAKE]: *stream*, flows 4.5 miles to Rice Fork 4.25 miles southwest of Potato Hill (lat. 39°18'50" N, long. 122°51'55" W; near W line sec. 22, T 17 N, R 9 W). Named on Elk Mountain (1967) and Potato Hill (1967) 7.5' quadrangles. Called Pamore Creek on Hullville (1922) 15' quadrangle.

Parramore Springs [LAKE]: *locality*, 2.25 miles east of Three Crossings (lat. 39°18'50" N, long. 122°52'45" W; sec. 21, T 17 N, R 9 W). Named on Elk Mountain (1967) 7.5' quadrangle. On Lake Pillsbury (1951) 15' quadrangle, the name applies to a spring at the site. Waring (p. 203) called the feature Paramore Spring.

Parry Gulch: see **Perry Gulch** [TRINITY].

Parsons Creek [MENDOCINO]: *stream*, flows 6.25 miles to Russian River 9 miles south-southeast of Ukiah (lat. 39°02'20" N, long. 123°07'35" W). Named on Purdys Gardens (1958) 7.5' quadrangle.

Pasture Gulch [TRINITY]: *canyon*, drained by a stream that flows 1.5 miles to Hayfork Creek 8 miles east of Hyampom (lat. 40°37'30" N, long. 123°17'50" W; sec. 20, T 3 N, R 8 E). Named on Hyampom (1951) 15' quadrangle.

Patrick Creek [DEL NORTE]:

(1) *stream*, formed by the confluence of East Fork and West Fork, flows 3.25 miles to Middle Fork Smith River 6.5 miles east-northeast of Gasquet (lat. 41°52'25" N, long. 123°50'35" W; near N line sec. 16, T 17 N, R 3 E). Named on Shelly Creek Ridge (1982) 7.5' quadrangle. East Fork is 4.5 miles long and West Fork is 2.5 miles long. Both forks are named on Shelly Creek Ridge (1982) 7.5' quadrangle.

(2) *locality*, 7 miles east-northeast of Gasquet (lat. 41°52'30" N, long. 123°50'35" W; near S line sec. 9, T 17 N, R 3 E). Named on Shelly Creek Ridge (1982) 7.5' quadrangle. Gasquet (1945) 15' quadrangle shows Old Patrick Creek Guard Station situated nearly 3 miles north-northwest of present Patrick Creek (2) at the forks of Patrick Creek (1)—Preston Peak (1922) 30'quadrangle shows Patrick Creek Station at this same site.

Patrick Creek [HUMBOLDT]: *stream*, flows 1.25 miles to the sea 8.5 miles north of Arcata (lat. 40°59'50" N, long. 124°06'55" W; sec. 18, T 7 N, R 1 E). Named on Arcata North (1959) 7.5' quadrangle.

Patrick Creek Campground [DEL NORTE]: *locality*, 6.5 miles east-southeast of Gasquet (lat. 41°52'20" N, long. 123°50'40" W; sec. 16, T 17 N, R 3 E); the place is along Middle Fork Smith River near the mouth of Patrick Creek (1). Named on Hurdygurdy Butte (1982) 7.5' quadrangle.

Patricks Point [HUMBOLDT]:

(1) *promontory*, 5.25 miles north of Trinidad along the coast (lat. 41°08'N, long. 124°09'30" W; sec. 27, 34, T 9 N, R 1 W). Named on Trinidad (1966) 7.5' quadrangle. This large promontory includes present Rocky Point, Abalone Point, and Palmers Point. On Trinidad (1952) 15' quadrangle, the name "Patricks Point" applies to present Palmers Point. Gudde (1949, p. 255) associated the name with Patrick Beegan, who had a ranch 6 miles north of Trinidad.

(2) *settlement*, 4.5 miles north of Trinidad (lat. 41°07'30" N, long. 124°09'20" W; on W line sec. 35, T 9 N, R 1 W); the place is just south of Patrick Point (1). Named on Trinidad (1966) 7.5' quadrangle.

Patsy Creek [MENDOCINO]: *stream*, flows 2.25 miles to North Fork Ten Mile Creek 6 miles south-southeast of Sherwood Peak (lat. 39°34'50" N, long. 123°34'20" W; near S line sec. 18, T 20 N, R 15 W). Named on Sherwood Peak (1967) 7.5' quadrangle.

Pattison Peak [TRINITY]: *peak*, 7 miles northeast of Hyampom (lat. 40°40'35" N, long. 123°20'40" W; near W line sec. 36, T 4 N, R 7 E). Altitude 5151 feet. Named on Hyampom (1951) 15' quadrangle.

Pauls Point [TRINITY]: *peak*, 4 miles east-northeast of Alderpoint [HUMBOLDT] (lat. 41°12'10" N, long. 123°32'25" W; near E line sec. 18, T 3 S, R 6 E). Named on Alderpoint (1969) 7.5' quadrangle.

Payne [TRINITY]: *locality,* 5 miles west-northwest of Black Rock Mountain (lat. 40°14'30" N, long. 123°05'30" W; sec. 27, T 28 N, R 11 W). Named on Black Rock Mountain (1954) 15' quadrangle.

Peachtree Crossing [LAKE]: *locality,* 3 miles northeast of the town of Lower Lake along Cache Creek (lat. 38°56'10" N, long. 122°34'W). Named on Lower Lake (1958) 7.5' quadrangle.

Peachtree Flat [MENDOCINO]: *area,* 12 miles southwest of Ornbaun Valley along North Fork Gualala River (lat. 38°48'15" N, long. 123°28'50" W; sec. 13, T 11 N, R 15 W). Named on Ornbaun Valley (1960) 15' quadrangle.

Peacock Creek [DEL NORTE]: *stream,* flows nearly 3 miles to Smith River 7 miles northeast of Crescent City (lat. 41°49'55" N, long. 124°06'40" W; sec. 30, T 17 N, R 1 E). Named on Hiouchi (1966) 7.5' quadrangle. Gold was discovered 6 miles from Crescent City in 1854 on a stream—presumably this one—that empties into Smith River at White and Miller Ferry, later known as Peacock's Ferry (Hoover, Rensch, and Rensch, p. 71).

Peacock Point [LAKE]: *peak,* 3.5 miles north-northwest of the town of Lower Lake (lat. 38°57'25" N, long. 122°38'30" W; sec. 21, T 13 N, R 7 W). Named on Clearlake Highlands (1958) 7.5' quadrangle.

Peacock's Ferry: see **Peacock Creek** [DEL NORTE].

Peaked Creek [HUMBOLDT]: *stream,* flows nearly 3 miles to Bear River 6 miles southwest of Scotia (lat. 40°26'N, long. 124°11'35" W; near SW cor. sec. 28, T 1 N, R 1 W). Named on Taylor Peak (1969) 7.5' quadrangle.

Peaked Prairie [HUMBOLDT]: *area,* 6 miles southwest of Scotia (lat. 40°25'10" N, long. 124°10'50" W; around SE cor. sec. 33, T 1 N, R 1 W); the place is east of Peaked Creek. Named on Taylor Peak (1969) 7.5' quadrangle.

Peaked Prairie: see **Upper Peaked Prairie** [HUMBOLDT].

Peak 8 [DEL NORTE]: *peak,* 11.5 miles east-northeast of Klamath Glen (lat. 41°33'05" N, long. 123°46'30" W). Altitude 5188 feet. Named on Summit Valley (1981) 7.5' quadrangle.

Peaks: see **The Peaks** [HUMBOLDT].

Peanut [TRINITY]: *village,* 6 miles north-northwest of Dubakella Mountain (lat. 40°28'N, long. 123°10'10" W; sec. 12, T 30 N, R 12 W). Named on Dubakella Mountain (1954) 15' quadrangle. Postal authorities established Peanut post office in 1900 and discontinued it in 1933; the community at the place was called Salt Creek, but postal officials rejected this name for the post office there—the postmaster of Weaverville claimed that he suggested the name "Peanut" for the post office in jest while he was eating peanuts, and postal authorities accepted it (Salley, p. 168).

Pearch Creek [HUMBOLDT]: *stream,* flows 4 miles to Klamath River 1 mile northeast of Orleans (lat. 41°18'45" N, long. 123°31'25" W). Named on Orleans (1978) and Orleans Mountain (1974) 7.5' quadrangles. Called Perch Creek on Orleans (1952) 15' quadrangle, and United States Board on Geographic Names (1977c, p. 5) gave this name as a variant. South Fork enters from the south less than 1 mile upstream from the mouth of the main creek; it is 2 miles long and is named on Orleans (1978) and Orleans Mountain (1974) 7.5' quadrangles.

Pearch Creek Campground [HUMBOLDT]: *locality,* 1 mile east-northeast of Orleans (lat. 41°18'35" N, long. 123°31'10" W); the place is along Pearch Creek. Named on Orleans (1978) 7.5' quadrangle. Called Perch Creek Campground on Orleans (1952) 15' quadrangle.

Pear Tree Gulch [TRINITY]: *canyon,* drained by a stream that flows less than 1 mile to Trinity River nearly 1 mile southeast of Helena (lat. 40°46'N, long. 123°06'50" W). Named on Helena (1951) 15' quadrangle.

Peat Pasture Gulch [MENDOCINO]: *canyon,* 0.5 mile long, 2 miles southeast of Navarro on upper reaches of Floodgate Creek (lat. 39°07'55" N, long. 123°31'15" W; sec. 28, T 15 N, R 15 W). Named on Navarro (1961) 15' quadrangle.

Peavine Ridge [HUMBOLDT]: *ridge,* generally west-northwest-trending, 3.25 miles long, 8.5 miles south-southeast of Scotia (lat. 40°22'35" N, long. 124°00'45" W). Named on Redcrest (1969), Scotia (1970), and Weott (1969) 7.5' quadrangles.

Peavine Ridge [LAKE]: *ridge,* southwest-trending, 1 mile long, 4 miles north-northeast of Crockett Peak (lat. 39°29'N, long. 122°45'15" W). Named on Crockett Peak (1967) 7.5' quadrangle.

Pebble Beach [DEL NORTE]: *beach,* 1.5 miles west-northwest of Crescent City along the coast (lat. 41°45'55" N, long. 124°13'50" W). Named on Crescent City (1966) 7.5' quadrangle.

Pecwan [HUMBOLDT]: *locality,* 1 mile east-southeast of Johnsons along Klamath River (lat. 41°20'40" N, long. 123°51'10" W; sec. 17, T 11 N, R 3 E); the place is near the mouth of Pecwan Creek. Named on Johnsons (1982) 7.5' quadrangle.

Pecwan Creek [HUMBOLDT]: *stream,* flows 6.5 miles to Klamath River 1 mile east-southeast of Johnsons (lat. 41°20'30" N, long. 123°51'10" W; sec. 17, T 11 N, R 3 E). Named on Blue Creek Mountain (1982) and Johnsons (1982) 7.5' quadrangles. The name "Pecwan" is from an Indian village that was situated near the mouth of the creek (Kroeber, p. 54). East Fork, which heads in Del Norte County, enters from the east 0.5 mile upstream from the mouth of the main creek and is 7.5 miles long. West Fork enters nearly 3 miles upstream from the mouth of the main creek and is 3.5 miles long. Both forks are named on Blue Creek Mountain (1982) and Johnsons (1982) 7.5' quadrangles. An early military post called Fort Capell was located on the west side of Klamath River opposite and a little south of the mouth of Pecwan Creek (Whiting and Whiting, p. 18).

Pecwan Ridge [HUMBOLDT]: *ridge,* generally northwest-trending, 3 miles long, 2.5 miles northwest of Johnsons (lat. 41°22'45" N, long. 123°53'50" W). Named on Ah Pah Ridge (1983) and Holter Ridge (1983) 7.5' quadrangles.

Pedro Opening [MENDOCINO]: *area,* 5.5 miles east-southeast of Leggett (lat. 39°49'05" N, long. 123°37'45" W; sec. 28, T 23 N, R 16 W). Named on Leggett (1969) 7.5' quadrangle.

Pedro Ridge [MENDOCINO]: *ridge,* generally north-trending, 2 miles long, 3.5 miles west-northwest of Eden Valley (lat. 39°39'15" N, long. 123°14'45" W). Named on Jamison Ridge (1967) 7.5' quadrangle.

Pegleg Camp [TRINITY]: *locality,* 7.25 miles south of Cecilville, which is in Siskiyou County, along North Fork Trinity River (lat. 41°01'40" N, long. 123°09'30" W). Site named on Cecil Lake (1979) 7.5' quadrangle.

Pelican Bay [DEL NORTE]: *embayment,* along the coast between Point Saint George and the mouth of Smith River (lat. 41°52'N, long. 124°13'W). Named on Crescent City (1966) and Smith River (1966) 7.5' quadrangles. Crescent City (1952) 15' quadrangle has the name at the south end of the embayment. Called B. del Pellicana on Ferry's (1851) map.

Pelican Rock [DEL NORTE]: *rock,* 1000 feet offshore at Crescent City (lat. 41°44'40" N, long. 124°11'05" W). Named on Sister Rocks (1966) 7.5' quadrangle.

Pelletreau Creek [TRINITY]:

(1) *stream,* flows 1.5 miles to Trinity River 7.5 miles east-southeast of Burnt Ranch (lat. 40°46'50" N, long. 123°20'W). Named on Ironside Mountain (1951) 15' quadrangle.

(2) *stream,* flows 6.5 miles to South Fork Trinity River 1.25 miles west-northwest of Hyampom (lat. 40°37'45" N, long. 123°28'25" W; sec. 23, T 3 N, R 6 E). Named on Hyampom (1951) 15' quadrangle, and on Blake Mountain (1979) 7.5' quadrangle.

Pelletreau Ridge [TRINITY]: *ridge,* generally north-trending, 3.5 miles long, 3 miles south-southwest of Hyampom (lat. 40°34'45" N, long. 123°28'15" W); the ridge is east of Pelletreau Creek (2). Named on Hyampom (1951) 15' quadrangle.

Pences: see **Bartlett Springs** [LAKE].

Peninsula: see **The Peninsula** [LAKE].

Penn Creek [HUMBOLDT]: *stream,* flows 1.5 miles to the sea 5 miles north of Trinidad (lat. 41°08'N, long. 124°09'35" W; sec. 27, T 9 N, R 1 W). Named on Trinidad (1966) 7.5' quadrangle.

Penney [TRINITY]: *locality,* 4.5 miles west of Black Rock Mountain along South Fork Trinity River (lat. 40°11'55" N, long. 123°05'45" W; sec. 10, T 27 N, R 11 W); the place is at the north end of Penney Ridge. Named on Black Rock Mountain (1954) 15' quadrangle.

Penney Glades [TRINITY]: *area,* 5.5 miles west of Black Rock Mountain (lat. 40°11'50" N, long. 123°06'45" W; sec. 9, T 27 N, R 11 W); the place is west of Penney. Named on Black Rock Mountain (1954) 15' quadrangle.

Penney Ridge [TRINITY]: *ridge,* north- to north-northwest-trending, 3.5 miles long, 4.5 miles west-southwest of Black Rock Mountain (lat. 40°10'15" N, long. 123°05'W). Named on Black Rock Mountain (1954) 15' quadrangle.

Penny: see **Little Penny** [MENDOCINO].

Pepper Gap [MENDOCINO]: *pass,* 11.5 miles southeast of Laytonville (lat. 39°33'25" N, long. 123°20'30" W; at N line sec. 31, T 20 N, R 13 W). Named on Willis Ridge (1966) 7.5' quadrangle.

Pepperwood [HUMBOLDT]: *village,* 3.5 miles northwest of Redcrest (lat. 40°26'45" N, long. 123°59'15" W; on S line sec. 19, T 1 N, R 2 E). Named on Redcrest (1969) 7.5' quadrangle. Postal authorities established Pepperwood post office in 1887, discontinued it in 1892, reestablished it in 1901, and discontinued it in 1965 (Salley, p. 169). The name is from a fine grove of California laurel, also called pepperwood (Gudde, 1949, p. 258). The place also was called Barkdull (Turner, p. 167).

Pepperwood Corrals [TRINITY]: *locality,* 9.5 miles south of Kettenpom (lat. 40°01'15" N, long. 123°26'50" W; sec. 13, T 5 S, R 6 E). Named on Lake Mountain (1967) 7.5' quadrangle.

Pepperwood Creek [MENDOCINO]: *stream,* flows 2 miles to Hulls Creek 9 miles north-northeast of Covelo (lat. 39°55'10" N, long. 123°11'45" W). Named on Bluenose Ridge (1967) 7.5' quadrangle.

Pepperwood Creek: see **Big Pepperwood Creek** [MENDOCINO].

Pepperwood Falls [HUMBOLDT]: *waterfall,* 3 miles west of Bridgeville (lat. 40°27'50" N, long. 123°51'15" W; near E line sec. 17, T 1 N, R 3 E). Named on Bridgeville (1969) 7.5' quadrangle.

Pepperwood Grove [LAKE]: *settlement,* 7.5 miles east of Lakeport along Clear Lake (lat. 39°03'30" N, long. 122°46'45" W; at SE cor. sec. 18, T 14 N, R 8 W). Named on Lucerne (1958) 7.5' quadrangle.

Pepperwood Gulch [MENDOCINO]: *canyon,* drained by a stream that flows nearly 1 mile to String Creek 6.5 miles north-northeast of Willits (lat. 39°29'10" N, long. 123°17'15" W; sec. 22, T 19 N, R 13 W). Named on Willits (1961) 15' quadrangle.

Pepperwood Spring [HUMBOLDT]: *spring,* 3 miles north-northeast of Point Delgada (lat. 40°03'40" N, long. 124°03'05" W; near N line sec. 3, T 5 S, R 1 E). Named on Shelter Cove (1969) 7.5' quadrangle.

Pepperwood Springs [HUMBOLDT]: *spring,* 5 miles west of Alderpoint (lat. 40°11'30" N, long. 123°42'10" W). Named on Fort Seward (1969) 7.5' quadrangle. On Alderpoint (1949) 15' quadrangle, the name applies to a locality at the site.

Perch Creek: see **Pearch Creek** [HUMBOLDT].

Perch Creek Campground: see **Pearch Creek Campground** [HUMBOLDT].

Peridotite Canyon [DEL NORTE]: *canyon,* drained by a stream that flows 5 miles to North Fork Smith River 3.5 miles north-northwest of Gasquet (lat. 41°53'45" N, long. 123°58'55" W; sec. 6, T 17 N, R 2 E). Named on Gasquet (1951) 15' quadrangle.

Perington Creek [HUMBOLDT]: *stream,* flows 3.5 miles to Jewett Creek (2) 5.25 miles south of Alderpoint (lat. 40°06'10" N, long. 123°37'35" W; sec. 21, T 4 S, R 5 E). Named on Harris (1969) 7.5' quadrangle. Called Purington Creek on Alderpoint (1949) 15' quadrangle. United States Board on Geographic Names (1973a, p. 3) gave the names "Durington Creek," "Parington Creek," and "Purington Creek" as variants.

Perini Creek [LAKE]: *stream,* flows nearly 2 miles to Seigler Canyon Creek 1.5 miles west-southwest of the town of Lower Lake (lat. 38°54'15" N, long. 122°38'15" W; sec. 9, T 12 N, R 7 W). Named on Clearlake Highlands (1958) 7.5' quadrangle.

Perini Hill [LAKE]: *peak,* 3.25 miles southwest of the town of Lower Lake (lat. 38°52'35" N, long. 122°39'05" W; near E line sec. 20, T 12 N, R 7 W). Named on Clearlake Highlands (1958) and Whispering Pines (1958) 7.5' quadrangles.

Perkins Creek [LAKE]: *stream,* flows 5 miles to North Fork Cache Creek 7 miles northeast of the town of Lower Lake (lat. 38°59'05" N, long. 122°31'10" W). Named on Lower Lake (1958) 7.5' quadrangle. G.F. Becker (p. 239) called the feature Perkins's Creek.

Perkins Creek Ridge [LAKE]: *ridge,* generally northeast-trending, 3 miles long, 5 miles northeast of the town of Lower Lake (lat. 38°37'45" N, long. 122°53'10" W); the ridge is southeast of Perkins Creek. Named on Lower Lake (1958) 7.5' quadrangle.

Perrott Creek [HUMBOLDT]: *stream,* flows nearly 1.5 miles to Eel River flood plain 2.5 miles north of Weott (lat. 40°21'30" N, long. 123°54'55" W; near S line sec. 23, T 1 S, R 2 E). Named on Weott (1969) 7.5' quadrangle.

Perry Gulch [MENDOCINO]: *canyon,* drained by a stream that flows nearly 3 miles to Navarro River 2.5 miles southwest of Navarro (lat. 39°07'40" N, long. 123°34'45" W; sec. 25, T 15 N, R 16 W). Named on Navarro (1961) 15' quadrangle.

Perry Gulch [TRINITY]: *canyon,* drained by a stream that flows 1.5 miles to Gratten Flat 20 miles north-northeast of Weaverville (lat. 40°58'30" N, long. 122°44'30" W; sec. 14, T 36 N, R 8 W). Named on Schell Mountain (1950) and Trinity Dam (1950) 15' quadrangles. United States Board on Geographic Names (1983d, p. 6) approved the name "Parry Gulch" for the canyon, and noted that the feature reportedly was named for John W. Parry, an early settler who mined there.

Perry Ridge [MENDOCINO]: *ridge,* south-trending, 1.25 miles long, 3.25 miles north-northwest of Covelo (lat. 39°50'20" N, long. 123°16'10" W; mainly in sec. 23, T 23 N, R 13 W). Named on Covelo West (1967) 7.5' quadrangle.

Perry Ridge Lake [MENDOCINO]: *intermittent lake,* 150 feet long, 4 miles north-northwest of Covelo (lat. 39°50'50" N, long. 123°16'05" W; near SE cor. sec. 14, T 23 N, R 13 W); the feature is near the north end of Perry Ridge. Named on Covelo West (1967) 7.5' quadrangle.

Perry Salt Log [TRINITY]: *locality,* nearly 4 miles south of Black Lassic (lat. 40°17'10" N, long. 123°31'45" W). Named on Black Lassic (1979) 7.5' quadrangle.

Perrys Knob [TRINITY]: *relief feature,* 9.5 miles east-northeast of Kettenpom (lat. 40°13'50" N, long. 123°18'25" W; near E line sec. 6, T 3 S, R 8 E). Named on Shannon Butte (1967) 7.5' quadrangle.

Perry Slough [HUMBOLDT]: *water feature,* joins Salt River 4.25 miles west of Fortuna (lat. 40°40'15" N, long. 124°14'W). Named on Fortuna (1959) 7.5' quadrangle.

Peter B Gulch [HUMBOLDT]: *canyon,* drained by a stream that flows nearly 1.5 miles to the sea 3.25 miles west of Petrolia (lat. 40°19'10" N, long. 124°20'15" W; sec. 1, T 2 S, R 3 W). Named on Petrolia (1969) 7.5' quadrangle. The name is for Peter B. Smith, who lived in the neighborhood of Petrolia (Turner, p. 168).

Peterptor Creek [TRINITY]: *stream,* flows 3.5 miles to Casoose Creek 17 miles south-southwest of Black Rock Mountain (lat. 40°00'20" N, long. 123°11'45" W; near W line sec. 22, T 25 N, R 12 W). Named on Black Rock Mountain (1954) 15' quadrangle.

Peters: see **Jack Peters Gulch** [MENDOCINO].

Peterson Creek [MENDOCINO]: *stream,* flows 2.5 miles to Tenmile Creek 10.5 miles southeast of Leggett (lat. 39°45'15" N, long. 123°35'05" W; near SW cor. sec. 18, T 22 N, R 15 W). Named on Cahto Peak (1967) and Tan Oak Park (1969) 7.5' quadrangles.

Peterson Gulch [MENDOCINO]:

(1) *canyon,* drained by a stream that flows less than 1 mile to South Fork Noyo River 10 miles north-northwest of Comptche (lat. 39°23'15" N, long. 123°40'50" W; near E line sec. 30, T 18 N, R 16 W). Named on Comptche (1960) 15' quadrangle.

(2) *canyon,* drained by a stream that flows 1.5 miles to Big River 4.25 miles northwest of Comptche (lat. 39°18'25" N, long. 123°38'40" W; near E line sec. 28, T 17 N, R 16 W). Named on Comptche (1960) 15' quadrangle.

Peterson Opening [HUMBOLDT-MENDOCINO]: *area,* 12.5 miles southwest of Alderpoint on Humboldt-Mendocino County line (lat. 40°00'10" N, long. 123°40'10" W; near SE cor. sec. 24, T 5 S, R 4 E). Named on Harris (1969) and Noble Butte (1969) 7.5' quadrangles.

Peterson Ridge [MENDOCINO]: *ridge,* west-trending, 2 miles long, 5.5 miles west-northwest of Boonville (lat. 39°02'30" N, long. 123°27'45" W). Named on Boonville (1959) 15' quadrangle.

Petes Pasture [TRINITY]: *area,* nearly 2 miles north-northeast of Forest Glen (lat. 40°23'55" N, long. 123°18'50" W; sec. 7, T 1 S, R 8 E). Named on Naufus Creek (1979) 7.5' quadrangle.

Petrified Canyon [LAKE]: *canyon,* drained by a stream that flows nearly 3 miles to Cache Creek 1.25 miles southeast of Wilson Valley (2) (lat. 38°57'25" N, long. 122°27'20" W; sec. 19, T 13 N, R 5 W). Named on Wilson Valley (1958) 7.5' quadrangle.

Petrolia [HUMBOLDT]: *village,* 10 miles southeast of Cape Mendocino near Mattole River (lat. 40°19'30" N, long. 124°17'05" W; sec. 3, T 2 S, R 2 W). Named on Petrolia (1969) 7.5' quadrangle. Postal authorities established Mattole post office in 1863, changed the name to Petrolea in 1865, and changed the name to Petrolia the same year (Salley, p. 135, 170). The place first was called "New Jerusalem," but in 1865 following shipment of crude oil from nearby oil wells—the first wells drilled for oil in California—the name was changed to Petrolia (Hoover, Rensch, and Rensch, p. 103.)

Petticoat Mountain [LAKE]: *peak,* 3.25 miles west-northwest of Jericho Valley (lat. 38°50'45" N, long. 122°29'30" W; sec. 35, T 12 N, R 6 W). Altitude 2121 feet. Named on Jericho Valley (1958) 7.5' quadrangle. The name is from the shape of the peak, which somewhat resembles an old-fashioned petticoat (Gudde, 1969, p. 244).

Pettijohn Basin [TRINITY]: *relief feature,* 1 mile east of Black Rock Mountain (lat. 40°12'10" N, long. 122°59'05" W; sec. 9, 10, T 27 N, R 10 W). Named on Yolla Bolly (1954) 15' quadrangle.

Pettijohn Mountain [TRINITY]: *peak,* 8 miles east-northeast of Weaverville (lat. 40°47'10" N, long. 122°48'30" W; sec. 19, T 34 N, R 8 W). Altitude 3590 feet. Named on Trinity Dam (1950) 15' quadrangle. Called Pettijohn Pk. on Weaverville (1913) 30'quadrangle.

Pettijohn Peak: see **Pettijohn Mountain** [TRINITY].

Petty Flat [HUMBOLDT]: *area,* 2 miles west-southwest of Bridgeville along Van Duzen River (lat. 40°27'45" N, long. 123°50'15" W; near E line sec. 16, T 1 N, R 3 E). Named on Bridgeville (1969) 7.5' quadrangle.

Pewetole Island [HUMBOLDT]: *island,* 550 feet long, 0.5 mile west-northwest of Trinidad, and 300 feet offshore (lat. 41°03'50" N, long. 124°09'05" W). Named on Trinidad (1966) 7.5' quadrangle.

Peyton Creek [TRINITY]: *stream,* flows 1.25 miles to South Fork Trinity River 4.5 miles southeast of Forest Glen (lat. 40°19'35" N, long. 123°16'10" W; near NE cor. sec. 4, T 2 S, R 8 E). Named on Forest Glen (1979) 7.5' quadrangle.

Pfeiffer Flat [TRINITY]: *area,* 8.5 miles south of Cecilville, which is in Siskiyou County, along North Fork Trinity River (lat. 41°01'25" N, long. 123°09'35" W). Named on Cecil Lake (1979) 7.5' quadrangle. Called Piper Flat on Cecilville (1955) 15' quadrangle, but United States Board on Geographic Names (1978a, p. 7) rejected this name for the feature.

Phelps: see **Dave Phelps Ridge** [LAKE].

Phelps Ridge [MENDOCINO]: *ridge,* north-northwest- to west-trending, 3 miles long, 6.5 miles west of Ornbaun Valley (lat. 38°54'30" N, long. 123°25'20" W). Named on Ornbaun Valley (1960) 15' quadrangle.

Philbrick Mill [MENDOCINO]: *locality,* 8.5 miles northwest of Boonville (lat. 39°04'55" N, long. 123°29'45" W; near SE cor. sec. 10, T 14 N, R 15 W). Named on Boonville (1959) 15' quadrangle.

Phillips Flat: see **Phillipsville** [HUMBOLDT].

Phillips Gulch [TRINITY]: *canyon,* drained by a stream that flows 3.5 miles to Grass Valley Creek 7 miles southeast of Weaverville (lat. 40°40'35" N, long. 122°49'50" W; sec. 36, T 33 N, R 9 W). Named on Weaverville (1950) 15' quadrangle.

Phillipsville [HUMBOLDT]: *village,* 7.5 miles north of Garberville along South Fork Eel River (lat. 40°12'35" N, long. 123°47'02" W; sec. 13, T 3 S, R 3 E). Named on Miranda (1970) 7.5' quadrangle. Postal authorities established Phillipsville post office in 1883, discontinued it in 1912, and reestablished it in 1948 (Salley, p. 170). United States Board on Geographic Names (1984b, p. 4) rejected the names "Kettintelbe," "Philippsville," and "Phillips Flat" for the place. After George Stump Phillips settled there about 1865, the site became known as Phillips Flat; C.

Hart Merriam changed the name to Kittinelbe for an Indian village that was at the place, but the name reverted to Phillipsville with the establishment of the post office in 1948 (Gudde, 1969, p. 244).

Philo [MENDOCINO]: *village*, 5.5 miles northwest of Boonville in Anderson Valley (lat. 39°03'55" N, long. 123°26'25" W; on S line sec. 18, T 14 N, R 14 W). Named on Boonville (1959) 15' quadrangle. Postal authorities established Philo post office in 1888 (Frickstad, p. 97). According to Gudde (1949, p. 260), Cornelius Prather, landowner and first postmaster, named the place for his favorite female cousin. According to Hanna (p. 234), Prather named the village for his former home, Philo, Illinois. California Mining Bureau's (1909c) map shows a place called Christine located 6.5 miles by stage line northwest of Philo. Postal authorities established Christine post office in 1874, discontinued it for a time in 1910, and discontinued it finally in 1912 (Frickstad, p. 94). Swiss settlers started the community, which was long known as Guntleys for one of the Swiss families, before it was renamed Christine for the daughter of another of the families (Carpenter, p. 50). O' Brien's (1953) map shows a place called Christine Junction situated about 8 miles northwest of Boonville.

Philpot Creek [TRINITY]: *stream*, flows 7.5 miles to Salt Creek (4) 6.5 miles north of Dubakella Mountain (lat. 40°28'10" N, long. 123°10'15" W; sec. 12, T 30 N, R 12 W). Named on Dubakella Mountain (1954) 15' quadrangle, and on Naufus Creek (1979) 7.5' quadrangle. North Fork enters from the north-northwest 1.25 miles upstream from the mouth of the main creek; it is 1.5 miles long and is named on Dubakella Mountain (1954) 15' quadrangle. North Fork is called N. Philpot Cr. on Hoaglin (1935) 30'quadrangle.

Phipps Creek [LAKE]: *stream*, flows 2.25 miles to North Fork Cache Creek 7 miles north-northeast of the town of Lower Lake (lat. 38°59'55" N, long. 122°33'15" W). Named on Lower Lake (1958) 7.5' quadrangle.

Phronies Flat [HUMBOLDT]: *area*, nearly 6 miles southeast of Honeydew (lat. 40°11'50" N, long. 124°01'50" W). Named on Honeydew (1970) 7.5' quadrangle.

Picayune Creek [TRINITY]: *stream*, flows 6 miles to Trinity River 6.5 miles south of China Mountain, which is in Siskiyou County (lat. 41°16'55" N, long. 122°35'20" W; near E line sec. 31, T 40 N, R 6 W); the stream heads at Picayune Lake. Named on Bonanza King (1955) and China Mountain (1955) 15' quadrangles. Called Picaune Cr. on Miller's (1890) map.

Picayune Creek: see **Little Picayune Creek** [TRINITY].

Picayune Lake [TRINITY]: *lake*, 1000 feet long, 17 miles north-northeast of Trinity Center (lat. 41°13'20" N, long. 122°31'25" W; sec. 23, T 39 N, R 6 W). Named on Bonanza King (1955) 15' quadrangle. Called Picaune Lake on Miller's (1890) map.

Pickett Creek [TRINITY]: *stream*, flows 1.5 miles to Ruth Reservoir 5 miles southwest of Forest Glen (lat. 40°19'25" N, long. 123°23'20" W; sec. 4, T 2 S, R 7 E); the stream heads near Pickett Peak. Named on Forest Glen (1979) and Ruth Reservoir (1978) 7.5' quadrangles.

Pickett Peak [TRINITY]: *peak*, nearly 3 miles southwest of Forest Glen (lat. 40°20'45" N, long. 123°21'45" W; near SW cor. sec. 26, T 1 S, R 7 E). Altitude 5774 feet. Named on Forest Glen (1979) 7.5' quadrangle.

Pickett Peak Campground [TRINITY]: *locality*, 3 miles west-southwest of Forest Glen (lat. 40°21'05" N, long. 123°22'20" W; sec. 27, T 1 S, R 7 E); the place is less than 1 mile northwest of Pickett Peak. Named on Forest Glen (1979) 7.5' quadrangle.

Pickle Spring [HUMBOLDT]: *spring*, 11 miles northeast of the town of Blue Lake (lat. 40°58'30" N, long. 123°48'50" W; near E line sec. 22, T 7 N, R 3 E). Named on Lord-Ellis Summit (1973) 7.5' quadrangle.

Pickrell Creek [MENDOCINO]: *stream*, flows nearly 1 mile to Middle Fork Eel River 1.5 miles east-southeast of Dos Rios (lat. 39°42'25" N, long. 123°19'25" W; near E line sec. 5, T 21 N, R 13 W). Named on Dos Rios (1967) 7.5' quadrangle.

Pictoe Hill: see **Pig Toe** [HUMBOLDT].

Pidgeon Point [HUMBOLDT]: *relief feature*, 6 miles south of Arcata (lat. 40°46'55" N, long. 124°06'W; near SW cor. sec. 29, T 5 N, R 1 E). Named on Arcata South (1959) 7.5' quadrangle.

Pierce: see **Mount Pierce** [HUMBOLDT].

Pierce Canyon [LAKE]: *canyon*, drained by a stream that flows 2 miles to Paradise Valley (1) 8.5 miles east of Lakeport (lat. 39°02'55" N, long. 122°45'25" W; sec. 21, T 14 N, R 8 W). Named on Lucerne (1958) 7.5' quadrangle.

Pierce Gulch [TRINITY]: *canyon*, drained by a stream that flows 1 mile to North Fork Coffee Creek 7 miles west-northwest of Billys Peak (1) (lat. 41°10'20" N, long. 122°53'05" W; near N line sec. 10, T 38 N, R 9 W). Named on Coffee Creek (1955) 15' quadrangle.

Piercy [MENDOCINO]: *village*, 9 miles north-northwest of Leggett along South Fork Eel River (lat. 39°57'55" N, long. 123°47'45" W; sec. 35, T 5 S, R 3 E). Named on Piercy (1969) 7.5' quadrangle. Postal authorities established Piercy post office in 1920 and named it for Sam Piercy, who settled at the site about 1900 (Salley, p. 171).

Piercy Creek [MENDOCINO]: *stream*, flows nearly 5 miles to South Fork Eel River 0.5 mile north-northwest of Piercy (lat. 39°58'25" N, long. 123°48'10" W; sec. 35, T 5 S, R 3 E). Named on Piercy (1969) 7.5' quadrangle.

Pierson Springs: see **Saratoga Springs** [LAKE].

Pieta [MENDOCINO]: *locality*, 5 miles southeast of Hopland (lat. 38°55'35" N, long. 123°03'10" W); the place is near the mouth of Pieta Creek. Named on Hopland (1944) 15' quadrangle. Postal authorities established Pieta post office, named for an Indian chief, in 1891 and discontinued it in 1897 (Salley, p. 171).

Pieta Creek [MENDOCINO]: *stream*, flows 11 miles to Coleman Creek 4.5 miles southeast of Hopland (lat. 38°55'25" N, long. 123°03'25" W; sec. 2, T 12 N, R 11 W). Named on Asti (1959), Highland Springs (1959), and Hopland (1960) 7.5' quadrangles.

Pigeon Rock [HUMBOLDT]: *relief feature*, 1.5 miles northwest of Yager Junction (lat. 40°33'40" N, long. 123°50'40" W; near N line sec. 16, T 2 N, R 3 E). Named on Yager Junction (1979) 7.5' quadrangle.

Pigeon Roost [DEL NORTE]: *relief feature*, 6.5 miles northwest of Buck Mountain (lat. 41°40'05" N, long. 123°58'25" W). Named on Cant Hook Mountain (1982) 7.5' quadrangle.

Pigeon Roost Spring [DEL NORTE]: *spring*, 6.25 miles northwest of Buck Mountain (lat. 41°40'N, long. 123°58'10" W); the spring is 0.25 mile east-southeast of Pigeon Roost. Named on Cant Hook Mountain (1982) 7.5' quadrangle. On Preston Peak (1922) 30'quadrangle, the name has the form "Pigeonroost Spring."

Piggy Springs [MENDOCINO]: *spring*, 2.5 miles east-southeast of Laytonville (lat. 39°40'15" N, long. 123°26'05" W). Named on Laytonville (1967) 7.5' quadrangle.

Pigpen Gulch [MENDOCINO]: *canyon*, drained by a stream that flows 1.5 miles to Big River 9 miles southwest of Willits (lat. 39°18'30" N, long. 123°27'45" W; near S line sec. 19, T 17 N, R 14 W). Named on Willits (1961) 15' quadrangle.

Pigtail Creek [MENDOCINO]: *stream*, flows 2 miles to Eden Creek less than 2 miles north-northwest of Eden Valley (lat. 39°39'10" N, long. 123°11'40" W; sec. 28, T 21 N, R 12 W). Named on Jamison Ridge (1967) 7.5' quadrangle.

Pig Toe [HUMBOLDT]: *ridge*, east-southeast-trending, 1 mile long, 8 miles southwest of Scotia (lat. 40°24'55" N, long. 124°13'10" W). Named on Taylor Peak (1969) 7.5' quadrangle. Called Pictoe Hill on Vander Leck's (1920b) map, and called Griffith Hill on Scotia (1950) 15' quadrangle. United States Board on Geographic Names (1974c, p. 4) gave the name "Griffith Hill" as a variant.

Pike: see **Billy Pike Creek** [MENDOCINO]; **Billy Pike Ridge** [MENDOCINO].

Pike County Bar: see **Browns Creek** [TRINITY].

Pillsbury: see **Lake Pillsbury** [LAKE].

Pilot Creek [HUMBOLDT]: *stream*, flows 13 miles to Mad River nearly 5 miles east-southeast of Showers Mountain (lat. 40°32'35" N, long. 123°37'10" W; sec. 21, T 2 N, R 5 E). Named on Blake Mountain (1979) and Sims Mountain (1979) 7.5' quadrangles.

Pilot Grove [LAKE]: *locality*, 5.5 miles northeast of the town of Upper Lake (lat. 39°13'35" N, long. 122°50'15" W). Named on Upper Lake (1958) 7.5' quadrangle.

Pilot Knob [LAKE]: *peak*, 3.5 miles southwest of Middletown (lat. 38°43'05" N, long. 122°40'W; at W line sec. 17, T 10 N, R 7 W). Named on Mount Saint Helena (1959) 7.5' quadrangle.

Pilot Peak [TRINITY]: *peak*, 9 miles south of Kettenpom (lat. 40°01'45" N, long. 123°26'35" W; at E line sec. 13, T 5 S, R 6 E). Altitude 4092 feet. Named on Lake Mountain (1967) 7.5' quadrangle.

Pilot Ridge [HUMBOLDT]: *ridge*, north-northwest-trending, 8 miles long, center 4.5 miles northeast of Showers Mountain (lat. 40°37'30" N, long. 123°38'15" W). Named on Blake Mountain (1979), Board Camp Mountain (1977), and Showers Mountain (1978) 7.5' quadrangles.

Pilot Rock [HUMBOLDT]:

(1) *rock*, 1.25 miles south-southwest of Trinidad, and 0.5 mile south of Trinidad Head (lat. 41°02'35" N, long. 124°09'05" W). Named on Trinidad (1966) 7.5' quadrangle. Captains of incoming schooners took their bearings for the anchorage from the feature (Waterman, p. 270).

(2) *relief feature*, 4 miles northeast of Showers Mountain (lat. 40°37'25" N, long. 123°38'45" W; sec. 19, T 3 N, R 5 E). Named on Showers Mountain (1978) 7.5' quadrangle.

Pilot Rock: see **Little Pilot Rock** [HUMBOLDT].

Pim Creek [MENDOCINO]: *stream*, flows 2 miles to Dutch Henry Creek 3 miles northwest of Longvale (lat. 39°35'N, long. 123°27'50" W; near W line sec. 18, T 20 N, R 14 W). Named on Longvale (1966) 7.5' quadrangle.

Pin Creek [TRINITY]: *stream*, flows 1.5 miles to Union Creek 7.5 miles west-southwest of Billys Peak (1) (lat. 41°05'N, long. 122°53'50" W; sec. 9, T 37 N, R 9 W). Named on Coffee Creek (1955) 15' quadrangle.

Pine Butte [HUMBOLDT]: *peak*, 6.5 miles northwest of Lone Star Junction (lat. 40°42'40" N, long. 123°56'55" W; at E line sec. 21, T 4 N, R 2 E). Named on Iaqua Buttes (1979) 7.5' quadrangle.

Pine Butte [TRINITY]: *peak*, 9 miles west of Forest Glen (lat. 40°24'N, long. 123°29'30" W; near SE cor. sec. 4, T 1 S, R 6 E). Named on

Sportshaven (1973) 7.5' quadrangle.

Pine Creek [HUMBOLDT]:

(1) *stream,* flows 18 miles to Klamath River 7.25 miles northeast of Coyote Peak (lat. 41°12'N, long. 123°45'05" W; near W line sec. 5, T 9 N, R 4 E). Named on French Camp Ridge (1983), Hoopa (1979), Hupa Mountain (1982), and Lord-Ellis Summit (1973) 7.5' quadrangles.

(2) *stream,* flows 2.25 miles to Long Prairie Creek 5 miles northeast of the town of Blue Lake (lat. 40°55'20" N, long. 123°54'20" W; near W line sec. 12, T 6 N, R 2 E). Named on Blue Lake (1979) 7.5' quadrangle.

Pine Creek [TRINITY]: *stream,* flows 3 miles to Eel River 12 miles south-southeast of Alderpoint [HUMBOLDT] (lat. 40°01'20" N, long. 123°30'45" W; sec. 16, T 5 S, R 6 E). Named on Bell Springs (1969) and Jewett Rock (1969) 7.5' quadrangles.

Pine Creek: see **Little Pine Creek** [HUMBOLDT].

Pine Flat [MENDOCINO]: *area,* about 10 miles east-northeast of Spyrock (2) (lat. 39°56'45" N, long. 123°17'05" W). Named on Mina (1967) 7.5' quadrangle.

Pine Flat [TRINITY]: *area,* 7.5 miles south of Kettenpom (lat. 40°02'55" N, long. 123°27'05" W; near S line sec. 1, T 5 S, R 6 E). Named on Lake Mountain (1967) 7.5' quadrangle.

Pine Flat: see **Little Pine Flat** [MENDOCINO].

Pine Flat Mountain [DEL NORTE]: *ridge,* south-trending, 3 miles long, 9.5 miles north of Gasquet (lat. 41°58'45" N, long. 123°59'15" W). Named on Gasquet (1951) 15' quadrangle.

Pine Grove [LAKE]: *settlement,* 1.5 miles northwest of Whispering Pines (lat. 38°49'40" N, long. 122°43'40" W; at and near N line sec. 10, T 11 N, R 8 W). Named on Whispering Pines (1958) 7.5' quadrangle.

Pine Grove [MENDOCINO]: *locality,* 3 miles north-northwest of Mendocino (lat. 39°20'55" N, long. 123°48'40" W; sec. 12, T 17 N, R 18 W). Named on Mendocino (1960) 7.5' quadrangle.

Pine Hill [HUMBOLDT]: *district,* 2.5 miles south of downtown Eureka (lat. 40°45'55" N, long. 124°10'20" W; near NE cor. sec. 3, T 4 N, R 1 W). Named on Eureka (1958) 7.5' quadrangle. The place also was called East Sunnyside and Tigerville, as well as Pine's Hill for Safford E. Pine, who had a dairy farm there (Turner, p. 171).

Pine Kop [LAKE]: *peak,* 11 miles east-northeast of Hull Mountain (lat. 39°34'25" N, long. 122°44'40" W; sec. 22, T 20 N, R 8 W). Altitude 5122 feet. Named on Felkner Hill (1968) 7.5' quadrangle.

Pine Lake Basin [MENDOCINO]: *relief feature,* 4.5 miles east-northeast of the town of Potter Valley (lat. 39°21'05" N, long. 123°11'W; near NW cor. sec. 10, T 17 N, R 12 W). Named on Redwood Valley (1960) 7.5' quadrangle.

Pine Mountain [HUMBOLDT]: *peak,* 4 miles east of Blocksburg (lat. 40°16'45" N, long. 123°33'40" W). Altitude 4760 feet. Named on Black Lassic (1979) 7.5' quadrangle.

Pine Mountain [LAKE]:

(1) *ridge,* 6 miles east-northeast of the town of Potter Valley [MENDOCINO] (lat. 39°21'50" N, long. 123°01'W). Named on Potter Valley (1960) 7.5' quadrangle. On Pomo (1943) 15' quadrangle, the name applies to the highest point on the ridge.

(2) *peak,* 9 miles north of Clearlake Oaks (lat. 39°08'50" N, long. 122°41'35" W; sec. 13, T 15 N, R 8 W). Altitude 4420 feet. Named on Clearlake Oaks (1960) 15' quadrangle.

(3) *peak,* 8 miles east of Lakeport (lat. 39°03'10" N, long. 122°46'05" W; sec. 20, T 14 N, R 8 W). Altitude 2533 feet. Named on Lucerne (1958) 7.5' quadrangle. Called Konokti Mountain on Lakeport (1938) 15' quadrangle.

(4) *peak,* 5 miles west-southwest of Middletown on Lake-Sonoma County line (lat. 38°43'55" N, long. 122°42'20" W; on E line sec. 11, T 10 N, R 8 W). Altitude 3614 feet. Named on Mount Saint Helena (1959) 7.5' quadrangle.

Pine Mountain [MENDOCINO]: *ridge,* generally east-trending, 1 mile long, nearly 4 miles south of Monument Peak (lat. 38°51'20" N, long. 123°57'10" W; sec. 26, 27, T 12 N, R 10 W). Named on Asti (1959) 7.5' quadrangle.

Pine Mountain Spring [LAKE]: *spring,* 6 miles east-northeast of the town of Potter Valley on Pine Mountain (1) (lat. 39°21'55" N, long. 123°00'55" W; near SW cor. sec. 32, T 18 N, R 10 W). Named on Potter Valley (1960) 7.5' quadrangle.

Pine Ridge [HUMBOLDT]: *ridge,* 10 miles long, center 6.25 miles south-southeast of Coyote Peak near Hoopa Mountain (lat. 41°04'N, long. 123°48'10" W); the ridge is west of Pine Creek (1). Named on Hupa Mountain (1982) and Lord-Ellis Summit (1973) 7.5' quadrangles.

Pine Ridge [MENDOCINO]:

(1) *ridge,* generally south-trending, 7 miles long, 10.5 miles northeast of Covelo (lat. 39°53'N, long. 123°05'15" W). Named on Leech Lake Mountain (1966) and Newhouse Ridge (1967) 7.5' quadrangles.

(2) *ridge,* north-northwest-trending, 4.5 miles long, 9 miles north-northeast of Boonville (lat. 39°08'N, long. 123°18'30" W). Named on Boonville (1959) 15' quadrangle.

Pine Ridge Summit [HUMBOLDT]: *locality,* 13 miles east-northeast of the town of Blue Lake (lat. 40°59'20" N, long. 123°46'35" W; sec. 13, T 7 N, R 3 E); the place is near the head of Pine Creek (1). Named on Lord-Ellis Summit (1973) 7.5' quadrangle.

Pine Root Spring [TRINITY]: *spring,* nearly 3 miles north of Forest Glen (lat. 40°24'50" N, long. 123°19'35" W; at NW cor. sec. 6, T 1 S, R 8 E). Named on Naufus Creek (1979) 7.5' quadrangle.

Pine Root Spring: see **Pine Root Spring Campground** [TRINITY].

Pine Root Spring Campground [TRINITY]: *locality,* 6 miles south-southeast of Dubakella Mountain (lat. 40°18'20" N, long. 123°06'W; near W line sec. 3, T 28 N, R 11 W). Named on Dubakella Mountain (1954) 15' quadrangle. Hoaglin (1935) 30'quadrangle shows Pine Root Spring at the site.

Pinkeye Lake [LAKE]: *intermittent lake,* 1200 feet long, 2.5 miles west of the town of Lower Lake (lat. 38°54'30" N, long. 122°39'25" W; sec. 8, T 12 N, R 7 W). Named on Clearlake Highlands (1958) 7.5' quadrangle.

Pinnacle Rock [LAKE]: *peak,* 8 miles east of the town of Upper Lake (lat. 39°08'50" N, long. 122°45'50" W; near W line sec. 16, T 15 N, R 8 W). Altitude 4618 feet. Named on Bartlett Mountain (1958) 7.5' quadrangle.

Pinnacle Spring [HUMBOLDT]: *spring,* 4.25 miles southwest of Honeydew (lat. 40°11'40" N, long. 124°10'20" W). Named on Shubrick Peak (1969) 7.5' quadrangle.

Pinto Creek [MENDOCINO]: *stream,* heads in Glenn County and flows 1.5 miles in Mendocino County to Atchison Creek 15 miles north of Hull Mountain (lat. 39°44'20" N, long. 122°56'W; near NE cor. sec. 26, T 22 N, R 10 W); the stream is south of Pinto Ridge. Named on Plaskett Ridge (1967) 7.5' quadrangle.

Pinto Ridge [MENDOCINO]: *ridge,* west-southwest-trending, 3.25 miles long, 15 miles north of Hull Mountain on Mendocino-Glenn County line (lat. 39°44'20" N, long. 122°54'30" W). Named on Plaskett Ridge (1967) 7.5' quadrangle.

Pip Creek [HUMBOLDT]: *stream,* flows 1.5 miles to Van Duzen River 3 miles west of Bridgville (lat. 40°27'40" N, long. 123°51'15" W; near E line sec. 17, T 1 N, R 3 E). Named on Bridgeville (1969) 7.5' quadrangle.

Pipe Creek [HUMBOLDT]: *stream,* flows 7.25 miles to Eel River 5 miles south-southeast of Alderpoint (lat. 40°06'40" N, long. 123°33'55" W; sec. 13, T 4 S, R 5 E). Named on Jewett Rock (1969) 7.5' quadrangle. Called Price Creek on Harris (1920) 15' quadrangle.

Pipe Line Creek [HUMBOLDT]: *stream,* flows 2.25 miles to lowlands along Eel River 2.25 miles northeast of Weott (lat. 40°20'25" N, long. 123°53'15" W). Named on Myers Flat (1969) and Weott (1969) 7.5' quadrangles.

Piper Flat: see **Pfeiffer Flat** [TRINITY].

Pirates Cove [LAKE]: *embayment,* 7 miles northwest of the town of Lower Lake along Clear Lake (lat. 38°59'20" N, long. 122°41'50" W; sec. 12, T 13 N, R 8 W). Named on Clearlake Highlands (1958) 7.5' quadrangle.

Pisgah View [DEL NORTE]: *locality,* 1.5 miles east of the mouth of Klamath River near the west end of Mynot Ridge (lat. 41°32'55" N, long. 124°02'50" W; sec. 3, T 13 N, R 1 E); the site overlooks the mouth of Klamath River. Named on Requa (1966) 7.5' quadrangle.

Pistol Spring [HUMBOLDT]: *spring,* 7.25 miles east of Showers Mountain (lat. 40°33'40" N, long. 123°33'45" W; near SW cor. sec. 12, T 2 N, R 5 E). Named on Blake Mountain (1979) 7.5' quadrangle.

Pitcher Creek [HUMBOLDT]: *stream,* flows 4.25 miles to Maple Creek (1) 6.5 miles north-northeast of Trinidad (lat. 41°09'N, long. 124°05'50" W; on W line sec. 20, T 9 N, R 1 E). Named on Rodgers Peak (1966) 7.5' quadrangle.

Pitney Ridge [LAKE]: *ridge,* generally southeast-trending, 5.5 miles long, 4 miles north-northeast of the town of Upper Lake (lat. 39°13'15" N, long. 122°53'10" W). Named on Bartlett Mountain (1958) and Upper Lake (1958) 7.5' quadrangles.

Pit Place Prairie [HUMBOLDT]: *area,* 9 miles north-northwest of Coyote Peak (lat. 41°14'50" N, long. 123°56'20" W; near NW cor. sec. 22, T 10 N, R 2 E). Named on Bald Hills (1982) and Holter Ridge (1983) 7.5' quadrangles. United States Board on Geographic Names (1983c, p. 6) approved the name "Pitt Place Prairie" for the feature, and rejected the names "Pit Place Prairie" and "Place Prairie." The name "Pitt" is for Joe Pitt, who lived at the site (Turner, p. 171).

Place Prairie: see **Pit Place Prairie** [HUMBOLDT].

Plank Cabin Spring [LAKE]: *spring,* 6 miles north-northwest of the town of Upper Lake (lat. 39°14'50" N, long. 122°57'W; sec. 15, T 16 N, R 10 W). Named on Upper Lake (1958) 7.5' quadrangle.

Plaskett Ridge [MENDOCINO]: *ridge,* mainly in Glenn County, but extends into Mendocino County 13 miles north of Hull Mountain (lat. 39°42'30" N, long. 122°53'35" W). Named on Plaskett Ridge (1967) 7.5' quadrangle.

Pleasant Valley [MENDOCINO]: *canyon,* drained by a stream that flows nearly 2 miles to Albion River 7.5 miles north of Elk (lat. 39°14'25" N, long. 123°42'30" W; at N line sec. 23, T 16 N, R 17 W). Named on Elk (1960) 7.5' quadrangle.

Plum Flat [LAKE]: *area,* 5.5 miles west-northwest of the town of Lower Lake (lat. 38°56'50" N, long. 122°42'20" W; near E line sec. 26, T 13 N, R 8 W). Named on Clearlake Highlands (1958) 7.5' quadrangle.

Plummer Creek [TRINITY]: *stream,* flows 7.5 miles to South Fork Trinity

River 9 miles northwest of Forest Glen (lat. 40°28'35" N, long. 123°25'05" W; at W line sec. 8, T 1 N, R 7 E); the stream heads at Bald Peaks of Plummer. Named on Naufus Creek (1979) and Sportshaven (1973) 7.5' quadrangles. On Hoaglin (1935) 30'quadrangle, the upper part of present Plummer Creek is called Naufus Creek, and present Naufus Creek is shown as the upper part of Plummer Creek.

Plummer Gulch [TRINITY]: *canyon,* drained by a stream that flows nearly 2 miles to Salt Creek (4) 6 miles north of Dubakella Mountain (lat. 40°27'35" N, long. 123°10'W; at N line sec. 13, T 30 N, R 12 W). Named on Dubakella Mountain (1954) 15' quadrangle.

Plummer Hill [TRINITY]: *ridge,* north-trending, 1.25 miles long, 3 miles east of Trinity Center (lat. 41°00'30" N, long. 122°38'W; in and near sec. 2, T 36 N, R 7 W). Named on Bonanza King (1955) and Schell Mountain (1950) 15' quadrangles.

Plummer Peak [TRINITY]: *peak,* 8 miles north-northwest of Dubakella Mountain (lat. 40°29'35" N, long. 123°12'W; near E line sec. 34, T 31 N, R 12 W). Altitude 4412 feet. Named on Dubakella Mountain (1954) 15' quadrangle.

Pocket: see **The Pocket** [LAKE].

Poe Mountain [LAKE]: *peak,* 3 miles southwest of the town of Upper Lake (lat. 39°07'35" N, long. 122°56'55" W; near NE cor. sec. 27, T 15 N, R 10 W). Named on Upper Lake (1958) 7.5' quadrangle.

Poge Creek [LAKE]: *stream,* flows nearly 3 miles to Alley Creek 1.5 miles north-northeast of the town of Upper Lake (lat. 39°11'N, long. 122°53'30" W). Named on Bartlett Mountain (1958) and Upper Lake (1958) 7.5' quadrangles.

Poges Peak [LAKE]: *peak,* 1.25 miles southeast of Three Crossings (lat. 39°18'20" N, long. 122°54'05" W; on N line sec. 29, T 17 N, R 9 W). Altitude 3422 feet. Named on Elk Mountain (1967) 7.5' quadrangle.

Pogie Point Campground [LAKE]: *locality,* 4.25 miles northwest of Bear Mountain at the northwest end of Lake Pillsbury (lat. 39°26'35" N, long. 122°58'05" W; sec. 3, T 18 N, R 10 W). Named on Lake Pillsbury (1967) 7.5' quadrangle. On Lake Pillsbury (1951) 15' quadrangle, the name has the form "Pogie Point Camp Ground."

Point Arena [MENDOCINO]:

(1) *promontory,* 4 miles northwest of the village of Point Arena (lat. 38°57'20" N, long. 123°44'25" W; at N line sec. 34, T 13 N, R 17 W). Named on Point Arena (1960) 7.5' quadrangle. Called Pt. Barra de Arena on Wilkes' (1841) map, and called Arena Pt. on Rogers and Johnson's (1857) map. Vancouver (p. 108) used the name "Point Barro de Arena" in 1793. United States Board on Geographic Names (1933, p. 102) rejected the form "Point Arenas" for the name. Wagner (p. 373) noted that Ferrer named the feature Cabo de Fortunas in 1543, Costanso called it Punta de Barrancas in 1770, and Bodega named it Delgada in 1775.

(2) *village,* 31 miles west of Hopland near the coast (lat. 38°54'35" N, long. 123°41'30" W; sec. 12, 13, T 12 N, R 17 W); the village is 4 miles southeast of Point Arena (1). Named on Point Arena (1960) 7.5' quadrangle. Postal authorities established Punta Arenas post office in 1858 and changed the name to Point Arena in 1889 (Frickstad, p. 97). United States Board on Geographic Names (1933, p. 611) rejected the name "Puntas Arenas" for the place. The first store at the site was built in 1859 (Hoover, Rensch, and Rensch, p. 196), and the community incorporated in 1908.

Point Arena Creek [MENDOCINO]: *stream,* flows 4 miles to the sea 1 mile west-northwest of the village of Point Arena (lat. 39°54'50" N, long. 123°42'30" W; sec. 11, T 12 N, R 17 W); the mouth of the stream is at Arena Cove. Named on Point Arena (1960) 7.5' quadrangle.

Point Arena Hot Springs: see **Garcia River** [MENDOCINO].

Point Bar: see **Limekiln Gulch** [TRINITY].

Point Barro de Arena: see **Point Arena** [MENDOCINO] (1).

Point Cabrillo [MENDOCINO]: *promontory,* 3.5 miles north-northwest of Mendocino (lat. 39°21' N, long. 123°49'35" W; sec. 12, T 17 N, R 18 W). Named on Mendocino (1960) 7.5' quadrangle. Called Cabrillo Point on Fort Bragg (1943) 15' quadrangle. Officials of United States Coast Survey named the feature to honor Juan Rodriquez Cabrillo (Wagner, p. 378).

Point Delgada [HUMBOLDT]: *promontory,* 34 miles south-southeast of Cape Mendocino along the coast (lat. 40°01'15" N, long. 124°04'W; sec. 16, T 5 S, R 1 E). Named on Shelter Cove (1969) 7.5' quadrangle. Wagner (p. 383) believed it probable that the name applied first to present Point Arena [MENDOCINO] and that it was transferred to present Point Delgada on some late Spanish map used by members of United States Coast Survey.

Point George: see **Point Saint George** [DEL NORTE].

Point Lakeview [LAKE]: *promontory,* 4.25 miles northwest of the town of Lower Lake along Clear Lake (lat. 38°56'50" N, long. 122°40'30" W; sec. 30, T 13 N, R 7 W). Named on Clearlake Highlands (1958) 7.5' quadrangle.

Point Mal Pass [HUMBOLDT]: *promontory,* 1.25 miles east of Point Delgada along the coast (lat. 40°01'10" N, long. 124°02'45" W). Named on Point Delgada (1920) 15' quadrangle.

Point No Pass [MENDOCINO]: *promontory,* 10 miles west of Piercy (lat. 39°58'15" N, long. 123°59'30" W; sec. 31, T 5 S, R 2 E). Named on Bear Harbor (1969) 7.5' quadrangle.

Point Saint George [DEL NORTE]: *promontory,* 3.25 miles northwest of Crescent City along the coast (lat. 41°47'N, long. 124°15'W). Named on Crescent City (1966) 7.5' quadrangle. United States Board on Geographic Names (1933, p. 657) rejected the form "St. George's " for the name. Called Pt. George on Parker's (1838) map. Scholfield's (1851) map shows Cape St. George, and has the name "St. Georges Reef" for offshore rocks there. According to United States Coast and Geodetic Survey (p. 149), St. George Reef consists of rocks and covered ledges extending 6.5 miles northwest and west from Point St. George. Wagner (p. 507) identified present Point Saint George as most probably the feature that Vizcaino called Cabo Blanco de San Sebastian in 1603. Vancouver gave the name "Point St. George" to the place on April 23, 1782, the day of the patron saint of England (Gudde, 1949, p. 294). At the same time Vancouver gave the name "Dragon Rocks" to rocks lying off the promontory—the name "Dragon" now applies to Dragon Channel, a water route through the rocks (Gudde, 1949, p. 99). Ferry's (1851) map has the name "B.S. Giorgie" for the site of the harbor at present Crescent City.

Poison Camp: see **Zenia** [TRINITY].

Poison Canyon [TRINITY]: *canyon,* 7 miles south of Billys Peak (1) along North Fork Swift Creek (1) (lat. 41°02'15" N, long. 122°47'35" W; sec. 28, 29, T 37 N, R 8 W). Named on Coffee Creek (1955) 15' quadrangle.

Poison Gulch [TRINITY]: *canyon,* drained by a stream that flows 1.5 miles to Oregon Gulch 15 miles northeast of Hayfork (lat. 40°43'50" N, long. 123°00'55" W; at W line sec. 9, T 33 N, R 10 W). Named on Hayfork (1951) 15' quadrangle.

Poison Oak Creek [HUMBOLDT]: *stream,* flows 2.5 miles to Eel River 1.5 miles northeast of Weott (lat. 40°20'20" N, long. 123°54'20" W; sec. 36, T 1 S, R 2 E). Named on Weott (1969) 7.5' quadrangle.

Poison Rock [MENDOCINO]: *peak,* 11 miles northeast of Eden Valley on Etsel Ridge (lat. 39°43'45" N, long. 123°01'45" W; near S line sec. 25, T 22 N, R 11 W). Named on Thatcher Ridge (1967) 7.5' quadrangle.

Poison Smith Spring [LAKE]: *spring,* 6 miles south-southeast of Kelseyville (lat. 38°53'50" N, long. 122°47'50" W; near SE cor. sec. 12, T 12 N, R 8 W). Named on Kelseyville (1959) 7.5' quadrangle.

Poison Spring [HUMBOLDT]: *spring,* 4 miles east of Showers Mountain (lat. 40°34'45" N, long. 123°37'25" W; near W line sec. 4, T 2 N, R 5 E). Named on Blake Mountain (1979) 7.5' quadrangle.

Poker Creek [DEL NORTE]: *stream,* flows 3 miles to Dunn Creek 8 miles northeast of Broken Rib Mountain (lat. 41°58'15" N, long. 123°34'45" W); the stream heads near Poker Flat, which is in Siskiyou County. Named on Polar Bear Mountain (1982) 7.5' quadrangle.

Polar Bear Mountain [DEL NORTE]: *peak,* 4.25 miles north of Preston Peak, which is in Siskiyou County, on Del Norte-Siskiyou County line (lat. 41°53'55" N, long. 123°35'50" W). Named on Polar Bear Mountain (1982) 7.5' quadrangle.

Pole Bars [MENDOCINO]: *relief feature,* 7.5 miles north of the town of Potter Valley (lat. 39°25'35" N, long. 123°05'30" W; on E line sec. 8, T 18 N, R 11 W). Named on Potter Valley (1960) 15' quadrangle.

Pole Garden [LAKE]: *locality,* 14 miles north of Clearlake Oaks near Lake-Colusa County line (lat. 39°13'10" N, long. 122°38'15" W; near SE cor. sec. 21, T 16 N, R 7 W). Named on Clearlake Oaks (1960) 15' quadrangle.

Pole Gulch [TRINITY]: *canyon,* drained by a stream that flows nearly 1 mile to Clair Engle Lake 14 miles northeast of Weaverville (lat. 40°53'30" N, long. 122°46'W; near W line sec. 15, T 35 N, R 8 W). Named on Trinity Dam (1950) 15' quadrangle.

Pole Point [MENDOCINO]: *peak,* 3.5 miles north of Hull Mountain (lat. 39°36'05" N, long. 122°55'20" W; sec. 11, T 20 N, R 10 W). Altitude 6163 feet. Named on Hull Mountain (1967) 7.5' quadrangle.

Police Camp [TRINITY]: *locality,* 13 miles south-southwest of Black Rock Mountain (lat. 40°02'20" N, long. 123°06'40" W; sec. 8, T 25 N, R 11 W). Named on Black Rock Mountain (1954) 15' quadrangle.

Pollack Creek: see **Pollock Creek** [HUMBOLDT].

Pollock Creek [HUMBOLDT]: *stream,* flows 2 miles to North Fork Mad River 4.25 miles east-northeast of the town of Blue Lake (lat. 40°54'25" N, long. 123°54'50" W; sec. 14, T 6 N, R 2 E). Named on Blue Lake (1979) 7.5' quadrangle. United States Board on Geographic Names (1978a, p. 7) rejected the form "Pollack Creek" for the name.

Pollock Creek: see **Bald Mountain Creek** [HUMBOLDT].

Poly Buttes [TRINITY]: *peaks,* 12 miles southeast of Salmon Mountain (lat. 41°03'30" N, long. 123°15'W). Named on Cecil Lake (1979) and Dees Peak (1978) 7.5' quadrangles.

Pomo [MENDOCINO]: *locality,* 1.25 miles southeast of the town of Potter Valley (lat. 39°18'10" N, long. 123°05'20" W; around NW cor. sec. 28, T 17 N, R 11 W). Named on Potter Valley (1960) 15' quadrangle. Postal authorities established Pomo post office in 1870, discontinued it in 1871, reestablished it in 1872, discontinued it in 1881, reestablished it in 1882, and discontinued it in 1911 (Frickstad, p. 97).

Pond Lily Creek [TRINITY]: *stream,* flows nearly 4 miles to East Fork Trinity River 10 miles northeast of Trinity Center (lat. 41°07'N, long. 122°34'W; near N line sec. 33, T 38 N, R 6 W); the stream heads at Pond Lily Lake.

Named on Bonanza King (1955) 15' quadrangle.

Pond Lily Lake [TRINITY]: *lake,* 500 feet long, 10 miles east-northeast of Trinity Center (lat. 41°04'50" N, long. 122°31'45" W; at W line sec. 11, T 37 N, R 6 W). Named on Bonanza King (1955) 15' quadrangle.

Pony Bar: see **Pony Creek** [TRINITY] (2).

Pony Buck Peak [TRINITY]: *peak,* 10.5 miles south-southeast of Dubakella Mountain (lat. 40°15'20" N, long. 123°02'40" W; at SW cor. sec. 19, T 28 N, R 10 W). Altitude 5610 feet. Named on Dubakella Mountain (1954) 15' quadrangle.

Pony Camp Meadows [TRINITY]: *area,* 13 miles north-northwest of Helena (lat. 40°56'45" N, long. 123°13'40" W); the place is just east-southeast of Pony Mountain. Named on Helena (1951) 15' quadrangle.

Pony Creek [TRINITY]:

(1) *stream,* flows nearly 5 miles to East Fork New River 14 miles south-southeast of Salmon Mountain (lat. 41°00'N, long. 123°17'W). Named on Dees Peak (1978) 7.5' quadrangle.

(2) *stream,* flows 1 mile to Trinity River 4 miles east-southeast of Salyer (lat. 40°51'55" N, long. 123°30'50" W). Named on Hennessy Peak (1979) 7.5' quadrangle. Gudde (1975, p. 272) listed a mining place called Pony Bar that was situated along Trinity River about 4 miles east of Salyer, presumably near the mouth of Pony Creek (2).

Pony Lake [TRINITY]: *lake,* 500 feet long, 8.5 miles southwest of Cecilville, which is in Siskiyou County (lat. 41°03'10" N, long. 123°14'40" W); the lake is south of Pony Buttes. Named on Cecil Lake (1979) 7.5' quadrangle.

Pony Meadows [MENDOCINO]: *area,* 8 miles north of Anthony Peak (lat. 39°57'20" N, long. 122°57'10" W; near N line sec. 10, T 24 N, R 10 W). Named on Buck Rock (1967) 7.5' quadrangle.

Pony Mountain [TRINITY]: *peak,* 13 miles north-northwest of Helena (lat. 40°56'50" N, long. 123°13'55" W). Altitude 7478 feet. Named on Helena (1951) 15' quadrangle.

Pony Point: see **Del Loma** [TRINITY]:

Pony Ridge [MENDOCINO]: *ridge,* southwest-trending, 2 miles long, 8.5 miles north of Anthony Peak (lat. 38°58'15" N, long. 122°56'30" W); Pony Meadows is at the southwest end of the ridge. Named on Buck Rock (1967) 7.5' quadrangle.

Pool Creek [LAKE]: *stream,* flows 1 mile to Scotts Valley 3 miles west-northwest of Lakeport (lat. 39°04'10" N, long. 122°57'40" W; at N line sec. 15, T 14 N, R 10 W). Named on Lakeport (1958) 7.5' quadrangle.

Poonkinny Creek [MENDOCINO]: *stream,* flows 2.5 miles to Goforth Creek less than 1 mile east of Dos Rios (lat. 39°43'10" N, long. 123°20'15" W; sec. 32, T 22 N, R 13 W). Named on Dos Rios (1967) 7.5' quadrangle. The name is of Indian origin (Kroeber, p. 56).

Poonkinny Lake [MENDOCINO]: *intermittent lake,* 750 feet long, 1 mile east of Dos Rios (lat. 39°43'N, long. 123°20" W; on S line sec. 32, T 22 N, R 13 W). Named on Dos Rios (1967) 7.5' quadrangle.

Poonkinny Ridge [MENDOCINO]: *ridge,* generally south-southeast-trending, 5.5 miles long, center 4.5 miles west of Covelo (lat. 39°47'20" N, long. 123°19'45" W). Named on Covelo West (1967) 7.5' quadrangle.

Poonkiny: see **Covelo** [MENDOCINO].

Poopoteyuk River: see **Black Butte River** [MENDOCINO].

Poorman Gulch [TRINITY]: *canyon,* drained by a stream that flows 0.5 mile to Coffee Creek 9 miles west of Billys Peak (1) (lat. 41°06'30" N, long. 122°56'W; sec. 31, T 38 N, R 9 W). Named on Coffee Creek (1955) 15' quadrangle.

Poor Mans Creek [MENDOCINO]: *stream,* flows 2.5 miles to Williams Creek (1) 6 miles east-northeast of Covelo (lat. 39°49'40" N, long. 123°08'30" W; sec. 25, T 23 N, R 12 W); the stream goes through Poor Mans Valley. Named on Covelo East (1967) 7.5' quadrangle.

Poor Mans Valley [MENDOCINO]: *valley,* 5 miles east-northeast of Covelo (lat. 39°49'35" N, long. 123°09'45" W; sec. 26, T 23 N, R 12 W). Named on Covelo East (1967) 7.5' quadrangle.

Porters Camp [DEL NORTE]: *locality,* 10 miles northeast of Broken Rib Mountain (lat. 41°58'05" N, long. 123°32'20" W). Named on Polar Bear Mountain (1982) 7.5' quadrangle.

Porter Spring [TRINITY]: *spring,* 4.5 miles north-northeast of Trinity Center (lat. 41°03'30" N, long. 122°38'30" W; near N line sec. 23, T 37 N, R 7 W). Named on Bonanza King (1955) 15' quadrangle.

Port Kenyon [HUMBOLDT]: *settlement,* 1.5 miles northwest of Ferndale near Salt River (lat. 40°35'40" N, long. 124°16'45" W; sec. 34, T 3 N, R 2 W). Named on Ferndale (1959) 7.5' quadrangle. Postal authorities established Port Kenyon post office in 1886, discontinued it in 1899, reestablished it in 1903, and discontinued it in 1913 (Frickstad, p. 45). John Gardner Kenyon laid out a townsite on his land at the place in 1876, when Salt River was navigable to the site, but floods and silting up of the river caused the port to decline by the late 1890's (Carlson, p. 25, 28; Edeline, p. 7, 9).

Port of Point Arena: see **Arena Cove** [MENDOCINO].

Port Trinidad: see **Trinidad** [HUMBOLDT].

Portuguese Gulch [MENDOCINO]: *canyon,* drained by a stream that flows 1 mile to Soda Spring Creek 2 miles north-northwest of Comptche (lat. 39°17'25" N, long. 123°36'25" W; near E line sec. 35, T 17 N, R 16 W). Named on Comptche (1960) 15' quadrangle.

Posey Gulch [TRINITY]: *canyon,* 2.25 miles long, 8 miles east-northeast of Weaverville (lat. 40°45'30" N, long. 122°47'40" W; mainly in sec. 32, T 34 N, R 8 W). Named on Trinity Dam (1950) 15' quadrangle.

Post Camp [MENDOCINO]: *locality,* 14 miles north-northwest of Hull Mountain (lat. 39°42'55" N, long. 122°59'50" W; sec. 32, T 22 N, R 10 W). Named on Plaskett Ridge (1967) 7.5' quadrangle.

Post Creek [TRINITY]: *stream,* flows about 6 miles to Rattlesnake Creek (2) 3 miles east-northeast of Forest Glen (lat. 40°23'30" N, long. 123°16'30" W; sec. 9, T 1 S, R 8 E). Named on Dubakella Mountain (1954) 15' quadrangle, and on Naufus Creek (1979) 7.5' quadrangle. United States Board on Geographic Names (1977c, p. 5) gave the name "Rattlesnake Creek" as a variant.

Post Creek: see **North Post Creek** [TRINITY]; **Rattlesnake Creek** [TRINITY] (2).

Potato Creek [TRINITY]: *stream,* flows 4.5 miles to East Fork Hayfork Creek 8 miles east-southeast of Hayfork (lat. 40°30'15" N, long. 123°02'30" W; at N line sec. 31, T 31 N, R 10 W). Named on Dubakella Mountain (1954) 15' quadrangle. Called South Fork [of East Fork Hayfork Creek] on Hoaglin (1935) 30'quadrangle.

Potato Hill [HUMBOLDT]: *peak,* 6.5 miles east-southeast of Board Camp Mountain (lat. 40°39'55" N, long. 123°36'15" W; at E line sec. 3, T 3 N, R 5 E). Named on Sims Mountain (1979) 7.5' quadrangle.

Potato Hill [LAKE]: *peak,* 6.5 miles southeast of Bear Mountain (lat. 39°21'10" N, long. 122°48'10" W; sec. 6, T 17 N, R 8 W). Altitude 4405 feet. Named on Potato Hill (1967) 7.5' quadrangle.

Potato Mountain [TRINITY]: *peak,* 8 miles east-southeast of Salmon Mountain (lat. 41°07'20" N, long. 123°17'05" W). Altitude 6698 feet. Named on Dees Peak (1978) 7.5' quadrangle.

Potato Patch [HUMBOLDT]:

(1) *area,* 3.5 miles south-southeast of Coyote Peak (lat. 41°05'15" N, long. 123°50'15" W; at N line sec. 16, T 8 N, R 3 E). Named on Hupa Mountain (1982) 7.5' quadrangle.

(2) *area,* 8.5 miles southwest of Dinsmore (lat. 40°25'05" N, long. 123°43'25" W; sec. 33, T 1 N, R 4 E). Named on Larabee Valley (1977) 7.5' quadrangle.

Potato Patch Creek [DEL NORTE-HUMBOLDT]: *stream,* heads in Del Norte County and flows 4 miles to West Fork Blue Creek 8 miles north of Johnsons in Humboldt County (lat. 41°27'40" N, long. 123°53'30" W; sec. 1, T 12 N, R 2 E). Named on Ah Pah Ridge (1983) and Klamath Glen (1982) 7.5' quadrangles.

Pothole Creek [MENDOCINO]: *stream,* flows 4 miles to Middle Fork Eel River 16 miles northeast of Covelo (lat. 39°56'55" N, long. 123°01'30" W; near E line sec. 12, T 24 N, R 11 W). Named on Leech Lake Mountain (1966) 7.5' quadrangle.

Pothole Crossing [MENDOCINO]: *locality,* 16 miles northeast of Covelo along Middle Fork Eel River (lat. 39°56'55" N, long. 123°01'30" W; near E line sec. 12, T 24 N, R 11 W); the place is at the mouth of Pothole Creek. Named on Leech Lake Mountain (1966) 7.5' quadrangle.

Potter Valley [MENDOCINO]:

(1) *valley,* 18 miles north-northeast of Ukiah on upper reaches of East Fork Russian River (lat. 39°19'N, long. 123°06'30" W). Named on Potter Valley (1960) and Redwood Valley (1960) 7.5' quadrangles. The name commemorates Thomas Potter and William Potter, who settled in the valley in the 1850's (Hanna, p. 243). Goodyear (1890c, p. 314) referred to Potter's Valley.

(2) *town,* 18 miles north-northeast of Ukiah in Potter Valley (1) (lat. 39°19'10" N, long. 123°06'30" W; around SW cor. sec. 17, T 17 N, R 11 W). Named on Potter Valley (1960) 7.5' quadrangle. Postal authorities established Potter Valley post office in 1870 (Frickstad, p. 97). California Mining Bureau's (1917c) map shows a place called Tompki located about 7 miles north-northwest of the town of Potter Valley. Postal authorities established Tomki post office 10 miles northwest of Potter Valley post office (NW quarter of SW quarter sec. 15, T 18 N, R 12 W) in 1912 and discontinued it the same year (Salley, p. 223).

Pound Gulch: see **Morrison Gulch** [MENDOCINO] (2).

Pou-Oup Ridge [DEL NORTE]: *ridge,* northwest-trending, 2 miles long, 4 miles northeast of the mouth of Klamath River (lat. 41°34'45" N, long. 124°01'05" W). Named on Requa (1966) 7.5' quadrangle.

Poverty Flat: see **Weaverville** [TRINITY].

Poverty Gulch [MENDOCINO]: *canyon,* drained by a stream that flows 1.25 miles to Mettick Creek 3.25 miles east of Comptche (lat. 39°15'45" N, long. 123°31'45" W; sec. 10, T 16 N, R 15 W). Named on Comptche (1960) 15' quadrangle.

Poverty Point [HUMBOLDT]: *peak,* 2 miles northeast of the town of Blue Lake (lat. 40°54'10" N, long. 123°57'25" W; sec. 16, T 6 N, R 2 E). Altitude 2032 feet. Named on Blue Lake (1979) 7.5' quadrangle.

Powder Flat [HUMBOLDT]: *area,* 16 miles south of Scotia (lat. 40°15'10" N, long. 124°07'W; near W line sec. 31, T 2 S, R 1 E). Named on Bull Creek (1969) 7.5' quadrangle.

Powell Ridge [TRINITY]: *ridge,* north-northwest-trending, 2.5 miles long,

3.5 miles south-southwest of Black Rock Mountain (lat. 40°09'15" N, long. 123°01'50" W). Named on Black Rock Mountain (1954) 15' quadrangle.

Powellville: see **Blocksburg** [HUMBOLDT].

Powerhouse Gulch [TRINITY]: *canyon*, 0.5 mile long, 4.5 miles north of Trinity Center (lat. 41°04'20" N, long. 122°42'25" W; on E line sec. 18, T 37 N, R 7 W). Named on Bonanza King (1955) 15' quadrangle.

Powers Creek [HUMBOLDT]:
(1) *stream*, flows 3 miles to lowlands along Mad River at the town of Blue Lake (lat. 40°53'N, long. 123°59'W; at SW cor. sec. 20, T 6 N, R 2 E). Named on Blue Lake (1979) 7.5' quadrangle.
(2) *stream*, flows nearly 3 miles to Steelhead Creek 2 miles west-southwest of Alderpoint (lat. 40°10'05" N, long. 123°38'45" W; near SW cor. sec. 29, T 3 S, R 5 E). Named on Fort Seward (1969) 7.5' quadrangle. Called Fort Seward Creek on Harris (1920) 15' quadrangle.

Prairie: see **Lake Prairie** [HUMBOLDT].

Prairie Creek [HUMBOLDT]: *stream*, flows 11.5 miles to Redwood Creek (1) 1 mile north-northeast of Orick (lat. 41°18'N, long. 124°02'55" W; sec. 34, T 11 N, R 1 E); the stream goes through Elk Prairie (1). Named on Fern Canyon (1966) and Orick (1966) 7.5' quadrangles.

Prairie Creek [TRINITY]: *stream*, flows 3 miles to Trinity River 10.5 miles east-southeast of Burnt Ranch (lat. 40°45'45" N, long. 123°17'W; sec. 33, T 5 N, R 8 E); the mouth of the stream is opposite Little Prairie. Named on Ironside Mountain (1951) 15' quadrangle.

Prather Flat [TRINITY]: *area*, 8 miles south of Kettenpom (lat. 40°02'35" N, long. 123°25'55" W; sec. 7, T 5 S, R 7 E). Named on Lake Mountain (1967) 7.5' quadrangle.

Prather Mill [LAKE]: *locality*, less than 1 mile south-southwest of Three Crossings (lat. 39°18'25" N, long. 122°55'35" W; at SE cor. sec. 24, T 17 N, R 10 W). Site named on Elk Mountain (1967) 7.5' quadrangle.

Pratt Mountain [HUMBOLDT]: *peak*, 6 miles southwest of Alderpoint (lat. 40°07'10" N, long. 123°41'30" W; near NE cor. sec. 14, T 4 S, R 4 E). Altitude 3892 feet. Named on Harris (1969) 7.5' quadrangle.

Preacher Gulch [HUMBOLDT]: *canyon*, drained by a stream that flows 2.25 miles to Bull Creek (1) 14 miles south-southeast of Scotia (lat. 40°17'20" N, long. 124°00'30" W). Named on Bull Creek (1969) and Weott (1969) 7.5' quadrangles.

Preacher Meadow [TRINITY]: *area*, 18 miles north-northeast of Weaverville along Swift Creek (1) (lat. 40°57'50" N, long. 122°47'50" W; on W line sec. 21, T 36 N, R 8 W). Named on Trinity Dam (1950) 15' quadrangle.

Preacher Meadow Camp Ground [TRINITY]: *locality*, 20 miles north-northeast of Weaverville along Swift Creek (1) (lat. 40°57'45" N, long. 122°43'50" W; sec. 24, T 36 N, R 8 W). Named on Schell Mountain (1950) 15' quadrangle.

Preachers Peak [TRINITY]: *peak*, 28 miles south of Etna, which is in Siskiyou County, on Trinity-Siskiyou County line (lat. 41°03'35" N, long. 122°55'W; sec. 17, T 37 N, R 9 W). Altitude 7180 feet. Named on Coffee Creek (1955) 15' quadrangle.

Pregnant Spring [MENDOCINO]: *spring*, 5 miles west-southwest of Hopland (lat. 38°57'10" N, long. 123°12'15" W; sec. 29, T 13 N, R 12 W). Named on Hopland (1960) 15' quadrangle.

Prescott Cabin [DEL NORTE]: *locality*, 5.25 miles south of Broken Rib Mountain (lat. 41°48'50" N, long. 123°42'30" W). Ruins named on Devils Punchbowl (1981) 7.5' quadrangle.

Prescott Fork [DEL NORTE]: *stream*, flows 7 miles to South Fork Smith River 7.5 miles northeast of Buck Mountain (lat. 41°42'05" N, long. 123°45'10" W); the stream is west of Prescott Mountain. Named on Devils Punchbowl (1981) and Prescott Mountain (1981) 7.5' quadrangles. United States Board on Geographic Names (1965d, p. 11) rejected the name "Prescott Fork Smith River" for the stream.

Prescott Lake [DEL NORTE]: *lake*, 350 feet long, 4.5 miles north of Harrington Mountain (lat. 41°44'15" N, long. 123°40'25" W); the lake is 1200 feet northwest of Prescott Mountain. Named on Prescott Mountain (1981) 7.5' quadrangle.

Prescott Mountain [DEL NORTE]: *peak*, 4.25 miles north of Harrington Mountain on Del Norte-Siskiyou County line (lat. 41°44'05" N, long. 123°40'20" W). Altitude 5871 feet. Named on Prescott Mountain (1981) 7.5' quadrangle.

Presswood [MENDOCINO]: *locality*, 1.25 miles north of Ukiah along Northwestern Pacific Railroad (lat. 39°10'05" N, long. 123°12'15" W). Named on Ukiah (1958) 7.5' quadrangle.

Preston Island [DEL NORTE]: *peninsula*, along the coast at Crescent City (lat. 41°45'05" N, long. 124°12'50" W). Named on Crescent City (1966) 7.5' quadrangle.

Preston Prairie [HUMBOLDT]: *area*, 7.25 miles south-southeast of Coyote Peak (lat. 41°02'05" N, long. 123°49'05" W). Named on Hupa Mountain (1982) 7.5' quadrangle.

Price Creek [HUMBOLDT]: *stream*, flows 8.5 miles to Eel River nearly 5 miles south of Fortuna (lat. 40°31'45" N, long. 124°09'40" W; sec. 27, T 2 N, R 1 W). Named on Ferndale (1959) and Fortuna (1959) 7.5' quadrangles. The name commemorates Isaac Price, who settled in the neighborhood in 1852 (Gudde, 1949, p. 273).

Price Creek [TRINITY]: *stream*, flows 7.5 miles to Trinity River 13 miles northeast of Hyampom (lat. 40°44'20" N, long. 123°15'W). Named on Hayfork (1951) and Hyampom (1951) 15' quadrangles. Called Coy Bar Creek on United States Geological Survey's (1915) map.

Price Creek: see **Pipe Creek** [HUMBOLDT].

Prince Island [DEL NORTE]: *island*, 0.25 mile long, 3.5 miles west-northwest of the town of Smith River, and 700 feet offshore (lat. 41°57'05" N, long. 124°12'50" W). Named on Smith River (1966) 7.5' quadrangle. Officials of United States Coast Survey named the feature about 1900, probably for Francis Prince, who came to the region before 1879 (Gudde, 1949, p. 273).

Princess Rock [HUMBOLDT]: *relief feature*, 9.5 miles east-northeast of the town of Blue Lake (lat. 40°54'50" N, long. 123°48'55" W; near SE cor. sec. 10, T 6 N, R 3 E). Named on Lord-Ellis Summit (1973) 7.5' quadrangle.

Pringle Ridge [HUMBOLDT]: *ridge*, east-southeast-trending, 1.5 miles long, 3.5 miles east-southeast of Honeydew (lat. 40°13'15" N, long. 124°03'30" W). Named on Honeydew (1970) 7.5' quadrangle.

Prisoner Rock [HUMBOLDT]: *rock*, 0.5 mile south of Trinidad in Trinidad Bay (lat. 41°03'10" N, long. 124°08'35" W). Named on Trinidad (1966) 7.5' quadrangle.

Pritchard Creek [HUMBOLDT]: *stream*, flows 4.5 miles to Mattole River 16 miles south-southwest of Scotia (lat. 40°15'40" N, long. 124°11'20" W; sec. 28, T 2 S, R 1 W). Named on Buckeye Mountain (1970) 7.5' quadrangle. Called Pritchett Creek on Scotia (1950) 15' quadrangle. James Pritchett settled by the stream in 1859 or 1860 (Turner, p. 175).

Pritchett Creek: see **Pritchard Creek** [HUMBOLDT].

Prospect Creek [TRINITY]: *stream*, flows 5.5 miles to East Fork of South Fork Trinity River 9.5 miles south of Dubakella Mountain (lat. 40°14'50" N, long. 120°06'45" W). Named on Dubakella Mountain (1954) 15' quadrangle.

Prosper Ridge [HUMBOLDT]: *ridge*, generally west-trending, 5.5 miles long, 3.5 miles south-southwest of Petrolia (lat. 40°16'30" N, long. 124°18'15" W). Named on Petrolia (1969) 7.5' quadrangle.

Pudding Creek [MENDOCINO]: *stream*, flows 14 miles to the sea 1 mile north-northwest of Fort Bragg (lat. 39°27'35" N, long. 123°48'30" W; near N line sec. 1, T 18 N, R 18 W). Named on Fort Bragg (1960) 7.5' quadrangle. According to Crump (p. 56), a station of California Western Railroad located 1 mile from Fort Bragg has the name "Pudding Creek."

Puerto de la Trinidad: see **Trinidad Bay** [HUMBOLDT].

Pularvasar Creek [HUMBOLDT]: *stream*, flows nearly 2 miles to Blue Creek 8.5 miles north-northwest of Johnsons (lat. 41°25'25" N, long. 123°55'30" W; near SE cor. sec. 15, T 12 N, R 2 E). Named on Ah Pah Ridge (1983) 7.5' quadrangle.

Pullen Creek [HUMBOLDT]: *stream*, flows 2.5 miles to Bear River 7 miles south of Scotia (lat. 40°23'05" N, long. 124°04'30" W). Named on Scotia (1970) 7.5' quadrangle.

Pumpkin Camp [HUMBOLDT]: *locality*, 1.5 miles southwest of Weitchpec (lat. 41°10'25" N, long. 123°43'50" W; sec. 9, T 9 N, R 4 E). Named on Weitchpec (1979) 7.5' quadrangle.

Punta Arenas: see **Point Arena** [MENDOCINO] (2).

Punta de Barrancas: see **Point Arena** [MENDOCINO] (1).

Punta Gorda [HUMBOLDT]: *promontory*, 6 miles southwest of Petrolia along the coast (lat. 40°15'45" N, long. 124°21'45" W; sec. 25, T 2 S, R 3 W). Named on Petrolia (1969) 7.5' quadrangle. Spaniards gave this name to a feature located farther north, but eventually the name shifted to the present place (Wagner, p. 390). The promontory had the local name "Windy Point" in the 1920's (Clark, p. 107).

Punta Gorda: see **Table Bluff** [HUMBOLDT] (1).

Puntas Arenas: see **Point Arena** [MENDOCINO] (2).

Purdys Gardens [MENDOCINO]: *locality*, 6.5 miles east-southeast of Ukiah (lat. 39°06'45" N, long. 123°05'35" W; near S line sec. 32, T 15 N, R 11 W). Named on Purdys Gardens (1958) 7.5' quadrangle.

Purington Creek: see **Perington Creek** [HUMBOLDT].

Puta Creek: see **Putah Creek** [LAKE].

Putah: see **Lower Lake** [LAKE].

Putah Creek [LAKE]: *stream*, flows 25 miles to Napa County 4.5 miles south-southeast of Jericho Valley (lat. 38°46'05" N, long. 122°24'55" W; near S line sec. 28, T 11 N, R 5 W). Named on Jericho Valley (1958), Middletown (1958), and Whispering Pines (1958) 7.5' quadrangles. Gibbs (p. 109) called the stream Putos creek, "or the Rio Dolores, as sometimes called." Tyson (p. 21) called it Puto Creek, and Whitney (p. 105) called it Puta Creek, but United States Board on Geographic Names (1933, p. 625) rejected the form "Puta Creek" for the name. According to Gudde (1949, p. 276), the name "Putah" is from the designation of Indians who lived along the stream, but Kroeber (p. 56) related the word to *puta*, which has the meaning "harlot" in Spanish.

Puter Creek [HUMBOLDT]: *stream*, flows nearly 2 miles to Mad River 2 miles southwest of Korbel (lat. 40°51'N, long. 123°59'25" W; sec. 6, T 5 N, R 2 E). Named on Arcata South (1959) and Korbel (1979) 7.5' quadrangles.

Putos Creek: see **Putah Creek** [LAKE].

Pyramid Point [DEL NORTE]: *promontory,* 3.25 miles west-northwest of the town of Smith River along the coast (lat. 41°56'45" N, long. 124°12'25" W; sec. 17, T 18 N, R 1 W). Named on Smith River (1966) 7.5' quadrangle.

Pyramid Ridge [MENDOCINO]: *ridge,* south-southwest- to west-trending, 1 mile long, 11 miles southeast of Ukiah (lat. 39°02'35" N, long. 123°03'35" W; sec. 27, 28, T 14 N, R 11 W). Named on Purdys Gardens (1958) 7.5' quadrangle.

—Q—

Quakenbush Mountain [LAKE]: *ridge,* west-trending, 1.5 miles long, 3.5 miles north of the town of Lower Lake (lat. 38°57'40" N, long. 122°36'W; mainly in sec. 23, 24, T 13 N, R 7 W). Named on Lower Lake (1958) 7.5' quadrangle.

Quarry Creek [HUMBOLDT]: *stream,* flows 3 miles to Mad River 0.5 mile southwest of the town of Blue Lake (lat. 40°52'30" N, long. 123°59'55" W; sec. 30, T 6 N, R 2 E). Named on Arcata South (1959) and Korbel (1979) 7.5' quadrangles.

Quartz Canyon [LAKE]: *canyon,* drained by a stream that flows 3.25 miles to Wolf Creek 6.25 miles north-northeast of Clearlake Oaks (lat. 39°05'55" N, long. 122°36'55" W). Named on Clearlake Oaks (1960) 15' quadrangle.

Quartz Creek [DEL NORTE]: *stream,* flows 8 miles to South Fork Smith River 2.25 miles northeast of Buck Mountain (lat. 41°39'10" N, long. 123°49'50" W). Named on Ship Mountain (1982) 7.5' quadrangle.

Quartz Spring [TRINITY]: *spring,* 21 miles northeast of Weaverville (lat. 40°55'N, long. 122°36'40" W; sec. 1, T 35 N, R 7 W). Named on Schell Mountain (1950) 15' quadrangle.

Queatchumpah Creek [TRINITY]: *stream,* flows 2.25 miles to Eel River 8 miles southeast of Alderpoint [HUMBOLDT] (lat. 40°05'20" N, long. 123°30'50" W; at E line sec. 29, T 4 S, R 6 E). Named on Jewett Rock (1969) 7.5' quadrangle.

Queen Peak [HUMBOLDT]: *peak,* 3.5 miles north-northeast of Point Delgada (lat. 40°04'N, long. 124°01'55" W; sec. 35, T 4 S, R 1 E). Named on Shelter Cove (1969) 7.5' quadrangle.

Quercus Point [LAKE]: *promontory,* 4.5 miles east-southeast of Lakeport along Clear Lake (lat. 39°01'50" N, long. 122°50'W; sec. 26, T 14 N, R 9 W). Named on Lucerne (1958) 7.5' quadrangle.

Quicksilver: see **Middletown** [LAKE].

Quigley Soda Springs: see **Arabella**, under **Long Valley** [LAKE] (2).

Quill Slough [HUMBOLDT]: *water feature,* joins Hawk Slough nearly 6 miles north of Ferndale (lat. 40°39'35" N, long. 124°15'50" W). Named on Cannibal Island (1959) 7.5' quadrangle.

Quinby: see **Denny** [TRINITY].

Quinby Creek [TRINITY]:

(1) *stream,* flows 3.25 miles to Trinity River 1.5 miles east of Salyer (lat. 40°53'35" N, long. 123°33'20" W; at E line sec. 13, T 6 N, R 5 E). Named on Salyer (1979) 7.5' quadrangle.

(2) *stream,* flows 4.5 miles to New River 11 miles north-northeast of Burnt Ranch (lat. 40°57'N, long. 123°23'W). Named on Ironside Mountain (1951) 15' quadrangle.

Quinliven Gulch [MENDOCINO]: *canyon,* drained by a stream that flows 1.25 miles to the sea 3.5 miles northwest of Gualala (lat. 38°48'05" N, long. 123°34'35" W; sec. 18, T 11 N, R 15 W). Named on Gualala (1960) 7.5' quadrangle. Called Quin Loven Gulch on Point Arena (1943) 15' quadrangle, but United States Board on Geographic Names (1962c p. 21) rejected the names "Quin Loven Gulch" and "Quinlivin Gulch" for the feature, and noted that the name "Quinliven" commemorates the Quinliven family, early settlers in the neighborhood.

Quin Loven Gulch: see **Quinliven Gulch** [MENDOCINO].

—R—

Rabbit: see **Jack Rabbit Valley** [HUMBOLDT].

Rabbit Glade Spring [LAKE]: *spring,* 7.5 miles south-southwest of Potato Hill (lat. 39°15'15" N, long. 122°51'25" W). Named on Potato Hill (1967) 7.5' quadrangle.

Rabbit Valley [LAKE]: *canyon,* drained by a stream that flows 1.5 miles to Kelsey Creek 7.5 miles south-southeast of Kelseyville (lat. 38°52'50" N, long. 122°47'50" W; at W line sec. 19, T 12 N, R 8 W). Named on The Geysers (1959) 7.5' quadrangle.

Racehorse Prairie [HUMBOLDT]: *area,* 6.5 miles south of Johnsons (lat. 41°15'35" N, long. 123°50'45" W; sec. 16, T 10 N, R 3 E). Named on Johnsons (1982) 7.5' quadrangle.

Race Track [TRINITY]: *area,* 11 miles northwest of Forest Glen (lat. 40°28'55" N, long. 123°28'50" W; sec. 10, T 1 N, R 6 E). Named on Sportshaven (1973) 7.5' quadrangle.

Rackerby Flat [TRINITY]: *area,* 19 miles northeast of Weaverville along Trinity River (lat. 40°56'10" N, long. 122°41'15" W; near E line sec. 32, T 36 N, R 7 W); the place is at the mouth of Rackerby Gulch. Named on Schell Mountain (1950) 15' quadrangle.

Rackerby Gulch [TRINITY]: *canyon,* drained by a stream that flows 1.5 miles to Rackerby Flat 19 miles northeast of Weaverville (lat. 40°56'N, long. 122°41'05" W; at E line sec. 32, T 36 N, R 7 W). Named on Schell Mountain (1950) 15' quadrangle.

Rackerby Ridge [TRINITY]: *ridge,* north-northeast- to south-trending, 2 miles long, 20 miles northeast of Weaverville (lat. 40°56'45" N, long. 122°40'W); the ridge is around the head of Rackerby Gulch. Named on Schell Mountain (1950) 15' quadrangle.

Rackout Spring [MENDOCINO]: *spring,* 5 miles south-southeast of Eden Valley (lat. 39°33'20" N, long. 123°09'25" W; near S line sec. 26, T 20 N, R 12 W). Named on Brushy Mountain (1966) 7.5' quadrangle.

Racoon Gulch: see **Coon Creek** [HUMBOLDT] (5).

Raff Creek [TRINITY]: *stream,* flows 1.5 miles to Eel River 11.5 miles south of Kettenpom (lat. 39°59'50" N, long. 123°28'50" W; at E line sec. 27, T 5 S, R 6 E). Named on Updegraff Ridge (1967) 7.5' quadrangle.

Ragged Gulch [TRINITY]: *canyon,* drained by a stream that flows 1 mile to East Fork Stuart Fork 13 miles northeast of Weaverville (lat. 40°51'35" N, long. 122°46'30" W; sec. 28, T 35 N, R 8 W). Named on Trinity Lake (1950) 15' quadrangle.

Raglan Flat [TRINITY]: *area,* 6 miles east-northeast of Kettenpom (lat. 40°11'15" N, long. 123°21'20" W; sec. 23, T 3 S, R 7 E). Named on Shannon Butte (1967) 7.5' quadrangle.

Raglan Gulch [TRINITY]: *canyon,* drained by a stream that flows 2.5 miles to North Fork Eel River 5.5 miles east of Kettenpom (lat. 40°10'10" N, long. 123°21'35" W; near SW cor. sec. 26, T 3 S, R 7 E). Named on Shannon Butte (1967) 7.5' quadrangle.

Rail Creek [MENDOCINO]: *stream,* mainly in Sonoma County, but flows for 1 mile in Mendocino County 11 miles south of Hopland (lat. 38°49'N, long. 123°08'25" W; sec. 12, T 11 N, R 12 W). Named on Hopland (1960) 15' quadrangle.

Rail Gulch [TRINITY]:

(1) *canyon,* drained by a stream that flows 1.25 miles to Indian Valley Creek 10.5 miles southeast of Hyampom (lat. 40°30'45" N, long. 123°18'30" W; near E line sec. 31, T 2 N, R 8 E). Named on Hyampom (1951) and Pickett Peak (1954) 15' quadrangles.

(2) *canyon,* drained by a stream that flows 1.25 miles to Salt Creek (4) 7.5 miles north of Dubakella Mountain (lat. 40°29'20" N, long. 123°09'50" W; at S line sec. 36, T 31 N, R 12 W). Named on Dubakella Mountain (1954) and Hayfork (1951) 15' quadrangles.

Rail Pile Ridge [HUMBOLDT]: *ridge,* west-trending, 1 mile long, 6.25 miles southeast of Honeydew (lat. 40°11'35" N, long. 124°01'20" W; on W line sec. 24, T 3 S, R 1 E). Named on Honeydew (1970) 7.5' quadrangle.

Railroad Creek [HUMBOLDT]:

(1) *stream,* flows nearly 3 miles to Little River 5.25 miles east-southeast of Trinidad (lat. 41°01'40" N, long. 124°02'55" W; at N line sec. 3, T 7 N, R 1 E). Named on Crannell (1966) 7.5' quadrangle.

(2) *stream,* flows nearly 2 miles to North Fork Mad River 5.5 miles north-northeast of the town of Blue Lake (lat. 40°57'15" N, long. 123°56'30" W; near NW cor. sec. 34, T 7 N, R 2 E). Named on Blue Lake (1979) 7.5' quadrangle.

Railroad Gulch [HUMBOLDT]: *canyon,* drained by a stream that flows 2 miles to South Fork Elk River (1) nearly 4 miles east-southeast of Fields Landing (lat. 40°42'05" N, long. 124°09'W; sec. 26, T 4 N, R 1 W). Named on Fields Landing (1959) 7.5' quadrangle.

Railroad Gulch [MENDOCINO]:

(1) *canyon,* drained by a stream that flows 2.25 miles to Big River 7.25 miles west-northwest of Comptche (lat. 39°18'55" N, long. 123°42'30" W; near S line sec. 24, T 17 N, R 17 W). Named on Comptche (1960) 15' quadrangle.

(2) *canyon,* drained by a stream that flows nearly 3 miles to Albion River 7.5 miles north of Elk (lat. 39°14'25" N, long. 123°42'30" W; at N line sec. 23, T 16 N, R 17 W). Named on Elk (1960) 7.5' quadrangle.

(3) *canyon,* drained by a stream that flows nearly 2 miles to Albion River 3 miles west of Comptche (lat. 39°15'45" N, long. 123°38'45" W; sec. 9, T 16 N, R 16 W). Named on Comptche (1960) 15' quadrangle.

Rainbow Peak [HUMBOLDT]: *peak,* 7 miles south-southwest of Scotia (lat. 40°23'40" N, long. 124°09'55" W; sec. 10, T 1 S, R 1 W); the peak is at the northwest end of Rainbow Ridge. Altitude 3364 feet. Named on Taylor Peak (1969) 7.5' quadrangle.

Rainbow Peak: see **South Rainbow Peak** [HUMBOLDT].

Rainbow Ridge [HUMBOLDT]: *ridge,* southeast- to south-trending, 7.5 miles long, 8.5 miles south-southwest of Scotia (lat. 40°21'45" N, long. 124°08'15" W). Named on Buckeye Mountain (1970), Bull Creek (1969), and Taylor Peak (1969) 7.5' quadrangles. According to Turner (p. 177), two trappers named the feature in the early 1860's when they saw a rainbow there.

Rainbow Ridge [TRINITY]: *ridge,* generally east-northeast-trending, 2 miles long, 6 miles west-southwest of Black Rock Mountain (lat. 40°10'45" N, long. 123°06'45" W). Named on Black Rock Mountain (1954) 15' quadrangle.

Rainbow Ridge: see **Little Rainbow Ridge** [HUMBOLDT].

Rainey Glades [TRINITY]: *area,* 5.5 miles west-southwest of Forest Glen (lat. 40°20'35" N, long. 123°25'20" W; on S line sec. 30, T 1 S, R 7 E). Named on Ruth Reservoir (1978) 7.5' quadrangle.

Rain Rock: see **The Rain Rock** [HUMBOLDT].

Ramon Creek [MENDOCINO]: *stream,* flows 4 miles to South Fork Big River 5 miles east of Comptche (lat. 39°16'20" N, long. 123°30'10" W; sec. 2, T 16 N, R 15 W). Named on Willits (1961) 15' quadrangle.

Ramon Opening: see **Clark Opening** [MENDOCINO].

Rams Creek: see **Ramshorn Creek** [TRINITY].

Ramsey [MENDOCINO]: *locality,* 6.5 miles north of Spyrock along Northwestern Pacific Railroad (lat. 39°58'20" N, long. 123°26'40" W). Named on Updegraff Ridge (1967) 7.5' quadrangle.

Ramsey Ridge [MENDOCINO]: *ridge,* southeast- to east-trending, 10 miles long, 15 miles north-northwest of Comptche (lat. 39°28'30" N, long. 123°40'W). Named on Comptche (1960) 15' quadrangle, and on Dutchmans Knoll (1966) 7.5' quadrangle.

Ramshorn Creek [TRINITY]: *stream,* flows 3.5 miles to Trinity River 10 miles north of Trinity Center (lat. 41°09'05" N, long. 122°40'W; at E line sec. 16, T 38 N, R 7 W). Named on Bonanza King (1955) 15' quadrangle. Called Rams Cr. on Miller's (1890) map. North Fork enters from the east-northeast 1 mile upstream from the mouth of the main creek and is 3.25 miles long. South Fork enters from the south-southeast 1.5 miles upstream from the mouth of the main creek and is 3.5 miles long. Both forks are named on Bonanza King (1955) 15' quadrangle.

Ramshorn Summit [TRINITY]: *pass,* 10.5 miles north-northeast of Trinity Center (lat. 41°08'20" N, long. 122°35'50" W; sec. 19, T 38 N, R 6 W); the pass is near the head of Ramshorn Creek. Named on Bonanza King (1955) 15' quadrangle.

Ram Spring [MENDOCINO]: *spring,* 7.5 miles east-northeast of Spyrock (2) (lat. 39°55'45" N, long. 123°19'10" W). Named on Mina (1967) 7.5' quadrangle.

Ram Spring Creek [MENDOCINO]: *stream,* flows 2.25 miles to North Fork Eel River 6.5 miles northeast of Spyrock (2) (lat. 39°56'10" N, long. 123°20'45" W); the stream heads near Ram Spring. Named on Mina (1967) 7.5' quadrangle.

Ranch [MENDOCINO]: *locality,* 13 miles north-northwest of Comptche along California Western Railroad (lat. 39°26'05" N, long. 123°42'15" W). Named on Comptche (1960) 15' quadrangle.

Rancheria Creek [HUMBOLDT]: *stream,* flows 3.5 miles to East Branch of South Fork Eel River 10 miles southwest of Alderpoint (lat. 40°03'35" N, long. 123°43'25" W; at E line sec. 4, T 5 S, R 4 E). Named on Harris (1969) 7.5' quadrangle.

Rancheria Creek [MENDOCINO]:

(1) *stream,* flows less than 1 mile to South Fork Eel River 2.5 miles north of Piercy (lat. 40°00'05" N, long. 123°46'35" W; sec. 24, T 5 S, R 3 E). Named on Piercy (1969) 7.5' quadrangle.

(2) *stream,* flows 33 miles to join Anderson Creek (2) and form Navarro River 5 miles west-northwest of Boonville (lat. 39°03'10" N, long. 123°26'25" W; near SE cor. sec. 19, T 14 N, R 14 W). Named on Boonville (1959), Hopland (1960), and Ornbaun Valley (1960) 15' quadrangles.

Rancheria Creek [TRINITY]:

(1) *stream,* flows 1 mile to New River 10 miles north-northeast of Burnt Ranch (lat. 40°56'20" N, long. 123°23'15" W). Named on Ironside Mountain (1951) 15' quadrangle.

(2) *stream,* flows 4 miles to Swift Creek (1) 21 miles northeast of Weaverville (lat. 40°59'15" N, long. 122°42'10" W; near SW cor sec. 8, T 36 N, R 7 W). Named on Bonanza King (1955) and Schell Mountain (1950) 15' quadrangles.

Ranch Opening: see **Upper Ranch Opening** [MENDOCINO].

Randall Creek [HUMBOLDT]: *stream,* flows 2 miles to the sea 8.5 miles south of Petrolia (lat. 40°12'N, long. 124°16'55" W; at S line sec. 15, T 3 S, R 2 W). Named on Cooskie Creek (1969) 7.5' quadrangle. Called Reynolds Creek on Gorda (1926) 15' quadrangle.

Ranger Mountain [HUMBOLDT]: *peak,* 4 miles east of Coyote Peak (lat. 41°07'35" N, long. 123°47'05" W; near N line sec. 36, T 9 N, R 3 E). Altitude 2690 feet. Named on Hupa Mountain (1982) 7.5' quadrangle.

Ranger Spring: see **Smith River** [DEL NORTE] (1).

Rarick Gulch [TRINITY]: *canyon,* drained by a stream that flows 3 miles to Canyon Creek (1) 4 miles east-northeast of Helena (lat. 40°48'05" N, long. 123°03'45" W; sec. 13, T 34 N, R 11 W). Named on Helena (1951) 15' quadrangle.

Raspberry Gulch [TRINITY]: *canyon,* drained by a stream that flows 2 miles to South Fork Trinity River 5.25 miles west of Black Rock Mountain (lat. 40°12'55" N, long. 123°06'30" W; sec. 4, T 27 N, R 11 W). Named on Black Rock Mountain (1954) 15' quadrangle.

Rattlesnake Camp [TRINITY]:

(1) *locality,* 9 miles south-southwest of Cecilville, which is in Siskiyou County (lat. 41°01'25" N, long. 123°11'35" W); the place is near Rattlesnake Lake. Site named on Cecil Lake (1979) 7.5' quadrangle.

(2) *locality,* 15 miles north of Helena along North Fork Trinity River (lat. 40°59'N, long. 123°09'30" W); the place is at the mouth of Rattlesnake Creek (1). Named on Helena (1951) 15' quadrangle.

Rattlesnake Creek [HUMBOLDT]:

(1) *stream,* flows 2.5 miles to East Creek 8 miles east-southeast of Showers Mountain (lat. 40°32'30" N, long. 123°33'20" W; sec. 24, T 2 N, R 5 E). Named on Blake Mountain (1979) 7.5' quadrangle.

(2) *stream,* flows 4.25 miles to join Oil Creek (3) and form Upper North Fork Mattole River 13 miles south of Scotia (lat. 40°17'25" N, long. 124°06'35" W; near N line sec. 19, T 2 S, R 1 E). Named on Bull Creek (1969) 7.5' quadrangle. According to Turner (p. 177), the name is from a winding road by the stream—the road was called Snake Road and Rattlesnake Road.

Rattlesnake Creek [LAKE]:

(1) *stream,* flows 5.5 miles to Eel River 6 miles northwest of Crockett Peak (lat. 39°29'35" N, long. 122°51'20" W; near N line sec. 22, T 19 N, R 9 W). Named on Crockett Peak (1967), Hull Mountain (1967), and Lake Pillsbury (1967) 7.5' quadrangles.

(2) *stream,* flows 2.5 miles to North Fork Cache Creek 8 miles northeast of the town of Upper Lake (lat. 39°14'40" N, long. 122°48'20" W). Named on Bartlett Mountain (1958) 7.5' quadrangle.

Rattlesnake Creek [MENDOCINO]: *stream,* flows 11 miles to South Fork Eel River 4.25 miles southeast of Leggett (lat. 39°49'25" N, long. 123°39'20" W; near W line sec. 20, T 23 N, R 16 W). Named on Iron Peak (1967), Leggett (1969), and Tan Oak Park (1969) 7.5' quadrangles.

Rattlesnake Creek [MENDOCINO-TRINITY]: *stream,* heads in Trinity County and flows 7.5 miles to Middle Fork Eel River 16 miles northeast of Covelo in Mendocino County (lat. 39°58'20" N, long. 123°03'20" W; near S line sec. 35, T 25 N, R 11 W). Named on Black Rock Mountain (1954) and Yolla Bolly (1954) 15' quadrangles, and on Leech Lake Mountain (1966) 7.5' quadrangle.

Rattlesnake Creek [TRINITY]:

(1) *stream,* flows 6.25 miles to North Fork Trinity River 15 miles north of Helena (lat. 40°59'N, long. 123°09'30" W). Named on Helena (1951) 15' quadrangle, and on Cecil Lake (1979) and Thompson Peak (1979) 7.5' quadrangles. Middle Fork is 3 miles long and enters 9.5 miles south of Cecilville, which is in Siskiyou County; it is named on Helena (1951) 15' quadrangle, and on Thompson Peak (1979) 7.5' quadrangle.

(2) *stream,* flows 10 miles to South Fork Trinity River less than 1 mile east-southeast of the center of Forest Glen (lat. 40°22'10" N, long. 123°18'40" W; sec. 19, T 1 S, R 8 E). Named on Dubakella Mountain (1954) 15' quadrangle, and on Forest Glen (1979) and Naufus Creek (1979) 7.5' quadrangles. United States Board on Geographic Names (1977c, p. 5) gave the name "Post Creek" as a variant.

Rattlesnake Creek: see **Little Rattlesnake Creek** [TRINITY]; **North Rattlesnake Creek** [TRINITY]; **Post Creek** [TRINITY].

Rattlesnake Flat [DEL NORTE]: *area,* 6 miles north-northwest of Buck Mountain along South Fork Smith River (lat. 41°41'25" N, long. 123°55'35" W; near SE cor. sec 15, T 15 N, R 2 E). Named on Cant Hook Mountain (1982) 7.5' quadrangle.

Rattlesnake Gap [TRINITY]: *pass,* 11.5 miles north-northeast of Hayfork (lat. 40°42'15" N, long. 123°05'40" W). Named on Hayfork (1951) 15' quadrangle.

Rattlesnake Island [LAKE]: *island,* 3000 feet long, less than 1 mile south of Clearlake Oaks in Clear Lake (lat. 39°00'40" N, long. 122°40'40" W). Named on Clearlake Oaks (1958) 7.5' quadrangle.

Rattlesnake Lake [DEL NORTE]: *lake,* 650 feet long, 7.25 miles northwest of Buck Mountain (lat. 41°42'05" N, long. 123°56'55" W; near N line sec. 16, T 15 N, R 2 E); the lake is near the head of Rattlesnake Slide. Named on Cant Hook Mountain (1982) 7.5' quadrangle.

Rattlesnake Lake [TRINITY]: *intermittent lake,* 150 feet long, 9 miles south-southwest of Cecilville, which is in Siskiyou County (lat. 41°01'30" N, long. 123°11'30" W). Named on Cecil Lake (1979) 7.5' quadrangle. United States Board on Geographic Names (1960a, p. 16) rejected the name "New River Lake" for the feature.

Rattlesnake Mountain [DEL NORTE]: *ridge,* generally south-southeast-trending, 5 miles long, 4.5 miles west-northwest of Buck Mountain (lat. 41°38'25" N, long. 123°57'05" W). Named on Cant Hook Mountain (1982) and Klamath Glen (1982) 7.5' quadrangles.

Rattlesnake Mountain: see **Little Rattlesnake Mountain** [DEL NORTE].

Rattlesnake Point [TRINITY]: *relief feature,* 4 miles southeast of Forest Glen along South Fork Trinity River (lat. 40°19'45" N, long. 123°16'45" W; on S line sec. 33, T 1 S, R 8 E). Named on Forest Glen (1979) 7.5' quadrangle.

Rattlesnake Ridge [HUMBOLDT]:

(1) *ridge,* northwest-trending, 1 mile long, 3 miles south-southwest of Orleans (lat. 41°15'35" N, long. 123°33'30" W). Named on Orleans (1978) 7.5' quadrangle.

(2) *ridge,* generally south-southwest-trending, 1.25 miles long, 6 miles south-southwest of Honeydew (lat. 40°09'30" N, long. 124°09'20" W). Named

on Shubrick Peak (1969) 7.5' quadrangle.

Rattlesnake Ridge [TRINITY]: *ridge*, generally east-trending, 4 miles long, 3.5 miles east-southeast of Forest Glen (lat. 40°20'50" N, long. 123°16'W). Named on Dubakella Mountain (1954) and Forest Glen (1979) 7.5' quadrangles.

Rattlesnake Rock [HUMBOLDT]: *relief feature*, 5 miles south-southeast of Showers Mountain (lat. 40°30'50" N, long. 123°38'50" W; near NE cor. sec. 31, T 2 N R 5 E). Named on Showers Mountain (1978) 7.5' quadrangle.

Rattlesnake Slide [DEL NORTE]: *relief feature*, 7 miles northwest of Buck Mountain (lat. 41°42'05" N, long. 123°56'25" W; near NW cor. sec. 15, T 15 N, R 2 E). Named on Cant Hook Mountain (1982) 7.5' quadrangle.

Rattlesnake Spring [MENDOCINO]: *spring*, 6 miles north of Eden Valley (lat. 39°42'45" N, long. 123°10'50" W; sec. 3, T 21 N, R 12 W). Named on Jamison Ridge (1967) 7.5' quadrangle.

Rattlesnake Summit [MENDOCINO]: *pass*, 10.5 miles east-southeast of Leggett (lat. 39°47'10" N, long. 123°32'35" W; sec. 4, T 22 N, R 15 W); the pass is at the head of a branch of Rattlesnake Creek (2). Named on Tan Oak Park (1969) 7.5' quadrangle.

Rawles Canyon [MENDOCINO]: *canyon*, drained by a stream that flows less than 1 mile to Rancheria Creek (2) 8 miles northwest of Ornbaun Valley (lat. 38°59'N, long. 123°25' 05" W; at E line sec. 17, T 13 N, R 14 W). Named on Ornbaun Valley (1960) 15' quadrangle.

Ray Gulch [MENDOCINO]: *canyon*, drained by a stream that flows 3.5 miles to Navarro River 4 miles northeast of Elk (lat. 39°10'10" N, long. 123°39'40" W; near E line sec. 7, T 15 N, R 16 W). Named on Navarro (1961) 15' quadrangle.

Raymond Flat [TRINITY]: *area*, 7 miles north-northwest of Helena along North Fork Trinity River (lat. 40°52'20" N, long. 123°09'45" W). Named on Helena (1951) 15' quadrangle.

Rays Creek [HUMBOLDT]: *stream*, flows 3 miles to East Branch of South Fork Eel River 10 miles south-southwest of Alderpoint (lat. 40°02'55" N, long. 123°42'20" W; near E line sec. 3, T 5 S, R 4 E). Named on Harris (1969) 7.5' quadrangle.

Rays Peak [TRINITY] *peak*, 5.5 miles south-southeast of Cecilville, which is in Siskiyou County, on Trinity-Siskiyou County line (lat. 41°03'55" N, long. 123°06'15" W). Altitude 7006 feet. Named on Thompson Peak (1979) 7.5' quadrangle.

Rays Peak [TRINITY]: *peak*, 3 miles northeast of Hyampom (lat. 40°38'50" N, long. 123°24'35" W; near S line sec. 8, T 3 N, R 7 E). Altitude 3920 feet. Named on Hyampom (1951) 15' quadrangle.

Ray Spring [MENDOCINO]: *spring*, 8 miles north-northeast of Covelo (lat. 39°53'50" N, long. 123°10'55" W). Named on Bluenose Ridge (1967) 7.5' quadrangle.

Rays Resort [MENDOCINO]: *locality*, 5.5 miles northwest of Boonville (lat. 39°03'30" N, long. 123°27'W). Named on Orrs (1944) 15' quadrangle.

Reading Bar [TRINITY]: *locality*, 6 miles south of Weaverville along Trinity River (lat. 40°38'35" N, long. 122°57'W; sec. 12, T 32 N, R 10 W); the place is at the mouth of Reading Creek. Named on Weaverville (1950) 15' quadrangle. United States Board on Geographic Names (1971a, p. 3) approved the name "Readings Bar" for the place, and gave the name "Reading Bar" as a variant; Major Pierson Barton Reading discovered gold at the site in 1848.

Reading Creek [TRINITY]: *stream*, flows 16 miles to Trinity River 6.25 miles south of Weaverville (lat. 40°38'35" N, long. 122°57'10" W; sec. 12, T 32 N, R 10 W); Reading Bar is at the mouth of the stream. Named on Weaverville (1950) 15' quadrangle. Called Reading's Creek on Miller's (1890) map, and called Reddings Cr. on Averill's (1940) map. United States Board on Geographic Names (1943, p. 12) rejected the names "Redding Creek" and "Reddings Creek" for the stream. A mining place of the 1850's called Turners Bar was situated 1 mile west of the mouth of Reading Creek on the south side of Trinity River (Gudde, 1975, p. 353). A mining place called Buck-Eye Bar was located along Trinity River 0.5 mile below Turners Bar, and a mining place called Cape Horn Bar was along the river opposite Turners Bar (Hoover, Rensch, and Rensch, p. 554).

Reading Rock: see **Redding Rock** [HUMBOLDT].

Readings Bar: see **Reading Bar** [TRINITY].

Reading's Creek: see **Reading Creek** [TRINITY].

Reas Creek [HUMBOLDT]: *stream*, flows 4.25 miles to Salt River 2 miles northwest of Ferndale (lat. 40°35'45" N, long. 124°17'30" W; near W line sec. 34, T 3 N, R 2 W). Named on Ferndale (1959) 7.5' quadrangle.

Red Alder Campground [DEL NORTE]: *locality*, 6.5 miles southeast of Crescent City along West Branch Mill Creek (lat. 41°42'10" N, long. 124°05'50" W; near SW cor. sec. 8, T 15 N, R 1 E). Named on Childs Hill (1966) 7.5' quadrangle.

Redbank Gorge [LAKE]: *relief feature*, 1 mile north-northeast of the town of Lower Lake along Cache Creek (lat. 38°55'20" N, long. 122°36'05" W; sec. 2, T 12 N, R 7 W). Named on Lower Lake (1958) 7.5' quadrangle.

Red Bluff [HUMBOLDT]: *hill*, 1 mile north-northeast of Fields Landing (lat. 40°44'30" N, long. 124°12'40" W; sec. 8, T 4 N, R 1 W). Named on Fields Landing (1959) 7.5' quadrangle. Called Humboldt Bluff on Rohnerville (1920) 15' quadrangle, but United States Board on Geographic Names (1943, p. 12) rejected this name for the feature. Turner (p. 177) gave the alternate names "Red Point" and "Howard's Bluff" for it.

Red Cap Creek [HUMBOLDT]: *stream*, flows 20 miles to Klamath River 4.5 miles southwest of Orleans (lat. 41°15'30" N, long. 123°36'15" W). Named on Hopkins Butte (1979), Orleans (1978), Salmon Mountain (1978), and Trinity Mountain (1979) 7.5' quadrangles. Called Redcap Creek on Sawyers Bar (1923) 30'quadrangle. The name recalls an Indian called Red Cap for the woollen hat that he wore (Gudde, 1949, p. 281). Middle Fork enters 10.5 miles upstream from the mouth of the main creek; it is 4.5 miles long and is named on Hopkins Butte (1979) and Salmon Mountain (1978) 7.5' quadrangles. North Fork enters from the northeast 8.5 miles upstream from the mouth of the main creek; it is 6.25 miles long and is named on Hopkins Butte (1979) and Salmon Mountain (1978) 7.5' quadrangles. South Fork enters from the south 7.5 miles upstream from the mouth of the main creek; it is 2.5 miles long and is named on Hopkins Butte (1979) 7.5' quadrangle.

Red Cap Glade [HUMBOLDT]: *area*, 5 miles west-southwest of Orleans (lat. 41°16'10" N, long. 123°37'30" W). Named on Fish Lake (1974) 7.5' quadrangle.

Red Cap Gulch [HUMBOLDT]: *canyon*, drained by a stream that flows 1 mile to Klamath River nearly 4 miles west-southwest of Orleans (lat. 41°16'30" N, long. 123°36'10" W). Named on Orleans (1978) 7.5' quadrangle.

Red Cap Gulch: see **Little Red Cap Gulch** [HUMBOLDT].

Red Cap Hole [HUMBOLDT]: *relief feature*, 7.25 miles northwest of Trinity Mountain (lat. 41°07'05" N, long. 123°29'50" W). Named on Trinity Mountain (1979) 7.5' quadrangle.

Red Cap Lake [HUMBOLDT]: *lake*, 550 feet long, less than 1 mile south-southwest of Salmon Mountain (lat. 41°10'20" N, long. 123°24'50" W). Named on Salmon Mountain (1978) 7.5' quadrangle. On Sawyers Bar (1923) 30'quadrangle, the name has the form "Redcap Lake."

Red Cap Prairie [HUMBOLDT]: *area*, 11.5 miles east-southeast of Weitchpec on Horse Trail Ridge (lat. 41°08'35" N, long. 123°30'W). Named on Hopkins Butte (1979) and Salmon Mountain (1978) 7.5' quadrangles. On Sawyers Bar (1923) 30'quadrangle, the name has the form "Redcap Prairie."

Red Chert Creek [MENDOCINO-TRINITY]: *stream*, heads in Trinity County and flows 4 miles, partly in Mendocino County, to Middle Fork Eel River 16 miles south-southwest of Black Rock Mountain in Trinity County (lat. 39°59'45" N, long. 123°06'25" W; near NE cor. sec. 29, T 25 N, R 11 W). Named on Bluenose Ridge (1967) 7.5' quadrangle.

Redcrest [HUMBOLDT]: *village*, 5.5 miles north of Weott (lat. 40°24'N, long. 123°56'55" W; near NE cor. sec. 9, T 1 S, R 2 E). Named on Redcrest (1969) 7.5' quadrangle. Postal authorities established Redcrest post office in 1965; the name is from redwood trees at the site (Salley, p. 182).

Redding Creek: see **Reading Creek** [TRINITY].

Redding Rock [HUMBOLDT]: *rock*, 7.25 miles west-northwest of Orick, and 5 miles offshore (lat. 41°20'25" N, long. 124°10'35" W). Named on Orick (1952) 15' quadrangle. Eureka (1949) 1° x 2° quadrangle shows Redding Rock lighthouse at the place. United States Board on Geographic Names (1971a, p. 3) approved the name "Reading Rock" for the feature, and gave the name "Redding Rock" as a variant; the Board pointed out that the name honors Major Pierson Barton Reading, who made a landing at the site in 1849.

Redeye Prairie [HUMBOLDT]: *area*, nearly 5 miles south-southeast of Coyote Peak (lat. 41°04'N, long. 123°49'55" W; near E line sec. 21, T 8 N, R 3 E). Named on Hupa Mountain (1982) 7.5' quadrangle.

Red Flat [TRINITY]: *area*, 7 miles northeast of Weaverville (lat. 40°47'15" N, long. 122°49'45" W; sec. 24, T 34 N, R 9 W). Named on Trinity Dam (1950) 15' quadrangle.

Red Hill [HUMBOLDT]: *ridge*, northeast-trending, less than 0.5 mile long, 3.5 miles east of Yager Junction (lat. 40°33'05" N, long. 123°45'25" W; sec. 17, T 2 N, R 4 E). Named on Yager Junction (1979) 7.5' quadrangle.

Red Hill Gulch [MENDOCINO]: *canyon*, drained by a stream that flows 1 mile to Mill Creek (9) 9.5 miles north-northwest of Boonville (lat. 39°07'15" N, long. 123°27'45" W; sec. 36, T 15 N, R 15 W). Named on Boonville (1959) 15' quadrangle.

Red Lassic [TRINITY]: *peak*, nearly 1 mile south of Black Lassic (lat. 40°19'40" N, long. 123°32'25" W); the peak is less than 1 mile east-southeast of Mount Lassic. Altitude 5898 feet. Named on Black Lassic (1979) 7.5' quadrangle.

Red Lassic: see **Mount Lassic** [HUMBOLDT].

Red Lassic Creek [TRINITY]: *stream*, flows nearly 2 miles to Van Duzen River 8 miles west-southwest of Forest Glen (lat. 40°20'35" N, long. 123°28'25" W; near SE cor. sec. 27, T 1 S, R 6 E). Named on Ruth Reservoir (1978) 7.5' quadrangle.

Red Mountain [DEL NORTE]: *peak*, 4.5 miles east of Klamath Glen (lat. 41°31'25" N, long. 123°54'25" W; at S line sec. 11, T 13 N, R 2 E). Altitude 4253 feet. Named on Klamath Glen (1982) 7.5' quadrangle. United States Board on Geographic Names (1943, p. 12) rejected the names "Mount Toorup," "Mount Turep" and "Red Mountain Ridge" for the feature.

Red Mountain [HUMBOLDT]: *peak,* 8 miles south of Dinsmore (lat. 40°22'40" N, long. 123°34'35" W; sec. 14, T 1 S, R 5 E). Named on Dinsmore (1977) 7.5' quadrangle.

Red Mountain [LAKE]: *peak,* nearly 6 miles north of Three Crossings (lat. 39°22'15" N, long. 122°55'25" W; near E line sec. 36, T 18 N, R 10 W). Altitude 2761 feet. Named on Elk Mountain (1967) 7.5' quadrangle.

Red Mountain [MENDOCINO]:
(1) *ridge,* generally north-trending, 4.25 miles long, 4.5 miles northeast of Leggett (lat. 39°55'50" N, long. 123°39'40" W). Named on Noble Butte (1969) 7.5' quadrangle.
(2) *ridge,* southeast-trending, 0.5 mile long, 8.5 miles southeast of Ukiah (lat. 39°04'N, long. 123°05'25" W; near S line sec. 17, T 14 N, R 11 W). Named on Purdys Gardens (1958) 7.5' quadrangle.

Red Mountain [TRINITY]:
(1) *peak,* 8 miles east-northeast of Trinity Center (lat. 41°03'30" N, long. 122°32'50" W; near NW cor. sec. 22, T 37 N, R 6 W). Altitude 6805 feet. Named on Bonanza King (1955) 15' quadrangle.
(2) *peak,* 5 miles south of Dubakella Mountain (lat. 40°18'55" N, long. 123°08'10" W; on W line sec. 32, T 29 N, R 11 W). Altitude 5637 feet. Named on Dubakella Mountain (1954) 15' quadrangle.
(3) *peak,* 13 miles north of Weaverville (lat. 40°54'45" N, long. 122°53'45" W). Altitude 7928 feet. Named on Trinity Dam (1950) 15' quadrangle.
(4) *peak,* 15 miles southwest of Black Rock Mountain (lat. 40°05'30" N, long. 123°14'10" W; sec. 20, T 26 N, R 12 W). Altitude 4173 feet. Named on Black Rock Mountain (1954) 15' quadrangle.

Red Mountain: see **Granite Peak** [TRINITY]; **Little Red Mountain** [MENDOCINO]; **South Red Mountain** [DEL NORTE].

Red Mountain Basin [LAKE]: *area,* 8.5 miles west of Lakeport (lat. 39°04'10" N, long. 123°04'15" W; sec. 16, T 14 N, R 11 W); the place is 1 mile east of Red Mountain [MENDOCINO]. Named on Purdys Gardens (1958) 7.5' quadrangle.

Red Mountain Camp [LAKE]: *locality,* 9.5 miles west-northwest of Lakeport (lat. 39°04'45" N, long. 123°05'15" W; near N line sec. 17, T 14 N, R 11 W); the place is less than 1 mile north of Red Mountain [MENDOCINO]. Named on Purdys Gardens (1958) 7.5' quadrangle.

Red Mountain Creek [HUMBOLDT]: *stream,* flows 2 miles to Bluff Creek [DEL NORTE-HUMBOLDT] 5 miles north-northeast of Weitchpec (lat. 41°14'55" N, long. 123°39'25" W). Named on Fish Lake (1974) and Weitchpec (1979) 7.5' quadrangles.

Red Mountain Creek [MENDOCINO]: *stream,* flows 6 miles to South Fork Eel River 3 miles southeast of Piercy (lat. 39°55'40" N, long. 123°45'40" W; sec. 17, T 24 N, R 17 W); the stream heads at Red Mountain (1). Named on Noble Butte (1969) and Piercy (1969) 7.5' quadrangles.

Red Mountain Creek [TRINITY]:
(1) *stream,* flows 3 miles to South Fork Trinity River 8 miles south-southwest of Dubakella Mountain (lat. 40°16'25" N, long. 123°10'55" W; sec. 14, T 28 N, R 12 W); the stream heads near Red Mountain (2). Named on Dubakella Mountain (1954) 15' quadrangle.
(2) *stream,* flows 6 miles to North Fork Eel River 11 miles southeast of Kettenpom (lat. 40°03'45" N, long. 123°18'15" W; sec. 5, T 5 S, R 8 E). Named on Black Rock Mountain (1954) 15' quadrangle, and on Long Ridge (1967) 7.5' quadrangle.

Red Mountain Creek: see **Little Red Mountain Creek** [TRINITY].

Red Mountain Field [TRINITY]: *area,* 15 miles southwest of Black Rock Mountain along Red Mountain Creek (2) (lat. 40°05' N, long. 123°14'50" W; near NW cor. sec. 29, T 26 N, R 12 W). Named on Black Rock Mountain (1954) 15' quadrangle.

Red Mountain Lake [HUMBOLDT]: *lake,* 950 feet long, 9 miles west-southwest of Orleans (lat. 41°15' 05" N, long. 123°41'25" W). Named on Fish Lake (1974) and Weitchpec (1979) 7.5' quadrangles.

Red Mountain Meadow [DEL NORTE]: *area,* 5 miles east of Klamath Glen (lat. 41°31'10" N, long. 123°54'W; near W line sec. 13, T 13 N, R 2 E); the place is 0.5 mile southeast of Red Mountain. Named on Klamath Glen (1982) 7.5' quadrangle.

Red Mountain Meadows [TRINITY]: *area,* 12.5 miles north of Weaverville (lat. 40°54'20" N, long. 122°53'05" W); the place is 0.5 mile east-southeast of Red Mountain (3). Named on Trinity Dam (1950) 15' quadrangle.

Red Mountain Pasture [TRINITY]: *area,* 6.5 miles south of Dubakella Mountain (lat. 40°17'35" N, long. 123°10'W; sec. 12, T 28 N, R 12 W); the place is near Red Mountain Creek (1). Named on Dubakella Mountain (1954) 15' quadrangle.

Red Mountain Ridge: see **Red Mountain** [DEL NORTE].

Red Peak: see **Mount Lassic** [HUMBOLDT].

Red Point: see **Red Bluff** [HUMBOLDT].

Red Ridge [LAKE]: *ridge,* south-trending, 1.5 miles long, 15 miles north-northeast of Clearlake Oaks on Lake-Colusa County line (lat. 39°12'05" N, long. 122°30'50" W. Named on Clearlake Oaks (1960) 15' quadrangle.

Red Rock [LAKE]: *peak,* 5.5 miles northeast of the town of Upper Lake (lat. 39°13'20" N, long. 122°49'40" W). Named on Bartlett Mountain (1958) 7.5' quadrangle.

Red Rock [HUMBOLDT]:
(1) *relief feature,* nearly 5 miles east-northeast of Cape Mendocino along Bear River (lat. 40°27'15" N, long. 124°19'15" W; sec. 20, T 1 N, R 2 W). Named on Capetown (1969) 7.5' quadrangle.
(2) *peak,* 7.5 miles south-southwest of Dinsmore (lat. 40°23'55" N, long. 123°39'45" W; near NW cor. sec. 7, T 1 S, R 5 E). Altitude 4225 feet. Named on Larabee Valley (1977) 7.5' quadrangle.

Red Rock [MENDOCINO]:
(1) *relief feature,* 12.5 miles northeast of Covelo (lat. 39°56'05" N, long. 123°06'55" W; sec. 17, T 24 N, R 11 W). Named on Leech Lake Mountain (1966) 7.5' quadrangle.
(2) *relief feature,* 10.5 miles northeast of Eden Valley (lat. 39°42'50" N, long. 123°01'35" W; near SE cor. sec. 36, T 22 N, R 11 W). Named on Thatcher Ridge (1967) 7.5' quadrangle.
(3) *relief feature,* 3 miles north-northeast of Hull Mountain (lat. 39°34'10" N, long. 122°55'10" W; near SE cor. sec. 23, T 20 N, R 10 W). Named on Hull Mountain (1967) 7.5' quadrangle.
(4) *peak,* 0.5 mile west-southwest of Monument Peak (lat. 38°54'30" N, long. 123°57'45" W; sec. 10, T 12 N, R 10 W). Named on Highland Springs (1959) 7.5' quadrangle.

Red Rock [TRINITY]: *relief feature,* nearly 2 miles east of Black Lassic (lat. 40°19'55" N, long. 123°30'30" W). Named on Black Lassic (1979) 7.5' quadrangle.

Red Rock Creek [MENDOCINO]: *stream,* flows 2 miles to Skunk Lake Creek 8.5 miles east-northeast of Eden Valley (lat. 39°41'20" N, long. 123°02'45" W); the stream heads near Red Rock (2). Named on Thatcher Ridge (1967) 7.5' quadrangle.

Red Rock Creek [TRINITY]: *stream,* flows 2.25 miles to Peterptor Creek 17 miles south-southwest of Black Rock Mountain (lat. 40°00'20" N, long. 123°11'20" W; sec. 22, T 25 N, R 12 W). Named on Black Rock Mountain (1954) 15' quadrangle, and on Bluenose Ridge (1967) 7.5' quadrangle.

Redrock Creek: see **Haynes Creek** [MENDOCINO].

Red Rock Gulch [HUMBOLDT]: *canyon,* drained by a stream that flows 1.5 miles to Bear River 5 miles east-northeast of Cape Mendocino (lat. 40°27'20" N, long. 124°19'10" W; sec. 20, T 1 N, R 2 W); the mouth of the canyon is at Red Rock (1). Named on Capetown (1969) 7.5' quadrangle.

Red Rock Mountain [TRINITY]: *peak,* 30 miles south of Etna, which is in Siskiyou County, on Trinity-Siskiyou County line (lat. 41°01'50" N, long. 122°53'50" W; near S line sec. 28, T 37 N, R 9 W). Altitude 7853 feet. Named on Coffee Creek (1955) 15' quadrangle.

Red Rock Mountain: see **Little Red Rock Mountain** [MENDOCINO].

Red Rock Place: see **Old Red Rock Place** [MENDOCINO].

Red Rock Ridge [MENDOCINO]: *ridge,* north-northeast-trending, 2.25 miles long, 2.25 miles north of Hull Mountain (lat. 39°33'15" N, long. 122°56'W). Named on Hull Mountain (1967) 7.5' quadrangle.

Red Rocks [LAKE]: *relief feature,* 8.5 miles east of Clearlake Oaks (lat. 39°01'40" N, long. 122°31'05" W; on E line sec. 28, T 14 N, R 6 W). Named on Clearlake Oaks (1960) 15' quadrangle.

Redway [HUMBOLDT]: *town,* 2.25 miles northwest of Garberville along South Fork Eel River (lat. 40°07'15" N, long. 123°49'15" W; around NE cor. sec. 15, T 4 S, R 3 E). Named on Garberville (1970) and Miranda (1970) 7.5' quadrangles. Charles Burris and Oscar Burris developed the place on land that they bought about 1923 (Turner, p. 178).

Redwine: see **Cummings** [MENDOCINO].

Redwine Spring [MENDOCINO]: *spring,* 8 miles north-northwest of Eden Valley (lat. 39°43'50" N, long. 123°14'20" W; near S line sec. 30, T 22 N, R 12 W). Named on Jamison Ridge (1967) 7.5' quadrangle.

Redwing Spring: see **Spiers Springs**, under **Bonanza Springs** [LAKE].

Redwood Creek [DEL NORTE]: *stream,* flows 2 miles to Craigs Creek 3 miles south of Gasquet (lat. 41°48'05" N, long. 123°58'20" W). Named on Gasquet (1981) 7.5' quadrangle.

Redwood Creek [HUMBOLDT]:
(1) *stream,* flows 64 miles to the sea 1.5 miles west-northwest of Orick (lat. 41°17'35" N, long. 124°05'25" W; sec. 32, T 11 N, R 1 E). Named on Bald Hills (1982), Board Camp Mountain (1977), Grouse Mountain (1979), Hupa Mountain (1982), Lord-Ellis Summit (1973), Maple Creek (1977), Orick (1966), Panther Creek (1982), and Rodgers Peak (1966) 7.5' quadrangles.
(2) *stream,* flows 9 miles to South Fork Eel River 2.5 miles west-northwest of Garberville (lat. 40°07'15" N, long. 123°50'10" W; near S line sec. 10, T 4 S, R 3 E). Named on Briceland (1969), Garberville (1970), and Miranda (1970) 7.5' quadrangles.

Redwood Creek [MENDOCINO]:
(1) *stream,* flows 3 miles to Hollow Tree Creek 14 miles south of Piercy (lat. 39°46'45" N, long. 123°45'10" W; sec. 9, T 22 N, R 17 W). Named on Hales Grove (1970) 7.5' quadrangle. South Fork enters from the south 0.5 mile upstream from the mouth of the main creek; it is nearly 2 miles long and is named on Hales Grove (1970) 7.5' quadrangle.
(2) *stream,* flows 3 miles to South Fork Eel River 2.5 miles northwest of Branscomb (lat. 39°40'50" N, long. 123°39'20" W; near N line sec. 16, T 21 N, R 16 W). Named on Lincoln Ridge (1966) 7.5' quadrangle. North Fork enters 1.25 miles upstream from the mouth of the main creek; it is 1

mile long and is named on Lincoln Ridge (1966) 7.5' quadrangle.

(3) *stream,* flows 4.5 miles to South Fork Tenmile River 16 miles north of Comptche (lat. 39°29'30" N, long. 123°36'20" W; near E line sec. 23, T 19 N, R 16 W). Named on Comptche (1960) 15' quadrangle, and on Sherwood Peak (1967) 7.5' quadrangle. North Fork enters from the north 1 mile upstream from the mouth of the main creek; it is 1.5 miles long and is named on Sherwood Peak (1967) 7.5' quadrangle. Branscomb (1921) 15' quadrangle shows North Fork as the main part of Redwood Creek.

(4) *stream,* flows 5 miles to Noyo River 8 miles west of Willits (lat. 39°25'20" N, long. 123°29'35" W; at E line sec. 11, T 18 N, R 15 W). Named on Willits (1961) 15' quadrangle.

(5) *stream,* flows 2.5 miles to Little North Fork Navarro River 15 miles north-northwest of Boonville (lat. 39°12'05" N, long. 123°30'W; sec. 35, T 16 N, R 15 W). Named on Boonville (1959) 15' quadrangle.

(6) *stream,* flows 2.5 miles to Mill Creek (12) 2.5 miles west of Ornbaun Valley (lat. 38°54'50" N, long. 123°21'10" W; sec. 7, T 12 N, R 13 W). Named on Ornbaun Valley (1960) 15' quadrangle

Redwood House [HUMBOLDT]: *locality,* 7 miles south-southwest of Lone Star Junction (lat. 40°32'05" N, long. 123°54'45" W; near SE cor. sec. 23, T 2 N, R 2 E). Named on Owl Creek (1979) 7.5' quadrangle.

Redwood Lodge [MENDOCINO]: *locality,* 13 miles north-northwest of Comptche along California Western Railroad (lat. 39°26'30" N, long. 123°41'15" W; on S line sec. 6, T 18 N, R 16 W). Named on Comptche (1960) 15' quadrangle.

Redwood Valley [MENDOCINO]:

(1) *valley,* 6 miles west-southwest of the town of Potter Valley along Russian River (lat. 39°18'N, long. 123°12'30" W). Named on Redwood Valley (1960) 7.5' quadrangle. Captain Edward Johnson, 6th United States Infantry, established a military post called Fort Weller in Redwood Valley (1) in 1859, and the facility was abandoned the same year; the name was for John B. Weller, governor of California (Frazer, p. 33).

(2) *town,* 6.5 miles southwest of the town of Potter Valley (lat. 39°15'55" N, long. 123°12'10" W); the town is near the south end of Redwood Valley (1). Named on Redwood Valley (1960) 7.5' quadrangle. Postal authorities established Redwood Valley post office in 1920 at a railroad station called Basil (Salley, p. 183).

Reed Mountain [HUMBOLDT]: *ridge,* generally southeast-trending, 4.5 miles long, 4.25 miles south-southeast of Garberville (lat. 40°02'15" N, long. 123°45' W). Named on Garberville (1970) and Harris (1969) 7.5' quadrangles. Ezra Reed settled in the neighborhood in 1860 and owned land on the ridge (Turner, p. 181).

Reeves Canyon [MENDOCINO]: *canyon,* drained by a stream that flows 2 miles to Outlet Creek 3.5 miles southeast of Longvale (lat. 39°30'40" N, long. 123°23'10" W; sec. 11, T 19 N, R 14 W). Named on Willits (1961) 15' quadrangle, and on Longvale (1966) and Willis Ridge (1966) 7.5' quadrangles.

Reeves Point [LAKE]: *promontory,* 2 miles east-southeast of Lakeport along Clear Lake (lat. 39°01'45" N, long. 122°52'50" W). Named on Lakeport (1958) 7.5' quadrangle.

Refuge Valley [TRINITY]: *valley,* 9 miles southwest of Forest Glen (lat. 40°16'50" N, long. 123°26'40" W; sec. 24, T 2 S, R 6 E). Named on Ruth Reservoir (1978) 7.5' quadrangle.

Regina Heights [MENDOCINO]: *locality,* 2 miles east of Ukiah (lat. 39°08'55" N, long. 123°10'20" W). Named on Ukiah (1958) 7.5' quadrangle.

Reiff: see **Lower Lake** [LAKE].

Reilly Heights [MENDOCINO]: *settlement,* 3 miles south-southeast of Navarro (lat. 39°06'40" N, long. 123°31'W; sec. 33, T 15 N, R 15 W). Named on Navarro (1961) 15' quadrangle.

Reister Canyon [LAKE]: *canyon,* drained by a stream that flows 1 mile to Wolf Creek 6.5 miles north-northeast of Clearlake Oaks (lat. 39°06'40" N, long. 122°37'50" W; near E line sec. 33, T 15 N, R 7 W); the canyon heads near Reister Knoll. Named on Clearlake Oaks (1958) 7.5' quadrangle.

Reister Knoll [LAKE]: *peak,* 7.25 miles north-northeast of Clearlake Oaks (lat. 39°07'15" N, long. 122°37'35" W; sec. 27, T 15 N, R 7 W). Altitude 2784 feet. Named on Clearlake Oaks (1958) 7.5' quadrangle.

Reister Rock [LAKE]: *relief feature,* 8 miles north of Clearlake Oaks (lat. 39°08'20" N, long. 122°38'35" W; near NW cor. sec. 21, T 15 N, R 7 W). Named on Clearlake Oaks (1960) 15' quadrangle.

Remington Canyon [LAKE]: *canyon,* drained by a stream that flows 1 mile to Grizzly Canyon (2) 5.25 miles south-southeast of Cold Spring Mountain (lat. 39°01'30" N, long. 122°28'05" W; near SE cor. sec. 25, T 14 N, R 6 W). Named on Wilbur Springs (1961) 15' quadrangle.

Renfroe Hole [HUMBOLDT]: *relief feature,* 3 miles east-southeast of Showers Mountain along Mad River (lat. 40°33'55" N, long. 123°38'25" W; sec. 8, T 2 N, R 5 E). Named on Showers Mountain (1978) 7.5' quadrangle.

Requa [DEL NORTE]: *village,* less than 1 mile east of the mouth of Klamath River on the north side of that river (lat. 41°32'50" N, long. 124°04'W; sec. 4, 5, T 13 N, R 1 E). Named on Requa (1966) 7.5' quadrangle. Postal authorities established Requa post office in 1878, discontinued it for a time in 1883, discontinued it again in 1883, reestablished it in 1888, moved it 0.5 mile west in 1895, moved it 0.5 mile east in 1898, and discontinued it in 1970 (Salley, p. 184). Kroeber (p. 56) thought that the name likely was from an Indian village at the mouth of Klamath River.

Rest: see **Camp Rest** [MENDOCINO].

Reynolds [MENDOCINO]: *locality,* 2.5 miles south-southeast of Piercy along South Fork Eel River (lat. 39°56'40" N, long. 123°46'45" W; sec. 7, T 24 N, R 17 W). Named on Piercy (1950) 15' quadrangle.

Reynolds Creek: see **Randall Creek** [HUMBOLDT].

Reynolds Rock [HUMBOLDT]: *rock,* 8.5 miles south of Petrolia, and 1250 feet offshore (lat. 40°12'05" N, long. 124°17'35" W); the rock is 3100 feet west of the mouth of Randall Creek, which is called Reynolds Cr. on Gorda (1926) 15' quadrangle. Named on Cooskie Creek (1969) 7.5' quadrangle.

Rice: see **Dan Rice Creek** [TRINITY].

Rice Creek [LAKE]: *stream,* flows 7.5 miles to Rice Fork 3.25 miles north-northeast of Three Crossings (lat. 39°21'20" N, long. 122°53'05" W; near W line sec. 4, T 17 N, R 9 W); the stream goes through Rice Valley. Named on Crockett Peak (1967), Elk Mountain (1967), and Potato Hill (1967) 7.5' quadrangles

Rice Creek [MENDOCINO]: *stream,* flows 2.5 miles to Big River 8 miles south-southwest of Willits (lat. 39°17'45" N, long. 123°24'05" W; sec. 27, T 17 N, R 14 W). Named on Willits (1961) 15' quadrangle.

Rice Fork [LAKE]: *stream,* flows 22 miles to Eel River nearly 3 miles west of Bear Mountain in Lake Allsbury (lat. 39°24'25" N, long. 122°57'10" W; near N line sec. 23, T 18 N, R 10 W). Named on Clearlake Oaks (1960) 15' quadrangle, and on Bartlett Mountain (1958), Elk Mountain (1967), Lake Pillsbury (1967), and Potato Hill (1967) 7.5' quadrangles. United States Board on Geographic Names (1933, p. 641) rejected the name "Rice Fork of Eel" for the feature.

Rice Lake [TRINITY]: *marsh,* 9.5 miles south of Kettenpom (lat. 40°01'40" N, long. 123°25'25" W; at E line sec. 18, T 5 S, R 7 E). Named on Lake Mountain (1967) 7.5' quadrangle.

Rice Valley [LAKE]: *valley,* 3 miles west of Potato Hill (lat. 39°20'50" N, long. 122°51'30" W; near N line sec. 10, T 17 N, R 9 W); the valley is along Rice Creek. Named on Potato Hill (1967) 7.5' quadrangle.

Richabaugh Glades [LAKE-MENDOCINO]: *area,* 11 miles southeast of Ukiah on Lake-Mendocino County line (lat. 39°02'55" N, long. 123°03'20" W; near N line sec. 27, T 14 N, R 11 W). Named on Purdys Gardens (1958) 7.5' quadrangle.

Richardson Creek [DEL NORTE]: *stream,* flows 1.25 miles to Klamath River 2.5 miles southeast of the mouth of that river (lat. 41°31'30" N, long. 124°02'40" W; at S line sec. 10, T 13 N, R 1 E). Named on Requa (1966) 7.5' quadrangle.

Richardson Glade [LAKE]: *area,* 7 miles south-southeast of Potato Hill (lat. 39°15'50" N, long. 122°44'55" W; sec. 3, T 16 N, R 8 W). Named on Lake Pillsbury (1951) 15' quadrangle, and on Fouts Springs (1968) 7.5' quadrangle.

Richardson Grove: see **Garberville** [HUMBOLDT].

Richardson's Springs: see **Grizzly Spring** [LAKE].

Rich Creek: see **Rich Gulch** [TRINITY] (2).

Rich Gulch [TRINITY]:

(1) *canyon,* drained by a stream that flows 1 mile to Clair Engle Lake 12 miles northeast of Weaverville (lat. 40°51'50" N, long. 122°47'45" W; sec. 29, T 35 N, R 8 W). Named on Trinity Dam (1950) 15' quadrangle.

(2) *canyon,* 3 miles long, opens into the canyon of East Fork of North Fork Trinity River 2.5 miles north of Helena (lat. 40°48'45" N, long. 123°07'10" W; sec. 9, T 34 N, R 11 W). Named on Helena (1951) 15' quadrangle. Miller's (1890) map shows Rich Cr. in the canyon.

Rider Creek: see **Rider Gulch** [MENDOCINO].

Rider Gulch [MENDOCINO]: *canyon,* drained by a stream that flows 1.25 miles to Wages Creek 1 mile northeast of Westport (lat. 39°38'50" N, long. 123°46'15" W; sec. 29, T 21 N, R 17 W). Named on Westport (1966) 7.5' quadrangle. The stream in the canyon is called Rider Creek on Cape Vizcaino (1950) 15' quadrangle.

Ridge [MENDOCINO]: *locality,* 6 miles south-southeast of Willits along Northwestern Pacific Railroad (lat. 39°20'10" N, long. 123°18'W; near SE cor. sec. 9, T 17 N, R 13 W). Named on Willits (1961) 15' quadrangle. Called Ridgewood on California Mining Bureau's (1909c) map. Postal authorities established Ridgewood post office 8 miles south of Willits in 1904 and discontinued it in 1914 (Salley, p. 185).

Ridge Point: see **Table Bluff** [HUMBOLDT] (1).

Ridgeville [TRINITY]: *locality,* 12 miles northeast of Weaverville (lat. 40°51'55" N, long. 122°48'05" W; sec. 29, T 35 N, R 8 W); the place is on the ridge that lies between Mule Creek and Digger Creek. Site named on Trinity Dam (1950) 15' quadrangle. The community, which also was called Golden City, began in 1855 (Bancroft, p. 370).

Ridgewood: see **Ridge** [MENDOCINO].

Ridgewood Heights [HUMBOLDT]: *settlement,* 3.5 miles east-northeast of Fields Landing (lat. 40°44'10" N, long. 124°08'45" W; sec. 11, 14, T 4 N, R 1 W). Named on Fields Landing (1959) 7.5' quadrangle.

Riley Ridge [MENDOCINO]:
(1) *ridge,* west-northwest-trending, 3.5 miles long, 11 miles north-northwest of Comptche (lat. 39°25'10" N, long. 123°38'20" W). Named on Comptche (1960) 15' quadrangle.
(2) *ridge,* southwest-trending, less than 1 mile long, 13 miles southeast of Ukiah (lat. 39°00'45" N, long. 123°03'15" W; sec. 3, T 13 N, R 11 W); the ridge is southwest of Riley Valley. Named on Purdys Gardens (1958) 7.5' quadrangle.

Riley Valley [LAKE-MENDOCINO]: *canyon,* less than 1 mile long, 7.25 miles west-southwest of Lakeport on Lake-Mendocino County line (lat. 39°01'15" N, long. 123°02'35" W). Named on Purdys Gardens (1958) 7.5' quadrangle.

Rio Albion: see **Albion River** [MENDOCINO].

Rio Dell [HUMBOLDT]: *town,* 1 mile north of Scotia on the west side of Eel River (lat. 40°29'45" N, long. 124°06'10" W; sec. 5, 6, T 1 N, R 1 E). Named on Hydesville (1979) and Scotia (1970) 7.5' quadrangles. Postal authorities established Rio Del post office in 1876 (Frickstad, p. 46), and the town incorporated in 1965. The place first was called Eagle Prairie (Gudde, 1949, p. 287). The name "Eagle Prairie" reportedly was from an old settler who had the nickname "Old Eagle Beak" (Ristow, p. 425).

Rio de los Tortolas: see **Little River** [HUMBOLDT].

Rio del Tlamachi: see **Klamath River** [DEL NORTE-HUMBOLDT].

Rio Dolores: see **Putah Creek** [LAKE].

Rio Grande: see **Big River** [MENDOCINO].

Rio Grando River: see **Noyo River** [MENDOCINO].

Ripple Creek [TRINITY]: *stream,* flows 3.25 miles to Trinity River 9 miles north of Trinity Center (lat. 41°08'15" N, long. 122°41'20" W; sec. 20, T 38 N, R 7 W). Named on Bonanza King (1955) 15' quadrangle.

Ripstein Camp [TRINITY]: *locality,* 9 miles northeast of Helena along Canyon Creek (1) (lat. 40°52'40" N, long. 123°01'40" W); the place is between the mouths of Ripstein Creek and Little Ripstein Creek. Named on Helena (1951) 15' quadrangle.

Ripstein Gulch [TRINITY]: *canyon,* drained by a stream that flows 2.5 miles to Canyon Creek (1) 9 miles northeast of Helena (lat. 40°52'45" N, long. 123°01'30" W). Named on Helena (1951) 15' quadrangle.

Ripstein Gulch: see **Little Ripstein Gulch** [TRINITY].

Ritmer Creek [DEL NORTE]: *stream,* flows 3.5 miles to Tillas Slough 2 miles west of the town of Smith River (lat. 41°55'55" N, long. 124°11'W; near S line sec. 21, T 18 N, R 1 W). Named on Smith River (1966) 7.5' quadrangle.

Riverdale [MENDOCINO]: *locality,* 2.25 miles northwest of Leggett (lat. 39°53'15" N, long. 123°44'45" W; near S line sec. 33, T 24 N, R 17 W); the place is along South Fork Eel River. Named on Noble Butte (1969) 7.5' quadrangle.

River Garden [MENDOCINO]: *area,* 3.5 miles south-southeast of Spyrock (2) (lat. 39°50'40" N, long. 123°25'10" W; near NE cor. sec. 21, T 23 N, R 14 W); the place is along Eel River. Named on Iron Peak (1967) 7.5' quadrangle. On Spyrock (1952) 15' quadrangle, the name applies to a locality along the railroad at the site. O' Brien's (1953) map has the form "River Gardens" for the name.

Riverside: see **Korbel** [HUMBOLDT].

Riverside Park [HUMBOLDT]: *settlement,* 7 miles north-northwest of Redcrest along Van Duzen River (lat. 40°29'45" N, long. 123°59'30" W; sec. 6, T 1 N, R 2 E). Named on Redcrest (1969) 7.5' quadrangle.

Riverview Camp [DEL NORTE]: *locality,* less than 1 mile east-southeast of Gasquet on the south side of Middle Fork Smith River (lat. 41°50'30" N, long. 123°57'10" W). Named on Gasquet (1945) 15' quadrangle.

Roach Creek [HUMBOLDT]: *stream,* flows 10 miles to Klamath River 5 miles south-southeast of Johnsons (lat. 41°16'35" N, long. 123°51'W; at E line sec. 8, T 10 N, R 3 E). Named on Bald Hills (1982), French Camp Ridge (1983), and Johnsons (1982) 7.5' quadrangles. According to Gannett (p. 264), the name is for a pioneer who drowned in the stream.

Roach Creek Hole [HUMBOLDT]: *area,* 4.5 miles north-northwest of Coyote Peak (lat. 41°11'05" N, long. 123°52'50" W; sec. 7, T 9 N, R 3 E); the place is southeast of the upper part of Roach Creek. Named on Bald Hills (1982) 7.5' quadrangle.

Road Gulch [TRINITY]: *canyon,* drained by a stream that flows 2 miles to Post Creek 5 miles west-northwest of Dubakella Mountain (lat. 40°25'20" N, long. 123°13'15" W; sec. 28, T 30 N, R 12 W). Named on Dubakella Mountain (1954) 15' quadrangle.

Roaring Gulch [HUMBOLDT]: *canyon,* drained by a stream that flows 1.25 miles to Redwood Creek (1) 7 miles south of Coyote Peak (lat. 41°01'50" N, long. 123°52'20" W; at N line sec. 6, T 7 N, R 3 E). Named on Hupa Mountain (1982) 7.5' quadrangle.

Roaring Soda Spring: see **Morton Soda Spring**, under **Soda Creek** [LAKE] (1).

Robbers Gulch [HUMBOLDT]: *canyon,* drained by a stream that flows 4 miles to Tully Creek 3.25 miles north-northeast of Coyote Peak (lat. 41°10'40" N, long. 123°50'10" W). Named on Bald Hills (1982) and French Camp Ridge (1983) 7.5' quadrangles.

Robbers Meadow [TRINITY]: *area,* 4.5 miles south-southwest of China Mountain, which is in Siskiyou County (lat. 41°19'20" N, long. 122°36'45" W; on N line sec. 24, T 40 N, R 7 W). Named on China Mountain (1955) 15' quadrangle.

Robbers Meadow Creek [TRINITY]: *stream,* flows 2.5 miles to Little Trinity River 6.5 miles south-southwest of China Mountain, which is in Siskiyou County (lat. 41°17'30" N, long. 122°37'45" W; at SE cor. sec. 26, T 40 N, R 7 W); the stream heads at Robbers Meadow. Named on China Mountain (1955) 15' quadrangle.

Robbers Roost [TRINITY]: *peak,* 1.5 miles southeast of Kettenpom (lat. 40°08'35" N, long. 123°26'25" W; near E line sec. 1, T 4 S, R 6 E). Named on Zenia (1967) 7.5' quadrangle. The name is of recent origin and has no historical basis (Jones, p. 353).

Robertson Creek: see **Robinson Creek** [MENDOCINO] (4).

Robinson Bar [TRINITY]: *locality,* 15 miles northeast of Weaverville along Trinity River (lat. 40°52'25" N, long. 122°43'W; sec. 24, T 35 N, R 8 W). Named on Schell Mountain (1950) 15' quadrangle.

Robinson Creek [HUMBOLDT]: *stream,* flows 1 mile to South Fork Eel River 1 mile south-southeast of Weott (lat. 40°18'35" N, long. 123°54'45" W; near NE cor. sec. 11, T 2 S, R 2 E). Named on Weott (1969) 7.5' quadrangle.

Robinson Creek [LAKE]: *stream,* flows 4 miles to Rodman Slough 1.5 miles south of the town of Upper Lake (lat. 39°08'40" N, long. 122°54'25" W; sec. 18, T 15 N, R 9 W). Named on Upper Lake (1958) 7.5' quadrangle.

Robinson Creek [MENDOCINO]:
(1) *stream,* flows 4.5 miles to Anderson Creek (2) at Boonville (lat. 39°00'50" N, long. 123°22'50" W; sec. 2, T 13 N, R 14 W). Named on Boonville (1959) and Ornbaun Valley (1960) 15' quadrangles.
(2) *stream,* flows 3.25 miles to North Fork Gualala River 7.25 miles southeast of Ornbaun Valley (lat. 38°50'50" N, long. 123°24'35" W; sec. 34, T 12 N, R 14 W). Named on Ornbaun Valley (1960) 15' quadrangle. Called Bear Creek on Ornbaun (1944) 15' quadrangle.
(3) *stream,* flows 2.5 miles to North Fork Gualala River 12 miles southwest of Ornbaun Valley (lat. 38°48'40" N, long. 123°28'50" W; sec. 12, T 11 N, R 15 W). Named on Ornbaun Valley (1960) 15' quadrangle.
(4) *stream,* flows 9 miles to Russian River 3.5 miles south-southeast of Ukiah (lat. 39°06'05" N, long. 123°10'55" W). Named on Boonville (1959) 15' quadrangle, and on Elledge Peak (1958) 7.5' quadrangle. United States Board on Geographic Names (1962a, p. 15) rejected the name "Robertson Creek" for the stream. According to Gudde (1969, p. 271), the name "Robertson Creek" commemorates William E. Robertson, who was in charge of the Indian agency at Ukiah in the 1870's . South Branch enters from the south 4.5 miles upstream from the mouth of the main creek; it is 3 miles long and is named on Boonville (1959) 15' quadrangle.

Robinson Creek [TRINITY]: *stream,* flows nearly 3 miles to Middle Fork Eel River 6.5 miles south of Black Rock Mountain (lat. 40°06'30" N, long. 122°59'25" W; near SE cor. sec. 9, T 26 N, R 10 W). Named on Yolla Bolly (1954) 15' quadrangle.

Robinson Gulch [MENDOCINO]: *canyon,* drained by a stream that flows 1.25 miles to the sea 0.5 mile northwest of Gualala (lat. 38°46'15" N, long. 123°32'10" W; sec. 28, T 11 N, R 15 W). Named on Gualala (1960) 7.5' quadrangle. Called School House Gulch on Point Arena (1943) 15' quadrangle, but United States Board on Geographic Names (1962c, p. 21) rejected this name for the feature, and pointed out that the name "Robinson" commemorates Cyrus D. Robinson, who settled at Gualala in 1858.

Robinson Point [MENDOCINO]: *promontory,* 0.5 mile west-northwest of Gualala along the coast (lat. 38°46'20" N, long. 123°32'25" W; sec. 28, T 11 N, R 15 W); the feature is 0.25 mile west-northwest of the mouth of Robinson Gulch. Named on Gualala (1960) 7.5' quadrangle. The name commemorates Cyrus D. Robinson of Robinson Gulch (Gudde, 1949, p. 288).

Robinson Reef [MENDOCINO]: *rock,* 0.5 mile west of Gualala (lat. 38°46'05" N, long. 123°32'20" W); the rock is 0.25 mile southwest of the mouth of Robinson Gulch. Named on Gualala (1960) 7.5' quadrangle. Officials of United States Coast Survey named the feature (Gudde, 1949, p. 288).

Robinson's Ferry: see **Scotia** [HUMBOLDT].

Robinsons Ferry: see **Bridgeville** [HUMBOLDT].

Rock Bar Creek [TRINITY]: *stream,* flows 1.5 miles to Trinity River 10 miles east-southeast of Burnt Ranch (lat. 40°46'N, long. 123°17'50" W; sec. 32, T 5 N, R 8 E). Named on Ironside Mountain (1951) 15' quadrangle.

Rock Cabin Camp [TRINITY]: *locality,* 14 miles south-southwest of Black Rock Mountain (lat. 40°00'35" N, long. 123°05' W; sec. 22, T 25 N, R 11 W). Named on Black Rock Mountain (1954) 15' quadrangle.

Rock Chute Creek [HUMBOLDT]: *stream,* flows 1.25 miles to Klamath River 7.5 miles northeast of Coyote Peak (lat. 41°12'40" N, long. 123°45'55" W; sec. 31, T 10 N, R 4 E). Named on French Camp Ridge (1983) and Weitchpec (1979) 7.5' quadrangles.

Rock Creek [DEL NORTE]:
(1) *stream,* flows 2.5 miles to Smith River 7.5 miles northeast of Crescent City (lat. 41°48'35" N, long. 124°04'50" W; near E line sec. 5, T 16 N, R

1 E). Named on Hiouchi (1966) 7.5' quadrangle.

(2) *stream,* flows 7.25 miles to South Fork Smith River 10 miles north-northwest of Buck Mountain (lat. 41°44'10" N, long. 123°58'55" W). Named on Cant Hook Mountain (1982) and Childs Hill (1966) 7.5' quadrangles.

Rock Creek [HUMBOLDT]: *stream,* flows 3.25 miles to Supply Creek 1 mile west of Hoopa (lat. 41°07'45" N, long. 123°41'40" W; sec. 26, T 8 N, R 4 E). Named on Hoopa (1979) 7.5' quadrangle.

Rock Creek [LAKE]: *stream,* flows nearly 4 miles to French Creek 5 miles south-southwest of Potato Hill (lat. 39°17'05" N, long. 122°50'10" W; sec. 35, T 17 N, R 9 W). Named on Potato Hill (1967) 7.5' quadrangle.

Rock Creek [MENDOCINO]:

(1) *stream,* flows 3.25 miles to Bell Springs Creek 12 miles east-northeast of Leggett (lat. 39°56'20" N, long. 123°31'10" W; sec. 10, T 24 N, R 15 W). Named on Bell Springs (1969) 7.5' quadrangle.

(2) *stream,* flows nearly 1 mile to Eel River 4 miles south of Dos Rios (lat. 39°39'40" N, long. 123°20'35" W; near E line sec. 19, T 21 N, R 13 W). Named on Dos Rios (1967) 7.5' quadrangle.

(3) *stream,* flows 1.5 miles to Howard Creek (2) 3.5 miles north-northeast of Westport (lat. 39°40'55" N, long. 123°45'20" W; at N line sec. 16, T 21 N, R 17 W). Named on Lincoln Ridge (1966) and Westport (1966) 7.5' quadrangles.

(4) *stream,* flows 3.5 miles to South Fork Eel River 2.5 miles northwest of Branscomb (lat. 39°40'55" N, long. 123°39'05" W; near S line sec. 9, T 21 N, R 16 W). Named on Cahto Peak (1967) and Lincoln Ridge (1966) 7.5' quadrangles.

Rock Creek [TRINITY]:

(1) *stream,* flows 2.5 miles to North Fork of Middle Fork Eel River 12 miles south-southwest of Black Rock Mountain (lat. 40°03'45" N, long. 123°07'55" W; sec. 32, T 26 N, R 11 W). Named on Black Rock Mountain (1954) 15' quadrangle.

(2) *stream,* flows 5 miles to North Fork Eel River 7.25 miles east-southeast of Kettenpom (lat. 40°07'25" N, long. 123°20'W; at S line sec. 12, T 4 S, R 7 E). Named on Shannon Butte (1967) 7.5' quadrangle.

(3) *stream,* flows 1.5 miles to Mad River 6.5 miles west-northwest of Forest Glen (lat. 40°26'N, long. 123°29'10" W; sec. 27, T 1 N, R 6 E). Named on Sportshaven (1973) 7.5' quadrangle.

Rock Creek: see **Big Rock Creek** [MENDOCINO]; **Little Rock Creek** [MENDOCINO]; **Yellowjacket Creek** [TRINITY] (2).

Rock Creek Butte Point [DEL NORTE]: *relief feature,* 9 miles south-southeast of Sawtooth Mountain (lat. 41°31'45" N, long. 123°39'35" W). Named on Chimney Rock (1981) 7.5' quadrangle.

Rock Creek Camp [DEL NORTE]: *locality,* 9 miles northwest of Buck Mountain along Rock Creek (2) (lat. 41°43'35" N, long. 123°59'30" W; sec. 6, T 15 N, R 2 E). Named on Ship Mountain (1952) 15' quadrangle.

Rock Gulch: see **Big Rock Gulch** [HUMBOLDT].

Rock Lake [HUMBOLDT]: *intermittent lake,* 250 feet long, 3.5 miles north-east of Showers Mountain (lat. 40°36'35" N, long. 123°38'45" W; sec. 30, T 3 N, R 5 E). Named on Showers Mountain (1978) 7.5' quadrangle.

Rockland [DEL NORTE]: *locality,* 9 miles north of Gasquet along North Fork Smith River 1 mile south of California-Oregon State line (lat. 41°58'55" N, long. 123°57'30" W). Named on Preston Peak (1922) 30'quadrangle.

Rockpile Creek [MENDOCINO]: *stream,* flows 14 miles to Sonoma County 11 miles south-southwest of Ornbaun Valley (lat. 38°46'40" N, long. 123°24'15" W; at S line sec. 22, T 11 N, R 14 W); the stream goes past Rockpile Peak. Named on Ornbaun Valley (1960) 15' quadrangle.

Rockpile Peak [MENDOCINO]: *peak,* 7.25 miles south-southwest of Ornbaun Valley (lat. 38°49'10" N, long. 123°21'25" W; near N line sec. 7, T 11 N, R 13 W). Altitude 1751 feet. Named on Ornbaun Valley (1960) 15' quadrangle.

Rockport [MENDOCINO]: *village,* 7.25 miles north-northwest of Westport (lat. 39°44'20" N, long. 123°49'W; near SW cor. sec. 24, T 22 N, R 18 W). Named on Westport (1966) 7.5' quadrangle. Postal authorities established Rockport post office in 1888, discontinued it in 1903, reestablished it in 1926, discontinued it in 1934, reestablished it in 1938, and discontinued it in 1957 (Salley, p. 187). The place also was called Cotineva; a chute and wharf were built there in 1876 (Gudde, 1949, p. 81, 289).

Rockport Bay [MENDOCINO]: *embayment,* 7 miles north-northwest of Westport along the coast at the mouth of Cottaneva Creek (lat. 39°44'05" N, long. 123°49'45" W; sec. 23, 26, T 22 N, R 18 W); the feature is less than 1 mile west-southwest of Rockport. Named on Westport (1966) 7.5' quadrangle.

Rockport Creek [MENDOCINO]: *stream,* flows 1.5 miles to South Fork Cottaneva Creek 7 miles north of Westport (lat. 39°44'10" N, long. 123°48'40" W; at N line sec. 25, T 22 N, R 18 W); Rockport is near the mouth of the stream. Named on Westport (1966) 7.5' quadrangle.

Rockport Creek: see **Cottaneva Creek** [MENDOCINO].

Rock Prairie [HUMBOLDT]: *area,* 8 miles west-northwest of Orleans (lat. 41°21'10" N, long. 123°41'50" W). Named on Fish Lake (1974) 7.5' quadrangle.

Rocktree Creek [MENDOCINO]: *stream,* flows 4 miles to Tomki Creek 12 miles northwest of the town of Potter Valley (lat. 39°27'20" N, long. 123°14'45" W; near SE cor. sec. 36, T 19 N, R 13 W); the stream heads at Rocktree Valley. Named on Willits (1961) 15' quadrangle.

Rocktree Valley [MENDOCINO]: *valley,* 4 miles northeast of Willits (lat. 39°27'15" N, long. 123°18'30" W; mainly in sec. 33, T 19 N, R 13 W). Named on Willits (1961) 15' quadrangle.

Rocky Basin Creek [MENDOCINO]: *stream,* heads in Glenn County and flows 1 mile in Mendocino County to Black Butte River 10 miles north of Hull Mountain (lat. 39°39'40" N, long. 122°54'25" W; near E line sec. 24, T 21 N, R 10 W). Named on Plaskett Ridge (1967) 7.5' quadrangle.

Rocky Basin Ridge [MENDOCINO]: *ridge,* west-southwest-trending, 2 miles long, 11 miles north-northwest of Hull Mountain on Mendocino-Glenn County line (lat. 39°40'15" N, long. 122°53'25" W). Named on Plaskett Ridge (1967) 7.5' quadrangle.

Rocky Camp: see **Rocky Saddle** [DEL NORTE].

Rocky Creek [LAKE]: *stream,* flows 8.5 miles to Cache Creek at the north end of Wilson Valley (2) (lat. 38°58'45" N, long. 122°28'30" W). Named on Wilson Valley (1958) 7.5' quadrangle.

Rocky Creek [MENDOCINO]:

(1) *stream,* flows 1 mile to Eel River 4 miles north of the town of Potter Valley (lat. 39°22'55" N, long. 123°05'35" W; near W line sec. 28, T 18 N, R 11 W). Named on Potter Valley (1960) 15' quadrangle.

(2) *stream,* flows nearly 3 miles to Russian River 6.25 miles west of the town of Potter Valley (lat. 39°19'05" N, long. 123°13'20" W; near W line sec. 20, T 17 N, R 12 W). Named on Potter Valley (1960) and Willits (1961) 15' quadrangles.

Rocky Glen Creek [HUMBOLDT]: *stream,* flows 3 miles to South Fork Eel River 1.5 miles south-southeast of Phillipsville (lat. 40°11'15" N, long. 123°46'15" W; sec. 19, T 3 S, R 4 E). Named on Fort Seward (1969) and Miranda (1970) 7.5' quadrangles.

Rocky Gulch [HUMBOLDT]: *canyon,* drained by a stream that flows 1.5 miles to lowlands along Arcata Bay 3.5 miles south of Arcata (lat. 40°49'15" N, long. 124°04'35" W; sec. 16, T 5 N, R 1 E). Named on Arcata South (1959) 7.5' quadrangle.

Rocky Gulch [MENDOCINO]: *canyon,* drained by a stream that flows 1 mile to Little North Fork Big River 7.5 miles northwest of Comptche (lat. 39°20'N, long. 123°42'W; near E line sec. 13, T 17 N, R 17 W). Named on Comptche (1960) 15' quadrangle.

Rocky Gulch [TRINITY]: *canyon,* drained by a stream that flows 1.5 miles to Coffee Creek 9 miles west-southwest of Billys Peak (1) (lat. 41°05'50" N, long. 122°56'05" W; sec. 6, T 37 N, R 9 W). Named on Coffee Creek (1955) 15' quadrangle.

Rocky Gulch: see **Hearn Gulch** [MENDOCINO].

Rocky Knob [DEL NORTE]: *peak,* 2.5 miles southeast of Broken Rib Mountain on Del Norte-Siskiyou County line (lat. 41°51'40" N, long. 123°38'55" W). Altitude 5716 feet. Named on Devils Punchbowl (1981) 7.5' quadrangle.

Rocky Lake [LAKE]: *lake,* 100 feet long, 7.5 miles west of Lakeport (lat. 39°03'30" N, long. 123°03'10" W; sec. 22, T 14 N, R 11 W). Named on Purdys Gardens (1958) 7.5' quadrangle.

Rocky Point [HUMBOLDT]: *promontory,* 5.5 miles north of Trinidad along the coast (lat. 41°08'20" N, long. 124°09'45" W; sec. 27, T 9 N, R 1 W); the promontory is part of a larger feature called Patricks Point (1). Named on Trinidad (1966) 7.5' quadrangle. According to Coy (1929, p. 26), Vancouver probably gave the name "Rocky Point" in 1792 to the feature later called Patrick's Point (present Palmers Point).

Rocky Point [LAKE]:

(1) *promontory,* 2.5 miles west of Bear Mountain along Lake Pillsbury (lat. 39°24'50" N, long. 122°56'45" W; sec. 14, T 18 N, R 10 W). Named on Lake Pillsbury (1967) 7.5' quadrangle.

(2) *relief feature,* 5 miles north of Cold Spring Mountain (lat. 39°10'N, long. 122°29'40" W; sec. 11, T 15 N, R 6 W). Named on Wilbur Springs (1961) 15' quadrangle.

(3) *promontory,* 3 miles north-northeast of Lakeport along Clear Lake (lat. 39°05'10" N, long. 122°53'55" W; sec. 6, T 14 N, R 9 W). Named on Lakeport (1958) 7.5' quadrangle.

(4) *promontory,* 4 miles northwest of the town of Lower Lake along Clear Lake (lat. 38°56'45" N, long. 122°40'W; near W line sec. 29, T 13 N, R 7 W). Named on Clearlake Highlands (1958) 7.5' quadrangle.

Rocky Point [MENDOCINO]: *relief feature,* 11 miles north of the town of Potter Valley (lat. 39°28'55" N, long. 123°05'50" W; near N line sec. 29, T 19 N, R 11 W). Named on Potter Valley (1960) 15' quadrangle.

Rocky Ridge [LAKE]: *ridge,* generally southeast-trending, 1.5 miles long, 8.5 miles north-northeast of Clearlake Oaks (lat. 39°07'50" N, long. 122°36'35" W). Named on Clearlake Oaks (1960) 15' quadrangle.

Rocky Ridge [MENDOCINO]: *ridge,* west-trending, 2 miles long, 8 miles north-northeast of Boonville (lat. 39°07'10" N, long. 123°19'15" W). Named on Boonville (1959) 15' quadrangle.

Rocky Saddle [DEL NORTE]: *pass,* 5 miles east-northeast of Klamath Glen (lat. 41°33'N, long. 123°54'45" W; near N line sec. 2, T 13 N, R 2 E).

Named on Klamath Glen (1982) 7.5' quadrangle. Ship Mountain (1952) 15' quadrangle shows Rocky Camp at the site.

Rodeo Creek [MENDOCINO]: *stream*, flows 2.5 miles to Eel River 4.5 miles south of Dos Rios (lat. 39°39'05" N, long. 123°20'35" W; near sec. 30, T 21 N, R 13 W); the stream goes through Rodeo Valley. Named on Dos Rios (1967) 7.5' quadrangle.

Rodeo Valley [MENDOCINO]: *valley*, 5.25 miles south-southeast of Dos Rios (lat. 39°38'50" N, long. 123°18'50" W; sec. 28, T 21 N, R 13 W). Named on Dos Rios (1967) 7.5' quadrangle.

Rodgers: see **Willits** [MENDOCINO].

Rodgers Break [HUMBOLDT]: *shoal*, 8.5 miles south of Petrolia, and 4000 feet offshore (lat. 40°12'N, long. 124°18'15" W). Named on Cooskie Creek (1969) 7.5' quadrangle.

Rodgers Mountain: see **Rodgers Peak** [HUMBOLDT].

Rodgers Peak [HUMBOLDT]: *ridge*, northwest-trending, 1 mile long, 9 miles northeast of Trinidad (lat. 41°09'45" N, long. 124°01'40" W). Named on Rodgers Peak (1966) 7.5' quadrangle. On Trinidad (1952) 15' quadrangle, the name refers to a peak on the ridge. United States Board on Geographic Names (1933, p. 647) approved the name "Rodgers Mountain" for the feature, but later (1968a, p. 7) approved the name "Rodgers Peak" for it, and rejected the names "Rodgers Mountain," "Rogers Peak," "Thornbury Mountain," and "Trinity Mountain."

Rodman Slough [LAKE]: *water feature*, formed by the confluence of Middle Creek (2) and Scotts Creek, flows 2.5 miles to Clear Lake 5 miles north-northeast of Lakeport (lat. 39°07'N, long. 122°53'05" W). Named on Lakeport (1958) and Upper Lake (1958) 7.5' quadrangles.

Rogers Creek [HUMBOLDT]: *stream*, flows 2.5 miles to Van Duzen River 3.5 miles west of Bridgeville (lat. 40°28'20" N, long. 123°51'45" W; near S line sec. 8, T 1 N, R 3 E). Named on Bridgeville (1969) 7.5' quadrangle.

Rogers Peak: see **Rodgers Peak** [HUMBOLDT].

Rohner Creek [HUMBOLDT]: *stream*, flows 2 miles to lowlands along Eel River at Fortuna (lat. 40°35'50" N, long. 124°08'55" W; sec. 35, T 3 N, R 1 W). Named on Fortuna (1959) and Hydesville (1979) 7.5' quadrangles.

Rohnerville [HUMBOLDT]: *town*, 2.25 miles southeast of Fortuna (lat. 40°34'15" N, long. 124°07'15" W; sec. 12, T 2 N, R 1 W). Named on Fortuna (1959) and Hydesville (1979) 7.5' quadrangles. Postal authorities established Eel River post office in 1857 and changed the name to Rohnerville in 1874 (Frickstad, p. 42). The name "Rohnerville" commemorates Henry Rohner, who founded the town (Bledsoe, p. 26).

Roller Gulch [MENDOCINO]: *canyon*, drained by a stream that flows 2 miles to Ray Gulch 4.5 miles northeast of Elk (lat. 39°10'25" N, long. 123°39'05" W; sec. 8, T 15 N, R 16 W). Named on Navarro (1961) 15' quadrangle.

Rolling Brook [MENDOCINO]: *stream*, flows nearly 3 miles to Garcia River 6 miles east-southeast of the village of Point Arena (lat. 38°53'N, long. 123°35'10" W; near S line sec. 24, T 12 N, R 16 W). Named on Point Arena (1960) 15' quadrangle.

Rolph: see **Fairhaven** [HUMBOLDT].

Rooster Rock [HUMBOLDT]: *relief feature*, 10 miles northeast of Lone Star Junction (lat. 40°44'25" N, long. 123°45' 05" W; sec. 8, T 4 N, R 4 E). Named on Mad River Buttes (1977) 7.5' quadrangle.

Root Creek [HUMBOLDT]: *stream*, flows 4.5 miles to Van Duzen River 5 miles north of Redcrest (lat. 40°28'30" N, long. 123°56'35" W; near N line sec. 15, T 1 N, R 2 E). Named on Redcrest (1969) 7.5' quadrangle.

Root Creek [LAKE]: *stream*, flows 2.5 miles to Wyman Creek 14 miles north-northwest of Clearlake Oaks (lat. 39°13'20" N, long. 122°43'35" W). Named on Clearlake Oaks (1960) 15' quadrangle.

Root Glade [LAKE]: *area*, 15 miles north of Clearlake Oaks (lat. 39°13'55" N, long. 122°42'55" W; near SE cor. sec. 14, T 16 N, R 8 W). Named on Clearlake Oaks (1960) 15' quadrangle.

Ropers Slough [HUMBOLDT]: *water feature*, 4.25 miles north of Ferndale (lat. 40°38'20" N, long. 124°16'15" W). Named on Cannibal Island (1959) 7.5' quadrangle.

Rosaleno Creek [HUMBOLDT]: *stream*, flows 2 miles to Klamath River 6 miles north-northwest of Orleans Mountain (lat. 41°21'45" N, long. 123°29'15" W). Named on Orleans (1978) and Orleans Mountain (1974) 7.5' quadrangles.

Rose Canyon [LAKE]: *canyon*, drained by a stream that flows 1.5 miles to Long Valley Creek 6.5 miles north-northwest of Clearlake Oaks (lat. 39°06'55" N, long. 122°42'20" W; near SE cor. sec. 26, T 15 N, R 8 W). Named on Clearlake Oaks (1958) 7.5' quadrangle.

Rose Creek [HUMBOLDT]: *stream*, flows 1.5 miles to Strawberry Creek 7.5 miles north of Arcata (lat. 40°59'05" N, long. 124°05'10" W; near N line sec. 20, T 7 N, R 1 E). Named on Arcata North (1959) 7.5' quadrangle.

Rose Creek [MENDOCINO]:

(1) *stream*, flows 2 miles to Middle Fork Eel River 10 miles east-northeast of Covelo (lat. 39°50'N, long. 123°04'W; sec. 22, T 23 N, R 11 W). Named on Newhouse Ridge (1967) 7.5' quadrangle.

(2) *stream*, flows 1.25 miles to South Branch of North Fork Navarro River 9 miles north of Boonville (lat. 39°08'25" N, long. 123°22'30" W; sec. 23, T 15 N, R 14 W). Named on Boonville (1959) 15' quadrangle.

Rose Gulch [TRINITY]: *canyon*, drained by a stream that flows 2 miles to East Fork Hayfork Creek 9.5 miles east-southeast of Hayfork (lat. 40°30'N, long. 123°01'05" W; sec. 32, T 31 N, R 10 W). Named on Hayfork (1951) 15' quadrangle.

Roseman Creek [MENDOCINO]: *stream*, flows 2.5 miles to the sea 6 miles northwest of Gualala (lat. 38°49'35" N, long. 123°36'30" W; near SE cor. sec. 2, T 11 N, R 16 W). Named on Gualala (1960) 7.5' quadrangle

Rose Peak [HUMBOLDT]: *peak*, 5 miles west-southwest of Garberville (lat. 40°04'40" N, long. 123°52'50" W; at SE cor. sec. 30, T 4 S, R 3 E). Altitude 2028 feet. Named on Briceland (1969) 7.5' quadrangle.

Rose Place [LAKE]: *locality*, 5 miles east of the town of Upper Lake in Tea Canyon (lat. 39°10'N, long. 122°49'W; at W line sec. 12, T 15 N, R 9 W). Named on Bartlett Mountain (1958) 7.5' quadrangle.

Rose Rock [MENDOCINO]: *relief feature*, 11 miles east-northeast of Eden Valley (lat. 39°42'N, long. 123°00'15" W; on E line sec. 6, T 21 N, R 10 W). Named on Thatcher Ridge (1967) 7.5' quadrangle.

Rosewood [HUMBOLDT]: *district*, 2.25 miles south of downtown Eureka (lat. 40°46'10" N, long. 124°09'50" W; near S line sec. 34, T 5 N, R 1 W). Named on Eureka (1958) 7.5' quadrangle. Called Stumpville on Eureka (1942) 15' quadrangle, but United States Board on Geographic Names (1950b, p. 6) rejected this name. Postal authorities established Stumpville post office, named for stumps left by logging operations, in 1930, changed the name to Rosewood in 1941, and discontinued it in 1955 (Salley, p. 189, 214).

Ross Creek [MENDOCINO]: *stream*, flows 2.5 miles to the sea 2.5 miles south-southeast of the village of Point Arena (lat. 38°52'35" N, long. 123°40'W; at W line sec. 29, T 12 N, R 16 W). Named on Point Arena (1960) 15' quadrangle. The name commemorates the Ross family, early residents of the neighborhood (Ross, p. 4-5).

Ross's Camp: see **Melbourne** [MENDOCINO].

Rough Canyon: see **Big Rough Canyon** [MENDOCINO].

Rough Gulch [HUMBOLDT]: *canyon*, drained by a stream that flows 1 mile to Van Duzen River 4 miles southwest of Showers Mountain (lat. 40°31'55" N, long. 123°44'30" W; near SW cor. sec. 21, T 2 N, R 4 E). Named on Showers Mountain (1978) 7.5' quadrangle.

Rough Gulch [TRINITY]: *canyon*, drained by a stream that flows 3 miles to South Fork Trinity River 7.5 miles south-southwest of Dubakella Mountain (lat. 40°17'35" N, long. 123°13'40" W; sec. 9, T 28 N, R 12 W). Named on Dubakella Mountain (1954) 15' quadrangle.

Round Knob [DEL NORTE]: *peak*, 10.5 miles northeast of Crescent City (lat. 41°52'20" N, long. 124°03'50" W; near N line sec. 16, T 17 N, R 1 E). Named on Hiouchi (1966) 7.5' quadrangle.

Round Mountain [LAKE]:

(1) *peak*, nearly 6 miles northeast of Hull Mountain (lat. 39°34'25" N, long. 122°51'10" W; sec. 22, T 20 N, R 9 W). Altitude 5062 feet. Named on Kneecap Ridge (1967) 7.5' quadrangle.

(2) *peak*, 4.25 miles east-southeast of the town of Upper Lake (lat. 39°08'50" N, long. 122°50' W). Altitude 3167 feet. Named on Bartlett Mountain (1958) 7.5' quadrangle.

(3) *peak*, nearly 3 miles northeast of Clearlake Oaks (lat. 39°02'55" N, long. 122°38'10" W; sec. 21, T 14 N, R 7 W). Named on Clearlake Oaks (1958) 7.5' quadrangle.

(4) *peak*, 1.25 miles north-northeast of Jericho Valley (lat. 38°51' N, long. 122°25'40" W). Named on Jericho Valley (1958) 7.5' quadrangle.

(5) *peak*, 2.25 miles southeast of Wilson Valley (2) (lat. 38°57'05" N, long. 122°26'10" W; at S line sec. 20, T 13 N, R 5 W). Altitude 1905 feet. Named on Wilson Valley (1958) 7.5' quadrangle.

Round Mountain [MENDOCINO]: *peak*, 6 miles north-northwest of Eden Valley (lat. 39°42'45" N, long. 123°12'35" W; on E line sec. 5, T 21 N, R 12 W). Altitude 2013 feet. Named on Jamison Ridge (1967) 7.5' quadrangle.

Round Mountain [TRINITY]:

(1) *peak*, 4.5 miles north of Kettenpom (lat. 40°13'35" N, long. 123°27'20" W; at SW cor. sec. 1, T 3 S, R 6 E). Named on Zenia (1967) 7.5' quadrangle.

(2) *ridge*, southwest-trending, 1.5 miles long, 15 miles southwest of Black Rock Mountain (lat. 40°02'20" N, long. 123°11'15" W; on N line sec. 10, T 25 N, R 12 W). Named on Black Rock Mountain (1954) 15' quadrangle.

Round Mountain: see **Little Round Mountain** [LAKE]; **Little Round Mountain** [TRINITY].

Round Mountain Creek: see **Little Round Mountain Creek** [LAKE].

Round Prairie [HUMBOLDT]:

(1) *area*, 8 miles south-southeast of Coyote Peak (lat. 41°01'40" N, long. 123°48'45" W; sec. 3, T 7 N, R 3 E). Named on Hupa Mountain (1982) 7.5' quadrangle.

(2) *area*, 7.5 miles northeast of the town of Blue Lake (lat. 40°57'40" N, long. 123°53'10" W; near SW cor. sec. 30, T 7 N, R 3 E). Named on Blue Lake (1979) 7.5' quadrangle.

Round Rock [DEL NORTE]: *rock*, 1.5 miles south-southeast of Crescent

City, and 1 mile offshore (lat. 41°43'55" N, long. 124°11'25" W). Named on Sister Rocks (1966) 7.5' quadrangle.

Roundtop Mountain [LAKE]: *peak*, nearly 2 miles west of the town of Lower Lake (lat. 38°55' N, long. 122°39'45" W; sec. 5, T 12 N, R 7 W). Altitude 2282 feet. Named on Clearlake Highlands (1958) 7.5' quadrangle.

Round Valley [MENDOCINO]: *valley*, 5 miles wide, at and around Covelo (lat. 39°47'30" N, long. 123°13'45" W). Named on Covelo East (1967), Covelo West (1967), and Jamison Ridge (1967) 7.5' quadrangles. Frank Asbill discovered the valley in 1854 and described it as round (Carranco and Beard, p. 41). The place also was called Nome Cult Valley, and the Indian farm and reservation there took that name (Keller, p. 5). Lieutenant Edward Dillon, 6th United States Infantry, established a camp called Nome Cult Indian Agency near the center of Round Valley in 1858; the facility was abandoned in 1861, but it was reoccupied in 1862 and renamed Fort Wright in honor of Brigadier General George Wright, commander of the department; after the Civil War the installation was called Camp Wright until it closed in 1875 (Frazer, p. 34).

Round Valley: see **Bohn Valley** [LAKE].

Round Valley Peak: see **Bohn Valley** [LAKE].

Rowdy Bar Creek [TRINITY]: *stream*, flows 1.5 miles to Trinity River 3.5 miles east-southeast of Burnt Ranch (lat. 40°47'25" N, long. 123°24'40" W). Named on Ironside Mountain (1951) 15' quadrangle.

Rowdy Creek [DEL NORTE]: *stream*, heads in the State of Oregon and flows 7 miles in Del Norte County to Smith River 1.5 miles southwest of the town of Smith River (lat. 41°54'40" N, long. 124°09'55" W; sec. 34, T 18 N, R 1 W). Named on High Divide (1966) and Smith River (1966) 7.5' quadrangles. South Fork enters from the southeast nearly 4 miles upstream from the mouth of the main creek; it is 3.25 miles long and is named on High Divide (1966) 7.5' quadrangle. On Point Saint George (1945) 15' quadrangle, present Savoy Creek has the name "South Fork Rowdy Creek."

Rowes Creek [MENDOCINO]: *stream*, flows nearly 4 miles to Sherwood Creek 5.5 miles north-northwest of Willits (lat. 39°29'05" N, long. 123°23'15" W; sec. 23, T 19 N, R 14 W). Named on Willits (1961) 15' quadrangle, and on Longvale (1966) 7.5' quadrangle.

Rowski Creek [TRINITY]: *stream*, flows 1 mile to South Fork Trinity River 3.5 miles southeast of Forest Glen (lat. 40°20'05" N, long. 123°17'05" W; sec. 33, T 1 S, R 8 E). Named on Forest Glen (1979) 7.5' quadrangle.

Royal Spring [LAKE]: *spring*, 15 miles north-northwest of Clearlake Oaks (lat. 39°13'55" N, long. 122°44'35" W; at S line sec. 15, T 16 N, R 8 W). Named on Clearlake Oaks (1960) 15' quadrangle.

Roycroft Gulch [TRINITY]: *canyon*, drained by a stream that flows 1.5 miles to Trinity River 10 miles east-northeast of Weaverville (lat. 40°47'30" N, long. 122°46' W; at W line sec. 22, T 34 N, R 8 W). Named on Trinity Dam (1950) 15' quadrangle.

Roycroft Gulch: see **Little Roycroft Gulch** [TRINITY].

Rube Creek [HUMBOLDT]: *stream*, flows 1.5 miles to Klamath River 8.5 miles north-northeast of Coyote Peak (lat. 41°14'25" N, long. 123°46'10" W; near W line sec. 19, T 10 N, R 4 E). Named on French Camp Ridge (1983) and Weitchpec (1979) 7.5' quadrangles.

Rube Ranch Creek [HUMBOLDT]: *stream*, flows less than 1 mile to Klamath River 8 miles north-northeast of Coyote Peak (lat. 41°13'40" N, long. 123°46'15" W; at W line sec. 30, T 10 N, R 4 E). Named on French Camp Ridge (1983) 7.5' quadrangle.

Ruby Creek [HUMBOLDT]: *stream*, flows 2.5 miles to Willow Creek (1) 5 miles west-southwest of the settlement of Willow Creek (lat. 40°54'30" N, long. 123°43' W; near NW cor. sec. 15, T 6 N, R 4 E). Named on Willow Creek (1979) 7.5' quadrangle.

Rumsey Bay [LAKE]: *embayment*, along Clear Lake near the north edge of Lakeport (lat. 39°03'20" N, long. 122°54'50" W; at NE cor. sec. 24, T 14 N, R 10 W). Named on Lakeport (1958) 7.5' quadrangle.

Rumsey Slough [LAKE]: *stream*, flows 1.5 miles to Clear Lake 2 miles southeast of Lakeport (lat. 39°01'25" N, long. 122°53'25" W; sec. 32, T 14 N, R 9 W). Named on Lakeport (1958) 7.5' quadrangle. On Lakeport (1938) 15' quadrangle, the part of present Rumsey Slough below its confluence with present Thompson Creek (2) has the name "Cole Creek."

Ruppert Point [LAKE]: *peak*, 9 miles north of Clearlake Oaks (lat. 39°09' N, long. 122°42' W; sec. 13, T 15 N, R 8 W); the peak is on Ruppert Ridge. Named on Clearlake Oaks (1960) 15' quadrangle.

Ruppert Ridge [LAKE]: *ridge*, east-southeast-trending, 9 miles north of Clearlake Oaks (lat. 39°09' N, long. 122°42' W). Named on Clearlake Oaks (1960) 15' quadrangle.

Rusch Creek [TRINITY]: *stream*, flows 6 miles to Hayfork Creek 10 miles east-southeast of Hyampom (lat. 40°35'20" N, long. 123°15'50" W). Named on Hyampom (1951) 15' quadrangle.

Rush Bottom [MENDOCINO]: *relief feature*, 4.5 miles north of Ornbaun Valley along Anderson Creek (2) (lat. 38°58'30" N, long. 123°18' W; sec. 21, T 13 N, R 13 W). Named on Ornbaun Valley (1960) 15' quadrangle.

Rush Creek [LAKE]: *stream*, flows 1 mile to Kelsey Creek 2.25 miles northwest of Whispering Pines in Cobb Valley (lat. 38°50'15" N, long. 122°44'25" W; near E line sec. 4, T 11 N, R 8 W). Named on Whispering Pines (1958) 7.5' quadrangle.

Rush Creek [TRINITY]: *stream*, flows 14 miles to Trinity River 5.5 miles east of Weaverville (lat. 40°43'15" N, long. 122°50' W; sec. 13, T 33 N, R 9 W). Named on Trinity Dam (1950) and Weaverville (1950) 15' quadrangles. Gudde (1975, p. 88) listed a mining place called Crows Bar that was situated opposite the confluence of Trinity River and Rush Creek.

Rush Creek Lakes [TRINITY]: *lakes*, largest 300 feet long, 7.5 miles north of Weaverville (lat. 40°50'15" N, long. 122°58' W); the lakes are near the head of Rush Creek. Named on Trinity Dam (1950) 15' quadrangle.

Rush Creek Public Camp [TRINITY]: *locality*, 6.5 miles north-northeast of Weaverville (lat. 40°49' N, long. 122°53'40" W; sec. 9, T 34 N, R 9 W); the place is along Rush Creek. Named on Trinity Dam (1950) 15' quadrangle.

Russ Creek [HUMBOLDT]; *stream*, flows 3.5 miles to lowlands 2.5 miles west of Ferndale (lat. 40°35'05" N, long. 124°18'40" W; at W line sec. 4, T 2 N, R 2 W). Named on Ferndale (1959) 7.5' quadrangle. The name is for Joseph Russ (Turner, p. 187).

Russell Brook [MENDOCINO]: *stream*, flows 4.5 miles to Big River 10.5 miles southwest of Willits (lat. 39°18'30" N, long. 123°29'55" W; at N line sec. 26, T 17 N, R 15 W). Named on Willits (1961) 15' quadrangle.

Russell Ridge [TRINITY]: *ridge*, generally south-trending, 1 mile long, 18 miles southwest of Black Rock Mountain (lat. 40°00'45" N, long. 123°14'55" W; sec. 23, 26, T 5 S, R 8 E). Named on Black Rock Mountain (1954) 15' quadrangle.

Russ Gulch [MENDOCINO]: *canyon*, drained by a stream that flows 1 mile to Flynn Creek 4.5 miles northwest of Navarro (lat. 39°11'45" N, long. 123°36'15" W; sec. 35, T 16 N, R 16 W). Named on Navarro (1961) 15' quadrangle.

Russian Gulch [MENDOCINO]:

(1) *canyon*, drained by a stream that flows 5 miles to the sea 1.5 miles north of Mendocino (lat. 39°19'45" N, long. 123°48'15" W; near SW cor. sec. 18, T 17 N, R 17 W). Named on Comptche (1960) 15' quadrangle, and on Mendocino (1960) 7.5' quadrangle.

(2) *canyon*, drained by a stream that flows 1.5 miles to Greenwood Creek 6 miles south of Navarro (lat. 39°03'50" N, long. 123°32'10" W; near N line sec. 21, T 14 N, R 15 W). Named on Navarro (1961) 15' quadrangle.

Russian River [MENDOCINO]: *stream*, flows 45 miles to Sonoma County 9.5 mile south-southeast of Hopland (lat. 38°51'10" N, long. 123°01'45" W; at S line sec. 25, T 12 N, R 11 W). Named on Potter Valley (1960) 15' quadrangle, and on Cloverdale (1960), Elledge Peak (1958), Hopland (1960), Purdys Gardens (1958), and Ukiah (1958) 7.5' quadrangles. East Fork enters from the northeast 3 miles north of Ukiah; it is 15 miles long and is named on Potter Valley (1960) 15' quadrangle, and on Cow Mountain (1958) and Ukiah (1958) 7.5' quadrangles.

Ruth [TRINITY]: *village*, 7 miles south of Forest Glen along Mad River (lat. 40°16'10" N, long. 123°19'15" W; at N line sec. 30, T 2 S, R 8 E). Named on Forest Glen (1979) 7.5' quadrangle. Pickett Peak (1954) 15' quadrangle shows the place located 4 miles farther northwest along Mad River at a site now under water of Ruth Reservoir (lat. 40°19' N, long. 123°22' W; near SW cor sec. 3, T 2 S, R 7 E). Postal authorities established Ruth post office in 1902 (Salley, p. 191). Jones, on a sketch map (p. 336), showed the site of Ruth from 1925 until 1960, and the new site of Ruth after 1960—the community moved upstream in 1960 to avoid inundation by water of Ruth Reservoir. Jones, on the same map, showed a place called Anada P.O. located about 2.5 miles southeast of the first site of Ruth, and a place called White Stump located about 1.5 miles west-northwest of the first site of Ruth. Postal authorities established Anada post office in 1898 and discontinued it in 1907, when they moved the service to Ruth (Frickstad, p. 206). John Jeans, who lived near the post office, suggested the name "Anada" for two girls, Ana and Ada, whom he had known in Missouri (Jones, p. 365). The name "White Stump" was given by an inebriated settler after lightning made a 20-foot stump out of a large pine tree at the site (Jones, p. 364). Postal authorities established Hetten post office 20 miles east of Blocksburg in 1890 and discontinued it in 1900, when they moved the service to Anada—the name "Hetten" is of Indian origin (Salley, p. 97). They established Kuntz post office 12 miles west of Ruth in 1906 and discontinued it in 1913—the name was for Charles F. Kuntz, first postmaster (Salley, p. 113).

Ruth Lake: see **Ruth Reservoir** [TRINITY].

Ruth Reservoir [TRINITY]: *lake*, behind a dam on Mad River nearly 6 miles west of Forest Glen (lat. 40°22'05" N, long. 123°25'55" W; near N line sec. 19, T 1 S, R 7 E); water of the lake covers the first site of Ruth. Named on Forest Glen (1979) and Ruth Reservoir (1978) 7.5' quadrangles. United States Board on Geographic Names (1986, p. 2) approved the name "Ruth Lake" for the feature, and rejected the names "New Ruth Reservoir" and "Ruth Reservoir."

Rutledge Opening [TRINITY]: *area*, 9 miles west-southwest of Forest Glen (lat. 40°20'40" N, long. 123°29'15" W; mainly in sec. 27, T 1 S, R 6 E). Named on Ruth Reservoir (1978) 7.5' quadrangle.

Ryan Creek [HUMBOLDT]: *stream*, flows 6.5 miles to Ryan Slough 6.5 miles south-southwest of Arcata (lat. 40°46'40" N, long. 124°07'05" W; near NW cor. sec. 31, T 5 N, R 1 E). Named on Arcata South (1959),

Eureka (1958), Fields Landing (1959), and McWhinney Creek (1979) 7.5' quadrangles. James Talbot Ryan bought property along the stream in 1853 (Turner, p. 187).

Ryan Creek [MENDOCINO]: *stream*, flows 2 miles to Outlet Creek 5 miles north-northwest of Willits (lat. 39°28'35" N, long. 123°22'35" W; near NE cor. sec. 26, T 19 N, R 14 W). Named on Willits (1961) 15' quadrangle.

Ryan Slough [HUMBOLDT]; *water feature*, joins Freshwater Slough nearly 6 miles south-southwest of Arcata (lat. 40°47'20" N, long. 124°06'50" W; sec. 30, T 5 N, R 1 E); the feature is the extension of Ryan Creek. Named on Arcata South (1959) 7.5' quadrangle.

– S –

Sacre Gap [LAKE]: *pass*, 4.5 miles south of Middletown on Lake-Sonoma County line (lat. 38°41'05" N, long. 122°38' W; sec. 28, T 10 N, R 7 W). Named on Mount Saint Helena (1959) 7.5' quadrangle.

Saddleback Opening [HUMBOLDT]: *area*, 7 miles east of Showers Mountain (lat. 40°34'50" N, long. 123°33'50" W; near W line sec. 1, T 2 N, R 5 E). Named on Blake Mountain (1979) 7.5' quadrangle.

Saddle Camp [TRINITY]: *locality*, 11 miles south-southwest of Black Rock MountaIn (lat. 40°03'45" N, long. 123°06'20" W; sec. 33, T 26 N, R 11 W). Named on Black Rock Mountain (1954) 15' quadrangle.

Saddle Gulch [TRINITY]:

(1) *canyon*, drained by a stream that flows 1.25 miles to South Fork Trinity River 6.5 miles north-northwest of Hyampom (lat. 40°41'55" N, long. 123°30'50" W). Named on Sims Mountain (1979) 7.5' quadrangle.

(2) *canyon*, drained by a stream that flows 1.5 miles to Hayfork Creek 3.5 miles east of Dubakella Mountain (lat. 41°22'30" N, long. 123°05' W; at NE cor. sec. 15, T 29 N, R 11 W). Named on Dubakella Mountain (1954) 15' quadrangle.

Saddle Mountain [HUMBOLDT]: *peak*, 8 miles south of Honeydew (lat. 40°07'35" N, long. 124°06' W; at E line sec. 7, T 4 S, R 1 E). Altitude 3292 feet. Named on Honeydew (1970) and Shelter Cove (1969) 7.5' quadrangles.

Saddle Opening [MENDOCINO]: *area*, 6 miles west of Ornbaun Valley (lat. 38°55'05" N, long. 123°24'45" W; sec. 3, T 12 N, R 14 W). Named on Ornbaun Valley (1960) 15' quadrangle.

Saddle Point [MENDOCINO]: *promontory*, 3.25 miles south-southeast of Albion along the coast (lat. 39°10'35" N, long. 123°45'10" W; sec. 9, T 15 N, R 17 W). Named on Albion (1960) 7.5' quadrangle.

Saddle Rock: see **Camel Rock** [MENDOCINO].

Saddle Spring [MENDOCINO]: *spring*, 3.25 miles south-southwest of Hopland (lat. 38°55'50" N, long. 123°08'50" W; sec. 1, T 12 N, R 12 W). Named on Hopland (1960) 15' quadrangle.

Sage Horn Creek [MENDOCINO]: *stream*, flows 2.5 miles to Salt Creek (2) 13 miles north-northwest of the town of Potter Valley (lat. 39°29' N, long. 123°18' W; sec. 20, T 19 N, R 12 W). Named on Brushy Mountain (1966) 7.5' quadrangle. On Potter Valley (1960) 15' quadrangle, the name applies to a nearby stream. United States Board on Geographic Names (1991, p. 6) approved the form "Sagehorn Creek" for the name.

Sailor Bar Creek [TRINITY]: *stream*, flows 3.5 miles to Trinity River 13 miles north of Hayfork (lat. 40°44'15" N, long. 123°11'10" W). Named on Hayfork (1951) 15' quadrangle.

Sail Rock [MENDOCINO]: *rock*, 6.25 miles south-southeast of village of Point Arena, and 0.5 mile offshore (lat. 38°49'55" N, long. 123°38' W). Named on Saunders Reef (1960) 7.5' quadrangle. To a viewer off of Point Arena, the pyramidal rock resembles a small vessel under sail (United States Coast and Geodetic Survey, p. 139).

Saint Albert: see **Camp Saint Albert** [MENDOCINO].

Saint Anthonys Point [MENDOCINO]: *promontory*, 0.5 mile north west of Elk along the coast (lat. 39°08'10" N, long. 123°43'20" W; at W line sec. 26, T 15 N, R 17 W). Named on Elk (1960) 7.5' quadrangle.

Saint George: see **Point Saint George** [DEL NORTE].

Saint George Channel [DEL NORTE]: *water feature*, 4 miles northwest of Crescent City (lat. 41°47'20" N, long. 124°16' W); the feature is less than 1 mile off the coast at Point Saint George. Named on Crescent City (1966) 7.5' quadrangle.

Saint George Reef: see **Point Saint George** [DEL NORTE].

Saint Helena Creek [LAKE]: *stream*, heads in Napa County and flows 9 miles to Putah Creek 1 mile north-northeast of Middletown (lat. 38°46' N, long. 122°36'15" W). Named on Detert Reservoir (1958) and Middletown (1958) 7.5' quadrangles.

Saint Helena Range: see **Mayacmas Mountains** [LAKE-MENDOCINO].

Saint John Canyon [MENDOCINO]: *canyon*, drained by a stream that flows 1 mile to North Fork Indian Creek (1) 5.5 miles north of Boonville (lat. 39°05'30" N, long. 123°22'45" W; near NW cor. sec. 11, T 14 N, R 14 W). Named on Boonville (1959) 15' quadrangle.

Saint Marys Creek [LAKE]: *stream*, flows 2.5 miles to Saint Helena Creek 2 miles south of Middletown (lat. 38°43'25" N, long. 122°36'50" W). Named on Detert Reservoir (1958) and Mount Saint Helena (1959) 7.5' quadrangles.

Saint Michael: see **Camp Saint Michael** [MENDOCINO].

Saint Orr Creek: see **Saint Orres Creek** [MENDOCINO].

Saint Orres Creek [MENDOCINO]: *stream*, flows nearly 2 miles to the sea 2.5 miles northwest of Gualala (lat. 38°47'35" N, long. 123°33'45" W; sec. 20, T 11 N, R 15 W). Named on Gualala (1960) 7.5' quadrangle. Called St. Orr Creek on Point Arena (1943) 15' quadrangle. United States Board on Geographic Names (1962c, p. 21) approved the name "Saint Orres Gulch" for the canyon of the stream, and rejected the name "Saint Orr Gulch" for the feature; the name reportedly is for the St. Orres family, early settlers in the neighborhood.

Saint Orres Gulch: see **Saint Orres Creek** [MENDOCINO].

Saints Rest Bar [HUMBOLDT]: *locality*, 1.5 miles east of Weitchpec along Klamath River (lat. 41°11'15" N, long. 123°40'45" W; sec. 11, T 9 N, R 4 E); the place is at the mouth of Saints Rest Creek. Named on Weitchpec (1979) 7.5' quadrangle.

Saints Rest Creek [HUMBOLDT]; *stream*, flows less than 1 mile to Klamath River 1.25 miles east of Weitchpec (lat. 41°11'15" N, long. 123°40'55" W; sec. 11, T 9 N, R 4 E). Named on Weitchpec (1979) 7.5' quadrangle.

Sallady Creek [MENDOCINO]: *stream*, flows nearly 4 miles to Black Butte River 12.5 miles east of Covelo (lat. 39°46'40" N, long. 123°00'55" W; sec. 7, T 22 N, R 10 W); the stream is west of Sallady Ridge. Named on Newhouse Ridge (1967) and Thatcher Ridge (1967) 7.5' quadrangles.

Sallady Ridge [MENDOCINO]: *ridge*, generally north-trending, 3 miles long, 12.5 miles northeast of Eden Valley (lat. 39°44'50" N, long. 123°00'50" W). Named on Newhouse Ridge (1967) and Thatcher Ridge (1967) 7.5' quadrangles.

Salminas Resort [LAKE]: *locality*, 7.5 miles west-southwest of the town of Lower Lake (lat. 38°52'35" N, long. 122°43'40" W; sec. 22, T 12 N, R 8 W). Named on Clearlake Highlands (1958) 7.5' quadrangle.

Salmon Alps: see **Salmon Mountains** [HUMBOLDT].

Salmon Creek [HUMBOLDT]:

(1) *stream*, flows about 12 miles to lowlands 3.5 miles south of Fields Landing (lat. 40°40'30" N, long. 124°12'05" W; sec. 5, T 3 N, R 1 W). Named on Fields Landing (1959), Hydesville (1979), and McWhinney Creek (1979) 7.5' quadrangles.

(2) *stream*, flows 1.25 miles to North Fork Yager Creek 1 mile south of Lone Star Junction (lat. 40°36'55" N, long. 123°52'20" W; at E line sec. 30, T 3 N, R 3 E). Named on Mad River Buttes (1977) and Yager Junction (1979) 7.5' quadrangles.

(3) *stream*, flows 12 miles to Eel River 3 miles northwest of Phillipsville (lat. 40°14'05" N, long. 123°49'50" W; sec. 3, T 3 S, R 3 E). Named on Ettersburg (1969) and Miranda (1970) 7.5' quadrangles. South Fork enters from the south 4.5 miles upstream from the mouth of the main creek; it is 5.5 miles long and is named on Ettersburg (1969) 7.5' quadrangle.

Salmon Creek [LAKE]: *stream*, formed by the confluence of Fuller Creek and Mill Creek (1), flows 2.5 miles to Lake Pillsbury 4.25 miles northwest of Bear Mountain (lat. 39°26'35" N, long. 122°57'55" W; sec. 3, T 18 N, R 10 W). Named on Lake Pillsbury (1967) 7.5' quadrangle. Called Fuller Creek on Lake Pillsbury (1951) 15' quadrangle.

Salmon Creek [MENDOCINO]:

(1) *stream*, flows nearly 2 miles to Middle Fork Eel River 5 miles north of Eden Valley (lat. 39°41'55" N, long. 123°10'20" W; at W line sec. 11, T 21 N, R 12 W). Named on Jamison Ridge (1967) 7.5' quadrangle.

(2) *stream*, flows 3.5 miles to Black Butte River 12.5 miles north of Hull Mountain (lat. 39°42' N, long. 122°55'25" W; sec. 1, T 21 N, R 10 W). Named on Plaskett Ridge (1967) 7.5' quadrangle.

(3) *stream*, flows 3.5 miles to Tomki Creek 7.5 miles north-northwest of the town of Potter Valley (lat. 39°25'10" N, long. 123°10'30" W; sec. 15, T 18 N, R 12 W). Named on Potter Valley (1960) 15' quadrangle.

(4) *stream*, flows 1.5 miles to Eel River 5 miles north of the town of Potter Valley (lat. 39°23'40" N, long. 123°06'50" W; near SE cor. sec. 19, T 18 N, R 11 W). Named on Potter Valley (1960) 15' quadrangle.

Salmon Creek: see **Beatrice** [HUMBOLDT]; **Big Salmon Creek** [MENDOCINO]; **Little Salmon Creek** [HUMBOLDT]; **Little Salmon Creek** [MENDOCINO]; **Whitesboro** [MENDOCINO].

Salmon Creek Bay: see **Whitesboro Cove** [MENDOCINO].

Salmon Creek Cove: see **Whitesboro Cove** [MENDOCINO].

Salmon Mountain [HUMBOLDT-TRINITY]: *peak*, 7 miles southwest of Forks of Salmon where Humboldt County, Trinity County, and Siskiyou County meet (lat. 41°11' N, long. 123°24'35" W); the peak is in Salmon Mountains. Altitude 6956 feet. Named on Salmon Mountain (1978) 7.5' quadrangle. United States Board on Geographic Names (1978b, p. 3) approved the name "Blacks Lake" for a feature, 250 feet long, located in Humboldt County 5 miles southwest of Salmon Mountain (lat. 41°08'09" N, long. 123°28'42" W).

Salmon Mountain Range: see **Salmon Mountains** [HUMBOLDT-TRINITY].

Salmon Mountains [HUMBOLDT-TRINITY]: *range*, in Humboldt Trinity, and Siskiyou Counties. United States Board on Geographic Names (1977b,

p. 5) gave the boundaries of the range as: on the north, Salmon River, North Fork Salmon River, North Russian Creek, and Etna Creek; on the east, Scott River, South Fork Scott River, Coffee Creek, North Fork Coffee Creek, Trinity River, Clair Engle Lake, and Lewiston Lake; on the south, Trinity River; and on the west, Trinity River and Klamath River—the Board gave the name "Salmon Alps" as a variant. Named on Weed (1963) 1° x 2° quadrangle. Hobson (p. 655, 656) referred to Salmon Mountain Range, and to Salmon River Range.

Salmon Point [MENDOCINO]: *promontory,* 1 mile southwest of Albion (lat. 39°12'50" N, long. 123°46'35" W; at S line sec. 29, T 16 N, R 17 W); the feature is south of Whitesboro Cove, which receives water of Big Salmon Creek and of Little Salmon Creek. Named on Albion (1960) 7.5' quadrangle.

Salmon River Range: see **Salmon Mountains** [HUMBOLDT-TRINITY].

Salmon Summit [TRINITY]: *pass,* 1.5 miles southeast of Salmon Mountain on Trinity-Siskiyou County line (lat. 41°10'05" N, long. 123°23'30" W). Named on Salmon Mountain (1978) 7.5' quadrangle.

Salmon Trinity Alps: see **Trinity Alps** [TRINITY].

Saloon Creek [TRINITY]: *stream,* flows 3.25 miles to North Fork Coffee Creek 6 miles west-northwest of Billys Peak (1) (lat. 41°10'15" N, long. 122°52'05" W; sec. 11, T 38 N, R 9 W). Named on Coffee Creek (1955) 15' quadrangle.

Salsig: see **Elk** [MENDOCINO].

Salt Canyon [LAKE]: *canyon,* less than 1 mile long, 4.5 miles east-northeast of Clearlake Oaks (lat. 39°03'10" N, long. 122°36'05" W; near N line sec. 23, T 14 N, R 7 W). Named on Clearlake Oaks (1960) 15' quadrangle.

Salt Canyon [MENDOCINO]: *canyon,* drained by a stream that flows 1.5 miles to Coleman Creek 4.5 miles east-southeast of Hopland (lat. 38°55'30" N, long. 123°02'30" W; near W line sec. 1, T 12 N, R 11 W). Named on Hopland (1960) 7.5 quadrangle.

Salt Creek [DEL NORTE]: *stream,* flows 3.25 miles to Hunter Creek 1 mile east of the mouth of Klamath River (lat. 41°32'50" N, long. 124°03'35" W; sec. 4, T 13 N, R 1 E). Named on Requa (1966) 7.5' quadrangle. On Klamath (1952) 15' quadrangle, present Salt Creek is called High Prairie Creek below the confluence of present Salt Creek and High Prairie Creek.

Salt Creek [LAKE]: *stream,* flows 3.25 miles to Rice Fork 4.5 miles south of Potato Hill (lat. 39°17'20" N, long. 122°49'10" W; near NE cor. sec. 36, T 17 N, R 9 W). Named on Potato Hill (1967) 7.5' quadrangle.

Salt Creek [MENDOCINO]:

(1) *stream,* flows 6 miles to Middle Fork Eel River 4.5 miles east-southeast of Dos Rios (lat. 39°41'55" N, long. 123°16'05" W; near NE cor. sec. 11, T 21 N, R 13 W). Named on Dos Rios (1967) 7.5' quadrangle.

(2) *stream,* flows 3.5 miles to Eel River 13 miles north-northwest of the town of Potter Valley (lat. 39°29'30" N, long. 123°12'50" W; sec. 20, T 19 N, R 12 W). Named on Potter Valley (1960) 15' quadrangle.

Salt Creek [TRINITY]:

(1) *stream,* flows nearly 3 miles to West Fork of North Fork Eel River (lat. 40°13'20" N, long. 123°25' W; near NW cor. sec. 8, T 3 S, R 6 E). Named Zenia (1967) 7.5' quadrangle.

(2) *stream,* flows 11 miles to North Fork Eel River 6 miles east-southeast of Kettenpom (lat. 40°08'05" N, long. 123°21'20" W; sec. 11, T 4 S, R 7 E). Named on Long Ridge (1967) and Shannon Butte (1967) 7.5' quadrangles.

(3) *stream,* flows 3 miles to Stuart Fork 15 miles north of Weaverville (lat. 40°56'45" N, long. 122°56'55" W; sec. 30, T 36 N, R 9 W). Named on Trinity Dam (1950) 15' quadrangle.

(4) *stream,* flows 15 miles to Hayfork Creek 1 mile west-southwest of Hayfork (lat. 40°33' N, long. 123°12'10" W; sec. 10, T 31 N, R 12 W). Named on Dubakella Mountain (1954) and Hayfork (1951) 15' quadrangles. West Fork enters from the west-southwest 3 miles northeast of Dubakella Mountain: it is 2 miles long and is named on Dubakella Mountain (1954) 15' quadrangle.

Salt Creek: see **Little Salt Creek** [MENDOCINO]; **Little Salt Creek** [TRINITY]; **Peanut** [TRINITY].

Salt Creek Campground [TRINITY]: *locality,* 3.5 miles north-northeast of Dubakella Mountain along Salt Creek (4) (lat. 40°25'30" N, long. 123°06'45" W; sec. 28, T 30 N, R 11 W). Named on Dubakella Mountain (1954) 15' quadrangle.

Salt Creek Divide [MENDOCINO]: *pass,* 3 miles north-northwest of Eden Valley (lat. 39°39'50" N, long. 123°12'30" W; near W line sec. 21, T 21 N, R 12 W). Named on Eden Valley (1952) 15' quadrangle.

Salt Flat [LAKE]: *area,* 5.25 miles northwest of the town of Upper Lake (lat. 39°13'35" N, long. 122°58'15" W; sec. 21, T 16 N, R 10 W). Named on Upper Lake (1958) 7.5' quadrangle.

Salt Flat [MENDOCINO]: *area,* 2.5 miles west of Eden Valley (lat. 39°37'15" N, long. 123°13'50" W; sec. 6, T 20 N, R 12 W). Named on Brushy Mountain (1966) 7.5' quadrangle.

Salt Flat [TRINITY]: *area,* 6 miles east-southeast of Weaverville along Trinity River (lat. 40°42'30" N, long. 122°50' W; at N line sec. 24, T 33 N, R 9 W). Named on Weaverville (1950) 15' quadrangle.

Salt Flat Creek [LAKE]: *stream,* flows 2 miles to Middle Creek (2) 4.5 miles north-northwest of the town of Upper Lake (lat. 39°13'35" N, long. 122°56'30" W; sec. 23, T 16 N, R 10 W). Named on Upper Lake (1958) 7.5' quadrangle.

Salt Glade [LAKE]: *area,* 2.5 miles north-northeast of Three Crossings (lat. 39°21' N, long. 122°53'55" W; sec. 5, T 17 N, R 9 W). Named on Elk Mountain (1967) 7.5' quadrangle.

Salt Glade Creek [LAKE]: *stream,* flows 1 mile to Rice Fork nearly 3 miles northeast of Three Crossings (lat. 39°20'55" N, long. 122°53'20" W; near SE cor. sec. 5, T 17 N, R 9 W); the stream goes through Salt Glade. Named on Elk Mountain (1967) 7.5' quadrangle.

Salt Gulch [TRINITY]: *canyon,* drained by a stream that flows 3.5 miles to Salt Creek (4) 4.25 miles north of Dubakella Mountain (lat. 40°26'45" N, long. 123°08'15" W; at SE cor. sec. 18, T 30 N, R 11 W). Named on Dubakella Mountain (1954) 15' quadrangle.

Salt Hollow Creek [MENDOCINO]: *stream,* flows 3 miles to Russian River 7 miles southwest of the town of Potter Valley (lat. 39°15'10" N, long. 123°12'10" W). Named on Redwood Valley (1960) 7.5' quadrangle.

Salt Lick Canyon [LAKE]: *canyon,* drained by a stream that flows nearly 2 miles to Wolf Creek 6 miles north-northeast of Clearlake Oaks (lat. 39°05'40" N, long. 122°36'40" W). Named on Clearlake Oaks (1960) 15' quadrangle.

Salt Lick Creek [TRINITY]: *canyon,* drained by a stream that flows 1 mile to High Camp Creek 3 miles south-southeast of China Mountain, which is in Siskiyou County (lat. 41°20'15" N, long. 122°33'05" W; sec. 9, T 40 N, R 6 W). Named on China Mountain (1955) 15' quadrangle.

Salt Log Spring [TRINITY]: *spring,* 7.5 miles east-northeast of Burnt Ranch (lat. 40°50'15" N, long. 123°20'05" W). Named on Ironside Mountain (1951) 15' quadrangle.

Salt River [HUMBOLDT]: *water feature,* 10.5 miles long, joins Eel River 4 miles northwest of Ferndale (lat. 40°37'20" N, long. 124°18'15" W. Named on Ferndale (1959) and Fortuna (1959) 7.5' quadrangles. Evanson (p. 6) described the feature as a major slough that is an abandoned channel of Eel River.

Salt Rock Camp [MENDOCINO]: *locality,* 10.5 miles northeast of Covelo (lat. 39°55'20" N, long. 123°08'30" W). Named on Bluenose Ridge (1967) 7.5' quadrangle.

Salt Spring Creek [LAKE]: *stream,* flows 2.25 miles to Lake Pillsbury 1.25 miles northwest of Bear Mountain (lat. 39°25' N, long. 122°54'55" W). Named on Lake Pillsbury (1967) 7.5' quadrangle.

Salt Spring Creek [MENDOCINO]: *stream,* flows 3.5 miles to Pieta Creek 7 miles southeast of Hopland (lat. 38°54'10" N, long. 123°01'10" W; sec. 7, T 12 N, R 10 W). Named on Asti (1959), Highland Springs (1959), and Hopland (1960) 7.5' quadrangles.

Salyer [TRINITY]: *village,* 35 miles west-northwest of Weaverville along Trinity River (lat. 40°53'30" N, long. 123°35' W; sec. 14, T 6 N, R 5 E). Named on Salyer (1979) 7.5' quadrangle. Postal authorities established Salyer post office in 1918 and named it for Charles M. Salyer, who had mining interests in the neighborhood (Salley, p. 192).

Sam Alley Ridge [LAKE]: *ridge,* generally southwest-trending, 2 miles long, 3 mile northeast of the town of Upper Lake (lat. 39°11'40" N, long. 122°52' W). Named on Bartlett Mountain (1958) and Upper Lake (1958) 7.5' quadrangles.

Samoa [HUMBOLDT]: *town,* 1.5 miles northwest of downtown Eureka (lat. 40°49'05" N, long. 124°11'05" W; sec. 16, T 5 N, R 1 W). Named on Eureka (1958) 7.5' quadrangle. Postal authorities established Samoa post office in 1894 (Frickstad, p. 46). The place first was called Brownsville, for James D.H. Brown, who started a dairy ranch in 1859; the name "Samoa" came at a time when the Samoan Islands were in the news—Humboldt Bay was assumed to be similar to Pago Pago harbor at Samoa (Gudde, 1949, p. 297).

Samoa Peninsula [HUMBOLDT]: *peninsula,* extends for 8 miles along the northwest side of Humboldt Bay and Arcata Bay, separating the bays from the sea; center 1.5 miles west-northwest of downtown Eureka (lat. 40°48'45" N, long. 124°11'30" W); the town of Samoa is on the feature. Named on Eureka (1958) 7.5' quadrangle.

Sam Watt Creek [MENDOCINO]: *stream,* flows 4.5 miles to Long Valley Creek 0.5 mile north-northwest of Longvale (lat. 39°33'40" N, long. 123°25'55" W; near NE cor. sec. 29, T 20 N, R 14 W); the stream goes past Sam Watt Rock. Named on Longvale (1966) 7.5' quadrangle.

Sam Watt Rock [MENDOCINO]: *relief feature,* 1 mile northwest of Longvale (lat. 39°33'50" N, long. 123°26'35" W; at N line sec. 29, T 20 N, R 14 W). Named on Longvale (1966) 7.5' quadrangle.

Sand Bank Creek [MENDOCINO]: *stream,* flows 2.5 miles to Middle Fork Eel River 3.5 miles east-southeast of Dos Rios (lat. 39°42'15" N, long. 123°17'05" W; near W line sec. 2, T 21 N, R 13 W); the stream heads near Sand Banks. Named on Dos Rios (1967) 7.5' quadrangle.

Sand Banks [MENDOCINO]: *relief feature,* 2.5 miles east-northeast of Dos Rios (lat. 39°43'40" N, long. 123°18'05" W; near NW cor. sec. 34, T 22 N, R 13 W). Named on Dos Rios (1967) 7.5' quadrangle.

Sandhill Lake [MENDOCINO]: *lake,* 600 feet long, 8.5 miles south of Westport (lat. 39°30'55" N, long. 123°46'25" W; sec. 17, T 19 N, R 17 W). Named on Inglenook (1966) 7.5' quadrangle.

Sand Rock [MENDOCINO]: *relief feature,* 6 miles north-northeast of Branscomb (lat. 39°43'40" N, long. 123°33'50" W; sec. 29, T 22 N, R 15 W). Named on Cahto Peak (1967) 7.5' quadrangle.

Sandy Bar [HUMBOLDT]:
(1) *locality,* 6 miles south of Coyote Peak (lat. 41°03' N, long. 123°52' W; at W line sec. 29, T 8 N, R 3 E). Named on Hupa Mountain (1982) 7.5' quadrangle.
(2) *locality,* 4.25 miles south-southeast of the settlement of Willow Creek along South Fork Trinity River (lat. 40°52'50" N, long. 123°36'20" W; sec. 22, T 6 N, R 5 E). Named on Salyer (1979) 7.5' quadrangle.

Sandy Bar [TRINITY]: *locality,* 4.25 miles east of Burnt Ranch along Trinity River (lat. 40°47'55" N, long. 123°23'40" W). Named on Ironside Mountain (1951) 15' quadrangle.

Sandy Bar Creek [TRINITY]: *stream,* flows 1.25 miles to Trinity River 4.25 miles east of Burnt Ranch (lat. 40°47'55" N, long. 123°23'30" W); Sandy Bar is at the mouth of the stream. Named on Ironside Mountain (1951) 15' quadrangle.

Sandy Bar Creek: see **Little Sandy Bar Creek** [TRINITY].

Sandy Canyon [TRINITY]: *canyon,* drained by a stream that flows 1 mile to Parker Creek 9 miles south-southwest of Billys Peak (1) (lat. 41°00'50" N, long. 122°49'50" W; near N line sec. 6, T 36 N, R 8 W). Named on Coffee Creek (1955) 15' quadrangle.

Sandy Prairie [HUMBOLDT]: *area,* 0.5 mile southwest of Fortuna along Eel River (lat. 40°35'30" N, long. 124°10' W). Named on Fortuna (1959) 7.5' quadrangle.

Sanel [MENDOCINO]: *land grant,* along Russian River at Largo and Hopland. Named on Elledge Peak (1958), Hopland (1960), and Purdys Gardens (1958) 7.5' quadrangles. Fernando Felix received 4 leagues in 1844 and claimed 17,754 acres patented in 1860 (Cowan, p. 89). The name is from an Indian village at the site (Hoover, Rensch, and Rensch, p. 196).

Sanel: see **Hopland** [MENDOCINO].

Sanel Mountain [MENDOCINO]: *peak,* 5.5 miles west-southwest of Hopland (lat. 38°56'55" N, long. 123°13' W; near NE cor. sec. 31, T 13 N, R 12 W). Altitude 3353 feet. Named on Hopland (1960) 15' quadrangle.

Sanel Valley [MENDOCINO]: *valley,* north of Hopland along Russian River (lat. 38°59' N, long. 123°06' W). Named on Hopland (1960) 7.5' quadrangle.

Sanger Canyon [DEL NORTE]: *canyon,* drained by a stream that flows 2.25 miles to East Fork Illinois River 5 miles northeast of Broken Rib Mountain (lat. 41°55'50" N, long. 123°37' W). Named on Broken Rib Mountain (1982) and Polar Bear Mountain (1982) 7.5' quadrangles.

Sanger Lake [DEL NORTE]: *lake,* 900 feet long, 2.5 miles east-northeast of Broken Rib Mountain (lat. 41°54'05" N, long. 123°38'45" W). Named on Broken Rib Mountain (1982) 7.5' quadrangle.

Sanger Peak [DEL NORTE]: *peak,* nearly 3 miles northeast of Broken Rib Mountain (lat. 41°55'10" N, long. 123°39'15" W). Altitude 5862 feet. Named on Broken Rib Mountain (1982) 7.5' quadrangle.

Sanger Peak: see **Little Sanger Peak** [DEL NORTE].

Sanhedrin: see **Hullville** [LAKE]; **Mount Sanhedrin**, under **Big Signal Peak** [MENDOCINO].

Sanhedrin Creek [MENDOCINO]: *stream,* flows 6.5 miles to Elk Creek 5 miles east-southeast of Eden Valley (lat. 39°36'45" N, long. 123°05'50" W). Named on Sanhedrin Mountain (1966) 7.5' quadrangle.

Sanhedrin Mountain [MENDOCINO]: *ridge,* generally west-northwest-trending, 2 miles long, 10 miles south-southeast of Eden Valley (lat. 39°30'45" N, long. 123°04'50" W). Named on Sanhedrin Mountain (1966) 7.5' quadrangle. United States Board on Geographic Names (1969a, p. 2) rejected the name Mount Sanhedrin for present Big Signal Peak.

Sapphire Lake [TRINITY]: *lake,* 0.5 mile long, 12 miles southeast of Cecilville, which is in Siskiyou County (lat. 41°00' N, long. 123°00'30" W). Named on Helena (1951) 15' quadrangle, and on Thompson Peak (1979) 7.5' quadrangle. Called Saphire L. on Averill's (1940) map.

Saratoga Springs [LAKE]: *locality,* 4 miles west of the town of Upper Lake (lat. 39°10'30" N, long. 122°58'50" W; near SW cor. sec. 4, T 15 N, R 10 W). Named on Upper Lake (1958) 7.5' quadrangle. Lakeport (1938) 15' quadrangle shows Bachelor post office at the site. Postal authorities established Bachelor post office in 1882, moved it 3.5 miles south in 1883, discontinued it in 1919, reestablished it in 1920, and discontinued it in 1940 (Salley, p. 13). The resort started at the site in the 1870's could accommodate 250 people by 1910 (Waring, p. 179). The resort also was called Pierson Springs (Bradley, p 221). California Mining Bureau's (1909c) map shows a place called Laurel Dell located 1.5 miles southwest of Balchelor. Postal authorities established Bertha post office in 1879 and discontinued it in 1900, when they moved it 1 mile southeast and changed the name to Laurel Dell; the name "Bertha" was from the given name of the wife of the first postmaster (Salley, p. 20). They discontinued Laurel Dell post office in 1922, reestablished it in 1925, and discontinued it in 1926 (Frickstad, p. 64). California Mining Bureau's (1909c) map shows a place called Midlakes situated 1 mile northwest of Laurel Dell near the west border of Lake County. Postal authorities established Midlake post office in 1900 and discontinued it in 1945 (Frickstad, p. 64). Bradley (p. 215) noted that Midlake post office was at a place called Blue Lakes located between present Blue Lakes and present Lower Blue Lake.

Sartori Gulch [MENDOCINO]: *canyon,* drained by a stream that flows nearly 2 miles to the sea 1.5 miles northwest of Elk (lat. 39°08'50" N, long. 123°44' W; sec. 22, T 15 N, R 17 W). Named on Elk (1960) 7.5' quadrangle.

Sarvorum Mountain [HUMBOLDT]: *ridge,* west-trending, 1.5 miles long, 3.5 miles southwest of Orleans (lat. 41°16'05" N, long. 123°35'10" W). Named on Orleans (1978) 7.5' quadrangle. The name is from an Indian rancheria that was located at the confluence of Boyce Creek and Klamath River (Gudde, 1969, p. 299).

Saugep Creek [DEL NORTE]: *stream,* flows 1.5 miles to Klamath River 3.25 miles southeast of the mouth of that river (lat. 41°30'55" N, long. 124°02'25" W; sec. 15, T 13 N, R 1 E). Named on Requa (1966) 7.5' quadrangle. The name is from an Indian word for coyote (Turner, p. 191).

Saunders Creek [HUMBOLDT]: *stream,* flows nearly 2 miles to Mattole River 16 miles south-southwest of Scotia (lat. 40°15'25" N, long. 124°11'05" W; sec. 33, T 2 S, R 1 W). Named on Buckeye Mountain (1970) and Shubrick Peak (1969) 7.5' quadrangles.

Saunders Landing [MENDOCINO]: *locality,* 4.5 miles south-southeast of the village of Point Arena (lat. 38°51'05" N, long. 123°38'55" W; sec. 4, T 11 N, R 16 W); the place is along the coast opposite Saunders Reef. Named on Saunders Reef (1960) 7.5' quadrangle.

Saunders Reef [MENDOCINO]: *shoal,* 4.5 miles south-southeast of Point Arena, and 0.5 mile offshore (lat. 38°51'10" N, long. 123°39'35" W). Named on Saunders Reef (1960) 7.5' quadrangle.

Savage Creek [HUMBOLDT]: *stream,* flows 1.5 miles to the sea 3.25 miles north of Trinidad (lat. 41°06' N, long. 124°09'35" W; sec. 3, T 8 N, R 1 W). Named on Trinidad (1966) 7.5' quadrangle.

Savoy Creek [DEL NORTE]: *stream,* flows 3 miles to South Fork Rowdy Creek 2.5 miles east-southeast of the town of Smith River (lat. 41°55'05" N, long. 124°06' W; sec. 30, T 18 N, R 1 E). Named on High Divide (1966) 7.5' quadrangle. Called South Fork Rowdy Creek on Point Saint George (1945) 15' quadrangle.

Sawmill Creek [HUMBOLDT]: *stream,* flows 2.25 miles to South Fork Eel River 3 miles south-southwest of Garberville (lat. 40°03'40" N, long. 123°49'25" W; near N line sec. 3, T 5 S, R 3 E). Named on Garberville (1970) 7.5' quadrangle.

Sawmill Flat [LAKE]: *area,* 8 miles east-southeast of the town of Upper Lake (lat. 39°08'15" N, long. 122°46' W; near E line sec. 20, T 15 N, R 8 W). Named on Bartlett Mountain (1958) 7.5' quadrangle.

Sawmill Gulch [HUMBOLDT]: *canyon,* drained by a stream that flows less than 1 mile to Wilson Creek (1) 2.25 miles north-northeast of Orleans (lat. 41°19'50" N, long. 123°31'10" W). Named on Orleans (1978) 7.5' quadrangle.

Sawmill Gulch [TRINITY]:
(1) *canyon,* drained by a stream that flows 1.5 miles to Trinity River 15 miles northeast of Weaverville (lat. 40°52'05" N, long. 122°43'15" W; near S line sec. 24, T 35 N, R 8 W). Named on Schell Mountain (1950) 15' quadrangle.
(2) *canyon,* drained by a stream that flows 1 mile to the canyon of Trinity River 21 miles northeast of Weaverville (lat. 40°57'45" N, long. 122°39'55" W; at W line sec. 22, T 36 N, R 7 W). Named on Schell Mountain (1950) 15' quadrangle.
(3) *canyon,* drained by a stream that flows 0.25 mile to Clair Engle Lake 14 miles northeast of Weaverville (lat. 40°52'10" N, long. 122°45'20" W; at S line sec. 22, T 35 N, R 8 W). Named on Trinity Dam (1950) 15' quadrangle.
(4) *canyon,* drained by a stream that flows 2.5 miles to Grass Valley Creek 6 miles southeast of Weaverville (lat. 40°40'35" N, long. 122°51'10" W; sec. 35, T 33 N, R 9 W). Named on Weaverville (1950) 15' quadrangle.
(5) *canyon,* drained by a stream that flows nearly 2 miles to Salt Creek (4) about 4 miles south of Hayfork (lat. 40°30' N, long. 123°10'30" W; sec. 36, T 31 N, R 12 W). Named on Dubakella Mountain (1954) and Hayfork (1951) 15' quadrangles.

Sawmill Point [HUMBOLDT]: *peak,* 1 mile west-northwest of Hoopa (lat. 41°03'10" N, long. 123°41'40" W; sec. 26, T 8 N, R 4 E). Altitude 1444 feet. Named on Hoopa (1979) 7.5' quadrangle.

Sawmill Ridge [HUMBOLDT]: *ridge,* generally east-trending, 3.25 miles long, 2.5 miles west-northwest of Hoopa (lat. 40°03'35" N, long. 123°43'20" W). Named on Hoopa (1979) 7.5' quadrangle.

Sawtelle Valley [LAKE]: *valley,* 5 miles north of Cold Spring Mountain (lat. 39°10'15" N, long. 122°29' W; around SW cor. sec. 1, T 15 N, R 6 W). Named on Wilbur Springs (1961) 15' quadrangle.

Sawtooth Mountain [DEL NORTE]: *peak,* 9 miles northwest of Dillon Mountain on Del Norte-Siskiyou County line (lat. 41°36'45" N, long. 123°42'40" W). Altitude 5781 feet. Named on Chimney Rock (1981) 7.5' quadrangle.

Sawtooth Mountain [TRINITY]: *peak,* 15 miles north-northeast of Helena (lat. 40°58'20" N, long. 123°00'10" W). Altitude 8886 feet. Named on Helena (1951) and Trinity Dam (1950) 15' quadrangles. United States Board on Geographic Names (1950a, p. 3) rejected the names "Thompson Mountain" and "Saw Tooth Mountain" for the feature.

Sawtooth Peak: see **Thompson Peak** [TRINITY] (2).

Sawtooth Ridge [TRINITY]: *ridge*, generally west-trending, 3.5 miles long, 31 miles south of Etna, which is in Siskiyou County, on Siskiyou-Trinity County line (lat. 41°00'45" N, long. 122°58'30" W). Named on Coffee Creek (1955) and Trinity Dam (1950) 15' quadrangles.

Sawyer Bar: see **Sawyers Bar Camp Ground** [DEL NORTE].

Sawyer Creek [MENDOCINO]: *stream*, flows 1.5 miles to Bottom Creek 15 miles north-northwest of Boonville (lat. 39°12'15" N, long. 123°28'45" W; sec. 36, T 16 N, R 15 W). Named on Boonville (1959) 15' quadrangle.

Sawyers: see **Hearst** [MENDOCINO].

Sawyers Bar Camp Ground [DEL NORTE]: *locality*, 7.5 miles east-northeast of Gasquet along Middle Fork Smith River (lat. 41°52'30" N, long. 123°49'50" W; at SE cor. sec. 9, T 17 N, R 3 E). Named on Gasquet (1951) 15' quadrangle. Wells' (1946) map shows a place called Sawyer Bar located along Middle Fork Smith River about 0.5 mile south of present Sawyers Bar Camp Ground at the mouth of Jones Creek (present Little Jones Creek). Preston Peak (1922) 30' quadrangle has the name "Lawyers Bar" at the site.

Scaath [DEL NORTE]: *locality*, 1.25 miles east of Klamath Glen (lat. 41°30'55" N, long. 123°58'05" W; sec. 17, T 13 N, R 2 E); the place is on the north side of Klamath River just west of Scaath Creek. Named on Klamath Glen (1982) 7.5' quadrangle.

Scaath Creek [DEL NORTE]: *stream*, flows 1 mile to Klamath River 1.5 miles east of Klamath Glen (lat. 41°30'45" N, long. 123°57'55" W). Named on Klamath Glen (1982) 7.5' quadrangle.

Schindler Creek [LAKE]: *stream*, enters Clear Lake 0.5 mile east-southeast of downtown Clearlake Oaks (lat. 39°01'20" N, long. 122°40' W; sec. 31, T 14 N, R 7 W). Named on Clearlake Oaks (1958) 7.5' quadrangle.

Schnable Diggings [HUMBOLDT]: *locality*, 8 miles east of Weitchpec along Red Cap Creek (lat. 41°12'30" N, long. 123°33'20" W). Named on Hopkins Butte (1979) 7.5' quadrangle. On Hoopa (1952) 15' quadrangle, the place has the designation "Schnable (placer diggings)."

Schneiders Bar [TRINITY]: *locality*, 5.5 miles east-southeast of Burnt Ranch (lat. 40°47'35" N, long. 123°22'15" W). Named on Ironside Mountain (1951) 15' quadrangle.

Schofield Gulch [TRINITY]: *canyon*, 0.5 mile long, opens into the canyon of East Weaver Creek nearly 4 miles north of Weaverville (lat. 40°46'55" N, long. 122°56'05" W; at S line sec. 19, T 34 N, R 9 W). Named on Trinity Dam (1950) 15' quadrangle.

Schofield Opening [HUMBOLDT]: *area*, 4 miles south-southwest of Garberville (lat. 40°02'30" N, long. 123°48'45" W; at NW cor. sec. 11, T 5 S, R 3 E). Named on Garberville (1970) 7.5' quadrangle.

Schofield Peak [HUMBOLDT]: *peak*, 4 miles south-southwest of Garberville (lat. 40°02'45" N, long. 123°48'35" W; near SW cor. sec. 2, T 5 S, R 3 E). Named on Garberville (1970) 7.5' quadrangle.

Schoolhouse Creek [HUMBOLDT]: *stream*, flows 2 miles to Trinity River 2.25 miles south-southeast of the settlement of Willow Creek (lat. 40°54'10" N, long. 123°36'45" W; at W line sec. 10, T 6 N, R 5 E). Named on Salyer (1979) and Willow Creek (1979) 7.5' quadrangles.

Schoolhouse Creek [MENDOCINO]: *stream*, flows 2.5 miles to the sea 3 miles south of Mendocino (lat. 39°15'40" N, long. 123°47'10" W; sec. 8, T 16 N, R 17 W). Named on Mendocino (1960) 7.5' quadrangle.

School House Gulch: see **Robinson Gulch** [MENDOCINO].

Schoolhouse Hill [HUMBOLDT]: *ridge*, northwest-trending, 1 mile long, 1.5 miles northwest of Bridgeville (lat. 40°29'15" N, long. 123°49'05" W; mainly in sec. 3, T 1 N, R 3 E). Named on Bridgeville (1969) 7.5' quadrangle.

Schoolhouse Opening [HUMBOLDT]: *area*, 5.25 miles southeast of Showers Mountain (lat. 40°31'25" N, long. 123°37'40" W; near E line sec. 29, T 2 N, R 5 E). Named on Showers Mountain (1978) 7.5' quadrangle.

Schoolhouse Pasture [HUMBOLDT]: *area*, 2 miles west-northwest of Coyote Peak (lat. 41°08'40" N, long. 123°53'50" W; sec. 25, T 9 N, R 2 E); the place is southwest of Schoolhouse Peak. Named on Bald Hills (1982) 7.5' quadrangle. Coyote Peak (1952) 15' quadrangle shows a feature called Schoolhouse Pasture Rock at the place.

Schoolhouse Pasture Rock: see **Schoolhouse Pasture** [HUMBOLDT].

Schoolhouse Peak [HUMBOLDT]: *peak*, nearly 2 miles northwest of Coyote Peak (lat. 41°09'15" N, long. 123°52'50" W; sec. 19, T 9 N, R 3 E). Altitude 3097 feet. Named on Bald Hills (1982) 7.5' quadrangle.

Schoolhouse Spring [TRINITY]: *spring*, 9 miles southeast of Kettenpom (lat. 40°04'30" N, long. 123°20' W; sec. 36, T 4 S, R 7 E). Named on Long Ridge (1967) 7.5' quadrangle.

Schoolmarm Creek [TRINITY]: *stream*, flows nearly 2 miles to Middle Fork Eel River 9 miles south-southwest of Black Rock Mountain (lat. 40°04'30" N, long. 123°02'55" W; sec. 25, T 26 N, R 11 W). Named on Black Rock Mountain (1954) 15' quadrangle.

Schoolmarm Ridge [TRINITY]: *ridge*, south-southeast- to southeast-trending, 2 miles long, 8 miles south-southwest of Black Rock Mountain (lat. 40°05'45" N, long. 123°03'45" W); the ridge is northeast of Schoolmarm Creek. Named on Black Rock Mountain (1954) 15' quadrangle.

School Section Creek [MENDOCINO]: *stream*, flows 1.5 miles to Elkhorn Creek (1) 6.25 miles northeast of Leggett (lat. 39°55'40" N, long. 123°37'35" W; sec. 16, T 24 N, R 16 W). Named on Noble Butte (1969) 7.5' quadrangle.

Schoolteacher Hill [LAKE]: *hill*, 3.25 miles north of the town of Lower Lake (lat. 38°57'30" N, long. 122°37'05" W; sec. 22, T 13 N, R 7 W). Named on Lower Lake (1958) 7.5' quadrangle.

Schooner Gulch [MENDOCINO]: *canyon*, 2.25 miles long, drained by a stream that enters the sea 3.5 miles southeast of the village of Point Arena (lat. 38°52' N, long. 123°39'15" W; near N line sec. 32, T 12 N, R 16 W). Named on Point Arena (1960) 15' quadrangle. The canyon splits at the head to form Hall Gulch and China Gulch (1). North Fork branches east-northeast 2000 feet upstream from the mouth of the main canyon; it is 2.5 miles long and is named on Point Arena (1960) 15' quadrangle.

Schroeder Rock [HUMBOLDT]: *peak*, 8 miles south-southeast of Alderpoint (lat. 40°04'15" N, long. 123°33'40" W; sec. 36, T 4 S, R 5 E). Altitude 2352 feet. Named on Jewett Rock (1969) 7.5' quadrangle.

Schuler Gulch [TRINITY]: *canyon*, drained by a stream that flows 1 mile to Granite Creek (1) 5.5 miles northwest of Billys Peak (1) (lat. 41°11'05" N, long. 122°50'40" W; sec. 1, T 38 N, R 9 W). Named on Coffee Creek (1955) 15' quadrangle.

Scorpion Creek [DEL NORTE]: *stream*, flows 2 miles to Bluff Creek 17 miles east-southeast of Klamath Glen (lat. 41°26'35" N, long. 123°41'15" W). Named on Lonesome Ridge (1974) 7.5' quadrangle.

Scorpion Creek [TRINITY]: *stream*, flows 4.5 mile to Trinity River 6.5 miles north of Trinity Center (lat. 41°06'05" N, long. 122°42'30" W; near NW cor. sec. 5, T 37 N, R 7 W); the stream heads near Scorpion Lake. Named on Bonanza King (1955) 15' quadrangle. North Fork enters from the north less than 1 mile upstream from the mouth of the main creek; it is 2.5 miles long and is named on Bonanza King (1955) 15' quadrangle.

Scorpion Lake [TRINITY]: *lake*, 300 feet long, 6 miles north-northeast of Trinity Center (lat. 41°05'15" N, long. 122°28'30" W; sec. 11, T 37 N, R 7 W). Named on Bonanza King (1955) 15' quadrangle.

Scotia [HUMBOLDT]: *town*, 8.5 miles south-southeast of Fortuna on the east side of Eel River (lat. 40°28'55" N, long. 124°06' W; on W line sec. 8, T 1 N, R 1 E). Named on Scotia (1970) 7.5' quadrangle. Postal authorities established Scotia post office in 1888 (Frickstad, p. 46). Pacific Lumber Company built a mill at the site in 1885; the town there first was called Forestville, and then Scotia for the many natives of Nova Scotia who worked in the mill (Gudde, 1969, p. 301). California Mining Bureau's (1917b) map shows a place called Robinson's Ferry located along the railroad on the north side of Eel River just north of Scotia.

Scotia Bluffs [HUMBOLDT]: *relief feature*, 7 miles south-southeast of Fortuna on the north side of Eel River opposite Rio Dell (lat. 40°30'40" N, long. 124°05'55" W; sec. 31, 32, T 2 N, R 1 E). Named on Hydesville (1979) 7.5' quadrangle.

Scotish Creek: see **Soctish Creek** [HUMBOLDT].

Scotish Point: see **Soctish Point** [HUMBOLDT].

Scott Creek [HUMBOLDT]:

(1) *stream*, flows 2.25 miles to Van Duzen River 2.5 miles south-southeast of Yager Junction (lat. 40°30'55" N, long. 123°42'30" W; near NW cor. sec. 36, T 2 N, R 3 E). Named on Yager Junction (1979) 7.5' quadrangle.

(2) *stream*, flows 2.5 miles to Larabee Creek 6 miles southwest of Bridgeville (lat. 40°24'20" N, long. 123°52'20" W; near E line sec. 6, T 1 S, R 3 E). Named on Bridgeville (1969) 7.5' quadrangle.

Scott Creek [MENDOCINO]: *stream*, flows 4 miles to Tomki Creek 9 miles northwest of the town of Potter Valley (lat. 39°25'30" N, long. 123°12'30" W; near S line sec. 8, T 18 N, R 12 W). Named on Potter Valley (1960) 15' quadrangle.

Scott Creek: see **Scotts Creek** [LAKE].

Scott Flat [TRINITY]: *area*, 1 mile southeast of Forest Glen along South Fork Trinity River (lat. 40°21'55" N, long. 123°18'25" W; on E line sec. 19, T 1 S, R 8 E). Named on Forest Glen (1979) 7.5' quadrangle.

Scott Glades [TRINITY]: *area*, 8.5 miles south-southeast of Dinsmore [HUMBOLDT] near Van Duzen River (lat. 40°23'35" N, long. 123°30'40" W; near E line sec. 8, T 1 S, R 6 E). Named on Dinsmore (1977) 7.5' quadrangle.

Scott Mountain [TRINITY]: *peak*, 17 miles southeast of Etna, which is in Siskiyou County, on Trinity-Siskiyou County line (lat. 41°16'45" N, long. 122°40'35" W; sec. 33, T 40 N, R 7 W); the peak is in Scott Mountains. Altitude 6829 feet. Named on China Mountain (1955) 15' quadrangle. Called Scotts Mtn. on Miller's (1890) map. Hobson (p. 655) called the feature Scott's Peak.

Scott Mountain Creek [TRINITY]: *stream*, flows 3.5 miles to Tangle Blue Creek 16 miles north of Trinity Center (lat. 41°14'15" N, long. 122°39'40" W; sec. 15, T 39 N, R 7 W). Named on Bonanza King (1955) and China Mountain (1955) 15' quadrangles.

Scott Mountains [TRINITY]: *range*, about 20 miles southwest of Weed, which is in Siskiyou County, on Trinity-Siskiyou County line (lat. 41°17' N, long. 122°41' W). Named on Weed (1963) 1° x 2° quadrangle. Hobson (p. 655) called the feature Scott's Mountains.

Scott Mountain Summit [TRINITY]: *pass,* 8 miles southwest of China Mountain, which is in Siskiyou County (lat. 41°16'35" N, long. 122°41'45" W; at N line sec. 5, T 39 N, R 7 W); the pass is at the head of Scott Mountain Creek. Named on China Mountain (1955) 15' quadrangle.

Scott Ridge [TRINITY]: *ridge,* west-southwest-trending, 1 mile long, 6.5 miles south-southeast of Black Rock Mountain (lat. 40°06'50" N, long. 122°58'30" W; sec. 10, T 26 N, R 10 W). Named on Yolla Bolly (1954) 15' quadrangle.

Scotts Creek [LAKE]: *stream,* flows about 30 miles to join Middle Creek (2) and form Rodman Slough 1.25 miles south of the town of Upper Lake (lat. 39°08'55" N, long. 122°54'40" W; at E line sec. 13, T 15 N, R 10 W). Named on Cow Mountain (1958), Lakeport (1958), Purdys Gardens (1958), and Upper Lake (1958) 7.5' quadrangles. Called Scott Creek on Lakeport (1938) and Ukiah (1920) 15' quadrangles. South Fork enters from the south 3.5 miles west of Lakeport; it is 7 miles long and is named on Highland Springs (1959) and Lakeport (1958) 7.5' quadrangles. United States Board on Geographic Names (1972a, p. 4) approved the name "Lakeport Lake" for a reservoir formed by a dam situated on Scotts Creek 2 miles west of Lakeport (lat. 39°03'05" N, long. 122°57'10" W; sec. 22, T 14 N, R 10 W), and rejected the name "Lakeport Reservoir" for the feature.

Scotts Gulch [TRINITY]: *canyon,* drained by a stream that flows 1 mile to Quimby Creek (2) 11 miles north-northeast of Burnt Ranch (lat. 40°57'15" N, long. 123°23'20" W). Named on Ironside Mountain (1951) 15' quadrangle.

Scotts Mountain [LAKE]: *peak,* 4.5 miles west-northwest of Lakeport (lat. 39°04'20" N, long. 122°59'45" W); the peak is 2 miles west of Scotts Valley. Altitude 2380 feet. Named on Lakeport (1958) 7.5' quadrangle.

Scotts Mountain: see **Scott Mountain** [TRINITY].

Scott's Mountains: see **Scott Mountains** [TRINITY].

Scott's Peak: see **Scott Mountain** [TRINITY].

Scotts Valley [LAKE]: *valley,* 1.5 miles northwest of Lakeport (lat. 39°04'30" N, long. 122°56'45" W); the valley is along Scotts Creek. Named on Lakeport (1958) 7.5' quadrangle.

Scottsville: see **Blue Lake** [HUMBOLDT] (2); **Four Corners** [MENDOCINO].

Scotty Point [HUMBOLDT]: *promontory,* 3 miles north-northwest of Trinidad along the coast (lat. 41°06'05" N, long. 124°09'45" W; on S line sec. 3, T 8 N, R 1 W). Named on Trinidad (1966) 7.5' quadrangle.

Scribner: see **Eureka** [HUMBOLDT].

Seabow: see **Camp Seabow** [MENDOCINO].

Sea Lion Gulch [HUMBOLDT]: *canyon,* drained by a stream that flows 1.25 miles to the sea 6.25 miles south-southwest of Petrolia (lat. 40°14'20" N, long. 124°19'50" W; sec. 6, T 3 S, R 2 W). Named on Cooskie Creek (1969) 7.5' quadrangle.

Sea Lion Rock [HUMBOLDT]: *rock,* 3.5 miles west-southwest of Petrolia, and 750 feet offshore (lat. 40°18'35" N, long. 124°21'10" W). Named on Petrolia (1969) 7.5' quadrangle.

Sea Lion Rock [MENDOCINO]:

(1) *rock,* 15 miles south of Piercy, and 550 feet offshore (lat. 39°45'35" N, long. 123°50'20" W). Named on Hales Grove (1970) 7.5' quadrangle.

(2) *rock,* 7.5 miles north-northwest of Westport, and 450 feet offshore (lat. 39°44'20" N, long. 123°50' W). Named on Cape Vizcaino (1950) 15' quadrangle.

Sea Lion Rocks [MENDOCINO]: *rocks,* nearly 3 miles northwest of the village of Point Arena, and 600 feet offshore (lat. 38°56'10" N, long. 123°43'45" W). Named on Point Arena (1960) 7.5' quadrangle.

Seal Rock [DEL NORTE]: *rock,* 8.5 miles west-northwest of Crescent City, and 5.25 miles off the coast at Point Saint George (lat. 41°48'50" N, long. 124°21' W). Named on Eureka (1958) 1° x 2° quadrangle.

Seal Rocks [MENDOCINO]: *rocks,* 8.5 miles southwest of Piercy at the coast (lat. 39°54'10" N, long. 123°55'35" W). Named on Bear Harbor (1969) 7.5' quadrangle.

Seaside Creek [MENDOCINO]: *stream,* flows 1.5 miles to the sea 5.5 miles south of Westport (lat. 39°33'35" N, long. 123°45'55" W; sec. 33, T 20 N, R 17 W). Named on Dutchmans Knoll (1966) and Inglenook (1966) 7.5' quadrangles.

Sebastapol [TRINITY]: *locality,* nearly 6 miles northeast of Weaverville (lat. 40°50'20" N, long. 122°46'20" W; near N line sec. 4, T 34 N, R 8 W). Site named on Trinity Lake (1950) 15' quadrangle. The community that John F. Chillis started at the place in 1853 was completely gone by 1900 (Jones, p. 43, 45). Water of Clair Engle Lake now covers the site.

Sebbas Creek [HUMBOLDT-MENDOCINO]: *stream,* heads in Humboldt County and flows about 3.5 miles to Indian Creek [MENDOCINO] (2) 4.5 miles west of Piercy in Mendocino County (lat. 39°58'05" N, long. 123°52'45" W; sec. 5, T 24 N, R 18 W). Named on Bear Harbor (1969) and Briceland (1969) 7.5' quadrangles.

Sebow: see **Camp Sebow**, under **Camp Seabow** [MENDOCINO].

Second Creek [HUMBOLDT]: *stream,* flows less than 1 mile to Camp Creek [HUMBOLDT] 4.5 miles northwest of Orleans (lat. 41°20'55" N, long. 123°35'55" W); the stream is between First Creek and Third Creek. Named on Orleans (1978) 7.5' quadrangle.

Secret Gulch [TRINITY]: *canyon,* drained by a stream that flows 1.5 miles to Mad River 12 miles west of Black Rock Mountain (lat. 40°10'20" N, long. 123°14' W; near SE cor. sec. 20, T 27 N, R 12 W). Named on Black Rock Mountain (1954) 15' quadrangle.

Section Four Creek [MENDOCINO]: *stream,* flows 2.5 miles to South Fork Eel River 5 miles east-southeast of Branscomb (lat. 39°37'25" N, long. 123°32'45" W; sec. 33, T 21 N, R 15 W). Named on Sherwood Peak (1967) 7.5' quadrangle.

Seely Creek [HUMBOLDT]: *stream,* flows 3 miles to Redwood Creek (2) 6.5 miles south-southwest of Phillipsburg (lat. 40°07'50" N, long. 123°51'30" W; sec. 9, T 4 S, R 3 E). Named on Ettersburg (1969) and Miranda (1970) 7.5' quadrangles.

Sego Ridge [TRINITY]: *ridge,* generally southwest-trending, 1 mile long, 5.5 miles south of Black Rock Mountain (lat. 40°07'20" N, long. 123°00'15" W; around SW cor. sec. 4, T 26 N, R 10 W). Named on Black Rock Mountain (1954) 15' quadrangle.

Seigler: see **Seigler Springs** [LAKE].

Seigler Canyon [LAKE]: *canyon,* nearly 3 miles long, along Seigler Canyon Creek above a point 2 miles west-southwest of the town of Lower Lake (lat. 38°53'55" N, long. 122°38'35" W; sec. 9, T 12 N, R 7 W). Named on Clearlake Highlands (1958) 7.5' quadrangle. United States Board on Geographic Names (1962b, p. 20) rejected the forms "Siegler Canyon" and "Sigler Canyon" for the name.

Seigler Canyon Creek [LAKE]: *stream,* flows 8 miles to Cache Creek 1 mile north of the town of Lower Lake (lat. 38°55'30" N, long. 122°36'40" W; near SW cor. sec. 35, T 13 N, R 7 W); the stream drains Seigler Canyon and goes past Seigler Springs. Named on Clearlake Highlands (1958) and Lower Lake (1958) 7.5' quadrangles. United States Board on Geographic Names (1962b, p. 20) rejected the names "Siegler Creek" and "Sigler Creek" for the stream.

Seigler Mountain [LAKE]: *peak,* 4 miles north of Whispering Pines (lat. 38°52'25" N, long. 122°42'30" W; sec. 23, T 12 N, R 8 W). Altitude 3692 feet. Named on Clearlake Highlands (1958) and Whispering Pines (1958) 7.5' quadrangles.

Seigler Springs [LAKE]: *locality,* nearly 5 miles west-southwest of the town of Lower Lake (lat. 38°52'30" N, long. 122°41'20" W; near E line sec. 24, T 12 N, R 8 W). Named on Clearlake Highlands (1958) and Whispering Pines (1958) 7.5' quadrangles. Postal authorities established Seigler post office in 1904, discontinued it in 1907, reestablished it in 1909, discontinued it in 1911, reestablished it with the name "Seigler Springs" in 1915, and discontinued it in 1969 (Salley, p. 201). Thomas Sigler discovered the springs at the site; the resort there was called Hot Sigler Springs in the 1870's (Gudde, 1949, p. 325). Goodyear (1890a, p. 230) called the place Seigler's Springs. United States Board on Geographic Names (1962b, p. 20) rejected the forms "Seigler Spring," "Siegler Springs," and "Sigler Springs" for the name.

Seigler Valley [LAKE]: *valley,* 4.25 miles north-northeast of Whispering Pines (lat. 38°52'15" N, long. 122°40'30" W; sec. 19, 30, T 12 N, R 7 W); the valley is less than 1 mile east of Seigler Springs. Named on Whispering Pines (1958) 7.5' quadrangle.

Semore Gulch [TRINITY]: *canyon,* drained by a stream that flows 1.5 miles to East Fork New River 17 miles northeast of Burnt Ranch (lat. 41°00' N, long. 123°16'25" W). Named on Ironside Mountain (1951) 15' quadrangle.

Senteney Creek [TRINITY]: *stream,* flows 2 miles to Van Duzen River 9 miles south-southeast of Dinsmore [HUMBOLDT] (lat. 40°22'50" N, long. 123°30'25" W; sec. 16, T 1 S, R 6 E). Named on Black Lassic (1979) and Dinsmore (1977) 7.5' quadrangles.

Senteney Rock [TRINITY]: *peak,* 1.5 miles north of Black Lassic near Humboldt-Trinity County line (lat. 40°21'35" N, long. 123°32'35" W). Altitude 5170 feet. Named on Black Lassic (1979) 7.5' quadrangle.

Sequoia: see **Whitlow** [HUMBOLDT].

Sequoia Creek [HUMBOLDT]: *stream,* flows 1 mile to Sonoma Creek 7 miles east-southeast of Weott (lat. 40°18' N, long. 123°47'45" W; at SW cor. sec. 12, T 2 S, R 3 E). Named on Myers Flat (1969) 7.5' quadrangle.

Serpentine Creek [HUMBOLDT]: *stream,* flows nearly 2 miles to Bluff Creek [DEL NORTE-HUMBOLDT] 7.5 miles west-southwest of Orleans (lat. 41°16'30" N, long. 123°40'40" W). Named on Fish Lake (1974) 7.5' quadrangle.

Seven Cedars: see **Hoaglin Valley** [TRINITY].

Sevenmile Slough [HUMBOLDT]: *water feature,* joins North Bay 6 miles north-northwest of Ferndale (lat. 40°39'40" N, long. 124°17'30" W). Named on Cannibal Island (1959) 7.5' quadrangle. The name is from the length of the feature (Turner, p. 192).

Seven Up Cedars Spring: see **Dubakella Mountain** [TRINITY].

Seven Up Peak [TRINITY]: *peak,* 16 miles north of Weaverville (lat. 40°57'30" N, long. 122°52'45" W; on S line sec. 22, T 36 N, R 9 W). Altitude 8132 feet. Named on Trinity Dam (1950) 15' quadrangle. Irvin Scott and Stanford Scott named the peak for the card game that they played while they were tending their cattle nearby (Jones, p. 12).

Severin Opening [HUMBOLDT]: *area,* 5.5 miles east-northeast of Showers Mountain (lat. 40°37'15" N, long. 123°36'35" W; near SE cor. sec. 21, T 3 N, R 5 E). Named on Blake Mountain (1979) 7.5' quadrangle.

Seward: see **Fort Seward** [HUMBOLDT].

Seward Creek [MENDOCINO]: *stream,* formed by the confluence of Jack Smith Creek and Eldridge Creek, flows 2 miles to Forsythe Creek 8 miles west-southwest of the town of Potter Valley (lat. 39°15'35" N, long. 123°13'25" W; at N line sec. 7, T 16 N, R 12 W). Named on Potter Valley (1960) and Willits (1961) 15' quadrangles. The name, given about 1880, commemorates Anson J. Seward (Gudde, 1949, p. 326).

Seward Creek: see **Jack Smith Creek** [MENDOCINO].

Shady Dell [MENDOCINO]: *canyon,* drained by a stream that flows 1.25 miles to Usal Creek 10.5 miles south of Piercy (lat. 39°49'55" N, long. 123°50'40" W; sec. 22, T 23 N, R 18 W). Named on Hales Grove (1970) 7.5' quadrangle.

Shady Gulch [TRINITY]: *canyon,* drained by a stream that flows 0.25 mile to Clair Engle Lake 13 miles northeast of Weaverville (lat. 40°51'30" N, long. 122°45'45" W; sec. 27, T 35 N, R 8 W). Named on Trinity Dam (1950) 15' quadrangle.

Shag Rock [LAKE]: *rock,* 8.5 miles east of Lakeport in Clear Lake (lat. 39°01'30" N, long. 122°45'40" W). Named on Lucerne (1958) 7.5' quadrangle.

Shake Cabin Flat [MENDOCINO]: *area,* 11 miles east of Covelo (lat. 39°47'55" N, long. 123°02'25" W; at SW cor. sec. 36, T 23 N, R 11 W). Named on Newhouse Ridge (1967) 7.5' quadrangle.

Shake City [MENDOCINO]: *locality,* 6.25 miles west-northwest of Willits along California Western Railroad (lat. 39°25'50" N, long. 123°27'50" W; at W line sec. 7, T 18 N, R 14 W). Named on Willits (1961) 15' quadrangle.

Shake Creek [MENDOCINO]: *stream,* flows 3 miles to Ellis Creek 4 miles east-southeast of Eden Valley (lat. 39°36'20" N, long. 123°06'50" W). Named on Brushy Mountain (1966) and Sanhedrin Mountain (1966) 7.5' quadrangles.

Shakesville: see **Smith River** [DEL NORTE] (2).

Shannon Butte [TRINITY]: *peak,* 5 miles east of Kettenpom (lat. 40°10' N, long. 123°22'15" W; at N line sec. 34, T 3 S, R 7 E). Altitude 3069 feet. Named on Shannon Butte (1967) 7.5' quadrangle. The name commemorates William Frederick Shannon, who homesteaded near the peak in 1902 (Jones, p. 359).

Shanty Creek [TRINITY]: *stream,* flows 3.5 miles to Van Duzen River 9 miles west of Forest Glen (lat. 40°22'10" N, long. 123°29'40" W; at N line sec. 21, T 1 S, R 6 E). Named on Black Lassic (1979) and Ruth Reservoir (1978) 7.5' quadrangles. The name is from bark-covered Indian huts (Gudde, 1949, p. 327).

Sharber Creek [TRINITY]: *stream,* flows 4.25 miles to Trinity River 1 mile east-northeast of Salyer (lat. 40°53'45" N, long. 123°33'50" W; sec. 13, T 6 N, R 5 E). Named on Salyer (1979) 7.5' quadrangle.

Sharp Point [HUMBOLDT]: *promontory,* 12.5 miles north of Trinidad along the coast (lat. 41°14'10" N, long. 124°06'30" W; sec. 19, T 10 N, R 1 E). Named on Rodgers Peak (1966) 7.5' quadrangle. Called Goat Rock on Trinidad (1945) 15' quadrangle, but United States Board on Geographic Names (1957, p. 3) rejected the names "Goat Rock" and "Conical Rock" for the feature. Waterman (p. 264) described the promontory as an extremely abrupt ridge that juts into the sea like a knife blade.

Sharp Point: see **Freshwater Rocks** [HUMBOLDT].

Sharp Rock [HUMBOLDT]: *rock,* 0.5 mile north-northwest of Cape Mendocino, and about 2000 feet offshore (lat. 40°26'45" N, long. 124°24'50" W). Named on Cape Mendocino (1969) 7.5' quadrangle.

Shasta Spring [TRINITY]: *spring,* 1.5 miles east of Weaverville (lat. 40°44' N, long. 122°54'30" W; sec. 8, T 33 N, R 9 W). Named on Weaverville (1950) 15' quadrangle.

Shaul Valley [LAKE]: *valley,* 3.25 miles southeast of Kelseyville (lat. 38°56'50" N, long. 122°47'30" W; sec. 30, T 13 N, R 8 W). Named on Kelseyville (1959) 7.5' quadrangle.

Shaw Creek [HUMBOLDT]: *stream,* flows 4 miles to Lawrence Creek 6 miles west of Lone Star Junction (lat. 40°37'10" N, long. 123°59'25" W; at S line sec. 19, T 3 N, R 2 E). Named on Iaqua Buttes (1979) and Owl Creek (1979) 7.5' quadrangles.

Shaw Gulch [HUMBOLDT]: *canyon,* drained by a stream that flows 1.25 miles to Elk River (1) 2.5 miles east-southeast of Fields Landing (lat. 40°42'50" N, long. 124°10'10" W; sec. 22, T 4 N, R 1 W). Named on Fields Landing (1959) 7.5' quadrangle.

Shearing Creek [MENDOCINO]: *stream,* flows 1.5 miles to Rancheria Creek (2) 2 miles north-northwest of Ornbaun Valley (lat. 38°56'30" N, long. 123°19' W; sec. 32, T 13 N, R 13 W). Named on Ornbaun Valley (1960) 15' quadrangle.

Sheep Camp Spring [TRINITY]: *spring,* 12 miles northwest of Forest Glen (lat. 40°29'25" N, long. 123°29'10" W; sec. 3, T 1 N, R 6 E). Named on Sportshaven (1973) 7.5' quadrangle.

Sheep Gulch [TRINITY]: *canyon,* drained by a stream that flows 1.5 miles to Indian Valley Creek 9.5 miles southeast of Hyampom (lat. 40°31' N, long. 123°19'30" W; at N line sec. 36, T 2 N, R 7 E). Named on Hyampom (1951) 15' quadrangle, and on Naufus Creek (1979) 7.5' quadrangle.

Sheep Pen Creek [DEL NORTE]: *stream,* flows 1.25 miles to Smith River 8 miles east-northeast of Crescent City (lat. 41°47'20" N, long. 124°03'15" W). Named on Hiouchi (1966) 7.5' quadrangle.

Sheep Ridge [MENDOCINO]: *ridge,* west- to southwest-trending, 1 mile long, 7.5 miles north of Anthony Peak (lat. 39°57'15" N, long. 122°56'10" W; sec. 2, 11, T 24 N, R 10 W). Named on Buck Rock (1967) 7.5' quadrangle.

Sheetiron Mountain [LAKE]: *peak,* 5 miles north-northeast of Crockett Peak (lat. 39°29'30" N, long. 122°44' W; near NE cor. sec. 22, T 19 N, R 8 W). Altitude 6503 feet. Named on Saint John Mountain (1968) 7.5' quadrangle. The name is from a sheet-iron hut built in the 1860's or 1870's (Gudde, 1969, p. 306).

Sheldon Creek [MENDOCINO]: *stream,* flows 2 miles to Vasser Creek 6.5 miles east-southeast of Hopland (lat. 38°56'40" N, long. 123°00'30" W; near W line sec. 27, T 13 N, R 10 W). Named on Highland Springs (1959) and Hopland (1960) 7.5' quadrangles

Shell Creek [MENDOCINO]: *stream,* flows 2 miles to Eel River 1 mile south-southeast of Spyrock (2) near Spyrock (1) (lat. 39°51'45" N, long. 123°26'05" W; near SE cor. sec. 8, T 23 N, R 14 W). Named on Iron Peak (1967) and Updegraff Ridge (1967) 7.5' quadrangles.

Shell Creek: see **Shell Mountain Creek** [TRINITY].

Shelley Creek: see **Shelly Creek** [DEL NORTE].

Shelley Creek Ridge: see **Shelly Creek Ridge** [DEL NORTE].

Shell Mountain [TRINITY]: *peak,* 7.5 miles south-southwest of Black Rock Mountain (lat. 40°06'45" N, long. 123°04'40" W; sec. 11, T 26 N, R 11 W). Altitude 6700 feet. Named on Black Rock Mountain (1954) 15' quadrangle.

Shell Mountain Creek [TRINITY]: *stream,* flows 4.5 miles to South Fork Trinity River 4.5 miles west of Black Rock Mountain (lat. 40°12' N, long. 123°05'45" W; sec. 10, T 27 N, R 11 W). Named on Black Rock Mountain (1954) 15' quadrangle. Called Shell Creek on Hoaglin (1935) 30' quadrangle.

Shell Peak [MENDOCINO]: *peak,* 8.5 miles east-northeast of Ukiah (lat. 39°11'25" N, long. 123°03'40" W; near N line sec. 3, T 15 N, R 11 W). Altitude 2704 feet. Named on Cow Mountain (1958) 7.5' quadrangle.

Shell Rock [MENDOCINO]: *relief feature,* 3.5 miles southwest of Spyrock (2) (lat. 39°50'35" N, long. 123°29'15" W; sec. 13, T 23 N, R 15 W). Named on Iron Peak (1967) 7.5' quadrangle.

Shell Rock Creek [MENDOCINO]: *stream,* flows 5 miles to Eel River 1.5 miles south-southeast of Spyrock (2) (lat. 39°51'25" N, long. 123°26' W; near E line sec. 17, T 23 N, R 14 E); the stream heads near Shell Rock. Named on Iron Peak (1967) 7.5' quadrangle.

Shelly Creek [DEL NORTE]: *stream,* flows 9 miles to Patrick Creek 7 miles northeast of Gasquet (lat. 41°54'05" N, long. 123°51'15" W; sec. 5, T 17 N, R 3 E). Named on Shelly Creek Ridge (1982) 7.5' quadrangle. Called Shelley Creek on Preston Peak (1922) 30' quadrangle.

Shelly Creek Camp Ground [DEL NORTE]: *locality,* 7 miles northeast of Gasquet (lat. 41°54'05" N, long. 123°51'10" W; sec. 5, T 17 N, R 3 E); the place is at the mouth of Shelly Creek. Named on Shelly Creek Ridge (1982) 7.5' quadrangle.

Shelly Creek Ridge [DEL NORTE]: *ridge,* generally south-trending, 5.5 miles long, 9 miles northeast of Gasquet (lat. 41°55' N, long. 123°49'10" W); the ridge is east of Shelly Creek. Named on Shelly Creek Ridge (1982) 7.5' quadrangle. Called Shelley Creek Ridge on Preston Peak (1922) 30' quadrangle.

Shelter Cove [HUMBOLDT]:

(1) *embayment,* east of Point Delgada along the coast (lat. 40°01'25" N, long. 124°03'40" W; sec. 15, 16, T 5 S, R 1 E). Named on Shelter Cove (1969) 7.5' quadrangle. Officials of United States Coast Survey named the feature in 1854 (Gudde, 1949, p. 328). The place was known as Stockton Harbor for a time after 1902 (Turner, p. 195).

(2) *village,* at Point Delgada (lat. 40°01'50" N, long. 124°04'15" W); the village is north of Shelter Cove (1). Named on Shelter Cove (1969) 7.5' quadrangle. Postal authorities established Shelter Cove post office in 1892, moved it 0.75 mile northeast in 1898, and discontinued it in 1933 (Salley, p. 203). Vander Leck's (1920b) map shows a place called Frank located 2 miles east-northeast of Shelter Cove. Postal authorities established Frank post office in 1892 and discontinued it in 1903; the name was for Frank McKee, first postmaster (Salley, p. 79).

Shelton Butte [HUMBOLDT]: *peak,* 5.25 miles northeast of Weitchpec (lat. 41°14'20" N, long. 123°37'55" W). Altitude 3568 feet. Named on Weitchpec (1979) 7.5' quadrangle.

Shelton Buttes [HUMBOLDT]: *ridge,* north-northwest-trending, 2 miles long, 5.5 miles north of Coyote Peak (lat. 41°12'35" N, long. 123°51'40" W). Named on French Camp Ridge (1983) 7.5' quadrangle.

Shelton Prairie [HUMBOLDT]: *area,* 4.25 miles north of Coyote Peak (lat. 41°11'50" N, long. 123°51'05" W; near SE cor. sec. 6, T 9 N, R 3 E); the place is near the south end of Shelton Buttes. Named on French Camp Ridge (1983) 7.5' quadrangle.

Shelving Rock Creek [MENDOCINO]: *stream,* flows 1.25 miles to Wheelbarrow Creek 6.5 miles southeast of Longvale (lat. 39°30'15" N, long. 123°19'35" W; sec. 17, T 19 N, R 13 W). Named on Willits (1961) 15' quadrangle, and on Willis Ridge (1966) 7.5' quadrangle. West Fork enters 0.25 mile upstream from the mouth of the main stream; it is 1 mile long and is named on Willits (1961) 15' quadrangle.

Shenanigan Ridge [HUMBOLDT]: *ridge*, generally northeast-trending, 1 mile long, 1.5 miles south-southeast of Petrolia (lat. 40°17'20" N, long. 124°16' W). Named on Petrolia (1969) 7.5' quadrangle.

Sherer Creek [TRINITY]: *stream*, flows 4.5 miles to Trinity River 8 miles south-southwest of China Mountain, which is in Siskiyou County (lat. 41°15'50" N, long. 122°36'45" W; sec. 1, T 39 N, R 7 W). Named on Bonanza King (1955) and China Mountain (1955) 15' quadrangles.

Sherer Ridge [TRINITY]: *ridge*, northwest-trending, 2.5 miles long, 16 miles north-northeast of Trinity Center (lat. 41°14'15" N, long. 122°36'45" W); the ridge is southwest of Sherer Creek. Named on Bonanza King (1955) 15' quadrangle.

Sheridan Creek [TRINITY]: *stream*, flows 2.5 miles to Trinity River 12 miles north-northeast of Hayfork (lat. 40°42'50" N, long. 123°02'45" W; sec. 18, T 33 N, R 10 W). Named on Hayfork (1951) 15' quadrangle.

Sherman Flat [HUMBOLDT]: *area*, 3.5 miles north of Blocksburg (lat. 40°19'30" N, long. 123°37'50" W; at NE cor. sec. 5, T 2 S, R 5 E). Named on Blocksburg (1969) 7.5' quadrangle.

Sherman Gulch [MENDOCINO]: *canyon*, drained by a stream that flows 1.25 miles to North Fork Indian Creek (1) 6.25 miles north of Boonville (lat. 39°06'05" N, long. 123°22'40" W; near W line sec. 2, T 14 N, R 14 W). Named on Boonville (1959) 15' quadrangle.

Sherman Ridge [MENDOCINO]: *ridge*, northwest-trending, 1.5 miles long, about 6.5 miles north of Boonville (lat. 39°06'15" N, long. 123°21'45" W); the ridge is northeast of Sherman Gulch. Named on Boonville (1959) 15' quadrangle.

Sherwood [MENDOCINO]: *locality*, 3 miles south-southwest of Longvale (lat. 39°31' N, long. 123°27' W). Named on Laytonville (1919) 15' quadrangle, which shows a post office at the place. Postal authorities established Sherwood Valley post office at the site in 1867 and discontinued it in 1881: They established Sherwood post office in 1883, discontinued it in 1898, reestablished it in 1900, and discontinued it in 1920 (Salley, p. 203). The name commemorates Alfred E. Sherwood, who settled at the place in 1853 (Hanna, p. 303). Postal authorities established Weltmer post office 3 miles south of Sherwood in 1908 and discontinued it in 1911 (Salley, p. 236).

Sherwood Creek [MENDOCINO]: *stream*, flows 9 miles to Outlet Creek 5.25 miles north-northwest of Willits (lat. 39°28'45" N, long. 123°23' W; sec. 23, T 19 N, R 14 W); the stream heads near Sherwood Peak and goes through Sherwood Valley. Named on Willits (1961) 15' quadrangle, and on Longvale (1966) 7.5' quadrangle.

Sherwood Creek [TRINITY]: *stream*, flows 2.25 miles to Battle Creek (1) 8.5 miles southeast of Salmon Mountain (lat. 41°05'10" N, long. 123°18'25" W). Named on Dees Peak (1978) 7.5' quadrangle, which shows Sherwood mine near the stream.

Sherwood Peak [MENDOCINO]: *peak*, 11.5 miles south-southeast of Branscomb (lat. 39°30'45" N, long. 123°30'35" W; sec. 10, T 19 N, R 15 W); the peak is near the east end of Sherwood Ridge. Altitude 3207 feet. Named on Sherwood Peak (1967) 7.5' quadrangle.

Sherwood Ridge [MENDOCINO]: *ridge*, generally south-trending, 5 miles long, 16 miles north of Comptche (lat. 39°29'45" N, long. 123°33'45" W). Named on Comptche (1960) 15' quadrangle, and on Sherwood Peak (1967) 7.5' quadrangle.

Sherwood Valley [MENDOCINO]: *valley*, 2 miles west-southwest of Longvale (lat. 39°31'50" N, long. 123°28'45" W); the valley is along Sherwood Creek. Named on Longvale (1966) 7.5' quadrangle.

Sherwood Valley: see **Sherwood** [MENDOCINO].

Shields Creek [MENDOCINO]: *stream*, flows 2.25 miles to Black Butte Creek 10 miles east of Covelo (lat. 39°48'20" N, long. 123°03'40" W; near E line sec. 34, T 23 N, R 11 W). Named on Newhouse Ridge (1967) 7.5' quadrangle. Called Billy Williams Creek on Covelo (1952) 15' quadrangle.

Shiell Gulch [TRINITY]: *canyon*, drained by a stream flows 2.25 miles to Hayfork Creek 7 miles northeast of Dubakella Mountain (lat. 40°27'20" N, long. 123°03'15" W; sec. 13, T 30 N, R 11 W). Named on Dubakella Mountain (1954) 15' quadrangle.

Shimmin Ridge [MENDOCINO]: *ridge*, generally south-trending, 3.5 miles long, 3.5 miles east-northeast of Longvale (lat. 39°34'50" N, long. 123°22'15" W). Named on Longvale (1966) and Willis Ridge (1966) 7.5' quadrangles.

Shimmy Lake [TRINITY]: *lake*, 600 feet long, 9 miles south-southwest of Billys Peak (1) (lat. 41°00'30" N, long. 122°48'15" W; sec. 5, T 36 N, R 8 W). Named on Coffee Creek (1955) 15' quadrangle.

Shinbone Ridge [TRINITY]: *ridge*, east-trending, 1.5 miles long, 12.5 miles southwest of Black Rock Mountain (lat. 40°03'30" N, long. 123°09' W). Named on Black Rock Mountain (1954) 15' quadrangle.

Shingle Mill Creek [MENDOCINO]: *stream*, flows 1.5 miles to South Branch of North Fork Navarro River 11 miles north-northwest of Boonville (lat. 39°09'35" N, long. 123°25'30" W; sec. 17, T 15 N, R 14 W). Named on Boonville (1959) 15' quadrangle.

Shinglemill Gulch [MENDOCINO]: *canyon*, drained by a stream that flows 2 miles to Schooner Gulch 4.5 miles southeast of the village of Point Arena (lat. 38°52'05" N, long. 123°37'40" W; near NW cor. sec. 34, T 12 N, R 16 W). Named on Gualala (1960) 7.5' quadrangle.

Shingle Shanty [TRINITY]: *locality*, 12 miles east-southeast of Weaverville (lat. 40°37'55" N, long. 122°44'15" W; sec. 14, T 32 N, R 8 W). Named on French Gulch (1979) 7.5' quadrangle.

Shin Skin Ridge [LAKE]: *ridge*, northeast-trending, 0.5 mile long, 6 miles west of Lakeport (lat. 39°03'30" N, long. 123°01'35" W; on E line sec. 23, T 14 N, R 11 W). Named on Purdys Gardens (1958) 7.5' quadrangle.

Shipman Creek [HUMBOLDT]: *stream*, flows nearly 3 miles to the sea about 9 miles south of Honeydew (lat. 40°07'05" N, long. 124°08'35" W; sec. 14, T 4 S, R 1 W). Named on Honeydew (1970) and Shubrick Peak (1969) 7.5' quadrangles.

Ship Mountain [DEL NORTE]: *ridge*, south-trending, 3 miles long, 7.5 miles north-northeast of Buck Mountain (lat. 41°43'30" N, long. 123°47'35" W). Named on Ship Mountain (1982) 7.5' quadrangle. William Lewis, first forest ranger in the Gasquet district, reportedly named the feature before 1914 (United States Board on Geographic Names, 1983a, p. 5). The peaks called Four Brothers are on the ridge.

Ship Mountain Lake [DEL NORTE]: *lake*, 300 feet long, 9 miles north-northeast of Buck Mountain (lat. 41°44'55" N, long. 123°47'30" W); the lake is near the north end of Ship Mountain. Named on Ship Mountain (1982) 7.5' quadrangle.

Shirley Slough [LAKE]: *stream*, flows less than 0.5 mile to Clear Lake 3.5 miles east-southeast of Lakeport (lat. 39°01'40" N, long. 122°51'10" W; sec. 27, T 14 N, R 9 W). Named on Lucerne (1958) 7.5' quadrangle.

Shively [HUMBOLDT]: *village*, 2.25 miles north-northwest of Redcrest (lat. 40°25'50" N, long. 123°58'05" W; near NE cor. sec. 32, T 1 N, R 2 E). Named on Redcrest (1969) 7.5' quadrangle. Postal authorities established Shively post office in 1906 and discontinued it in 1965; the name was for William R. Shively, an early settler (Salley, p. 203). The place also was called Bluff Prairie and Paradise (Turner, p. 195).

Shively Creek [HUMBOLDT]: *stream*, flows 4 miles to Eel River 3.5 miles north-northwest of Redcrest (lat. 40°26'40" N, long. 123°58'55" W; at N line sec. 29, T 1 N, R 2 E). Named on Redcrest (1969) 7.5' quadrangle.

Shively Flat [HUMBOLDT]: *area*, 2.5 miles north-northwest of Redcrest (lat. 40°26' N, long. 123°58'25" W; sec. 29, 32, T 1 N, R 2 E); the place is at the village of Shively. Named on Redcrest (1969) 7.5' quadrangle.

Shock Creek [TRINITY]: *stream*, flows 2.5 miles to Summit Creek 7.5 miles east of Hayfork (lat. 40°34'40" N, long. 123°02'40" W; near SW cor. sec. 31, T 32 N, R 10 W). Named on Hayfork (1951) 15' quadrangle.

Shoemake Opening [MENDOCINO]: *area*, 6 miles northeast of Boonville (lat. 39°04'45" N, long. 123°17'40" W; near N line sec. 16, T 14 N, R 13 W). Named on Boonville (1959) 15' quadrangle.

Shoemaker Bally [TRINITY]: *peak*, 17 miles southeast of Weaverville on Trinity-Shasta County line (lat. 40°34'10" N, long. 122°41'50" W). Altitude 5955 feet. Named on Shasta Bally (1978) 7.5' quadrangle.

Shoemaker Gulch [TRINITY]: *canyon*, drained by a stream that flows 1 mile to Reading Creek 13 miles south-southeast of Weaverville (lat. 40°33'35" N, long. 122°51'30" W; at SE cor. sec. 3, T 31 N, R 9 W). Named on Weaverville (1950) 15' quadrangle.

Sholes Creek [HUMBOLDT]: *stream*, flows 4.5 miles to Mattole River 6 miles southeast of Honeydew (lat. 40°11'50" N, long. 124°02'05" W). Named on Honeydew (1970) 7.5' quadrangle.

Shoreline Rock [MENDOCINO]: *rock*, 11 miles south-southwest of Piercy, and just offshore (lat. 39°49'15" N, long. 123°50'50" W). Named on Hales Grove (1970) 7.5' quadrangle.

Short Creek [MENDOCINO]: *stream*, flows about 11 miles to Mill Creek (1) 2 miles east of Covelo in Round Valley (lat. 39°47'20" N, long. 123°12'35" W; near SW cor. sec. 4, T 22 N, R 12 W). Named on Covelo East (1967), Covelo West (1967), and Mina (1967) 7.5' quadrangles.

Short Gulch [TRINITY]: *canyon*, drained by a stream that flows 1 mile to Tom Lang Gulch 7 miles southeast of Weaverville (lat. 40°39'10" N, long. 122°51'50" W; near SE cor. sec. 3, T 32 N, R 9 W). Named on Weaverville (1950) 15' quadrangle.

Short Ridge [MENDOCINO]:

(1) *ridge*, east-northeast-trending, less than 1 mile long, 11 miles east-southeast of Covelo (lat. 39°45'15" N, long. 123°02'45" W; at N line sec. 23, T 22 N, R 11 W). Named on Newhouse Ridge (1967) 7.5' quadrangle.

(2) *ridge*, southwest-trending, 0.25 mile long, 9.5 miles southeast of Ukiah (lat. 39°03'45" N, long. 123°04'20" W; sec. 21, T 14 N, R 11 W). Named on Purdys Gardens (1958) 7.5' quadrangle.

Shotgun Pass [HUMBOLDT]: *pass*, 7.5 miles west of Coyote Peak (lat. 41°06'50" N, long. 123°59'40" W). Named on Panther Creek (1982) 7.5' quadrangle.

Showers Creek [HUMBOLDT]: *stream*, flows 3.25 miles to Mad River 2 miles north of Showers Mountain (lat. 40°36'25" N, long. 123°41'30" W). Named on Showers Mountain (1978) 7.5' quadrangle.

Showers Mountain [HUMBOLDT]: *peak*, 26 miles southeast of the town of Blue Lake (lat. 40°34'45" N, long. 123°41'45" W; sec. 2, T 2 N, R 4 E). Altitude 4410 feet. Named on Showers Mountain (1978) 7.5' quadrangle.

Showers Pass [HUMBOLDT]: *pass*, 1.5 miles west-southwest of Showers Mountain (lat. 40°44'15" N, long. 123°43'40" W; near NE cor. sec. 9, T 2 N, R 4 E). Named on Showers Mountain (1978) 7.5' quadrangle. According to local tradition, the name commemorates Jacob O. Showers, who once rode through the pass at breakneck speed to escape from Indians (Gudde, 1969, p. 308).

Showers Pass: see **Maple Creek** [HUMBOLDT] (3).

Showers Rock [HUMBOLDT]: *relief feature*, 1.5 miles west-southwest of Showers Mountain (lat. 40°34'15" N, long. 123°43'15" W; sec. 10, T 2 N, R 4 E); the feature is less than 0.5 mile east of Showers Mountain. Named on Showers Mountain (1978) 7.5' quadrangle.

Shubrick: see **Shubrick Rock** [HUMBOLDT].

Shubrick Peak [HUMBOLDT]: *peak*, 7 miles south-southwest of Honeydew (lat. 40°09'20" N, long. 124°11'15" W; near S line sec. 33, T 3 S, R 1 W). Altitude 2797 feet. Named on Shubrick Peak (1969) 7.5' quadrangle. The name is from *U.S.S. Shubrick*, the first lighthouse-tending ship on the Pacific Coast (Turner, p. 196).

Shubrick Rock [HUMBOLDT]: *rock*, 9 miles south-southwest of Honeydew (lat. 40°07'20" N, long. 124°10'10" W); the feature is 2.5 miles south-southeast of Shubrick Peak. Named on Shubrick Peak (1969) 7.5' quadrangle. Point Delgada (1920) 15' quadrangle has the name "Shubrick" for a place on the coast opposite Shubrick Rock.

Sidehill Prairie [HUMBOLDT]:

(1) *area*, 5.5 miles north of Coyote Peak (lat. 41°12'55" N, long. 123°52'45" W; sec. 31, T 10 N, R 3 E). Named on Bald Hills (1982) 7.5' quadrangle.

(2) *area*, 8 miles south-southeast of Coyote Peak (lat. 41°01'35" N, long. 123°47'30" W; near E line sec. 2, T 7 N, R 3 E). Named on Hupa Mountain (1982) 7.5' quadrangle.

(3) *area*, 2.5 miles west-northwest of Scotia (lat. 40°29'20" N, long. 124°08'45" W; on N line sec. 11, T 1 N, R 1 W). Named on Taylor Peak (1969) 7.5' quadrangle.

Sidney Gulch [TRINITY]: *canyon*, drained by a stream that flows 3 miles to Ten Cent Gulch in Weaverville (lat. 40°43'45" N, long. 122°56'15" W; at W line sec. 7, T 33 N, R 9 W). Named on Trinity Dam (1950) and Weaverville (1950) 15' quadrangles.

Siegler Canyon: see **Seigler Canyon** [LAKE].

Siegler Creek: see **Seigler Canyon Creek** [LAKE].

Siegler Springs: see **Seigler Springs** [LAKE].

Sigler Canyon: see **Seigler Canyon** [LAKE].

Sigler Creek: see **Seigler Canyon Creek** [LAKE].

Sigler Springs: see **Seigler Springs** [LAKE].

Signal: see **Little Signal** [LAKE]; **Signal Port Creek** [MENDOCINO].

Signal Creek [MENDOCINO]: *stream*, flows 4 miles to Garcia River 11 miles west-southwest of Ornbaun Valley (lat. 38°52'45" N, long. 123°30'05" W; near NW cor. sec. 26, T 12 N, R 15 W); the stream heads on Signal Ridge. Named on Ornbaun Valley (1960) 15' quadrangle.

Signal Peak [DEL NORTE]: *peak*, 10.5 miles northeast of Crescent City (lat. 41°50'40" N, long. 124°02'25" W). Altitude 2048 feet. Named on Hiouchi (1966) 7.5' quadrangle.

Signal Peak [LAKE]: *peak*, nearly 3 miles south-southeast of Crockett Peak (lat. 39°23'25" N, long. 122°45'45" W; on N line sec. 28, T 18 N, R 8 W). Altitude 6684 feet. Named on Crockett Peak (1967) 7.5' quadrangle. This apparently is the feature that Goodyear (1890b, p. 154) called Mount John.

Signal Peak [MENDOCINO]: *peak*, 4.25 miles north-northeast of Branscomb (lat. 39°42'10" N, long. 123°34'45" W; sec. 6, T 21 N, R 15 W). Altitude 4114 feet. Named on Cahto Peak (1967) 7.5' quadrangle.

Signal Peak: see **Big Signal Peak** [MENDOCINO]; **Little Signal Peak** [MENDOCINO]; **Mount Lassic** [HUMBOLDT].

Signal Port: see **Signal Port Creek** [MENDOCINO].

Signal Port Creek [MENDOCINO]: *stream*, flows nearly 3 miles to the sea 6.25 miles northwest of Gualala, and 2.5 miles northwest of Fish Rock (lat. 38°49'40" N, long. 123°36'55" W; sec. 2, T 11 N, R 16 W). Named on Gualala (1960) 7.5' quadrangle. Postal authorities established Signal post office 3.5 miles northwest of Fish Rock in 1882 and discontinued it the same year; they reestablished it with the name "Signal Port" in 1888 and discontinued it in 1890—the name is from signals made to ships waiting to take a load of lumber (Salley, p. 204).

Signal Ridge [MENDOCINO]: *ridge*, generally southwest-trending, 14 miles long, center about 8.5 miles west-southwest of Ornbaun Valley (lat. 38°51' N, long. 123°26'30" W). Named on Ornbaun Valley (1960) and Point Arena (1960) 15' quadrangles.

Siligo Meadows [TRINITY]: *area*, 15 miles north of Weaverville (lat. 40°56'10" N, long. 122°53'05" W; sec. 34, T 36 N, R 9 W); the place is 1.25 miles southeast of Siligo Peak. Named on Trinity Dam (1950) 15' quadrangle. The name commemorates Louis Siligo, a Lewiston cattleman (Jones, p. 10).

Siligo Peak [TRINITY]: *peak*, 15 miles north of Weaverville (lat. 40°56'40" N, long. 122°53'55" W; near S line sec. 28, T 36 N, T 9 W). Named on Trinity Dam (1950) 15' quadrangle. The name commemorates Louis Siligo of Siligo Meadows (Jones, p. 10).

Silverado: see **Camp Silverado** [MENDOCINO].

Silver Creek [MENDOCINO]: *stream*, flows 2.5 miles to Middle Fork Eel River 6 miles east of Covelo (lat. 39°48'30" N, long. 123°08'20" W; sec. 36, T 23 N, R 12 W). Named on Covelo East (1967) 7.5' quadrangle.

Silver Creek [TRINITY]: *stream*, flows 3.5 miles to South Fork Trinity River 7.25 miles southwest of Dubakella Mountain (lat. 40°18'45" N, long. 123°14'45" W; near N line sec. 5, T 28 N, R 12 W). Named on Dubakella Mountain (1954) 15' quadrangle.

Silver Flat [TRINITY]: *area*, 5.5 miles southeast of Forest Glen (lat. 40°19' N, long. 123°15'10" W; near S line sec. 31, T 29 N, R 12 W). Named on Forest Glen (1979) 7.5' quadrangle.

Silver Spring [TRINITY]: *spring*, 6 miles southwest of Dubakella Mountain (lat. 40°20'15" N, long. 123°14'10" W; sec. 29, T 29 N, R 12 W); the spring is near Silver Creek. Named on Dubakella Mountain (1954) 15' quadrangle.

Simerson [MENDOCINO]: *locality*, 1 mile north of downtown Willits (lat. 39°25'15" N, long. 123°21'10" W; at SW cor. sec. 7, T 18 N, R 13 W). Named on Willits (1942) 15' quadrangle.

Simmerley Flat [MENDOCINO]: *area*, 4.5 miles east of Covelo (lat. 39°47'50" N, long. 123°09'50" W; sec. 2, T 22 N, R 12 W). Named on Covelo East (1967) 7.5' quadrangle.

Simmerly Creek [MENDOCINO]: *stream*, flows 3 miles to Middle Fork Eel River 4.5 miles north of Eden Valley (lat. 39°41'40" N, long. 123°10'15" W; near W line sec. 11, T 21 N, R 12 W). Named on Jamison Ridge (1967) 7.5' quadrangle.

Simmons Camp [TRINITY]: *locality*, 4 miles east of Dinsmore [HUMBOLDT] along Mad River (lat. 40°28'50" N, long. 123°31'45" W; near W line sec. 8, T 1 N, R 6 E). Named on Blocksburg (1949) 15' quadrangle.

Simmons Creek [TRINITY]: *stream*, flows 2.5 miles to East Fork Hayfork Creek 10 miles east-southeast of Hayfork (lat. 40°30'20" N, long. 123°00'35" W; near SE cor. sec. 29, T 31 N, R 10 W). Named on Hayfork (1951) 15' quadrangle. Called Sims Creek on Chanchelulla Peak (1951) 15' quadrangle.

Simms Camp [LAKE]: *locality*, nearly 7 miles west of Lakeport (lat. 39°02'45" N, long. 123°02'30" W; sec. 26, T 14 N, R 11 W). Named on Purdys Gardens (1958) 7.5' quadrangle.

Simpson Creek [HUMBOLDT]: *stream*, flows 3 miles to Mad River 4 miles south-southeast of Korbel (lat. 40°48'45" N, long. 123°55'10" W; near S line sec. 14, T 5 N, R 2 E). Named on Korbel (1979) 7.5' quadrangle.

Sims Creek [HUMBOLDT]: *stream*, flows 2.25 miles to Grouse Creek (2) 7.5 miles east of Board Camp Mountain (lat. 40°42'50" N, long. 123°34'45" W); the stream heads at Sims Mountain. Named on Sims Mountain (1979) 7.5' quadrangle. Called Wises Creek on Pilot Creek (1922) 15' quadrangle. The name "Wises Creek" recalls Jessie Wise, who took a homestead along present Sims Creek in 1904 and ran Wise Station, a pack-horse stopping place (Rowley, p. 90).

Sims Creek: see **Simmons Creek** [TRINITY].

Sims Gap [TRINITY]: *pass*, 5 miles north-northwest of Hayfork (lat. 40°37'15" N, long. 123°13'20" W). Named on Hayfork (1951) 15' quadrangle.

Sims Gulch [HUMBOLDT]: *canyon*, drained by a stream that flows 1.5 miles to Camp Creek 1 mile northwest of Orleans (lat. 41°18'40" N, long. 123°33'25" W). Named on Orleans (1978) 7.5' quadrangle.

Sims Mountain [HUMBOLDT]: *peak*, nearly 7 miles east-northeast of Board Camp Mountain (lat. 40°44'40" N, long. 123°36'25" W). Altitude 4478 feet. Named on Sims Mountain (1979) 7.5' quadrangle. On China Flat (1922) 15' quadrangle, the name applies to a peak situated 14 miles south of the present settlement of Willow Creek (lat. 40°45'20" N, long. 123°34'25" W; sec. 1, T 4 N, R 5 E).

Sindel Gulch [MENDOCINO]: *canyon*, drained by a stream that flows 1 mile to James Creek 8 miles northeast of Comptche (lat. 39°21'45" N, long. 123°30'30" W; sec. 2, T 17 N, R 15 W). Named on Comptche (1960) 15' quadrangle.

Singleton Butte [HUMBOLDT]: *peak*, 4 miles east-northeast of Showers Mountain (lat. 40°36' N, long. 123°37'50" W; sec. 32, T 3 N, R 5 E). Named on Showers Mountain (1978) 7.5' quadrangle, which shows Singleton ranch situated 0.5 mile west-southwest of Singleton Butte.

Singley Bar [HUMBOLDT]: *locality*, 3.25 miles west-northwest of Fortuna on the north side of Eel River (lat. 40°36'55" N, long. 124°12'45" W; sec. 29, 30, T 3 N, R 1 W). Named on Fortuna (1959) 7.5' quadrangle. The name recalls George A. Singley, who took over operation of Singley's Ferry on Eel River (near SW cor. sec. 20, T 3 N, R 1 W) in 1873, and who operated the ferry until 1880; the ferry was moved down the river to the county road in 1890, where a bridge was built in 1911 (Edeline, p. 107-108). Eel River and Eureka Railroad Company established a shipping point called Singley's Station in 1884 near the north landing of Singley's Ferry (Carlson, p. 93; Edeline, p. 107-108).

Singley Creek [HUMBOLDT]: *stream*, flows about 5 miles to reach the sea

0.5 mile south-southeast of Cape Mendocino (lat. 40°25'55" N, long. 124°24'10" W; sec. 34, T 1 N, R 3 E). Named on Cape Mendocino (1969) and Capetown (1969) 7.5' quadrangles. Called Stingley Creek on Cape Mendocino (1921) 15' quadrangle, but United States Board on Geographic Names (1940, p. 39) rejected this name for the stream.

Singley's Ferry: see **Singley Bar** [HUMBOLDT].

Singleys Soda Spring: see **Soda Spring** [MENDOCINO] (4).

Singley's Station: see **Singley Bar** [HUMBOLDT].

Siskiyou Fork: see **Smith River** [DEL NORTE] (1).

Siskiyou Mountains [DEL NORTE-HUMBOLDT]: *range*, north and west of Klamath River in Del Norte, Humboldt, and Siskiyou Counties; extends north into the State of Oregon. Named on Weed (1963) 1° x 2° quadrangle. Hudson's Bay Company trappers first used the name "Siskiyou" in the region about 1828 (Gudde, 1949, p. 333).

Siskiyou Pass [DEL NORTE]: *pass*, 4.5 miles south of Broken Rib Mountain on Del Norte-Siskiyou County line (lat. 41°49'05" N, long. 123°41'50" W); the pass is in Siskiyou Mountains near the head of South Siskiyou Fork. Named on Devils Punchbowl (1981) 7.5' quadrangle.

Sister Rocks [DEL NORTE]: *rocks*, 7 miles south-southeast of Crescent City, and 0.5 mile offshore at Midway Point (lat. 41°39'30" N, long. 124°08'40" W). Named on Sister Rocks (1966) 7.5' quadrangle.

Sitsetalko Creek: see **Decker Creek** [HUMBOLDT].

Sixmile Creek [TRINITY]: *stream*, flows 2 miles to Virgin Creek 9 miles south of Salmon Mountain (lat. 41°03'25" N, long. 123°23'05" W). Named on Trinity Mountain (1979) 7.5' quadrangle.

Sixmile Spring [HUMBOLDT]: *spring*, 4.25 miles north of Hoopa (lat. 41°06'35" N, long. 123°40'15" W; sec. 1, T 8 N, R 4 E). Named on Hoopa (1979) 7.5' quadrangle.

Skeleton Creek [LAKE]: *stream*, flows 3 miles to Eel River 4.25 miles west of Crockett Peak (lat. 39°26'05" N, long. 122°51'20" W). Named on Crockett Peak (1967) 7.5' quadrangle.

Skeleton Glade [LAKE]: *area*, 4.25 miles west-northwest of Crockett Peak (lat. 39°26'45" N, long. 122°51'10" W); the place is north of Skeleton Creek. Named on Crockett Peak (1967) 7.5' quadrangle.

Skelly: see **Holmes** [HUMBOLDT].

Skid Gulch [MENDOCINO]: *canyon*, drained by a stream that flows 0.5 mile to Navarro River 2.5 miles southwest of Navarro (lat. 39°07'15" N, long. 123°34' W; near W line sec. 31, T 15 N, R 15 W). Named on Navarro (1961) 15' quadrangle.

Skidmore Creek [MENDOCINO]: *stream*, flows nearly 6 miles to Black Butte River just inside Glenn County (lat. 39°38'20" N, long. 122°53'15" W). Named on Hull Mountain (1967) and Plaskett Ridge (1967) 7.5' quadrangles.

Skidmore Ridge [MENDOCINO]: *ridge*, generally east-northeast-trending, 1.25 miles long, 8 miles north of Hull Mountain (lat. 39°38'20" N, long. 122°55'20" W); the ridge is northwest of Skidmore Creek. Named on Plaskett Ridge (1967) 7.5' quadrangle.

Skookum Prairie [HUMBOLDT]; *area*, nearly 2 miles north-northwest of Coyote Peak (lat. 41°09'30" N, long. 123°52'05" W; sec 19, 20, T 9 N, R 3 E). Named on French Camp Ridge (1983) 7.5' quadrangle

Skull Camp [TRINITY]: *locality*, 6.5 miles southwest of Hyampom (lat. 40°32'35" N, long. 123°32'10" W; near NE cor. sec. 19, T 2 N, R 6 E). Named on Blake Mountain (1979) 7.5' quadrangle.

Skunk Cabbage Creek [HUMBOLDT]: *stream*, flows 2.5 miles to Prairie Creek 1.5 miles north-northeast of Orick (lat. 41°18'20" N, long. 124°02'35" W; sec. 27, T 11 N, R 1 E). Named on Orick (1966) 7.5' quadrangle.

Skunk Creek [HUMBOLDT]: *stream*, flows 1 mile to Trinity River 3 miles south-southeast of Weitchpec (lat. 41°09'05" N, long. 123°40'55" W; near E line sec. 23, T 9 N, R 4 E). Named on Weitchpec (1979) 7.5' quadrangle.

Skunk Creek [MENDOCINO]: *stream*, flows 1.5 miles to Robinson Creek (4) 9 miles northeast of Boonville (lat. 39°06'50" N, long. 123°16'20" W; sec. 34, T 15 N, R 13 W). Named on Boonville (1959) 15' quadrangle.

Skunk Flat [MENDOCINO]: *area*, 5.25 miles west of Covelo (lat. 39°47'10" N, long. 123°20'45" W; at N line sec. 7, T 22 N, R 13 W). Named on Covelo West (1967) 7.5' quadrangle.

Skunk Flat [TRINITY]: *area*, 14 miles southeast of Weaverville (lat. 40°32'55" N, long. 122°49'30" W; near SE cor. sec. 12, T 31 N, R 9 W); the place is near Skunk Gulch. Named on Weaverville (1950) 15' quadrangle.

Skunk Gulch [TRINITY]: *canyon*, drained by a stream that flows nearly 3 miles to Reading Creek 14 miles south-southeast of Weaverville (lat. 40°32'30" N, long. 122°51' W; sec. 14, T 31 N, R 9 W). Named on Weaverville (1950) 15' quadrangle.

Skunk Lake [MENDOCINO]: *lake*, 350 feet long, 9.5 miles northeast of Eden Valley (lat. 39°42'45" N, long. 123°02'40" W; on S line sec. 35, T 22 N, R 11 W). Named on Thatcher Ridge (1967) 7.5' quadrangle.

Skunk Lake Creek [MENDOCINO]: *stream*, flows 3.5 miles to Haynes Creek 8.5 miles east-northeast of Eden Valley (lat. 39°41'20" N, long. 123°02'45" W); Skunk Lake is at the head of a branch of the stream. Named on Thatcher Ridge (1967) 7.5' quadrangle. On Eden Valley (1952) 15' quadrangle, present Skunk Lake Creek is shown as part of Haynes Creek, but United States Board on Geographic Names (1969a, p. 4) rejected the names "Haynes Creek" and "Bed Rock Creek" for present Skunk Lake Creek.

Skunk Rock [MENDOCINO]: *peak*, 10 miles northeast of Eden Valley (lat. 39°43'10" N, long. 123°02'50" W; sec. 35, T 22 N, R 11 W); the peak is 0.5 mile north of Skunk Lake. Altitude 5056 feet. Named on Thatcher Ridge (1967) 7.5' quadrangle.

Sky High [LAKE]: *peak*, 5.25 miles east of the town of Lower Lake (lat. 38°54'45" N, long. 122°30'40" W; sec. 3, T 12 N, R 6 W). Altitude 2833 feet. Named on Lower Lake (1958) 7.5' quadrangle.

Skylight Ridge [TRINITY]: *ridge*, southwest-trending, 1.5 miles long, 5 miles south of Black Rock Mountain (lat. 40°08' N, long. 123°00' W). Named on Black Rock Mountain (1954) and Yolla Bolly (1954) 15' quadrangles.

Sky Rock [LAKE]: *peak*, 5.5 miles northeast of the town of Upper Lake (lat. 39°12'55" N, long. 122°49'45" W). Altitude 4067 feet. Named on Bartlett Mountain (1958) 7.5' quadrangle.

Slate Bar: see **Steiner Flat** [TRINITY].

Slate Creek [HUMBOLDT]: *stream*, flows 7.5 miles to Klamath River 6.5 miles southwest of Orleans (lat. 41°15'05" N, long. 123°38'30" W). Named on Fish Lake (1974) 7.5' quadrangle.

Slate Creek [TRINITY]: *stream*, flows 4 miles to Clair Engle Lake 8.5 miles north-northeast of Weaverville (lat. 40°50'15" N, long. 122°51'30" W; near N line sec. 2, T 34 N, R 9 W). Named on Trinity Dam (1950) 15' quadrangle.

Slate Creek Butte [HUMBOLDT]; *peak*, 8 miles west-northwest of Orleans (lat. 41°21'05" N, long. 123°40'30" W); the peak is near the head of Slate Creek. Altitude 4851 feet. Named on Fish Lake (1974) 7.5' quadrangle. United States Board on Geographic Names (1977a, p. 6) gave the variant name "Fish Creek Butte" for the feature.

Slate Gap [TRINITY]: *pass*, 3 miles east-southeast of Salmon Mountain on Trinity-Siskiyou County line (lat. 41°09'40" N, long. 123°21'45" W). Named on Youngs Peak (1979) 7.5' quadrangle.

Slate Mountain [TRINITY]: *peak*, 8 miles east of Trinity Center on Trinity-Shasta County line (lat. 41°00'10" N, long. 122°32'15" W; near SE cor. sec. 3, T 36 N, R 6 W). Altitude 5520 feet. Named on Bonanza King (1955) 15' quadrangle.

Slater Creek [HUMBOLDT]: *stream*, flows 2.5 miles to Eel River 6 miles south of Fortuna (lat. 40°30'35" N, long. 124°08'35" W). Named on Fortuna (1959) and Taylor Peak (1969) 7.5' quadrangles. Carranco and Sorensen (p. 157) noted the alternate name "Metropolitan Creek" for the feature—Metropolitan Redwood Company had timber along the stream.

Slater Island [LAKE]: *island*, 1400 feet long, 1.5 miles northwest of the town of Lower Lake in Clear Lake (lat. 38°55'50" N, long. 122°37'50" W; on W line sec. 34, T 13 N, R 7 W). Named on Clearlake Highlands (1958) 7.5' quadrangle.

Slattery Gulch [TRINITY]: *canyon*, drained by a stream that flows 1 mile to Slattery Pond 16 miles north-northeast of Hayfork (lat. 40°44'20" N, long. 123°01' W; near SE cor. sec. 5, T 33 N, R 10 W). Named on Hayfork (1951) 15' quadrangle. The Slattery family had ranches on both sides of the canyon (Jones, p. 174).

Slattery Pond [TRINITY]: *lake*, 1500 feet long, 15 miles north-northeast of Hayfork at the lower end of Slattery Gulch (lat. 40°44'15" N, long. 123°01'10" W; near NE cor. sec. 8, T 33 N, R 10 W). Named on Hayfork (1951) 15' quadrangle.

Slaughterhouse Gulch [MENDOCINO]:

(1) *canyon*, drained by a stream that flows 2 miles to South Fork Cottaneva Creek 7.5 miles north of Westport (lat. 39°44'40" N, long. 123°48' W; near W line sec. 19, T 22 N, R 17 W). Named on Hales Grove (1970) and Westport (1966) 7.5' quadrangles.

(2) *canyon*, drained by a stream that flows less than 1 mile to the sea 0.5 mile north of downtown Mendocino at Agate Beach (lat. 39°18'55" N, long. 123°47'55" W; near S line sec. 19, T 17 N, R 17 W). Named on Mendocino (1960) 7.5' quadrangle.

Sled Creek [MENDOCINO]: *stream*, flows 1 mile to Mill Creek (12) 0.5 mile southwest of Ornbaun Valley (lat. 38°54'50" N, long. 123°18'50" W; sec. 9, T 12 N, R 13 W). Named on Ornbaun Valley (1960) 15' quadrangle.

Sled Ridge [LAKE]: *ridge*, southwest-trending, 1.25 miles long, 3.5 miles south of Elk Mountain (lat. 39°15'45" N, long. 122°55'15" W). Named on Elk Mountain (1967) 7.5' quadrangle.

Sleeper Peak [LAKE]: *peak*, 2.25 miles northwest of the town of Upper Lake (lat. 39°11'35" N, long. 122°55'50" W; near SE cor. sec. 35, T 16 N, R 10 W). Named on Upper Lake (1958) 7.5' quadrangle.

Sleepy Hollow [HUMBOLDT]: *relief feature*, 4.5 miles south of Ferndale (lat. 30°30'45" N, long. 124°16'25" W; near E line sec. 34, T 2 N, R 2 W). Named on Ferndale (1959) 7.5' quadrangle.

Slick Rock Creek [MENDOCINO]: *stream*, flows 3 miles to the sea 6 miles southeast of the village of Point Arena (lat. 38°50'10" N, long. 123°37'40" W; sec. 3, T 11 N, R 16 W). Named on Gualala (1960) 7.5' quadrangle.

Slide: see **Fortuna** [HUMBOLDT].
Slide Camp: see **Biggs Gulch** [MENDOCINO].
Slide Creek [HUMBOLDT]:
(1) *stream*, flows 4.5 miles to Blue Creek 7.5 miles north-northeast of Johnsons (lat. 41°27'05" N, long. 123°49'30" W). Named on Blue Creek Mountain (1982) 7.5' quadrangle.
(2) *stream*, flows 2.25 miles to Bluff Creek 4.5 miles northeast of Weitchpec (lat. 41°14'35" N, long. 123°39'25" W). Named on Weitchpec (1979) 7.5' quadrangle.
(3) *stream*, flows 1.5 miles to Bull Creek (1) 13 miles south-southeast of Scotia (lat. 40°18'20" N, long. 124°01'45" W; near NE cor. sec. 14, T 2 S, R 1 E). Named on Bull Creek (1969) 7.5' quadrangle.
Slide Creek [TRINITY]: *stream*, flows 8 miles to join Virgin Creek and form New River 11 miles south-southeast of Salmon Mountain (lat. 41°01'50" N, long. 123°20'50" W). Named on Dees Peak (1978) 7.5' quadrangle. United States Board on Geographic Names (1977b, p. 5) gave the variant name "New River" for present Slide Creek.
Slide Gulch [HUMBOLDT]: *canyon*, drained by a stream that flows 1 mile to Camp Creek 2.5 miles northwest of Orleans (lat. 41°19'55" N, long. 123°34'10" W). Named on on Orleans (1978) 7.5' quadrangle.
Slide Gulch [TRINITY]: *canyon*, drained by a stream that flows 1 mile to Coffee Creek 2.25 miles west-southwest of Billys Peak (1) (lat. 41°07' N, long. 122°48'30" W; near SW cor. sec. 29, T 38 N, R 8 W). Named on Coffee Creek (1955) 15' quadrangle.
Slide Lake [TRINITY]: *lake*, 500 feet long, 5.5 miles south of China Mountain, which is in Siskiyou County (lat. 41°18' N, long. 122°35' W; sec. 29, T 40 N, R 6 W). Named on China Mountain (1955) 15' quadrangle.
Slide Peak: see **North Slide Peak** [HUMBOLDT].
Slides: see **The Slides** [LAKE].
Smith [HUMBOLDT]: *locality*, 8.5 miles east of Weott along Northwestern Pacific Railroad (lat. 40°18'30" N, long. 123°45'45" W; sec. 7, T 2 S, R 4 E). Named on Weott (1949) 15' quadrangle.
Smith: see **Jack Smith Creek** [MENDOCINO]; **John Smith Creek** [MENDOCINO]; **Poison Smith Spring** [LAKE].
Smith Canyon [LAKE]: *canyon*, drained by a stream that flows 2.25 miles to Alley Creek nearly 2 miles east-northeast of the town of Upper Lake (lat. 39°10'50" N, long. 122°52'40" W; sec. 5, T 15 N, R 9 W). Named on Bartlett Mountain (1958) and Upper Lake (1958) 7.5' quadrangles.
Smith Creek [HUMBOLDT]:
(1) *stream*, flows 4.5 miles to Cutoff Slough 4 miles northwest of Ferndale (lat. 40°37' N, long. 124°19' W). Named on Ferndale (1959) 7.5' quadrangle.
(2) *stream*, flows 2 miles to Larabee Creek 5.25 miles southwest of Bridgeville (lat. 40°24'25" N, long. 123°51'20" W; sec. 5, T 1 S, R 3 E). Named on Bridgeville (1969) 7.5' quadrangle.
Smith Creek [MENDOCINO]:
(1) *stream*, flows 5.5 miles to South Fork Ten Mile River 10.5 miles south-southwest of Branscomb (lat. 39°31'30" N, long. 123°43'45" W; near W line sec. 11, T 19 N, R 17 W); the stream is south of Smith Ridge. Named on Dutchmans Knoll (1966) 7.5' quadrangle.
(2) *stream*, flows less than 1 mile to the sea 1.25 miles north-northwest of Albion (lat. 39°14'25" N, long. 123°46'30" W; near N line sec. 20, T 16 N, R 17 W). Named on Albion (1960) 7.5' quadrangle.
Smith Creek [TRINITY]:
(1) *stream*, flows 3 miles to Baker Creek 13 miles northeast of Trinity Center (lat. 41°07'10" N, long. 122°29'50" W; sec. 25, T 38 N, R 6 W). Named on Bonanza King (1955) and Dunsmuir (1954) 15' quadrangles.
(2) *stream*, flows 2 miles to Mad River 9.5 miles east-northeast of Kettenpom (lat. 40°13'50" N, long. 123°18'15" W; near W line sec. 5, T 3 S, R 8 E); the stream heads near Smith Peak. Named on Shannon Butte (1967) 7.5' quadrangle.
Smith Flat: see **Douglas City** [TRINITY].
Smith Gulch [HUMBOLDT]: *canyon*, drained by a stream that flows 1 mile to the sea 5.5 miles southwest of Petrolia (lat. 40°16'20" N, long. 124°21'40" W; at S line sec. 24, T 2 S, R 3 W). Named on Petrolia (1969) 7.5' quadrangle.
Smith Gulch [TRINITY]:
(1) *canyon*, drained by a stream that flows 1.25 miles to Clair Engle Lake 14 miles northeast of Weaverville (lat. 40°53'05" N, long. 122°45'35" W; near S line sec. 15, T 35 N, R 8 W). Named on Schell Mountain (1950) and Trinity Dam (1950) 15' quadrangles.
(2) *canyon*, drained by a stream that flows 2.25 miles to Clair Engle Lake 9.5 miles northeast of Weaverville (lat. 40°49'30" N, long. 122°48'30" W; at S line sec. 6, T 34 N, R 8 W). Named on Trinity Dam (1950) 15' quadrangle.
Smith Lake [TRINITY]: *lake*, 1600 feet long, 16 miles north of Weaverville (lat. 40°57'50" N, long. 122°59'35" W; on E line sec. 22, T 36 N, R 10 W). Named on Trinity Dam (1950) 15' quadrangle.
Smith Opening [HUMBOLDT]: *area*, 8 miles east-southeast of Board Camp Mountain (lat. 40°38'10" N, long. 123°35'10" W; near SE cor. sec. 15, T 3 N, R 5 E). Named on Sims Mountain (1979) 7.5' quadrangle.
Smith Peak [TRINITY]: *peak*, 8 miles northeast of Kettenpom (lat. 40°13'45" N, long. 123°20'20" W; sec. 1, T 3 S, R 7 E). Altitude 4216 feet. Named on Shannon Butte (1967) 7.5' quadrangle.
Smith Prairie [HUMBOLDT]: *area*, 7.5 miles north-northwest of Coyote Peak (lat. 41°14'15" N, long. 123°54'35" W; sec. 23, 26, T 10 N, R 2 E). Named on Bald Hills (1982) 7.5' quadrangle.
Smith Ridge [MENDOCINO]: *ridge*, generally west-trending, 12 miles long, center 8.5 miles south of Branscomb (lat. 39°31'30" N, long. 123°37' W). Named on Dutchmans Knoll (1966) and Sherwood Peak (1967) 7.5' quadrangles.
Smith River [DEL NORTE]:
(1) *stream*, formed by the confluence of Middle Fork and North Fork at Gasquet, flows 25 miles to the sea 3 miles west of the town of Smith River (lat. 41°56'10" N, long. 124°12'10" W; sec. 20, T 18 N, R 1 W). Named on Gasquet (1981), High Divide (1966), Hiouchi (1966), and Smith River (1966) 7.5' quadrangles. Called Smith's R. on United States Coast Survey's (1854) map, and called Smiths R. on Bancroft's (1864) map, but United States Board on Geographic Names (1954, p. 4) rejected the name "Smith's River" for the feature, and noted that the name "Smith" is for Jedediah Strong Smith, who explored the region in 1828. Smith or his cartographer applied the name first to the lower part of present Klamath River, but George Gibbs gave Smith's name to present Smith River in 1851 (Gudde, 1969, p. 313-314). Middle Fork is 25 miles long and is named on Broken Rib Mountain (1982), Devils Punchbowl (1981), Gasquet (1981), Hurdygurdy Butte (1982), and Shelly Creek Ridge (1982) 7.5' quadrangles. North Fork, which heads in the State of Oregon, is 14 miles long and is named on Gasquet (1951) 15' quadrangle. South Fork enters 16 miles upstream from the mouth of the main stream; it is 40 miles long and is named on Cant Hook Mountain (1982), Devils Punchbowl (1981), Gasquet (1981), Hiouchi (1966), Prescott Mountain (1981), and Ship Mountain (1982) 7.5' quadrangles. California Mining Bureau's (1917a) map shows a locality called South Fork situated on the east side of Smith River just south of the mouth of South Fork Smith River. Siskiyou Fork enters from the south-southeast just west of Washington Flat; it is 9.5 miles long and is named on Broken Rib Mountain (1982), Devils Punchbowl (1981), Hurdygurdy Butte (1982), and Shelly Creek Ridge (1982) 7.5' quadrangles. United States Board on Geographic Names (1983c, p. 6) rejected the names "Siskiyou Fork of Middle Fork Smith River," "Siskiyou Fork Smith River," and "Twin Peak Branch" for present Siskiyou Fork. South Siskiyou Fork heads at Siskiyou Pass and enters Siskiyou Fork 3.5 miles upstream from the mouth of that stream; it is 5 miles long and is named on Devils Punchbowl (1981) and Hurdygurdy Butte (1982) 7.5' quadrangles. United States Board on Geographic Names (1983c, p. 7) rejected the names "Siskiyou Fork," "South Siskiyou Fork Middle Smith River," and "South Siskiyou Fork Smith River" for present South Siskiyou Fork. Wells' (1946) map shows a feature called Ranger Spring located near the head of an unnamed branch of South Siskiyou Fork (lat. 41°50'50" N, long. 123°46'40" W; sec. 24, T 17 N, R 3 E).
(2) *town*, 12 miles north-northeast of Crescent City (lat. 41°55'45" N, long. 124°08'50" W; in and near sec. 26, T 18 N, R 1 W); the town is 3 miles east of the mouth of Smith River (1). Named on Smith River (1966) 7.5' quadrangle. Postal authorities established Smith River post office in 1863 (Frickstad, p. 25). Chase (p. 310) called the place Smith River Corners, but United States Board on Geographic Names (1954, p. 4) rejected the names "Smith River Corners" and "Smith's River" for the community. Postal authorities established Shakesville post office 5 miles south of Smith River post office in 1893 and discontinued it in 1894 (Salley, p. 202).
Smith River Corners: see **Smith River** [DEL NORTE] (2).
Smith Rock [HUMBOLDT]: *relief feature*, 5 miles east-northeast of Cape Mendocino (lat. 40°27'40" N, long. 124°19'10" W; at N line sec. 20, T 1 N, R 2 W). Named on Capetown (1969) 7.5' quadrangle.
Smith's River: see **Klamath River** [DEL NORTE-HUMBOLDT]; **Smith River** [DEL NORTE] (1); **Smith River** [DEL NORTE] (2).
Smokehouse Creek [HUMBOLDT]: *stream*, flows 1.25 miles to Snow Camp Creek (2) 3 miles north of Board Camp Mountain (lat. 40°44'30" N, long. 123°43'20" W; at E line sec. 9, T 4 N, R 4 E). Named on Board Camp Mountain (1977) 7.5' quadrangle.
Smokehouse Creek [LAKE]: *stream*, flows 9 miles to Lake Pillsbury 4.25 miles northwest of Bear Mountain (lat. 39°26'35" N, long. 122°57'55" W; sec. 3, T 18 N, R 10 W). Named on Hull Mountain (1967), Lake Pillsbury (1967), and Sanhedrin Mountain (1966) 7.5' quadrangles. The name is from a crude smokehouse built about 1870 for smoking salmon (Gudde, 1969, p. 314).
Smokehouse Creek [MENDOCINO-TRINITY]: *stream*, heads in Trinity County and flows 4 miles to Beaver Creek nearly 7 miles north of Anthony Peak in Mendocino County (lat. 39°56'30" N, long. 122°57'15" W; near N line sec. 15, T 24 N, R 10 W); the stream is east of Smokehouse Ridge. Named on Buck Rock (1967) 7.5' quadrangle.
Smokehouse Ridge [MENDOCINO-TRINITY]: *ridge*, south- to west-trending, 3 miles long, 9 miles north of Anthony Peak on Mendocino-Trinity County line (lat. 39°58'15" N, long. 122°58'20" W). Named on Buck Rock

(1967) 7.5' quadrangle.

Smoky Camp Creek [TRINITY]: *stream,* flows less than 1 mile to Don Juan Creek 3.25 miles east of Burnt Ranch (lat. 40°48'45" N, long. 123°24'45" W). Named on Ironside Mountain (1951) 15' quadrangle.

Smoky Creek [TRINITY]: *stream,* flows 5.5 miles to South Fork Trinity River 7.5 miles southwest of Dubakella Mountain (lat. 40°18'15" N, long. 123°14'10" W; sec. 5, T 28 N, R 12 W). Named on Dubakella Mountain (1954) 15' quadrangle. East Fork enters from the east 2.5 miles upstream from the mouth of the main creek, and North Fork enters from the north 1.25 miles upstream from the mouth of the main creek; each fork is 2.5 miles long, and each is named on Dubakella Mountain (1954) 15' quadrangle.

Snelly Peak [LAKE]: *peak,* 2.25 miles south-southeast of Middletown (lat. 38°43'30" N, long. 122°35'45" W; near E line sec. 11, T 10 N, R 7 W). Altitude 2123 feet. Named on Detert Reservoir (1958) 7.5' quadrangle.

Snipe Gulch [TRINITY]: *canyon,* drained by a stream that flows 1 mile to the canyon of Trinity River 5.5 miles southeast of Weaverville (lat. 40°41'15" N, long. 122°51'10" W; sec. 26, T 33 N, R 9 W). Named on Weaverville (1950) 15' quadrangle.

Snook Mountain [MENDOCINO]: *peak,* 5 miles south of Ornbaun Valley (lat. 38°50'40" N, long. 123°19'25" W; sec. 32, T 12 N, R 13 W). Altitude 2453 feet. Named on Ornbaun Valley (1960) 15' quadrangle.

Snow Camp [TRINITY]: *locality,* 7.5 miles south-southeast of Hyampom (lat. 41°31'15" N, long. 123°22'45" W; near W line sec. 27, T 2 N, R 7 E). Named on Hyampom (1951) 15' quadrangle. The name is from a cabin that was buried under 8 feet of snow about 1904 (Turner, p. 198).

Snow Camp Creek [HUMBOLDT]:

(1) *stream,* flows 2.5 miles to Pine Creek (1) 4.5 miles east-northeast of Coyote Peak (lat. 41°09'30" N, long. 123°46'50" W; at S line sec. 13, T 9 N, R 3 E). Named on French Camp Ridge (1983) and Weitchpec (1979) 7.5' quadrangles.

(2) *stream,* flows 2.25 miles to Twin Lakes Creek 3 miles north of Board Camp Mountain (lat. 40°44'30" N, long. 123°43'15" W; near W line sec. 10, T 4 N, R 4 E). Named on Board Camp Mountain (1977) and Mad River Buttes (1977) 7.5' quadrangles.

Snow Camp Lake [HUMBOLDT]: *lake,* 1200 feet long, 10 miles northeast of Lone Star Junction (lat. 40°44'50" N, long. 123°45'30" W; near NW cor. sec. 8, T 4 N, R 4 E); the lake is at the head of Snow Camp Creek (2). Named on Mad River Buttes (1977) 7.5' quadrangle.

Snow Camp Mountain [HUMBOLDT]: *ridge,* southeast-trending, 1.5 miles long, 10 miles northeast of Lone Star Junction (lat. 40°45' N, long. 123°46'15" W). Named on Mad River Buttes (1977) and Maple Creek (1977) 7.5' quadrangles.

Snow Gap [TRINITY]: *pass,* nearly 6 miles south-southwest of Dubakella Mountain (lat. 40°18'20" N, long. 123°10'50" W; sec. 2, T 28 N, R 12 W). Named on Dubakella Mountain (1954) 15' quadrangle.

Snow Glade [HUMBOLDT]: *area,* 2.5 miles east-northeast of Showers Mountain (lat. 40°35'35" N, long. 123°39'10" W; sec. 31, T 3 N, R 5 E). Named on Showers Mountain (1978) 7.5' quadrangle.

Snow Gulch [TRINITY]:

(1) *canyon,* drained by a stream that flows 1.5 miles to Trinity River 2.25 miles north of Trinity Center (lat. 41°02'20" N, long. 122°41'20" W; near E line sec. 29, T 37 N, R 7 W). Named on Bonanza King (1955) 15' quadrangle.

(2) *canyon,* drained by a stream that flows 1 mile to Rush Creek 5.5 miles east of Weaverville (lat. 40°43'30" N, long. 122°50'10" W; near S line sec. 12, T 33 N, R 9 W). Named on Weaverville (1950) 15' quadrangle.

Snow Mountain [HUMBOLDT]: *peak,* 3 miles south-southwest of Hoopa (lat. 41°00'20" N, long. 123°41'45" W; sec. 11, T 7 N, R 4 E). Altitude 3705 feet. Named on Hoopa (1979) 7.5' quadrangle.

Snow Mountain [LAKE]: *ridge,* generally west-northwest-trending, 1.5 miles long, 3.25 miles south of Crockett Peak on Lake-Colusa County line (lat. 39°23' N, long. 122°45'45" W; in and near sec. 28, T 18 N, R 8 W). Named on Crockett Peak (1967) 7.5' quadrangle.

Snow Mountain [MENDOCINO]: peak, 5.25 miles west-southwest of Hopland (lat. 38°56'15" N, long. 123°11'50" W; sec. 32, T 13 N, R 12 W). Altitude 3140 feet. Named on Hopland (1960) 15' quadrangle.

Snow Mountain East [LAKE]: *peak,* 4.5 miles south-southeast of Crockett Peak on Lake-Colusa County line (lat. 39°23' N, long. 122°45'05" W; sec. 27, T 18 N, R 8 W); the peak is on Snow Mountain 0.5 mile north of Snow Mountain West. Altitude 7056 feet. Named on Crockett Peak (1967) 7.5' quadrangle.

Snow Mountain West [LAKE]: *peak,* 3.5 miles south-southeast of Crockett Peak on Lake-Colusa County line (lat. 39°22'40" N, long. 122°45'30" W; near SE cor. sec. 28, T 18 N, R 8 W); the peak is on Snow Mountain 0.5 mile south of Snow Mountain East. Altitude 7038 feet. Named on Crockett Peak (1967) 7.5' quadrangle.

Snow Prairie [HUMBOLDT]: *area,* 7.5 miles south-southeast of Scotia (lat. 40°23' N, long. 124°02'30" W). Named on Scotia (1970) 7.5' quadrangle.

Snows Lake [LAKE]: *lake,* 1400 feet long, 5.25 miles northeast of Whispering Pines (lat. 38°52'05" N, long. 122°38'40" W; on S line sec. 21, T 12 N, R 7 W). Named on Whispering Pines (1958) 7.5' quadrangle.

Snowslide Gulch [TRINITY]:

(1) *canyon,* drained by a stream that flows 1 mile to North Fork Coffee Creek 7 miles west-northwest of Billys Peak (1) (lat. 41°10'20" N, long. 122°53'05" W; near N line sec. 10, T 38 N, R 9 W). Named on Coffee Creek (1955) 15' quadrangle.

(2) *canyon,* drained by a stream that flows 1.5 miles to Trinity River 7.5 miles north of Trinity Center (lat. 41°06'50" N, long. 122°42'15" W; near W line sec. 32, T 38 N, R 7 W). Named on Bonanza King (1955) 15' quadrangle.

(3) *canyon,* drained by a stream that flows 1.25 miles to Mule Creek 12 miles north-northeast of Weaverville (lat. 40°53'15" N, long. 122°49'45" W; sec. 13, T 35 N, R 9 W). Named on Trinity Dam (1950) 15' quadrangle.

(4) *canyon,* drained by a stream that flows 1.5 miles to Stuart Fork 9 miles north-northeast of Weaverville (lat. 40°51'35" N, long. 122°53'30" W; sec. 28, T 35 N, R 9 W). Named on Trinity Dam (1950) 15' quadrangle.

Snowslide Peak [TRINITY]: *peak,* about 11 miles southwest of Billys Peak (1) (lat. 41°00'15" N, long. 122°54' W; sec. 4, T 36 N, R 9 W). Named on Coffee Creek (1955) 15' quadrangle.

Snuffins Creek [MENDOCINO]: *stream,* flows 2.5 miles to Daugherty Creek 11.5 miles north of Boonville (lat. 39°10'35" N, long. 123°23'40" W; sec. 10, T 15 N, R 14 W). Named on Boonville (1959) 15' quadrangle

Soap Creek [LAKE]: *stream,* flows 2.5 miles to North Fork Cache Creek 15 miles north of Clearlake Oaks (lat. 39°12' N, long. 122°42'30" W). Named on Clearlake Oaks (1960) 15' quadrangle. The name is from borax in the water (Bradley, p. 221).

Soap Creek [TRINITY]: *stream,* flows 1.5 miles to South Fork Trinity River 9 miles south of Dubakella Mountain (lat. 40°15'30" N, long. 123°09' W; sec. 19, T 28 N, R 11 W). Named on Dubakella Mountain (1954) 15' quadrangle.

Soap Creek Springs: see **Newman Springs** [LAKE].

Soapstone Gulch [DEL NORTE-HUMBOLDT]: *canyon,* drained by a stream that heads in Del Norte County and flows 2 miles to Nickowitz Creek 8.5 miles northeast of Johnsons in Humboldt County (lat. 41°26'55" N, long. 123°46'20" W). Named on Blue Creek Mountain (1982) and Lonesome Ridge (1974) 7.5' quadrangles.

Soctish Creek [HUMBOLDT]: *stream,* flows 4.5 miles to Trinity River 3.25 miles north-northwest of Hoopa (lat. 41°05'25" N, long. 123°42'15" W; sec. 10, T 8 N, R 4 E). Named on Hoopa (1979) 7.5' quadrangle. North Fork enters from the northwest 1.5 miles upstream from the mouth of the main creek; it is nearly 4 miles long and is named on Hoopa (1979) and Hupa Mountain (1982) 7.5' quadrangles. United States Board on Geographic Names (1980, p. 5) rejected the name "Scotish Creek" for the stream.

Soctish Point [HUMBOLDT]: *peak,* 2.25 miles west-northwest of Hoopa (lat. 41°04' N, long. 123°42'55" W; sec. 22, T 8 N, R 4 E). Altitude 1936 feet. Named on Hoopa (1979) 7.5' quadrangle. United States Board on Geographic Names (1980, p. 5) rejected the name "Scotish Point" for the feature.

Soda Basin [MENDOCINO]: *relief feature,* 6 miles west of Willits (lat. 39°25' N, long. 123°27'50" W; on E line sec. 13, T 18 N, R 15 W). Named on Willits (1961) 15' quadrangle.

Soda Bay [LAKE]:

(1) *embayment,* 7.25 miles east-southeast of Lakeport along Clear Lake (lat. 39°00'15" N, long. 122°47'30" W; sec. 6, T 13 N, R 8 W). Named on Lucerne (1958) 7.5' quadrangle. Soda water bubbles up from springs in the embayment and on nearby land (Menefee, p. 244).

(2) *town,* 7.5 miles east-southeast of Lakeport (lat. 39°00'05" N, long. 122°47'20" W; sec. 6, T 13 N, R 8 W); the town is along Soda Bay (1). Named on Kelseyville (1959) and Lucerne (1958) 7.5' quadrangles. A boating and fishing resort called Soda Bay Springs provided accommodations for about 150 people at the place in 1910 (Waring, p. 191).

Soda Bay Springs: see **Soda Bay** [LAKE] (2)

Soda Canyon [LAKE]: *canyon,* drained by a stream that flows 1.5 miles to Phipps Creek 5.5 miles north-northeast of the town of Lower Lake (lat. 38°59'20" N, long. 122°34'20" W). Named on Clearlake Oaks (1960) 15' quadrangle, and on Lower Lake (1958) 7.5' quadrangle.

Soda Creek [HUMBOLDT]: *stream,* flows nearly 3 miles to Eel River 2.5 miles northwest of Alderpoint (lat. 40°11'55" N, long. 123°39'05" W; near SE cor. sec. 18, T 3 S, R 5 E). Named on Fort Seward (1969) 7.5' quadrangle. On Alderpoint (1949) 15' quadrangle, nearby Jackass Creek is called Soda Creek.

Soda Creek [LAKE]:

(1) *stream,* formed by the confluence of Panther Creek (1) and Welch Creek, flows 2.5 miles to Eel River 4 miles west of Bear Mountain (lat. 39°24'35" N, long. 122°58'40" W; near SW cor. sec. 15, T 18 N, R 10 W). Named on Lake Pillsbury (1967) 7.5' quadrangle. On Hullville (1922) 15' quadrangle, present Welch Creek is called Soda Creek. Waring (p. 204) listed Morton Soda Spring, located near the mouth of Soda Creek. Bradley (p. 224) gave the name "Roaring Soda Spring" for the same feature.

(2) *stream,* flows 10 miles to Putah Creek 4 miles southwest of Jericho Valley (lat. 38°47'45" N, long. 122°29'15" W; near N line sec. 23, T 11 N, R 6 W). Named on Jericho Valley (1958), Lower Lake (1958), and Middletown (1958) 7.5' quadrangles. United States Board on Geographic Names (1962b, p. 20) rejected the name "Jerusalem Valley Creek" for the feature.

Soda Creek [MENDOCINO]:

(1) *stream,* flows less than 1 mile to Hayworth Creek 8.5 miles west-northwest of Willits (lat. 39°28'40" N, long. 123°28'55" W; near NW cor. sec. 25, T 19 N, R 15 W). Named on Willits (1961) 15' quadrangle.

(2) *stream,* flows 2.25 miles to Daugherty Creek 15 miles north-northwest of Boonville (lat. 39°12'50" N, long. 123°26'30" W; sec. 29, T 16 N, R 14 W). Named on Boonville (1959) 15' quadrangle.

(3) *stream,* flows 2.5 miles to North Fork Navarro River 1.5 miles west-northwest of Navarro (lat. 39°09'35" N, long. 123°34' W; near W line sec. 18, T 15 N, R 15 W). Named on Navarro (1961) 15' quadrangle.

(4) *stream,* flows 2.25 miles to Low Gap Creek (3) 10 miles north of Boonville (lat. 39°09'15" N, long. 123°22'20" W; near S line sec. 14, T 15 N, R 14 W). Named on Boonville (1959) 15' quadrangle.

(5) *stream,* flows 6 miles to Anderson Creek less than 1 mile east-southeast of Boonville (lat. 39°00'15" N, long. 123°21'10" W; sec. 12, T 13 N, R 14 W). Named on Boonville (1959) 15' quadrangle.

(6) *stream,* flows 4 miles to Dry Creek (2) 10 miles south-southwest of Hopland (lat. 38°49'50" N, long. 123°10' W; sec. 2, T 11 N, R 12 W). Named on Hopland (1960) 15' quadrangle.

Soda Creek: see **Little Soda Creek** [LAKE]; **Welch Creek** [LAKE].

Soda Fork [MENDOCINO]: *stream,* flows 2.5 miles to Elk Creek (4) 8.5 miles south of Navarro (lat. 39°01'45" N, long. 123°34' W; sec. 31, T 14 N, R 15 W). Named on Navarro (1961) 15' quadrangle.

Soda Gulch [MENDOCINO]: *canyon,* drained by a stream that flows 1 mile to Flume Gulch 3 miles northeast of Elk (lat. 39°09'20" N, long. 123°40' W; sec. 18, T 15 N, R 16 W). Named on Elk (1960) 7.5' quadrangle.

Soda Spring [MENDOCINO]:

(1) *spring,* 5.5 miles north-northwest of the town of Potter Valley (lat. 39°23'20" N, long. 123°09'40" W; sec. 26, T 18 N, R 12 W). Named on Potter Valley (1960) 15' quadrangle.

(2) *spring,* 1.5 miles north-northwest of Comptche (lat. 39°17' N, long. 123°36'20" W; near SE cor. sec. 35, T 17 N, R 16 W). Named on Comptche (1960) 15' quadrangle.

(3) *spring,* 8.5 miles south of Navarro (lat. 39°01'40" N, long. 123°33'20" W; sec. 31, T 14 N, R 15 W). Named on Navarro (1961) 15' quadrangle.

(4) *spring,* 3 miles east-northeast of Boonville (lat. 39°01'25" N, long. 123°18'50" W; near S line sec. 32, T 14 N, R 13 W). Named on Boonville (1959) 15' quadrangle. Waring (p. 171) described Singleys Soda Spring, located about 5 miles by road northeast of Boonville.

(5) *spring,* 1.5 miles east of Branscomb along Mud Creek (3) (lat. 39°39'15" N, long. 123°36'15" W). Named on Branscomb (1921) 15' quadrangle.

Soda Spring: see **Big Soda Spring** [LAKE].

Soda Spring Creek [MENDOCINO]: *stream,* flows 1.5 miles to North Fork Albion River 1.5 miles north-northwest of Comptche (lat. 39°17' N, long. 123°36'20" W; near SE cor. sec. 35, T 17 N, R 16 W); Soda Spring (2) is at the mouth of the stream. Named on Comptche (1960) 15' quadrangle.

Soda Spring Gulch [MENDOCINO]: *canyon,* drained by a stream that flows less than 1 mile to Little North Fork Albion River 8 miles north-northeast of Elk (lat. 39°14'05" N, long. 123°38'30" W; at E line sec. 21, T 16 N, R 16 W). Named on Elk (1960) 7.5' quadrangle.

Soda Springs [MENDOCINO]: *locality,* 4.5 miles west of Willits along California Western Railroad (lat. 39°25'15" N, long. 123°25'55" W; near S line sec. 8, T 18 N, R 14 W). Named on Willits (1961) 15' quadrangle.

Soldier Basin [TRINITY]: *relief feature,* 5.5 miles east-northeast of Kettenpom along North Fork Eel River (lat. 40°12'10" N, long. 123°22'20" W; sec. 15, T 3 S, R 7 E); the feature is at the mouth of Soldier Creek (2). Named on Shannon Butte (1967) 7.5' quadrangle. Soldiers camped at the place when they were rounding up Indians in the 1860's (Jones, p. 359).

Soldier Creek [MENDOCINO]: *stream,* flows 2.25 miles to Usal Creek 9 miles south of Piercy (lat. 39°50'55" N, long. 123°49'50" W). Named on Hales Grove (1970) 7.5' quadrangle.

Soldier Creek [TRINITY]:

(1) *stream,* flows 4.5 miles to Virgin Creek 8 miles south of Salmon Mountain (lat. 41°04'25" N, long. 123°22'55" W). Named on Trinity Mountain (1979) 7.5' quadrangle.

(2) *stream,* flows 4.5 miles to North Fork Eel River 5.5 miles east-northeast of Kettenpom (lat. 40°12'10" N, long. 123°22'20" W; sec. 15, T 3 S, R 7 E); Soldier Basin is at the mouth of the stream. Named on Ruth Reservoir (1978), Shannon Butte (1967), and Zenia (1967) 7.5' quadrangles.

(3) *stream,* flows 5 miles to Trinity River 12.5 miles northeast of Hayfork (lat. 40°41'25" N, long. 123°01'35" W; sec. 29, T 33 N, R 10 W). Named on Hayfork (1951) 15' quadrangle.

Soldier Frank Hill [MENDOCINO]: *peak,* 15 miles south of Piercy (lat. 39°45'40" N, long. 123°49'55" W; sec. 14, T 22 N, R 18 W); the peak is 0.5 mile northeast of Soldier Frank Point. Altitude 728 feet. Named on Hales Grove (1970) 7.5' quadrangle.

Soldier Frank Point [MENDOCINO]: *promontory,* 15 miles south of Piercy along the coast (lat. 39°45'25" N, long. 123°50'15" W; sec. 14, T 22 N, R 18 W); the feature is 0.5 mile southwest of Soldier Frank Peak. Named on Hales Grove (1970) 7.5' quadrangle.

Soldier Point [MENDOCINO]: *promontory,* less than 1 mile west-southwest of downtown Fort Bragg along the coast (lat. 39°26'25" N, long. 123°49'05" W; sec. 12, T 18 N, R 18 W). Named on Fort Bragg (1960) 7.5' quadrangle. The embayment along the coast at Fort Bragg was known as Soldiers Harbor (United States Coast and Geodetic Survey, p. 142).

Soldiers Grove [HUMBOLDT]: *locality,* 1.25 miles south of Showers Mountain (lat. 40°33'35" N, long. 123°41'40" W; near S line sec. 11, T 2 N, R 4 E). Named on Showers Mountain (1978) 7.5' quadrangle.

Soldiers Harbor: see **Soldier Point** [MENDOCINO].

Soldier Well [DEL NORTE]: *well,* 7 miles northwest of Buck Mountain on Little Rattlesnake Mountain (lat. 41°41'20" N, long. 123°57'40" W; near NW cor. sec. 21, T 15 N, R 2 E). Named on Cant Hook Mountain (1982) 7.5' quadrangle.

Solomon Peak [TRINITY]: *peak,* 13 miles south-southeast of Black Rock Mountain on Trinity-Tehama County line (lat. 40°01'15" N, long. 122°57'15" W; sec. 15, T 25 N, R 10 W). Altitude 7581 feet. Named on Yolla Bolly (1954) 15' quadrangle.

Somerville Creek [HUMBOLDT]: *stream,* flows 3 miles to Redwood Creek (2) 5.5 miles west of Garberville at Briceland (lat. 40°06'30" N, long. 123°53'45" W; sec. 18, T 4 S, R 3 E). Named on Briceland (1969) 7.5' quadrangle.

Somes Mountain [HUMBOLDT]: *peak,* 3 miles north of Orleans Mountain on Humboldt-Siskiyou County line (lat. 41°19'10" N, long. 123°27'50" W); the peak is at the head of Somes Creek. Altitude 5305 feet. Named on Orleans Mountain (1974) 7.5' quadrangle.

Sonoma Creek [HUMBOLDT]: *stream,* flows 3.25 miles to Eel River 6.5 miles east of Weott (lat. 40°18'50" N, long. 123°48'05" W; near S line sec. 2, T 2 S, R 3 E). Named on Myers Flat (1969) 7.5' quadrangle.

Sotsin Point [HUMBOLDT]: *promontory,* 1.25 miles southeast of Trinidad along the coast (lat. 41°02'50" N, long. 124°07'25" W; sec. 25, T 8 N, R 1 W). Named on Crannell (1966) 7.5' quadrangle.

South Bay [HUMBOLDT]: *bay;* the southernmost part of Humboldt Bay. Named on Cannibal Island (1959) and Fields Landing (1959) 7.5' quadrangles.

South Bay Station: see **Fields Landing** [HUMBOLDT].

South Channel [HUMBOLDT]: *channel,* joins Hookton Channel nearly 1.5 miles north-northwest of Fields Landing (lat. 40°44'30" N, long. 124°13'35" W); the feature heads near Southport Landing. Named on Fields Landing (1959) 7.5' quadrangle.

South Dobbyn Creek [HUMBOLDT-TRINITY]: *stream,* heads in Trinity County and flows 10 miles to join North Dobbyn Creek and form Dobbyn Creek 3 miles north of Alderpoint in Humboldt County (lat. 40°13'20" N, long. 123°36'05" W; sec. 10, T 3 S, R 5 E). Named on Alderpoint (1969) 7.5' quadrangle.

South Eel River: see **Eel River** [HUMBOLDT-LAKE-MENDOCINO-TRINITY].

South Fork [HUMBOLDT]: *locality,* 1.5 miles north of Weott along Northwestern Pacific Railroad (lat. 40°20'40" N, long. 123°54'50" W; sec. 26, T 1 S, R 2 E); the place is 1 mile south of the confluence of Eel River with its South Fork. Named on Weott (1969) 7.5' quadrangle. The railroad station at the place first was called Dyerville for the nearby locality, but the name was changed to South Fork for South Fork Eel River (Gudde, 1969, p. 317). Postal authorities established South Fork post office in 1861, discontinued it in 1862, reestablished it in 1933 when Dyerville post office was destroyed by a flood, and discontinued it in 1965 (Salley, p. 208).

South Fork [MENDOCINO]: *locality,* 13 miles north-northwest of Comptche along California Western Railroad (lat. 39°25'30" N, long. 123°43'30" W; sec. 14, T 18 N, R 17 W). Named on Comptche (1960) 15' quadrangle.

South Fork: see **Smith River** [DEL NORTE].

South Fork Camp [MENDOCINO]: *locality,* 3.25 miles northeast of Comptche (lat. 39°18' N, long. 123°33' W; near W line sec. 28, T 17 N, R 15 W); the place is along Big River about 1.25 miles downstream from the mouth of South Fork Big River. Named on Comptche (1960) 15' quadrangle.

South Fork Mountain [HUMBOLDT-TRINITY]: *ridge,* south-southwest- to southwest-trending, 37 miles long, on Humboldt-Trinity County line, mainly in Trinity County. Named on Redding (1958) 1° x 2° quadrangle.

South Kelsey Peak [TRINITY]: *peak,* 7.5 miles west of Black Rock Mountain (lat. 40°12'15" N, long. 123°08'45" W; sec. 7, T 27 N, R 11 W); the peak is 1 mile east-southeast of North Kelsey Peak. Named on Black Rock Mountain (1954) 15' quadrangle. The name commemorates Samuel Kelsey, an early explorer and guide in the region (Jones, p. 366).

South Leggett [MENDOCINO]: *settlement,* 1 mile south-southeast of Leggett (lat. 39°51' N, long. 123°42'15" W; sec. 14, T 23 N, R 17 W). Named on Leggett (1969) 7.5' quadrangle.

Southmayd Ridge [HUMBOLDT]: *ridge,* generally west-trending, 3.5 miles long, 8 miles east of Cape Mendocino (lat. 40°26'15" N, long. 124°15'15" W). Named on Capetown (1969) and Taylor Peak (1969) 7.5' quadrangles.

South Mickey Ridge [TRINITY]: *ridge*, east-southeast-trending, 1.5 miles long, 7.5 miles south-southwest of Black Rock Mountain (lat. 40°06'15" N, long. 123°03' W; mainly in sec. 13, T 26 N, R 11 W); the ridge is 1 mile south of North Mickey Ridge. Named on Black Rock Mountain (1954) 15' quadrangle.

South Peak [LAKE]: *peak*, 3.5 miles east of Kelseyville (lat. 38°58'10" N, long. 122°46'15" W; on N line sec. 20, T 13 N, R 8 W). Named on Kelseyville (1959) 7.5' quadrangle.

Southport Landing [HUMBOLDT]: *locality*, 2.5 miles southwest of Fields Landing (lat. 40°41'40" N, long. 124°14'50" W; at S line sec. 25, T 4 N, R 2 W). Named on Fields Landing (1959) 7.5' quadrangle. Called Meyers Landing on Rohnerville (1920) 15' quadrangle, but United States Board on Geographic Names (1940, p. 39) rejected the names "Meyers Landing" and "Heneys Landing" for the place. Coy (1929, p. 200, 223) used the forms "Myers Landing" and "Myer's Landing" for the name. The name "Myers" was from Jacob Myers, a prominent citizen of the Humboldt Bay neighborhood in the 1850's (Turner, p. 154).

South Rainbow Peak [HUMBOLDT]: *peak*, 9.5 miles south of Scotia and 4.25 miles southeast of Rainbow Peak (lat. 40°20'40" N, long. 124°06'55" W; near NW cor. sec. 31, T 1 S, R 1 E); the peak is on Rainbow Ridge. Named on Bull Creek (1969) 7.5' quadrangle.

South Red Mountain [DEL NORTE]: *ridge*, generally southeast-trending, 1.5 mile long, 6.5 miles east of Klamath Glen (lat. 41°29'45" N, long. 123°52' W). Named on Ah Pah ridge (1983), Blue Creek Mountain (1982), and Klamath Glen (1982) 7.5' quadrangles.

South Ridge [LAKE]: *ridge*, southeast- to east-trending, less than 1 mile long, 5 miles west of Bear Mountain (lat. 39°25'05" N, long. 122°35' W; sec. 16, T 18 N, R 10 W); the feature is 1 mile south of North Ridge (1). Named on Lake Pillsbury (1967) 7.5' quadrangle.

South Ridge [MENDOCINO]: *ridge*, south-southeast-trending, 0.5 mile long, 6.25 miles north-northeast of Boonville (lat. 39°05'45" N, long. 123°20'30" W); the feature is south of North Ridge. Named on Boonville (1959) 15' quadrangle.

South Siskiyou Fork: see **Smith River** [DEL NORTE] (1).

South Spit [HUMBOLDT]: *peninsula*, extends for 4 miles south-southwest from the entrance to Humboldt Bay, where it separates the south part of Humboldt Bay from the sea; center 2 miles west of Fields Landing (lat. 40°43'45" N, long. 124°15' W). Named on Cannibal Island (1959), Eureka (1958), and Fields Landing (1959) 7.5' quadrangles.

South Twin Gulch [TRINITY]: *canyon*, drained by a stream that flows 1 mile to Trinity River 20 miles northeast of Weaverville (lat. 40°56'40" N, long. 122°41'15" W; near SE cor. sec. 29, T 36 N, R 7 W); the mouth of the canyon is 600 feet south of the mouth of North Twin Gulch. Named on Schell Mountain (1950) 15' quadrangle.

South Willow Creek Camp [LAKE]: *locality*, 6.5 miles west of Lakeport (lat. 39°03'50" N, long. 123°02'05" W; near N line sec. 23, T 14 N, R 11 W); the place is along a branch of Willow Creek (2). Named on Purdys Gardens (1958) 7.5' quadrangle.

Spanish Creek [HUMBOLDT]: *stream*, flows 2.25 miles to the sea 10 miles south of Petrolia (lat. 40°11' N, long. 124°15'20" W; sec. 26, T 3 S, R 2 W). Named on Cooskie Creek (1969) and Shubrick Peak (1969) 7.5' quadrangles.

Spanish Creek [LAKE]: *stream*, formed by the confluence of East Fork and West Fork, flows 1.5 miles to North Fork Cache Creek 11 miles north-northeast of Clearlake Oaks (lat. 39°10'10" N, long. 122°36'55" W; near N line sec. 10, T 15 N, R 7 W); the stream is east of Spanish Ridge. Named on Clearlake Oaks (1960) 15' quadrangle. East Fork is 2.5 miles long, and West Fork is 3 miles long; both forks are named on Clearlake Oaks (1960) 15' quadrangle.

Spanish Creek [MENDOCINO]: *stream*, flows 2 miles to Brush Creek 4.5 miles north of the village of Point Arena (lat. 38°58'20" N, long. 123°40'30" W; sec. 19, T 13 N, R 16 W). Named on Point Arena (1960) 7.5' quadrangle.

Spanish Flat [HUMBOLDT]: *area*, 9.5 miles south of Petrolia along the coast (lat. 40°11'20" N, long. 124°15'45" W; sec. 23, T 3 S, R 2 W); the place is northwest of the mouth of Spanish Creek. Named on Cooskie Creek (1969) 7.5' quadrangle. The name is from a legend concerning Spanish treasure hidden in a cave near the place (Turner, p. 202).

Spanish Ridge [HUMBOLDT]: *ridge*, west-trending, nearly 2 miles long, 8 miles west-southwest of Honeydew (lat. 40°12'10" N, long. 124°15'30" W). Named on Cooskie Creek (1969) and Shubrick Peak (1969) 7.5' quadrangles.

Spanish Ridge [LAKE]: *ridge*, south-southeast-trending, 3.5 miles long, 12 miles north of Clearlake Oaks (lat. 39°11'30" N, long. 122°38'30" W); the feature is west of Spanish Creek. Named on Clearlake Oaks (1960) 15' quadrangle.

Specimen Creek [TRINITY]: *stream*, flows nearly 2 miles to Grizzly Creek 7.25 miles south of Cecilville, which is in Siskiyou County (lat. 41°02'20" N, long. 123°06'30" W). Named on Thompson Peak (1979) 7.5' quadrangle.

Spiers Springs: see **Bonanza Springs** [LAKE].

Spike Buck Creek [HUMBOLDT]: *stream*, flows 2.5 miles to Barney Creek 11 miles south of the settlement of Willow Creek (lat. 40°46'50" N, long. 123°38'30" W); the stream heads near Spike Buck Mountain. Named on Grouse Mountain (1979) 7.5' quadrangle.

Spike Buck Gulch [TRINITY]: *canyon*, drained by a stream that flows 2 miles to Mumbo Creek 13 miles north-northeast of Trinity Center (lat. 41°10'30" N, long. 122°34'45" W; near N line sec. 8, T 38 N, R 6 W). Named on Bonanza King (1955) 15' quadrangle.

Spike Buck Mountain [HUMBOLDT]: *peak*, 11.5 miles south of the settlement of Willow Creek (lat. 40°46'45" N, long. 123°39'55" W; near NE cor. sec. 30, T 5 N, R 4 E). Altitude 5484 feet. Named on Grouse Mountain (1979) 7.5' quadrangle.

Spikenard Creek [LAKE]: *stream*, flows 2 miles to Big Canyon Creek 3 miles northeast of Whispering Pines (lat. 38°51' N, long. 122°40'25" W; sec. 31, T 12 N, R 7 W). Named on Whispering Pines (1958) 7.5' quadrangle.

Split Rock [DEL NORTE]: *promontory*, 3.5 miles south of the mouth of Klamath River along the coast (lat. 41°29'40" N, long. 124°04'25" W; at N line sec. 29, T 13 N, R 1 E). Named on Fern Canyon (1966) 7.5' quadrangle. The name is from a cut on the north face of the promontory (United States Coast and Geodetic Survey, p. 148). Wells' (1946) map shows a relief feature called Alder Butte situated near the coast 1.5 miles south-southeast of Split Rock (lat. 41°28'30" N, long, 124°03'45" W; sec. 33, T 13 N, R 1 E).

Split Rock [LAKE]:
(1) *relief feature*, 2.25 miles west-southwest of Bear Mountain along Rice Fork (lat. 39°23'25" N, long. 122°56'05" W; sec. 25, T 18 N, R 10 W). Named on Lake Pillsbury (1967) 7.5' quadrangle.
(2) *relief feature*, 11.5 miles north-northeast of Clearlake Oaks (lat. 39°10'30" N, long. 122°35'10" W). Named on Clearlake Oaks (1960) 15' quadrangle.

Split Rock [MENDOCINO]: *narrows*, about 5.5 miles northeast of Spyrock (2) along North Fork Eel River (lat. 39°56'20" N, long. 123°22'20" W; sec. 12, T 24 N, R 14 W). Named on Mina (1967) 7.5' quadrangle.

Spooner Creek [MENDOCINO]: *stream*, flows 2 miles to Bottom Creek 15 miles north-northwest of Boonville (lat. 39°12'30" N, long. 123°28'20" W; near NW cor. sec. 31, T 16 N, R 14 W). Named on Boonville (1959) 15' quadrangle.

Sportshaven [TRINITY]: *locality*, 9 miles west-northwest of Forest Glen (lat. 40°25'50" N, long. 123°28'30" W; near SW cor. sec. 26, T 1 N, R 6 E). Named on Sportshaven (1973) 7.5' quadrangle.

Sportsman Creek [MENDOCINO]: *stream*, flows nearly 3 miles to Elk Creek (2) 11 miles east-southeast of Eden Valley (lat. 39°32'40" N, long. 123°00'55" W; at W line sec. 31, T 20 N, R 10 W). Named on Sanhedrin Mountain (1966) 7.5' quadrangle. The canyon of the stream is called Dead Horse Canyon on Eden Valley (1952) 15' quadrangle, but United States Board on Geographic Names (1969a, p. 4) rejected this name and the name "Mendenhall Creek" for the stream.

Sportsman Glade [MENDOCINO]: *relief feature*, 11 miles southeast of Eden Valley (lat. 39°31'35" N, long. 123°01'40" W; near S line sec. 1, T 19 N, R 11 W). Named on Sanhedrin Mountain (1966) 7.5' quadrangle.

Spot Creek [TRINITY]: *stream*, flows less than 1 mile to South Fork Trinity River 4 miles southeast of Forest Glen (lat. 40°19'45" N, long. 123°16'25" W; at S line sec. 33, T 1 S, R 8 E). Named on Forest Glen (1979) 7.5' quadrangle.

Spotted Rock [HUMBOLDT]: *relief feature*, about 2.5 miles north-northeast of Showers Mountain (lat. 40°36'50" N, long. 123°40'25" W; sec. 25, T 3 N, R 4 E). Named on Showers Mountain (1978) 7.5' quadrangle.

Spring Camp [MENDOCINO]: *locality*, 4.25 miles south of Eden Valley (lat. 39°33'50" N, long. 123°10'25" W; sec. 27, T 20 N, R 12 W). Named on Brushy Mountain (1966) 7.5' quadrangle. United States Board on Geographic Names (1992, p. 4) approved the name "Summer Camp" for the place.

Spring Creek [HUMBOLDT]: *stream*, flows 1.25 miles to Trinity River 1.5 miles north-northwest of Hoopa (lat. 41°04'15" N, long. 123°41'30" W; sec. 14, T 8 N, R 4 E). Named on Hoopa (1979) 7.5' quadrangle.

Spring Creek [MENDOCINO]: *stream*, flows 1.5 miles to Tenmile Creek 11.5 southeast of Leggett (lat. 39°46'05" N, long. 123°32'35" W; at N line sec. 16, T 22 N, R 15 W). Named on Tan Oak Park (1969) 7.5' quadrangle.

Spring Creek: see **Spring Gulch** [TRINITY] (2).

Springer Flat [LAKE]: *area*, 6.5 miles north-northeast of Clearlake Oaks along Wolf Creek (lat. 39°06'35" N, long. 122°37'50" W; near E line sec. 33, T 15 N, R 7 W). Named on Clearlake Oaks (1958) 7.5' quadrangle.

Spring Gulch [TRINITY]:
(1) *canyon*, drained by a stream that flows less than 1 mile to Coffee Creek 5.5 miles north-northwest of Trinity Center (lat. 41°05' N, long. 122°43'30" W; near W line sec. 7, T 37 N, R 7 W). Named on Bonanza King (1955) 15' quadrangle.
(2) *canyon*, drained by a stream that flows about 3.5 miles to Indian Creek (2) 9.5 miles south-southeast of Weaverville (lat. 40°36'20" N, long. 122°52'05" W; near N line sec. 27, T 32 N, R 9 W). Named on Weaverville

(1950) 15' quadrangle. Miller's (1890) map shows Spring Cr. in the canyon.

(3) *canyon,* drained by a stream that flows 1.5 miles to Browns Creek 13 miles south of Weaverville (lat. 40°32'35" N, long. 122°56' W; near SE cor. sec. 12, T 31 N, R 10 W). Named on Weaverville (1950) 15' quadrangle.

Spring Prairie [HUMBOLDT]:

(1) *area,* 5 miles south of Coyote Peak (lat. 41°03'45" N, long. 123°51'50" W; near SW cor. sec. 20, T 8 N, R 3 E). Named on Hupa Mountain (1982) 7.5' quadrangle.

(2) *area,* 6.25 miles south-southeast of Korbel (lat. 40°47'15" N, long. 123°54'25" W; near W line sec. 25, T 5 N, R 2 E). Named on Korbel (1979) 7.5' quadrangle.

Spring Rock [TRINITY]: *relief feature,* 7.5 miles south of Black Rock Mountain (lat. 40°05'40" N, long. 122°59'50" W; near N line sec. 21, T 26 N, R 10 W). Named on Yolla Bolly (1954) 15' quadrangle.

Springs: see **The Springs** [HUMBOLDT].

Springtime Flat [TRINITY]: *area,* 12.5 miles southeast of Hyampom (lat. 40°30'45" N, long. 123°15'10" W; sec. 29, T 31 N, R 12 W). Named on Hyampom (1951) 15' quadrangle.

Spring Valley Creek [HUMBOLDT]: *stream,* flows 1 mile to Showers Creek 1.25 miles north-northwest of Showers Mountain (lat. 40°35'40" N, long. 123°42'35" W; sec. 34, T 3 N, R 4 E). Named on Showers Mountain (1978) 7.5' quadrangle.

Springville: see **Fortuna** [HUMBOLDT].

Sproul Creek [HUMBOLDT]: *stream,* flows 7.5 miles to South Fork Eel River 2.5 miles southwest of Garberville (lat. 40°04'10" N, long. 123°49'35" W; sec. 34, T 4 S, R 3 E). Named on Garberville (1970) 7.5' quadrangle. Called Sprowl Creek on Garberville (1949) 15' quadrangle, called Sproule Creek on Briceland (1921) 15' quadrangle, and called Sprout Cr. on Vander Leck's (1920b) map. United States Board on Geographic Names (1973b, p. 3) gave the names "Sprowell Creek" and "Sprowl Creek" as variants; the name commemorates brothers Atwood Sproul and Gilbert Sproul, pioneers in the neighborhood. West Fork enters from the west 3.5 miles upstream from the mouth of the main creek; it is 5.25 miles long and is named on Briceland (1969) and Garberville (1970) 7.5' quadrangles.

Sproul Creek: see **Little Sproul Creek** [HUMBOLDT].

Sproule Creek: see **Sproul Creek** [HUMBOLDT].

Sprout Creek: see **Sproul Creek** [HUMBOLDT].

Sprowell Creek: see **Sproul Creek** [HUMBOLDT].

Sprowl Creek: see **Sproul Creek** [HUMBOLDT].

Spruce Acres [HUMBOLDT]: *locality,* 5.5 miles south-southwest of Orick (lat. 41°12'45" N, long. 124°06'10" W). Named on Eureka (1958) 1° x 2° quadrangle.

Spruce Canyon [LAKE]: *canyon,* drained by a stream that flows 2.25 miles to Scotts Creek 4.5 miles west of Lakeport (lat. 39°03'45" N, long. 123°00' W; sec. 17, T 14 N, R 10 W); the upper part of the canyon is west of Spruce Ridge. Named on Purdys Gardens (1958) 7.5' quadrangle.

Spruce Creek [DEL NORTE]: *stream,* flows 1.25 miles to Hunter Creek 1.25 miles east of the mouth of Klamath River (lat. 41°32'55" N, long. 124°03'25" W; sec. 4, T 13 N, R 1 E). Named on Requa (1966) 7.5' quadrangle.

Spruce Grove [HUMBOLDT]: *peak,* 7 miles south-southwest of Alderpoint (lat. 40°05'35" N, long. 123°40'45" W; near S line sec. 24, T 4 S, R 4 E). Altitude 3082 feet. Named on Harris (1969) 7.5' quadrangle. On Alderpoint (1949) 15' quadrangle, the name applies to a locality near the peak.

Spruce Grove: see **Harris** [HUMBOLDT]; **Spruce Grove Campground** [MENDOCINO].

Spruce Grove Campground [MENDOCINO]: *locality,* 4 miles north of Hull Mountain (lat. 39°34'55" N, long. 122°56'05" W; at S line sec. 14, T 20 N, R 10 W). Named on Hull Mountain (1967) 7.5' quadrangle. Hull Mountain (1952) 15' quadrangle shows a place called Spruce Grove situated near present Spruce Grove Campground.

Spruce Point [HUMBOLDT]:

(1) *ridge,* north-northwest-trending, 0.5 mile long, 1.5 miles northeast of Fields Landing (lat. 40°44'25" N, long. 124°11'40" W; at SW cor. sec. 9, T 4 N, R 1 W). Named on Fortuna (1944) 15' quadrangle.

(2) *locality,* 1.5 miles northeast of Fields Landing (lat. 40°44'35" N, long. 124°11'50" W; near E line sec. 8, T 4 N, R 1 W); the place is near Spruce Point (1). Named on Fields Landing (1959) 7.5' quadrangle.

Spruce Ridge [LAKE]: *ridge,* north-trending, nearly 1 mile long, 5.5 miles west of Lakeport (lat. 39°03'25" N, long. 123°01'05" W; sec. 24, T 14 N, R 11 W); the ridge is east of the upper part of Spruce Canyon. Named on Purdys Gardens (1958) 7.5' quadrangle.

Spyrock [MENDOCINO]:

(1) *relief feature,* 1 mile south-southeast of Spyrock (2) near Eel River (lat. 39°51'55" N, long. 123°26'15" W; near SE cor. sec. 8, T 23 N, R 14 W). Named on Iron Peak (1967) 7.5' quadrangle. Indians sent smoke signals from the place in the early days (Hoover, Rensch, and Rensch, p. 198).

(2) *locality,* 14 miles east of Leggett along Northwestern Pacific Railroad (lat. 39°52'45" N, long. 123°26'35" W; sec. 32, T 24 N, R 14 W); the place is 1 mile north-northwest of Spyrock (1). Named on Updegraff Ridge (1967) 7.5' quadrangle. O'Brien's (1953) map has the form "Spy Rock" for the name. Postal authorities established Spyrock post office in 1910, discontinued it in 1911, reestablished it in 1915, and discontinued it in 1967 (Salley, p. 211). They established Bentley post office 4.5 miles north of Spyrock post office in 1939, moved it 0.75 mile west in 1940, and discontinued it that same year (Salley, p. 19).

Squashan Creek [HUMBOLDT]: *stream,* flows 2.5 miles to the sea 7.25 miles north of Orick (lat. 41°23'20" N, long. 124°04'10" W; sec. 33, T 12 N, R 1 E). Named on Fern Canyon (1966) and Orick (1966) 7.5' quadrangles. Gudde (1949, p. 341) called the feature Squash Ann Creek, and noted that the name is of Indian origin.

Squaw Camp [TRINITY]: *locality,* 11.5 miles north-northeast of Hayfork (lat. 40°42'50" N, long. 123°07'50" W). Named on Hayfork (1951) 15' quadrangle.

Squaw Creek [HUMBOLDT]:

(1) *stream,* flows 3.5 miles to Lindsay Creek 5 miles north-northeast of Arcata (lat. 40°56'05" N, long. 124°02'10" W; sec. 2, T 6 N, R 1 E). Named on Arcata North (1959) and Blue Lake (1979) 7.5' quadrangles.

(2) *stream,* flows 3.5 miles to Bull Creek (2) 4 miles west-northwest of Weott (lat. 40°20'55" N, long. 123°59'15" W; at E line sec. 30, T 1 S, R 2 E). Named on Bull Creek (1969) 7.5' quadrangle.

(3) *stream,* flows 11.5 miles to Mattole River 16 miles south-southwest of Scotia (lat. 40°16'05" N, long. 124°13'30" W; sec. 30, T 2 S, R 1 W). Named on Buckeye Mountain (1970) and Shubrick Peak (1969) 7.5' quadrangles.

(4) *stream,* flows 4.5 miles to East Branch of South Fork Eel River 10.5 miles southwest of Alderpoint (lat. 40°03'55" N, long. 123°44'20" W; near S line sec. 33, T 4 S, R 4 E). Named on Harris (1969) 7.5' quadrangle.

Squaw Creek [MENDOCINO]: *stream,* flows 1 mile to Rattlesnake Creek (2) 4.25 miles southeast of Leggett (lat. 39°49'50" N, long. 123°38'50" W; sec. 20, T 23 N, R 16 W). Named on Leggett (1969) 7.5' quadrangle.

Squaw Creek [TRINITY]: *stream,* flows 1 mile to New River 10.5 miles north-northeast of Burnt Ranch (lat. 40°56'30" N, long. 123°23' W). Named on Ironside Mountain (1951) 15' quadrangle.

Squaw Creek: see **Squaw Gulch** [TRINITY].

Squaw Creek Ridge [HUMBOLDT]: *ridge,* generally north-trending, 2.25 miles long, 11.5 miles south-southeast of Scotia (lat. 40°19'45" N, long. 124°00'35" W). Named on Bull Creek (1969) 7.5' quadrangle.

Squaw Flat [TRINITY]: *area,* 14 miles south of Weaverville (lat. 40°31'30" N, long. 122°57' W; near W line sec. 24, T 31 N, R 10 W). Named on Weaverville (1950) 15' quadrangle.

Squaw Gulch [TRINITY]: *canyon,* drained by a stream that flows 2.5 miles to East Fork of North Fork Trinity River 6 miles north of Helena (lat. 40°51'45" N, long. 123°08' W; sec. 29, T 35 N, R 11 W). Named on Helena (1951) 15' quadrangle. Miller's (1890) map has the name "Squaw Cr." for the stream in the canyon.

Squaw Opening [MENDOCINO]: *area,* 14 miles north of Boonville along Gates Creek (lat. 39°12'30" N, long. 123°25'15" W; at N line sec. 33, T 16 N, R 14 W). Named on Boonville (1959) 15' quadrangle.

Squaw Prairie [HUMBOLDT]: *area,* 3.25 miles south-southwest of Coyote Peak (lat. 41°05'15" N, long. 123°52'55" W; sec. 18, T 8 N, R 3 E). Named on Panther Creek (1982) 7.5' quadrangle.

Squaw Rock [MENDOCINO]:

(1) *relief feature,* 7 miles west-southwest of Ornbaun Valley (lat. 38°52'10" N, long. 123°25'10" W; sec. 21, T 12 N, R 14 W). Named on Ornbaun Valley (1960) 15' quadrangle.

(2) *relief feature,* 5.25 miles southeast of Hopland on the west side of Russian River (lat. 38°54'45" N, long. 123°03'15" W; near S line sec. 2, T 12 N, R 11 W). Named on Hopland (1960) 7.5' quadrangle. The feature, which also is called Lover's Leap, is associated with an Indian legend (Hoover, Rensch, and Rensch, p. 196).

Squaw Rock Slide [MENDOCINO]: *relief feature,* 5.25 miles southeast of Hopland on the west side of Russian River (lat. 38°54'45" N, long. 123°03' W; near S line sec. 2, T 12 N, R 11 W); the feature is across Russian River from Squaw Rock (2). Named on Hopland (1960) 7.5' quadrangle.

Squaw Tit [HUMBOLDT]: *peak,* 7.5 miles west-southwest of Coyote Peak (lat. 41°04'25" N, long. 123°58'50" W; near SW cor. sec. 17, T 8 N, R 2 E). Altitude 2105 feet. Named on Panther Creek (1982) 7.5' quadrangle.

Squaw Valley: see **Big Squaw Valley** [LAKE]; **Little Squaw Valley** [LAKE].

Squaw Valley Creek [LAKE]: *stream,* flows 3.25 miles to Lake Pillsbury 2.5 miles northwest of Bear Mountain (lat. 39°26'10" N, long. 122°56'05" W; at N line sec. 12, T 18 N, R 10 W); the stream goes through Big Squaw Valley. Named on Lake Pillsbury (1967) 7.5' quadrangle.

Squirrel Creek [TRINITY]: *stream,* flows 4.5 miles to the canyon of Trinity River 22 miles northeast of Weaverville (lat. 40°58'45" N, long. 122°40' W; at W line sec. 15, T 36 N, R 7 W). Named on Bonanza King (1955) and Schell Mountain (1950) 15' quadrangles.

Squirrel Creek: see **Squirrel Gulch** [TRINITY].

Squirrel Flat [TRINITY]: *area,* 2.25 miles east of Trinity Center (lat. 41°00'25" N, long. 122°38'45" W; near W line sec. 2, T 36 N, R 7 W); the place is along Squirrel Creek at the mouth of Squirrel Gulch. Named on Bonanza King (1955) 15' quadrangle.

Squirrel Gulch [TRINITY]: *canyon,* drained by a stream that flows 4 miles to Squirrel Creek 2.25 miles east of Trinity Center (lat. 41°00'20" N, long. 122°38'50" W; at W line sec. 2, T 36 N, R 7 W). Named on Bonanza King (1955) 15' quadrangle. On Etna (1934) 30' quadrangle, the stream in the canyon is called Squirrel Creek.

Squirrel Tail Ridge [HUMBOLDT]: *ridge,* generally southwest-trending, 1.5 miles long, 11 miles east of the town of Blue Lake (lat. 40°52'30" N, long. 123°46'50" W). Named on Lord-Ellis Summit (1973) and Maple Creek (1977) 7.5' quadrangles.

Stafford [HUMBOLDT]: *village,* 3 miles southeast of Scotia on the south side of Eel River (lat. 40°27'15" N, long. 124°03'20" W; sec. 22, T 1 N, R 1 E). Named on Scotia (1970) 7.5' quadrangle. The community began in 1895 or 1896 and was named for Judge Cyrus G. Stafford; the place also was called Brown's Mill and Brown's Camp, for Percy Brown, owner of a lumber plant there in 1908 (Turner, p. 203).

Stag Canyon [LAKE]: *canyon,* drained by a stream that flows 1.25 miles to Cache Creek 4.5 miles northeast of the town of Lower Lake (lat. 38°57'15" N, long. 122°32'55" W). Named on Lower Lake (1958) 7.5' quadrangle.

Stanley Creek [HUMBOLDT]: *stream,* flows 2 miles to Mattole River 9.5 miles southwest of Garberville (lat. 40°01' N, long. 123°56'05" W). Named on Briceland (1969) 7.5' quadrangle.

Stanley Creek [MENDOCINO]:

(1) *stream,* flows 5 miles to South Fork Eel River 0.5 mile southwest of Piercy (lat. 39°57'35" N, long. 123°48' W; near SE cor. sec. 1, T 24 N, R 18 W). Named on Piercy (1969) 7.5' quadrangle.

(2) *stream,* flows 1.5 miles to North Fork Ten Mile River 6.5 miles southeast of Branscomb (lat. 39°35'15" N, long. 123°32'35" W; sec. 17, T 20 N, R 15 W). Named on Sherwood Peak (1967) 7.5' quadrangle.

Stansberry Creek [HUMBOLDT]: *stream,* flows nearly 2 miles to Mattole River 3.5 miles southwest of Petrolia (lat. 40°17'20" N, long. 124°20' W; near S line sec. 18, T 2 S, R 2 W). Named on Petrolia (1969) 7.5' quadrangle.

Stansbury Spring [MENDOCINO]: *spring,* 9.5 miles west of Ornbaun Valley (lat. 38°56'15" N, long. 123°28'45" W; sec. 1, T 12 N, R 15 W). Named on Ornbaun Valley (1960) 15' quadrangle.

Stanton Creek [LAKE]: *stream,* flows 5.5 miles to North Fork Cache Creek 10.5 miles northeast of Clearlake Oaks (lat. 39°07'45" N, long. 122°32'15" W; near W line sec. 21, T 15 N, R 6 W). Named on Clearlake Oaks (1960) 15' quadrangle.

Stanton Glade [LAKE]: *area,* 15 miles north-northeast of Clearlake Oaks (lat. 39°12'05" N, long. 122°31'35" W); the place is at the head of Stanton Creek. Named on Clearlake Oaks (1960) 15' quadrangle.

Stapp Creek [MENDOCINO]: *stream,* flows less than 1 mile to Tenmile Creek 8 miles northeast of Branscomb (lat. 39°43'55" N, long. 123°30'40" W; near W line sec. 26, T 22 N, R 15 W). Named on Cahto Peak (1967) 7.5' quadrangle.

Star Creek [TRINITY]: *stream,* flows 1 mile to North Fork Swift Creek (1) 21 miles north-northeast of Weaverville (lat. 40°59'40" N, long. 122°43'45" W; sec. 12, T 36 N, R 8 W). Named on Schell Mountain (1950) 15' quadrangle.

Star Gulch [TRINITY]: *canyon,* drained by a stream that flows 1 mile to Middle Fork Kingsbury Gulch 4 miles southeast of Hayfork (lat. 40°30'55" N, long. 123°07'30" W). Named on Hayfork (1951) 15' quadrangle.

Star Mountain [TRINITY]: *peak,* 11.5 miles southeast of Dubakella Mountain on Trinity-Tehama County line (lat. 40°15'30" N, long. 123°00'30" W; on W line sec. 21, T 28 N, R 10 W). Named on Chanchelulla Peak (1951) and Dubakella Mountain (1954) 15' quadrangles.

Star Rock [DEL NORTE]: *rock,* 5.5 miles west-northwest of Crescent City, and 2 miles offshore at Point Saint George (lat. 41°46'30" N, long. 124°17'20" W). Named on Eureka (1958) 1° x 2° quadrangle. A water-covered ledge called Mansfield Break is located nearly 3.5 miles northwest of Star Rock and is about 100 yards in extent; a water-covered ledge called Brother Jonathan Rock, or Jonathan Rock, is situated 2.5 miles northwest of Star Rock—it was named for the steamer *Brother Jonathan,* which was wrecked there in 1865 (Gudde, 1969, p. 39; United States Coast and Geodetic Survey, p. 149-150).

Starvation Flat [TRINITY]: *area,* 8 miles east of Weaverville along Trinity River (lat. 40°45' N, long. 122°47' W); water of Lewiston Lake now partly covers the place. Named on Trinity Lake (1950) and Weaverville (1950) 15' quadrangles.

Starvation Opening [HUMBOLDT]: *area,* 5 miles south-southeast of Board Camp Mountain (lat. 40°38' N, long. 123°40'10" W; on S line sec. 13, T 3 N, R 4 E). Named on Board Camp Mountain (1977) 7.5' quadrangle.

Starwein Flat [DEL NORTE]: *area,* 3 miles east-southeast of Klamath Glen on the east side of Klamath River (lat. 41°29'50" N, long. 123°57'45" W; sec. 20, 29, T 13 N, R 2 E). Named on Ah Pah Ridge (1983) and Klamath Glen (1982) 7.5' quadrangles.

Starwein Ridge [DEL NORTE-HUMBOLDT]: *ridge,* generally south-trending, 6 miles long, 5 miles east-southeast of Klamath Glen on Del Norte-Humboldt County line (lat. 41°28' N, long. 123°55'05" W). Named on Ah Pah Ridge (1983) and Klamath Glen (1982) 7.5' quadrangles. The name is from an Indian word (Stewart, G.R., p. 459).

Steamboat Rock [DEL NORTE]: *rock,* just south of Crescent City, and 0.5 mile offshore (lat. 41°44'20" N, long. 124°11'55" W). Named on Sister Rocks (1966) 7.5' quadrangle.

Steamboat Rock [HUMBOLDT]: *rock,* 1.5 miles south of Cape Mendocino, and 1450 feet offshore (lat. 40°24'55" N, long. 124°24'10" W). Named on Cape Mendocino (1969) 7.5' quadrangle. The upper part of the feature is white and the lower part is black, making the whole resemble a steamship that has a black hull and white upper part (United States Coast and Geodetic Survey, p. 144).

Steel Bench [MENDOCINO]: *area,* 14 miles northeast of Covelo (lat. 39°54'25" N, long. 123°01'35" W; near E line sec. 25, T 24 N, R 11 W). Named on Leech Lake Mountain (1966) 7.5' quadrangle.

Steelhead [HUMBOLDT]: *locality,* nearly 2 miles west-southwest of Alderpoint along Northwestern Pacific Railroad (lat. 40°10'10" N, long. 123°38'40" W; near W line sec. 29, T 3 S, R 5 E); the place is near the mouth of Steelhead Creek. Named on Fort Seward (1969) 7.5' quadrangle.

Steelhead Creek [HUMBOLDT]: *stream,* flows 4.5 miles to Eel River 2 miles west of Alderpoint (lat. 40°10'20" N, long. 123°38'45" W; near W line sec. 29, T 3 S, R 5 E). Named on Fort Seward (1969) 7.5' quadrangle. On Alderpoint (1949) 15' quadrangle, the part of the stream that is above a point 2 miles upstream from its mouth is called South Fork, and an unnamed branch of present Steelhead Creek is considered the main stream.

Steens Landing [MENDOCINO]: *locality,* 6.25 miles northwest of Gualala (lat. 38°49'40" N, long. 123°37' W; sec. 2, T 11 N, R 16 W). Named on Gualala (1960) 7.5' quadrangle.

Steep Gulch [MENDOCINO]: *canyon,* drained by a stream that flows nearly 4 miles to Tenmile Creek 12 miles southeast of Leggett (lat. 39°45'40" N, long. 123°30' W; sec. 16, T 22 N, R 15 W). Named on Tan Oak Park (1969) 7.5' quadrangle.

Steep Gulch: see **Getchell Gulch** [MENDOCINO].

Steep Village [HUMBOLDT]: *locality,* nearly 2 miles west-northwest of Orick along the coast (lat. 41°17'45" N, long. 124°05'25" W; sec. 32, T 11 N, R 1 E). Named on Orick (1952) 15' quadrangle, which indicates Indian ruins at the place.

Steer Creek [TRINITY]: *stream,* flows 1 mile to Swift Creek (1) 20 miles north-northeast of Weaverville (lat. 40°59'50" N, long. 122°49'35" W; sec. 7, T 36 N, R 8 W). Named on Coffee Creek (1955) and Trinity Dam (1950) 15' quadrangles.

Steiner Flat [TRINITY]: *area,* 4.5 miles south-southwest of Weaverville along Trinity River (lat. 40°40'20" N, long. 122°57'50" W; sec. 35, T 33 N, R 10 W). Named on Weaverville (1950) 15' quadrangle. Benjamin Steiner started a ranch at the site in 1850 (Jones, p. 296). The place also was called Steinerville (Hanna, p. 316). United States Board on Geographic Names (1972b, p. 3) approved the name "Lorenz Gulch" for a ravine that trends south-southwest for 1 mile to Steiner Flat. Gudde (1975, p. 322) listed a mining place of 1850 called Slate Bar that was on the north side of Trinity River west of Steiner Flat.

Steinerville: see **Steiner Flat** [TRINITY].

Stemple Canyon [LAKE]: *canyon,* drained by a stream that flows 3 miles to Cache Creek 1 mile northwest of Wilson Valley (2) (lat. 38°59'10" N, long. 122°29' W). Named on Wilbur Springs (1961) 15' quadrangle, and on Wilson Valley (1958) 7.5' quadrangle.

Stephens Creek: see **Idlewild** [DEL NORTE].

Stetson Creek [TRINITY]: *stream,* flows 1.5 miles to Trinity River 3.5 miles east-southeast of Burnt Ranch (lat. 40°47'05" N, long. 123°25' W). Named on Ironside Mountain (1951) 15' quadrangle.

Steveale Creek [TRINITY]: *stream,* flows 1.5 miles to South Fork Coffee Creek 8.5 miles west of Billys Peak (1) (lat. 41°08'45" N, long. 123°55'05" W; sec. 17, T 38 N, R 9 W); the stream heads at Steveale Meadow. Named on Coffee Creek (1955) 15' quadrangle.

Steveale Meadow [TRINITY]: *area,* 8 miles west-northwest of Billys Peak (1) (lat. 41°09'45" N, long. 122°54'50" W; sec. 8, T 38 N, R 9 W). Named on Coffee Creek (1955) 15' quadrangle.

Stevens Camp [DEL NORTE]: *locality,* 2.25 miles east-northeast of Broken Rib Mountain (lat. 41°53'50" N, long. 123°38'45" W). Named on Broken Rib Mountain (1982) 7.5' quadrangle.

Stevens Creek [HUMBOLDT]: *stream,* flows 4 miles to Grizzly Creek 6.5 miles north-northeast of Redcrest (lat. 40°29'30" N, long. 123°54'20" W; near SW cor. sec. 1, T 1 N, R 2 E). Named on Owl Creek (1979) 7.5' quadrangle.

Stevens Mountain [DEL NORTE]: *peak,* 1 mile north-northwest of Harrington Mountain (lat. 41°41'10" N, long. 123°41'25" W). Named on Prescott Mountain (1981) 7.5' quadrangle. Officials of the Forest Service named the feature for Phil Stevens, who drove a stage between Crescent City and Grants Pass, Oregon (Gudde, 1969, p. 321).

Stevens Prairie [DEL NORTE]: *area,* 7.5 miles east-southeast of Klamath Glen (lat. 41°28'30" N, long. 123°51'30" W). Named on Blue Creek Mountain (1982) 7.5' quadrangle.

Stewart Creek [MENDOCINO]: *stream,* flows 3 miles to North Fork Gualala River 9 miles southwest of Ornbaun Valley (lat. 38°49'05" N, long. 123°25'20" W; near NE cor. sec. 9, T 11 N, R 14 W). Named on Ornbaun Valley (1960) 15' quadrangle.

Stewart Creek: see **Mills Creek** [MENDOCINO]; **Stuart Fork** [TRINITY].

Stewart Ridge [HUMBOLDT]: *ridge,* southwest-trending, 1.5 miles long, 4.5 miles east of Honeydew (lat. 40°14'15" N, long. 124°02'05" W). Named on Honeydew (1970) 7.5' quadrangle.

Stewart's Fork: see **Stuart Fork** [TRINITY].

Stick Lake [MENDOCINO]: *intermittent lake,* 250 feet long, 13 miles northeast of Covelo (lat. 39°56'10" N, long. 123°05'05" W; near W line sec. 15, T 24 N, R 11 W). Named on Leech Lake Mountain (1966) 7.5' quadrangle.

Stick Lake Canyon [MENDOCINO]: *canyon,* drained by a stream that flows 3.25 miles to Middle Fork Eel River 16 miles northeast of Covelo (lat. 39°58'40" N, long. 123°05' W; sec. 34, T 25 N, R 11 W); Stick Lake is at the head of a branch of the canyon. Named on Leech Lake Mountain (1966) 7.5' quadrangle.

Stienhart Lakes [LAKE]: *dry lakes,* four, 7.5 miles northeast of Middletown (lat. 38°50'30" N, long. 122°32' W; in and near sec. 32, 33, T 12 N, R 6 W). Named on Middletown (1958) 7.5' quadrangle. On Lower Lake (1945) 15' quadrangle, all but the largest of the four features are shown as intermittent lakes.

Still Creek [DEL NORTE]: *stream,* flows nearly 3 miles to North Fork Smith River 7.25 miles north-northwest of Gasquet (lat. 41°56'50" N, long. 123°59'20" W; near S line sec. 18, T 18 N, R 2 E). Named on Gasquet (1981) and High Divide (1966) 7.5' quadrangles.

Stiller Gulch [TRINITY]: *canyon,* drained by a stream that flows 0.5 mile to East Fork Stuart Fork 14 miles northeast of Weaverville (lat. 40°52'40" N, long. 122°45'50" W; sec. 22, T 35 N, R 8 W). Named on Trinity Lake (1950) 15' quadrangle.

Stillwell Point [MENDOCINO]: *promontory,* 3.5 miles south of Mendocino along the coast (lat. 39°15'10" N, long. 123°47'10" W; sec. 17, T 16 N, R 17 W). Named on Mendocino (1960) 7.5' quadrangle.

Stingley Creek: see **Singley Creek** [HUMBOLDT].

Stitz Creek [HUMBOLDT]: *stream,* flows nearly 4 miles to Eel River 3 miles east-southeast of Scotia (lat. 40°27'40" N, long. 124°03'10" W; at N line sec. 22, T 1 N, R 1 E). Named on Scotia (1970) 7.5' quadrangle.

Stockton Flat [TRINITY]: *area,* 4.25 miles southeast of Forest Glen along South Fork Trinity River (lat. 40°19'40" N, long. 123°16'15" W; near NE cor. sec. 4, T 2 S, R 8 E). Named on Forest Glen (1979) 7.5' quadrangle. The name is from the annual use of the place as a camping spot by a group of hunters from Stockton, California (Jones, p. 373).

Stockton Flat: see **Hoffman Flat** [TRINITY].

Stockton Harbor: see **Shelter Cove** [HUMBOLDT].

Stockton Ridge [TRINITY]: *ridge,* south-trending, 1.5 miles long, 5.5 miles south of Black Rock Mountain (lat. 40°07'30" N, long. 123°01'30" W). Named on Black Rock Mountain (1954) 15' quadrangle.

Stoddard Lake [TRINITY]: *lake,* 1700 feet long, 1.25 miles north-northeast of Billys Peak (1) (lat. 41°09'10" N, long. 122°45'20" W; on W line sec. 14, T 38 N, R 8 W); the lake is 1 mile south of Stoddard Meadow. Named on Coffee Creek (1955) 15' quadrangle.

Stoddard Lake: see **Middle Stoddard Lake**, under **McDonald Lake** [TRINITY].

Stoddard Meadow [TRINITY]: *area,* about 2.25 miles north of Billys Peak (1) (lat. 41°10' N, long. 122°45'30" W; sec. 10, T 38 N, R 8 W). Named on Coffee Creek (1955) 15' quadrangle, which shows Stoddard cabin at the place. The name commemorates John Stoddard, a cattleman and miner who had a ranch along Trinity River near Ripple Creek (Jones, p. 10)).

Stone [HUMBOLDT]: *locality,* 6.5 miles south-southeast of Fortuna along Northwestern Pacific Railroad (lat. 40°30'45" N, long. 134°06'50" W; sec. 31, T 2 N, R 1 E). Named on Hydesville (1979) 7.5' quadrangle.

Stone Corral [DEL NORTE]: *locality,* nearly 7 miles east of the town of Smith River (lat. 41°56' N, long. 124°01' W; at SE cor. sec. 23, T 18 N, R 1 E). Site named on High Divide (1966) 7.5' quadrangle.

Stone Creek [TRINITY]: *stream,* flows 1.5 miles to Browns Creek 3.25 miles south-southeast of Chanchelulla Peak (lat. 40°25'50" N, long. 122°57'4" W; near N line sec. 26, T 30 N, R 10 W); the stream is east of Stone Ridge. Named on Chanchelulla Peak (1951) 15' quadrangle.

Stonehouse [TRINITY]: *locality,* 15 miles north-northeast of Helena along Canyon Creek (1) (lat. 40°58' N, long. 123°01'15" W). Named on Helena (1951) 15' quadrangle.

Stonehouse Gulch [TRINITY]: *canyon,* drained by a stream that flows 1.25 miles to Canyon Creek (1) 14 miles north-northeast of Helena (lat. 40°57'30" N, long. 123°01'15" W); the mouth of the canyon is 0.5 mile downstream along Canyon Creek (1) from Stonehouse. Named on Helena (1951) 15' quadrangle.

Stone Lagoon [HUMBOLDT]: *lake,* 2 miles long, 13 miles north of Trinidad near the coast, and separated from the sea by a sandy beach (lat. 41°14'35" N, long. 124°05'30" W). Named on Orick (1966) and Rodgers Peak (1966) 7.5' quadrangles.

Stone Opening [HUMBOLDT]: *area,* 6.5 miles south-southwest of Garberville (lat. 40°01'30" N, long. 123°49'25" W; sec. 15, T 5 S, R 3 E). Named on Garberville (1970) 7.5' quadrangle.

Stoner Creek [MENDOCINO]: *stream,* flows 3 miles to Eel River 7.5 miles west-southwest of Covelo (lat. 39°45'40" N, long. 123°22'50" W; sec. 13, T 22 N, R 14 W). Named on Covelo West (1967) and Iron Peak (1967) 7.5' quadrangles.

Stone Ridge [TRINITY]: *ridge,* south-southeast-trending, 1.5 miles long, 2 miles south-southeast of Chanchelulla Peak (lat. 40°26'40" N, long. 122°58'50" W; sec. 15, 22, T 30 N, R 10 W); the ridge is west of Stone Creek. Named on Chanchelulla Peak (1951) 15' quadrangle.

Stonewall Pass [TRINITY]: *pass,* 13 miles north of Weaverville (lat. 40°54'45" N, long. 122°53'20" W). Named on Trinity Dam (1950) 15' quadrangle. The name is from a wall of boulders that cattlemen built to keep their stock from drifting across the pass (Jones, p. 12).

Stonewall Pass: see **Little Stonewall Pass** [TRINITY].

Stoney Creek [MENDOCINO]: *stream,* flows 2 miles to Eel River 7.5 miles west-southwest of Covelo (lat. 39°45'05" N, long. 123°22'45" W; near N line sec. 24, T 22 N, R 14 W). Named on Iron Peak (1967) and Laytonville (1967) 7.5' quadrangles.

Stoney Creek [TRINITY]: *stream,* flows 5 miles to Clair Engle Lake 10 miles north-northeast of Weaverville (lat. 40°51'25" N, long. 122°51' W; near S line sec. 26, T 35 N, R 9 W). Named on Trinity Dam (1950) 15' quadrangle.

Stoney Creek Ridge: see **Stoney Ridge** [TRINITY].

Stoney Ridge [TRINITY]: *ridge,* south-southeast-trending, 1.5 miles long, 12 miles north-northeast of Weaverville (lat. 40°53'30" N, long. 122°52'35" W; mainly in sec. 15, T 35 N, R 9 W); the ridge is west of Stoney Creek. Named on Trinity Dam (1950) 15' quadrangle. Called Stoney Cr. Ridge on Averill's (1940) map.

Stony Creek [DEL NORTE]: *stream,* flows 6.25 miles to North Fork Smith River 1 mile north-northwest of Gasquet (lat. 41°51'40" N, long. 123°57'45" W; at W line sec. 16, T 17 N, R 2 E). Named on Gasquet (1951) 15' quadrangle.

Stony Creek [MENDOCINO]: *stream,* flows 2 miles to Eel River 7 miles northeast of Laytonville (lat. 39°45'05" N, long. 123°22'45" W; near N line sec. 24, T 22 N, R 14 W). Named on Iron Peak (1967) and Laytonville (1967) 7.5' quadrangles.

Stony Creek, Middle Fork [LAKE]: *stream,* flows 7.5 miles to Glenn County 2 miles east-southeast of Crockett Peak (lat. 39°25'05" N, long. 122°44'20" W). Named on Crockett Peak (1967) and Saint John Mountain (1968) 7.5' quadrangles.

Stony Top [LAKE]: *relief feature,* 7 miles east-northeast of Clearlake Oaks (lat. 39°04'20" N, long. 122°34' W). Named on Clearlake Oaks (1960) 15' quadrangle.

Store Gulch [TRINITY]: *canyon,* drained by a stream that flows 0.5 mile to East Fork of North Fork Trinity River 2.5 miles north of Helena (lat. 40°48'45" N, long. 123°07'10" W; sec. 9, T 34 N, R 11 W). Named on Helena (1951) 15' quadrangle.

Storm Canyon [LAKE]: *canyon,* drained by a stream that flows less than 1 mile to Kelsey Creek 5.5 miles south of Kelseyville (lat. 38°53'50" N, long. 122°51'15" W; near SW cor. sec. 10, T 12 N, R 9 W). Named on Kelseyville (1959) 7.5' quadrangle.

Stoten Opening [MENDOCINO]: *area,* 4.25 miles northeast of Branscomb (lat. 39°42'05" N, long. 123°34'30" W; sec. 6, T 21 N, R 15 W). Named on Cahto Peak (1967) 7.5' quadrangle.

Stove Camp [TRINITY]: *locality,* 12.5 miles east-northeast of Burnt Ranch (lat. 40°53'55" N, long. 123°16'10" W). Named on Ironside Mountain (1951) 15' quadrangle.

Stove Glade [LAKE]: *area,* 14 miles north-northeast of Clearlake Oaks (lat. 39°11'10" N, long. 122°31'15" W; near NE cor. sec. 4, T 15 N, R 6 W). Named on Clearlake Oaks (1960) 15' quadrangle.

Stoveleg Gap [TRINITY]: *pass,* 7.5 miles north of Helena (lat. 40°52'50" N, long. 123°08'40" W; near SE cor. sec. 18, T 35 N, R 11 W). Named on Helena (1951) 15' quadrangle.

Stover Creek [HUMBOLDT]: *stream,* flows 1.5 miles to Redwood Creek (1) 6 miles south of Coyote Peak (lat. 41°02'55" N, long. 123°52'20" W; near SE cor. sec. 30, T 8 N, R 3 E). Named on Hupa Mountain (1982) 7.5' quadrangle.

Strause Gulch [TRINITY]: *canyon,* drained by a stream that flows 2 miles to Rattlesnake Creek (1) 9.5 miles south of Cecilville, which is in Siskiyou County (lat. 41°00'20" N, long. 123°07'40" W). Named on Helena (1951) 15' quadrangle, and on Thompson Peak (1979) 7.5' quadrangle.

Strauss Orchard [MENDOCINO]: *area,* 6.5 miles west-southwest of Branscomb (lat. 39°37'55" N, long. 123°44'30" W; sec. 34, T 21 N, R 17 W). Named on Lincoln Ridge (1966) 7.5' quadrangle.

Strawberry Creek [HUMBOLDT]: *stream,* flows 3.5 miles to the sea 8.5 miles north of Arcata (lat. 40°59'40" N, long. 124°06'55" W; sec. 18, T 7 N, R 1 E). Named on Arcata North (1959) 7.5' quadrangle.

Strawberry Rock [HUMBOLDT]: *relief feature,* 4.5 miles southwest of Petrolia (lat. 40°16'50" N, long. 124°21' W; sec. 24, T 2 S, R 3 W). Named on Petrolia (1969) 7.5' quadrangle.

Streeter Creek [MENDOCINO]: *stream,* flows 3.5 miles to Tenmile Creek 8 miles northeast of Branscomb (lat. 39°44'45" N, long. 123°31'40" W; sec. 22, T 22 N, R 15 W). Named on Cahto Peak (1967) 7.5' quadrangle.

Streeter Ridge [LAKE]: *ridge,* north-northwest-trending, 1.5 miles long, 3.25 miles west of Three Crossings (lat. 39°19'25" N, long. 122°58'45" W). Named on Elk Mountain (1967) 7.5' quadrangle.

Stribling Gulch [TRINITY]: *canyon,* drained by a stream that flows 1 mile to Grizzly Creek 7.25 miles south of Cecilville, which is in Siskiyou County (lat. 41°02'20" N, long. 123°07'10" W). Named on Thompson Peak (1979) 7.5' quadrangle.

String Bean Creek [TRINITY]: *stream,* flows 2 miles to Hayfork Creek 3.5 miles east-southeast of Dubakella Mountain (lat. 40°22'15" N, long. 123°04'50" W; near W line sec. 14, T 29 N, R 11 W). Named on Dubakella Mountain (1954) 15' quadrangle.

String Creek [MENDOCINO]:*stream,* flows 4.5 miles to Rocktree Creek 6 miles northeast of Willits (lat. 39°27'50" N, long. 123°16'20" W; sec. 35, T 19 N, R 13 W). Named on Willits (1961) 15' quadrangle. Middle Fork enters 4 miles upstream from the mouth of the main creek and is nearly 1 mile long. North Fork enters from the northwest 900 feet downstream from the mouth of Middle Fork and is less than 1 mile long. Both forks are named on Willits (1961) 15' quadrangle.

Stringtown [TRINITY]: *locality,* 2.5 miles north of Trinity Center along Trinity River (lat. 41°02'25" N, long. 122°41'55" W; sec. 29, T 37 N, R 7 W). Named on Bonanza King (1955) 15' quadrangle.

Strong Mountain [MENDOCINO]: *peak,* 8.5 miles southeast of Branscomb (lat. 39°33'55" N, long. 123°30'50" W; at S line sec. 22, T 20 N, R 15 W). Altitude 3240 feet. Named on Sherwood Peak (1967) 7.5' quadrangle.

Strongs Creek [HUMBOLDT]: *stream,* flows 5.25 miles to lowlands along Eel River 1.25 miles south-southeast of Fortuna (lat. 40°34'45" N, long. 124°08'50" W; sec. 2, T 2 N, R 1 W). Named on Fortuna (1959) and Hydesville (1979) 7.5' quadrangles. North Fork enters from the northeast 2.25 miles upstream from the mouth of the main creek; it is nearly 3 miles long and is named on Hydesville (1979) 7.5' quadrangle.

Strongs Station [HUMBOLDT]: *locality,* 7 miles north of Redcrest along Van Duzen River (lat. 40°29'55" N, long. 123°58'15" W; sec. 5, T 1 N, R 2 E). Site named on Redcrest (1969) 7.5' quadrangle. The name is for Samuel Strong, who started a hotel at the place between 1866 and 1875 (Turner,. 207).

Strope Creek [TRINITY]: *stream,* flows 3.5 miles to Clair Engle Lake 14 miles north-northeast of Weaverville (lat. 40°53'10" N, long. 122°46'45" W; sec. 16, T 35 N, R 8 W). Named on Trinity Dam (1950) 15' quadrangle. According to Gudde (1975, p. 338), the stream also was called Stroup Creek. Gudde (1975, p. 247) mentioned a mining place called Norton Diggings that was located at the confluence of Strope Creek and East Branch Stuarts Fork; water of Clair Engle Lake now covers the site.

Stroup Creek: see **Strope Creek** [TRINITY].

Stuart Creek: see **Stuart Fork** [TRINITY].

Stuart Fork [TRINITY]: *stream,* flows 14 miles to Clair Engle Lake 9.5 miles north-northeast of Weaverville (lat. 40°51'25" N, long. 122°52'45" W; sec. 27, T 35 N, R 9 W). Named on Coffee Creek (1955) and Trinity Dam (1950) 15' quadrangles. Called Stewart's Fork on Red Bluff (1894) 1° quadrangle, and called Stuart Cr. on Averill's (1940) map. United States Board on Geographic Names (1965b, p. 16) rejected the names "Stewart Creek," "Stewart's Creek," "Stewarts Creek," "Stuart Fork Creek," "Stuart Fork of Trinity River," "Stuart's Creek," and "Stuarts Creek" for the stream. East Fork enters Clair Engle Lake 15 miles northeast of Weaverville; it is 7 miles long and is named on Trinity Dam (1950) 15' quadrangle. Present East Fork is called East Fork of Stewart's Fork on Red Bluff (1894) 1° quadrangle; United States Board on Geographic Names (1965b, p. 13) rejected the form "East Fork of Stuart Fork" for the name.

Stuart Fork Creek: see **Stuart Fork** [TRINITY].

Stuart Gap [TRINITY]: *pass,* 2.5 miles northeast of Black Rock Mountain on Trinity-Tehama County line (lat. 40°13'45" N, long. 122°58'30" W; sec. 34, T 28 N, R 10 W). Named on Yolla Bolly (1954) 15' quadrangle.

Stubbs: see **Clearlake Oaks** [LAKE].

Stubbs Island [LAKE]: *island,* 2350 feet long, 0.5 mile southeast of downtown Clearlake Oaks in Clear Lake (lat. 39°01'05" N, long. 122°40'10" W); present Clearlake Oaks was called Stubbs before 1935. Named on Clearlake Oaks (1958) 7.5' quadrangle.

Studhorse Prairie [HUMBOLDT]: *area,* 9 miles south of Coyote Peak (lat. 41°00'20" N, long. 123°50'10" W; sec. 9, T 7 N, R 3 E). Named on Hupa Mountain (1982) 7.5' quadrangle.

Stumpville: see **Rosewood** [HUMBOLDT].

Sucker Lake [HUMBOLDT]: *lake,* 750 feet long, 8.5 miles south of the settlement of Willow Creek (lat. 40°49'10" N, long. 123°36'50" W). Named on Hennessy Peak (1979) 7.5' quadrangle.

Sugar Loaf: see **Sugarloaf Island** [HUMBOLDT].

Sugarloaf [LAKE]:

(1) *peak,* 5.25 miles east-southeast of Kelseyville (lat. 38°56'25" N, long. 122°45' W; on S line sec. 28, T 13 N, R 8 W). Named on Clearlake Highlands (1958) and Kelseyville (1959) 7.5' quadrangles.

(2) *peak,* 5 miles southeast of Whispering Pines (lat. 38°45'15" N, long. 122°39'20" W; sec. 5, T 10 N, R 7 W). Named on Whispering Pines (1958) 7.5' quadrangle.

Sugarloaf [MENDOCINO]: *peak,* 11 miles west-northwest of Ornbaun Valley (lat. 38°59' N, long. 123°29' W; on S line sec. 14, T 13 N, R 15 W). Named on Ornbaun Valley (1960) 15' quadrangle.

Sugarloaf Island [HUMBOLDT]: *island,* 750 feet long, 800 feet west of Cape Mendocino (lat. 40°26'20" N, long. 124°24'45" W). Named on Cape Mendocino (1969) 7.5' quadrangle. United States Board on Geographic Names (1973a, p. 3) gave the name "Sugar Loaf" as a variant.

Sugarloaf Mountain [DEL NORTE]: *peak,* 4.25 miles northeast of Buck Mountain (lat. 41°40'30" N, long. 123°48'05" W). Altitude 2918 feet. Named on Ship Mountain (1982) 7.5' quadrangle.

Sugarloaf Mountain [HUMBOLDT]:

(1) *peak,* 1 mile south of Ferndale (lat. 40°33'40" N, long. 124°15'50" W; near N line sec. 14, T 2 N, R 2 W). Altitude 765 feet. Named on Ferndale (1959) 7.5' quadrangle.

(2) *peak,* 12 miles south of the settlement of Willow Creek (lat. 40°46'15" N, long. 123°36'40" W). Altitude 3897 feet. Named on Hennessy Peak (1979) 7.5' quadrangle.

Sugarloaf Mountain [TRINITY]: *peak,* 11.5 miles south-southeast of Black Rock Mountain on Trinity-Tehama County line (lat. 40°02'45" N, long. 122°57'05" W; sec. 3, T 25 N, R 10 W). Altitude 7367 feet. Named on Yolla Bolly (1954) 15' quadrangle.

Sugarloaf Peak [TRINITY]: *peak,* 16 miles south of Weaverville (lat. 40°30'30" N, long. 122°55'50" W; sec. 30, T 31 N, R 9 W). Altitude 4004 feet. Named on Weaverville (1950) 15' quadrangle.

Sugar Pine Butte [TRINITY]: *peak,* 6.5 miles southwest of Billys Peak (1) (lat. 41°03'30" N, long. 122°50'30" W; at N line sec. 24, T 37 N, R 9 W); the peak is 0.5 mile southeast of Sugar Pine Lake. Altitude 7861 feet. Named on Coffee Creek (1955) 15' quadrangle.

Sugar Pine Creek [TRINITY]: *stream,* flows 4.5 miles to Coffee Creek 2.25 miles southwest of Billys Peak (1) (lat. 41°06'45" N, long. 122°48'15" W; sec. 32, T 38 N, R 8 W); the stream heads at Sugar Pine Lake. Named on Coffee Creek (1955) 15' quadrangle. On Etna (1934) 30' quadrangle, the name has the form "Sugarpine Creek."

Sugar Pine Lake [TRINITY]: *lake,* 800 feet long, 6.5 miles southwest of Billys Peak (1) (lat. 41°03'45" N, long. 122°51'10" W; sec. 14, T 37 N, R 9 W). Named on Coffee Creek (1955) 15' quadrangle.

Sugar Pine Mountain [HUMBOLDT]: *ridge,* generally north-northwest-trending, 2.5 miles long, 8 miles southeast of Coyote Peak (lat. 41°02'50" N, long. 123°45'20" W). Named on Hoopa (1979) and Hupa Mountain (1982) 7.5' quadrangles.

Sugar Ridge [MENDOCINO-TRINITY]: *ridge,* southwest-trending, 1.5 miles long, 9.5 miles north of Anthony Peak on Mendocino-Trinity County line (lat. 39°58'50" N, long. 122°56'45" W). Named on Buck Rock (1967) 7.5' quadrangle.

Suicide Rock [HUMBOLDT]: *relief feature,* 5 miles south-southeast of Showers Mountain (lat. 40°30'35" N, long. 123°39'35" W; sec. 31, T 2 N, R 5 E). Named on Showers Mountain (1978) 7.5' quadrangle.

Sullivan Gulch [HUMBOLDT]: *canyon,* drained by a stream that flows 3.5 miles to North Fork Mad River at Korbel (lat. 40°52'05" N, long. 123°57'35" W; near S line sec. 28, T 6 N, R 2 E). Named on Korbel (1979) 7.5' quadrangle.

Sulphur Bank [LAKE]: *settlement,* 7 miles north-northwest of the town of Lower Lake along Clear Lake (lat. 38°59'55" N, long. 122°40'25" W; in and near sec. 6, T 13 N, R 7 W). Named on Clearlake Highlands (1958) and Clearlake Oaks (1958) 7.5' quadrangles. Clearlake Oaks (1958) 7.5' quadrangle also shows Sulphur Bank mine located just northeast of the settlement (lat. 39°00'10" N, long. 122°39'50" W). The name is from the "low, rounded hill" called Sulphur Bank, where sulphur was produced from 1865 to 1868; the mine there was reopened and developed for quicksilver in 1873 (Bradley, p. 234, 236). A mining village called Eastlake sprang up at Sulphur Bank; it was named for the part of Clear Lake that extends eastward just east of The Narrows (2) (Palmer, p. 146). Postal authorities established Eastlake post office in 1877 and discontinued it in 1884 (Frickstad, p. 63). Irelan (p. 327) noted that Borax Springs, named for the borate content of the water, were situated on the edge of Clear Lake near Sulphur Banks. G.F. Becker (p. 264) mentioned that a feature called Little Sulphur Bank was situated a few hundred feet east of the mud flat of Borax Lake.

Sulphur Bank Point [LAKE]: *promontory,* 2.5 miles west-southwest of Clearlake Oaks along Clear Lake (lat. 39°00'30" N, long. 122°43'20" W; on W line sec. 2, T 13 N, R 8 W). Named on Clearlake Oaks (1958) 7.5' quadrangle.

Sulphur Bank Ridge [LAKE]: *ridge,* east-trending, 2 miles long, 6.5 miles north-northeast of the town of Lower Lake (lat. 38°59'40" N, long. 122°40'10" W); the ridge is just south of the settlement of Sulphur Bank. Named on Clearlake Highlands (1958) 7.5' quadrangle.

Sulphur Camp [TRINITY]: *locality,* 9.5 miles southwest of Black Rock

Mountain (lat. 40°06' N, long. 123°07' W; near SW cor. sec. 16, T 26 N, R 11 W). Named on Black Rock Mountain (1954) 15' quadrangle.

Sulphur Canyon [LAKE]: *canyon,* drained by a stream that flows nearly 5 miles to Long Valley Creek 4.5 miles north of Clearlake Oaks (lat. 39°05'20" N, long. 122°40'10" W; sec. 6, T 14 N, R 7 W). Named on Clearlake Oaks (1958) 7.5' quadrangle.

Sulphur Creek [HUMBOLDT]:

(1) *stream,* flows 3.5 miles to Van Duzen River 0.5 mile west of Dinsmore (lat. 40°29'20" N, long. 123°37' W; sec. 4, T 1 N, R 5 E). Named on Dinsmore (1977) 7.5' quadrangle.

(2) *stream,* flows 2.25 miles to East Branch of North Fork Mattole River 10 miles south-southwest of Scotia (lat. 40°20'50" N, long. 123°10'15" W; near S line sec. 27, T 1 S, R 1 W). Named on Buckeye Mountain (1970) 7.5' quadrangle.

Sulphur Creek [LAKE]: *stream,* flows 2 miles to Kelsey Creek 9 miles south-southeast of Kelseyville (lat. 38°51'20" N, long. 122°45'45" W; near SE cor. sec. 29, T 12 N, R 8 W). Named on The Geysers (1959) and Whispering Pines (1958) 7.5' quadrangles.

Sulphur Creek [MENDOCINO]: *stream,* flows nearly 7 miles to Russian River 1.25 miles northeast of Ukiah (lat. 39°09'35" N, long. 123°11'15" W). Named on Cow Mountain (1958) and Ukiah (1958) 7.5' quadrangles.

Sulphur Fork [MENDOCINO]: *stream,* flows nearly 2 miles to Elk Creek (4) 8 miles south-southwest of Navarro (lat. 39°02'15" N, long. 123°34'40" W; near E line sec. 36, T 14 N, R 16 W). Named on Navarro (1961) 15' quadrangle.

Sulphur Glade Creek [TRINITY]: *stream,* flows 3.25 miles to South Fork Trinity River nearly 7 miles south of Hyampom (lat. 40°31'10" N, long. 123°26'45" W; sec. 25, T 2 N, R 6 E). Named on Hyampom (1951) 15' quadrangle, and on Sportshaven (1973) 7.5' quadrangle.

Sulphur Glade Ridge [TRINITY]: *ridge,* east-northeast-trending, 3 miles long, 8 miles south of Hyampom (lat. 40°30' N, long. 123°28' W); the ridge is south of Sulphur Glade Creek. Named on Hyampom (1951) 15' quadrangle, and on Sportshaven (1973) 7.5' quadrangle.

Sulphur Gulch [TRINITY]:

(1) *canyon,* drained by a stream that flows 1 mile to Browns Creek 15 miles south of Weaverville (lat. 40°30'50" N, long. 122°56'40" W; sec. 25, T 31 N, R 10 W). Named on Weaverville (1950) 15' quadrangle.

(2) *canyon,* drained by a stream that flows 0.5 mile to East Fork Hayfork Creek 9 miles north-northeast of Dubakella Mountain (lat. 40°29'40" N, long. 123°03'15" W). Named on Dubakella Mountain (1954) 15' quadrangle.

Sulphur Spring [HUMBOLDT]: *spring,* 1.5 miles east of Weitchpec (lat. 41°11'30" N, long. 123°40'35" W). Named on Weitchpec (1979) 7.5' quadrangle.

Sulphur Spring [LAKE]:

(1) *spring,* 5.5 miles east of the town of Upper Lake (lat. 39°08'55" N, long. 122°48'30" W; sec. 13, T 15 N, R 9 W). Named on Bartlett Mountain (1958) 7.5' quadrangle.

(2) *spring,* 9.5 miles east-northeast of Clearlake Oaks (lat. 39°05'15" N, long. 122°31'30" W; sec. 4, T 14 N, R 6 W). Named on Clearlake Oaks (1960) 15' quadrangle.

(3) *spring,* 3 miles southwest of Lakeport (lat. 39°00'40" N, long. 122°57'05" W; at N line sec. 3, T 13 N, R 10 W). Named on Lakeport (1958) 7.5' quadrangle.

Sulphur Spring [TRINITY]: *spring,* 6.5 miles south of Hyampom near South Fork Trinity River (lat. 40°31'15" N, long. 123°26'55" W; sec. 25, T 2 N, R 6 E). Named on Hyampom (1951) 15' quadrangle.

Sulphur Spring Creek [MENDOCINO]: *stream,* flows 4.5 miles to Elk Creek (2) 9.5 miles east-southeast of Eden Valley (lat. 39°33'25" N, long. 123°01'55" W). Named on Sanhedrin Mountain (1966) 7.5' quadrangle.

Sulphur Valley [HUMBOLDT]: *area,* 2 miles south-southwest of Dinsmore (lat. 40°27'55" N, long. 123°37' W; sec. 16, T 1 N, R 5 E). Named on Dinsmore (1977) 7.5' quadrangle.

Sultan Creek [DEL NORTE]: *stream,* flows 2.5 miles to Smith River 8.5 miles north-northeast of Crescent City (lat. 41°51'35" N, long. 124°07'10" W; near S line sec. 13, T 17 N, R 1 W). Named on Hiouchi (1966) 7.5' quadrangle.

Summer Camp: see **Spring Camp** [MENDOCINO].

Summit [LAKE]: *locality,* 7 miles west-northwest of the town of Upper Lake (lat. 39°11'30" N, long. 123°02' W; near NE cor. sec. 2, T 15 N, R 11 W). Named on Cow Mountain (1958) 7.5' quadrangle.

Summit [MENDOCINO]: *locality,* 3.25 miles west of Willits along California Western Railroad (lat. 39°24'10" N, long. 123°24'50" W; sec. 21, T 18 N, R 14 W). Named on Willits (1961) 15' quadrangle.

Summit Camp: see **Summit Flat** [TRINITY].

Summit Creek [HUMBOLDT]: *stream,* flows 1.5 miles to Three Creeks nearly 5 miles west of the settlement of Willow Creek (lat. 40°56'10" N, long. 123°43'05" W; near NE cor. sec. 4, T 6 N, R 4 E). Named on Willow Creek (1979) 7.5' quadrangle.

Summit Creek [TRINITY]: *stream,* flows 5 miles to Carr Creek (2) 6.25 miles east-northeast of Hayfork (lat. 40°35' N, long. 123°04'20" W; sec. 35, T 32 N, R 11 W). Named on Hayfork (1951) 15' quadrangle.

Summit Flat [TRINITY]: *area,* 4.5 miles south-southeast of Black Lassic (lat. 40°16'30" N, long. 123°30'55" W). Named on Black Lassic (1979) 7.5' quadrangle. Blocksburg (1949) 15' quadrangle shows Summit Camp at the place.

Summit Lake [LAKE]: *lake,* 250 feet long, 4.5 miles east of Big Signal Peak [MENDOCINO] (lat. 39°30'45" N, long. 123°00'40" W; near SW cor. sec, 7, T 19 N, R 10 W). Named on Sanhedrin Mountain (1966) 7.5' quadrangle.

Summit Lake [TRINITY]: *lake,* 950 feet long, 15 miles north of Weaverville (lat. 40°51'20" N, long. 122°53'45" W; sec. 33, T 36 N, R 9 W). Named on Trinity Dam (1950) 15' quadrangle.

Summit Lake: see **Tule Lake** [LAKE] (1).

Summit Rock [LAKE]: *relief feature,* 9.5 miles north-northwest of Clearlake Oaks (lat. 39°09' N, long. 122°44'50" W; sec. 16, T 15 N, R 8 W). Named on Clearlake Oaks (1958) 7.5' quadrangle.

Summit Spring [MENDOCINO]: *spring,* 10 miles west-northwest of Ornbaun Valley (lat. 38°58'25" N, long. 123°28'30" W; near W line sec. 24, T 13 N, R 15 W). Named on Ornbaun Valley (1960) 15' quadrangle.

Summit Valley [DEL NORTE]: *area,* 4 miles southeast of Buck Mountain (lat. 41°35'40" N, long. 123°48'35" W). Named on Ship Mountain (1982) 7.5' quadrangle.

Summit Valley [MENDOCINO]: *valley,* 7.5 miles east-northeast of Spyrock (2) (lat. 39°54'15" N, long. 123°18'30" W). Named on Mina (1967) 7.5' quadrangle.

Sumner Ridge [LAKE]: *ridge,* generally northwest-trending, 1.5 miles long, 6.5 miles south-southwest of Potato Hill (lat. 39°15'45" N, long. 122°51'05" W). Named on Potato Hill (1967) 7.5' quadrangle.

Sunday Creek [TRINITY]: *stream,* flows 2 miles to Stuart Fork 11 miles north of Weaverville (lat. 40°53' N, long. 122°55'40" W; at S line sec. 18, T 35 N, R 9 W). Named on Trinity Dam (1950) 15' quadrangle.

Sunflower Creek [TRINITY]: *stream,* flows 3 miles to Trinity River 15 miles north of Trinity Center (lat. 41°12'45" N, long. 122°38'45" W; near W line sec. 26, T 39 N, R 7 W); Sunflower Flat is at the mouth of the creek. Named on Bonanza King (1955) 7.5' quadrangle.

Sunflower Flat [TRINITY]: *area,* 15 miles north of Trinity Center along Trinity River (lat. 41°12'55" N, long. 122°38'50" W; near NW cor. sec. 26, T 39 N, R 7 W). Named on Bonanza King (1955) 15' quadrangle.

Sunflower Glade [TRINITY]: *area,* 13 miles south of Black Rock Mountain (lat. 40°00'40" N, long. 123°00'45" W, near N line sec. 19, T 25 N, R 10 W). Named on Black Rock Mountain (1954) 15' quadrangle.

Sunny Brae [HUMBOLDT]: *town,* about 1 mile southeast of downtown Arcata (lat. 40°51'35" N, long. 124°03'55" W; sec. 33, 34, T 6 N, R 1 E). Named on Arcata South (1959) 7.5' quadrangle.

Sunny Flat [TRINITY]: *area,* 8.5 miles north of Trinity Center along Trinity River (lat. 41°07'55" N, long. 122°41'55" W; on S line sec. 20, T 38 N, R 7 W). Named on Bonanza King (1955) 15' quadrangle.

Sunnyside [MENDOCINO]: *locality,* 10 miles north-northeast of Covelo (lat. 39°56' N, long. 123°12'30" W; sec. 17, T 24 N, R 12 W). Named on Covelo (1952) 15' quadrangle.

Sunnyside: see **East Sunnyside**, under **Pine Hill** [HUMBOLDT].

Sunrise Creek [TRINITY]: *stream,* flows 1 mile to Landers Creek 9.5 miles southwest of Billy Peak (1) (lat. 41°01'15" N, long. 122°52'30" W; sec. 34, T 37 N, R 9 W). Named on Coffee Creek (1955) 15' quadrangle.

Sunrise Vista [LAKE]: *locality,* 7 miles west-southwest of the town of Lower Lake (lat. 38°52'50" N, long. 122°44' W; near N line sec. 22, T 12 N, R 8 W). Named on Clearlake Highlands (1958) 7.5' quadrangle.

Sunset Gap [LAKE-MENDOCINO]: *pass,* 9 miles north-northeast of the town of Potter Valley on Mendocino-Lake County line (lat. 39°26'45" N, long. 123°04'15" W; sec. 3, T 18 N, R 11 W). Named on Potter Valley (1960) 15' quadrangle.

Sunset Point Campground [LAKE]: *locality,* 3 miles northwest of Bear Mountain on the north side of Lake Pillsbury (lat. 39°26'20" N, long. 122°56'20" W; near SW cor. sec. 1, T 18 N, R 10 W). Named on Lake Pillsbury (1967) 7.5' quadrangle.

Sunset Spring [HUMBOLDT]: *spring,* 2 miles south-southeast of Orleans (lat. 41°16'40" N, long. 123°31'20" W). Named on Orleans (1978) 7.5' quadrangle.

Supply Creek [HUMBOLDT]: *stream,* flows 9 miles to Trinity River 0.25 mile north of Hoopa (lat. 41°03'15" N, long. 123°40'30" W; sec. 25, T 8 N, R 4 E). Named on Hoopa (1979) and Willow Creek (1979) 7.5' quadrangles.

Surgone [HUMBOLDT]: *locality,* 1.5 miles southeast of Johnsons along Klamath River (lat. 41°20'05" N, long. 123°51'15" W; near S line sec. 17, T 11 N, R 3 E). Named on Johnsons (1982) 7.5' quadrangle.

Surprise Creek [TRINITY]: *stream,* flows 2 miles to South Fork Trinity River 7.5 miles south of Salyer (lat. 41°47'10" N, long. 123°33'25" W). Named on Hennessy Peak (1979) 7.5' quadrangle.

Surpur Creek [HUMBOLDT]: *stream,* flows 4.25 miles to Klamath River 3.25 miles northwest of Johnsons (lat. 41°22'50" N, long. 123°55'05" W; sec. 35, T 12 N, R 2 E). Named on Ah Pah Ridge (1983) and Holter Ridge

(1983) 7.5' quadrangles. The name is from an Indian village called Serper that formerly was at the site (Kroeber, p. 60).

Surrender Creek [MENDOCINO]: *stream,* flows 1 mile to Soda Creek (3) at Navarro (lat. 39°09'15" N, long. 123°32'30" W; near N line sec. 20, T 15 N, R 15 W). Named on Navarro (1961) 15' quadrangle.

Surveyor Campground [MENDOCINO]: *locality,* 2 miles south-southwest of Anthony Peak (lat. 39°49'10" N, long. 122°58'15" W; sec. 28, T 23 N, R 10 W). Named on Mendocino Pass (1967) 7.5' quadrangle.

Surveyors Canyon [MENDOCINO]: *canyon,* drained by a stream that flows 1 mile to South Fork Eel River 6.5 miles southeast of Leggett (lat. 39°46'20" N, long. 123°39'05" W; sec. 8, T 22 N, R 16 W). Named on Leggett (1969) 7.5' quadrangle.

Surveyors Flat [MENDOCINO]: *area,* 10 miles north of Hull Mountain (lat. 39°39'40" N, long. 122°57'40" W; sec. 22, T 21 N, R 10 W). Named on Plaskett Ridge (1967) 7.5' quadrangle.

Surveyor Spring [TRINITY]: *spring,* 7.5 miles northeast of Kettenpom (lat. 40°13'55" N, long. 123°21'30" W; sec. 2, T 3 S, R 7 E). Named on Kettenpom (1955) 15' quadrangle.

Swains Flat [HUMBOLDT]: *area,* 3.5 miles west of Bridgeville along Van Duzen River (lat. 40°28'10" N, long. 123°52' W; near NW cor. sec. 17, T 1 N, R 3 E). Named on Bridgeville (1969) 7.5' quadrangle.

Swain Slough [HUMBOLDT]: *stream,* flows 1 mile to Elk River (1) 2.5 miles south-southwest of downtown Eureka (lat. 40°45'20" N, long. 124°11'20" W; sec. 4, T 4 N, R 1 W). Named on Eureka (1958) and Fields Landing (1959) 7.5' quadrangles.

Swallow Rock [LAKE]: *relief feature,* 2.5 miles southwest of Bear Mountain along Rice Fork (lat. 39°23'05" N, long. 122°56'05" W; sec. 25, T 18 N, R 10 W). Named on Lake Pillsbury (1967) 7.5' quadrangle.

Swallow Rock [MENDOCINO]: *relief feature,* 7.5 miles north-northwest of Hull Mountain (lat. 39°37'15" N, long. 122°59'30" W; sec. 5, T 20 N, R 10 W). Named on Hull Mountain (1967) 7.5' quadrangle.

Swamp Gulch [MENDOCINO]: *canyon,* 0.5 mile long, 7.5 miles northwest of Willits (lat. 39°29'30" N, long. 123°25'15" W; sec. 17, 20, T 19 N, R 14 W). Named on Willits (1961) 15' quadrangle.

Swauger: see **Loleta** [HUMBOLDT].

Swayback Ridge [HUMBOLDT-TRINITY]: *ridge,* south-southeast-trending, 4 miles long, 7 miles south-southeast of Dinsmore on Humboldt-Trinity County line, mainly in Humboldt County (lat. 40°23'40" N, long. 123°33'55" W). Named on Black Lassic (1979) and Dinsmore (1977) 7.5' quadrangles.

Sweasey Lake [HUMBOLDT]: *lake,* 1000 feet long, 4 miles west-southwest of Dinsmore (lat. 40°28'05" N, long. 123°40'25" W; sec. 13, T 1 N, R 4 E). Named on Larabee Valley (1977) 7.5' quadrangle.

Sweathouse Creek [HUMBOLDT]: *stream,* flows 1.5 miles to Redwood Creek (1) 9 miles east-northeast of the town of Blue Lake (lat. 40°55'50" N, long. 123°49'25" W; sec. 3, T 6 N, R 3 E). Named on Lord-Ellis Summit (1973) 7.5' quadrangle.

Swede Canyon [LAKE]: *canyon,* drained by a stream that flows nearly 1 mile to North Fork Cache Creek 8.5 miles northeast of the town of Upper Lake (lat. 39°14' N, long. 122°46'20" W). Named on Bartlett Mountain (1958) 7.5' quadrangle.

Swede Creek [TRINITY]: *stream,* flows 3.5 miles to Trinity River 6.25 miles east of Burnt Ranch (lat. 40°47'35" N, long. 123°21'20" W). Named on Ironside Mountain (1951) 15' quadrangle. Called Sweede Cr. on Miller's (1890) map.

Swede Creek: see **Little Swede Creek** [TRINITY].

Sweepstake Flat [TRINITY]: *area,* 3 miles west-southwest of Weaverville (lat. 40°43' N, long. 122°59'20" W; sec. 15, T 33 N, R 10 W). Named on Weaverville (1950) 15' quadrangle.

Sweet Creek [HUMBOLDT]: *stream,* flows 2.25 miles to Price Creek 7 miles south-southwest of Fortuna (lat. 40°30'05" N, long. 124°12'10" W; near N line sec. 5, T 1 N, R 1 W). Named on Fortuna (1959) and Taylor Peak (1969) 7.5' quadrangles.

Sweet Hollow Creek [LAKE]: *canyon,* drained by a stream that flows 2.5 miles to North Fork Cache Creek 6 miles east of Clearlake Oaks (lat. 39°01'10" N, long. 122°34' W). Named on Clearlake Oaks (1960) 15' quadrangle.

Sweet Springs Creek [LAKE]: *stream,* flows 1.25 miles to Copsey Creek 5 miles northeast of Whispering Pines (lat. 38°51'20" N, long. 122°38' W; near SE cor. sec. 28, T 12 N, R 7 W). Named on Whispering Pines (1958) 7.5' quadrangle.

Sweetwater Creek [LAKE]: *stream,* flows 4.25 miles to Kelsey Creek 5 miles south of Kelseyville (lat. 38°54'20" N, long. 122°51'05" W; sec. 10, T 12 N, R 9 W). Named on Kelseyville (1959) 7.5' quadrangle.

Swift Creek [HUMBOLDT]: *stream,* flows about 2.5 miles to Butte Creek (2) nearly 6 miles southwest of Dinsmore (lat. 40°25'45" N, long. 123°40'20" W; at S line sec. 25, T 1 N, R 4 E). Named on Larabee Valley (1977) 7.5' quadrangle.

Swift Creek [TRINITY]:

(1) *stream,* flows 16 miles to Trinity River 22 miles north-northeast of Weaverville (lat. 40°59'15" N, long. 122°40'05" W; at SE cor. sec. 9, T 36 N, R 7 W). Named on Coffee Creek (1955), Schell Mountain (1950), and Trinity Dam (1950) 15' quadrangles. North Fork enters from the north-northwest 20 miles north-northeast of Weaverville; it is 7.5 miles long and is named on Bonanza King (1955), Coffee Creek (1955), and Schell Mountain (1950) 15' quadrangles.

(2) *stream,* flows 2 miles to South Fork Trinity River 2.5 miles west-northwest of Forest Glen (lat. 40°23'05" N, long. 123°22'05" W; sec. 15, T 1 S, R 7 E). Named on Naufus Creek (1979), Ruth Reservoir (1978), and Sportshaven (1973) 7.5' quadrangles.

Swim Meadow [TRINITY]: *area,* 4.5 miles west-southwest of Dubakella Mountain (lat. 40°21'05" N, long. 123°13'20" W; sec. 21, T 29 N, R 12 W). Named on Dubakella Mountain (1954) 15' quadrangle.

Swim Ridge [TRINITY]: *ridge,* south-trending, 5.5 miles long, 9 miles west-southwest of Black Rock Mountain (lat. 40°10' N, long. 123°10'30" W). Named on Black Rock Mountain (1954) 15' quadrangle.

Switzer Rock [MENDOCINO]: *rock,* less than 1 mile north-northwest of Westport, and 1850 feet offshore (lat. 39°38'50" N, long. 123°47'25" W). Named on Westport (1966) 7.5' quadrangle.

Sylar Spring [LAKE]: *spring,* 7 miles south-southeast of Potato Hill (lat. 39°15'30" N, long. 122°45'35" W). Named on Potato Hill (1967) 7.5' quadrangle.

Sylvandale [MENDOCINO]: *locality,* 7.5 miles north-northwest of Willits (lat. 39°29'20" N, long. 123°25'20" W). Named on Willits (1942) 15' quadrangle. Postal authorities established Sylvandale post office in 1911 and discontinued it in 1918 (Salley, p. 217). California Mining Bureau's (1917c) map shows a place called En Cimo located about 3 miles north-northwest of Sylvandale at the end of a railroad spur line.

—T—

Table Bluff [HUMBOLDT]:

(1) *ridge,* east-southeast- to southeast-trending, 4 miles long, center 3.5 miles south-southwest of Fields Landing (lat. 40°40'40" N, long. 124°14'20" W). Named on Cannibal Island (1959) and Fields Landing (1959) 7.5' quadrangles. S.W. Shaw named the feature in 1851 (Turner, p. 211). On Fortuna (1944) 15' quadrangle, application of the name extends southeast to include present Tompkins Hill. According to Wagner (p. 458), present Table Bluff (1) probably is the feature that Hezeta named Punta Gorda in 1775. The exploring party on the *Laura Virginia* called it Ridge Point in 1850, and the expedition under Samuel Brannan called it Brannan Bluff the same year; the present name is from the appearance of the feature (Coy, 1929, p. 45, 48, 97).

(2) *locality,* 4.5 miles south of Fields Landing (lat. 40°39'30" N, long. 124°12'55" W; on E line sec. 7, T 3 N, R 1 W); the place is at the southeast end of Table Bluff (1). Named on Fields Landing (1959) 7.5' quadrangle. Postal authorities established Table Bluff post office in 1861, discontinued it in 1862, reestablished it in 1867, discontinued it in 1868, reestablished it in 1870, discontinued it in 1891, reestablished it in 1892, discontinued it the same year, reestablished it in 1900, and discontinued it in 1901 (Frickstad, p. 46).

Table Mountain [DEL NORTE]: *ridge,* west-trending, 1.5 miles long, 10.5 miles west-southwest of Gasquet (lat. 41°46'50" N, long. 123°47'25" W). Named on Hurdygurdy Butte (1982) 7.5' quadrangle.

Table Mountain [MENDOCINO]: *ridge,* west-northwest-trending, 1.5 miles long, 7.25 miles north of Elk (lat. 39°14'10" N, long. 123°47'15" W; mainly in sec. 24, T 16 N, R 17 W). Named on Elk (1960) 7.5' quadrangle.

Table Rock [MENDOCINO]:

(1) *relief feature,* 10 miles northeast of Eden Valley (lat. 39°44'20" N, long. 123°04'20" W; sec. 27, T 22 N, R 11 W). Named on Thatcher Ridge (1967) 7.5' quadrangle.

(2) *peak,* 10.5 miles northeast of Spyrock (2) (lat. 39°58'25" N, long. 123°17'45" W). Named on Mina (1967) 7.5' quadrangle.

Talawa Lake: see **Lake Earl** [DEL NORTE]; **Lake Talawa** [**DEL NORTE**].

Talawa Slough [DEL NORTE]: stream, flows 2..25 miles to Lake Earl 7 miles north of Crescent City (lat. 41°51'25" N, long. 124°11'30" W; sec. 21, T 17 N, R 1 W). Named on Crescent City (1966) 7.5' quadrangle. The name i s of Indian origin (Gudde, 1949, p. 352).

Taliaferro Ridge [MENDOCINO]: *ridge,* east- to east-northeast-trending, 3.5 miles long, 14 miles northeast of Covelo (lat. 39°55' N, long. 123°02'45" W). Named on Leech Lake Mountain (1966) 7.5' quadrangle. United States Board on Geographic Names (1969a, p. 4) approved the name to honor Professor Nicholas Lloyd Taliaferro of University of California, who studied geology of the region.

Talmadge: see **Talmage** [MENDOCINO].

Talmage [MENDOCINO]: *locality,* 2.5 miles east-southeast of Ukiah (lat. 39°07'50" N, long. 123°09'50" W). Named on Ukiah (1958) 7.5' quadrangle. Postal authorities established Talmage post office in 1891; the name commemorates Junius Talmage, a pioneer settler (Salley, p. 218). United States Board on Geographic Names (1962a, p. 17) rejected the form "Talmadge" for the name.

Tamarack Creek [TRINITY]: *stream,* flows 1.5 miles to East Fork Trinity River 16 miles northeast of Trinity Center (lat. 41°09'15" N, long. 122°27'35" W; sec. 17, T 38 N, R 5 W). Named on Dunsmuir (1954) 15' quadrangle.

Tamarack Lake [TRINITY]: *lake,* 1500 feet long, 14 miles east-northeast of Trinity Center (lat. 41°06'10" N, long. 122°27'40" W; on S line sec. 32, T 38 N, R 5 W). Named on Dunsmuir (1954) 15' quadrangle.

Tangle Blue Creek [TRINITY]: *stream,* flows nearly 7 miles to Trinity River 16 miles north of Trinity Center (lat. 41°13'35" N, long. 122°38'40" W; sec. 23, T 39 N, R 7 W); the stream heads at Tangle Blue Lake. Named on Bonanza King (1955) 15' quadrangle.

Tangle Blue Lake [TRINITY]: *lake,* 1300 feet long, 14 miles north of Trinity Center (lat. 41°12'25" N, long. 122°44'35" W; at SE cor. sec. 26, T 39 N, R 8 W). Named on Bonanza King (1955) 15' quadrangle.

Tank Creek [MENDOCINO]: *stream,* flows nearly 3 miles to Short Creek 5 miles north-northeast of Covelo (lat. 39°51'10" N, long. 123°12' W; sec. 16, T 23 N, R 12 W). Named on Bluenose Ridge (1967) and Covelo East (1967) 7.5' quadrangles.

Tank 4 Gulch [MENDOCINO]: *canyon,* drained by a stream that flows 1.5 miles to Flynn Creek 5 miles northwest of Navarro (lat. 39°12'10" N, long. 123°36'15" W; at W line sec. 36, T 16 N, R 16 W). Named on Navarro (1961) 15' quadrangle.

Tank Gulch [HUMBOLDT]:

(1) *canyon,* drained by a stream that flows 1 mile to Eel River 1.25 miles north-northeast of Scotia (lat. 40°29'50" N, long. 124°05'20" W; sec. 5, T 1 N, R 1 E). Named on Scotia (1970) 7.5' quadrangle.

(2) *canyon,* drained by a stream that flows 21 miles to Redwood Creek (2) 5.5 miles west of Garberville (lat. 40°06'35" N, long. 123°54'35" W; sec. 18, T 4 S, R 3 E). Named on Briceland (1969) 7.5' quadrangle.

Tank Ridge [HUMBOLDT]: *ridge,* south- to southeast-trending, less than 1 mile long, 6 miles west of Garberville (lat. 40°06'50" N, long. 123°54'15" W; near E line sec. 13, T 4 S, R 2 E); the ridge is west of Tank Gulch (2). Named on Briceland (1969) 7.5' quadrangle.

Tannery Gulch [TRINITY]: *canyon,* drained by a stream that flows nearly 2 miles to Clair Engle Lake 8.5 miles north-northeast of Weaverville (lat. 40°50'05" N, long. 122°51' W; sec. 2, T 34 N, R 9 W). Named on Trinity Dam (1950) 15' quadrangle. The name is for the tannery of Bartlett and Company, built at the mouth of the canyon in 1856 (Jones, p. 47).

Tannery Ridge [TRINITY]: *ridge,* east-northeast-trending, 2 miles long, 8 miles north-northeast of Weaverville (lat. 40°49'35" N, long. 122°52'15" W); the ridge is north of Tannery Gulch. Named on Trinity Dam (1950) 15' quadrangle.

Tanoak [HUMBOLDT]: *locality,* 8 miles east of Weott along Northwestern Pacific Railroad (lat. 40°19'05" N, long. 123°46'15" W; sec. 6, T 2 S, R 4 E). Named on Weott (1949) 15' quadrangle.

Tan Oak Park [MENDOCINO]: *locality,* 6.5 miles east-southeast of Leggett (lat. 39°49'40" N, long. 123°36'15" W; sec. 22, T 23 N, R 16 W). Named on Tan Oak Park (1969) 7.5' quadrangle.

Tan Oak Ridge [HUMBOLDT]: *ridge,* northeast-trending, nearly 2 miles long, 4.25 mile south-southwest of Honeydew (lat. 40°11 '15" N, long. 124°09' W). Named on Shubrick Peak (1969) 7.5' quadrangle.

Tantrum Glade [MENDOCINO]: *area,* 7 miles north-northeast of Anthony Peak (lat. 39°56'20" N, long. 122°55'30" W; near SW cor. sec. 12, T 24 N, R 10 W). Named on Buck Rock (1967) 7.5' quadrangle. The name was given after a crazed mule upset a camp at the place (Gudde, 1949, p. 354).

Tapie Lake [TRINITY]: *lake,* 450 feet long, 6.5 miles south-southwest of Billys Peak (1) (lat. 41°02'45" N, long. 122°48'45" W; near SW cor. sec. 20, T 37 N, R 8 W). Named on Coffee Creek (1955) 15' quadrangle. The name commemorates Raymond Eugene Tapie, who stocked the lake with trout (United States Board on Geographic Names, 1954, p. 4).

Tartar Creek [MENDOCINO]: *stream,* flows 1.5 miles to String Creek 6.25 miles northeast of Willits (lat. 39°28'40" N, long. 123°16'40" W; near NW cor. sec. 26, T 19 N, T 13 W). Named on Willits (1961) 15' quadrangle.

Tarup Creek [DEL NORTE-HUMBOLDT]: *stream,* heads in Humboldt County and flows 4.5 miles to lowlands along Klamath River 1.5 miles east-southeast of Klamath Glen in Del Norte County (lat. 41°30'15" N, long. 123°58' W; sec. 20, T 13 N, R 2 E). Named on Ah Pah Ridge (1983) and Klamath Glen (1982) 7.5' quadrangles. According to Kroeber (p. 64), who used the form "Turup Creek," the name is from an Indian village located on the south side of Klamath River.

Tatu [MENDOCINO]: *locality,* 4 miles south of Dos Rios along Northwestern Pacific Railroad (lat. 39°39'30" N, long. 123°20'40" W; near SE cor. sec. 19, T 21 N, R 13 W); the place is at the mouth of Tatu Creek. Named on Dos Rios (1967) 7.5' quadrangle.

Tatu Creek [MENDOCINO]: *stream,* flows 1.5 miles to Eel River 4.25 miles south of Dos Rios (lat. 39°39'25" N, long. 123°20'40" W; near SE cor. sec. 19, T 21 N, R 13 W). Named on Dos Rios (1967) 7.5' quadrangle.

Taylor Creek [MENDOCINO]: *stream,* flows 1.25 miles to South Fork Eel River 1.5 miles east-southeast of Branscomb (lat. 39°38'30" N, long. 123°36'10" W; sec. 25, T 21 N, R 16 W). Named on Cahto Peak (1967) 7.5' quadrangle. Called Bear Creek on Branscomb (1951) 15' quadrangle, where present Bear Creek (5) is called Taylor Creek.

Taylor Flat [TRINITY]: *area,* 0.25 mile southeast of the center of Forest Glen along South Fork Trinity River (lat. 40°23'10" N, long. 123°19'10" W; sec. 19, T 1 S, R 8 E). Named on Forest Glen (1979) 7.5' quadrangle.

Taylor Flat: see **Del Loma** [TRINITY].

Taylor Gulch [MENDOCINO]: *canyon,* drained by a stream that flows 0.5 mile to Little Salmon Creek 6 miles north of Elk (lat. 39°12'50" N, long. 123°44'20" W; sec. 27, T 16 N, R 17 W). Named on Elk (1960) 7.5' quadrangle.

Taylor Gulch [TRINITY]: *canyon,* drained by a stream that flows 1 mile to Greenhorn Gulch 15 miles north-northeast of Weaverville (lat. 40°54'50" N, long. 122°47' W; sec. 9, T 35 N, R 8 W). Named on Trinity Dam (1950) 15' quadrangle.

Taylor Peak [HUMBOLDT]: *peak,* 9.5 miles southwest of Scotia (lat. 40°22'40" N, long. 124°13'10" W; near SE cor. sec. 18, T 1 S, R 1 W). Altitude 3374 feet. Named on Taylor Peak (1969) 7.5' quadrangle. Manon Taylor owned the feature in the 1870's (Turner, p. 212).

Taylor Ridge [HUMBOLDT]: *ridge,* southwest-trending, 1.25 miles long, 3 miles south of Board Camp Mountain (lat. 40°39'15" N, long. 123°42'55" W; mainly in sec. 10, T 3 N, R 4 E). Named on Board Camp Mountain (1977) 7.5' quadrangle.

Taylors Flat: see **Forest Glen** [TRINITY].

Tea Canyon [LAKE]: *canyon,* drained by a stream that flows 1.5 miles to Clover Creek 4.25 miles east of the town of Upper Lake (lat. 39°09'40" N, long. 122°49'55" W; sec. 11, T 15 N, R 9 W). Named on Bartlett Mountain (1958) 7.5' quadrangle.

Tectah Creek [HUMBOLDT]: *stream,* flows 13 miles to Klamath River 1.5 miles northwest of Johnsons (lat. 41°22' N, long. 123°54' W; sec. 1, T 11 N, R 2 E). Named on Bald Hills (1982) and Holter Ridge (1983) 7.5' quadrangles. The name is of Indian origin (Gudde, 1949, p. 355).

Teds Ridge [DEL NORTE]: *ridge,* north-northwest-trending, 1.25 miles long, 4.25 miles north of the mouth of Klamath River (lat. 41°36'30" N, long. 124°04' W). Named on Requa (1966) 7.5' quadrangle.

Telegraph Creek [HUMBOLDT]: *stream,* flows 2.5 miles to the sea 2 miles north-northwest of Point Delgada (lat. 40°02'50" N, long. 124°04'45" W; at S line sec. 4, T 5 S, R 1 E). Named on Shelter Cove (1969) 7.5' quadrangle.

Telegraph Ridge [HUMBOLDT]:

(1) *ridge,* southeast-trending, 2 miles long, nearly 6 miles southwest of Honeydew (lat. 40°11'30" N, long. 124°12'30" W). Named on Shubrick Peak (1969) 7.5' quadrangle.

(2) *ridge,* southeast-trending, 3.5 miles long, 9 miles west of Garberville (lat. 40°06'35" N, long. 123°57'30" W). Named on Briceland (1969) and Ettersburg (1969) 7.5' quadrangles.

Telegraph Rock [LAKE]: *relief feature,* 4.25 miles east of the town of Upper Lake (lat. 39°09'45" N, long. 122°50' W; near W line sec. 11, T 15 N, R 9 W). Named on Bartlett Mountain (1958) 7.5' quadrangle.

Telephone Ridge [TRINITY]: *ridge,* northeast-trending, 1.5 mile long, 2 miles northeast of Dubakella Mountain (lat. 40°24'30" N, long. 123°07'30" W; sec. 32, T 30 N, R 11 W). Named on Dubakella Mountain (1954) 15' quadrangle.

Telescope Peak [HUMBOLDT]: *peak,* 3.5 miles south-southwest of Hoopa (lat. 41°00'10" N, long. 123°42'50" W; sec. 10, T 7 N, R 4 E). Altitude 4148 feet. Named on Hoopa (1979) 7.5' quadrangle.

Ten Cent Gulch [TRINITY]: *canyon,* drained by a stream that flows 3 miles to East Weaver Creek 0.5 mile south of the center of Weaverville (lat. 40°43'20" N, long. 122°56'20" W; near NW cor. sec. 18, T 33 N, R 9 W); the canyon is west of Five Cent Gulch. Named on Trinity Dam (1950) and Weaverville (1950) 15' quadrangles.

Tenmile Creek [DEL NORTE]: *stream,* flows 1 mile to West Fork Patrick Creek 7.25 miles northeast of Gasquet (lat. 41°54'25" N, long. 123°51'15" W; sec. 32, T 18 N, R 3 E). Named on Shelly Creek Ridge (1982) 7.5' quadrangle.

Tenmile Creek [MENDOCINO]: *stream,* flows 21 miles to South Fork Eel River 9 miles south-southeast of Leggett (lat. 39°45'15" N, long. 123°37'50" W; sec. 16, T 22 N, R 16 W). Named on Cahto Peak (1967), Laytonville (1967), Leggett (1969), and Tan Oak Park (1969) 7.5' quadrangles.

Ten Mile River [MENDOCINO]: *stream,* formed by the confluence of Middle Fork and North Fork, flows nearly 7 miles to the sea 6 miles south of Westport (lat. 39°33'10" N, long. 123°45'55" W; sec. 33, T 20 N, R 17 W). Named on Dutchmans Knoll (1966) and Inglenook (1966) 7.5' quadrangles. The stream, which is 10 miles north of Noyo, was named for this distance from Noyo in the 1850's (Gudde, 1949, p. 214). United States Board on Geographic Names (1961c, p. 17) rejected the forms "Tenmile," "Ten Mile Creek," and "Tenmile River" for the name. Middle Fork and North Fork each are 15 miles long; both forks are named on Dutchmans Knoll (1966) and Sherwood Peak (1967) 7.5' quadrangles. Little North Fork enters North Fork nearly 2 miles upstream from the confluence of North Fork and Middle Fork; it is 4 miles long and is named on Dutchmans Knoll (1966) 7.5' quadrangle. South Fork enters from the southeast 1.5 miles upstream from the mouth of the main stream; it is 17 miles long and is named on Comptche

(1960) 15' quadrangle, and on Dutchmans Knoll (1966) and Sherwood Peak (1967) 7.5' quadrangles.

Tenmile River Bluff [MENDOCINO]: *promontory*, 5.25 miles south of Westport along the coast (lat. 39°33'45" N, long. 123°46'05" W; sec. 29, T 20 N, R 17 W); the feature is less than 1 mile north of the mouth of Ten Mile River. Named on Inglenook (1966) 7.5' quadrangle.

Tenmile Spring [HUMBOLDT]: *spring*, 6 miles east of Weitchpec (lat. 41°10'15" N, long. 123°35'45" W; at N line sec. 15, T 9 N, R 5 E). Named on Hopkins Butte (1979) 7.5' quadrangle.

Tenney Peak [MENDOCINO]: *peak*, 6 miles northeast of Willits (lat. 39°28'05" N, long. 123°16' W; sec. 35, T 19 N, R 13 W). Named on Willits (1961) 15' quadrangle.

Tepee Creek [HUMBOLDT]: *stream*, flows 1.5 miles to Bull Creek (2) 2 miles northwest of Weott (lat. 40°20'30" N, long. 123°57' W; near NE cor. sec. 33, T 1 S, R 2 E). Named on Weott (1969) 7.5' quadrangle.

Tepee Gulch Camp [TRINITY]: *locality*, 21 miles northeast of Weaverville (lat. 40°57'15" N, long. 122°38'40" W; sec. 26, T 36 N, R 7 W). Named on Schell Mountain (1950) 15' quadrangle.

Tepona Point [HUMBOLDT]: *promontory*, nearly 2 miles southeast of Trinidad along the coast (lat. 41°02'20" N, long. 124°07'15" W; sec. 36, T 8 N, R 1 W). Named on Crannell (1966) 7.5' quadrangle.

Tepo Ridge [DEL NORTE]: *ridge*, northeast-trending, 2 miles long, 2.5 miles northeast of the mouth of Klamath River (lat. 41°34'05" N, long. 124°02'15" W). Named on Requa (1966) 7.5' quadrangle.

Terwah: see **Turwar Valley** [DEL NORTE].

Terwah Creek: see **Turwar Creek** [DEL NORTE].

Texas Bar: see **Douglas City** [TRINITY].

Texas Chow Creek [TRINITY]: *stream*, flows 3.5 miles to Prospect Creek 9 miles south-southeast of Dubakella Mountain (lat. 40°15'15" N, long. 123°06'20" W; near SE cor. sec. 21, T 28 N, R 11 W). Named on Dubakella Mountain (1954) 15' quadrangle.

Thatcher Butte [MENDOCINO]: *peak*, 8.5 miles east of Eden Valley (lat. 39°37'35" N, long. 123°01'50" W); the peak is near the head of Thatcher Creek. Named on Thatcher Ridge (1967) 7.5' quadrangle. The name recalls the two Thatcher brothers who wintered near the feature in 1856; Indians killed one of the brothers there (Keller, p. 7).

Thatcher Creek [MENDOCINO]: *stream*, flows 8 miles to Middle Fork Eel River 5.5 miles northeast of Eden Valley (lat. 39°41'20" N, long. 123°07' W; at E line sec. 7, T 21 N, R 11 W); the stream heads near Thatcher Butte and flows south of Thatcher Ridge. Named on Thatcher Ridge (1967) 7.5' quadrangle.

Thatcher Creek: see **Little Thatcher Creek** [MENDOCINO].

Thatcher Ridge [MENDOCINO]: *ridge*, north-northeast-trending, 1.5 miles long, 8.5 miles northeast of Eden Valley (lat. 39°42'10" N, long. 123°03'45" W). Named on Thatcher Ridge (1967) 7.5' quadrangle.

The Basin [HUMBOLDT]: *valley*, 7.5 miles north-northeast of the town of Blue Lake (lat. 40°59'10" N, long. 123°57'30" W; sec. 16, 21, T 7 N, R 2 E). Named on Blue Lake (1979) 7.5' quadrangle. Marsh covers most of the valley.

The Bedstead [TRINITY]: *relief feature*, 10.5 miles north-northeast of Trinity Center (lat. 41°08'45" N, long. 122°36'15" W; at S line sec. 18, T 38 N, R 6 W). Named on Bonanza King (1955) 15' quadrangle.

The Big Bend [MENDOCINO]: *bend*, 6.5 miles west-northwest of Boonville along Rancheria Creek (2) (lat. 39°02'30" N, long. 123°28'45" W; sec. 26, T 14 N, R 15 W). Named on Boonville (1959) 15' quadrangle.

The Brothers [HUMBOLDT]: *rocks*, 4.25 miles west of Petrolia, and nearly 0.5 mile offshore (lat. 40°20' N, long. 124°21'55" W). Named on Petrolia (1969) 7.5' quadrangle.

The Cedars [LAKE]: *area*, 3 miles south of Jericho Valley (lat. 38°47'25" N, long. 122°26' W; in and near sec. 20, T 11 N, R 5 W). Named on Jericho Valley (1958) 7.5' quadrangle.

The Cedars [TRINITY]: *locality*, 2.25 miles southwest of Billys Peak (1) along Coffee Creek (lat. 41°06'30" N, long. 122°48' W; sec. 32, T 38 N, R 8 W). Named on Coffee Creek (1955) 15' quadrangle.

The Corners: see **Boonville** [MENDOCINO].

The Cove: see **Helena** [TRINITY].

The Dell [LAKE]: *canyon*, less than 1 mile long, 2 miles west-northwest of the town of Lower Lake (lat. 39°55'10" N, long. 122°38'55" W; on E line sec. 5, T 12 N, R 7 W). Named on Clearlake Highlands (1958) 7.5' quadrangle.

The Eddys [TRINITY]: *area*, west of the town of Mount Shasta, which is in Siskiyou County, on Trinity-Siskiyou County line; the place is around Mount Eddy. Named on Bonanza King (1955), China Mountain (1955), Dunsmuir (1954), and Weed (1954) 15' quadrangles.

The Forks [MENDOCINO]: *locality*, 3 miles north of Ukiah (lat. 39°11'35" N, long. 123°12'20" W). Named on Ukiah (1958) 7.5' quadrangle.

The Gap [HUMBOLDT]: *pass*, 5.5 miles east-northeast of Trinidad (lat. 41°05'45" N, long. 124°02'50" W; sec. 10, T 8 N, R 1 E). Named on Crannell (1966) 7.5' quadrangle.

The Great Break [HUMBOLDT]: *shoal*, 3.25 miles west of Cape Mendocino (lat. 40°26'10" N, long. 124°28'15" W). Named on Cape Mendocino (1969) 7.5' quadrangle.

The Hermitage [MENDOCINO]: *locality*, 4.25 miles southeast of Leggett (lat. 39°49'25" N, long. 123°39'20" W; at W line sec. 20, T 23 N, R 16 W). Named on Leggett (1969) 7.5' quadrangle.

The H.J. [HUMBOLDT]: *ridge*, west-trending, 1 mile long, 5 miles south-southwest of Petrolia (lat. 40°15'10" N, long. 124°19' W; sec. 32, T 2 S, R 2 W). Named on Petrolia (1969) 7.5' quadrangle.

The Island [HUMBOLDT]: *peak*, 15 miles south-southeast of Scotia (lat. 40°16'50" N, long. 124°00'30" W; on E line sec. 24, T 2 S, R 1 E). Altitude 1699 feet. Named on Bull Creek (1969) 7.5' quadrangle.

The Island [LAKE]: *peaks*, two, 4.5 miles east of Big Signal Peak [MENDOCINO] near Lake-Mendocino County line (lat. 39°30'45" N, long. 123°00'25" W; at S line sec. 7, T 19 N, R 10 W). Named on Sanhedrin Mountain (1966) 7.5' quadrangle.

The Island [MENDOCINO]: *hill*, 6 miles north of Willits (lat. 39°29'35" N, long. 123°20'20" W; on S line sec. 18, T 19 N, R 13 W). Named on Willits (1961) 15' quadrangle.

The Knob [TRINITY]: *peak*, 8 miles south-southeast of Black Rock Mountain (lat. 40°05'20" N, long. 122°58' W; on E line sec. 22, T 26 N, R 10 W). Altitude 6486 feet. Named on Yolla Bolly (1954) 15' quadrangle.

The Lagoon [MENDOCINO]: *lake*, 7.5 miles north of Elk (lat. 39°14'15" N, long. 123°44'25" W; sec. 22, T 16 N, R 17 W). Named on Elk (1960) 7.5' quadrangle. The feature is a cutoff bend of Albion River

The Narrows [HUMBOLDT]: *narrows*, about 12 miles south-southeast of Scotia along Bull Creek (1) (lat. 40°18'50" N, long. 124°01'55" W; sec. 11, T 2 S, R 1 E). Named on Bull Creek (1969) 7.5' quadrangle.

The Narrows [LAKE]:

(1) *narrows*, 6 miles west of the town of Upper Lake between two parts of Blue Lake (lat. 39°10'35" N, long. 123°00'55" W; sec. 6, T 15 N, R 10 W). Named on Cow Mountain (1958) 7.5' quadrangle.

(2) *narrows*, 8.5 miles east of Lakeport between the east and west parts of Clear Lake (lat. 39°02' N, long. 122°45'30" W). Named on Clearlake Oaks (1958) and Lucerne (1958) 7.5' quadrangles.

The Oaks [MENDOCINO]: *locality*, 7.5 miles southwest of Hopland (lat. 38°54'15" N, long. 123°13'30" W; sec. 8, T 12 N, R 12 W). Named on Hopland (1960) 15' quadrangle.

The Outlet [MENDOCINO]: *canyon*, 2 miles long, 8 miles north of Eden Valley along lower reaches of Mill Creek (1) (lat. 39°44'50" N, long. 123°09'30" W). Named on Jamison Ridge (1967) 7.5' quadrangle.

The Peaks [HUMBOLDT]: *peaks*, three, 9 miles east-northeast of Weott (lat. 40°21'50" N, long. 123°47' W; sec. 24, T 1 S, R 3 E). Named on Myers Flat (1969) 7.5' quadrangle.

The Peninsula [LAKE]: *ridge*, east-southeast-trending, 1.25 miles long, 7.25 miles northeast of the town of Lower Lake between Cache Creek and North Fork Cache Creek (lat. 38°58'45" N, long. 122°30'30" W). Named on Lower Lake (1958) and Wilson Valley (1958) 7.5' quadrangles.

The Pocket [LAKE]: *area*, 5.25 miles east of the town of Upper Lake (lat. 39°10'40" N, long. 122°48'55" W; near W line sec. 1, T 15 N, R 9 W). Named on Bartlett Mountain (1958) 7.5' quadrangle.

The Rain Rock [HUMBOLDT]: *locality*, 2.5 miles southeast of Hoopa along Trinity River (lat. 41°00'30" N, long. 123°38'30" W). Named on Hoopa (1979) 7.5' quadrangle, which identifies the place as an Indian ceremonial site. Ceremonies that Indians held there were meant to appease the weather deity (Turner, p. 177).

The Slides [LAKE]: *relief feature*, 9 miles north-northeast of the town of Potter Valley [MENDOCINO] (lat. 39°25'15" N, long. 123°00'30" W; on S line sec. 8, T 18 N, R 10 W). Named on Potter Valley (1960) 15' quadrangle.

The Springs [HUMBOLDT]: *locality*, 6 miles south-southeast of Arcata (lat. 40°47'55" N, long. 124°02' W; near S line sec. 23, T 5 N, R 1 E). Named on Eureka (1942) 15' quadrangle. Arcata South (1959) 7.5' quadrangle shows a spring at the place.

The Turtles: see **Turtle Rocks** [HUMBOLDT].

Third Creek [HUMBOLDT]: *stream*, flows less than 1 mile to Camp Creek 7 miles northwest of Orleans (lat. 41°20'50" N, long. 123°35'20" W); the mouth of the creek is 3500 feet downstream from the mouth of Second Creek. Named on Orleans (1978) 7.5' quadrangle.

Thistle Glade Campground [LAKE]: *locality*, 5.5 miles west-southwest of Crockett Peak (lat. 39°23'35" N, long. 122°52' W); the place is south of Thistle Glade Creek. Named on Crockett Peak (1967) 7.5' quadrangle.

Thistle Glade Creek [LAKE]: *stream*, flows 5.5 miles to Eel River 1.25 miles southeast of Bear Mountain (lat. 39°23'45" N, long. 122°52'50" W). Named on Crockett Peak (1967) 7.5' quadrangle.

Thistle Glen Camp [LAKE]: *locality*, 1.25 miles west-southwest of Bear Mountain along Eel River (lat. 39°23'45" N, long. 122°52'45" W); the place is at the mouth of Thistle Glade Creek. Named on Lake Pillsbury (1967) 7.5' quadrangle.

Thistle Spring [MENDOCINO]: *spring*, 11 miles northeast of Covelo (lat. 39°53'45" N, long. 123°05'20" W; sec. 33, T 24 N, R 11 W). Named on Leech Lake Mountain (1966) 7.5' quadrangle.

Thomas: see **John Thomas Creek** [LAKE].

Thomas Creek [MENDOCINO]: *stream,* flows 5.25 miles to Eel River 11 miles north of the town of Potter Valley (lat. 39°28'30" N, long. 123°09' W; near E line sec. 26, T 19 N, R 12 W). Named on Potter Valley (1960) 15' quadrangle.

Thomas Hill [HUMBOLDT]: *peak,* 9 miles south of Scotia (lat. 40°21'25" N, long. 124°04'20" W). Named on Bull Creek (1969) 7.5' quadrangle.

Thompson Bluff [HUMBOLDT]: *relief feature,* 3.25 miles east-northeast of Weott on the south side of Eel River (lat. 40°20'20" N, long. 123°52'05" W; at W line sec. 32, T 1 S, R 3 E); the feature is nearly 1 mile west-southwest of the mouth of Thompson Creek (2). Named on Myers Flat (1969) 7.5' quadrangle.

Thompson Creek [HUMBOLDT]:
(1) *stream,* flows 3 miles to Little Van Duzen River 5 miles south of Dinsmore (lat. 40°25'05" N, long. 123°37'25" W; sec. 33, T 1 N, R 5 E). Named on Dinsmore (1977) 7.5' quadrangle.
(2) *stream,* flows 2.5 miles to Eel River 4 miles east-northeast of Weott (lat. 40°20'40" N, long. 123°51'10" W; near SE cor. sec. 29, T 1 S, R 3 E). Named on Myers Flat (1969) 7.5' quadrangle.

Thompson Creek [HUMBOLDT-MENDOCINO]: *stream,* flows 3.5 miles, partly in Humboldt County, to Mattole River 7 miles west of Piercy in Mendocino County (lat. 39°59'55" N, long. 123°55'40" W). Named on Bear Harbor (1969) and Briceland (1969) 7.5' quadrangles.

Thompson Creek [LAKE]:
(1) *stream,* flows 2.5 miles to Manning Creek 23 miles south-southeast of Lakeport (lat. 39°00'25" N, long. 122°53'45" W; sec. 6, T 13 N, R 9 W). Named on Highland Springs (1959) and Lakeport (1958) 7.5' quadrangles.
(2) *stream,* flows 1.25 miles to Rumsey Slough 2.25 miles southeast of Lakeport (lat. 39°01'05" N, long. 122°53'30" W; sec. 32, T 14 N, R 9 W). Named on Lakeport (1958) 7.5' quadrangle. On Lakeport (1938) 15' quadrangle, this stream and the part of present Rumsey Slough below the entrance of this stream are called Cole Creek, and the whole is shown as a continuation of present Thompson Creek (1).

Thompson Creek [MENDOCINO]: *stream,* flows 1 mile to Dutch Charlie Creek 3.5 miles northwest of Branscomb (lat. 39°41'20" N, long. 123°40'35" W; near W line sec. 8, T 21 N, R 16 W). Named on Lincoln Ridge (1966) 7.5' quadrangle.

Thompson Field [HUMBOLDT]: *area,* 5 miles east of Weott on the north side of Eel River (lat. 40°19'45" N, long. 123°50'10" W; at SE cor. sec. 33, T 1 S, R 3 E). Named on Myers Flat (1969) 7.5' quadrangle.

Thompson Gulch [MENDOCINO]: *canyon,* drained by a stream that flows 1.5 miles to Little North Fork Big River 7.5 miles northwest of Comptche (lat. 39°20'25" N, long. 123°41'30" W; near N line sec. 18, T 17 N, R 16 W). Named on Comptche (1960) 15' quadrangle.

Thompson Gulch [TRINITY]:
(1) *canyon,* drained by a stream that flows less than 1 mile to Coffee Creek 9 miles west of Billys Peak (1) (lat. 41°06'20" N, long. 122°56' W; sec. 31, T 38 N, R 9 W). Named on Coffee Creek (1955) 15' quadrangle.
(2) *canyon,* drained by a stream that flows 3.5 miles to Carter Gulch 0.5 mile north of Hayfork (lat. 40°33'40" N, long. 123°10'45" W; at NW cor. sec. 12, T 31 N, R 12 W); the canyon heads at Thompson Peak (1). Named on Hayfork (1951) 15' quadrangle.

Thompson Mountain: see **Sawtooth Mountain** [TRINITY].

Thompson Peak [TRINITY]:
(1) *peak,* 4 miles north of Hayfork (lat. 40°36'40" N, long. 123°11'05" W); the peak is at the head of Thompson Gulch (2). Altitude 4957 feet. Named on Hayfork (1951) 15' quadrangle.
(2) *peak,* 11 miles south-southeast of Cecilville, which is in Siskiyou County (lat. 41°00'05" N, long. 123°02'50" W). Altitude 8994 feet. Named on Helena (1951) 15' quadrangle, and on Thompson Peak (1978) 7.5' quadrangle. A packer named Thompson climbed the peak in the 1870's and chiseled his name on the summit (Gudde, 1949, p. 360). United States Board on Geographic Names (1950a, p. 3) rejected the names "Thompson's Peak" and "Sawtooth Peak" for the feature. The Board (1967, p. 9) approved the name "Mount Hilton" for a peak, altitude 8964 feet, situated 3 miles south of Thompson Peak (2) (lat. 40°57'25" N, long. 123°03'14" W); the name is for James Hilton, author of *Lost Horizon,* who visited the region and stated that it was his idea of Shangri-La.

Thompson Peak: see **Gibson Peak** [TRINITY].

Thompson Prairie [HUMBOLDT]: *area,* 8 miles north-northwest of Coyote Peak (lat. 41°14' N, long. 123°55'55" W; at N line sec. 27, T 10 N, R 2 E). Named on Bald Hills (1982) 7.5' quadrangle.

Thorn: see **Thorn Junction** [HUMBOLDT]; **Whitethorn** [HUMBOLDT].

Thornbury Mountain: see **Rodgers Peak** [HUMBOLDT].

Thorne Gulch [TRINITY]: *canyon,* drained by a stream that flows 1 mile to Deadwood Creek 11 miles east of Weaverville (lat. 40°43'05" N, long. 122°43'55" W; near E line sec. 14, T 33 N, R 8 W). Named on French Gulch (1979) 7.5' quadrangle.

Thorn Junction [HUMBOLDT]: *locality,* 9 miles west-southwest of Garberville (lat. 40°03'50" N, long. 123°57'45" W; near SW cor. sec. 33, T 4 S, R 2 E). Named on Briceland (1969) 7.5' quadrangle. Called Thorn on Briceland (1921) 15' quadrangle.

Thorn Siding [MENDOCINO]: *locality,* 6.5 miles south-southeast of Hopland along Northwestern Pacific Railroad (lat. 38°53'45" N, long. 123°03'15" W). Named on Hopland (1944) 15' quadrangle.

Three Brothers [HUMBOLDT]: *rocks,* nearly 4 miles west of Petrolia, and 1900 feet offshore (lat. 40°19'35" N, long. 124°21'25" W). Named on Petrolia (1969) 7.5' quadrangle.

Three Cabins: see **Blue Lake** [HUMBOLDT] (2).

Three Chop Ridge [MENDOCINO]: *ridge,* generally west-trending, 9 miles long, center 10 miles north-northeast of Comptche (lat. 39°24' N, long. 123°33' W). Named on Comptche (1960) and Willits (1961) 15' quadrangles.

Three Creeks [HUMBOLDT]: *stream,* flows 4.5 miles to Willow Creek (1) 3.5 miles west-southwest of the settlement of Willow Creek (lat. 40°55'15" N, long. 123°41'45" W; sec. 11, T 6 N, R 4 E). Named on Willow Creek (1979) 7.5' quadrangle.

Three Creeks Summit [HUMBOLDT]: *locality,* 4 miles west of the settlement of Willow Creek (lat. 40°57' N, long. 123°42'25" W; sec. 34, T 7 N, R 4 E). Named on Willow Creek (1979) 7.5' quadrangle.

Three Crossings [LAKE]: *locality,* 6.25 miles south of Bear Mountain along Parramore Creek (lat. 39°19' N, long. 122°55'15" W; sec. 19, T 17 N, R 9 W). Named on Elk Mountain (1967) 7.5' quadrangle.

Three Forks [TRINITY]: *locality,* 12 miles west-southwest of Black Rock Mountain along Mad River (lat. 40°09'55" N, long. 123°13'35" W; sec. 28, T 27 N, R 12 W); the place is near the entrance of North Fork and South Fork into Mad River. Named on Black Rock Mountain (1954) 15' quadrangle.

Three Peaks [LAKE]: *peaks,* three, 5 miles south-southeast of Middletown (lat. 38°41'15" N, long. 122°34'30" W; on E line sec. 25, T 10 N, R 7 W). Named on Detert Reservoir (1958) 7.5' quadrangle.

Three Peaks: see **King Peak** [HUMBOLDT].

Three Sisters Gulch [TRINITY]: *canyon,* drained by a stream that flows 1 mile to Coffee Creek 5.5 miles west-southwest of Billys Peak (1) (lat. 41°06'45" N, long. 122°51'20" W; sec. 34, T 38 N, R 9 W). Named on Coffee Creek (1955) 15' quadrangle.

Three Springs [MENDOCINO]: *spring,* 6.5 miles south of Navarro (lat. 39°03'15" N, long. 123°33' W; near S line sec. 20, T 14 N, R 15 W). Named on Navarro (1961) 15' quadrangle.

Three Springs Creek [MENDOCINO]: *stream,* flows 2.5 miles to Elk Creek (4) 8 miles south-southwest of Navarro (lat. 39°02'45" N, long. 123°35'20" W; sec. 25, T 14 N, R 16 W); the feature called Three Springs is near the head of the stream. Named on Navarro (1961) 15' quadrangle. Called North Fork [Elk Creek] on Navarro (1943) 15' quadrangle.

Thumb Rock [TRINITY]: *relief feature,* 8 miles south-southwest of Billys Peak (1) (lat. 41°01'30" N, long. 122°49'10" W; sec. 31, T 37 N, R 8 W). Named on Coffee Creek (1955) 15' quadrangle.

Thurman Creek [HUMBOLDT]: *stream,* flows 4 miles to Larabee Creek 4.25 miles north-northwest of Blocksburg (lat. 40°20'05" N, long. 123°40'05" W; near E line sec. 36, T 1 S, R 4 E). Named on Blocksburg (1969) and Larabee Valley (1977) 7.5' quadrangles.

Thurmon Rock [MENDOCINO]: *relief feature,* 12.5 miles north-northwest of Hull Mountain (lat. 39°41'30" N, long. 122°59'55" W; near W line sec. 8, T 21 N, R 10 W). Named on Plaskett Ridge (1967) 7.5' quadrangle.

Thurston Creek [LAKE]: *stream,* flows 9 miles to Thurston Lake 4.5 miles west-northwest of the town of Lower Lake (lat. 38°56'10" N, long. 122°41'25" W; sec. 36, T 13 N, R 8 W). Named on Clearlake Highlands (1958) 7.5' quadrangle. Upson and Kunkel's (1955) map shows a valley called Bonfield Flat located near the head of Thurston Creek.

Thurston Gulch [TRINITY]: *canyon,* drained by a stream that flows 2.5 miles to North Fork Trinity River 9 miles north-northwest of Helena (lat. 40°54' N, long. 123°10' W); the canyon heads near Thurston Peaks. Named on Helena (1951) 15' quadrangle.

Thurston Lake [LAKE]: *lake,* 1.5 miles long, 3.5 miles west-northwest of the town of Lower Lake (lat. 38°55'55" N, long. 122°40'40" W; in and near sec. 31, T 13 N, R 7 W). Named on Clearlake Highlands (1958) 7.5' quadrangle.

Thurston Peaks [TRINITY]: *peaks,* 11 miles north-northwest of Helena (lat. 40°55' N, long. 123°13' W). Altitude of highest 7591 feet. Named on Helena (1951) 15' quadrangle.

Ticknor Creek [HUMBOLDT]: *stream,* flows 3 miles to Eel River 3.5 miles south-southeast of Alderpoint (lat. 40°07'45" N, long. 123°34'40" W; sec. 11, T 4 S, R 5 E). Named on Alderpoint (1969) 7.5' quadrangle.

Tick Prairie [HUMBOLDT]: *area,* 4 miles west of Coyote Peak (lat. 41°08'35" N, long. 123°55'35" W; near E line sec. 27, T 9 N, R 2 E). Named on Bald Hills (1982) 7.5' quadrangle.

Tie Camp [MENDOCINO]: *locality,* 6 miles west-southwest of present Piercy (lat. 39°37' N, long. 123°54'25" W). Named on Kenny (1920) 15' quadrangle.

Tierney Canyon [HUMBOLDT-TRINITY]: *canyon,* drained by a stream that heads in Humboldt County and flows 2.25 miles to Van Duzen River 5.5 miles southeast of Dinsmore in Trinity County (lat. 40°26'40" N, long. 123°31'45" W, near NW cor. sec. 29, T 1 N, R 6 E); the canyon heads near

Tierney Peak. Named on Dinsmore (1977) 7.5' quadrangle.

Tierney Peak [HUMBOLDT]: *peak*, 4.5 miles south-southeast of Dinsmore (lat. 40°26'10" N, long. 123°33'50" W; sec. 25, T 1 N, R 5 E). Altitude 5179 feet. Named on Dinsmore (1977) 7.5' quadrangle.

Tigerville: see **Pine Hill** [HUMBOLDT].

Tighe: see **Burlington** [HUMBOLDT].

Tillas Island [DEL NORTE]: *peninsula*, 2.5 miles west of the town of Smith River (lat. 41°55'55" N, long. 124°11'35" W); the feature is west of the lower part of Tillas Slough. Named on Smith River (1966) 7.5' quadrangle. Crescent City (1952) 15' quadrangle shows the feature as an island.

Tillas Slough [DEL NORTE]: *water feature*, 3 miles long, 2 miles west of the town of Smith River (lat. 41°55'55" N, long. 124°11'10" W). Named on Smith River (1966) 7.5' quadrangle.

Tilly: see **Laytonville** [MENDOCINO].

Timbered Ridge [MENDOCINO]: *ridge*, generally west-trending, 1.5 miles long, 9.5 miles north-northeast of Eden Valley (lat. 39°45' N, long. 123°06'15" W). Named on Newhouse Ridge (1967) and Thatcher Ridge (1967) 7.5' quadrangles.

Timber Lake [LAKE]: *lake*, 350 feet long, 1.5 miles east-northeast of Potato Hill (lat. 39°21'50" N, long. 122°46'35" W; at SE cor. sec. 32, T 18 N, R 8 W). Named on Potato Hill (1967) 7.5' quadrangle.

Timberline Camp [LAKE]: *locality*, nearly 1 mile south of Hull Mountain on Boardman Ridge (lat. 39°30'35" N, long. 122°56'05" W; near S line sec. 11, T 19 N, R 10 W). Named on Hull Mountain (1967) 7.5' quadrangle.

Timber Point [MENDOCINO]: *ridge*, west-trending, 0.5 mile long, 10 miles south-southwest of Piercy (lat. 39°50'50" N, long. 123°52'40" W; on E line sec. 17, T 23 N, R 18 W). Named on Hales Grove (1970) and Mistake Point (1969) 7.5' quadrangles.

Timber Ridge [MENDOCINO]: *ridge*, northwest-trending, 3 miles long, 9 miles south-southwest of Piercy (lat. 39°51'30" N, long. 123°51'35" W). Named on Hales Grove (1970) and Mistake Point (1969) 7.5' quadrangles.

Tin Cabin Creek [MENDOCINO]: *stream*, flows 4 miles to Eel River 3.5 miles south-southeast of Spyrock (2) (lat. 39°50'40" N, long. 123°24'55" W; near E line sec. 21, T 23 N, R 14 W). Named on Covelo West (1967) and Iron Peak (1967) 7.5' quadrangles.

Tin Can Creek [MENDOCINO]: *stream*, flows 3 miles to Alder Creek (3) 10.5 miles south-southwest of Navarro (lat. 39°00'10" N, long. 123°36'35" W; near W line sec. 11, T 13 N, R 16 W). Named on Navarro (1961) and Point Arena (1960) 15' quadrangles.

Tindall Camp [MENDOCINO]: *locality*, 10 miles west-southwest of Ornbaun Valley (lat. 38°51'25" N, long. 123°28'40" W; at E line sec. 36, T 12 N, R 15 W). Named on Ornbaun Valley (1960) 15' quadrangle.

Tip Top Ridge [HUMBOLDT]: *ridge*, generally south-southeast-trending, 8.5 miles long, center about 5 miles north of the town of Blue Lake (lat. 40°57'30" N, long. 123°59'15" W). Named on Arcata North (1959), Blue Lake (1979), and Crannell (1966) 7.5' quadrangles. Called Tiptop Ridge on Trinidad (1952) 15' quadrangle, but United States Board on Geographic Names (1968a, p. 8) rejected this form for the name.

Tish Tang a Tang Creek [HUMBOLDT]: *stream*, flows 12 miles to Trinity River 2.5 miles southeast of Hoopa (lat. 41°01'35" N, long. 123°38'20" W; sec. 5, T 7 N, R 5 E). Named on Hoopa (1979), Tish Tang Point (1978), and Trinity Mountain (1979) 7.5' quadrangles. Called Tish Tang-a-Tang Cr. (with hyphens) on Hoopa (1935) 30' quadrangle. The name is the Americanization of the Indian designation of a village at the mouth of the stream (Kroeber, p. 62). South Fork enters 6 miles east of Hoopa; it is 4.25 miles long and is named on Tish Tang Point (1978) and Trinity Mountain (1979) 7.5' quadrangles.

Tish Tang a Tang Ridge [HUMBOLDT]: *ridge*, generally west-trending, 7.5 miles long, center 7 miles east of Hoopa (lat. 41°02'25" N, long. 123°32'30" W). Named on Tish Tang Point (1978) and Trinity Mountain (1979) 7.5' quadrangles. United States Board on Geographic Names (1983a, p. 4) approved the name "Graveyard Prairie" for a meadow located on the south slope of Tish Tang a Tang Ridge (lat. 41°02'20" N, long. 123°29'15" W); the place reportedly has the graves of two soldiers accused of murder and caught by the army in 1864.

Tish Tang Campground [HUMBOLDT]: *locality*, 2.5 miles southeast of Hoopa along Trinity River (lat. 41°01'25" N, long. 123°38'15" W); the place is opposite the mouth of Tish Tang a Tang Creek. Named on Hoopa (1979) 7.5' quadrangle.

Tish Tang Point [HUMBOLDT]: *peak*, 8 miles east of Hoopa (lat. 41°03'35" N, long. 123°31'40" W); the peak is south of Tish Tang a Tang Creek. Altitude 4963 feet. Named on Tish Tang Point (1978) 7.5' quadrangle.

Titlow Hill [HUMBOLDT]: *peak*, 8 miles south-southwest of the settlement of Willow Creek (lat. 40°50'20" N, long. 123°42'40" W; at S line sec. 3, T 5 N, R 4 E). Named on Grouse Mountain (1979) 7.5' quadrangle.

Tlamath River: see **Klamath River** [DEL NORTE-HUMBOLDT].

Tolcan Campground [HUMBOLDT]: *locality*, 4.25 miles north of Point Delgada (lat. 40°05' N, long. 124°03'20" W; sec. 27, T 4 S, R 1 E). Named on Shelter Cove (1969) 7.5' quadrangle.

Tolson: see **Hales Grove** [MENDOCINO].

Tom Bell Creek [MENDOCINO]: *stream*, flows 2.5 miles to Albion River 3 miles west of Comptche (lat. 39°16'05" N, long. 123°38'30" W; near NE cor. sec. 9, T 16 N, R 16 W). Named on Camptche (1960) 15' quadrangle.

Tom Bell Flat [MENDOCINO]: *area*, 3 miles west of Comptche (lat. 39°16'10" N, long. 123°38'30" W; at SE cor. sec. 4, T 16 N, R 16 W); the place is at the mouth of Tom Bell Creek. Named on Comptche (1960) 15' quadrangle.

Tombstone Rock [TRINITY]: *relief feature*, 7.25 miles southwest of Black Rock Mountain (lat. 40°08'15" N, long. 123°06'50" W; near S line sec. 33, T 27 N, R 11 W). Named on Black Rock Mountain (1954) 15' quadrangle.

Tom Creek [HUMBOLDT]: *stream*, flows 2 miles to Big Lagoon 8.5 miles north-northeast of Trinidad (lat. 41°10'30" N, long. 124°06'10" W; sec. 7, T 9 N, R 1 E); the stream heads opposite the source of Tom McDonald Creek. Named on Rodgers Peak (1966) 7.5' quadrangle.

Tom Dye Rock [LAKE]: *relief feature*, 4.5 miles south-southwest of Middletown (lat. 38°41'25" N, long. 122°38'05" W; near NE cor. sec. 28, T 10 N, R 7 W). Named on Mount Saint Helena (1959) 7.5' quadrangle. Tom Dye of Middletown hid out at the place after he killed a man in 1878 (Gudde, 1969, p. 341).

Tom Gulch [HUMBOLDT]: *canyon*, drained by a stream that flows 2 miles to South Fork Elk River (1) 4.5 miles east-southeast of Fields Landing (lat. 40°41'35" N, long. 124°08'35" W; near NE cor. sec. 35, T 4 N, R 1 W). Named on Fields Landing (1959) 7.5' quadrangle.

Tomki: see **Potter Valley** [MENDOCINO] (2).

Tomkiah: see **Willits** [MENDOCINO].

Tomki Creek [MENDOCINO]: *stream*, flows 21 miles to Eel River 7.5 miles north-northwest of the town of Potter Valley (lat. 39°25'30" N, long. 123°08'30" W; sec. 12, T 18 N, R 12 W). Named on Potter Valley (1960) and Willits (1961) 15' quadrangles, and on Longvale (1966) and Willis Ridge (1966) 7.5' quadrangles. The name is of Indian origin (Gudde, 1969, p. 341).

Tom Lang Gulch [TRINITY]: *canyon*, drained by a stream that flows 3.25 miles to Trinity River 4.5 miles southeast of Weaverville (lat. 40°41'05" N, long. 122°52'15" W; sec. 27, T 33 N, R 9 W). Named on Weaverville (1950) 15' quadrangle. Called Tom Long Gulch on Weaverville (1913) 30' quadrangle.

Tom Long Creek [HUMBOLDT-MENDOCINO]: *stream*, heads in Mendocino County and flows 7.25 miles to East Branch of South Fork Eel River 11 miles south-southwest of Alderpoint in Humboldt County (lat. 40°01'40" N, long. 123°41'55" W; at N line sec. 14, T 5 S, R 4 E). Named on Bell Springs (1969), Harris (1969), Jewett Rock (1969), and Noble Butte (1969) 7.5' quadrangles.

Tom Long Gulch: see **Tom Lang Gulch** [TRINITY].

Tom McDonald Creek [HUMBOLDT]: *stream*, flows 4.5 miles to Redwood Creek (1) 12.5 miles north-northeast of Trinidad (lat. 41°12'25" N, long. 124°00'35" W; near N line sec. 1, T 9 N, R 1 E). Named on Rodgers Peak (1966) 7.5' quadrangle.

Tompkins Creek [TRINITY]: *stream*, flows 2.5 miles to Mad River 6.5 miles south of Forest Glen (lat. 40°16'40" N, long. 123°19'55" W; sec. 24, T 2 S, R 7 E). Named on Forest Glen (1979) 7.5' quadrangle.

Tompkins Hill [HUMBOLDT]: *ridge*, generally west-trending, 7 miles south-southeast of Fields Landing (lat. 40°37'40" N, long. 124°10'45" W; sec. 21, 22, T 3 N, R 1 W). Named on Fields Landing (1959) 7.5' quadrangle. On Fortuna (1944) 15' quadrangle, the ridge is the southeast extension of present Table Bluff (1). The name is for Nicholas Tompkins, who settled at the place in 1850 (Turner, p. 217).

Toney Creek [MENDOCINO]: *stream*, flows 3 miles to Eden Creek at the north edge of Eden Valley (lat. 39°38'15" N, long. 123°10'55" W; sec. 34, T 21 N, R 12 W). Named on Brushy Mountain (1966) and Jamison Ridge (1967) 7.5' quadrangles.

Tonys Point [TRINITY]: *relief feature*, 7 miles east-southeast of Burnt Ranch along Trinity River (lat. 41°47' N, long. 123°20'45" W). Named on Ironside Mountain (1951) 15' quadrangle.

Toorup: see **Mount Toorup**, under **Red Mountain** [DEL NORTE].

Too too tut na: see **Klamath River** [DEL NORTE-HUMBOLDT].

Torrey Corrals [HUMBOLDT]: *locality*, nearly 6 miles east-northeast of Showers Mountain lat. 40°36'50" N, long. 123°36' W; sec. 27, T 3 N, R 5 E); the place is 0.5 mile north-northwest of Torrey Crossing. Named on Blake Mountain (1979) 7.5' quadrangle.

Torrey Crossing [HUMBOLDT]: *locality*, nearly 6 miles east-northeast of Showers Mountain along Pilot Creek (lat. 40°36'30" N, long. 123°35'45" W; sec. 27, T 3 N, R 5 E). Named on Blake Mountain (1979) 7.5' quadrangle.

Torrey Ridge [HUMBOLDT]: *ridge*, southwest-trending, 1.25 miles long, 6.5 miles east-northeast of Showers Mountain (lat. 40°37' N, long. 123°35'10" W); the ridge is northeast of Torrey Crossing. Named on Blake Mountain (1979) 7.5' quadrangle. The name is for Abner Wood Torrey, who settled in the neighborhood in 1877 (Turner, p. 217).

Toss-up Creek [HUMBOLDT]: *stream*, flows 3 miles to Redwood Creek (1) 10.5 miles northeast of the town of Blue Lake (lat. 40°59'10" N, long.

123°51' W; near NW cor. sec. 21, T 7 N, R 3 E). Named on Blue Lake (1979) and Lord-Ellis Summit (1973) 7.5' quadrangles.

Tostin Creek [HUMBOLDT]: *stream,* flows 3.5 miles to South Fork Salmon Creek 6 miles west-southwest of Phillipsburg (lat. 40°10'50" N, long. 123°53'20" W; near SW cor. sec. 19, T 3 S, R 3 E). Named on Ettersburg (1969) and Miranda (1970) 7.5' quadrangles.

Towhead Flat [LAKE]: *area,* 11 miles north-northeast of the town of Potter Valley [MENDOCINO] (lat. 39°28'05" N, long. 123°02'05" W; at SE cor. sec. 26, T 19 N, R 11 W). Named on Potter Valley (1960) 7.5' quadrangle.

Town Creek [MENDOCINO]: *stream,* flows 6.5 miles to Grist Creek 0.5 mile south-southeast of Covelo (lat. 39°47' N, long. 123°14'35" W; sec. 7, T 22 N, R 12 W). Named on Covelo East (1967) and Covelo West (1967) 7.5' quadrangles.

Township Gulch [MENDOCINO]: *canyon,* drained by a stream that flows less than 1 mile to Rancheria Creek (2) 5.25 miles west-northwest of Boonville (lat. 39°02' N, long. 123°27'30" W; near E line sec. 36, T 14 N, R 15 W). Named on Boonville (1959) 15' quadrangle.

Traft Ridge [LAKE]: *ridge,* north-northwest- to northwest-trending, 1 mile long, nearly 5 miles west of Lakeport (lat. 39°03'10" N, long. 123°00'10" W). Named on Purdys Gardens (1958) 7.5' quadrangle.

Trail Creek [HUMBOLDT]: *stream,* flows less than 1 mile to Little South Fork Boise Creek (1) 3.5 miles south-southeast of Orleans (lat. 41°15'15" N, long. 123°30'40" W). Named on Hopkins Butte (1979) and Orelans (1978) 7.5' quadrangles.

Trail Ridge [HUMBOLDT]: *ridge,* southeast- to south-trending, 1.5 miles long, 2.25 miles south-southeast of Coyote Peak (lat. 41°06'20" N, long. 123°50'25" W). Named on Hupa Mountain (1982) 7.5' quadrangle.

Tramp Creek [MENDOCINO]: *stream,* flows nearly 2 miles to Middle Fork Eel River 7.5 miles east-northeast of Covelo (lat. 39°49'25" N, long. 123°07' W; at E line sec. 30, T 23 N, R 11 W). Named on Newhouse Ridge (1967) 7.5' quadrangle.

Tramway Camp: see **Wheel Gulch** [MENDOCINO].

Tramway Gulch [MENDOCINO]:

(1) *canyon,* drained by a stream that flows 1.5 miles to Big River 3.5 miles north of Comptche (lat. 39°18'45" N, long. 123°36'10" W; near NW cor. sec. 5, T 17 N, R 16 W). Named on Comptche (1960) 15' quadrangle.

(2) *canyon,* drained by a stream that flows 1.5 miles to North Fork Navarro River 3.5 miles west of Navarro (lat. 39°09'20" N, long. 123°39'15" W; near SW cor. sec. 14, T 15 N, R 16 W). Named on Navarro (1961) 15' quadrangle.

Tramway Gulch: see **Wheel Gulch** [MENDOCINO].

Trappers Creek [HUMBOLDT]: *stream,* flows 1 mile to Grouse Creek (2) 7 miles east of Board Camp Mountain (lat. 40°42'20" N, long. 123°35'20" W). Named on Sims Mountain (1979) 7.5' quadrangle.

Travelers Home [MENDOCINO]: *area,* 12 miles east-northeast of Covelo (lat. 39°52'50" N, long. 123°03'35" W; near E line sec. 3, T 23 N, R 11 W). Named on Leech Lake Mountain (1966) 7.5' quadrangle. On Covelo (1952) 15' quadrangle, the name applies to the canyon in which the place lies.

Travelers Home: see **Hearst** [MENDOCINO].

Tree House [MENDOCINO]: *locality,* nearly 5 miles south-southeast of Piercy along South Fork Eel River (lat. 39°55' N, long. 123°45'50" W; sec. 20, T 24 N, R 17 W). Named on Piercy (1950) 15' quadrangle.

Treloar Creek [TRINITY]: *stream,* flows 4 miles to Trinity River 14 miles northeast of Hyampom (lat. 40°44'20" N, long. 123°15'10" W). Named on Helena (1951) and Hyampom (1951) 15' quadrangles.

Treloar Ridge [TRINITY]: *ridge,* south-trending, 5.5 miles long, 6 miles west of Helena (lat. 40°47' N, long. 123°14'15" W). Named on Hayfork (1951) and Helena (1951) 15' quadrangles.

Tri Board Camp [HUMBOLDT]: *locality,* at the top of Board Camp Mountain (lat. 40°41'50" N, long. 123°43' W; sec. 27, T 4 N, R 4 E). Named on Board Camp Mountain (1977) 7.'5' quadrangle.

Tri-Forest Peak [TRINITY]: *peak,* 18 miles north of Weaverville on Trinity-Siskiyou County line (lat. 40°59'40" N, long. 122°55' W; near E line sec. 8, T 36 N, R 9 W); Klamath National Forest, Shasta National Forest, and Trinity National Forest meet at the place. Altitude 7681 feet. Named on Trinity Dam (1950) 15' quadrangle.

Trinidad [HUMBOLDT]: *village,* 18 miles north of Eureka along the coast (lat. 41°03'35" N, long. 124°08'25" W; sec. 23, 26, T 8 N, R 1 W). Named on Trinidad (1966) 7.5' quadrangle. Called Port Trinidad on Gibbes' (1852) map. Postal authorities established Trinidad post office in 1851 (Frickstad, p. 47), and the community incorporated in 1870. A group of men arrived at the site in 1850 aboard the schooner *James R. Whiting* and laid out the town (Coy, 1929, p. 49). The place first was called Warnersville to honor R.V. Warner, an original settler (Hanna, p. 333). Postal authorities established Hadley post office 27 miles northeast of Trinidad in 1880 and discontinued it in 1881 (Salley, p. 91). California Mining Bureau's (1909b) map shows a place called Luffenholtz located nearly 5 miles southeast of Trinidad along the railroad. Postal authorities established Luffenholtz post office in 1904 and discontinued it in 1909 (Salley, p. 129). The name "Luffenholtz" was for an early settler who built a mill at the place, and who used the form "Luffelholz" for his name (Coy, 1929, p. 96). California Mining Bureau's (1917b) map shows a place called Camp 19 located about 6 miles east of Luffenholtz.

Trinidad Bay [HUMBOLDT]: *embayment,* at Trinidad along the coast (lat. 41°03'15" N, long. 124°08'25" W; sec. 25, 26, T 8 N, R 1 W); the feature is east of Trinidad Head. Named on Trinidad (1966) 7.5' quadrangle. Bruno de Hezeta entered the embayment in 1775 and gave it the name "Puerto de la Trinidad" because he took possession on Trinity Sunday (Gudde, 1949, p. 368). United States Coast and Geodetic Survey (p. 147) referred to Trinidad Harbor, "a small cove eastward of Trinidad Head."

Trinidad Harbor: see **Trinidad Bay** [HUMBOLDT].

Trinidad Head [HUMBOLDT]: *promontory,* 0.5 mile southwest of Trinidad along the coast (lat. 41°03'15" N, long. 124°09' W; sec. 26, T 8 N, R 1 W); the feature is at the west end of Trinidad Bay. Named on Trinidad (1966) 7.5' quadrangle. Members of the Gregg party gave the name "Gregg's Point" to the feature in 1849 (Bancroft, p. 501.)

Trinidad Head: see **Little Trinidad Head**, under **Little Head** [HUMBOLDT].

Trinity: see **Camp Trinity** [TRINITY]; **Junction City** [TRINITY].

Trinity Alps [TRINITY]:

(1) *range,* 11 miles southeast of Cecilville, which is in Siskiyou County, on Trinity-Siskiyou County line (lat. 41°00'45" N, long. 123°00' W). Named on Cecilville (1955), Coffee Creek (1955), and Trinity Lake (1950) 15' quadrangles. United States Board on Geographic Names (1960a, p. 18) rejected the name "Salmon Trinity Alps" for the feature.

(2) *locality,* 9 miles north-northeast of Weaverville (lat. 40°51'25" N, long. 122°53'15" W; sec. 28, T 35 N, R 9 W). Named on Trinity Dam (1950) 15' quadrangle. Postal authorities established Trinity Alps post office in 1928 and discontinued it in 1954 (Frickstad, p. 208).

Trinity Alps Creek [TRINITY]: *stream,* flows 3.5 miles to Stuart Fork 9.5 miles north-northeast of Weaverville (lat. 40°51'35" N, long. 122°53'30" W; sec. 28, T 35 N, R 9 W); the mouth of the creek is near Trinity Alps (2). Named on Trinity Dam (1950) 15' quadrangle. On Weaverville (1913) 30' quadrangle, the canyon of the stream is called Deep Gulch.

Trinity Bay: see **Humboldt Bay** [HUMBOLDT].

Trinity Center [TRINITY]: *village,* 21 miles north-northeast of Weaverville along Trinity River (lat. 41°00'20" N, long. 122°41'20" W; near E line sec. 5, T 36 N, R 7 W). Named on Bonanza King (1955) 15' quadrangle. Water of Clair Engle Reservoir now covers the original site of Trinity Center; a new community called Trinity Center was built in 1959 a short distance south of the old site (Jones, p. 35). Postal authorities established Trinity Centre post office in 1855, discontinued it in 1872, reestablished it in 1873, and changed the name to Trinity Center in 1894 (Salley, p. 224). They established Altoona post office 11 miles north of Trinity Center in 1876, discontinued it for a time the same year, and discontinued it finally in 1880 (Salley, p. 6). Bonanza King (1955) 15' quadrangle shows Altoona mine situated 12 miles northeast of Trinity Center.

Trinity House Gulch [TRINITY]: *canyon,* drained by a stream that flows 3 miles to Trinity River 4.5 miles east-southeast of Weaverville (lat. 40°41'40" N, long. 122°51'50" W; near NE cor. sec. 2, T 33 N, R 9 W). Named on Weaverville (1950) 15' quadrangle.

Trinity Lake: see **Clair Engle Lake** [TRINITY].

Trinity Mountain [HUMBOLDT-TRINITY]: *peak,* 14 miles east of Hoopa on Humboldt-Trinity County line (lat. 41°01'55" N, long. 123°24'45" W). Altitude 6094 feet. Named on Trinity Mountain (1979) 7.5' quadrangle.

Trinity Mountain: see **Hoadley Peaks** [TRINITY]; **North Trinity Mountain** [HUMBOLDT]; **Rodgers Peak** [HUMBOLDT].

Trinity Mountains [TRINITY]: *range,* west of Trinity River on Trinity-Shasta County line. Named on Redding (1958) 1° x 2° quadrangle. Called Bully Choop Mountains on Red Bluff (1894) 1° quadrangle.

Trinity Reservoir: see **Clair Engle Lake** [TRINITY].

Trinity River [HUMBOLDT-TRINITY]: *stream,* formed by the confluence of High Camp Creek and Bear Creek (1) in Trinity County, flows 145 miles to Klamath River at Weitchpec in Humboldt County (lat. 41°11'05" N, long. 123°42'25" W; sec. 10, T 9 N, R 4 E). Named on Redding (1958) and Weed (1963) 1° x 2° quadrangles. P.B. Reading discovered the river in 1845 while on a trapping expedition; he gave it the name "Trinity" in the mistaken belief that it flowed to the coast at Trinidad Bay (Bledsoe, p. 62). East Fork enters the main stream from the northeast 22 miles northeast of Weaverville; it is 20 miles long and is named on Bonanza King (1955), Dunsmuir (1954), and Schell Mountain (1950) 15' quadrangles. Present Mumbo Creek [TRINITY] is called N. Fk. [of E. Fk. Trinity River] on Miller's (1890) map. North Fork enters the main stream from the north near Helena; it is 26 miles long and is named on Helena (1951) 15' quadrangle, and on Cecil Lake (1979) 7.5' quadrangle. East Fork of North Fork enters North Fork 1.25 miles upstream from the mouth of North Fork; it is 17 miles long and is named on Helena (1951) 15' quadrangle. East Branch of East Fork of North Fork enters East Fork of North Fork from the northeast 8 miles north of Helena; it is 5 miles long and is named on Helena (1951) 15' quadrangle. South Fork enters the main stream from the south 1 mile west of Salyer; it is 70 miles long and is named on Redding (1958)

1° x 2° quadrangle. East Fork of South Fork enters South Fork from the east 7 miles west-northwest of Black Rock Mountain; it is 10.5 miles long and is named on Black Rock Mountain (1954) and Yolla Bolly (1954) 15' quadrangles.

Trinity River: see **Little Trinity River** [TRINITY].

Trinity River Campground [TRINITY]: *locality*, 7.5 miles north of Trinity Center (lat. 41°06'45" N, long. 122°41'20" W; on W line sec. 32, T 38 N, R 7 W); the place is along Trinity River. Named on Bonanza King (1955) 15' quadrangle.

Trinity Village [TRINITY]: *settlement*, 3.25 miles east-southeast of Salyer (lat. 40°52'35" N, long. 123°31'30" W). Named on Salyer (1979) 7.5' quadrangle.

Triplett Gulch [MENDOCINO]: *canyon*, drained by a stream that flows 1.25 miles to the sea 5 miles northwest of Gualala (lat. 38°48'45" N, long. 123°35'55" W; sec. 12, T 11 N, R 16 W). Named on Gualala (1960) 7.5' quadrangle.

Trough Ridge [TRINITY]: *ridge*, east-trending, 2.5 miles long, 6 miles west of Black Rock Mountain (lat. 40°11'55" N, long. 123°07'20" W). Named on Black Rock Mountain (1954) 15' quadrangle.

Trout Creek [LAKE]:

(1) *stream*, flows 4 miles to Eel River 4.25 miles east-northeast of Hull Mountain (lat. 39°32'20" N, long. 122°51'30" W; near S line sec. 34, T 20 N, R 9 W). Named on Hull Mountain (1967) and Kneecap Ridge (1967) 7.5' quadrangles.

(2) *stream*, flows 2 miles to Cache Creek 1.5 miles south-southeast of Wilson Valley (2) (lat. 38°57'05" N, long. 122°27'10" W; near S line sec. 19, T 13 N, R 5 W). Named on Wilson Valley (1958) 7.5' quadrangle.

Trout Creek [MENDOCINO]: *stream*, flows 2.25 miles to Eel River 4.5 miles north-northeast of the town of Potter Valley (lat. 39°22'30" N, long. 123°03'45" W; sec. 34, T 18 N, R 11 W). Named on Potter Valley (1960) 15' quadrangle.

Trout Creek [TRINITY]: *stream*, flows 2.5 miles to Mad River 11 miles west-southwest of Black Rock Mountain (lat. 40°08'15" N, long. 123°11'55" W; sec. 3, T 26 N, R 12 W). Named on Black Rock Mountain (1954) 15' quadrangle.

Troutdale Creek [LAKE]: *stream*, flows 1 mile to Napa County 5.5 miles south of Middletown (lat. 38°40'25" N, long. 122°36'15" W; sec. 35, T 10 N, R 7 W). Named on Detert Reservoir (1958) 7.5' quadrangle.

Truss Creek [HUMBOLDT]; *stream*, flows 0.5 mile to South Fork Eel River 3 miles south-southeast of Weott (lat. 40°17'05" N, long. 123°53'25" W; near NW cor. sec. 19, T 2 S, R 3 E). Named on Weott (1969) 7.5' quadrangle.

Tryon Corner [DEL NORTE]: *locality*, 3.5 miles south of the town of Smith River (lat. 41°52'50" N, long. 124°08'40" W; sec. 11, T 17 N, R 1 W). Named on Smith River (1966) 7.5' quadrangle.

Tryon Creek [DEL NORTE]: *stream*, flows 3.25 miles to end 3 miles southwest of the town of Smith River near Yontocket Slough (lat. 41°53'45" N, long. 124°10'55" W; sec. 4, T 17 N, R 1 W). Named on Crescent City (1966) and Smith River (1966) 7.5' quadrangles.

Tub Creek [TRINITY]: *stream*, flows 2.5 miles to Cox Creek 6.25 miles east of Kettenpom (lat. 40°10'05" N, long. 123°20'40" W; at SE cor. sec. 26, T 3 S, R 7 E); the stream heads near Tub Spring. Named on Shannon Butte (1967) 7.5' quadrangle.

Tub Spring [TRINITY]: *spring*, 8 miles east-northeast of Kettenpom (lat. 40°11'15" N, long. 123°18'45" W; sec. 19, T 3 S, R 8 E). Named on Shannon Butte (1967) 7.5' quadrangle. The name is from a barrel that was cut in half and set in the spring (Gudde, 1949, p. 370).

Tucker Camp [LAKE]: *locality*, 6.25 miles west of Lakeport (lat. 39°03'05" N, long. 123°01'50" W); the place is near southeast end of Tucker Ridge. Named on Purdys Gardens (1958) 7.5' quadrangle.

Tucker Ridge [LAKE]: *ridge*, northwest-trending, 0.5 mile long, 6.5 miles west of Lakeport (lat. 39°03'10" N, long. 123°02'05" W; sec. 23, T 14 N, R 11 W). Named on Purdys Gardens (1958) 7.5' quadrangle.

Tucker Rock: see **Klamath River** [DEL NORTE-HUMBOLDT].

Tule Creek [TRINITY]: *stream*, flows 8 miles to Hayfork Creek 1.5 miles west of Hayfork (lat. 40°33'05" N, long. 123°12'50" W; sec. 10, T 31 N R 12 W). Named on Hayfork (1951) and Hyampom (1951) 15' quadrangles, and on Naufus Creek (1979) 7.5' quadrangle. Called Main Tule Cr. on Averill's (1940) map.

Tule Creek: see **East Tule Creek** [TRINITY]; **West Tule Creek** [TRINITY].

Tule Island [LAKE]: *island*, 700 feet long, 5 miles north-northeast of Lakeport in Clear Lake (lat. 39°06'55" N, long. 122°52'35" W). Named on Lakeport (1958) 7.5' quadrangle.

Tule Lake [LAKE]:

(1) *lake*, 600 feet long, 12.5 miles north-northeast of the town of Potter Valley [MENDOCINO] (lat. 39°29'20" N, long. 123°02' W; on E line sec. 23, T 19 N, R 11 W). Named on Potter Valley (1960) 15' quadrangle. Called Summit Lake on Pomo (1943) 15' quadrangle.

(2) *intermittent lake*, 2 miles long, 2 miles west of the town of Upper Lake (lat. 39°09'40" N, long. 122°56'40" W); the feature is formed by the widening of Scott Creek. Named on Upper Lake (1958) 7.5' quadrangle. Chandler (p. 32) called Tule Lake "a small, marshy depression."

Tule Spring [HUMBOLDT]: *spring*, 2.5 miles southwest of Showers Mountain (lat. 40°33'20" N, long. 123°44' W; sec. 16, T 2 N, R 4 E). Named on Showers Mountain (1978) 7.5' quadrangle.

Tully Creek [HUMBOLDT]: *stream*, flows 9.5 miles to Klamath River 8 miles north-northeast of Coyote Peak (lat. 41°13'45" N, long. 123°46'20" W; near E line sec. 25, T 10 N, R 3 E). Named on French Camp Ridge (1983) 7.5' quadrangle.

Tunnel Creek [TRINITY]: *canyon*, drained by a stream that flows 3.25 miles to Eel River 9 miles south of Kettenpom (lat. 40°01'50" N, long. 123°29'30" W; sec. 15, T 5 S, R 6 E); the mouth of the creek is just east of a tunnel along Northwestern Pacific Railroad. Named on Lake Mountain (1967) 7.5' quadrangle. Called Copper Mine Creek on Island Mountain (1922) 15' quadrangle.

Tunnel Ridge [TRINITY]: *ridge*, south-trending, 2 miles long, 5 miles east of Helena (lat. 40°46'30" N, long. 123°02' W). Named on Helena (1951) 15' quadrangle.

Tunnel Spring: see **Astorg Spring**, under **Glenbrook** [LAKE].

Turep: see **Mount Turep**, under **Red Mountain** [DEL NORTE].

Turner: see **Brad Turner Creek** [MENDOCINO].

Turner Creek [MENDOCINO]: *stream*, flows nearly 5 miles to Mill Creek (1) 4 miles southeast of Covelo (lat. 39°45'15" N, long. 123°11'20" W; near W line sec. 22, T 22 N, R 12 W). Named on Covelo East (1967) and Jamison Ridge (1967) 7.5' quadrangles.

Turner Flat [LAKE]: *area*, 4.25 miles west-southwest of Middletown (lat. 38°44'10" N, long. 122°41'30" W; on S line sec. 1, T 10 N, R 8 W). Named on Mount Saint Helena (1959) 7.5' quadrangle.

Turner Opening [HUMBOLDT]: *area*, 6.5 miles south-southeast of Scotia (lat. 40°23'25" N, long. 124°03'25" W). Named on Scotia (1970) 7.5' quadrangle.

Turners Bar: see **Reading Creek** [TRINITY].

Turney Spring [TRINITY]: *spring*, 13 miles south-southeast of Salmon Mountain (lat. 41°01'20" N, long. 123°16'50" W). Named on Dees Peak (1978) 7.5' quadrangle.

Turtle Lake [HUMBOLDT]:

(1) *lake*, 250 feet long, 3 miles north-northwest of Weitchpec (lat. 41°13'45" N, long. 123°43'15" W). Named on Weitchpec (1979) 7.5' quadrangle.

(2) *intermittent lake*, 650 feet long, 5.5 miles west of Dinsmore (lat. 40°29'30" N, long. 123°42'45" W; sec. 3, T 1 N, R 4 E). Named on Larabee Valley (1977) 7.5' quadrangle.

Turtle Lake [MENDOCINO]: *lake*, 150 feet long, nearly 4 miles northeast of Hull Mountain (lat. 39°33'55" N, long. 122°53'25" W; near N line sec. 29, T 20 N, R 9 W). Named on Hull Mountain (1967) 7.5' quadrangle.

Turtle Lake [TRINITY]: *intermittent lake*, 150 feet long, 6 miles south of Kettenpom (lat. 40°04'35" N, long. 123°26' W; near N line sec. 31, T 4 S, R 7 E). Named on Lake Mountain (1967) 7.5' quadrangle.

Turtle Rocks [HUMBOLDT]: *rocks*, 5.5 miles north-northwest of Trinidad, and 1 mile offshore at Patricks Point (1) (lat. 41°08' N, long. 124°11' W). Named on Trinidad (1966) 7.5' quadrangle. Called The Turtles on Gibbes' (1852) map. California Mining Bureau's (1917b) map shows Turtle Rock at the place.

Turtles: see **The Turtles**, under **Turtle Rocks** [HUMBOLDT].

Turup Creek: see **Tarup Creek** [DEL NORTE].

Turwah: see **Turwar Valley** [DEL NORTE].

Turwar: see **Fort Turwar**, under **Turwar Valley** [DEL NORTE].

Turwar Creek [DEL NORTE]: *stream*, flows 14 miles to Klamath River 0.5 mile northwest of Klamath Glen (lat. 41°31'15" N, long. 124°00' W; sec. 13, T 13 N, R 1 E). Named on Cant Hook Mountain (1982) and Klamath Glen (1982) 7.5' quadrangles. United States Board on Geographic Names (1943, p. 14) rejected the forms "Terwah Creek," "Terwer Creek," "Turwah Creek," and "Turwur Creek" for the name, which is of Indian origin (Kroeber, p. 62).

Turwar Riffle [DEL NORTE]: *water feature*, less than 1 mile southeast of Klamath Glen along Klamath River (lat. 41°30'10" N, long. 123°59'05" W; sec. 19, T 13 N, R 2 E). Named on Klamath Glen (1982) 7.5' quadrangle.

Turwar Valley [DEL NORTE]: *valley*, 1 mile north-northeast of Klamath Glen (lat. 41°31'05" N, long. 123°59'15" W); the valley is along Turwar Creek. Named on Klamath Glen (1982) 7.5' quadrangle. Lieutenant Crook established Fort Turwar at the valley in 1857 to control and protect Indians of the region; the name, which also had the spellings "Ter-Waw," "Ter a wa", "Ter-wau," and "Terwah," reportedly was from the Indian designation of the place (Frazer, p. 33; Whiting and Whiting, p. 83). The garrison was withdrawn in 1861, but returned the same year; Klamath River flooded the place four times during the winter of 1861 and 1862, and the facility was abandoned finally in 1862 (Frazer, p. 33). Postal authorities established Turwah post office 7 miles east of Requa—presumably in Turwar Valley—in 1898 and discontinued it in 1899; they reestablished it with the name "Terwah" in 1905 and discontinued it the same year (Salley, p. 220).

Tuttle Buttes [HUMBOLDT]: *peaks*, two, 6 miles west of Alderpoint (lat. 40°09'45" N, long. 123°43'05" W). Named on Fort Seward (1969) 7.5' quadrangle. Called Tuttle Butte on Alderpoint (1949) 15' quadrangle. United States Board on Geographic Names (1973b, p. 3) approved the name "Tuttle Buttes" for the feature, and gave the form "Tuttle Butte" as a variant. The name commemorates either Lucius C. Tuttle, or his son Frederick A. Tuttle, both ranchers in the neighborhood (Turner, p. 219).

Tuttle Creek [HUMBOLDT]: *stream*, flows 1.5 miles to South Fork Eel River 3 miles south of Phillipsville (lat. 40°10'05" N, long. 123°46'50" W). Named on Miranda (1970) 7.5' quadrangle.

Tuttle Creek [MENDOCINO]: *stream*, flows 1.25 miles to Case Creek 7 miles east-northeast of Branscomb (lat. 39°41'15" N, long. 123°30'45" W; sec. 11, T 21 N, R 15 W). Named on Cahto Peak (1967) 7.5' quadrangle.

Twelvemile Creek [DEL NORTE]: *stream*, flows 1.5 miles to Patrick Creek 6.5 miles east-northeast of Gasquet (lat. 41°53'10" N, long. 123°51'10" W; sec. 8, T 17 N, R 3 E). Named on Shelly Creek Ridge (1982) 7.5' quadrangle.

Twentyone Rock [HUMBOLDT]: *relief feature*, nearly 3 miles east of Trinidad (lat. 41°03'55" N, long. 124°05'25" W; sec. 20, T 8 N, R 1 E). Named on Crannell (1966) 7.5' quadrangle.

Twin Bridges Creek [MENDOCINO]: *stream*, flows nearly 4 miles to Eel River 7 miles south-southwest of Eden Valley (lat. 39°31'55" N, long. 123°13'40" W). Named on Brushy Mountain (1966) 7.5' quadrangle. Called Bridges Creek on Eden Valley (1929) 15' quadrangle.

Twin Creek [HUMBOLDT]: *stream*, flows 2.5 miles to Eel River 2.5 miles southeast of Scotia (lat. 40°27'15" N, long. 124°04'10" W; sec. 21, T 1 N, R 1 E). Named on Scotia (1970) 7.5' quadrangle.

Twin Creeks: see **Dinner Creek** [HUMBOLDT] (1).

Twin Gulch: see **North Twin Gulch** [TRINITY]; **South Twin Gulch** [TRINITY].

Twin Knobs [LAKE]: *relief feature*, 8.5 miles north-northwest of the town of Upper Lake (lat. 39°14'50" N, long. 122°56'15" W; sec. 14, T 16 N, R 10 W). Named on Upper Lake (1958) 7.5' quadrangle.

Twin Lakes [HUMBOLDT]:

(1) *intermittent lakes*, two, largest 300 feet long, 2.25 miles northwest of Board Camp Mountain (lat. 40°43'25" N, long. 123°44'40" W; near SE cor. sec. 17, T 4 N, R 4 E). Named on Board Camp Mountain (1977) 7.5' quadrangle.

(2) *lakes*, two, each 900 feet long, 7 miles west of Orleans (lat. 41°19'15" N, long. 123°40" W). Named on Fish Lake (1974) 7.5' quadrangle.

Twin Lakes [MENDOCINO]:

(1) *lakes*, two, largest 900 feet long, 4.25 miles south-southeast of Laytonville (lat. 39°37'55" N, long. 123°26'15" W; at W line sec. 33, T 21 N, R 14 W). Named on Laytonville (1967) 7.5' quadrangle.

(2) *lakes*, largest 1300 feet long, 2 miles north-northwest of Willits (lat. 39°25'50" N, long. 123°22'10" W; near NW cor. sec. 12, T 18 N, R 14 W). Named on Willits (1961) 15' quadrangle.

Twin Lakes [TRINITY]:

(1) *lakes*, two, largest 1000 feet long, 13 miles east-northeast of Trinity Center (lat. 41°06'10" N, long. 122°28'15" W; near SW cor. sec. 32, T 38 N, R 5 W). Named on Dunsmuir (1954) 15' quadrangle.

(2) *lakes*, two, largest 300 feet long, 19 miles north-northeast of Weaverville (lat. 40°59'35" N, long. 122°49'05" W; near E line sec. 7, T 36 N, R 8 W). Named on Trinity Dam (1950) 15' quadrangle.

Twin Lakes Creek [HUMBOLDT]: *stream*, flows 2.5 miles to Redwood Creek (1) 3 miles north of Board Camp Mountain (lat. 40°44'35" N, long. 123°43'10" W; near W line sec. 10, T 4 N, R 4 E). Named on Board Camp Mountain (1977) 7.5' quadrangle.

Twin Lakes Creek [TRINITY]: *stream*, flows 1 mile to South Fork Trinity River 5.5 miles north-northwest of Hyampom (lat. 40°41' N, long. 123°30'10" W). Named on Hyampom (1951) 15' quadrangle.

Twin Peak Branch: see **Siskiyou Fork**, under **Smith River** [DEL NORTE] (1).

Twin Peaks [DEL NORTE]: *peak*, 2.5 miles south of Broken Rib Mountain on Del Norte-Siskiyou County line (lat. 41°50'15" N, long. 123°40'50" W). Altitude 5944 feet. Named on Devils Punchbowl (1981) 7.5' quadrangle. Preston Peak (1922) 30' quadrangle shows two peaks close together at the summit of the feature.

Twin Peaks [HUMBOLDT]: *peaks*, two, 5 miles east-southeast of Cape Mendocino on Branstetter Ridge (lat. 40°24'40" N, long. 124°19'10" W; sec. 5, T 1 S, R 2 W). Altitude of highest 2662 feet. Named on Capetown (1969) 7.5' quadrangle.

Twin Rock Ridge [MENDOCINO]: *ridge*, generally west-trending, 1.5 miles long, 6.5 miles east of Covelo (lat. 39°47'15" N, long. 123°07'30" W). Named on Covelo East (1967) and Newhouse Ridge (1967) 7.5' quadrangles.

Twin Rocks [HUMBOLDT]: *rocks*, 3700 feet northwest of Cape Mendocino, and 3000 feet offshore (lat. 40°26'45" N, long. 124°25'05" W). Named on Cape Mendocino (1969) 7.5' quadrangle.

Twin Rocks [MENDOCINO]:

(1) *peaks*, two, 1700 feet apart, the westernmost is 10.5 miles east of Leggett (lat. 39°50'50" N, long. 123°31'15" W; at N line sec. 15, T 23 N, R 15 W). Named on Tan Oak Park (1969) 7.5' quadrangle.

(2) *relief feature*, 6 miles north-northwest of Willits (lat. 39°29'10" N, long. 123°23'45" W; near E line sec. 22, T 19 N, R 14 W). Named on Willits (1961) 15' quadrangle.

Twin Rocks: see **Twin Rocks Creek** [MENDOCINO] (1).

Twin Rocks Creek [MENDOCINO]:

(1) *stream*, flows 4 miles to Rattlesnake Creek (2) 8.5 miles east-southeast of Leggett (lat. 39°49'25" N, long. 123°33'55" W; sec. 29, T 23 N, R 15 W); the stream goes between Twin Rocks (1). Named on Tan Oak Park (1969) 7.5' quadrangle. O'Brien's (1953) map shows a locality called Twin Rock just south of the mouth of Twin Rocks Creek (1).

(2) *stream*, flows 2.5 miles to Jumpoff Creek 3.5 miles south-southwest of Anthony Peak (lat. 39°48'10" N, long. 122°59'30" W; sec. 32, T 23 N, R 10 W); the stream is north of Twin Rocks Ridge (2). Named on Mendocino Pass (1967) 7.5' quadrangle.

Twin Rocks Ridge [MENDOCINO]:

(1) *ridge*, generally west-trending, 1.5 miles long, 6.5 miles east of Covelo (lat. 39°47'15" N, long. 123°07'30" W). Named on Covelo East (1967) and Newhouse Ridge (1967) 7.5' quadrangles.

(2) *ridge*, 4.5 miles long, 14 miles east of Covelo (lat. 39°47'25" N, long. 123°59' W). Named on Mendocino Pass (1967) and Newhouse Ridge (1967) 7.5' quadrangles.

Twin Sisters [LAKE]: *peaks*, 7 miles south-southeast of Wilson Valley (2) on Lake-Yolo County line (lat. 38°53'05" N, long. 122°24'25" W). Named on Wilson Valley (1958) 7.5' quadrangle.

Twin Sisters Mountain [TRINITY]: *peak*, 6 miles northwest of Helena (lat. 40°50'10" N, long. 123°12'20" W). Altitude 5932 feet. Named on Helena (1951) 15' quadrangle.

Twin Springs [LAKE]: *springs*, 2 miles west-northwest of Crockett Peak (lat. 39°26'40" N, long. 122°48'30" W). Named on Crockett Peak (1967) 7.5' quadrangle.

Twin Springs [MENDOCINO]: *springs*, 3.5 miles northeast of Laytonville (lat. 39°43'10" N, long. 123°25'45" W; sec. 33, T 22 N, R 14 W). Named on Laytonville (1967) 7.5' quadrangle.

Twin Valley [LAKE]: *valleys*, two, 8.5 miles east-northeast of the town of Upper Lake (lat. 39°13'15" N, long. 122°46' W). Named on Bartlett Mountain (1958) 7.5' quadrangle. Called Twin Valleys on Lakeport (1938) 15' quadrangle, but United States Board on Geographic Names (1962c, p. 22) rejected this form for the name.

Twin Valley Creek [LAKE]: *stream*, flows 5.25 miles to North Fork Cache Creek 14 miles north-northwest of Clearlake Oaks (lat. 39°13'15" N, long. 122°44' W; sec. 22, T 16 N, R 8 W); the stream flows through Twin Valley. Named on Clearlake Oaks (1960) 15' quadrangle, and on Bartlett Mountain (1958) 7.5' quadrangle. United States Board on Geographic Names (1962c, p. 22) rejected the form "Twin Valleys Creek" for the name.

Twobit Gulch [TRINITY]: *canyon*, drained by a stream that flows 0.5 mile to East Fork Hayfork Creek 9 miles north-northeast of Dubakella Mountain (lat. 40°29'30" N, long. 123°03'35" W); the mouth of the canyon is 800 feet downstream from the mouth of Fourbit Gulch. Named on Dubakella Mountain (1954) 15' quadrangle.

201 Spur [TRINITY]: *locality*, 6.5 miles southeast of Alderpoint [HUMBOLDT] along Northwestern Pacific Railroad (lat. 40°06'05" N, long. 123°31'55" W; near W line sec. 20, T 4 S, R 6 E). Named on Jewett Rock (1969) 7.5' quadrangle.

Two Log Creek [MENDOCINO]: *stream*, flows 3.5 miles to Big River 4 miles north-northwest of Comptche (lat. 39°19'10" N, long. 123°36'50" W; sec. 23, T 17 N, R 16 W). Named on Comptche (1960) 15' quadrangle.

Twomile Creek [HUMBOLDT]: *stream*, flows nearly 1 mile to Supply Creek 2 miles southwest of Hoopa (lat. 41°02' N, long. 123°42'15" W; sec. 34, T 8 N, R 4 E). Named on Hoopa (1979) 7.5' quadrangle.

Twomile Creek [TRINITY]: *stream*, flows 1.5 miles to Virgin Creek 10 miles south-southeast of Salmon Mountain (lat. 41°02'30" N, long. 123°21'40" W). Named on Dees Peak (1978) and Trinity Mountain (1979) 7.5' quadrangles.

Two Rivers: see **Dos Rios** [MENDOCINO].

Two Rock [MENDOCINO]: *peak*, 6 miles southwest of Willits (lat. 39°20'40" N, long. 123°26'40" W; at N line sec. 5, T 17 N, R 14 W). Named on Willits (1961) 15' quadrangle.

Tyee City [HUMBOLDT]: *locality*, 4 miles north-northwest of Arcata along Mad River (lat. 40°55'20" N, long. 124°07'35" W; sec. 12, T 6 N, R 1 W). Named on Tyee City (1959) 7.5' quadrangle.

Tyler Creek [MENDOCINO]: *stream*, flows nearly 7 miles to Pieta Creek 1.5 miles south-southwest of Monument Peak (lat. 38°53'15" N, long. 123°57'50" W; sec. 15, T 12 N, R 10 W). Named on Asti (1959) and Highland Springs (1959) 7.5' quadrangles.

Tyler Valley [MENDOCINO]: *valley*, 4.5 miles southeast of Monument Peak (lat. 38°52'15" N, long. 123°53'45" W; sec. 19, 20, T 12 N, R 9 W); the valley is along Tyler Creek. Named on Asti (1959) and Highland Springs (1959) 7.5' quadrangles.

Tyson Creek [HUMBOLDT]: *stream,* flows 1 mile to North Fork Mad River 6.5 miles north of the town of Blue Lake (lat. 40°58'35" N, long. 123°57'40" W; near W line sec. 21, T 7 N, R 2 E). Named on Blue Lake (1979) 7.5' quadrangle.

—U—

Uhl Basin [TRINITY]: *relief feature,* 9 miles south of Black Rock Mountain (lat. 40°04'30" N, long. 123°00'50" W; sec. 29, T 26 N, R 10 W); the feature is at the head of Uhl Creek. Named on Black Rock Mountain (1954) 15' quadrangle.

Uhl Creek [TRINITY]: *stream,* flows 1.5 miles to Middle Fork Eel River 9 miles south of Black Rock Mountain (lat. 40°04'30" N, long. 123°02'30" W; at W line sec. 30, T 26 N, R 10 W). Named on Black Rock Mountain (1954) 15' quadrangle.

Uhl Peak [MENDOCINO]: *peak,* 1.25 miles north-northeast of Anthony Peak on Mendocino-Tehama County line (lat. 39°51'45" N, long. 122°57'05" W; sec. 10, T 23 N, R 10 W). Named on Mendocino Pass (1967) 7.5' quadrangle.

Ukiah [MENDOCINO]: *town,* in the central part of the south half of Mendocino County along Russian River (lat. 39°09' N, long. 123°12'30" W); the town is on Yokaya grant. Named on Elledge Peak (1958) and Ukiah (1958) 7.5' quadrangles. Called Ukiah City on Bancroft's (1864) map. Postal authorities established Ukiah post office in 1858 (Frickstad, p. 98), and the town incorporated in 1876. The first settler, Mr. S. Lowry, came to the site in 1856; the name "Ukiah" is derived from Yokaya grant (Hoover, Rensch, and Rensch, p. 196). Postal authorities established Arthur post office 3 miles south of Ukiah in 1903 and discontinued it in 1905 (Salley, p. 11). Crawford (1896, p. 512) noted that water from Garby's Spring, located at the base of the foothills 1 mile west of Ukiah, was highly prized by invalids. This appears to be the feature that Waring (p. 173) called Gobbis Soda Spring.

Ulco: see **Fort Bragg** [MENDOCINO].

Ullathorne Creek [HUMBOLDT]: *stream,* flows 2.25 miles to Klamath River 1.5 miles west-southwest of Orleans (lat. 41°17'30" N, long. 123°34'10" W; sec. 2, T 10 N, R 5 E). Named on Orleans (1978) 7.5' quadrangle.

Umbrella Butte [MENDOCINO]: *peak,* 7.5 miles north-northeast of Hull Mountain (lat. 39°37'35" N, long. 122°53'45" W). Altitude 3739 feet. Named on Plaskett Ridge (1967) 7.5' quadrangle.

Umbrella Butte [MENDOCINO]: see **Dicks Butte** [MENDOCINO].

Umbrella Creek [MENDOCINO]: *stream,* flows 3.25 miles to Black Butte River 8 miles north-northeast of Hull Mountain just inside Glenn County (lat. 39°27'45" N, long. 122°52'40" W). Named on Hull Mountain (1967) and Plaskett Ridge (1967) 7.5' quadrangles.

Uncle Sam: see **Kelseyville** [LAKE].

Uncle Sam Mountain: see **Mount Konocti** [LAKE].

Uncle Tommy [HUMBOLDT]: *peak,* nearly 4 miles south-southwest of Petrolia (lat. 40°16'25" N, long. 124°18'30" W; at SW cor. sec. 21, T 2 S, R 2 W). Altitude 2131 feet. Named on Petrolia (1969) 7.5' quadrangle. The name recalls two Indians, Tommy Scott and Tommy Jack (Turner, p. 220).

Underwood Creek [TRINITY]: *stream,* flows 2.5 miles to South Fork Trinity River 8 miles north-northwest of Hyampom (lat. 40°43'10" N, long. 123°31'15" W); the stream heads at Underwood Mountain. Named on Hyampom (1951) 15' quadrangle, and on Sims Mountain (1979) 7.5' quadrangle.

Underwood Mountain [TRINITY]: *ridge,* south-southwest-trending, 3 miles long, 8 miles north of Hyampom (lat. 40°43'45" N, long. 123°28'50" W). Named on Hyampom (1951) 15' quadrangle.

Underwood Park [MENDOCINO]: *locality,* 0.25 mile south-southwest of Leggett (lat. 39°51'35" N, long. 123°43' W; on W line sec. 11, T 23 N, R 17 W). Named on Leggett (1969) 7.5' quadrangle.

Union: see **Arcata** [HUMBOLDT].

Union Creek [TRINITY]: *stream,* flows 6 miles to Coffee Creek 6.25 miles west-southwest of Billys Peak (1) (lat. 41°06'50" N, long. 122°53'05" W; near N line sec. 34, T 38 N, R 9 W). Named on Coffee Creek (1955) 15' quadrangle.

Union Gulch [TRINITY]: *canyon,* drained by a stream that flows 2 miles to Little Browns Creek 2.5 miles east of Weaverville (lat. 40°44'10" N, long. 122°53'35" W; near N line sec. 9, T 33 N, R 9 W). Named on Weaverville (1950) 15' quadrangle.

Union Lake [TRINITY]: *lake,* 1000 feet long, 8.5 miles southwest of Billys Peak (1) (lat. 41°02'35" N, long. 122°53' W; on N line sec. 27, T 37 N, R 9 W); the lake is at the head of a branch of Union Creek. Named on Coffee Creek (1955) 15' quadrangle.

Union Landing [MENDOCINO]: *locality,* 4.25 miles north of Westport along the coast (lat. 39°42' N, long. 123°48'05" W; on E line sec. 1, T 21 N, R 18 W). Named on Westport (1966) 7.5' quadrangle. Cape Vizcaino (1921) 15' quadrangle shows a pier at the place.

Union Town: see **Arcata** [HUMBOLDT].

Unity Gulch [TRINITY]: *canyon,* drained by a stream that flows 0.5 mile to Clair Engle Lake 14 miles northeast of Weaverville (lat. 40°52'40" N, long. 122°45'30" W; sec. 22, T 35 N, R 8 W). Named on Trinity Dam (1950) 15' quadrangle.

Updegraff Ridge [MENDOCINO]: *ridge,* north-northwest-trending, 3.5 miles long, 3 miles east-northeast of Spyrock (lat. 39°54' N, long. 123°23'45" W). Named on Updegraff Ridge (1967) 7.5' quadrangle.

Upp [MENDOCINO]: *locality,* 1.25 miles north of downtown Willits along present Upp Creek (lat. 39°25'35" N, long. 123°21'20" W; near E line sec. 12, T 18 N, R 14 W). Named on Willits (1942) 15' quadrangle.

Up-pa Mountain: see **Hupa Mountain** [HUMBOLDT].

Upp Creek [MENDOCINO]: *stream,* flows 2.5 miles to Little Lake Valley 1.25 miles north of Willits (lat. 39°25'40" N, long. 123°21'20" W; near E line sec. 12, T 18 N, R 14 W). Named on Willits (1961) 15' quadrangle.

Upper Bohn Lake [LAKE]: *lake,* 1650 feet long, 9 miles east of Middletown (lat. 38°44' N, long. 122°26'45" W; at NE cor. sec. 7, T 10 N, R 5 W); the lake is 1 mile east-southeast of Lower Bohn Lake. Named on Aetna Springs (1958) 7.5' quadrangle. United States Board on Geographic Names (1991, p. 7) rejected the name "Eaton H. Magoon Lake" for the feature.

Upper Bull Creek Flat [HUMBOLDT]: *area,* 2.5 miles northwest of Weott along Bull Creek (1) (lat. 40°20'50" N, long. 120°57'20" W; sec. 28, T 1 S, R 2 E). Named on Weott (1969) 7.5' quadrangle. Present Upper Bull Creek Flat and Lower Bull Creek Flat together have the name "Bull Creek Flat" on Weott (1949) 15' quadrangle.

Upper Canyon Creek Meadows [TRINITY]: *area,* 13 miles north-northeast of Helena (lat. 40°56'35" N, long. 123°01'10" W); the place is along Canyon Creek (1). Named on Helena (1951) 15' quadrangle.

Upper Clear Lake: see **Upper Lake** [LAKE].

Upper Coon Mountain [DEL NORTE]: *ridge,* west- to southwest-trending, 3.5 miles long, 6 miles east-southeast of Gasquet (lat. 41°49' N, long. 123°51'45" W); the ridge is east of Lower Coon Mountain. Named on Gasquet (1981) and Hurdygurdy Butte (1982) 7.5' quadrangles.

Upper Glade Camp [TRINITY]: *locality,* 12 miles south-southwest of Black Rock Mountain (lat. 40°02'15" N, long. 123°03'55" W; near E line sec. 10, T 25 N, R 11 W); the place is about 1 mile northwest of Lower Glade Camp. Named on Black Rock Mountain (1954) 15' quadrangle. Hoaglin (1935) 30' quadrangle shows Glade Camp at or near the site of present Upper Glade Camp.

Upper Indian Valley: see **Little Indian Valley** [LAKE].

Upper Lake [LAKE]: *town,* 8 miles north of Lakeport (lat. 39°09'55" N, long. 122°54'25" W; sec. 7, T 15 N, R 9 W). Named on Upper Lake (1958) 7.5' quadrangle. Postal authorities established Upper Clear Lake post office in 1858, changed the name to Upper Lake in 1875, changed it to Upperlake in 1895, and changed it back to Upper Lake in 1906 (Salley, p. 228). The community began when William B. Elliott started a blacksmith shop at the site about 1856 (Hanna, p. 340). A body of water called Upper Lake was near the town before the 1920's, when a reclamation effort left it dry (Hoover, Rensch, and Rensch, p. 139). Waring (p. 268) noted that a feature called Hayville Sulphur Spring was situated 5 miles northwest of the town of Upper Lake; water from the spring was used to some extent for bathing and drinking.

Upper Lake [TRINITY]: *lake,* 300 feet long, 10.5 miles south of Kettenpom (lat. 40°00'35" N, long. 123°28'15" W; sec. 23, T 5 S, R 6 E); the lake is 1 mile east-southeast of Lower Lake. Named on Lake Mountain (1967) 7.5' quadrangle.

Upper Lake: see **Clear Lake** [LAKE].

Upper Mattole [HUMBOLDT]: *locality,* 16 miles south-southwest of Scotia along Mattole River (lat. 40°15'30" N, long. 124°11'30" W). Named on Glynn (1919) 15' quadrangle. Postal authorities established Upper Mattole post office in 1871 and discontinued it in 1943 (Frickstad, p. 47).

Upper Mumbo Lake [TRINITY]: *lake,* 600 feet long, 16 miles northeast of Trinity Center (lat. 41°11'30" N, long. 122°30'15" W; sec. 36, T 39 N, R 6 W); the lake is at the head of Mumbo Creek. Named on Bonanza King (1955) 15' quadrangle.

Upper Nye Camp [LAKE]: *locality,* 1.5 miles east-northeast of Crockett Peak (lat. 39°26'05" N, long. 122°44'50" W). Named on Saint John Mountain (1968) 7.5' quadrangle.

Upper Peaked Prairie [HUMBOLDT]: *area,* 7 miles southwest of Scotia (lat. 40°24'25" N, long. 124°10'35" W; near SE cor. sec. 4, T 1 S, R 1 W); the place is less than 1 mile south of Peaked Prairie. Named on Taylor Peak (1969) 7.5' quadrangle.

Upper Ranch Opening [MENDOCINO]: *area,* 9 miles southwest of Willits near Big River (lat. 39°18'45" N, long. 123°28'10" W; near SW cor. sec. 19, T 17 N, R 14 W). Named on Willits (1961) 15' quadrangle.

Usal [MENDOCINO]: *locality,* 10 miles south of Piercy (lat. 39°50'05" N, long. 123°50'35" W; sec. 22, T 23 N, R 18 W); the place is along Usal Creek. Named on Hales Grove (1970) 7.5' quadrangle. Postal authorities established Usal post office in 1890 and discontinued it in 1903 (Frickstad, p. 98). The community began with construction of a lumber mill at the site (Gudde, 1969, p. 350-351).. The name is of Indian origin (Kroeber, p. 65-66).

Usal Creek [MENDOCINO]: *stream,* flows 9 miles to the sea 10.5 miles south-southwest of Piercy (lat. 39°49'55" N, long. 123°51' W; sec. 27, T 23 N, R 18 W). Named on Bear Harbor (1969), Hales Grove (1970), and Piercy (1969) 7.5' quadrangles. South Fork enters 1.5 miles upstream from the mouth of the main creek; it is 4.5 miles long and is named on Hales Grove (1970) 7.5' quadrangle. Kenny (1920) 15' quadrangle shows a water feature called Usal Lagoon situated along lower reaches of Usal Creek in Usal Valley.

Usal Lagoon: see **Usal Creek** [MENDOCINO].

Usal Rock [MENDOCINO]: *rock,* 12.5 miles south of Pierce, and 550 feet offshore (lat. 39°48'15" N, long. 123°50'40" W); the rock is 2 miles south of the mouth of Usal Creek. Named on Hales Grove (1970) 7.5' quadrangle.

Usal Valley: see **Usal Creek** [MENDOCINO].

Usher Gulch [TRINITY]: *canyon,* drained by a stream that flows 1 mile to the canyon of Trinity River 3.5 miles north of Trinity Center (lat. 41°03'30" N, long. 122°42'15" W; near NW cor. sec. 20, T 37 N, R 7 W). Named on Bonanza King (1955) 15' quadrangle.

—V—

Valdor Gulch: see **East Valdor Gulch** [TRINITY]; **West Valdor Gulch** [TRINITY].

Valentine Creek [MENDOCINO]: *area,* flows 2.5 miles to Big River 9 miles south-southwest of Willits (lat. 39°17'25" N, long. 123°25'15" W; near N line sec. 33, T 17 N, R 14 W). Named on Willits (1961) 15' quadrangle.

Vallejo Gulch [MENDOCINO]: *canyon,* drained by a stream that flows 1.5 miles to Ten Mile River 7.5 miles southwest of Branscomb (lat. 39°34'20" N, long. 123°43'05" W; near N line sec. 26, T 20 N, R 17 W). Named on Dutchmans Knoll (1966) 7.5' quadrangle.

Vananken Creek: see **Vanauken Creek** [HUMBOLDT].

Van Arsdale Reservoir [MENDOCINO]: *lake,* behind Cape Horn Dam on Eel River 4.5 miles north of the town of Potter Valley (lat. 39°23'10" N, long. 123°06'55" W; sec. 30, T 18 N, R 11 W). Named on Potter Valley (1960) 15' quadrangle. The name, given in 1905, honors W.W. Van Arsdale, president of Eel River Power and Irrigation Company (Gudde, 1949, p. 376). Postal authorities established Capehorn post office 6 miles north of the town of Potter Valley in 1894 and discontinued it the same year (Salley, p. 37).

Vanauken Creek [HUMBOLDT]: *stream,* flows 2 miles to Mattole River 9.5 miles west-southwest of Garberville (lat. 40°03'05" N, long. 123°57'20" W). Named on Briceland (1969) 7.5' quadrangle. Called Vananken Creek on Garberville (1949) 15' quadrangle. United States Board on Geographic Names (1974a, p. 3) gave the names "Vananken Creek," "Van Arken Creek," "Van Arkin Creek," and "Vanarkin Creek" as variants.

Vance Gulch [TRINITY]: *canyon,* 0.5 mile long, opens into the canyon of Trinity River 5 miles east of Burnt Ranch (lat. 40°47'45" N, long. 123°22'45" W). Named on Ironside Mountain (1951) 15' quadrangle.

Vance's Bar: see **Big Bar** [TRINITY].

Van Choick Ridge [HUMBOLDT]: *ridge,* southeast-trending, 1 mile long, 12 miles south-southwest of Scotia (lat. 40°19' N, long. 124°09'30" W). Named on Buckeye Mountain (1970) 7.5' quadrangle. Called Van Schoaick Ridge on Scotia (1950) 15' quadrangle.

Van Damme Beach [MENDOCINO]: *beach,* 2.25 miles south of Mendocino along the coast at the mouth of Little River (lat. 39°16'25" N, long. 123°47'30" W; sec. 6, T 16 N, R 17 W). Named on Mendocino (1960) 7.5' quadrangle.

Vandenburg Ridge [LAKE-MENDOCINO]: *ridge,* northwest-trending, less than 1 mile long, 8.5 miles east-southeast of Ukiah on Lake-Mendocino County line (lat. 39°04'50" N, long. 123°05'30" W; on S line sec. 8, T 14 N, R 11 W). Named on Purdys Gardens (1958) 7.5' quadrangle.

Van Dusen's Fork: see **Van Duzen River** [HUMBOLDT-TRINITY].

Van Duzen Public Camp [HUMBOLDT]: *locality,* less than 1 mile southeast of Dinsmores (present Dinsmore) along Van Duzen River (lat. 40°29'10" N, long. 123°35'35" W; at N line sec. 10, T 1 N, R 5 E). Named on Blocksburg (1949) 15' quadrangle.

Van Duzen River [HUMBOLDT-TRINITY]: *stream,* heads in Trinity County and flows 60 miles to Eel River 4 miles south of Fortuna in Humboldt County (lat. 40°32'30" N, long. 124°09'25" W; at W line sec. 23, T 2 N, R 1 W). Named on Eureka (1958) and Redding (1958) 1° x 2° quadrangles. Members of the Gregg party named the stream Van Dusen's Fork in 1851 for a member of their group (Gibbs, p. 125, 132). United States Board on Geographic Names (1933, p. 787) rejected the name "Van Duzen Fork of Eel River" for the stream. West Fork enters 9 miles southwest of Forest Glen; it is 5.5 miles long and is named on Black Lassic (1979) and Ruth Reservoir (1978) 7.5' quadrangles. United States Board on Geographic Names (1977c, p. 6) gave the name "West Fork Van Duzen Creek" as a variant of "West Fork Van Duzen River."

Van Duzen River: see **Little Van Duzen River** [HUMBOLDT].

Van Horn Creek [MENDOCINO]: *stream,* flows 2.5 miles to Black Butte Creek 9.5 miles east of Covelo (lat. 39°49'05" N, long. 123°04'30" W; near SW cor. sec. 27, T 23 N, R 11 W). Named on Newhouse Ridge (1967) 7.5' quadrangle.

Van Horn Creek [TRINITY]: *stream,* flows nearly 3 miles to Mad River 10.5 miles east of Kettenpom (lat. 40°11'30" N, long. 123°16'05" W; at W line sec. 18, T 27 N, R 12 W). Named on Shannon Butte (1967) 7.5' quadrangle.

Van Horn Peak [TRINITY]: *peak,* 12 miles west of Black Rock Mountain (lat. 40°12'25" N, long. 123°14'10" W; near E line sec. 8, T 27 N, R 12 W); the peak is at the north end of Van Horn Ridge. Named on Black Rock Mountain (1954) 15' quadrangle.

Van Horn Ridge [TRINITY]: *ridge,* south-southwest- to south-trending, 3 miles long, 11.5 miles west of Black Rock Mountain (lat. 40°11'30" N, long. 123°13'30" W); Van Horn Peak is at the north end of the ridge. Named on Black Rock Mountain (1954) 15' quadrangle.

Van Matre Creek [TRINITY]: *stream,* flows 3.5 miles to Stuart Fork 10 miles north of Weaverville (lat. 40°52'30" N, long. 122°55'10" W; near W line sec. 20, T 35 N, R 9 W). Named on Trinity Dam (1950) 15' quadrangle. The name commemorates Mart Van Matre, a Lewiston cattleman (Jones, p. 10).

Van Matre Meadows [TRINITY]: *area,* 13 miles north of Weaverville (lat. 40°55'05" N, long. 122°53'35" W). Named on Trinity Dam (1950) 15' quadrangle. The name commemorates Mart Van Matre of Van Matre Creek (Jones, p. 10).

Van Ness Creek [TRINITY]: *stream,* flows 4 miles to Feeny Gulch 16 miles northeast of Weaverville (lat. 40°52'30" N, long. 122°42'05" W; sec. 19, T 35 N, R 7 W). Named on Schell Mountain (1950) 15' quadrangle, which shows Five Pines mine along the stream—H.J. Van Ness discovered the mine in 1895 (Jones, p. 41).

Vans Camp: see **Hurdygurdy Creek** [DEL NORTE].

Van Schoaick Ridge: see **Van Choick Ridge** [HUMBOLDT].

Van Zandts Resort [MENDOCINO]: *locality,* 5 miles northwest of Boonville (lat. 39°03'05" N, long. 123°26'15" W). Named on Orrs (1944) 15' quadrangle.

Vasser Creek [MENDOCINO]: *stream,* flows 5 miles to Coleman Creek 4.5 miles east-southeast of Hopland (lat. 38°56'30" N, long. 123°02'35" W; near W line sec. 35, T 13 N, R 11 W). Named on Highland Springs (1959) and Hopland (1960) 7.5' quadrangles.

Vaughn Spring [TRINITY]: *spring,* 10 miles southeast of Hyampom (lat. 40°30'55" N, long. 123°19'30" W; on W line sec. 31, T 2 N, R 8 E). Named on Hyampom (1951) 15' quadrangle.

Vichy Springs [MENDOCINO]: *locality,* 3 miles east-northeast of Ukiah along Sulphur Creek (lat. 39°10' N, long. 123°09'25" W). Named on Ukiah (1958) 7.5' quadrangle. Postal authorities established Vichy Springs post office in 1893 and discontinued it in 1936 (Frickstad, p. 98). Anderson (p. 257, 259) called the place Doolan's Ukiah Vichy Springs. It was a resort that in 1909 had a small hotel and several guest cottages (Waring, p. 171). The name is from the similarity of the water at the site to the water of the celebrated Vichy Springs of Germany (Carpenter, p. 93).

Victor Creek [HUMBOLDT]: *stream,* flows 1.5 miles to Bloody Nose Creek in the settlement of Willow Creek (lat. 40°56'20" N, long. 123°37'20" W; sec. 33, T 7 N, R 5 E). Named on Willow Creek (1979) 7.5' quadrangle.

Villardville: see **Crescent City** [DEL NORTE].

Vincent Creek [HUMBOLDT]: *stream,* flows less than 1 mile to Mad River 2.5 miles south-southeast of Korbel (lat. 40°50'10" N, long. 123°56'35" W; sec. 10, T 5 N, R 2 E). Named on Korbel (1979) 7.5' quadrangle.

Vinegar Peak [TRINITY]: *peak,* 9.5 miles south-southeast of Black Rock Mountain on Trinity-Tehama County line (lat. 40°04'15" N, long. 122°58' W; at NE cor. sec. 34, T 26 N, R 10 W). Altitude 6549 feet. Named on Yolla Bolly (1954) 15' quadrangle.

Vinton Lake [MENDOCINO]: *lake,* 225 feet long, 1 mile west-northwest of Dos Rios (lat. 39°43'25" N, long. 123°22'25" W; at N line sec. 36, T 22 N, R 14 W). Named on Dos Rios (1967) 7.5' quadrangle.

Violet Spring [LAKE]: *spring,* 5 miles northwest of Three Crossings (lat. 39°21'50" N, long. 122°59'25" W; on N line sec. 4, T 17 N, R 10 W). Named on Elk Mountain (1967) 7.5' quadrangle.

Virgin Buttes: see **Virgin Creek Buttes** [TRINITY].

Virgin Creek [MENDOCINO]: *stream,* flows nearly 3 miles to the sea 2 miles north of Fort Bragg (lat. 39°28'20" N, long. 123°48'15" W; sec. 31, T 19 N, R 17 W). Named on Fort Bragg (1960) 7.5' quadrangle.

Virgin Creek [TRINITY]: *stream,* flows 12 miles to join Slide Creek and form New River 11 miles south-southeast of Salmon Mountain (lat. 41°01'50" N, long. 123°20'50" W). Named on Dees Peak (1978), Salmon Mountain (1978), Trinity Mountain (1979), and Youngs Peak (1979) 7.5' quadrangles.

Virgin Creek Buttes [TRINITY]: *peak,* 9 miles south-southeast of Salmon Mountain (lat. 41°03'40" N, long. 123°20'50" W); the feature is northeast of Virgin Creek. Altitude 4712 feet. Named on Dees Peak (1978) 7.5' quadrangle. United States Board on Geographic Names (1977b, p. 6) gave the name "Virgin Buttes" as a variant.

Vitzthum Gulch [TRINITY]: *canyon,* drained by a stream that flows 1 mile to Trinity River 6.5 miles south-southeast of Weaverville (lat. 40°44'20" N, long. 122°53'40" W; near NW cor. sec. 4, T 32 N, R 9 W). Named on Weaverville (1950) 15' quadrangle.

Vizcaino: see **Cape Vizcaino** [MENDOCINO].

V Spring [TRINITY]: *spring*, 5.5 miles north-northeast of Forest Glen (lat. 40°26'55" N, long. 123°17'30" W; sec. 20, T 1 N, R 8 E). Named on Naufus Creek (1979) 7.5' quadrangle.

Vulture Spring [MENDOCINO]: *spring*, 8.5 miles south-southeast of Eden Valley (lat. 39°31'10" N, long. 123°06'05" W; sec. 8, T 19 N, R 11 W). Named on Sanhedrin Mountain (1966) 7.5' quadrangle.

—W—

Wacket Creek: see **Hoppaw Creek** [DEL NORTE].

Waddington [HUMBOLDT]: *locality*, 3.25 miles southwest of Fortuna (lat. 40°34' N, long. 124°12'15" W; sec. 8, T 2 N, R 1 W). Named on Fortuna (1959) 7.5' quadrangle. Postal authorities established Waddington post office in 1891 and discontinued it in 1940 (Frickstad, p. 47). Alexander Waddington, a merchant who came to Humboldt County in 1875, founded the place (Carlson, p. 34); it originally was called Waddington Corners (Turner, p. 223).

Waddington Corners: see **Waddington** [HUMBOLDT].

Wages Creek [MENDOCINO]: *stream*, flows 8.5 miles to the sea 1 mile north of Westport (lat. 39°39'05" N, long. 123°47'05" W; near N line sec. 30, T 21 N, R 17 W). Named on Lincoln Ridge (1966) and Westport (1966) 7.5' quadrangles. The misspelled name is for Alfred Weges, who settled by the stream in 1864 (Carpenter, p. 129). North Fork enters from the north-northeast 4.5 miles upstream from the mouth of the main creek and is nearly 2 miles long. South Fork enters from the southeast 6 miles upstream from the mouth of the main creek and is 1.5 miles long. Both forks are named on Lincoln Ridge (1966) 7.5' quadrangle.

Waggit Spring [TRINITY]: *spring*, 7 miles southwest of Forest Glen (lat. 40°18'35" N, long. 123°25'35" W; sec. 7, T 2 S, R 7 E). Named on Ruth Reservoir (1978) 7.5' quadrangle.

Wagner Creek [TRINITY]: *stream*, flows 2.5 miles to Coffee Creek 2.5 miles south of Billys Peak (1) (lat. 41°05'50" N, long. 122°46'20" W; at W line sec. 3, T 37 N, R 8 W). Named on Coffee Creek (1955) 15' quadrangle.

Wailaki Campground [HUMBOLDT]: *locality*, 3.5 miles east of Point Delgada along South Fork Bear Creek (7) (lat. 40°01'05" N, long. 124°00'05" W). Named on Shelter Cove (1969) 7.5' quadrangle.

Waite's Slough: see **McNultys Slough** [HUMBOLDT].

Wakefield: see **Crescent City** [DEL NORTE].

Wakell Flat: see **Waukell Flat** [DEL NORTE].

Waldorff Crossing [TRINITY]: *locality*, 4.5 miles north-northwest of Helena along North Fork Trinity River (lat. 40°50'05" N, long. 123°09'35" W; near NW cor. sec. 6, T 34 N, R 11 W). Named on Helena (1951) 15' quadrangle. United States Geological Survey's (1915) map has the form "Waldorf Crossing" for the name.

Waldorff Flat [TRINITY]: *area*, 2.25 miles south of Hyampom along South Fork Trinity River (lat. 40°34'15" N, long. 123°26'30" W; sec. 12, T 2 N, R 6 E). Named on Hyampom (1951) 15' quadrangle.

Waldron Creek [MENDOCINO]: *stream*, flows 2.5 miles to Hollow Tree Creek 7.5 miles south of Leggett (lat. 39°45'20" N, long. 123°43'25" W; near W line sec. 14, T 22 N, R 17 W). Named on Leggett (1969), Lincoln Ridge (1966), and Westport (1966) 7.5' quadrangles.

Waldron Pass [MENDOCINO]: *pass*, 7.5 miles north of Westport (lat. 39°44'35" N, long. 123°45'25" W; sec. 21, T 22 N, R 17 W); the pass is near the head of Waldron Creek. Named on Westport (1966) 7.5' quadrangle.

Walhalla: see **Gualala** [MENDOCINO].

Walker Butte [HUMBOLDT]: *peak*, 10 miles south of Alderpoint (lat. 40°02'10" N, long. 123°35'30" W; near SW cor. sec. 11, T 5 S, R 5 E); the peak is on Walker Ridge (2). Named on Jewett Rock (1969) 7.5' quadrangle. United States Board on Geographic Names (1973a, p. 3) gave the name "Walker Buttes" as a variant.

Walker Creek [MENDOCINO]: *stream*, flows 5 miles to Forsythe Creek 7 miles south-southeast of Willits in Walker Valley (lat. 39°18'50" N, long. 123°18'45" W; near W line sec. 21, T 17 N, R 13 W). Named on Willits (1961) 15' quadrangle.

Walker Creek: see **Waukell Creek** [DEL NORTE].

Walker Gulch [MENDOCINO]: *canyon*, drained by a stream that flows 1 mile to the sea 5.5 miles south-southeast of the village of Point Arena (lat. 38°50'40" N, long. 123°38'15" W; sec. 3, T 11 N, R 16 W). Named on Saunders Reef (1960) 7.5' quadrangle.

Walker Lake [MENDOCINO]: *lake*, 3100 feet long, behind a dam on Walker Creek 6 miles south of Willits (lat. 39°19'15" N, long. 123°20'20" W; near S line sec. 18, T 17 N, R 13 W). Named on Willits (1961) 15' quadrangle.

Walker Ridge [HUMBOLDT]:

(1) *ridge*, generally west-trending, 3.5 miles long, center 6.25 miles south-east of Cape Mendocino (lat. 40°23' N, long. 124°18'50" W). Named on Capetown (1969) 7.5' quadrangle.

(2) *ridge*, generally northeast-trending, 3.5 miles long, 9 miles south-south-east of Aldrpoint (lat. 40°03' N, long. 123°34'30" W). Named on Jewett Rock (1969) 7.5' quadrangle.

Walker Ridge [LAKE]: *ridge*, south-trending, 4 miles long, south of Cold Spring Mountain on Lake-Colusa County line (lat. 39°05' N, long. 122°29'10" W). Named on Wilbur Springs (1961) 15' quadrangle.

Walker Valley [MENDOCINO]: *valley*, 7 miles south-southeast of Willits (lat. 39°18'50" N, long. 123°18'30" W; in and near sec. 21, T 17 N, R 13 W); the valley is at the mouth of Walker Creek. Named on Willits (1961) 15' quadrangle.

Wallholla: see **Gualala** [MENDOCINO].

Wallholla River: see **Gualala River** [MENDOCINO].

Walters Creek [MENDOCINO]: *stream*, flows 1.25 miles to Hollow Tree Creek 5.25 miles south of Leggett (lat. 39°47'20" N, long. 123°43'55" W; sec. 3, T 22 N, R 17 W). Named on Leggett (1969) 7.5' quadrangle.

Warden Creek [HUMBOLDT]: *stream*, flows 2.25 miles to Sproul Creek 4.25 miles southwest of Garberville (lat. 40°03'20" N, long. 123°51'05" W). Named on Briceland (1969) and Garberville (1970) 7.5' quadrangles.

Ward Lake [TRINITY]: *lake*, 1000 feet long, 11.5 miles southwest of Billys Peak (1) (lat. 41°00'15" N, long. 122°54'30" W; sec. 4, T 36 N, R 9 W). Named on Coffee Creek (1955) 15' quadrangle. The name commemorates a cowhand named Whit Ward (Jones, p. 10).

Wardlow Rock [LAKE]: *relief feature*, 3.25 miles south of Whispering Pines (lat. 38°46' N, long. 122°43'10" W; near W line sec. 35, T 11 N, R 8 W). Named on Whispering Pines (1958) 7.5' quadrangle.

Ward Mountain [MENDOCINO]: *peak*, 5 miles southwest of Hopland (lat. 38°55'30" N, long. 123°10'45" W; sec. 3, T 12 N, R 12 W). Altitude 3043 feet. Named on Hopland (1960) 15' quadrangle.

Warnersville: see **Trinidad** [HUMBOLDT].

Warren Creek [HUMBOLDT]: *stream*, flows 2.25 miles to Mad River 3 miles northeast of Arcata (lat. 40°54'15" N, long. 124°02'35" W; near E line sec. 15, T 6 N, R 1 E). Named on Arcata North (1959) 7.5' quadrangle. J.P. Warren settled on a claim by the stream in the 1860's (Cullberg, p. 60).

Waseck [HUMBOLDT]: *locality*, 8 miles northeast of Coyote Peak along Klamath River (lat. 41°12'55" N, long. 123°45'30" W; sec. 31, T 10 N, R 4 E). Named on Coyote Peak (1952) 15' quadrangle.

Washington Corners: see **Arlynda Corners** [HUMBOLDT].

Washington Flat [DEL NORTE]: *locality*, 9 miles east-northeast of Gasquet along Middle Fork Smith River (lat. 41°53'15" N, long. 123°48' W). Named on Shelly Creek Ridge (1982) 7.5' quadrangle. Preston Peak (1922) 30' quadrangle shows Washington ranch at the site. The name commemorates a pioneer hunter and trapper named George Washington, who was killed by a landslide at the place (Gudde, 1949, p. 384).

Washington Gulch [HUMBOLDT]: *canyon*, drained by a stream that flows 1.5 miles to lowlands 2.5 miles south-southeast of Arcata (lat. 40°50' N, long. 124°03'50" W; near E line sec. 9, T 5 N, R 1 E). Named on Arcata South (1959) 7.5' quadrangle. The name commemorates Henry Washington, who set up Humboldt Base and Meridian in 1853 (Turner, p. 224).

Washington Inlet: see **Big Lagoon** [HUMBOLDT] (1).

Washington Peak [DEL NORTE]: *peak*, 10.5 miles east-northeast of Gasquet (lat. 41°52'55" N, long. 123°46'20" W; at E line sec. 12, T 17 N, R 3 E). Altitude 2918 feet. Named on Shelly Creek Ridge (1982) 7.5' quadrangle.

Washington Rock [TRINITY]: *peak*, 11 miles southwest of Black Rock Mountain (lat. 40°05'05" N, long. 123°08'30" W; near S line sec. 19, T 26 N, R 11 W). Altitude 5212 feet. Named on Black Rock Mountain (1954) 15' quadrangle.

Waterbarrel Opening [HUMBOLDT]: *area*, 6.5 miles east-southeast of Board Camp Mountain (lat. 40°39'30" N, long. 123°36'05" W; near NW cor. sec. 10, T 3 N, R 5 E). Named on Sims Mountain (1979) 7.5' quadrangle.

Water Canyon: see **Big Water Canyon** [MENDOCINO]; **Little Water Canyon** [MENDOCINO].

Water Dog Lakes [HUMBOLDT]: *lakes*, two, largest 350 feet long, 6.25 miles northwest of Trinity Mountain (lat. 41°06'25" N, long. 123°28'45" W). Named on Trinity Mountain (1979) 7.5' quadrangle.

Waterfall Gulch [MENDOCINO]: *canyon*, drained by a stream that flows 1 mile to Usal Creek 7 miles south-southwest of Piercy (lat. 39°52'45" N, long. 123°51'50" W). Named on Piercy (1969) 7.5' quadrangle.

Water Gulch [HUMBOLDT]: *canyon*, drained by a stream that flows 0.5 mile to Little River 5.25 miles southeast of Trinidad (lat. 41°00'50" N, long. 124°03'35" W; near NW cor. sec. 10, T 7 N, R 1 E). Named on Crannell (1966) 7.5' quadrangle.

Water Gulch [MENDOCINO]: *canyon*, drained by a stream that flows 2 miles to Chamberlain Creek 6.5 miles north-northeast of Comptche (lat. 39°21'20" N, long. 123°33'15" W; sec. 5, T 17 N, R 15 W). Named on Comptche (1960) 15' quadrangle. The stream in the canyon is called Freathy Creek on Glenblair (1943) 15' quadrangle.

Water Hole [DEL NORTE]: *lake*, 200 feet long, 10.5 miles east of Klamath

Glen (lat. 41°31'50" N, long. 123°47'30" W). Named on Ship Mountain (1952) 15' quadrangle.

Waterman Ridge [HUMBOLDT]: *ridge*, north- to west-trending, 3.5 miles long, center 4 miles northeast of the settlement of Willow Creek (lat. 40°58'30" N, long. 123°34' W). Named on Salyer (1979) 7.5' quadrangle.

Waters Camp [LAKE]: *locality*, 1.25 miles east-northeast of Crockett Peak (lat. 39°26'20" N, long. 122°45'10" W). Named on Crockett Peak (1967) 7.5' quadrangle.

Waterspout [TRINITY]: *spring*, 9.5 miles southeast of Black Rock Spring (lat. 40°07'40" N, long. 123°09'15" W; at NW cor. sec. 7, T 26 N, R 11 W). Named on Black Rock Mountain (1954) 15' quadrangle. United States Board on Geographic Names (1982a, p. 3) rejected the names "Water Spout" and "Waterspout Spring" for the feature. The name is from a hewn pole used as a spout to gather water from the spring (Jones, p. 363).

Waterspout Spring: see **Waterspout** [TRINITY].

Watertrough Camp [TRINITY]: *locality*, 10 miles south-southwest of Black Rock Mountain (lat. 40°04'45" N, long. 123°05' W; sec. 27, T 26 N, R 11 W). Named on Black Rock Mountain (1954) 15' quadrangle.

Water Trough Spring [TRINITY]: *spring*, 11.5 miles east-northeast of Kettenpom (lat. 40°14'30" N, long. 123°16'35" W; near S line sec. 33, T 2 S, R 8 E). Named on Shannon Butte (1967) 7.5' quadrangle.

Watson Bar: see **Del Loma** [TRINITY].

Watson Creek [TRINITY]: *stream*, flows 2.5 miles to East Fork Trinity River 5 miles east-northeast of Trinity Center (lat. 41°02' N, long. 122°36' W; sec. 30, T 37 N, R 6 W). Named on Bonanza King (1955) 15' quadrangle.

Watson Range [LAKE]: *ridge*, east-trending, 1 mile long, 3.25 miles southwest of Jericho Valley (lat. 38°47'45" N, long. 122°28'15" W; at N line sec. 24, T 11 N, R 6 W). Named on Jericho Valley (1958) 7.5' quadrangle.

Watt: see **Sam Watt Creek** [MENDOCINO]; **Sam Watt Rock** [MENDOCINO].

Watts Lake [TRINITY]: *lake*, 175 feet long, 12.5 miles southwest of Forest Glen (lat. 40°15'05" N, long. 123°29'45" W; near E line sec. 33, T 2 S, R 6 E). Named on Ruth Reservoir (1978) 7.5' quadrangle.

Waukell Creek [DEL NORTE]: *stream*, flows 3 miles to lowlands along Klamath River 3.5 miles southeast of the mouth of that river (lat. 41°30'45" N, long. 124°01'35" W; sec. 14, T 13 N, R 1 E); Waukell Flat is at the mouth of the stream. Named on Fern Canyon (1966) and Requa (1966) 7.5' quadrangles. Called Walker Creek on O'Brien's (1952) map. The name "Waukell" is from an Indian village (Kroeber, p. 66).

Waukell Creek [HUMBOLDT]: *stream*, flows nearly 2 miles to Klamath River 8.5 miles southeast of Johnsons (lat. 41°15'05" N, long. 123°46'30" W; sec. 13, T 10 N, R 3 E). Named on French Camp Ridge (1983) and Johnsons (1982) 7.5' quadrangles.

Waukell Flat [DEL NORTE]: *area*, 4.25 miles east-southeast of the mouth of Klamath River on the south side of that river (lat. 41°31'05" N, long. 124°00'30" W; sec. 14, T 13 N, R 1 E); the place is at the mouth of Waukell Creek. Named on Requa (1966) 7.5' quadrangle. Klamath (1952) 15' quadrangle shows a locality called Waukell Flat at the site. Goddard's (1857) map shows Wakell Flat.

Weaver Bally: see **Monument Peak** [TRINITY] (1); **Weaver Bally Mountain** [TRINITY].

Weaver Bally Mountain [TRINITY]: *ridge*, generally south-southwest-trending, 3 miles long, 7 miles north-northwest of Weaverville (lat. 40°49'15" N, long. 122°59'10" W). Named on Helena (1951) and Trinity Dam (1950) 15' quadrangles. Called Weaver Bollo on California Mining Bureau's (1917b) map, and called Weaver Bally on Averill's (1940) map. United States Board on Geographic Names (1983d, p. 7) approved the name "Weaver Bally" for the feature, and rejected the names "Mount Baldy," "Mount Bally," "Weaver Bally Mountain," "Weaver Bully," and "West Weaver Bally."

Weaver Bally Mountain: see **Monument Peak** [TRINITY] (1).

Weaver Bully: see **Weaver Bally Mountain** [TRINITY].

Weaver Creek [TRINITY]: *stream*, formed by the confluence of East Weaver Creek and West Weaver Creek, flows 6 miles to Trinity River 5.5 miles south of Weaverville (lat. 40°39'05" N, long. 122°56'25" W; at SE cor. sec. 1, T 32 N, R 10 W). Named on Weaverville (1950) 15' quadrangle.

Weaver Creek: see **East Weaver Creek** [TRINITY]; **Little Weaver Creek**, under **Big Bar Creek** [TRINITY]; **West Weaver Creek** [TRINITY].

Weaver Lake: see **East Weaver Lake** [TRINITY].

Weaverville [TRINITY]: *town*, in the east-central part of Trinity County (lat. 40°44' N, long. 122°56'15" W; on W line sec. 7, T 33 N, R 9 W); the town is along Weaver Creek. Named on Weaverville (1950) 15' quadrangle. Postal authorities established Weaverville post office in 1850 (Frickstad, p. 209). According to Gudde (1949, p. 385), the name is for George Weaver, a prospector who built the first cabin at the place in 1850. According to Hanna (p. 351), the name is for William Weaver, who came to the site to mine gold in 1849. Gudde (1975, p. 113, 125) mentioned places called Fagg Town and French Town that were part of Weaverville in the 1850's. Gudde (1975, p. 22) also listed a mining place called Arkansas Bar that was situated just south of Weaverville, and (1975, p. 275) a mining place called Poverty Flat that was located 3.5 miles southeast of Weaverville.

Weber Creek [HUMBOLDT]: *stream*, flows 2.5 miles to Eel River 2.25 miles southeast of Redcrest (lat. 40°22'40" N, long. 123°55'05" W; sec. 14, T 1 S, R 2 E). Named on Redcrest (1969) 7.5' quadrangle.

Weber Flat [TRINITY]: *area*, 10 miles north of Weaverville (lat. 40°52' N, long. 122°53'35" W; near N line sec. 28, T 35 N, R 9 W). Named on Trinity Dam (1950) 15' quadrangle.

Wedding Cake [TRINITY]: *relief feature*, 16 miles north-northeast of Helena (lat. 40°59'30" N, long. 123°02'50" W). Named on Helena (1951) 15' quadrangle. James King and his new wife named the feature about 1870 for its fancied resemblance to a wedding cake (Gudde, 1949, p. 385-386).

Wedding Rock [HUMBOLDT]: *rock*, 5.5 miles north of Trinidad, and 650 feet offshore (lat. 41°08'30" N, long. 124°09'50" W). Named on Trinidad (1966) 7.5' quadrangle.

Weekend Island [LAKE]: *island*, 700 feet long, 3.25 miles west-southwest of Clearlake Oaks in Clear Lake (lat. 39°01'35" N, long. 122°44'05" W). Named on Clearlake Oaks (1958) 7.5' quadrangle.

Weir: see **Harry Weir Creek** [HUMBOLDT].

Weitchpec [HUMBOLDT]: *village*, 35 miles northeast of Eureka at the confluence of Trinity River and Klamath River (lat. 41°11'15" N, long. 123°42'20" W; sec. 10, T 9 N, R 4 E). Named on Weitchpec (1979) 7.5' quadrangle. Postal authorities established Weitchpec post office in 1858, discontinued it in 1860, reestablished it in 1891, and discontinued it in 1962 (Salley, p. 236). The name is of Indian origin (Kroeber, p. 66). Gudde (1975, p. 367) listed Weitchpec Bar, a mining place situated at the junction of Klamath River and Trinity River. Coy (1929, p. 69) mentioned Durkee's Ferry, located at the same site; Clark W. Durkee operated the ferry about 1851 (Turner, p. 64). Whiting and Whiting (p. 86) noted that a military post called Fort Wool was located at the mouth of Trinity River.

Weitchpec Bar: see **Weitchpec** [HUMBOLDT].

Weitchpec Creek [HUMBOLDT]: *stream*, flows 0.5 mile to Klamath River at Weitchpec (lat. 41°11'15" N, long. 123°42'30" W; sec. 10, T 9 N, R 4 E). Named on Weitchpec (1979) 7.5' quadrangle.

Welch Creek [LAKE]: *stream*, flows about 3 miles to join Panther Creek (1) and form Soda Creek (1) 5 miles west-northwest of Bear Mountain (lat. 39°26'20" N, long. 122°59'05" W). Named on Lake Pillsbury (1951) and Potter Valley (1960) 15' quadrangles. Called Soda Creek on Hullville (1922) 15' quadrangle.

Weller: see **Fort Weller**, under **Redwood Valley** [MENDOCINO] (1).

Wells Mountain [TRINITY]: *ridge*, generally north-northeast-trending, 2 miles long, 9 miles east of Hayfork (lat. 40°32'35" N, long. 123°00'55" W). Named on Hayfork (1951) 15' quadrangle.

Weltmer: see **Sherwood** [MENDOCINO].

Wendling: see **Navarro** [MENDOCINO].

Weonme Flat [HUMBOLDT]: *area*, 6 miles north-northeast of Redcrest (lat. 40°28'30" N, long. 123°53' W; near W line sec. 7, T 1 N, R 3 E). Named on Redcrest (1969) 7.5' quadrangle.

Weott [HUMBOLDT]: *village*, 17 miles north-northwest of Garberville (lat. 40°19'20" N, long. 123°55'15" W; sec. 2, T 2 S, R 2 E). Named on Weott (1969) 7.5' quadrangle. Postal authorities established Weott post office in 1925 (Frickstad, p. 47). The name is of Indian origin (Gudde, 1949, p. 386).

Weott: see **Camp Weott** [HUMBOLDT]:

Wescott Creek [LAKE]: *stream*, heads in Glenn County and flows nearly 2 miles in Lake County to Corbin Creek 9.5 miles east-northeast of Hull Mountain (lat. 39°33'20" N, long. 122°46' W; sec. 28, T 20 N, R 8 W). Named on Kneecap Ridge (1967) 7.5' quadrangle.

Wesley Ives Creek [MENDOCINO]: *stream*, flows 3.5 miles to Hull Creek 3.25 miles north-northeast of Hull Mountain (lat. 39°33'45" N, long. 122°54'10" W; sec. 25, T 20 N, R 10 W). Named on Hull Mountain (1967) 7.5' quadrangle.

West Crockett Camp [LAKE]: *locality*, 0.5 mile northwest of Crockett Peak (lat. 39°26'10" N, long. 122°46'50" W). Named on Crockett Peak (1967) 7.5' quadrangle.

Westhaven [HUMBOLDT]: *settlement*, 2.5 miles southeast of Trinidad (lat. 41°02'10" N, long. 124°06'30" W; sec. 31, T 8 N, R 1 E). Named on Crannell (1966) 7.5' quadrangle.

West Hayshed Creek [TRINITY]: *stream*, flows 2 miles to Hayshed Creek 8 miles north-northeast of Hyampom (lat. 40°43'10" N, long. 123°22'10" W; sec. 15, T 4 N, R 7 E). Named on Hyampom (1951) 15' quadrangle.

West Low Gap: see **Martin Gap** [TRINITY].

Westlund Creek [HUMBOLDT]: *stream*, flows 4 miles to Mattole River 4.5 miles east-southeast of Honeydew (lat. 40°13'40" N, long. 124°02'25" W). Named on Ettersburg (1969), Honeydew (1970), and Weott (1969) 7.5' quadrangles.

Westport [MENDOCINO]: *village*, 13 miles north of Fort Bragg along the coast (lat. 39°38'15" N, long. 123°47' W; around NW cor. sec. 32, T 21 N, R 17 W). Named on Westport (1966) 7.5' quadrangle. Postal authorities established Westport post office in 1879 (Frickstad, p. 98). The place first was called Beal's Landing for Samuel Beal, the first settler there; James T. Rodgers started building a chute at the site in 1877, and renamed the place Westport to contrast with the name of his hometown, Eastport, Maine

(Gudde, 1949, p. 387).

West Side Creek [HUMBOLDT]: *stream*, flows 3 miles to Bear River 8 miles east of Cape Mendocino (lat. 40°27'05" N, long. 124°15'10" W; at W line sec. 24, T 1 N, R 2 W). Named on Capetown (1969) and Taylor Peak (1969) 7.5' quadrangles.

West Tule Creek [TRINITY]: *stream*, flows 3 miles to Tule Creek 3 miles southwest of Hayfork (lat. 40°31'30" N, long. 123°13'30" W; sec. 21, T 31 N, R 12 W). Named on Hayfork (1951) and Hyampom (1951) 15' quadrangles.

West Valdor Gulch [TRINITY]: *canyon*, 0.5 mile long, opens into East Valdor Gulch 2.25 miles east of Helena (lat. 40°46'10" N, long. 123°05' W; near SW cor. sec. 26, T 34 N, R 11 W). Named on Helena (1951) 15' quadrangle.

West Weaver Bally: see **Weaver Bally Mountain** [TRINITY].

West Weaver Creek [TRINITY]: *stream*, flows 7 miles to join East Weaver Creek and form Weaver Creek less than 1 mile south of the center of Weaverville (lat. 40°43'20" N, long. 122°56'20" W; near NW cor. sec. 18, T 33 N, R 9 W). Named on Trinity Dam (1950) and Weaverville (1950) 15' quadrangles. Called West Fork [Weaver Creek] on Weaverville (1913) 30' quadrangle, but United States Board on Geographic Names (1983d, p. 7) rejected this name for the stream. The Board at the same time (p. 4) approved the name "Austrian Gulch" for a ravine, 1 mile long, that opens into the canyon of West Weaver Creek 3.6 miles northwest of Weaverville (lat. 40'46'55" N, long. 122°59'10" W; sec. 22, T 34 N, R 10 W).

Weymouth Inn [HUMBOLDT]: *locality*, nearly 5 miles south of Fortuna (lat. 40°31'45" N, long. 124°09'55" W; sec. 27, T 2 N, R 1 W). Named on Fortuna (1959) 7.5' quadrangle.

Whalan Station [TRINITY]: *locality*, 16 miles northeast of Trinity Center (lat. 41°09'15" N, long. 122°27'30" W; sec. 17, T 38 N, R 5 W). Named on Dunsmuir (1954) 15' quadrangle.

Whale Gulch [HUMBOLDT-MENDOCINO]: *canyon*, drained by a stream that heads in Humboldt County and flows 4 miles to the sea 9.5 miles west of Piercy in Mendocino County (lat. 39°57'40" N, long. 123°58'40" W; at S line sec. 4, T 24 N, R 19 W). Named on Bear Harbor (1969) and Briceland (1969) 7.5' quadrangles.

Whaler Island [DEL NORTE]: *island*, 850 feet long, 1600 feet offshore at Crescent City (lat. 41°44'25" N, long. 124°11' W). Named on Sister Rocks (1966) 7.5' quadrangle. The island is connected to land by a breakwater.

Whale Rock [DEL NORTE]: *rock*, 7.5 miles west-northwest of Crescent City, and 4.5 miles offshore from Point Saint George (lat. 41°47'10" N, long. 124°20'50" W). Named on Eureka (1958) 1° x 2° quadrangle.

Wharf Rock [MENDOCINO]: *rock*, 0.25 mile west of Elk, and 350 feet offshore (lat. 39°07'50" N, long. 123°43'20" W). Named on Elk (1960) 7.5' quadrangle.

Wheelbarro Creek [MENDOCINO]: *stream*, flows 3.25 miles to Tomki Creek 6.5 miles east-southeast of Longvale (39°31'05" N, long. 123°18'45" W; sec. 9, T 19 N, R 13 W). Named on Willits (1961) 15' quadrangle, and on Willis Ridge (1966) 7.5' quadrangle.

Wheelbarro Valley [MENDOCINO]: *canyon*, 1 mile long, 6 miles north of Willits (lat. 39°29'45" N, long. 123°20'30" W; sec. 18, T 19 N, R 13 W). Named on Willits (1961) 15' quadrangle, and on Willis Ridge (1966) 7.5' quadrangle.

Wheeler [MENDOCINO]: *locality*, 8.5 miles southwest of Piercy (lat. 39°53'10" N, long. 123°54'40" W; near NW cor. sec. 6, T 23 N, R 18 W). Site named on Bear Harbor (1969) 7.5' quadrangle.

Wheeler Point [LAKE]: *promontory*, 6.5 miles northwest of the town of Lower Lake along Clear Lake (lat. 38°58'05" N, long. 122°42'35" W; sec. 23, T 13 N, R 8 W). Named on Clearlake Highlands (1958) 7.5' quadrangle.

Wheel Gulch [MENDOCINO]: *canyon*, drained by a stream that flows 0.5 mile to Big River nearly 6 miles northwest of Comptche (lat. 39°19' N, long. 123°40'20" W; sec. 20, T 17 N, R 16 W). Named on Comptche (1960) 15' quadrangle. The name is from wheels used for moving logs; the canyon also was called Tramway Gulch, and a place in the canyon was called Tramway Camp, or Gas Camp for gasoline-operated machinery there (Jackson, Francis, p. 88).

Wheel Gulch [TRINITY]:

(1) *canyon*, drained by a stream that flows 1 mile to Trinity River 3 miles east-southeast of Helena (lat. 40°45'50" N, long. 123°04'30" W; sec. 35, T 34 N, R 11 W). Named on Helena (1951) 15' quadrangle.

(2) *canyon*, drained by a stream that flows 3 miles to Trinity River 13 miles north of Hayfork (lat. 40°44'05" N, long. 123°12' W). Named on Hayfork (1951) and Helena (1951) 15' quadrangles.

Whipple Ridge [MENDOCINO]: *ridge*, northwest-tending, 1.5 miles long, 7 miles northwest of Boonville (lat. 39°05'40" N, long. 123°26'30" W). Named on Boonville (1959) 15' quadrangle.

Whiskey Creek [TRINITY]: *stream*, flows 1.5 miles to North Fork Trinity River 10 miles south of Cecil Lake (lat. 41°00'15" N, long. 123°09'30" W). Named on Cecil Lake (1979) 7.5' quadrangle.

Whiskey Lake [DEL NORTE]: *lake*, 350 feet long, 3.25 miles northeast of Broken Rib Mountain (lat. 41°55'20" N, long. 123°38'40" W). Named on Broken Rib Mountain (1982) 7.5' quadrangle.

Whiskey Springs [MENDOCINO]: *locality*, 8 miles north-northwest of Comptche (lat. 39°21'50" N, long. 123°39'50" W; near E line sec. 5, T 17 N, R 16 W). Named on Comptche (1960) 15' quadrangle.

Whisky Bill Peak [TRINITY]: *peak*, 11 miles northeast of Trinity Center (lat. 41°06'10" N, long. 122°31'30" W; near S line sec. 35, T 38 N, R 6 W). Altitude 6351 feet. Named on Bonanza King (1955) 15' quadrangle.

Whisky Creek [TRINITY]: *stream*, flows 1 mile to East Fork New River 15 miles north-northeast of Ironside Mountain (lat. 40°59'10" N, long. 123°18'30" W). Named on Ironside Mountain (1951) 15' quadrangle.

Whispering Pines [LAKE]: *settlement*, 8.5 miles southwest of the town of Lower Lake (lat. 38°48'50" N, long. 122°42'40" W; sec. 14, T 11 N, R 8 W). Named on Whispering Pines (1958) 7.5' quadrangle.

White: see **Widow White Creek** [HUMBOLDT].

White and Miller Ferry: see **Peacock Creek** [DEL NORTE].

White Creek [MENDOCINO]: *stream*, flows 4 miles to East Fork Russian River 3.5 miles south of the town of Potter Valley (lat. 39°16'25" N, long. 123°06'05" W; sec. 5, T 16 N, R 11 W). Named on Potter Valley (1960) and Redwood Valley (1960) 7.5' quadrangles.

White Creek [TRINITY]: *stream*, flows 1.5 miles to East Fork New River 16 miles northeast of Burnt Ranch (lat. 40°59'30" N, long. 123°17'35" W). Named on Ironside Mountain (1951) 15' quadrangle.

White Gulch [MENDOCINO]: *canyon*, drained by a stream that flows nearly 1 mile to Ray Gulch 5.5 miles northeast of Elk (lat. 39°11'20" N, long. 123°38'20" W; sec. 4, T 15 N, R 15 W). Named on Elk (1960) 7.5' quadrangle.

Whitehall: see **Yorkville** [MENDOCINO].

White Hawk Creek [MENDOCINO]: *stream*, flows 3.25 miles to Black Butte River 6 miles south of Anthony Peak (lat. 39°45'40" N, long. 122°58'15" W; sec. 16, T 22 N, R 10 W). Named on Mendocino Pass (1967) 7.5' quadrangle.

White Hawk Ridge [MENDOCINO]: *ridge*, south-trending, 2 miles long, 5 miles south of Anthony Peak (lat. 39°46'45" N, long. 122°58'30" W); the ridge is west of White Hawk Creek. Named on Mendocino Pass (1967) 7.5' quadrangle.

White Horse Creek [MENDOCINO]: *stream*, flows 1.5 miles to Glenn County 6.5 miles north-northeast of Hull Mountain (lat. 39°36'25" N, long. 122°53'05" W; at E line sec. 8, T 20 N, R 9 W). Named on Hull Mountain (1967) 7.5' quadrangle.

White Oak Creek [HUMBOLDT]: *stream*, flows 2.25 miles to Grouse Creek (2) 3.25 miles east-northeast of Board Camp Mountain (lat. 40°43'05" N, long. 123°40'15" W; sec. 24, T 4 N, R 4 E). Named on Board Camp Mountain (1977) 7.5' quadrangle.

White Oak Gulch [TRINITY]: *canyon*, drained by a stream that flows 0.5 mile to Trinity River 20 miles northeast of Weaverville (lat. 40°57' N, long. 122°40'50" W; sec. 28, T 36 N, R 7 W). Named on Schell Mountain (1950) 15' quadrangle.

White Oak Opening [HUMBOLDT]: *area*, 1.5 miles northeast of Board Camp Mountain (lat. 40°42'55" N, long. 123°41'50" W; sec. 23, T 4 N, R 4 E); the place is near the head of a branch of White Oak Creek. Named on Board Camp Mountain (1977) 7.5' quadrangle.

White Pebble Spring [LAKE]: *spring*, 5 miles northwest of Three Crossings (lat. 39°22' N, long. 122°59'30" W; sec. 33, T 18 N, R 10 W). Named on Elk Mountain (1967) 7.5' quadrangle.

White Plains: see **Fort Bragg** [MENDOCINO].

White Point [LAKE]: *relief feature*, 5.25 miles south-southeast of Middletown (lat. 38°41' N, long. 122°34'10" W; sec. 30, T 10 N, R 8 W). Named on Detert Reservoir (1958) 7.5' quadrangle.

White Ranch Glades [LAKE]: *areas*, 14 miles north of Clearlake Oaks (lat. 39°13'25" N, long. 122°42'50" W). Named on Clearlake Oaks (1960) 15' quadrangle.

White Rock [DEL NORTE]:

(1) *rock*, 3.5 miles northwest of Crescent City, and 1100 feet offshore at Point Saint George (lat. 41°47' N, long. 124°15'30" W). Named on Crescent City (1966) 7.5' quadrangle.

(2) *rock*, 1.5 miles west-southwest of Crescent City, and 3900 feet offshore (lat. 41°44'50" N, long. 124°13'40" W). Named on Sister Rocks (1966) 7.5' quadrangle.

(3) *rock*, 2.25 miles south of the mouth of Klamath River, and 850 feet offshore (lat. 41°30'55" N, long. 124°05'05" W). Named on Requa (1966) 7.5' quadrangle.

White Rock [HUMBOLDT]: *rock*, 2 miles north-northwest of Trinidad, and 650 feet offshore (lat. 41°05'15" N, long. 124°09'35" W). Named on Trinidad (1966) 7.5' quadrangle.

White Rock [MENDOCINO]:

(1) *relief feature*, nearly 6 miles south-southwest of Spyrock (2) (lat. 39°48'15" N, long. 123°29'35" W; at SE cor.sec. 26, T 23 N, R 15 W). Named on Iron Peak (1967) 7.5' quadrangle.

(2) *rock*, 2.5 miles south of Elk, and 3000 feet offshore (lat. 39°05'40" N, long. 123°43'05" W). Name on Mallo Pass Creek (1960) 7.5' quadrangle.

White Rock [TRINITY]: *peak*, 11 miles southeast of Dubakella Mountain on Trinity-Tehama County line (lat. 40°15'50" N, long. 123°01'10" W; sec. 20, T 28 N, R 10 W). Named on Dubakella Mountain (1954) 15' quadrangle.

White Rock: see **Big White Rock** [MENDOCINO].

White Rock Canyon [LAKE]:

(1) *canyon,* drained by a stream that flows about 1 mile to Middle Creek (2) 4 miles north-northwest of the town of Upper Lake (lat. 39°13'10" N, long. 122°55'50" W; near NE cor. sec. 26, T 16 N, R 10 W). Named on Upper Lake (1958) 7.5' quadrangle.

(2) *canyon,* drained by a stream that flows 2 miles to the canyon of Scotts Creek 5 miles west-southwest of the town of Upper Lake (lat. 39°07'30" N, long. 122°59'10" W; near NE cor. sec. 29, T 15 N, R 10 W); the canyon heads near White Rock Mountain. Named on Upper Lake (1958) 7.5' quadrangle.

White Rock City [TRINITY]: *locality,* 9 miles southeast of Salmon Mountain (lat. 41°05'20" N, long. 123°16'50" W). Site named on Dees Peak (1978) 7.5' quadrangle. White Rock City was at the site of Couer post office, and was one of three rival townsites near one another; it was abandoned in 1904 (Jones, p. 264-265). Postal authorities established Coeur post office in 1885 and discontinued it in 1896; the name was for Alexander Coeur, first postmaster (Salley, p. 47). They established Francis post office 20 miles south of Coeur post office in 1881, discontinued it for a time in 1887, and discontinued it finally in 1897; the name was for Joseph M. Francis, first postmaster (Salley, p. 79).

White Rock Creek [MENDOCINO]: *stream,* flows 5.25 miles to Iron Creek 8 miles south of Spyrock (2) (lat. 39°45'50" N, long. 123°26' W; near N line sec. 16, T 22 N, R 14 W); the stream heads south of White Rock (1). Named on Iron Peak (1967) 7.5' quadrangle.

White Rock Mountain [LAKE]: *peak,* 4 miles west-southwest of the town of Little Lake (lat. 39°08'50" N, long. 122°58'45" W; sec. 16, T 15 N, R 10 W). Altitude 2690 feet. Named on Upper Lake (1958) 7.5' quadrangle.

White Rocks [HUMBOLDT]: *relief feature,* 4.5 miles south-southeast of Coyote Peak (lat. 41°04'20" N, long. 123°49'10" W). Named on Hupa Mountain (1982) 7.5' quadrangle.

White Rock Spring [HUMBOLDT]: *spring,* 9.5 miles south-southwest of the settlement of Willow Creek (lat. 40°48'50" N, long. 123°41'40" W; sec. 14, T 5 N, R 4 E). Named on Grouse Mountain (1979) 7.5' quadrangle.

Whites Bar Creek [TRINITY]: *stream,* flows 1 mile to Trinity River 11 miles east-southeast of Burnt Ranch (lat. 40°45'40" N, long. 123°16'50" W; sec. 33, T 5 N, R 8 E). Named on Ironside Mountain (1951) 15' quadrangle.

Whitesboro [MENDOCINO]: *locality,* less than 1 mile south-southeast of Albion (lat. 39°12'50" N, long. 123°45'45" W; near S line sec. 28, T 16 N, R 17 W). Site named on Albion (1960) 7.5' quadrangle. Postal authorities established Whitesboro post office in 1881 and discontinued it in 1899 (Frickstad, p. 98). The name, given in 1876, commemorates Lorenzo E. White, principal owner of Salmon Creek Mill Company (Gudde, 1969, p. 363). Carpenter (p. 67) referred to a village called Salmon Creek that was situated at or near the place.

Whitesborro Bay: see **Whitesboro Cove** [MENDOCINO].

Whitesboro Cove [MENDOCINO]: *embayment,* 0.5 mile southwest of Albion at the mouth of Big Salmon Creek (lat. 39°13' N, long. 123°46'15" W); the embayment is west of the site of Whitesboro. Named on Albion (1960) 7.5' quadrangle. United States Board on Geographic Names (1943, p. 14) rejected the names "Salmon Creek Bay," "Salmon Creek Cove," and "Whitesboro Bay" for the feature.

Whites Creek [TRINITY]: *stream,* flows 5 miles to North Fork Trinity River 12 miles north of Helena (lat. 40°56'40" N, long. 123°09'15" W). Named on Helena (1951) 15' quadrangle. Called White's Cr. on Miller's (1890) map.

Whites Creek Lake [TRINITY]: *lake,* 200 feet long, 14 miles north-northwest of Helena (lat. 40°57'20" N, long. 123°13'20" W); the lake is along a branch of Whites Creek. Named on Helena (1951) 15' quadrangle.

White Slide [MENDOCINO]: *relief feature,* 10 miles northeast of Leggett (lat. 39°57'45" N, long. 123°34'30" W; sec. 6, T 24 N, R 15 W). Named on Bell Springs (1969) 7.5' quadrangle.

White Stump: see **Ruth** [TRINITY].

Whitethorn [HUMBOLDT]: *locality,* 9.5 miles southwest of Garberville (lat. 40°01'20" N, long. 123°56'15" W). Named on Briceland (1969) 7.5' quadrangle. Called Thorn on Garberville (1949) 15' quadrangle. Postal authorities established Thorn post office in 1888, discontinued it in 1923, reestablished it in 1951, and changed the name to Whitethorn in 1961—this name is from the abundance of native thornbush in the neighborhood (Salley, p. 239).

Whiteys Gulch [HUMBOLDT]: *canyon,* drained by a stream that flows 1.25 miles to Klamath River 1.25 miles southwest of Orleans (lat. 41°17'15" N, long. 123°33'15" W). Named on Orleans (1978) 7.5' quadrangle.

Whiteys Peak [HUMBOLDT] *peak,* 2.25 miles north-northwest of Salmon Mountain on Humboldt-Siskiyou County line (lat. 41°12'45" N, long. 123°26' W). Named on Salmon Mountain (1978) 7.5' quadrangle.

Whiting Ridge [HUMBOLDT]: *ridge,* south-trending, 3 miles long, 5 miles east-southeast of Board Camp Mountain (lat. 40°39'30" N, long. 123°38'05" W). Named on Board Camp Mountain (1977) 7.5' quadrangle.

Whiting Spring [HUMBOLDT]: *spring,* 5.25 mile east-southeast of Board Camp Mountain (lat. 40°39'30" N, long. 123°37'50" W; sec. 8, T 3 N, R 5 E). Named on Board Camp Mountain (1977) 7.5' quadrangle.

Whitlow [HUMBOLDT]: *locality,* 7 miles east of Weott along Northwestern Pacific Railroad (lat. 40°18'55" N, long. 123°47'40" W; at E line sec. 2, T 2 S, R 3 E). Named on Myers Flat (1969) 7.5' quadrangle. Called Sequoia on Weott (1949) 15' quadrangle, which also shows Whitlow P.O. at the site. Postal authorities established Whitlow post office in 1927 and discontinued it in 1965; the name was for Albert Whitlow, first postmaster (Salley, p. 240).

Whitmore Creek [HUMBOLDT]: *stream,* flows 1.5 miles to Klamath River 3 miles north-northeast of Orleans (lat. 41°20'10" N, long. 123°30'35" W). Named on Orleans (1978) and Orleans Mountain (1974) 7.5' quadrangles.

Whitney Creek [MENDOCINO]: *stream,* flows 2.5 miles to Eel River 7 miles north of the town of Potter Valley (lat. 39°10'05" N, long. 123°07'40" W; near W line sec. 14, T 18 N, R 11 W). Named on Potter Valley (1960) 15' quadrangle.

Whitney Gulch [TRINITY]: *canyon,* drained by a stream that flows 2 miles to Buckeye Creek (2) 8 miles northeast of Weaverville (lat. 40°48'05" N, long. 122°49'10" W; sec. 18, T 34 N, R 8 W). Named on Trinity Dam (1950) 15' quadrangle.

Who Who Creek [MENDOCINO]: *stream,* formed by the confluence of North Branch and South Branch, flows 0.5 mile to Hulls Creek 10.5 miles north-northeast of Spyrock (2) (lat. 39°55' N, long. 123°15'10" W). Named on Mina (1967) 7.5' quadrangle. North Branch is 1.5 miles long, and South Branch is nearly 1 mile long; both branches are named on Mina (1967) 7.5' quadrangle.

Who Who Lake [MENDOCINO]: *intermittent lake,* 350 feet long, 8 miles east-northeast of Spyrock (2) (lat. 39°55'05" N, long. 123°17'55" W). Named on Mina (1967) 7.5' quadrangle.

Widow Creek [LAKE]: *stream,* flows 1.5 miles to Kelsey Creek 5 miles south of Kelseyville (lat. 38°54'30" N, long. 122°51'20" W; near NW cor. sec. 10, T 12 N, R 9 W). Named on Kelseyville (1959) 7.5' quadrangle.

Widow White Creek [HUMBOLDT]: *stream,* flows 3 miles to the sea 6.5 miles north-northwest of Arcata (lat. 40°57'50" N, long. 124°07'25" W; sec. 25, T 7 N, R 1 W). Named on Arcata North (1959) 7.5' quadrangle. The name is for Asa White's widow (Turner, p. 231).

Wilcox Ridge [TRINITY]: *ridge,* generally north-trending, 3.5 miles long, 9.5 miles west-northwest of Black Rock Mountain (lat. 40°14'45" N, long. 123°10'45" W). Named on Black Rock Mountain (1954) and Dubakella Mountain (1954) 15' quadrangles.

Wild Bill Creek [LAKE]: *stream,* flows 2.25 miles to North Fork Cache Creek 8.5 miles northeast of the town of Upper Lake (lat. 39°14'05" N, long. 122°46'45" W). Named on Bartlett Mountain (1958) 7.5' quadrangle, which shows Wild Bill place near the stream.

Wild Bill Ridge [LAKE]: *ridge,* northwest-to north-northwest-trending, 2 miles long, 7.25 miles northeast of the town of Upper Lake (lat. 39°13' N, long. 122°47'45" W); the ridge is southeast of Wild Bill Creek. Named on Bartlett Mountain (1958) 7.5' quadrangle.

Wildcat Butte [HUMBOLDT]: *peak,* 6 miles northwest of Alderpoint (lat. 40°13'50" N, long. 123°41'40" W; sec. 2, T 3 S, R 4 E). Altitude 1739 feet. Named on Fort Seward (1969) 7.5' quadrangle.

Wildcat Canyon [LAKE]: *canyon,* drained by a stream that flows 2.25 miles to Seigler Canyon 3 miles west-southwest of the town of Lower Lake (lat. 38°53'40" N, long. 122°39'40" W; sec. 17, T 12 N, R 7 W). Named on Clearlake Highlands (1958) 7.5' quadrangle.

Wildcat Creek [DEL NORTE]: *stream,* flows 2.5 miles to East Fork Blue Creek 15 miles east of Klamath Glen (lat. 41°29'25" N, long. 123°42'35" W). Named on Lonesome Ridge (1974) 7.5' quadrangle.

Wildcat Creek [HUMBOLDT]: *stream,* flows 2 miles to Mad River 3.5 miles east-southeast of Showers Mountain (lat. 40°33'50" N, long. 123°37'50" W; sec. 8, T 2 N, R 5 E). Named on Blake Mountain (1979) and Showers Mountain (1978) 7.5' quadrangles.

Wildcat Creek [MENDOCINO]: *stream,* flows 4 miles to South Fork Eel River 4 miles south-southeast of Piercy (lat. 39°54'45" N, long. 123°45'35" W; sec. 20, T 24 N, R 17 W). Named on Piercy (1969) 7.5' quadrangle.

Wildcat Lake [LAKE]: *intermittent lake,* 225 feet long, 3.25 miles south-southwest of Jericho Valley (lat. 38°46'10" N, long. 122°29'20" W; near S line sec. 26, T 11 N, R 6 W). Named on Jericho Valley (1958) 7.5' quadrangle.

Wildcat Peak [TRINITY]: *peak,* 6.5 miles east-northeast of Trinity Center (lat. 41°02'50" N, long. 122°34'40" W; near S line sec. 20, T 37 N, R 6 W). Altitude 5576 feet. Named on Bonanza King (1955) 15' quadrangle.

Wildcat Ridge [HUMBOLDT]: *ridge,* generally north-trending, 2.5 miles long, center 1.5 miles south-southwest of Ferndale (lat. 40°33'30" N, long. 124°16'25" W). Named on Ferndale (1959) 7.5' quadrangle.

Wilder: see **Ettersburg** [HUMBOLDT].

Wilder Creek [HUMBOLDT]: *stream,* flows 4 miles to Camp Creek 3 miles north-northwest of Orleans (lat. 41°20'15" N, long. 123°34'10" W). Named on Bark Shanty Gulch (1974) and Orleans (1978) 7.5' quadrangles.

Wilder Gulch [HUMBOLDT]: *canyon,* drained by a stream that flows 1.25 miles to Klamath River at Orleans (lat. 41°18'05" N, long. 123°32'15" W). Named on Orleans (1978) 7.5' quadrangle.

Wilderness Lodge [MENDOCINO]: *locality,* 6 miles north of Branscomb along South Fork Eel River (lat. 39°44'25" N, long. 123°37'50" W; sec. 21, T 22 N, R 16 W). Named on Lincoln Ridge (1966) 7.5' quadrangle.

Wilder Ridge [HUMBOLDT]: *ridge,* north-northeast-trending, 3.25 miles long, 4.5 miles south-southeast of Honeydew (lat. 40°11'05" N, long. 124°05'20" W). Named on Honeydew (1970) 7.5' quadrangle.

Wildhorse Creek [LAKE-MENDOCINO]: *stream,* heads in Mendocino County and flows 1.25 miles in Lake and Mendocino Counties to Sonoma County 8 miles east-southeast of Monument Peak (lat. 38°51' N, long. 123°50'05" W; at S line sec. 26, T 12 N, R 9 W). Named on The Geysers (1959) 7.5' quadrangle.

Wild Horse Opening [MENDOCINO]: *area,* 4.5 miles northeast of Comptche along Big River (lat. 39°18'15" N, long. 123°31'20" W; sec. 27, T 17 N, R 15 W). Named on Comptche (1960) 15' quadrangle.

Wildhorse Peak [TRINITY]: *peak,* 15 miles southeast of Kettenpom near or on Mendocino-Trinity-County line (lat. 39°58'40" N, long. 123°17'50" W; sec. 36, T 5 S, R 8 E). Altitude 3564 feet. Named on Mina (1967) 7.5' quadrangle.

Wild Oat Canyon [MENDOCINO]: *canyon,* drained by a stream that flows 1 mile to Little Lake Valley 2.5 miles north of Willits (lat. 39°26'45" N, long. 123°21'15" W; near NW cor. sec. 6, T 18 N, R 13 W). Named on Willits (1961) 15' quadrangle.

Wildwood [TRINITY]: *locality,* 5 miles east of Dubakella Mountain along Hayfork Creek (lat. 40°24' N, long. 123°03'10" W; near N line sec. 1, T 29 N, R 11 W). Named on Dubakella Mountain (1954) 15' quadrangle. Postal authorities established Wildwood post office in 1888, discontinued it in 1893, reestablished it in 1958, discontinued it in 1961, and reestablished it in 1966 (Salley, p. 240). United States Board on Geographic Names (1978c, p. 2) approved the name "Hackney Spring" for a feature located 6 miles southwest of Wildwood (lat. 40°19'31" N, long. 123°06'31" W), and approved the name "Hell to Find Lake" for a feature located 5.5 miles southwest of Wildwood—cattlemen gave this descriptive name before 1900. The Board (1979, p. 4) also approved the name "McFarland Ridge" for a feature, 3 miles long, located 2.5 miles southeast of Wildwood on Trinity-Shasta County line (lat. 40°22'40" N, long. 123°01' W, at the north-east end).

Wilkinson Creek [LAKE]: *stream,* flows 2 miles to Saint Helena Creek 2.5 miles south of Middletown (lat. 38°42'50" N, long. 122°36'35" W). Named on Detert Reservoir (1958) 7.5' quadrangle.

Williams: see **Billy Williams Creek** [MENDOCINO]; **Billy Williams Ridge** [MENDOCINO].

Williams Creek [DEL NORTE]: *stream,* flows 5 miles to Eightmile Creek 4.5 miles east of Buck Mountain (lat. 41°37'25" N, long. 123°46'55" W). Named on Summit Valley (1981) 7.5' quadrangle.

Williams Creek [HUMBOLDT]:

(1) *stream,* flows 6 miles to Salt River 4.5 miles west of Fortuna (lat. 40°35'20" N, long. 124°14'15" W; sec. 1, T 2 N, R 2 W). Named on Ferndale (1959) and Fortuna (1959) 7.5' quadrangles.

(2) *stream,* flows nearly 2 miles to South Fork Eel River 2.5 miles south of Phillipsville (lat. 40°10'25" N, long. 123°46'50" W). Named on Miranda (1970) 7.5' quadrangle.

Williams Creek [MENDOCINO]:

(1) *stream,* flows 9.5 miles to Middle Fork Eel River 6.25 miles east-north-east of Covelo (lat. 39°48'55" N, long. 123°07'55" W; near NW cor. sec. 31, T 23 N, R 11 W). Named on Covelo East (1967), Leech Lake Mountain (1966), and Newhouse Ridge (1967) 7.5' quadrangles.

(2) *stream,* flows 5 miles to East Fork Russian River at the town of Potter Valley (lat. 39°19'30" N, long. 123°06'20" W; sec. 17, T 17 N, R 11 W). Named on Potter Valley (1960) and Redwood Valley (1960) 7.5' quadrangles.

Williams Peak [MENDOCINO]: *peak,* 7.25 miles south-southwest of Willits (lat. 39°19' N, long. 123°24'45" W; near W line sec. 22, T 17 N, R 14 W). Altitude 2724 feet. Named on Willits (1961) 15' quadrangle.

Williams Point [MENDOCINO]: *promontory,* 16 miles south of Piercy along the coast (lat. 39°45'10" N, long. 123°50'15" W; sec. 14, T 22 N, R 18 W). Named on Hales Grove (1970) 7.5' quadrangle

Williams Ridge [HUMBOLDT]: *ridge,* generally northeast-trending, 5 miles long, 3.5 miles north of Coyote Peak (lat. 41°11'10" N, long. 123°51'35" W). Named on Bald Hills (1982) 7.5' quadrangle.

Williams Valley [MENDOCINO]: *valley,* 5 miles northeast of Covelo along Short Creek (lat. 39°50'45" N, long. 123°11'15" W). Named on Covelo East (1967) 7.5' quadrangle.

Willis Ridge [MENDOCINO]: *ridge,* north-northwest-trending, 7 miles long, center 6 miles east of Longvale (lat. 39°33'30" N, long. 123°19' W). Named on Willis Ridge (1966) 7.5' quadrangle.

Willits [MENDOCINO]: *town,* 20 miles north-northwest of Ukiah in Little Lake Valley (lat. 39°24'30" N, long. 123°21'10" W; around SW cor. sec. 18, T 18 N, R 13 W). Named on Willits (1961) 15' quadrangle. Postal authorities established Little Lake post office, named for its location in Little Lake Valley, in 1861 and changed the name to Willits in 1874 (Salley, p. 123). The town incorporated in 1888. The name commemorates Hiram Willits, who came to the site in 1857 and owned the land upon which Kirk Brier started the town in the 1860's; the community first was known as Willitsville (Hanna, p. 355). California Mining Bureau's (1909c) map shows a place called Northwestern located along the railroad about 3 miles northwest of Willits. Postal authorities established Northwestern post office in 1906 and discontinued it in 1927; the name was for the location of the place northwest of Willits along California Western Railroad (Salley, p. 157). California Mining Bureau's (1917c) map shows a place called Rodgers located 3 miles west of Willits along the railroad. Postal authorities established Tomkiah post office 10 miles northeast of Little Lake post office (SW quarter sec. 31, T 19 N, R 12 W) in 1872, changed the name to Glenmark in 1873, and discontinued it in 1874 (Salley, p. 86, 223). Waring (p. 259) listed Muir Springs, located on the edge of Little Lake Valley about 4 miles northeast of Willits; the feature produced mildly sulphureted water and natural gas—Willits (1942) 15' quadrangle shows Muir ranch situated nearly 4 miles northeast of Willits (near N line sec. 9, T 18 N, R 13 W).

Willits Creek [MENDOCINO]: *stream,* flows 6.5 miles to Little Lake Valley at Willits (lat. 39°24'50" N, long. 123°21'45" W; sec. 13, T 18 N, R 14 W). Named on Willits (1961) 15' quadrangle.

Willits Ravine [TRINITY]: *canyon,* drained by a stream that flows 1.5 miles to Crow Creek 13 miles northeast of Trinity Center (lat. 41°09' N, long. 122°31'15" W; sec. 14, T 38 N, R 6 W). Named on Bonanza King (1955) 15' quadrangle.

Willitsville: see **Willits** [MENDOCINO].

Willow Basin [TRINITY]: *relief feature,* 9 miles south of Black Rock Mountain (lat. 40°04'45" N, long. 122°59'25" W; near N line sec. 28, T 26 N, R 10 W). Named on Yolla Bolly (1954) 15' quadrangle.

Willow Basin Creek [TRINITY]: *stream,* flows 1.5 miles to Middle Fork Eel River 7.5 miles south-southeast of Black Rock Mountain (lat. 40°06' N, long. 122°58'45" W; sec. 15, T 26 N, R 10 W); the stream heads at Willow Basin. Named on Yolla Bolly (1954) 15' quadrangle.

Willow Brook [HUMBOLDT]: *stream,* flows 1 mile to lowlands near Humboldt Bay 2.5 miles south-southeast of Fields Landing (lat. 40°41'30" N, long. 124°11'40" W; near NW cor. sec. 33, T 4 N, R 1 W). Named on Fields Landing (1959) 7.5' quadrangle.

Willow Creek [HUMBOLDT]:

(1) *stream,* flows 11 miles to Trinity River less than 0.5 mile north of the settlement of Willow Creek (lat. 40°56'40" N, long. 123°37'45" W; at E line sec. 29, T 7 N, R 5 E). Named on Lord-Ellis Summit (1973) and Willow Creek (1979) 7.5' quadrangles. East Fork enters 4.5 miles west-southwest of the settlement of Willow Creek; it is 7.5 miles long and is named on Grouse Mountain (1979) and Willow Creek (1979) 7.5' quadrangles.

(2) *stream,* flows 1 mile to the sea 6.25 miles southwest of Petrolia (lat. 40°14'40" N, long. 124°20'30" W). Named on Cooskie Creek (1969) and Petrolia (1969) 7.5' quadrangles.

(3) *settlement,* near the mouth of Willow Creek (1) (lat. 40°56'20" N, long. 123°37'45" W; on W line sec, 33, T 7 N, R 5 E). Named on Willow Creek (1979) 7.5' quadrangle. China Flat (1922) 15' quadrangle has the name "Willow Creek" for a community situated nearly 0.5 mile farther north-west across Willow Creek (1) (sec. 29, T 7 N, R 5 E), and has the name "China Flat P.O." at the site of present Willow Creek (3). Postal authorities established China Flat post office in 1878 and changed the name to Willow Creek in 1915 (Frickstad, p. 42). The first settlers were Chinese people from the mines and lumber camps (Turner, p. 49).

Willow Creek [LAKE]:

(1) *stream,* flows 5 miles to Rice Fork 2.25 miles south-southwest of Lake Pillsbury (lat. 39°22'35" N, long. 122°54'35" W). Named on Elk Mountain (1967) and Lake Pillsbury (1967) 7.5' quadrangles.

(2) *stream,* flows nearly 4 miles to Scotts Creek 8 miles west-northwest of Lakeport (lat. 39°06'10" N, long. 123°02'30" W; sec. 2, T 14 N, R 11 W). Named on Purdy's Gardens (1958) 7.5' quadrangle.

Willow Creek [MENDOCINO]: *stream,* flows about 2 miles to Mill Creek (13) 5 miles east of Ukiah (lat. 39°08'30" N, long. 123°06'45" W). Named on Cow Mountain (1958) and Purdys Gardens (1958) 7.5' quadrangles.

Willow Creek [TRINITY]:

(1) *stream,* flows 1.5 miles to Deer Creek (1) 17 miles north of Weaverville (lat. 40°58'10" N, long. 122°55'10" W; sec. 17, T 36 N, R 9 W). Named on Trinity Dam (1950) 15' quadrangle.

(2) *stream,* flows 3 miles to North Fork of Middle Fork Eel River 11.5 miles southwest of Black Rock Mountain (lat. 40°04'20" N, long. 123°08'10" W; near W line sec. 29, T 26 N, R 11 W). Named on Black Rock Mountain (1954) 15' quadrangle.

(3) *stream,* flows 3.5 miles to North Fork Eel River 8 miles east-northeast

of Kettenpom (lat. 40°06'15" N, long. 123°19'20" W; near W line sec. 19, T 4 S, R 8 E). Named on Long Ridge (1967) 7.5' quadrangle.

(4) *stream*, flows 2.5 miles to Eel River 11.5 miles south of Kettenpom (lat. 39°59'35" N, long. 123°28'05" W; sec. 26, T 5 S, R 6 E). Named on Lake Mountain (1967) and Updegraff Ridge (1967) 7.5' quadrangles.

Willow Creek Camp: see **South Willow Creek Camp** [LAKE].

Willow Draw Creek [HUMBOLDT]: *stream*, flows 2.5 miles to Eel River nearly 6 miles northwest of Alderpoint (lat. 40°14'20" N, long. 123°40'55" W; near N line sec. 1, T 3 S, R 4 E). Named on Fort Seward (1969) 7.5' quadrangle.

Willow Flat [LAKE]: *area*, 4.5 miles east-northeast of the town of Upper Lake (lat. 39°10'55" N, long. 122°49'45" W; sec. 2, T 15 N, R 9 W). Named on Bartlett Mountain (1958) 7.5' quadrangle.

Willow Gulch [TRINITY]:

(1) *canyon*, drained by a stream that flows 3.5 miles to Big French Creek 11 miles east-northeast of Burnt Ranch (lat. 40°51'35" N, long. 123°16'25" W). Named on Ironside Mountain (1951) 15' quadrangle.

(2) *canyon*, drained by a stream that flows 1 mile to Salt Creek (4) 5.25 miles north of Dubakella Mountain (lat. 40°27'10" N, long. 123°09'25" W; near E line sec. 13, T 30 N, R 12 W). Named on Dubakella Mountain (1954) 15' quadrangle.

(3) *canyon*, drained by a stream that flows 2.5 miles to Duncan Creek 6.25 miles east of Hayfork (lat. 40°34'15" N, long. 123°04' W; sec. 1, T 31 N, R 11 W). Named on Hayfork (1951) 15' quadrangle.

Willow Point [LAKE]: *promontory*, along Clear Lake at Lakeport (lat. 39°02'55" N, long. 122°54'40" W; near SE cor. sec. 24, T 14 N, R 10 W). Named on Lakeport (1958) 7.5' quadrangle.

Willow Ridge [LAKE]: *ridge*, northwest-trending, 1.5 miles long, 7 miles west of Lakeport (lat. 39°04'10" N, long. 123°02'50" W); the ridge is southwest of Willow Creek (2). Named on Purdy's Gardens (1958) 7.5' quadrangle.

Willow Spring [MENDOCINO]: *spring*, 10 miles northeast of Spyrock (2) (lat. 39°58'15" N, long. 123°17'50" W). Named on Mina (1967) 7.5' quadrangle.

Willsey Creek [MENDOCINO]: *stream*, flows 2 miles to Cold Creek (4) 5.25 miles north-northwest of Covelo (lat. 39°51'05" N, long. 123°17'40" W; near S line sec. 10, T 23 N, R 13 W). Named on Covelo West (1967) 7.5' quadrangle.

Wilson: see **Jim Wilson Flat** [TRINITY]; **Lousy Creek** [TRINITY].

Wilson Creek [DEL NORTE]: *stream*, flows 8.5 miles to the sea 4 miles north-northwest of the mouth of Klamath River (lat. 41°36'20" N, long. 124°06'05" W; sec. 18, T 14 N, R 1 E). Named on Childs Hill (1966) and Requa (1966) 7.5' quadrangles. Called Wilsons C. on Colton's (1863) map.

Wilson Creek [HUMBOLDT]:

(1) *stream*, flows 2.25 miles to Klamath River 2.25 miles north-northeast of Orleans (lat. 41°19'50" N, long. 123°31'10" W). Named on Orleans (1978) 7.5' quadrangle.

(2) *stream*, flows 3.25 miles to Mad River 4 miles east-northeast of Lone Star Junction (lat. 40°38'45" N, long. 123°48' W; sec. 14, T 3 N, R 3 E). Named on Mad River Buttes (1977) 7.5' quadrangle. The name is for either Jerry Wilson or Stanley Wilson, both of whom settled by the stream (Turner, p. 235.

(3) *stream*, flows 3.25 miles to Yager Creek 6.5 miles southeast of Fortuna (lat. 40°31'50" N, long. 124°04' W; sec. 28, T 2 N, R 1 E). Named on Hydesville (1979) 7.5' quadrangle.

Wilson Creek [MENDOCINO]:

(1) *stream*, flows 1.5 miles to Rattlesnake Creek (2) 5 miles east-southeast of Leggett (lat. 39°49'55" N, long. 123°37'45" W; sec. 21, T 23 N, R 16 W). Named on Leggett (1969) 7.5' quadrangle.

(2) *stream*, flows 2 miles to Tenmile Creek 8 miles northeast of Branscomb (lat. 39°43'05" N, long. 123°30'15" W; sec. 35, T 22 N, R 15 W). Named on Cahto Peak (1967) and Laytonville (1967) 7.5' quadrangles. Called Jno. Wilson Creek on Laytonville (1919) 15' quadrangle.

Wilson Creek [MENDOCINO-TRINITY]: *stream*, heads in Trinity County and flows nearly 7 miles to North Fork Eel River 5.25 miles northeast of Spyrock (2) in Mendocino County (lat. 39°56'20" N, long. 123°22'50" W; sec. 12, T 24 N, R 14 W). Named on Lake Mountain (1967) and Updegraff Ridge (1967) 7.5' quadrangles.

Wilson Creek [TRINITY]:

(1) *stream*, flows 3.5 miles to Hayfork Creek 5.25 miles east-northeast of Dubakella Mountain (lat. 40°24'45" N, long. 123°03'20" W; sec. 36, T 30 N, R 11 W). Named on Dubakella Mountain (1954) 15' quadrangle.

(2) *stream*, flows 2 miles to Kettenpom Creek 4 miles east of Kettenpom (lat. 40°09'05" N, long. 123°23'10" W; at E line sec. 4, T 4 S, R 7 E). Named on Zenia (1967) 7.5' quadrangle.

Wilson Glade [LAKE]: *area*, 7.25 miles northeast of Clearlake Oaks (lat. 39°05'30" N, long. 122°34'30" W). Named on Clearlake Oaks (1960) 15' quadrangle.

Wilson Glade Canyon [LAKE]: *canyon*, drained by a stream that flows 2.5 miles to North Fork Cache Creek 9 miles east-northeast of Clearlake Oaks (lat. 39°05'05" N, long. 122°32'10" W; sec. 4, T 14 N, R 6 W); the canyon heads at Wilson Glade. Named on Clearlake Oaks (1960) 15' quadrangle.

Wilson Gulch [MENDOCINO]: *canyon*, drained by a stream that flows 2 miles to Long Valley Creek 4.25 miles north-northwest of Longvale (lat. 39°35'55" N, long. 123°27'10" W; sec. 7, T 20 N, R 14 W). Named on Longvale (1966) 7.5' quadrangle.

Wilson Point [TRINITY]: *peak*, 5.5 miles east-northeast of Dubakella Mountain (lat. 40°24'45" N, long. 123°01'45" W; sec. 31, T 30 N, R 10 W). Named on Dubakella Mountain (1954) 15' quadrangle.

Wilson Rock [DEL NORTE]: *rock*, nearly 3 miles north-northwest of the mouth of Klamath River, and 0.5 mile offshore (lat. 41°35'50" N, long. 124°06'40" W); the rock is less than 1 mile southwest of the mouth of Wilson Creek. Named on Requa (1966) 7.5' quadrangle.

Wilson Valley [LAKE]:

(1) *valley*, 5.5 miles east-southeast of the town of Upper Lake (lat. 39°08'35" N, long. 122°48'20" W; near S line sec. 13, T 15 N, R 9 W). Named on Bartlett Mountain (1958) 7.5' quadrangle.

(2) *valley*, 8.5 miles east-northeast of the town of Lower Lake along Cache Creek (lat. 38°58'20" N, long. 122°28'10" W). Named on Wilson Valley (1958) 7.5' quadrangle.

Wimer Creek [DEL NORTE]: *stream*, heads in the State of Oregon and flows 1.5 miles to Diamond Creek 9.5 miles north-northeast of Gasquet (lat. 41°58'35" N, long. 123°54'30" W; sec. 2, T 18 N, R 2 E). Named on Gasquet (1951) 15' quadrangle.

Wimer Spring [DEL NORTE]: *spring*, 6.5 miles east-northeast of the town of Smith River (lat. 41°57'25" N, long. 124°01'40" W; sec. 14, T 18 N, R 1 E). Named on Crescent City (1952) 15' quadrangle.

Winchester Ridge [HUMBOLDT]: *ridge*, east-trending, 2.5 miles long, 3.5 miles west of Alderpoint (lat. 40°11'05" N, long. 123°40'30" W). Named on Fort Seward (1969) 7.5' quadrangle.

Winchuck River, South Fork [DEL NORTE]: *stream*, flows 7 miles to Winchuck River 5.25 miles north-northwest of the town of Smith River (lat. 41°59'50" N, long. 124°11'35" W; near NW cor. sec. 33, T 10 N, R 1 W). Named on High Divide (1966) and Smith River (1966) 7.5' quadrangles. Winchuck River is mainly in the State of Oregon, but it loops south across California-Oregon State line at the confluence with its South Fork. The name "Winchuck" may be of Indian origin (McArthur, p. 802).

Windem Creek [MENDOCINO]: *stream*, flows 1.5 miles to South Fork Eel River 5 miles east-southeast of Branscomb (lat. 39°37'40" N, long. 123°32'30" W; sec. 33, T 21 N, R 15 W). Named on Cahto Peak (1967) 7.5' quadrangle.

Windy Creek [HUMBOLDT]: *stream*, flows 1.5 miles to Redwood Creek (1) 9.5 miles east of Blue Lake (2) (lat. 40°52'55" N, long. 123°48'05" W; at N line sec. 26, T 6 N, R 3 E). Named on Lord-Ellis Summit (1973) 7.5' quadrangle.

Windy Gap [MENDOCINO]:

(1) *pass*, 2.5 miles north of Leggett (lat. 39°54'05" N, long. 123°43'05" W; near E line sec. 27, T 24 N, R 17 W). Named on Noble Butte (1969) 7.5' quadrangle.

(2) *pass*, less than 1 mile northwest of Hull Mountain (lat. 39°31'45" N, long. 122°56'50" W; sec. 3, T 19 N, R 10 W). Named on Hull Mountain (1967) 7.5' quadrangle.

Windy Mountain [TRINITY]: *peak*, 9 miles south of Black Rock Mountain (lat. 40°04'45" N, long. 122°59'45" W; sec. 28, T 26 N, R 10 W). Altitude 5989 feet. Named on Black Rock Mountain (1954) and Yolla Bolly (1954) 15' quadrangles.

Windy Nip [TRINITY]: *pass*, 12 miles northwest of Forest Glen (lat. 40°29'25" N, long. 123°29'20" W; sec. 3, T 1 N, R 6 E). Named on Sportshaven (1973) 7.5' quadrangle.

Windy Nip Gap [HUMBOLDT]: *pass*, 15 miles south of Scotia (lat. 40°16' N, long. 124°05'15" W; near SE cor. sec. 29, T 2 S, R 1 E). Named on Bull Creek (1969) 7.5' quadrangle.

Windy Point [LAKE]: *peak*, 7 miles east of the town of Upper Lake (lat. 39°10'55" N, long. 122°46'55" W; on W line sec. 5, T 15 N, R 8 W); the peak is at the southeast end of Windy Ridge. Altitude 4772 feet. Named on Bartlett Mountain (1958) 7.5' quadrangle.

Windy Point [MENDOCINO]:

(1) *relief feature*, 5.25 miles east-northeast of Laytonville (lat. 39°42'35" N, long. 123°23'05" W; at SW cor. sec. 36, T 22 N, R 14 W). Named on Laytonville (1967) 7.5' quadrangle.

(2) *relief feature*, 2.5 miles east-southeast of Dos Rios on the north side of Middle Fork Eel River (lat. 39°42'15" N, long. 123°18'30" W). Named on Dos Rios (1967) 7.5' quadrangle.

(3) *peak*, 1.5 miles west of Hull Mountain (lat. 39°31'25" N, long. 122°57'45" W; sec. 9, T 19 N, R 10 W). Altitude 5982 feet. Named on Hull Mountain (1967) 7.5' quadrangle.

Windy Point: see **Punta Gorda** [HUMBOLDT].

Windy Ridge [HUMBOLDT]: *ridge*, west-southwest-trending, 2 miles long, 3.25 mile north-northeast of Showers Mountain (lat. 40°37'25" N, long. 123°40'15" W). Named on Board Camp Mountain (1977) and Showers Mountain (1978) 7.5' quadrangles.

Windy Ridge [LAKE]: *ridge*, west-northwest-trending, 1.5 miles long, 6.5

miles east-northeast of the town of Upper Lake (lat. 39°11'25" N, long. 122°47'45" W); Windy Point is at the southeast end of the ridge. Named on Bartlett Mountain (1958) 7.5' quadrangle.

Windy Ridge [MENDOCINO]: *ridge*, generally west-trending, 1.25 miles long, 6 miles west-southwest of Covelo (lat. 39°45'35" N, long. 123°21'20" W; at S line sec. 18, T 22 N, R 13 W). Named on Covelo West (1967) 7.5' quadrangle.

Windy Ridge: see **Little Windy Ridge** [HUMBOLDT].

Winery Gulch [MENDOCINO]: *canyon*, drained by a stream that flows 1 mile to South Fork Albion River 7 miles north-northwest of Navarro (lat. 39°14'15" N, long. 123°36'20" W; near NE cor. sec. 23, T 16 N, R 16 W). Named on Navarro (1961) 15' quadrangle.

Winkie Flat [MENDOCINO]: *area*, 1.5 miles south of Leggett (lat. 39°50'40" N, long. 123°43'15" W; sec. 15, T 23 N, R 17 W). Named on Leggett (1969) 7.5' quadrangle.

Winton Corners [DEL NORTE]: *locality*, about 1 mile west-southwest of the town of Smith River (lat. 41°55'35" N, long. 124°09'20" W; sec. 27, T 18 N, R 1 W). Named on Smith River (1966) 7.5' quadrangle.

Wintoon Flat [TRINITY]: *area*, 2.5 miles south of Hyampom along South Fork Trinity River (lat. 40°34'15" N, long. 123°26'30" W; sec. 12, T 2 N, R 6 E). Named on Hyampom (1951) 15' quadrangle.

Wire Fence Opening [HUMBOLDT]: *area*, 11.5 miles south-southwest of Scotia (lat. 40°20' N, long. 124°11'55" W). Named on Buckeye Mountain (1970) 7.5' quadrangle.

Wiregrass Prairie [HUMBOLDT]: *area*, 5.25 miles north-northeast of Coyote Peak (lat. 41°11'50" N, long. 123°48'15" W). Named on French Camp Ridge (1983) 7.5' quadrangle.

Wiregrass Ridge [HUMBOLDT]: *ridge*, generally north-northwest-trending, 6 miles long, center 8 miles northeast of the town of Blue Lake (lat. 40°58'15" N, long. 123°53'15" W). Named on Blue Lake (1979), Lord-Ellis Summit (1973), and Panther Creek (1982) 7.5' quadrangles.

Wiregrass Spring [TRINITY]: *spring*, 8.5 miles east of Kettenpom (lat. 40°10'45" N, long. 123°18'25" W; near NE cor. sec. 30, T 3 S, R 8 E). Named on Shannon Butte (1967) 7.5' quadrangle.

Wiregrass Springs [TRINITY]: *springs*, 6.5 miles south-southeast of Forest Glen (lat. 40°16'55" N, long. 123°17'30" W; sec. 20, T 2 S, R 8 E). Named on Forest Glen (1979) 7.5' quadrangle.

Wise Gulch [MENDOCINO]: *canyon*, drained by a stream that flows nearly 1 mile to South Fork Eel River 3 miles southeast of Branscomb (lat. 39°37'35" N, long. 123°34'50" W; sec. 31, T 21 N, R 15 W). Named on Cahto Peak (1967) 7.5' quadrangle.

Wises Creek: see **Sims Creek** [HUMBOLDT].

Witherell Creek [MENDOCINO]: *stream*, flows 2 miles to Anderson Creek (2) 1.5 miles northwest of Boonville (lat. 39°01'40" N, long. 123°23'10" W; sec. 34, T 14 N, R 14 W). Named on Boonville (1959) 15' quadrangle.

Witter: see **Witter Springs Post Office** [LAKE].

Witter Springs [LAKE]: *spring*, nearly 5 miles west-northwest of the town of Upper Lake along Dayle Creek (lat. 39°11'20" N, long. 122°59'30" W; near N line sec. 5, T 15 N, R 10 W). Named on Upper Lake (1958) 7.5' quadrangle. The name recalls Dr. Dexter Witter, who with W.P. Radcliff, purchased the property in 1871 and built a hotel there in 1873 (Palmer, p. 205).

Witter Springs Post Office [LAKE]: *locality*, 3 miles west-northwest of the town of Upper Lake in Bachelor Valley (lat. 39°10'50" N, long. 122°57'45" W; sec. 3, T 15 N, R 10 W). Named on Upper Lake (1958) 7.5' quadrangle. Postal authorities established Witter's Springs post office in 1873, discontinued it in 1880, reestablished it with the name "Witter" in 1901, and moved it 1.5 miles southeast in 1913, when they changed the name to Witter Springs (Salley, p. 242).

Wohlys Pass [MENDOCINO]: *pass*, 12 miles north-northwest of Boonville (lat. 39°10'40" N, long. 123°24'45" W; near NW cor. sec. 9, T 15 N, R 14 W). Named on Boonville (1959) 15' quadrangle.

Wolf Creek [LAKE]: *stream*, formed by the confluence of North Fork and South Fork, flows 5.5 miles to North Fork Cache Creek 6 miles east-northeast of Clearlake Oaks (lat. 39°04'10" N, long. 122°35' W; at N line sec. 13, T 14 N, R 7 W). Named on Clearlake Oaks (1960) 15' quadrangle. North Fork and South Fork each are 3 miles long, and both are named on Clearlake Oaks (1960) 15' quadrangle. Waring (p. 196) listed Dinsmore Soda Spring, which issued at the west edge of Wolf Creek on Dinsmore ranch. Bradley (p. 224) gave a location for Dinsmore Spring (sec. 11, T 14 N, R 7 W) that places it between 0.5 mile and 1.5 miles upstream from the mouth of Wolf Creek.

Wolf Creek Ridge [LAKE]: *ridge*, generally southeast-trending, 2.5 miles long, 5 miles north-northeast of Clearlake Oaks (lat. 39°05'20" N, long. 122°38'30" W). Named on Clearlake Oaks (1958) 7.5' quadrangle.

Wolfey Gulch [MENDOCINO]: *canyon*, drained by a stream that flows 1.25 miles to Flynn Creek 5.25 miles northwest of Navarro (lat. 39°12'30" N, long. 123°36'15" W; near NW cor. sec. 36, T 16 N, R 16 W). Named on Navarro (1961) 15' quadrangle.

Wolford Creek: see **Wolford Gulch** [TRINITY].

Wolford Gulch [TRINITY]: *canyon*, drained by a stream that flows about 1.5 miles to Granite Creek (1) 5.25 miles northwest of Billys Peak (1) (lat. 41°11'10" N, long. 122°50'15" W; sec. 1, T 38 N, R 9 W). Named on Coffee Creek (1955) 15' quadrangle, which shows Wolford cabin in the canyon. On Etna (1934) 30' quadrangle, the stream in the canyon is called Wolford Creek.

Wolf Valley [MENDOCINO]: *valley*, 6.5 miles north of the town of Potter Valley (lat. 39°24'40" N, long. 123°05' W; mainly in sec. 16, T 18 N, R 11 W). Named on Potter Valley (1960) 15' quadrangle.

Wolverton Gulch [HUMBOLDT]: *canyon*, drained by a stream that flows 3.5 miles to lowlands along Van Duzen River 4.25 miles south-southeast of Fortuna (lat. 40°32'45" N, long. 124°06'50" W; sec. 19, T 2 N, R 1 E). Named on Hydesville (1979) 7.5' quadrangle. The name commemorates Alfred Wolverton, a farmer in the neighborhood before 1870 (Turner, p. 235).

Woodin: see **Johnny Woodin Ridge** [MENDOCINO].

Woodley Island [HUMBOLDT]: *island*, 3300 feet long, just north of downtown Eureka in Humboldt Bay (lat. 40°48'35" N, long. 124°09'35" W). Named on Eureka (1958) 7.5' quadrangle. Captain William J. Woodley received the land in 1869 under the Swamp and Overflowed Lands Act (Turner, p. 236).

Woodman [MENDOCINO]: *locality*, 8 miles west-southwest of Covelo along Northwestern Pacific Railroad (lat. 39°46'15" N, long. 123°23'20" W; sec. 11, T 22 N, R 14 W); the place is less than 0.5 mile south of the mouth of Woodman Creek. Named on Iron Peak (1967) 7.5' quadrangle. Postal authorities established Woodman post office in 1922 and discontinued it in 1925 (Frickstad, p. 99).

Woodman Creek [MENDOCINO]: *stream*, flows nearly 7 miles to Eel River about 8 miles west of Covelo (lat. 39°46'20" N, long. 123°23'25" W; sec. 11, T 22 N, R 14 W); the stream heads near Woodman Peak. Named on Iron Peak (1967) and Laytonville (1967) 7.5' quadrangles. Iron Creek is called North Fork [Woodman Creek] on Spyrock (1952) 15' quadrangle.

Woodman Peak [MENDOCINO]: *peak*, 2 miles northeast of Laytonville (lat. 39°42'40" N, long. 123°27'20" W; near SW cor. sec. 32, T 22 N, R 14 W). Altitude 2949 feet. Named on Laytonville (1967) 7.5' quadrangle.

Woods Camp [LAKE]: *locality*, 5.5 miles west of Lakeport (lat. 39°03'05" N, long. 123°01' W; at S line sec. 24, T 14 N, R 11 W). Named on Purdys Gardens (1958) 7.5' quadrangle.

Woods Creek [HUMBOLDT]: *stream*, flows 2.5 miles to Mattole River 1.5 miles west-southwest of Honeydew (lat. 40°13'50" N, long. 124°16'25" W; near S line sec. 2, T 3 S, R 1 W). Named on Shubrick Peak (1969) 7.5' quadrangle. The name commemorates John Woods, a local pioneer (Turner, p. 236).

Woodtick Gulch [DEL NORTE]: *canyon*, drained by a stream that flows nearly 2 miles to Nickowitz Creek 13 miles east of Klamath Glen (lat. 41°27'50" N, long. 123°43'25" W). Named on Lonesome Ridge (1974) 7.5' quadrangle.

Wool: see **Fort Wool**, under **Weitchpec** [HUMBOLDT].

Wooley Bear Spring [DEL NORTE]: *spring*, 1.25 miles south of Buck Mountain on the west side of Lems Ridge (lat. 41°36'50" N, long. 123°51'50" W). Named on Summit Valley (1981) 7.5' quadrangle.

Wool Mountain [HUMBOLDT]: *peak*, 3.5 miles east-southeast of Alderpoint near Humboldt-Trinity County line (lat. 40°09'45" N, long. 123°32'45" W; sec. 31, T 3 S, R 6 E). Altitude 3498 feet. Named on Alderpoint (1969) 7.5' quadrangle.

Worswick [HUMBOLDT]: *locality*, 2 miles west-northwest of Fortuna along Northwestern Pacific Railroad (lat. 40°36'55" N, long. 124°11'25" W; sec. 28, T 3 N, R 1 W). Named on Fortuna (1959) 7.5' quadrangle.

Worthla Creek [DEL NORTE]: *stream*, flows 1 mile to Klamath River 1.5 miles east-southeast of Klamath Glen (lat. 41°30'20" N, long. 123°57'40" W; sec. 20, T 13 N, R 2 E). Named on Klamath Glen (1982) 7.5' quadrangle. The name is of Indian origin (Gudde, 1949, p. 393).

Wounded Knee Mountain [DEL NORTE]: *peak*, 1.5 miles west of Broken Rib Mountain (lat. 41°53'10" N, long. 123°43'10" W). Named on Broken Rib Mountain (1982) 7.5' quadrangle. The name is from an incident suffered by an employee of United States Geological Survey who was working in the neighborhood in 1915 (Gudde, 1949, p. 41).

Wrangletown: see **Freshwater** [HUMBOLDT].

Wright: see **Camp Wright** and **Fort Wright**, under **Round Valley** [MENDOCINO].

Wright Peak [LAKE]: *peak*, 4 miles east of Kelseyville on Mount Konocti. (lat. 38°58'30" N, long. 122°45'50" W; sec. 17, T 13 N, R 8 W). Altitude 4299 feet. Named on Kelseyville (1959) 7.5' quadrangle. United States Board on Geographic Names (1962b, p. 21) rejected the names "East Peak" and "Mathews Peak" for the feature.

Wrights Ridge [TRINITY]: *ridge*, northeast-trending, 4.5 miles long, 10.5 miles south of Black Rock Mountain (lat. 40°03'15" N, long. 123°02' W). Named on Black Rock Mountain (1954) 15' quadrangle. Called Wright Ridge on Hoaglin (1935) 30' quadrangle.

Wrights Valley [TRINITY]: *relief feature*, 12 miles south-southwest of Black Rock Mountain (lat. 40°02'30" N, long. 123°04'50" W; at NE cor. sec. 9, T 25 N, R 11 W); the feature is at the west end of Wrights Ridge. Named on Black Rock Mountain (1954) 15' quadrangle.

Wylettie Flat [MENDOCINO]: *area,* 6.5 miles east of Spyrock (2) (lat. 39°52'35" N, long. 123°19'15" W; at and near SE cor. sec. 5, T 23 N, R 13 W). Named on Covelo West (1967) and Mina (1967) 7.5' quadrangles.

Wyley Glade [LAKE]: *area,* 12.5 miles north of Clearlake Oaks (lat. 39°11'40" N, long. 122°37'10" W). Named on Clearlake Oaks (1960) 15' quadrangle.

Wyman Creek [LAKE]: *stream,* flows 2.5 miles to North Fork Cache Creek 14 miles north-northwest of Clearlake Oaks (lat. 39°13'05" N, long. 122°43'50" W; near SE cor. sec. 22, T 16 N, R 8 W); the stream heads near Wyman Flat. Named on Clearlake Oaks (1960) 15' quadrangle.

Wyman Flat [LAKE]: *area,* 15 miles north of Clearlake Oaks (lat. 39°14' N, long. 122°42' W; sec. 13, T 16 N, R 8 W). Named on Clearlake Oaks (1960) 15' quadrangle.

Wyman Glade [LAKE]: *area,* 4 miles north-northeast of the town of Upper Lake (lat. 39°12'50" N, long. 122°52'50" W; sec. 28, 29, T 16 N, R 9 W). Named on Bartlett Mountain (1958) and Upper Lake (1958) 7.5' quadrangles.

– X - Y –

Yager: see **Yager Valley** [HUMBOLDT].

Yager Camp [HUMBOLDT]: *locality,* nearly 6 miles east-southeast of Fortuna (lat. 40°33'45" N, long. 124°03'35" W; near NW cor. sec. 15, T 2 N, R 1 E); the place is along Yager Creek. Named on Hydesville (1979) 7.5' quadrangle.

Yager Creek [HUMBOLDT]: *stream,* formed by the confluence of Middle Fork and North Fork 4.5 miles south-southwest of Lone Star Junction, flows 14 miles to Van Duzen River 6.5 miles southeast of Fortuna (lat. 40°31'30" N, long. 124°04'30" W; sec. 28, T 2 N, R 1 E). Named on Hydesville (1979) 7.5' quadrangle, and called Yeager Creek on Owl Creek (1979) 7.5' quadrangle. North Fork, which is formed by the confluence of Freese Creek and Indian Creek (3), is 11 miles long and Middle Fork is 5.5 miles long. South Fork enters the main creek 1 mile downstream from the confluence of Middle Fork and North Fork, and is 9.5 miles long. All three forks are named on Owl Creek (1979) and Yager Junction (1979) 7.5' quadrangles. Waring (p. 261) listed a feature called Cook Spring located near the north bank of North Yager Creek (present North Fork Yager Creek) 0.25 mile east of Iaqua.

Yager Junction [HUMBOLDT]: *locality,* 6.5 miles south-southeast of Lone Star Junction (lat. 40°32'55" N, long. 123°49'25" W; near S line sec. 15, T 2 N, R 3 E); the place is near the east end of Yager Valley. Named on Yager Junction (1979) 7.5' quadrangle.

Yager Valley [HUMBOLDT]: *valley,* along South Fork Yager Creek west of Yager Junction (center near lat. 40°33'10" N, long. 123°50'20" W). Named on Yager Junction (1979) 7.5' quadrangle. Kneeland (1922) 15' quadrangle shows a place called Yager located in present Yager Valley (sec. 16, T 2 N, R 3 E). Postal authorities established Yagerville post office in 1872, discontinued it in 1874, reestablished it with the name "Yager" in 1880, and discontinued it 1932 (Salley, p. 244.)

Yagerville: see **Yager Valley** [HUMBOLDT].

Yale Creek [MENDOCINO]: *stream,* flows 2.25 miles to Rancheria Creek (2) 3 miles southeast of Ornbaun Valley (lat. 38°53'10" N, long. 123°15'50" W; at E line sec. 14, T 12 N, R 13 W). Named on Ornbaun Valley (1960) 15' quadrangle.

Yates' Beach: see **Crescent City** [DEL NORTE].

Ycatapom Peak [TRINITY]: *peak,* 7.5 miles south of Billys Peak (1) (lat. 41°01'45" N, long. 122°47'40" W; at NW cor. sec. 33, T 37 N, R 8 W). Altitude 7596 feet. Named on Coffee Creek (1955) 15' quadrangle.

Yeager Creek: see **Yager Creek** [HUMBOLDT].

Yellow Hound Ridge [MENDOCINO]: *ridge,* generally west-trending, 2 miles long, 10 miles southwest of Ornbaun Valley (lat. 38°49'50" N, long. 123°27'15" W; sec. 5, 6, T 11 N, R 14 W). Named on Ornbaun Valley (1960) 15' quadrangle.

Yellow Jacket: see **Yellowjacket Place** [TRINITY].

Yellow Jacket Butte [HUMBOLDT]: *peak,* 3.25 miles southwest of Blocksburg (lat. 40°15' N, long. 123°41'20" W; sec. 35, T 2 S, R 4 E). Named on Blocksburg (1969) and Fort Seward (1969) 7.5' quadrangles.

Yellowjacket Campground: see **Yellowjacket Place** [TRINITY].

Yellow Jacket Creek [TRINITY]: *stream,* flows 4.25 miles to East Fork of North Fork Trinity River 7.25 miles north of Helena (lat. 40°52' N, long. 123°07'45" W; sec. 20, T 35 N, R 11 W). Named on Helena (1951) 15' quadrangle. Called Yellowjacket Creek on United States Geological Survey's (1915) map. According to Gudde (1949, p. 395), the stream is named for an Indian family.

Yellowjacket Creek [DEL NORTE]: *stream,* flows 1 mile to South Fork Smith River 1.25 miles northeast of Buck Mountain (lat. 41°39'05" N, long. 123°51'20" W). Named on Ship Mountain (1982) 7.5' quadrangle.

Yellowjacket Creek [TRINITY]:

(1) *stream,* flows 3.5 miles to North Fork of Middle Fork Eel River 10 miles southwest of Black Rock Mountain (lat. 40°05'50" N, long. 123°07'40" W; at S line sec. 17, T 26 N, R 11 W). Named on Black Rock Mountain (1954) 15' quadrangle.

(2) *stream,* flows 2.5 miles to North Fork Eel River 6 miles east-southeast of Kettenpom (lat. 40°08'25" N, long. 123°21'15" W; at N line sec. 11, T 4 S, R 7 E). Named on Shannon Butte (1967) 7.5' quadrangle. Called Rock Creek on Island Mountain (1922) 15' quadrangle.

Yellowjacket Place [TRINITY]: *locality,* 7.5 miles east of Kettenpom (lat. 40°10'15" N, long. 123°19'20" W; near W line sec. 30, T 3 S, R 8 E). Named on Shannon Butte (1967) 7.5' quadrangle. Kettenpom (1955) 15' quadrangle has the name "Yellowjacket Campground" at the place, and Island Mountain (1922) 15' quadrangle has the name "Yellow Jacket" there.

Yellow Jacket Spring [HUMBOLDT]: *spring,* 6 miles southeast of Board Camp Mountain (lat. 40°37'45" N, long. 123°38'50" W; sec. 19, T 3 N, R 5 E). Named on Board Camp Mountain (1977) 7.5' quadrangle.

Yellowjacket Spring [MENDOCINO]: *spring,* 6.25 miles north of Eden Valley (lat. 39°42'55" N, long. 123°09'25" W; near SE cor. sec. 35, T 22 N, R 12 W). Named on Jamison Ridge (1967) 7.5' quadrangle.

Yew Wood Creek [TRINITY]: *stream,* flows 2.5 miles to Hembrey Creek 2.5 miles northwest of Kettenpom (lat. 40°11'05" N, long. 123°29'50" W; sec. 21, T 3 S, R 6 E). Named on Zenia (1967) 7.5' quadrangle.

Yew Wood Creek: see **Line Gulch** [TRINITY].

Yokaya [MENDOCINO]: *land grant,* in Redwood Valley (1) and south along Russian River past Ukiah. Named on Potter Valley (1960) 15' quadrangle, and on Elledge Peak (1958) 7.5' quadrangle. Cayetano Juarez received 8 leagues in 1845 and claimed 35,541 acres patented in 1867 (Cowan, p. 108). The name is of Indian origin (Hoover, Rensch, and Rensch, p. 196).

Yolla Bolly Mountains: see **North Yolla Bolly Mountains** [TRINITY].

Yontocket [DEL NORTE]: *locality,* 3 miles west-southwest of the town of Smith River (lat. 41°54'25" N, long. 124°11'50" W; sec. 32, T 18 N, R 1 W). Site named on Smith River (1966) 7.5' quadrangle. The name seems to be from the designation of an Indian village (Kroeber, p. 68).

Yontocket Slough [DEL NORTE]: *water feature,* 2.5 miles southwest of the town of Smith River (lat. 41°54'10" N, long. 124°11'05" W; mainly in sec. 33, T 18 N, R 1 W); the feature is east of the site of Yontocket. Named on Smith River (1966) 7.5' quadrangle.

York Creek [MENDOCINO]: *stream,* flows 8 miles to Russian River 3.5 miles north of Ukiah (lat. 39°12'10" N, long. 123°12'05" W). Named on Boonville (1959) 15' quadrangle, and on Ukiah (1958) 7.5' quadrangle.

Yorkville [MENDOCINO]: *village,* 7.5 miles southwest of Hopland (lat. 38°54' N, long. 123°13' W; near SE cor. sec. 8, T 12 N, R 12 W). Named on Hopland (1960) 15' quadrangle. Ornbaun (1944) 15' quadrangle shows Yorkville located 2.5 miles farther west-northwest (lat. 38°54'50" N, long. 123°15'40" W), and shows Yorkville P.O. at present Yorkville. Postal authorities established Yorkville post office in 1868 and moved it 3.5 miles southeast in 1937 (Salley, p. 245). The name commemorates R.H. York, founder of the community (Carpenter, p. 51). California Mining Bureau's (1917c) map shows a place called Hermitage located about 6 miles east-southeast of the first site of Yorkville. Postal authorities established Hermitage post office 8 miles southeast of Yorkville in 1860, moved it 1.5 miles east on 1901, and discontinued it in 1902 (Salley, p. 96). S.W. Knowles settled at Hermitage in 1858 and named it (Carpenter, p. 101). Postal authorities established Whitehall post office 4 miles northwest of Hermitage post office in 1875 and discontinued it in 1876 (Salley, p. 239).

Young Creek [MENDOCINO]: *stream,* flows 2.5 miles to Feliz Creek 5.5 miles west-northwest of Hopland (lat. 38°59'35" N, long. 123°12'45" W; at SE cor. sec. 7, T 13 N, R 12 W). Named on Hopland (1960) 15' quadrangle.

Young Gulch [TRINITY]: *canyon,* drained by a stream that flows 2 miles to Hyampom Valley 2.25 miles northwest of Hyampom (lat. 40°38'35" N, long. 123°28'30" W; near NW cor. sec. 11, T 3 N, R 6 E). Named on Hyampom (1951) 15' quadrangle.

Youngs: see **Dyerville** [HUMBOLDT].

Youngs Corral Spring [LAKE]: *spring,* 6 miles south-southeast of Potato Hill (lat. 39°16'35" N, long. 122°45'05" W; near SW cor. sec. 34, T 17 N, R 9 W). Named on Potato Hill (1967) 7.5' quadrangle. Lake Pillsbury (1951) 15' quadrangle shows Youngs Corral at the site.

Young's Creek: see **Doyle Creek** [MENDOCINO].

Youngs Lake [HUMBOLDT]: *lake,* 200 feet long, 3.25 miles north of Weitchpec (lat. 41°13'15" N, long. 123°42'55" W). Named on Weitchpec (1979) 7.5' quadrangle.

Young's Natural Gas Well and Mineral Springs: see **Kelseyville** [LAKE].

Youngs Peak [DEL NORTE]: *peak,* 2.5 miles east of Broken Rib Mountain on Del Norte-Siskiyou County line (lat. 41°53'25" N, long. 123°38'20" W). Altitude 6308 feet. Named on Broken Rib Mountain (1982) 7.5' quadrangle. Called Broken Rib Peak on Weed (1963) 1° x 2° quadrangle.

Youngs Peak [LAKE]: *peak,* 4 miles north-northeast of the town of Upper Lake (lat. 39°13'20" N, long. 122°53'10" W; at N line sec. 29, T 16 N, R 9 W). Altitude 3683 feet. Named on Upper Lake (1958) 7.5' quadrangle.

Youngs Peak [TRINITY]: *peak,* 4 miles east-southeast of Salmon Mountain on Trinity-Siskiyou County line (lat. 41°09'25" N, long. 123°20'25" W).

Altitude 6329 feet. Named on Youngs Peak (1979) 7.5' quadrangle.

– Z –

Zeigler Point [TRINITY]: *peak,* 3.5 miles east-northeast of Salyer (lat. 40°54'40" N, long. 123°31'10" W). Altitude 3725 feet. Named on Salyer (1979) 7.5' quadrangle.

Zeigler Spring [TRINITY]: *spring,* 2.5 miles northeast of Burnt Ranch (lat. 40°50' N, long. 123°26'25" W). Named on Ironside Mountain (1951) 15' quadrangle.

Zenia [TRINITY]: *village,* 3.5 miles north-northwest of Kettenpom (lat. 40°12'20" N, long. 123°29'25" W; sec. 15, T 3 S, R 6 E). Named on Zenia (1967) 7.5' quadrangle. Postal authorities established Zenia post office in 1899 (Salley, p. 246); George Croyden, first postmaster, named it for a girl (Gudde, 1949, p. 399). The men who came to the place about 1860 called it Poison Camp because larkspur growing there poisoned their cattle (Jones, p. 354). Postal authorities established Grouse post office 8 miles southeast of Zenia in 1905 and discontinued it in 1907 (Salley, p. 90).

Zenia Bluffs [TRINITY]: *relief feature,* 4 miles east-northeast of Alderpoint [HUMBOLDT] on the north side of South Dobbyn Creek (lat. 40°11'35" N, long. 123°32'15" W). Named on Alderpoint (1969) 7.5' quadrangle.

Zeni Ridge [MENDOCINO]: *ridge,* generally east-southeast-trending, 3.5 miles long, 9 miles west-southwest of Ornbaun Valley (lat. 38°53' N, long. 123°28' W). Named on Ornbaun Valley (1960) 15' quadrangle.

Zimory Canyon [LAKE]: *canyon,* drained by a stream that flows 2.5 miles to Little Indian Valley 10 miles northeast of Clearlake Oaks (lat. 39°06'55" N, long. 122°32'05" W; sec. 28, T 15 N, R 6 W). Named on Clearlake Oaks (1960) 15' quadrangle.

NORTH COAST REGION
DEL NORTE, HUMBOLDT, LAKE, MENDOCINO AND TRINITY COUNTIES

REFERENCES CITED

BOOKS AND ARTICLES

Anderson, Winslow. 1892. *Mineral springs and health resorts of California*. San Francisco: The Bancroft Company, 347 p.

Averill, Chas. Volney. 1929. "Lake County." *Mining in California*, v. 25, no. 3, p. 337-365.

_____1935. "Redding field district (Mines and mineral resources of Siskiyou County)." *California Journal of Mines and Geology*, v. 31, no. 3, p. 255-338.

_____1941. "Redding field district (Mineral resources of Trinity County)." *California Journal of Mines and Geology*, v. 37, no. 1, p. 8-89.

Bancroft, Hubert Howe. 1888. *History of California, Volume VI, 1848-1859*. San Francisco: The History Company, Publishers., 787 p.

Becker, George F. 1888. *Geology of the quicksilver deposits of the Pacific slope*. (United States Geological Survey Monograph XIII.) Washington: Government Printing Office, 486 p.

Becker, Robert H. 1964. *Diseños of California ranchos*. San Francisco: The Book Club of California, (no pagination).

_____1969. *Designs on the land*. San Francisco: The Book Club of California, (no pagination).

Bledsoe, A.J. 1956. *Indian wars of the northwest, A California sketch*. Oakland, California: Biobooks, 292 p.

Bradley, Walter W. 1915. "The counties of Colusa, Glenn, Lake, Marin, Napa, Solano, Sonoma, Yolo." *Report XIV of the State Mineralogist*. Sacramento: California State Mining Bureau, p. 173-370.

Brereton, John V. 1973. *In the Round Valley area sixty years ago*. Ukiah, California: Mendocino County Historical Society, Inc., 27 p.

Brewer, William H. 1949. *Up and down California in 1860-1864*. Berkeley and Los Angeles: University of California Press, 583 p.

Brown, G. Chester. 1915. "The counties of Shasta, Siskiyou, Trinity." *Report XIV of the State Mineralogist*. Sacramento: California State Printing Office, p. 745-925.

Browne, J. Ross, and Taylor, James W. 1867. *Reports upon the mineral resources of the United States*. Washington: Government Printing Office, 360 p.

California Division of Highways. 1934. *California highway transportation survey, 1934*. Sacramento: Department of Public Works, Division of Highways, 130 p. + appendices.

Cargill, Hazel. 1983. "The Fieldbrook story—(1856)." *Golden adventures from The Humboldt Historian*. Eureka, California: Humboldt County Historical Society, p. 16-20.

Carlson, Beverly (compiler). 1976. *Where the ferns grew tall, An early history of Ferndale*. (Written by the Class of 1977, Ferndale Union High School.) (Privately printed), 378 p.

Carpenter, Aurelius O. 1977. *A history of Mendocino County*. (Originally published by Historic Record Company, Los Angeles, California, 1914.) Mendocino, California: Pacific Rim Research, 144 p.

Carranco, Lynwood, and Beard, Estle. 1981. *Genocide and vendetta, The Round Valley wars of northern California*. Norman: University of Oklahoma Press, 403 p.

Carranco, Lynwood, and Sorensen, Henry L. 1988. *Steam in the redwoods*. Caldwell, Idaho: The Caxton Printers, Ltd., 224 p.

Chandler, Albert E. 1901. *Water storage, Cache Creek, California*. (United States Geological Survey Water-Supply and Irrigation Papers No. 45.) Washington: Government Printing Office, 48 p.

Chase, J. Smeaton. 1913. *California coast trails*. Boston and New York: Houghton Mifflin Company, 326 p.

Clark, T.K. 1983. *Regional history of Petrolia and the Mattole Valley*. Eureka, California: Miller Press, 191 p.

Cowan, Robert G. 1956. *Ranchos of California*. Fresno, California: Academy Library Guild, 151 p.

Coy, Owen C. 1923. *California county boundaries*. Berkeley: California Historical Survey Commission, 335 p.

_____1929. *The Humboldt Bay region, 1850-1875*. Los Angeles: The California State Historical Association, 346 p.

Crawford, J.J. 1894. "Report of the State Mineralogist." *Twelfth report of the State Mineralogist, (Second Biennial,) two years ending September 15, 1894*. Sacramento: California State Mining Bureau, p. 8-412.

_____1896. "Report of the State Mineralogist." *Thirteenth report (Third Biennial) of the State Mineralogist for the two years ending September 15, 1896*. Sacramento: California State Mining Bureau, p. 10-646.

Crump, Spencer. 1975. *Redwoods, iron horses, and the Pacific, The story of the California Western "Skunk" Railroad*. (Fourth edition, revised.) Corona del Mar, California: Trans-Anglo Books, 176 p.

Cullberg, Isaac. 1983. "Turning leaves of memory—(1885)." *Golden adventures from The Humboldt Historian*. Eureka, California: Humboldt County Historical Society, p. 60-64.

Edeline, Denis P. 1983. *Along the banks of Salt River*. (Author), 167 p.

Eich, Glenyth L. 1983. "'Pumpkin Center' revisited—(1905)." *Golden Adventures from The Humboldt Historian*. Eureka, California: Humboldt County Historical Society, p. 92-100.

Evanson, R.E. 1959. *Geology and ground-water features of the Eureka area, Humboldt County, California*. (United States Geological Survey Water-Supply Paper 1470.) Washington: United States Government Printing Office, 86 p.

Frazer, Robert W. 1965. *Forts of the West*. Norman: University of Oklahoma Press, 246 p.

Frickstad, Walter N. 1955. *A century of California post offices, 1848 to 1954*. Oakland, California: Philatelic Research Society, 395 p.

Gannett, Henry. 1905. *The origin of certain place names in the United States*. (Second edition.) (United States Geological Survey Bulletin No. 258.) Washington: Government Printing Office, 334 p.

Gibbs, George. 1972. *George Gibb's journal of Redick McKee's expedition through northwestern California in 1851*. Berkeley: University of California, Department of Anthropology, Archeological Research Facility, 88 p.

Goodyear, W.A. 1890a. "Lake County." *Tenth annual report of the State Mineralogist, for the year ending December 1, 1890*. Sacramento: California State Mining Bureau, p. 227-271.

_____1890b. "Colusa County." *Tenth annual report of the State Mineralogist, for the year ending December 1, 1890*. Sacramento: California State Mining Bureau, p. 153-164.

_____1890c. "Mendocino County." *Tenth annual report of the State Mineralogist, for the year ending December 1, 1890*. Sacramento: California State Mining Bureau, p. 314-322.

Gudde, Erwin G. 1949. *California place names*. Berkeley and Los Angeles: University of California Press, 431 p.

_____1969. *California place names*. Berkeley and Los Angeles: University of California Press, 416 p.

_____1975. *California gold camps*. Berkeley, Los Angeles, London: University of California Press, 467 p.

Hanna, Phil Townsend. 1951. *The dictionary of California land names*. Los Angeles: The Automobile Club of Southern California, 392 p.

Hobson, J.B. 1890. "Siskiyou County." *Tenth annual report of the State Mineralogist, for the year ending December 1, 1890*. Sacramento: California State Mining Bureau, p. 655-658.

Hoover, Mildred Brooke, Rensch, Hero Eugene, and Rensch, Ethel Grace. 1966. *Historic spots in California*. (Third edition, revised by William N. Abeloe.) Stanford, California: Stanford University Press, 642 p.

Irelan, William, Jr. 1888. "Report of the State Mineralogist." *Eighth annual report of the State Mineralogist. for the year ending October 1, 1888*. Sacramento: California State Mining Bureau, p. 12-695.

Jackson, Francis. 1975. *Big River was dammed*. Mendocino, California: (Author), 138 p.

Jackson, Walter. 1976. *Bridgeport, Mendocino County, California*. Ukiah, California: Mendocino County Historical Society, Inc., 16 p.

Jennings, C.W. 1968. "Point Arena Hot Springs." *Mineral Information Service*, v. 21, no. 4, p. 61.

Johnson, Bertha E. 1982. "The town of Hookton—(1858)." *Frontier moments from the Humboldt Historian*. Eureka, California: Humboldt County Historical Society, p. 24-26.

Jones, Alice Goen (editor). 1981. *Trinity County historic sites*. Weaverville, California: Trinity County Historical Society, 422 p.

Keller, John E. 1976. *The saga of Round Valley, The last of the West*. (Second printing.) Ukiah, California: Mendocino County Historical Society, 28 p.

Kroeber, A.L. 1916. "California place names of Indian origin." *University of California Publications in American Archæology and Ethnology*, v. 12, no. 2, p. 31-69.

Laizure, C. McK. 1925. "San Francisco field division (Del Norte County)." *Mining in California*, v. 21, no. 3, p. 281-324.

Landsman, David (editor). 1977a. *Mendocino County historic annals—No. 1*. Mendocino, California: Pacific Rim Research, 96 p.

_____(editor). 1977b. *Mendocino County historic annals—No. 2*. Mendocino, California: Pacific Rim Research, 96 p.

Lanphere, Marvin A., and Irwin, William P. 1987. "In search of the Abrams post office." *California Geology*, v. 40, no. 5, p. 99-103.

Lowell, F.L. 1915. "The counties of Del Norte, Humboldt, Mendocino." *Report XIV of the State Mineralogist*. Sacramento: California State Mining Bureau, 371-425.

Manning, George A., and Ogle, Burdette A. 1950. *Geology of the Blue Lake quadrangle, California*. (California Division of Mines Bulletin 148.) San Francisco: Division of Mines, 36 p.

McArthur, Lewis A. 1974. *Oregon geographic names*. (Fourth edition, revised and enlarged by Lewis L. McArthur.) Portland, Oregon: Oregon Historical Society, 835 p.

McBeth, Frances Turner. 1950. *Lower Klamath country*. Berkeley: Anchor Press, 76 p.

Menefee, C.A. 1873. *Historical and descriptive sketch book of Napa, Sonoma, Lake and Mendocino*. Napa City: Reporter Publishing House, 356 p.

Miller, Wm. P. 1890. "Trinity County." *Tenth annual report of the State Mineralogist, for the year ending December 1, 1890*. Sacramento: California State Mining Bureau, p. 695-727.

Mosier, Dan L. 1979. *California coal towns, coaling stations, & landings*. San Leandro, California: Mines Road Books, 8 p.

O'Brien, J.C. 1952. "Mines and mineral resources of Del Norte County, California." *California Journal of Mines and Geology*, v. 48, no. 4, p. 261-309.

_____1953. "Mines and mineral resources of Mendocino County, California." *California Journal of Mines and Geology*, v. 49, no. 4, p. 347-398.

Palais, Hyman. 1958. "The history of northwestern California." *Natural Resources of northwestern California, Preliminary report. Appendix, Recreation resources, Supplement, History and Archaeology*. Washington: United States Department of the Interior, Pacific Southwest Field Committee, p. 5-62.

Palmer, Lyman L. 1974. *History of Lake County, California*. (Reprinted from *History of Napa and Lake Counties, California*, published in 1881 by Slocum, Bowen & Co., San Francisco.) Fresno, California: Valley Publishers, 328 p.

Perez, Crisostomo N. 1996. *Land grants in Alta California*. Rancho Cordova, California: Landmark Enterprises, 264 p.

Quimby, Myron J. 1969. *Scratch Ankle, U.S.A., American place names and their derivation*. New York: A.S. Barnes and Company, 390 p.

Ristow, Walter W. 1970. "A covey of names." *Surveying and Mapping*, v. 30, no. 3, p. 419-426.

Ross, Frederick G. 1977. *The actor from Point Arena, Excerpts taken from the "Memories of an old theatrical man."* Berkeley: The Friends of the Bancroft Library, 38 p.

Rowley, Maxwell C. 1982. "Wise Station—Landmarks from days of packtrains, prospectors—(1904)." *Frontier moments from The Humboldt Historian*. Eureka, California: Humboldt County Historical Society, p. 90-93.

Salley, H.E. 1977. *History of California post offices, 1849-1976*. La Mesa, California: Postal History Associates, Inc., 300 p.

Simoons, Frederick J. 1954. "Nineteenth century mines and mineral spring resorts of Lake County, California." *California Journal of Mines and Geology*, v. 50, no. 2, p. 295-319.

Stewart, Charles L. 1934. "Early ascents of Mount Shasta." *Sierra Club Bulletin*, v. 19, no. 3, p. 58-70.

Stewart, George R. 1970. *American place-names, A concise and selective dictionary for the continental United States of America*. New York: Oxford University Press, 550 p.

Trexler, James H., Jr. 1989. "Ancestral Klamath River deposits at Gold Bluffs, Prairie Creek Redwoods State Park." *California Geology*, v. 42, no. 7, p. 147-154.

Turner, Dennis W. 1993. *Place names of Humboldt County, California*. Orangevale, California: (Author), 280 p.

Tyson, Philip T. 1850. "Report of P.T. Tyson, esq., upon the geology of California." *Report of the Secretary of War, communicating information in relation to the geology and topography of California*. (31st Cong., 1st Sess., Sen. Ex. Doc. No. 47.) Washington: Government Printing Office, p. 3-74.

United States Board on Geographic Names (under name "United States Geographic Board"). 1933. *Sixth report of the United States Geographic Board, 1890 to 1932*. Washington: United States Government Printing Office, 834 p.

_____(under name "United States Board on Geographical Names"). 1939. *Decisions of the United States Board on Geographical Names, Decisions rendered between July 1, 1938, and June 30, 1939*. Washington: Government Printing Office, 41 p.

_____(under name "United States Board on Geographical Names"). 1940. *Decisions of the United States Board on Geographical Names, Decisions rendered between July 1, 1939, and June 30, 1940*. Washington: Government Printing Office, 46 p.

_____(under name "United States Board on Geographical Names"). 1942. *Decisions of the United States Board on Geographical Names, Decisions rendered between July 1, 1940, and June 30, 1941*. Washington: Government Printing Office, 89 p.

_____(under name "Board on Geographical Names"). 1943. *Decisions rendered between July 1, 1941, and June 30, 1943*. Washington: Department of the Interior, 104 p.

_____1949. *Decision lists nos. 4905, 4906, May, June, 1949*. Washington: Department of the Interior, 10 p.

_____1950a. *Decision list no. 5003, January, February, March, 1950*. Washington: Department of the Interior, 24 p.

_____1950b. *Decisions on names in the United States and Alaska rendered during April, May, and June 1950*. (Decision list no. 5006.) Washington: Department of the Interior, 47 p.

_____1954. *Decisions on names in the United States, Alaska and Puerto Rico, Decisions rendered from July 1950 to May 1954*. (Decision list no. 5401.) Washington: Department of the Interior, 115 p.

_____1957. *Decision on names in the United States, Alaska and Hawaii, Decisions rendered from May 1954 through March 1957*. (Decision list no. 5701.) Washington: Department of the Interior, 23 p.

_____1960a. *Decisions on names in the Unites States and Puerto Rico, Decisions rendered in May, June, July, and August, 1959*. (Decision list no. 5903.) Washington: Department of the Interior, 79 p.

_____1960b. *Decisions on names in the United States, Decisions rendered from September 1959 through December 1959*. (Decision list no. 5904.) Washington: Department of the Interior, 68 p.

_____1961a. *Decisions on names in the United States, Decisions rendered from September through December 1960*. (Decision list no. 6003.) Washington: Department of the Interior, 73 p.

_____1961b. *Decisions on names in the United States, Decisions rendered from January through April 1961*. (Decision list no. 6101.) Washington: Department of the Interior, 74 p.

_____1961c. *Decisions on names in the United States, Decisions rendered from May through August 1961*. (Decision list no. 6102.) Washington: Department of the Interior, 81 p.

_____1962a. *Decisions on names in the United States, Decisions rendered from September through December 1961*. (Decision list no. 6103.) Washington: Department of the Interior, 75 p.

_____1962b. *Decisions on names in the United States, Decisions rendered from January through April 1962*. (Decision list no. 6201.) Washington: Department of the Interior, 72 p.

_____1962c. *Decisions on names in the United States, Decisions rendered from May through August 1962*. (Decision list no. 6202.) Washington: Department of the Interior, 81 p.

_____1963. *Decisions on names in the United States, Decisions rendered from September through December 1962*. (Decision list no. 6203.) Washington: Department of the Interior, 59 p.

_____1964. *Decisions on geographic names in the United States, September through December 1963*. (Decision list no. 6303.) Washington: Department of the Interior, 66 p.

_____1965a. *Decisions on geographic names in the United States, September through December 1964*. (Decision list no. 6403.) Washington: Department of the Interior, 66 p.

_____1965b. *Decisions on geographic names in the United States, January through March 1965*. (Decision list No. 6501.) Washington: Department of the Interior, 85 p.

_____1965c. *Decisions on geographic names in the United States, April through June 1965*. (Decision list no. 6502.) Washington: Department of the Interior, 39 p.

_____1965d. *Decisions on geographic names in the United States, July through September 1965*. (Decision list No. 6503.) Washington: Department of the Interior, 74 p.

_____1967. *Decisions on geographic names in the United States, July through September 1966*. (Decision list no. 6603.) Washington: Department of the Interior, 38 p.

_____1968a. *Decisions on geographic names in the United States, October through December 1967*. (Decision list no. 6704.) Washington: Department of the Interior, 46 p.

_____1968b. *Decisions on geographic names in the United States, April through June 1968*. (Decision list no. 6802.) Washington: Department of

the Interior, 42 p.
_____1969a. *Decisions on geographic names in the United States, October through December 1968*. (Decision list no. 6804.) Washington: Department of the Interior, 33 p.
_____1969b. *Decisions on geographic names in the United States, January through March 1969*. (Decision list no. 6901.) Washington: Department of the Interior, 31 p.
_____1970. *Decisions on geographic names in the United States, July through September 1970*. (Decision list no. 7003.) Washington: Department of the Interior, 15 p.
_____1971a. *Decisions on geographic names in the United States, October through December 1970*. (Decision list no. 7004.) Washington: Department of the Interior, 28 p.
_____1971b. *Decisions on geographic names in the United States, January through March 1971*. (Decision list no. 7101.) Washington: Department of the Interior, 19 p.
_____1972a. *Decisions on geographic names in the United States, January through March 1972*. (Decision list no. 7201.) Washington: Department of the Interior, 32 p.
_____1972b. *Decisions on geographic names in the United States, July through September 1972*. (Decision list no. 7203.) Washington: Department of the Interior, 17 p.
_____1973a. *Decisions on geographic names in the United States, April through June 1973*. (Decision list no. 7302.) Washington: Department of the Interior, 16 p.
_____1973b. *Decisions on geographic names in the United States, July through September 1973*. (Decision list no. 7303.) Washington: Department of the Interior, 14 p.
_____1974a. *Decisions on geographic names in the United States, October through December 1973*. (Decision list no. 7304.) Washington: Department of the Interior, 15 p.
_____1974b. *Decisions on geographic names in the United States, January through March 1974*. (Decision list no. 7401.) Washington: Department of the Interior, 27 p.
_____1974c. *Decisions on geographic names in the United States, April through June 1974*. (Decision list no. 7402.) Washington: Department of the Interior, 27 p.
_____1975. *Decisions on geographic names in the United States, April through June 1975*. (Decision list no. 7502.) Washington: Department of the Interior, 32 p.
_____1976a. *Decisions on geographic names in the United States, April through June 1976*. (Decision list no. 7602.) Washington: Department of the Interior, 26 p.
_____1976b. *Decisions on geographic names in the United States, July through September 1976*. (Decision list no. 7603.) Washington: Department of the Interior, 25 p.
_____1977a. *Decisions on geographic names in the United States, October through December 1976*. (Decision list no. 7604.) Washington: Department of the Interior, 34 p.
_____1977b. *Decisions on geographic names in the United States, January through March 1977*. (Decision list no. 7701.) Washington: Department of the Interior, 32 p.
_____1977c. *Decisions on geographic names in the United States, April through June 1977*. (Decision list no. 7702.) Washington: Department of the Interior, 40 p.
_____1978a. *Decisions on geographic names in the United States, October through December 1977*. (Decision list no. 7704.) Washington: Department of the Interior, 29 p.
_____1978b. *Decisions on geographic names in the United States, July through September 1978*. (Decision list no. 7803.) Washington: Department of the Interior, 32 p.
_____1978c. *Decisions on geographic names in the United States, October through December 1978*. (Decision list no. 7804.) Washington: Department of the Interior, 48 p.
_____1979. *Decisions on geographic names in the United States, January through March 1979*. (Decision list no. 7901.) Washington: Department of the Interior, 27 p.
_____1980. *Decisions on geographic names in the United States, April through June 1980*. (Decision list no. 8002.) Washington: Department of the Interior, 33 p.
_____1981a. *Decisions on geographic names in the United States, October through December 1980*. (Decision list no. 8004.) Washington: Department of the Interior, 21 p.
_____1981b. *Decisions on geographic names in the United States, January through March 1981*. (Decision list no. 8101.) Washington: Department of the Interior, 23 p.
_____1981c. *Decisions on geographic names in the United States, April through June 1981*. (Decision list no. 8102.) Washington: Department of the Interior, 28 p.
_____1982a. *Decisions on geographic names in the United States, October through December 1981*. (Decision list no. 8104.) Washington: Department of the Interior, 26 p.
_____1982b. *Decisions on geographic names in the United States, January through March 1982*. (Decision list no. 8201.) Washington: Department of the Interior, 17 p.
_____1982c. *Decisions on geographic names in the United States, April through June 1982*. (Decision list no. 8202.) Washington: Department of the Interior, 21 p.
_____1983a. *Decisions on geographic names in the United States, July through September 1982*. (Decision list no. 8203.) Washington: Department of the Interior, 25 p.
_____1983b. *Decisions on geographic names in the United States, October through December 1982*. (Decision list no. 8204.) Washington: Department of the Interior, 26 p.
_____1983c. *Decisions on geographic names in the United States, January through March 1983*. (Decision list no. 8301.) Washington: Department of the Interior, 33 p.
_____1983d. *Decisions on geographic names in the United States, April through June 1983*. (Decision list no. 8302.) Washington: Department of the Interior, 29 p.
_____1984a. *Decisions on geographic names in the United States, January through March 1984*. (Decision list no. 8401.) Washington: Department of the Interior, 29 p.
_____1984b. *Decisions on geographic names in the United States, April through June 1984*. (Decision list no. 8402.) Washington: Department of the Interior, 22 p.
_____1984c. *Decisions on geographic names in the United States, October through December 1984*. (Decision list no. 8404.) Washington: Department of the Interior, 18 p.
_____1986. *Decisions on geographic names in the United States, July through September 1986*. (Decision list no. 8603.) Washington: Department of the Interior, 11 p.
_____1991. *Decisions on geographic names in the United States*. (Decision list 1991.) Washington: Department of the Interior, 40 p.
_____1992. *Decisions on geographic names in the United States*. (Decision list 1992.) Washington: Department of the Interior, 21 p.
United States Coast and Geodetic Survey. 1963. *United States Coast Pilot 7, Pacific Coast, California, Oregon, Washington, and Hawaii*. (Ninth edition.) Washington: United States Government Printing Office, 336 p.
United States Coast Survey. 1855. *Report of the Superintendent of the Coast Survey, showing the progress of the Survey during the year 1854*. Washington: Beverley Tucker, Public Printer.
Upson, J.E., and Kunkel, Fred. 1955. *Ground water of the Lower Lake-Middletown area, Lake County, California*. (United States Geological Survey Water-Supply Paper 1297.) Washington: Government Printing Office, 83 p.
Vancouver, George. 1953. *Vancouver in California, 1792-1794*. (The original account edited and annotated by Marguerite Eyer Wilbur.) Los Angeles: Glen Dawson, 274 p.
Vander Leck, Lawrence. 1921. *Petroleum resources of California*. (California State Mining Bureau Bulletin no. 89.) Sacramento: California State Printing Office, 186 p.
Wagner, Henry R. 1968. *The cartography of the Northwest Coast of America to the year 1800*. (One-volume reprint of the 1937 edition.) Amsterdam: N. Israel, 543 p.
Waring, Gerald A. 1915. *Springs of California*. (United States Geological Survey Water-Supply Paper 338.) Washington: Government Printing Office, 410 p.
Waterman, T.T. 1920. "Yurok geography." *University of California Publications in American Archæology and Ethnology*, v. 16, no. 5, p. 177-314.
Wells, Francis G., Cater, Fred W., Jr., and Rynearson, Garn A. 1946. "Chromite deposits of Del Norte County, California." *Geological investigations of chromite in California*. (Division of Mines Bulletin 134.) San Francisco: California Division of Mines, p. 1-76.
Whiting, J.S., and Whiting, Richard J. 1960. *Forts of the State of California*. (Authors), 90 p.
Whitney, J.D. 1865. *Report of progress and synopsis of the field-work, from 1860 to 1864*. (Geological Survey of California, Geology, Volume I.) Published by authority of the Legislature of California, 498 p.

QUADRANGLE MAPS

(All maps published by United States Geological Survey, except as noted. Dates identify the editions of the maps. If a reprinted or revised map was used, the year of reprinting or revision is given in parentheses, unless the reprinted or revised map is cited specifically in the text.)

Aetna Springs 7.5'—1958.
Ah Pah Ridge 7.5'—1983.
Albion 7.5'—1960.
Alderpoint 15' (same area as Harris 15')—1949.
7.5'—1969.

Anada 15' (same area as Pickett Peak 15')—1918 (Army).
Arcata North 7.5'—1959.
Arcata South 7.5'—1959.
Asti 7.5'—1959.
Bald Hills 7.5'—1982.
Bark Shanty Gulch 7.5'—1974.
Bartlett Mountain 7.5'—1958.
Bartlett Springs 15' (same area as Clearlake Oaks 15')—1944.
Bear Harbor 7.5'—1969.
Bell Springs 7.5'—1969.
Black Lassic 7.5'—1979.
Black Rock Mountain 15'—1954.
Blake Mountain 7.5'—1979.
Blocksburg 15' (same area as South Fork Peak 15')—1949.
7.5'—1969.
Blue Creek Mountain 7.5'—1982.
Blue Lake 15'—1951.
7.5'—1979.
Bluenose Ridge 7.5'—1967.
Board Camp Mountain 7.5'—1977.
Bonanza King 15'—1955.
Boonville 15' (same area as Orrs 15')—1943; 1959.
Branscomb 15'—1921 (Army); 1951.
Briceland 15' (same area as Garberville 15')—1921 (Army).
7.5'—1969.
Bridgeville 7.5'—1969.
Broken Rib Mountain 7.5'—1982.
Brushy Mountain 7.5'—1966.
Buckeye Mountain 7.5'—1970.
Buck Rock 7.5'—1967.
Bull Creek 7.5'—1969.
Cahto Peak 7.5'—1967.
Cannibal Island 7.5'—1959.
Cant Hook Mountain 7.5'—1982.
Cape Fortunas 15' (same area as Ferndale 15')—1920 (Army).
Cape Mendocino 15'—1921 (Army); 1950.
7.5'—1969.
Capetown 7.5'—1969.
Cape Vizcaino 15'—1921 (Army); 1950.
Cecil Lake 7.5'—1979.
Cecilville 15'—1955.
Chanchelulla Peak 15'—1951.
Childs Hill 7.5'—1966.
Chimney Rock 7.5'—1981.
China Flat 15' (same area as Willow Creek 15')—1922 (Army).
China Mountain 15'—1955.
Clearlake Highlands 7.5'—1958.
Clearlake Oaks 15' (same area as Bartlett Springs 15')—1960.
7.5'—1958.
Cloverdale 7.5'—1960.
Coffee Creek 15'—1955.
Comptche 15' (same area as Glenblair 15')—1960.
Cooskie Creek 7.5'—1969.
Covelo 15'—1926 (reprinted 1944); 1952.
Covelo East 7.5'—1967.
Covelo West 7.5'—1967.
Cow Mountain 7.5'—1958.
Coyote Peak 15'—1945 (Army); 1952.
Crannell 7.5'—1966.
Crescent City 15' (same area as Point Saint George 15')—1952.
7.5'—1966.
Crockett Peak 7.5'—1967.
Dees Peak 7.5'—1978.
Detert Reservoir 7.5'—1958.
Devils Punchbowl 7.5'—1981.
Dinsmore 7.5'—1977.
Dos Rios 7.5'—1967.
Dubakella Mountain 15'—1954.
Dunsmuir 15'—1954.
Dutchmans Knoll 7.5'—1966.
Dyerville 15' (same area as Weott 15')—1921 (Army).
Eden Valley 15'—1929; 1952.
Elk 7.5'—1960.
Elk Mountain 7.5'—1967.
Elledge Peak 7.5'—1958.
Etna 30'—1934.
Ettersburg 7.5'—1969.
Eureka 1°x 2°—1949 (Army); 1958 (limited revision 1966).
15'—1942 (reprinted 1948).
7.5'—1958.
Felkner Hill 7.5'—1968.
Fern Canyon 7.5'—1966.
Ferndale 15' (same area as Cape fortunas 15')—1943.
7.5'—1959.
Fields Landing 7.5'—1959.
Fish Lake 7.5'—1974.
Forest Glen 7.5'—1979.
Fort Bragg 15'—1943 (Army).
7.5'—1960.
Fort Seward 7.5'—1969.
Fortuna 15' (same area as Rohnerville 15')—1944.
7.5'—1959.
Fouts Springs 7.5'—1968.
French Camp Ridge 7.5'—1983.
French Gulch 7.5'—1979.
Garberville 15' (same area as Briceland 15')—1949.
7.5'—1970.
Gasquet 15'—1945 (Army); 1951.
7.5'—1981.
Glascock Mountain 7.5'—1958.
Glenblair 15' (same area as Comptche 15')—1943 (Army).
Glynn 15' (same area as Scotia 15')—1919.
Gorda 15'—1926 (reprinted 1936) (Army).
Grouse Mountain 7.5'—1979.
Gualala 7.5'—1960.
Hales Grove 7.5'—1970.
Harris 15' (same area as Alderpoint 15')—1920 (Army).
7.5'—1969.
Hayfork 15'—1951.
Helena 15'—1951.
Hennessy Peak 7.5'—1979.
High Divide 7.5'—1966.
Highland Springs 7.5'—1959.
Hiouchi 7.5'—1966.
Hoaglin 30'—1935 (reprinted 1944).
Holter Ridge 7.5'—1983.
Honeydew 7.5'—1970.
Hoopa 30'—1935 (advance sheet) (Army).
15'—1952.
7.5'—1979.
Hopkins Butte 7.5'—1979.
Hopland 15'—1944 (Army); 1960.
7.5'—1960.
Hull Mountain 15'—1952.
7.5'—1967.
Hullville 15' (same area as Lake Pillsbury 15')—1922 (Army).
Hupa Mountain 7.5'—1982.
Hurdygurdy Butte 7.5'—1982.
Hyampom 15'—1951.
Hydesville 7.5'—1979.
Iaqua Buttes 15' (same area as Kneeland 15')—1950.
7.5'—1979.
Inglenook 7.5'—1966.
Iron Peak 7.5'—1967.
Ironside Mountain 15'—1951.
Island Mountain 15' (same area as Kettenpom 15')—1922 (Army).
Jamison Ridge 7.5'—1967.
Jericho Valley 7.5'—1958.
Jewett Rock 7.5'—1969.
Johnsons 7.5'—1982.
Kelseyville 15'—1944 (Army).
7.5'—1959.
Kenny 15' (same area as Piercy 15')—1920 (Army).
Kettenpom 15' (same area as Island Mountain 15')—1955.
Klamath 15' (same area as Requa 15')—1952.
Klamath Glen 7.5'—1982.
Kneecap Ridge 7.5'—1967.
Kneeland 15' (same area as Iaqua Buttes 15')—1922 (reprint 1938) (Army).
Knoxville 7.5'—1958.
Korbel 7.5'—1979.
Lake Mountain 7.5'—1967.
Lake Pillsbury 15' (same area as Hullville 15')—1951.
7.5'—1967.
Lakeport 15'—1938 (reprinted 1948).
7.5'—1958.
Larabee Valley 7.5'—1977.
Laytonville 15'—1919 (Army); 1951.
7.5'—1967.
Leech Lake Mountain 7.5'—1966.
Leggett 15'—1952.
7.5'—1969.
Lincoln Ridge 7.5'—1966.

Lonesome Ridge 7.5'—1974.
Long Ridge 7.5'—1967.
Longvale 7.5'—1966.
Lord-Ellis Summit 7.5'—1973.
Lower Lake 15'—1945 (Army).
7.5'—1958 (photorevised 1975).
Lucerne 7.5'—1958.
Mad River Buttes 7.5'—1977.
Mallo Pass Creek 7.5'—1960.
Maple Creek 7.5'—1977.
McWhinney Creek 7.5'—1979.
Mendocino 7.5'—1960.
Mendocino Pass 7.5'—1967.
Middletown 7.5'—1958.
Mina 7.5'—1967.
Miranda 7.5'—1970.
Mistake Point 7.5'—1969.
Morgan Valley 15'—1944.
Mount Saint Helena 7.5'—1959.
Myers Flat 7.5'—1969.
Naufus Creek 7.5'—1979.
Navarro 15' (same area as Saddle Point 15)—1943; 1961.
Newhouse Ridge 7.5'—1967.
Noble Butte 7.5'—1969.
Orick 15'—1952.
7.5'—1966.
Orleans 15'—1952.
7.5'—1978.
Orleans Mountain 7.5'—1974.
Ornbaun 15' (same area as Ornbaun Valley 15')—1944 (Army).
Ornbaun Valley 15' (same area as Ornbaun 15')—1960.
Orrs 15' (same area as Boonville 15')—1944 (Army).
Owl Creek 7.5'—1979.
Panther Creek 7.5'—1982.
Petrolia 7.5'—1969.
Pickett Peak 15' (same area as Pickett Peak 15')—1954.
Piercy 15' (same area as Kenny 15')—1950.
7.5'—1969.
Pilot Creek 15'—1922 (Army).
Plaskett Ridge 7.5'—1967.
Point Arena 15'—1943 (Army); 1960.
7.5'—1960 (photorevised 1978).
Point Delgada 15'—1920 (Army); 1949.
Point Saint George 15' (same area as Crescent City 15')—1945 (Army).
Polar Bear Mountain 7.5'—1982.
Pomo 15' (same area as Potter Valley 15')—1943.
Pope Valley 15' (same area as Saint Helena 15')—1921 (Army).
Potato Hill 7.5'—1967.
Potter Valley 15' (same area as Pomo 15')—1960.
7.5'—1960.
Prescott Mountain 7.5'—1981.
Preston Peak 30'—1922 (reprinted 1944).
15'—1956.
Purdys Gardens 7.5'—1958.
Red Bluff 1°—1894 (reprinted 1899).
Redcrest 7.5'—1969.
Redding 1°x 2°—1958 (limited revision 1964).
Redwood Valley 7.5'—1960.
Requa 7.5'—1966.
Rodgers Peak 7.5'—1966.
Rohnerville 15' (same area as Fortuna 15')—1920 (reprinted 1938) (Army).
Ruth Reservoir 7.5'—1978.
Saddle Point 15' (same area as Navarro 15')—1944.
Saint John Mountain 7.5'—1968.
Salmon Mountain 15'—1955.
7.5'—1978.
Salyer 7.5'—1979.
Sanhedrin Mountain 7.5'—1966.
Santa Rosa 1°x 2°—1958.
Saunders Reef 7.5'—1960.
Sawyers Bar 30'—1923 (reprinted 1945).
Schell Mountain 15'—1950.
Scotia 15' (same area as Glynn 15')—1950.
7.5'—1970.
Shannon Butte 7.5'—1967.
Shasta 1°—1894.
Shasta Bally 7.5'—1978.
Shelly Creek Ridge 7.5'—1982.
Shelter Cove 7.5'—1969.
Sherwood Peak 7.5'—1967.
Ship Mountain 15'—1952.
7.5'—1982.
Showers Mountain 7.5'—1978.
Shubrick Peak 7.5'—1969.
Sims Mountain 7.5'—1979.
Sister Rocks 7.5'—1966.
Smith River 7.5'—1966.
South Fork Peak 15' (same area as Blocksburg 15')—1929 (Army).
Sportshaven 7.5'—1973.
Spyrock 15'—1920 (Army); 1952.
Stonyford 15'—1951.
Summit Valley 7.5'—1981.
Tan Oak Park 7.5'—1969.
Taylor Peak 7.5'—1969.
Tectah Creek 15'—1945 (Army); 1952.
Thatcher Ridge 7.5'—1967.
The Geysers 7.5'—1959.
Thompson Peak 7.5'—1979.
Tish Tang Point 7.5'—1978.
Trinidad 15'—1945 (Army); 1952.
7.5'—1966.
Trinity Dam 15' (same area as Trinity Lake 15')—1950 (minor corrections 1964, 1968).
Trinity Lake 15' (same area as Trinity Dam 15')—1950 (minor revisions 1962).
Trinity Mountain 7.5'—1979.
Tyee City 7.5'—1959.
Ukiah 1°x 2°—1957.
15'—1920 (Army); 1944 (Army).
7.5'—1958.
Updegraff Ridge 7.5'—1967.
Upper Lake 7.5'—1958.
Weaverville 30'—1913 (reprinted 1947).
15'—1950.
Weed 1°x 2°—1963.
15'—1954.
Weitchpec 7.5'—1979.
Weott 15' (same area as Dyerville 15')—1949.
7.5'—1969.
Westport 7.5'—1966.
Whispering Pines 7.5'—1958.
Wilbur Springs 15' (same area as Venado 15')—1961.
Willis Ridge 7.5'—1966.
Willits 15'—1942; 1961.
Willow Creek 15' (same area as China Flat 15')—1952.
7.5'—1979.
Wilson Valley 7.5'—1958.
Yager Junction 7.5'—1979.
Yolla Bolly 15'—1954.
Youngs Peak 7.5'—1979.
Zenia 7.5'—1967.

MISCELLANEOUS MAPS

Averill. 1940. "Map of Trinity County showing locations of principal mineral deposits." (Plate I *in* Averill, 1941.)

Bancroft. 1864. "Bancroft's map of the Pacific States." Compiled by Wm. H. Knight. Published by H.H. Bancroft & Co., Booksellers and Stationers, San Francisco, Cal.

Burr. 1839. "Map of the United States of North America with parts of the adjacent countries." By David N. Burr. (Late Topographer to the Post Office.) Geographer to the House of Representatives of the U.S.

California Division of Highways. 1934. (Appendix "A" *of* California Division of Highways.)

California Mining Bureau. 1909a. "Del Norte and Siskiyou Counties." (*In* California State Mining Bureau Bulletin 56.)

_____1909b. "Humboldt and Trinity Counties." (*In* California State Mining Bureau Bulletin 56.)

_____1909c. "Mendocino, Glenn, Lake, and Colusa Counties." (*In* California State Mining Bureau Bulletin 56.)

_____1917a. (Untitled map *in* California State Mining Bureau Bulletin 74, p. 158.)

_____1917b. (Untitled map *in* California State Mining Bureau Bulletin 74, p. 160.)

_____1917c. (Untitled map *in* California State Mining Bureau Bulletin 74, p. 162.)

Chandler. 1901. "Map of Cache Creek Basin." (Plate I *in* Chandler.)

Colton. 1863. "Colton's map of California, Nevada, Utah, Colorado, Arizona, & New Mexico." Published by J.H. Colton, 172 William St., New York.

Eddy. 1854. "Approved and declared to be the official map of the State of California by an act of the Legislature passed March 25th 1853." Compiled by W.M. Eddy, State Surveyor General. Published for R.A. Eddy,

Marysville, California, by J.H. Colton, New York.
Ferry. 1851. "Nuova California." By Hypolite Ferry.
Fremont. 1845. "Map of an exploring expedition to the Rocky Mountains in the year 1842 and to Oregon & North California in the years 1843-44." By Brevet Capt. J.C. Frémont.
Gibbes. 1852. "A new map of California." By Charles Drayton Gibbes, from his own and other recent surveys and explorations. Published by C.D. Gibbes, Stockton, Cal.
Goddard. 1857. "Britton & Rey's map of the State of California." By George H. Goddard.
Manning and Ogle. 1950. "Economic map of the Blue Lake quadrangle, California." (Plate 2 *in* Manning and Ogle.)
Miller. 1890. "Geological map of Trinity County, Cal." (*In* Miller.)
O'Brien. 1952. "Map of Del Norte County, California, showing distribution of peridotite and locations of mineral deposits." (Plate 13 *in* O'Brien, 1952.)
_____1953. "Mines and claims of Mendocino County." (Plate 10a *in* O'Brien, 1953.)
Parker. 1838. "Map of Oregon Territory." By Samuel Parker.
Rogers and Johnston. 1857. "State of California." By Prof. H.D. Rodgers & A. Keith Johnston.
Scholfield. 1851. "Map of southern Oregon and northern California." Compiled from the best authorities, and from personal surveys and explorations, by N. Scholfield, Civil Engineer. Published by Marvin & Hitchcock, San Francisco.
Tanner. 1849. "Map of California, New Mexico, Texas, &c." Published by H.S.Tanner.
Upson and Kunkel. 1955. "Ground-water basins of the Lower Lake-Middletown area, Lake County, California." (Plate I *in* Upson and Kunkel.)
United States Coast Survey. 1854. "Reconnaissance of the Western Coast of the United States, Middle Sheet, from San Francisco to Umpquah River." Scale 1:1,200,000. 1854. (*In* United States Coast Survey.)
United States Geological Survey. 1915. "Big Bar and vicinity."
Vander Leck. 1920a. "Geological map of Pt. Arena district." (Plate III *in* Vander Leck.)
_____1920b. "Map of southwestern Humboldt County." (Plate IV *in* Vander Leck.)
Wells. 1946. "Topographic map of Del Norte County, California, showing distribution of peridotite and location of chromite deposits." By Francis G. Wells. (Plate I *in* Wells, Cater, and Rynearson, 1946.)
Wilkes. 1841. "Map of Upper California." By the U.S. Ex. Ex. and best authorities.

Part Two

North Sacramento Valley Region

Butte, Glenn, Shasta, Siskiyou and Tehama Counties

Part Two—North Sacramento Valley Region

North Sacramento Valley Region
Butte, Glenn, Shasta, Siskiyou and Tehama Counties

Regional Setting

General.—This section concerns geographic features in five counties—Butte, Glenn, Shasta, Siskiyou, and Tehama—that lie in and around the north part of Sacramento Valley. All Townships (T) and Ranges (R) refer to Mount Diablo Base and Meridian, except in westernmost Siskiyou County, where they refer to Humboldt Base and Meridian. Sacramento Valley is the north part of the Central Valley, or Great Valley, of California, and takes its name from the river that drains it. The whole Central Valley is called Buena Ventura Valley on Wilkes' (1841) map. Highlands east of the valley as far south as Lassen Peak belong to the Cascade Range of Oregon and California, and highlands east of the valley and south of Lassen Peak are the northernmost part of the Sierra Nevada of California. Garces gave the name "Sierra de San Marcos" to the present Sierra Nevada in 1776 (Boyd, p. 3), Wilkes (p. 44) called the feature California Range in 1841, Lyman (p. 307) called it "Sierra Nevada, or Snowy Mountains" in 1849, and Kip (p. 46) called it Snowy Range in 1850. United States Board on Geographic Names (1933, p. 692) ruled against the form "Sierra Nevadas" for the name of the range. Whitney (p. 2) pointed out that the feature long was known to the Spaniards as Sierra Nevada, or Snowy Range, because "the most distant and loftiest elevations are never entirely bare of snow, and for a large portion of the year are extensively covered with it." The map on the facing page shows the location of the North Sacramento Valley Region and the counties in it.

Butte County.—Butte County is east of Sacramento River in Sacramento Valley and in the adjacent part of the Sierra Nevada. It includes Lake Oroville, formed by a great dam on Feather River. Butte County is one of the counties that the state legislature created in 1850; more than half of the original county territory was lost in 1854 when Plumas County was organized, and numerous boundary adjustments have been made with neighboring counties over the years (Coy, p. 69-79). The county seat first was at Hamilton, it moved in 1850 to Bidwell Bar, and moved in 1856 to Oroville; the county name is from Sutter Buttes, which are in Sutter County (Hoover, Rensch, and Rensch, p. 35).

Glenn County.—Glenn County lies in Sacramento Valley and in highlands to the west; all but the southeasternmost corner of the county is west of Sacramento River. Most of the residents of the county live in the valley. Glenn county was organized in 1891 from territory of Colusa County; changes in the original county boundaries have been minor (Coy, p. 107-109). The county name is from Dr. Hugh James Glenn, who came to the region in 1867 and had large landholdings there; Willows is the county seat (Hoover, Rensch, and Rensch, p. 96, 97).

Shasta County.—Shasta County is near the north end of Sacramento Valley, and includes highlands both to the east and west. The name is from Mount Shasta, which was in the original territory of the county (Irelan, p. 562). The major population centers are along Sacramento River. The Shasta County that was created in 1850 was much larger than the present county; the north half of the original county was lost in 1852 with thc crcation of Siskiyou County, and about half of what was lcft was lost in 1864 with the creation of Lassen County; small parts of the Shasta County were detached in 1851 and 1857 when adjustments were made to the south boundary (Coy, p. 250-252). The county seat first was at Reading's Ranch, it moved to Shasta in 1851, and moved finally to Redding in 1888 (Hoover, Rensch, and Rensch, p. 482).

Siskiyou County.—Siskiyou County occupies the central part of northernmost California, where it includes Siskiyou Mountains and upper reaches of Sacramento River. Mount Shasta is a conspicuous feature of the county. The population centers are mainly in Shasta Valley and along Sacramento River. The state legislature created the county in 1852 from parts of previously formed Shasta County and Klamath County; the principal boundary changes of Siskiyou County came in 1874, when present Modoc County was detached from Siskiyou County, and in 1874 and 1875, when Klamath County was abolished and part of its territory added to Siskiyou County (Coy, p. 256-257). Yreka has always been the seat of government (Hoover, Rensch, and Rensch, p. 497).

Tehama County.—Sacramento River divides Tehama County into nearly equal parts to the east and west. The county was organized in 1856 from parts of previously existing Butte County, Colusa County, and Shasta County; adjustments to the county boundaries were made in 1857 and 1859 (Coy, p. 276-277). The county seat first was at Tehama and it moved to Red Bluff in 1857, where it remains (Hoover, Rensch, and Rensch, p. 547).

North Sacramento Valley Region
Butte, Glenn, Shasta, Siskiyou and Tehama Counties

— A —

Abbott Lake [SISKIYOU]: *lake,* 1250 feet long, 8.5 miles north-northwest of Sawyers Bar (lat. 41°25' N, long. 123°11'05" W). Named on English Peak (1977) 7.5' quadrangle.

Abertine: see **Butte Creek House** [BUTTE].

Abner: see **Grass Lake** [SISKIYOU] (2).

Abney Butte [SISKIYOU]: *peak,* 9.5 miles north of the village of Seiad Valley (lat. 41°58'35" N, long. 123°09'25" W). Altitude 4403 feet. Named on Kangaroo Mountain (1980) 7.5' quadrangle. Called Ahney Butte on Seiad Valley (1955) 15' quadrangle.

Abraham Plains [TEHAMA]: *area,* 10 miles east of Red Bluff (lat. 40°11'50" N, long. 122°03'15" W). Named on Tuscan Springs (1951) 7.5' quadrangle.

Abrams Lake [SISKIYOU]: *lake,* 400 feet long, 3 miles northwest of the town of Mount Shasta (lat. 41°20'15" N, long. 122°21'15" W; sec. 6, T 40 N, R 4 W). Named on Weed (1954) 15' quadrangle.

Acme: see **Black Butte** [SISKIYOU] (2).

Acorn Hollow [TEHAMA]: *canyon,* drained by a stream that flows 10 miles to Toomes Creek 4 miles north of Vina (lat. 39°59'25" N, long. 122°02'30" W; near SW cor. sec. 25, T 25 N, R 2 W). Named on Panther Spring (1953) 15' quadrangle, and on Vina (1950) 7.5' quadrangle.

Acorn Spring [SISKIYOU]: *spring,* 1.5 miles west of Forks of Salmon (lat. 41°15'20" N, long. 123°20'55" W). Named on Forks of Salmon (1978) 7.5' quadrangle.

Acorn Springs Flat: see **Bull Barn Flat** [SISKIYOU].

Adams: see **John Adams**, under **Centerville** [BUTTE].

Adams Bar: see **Oroville** [BUTTE].

Adams Creek [BUTTE]: *stream,* flows 1.5 miles to Brush Creek (1) 2 miles southeast of the village of Brush Creek (lat. 39°40'20" N, long. 121°18'35" W). Named on Brush Creek (1970) 7.5' quadrangle.

Adam's Ferry: see **Logan's Ferry** [SHASTA].

Adamstown: see **Oroville** [BUTTE].

Adamsville: see **Oroville** [BUTTE].

Adler Creek [SHASTA]: *stream,* flows 0.5 mile to Sacramento River Arm Shasta Lake 13 miles south of Lamoine (lat. 40°47'25" N, long. 121°23'55" W; sec. 23, T 34 N, R 5 W). Named on Lamoine (1957) 15' quadrangle.

Adobe Ferry: see **Red Bluff** [TEHAMA].

Adobe Flat [SISKIYOU]: *area,* 15 miles east of Bartle (lat. 41°13'55" N, long. 121°29'45" W; sec. 10, T 39 N, R 4 E). Named on Fall River Mills (1961) 15' quadrangle.

Afton [GLENN]: *locality,* 3.25 miles south-southeast of Butte City (lat. 39°25'10" N, long. 121°57'55" W; at NW cor. sec. 15, T 18 N, R 1 W). Named on Butte City (1952) 7.5' quadrangle. Postal authorities established Afton post office in 1887, discontinued it in 1910, reestablished it in 1915, and discontinued it in 1923 (Frickstad, p. 40).

Agate Flat [SISKIYOU]: *area,* 23 miles west-northwest of Macdoel (lat. 42°00'15" N, long. 122°23'15" W; near N line sec. 23, T 48 N, R 5 W). Named on Copco (1954) 15' quadrangle.

Ager [SISKIYOU]: *locality,* 24 miles west of Macdoel (lat. 41°52' N, long. 122°27'30" W; at E line sec. 6, T. 46 N, R 5 W); the place is along Willow Creek (3). Named on Copco (1954) 15' quadrangle. Postal authorities established Willow Creek post office in 1876, moved it 1.5 miles northeast in 1888 when they changed the name to Ager, and discontinued it in 1940; the name "Ager" was for Judson A. Ager, a pioneer settler (Salley, p. 2, 241). Diller and others' (1915) map shows a place called Thrall situated along the railroad about 3 miles north-northwest of Ager. Postal authorities established Thrall post office in 1904, discontinued it the same year, reestablished it in 1905, and discontinued it in 1914; the name was for Will Thrall, a pioneer mountain man (Salley, p. 221).

Aguas Frias [BUTTE-GLENN]: *land grant,* 10 miles south of Chico on Butte-Glenn County line. Named on Butte City (1952), Llano Seco (1948), Nelson (1948), and West of Biggs (1952) 7.5' quadrangles. Salvador Osio received 6 leagues in 1844; Samuel Todd and Andrew Randall claimed 26,761 acres patented in 1860 (Cowan, p. 13; Perez, p. 52).

Ah-Di-Na [SHASTA]: *locality,* 3.25 miles north-northwest of Shoeinhorse Mountain along McCloud River [SHASTA-SISKIYOU] (lat. 41°06'45" N, long. 122°05'45" W). Named on Shoeinhorse Mountain (1954) 15' quadrangle.

Ah Moon Bar: see **Swayne Hill** [BUTTE].

Ahney Butte: see **Abney Butte** [SISKIYOU].

Aiken Gulch [SHASTA]: *canyon,* drained by a stream that flows 7 miles to Middle Fork Cottonwood Creek [SHASTA-TEHAMA] 8 miles south of Ono (lat. 40°21'35" N, long. 122°35'20" W; at N line sec. 19, T 29 N, R 6 W). Named on Ono (1952) 15' quadrangle.

Ainsworth Corner [SISKIYOU]: *locality,* 15 miles northeast of Mount Dome near California-Oregon State line (lat. 41°59'55" N, long. 121°33'25" W; sec. 18, T 48 N, R 4 E). Named on Mount Dome (1950) 15' quadrangle.

Alamine Peak [SHASTA]: *peak,* 3.5 miles south-southeast of Whitmore (lat. 40°35' N, long. 121°52'40" W; on E line sec. 32, T 32 N, R 1 E). Altitude 3031 feet. Named on Whitmore (1956) 15' quadrangle.

Alberry Creek: see **Aubrey Creek** [SISKIYOU].

Albers Meadow [SISKIYOU]: *area,* 6.25 miles south-southwest of Ukonom Lake (lat. 41°30'20" N, long. 123°25'30" W). Named on Ukonom Mountain (1980) 7.5' quadrangle.

Albert Creek [SHASTA]: *stream,* flows 2 miles to Middle Salt Creek 5.25 miles southeast of Lamoine (lat. 40°56'15" N, long. 122°20'40" W; near E line sec. 32, T 36 N, R 4 W). Named on Lamoine (1957) 15' quadrangle.

Albert Lake [SISKIYOU]: *lake,* 450 feet long, 9 miles south-southwest of Etna (lat. 41°20'40" N, long. 122°58'05" W; sec. 12, T 40 N, R 10 W). Named on Etna (1955) 15' quadrangle.

Albert Lake: see **Upper Albert Lake** [SISKIYOU].

Albertson: see **Palo Cedro** [SHASTA].

Alcohol Jacks Reservoir [SHASTA]: *lake,* 200 feet long, 5.5 miles south-southwest of Coble Mountain along Procter Creek (lat. 40°48'25" N, long. 121°22'45" W; sec. 14, T 34 N, R 5 E). Named on Jellico (1957) 15' quadrangle.

Alder Campground [TEHAMA]: *locality,* 4.5 miles south-southwest of Deer Creek Station along Deer Creek (2) (lat. 40°12'40" N, long. 121°29'40" W; sec. 11, T 27 N, R 4 E). Named on Jonesville (1958) 15' quadrangle.

Alder Creek [SHASTA]:

(1) *stream,* flows 2.5 miles to Devils Canyon (1) 6.5 miles north of the village of Big Bend (lat. 41°07' N, long. 121°55'25" W). Named on Big Bend (1961) 15' quadrangle.

(2) *stream,* flows 0.5 mile to Sacramento River Arm Shasta Lake 12.5 miles south of Lamoine (lat. 40°48' N, long. 122°24' W; near S line sec. 14, T 34 N, R 5 W). Named on Lamoine (1957) 15' quadrangle.

(3) *stream,* flows 0.5 mile to Sacramento River Arm Shasta Lake 13 miles south of Lamoine (lat. 40°47'25" N, long. 122°24' W; sec. 23, T 34 N, R 5 W). Named on Lamoine (1957) 15' quadrangle.

Alder Creek [SISKIYOU]:

(1) *stream,* flows 3 miles to Sniktaw Creek 7.25 miles west of Fort Jones (lat. 41°36'55" N, long. 122°58'50" W; near S line sec. 34, T 44 N, R 10 W). Named on Fort Jones (1955) 15' quadrangle, and on Boulder Peak (1981) 7.5' quadrangle.

(2) *stream,* flows 2 miles to Etna Creek nearly 3 miles southwest of Etna

(lat. 41°25'30" N, long. 122°55'35" W; near S line sec. 6, T 41 N, R 9 W). Named on Etna (1955) 15' quadrangle.

(3) *stream,* flows 4.5 miles to Butte Creek [BUTTE-GLENN] 20 miles south of Macdoel (lat. 41°32'35" N, long. 122°03'40" W; sec. 27, T 43 N, R 2 W). Named on The Whaleback (1954) 15' quadrangle.

Alder Creek [TEHAMA]:

(1) *stream,* flows 1 mile to Deer Creek (2) at Deer Creek Station (lat. 40°15'55" N, long. 121°27' W; at S line sec. 20, T 28 N, R 5 E). Named on Mount Harkness (1956) 15' quadrangle.

(2) *stream,* flows nearly 2 miles to Red Bank Creek 4 miles south-southwest of Wakefield Flat (lat. 40°04'35" N, long. 122°40'40" W; sec. 29, T 26 N, R 7 W). Named on Raglin Ridge (1967) 7.5' quadrangle.

(3) *stream,* flows 3 miles to Thomes Creek 7 miles northwest of Ball Mountain (lat. 39°59'35" N, long. 122°52'50" W; near NW cor. sec. 28, T 25 N, R 9 W). Named on Buck Rock (1967) 7.5' quadrangle.

Alder Flat [GLENN]: *area,* 10 miles west-northwest of the village of Elk Creek (lat. 39°38'30" N, long. 122°43'15" W; near SW cor. sec. 25, T 21 N, R 8 W); the place is less than 1 mile south-southeast of Alder Springs. Named on Alder Springs (1967) 7.5' quadrangle. Called Alder Flats on Elk Creek (1918) 15' quadrangle.

Alder Gulch [SHASTA]:

(1) *canyon,* drained by a stream that flows 0.5 mile to East Fork Clear Creek 5.5 miles south of Schell Mountain (lat. 40°46'30" N, long. 122°32'55" W; sec. 28, T 34 N, R 6 W). Named on Schell Mountain (1950) 15' quadrangle.

(2) *canyon,* drained by a stream that flows 1.5 miles to Middle Fork Cottonwood Creek [SHASTA-TEHAMA] 2 miles southwest of Arbuckle Mountain (lat. 40°22'45" N, long. 122°53'10" W; sec. 9, T 29 N, R 9 W). Named on Chanchelulla Peak (1951) 15' quadrangle.

Alder Gulch [SISKIYOU]: *canyon,* drained by a stream that flows 1 mile to Shackleford Creek 10.5 miles south of Scott Bar (lat. 41°35'25" N, long. 123°00'05" W; sec. 9, T 43 N, R 10 W). Named on Boulder Peak (1981) 7.5' quadrangle.

Alder Spring [SHASTA]: *spring,* 7.5 miles southeast of Bollibokka Mountain (lat. 40°52'15" N, long. 122°05'50" W; sec. 21, T 35 N, R 2 W). Named on Bollibokka Mountain (1957) 15' quadrangle.

Alder Spring [SISKIYOU]: *spring,* 3.5 miles northeast of the village of Seiad Valley (lat. 41°52'55" N, long. 123°08'50" W). Named on Kangaroo Mountain (1980) 7.5' quadrangle.

Alder Springs [GLENN]: *village,* 10.5 miles west-northwest of the village of Elk Creek (lat. 39°39'05" N, long. 122°43'30" W; at NE cor. sec. 26, T 21 N, R 8 W). Named on Alder Springs (1967) 7.5' quadrangle. On Elk Creek (1918) 15' quadrangle, the village has the designation "Oriental (Alder Springs)," but United States Board on Geographic Names (1933, p. 87) rejected the name "Oriental" for the place. Postal authorities established Oriental post office in 1888, changed the name to Alder Springs in 1917, and discontinued it in 1940 (Salley, p. 4, 162).

Alex Creek [SISKIYOU]: *stream,* flows 3.5 mile to Elliot Creek 3.25 miles north of Condrey Mountain (lat. 41°59' N, long. 122°58'45" W; sec. 26, T 48 N, R 10 W); the stream heads at Alex Hole. Named on Condrey Mountain (1955) 15' quadrangle. Yreka (1939) 30' quadrangle shows Alex Creek joining Studhorse Creek, and Studhorse Creek joining Elliot Creek.

Alex Hole [SISKIYOU]: *relief feature,* 0.5 mile east of Condrey Mountain (lat. 41°56'15" N, long. 122°58' W; near E line sec. 11, T 47 N, R 10 W); the feature is at the head of Alex Creek. Named on Condrey Mountain (1955) 15' quadrangle.

Alfa: see **Glenburn** [SHASTA].

Algoma [SISKIYOU]: *locality,* 3.25 miles west of Bartle along McCloud River [SHASTA-SISKIYOU] (lat. 41°15'20" N, long. 121°53' W; sec. 5, T 39 N, R 1 E). Named on Bartle (1961) 15' quadrangle. Postal authorities established Algomah (with the final "h") post office in 1902 and discontinued it in 1909; Algomah Lumber Company had a sawmill at the site (Salley, p. 4).

Allen: see **Baird** [SHASTA]; **George Allen Gulch** [SISKIYOU].

Allentown: see **Toadtown** [BUTTE].

Allgood: see **Jake Allgood Gulch** [SISKIYOU].

Allie Cove [SHASTA]: *embayment,* 17 miles south-southeast of Lamoine along Pit River Arm Shasta Lake (lat. 40°45'35" N, long. 122°17'20" W; sec. 35, T 34 N, R 4 W). Named on Lamoine (1957) 15' quadrangle.

All Top [TEHAMA]: *peak,* 9 miles west of Paskenta (lat. 39°52'55" N, long. 122°42'35" W; sec. 1, T 23 N, R 8 W). Altitude 5164 feet. Named on Riley Ridge (1967) 7.5' quadrangle.

Al Smith Gulch [SHASTA]: *canyon,* drained by a stream that flows 1.5 miles to Clear Creek 8 miles southwest of Schell Mountain (lat. 40°45'40" N, long. 122°36'45" W; near W line sec. 36, T 34 N, R 7 W). Named on Schell Mountain (1950) 15' quadrangle.

Al Smith Gulch: see **George Williams Gulch** [SHASTA].

American Bar [BUTTE]: *locality,* 3.5 miles east of the village of Brush Creek along Middle Fork Feather River (lat. 39°41'35" N, long. 121°16'15" W). Named on Brush Creek (1970) 7.5' quadrangle.

American Ranch: see **Anderson** [SHASTA].

Ananias Camp [SISKIYOU]: *locality,* 17 miles south-southwest of Scott Bar (lat. 41°32'45" N, long. 123°12' W). Named on Marble Mountain (1980) 7.5' quadrangle.

Anderson [SHASTA]: *town,* 10 miles south-southeast of Redding (lat. 40°27' N, long. 122°18' W). Named on Cottonwood (1965) 7.5' quadrangle. Postal authorities established American Ranch post office in 1855 and moved it to nearby Anderson townsite in 1878, when they changed the name to Anderson (Salley, p. 7). The town incorporated in 1956. The name "Anderson" commemorates Elias Anderson, who purchased land at the place in 1856 and ran a travelers stop called American Ranch (Giles, p. 197). When the railroad arrived in 1872, railroad officials named the station for Anderson, who granted right of way across his land (Gudde, 1949, p. 11). A place called Dersch Station, or Bakers, was 10 miles northeast of Anderson; it was a travelers stop owned in 1850 by a man named Baker, and later owned by George Dersch and Mary Dersch, who purchased the property in 1861 (Steger, p. 28).

Anderson Creek [GLENN]: *stream,* flows nearly 1 mile to Lake County 12.5 miles west-southwest of the village of Elk Creek (lat. 39°30'20" N, long. 122°44'05" W). Named on Felkner Hill (1968) 7.5' quadrangle.

Anderson Creek [SHASTA]: *stream,* flows 16 miles to Sacramento River 2.25 miles south of Balls Ferry (lat. 40°23'05" N, long. 122°11'50" W). Named on Balls Ferry (1965), Cottonwood (1965), and Olinda (1964) 7.5' quadrangles.

Anderson Fork [BUTTE]: *stream,* flows 7.25 miles to Rock Creek [BUTTE-TEHAMA] 8.5 miles north of Chico (lat. 39°51'05" N, long. 121°49'25" W; near W line sec. 13, T 23 N, R 1 E). Named on Campbell Mound (1952), Cohasset (1979) and Richardson Springs (1951) 7.5' quadrangles.

Anderson Mill [BUTTE]: *locality,* 10 miles north-northwest of Paradise (lat. 39°58'50" N, long. 121°42' W; sec. 36, T 25 N, R 2 E). Site named on Cohasset (1979) 7.5' quadrangle.

Anderson Peak [SISKIYOU]: *peak,* 5 miles south-southwest of Scott Bar (lat. 41°40'35" N, long. 123°02'20" W; near S line sec. 7, T 44 N, R 10 W). Altitude 5910 feet. Named on Scott Bar (1980) 7.5' quadrangle.

Anderson Point [SHASTA]: *peak,* 3.25 miles north of Arbuckle Mountain (lat. 40°26'45" N, long. 122°51'55" W; on S line sec. 15, T 30 N, R 9 W); the peak is on Anderson Spring Ridge. Named on Chanchelulla Peak (1951) 15' quadrangle.

Anderson Spring Ridge [SHASTA]: *ridge,* southeast-trending, 3 miles long, 3.5 miles north of Arbuckle Mountain (lat. 40°26'50" N, long. 122°52' W). Named on Chanchelulla Peak (1951) 15' quadrangle

Andesite [SISKIYOU]: *locality,* 22 miles south-southwest of Macdoel (lat. 41°32' N, long. 122°12'05" W; near NW cor. sec. 33, T 43 N, R 3 W). Named on The Whaleback (1954) 15' quadrangle.

Andrews Creek [SHASTA]: *stream,* flows nearly 4 miles to South Fork Clear Creek 1.5 miles northwest of Igo (lat. 40°31'20" N, long. 122°33'25" W; near SW cor. sec. 21, T 31 N, R 6 W). Named on Igo (1979) 7.5' quadrangle. The name commemorates Alex R. Andrews, who had mining claims along the stream (Steger, p. 13).

Angel Creek [SISKIYOU]: *stream,* flows 10.5 miles to McCloud River [SHASTA-SISKIYOU] 6 miles southeast of McCloud (lat. 41°11'40" N, long. 122°03'40" W; near E line sec. 27, T 39 N, R 2 W). Named on Big Bend (1961) and Shoeinhorse Mountain (1954) 15' quadrangles. Called Willow Creek on Shasta (1894) 1° quadrangle.

Angel Lake [SISKIYOU]: *lake,* 400 feet long, 16 miles south-southwest of Scott Bar (lat. 41°31'40" N, long. 123°07'05" W). Named on Boulder Peak (1981) 7.5' quadrangle.

Angel Meadow [SISKIYOU]: *area,* 8 miles west-southwest of Bartle (lat. 41°12'20" N, long. 121°57'15" W; near S line sec. 22, T 39 N, R 1 W); the place is along Angel Creek. Named on Big Bend (1961) 15' quadrangle.

Angel Slough [BUTTE-GLENN]: *water feature,* heads in Butte County and extend for 21 miles in Butte and Glenn Counties to Colusa County 7 miles southeast of Butte City (lat. 39°23'05" N, long. 121°54'40" W; at E line sec. 25, T 18 N, R 1 W); the feature is east of and generally parallel to Sacramento River. Named on Butte City (1952), Llano Seco (1948) and Ord Ferry (1949) 7.5' quadrangles.

Anita [BUTTE]: *locality,* 2.5 mile north-northwest of Nord along Southern Pacific Railroad (lat. 39°48'40" N, long. 121°58'35" W). Named on Nord (1951) 7.5' quadrangle.

Ankeny Gulch [SISKIYOU]: *canyon,* drained by a stream that flows 1 mile to Wildcat Creek 11 miles south-southeast of Etna (lat. 41°18'30" N, long. 122°50' W; at S line sec. 13, T 40 N, R 9 W). Named on Etna (1955) 15' quadrangle.

Anklin Meadows [SHASTA]: *area,* 3.25 miles north-northeast of Lassen Peak (lat. 40°32' N, long. 121°29'25" W; sec. 14, T 31 N, R 4 E). Named on Prospect Peak (1957) 15' quadrangle. L.W. Collins, superintendent of Lassen Volcanic National Park, recommended the name in 1931 to honor Richard Anklin, who homesteaded at the place; a mudflow caused by the 1915 eruption of Lassen Peak devastated the area (Schulz, p. 1).

Antelope Campground: see **South Antelope Campground** [TEHAMA].

Antelope Creek [SHASTA]: *stream,* flows 7 miles to Cottonwood Creek [SHASTA-TEHAMA] 5 miles south-southwest of Olinda (lat. 40°22'25" N, long. 122°26'05" W; at S line sec. 9, T 29 N, R 5 W). Named on Ono (1952) 15' quadrangle, and on Olinda (1964) 7.5' quadrangle.

Antelope Creek [SISKIYOU]: *stream,* flows 19 miles to Antelope Sink 4.25 miles northeast of Bray (lat. 41°40'50" N, long. 122°53'50" W; sec. 6, T 44 N, R 1 E). Named on Bartle (1961) and Bray (1950) 15' quadrangles.

Antelope Creek [TEHAMA]: *stream,* formed by the confluence of North Fork and South Fork, flows 28 miles to Sacramento River 5.25 miles north-northwest of Los Molinos (lat. 40°05'45" N, long. 122°07' W). Named on Panther Spring (1953) 15' quadrangle, and on Los Molinos (1952, photorevised 1969), Red Bluff East (1951), and Tuscan Springs (1951) 7.5' quadrangles. The name is a translation of the Spanish term *Arroyo de los Berrendos* (Gudde, 1949, p. 12). North Fork is 15 miles long and is named on Lassen Peak (1956), Manton (1956), and Panther Spring (1953) 15' quadrangles. South Fork is 16 miles long and is named on Butte Meadows (1958), Lassen Peak (1956), Manton (1956), and Panther Spring (1953) 15' quadrangles. Middle Fork joins North Fork 12 miles south-southeast of Manton; it is 9.5 miles long and is named on Lassen Peak (1956) and Manton (1956) 15' quadrangles.

Antelope Creek: see **Little Antelope Creek** [TEHAMA].

Antelope Creek Lakes [SISKIYOU]: *lakes,* two, largest 600 feet long, 17 miles north-northwest of Bartle (lat. 41°28' N, long. 121°58'50" W; near SE cor. sec. 20, T 42 N, R 1 W); the lakes are at the head of Antelope Creek. Named on Bartle (1961) 15' quadrangle.

Antelope Mountain [SISKIYOU]: *ridge,* southwest- to south-trending, 2 miles long, 9.5 miles south of Yreka (lat. 41°36' N, long. 122°38'10" W). Named on Yreka (1954) 15' quadrangle.

Antelope Sink [SISKIYOU]: *intermittent lake,* 4.25 miles northeast of Bray (lat. 41°41' N, long. 121°54' W; sec. 6, T 44 N, R 1 E); the feature is at the mouth of Antelope Creek. Named on Bray (1950) 15' quadrangle.

Antelope Springs: see **Wicks Corner** [BUTTE].

Antelope Valley [GLENN]: *valley,* mainly in Colusa County, but extends north into Glenn County 4.5 miles southeast of High Peak (lat. 39°23'05" N, long. 122°21'30" W). Named on Logan Ridge (1958) 7.5' quadrangle.

Antelope Well [SISKIYOU]: *well,* 10.5 miles northwest of Medicine Lake (lat. 41°40'45" N, long. 121°45' W; near S line sec. 4, T 44 N, R 2 E). Named on Medicine Lake (1952) 15' quadrangle.

Ant Flat [TEHAMA]: *area,* 2.5 miles north-northeast of Wakefield Flat along South Fork Cottonwood Creek [SHASTA-TEHAMA] (lat. 40°09'15" N, long. 122°36'55" W; near NE cor. sec. 35, T 37 N, R 7 W). Named on Oxbow Bridge (1967) 7.5' quadrangle.

Anthony Milne Camp [SISKIYOU]: *locality,* 20 miles south-southwest of Scott Bar along Wooley Creek (lat. 41°30'05" N, long. 123°12'40" W). Named on Marble Mountain (1980) 7.5' quadrangle.

Antler: see **Gregory** [SHASTA].

Antlers [SHASTA]: *locality,* 6.5 miles south-southeast of Lamoine (lat. 40°53'40" N, long. 122°22'15" W; at NW cor. sec. 18, T 35 N, R 4 W). Named on Lamoine (1957) 15' quadrangle.

Apperson Cow Camp [TEHAMA]: *locality,* 14 miles south of Panther Spring along Deer Creek (2) (lat. 40°02'30" N, long. 121°47'50" W; sec. 7, T 25 N, R 2 E). Named on Panther Spring (1953) 15' quadrangle. Called Apperson place on Mineral (1941) 30' quadrangle.

Apperson Winter Camp [TEHAMA]: *locality,* 15 miles southwest of Panther Spring (lat. 40°05'45" N, long. 121°59'40" W; at W line sec. 21, T 26 N, R 1 W). Named on Mineral (1941) 30' quadrangle.

Applegate River [SISKIYOU]: *stream,* formed by the confluence of Middle Fork and Butte Fork, flows 3.5 miles to the State of Oregon 12 miles north of the village of Seiad Valley (lat. 42°00'30" N, long. 123°09'10" W; sec. 17, T 48, R 11 W). Named on Seiad Valley (1955) 15' quadrangle. The name commemorates Lindsay Applegate, Oregon pioneer who prospected for gold in the river in 1848 (McArthur, p. 21). Butte Fork is 9 miles long and Middle Fork is 8.5 miles long; both forks are named on Figurehead Mountain (1980) and Kangaroo Mountain (1980) 7.5' quadrangles.

Applesass Bar: see **Eddy Gulch** [SISKIYOU].

Applesauce Bar: see **Eddy Gulch** [SISKIYOU].

Applesauce Creek: see **Hickey Gulch** [SISKIYOU].

Applesauce Gulch [SISKIYOU]: *canyon,* drained by a stream that flows nearly 2 miles to North Fork Salmon River 3.5 miles east-northeast of Sawyers Bar (lat. 41°18'35" N, long. 123°04'05" W). Named on Tanners Peak (1977) 7.5' quadrangle. On Sawyers Bar (1923) 30' quadrangle, the name "Applesauce Cr." applies to the stream in nearby Hickey Gulch.

Appleton: see **Magalia** [BUTTE].

Appletree Glade [TEHAMA]: *area,* 1.5 miles east-northeast of Tomhead Mountain (lat. 40°09' N, long. 122°47'20" W; sec. 32, T 27 N, R 8 W). Named on Yolla Bolly (1954) 15' quadrangle.

Arastra Creek [SISKIYOU]: *stream,* flows 1.5 miles to Hungry Creek 10 miles west-northwest of Hornbrook (lat. 41°58'40" N, long. 122°43'50" W; sec. 26, T 48 N, R 8 W). Named on Hornbrook (1955) 15' quadrangle.

Arbuckle Basin [SHASTA]: *relief feature,* 2.25 miles east-southeast of Arbuckle Mountain (lat. 40°23'30" N, long. 122°49'30" W; near SE cor. sec. 1, T 29 N, R 9 W); the feature is near the head of Arbuckle Creek. Named on Chanchelulla Peak (1951) 15' quadrangle.

Arbuckle Creek [SHASTA]: *stream,* flows 1.25 miles to Pit River Arm Shasta Lake 12 miles south-southeast of Bollibokka Mountain (lat. 40°46'30" N, long. 122°07'40" W; near W line sec. 29, T 34 N, R 2 W). Named on Bollibokka Mountain (1957) 15' quadrangle.

Arbuckle Flat [SHASTA]: *area,* 13 miles south-southeast of Bollibokka Mountain (lat. 40°45'45" N, long. 122°06'45" W; near NE cor. sec. 32, T 34 N, R 2 W). Named on Bollibokka Mountain (1957) 15' quadrangle.

Arbuckle Gulch [SHASTA]: *canyon,* drained by a stream that flows 4 miles to Rocky Creek 5.5 miles east of Arbuckle Mountain (lat. 40°23'10" N, long. 122°46' W; at E line sec. 9, T 29 N, R 8 W). Named on Chanchelulla Peak (1951) 15' quadrangle.

Arbuckle Mountain [SHASTA]: *peak,* 28 miles west-southwest of Redding (lat. 40°24' N, long. 122°52' W; at N line sec. 3, T 29 N, R 9 W). Altitude 3715 feet. Named on Chanchelulla Peak (1951) 15' quadrangle. The name is for Mr. A. Arbuckle, a prospector in the early 1850's (Gudde, 1949, p. 13).

Arch Rock [BUTTE]: *relief feature,* 4.5 miles northeast of Pulga along North Fork Feather River (lat. 39°51'10" N, long. 121°23'25" W; sec. 14, T 23 N, R 5 E). Named on Pulga (1979) 7.5' quadrangle.

Argus Gulch [SISKIYOU]: *canyon,* drained by a stream that flows 1 mile to Black Bear Creek 4 miles south-southwest of Sawyers Bar (lat. 41°14'55" N, long. 123°10'10" W). Named on Sawyers Bar (1979) 7.5' quadrangle.

Arkright Flat [SHASTA]: *area,* 2.5 miles east-southeast of Burney Falls (lat. 41°00' N, long. 121°36' W; sec. 2, 11, T 36 N, R 3 E). Named on Burney (1957) and Pondosa (1961) 15' quadrangles.

Arnica Sink [SISKIYOU]: *area,* 1.5 miles northeast of Medicine Lake (lat. 41°35'45" N, long. 121°34'25" W; sec. 1, T 43 N, R 3 E). Named on Medicine Lake (1952) 15' quadrangle.

Arroyo Arenoso: see **Thomes Creek** [TEHAMA].

Arroyo Chico [BUTTE]: *land grant,* at and around Chico. Named on Nord (1951), Ord Ferry (1949), Paradise West (1980), and Richardson Springs (1951) 7.5' quadrangles. Called Rancho de Farwell on Chico (1948), Llano Seco (1948), and Ord Ferry (1949) 7.5' quadrangles. According to Cowan (p. 36), who gave the alternate name "Farwell" for the grant, Edward A. Farwell received 5 leagues in 1844, and Jas. Williams claimed 22,194 acres patented in 1863. According to Perez (p. 53), William Dickey received the grant in 1844, and John Bidwell patented it in 1860.

Arroyo Chico: see **Big Chico Creek** [BUTTE-TEHAMA].

Arroyo de los Picos: see **Butte Creek** [BUTTE-GLENN].

Arroyo de los Saucos: see **Elder Creek** [TEHAMA].

Arthur Lake [SHASTA]: *lake,* 900 feet long, 8.5 miles north-northeast of Whitmore (lat. 40°43'50" N, long. 121°49'45" W; sec. 11, T 33 N, R 1 E). Named on Whitmore (1956) 15' quadrangle.

Artois [GLENN]: *village,* nearly 5 miles north of Willows (lat. 39°37'15" N, long. 122°11'35" W; sec. 3, 4, T 20 N, R 3 W). Named on Willows (1951) 7.5' quadrangle. Called Germantown on Willows (1906) 15' quadrangle. Postal authorities established Germantown post office in 1877 and changed the name to Artois in 1918; the place was renamed for a province in France because of anti-German feeling during World War I (Salley, p. 11, 84).

Arvison Flat [SHASTA]: *area,* 4 miles north of the village of Big Bend (lat. 41°04'35" N, long. 121°55'25" W; sec. 12, T 37 N, R 1 W). Named on Big Bend (1961) 15' quadrangle.

Asbury Peak: see **Black Butte** [SHASTA].

Ash Camp [SHASTA]: *locality,* 3.5 miles north of Shoeinhorse Mountain along McCloud River [SHASTA-SISKIYOU] (lat. 41°07' N, long. 122°03'40" W). Named on Shoeinhorse Mountain (1954) 15' quadrangle.

Ash Creek [SHASTA]:

(1) *stream,* flows nearly 1 mile to Squaw Creek (2) 6 miles east-southeast of Bollibokka Mountain (lat. 40°53'50" N, long. 122°06'50" W; near SE cor. sec. 8, T 35 N, R 2 W). Named on Bollibokka Mountain (1957) 15' quadrangle.

(2) *stream,* flows 22 miles to Sacramento River 1 mile north of Balls Ferry (lat. 40°25'50" N, long. 122°11'45" W). Named on Manton (1956) and Whitmore (1956) 15' quadrangles, and on Balls Ferry (1965) and Tuscan Buttes NE (1965) 7.5' quadrangles. Called Shingle Creek on Mineral (1941) 30' quadrangle.

Ash Creek [SISKIYOU]:

(1) *stream,* flows 4.5 miles to Klamath River 6.25 miles south-southwest of Hornbrook (lat. 41°50' N, long. 122°37'10" W; sec. 13, T 46 N, R 7 W). Named on Hornbrook (1955) 15' quadrangle.

(2) *stream,* flows 20 miles to McCloud River [SHASTA-SISKIYOU] 6.25 miles west of Bartle (lat. 41°15'20" N, long. 121°56'20" W; near W line sec. 2, T 39 N, R 1 W). Named on Bartle (1961) and Shasta (1954) 15' quadrangles. Bartle (1939) 30' quadrangle shows the stream ending at Ash Creek Sink.

Ash Creek: see **Little Dry Creek** [BUTTE].

Ash Creek Butte [SISKIYOU]: *peak,* 14 miles north-northeast of McCloud (lat. 41°26'50" N, long. 122°02'45" W; sec. 35, T 42 N, R 2 W); the peak is north of Ash Creek (2). Altitude 8378 feet. Named on Shasta (1954) 15' quadrangle.

Ash Creek Junction [SISKIYOU]: *locality,* 2.25 miles east-northeast of McCloud along McCloud River Railroad (lat. 41°15'05" N, long. 122°04'40" W; on E line sec. 33, T 40 N, R 2 W). Named on Shasta (1954) 15' quadrangle.

Ash Creek Sink [SISKIYOU]: *area,* 7.25 miles west-northwest of Bartle (lat. 41°18'10" N, long. 121°56'45" W; sec. 22, T 40 N, R 1 W); the place is along Ash Creek (2). Named on Bartle (1961) 15' quadrangle. Bartle (1939) 30' quadrangle has the name "Ash Creek Sink" at the end of Ash Creek (2).

Ash Creek Station [SISKIYOU]: *locality,* about 7.25 miles west of Bartle along McCloud River Railroad near the rail crossing of Ash Creek (2) (lat. 41°16'05" N, long. 121°56'55" W; sec. 34, T 40 N, R 1 W). Named on Bartle (1961) 15' quadrangle.

Ashpan Butte [SHASTA]: *peak,* 8.5 miles north-northwest of Lassen Peak (lat. 40°36'20" N, long. 121°33' W; sec. 20, T 32 N, R 4 E); the peak is less than 0.5 mile east of Ashpan Flat. Named on Manzanita Lake (1956) 15' quadrangle.

Ashpan Flat [SHASTA]: *area,* 9 miles north-northwest of Lassen Peak (lat. 40°36'30" N, long. 121°33'20" W; sec. 19, T 32 N, R 4 E); the place is less than 0.5 mile west of Ashpan Butte. Named on Manzanita Lake (1956) 15' quadrangle.

Aspen Butte: see **Asperin Butte** [SISKIYOU].

Aspen Lake [SISKIYOU]: *lake,* 750 feet long, 13 miles south-southwest of Scott Bar (lat. 41°33'55" N, long. 123°06'25" W). Named on Boulder Peak (1981) 7.5' quadrangle.

Asperin Butte [SISKIYOU]: *hill,* 16 miles north of Bray (lat. 41°29'50" N, long. 121°49' W; near SE cor. sec. 11, T 42 N, R 1 E). Altitude 6087 feet. Named on Bartle (1961) 15' quadrangle. United States Board on Geographic Names (1964, p. 7) rejected the name "Aspen Butte" for the feature.

Atchison Campground [GLENN]: *locality,* 3.25 miles west-northwest of Black Butte (lat. 39°45' N, long. 122°55'30" W; sec. 24, T 22 N, R 10 W); the place is along Atchison Creek. Named on Mendocino Pass (1967) 7.5' quadrangle.

Atchison Creek [GLENN]: *stream,* flows 4.25 miles to Mendocino County 3.25 miles west-northwest of Black Butte (lat. 39°44'50" N, long. 122°55'40" W; sec. 23, T 22 N, R 10 W). Named on Mendocino Pass (1967) and Plaskett Ridge (1967) 7.5' quadrangles.

Athena [GLENN]: *locality,* 3.25 miles east of Fruto along Southern Pacific Railroad (lat. 39°34'55" N, long. 122°23'30" W; near N line sec. 23, T 20 N, R 5 W). Named on Fruto (1944) 15' quadrangle.

Atkins Creek [SHASTA]: *stream,* flows 8 miles to South Cow Creek 5 miles east-southeast of Whitmore (lat. 40°36'35" N, long. 121°49'20" W; sec. 23, T 32 N, R 1 E). Named on Manzanita Lake (1956) and Whitmore (1956) 15' quadrangles. Steger (p. 13-14) associated the name with Quint N. Atkins, who was county surveyor in the 1870's, and noted that the site of Atkins Mill is along the stream about 8 miles east of Whitmore.

Atkins Creek [SISKIYOU]: *stream,* flows 2.5 miles to North Fork Salmon River 7.25 miles north-northeast of Sawyers Bar (lat. 41°24'05" N, long. 123°05'45" W). Named on English Peak (1977) and Yellow Dog Peak (1977) 7.5' quadrangles.

Atkins Meadows [SISKIYOU]: *area,* 2.5 miles east of Bartle along North Fork Creek (lat. 41°15' N, long. 121°46' W). Named on Bartle (1961) and Big Bend (1961) 15' quadrangles. United States Board on Geographic Names (1964, p. 7) rejected the form "Atkins Meadow" for the name.

Atkins Mill: see **Atkins Creek** [SHASTA].

Attebery Bar [SISKIYOU]: *locality,* 7.5 miles northwest of Ukonom Lake along Klamath River (lat. 41°40'05" N, long. 123°26'10" W). Named on Clear Creek (1981) 7.5' quadrangle.

Attlebury Glade [TEHAMA]: *area,* 3 miles east of Tomhead Mountain (lat. 40°08'10" N, long. 122°45'30" W; near W line sec. 3, T 26 N, R 8 W). Named on Yolla Bolly (1954) 15' quadrangle.

Aubrey Creek [SISKIYOU]: *stream,* flows 2.5 miles to Klamath River 5 miles northeast of Dillon Mountain (lat. 41°35'10" N, long. 123°30'50" W). Named on Dillon Mountain (1983) 7.5' quadrangle. Called Alberry Creek on Preston Peak (1922) 30' quadrangle, but United States Board on Geographic Names (1960a, p. 11) rejected this designation for the feature.

Aubrey Ridge [SHASTA]: *ridge,* west-southwest-trending, 3 miles long, 4.5 miles west-northwest of Burney (lat. 40°54'30" N, long. 121°44'30" W). Named on Burney (1957) and Montgomery Creek (1956) 15' quadrangles.

Auger Creek [TEHAMA]: *stream,* flows 3.25 miles to Thomes Creek 4 miles west of Ball Mountain (lat. 39°55'15" N, long. 122°51'35" W; sec. 22, T 24 N, R 9 W). Named on Ball Mountain (1967) and Buck Rock (1967) 7.5' quadrangles.

Auk Auk Ridge [GLENN]: *ridge,* southeast-trending, less than 1 mile long, 6 miles east-southeast of Saint John Mountain (lat. 39°23'35" N, long. 122°35'40" W). Named on Stonyford (1968) 7.5' quadrangle.

Ault Gulch [SISKIYOU]: *canyon,* drained by a stream that flows nearly 2 miles to Garden Gulch (2) 4 miles east-southeast of Cecilville (lat. 41°06'50" N, long. 123°04'10" W). Named on Thompson Peak (1979) 7.5' quadrangle.

Avalanche Gulch [SISKIYOU]:
(1) *canyon,* drained by a stream that flows 1 mile to Butte Fork Applegate River 8 miles north of the village of Seiad Valley (lat. 41°57'25" N, long. 123°13'05" W). Named on Kangaroo Mountain (1980) 7.5' quadrangle.
(2) *canyon,* drained by a stream that flows 3 miles to Bunny Flat 8.5 miles north-northwest of McCloud (lat. 41°21'30" N, long. 122°14' W; sec. 31, T 41 N, R 3 W). Named on Shasta (1954) 15' quadrangle.

Avery Creek [TEHAMA]: *stream,* flows 1.5 miles to Mill Creek (3) 3.5 miles south of Panther Spring (lat. 40°10'55" N, long. 121°47' W; sec. 19, T 27 N, R 2 E). Named on Panther Spring (1953) 15' quadrangle, which shows Avery place near the mouth of the stream. Called Squaw Cr. on Mineral (1941) 30' quadrangle.

Avon: see **Biggs** [BUTTE].

Azalea [SISKIYOU]: *locality,* 2.5 miles south-southeast of the town of Mount Shasta along Southern Pacific Railroad (lat. 41°16'40" N, long. 122°18' W; sec. 27, T 40 N, R 4 W). Named on Weed (1954) 15' quadrangle.

Azalea Lake [SISKIYOU]: *lake,* 650 feet long, 13 miles north-northeast of Happy Camp (lat. 41°58'10" N, long. 123°18' W). Named on Figurehead Mountain (1980) 7.5' quadrangle. United States Board on Geographic Names (1960b, p. 5) rejected the name "Elk Lake" for the feature.

Azelle Creek [SHASTA]: *stream,* flows 1 mile to Pit River Arm Shasta Lake 17 miles southeast of Lamoine (lat. 40°46'40" N, long. 122°15'15" W; sec. 30, T 34 N, R 3 W). Named on Lamoine (1957) 15' quadrangle.

—B—

Babs Fork: see **Kidder Creek** [SISKIYOU].

Babs Lake [SISKIYOU]: *lake,* 4.25 miles long, 12.5 miles north-northeast of Sawyers Bar (lat. 41°27'25" N, long. 123°01'05" W; near S line sec. 29, T 42 N, R 10 W); the lake is at the head of a branch of Babs Fork Kidder Creek. Named on Yellow Dog Peak (1977) 7.5' quadrangle.

Back Action Flat: see **Hillcrest** [SHASTA].

Backbone Creek [SHASTA]: *stream,* flows nearly 7 miles to Backbone Creek Inlet Shasta Lake 11.5 miles south of Lamoine (lat. 40°48'45" N, long. 122°26'05" W; at N line sec. 16, T 34 N, R 5 W); the stream is southwest of Backbone Ridge (1). Named on Lamoine (1957) and Schell Mountain (1950) 15' quadrangles. Called Big Backbone Creek on Averill's (1939) map. Red Bluff (1894) 1° quadrangle has the form "Back Bone Creek" for the name. North Fork enters from the northwest 2.5 miles upstream from the mouth of the main creek; it is 5.5 miles long and is named on Lamoine (1957) and Schell Mountain (1950) 15' quadrangles. South Fork enters from the southwest 2.5 miles south-southeast of Schell Mountain; it is 2 miles long and is named on Schell Mountain (1950) 15' quadrangle.

Backbone Creek: see **Little Backbone Creek** [SHASTA].

Backbone Creek Inlet [SHASTA]: *embayment,* 14 miles south of Lamoine along Shasta Lake (lat. 40°45'30" N, long. 122°24'45" W); the feature is the flooded lower part of the canyon of Backbone Creek. Named on Lamoine (1957) 15' quadrangle. United States Board on Geographic Names (1990, p. 5) approved the name "Big Backbone Creek Inlet" for the embayment.

Backbone Lake [SHASTA]: *lake,* 200 feet long, 16 miles northwest of Lassen Peak (lat. 40°40'35" N, long. 121°10'25" W; sec. 31, T 33 N, R 3 E); the lake is on the northeast side of Jacks Backbone. Named on Manzanita Lake (1956) 15' quadrangle.

Backbone Ridge [SHASTA]:
(1) *ridge,* southeast-trending, 8 miles long, 10 miles south of Lamoine (lat. 40°50' N, long. 122°27'15" W). Named on Lamoine (1957) 15' quadrangle. Steger (p. 14) noted the old name "Devil's Backbone" for the feature, given because the trail there was steep, narrow, and rough.
(2) *ridge,* generally east-trending, 5 miles long, 12 miles north of Millville (lat. 40°43'15" N, long. 122°11'15" W). Named on Bella Vista (1965) 7.5' quadrangle.

Back Meadows [SISKIYOU]: *area,* 12 miles south-southwest of Scott Bar (lat. 41°34'25" N, long. 123°04'50" W). Named on Boulder Peak (1981) 7.5' quadrangle. Called Black Meadows on Scott Bar (1955) 15' quadrangle, but United States Board on Geographic Names (1981c, p. 3) rejected this name for the feature.

Back Meadows Creek [SISKIYOU]: *stream,* flows nearly 2 miles to Shackleford Creek 13 miles south-southwest of Scott Bar (lat. 41°33'35" N, long. 123°03'35" W); the stream heads at Back Meadows. Named on Boulder Peak (1981) 7.5' quadrangle. Called Black Meadows Creek on Scott Bar (1955) 15' quadrangle, but United States Board on Geographic Names (1981c, p. 3) rejected this name for the feature.

Bacon Creek [SHASTA]: *stream,* flows nearly 4 miles to Salt Creek (3) 9 miles north of Millville (lat. 40°40'35" N, long. 122°11'10" W; near NE cor. sec. 34, T 33 N, R 3 W). Named on Bella Vista (1965) 7.5' quadrangle. Called Willow Creek on Redding (1901) 30' quadrangle, but United

States Board on Geographic Names (1966, p. 6) rejected this name.

Bacon Rind Campground [SISKIYOU]: *locality,* 5.5 miles north of Cecilville (lat. 41°13'20" N, long. 123°08'15" W). Named on Cecilville (1979) 7.5' quadrangle.

Badger Creek [SISKIYOU]: *stream,* flows 2 miles to Klamath River 7 miles north of Yreka (lat. 41°49'50" N, long. 122°37'45" W; at S line sec. 14, T 46 N, R 7 W); the stream heads at Badger Mountain. Named on Hornbrook (1955) 15' quadrangle.

Badger Flat [SHASTA]: *area,* 7 miles northeast of Lassen Peak (lat. 40°33'35" N, long. 121°24'35" W; sec. 10, T 31 N, R 5 E). Named on Prospect Peak (1957) 15' quadrangle. The place was called Pine Meadows in the 1850's, and was called Booker Flat in the early 1880's for John R. Booker, who drove a freight wagon pulled by oxen (Schulz, p. 1-2)

Badger Mountain [SHASTA]: *ridge,* west-trending, 1 mile long, 7 miles north-northeast of Lassen Peak (lat. 40°34'30" N, long. 121°26' W; sec. 4, 5, T 31 N, R 5 E); the ridge is 1.5 miles northwest of Badger Flat. Named on Prospect Peak (1957) 15' quadrangle. The name is from Badger Flat (Steger, p. 14). United States Board on Geographic Names (1986c, p. 4) approved the name "Rail Canyon" for a feature, 2 miles long, situated halfway between Badger Mountain and West Prospect Peak (lat. 40°35'59" N, long. 121°24'28" W at the north end), and rejected the name "Box Canyon" for it.

Badger Mountain [SISKIYOU]: *peak,* 9 miles south-southwest of Hornbrook (lat. 41°48' N, long. 122°38'10" W; at NW cor. sec. 35, T 46 N, R 7 W); the peak is at the head of Badger Creek. Named on Hornbrook (1955) 15' quadrangle.

Badger Peak [SISKIYOU]: *peak,* 2 miles northwest of Medicine Lake (lat. 41°35'55" N, long. 121°37'45" W; sec. 4, T 43 N, R 3 E). Altitude 7354 feet. Named on Medicine Lake (1952) 15' quadrangle.

Badger Peak: see **Paradise Craggy** [SISKIYOU].

Bagdad: see **Oroville** [BUTTE].

Bagley Flat [SHASTA]: *area,* 12 miles east-northeast of Bollibokka Mountain (lat. 40°58'45" N, long. 122°00' W; sec. 17, T 36 N, R 1 W); the place is 2 miles southeast of Bagley Mountain. Named on Bollibokka Mountain (1957) and Montgomery Creek (1956) 15' quadrangles.

Bagley Mountain [SHASTA]: *peak,* 5 miles south-southeast of Shoeinhorse Mountain (lat. 41°00'10" N, long. 122°01'40" W); the peak is 2 miles northwest of Bagley Flat. Named on Bollibokka Mountain (1957) and Shoeinhorse Mountain (1954) 15' quadrangles.

Bagley Mountain: see **Little Bagley Mountain** [SHASTA].

Bailey: see **Camp Bailey**, under **Motion** [SHASTA].

Bailey Cove [SHASTA]: *embayment,* 14 miles south-southeast of Lamoine along McCloud River Arm Shasta Lake (lat. 40°48' N, long. 122°18'30" W; sec. 15, T 34 N, R 4 W). Named on Lamoine (1957) 15' quadrangle. The feature is the flooded canyon of former Bailey Creek, which is named on Lamoine (1946) 15' quadrangle.

Bailey Creek [SHASTA]: *stream,* formed by the confluence of North Fork and South Fork, flows 14 miles to North Fork Battle Creek [SHASTA-TEHAMA] 3 miles southeast of Shingletown (lat. 40°27'20" N, long. 121°51'30" W; sec. 15, T 30 N, R 1 E). Named on Manton (1956), Manzanita Lake (1956), and Lassen Peak (1956) 15' quadrangles. The name commemorates Joel Bailey, a pioneer settler near Viola (Hanna, p. 22). North Fork is 5.5 miles long and South Fork is 5 miles long; both forks are named on Lassen Peak (1956) 15' quadrangle.

Bailey Creek: see **Bailey Cove** [SHASTA].

Bailey Creek Meadows [SHASTA]: *area,* 8.5 miles west of Lassen Peak (lat. 40°30'10" N, long. 121°39'45" W; sec. 29, T 31 N, R 3 E); the place is along Bailey Creek. Named on Manzanita Lake (1956) 15' quadrangle.

Bailey Hill [SISKIYOU]: *peak,* 5.5 miles north-northwest of Hornbrook (lat. 41°59'15" N, long. 122°35'45" W; near NE cor. sec. 25, T 48 N, R 7 W). Altitude 4123 feet. Named on Hornbrook (1955) 15' quadrangle. United States Board on Geographic Names (1985a, p. 3) rejected the name "Shelton Rock" for the feature.

Bainbridge Reservoir [SHASTA]: *lake,* 700 feet long, 6.25 miles south of Coble Mountain along Procter Creek (lat. 40°47'50" N, long. 121°22'20" W; at N line sec. 24, T 34 N, R 5 E). Named on Jellico (1957) 15' quadrangle.

Baird [SHASTA]: *locality,* 15 miles south-southeast of Lamoine along McCloud River [SHASTA-SISKIYOU] (lat. 40°47'15" N, long. 122°17'45" W; near E line sec. 23, T 34 N, R 4 W); water of Lake Shasta now covers the site. Named on Redding (1901) 30' quadrangle, which also has the name "Gregory" at or near the place. Postal authorities established Baird post office in 1878, discontinued it in 1920, reestablished it in 1929, and discontinued it in 1933 (Frickstad, p. 178). The name was for Spencer E. Baird, who was appointed the first fish commissioner of California in 1872 (Steger, p. 14). Averill's (1939) map shows a place called Heroult located along the railroad about 2.25 miles southeast of Baird. Postal authorities established Heroult post office in 1907 and discontinued it in 1928 (Frickstad, p. 180). The name "Heroult" was for Dr. Heroult of Paris, whom H.H. Noble of Northern California Power Company engaged to develop an electrolytic smelter that operated from 1907 until 1919 (Steger, p. 39). Averill's (1939) map also shows a place called Wyndham located less than 2 miles south-southwest of Baird along the railroad near the confluence of Pitt River and McCloud River [SHASTA-SISKIYOU]. Red Bluff (1894) 1° quadrangle has the name "Allen" at a place situated about 1 mile northwest of the site of Baird. Baird Caves are located northeast of Baird on the east side of McCloud River [SHASTA-SISKIYOU] (sec. 13, T 34 N, R 4 W); the caves also are known as Stoneman Caves because a skeleton found there appeared to belong to the Stone Age (Steger, p. 14).

Baird Caves: see **Baird** [SHASTA].

Baird Springs [SISKIYOU]: *spring,* 8 miles southeast of Bray (lat. 41°34'15" N, long. 121°51' W; sec. 15, T 43 N, R 1 E). Named on Bray (1950) 15' quadrangle.

Baker Creek [BUTTE]: *stream,* flows 3.5 miles to Clear Creek (2) 5 miles east-southeast of Pulga (lat. 39°46'40" N, long. 121°21'40" W; sec. 12, T 22 N, R 5 E). Named on Soapstone Hill (1979) 7.5' quadrangle.

Baker Creek [SHASTA]:

(1) *stream,* flows 2.5 miles to Kosk Creek 2.5 miles north-northwest of Big Bend (lat. 41°03'20" N, long. 121°55'30" W; sec. 24, T 37 N, R 1 W). Named on Big Bend (1961) 15' quadrangle. Called Bakers Cr. on Averill's (1939) map.

(2) *stream,* flows nearly 2 miles to Duncan Creek 6.25 miles northeast of Arbuckle Mountain (lat. 40°28'20" N, long. 122°47'50" W; near NW cor. sec. 8, T 30 N, R 8 W). Named on Chanchelulla Peak (1951) 15' quadrangle.

Baker Flat [SISKIYOU]: *area,* 8 miles north-northwest of Fort Jones (lat. 41°43'05" N, long. 122°53'20" W; sec. 28, T 45 N, R 9 W). Named on Fort Jones (1955) 15' quadrangle, which shows Baker cabin near the site.

Baker Flat Creek [SHASTA]: *stream,* flows 4 miles to Middle Fork Cottonwood Creek [SHASTA-TEHAMA] 7.25 miles west-southwest of Arbuckle Mountain (lat. 40°20'50" N, long. 122°59' W; near SW cor. sec. 22, T 29 N, R 10 W). Named on Chanchelulla Peak (1951) and Dubakella Mountain (1954) 15' quadrangles. Called Bakers Flat Cr. on Hoaglin (1935) 30' quadrangle.

Baker Gulch [SHASTA]:

(1) *canyon,* drained by a stream that flows 0.5 mile to East Fork Clear Creek nearly 5.5 miles south of Schell Mountain (lat. 40°46'45" N, long. 122°32'30" W; near W line sec. 27, T 34 N, R 6 W). Named on Schell Mountain (1950) 15' quadrangle, which shows Baker mine in the canyon.

(2) *canyon,* drained by a stream that flows 1.25 miles to the canyon of Dry Creek (5) nearly 3 miles south-southwest of Olinda (lat. 40°24'25" N, long. 122°26' W; sec. 33, T 30 N, R 5 W). Named on Olinda (1964) 7.5' quadrangle.

Baker Gulch [SISKIYOU]:

(1) *canyon,* drained by a stream that flows nearly 2 miles to Indian Creek (1) 5 miles north-northwest of Happy Camp (lat. 41°51'50" N, long. 123°24'05" W; at W line sec. 15, T 17 N, R 7 E). Named on Deadman Point (1981) and Happy Camp (1980) 7.5' quadrangles.

(2) *canyon,* drained by a stream that flows 0.5 mile to McAdam Creek 6.5 miles north of Fort Jones (lat. 41°42'10" N, long. 122°48'55" W; sec. 31, T 45 N, R 8 W). Named on Fort Jones (1955) 15' quadrangle.

Baker Gulch [TEHAMA]: *canyon,* drained by a stream that flows 1.5 miles to Cottonwood Creek [SHASTA-TEHAMA] 6.5 miles north of Rosewood (lat. 40°21'40" N, long. 122°35' W; near S line sec. 18, T 29 N, R 6 W). Named on Ono (1952) 15' quadrangle.

Baker Lake [SHASTA]: *lake,* 900 feet long, 13 miles north-northeast of Lassen Peak (lat. 40°38'50" N, long. 121°22'35" W; on W line sec. 12, T 32 N, R 5 E). Named on Prospect Peak (1957) 15' quadrangle.

Bakers: see **Anderson** [SHASTA].

Baker Slough [GLENN]: *stream,* flows 4 miles to Logan Creek 9 miles east of High Peak (lat. 39°25'25" N, long. 122°15'05" W; sec. 12, T 18 N, R 4 W). Named on Logan Ridge (1958) 7.5' quadrangle.

Balcony Cave [SISKIYOU]: *cave,* 12 miles north-northeast of Medicine Lake (lat. 41°44'45" N, long. 121°32'40" W; near W line sec. 17, T 45 N, R 4 E). Named on Medicine Lake (1952) 15' quadrangle.

Bald Butte [SISKIYOU]: *peak,* 17 miles north-northwest of Forks of Salmon (lat. 41°28'40" N, long. 123°28'15" W). Named on Somes Bar (1979) 7.5' quadrangle.

Bald Hill [GLENN]: *peak,* 8.5 miles north-northwest of the village of Elk Creek (lat. 39°43'25" N, long. 122°34'55" W; sec. 31, T 22 N, R 6 W). Altitude 1839 feet. Named on Chrome (1968) 7.5' quadrangle.

Bald Hill [TEHAMA]: *ridge,* north-trending, less than 0.5 mile long, 1.5 miles east of Bend (lat. 40°15'05" N, long. 122°10'35" W; near W line sec. 26, T 28 N, R 3 W). Named on Bend (1965) and Red Bluff East (1951) 7.5' quadrangles.

Bald Hill: see **Bald Mountain** [BUTTE].

Bald Hills [SHASTA]: *range,* center 6 miles south of Ono between North Fork and Middle Fork Cottonwood Creek [SHASTA-TEHAMA] (lat. 40°24' N, long. 122°38' W). Named on Ono (1952) 15' quadrangle. Whitney (p. 320) reported in 1865 that the range has a peculiar appearance because it is destitute of trees and shrubs.

Bald Hornet Creek [SISKIYOU]: *stream,* flows nearly 2 miles to South

Fork Indian Creek (1) 6.5 miles north-northwest of Happy Camp (lat. 41°52'35" N, long. 123°26'40" W). Named on Happy Camp (1980) 7.5' quadrangle.

Bald Knob [TEHAMA]: *peak,* 18 miles west-southwest of Panther Spring (lat. 40°00'30" N, long. 121°55'05" W; on E line sec. 24, T 25 N, R 1 W). Altitude 1498 feet. Named on Panther Spring (1953) 15' quadrangle.

Bald Mountain [BUTTE]: *peak,* 10.5 miles north of Pulga (lat. 39°57'10" N, long. 121°28'55" W; near W line sec. 12, T 24 N, R 4 E). Altitude 5778 feet. Named on Kimshew Point (1979) 7.5' quadrangle. Called Bald Hill on Bidwell Bar (1897) 30' quadrangle

Bald Mountain [SHASTA]:

(1) *peak,* 5.25 miles west-northwest of Shoeinhorse Mountain (lat. 41°06' N, long. 122°09'50" W; sec. 35, T 38 N, R 3 W). Altitude 4697 feet. Named on Shoeinhorse Mountain (1954) 15' quadrangle.

(2) *peak,* 6 miles north-northeast of Big Bend (lat. 41°05'50" N, long. 121°51'10" W; near W line sec. 3, T 37 N, R 1 E). Altitude 5536 feet. Named on Big Bend (1961) 15' quadrangle.

(3) *mountain,* 2 miles northwest of Coble Mountain (lat. 40°54' N, long. 121°22'35" W). Altitude 5578 feet. Named on Jellico (1957) 15' quadrangle.

Bald Mountain [SISKIYOU]:

(1) *peak,* 6.5 miles north-northwest of Orleans, which is in Humboldt County (lat. 41°23'35" N, long. 123°34'30" W). Named on Bark Shanty Gulch (1974) 7.5' quadrangle.

(2) *peak,* 11.5 miles south of Condrey Mountain (lat. 41°46'30" N, long. 122°57' W; sec. 35, T 46 N, R 10 W). Altitude 5493 feet. Named on Condrey Mountain (1955) 15' quadrangle.

Bald Mountain Creek [SHASTA]: *stream,* flows 1.5 miles to McCloud River [SHASTA-SISKIYOU] 4 miles west-northwest of Shoeinhorse Mountain (lat. 41°05'45" N, long. 122°08'10" W); the stream is 1.5 miles east of Bald Mountain (1). Named on Shoeinhorse Mountain (1954) 15' quadrangle.

Bald Mountain Reservoir [SHASTA]: *lake,* 1200 feet long, 2.5 miles west-southwest of Coble Mountain (lat. 40°52'25" N, long. 121°23'35" W; at SW cor. sec. 23, T 35 N, R 5 E); the lake is 2 miles south-southwest of Bald Mountain (3). Named on Jellico (1957) 15' quadrangle.

Bald Mountain Ridge [SISKIYOU]: *ridge,* south-southeast trending, 5 miles long, center 5.5 miles west-southwest of Happy Camp (lat. 41°46'15" N, long. 123°29'05" W); Baldy Mountain is at the north end of the ridge. Named on Clear Creek (1981) and Happy Camp (1980) 7.5' quadrangles.

Bald Rock: see **Big Bald Rock** [BUTTE]; **Little Bald Rock** [BUTTE].

Bald Rock Canyon [BUTTE]: *canyon,* about 4 miles long, along Middle Fork Feather River 3.25 miles southeast of the village of Brush Creek (lat. 39°39'05" N, long. 121°17'45" W). Named on Brush Creek (1970) 7.5' quadrangle.

Bald Rock Dome [BUTTE]: *relief feature,* 3 miles south-southeast of the village of Brush Creek (lat. 39°39'15" N, long. 121°18'25" W). Named on Brush Creek (1970) 7.5' quadrangle.

Baldwin Creek [SHASTA]: *stream,* flows 9 miles to Battle Creek [SHASTA-TEHAMA] 10 miles east of Balls Ferry (lat. 40°25'35" N, long. 122°00'25" W; at W line sec. 29, T 30 N, R 1 W). Named on Manton (1956) 15' quadrangle, and on Tuscan Buttes NE (1965) 7.5' quadrangle. Called Woodhall Creek on Averill's (1939) map. Steger (p. 15) associated the name "Baldwin" with J.H. Baldwin, who homesteaded in the neighborhood in 1872. Steger (p. 66) described Woodall Creek as a branch of Baldwin Creek, and associated the name "Woodall" with George Woodall, who owned a mill at Shingletown.

Baldwin Reservoir [SHASTA]: *lake,* 1400 feet long, 1.5 miles east-northeast of Shingletown (lat. 40°29'50" N, long. 121°51'50" W; sec. 33, T 31 N, R 1 E). Named on Mineral (1941) 30' quadrangle. Northern California Power Company built the reservoir in 1911 (Steger, p. 15).

Baldy: see **Little Baldy** [SISKIYOU].

Baldy Gap [SISKIYOU]: *pass,* 9.5 miles north of Fort Jones (lat. 41°44'45" N, long. 122°50'05" W; near W line sec. 13, T 45 N, R 9 W); the pass is just north-northwest of Indian Creek Baldy. Named on Fort Jones (1955) 15' quadrangle.

Baldy Mountain [SISKIYOU]: *peak,* 6.25 miles west of Happy Camp (lat. 41°48'10" N, long. 123°29'50" W). Altitude 5745 feet. Named on Happy Camp (1980) 7.5' quadrangle. United States Board on Geographic Names (1967b, p. 2) approved the name "Baldy Mountain Ridge" for a ridge, 5 miles long, that trends south from Baldy Mountain.

Baldy Mountain Ridge: see **Baldy Mountain** [SISKIYOU].

Bales Mountain [SHASTA]: *peak,* 8 miles north-northeast of the village of Montgomery Creek (lat. 40°56'15" N, long. 121°50'15" W). Altitude 5105 feet. Named on Montgomery Creek (1956) 15' quadrangle.

Ball: see **Mount Hebron** [SISKIYOU] (2).

Ball Mountain [TEHAMA]: *peak,* 32 miles west of Corning (lat. 39°55'55" N, long. 122°47' W; near S line sec. 17, T 24 N, R 8 W). Altitude 6557 feet. Named on Ball Mountain (1967) 7.5' quadrangle.

Ball Rock [TEHAMA]: *peak,* 12 miles west-northwest of Paskenta (lat. 39°58' N, long. 122°44'15" W; near E line sec. 3, T 24 N, R 8 W). Altitude 6663 feet. Named on Riley Ridge (1967) 7.5' quadrangle.

Balls Camp [TEHAMA]: *locality,* 6 miles southwest of Mineral along Deadhorse Creek (lat. 40°17'55" N, long. 121°41'25" W; sec. 12, T 28 N, R 2 E). Site named on Lassen Peak (1956) 15' quadrangle.

Balls Ferry [SHASTA]: *locality,* 6 miles east-southeast of Anderson on the west side of Sacramento River (lat. 40°25'05" N, long. 122°11'40" W). Named on Balls Ferry (1965) 7.5' quadrangle. Called Ball's Ferry on Red Bluff (1894) 1° quadrangle. Major P.B. Reading moved his ferry to the place in 1868 and sold it to William Ball the same year; the community of Ball's Ferry is gone, but the name is retained by present Balls Ferry, a fishing resort across the river from the old townsite (Steger, p. 15). Postal authorities established Parkville post office in 1871, moved it 1 mile south and changed the name to Ball's Ferry in 1875, and discontinued it in 1916; the name "Parkville" was for John W. Park, a settler of 1850 (Salley, 14, 167). They established Battle Creek post office 3 miles south of Ball's Ferry post office in Tehama County in 1865 and discontinued in 1877 (Salley, p. 16).

Ball's Ranch: see **Mount Hebron** [SISKIYOU] (2).

Bally Mountain [SISKIYOU]: *peak,* 8 miles south-southwest of Yreka (lat. 41°37'45" N, long. 122°41'15" W; near W line sec. 29, T 44 N, R 7 W). Altitude 5512 feet. Named on Yreka (1954) 15' quadrangle.

Bally Mountain: see **Shasta Bally** [SHASTA].

Balsam Creek [BUTTE]: *stream,* flows 2.5 miles to Big Kimshew Creek 10.5 miles north of Pulga (lat. 39°57'25" N, long. 121°27' W; near NE cor. sec. 7, T 24 N, R 5 E). Named on Kimshew Point (1979) 7.5' quadrangle.

Balsum Hill: see **Big Kimshew Creek** [BUTTE].

Bangor [BUTTE]: *village,* 11.5 miles southeast of Oroville (lat. 39°23'20" N, long. 121°24'15" W; mainly in sec. 27, T 18 N, R 5 E). Named on Bangor (1947) 7.5' quadrangle. Postal authorities established Bangor post office in 1857 (Frickstad, p. 8). J.R. Lambert and his brother opened a store at the place in 1855, and the mining camp that developed there took the name of their hometown in Maine (Wells and Chambers, p. 264). Postal authorities established Millers Ranch post office 7 miles northeast of Bangor in 1862 and discontinued it in 1865 (Salley, p. 140). L.C. Hyland opened a store about a quarter of a mile from the site of Bangor in 1855 and laid out a town there that he called Hylandville, but the town failed to develop (Wells and Chambers, p. 264).

Baranca Colorada: see **Red Bank Creek** [TEHAMA].

Barber [BUTTE]: *locality,* 1 mile south of downtown Chico along Southern Pacific Railroad (lat. 39°42'50" N, long. 121°50'05" W; sec. 35, T 22 N, R 1 E). Named on Chico (1948) 7.5' quadrangle. The name is for O.C. Barber, president of Diamond Match Company, which had a plant at the place (Dunn, F.D., p. 5).

Barber Gulch [SHASTA]: *canyon,* drained by a stream that flows 0.5 mile to Dog Creek 2.25 miles south of Lamoine (lat. 40°56'30" N, long. 122°26'10" W). Named on Lamoine (1957) 15' quadrangle.

Barb Ridge [GLENN]: *ridge,* west-northwest-trending, 1 mile long, 2.5 miles south of Black Butte (lat. 39°41'15" N, long. 122°52'10" W). Named on Plaskett Meadows (1967) 7.5' quadrangle.

Bardees Bar [BUTTE]: *locality,* 2.5 miles south of Pulga along North Fork Feather River (lat. 39°46'05" N, long. 121°27'30" W; at N line sec. 18, T 22 N, R 5 E). Named on Pulga (1979) 7.5' quadrangle. F.D. Dunn (p. 5) gave the names "Bardee Bar," "Barteece Bar," and "Burdys Bar" as alternate names for the place.

Bare Mountain [SISKIYOU]: *peak,* 13 miles north-northwest of Happy Camp (lat. 41°59'10" N, long. 123°26'40" W). Altitude 5995 feet. Named on Deadman Point (1981) 7.5' quadrangle.

Bare Rock [SHASTA]: *peak,* 10.5 miles north-northeast of the village of Big Bend (lat. 41°09' N, long. 121°48'35" W). Altitude 4239 feet. Named on Big Bend (1961) 15' quadrangle.

Barker Camp [TEHAMA]: *locality,* 7.25 miles west-northwest of Tomhead Mountain (lat. 40°11'10" N, long. 122°56' W; near E line sec. 13, T 27 N, R 10 W). Named on Yolla Bolly (1954) 15' quadrangle.

Barkhouse Creek [SISKIYOU]: *stream,* flows 6 miles to Klamath River 10 miles southeast of Condrey Mountain (lat. 41°49'50" N, long. 122°50'45" W; sec. 13, T 46 N, R 9 W). Named on Condrey Mountain (1955) 15' quadrangle. Crawford (1894, p. 286) used the form "Barkehouse Creek" for the name.

Barkhouse Gulch: see **Little Barkhouse Gulch** [SISKIYOU].

Barkley Mountain [TEHAMA]: *peak,* 3.25 miles north-northwest of Polk Springs (lat. 40°09'35" N, long. 121°41'25" W; near SE cor. sec. 25, T 27 N, R 2 E). Altitude 4488 feet. Named on Butte Meadows (1958) 15' quadrangle.

Bark Shanty Camp [SISKIYOU]: *locality,* 9 miles north of Orleans, which is in Humboldt County (lat. 41°26'05" N, long. 123°33'25" W); the place is near the head of Bark Shanty Gulch. Named on Bark Shanty Gulch (1974) 7.5' quadrangle.

Bark Shanty Creek [SISKIYOU]:

(1) *stream,* flows 2 miles to Grider Creek 5.25 miles south-southwest of the village of Seiad Valley (lat. 44°46' N, long. 123°13'20" W). Named on Seiad Valley (1980) 7.5' quadrangle.

(2) *stream,* flows less than 1 mile to Taylor Creek (1) 7.25 miles east-northeast of Cecilville (lat. 41°10'45" N, long. 123°00'20" W). Named on Grasshopper Ridge (1979) 7.5' quadrangle.

Bark Shanty Gulch [SISKIYOU]: *canyon,* drained by a stream that flows 5.25 miles to Rock Creek [BUTTE-TEHAMA] (1) 13 miles north of Orleans, which is in Humboldt County (lat. 41°29'45" N, long. 123°34' W). Named on Bark Shanty Gulch (1974) 7.5' quadrangle.

Barn Gulch [SISKIYOU]: *canyon,* 1 mile long, opens into the canyon of Moffett Creek 12 miles south-southwest of Yreka (lat. 41°33'50" N, long. 122°41'15" W). Named on Yreka (1954) 15' quadrangle.

Barn Hollow [TEHAMA]: *canyon,* 1.5 miles long, 4 miles south-southwest of Campbell Mound (lat. 39°55'40" N, long. 121°51'40" W). Named on Campbell Mound (1952) 7.5' quadrangle.

Barntop Mountain [SISKIYOU]: *peak,* 8 miles northeast of Mount Dome (lat. 41°52'45" N, long. 121°34'20" W; sec. 25, T 47 N, R 3 E). Altitude 5122 feet. Named on Mount Dome (1950) 15' quadrangle.

Barnum Flat Reservoir [SISKIYOU]: *intermittent lake,* 1.5 miles long, 18 miles east-northeast of Bartle (lat. 41°19'15" N, long. 121°28'15" W; mainly in sec. 11, T 40 N, R 4 E). Named on White Horse (1962) 15' quadrangle.

Barnum Mill [BUTTE]: *locality,* 17 miles north-northeast of Paradise (lat. 39°59'55" N, long. 121°31'40" W). Named on Chico (1895) 30' quadrangle.

Barrel Gulch [SHASTA]: *canyon,* 0.5 mile long, 5.5 miles north of Schell Mountain (lat. 40°56'05" N, long. 122°31'15" W; sec. 35, T 36 N, R 6 W). Named on Schell Mountain (1950) 15' quadrangle.

Barrel Spring [SISKIYOU]: *spring,* 3.25 miles north of Forks of Salmon (lat. 41°18'20" N, long. 123°20'05" W). Named on Forks of Salmon (1978) 7.5' quadrangle.

Barrett Lake [SHASTA]: *lake,* 700 feet long, 16 miles north of Lassen Peak (lat. 40°43' N, long. 121°34'30" W; near W line sec. 18, T 33 N, R 4 E). Named on Manzanita Lake (1956) 15' quadrangle.

Barrier Peak: see **Raker Peak** [SHASTA].

Bars Creek [SHASTA]: *stream,* flows 1 mile to Squaw Creek (2) 7.25 miles southeast of Bollibokka Mountain (lat. 40°51'15" N, long. 122°07'30" W; near S line sec. 29, T 35 N, R 2 W). Named on Bollibokka Mountain (1957) 15' quadrangle.

Barteece Bar: see **Bardees Bar** [BUTTE].

Bartle [SISKIYOU]: *locality,* 25 miles south-southwest of Medicine Lake along McCloud River Railroad (lat. 41°15'25" N, long. 121°49'15" W; sec. 2, T 39 N, R 1 E). Named on Bartle (1961) 15' quadrangle. California Mining Bureau's (1917a) map shows a place called Glazier located 4 miles west of Bartle along the railroad. Postal authorities established Glazier post office in 1888, moved it 0.5 mile northeast in 1906 when they changed the name to Bartle, discontinued it in 1911, reestablished it in 1915, and discontinued it in 1924—the name "Bartle" was for Abraham Bartle and Jerome Bartle, cattlemen and operators of a resort (Salley, p. 15, 85). California Mining Bureau's (1917a) map shows a place called McGavis located about 17 miles north of Bartle at the end of a rail line.

Bartle Creek [SISKIYOU]: *stream,* flows 6 miles to end near Bartle (lat. 41°15'45" N, long. 121°49'15" W; near N line sec. 2, T 39 N, R 1 E). Named on Bartle (1961) 15' quadrangle.

Bartle Gap [SHASTA]: *pass,* 11.5 miles north-northeast of the village of Big Bend (lat. 41°10'10" N, long. 121°49'10" W; near S line sec. 35, T 39 N, R 1 E). Named on Big Bend (1961) 15' quadrangle.

Basin: see **The Basin** [GLENN].

Basin Cedar: see **Cedar Basin** [SISKIYOU] (1).

Basin Creek [GLENN]: *stream,* flows 1 mile to Middle Creek 9 miles south of Black Butte (lat. 39°35'35" N, long. 122°51'30" W; near N line sec. 15, T 20 N, R 9 W); the feature called The Basin is near the mouth of the creek. Named on Kneecap Ridge (1967) 7.5' quadrangle.

Basin Creek [TEHAMA]: *stream,* flows 2.5 miles to North Fork Elder Creek 7 miles south-southwest of Wakefield Flat (lat. 40°01'55" N, long. 122°41'10" W; sec. 7, T 25 N, R 7 W). Named on Raglin Ridge (1967) 7.5' quadrangle.

Basin Creek: see **Little Basin Creek** [TEHAMA].

Basin Gulch [SHASTA]: *canyon,* drained by a stream that flows 3 miles to Harrison Gulch 6 miles southwest of Arbuckle Mountain (lat. 40°21'20" N, long. 122°57'40" W; sec. 23, T 29 N, R 10 W). Named on Chanchelulla Peak (1951) and Dubakella Mountain (1954) 15' quadrangles.

Basin Gulch [TEHAMA]: *canyon,* drained by a stream that flows less than 1 mile to Wells Creek nearly 5 miles south-southeast of Beegum Peak (lat. 40°15'15" N, long. 122°50'40" W; near N line sec. 26, T 28 N, R 9 W). Named on Chanchelulla Peak (1951) 15' quadrangle.

Basin Hollow [SHASTA]: *locality,* about 5 miles east-northeast of Millville (lat. 40°35' N, long. 122°05' W). Named on Red Bluff (1894) 1° quadrangle.

Basin Hollow Creek [SHASTA]: *stream,* flows 7.5 miles to Cow Creek 1.25 miles east of Millville (lat. 40°32'40" N, long. 122°09' W; sec. 13, T 31 N, R 3 W). Named on Palo Cedro (1965) 7.5' quadrangle.

Bass: see **Mountain Gate** [SHASTA].

Bass Mountain [SHASTA]: *peak,* 3.5 miles north of the town of Central Valley (lat. 40°43'35" N, long. 122°22' W; sec. 7, T 33 N, R 4 W); the peak is 0.5 mile north of present Saddle Back. Altitude 2784 feet. Named on Project City (1957) 7.5' quadrangle. The feature first was called Saddle Back Mountain, but the name was changed in 1911 to honor John S.P. Bass, an early settler and assemblyman from Shasta County and Trinity County (Steger, p. 16).

Bastard Canyon [SHASTA]: *canyon,* drained by a stream that flows 1 mile to Salt Creek (6) 9 miles southeast of Lamoine (lat. 40°54' N, long. 122°17'25" W; sec. 11, T 35 N, R 4 W). Named on Lamoine (1957) 15' quadrangle.

Bat Butte [SISKIYOU]: *relief feature,* 11 miles north-northeast of Medicine Lake (lat. 41°44'20" N, long. 121°33'10" W; sec. 18, T 45 N, R 4 E). Named on Medicine Lake (1952) 15' quadrangle.

Batchelor Point [BUTTE]: *peak,* 1.25 miles southwest of Pulga (lat. 39°47'35" N, long. 121°28' W; at W line sec. 6, T 22 N, R 5 E). Altitude 3466 feet. Named on Pulga (1979) 7.5' quadrangle.

Bathtub Spring [BUTTE]: *spring,* 10 miles northwest of the village of Elk Creek (lat. 39°42'30" N, long. 122°39'05" W). Named on Alder Springs (1967) 7.5' quadrangle.

Battle Creek [SHASTA]: *stream,* flows 2.25 miles to McCloud River [SHASTA-SISKIYOU] 5 miles north of Shoeinhorse Mountain (lat. 41°08'20" N, long. 122°04'55" W). Named on Shoeinhorse Mountain (1954) 15' quadrangle. Called Buck Cr. on Dunsmuir (1935) 30' quadrangle.

Battle Creek [SHASTA-TEHAMA]: *stream,* formed by the confluence of North Fork and South Fork, flows 16 miles, mainly along Shasta-Tehama County line, to Sacramento River 7.25 miles north-northeast of Bend (lat. 40°21'20" N, long. 122°10'25" W). Named on Manton (1956) 15' quadrangle, and on Balls Ferry (1965), Bend (1965), and Tuscan Buttes NE (1965) 7.5' quadrangles. Work called the stream Sycamore Creek in 1832, and Fremont called it Noza Creek; the name "Battle Creek" came in 1849 after a bloody battle between trappers and Indians (Steger, p. 16). North Fork, which heads in Shasta County, is 29 miles long and is named on Manton (1956), Manzanita Lake (1956), and Whitmore (1956) 15' quadrangles; it forms part of Shasta-Tehama County line. South Fork, which is in Tehama County, is formed by the confluence of Nanny Creek and Summit Creek; it is 27 miles long and is named on Lassen Peak (1956) and Manton (1956) 15' quadrangles.

Battle Creek: see **Balls Ferry** [SHASTA].

Battle Creek Meadows [TEHAMA]: *area,* along South Fork Battle Creek [SHASTA-TEHAMA] at Mineral (lat. 40°20'15" N, long. 121°36' W). Named on Lassen Peak (1956) 15' quadrangle.

Battle Creek Reservoir: see **North Battle Creek Reservoir** [SHASTA].

Baum Lake [SHASTA]: *lake,* 8 miles east-northeast of Burney along Hat Creek (lat. 40°56'20" N, long. 121°32'40" W; sec. 29, 32, T 36 N, R 4 E). Named on Burney (1957) 15' quadrangle.

Baxters Gulch [SHASTA]: *canyon,* drained by a stream that flows less than 1 mile to Squaw Creek Arm Shasta Lake 10.5 miles south of Bollibokka Mountain (lat. 40°47' N, long. 122°13'10" W; near SW cor. sec. 21, T 34 N, R 3 W). Named on Bollibokka Mountain (1957) 15' quadrangle.

Bayes: see **Jerome** [SISKIYOU].

Bayha [SHASTA]: *locality,* 10.5 miles north-northeast of Redding (lat. 40°43'40" N, long. 122°19'30" W; sec. 9, T 33 N, R 4 W). Named on Redding (1901) 30' quadrangle. Postal authorities established Bayha post office in 1900 and discontinued it in 1907 (Frickstad, p. 178). The place was the headquarters of an unsuccessful mining company organized by George Bayha (Steger, p. 16).

Bayles: see **Delta** [SHASTA].

Bayliss [GLENN]: *locality,* 9 miles east-northeast of Willows (lat. 39°34'55" N, long. 122°02'45" W). Named on Glenn (1951) 7.5' quadrangle.

Beal Creek [SHASTA]: *stream,* flows 4.5 miles to South Cow Creek 6.25 miles east-southeast of Whitmore (lat. 40°36'15" N, long. 121°47'50" W; near SW cor. sec. 19, T 32 N, R 2 E). Named on Manzanita Lake (1956) and Whitmore (1956) 15' quadrangles. Called Beale Creek by Steger (p. 16), who noted that Joe Beale and Cynthia Beale homesteaded near the stream.

Bean Creek [BUTTE]: *stream,* flows 3.5 miles to Middle Fork Feather River 7 miles north-northwest of Forbestown (lat. 39°36'35" N, long. 121°19'40" W; sec. 8, T 20 N, R 6 E). Named on Brush Creek (1970) and Forbestown (1970) 7.5' quadrangles.

Bean Creek Bar [BUTTE]: *locality,* 7 miles north-northwest of Forbestown along Middle Fork Feather River (lat. 39°36'30" N, long. 121°19'20" W; sec. 8, T 20 N, R 6 E); the place is at the mouth of Bean Creek. Named on Big Bend Mountain (1948) 15' quadrangle. Water of Lake Oroville now covers the site.

Bean Gulch [SISKIYOU]: *canyon,* drained by a stream that heads in the State of Oregon and flows nearly 1 mile in Siskiyou County to Middle Fork Applegate River 15 miles north-northeast of Happy Camp (lat. 41°59'40" N, long. 123°16'33" W). Named on Figurehead Mountain (1980) 7.5' quadrangle.

Beans Camp [SISKIYOU]:

(1) *locality,* 5.5 miles west of Happy Camp (lat. 41°47'30" N, long. 123°29'30" W). Named on Happy Camp (1980) 7.5' quadrangle.
(2) *locality,* 10.5 miles north-northwest of Orleans, which is in Humboldt County (lat. 41°26'40" N, long. 123°36'40" W); the place is near the head of Beans Gulch. Named on Bark Shanty Gulch (1974) 7.5' quadrangle.

Beans Gulch [SISKIYOU]: *canyon,* drained by a stream that flows 4.5 miles to Bark Shanty Gulch 12.5 miles north of Orleans, which is in Humboldt County (lat. 41°28'40" N, long. 123°33'20" W); the canyon is southeast of Beans Ridge. Named on Bark Shanty Gulch (1974) 7.5' quadrangle.

Beansoup Bar [BUTTE]: *locality,* 6.5 miles north-northeast of Paradise along West Branch Feather River at the mouth of Little West Fork (lat. 39°50'30" N, long. 121°33'30" W; near NW cor. sec. 20, T 23 N, R 4 E). Named on Paradise East (1980) 7.5' quadrangle.

Beans Ridge [SISKIYOU]: *ridge,* northeast-trending, 3.25 miles long, 12 miles north of Orleans, which is in Humboldt County (lat. 41°28'15" N, long. 123°35'10" W); the ridge is northwest of Beans Gulch. Named on Bark Shanty Gulch (1974) 7.5' quadrangle.

Bear Butte: see **Signal Butte** [SISKIYOU] (1).

Bear Camp [SHASTA]: *locality,* 6.5 miles north of the village of Big Bend along Kosk Creek (lat. 41°06'55" N, long. 121°54' W; at N line sec. 31, T 38 N, R 1 E). Named on Big Bend (1961) 15' quadrangle.

Bear Canyon [GLENN]: *canyon,* drained by a stream that flows 3.25 miles to Grindstone Creek [GLENN-TEHAMA] 13 miles northwest of the village of Elk Creek (lat. 39°44'15" N, long. 122°43' W). Named on Alder Springs (1967) 7.5' quadrangle.

Bear Canyon [SHASTA]: *canyon,* drained by a stream that flows 3.5 miles to Pit River 13 miles southeast of Bollibokka Mountain (lat. 40°49'05" N, long. 122°01'25" W; sec. 7, T 34 N, R 1 W). Named on Bollibokka Mountain (1957) and Montgomery Creek (1956) 15' quadrangles. Averill's (1939) map has the name "Bear Cr." for the stream in the canyon.

Bear Canyon [SISKIYOU]: *canyon,* drained by a stream that flows 5.5 miles to Shovel Creek 15 miles northwest of Macdoel (lat. 47°57'10" N, long. 122°10'40" W; at S line sec. 35, T 48 N, R 3 W). Named on Macdoel (1954) 15' quadrangle.

Bear Canyon [TEHAMA]: *canyon,* drained by a stream that flows 2 miles to Mill Creek (3) nearly 7 miles south-southwest of Panther Spring (lat. 40°09'20" N, long. 121°48'55" W). Named on Panther Spring (1953) 7.5' quadrangle.

Bear Canyon Campground [SISKIYOU]: *locality,* 12.5 miles west-northwest of Macdoel (lat. 41°53'30" N, long. 122°13'30" W; near NW cor. sec. 28, T 47 N, R 3 W); the place is near the head of Bear Canyon. Named on Macdoel (1954) 15' quadrangle.

Bearcap Mountain [SISKIYOU]: *peak,* 12 miles south-southeast of Condrey Mountain (lat. 41°47'45" N, long. 122°50'20" W; sec. 36, T 46 N, R 9 W). Altitude 4173 feet. Named on Condrey Mountain (1955) 15' quadrangle.

Bear Corral Gulch [SISKIYOU]: *canyon,* 1 mile long, opens into the canyon of Moffett Creek 11 miles south-southwest of Yreka (lat. 41°35'05" N, long. 122°42'10" W; near SE cor. sec. 12, T 43 N, R 8 W). Named on Yreka (1954) 15' quadrangle.

Bear Creek [SHASTA]:
(1) *stream,* flows 2 miles to Clear Creek 4.25 miles west-southwest of Schell Mountain (lat. 40°49'50" N, long. 122°36'20" W; sec. 1, T 34 N, R 7 W). Named on Schell Mountain (1950) 15' quadrangle.
(2) *stream,* formed by the confluence of North Fork and South Fork, flows 20 miles to Sacramento River 1.5 miles north-northwest of Balls Ferry (lat. 40°26'10" N, long. 122°12'10" W; sec. 21, T 30 N, R 3 W). Named on Millville (1953) 15' quadrangle, and on Balls Ferry (1965) 7.5' quadrangle. North Fork is 8 miles long and South Fork is 14 miles long; both forks are named on Whitmore (1956) 15' quadrangle. On Lassen Peak (1894) 1° quadrangle, present South Fork is called Bear Creek.

Bear Creek [SHASTA-SISKIYOU]: *stream,* heads in Shasta County and flows 21 miles, partly in Siskiyou County, to Fall River 9 miles north-northeast of Burney Falls in Shasta County (lat. 41°06'50" N, long. 121°33'20" W; sec. 19, T 38 N, R 4 E). Named on Pondosa (1961) 15' quadrangle. North Fork enters from the northwest 1 mile west-southwest of Pondosa; it is 3 miles long and is named on Pondosa (1961) 15' quadrangle. United States Board on Geographic Names (1964) rejected the name "North Fork Bear Creek" for present North Fork Creek [SISKIYOU], which is a tributary to North Fork Bear Creek [SHASTA-SISKIYOU].

Bear Creek [SISKIYOU]:
(1) *stream,* flows about 5.5 miles to Elk Creek 5 miles north-northeast of Okonom Lake (lat. 41°38'40" N, long. 123°18'25" W); the stream heads at Bear Lake (2) and goes through Bear Valley (2). Named on Grider Valley (1981) and Huckleberry Mountain (1980) 7.5' quadrangles.
(2) *stream,* heads in the State of Oregon and flows 4.5 miles in Siskiyou County to West Fork Beaver Creek (1) 7.25 miles east-northeast of Condrey Mountain (lat. 41°57' N, long. 122°50'30" W; sec. 1, T 47 N, R 9 W). Named on Condrey Mountain (1955) 15' quadrangle.
(3) *stream,* flows 2.5 miles to Dutch Creek (4) 7.5 miles west of Hornbrook (lat. 41°53'45" N, long. 122°41'50" W; near E line sec. 30, T 47 N, R 7 W). Named on Hornbrook (1955) 15' quadrangle.
(4) *stream,* flows nearly 2 miles to Sacramento River at Dunsmuir (lat. 41°13'50" N, long. 122°16'30" W; sec. 13, T 39 N, R 4 W). Named on Dunsmuir (1954) 15' quadrangle.

Bear Creek [TEHAMA]: *stream,* flows 2 miles to Deer Creek (2) 2.5 miles south-southwest of Polk Springs (lat. 40°05' N, long. 121°40'50" W; sec. 30, T 26 N, R 3 E). Named on Butte Meadows (1958) 15' quadrangle.

Bear Creek: see **Bear Canyon** [SHASTA]; **Big Bear Creek** [TEHAMA]; **Little Bear Creek** [TEHAMA].

Bear Creek Canyon [SHASTA]: *canyon,* 9 miles long, along Bear Creek (2) above a point about 4 miles east-southeast of Millville (lat. 40°31'45" N, long. 122°06'20" W; near W line sec. 21, T 31 N, R 2 W). Named on Millville (1953) and Whitmore (1956) 15' quadrangles.

Bear Creek Falls [SHASTA]: *waterfall,* 7 miles south-southwest of Whitmore (lat. 40°31'55" N, long. 121°56'45" W; near N line sec. 23, T 31 N, R 1 W); the feature is along South Fork Bear Creek (2). Named on Whitmore (1956) 15' quadrangle.

Bear Creek Ridge [SHASTA]: *ridge,* southwest-trending, 3 miles long, 6 miles south-southwest of Whitmore (lat. 40°33' N, long. 121°57'30" W); the ridge is northwest of North Fork Bear Creek (2). Named on Whitmore (1956) 15' quadrangle.

Bear Den [TEHAMA]: *peak,* 9 miles west of Paskenta (lat. 39°52' N, long. 122°42'45" W; sec. 12, T 23 N, R 8 W). Named on Hall Ridge (1967) 7.5' quadrangle.

Bear Flat: see **Big Bear Flat** [SISKIYOU]; **Little Bear Flat** [SHASTA].

Bearground Gulch [SISKIYOU]: *canyon,* drained by a stream that flows 1.5 miles to Jaynes Canyon 3.5 miles east-northeast of Condrey Mountain (lat. 41°57' N, long. 122°54'40" W; near E line sec. 5, T 47 N, R 9 W). Named on Condrey Mountain (1955) 15' quadrangle.

Bearground Spring [SISKIYOU]: *spring,* 3.25 miles northeast of Condrey Mountain (lat. 41°58'10" N, long. 122°55'45" W; at E line sec. 31, T 48 N, R 9 W). Named on Condrey Mountain (1955) 15' quadrangle.

Bear Gulch [BUTTE]:
(1) *canyon,* drained by a stream that heads in Plumas County and flows 1 mile to Little North Fork [of Middle Fork Feather River] 6 miles northeast of the village of Brush Creek in Butte County (lat. 39°44'50" N, long. 121°15'05" W). Named on Brush Creek (1970) and Cascade (1948) 7.5' quadrangles.
(2) *canyon,* drained by a stream that flows 1 mile to Lost Creek 2.5 miles northwest of Clipper Mills (lat. 39°33'45" N, long. 121°11'05" W; near W line sec. 27, T 20 N, R 7 E). Named on Clipper Mills (1948) 7.5' quadrangle.

Bear Gulch [SHASTA]:
(1) *canyon,* drained by a stream that flows 2 miles to Clear Creek 8 miles north-northwest of Schell Mountain (lat. 40°57'30" N, long. 122°35' W; at S line sec. 20, T 36 N, R 6 W). Named on Schell Mountain (1950) 15' quadrangle.
(2) *canyon,* drained by a stream that flows less than 1 mile to Damnation Creek 6 miles north of Schell Mountain (lat. 40°56'25" N, long. 122°33' W; near NW cor. sec. 34, T 36 N, R 6 W). Named on Schell Mountain (1950) 15' quadrangle.
(3) *canyon,* drained by a stream that flows nearly 2 miles to Cedar Creek 16 miles southeast of Bollibokka Mountain (lat. 40°46'15" N, long. 122°00'20" W; near W line sec. 29, T 34 N, R 1 W). Named on Bollibokka Mountain (1957) 15' quadrangle.
(4) *canyon,* drained by a stream that flows less than 1 mile to Clear Creek 7.25 miles south-southwest of Schell Mountain (lat. 40°46'10" N, long. 122°36'25" W; near S line sec. 25, T 34 N, R 7 W). Named on Schell Mountain (1950) 15' quadrangle.
(5) *canyon,* drained by a stream that flows about 2 miles to Willow Creek (4) 3.5 miles southwest of the village of French Creek (lat. 40°40'10" N, long. 122°41'10" W; near SE cor. sec. 31, T 33 N, R 7 W). Named on French Gulch (1979) 7.5' quadrangle.

Bear Gulch [SISKIYOU]:
(1) *canyon,* drained by a stream that flows 3.5 miles to Rock Creek [BUTTE-TEHAMA] (1) 1.5 miles southwest of Dillon Mountain (lat. 41°30'40" N, long. 123°35'25" W). Named on Dillon Mountain (1983) 7.5' quadrangle.
(2) *canyon,* drained by a stream that flows 1.5 miles to Little South Fork Indian Creek (1) 7.5 miles northwest of Happy Camp (lat. 41°51'20" N, long. 123°29'50" W). Named on Happy Camp (1980) 7.5' quadrangle.
(3) *canyon,* drained by a stream that flows 1 mile to Ash Creek (1) 4.5 miles southwest of Hornbrook (lat. 41°51'55" N, long. 122°37'10" W; at W line sec. 1, T 46 N, R 7 W). Named on Hornbrook (1955) 15' quadrangle.
(4) *canyon,* drained by a stream that flows 1.5 miles to Cook and Green Creek 9 miles north-northeast of the village of Seiad Valley (lat. 41°57'30" N, long. 123°08' W). Named on Kangaroo Mountain (1980) 7.5' quadrangle.

Bear Gulch [TEHAMA]:
(1) *canyon,* drained by a stream that flows 1.25 miles to Beegum Creek [SHASTA-TEHAMA] 1 mile west of Beegum Peak (lat. 40°19' N, long. 122°54'10" W; near S line sec. 32, T 29 N, R 9 W). Named on Chanchelulla Peak (1951) 15' quadrangle.

(2) *canyon,* drained by a stream that flows 1.5 miles to Wells Creek 5 miles south-southeast of Beegum Peak (lat. 40°14'55" N, long. 122°51'15" W; sec. 26, T 28 N, R 9 W). Named on Chanchelulla Peak (1951) 15' quadrangle.

(3) *canyon,* drained by a stream that flows 2 miles to South Fork Cottonwood Creek [SHASTA-TEHAMA] 7 miles west-northwest of Tomhead Mountain (lat. 40°09'30" N, long. 122°56'30" W; sec. 25, T 27 N, R 10 W). Named on Yolla Bolly (1954) 15' quadrangle.

Bear Gulch: see **Big Bear Gulch** [SHASTA]; **Little Bear Gulch** [SHASTA].

Bear Lake [BUTTE]: *lake,* 150 feet long, 11.5 miles north-northwest of Paradise along Big Chico Creek [BUTTE-TEHAMA] (lat. 39°55'05" N, long. 121°40'50" W; at S line sec. 19, T 24 N, R 3 E). Named on Cohasset (1979) 7.5' quadrangle.

Bear Lake [SISKIYOU]:

(1) *lake,* 900 feet long, 0.5 mile west-northwest of Bear Peak (lat. 41°41'40" N, long. 123°35' W). Named on Bear Peak (1982) 7.5' quadrangle.

(2) *lake,* 650 feet long, 14 miles southwest of Scott Bar (lat. 41°37'45" N, long. 123°13'20" W); the lake is at the head of Bear Creek (1). Named on Grider Valley (1981) 7.5' quadrangle.

(3) *intermittent lake,* 1000 feet long, 5 miles east-northeast of Bartle (lat. 41°16'15" N, long. 121°43'30" W; sec. 27, T 40 N, R 2 E); the feature is 2 miles south of Bear Mountain. Named on Hambone (1961) 15' quadrangle.

Bear Lake: see **Big Bear Lake** [SHASTA]; **Little Bear Lake** [SHASTA]; **Lower Bear Lake** [SISKIYOU].

Bear Mountain [SHASTA]: *peak,* 6.5 miles east-northeast of the town of Central Valley (lat. 40°43'35" N, long. 122°15'30" W; near SW cor. sec. 7, T 33 N, R 3 W). Altitude 2625 feet. Named on Project City (1957) 7.5' quadrangle.

Bear Mountain [SISKIYOU]:

(1) *peak,* 6 miles east-northeast of Bartle (lat. 41°18'05" N, long. 121°43'05" W; near E line sec. 15, T 40 N, R 2 E). Altitude 5831 feet. Named on Hambone (1961) 15' quadrangle.

(2) *peak,* 4.25 miles southwest of Preston Peak on Siskiyou-Del Norte County line (lat. 41°47'45" N, long. 123°40'15" W). Altitude 6411 feet. Named on Devils Punchbowl (1981) 7.5' quadrangle.

Bear Mountain: see **Bear Peak** [SISKIYOU].

Bear Paw [SISKIYOU]: *ridge,* 2 miles long, 7.25 miles south of Broken Rib Mountain, which is in Del Norte County (lat. 41°47'10" N, long. 123°40'15" W); the ridge is less than 1 mile south of Bear Mountain (2). Named on Devils Punchbowl (1981) 7.5' quadrangle. United States Board on Geographic Names (1965c, p. 7) noted that the ridge is linked to Bear Mountain (2) as the paw of a bear is linked to the bear.

Bearpaw Butte [SISKIYOU]: *hill,* 10 miles north-northeast of Medicine Lake (lat. 41°43'20" N, long. 121°33'10" W; near S line sec. 19, T 45 N, R 4 E). Named on Medicine Lake (1952) 15' quadrangle. The name is from the bear paws that trappers nailed to a tree near the hill in the 1880's (Knox, p. 55). A map of Lava Beds National Monument prepared by the Park Service shows Merrill Ice Cave situated just northeast of Bearpaw Butte. United States Board on Geographic Names (1949, p. 4) approved the name "Merrill Ice Cave" and rejected the name "Bearpaw Ice Cave" for this feature; the Board also noted that the name "Merrill" commemorates Charles Henry Merrill, who homesteaded at the site of the cave.

Bear Paw Ice Cave: see **Merrill Ice Cave**, under **Bear Paw Butte** [SISKIYOU].

Bear Peak [SISKIYOU]: *peak,* 12.5 miles southwest of Happy Camp (lat. 41°41'30" N, long. 123°34'30" W). Altitude 5740 feet. Named on Bear Peak (1982) 7.5' quadrangle. Called Bear Mountain on Preston Peak (1922) 30' quadrangle, but United States Board on Geographic Names (1960a, p. 11) rejected this name for the feature.

Bear Pen Creek [SISKIYOU]: *stream,* flows about 2 miles to Clear Creek (1) 3.5 miles north-northwest of Bear Peak (lat. 41°44'30" N, long. 123°35'50" W). Named on Bear Peak (1982) and Preston Peak (1982) 7.5' quadrangles.

Bear Pen Springs [SHASTA]: *spring,* 6 miles south-southeast of Whitmore (lat. 40°33'30" N, long. 121°51'35" W; near E line sec. 9, T 31 N, R 1 E). Named on Whitmore (1956) 15' quadrangle.

Bear Ranch Creek [BUTTE]: *stream,* flows 3 miles to North Fork Feather River 4 miles northeast of Pulga (lat. 39°50'35" N, long. 121°23'45" W; near SW cor. sec. 14, T 23 N, R 5 E); the stream heads south of Bear Ranch Hill. Named on Pulga (1979) and Soapstone Hill (1979) 7.5' quadrangles.

Bear Ranch Hill [BUTTE]: *peak,* 5.25 miles north of Pulga (lat. 39°50'45" N, long. 121°22' W; sec. 13, T 23 N, R 5 E). Altitude 4853 feet. Named on Soapstone Hill (1979) 7.5' quadrangle.

Bear Ridge [SISKIYOU]: *ridge,* generally west-southwest-trending, 3.25 miles long, 11.5 miles west of Dunsmuir (lat. 41°13'50" N, long. 122°29'15" W). Named on Bonanza King (1955) and Dunsmuir (1954) 15' quadrangles.

Bear Skull Camp [SISKIYOU]: *locality,* 14 miles north of Forks of Salmon along Wooley Creek lat. 41°27'35" N, long. 123°17'50" W); the place is 3000 feet downstream from the mouth of Bear Skull Creek. Named on Medicine Mountain (1978) 7.5' quadrangle. Forks of Salmon (1955) 15' quadrangle shows the place situated upstream from the mouth of Bear Skull Creek.

Bear Skull Creek [SISKIYOU]: *stream,* flows 1 mile to Wooley Creek 14 miles north of Forks of Salmon (lat. 41°27'55" N, long. 123°17'20" W). Named on Medicine Mountain (1978) 7.5' quadrangle.

Bear Spring [SHASTA]: *spring,* 7 miles northeast of the village of Montgomery Creek (lat. 40°54'40" N, long. 121°49'45" W; on N line sec. 11, T 35 N, R 1 E). Named on Montgomery Creek (1956) 15' quadrangle.

Bear Spring [SISKIYOU]:

(1) *spring,* 6.25 miles northwest of McCloud (lat. 41°18'20" N, long. 122°13'50" W; near SE cor. sec. 18, T 40 N, R 3 W). Named on Shasta (1954) 15' quadrangle.

(2) *spring,* 14 miles north of Bartle (lat. 41°27'25" N, long. 121°48'15" W; sec. 25, T 42 N, R 1 E). Named on Bartle (1961) 15' quadrangle.

Beartrap Creek [SHASTA]:

(1) *stream,* flows 1.5 miles to Squaw Valley Creek [SHASTA-SISKIYOU] 7 miles west-northwest of Shoeinhorse Mountain (lat. 41°06'45" N, long. 122°11'15" W; sec. 27, T 38 N, R 3 W). Named on Shoeinhorse Mountain (1954) 15' quadrangle.

(2) *stream,* flows 1.5 miles to Squaw Creek (2) 6.5 miles east of Bollibokka Mountain (lat. 40°55'55" N, long. 122°05'25" W; near SE cor. sec. 33, T 36 N, R 2 W). Named on Bollibokka Mountain (1957) 15' quadrangle.

(3) *stream,* flows less than 1 mile to Backbone Creek 11 miles south of Lamoine (lat. 40°49'30" N, long. 122°28'30" W; near N line sec. 7, T 34 N, R 5 W). Named on Lamoine (1957) 15' quadrangle.

Beartrap Gulch [SHASTA]: *canyon,* drained by a stream that flows nearly 1 mile to Brandy Creek 1.5 miles southeast of Shasta Bally (lat. 40°35'15" N, long. 122°37'40" W; sec. 35, T 32 N, R 7 W). Named on Shasta Bally (1978) 7.5' quadrangle.

Bear Valley [SHASTA]: *valley,* 12 miles north-northwest of Millville (lat. 40°43' N, long. 122°14'30" W; sec. 18, T 33 N, R 3 W). Named on Millville (1953) 15' quadrangle.

Bear Valley [SISKIYOU]:

(1) *relief feature,* 0.5 mile east-northeast of Bear Peak (lat. 41°41'40" N, long. 123°33'50" W). Named on Bear Peak (1982) 7.5' quadrangle.

(2) *valley,* 14 miles southwest of Scott Bar (lat. 41°38'05" N, long. 123°13'45" W); the valley is along Bear Creek (1). Named on Grider Valley (1981) 7.5' quadrangle.

(3) *canyon,* 5.5 miles southwest of Cecilville (lat. 41°04'40" N, long. 123°12' W). Named on Cecil Lake (1979) 7.5' quadrangle.

Bear Valley: see **Little Bear Valley** [SISKIYOU].

Bear Valley Creek [SISKIYOU]:

(1) *stream,* flows 3 miles to Clear Creek (1) 3 miles north-northeast of Bear Peak (lat. 41°44' N, long. 123°33'40" W); the stream heads at Bear Valley (1). Named on Bear Peak (1982) 7.5' quadrangle.

(2) *stream,* flows 2.5 miles to Thompson Creek 9 miles north of Happy Camp (lat. 41°55'10" N, long. 123°20'50" W). Named on Figurehead Mountain (1980) 7.5' quadrangle.

Bear Valley Creek: see **Little Bear Valley Creek** [SISKIYOU].

Bear Wallow [SHASTA]: *relief feature,* 11.5 miles north-northwest of the village of Big Bend (lat. 41°10'30" N, long. 121°59'30" W; on S line sec. 32, T 39 N, R 1 W). Named on Big Bend (1961) 15' quadrangle.

Bear Wallow [SISKIYOU]:

(1) *area,* 10 miles north-northeast of Happy Camp (lat. 41°55' N, long. 123°16'45" W). Named on Figurehead Mountain (1980) 7.5' quadrangle. Happy Camp (1956) 15' quadrangle shows Bear Wallow Camp at the place.

(2) *relief feature,* 9 miles west of Macdoel (lat. 41°49'10" N, long. 122°10'15" W; near NE cor. sec. 23, T 46 N, R 3 W). Named on Macdoel (1954) 15' quadrangle. United States Board on Geographic Names (1986c, p. 2) approved the name "Bear Wallow" for springs situated about 0.5 mile east of Bear Wallow (2) (lat. 41°48'53" N, long. 122°09'35" W).

(3) *spring,* 6 miles northwest of Bartle (lat. 41°19'10" N, long. 121°54' W; near NW cor. sec. 18, T 40 N, R 1 E). Named on Bartle (1961) 15' quadrangle.

Bear Wallow [TEHAMA]:

(1) *relief feature,* 9 miles west-southwest of Ball Mountain (lat. 39°53'25" N, long. 122°52'50" W; sec. 33, T 24 N, R 9 W). Named on Buck Rock (1967) 7.5' quadrangle.

(2) *relief feature,* 4.5 miles southwest of Wakefield Flat (lat. 40°04'50" N, long. 122°42'10" W; near W line sec. 30, T 26 N, R 7 W). Named on Raglin Ridge (1967) 7.5' quadrangle. On Colyear Springs (1957) 15' quadrangle, the name applies to a spring situated a little west of present Bear Wallow (2).

Bear Wallow: see **Bear Wallow Spring** [TEHAMA].

Bear Wallow Butte [SHASTA]: *peak,* 10 miles north of Lassen Peak (lat. 40°38' N, long. 121°32'10" W; near SW cor. sec. 9, T 32 N, R 4 E). Named on Manzanita Lake (1956) 15' quadrangle.

Bear Wallow Camp: see **Bear Wallow** [SISKIYOU] (1)

Bear Wallow Campground [TEHAMA]: *locality,* 1.5 miles south-southeast of Mineral (lat. 40°19'50" N, long. 121°34'45" W; sec. 31, T 29 N, R

4 E). Named on Lassen Peak (1956) 15' quadrangle.

Bear Wallow Creek [GLENN]: *stream,* flows 3 miles to Middle Fork Stony Creek [GLENN-TEHAMA] 1.5 miles south-southwest of Saint John Mountain (lat. 39°24'50" N, long. 122°42'40" W). Named on Saint John Mountain (1968) 7.5' quadrangle.

Bear Wallow Creek [SISKIYOU]: *stream,* flows 3.5 miles to Grass Lake (1) 14 miles southwest of Macdoel (lat. 41°39'15" N, long. 122°10'30" W; at S line sec. 15, T 44 N, R 3 W). Named on The Whaleback (1954) 15' quadrangle.

Bear Wallow Gulch [SHASTA]: *canyon,* drained by a stream that flows less than 1 mile to Duncan Creek 6 miles northeast of Arbuckle Mountain (lat. 40°28' N, long. 122°47'55" W; near W line sec. 8, T 30 N, R 8 W). Named on Chanchelulla Peak (1951) 15' quadrangle.

Bear Wallow Gulch [SISKIYOU]: *canyon,* drained by a stream that flows 1 mile to Right Hand Fork of North Fork Salmon River 10 miles north of Sawyers Bar (lat. 41°26'25" N, long. 123°06'15" W). Named on Yellow Dog Peak (1977) 7.5' quadrangle.

Bear Wallow Peak [SISKIYOU]: *peak,* 11.5 miles north of Sawyers Bar (lat. 41°28' N, long. 123°07'20" W). Altitude 7048 feet. Named on Yellow Dog Peak (1977) 7.5' quadrangle.

Bear Wallow Ridge [GLENN]: *ridge,* west- to southwest-trending, nearly 3 miles long, 8 miles south-southeast of Black Butte (lat. 39°36'55" N, long. 122°49'15" W). Named on Kneecap Ridge (1967) 7.5' quadrangle.

Bearwallow Spring [GLENN]: *spring,* 8 miles northwest of the village of Elk Creek (lat. 39°41'50" N, long. 122°37'45" W). Named on Alder Springs (1967) 7.5' quadrangle.

Bear Wallow Spring [SISKIYOU]:

(1) *spring,* 11.5 miles northwest of Macdoel (lat. 41°56'55" N, long. 122°09' W; near W line sec. 6, T 47 N, R 2 W). Named on Macdoel (1954) 15' quadrangle.

(2) *spring,* 7.5 miles southwest of Macdoel (lat. 41°41'45" N, long. 121°14'15" W; sec. 6, T 44 N, R 3 E). Named on Macdoel (1941) 30' quadrangle.

Bear Wallow Spring [TEHAMA]: *spring,* 9 miles south-southwest of Wakefield Flat (lat. 40°00'35" N, long. 122°42'50" W; sec. 24, T 25 N, R 8 W). Named on Raglin Ridge (1967) 7.5' quadrangle. Colyear Springs (1957) 15' quadrangle has the name "Bear Wallow" at the site.

Beatson Hollow [BUTTE]: *canyon,* 4.25 miles long, along Campbell Creek above a point 5 miles north-northwest of Oroville (lat. 39°34'20" N, long. 121°36' W; sec. 23, T 20 N, R 3 E). Named on Oroville (1970) 7.5' quadrangle.

Beaughton Creek [SISKIYOU]: *stream,* flows 5.5 miles to Shasta River nearly 4 miles northwest of Weed (lat. 41°27'35" N, long. 122°26'10" W; near W line sec. 28, T 42 N, R 5 W). Named on Weed (1954) 15' quadrangle.

Beauty Flat [SISKIYOU]: *area,* 7.5 miles southwest of Scott Bar (lat. 41°39'15" N, long. 123°05'25" W). Named on Scott Bar (1980) 7.5' quadrangle.

Beauty Peak [BUTTE]: *peak,* 7.5 miles south-southwest of Paradise (lat. 39°38'55" N, long. 121°40'10" W; sec. 29, T 21 N, R 3 E). Altitude 570 feet. Named on Hamlin Canyon (1951) 7.5' quadrangle.

Beaver Basin [SISKIYOU]: *relief feature,* 19 miles northwest of Macdoel, where East Fork and West Fork join Beaver Creek (2) (lat. 41°59'50" N, long. 122°18'30" W; sec. 21, T 48 N, R 4 W). Named on Copco (1954) 15' quadrangle.

Beaver Creek [SHASTA]: *stream,* heads in Lassen County and flows 3 miles in Shasta County to Pit River 5.5 miles northeast of Fall River Mills (lat. 41°03' N, long. 121°21' W; near NE cor. sec. 14, T 37 N, R 5 E). Named on Fall River Mills (1961) 15' quadrangle. Major Reading named the stream in 1843 for the numerous beaver dams there (Steger, p. 17).

Beaver Creek [SISKIYOU]:

(1) *stream,* formed by the confluence of Cow Creek (2) and Grouse Creek (1), flows 11 miles to Klamath River 10 miles east-southeast of Condrey Mountain (lat. 41°52'15" N, long. 122°49' W; sec. 6, T 46 N, R 8 W). Named on Condrey Mountain (1955) 15' quadrangle. West Fork enters from the northwest 5.5 miles upstream from the mouth of the main creek; it is 7 miles long and is named on Condrey Mountain (1955) 15' quadrangle. Yreka (1939) 30' quadrangle has the name "West Beaver Creek" for present West Fork.

(2) *stream,* heads in the State of Oregon and flows 1 mile in Siskiyou County to Copco Lake 19 miles west-northwest of Macdoel (lat. 41°59'35" N, long. 122°18'30" W; sec. 21, T 48 N, R 4 W). Named on Copco (1954) 15' quadrangle. East Fork enters from the northeast 800 feet upstream from the mouth of the main creek; it heads in the State of Oregon and is 1.5 miles long in Siskiyou County. West Fork enters 1300 feet upstream from the mouth of the main creek; it heads in the State of Oregon and is 1.25 miles long in Siskiyou County. Both forks are named on Copco (1954) 15' quadrangle.

Beaver Creek [TEHAMA]: *stream,* flows 2.5 miles to Deer Creek (2) 3 miles south-southwest of Polk Springs (lat. 40°04'55" N, long. 121°41'30" W; near NE cor. sec. 25, T 26 N, R 2 E). Named on Butte Meadows (1958) 15' quadrangle.

Beaver Creek: see **Jenny Creek** [SISKIYOU].

Beaver Creek Campground [SISKIYOU]: *locality,* 8 miles east of Condrey Mountain (lat. 41°55'40" N, long. 122°49'45" W; near W line sec. 18, T 47 N, R 8 W); the place is along Beaver Creek (1). Named on Condrey Mountain (1955) 15' quadrangle.

Beaver Island: see **Bridge Bay Resort** [SHASTA].

Beaver River: see **Scott River** [SISKIYOU].

Bedford Creek [GLENN]:*stream,* flows 5 miles to North Fork (2) Stony Creek [GLENN-TEHAMA] 15 miles west of Orland (lat. 39°47'05" N, long. 122°28'35" W; at NW cor. sec. 7, T 22 N, R 5 W). Named on Chrome (1968), Newville (1967), and Sehorn Creek (1967) 7.5' quadrangles.

Bedrock Spring [SHASTA]: *spring,* 10 miles north-northeast of the village of Montgomery Creek (lat. 40°58'10" N, long. 121°50'45" W). Named on Montgomery Creek (1956) 7.5' quadrangle.

Bed Spring [SISKIYOU]: *spring,* 8 miles east of the village of Seiad Valley (lat. 41°51'40" N, long. 123°02'25" W; near E line sec. 6, T 46 N, R 10 W). Named on Hamburg (1980) 7.5' quadrangle.

Beebee Bar: see **Scott Bar** [SISKIYOU].

Bee Camp [SISKIYOU]: *locality,* 8 miles north of the village of Seiad Valley (lat. 41°55'40" N, long. 123°10'35" W). Named on Kangaroo Mountain (1980) 7.5' quadrangle.

Bee Creek [SHASTA]: *stream,* flows 4.5 miles to North Fork Cottonwood Creek [SHASTA-TEHAMA] 2.25 miles southeast of Ono (lat. 40°27' N, long. 122°35'20" W; sec. 18, T 30 N, R 6 W). Named on Ono (1952) 15' quadrangle.

Beef Corral Gulch [SISKIYOU]: *canyon,* 1 mile long, 11 miles south-southwest of Yreka (lat. 41°35'15" N, long. 122°42'15" W; mainly in sec. 7, T 43 N, R 7 W). Named on Yreka (1954) 15' quadrangle.

Bee Flat [SISKIYOU]: *area,* 15 miles north-northeast of Happy Camp (lat. 42°00' N, long. 123°18' W). Named on Figurehead Mountain (1980) 7.5' quadrangle.

Beegum [SHASTA]: *locality,* nearly 4 miles south of Arbuckle Mountain (lat. 40°20'45" N, long. 122°51'20" W; near SW cor. sec. 23, T 29 N, R 9 W); the place is along Beegum Creek [SHASTA-TEHAMA]. Named on Chanchelulla Peak (1951) 15' quadrangle.

Beegum Basin [TEHAMA]: *relief feature,* 8.5 miles west-northwest of Tomhead Mountain (lat. 40°11'30" N, long. 122°57'35" W; on N line sec. 14, T 27 N, R 10 W); the feature is at the head of South Fork Beegum Creek [SHASTA-TEHAMA]. Named on Yolla Bolly (1954) 15' quadrangle.

Beegum Creek [SHASTA-TEHAMA]: *stream,* formed by the confluence of Middle Fork and North Fork, flows 16 miles to Middle Fork Cottonwood Creek [SHASTA-TEHAMA] 10 miles southwest of Ono (lat. 40°21'50" N, long. 122°44'15" W; sec. 14, T 29 N, R 8 W). Named on Chanchelulla Peak (1951) and Ono (1952) 15' quadrangles. Middle Fork is nearly 7 miles long and forms part of Shasta-Tehama County line. North Fork is nearly 6 miles long. Both forks are named on Chanchelulla Peak (1951) and Dubakella Mountain (1954) 15' quadrangles. On Hoaglin (1935) 30' quadrangle, present North Fork is called Beegum Creek. South Fork enters the main stream from the south nearly 2 miles west-southwest of Beegum Peak; it is 9.5 miles long and is named on Chanchelulla Peak (1951) and Yolla Bolly (1954) 15' quadrangles.

Beegum Gorge [SHASTA-TEHAMA]: *canyon,* 5 miles long, 5 miles south-southwest of Arbuckle Mountain on Shasta-Tehama County line (lat. 40°19'50" N, long. 122°53'30" W); the canyon is along Beegum Creek [SHASTA-TEHAMA] above Beegum. Named on Chanchelulla Peak (1951) 15' quadrangle.

Beegum Peak [TEHAMA]: *peak,* 35 miles west-northwest of Red Bluff (lat. 40°18'50" N, long. 122°53'10" W; on S line sec. 33, T 29 N, R 9 W); the peak is 2.5 miles southwest of Beegum [SHASTA]. Altitude 4098 feet. Named on Chanchelulla Peak (1951) 15' quadrangle.

Beehive Bend [BUTTE]: *water feature,* cutoff meander of Sacramento River 10.5 miles east-southeast of Willows (lat. 39°29'15" N, long. 122°00'30" W). Named on Princeton (1952) 7.5' quadrangle.

Beehive Flat [TEHAMA]: *area,* 3.5 miles northwest of Paskenta (lat. 39°53'20" N, long. 122°38'05" W; near S line sec. 34, T 24 N, R 7 W). Named on Riley Ridge (1967) 7.5' quadrangle.

Bee Knoll [SHASTA]: *peak,* 10 miles north-northeast of the village of Montgomery Creek (lat. 40°58'45" N, long. 121°51'05" W). Named on Montgomery Creek (1956) 15' quadrangle.

Bee Lake: see **Lower Twin Lake** [SHASTA] (2).

Beetle Butte [SHASTA]: *peak,* 3.25 miles west of Shoeinhorse Mountain (lat. 41°04' N, long. 122°08'05" W). Named on Shoeinhorse Mountain (1954) 15' quadrangle.

Belfast Meadows [TEHAMA]: *area,* 5.5 miles south-southwest of Mineral (lat. 40°16'15" N, long. 121°37'30" W; near N line sec. 22, T 28 N, R 3 E). Named on Lassen Peak (1956) 15' quadrangle.

Bell: see **Henry Bell Creek**, under **Negro Creek** [SISKIYOU] (1); **Henry Bell Gulch** [SISKIYOU].

Bella Vista [SHASTA]: *village,* 7 miles north-northwest of Millville (lat.

40°38'20" N, long. 122°13'14" W; near S line sec. 8, T 32 N, R 3 W). Named on Bella Vista (1965) 7.5' quadrangle. On Redding (1901) 30' quadrangle, the name "Bellavista" applies to a community located less than 1 mile southeast of present Bella Vista (sec. 17, T 32 N, R 3 W), and the name "Frazier Corners" is at or near the site of present Bella Vista. Postal authorities established Bella Vista post office in 1893, discontinued it in 1918, reestablished it at a new site in 1920, and moved it 0.5 mile east in 1937 (Salley, p. 17). Steger (p. 17, 33) noted that Shasta Lumber Company started the village of Bella Vista about 1888, and that in 1920 postal authorities moved Bella Vista post office to a spot near Fraser's Corner, where Daniel A. Fraser had a blacksmith shop.

Bell Echo Camp [SISKIYOU]: *locality,* nearly 3 miles north of Preston Peak (lat. 41°52'35" N, long. 123°37'15" W). Named on Polar Bear Mountain (1982) 7.5' quadrangle.

Belle Mill [TEHAMA]: *locality,* 9 miles south-southeast of Manton (lat. 40°18'30" N, long. 121°45'30" W). Named on Lassen Peak (1894) 1° quadrangle.

Bell's Bridge: see **Redding** [SHASTA].

Bell Spring [TEHAMA]: *spring,* 2.5 miles east-northeast of Campbell Mound (lat. 39°58'50" N, long. 121°46'25" W; near SE cor. sec. 32, T 25 N, R 2 E). Named on Campbell Mound (1952) 7.5' quadrangle.

Belnap Spring [SISKIYOU]: *spring,* 7 miles north of Bartle (lat. 41°23'50" N, long. 121°47'40" W; on E line sec. 13, T 41 N, R 1 E). Named on Bartle (1961) 15' quadrangle.

Belvedere: see **Willows** [GLENN].

Bench Lake [SHASTA]: *lake,* 400 feet long, 4.5 miles east-southeast of Lassen Peak (lat. 40°27'10" N, long. 121°26'10" W; at N line sec. 21, T 30 N, R 5 E). Named on Mount Harkness (1956) 15' quadrangle. The name is from the position of the lake on a topographic bench (Schulz, p. 3).

Bend [TEHAMA]: *village,* 6 miles north-northeast of Red Bluff (lat. 40°15'20" N, long. 122°12'25" W; sec. 28, T 28 N, R 3 W); the village is at Big Bend (1). Named on Bend (1965) 7.5' quadrangle. Postal authorities established Bend post office in 1897 and discontinued it in 1935 (Frickstad, p. 203). The place first was called Horsethief Bend, and later Sander's Bend for an early settler (Gudde, 1949, p. 28).

Bend: see **The Bend** [SHASTA].

Benjamin Creek [SISKIYOU]: *stream,* flows 1.5 miles to Klamath River 2.25 miles south-southwest of Happy Camp (lat. 41°46'10" N, long. 123°24'05" W). Named on Happy Camp (1980) 7.5' quadrangle.

Bennet Springs [TEHAMA]: *spring,* 7.5 miles west-southwest of Paskenta (lat. 39°49'50" N, long. 122°39'40" W; near SE cor. sec. 20, T 23 N, R 7 W). Named on Paskenta (1920) 15' quadrangle.

Bennett Creek [TEHAMA]: *stream,* flows 5.25 miles to Thomes Creek 4.5 miles west-southwest of Paskenta (lat. 39°51'10" N, long. 122°37'20" W; sec. 14, T 23 N, R 7 W). Named on Hall Ridge (1967) and Newville (1967) 7.5' quadrangles.

Bennett's: see **Forks of Salmon** [SISKIYOU].

Bennett Spring [TEHAMA]: *spring,* 7.25 miles south-southwest of Polk Springs (lat. 40°01'15" N, long. 121°43'15" W; at S line sec. 14, T 25 N, R 2 E). Named on Butte Meadows (1958) 15' quadrangle.

Benton City: see **Vina** [TEHAMA].

Berdan: see **Forest Ranch** [BUTTE].

Berry: see **Bill Berry Creek**, under **Scott Bar** [SISKIYOU].

Berry Canyon [BUTTE]: *canyon,* drained by Little Dry Creek, which flows 9 miles to lowlands 11 miles northwest of Oroville (lat. 39°37'55" N, long. 121°41' W; sec. 31, T 21 N, R 3 E). Named on Cherokee (1970) and Hamlin Canyon (1951) 7.5' quadrangles.

Berry Creek [BUTTE]:

(1) *stream,* flows 7.25 miles to North Fork Feather River 2.25 miles northwest of the village of Berry Creek (lat. 39°40'10" N, long. 121°25'50" W; near SE cor. sec. 17, T 21 N, R 5 E). Named on Berry Creek (1970) and Brush Creek (1970) 7.5' quadrangles. South Fork enters 1.5 miles east of the village of Berry Creek; it is nearly 2 miles long and is named on Brush Creek (1970) 7.5' quadrangle.

(2) *village,* 11.5 miles northeast of Oroville (lat. 39°38'40" N, long. 121°24'05" W; sec. 27, T 21 N, R 5 E); the place is along Berry Creek (1). Named on Berry Creek (1970) 7.5' quadrangle. The village is at what was called Berry Valley on a map of 1854 (Dunn, F.D., p. 7). Postal authorities established Oak Arbor post office in 1874, moved it and changed the name to Berry Creek in 1875, moved it 1 mile northeast in 1893, moved it 1 mile south in 1908, discontinued it in 1912, reestablished it in 1913, discontinued it in 1926, and reestablished it in 1927 (Salley, p. 19, 157). Berry Creek post office was at a place called Virginia Mills, but the post office took its name from the nearby stream (Gudde, 1949, p. 29).

Berry Creek [SHASTA]: *stream,* flows nearly 3 miles to Millseat Creek 2 miles east-southeast of Shingletown (lat. 40°28'50" N, long. 121°51'05" W; sec. 3, T 30 N, R 1 E); the stream heads at Berry Spring. Named on Manton (1956) and Whitmore (1956) 15' quadrangles.

Berry Creek [TEHAMA]: *stream,* flows 2.25 miles to Cold Spring Creek 2.5 miles north-northwest of Ball Mountain (lat. 39°57'55" N, long. 122°48'10" W; sec. 6, T 24 N, R 8 W). Named on Ball Mountain (1967) 7.5' quadrangle.

Berry Creek Bar [BUTTE]: *locality,* 2.5 miles northwest of the village of Berry Creek along North Fork Feather River (lat. 39°40'20" N, long. 121°26'05" W; sec. 17, T 21 N, R 5 E); the place is at the mouth of Berry Creek (1). Named on Big Bend Mountain (1948) 15' quadrangle.

Berry Creek Station [BUTTE]: *locality,* 2.5 miles northwest of the village of Berry Creek along Western Pacific Railroad (lat. 39°40'15" N, long. 121°26'10" W; near SE cor. sec. 17, T 21 N, R 5 E); the place is near the mouth of Berry Creek (1). Named on Big Bend Mountain (1948) 15' quadrangle

Berry Ridge [TEHAMA]: *ridge,* generally north-trending, 1.25 miles long, center 1 mile north of Ball Mountain (lat. 39°56'45" N, long. 122°46'50" W; sec. 8, 17, T 24 N, R 8 W); the ridge is east of Berry Creek. Named on Ball Mountain (1967) 7.5' quadrangle.

Berry Spring [SHASTA]: *spring,* 10 miles south-southeast of Whitmore (lat. 40°30'15" N, long. 121°48'50" W; near S line sec. 25, T 31 N, R 1 E); the spring is at the head of Berry Creek. Named on Whitmore (1956) 15' quadrangle.

Berryvale: see **Mount Shasta** [SISKIYOU] (2).

Berry Valley: see **Berry Creek** [BUTTE] (2).

Berthas Cupboard Cave [SISKIYOU]: *cave,* 8 miles north-northeast of Medicine Lake (lat. 41°41'20" N, long. 121°31'45" W; sec. 5, T 44 N, R 4 E). Named on Medicine Lake (1952) 15' quadrangle.

Bestville [SISKIYOU]: *locality,* 0.5 mile west of Sawyers Bar along North Fork Salmon River (lat. 41°18'05" N, long. 123°08'25" W). Site named on Sawyers Bar (1979) 7.5' quadrangle. The former community at the place was named for Captain Best, who led the first prospectors into the neighborhood in 1850 (Gudde, 1949, p. 30).

Beswick [SISKIYOU]: *locality,* 15 miles northwest of Macdoel along Klamath River (lat. 41°58' N, long. 122°13'10" W; at N line sec. 33, T 48 N, R 3 W). Named on Macdoel (1954) 15' quadrangle. On Macdoel (1941) 30' quadrangle, the name applies to a place situated 1 mile farther east-northeast along Klamath River near the mouth of Shovel Creek. United States Board on Geographic Names (1986c, p. 2) gave this second place as the site of Beswick (lat. 41°58' N, long. 122°12'07" W; sec. 27, T 48 N, R 3 W), and noted that Richard Beswick started a community there in 1869. Postal authorities established Beswick post office in 1882, moved it 1.25 miles northeast in 1890, and discontinued it in 1947 (Salley, p. 20). Waring (p. 120) listed Klamath Hot Springs, also located along Klamath River near the mouth of Shovel Creek—the place was a resort that formerly was known as Shovel Creek Mud Springs. Diller and others (p. 60) noted the name "Shovel Creek Springs" for the resort.

Beverly Spring [TEHAMA]: *spring,* 8 miles south-southwest of Ball Mountain (lat. 39°49'55" N, long. 122°50'40" W; near W line sec. 23, T 23 N, R 9 W). Named on Log Spring (1967) 7.5' quadrangle.

Bidwell [BUTTE]: *locality,* 1.25 miles west of Bidwell Bar along Western Pacific Railroad (lat. 39°33'30" N, long. 121°27'50" W; at W line sec. 30, T 20 N, R 5 E). Named on Big Bend Mountain (1948) 15' quadrangle. Water of Lake Oroville now covers the site.

Bidwell Bar [BUTTE]: *locality,* 6.5 miles east-northeast of Oroville along Feather River (lat. 39°33'30" N, long. 121°26'25" W; sec. 29, T 20 N, R 5 E). Named on Big Bend Mountain (1948) 15' quadrangle. Water of Lake Oroville now covers the site. Postal authorities established Bidwell's Bar post office in 1851, discontinued it in 1864, reestablished it in 1865, and discontinued it in 1900 (Salley, p. 20). John Bidwell started a mining camp at the site in 1848 (Wells and Chambers, p. 254). The lower end of Bidwell Bar was known as Dawlytown in 1849 for a merchant who opened a store there (Delano, p. 255). A mining camp called Potter's Bar for its first settler was situated 2 miles above Bidwell Bar (Wells and Chambers, p. 254).

Bidwell Bar Canyon [BUTTE]: *canyon,* 2.5 miles long, opens into the canyon of Feather River about 0.25 mile southwest of Bidwell Bar (lat. 39°33'15" N, long. 121°26'45" W; near NE cor. sec. 31, T 20 N, R 5 E). Named on Big Bend Mountain (1948) 15' quadrangle.

Bidwell Canyon Campground [BUTTE]: *locality,* 1.5 miles east of Oroville Dam along Lake Oroville (lat. 39°32' N, long. 121°27'30" W; sec. 6, T 19 N, R 5 E). Named on Oroville (1970) 7.5' quadrangle.

Bidwell Creek [BUTTE]: *stream,* flows nearly 2 miles to French Creek 5 miles north-northeast of the village of Berry Creek (lat. 39°43'35" N, long. 121°22'40" W; near S line sec. 26, T 22 N, R 5 E). Named on Berry Creek (1970) 7.5' quadrangle.

Bidwell Hill: see **North Bidwell Hill** [BUTTE]; **South Bidwell Hill** [BUTTE].

Bidwell Point [GLENN]: *peak,* 0.5 mile east-southeast of the village of Elk Creek (lat. 39°36'05" N, long. 122°31'55" W; near E line sec. 9, T 20 N, R 6 W). Named on Elk Creek (1968) 7.5' quadrangle. John Bidwell camped at the site in 1844 (Hoover, Rensch, and Rensch, p. 98).

Bidwell's Landing: see **Chico Landing** [BUTTE].

Big Backbone Creek: see **Backbone Creek** [SHASTA].

Big Backbone Creek Inlet: see **Backbone Creek Inlet** [SHASTA].

Big Bald Rock [BUTTE]: *relief feature,* 3 miles south of the village of Brush

Creek (lat. 39°38'40" N, long. 121°20'40" W; sec. 30, T 21 N, R 6 E); the feature is 1 mile southwest of Little Bald Rock. Named on Brush Creek (1970) 7.5' quadrangle. Called Bald Rock on Bidwell Bar (1897) 30' quadrangle.

Big Bar [BUTTE]: *locality,* 0.5 mile east of present Pulga along North Fork Feather River (lat. 39°48'20" N, long. 121°26'10" W). Named on Bidwell Bar (1897) 30' quadrangle. The place also was known as Pulga Bar and Montreal Bar (Dunn, F.D., p. 8).

Big Bar Hill: see **Big Bar Mountain** [BUTTE].

Big Bar Mountain [BUTTE]: *peak,* 2 miles southeast of Pulga (lat. 39°46'40" N, long. 121°25'35" W; near W line sec. 9, T 22 N, R 5 E); the peak is 2 miles southeast of the site of Big Bar. Altitude 4377 feet. Named on Pulga (1979) 7.5' quadrangle. United States Board on Geographic Names (1960b, p. 6) rejected the name "Big Bar Hill" for the feature.

Big Basin Creek [SHASTA]: *stream,* flows 2 miles to Star City Creek 11 miles north-northwest of the village of Big Bend (lat. 41°10'10" N, long. 121°59'30" W). Named on Big Bend (1961) 15' quadrangle.

Big Bear Creek [TEHAMA]: *stream,* flows 2.5 miles to Big Chico Creek [BUTTE-TEHAMA] 6.5 miles south of Polk Springs (lat. 40°01'20" N, long. 121°38'40" W; sec. 16, T 25 N, R 3 E); the mouth of the creek is 1 mile upstream from the mouth of Little Bear Creek. Named on Butte Meadows (1958) 15' quadrangle.

Big Bear Flat [SISKIYOU]: *area,* 6.5 miles southeast of Bartle along North Fork Bear Creek [SHASTA-SISKIYOU] (lat. 41°11'45" N, long. 121°43' W). Named on Pondosa (1961) 15' quadrangle. Called Bear Flat on Bartle (1939) 30' quadrangle, but United States Board on Geographic Names (1964, p. 8) rejected this name for the feature.

Big Bear Gulch [SHASTA]: *canyon,* drained by a stream that flows 1 mile to Middle Fork Cottonwood Creek [SHASTA-TEHAMA] 1 mile northeast of Arbuckle Mountain (lat. 40°24'35" N, long. 122°51' W). Named on Chanchelulla Peak (1951) 15' quadrangle.

Big Bear Lake [SHASTA]: *lake,* 1000 feet long, 6 miles east-northeast of Lassen Peak (lat. 40°31'30" N, long. 121°24' W; at NW cor. sec. 27, T 31 N, R 5 E); the lake 0.25 mile east-northeast of Little Bear Lake. Named on Prospect Peak (1957) 15' quadrangle. The feature is one of the group called Cluster Lakes.

Big Bend [BUTTE]: *locality,* nearly 5 miles northwest of the village of Berry Creek (lat. 39°41'55" N, long. 121°27'30" W; at S line sec. 6, T 21 N, R 5 E); the place is on Big Bend Mountain. Named on Berry Creek (1970) 7.5' quadrangle. On Bidwell Bar (1897) 30' quadrangle, the name applies to a place located about 1 mile farther west. Postal authorities established Bigbend post office in 1883 and discontinued it in 1891 (Frickstad, p. 8).

Big Bend [SHASTA]: *village,* 25 miles west of Fall River Mills along Pit River (lat. 41°01'15" N, long. 121°54'30" W; at W line sec. 31, T 37 N, R 1 E). Named on Big Bend (1961) 15' quadrangle. Postal authorities established Henderson post office in 1906 and changed the name to Big Bend in 1922; the name "Henderson" was for Thomas J. Henderson, first postmaster, and the name "Big Bend" is for a 10-mile bend in Pit River (Salley, p. 21, 96).

Big Bend [TEHAMA]:

(1) *bend,* 4.5 miles north-northeast of Red Bluff along Sacramento River (lat. 40°14'15" N, long. 122°12'45" W). Named on Red Bluff East (1951) 7.5' quadrangle.

(2) *locality,* 5.5 miles south-southeast of Mineral along Mill Creek (3) (lat. 40°15'30" N, long. 121°33'30" W). Named on Lassen Peak (1956) 15' quadrangle. Called Big Bend Camp on Mineral (1941) 30' quadrangle.

Big Bend Camp: see **Big Bend** [TEHAMA] (2).

Big Bend Creek [SISKIYOU]: *stream,* flows 3.5 miles to South Fork Salmon River nearly 7 miles southeast of Cecilville (lat. 41°04'50" N, long. 123°01'50" W); the stream heads near Coyote Peak. Named on Coffee Creek (1955) 15' quadrangle, and on Thompson Peak (1979) 7.5' quadrangle. Called Coyote Cr. on Etna (1934) 30' quadrangle. A place called Buells Flat was situated along South Fork Salmon River at the mouth of Big Bend Creek; the name was for William M. Buell, who came to the neighborhood in 1850 and had a trading post at the site until about 1860 (Gudde, 1975, p. 51).

Big Bend Mountain [BUTTE]: *ridge,* east-trending, 4 mile long, 4.25 miles north-northwest of the village of Berry Creek (lat. 39°42' N, long. 121°26'30" W); the course of North Fork Feather River takes a great bend to the east to go around the ridge. Named on Berry Creek (1970) 7.5' quadrangle.

Big Blue Lake [SISKIYOU]: *lake,* 1800 feet long, 9 miles south-southwest of Etna (lat. 41°20'35" N, long. 122°58'50" W; sec. 11, T 40 N, R 10 W). Named on Etna (1955) 15' quadrangle.

Big Bollibokka Creek [SHASTA]: *stream,* flows 1.5 miles to McCloud River [SHASTA-SISKIYOU] nearly 2 miles north of Bollibokka Mountain (lat. 40°57'30" N, long. 122°12'55" W; near N line sec. 28, T 36 N, R 3 W); the mouth of the creek is 1000 feet downstream from the mouth of Little Bollibokka Creek. Named on Bollibokka Mountain (1957) 15' quadrangle.

Big Brushy Gulch [SISKIYOU]: *canyon,* drained by a stream that flows 0.5 mile to Indian Creek (3) 8 miles north of Fort Jones (lat. 41°43'10" N, long. 122°50'55" W; sec. 26, T 45 N, R 9 W); the mouth of the canyon is 0.5 mile upstream from the mouth of Little Brushy Gulch. Named on Fort Jones (1955) 15' quadrangle.

Big Buck Ridge [SISKIYOU]: *ridge,* north-trending, 2.5 miles long, 4.5 miles east of Preston Peak (lat. 41°50'15" N, long. 123°31'25" W); the feature is west of Little Buck Ridge. Named on Preston Peak (1982) 7.5' quadrangle.

Big Butte Creek: see **Butte Creek** [BUTTE-GLENN].

Big Butte Creek, East Fork: see **Varey Creek** [BUTTE].

Big Camp [SISKIYOU]: *locality,* 10.5 miles northeast of Happy Camp (lat. 41°55' N, long. 123°15'45" W). Named on Figurehead Mountain (1980) 7.5' quadrangle.

Big Canon [SISKIYOU]: *locality,* 3 miles east-southeast of the town of Mount Shasta along Southern Pacific Railroad (lat. 41°17'45" N, long. 122°15'30" W; sec. 24, T 40 N, R 4 W). Named on Weed (1954) 15' quadrangle.

Big Canyon Creek [SISKIYOU]: *stream,* flows 7 miles to Sacramento River 2.5 miles south-southeast of the town of Mount Shasta (lat. 41°15'50" N, long. 122°17'20" W; near SE cor. sec. 34, T 40 N, R 4 W). Named on Weed (1954) 15' quadrangle.

Big Carmen Creek [SISKIYOU]: *stream,* flows 2 miles to Grouse Creek (3) 14 miles southeast of Etna (lat. 41°18'50" N, long. 122°42'15" W; at W line sec. 20, T 40 N, R 7 W); the stream heads at Big Carmen Lake. Named on China Mountain (1955) 15' quadrangle. Called Carmen Cr. on Etna (1934) 30' quadrangle.

Big Carmen Lake [SISKIYOU]: *lake,* 700 feet long, 16 miles southeast of Etna (lat. 41°17'30" N, long. 122°41'15" W; on S line sec. 29, T 40 N, R 7 W); the lake is 0.25 mile northwest of Little Carmen Lake at the head of Big Carmen Creek. Named on China Mountain (1955) 15' quadrangle.

Big Cave [SHASTA]: *cave,* 5 miles north-northwest of Coble Mountain (lat. 40°57' N, long. 121°22'15" W; on S line sec. 15, T 36 N, R 5 E). Named on Jellico (1957) 15' quadrangle.

Big Cedar Camp [SHASTA]: *locality,* 7.25 miles north-northeast of the village of Big Bend along Kosk Creek (lat. 41°07'20" N, long. 121°52'30" W; on E line sec. 29, T 38 N, R 1 E). Named on Bartle (1939) 30' quadrangle.

Big Chico Creek [BUTTE-TEHAMA]: *stream,* heads just inside Tehama County and flows 38 miles to Sacramento River 6 miles west-southwest of Chico in Butte County (lat. 39°42' N, long. 121°56'25" W). Named on Butte Meadows (1958) 15' quadrangle, and on Chico (1948), Cohasset (1979), Ord Ferry (1949), and Richardson Springs (1951) 7.5' quadrangles. Called Chico Creek on Chico Landing (1912) and Durham (1912) 7.5' quadrangles. William Dickey and Edward A. Farley gave the name "Arroyo Chico" to the stream in 1843 (Hanna, p. 62).

Big Conrad Gulch [SISKIYOU]: *canyon,* drained by a stream that flows 1.5 miles to South Fork Salmon River 27 miles south of Etna (lat. 41°03'55" N, long. 122°57'35" W); the canyon is east of Little Conrad Gulch. Named on Coffee Creek (1955) 15' quadrangle. Called Conrad Gulch on Etna (1934) 30' quadrangle.

Big Crane Creek [TEHAMA]: *stream,* flows 7.5 miles to Dry Creek (1) nearly 3 miles east-northeast of Rosewood (lat. 40°16'50" N, long. 122°30'10" W; near E line sec. 14, T 28 N, R 6 W). Named on Ono (1952) 15' quadrangle, and on Oxbow Bridge (1967) 7.5' quadrangle.

Big Creek [SHASTA]: *stream,* flows nearly 2 miles to North Fork Backbone Creek 9 miles south-southwest of Lamoine (lat. 40°51'25" N, long. 122°29'20" W). Named on Lamoine (1957) and Schell Mountain (1950) 15' quadrangles.

Big Creek [SISKIYOU]:

(1) *stream,* flows 2.5 miles to North Fork Salmon River 4.25 miles east-northeast of Forks of Salmon (lat. 41°17'10" N, long. 123°14'55" W). Named on Forks of Salmon (1978) 7.5' quadrangle.

(2) *stream,* flows 3.25 miles to North Fork Salmon River 7 miles north-northeast of Sawyers Bar (lat. 41°23'40" N, long. 123°05'30" W). Named on Yellow Dog Peak (1977) 7.5' quadrangle.

Big Dry Creek [TEHAMA]: *stream,* flows 17 miles to join Little Dry Creek and form Dry Creek (3) 18 miles southwest of Panther Spring (lat. 40°02'15" N, long. 121°58'35" W; near E line sec. 9, T 25 N, R 1 W). Named on Butte Meadows (1958) and Panther Spring (1953) 15' quadrangles. Called Dry Creek on Mineral (1941) 30' quadrangle.

Big Duck Lake [SISKIYOU]: *lake,* 1800 feet long, 10.5 miles south-southwest of Etna (lat. 41°18'30" N, long. 122°56'25" W; at N line sec. 19, T 40 N, R 9 W); the feature is nearly 0.5 mile east of Little Duck Lake. Named on Etna (1955) 15' quadrangle. Called Duck Lake on Etna (1934) 30' quadrangle.

Big Elk Fork: see **Wooley Creek** [SISKIYOU].

Big Elk Lake [SISKIYOU]: *lake,* 650 feet long, 18 miles southwest of Scott Bar (lat. 41°32'45" N, long. 123°13'25" W). Named on Marble Mountain (1980) 7.5' quadrangle

Bigelow Gulch [SISKIYOU]: *canyon,* drained by a stream that flows 2.25 miles to McCloud River [SHASTA-SISKIYOU] 7.5 miles east-southeast of McCloud (lat. 41°13'20" N, long. 122°00'10" W; sec. 18, T 39 N, R 1 W). Named on Big Bend (1961) 15' quadrangle.

Bigelow Meadow [SISKIYOU]: *area,* 7.25 miles east-northeast of McCloud (lat. 41°13'20" N, long. 122°00'20" W; sec. 18, T 39 N, R 1 W); the place is at the mouth of Bigelow Gulch. Named on Shoeinhorse (1954) 15' quadrangle.

Big Ferry Creek [SISKIYOU]: *stream,* flows 3.5 miles to Scott River 2 miles south-southwest of Scott Bar (lat. 41°42'45" N, long. 123°01'05" W; near N line sec. 32, T 45 N, R 10 W); the mouth of the stream is 1200 feet downstream from the mouth of Little Ferry Creek. Named on Fort Jones (1955) 15' quadrangle, and on Scott Bar (1980) 7.5' quadrangle. Called Ferry Creek on Seiad (1922) 30' quadrangle.

Big Flat [SHASTA]: *area,* 3 miles north-northeast of the village of Big Bend (lat. 41°03'30" N, long. 121°53' W; sec. 17, 20, T 37 N, R 1 E). Named on Big Bend (1961) 15' quadrangle.

Big Flat: see **Cecilville** [SISKIYOU].

Biggs [BUTTE]: *town,* 11 miles southwest of Oroville (lat. 39°24'45" N, long. 121°42'40" W; mainly in sec. 14, T 18 N, R 2 E). Named on Biggs (1970) 7.5' quadrangle. Postal authorities established Biggs Station post office in 1871 and changed the name to Biggs in 1884 (Frickstad, p. 8). The town incorporated in 1903. The name commemorates Major Marion Biggs, who made the first shipment of grain sent by railroad from the place (Wells and Chambers, p. 246). Postal authorities established Avon post office 7.5 miles north of Biggs in 1889 and discontinued it in 1899 (Salley, p. 12).

Biggs: see **East Biggs** [BUTTE].

Biggs Station: see **Biggs** [BUTTE]; **East Biggs** [BUTTE].

Big Gulch [SHASTA]: *canyon,* drained by a stream that flows 4.5 miles to Clear Creek nearly 5 miles southwest of Schell Mountain (lat. 40°49'50" N, long. 122°36'20" W; sec. 1, T 34 N, R 7 W). Named on Schell Mountain (1950) 15' quadrangle.

Big Hot Spring Valley: see **Morgan Hot Spring** [TEHAMA].

Big Kimshew Creek [BUTTE]: *stream,* flows 12 miles to West Branch Feather River 2 miles south-southeast of Stirling City (lat. 39°52'50" N, long. 121°30'20" W; sec. 3, T 23 N, R 4 E). Named on Kimshew Point (1979) and Stirling City (1979) 7.5' quadrangles. Called Kimshew Creek on Bidwell Bar (1897) 30' quadrangle, but United States Board on Geographic Names (1960b, p. 6) rejected this name for the stream. The word "Kimshew" is attributed to Indians (Gudde, 1949, p. 174). F.D. Dunn (p. 4) listed an inhabited place called Balsum Hill that was located on the east side of Big Kimshew Creek about 1 mile west of Table Mountain (sec. 32, T 25 N, R 5 E).

Big Lake [SHASTA]:
(1) *lake,* about 2 miles long, 8 miles north-northeast of Fall River Mills at the head of Tule River (lat. 41°07' N, long. 121°24' W). Named on Fall River Mills (1961) 15' quadrangle.
(2) *lake,* 500 feet long, 12 miles northwest of Lassen Peak (lat. 40°37'50" N, long. 121°37'40" W; on N line sec. 15, T 32 N, R 3 E). Named on Manzanita Lake (1956) 15' quadrangle.

Bigland Gulch [SISKIYOU]: *canyon,* drained by a stream that flows 1 mile to Indian Creek (3) 5.5 miles north of Fort Jones (lat. 41°41'15" N, long. 122°51'15" W; near SW cor. sec. 2, T 44 N, R 9 W). Named on Fort Jones (1955) 15' quadrangle.

Big Meadow [SISKIYOU]: *area,* 5.5 miles south-southwest of Ukonom Lake (lat. 41°30'35" N, long. 123°24' W). Named on Ukonom Mountain (1980) 7.5' quadrangle.

Big Meadows [SISKIYOU]:
(1) *area,* 11 miles south-southwest of Scott Bar (lat. 41°35'05" N, long. 123°03'25" W). Named on Boulder Peak (1981) 7.5' quadrangle.
(2) *area,* 11.5 miles north-northwest of Sawyers Bar (lat. 41°27'30" N, long. 123°11'30" W). Named on English Peak (1977) 7.5' quadrangle.
(3) *area,* 8.5 miles northwest of Fort Jones (lat. 41°41'25" N, long. 122°57'15" W; sec. 1, 2, T 44 N, R 10 W). Named on Fort Jones (1955) 15' quadrangle. United States Board on Geographic Names (1984c, p. 2) approved the name "Milk Ranch Meadows" for the feature, and rejected the names "Big Meadows" and "Milk Ranch Meadow."

Big Meadows Creek [SISKIYOU]:
(1) *stream,* flows 2.25 miles to Shackleford Creek 12 miles south of Scott Bar (lat. 41°34'20" N, long. 123°01'15" W; near S line sec. 17, T 43 N, R 10 W); the stream heads at Big Meadows (1). Named on Boulder Peak (1981) 7.5' quadrangle.
(2) *stream,* flows 4 miles to Wooley Creek 14 miles north-northwest of Sawyers Bar (lat. 41°29'20" N, long. 123°14'30" W); the stream heads at Big Meadows (2). Named on English Peak (1977) 7.5' quadrangle.

Big Medicine Creek [SISKIYOU]: *stream,* flows 2 miles to North Fork Wooley Creek 16 miles north of Forks of Salmon (lat. 41°29'05" N, long. 123°16'45" W); heads at Medicine Mountain—the mouth of the stream is 1500 feet upstream from the mouth of Little Medicine Creek. Named on Medicine Mountain (1978) 7.5' quadrangle.

Big Mill Creek [SISKIYOU]: *stream,* flows 5.5 miles to East Fork Scott River 12.5 miles south-southeast of Etna (lat. 41°18'40" N, long. 122°45'40" W; near W line sec. 14, T 40 N, R 8 W). Named on China Mountain (1955) and Etna (1955) 15' quadrangles. Called Mill Creek on Etna (1934) 30' quadrangle.

Big Ridge [BUTTE]: *ridge,* generally south-trending, 2.25 miles long, 7 miles northeast of Oroville Dam (lat. 39°37' N, long. 121°24'35" W). Named on Berry Creek (1970) and Oroville Dam (1970) 7.5' quadrangles.

Big Ridge [SISKIYOU]: *ridge,* generally southeast-trending, 4.5 miles long, 13 miles west-southwest of Scott Bar (lat. 41°39'30" N, long. 123°13'45" W). Named on Grider Valley (1981) and Huckleberry Mountain (1980) 7.5' quadrangles.

Big Ripples [BUTTE]: *locality,* nearly 6 miles north-northwest of Bidwell Bar along North Fork Feather River (lat. 39°37'30" N, long. 121°29'10" W); water of Lake Oroville now covers the site. Named on Bidwell Bar (1897) 30' quadrangle.

Big Rock [SISKIYOU]:
(1) *peak,* nearly 3 miles northeast of Condrey Mountain (lat. 41°57'55" N, long. 122°56'30" W; sec. 31, T 48 N, R 9 W). Altitude 6852 feet. Named on Condrey Mountain (1955) 15' quadrangle.
(2) *relief feature,* 9.5 miles north-northwest of Fort Jones (lat. 41°43'50" N, long. 122°54'50" W; on E line sec. 19, T 45 N, R 9 W). Named on Fort Jones (1955) 15' quadrangle.

Big Rock Camp [SISKIYOU]: *locality,* 15 miles southwest of Scott Bar (lat. 41°35'10" N, long. 123°12' W); the place is near the head of Big Rock Fork [of] Canyon Creek (3). Named on Marble Mountain (1980) 7.5' quadrangle.

Big Rock Fork: see **Canyon Creek** [SISKIYOU] (3).

Big Salt Creek [TEHAMA]: *stream,* flows 8 miles to Cottonwood Creek [SHASTA-TEHAMA] 8.5 miles northwest of Rosewood (lat. 40°20'20" N, long. 122°41'20" W; at W line sec. 29, T 29 N, R 7 W); the mouth of the creek is 2.5 miles downstream from the mouth of Little Salt Creek (1). Named on Chanchelulla Peak (1951) and Ono (1952) 15' quadrangles.

Big Sand Flat [SISKIYOU]: *area,* 8.5 miles north-northeast of Bartle (lat. 41°22'05" N, long. 121°45'35" W; in and near sec. 29, T 41 N, R 2 E). Named on Bartle (1961) 15' quadrangle.

Big Smoky Creek [TEHAMA]: *stream,* flows 7.25 miles to Deer Creek (2) 1.25 miles south-southwest of Polk Springs (lat. 40°06' N, long. 121°40'10" W; near NW cor. sec. 20, T 26 N, R 3 E). Named on Butte Meadows (1958) 15' quadrangle. Called Smoky Creek on Mineral (1941) 30' quadrangle.

Big Spring [GLENN]: *spring,* 9 miles south of Black Butte (lat. 39°35'25" N, long. 122°52'55" W; sec. 16, T 20 N, R 9 W). Named on Hull Mountain (1967) 7.5' quadrangle.

Big Spring [SHASTA]:
(1) *spring,* 3.5 miles southeast of Castella (lat. 41°06'20" N, long. 122°16'15" W; sec. 36, T 38 N, R 4 W). Named on Dunsmuir (1954) 15' quadrangle.
(2) *spring,* 11 miles north of Lassen Peak (lat. 40°38'40" N, long. 121°28' W; near N line sec. 12, T 32 N, R 4 E). Named on Prospect Peak (1957) 15' quadrangle. Lassen Peak (1894) 1° quadrangle has the name "Great Spring" for a locality situated near present Big Spring (2).

Big Springs [SISKIYOU]:
(1) *spring,* 1.25 miles northwest of the town of Mount Shasta (lat. 41°19'45" N, long. 122°19'35" W; near E line sec. 8, T 40 N, R 4 W). Named on Weed (1954) 15' quadrangle.
(2) *springs,* 5.5 miles east-southeast of McCloud along McCloud River [SHASTA-SISKIYOU] (lat. 41°13'45" N, long. 122°02'20" W; near E line sec. 14, T 39 N, R 2 W). Named on Shoeinhorse Mountain (1954) 15' quadrangle.
(3) *locality,* 26 miles southwest of Macdoel (lat. 41°35'45" N, long. 122°24'05" W; near SE cor. sec. 3, T 43 N, R 5 W). Named on Lake Shastina (1954) 15' quadrangle.

Big Springs Campground [SHASTA]: *locality,* 10.5 miles north-northeast of Lassen Peak along Hat Creek (lat. 40°38' N, long. 121°27'50" W; near SE cor. sec. 12, T 32 N, R 4 E); the place is less than 1 mile south-southeast of Big Spring (2). Named on Prospect Peak (1957) 15' quadrangle.

Big Springs Creek [SISKIYOU]: *stream,* flows 2 miles to Cold Creek (4) less than 1 mile southwest of the town of Mount Shasta (lat. 41°18'20" N, long. 122°19'30" W; near SW cor. sec. 16, T 40 N, R 4 W); the stream heads at Big Springs (1). Named on Weed (1954) 15' quadrangle.

Big Stony Bar: see **Kanaka Bar** [BUTTE].

Big Stump Camp [TEHAMA]: *locality,* 1.25 miles northeast of Ball Mountain (lat. 39°56'35" N, long. 122°45'50" W; near N line sec. 16, T 24 N, R 8 W). Named on Ball Mountain (1967) 7.5' quadrangle.

Big Tableland [SISKIYOU]: *relief feature,* mesalike elevation 10.5 milcs southeast of Dorris (lat. 41°53' N, long. 121°45' W). Named on Dorris (1950) and Mount Dome (1950) 15' quadrangles.

Big Twin Creek [SISKIYOU]: *stream,* flows 1.5 miles to North Fork Salmon River 6.25 miles north-northeast of Sawyers Bar (lat. 41°22'55" N, long. 123°05'10" W); the mouth of the stream is 650 feet downstream from the mouth of Little Twin Creek. Named on Tanners Peak (1977) and Yellow Dog Peak (1977) 7.5' quadrangles.

Big Wheel Gulch [SISKIYOU]: *canyon,* drained by a stream that flows 1.5 miles to McAdam Creek 4.5 miles north of Fort Jones (lat. 41°40'15" N, long. 122°49'40" W; at N line sec. 13, T 44 N, R 9 W). Named on Fort

Jones (1955) 15' quadrangle. United States Board on Geographic Names (1985c, p. 2, 3) approved the name "Soares Gulch" for the feature, and applied the name "Big Wheel Gulch" to a nearby canyon that opens into the canyon of McAdam Creek 3.5 miles north of Fort Jones (lat. 41°39'38" N, long. 122°49'57" W; sec. 13, T 44 N, R 9 W).

Big Winters Creek [BUTTE]: *stream,* flows 1.5 miles to Sucker Run 5.5 miles north-northwest of Clipper Mills (lat. 39°36'05" N, long. 121°13'05" W; at S line sec. 8, T 20 N, R 7 E); the mouth of the stream is less than 1 mile upstream from the mouth of Winters Creek. Named on Clipper Mills (1948) 7.5' quadrangle.

Bill Berry Creek: see **Scott Bar** [SISKIYOU].

Bills Creek [SHASTA]: *stream,* flows 2 miles to Squirrel Creek 6 miles east of Bollibokka Mountain (lat. 40°55'15" N, long. 122°06'05" W; sec. 4, T 35 N, R 2 W). Named on Bollibokka Mountain (1957) 15' quadrangle. The canyon of the stream is called Timber Canyon on Redding (1901) 30' quadrangle.

Bingham Lake [SISKIYOU]: *lake,* 900 feet long, 13 miles south-southwest of Etna (lat. 41°16'35" N, long. 122°56'55" W; near NW cor. sec. 31, T 40 N, R 9 W). Named on Etna (1955) 15' quadrangle.

Bird Flat [SHASTA]: *area,* nearly 4 miles northwest of Burney Falls (lat. 41°03'15" N, long. 121°42' W; sec. 23, T 37 N, R 2 E). Named on Pondosa (1961) 15' quadrangle. Steger (p. 18), who used the form "Bird's Flat" for the name, noted that the area is a nesting place for migratory birds.

Biscuit Flat [TEHAMA]: *area,* 3 miles west of Wakefield Flat along South Fork Cottonwood Creek [SHASTA-TEHAMA] (lat. 40°07'15" N, long. 122°41'50" W; sec. 7, T 26 N, R 7 W). Named on Raglin Ridge (1967) 7.5' quadrangle.

Bishop Creek [SISKIYOU]: *stream,* flows 2.5 miles to Elk Creek 6.5 miles north of Ukonom Lake (lat. 41°40'25" N, long. 123°20'45" W). Named on Clear Creek (1981) and Huckleberry Mountain (1980) 7.5' quadrangles.

Bittenbender Creek [SISKIYOU]: *stream,* flows 1 mile to Klamath River 2.25 miles west-northwest of the village of Seiad Valley (lat. 41°51'35" N, long. 123°14'05" W). Named on Seiad Valley (1980) 7.5' quadrangle.

Black Bear [SISKIYOU]: *locality,* 7 miles north-northwest of Cecilville (lat. 41°14'30" N, long. 123°10'35" W); the place is along Black Bear Creek. Named on Cecilville (1979) 7.5' quadrangle. Postal authorities established Black Bear post office in 1869 and discontinued it in 1941; the post office name had both the forms "Black Bear" and "Blackbear" (Salley, p. 22).

Black Bear Camp [TEHAMA]: *locality,* 8.5 miles west-southwest of Paskenta (lat. 39°49'25" N, long. 122°40'35" W; near W line sec. 29, T 23 N, R 7 W). Named on Hall Ridge (1967) 7.5' quadrangle.

Black Bear Creek [SISKIYOU]: *stream,* flows 6 miles to South Fork Salmon River 6 miles northwest of Cecilville (lat. 41°12'15" N, long. 123°13'25" W. Named on Cecilville (1979) and Sawyers Bar (1979) 7.5' quadrangles.

Black Bear Summit [SISKIYOU]: *pass,* 2.5 miles south-southwest of Sawyers Bar (lat. 41°15'50" N, long. 123°08'45" W); the pass is at the head of Black Bear Creek. Named on Sawyers Bar (1979) 7.5' quadrangle.

Blackberry Creek [SHASTA]: *stream,* flows 1.5 miles to Pit River 10 miles north-northeast of the village of Montgomery Creek (lat. 40°57'55" N, long. 121°49'40" W). Named on Montgomery Creek (1956) 15' quadrangle.

Blackberry Creek [SISKIYOU]: *stream,* flows 1.25 miles to West Fork Knownothing Creek nearly 6 miles east-northeast of Salmon Mountain (lat. 41°12'45" N, long. 123°18'30" W). Named on Youngs Peak (1979) 7.5' quadrangle.

Blackberry Island [TEHAMA]: *island,* 5.5 miles east-southeast of Red Bluff along Sacramento River (lat. 40°08'35" N, long. 122°08'35" W; at SE cor. sec. 36, T 27 N, R 3 W). Named on Red Bluff East (1951) 7.5' quadrangle.

Black Butte [GLENN]: *peak,* 19 miles west-southwest of Newville (lat. 39°43'35" N, long. 122°52'20" W; sec. 27, T 22 N, R 9 W). Altitude 7448 feet. Named on Plaskett Meadows (1967) 7.5' quadrangle.

Black Butte [SHASTA]: *crater,* 6.5 miles west-southwest of Shingletown (lat. 40°27'15" N, long. 121°59'50" W; sec. 17, T 30 N, R 1 W). Named on Manton (1956) 15' quadrangle, and on Tuscan Buttes NE (1965) 7.5' quadrangle. On Red Bluff (1894) 1° quadrangle, the crater has the label "Cone." The feature also is known as Asbury Peak, for William Asbury, who homesteaded on its south slope (Steger, p. 18).

Black Butte [SISKIYOU]:

(1) *mountain,* 4.5 miles south-southeast of Weed (lat. 41°22' N, long. 122°20'50" W). Altitude 6325 feet. Named on Weed (1954) 15' quadrangle. Called Wintoon Butte on Shasta (1894) 1° quadrangle, called Cone Mountain on Diller's (1895) map, and called Sugarloaf on Diller and others' (1915) map, but United States Board on Geographic Names (1933, p. 232; 1936, p. 9) rejected the names "Wintoon Butte," "Cone Mountain," "Sugar Loaf," and "Muir Butte" for the feature. Beckwith (p. 50) used the name "Black Butte" in the 1850's, and noted that the mountain was as "black as the darkest iron ore."

(2) *locality,* 2.5 miles south-southeast of Weed along Southern Pacific Railroad (lat. 41°23'30" N, long. 122°21'35" W; at NW cor. sec. 19, T 41 N, R 4 W); the place is 2 miles north-northwest of Black Butte (1). Named on Weed (1954) 15' quadrangle. Diller's (1895) map shows a place called Acme located along the railroad at or near present Black Butte (2).

Black Butte [TEHAMA]:

(1) *peak,* 0.5 mile north-northwest of Panther Spring (lat. 40°15'20" N, long. 121°46'40" W). Altitude 3555 feet. Named on Manton (1956) 15' quadrangle.

(2) *peak,* 9 miles south-southeast of Flournoy (lat. 39°48'55" N, long. 122°21'05" W; near SE cor. sec. 30, T 23 N, R 4 W). Named on Black Butte Dam (1967) 7.5' quadrangle. On Flournoy (1958) 15' quadrangle, the name applies to the ridge on which present Black Butte (2) is the high point.

Black Butte: see **Mount Conard** [TEHAMA]; **Prospect Peak** [SHASTA].

Black Butte Creek: see **Butte Creek** [SHASTA].

Black Butte Lake: see **Black Butte Reservoir** [GLENN-TEHAMA].

Black Butte Meadows: see **Conard Meadows** [TEHAMA].

Black Butte Reservoir [GLENN-TEHAMA]: *lake,* on Glenn-Tehama County line behind a dam 9 miles southeast of Flournoy on Stony Creek [GLENN-TEHAMA] (lat. 39°49' N, long. 122°20'10" W; sec. 29, T 23 N, R 4 W); Black Butte [TEHAMA] (2) is near the dam that forms the lake. Named on Black Butte Dam (1967), Julian Rocks (1968), and Sehorn Creek (1967) 7.5' quadrangles. United States Board on Geographic Names (1972a, p. 4) approved the name "Black Butte Lake" for the feature, and gave the name "Black Butte Reservoir" as a variant.

Black Butte River [GLENN]: *stream,* formed by the confluence of Estell Creek and Middle Creek, flows 4.25 miles to Mendocino County nearly 6 miles south of Black Butte (lat. 39°38'40" N, long. 122°53'25" W). Named on Kneecap Ridge (1967) and Plaskett Ridge (1967) 7.5' quadrangles. United States Board on Geographic Names (1933, p. 148) rejected the names "Poopoteyuk River" and "South Fork of Middle Fork Eel River" for the stream.

Black Butte Spring [SISKIYOU]: *spring,* 2.5 miles southeast of Weed (lat. 41°23'45" N, long. 122°21'25" W; sec. 18, T 41 N, R 4 W); the spring is 2 miles north-northwest of Black Butte (1). Named on Weed (1954) 15' quadrangle.

Black Crater [SISKIYOU]: *relief feature,* 8 miles east-southeast of Mount Dome (lat. 41°46' N, long. 121°33' W; near SE cor. sec. 6, T 45 N, R 4 E). Named on Mount Dome (1950) 15' quadrangle.

Black Crater: see **The Whaleback** [SISKIYOU].

Black Diamond Creek [BUTTE]: *stream,* flows 2 miles to Dry Creek 6.25 miles east-southeast of Saint John Mountain (lat. 39°24'45" N, long. 122°34'45" W; at W line sec. 18, T 18 N, R 6 W). Named on Stonyford (1968) 7.5' quadrangle.

Black Diamond Glades [GLENN]: *area,* 5.25 miles east-southeast of Saint John Mountain (lat. 39°24'15" N, long. 122°36'30" W; sec. 23, T 18 N, R 7 W); the place is at the head of Black Diamond Creek. Named on Stonyford (1968) 7.5' quadrangle.

Black Diamond Ridge [GLENN]: *ridge,* generally south-trending, 3 miles long, 4 miles east-southeast of Saint John Mountain (lat. 39°24'35" N, long. 122°37'15" W). Named on Saint John Mountain (1968) and Stonyford (1968) 7.5' quadrangles.

Black Flat [TEHAMA]: *area,* 3.5 miles north-northwest of Ball Mountain (lat. 40°58'45" N, long. 122°48'45" W; near E line sec. 36, T 25 N, R 9 W). Named on Ball Mountain (1967) 7.5' quadrangle.

Black Fox Mountain [SISKIYOU]: *peak,* 7.25 miles north-northwest of Bartle (lat. 41°20'45" N, long. 121°53'25" W; near E line sec. 6, T 40 N, R 1 E). Altitude 6502 feet. Named on Bartle (1961) 15' quadrangle.

Black Fox Mountain: see **Little Black Fox Mountain** [SISKIYOU].

Black Gulch [SISKIYOU]: *canyon,* drained by a stream that flows 3.25 miles to South Fork Salmon River 3 miles southeast of Cecilville (lat. 41°06'45" N, long. 123°05'15" W). Named on Thompson Peak (1979) 7.5' quadrangle.

Blackjack Spring [TEHAMA]: *spring,* 8.5 miles south-southwest of Ball Mountain (lat. 39°49'50" N, long. 122°51'50" W; near SW cor. sec. 22, T 23 N, R 9 W). Named on Log Spring (1967) 7.5' quadrangle.

Black Marble Mountain [SISKIYOU]: *peak,* 15 miles southwest of Scott Bar (lat. 41°34'40" N, long. 123°12'10" W); the peak is in Marble Mountains. Altitude 7442 feet. Named on Marble Mountain (1980) 7.5' quadrangle. Called Black Mtn. on Scott Bar (1955) 15' quadrangle, but United States Board on Geographic Names (1981c, p. 3) rejected this name for the feature.

Black Meadows: see **Back Meadows** [SISKIYOU].

Black Meadows Creek: see **Back Meadows Creek** [SISKIYOU].

Black Mountain [SISKIYOU]:

(1) *peak,* 14 miles north of Forks of Salmon (lat. 41°27'40" N, long. 123°22'35" W). Altitude 5022 feet. Named on Somes Bar (1979) 7.5' quadrangle.

(2) *peak,* 10.5 miles northeast of the village of Seiad Valley (lat. 41°57'15" N, long. 123°03'50" W; at W line sec. 6, T 47 N, R 10 W); the peak is 2200 feet west of White Mountain. Named on Dutch Creek (1980) 7.5' quadrangle.

(3) *peak,* 4.5 miles south-southeast of Hornbrook (lat. 41°51'30" N, long. 122°30'30" W; at N line sec. 11, T 46 N, R 6 W). Altitude 5118 feet.

Named on Hornbrook (1955) 15' quadrangle. Called Round Hill on Shasta (1894) 1° quadrangle.
(4) *peak,* 7 miles east-southeast of Medicine Lake (lat. 41°31'50" N, long. 121°28'30" W). Altitude 6984 feet. Named on Timber Mountain (1952) 15' quadrangle.

Black Mountain [SISKIYOU]: *peak,* 31 miles south of Etna on Siskiyou-Trinity County line (lat. 41°00'30" N, long. 122°54'45" W; near E line sec. 5, T 36 N, R 9 W). Altitude 8019 feet. Named on Coffee Creek (1955) 15' quadrangle.

Black Mountain: see **Black Marble Mountain** [SISKIYOU].

Black Oak Campground [TEHAMA]: *locality,* 1.25 miles northwest of Mineral (lat. 40°21'35" N, long. 121°36'35" W; at E line sec. 23, T 29 N, R 3 E). Named on Lassen Peak (1956) 15' quadrangle.

Black Oak Grove [TEHAMA]: *locality,* 5 miles southwest of Panther Spring (lat. 40°11'40" N, long. 121°50'30" W). Named on Panther Spring (1953) 15' quadrangle.

Black Rock [SISKIYOU]:
(1) *relief feature,* 16 miles south-southeast of Etna (lat. 41°15'05" N, long. 122°44'30" W; sec. 12, T 39 N, R 8 W). Named on Bonanza King (1955) and China Mountain (1955) 15' quadrangles.
(2) *peak,* 13 miles west of Macdoel (lat. 41°52' N, long. 122°14'55" W; near E line sec. 1, T 46 N, R 4 W). Altitude 6894 feet. Named on Copco (1954) and Macdoel (1954) 15' quadrangles.

Black Rock [TEHAMA]: *relief feature,* 5.25 miles north-northwest of Polk Springs (lat. 40°11' N, long. 121°42'30" W; near NE cor. sec. 23, T 27 N, R 2 E). Named on Butte Meadows (1958) 15' quadrangle.

Black Rock: see **Little Black Rock** [SHASTA].

Black Rock Peak: see **Freaner Peak** [SHASTA].

Blacks Gulch [SISKIYOU]:
(1) *canyon,* drained by a stream that flows about 1.5 miles to Indian Creek (3) 8.5 miles north of Fort Jones (lat. 41°43'45" N, long. 122°50'50" W; at S line sec. 23, T 45 N, R 9 W). Named on Fort Jones (1955) 15' quadrangle.
(2) *canyon,* drained by a stream that flows 1.5 miles to Yreka Creek 5.5 miles south-southwest of Yreka (lat. 41°40'05" N, long. 122°41'45" W; near N line sec. 18, T 44 N, R 7 W). Named on Yreka (1954) 15' quadrangle.

Blaine: see **Mary Blaine Mountain** [SISKIYOU].

Blair: see **Whiskeytown** [SHASTA].

Blair Ravine [BUTTE]: *canyon,* drained by a stream that flows less than 1 mile to Concow Creek 5.5 miles east-southeast of Paradise (lat. 39°44' N, long. 121°32'25" W; at W line sec. 28, T 22 N, R 4 E). Named on Cherokee (1970) 7.5' quadrangle.

Blakes Fork: see **South Russian Creek** [SISKIYOU].

Blanche Lake [SISKIYOU]: *lake,* 2.25 miles southeast of Medicine Lake (lat. 41°33'25" N, long. 121°34'10" W; sec. 24, T 43 N, R 3 E). Named on Medicine Lake (1952) 15' quadrangle.

Blavo [BUTTE]: *locality,* 10 miles west-northwest of Oroville along Sacramento Northern Railroad (lat. 39°34'15" N, long. 121°43'50" W). Named on Shippee (1948) 7.5' quadrangle.

Blethen Island [TEHAMA]: *island,* 2.5 miles northwest of Vina in Sacramento River (lat. 39°57'45" N, long. 122°05' W). Named on Vina (1904) 15' quadrangle.

Blind Horse Creek [SISKIYOU]: *stream,* flows 2.5 miles to South Fork Salmon River 5.5 miles southeast of Cecilville (lat. 41°05'30" N, long. 123°03'10" W). Named on Thompson Peak (1979) 7.5' quadrangle.

Blinzig [BUTTE]: *locality,* 5 miles north of the village of Berry Creek along Western Pacific Railroad (lat. 39°42'45" N, long. 121°24'40" W; near SW cor. sec. 34, T 22 N, R 5 E). Named on Big Bend Mountain (1948) 15' quadrangle. Water of Lake Oroville now covers the site. From 1909 until 1912 the place was a railroad siding that served Camp Enjoyment, one of the first summer resorts opened along Feather River (NE cor. sec. 34, T 22 N, R 5 E) (Dunn, F.D., p. 10, 18).

Blinzig: see **New Blinzig** [BUTTE].

Blodgett Creek [SHASTA]: *stream,* flows 1.5 miles to Clear Creek 8 miles north of Schell Mountain (lat. 40°58'15" N, long. 122°33'35" W; near N line sec. 21, T 36 N, R 6 W). Named on Schell Mountain (1950) 15' quadrangle.

Bloody Gulch [SISKIYOU]: *canyon,* less than 1 mile long, opens into the canyon of Indian Creek (3) 3 miles north-northwest of Fort Jones (lat. 41°39'05" N, long. 122°51'40" W; sec. 22, T 44 N, R 9 W). Named on Fort Jones (1955) 15' quadrangle.

Bloody Island [TEHAMA]: *area,* 8 miles north of Bend between Sacramento River and Battle Creek [SHASTA-TEHAMA] (lat. 40°22'15" N, long. 122°10'45" W). Named on Balls Ferry (1965) and Bend (1965) 7.5' quadrangles. Samuel J. Hensley named the feature after he had an encounter with some Indians there in 1844 (Hoover, Rensch, and Rensch, p. 548).

Bloomer [BUTTE]: *locality,* 5.5 miles north-northwest of Bidwell Bar along Western Pacific Railroad (lat. 39°37'35" N, long. 121°29'30" W; near S line sec. 35, T 21 N, R 4 E); the place is 2.5 miles southwest of Bloomer Mountain. Named on Big Bend Mountain (1948) 15' quadrangle. Water of Lake Oroville now covers the site.

Bloomer Bar: see **Bloomer Hill** [BUTTE].

Bloomer Hill [BUTTE]: *peak,* 3.25 miles west of the village of Berry Creek (lat. 39°39'10" N, long. 121°27'45" W; sec. 30, T 21 N, R 5 E). Altitude 3005 feet. Named on Berry Creek (1970) 7.5' quadrangle. Wells and Chambers' (1882) map shows a place called Bloomer Bar located along North Fork Feather River about 2 miles northwest of present Bloomer Hill. F.D. Dunn (p. 73) listed a place called Mugginsville that was located on the west bank of North Fork Feather River opposite Bloomer Hill (sec. 26, T 21 N, R 4 E), and (p. 60) listed a place called Lattimores Bar, or Latimer Bar, that was situated along the south side of North Fork Feather River about 1.5 miles north of present Bloomer Hill (sec. 18, T 21 N, R 5 E).

Bloomer Ravine [BUTTE]: *canyon,* drained by a stream that flows 1.25 miles to Lake Oroville 4 miles west of the village of Berry Creek (lat. 39°38' N, long. 121°28'35" W; sec. 36, T 21 N, R 4 E); the canyon heads near Bloomer Hill. Named on Berry Creek (1970) 7.5' quadrangle.

Bloomfield Pass [SISKIYOU]: *pass,* 9 miles north-northeast of the village of Seiad Valley (lat. 41°57'50" N, long. 123°07'20" W). Named on Dutch Creek (1980) 7.5' quadrangle.

Bloomingdale: see **Oregon City** [BUTTE].

Blossom [TEHAMA]: *locality,* 5.5 miles north of Red Bank (lat. 40°10'30" N, long. 122°25'25" W; near SW cor. sec. 22, T 27 N, R 5 W). Named on Blossom (1952) 7.5' quadrangle.

Blowhard Ravine: see **Inskip** [BUTTE].

Blueberry Lake [SISKIYOU]: *lake,* 500 feet long, 14 miles north of Sawyers Bar (lat. 41°29'50" N, long. 123°08'20" W). Named on English Peak (1977) 7.5' quadrangle.

Blue Canyon [SHASTA]: *canyon,* drained by a stream that flows 1 mile to Shasta Lake 13 miles north of Millville (lat. 40°44'05" N, long. 122°09'15" W; near N line sec. 12, T 33 N, R 3 W). Named on Bella Vista (1965) 7.5' quadrangle. Called Long Gulch on Millville (1953) 15' quadrangle, but United States Board on Geographic Names (1966, p. 6) rejected this name for the feature.

Blue Canyon [TEHAMA]: *canyon,* drained by a stream that flows 1.5 miles to Middle Fork Elder Creek 8 miles north-northwest of Paskenta (lat. 39°59'40" N, long. 122°35'35" W; near E line sec. 25, T 25 N, R 7 W). Named on Paskenta (1967) 7.5' quadrangle.

Bluedoor Flat [TEHAMA]: *area,* 4.25 miles east of Wakefield Flat (lat. 40°07'10" N, long. 122°33'40" W; sec. 8, T 26 N, R 6 W). Named on Lowrey (1967) 7.5' quadrangle.

Blue Granite Lake [SISKIYOU]: *lake,* 1250 feet long, 2.5 miles east-southeast of Ukonom Lake (lat. 41°34' N, long. 123°18'35" W). Named on Ukonom Lake (1980) 7.5' quadrangle. The lake, which is at the head of a branch of Granite Creek (2), is one of the group called Granite Lakes on Seiad (1922) 30' quadrangle.

Blue Gulch [SISKIYOU]:
(1) *canyon,* drained by a stream that flows 1 mile to South Fork Salmon River 2.5 miles southeast of Cecilville (lat. 41°07'05" N, long. 123°05'35" W). Named on Thompson Peak (1979) 7.5' quadrangle.
(2) *canyon,* drained by a stream that flows 1.5 miles to Klamath River 1.5 miles south-southeast of Hornbrook (lat. 41°53'15" N, long. 122°32'35" W; at N line sec. 33, T 47 N, R 6 W). Named on Hornbrook (1955) 15' quadrangle.

Blue Heron Creek [SISKIYOU]: *stream,* flows 2.25 miles to McCloud River [SHASTA-SISKIYOU] 7.5 miles west of Bartle (lat. 41°14'25" N, long. 121°57'45" W; near E line sec. 9, T 39 N, R 1 W). Named on Big Bend (1961) 15' quadrangle.

Blue Jay Creek [SHASTA]: *stream,* flows 2.5 miles to Kosk Creek 1.25 miles west-northwest of the village of Big Bend (lat. 41°01'45" N, long. 121°55'50" W; near SE cor. sec. 26, T 37 N, R 1 W). Named on Big Bend (1961) 15' quadrangle.

Blue Jay Creek [SISKIYOU]: *stream,* flows 1 mile to Scott River 12.5 miles south of Etna (lat. 41°16'35" N, long. 122°51'30" W; near W line sec. 35, T 40 N, R 9 W). Named on Etna (1955) 15' quadrangle.

Bluejay Mountain [SHASTA]: *peak,* 11 miles east-southeast of Bollibokka Mountain (lat. 40°53' N, long. 122°01'15" W; on N line sec. 19, T 35 N, R 1 W). Altitude 3276 feet. Named on Bollibokka Mountain (1957) 15' quadrangle.

Blue Jay Ridge [SISKIYOU]: *ridge,* north-northeast-trending, 1.5 miles long, 15 miles south of Etna (lat. 41°14'30" N, long. 122°51'30" W). Named on Coffee Creek (1955) 15' quadrangle.

Blue Lake [SHASTA]:
(1) *lake,* 400 feet long, 5 miles north-northeast of Burney (lat. 40°56'50" N, long. 121°37'20" W; sec. 27, T 36 N, R 3 E). Named on Burney (1939) 30' quadrangle.
(2) *lake,* 800 feet long, 10 miles north-northeast of Whitmore (lat. 40°45' N, long. 121°48'10" W; near NE cor. sec. 1, T 33 N, R 1 E). Named on Montgomery Creek (1956) and Whitmore (1956) 15' quadrangles.
(3) *lake,* 350 feet long, 2.5 miles west-southwest of Lassen Peak (lat. 40°28'05" N, long. 121°33'05" W; at E line sec. 8, T 30 N, R 4 E). Named

on Lassen Peak (1956) 15' quadrangle. The name is from the color of the lake as seen from the west side of Mount Diller (Schulz, p. 4).

Blue Lake: see **Big Blue Lake** [SISKIYOU].

Blue Lake Canyon [SHASTA]: *canyon,* 5 miles long, along North Fork Bailey Creek above a point 6 miles west of Lassen Peak (lat. 40°29'35" N, long. 121°37'30" W; sec. 34, T 31 N, R 3 E); Blue Lake (3) is near the head of the canyon. Named on Lassen Peak (1956) 15' quadrangle.

Blue Mountain [SHASTA]:

(1) *peak,* 5 miles northwest of Schell Mountain on Shasta-Trinity County line (lat. 40°54' N, long. 122°36' W; on W line sec. 7, T 35 N, R 6 W). Named on Schell Mountain (1950) 15' quadrangle.

(2) *ridge,* east-trending, 2 miles long, 4.5 miles south of Whitmore (lat. 40°34' N, long. 121°55'15" W). Named on Whitmore (1956) 15' quadrangle.

Blue Mountain [SISKIYOU]: *peak,* 4.25 miles south of the village of Seiad Valley (lat. 41°46'50" N, long. 123°11'40" W). Altitude 5260 feet. Named on Seiad Valley (1980) 7.5' quadrangle.

Blue Nose: see **Blue Nose Bluff** [SISKIYOU].

Blue Nose Bluff [SISKIYOU]: *relief feature,* 3.5 miles northeast of Dillon Mountain along the west side of Klamath River (lat. 41°34'05" N, long. 123°31'50" W). Named on Dillon Mountain (1983) 7.5' quadrangle. Dillon Mountain (1955) 15' quadrangle shows Blue Nose mine situated across Klamath River from Blue Nose Bluff. Postal authorities established Blue Nose post office, named for the mine, in 1917 and discontinued it in 1927 (Salley, p. 23). Nova Scotians, sometimes known as Blue Noses, started the mine (Gudde, 1969, p. 32).

Bluenose Peak [SHASTA]: *peak,* 11.5 miles southwest of Shasta Bally on Shasta-Trinity County line (lat. 40°30' N, long. 122°51' W; near N line sec. 35, T 31 N, R 9 W). Named on Weaverville (1950) 15' quadrangle.

Blue Pond [SISKIYOU]: *lake,* 700 feet long, 6 miles west of Fort Jones (lat. 41°35'30" N, long. 122°57'15" W; on W line sec. 12, T 43 N, R 10 W). Named on Fort Jones (1955) 15' quadrangle.

Blue Ridge [SHASTA]:

(1) *ridge,* generally northeast-trending, 2 miles long, 5 miles west-southwest of Shasta Bally on Shasta-Trinity County line (lat. 40°34'15" N, long. 122°43'55" W). Named on Shasta Bally (1978) 7.5' quadrangle.

(2) *ridge,* south-trending, 2.5 miles long, 5.5 miles northeast of the town of Central Valley (lat. 40°44' N, long. 122°17' W). Named on Project City (1957) 7.5' quadrangle.

Blue Ridge [SISKIYOU]: *ridge,* west-trending, 9.5 miles long, center 5 miles west-southwest of Sawyers Bar (lat. 41°16'15" N, long. 123°13'15" W). Named on Forks of Salmon (1978) and Sawyers Bar (1979) 7.5' quadrangles.

Blue Ridge [TEHAMA]: *ridge,* west-southwest-trending, 7 miles long, 8 miles west-northwest of Mineral (lat. 40°24' N, long. 121°43'45" W). Named on Lassen Peak (1956) and Manton (1956) 15' quadrangles.

Blue Ridge Springs [TEHAMA]: *springs,* 7.5 miles west-northwest of Mineral (lat. 40°23'35" N, long. 121°43'25" W; at W line sec. 2, T 29 N, R 2 E); the springs are on the southeast side of Blue Ridge. Named on Lassen Peak (1956) 15' quadrangle.

Blue Slide Creek [GLENN]: *stream,* flows 1 mile to Mendocino County nearly 5 miles northwest of Black Butte (lat. 39°46'25" N, long. 122°56'10" W; sec. 11, T 22 N, R 10 W). Named on Mendocino Pass (1967) 7.5' quadrangle.

Blue Tent Creek [TEHAMA]: *stream,* flows 9.5 miles to Sacramento River 2.25 miles north-northeast of downtown Red Bluff (lat. 40°12'20" N, long. 122°12'50" W; sec. 9, T 27 N, R 3 W). Named on Hooker (1965), Red Bluff East (1951), and Red Bluff West (1951) 7.5' quadrangles.

Bluff Falls [TEHAMA]: *waterfall,* 5.5 miles north-northeast of Mineral (lat. 40°24'50" N, long. 121°32' W; near W line sec. 34, T 30 N, R 4 E). Named on Lassen Peak (1956) 15' quadrangle.

Bluff Falls Campground [TEHAMA]: *locality,* nearly 6 miles northeast of Mineral (lat. 40°24'45" N, long. 121°31'50" W; near SW cor. sec. 34, T 30 N, R 4 E); the place is near Bluff Falls. Named on Lassen Peak (1956) 15' quadrangle.

Bluff Lake [SHASTA]: *lake,* 400 feet long, 8 miles east-southeast of Lassen Peak (lat. 40°27'50" N, long. 121°21'30" W; sec. 18, T 30 N, R 6 E). Named on Mount Harkness (1956) 15' quadrangle.

Bluff Springs [TEHAMA]: *springs,* 4 miles southeast of Manton (lat. 40°24'10" N, long. 121°48'45" W; sec. 1, T 29 N, R 1 E). Named on Manton (1956) 15' quadrangle. Called Bluff Spring on Mineral (1941) 30' quadrangle.

Bluford Gulch [SHASTA]: *canyon,* drained by a stream that flows 3.25 miles to Knob Gulch 1.5 miles west-northwest of Arbuckle Mountain (lat. 40°24'30" N, long. 122°53'45" W; near E line sec. 32, T 30 N, R 9 W). Named on Chanchelulla Peak (1951) 15' quadrangle.

Blunkall Crosing [TEHAMA]: *locality,* 8.5 miles south-southwest of Panther Spring along Mill Creek (3) (lat. 40°08'30" N, long. 121°51'05" W). Named on Panther Spring (1953) 15' quadrangle.

Blunt [TEHAMA]: *locality,* 3.5 miles south-southeast of Hooker (lat. 40°15'05" N, long. 122°18'20" W; sec. 27, T 28 N, R 4 W). Named on Hooker (1965) 7.5' quadrangle. On Red Bank (1952) 15' quadrangle, the name applies to a place situated 1 mile farther east-southeast along the railroad (near NW cor. sec. 35, T 28 N, R 4 W).

Board Creek [TEHAMA]: *stream,* flows 4.5 miles to Grindstone Creek [GLENN-TEHAMA] 10 miles south-southwest of Ball Mountain (lat. 39°48'35" N, long. 122°52'25" W; sec. 33, T 23 N, R 9 W). Named on Mendocino Pass (1967) 7.5' quadrangle.

Boardman Gulch [SISKIYOU]: *canyon,* drained by a stream that flows 1 mile to the canyon of Indian Creek (3) 3.5 miles north-northwest of Fort Jones (lat. 41°39'20" N, long. 122°51'30" W; at S line sec. 15, T 44 N, R 9 W). Named on Fort Jones (1955) 15' quadrangle.

Board Ridge [TEHAMA]: *ridge,* generally east-trending, 1.25 miles long, 11.5 miles southwest of Ball Mountain (lat. 39°48'40" N, long. 122°55'45" W; sec. 35, 36, T 23 N, R 10 W); the ridge is southwest of Board Creek. Named on Mendocino Pass (1967) 7.5' quadrangle.

Board Tree Campground [GLENN]: *locality,* 5.25 miles south-southeast of Black Butte (lat. 39°39'15" N, long. 121°50'05" W; near NE cor. sec. 26, T 21 N, R 9 W). Named on Plaskett Meadows (1967) 7.5' quadrangle. On Hull Mountain (1952) 15' quadrangle, the name has the form "Board Tree Camp."

Boardtree Gulch [SISKIYOU]: *canyon,* drained by a stream that flows 1.25 miles to South Fork Salmon River 4.5 miles southeast of Cecilville (lat. 41°05'55" N, long. 123°04'15" W). Named on Thompson Peak (1979) 7.5' quadrangle.

Boat Gunwale Creek [TEHAMA]: *stream,* flows nearly 7 miles to Mill Creek (3) 6.5 miles south-southwest of Panther Spring (lat. 40°09'35" N, long. 12148'45" W). Named on Butte Meadows (1958) and Panther Spring (1953) 15' quadrangles.

Boga [BUTTE]: *land grant,* south-southeast of Gridley and west of Feather River on Butte-Sutter County line. Named on Biggs (1970), Gridley (1952), and Honcut (1952) 7.5' quadrangles. Charles W. Flügge received 5 leagues in 1844 and Thomas O. Larkin claimed 22,185 acres patented in 1865 (Cowan, p. 19; Cowan gave the grant name "Flügge" as an alternate).

Bogard Gulch [SISKIYOU]: *canyon,* drained by a stream that flows nearly 2 miles to West Fork Cottonwood Creek (1) 6.5 miles west-northwest of Hornbrook (lat. 41°57'20" N, long. 122°40' W; sec. 4, T 47 N, R 7 W). Named on Hornbrook (1955) 15' quadrangle.

Bogus [SISKIYOU]: *locality,* 20 miles northeast of Yreka along Cold Creek (2) above its confluence with Bogus Creek (lat. 41°55'55" N, long. 122°21'15" W). Named on Shasta (1894) 1° quadrangle, which shows the place near the site of Bogus school shown on Copco (1954) 15' quadrangle. Postal authorities established Bogus post office in 1876 and discontinued it in 1913 (Frickstad, p. 186).

Bogus Creek [SISKIYOU]: *stream,* flows 14 miles to Klamath River 23 miles west-northwest of Macdoel (lat. 41°50'50" N, long. 122°26'30" W; near NE cor. sec. 17, T 47 N, R 5 W). Named on Copco (1954) 15' quadrangle. Gudde (1949, p. 36) attributed the name "Bogus" in the region to the activity of counterfeiters.

Bogus Creek: see **Little Bogus Creek** [SISKIYOU].

Bogus Gulch [SHASTA]: *canyon,* drained by a stream that flows less than 1 mile to South Fork Clear Creek 2 miles north-northwest of Igo (lat. 40°32' N, long. 122°33'20" W; near N line sec. 21, T 31 N, R 6 W). Named on Igo (1979) 7.5' quadrangle.

Bogus Mountain [SISKIYOU]: *peak,* 20 miles west of Macdoel (lat. 41°51'30" N, long. 122°23'30" W; at N line sec. 11, T 46 N, R 5 W). Altitude 4501 feet. Named on Copco (1954) 15' quadrangle.

Bohemotash Mountain [SHASTA]: *peak,* 14 miles south of Lamoine (lat. 40°47'05" N, long. 122°28'25" W; near S line sec. 19, T 34 N, R 5 W). Altitude 4432 feet. Named on Lamoine (1957) 15' quadrangle. The name is of Indian origin (Kroeber, p. 35).

Bolam Creek [SISKIYOU]: *stream,* flows 6.25 miles to Whitney Creek 8 miles northeast of Weed (lat. 41°29'55" N, long. 122°15'40" W; sec. 12, T 42 N, R 4 W). Named on Shasta (1954) and Weed (1954) 15' quadrangles. United States Board on Geographic Names (1933, p. 155) rejected the form "Bulam Creek" for the name.

Bolam Glacier [SISKIYOU]: *glacier,* 12 miles north-northwest of McCloud on Mount Shasta (1) (lat. 41°25'15" N, long. 122°12' W; sec. 4, 9, T 41 N, R 3 W); the glacier is at the head of Bolam Creek. Named on Shasta (1954) 15' quadrangle. Called Bulam Glacier on Russell's (1883) map, but United States Board on Geographic Names (1933, p. 155) rejected this name for the feature

Boles Creek [SISKIYOU]: *stream,* flows 4.5 miles to Shasta River 3 miles west-northwest of Weed (lat. 41°26'45" N, long. 122°25'50" W; sec. 33, T 42 N, R 5 W). Named on Weed (1954) 15' quadrangle.

Bolivar Peak: see **Craggy Peak** [SISKIYOU].

Bollibokka Creek: see **Big Bollibokka Creek** [SHASTA]; **Little Bollibokka Creek** [SHASTA].

Bollibokka Mountain [SHASTA]: *peak,* 25 miles north-northeast of Redding (lat. 40°56' N, long. 122°12'50" W; sec. 33, T 36 N, R 3 W). Altitude 4079 feet. Named on Bollibokka Mountain (1957) 15' quadrangle. On Redding (1901) 30' quadrangle, the name applies to a ridge, 3 miles long, that has present Bollibokka Mountain at the southwest end. The name "Bollibokka" is of Indian origin (Gudde, 1949, p. 36). United States Board on Geographic Names (1982b, p. 2) approved the name "Forks Flat" for a place located 3.5 miles northeast of Bollibokka Mountain on the right bank of Chatterdown Creek near the mouth of South Fork of that creek (lat. 40°58'53" N, long. 122°10'52" W; sec. 14, T 36 N, R 3 W).

Bolt Creek [BUTTE]: *stream,* flows 5.5 miles to Big Butte Creek less than 1 mile east of Butte Meadows (lat. 40°04'45" N, long. 121°32'15" W; at W line sec. 28, T 26 N, R 4 E). Named on Butte Meadows (1958) and Jonesville (1958) 15' quadrangles.

Bone Gulch [TEHAMA]: *canyon,* drained by a stream that flows nearly 4 miles to Weemasoul Creek 7.5 miles north-northwest of Wakefield Flat (lat. 40°13'50" N, long. 122°41' W; near S line sec. 32, T 28 N, R 7 W). Named on Cold Fork (1967) 7.5' quadrangle.

Bones Gulch [SHASTA]: *canyon,* drained by a stream that flows 1.5 miles to McCloud River [SHASTA-SISKIYOU] 3 miles northwest of Shoeinhorse Mountain (lat. 41°05'40" N, long. 122°06'45" W). Named on Shoeinhorse Mountain (1954) 15' quadrangle.

Bonita Butte [SISKIYOU]: *hill,* 11 miles north-northwest of Medicine Lake (lat. 41°44'15" N, long. 121°39'30" W; at SW cor. sec. 17, T 45 N, R 3 E). Altitude 5006 feet. Named on Medicine Lake (1952) 15' quadrangle.

Bonita Lake [SISKIYOU]: *intermittent lake,* 1200 feet long, 4 miles south-southeast of Mount Dome (lat. 41°45'20" N, long. 121°40'05" W; sec. 7, T 45 N, R 3 E). Named on Mount Dome (1950) 15' quadrangle.

Bonnet Rock [SISKIYOU]: *relief feature,* 15 miles south of Yreka (lat. 41°30'50" N, long. 122°34'25" W; near E line sec. 6, T 42 N, R 6 W). Named on Yreka (1954) 15' quadrangle.

Bonnie Crags [SHASTA]: *relief feature,* 5.5 miles south of Whitmore (lat. 40°33'10" N, long. 121°54' W; sec. 7, T 31 N, R 1 E). Named on Whitmore (1956) 15' quadrangle. United States Board on Geographic Names (1986c, p. 3) approved the form "Bonnie Craigs" for the name.

Bonnie Craigs: see **Bonnie Crags** [SHASTA].

Bontabile Creek [SHASTA]: *stream,* flows 1 mile to Shasta Lake 4.5 miles north-northeast of the town of Central Valley (lat. 40°44'30" N, long. 122°20'10" W; at W line sec. 4, T 33 N, R 4 W). Named on Project City (1957) 7.5' quadrangle.

Booker Flat: see **Badger Flat** [SHASTA].

Boomer Creek [BUTTE]: *stream,* flows 3.5 miles to Fall River 8.5 miles north of Clipper Mills (lat. 39°38'55" N, long. 121°10'35" W; sec. 27, T 21 N, R 7 E). Named on Cascade (1948) 7.5' quadrangle.

Boots Bend [TEHAMA]: *locality,* a bend in the road 7.25 miles west-southwest of Mineral (lat. 40°17'50" N, long. 121°43' W; sec. 11, T 28 N, R 2 E). Named on Lassen Peak (1956) 15' quadrangle.

Boozey Lake [SISKIYOU]: *intermittent lake,* 900 feet long, 6.5 miles north-east of Mount Dome (lat. 41°52'20" N, long. 121°35'40" W; sec. 35, T 47 N, R 3 E). Named on Mount Dome (1950) 15' quadrangle.

Boralma [SHASTA]: *locality,* 11 miles north-northwest of Redding (lat. 40°43'30" N, long. 122°29'30" W; sec. 12, T 33 N, R 6 W). Named on Redding (1901) 30' quadrangle. Postal authorities established Boralma post office in 1901 and discontinued it in 1906 (Frickstad, p. 178).

Border Mountain [SISKIYOU]: *mountain,* 9 miles southeast of Medicine Lake (lat. 41°29'30" N, long. 121°28' W; on E line sec. 11, T 42 N, R 4 E). Altitude 6260 feet. Named on Timber Mountain (1952) and White Horse (1962) 15' quadrangles.

Bosquejo [BUTTE-TEHAMA]: *land grant,* on the east side of Sacramento River at and south of Vina. Named on Foster Island (1950), Nord (1951), and Vina (1950) 7.5' quadrangles. Peter Lassen received 5 leagues in 1844 and claimed 22,206 acres patented in 1862 (Cowan, p. 20).

Boswell Gulch [SHASTA]: *canyon,* drained by a stream that flows 1 mile to Right Fork 2.5 miles northwest of the village of French Gulch (lat. 40°43'30" N, long. 122°40'30" W; near SE cor. sec. 8, T 33 N, R 7 W). Named on French Gulch (1979) 7.5' quadrangle.

Boswell Ridge [TEHAMA]: *ridge,* generally south-trending, 5 miles long, 5 miles north-northwest of Ball Mountain (lat. 39°59'30" N, long. 122°50' W). Named on Yolla Bolly (1954) 15' quadrangle, and on Ball Mountain (1967) 7.5' quadrangle.

Bosworth Meadow [SHASTA]: *area,* 8.5 miles north-northwest of Burney Falle (lat. 41°07'30" N, long. 121°42' W; near SE cor. sec. 14, T 38 N, R 2 E). Named on Pondosa (1961) 15' quadrangle.

Bottle Creek [BUTTE]: *stream,* flows 3 miles to Bull Creek 5.25 miles south of Butte Meadows (lat. 40°00'25" N, long. 121°34'15" W; sec. 19, T 25 N, R 4 E); the stream heads north of Bottle Hill. Named on Butte Meadows (1958) 15' quadrangle.

Bottle Hill [BUTTE]: *peak,* 4.5 miles southeast of Butte Meadows (lat. 40°01'05" N, long. 121°32' W; near S line sec. 16, T 25 N, R 4 E). Altitude 5307 feet. Named on Butte Meadows (1958) 15' quadrangle.

Boulder Creek [SHASTA]:

(1) *stream,* flows 4.5 miles to Sacramento River 10 miles south-southwest of Castella (lat. 41°01' N, long. 122°24'15" W; at S line sec. 35, T 37 N, R 5 W). Named on Dunsmuir (1954) 15' quadrangle.

(2) *stream,* flows 5 miles to Chum Creek 3 miles east-northeast of Redding (lat. 40°35'55" N, long. 122°20'25" W; sec. 29, T 32 N, R 4 W). Named on Enterprise (1957), Redding (1957), and Shasta Dam (1956) 7.5' quadrangles.

(3) *stream,* flows 4.25 miles to Whiskeytown Lake nearly 5 miles south-southeast of the village of French Gulch (lat. 40°38'30" N, long. 122°35'35" W; sec. 7, T 32 N, R 6 W). Named on French Gulch (1979), Shasta Bally (1978), and Whiskeytown (1979) 7.5' quadrangles.

(4) *stream,* flows 3.5 miles to Spring Creek (6) 5.25 miles west-southwest of Summit City (lat. 40°39'35" N, long. 122°32'15" W; sec. 1, T 32 N, R 6 W). Named on Shasta Dam (1956) and Whiskeytown (1979) 7.5' quadrangles.

Boulder Creek [SISKIYOU]:

(1) *stream,* flows nearly 4 miles to Scott River 9 miles south-southwest of Scott Bar (lat. 41°38'05" N, long. 123°05'50" W); the stream heads near Boulder Peak (2). Named on Boulder Peak (1981) and Scott Bar (1980) 7.5' quadrangles.

(2) *stream,* flows 1.5 miles to North Fork Salmon River 10 miles north of Sawyers Bar (lat. 41°26'15" N, long. 123°09'40" W). Named on English Peak (1977) 7.5' quadrangle.

(3) *stream,* formed by the confluence of West Boulder Creek and Wolf Creek (2), flows 2.5 miles to Scott River 12 miles south-southeast of Etna (lat. 41°17'40" N, long. 122°49'30" W; at N line sec. 25, T 40 N, R 9 W). Named on Etna (1955) 15' quadrangle.

Boulder Creek: see **East Boulder Creek** [SISKIYOU]; **Fivemile Creek** [SISKIYOU]; **Paige Boulder Creek** [SHASTA]; **West Boulder Creek** [SISKIYOU].

Boulder Gulch [SISKIYOU]: *canyon,* drained by a stream that flows nearly 1 mile to North Fork Salmon River 3.5 miles west of Sawyers Bar (lat. 41°18'25" N, long. 123°12'05" W). Named on Sawyers Bar (1979) 7.5' quadrangle. Called Cronan Gulch on Sawyers Bar (1923) 30' quadrangle, but United States Board on Geographic Names (1960a, p. 12) rejected this name for the canyon.

Boulder Gulch: see **Kanaka Gulch** [SISKIYOU].

Boulder Lake: see **East Boulder Lake** [SISKIYOU]; **Lower Boulder Lake** [SISKIYOU]; **Middle Boulder Lake** [SISKIYOU]; **West Boulder Lake** [SISKIYOU].

Boulder Peak [SHASTA]: *peak,* 9 miles west-northwest of Castella on Shasta-Trinity County line (lat. 41°10'45" N, long. 122°28'30" W; near E line sec. 6, T 38 N, R 5 W). Altitude 6968 feet. Named on Dunsmuir (1954) 15' quadrangle.

Boulder Peak [SISKIYOU]:

(1) *peak,* 5.25 miles east-southeast of Preston Peak (lat. 41°48'25" N, long. 123°31' W). Altitude 6014 feet. Named on Preston Peak (1982) 7.5' quadrangle.

(2) *peak,* 12 miles south-southwest of Scott Bar (lat. 41°34'45" N, long. 123°05'25" W); the peak is on the ridge called Red Mountain. Altitude 8299 feet. Named on Boulder Peak (1981) 7.5' quadrangle. Called Red Mountain on Seiad (1922) 30' quadrangle, but United States Board on Geographic Names (1960a, p. 12) rejected this name for the peak.

Boulder Point [TEHAMA]: *relief feature,* 1 mile east-northeast of Wakefield Flat (lat. 40°07'45" N, long. 122°37'15" W; at S line sec. 2, T 26 N, R 7 W). Named on Oxbow Bridge (1967) 7.5' quadrangle.

Boulevard Cave [SISKIYOU]: *cave,* 12 miles north-northeast of Medicine Lake (lat. 41°44'50" N, long. 121°32'40" W; near W line sec. 17, T 45 N, R 4 E). Named on Medicine Lake (1952) 15' quadrangle.

Bowers Creek [TEHAMA]: *stream,* flows 5 miles to Thomes Creek 6 miles west-southwest of Paskenta (lat. 39°51'05" N, long. 122°38'50" W; sec. 16, T 23 N, R 7 W). Named on Hall Ridge (1967) 7.5' quadrangle.

Bowman Canyon [GLENN]: *canyon,* drained by a stream that flows 4.25 miles to North Fork Elk Creek 3 miles west of the village of Elk Creek (lat. 39°36'15" N, long. 122°35'40" W; sec. 12, T 20 N, R 7 W). Named on Elk Creek (1968) and Felkner Hill (1968) 7.5' quadrangles.

Bowman Ridge [GLENN]: *ridge,* generally east-trending, 3 miles long, 5.5 miles west of the village of Elk Creek (lat. 39°36'35" N, long. 122°38'15" W); the ridge is north of Bowman Canyon. Named on Elk Creek (1968) and Felkner Hill (1968) 7.5' quadrangles.

Box Camp [SISKIYOU]:

(1) *locality,* 12.5 miles southwest of Scott Bar (lat. 41°36'15" N, long. 123°09'25" W; sec. 6, T 43 N, R 11 W). Named on Scott Bar (1955) 15' quadrangle.

(2) *locality,* 7 miles west-northwest of Sawyers Bar (lat. 41°21'20" N, long. 123°14'45" W). Named on Sawyers Bar (1979) 7.5' quadrangle.

Box Camp Mountain [SISKIYOU]: *ridge,* east- to northeast-trending, 2 miles long, 13 miles southwest of Scott Bar (lat. 41°35'55" N, long. 123°10'05" W); Box Camp (1) was on the ridge. Named on Marble Mountain (1980) 7.5' quadrangle.

Box Canyon [SHASTA]: *canyon,* drained by a stream that flows 1 mile to Backbone Creek 11 miles south-southwest of Lamoine (lat. 40°49'30" N, long. 122°29'45" W; at N line sec. 12, T 34 N, R 6 W). Named on Lamoine (1957) and Schell Mountain (1950) 15' quadrangles.

Box Canyon [SISKIYOU]: *canyon,* about 1 mile long, 2 miles south-southwest of Mount Dome along Willow Creek (4) (lat. 41°47' N, long. 122°42'15" W; on E line sec. 35, T 46 N, R 2 E). Named on Mount Dome (1950) 15' quadrangle.

Box Canyon: see **Rail Canyon**, under **Badger Mountain** [SHASTA].

Box Hall Flat [BUTTE]: *area,* 3.25 miles north of Oroville Dam (lat. 39°35'05" N, long. 121°29'30" W; near S line sec. 14, T 20 N, R 4 E). Named on Oroville Dam (1970) 7.5' quadrangle.

Box Lake [SHASTA]: *lake,* 2000 feet long, 16 miles north of Lassen Peak (lat. 40°43'15" N, long. 121°34'10" W; sec. 18, T 33 N, R 4 E). Named on Manzanita Lake (1956) 15' quadrangle.

Boya Gulch: see **Boyd Gulch** [SISKIYOU].

Boyce [SHASTA]: *locality,* 6 miles east-northeast of Millville (lat. 40°35'50" N, long. 122°03'55" W). Named on Red Bluff (1894) 1° quadrangle.

Boyd Gulch [SISKIYOU]: *canyon,* drained by a stream that flows 1.5 miles to Salmon River 2.25 miles northwest of Forks of Salmon (lat. 41°17' N, long. 123°21'05" W). Named on Forks of Salmon (1978) 7.5' quadrangle. Called Boya Gulch on Forks of Salmon (1955) 15' quadrangle, and United States Board n Geographic Names (1977b, p. 4) gave this name as a variant.

Bradley: see **Mount Bradley** [SISKIYOU].

Brandons Bar: see **Happy Camp** [SISKIYOU].

Brand Spring [SHASTA]: *spring,* 9 miles south-southeast of Whitmore (lat. 40°30'30" N, long. 121°51'30" W; at E line sec. 28, T 31 N, R 1 E). Named on Whitmore (1956) 15' quadrangle.

Brandy Creek [SHASTA]: *stream,* flows 6 miles to Whiskeytown Lake 8 miles north-northwest of Igo (lat. 40°37' N, long. 122°34'20" W; sec. 20, T 32 N, R 6 W). Named on Igo (1979) and Shasta Bally (1978) 7.5' quadrangles.

Brandy Creek Campground [SHASTA]: *locality,* 8 miles north-northwest of Igo along Whiskeytown Lake (lat. 40°36'55" N, long. 122°34'25" W; sec. 20, T 32 N, R 6 W); the place is near the mouth of Brandy Creek. Named on Igo (1979) 7.5' quadrangle.

Brannin Creek [TEHAMA]: *stream,* flows 13 miles to Burch Creek 3.5 miles south of Corning (lat. 39°52'30" N, long. 122°10'20" W; sec. 2, T 23 N, R 3 W). Named on Black Butte Dam (1967), Corning (1951), and Kirkwood (1949) 7.5' quadrangles.

Braselton Hill [BUTTE]: *peak,* less than 2 miles east of Palermo (lat. 39°26'15" N, long. 121°31'45" W). Named on Marysville (1895) 30' quadrangle. F.D. Dunn (p. 44) gave the alternate names "Gibralter Hill" and "Watertank Hill" for the feature.

Bray [SISKIYOU]: *locality,* 22 miles south of Dorris along Southern Pacific Railroad (lat. 41°38'45" N, long. 121°58' W; sec. 21, T 44 N, R 1 W). Named on Bray (1950) 15' quadrangle. Postal authorities established Bray post office in 1909 and discontinued it in 1967; the name was for William J. Bray, pioneer settler and first postmaster (Salley, p. 26).

Brazell Meadows [TEHAMA]: *area,* 9 miles west-southwest of Mineral (lat. 40°17'45" N, long. 121°44'45" W; sec. 9, 10, T 28 N, R 2 E). Named on Lassen Peak (1956) and Manton (1956) 15' quadrangles.

Brazille Flat [SISKIYOU]: *area,* 1 mile northwest of Forks of Salmon along Salmon River (lat. 41°16'05" N, long. 123°20'15" W). Named on Forks of Salmon (1978) 7.5' quadrangle.

Break Neck Canyon: see **Cold Creek** [BUTTE].

Breakneck Canyon [BUTTE]: *canyon,* drained by a stream that flows 2.25 miles to Big Kimshew Creek 7.5 miles north-northwest of Pulga (lat. 39°54'30" N, long. 121°29' W; near W line sec. 25, T 24 N, R 4 E). Named on Kimshew Point (1979) 7.5' quadrangle. United States Board on Geographic Names (1960b, p. 6) rejected the form "Break Neck Canyon" for the name.

Breedlove Reservoir [BUTTE]: *lake,* 500 feet long, 1 mile north of Stirling City (lat. 39°55'20" N, long. 121°31'55" W; sec. 21, T 24 N, R 4 E). Named on Stirling City (1979) 7.5' quadrangle.

Brewer Creek [SISKIYOU]: *stream,* flows 7 miles to lowlands 11.5 miles north-northeast of McCloud (lat. 41°24'20" N, long. 122°03'20" W; near NW cor. sec. 14, T 41 N, R 2 W). Named on Shasta (1954) 15' quadrangle.

Brewery Creek [TEHAMA]: *stream,* flows 2.25 miles to Sacramento River 0.5 mile north of downtown Red Bluff (lat. 40°11'05" N, long. 122°14'10" W; at E line sec. 19, T 27 N, R 3 W). Named on Red Bluff East (1951) and Red Bluff West (1951) 7.5' quadrangles.

Brewster: see **Castella** [SHASTA].

Brickyard Creek [TEHAMA]: *stream,* flows 9 miles to Reeds Creek less than 0.5 mile south of downtown Red Bluff (lat. 40°10'10" N, long. 122°14' W; near NE cor. sec. 29, T 27 N, R 3 W). Named on Red Bluff East (1951) and Red Bluff West (1951) 7.5' quadrangles.

Bridge Bay Resort [SHASTA]: *locality,* 17 miles south-southeast of Lamoine along Shasta Lake (lat. 40°45'20" N, long. 122°19'15" W; sec. 33, T 34 N, R 4 W). Named on Lamoine (1957) 15' quadrangle. United States Board on Geographic Names (1972c, p. 2) approved the name "Beaver Island" for an island, 0.3 mile long, situated 0.5 mile west of Bridge Bay Resort in Shasta Lake.

Bridge Campground [SHASTA]: *locality,* 17 miles north-northeast of Lassen Peak along Hat Creek (lat. 40°43'50" N, long. 121°26'05" W; on E line sec. 8, T 33 N, R 5 E). Named on Prospect Peak (1957) 15' quadrangle.

Bridge Creek [SISKIYOU]: *stream,* flows 9 miles to Wooley Creek 13 miles north of Forks of Salmon (lat. 41°26'25" N, long. 123°21'25" W). Named on Medicine Mountain (1978) and Ukonom Lake (1980) 7.5' quadrangles. Smith Fork enters nearly 5 miles south of Ukonom Lake; it is 1.25 miles long and is named on Ukonom Lake (1980) 7.5' quadrangle.

Bridge Flat: see **Bridge Flat Campground** [SISKIYOU].

Bridge Flat Campground [SISKIYOU]: *locality,* 8.5 miles southwest of Scott Bar (lat. 41°39' N, long. 123°06'45" W). Named on Scott Bar (1980) 7.5' quadrangle. Scott Bar (1955) 15' quadrangle shows Bridge Flat at the place.

Bridge Gulch [SISKIYOU]: *canyon,* drained by a stream that flows 0.5 mile to Indian Creek (3) 3.5 miles north of Fort Jones (lat. 41°39'40" N, long. 122°51'05" W; sec. 14, T 44 N, R 9 W). Named on Fort Jones (1955) 15' quadrangle.

Bridgeport: see **Elk Creek** [GLENN] (2).

Bridges Creek [SHASTA]: *stream,* flows 3.5 miles to North Fork Battle Creek [SHASTA-TEHAMA] 12.5 miles west-northwest of Lassen Peak (lat. 40°33'15" N, long. 121°43'20" W; near NW cor. sec. 11, T 31 N, R 2 E). Named on Manzanita Lake (1956) 15' quadrangle.

Briggsville: see **Reading Bar** [SHASTA].

Brincard: see **Redding** [SHASTA].

Briscoe Creek [GLENN]: *stream,* flows 11 miles to Stony Creek [GLENN-TEHAMA] less than 1 mile south of the village of Elk Creek (lat. 39°35'35" N, long. 122°32'20" W; near N line sec. 16, T 20 N, R 6 W). Named on Elk Creek (1968) and Felkner Hill (1968) 7.5' quadrangles. The name commemorates Watt Briscoe, a stockman in the neighborhood in the early 1850's (Gudde, 1949, p. 40). North Fork enters 7.25 miles south-southwest of the village of Elk Creek; it is 4.25 miles long and is named on Elk Creek (1968) and Felkner Hill (1968) 7.5' quadrangles. On Elk Creek (1918) 15' quadrangle, present North Fork has the designation "North Branch Brisco Cr."

Briscoe Rocks [BUTTE]: *narrows,* 3.25 miles south-southwest of the village of Elk Creek (lat. 39°33'35" N, long. 122°33'45" W; sec. 29, T 20 N, R 6 W); the feature is along Briscoe Creek. Named on Elk Creek (1968) 7.5' quadrangle.

Britton: see **Camp Britton** [SHASTA]; **Lake Britton** [SHASTA].

Brock Butte [SHASTA]: *peak,* 7.5 miles east-southeast of Bollibokka Mountain (lat. 40°53'05" N, long. 122°05'05" W; sec. 15, T 35 N, R 2 W). Altitude 3459 feet. Named on Bollibokka Mountain (1957) 15' quadrangle. The name is for Dave Brock, Sr. (Steger, p. 19).

Brock Creek [SHASTA]: *stream,* flows 1.5 miles to Pit River Arm Shasta Lake 11 miles southeast of Bollibokka Mountain (lat. 40°48'35" N, long. 122°05'30" W; near SE cor. sec. 9, T 34 N, R 2 W). Named on Bollibokka Mountain (1957) 15' quadrangle. The name commemorates Dave Brock, Sr. (Steger, p. 19).

Brock Mountain [SHASTA]: *ridge,* generally south-southeast-trending, 3 miles long, 10.5 miles south-southeast of Bollibokka Mountain (lat. 40°47'55" N, long. 122°07'45" W). Named on Bollibokka Mountain (1957) 15' quadrangle. The name commemorates Dave Brock, Sr. (Steger, p. 19).

Broken Rib Peak: see **Youngs Peak** [SISKIYOU] (1).

Brokeoff Meadows [SHASTA]: *area,* 4.5 miles west of Lassen Peak (lat. 40°28'30" N, long. 121°35'20" W; near W line sec. 7, T 30 N, R 3 E); the place is 2.5 miles north-northwest of Brokeoff Mountain. Named on Lassen Peak (1956) 15' quadrangle. The feature also was known as Hollensworth Flat for a herder (Steger, p. 20).

Brokeoff Mountain [SHASTA]: *peak,* 4 miles southwest of Lassen Peak near Shasta-Tehama County line (lat. 40°26'50" N, long. 121°33'45" W; sec. 20, T 30 N, R 4 E). Named on Lassen Peak (1956) 15' quadrangle. United States Board on Geographic Names (1933, p. 166) rejected the name "Mount Lassen" for the peak. The feature is the remains of a collapsed volcano (Schulz, p. 6).

Brown Butte [SHASTA]: *peak,* 8 miles east-southeast of Burney (lat. 40°50'05" N, long. 121°31'45" W; sec. 4, T 34 N, R 4 E). Altitude 4643 feet. Named on Burney (1957) 15' quadrangle.

Brown Creek [SISKIYOU]: *stream,* heads in Siskiyou County and flows 3 miles to Wilder Creek nearly 4 miles north-northwest of Orleans in Humboldt County (lat. 41°21'10" N, long. 123°34' W). Named on Bark Shanty Gulch (1974) 7.5' quadrangle.

Brownell: see **Dorris** [SISKIYOU].

Brownell Camp [GLENN]: *locality,* 4.5 miles southeast of Black Butte (lat. 39°39' N, long. 122°48'15" W; sec. 30, T 21 N, R 8 W). Named on Plaskett Meadows (1967) 7.5' quadrangle.

Brownell Meadow [SISKIYOU]: *area,* just south of Medicine Lake (lat. 41°34'30" N, long. 122°36'15" W; at NE cor. sec. 15, T 43 N, R 3 E). Named on Medicine Lake (1952) 15' quadrangle.

Brown Gulch [TEHAMA]: *canyon,* less than 0.5 mile long, 6 miles northeast of Los Molinos (lat. 40°04'15" N, long. 122°00'20" W; on S line sec. 29, T 26 N, R 1 W). Named on Los Molinos (1952) 7.5' quadrangle.

Brownharts: see **Coutolenc** [BUTTE].

Brown Mountain [SHASTA]: *peak,* 7.5 miles north-northwest of Schell Mountain (lat. 40°57'15" N, long. 122°35'40" W; sec. 30, T 36 N, R 6 W). Altitude 4711 feet. Named on Schell Mountain (1950) 15' quadrangle.

Brown Ravine [BUTTE]: *canyon,* 3.25 miles long, drained by Last Chance Creek (1) above a point 13 miles north of Pulga (lat. 39°59'35" N, long. 121°28'35" W). Named on Jonesville (1958) 15' quadrangle, and on Kimshew Point (1979) 7.5' quadrangle.

Browns Camp [TEHAMA]:

(1) *locality,* 3.25 miles north-northeast of Bear Creek Station along Guernsey Creek (lat. 40°18'40" N, long. 121°26'10" W; near W line sec. 4, T 28 N, R 5 E). Named on Mount Harkness (1956) 15' quadrangle.

(2) *locality,* 6.5 miles south of Tomhead Mountain (lat. 40°02'45" N, long. 122°48'20" W; at S line sec. 6, T 25 N, R 8 W). Named on Yolla Bolly (1954) 15' quadrangle.

Browns Canyon [GLENN]: *canyon,* drained by a stream that flows 4.25 miles to Grindstone Creek [GLENN-TEHAMA] 14 miles northwest of the village of Elk Creek (lat. 39°44'50" N, long. 122°43'20" W). Named on Alder Springs (1967) and Hall Ridge (1967) 7.5' quadrangles.

Browns Canyon [SHASTA]: *canyon,* drained by a stream that flows 0.5 mile to Pit River Arm Shasta Lake 12.5 miles south-southeast of Bollibokka Mountain (lat. 40°46'30" N, long. 122°06'30" W; at E line sec. 28, T 34 N, R 2 W). Named on Bollibokka Mountain (1957) 15' quadrangle.

Browns Creek [SISKIYOU]: *stream,* flows 1.25 miles to Klamath River 7.5 miles northwest of Ukonom Lake (lat. 41°40' N, long. 123°26'45" W). Named on Clear Creek (1981) 7.5' quadrangle.

Browns Gulch [SISKIYOU]:

(1) *canyon,* 0.5 mile long, 1.5 miles east-southeast of Cecilville (lat. 41°07'50" N, long. 123°06'55" W). Named on Grasshopper Ridge (1979) 7.5' quadrangle.

(2) *canyon,* drained by a stream that flows 1 mile to South Fork Salmon River 27 miles south of Etna (lat. 41°04'10" N, long. 122°58'10" W). Named on Coffee Creek (1955) 15' quadrangle.

Browns Knob [SISKIYOU]: *peak,* 8.5 miles southeast of the village of Seiad Valley (lat. 41°45'05" N, long. 123°05'35" W). Named on Hamburg (1980) 7.5' quadrangle.

Browns Lake [SISKIYOU]: *lake,* 800 feet long, 1 mile southwest of the town of Mount Shasta (lat. 41°18'05" N, long. 122°19'40" W; near NE cor. sec. 20, T 40 N, R 4 W). Named on Weed (1954) 15' quadrangle.

Browns Meadow [SISKIYOU]: *area,* 28 miles south of Etna (lat. 41°03' N, long. 122°58'20" W). Named on Coffee Creek (1955) 15' quadrangle.

Browns Resort: see **Klamath River Post Office** [SISKIYOU].

Brownsville: see **Cecilville** [SHASTA]; **Copper City** [SHASTA].

Bruces Gulch [SISKIYOU]: *canyon,* drained by a stream that flows 1 mile to Hi-you Gulch 7.25 miles north of Fort Jones (lat. 41°42'40" N, long. 122°49'10" W; near NW cor. sec. 31, T 45 N, R 8 W). Named on Fort Jones (1955) 15' quadrangle.

Bruin Flat [SISKIYOU]: *area,* 4 miles south of Medicine Lake (lat. 41°31'25" N, long. 121°35'35" W; sec. 35, T 43 N, R 3 E). Named on Medicine Lake (1952) 15' quadrangle.

Brunswick Ridge [SHASTA]: *ridge,* east-southeast- to south-southeast-trending, 3 miles long, 2.5 miles west of the village of French Gulch (lat. 40°41'45" N, long. 122°41' W). Named on French Gulch (1979) 7.5' quadrangle, which shows Brunswick mine on the ridge.

Brush [BUTTE]: *locality,* 3.5 miles north of the village of Berry Creek along Western Pacific Railroad (lat. 39°41'45" N, long. 121°24'15" W; near N line sec. 10, T 21 N, R 5 E). Named on Big Bend Mountain (1948) 15' quadrangle.

Brush Camp [TEHAMA]: *locality,* 12 miles south of Panther Spring along Little Dry Creek (lat. 40°04'30" N, long. 121°48'10" W; near W line sec. 30, T 26 N, R 2 E). Named on Panther Spring (1953) 15' quadrangle.

Brush Creek [BUTTE]:

(1) *stream,* flows 3 miles to Middle Fork Feather River 2.5 miles southeast of the village of Brush Creek (lat. 39°40'10" N, long. 121°18'10" W). Named on Brush Creek (1970) 7.5' quadrangle.

(2) *village,* 4.5 miles northeast of the village of Berry Creek (lat. 39°41'25" N, long. 121°20'15" W; on E line sec. 7, T 21 N, R 6 E). Named on Brush Creek (1970) 7.5' quadrangle. Bidwell Bar (1897) 30' quadrangle has the name "Brush Creek" at the site of present Mountain House. Postal authorities established Brush Creek post office in 1856, moved it 1 mile south in 1902, and discontinued it in 1916 (Salley, p. 28). California Mining Bureau's (1909d) map shows a place called Stanwood located 3 miles northwest of the village of Berry Creek. Postal authorities established Stanwood post office in 1905 and discontinued it in 1915 (Salley, p. 212); Swayne Lumber Company had a mill at the site (Dunn, F.D., p. 101). They established Tilden post office 2.5 miles northwest of Stanwood in 1910 and moved it in 1914, when they changed the name to Swayne (Salley, p. 222). The name "Tilden" was for a vice president of Swayne Lumber Company (Dunn, F.D., p. 106). California Mining Bureau's (1917c) map shows Swayne located about 4 miles north of the village of Berry Creek. Postal authorities established Swayne post office 8 miles by railroad southeast of Pulga in 1914 and discontinued it in 1917; the name was for Warren H. Swayne, first postmaster (Salley, p. 217).

Brush Creek [SHASTA]:

(1) *stream,* flows 3 miles to Clear Creek 3 miles west of Schell Mountain (lat. 40°51'30" N, long. 122°35' W). Named on Schell Mountain (1950) 15' quadrangle.

(2) *stream,* flows 4 miles to North Fork Battle Creek [SHASTA-TEHAMA] 3.5 miles south of Shingletown (lat. 40°26'35" N, long. 121°52'30" W). Named on Manton (1956) 15' quadrangle.

Brush Creek [SISKIYOU]: *stream,* flows 3.25 miles to Klamath River 23 miles west-northwest of Macdoel (lat. 41°55'55" N, long. 122°26'20" W; at SE cor. sec. 8, T 47 N, R 5 W). Named on Copco (1954) 15' quadrangle.

Brush Creek [TEHAMA]:

(1) *stream,* flows 8 miles to Reeds Creek 4 miles west-southwest of downtown Red Bluff (lat. 40°09'25" N, long. 122°18'15" W; at S line sec. 27, T 27 N, R 4 W). Named on Blossom (1952) and Red Bluff West (1951) 7.5' quadrangles.

(2) *stream,* flows 3.5 miles to South Fork Cottonwood Creek [SHASTA-TEHAMA] 3.25 miles west of Wakefield Flat (lat. 40°07'15" N, long. 122°42'05" W). Named on Raglin Ridge (1967) 7.5' quadrangle.

(3) *stream,* flows 8.5 miles to Singer Creek [BUTTE-TEHAMA] 8.5 miles west-southwest of Campbell Mound (lat. 39°55'10" N, long. 121°57'35" W; sec. 22, T 24 N, R 1 W). Named on Richardson Springs NW (1952) 7.5' quadrangle. West Fork enters 3.25 miles upstream from the mouth of the main creek and is 4.25 miles long. Middle Fork enters West Fork less than 0.25 mile upstream from the mouth of West Fork and is 5 miles long. Both forks are named on Panther Spring (1953) 15' quadrangle, and on Richardson Springs NW (1952) 7.5' quadrangle.

Brush Creek: see **Bush Creek** [BUTTE]; **Mountain House** [BUTTE].

Brush Gulch [SHASTA]: *canyon,* drained by a stream that flows 1 mile to Clear Creek 2.5 miles west-northwest of Schell Mountain (lat. 40°52'30" N, long. 122°34'25" W). Named on Schell Mountain (1950) 15' quadrangle.

Brush Mountain [SHASTA]: *peak,* 5.5 miles northeast of Burney (lat. 40°55'40" N, long. 121°35'10" W; on N line sec. 7, T 35 N, R 3 E). Altitude 3812 feet. Named on Burney (1957) 15' quadrangle.

Brush Mountain [TEHAMA]: *peak,* 9 miles northwest of Paskenta (lat. 39°59' N, long. 122°39'35" W; sec. 33, T 25 N, R 7 W). Named on Riley Ridge (1967) 7.5' quadrangle.

Brush Patch [SHASTA]: *area,* 2.5 miles west of the village of Montgomery Creek (lat. 40°50'10" N, long. 121°58'10" W; around NW cor. sec. 3, T 34 N, R 1 W). Named on Montgomery Creek (1956) 15' quadrangle.

Brushy Butte [SHASTA]:

(1) *peak,* 12 miles north of Fall River Mills (lat. 41°10'45" N, long. 121°26'30" W). Altitude 3853 feet. Named on Fall River Mills (1961) 15' quadrangle

(2) *peak,* 4 miles northeast of Shoeinhorse Mountain (lat. 41°06'45" N, long. 122°00'15" W). Altitude 5194 feet. Named on Big Bend (1961) and Shoeinhorse Mountain (1954) 15' quadrangles.

Brushy Camp Ridge [GLENN]: *ridge,* mainly in Lake County, but extends east into Glenn County 12 miles west-southwest of the village of Elk Creek (lat. 39°30'45" N, long. 122°44'10" W). Named on Felkner Hill (1968) 7.5' quadrangle.

Brushy Canyon [SHASTA]: *canyon,* drained by a stream that flows 0.5 mile to Shasta Lake (lat. 40°45'30" N, long. 122°11'10" W; sec. 34, T 34 N, R 2 W). Named on Bollibokka Mountain (1957) 15' quadrangle

Brushy Gulch [SISKIYOU]:

(1) *canyon,* drained by a stream that flows 1 mile to Rattlesnake Creek 6.25 miles north-northwest of Fort Jones (lat. 41°41'15" N, long. 122°53'45" W; near SE cor. sec. 5, T 44 N, R 9 W). Named on Fort Jones (1955) 15' quadrangle.

(2) *canyon,* drained by a stream that flows 1.5 miles to Klamath River 8 miles southwest of Hornbrook (lat. 41°50'30" N, long. 122°40'15" W; sec. 16, T 46 N, R 7 W). Named on Hornbrook (1955) 15' quadrangle.

(3) *canyon,* drained by a stream that flows about 2.5 miles to Slide Creek (4) 27 miles west-northwest of Macdoel (lat. 41°59'15" N, long. 122°28'55" W; near N line sec. 25, T 48 N, R 6 W). Named on Copco (1954) and Hornbrook (1955) 15' quadrangles.

Brushy Gulch: see **Big Brushy Gulch** [SISKIYOU]; **Little Brushy Gulch** [SISKIYOU].

Brushy Hollow [TEHAMA]: *canyon,* drained by a stream that flows 1 mile to Big Crane Creek 9.5 miles north-northeast of Wakefield Flat (lat. 40°14'55" N, long. 122°33'50" W; sec. 29, T 28 N, R 6 W). Named on Oxbow Bridge (1967) 7.5' quadrangle.

Brushy Hollow Spring [TEHAMA]: *spring,* 9 miles north-northeast of Wakefield Flat (lat. 40°14'50" N, long. 122°34'30" W; on E line sec. 30, T 28 N, R 6 W); the spring is in Brushy Hollow. Named on Oxbow Bridge (1967) 7.5' quadrangle.

Brushy Mountain [GLENN]: *ridge,* north-trending, 2.25 miles long, 3.5 miles south-southeast of Black Butte (lat. 39°40'45" N, long. 122°51'15" W). Named on Plaskett Meadows (1967) 7.5' quadrangle.

Brushy Mountain [SHASTA]: *ridge,* north-trending, 2.25 miles long, 12.5 miles west-southwest of Arbuckle Mountain on Shasta-Trinity County line (lat. 40°18' N, long. 123°03'55" W; sec. 2, 11, T 28 N, R 11 W). Named on Dubakella Mountain (1954) 15' quadrangle.

Brushy Mountain [TEHAMA]: *peak,* 17 miles south of Panther Spring (lat. 40°00'30" N, long. 121°47'10" W; at SW cor. sec. 20, T 25 N, R 2 E). Named on Panther Spring (1953) 15' quadrangle.

Brushy Ridge [GLENN]: *ridge,* north-trending, 2.25 miles long, nearly 6 miles northeast of Saint John Mountain (lat. 39°29'10" N, long. 122°36'20" W). Named on Stonyford (1968) 7.5' quadrangle.

Brushy Ridge [TEHAMA]: *ridge,* generally east-trending, 3 miles long, 3.25 miles north of Tomhead Mountain (lat. 40°10'50" N, long. 122°50' W). Named on Yolla Bolly (1954) 15' quadrangle.

Bryant Ravine [BUTTE]: *canyon,* drained by a stream that flows 2 miles to Frey Creek 7 miles north of Forbestown (lat. 39°37'20" N, long. 121°16'10" W; sec. 2, T 20 N, R 6 E). Named on Forbestown (1970) 7.5' quadrangle.

Bryant Ridge [TEHAMA]: *ridge,* west-southwest-trending, 2.5 miles long, 7 miles west-southwest of Mineral (lat. 40°18'10" N, long. 121°42'45" W). Named on Lassen Peak (1956) 15' quadrangle.

Buck Butte [SISKIYOU]: *hill,* 10 miles southeast of Medicine Lake (lat. 41°28'30" N, long. 121°28'05" W; at SE cor. sec. 14, T 42 N, R 4 E). Altitude 5367 feet. Named on White Horse (1962) 15' quadrangle.

Buck Camp [TEHAMA]: *locality,* 3000 feet south-southeast of Tomhead Mountain (lat. 40°07'45" N, long. 122°48'45" W; near SW cor. sec. 6, T 26 N, R 8 W). Named on Yolla Bolly (1954) 15' quadrangle.

Buck Creek [TEHAMA]:

(1) *stream,* flows 6 miles to Harvey Creek 4 miles southwest of Tomhead Mountain (lat. 40°05'45" N, long. 122°51'50" W; at N line sec. 22, T 26 N, R 9 W). Named on Yolla Bolly (1954) 15' quadrangle.

(2) *stream,* flows nearly 5 miles to Cottonwood Creek [SHASTA-TEHAMA] 3 miles west of Wakefield Flat (lat. 40°07'20" N, long. 122°41'40" W; sec. 7, T 26 N, R 7 W). Named on Raglin Ridge (1967) 7.5' quadrangle.

Buck Creek: see **Battle Creek** [SHASTA].

Buckeye [SHASTA]: *village,* nearly 3 miles south of Summit City (lat. 40°39'25" N, long. 122°23'50" W; sec. 2, T 32 N, R 5 W). Named on Shasta Dam (1956) 7.5' quadrangle. Postal authorities established Buckeye post office in 1880, discontinued it in 1918, reestablished it in 1938, and discontinued it in 1943 (Frickstad, p. 178). The place began in the early 1850's as a mining camp settled by people from Ohio, the Buckeye state; it first was known locally as Ohio City (Hanna, p. 43).

Buckeye Creek [BUTTE]: *stream,* flows 1 mile to Winters Creek 5.5 miles northwest of Clipper Mills (lat. 39°35'35" N, long. 121°13'40" W; sec. 18, T 20 N, R 7 E). Named on Clipper Mills (1948) 7.5' quadrangle.

Buckeye Creek [SHASTA]: *stream,* flows 3.25 miles to Churn Creek 3 miles south of the town of Central Valley (lat. 40°38'10" N, long. 122°21'55" W; near N line sec. 18, T 32 N, R 4 W); the stream flows past Buckeye. Named on Project City (1957) and Shasta Dam (1956) 7.5' quadrangles.

Buckeye Creek: see **Little Buckeye Creek** [BUTTE].

Buck Gulch [SHASTA]: *canyon,* drained by a stream that flows 1 mile to Backbone Creek 11 miles south-southwest of Lamoine (lat. 40°49'35" N, long. 122°29'20" W; near N line sec. 12, T 34 N, R 6 W). Named on Lamoine (1957) 15' quadrangle.

Buck Hollow [SHASTA]: *canyon,* drained by a stream that flows 1.25 miles to Salt Creek (5) nearly 5 miles north of Igo (lat. 40°34'25" N, long. 122°31'10" W; near E line sec. 3, T 31 N, R 6 W). Named on Igo (1979) 7.5' quadrangle.

Buckhorn Bally [SHASTA]: *peak,* 3.5 miles west-northwest of Shasta Bally on Shasta-Trinity County line (lat. 40°37'05" N, long. 122°42'35" W; near E line sec. 24, T 32 N, R 8 W). Named on Shasta Bally (1978) 7.5' quadrangle.

Buckhorn Bally [SISKIYOU]: *peak,* 9.5 miles east of Condrey Mountain (lat. 41°55'10" N, long. 122°47'45" W; near S line sec. 17, T 47 N, R 8 W). Altitude 5157 feet. Named on Condrey Mountain (1955) 15' quadrangle.

Buckhorn Camp [SISKIYOU]: *locality,* 0.5 mile southeast of Condrey Mountain (lat. 41°55'50" N, long. 122°58'10" W; near N line sec. 14, T 47 N, R 10 W); the place is at the head of Buckhorn Creek (2). Named on Condrey Mountain (1955) 15' quadrangle, which shows an unnamed spring at the place. United States Board on Geographic Names (1978b, p. 3) approved the name "Buckhorn Spring" for this spring.

Buckhorn Creek [SISKIYOU]:

(1) *stream,* flows 2.25 miles to Bear Creek (1) 6 miles northeast of Ukonom Lake (lat. 41°39'10" N, long. 123°17'05" W); the stream heads at Buckhorn Spring (1). Named on Huckleberry Mountain (1980) 7.5' quadrangle.

(2) *stream,* flows 7.5 miles to Horse Creek (2) 10 miles east of the village of Seiad Valley (lat. 41°50' N, long. 123°00'30" W; sec. 16, T 46 N, R 10 W). Named on Condrey Mountain (1955) 15' quadrangle, and on Hamburg (1980) 7.5' quadrangle.

Buckhorn Gulch [SISKIYOU]: *canyon,* drained by a stream that flows 2 miles to the canyon of Beaver Creek (1) nearly 7 miles east-southeast of Condrey Mountain (lat. 41°53'45" N, long. 122°49'15" W; sec. 30, T 47 N, R 8 W); the canyon heads near Buckhorn Bally. Named on Condrey Mountain (1955) 15' quadrangle.

Buckhorn Gulch [TEHAMA]: *canyon,* drained by a stream that flows 1.25 miles to Mill Creek (3) 7.5 miles south-southwest of Panther Spring (lat. 40°09'10" N, long. 121°50'35" W). Named on Panther Spring (1953) 15' quadrangle.

Buckhorn Lake [SHASTA]: *lake,* 1300 feet long, 8 miles northeast of Whitmore (lat. 40°42'05" N, long. 121°47'35" W; sec. 19, T 33 N, R 2 E). Named on Whitmore (1956) 15' quadrangle. Called Buckhorn Lake Resvr. on Averill's (1939) map. The name is from skeletons of two deer with locked antlers that David B. Brandstatter found by the lake (Steger, p. 20).

Buckhorn Lake [SISKIYOU]: *lake,* 325 feet long, 13 miles south-southwest of Scott Bar (lat. 41°33'50" N, long. 123°06'30" W). Named on Boulder Peak (1981) 7.5' quadrangle.

Buckhorn Lake Reservoir: see **Buckhorn Lake** [SHASTA].

Buckhorn Mountain [SISKIYOU]: *peak,* 14 miles west-southwest of Scott Bar (lat. 41°40'25" N, long. 123°14'55" W). Altitude 6900 feet. Named on Grider Valley (1981) 7.5' quadrangle.

Buckhorn Ridge [SISKIYOU]: *ridge,* south-southeast-trending, 5 miles long, 4.5 miles south of Condrey Mountain (lat. 41°52'30" N, long. 122°57'30" W). Named on Condrey Mountain (1955) 15' quadrangle, which shows Dry Lake lookout at the northeast end of the ridge, and an intermittent lake near the lookout—United States Board on Geographic Names (1978c, p. 2) approved the name "Dry Lake" for this intermittent lake.

Buckhorn Spring [SISKIYOU]:

(1) *spring,* 8 miles northeast of Ukonom Lake (lat. 41°40'15" N, long. 123°15'05" W). Named on Huckleberry Mountain (1980) 7.5' quadrangle. Called Summit Spring on Seiad (1922) 30' quadrangle.

(2) *spring,* 10 miles east of Condrey Mountain (lat. 41°50'05" N, long. 122°47'35" W; near S line sec. 17, T 47 N, R 8 W). Named on Condrey Mountain (1955) 15' quadrangle.

Buckhorn Spring: see **Buckhorn Camp** [SISKIYOU].

Buckhorn Summit [SHASTA]: *pass,* nearly 7 miles southwest of the village of French Gulch on Shasta-Trinity County line (lat. 40°38'05" N, long. 122°44' W; sec. 14, T 32 N, R 8 W). Named on French Gulch (1979) 7.5' quadrangle.

Buck Lake [SISKIYOU]: *lake,* 750 feet long, 4.25 miles west-southwest of Preston Peak (lat. 41°48'55" N, long. 123°41'15" W); the lake is at the head of a branch of Doe Creek. Named on Devils Punchbowl (1981) 7.5' quadrangle.

Buck Mountain [SHASTA]: *peak,* 10 miles east-southeast of Bollibokka Mountain (lat. 40°53'45" N, long. 122°00'30" W; at SW cor. sec. 8, T 35 N, R 1 W). Named on Bollibokka Mountain (1957) and Montgomery Creek (1956) 15' quadrangles.

Buck Mountain [SISKIYOU]: *peak,* 8 miles north of Bartle (lat. 41°22'30" N, long. 121°50' W; at E line sec. 27, T 41 N, R 1 E). Altitude 6525 feet. Named on Bartle (1961) 15' quadrangle.

Buck Mountain: see **Buck Peak** [SISKIYOU].

Buck Mountain Spring [SISKIYOU]: *spring,* 6.25 miles north of Bartle (lat. 41°20'50" N, long. 121°49'30" W; sec. 2, T 40 N, R 1 E); the spring is 2 miles south of Buck Mountain. Named on Bartle (1961) 15' quadrangle.

Buck Peak [SISKIYOU]: *peak,* 13 miles north-northwest of Happy Camp (lat. 41°58'30" N, long. 123°18'30" W). Named on Figurehead Mountain (1980) 7.5' quadrangle. Called Buck Mtn. on Happy Camp (1956) 15' quadrangle, but United States Board on Geographic Names (1981c, p. 3) rejected this name for the feature.

Buck Point [GLENN]: *peak,* 11 miles northwest of the village of Elk Creek (lat. 39°44'15" N, long. 122°39' W); the peak is 2 miles north of Doe Peak. Altitude 4073 feet. Named on Alder Springs (1967) 7.5' quadrangle.

Buck Point [SHASTA]: *peak,* 13 miles north of Millville (lat. 40°44'20" N, long. 122°12' W; near SW cor. sec. 3, T 33 N, R 3 W). Altitude 1679 feet. Named on Bella Vista (1965) 7.5' quadrangle.

Buck Ridge [GLENN]: *ridge,* southwest-trending, 2 miles long, nearly 7 miles south-southeast of Black Butte (lat. 39°38'15" N, long. 122°48'55" W). Named on Plaskett Meadows (1967) 7.5' quadrangle.

Buck Ridge [SHASTA]: *ridge,* generally west-trending, 2 miles long, 2.5 miles west of Shoeinhorse Mountain (lat. 41°04'15" N, long. 122°07'10" W). Named on Shoeinhorse Mountain (1954) 15' quadrangle.

Buck Ridge: see **Big Buck Ridge** [SISKIYOU]; **Little Buck Ridge** [SISKIYOU].

Buck Rock [TEHAMA]: *peak,* 9 miles west of Ball Mountain on Tehama-Mendocino County line (lat. 39°54'30" N, long. 122°56'50" W; near E line sec. 27, T 24 N, R 10 W). Altitude 6658 feet. Named on Buck Rock (1967) 7.5' quadrangle.

Bucks Flat [TEHAMA]: *area,* 2 miles southwest of Panther Spring (lat. 40°13'55" N, long. 121°48' W; at SE cor. sec. 36, T 28 N, R 1 E). Named on Panther Spring (1953) 15' quadrangle. The name recalls an ox called Buck that Indians stole and killed (Gudde, 1949, p. 42).

Bucks Peak [SHASTA]: *peak,* 7 miles southeast of Lamoine (lat. 40°54'50" N, long. 122°19'30" W; sec. 4, T 35 N, R 4 W). Altitude 4092 feet. Named on Lamoine (1957) 15' quadrangle.

Buck Spring [GLENN]: *spring,* 7.5 miles west-northwest of the village of Elk Creek (lat. 39°39'05" N, long. 122°39'50" W). Named on Alder Springs (1967) 7.5' quadrangle.

Buck Spring [TEHAMA]: *spring,* 10.5 miles west-southwest of Paskenta (lat. 39°49'05" N, long. 122°43'10" W; near E line sec. 26, T 23 N, R 8 W). Named on Hall Ridge (1967) 7.5' quadrangle.

Budden Canyon [TEHAMA]: *canyon,* drained by a stream that flows 6.25 miles to Dry Creek (1) 8 miles west-northwest of Rosewood (lat. 40°18' N, long. 122°42' W; at N line sec. 7, T 28 N, R 7 W). Named on Chanchelulla Peak (1951) and Ono (1952) 15' quadrangles.

Budwiser Gap [SHASTA]: *pass,* 10 miles north of Schell Mountain (lat. 41°00' N, long. 122°31'15" W; at N line sec. 11, T 36 N, R 6 W). Named on Schell Mountain (1950) 15' quadrangle.

Buells Flat: see **Big Bend Creek** [SISKIYOU].

Buena Ventura Valley: see "Regional setting."

Buena Vista [TEHAMA]: *locality,* 14 miles south-southwest of Panther Spring (lat. 40°03'25" N, long. 121°52'05" W; at N line sec. 4, T 25 N, R 1 E). Named on Panther Spring (1953) 15' quadrangle. Called Buenavista on Mineral (1941) 30' quadrangle.

Buffom Creek [SHASTA]: *stream,* flows 1.5 miles to Hatchet Creek 4 miles northwest of the village of Montgomery Creek (lat. 40°52'35" N, long. 121°51'35" W; near W line sec. 22, T 35 N, R 1 E). Named on Montgomery Creek (1956) 15' quadrangle. United States Board on Geographic Names (1991, p. 3) approved the form "Buffum Creek" for the name, and noted that it commemorates Frank Buffum, who settled along the creek in 1888.

Buffum Creek: see **Buffom Creek** [SHASTA].

Bug Creek [SISKIYOU]: *stream,* flows 1.25 miles to Thompson Creek 6.5 miles north-northeast of Happy Camp (lat. 41°52'40" N, long. 123°19'10" W). Named on Figurehead Mountain (1980) 7.5' quadrangle.

Bug Gulch [SISKIYOU]: *canyon,* 1.5 miles long, along Right Hand Fork of North Fork Salmon Creek above a point 12.5 miles north of Sawyers Bar (lat. 41°28'20" N, long. 123°04'50" W). Named on Yellow Dog Peak (1977) 7.5' quadrangle.

Bug Lake [SISKIYOU]: *lake,* 150 feet long, 12 miles north of Sawyers Bar (lat. 41°28'25" N, long. 123°07' W); the lake is at the head of Bug Gulch. Named on Yellow Dog Peak (1977) 7.5' quadrangle.

Bulam Creek: see **Bolam Creek** [SISKIYOU].

Bulam Glacier: see **Bolam Glacier** [SISKIYOU].

Buljon Gulch: see **Bullion Gulch** [SHASTA].

Bull: see **Johnny Bull Creek** [SISKIYOU].

Bull Barn Flat [SISKIYOU]: *area,* just south of Forks of Salmon (lat. 41°15'20" N, long. 123°19'20" W). Named on Forks of Salmon (1978) 7.5' quadrangle. Called Acorn Springs Flat on Forks of Salmon (1955) 15' quadrangle, but United States Board on Geographic Names (1978a, p. 5) rejected this name for the feature.

Bull Canyon [SHASTA]: *canyon,* drained by a stream that flows 3 miles to Kosk Creek 8 miles north-northeast of the village of Big Bend (lat. 41°07'30" N, long. 121°53'15" W; sec. 29, T 38 N, R 1 E). Named on Big Bend (1961) 15' quadrangle.

Bull Creek [BUTTE]: *stream,* flows 7 miles to Butte Creek [BUTTE-GLENN] 5.5 miles south-southwest of Butte Meadows (lat. 40°00'15" N, long. 121°35' W; at S line sec. 24, T 25 N, R 3 E). Named on Butte Meadows (1958) 15' quadrangle.

Bull Creek [SHASTA]:

(1) *stream,* flows 1.25 miles to Nelson Creek (1) nearly 3 miles northeast of the village of Big Bend (lat. 41°02'50" N, long. 121°52'15" W; near W line sec. 21, T 37 N, R 1 E). Named on Big Bend (1961) 15' quadrangle.

(2) *stream,* flows less than 1 mile to Backbone Creek Inlet 12 miles south of Lamoine (lat. 40°48'30" N, long. 122°25'45" W; at E line sec. 16, T 34 N, R 5 W). Named on Lamoine (1957) 15' quadrangle.

Bull Creek [SISKIYOU]: *stream,* flows 6 miles to McCloud River [SHASTA-SISKIYOU] 4 miles west of Bartle (lat. 41°15'20" N, long. 121°52'40" W; sec. 5, T 39 N, R 1 E). Named on Bartle (1961) and Big Bend (1961) 15' quadrangles.

Bullet Chup: see **Bully Choop Mountain** [SHASTA].

Bull Flat [TEHAMA]: *area,* 5.25 miles northwest of Ball Mountain (lat. 39°58'50" N, long. 122°51'35" W; on S line sec. 27, T 25 N, R 9 W). Named on Ball Mountain (1967) 7.5' quadrangle.

Bull Gulch [SHASTA]: *canyon,* drained by a stream that flows 1.5 miles to Whiskeytown Lake 4 miles south-southeast of the village of French Creek (lat. 40°38'55" N, long. 122°36'40" W; near N line sec. 12, T 32 N, R 7 W). Named on Whiskeytown (1979) 7.5' quadrangle.

Bullhead Creek [SISKIYOU]: *stream,* flows 4 miles to Bogus Creek 22 miles west-northwest of Macdoel (lat. 41°55'40" N, long. 122°24'15" W; sec. 15, T 47 N, R 5 W). Named on Copco (1954) 15' quadrangle.

Bull Hill [BUTTE]: *ridge,* northwest-trending, about 1 mile long, 2 miles southwest of Butte Meadows (lat. 40°03'45" N, long. 121°31'30" W; sec. 33, T 26 N, R 4 E). Named on Butte Meadows (1958) 15' quadrangle

Bullion Gulch [SHASTA]: *canyon,* drained by a stream that flows nearly 2 miles to Ditch Fork Duncan Creek 4 miles northeast of Arbuckle Mountain (lat. 40°26'50" N, long. 122°49'15" W; near SE cor. sec. 13, T 30 N, R 9 W). Named on Chanchelulla Peak (1951) 15' quadrangle. The canyon also was called Buljon Gulch (Steger, p. 20).

Bullion Mountain [SISKIYOU]: *peak,* 10 miles north-northwest of Hornbrook (lat. 41°57' N, long. 122°43'55" W; sec. 2, T 47 N, R 8 W). Altitude 5535 feet. Named on Hornbrook (1955) 15' quadrangle.

Bull Meadow [SISKIYOU]: *area,* 10 miles southwest of Macdoel (lat. 41°44'40" N, long. 122°09' W; sec. 14, T 45 N, R 3 W). Named on The Whaleback (1954) 15' quadrangle.

Bullock Creek [SHASTA]: *stream,* flows 2 miles to South Cow Creek 15 miles northwest of Lassen Peak (lat. 40°37'30" N, long. 121°42'45" W). Named on Manzanita Lake (1956) 15' quadrangle.

Bullseye Lake [SISKIYOU]: *lake,* 700 feet long, 2.25 miles southeast of Medicine Lake (lat. 41°33'20" N, long. 121°34'30" W; sec. 24, T 43 N, R 3 E). Named on Medicine Lake (1952) 15' quadrangle.

Bullskin: see **Round Mountain** [SHASTA] (3).

Bullskin Ridge [SHASTA]: *ridge,* generally west-trending, 9 miles long, center about 15 miles northeast of Millville (lat. 40°43' N, long. 122°00' W). Named on Millville (1953) and Whitmore (1956) 15' quadrangles. The name is from "Bullskin Jack," a saloonkeeper who received his nickname from a bull skin that he had drying on a fence at his saloon (Gudde, 1949, p. 44).

Bully Choop Mountain [SHASTA]: *peak,* 7 miles west-southwest of Shasta Valley on Shasta-Trinity County line (lat. 40°33'20" N, long. 122°46' W; near E line sec. 9, T 31 N, R 8 W). Altitude 6974 feet. Named on Weaverville (1950) 15' quadrangle. According to Goodyear (p. 255), the name means "needle peak" in an Indian dialect. Whitney (p. 323) called the feature Bullet Chup.

Bully Choop Mountains: see **Trinity Mountains** [SHASTA-SISKIYOU].

Bully Hill [SHASTA]:

(1) *peak,* 9.5 miles south of Bollibokka Mountain (lat. 40°48' N, long. 122°12'30" W; sec. 16, T 34 N, R 3 W). Altitude 2030 feet. Named on Bollibokka Mountain (1957) 15' quadrangle.

(2) *locality,* 9.5 miles south of Bollibokka Mountain (lat. 40°47'50" N, long. 122°11'30" W; near S line sec. 15, T 34 N, R 3 W); the place is less than 1 mile east of Bully Hill (1). Site named on Bollibokka Mountain (1957) 15' quadrangle. The community started in 1862 when gold and silver ore were discovered there (Brown, p. 774). An early trading center called Pittsburg was situated along Town Creek 1 mile east of Bully Hill (2) (Steger, p. 20, 52-53).

Bumblebee Creek [SISKIYOU]: *stream,* flows 2.5 miles to Beaver Creek (1) 9.5 miles east of Condrey Mountain (lat. 41°57'10" N, long. 122°47'40" W; sec. 5, T 47 N, R 8 W). Named on Condrey Mountain (1955) and Hornbrook (1955) 15' quadrangles.

Bumpass Hell [SHASTA]: *area,* 2.5 miles south of Lassen Peak (lat. 40°27'25" N, long. 121°30' W; sec. 14, T 30 N, R 4 E). Named on Lassen Peak (1956) and Mount Harkness (1956) 15' quadrangles. Called Bumpass Hot Sprs. on Lassen Peak (1894) 1° quadrangle. United States Board on Geographic Names (1948a, p. 4) approved the designation "Bumpass Hell" for this crater-shaped basin of hot springs, and noted that the name is for Kendall Vanhook Bumpass, who discovered the spot; at the same time the Board rejected the forms "Bumpers Hell," "Bumpas Hell," "Bumpas Hot Springs," "Bumpass Hot Springs," "Bumpass Inferno," and "Bumpass's Hell" for the name

Bumpass Hot Springs: see **Bumpass Hell** [SHASTA].

Bumpass Inferno: see **Bunpass Hell** [SHASTA].

Bumpass Mountain [SHASTA]: *peak,* nearly 2 miles south-southeast of Lassen Peak (lat. 40°27'40" N, long. 121°29'50" W; near E line sec. 14, T 30 N, R 4 E); the peak is north of Bumpass Hell. Altitude 8753 feet. Named on Mount Harkness (1956) 15' quadrangle. United States Board on Geographic Names (1948b, p. 1) rejected the form "Bumpas Mountain" for the name.

Bunchgrass Campground [SHASTA]: *locality,* 12 miles north-northwest of Lassen Peak (lat. 40°38'30" N, long. 121°36'30" W; near NW cor. sec. 11, T 32 N, R 3 E); the place is along Bunchgrass Creek. Named on Manzanita Lake (1956) 15' quadrangle.

Bunchgrass Creek [SHASTA]: *stream,* flows 2 miles to Bunchgrass Valley 12 miles north-northwest of Lassen Peak (lat. 40°38'20" N, long. 121°36' W; sec. 11, T 32 N, R 3 E). Named on Manzanita Lake (1956) 15' quadrangle.

Bunch Grass Meadow: see **Little Bunch Grass Meadow** [SHASTA].

Bunchgrass Mountain [SHASTA]: *peak,* 8 miles northeast of the village of Montgomery Creek (lat. 40°55'40" N, long. 121°49'35" W). Altitude 5496 feet. Named on Montgomery Creek (1956) 15' quadrangle.

Bunchgrass Valley [SHASTA]: *valley,* 11 miles north-northwest of Lassen Peak (lat. 40°38' N, long. 121°35' W). Named on Manzanita Lake (1956) 15' quadrangle. Averill's (1939) map has the form "Bunch Grass Valley" for the name.

Bunch Grass Valley: see **Little Bunch Grass Valley**, under **Little Bunch Grass Meadow** [SHASTA].

Bundoora Spring [SISKIYOU]: *spring,* 9 miles west of Bartle along

McCloud River [SHASTA-SISKIYOU] (lat. 41°14' N, long. 121°59'30" W; at S line sec. 8, T 39 N, R 1 W). Named on Big Bend (1961) 15' quadrangle.

Bunny Flat [SISKIYOU]: *area,* 8.5 miles north-northwest of McCloud (lat. 41°21'20" N, long. 122°13'55" W; sec. 31, T 41 N, R 3 W). Named on Shasta (1954) 15' quadrangle.

Buns Basin [SISKIYOU]: *relief feature,* 5.5 miles south-southeast of Ukonom Lake (lat. 41°30'05" N, long. 123°19'05" W). Named on Ukonom Lake (1980) 7.5' quadrangle.

Bunton Hollow Creek [SISKIYOU]: *stream,* flows 2.25 miles to Shasta Valley 9.5 miles south of Hornbrook (lat. 41°46'35" N, long. 122°31'30" W; sec. 3, T 45 N, R 6 W). Named on Hornbrook (1955) 15' quadrangle.

Burch Creek [TEHAMA]: *stream,* formed by the confluence of Elmore Creek and Jackson Spring Creek, flows 23 miles to Sacramento River 10 miles southeast of Corning (lat. 39°48'55" N, long. 122°03'50" W). Named on Black Butte Dam (1967), Corning (1951), Foster Island (1950), Henleyville (1967), and Kirkwood (1949) 7.5' quadrangles. On Corning (1951) 15' quadrangle, present Burch Creek below Brannen Creek is called Rice Creek

Burdys Bar: see **Bardees Bar** [BUTTE].

Burgess: see **Montgomery Creek** [SHASTA] (2).

Burgess Creek: see **Cape Horn Creek** [SHASTA].

Burgettville: see **Glenburn** [SHASTA].

Burn: see **The Burn** [TEHAMA].

Burney [SHASTA]: *town,* 43 miles east-northeast of Redding (lat. 40°52'55" N, long, 121°40'05" W). Named on Burney (1957) 15' quadrangle. Called Burney Valley on Lassen Peak (1894) 1° quadrangle. Postal authorities established Burney Valley post office in 1872 and changed the name to Burney in 1894 (Frickstad, p. 178). The name commemorates Samuel Burney, who came to the place in 1857 and built a log cabin, barn, and corral 1 mile north of the present town (Hoover, Rensch, and Rensch, p., 486).

Burney Butte: see **Burney Mountain** [SHASTA].

Burney Creek [SHASTA]: *stream,* flows 30 miles to Lake Britton less than 1 mile north of Burney Falls (lat. 41°01'15" N, long. 121°39'15" W; near NW cor. sec. 29, T 37 N, R 3 E). Named on Burney (1957), Manzanita Lake (1956), and Pondosa (1961) 15' quadrangles.

Burney Falls [SHASTA]: *waterfall,* 11 miles west of Fall River Mills (lat. 41°00'40" N, long. 121°39'05" W; near E line sec. 5, T 36 N, R 3 E); the feature is along Burney Creek. Named on Pondosa (1961) 15' quadrangle.

Burney Lake [SISKIYOU]: *lake,* 1000 feet long, 3.5 miles east-southeast of Ukonom Lake (lat. 41°33'45" N, long. 123°17'25" W); the lake is at the head of Burney Valley Creek. Named on Ukonom Lake (1980) 7.5' quadrangle.

Burney Mountain [SHASTA]: *mountain,* nearly 6 miles south-southeast of Burney (lat. 40°48'30" N, long. 121°37'30" W; sec. 15, T 34 N, R 3 E). Altitude 7863 feet. Named on Burney (1957) 15' quadrangle. Called Burney Butte on Lassen Peak (1894) 1° quadrangle, and called Burney Pk. on California Mining Bureau's (1917b) map.

Burney Peak: see **Burney Mountain** [SHASTA].

Burney Spring [SHASTA]: *spring,* 7.5 miles south-southeast of Burney (lat. 40°46'50" N, long. 121°37'20" W; near N lines sec. 27, T 34 N, R 3 E); the spring is 2 miles south of the top of Burney Mountain. Named on Burney (1957) 15' quadrangle.

Burney Spring Mountain [SHASTA]: *peak,* 8 mile north of Burney (lat. 40°59'45" N, long. 121°39'55" W; near W line sec. 8, T 36 N, R 3 E). Named on Burney (1957) 15' quadrangle.

Burney Valley [SISKIYOU]: *valley,* 3.5 miles east of Ukonom Lake (lat. 41°35' N, long. 123°17'30" W). Named on Ukonom Lake (1980) 7.5' quadrangle.

Burney Valley: see **Burney** [SHASTA].

Burney Valley Creek [SISKIYOU]: *stream,* flows 3.5 miles to Granite Creek (2) 4 miles northeast of Ukonom Lake (lat. 41°36'45" N, long. 123°17'25" W); the stream heads at Burney Lake and flows through Burney Valley. Named on Ukonom Lake (1980) 7.5' quadrangle.

Burns Creek [SISKIYOU]: *stream,* flows 2.5 miles to Klamath River 3.25 miles northeast of Dillon Mountain (lat. 41°33'35" N, long. 123°31'20" W). Named on Dillon Mountain (1983) and Ukonom Mountain (1980) 7.5' quadrangles.

Burnt Camp [TEHAMA]:

(1) *locality,* nearly 6 miles west of Tomhead Mountain along South Fork Cottonwood Creek [SHASTA-TEHAMA] (lat. 40°08'40" N, long. 122°55'25" W; sec. 31, T 27 N, R 9 W); the place is near the mouth of Burnt Canyon. Named on Yolla Bolly (1954) 15' quadrangle.

(2) *locality,* 6.25 miles south-southwest of Tomhead Mountain along Slides Creek (lat. 40°03' N, long. 122°51'20" W; sec. 3, T 25 N, R 9 W). Named on Yolla Bolly (1954) 15' quadrangle.

Burnt Canyon [TEHAMA]: *canyon,* drained by a stream that flows 1.25 miles to South Fork Cottonwood Creek [SHASTA-TEHAMA] nearly 6 miles west of Tomhead Mountain (lat. 40°08'40" N, long. 122°55'25" W; sec. 31, T 27 N, R 9 W). Named on Yolla Bolly (1954) 15' quadrangle.

Burnt Creek [TEHAMA]: *stream,* flows nearly 2 miles to Grindstone Creek [GLENN-TEHAMA] 9.5 miles southwest of Ball Mountain (lat. 39°50'35" W, long. 122°54'50" W; at E line sec. 13, T 23 N, R 10 W). Named on Mendocino Pass (1967) 7.5' quadrangle.

Buroughs Pinery [TEHAMA]: *area,* 3 miles east-northeast of Campbell Mound (lat. 39°59'40" N, long. 121°46' W; near SW cor. sec. 28, T 25 N, R 2 E). Named on Campbell Mound (1952) 7.5' quadrangle.

Burris Creek [GLENN]: *stream,* flows 8.5 miles to Black Butte Reservoir 12 miles west-northwest of Orland (lat. 39°48' N, long. 122°24'15" W; at SW cor. sec. 35, T 23 N, R 5 W). Named on Chrome (1968), Julian Rocks (1968), and Sehorn Creek (1967) 7.5' quadrangles.

Burrows Gap [GLENN]: *pass,* 3 miles south of Newville (lat. 39°45' N, long. 122°31'40" W; near W line sec. 22, T 22 N, R 6 W). Named on Chrome (1968) and Newville (1967) 7.5' quadrangles.

Burr Valley [TEHAMA]: *valley,* 9 miles long, center 3.25 miles north of Red Bank along Reeds Creek (lat. 40°08'40" N, long. 122°26' W). Named on Blossom (1952) 7.5' quadrangle.

Burts Ferry [BUTTE]: *locality,* 4 miles east-northeast of Gridley along Feather River (lat. 39°23'05" N, long. 121°37'30" W). Named on Marysville (1895) 30' quadrangle. A settlement called Cordelia was situated on the east bank of Feather River opposite Burts Ferry in 1851 (Dunn, F.D., p. 27).

Bush Bar [SHASTA]: *locality,* 11 miles north-northwest of the village of Montgomery Creek along Pit River (lat. 40°59'50" N, long. 121°58'05" W; near NE cor. sec. 9, T 36 N, R 1 W). Named on Montgomery Creek (1956) 15' quadrangle.

Bush Creek [BUTTE]: *stream,* flows 4 miles to French Creek 4 miles north-northwest of the village of Brush Creek (lat. 39°44'30" N, long. 121°21'35" W). Named on Brush Creek (1970) and Pulga (1979) 7.5' quadrangles. United States Board on Geographic Names (1960b, p. 6) rejected the name "Brush Creek" for the feature.

Busombe: see **Millville** [SHASTA].

Butcher Creek [SHASTA]: *stream,* flows 1.25 miles to Shasta Lake 4.5 miles north-northwest of Summit City (lat. 40°44'45" N, long. 122°26'10" W; sec. 4, T 33 N, R 5 W). Named on Lamoine (1957) 15' quadrangle, and on Shasta Dam (1956) 7.5' quadrangle.

Butcher Gulch [SHASTA]: *canyon,* drained by a stream that flows 1 mile to Atkins Creek 17 miles northwest of Lassen Peak (lat. 40°39'50" N, long. 121°44' W; sec. 3, T 32 N, R 2 E). Named on Manzanita Lake (1956) 15' quadrangle.

Butcher Gulch [SISKIYOU]:

(1) *canyon,* drained by a stream that flows 1.5 miles to South Fork Salmon River nearly 4 miles west-northwest of Cecilville (lat. 41°09'35" N, long. 123°12'25" W). Named on Cecilville (1979) 7.5' quadrangle.

(2) *canyon,* drained by a stream that flows nearly 2 miles to Humbug Creek 8.5 miles southwest of Hornbrook (lat. 41°49'30" N, long. 122°40'30" W; sec. 21, T 46 N, R 7 W). Named on Hornbrook (1955) 15' quadrangle.

Butcher Gulch Campground [SHASTA]: *locality,* 16 miles northwest of Lassen Peak (lat. 40°39' N, long. 121°43'40" W; near E line sec. 3, T 32 N, R 2 E); the place is at the head of Butcher Gulch. Named on Manzanita Lake (1956) 15' quadrangle.

Butcherknife Creek [SHASTA]: *stream,* flows 2 miles to Hawkins Creek 3.5 miles north-northeast of Shoeinhorse Mountain (lat. 41°06'55" N, long. 122°07'05" W). Named on Shoeinhorse Mountain (1954) 15' quadrangle.

Butler Camp [GLENN]: *locality,* 10 miles south-southwest of the village of Elk Creek (lat. 39°30'50" N, long. 122°40'50" W). Named on Felkner Hill (1968) 7.5' quadrangle.

Butler Creek [SISKIYOU]: *stream,* flows 4.25 miles to Salmon River 7 miles northwest of Forks of Salmon (lat. 41°20'10" N, long. 123°24'25" W). Named on Orleans Mountain (1974) 7.5' quadrangle.

Butler Flat [SISKIYOU]: *area,* 7 miles northwest of Forks of Salmon (lat. 41°20'10" N, long. 123°24'30" W); the place is along Salmon River at the mouth of Butler Creek. Named on Orleans Mountain (1974) 7.5' quadrangle.

Butler Mountain [SISKIYOU]: *peak,* 6 miles northwest of Forks of Salmon (lat. 41°19'10" N, long. 123°23'45" W). Altitude 3481 feet. Named on Orleans Mountain (1974) 7.5' quadrangle.

Butler Slough [TEHAMA]: *stream,* flows nearly 5 miles to Sacramento River 3.5 miles north-northeast of Gerber (lat. 40°06'10" N, long. 122°07'40" W). Named on Gerber (1950), Los Molinos (1952), Red Buff East (1951), and Tuscan Springs (1951) 7.5' quadrangles.

Butte: see **Butte City** [GLENN].

Butte City [GLENN]: *village,* 11 miles east-southeast of Williams on the east side of Sacramento River (lat. 39°27'50" N, long. 121°59'25" W; at N line sec. 32, T 19 N, R 1 W). Named on Butte City (1952) 7.5' quadrangle. Called Butte on Eddy's (1854) map. Postal authorities established Butte City post office in 1873 (Frickstad, p. 40).

Butte Creek [BUTTE-GLENN]: *stream,* flows 70 miles to Sutter and Colusa Counties 13 miles southwest of Biggs (lat. 39°18'15" N, long. 121°54'25" W); the lower part of the stream forms Butte-Glenn County line and Butte-Colusa County line. Named on Chico (1958) and Susanville (1962) 1°x 2° quadrangles. Called Big Butte Creek on Chico (1895)

30' quadrangle, and called Arroyo de los Picos on a diseño of Larkins Childrens Rancho of 1844, where present Sutter Buttes in Sutter County is called Los Picos de Sutter (Becker, 1969). A survey of 1867 used the name "Tres Picos" for the stream (Dunn, F.D., p. 107). West Branch enters 4.5 miles west of Stirling City at Forks of Butte; it is 10 miles long and is named on Butte Meadows (1958) 15' quadrangle, and on Cohasset (1979) and Stirling City (1979) 7.5' quadrangles. West Branch is called West Fork on Chico (1895) 30' quadrangle.

Butte Creek [GLENN]: *stream,* flows 2.5 miles to Mendocino County 2 miles west of Black Butte (lat. 39°43'45" N, long. 122°54'40" W; at W line sec. 29, T 22 N, R 9 W). Named on Plaskett Meadows (1967) and Plaskett Ridge (1967) 7.5' quadrangles.

Butte Creek [SHASTA]: *stream,* heads in Lassen County and flows 3 miles in Shasta County to end 20 miles north-northeast of Lassen Peak (lat. 40°44'40" N, long. 121°19'45" W; near S line sec. 5, T 33 N, R 6 E). Named on Prospect Peak (1957) 15' quadrangle. The stream was called Black Butte Creek in the early days (Steger, p. 21).

Butte Creek [SISKIYOU]: *stream,* flows about 32 miles to Butte Valley 6.5 miles south of Macdoel (lat. 41°44'30" N, long. 122°00'10" W). Named on Bartle (1961), Bray (1950), Macdoel (1954), Shasta (1954), and The Whaleback (1954) 15' quadrangles.

Butte Creek: see **Chico** [BUTTE]; **Helltown** [BUTTE]; **Little Butte Creek** [BUTTE]; **Little Butte Creek** [BUTTE-GLENN]; **Middle Butte Creek** [BUTTE].

Butte Creek Cabin [SHASTA]: *locality,* 19 miles north-northeast of Lassen Peak (lat. 40°43'30" N, long. 121°19'30" W; sec. 17, T 33 N, R 6 E); the place is along Butte Creek. Named on Prospect Peak (1957) 15' quadrangle.

Butte Creek House [BUTTE]: *locality,* 3.25 miles east-southeast of Jonesville (lat. 40°05'15" N, long. 121°24'55" W; near S line sec. 21, T 26 N, R 5 E). Named on Jonesville (1958) 15' quadrangle. Postal authorities established Abertine post office 13 miles north of Inskip post office in 1910 and discontinued it in 1914 (Salley, p. 1)—it is believed that the post office was at Butte Creek House, where it served tree tappers who gathered pine pitch to distill and use in a patent medicine made by Abertine Medical Company (Dunn, F.D., p. 1).

Butte Creek Rim [SHASTA]: *escarpment,* generally north-trending, 14 miles long, center about 6 miles south of Coble Mountain (lat. 40°47'30" N, long. 121°20'50" W); the feature extends south into Lassen County. Named on Jellico (1957) and Prospect Peak (1957) 15' quadrangles.

Butte Fork: see **Applegate River** [SISKIYOU].

Butte Fork Slide [SISKIYOU]: *relief feature,* 8.5 miles north of the village of Seiad Valley (lat. 41°57'40" N, long. 123°10'30" W); the feature is along a tributary of Butte Fork Applegate River. Named on Kangaroo Mountain (1980) 7.5' quadrangle.

Butte Meadows [BUTTE]: *village,* 29 miles north-northeast of Chico (lat. 40°04'50" N, long. 121°33' W; mainly in sec. 29, T 26 N, R 33 W); the village is along Butte Creek [BUTTE-GLENN]. Named on Butte Meadows (1958) 15' quadrangle. Postal authorities established Butte Meadows post office in 1878 in Tehama County, moved it 1 mile east into Butte County the same year, moved it 1 mile west back into Tehama County in 1880, and moved it 1 mile east into Butte County in 1888 (Salley, p. 30).

Butte Mills: see **Magalia** [BUTTE].

Butter Creek [SHASTA]: *stream,* flows 1.5 miles to Richardson Creek 1.5 miles north of the village of Montgomery Creek (lat. 40°54'15" N, long. 121°54'30" W; near W line sec. 7, T 35 N, R 1 E). Named on Montgomery Creek (1956) 15' quadrangle.

Butte Reservoir: see **Meiss Lake** [SISKIYOU].

Buttermilk Creek [TEHAMA]: *stream,* flows 2 miles to Willow Creek (2) 5.5 miles south-southwest of Ball Mountain (lat. 39°51'55" N, long. 122°50'45" W; near W line sec. 11, T 23 N, R 9 W). Named on Log Spring (1967) 7.5' quadrangle.

Buttermilk Spring [TEHAMA]: *spring,* 8 miles south-southwest of Ball Mountain (lat. 39°50'15" N, long. 122°51'45" W; near W line sec. 22, T 23 N, R 9 W); the spring is less than 0.5 mile south of the head of Buttermilk Creek. Named on Log Spring (1967) 7.5' quadrangle.

Butte Sink [BUTTE]: *marsh,* 12.5 miles southwest of Biggs on Butte-Sutter County line (lat. 39°18'15" N, long. 121°53'45" W); the feature is east of Butte Creek [BUTTE-GLENN]. Named on Sanborn Slough (1952) 7.5' quadrangle.

Butte Valley [SISKIYOU]: *valley,* at and around Macdoel. Named on Dorris (1950), Macdoel (1954), and The Whaleback (1954) 15' quadrangles.

Butte Valley: see **Durham** [BUTTE].

Butteville: see **Edgewood** [SISKIYOU].

Butt Mountain [TEHAMA]: *peak,* 4.5 miles southeast of Deer Creek Station (lat. 40°13' N, long. 121°23'05" W). Altitude 7866 feet. Named on Jonesville (1958) 15' quadrangle.

Buzzard Creek [SISKIYOU]: *stream,* flows 2.25 miles to Klamath River 11 miles north-northwest of Ukonom Lake (lat. 41°43'50" N, long. 123°25'45" W). Named on Clear Creek (1981) 7.5' quadrangle.

Buzzard Lake [SISKIYOU]: *lake,* 300 feet long, 16 miles south-southwest of Scott Bar (lat. 41°31'30" N, long. 123°05'40" W). Named on Boulder Peak (1981) 7.5' quadrangle.

Buzzard Roost: see **Round Mountain** [SHASTA] (3).

By Gonney Spring [SHASTA]: *spring,* 1.5 miles north-northeast of the village of Montgomery Creek (lat. 40°51'45" N, long. 121°54'15" W; sec. 30, T 35 N, R 1 E). Named on Montgomery Creek (1956) 15' quadrangle.

— C —

Cabin Butte [SISKIYOU]: *peak,* 6.5 miles north of Bartle (lat. 41°21' N, long. 121°50'30" W; on S line sec. 34, T 41 N, R 1 E). Altitude 5709 feet. Named on Bartle (1961) 15' quadrangle, which shows Snow Survey cabin near the peak.

Cabin Creek [SHASTA]: *stream,* flows 2 miles to Squaw Valley Creek [SHASTA-SISKIYOU] 7.5 miles northwest of Shoeinhorse Mountain (lat. 41°08'35" N, long. 122°10'10" W). Named on Shoeinhorse Mountain (1954) 15' quadrangle.

Cabin Gulch [SISKIYOU]: *canyon,* drained by a stream that flows 2 miles to Bug Gulch 12.5 miles north of Sawyers Bar (lat. 41°28'35" N, long. 123°06' W). Named on Yellow Dog Peak (1977) 7.5' quadrangle.

Cabin Hollow [BUTTE]: *canyon,* drained by a stream that flows 3.5 miles to Sycamore Creek (1) 4.5 miles north-northeast of Chico (lat. 39°47'05" N, long. 121°47'40" W). Named on Richardson Springs (1951) 7.5' quadrangle.

Cabin Meadow Creek [SISKIYOU]: *stream,* flows 4.5 miles to Houston Creek 14 miles east-southeast of Etna (lat. 41°23'10" N, long. 122°37'45" W; near W line sec. 23, T 41 N, R 7 W). Named on China Mountain (1955) 15' quadrangle.

Cabin Meadow Lake [SISKIYOU]: *lake,* 450 feet long, 18 miles east-southeast of Etna (lat. 41°20'25" N, long. 122°35'15" W; at W line sec. 8, T 40 N, R 6 W); the lake is near the head of Cabin Meadow Creek. Named on China Mountain (1955) 15' quadrangle.

Cabin Spring [SHASTA]: *spring,* 7 miles west-southwest of Lassen Peak (lat. 40°27'30" N, long. 121°37'40" W). Named on Lassen Peak (1956) 15' quadrangle.

Cable Mountain: see **Coble Mountain** [SHASTA].

Cable Spring: see **Coble Spring** [SHASTA].

Cache Cabin [SHASTA]: *locality,* 18 miles north-northeast of Lassen Peak (lat. 40°44'15" N, long. 121°20'40" W; sec. 7, T 33 N, R 6 E). Named on Prospect Peak (1957) 15' quadrangle.

Cade Creek [SISKIYOU]: *stream,* flows nearly 4 miles to Klamath River less than 2 miles east-northeast of Happy Camp (lat. 41°48'25" N, long. 123°20'50" W; sec. 1, T 16 N, R 7 E); the stream is west of Cade Mountain. Named on Slater Butte (1980) 7.5' quadrangle.

Cade Mountain [SISKIYOU]: *peak,* 4 miles northeast of Happy Camp (lat. 41°50'15" N, long. 123°19'30" W); the peak is at the head of a branch of Cade Creek. Altitude 3965 feet. Named on Slater Butte (1980) 7.5' quadrangle.

Cadillac: see **Hornbrook** [SISKIYOU].

Caesar Peak [SISKIYOU]: *peak,* 11 miles south-southeast of Cecilville on Siskiyou-Trinity County line (lat. 41°00'15" N, long. 123°02'10" W). Altitude 8920 feet. Named on Thompson Peak (1979) 7.5' quadrangle.

Caldwell Butte [SISKIYOU]: *crater,* 10 miles north-northeast of Medicine Lake (lat. 41°42' N, long. 121°29' W; sec. 35, T 45 N, R 4 E). Named on Timber Mountain (1952) 15' quadrangle. The name recalls an early sheep rancher who had a cabin near the crater (Knox, p. 57).

Caldwell Ice Caves [SISKIYOU]: *caves,* 10 miles north-northeast of Medicine Lake (lat. 41°41'30" N, long. 121°28'30" W; near SE cor. sec. 35, T 45 N, R 4 E); the caves are just southeast of Caldwell Butte. Named on Timber Mountain (1952) 15' quadrangle. Mr. Caldwell of Caldwell Butte supplied his sheep with water from the caves (Knox, p. 57).

Caldwell Lakes [SISKIYOU]: *lakes,* three, largest 400 feet long, 19 miles east-southeast of Etna (lat. 41°22'20" N, long. 122°33'20" W; on and near E line sec. 29, T 41 N, R 6 W). Named on China Mountain (1955) 15' quadrangle.

Caldwell Minor [SISKIYOU]: *relief feature,* 10 miles north-northeast of Medicine Lake (lat. 41°42'20" N, long. 121°28'50" W; at N line sec. 35, T 45 N, R 4 E); the feature is at the north edge of Caldwell Butte. Named on Timber Mountain (1952) 15' quadrangle.

Calf Creek [TEHAMA]:

(1) *stream,* formed by the confluence of North Fork and South Fork, flows 0.25 mile to Deer Creek (2) 6.5 miles northeast of Polk Springs (lat. 40°10'10" N, long. 121°33'50" W). Shown, but unnamed, on Butte Meadows (1958) 15' quadrangle. North Fork is 3.5 miles long and South Fork is 2 miles long; both forks are named on Butte Meadows (1958) 15' quadrangle. North Fork is called Calf Cr. on Mineral (1941) 30' quadrangle.

(2) *stream,* flows 2.25 miles to Deer Creek (2) 1.25 miles north-northeast of Polk Springs (lat. 40°08' N, long. 121°39'05" W; at E line sec. 5, T 26 N, R 3 E). Named on Butte Meadows (1958) 15' quadrangle.

Calf Lake [SISKIYOU]: *lake,* 650 feet long, 13 miles south-southwest of

Scott Bar (lat. 41°33'40" N, long. 123°05'45" W). Named on Boulder Peak (1981) 7.5' quadrangle. This lake and nearby Long High Lake have the name "Calf Lakes" on Seiad (1922) 30' quadrangle.

Calf Lakes: see **Calf Lake** [SISKIYOU].

California Bar: see **Jims Camp** [SISKIYOU].

California Island [GLENN]: *island,* 18 miles north of Butte City in Sacramento River (lat. 39°44'15" N, long. 121°57'45" W). Named on Chico Landing (1912) 7.5' quadrangle.

California Nutmeg Spring [BUTTE]: *spring,* 5 miles southeast of the village of Brush Creek (lat. 39°58'35" N, long. 121°16'15" W). Named on Brush Creek (1970) 7.5' quadrangle.

California Range: see **Sierra Nevada**, under "Regional setting."

Calkins [SHASTA]: *locality,* 8 miles north of Millville (lat. 40°39'40" N, long. 122°10'55" W; near NW cor. sec. 2, T 32 N, R 3 W). Named on Redding (1901) 30' quadrangle.

Callahan [SISKIYOU]: *village,* 11.5 miles south-southeast of Etna along Scott River (lat. 41°18'30" N, long. 122°48' W; at NW cor. sec. 21, T 40 N, R 8 W). Named on Etna (1955) 15' quadrangle. Postal authorities established Callahan's Ranch post office in 1858, changed the name to Callahans Ranch in 1882, and changed it to Callahan in 1892 (Salley, p. 32). The name is for M.B. Callahan, who came to the place in 1851, opened a travelers stop, and sold out in 1855 (Denny, p. 41). Postal authorities established Schneider post office 5 miles northeast of Callahan in 1902 and discontinued it the same year (Salley, p. 199). Alber H. Denny built a trading post that he called Fort Denny at Callahans in 1851 (Whiting and Whiting, p. 23). Gudde (1975, p. 333) listed a place called Springtown that was along South Fork Salmon River about 3 miles above present Callahan. United States Board on Geographic Names (1967b, p. 3) approved the name "Hayden Ridge" for a feature that extends north for 3.5 miles from a point 1.5 miles northeast of Callahan (lat. 41°22'20" N, long. 122°46'35" W).

Callahan Camp [SISKIYOU]: *locality,* 12 miles south-southeast of Etna (lat. 41°17'50" N, long. 122°48' W; at E line sec. 20, T 40 N, R 8 W); the place is less than 1 mile south of Callahan. Named on Etna (1955) 15' quadrangle.

Callahan Gulch [SISKIYOU]: *canyon,* drained by a stream that flows 3 miles to Black Bear Creek 7 miles north-northwest of Cecilville (lat. 41°14'30" N, long. 123°10'35" W). Named on Cecilville (1979) 7.5' quadrangle.

Callahan's Ranch: see **Callahan** [SISKIYOU].

Calls Bend [GLENN]: *bend,* 1.5 miles north of Butte City along Sacramento River (lat. 39°29'05" N, long. 121°59'45" W). Named on Butte City (1912) 7.5' quadrangle.

Calor: see **Dorris** [SISKIYOU].

Camel Creek: see **Campbell Creek** [SHASTA] (1); **Campbell Creek** [TEHAMA] (1).

Camel Mound: see **Campbell Mound** [TEHAMA].

Cameron Creek [TEHAMA]: *stream,* flows nearly 4 miles to Antelope Creek 9 miles west of Panther Spring (lat. 40°14'50" N, long. 121°56'45" W; sec. 26, T 28 N, R 1 W). Named on Manton (1956) 15' quadrangle.

Cameron Meadow [SISKIYOU]: *area,* 8.5 miles north of the village of Seiad Valley (lat. 41°57'50" N, long. 123°12' W). Named on Kangaroo Mountain (1980) 7.5' quadrangle.

Cameron Meadows [SISKIYOU]: *area,* 13 miles north-northeast of Happy Camp (lat. 41°58'10" N, long. 123°15'10" W). Named on Figurehead Mountain (1980) 7.5' quadrangle. Happy Camp (1956) 15' quadrangle shows the feature situated nearly 1 mile farther west.

Camp Bailey: see **Motion** [SHASTA].

Campbell Creek [BUTTE]: *stream,* flows 6.5 miles to Cottonwood Creek 5 miles northwest of Oroville (lat. 39°34'35" N, long. 121°37'50" W; near W line sec. 22, T 20 N, R 3 E). Named on Oroville (1970) 7.5' quadrangle.

Campbell Creek [SHASTA]:

(1) *stream,* flows 2.25 miles to Sacramento River 3 miles south-southeast of Lamoine (lat. 40°56'55" N, long. 122°24'40" W; sec. 35, T 36 N, R 5 W). Named on Lamoine (1957) 15' quadrangle. Called Camel Cr. on Averill's (1939) map.

(2) *stream,* flows 2.5 miles to McCloud River Arm Shasta Lake 5.5 miles south of Bollibokka Mountain (lat. 40°51'10" N, long. 122°14' W; near S line sec. 29, T 35 N, R 3 W). Named on Bollibokka Mountain (1957) 15' quadrangle. Steger (p. 22) associated the name with Jeremiah B. Campbell, who settled by the stream in 1855.

Campbell Creek [TEHAMA]:

(1) *stream,* flows 20 miles to Pine Creek (3) 7 miles north of Nord [BUTTE] (lat. 39°52'30" N, long. 121°58'45" W). Named on Panther Spring (1953) and Richardson Springs (1952) 15' quadrangles. Called Camel Creek on Chico (1895) 30' quadrangle.

(2) *stream,* flows 4.25 miles to Big Chico Creek [BUTTE-TEHAMA] 8 miles east of Campbell Mound (lat. 39°59'40" N, long. 121°39'35" W). Named on Butte Meadows (1958) 15' quadrangle, and on Cohasset (1979) 7.5' quadrangle.

Campbell Creek: see **Nelson Ravine** [BUTTE] (1).

Campbell Flat [BUTTE]: *area,* 10 miles south-southeast of Paradise (lat. 39°37'25" N, long. 121°31'50" W; mainly in sec. 33, T 21 N, R 4 E); the place is about 1 mile south-southeast of Cherokee. Named on Cherokee (1970) and Oroville (1970) 7.5' quadrangles. F.D. Dunn (p. 22) listed a place called Cherokee Camp that was situated at Campbell Flat.

Campbell Hills [BUTTE]: *ridge,* west-southwest-trending, 2.5 miles long, 2.25 miles west-northwest of Oroville (lat. 39°32' N, long. 121°36'40" W). Named on Oroville (1970) and Shippee (1948) 7.5' quadrangles. On Dry Creek (1912) and Oroville (1912) 7.5' quadrangles, the ridge is shows as part of South Table Mountain.

Campbell Lake [SISKIYOU]: *lake,* 2000 feet long, 15 miles south-southwest of Scott Bar (lat. 41°32' N, long. 123°06'15" W). Named on Boulder Peak (1981) 7.5' quadrangle. Seiad (1922) 30' quadrangle has the name "Campbell Lakes" for present Campbell Lake and nearby Cliff Lake (1) together, but United States Board on Geographic Names (1960a, p. 13) rejected the name "Campbell Lakes" for the pair

Campbell Lakes: see **Campbell Lake** [SISKIYOU].

Campbell Meadow [BUTTE]: *area,* 1.5 miles north-northwest of Pulga (lat. 39°49'35" N, long. 121°27'45" W; sec. 30, T 23 N, R 5 E). Named on Pulga (1979) 7.5' quadrangle.

Campbell Mound [TEHAMA]: *peak,* 20 miles east of Corning (lat. 39°58'25" N, long. 121°49'05" W). Altitude 2349 feet. Named on Campbell Mound (1952) 7.5' quadrangle. Called Camel Mound on Chico (1895) 30' quadrangle.

Campbell Pinery: see **Cohasset Ridge** [BUTTE].

Campbell Ridge [TEHAMA]: *ridge,* southwest-trending, 2 miles long, 8.5 miles south-southwest of Polk Springs (lat. 40°01'35" N, long. 121°44'15" W). Named on Butte Meadows (1958) 15' quadrangle.

Campbell Slough [GLENN]: *water feature,* distributary of Angel Slough, flows 9 miles to Howard Slough 6 miles east-southeast of Butte City (lat. 39°25'15" N, long. 121°53'30" W; at SE cor. sec. 7, T 18 N, R 1 E). Named on Butte City (1952, photorevised 1973) and Llano Seco (1948) 7.5' quadrangles.

Campbell Spring [SISKIYOU]: *spring,* 7.25 miles north-northeast of Cecilville (lat. 41°14'35" N, long. 123°05'50" W). Named on Grasshopper Ridge (1979) 7.5' quadrangle.

Campbell Station: see **Mountain House** [BUTTE].

Campbells Soda Spring: see **Upper Soda Spring** [SISKIYOU].

Campbellville [TEHAMA]: *settlement,* 7 miles south-southwest of Polk Springs (lat. 40°01'30" N, long. 121°43'40" W; sec. 14, T 25 N, R 2 E); the place is near the northeast end of Campbell Ridge. Named on Butte Meadows (1958) 15' quadrangle.

Camp Britton [SHASTA]: *locality,* less than 1 mile north of Burney Falls along Lake Britton (lat. 41°01'20" N, long. 121°39'15" W; near SW cor. sec. 20, T 37 N, R 3 E). Named on Pondosa (1961) 15' quadrangle.

Camp Creek [BUTTE]: *stream,* flows 7 miles to North Fork Feather River 2 miles northeast of Pulga (lat. 39°49'20" N, long. 121°25'15" W; sec. 28, T 23 N, R 5 E). Named on Kimshew Point (1979) and Pulga (1979) 7.5' quadrangles.

Camp Creek [SISKIYOU]:

(1) *stream,* heads in the State of Oregon and flows 4.25 miles in Siskiyou County to Klamath River 24 miles north of Macdoel (lat. 41°57'30" N, long. 122°25'50" W; sec. 4, T 47 N, R 5 W). Named on Copco (1954) 15' quadrangle.

(2) *stream,* heads in Siskiyou County and flows 15 miles to Klamath River 1.25 miles west-southwest of Orleans in Humboldt County (lat. 41°17'35" N, long. 123°33'40" W). Named on Bark Shanty Gulch (1974) 7.5' quadrangle.

Camp Creek: see **Hines Creek** [SISKIYOU].

Camp Digger Butte [SHASTA]: *locality,* 4.5 miles east-southeast of Shingletown (lat. 40°27'35" N, long. 121°48'55" W; sec. 18, T 30 N, R 2 E). Named on Mineral (1941) 30' quadrangle.

Camp Eden [SISKIYOU]: *locality,* 13 miles south of Etna (lat. 41°16'05" N, long. 122°52'50" W; near SE cor. sec. 33, T 40 N, R 9 W); the place is near the mouth of Grizzly Creek. Named on Etna (1955) 15' quadrangle. According to Denny (p. 43), a community called Gasburg was situated at the mouth of Grizzly Creek. United States Board on Geographic Names (1987c, p. 2) approved the name Osterried Gulch for a ravine, 1.8 miles long, that opens into the canyon of Wildcat Creek 2 miles north-northeast of Camp Eden; the name is for Peter Osterried, who had mining claims in the neighborhood in the 1890's.

Camp Eighteen [BUTTE]: *locality,* 7 miles north of Clipper Mills (lat. 39°37'40" N, long. 121°10'15" W; at and around SE cor. sec. 34, T 21 N, R 7 E). Named on Cascade (1948) 7.5' quadrangle. A railroad siding called Ward was situated 0.5 mile from Camp Eighteen (Dunn, F.D., p. 109).

Camp Ellendale [GLENN]: *locality,* 9.5 miles west-northwest of the village of Elk Creek (lat. 39°40'25" N, long. 122°41'45" W). Named on Alder Springs (1967) 7.5' quadrangle.

Camp Enjoyment: see **Blinzig** [BUTTE].

Camp Five [TEHAMA]: *locality,* 7.5 miles south-southwest of Mineral (lat.

40°15'30" N, long. 121°39'50" W; near W line sec. 29, T 28 N, R 3 E). Site named on Lassen Peak (1956) 15' quadrangle.

Camp Forward [SHASTA]: *locality,* 13 miles west-southwest of Lassen Peak (lat. 40°26'15" N, long. 121°44'15" W; on S line sec. 23, T 30 N, R 2 E). Named on Lassen Peak (1956) 15' quadrangle.

Camp Four Campsite [SISKIYOU]: *locality,* 16 miles north-northwest of Forks of Salmon along Haypress Creek (lat. 41°28'40" N, long. 123°23'55" W). Named on Somes Bar (1979) 7.5' quadrangle.

Camp Gulch [SISKIYOU]: *canyon,* drained by a stream that heads in the State of Oregon and flows less than 0.25 mile in Siskiyou County to Middle Fork Applegate River 15 miles north-northeast of Happy Camp (lat. 42°00' N, long. 123°16'05" W). Named on Figurehead Mountain (1980) 7.5' quadrangle.

Camp Hollenbush: see **Fall River Valley** [SHASTA].

Camp Lassen [BUTTE]: *locality,* less than 1 mile north-northwest of Butte Meadows (lat. 40°05'35" N, long. 121°33'15" W; near W line sec. 20, T 26 N, R 4 E). Named on Butte Meadows (1958) 15' quadrangle.

Camp Lowe [SISKIYOU]: *locality,* nearly 2 miles south of Hornbrook (lat. 41°53'15" N, long. 122°33'10" W; near NW cor. sec. 33, T 47 N, R 6 W). Named on Yreka (1939) 30' quadrangle.

Camp McCumber [SHASTA]: *locality,* 12.5 miles west-northwest of Lassen Peak (lat. 40°32'25" N, long. 121°43'40" W; near NE cor. sec. 15, T 31 N, R 2 E). Named on Manzanita Lake (1956) 15' quadrangle.

Camp Moses: see **Shasta Alpine Lodge** [SISKIYOU].

Camp Nine Flat [SHASTA]: *area,* 3.5 miles west of Burney Falls along Pit River (lat. 41°00'30" N, long. 121°43' W). Named on Pondosa (1961) 15' quadrangle.

Camp One [BUTTE]: *locality,* 6.5 miles northwest of Clipper Mills (lat. 39°36'30" N, long. 121°13'45" W; sec. 7, T 20 N, R 7 E). Named on Clipper Mills (1948) 7.5' quadrangle.

Campo Seco Ridge [TEHAMA]: *ridge,* south-southwest- to west-trending, 4.5 miles long, 15 miles southwest of Panther Spring (lat. 40°06'30" N, long. 121°58'30" W). Named on Panther Spring (1953) 15' quadrangle, and on Los Molinos (1952) 7.5' quadrangle.

Camp Ross: see **Shasta Alpine Lodge** [SISKIYOU].

Camp Shasta [SHASTA]: *locality,* 1.5 miles west-northwest of Burney Falls near Pit River (lat. 41°01'15" N, long. 121°40'45" W; near E line sec. 36, T 37 N, R 2 E). Named on Pondosa (1961) 15' quadrangle.

Camp Tehama [TEHAMA]: *locality,* 4 miles east of Mineral along Mill Creek (3) (lat. 40°20'50" N, long. 121°31'10" W; sec. 27, T 29 N, R 4 E). Named on Lassen Peak (1956) 15' quadrangle.

Camp Three: see **Camp Three Campground** [SISKIYOU].

Camp Three Campground [SISKIYOU]: *locality,* 14 miles north-northwest of Forks of Salmon along Rogers Creek (lat. 41°26'30" N, long. 123°25'15" W). Named on Somes Bar (1979) 7.5' quadrangle. Forks of Salmon (1955) 15' quadrangle shows Camp Three at the place.

Cana [BUTTE]: *locality,* 4.5 miles north-northwest of Nord (lat. 39°50'25" N, long. 121°59'35" W; at NE cor. sec. 20, T 23 N, R 1 W). Named on Nord (1951) 7.5' quadrangle. Postal authorities established Cana post office in 1871, discontinued it for a time in 1895, discontinued it again for a time in 1900, and discontinued it finally in 1913 (Frickstad, p. 8).

Canaan Gulch [SISKIYOU]: *canyon,* drained by a stream that flows 2 miles to Yreka Creek 4.5 miles south-southwest of Yreka (lat. 41°40'30" N, long. 122°40'30" W; sec. 8, T 44 N, R 7 W). Named on Yreka (1954) 15' quadrangle. United States Board on Geographic Names (1985b, p. 1) rejected the names "Cannon Gulch" and "Left Fork Canaan Gulch" for the feature.

Canal Gulch [SISKIYOU]: *canyon,* drained by a stream that flows 3 miles to Yreka Creek 11 miles south-southwest of Hornbrook (lat. 41°45'35" N, long. 122°37'20" W; sec. 11, T 45 N, R 7 W). Named on Hornbrook (1955) 15' quadrangle.

Canby Bay [SISKIYOU]: *area,* 8 miles east of Mount Dome (lat. 41°49'20" N, long. 121°32' W; around SE cor. sec. 17, T 46 N, R 4 E). Named on Mount Dome (1950) 15' quadrangle.

Cannon Gulch: see **Canaan Gulch** [SISKIYOU].

Cannon Reservoir [BUTTE]: *lake,* 0.25 mile long, 7 miles north of Oroville (lat. 39°36'50" N, long. 121°31'55" W; on S line sec. 4, T 20 N, R 4 E). Named on Oroville (1970) 7.5' quadrangle. Called Hendrick Reservoir on California Division of Highways' (1934) map.

Canoe Creek: see **Hat Creek** [SHASTA]; **Lost Creek** [SHASTA] (2).

Cantara [SISKIYOU]: *locality,* 4 miles south-southeast of the town of Mount Shasta along Southern Pacific Railroad (lat. 41°15'55" N, long. 122°17'30" W; near SE cor. sec. 34, T 40 N, R 4 W). Named on Dunsmuir (1935) 30' quadrangle. Postal authorities established Cantara post office in 1902 and discontinued it in 1916 (Frickstad, p. 186).

Cantrall Creek [SHASTA]: *stream,* flows 0.5 mile to Pit River 10.5 miles north-northeast of the village on Montgomery Creek (lat. 40°59' N, long. 121°50'55" W). Named on Montgomery Creek (1956) 15' quadrangle. United States Board on Geographic Names (1990, p. 6) approved the name "Cantrell Creek" for the stream.

Cantrell Creek: see **Cantrall Creek** [SHASTA].

Canyon Creek [BUTTE]: *stream,* flows nearly 4 miles to Lake Oroville 4.5 miles north-northeast of Oroville Dam (lat. 39°35'35" N, long. 121°26'35" W; near W line sec. 17, T 20 N, R 5 E). Named on Berry Creek (1970) and Oroville Dam (1970) 7.5' quadrangles. East Fork enters Lake Oroville 1 mile east of the mouth of the main stream; it is nearly 4 miles long and is named on Forbestown (1970) and Oroville Dam (1970) 7.5' quadrangles.

Canyon Creek [SHASTA]:

(1) *stream,* flows 3 miles to Rock Creek (3) 6 miles east-southeast of Shingletown (lat. 40°27'05" N, long. 121°46'20" W; near E line sec. 17, T 30 N, R 2 E). Named on Lassen Peak (1956) and Manton (1956) 15' quadrangles.

(2) *stream,* flows 3 miles to Pit River 10 miles northeast of the village of Montgomery Creek (lat. 40°57'25" N, long. 121°48'05" W). Named on Montgomery Creek (1956) 15' quadrangle.

Canyon Creek [SISKIYOU]:

(1) *stream,* flows nearly 2 miles to Wooley Creek 13 miles north of Forks of Salmon (lat. 41°26'35" N, long. 123°20'20" W). Named on Medicine Mountain (1978) 7.5' quadrangle.

(2) *stream,* flows 5.5 miles to Seiad Creek nearly 2 miles east-northeast of the village of Seiad Valley (lat. 41°51'20" N, long. 123°09'55" W). Named on Kangaroo Mountain (1980) and Seiad Valley (1980) 7.5' quadrangles.

(3) *stream,* flows 7.5 miles to Scott River 9 miles southwest of Scott Bar (lat. 41°38' N, long. 123°06'10" W). Named on Boulder Peak (1981), Marble Mountain (1980), and Scott Bar (1980) 7.5' quadrangles. Big Rock Fork enters 15 miles southwest of Scott Bar; it is 1.5 miles long and is named on Marble Mountain (1980) 7.5' quadrangle.

Canyon Creek [TEHAMA]: *stream,* flows 3.5 miles to Mill Creek (3) 5.5 miles northeast of Lassen Peak (lat. 40°22'50" N, long. 121°30'40" W; at S line sec. 11, T 29 N, R 4 E). Named on Lassen Peak (1956) and Mount Harkness (1956) 15' quadrangles.

Canyon Creek: see **Big Canyon Creek** [SISKIYOU].

Canyon Hill Gulch [SHASTA]: *canyon,* drained by a stream that flows 0.5 mile to Clear Creek 7 miles southwest of Schell Mountain (lat. 40°46'30" N, long. 122°36'40" W; near N line sec. 25, T 34 N, R 7 W). Named on Schell Mountain (1950) 15' quadrangle.

Canyon Hollow [SHASTA]: *canyon,* drained by a stream that flows 2.5 miles to lowlands along Sacramento River 2 miles south of Redding (lat. 40°33'10" N, long. 122°23'20" W). Named on Redding (1957) 7.5' quadrangle.

Canyon Mountain [SISKIYOU]: *peak,* 2 miles northwest of Cecilville (lat. 41°09'35" N, long. 123°10'20" W). Named on Cecilville (1979) 7.5' quadrangle.

Capay [GLENN]: *locality,* 7 miles east-northeast of Orland (lat. 39°47'50" N, long. 122°05'05" W); the place is on Capay grant. Named on Foster Island (1950) 7.5' quadrangle.

Capay [GLENN-TEHAMA]: *land grant,* southeast of Kirkwood on the west side of Sacramento River. Named on Foster Island (1950), Hamilton City (1949), Kirkwood (1949), Ord Ferry (1949), and Nord (1951) 7.5' quadrangles. Josefa Soto received 10 leagues in 1844 and claimed 44,388 acres patented in 1859 (Cowan, p. 23).

Cape Horn [BUTTE]:

(1) *relief feature,* 5.25 miles northwest of Stirling City along Butte Creek [BUTTE-GLENN] (lat. 39°58' N, long. 121°35'30" W; sec. 1, T 24 N, R 3 E). Named on Stirling City (1979) 7.5' quadrangle.

(2) *peak,* 4.5 miles southeast of Paradise (lat. 39°42'40" N, long. 121°33'30" W; near NW cor. sec. 5, T 21 N, R 4 E). Named on Cherokee (1970) 7.5' quadrangle.

Cape Horn Creek [SHASTA]: *stream,* flows nearly 2 miles to Pit River 8 miles northwest of the village on Montgomery Creek (lat. 40°54'40" N, long. 121°59' W; near SW cor. sec. 4, T 35 N, R 1 W). Named on Montgomery Creek (1956) 15' quadrangle. Old settlers in the neighborhood call the stream Burgess Creek (Steger, p. 22).

Cape Horn Creek [SISKIYOU]: *stream,* flows 2.5 miles to Klamath River 2.5 miles east-southeast of Hornbrook (lat. 41°54' N, long. 122°30'30" W; near N line sec. 26, T 47 N, R 6 W). Named on Hornbrook (1955) 15' quadrangle.

Captain Jacks Bridge [SISKIYOU]: *relief feature,* 12.5 miles north-northeast of Medicine Lake (lat. 41°44'45" N, long. 121°29'30" W; sec. 15, T 45 N, R 4 E); the feature is near Captain Jacks Ice Cave. Named on Timber Mountain (1952) 15' quadrangle.

Captain Jacks Ice Cave [SISKIYOU]: *cave,* 12.5 miles north-northeast of Medicine Lake (lat. 41°44'50" N, long. 121°29'35" W; sec. 15, T 45 N, R 4 E). Named on Timber Mountain (1952) 15' quadrangle.

Captain Jacks Stronghold [SISKIYOU]: *area,* 9.5 miles east of Mount Dome (lat. 41°49'25" N, long. 121°30'30" W; sec. 15, T 46 N, R 4 E). Named on Mount Dome (1950) 15' quadrangle. The name is from the Indian leader in the Modoc War (Gudde, 1969, p. 53).

Captain Jones Rapids [TEHAMA]: *water feature,* 1.5 miles west-southwest of Vina along Sacramento River (lat. 39°55'30" N, long. 122°04'55" W). Named on Vina (1904) 15' quadrangle.

Carberry Flat [SHASTA]: *area,* 7.5 miles east of the village of Montgomery Creek (lat. 40°51'10" N, long. 121°46'45" W; at N line sec. 32, T 35 N, R 2 E); the place is nearly 2 miles north-northeast of Carberry Mountain. Named on Montgomery Creek (1956) 15' quadrangle.

Carberry Mountain [SHASTA]: *peak,* nearly 7 miles east of the village of Montgomery Creek (lat. 40°49'55" N, long. 121°47'45" W; near W line sec. 6, T 34 N, R 2 E). Named on Montgomery Creek (1956) 15' quadrangle.

Carbon [SHASTA]: *locality,* 8 miles northeast of Burney Valley (present Burney) (lat. 40°55'30" N, long. 121°33' W). Named on Lassen Peak (1894) 1° quadrangle. Postal authorities established Carbon post office in 1885, moved it 1 mile east in 1910, and discontinued it in 1923; the name was from the color of the soil at the place (Salley, p. 37).

Carey Gulch [BUTTE]: *canyon,* drained by a stream that flows 2.25 miles to Get Up and Get Creek 3.5 miles north-northeast of the village of Brush Creek (lat. 39°44'15' N, long. 121°18'55" W; near N line sec. 28, T 22 N, R 6 E). Named on Brush Creek (1970) 7.5' quadrangle.

Caribou Creek [SISKIYOU]: *stream,* flows nearly 3 miles to Little South Fork Salmon River 8 miles southeast of Cecilville (lat. 41°03'45" N, long. 123°00'55" W); the stream heads west of Caribou Mountain. Named on Coffee Creek (1955) 15' quadrangle, and on Thompson Peak (1979) 7.5' quadrangle.

Caribou Gulch [SISKIYOU]: *canyon,* drained by a stream that flows 1 mile to South Fork Salmon River 27 miles south of Etna (lat. 41°04' N, long. 122°57'15" W). Named on Coffee Creek (1955) 15' quadrangle.

Caribou Lake [SISKIYOU]: *lake,* 2600 feet long, 30 miles south of Etna (lat. 41°01'15" N, long. 122°58'30" W); the lake is 1 mile southwest of Caribou Mountain. Named on Coffee Creek (1955) 15' quadrangle.

Caribou Lake: see **Little Caribou Lake** [SISKIYOU]; **Lower Caribou Lake** [SISKIYOU].

Caribou Mountain [SISKIYOU]: *peak,* 30 miles south of Etna (lat. 41°01'45" N, long. 122°57'30" W). Altitude 8575 feet. Named on Coffee Creek (1955) 15' quadrangle.

Carmen Creek: see **Big Carmen Creek** [SISKIYOU]; **Little Carmen Creek** [SISKIYOU].

Carmen Lake: see **Big Carmen Lake** [SISKIYOU]; **Little Carmen Lake** [SISKIYOU].

Carmina [BUTTE]: *locality,* less than 4 miles north of Durham along Northern Electric Railroad (lat. 39°41'05" N, long. 121°47'45" W). Named on Durham (1912) 7.5' quadrangle.

Carobe Lake [SHASTA]: *lake,* 500 feet long, 5.5 miles east-southeast of Shingletown (lat. 40°27'10" N, long. 121°48' W; at SE cor. sec. 18, T 30 N, R 2 E). Named on Manton (1956) 15' quadrangle.

Caroline Creek [SISKIYOU]: *stream,* flows 0.5 mile to Klamath River 1 mile south-southeast of the village of Seiad Valley (lat. 41°49'40" N, long. 123°11'20" W). Named on Seiad Valley (1980) 7.5' quadrangle.

Carpenter Ridge [BUTTE]: *ridge,* south-trending, 11 miles long, center 7.5 miles north-northwest of Stirling City (lat. 40°00' N, long. 121°36'15" W). Named on Butte Meadows (1958) 15' quadrangle, and on Stirling City (1979) 7.5' quadrangle.

Carrick Creek: see **Garrick Creek** [SISKIYOU].

Carson Gulch [SISKIYOU]: *canyon,* drained by a stream that flows 2 miles to Klamath River 2.25 miles south of Hornbrook (lat. 41°51'50" N, long. 122°33'45" W; sec. 5, T 46 N, R 6 W). Named on Hornbrook (1955) 15' quadrangle.

Carson Spring [BUTTE]: *spring,* 4 miles west-southwest of Paradise along Butte Creek [BUTTE-GLENN] (lat. 39°44'20" N, long. 121°41'55" W; near N line sec. 25, T 22 N, R 2 E). Named on Hamlin Canyon (1951) 7.5' quadrangle.

Carter Creek [SISKIYOU]: *stream,* flows 2.5 miles to Klamath River 3.5 miles northeast of Dillon Mountain (lat. 41°33'45" N, long. 123°31'25" W). Named on Dillon Mountain (1983) and Ukonom Mountain (1980) 7.5' quadrangles.

Carter Creek [TEHAMA]: *stream,* flows about 4.25 miles to Deer Creek (2) 2.5 miles east of Deer Creek Station (lat. 40°15'40" N, long. 121°24'05" W; at E line sec. 27, T 28 N, R 5 E). Named on Jonesville (1958) and Mount Harkness (1956) 15' quadrangles.

Carter Meadow [SISKIYOU]: *area,* 16 miles south of Etna along East Fork of South Fork Salmon River (lat. 41°13'20" N, long. 122°55'45" W; near SW cor. sec. 20, T 39 N, R 9 W). Named on Coffee Creek (1955) 15' quadrangle. United States Board on Geographic Names (1967b, p. 2) approved the name "Carter Meadows Summit" for a pass situated about 1.5 miles east of Carter Meadow (sec. 21, 28, T 39 N, R 9 W).

Carter Meadow [TEHAMA]: *marsh,* 3.5 miles southeast of Deer Creek Station (lat. 40°13'20" N, long. 121°24'25" W). Named on Jonesville (1958) 15' quadrangle.

Carter Meadows Summit: see **Carter Meadow** [SISKIYOU].

Cary Pasture Creek [TEHAMA]: *stream,* flows nearly 3 miles to Thomes Creek 4.25 miles south-southwest of Ball Mountain (lat. 39°52'20" N, long. 122°48'25" W; at S line sec. 6, T 23 N, R 8 W). Named on Ball Mountain (1967) and Log Spring (1967) 7.5' quadrangles.

Cascade Creek [BUTTE]: *stream,* heads in Plumas County and flows 5.5 miles, almost entirely in Plumas County, to South Branch of Middle Fork Feather River 12 miles north-northwest of Clipper Mills in Butte County (lat. 39°42'05" N, long. 121°12'40" W; near SE cor. sec. 5, T 21 N, R 7 E). Named on Cascade (1948) 7.5' quadrangle.

Cascade Creek [BUTTE-TEHAMA]: *stream,* heads in Tehama County and flows 5.5 miles to Big Chico Creek [BUTTE-TEHAMA] 2 miles west-northwest of Butte Meadows in Butte County (lat. 40°05'15" N, long. 121°35' W; near S line sec. 28, T 26 N, R 3 E). Named on Butte Meadows (1958) 15' quadrangle.

Cascade Gulch [SISKIYOU]: *canyon,* drained by a stream that flows 6 miles to lowlands 2 miles north-northwest of the town of Mount Shasta (lat. 41°20'30" N, long. 122°17'20" W; sec. 3, T 40 N, R 4 W). Named on Shasta (1954) 15' quadrangles.

Cascade Range [SISKIYOU]: *range,* extends south from the State of Oregon into Siskiyou County east of Shasta Valley and Sacramento River; Mount Shasta is part of the range. Named on Weed (1963) 1°x 2° quadrangle. The name was in use in the State of Oregon as early as the 1820's (McArthur, p. 133.)

Cascade Springs [SHASTA]: *spring,* 3.5 miles east of Mount Lassen (lat. 40°29'30" N, long. 121°26'15" W; near SE cor. sec. 4, T 30 N, R 5 E). Named on Mount Harkness (1956) 15' quadrangle.

Cassel [SHASTA]: *village,* 7 miles east-northeast of Burney along Hat Creek (lat. 40°55'10" N, long. 121°33' W; sec. 5, T 35 N, R 4 E). Named on Burney (1957) 15' quadrangle. Lassen Peak (1894) 1° quadrangle has the designation "Hat Creek (Cassel P.O.)" at the place. Postal authorities moved Hat Creek post office 10 miles north in 1887 and changed the name to Cassel (Salley, p. 39). The village, which first was settled by Germans, was called Fiddleburg; later the name was changed to Cassel for the German town of Kassel (Giles, p. 235).

Castella [SHASTA]: *village,* 39 miles north of Redding (lat. 41°08'25" N, long. 122°19' W; sec. 22, T 38 N, R 4 W). Named on Dunsmuir (1954) 15' quadrangle. The place first was called Castle Rock (Steger, p. 23). Postal authorities established Leland post office in 1890 and changed the name to Castella in 1892; the name "Leland" was for Leland Stanford, who had a vacation home in the vicinity (Salley, p. 120). California Mining Bureau's (1909b) map shows a place called Eubanks located along the railroad 1 mile north of Castella. Postal authorities established Eubanks post office in 1905 and discontinued it in 1918; the name was for J. Cal Eubanks, a pioneer (Salley, p. 71). They established Brewster post office 8 miles south of Dunsmuir [SISKIYOU] in 1893 and discontinued it in 1895, when they moved the service to Castella (Salley, p. 26).

Castillo del Diablo: see **Castle Crags** [SISKIYOU-SHASTA].

Castle Crag [SHASTA]: *locality,* 2 miles northeast of Castella (lat. 41°09'45" N, long. 122°17'30" W; sec. 11, T 38 N, R 4 W); the place is 3 miles southeast of Castle Crags [SHASTA-SISKIYOU]. Named on Dunsmuir (1954) 15' quadrangle. Shasta (1894) 1° quadrangle shows a place called Lower Soda Spring located at or near present Castle Crag. Postal authorities established Castle Crag post office in 1892, discontinued it in 1901, reestablished it in 1909 with the name "Castle Crags," and discontinued it in 1930 (Salley, p. 40).

Castle Crags [SHASTA-SISKIYOU]: *relief feature,* 4.5 miles southwest of Dunsmuir on Siskiyou-Shasta County line (lat. 41°11'10" N, long. 122°20'45" W). Named on Dunsmuir (1954) 15' quadrangle. Called Castle Rock on Shasta (1894) 1° quadrangle. Baker's (1855) map shows Devil's Castle at the place, and Bancroft's (1864) map has the form "Devils Castle" for the name. The feature also was known as Castillo del Diablo (Hanna, p. 59).

Castle Crags: see **Castle Crag** [SHASTA].

Castle Crag Spring: see **Soda Spring** [SHASTA] (1).

Castle Creek [SHASTA-SISKIYOU]: *stream,* flows 9.5 miles to Sacramento River less than 0.5 mile north-northeast of Castella (lat. 41°08'45" N, long. 122°18'20" W; at N line sec. 22, T 38 N, R 4 W). Named on Dunsmuir (1954) 15' quadrangle. North Fork enters from the north 2.5 miles upstream from the mouth of the main creek; it heads in Siskiyou County and is 5 miles long. South Fork enters from the southwest 4.5 miles upstream from the mouth of the main creek and is 3 miles long. Both forks are named on Dunsmuir (1954) 15' quadrangle.

Castle Creek: see **Castle Lake Creek** [SISKIYOU]; **Little Castle Creek** [SISKIYOU].

Castle Creek Campground [SHASTA]: *locality,* 2.5 miles west-northwest of Castella along Castle Creek (lat. 41°09'20" N, long. 122°21'45" W; near E line sec. 18, T 38 N, R 4 W). Named on Dunsmuir (1954) 15' quadrangle.

Castle Dome [SHASTA]: *peak,* 2.25 miles north-northwest of Castella near the southeast end of Castle Crags (lat. 41°10'30" N, long. 122°19'30" W). Altitude 4966 feet. Named on Dunsmuir (1954) 15' quadrangle.

Castle Lake [SISKIYOU]: *lake,* nearly 0.5 mile long, 6 miles west of Dunsmuir (lat. 41°13'40" N, long. 122°22'55" W; on E line sec. 24, T 39 N, R 5 W). Named on Dunsmuir (1954) 15' quadrangle.

Castle Lake: see **Little Castle Lake** [SISKIYOU].

Castle Lake Creek [SISKIYOU]: *stream,* flows 5 miles to Scott Camp Creek

3 miles south-southwest of the town of Mount Shasta (lat. 41°16'30" N, long. 122°20'10" W; sec. 32, T 40 N, R 4 W); the stream heads at Castle Lake. Named on Dunsmuir (1954) and Weed (1954) 15' quadrangles. Called Castle Creek on Dunsmuir (1935) 30' quadrangle.

Castle Lake Creek: see **Little Castle Lake Creek**, under **Ney Springs Creek** [SISKIYOU].

Castle Rock [BUTTE]: *peak*, 3.25 miles west-southwest of Paradise (lat. 39°44'30" N, long. 121°41' W; at S line sec. 19, T 22 N, R 3 E). Named on Hamlin Canyon (1951) 7.5' quadrangle.

Castle Rock: see **Castella** [SHASTA]; **Castle Crags** [SHASTA-SISKIYOU].

Castles: see **The Castles** [SISKIYOU].

Castle Springs: see **Shasta Springs** [SISKIYOU].

Cataract: see **Klamathon** [SISKIYOU].

Cat Ridge [TEHAMA]: *ridge*, south-southeast-trending, 1.5 miles long, 5 miles northwest of Paskenta (lat. 39°56'05" N, long. 122°36'30" W). Named on Paskenta (1967) 7.5' quadrangle.

Catsup Creek [SISKIYOU]: *stream*, flows about 3 miles to Camp Creek (2) 7.25 miles north-northwest of Orleans, which is in Humboldt County (lat. 41°23'40" N, long. 123°36'15" W). Named on Bark Shanty Gulch (1974) 7.5' quadrangle.

Cattle Ridge [TEHAMA]: *ridge*, southeast-trending, 2.25 miles long, 10 miles southwest of Ball Mountain (lat. 39°49'45" N, long. 122°55' W). Named on Mendocino Pass (1967) 7.5' quadrangle.

Cavanaugh Canyon [SHASTA]: *canyon*, drained by a stream that flows 2 miles to Dog Creek 3.5 miles south-southwest of Lamoine (lat. 40°55'55" N, long. 122°27'40" W; near S line sec. 32, T 36 N, R 5 W). Named on Lamoine (1957) 15' quadrangle.

Cave Campground [SHASTA]: *locality*, 14 miles north-northeast of Lassen Peak along Hat Creek (lat. 40°41' N, long. 121°25'25" W; near S line sec. 28, T 33 N, R 5 E); the place is near Subway Cave. Named on Prospect Peak (1957) 15' quadrangle.

Cave Creek [BUTTE]: *stream*, flows 3.5 miles to Mud Creek 8.5 miles north-northeast of Chico at Richardson Springs (lat. 39°50'25" N, long. 121°46'35" W; near N line sec. 20, T 23 N, R 2 E). Named on Campbell Mound (1952) and Richardson Springs (1951) 7.5' quadrangles. On Richardson Springs (1944) 15' quadrangle, the stream is shown as the upper part of present Mud Creek.

Caves: see **The Caves**, under **Pluto Cave** [SISKIYOU].

Cave Spring [TEHAMA]: *spring*, 8 miles south of Panther Spring (lat. 40°08'05" N, long. 121°46'45" W; sec. 5, T 26 N, R 2 E). Named on Panther Spring (1953) 15' quadrangle.

Cave Spring: see **Upper Soda Spring** [SISKIYOU].

Cayenne Ridge [SISKIYOU]: *ridge*, generally northeast-trending, 3 miles long, 12 miles southwest of Scott Bar (lat. 41°38' N, long. 123°11' W). Named on Grider Valley (1981) and Marble Mountain (1980) 7.5' quadrangles.

Cayton [SHASTA]: *locality*, 3.25 miles north-northeast of Burney Falls (lat. 41°03'35" N, long. 121°38' W; sec. 9, T 37 N, R 3 E); the place is in Cayton Valley. Named on Bartle (1939) 30' quadrangle. Postal authorities established Cayton post office in 1884 and discontinued it in 1951 (Salley, p. 40).

Cayton Creek [SHASTA]: *stream*, flows 3 miles to Lake Britton 2 miles north-northeast of Burney Falls (lat. 41°02'10" N, long. 121°38'15" W; at SE cor. sec. 17, T 37 N, R 3 E); the stream heads in Cayton Valley. Named on Pondosa (1961) 15' quadrangle.

Cayton Valley [SHASTA]: *valley*, 3.5 miles north-northeast of Burney Falls (lat. 41°03'30" N, long. 121°37'30" W). Named on Pondosa (1961) 15' quadrangle. William Cayton settled in the valley in 1855 (Steger, p. 23).

Cayuse Gulch [SISKIYOU]: *canyon*, drained by a stream that flows 2 miles to Klamath River 8.5 miles west-southwest of Hornbrook (lat. 41°51'15" N, long. 122°41'45" W; near E line sec. 7, T 46 N, R 7 W). Named on Hornbrook (1955) 15' quadrangle.

Cecil Creek [SISKIYOU]: *stream*, flows 5 miles to South Fork Salmon River 0.5 mile east-southeast of Cecilville (lat. 41°08'20" N, long. 123°07'35" W). Named on Cecil Lake (1979) and Cecilville (1979) 7.5' quadrangles. The name commemorates John B. Cecil (Ball, p. 20).

Cecil Lake [SISKIYOU]: *lake*, 400 feet long, 4.25 miles south of Cecilville (lat. 41°04'50" N, long. 123°08'10" W); the lake is at the head of Cecil Creek. Named on Cecil Lake (1979) 7.5' quadrangle.

Cecil Point [SISKIYOU]: *relief feature*, 3.5 miles south of Cecilville (lat. 41°05'30" N, long. 123°07'35" W). Named on Cecil Lake (1979) 7.5' quadrangle.

Cecilville [SISKIYOU]: *village*, 10.5 miles south of Sawyers Bar (lat. 41°08'35" N, long. 123°08'20" W). Named on Cecilville (1979) 15' quadrangle. Postal authorities established Cecilville post office in 1879 and discontinued it in 1972 (Salley, p. 40). The misspelled name commemorates John Baker Sissel, who came to the region before 1849 (Gudde, 1949, p. 62). Ball (p. 20) used the form "Cecil" for Sissel's name. Postal authorities established Dagget post office in 1881, moved it and changed the name to Jordan in 1883, and discontinued it in 1888, when they moved it to Cecilville; the name "Dagget" was for Miss Leslie Dagget, first postmaster; the name Jordan was for Joseph Jordan, first postmaster (Salley, p. 54, 108). They established Matthews post office 4.5 miles southeast of Cecilville in 1899 and discontinued it in 1900 (Salley, p. 135). They established Big Flat post office at a vacation resort located 16 miles by trail southeast of Cecilville (SW quarter sec. 7, T 37 N, R 9 W) in 1935 and discontinued it in 1941 (Salley, p. 21). A place called Brownsville was situated along East Fork of South Fork Salmon River; a man named George Green Brown lived there in the 1890's (Ball, p. 20).

Cedar Basin [SISKIYOU]:

(1) *relief feature*, 4 miles south-southeast of Preston Peak (lat. 41°46'40" N, long. 123°35'30" W); the feature is at the head of Cedar Creek (1) on the west side of Cedar Crest. Named on Preston Peak (1982) 7.5' quadrangle. Called Basin Cedar on Preston Peak (1956) 15' quadrangle, but United States Board on Geographic Names (1983a, p. 3) rejected this name for the feature.

(2) *area*, 13 miles north-northeast of Happy Camp (lat. 41°57'55" N, long. 123°17'15" W). Named on Figurehead Mountain (1980) 7.5' quadrangle.

Cedar Basin [TEHAMA]: *relief feature*, 7.25 miles south-southwest of Tomhead Mountain (lat. 40°02'40" N, long. 122°52'30" W; sec. 4, T 25 N, R 9 W). Named on Yolla Bolly (1954) 15' quadrangle.

Cedar Basin Camp [TEHAMA]: *locality*, nearly 7 miles south-southwest of Tomhead Mountain (lat. 40°03' N, long. 122°52'15" W; sec. 4, T 25 N, R 9 W); the place is near Cedar Basin. Named on Yolla Bolly (1954) 15' quadrangle.

Cedar Camp [SISKIYOU]: *locality*, 3.25 miles northwest of Dillon Mountain (lat. 41°33'25" N, long. 123°37'25" W); the place is near the head of Cedar Creek (2). Named on Dillon Mountain (1983) 7.5' quadrangle.

Cedar Camp: see **Big Cedar Camp** [SHASTA].

Cedar Cove [SISKIYOU]: *canyon*, drained by a stream that flows 1 mile to Klamath River 8.5 miles southeast of Condrey Mountain (lat. 41°50'30" N, long. 122°52'20" W; near E line sec. 10, T 46 N, R 9 W). Named on Condrey Mountain (1955) 15' quadrangle.

Cedar Creek [BUTTE]:

(1) *stream*, flows 3.5 miles to West Branch Butte Creek [BUTTE-GLENN] 6.25 miles south-southwest of Butte Meadows (lat. 40°00'10" N, long. 121°36'45" W; near NW cor. sec. 26, T 25 N, R 3 E). Named on Butte Meadows (1958) 15' quadrangle.

(2) *stream*, heads in Plumas County and flows 2.5 miles to North Fork Feather River 3.5 miles northeast of Pulga in Butte County (lat. 39°51'05" N, long. 121°24'20" W; near S line sec. 15, T 23 N, R 5 E). Named on Pulga (1979) 7.5' quadrangle.

Cedar Creek [SHASTA]: *stream*, flows 13 miles to Little Cow Creek 16 miles southeast of Bollibokka Mountain (lat. 40°45'15" N, long. 122°01'45" W; near SE cor. sec. 36, T 34 N, R 2 W). Named on Bollibokka Mountain (1957) and Montgomery Creek (1956) 15' quadrangles.

Cedar Creek [SISKIYOU]:

(1) *stream*, flows 2.5 miles to Preston Creek 2.5 miles south of Preston Peak (lat. 41°47'45" N, long. 123°37' W); the creek heads at Cedar Crest. Named on Preston Peak (1982) 7.5' quadrangle.

(2) *stream*, flows 4 miles to Dillon Creek 3.5 miles north of Dillon Mountain (lat. 41°34'45" N, long. 123°34'15" W). Named on Dillon Mountain (1983) 7.5' quadrangle.

(3) *stream*, flows 3.5 miles to Thompson Creek 10 miles north of Happy Camp (lat. 41°56'15" N, long. 123°21'25" W). Named on Figurehead Mountain (1980) 7.5' quadrangle.

Cedar Creek [TEHAMA]: *stream*, flows 4 miles to Cold Fork (1) nearly 4 miles north-northeast of Tomhead Mountain (lat. 40°11'15" N, long. 122°46'50" W; sec. 17, T 27 N, R 8 W). Named on Yolla Bolly (1954) 15' quadrangle.

Cedar Crest [SISKIYOU]: *ridge*, generally north-trending, 5.5 miles long, center about 3 miles south-southeast of Preston Peak (lat. 41°47'45" N, long. 123°34'50" W). Named on Preston Peak (1982) 7.5' quadrangle. United States Board on Geographic Names (1965c, p. 8) pointed out that cedars are characteristic trees on the ridge.

Cedar Flat [SISKIYOU]:

(1) *area*, nearly 5 miles south of Ukonom Lake along Bridge Creek (lat. 41°30'50" N, long. 123°20' W). Named on Ukonom Lake (1980) 7.5' quadrangle. Ukonom Lake (1955) 15' quadrangle shows Cedar Flat cabin at the place.

(2) *area*, 11.5 miles southeast of Condrey Mountain (lat. 41°50'10" N, long. 122°48'30" W; sec. 17, T 46 N, R 8 W). Named on Condrey Mountain (1955) 15' quadrangle.

Cedar Gulch [SHASTA]:

(1) *canyon*, drained by a stream that flows 1.25 miles to Clear Creek 5.5 miles southwest of Schell Mountain (lat. 40°47'50" N, long. 122°36'20" W; sec. 13, T 34 N, R 7 W). Named on Schell Mountain (1950) 15' quadrangle.

(2) *canyon*, drained by a stream that flows 1 mile to East Fork Clear Creek 5.5 miles south of Schell Mountain (lat. 40°46'35" N, long. 122°32'40" W; sec. 28, T 34 N, R 6 W). Named on Schell Mountain (1950) 15' quadrangle.

Cedar Gulch [SISKIYOU]:
(1) *canyon,* drained by a stream that flows 1.5 miles to Scott Valley 8.5 miles south-southeast of Etna (lat. 41°20'40" N, long. 122°49'45" W; sec. 1, T 40 N, R 9 W). Named on Etna (1955) 15' quadrangle.
(2) *canyon,* drained by a stream that flows 2 miles to Moffett Creek 11.5 miles south-southwest of Yreka (lat. 41°34'35" N, long. 122°41'40" W; sec. 18, T 43 N, R 7 W). Named on Yreka (1954) 15' quadrangle.
(3) *canyon,* drained by a stream that flows nearly 2 miles to Klamath River 12.5 miles west of Macdoel (lat. 41°54'10" N, long. 122°28'30" W; near SW cor. sec. 19, T 47 N, R 5 W). Named on Copco (1954) 15' quadrangle.

Cedar Lake [SISKIYOU]:
(1) *lake,* 800 feet long, 12 miles west of Dunsmuir (lat. 41°12'30" N, long. 122°29'45" W; sec. 25, T 39 N, R 6 W). Named on Dunsmuir (1954) 15' quadrangle.
(2) *lake,* 1700 feet long, 2400 feet west-southwest of Macdoel (lat. 41°39'50" N, long. 122°24'20" W; sec. 15, T 44 N, R 5 W). Named on Lake Shastina (1954) 15' quadrangle.

Cedar Mountain [SISKIYOU]: *mountain,* 5.5 miles north-northeast of Bray (lat. 41°42'35" N, long. 121°54'15" W; near NE cor. sec. 36, T 45 N, R 1 W). Altitude 5990 feet. Named on Bray (1950) 15' quadrangle.

Cedar Point [SISKIYOU]: *promontory,* 2.5 miles south of Dorris along the east side of Butte Valley (lat. 41°55'45" N, long. 121°54'30" W; sec. 7, T 47 N, R 1 W). Named on Dorris (1950) 15' quadrangle.

Cedar Ravine [BUTTE]: *canyon,* drained by a stream that flows less than 1 mile to Middle Fork Feather River 6 miles north-northwest of Forbestown (lat. 39°36' N, long. 121°19' W; near SE cor. sec. 8, T 20 N, R 8 E). Named on Forbestown (1970) 7.5' quadrangle.

Cedar Ridge [GLENN]: *ridge,* south-trending, 2 miles long, 11 miles west of the village of Elk Creek (lat. 39°35'55" N, long. 122°44'40" W; mainly in sec. 10, 11, T 20 N, R 8 W). Named on Felkner Hill (1968) 7.5' quadrangle.

Cedars: see **The Cedars** [SISKIYOU].

Cedar Salt Log Creek [SHASTA]: *stream,* flows 8.5 miles to Pit River 10 miles north-northwest of the village of Montgomery Creek (lat. 40°59' N, long. 121°58'45" W; near N line sec. 16, T 36 N, R 1 W); the creek goes through Iron Canyon. Named on Big Bend (1961) 15' quadrangle. United States Board on Geographic Names (1972b, p. 3) approved the name "Iron Canyon Creek" for the stream, and gave the name "Cedar Salt Log Creek" as a variant.

Cedar Spring [SISKIYOU]: *spring,* 13 miles north-northwest of Happy Camp (lat. 41°58'35" N, long. 123°26' W; sec. 5, T 18 N, R 7 E). Named on Happy Camp (1956) 15' quadrangle.

Cedar Spring [TEHAMA]: *spring,* nearly 4 miles north of Polk Springs (lat. 40°10'15" N, long. 121°39'50" W; near NW cor. sec. 29, T 27 N, R 3 E). Named on Butte Meadows (1958) 15' quadrangle

Cedar Well [SISKIYOU]: *well,* 6 miles east-northeast of Bray (lat. 41°41'15" N, long. 121°52'20" W; near NW cor. sec. 4, T 44 N, R 1 E); the well is 2.25 miles southeast of Cedar Mountain. Named on Bray (1950) 15' quadrangle.

Cement Banks [SISKIYOU]: *relief feature,* 15 miles south-southeast of Etna (lat. 41°14'25" N, long. 122°48' W; sec. 17, T 39 N, R 8 W). Named on Coffee Creek (1955) 15' quadrangle.

Cement Creek [SISKIYOU]: *stream,* flows 1 mile to West Boulder Creek 15 miles south-southeast of Etna (lat. 41°15' N, long. 122°49' W; at NW cor. sec. 17, T 39 N, R 8 W); the stream heads near Cement Banks. Named on Coffee Creek (1955) 15' quadrangle.

Cement Creek [TEHAMA]: *stream,* flows 2.5 miles to Panther Creek (2) 6 miles northeast of Polk Springs (lat. 40°10'45" N, long. 121°35'10" W; sec. 24, T 27 N, R 3 E). Named on Butte Meadows (1958) 15' quadrangle.

Centennial Gulch [SHASTA]: *canyon,* drained by a stream that flows 1.5 miles to Right Fork 2.5 miles west-northwest of the village of French Gulch (lat. 40°43'45" N, long. 122°41'35" W; sec. 7, T 33 N, R 7 W). Named on French Gulch (1979) 7.5' quadrangle.

Center Ville: see **Oroville** [BUTTE].

Centerville [BUTTE]: *locality,* 2.5 miles northwest of Paradise along Butte Creek [BUTTE-GLENN] (lat. 39°47'15" N, long. 121°39'20" W; at E line sec. 5, T 22 N, R 3 E). Named on Paradise West (1980) 7.5' quadrangle. The name is from the position of the place halfway between Helltown and Diamondville; John Adams post office was at the site (Dunn, F.D., p. 20). Postal authorities established John Adams post office in 1880 and discontinued it in 1913; the name was for the first postmaster (Salley, p. 107).

Centerville [SHASTA]: *locality,* 6.5 miles southwest of Redding (lat. 40°31'05" N, long. 122°29'05" W; around SW cor. sec. 19, T 31 N, R 5 W). Named on Redding (1957) 7.5' quadrangle. Called Larkin on Redding (1901) 30' quadrangle. Postal authorities established Larkin post office in 1899 and discontinued it in 1912 (Frickstad, p. 181). The name "Larkin" was for John Larkin, who had a store and saloon at Centerville, and who was coroner of Shasta County from 1911 until 1929 (Steger, p. 43).

Centipede Creek [SHASTA]: *stream,* flows 1.5 miles to McCloud River [SHASTA-SISKIYOU] 3.5 miles north of Shoeinhorse Mountain (lat. 41°07'05" N, long. 122°03'35" W). Named on Shoeinhorse Mountain (1954) 15' quadrangle.

Central House [BUTTE]: *locality,* 4 miles west-northwest of Honcut (lat. 39°21'20" N, long. 121°36'15" W; sec. 2, T 17 N, R 3 E). Named on Honcut (1912) 7.5' quadrangle. Postal authorities established Central House post office in 1859 and discontinued it in 1909 (Frickstad, p. 8).

Central Valley [SHASTA]: *town,* 6.5 miles north of Redding (lat. 40°40'50" N, long. 122°22'05" W; on N line sec. 31, T 33 N, R 4 W). Named on Project City (1957) and Shasta Dam (1956) 7.5' quadrangles. Central Valley post office was established in 1938 (Frickstad, p. 179). The town began when construction started in 1938 on nearby Shasta Dam, the principal unit of Central Valley Project (Gudde, 1949, p. 62).

Central Valley: see "Regional setting."

Chain Gang Gulch [SHASTA]: *canyon,* drained by a stream that flows less than 1 mile to Squaw Creek Arm Shasta Lake 9.5 miles south-southeast of Bollibokka Mountain (lat. 40°48'25" N, long. 122°09' W; sec. 13, T 34 N, R 3 W). Named on Bollibokka Mountain (1957) 15' quadrangle.

Chalk Bank Landing [SISKIYOU]: *locality,* 7.5 miles north-northeast of Mount Dome along Lower Klamath Lake (lat. 41°54'45" N, long. 121°38'30" W; at E line sec. 17, T 47 N, R 3 E). Named on Mount Dome (1950) 15' quadrangle.

Chalk Mountain [SHASTA]:
(1) *peak,* 12 miles north-northeast of the village of Montgomery Creek (lat. 40°59'40" N, long. 121°48'30" W). Altitude 5880 feet. Named on Big Bend (1961) and Montgomery Creek (1956) 15' quadrangles.
(2) *peak,* 5.5 miles south-southeast of Whitmore (lat. 40°33'20" N, long. 121°52'15" W; sec. 9, T 31 N, R 1 E). Altitude 3373 feet. Named on Whitmore (1956) 15' quadrangle.

Chalk Reservoir [SHASTA]: *lake,* 300 feet long, 11 miles northeast of Burney (lat. 40°59'55" N, long. 121°32'15" W; near W line sec. 32, T 37 N, R 4 E). Named on Burney (1957) 15' quadrangle.

Chambers Ravine: see **Schirmer Ravine** [BUTTE].

Chamise Peak [SHASTA]: *peak,* nearly 2 miles west of Summit City (lat. 40°41'15" N, long. 122°26'10" W; sec. 28, T 33 N, R 5 W). Altitude 1628 feet. Named on Shasta Dam (1956) 7.5' quadrangle.

Champlin Slough [TEHAMA]: *stream,* flows 8.5 miles to Toomes Creek 3 miles north-northwest of Vina (lat. 39°58'10" N, long. 122°04'50" W). Named on Los Molinos (1952) and Vina (1950) 7.5' quadrangles.

Chandler Glade [SISKIYOU]: *area,* 13 miles west of Macdoel (lat. 41°50'15" N, long. 122°15'40" W; near W line sec. 13, T 46 N, R 4 W). Named on Copco (1954) 15' quadrangle.

Chandon [BUTTE]: *locality,* 2 miles south-southeast of Gridley along Northern Electric Railroad (lat. 39°18'55" N, long. 121°39'45" W). Named on Gridley (1912) 7.5' quadrangle. Officials of the railroad named the place for the landowner there (Gudde, 1949, p. 63-64).

Channel: see **Magalia** [BUTTE].

Channel Creek: see **Chino Creek** [BUTTE].

Channel Slough [BUTTE]: *stream,* 2.5 miles long, joins Mud Creek 5 miles west of Chico (lat. 39°44' N, long. 121°55'45" W). Named on Ord Ferry (1949) 7.5' quadrangle, which shows the feature as a distributary of Lindo Channel.

Chaos Crags [SHASTA]: *relief feature,* 2.5 miles north-northwest of Lassen Peak (lat. 40°31'15" N, long. 121°31'05" W). Named on Manzanita Lake (1956) 15' quadrangle. The name is from Chaos Jumbles, which is situated just north of Chaos Crags (Schulz, p. 9).

Chaos Crater [SHASTA]: *crater,* 3.25 miles north-northwest of Lassen Peak (lat. 40°32' N, long. 121°31'45" W; sec. 16, T 31 N, R 4 E). Named on Manzanita Lake (1956) 15' quadrangle.

Chaos Jumbles [SHASTA]: *relief feature,* 4.5 miles north-northwest of Lassen Peak (lat. 40°32'30" N, long. 121°33' W; near N line sec. 17, T 31 N, R 4 E). Named on Manzanita Lake (1956) 15' quadrangle. United States Board on Geographic Names (1943, p. 10) rejected the name "Chaos Lava Beds" for the feature. The name refers to the jumbled debris of an avalanche that followed uplift of Chaos Crags (Schulz, p. 10).

Chaos Lava Beds: see **Chaos Jumbles** [SHASTA].

Chaparral [BUTTE]: *locality,* 3.5 miles southeast of Butte Meadows (lat. 40°02'20" N, long. 121°31' W). Named on Mineral (1941) 30' quadrangle. Butte Meadows (1958) 15' quadrangle shows Chaparral Guard Sta. at the site. Postal authorities established Chaparral post office in 1888 and discontinued it in 1894 (Frickstad, p. 8). F.D. Dunn (p. 21) gave the alternate names "Chaparral House," "Chaparal House," and "Chaparral Hill House" for the place.

Chaparral Hill [SISKIYOU]: *mountain,* 2.5 miles west-southwest of Fort Jones (lat. 41°35'15" N, long. 122°53' W). Named on Fort Jones (1955) 15' quadrangle. Called Chapparal Hill on Averill's (1935) map.

Chaparral Hill House: see **Chaparral** [BUTTE].

Chaparral House: see **Chaparral** [BUTTE].

Chapman Gulch [TEHAMA]: *canyon,* drained by a stream that flows 3.5 miles to Paynes Creek (1) 8 miles south-southeast of Manton (lat. 40°20' N, long. 121°47'30" W; sec. 30, T 29 N, R 2 E). Named on Lassen Peak (1956) and Manton (1956) 15' quadrangles.

Chapmans Mill [BUTTE]: *locality,* 13 miles north of Paradise (lat. 39°56'50"

N, long. 121°34'45" W). Named on Chico (1895) 30' quadrangle.

Chapmantown [BUTTE]: *district,* 1 mile east-southeast of downtown Chico (lat. 39°43'20" N, long. 121°49'15" W). Named on Chico (1948) 7.5' quadrangle.

Chardon: see **Oroville** [BUTTE].

Charles Creek: see **Charlie Creek** [SHASTA].

Charley's Ranch: see **Honcut Creek** [BUTTE].

Charlie Creek [SHASTA]: *stream,* flows 3.5 miles to Sacramento River Arm Shasta Lake 7.25 miles south of Lamoine (lat. 40°52'20" N, long. 122°24'10" W; sec. 23, T 35 N, R 5 W). Named on Lamoine (1957) 15' quadrangle. Steger (p. 24) called the stream Charles Creek, and associated the name with Charles Kluchi, who was the grandson of an Indian doctor.

Charlies Rock [GLENN]: *relief feature,* 2.5 miles east of Black Butte (lat. 39°43'50" N, long. 122°49'25" W; sec. 25, T 22 N, R 9 W). Named on Plaskett Meadows (1967) 7.5' quadrangle.

Charmaine Lake [SISKIYOU]: *lake,* 350 feet long, 9 miles north-northwest of Sawyers Bar (lat. 41°24'50" N, long. 123°12' W). Named on English Peak (1977) 7.5' quadrangle.

Chase Gulch [SHASTA]: *canyon,* drained by a stream that flows nearly 1 mile to Dog Creek 4.25 miles southwest of Lamoine (lat. 40°55'45" N, long. 122°28'50" W; near N line sec. 6, T 35 N, R 5 W). Named on Lamoine (1957) 15' quadrangle.

Chase Gulch: see **Kohl Creek** [SISKIYOU].

Chasta Butte: see **Mount Shasta** [SISKIYOU] (1).

Chatterdown Creek [SHASTA]: *stream,* flows 5.5 miles to McCloud River [SHASTA-SISKIYOU] 3.5 miles north-northeast of Bollibokka Mountain (lat. 40°58'45" N, long. 122°11'45" W; sec. 15, T 36 N, R 3 W). Named on Bollibokka Mountain (1957) and Shoeinhorse Mountain (1954) 15' quadrangles. Called Chatterdowen Creek on Redding (1901) 30' quadrangle, but United States Board on Geographic Names (1991, p. 3) rejected the designations "Chatterdowen Creek" and "Chattidown Creek" for the feature. The name is of Indian origin (Steger, p. 24). East Fork enters from the southeast 2.5 miles upstream from the mouth of the main creek; it is nearly 2 miles long and is named on Bollibokka Mountain (1957) 15' quadrangle. North Fork enters from the north less than 1 mile upstream from the mouth of the main creek; it is 3 miles long and is named on Bollibokka Mountain (1957) and Shoeinhorse Mountain (1954) 15' quadrangles. South Fork enters from the southeast less than 1 mile upstream from the mouth of the main creek; it is 3 miles long and is named on Bollibokka Mountain (1957) 15' quadrangle.

Cheeseville [SISKIYOU]: *locality,* 6.5 miles south-southwest of Fort Jones in Scott Valley (lat. 41°31'20" N, long. 122°53'55" W; sec. 5, T 42 N, R 9 W). Named on Fort Jones (1955) 15' quadrangle.

Cheno Creek: see **Chino Creek** [BUTTE].

Cherokee [BUTTE]: *locality,* 9 miles south-southeast of Paradise (lat. 39°31'15" N, long. 121°32'15" W; sec. 28, T 21 N, R 4 E). Named on Cherokee (1970) 7.5' quadrangle. Postal authorities established Cherokee post office in 1854 and discontinued it in 1912 (Frickstad, p. 9). The name is from Cherokee Indians who worked gold deposits at the site in 1853 (Wells and Chambers, p. 251). F.D. Dunn (p. 21) gave the alternate names "Cherokee Flat" and "Drytown" for the place.

Cherokee Camp: see **Campbell Flat** [BUTTE].

Cherokee Creek: see **Vinton Gulch** [BUTTE].

Cherokee Flat: see **Cherokee** [BUTTE].

Cherry Creek [SISKIYOU]:

(1) *stream,* flows 1 mile to Little North Fork Salmon River 5.25 miles north-northwest of Sawyers Bar (lat. 41°21'55" N, long. 123°11'10" W). Named on Sawyers Bar (1979) 7.5' quadrangle.

(2) *stream,* flows 3 miles to join Deadwood Creek and form McAdam Creek 8 miles north-northeast of Fort Jones (lat. 41°42'50" N, long. 122°48'10" W; near SW cor. sec. 29, T 45 N, R 8 W). Named on Fort Jones (1955) 15' quadrangle, which shows Cherry Hill mine located about 8 miles by road from Yreka near the head of Cherry Creek (2). Postal authorities established Cherryhill post office 8 miles west of Yreka in 1902 and discontinued it the same year (Salley, p. 42).

Cherry Flat [SISKIYOU]: *area,* 7.25 miles south of Condrey Mountain (lat. 41°50' N, long. 122°58'45" W; sec. 14, T 46 N, R 10 W). Named on Condrey Mountain (1955) 15' quadrangle.

Cherry Hill [BUTTE]: *ridge,* west-southwest-trending, 1 mile long, 1.5 miles southwest of Jonesville (lat. 40°05'55" N, long. 121°29'30" W; near N line sec. 23, T 26 N, R 4 E). Named on Jonesville (1958) 15' quadrangle.

Cherryhill: see **Cherry Creek** [SISKIYOU] (2).

Cherry Thicket [SHASTA]: *area,* 9.5 miles west-northwest of Lassen Peak (lat. 40°33' N, long. 121°39'30" W; sec. 8, T 31 N, R 3 E). Named on Burney (1939) 30' quadrangle.

Chickabally Mountain [SHASTA]: *peak,* 10 miles south-southwest of Ono (lat. 40°20'50" N, long. 122°42' W; sec. 19, T 29 N, R 7 W). Altitude 1335 feet. Named on Ono (1952) 15' quadrangle.

Chickatee Gulch [TEHAMA]: *canyon,* drained by a stream that flows 1 mile to Wells Creek 6 miles southeast of Beegum Peak (lat. 40°15'40" N, long. 122°48' W; at W line sec. 20, T 28 N, R 8 W). Named on Chanchelulla Peak (1951) 15' quadrangle.

Chicken Hawk Hill [SHASTA]: *peak,* 9.5 miles west-southwest of Castella (lat. 41°04'30" N, long. 122°28'30" W; at NW cor. sec. 17, T 37 N, R 5 W). Altitude 6154 feet. Named on Dunsmuir (1954) 15' quadrangle.

Chicken Hollow [TEHAMA]: *canyon,* drained by a stream that flows 1 mile to Juniper Gulch (1) 5.5 miles west-southwest of Manton (lat. 40°25' N, long. 121°58'15" W; near NE cor. sec. 33, T 30 N, R 1 W). Named on Manton (1956) 15' quadrangle.

Chico [BUTTE]: *city,* 22 miles northwest of Oroville (lat. 39°43'45" N, long. 121°50'15" W). Named on Chico (1948) and Richardson Springs (1951) 7.5' quadrangles. Postal authorities established Chico post office in 1851 (Frickstad, p. 9), and the city incorporated in 1872. J.S. Henning, county surveyor, laid out the community for General Bidwell in 1860 on Bidwell's land (Wells and Chambers, p. 223). California Division of Highways' (1934) map shows a place called Mulberry located 1.25 miles southeast of downtown Chico along Northern Pacific Railroad, and a place called Speedway located nearly 3 miles southeast of Chico along the same railroad (near W line sec. 6, T 21 N, R 2 E)—according to F.D. Dunn (p. 100), Speedway first had the name "Speed." Dunn also noted (p. 96) that a place called Savona was located just south of Speed along the railroad (sec. 7, T 21 N, R 2 E). California Division of Highways' (1934) map shows a place called Butte Creek situated 4 miles east-southeast of downtown Chico along Southern Pacific Railroad (sec. 5, T 21 N, R 2 E), and a place called Dredge located less than 1 mile east of the place called Butte Creek (sec. 4, T 21 N, R 2 E). The same map shows a place called Crouch situated about 7 miles east of Chico along Southern Pacific Railroad (at W line sec. 1, T 21 N, R 2 E). Postal authorities established Greenland post office 5 miles north of Chico in 1863 and discontinued it in 1864. They established Johnson post office 5.5 miles southeast of Chico (SE quarter sec. 17, T 21 N, R 2 E) in 1881 and discontinued it in 1882 (Salley, p. 89, 107). They established Dodgeland post office 15 miles southwest of Chico (NW quarter sec. 31, T 20 N, R 1 E) in 1918 and discontinued it in 1923 (Salley, p. 60). They established Rock Creek post office 7 miles northwest of Chico (sec. 25, T 23 N, R 1 W) in 1858 and discontinued it in 1871—James L. Keefer was the first postmaster (Salley, p. 187); the place also was known as Keefers Station (Dunn, F.D., p. 94). Colbys Landing, named for the proprietor, was a shipping point situated about 7 miles northwest of Chico along Sacramento River; it operated from 1858 until the railroad came to Nord in 1870 (Dunn, F.D., p. 25).

Chico Creek: see **Big Chico Creek** [BUTTE-TEHAMA]; **Little Chico Creek** [BUTTE].

Chico Landing [BUTTE]: *locality,* 6 miles west of Chico along Sacramento River (lat. 39°42'45" N, long. 121°56'40" W). Site named on Ord Ferry (1949) 7.5' quadrangle. The place first was known as Bidwell's Landing (Hoover, Rensch, and Rensch, p. 36). Reavis Ferry was located just above Chico Landing (Dunn, F.D., p. 90).

Chico Meadows [BUTTE]: *area,* about 1 mile north of Butte Meadows along Big Chico Creek [BUTTE-TEHAMA] (lat. 40°05'40" N, long. 121°33' W; sec. 20, T 26 N, R 4 E). Named on Butte Meadows (1958) 15' quadrangle.

Chico Vecino [BUTTE]: *district,* 1 mile north-northwest of downtown Chico (lat. 39°44'35" N, long. 121°51' W). Named on Durham (1912) 7.5' quadrangle.

Chilcoot Pass: see **Chilkoot Pass** [SISKIYOU].

Childs Meadows [TEHAMA]:

(1) *valley,* 5.5 miles north-northwest of Deer Creek Station (lat. 40°20'30" N, long. 121°29' W). Named on Mount Harkness (1956) 15' quadrangle.

(2) *locality,* 7 miles north-northwest of Deer Creek Station (lat. 40°21'40" N, long. 121°29'35" W; sec. 24, T 29 N, R 4 E); the place is near the north end of Childs Meadows (1). Named on Mount Harkness (1956) 15' quadrangle.

Chilkoot Pass [SISKIYOU]: *pass,* 5 miles south-southwest of Cecilville on Siskiyou-Trinity County line (lat. 41°04'55" N, long. 123°09'55" W). Named on Cecil Lake (1979) 7.5' quadrangle. United States Board on Geographic Names (1979a, p. 3) approved the name "Chilcoot Pass" for a feature on Siskiyou-Trinity County line at the head of Chilcoot Creek, which is in Trinity County (lat. 41°19'50" N, long. 122°35'12" W; sec. 17, T 40 N, R 6 W).

Chimney Crater [SISKIYOU]: *crater,* 5 miles south-southwest of Medicine Lake (lat. 41°30'50" N, long. 121°37'40" W). Named on Medicine Lake (1952) 15' quadrangle.

Chimney Rock [GLENN]: *relief feature,* 2.25 miles southeast of Black Butte (lat. 39°42'35" N, long. 122°50'15" W). Named on Plaskett Meadows (1967) 7.5' quadrangle.

Chimney Rock [SISKIYOU]: *peak,* 8 miles north-northeast of Forks of Salmon (lat. 41°21'55" N, long. 123°16'15" W). Altitude 6870 feet. Named on Forks of Salmon (1978) 7.5' quadrangle.

Chimney Rock Lake [SISKIYOU]: *lake,* 600 feet long, 8 miles north-northeast of Forks of Salmon (lat. 41°21'55" N, long. 123°16'15" W); the lake is 1800 feet north-northwest of Chimney Rock. Altitude 6870 feet. Named on Forks of Salmon (1978) 7.5' quadrangle.

China Creek [SISKIYOU]:

(1) *stream,* flows 4.25 miles to Klamath River 3.25 miles east of Happy Camp (lat. 41°47'55" N, long. 123°18'45" W; at N line sec. 8, T 16 N, R 8 E). Named on Slater Butte (1980) 7.5' quadrangle. South Fork enters from the south-southeast 1.5 miles upstream from the mouth of the main stream; it is 3.25 miles long and is named on Slater Butte (1980) 7.5' quadrangle.

(2) *stream,* flows 3.25 miles to Nordheimer Creek 4 miles north of Salmon Mountain (lat. 41°14'30" N, long. 123°23'30" W). Named on Salmon Mountain (1978) 7.5' quadrangle.

(3) *stream,* flows 2.5 miles to Blind Horse Creek 5.5 miles southeast of Cecilville (lat. 41°05'10" N, long. 123°03'10" W). Named on Thompson Peak (1979) 7.5' quadrangle.

(4) *stream,* flows less than 1 mile to Humboldt County 7.25 miles northwest of Orleans, which is in Humboldt County (lat. 41°22'55" N, long. 123°37'40" W). Named on Lonesome Ridge (1974) 7.5' quadrangle.

China Creek: see **Chino Creek** [BUTTE].

China Doctor Creek [SISKIYOU]: *stream,* flows 1 mile to Klamath River 10.5 miles southeast of the village of Seiad Valley (lat. 41°45'25" N, long. 123°00'45" W; near S line sec. 8, T 45 N, R 10 W). Named on Hamburg (1980) 7.5' quadrangle.

China Garden [SHASTA]: *area,* 2.5 miles north-northwest of Balls Ferry along the east side of Sacramento River (lat. 40°27'40" N, long. 122°13'20" W). Named on Balls Ferry (1965) 7.5' quadrangle.

China Gulch [BUTTE]: *canyon,* drained by a stream that flows 1.25 miles to North Fork Feather River 5.5 miles north-northwest of the village of Berry Creek (lat. 39°42'55" N, long. 121°27'15" W; sec. 31, T 22 N, R 5 E). Named on Berry Creek (1970) 7.5' quadrangle. On Bidwell Bar (1897) 30' quadrangle, the stream in the canyon is called Rock Creek. Wells and Chambers' (1882) map shows a place called Whiskey Bar situated along North Fork Feather River at the mouth of present China Gulch.

China Gulch [SHASTA]: *canyon,* drained by a stream that flows nearly 5.5 miles to Dry Creek (5) 3 miles southwest of Olinda (lat. 40°24'45" N, long. 122°26'35" W; near W line sec. 33, T 30 N, R 5 W). Named on Olinda (1964) 7.5' quadrangle.

China Gulch [SISKIYOU]:

(1) *canyon,* drained by a stream that flows 1.25 miles to North Fork Salmon River 3.5 miles east-northeast of Forks of Salmon (lat. 41°16'55" N, long. 123°15'45" W). Named on Forks of Salmon (1978) 7.5' quadrangle.

(2) *canyon,* drained by a stream that flows 1.25 miles to North Russian Creek 5.5 miles northeast of Sawyers Bar (lat. 41°20'40" N, long. 123°02'30" W). Named on Tanners Peak (1977) 7.5' quadrangle.

(3) *canyon,* drained by a stream that flows 0.5 mile to Humbug Creek 15 miles southeast of Condrey Mountain (lat. 41°46'35" N, long. 122°47'45" W; sec. 5, T 45 N, R 8 W). Named on Condrey Mountain (1955) 15' quadrangle.

(4) *canyon,* drained by a stream that flows 0.25 mile to Indian Creek (3) 6 miles north of Fort Jones (lat. 41°41'35" N, long. 122°51'20" W; at W line sec. 2, T 44 N, R 9 W). Named on Fort Jones (1955) 15' quadrangle.

(5) *canyon,* drained by a stream that flows 2.25 miles to Klamath River 10.5 miles west-southwest of Hornbrook (lat. 41°51'50" N, long. 122°44'35" W; sec. 2, T 46 N, R 8 W); the canyon heads near China Peak (2). Named on Hornbrook (1955) 15' quadrangle.

China Gulch [TEHAMA]:

(1) *canyon,* drained by a stream that flows 4 miles to the head of Little Dry Creek (1) 9 miles west of Hooker (lat. 40°19'05" N, long. 122°29'10" W; near S line sec. 36, T 29 N, R 6 W); the canyon divides at the head into North Fork and South Fork. Named on Ono (1952) 15' quadrangle, and on Mitchell Gulch (1965) 7.5' quadrangle. On Anderson (1947) 15' quadrangle, the name "China Gulch" applies to the canyon of present Little Dry Creek (1) to the mouth of Devils Gulch, and United States Board on Geographic Names (1983a, p. 3) accepted this nomenclature. North Fork is 3 miles long and South Fork is 3.5 miles long; both forks are named on Ono (1952) 15' quadrangle.

(2) *canyon,* drained by a stream that flows 1.5 miles to Bowers Creek 6.5 miles west-southwest of Paskenta (lat. 39°50'25" N, long. 122°39'15" W; sec. 21, T 23 N, R 7 W). Named on Hall Ridge (1967) 7.5' quadrangle.

China Gulch: see **Little China Gulch** [SISKIYOU].

China Mountain [SISKIYOU]: *peak,* 17 miles east-southeast of Etna (lat. 41°22'40" N, long. 122°34'30" W; at NE cor. sec. 30, T 41 N, R 6 W). Altitude 8542 feet. Named on China Mountain (1955) 15' quadrangle.

China Mountain: see **South China Mountain** [SISKIYOU].

China Peak [SISKIYOU]:

(1) *peak,* 6 miles east-northeast of Happy Camp (lat. 41°50'10" N, long. 123°16'30" W). Altitude 4169 feet. Named on Slater Butte (1980) 7.5' quadrangle.

(2) *peak,* 10.5 miles west-southwest of Hornbrook (lat. 41°50'05" N, long. 122°43'30" W; sec. 13, T 46 N, R 8 W); the peak is at the head of China Gulch (5). Altitude 4810 feet. Named on Hornbrook (1955) 15' quadrangle.

China Point [SISKIYOU]:

(1) *relief feature,* 3 miles east of Happy Camp along Klamath River (lat. 41°48'10" N, long. 123°18'55" W; sec. 5, T 16 N, R 8 E); the feature is opposite the mouth of China Creek (1). Named on Slater Butte (1980) 7.5' quadrangle.

(2) *relief feature,* 6 miles west of Sawyers Bar along North Fork Salmon River (lat. 41°17'45" N, long. 123°14'45" W). Named on Sawyers Bar (1979) 7.5' quadrangle.

China Point: see **East China Point** [BUTTE]; **West China Point** [BUTTE].

China Slough [TEHAMA]: *stream,* flows nearly 5 miles to Deer Creek (2) 1.5 miles west-southwest of Vina (lat. 39°55'30" N, long. 122°04'50" W). Named on Vina (1950) 7.5' quadrangle.

Chinese Rapids [TEHAMA]: *water feature,* 0.5 mile east of Bend along Sacramento River (lat. 40°15'20" N, long. 122°11'50" W; on W line sec. 27, T 28 N, R 3 W). Named on Bend (1965) 7.5' quadrangle.

Chino Creek [BUTTE]: *stream,* flows 5 miles to North Fork Feather River 8 miles north of the village of Berry Creek (lat. 39°43'10" N, long. 121°25'20" W; sec. 33, T 22 N, R 5 E). Named on Berry Creek (1970) and Pulga (1979) 7.5' quadrangles. Wells and Chambers' (1882) map has the designation "Cheno or Channel Creek" for the feature. F.D. Dunn (p. 23) listed the alternate name "China Creek" for the stream.

Chino Ridge [BUTTE]: *ridge,* south-trending, 1.25 miles long, 6.5 miles north of the village of Berry Creek (lat. 39°44'25" N, long. 121°24'30" W); the ridge is north and west of Chino Creek. Named on Berry Creek (1970) 7.5' quadrangle.

Chinquapin Lake [SISKIYOU]: *lake,* 450 feet long, 14 miles south-southwest of Scott Bar (lat. 41°33'45" N, long. 123°06'35" W). Named on Boulder Peak (1981) 7.5' quadrangle.

Chipmunk Lake [SISKIYOU]: *lake,* 400 feet long, 10.5 miles west-southwest of the town of Mount Shasta (lat. 41°15'10" N, long. 122°29'35" W; sec. 12, T 39 N, R 6 W). Named on Weed (1954) 15' quadrangle.

Chippy Spur [SISKIYOU]: *locality,* 12.5 miles northeast of Bartle along the railroad (lat. 41°23'15" N, long. 121°39'30" W). Named on Hambone (1961) 15' quadrangle.

Chiquito Creek [SHASTA]: *stream,* flows 2 miles to McCloud River [SHASTA-SISKIYOU] 8.5 miles west-southwest of Shoeinhorse Mountain (lat. 41°01'05" N, long. 122°13'10" W). Named on Shoeinhorse Mountain (1954) 15' quadrangle.

Chirpchatter Mountain [SHASTA]: *peak,* nearly 7 miles southeast of Bollibokka Mountain (lat. 40°51'45" N, long. 122°07'45" W; on E line sec. 30, T 35 N, R 2 W). Named on Bollibokka Mountain (1957) 15' quadrangle.

Christie Hill [TEHAMA]: *peak,* 4 miles northeast of Mineral (lat. 40°23'15" N, long. 121°32'25" W; sec. 9, T 29 N, R 4 E). Altitude 6559 feet. Named on Lassen Peak (1956) 15' quadrangle.

Chrome [GLENN]: *locality,* 9 miles north of the village of Elk Creek (lat. 39°43'50" N, long. 122°32'40" W; on W line sec. 28, T 22 N, R 6 W). Named on Chrome (1968) 7.5' quadrangle. According to Dillon (1971, p. 69), Millsaps post office was located at Chrome. Postal authorities established Millsaps post office in 1894 and discontinued in 1927; the name was for George W. Millsaps, a settler of 1854 (Salley, p. 14).

Chrome Creek [GLENN]: *stream,* flows nearly 4 miles to Heifer Camp Creek 2 miles southwest of Newville (lat. 39°46'05" N, long. 122°32'50" W; near NW cor. sec. 16, T 22 N, R 6 W); the stream heads near Chrome. Named on Chrome (1968) and Newville (1967) 7.5' quadrangles.

Chummy Meadows [TEHAMA]: *area,* 10 miles north of Deer Creek Station (lat. 40°24'25" N, long. 121°29'10" W; at N line sec. 1, T 29 N, R 4 E). Named on Mount Harkness (1956) 15' quadrangle.

Churn Creek [SHASTA]: *stream,* flows 20 miles to Sacramento River 1.5 miles north of Anderson (lat. 40°28'25" N, long. 122°18'05" W; sec. 10, T 30 N, R 4 W). Named on Cottonwood (1965), Enterprise (1957), Project City (1957), and Shasta Dam (1956) 7.5' quadrangles. The name is from a churnlike hole formed by a waterfall (Steger, p. 24).

Churn Creek: see **Little Churn Creek** [SHASTA].

Churn Creek Bottom [SHASTA]: *area,* 6 miles south-southeast of Redding (lat. 40°30'45" N, long. 122°20' W); the place is along the lower reaches of Churn Creek. Named on Cottonwood (1965) and Enterprise (1957) 7.5' quadrangles.

Churntown [SHASTA]: *locality,* 6.25 miles north of Redding (lat. 40°40'30" N, long. 122°24'25' W; sec. 35, T 33 N, R 5 W); the place is along upper reaches of Churn Creek (present Little Churn Creek). Named on Redding (1901) 30' quadrangle. Postal authorities established Churntown post office in 1863 and discontinued it in 1866 (Frickstad, p. 179). Gudde (1975, p. 206) listed a mining camp called Mankinsville that was located 1.5 miles below Churntown along Churn Creek.

Cinder Butte [SHASTA]:

(1) *peak,* 7.5 miles west of Coble Mountain (lat. 40°52'05" N, long. 121°29'20" W; sec. 26, T 35 N, R 4 E). Altitude 4388 feet. Named on Jellico (1957) 15' quadrangle.

(2) *peak,* 8.5 miles southeast of Burney (lat. 40°48' N, long. 121°33'10" W; near SW cor. sec. 17, T 34 N, R 4 E). Altitude 5075 feet. Named on Burney (1957) 15' quadrangle.

Cinder Butte [SISKIYOU]: *crater,* 7.25 miles north of Medicine Lake (lat.

41°41'10" N, long. 121°36' W; near W line sec. 2, T 44 N, R 3 E). Named on Medicine Lake (1952) 15' quadrangle.

Cinder Cone [SHASTA]: *peak,* 3.25 miles north of Coble Mountain (lat. 40°55'55" N, long. 121°21'45" W; near NW cor. sec. 26, T 36 N, R 5 E). Named on Jellico (1957) 15' quadrangle.

Cinder Cone [SISKIYOU]:
(1) *relief feature,* 6 miles northeast of Weed (lat. 41°28'40" N, long. 122°17'20" W; near NE cor. sec. 22, T 42 N, R 4 W). Altitude 5480 feet. Named on Weed (1954) 15' quadrangle.
(2) *crater,* 4.5 miles south-southwest of Medicine Lake (lat. 41°31'45" N, long. 121°38'40" W). Altitude 6322 feet. Named on Medicine Lake (1952) 15' quadrangle.

Cinnabar Camp [SISKIYOU]: *locality,* 9 miles west of Hornbrook (lat. 41°54'40" N, long. 122°43'40" W; sec. 24, T 47 N, R 8 W). Named on Hornbrook (1955) 15' quadrangle.

Cinnabar Springs [SISKIYOU]: *spring,* 6 miles east-northeast of Condrey Mountain (lat. 41°58' N, long. 122°52'10" W; sec. 34, T 48 N, R 9 W). Named on Condrey Mountain (1955) 15' quadrangle, which shows a cinnabar mine near the spring. Job Garretson had a resort at the site from 1908 until 1910; the place had both the names "Cinnabar Springs," for nearby cinnabar prospects, and "Garretson Soda Springs," for Job Garretson (Hanna, p. 64). Brown (p. 869) listed a place called Siskiyou Mineral Springs situated at or near present Cinnabar Springs (sec. 33, 34, T 48 N, R 9 W). Waring (p. 217) listed Keller Soda Spring, located 4.5 miles below Garretson Soda Spring on the north side of West Fork Beaver Creek (1) near the home of Alex Keller.

Cirby Creek [BUTTE]: *stream,* flows 2.5 miles to Concow Creek 6.25 miles east-northeast of Paradise (lat. 39°47'10" N, long. 121°30'35" W; near SE cor. sec. 3, T 22 N, R 4 E). Named on Paradise East (1980) and Pulga (1979) 7.5' quadrangles.

Cirby Meadow [BUTTE]: *area,* 4.5 miles east-southeast of Jonesville (lat. 40°04'55" N, long. 121°23'15" W; at E line sec. 27, T 26 N, R 5 E). Named on Jonesville (1958) 15' quadrangle.

Claiborne Creek [SHASTA]: *stream,* flows 6.5 miles to McCloud River [SHASTA-SISKIYOU] nearly 7 miles west-southwest of Shoeinhorse Mountain (lat. 41°02'40" N, long. 122°10'35" W). Named on Shoeinhorse Mountain (1954) 15' quadrangle. Sim Southern named the stream for G.B. Claiborne, president of San Joaquin Bank in Stockton, who was with the first fishing party on McCloud River [SHASTA-SISKIYOU] in the 1860's (Steger, p. 24). South Fork enters 1.25 miles upstream from the mouth of the main creek; it is 4.5 miles long and is named on Shoeinhorse Mountain (1954) 15' quadrangle.

Claiborne Peak [SHASTA]: *peak,* 6 miles west-southwest of Shoeinhorse Mountain (lat. 41°01'55" N, long. 122°10'15" W); the peak is less than 1 mile south of the mouth of Claiborne Creek. Named on Shoeinhorse Mountain (1954) 15' quadrangle.

Clamitte River: see **Klamath River** [SISKIYOU].

Clapboard Gulch [SISKIYOU]: *canyon,* drained by a stream that flows 2 miles to Duzel Creek 13 miles south-southwest of Yreka (lat. 41°33'10" N, long. 123°43'55" W; sec. 23, T 43 N, R 8 W). Named on Yreka (1954) 15' quadrangle.

Clarenback Point [BUTTE]: *relief feature,* 7 miles south-southwest of Paradise (lat. 39°39'30" N, long. 121°40'25" W; on W line sec. 20, T 21 N, R 3 E). Named on Hamlin Canyon (1951) 7.5' quadrangle. Called Clarenbach Point on Oroville (1942) 15' quadrangle.

Clarence King Lake [SISKIYOU]: *lake,* 600 feet long, 12 miles north-northwest of McCloud (lat. 41°24'45" N, long. 122°13'25" W; sec. 8, T 41 N, R 3 W). Named on Shasta (1954) 15' quadrangle.

Clark Creek [SHASTA]: *stream,* flows 10 miles to Lake Britton 2 miles north-northwest of Burney Falls (lat. 41°02'15" N, long. 121°40'05" W; sec. 18, T 37 N, R 3 E). Named on Big Bend (1961) and Pondosa (1961) 15' quadrangles. The name is for Alex Clark, a pioneer in the region (Hanna, p. 65). North Fork enters from the north 5 miles upstream from the mouth of the main creek; it is 3.5 miles long and is named on Pondosa (1961) 15' quadrangle.

Clark Creek [SISKIYOU]: *stream,* flows 6 miles to Scott River 3.5 miles southeast of Etna (lat. 41°25'20" N, long. 122°50'45" W; near N line sec. 11, T 41 N, R 9 W). Named on Etna (1955) 15' quadrangle. Averill's (1935) map has the form "Clarks Cr." for the name.

Clark Creek: see **Deadman Creek** [SHASTA].

Clark Creek Camp [SHASTA]: *locality,* 2.25 miles north-northwest of Burney Falls (lat. 41°02'35" N, long. 121°40'15" W); the place is along Clark Creek. Named on Bartle (1939) 30' quadrangle.

Clarks Gulch [SHASTA]: *canyon,* drained by a stream that flows 1 mile to Sacramento River 1 mile south-southwest of Lamoine (lat. 40°57'45" N, long. 122°25'50" W; near W line sec. 22, T 36 N, R 5 W). Named on Lamoine (1957) 15' quadrangle.

Clark Slough: see **McClure Creek** [TEHAMA] (2).

Clark Valley [GLENN]: *canyon,* 7 miles long, along South Fork Willow Creek above a point 2.5 miles south-southeast of Fruto (lat. 39°33'15" N, long. 122°26'15" W). Named on Lodoga (1960) 15' quadrangle, and on Fruto (1968) 7.5' quadrangle.

Clauson Creek [SISKIYOU]: *stream,* flows 2.5 miles to South Fork Indian Creek (1) 6.5 miles north-northwest of Happy Camp (lat. 41°52'35" N, long. 123°26'40" W). Named on Happy Camp (1980) 7.5' quadrangle.

Clear Creek [BUTTE]:
(1) *stream,* flows 4 miles to Butte Creek [BUTTE-GLENN] 4.25 miles northwest of Stirling City (lat. 39°56'45" N, long. 121°35'35" W; near S line sec. 12, T 24 N, R 3 E). Named on Stirling City (1979) 7.5' quadrangle.
(2) *stream,* flows 2.5 miles to West Branch French Creek 5 miles east-southeast of Pulga (lat. 39°46'45" N, long. 121°22' W; sec. 12, T 22 N, R 5 E). Named on Soapstone Hill (1979) 7.5' quadrangle.
(3) *stream,* flows 12.5 miles to Dry Creek 9.5 miles northwest of Oroville (lat. 39°36'20" N, long. 121°41' W; at W line sec. 7, T 20 N, R 3 E). Named on Cherokee (1970), Hamlin Canyon (1951), and Shippee (1948) 7.5' quadrangles. West Branch enters 8 miles south of Paradise; it is 5.5 miles long and is named on Cherokee (1970) and Hamlin Canyon (1951) 7.5 quadrangles.

Clear Creek [SHASTA]: *stream,* flows 57 miles to Sacramento River 5.5 miles south-southeast of Redding (lat. 40°30'20" N, long. 122°22' W). Named on Schell Mountain (1950) 15' quadrangle, and on Enterprise (1957), French Gulch (1979), Igo (1979), Olinda (1964), Redding (1957, photorevised 1969), and Whiskeytown (1979) 7.5' quadrangles. East Fork enters from the east 8.5 miles south-southwest of Schell Mountain; it is 6.5 miles long and is named on Schell Mountain (1950) 15' quadrangle. First South Fork of East Fork enters East Fork from the southeast 2 miles upstream from the mouth of East Fork; it is 2.5 miles long and is named on Schell Mountain (1950) 15' quadrangle, and on Whiskeytown (1979) 7.5' quadrangle. Second South Fork of East Fork enters East Fork from the southeast 3 miles upstream from the mouth of East Fork; it is 1.5 miles long and is named on Schell Mountain (1950) 15' quadrangle. Third South Fork of East Fork enters East Fork 3.5 miles upstream from the mouth of East Fork; it is 2 miles long and is named on Schell Mountain (1950) 15' quadrangle. North Fork of East Fork enters East Fork from the north 2.5 miles upstream from the mouth of East Fork; it is 2 miles long and is named on Schell Mountain (1950) 15' quadrangle. South Fork Clear Creek enters Clear Creek 1 mile northeast of Igo; it is 7.5 miles long and is named on Igo (1979) 7.5' quadrangle.

Clear Creek [SISKIYOU]:
(1) *stream,* flows 24 miles to Klamath River 10 miles north-northwest of Ukonom Lake (lat. 41°42'35" N, long. 123°26'50" W). Named on Bear Peak (1982), Broken Rib Mountain (1982), Clear Creek (1981), Devils Punchbowl (1981), and Prescott Mountain (1981) 7.5' quadrangles. South Fork enters 0.5 mile upstream from the mouth of the main creek; it is nearly 6 miles long and is named on Bear Peak (1982) and Clear Creek (1981) 7.5' quadrangles. West Fork enters from the west 6 miles south-southwest of Preston Peak; it is 5.25 miles long and is named on Devils Punchbowl (1981) and Prescott Mountain (1981) 7.5' quadrangles.
(2) *stream,* formed by the confluence of North Fork and South Fork, flows 1 mile to McAdam Creek 5 miles north of Fort Jones (lat. 41°40'45" N, long. 122°49'35" W; sec. 12, T 44 N, R 9 W). Named on Fort Jones (1955) 15' quadrangle. North Fork is 1.5 miles long and South Fork is 1.5 miles long. Middle Fork, which is 1 mile long, enters South Fork from the east 400 feet upstream from the confluence of North Fork and South Fork. All three forks are named on Fort Jones (1955) 15' quadrangle.
(3) *stream,* flows 4 miles to Humbug Creek 8 miles southwest of Hornbrook (lat. 41°49'45" N, long. 122°40'10" W; sec. 21, T 46 N, R 7 W). Named on Hornbrook (1955) 15' quadrangle.
(4) *stream,* flows 1.5 miles to Mud Creek (2) 8.5 miles north of McCloud (lat. 41°22'30" N, long. 122°08'25" W; sec. 25, T 41 N, R 3 W). Named on Shasta (1954) 15' quadrangle.
(5) *locality,* 10 miles north-northwest of Ukonom Lake at the mouth of Clear Creek (1) (lat. 41°42'35" N, long. 123°26'55" W). Named on Clear Creek (1981) 7.5' quadrangle. Postal authorities established Clear Creek post office in 1934 and discontinued it in 1963 (Salley, p. 45).

Clear Creek: see **Pentz** [BUTTE].

Clear Creek Camp Ground [SHASTA]: *locality,* 6.25 miles north-northwest of Schell Mountain (lat. 40°56' N, long. 122°35'10" W; sec. 32, T 36 N, R 6 W); the place is along Clear Creek. Named on Schell Mountain (1950) 15' quadrangle.

Clear Creek Diggings: see **Reading Bar** [SHASTA].

Clear Lake [SISKIYOU]: *lake,* 700 feet long, 9 miles north-northeast of Forks of Salmon (lat. 41°23'05" N, long. 123°16'25" W). Named on Medicine Mountain (1978) 7.5' quadrangle.

Cleghorn Meadow [SISKIYOU]: *area,* 5 miles east of Condrey Mountain (lat. 41°55'20" N, long. 122°52'15" W; sec. 15, T 47 N, R 9 W). Named on Condrey Mountain (1955) 15' quadrangle.

Clements Ridge [BUTTE]: *ridge,* generally south-southwest-trending, 2.5 miles long, 2.5 miles south of Paradise (lat. 39°42'45" N, long. 121°36'55" W). Named on Cherokee (1970) and Hamlin Canyon (1951) 7.5' quadrangles.

Clendenning Creek: see **Glendenning Creek** [SHASTA].

Cleveland Hill [BUTTE]: *ridge,* north-trending, 2.25 miles long, 5 miles north-northwest of Bangor (lat. 39°27' N, long. 121°27'15" W; on N line sec. 6, T 18 N, R 5 E). Named on Bangor (1947) 7.5' quadrangle.

Cliff Lake [SHASTA]: *lake,* 800 feet long, 3 miles east-southeast of Mount Lassen (lat. 40°28'35" N, long. 121°27'20" W; sec. 8, T 30 N, R 5 E). Named on Mount Harkness (1956) 15' quadrangle.

Cliff Lake [SISKIYOU]:

(1) *lake,* 2500 feet long, 16 miles south-southwest of Scott Bar (lat. 41°31'25" N, long. 123°06'45" W). Named on Boulder Peak (1981) 7.5' quadrangle. This lake and nearby Campbell Lake together are called Campbell Lakes on Seiad (1922) 30' quadrangle, but United States Board on Geographic Names (1960a, p. 13) rejected this name for present Cliff Lake (1).

(2) *lake,* 1200 feet long, 11.5 miles west of Dunsmuir (lat. 41°12' N, long. 122°29'25" W; on W line sec. 31, T 39 N, R 5 W). Named on Dunsmuir (1954) 15' quadrangle.

Cliff Lake: see **Lower Cliff Lake** [SISKIYOU]; **Upper Cliff Lake** [SISKIYOU].

Cliff Valley [SISKIYOU]: *canyon,* drained by a stream that flows 4 miles to Grider Creek 12 miles west of Scott Bar (lat. 41°43'45" N, long. 123°14'05" W). Named on Grider Valley (1981) 7.5' quadrangle.

Clifton Ridge [GLENN]: *ridge,* southwest- to south-southwest-trending, 2.5 miles long, 4 miles west-northwest of Black Butte on Glenn-Mendocino County line (lat. 39°44'45" N, long. 122°56'15" W). Named on Mendocino Pass (1967) and Plaskett Ridge (1967) 7.5' quadrangles.

Clikapudi Creek [SHASTA]: *stream,* flows 1.5 miles to Shasta Lake 13 miles north of Millville (lat. 40°43'50" N, long. 122°11'50" W; sec. 10, T 33 N, R 3 W). Named on Bella Vista (1965) 7.5' quadrangle. The name has an Indian origin (Steger, p. 25).

Cline Gulch [SHASTA]: *canyon,* drained by a stream that flows 4.5 miles to Clear Creek 1 mile north of the village of French Gulch (lat. 40°43' N, long. 122°37'55" W; near W line sec. 14, T 33 N, R 7 W). Named on French Gulch (1979) and Whiskeytown (1979) 7.5' quadrangles. The name recalls John Cline, who filed on land in the canyon in 1852 (Steger, p. 25). Gudde (1975, p. 177) listed a mining camp called Jillsonville that was built for Gladstone mine in 1912 at the upper end of Cline Gulch. Whiskeytown (1979) 7.5' quadrangle shows Gladstone mine in Cline Gulch (sec. 18, T 33 N, R 6 W).

Clinton Draw: see **Hardin Butte** [SISKIYOU].

Clipper Mills [BUTTE]: *village,* 21 miles east of Oroville (lat. 39°32' N, long. 121°09'20" W; sec. 2, T 19 N, R 7 E). Named on Clipper Mills (1948) 7.5' quadrangle. Called Clipper Mill on Bidwell Bar (1897) 30' quadrangle. Postal authorities established Clipper Mills post office in 1861 and moved it 2.5 miles northeast in 1891 (Salley, p. 46). Sawmills began operating at the place in 1855 (Hanna, p. 66). Lumbermen had built a small water-driven mill called Pine Grove Mill along Grizzly Creek 0.75 mile north of present Clipper Mills in 1852 (Wells and Chambers, p. 263).

Cloak Lake [SISKIYOU]: *lake,* 26 miles west-southwest of Macdoel (lat. 41°38'30" N, long. 122°26'10" W; on W line sec. 21, T 44 N, R 5 W). Named on Lake Shastina (1954) 15' quadrangle.

Close Butte: see **Sloan Butte** [SISKIYOU].

Clough: see **Clough Creek** [SHASTA].

Clough Camp: see **Lee Camp** [TEHAMA].

Clough Creek [SHASTA]: *stream,* flows 7 miles to Stillwater Creek (lat. 40°33'05" N, long. 122°17'05" W; sec. 11, T 31 N, R 4 W). Named on Enterprise (1957) and Project City (1957) 7.5' quadrangles. Red Bluff (1894) 1° quadrangle has the name "Clough" at the mouth of present Clough Creek. The name commemorates Noah Clough, who settled by the stream in the 1850's (Gudde, 1949, p. 71).

Clough Gulch [SHASTA]: *canyon,* drained by a stream that flows 4.5 miles to South Cow Creek 5.25 miles east of Millville (lat. 40°33' N, long. 122°04'45" W; at N line sec. 15, T 31 N, R 2 W). Named on Millville (1953) 15' quadrangle. The name commemorates Noah Clough of Clough Creek (Gudde, 1949, p. 71).

Clover Creek [GLENN]: *stream,* flows 6 miles to Briscoe Creek 4 miles south-southwest of the village of Elk Creek (lat. 39°33'20" N, long. 122°34'05" W; near E line sec. 30, T 20 N, R 6 W). Named on Elk Creek (1968) and Felkner Hill (1968) 7.5' quadrangles.

Clover Creek [SHASTA]:

(1) *stream,* flows 28 miles to Cow Creek 0.5 mile west-northwest of Millville (lat. 40°33'15" N, long. 122°11'10" W; sec. 10, T 31 N, R 3 W). Named on Millville (1953) and Whitmore (1956) 15' quadrangles. Red Bluff (1894) 1° quadrangle shows Clover Creek Valley situated about 8 miles northeast of Millville along Clover Creek (1).

(2) *stream,* flows 9 miles to Sacramento River 1.5 miles north of Anderson (lat. 40°28'25" N, long. 122°17'30" W; at W line sec. 11, T 30 N, R 4 W). Named on Cottonwood (1965) and Enterprise (1957) 7.5' quadrangles.

Clover Creek [TEHAMA]: *stream,* flows nearly 6 miles to Red Bank Creek 1.5 miles north-northwest of Red Bank (lat. 40°07' N, long. 122°27'35" W; near S line sec. 8, T 26 N, R 5 W). Named on Lowrey (1967) and Red Bank (1952) 7.5' quadrangles.

Clover Creek Mountain: see **Clover Mountain** [SHASTA].

Clover Creek Springs [SHASTA]: *springs,* 9.5 miles northeast of Whitmore (lat. 40°43'30" N, long. 121°47'20" W; at N line sec. 18, T 33 N, R 2 E); the springs are at the head of Clover Creek (1). Named on Whitmore (1956) 15' quadrangle.

Clover Creek Valley: see **Clover Creek** [SHASTA] (1).

Cloverdale [SHASTA]: *settlement,* 4.25 miles west-northwest of Olinda (lat. 40°28'25" N, long. 122°28'30" W; on S line sec. 6, T 30 N, R 5 W). Named on Olinda (1964) 7.5' quadrangle.

Clover Mountain [SHASTA]: *peak,* 10.5 miles northeast of Whitmore (lat. 40°44'30" N, long. 121°47'20" W; sec. 6, T 33 N, R 2 E). Named on Whitmore (1956) 15' quadrangle. Called Clover Cr. Mt. on Averill's (1939) map.

Cluster Lakes [SHASTA]: *lakes,* 6.5 miles east-northeast of Lassen Peak (lat. 40°31'40" N, long. 121°23'15" W). Named on Prospect Peak (1957) 15' quadrangle.

Coal Canyon [BUTTE]: *canyon,* 3.5 miles long, along Gold Run above a point 6.5 miles north-northwest of Oroville (lat. 39°36' N, long. 121°35'45" W; sec. 12, T 20 N, R 3 E). Named on Oroville (1970) 7.5' quadrangle. Low-quality coal mined in the canyon in the 1860's was used to make illuminating gas in Oroville (Dunn, F.D., p. 25).

Coal Creek [SHASTA]:

(1) *stream,* flows 1.5 miles to Kosk Creek 8.5 miles north-northeast of the village of Big Bend (lat. 41°07'55" N, long. 121°50'50" W; sec. 22, T 38 N, R 1 E). Named on Big Bend (1961) 15' quadrangle, which shows a coal mine near the stream.

(2) *stream,* flows 1.5 miles to Salt Creek Inlet 10 miles south-southeast of Lamoine (lat. 40°50'55" N, long. 122°20'05" W; near NE cor. sec. 32, T 35 N, R 4 W). Named on Lamoine (1957) 15' quadrangle.

(3) *stream,* flows 2 miles to Clover Creek (1) 12.5 miles northeast of Millville (lat. 40°40'30" N, long. 122°00'20" W; sec. 32, T 33 N, R 1 W). Named on Millville (1953) and Whitmore (1956) 15' quadrangles.

Coal Gulch [SHASTA]: *canyon,* drained by a stream that flows 5 miles to Old Cow Creek 2.5 miles west of Whitmore (lat. 40°37'45" N, long. 121°57'35" W; sec. 15, T 32 N, R 1 W). Named on Whitmore (1956) 15' quadrangle. Diller (1889, p. 408) noted that coal was found in the canyon.

Coal Pit Gulch [SHASTA]:

(1) *canyon,* drained by a stream that flows less than 1 mile to Slate Creek (1) 1.5 miles west of Lamoine (lat. 40°58'35" N, long. 122°27'30" W; at E line sec. 17, T 36 N, R 5 W). Named on Lamoine (1957) 15' quadrangle.

(2) *canyon,* drained by a stream that flows 3.5 miles to Dry Creek (5) 4 miles west of Olinda (lat. 40°27'10" N, long. 122°28'40" W; sec. 18, T 30 N, R 5 W). Named on Ono (1952) 15' quadrangle, and on Olinda (1964) 7.5' quadrangle.

Coats Creek [SISKIYOU]: *stream,* flows 2.5 miles to Mill Creek (5) 13 miles south-southeast of Condrey Mountain (lat. 41°45'15" N, long. 122°55'10" W; sec. 18, T 45 N, R 7 W). Named on Condrey Mountain (1955) and Fort Jones (1955) 15' quadrangles.

Cobb Flat [TEHAMA]: *valley,* 3.25 miles north of Wakefield Flat along Guyre Creek (lat. 40°10'25" N, long. 122°38'30" W; near S line sec. 22, T 27 N, R 7 W). Named on Cold Fork (1967) 7.5' quadrangle.

Coble Mountain [SHASTA]: *peak,* 17 miles east of Burney (lat. 40°53' N, long. 121°21' W; sec. 19, T 35 N, R 6 E). Altitude 5125 feet. Named on Jellico (1957) 15' quadrangle. United States Board on Geographic Names (1984a, p. 3) rejected the name "Cable Mountain" for the feature.

Coble Spring [SHASTA]: *spring,* 2 miles south-southeast of Coble Mountain (lat. 40°51'20" N, long. 121°20' W; sec. 32, T 35 N, R 6 E). Named on Jellico (1957) 15' quadrangle. United States Board on Geographic Names (1984a, p. 3) rejected the name "Cable Spring" for the feature.

Codora [GLENN]: *locality,* 10.5 miles east-southeast of Willows along Southern Pacific Railroad (lat. 39°27'30" N, long. 122°01'15" W). Named on Princeton (1952) 7.5' quadrangle.

Codora Four Corners [GLENN]: *locality,* 10.5 miles east-southeast of Willows (lat. 39°27'25" N, long. 122°01' W); the place is 0.25 mile east of Codora. Named on Princeton (1952) 7.5' quadrangle.

Cody Bar [SISKIYOU]: *locality,* 4.25 miles west-northwest of Cecilville (lat. 41°09'55" N, long. 123°12'50" W). Named on Cecilville (1979) 7.5' quadrangle.

Cody Creek [SISKIYOU]: *stream,* flows 1.5 miles to South Fork Salmon River 4.5 miles west-northwest of Cecilville (lat. 41°10'05" N, long. 123°13'05" W). Named on Cecilville (1979) 7.5' quadrangle.

Coffee Can Creek [SISKIYOU]: *stream,* flows 2 miles to Dillon Creek 4.5 miles north-northwest of Dillon Mountain (lat. 41°35'35" N, long. 123°36' W). Named on Dillon Mountain (1983) 7.5' quadrangle.

Coggins: see **Weed** [SISKIYOU].

Coggins Park [SHASTA]: *area,* 3.5 miles west of Shasta Bally (lat. 40°36' N, long. 122°41'50" W; sec. 30, T 32 N, R 7 W). Named on Shasta Bally (1978) 7.5' quadrangle.

Cohasset [BUTTE]: *village,* 13 miles north-northwest of Paradise (lat. 39°55'35" N, long. 121°43'50" W); the place is on Cohasset Ridge. Named on Cohasset (1979) 7.5' quadrangle. Postal authorities established Cohasset post office in 1888 and discontinued it in 1920 (Frickstad, p. 9). The place was known as Keefers Ridge in the 1860's, and then was called North Point, after a school district, before the name was changed to accommodate postal officials; the present name is from a town in Massachusetts (Dunn, F.D., p. 25).

Cohasset Ridge [BUTTE-TEHAMA]: *ridge,* 15 miles long, about 12 miles north-northwest of Paradise on Butte-Tehama County line, mainly in Butte County (center near lat. 39°54' N, long. 121°44'30" W); Cohasset is on the ridge. Named on Butte Meadows (1958) 15' quadrangle, and on Campbell Mound (1952), Cohasset (1979), and Richardson Springs (1951) 7.5' quadrangles. Called Keefer Ridge on Mineral (1941) 30' quadrangle. The feature had the early names "Campbell Pinery," "Keefer Pinery," and "Hogs Back" (Dunn, F.D., p. 25, 51).

Colby Creek [BUTTE-TEHAMA]: *stream,* heads in Tehama County and flows 3 miles to Butte Creek [BUTTE-GLENN] 1 mile west of Jonesville in Butte County (lat. 40°06'40" N, long. 121°29' W; sec. 14, T 26 N, R 4 E); the stream heads near Colby Mountain. Named on Butte Meadows (1958) and Jonesville (1958) 15' quadrangles.

Colby Meadow [SISKIYOU]: *area,* 4.5 miles south-southeast of Bartle (lat. 41°11'45" N, long. 121°46'45" W; on S line sec. 19, T 39 N, R 2 E). Named on Big Bend (1961) 15' quadrangle.

Colby Mountain [TEHAMA]: *peak,* 8 miles east-northeast of Polk Springs (lat. 40°08'45" N, long. 121°31'15" W; near SE cor. sec. 33, T 27 N, R 4 E). Altitude 6002 feet. Named on Butte Meadows (1958) 15' quadrangle.

Colbys Landing: see **Chico** [BUTTE].

Cold Boiling Lake [SHASTA]: *lake,* 450 feet long, 2.5 miles south-southeast of Lassen Peak (lat. 40°27'20" N, long. 121°29' W; near SE cor. sec. 13, T 30 N, R 4 E). Named on Mount Harkness (1956) 15' quadrangle. Schulz (p. 11-12) noted that the name is from gas bubbles that rise in the water. United States Board on Geographic Names (1933, p. 228) rejected the name "Soda Lake" for the feature.

Cold Creek [BUTTE]: *stream,* flows 3 miles to West Branch Feather River 1 mile east of Stirling City (lat. 39°54'25" N, long. 121°30'40" W; sec. 27, T 24 N, R 4 E). Named on Kimshew Point (1979) and Stirling City (1979) 7.5' quadrangles. On Bidwell Bar (1897) 30' quadrangle, the canyon of the stream is called Break Neck Canyon; United States Board on Geographic Names (1960b, p. 7) rejected the name "Breakneck Canyon" for the feature.

Cold Creek [GLENN]: *stream,* flows 9 miles to Mendocino County 2.5 miles south-southwest of Black Butte (lat. 39°41'40" N, long. 122°53'25" W). Named on Plaskett Meadows (1967) and Plaskett Ridge (1967) 7.5' quadrangles.

Cold Creek [SISKIYOU]:

(1) *stream,* flows 5.25 miles to Bogus Creek 20 miles west-northwest of Macdoel (lat. 41°55'40" N, long. 122°21'50" W; near E line sec. 13, T 47 N, R 5 W). Named on Copco (1954) 15' quadrangle.

(2) *stream,* flows 4 miles to Bogus Creek 16 miles west of Macdoel (lat. 41°51'50" N, long. 122°19'20" W; near E line sec. 8, T 46 N, R 4 W). Named on Copco (1954) 15' quadrangle.

(3) *stream,* flows 6.5 miles to Ash Creek (2) 10.5 miles north-northeast of McCloud (lat. 41°23'10" N, long. 122°02' W; sec. 24, T 41 N, R 2 W). Named on Shasta (1954) 15' quadrangle.

(4) *stream,* flows 2.25 miles to Wagon Creek 2 miles south-southwest of the town of Mount Shasta (lat. 41°17'15" N, long. 122°19'35" W). Named on Weed (1954) 15' quadrangle.

Cold Creek [TEHAMA]: *stream,* flows 2.5 miles to South Fork Battle Creek [SHASTA-TEHAMA] 3 miles west of Mineral (lat. 40°21'05" N, long. 121°39'10" W; near N line sec. 28, T 29 N, R 3 E). Named on Lassen Peak (1956) 15' quadrangle.

Cold Creek Butte [TEHAMA]: *peak,* 2.5 miles west of Mineral (lat. 40°20'50" N, long. 121°38'40" W; near W line sec. 27, T 29 N, R 3 E); the peak is 0.5 mile east-southeast of the mouth of Cold Creek. Named on Lassen Peak (1956) 15' quadrangle.

Cold Creek Meadows [TEHAMA]: *area,* 2 miles west-southwest of Mineral (lat. 40°20'20" N, long. 121°37'55" W; near SE cor. sec. 27, T 29 N, R 3 E); the place is along Cold Creek. Named on Lassen Peak (1956) 15' quadrangle.

Cold Fork [TEHAMA]:

(1) *stream,* flows 27 miles to South Fork Cottonwood Creek [SHASTA-TEHAMA] 8 miles northeast of Wakefield Flat (lat. 40°12'40" N, long. 122°32'30" W). Named on Yolla Bolly (1954) 15' quadrangle, and on Cold Fork (1967) and Oxbow Bridge (1967) 7.5' quadrangles.

(2) *locality,* 3.5 miles north-northwest of Wakefield Flat (lat. 40°10'20" N, long. 122°40'25" W; near S line sec. 20, T 27 N, R 7 W); the place is along Cold Fork (1). Named on Cold Fork (1967) 7.5' quadrangle. Postal authorities established Cold Fork post office in 1915 and discontinued it in 1920 (Frickstad, p. 203).

Cold Spring Creek [TEHAMA]: *stream,* flows 4.5 miles to Fish Creek 3.25 miles north-northwest of Ball Mountain (lat. 39°58'20" N, long. 122°48'45" W; at N line sec. 1, T 24 N, R 9 W). Named on Ball Mountain (1967) and Riley Ridge (1967) 7.5' quadrangles. United States Board on Geographic Names (1969b, p. 4) rejected the form "Cold Springs Creek" for the name. On Anthony Peak (1952) 15' quadrangle, present Griffin Creek is considered part of Cold Spring Creek.

Cold Spring Gulch [SHASTA]:

(1) *canyon,* 1.5 miles long, opens into the canyon of Middle Fork Cottonwood Creek [SHASTA-TEHAMA] 3.5 miles southwest of Arbuckle Mountain (lat. 40°21'35" N, long. 122°54'35" W; at SW cor. sec. 17, T 29 N, R 9 W). Named on Chanchelulla Peak (1951) 15' quadrangle.

(2) *canyon,* 0.5 mile long, opens into the canyon of Whiskey Creek 4.25 miles east-southeast of the village of French Gulch (lat. 40°40'25" N, long. 122°33'50" W). Named on French Gulch (1944) 15' quadrangle.

Cold Spring Hill [TEHAMA]: *peak,* 4.25 miles south of Polk Springs (lat. 40°03'20" N, long. 121°39'45" W; sec. 5, T 25 N, R 3 E). Named on Butte Meadows (1958) 15' quadrangle.

Cold Spring Ridge [TEHAMA]: *ridge,* north-northwest- to west-trending, 1.25 miles long, 2.25 miles north-northeast of Ball Mountain (lat. 39°57'40" N, long. 122°45'25" W); the ridge is north of the upper reaches of Cold Spring Creek. Named on Ball Mountain (1967) 7.5' quadrangle.

Cold Springs Creek [SISKIYOU]: *stream,* flows 1.5 miles to Boulder Creek (2) 10 miles north of Sawyers Bar (lat. 41°26'30" N, long. 123°10' W). Named on English Peak (1977) 7.5' quadrangle.

Cole [SISKIYOU]: *locality,* 7.5 miles north-northwest of Hornbrook (lat. 42°00'10" N, long. 122°38'20" W; on S line sec. 15, T 48 N, R 7 W). Named on Hornbrook (1955) 15' quadrangle. Diller and others' (1915) map shows a place called Zuleka along the railroad 4 miles southeast of Cole.

Cole Creek [SISKIYOU]: *stream,* flows nearly 4 miles to South Fork Indian Creek (1) 8 miles northwest of Happy Camp (lat. 41°52'25" N, long. 123°29'25" W). Named on Deadman Point (1981), Happy Camp (1980), and Polar Bear Mountain (1982) 7.5' quadrangles.

Coleman Forebay [SHASTA]: *lake,* 1000 feet long, 4.25 miles east of Balls Ferry (lat. 40°24'50" N, long. 122°06'45" W; sec. 32, T 30 N, R 2 W). Named on Tuscan Buttes NE (1965) 7.5' quadrangle.

Coles: see **Hilt** [SISKIYOU].

Collins Creek [SISKIYOU]: *stream,* flows 3.5 miles to Klamath River 8 miles south of Condrey Mountain (lat. 41°49'25" N, long. 122°58'20" W; near S line sec. 14, T 46 N, R 10 W). Named on Condrey Mountain (1955) 15' quadrangle.

Collins Spring [SISKIYOU]: *spring,* nearly 6 miles north of Hornbrook (lat. 41°59'45" N, long. 122°34'20" W; near W line sec. 20, T 48 N, R 6 W). Named on Hornbrook (1955) 15' quadrangle.

Colusa Drain [GLENN]: *water feature,* enters Colusa County 11 miles southeast of Willows (lat. 39°24'50" N, long. 122°03'05" W). Named on Glenn (1951) and Princeton (1952) 7.5' quadrangles.

Colyear: see **Red Bank** [TEHAMA].

Colyear Springs [TEHAMA]: *spring,* 5 miles southwest of Wakefield Flat (lat. 40°04'10" N, long. 122°41'35" W; near N line sec. 31, T 26 N, R 7 W). Named on Raglin Ridge (1967) 7.5' quadrangle. Called Colyer's Springs on Red Bluff (1894) 1° quadrangle. United States Board on Geographic Names (1968c, p. 5) rejected the name Colyer Springs for the feature. Mr. J. Colyear of Red Bluff owned the place (Crawford, 1896, p. 522). An early attempt to start a resort at the site met with little success (Waring, p. 266).

Comanche Creek [BUTTE]: *stream,* flows 13 miles to a ditch 5 miles southwest of Chico (lat. 39°40'45" N, long. 121°53'45" W). Named on Chico (1948) and Ord Ferry (1949) 7.5' quadrangles. Called Edgar Slough on Chico Landing (1912) and Durham (1912) 7.5' quadrangles, but United States Board on Geographic Names (1961, p. 17) rejected this name for the feature.

Commissary Spring [TEHAMA]: *spring,* 10 miles west-southwest of Paskenta (lat. 39°48'35" N, long. 122°42'35" W; sec. 36, T 23 N, R 8 W). Named on Hall Ridge (1967) 7.5' quadrangle.

Comosa: see **Tehama** [TEHAMA].

Compressor Gulch [SISKIYOU]: *canyon,* drained by a stream that flows 1.25 miles to East Fork Salmon River 2.5 miles south-southeast of Sawyers Bar (lat. 41°15'45" N, long. 123°06'45" W). Named on Tanners Peak (1977) 7.5' quadrangle.

Conant [SHASTA]: *locality,* 2 miles south of Castella along Southern Pacific Railroad (lat. 41°06'45" N, long. 122°19'30" W; near E line sec. 33, T 38 N, R 4 W). Named on Dunsmuir (1954) 15' quadrangle. The name is for W. Conant, who lived at the place (Steger, p. 25).

Conard: see **Mount Conard** [TEHAMA].

Conard Lake [TEHAMA]: *lake,* 200 feet long, 4.25 miles northeast of Mineral (lat. 40°26'30" N, long. 121°29'50" W; near E line sec. 23, T 30 N, R 4 E); the lake is north of Mount Conard. Named on Mount Harkness (1956) 15' quadrangle.

Conard Meadows [TEHAMA]: *area,* 8 miles northeast of Mineral (lat. 40°26'30" N, long. 121°30'15" W; sec. 23, T 30 N, R 4 E); the place is less than 1 mile north of Mount Conard, which is called Black Butte on Mineral (1941) 30' quadrangle. Named on Lassen (1956) 15' quadrangle. United States Board on Geographic Names (1948a, p. 5) rejected the name "Black Butte Meadows" for the area.

Concow [BUTTE]: *locality,* 4.5 miles east of Paradise (lat. 39°46' N, long. 121°30'45" W). Named on Chico (1895) 30' quadrangle. Postal authorities established Con Cow post office in 1882, changed the name to Concow in 1895, moved it 1 mile south in 1903, moved it 1 mile north in 1906, and discontinued it that same year (Salley, p. 49). The first settlers arrived at the place in 1856 (Dunn, F.D., p. 26). The name is of Indian origin (Kroeber, p. 40).

Concow Creek [BUTTE]: *stream,* flows 11 miles to West Branch Feather River 4.5 miles east-southeast of Paradise (lat. 39°43'15" N, long. 121°33'15" W; sec. 32, T 22 N, R 4 E). Named on Cherokee (1970), Paradise East (1980), and Pulga (1979) 7.5 quadrangles. The stream was called East Branch of Feather River on some early maps (Dunn, F.D., p. 26).

Concow Reservoir [BUTTE]: *lake,* behind a dam on Concow Creek 5 miles east of Paradise (lat. 39°45'50" N, long. 121°31'35" W; sec. 16, T 22 N, R 4 E). Named on Paradise East (1980) 7.5' quadrangle. Called Spring Valley Reservoir on Chico (1895) 30' quadrangle. Spring Valley Hydraulic Gold Company was organized in Concow Valley to furnish water for hydraulic mining (Wells and Chambers, p. 254).

Concow Valley: see **Concow Reservoir** [BUTTE].

Condrey Mountain [SISKIYOU]: *peak,* 22 miles northwest of Yreka (lat. 41°56'15" N, long. 122°58'40" W). Altitude 7112 feet. Named on Condrey Mountain (1955) 15' quadrangle.

Cone Mountain: see **Black Butte** [SISKIYOU] (1).

Cone Point [SISKIYOU]: *relief feature,* 6.5 miles southeast of McCloud (lat. 41°11'25" N, long. 122°03'15" W; near SW cor. sec. 26, T 39 N, R 2 W). Named on Shoeinhorse Mountain (1954) 15' quadrangle.

Cone Reservoir: see **Porcupine Reservoir** [SHASTA].

Coney Island [SISKIYOU]: *locality,* 0.5 mile west of Bartle (lat. 41°15'20" N, long. 121°50' W; near E line sec. 3, T 39 N, R 1 E). Named on Bartle (1961) 15' quadrangle.

Connor Creek [SHASTA-SISKIYOU]: *stream,* heads in Siskiyou County and flows 2 miles to Squaw Valley Creek 8 miles north-northwest of Shoeinhorse Mountain in Shasta County (lat. 41°10'35" N, long. 122°08'15" W; near SE cor. sec. 36, T 39 N, R 3 W). Named on Shoeinhorse Mountain (1954) 15' quadrangle.

Conrad Gulch: see **Big Conrad Gulch** [SISKIYOU]; **Little Conrad Gulch** [SISKIYOU].

Constant Flow Gulch [SHASTA]: *canyon,* drained by a stream that flows 0.5 mile to Pit River 12 miles east-southeast of Bollibokka Mountain (lat. 40°50'50" N, long. 122°00'45" W; sec. 31, T 35 N, R 1 W). Named on Bollibokka Mountain (1957) 7.5' quadrangle.

Cook and Green Butte: see **Red Butte** [SISKIYOU] (1).

Cook and Green Campground [SISKIYOU]: *locality,* 9 miles north of the village of Seiad Valley (lat. 41°58'25" N, long. 123°10'40" W); the place is near the mouth of Cook and Green Creek. Named on Kangaroo Mountain (1980) 7.5' quadrangle.

Cook and Green Creek [SISKIYOU]: *stream,* flows 4.5 miles to Applegate River 9 miles north of the village of Seiad Valley (lat. 41°58'35" N, long. 123°10'40" W). Named on Dutch Creek (1980) and Kangaroo Mountain (1980) 7.5' quadrangles.

Cook and Green Pass [SISKIYOU]: *pass,* 7.5 miles north-northeast of the village of Seiad Valley (lat. 41°56'30" N, long. 123°08'40" W); the pass is at the head of a tributary to Cook and Green Creek. Named on Kangaroo Mountain (1980) 7.5' quadrangle.

Cooks Flat [TEHAMA]: *area,* nearly 2 miles north-northeast of Wakefield Flat along South Fork Cottonwood Creek [SHASTA-TEHAMA] (lat. 40°09' N, long. 122°37'30" W). Named on Cold Fork (1967) 7.5' quadrangle.

Cooks Ridges [TEHAMA]: *ridge,* generally southeast-trending, 1.5 miles long, 2.5 miles north of Wakefield Flat (lat. 40°09'45" N, long. 122°38'15" W; mainly in sec. 27, T 27 N, R 7 W). Named on Cold Fork (1967) 7.5' quadrangle.

Coon Creek [BUTTE]:

(1) *stream,* flows 2 miles to Bull Creek 3.25 miles south-southeast of Butte Meadows (lat. 40°02'10" N, long. 121°32'10" W; sec. 9, T 25 N, R 4 E). Named on Butte Meadows (1958) 15' quadrangle.

(2) *stream,* flows 2.25 miles to Peavine Creek nearly 4 miles north-northeast of the village of Brush Creek (lat. 39°44'35" N, long. 121°19' W; sec. 21, T 22 N, R 6 E). Named on Brush Creek (1970) and Soapstone Hill (1979) 7.5' quadrangles.

Coon Creek [SISKIYOU]: *stream,* flows 3.5 miles to Klamath River 7.5 miles west-northwest of Ukonom Lake (lat. 41°36'45" N, long. 123°29'45" W). Named on Bear Peak (1982) and Ukonom Mountain (1980) 7.5' quadrangles.

Coon Hollow [BUTTE]:

(1) *canyon,* drained by a stream that flows 4.25 miles to West Branch Feather River 3.5 miles south of Jonesville (lat. 40°03'45" N, long. 121°28'15" W; sec. 36, T 26 N, R 4 E). Named on Jonesville (1958) 15' quadrangle.

(2) *canyon,* drained by a stream that flows 1.25 miles to Schirmer Ravine 3.5 miles north of Oroville (lat. 39°33'50" N, long. 121°34'05" W; sec. 30, T 20 N, R 4 E). Named on Oroville (1970) 7.5' quadrangle.

Coon Hollow [SISKIYOU]: *canyon,* drained by a stream that flows 4.25 miles to Independence Creek 5.25 miles northwest of Ukonom Lake (lat. 41°38'05" N, long. 123°25'35" W). Named on Clear Creek (1981) and Huckleberry Mountain (1980) 7.5' quadrangles.

Coon Ravine [BUTTE]: *canyon,* drained by a stream that flows 0.5 mile to South Fork Feather River 5.25 miles west-northwest of Forbestown (lat. 39°32'35" N, long. 121°19'30" W; near S line sec. 32, T 20 N, R 6 E). Named on Forbestown (1970) 7.5' quadrangle.

Coon Ridge [BUTTE]: *ridge,* southwest-trending, 5 miles long, 6 miles southwest of Paradise (lat. 39°41'45" N, long. 121°43'30" W). Named on Chico (1948) and Hamlin Canyon (1951) 7.5' quadrangles.

Coonrod Flat [SISKIYOU]: *area,* 10 miles northwest of Bartle (lat. 41°20'15" N, long. 121°58'15" W; sec. 4, T 40 N, R 1 W). Named on Bartle (1961) 15' quadrangle.

Coon Run [SISKIYOU]: *stream,* flows 1.25 miles to Indian Creek (1) 9.5 miles north-northwest of Happy Camp (lat. 41°54'50" N, long. 123°27'50" W; sec. 25, T 18 N, R 6 E). Named on Deadman Point (1981) 7.5' quadrangle.

Cooper Canyon [TEHAMA]: *canyon,* drained by a stream that flows nearly 2 miles to Smallwood Gulch 8.5 miles southeast of Wakefield Flat (lat. 40°01'55" N, long. 122°32'55" W; sec. 16, T 25 N, R 6 W). Named on Lowrey (1967) 7.5' quadrangle.

Cooper Meadow [SISKIYOU]: *area,* 15 miles southeast of Etna (lat. 41°19'55" N, long. 122°39'10" W; near NE cor. sec. 15, T 40 N, R 7 W). Named on China Mountain (1955) 15' quadrangle.

Copco [SISKIYOU]: *village,* 21 miles west-northwest of Macdoel (lat. 41°59'10" N, long. 122°21'30" W; at W line sec. 30, T 48 N, R 4 W). Named on Copco (1954) 15' quadrangle. Postal authorities established Copco post office in 1914 and discontinued it in 1954 (Frickstad, p. 186). The name is from California Oregon Power Company (Stewart, G.R., p. 112).

Copco Lake [SISKIYOU]: *lake,* behind a dam on Klamath River 20 miles west-northwest of Macdoel (lat. 41°58'45" N, long. 122°20' W; sec. 29, T 48 N, R 4 W). Named on Copco (1954) 15' quadrangle.

Copeland [TEHAMA]: *locality,* 1.5 miles north-northwest of Vina (lat. 39°57'20" N, long. 122°03'45" W). Named on Vina (1904) 15' quadrangle.

Copeland Bar [TEHAMA]: *locality,* 2 miles west of Vina on the east side of Sacramento River (lat. 39°55'50" N, long. 122°05'25" W; on S line sec. 16, T 24 N, R 2 W). Named on Vina (1950) 7.5' quadrangle.

Copley: see **Motion** [SHASTA].

Copley Mountain [SHASTA]: *peak,* 4.5 miles west of Summit City (lat. 40°40'55" N, long. 122°29'15" W; at S line sec. 25, T 33 N, R 6 W). Named on Shasta Dam (1956) 7.5' quadrangle.

Copper: see **Eileen** [SISKIYOU].

Copper Butte [SISKIYOU]: *peak,* 8 miles north-northeast of the village of Seiad Valley (lat. 41°56'15" N, long. 123°06'45" W). Named on Dutch Creek (1980) 7.5' quadrangle.

Copper City [GLENN]: *locality,* 3.25 miles east of Black Butte (lat. 39°43'20" N, long. 122°48'30" W; sec. 31, T 22 N, R 8 E). Named on Plaskett Meadows (1967) 7.5' quadrangle. Hull Mountain (1952) 15' quadrangle shows Copper City Campground at the site.

Copper City [SHASTA]: *locality,* 10.5 miles south of present Bollibokka Mountain along Squaw Creek (2) (lat. 40°46'30" N, long. 122°13' W; sec. 28, T 34 N, R 3 W). Named on Redding (1901) 30' quadrangle, which also has the name "Ydalpom" at the place. Postal authorities established Copper City post office in 1878 and discontinued it in 1880; the name was from Gold Silver and Copper Company (Salley, p. 50). They established Ydalpom post office in 1888 and discontinued it in 1943 (Salley, p. 244). Copper City first was known as Williams and as Brownsville; the name "Ydalpom" is of Indian origin (Steger, p. 26, 67).

Copper City Campground: see **Copper City** [GLENN].

Copper Creek [SISKIYOU]:

(1) *stream,* flows 5.25 miles to Twin Valley Creek 5 miles northeast of Preston Peak (lat. 41°52'45" N, long. 123°32'15" W); the stream heads at Copper Mountain. Named on Polar Bear Mountain (1982) and Preston Peak (1982) 7.5' quadrangles.

(2) *stream,* flows nearly 6 miles to Dillon Creek 5.5 miles north-northwest of Dillon Mountain (lat. 41°35'55" N, long. 123°37'35" W). Named on Chimney Rock (1981) 7.5' quadrangle.

(3) *stream,* flows 1.5 miles to Elk Creek 11 miles north of Ukonom Lake (lat. 41°44'30" N, long. 123°21'15" W). Named on Huckleberry Mountain (1980) 7.5' quadrangle.

(4) *stream,* flows nearly 3 miles to Soap Creek 7.5 miles southwest of Yreka (lat. 41°39'40" N, long. 122°44'30" W; sec. 14, T 44 N, R 8 W). Named on Fort Jones (1955) and Yreka (1954) 15' quadrangles.

Copper Mountain [SISKIYOU]: *peak,* 1 mile northwest of Preston Peak (lat. 41°51' N, long. 123°36'40" W). Altitude 6334 feet. Named on Preston Peak (1982) 7.5' quadrangle. Called Copper Peak on Preston Peak (1922) 30' quadrangle.

Copper Peak: see **Copper Mountain** [SISKIYOU].

Coquette Falls [SISKIYOU]: *waterfall,* 14 miles north-northwest of McCloud (lat. 41°26'50" N, long. 122°12'50" W; sec. 32, T 42 N, R 3 W). Named on Shasta (1954) 15' quadrangle.

Coram [SHASTA]: *locality,* 2.5 miles northwest of Summit City along Southern Pacific Railroad (lat. 40°42'40" N, long. 122°26'25" W; near NW cor. sec. 21, T 33 N, R 5 W). Named on Shasta Dam (1956) 7.5' quadrangle, which shows Balaklala mine located 3 miles west of Coram (near S line sec. 12, T 33 N, R 6 W). Postal authorities established Coram post office in 1906 and discontinued it in 1922 (Frickstad, p. 179). The name recalls Joseph Coram, who had an interest in Balaklala mine and smelter (Steger, p. 26). California Mining Bureau's (1909b) map shows a place called Kimberly located 6 miles by stage line northwest of Coram. Postal authorities established Kimberly post office in 1907 and discontinued it in 1913; the name was for the owner of Balaklala Consolidated Mining Company—the post office was on company property (Salley, p. 111).

Corbett: see **Dorris** [SISKIYOU].

Corbin Creek [GLENN]: *stream,* flows 5.5 miles to Lake County 11 miles south-southwest of the village of Elk Creek (lat. 39°32'55" N, long. 122°44'05" W; at W line sec. 35, T 20 N, R 8 W). Named on Felkner Hill (1968) 7.5' quadrangle. North Fork enters from the north 11 miles west-southwest of the village of Elk Creek near Glenn-Lake County line; it is 5 miles long and is named on Felkner Hill (1968) 7.5' quadrangle.

Cordelia: see **Burts Ferry** [BUTTE].

Corduroy: see **The Corduroy** [SHASTA].

Corey Peak [SISKIYOU]: *peak,* 17 miles east-southeast of Etna on Siskiyou-Trinity County line (lat. 41°19'45" N, long. 122°36'10" W; sec. 18, T 40 N, R 6 W). Altitude 7737 feet. Named on China Mountain (1955) 15' quadrangle.

Cornaz Lake [SHASTA]: *intermittent lake,* 9 miles southeast of Burney (lat. 40°47'25" N, long. 121°32'35" W; sec. 20, T 34 N, R 4 E). Named on Burney (1957) 15' quadrangle. The name recalls Julius Cornaz, who came to Shasta County in 1858 and was the third settler in the neighborhood of Burney; the feature is called Lake Freanor on a map of 1853 (Steger, p. 26).

Cornaz Peak [SHASTA]: *peak,* 9 miles southeast of Burney (lat. 40°48'15" N, long. 121°32'30" W; near E line sec. 17, T 34 N, R 4 E); the peak is less than 1 mile north of Cornaz Lake. Named on Burney (1957) 15' quadrangle.

Cornaz Spring [SHASTA]: *spring,* 8.5 miles southeast of Burney (lat. 40°47'35" N, long. 121°33'20" W; at E line sec. 19, T 34 N, R 4 E); the spring is 0.5 mile west of Cornaz Lake. Named on Burney (1957) 15' quadrangle.

Cornaz Spring: see **Cornez Spring** [SHASTA].

Cornez Spring [SHASTA]: *spring,* 15 miles north of Lassen Peak (lat. 40°42'25" N, long. 121°32'55" W; sec. 20, T 33 N, R 4 E). Named on Manzanita Lake (1956) 15' quadrangle. United States Board on Geographic Names (1986a, p. 1) rejected the form "Cornaz Spring" for the name.

Corning [TEHAMA]: *town,* 17 miles south of Red Bluff (lat. 39°55'40" N, long. 122°10'45" W; around NE cor. sec. 22, T 24 N, R 3 W). Named on Corning (1951) 7.5' quadrangle. Postal authorities established Riceville post office in 1881; they moved it 1 mile east to the railroad in 1882 when they renamed it Corning (Salley, p. 184). The town incorporated in 1907. Pacific Improvement Company, a subsidiary of Central Pacific Railroad, started the community in 1882 and named it in memory of John Corning, a former railroad official (Gudde, 1949, p. 79).

Cornish Creek [SHASTA]: *stream,* flows 1 mile to Sacramento River 2.5 miles west of Summit City (lat. 40°41'40" N, long. 122°26'45" W; at W line sec. 28, T 33 N, R 5 W). Named on Shasta Dam (1956) 7.5' quadrangle.

Corral Gulch [TEHAMA]: *canyon,* drained by a stream that flows 4.5 miles to Big Salt Creek 9 miles west-northwest of Rosewood (lat. 40°20'10" N, long. 122°42'10" W; sec. 30, T 29 N, R 7 W). Named on Chanchelulla Peak (1951) and Ono (1952) 15' quadrangles.

Corral Meadow [SHASTA]: *area,* 6 miles east-southeast of Lassen Peak (lat. 40°27'40" N, long. 121°23'50" W; sec. 14, 15, T 30 N, R 5 E). Named on Mount Harkness (1956) 15' quadrangle. George La Pie built a log corral at the place (Schulz, p. 12).

Cory [GLENN]: *locality,* 3 miles northeast of Orland along Southern Pacific Railroad (lat. 39°46'05" N, long. 122°09' W; at N line sec. 13, T 22 N, R 3 W). Named on Kirkwood (1949) 7.5' quadrangle.

Cory Canyon [BUTTE]: *canyon,* drained by a stream that flows 2.5 miles to Little Dry Creek 7 miles south-southwest of Paradise (lat. 39°38'55" N, long. 121°39'35" W; sec. 29, T 21 N, R 3 E). Named on Hamlin Canyon (1951) 7.5' quadrangle.

Cosecha [BUTTE]: *locality,* 3.5 miles west-southwest of Chico along Northern Electric Railroad (lat. 39°42'50" N, long. 121°53'45" W). Named on Chico Landing (1912) 7.5' quadrangle.

Costa Gulch [SISKIYOU]: *canyon,* drained by a stream that flows 3 miles to Moffett Creek 5 miles east-northeast of Fort Jones (lat. 41°38' N, long. 122°45'10" W; sec. 27, T 44 N, R 8 W). Named on Fort Jones (1955) 15' quadrangle.

Cosy Dell [SHASTA]: *area,* 6.25 miles southwest of Schell Mountain (lat. 40°47'25" N, long. 122°36'40" W; sec. 24, T 34 N, R 7 W). Named on Schell Mountain (1950) 15' quadrangle.

Cottage Grove [SISKIYOU]: *locality,* 6 miles north-northeast of Dillon Mountain along Klamath River (lat. 41°36'10" N, long. 123°30'15" W). Site named on Dillon Mountain (1983) 7.5' quadrangle. Postal authorities established Cottage Grove post office in 1857, discontinued it in 1872, reestablished it in 1875, and discontinued it in 1898 (Frickstad, p. 186). The place was a mining camp at times from 1852 until the 1930's (Gudde, 1975, p. 83). Postal authorities established Tomar post office 25 miles south of Cottage Grove in 1892 and discontinued it in 1894 (Salley, p. 223).

Cottonwood [SHASTA]: *town,* 4.5 miles south of Anderson (lat. 40°23'15" N, long. 122°16'45" W; mainly in sec. 11, T 29 N, R 4 W); the town is on the north side of Cottonwood Creek [SHASTA-TEHAMA]. Named on Cottonwood (1965) 7.5' quadrangle. Postal authorities established Cottonwood post office in 1852 (Frickstad, p. 179). They established Elderton post office 4 miles west of Cottonwood in 1860 and discontinued it in 1862 (Salley, p. 66). They established Riley post office 20 miles southwest of Cottonwood in Tehama County in 1881 and discontinued it in 1893 (Salley, p. 185).

Cottonwood: see **Henly** [SISKIYOU].

Cottonwood Creek [BUTTE]: *stream,* flows 8 miles to a canal 8 miles west of Oroville (lat. 39°31'20" N, long. 121°42'20" W; at NW cor. sec. 12, T 19 N, R 2 E). Named on Shippee (1948) 7.5' quadrangle.

Cottonwood Creek [GLENN]: *stream,* flows 2 miles to Cold Creek 3.5 miles east-southeast of Black Butte (lat. 39°42'05" N, long. 122°48'45" W; sec. 6, T 21 N, R 8 W). Named on Plaskett Meadows (1967) 7.5' quadrangle.

Cottonwood Creek [SHASTA]:

(1) *stream,* flows 1 mile to Squaw Valley Creek [SHASTA-SISKIYOU] 8 miles north-northwest of Shoeinhorse Mountain (lat. 41°10'30" N, long. 122°08'15" W; at N line sec. 1, T 38 N, R 3 W). Named on Shoeinhorse Mountain (1954) 15' quadrangle.

(2) *stream,* flows 2 miles to Sacramento River 2.5 miles west-northwest of Summit City (lat. 40°42'10" N, long. 122°26'50" W; near E line sec. 20, T 33 N, R 5 W). Named on Shasta Dam (1956) 7.5' quadrangle.

Cottonwood Creek [SHASTA-TEHAMA]: *stream,* formed by the confluence of Middle Fork and North Fork 7.5 miles southeast of Ono, flows 20 miles to Sacramento River nearly 3 miles south of Balls Ferry (lat. 40°22'40" N, long. 122°11'55" W). Named on Balls Ferry (1965), Cottonwood (1965), Hooker (1965), Mitchell Gulch (1965), and Olinda (1964) 7.5' quadrangles. The stream forms part of Shasta-Tehama County line. Middle Fork, which also forms part of Shasta-Tehama County line, is 41 miles long and is named on Chanchelulla Peak (1951), Dubakella Mountain (1954), and Ono (1952) 15' quadrangles. United States Board on Geographic Names (1983b, p. 6) rejected the name "Cottonwood Creek" for Middle Fork. California Mining Bureau's (1917b) map shows a place called Middlefork located along Middle Fork Cottonwood Creek about halfway between Knob and Beegum. Postal authorities established Middlefork post office in 1888 and discontinued it in 1898 (Frickstad, p. 181). North Fork is 25 miles long and is named on Ono (1952) 15' quadrangle, and on Shasta Bally (1978) 7.5' quadrangle. Moon Fork joins North Fork in Rainbow Lake; it is 5.5 miles long and is named on Shasta Bally (1978) 7.5' quadrangle. South Fork, which is entirely in Tehama County, enters the main stream from the southwest 5 miles north of Hooker; it is 60 miles long and is named on Yolla Bolly (1954) 15' quadrangle, and on Blossom (1952), Cold Fork (1967), Hooker (1965), Mitchell Gulch (1965), Oxbow Bridge (1967) and Raglin Ridge (1967) 7.5' quadrangles.

Cottonwood Creek [SISKIYOU]:

(1) *stream,* heads in the State of Oregon and flows 11 miles in Siskiyou County to Klamath River 1.5 miles southeast of Hornbrook (lat. 41°53'20" N, long. 122°32'35" W; sec. 28, T 47 N, R 6 W). Named on Hornbrook (1955) 15' quadrangle. West Fork enters from the southwest 6 miles northwest of Hornbrook; it is 5 miles long and is named on Hornbrook (1955) 15' quadrangle. Whitney (p. 353) used the name "Cottonwood Valley" for the valley of the stream.

(2) *stream,* flows 5 miles to Moffett Creek 11 miles south-southwest of Yreka (lat. 41°35'10" N, long. 122°43'10" W; sec. 12, T 43 N, R 8 W). Named on Yreka (1954) 15' quadrangle.

(3) *stream,* flows 2.5 miles to Oklahoma Flat 7.5 miles southeast of Dorris (lat. 41°54'30" N, long. 121°47'40" W; near N line sec. 19, T 47 N, R 2 E). Named on Dorris (1950) 15' quadrangle.

Cottonwood Creek [TEHAMA]: *stream,* flows 9 miles to Little Antelope Creek 12.5 miles east of Red Bluff (lat. 40°11'55" N, long. 122°00'25" W; near N line sec. 17, T 27 N, R 1 W). Named on Panther Spring (1953) 15' quadrangle, and on Tuscan Springs (1951) 7.5' quadrangle.

Cottonwood Creek: see **Little Cottonwood Creek** [BUTTE].

Cottonwood Glade [GLENN]: *area,* 3.5 miles east-southeast of Black Butte (lat. 39°42' N, long. 122°48'35" W; near S line sec. 6, T 21 N, R 8 W); the place is at the mouth of Cottonwood Creek. Named on Plaskett Meadows (1967) 7.5' quadrangle. Hull Mountain (1952) 15' quadrangle shows Cottonwood Glade Campground at the site.

Cottonwood Glade Campground: see **Cottonwood Glade** [GLENN].

Cottonwood Gulch [SHASTA]: *canyon,* drained by a stream that flows 2 miles to South Cow Creek 3 miles south of Whitmore (lat. 40°35'15" N, long. 121°55'30" W; sec. 36, T 32 N, R 1 W). Named on Whitmore (1956) 15' quadrangle.

Cottonwood Peak [SISKIYOU]: *peak,* 5 miles west-southwest of Hornbrook (lat. 41°53'15" N, long. 122°38'40" W; at S line sec. 27, T 47 N, R 7 W). Named on Hornbrook (1955) 15' quadrangle. United States Board on Geographic Names (1967b, p. 3) approved the name "Little Cottonwood Peak" for a feature located 2 miles south of Cottonwood Peak (lat. 41°51'25" N, long. 122°38'42" W; sec. 10, T 46 N, R. 7 W).

Cottonwood Spring [GLENN]: *spring,* 12 miles northwest of the village of Elk Creek (lat. 39°43'35" N, long. 122°41'45" W). Named on Alder Springs (1967) 7.5' quadrangle.

Cottonwood Spring [TEHAMA]: *spring,* 4.25 miles north-northeast of Dales (lat. 40°22'20" N, long. 122°03' W; near N line sec. 14, T 29 N, R 2 W). Named on Dales (1965) 7.5' quadrangle.

Cottonwood Spring Gulch [TEHAMA]: *canyon,* drained by a stream that flows 1 mile to Green Gulch 7.5 miles east-southeast of Beegum Peak (lat. 40°15'50" N, long. 122°45'30" W; sec. 22, T 28 N, R 8 W). Named on Chanchelulla Peak (1951) 15' quadrangle.

Cottonwood Valley: see **Cottonwood Creek** [SISKIYOU] (1).

Cougar [SISKIYOU]: *locality,* 19 miles south-southwest of Macdoel along Southern Pacific Railroad (lat. 41°35' N, long. 122°11' W; near W line sec. 10, T 43 N, R 3 W). Named on The Whaleback (1954) 15' quadrangle. Averill's (1935) map shows a place called Pineland located just south of Couger.

Cougar Butte [SISKIYOU]: *crater,* 8.5 miles northeast of Medicine Lake (lat. 41°39'20" N, long. 121°28'05" W; on E line sec. 14, T 44 N, R 4 E). Named on Timber Mountain (1952) 15' quadrangle.

Cougar Creek [SISKIYOU]: *stream,* flows 2.5 miles to Elk Creek 8.5 miles north of Ukonom Lake (lat. 41°42'10" N, long. 123°21'10" W). Named on Huckleberry Mountain (1980) 7.5' quadrangle.

Cougar Gulch [SISKIYOU]: *canyon,* drained by a stream that flows 1 mile to Klamath River 11 miles east-southeast of Condrey Mountain (lat. 41°51'55" N, long. 122°47'25" W; near W line sec. 4, T 46 N, R 8 W). Named on Condrey Mountain (1955) 15' quadrangle.

Counts Gulch [SISKIYOU]: *canyon,* drained by a stream that flows 1.5 miles to Whites Gulch (1) 2.5 miles east of Sawyers Bar (lat. 41°17'35" N, long. 123°04'55" W). Named on Tanners Peak (1977) 7.5' quadrangle.

Cousins Gulch [SISKIYOU]: *canyon,* drained by a stream that flows 0.5 mile to Humbug Creek 15 miles southeast of Condrey Mountain (lat. 41°46'40" N, long. 122°47'20" W; sec. 5, T 45 N, R 8 W). Named on Condrey Mountain (1955) 15' quadrangle.

Coutolenc [BUTTE]: *locality,* 8.5 miles northeast of Paradise (lat. 39°52'25" N, long. 121°34'40" W; near SE cor. sec. 1, T 23 N, R 3 E). Named on Paradise East (1980) 7.5' quadrangle. Chico (1895) 30' quadrangle shows Old Lovelock at or near the place. Postal authorities established Coutolenc post office in 1890 and discontinued it in 1937 (Frickstad, p. 9). The name commemorates Eugene Fortune Coutolenc, who came to the site about 1885 and started a general mercantile and meat packing business that became the nucleus of the community (Hanna, p. 75). F.D. Dunn (p. 28) gave the alternate names "Musselmans," "Brownharts," and "Old Lovelock" for the place. The name "Lovelock" recalls George Lovelock, who had a hotel and store 5 miles above Dogtown in 1855 (Wells and Chambers, p. 260).

Cove: see **The Cove** [SHASTA].

Cove Creek [SHASTA]: *stream,* flows 1 mile to Pit River 17 miles south-southeast of Lamoine (lat. 40°45'50" N, long. 122°16'10" W; sec. 36, T 34 N, R 4 W). Named on Lamoine (1946) 15' quadrangle. Water of McClure River Arm Shasta Lake now floods the canyon of the stream

Covertsburg: see **Red Bluff** [TEHAMA].

Covey: see **Dan Covey Butte** [SHASTA].

Cow Camp [TEHAMA]: *locality,* 3 miles south of Ball Mountain (lat. 39°53'20" N, long. 122°46'30" W; near SE cor. sec. 32, T 24 N, R 8 W). Named on Ball Mountain (1967) 7.5' quadrangle.

Cow Canyon [SHASTA]: *canyon,* drained by a stream that flows 3 miles to Pit River 12.5 miles east-southeast of Bollibokka Mountain (lat. 40°50'45" N, long. 122°00'25" W; near W line sec. 32, T 35 N, R 1 W). Named on Bollibokka Mountain (1957) 15' quadrangle.

Cow Creek [SHASTA]: *stream,* formed by the confluence of Old Cow Creek and South Cow Creek, flows 14 miles to Sacramento River nearly 4 miles north-northwest of Balls Ferry (lat. 40°27'50" N, long. 121°13'45" W; sec. 8, T 30 N, R 3 W). Named on Balls Ferry (1965) and Palo Cedro (1965) 7.5' quadrangles. Fremont named the stream in 1846 for wild cattle (Steger, p. 26). On Lassen Peak (1894) 1° quadrangle, present Dry Clover Creek is called North Fork Cow Creek, and present South Cow Creek is called South Fork Cow Creek. D.D. Harrill and Company received a license in 1852 to operate a ferry, known as Emigrant Ferry, on Sacramento River at the mouth of Cow Creek (Amesbury, p. 35).

Cow Creek [SISKIYOU]:

(1) *stream,* flows 1.25 miles to North Russian Creek 6.5 miles northeast of Sawyers Bar (lat. 41°21'35" N, long. 123°01'55" W). Named on Tanners Peak (1977) 7.5' quadrangle.

(2) *stream,* heads in the State of Oregon and flows 1 mile in Siskiyou County to join Grouse Creek (1) and form Beaver Creek (1) 11.5 miles east-northeast of Condrey Mountain (lat. 41°59'45" N, long. 122°46'10" W; sec. 21, T 48 N, R 8 W). Named on Condrey Mountain (1955) 15' quadrangle.

(3) *stream,* flows 3 miles to McCloud River [SHASTA-SISKIYOU] 2.5 miles south-southeast of Bartle (lat. 41°13'20" N, long. 121°48'30" W; near NW cor. sec. 13, T 39 N, R 1 E). Named on Big Bend (1961) 15' quadrangle.

Cow Creek: see **Little Cow Creek** [SHASTA]; **Old Cow Creek** [SHASTA]; **South Cow Creek** [SHASTA].

Cow Creek Forebay [SHASTA]: *lake,* 300 feet long, 9 miles east-northeast of Millville (lat. 40°34'50" N, long. 122°00'40" W; near SE cor. sec. 31, T 32 N, R 1 W). Named on Millville (1953) 15' quadrangle.

Cow Creek Meadows [SHASTA]: *area,* 15 miles northwest of Lassen Peak (lat. 40°39'45" N, long. 121°40'15" W; on W line sec. 5, T 32 N, R 3 E); the place is along Old Cow Creek. Named on Manzanita Lake (1956) 15' quadrangle. United States Board on Geographic Names (1986c, p. 4) approved the name "Old Cow Creek Meadows" for the place.

Cow Gulch [SHASTA]: *canyon,* drained by a stream that flows 3.5 miles to Middle Fork Cottonwood Creek [SHASTA-TEHAMA] 2 miles south-southwest of Arbuckle Mountain (lat. 40°22'40" N, long. 122°53'15" W; sec. 9, T 29 N, R 9 W). Named on Chanchelulla Peak (1951) 15' quadrangle.

Cow Gulch: see **Little Cow Gulch** [SHASTA].

Cowslip Campground [TEHAMA]: *locality,* 2.5 miles north-northwest of Mineral (lat. 40°22'45" N, long. 121°37' W; near N line sec. 14, T 29 N, R 3 E). Named on Lassen Peak (1956) 15' quadrangle.

Cox Glade [TEHAMA]: *area,* 3.5 miles northwest of Tomhead Mountain (lat. 40°10'35" N, long. 122°51'15" W; near W line sec. 29, T 27 N, R 9 W). Named on Yolla Bolly (1954) 15' quadrangle.

Coxs Bend [GLENN]: *bend,* 1 mile north-northwest of Butte City along Sacramento River (lat. 39°28'15" N, long. 121°59'30" W). Named on Butte City (1912) 7.5' quadrangle. Called Cox Bend on Marysville (1895) 30' quadrangle.

Coyote Creek [TEHAMA]: *stream,* flows 18 miles to Oat Creek 1.5 miles north-northeast of Gerber (lat. 40°04'40" N, long. 122°08'10" W). Named on Gerber (1950), Henleyville (1967), and West of Gerber (1951) 7.5' quadrangles.

Coyote Creek: see **Big Bend Creek** [SISKIYOU].

Coyote Flat [SHASTA]: *area,* 9 miles southeast of Whitmore (lat. 40°32'15" N, long. 121°47'30" W; sec. 18, T 31 N, R 2 E). Named on Whitmore (1956) 15' quadrangle.

Coyote Flat Reservoir [SHASTA]: *intermittent lake,* 550 feet long, 4 miles east-northeast of Burney Falls (lat. 41°02'20" N, long. 121°15'20" W; sec. 14, T 37 N, R 3 E). Named on Pondosa (1961) 15' quadrangle.

Coyote Gap [BUTTE]: *pass,* 1.5 miles east of Pulga (lat. 39°47'55" N, long. 121°22'40" W; near E line sec. 35, T 23 N, R 5 E). Named on Pulga (1979) 7.5' quadrangle.

Coyote Gulch [SISKIYOU]:

(1) *canyon,* drained by a stream that flows about 1 mile to Indian Creek (3) nearly 5 miles north of Fort Jones (lat. 41°40'35" N, long. 122°50'55" W; sec. 11, T 44 N, R 9 W). Named on Fort Jones (1955) 15' quadrangle.

(2) *canyon,* drained by a stream that flows 2.5 miles to Angel Creek 6.25 miles southeast of McCloud (lat. 41°12'05" N, long. 122°02'40" W; sec. 26, T 39 N, R 2 W). Named on Shoeinhorse Mountain (1954) 15' quadrangle.

Coyote Hill: see **Dorris** [SISKIYOU].

Coyote Peak [SHASTA]: *peak,* 3 miles east-southeast of Shoeinhorse Mountain (lat. 41°03'10" N, long. 122°01' W). Named on Shoeinhorse Mountain (1954) 15' quadrangle.

Coyote Peak [SISKIYOU]: *peak,* 25 miles south of Etna on Siskiyou-Trinity County line (lat. 41°05'45" N, long. 122°58'10" W). Named on Coffee Creek (1955) 15' quadrangle.

Coyote Ridge: see **Dorris** [SISKIYOU].

Coyote Spring [SHASTA]: *spring,* 17 miles north-northeast of Lassen Peak (lat. 40°42'20" N, long. 121°22'15" W; sec. 24, T 33 N, R 5 E). Named on Prospect Peak (1957) 15' quadrangle.

Cracker Canyon [TEHAMA]: *canyon,* drained by a stream that flows 1 mile to South Fork Cottonwood Creek [SHASTA-TEHAMA] 2.25 miles north-northeast of Wakefield Flat (lat. 40°09'15" N, long. 122°37' W; sec. 35, T 27 N, R 7 W). Named on Cold Fork (1967) and Oxbow Bridge (1967) 7.5' quadrangles.

Cracker Meadows [SISKIYOU]: *area,* 3.5 miles north-northwest of Preston Peak (lat. 41°52'40" N, long. 123°38'20" W). Named on Broken Rib Mountain (1982) 7.5' quadrangle.

Craddock Gulch [SHASTA]: *canyon,* drained by a stream that flows nearly 1 mile to Whiskeytown Lake 7.5 miles southeast of the village of French Gulch (lat. 40°37'35" N, long. 122°31'55" W; sec. 15, T 32 N, R 6 W).

Named on Whiskeytown (1979) 7.5' quadrangle.

Craggy: see **Paradise Craggy** [SISKIYOU].

Craggy Mountain [SISKIYOU]: *peak*, 12.5 miles southwest of Hornbrook (lat. 41°48'45" N, long. 122°44'50" W). Altitude 5575 feet. Named on Condrey Mountain (1955) and Hornbrook (1955) 15' quadrangles.

Craggy Peak [SISKIYOU]: *peak*, 15 miles south-southeast of Etna (lat. 41°15'30" N, long. 122°46'45" W; on E line sec. 9, T 39 N, R 8 W). Altitude 8098 feet. Named on Etna (1955) 15' quadrangle. Called Scott Mt. on Shasta (1894) 1° quadrangle. Gudde (1949, p. 36) noted that the feature had the old name "Bolivar" from the South American leader, Simon Bolivar. Etna (1934) 30' quadrangle shows Bolivar lookout on the peak.

Crags Lake [SHASTA]: *lake*, 400 feet long, 3.25 miles north-northwest of Lassen Peak in Chaos Crater (lat. 40°32' N, long. 121°31'45" W; sec. 16, T 31 N, R 4 E); the lake is at the northeast end of Chaos Crags. Named on Manzanita Lake (1956) 15' quadrangle.

Craig [BUTTE]:

(1) *locality*, 3 miles east-southeast of Bidwell Bar along Feather River Railway (lat. 39°32'50" N, long. 121°23'10" W; near W line sec. 35, T 20 N, R 5 E). Named on Big Bend Mountain (1948) 15' quadrangle.

(2) *locality*, nearly 2 miles west-northwest of Honcut along Western Pacific Railroad (lat. 39°20'15" N, long. 121°33'50" W; near S line sec. 7, T 17 N, R 4 E). Named on Honcut (1952) 7.5' quadrangle. The place first was called Marston, for a railroad official, and then named Craig in 1911 to honor another railroad official (Dunn, F.D., p. 29, 66).

Craig Cave [SISKIYOU]: *cave*, 13 miles north-northeast of Medicine Lake (lat. 41°43'10" N, long. 121°27'15" W; near NE cor. sec. 25, T 45 N, R 4 E). Named on Timber Mountain (1952) 15' quadrangle.

Craig Creek [TEHAMA]: *stream*, diverges from Antelope Creek and flows 1.5 miles to Sacramento River 3.5 miles east-southeast of Red Bluff (lat. 40°08'20" N, long. 122°08'25" W). Named on Red Bluff East (1951) 7.5' quadrangle.

Crain Mill [BUTTE]: *locality*, 3.5 miles south-southwest of Pulga (lat. 39°45'40" N, long. 121°29'30" W; sec. 14, T 22 N, R 4 E). Site named on Pulga (1979) 7.5' quadrangle.

Cramer Spring [SISKIYOU]: *spring*, 12 miles northwest of Bartle (lat. 41°23'45" N, long. 121°57'30" W; near SW cor. sec. 15, T 41 N, R 1 W). Named on Bartle (1961) 15' quadrangle.

Cram Gulch [SISKIYOU]: *canyon*, 4.5 miles long, opens into Shasta Valley 8 miles south-southeast of Yreka (lat. 41°37'45" N, long. 122°34' W; sec. 29, T 44 N, R 6 W). Named on Yreka (1954) 15' quadrangle.

Crane Creek: see **Big Crane Creek** [TEHAMA]; **Little Crane Creek** [TEHAMA].

Crane Mountain [SHASTA]: *peak*, 3.5 miles east of Lamoine (lat. 40°58' N, long. 122°22' W; sec. 19, T 36 N, R 4 W). Named on Lamoine (1957) 15' quadrangle. On Lamoine (1946) 15' quadrangle, the name applies to the ridge on which present Crane Mountain is the high point.

Crane Valley [BUTTE]: *valley*, 11 miles north of Pulga along Big Kimshew Creek (lat. 39°57'40" N, long. 121°26'50" W). Named on Kimshew Point (1979) 7.5' quadrangle.

Cranston Knob: see **Hardin Butte** [SISKIYOU].

Crapo Creek [SISKIYOU]: *stream*, flows 7.5 miles to Salmon River 3 miles northwest of Forks of Salmon (lat. 41°17'35" N, long. 123°21'40" W); the stream heads near Crapo Meadows. Named on Forks of Salmon (1978) 7.5' quadrangle.

Crapo Meadows [SISKIYOU]: *area*, 7.5 miles north-northeast of Forks of Salmon (lat. 41°21'35" N, long. 123°16'30" W); the place is near the head of Crapo Creek. Named on Forks of Salmon (1978) 7.5' quadrangle.

Crapo Mountain [SISKIYOU]: *peak*, 6 miles northwest of Sawyers Bar (lat. 41°21'05" N, long. 123°13'10" W); the peak is at the northeast end of Yellow Jacket Ridge. Altitude 6885 feet. Named on Sawyers Bar (1979) 7.5' quadrangle. The whole of present Yellow Jacket Ridge is called Crapo Mountain on Sawyers Bar (1923) 30' quadrangle.

Crater Butte [SHASTA]: *crater*, 8 miles east of Mount Lassen (lat. 40°29'20" N, long. 121°21'20" W; sec. 6, T 30 N, R 6 E). Named on Mount Harkness (1956) 15' quadrangle, which shows a lake in the crater. The lake is called Crater Pool (Schulz, p. 13).

Crater Creek [SISKIYOU]: *stream*, flows 3 miles to East Fork Scott River 14 miles east-southeast of Etna (lat. 41°24'10" N, long. 122°38'15" W; sec. 15, T 41 N, R 7 W). Named on China Mountain (1955) 15' quadrangle.

Crater Lake [SISKIYOU]: *lake*, 700 feet long, 17 miles east-southeast of Etna (lat. 41°23' N, long. 122°34'45" W; sec. 19, T 41 N, R 6 W); the lake is above the head of Crater Creek. Named on China Mountain (1955) 15' quadrangle.

Crater Lake: see **Little Crater Lake** [SISKIYOU].

Crater Peak [SHASTA]: *peak*, 16 miles north-northwest of Lassen Peak (lat. 40°41'50" N, long. 121°37' W; near S line sec. 22, T 33 N, R 3 E). Altitude 8677 feet. Named on Manzanita Lake (1956) 15' quadrangle.

Crater Pool: see **Crater Butte** [SHASTA].

Crawfish Gulch [SISKIYOU]: *canyon*, drained by a stream that flows nearly 1 mile to Horse Creek (2) 6 miles east-northeast of the village of Seiad Valley (lat. 41°51'35" N, long. 123°05'15" W; sec. 2, T 46 N, R 11 W). Named on Hamburg (1980) 7.5' quadrangle.

Crawford Creek [SISKIYOU]:

(1) *stream*, flows 2 miles to Klamath River 7.25 miles northwest of Ukonom Lake (lat. 41°38'55" N, long. 123°27'45" W). Named on Clear Creek (1981) 7.5' quadrangle.

(2) *stream*, flows 7.5 miles to South Fork Salmon River near Cecilville (lat. 41°08'20" N, long. 123°08'20" W). Named on Cecilville (1979) and Grasshopper Ridge (1979) 7.5' quadrangles. West Fork enters from the north 3 miles upstream from the mouth of the main stream; it is 2.5 miles long and is named on Cecilville (1979) 7.5' quadrangle.

Crazy Canyon [TEHAMA]: *canyon*, drained by a stream that flows 4.25 miles to South Fork Antelope Creek 2 miles west-southwest of Panther Spring (lat. 40°14'25" N, long. 121°48'20" W; sec. 36, T 28 N, R 1 E). Named on Panther Spring (1953) 15' quadrangle.

Creole Belle Gulch [SISKIYOU]: *canyon*, drained by a stream that flows 1 mile to South Russian Creek nearly 7 miles east of Sawyers Bar (lat. 41°18'30" N, long. 123°00'05" W). Named on Tanners Peak (1977) 7.5' quadrangle.

Crescent Butte [SISKIYOU]: *hill*, 10.5 miles north-northeast of Medicine Lake (lat. 41°43'05" N, long. 121°30'50" W; sec. 28, T 45 N, R 4 E). Named on Medicine Lake (1952) 15' quadrangle.

Crescent Cliff [SHASTA]: *relief feature*, 1.25 miles west of Lassen Peak (lat. 40°29'15" N, long. 121°31'45" W; near S line sec. 33, T 31 N, R 4 E). Named on Lassen Peak (1956) 15' quadrangle.

Crescent Crater [SHASTA]: *relief feature*, 1.25 miles north-northeast of Lassen Peak (lat. 40°30'20" N, long. 121°29'35" W; sec. 26, T 31 N, R 4 E). Named on Prospect Peak (1957) 15' quadrangle.

Crescent Falls: see **Mossbrae Falls** [SISKIYOU].

Cresta [BUTTE]: *locality*, 3.5 miles northeast of Pulga along Western Pacific Railroad (lat. 39°50'35" N, long. 121°24'15" W; sec. 15, T 23 N, R 5 E). Named on Pulga (1979) 7.5' quadrangle.

Creums Lake: see **Crumes Lake** [SISKIYOU].

Croaks Gulch [SISKIYOU]: *canyon*, drained by a stream that flows 0.5 mile to North Fork Salmon River 0.5 mile west of Sawyers Bar (lat. 41°18'05" N, long. 123°08'20" W). Named on Sawyers Bar (1979) 7.5' quadrangle.

Cronan Gulch [SISKIYOU]: *canyon*, drained by a stream that flows 2 miles to North Fork Salmon River 3.25 miles west-northwest of Sawyers Bar (lat. 41°18'50" N, long. 123°11'25" W). Named on Sawyers Bar (1979) 7.5' quadrangle. Called Garden Gulch on Sawyers Bar (1923) 30' quadrangle, but United States Board on Geographic Names (1960a, p. 13) rejected this name.

Cronan Gulch: see **Boulder Gulch** [SISKIYOU].

Croney Creek [TEHAMA]: *stream*, flows 3.5 miles to Thomes Creek 5.5 miles northwest of Ball Mountain (lat. 39°58'40" N, long. 122°52' W; sec. 33, T 25 N, R 9 W). Named on Ball Mountain (1967) and Buck Rock (1967) 7.5' quadrangles.

Croney Ridge [TEHAMA]: *ridge*, east-trending, 3.25 miles long, 7.5 miles west-northwest of Ball Mountain (lat. 39°59'10" N, long. 122°54'10" W); the ridge is north of Croney Creek. Named on Buck Rock (1967) 7.5' quadrangle.

Crook: see **Fort Crook**, under **Fall River Valley** [SHASTA].

Crooked Bar [BUTTE]: *locality*, 4.25 miles east-northeast of the village of Brush Creek along Middle Fork Feather River (lat. 39°42'50" N, long. 121°15'55" W; near SE cor. sec. 35, T 22 N, R 6 E). Named on Brush Creek (1970) 7.5' quadrangle.

Crooked Gulch [SISKIYOU]: *canyon*, drained by a stream that flows 2.5 miles to Moffett Creek 9 miles south-southwest of Yreka (lat. 41°37'10" N, long. 122°43' W; sec. 36, T 44 N, R 8 W). Named on Yreka (1954) 15' quadrangle.

Crooker Gulch [SISKIYOU]: *canyon*, drained by a stream that flows nearly 1 mile to Walla Walla Creek 6.5 miles north-northwest of Fort Jones (lat. 41°42'05" N, long. 122°52'35" W; near SW cor. sec. 34, T 45 N, R 9 W). Named on Fort Jones (1955) 15' quadrangle.

Crooks Creek [SHASTA]: *stream*, flows 2.25 miles to Squaw Creek (2) 7 miles east of Bollibokka Mountain (lat. 40°56'30" N, long. 122°04'50" W; sec. 34, T 36 N, R 2 W). Named on Bollibokka Mountain (1957) 15' quadrangle.

Crook Springs [SHASTA]: *springs*, 9.5 miles south-southeast of Whitmore (lat. 40°30'55" N, long. 121°49'10" W; near NW cor. sec. 25, T 31 N, R 1 E). Named on Whitmore (1956) 15' quadrangle.

Crouch: see **Chico** [BUTTE].

Crouch Ravine [BUTTE]: *canyon*, drained by a stream that flows 4 miles to lowlands 5.5 miles southeast of Chico (lat. 39°40'35" N, long. 121°45'50" W). Named on Chico (1948) and Hamlin Canyon (1951) 7.5' quadrangles.

Crow Creek [SHASTA]: *stream*, flows 7 miles to Roaring River 7.25 miles southeast of Ono (lat. 40°23'50" N, long. 122°31'15" W; sec. 3, T 29 N, R 6 W). Named on Ono (1952) 15' quadrangle. Isaac Crow lived by the stream in the late 1860's (Steger, p. 27).

Crow Flat [SHASTA]: *area*, 10 miles south-southwest of Ono along Middle

Fork Cottonwood Creek [SHASTA-TEHAMA] (lat. 40°20' N, long. 122°40'10" W; sec. 28, 29, T 29 N, R 7 W). Named on Ono (1952) 15' quadrangle.

Crowfoot Point [TEHAMA]: *locality,* 4.5 miles west of Paskenta (lat. 39°52'40" N, long. 122°37'35" W; near E line sec. 3, T 23 N, R 7 W). Named on Riley Ridge (1967) 7.5' quadrangle.

Crow Gulch [SHASTA]: *canyon,* drained by a stream that flows nearly 4 miles to Beegum Creek [SHASTA-TEHAMA] 5 miles southeast of Arbuckle Mountain (lat. 40°21'20" N, long. 122°47'30" W; near N line sec. 20, T 29 N, R 8 W). Named on Chanchelulla Peak (1951) 15' quadrangle. West Fork branches west 0.5 mile above the mouth of the main canyon; it is 2.5 miles long and is named on Chanchelulla Peak (1951) 15' quadrangle.

Crow Gulch [TEHAMA]: *canyon,* drained by a stream that flows 1.5 miles to Middle Fork Cottonwood Creek [SHASTA-TEHAMA] 7.5 miles northwest of Rosewood (lat. 40°19'45" N, long. 122°40'20" W; at NE cor. sec. 32, T 29 N, R 7 W). Named on Ono (1952) 15' quadrangle.

Croy: see **Croy Gulch** [SISKIYOU].

Croy Gulch [SISKIYOU]: *canyon,* drained by a stream that flows 1.25 miles to Klamath River 7 miles southwest of Hornbrook (lat. 41°50' N, long. 122°38'20" W; near W line sec. 14, T 46 N, R 7 W). Named on Hornbrook (1955) 15' quadrangle. Postal authorities established Croy post office 9 miles southwest of Hornbrook in 1907 and discontinued it in 1913; the name was for Jefferson P. Croy, first postmaster (Salley, p. 53).

Crumbaugh Lake [SHASTA]: *lake,* 1100 feet long, 3 miles south-southeast of Lassen Peak (lat. 40°26'50" N, long. 121°29'20" W; sec. 24, T 30 N, R 4 E). Named on Mount Harkness (1956) 15' quadrangle. Called Crumbo Lake on Lassen Peak (1894) 1° quadrangle, but United States Board on Geographic Names (1933, p. 246) rejected this name for the feature. Steger (p. 27) associated the name with Peter C. Crumbaugh, a pioneer sheepman.

Crumbo Lake: see **Crumbaugh Lake** [SHASTA].

Crumes Lake [SISKIYOU]: *intermittent lake,* 3600 feet long, 3.5 miles north-northeast of Mount Dome (lat. 41°49'40" N, long. 121°37'15" W; sec. 15, T 46 N, R 3 E). Named on Mount Dome (1950) 15' quadrangle. United States Board on Geographic Names (1987a, p. 2) rejected the name "Creums Lake" for the feature.

Crystal Clear Creek [SISKIYOU]: *stream,* flows 1 mile to Cold Springs Creek 11 miles north of Sawyers Bar (lat. 41°26'30" N, long. 123°10'15" W). Named on English Peak (1977) 7.5' quadrangle.

Crystal Creek [SHASTA]: *stream,* flows 8 miles to Willow Creek (4) 2.5 miles south of the village of French Gulch (lat. 40°40'05" N, long. 122°38'40" W; near S line sec. 34, T 33 N, R 7 W). Named on French Gulch (1979) and Shasta Bally (1978) 7.5' quadrangles. Steger (p. 27) noted that quartz crystals have been found along the stream.

Crystal Creek [SISKIYOU]: *stream,* flows 3 miles to Scott Valley 2.25 miles north-northwest of Etna (lat. 41°29'20" N, long. 122°54'15" W; sec. 17, T 42 N, R 9 W). Named on Etna (1955) 15' quadrangle.

Crystal Creek: see **Etna** [SISKIYOU].

Crystal Creek Conservation Camp [SHASTA]: *locality,* 5 miles south-southwest of the village of French Gulch (lat. 40°38'05" N, long. 122°40'30" W; near NE cor. sec. 17, T 32 N, R 7 W); the place is along Crystal Creek. Named on French Gulch (1979) 7.5' quadrangle.

Crystal Creek Rock [SISKIYOU]: *relief feature,* 2.25 miles north-northwest of Etna (lat. 41°29'10" N, long. 122°54'55" W; at E line sec. 18, T 42 N, R 9 W); the feature is by Crystal Creek. Named on Etna (1955) 15' quadrangle.

Crystal Hill [BUTTE]: *peak,* 6 miles northwest of Forbestown (lat. 39°34'05" N, long. 121°22'10" W; at W line sec. 25, T 20 N, R 5 E). Named on Forbestown (1970) 7.5' quadrangle.

Crystal Lake [SHASTA]: *lake,* 4500 feet long, 7 miles east-northeast of Burney (lat. 40°56'15" N, long. 121°33'30" W; sec. 31, 32, T 36 N, R 4 E). Named on Burney (1957) 15' quadrangle.

Crystal Lake: see **Medicine Lake** [SISKIYOU].

Crystal Springs [SHASTA]: *spring,* 7.5 miles north of Fall River Mills (lat. 41°06'45" N, long. 121°26'50" W). Named on Fall River Mills (1961) 15' quadrangle.

Crystal Springs [SISKIYOU]: *spring,* 0.5 mile southwest of Medicine Lake (lat. 41°34'20" N, long. 121°36'30" W; near NE cor. sec. 14, T 43 N, R 3 E). Named on Medicine Lake (1952) 15' quadrangle.

Cub Creek [SISKIYOU]: *stream,* flows 4.25 miles to Ukonom Creek 4 miles west of Ukonom Lake (lat. 41°34'15" N, long. 123°25'55" W). Named on Ukonom Mountain (1980) 7.5' quadrangle.

Cub Creek [TEHAMA]: *stream,* flows 5 miles to Deer Creek (2) 10.5 miles northeast of Polk Springs (lat. 40°12'15" N, long. 121°30'30" W; at S line sec. 10, T 27 N, R 4 E). Named on Butte Meadows (1958) and Jonesville (1958) 15' quadrangles.

Cub Hill [SISKIYOU]: *hill,* 14 miles north of Bartle (lat. 41°28' N, long. 121°47'30" W; near W line sec. 19, T 42 N, R 2 E). Altitude 5453 feet. Named on Bartle (1961) 15' quadrangle.

Cub Spring [SISKIYOU]: *spring,* 2.5 miles southeast of Bartle (lat. 41°13'30" N, long. 121°46'35" W; sec. 7, T 39 N, R 2 W). Named on Big Bend (1961) 15' quadrangle.

Cuddihy Fork: see **Wooley Creek** [SISKIYOU].

Cuddihy Lakes [SISKIYOU]: *lakes,* largest 1200 feet long, 3 miles southeast of Ukonom Lake (lat. 41°32'50" N, long. 123°19'15" W); the lakes are near the head of Cuddihy Fork [of North Fork Wooley Creek]. Named on Ukonom Lake (1980) 7.5' quadrangle.

Cuddihy Valley [SISKIYOU]: *canyon,* 3.25 miles southeast of Ukonom Lake (lat. 41°33' N, long. 123°18'30" W); the canyon is along Cuddihy Fork [of North Fork Wooley Creek]. Named on Ukonom Lake (1980) 7.5' quadrangle.

Cuddleback Flat [BUTTE]: *area,* 3.25 miles southeast of Butte Meadows (lat. 40°02'50" N, long. 121°30'20" W; sec. 3, T 25 N, R 4 E). Named on Butte Meadows (1958) 15' quadrangle.

Culp: see **Panorama Point** [SHASTA].

Cunningham Creek [SHASTA]: *stream,* flows 1 mile to North Fork Backbone Creek 10 miles south-southwest of Lamoine (lat. 40°50'10" N, long. 122°28'35" W; at N line sec. 6, T 34 N, R 5 W). Named on Lamoine (1957) 15' quadrangle.

Cunningham Ravine [BUTTE]: *canyon,* drained by a stream that flows 2.25 miles to Little West Fork [of West Fork Feather River] 2.25 miles west of Stirling City (lat. 39°53'55" N, long. 121°34'10" W; near S line sec. 30, T 24 N, R 4 E). Named on Stirling City (1979) 7.5' quadrangle.

Curargo: see **Motion** [SHASTA].

Curl Creek [SHASTA]: *stream,* flows 1.25 miles to McCloud River Arm Shasta Lake 14 miles southeast of Lamoine (lat. 40°48'55" N, long. 122°16'10" W; sec. 12, T 34 N, R 4 W). Named on Lamoine (1957) 15' quadrangle.

Curley Jack Campground [SISKIYOU]: *locality,* 1 mile southwest of Happy Camp along Klamath River (lat. 41°47'05" N, long. 123°23'20" W; near S line sec. 10, T 16 N, R 7 E); the place is opposite the mouth of Curly Jack Creek. Named on Happy Camp (1956) 15' quadrangle.

Curley Jack Creek [SISKIYOU]: *stream,* flows 1.25 miles to Klamath River less than 1 mile southwest of Happy Camp (lat. 41°47'10" N, long. 123°23'30" W; near S line sec. 10, T 16 N, R 7 E). Named on Happy Camp (1980) 7.5' quadrangle.

Curl Ridge [SHASTA]: *ridge,* generally north-trending, 8.5 miles long, center 4 miles east of Bollibokka Mountain (lat. 40°56'30" N, long. 122°08'30" W). Named on Bollibokka Mountain (1957) 15' quadrangle.

Curtis [SISKIYOU]: *locality,* 5 miles southeast of Bartle along McCloud River Railroad (lat. 41°12' N, long. 121°45'50" W; sec. 20, T 39 N, R 2 E). Named on Big Bend (1961) 15' quadrangle.

Curtis Lake [SHASTA]: *lake,* 250 feet long, 11 miles northeast of the village of Big Bend (lat. 41°08'45" N, long. 121°47'15" W; sec. 7, T 38 N, R 2 E). Named on Big Bend (1961) 15' quadrangle.

Curtis Meadows [SISKIYOU]: *area,* 0.5 mile southwest of Bartle along McCloud River [SHASTA-SISKIYOU] (lat. 41°15' N, long. 121°49'30" W; on E line sec. 3, T 39 N, R 1 E). Named on Bartle (1961) and Big Bend (1961) 15' quadrangles.

Cutter Butte [SHASTA]: *peak,* 9 miles east-northeast of Whitmore (lat. 41°40'10" N, long. 121°45'05" W; near S line sec. 33, T 33 N, R 2 E). Named on Manzanita Lake (1956) and Whitmore (1956) 15' quadrangles.

Cutter Place Campground [SHASTA]: *locality,* 16 miles northwest of Lassen Peak (lat. 40°39'45" N, long. 121°43'30" W; at E line sec. 3, T 32 N, R 2 E). Named on Manzanita Lake (1956) 15' quadrangle.

Cut-throat Gulch [SHASTA]: *canyon,* drained by a stream that flows 3 miles to Ditch Fork Duncan Creek 4 miles north-northeast of Arbuckle Mountain (lat. 40°27' N, long. 122°49'50" W; sec. 13, T 30 N, R 9 W). Named on Chanchelulla Peak (1951) 15' quadrangle.

Cyclone Gap [SISKIYOU]: *pass,* 2 miles north-northwest of Preston Peak (lat. 41°51'45" N, long. 123°37'10" W). Named on Preston Peak (1982) 7.5' quadrangle.

Cyclorama Peak: see **Ski Heil Peak** [SHASTA].

Cypress Campground [SHASTA]: *locality,* 19 miles north-northwest of Lassen Peak (lat. 40°44'35" N, long. 121°36'35" W; sec. 2, T 33 N, R 3 E). Named on Manzanita Lake (1956) 15' quadrangle.

Cypress Ridge [SISKIYOU]: *ridge,* generally south-trending, 2 miles long, 4.25 miles north-northeast of the village of Seiad Valley (lat. 41°53'45" N, long. 123°09'20" W). Named on Kangaroo Mountain (1980) 7.5' quadrangle.

— D —

Dad Lofton Spring [SHASTA]: *spring,* 9.5 miles north-northwest of the village of Big Bend (lat. 41°08'35" N, long. 121°58'50" W). Named on Big Bend (1961) 15' quadrangle.

Dads Pocket [SISKIYOU]: *relief feature,* 19 miles southwest of Scott Bar (lat. 41°32' N, long. 123°14'15" W; near W line sec. 33, T 43 N, R 12 W). Named on Scott Bar (1955) 15' quadrangle.

Dagget: see **Cecilville** [SISKIYOU].

Daggett Creek [SISKIYOU]: *stream,* flows about 1.5 miles to Clear Creek

(1) 11.5 miles north-northwest of Ukonom Lake (lat. 41°42'45" N, long. 123°28'15" W). Named on Clear Creek (1981) 7.5' quadrangle.

Daggett Mountain [SISKIYOU]: *peak,* 20 miles west-northwest of Macdoel (lat. 41°58'10" N, long. 122°20'30" W; on E line sec. 31, T 48 N, R 4 W). Altitude 3533 feet. Named on Copco (1954) 15' quadrangle.

Dairy Creek [SHASTA-SISKIYOU]: *stream,* flows 2.5 miles, partly in Siskiyou County, to Squaw Valley Creek [SHASTA-SISKIYOU] 9 miles north-northwest of Shoeinhorse Mountain in Shasta County (lat. 41°10'50" N, long. 122°08'45" W; sec. 36, T 39 N, R 3 W). Named on Shoeinhorse Mountain (1954) 15' quadrangle.

Dairy Creek [SISKIYOU]: *stream,* flows 1 mile to Bear Wallow Creek 14 miles southwest of Macdoel (lat. 41°39'45" N, long. 122°10'50" W; sec. 15, T 44 N, R 3 W). Named on The Whaleback (1954) 15' quadrangle.

Dairyville [TEHAMA]: *village,* 7 miles east-southeast of Red Bluff (lat. 40°07'50" N, long. 122°07'20" W). Named on Tuscan Springs (1951) 7.5' quadrangle.

Dale Creek [SISKIYOU]: *stream,* flows 6.5 miles to Shasta River 3 miles southwest of Weed (lat. 41°24'10" N, long. 122°26' W; sec. 16, T 41 N, R 5 W). Named on Weed (1954) 15' quadrangle. Called Middle Fork Shasta River on Shasta (1894) 1° quadrangle.

Dales [TEHAMA]: *village,* 8.5 miles east-northeast of Bend (lat. 40°18'50" N, long. 122°04'10" W; near NE cor. sec. 3, T 28 N, R 2 W). Named on Dales (1965) 7.5' quadrangle.

Dales Lake [TEHAMA]: *lake,* 0.25 mile long, 1.25 miles north-northeast of Dales (lat. 40°19'55" N, long. 122°03'40" W; on S line sec. 26, T 29 N, R 2 W). Named on Dales (1965) 7.5' quadrangle.

Dam Gulch [SHASTA]: *canyon,* drained by a stream that flows 0.5 mile to Slate Creek (1) 2 miles west of Lamoine (lat. 40°58'40" N, long. 122°28'05" W; sec. 17, T 36 N, R 5 W). Named on Lamoine (1957) 15' quadrangle.

Damnation Creek [SHASTA]: *stream,* flows 3 miles to Clear Creek 6 miles north-northwest of Schell Mountain (lat. 40°55'45" N, long. 122°35'05" W; near S line sec. 32, T 36 N, R 6 W). Named on Schell Mountain (1950) 15' quadrangle.

Damnation Pass [SHASTA]: *pass,* 6 miles north of Schell Mountain (lat. 40°56'30" N, long. 122°30'15" W; near N line sec. 34, T 36 N, R 6 W); the feature is 1.5 miles south-southwest of Damnation Peak. Named on Schell Mountain (1950) 15' quadrangle.

Damnation Peak [SHASTA]: *peak,* 7.25 miles north of Schell Mountain (lat. 40°57'35" N, long. 122°31'35" W; sec. 23, T 36 N, R 6 W); the peak is 1.5 miles north-northeast of Damnation Pass. Named on Schell Mountain (1950) 15' quadrangle.

Dana [SHASTA]: *village,* 8.5 miles north-northeast of Burney Falls (lat. 41°06'10" N, long. 121°33'45" W; at SE cor. sec. 24, T 38 N, R 3 E). Named on Pondosa (1961) 15' quadrangle. Postal authorities established Dana post office in 1888 and discontinued it in 1951 (Frickstad, p. 179). Loren Dana settled at the site in the 1860's and built a sawmill there (Steger, p. 27).

Dan Covey Butte [SHASTA]: *peak,* 11 miles northeast of Whitmore (lat. 40°43'45" N, long. 121°45'15" W; sec. 9, T 33 N, R 2 E). Altitude 6163 feet. Named on Manzanita Lake (1956) and Whitmore (1956) 15' quadrangles.

Dangerfields Ferry: see **Fort Reading** [SHASTA].

Dan Hunt Meadows [SHASTA]: *area,* 10 miles east-northeast of Whitmore (lat. 40°42'15" N, long. 121°45'25" W; sec. 21, T 33 N, R 2 E); the place is 2.25 miles south-southeast of Dan Hunt Mountain. Named on Whitmore (1956) 15' quadrangle. Called Hunt Meadows on Burney (1939) 30' quadrangle.

Dan Hunt Mountain [SHASTA]: *ridge,* west-southwest-trending, 2.5 miles long, 11 miles northeast of Whitmore (lat. 40°44'15" N, long. 121°45'45" W). Named on Manzanita Lake (1956) and Whitmore (1956) 15' quadrangles. The name commemorates Dan Hunt, a pioneer cattleman (Steger, p. 27).

Dark Canyon [BUTTE]:

(1) *canyon,* 4 miles long, opens into the canyon of West Branch Feather River 5.5 miles west-northwest of the village of Berry Creek (lat. 39°40'10" N, long. 121°30'05" W; at S line sec. 14, T 21 N, R 4 E). Named on Berry Creek (1970) 7.5' quadrangle. Water of Lake Oroville floods the lower part of the canyon.

(2) *canyon,* drained by a stream that heads in Plumas County and flows 2.25 miles to Fall River 9 miles north of Clipper Mills (lat. 39°39'35" N, long. 121°11'35" W; near SE cor. sec. 21, T 21 N, R 7 E). Named on Cascade (1948) 7.5' quadrangle.

Dark Canyon [SHASTA]:

(1) *canyon,* drained by a stream that flows 0.25 mile to Backbone Creek Inlet 15 miles south of Lamoine (lat. 40°45'55" N, long. 122°25' W; sec. 34, T 34 N, R 5 W). Named on Lamoine (1957) 15' quadrangle.

(2) *canyon,* drained by a stream that flows 0.5 mile to Squaw Creek Arm Shasta Lake 8 miles south-southeast of Bollibokka Mountain (lat. 40°49'50" N, long. 122°08'35" W; near W line sec. 6, T 34 N, R 2 W). Named on Bollibokka Mountain (1957) 15' quadrangle.

(3) *canyon,* drained by a stream that flows less than 1 mile to Shasta Lake 13 miles north of Millville (lat. 40°44'15" N, long. 122°08'20" W; at S line sec. 6, T 33 N, R 2 W). Named on Bella Vista (1965) 7.5' quadrangle.

Dark Canyon [SISKIYOU]: *canyon,* drained by a stream that flows 1.5 miles to Dillon Creek 4.25 miles north of Dillon Mountain (lat. 41°35'35" N, long. 123°34'55" W). Named on Dillon Mountain (1983) 7.5' quadrangle.

Dark Canyon [TEHAMA]: *canyon,* drained by a stream that flows 5 miles to Thomes Creek 11 miles west of Paskenta (lat. 39°52'25" N, long. 122°44'45" W; at S line sec. 3, T 23 N, R 8 W). Named on Ball Mountain (1967), Hall Ridge (1967), and Riley Ridge (1967) 7.5' quadrangles.

Darkey Creek [SISKIYOU]: *stream,* flows 2.5 miles to Seiad Creek 1.25 miles east-northeast of the village of Seiad Valley (lat. 41°50'55" N, long. 123°10'20" W). Named on Seiad Valley (1980) 7.5' quadrangle. Called Darky Cr. on Seiad (1922) 30' quadrangle.

Dark Gulch [SISKIYOU]: *canyon,* drained by a stream that flows 2 miles to East Fork of South Fork Salmon River 16 miles south of Etna (lat. 41°13'30" N, long. 122°56'35" W; sec. 19, T 39 N, R 9 W). Named on Coffee Creek (1955) 15' quadrangle.

Dark Hollow Creek [GLENN]: *stream,* heads in Colusa County and flows 2 miles in Glenn County to Middle Fork Stony Creek [GLENN-TEHAMA] 2.5 miles south of Saint John Mountain (lat. 39°24' N, long. 122°41'05" W). Named on Saint John Mountain (1968) 7.5' quadrangle.

Darky Creek: see **Darkey Creek** [SISKIYOU].

Darling Ravine: see **Sand Spring Canyon** [TEHAMA].

Date Creek: see **Wilson Creek** [BUTTE].

Daves Ridge [GLENN-TEHAMA]: *ridge,* south-trending, 3.25 miles long, 10.5 miles west of Newville [GLENN] on Glenn-Tehama County line (lat. 39°47'30" N, long. 122°43' W). Named on Hall Ridge (1967) 7.5' quadrangle.

Daves Spring [GLENN]: *spring,* 10 miles west of Newville (lat. 39°46'50" N, long. 122°42'55" W); the spring is on the east side of Daves Ridge. Named on Hall Ridge (1967) 7.5' quadrangle.

David [BUTTE]: *locality,* nearly 6 miles north-northwest of the village of Berry Creek along Western Pacific Railroad (lat. 39°43' N, long. 121°27'30" W; sec. 31, T 22 N, R 5 E). Named on Big Bend Mountain (1948) 15' quadrangle.

Davis Creek [SISKIYOU]: *stream,* flows 2 miles to Klamath River 7.5 miles north-northeast of Orleans, which is in Humboldt County (lat. 41°24'15" N, long. 123°30'05" W). Named on Somes Bar (1979) 7.5' quadrangle.

Davis Flat Creek [TEHAMA]: *stream,* flows 1 mile to Wells Creek nearly 5 miles southeast of Beegum Peak (lat. 40°15'50" N, long. 122°49'40" W; sec. 24, T 28 N, R 9 W). Named on Chanchelulla Peak (1951) 15' quadrangle.

Davis Gulch [SHASTA]: *canyon,* drained by a stream that flows 1 mile to Clear Creek 7 miles southeast of the village of French Gulch (lat. 40°37'15" N, long. 121°33'20" W). Named on French Gulch (1944) 15' quadrangle. Water of Whiskeytown Lake now floods the canyon.

Davis Gulch [SISKIYOU]:

(1) *canyon,* drained by a stream that flows 1.5 miles to Empire Creek 9 miles west of Hornbrook (lat. 41°53'50" N, long. 122°43'45" W; sec. 25, T 47 N, R 8 W). Named on Hornbrook (1955) 15' quadrangle.

(2) *canyon,* drained by a stream that flows 5.5 miles to lowlands 19 miles west-southwest of Macdoel (lat. 41°41'10" N, long. 122°20'45" W; sec. 6, T 44 N, R 4 W). Named on Lake Shastina (1954) 15' quadrangle.

Davis Mountain [SHASTA]: *peak,* 6 miles east of Whitmore (lat. 40°38'20" N, long. 121°48'20" W; sec. 12, T 32 N, R 1 E). Named on Whitmore (1956) 15' quadrangle.

Davison Spring [TEHAMA]: *spring,* 3.25 miles south-southwest of Panther Spring (lat. 40°12'30" N, long. 121°48'45" W). Named on Panther Spring (1953) 15' quadrangle.

Dawleytown: see **Bidwell Bar** [BUTTE].

Dayton [BUTTE]: *village,* 5.5 miles south-southwest of Chico (lat. 39°38'55" N, long. 121°52'15" W). Named on Chico (1948) 7.5' quadrangle. Postal authorities established Grainland post office at Dayton in 1867, discontinued it the same year, reestablished it in 1873, discontinued it in 1892, reestablished it in 1893, and discontinued it in 1902 (Frickstad, p. 9; Wells and Chambers, p. 250). The place first was called Day Town by teamsters because it was one day of travel from Marysville and Red Bluff (Dunn, F.D., p. 31).

Dayton Landing [BUTTE]: *locality,* 9.5 miles west of Durham along Sacramento River (lat. 39°37'45" N, long. 121°59' W); the place is 6 miles west of Dayton. Named on Chico (1895) 30' quadrangle. Grain was shipped from the place before the railroad reached the neighborhood (Dunn, F.D., p. 31).

Day Town: see **Dayton** [BUTTE].

D Camp [TEHAMA]: *locality,* 8.5 miles southwest of Tomhead Mountain (lat. 40°03'05" N, long. 122°56' W; sec. 2, T 25 N, R 10 W). Named on Yolla Bolly (1954) 15' quadrangle.

Dead Cow Creek [SISKIYOU]: *stream,* flows 3 miles to Jaynes Canyon 3.25 miles east of Condrey Mountain (lat. 41°56'45" N, long. 122°55' W; near N line sec. 8, T 47 N, R 9 W). Named on Condrey Mountain (1955) 15' quadrangle.

Dead Horse Canyon [SISKIYOU]: *canyon,* 1 mile long, 4 miles southeast of Big Bend (lat. 41°12'30" N, long. 121°46'30" W). Named on Big Bend (1961) 15' quadrangle.

Dead Horse Creek [SHASTA]:
(1) *stream,* flows 1 mile to Salt Creek (6) 10 miles southeast of Lamoine (lat. 40°51'50" N, long. 122°18'45" W; near NW cor. sec. 27, T 35 N, R 4 W). Named on Lamoine (1957) 15' quadrangle.
(2) *stream,* flows 1.5 miles to Pit River Arm Shasta Lake 12 miles south-southeast of Bollibokka Mountain (lat. 40°46'10" N, long. 122°09' W; sec. 30, T 34 N, R 2 W). Named on Bollibokka Mountain (1957) 15' quadrangle.

Dead Horse Creek [SISKIYOU]: *stream,* flows 2 miles to Wooley Creek 13 miles north of Forks of Salmon (lat. 41°27'10" N, long. 123°18'30" W). Named on Medicine Mountain (1978) 7.5' quadrangle.

Dead Horse Creek [TEHAMA]: *stream,* flows 3.5 miles to Deer Creek (2) 4.5 miles northeast of Polk Springs (lat. 40°10' N, long. 121°36'45" W; near W line sec. 26, T 27 N, R 3 E). Named on Butte Meadows (1958) 15' quadrangle. Mineral (1941) 30' quadrangle had the form "Deadhorse Cr." for the name.

Deadhorse Creek [TEHAMA]: *stream,* flows 6 miles to North Fork Antelope Creek 12 miles south-southeast of Manton (lat. 40°16'50" N, long. 121°45'30" W; sec. 16, T 28 N, R 2 E). Named on Lassen Peak (1956) and Manton (1956) 15' quadrangles.

Deadhorse Falls [TEHAMA]: *waterfall,* 4.5 miles west-southwest of Mineral (lat. 40°18'40" N, long. 121°40'05" W; near E line sec. 6, T 28 N, R 3 E); the feature is along Deadhorse Creek. Named on Lassen Peak (1956) 15' quadrangle.

Dead Horse Gulch [SISKIYOU]: *canyon,* drained by a stream that flows 1 mile to North Fork Salmon River 2.5 miles east-northeast of Forks of Salmon (lat. 41°16'35" N, long. 123°16'35" W). Named on Forks of Salmon (1978) 7.5' quadrangle.

Dead Horse Ridge [SHASTA]: *ridge,* east-southeast-trending, 2.25 miles long, about 10 miles west-southwest of Arbuckle Mountain (lat. 40°20'15" N, long. 123°02' W). Named on Dubakella Mountain (1954) 15' quadrangle.

Dead Horse Ridge [TEHAMA]: *ridge,* south- to southeast-trending, 1 mile long, 8 miles west-northwest of Tomhead Mountain (lat. 40°10' N, long. 122°57'50" W). Named on Yolla Bolly (1954) 15' quadrangle.

Dead Horse Slough [BUTTE]: *stream,* flows nearly 6 miles to Little Chico Creek in Chico (lat. 39°43'50" N, long. 121°49'20" W; near W line sec. 25, T 22 N, R 1 E). Named on Richardson Springs (1952) 15' quadrangle, and on Chico (1948) 7.5' quadrangle.

Dead Horse Summit [SISKIYOU]: *pass,* 4.5 miles southeast of Bartle (lat. 41°12'10" N, long. 121°45'50" W; sec. 20, T 39 N, R 2 E). Named on Big Bend (1961) 15' quadrangle.

Deadlun Creek [SHASTA]: *stream,* flows 4 miles to Cedar Salt Log Creek 4.25 miles west-northwest of the village of Big Bend (lat. 41°03'45" N, long. 121°58'50" W; sec. 21, T 37 N, R 1 W). Named on Big Bend (1961) 15' quadrangle.

Deadman Creek [SHASTA]: *stream,* flows 2 miles to Clark Creek 11 miles northeast of the village of Big Bend (lat. 41°07' N, long. 121°45' W; near W line sec. 21, T 38 N, R 2 E). Named on Big Bend (1961) 15' quadrangle. United States Board on Geographic Names (1964, p. 9) rejected the name "Clark Creek" for the stream.

Deadman Crossing [TEHAMA]: *locality,* 4 miles northeast of Wakefield Flat along South Fork Cottonwood Creek [SHASTA-TEHAMA] (lat. 40°09'25" N, long. 122°34'50" W; near N line sec. 31, T 27 N, R 6 W). Named on Oxbow Bridge (1967) 7.5' quadrangle, which shows a grave at the place.

Deadman Gulch [SISKIYOU]:
(1) *canyon,* drained by a stream that flows 2.25 miles to North Fork Salmon River 9 miles north of Sawyers Bar (lat. 41°25'50" N, long. 123°06'45" W). Named on English Peak (1977) and Yellow Dog Peak (1977) 7.5' quadrangles.
(2) *canyon,* drained by a stream that flows 1.25 miles to Klamath River 8.5 miles west-southwest of Hornbrook (lat. 41°51'50" N, long. 122°42'20" W; sec. 6, T 46 N, R 7 W). Named on Hornbrook (1955) 15' quadrangle.

Deadman Gulch [TEHAMA]: *canyon,* drained by a stream that flows 1.5 miles to Mill Creek (3) 8 miles south-southwest of Panther Spring (lat. 40°08'55" N, long. 121°50'50" W). Named on Panther Spring (1953) 15' quadrangle.

Deadman Lake [SISKIYOU]: *lake,* 1000 feet long, 3.5 miles southeast of Ukonom Lake (lat. 41°32'25" N, long. 123°18'50" W). Named on Ukonom Lake (1980) 7.5' quadrangle.

Deadman Peak [SISKIYOU]: *peak,* 20 miles south of Etna on Siskiyou-Trinity County line (lat. 41°10'40" N, long. 122°56' W; sec. 6, T 38 N, R 9 W). Named on Coffee Creek (1955) 15' quadrangle. On Etna (1934) 30' quadrangle, the name applies to a peak located about 2 miles farther west.

Deadman Point [SISKIYOU]: *peak,* 7.5 miles north-northwest of Happy Camp (lat. 41°53'35" N, long. 123°26'50" W). Altitude 3405 feet. Named on Deadman Point (1981) 7.5' quadrangle.

Deadman Ravine [BUTTE]: *canyon,* drained by a stream that flows 0.5 mile to Lake Oroville 2 miles southeast of Oroville Dam (lat. 39°30'50" N, long. 121°27'25" W; near S line sec. 7, T 19 N, R 5 E). Named on Oroville Dam (1970) 7.5' quadrangle.

Deadman Spring [BUTTE]: *spring,* 4 miles south of Paradise (lat. 39°42' N, long. 121°28' W; near SW cor. sec. 3, T 21 N, R 3 E). Named on Hamlin Canyon (1951) 7.5' quadrangle.

Deadmans Reach [BUTTE]: *water feature,* abandoned course of part of Sacramento River 10 miles southwest of Chico (lat. 39°38'15" N, long. 121°59' W). Named on Ord Ferry (1949) 7.5' quadrangle.

Dead Mole Spring [SISKIYOU]: *spring,* 8 miles east of the village of Seiad Valley (lat. 41°51'40" N, long. 123°02'30" W; near E line sec. 6, T 46 N, R 10 W). Named on Hamburg (1980) 7.5' quadrangle.

Dead Mule Camp [TEHAMA]: *locality,* 6.25 miles south-southwest of Ball Mountain (lat. 39°50'45" N, long. 122°49'40" W; near W line sec. 13, T 23 N, R 9 W). Named on Log Spring (1967) 7.5' quadrangle. Anthony Peak (1952) 15' quadrangle shows Dead Mule Spring at the site.

Dead Mule Gulch [SISKIYOU]: *canyon,* drained by a stream that flows nearly 1 mile to Salmon River less than 1 mile northwest of Forks of Salmon (lat. 41°15'50" N, long. 123°19'55" W). Named on Forks of Salmon (1978) 7.5' quadrangle.

Dead Mule Spring: see **Dead Mule Camp** [TEHAMA].

Dead Rabbit [TEHAMA]: *relief feature,* 7.25 miles west-southwest of Paskenta (lat. 39°50'45" N, long. 122°40'15" W; near S line sec. 17, T 23 N, R 7 W). Named on Hall Ridge (1967) 7.5' quadrangle.

Deadwood [BUTTE]: *locality,* 5.5 miles east of Paradise (lat. 39°44'35" N, long. 121°31'25" W; at SE cor. sec. 21, T 22 N, R 4 E); the place is along Deadwood Creek. Named on Cherokee (1970) 7.5' quadrangle.

Deadwood [SISKIYOU]: *locality,* 8 miles north-northeast of Fort Jones (lat. 41°42'55" N, long. 122°48'05" W; near E line sec. 29, T 45 N, R 8 W); the place is at the mouth of Deadwood Creek. Site named on Fort Jones (1955) 15' quadrangle.

Deadwood Baldy Peak: see **Deadwood Creek** [SISKIYOU].

Deadwood Creek [BUTTE]: *stream,* flows 2.5 miles to Concow Creek 5 miles east of Paradise (lat. 39°44'25" N, long. 121°32'05" W; sec. 28, T 22 N, R 4 E). Named on Berry Creek (1970) and Cherokee (1970) 7.5' quadrangles.

Deadwood Creek [SISKIYOU]: *stream,* flows 4 miles to join Cherry Creek (2) and form McAdam Creek 8 miles north-northeast of Fort Jones (lat. 41°42'50" N, long. 122°48'10" W; near SW cor. sec. 29, T 45 N, R 8 W); the mouth of the stream is at the site of Deadwood. Named on Condrey Mountain (1955) and Fort Jones (1955) 15' quadrangles. East Fork enters from the east 1.5 miles upstream from the mouth of the main stream; it is 2 miles long and is named on Fort Jones (1955) 15' quadrangle. United States Board on Geographic Names (1979a, p. 3) approved the name "Deadwood Baldy Peak" for a feature, altitude 5693 feet, located 9.7 miles west-northwest of Yreka near the head of Deadwood Creek (lat. 41°46'07" N, long. 122°49'05" W; sec. 7, T 45 N, R 8 W)—the name is from a fire tower that was on the peak.

Deadwood Gulch [SHASTA]: *canyon,* drained by a stream that flows 1 mile to Whiskey Creek 4 miles east-southeast of the village of French Gulch (lat. 40°40'35" N, long. 122°34' W; sec. 32, T 33 N, R 6 W). Named on Whiskeytown (1979) 7.5' quadrangle.

Deason Flat [SISKIYOU]: *area,* nearly 2 miles southwest of Happy Camp along Klamath River (lat. 41°46'30" N, long. 123°24' W; mainly in sec. 15, T 16 N, R 7 E). Named on Happy Camp (1980) 7.5' quadrangle.

Death Valley [SISKIYOU]: *area,* 14 miles southwest of Scott Bar (lat. 41°35'30" N, long. 123°10'30" W). Named on Scott Bar (1980) 7.5' quadrangle.

Death Valley Creek [SISKIYOU]: *stream,* flows 1.5 miles to Canyon Creek (3) 14 miles southwest of Scott Bar (lat. 41°34'55" N, long. 123°09'25" W); the stream goes though Death Valley. Named on Marble Mountain (1980) 7.5' quadrangle.

Deep Crater [SISKIYOU]: *crater,* 20 miles northeast of Bartle (lat. 41°27'20" N, long. 121°32'35" W; on E line sec. 30, T 42 N, R 4 E). Named on Hambone (1961) 15' quadrangle.

Deep Creek [SHASTA]: *stream,* flows 2.25 miles to Pit River 10 miles north-northeast of the village of Montgomery Creek (lat. 40°58'50" N, long. 121°50'10" W). Named on Montgomery Creek (1956) 15' quadrangle.

Deep Creek [SISKIYOU]: *stream,* flows 2.5 miles to Scott River 7.5 miles southwest of Scott Bar (lat. 41°39'55" N, long. 123°06'40" W). Named on Grider Valley (1981) and Scott Bar (1980) 7.5' quadrangles.

Deep Creek Campground [SHASTA]: *locality,* 10 miles north-northeast of the village of Montgomery Creek along Pit River (lat. 40°58' N, long. 122°50'10" W); the place is at the mouth of Deep Creek. Named on Montgomery Creek (1956) 15' quadrangle.

Deep Hole [SHASTA]: *crater,* 5.5 miles west-northwest of Lassen Peak (lat. 40°31' N, long. 121°36'10" W; at S line sec. 23, T 31 N, R 3 E). Named on Manzanita Lake (1958) 15' quadrangle. Called Hole in the Ground on Burney (1939) 30' quadrangle.

Deep Hole Camp [TEHAMA]: *locality,* 11 miles south of Panther Spring (lat. 40°05'20" N, long. 121°45'45" W; sec. 21, T 26 N, R 2 E). Named on Panther Spring (1953) 15' quadrangle.

Deep Hole Creek [SHASTA]: *stream,* flows 3.25 miles to East Fork Stillwater Creek 3.5 miles east of the town of Central Valley (lat. 40°40'35" N, long. 122°18'05" W; sec. 34, T 33 N, R 4 W). Named on Project City (1957) 7.5' quadrangle.

Deep Ice Caves [SISKIYOU]: *caves,* 19 miles north-northeast of Bartle (lat. 41°29'45" N, long. 121°36'45" W). Named on Hambone (1961) 15' quadrangle.

Deep Lake [SISKIYOU]:
(1) *lake,* 1250 feet long, 13 miles south-southwest of Scott Bar (lat. 41°34'10" N, long. 123°06'40" W). Named on Boulder Peak (1981) 7.5' quadrangle.
(2) *intermittent lake,* 2.5 miles east-northeast of Mount Dome (lat. 41°49'30" N, long. 121°38'40" W; on E line sec. 17, T 46 N, R 3 E). Named on Mount Dome (1950) 15' quadrangle.

Deep Lake Creek [SISKIYOU]: *stream,* flows nearly 3 miles to Canyon Creek (3) 11.5 miles south-southwest of Scott Bar (lat. 41°36'25" N, long. 123°07'25" W); Deep Lake (1) is along the stream. Named on Boulder Peak (1981) 7.5' quadrangle. Called Little Elk Lake Creek on Seiad (1922) 30' quadrangle, where present Seiad Valley Creek is called Deep Lake Cr., but United States Board on Geographic Names (1960a, p. 13) rejected the name "Little Elk Lake Creek" for present Deep Lake Creek.

Deer Basin [TEHAMA]: *relief feature,* 2.25 miles southeast of Beegum Peak (lat. 40°17'30" N, long. 122°51'20" W; at W line sec. 11, T 28 N, R 9 W). Named on Chanchelulla Peak (1951) 15' quadrangle.

Deer Camp [SISKIYOU]: *locality,* 4 miles southeast of Condrey Mountain (lat. 41°53'50" N, long. 122°55'45" W; sec. 30, T 47 N, R 9 W). Named on Condrey Mountain (1955) 15' quadrangle. United States Board on Geographic Names (1978b, p. 3) approved the name "Deer Camp Meadows" for meadows at the place.

Deer Camp Meadows: see **Deer Camp** [SISKIYOU].

Deer Creek [SHASTA]:
(1) *stream,* flows 2.5 miles to North Fork Battle Creek [SHASTA-TEHAMA] 12.5 miles west-northwest of Lassen Peak (lat. 40°32' N, long. 121°44' W; sec. 15, T 31 N, R 2 E); the stream goes through Deer Flat. Named on Manzanita Lake (1956) 15' quadrangle.
(2) *stream,* flows 4 miles to Hawkins Creek 4 miles north-northeast of Shoeinhorse Mountain (lat. 41°06'50" N, long. 122°01'45" W). Named on Big Bend (1961) and Shoeinhorse Mountain (1954) 15' quadrangles.

Deer Creek [SISKIYOU]:
(1) *stream,* flows 3.25 miles to Beaver Creek (1) 11 miles east-northeast of Condrey Mountain (lat. 41°59' N, long. 122°46'15" W; sec. 28, T 48 N, R 8 W). Named on Condrey Mountain (1955) 15' quadrangle.
(2) *stream,* flows 6.5 miles to Copco Lake 18 miles west-northwest of Macdoel (lat. 41°58'25" N, long. 122°17'55" W; sec. 34, T 48 N, R 4 W). Named on Copco (1954) 15' quadrangle.
(3) *stream,* flows 4.25 miles to Sacramento River 3.5 miles west-southwest of the town of Mount Shasta (lat. 41°17'30" N, long. 122°22'15" W; at S line sec. 24, T 40 N, R 5 W). Named on Weed (1954) 15' quadrangle.

Deer Creek [TEHAMA]:
(1) *stream,* flows 1.5 miles to South Fork Cottonwood Creek [SHASTA-TEHAMA] 6.5 miles west of Tomhead Mountain (lat. 40°09'20" N, long. 122°56' W; near W line sec. 25, T 27 N, R 10 W); the stream is west of Deer Ridge. Named on Yolla Bolly (1954) 15' quadrangle.
(2) *stream,* flows 58 miles to Sacramento River 1.5 miles west-southwest of Vina (lat. 39°55'30" N, long. 122°04'50" W). Named on Butte Meadows (1958), Jonesville (1958), Mount Harkness (1956), and Panther Spring (1953) 15' quadrangles, and on Richardson Springs NW (1952) and Vina (1950) 7.5' quadrangles.
(3) *locality,* 3 miles east of Deer Creek Station (lat. 40°15'35" N, long. 121°23'30" W; sec. 26, T 28 N, R 5 E); the place is along Deer Creek (2). Named on Mount Harkness (1956) 15' quadrangle.

Deer Creek Crossing [TEHAMA]: *locality,* 13 miles south of Panther Spring (lat. 40°03'10" N, long. 121°47'05" W; sec. 5, T 25 N, R 2 E); the place is along Deer Creek (2). Named on Panther Spring (1953) 15' quadrangle. Called Graham Crossing on Mineral (1941) 30' quadrangle.

Deer Creek Falls [TEHAMA]: *waterfall,* 10 miles east-northeast of Polk Spring (lat. 40°12' N, long. 121°30'45" W; near NW cor. sec. 15, T 27 N, R 4 E); the feature is along Deer Creek (2). Named on Butte Meadows (1958) 15' quadrangle.

Deer Creek Flat [TEHAMA]: *area,* 16 miles south of Panther Spring (lat. 40°01'10" N, long. 121°50' W); the place is south of Deer Creek (2). Named on Panther Spring (1953) 15' quadrangle.

Deer Creek Meadows [TEHAMA]: *area,* 1.5 miles east of Deer Creek Station (lat. 40°16'10" N, long. 121°25'20" W; sec. 21, 22, T 28 N, R 5 E); the place is along Deer Creek (2). Named on Mount Harkness (1956) 15' quadrangle.

Deer Creek Pass [TEHAMA]: *pass,* 5 miles east of Deer Creek Station on Tehama-Plumas County line (lat. 40°15'10" N, long. 121°21'45" W; near W line sec. 30, T 28 N, R 6 E). Named on Mount Harkness (1956) 15' quadrangle.

Deer Creek Station [TEHAMA]: *locality,* 9.5 miles southeast of Mineral (lat. 40°16' N, long. 121°27' W; near S line sec. 20, T 28 N, R 5 E); the place is along Deer Creek (2). Named on Mount Harkness (1956) 15' quadrangle.

Deer Flat [SHASTA]: *marsh,* 10.5 miles west-northwest of Lassen Peak (lat. 40°31'50" N, long. 121°41'45" W; at S line sec. 13, T 31 N, R 2 E); the feature is along Deer Creek (1). Named on Manzanita Lake (1956) 15' quadrangle.

Deerhaven: see **Sims** [SHASTA].

Deer Lake [SHASTA]: *lake,* 300 feet long, 6.25 miles east of Lassen Peak (lat. 40°29' N, long. 121°23'15" W; at S line sec. 2, T 30 N, R 5 E). Named on Mount Harkness (1956) 15' quadrangle.

Deer Lick Creek [SISKIYOU]:
(1) *stream,* flows 1.25 miles to Indian Creek (1) 4 miles north of Happy Camp (lat. 41°51'05" N, long. 123°23'15" W). Named on Happy Camp (1980) and Slater Butte (1980) 7.5' quadrangles.
(2) *stream,* flows 2.25 miles to Wooley Creek 11 miles north-northwest of Forks of Salmon (lat. 41°23'50" N, long. 123°24'35" W). Named on Somes Bar (1979) 7.5' quadrangle.
(3) *stream,* flows nearly 2 miles to North Fork Salmon River 10 miles north of Sawyers Bar (lat. 41°26'30" N, long. 123°08'10" W). Named on English Peak (1977) 7.5' quadrangle.

Deer Mountain [GLENN]: *peak,* nearly 6 miles west of Newville (lat. 39°47'05" N, long. 122°37'55" W; at N line sec. 10, T 22 N, R 7 W). Altitude 3014 feet. Named on Hall Ridge (1967) 7.5' quadrangle.

Deer Mountain [SISKIYOU]: *peak,* 16 miles south-southwest of Macdoel (lat. 41°36'25" N, long. 122°07'40" W; near NE cor. sec. 1, T 43 N, R 3 W). Altitude 7006 feet. Named on The Whaleback (1954) 15' quadrangle.

Deer Mountain: see **Little Deer Mountain** [SISKIYOU].

Deer Park [BUTTE]: *locality,* 10 miles east-southeast of Pulga on Butte-Plumas County line (lat. 39°46'05" N, long. 121°16' W; at NE cor. sec. 14, T 22 N, R 6 E). Named on Soapstone Hill (1979) 7.5' quadrangle.

Deer Peak [BUTTE]: *peak,* 8 miles southeast of Paradise (lat. 39°40'10" N, long. 121°31'40" W; near SE cor. sec. 16, T 21 N, R 4 E). Named on Cherokee (1970) 7.5' quadrangle.

Deer Pen Creek [SISKIYOU]: *stream,* flows 1 mile to North Fork Salmon River 8.5 miles north of Sawyers Bar (lat. 41°25' N, long. 123°06'10" W). Named on Yellow Dog Peak (1977) 7.5' quadrangle.

Deer Ridge [TEHAMA]: *ridge,* southwest-trending, 1.5 miles long, nearly 6 miles west-northwest of Tomhead Mountain (lat. 40°09'45" N, long. 122°55'15" W; mainly in sec. 30, T 27 N, R 9 W); the feature is east of Deer Creek (1). Named on Yolla Bolly (1954) 15' quadrangle.

Deer Spring [SISKIYOU]: *spring,* 4 miles east-southeast of Bartle (lat. 41°14'10" N, long. 121°44'30" W; sec. 9, T 39 N, R 2 E). Named on Pondosa (1961) 15' quadrangle.

Deer Springs [SHASTA]: *springs,* 11.5 miles north of the village of Big Bend (lat. 41°10'55" N, long. 121°52'50" W; on N line sec. 32, T 39 N, R 1 E). Named on Big Bend (1961) 15' quadrangle.

Dees Peak [SISKIYOU]: *peak,* 9.5 miles southeast of Salmon Mountain on Siskiyou-Trinity County line (lat. 41°06'15" N, long. 123°15'40" W). Altitude 6904 feet. Named on Dees Peak (1978) 7.5' quadrangle.

Deetz [SISKIYOU]: *locality,* 5 miles northwest of the town of Mount Shasta along Southern Pacific Railroad (lat. 41°21'30" N, long. 122°22'55" W; at E line sec. 35, T 41 N, R 5 W). Named on Weed (1954) 15' quadrangle.

Defiance Mill: see **Old Defiance Mill** [BUTTE].

De Haven Gulch [TEHAMA]:
(1) *canyon,* drained by a stream that flows 8 miles to Paynes Creek (1) at Dales (lat. 40°18'50" N, long. 122°04'20" W; near N line sec. 3, T 28 N, R 2 W). Named on Manton (1956) 15' quadrangle, and on Dales (1965) 7.5' quadrangle.
(2) *canyon,* drained by a stream that flows nearly 2 miles to the canyon of North Fork Elder Creek 7.5 miles south-southeast of Wakefield Flat (lat. 40°01'30" N, long. 122°35'30" W; at E line sec. 13, T 25 N, R 7 W). Named on Lowrey (1967) 7.5' quadrangle.

Dehaven Gulch [TEHAMA]: *canyon,* drained by a stream that flows 3.5 miles to Little Antelope Creek 7.5 miles east of Red Bluff (lat. 40°10'50" N, long. 122°05'40" W). Named on Tuscan Springs (1951) 7.5' quadrangle.

Dekkas Creek [SHASTA]: *stream,* flows 2 miles to McCloud River Arm Shasta Lake 4.25 miles south of Bollibokka Mountain (lat. 40°52'15" N, long. 122°12'55" W; near S line sec. 21, T 35 N, R 3 W). Named on Bollibokka Mountain (1957) 15' quadrangle. The name is of Indian origin (Steger, p. 28).

Dekkas Creek Saddle [SHASTA]: *pass,* 5.5 miles south-southeast of Bollibokka Mountain (lat. 40°51'35" N, long. 122°10'30" W; sec. 26, T 35 N, R 3 W); the pass is near the head of Dekkas Creek. Named on Bollibokka Mountain (1957) 15' quadrangle.

Delamar [SHASTA]: *locality,* 10 miles south of present Bollibokka Mountain along Squaw Creek (2) (lat. 40°47'30" N, long. 122°11'15" W; sec. 22, T 34 N, R 3 W). Named on Redding (1901) 30' quadrangle, which also has the names "Winthrop" and "Salee" at the place. The name "Salee" is from James Salee, who bought Bully Hill mine in 1897; the name

"Delamar" is from J.F. Delamar, who purchased the mine from Salee that same year (Steger, p. 28, 57). Postal authorities established Winthrop post office at the place in 1900 and discontinued it in 1932; the name was for Winthrop Mining Company (Salley, p. 242).

Delaney: see **Weed** [SISKIYOU].

Delaney Slough [TEHAMA]: *water feature,* joins Deer Creek (2) less than 1 mile north of Vina (lat. 39°56'45" N, long. 122°03'10" W). Named on Richardson Springs NW (1952) and Vina (1950) 7.5' quadrangles.

Delay Camp [TEHAMA]: *locality,* 16 miles south-southwest of Panther Spring (lat. 40°03' N, long. 121°54'15" W; sec. 6, T 25 N, R 1 E). Named on Panther Spring (1953) 15' quadrangle.

Del Harleson Camp [GLENN]: *locality,* 8.5 miles west of Newville (lat. 39°47'15" N, long. 122°40'50" W; near SE cor. sec. 6, T 22 N, R 7 W). Named on Hall Ridge (1967) 7.5' quadrangle.

Delta [SHASTA]: *locality,* 2.5 miles south of Lamoine (lat. 40°56'35" N, long. 122°25'20" W; near NE cor. sec. 34, T 36 N, R 5 W); the place is near the mouth of Dog Creek. Named on Lamoine (1957) 15' quadrangle. According to Giles (p. 80), the locality also was called Dog Creek. Postal authorities established Delta post office in 1875 and moved it 4 miles north in 1880, when they changed the name to Slate Creek; they established Bayles post office, named for Abraham M. Bayles, first postmaster, 5 miles south of Slate Creek post office in 1884, changed the name to Delta in 1948, and discontinued it in 1954 (Salley, p. 16, 57). Railroad workers gave the name "Delta" to the place because Sacramento River, Dog Creek, and level land there form the Greek letter "delta" (Steger, p. 28). California Division of Highways' (1934) map shows a place called Smithson located 4.25 miles southeast of Delta along Southern Pacific Railroad (near SW cor. sec. 7, T 35 N, R 4 W). Postal authorities established Halcyon post office in 1882, moved it 300 yards south in 1883 when they changed the name to Smithson, and discontinued it in 1892; the name "Smithson" was for for James Smithson, who operated the hotel and stage stop at Sacramento River bridge in 1879 (Salley, p. 92, 207). They established Mabel post office 8 miles south of Smithson post office in 1885 and discontinued it in 1903 (Salley, p. 130).

Delta Point [SHASTA]: *peak,* 1.25 miles southeast of Lamoine (lat. 40°57'50" N, long. 122°24'45" W; sec. 23, T 36 N, R 5 W); the peak is 1.5 miles north-northeast of Delta. Altitude 3079 feet. Named on Lamoine (1957) 15' quadrangle.

Delucci Ridge [SHASTA]: *ridge,* south-southeast-trending, 0.5 mile long, 2.25 miles west of Burney Falls (lat. 41°00'40" N, long. 121°41'30" W). Named on Pondosa (1961) 15' quadrangle.

Democrat Mountain [SHASTA]: *ridge,* generally east-southeast-trending, 2 miles long, 5 miles west-southwest of Summit City (lat. 40°39' N, long. 122°29' W). Named on Shasta Dam (1956) 7.5' quadrangle.

Denny: see **Fort Denny**, under **Callahan** [SISKIYOU].

Derby Ridge: see **Timber Ridge** [TEHAMA].

Dersch Meadows [SHASTA]:

(1) *area,* 3.5 miles east-northeast of Lassen Peak (lat. 40°30'10" N, long. 121°26'35" W; sec. 32, T 31 N, R 5 E). Named on Mount Harkness (1956) and Prospect Peak (1957) 15' quadrangles. The name commemorates Fred Dersch, who had a cabin and corral at the place (Schulz, p. 15).

(2) *area,* 9.5 miles east-southeast of Whitmore (lat. 40°34'10" N, long. 121°45'15" W; sec. 4, T 31 N, R 2 E). Named on Whitmore (1956) 15' quadrangle.

Dersch Station: see **Anderson** [SHASTA].

De Sabla [BUTTE]: *locality,* 5 miles west-southwest of Stirling City (lat. 39°52'30" N, long. 121°36'45" W; sec. 2, T 23 N, R 3 E). Named on Paradise East (1980) and Stirling City (1979) 7.5' quadrangles. Called Hupps Mill on Chico (1895) 30' quadrangle. Postal authorities established Hupp post office in 1909, changed the name to De Sabla in 1911, and discontinued it in 1942 (Frickstad, p. 9, 10). The name "Hupp" was for John Hupp, an early sawmill operator, miner, and community leader (Dunn, F.D., p. 53). The name "De Sabla" is for Eugene De Sabla, who was involved in construction of a power plant at the site in 1903 (Gudde, 1949, p. 93).

De Sabla Reservoir: see **Lake De Sabla** [BUTTE].

Des Moines Creek [SISKIYOU]: *stream,* flows 1.5 miles to Indian Creek (1) 14 miles north-northwest of Happy Camp (lat. 41°58'35" N, long. 123°29'50" W). Named on Polar Bear Mountain (1982) 7.5' quadrangle.

Desolation Canyon: see **Desolation Gulch** [SISKIYOU].

Desolation Gulch [SISKIYOU]: *canyon,* drained by a stream that flows 1.5 miles to Butte Fork Applegate River 7.5 miles north of the village of Seiad Valley (lat. 41°56'50" N, long. 123°13'15" W). Named on Kangaroo Mountain (1980) 7.5' quadrangle. United States Board on Geographic Names (1983c, p. 5) rejected the form "Desolation Canyon" for the name.

Desolation Peak: see **Red Butte** [SISKIYOU] (1).

Destruction River: see **Sacramento River**.

Deter Camp [SISKIYOU]: *locality,* 11.5 miles north-northeast of McCloud (lat. 41°24'55" N, long. 122°04'15" W; sec. 10, T 41 N, R 2 W). Named on Dunsmuir (1935) 30' quadrangle.

Deter Spring [SISKIYOU]: *spring,* 10 miles north of Bartle (lat. 41°23' N, long. 121°50'05" W; near E line sec. 15, T 41 N, R 1 E). Named on Bartle (1961) 15' quadrangle.

Deter Well [SISKIYOU]: *well,* 11 miles north-northwest of Bartle (lat. 41°24'30" N, long. 121°52'50" W; on S line sec. 8, T 41 N, R 1 E). Named on Bartle (1939) 30' quadrangle.

Devastated Area [SHASTA]: *area,* center about 2 miles northeast of Lassen Peak (lat. 40°30'20" N, long. 121°29'25" W). Named on Mount Harkness (1956) and Prospect Peak (1957) 15' quadrangles. L.W. Collins, superintendent of Lassen Volcanic National Park, recommended the name for this area of forest that was destroyed by the eruption of Lassen Peak in 1915; debris in the area covers Jessen Meadows, once owned by Andrew Jessen and Nelson Stewart, who had a summer cow camp at the place (Schulz, p. 15, 29).

Devil Canyon [BUTTE]: *canyon,* about 3 miles long, 14 miles north-northwest of Clipper Mills along Middle Fork Feather River on Butte-Plumas County line (lat. 39°43'30" N, long. 121°13'30" W). Named on Cascade (1948) 7.5' quadrangle.

Devil's Backbone: see **Backbone Ridge** [SHASTA] (1).

Devils Basin [TEHAMA]: *relief feature,* 9.5 miles west of Paskenta (lat. 39°51'20" N, long. 122°43'05" W; at NE cor. sec. 14, T 23 N, R 8 W). Named on Hall Ridge (1967) 7.5' quadrangle.

Devils Canyon [SHASTA]:

(1) *canyon,* drained by a stream that flows 4 miles to Kosk Creek 6 miles north of the village of Big Bend (lat. 41°06'30" N, long. 121°55' W). Named on Big Bend (1961) 15' quadrangle.

(2) *canyon,* drained by a stream that flows 3 miles to Pit River 5.25 miles northwest of the village of Montgomery Creek (lat. 40°54'10" N, long. 121°58'55" W; sec. 9, T 35 N, R 1 W). Named on Bollibokka Mountain (1957) and Montgomery Creek (1956) 15' quadrangles.

Devils Canyon [SISKIYOU]: *canyon,* drained by a stream that flows 2.5 miles to Little North Fork Salmon River 7 miles northwest of Sawyers Bar (lat. 41°22'40" N, long. 123°12'50" W). Named on English Peak (1977) and Sawyers Bar (1979) 7.5' quadrangles.

Devils Canyon: see **Little Devils Canyon** [SHASTA].

Devil's Castle: see **Castle Crags** [SHASTA-SISKIYOU].

Devils Den [TEHAMA]: *area,* 6 miles south-southwest of Polk Springs (lat. 40°02'45" N, long. 121°43'15" W; sec. 11, T 25 N, R 2 E). Named on Butte Meadows (1958) 15' quadrangle.

Devils Gate [SISKIYOU]: *relief feature,* 12 miles south of Macdoel (lat. 41°39'10" N, long. 122°00'45" W; at N line sec. 19, T 44 N, R 1 W). Named on The Whaleback (1954) 15' quadrangle.

Devils Gulch [BUTTE]: *canyon,* drained by a stream that heads in Plumas County and flows 1.5 miles to Middle Fork Feather River 14 miles north-northwest of Clipper Mills in Butte County (lat. 39°43'20" N, long. 121°14'55" W; near E line sec. 36, T 22 N, R 6 E). Named on Cascade (1948) 7.5' quadrangle.

Devils Gulch [SISKIYOU]:

(1) *canyon,* drained by a stream that flows 1.5 miles to Empire Creek 9 miles west of Hornbrook (lat. 41°53'25" N, long. 122°43'45" W; sec. 25, T 47 N, R 8 W). Named on Hornbrook (1955) 15' quadrangle.

(2) *canyon,* 1 mile long, 10 miles west of Dunsmuir (lat. 41°12'15" N, long. 122°27'35" W; sec. 29, 32, T 39 N, R 5 W); the canyon heads at Devils Pocket. Named on Dunsmuir (1954) 15' quadrangle.

(3) *canyon,* drained by a stream that flows 1.5 miles to Taylor Creek (1) 7.5 miles east-northeast of Cecilville (lat. 41°10'50" N, long. 123°00'10" W). Named on Grasshopper Ridge (1979) 7.5' quadrangle.

Devils Gulch [TEHAMA]:

(1) *canyon,* drained by a stream that flows nearly 3.5 miles to Little Dry Creek (1) 9 miles west-northwest of Hooker (lat. 40°20'20" N, long. 122°28'50" W; at E line sec. 25, T 29 N, R 6 W). Named on Ono (1952) 15' quadrangle, and on Mitchell Gulch (1965) 7.5' quadrangle. On Anderson (1947) 15' quadrangle, the name "China Gulch" applies to present Little Dry Creek (1) up to the mouth of Devils Gulch (1), and United States Board on Geographic Names (1983a, p. 3) accepted this nomenclature. The canyon divides at the head into North Fork and South Fork. North Fork is 3 miles long and South Fork is 3.5 miles long; both forks are named on Ono (1952) 15' quadrangle. United States Board on Geographic Names (1983a, p. 5) rejected the name "Devils Gulch" for South Fork.

(2) *canyon,* drained by a stream that flows 1 mile to Initial Gulch 4.25 miles southeast of Manton (lat. 40°22'40" N, long. 121°48'30" W; sec. 12, T 29 N, R 1 E). Named on Manton (1956) 15' quadrangle.

Devils Half Acre [SHASTA]: *area,* 15 miles north-northeast of Lassen Peak (lat. 40°41'10" N, long. 121°24'45" W; sec. 27, 28, T 33 N, R 5 E). Named on Prospect Peak (1957) 15' quadrangle.

Devils Half Acre [TEHAMA]: *area,* 12.5 miles east-northeast of Red Bluff (lat. 40°13'10" N, long. 122°00'30" W; sec. 5, 6, T 27 N, R 1 W). Named on Tuscan Springs (1951) 7.5' quadrangle.

Devils Hole Gulch [TEHAMA]: *canyon,* drained by a stream that flows 4 miles to South Fork Cottonwood Creek [SHASTA-TEHAMA] 5.5 miles west of Tomhead Mountain (lat. 40°08'15' N, long. 122°55'10" W; at S line sec. 31, T 27 N, R 9 W). Named on Yolla Bolly (1954) 15' quadrangle.

Devils Hole Ridge [TEHAMA]: *ridge,* south-southeast-trending, 3.5 miles long, 8 miles west of Tomhead Mountain on Tehama-Trinity County line (lat. 40°07' N, long. 122°58'05" W); the ridge is west of Devils Hole Gulch. Named on Yolla Bolly (1954) 15' quadrangle.

Devils Homestead [SISKIYOU]: *area,* 7 miles east of Mount Dome at the base of Gillem Bluff (lat. 41°47'35" N, long. 121°33'30" W; sec. 30, 31, T 46 N, R 4 E). Named on Mount Dome (1950) 15' quadrangle.

Devils Kitchen [TEHAMA]: *area,* 4 miles south-southwest of Polk Springs (lat. 40°03'50" N, long. 121°41'15" W; on E line sec. 36, T 26 N, R 2 E). Named on Butte Meadows (1958) 15' quadrangle.

Devils Mountain [SHASTA]: *peak,* 7 miles north of Big Bend (lat. 41°07'10" N, long. 121°54'45" W). Altitude 3757 feet. Named on Big Bend (1961) 15' quadrangle.

Devils Mountain: see **Little Devils Mountain** [SHASTA].

Devils Parade Ground [TEHAMA]: *area,* 2 miles south of Polk Springs (lat. 40°05' N, long. 121°40' W). Named on Butte Meadows (1958) 15' quadrangle.

Devils Peak: see **Lower Devils Peak** [SISKIYOU]; **Middle Devils Peak** [SISKIYOU]; **Upper Devils Peak** [SISKIYOU].

Devils Pocket [SISKIYOU]: *relief feature,* 10 miles west of Dunsmuir (lat. 41°11'40" N, long. 122°27'45" W; sec. 32, T 39 N, R 5 W); the feature is at the head of Devils Gulch (2). Named on Dunsmuir (1954) 15' quadrangle.

Devils Punchbowl [SISKIYOU]: *relief feature,* 4 miles southwest of Preston Peak (lat. 41°48'10" N, long. 123°40'15" W). Named on Preston Peak (1956) 15' quadrangle. Averill's (1935) map has the form "Devils Punch Bowl" for the name.

Devils Rock [SHASTA]: *peak,* 8 miles southeast of Bollibokka Mountain (lat. 40°50'50" N, long. 122°06'30" W; sec. 33, T 35 N, R 2 W). Altitude 3263 feet. Named on Bollibokka Mountain (1957) 15' quadrangle.

Devils Rock Garden [SHASTA]: *area,* 12 miles north-northwest of Lassen Peak (lat. 40°39'15" N, long. 121°33' W). Named on Manzanita Lake (1956) 15' quadrangle.

Dewey Gulch [SISKIYOU]: *canyon,* drained by a stream that flows 2.5 miles to Little Shasta River 16 miles west-southwest of Macdoel (lat. 41°45'15" N, long. 122°18'15" W; near N line sec. 16, T 45 N, R 4 W). Named on Copco (1954) 15' quadrangle.

Dewitt Gulch [TEHAMA]: *canyon,* drained by a stream that flows nearly 6 miles to Little Antelope Creek 10.5 miles east of Red Bluff (lat. 40°11' N, long. 122°02'10" W; sec. 24, T 27 N, R 2 W); the canyon heads at Dewitt Peak. Named on Panther Spring (1953) 15' quadrangle, and on Tuscan Springs (1951) 7.5' quadrangle.

Dewitt Peak [TEHAMA]: *peak,* 11 miles southwest of Panther Spring (lat. 40°09'30" N, long. 121°56'45" W; at N line sec. 35, T 27 N, R 1 W). Named on Panther Spring (1953) 15' quadrangle.

Dexter Gulch [TEHAMA]: *canyon,* drained by a stream that flows 3 miles to Salt Creek (1) 5 miles west-southwest of Rosewood (lat. 40°15'10" N, long. 122°38'40" W; sec. 27, T 28 N, R 7 W). Named on Ono (1952) 15' quadrangle.

Diamond Lake [SISKIYOU]: *lake,* 250 feet long, 9 miles north-northwest of Sawyers Bar (lat. 41°24'40" N, long. 123°13'05" W). Named on English Peak (1977) 7.5' quadrangle.

Diamond Lake [TEHAMA]: *lake,* 700 feet long, 4.25 miles south-southwest of Mineral (lat. 40°17'30" N, long. 121°17'40" W; near W line sec. 10, T 28 N, R 3 E). Named on Lassen Peak (1956) 15' quadrangle.

Diamond Peak [SHASTA]: *peak,* 2 miles south-southwest of Lassen Peak (lat. 40°27' N, long. 121°31'20" W; near N line sec. 22, T 30 N, R 4 E). Named on Lassen Peak (1956) 15' quadrangle. Steger (p. 29) attributed the name to small quartz crystals that resemble diamonds.

Diamondville [BUTTE]: *locality,* 4 miles west of Paradise along Big Butte Creek (Butte Creek [BUTTE-GLENN] of more recent maps) (lat. 39°45'35" N, long. 121°40'30" W). Named on Chico (1895) 30' quadrangle. The place first was called Rich Bar and then Goatville, before it was renamed Diamondville to honor James Diamond (Dunn, F.D., p. 32).

Dibble Creek [TEHAMA]: *stream,* flows 15 miles to Sacramento River 1.25 miles north-northeast of downtown Red Bluff (lat. 40°11'35" N, long. 122°13'35" W; sec. 17, T 27 N, R 3 W). Named on Blossom (1952), Red Bluff East (1951), and Red Bluff West (1951) 7.5' quadrangles. North Fork enters from the northwest nearly 3 miles northwest of downtown Red Bluff; it is 11 miles long and is named on Blossom (1952) and Red Bluff West (1951) 7.5' quadrangles. South Fork enters 3 miles northwest of downtown Red Bluff; it is 5 miles long and is named on Red Bluff West (1951) 7.5' quadrangle.

Dickerson Creek [SHASTA]: *stream,* flows 4.5 miles to North Fork Bear Creek (2) 4.5 miles south-southeast of Whitmore (lat. 40°34'25" N, long. 121°52' W; sec. 4, T 31 N, R 1 E). Named on Whitmore (1956) 15' quadrangle.

Dickson Flat [SHASTA]: *area,* 10.5 miles north of Burney Falls (lat. 41°09'45" N, long. 121°40' W; at N line sec. 6, T 38 N, R 3 E). Named on Pondosa (1961) 15' quadrangle.

Dicus Slough [BUTTE]: *water feature,* joins Sacramento River 13 miles west-northwest of Chico (lat. 39°49'45" N, long. 122°03'20" W). Named on Foster Island (1950) 7.5' quadrangle.

Didallas Creek [SHASTA]: *stream,* flows nearly 2 miles to Squaw Creek Arm Shasta Lake 8.5 miles south-southeast of Bollibokka Mountain (lat. 40°49'50" N, long. 122°09'15" W; at N line sec. 12, T 34 N, R 3 W). Named on Bollibokka Mountain (1957) 15' quadrangle. The name is of Indian origin (Steger, p. 29). West Fork enters from the west 0.25 mile upstream from the mouth of the main creek; it is 2 miles long and is named on Bollibokka Mountain (1957) 15' quadrangle.

Digger Bay [SHASTA]: *embayment,* 3 miles north-northeast of Summit City along Shasta Lake (lat. 40°43'35" N, long. 122°23'20" W; sec. 12, T 33 N, R 5 W); the feature is the flooded lower part of the canyon of Digger Creek. Named on Shasta Dam (1956) 7.5' quadrangle.

Digger Butte [TEHAMA]: *peak,* 4.5 miles east of Manton (lat. 40°25'50" N, long. 121°47'05" W; sec. 29, T 30 N, R 2 E); the feature is near Digger Creek [SHASTA-TEHAMA]. Altitude 4018 feet. Named on Manton (1956) 15' quadrangle.

Digger Butte: see **Camp Digger Butte** [SHASTA].

Digger Creek [SHASTA]: *stream,* flows 1 mile to Digger Bay 3 miles north-northeast of Summit City (lat. 40°43'35" N, long. 122°23'05" W; near S line sec. 12, T 33 N, R 5 W). Named on Project City (1957) and Shasta Dam (1956) 7.5' quadrangles.

Digger Creek [SHASTA-TEHAMA]: *stream,* flows 19 miles to North Fork Battle Creek [SHASTA-TEHAMA] 2.5 miles west-southwest of Manton (lat. 40°25'30" N, long. 121°55' W; near E line sec. 25, T 30 N, R 1 W). Named on Lassen Peak (1956) and Manton (1956) 15' quadrangles. The stream forms part of Shasta-Tehama County line. South Fork enters 9.5 miles northwest of Mineral; it is 7.25 miles long and is named on Lassen Peak (1956) 15' quadrangle. South Fork is called Dry Creek on Mineral (1941) 30' quadrangle, but United States Board on Geographic Names (1959, p. 7) rejected the names "Dry Creek" and "South Digger Creek" for South Fork.

Digger Creek [TEHAMA]:

(1) *stream,* flows 7.25 miles to Thomes Creek just east of Paskenta (lat. 39°53' N, long. 122°32'40" W; sec. 4, T 23 N, R 6 W). Named on Paskenta (1967) and Riley Ridge (1967) 7.5' quadrangles.

(2) *stream,* flows 3 miles to Cold Fork (1) 4 miles north-northeast of Tomhead Mountain (lat. 40°11'15" N, long. 122°46'45" W; near W line sec. 16, T 27 N, R 8 W). Named on Yolla Bolly (1954) 15' quadrangle.

(3) *stream,* flows 5.25 miles to Elder Creek 5 miles south-southwest of Red Bank (lat. 40°01'50" N, long. 122°28'45" W; near NE cor. sec. 13, T 25 N, R 6 W). Named on Lowrey (1967), Paskenta (1967), and Red Bank (1952) 7.5' quadrangles.

Digger Pine Camp [TEHAMA]: *locality,* 13 miles south of Panther Spring (lat. 40°03'10" N, long. 121°49'15" W); the place is just west of Digger Pine Flat. Named on Mineral (1941) 30' quadrangle.

Digger Pine Flat [TEHAMA]: *area,* 14 miles south of Panther Spring (lat. 40°03'05" N, long. 121°48'15" W). Named on Panther Spring (1953) 15' quadrangle.

Digger Pine Hill [TEHAMA]: *ridge,* generally northeast-trending, 1 mile long, 2.5 miles west of Paskenta (lat. 39°53' N, long. 122°35'30" W). Named on Paskenta (1967) 7.5' quadrangle.

Digger Ravine [BUTTE]: *canyon,* drained by a stream that flows less than 0.5 mile to Oregon Gulch (2) 5 miles north-northeast of Oroville (lat. 39°35' N, long. 121°31'40" W; at S line sec. 16, T 20 N, R 4 E). Named on Oroville (1970) 7.5' quadrangle.

Digger Ridge [GLENN]: *ridge,* east-trending, 3.5 miles long, 7 miles west of Newville (lat. 39°47' N, long. 122°38'30" W). Named on Hall Ridge (1967) and Newville (1967) 7.5' quadrangles.

Diggles Gulch [SISKIYOU]: *canyon,* drained by a stream that flows 1.5 miles to Cherry Creek (2) 8 miles north-northeast of Fort Jones (lat. 41°42'55" N, long. 122°46'50" W; sec. 28, T 45 N, R 8 W). Named on Fort Jones (1955) 15' quadrangle.

Di Hill [SHASTA]: *peak,* 6 miles south of Whitmore (lat. 40°32'35" N, long. 121°55'15" W; sec. 13, T 31 N, R 1 W). Named on Whitmore (1956) 15' quadrangle.

Dillberry Gulch [SISKIYOU]: *canyon,* drained by a stream that flows 2 miles to Scott River at Scott Bar (lat. 41°44'25" N, long. 123°00'10" W; sec. 21, T 45 N, R 10 W). Named on Scott Bar (1980) 7.5' quadrangle.

Diller: see **Mount Diller** [SHASTA].

Diller Canyon [SISKIYOU]: *canyon,* 3 miles long, 6.5 miles east of Weed on the west side of Shastina (lat. 41°24'30" N, long. 122°15'30" W). Named on Shasta (1954) and Weed (1954) 15' quadrangles.

Dillon Camp [SISKIYOU]: *locality,* 4 miles west of Dillon Mountain (lat. 41°32'30" N, long. 123°38'45" W). Site named on Chimney Rock (1981) 7.5' quadrangle.

Dillon Cove [TEHAMA]: *relief feature,* 13 miles south of Panther Spring (lat. 40°03'40" N, long. 121°47'35" W; sec. 31, T 26 N, R 2 E). Named on Panther Spring (1953) 15' quadrangle.

Dillon Creek [SISKIYOU]: *stream,* flows 14 miles to Klamath River 3.5 miles north-northeast of Dillon Mountain (lat. 41°34'35" N, long. 123°32'15" W). Named on Chimney Rock (1981) and Dillon Mountain (1983) 7.5' quadrangles. North Fork enters from the north 4.5 miles north of Dillon Mountain; it is 11 miles long and is named on Bear Peak (1982), Dillon Mountain (1983), and Prescott Mountain (1981) 7.5' quadrangles.

Dillon Creek Campground [SISKIYOU]: *locality,* 3.5 miles north-northeast of Dillon Mountain (lat. 41°34'25" N, long. 123°32'35" W); the place is along Dillon Creek 2000 feet above the mouth of that stream. Named on Dillon Mountain (1983) 7.5' quadrangle.

Dillon Divide [SISKIYOU]: *ridge,* northeast- to east-trending, 5 miles long, center about 4 miles south-southwest of Bear Peak (lat. 41°38'50" N, long. 123°38'30" W); the ridge is south of North Fork Dillon Creek. Named on Bear Peak (1982) and Prescott Mountain (1981) 7.5' quadrangles.

Dillon Mountain [SISKIYOU]: *peak,* 21 miles south-southwest of Happy Camp (lat. 41°31'50" N, long. 123°34'20" W). Altitude 4668 feet. Named on Dillon Mountain (1983) 7.5' quadrangle.

Dinner Gulch [SHASTA]: *canyon,* drained by a stream that flows less than 1 mile to Squaw Creek (2) 7.5 miles southeast of Bollibokka Mountain (lat. 40°51' N, long. 122°07'40" W; at W line sec. 32, T 35 N, R 2 W). Named on Bollibokka Mountain (1957) 15' quadrangle.

Dipping Vat Flat [TEHAMA]: *area,* 2.5 miles northeast of Wakefield Flat along South Fork Cottonwood Creek [SHASTA-TEHAMA] (lat. 40°09'05" N, long. 122°36'35" W; sec. 36, T 27 N, R 7 W). Named on Oxbow Bridge (1967) 7.5' quadrangle. Colyrear Springs (1957) 15' quadrangle has the form "Dippingvat Flat" for the name.

Dirigo [SHASTA]: *locality,* less than 1 mile north-northeast of Castella along Southern Pacific Railroad (lat. 41°09' N, long. 122°18'30" W; sec. 15, T 38 N, R 4 W). Named on Dunsmuir (1954) 15' quadrangle.

Dirty Gulch [TEHAMA]: *canyon,* drained by a stream that flows 1 mile to Little Dry Creek 9 miles west-northwest of Hooker (lat. 40°20' N, long. 122°29'10" W; near S line sec. 25, T 29 N, R 6 W). Named on Mitchell Gulch (1965) 7.5' quadrangle.

Discovery Creek [BUTTE]: *stream,* flows 2.5 miles to Last Chance Creek (1) 4 miles north-northeast of Stirling City (lat. 39°57'50" N, long. 121°30'15" W; near E line sec. 3, T 24 N, R 4 E). Named on Kimshew Point (1979) and Stirling City (1979) 7.5' quadrangles. Called Fish Creek on Bidwell Bar (1897) 30' quadrangle, but United States Board on Geographic Names (1960b, p. 7) rejected this name for the stream.

Ditch Creek [SHASTA]: *stream,* flows 4 miles to Cayton Valley 4.5 miles north-northeast of Burney Falls (lat. 41°04'25" N, long. 121°38' W; sec. 4, T 37 N, R 3 E); a ditch that takes water from North Fork Clark Creek brings water to the head of the stream. Named on Pondosa (1961) 15' quadrangle.

Ditch Creek [SISKIYOU]: *stream,* flows 5.5 miles to Cottonwood Creek (1) 1.25 miles north-northwest of Hornbrook (lat. 41°55'35" N, long. 122°34'15" W; sec. 17, T 47 N, R 6 W). Named on Hornbrook (1955) 15' quadrangle. North Fork enters from the northwest 3.5 miles west of Hornbrook; it is 1.5 miles long and is named on Hornbrook (1955) 15' quadrangle.

Ditch Creek [TEHAMA]: *stream,* flows 4.5 miles to Deer Creek (2) less than 0.5 mile south-southwest of Polk Springs (lat. 40°06'45" N, long. 121°40'05" W; near NW cor. sec. 17, T 26 N, R 3 E). Named on Butte Meadows (1958) 15' quadrangle.

Ditch Creek: see **Fox Creek** [BUTTE].

Ditch Fork: see **Duncan Creek** [SHASTA].

Divide Peak: see **Raker Peak** [SHASTA].

Dixon Ravine [BUTTE]: *canyon,* drained by a stream that flows less than 0.5 mile to Oregon Gulch (2) 5.25 miles north-northeast of Oroville (lat. 39°35'15" N, long. 121°31'55" W; sec. 16, T 20 N, R 4 E). Named on Oroville (1970) 7.5' quadrangle.

Dobbins Creek [SISKIYOU]: *stream,* flows nearly 2 miles to Klamath River 2.5 miles east-northeast of Dillon Mountain (lat. 41°32'25" N, long. 123°31'35" W). Named on Dillon Mountain (1983) 7.5' quadrangle.

Dobkins Lake [SISKIYOU]: *lake,* 1300 feet long, 9 miles west-northwest of the town of Mount Shasta (lat. 41°20'30" N, long. 122°28'45" W; sec. 6, T 40 N, R 5 W). Named on Weed (1954) 15' quadrangle.

Dobson: see **Red Bluff** [TEHAMA].

Doby Creek [SHASTA]: *stream,* flows 4 miles to North Fork Cottonwood Creek [SHASTA-TEHAMA] 1.5 miles west-southwest of Ono (lat. 40°28'10" N, long. 122°38'50" W; sec. 10, T 30 N, R 7 W). Named on Ono (1952) 15' quadrangle, and on Shasta Bally (1978) 7.5' quadrangle.

Dockery Gulch [SISKIYOU]: *canyon,* drained by a stream that flows 2 miles to the stream in McConaughy Gulch nearly 6 miles east-southeast of Etna (lat. 41°25'30" N, long. 122°47'30" W; sec. 8, T 41 N, R 8 W). Named on Etna (1955) 15' quadrangle.

Dock Well [SISKIYOU]: *well,* 8 miles northwest of Medicine Lake (lat. 41°39' N, long. 121°43'20" W; near SE cor. sec. 15, T 44 N, R 2 E). Named on Medicine Lake (1952) 15' quadrangle.

Dodge Creek [SHASTA]: *stream,* flows 3.5 miles to Clear Creek 5 miles southwest of Schell Mountain (lat. 40°48'35" N, long. 122°36'30" W; sec. 12, T 34 N, R 7 W). Named on Schell Mountain (1950) 15' quadrangle.

Dodgeland: see **Chico** [BUTTE].

Doe Creek [SISKIYOU]: *stream,* flows 2.5 miles to Clear Creek (1) 2.25 miles west-southwest of Preston Peak (lat. 41°49'15" N, long. 123°39'10" W); the stream heads at Doe Flat. Named on Devils Punchbowl (1981) 7.5' quadrangle.

Doe Flat [SHASTA]: *area,* 2 miles south-southeast of Schell Mountain (lat. 40°49'15" N, long. 122°30'35" W; sec. 2, T 34 N, R 6 W); the place is near the head of Doe Gulch (2). Named on Schell Mountain (1950) 15' quadrangle.

Doe Flat [SISKIYOU]: *area,* 4.25 miles west-southwest of Preston Peak (lat. 41°49'15" N, long. 123°41'40" W). Named on Devils Punchbowl (1981) 7.5' quadrangle.

Doe Gulch [SHASTA]:

(1) *canyon,* drained by a stream that flows 1.25 miles to Salt Creek (6) 9 miles east-southeast of Lamoine (lat. 40°54'45" N, long. 122°17'05" W; at E line sec. 2, T 35 N, R 4 W). Named on Lamoine (1957) 15' quadrangle.

(2) *canyon,* drained by a stream that flows less than 1 mile to Backbone Creek 11 miles south-southwest of Lamoine (lat. 40°49'30" N, long. 122°29'50" W; at N line sec. 12, T 34 N, R 6 W). Named on Lamoine (1957) 15' quadrangle.

Doe Mill Ridge [BUTTE]: *ridge,* generally southwest-trending, about 16 miles long, lies between Butte Creek [BUTTE-GLENN] and Little Chico Creek. Named on Chico (1948), Cohasset (1979), Hamlin Canyon (1951), and Paradise West (1980) 7.5' quadrangles.

Doe Mountain [TEHAMA]: *peak,* nearly 5 miles east of Mineral (lat. 40°20'55" N, long. 121°30'20" W; near N line sec. 26, T 29 N, R 4 E). Altitude 5968 feet. Named on Lassen Peak (1956) 15' quadrangle.

Doe Peak [GLENN]: *peak,* 10 miles northwest of the village of Elk Creek (lat. 39°42'40" N, long. 122°39'20" W); the peak is 2 miles south of Buck Point. Altitude 3557 feet. Named on Alder Springs (1967) 7.5' quadrangle.

Doe Peak [SISKIYOU]: *peak,* 9 miles southwest of Medicine Lake (lat. 41°30'20" N, long. 121°44'25" W; sec. 4, T 42 N, R 2 E). Altitude 6152 feet. Named on Medicine Lake (1952) 15' quadrangle.

Doe Spring [GLENN]: *spring,* 10 miles northwest of the village of Elk Creek (lat. 39°42'30" N, long. 122°39'20" W); the spring is 900 feet south of Doe Peak. Named on Alder Springs (1967) 7.5' quadrangle.

Dog Camp [TEHAMA]: *locality,* 6.5 miles west of Paskenta (lat. 39°52'40" N, long. 122°39'45" W; on E line sec. 5, T 23 N, R 7 W). Named on Riley Ridge (1967) 7.5' quadrangle.

Dog Creek [SHASTA]: *stream,* flows 7.5 miles to Sacramento River nearly 3 miles south-southeast of Lamoine (lat. 40°56'30" N, long. 122°25'20" W; sec. 34, T 36 N, R 5 W). Named on Lamoine (1957) and Schell Mountain (1950) 15' quadrangles. Little South Fork enters from the south 4 miles upstream from the mouth of the main creek; it is 2.5 miles long and is named on Lamoine (1957) 15' quadrangle. Little South Fork is called Middle Fork on Redding (1901) 30' quadrangle. North Fork enters from the northwest 5.5 miles north-northeast of Schell Mountain; it is 2.5 miles long and is named on Schell Mountain (1950) 15' quadrangle. North Fork is called Dog Creek on Weaverville (1913) 30' quadrangle.

Dog Creek: see **Delta** [SHASTA]; **Little Dog Creek** [SHASTA].

Dog Creek Mountain [SHASTA]: *peak,* 3 miles north of Schell Mountain (lat. 40°53'50" N, long. 122°31'15" W; sec. 11, T 35 N, R 6 W); the peak is near the head of Dog Creek. Named on Schell Mountain (1950) 15' quadrangle.

Dog Fork: see **Elliot Creek** [SISKIYOU].

Dog Fork Creek: see **Elliot Creek** [SISKIYOU].

Doggett Creek [SISKIYOU]: *stream,* flows 5.5 miles to Klamath River 8 miles southeast of Condrey Mountain (lat. 41°50'40" N, long. 122°53'15" W; sec. 10, T 46 N, R 9 W). Named on Condrey Mountain (1955) 15' quadrangle.

Dog Gulch [SHASTA]: *canyon,* drained by a stream that flows 1.25 miles to Clear Creek 6 miles north of Igo (lat. 40°35'35" N, long. 122°32'35" W; near SE cor. sec. 28, T 32 N, R 6 W). Named on Igo (1979) 7.5' quadrangle.

Dog Paw [SISKIYOU]: *relief feature,* 16 miles south-southwest of Etna (lat. 41°13'35" N, long. 122°59'45" W; sec. 22, T 39 N, R 10 W). Named on Coffee Creek (1955) 15' quadrangle.

Dogtown [GLENN]: *locality,* 9.5 miles west of the village of Elk Creek (lat. 39°35'20" N, long. 122°42'45" W; sec. 13, T 20 N, R 8 W). Named on Felkner Hill (1968) 7.5' quadrangle.

Dogtown: see **Magalia** [BUTTE].

Dogtown Peak: see **Sawmill Peak** [BUTTE].

Dogwood Butte [SISKIYOU]: *peak,* 1.5 miles west of McCloud (lat. 41°15' N, long. 122°10'05" W; sec. 2, T 39 N, R 3 W). Named on Shasta (1954) and Shoeinhorse Mountain (1954) 15' quadrangles.

Dogwood Creek [BUTTE]: *stream,* flows 4.5 miles to North Fork Feather River 1.5 miles northeast of Pulga (lat. 39°48'55" N, long. 121°25'35" W; near SW cor. sec. 28, T 23 N, R 5 E). Named on Pulga (1979) 7.5' quadrangle.

Dogwood Gulch [SHASTA]: *canyon,* drained by a stream that flows 1.5

miles to Middle Fork Cottonwood Creek [SHASTA-TEHAMA] 4 miles east-northeast of Arbuckle Mountain (lat. 40°25'15" N, long. 122°47'25" W; near W line sec. 29, T 30 N, R 8 W). Named on Chanchelulla Peak (1951) 15' quadrangle.

Dogwood Lake [SISKIYOU]: *lake,* 300 feet long, 14 miles south-southwest of Scott Bar (lat. 41°33'35" N, long. 123°06'35" W). Named on Boulder Peak (1981) 7.5' quadrangle.

Dolde: see **Redding** [SHASTA].

Dollar Creek [SISKIYOU]: *stream,* flows 1.5 miles to Little North Fork Salmon River 8 miles northwest of Sawyers Bar (lat. 41°22'35" N, long. 123°14'30" W); the stream goes past Dollar Meadows. Named on English Peak (1977), Forks of Salmon (1978), and Sawyers Bar (1979) 7.5' quadrangles.

Dollar Meadows [SISKIYOU]: *area,* 8.5 miles north-northeast of Forks of Salmon (lat. 41°22'15" N, long. 123°15'20" W); the place is near Dollar Creek. Named on Forks of Salmon (1978) 7.5' quadrangle.

Doll Camp [TEHAMA]: *locality,* 7.25 miles west-southwest of Ball Mountain (lat. 39°53'20" N, long. 122°54'25" W; sec. 31, T 24 N, R 9 W); the place is on the north side of Doll Ridge. Named on Buck Rock (1967) 7.5' quadrangle.

Doll Creek [TEHAMA]: *stream,* flows 2 miles to Willow Creek (2) 7 miles west-southwest of Ball Mountain (lat. 39°53'35" N, long. 122°54'15" W; near E line sec. 31, T 24 N, R 9 W); the stream is north of Doll Ridge. Named on Buck Rock (1967) 7.5' quadrangle.

Doll Ridge [TEHAMA]: *ridge,* east-trending, 2.5 miles long, 8 miles west-southwest of Ball Mountain (lat. 39°53'10" N, long. 122°55'30" W). Named on Buck Rock (1967) 7.5' quadrangle.

Dome Mountain: see **Mount Dome** [SISKIYOU].

Dona Creek [SISKIYOU]: *stream,* flows 4.5 miles to Klamath River 7.5 miles south-southeast of Condrey Mountain (lat. 41°50'30" N, long. 122°55'15" W; sec, 8, T 46 N, R 9 W). Named on Condrey Mountain (1955) 15' quadrangle.

Doney Creek [SHASTA]: *stream,* flows 2.5 miles to Sacramento River Arm Shasta Lake 6.25 miles south of Lamoine (lat. 40°53'30" N, long. 122°24'10" W; near N line sec. 14, T 35 N, R 5 W). Named on Lamoine (1957) 15' quadrangle. Red Bluff (1894) 1° quadrangle has the name "Doney" at a site just west of Sacramento River about 2.5 miles north of the mouth of present Doney Creek, and opposite the mouth of Middle Salt Creek. Steger (p. 29) associated the name with William K. Doney, who settled in the neighborhood in 1860.

Donomore Creek [SISKIYOU]: *stream,* flows 2 miles to Elliot Creek 4.5 miles north-northeast of Condrey Mountain (lat. 41°59'30" N, long. 122°55'45" W); the stream heads at Donomore Meadows. Named on Condrey Mountain (1955) 15' quadrangle.

Donomore Creek: see **Wards Fork**, under **Elliot Creek** [SISKIYOU].

Donomore Meadows [SISKIYOU]: *area,* 5.5 miles northeast of Condrey Mountain (lat. 41°59'45" N, long. 122°54'30" W). Named on Condrey Mountain (1955) 15' quadrangle.

Doodlebug Gulch [SHASTA]: *canyon,* drained by a stream that flows 0.5 mile to Hawkins Creek 3.25 miles north-northeast of Shoeinhorse Mountain (lat. 41°06'45" N, long. 122°02'40" W). Named on Shoeinhorse Mountain (1954) 15' quadrangle.

Dooles Creek [SHASTA]: *stream,* flows 2 miles to McCloud River Arm Shasta Lake nearly 3 miles south of Bollibokka Mountain (lat. 40°53'10" N, long. 122°13'15" W; at W line sec. 16, T 35 N, R 3 W). Named on Bollibokka Mountain (1957) 15' quadrangle.

Doolittle Creek [SISKIYOU]:

(1) *stream,* flows 6.5 miles to Indian Creek (1) 1.5 miles north of Happy Camp (lat. 41°49' N, long. 123°22'55" W; at E line sec. 34, T 17 N, R 7 E). Named on Happy Camp (1980) 7.5' quadrangle.

(2) *stream,* flows nearly 6 miles to Elk Creek 7.5 miles north of Ukonom Lake (lat. 41°41'15" N, long. 123°21'10" W). Named on Huckleberry Mountain (1980) 7.5' quadrangle.

(3) *stream,* flows about 1 mile to Klamath River 11 miles north-northwest of Ukonom Lake (lat. 41°44'50" N, long. 123°24'30" W). Named on Clear Creek (1981) and Happy Camp (1980) 7.5' quadrangles.

Doon Camp [BUTTE]: *locality,* 2 miles west-southwest of Stirling City along Little West Fork [of West Fork Feather River] (lat. 39°53'50" N, long. 121°33'50" W; sec. 31, T 24 N, R 4 E). Named on Stirling City (1979) 7.5' quadrangle.

Doons Mill [BUTTE]: *locality,* 10.5 miles north-northeast of Paradise, and just south of present Stirling City (lat. 39°53'50" N, long. 121°31'30" W). Named on Chico (1895) 30' quadrangle.

Dorris [SISKIYOU]: *town,* 10 miles north-northeast of Macdoel (lat. 41°58' N, long. 121°55' W; around NW cor. sec. 31, T 48 N, R 1 E). Named on Dorris (1950) 15' quadrangle. The name commemorates Presley A. Dorris and his brother Carlos J. Dorris, stockmen in the 1860's (Gudde, 1949, p. 98). The town incorporated in 1908. Postal authorities established Picard post office in 1888 and moved it 3 miles east in 1907 when they changed the name to Dorris; the name "Picard" was for Francis Picard, first postmaster (Salley, p. 171). They established Otey's Ranch post office, named for J. Otey, in 1888, moved it 0.25 mile south and changed the name to Corbett in 1892, and discontinued it in 1896, when they moved the service to Picard (Salley, p. 50, 164). California Mining Bureau's (1909a) map shows a place called Brownell situated at the end of a stage line 17.25 miles southeast of Dorris. Postal authorities established Brownell post office in 1892, moved it 0.75 mile southwest in 1899, moved it 2.5 miles north in 1902, moved it 1 mile southeast in 1908, and discontinued it in 1912 when the post office was located 10 miles southeast of Dorris; the name was for Sarah M. Brownell, first postmaster (Salley, p. 27). They established Calor post office 8 miles east of Dorris in 1918 and discontinued it in 1930; the name was from the location of the post office near California-Oregon State line (Salley, p. 32). United States Board on Geographic Names (1986b, p. 2) approved the name "Coyote Ridge" for a feature, 6.2 miles long, situated 10 miles southeast of Dorris (lat 41°50'55" N, long. 121°48'35" W, at northwest end), and rejected the name "Coyote Hill" for the ridge.

Dorris Hill [SISKIYOU]: *hill,* 22 miles west-southwest of Macdoel (lat. 41°41'35" N, long. 122°23'40" W; at W line sec. 2, T 44 N, R 5 W). Altitude 3100 feet. Named on Lake Shastina (1954) 15' quadrangle.

Dorris Spring [SISKIYOU]: *spring,* 6.25 miles southwest of Macdoel (lat. 41°45'35" N, long. 122°05' W; sec. 9, T 45 N, R 2 W). Named on Macdoel (1954) 15' quadrangle.

Dotys Camp [TEHAMA]: *locality,* 9 miles southwest of Mineral (lat. 40°15'55" N, long. 121°43'10" W; near W line sec. 23, T 28 N, R 2 E); the place is 0.5 mile southwest of Doty Spring. Site named on Lassen Peak (1956) 15' quadrangle.

Doty Spring [TEHAMA]: *spring,* 9.5 miles southwest of Mineral (lat. 40°15'30" N, long. 121°43'40" W; near SE cor. sec. 22, T 28 N, R 2 E). Named on Lassen Peak (1956) 15' quadrangle.

Double Spring [SISKIYOU]: *spring,* 17 miles south of Macdoel (lat. 41°35'25" N, long. 122°04' W; sec. 3, T 43 N, R 2 W). Named on The Whaleback (1954) 15' quadrangle.

Dougherty Bluff [SISKIYOU]: *relief feature,* 3.5 miles east-northeast of Forks of Salmon along North Fork Salmon River (lat. 41°17' N, long. 123°15'30" W). Named on Forks of Salmon (1978) 7.5' quadrangle.

Douglas Creek [SISKIYOU]: *stream,* flows 2 miles to Klamath River 9 miles north-northwest of Ukonom Lake (lat. 41°41'30" N, long. 123°26'35" W). Named on Clear Creek (1981) 7.5' quadrangle.

Dover Cut off [BUTTE-GLENN]: *water feature,* 7 miles west-southwest of Chico along Sacramento River on Butte-Glen County line (lat. 39°41' N, long. 121°57'30" W). Named on Chico (1895) 30' quadrangle

Dow: see **Tom Dow Creek** [SHASTA].

Dowling Gulch [SISKIYOU]: *canyon,* drained by a stream that flows 2 miles to Humbug Creek 12 miles southwest of Hornbrook (lat. 41°47' N, long. 122°42'15" W; sec. 6, T 45 N, R 7 W). Named on Hornbrook (1955) 15' quadrangle.

Doyle Butte [SHASTA]: *peak,* 6 miles southeast of Burney (lat. 40°49'35" N, long. 121°35'20" W; at N line sec. 12, T 34 N, R 3 E). Altitude 5498 feet. Named on Burney (1957) 15' quadrangle.

Doyles Corner [SHASTA]: *locality,* 6 miles east of Burney (lat. 40°52'40" N, long. 121°33'30" W; sec. 19, T 35 N, R 4 E). Named on Burney (1957) 15' quadrangle. Dave Doyle settled at the place (Steger, p. 29).

Draper: see **Hooker** [TEHAMA].

Dredge: see **Chico** [BUTTE].

Drennan Camp [TEHAMA]: *locality,* 12 miles south of Panther Spring along Little Dry Creek (lat. 40°05'30" N, long. 121°48'30" W). Named on Panther Spring (1953) 15' quadrangle.

Dresser Camp [BUTTE]: *locality,* 7.5 miles south of Jonesville (lat. 40°00'15" N, long. 121°26'45" W; near SW cor. sec. 20, T 25 N, R 5 E). Named on Jonesville (1958) 15' quadrangle.

Dripping Springs [SHASTA]: *spring,* 9.5 miles southwest of Shasta Bally (lat. 40°30'10" N, long. 122°46'45" W; on N line sec. 33, T 31 N, R 8 W). Named on Weaverville (1950) 15' quadrangle.

Dropoff Creek [SHASTA]: *stream,* flows 2.25 miles to Star City Creek 7 miles north-northeast of Shoeinhorse Mountain (lat. 41°09'45" N, long. 122°01' W). Named on Big Bend (1961) and Shoeinhorse Mountain (1954) 15' quadrangles. United States Board on Geographic Names (1964, p. 9) rejected the name "Fools Creek" for the stream.

Drumheller Slough [GLENN]: *water feature,* enters Colusa County 5.5 miles south-southeast of Butte City (lat. 39°23'05" N, long. 121°57'45" W; near W line sec. 27, T 18 N, R 1 W). Named on Butte City (1952) 7.5' quadrangle.

Drunken Gulch [SHASTA]: *canyon,* drained by a stream that flows 1.5 miles to Clear Creek 4.25 miles north-northeast of the village of French Gulch (lat. 40°44'50" N, long. 122°37'15" W; sec. 2, T 33 N, R 7 W). Named on Whiskeytown (1979) 7.5' quadrangle.

Dry Burney Creek [SHASTA]: *stream,* flows 6 miles to Burney Creek 19 miles north-northwest of Lassen Peak (lat. 40°43'35" N, long. 121°42'50" W; near S line sec. 11, T 33 N, R 2 E). Named on Manzanita Lake (1956) 15' quadrangle.

Dry Clover Creek [SHASTA]: *stream,* flows 9.5 mile to Clover Creek (1)

10 miles east-northeast of Millville (lat. 40°37'50" N, long. 122°01'45" W; at W line sec. 18, T 32 N, R 1 W). Named on Millville (1953) and Whitmore (1956) 15' quadrangles. Called North Fork Cow Creek on Lassen Peak (1894) 1° quadrangle.

Dry Creek [BUTTE]: *stream,* flows 22 miles to a canal 8.5 miles west-northwest of Oroville (lat. 39°33'15" N, long. 121°42'20" W; near SW cor. sec. 25, T 20 N, R 2 E). Named on Cherokee (1970), Hamlin Canyon (1951), Paradise East (1980), and Shippee (1948) 7.5' quadrangles. The stream had the early names "Table Mountain Creek" and "Tablemount Creek" (Dunn, F.D., p. 105).

Dry Creek [GLENN]: *stream,* flows 8 miles to Stony Creek [GLENN-TEHAMA] 8.5 miles east of Saint John Mountain (lat. 39°25'05" N, long. 122°32'05" W; sec. 16, T 18 N, R 6 W). Named on Stonyford (1968) 7.5' quadrangle.

Dry Creek [SHASTA]:

(1) *stream,* flows 11 miles to Little Cow Creek 5.25 miles north-northwest of Millville (lat. 40°36'55" N, long. 122°13'35" W; sec. 20, T 32 N, R 3 W). Named on Bella Vista (1965) and Project City (1957) 7.5' quadrangles.

(2) *stream,* flows 4.5 miles to Oak Run Creek 8 miles northeast of Millville (lat. 40°38'15" N, long. 122°05'10" W; at NW cor. sec. 15, T 32 N, R 2 W). Named on Millville (1953) 15' quadrangle.

(3) *stream,* flows 5 miles to Oak Run Creek 1.5 miles northwest of Millville (lat. 40°33'50" N, long. 122°11'35" W; at S line sec. 3, T 31 N, R 3 W). Named on Palo Cedro (1965) 7.5' quadrangle.

(4) *stream,* flows nearly 7.5 miles to Bear Creek (2) 2 miles north of Balls Ferry (lat. 40°26'45" N, long. 122°12'05" W). Named on Balls Ferry (1965) and Palo Cedro (1965) 7.5' quadrangles.

(5) *stream,* flows 12 miles to Cottonwood Creek [SHASTA-TEHAMA] 4.5 miles south of Olinda (lat. 40°22'45" N, long. 122°25'15" W; near W line sec. 10, T 29 N, R 5 W). Named on Ono (1952) 15' quadrangle, and on Olinda (1964) 7.5' quadrangle.

(6) *stream,* flows less than 1 mile to Whiskeytown Lake 6 mile south-southeast of the village of French Gulch (lat. 40°37'35" N, long. 122°35' W; sec. 18, T 32 N, R 6 W). Named on Whiskeytown (1979) 7.5' quadrangle.

Dry Creek [SISKIYOU]:

(1) *stream,* flows 6.5 miles to Klamath River 24 miles west-northwest of Macdoel (lat. 41°50' N, long. 122°27' W; at SE cor. sec. 18, T 47 N, R 5 W). Named on Copco (1954) and Hornbrook (1955) 15' quadrangles.

(2) *stream,* flows 4 miles to Little Shasta River 15 miles west-southwest of Macdoel (lat. 41°45'15" N, long. 122°18'20" W; near N line sec. 16, T 45 N, R 4 W). Named on Copco (1954) 15' quadrangle.

(3) *stream,* flows 13 miles to Ash Creek (2) 7 miles west-northwest of Bartle (lat. 41°17'50" N, long. 121°56'30" W; at W line sec. 23, T 40 N, R 1 W). Named on Bartle (1961) 15' quadrangle.

(4) *stream,* flows 5.5 miles to McCloud River [SHASTA-SISKIYOU] 0.5 mile west-southwest of Bartle (lat. 41°15'10" N, long. 121°49'50" W; at W line sec. 2, T 39 N, R 1 E). Named on Big Bend (1961) 15' quadrangle.

Dry Creek [TEHAMA]:

(1) *stream,* flows 30 miles to South Fork Cottonwood Creek [SHASTA-TEHAMA] nearly 7 miles west-northwest of Hooker (lat. 40°19'30" N, long. 122°26'40" W; near E line sec. 32, T 29 N, R 5 W). Named on Chanchelulla Peak (1951) and Ono (1952) 15' quadrangles, and on Mitchell Gulch (1965) 7.5' quadrangle.

(2) *stream,* formed by the confluence of North Fork and South Fork, flows 4.5 miles to Red Bank Creek 4.5 miles east-southeast of Wakefield Flat (lat. 40°05'40" N, long. 122°34'10" W; sec. 20, T 26 N, R 6 W). Named on Lowrey (1967) and Raglin Ridge (1967) 7.5' quadrangles. North Fork and South Fork each are 2.5 miles long; both forks are named on Raglin Ridge (1967) 7.5' quadrangle.

(3) *stream,* formed by the confluence of Big Dry Creek and Little Dry Creek, flows nearly 6 miles to Toomes Creek 4 miles north of Vina (lat. 39°59'15" N, long. 122°02'45" W; near W line sec. 25, T 25 N, R 2 W). Named on Panther Spring (1953) 15' quadrangle, and on Los Molinos (1952) and Vina (1950) 7.5' quadrangles. Called Toomes Creek on Mineral (1941) 30' quadrangle, and on Tehama (1905) 15' quadrangle.

Dry Creek: see **Big Dry Creek** [TEHAMA]; **Digger Creek** [SHASTA-TEHAMA], **East Dry Creek** [SHASTA]; **Little Dry Creek** [BUTTE]; **Little Dry Creek** [TEHAMA]; **Oak Run Creek** [SHASTA].

Dry Creek Campground [SHASTA]: *locality,* 6 miles south-southeast of the village of French Gulch along Whiskeytown Lake (lat. 40°37'35" N, long. 122°34'50" W; near E line sec. 18, T 32 N, R 6 W); the place is at the mouth of Dry Creek (6). Named on Igo (1979) and Whiskeytown (1979) 7.5' quadrangles.

Dry Creek Hill [GLENN]: *peak,* 3.5 miles east-northeast of Saint John Mountain (lat. 39°27'25" N, long. 122°37'55" W; sec. 34, T 19 N, R 7 W); the peak is at the head of Dry Creek. Altitude 3175 feet. Named on Saint John Mountain (1968) 7.5' quadrangle.

Dry Creek Peak [SISKIYOU]: *peak,* 16 miles north-northwest of Bartle (lat. 41°27'45" N, long. 121°58'20" W; sec. 28, T 42 N, R 1 W); the peak is at the head of Dry Creek (3). Named on Bartle (1961) 15' quadrangle.

Dry Creek Spring [SISKIYOU]: *spring,* 14 miles north-northwest of Bartle (lat. 41°26'05" N, long. 121°57'45" W; near NE cor. sec. 4, T 41 N, R 1 W); the spring is along a branch of Dry Creek (3). Named on Bartle (1961) 15' quadrangle.

Dry Fork: see **Squaw Creek** [SHASTA] (3).

Dry Gulch [SISKIYOU]:

(1) *canyon,* drained by a stream that flows nearly 2 miles to Crawford Creek 1.25 miles north-northeast of Cecilville (lat. 41°09'30" N, long. 123°07'40" W). Named on Grasshopper Ridge (1979) 7.5' quadrangle.

(2) *canyon,* drained by a stream that flows 2 miles to Shasta Creek 8 miles south-southwest of Hornbrook (lat. 41°48'10" N, long. 122°35'50" W; near SE cor. sec. 25, T 46 N, R 7 W). Named on Hornbrook (1955) 15' quadrangle.

(3) *canyon,* drained by a stream that flows less than 1 mile to Angel Creek 10 miles west-southwest of Bartle (lat. 41°11'55" N, long. 121°59'55" W; at W line sec. 29, T 39 N, R 1 W). Named on Big Bend (1961) 15' quadrangle.

Dry Gulch [TEHAMA]: *canyon,* drained by a stream that flows 6 miles to Love Branch 6 miles east of Manton (lat. 40°26' N, long. 121°45'20" W). Named on Lassen Peak (1956) and Manton (1956) 15' quadrangles.

Dry Lake [SHASTA]: *intermittent lake,* 0.5 mile long, 5.5 mile south-southwest of Burney (lat. 40°48'20" N, long. 121°42'05" W; sec. 13, T 34 N, R 2 E). Named on Burney (1957) 15' quadrangle.

Dry Lake [SISKIYOU]:

(1) *lake,* 125 feet long, 3.25 miles southeast of Bear Peak (lat. 41°39'30" N, long. 123°31'40" W). Named on Bear Peak (1982) 7.5' quadrangle.

(2) *lake,* 250 feet long, 8 miles north-northwest of Sawyers Bar (lat. 41°23'55" N, long. 123°12'35" W). Named on English Peak (1977) 7.5' quadrangle.

Dry Lake [TEHAMA]: *dry lake,* 6.5 miles southwest of Wakefield Flat (lat. 40°03'20" N, long. 122°43'40" W; near N line sec. 2, T 25 N, R 8 W). Named on Raglin Ridge (1967) 7.5' quadrangle.

Dry Lake: see **Buckhorn Ridge** [SISKIYOU].

Dry Lake Campground [TEHAMA]: *locality,* 3 miles north-northwest of Mineral (lat. 40°23'25" N, long. 121°37'10" W; sec. 11, T 29 N, R 3 E). Named on Lassen Peak (1956) 15' quadrangle, which shows an unnamed dry lake at the site.

Dry Lake Reservoir [GLENN]: *intermittent lake,* 150 feet long, 7.5 miles north-northwest of the village of Elk Creek (lat. 39°41'20" N, long. 122°36'45" W). Named on Chrome (1968) 7.5' quadrangle.

Drytown: see **Cherokee** [BUTTE].

Dubock Slough [BUTTE]: *stream,* flows 5.5 miles to a ditch 6.5 miles southwest of Chico (lat. 39°39'10" N, long. 121°54'40" W). Named on Chico (1949) 15' quadrangle.

Duck Creek: see **Ducket Creek** [SHASTA]; **Summit Creek** [SHASTA].

Ducket Creek [SHASTA]: *stream,* flows 6.5 miles to North Fork Cottonwood Creek [SHASTA-TEHAMA] 2.5 miles west-southwest of Ono (lat. 40°27'45" N, long. 122°39'50" W; near S line sec. 9, T 30 N, R 7 W); the stream heads near Ducket Peak. Named on Ono (1952) 15' quadrangle, and on Shasta Bally (1978) 7.5' quadrangle. Called Duck Creek on Averill's (1939) map. H.P. Ducket camped by the stream in the late 1890's and made a painting of it that was exhibited; a map of 1884 had the names "Numhebe Creek" and "Hoover Creek" for the stream (Steger, p. 30).

Ducket Peak [SHASTA]: *peak,* 4 miles south of Shasta Bally (lat. 40°32'40" N, long. 122°38'35" W). Altitude 4623 feet. Named on Shasta Bally (1978) 7.5' quadrangle. Called Eagle Creek Peak on French Gulch (1944) 15' quadrangle, where present Rector Peak is called Ducket Peak.

Duck Lake [SISKIYOU]: *intermittent lake,* 500 feet long, 9 miles south of Bray (lat. 41°31'05" N, long. 121°59'30" W; sec. 5, T 42 N, R 1 W). Named on Bray (1950) 15' quadrangle.

Duck Lake: see **Big Duck Lake** [SISKIYOU]; **Little Duck Lake** [SISKIYOU]; **Summit Lake** [SHASTA] (3).

Duck Lake Creek [SISKIYOU]: *stream,* flows 4 miles to French Creek (2) 8 miles south of Etna (lat. 41°20'40" N, long. 122°54'15" W; sec. 5, T 40 N, R 9 W); the stream heads at Big Duck Lake and Little Duck Lake. Named on Etna (1955) 15' quadrangle.

Dudgen Butte [SHASTA]: *peak,* 7.5 miles east-southeast of Burney (lat. 40°50' N, long. 121°32'40" W; sec. 5, T 34 N, R 4 E). Named on Burney (1957) 15' quadrangle.

Duncan Canyon [TEHAMA]: *canyon,* 1 mile long, 4.5 miles northwest of Paskenta (lat. 39°56'15" N, long. 122°35'50" W; sec. 13, T 24 N, R 7 W). Named on Paskenta (1967) 7.5' quadrangle.

Duncan Creek [SHASTA]: *stream,* flows 9.5 miles to Middle Fork Cottonwood Creek [SHASTA-TEHAMA] 4.5 miles east of Arbuckle Mountain (lat. 40°24'05" N, long. 122°46'40" W; at N line sec. 4, T 29 N, R 8 W). Named on Chanchelulla Peak (1951) 15' quadrangle. On Averill's (1939) map, the part of the stream above present Ditch Fork is called Middle Fork. The name "Duncan" commemorates the Duncan brothers, who settled by the stream and operated one of the first sawmills in southwestern Shasta County (Steger, p. 30). East Fork enters from the northeast 3 miles upstream from the mouth of the main creek and is 5.5 miles long. Ditch Fork enters nearly 4 miles upstream from the mouth of the main creek and is

6.5 miles long. Both forks are named on Chanchelulla Peak (1951) 15' quadrangle. On Averill's (1939) map, present Ditch Fork is called West Branch.

Duncan Creek [SISKIYOU]: *stream,* flows 2.5 miles to Salmon River 7.5 miles northwest of Forks of Salmon (lat. 41°20'55" N, long. 123°24'20" W). Named on Orleans Mountain (1974) 7.5' quadrangle.

Dunning Slough [GLENN]: *water feature,* cutoff meander of Sacramento River 18 miles north of Butte City (lat. 39°44' N, long. 121°59'40" W). Named on Ord Ferry (1949) 7.5' quadrangle.

Dunns Gulch [SISKIYOU]: *canyon,* drained by a stream that flows 1 mile to Humbug Creek 9.5 miles southwest of Hornbrook (lat. 41°48'45" N, long. 122°40'50" W; sec. 29, T 46 N, R 7 W). Named on Hornbrook (1955) 15' quadrangle.

Dunsmuir [SISKIYOU]: *town,* 7 miles south-southeast of the town of Mount Shasta along Sacramento River (lat. 41°12'45" N, long. 122°16'15" W; in and near sec. 25, T 39 N, R 4 W). Named on Dunsmuir (1954) 15' quadrangle. The town incorporated in 1909. Postal authorities established Mannon post office in 1886 and moved it 1 mile south in 1887, when they changed the name to Dunsmuir; the name "Mannon" was for Dick Mannon, pioneer owner of Soda Springs and the hotel there (Salley, p. 131). The name "Dunsmuir" commemorates Alexander Dunsmuir, who passed through the place and promised the settlers there that he would give a fountain to them if they would name the community for him; the site previously had the name "Pusher" (Gudde, 1949, p. 101). Postal authorities established Pebble post office 6 miles by rail east of Dunsmuir in 1889, discontinued it in 1890, reestablished it in 1893, and discontinued it in 1895 (Salley, p. 169).

Dunsmuir Rock: see **Mount Bradley** [SISKIYOU].

Durbin Lake [SHASTA]: lake, 700 feet long, 16 miles north-northwest of Lassen Peak (lat. 40°42'35" N, long. 121°34'15" W; near NW cor. sec. 19, T 33 N, R 4 E). Named on Manzanita Lake (1956) 15' quadrangle. Steger (p. 30) associated the name with William G. Durbin, who supervised Lassen National Forest from 1923 until 1936.

Durbin Spring [BUTTE]: *spring,* 12 miles north-northwest of Paradise (lat. 39°54'40" N, long. 121°42'05" W; sec. 25, T 24 N, R 2 E). Named on Cohasset (1979) 7.5' quadrangle.

Durham [BUTTE]: *town,* 6 miles south-southeast of Chico (lat. 39°38'40" N, long. 121°47'55" W; mainly in sec. 30, T 21 N, R 2 E). Named on Chico (1948) 7.5' quadrangle. Postal authorities established Butte Valley post office 5.5 miles southeast of Chico in 1861; they moved it to a site 7 miles south of Chico and changed the name to Durham in 1871 (Salley, p. 30, 63). The name "Durham" commemorates W.W. Durham, who represented Butte County in the state legislature in 1879 and 1880 (Wells and Chambers, p. 249). F.D. Dunn (p. 93) listed a place called Roble, Robles, or Roble Station that was situated about 1.25 miles north of Durham along the railroad (sec. 24, T 21 N, R 1 E).

Durham Slough [BUTTE]: *stream,* flows 7.5 miles to Butte Creek [BUTTE-GLENN] 8 miles south-southwest of Durham (lat. 39°32'15" N, long. 121°51'05" W). Named on Chico (1948) and Nelson (1948) 7.5' quadrangles.

Durley Flat [TEHAMA]: *area,* 6.5 miles west of Panther Spring (lat. 40°15' N, long. 121°53'30" W). Named on Manton (1956) and Panther Spring (1953) 15' quadrangles.

Durney Lake [SISKIYOU]: *lake,* 600 feet long, 9 miles west of the town of Mount Shasta (lat. 40°20'05" N, long. 122°28'35" W; on S line sec. 6, T 40 N, R 5 W). Named on Weed (1954) 15' quadrangle.

Dutch Butte [SHASTA]: *relief feature,* 8 mile southeast of Burney (lat. 40°48'30" N, long. 121°33'10" W; near NW cor. sec. 17, T 34 N, R 4 E); the feature is 1.25 miles south-southwest of Dutch Flat. Named on Burney (1957) 15' quadrangle.

Dutch Creek [SHASTA]: *stream,* flows 3 miles to Squaw Valley Creek nearly 7 miles west of Shoeinhorse Mountain (lat. 41°03'50" N, long. 122°12' W; sec. 15, T 37 N, R 3 W). Named on Shoeinhorse Mountain (1954) 15' quadrangle. Sim Southern named the stream for Dr. Dutch, a dentist from San Francisco who was a frequent visitor to Sims Station in the 1860's (Steger, p. 30).

Dutch Creek [SISKIYOU]:

(1) *stream,* flows 4.5 miles to Elliot Creek 12.5 miles north-northeast of the village of Seiad Valley (lat. 41°59'50" N, long. 123°04'25" W). Named on Dutch Creek (1980) 7.5' quadrangle. West Fork enters from the south-southwest 0.5 mile upstream from the mouth of the main stream; it is nearly 2 miles long and is named on Dutch Creek (1980) 7.5' quadrangle.

(2) *stream,* flows nearly 1.5 miles to Klamath River 6.5 miles northwest of Ukonom Lake (lat. 41°37'55" N, long. 123°27'35" W). Named on Clear Creek (1981) 7.5' quadrangle.

(3) *stream,* flows 3 miles to Beaver Creek (1) 7.5 miles east-southeast of Condrey Mountain (lat. 41°55' N, long. 122°50'10" W; at S line sec. 13, T 47 N, R 9 W). Named on Condrey Mountain (1955) 1.5' quadrangle.

(4) *stream,* flows 5.5 miles to Klamath River 9.5 miles west-southwest of Hornbrook (lat. 41°51'50" N, long. 122°43'35" W; sec. 1, T 46 N, R 8 W). Named on Hornbrook (1955) 15' quadrangle.

(5) *stream,* flows 3 miles to Camp Creek 24 miles west-northwest of Macdoel (lat. 41°58'30" N, long. 122°26' W; sec. 33, T 48 N, R 5 W). Named on Copco (1954) 15' quadrangle.

Dutch Creek: see **Little Dutch Creek** [SISKIYOU].

Dutch Flat [SHASTA]: *area,* 8 miles east-southeast of Burney (lat. 40°49'25" N, long. 121°32'20" W; near NE cor. sec. 8, T 34 N, R 4 E); the place is 1.25 miles north-northeast of Dutch Butte. Named on Burney (1957) 15' quadrangle.

Dutch Gulch [SHASTA]:

(1) *canyon,* drained by a stream that flows 5.5 miles to Cottonwood Creek [SHASTA-TEHAMA] 6 miles southwest of Olinda (lat. 40°23'05" N, long. 122°29'25" W). Named on Ono (1952) 15' quadrangle, and on Olinda (1964) 7.5' quadrangle.

(2) *canyon,* drained by a stream that flows 2.5 miles to French Gulch (2) 1 mile west-northwest of the village of French Gulch (lat. 40°42'25" N, long. 122°39'10" W; at W line sec. 22, T 33 N, R 7 W). Named on French Gulch (1979) 7.5' quadrangle.

Dutch Henry Creek [GLENN]: *stream,* flows 2.5 miles to Minton Creek 3 miles northeast of High Peak (lat. 39°27'35" N, long. 122°23'20" W; sec. 35, T 19 N, R 5 W). Named on Lodoga (1960) 15' quadrangle.

Dutchman Gulch [TEHAMA]: *canyon,* drained by a stream that flows 4.5 miles to South Fork Dry Creek (1) 3.25 miles southwest of Beegum Peak (lat. 40°16'35" N, long. 122°55'30" W; sec. 18, T 28 N, R 9 W). Named on Chanchelulla Peak (1951) 15' quadrangle.

Dutchman Peak [SHASTA]: *peak,* 6.5 miles northwest of Big Bend (lat. 41°05'30" N, long. 121°59'35" W; sec. 5, T 37 N, R 1 W). Altitude 4555 feet. Named on Big Bend (1961) 15' quadrangle.

Dutch Owen Creek [GLENN]: *stream,* flows nearly 1 mile to Lake County 12 miles west-southwest of the village of Elk Creek (lat. 39°31'40" N, long. 122°44'05" W). Named on Felkner Hill (1968) 7.5' quadrangle.

Dutch Pete Spring [BUTTE]: *spring,* 7.5 miles north-northeast of Oroville (lat. 39°37'05" N, long. 121°31'35" W; sec. 4, T 20 N, R 4 E). Named on Oroville (1970) 7.5' quadrangle.

Dutch Ravine [BUTTE]: *canyon,* drained by a stream that flows 1.25 miles to Rocky Honcut Creek 3.5 miles north of Bangor (lat. 39°26'30" N, long. 121°29' W; near S line sec. 3, T 18 N, R 5 E). Named on Bangor (1947) 7.5' quadrangle.

Duzel Creek [SISKIYOU]: *stream,* flows 9 miles to Moffett Creek 11 miles south-southwest of Yreka (lat. 41°34'50" N, long. 122°42'40" W; near NE cor. sec. 13, T 43 N, R 8 W). Named on China Mountain (1955), Fort Jones (1955), and Yreka (1954) 15' quadrangles.

Duzel Rock [SISKIYOU]: *peak,* 15 miles south-southwest of Yreka (lat. 41°31'40" N, long. 122°43'20" W; sec. 36, T 43 N, R 8 W). Altitude 6039 feet. Named on Yreka (1954) 15' quadrangle. Called Skukum Rock on Shasta (1894) 1° quadrangle. The name "Skukum" is of Indian origin (Kroeber, p. 58).

Dwinnell Lake: see **Lake Shastina** [SISKIYOU].

Dwinnell Reservoir: see **Lake Shastina** [SISKIYOU].

Dye: see **Ike Dye Hill** [TEHAMA].

Dye Creek [TEHAMA]: *stream,* flows 15 miles to Sacramento River 3.25 miles north-northwest of Los Molinos (lat. 40°04'05" N, long. 122°06'35" W). Named on Panther Spring (1953) 15' quadrangle, and on Los Molinos (1952, photorevised 1969) 7.5' quadrangle. Called Rio de los Berrendos on Tehama (1905) 15' quadrangle. North Fork enters 7.25 miles north-northeast of Los Molinos; it is 4 miles long and is named on Panther Spring (1953) 15' quadrangle, and on Los Molinos (1952) 7.5' quadrangle. Little North Fork enters North Fork from the north 15 miles southwest of Panther Spring; it is 2.5 miles long and in named on Panther Spring (1953) 15' quadrangle.

— E —

Eagle Canyon [SHASTA-TEHAMA]: *canyon,* about 2.5 miles long, 2.5 miles west-southwest of Manton along North Fork Battle Creek [SHASTA-TEHAMA] on Shasta-Tehama County line (lat. 40°25'25" N, long. 121°55'05" W). Named on Manton (1956) 15' quadrangle.

Eagle Creek [SHASTA]: *stream,* flows nearly 7 miles to North Fork Cottonwood Creek [SHASTA-TEHAMA] (lat. 40°27'55" N, long. 122°36'40" W; near W line sec. 12, T 30 N, R 7 W). Named on Ono (1952) 15' quadrangle, and on Igo (1979) and Shasta Bally (1978) 7.5' quadrangles.

Eagle Creek: see **Ono** [SHASTA].

Eagle Creek Peak: see **Ducket Peak** [SHASTA].

Eagle Gulch [BUTTE]: *canyon,* drained by a stream that heads in Yuba County and flows less than 1 mile to Lost Creek Reservoir 3 miles north-northeast of Clipper Mills in Butte County (lat. 39°34'10" N, long. 121°07'50" W; near NE cor. sec. 25, T 20 N, R 7 E). Named on Clipper Mills (1948) and Strawberry Valley (1948) 7.5' quadrangles.

Eagle Nest Butte [SISKIYOU]: *hill,* 8.5 miles north of Medicine Lake (lat. 41°42'15" N, long. 121°34' W; near NE cor. sec. 36, T 45 N, R 3 E). Altitude 5477 feet. Named on Medicine Lake (1952) 15 quadrangle.

Eagle Peak [SHASTA]: *peak,* 1 mile southwest of Lassen Peak (lat. 40°28'40" N, long. 121°31' W; sec. 10, T 30 N, R 4 E). Altitude 9222 feet. Named on Lassen Peak (1956) 15' quadrangle.

Eagle Peak [SISKIYOU]: *peak,* 18 miles south-southeast of Etna on Siskiyou-Trinity County line (lat. 41°12'15" N, long. 122°48' W; at N line sec. 32, T 39 N, R 8 W); the peak is near the head of Eagle Creek in Trinity County. Altitude 7789 feet. Named on Coffee Creek (1955) 15' quadrangle.

Eagle Peak [TEHAMA]: *peak,* 6 miles west-northwest of Paskenta (lat. 39°55'40" N, long. 122°38'25" W; near N line sec. 22, T 24 N, R 7 W). Named on Riley Ridge (1967) 7.5' quadrangle.

Eagle Point: see **Gibson** [SHASTA].

Eagle Rock [SISKIYOU]: *peak,* 13 miles west-northwest of Macdoel (lat. 41°52'40" N, long. 122°14'30" W; near NW cor. sec. 32, T 47 N, R 3 W). Altitude 6993 feet. Named on Macdoel (1954) 15' quadrangle.

Eagle Rock [TEHAMA]: *relief feature,* 7.25 miles west-northwest of Paskenta (lat. 39°55'40" N, long. 122°40'05" W; near N line sec. 20, T 24 N, R 7 W). Named on Riley Ridge (1967) 7.5' quadrangle.

Eagle Rock Camp [TEHAMA]: *locality,* 7.5 miles west-northwest of Paskenta (lat. 39°55'55" N, long. 122°40'10" W; near S line sec. 17, T 24 N, R 7 W); the place is 0.25 mile north-northwest of Eagle Rock. Named on Riley Ridge (1967) 7.5' quadrangle.

Eagle Spring [SISKIYOU]: *spring,* 5.5 miles west of Scott Bar (lat. 41°44'50" N, long. 123°06'40" W). Named on Scott Bar (1980) 7.5' quadrangle. Scott Bar (1955) 15' quadrangle shows Eagle Spring Camp at the place.

Eagle Spring Camp: see **Eagle Spring** [SISKIYOU].

East Biggs [BUTTE]: *settlement,* 3 miles east of Biggs (lat. 39°24'55" N, long. 121°39'15" W). Named on Biggs (1970) 7.5' quadrangle. Biggs (1912) 7.5' quadrangle shows Biggs Station along Northern Electric Railroad at the site. Marysville (1895) 30' quadrangle shows a place called Rio Bonito situated at or near present East Biggs. Postal authorities established Rio Bonito post office in 1909 and discontinued it in 1914 (Frickstad, p. 12).

East Boulder Creek [SISKIYOU]: *stream,* flows nearly 4 miles to West Boulder Creek 14 miles south-southeast of Etna (lat. 41°15'35" N, long. 122°41'10" W; at E line sec. 7, T 39 N, R 8 W); East Boulder Lake is near the head of the stream. Named on Coffee Creek (1955) and Etna (1955) 15' quadrangles.

East Boulder Lake [SISKIYOU]: *lake,* 1700 feet long, 16 miles south-southeast of Etna (lat. 41°13'55" N, long. 122°47' W; near N line sec. 21, T 39 N, R 8 W); the lake is along upper reaches of East Boulder Creek. Named on Coffee Creek (1955) 15' quadrangle.

East China Point [BUTTE]: *ridge,* south-southwest-trending, 1.25 miles long, 1.5 miles south of Stirling City (lat. 39°52'50" N, long. 121°31'50" W; mainly in sec. 4, T 23 N, R 4 E). Named on Paradise East (1980) and Stirling City (1979) 7.5' quadrangles.

East Creek: see **Pinkard Creek** [BUTTE].

East Dog Fork: see **Elliot Creek** [SISKIYOU].

East Dry Creek [SHASTA]: *stream,* flows 4 miles to Dry Creek (1) 10 miles north-northwest of Millville (lat. 40°41'10" N, long. 122°14'45" W; sec. 30, T 33 N, R 3 W). Named on Bella Vista (1965) 7.5' quadrangle.

East Fork Campground [SISKIYOU]: *locality,* nearly 2 miles east-northeast of Cecilville (lat. 41°09'10" N, long. 123°06'35" W); the place is near the mouth of East Fork of South Fork Salmon River. Named on Grasshopper Ridge (1979) 7.5' quadrangle.

East Fork Mountain [SHASTA]: *ridge,* north-northwest-trending, 1.5 miles long, 9 miles east of Bollibokka Mountain (lat. 40°55'45" N, long. 122°02'45" W; on N line sec. 1, T 35 N, R 2 W); the ridge is south of East Fork Squaw Creek (2). Named on Bollibokka Mountain (1957) 15' quadrangle.

East Fork Ridge [SISKIYOU]: *ridge,* generally south-trending, 8 miles long, center 11 miles north-northwest of Happy Camp (lat. 41°57' N, long. 123°25'45" W); the ridge is west of East Fork Indian Creek (1). Named on Deadman Point (1981) 7.5' quadrangle.

East Gridley [BUTTE]: *settlement,* 2 miles east of Gridley (lat. 39°21'50" N, long. 121°39'40" W). Named on Gridley (1952) 7.5' quadrangle. Gridley (1912) 7.5' quadrangle shows Gridley Sta. located along Sacramento Northern Railroad at the site.

East Gulch [SISKIYOU]: *canyon,* drained by a stream that flows 2.5 miles to Moffett Creek 13 miles south of Yreka (lat. 41°32'25" N, long. 122°40'45" W; sec. 29, T 43 N, R 7 W). Named on Yreka (1954) 15' quadrangle.

East Jerome Butte: see **Jerome** [SISKIYOU].

East Low Gap: see **Low Gap** [TEHAMA].

Eastman Lake [SHASTA]: *marsh,* 7.5 miles north-northwest of Fall River Mills (lat. 41°06'35" N, long. 121°28'55" W; near SW cor. sec. 23, T 38 N, R 4 E). Named on Fall River Mills (1961) 15' quadrangle.

Eastman Lake: see **Little Tule River** [SHASTA].

East Peak [SISKIYOU]: *peak,* 11 miles north-northwest of Forks of Salmon (lat. 41°23'45" N, long. 123°26'15" W). Altitude 3900 feet. Named on Somes Bar (1979) 7.5' quadrangle.

East Prospect Peak: see **Prospect Peak** [SHASTA].

East Reservoir [GLENN]: *intermittent lake,* 150 feet long, 7.5 miles north-northwest of the village of Elk Creek (lat. 39°41'35" N, long. 122°36'50" W). Named on Chrome (1968) 7.5' quadrangle.

East Sand Slough [TEHAMA]: *water feature,* joins Sacramento River 1 mile southeast of downtown Red Bluff (lat. 40°09'55" N, long. 122°13'05" W; at E line sec. 29, T 27 N, R 3 W). Named on Red Bluff East (1951) 7.5' quadrangle.

East Sulphur Creek [SHASTA-TEHAMA]: *stream,* heads in Shasta County and flows 3 miles to join West Sulphur Creek [SHASTA-TEHAMA] and form Mill Creek (3) 7 miles northeast of Mineral in Tehama County (lat. 40°25'45" N, long. 121°31'20" W; sec. 27, T 30 N, R 4 E). Named on Lassen Peak (1956) 15' quadrangle.

East Valley Creek [SHASTA]: *stream,* flows 5 miles to East Fork Stillwater Creek 4.5 miles east-southeast of the town of Central Valley (lat. 40°39' N, long. 122°17'30" W; near N line sec. 11, T 32 N, R 4 W). Named on Project City (1957) 7.5' quadrangle.

East Walker Creek [SISKIYOU]: *stream,* flows nearly 2 miles to Walker Creek 3.5 miles south-southeast of the village of Seiad Valley (lat. 41°47'50" N, long. 123°09'55" W; sec. 30, T 46 N, R 11 W). Named on Seiad Valley (1980) 7.5' quadrangle.

Eaton Lakes [SISKIYOU]: *lakes,* three, largest 1200 feet long, 10 miles south of Etna (lat. 41°18'55" N, long. 122°55'30" W; sec. 18, T 40 N, R 9 W); the lakes are less than 1 mile north-northeast of Eaton Peak. Named on Etna (1955) 15' quadrangle.

Eaton Peak [SISKIYOU]: *peak,* 11 miles south of Etna (lat. 41°18'15" N, long. 122°55'55" W; sec. 19, T 40 N, R 9 W); the peak is less than 1 mile south-southwest of Eaton Lakes. Altitude 7609 feet. Named on Etna (1955) 15' quadrangle.

Eby: see **Red Bank** [TEHAMA].

Echo Canyon [SISKIYOU]: *canyon,* drained by a stream that flows 2 miles to Butte Fork Applegate River 8.5 miles north of the village of Seiad Valley (lat. 41°57'50" N, long. 123°11'15" W). Named on Kangaroo Mountain (1980) 7.5' quadrangle.

Echo Lake [SHASTA]:
(1) *lake,* 1300 feet long, 9 miles west-northwest of Castella (lat. 41°10'50" N, long. 122°28'25" W; sec. 5, 6, T 38 N, R 5 W). Named on Dunsmuir (1954) 15' quadrangle.
(2) *lake,* 1250 feet long, 6 miles east of Lassen Peak (lat. 40°29'45" N, long. 121°23'30" W; on N line sec. 2, T 30 N, R 5 E). Named on Mount Harkness (1956) 15' quadrangle.

Echo Lake [SISKIYOU]: *lake,* 350 feet long, 6.5 miles north of the village of Seiad Valley (lat. 41°56'10" N, long. 123°10'20" W); the lake is at the head of Echo Canyon. Named on Kangaroo Mountain (1980) 7.5' quadrangle.

Eddy Creek [SISKIYOU]: *stream,* flows 7.5 miles to Shasta Creek 3 miles west-southwest of Weed (lat. 41°24'15" N, long. 122°26' W; sec. 16, T 41 N, R 5 W). Named on China Mountain (1955) and Weed (1954) 15' quadrangles.

Eddy Gulch [SISKIYOU]: *canyon,* drained by a stream that flows 3 miles to North Fork Salmon River 0.5 mile east-southeast of Sawyers Bar (lat. 41°17'50" N, long. 123°07'10" W). Named on Sawyers Bar (1979) and Tanners Peak (1977) 7.5' quadrangles. Called Eddys Gulch on Sawyers Bar (1923) 30' quadrangle, and Crawford (1894, p. 285) used the form "Eddy's Gulch" for the name. East Fork branches southeast from the main canyon 2.5 miles south-southeast of Sawyers Bar; it is 1.5 miles long and is named on Grasshopper Ridge (1979) and Sawyers Bar (1979) 7.5' quadrangles. West Fork branches southwest from the main canyon 2.25 miles south of Sawyers Bar; it is 0.5 mile long and is named on Sawyers Bar (1979) 7.5' quadrangle. Daggett (1957b, p. 8) noted that places called Slapjack Bar and Applesass Bar were located along North Fork Salmon River opposite Eddy's Gulch. Gudde (1975, p. 20) used the form "Applesauce Bar" instead of "Applesass Bar."

Eddy Lake [BUTTE]: *water feature,* 11 miles southwest of Durham (lat. 39°33' N, long. 121°58' W). Named on Llano Seco (1948) 7.5' quadrangle.

Eddy Mountain: see **Mount Eddy** [SISKIYOU].

Eddys: see **The Eddys** [SISKIYOU].

Eddy's Gulch: see **Eddy Gulch** [SISKIYOU].

Eden: see **Camp Eden** [SISKIYOU].

Edgar Slough: see **Comanche Creek** [BUTTE].

Edge Cabin Spring [TEHAMA]: *spring,* 5.5 miles northeast of Deer Creek Station (lat. 40°19' N, long. 121°22'30" W; sec. 1, T 28 N, R 5 E). Named on Mount Harkness (1956) 15' quadrangle.

Edge Creek [SISKIYOU]: *stream,* heads in the State of Oregon and flows 3 miles to Klamath River 14 miles northwest of Macdoel (lat. 41°58'05" N, long. 122°12'50" W; near S line sec. 28, T 48 N, R 3 W). Named on Macdoel (1954) 15' quadrangle.

Edgewood [SISKIYOU]: *village,* 3.5 miles northwest of Weed (lat. 41°27'30" N, long. 122°25'45" W; sec. 28, T 42 N, R 5 W). Named on Weed (1954) 15' quadrangle. Shasta (1894) 1° quadrangle shows a place called Butteville at or near the site. Postal authorities established Edgwood post office in 1870 and changed the name to Edgewood in 1902 (Frickstad, p. 187).

William Brown and Jackson Brown settled at the site in 1851, and Joseph Cavanaugh opened a hotel there in 1860; the place also was known as Butteville (Hanna, p. 95).

Edgwood: see **Edgewood** [SISKIYOU].

Edson Creek [SISKIYOU]: *stream,* flows 9 miles to Dry Creek (3) 7 miles northwest of Bartle (lat. 41°18'45" N, long. 121°56' W; sec. 14, T 40 N, R 1 W). Named on Bartle (1961) 15' quadrangle.

Edsons: see **Gazelle** [SISKIYOU].

Edwards Lake: see **Hemlock Lake** [SHASTA].

Eel River, South Fork of Middle Fork: see **Black Butte River** [GLENN].

Eileen [SISKIYOU]: *locality,* 9.5 miles north-northeast of the village of Seiad Valley (lat. 41°57'45" N, long. 123°06'15" W). Site named on Dutch Creek (1980) 7.5' quadrangle. Postal authorities established Eileen post office in 1907 and discontinued it in 1909; the name was for the postmaster's wife (Salley, p. 66). They established Hutton post office 4 miles northwest of Eileen in 1906 and discontinued it in 1914; the name was for the operator of a resort at the site (Salley, p. 102). California State Mining Bureau's (1917a) map shows a place called Copper located just west of Hutton near California-Oregon State line. Postal authorities established Copper post office in 1914 and discontinued it in 1924 (Salley, p. 50).

Eiler: see **Lake Eiler** [SHASTA].

Eiler Butte [SHASTA]: *peak,* 17 miles north of Lassen Peak (lat. 40°43'20" N, long. 121°33'15" W; near N line sec. 18, T 33 N, R 4 E); the peak is southeast of Lake Eiler. Named on Manzanita Lak (1956) 15' quadrangle.

Eiler Gulch [SHASTA]: *canyon,* drained by a stream that flows 5 miles before ending 9.5 miles south-southeast of Burney (lat. 40°45'55" N, long. 121°35' W; sec. 36, T 34 N, R 3 E). Named on Burney (1957) and Manzanita Lake (1956) 15' quadrangles.

Eilers: see **Round Mountain** [SHASTA] (3).

Elam Campground [TEHAMA]: *locality,* 1.25 miles south of Deer Creek Station (lat. 40°14'45" N, long. 121°26'50" W; sec. 32, T 28 N, R 5 E). Named on Jonesville (1958) 15' quadrangle.

Elam Creek [TEHAMA]: *stream,* flows nearly 6 miles to Deer Creek (2) 1.25 miles south of Deer Creek Station (lat. 40°15' N, long. 121°26'45" W; at S line sec. 29, T 28 N, R 5 E). Named on Jonesville (1958) and Mount Harkness (1956) 15' quadrangles.

Elbow Spring [SISKIYOU]: *spring,* 1.5 miles south-southeast of Bear Peak (lat. 41°40'30" N, long. 123°33'45" W). Named on Bear Peak (1982) 7.5' quadrangle.

El Camino [TEHAMA]: *locality,* 1.5 miles southwest of Gerber (lat. 40°02'25" N, long. 122°10'10" W). Named on Gerber (1950) 7.5' quadrangle.

El Capitan [SISKIYOU]: *peak,* nearly 2.5 miles north of Preston Peak (lat. 41°52'10" N, long. 123°36'40" W). Altitude 6813 feet. Named on Preston Peak (1982) 7.5' quadrangle.

Elder Creek [TEHAMA]: *stream,* formed by the confluence of North Fork and South Fork, flows 22 miles to Sacramento River nearly 2 miles north-northwest of Los Molinos (lat. 40°02'35" N, long. 122°06'50" W). Named on Gerber (1950), Los Molinos (1952), Lowrey (1967), Red Bank (1952), and West of Gerber (1951) 7.5' quadrangles. Called Arro. de los Saucos on a diseño of Las Flores grant in 1844 (Becker, 1964). North Fork is 15 miles long and is named on Yolla Bolly (1954) 15' quadrangle, and on Lowrey (1967) and Raglin Ridge (1967) 7.5' quadrangles. South Fork is 17 miles long and is named on Lowrey (1967), Paskenta (1967), and Riley Ridge (1967) 7.5' quadrangles. South Fork of South Fork enters South Fork 6.5 miles northwest of Paskenta; it is 5.5 miles long and is named on Riley Ridge (1967) 7.5' quadrangle. Middle Fork enters South Fork 1800 feet upstream from the confluence of North Fork and South Fork; it is nearly 7 miles long and is named on Lowrey (1967), Paskenta (1967), and Riley Ridge (1967) 7.5' quadrangles.

Elder Creek: see **Red Bluff** [TEHAMA].

Elderton: see **Cottonwood** [SHASTA].

Election Gap [SISKIYOU]: *pass,* 7.25 miles southwest of Cecilville on Siskiyou-Trinity County line (lat. 41°04'35" N, long. 123°14'15" W). Named on Cecil Lake (1979) 7.5' quadrangle.

Elena: see **Montgomery Creek** [SHASTA] (2).

Elephant Hill [GLENN]: *ridge,* northwest-trending, 1 mile long, 5.25 miles east-northeast of Saint John Mountain (lat. 39°27'30" N, long. 122°36'20" W; sec. 35, T 19 N, R 7 W). Named on Stonyford (1968) 7.5' quadrangle.

Eliza Gulch [SISKIYOU]: *canyon,* drained by a stream that flows 1.5 miles to Humbug Creek 15 miles southeast of Condrey Mountain (lat. 41°46'45" N, long. 122°46'40" W). Named on Condrey Mountain (1955) 15' quadrangle.

Elk Creek [GLENN]:

(1) *stream,* formed by the confluence of North Fork and South Fork, flows 2.5 miles to Stony Creek [GLENN-TEHAMA] at the village of Elk Creek (lat. 39°36'10" N, long. 122°32'05" W; sec. 9, T 20 N, R 6 W). Named on Elk Creek (1968) 7.5' quadrangle. North Fork is 9 miles long, and South Fork is 7.5 miles long; both forks are named on Elk Creek (1968) and Felkner Hill (1968) 7.5' quadrangles. On Elk Creek (1918) 15' quadrangle, present North Fork is called Elk Creek.

(2) *village,* 19 miles west-northwest of Willows (lat. 39°36'15" N, long. 122°32'15" W; sec. 9, T 20 N, R 6 W); the village is at the mouth of Elk Creek (1). Named on Elk Creek (1968) 7.5' quadrangle. Postal authorities established Elk Creek post office in 1872 (Frickstad, p. 40). California Mining Bureau's (1909d) map shows a place called Winslow located 1 mile east of the village of Elk Creek. Postal authorities established Winslow post office in 1901 and discontinued it in 1915; the site also was known as Bridgeport (Salley, p. 242).

Elk Creek [SISKIYOU]: *stream,* flows 14 miles to Klamath River 1.25 miles southwest of Happy Camp (lat. 41°46'50" N, long. 123°23'35" W; sec. 15, T 16 N, R 7 E); the stream heads at Elk Valley. Named on Happy Camp (1980), Huckleberry Mountain (1980), Marble Mountain (1980), Slater Butte (1980), and Ukonom Lake (1980) 7.5' quadrangles. East Fork enters from the east 11 miles north of Ukonom Lake; it is nearly 7 miles long and is named on Huckleberry Mountain (1980) 7.5' quadrangle.

Elk Creek: see **Little Elk Creek** [SISKIYOU]; **Mud Creek** [SISKIYOU] (2).

Elk Flat [SISKIYOU]: *area,* 11 miles northwest of Bartle (lat. 41°22'15" N, long. 121°58'20" W; sec. 28, T 41 N, R 1 W). Named on Bartle (1961) 15' quadrangle.

Elk Flat [TEHAMA]: *area,* 3 miles west-northwest of Red Bank (lat. 40°06'45" N, long. 121°30' W). Named on Lowrey (1967) and Red Bank (1952) 7.5' quadrangles.

Elk Fork: see **Big Elk Fork**, under **Wooley Creek** [SISKIYOU].

Elk Hole [SISKIYOU]: *lake,* 125 feet long, 9 miles northwest of Dillon Mountain (lat. 41°36'40" N, long. 123°42'25" W). Named on Chimney Rock (1981) 7.5' quadrangle.

Elkhorn Creek [TEHAMA]:

(1) *stream,* flows 2 miles to Cottonwood Creek [SHASTA-TEHAMA] 3 miles south-southeast of Tomhead Mountain (lat. 40°06' N, long. 122°47'10" W; near SE cor. sec. 17, T 26 N, R 8 W); the stream heads at Elkhorn Ridge. Named on Yolla Bolly (1954) 15' quadrangle.

(2) *stream,* flows 1.25 miles to South Fork Cottonwood Creek [SHASTA-TEHAMA] 4.5 miles west of Wakefield Flat (lat. 40°07'25" N, long. 122°43'25" W). Named on Raglin Ridge (1967) 7.5' quadrangle. Called Quail Creek on Colyear Springs (1957) 15' quadrangle, but United States Board on Geographic Names (1968c, p. 5) rejected this name for the stream.

Elkhorn Peak [TEHAMA]: *peak,* 4.25 miles east-southeast of Tomhead Mountain (lat. 40°06'15" N, long. 122°45'05" W; sec. 15, T 26 N, R 8 W); the peak is at the north end of Elkhorn Ridge. Altitude 5174 feet. Named on Yolla Bolly (1954) 15' quadrangle.

Elkhorn Ridge [TEHAMA]: *ridge,* north-trending, nearly 2 miles long, 4.5 miles west-southwest of Wakefield Flat (lat. 40°04'45" N, long. 122°44'45" W). Named on Yolla Bolly (1954) 15' quadrangle, and on Raglin Ridge (1967) 7.5' quadrangle.

Elk Lake [SISKIYOU]: *lake,* 600 feet long, 6.5 miles north of the village of Seiad Valley (lat. 41°56'10" N, long. 123°11'05" W). Named on Kangaroo Mountain (1980) 7.5' quadrangle. United States Board on Geographic Names (1983c, p. 5) rejected the name "Moraine Lake" for the feature.

Elk Lake [TEHAMA]: *lake,* 400 feet long, 9 miles west-northwest of Ball Mountain (lat. 39°59'55" N, long. 122°55'25" W; on S line sec. 24, T 25 N, R 10 W). Named on Buck Rock (1967) 7.5' quadrangle.

Elk Lake: see **Azalea Lake** [SISKIYOU]; **Big Elk Lake** [SISKIYOU]; **Little Elk Lake** [SISKIYOU].

Elk Lake Creek: see **Little Elk Lake Creek** [SISKIYOU]; **Little Elk Lake Creek**, under **Deep Lake Creek** [SISKIYOU].

Elklawn: see **Soda Springs** [SISKIYOU] (3).

Elk Lick [SISKIYOU]: *lake,* 2.5 miles east-northeast of Preston Peak (lat. 41°50'40" N, long. 123°33'35" W). Named on Preston Peak (1982) 7.5' quadrangle, which shows a marshy lake.

Elk Lick Ridge [SISKIYOU]: *ridge,* generally west-trending, 2.5 miles long, 3.25 miles east-southeast of Preston Peak (lat. 41°49'25" N, long. 123°32'50" W); the ridge is 1.5 miles south-southeast of Elk Lick. Named on Preston Peak (1982) 7.5' quadrangle.

Elk Meadow [SISKIYOU]: *area,* 7.25 miles north-northeast of the village of Seiad Valley (lat. 41°56'25" N, long. 123°09'25" W). Named on Kangaroo Mountain (1980) 7.5' quadrangle.

Elk Peak [SISKIYOU]: *peak,* 18 miles southwest of Scott Bar (lat. 41°34'10" N, long. 123°14'55" W). Altitude 6992 feet. Named on Marble Mountain (1980) 7.5' quadrangle.

Elk Ridge [GLENN]: *ridge,* east-southeast-trending, 1.5 miles long, 4.5 miles east of Black Butte (lat. 39°43'25" N, long. 122°47' W; mainly in sec. 32, T 22 N, R 8 W). Named on Plaskett Meadows (1967) 7.5' quadrangle.

Elk Ridge [TEHAMA]: *ridge,* generally east-trending, 3.5 miles long, 5.25 miles west of Ball Mountain (lat. 39°56'30" N, long. 122°52'40" W). Named on Ball Mountain (1967) and Buck Rock (1967) 7.5' quadrangles.

Elks Lake [SHASTA]: *lake,* 750 feet long, 8.5 miles north-northwest of Millville (lat. 40°39'50" N, long. 122°14' W; near N line sec. 5, T 32 N, R 3 W). Named on Bella Vista (1965) 7.5' quadrangle.

Elk Spring [SISKIYOU]: *spring,* 5 miles north-northeast of McCloud (lat. 41°18'50" N, long. 122°05'10" W; sec. 16, T 40 N, R 2 W). Named on

Shasta (1954) 15' quadrangle.

Elks Retreat [BUTTE]: *locality,* 8 miles east of Pulga (lat. 39°46'55" N, long. 121°18'10" W; at NE cor. sec. 9, T 22 N, R 6 E). Named on Pulga (1957) 15' quadrangle.

Elk Valley [SISKIYOU]: *valley,* 16 miles southwest of Scott Bar (lat. 41°35'15" N, long. 123°13'05" W); the valley is along upper reaches of Elk Creek. Named on Marble Mountain (1980) 7.5' quadrangle.

Ellendale: see **Camp Ellendale** [GLENN].

Ellery Creek [SHASTA]: *stream,* flows 1.5 miles to McCloud River Arm Shasta Lake 2 miles southwest of Bollibokka Mountain (lat. 40°55' N, long. 122°14'35" W; near E line sec. 6, T 35 N, R 3 W). Named on Bollibokka Mountain (1957) and Lamoine (1957) 15' quadrangles. Steger (p. 31) associated the name with William Ellery of San Francisco, who built a lodge along McCloud River [SHASTA-SISKIYOU].

Elliot Creek [SISKIYOU]: *stream,* formed by the confluence of Dog Fork and Wards Fork, flows 12 miles to the State of Oregon 12 miles north of the village of Seiad Valley (lat. 42°15' N, long. 123°09'15" W; sec. 17, T 48 N, R 11 W). Named on Condrey Mountain (1955) and Seiad Valley (1955) 15' quadrangles. United States Board on Geographic Names (1978b, p. 4) approved the form "Elliott Creek" for the name. Dog Fork is 2.5 miles long and is named on Condrey Mountain (1955) 15' quadrangle. Present Dog Fork is called Middleshell Creek on Yreka (1939) 30' quadrangle, but United States Board on Geographic Names (1984b, p. 4) rejected the designations "Middleshell Creek" and "Dog Fork Creek" for the stream. The Board (p. 4) at the same time approved the name "East Dog Fork" for a stream, 0.8 mile long, that joins Dog Fork 0.5 mile west of Miller Glade (lat. 41°58'47" N, long. 122°57'02" W; sec. 25, T 48 N, R 10 W); present East Dog Fork has the name "Dog Fork" on Condrey Mountain (1955) 15' quadrangle, but the Board rejected this name for the stream. Wards Fork is 2 miles long and is named on Condrey Mountain (1955) 15' quadrangle. United States Board on Geographic Names (1978c, p. 4) rejected the names "Donomore Creek" and "Wards Creek" for present Wards Fork. The Board (1978b, p. 5) approved the name "Wards Fork Gap" for a pass at the head of Wards Fork (lat. 41°58'52" N, long. 122°55' W; sec. 29, T 48 N, R 9 W). Silver Fork enters 0.25 mile downstream from the confluence of Dog Fork and Wards Fork; it heads in the State of Oregon, is 0.5 mile long in Siskiyou County, and is named on Condrey Mountain (1955) 15' quadrangle.

Elliot Spring House [BUTTE]: *locality,* 15 miles north-northwest of Oroville (lat. 39°42'35" N, long. 121°40'20" W; near W line sec. 5, T 21 N, R 3 E). Named on Hamlin Canyon (1951) 7.5' quadrangle. Called Spring House on Oroville (1942) 15' quadrangle.

Elliott Creek [SISKIYOU]: *stream,* flows 3.5 miles to Klamath River 5.5 miles northeast of Dillon Mountain (lat. 41°35'40" N, long. 123°30'25" W). Named on Dillon Mountain (1983) 7.5' quadrangle.

Elliott Creek: see **Elliot Creek** [SISKIYOU].

Ellis [SHASTA]: *locality,* 7 miles east of Millville (lat. 40°33'30" N, long. 122°02'30" W; sec. 12, T 31 N, R 2 W). Named on Redding (1901) 30' quadrangle.

Elmo Gulch [SISKIYOU]: *canyon,* drained by a stream that flows less than 0.5 mile to Humbug Creek 15 miles southeast of Condrey Mountain (lat. 41°46'50" N, long. 122°47'55" W; sec. 5, T 45 N, R 8 W). Named on Condrey Mountain (1955) 15' quadrangle.

Elmore [SHASTA]: *locality,* 11.5 miles south of Lamoine along Southern Pacific Railroad (lat. 40°48'40" N, long. 122°23'30" W; near NE cor. sec. 14, T 34 N, R 5 W); the place is just south of the mouth of Elmore Creek. Named on Redding (1901) 30' quadrangle.

Elmore Bay [SHASTA]: *embayment,* 10.5 miles south of Lamoine along Sacramento River Arm Shasta Lake (lat. 40°49'45" N, long. 122°23'15" W; in and near sec. 1, T 34 N, R 5 W); the feature is 0.5 mile south-southeast of Elmore Mountain. Named on Lamoine (1957) 15' quadrangle. Lamoine (1946) 15' quadrangle shows Elmore Valley at the place—water of Shasta Lake flooded the valley to form the embayment.

Elmore Creek [SHASTA]: *stream,* flows 0.5 mile to Sacramento River Arm Shasta Lake 11.5 miles south of Lamoine (lat. 40°48'55" N, long. 122°24'30" W; sec. 11, T 34 N, R 5 W). Named on Lamoine (1957) 15' quadrangle.

Elmore Creek [TEHAMA]: *stream,* flows 10.5 miles to join Jackson Spring Creek and form Burch Creek 6 miles southeast of Flournoy (lat. 39°51'50" N, long. 122°21' W; sec. 7, T 23 N, R 4 W). Named on Black Butte Dam (1967), Newville (1967), and Sehorn Creek (1967) 7.5' quadrangles.

Elmore Mountain [SHASTA]: *peak,* 10 miles south of Lamoine (lat. 40°50'25" N, long. 122°23'35" W; near SE cor. sec. 35, T 35 N, R 5 W). Altitude 2452 feet. Named on Lamoine (1957) 15' quadrangle.

Elmore Valley: see **Elmore Bay** [SHASTA].

El Primer Cañon or Rio de los Berrendo [TEHAMA]: *land grant,* on the east side of Sacramento River southeast of Red Bluff. Named on Gerber (1950), Los Molinos (1952), Red Bluff East (1951), and Tuscan Springs (1951) 7.5' quadrangles. Tehama (1905) 15' quadrangle has the form "El Primer Canyon or Rio de los Berrendos" for the name. According to Cowan (p. 64), Job F. Dye received 6 leagues in 1844 and claimed 26,637 acres patented in 1871; according to Perez (p. 83), the grantee was Francisco Dye.

El Rio de las Plumas: see **Feather River** [BUTTE].

Elsey [BUTTE]: *locality,* 7 miles north-northwest of Oroville along Western Pacific Railroad (lat. 39°36'25" N, long. 121°35'35" W; sec. 12, T 20 N, R 3 E). Named on Oroville (1970) 7.5' quadrangle.

Emerald Lake [SHASTA]: *lake,* 600 feet long, 1.5 miles south-southwest of Lassen Peak (lat. 40°28'05" N, long. 121°31' W; on N line sec. 15, T 30 N, R 4 E). Named on Lassen Peak (1956) 15' quadrangle. The name is from the green color of the water (Schulz, p. 18).

Emery and Mitchell Island [BUTTE]: *area,* 10 miles west-northwest of Chico on the east side of Sacramento River (lat. 39°46'45" N, long. 122°01'20" W). Named on McIntosh Landing (1914) 7.5' quadrangle.

Emigrant Creek [SISKIYOU]: *stream,* flows nearly 4 miles to Mill Creek (6) 6.5 miles west-southwest of Fort Jones (lat. 41°34'25" N, long. 122°57'30" W; sec. 14, T 43 N, R 10 W). Named on Fort Jones (1955) 15' quadrangle. Called Evans Cr. on Yreka (1939) 30' quadrangle.

Emigrant Ferry: see **Cow Creek** [SHASTA].

Emigrant Ford Campground [SHASTA]: *locality,* 7 miles north-northeast of Lassen Peak (lat. 40°35'10" N, long. 121°28'15" W; near N line sec. 36, T 32 N, R 4 E). Named on an old emigrant trail.

Emigrant Lake [SHASTA]: *lake,* 900 feet long, 8 miles east-northeast of Lassen Peak (lat. 40°32'40" N, long. 121°22'30" W; near SW cor. sec. 13, T 31 N, R 5 E). Named on Prospect Peak (1957) 15' quadrangle. The name is from the proximity of the lake to the old emigrant trail (United States Board on Geographic Names, 1937, p. 11).

Emigrant Pass [SHASTA]: *pass,* 3 miles northeast of Lassen Peak (lat. 40°30'50" N, long. 121°27'50" W). Named on Prospect Peak (1957) 15' quadrangle, which shows the pass along the emigrant trail.

Emigrant Spring [TEHAMA]: *spring,* 8 miles south of Panther Spring (lat. 40°07'55" N, long. 121°47'10" W; sec. 6, T 26 N, R 2 E). Named on Panther Spring (1953) 15' quadrangle.

Emily: see **Mount Emily** [SISKIYOU].

Empire Creek [BUTTE]: *stream,* flows 3.5 miles to West Branch Feather River 6 miles north-northeast of Paradise (lat. 39°49'50" N, long. 121°33'45" W; near SW cor. sec. 19, T 23 N, R 4 E). Named on Paradise East (1980) 7.5' quadrangle.

Empire Creek [SISKIYOU]: *stream,* flows 6.5 miles to Klamath River 10 miles west-southwest of Hornbrook (lat. 41°52'05" N, long. 122°44'15" W; sec. 2, T 46 N, R 8 W). Named on Hornbrook (1955) 15' quadrangle.

Empire Creek: see **Gottville** [SISKIYOU].

Empire Mill: see **Gottville** [SISKIYOU].

English Lake [SISKIYOU]: *lake,* 1100 feet long, 9 miles north-northwest of Sawyers Bar (lat. 41°24'50" N, long. 123°12'30" W); the lake is nearly 1 mile north-northeast of English Peak. Named on English Peak (1977) 7.5' quadrangle.

English Lake: see **Upper English Lake** [SISKIYOU].

English Peak [SISKIYOU]: *peak,* 8.5 miles north-northwest of Sawyers Bar (lat. 41°24'05" N, long. 123°12'50" W). Altitude 7322 feet. Named on English Peak (1977) 7.5' quadrangle.

Enjoyment: see **Camp Enjoyment**, under **Blinzig** [BUTTE].

Ensign [TEHAMA]: *locality,* 4 miles north-northwest of Vina along Southern Pacific Railroad (lat. 39°59'20" N, long. 122°05' W). Named on Vina (1904) 15' quadrangle.

Enterprise [BUTTE]: *locality,* 5 miles west-northwest of Forbestown along South Fork Feather River (lat. 39°32'05" N, long. 121°21'45" W; sec. 1, T 19 N, R 5 E). Named on Big Bend Mountain (1948) 15' quadrangle. Water of Lake Oroville now covers the site. Postal authorities established Enterprise post office in 1878, discontinued it for a time in 1903, and discontinued it finally in 1926 (Frickstad, p. 9). The place, which also was known as Mountain Spring, began in 1852 as a construction camp for Union Enterprise fluming operation (Dunn, F.D., p. 37). A mining place called Yankee Flat was located 5 miles southeast of Enterprise (Gudde, 1975, p. 377).

Enterprise [SHASTA]: *district,* 3 miles east-southeast of downtown Redding (lat. 40°34' N, long. 122°20'15" W; in and near sec. 5, T 31 N, R 4 W). Named on Enterprise (1957) 7.5' quadrangle.

Enterprise Gulch [SISKIYOU]: *canyon,* drained by a stream that flows 0.5 mile to McAdam Creek 6.25 miles north of Fort Jones (lat. 41°41'50" N, long. 122°49'05" W; near NW cor. sec. 6, T 44 N, R 8 W). Named on Fort Jones (1955) 15' quadrangle.

Erickson [SISKIYOU]: *locality,* 13 miles south-southwest of Macdoel along Southern Pacific Railroad (lat. 41°39' N, long. 122°06'35" W; sec. 20, T 44 N, R 2 W). Named on The Whaleback (1954) 15' quadrangle.

Eskimo Hill [SHASTA]: *peak,* 6.5 miles northwest of Manzanita Lake (lat. 40°33'40" N, long. 121°34'45" W; near SE cor. sec. 1, T 31 N, R 3 E). Named on Manzanita Lake (1956) 15' quadrangle.

Esperanza [SISKIYOU]: *locality,* 4.5 miles east of McCloud along McCloud River Railroad (lat. 41°15'50" N, long. 122°03'15" W; near SW cor. sec. 35, T 40 N, R 2 W); the place is near present Esperanza Spring. Named on Dunsmuir (1935) 30' quadrangle.

Esperanza Spring [SISKIYOU]: *spring,* 5 miles east-northeast of McCloud (lat. 41°16'20" N, long. 122°02'45" W; sec. 35, T 40 N, R 2 W). Named on Shasta (1954) 15' quadrangle.

Esquon [BUTTE]:
(1) *land grant,* 10 miles south-southeast of Chico. Named on Chico (1948), Hamlin Canyon (1951), Nelson (1948), and Shippee (1948) 7.5' quadrangles. According to Cowan (p. 35), Samuel Neal received 5 leagues in 1844 and claimed 22,194 acres patented in 1860. According to Perez (p. 66), Samuel Neal and John A. Sutter were the grantees.
(2) *locality,* 3 miles south-southeast of Durham along Sacramento Northern Railroad (lat. 39°36'20" N, long. 121°46' W); the place is on Esquon grant. Named on Nelson (1948) 7.5' quadrangle.

Estell Creek [GLENN]: *stream,* flows 4 miles to join Middle Creek and form Black Butte River 9 miles south of Black Butte (lat. 39°35'40" N, long. 122°51'25" W; at N line sec. 15, T 20 N, R 9 W). Named on Kneecap Ridge (1967) 7.5' quadrangle.

Estep [SHASTA]: *locality,* 12.5 miles north-northeast of Millville (lat. 40°41'45" N, long. 122°02'30" W; at S line sec. 24, T 33 N, R 2 W). Site named on Millville (1953) 15' quadrangle.

Ethel: see **Lake Ethel** [SISKIYOU].

Etna [SISKIYOU]: *town,* 23 miles southwest of Yreka in Scott Valley (lat. 41°27'25" N, long. 122°53'45" W; mainly in sec. 28, 29, T 42 N, R 9 W). Named on Etna (1955) 15' quadrangle. Postal authorities established Etna Mills post office in 1861, moved it 2 miles north in 1863, and changed the name to Etna in 1924—the state legislature dropped the word "Mills" from the name of the town in 1874 (Salley, p. 71), and the town incorporated in 1878. The mining camp at the site first was known as Rough and Ready, and when a flour mill was built there in 1856 the name of the place became Rough and Ready Mills; a nearby flour mill was called Etna Mills, and when postal authorities moved the post office at Etna Mills to Rough and Ready in 1863, the post office name came too (Hanna, p. 100). Postal authorities established Crystal Creek post office 4 miles north of Etna Mills post office in 1871 and discontinued it in 1873 (Salley, p. 53).

Etna Creek [SISKIYOU]: *stream,* flows 10.5 miles to Scott River 3 miles east-northeast of Etna (lat. 41°28'40" N, long. 122°50'50" W; sec. 23, T 42 N, R 9 W). Named on Etna (1955) 15' quadrangle. On Averill's (1935) map, present Etna Creek is called Mill Creek below the confluence of Etna Creek and present Mill Creek (7). United States Board on Geographic Names (1968a, p. 4) approved the name "Etna Summit" for a pass 6.7 miles southwest of Etna near the head of Etna Creek (lat. 41°23'43" N, long. 122°59'35" W; sec. 21, T 41 N, R 10 W).

Etna Mills: see **Etna** [SISKIYOU].

Etna Mountain [SISKIYOU]: *peak,* 6 miles south-southwest of Etna (lat. 41°23'15" N, long. 122°57'10" W; on E line sec. 23, T 41 N, R 10 W). Altitude 7528 feet. Named on Etna (1955) 15' quadrangle.

Etna Summit: see **Etna Creek** [SISKIYOU].

Etzler Creek [TEHAMA]: *stream,* flows nearly 4 miles to North Fork Red Bank Creek 4 miles northwest of Red Bank (lat. 40°08'40" N, long. 122°29'15" W; near SE cor. sec. 36, T 27 N, R 6 W). Named on Blossom (1952) and Oxbow Bridge (1967) 7.5' quadrangles.

Eubanks: see **Castella** [SHASTA].

Euchre Glade [GLENN]: *area,* 6 miles northeast of Black Butte (lat. 39°47'05" N, long. 122°47'15" W; on S line sec. 5, T 22 N, R 8 W). Named on Log Spring (1967) 7.5' quadrangle.

Eureka Mill [SHASTA]: *locality,* 13 miles west of Lassen Peak (lat. 40°31'45" N, long. 121°44'50" W). Named on Lassen Peak (1894) 1° quadrangle. California Mining Bureau's (1917b) map has the name "Eureka Mills" at the place.

Eury Glade [TEHAMA]: *area,* 4.25 miles south-southwest of Ball Mountain (lat. 39°52'35" N, long. 122°49'20" W; sec. 1, T 23 N, R 9 W). Named on Ball Mountain (1967) 7.5' quadrangle.

Evans: see **Weed** [SISKIYOU]; **Yankee Hill** [BUTTE].

Evans Bar [BUTTE]: *locality,* 4 miles southeast of the village of Brush Creek along Middle Fork Feather River (lat. 39°38'50" N, long. 121°17'20" W). Named on Brush Creek (1970) 7.5' quadrangle.

Evans Creek [SISKIYOU]: *stream,* flows 1 mile to an unnamed canyon that opens into the canyon of Emigrant Creek 8 miles southwest of Fort Jones (lat. 41°32'30" N, long. 122°58' W; near S line sec. 26, T 43 N, R 10 W). Named on Fort Jones (1955) 15' quadrangle. Present Emigrant Creek is called Evans Cr. on Yreka (1939) 30' quadrangle.

Evans Mountain [SISKIYOU]: *peak,* 6.25 miles east-northeast of Happy Camp (lat. 41°50' N, long. 123°16' W; sec. 17, T 46 N, R 12 W). Altitude 4269 feet. Named on Slater Butte (1980) 7.5' quadrangle.

Evansville: see **Forbestown** [BUTTE].

Everett Lake [SHASTA]: *lake,* 1100 feet long, 16 miles north-northwest of Lassen Peak (lat. 40°42'05" N, long. 121°35'55" W). Named on Manzanita Lake (1956) 15' quadrangle. Called Everitt L. on Burney (1939) 30' quadrangle.

Everill Creek [SISKIYOU]: *stream,* flows 2.5 miles to Klamath River 10 miles east of the village of Seiad Valley (lat. 41°48'45" N, long. 123°00'35" W; sec. 21, T 46 N, R 10 W). Named on Condrey Mountain (1955) 15' quadrangle, and on Hamburg (1980) 7.5' quadrangle.

Everitt Hill [SISKIYOU]: *peak,* 5.25 miles northwest of McCloud (lat. 41°17'55" N, long. 122°13' W; sec. 20, T 40 N, R 3 W). Altitude 5709 feet. Named on Shasta (1954) 15' quadrangle. The name commemorates John Samuel Everitt, supervisor of Shasta National Forest, who died in 1934 in a forest fire on the peak (Gudde, 1969, p. 105).

Everitt Lake: see **Everett Lake** [SHASTA].

Ewalt Camp [BUTTE]: *locality,* 7 miles northwest of Stirling City along West Branch Butte Creek [BUTTE-GLENN] (lat. 39°58'50" N, long. 121°37' W). Named on Stirling City (1979) 7.5' quadrangle.

Eye Creek [SHASTA]: *stream,* flows 2.5 miles to Middle Salt Creek 5.25 miles east-southeast of Lamoine (lat. 40°56'30" N, long. 122°20'30" W; near W line sec. 33, T 36 N, R 4 W). Named on Lamoine (1957) 15' quadrangle. Called North Fork Middle Salt Creek on Redding (1901) 30' quadrangle.

Eyese Bar [SISKIYOU]: *locality,* 3 miles southeast of Dillon Mountain along Klamath River (lat. 41°30'15" N, long. 123°31'35" W); the place is just above the mouth of Eyese Creek. Named on Dillon Mountain (1983) 7.5' quadrangle.

Eyese Creek [SISKIYOU]: *stream,* flows 1.25 miles to Klamath River 3 miles southeast of Dillon Mountain (lat. 41°30'25" N, long. 123°31'30" W). Named on Dillon Mountain (1983) 7.5' quadrangle. The name is from an Indian village that was situated along the stream (Stewart, G.R., p. 160).

— F —

Facey Gulch [SISKIYOU]: *canyon,* drained by a stream that flows 2.5 miles to Scott Valley 7.25 miles south-southeast of Etna (lat. 41°22'15" N, long. 122°49'15" W; at W line sec. 30, T 41 N, R 8 W). Named on Etna (1955) 15' quadrangle.

Fagan [BUTTE]: *locality,* 2 miles south-southeast of Gridley along Southern Pacific Railroad (lat. 39°20'10" N, long. 121°41' W; sec. 7, T 17 N, R 3 E). Named on Gridley (1952) 7.5' quadrangle. Railroad officials named the place for Edward Fagan, owner of land at the site (Gudde, 1949, p. 112).

Fairfield Bar [BUTTE]: *locality,* 6.5 miles northwest of Forbestown (lat. 39°34'45" N, long. 121°21'30" W; sec. 24, T 20 N, R 5 E); water of Lake Oroville now covers the site. Named on Big Bend Mountain (1948) 15' quadrangle.

Fairfield Peak [SHASTA]: *crater,* 8.5 miles east-northeast of Lassen Peak (lat. 40°31'05" N, long. 121°21'10" W; sec. 30, T 31 N, R 6 E). Named on Prospect Peak (1957) 15' quadrangle. The name honors Asa M. Fairfield (United States Board on Geographic Names, 1933, p. 295).

Falks Lake [SHASTA]: *lake,* 1150 feet long, 2 miles west-southwest of Redding (lat. 40°34'30" N, long. 122°25'55" W; near N line sec. 4, T 31 N, R 5 W). Named on Redding (1957, photorevised 1969) 7.5' quadrangle.

Fallager Creek [BUTTE]: *stream,* flows 4.5 miles to Dry Creek 8.5 miles northwest of Oroville (lat. 39°36'40" N, long. 121°39'20" W; near S line sec. 5, T 20 N, R 3 E). Named on Cherokee (1970), Hamlin Canyon (1951), and Shippee (1948) 7.5' quadrangles.

Fall City: see **Fall River Mills** [SHASTA].

Fall Creek [BUTTE]: *stream,* flows 3.5 miles to West Branch Feather River 9 miles northeast of Paradise (lat. 39°51'35" N, long. 121°30'50" W; near S line sec. 10, T 23 N, R 4 E). Named on Paradise East (1980) and Pulga (1979) 7.5' quadrangles.

Fall Creek [SHASTA]:
(1) *stream,* flows 3 miles to Sacramento River nearly 2 miles northeast of Castella (lat. 41°09'10" N, long. 122°17'20" W; sec. 14, T 38 N, R 4 W). Named on Dunsmuir (1954) and Shoeinhorse Mountain (1954) 15' quadrangles.
(2) *stream,* flows 1.5 miles to Salt Creek (6) 10 miles southeast of Lamoine (lat. 40°51'35" N, long. 122°19' W; at E line sec. 28, T 35 N, R 4 W). Named on Lamoine (1957) 15' quadrangle.
(3) *stream,* flows 3.5 miles to Backbone Creek 11 miles south of Lamoine (lat. 40°49'10" N, long. 122°27'15" W; sec. 8, T 34 N, R 5 W). Named on Lamoine (1957) 15' quadrangle.

Fall Creek [SISKIYOU]: *stream,* heads in the State of Oregon and flows 3 miles to Klamath River 22 miles west-northwest of Macdoel (lat. 41°58'20" N, long. 122°22' W; sec. 36, T 48 N, R 5 W). Named on Copco (1954) 15' quadrangle. California Mining Bureau's (1917a) map shows a place called Fall Creek along Klamath Lake Railroad near the mouth of the stream called Fall Creek.

Fall River [BUTTE]: *stream,* heads in Plumas County and flows 12 miles in Butte County to Middle Fork Feather River 4.5 miles southeast of the village of Brush Creek (lat. 39°38'15" N, long. 121°16'45" W); Feather Falls (1) is along the stream. Named on Brush Creek (1970) and Cascade (1948) 7.5' quadrangles

Fall River [SHASTA]: *stream,* flows 23 miles to Pit River at Fall River Mills (lat. 41°00'05" N, long. 121°26'10" W; sec. 31, T 37 N, R 5 E). Named on

Fall River Mills (1961) and Pondosa (1961) 15' quadrangles. Fremont named the stream in 1846 for the numerous falls and cascades along it (Steger, p. 31).

Fall River Camp Ground [BUTTE]: *locality,* 8.5 miles north of Clipper Mills (lat. 39°39'05" N, long. 121°10'50" W; sec. 27, T 21 N, R 7 E); the place is along Fall River. Named on Cascade (1948) 7.5' quadrangle.

Fall River Mills [SHASTA]: *town,* 58 miles east-northeast of Redding (lat. 41°00'20" N, long. 121°26'15" W; sec. 30, 31, T 37 N, R 5 E); the town is at the mouth of Fall River. Named on Fall River Mills (1961) 15' quadrangle. Postal authorities established Fall River Mills post office in 1873 (Frickstad, p. 179). W.H. Winters built lumber and flour mills for which the place was named; the community also was called Fall City (Steger, p. 31).

Fall River Valley [SHASTA]: *valley,* north of Fall River Mills and McArthur (lat. 41°04' N, long. 121°27' W). Named on Fall River Mills (1961) and Pondosa (1961) 15' quadrangles. Captain John W.T. Gardiner established a military post called Camp Hollenbush, for assistant surgeon Calvin G. Hollenbush, in 1857 on the north bank of Fall River at the upper end of Fall River Valley about 10 miles northwest of Fall River Mills; the name of the post was changed the same year to Fort Crook, for Lieutenant George Crook—the army abandoned the facility in 1869 (Frazer, p. 22; Hoover, Rensch, and Rensch, p. 489).

False Gap [SISKIYOU]: *pass,* 10 miles south-southeast of Bray (lat. 41°30'50" N, long. 121°54' W; sec. 6, T 42 N, R 1 E). Named on Bray (1950) 15' quadrangle.

Falvey Lake [SISKIYOU]: *intermittent lake,* 1200 feet long, 5.25 miles north-northeast of Mount Dome (lat. 41°52'35" N, long. 121°38'30" W; at NW cor. sec. 33, T 47 N, R 3 E). Named on Mount Dome (1950) 15' quadrangle.

Fan Gulch [SISKIYOU]: *canyon,* drained by a stream that flows 1.5 miles to Angel Creek 6 miles southeast of McCloud (lat. 41°11'15" N, long. 122°03'20" W; near W line sec. 26, T 39 N, R 2 W). Named on Shoeinhorse Mountain (1954) 15' quadrangle.

Fannie Creek [SHASTA]: *stream,* flows 2 miles to Middle Salt Creek 5 miles southeast of Lamoine (lat. 40°55'50" N, long. 122°21'45" W; near N line sec. 6, T 35 N, R 4 W). Named on Lamoine (1957) 15' quadrangle.

Farley Gulch [SISKIYOU]: *canyon,* drained by a stream that flows 1.25 mile to Moffett Creek 15 miles south of Yreka (lat. 41°31'25" N, long. 122°41'20" W; at SW cor. sec. 32, T 43 N, R 7 W). Named on Yreka (1954) 15' quadrangle.

Farwell: see **Arroyo Chico** [BUTTE].

Fat Doe Gulch [SISKIYOU]: *canyon,* drained by a stream that flows 1.5 miles to Bear Creek (2) 7.25 miles east-northeast of Condrey Mountain (lat. 41°58'15" N, long. 122°50'40" W; sec. 36, T 48 N, R 9 W). Named on Condrey Mountain (1955) 15' quadrangle.

Faulkstein Camp: see **Faulkstine Spring** [SISKIYOU].

Faulkstein Spring [SISKIYOU]: *spring,* 9.5 miles west-southwest of Scott Bar (lat. 41°42'35" N, long. 123°10'50" W). Named on Grider Valley (1981) 7.5' quadrangle. Scott Bar (1955) 15' quadrangle shows Faulkstein Camp at the place.

Fauries Peak [SHASTA]: *peak,* 5 miles east of the village of Montgomery Creek (lat. 40°50'05" N, long. 121°49'45" W; sec. 2, T 34 N, R 1 E). Named on Montgomery Creek (1956) 15' quadrangle.

Fawn Creek [SISKIYOU]: *stream,* flows 3.5 miles to Sacramento River 9 miles west of Dunsmuir (lat. 41°14' N, long. 122°26'30" W; near S line sec. 16, T 39 N, R 5 W). Named on Dunsmuir (1954) 15' quadrangle.

Feather Falls [BUTTE]:

(1) *waterfall,* 4.5 miles southeast of the village of Brush Creek along Fall River (lat. 39°37'35" N, long. 121°16'25" W). Named on Brush Creek (1970) 7.5' quadrangle.

(2) *village,* 5.25 miles north of Forbestown (lat. 39°35'40" N, long. 121°15'20" W; at W line sec. 13, T 20 N, R 6 E). Named on Clipper Mills (1948) and Forbestown (1970) 7.5' quadrangles. Bidwell Bar (1897) 30' quadrangle shows a place called Mooretown located at or near present Feather Falls (2). Postal authorities established Feather River post office in 1919, discontinued it the same year, reestablished it in 1921, changed the name to Feather Falls in 1921, and moved it 2.5 miles southwest in 1938 (Salley, p. 73). They established Mooretown post office in 1888 and discontinued it in 1913 (Frickstad, p. 11). The name of the community of Mooretown was changed to Feather Falls when postal authorities moved Feather Falls post office to the place in 1938 (Dunn, F.D., p. 70).

Feather Lake [SHASTA]: *lake,* 900 feet long, 7.25 miles east-northeast of Lassen Peak (lat. 40°31'30" N, long. 121°22'45" W; at NW cor. sec. 25, T 31 N, R 5 E). Named on Prospect Peak (1957) 15' quadrangle. The lake is one of the group called Cluster Lakes.

Feather River [BUTTE]: *stream,* formed by the confluence of Middle Fork and South Fork 3.5 miles east-northeast of Oroville Dam in Lake Oroville, flows 30 miles to Yuba County and Sutter County 5.25 miles west-southwest of Honcut (lat. 39°17'45" N, long. 121°37'20" W). Named on Biggs (1970), Gridley (1952), Honcut (1952), Oroville (1970), and Oroville Dam (1970) 7.5' quadrangles. Called Rio de las Plumas on Fremont's (1845) map, and called Rio del Plumas on Sage's (1846) map. Luis Arguello is said to have given the name "El Rio de las Plumas" to the stream in 1817 because he saw bird feathers on the water there (Hart, p. 135)—*las plumas* means "the feathers" in Spanish. Middle Fork enters Butte County from Plumas County and flows 22 miles to join South Fork; it is named on Brush Creek (1970), Cascade (1948), Forbestown (1970), and Oroville Dam (1970) 7.5' quadrangles. South Branch of Middle Fork enters Butte County from Plumas County and flows 4 miles to Middle Fork nearly 4 miles east-northeast of the village of Brush Creek; it is named on Brush Creek (1970) and Cascade (1948) 7.5' quadrangles. North Fork enters Butte County from Plumas County and flows 33 miles to Feather River 1.5 miles north-northeast of Oroville Dam in Lake Oroville; it is named on Berry Creek (1970), Oroville Dam (1970), and Pulga (1979) 7.5' quadrangles. South Fork enters Butte County from Plumas County and flows 22 miles to join Middle Fork; it is named on Cascade (1948), Clipper Mills (1948), Forbestown (1970), and Oroville Dam (1970) 7.5' quadrangles. West Branch enters North Fork Feather River from the west 5 miles west-northwest of the village of Berry Creek; it is 54 miles long and is named on Butte Meadows (1958) and Jonesville (1958) 15' quadrangles, and on Berry Creek (1970), Cherokee (1970), Paradise East (1980), and Stirling City (1979) 7.5' quadrangles. Little North Fork heads in Plumas County and flows 7 miles in Butte County to Middle Fork Feather River 4 miles east-northeast of the village of Brush Creek; it is named on Brush Creek (1970) 7.5' quadrangle, and is called Little North Fork Middle Fork Feather River on Soapstone Hill (1979) 7.5' quadrangle. Little West Fork flows 7 miles to join West Branch Feather River 6.5 miles north-northeast of Paradise; it is named on Paradise East (1980) and Stirling City (1979) 7.5' quadrangles, and is called Little West Branch on Chico (1895) 30' quadrangle.

Feather River: see **Feather Falls** [BUTTE] (2).

Feather River, East Branch: see **Concow Creek** [BUTTE].

Felkner Hill [GLENN]: *peak,* 9.5 miles southwest of the village of Elk Creek (lat. 39°31'15" N, long. 122°40'50" W); the peak is near the northwest end of Felkner Ridge. Altitude 5656 feet. Named on Felkner Hill (1968) 7.5' quadrangle.

Felkner Ridge [GLENN]: *ridge,* generally southeast-trending, 3 miles long, 10 miles southwest of the village of Elk Creek (lat. 39°30'20" N, long. 122°40' W). Named on Felkner Hill (1968) and Saint John Mountain (1968) 7.5' quadrangles.

Fender Ferry: see **Fenders Flat** [SHASTA].

Fenders Flat [SHASTA]: *area,* 12.5 miles east-southeast of Bollibokka Mountain along Pit River (lat. 40°50'45" N, long. 122°00'45" W; sec. 31, T 35 N, R 1 W); the place is 0.5 mile north-northeast of the mouth of Potem Creek. Named on Bollibokka Mountain (1957) 15' quadrangle. The name recalls the Fender brothers, who started Fender Ferry on Pit River near Potem Creek in 1860—a bridge replaced the ferry in 1914 (Steger, p. 31).

Fern [SHASTA]: *locality,* 4.25 miles north of Whitmore (lat. 40°41'20" N, long. 121°55'45" W; near W line sec. 25, T 33 N, R 1 W). Named on Whitmore (1956) 15' quadrangle. Postal authorities established Fern post office in 1898 and discontinued it in 1945 (Frickstad, p. 179).

Fernandez [BUTTE]: *land grant,* southwest of Oroville. Named on Biggs (1970), Oroville (1970), and Palermo (1970) 7.5' quadrangles. Dionisio Fernandez and Maximo Fernandez received 4 leagues in 1846 and claimed 17,806 acres patented in 1867 (Cowan, p. 36). According to Perez (p. 67), the patent was given in 1857.

Fern Spring [SHASTA]: *spring,* 2 miles west-southwest of Whitmore (lat. 40°37'05" N, long. 121°57' W; near W line sec. 23, T 32 N, R 1 W). Named on Whitmore (1956) 15' quadrangle.

Fern Spring [SISKIYOU]: *spring,* less than 1 mile west-northwest of the village of Seiad Valley (lat. 41°50'55" N, long. 123°12'35" W). Named on Seiad Valley (1980) 7.5' quadrangle.

Fern Springs [TEHAMA]: *springs,* 3.5 miles northeast of Deer Creek Station (lat. 40°18'20" N, long. 121°24'35" W; near N line sec. 10, T 28 N, R 5 E). Named on Mount Harkness (1956) 15' quadrangle.

Ferrils Gulch: see **O'Farrill Gulch** [SISKIYOU].

Ferry Creek: see **Big Ferry Creek** [SISKIYOU]; **Little Ferry Creek** [SISKIYOU].

Ferry Point [SISKIYOU]: *relief feature,* 7.5 miles north-northwest of Ukonom Lake along Klamath River (lat. 41°40'20" N, long. 123°25'45" W). Named on Clear Creek (1981) 7.5' quadrangle. Seiad (1922) 30' quadrangle has the name "Ferry Point" for a locality on the east side of Klamath River opposite present Ferry Point. Postal authorities established Ferry Point post office at a ferry crossing of Klamath River in 1858 and discontinued it in 1867; the post office was in Del Norte County, but the site now is in Siskiyou County (Salley, p. 74).

Fiddleburg: see **Cassel** [SHASTA].

Fiddler Creek: see **Fiddlers Creek** [SHASTA].

Fiddlers Creek [SHASTA]: *stream,* flows 7 miles to Middle Fork Cottonwood Creek [SHASTA-TEHAMA] 10 miles south-southwest of Ono (lat. 40°20'30" N, long. 122°41'30" W; near NE cor. sec. 30, T 29 N, R 7 W).

Named on Chanchelulla Peak (1951) and Ono (1952) 15' quadrangles. Called Fiddler Creek on Red Bluff (1894) 1° quadrangle. United States Board on Geographic Names (1982a, p. 3) approved the name "Fidler Creek" for the stream, and rejected the names "Fiddler Creek" and "Fiddlers Creek" for it—the Board pointed out that the name commemorates Captain Hercules Fidler, who settled near the stream in the 1860's.

Fiddlers Green [GLENN]: *area,* 13 miles northwest of the village of Elk Creek (lat. 39°43'45" N, long. 122°42'50" W). Named on Alder Springs (1967) 7.5' quadrangle.

Fidler Creek: see **Fiddlers Creek** [SHASTA].

Fielding: see **Keswick** [SHASTA].

Fields: see **Obe Fields Spring** [TEHAMA].

Fields Ridge [BUTTE]: *ridge,* south- to west-trending, 6 miles long, 3.5 miles northwest of Clipper Mills (lat. 39°34'30" N, long. 121°12' W). Named on Clipper Mills (1948) 7.5' quadrangle.

Figurehead Mountain [SISKIYOU]: *peak,* 12 miles north-northeast of Happy Camp (lat. 41°57'45" N, long. 123°18'10" W). Altitude 6374 feet. Named on Figurehead Mountain (1980) 7.5' quadrangle.

Fillippi Creek [GLENN]: *stream,* flows nearly 3 miles to South Fork Willow Creek 5 miles south of Fruto (lat. 39°30'45" N, long. 122°27'10" W; near W line sec. 8, T 19 N, R 5 W). Named on Lodoga (1960) 15' quadrangle, and on Fruto (1968) 7.5' quadrangle.

Filson Spring [SISKIYOU]: *spring,* 18 miles south of Macdoel (lat. 41°33'50" N, long. 122°00'50" W; near N line sec. 19, T 43 N, R 1 W). Named on The Whaleback (1954) 15' quadrangle.

Fine Gold Gulch [BUTTE]: *canyon,* drained by a stream that flows 3.25 miles to North Honcut Creek 3 miles west-northwest of Bangor (lat. 39°24'25" N, long. 121°27'10" W; sec. 19, T 18 N, R 5 E). Named on Bangor (1947) 7.5' quadrangle.

Finley Butte [TEHAMA]: *peak,* 11 miles south of Manton (lat. 40°16'45" N, long. 121°52' W; sec. 16, T 28 N, R 1 E). Altitude 2829 feet. Named on Manton (1956) 15' quadrangle.

Finley Camp [SISKIYOU]: *locality,* 4 miles east-northeast of Sawyers Bar along North Fork Salmon River (lat. 41°19'40" N, long. 123°03'40" W). Named on Tanners Peak (1977) 7.5' quadrangle. Called Finleys Camp on Sawyers Bar (1923) 30' quadrangle.

Finley Gulch [SISKIYOU]: *canyon,* drained by a stream that flows 1 mile to Hungry Creek 11 miles east of Condrey Mountain (lat. 41°58'50" N, long. 123°46'10" W; near NE cor. sec. 33, T 48 N, R 8 W). Named on Condrey Mountain (1955) 15' quadrangle.

Finley Lake [TEHAMA]: *lake,* 1000 feet long, 11.5 miles south of Manton (lat. 40°16'15" N, long. 121°51'05" W; near NW cor. sec. 22, T 28 N, R 1 E). Named on Manton (1956) 15' quadrangle.

Finleys Camp: see **Finley Camp** [SISKIYOU].

Fire Mountain [TEHAMA]: *locality,* 2.5 miles north-northeast of Deer Creek Station along Guernsey Creek (lat. 40°03'15" N, long. 121°25'10" W; at W line sec. 10, T 28 N, R 5 E). Named on Mount Harkness (1956) 15' quadrangle.

Fir Glade [SISKIYOU]: *area,* 14 miles north-northeast of Happy Camp (lat. 41°59'45" N, long. 123°18'30" W). Named on Figurehead Mountain (1980) 7.5' quadrangle. United States Board on Geographic Names (1960b, p. 8) rejected the name "Fir Glade Swamp" for the feature.

Fir Glade Swamp: see **Fir Glade** [SISKIYOU].

Fir Gulch [SHASTA]: *canyon,* drained by a stream that flows 1.5 miles to Middle Fork Cottonwood Creek [TEHAMA] 6.25 miles west-southwest of Arbuckle Mountain (lat. 40°21' N, long. 121°57'45" W). Named on Chanchelulla Peak (1951) 15' quadrangle.

First Creek [SHASTA]: *stream,* flows 1 mile to Squaw Creek Arm Shasta Lake 9.5 miles south of Bollibokka Mountain (lat. 40°47'45" N, long. 122°11'20" W; at S line sec. 15, T 34 N, R 3 W). Named on Bollibokka Mountain (1957) 15' quadrangle.

First Creek [SISKIYOU]: *stream,* flows 4.5 miles to lowlands 11.5 miles south-southwest of Macdoel (lat. 41°40'30" N, long. 122°04'55" W; near E line sec. 9, T 44 N, R 2 W); the stream heads at First Spring. Named on The Whaleback (1954) 15' quadrangle.

First Spring [SISKIYOU]: *spring,* 10 miles southwest of Macdoel (lat. 41°43'15" N, long. 122°07'50" W; sec. 25, T 45 N, R 3 W). Named on The Whaleback (1954) 15' quadrangle.

Fish Camp Flat [BUTTE]: *area,* 1.25 miles south-southeast of Pulga (lat. 39°47'05" N, long. 121°26'20" W; near S line sec. 5, T 22 N, R 5 E). Named on Pulga (1979) 7.5' quadrangle.

Fish Creek [BUTTE]: *stream,* flows 6.25 miles to West Branch Feather River 2.5 miles north of Stirling City (lat. 39°56'45" N, long. 121°31'55" W; sec. 9, T 24 N, R 4 E). Named on Stirling City (1979) 7.5' quadrangle. Called Last Chance Creek on Chico (1895) 30' quadrangle, where present Last Chance Creek (1) is called Fish Creek. West Branch enters 2.5 miles upstream from the mouth of the main creek, it is 3 miles long and is named on Stirling City (1979) 7.5' quadrangle.

Fish Creek [SHASTA]: *stream,* flows 2.5 miles to Squaw Creek (1) nearly 5 miles south of Shoeinhorse Mountain (lat. 41°00'05" N, long. 122°03'35" W). Named on Shoeinhorse Mountain (1954) 15' quadrangle.

Fish Creek [SISKIYOU]: *stream,* flows 3 miles to Grider Creek 11.5 miles west of Scott Bar (lat. 41°43'10" N, long. 123°13'30" W). Named on Grider Valley (1981) 7.5' quadrangle.

Fish Creek [TEHAMA]: *stream,* flows 10.5 miles to Thomes Creek 3.5 miles west-northwest of Ball Mountain (lat. 39°56'45" N, long. 122°50'55" W; near E line sec. 10, T 24 N, R 9 W). Named on Yolla Bolly (1954) 15' quadrangle, and on Ball Mountain (1967) 7.5' quadrangle.

Fish Creek: see **Discovery Creek** [BUTTE].

Fisher [SHASTA]: *locality,* 8 miles south-southwest of Castella along Southern Pacific Railroad (lat. 41°02'10" N, long. 122°23'30" W; sec. 25, T 37 N, R 5 W). Named on Dunsmuir (1954) 15' quadrangle. The name commemorates Simeon Fisher Southern, a pioneer settler (Hanna, p. 106).

Fish Gulch [SISKIYOU]:

(1) *canyon,* drained by a stream that flows nearly 2 miles to Horse Creek (2) 6.5 miles east of the village of Seiad Valley (lat. 41°51' N, long. 123°04'20" W; sec. 12, T 46 N, R 11 W). Named on Hamburg (1980) 7.5' quadrangle.

(2) *canyon,* drained by a stream that flows 2.5 miles to Beaver Creek (1) 9 miles east-southeast of Condrey Mountain (lat. 41°52'50" N, long. 122°49'10" W; sec. 31, T 47 N, R 8 W). Named on Condrey Mountain (1955) 15' quadrangle.

Fish Lake [SISKIYOU]: *lake,* 650 feet long, 18 miles south of Etna (lat. 41°11'40" N, long. 122°57'40" W; sec. 36, T 39 N, R 10 W); the lake is at the head of Fish Lake Creek. Named on Coffee Creek (1955) 15' quadrangle.

Fish Lake: see **Lonesome Lake** [SISKIYOU].

Fish Lake Creek [SISKIYOU]: *stream,* flows nearly 3 miles to East Fork of South Fork Salmon River 16 miles south-southwest of Etna (lat. 41°13'40" N, long. 122°58'50" W; sec. 23, T 39 N, R 10 W); the stream heads at Fish Lake. Named on Coffee Creek (1955) 15' quadrangle.

Fish Meadow [SISKIYOU]: *area,* 9 miles east-northeast of the village of Seiad Valley (lat. 41°52'30" N, long. 123°01'30" W). Named on Dutch Creek (1980) and Hamburg (1980) 7.5' quadrangles.

Fish Mountain [SHASTA]: *peak,* 2 miles east-northeast of the town of central Valley (lat. 40°41'40" N, long. 122°20' W; near NW cor. sec. 28, T 33 N, R 4 W). Altitude 1421 feet. Named on Project City (1957) 7.5' quadrangle.

Fish Ridge [TEHAMA]: *ridge,* west-southwest-trending, 1.5 miles long, 9.5 miles south-southeast of Tomhead Mountain (lat. 40°00'15" N, long. 122°47' W); the ridge is east of Fish Creek. Named on Yolla Bolly (1954) 15' quadrangle.

Fishtrap Creek [SISKIYOU]: *stream,* flows less than 2 miles to Beaver Creek (1) 9.5 miles east of Condrey Mountain (lat. 41°56'45" N, long. 122°48' W; at N line sec. 8, T 47 N, R 8 W). Named on Condrey Mountain (1955) 15' quadrangle. Averill's (1935) map has the form "Fish Trap Cr." for the name.

Fisk Ridge [SISKIYOU]: *ridge,* southwest-trending, 3 miles long, 12.5 miles southeast of Bray (lat. 41°30'45" N, long. 121°48'15" W). Named on Bray (1950) 15' quadrangle.

Fitzhugh Gulch [SHASTA]: *canyon,* drained by a stream that flows 1 mile to McCloud River [SHASTA-SISKIYOU] 3.25 miles north-northwest of Shoeinhorse Mountain (lat. 41°06'45" N, long. 122°05'20" W). Named on Shoeinhorse Mountain (1954) 15' quadrangle.

Fitzpatrick [SHASTA]: *locality,* 11 miles north of Millville (lat. 40°42'15" N, long. 122°09' W; near NE cor. sec. 24, T 33 N, R 3 W). Named on Redding (1901) 30' quadrangle.

Five and Ten Divide [SISKIYOU]: *ridge,* north-trending, 5 miles long, 6.5 miles southeast of Preston Peak (lat. 41°46' N, long. 123°31'25" W); the ridge is between Fivemile Creek and Tenmile Creek. Named on Bear Peak (1982) and Preston Peak (1982) 7.5' quadrangles.

Five Corners [BUTTE]: *locality,* 5 miles north-northwest of Pulga (lat. 39°52' N, long. 121°29'45" W; at N line sec. 11, T 23 N, R 4 E). Named on Pulga (1979) 7.5' quadrangle.

Five Dollar Camp [SISKIYOU]: *locality,* 4.5 miles south of Cecilville (lat. 41°04'40" N, long. 123°09'10" W). Site named on Cecil Lake (1979) 7.5' quadrangle.

Fivemile Creek [SISKIYOU]: *stream,* flows about 6 miles to Clear Creek (1) 4 miles northeast of Bear Peak (lat. 41°43'30" N, long. 123°30'50" W). Named on Bear Peak (1982), Happy Camp (1980), and Preston Peak (1982) 7.5' quadrangles. Called Boulder Cr. on Preston Peak (1922) 30' quadrangle, and called Five Mile Cr. on Averill's (1935) map, but United States Board on Geographic Names (1960a, p. 14) rejected the names "Boulder Creek" and "Five Mile Creek" for the feature.

Fivemile Gulch [SHASTA]: *canyon,* drained by a stream that flows 4 miles to Clear Creek nearly 3 miles north-northeast of the village of French Gulch (lat. 40°44'30" N, long. 122°37'25" W). Named on Schell Mountain (1950) 15' quadrangle, and on French Gulch (1979) 7.5' quadrangle. Irish Placer Mining Company brought water for placer mining from the canyon through a ditch 5 miles long (Steger, p. 32). North Fork enters from the north 9.5 miles southwest of Schell Mountain; it is 2.25 miles long and is named on Schell Mountain (1950) 15' quadrangle.

Flag Canyon [BUTTE]: *canyon,* drained by a stream that flows 3.5 miles to Dry Creek 8.5 miles north-northwest of Oroville (lat. 39°38'05" N, long. 121°35'50" W; at W line sec. 36, T 21 N, R 3 E). Named on Cherokee (1970) and Oroville (1970) 7.5' quadrangles.

Flapjack Bar[SISKIYOU]: *locality,* 1 mile east-southeast of Sawyers Bar along North Fork Salmon River (lat. 41°17'40" N, long. 123°06'40" W). Named on Tanners Peak (1977) 7.5' quadrangle.

Flat Creek [SHASTA]:

(1) *stream,* flows 4.5 miles to Pit River Arm Shasta Lake 11 miles southeast of Bollibokka Mountain (lat. 40°48'45" N, long. 122°04'30" W; sec. 10, T 34 N, R 2 W). Named on Bollibokka Mountain (1957) 15' quadrangle.

(2) *stream,* flows 3.5 miles to Sacramento River 4 miles southwest of Summit City (lat. 40°38'15" N, long. 122°26'55" W; near W line sec. 9, T 32 N, R 5 W). Named on Shasta Dam (1956) 7.5' quadrangle.

(3) *stream,* flows 4 miles to Tadpole Creek 5 miles southwest of Redding (lat. 40°31'30" N, long. 122°26'55" W; near E line sec. 20, T 31 N, R 5 W). Named on Redding (1957) 7.5' quadrangle.

Flatiron [BUTTE]: *peak,* 3.5 miles west-southwest of Paradise (lat. 39°44'15" N, long. 121°41'30" W; at W line sec. 30, T 22 N, R 3 E). Named on Hamlin Canyon (1951) 7.5' quadrangle.

Flatiron Hill: see **Flatiron Mountain** [TEHAMA].

Flatiron Mountain [TEHAMA]: *peak,* nearly 3 miles north of Polk Springs (lat. 40°09'30" N, long. 121°40' W; at N line sec. 32, T 27 N, R 3 E). Altitude 4400 feet. Named on Butte Meadows (1958) 15' quadrangle. Called Flatiron Hill on Lassen Peak (1894) 1° quadrangle.

Flatiron Ridge [SHASTA]: *ridge,* east-southeast-trending, 2.5 miles long, 7 miles east-southeast of Lassen Peak (lat. 40°27' N, long. 121°23'15" W). Named on Mount Harkness (1956) 15' quadrangle. The name is from the shape of the feature (Schulz, p. 20). The southeast end of the ridge is on Shasta-Plumas County line

Flat Springs Canyon [SISKIYOU]: *canyon,* drained by a stream that flows nearly 2 miles to Bogus Creek 17 miles west-northwest of Macdoel (lat. 41°53'55" N, long. 122°19'55" W; sec. 29, T 47 N, R 4 W). Named on Copco (1954) 15' quadrangle.

Flat Top [SHASTA]: *peak,* 15 miles northwest of Lassen Peak (lat. 40°39'15" N, long. 121°40'45" W; sec. 6, T 32 N, R 3 E). Named on Manzanita Lake (1956) 15' quadrangle. United States Board on Geographic Names (1987b, p. 1) rejected the name "Table Mountain" for the feature.

Flat Woods [SHASTA]: *area,* 8.5 miles north-northwest of the village on Montgomery Creek (lat. 40°57'15" N, long. 121°57'45" W). Named on Montgomery Creek (1956) 15' quadrangle.

Flea Mountain [BUTTE]: *peak,* 2.25 miles northwest of Pulga (lat. 39°49'45" N, long. 121°28'15" W; at S line sec. 24, T 23 N, R 4 E). Named on Pulga (1979) 7.5' quadrangle.

Flea Valley [BUTTE]: *valley,* 3 miles northwest of Pulga (lat. 39°49'50" N, long. 121°29'10" W; at SE cor. sec. 23, T 23 N, R 4 E); the valley is less than 1 mile west of Flea Mountain. Named on Pulga (1979) 7.5' quadrangle. Bidwell Bar (1897) 30' quadrangle shows a community called Flea Valley at the place.

Flea Valley Creek [BUTTE]: *stream,* flows nearly 3 miles to North Fork Feather River at Pulga (lat. 39°48'10" N, long. 121°26'45" W; near W line sec. 32, T 23 N, R 5 E); the stream heads at Flea Valley. Named on Pulga (1979) 7.5' quadrangle.

Fleener Chimneys [SISKIYOU]: *relief feature,* 7.25 miles east-southeast of Mount Dome (lat. 41°45'30" N, long. 121°34' W; near E line sec. 12, T 45 N, R 3 E). Named on Mount Dome (1950) 15' quadrangle. United States Board on Geographic Names (1949, p. 4) rejected the names "Fleener's Chimney" and "Fleeners Chimneys," and noted that the name "Fleener" commemorates Sam Fleener, who homesteaded near the feature.

Flems Fork: see **Ukonom Creek** [SISKIYOU].

Flint Valley [SISKIYOU]: *relief feature,* 6 miles west-northwest of Dillon Mountain (lat. 41°33'05" N, long. 123°40'50" W). Named on Chimney Rock (1981) 7.5' quadrangle.

Flood Creek [TEHAMA]: *stream,* flows 3 miles to Thomes Creek 3.25 miles west of Ball Mountain (lat. 39°56'10" N, long. 122°50'45" W; at W line sec. 14, T 24 N, R 9 W). Named on Ball Mountain (1967) 7.5' quadrangle.

Florin Crossing [SISKIYOU]: *locality,* 11 miles east-southeast of Bartle along Bear Creek [SHASTA-SISKIYOU] (lat. 41°11'05" N, long. 121°37'40" W; sec. 28, T 39 N, R 3 E). Named on Pondosa (1961) 15' quadrangle.

Flournoy [TEHAMA]: *village,* 13 miles west of Corning (lat. 39°55'15" N, long. 122°26'05" W; sec. 21, T 24 N, R 5 W). Named on Flournoy (1967) 7.5' quadrangle. Postal authorities established Flournoy post office in 1908 (Frickstad, p. 204). The name commemorates the Flournoy family, residents of the neighborhood since the 1870's (Gudde, 1949, p. 117).

Flower Gulch [SISKIYOU]: *canyon,* drained by a stream that flows 2 miles to Right Hand Fork of North Fork Salmon River 10 miles north of Forks of Salmon (lat. 41°26'25" N, long. 123°06'05" W). Named on Yellow Dog Peak (1977) 7.5' quadrangle.

Flowers Ridge [GLENN]: *ridge,* north-northeast-trending, nearly 2 miles long, 4.5 miles north-northeast of Black Butte (lat. 39°46'35" N, long. 122°39'35" W). Named on Log Spring (1967) 7.5' quadrangle.

Floyd: see **Orland** [GLENN].

Flügge: see **Boga** [BUTTE].

Fluhart Basin [SHASTA]: *relief feature,* 3.25 miles south-southwest of Whitmore (lat. 40°35' N, long. 121°55'45" W; near W line sec. 36, T 32 N, R 1 W). Named on Whitmore (1956) 15' quadrangle. United States Board on Geographic Names (1986c, p. 3) approved the name "Fluhart Gap" for a pass situated 1 mile south-southwest of Fluhart Basin (lat. 40°34'07" N, long. 121°56'26" W; sec. 2, T 31 N, R 1 W).

Fluhart Gap: see **Fluhart Basin** [SHASTA].

Flume: see **Sims** [SHASTA].

Flume Canyon [SHASTA]: *canyon,* drained by a stream that flows 0.5 mile to Squaw Creek Arm Shasta Lake 10.5 miles south of Bollibokka Mountain (lat. 40°47'25" N, long. 122°10'20" W; sec. 23, T 34 N, R 3 W). Named on Bollibokka Mountain (1957) 15' quadrangle.

Flume Canyon [SISKIYOU]: *canyon,* drained by a stream that flows 1.5 miles to Shovel Creek 9 miles west-northwest of Macdoel (lat. 41°52'55" N, long. 122°09'40" W; near S line sec. 25, T 47 N, R 3 W). Named on Macdoel (1954) 15' quadrangle.

Flume Creek [SHASTA]: *stream,* flows 4.5 miles to Sacramento River 3.5 miles south-southwest of Castella (lat. 41°05'40" N, long. 122°20'35" W; at E line sec. 5, T 37 N, R 4 E). Named on Dunsmuir (1954) 15' quadrangle. The stream has worn a natural flume, 75 to 100 feet long, in bedrock (Steger, p. 32).

Flume Creek [TEHAMA]: *stream,* flows 5.5 miles to Salt Creek (2) 8.5 miles east-northeast of Red Bluff (lat. 40°13'55" N, long. 122°05'40" W; near S line sec. 33, T 28 N, R 2 W). Named on Tuscan Springs (1951) 7.5' quadrangle.

Flume Creek Ridge [SHASTA]: *ridge,* generally east-trending, 4.5 miles long, 3 miles west of Castella (lat. 41°07'55" N, long. 122°22'30" W); the ridge is north of Flume Creek. Named on Dunsmuir (1954) 15' quadrangle.

Fly Stain Creek [SISKIYOU]: *stream,* flows about 1 mile to Beaver Creek (1) 12 miles east-northeast of Condrey Mountain (lat. 41°59'05" N, long. 123°46'15" W). Named on Condrey Mountain (1955) 15' quadrangle.

Fogg Gulch [SISKIYOU]: *canyon,* drained by a stream that flows 2.5 miles to Little Shasta River 9.5 miles west-southwest of Macdoel (lat. 41°44'05" N, long. 122°20'45" W). Named on Copco (1954) and Lake Shastina (1954) 15' quadrangles.

Fong Wah Bar [SISKIYOU]: *locality,* 1.5 miles northwest of Forks of Salmon along Salmon River (lat. 41°16'30" N, long. 123°20'40" W); the place is less than 0.5 mile downstream from the mouth of Fong Wah Gulch. Named on Forks of Salmon (1978) 7.5' quadrangle.

Fong Wah Gulch [SISKIYOU]: *canyon,* drained by a stream that flows 1.5 miles to Salmon River 1.25 miles northwest of Forks of Salmon (lat. 41°16'10" N, long. 123°20'25" W). Named on Forks of Salmon (1978) 7.5' quadrangle.

Fons Butte [SISKIYOU]: *hill,* 14 miles north-northwest of Bartle (lat. 41°24'45" N, long. 121°59'30" W; sec. 8, T 41 N, R 1 W). Altitude 5470 feet. Named on Bartle (1961) 15' quadrangle.

Fools Creek: see **Dropoff Creek** [SHASTA].

Fools Gulch [SHASTA]: *canyon,* drained by a stream that flows nearly 2 miles to Star City Creek 7 miles north-northeast of Shoeinhorse Mountain (lat. 41°09'40" N, long. 122°01'35" W). Named on Shoeinhorse Mountain (1954) 15' quadrangle.

Fools Paradise: see **Paradise Craggy** [SISKIYOU].

Forbestown [BUTTE]: *village,* 14 miles east of Oroville (lat. 39°31'05" N, long. 121°16'15" W; sec. 11, T 19 N, R 6 E). Named on Forbestown (1970) 7.5' quadrangle. Postal authorities established Forbestown post office in 1854, discontinued it in 1925, and reestablished it in 1936 (Frickstad, p. 9). B.F. Forbes opened a small store at the place in 1850; a man named Tolle began mining and trading at a site located about 0.5 mile downstream from present Forbestown—this place was known as Tolle's Old Diggings to distinguish it from other diggings that Tolle owned (Wells and Chambers, p. 261). A place called Evansville was situated 5 miles southwest of Forbestown—the name was for the first settler (Gudde, 1975, p. 113).

Forbestown: see **Old Forbestown** [BUTTE].

Forbestown Ravine [BUTTE]: *canyon,* drained by a stream that flows 1.5 miles to South Fork Feather River 1.5 miles north of Forbestown (lat. 39°32'35" N, long. 121°16' W; near S line sec. 35, T 20 N, R 6 E); the canyon heads at Old Forbestown. Named on Forbestown (1970) 7.5' quadrangle.

Ford: see **Pat Ford Creek** [SISKIYOU].

Ford Hill [GLENN]: *peak,* 5 miles southeast of Black Butte (lat. 39°40'30" N, long. 122°48'30" W; sec. 18, T 21 N, R 8 W). Named on Plaskett Meadows (1967) 7.5' quadrangle.

Foreman Creek [BUTTE]:

(1) *stream,* heads just inside Plumas County and flows 2 miles to Baker Creek 6 miles east-southeast of Pulga (lat. 39°47'05" N, long. 121°20'20" W; near E line sec. 6, T 22 N, R 6 E). Named on Soapstone Hill (1979)

7.5' quadrangle.

(2) *stream,* flows less than 1 mile to Lake Oroville nearly 4 miles north-northeast of Oroville Dam (lat. 39°35'15" N, long. 121°27'15" W; sec. 18, T 20 N, R 5 E). Named on Oroville Dam (1970) 7.5' quadrangle.

Foreman Glade [TEHAMA]: *area,* 4.25 miles west of Ball Mountain (lat. 39°56'10" N, long. 122°51'40" W; near NW cor. sec. 15, T 24 N, R 9 W). Named on Ball Mountain (1967) 7.5' quadrangle. Anthony Peak (1952) 15' quadrangle has the name at a site about 2 miles north-northeast of present Foreman Glade (near NE cor. sec. 3, T 24 N, R 9 W), but United States Board on Geographic Names (1969c, p. 4) approved the name for the place shown on Ball Mountain (1967) 7.5' quadrangle.

Foreman Spring [GLENN]: *spring,* 10 miles west of the village of Elk Creek (lat. 39°36'30" N, long. 122°43'25" W; near N line sec. 11, T 20 N, R 8 W). Named on Felkner Hill (1968) 7.5' quadrangle.

Forest House [SISKIYOU]: *locality,* 5 miles south-southwest of Yreka along Yreka Creek (lat. 41°40'25" N, long. 122°41'05" W; sec. 8, T 44 N, R 7 W). Named on Yreka (1954) 15' quadrangle.

Forest Lake [TEHAMA]: *lake,* 300 feet long, 7 miles north-northeast of Mineral (lat. 40°26'30" N, long. 121°32'45" W; near SW cor. sec. 21, T 30 N, R 4 E). Named on Lassen Peak (1956) 15' quadrangle.

Forest Ranch [BUTTE]: *village,* 8.5 miles north-northwest of Paradise (lat. 39°52'25" N, long. 121°40'45" W; at E line sec. 6, 7, T 23 N, R 3 E). Named on Cohasset (1979) and Paradise West (1980) 7.5' quadrangles. Postal authorities established Forest Ranch post office in 1878, discontinued it in 1926, reestablished it in 1932, moved it 0.5 mile north in 1937, and moved it 1.5 miles southwest the same year (Salley, p. 77). California Mining Bureau's (1909d) map shows a place called Berdan located between Forest Ranch and Westbranch. Postal authorities established Berdan post office 8 miles north of Forest Ranch in 1878, moved it 1.25 miles south in 1909, and discontinued it in 1916; the name was for Myron G. Berdan, first postmaster (Salley, p. 19). F.D. Dunn (p. 86) listed a stage stop called Platts that was located between Berdan and Westbranch (about sec. 9, T 24 N, R 5 E).

Forestvale: see **Mount Shasta** [SISKIYOU] (2).

Forked Creek [TEHAMA]: *stream,* flows 4 miles to Deer Creek (2) 9.5 miles northeast of Polk Springs (lat. 40°11'50" N, long. 121°31'05" W; at E line sec. 16, T 27 N, R 4 E). Named on Butte Meadows (1958) 15' quadrangle. Called Onion Creek on Lassen Peak (1894) 1° quadrangle.

Forks Flat: see **Bollibokka Mountain** [SHASTA].

Forks of Butte [BUTTE]: *locality,* 4.5 miles west of Stirling City (lat. 39°54'55" N, long. 121°36'55" W; near NE cor. sec. 27, T 24 N, R 3 E); West Branch joins Butte Creek [BUTTE-GLENN] at the site. Named on Stirling City (1979) 7.5' quadrangle.

Forks of Salmon [SISKIYOU]: *village,* 48 miles southeast of Yreka (lat. 41°15'30" N, long. 123°19'15" W); the village is at the confluence of North Fork Salmon River and South Fork Salmon River. Named on Forks of Salmon (1978) 7.5' quadrangle. Postal authorities established Forks of Salmon post office in 1858, discontinued it in 1871, and reestablished it in 1872 (Frickstad, p. 187). The place commonly was known as Bennett's (Dunn, R.L., p. 426). Postal authorities established Novelty post office 9 miles southeast of Forks of Salmon in 1888 and discontinued it in 1893 (Salley, p. 157).

Forks Reservoir [GLENN]: *intermittent lake,* 200 feet long, 8.5 miles northwest of the village of Elk Creek (lat. 39°41'35" N, long. 122°38'50" W). Named on Alder Springs (1967) 7.5' quadrangle.

Forks Ridge [TEHAMA]: *ridge,* east-southeast- to south-southeast-trending, 5 miles long, 5.5 miles west-southwest of Ball Mountain (lat. 39°53'45" N, long. 122°52'45" W). Named on Ball Mountain (1967) and Buck Rock (1967) 7.5' quadrangles.

Fort Creek [SHASTA]: *stream,* flows 0.5 mile to Shasta Lake 12 miles south of Bollibokka Mountain (lat. 40°45'55" N, long. 122°11'55" W; near N line sec. 34, T 34 N, R 3 W). Named on Bollibokka Mountain (1957) 15' quadrangle.

Fort Crook: see **Fall River Valley** [SHASTA].

Fort Denny: see **Callahan** [SISKIYOU].

Fort Goff [SISKIYOU]: *locality,* 8 miles northeast of Happy Camp along Klamath River (lat. 41°51'20" N, long. 123°15'25" W). Named on Slater Butte (1980) 7.5' quadrangle. Postal authorities established Fort Goff post office in 1858 and discontinued it in 1862 (Frickstad, p. 187).

Fort Goff Creek [SISKIYOU]: *stream,* formed by the confluence of East Fork and Middle Fork, flows 4.5 miles to Klamath River 8 miles northeast of Happy Camp (lat. 41°51'50" N, long. 123°15'25" W); the stream joins Klamath River at Fort Goff. Named on Figurehead Mountain (1980) and Slater Butte (1980) 7.5' quadrangles. Called Goff Creek on Averill's (1935) map. East Fork is 1.25 miles long and Middle Fork is nearly 3 miles long. West Fork, which enters from the northwest less that 1 mile downstream from the confluence of East Fork and Middle Fork, is 2.25 miles long. All three forks are named on Figurehead Mountain (1980) 7.5' quadrangle.

Fort Hooper: see **Hooperville** [SISKIYOU].

Fort Jones [SISKIYOU]: *town,* 13 miles southwest of Yreka (lat. 41°36'30" N, long. 122°50'30" W; in and near sec. 2, T 43 N, R 9 W). Named on Fort Jones (1955) 15' quadrangle. Postal authorities established Ottitiewa post office, named for Indians of the neighborhood, in 1854, and changed the name to Fort Jones in 1860 (Salley, p. 164). The town incorporated in 1872. The community began in 1851 as a hotel and stage station; it was known as Wheelock for its founder, and also was known as Scottsburg and Ottitiewa before the name was changed in 1862 to Fort Jones for an army camp that was situated 1 mile to the south (Hanna, p. 156; Hoover, Rensch, and Rensch, p. 506). The military post was built in 1852 to protect the region from depredations by Indians—the name honored Colonel Roger Jones, Adjutant General, United States Army, who died in 1852; the post was abandoned in 1858 (Frazer, p. 24-25).

Fort Mountain [SHASTA]: *peak,* 5 miles northeast of Burney Falls (lat. 41°04' N, long. 121°35'30" W; near S line sec. 2, T 37 N, R 3 E); the peak stands above the site of Fort Crook (Steger, p. 32). Altitude 4858 feet. Named on Pondosa (1961) 15' quadrangle..

Fort Reading [SHASTA]: *locality,* 5.25 miles north-northwest of present Balls Ferry along Cow Creek (lat. 40°29'10" N, long. 122°13'50" W; sec. 5, T 30 N, R 3 W). Site named on Tuscan Buttes (1944) 15' quadrangle. Lieutenant Nelson H. Davis established a military post at the site in 1852 for protection from Indians; the garrison was withdrawn in 1856, and thereafter the post was occupied only occasionally before it was abandoned in 1870—the name was for P.B. Reading (Frazer, p. 29). Goddard's (1857) map shows Dangerfields Ferry on Sacramento River near Fort Reading.

Fortyniner Gulch [BUTTE]: *canyon,* drained by a stream that flows 1.5 miles to West Branch Feather River 4 miles northeast of Paradise (lat. 39°47'35" N, long. 121°33'40" W; at E line sec. 6, T 22 N, R 4 E). Named on Paradise East (1980) 7.5' quadrangle.

Forward: see **Camp Forward** [SHASTA].

Forward Mill [TEHAMA]: *locality,* 9.5 miles northwest of Mineral (lat. 40°26'05" N, long. 121°43'55" W; near N line sec. 26, T 30 N, R 2 E); the place is across Digger Creek [SHASTA-TEHAMA] from Camp Forward [SHASTA]. Named on Lassen Peak (1956) 15' quadrangle.

Fossil Cave [SISKIYOU]: *cave,* 11 miles south of Tulelake (lat. 41°46'05" N, long. 121°28'35" W; sec. 26, T 48 N, R 4 E). Named on Tulelake (1951) 15' quadrangle.

Foster [SISKIYOU]: *locality,* 14 miles south-southwest of Etna (lat. 41°15'15" N, long. 122°57'30" W; sec. 12, T 39 N, R 10 W). Named on Etna (1955) 15' quadrangle. Etna (1934) 30' quadrangle shows the Foster mine at the place.

Foster Island [TEHAMA]: *island,* 8 miles southeast of Corning in Sacramento River (lat. 39°51'20" N, long. 121°03'40" W). Named on Foster Island (1950) 7.5' quadrangle. Called Gazelle I. on Vina (1904) 15' quadrangle, where present Lower Foster Island is called Foster I.

Fountain of Youth Spring [SISKIYOU]: *spring,* 9.5 miles west-northwest of Hornbrook (lat. 41°58'45" N, long. 122°42'40" W; near E line sec. 25, T 48 N, R 8 W). Named on Hornbrook (1955) 15' quadrangle.

Four Bit Gulch [SISKIYOU]: *canyon,* drained by a stream that flows less than 1 mile to Green Creek 15 miles north-northwest of Happy Camp (lat. 41°59'20" N, long. 123°29'30" W; near SW cor. sec. 35, T 19 N, R 6 E); the canyon is west of Two Bit Gulch. Named on Deadman Point (1981) and Polar Bear Mountain (1982) 7.5' quadrangles.

Four Corners [BUTTE]: *locality,* 4.25 miles north-northwest of Chico (lat. 39°46'45" N, long. 121°53' W). Named on Chico (1895) 30' quadrangle.

Four Corners [SHASTA]: *locality,* 1.25 miles southeast of Burney Falls (lat. 41°00'05" N, long. 121°37'50" W; at SE cor. sec. 4, T 36 N, R 3 E). Named on Pondosa (1961) 15' quadrangle. United States Board on Geographic Names (1964, p. 10) rejected the name "Old Four Corners" for the place.

Four Corners [SISKIYOU]:

(1) *locality,* 25 miles southwest of Macdoel (lat. 41°37'25" N, long. 122°23'55" W; at NW cor. sec. 35, T 44 N, R 5 W). Named on Lake Shastina (1954) 15' quadrangle.

(2) *locality,* 4 miles north-northwest of Bartle (lat. 41°18'40" N, long. 121°51'30" W; sec. 16, T 40 N, R 1 E). Named on Bartle (1961) 15' quadrangle.

Four Lantern Flat [TEHAMA]: *area,* 2.5 miles northwest of Polk Springs (lat. 40°08'35" N, long. 121°21'55" W; on S line sec. 36, T 27 N, R 2 E). Named on Butte Meadows (1958) 15' quadrangle.

Fourmile Butte [SISKIYOU]: *peak,* 9 miles north-northeast of Happy Camp (lat. 41°55'05" N, long. 123°18'50" W); the peak is near the head of Fourmile Creek (1). Altitude 5488 feet. Named on Figurehead Mountain (1980) 7.5' quadrangle.

Fourmile Creek [SISKIYOU]:

(1) *stream,* flows nearly 2 miles to Thompson Creek 7.25 miles north-northeast of Happy Camp (lat. 41°53'45" N, long. 123°19'55" W). Named on Figurehead Mountain (1980) 7.5' quadrangle. O'Brien's (1947) map has the form "4 Mile Cr." for the name.

(2) *stream,* flows 2.25 miles to Clear Creek (1) 12 miles northwest of Ukonom Lake (lat. 41°43'10" N, long. 123°29'55" W). Named on Clear Creek (1981) 7.5' quadrangle. Called Four Mile Cr. on Averill's (1935) map, but United States Board on Geographic Names (1965c, p. 9) re-

jected this form of the name.

Fourmile Flat [SISKIYOU]: *area,* 4.5 miles west of Bartle along McCloud River [SHASTA-SISKIYOU] (lat. 41°15'55" N, long. 121°54'15" W; near SE cor. sec. 36, T 40 N, R 1 W). Named on Bartle (1961) 15' quadrangle.

Fourmile Hill [SISKIYOU]: *hill,* 4.25 miles north of Medicine Lake (lat. 41°38'30" N, long. 121°36'45" W; sec. 22, T 44 N, R 3 E). Altitude 7063 feet. Named on Medicine Lake (1952) 15' quadrangle. United States Board on Geographic Names (1967b, p. 4) approved the name "Lookout Butte" for a feature located 0.5 mile northwest of Fourmile Hill (sec. 15, 16, T 44 N, R 3 E).

Fourteenmile House [BUTTE]: *locality,* 7.5 miles north-northwest of Paradise (lat. 39°51' N, long. 121°41'40" W; at E line sec. 13, T 23 N, R 2 E). Site named on Paradise (1953) 15' quadrangle. Called 14 M. House on Chico (1895) 30' quadrangle.

Fourth of July Gulch [SISKIYOU]: *canyon,* drained by a stream that flows nearly 1 mile to West Fork Crawford Creek (2) 2.5 miles north of Cecilville (lat. 41°10'50" N, long. 123°08'15" W). Named on Cecilville (1979) 7.5' quadrangle.

Fowler Camp [SISKIYOU]: *locality,* 6.25 miles west of McCloud along McCloud River [SHASTA-SISKIYOU] (lat. 41°14'40" N, long. 122°01'20" W; sec. 12, T 39 N, R 2 W). Named on Shoeinhorse Mountain (1954) 15' quadrangle.

Fowler Gulch [SHASTA]: *canyon,* drained by a stream that flows nearly 1 mile to Squaw Creek Arm Shasta Lake 8.5 miles south-southeast of Bollibokka Mountain (lat. 40°49'15" N, long. 122°08'55" W; near NE cor. sec. 12, T 34 N, R 3 W). Named on Bollibokka Mountain (1957) 15' quadrangle.

Fox Creek [BUTTE]: *stream,* flows nearly 2 miles to West Branch French Creek 6 miles southeast of Pulga (lat. 39°45'05" N, long. 121°21'30" W; at E line sec. 24, T 22 N, R 5 E). Named on Soapstone Hill (1979) 7.5' quadrangle. The stream was called Ditch Creek on a map of 1877 (Dunn, F.D., p. 42).

Fox Creek [SHASTA]: *stream,* flows 2 miles to Pit River 10 miles north-northeast of the village of Montgomery Creek (lat. 40°58'30" N, long. 121°50'50" W). Named on Montgomery Creek (1956) 15' quadrangle.

Fox Creek [SISKIYOU]: *stream,* flows 6 miles to Scott River 12.5 miles south of Etna (lat. 41°16'50" N, long. 122°51'05" W; at S line sec. 26, T 40 N, R 9 W). Named on Coffee Creek (1955) and Etna (1955) 15' quadrangles. United States Board on Geographic Names (1967b, p. 3) approved the name "Fox Creek Ridge" for a feature, 2 miles long, that is located east of Fox Creek (lat. 41°15'55" N, long. 122°50'05" W, at north end).

Fox Creek Lake [SISKIYOU]: *lake,* 900 feet long, 17 miles south of Etna (lat. 41°12'40" N, long. 122°50'55" W; sec. 25, T 39 N, R 9 W); the lake is at the head of a branch of Fox Creek. Named on Coffee Creek (1955) 15' quadrangle.

Fox Creek Ridge: see **Fox Creek** [SISKIYOU].

Franklin City: see **Whiskeytown** [SHASTA].

Franklin Gulch [SHASTA]: *canyon,* drained by a stream that flows 1 mile to Right Fork nearly 2.5 miles northwest of the village of French Gulch (lat. 40°43'25" N, long. 122°40'15" W). Named on French Gulch (1979) 7.5' quadrangle, which shows Franklin mine near the canyon.

Franklin Gulch [SISKIYOU]: *canyon,* drained by a stream that flows 3.25 mile to Scott River 11 miles east-southeast of the village of Seiad Valley (lat. 41°45'30" N, long. 123°00'45" W; sec. 17, T 45 N, R 10 W). Named on Condrey Mountain (1955) 15' quadrangle, and on Hamburg (1980) 7.5' quadrangle.

Franklin Gulch: see **Slug Gulch** [SISKIYOU] (1).

Franklin Point [TEHAMA]: *peak,* nearly 5 miles west-southwest of Wakefield Flat (lat. 40°02'50" N, long. 122°40'45" W; sec. 5, T 25 N, R 7 W). Altitude 3482 feet. Named on Raglin Ridge (1967) 7.5' quadrangle.

Franks Meadows: see **Franks Valley** [SISKIYOU].

Franks Valley [SISKIYOU]: *canyon,* 4.5 miles southeast of Ukonom Lake (lat. 41°33' N, long. 123°16'40" W). Named on Ukonom Lake (1980) 7.5' quadrangle. Averill's (1935) map has the name "Franks Mdws." at the place.

Fraser's Corner: see **Bella Vista** [SHASTA].

Frazier Corners: see **Bella Vista** [SHASTA].

Frazier Creek [BUTTE]: *stream,* flows 2.25 miles to North Fork Feather River 2.5 miles northwest of the village of Berry Creek (lat. 39°40'30" N, long. 121°26' W; sec. 17, T 21 N, R 5 E). Named on Berry Creek (1970) 7.5' quadrangle. Water of Lake Oroville now floods the lower part of the stream course.

Frazier Creek [TEHAMA]: *stream,* flows 3.25 miles to Sacramento River 4.5 miles north of Bend (lat. 40°19'15" N, long. 122°12'25" W; sec. 33, T 29 N, R 3 W). Named on Bend (1965) 7.5' quadrangle.

Freaner Butte: see **Freaner Peak** [SHASTA].

Freaner Peak [SHASTA]: *peak,* 18 miles north of Lassen Peak (lat. 40°44'15" N, long. 121°34' W; near N line sec. 7, T 33 N, R 4 E). Altitude 7485 feet. Named on Manzanita Lake (1956) 15' quadrangle. Called Magee Peak on Lassen Peak (1894) 1° quadrangle, called Stoney Peak on Burney (1939) 30' quadrangle, and called Tamarack Pk. on Averill's (1939) map. United States Board on Geographic Names (1947, p. 2) rejected the names "Black Rock Peak," "Freaner Butte," "Magee Peak," "Stoney Peak," "Stony Butte," "Stony Peak," "Tamarack Mountain," and "Tamarack Peak" for the feature. Members of Shasta Historical Society requested the name "Freanor" for the peak to commemorate James L. Freanor, whom Indians killed along Pit River in 1852 (Steger, p. 33).

Freanor: see **Lake Freanor**, under **Cornaz Lake** [SHASTA].

Fredonia: see **Honcut Creek** [BUTTE].

Fredonyer Peak [SHASTA]: *peak,* 15 miles north-northwest of Lassen Peak (lat. 40°41'10" N, long. 121°15'45" W; near SE cor. sec. 26, T 33 N, R 3 E). Altitude 8054 feet. Named on Manzanita Lake (1956) 15' quadrangle.

Freetown: see **Humbug Creek** [SISKIYOU].

French Bar: see **Scott Bar** [SISKIYOU].

French Creek [BUTTE]: *stream,* flows 12.5 miles to North Fork Feather River 3.5 miles north of the village of Berry Creek (lat. 39°41'45" N, long. 121°24'15" W; near N line sec. 10, T 21 N, R 5 E). Named on Berry Creek (1970), Brush Creek (1970), and Soapstone Hill (1979) 7.5' quadrangles. Wells and Chambers' (1882) map shows a place called French Creek Bar located along North Fork Feather River at the mouth of French Creek.

French Creek [GLENN]:

(1) *stream,* flows 1.25 miles to Black Butte River 7 miles south of Black Butte (lat. 39°37'45" N, long. 122°52'40" W). Named on Plaskett Meadows (1967) 7.5' quadrangle.

(2) *stream,* flows 15 miles to South Fork Willow Creek 3 miles north-northwest of Willows (lat. 39°33'40" N, long. 122°13'20" W; sec. 29, T 20 N, R 3 W). Named on Julian Rocks (1968), Stone Valley (1952, photorevised 1969), and Willows (1951, photorevised 1969) 7.5' quadrangles.

French Creek [SHASTA]: *stream,* flows 7.5 miles to Little Cow Creek 4.25 miles northwest of Millville (lat. 40°36'05" N, long. 122°13'30" W; sec. 29, T 32 N, R 3 W). Named on Bella Vista (1965) and Palo Cedro (1965) 7.5' quadrangles. Called Swede Creek on Millville (1953) 15' quadrangle, where present Swede Creek is called French Creek. United States Board on Geographic Names (1965b, p. 11) rejected the name "Swede Creek" for present French Creek.

French Creek [SISKIYOU]:

(1) *stream,* flows 3 miles to South Fork Salmon River 3 miles west of Cecilville (lat. 41°08'45" N, long. 123°11'50" W). Named on Cecil Lake (1979) and Cecilville (1979) 7.5' quadrangles.

(2) *stream,* flows 9 miles to Scott River 3.5 miles southeast of Etna (lat. 41°25' N, long. 122°50'45" W; sec. 11, T 41 N, R 9 W). Named on Etna (1955) 15' quadrangle. North Fork enters 5.25 miles south of Etna; it is 4.5 miles long and is named on Etna (1955) 15' quadrangle.

French Creek Bar: see **French Creek** [BUTTE].

French Crossing [BUTTE]: *locality,* 10.5 miles west-southwest of Biggs along Butte Creek [BUTTE-GLENN] on Butte-Colusa County line (lat. 39°20'15" N, long. 121°53'20" W). Named on Marysville (1895) 30' quadrangle. The name is for a French trapper (Dunn, F.D., p. 43).

French Flat [SISKIYOU]: *area,* 12 miles south-southeast of Etna (lat. 41°17'40" N, long. 122°50' W; at N line sec. 25, T 40 N, R 9 W). Named on Etna (1955) 15' quadrangle.

French Gulch [SHASTA]:

(1) *canyon,* drained by a stream that flows nearly 1 mile to Slate Creek (1) 1 mile west-southwest of Lamoine (lat. 40°58'30" N, long. 122°26'50" W; near S line sec. 16, T 36 N, R 5 W). Named on Lamoine (1957) 15' quadrangle.

(2) *canyon,* drained by a stream that flows 2.25 miles to Clear Creek at the village of French Gulch (lat. 40°41'50" N, long. 122°38'10" W; near SE cor. sec. 23, T 33 N, R 7 W). Named on French Gulch (1979) 7.5' quadrangle.

(3) *village,* 16 miles west-northwest of Redding (lat. 40°42'05" N, long. 122°38'10" W; sec. 22, T 33 N, R 7 W); the village is along Clear Creek just north of the mouth of French Gulch (2). Named on French Gulch (1979) 7.5' quadrangle. Postal authorities established French Gulch post office in 1856 (Frickstad, p. 179). A place called Morrowville was situated 1.5 miles west of the present village of French Gulch in the early 1850's (Steger, p. 33); the name was from H.B. Morrow, a miner (Giles, p. 175).

French Gulch [SISKIYOU]:

(1) *canyon,* drained by a stream that flows nearly 2 miles to Middle Fork Applegate River 10.5 miles north of the village of Seiad Valley (lat. 41°59'05" N, long. 123°13'50" W). Named on Figurehead Mountain (1980) and Kangaroo Mountain (1980) 7.5' quadrangles.

(2) *canyon,* drained by a stream that flows less than 1 mile to Klamath River 7.5 miles south of Condrey Mountain (lat. 41°49'55" N, long. 122°56'50" W; near E line sec. 13, T 46 N, R 10 W). Named on Condrey Mountain (1955) 15' quadrangle.

(3) *canyon,* drained by a stream that flows about 1.5 miles to Indian Creek (3) 6.25 miles north of Fort Jones (lat. 41°41'40" N, long. 122°51'30" W; near E line sec. 3, T 44 N, R 9 W). Named on Fort Jones (1955) 15' quadrangle.

Frenchman Gulch [SHASTA]: *canyon,* drained by a stream that flows 0.5 mile to Squaw Creek Arm Shasta Lake 11 miles south of Bollibokka Mountain (lat. 40°46'50" N, long. 122°10'45" W; near N line sec. 26, T 34 N, R 3 W). Named on Bollibokka Mountain (1957) 15' quadrangle.

French Ravine [BUTTE]: *canyon,* drained by a stream that flows nearly 2 miles to Rocky Honcut Creek 2.5 miles north-northwest of Bangor (lat. 39°25'20" N, long. 121°25'45" W; near NE cor. sec. 17, T 18 N, R 5 E). Named on Bangor (1947) 7.5' quadrangle.

French Ridge [GLENN]: *ridge,* south-southwest- to west-trending, 1 mile long, nearly 6 miles south of Black Butte (lat. 39°38'35" N, long. 122°52' W). Named on Plaskett Meadows (1967) 7.5' quadrangle.

French Ridge [SHASTA]: *ridge,* north- to northeast-trending, 2.25 miles long, 4.5 miles north-northeast of Schell Mountain (lat. 40°49'45" N, long. 122°30'30" W). Named on Lamoine (1957) and Schell Mountain (1950) 15' quadrangles.

French Town [SISKIYOU]: *locality,* 4.5 miles northwest of Yreka along Humbug Creek (lat. 41°47' N, long. 122°42' W). Named on Shasta (1894) 1° quadrangle. The place began as a mining camp in the early 1850's; it also was known as Riderville, Plugtown, and Mowry Flat (Hanna, p. 113). The name "French Town" was for the numerous Frenchmen mining at the place in 1864, and the name "Plugtown" was for old Dr. Nichols, who wore a plug hat (Hoover, Rensch, and Rensch, p. 508). The name "Riderville" was for W.G. Rider, who had a mining claim at Rider Gulch (Gudde, 1975, p. 292).

Freshwater Creek [GLENN]: *stream,* flows 3 miles to Salt Creek [GLENN-TEHAMA] 5 miles west of Newville (lat. 39°47'55" N, long. 122°37' W; at N line sec. 2, T 22 N, R 7 W). Named on Hall Ridge (1967) and Newville (1967) 7.5' quadrangles.

Freshwater Gulch [TEHAMA]: *canyon,* drained by a stream that flows 1.5 miles to Salt Gulch 4.5 miles west-northwest of Wakefield Flat (lat. 40°09'30" N, long. 122°43' W). Named on Cold Fork (1967) 7.5' quadrangle. On Colyear Springs (1957) 15' quadrangle, the lower part of present Salt Gulch is considered part of Freshwater Gulch.

Frey Creek [BUTTE]: *stream,* flows 6 miles to Middle Fork Feather River 5 miles southeast of the village of Brush Creek (lat. 39°37'50" N, long. 121°16'55" W). Named on Brush Creek (1970), Cascade (1948), and Forbestown (1970) 7.5' quadrangles.

Frey Creek: see **Little Frey Creek** [BUTTE].

Freys Soda Spring: see **Upper Soda Spring** [SISKIYOU].

Frog Lake [SISKIYOU]: *intermittent lake,* 17 miles north-northwest of Bartle (lat. 41°29'45" N, long. 121°55' W; sec. 12, T 42 N, R 1 W). Named on Bartle (1961) 15' quadrangle.

Frog Lake: see **Little South Fork Lake** [SISKIYOU].

Frog Pond: see **The Frog Pond** [SISKIYOU].

Frog Pond Gulch [SISKIYOU]: *canyon,* drained by a stream that flows 1 mile to Middle Fork Applegate River 15 miles north-northeast of Happy Camp (lat. 41°59'40" N, long. 123°14'55" W). Named on Figurehead Mountain (1980) 7.5' quadrangle.

Frogtown: see **Hawkinsville** [SISKIYOU].

Frolic Spring [GLENN]: *spring,* 4 miles east-northeast of Black Butte (lat. 39°44'45" N, long. 122°47'25" W; sec. 19, T 22 N, R 8 W). Named on Hull Mountain (1952) 15' quadrangle.

Frost Gulch [SHASTA]: *canyon,* drained by a stream that flows 0.5 mile to Shasta Lake 4 miles north-northeast of Summit City (lat. 40°44'25" N, long. 122°22'35" W; sec. 1, T 33 N, R 5 W). Named on Project City (1957) and Shasta Dam (1956) 7.5' quadrangles.

Frozen River Cave [SISKIYOU]: *cave,* 12.5 mile north-northeast of Medicine Lake (lat. 41°44'30" N, long. 121°29'45" W; sec. 15, T 45 N, R 4 E). Named on Timber Mountain (1952) 15' quadrangle.

Fruit Mountain [SISKIYOU]: *peak,* 8.5 miles north-northwest of the village of Seiad Valley (lat. 41°57'40" N, long. 123°14'45" W). Altitude 5932 feet. Named on Kangaroo Mountain (1980) 7.5' quadrangle.

Fruto [GLENN]: *village,* 14 miles west-northwest of Willows (lat. 39°35'20" N, long. 122°27' W; sec. 17, T 20 N, R 5 W). Named on Fruto (1968) 7.5' quadrangle. Postal authorities established Fruto post office in 1888 and discontinued it in 1953 (Frickstad, p. 40).

Fryingpan Creek [SISKIYOU]: *stream,* flows 2 miles to Klamath River 2.5 miles east-southeast of Happy Camp (lat. 41°46'40" N, long. 123°19'40" W; near E line sec. 18, T 16 N, R 8 E); the stream heads on Fryingpan Ridge. Named on Slater Butte (1980) 7.5' quadrangle.

Frying Pan Lake [SISKIYOU]: *lake,* 650 feet long, 16 miles south-southwest of Scott Bar (lat. 41°33'10" N, long. 123°10'45" W). Named on Marble Mountain (1980) 7.5' quadrangle, where the outline of the lake somewhat resembles a frying pan.

Fryingpan Ridge [SISKIYOU]: *ridge,* southeast- to east-trending, 7.5 miles long, center about 4 miles southeast of Happy Camp (lat. 41°45'20" N, long. 123°18'45" W). Named on Huckleberry Mountain (1980) and Slater Butte (1980) 7.5' quadrangles.

Fuller Flat [SHASTA]: *area,* 5 miles east-northeast of the village of Montgomery Creek along Hatchet Creek (lat. 40°51'25" N, long. 121°47'45" W; near NE cor. sec. 26, T 35 N, R 1 E); the place is north of Fuller Mountain. Named on Montgomery Creek (1956) 15' quadrangle.

Fuller Mountain [SHASTA]: *peak,* 5.25 miles east of the village of Montgomery Creek (lat. 40°51'15" N, long. 121°49'25" W; near SW cor. sec. 25, T 35 N, R 1 E); the peak is south of Fuller Flat. Altitude 4547 feet. Named on Montgomery Creek (1956) 15' quadrangle.

Funks Creek [GLENN]: *stream,* flows 4.25 miles to Colusa County 4.5 miles southeast of High Peak (lat. 39°23'05" N, long. 122°21'25" W; near W line sec. 30, T 18 N, R 4 W). Named on Lodoga (1960) 15' quadrangle.

Furnaceville [SHASTA]: *locality,* 15 miles north-northeast of Millville (lat. 40°44'30" N, long. 122°03'50" W; sec. 2, T 33 N, R 2 W). Named on Redding (1901) 30' quadrangle. Marcus H. Peck built furnaces at the place during early development of copper mines that he bought in 1873 (Steger, p. 33).

— G —

Galen Creek [BUTTE]: *stream,* flows 4.5 miles to Madrone Lake at the village of Berry Creek (lat. 39°38'55" N, long. 121°24'05" W; sec. 27, T 21 N, R 5 E). Named on Berry Creek (1970) and Brush Creek (1970) 7.5' quadrangles.

Galen Ridge [BUTTE]: *ridge,* west-southwest- to southwest-trending, 8 mile long, center 2 miles north of the village of Berry Creek (lat. 39°39'55" N, long. 121°22'30" W); the ridge is south of Galen Creek. Named on Berry Creek (1970) and Brush Creek (1970) 7.5' quadrangles.

Gap Creek [SHASTA]: *stream,* flows 2.5 miles to Cedar Salt Log Creek 4.25 miles west-northwest of the village of Big Bend (lat. 41°02'35" N, long. 121°59' W; near SW cor. sec. 21, T 37 N, R 1 W). Named on Big Bend (1961) and Shoeinhorse Mountain (1954) 15' quadrangles.

Gap Creek: see **Little Gap Creek** [SHASTA].

Gard Creek [SISKIYOU]: stream, flows 1.5 miles to Klamath River 1 mile south-southeast of the village of Seiad Valley (lat. 41°49'50" N, long. 123°10'45" W; sec. 13, T 46 N, R 12 W). Named on Seiad Valley (1980) 7.5' quadrangle.

Garden Creek [SHASTA]: stream, flows about 1.5 miles to Squaw Creek (2) 8.5 miles east-northeast of Bollibokka Mountain (lat. 40°57'45" N, long. 122°03'45" W; sec. 23, T 36 N, R 2 W). Named on Bollibokka Mountain (1957) 15' quadrangle.

Garden Gulch [SISKIYOU]:

(1) *canyon,* drained by a stream that flows 2.25 miles to Little North Fork Salmon River 3 miles northwest of Sawyers Bar (lat. 41°19'25" N, long. 123°10'45" W). Named on Sawyers Bar (1979) 7.5' quadrangle.

(2) *canyon,* drained by a stream that flows 5.5 miles to South Fork Salmon River 4 miles southeast of Cecilville (lat. 41°06'05" N, long. 123°04'35" W). Named on Grasshopper Ridge (1979) and Thompson Peak (1979) 7.5' quadrangles.

Garden Gulch: see **Cronan Gulch** [SISKIYOU].

Garden Ridge [SHASTA]: *ridge,* generally south-southeast-trending, 1.5 miles long, 4.25 miles south-southwest of Shoeinhorse Mountain (lat. 41°00'30" N, long. 122°05'30" W). Named on Shoeinhorse Mountain (1954) 15' quadrangle.

Gardens: see **The Gardens** [SHASTA].

Garner Butte [SISKIYOU]: *hill,* 5.5 miles east-southeast of Bray (lat. 41°37'30" N, long. 121°52' W; sec. 28, T 44 N, R 1 E). Altitude 5043 feet. Named on Bray (1950) 15' quadrangle.

Garner Mountain [SISKIYOU]: *mountain,* 9 miles east-southeast of Bray (lat. 41°35'30" N, long. 121°48'30" W; near N line sec. 12, T 43 N, R 1 E). Altitude 7248 feet. Named on Bray (1950) 15' quadrangle. United States Board on Geographic Names (1967b, p. 4) approved the name "Squaw Peak" for a feature, altitude 6914 feet, located 3 miles southeast of Garner Mountain (lat. 41°33'27" N, long. 121°45'45" W). At the same time, the Board (p. 5) approved the name "Typhoon Mesa" for a flat-topped elevation located 4 miles south of Garner Mountain (sec, 25, 26, 35, 36, T 43 N, R 1 E), and approved the name "Tamarack Lake" for a lake, 0.1 mile long, located 3 miles south-southeast of Garner Mountain (lat. 41°32'43" N, long. 121°47'30" W).

Garnett Camp [GLENN]: *locality,* 3 miles south-southeast of Black Butte (lat. 39°41'30" N, long. 121°50'45" W). Named on Plaskett Meadows (1967) 7.5' quadrangle.

Garret Flat [SHASTA]: *area,* 6.5 miles west of Shoeinhorse Mountain along Squaw Valley Creek (lat. 41°03'55" N, long. 122°11'45" W; sec. 15, T 37 N, R 3 W). Named on Shoeinhorse Mountain (1954) 15' quadrangle.

Garretson Soda Springs: see **Cinnabar Springs** [SISKIYOU].

Garrick Creek [SISKIYOU]: *stream,* flows 6.5 miles to Lake Shastina 30 miles southwest of Macdoel (lat. 41°30'20" N, long. 122°24' W; at W line sec. 11, T 42 N, R 5 W). Named on Lake Shastina (1954) and Weed (1954) 15' quadrangles. United States Board on Geographic Names (1984b, p. 3) approved the name "Carrick Creek" for the stream.

Garvey Bar [SISKIYOU]: *locality,* 8 miles southwest of Hornbrook (lat. 41°49'45" N, long. 122°39'20" W; near N line sec. 22, T 46 N, R 7 W); the place is near the mouth of Garvey Creek. Named on Hornbrook (1955)

15' quadrangle.

Garvey Glade [SISKIYOU]: *relief feature,* 11.5 miles west-northwest of Macdoel (lat. 41°52'30" N, long. 122°12'45" W; near E line sec. 33, T 47 N, R 3 W). Named on Macdoel (1954) 15' quadrangle.

Garvey Gulch [SISKIYOU]: *canyon,* drained by a stream that flows 1.5 miles to Klamath River 8 miles southwest of Hornbrook (lat. 41°49'35" N, long. 122°39'20" W; sec. 22, T 46 N, R 7 W). Named on Hornbrook (1955) 15' quadrangle.

Gasburg: see **Camp Eden** [SISKIYOU].

Gas Point [SHASTA]: *locality,* 6 miles southeast of Ono (lat. 40°25' N, long. 122°32' W; near NW cor. sec. 34, T 30 N, R 6 W). Named on Ono (1952) 15' quadrangle. Called Gas Point P.O. on Red Bluff (1894) 1° quadrangle. Postal authorities established Gas Point post office in 1875, discontinued it for a time in 1881, and discontinued it finally in 1933 (Salley, p. 83). According to Steger (p. 33), the name is from the custom of old prospectors to gather at the place and "gas and spin yarns." Postal authorities established Pinckney post office 2 miles southeast of Gas Point in 1881 and discontinued it in 1890 (Salley, p. 171).

Gasquet Gulch [SISKIYOU]: *canyon,* drained by a stream that flows 1.5 miles to South Fork Clear Creek (1) 10.5 miles north-northwest of Ukonom Lake (lat. 41°42'25" N, long. 123°28' W). Named on Clear Creek (1981) 7.5' quadrangle.

Gate: see **The Gate** [SISKIYOU].

Gate Creek: see **Gates Creek** [SISKIYOU].

Gate Lake [SISKIYOU]: *lake,* 200 feet long, 16 miles southwest of Scott Bar (lat. 41°33'30" N, long. 123°10'55" W). Named on Marble Mountain (1980) 7.5' quadrangle.

Gates: see **Ross Gates Spring** [TEHAMA].

Gates Creek [SISKIYOU]: *stream,* flows 1 mile to Wooley Creek 11.5 miles north-northwest of Forks of Salmon (lat. 41°24'50" N, long. 123°23'45" W). Named on Somes Bar (1979) 7.5' quadrangle. Called Gate Cr. on Sawyers Bar (1923) 30' quadrangle.

Gay Creek [GLENN-TEHAMA]: *stream,* flows 9 miles, mainly in Tehama County, but partly in Glenn County, to Moore Creek 3.25 miles south-southwest of Kirkwood (lat. 39°48'50" N, long. 122°10'55" W; near S line sec. 27, T 23 N, R 3 W). Named on Black Butte Dam (1967) and Kirkwood (1949) 7.5' quadrangles.

Gazelle [SISKIYOU]: *village,* 16 miles south-southeast of Yreka (lat. 41°31'15" N, long. 122°31'10" W; on and near N line sec. 3, T 42 N, R 6 W). Named on Yreka (1954) 15' quadrangle. Postal authorities established Gazelle post office in 1870, discontinued it in 1872, and reestablished it the same year (Frickstad, p. 187). The village began as a station on the California-Oregon trail; E.B. Edson and J.R. Edson acquired the property in 1853—the place was known as Edsons until 1870 (Hanna, p. 119).

Gazelle Island: see **Foster Island** [TEHAMA].

Gazelle Mountain [SISKIYOU]: *peak,* 12 miles east-southeast of Etna (lat. 41°24'45" N, long. 122°40'15" W; near E line sec. 8, T 41 N, R 7 W). Named on China Mountain (1955) 15' quadrangle.

Geagan: see **Weed** [SISKIYOU].

Geary Spring [TEHAMA]: *spring,* 13 miles east-southeast of Red Bluff (lat. 40°08' N, long. 122°00'30" W; sec. 5, T 26 N, R 1 W). Named on Tehama (1905) 15' quadrangle. Travelers and stockmen used the place for camping and watering (Waring, p. 335).

Gem Lake [SISKIYOU]: *lake,* 100 feet long, 15 miles south-southwest of Scott Bar (lat. 41°32'35" N, long. 123°07'55" W); the feature is near Jewel Lake. Named on Marble Mountain (1980) 7.5' quadrangle.

Genot: see **Mose Genot Glade** [TEHAMA].

George Allen Gulch [SISKIYOU]: *canyon,* drained by a stream that flows 1.5 miles to Scott River 3.5 miles south-southwest of Scott Bar (lat. 41°42' N, long. 123°02'15" W; at N line sec. 6, T 44 N, R 10 W). Named on Scott Bar (1980) 7.5' quadrangle.

George Williams Gulch [SHASTA]: *canyon,* drained by a stream that flows 2 miles to Clear Creek 1.5 miles south of the village of French Gulch (lat. 40°40'55" N, long. 122°38'15" W; at S line sec. 27, T 33 N, R 7 W). Named on French Gulch (1979) and Whiskeytown (1979) 7.5' quadrangles. Called Al Smith Gulch on French Gulch (1944) 15' quadrangle, but United States Board on Geographic Names (1978a, p. 5) rejected this name for the feature.

Gerber [TEHAMA]: *town,* 9.5 miles south-southeast of Red Bluff (lat. 40°03'20" N, long. 122°09' W). Named on Gerber (1950) 7.5' quadrangle. Postal authorities established Gerber post office in 1916 (Frickstad, p. 204). Officials of Southern Pacific Railroad named the place for H.E. Gerber, who sold land there to the railroad (Gudde, 1949, p. 126).

Germantown: see **Artois** [GLENN].

Get Up and Get Creek [BUTTE]: *stream,* flows 2 miles to Peavine Creek 3.5 miles north-northeast of the village of Brush Creek (lat. 39°44'15" N, long. 121°19'15" W; at E line sec. 29, T 22 N, R 6 E). Named on Brush Creek (1970) and Soapstone Hill (1979) 7.5' quadrangles.

Ghost Camp [SHASTA]: *locality,* 3.5 miles north-northeast of Shoeinhorse Mountain along Hawkins Creek (lat. 41°06'55" N, long. 122°07'05" W). Named on Shoeinhorse Mountain (1954) 15' quadrangle.

Giant Crater [SISKIYOU]: *crater,* 5.5 miles south-southwest of Medicine Lake (lat. 41°30'30" N, long. 121°38'25" W). Named on Medicine Lake (1952) 15' quadrangle.

Gibraltar Hill: see **Braselton Hill** [BUTTE].

Gibson [SHASTA]: *locality,* 10 miles south-southwest of Castella along Southern Pacific Railroad (lat. 41°00'40" N, long. 122°24'30" W; sec. 2, T 36 N, R 5 W). Named on Dunsmuir (1954) 15' quadrangle. The name commemorates Reuben Gibson, who led white men and Indians in a battle against Modoc Indians in 1855 (Steger, p. 33-34). Shasta (1894) 1° quadrangle shows a place called Portuguese Flat situated at or near present Gibson, and California Division of Highways' (1934) map shows a place called Eagle Point located about 0.5 mile south of Gibson along Southern Pacific Railroad.

Gibson Creek [SHASTA]: *stream,* flows 1.5 miles to Sacramento River Arm Shasta Lake 5 miles southeast of Lamoine (lat. 40°55'10" N, long. 122°22'45" W; sec. 1, T 35 N, R 5 W). Named on Lamoine (1957) 15' quadrangle.

Gibson Gulch [SISKIYOU]: *canyon,* drained by a stream that flows 2 miles to South Fork Salmon Creek 2 miles east of Cecilville (lat. 41°08'35" N, long. 123°06'05" W). Named on Grasshopper Ridge (1979) 7.5' quadrangle.

Gillem Bluff [SISKIYOU]: *escarpment,* south-trending, 3.5 miles long, center 6.5 miles east of Mount Dome (lat. 41°48'15" N, long. 121°33'45" W). Named on Mount Dome (1950) 15' quadrangle. Colonel Alvan C. Gillem, commander of troops during the Modoc War, had a camp at the base of the bluff in 1873 (Thompson, p. 130).

Gillem Lakes [SISKIYOU]: *intermittent lakes,* two, largest nearly 1 mile long, 5.25 miles east-northeast of Mount Dome (lat. 41°49'40" N, long. 121°35'15" W). Named on Mount Dome (1950) 15' quadrangle.

Gillis [SISKIYOU]: *locality,* 10 miles north-northwest of Macdoel (lat. 41°57'30" N, long. 122°05'40" W; sec. 33, T 48 N, R 2 W). Named on Macdoel (1954) 15' quadrangle.

Gilroy Flat [SHASTA]: *area,* 2.5 miles west-northwest of Schell Mountain along Clear Creek (lat. 40°51'55" N, long. 122°34'35" W). Named on Schell Mountain (1950) 15' quadrangle.

Gilta [SISKIYOU]: *locality,* 4.25 miles south of Forks of Salmon (lat. 41°11'50" N, long. 123°19'40" W). Named on Sawyers Bar (1923) 30' quadrangle. Salmon Mountain (1955) 15' quadrangle shows Gilta mine at the place. Postal authorities established Gilta post office, named for the mine, in 1892 and discontinued it in 1915 (Salley, p. 85).

Gimbal: see **Nord** [BUTTE].

Gimblin Creek [SHASTA]: *stream,* flows 1.5 miles to North Fork Cottonwood Creek [SHASTA-TEHAMA] 4 miles south-southwest of Shasta Bally (lat. 40°32'50" N, long. 122°39'55" W). Named on Shasta Bally (1978) 7.5' quadrangle.

Girard Ridge [SHASTA]: *ridge,* south- to west-trending, 8 miles long, 10 miles west-northwest of Shoeinhorse Mountain (lat. 41°08'45" N, long. 122°14' W). Named on Dunsmuir (1954) and Shoeinhorse Mountain (1954) 15' quadrangles. The name is for Louis Girard, a French Canadian (Steger, p. 34).

Girvan [SHASTA]: *locality,* 3 miles south of Redding along Southern Pacific Railroad (lat. 40°30'45" N, long. 122°22'45" W). Named on Redding (1957) 7.5' quadrangle.

Glacier Spring: see **Shasta Springs** [SISKIYOU].

Glasgow Bar [SISKIYOU]: *locality,* 1 mile east-southeast of Forks of Salmon (lat. 41°15'05" N, long. 123°18'15" W). Named on Forks of Salmon (1978) 7.5' quadrangle.

Glasgow Gulch [SISKIYOU]: *canyon,* drained by a stream that flows 1.5 miles to North Fork Salmon River 2 miles west-northwest of Sawyers Bar (lat. 41°18'25" N, long. 123°09'55" W). Named on Sawyers Bar (1979) 7.5' quadrangle.

Glassburner Meadows [TEHAMA]: *area,* 4.5 miles north-northeast of Mineral (lat. 40°24'40" N, long. 121°34' W; near SW cor. sec. 32, T 30 N, R 4 E). Named on Lassen Peak (1956) 15' quadrangle.

Glass Mountain [SISKIYOU]: *peak,* about 5 miles west-northwest of Medicine Lake (lat. 41°36'15" N, long. 121°30'15" W). Altitude 7622 feet. Named on Medicine Lake (1952) and Timber Mountain (1952) 15' quadrangles.

Glass Mountain: see **Little Glass Mountain** [SISKIYOU].

Glass Springs [SHASTA]: *springs,* 10.5 miles southeast of Whitmore (lat. 40°30'50" N, long. 121°46'50" W; sec 29, 30, T 31 N, R 2 E). Named on Whitmore (1956) 15' quadrangle.

Glazer Ridge [BUTTE]: *ridge,* mainly in Plumas County, but extends south into Butte County 11 miles east-southeast of Pulga (lat. 39°45'10" N, long. 121°15'10" W; on N line sec. 24, T 22 N, R 6 E). Named on Pulga (1957) 15' quadrangle.

Glazier: see **Bartle** [SISKIYOU].

Gleason Peak [TEHAMA]: peak, 9.5 miles southeast of Wakefield Flat (lat. 40°02' N, long. 122°30'30" W; near S line sec. 11, T 25 N, R 6 W). Altitude 1165 feet. Named on Lwrey (1967) 7.5' quadrangle.

Glenburn [SHASTA]: *village,* nearly 5 miles north-northwest of Fall River

Mills (lat. 41°03'40" N, long. 121°29'20" W; sec. 10, T 37 N, R 4 E). Named on Fall River Mills (1961) 15' quadrangle. Called Burgettville on Modoc Lava Bed (1892) 1° quadrangle—Bill Burgett operated a blacksmith shop at the place (Giles, p. 230). Postal authorities established Burgettville post office in 1871, discontinued it in 1876, reestablished it in 1877, and discontinued it in 1888, when they moved it 1 mile west and changed the name to Swasey—H.M. Swasey had a mill at the site (Salley, p. 29, 217); they changed the post office name to Glenburn in 1892 at the request of Mrs. Moores, the postmaster, who wanted the name of her old home (Salley, p. 217; Steger, p. 34). They established Alfa post office 7 miles northwest of Bugettville in 1888 and discontinued it in 1895; the name was from alfalfa grown on the neighboring farms (Salley, p. 4).

Glen Cove [GLENN]: *locality,* 13 miles north of Butte City on the west side of Sacramento River (lat. 39°39' N, long. 121°59'30" W). Named on Chico (1895) 30' quadrangle.

Glendenning Creek [SHASTA]: *stream,* flows 6.25 miles to Old Cow Creek 1 mile north-northeast of Whitmore (lat. 40°38'40" N, long. 121°54'30" W; sec. 7, T 32 N, R 1 E). Named on Whitmore (1956) 15' quadrangle. Called Clendenning Creek on Burney (1939) 30' quadrangle.

Glendenning Fork: see **Kidder Creek** [SISKIYOU].

Glendenning Gulch [SISKIYOU]: *canyon,* drained by a stream that flows 2.5 miles to Moffett Creek 12.5 miles south-southwest of Yreka (lat. 41°33'25" N, long. 122°41'10" W; sec. 20, T 43 N, R 7 W). Named on Yreka (1954) 15' quadrangle.

Glenn [GLENN]: *village,* 10 miles east of Willows (lat. 39°31'20" N, long. 122°00'50" W). Named on Glenn (1951) 7.5' quadrangle. Postal authorities established Glenn post office in 1903 (Frickstad, p. 40).

Glenn Siding [GLENN]: *locality,* 9.5 miles east of Willows along Southern Pacific Railroad (lat. 39°32'05" N, long. 122°01'05" W); the place is 1 mile north of Glenn. Named on Glenn (1951) 7.5' quadrangle.

Glenn Spring [GLENN]: *spring,* 4 miles north of High Peak (lat. 39°28'45" N, long. 122°26'10" W; at SW cor. sec. 21, T 19 N, R 5 W). Named on Lodoga (1960) 15' quadrangle.

Glover: see **Julia Glover Flat** [SISKIYOU].

Glover Ridge [BUTTE]: *ridge,* east-trending, 1 mile long, 7.5 miles southeast of Paradise (lat. 39°39'55" N, long. 121°32'50" W; sec. 20, 21, T 21 N, R 4 E). Named on Cherokee (1970) 7.5' quadrangle.

Goat Camp [SHASTA]: *locality,* 11.5 miles west-southwest of Arbuckle Mountain (lat. 40°19'20" N, long. 123°03'50" W; at E line sec. 35, T 29 N, R 11 W). Named on Dubakella Mountain (1954) 15' quadrangle.

Goat Camp [TEHAMA]:

(1) *locality,* 8 miles northwest of Wakefield Flat (lat. 40°12'55" N, long. 122°44'05" W; sec. 2, T 27 N, R 8 W). Named on Cold Fork (1967) 7.5' quadrangle.

(2) *locality,* 6.5 miles west-northwest of Wakefield Flat (lat. 40°10'30" N, long. 122°44'55" W; sec. 22, T 27 N, R 8 W). Named on Colyear Springs (1957) 15' quadrangle.

(3) *locality,* 5 miles south of Wakefield Flat (lat. 40°03'10" N, long. 122°39' W; sec. 4, T 25 N, R 7 W). Named on Raglin Ridge (1967) 7.5' quadrangle.

(4) *locality,* 12.5 miles south-southwest of Panther Spring (lat. 40°05'15" N, long. 121°52'30" W). Named on Panther Spring (1953) 15' quadrangle. Called Ward Goat Camp on Mineral (1941) 30' quadrangle.

Goat Creek [SHASTA]:

(1) *stream,* flows 3 miles to Hatchet Creek 4.5 miles west-northwest of the village of Montgomery Creek (lat. 40°51'40" N, long. 121°50'45" W; near E line sec. 27, T 35 N, R 1 E). Named on Montgomery Creek (1956) 15' quadrangle.

(2) *stream,* flows 0.5 mile to Pit River Arm Shasta Lake 15 miles south-southeast of Lamoine (lat. 40°46'20" N, long. 122°19'15" W; sec. 28, T 34 N, R 4 W). Named on Lamoine (1957) 15' quadrangle.

Goat Hill [TEHAMA]: *peak,* 7.5 miles south of Ball Mountain (lat. 39°49'50" N, long. 122°45'35" W; at S line sec. 21, T 23 N, R 8 W). Altitude 6116 feet. Named on Log Spring (1957) 7.5' quadrangle. On Anthony Peak (1952) and Paskenta (1952) 15' quadrangles, the name applies to the ridge on which present Goat Hill is a high point.

Goat Island [SHASTA]: *island,* 2 miles long, center 1.25 miles south of Balls Ferry between Sacramento River and an unnamed stream that diverges from Sacramento River, and then rejoins the river 2 miles farther downstream (lat. 40°24' N, long. 122°11'35" W). Named on Balls Ferry (1965) 7.5' quadrangle. United States Board on Geographic Names (1971b, p. 3) approved the name "Rancherie Island" for an island bounded on the east by Sacramento River, on the west by Anderson Creek, and on the south by Reading Island; the Board gave the variant name "Goat Island" for the feature. At the same time, the Board approved the name "Reading Island" for an island, 0.6 mile long, bounded on the east by Sacramento River, on the west by Anderson Creek, and on the north by Rancherie Island; the Board gave the variant name "Goat Island" for this island.

Goat Point [BUTTE]: *relief feature,* 9, miles southeast of Paradise (lat. 39°39'40" N, long. 121°30'35" W; sec. 22, T 21 N, R 4 E). Named on Cherokee (1970) 7.5' quadrangle.

Goatville: see **Diamondville** [BUTTE].

Goering: see **Redding** [SHASTA].

Goff: see **Fort Goff** [SISKIYOU].

Goff Butte [SISKIYOU]: *peak,* 12 miles north-northeast of Happy Camp (lat. 41°56'55" N, long. 123°16'30" W); the feature is near the head of Middle Fork Fort Goff Creek. Altitude 5593 feet. Named on Figurehead Mountain (1980) 7.5' quadrangle.

Goff Creek: see **Fort Goff Creek** [SISKIYOU].

Gold Creek [SHASTA]: *stream,* flows 1.25 miles to Star City Creek 11 miles north-northwest of the village of Big Bend (lat. 41°10'20" N, long. 121°58'20" W). Named on Big Bend (1961) 15' quadrangle.

Gold Digger Pass [SISKIYOU]: *pass,* 4.5 miles east-southeast of Mount Dome (lat. 41°47' N, long. 121°36'10" W; near W line sec. 35, T 46 N, R 3 E). Named on Mount Dome (1950) 15' quadrangle.

Golden Russian Lake: see **Russian Peak** [SISKIYOU].

Golden State Island [BUTTE]: *island,* 7.5 miles southwest of Chico between Sacramento River and Murphy Slough (lat. 39°40'15" N, long. 121°57'45" W). Named on Ord Ferry (1949) 7.5' quadrangle.

Golden Trout Crossing [BUTTE]: *locality,* 5 miles north of Clipper Mills along South Fork Feather River (lat. 39°36'25" N, long. 121°09'05" W; near E line sec. 11, T 20 N, R 7 E). Named on Clipper Mills (1948) 7.5' quadrangle.

Gold Flat [BUTTE]: *area,* 5.25 miles southeast of Paradise (lat. 39°42'30" N, long. 121°32'45" W; mainly in sec. 5, T 21 N, R 4 E). Named on Cherokee (1970) 7.5' quadrangle.

Gold Flat [SISKIYOU]: *area,* 6 miles southwest of Scott Bar along Scott River (lat. 41°41'05" N, long. 123°05'25" W). Named on Scott Bar (1980) 7.5' quadrangle.

Gold Granite Lake [SISKIYOU]: *lake,* 400 feet long, 2 miles southeast of Ukonom Lake (lat. 41°33'40" N, long. 123°19'25" W). Named on Ukonom Lake (1980) 7.5' quadrangle. The lake is one of the group called Granite Lakes on Seiad (1922) 30' quadrangle.

Gold Hill [BUTTE]: *peak,* 5.5 miles south of Butte Meadows (lat. 40°00' N, long. 121°32'15" W; at and near NW cor. sec. 28, T 25 N, R 4 E). Named on Butte Meadows (1958) 15' quadrangle.

Gold Lake [BUTTE]: *locality,* 17 miles north-northeast of Bidwell Bar (lat. 39°46'50" N, long. 121°19'20" W). Named on Bidwell Bar (1897) 30' quadrangle.

Gold Run [BUTTE]: *stream,* flows 10.5 miles to Dry Creek 9 miles west-northwest of Oroville (lat. 39°34'50" N, long. 121°41'50" W; near N line sec. 24, T 20 N, R 2 E). Named on Oroville (1970) and Shippee (1948) 7.5' quadrangles.

Goldsborough Gulch [SHASTA]: *canyon,* drained by a stream that flows 1.5 miles to Beegum Creek [SHASTA-TEHAMA] 3.5 miles south of Arbuckle Mountain (lat. 40°20'50" N, long. 122°51'50" W; sec. 22, T 29 N, R 9 W). Named on Chanchelulla Peak (1951) 15' quadrangle.

Goodbye Lake [SISKIYOU]: *lake,* 225 feet long, 5.25 miles north-northeast of the village of Seiad Valley (lat. 41°54'55" N, long. 123°10'30" W). Named on Kangaroo Mountain (1980) 7.5' quadrangle.

Goods Mountain [SHASTA]: *peak,* 7.5 miles west of Arbuckle Mountain on Shasta-Trinity County line (lat. 40°23'25" N, long. 123°00'15" W; near SW cor. sec. 4, T 29 N, R 10 W). Named on Dubakella Mountain (1954) 15' quadrangle.

Gooey Gulch [SISKIYOU]: *canyon,* drained by a stream that flows 1.25 miles to East Fork of South Fork Salmon River 4.5 miles northeast of Cecilville (lat. 41°11'10" N, long. 123°04'35" W). Named on Grasshopper Ridge (1979) 7.5' quadrangle.

Goose Creek [SHASTA]: *stream,* flows 9 miles to Burney Creek 3 miles north-northeast of Burney (lat. 40°55'25" N, long. 121°39'10" W; sec. 5, T 35 N, R 3 E); the stream heads near Goose Mountain and goes through Goose Valley. Named on Burney (1957) and Montgomery Creek (1956) 15' quadrangles.

Goose Gap [SHASTA]: *pass,* 7.5 miles east of Bollibokka Mountain (lat. 40°54'45" N, long. 122°04'20" W; at SE cor. sec. 3, T 35 N, R 2 W). Named on Bollibokka Mountain (1957) 15' quadrangle.

Goose Lake [BUTTE]: *intermittent lake,* 13 miles northwest of Chico (lat. 39°52'25" N, long. 122°00'40" W). Named on McIntosh Landing (1914) 7.5' quadrangle.

Goose Mountain [SHASTA]: *peak,* 9.5 miles northeast of the village of Montgomery Creek (lat. 40°55'35" N, long. 121°47' W; at NW cor. sec. 5, T 35 N, R 2 E). Altitude 4935 feet. Named on Montgomery Creek (1956) 15' quadrangle.

Goosenest [SISKIYOU]: *peak,* 13 miles southwest of Macdoel (lat. 41°43'15" N, long. 122°13'15" W; at W line sec. 29, T 45 N, R 3 W). Altitude 8280 feet. Named on The Whaleback (1954) 15' quadrangle. Diller and others' (1915) map has the form "Goose Nest" for the name.

Goosenest Butte: see **Hardin Butte** [SISKIYOU].

Goose Nest Mountain [SISKIYOU]: see **Hardin Butte** [SISKIYOU].

Goose Valley [SHASTA]: *valley,* 4.5 miles north-northwest of Burney (lat. 40°56'30" N, long. 121°42'30" W). Named on Burney (1957) 15' quadrangle. Lassen Peak (1894) 1° quadrangle shows marsh at the place. Wild geese and ducks nest at the site (Steger, p. 34).

Gopher Creek [GLENN]: *stream,* flows 5.5 miles to Nye Creek 3 miles east of Fruto (lat. 39°34'55" N, long. 122°23'40" W; at N line sec. 23, T 20 N, R 5 W). Named on Fruto (1968) 7.5' quadrangle.

Gopher Gulch [SISKIYOU]: *canyon,* 1 mile long, 8 miles west-southwest of Bartle (lat. 41°13'45" N, long. 121°57'55" W; sec. 9, 16, T 39 N, R 1 W). Named on Big Bend (1961) 15' quadrangle.

Gordon Canyon [TEHAMA]: *canyon,* drained by a stream that flows nearly 2 miles to Hull Canyon 4 miles northwest of Paskenta (lat. 39°55'15" N, long. 122°35'55" W; sec. 24, T 24 N, R 7 W). Named on Paskenta (1967) 7.5' quadrangle.

Gordons Ferry [SISKIYOU]: *locality,* 2.5 miles east-southeast of Happy Camp along Klamath River (lat. 41°46'40" N, long. 123°19'40" W). Named on Seiad (1922) 30' quadrangle.

Gorge: see **The Gorge** [TEHAMA].

Gottville [SISKIYOU]: *locality,* 10 miles west-southwest of Hornbrook along Klamath River at the mouth of Empire Creek (lat. 41°52'05" N, long. 122°44'20" W; sec. 2, T 46 N, R 8 W). Named on Hornbrook (1955) 15' quadrangle, which shows Honolulu school at the place. Called Klamath River on Yreka (1939) 30' quadrangle, and Shasta (1894) 1° quadrangle shows Empire Mill at the site. Postal authorities established Honolulu post office in 1881 and discontinued it in 1885; the place also was known as Empire Creek (Salley, p. 99). They established Gottville post office, which previously was called Honolulu post office, in 1887, and discontinued it in 1934; the name was for William N. Gott, first postmaster (Salley, p. 87).

Gould Gulch [SISKIYOU]: *canyon,* drained by a stream that flows 2.25 miles to East Fork of South Fork Salmon River 5.5 miles northeast of Cecilville (lat. 41°12'10" N, long. 123°03'50" W). Named on Grasshopper Ridge (1979) 7.5' quadrangle.

Goulding Creek [GLENN]: *stream,* flows 3.25 miles to North Fork (1) Stony Creek [GLENN-TEHAMA] 3.25 miles east-southeast of Saint John Mountain (lat. 39°25' N, long. 122°38' W). Named on Saint John Mountain (1968) 7.5' quadrangle.

Gout Rock [GLENN]: *peak,* 8.5 miles east-northeast of Saint John Mountain on Gravelly Ridge (lat. 39°28'40" N, long. 122°32'35" W; at NE cor. sec. 29, T 19 N, R 6 W). Altitude 1670 feet. Named on Stonyford (1968) 7.5' quadrangle.

Government Camp [SHASTA]: *locality,* 0.5 mile northeast of Summit City (lat. 40°42' N, long. 122°23'20" W; on E line sec. 26, T 33 N, R 5 W). Named on Shasta Dam (1956) 7.5' quadrangle. Steger (p. 34) referred to the place as Government City, and gave it the alternate name "Toyon"—it was established in 1938 as headquarters for officials of Shasta Dam.

Government City: see **Government Camp** [SHASTA].

Government Flat [TEHAMA]: *area,* 10 miles southwest of Ball Mountain (lat. 39°51'40" N, long. 122°56'25" W; sec. 11, T 23 N, R 10 W). Named on Mendocino Pass (1967) 7.5' quadrangle.

Government Gulch [TEHAMA]: *canyon,* drained by a stream that flows 7.25 miles to Elder Creek 6.5 miles south-southeast of Red Bank (lat. 40°01' N, long. 122°22'40" W; near S line sec. 13, T 25 N, R 5 W). Named on Flournoy (1967) and Red Bank (1952) 7.5' quadrangles.

Government Lake [SHASTA]: *intermittent lake,* 3000 feet long, 7 miles south of Coble Mountain (lat. 40°47'05" N, long. 121°22'35" W; at SW cor. sec. 24, T 34 N, R 5 E); the feature is 0.5 mile northeast of Government Well. Named on Jellico (1957) 15' quadrangle, which shows a small permanent lake in the larger intermittent lake.

Government Spring [TEHAMA]: *spring,* 7.5 miles west-northwest of Paskenta (lat. 39°54'50" N, long. 122°40'55" W; near NW cor. sec. 29, T 24 N, R 7 W). Named on Riley Ridge (1967) 7.5' quadrangle.

Government Well [SHASTA]: *well,* 7.5 miles south-southwest of Coble Mountain (lat. 40°46'50" N, long. 121°23'05" W; near N line sec. 26, T 34 N, R 5 E). Named on Jellico (1957) 15' quadrangle. Soldiers dug the well in the late 1850's to furnish water to an army camp near Government Lake (Steger, p. 34). United States Board on Geographic Names (1983b, p. 7) approved the name "Ward Spring" for a feature situated 2 miles east of Government Well (lat. 40°47' N, long. 121°20'25" W; sec. 30, T 34 N, R 6 E).

Grace Lake [SHASTA]: *lake,* 1100 feet long, 1.5 miles east-southeast of Shingletown (lat. 40°29' N, long. 121°51'45" W; near E line sec. 4, T 30 N, R 1 E). Named on Manton (1956) 15' quadrangle. The name commemorates the daughter of H.H. Noble of Shasta Power Company (Steger, p. 34).

Graham [SISKIYOU]: *locality,* 26 miles south-southwest of Macdoel (lat. 41°30'30" N, long. 122°16'10" W; near N line sec. 11, T 42 N, R 4 W). Named on Macdoel (1941) 30' quadrangle.

Graham Creek [SISKIYOU]:

(1) *stream,* flows 1 mile to North Hungry Creek 11.5 miles west-northwest of Hornbrook (lat. 41°59'40" N, long. 122°44'35" W; sec. 23, T 48 N, R 8 W). Named on Hornbrook (1955) 15' quadrangle.

(2) *stream,* flows 6.5 miles to Whitney Creek 26 miles south-southwest of Macdoel (lat. 4130'40" N, long. 122°16'15" W; sec. 2, T 42 N, R 4 W). Named on Lake Shastina (1954), Shasta (1954), and Weed (1954) 15' quadrangles.

Graham Crossing: see **Deer Creek Crossing** [TEHAMA].

Graham Gulch [SISKIYOU]: *canyon,* drained by a stream that flows 1 mile to South Fork Salmon River 7.25 miles northwest of Cecilville (lat. 41°13'05" N, long. 123°14'10" W). Named on Cecilville (1979) 7.5' quadrangle.

Graham Pinery [TEHAMA]: *area,* 13 miles south of Panther Spring (lat. 40°03'30" N, long. 121°45'30" W); the place is north-northeast of present Deer Creek Crossing, which is called Graham Crossing on Mineral (1941) 30' quadrangle.. Named on Butte Meadows (1958) and Panther Spring (1953) 15' quadrangles.

Grainland: see **Dayton** [BUTTE].

Granite Creek [SISKIYOU]:

(1) *stream,* flows 2.25 miles to Indian Creek (1) 13 miles north-northwest of Happy Camp (lat. 41°57'55" N, long. 123°29'20" W). Named on Deadman Point (1981) and Polar Bear Mountain (1982) 7.5' quadrangles.

(2) *stream,* flows 5.25 miles to Elk Creek 4.5 miles northeast of Ukonom Lake (lat. 41°37'05" N, long. 123°17'05" W). Named on Ukonom Lake (1980) 7.5' quadrangle.

(3) *stream,* flows 3.25 miles to Nordheimer Creek 4 miles west of Forks of Salmon (lat. 41°15'25" N, long. 123°23'50" W). Named on Orleans Mountain (1974) and Salmon Mountain (1978) 7.5' quadrangles.

Granite Gulch [SISKIYOU]: *canyon,* drained by a stream that flows 3.5 miles to East Fork Knownothing Creek nearly 6 miles east of Salmon Mountain (lat. 41°11'40" N, long. 123°18'05" W). Named on Youngs Peak (1979) 7.5' quadrangle.

Granite Lakes [SISKIYOU]: *lakes,* 16 miles south of Happy Camp (lat. 41°34' N, long. 123°20' W). Named on Seiad (1922) 30' quadrangle. This group of lakes includes present Blue Granite Lake, Gold Granite Lake, and Green Granite Lake.

Granite Meadow [SISKIYOU]: *area,* 1.5 miles east-southeast of Ukonom Lake (lat. 41°34'05" N, long. 123°19'40" W); the place is near the head of Granite Creek (2). Named on Ukonom Lake (1980) 7.5' quadrangle.

Granite Point [SISKIYOU]: *relief feature,* 3 miles east-southeast of the village of Seiad Valley along Klamath River (lat. 41°49'35" N, long. 123°08'15" W; near SE cor. sec. 17, T 46 N, R 11 W). Named on Seiad Valley (1980) 7.5' quadrangle.

Granite Ridge [BUTTE]: *ridge,* north-northeast-trending, less than 1 mile long, 6 miles north of Pulga (lat. 39°53'10" N, long. 121°27'30" W; on S line sec. 31, T 24 N, R 5 E). Named on Kimshew Point (1979) 7.5' quadrangle.

Granite Spring [BUTTE]: *spring,* 7 miles north of Pulga (lat. 39°54'05" N, long. 121°26'40" W; near SW cor. sec. 29, T 24 N, R 5 E). Named on Kimshew Point (1979) 7.5' quadrangle.

Grant Bluffs [SISKIYOU]: *relief feature,* 7 miles northwest of Forks of Salmon along Salmon River (lat. 41°20'20" N, long, 123°23'50" W); the feature is 0.25 mile downstream from the mouth of Grant Creek (1). Named on Orleans Mountain (1974) 7.5' quadrangle.

Grant Creek [SISKIYOU]:

(1) *stream,* flows nearly 1 mile to Salmon River 6.5 miles northwest of Forks of Salmon (lat. 41°20'10" N, long. 123°23'40" W). Named on Orleans Mountain (1974) 7.5' quadrangle.

(2) *stream,* flows nearly 3 miles to North Fork Salmon River 10 miles north of Sawyers Bar (lat. 41°26'50" N, long. 123°08'35" W); the stream heads at Grants Meadows. Named on English Peak (1977) 7.5' quadrangle.

Grants Meadows [SISKIYOU]: *area,* 12.5 miles north of Sawyers Bar (lat. 41°28'55" N, long. 123°07'50" W). Named on English Peak ·(1977) 7.5' quadrangle.

Grapevine Canyon [TEHAMA]: *canyon,* 0.5 mile long, 6.5 miles southeast of Manton (lat. 40°22' N, long. 121°47' W; on E line sec. 18, T 29 N, R 2 E). Named on Manton (1956) 15' quadrangle.

Grapevine Creek: see **Little Grapevine Creek** [TEHAMA].

Grapevine Crossing [TEHAMA]: *locality,* 10 miles south of Panther Spring along Big Dry Creek (lat. 40°06'25" N, long. 121°46'45" W; sec. 17, T 26 N, R 2 E). Named on Panther Spring (1953) 15' quadrangle.

Grapevine Gulch [TEHAMA]: *canyon,* drained by a stream that flows nearly 1 mile to Dry Creek (1) 7.5 miles east-southeast of Beegum Peak (lat. 40°46'50" N, long. 122°45'10" W; sec. 15, T 28 N, R 8 W). Named on Chanchelulla Peak (1951) 15' quadrangle.

Grapevine Spring [TEHAMA]: *spring,* nearly 7 miles southeast of Manton (lat. 40°22'10" N, long. 121°46'30" W; near W line sec. 17, T 29 N, R 2 E); the spring is at the head of Grapevine Canyon. Named on Manton (1956) 15' quadrangle.

Grapit [GLENN]: *locality,* 4.5 miles south of Orland along Southern Pacific Railroad (lat. 39°40'50" N, long. 122°11'35" W; near NW cor. sec. 15, T 21 N, R 3 W). Named on Orland (1951) 7.5' quadrangle, which shows a gravel pit near the place.

Grasshopper Flat [SHASTA]: *area,* 2.25 miles east-northeast of the village of Big Bend (lat. 41°02'15" N, long. 121°52'25" W; on W line sec. 28, T 37 N, R 1 E). Named on Big Bend (1961) 15' quadrangle.

Grasshopper Flat [SISKIYOU]: *area,* 6.25 miles southwest of Medicine Lake (lat. 41°31'35" N, long. 121°41'35" W). Named on Medicine Lake (1952) 15' quadrangle.

Grasshopper Ridge [SISKIYOU]: *ridge,* south- to southwest-trending, 3.5 miles long, 8 miles northeast of Cecilville (lat. 41°13'45" N, long. 123°02'10" W). Named on Grasshopper Ridge (1979) 7.5' quadrangle.

Grass Lake [SISKIYOU]:

(1) *marsh,* 15 miles south-southwest of Macdoel (lat. 41°38'45" N, long. 122°10'15" W). Named on The Whaleback (1954) 15' quadrangle. Shasta (1894) 1° quadrangle has the name "Grass Valley" at the place.

(2) *locality,* 16 miles south-southwest of Macdoel (lat. 41°38'15" N, long. 122°11'05" W; near NE cor. sec. 28, T 44 N, R 3 W); the site is at the southwest end of Grass Lake (1). Named on The Whaleback (1954) 15' quadrangle. Postal authorities established Grass Lake post office in 1906 and discontinued it the same year (Frickstad, p. 187). Diller and others' (1915) map shows the following places: Abner, located along Southern Pacific Railroad nearly 3 miles east of Grass Lake (2); Swanston, located along the railroad 4 miles south of Grass Lake (2) at or near present Cougar; Morrison, located 6.5 miles south of Grass Lake (2) along the railroad; and Hoey, located about 8 miles south-southwest of Grass Lake (2) along the railroad at or near present Bolam.

Grass Lake: see **Grassy Lake** [SHASTA].

Grass Spring [SHASTA]: *spring* 11.5 miles north-northwest of the village of Big Bend (lat. 41°10'40" N, long. 121°59'05" W; near SE cor. sec. 32, T 39 N, R 1 W). Named on Big Bend (1961) 15' quadrangle.

Grass Valley: see **Grass Lake** [SISKIYOU] (1).

Grassy Creek [SHASTA]: *stream,* flows 0.5 mile to Lassen County 9.5 miles east of Lassen Peak (lat. 40°28'35" N, long. 121°19'35" W; at E line sec. 8, T 30 N, R 6 E); the stream heads at Horseshoe Lake, which formerly was called Grassy Lake. Named on Mount Harkness (1956) 15' quadrangle.

Grassy Lake [SHASTA]: *dry lake,* 0.5 mile long, 10 miles south-southwest of Coble Mountain (lat. 40°45' N, long. 121°24' W; sec. 3, T 33 N, R 5 E). Named on Jellico (1957) and Prospect Peak (1957) 15' quadrangles. Called Grass Lake on Halls Flat (1939) 30' quadrangle, but United States Board on Geographic Names (1960b, p. 8) rejected this name for the feature.

Grassy Lake: see **Horseshoe Lake** [SHASTA].

Grassy Patch [GLENN]: *area,* 8.5 miles west-northwest of the village of Elk Creek (lat. 39°39'10" N, long. 122°40'50" W). Named on Alder Springs (1967) 7.5' quadrangle.

Grassy Swale [SHASTA]: *canyon,* drained by a stream that flows 3 miles to Kings Creek nearly 6 miles east-southeast of Lassen Peak (lat. 40°27'50" N, long. 121°27'50" W; at E line sec. 15, T 30 N, R 5 E); the canyon heads near Horseshoe Lake, which formerly was called Grassy Lake. Named on Mount Harkness (1956) 15' quadrangle.

Gravel Creek [SISKIYOU]: *stream,* flows 5 miles to lowlands 15 miles north of McCloud (lat. 41°28' N, long. 122°05'30" W; near S line sec. 21, T 42 N, R 2 W). Named on Shasta (1954) 15' quadrangle.

Gravelly Flat [GLENN]: *area,* 12 miles south-southeast of Black Butte along Wescott Creek (lat. 39°35'15" N, long. 122°45'40" W; sec. 16, T 20 N, R 8 W). Named on Kneecap Ridge (1967) 7.5' quadrangle.

Gravelly Ridge [GLENN]: *ridge,* north- to north-northwest-trending, 14 miles long, 8.5 miles east-northeast of Saint John Mountain (center near lat. 39°29'30" N, long. 122°33'10" W). Named on Elk Creek (1968) and Stony Ford (1968) 7.5' quadrangles. The ridge extends south into Colusa County.

Graveyard Gulch [SISKIYOU]: *canyon,* drained by a stream that flows 3.5 miles to Scott River 7.5 miles west-northwest of Fort Jones (lat. 41°38'15" N, long. 122°58'50" W; sec. 27, T 44 N, R 10 W). Named on Fort Jones (1955) 15' quadrangle.

Gray : see **Nellie Gray Gulch** [SISKIYOU]; **Tom Gray Gulch** [SISKIYOU].

Grayback: see **Little Grayback** [SISKIYOU].

Grayback Ridge [SHASTA]: *ridge,* northwest-trending, 3 miles long, 10.5 miles north-northwest of Lassen Peak (lat. 40°37'15" N, long. 121°35'45" W). Named on Manzanita Lake (1956) 15' quadrangle.

Gray Butte [SISKIYOU]: *peak,* 7.25 miles north-northwest of McCloud (lat. 41°20'55" N, long. 122°11'30" W; at SE cor. sec. 33, T 41 N, R 3 W). Altitude 8119 feet. Named on Shasta (1954) 15' quadrangle.

Gray Cliff [SHASTA]: *relief feature,* 15 miles north-northwest of Lassen Peak on the north side of Magee Peak (lat. 40°41'30" N, long. 121°37'05" W; sec. 27, T 33 N, R 3 E). Named on Manzanita Lake (1956) 15' quadrangle.

Gray Rock Lake [SISKIYOU]: *lake,* 1100 feet long, 8.5 miles west of Dunsmuir (lat. 41°12'55" N, long. 122°25'55" W; near NW cor. sec. 27, T 39 N, R 5 W). Named on Dunsmuir (1954) 15' quadrangle. This lake is the largest of the group called Gray Rock Lakes on Dunsmuir (1935) 30' quadrangle.

Gray Rock Lake: see **Upper Gray Rock Lake** [SISKIYOU].

Gray Rock Lakes: see **Gray Rock Lake** [SISKIYOU]; **Timber Lake** [SISKIYOU]; **Upper Gray Rock Lake** [SISKIYOU].

Gray Rocks [SHASTA]:

(1) *relief feature,* 9 miles southeast of Bollibokka Mountain (lat. 40°49'40" N, long. 122°06'45" W; near E line sec. 5, T 34 N, R 2 W). Named on Bollibokka Mountain (1957) 15' quadrangle.

(2) *relief feature,* 9 miles northeast of the town of Central Valley (lat. 40°44'45" N, long. 122°17'55" W; at E line sec. 3, T 33 N, R 4 W). Named on Project City (1957) 7.5' quadrangle.

Gray Rocks: see **North Gray Rocks** [SHASTA].

Grays Peak [TEHAMA]: *peak,* 4.25 miles northwest of Mineral (lat. 40°23'55" N, long. 121°38'10" W; sec. 3, T 29 N, R 3 E). Altitude 6370 feet. Named on Lassen Peak (1956) 15' quadrangle.

Greasewood Basin [TEHAMA]: *relief feature,* 2.5 miles northeast of Tomhead Mountain (lat. 40°09'50" N, long. 122°46'45" W; sec. 28, 29, T 27 N, R 8 W). Named on Yolla Bolly (1954) 15' quadrangle.

Greasewood Hill [TEHAMA]: *peak,* 5.5 miles west-northwest of Wakefield Flat (lat. 40°09'30" N, long. 122°44'20" W). Altitude 2738 feet. Named on Cold Fork (1967) 7.5' quadrangle.

Great Spring: see **Big Spring** [SHASTA] (2).

Great Valley: see "Regional setting."

Greek Ranch Camp [BUTTE]: *locality,* 1.25 miles southwest of Stirling City (lat. 39°53'45" N, long. 121°33'30" W; sec. 32, T 24 N, R 4 E). Named on Stirling City (1979) 7.5' quadrangle.

Green: see **Cook and Green Butte**, under **Red Butte** [SISKIYOU] (1); **Cook and Green Campground** [SISKIYOU]; **Cook and Green Creek** [SISKIYOU]; **Cook and Green Pass** [SISKIYOU].

Green Burney Camp: see **Old Green Burney Camp** [SHASTA].

Green Burney Creek [SHASTA]: *stream,* flows 6.5 miles to Burney Creek 6.5 miles south-southwest of Burney (lat. 40°48'45" N, long. 121°43'10" W; near S line sec. 11, T 34 N, R 2 E). Named on Burney (1957), Montgomery Creek (1956), and Whitmore (1956) 15' quadrangles.

Green Butte [SISKIYOU]: *relief feature,* 9 miles north-northwest of McCloud (lat. 41°22'20" N, long. 122°12'20" W; sec. 28, T 41 N, R 3 W). Named on Shasta (1954) 15' quadrangle.

Green Creek [SISKIYOU]: *stream,* heads in the State of Oregon and flows 2 miles to Indian Creek (1) 14 miles north-northwest of Happy Camp (lat. 41°58'30" N, long. 123°29'45" W). Named on Deadman Point (1981) 7.5' quadrangle.

Green Granite Lake [SISKIYOU]: *lake,* 750 feet long, 2 miles southeast of Ukonom Lake (lat. 41°33'40" N, long. 123°19'40" W). Named on Ukonom Lake (1980) 7.5' quadrangle. This is one of the group called Granite Lakes on Seiad (1922) 30' quadrangle.

Green Gulch [TEHAMA]: *canyon,* drained by a stream that flows 2.25 miles to Dry Creek (1) 7.5 miles east-southeast of Beegum Peak (lat. 40°46'50" N, long. 122°45'10" W; sec. 15, T 28 N, R 8 W). Named on Chanchelulla Peak (1951) 15' quadrangle.

Greenhorn Creek [SISKIYOU]: *stream,* flows 8.5 miles to the canyon of Yreka Creek 1.5 miles south of Yreka (lat. 41°42'40" N, long. 122°38'45" W; near NW cor. sec. 34, T 45 N, R 7 W). Named on Yreka (1954) 15' quadrangle. The lower course of the stream is obscured by mine tailings. The name is from an inexperienced prospector, called a greenhorn, who struck it rich at the stream (Herzog, p. 66-67).

Greenland: see **Chico** [BUTTE].

Green Mountain [SHASTA]:

(1) *peak,* 6 miles east of Lamoine (lat. 40°58'05" N, long. 122°18'55" W; sec. 22, T 36 N, R 4 W). Altitude 4059 feet. Named on Lamoine (1957) 15' quadrangle. On Lamoine (1946) 15' quadrangle, the name applies to the ridge on which present Green Mountain is the high point.

(2) *peak,* 11 miles south-southeast of Bollibokka Mountain (lat. 40°46'45" N, long. 122°09'20" W; near N line sec. 25, T 34 N, R 3 W). Altitude 2247 feet. Named on Bollibokka Mountain (1957) 15' quadrangle.

(3) *peak,* 9.5 miles east-southeast of the village of Montgomery Creek (lat. 40°47' N, long. 121°45'30" W; near N line sec. 28, T 34 N, R 2 E). Altitude 6041 feet. Named on Montgomery Creek (1956) 15' quadrangle.

Greens Creek [SHASTA]: *stream,* flows 1.5 miles to McCloud River Arm Shasta Lake 14 miles southeast of Lamoine (lat. 40°49'35" N, long. 122°15'15" W; sec. 6, T 34 N, R 3 W). Named on Bollibokka Mountain (1957) and Lamoine (1957) 15' quadrangles.

Green Valley [GLENN]:

(1) *valley,* 5.25 miles south-southwest of the village of Elk Creek along Mad Creek (lat. 39°32'30" N, long. 122°35'25" W). Named on Elk Creek (1968) 7.5' quadrangle.

(2) *valley,* 9 miles east of Saint John Mountain (lat. 39°27'15" N, long. 122°32'05" W). Named on Stonyford (1968) 7.5' quadrangle.

Green Valley [SISKIYOU]: *canyon,* 6.25 miles northeast of Ukonom Lake (lat. 41°38'10" N, long. 123°15'10" W; sec. 29, T 44 N, R 12 W). Named on Ukonom Lake (1955) 15' quadrangle.

Green Valley Creek [SISKIYOU]: *stream,* flows 2 miles to Bear Creek (1) 6.5 miles northeast of Ukonom Lake (lat. 41°38'40" N, long. 123°15'40" W); the stream goes through Green Valley. Named on Grider Valley (1981) and Huckleberry Mountain (1980) 7.5' quadrangles.

Greenview [SISKIYOU]: *town,* 5.25 miles southwest of Fort Jones (lat. 41°33' N, long. 122°54'20" W; sec. 29, T 43 N, R 9 W). Named on Fort Jones

(1955) 15' quadrangle. Postal authorities established Greenview post office in 1900; the name is for both the Green family and the view at the place (Salley, p. 89).

Greenwood [GLENN]: *locality,* 3.5 miles south of Orland along Southern Pacific Railroad (lat. 39°41'45" N, long. 122°11'40" W; near NW cor. sec. 10, T 21 N, R 3 W). Named on Orland (1951) 7.5' quadrangle.

Gregory [SHASTA]: *locality,* 7 miles south-southeast of Lamoine (lat. 40°53' N, long. 122°22'45" W; near SE cor. sec. 13, T 35 N, R 5 W). Named on Redding (1901) 30' quadrangle, which also has the name "Baird" at or near the site. Postal authorities established Gregory post office in 1900, changed the name to Antler in 1908, and discontinued it in 1914; the name "Gregory" was for James F. Gregory, first postmaster, and the name "Antler" was for antelope antlers that decorated the hotel where the post office was located (Salley, p. 8, 90). Red Bluff (1894) 1° quadrangle has the name "Whitney" at a place situated less than 1 mile southeast of the site of Gregory.

Gregory Creek [SHASTA]: *stream,* flows 1.5 miles to Sacramento River Arm Shasta Lake 8 miles south-southeast of Lamoine (lat. 40°52'40" N, long. 122°22' W; sec. 19, T 35 N, R 4 W). Named on Lamoine (1957) 15' quadrangle. Steger (p. 35) associated the name with Martha Gregory, who owned property along the stream.

Gregory Mountain [SISKIYOU]: *hill,* 6.5 miles east of Yreka in Shasta Valley (lat. 41°42'50" N, long. 122°30'50" W; at SW cor. sec. 26, T 45 N, R 6 W). Named on Yreka (1954) 15' quadrangle.

Grenada [SISKIYOU]: *town,* 8.5 miles southeast of Yreka in Shasta Valley (lat. 41°38'45" N, long. 122°31'20" W; sec. 22, T 44 N, R 6 W). Named on Yreka (1954) 15' quadrangle. Postal authorities established Grenada post office in 1917; railroad officials named the place for Grenada County, Mississippi (Salley, p. 90). The neighborhood of the town first was called Starve-Out because of the poor land there (Gudde, 1949, p. 135).

Grey Rock Lake [SHASTA]: *lake,* 700 feet long, 6 miles west-southwest of Castella (lat. 41°07'15" N, long. 122°25'30" W; sec. 27, T 38 N, R 5 W); the lake is 1.25 miles east-southeast of Grey Rocks. Named on Dunsmuir (1954) 15' quadrangle.

Grey Rocks [SHASTA]: *relief feature,* north-trending, 2 miles long, 7 miles west of Castella on Shasta-Trinity County line (lat. 41°07'45" N, long. 122°26'45" W). Named on Dunsmuir (1954) 15' quadrangle.

Grider Creek [SISKIYOU]: *stream,* flows 16 miles to Klamath River 0.5 mile west of the village of Seiad Valley (lat. 41°50'30" N, long. 123°12'20" W); the stream heads at Grider Valley. Named on Grider Valley (1981) and Seiad Valley (1980) 7.5' quadrangles.

Grider Creek: see **Little Grider Creek** [SISKIYOU]; **West Grider Creek** [SISKIYOU].

Grider Ridge [SISKIYOU]: *ridge,* generally south-trending, 6 miles long, 5.5 miles south-southwest of the village of Seiad Valley (lat. 41°46'20" N, long. 123°14'45" W). Named on Grider Valley (1981), Huckleberry Mountain (1980), and Seiad Valley (1980) 7.5' quadrangles. The name commemorates William T. Grider, who settled at the mouth of Grider Creek in 1890 (United States Board on Geographic Names, 1967b, p. 3).

Grider Valley [SISKIYOU]: *canyon,* 12.5 miles west-southwest of Scott Bar (lat. 41°40' N, long. 123°12' W); the canyon is at the head of Grider Creek. Named on Grider Valley (1981) 7.5' quadrangle.

Gridley [BUTTE]: *town,* 13 miles southwest of Oroville (lat. 39°21'45" N, long. 121°41'50" W; on N line sec. 1, T 17 N, R 2 E). Named on Gridley (1952) 7.5' quadrangle. Postal authorities established Martinsburgh post office in 1865, discontinued it in 1866, reestablished it in 1868, and changed the name to Gridley in 1870 (Salley, p. 134). According to F.D. Dunn (p. 66), Martinsburgh was near present Peachton (sec. 29, T 18 N, R 3 E). Gridley incorporated in 1905. The community was laid out when the railroad came to the place in 1870 and named for George W. Gridley, who owned the land there (Wells and Chambers, p. 248).

Gridley Station: see **East Gridley** [BUTTE].

Griffin Creek [TEHAMA]: *stream,* flows 2.25 miles to Cold Spring Creek 2.5 miles north of Ball Mountain (lat. 39°57'55" N, long. 122°46'50" W; sec. 5, T 24 N, R 8 W). Named on Ball Mountain (1967) 7.5' quadrangle. On Anthony Peak (1952) 15' quadrangle, present Griffin Creek is shown as part of Cold Spring Creek, but United States Board on Geographic Names (1969b, p. 4) rejected this nomenclature.

Griffin Gulch [BUTTE]: *canyon,* drained by a stream that flows 2.5 miles to West Branch Feather River 3.5 miles east-northeast of Paradise (lat. 39°46'50" N, long. 121°33'30" W; near W line sec. 8, T 22 N, R 4 E). Named on Paradise East (1980) 7.5' quadrangle.

Grindstone Camp [SISKIYOU]: *locality,* 13 miles southwest of Scott Bar (lat. 41°35'10" N, long. 123°09'35" W; at S line sec. 7, T 43 N, R 11 W). Named on Scott Bar (1955) 15' quadrangle.

Grindstone Creek [GLENN-TEHAMA]: *stream,* heads in Tehama County and flows 32 miles to Stony Creek [GLENN-TEHAMA] 4.5 miles north of the village of Elk Creek in Glenn County (lat. 39°40'15" N, long. 122°31'25" W; at S line sec. 15, T 21 N, R 6 W). Named on Alder Springs (1967), Chrome (1968), Hall Ridge (1967), Log Spring (1967), and Mendocino Pass (1967) 7.5' quadrangles. The name is from grindstones quarried along the stream in 1845 (Hoover, Rensch, and Rensch, p. 98). Present Mill Creek [GLENN] is called South Fork Grindstone Creek on Elk Creek (1918) 15' quadrangle.

Grizzly Butte [SISKIYOU]: *peak,* 8 miles south-southeast of Cecilville [SISKIYOU] on Siskiyou-Trinity County line (lat. 41°02'45" N, long. 123°03'15" W). Altitude 6990 feet. Named on Thompson Peak (1979) 7.5' quadrangle.

Grizzly Creek [BUTTE]:
(1) *stream,* flows 3 miles to Dark Canyon 5.5 miles west-northwest of the village of Berry Creek (lat. 39°40'45" N, long. 121°29'50" W; sec. 14, T 21 N, R 4 E). Named on Berry Creek (1970) and Cherokee (1970) 7.5' quadrangles.
(2) *stream,* heads in Yuba County and flows nearly 3 miles to Oroleve Creek 1 mile west of Clipper Mills in Butte County (lat. 39°32'15" N, long. 121°10'35" W; sec. 3, T 19 N, R 7 E). Named on Clipper Mills (1948) 7.5' quadrangle.

Grizzly Creek [SISKIYOU]: *stream,* flows 2.5 miles to Scott River 13 miles south of Etna (lat. 41°16' N, long. 122°52'45" W; near SW cor. sec. 34, T 40 N, R 9 W); the stream heads near Grizzly Peak. Named on Etna (1955) 15' quadrangle.

Grizzly Creek [TEHAMA]: *stream,* flows 9 miles to Red Bank Creek 5.25 miles east-southeast of Wakefield Flat (lat. 40°06'10" N, long. 122°32'45" W; sec. 16, T 26 N, R 6 W). Named on Lowrey (1967) and Raglin Ridge (1967) 7.5' quadrangles.

Grizzly Creek: see **Jenny Creek** [SISKIYOU]; **Little Grizzly Creek** [SISKIYOU]; **Little Grizzly Creek** [TEHAMA].

Grizzly Gulch [SHASTA]: *canyon,* drained by a stream that flows nearly 3 miles to Whiskeytown Lake 3.5 miles south-southeast of the village of French Creek (lat. 40°39'25" N, long. 122°35'55" W; sec. 1, T 32 N, R 7 W). Named on Whiskeytown (1979) 7.5' quadrangle.

Grizzly Gulch [SISKIYOU]: *canyon,* drained by a stream that flows 1 mile to Indian Creek (3) 6.25 miles north of Fort Jones (lat. 41°41'45" N, long. 122°51'30" W; near E line sec. 3, T 44 N, R 9 W). Named on Fort Jones (1955) 15' quadrangle.

Grizzly Lodge [BUTTE]: *locality,* nearly 1 mile north of Clipper Mills (lat. 39°32'40" N, long. 121°09'20" W; sec. 35, T 20 N, R 7 E); the place is north of Grizzly Creek (2). Named on Clipper Mills (1948) 7.5' quadrangle.

Grizzly Peak [SHASTA]: *peak,* 9.5 miles north-northwest of the village of Big Bend (lat. 41°08'45" N, long. 121°58'40" W). Altitude 6252 feet. Named on Big Bend (1961) 15' quadrangle.

Grizzly Peak [SISKIYOU]: *peak,* 13 miles south of Etna (lat. 41°16'25" N, long. 122°55'50" W; sec. 31, T 40 N, R 9 W); the peak is near the head of Grizzly Creek. Altitude 7930 feet. Named on Etna (1955) 15' quadrangle.

Grouse Creek [SISKIYOU]:
(1) *stream,* heads in the State of Oregon and flows 1 mile in Siskiyou County to join Cow Creek (2) and form Beaver Creek (1) 11.5 miles east-northeast of Condrey Mountain (lat. 41°59'45" N, long. 122°46'10" W; sec. 21, T 48 N, R 8 W). Named on Condrey Mountain (1955) 15' quadrangle.
(2) *stream,* flows 3.5 miles to Barkhouse Creek 10.5 miles southeast of Condrey Mountain (lat. 41°49'10" N, long. 122°50'50" W; sec. 24, T 46 N, R 9 W). Named on Condrey Mountain (1955) 15' quadrangle.
(3) *stream,* flows 5 miles to East Fork Scott River 13 miles southeast of Etna (lat. 41°19' N, long. 122°43'40" W; near E line sec. 13, T 40 N, R 8 W). Named on China Mountain (1955) 15' quadrangle.

Grouse Creek Lake [SISKIYOU]: *lake,* 700 feet long, 16 miles southeast of Etna (lat. 41°17'20" N, long. 122°40'20" W; near N line sec. 33, T 40 N, R 7 W); the lake is at the head of Grouse Creek (3). Named on China Mountain (1955) 15' quadrangle.

Grouse Hill [SISKIYOU]: *hill,* 2.5 miles north-northwest of Medicine Lake (lat. 41°36'45" N, long. 121°37'40" W; sec. 33, T 44 N, R 3 E). Named on Medicine Lake (1952) 15' quadrangle.

Grouse Mountain [SHASTA]: *peak,* 3.5 miles west-northwest of Igo (lat. 40°31'40" N, long. 122°36'05" W; near E line sec. 24, T 31 N, R 7 W). Altitude 2861 feet. Named on Igo (1979) 7.5' quadrangle.

Grouse Point [SISKIYOU]: *peak,* 4.25 miles north-northwest of Cecilville (lat. 41°11'50" N, long. 123°05'50" W). Named on Grasshopper Ridge (1979) 7.5' quadrangle.

Grouse Spring [GLENN]: *spring,* 7.5 miles southeast of Black Butte (lat. 39°38'25" N, long. 122°46'55" W; near SE cor. sec. 29, T 21 N, R 8 W). Named on Plaskett Meadows (1967) 7.5' quadrangle.

Grouse Spring [SHASTA]:
(1) *spring,* 5 miles north of Schell Mountain (lat. 40°50'45" N, long. 122°31'55" W; on N line sec. 3, T 35 N, R 6 W). Named on Schell Mountain (1950) 15' quadrangle.
(2) *spring,* 15 miles northwest of Lassen Peak (lat. 40°38'25" N, long. 121°42'20" W; at W line sec. 12, T 32 N, R 2 E). Named on Manzanita Lake (1956) 15' quadrangle.

Grouse Spring [SISKIYOU]: *spring,* 12.5 miles west-northwest of Macdoel (lat. 41°55'50" N, long. 122°12'30" W; near NW cor. sec. 15, T 47 N, R 3 W). Named on Macdoel (1954) 15' quadrangle.

Grove City: see **Vina** [TEHAMA].

Growler Hot Spring [TEHAMA]: *spring,* 5.5 miles east-northeast of Mineral (lat. 40°23'40" N, long. 121°30'20" W; near N line sec. 11, T 29 N, R 4 E). Named on Lassen Peak (1956) 15' quadrangle.

Grubbes Creek [BUTTE]: *stream,* flows 1.25 miles to Frey Creek 6 miles southeast of the village of Brush Creek (lat. 39°38'05" N, long. 121°15'10" W). Named on Brush Creek (1970) and Cascade (1948) 7.5' quadrangles.

Grub Flat Reservoir [BUTTE]: *lake,* 550 feet long, 9 miles south-southeast of Paradise (lat. 39°38'20" N, long. 121°31'55" W; at N line sec. 33, T 21 N, R 4 E). Named on Cherokee (1970) 7.5' quadrangle.

Guano Bridge [SISKIYOU]: *relief feature,* 11 miles south of Tulelake (lat. 41°48'05" N, long. 121°28'55" W; sec. 26, T 46 N, R 4 E). Named on Tulelake (1951) 15' quadrangle.

Gulick Creek [SISKIYOU]: *stream,* flows 1.5 miles to South Fork Salmon River 29 miles south of Etna (lat. 41°02'15" N, long. 122°55'50" W; sec. 30, T 37 N, R 9 W). Named on Coffee Creek (1955) 15' quadrangle.

Gum Boot Creek [SISKIYOU]:

(1) *stream,* flows nearly 2 miles to South Fork Clear Creek (1) 3.5 miles east of Bear Peak (lat. 41°41'20" N, long. 123°30'10" W). Named on Bear Peak (1982) 7.5' quadrangle.

(2) *stream,* flows 1.5 miles to Mill Creek (5) 13 miles south-southeast of Condrey Mountain (lat. 41°45'20" N, long. 122°53'30" W; sec. 16, T 45 N, R 9 W). Named on Condrey Mountain (1955) and Fort Jones (1955) 15' quadrangles.

Gumboot Lake [SISKIYOU]: *lake,* 800 feet long, 26 miles southeast of Etna (lat. 41°12'45" N, long. 122°30'35" W; on E line sec. 26, T 39 N, R 6 W). Named on Bonanza King (1955) 15' quadrangle.

Gumboot Lake: see **Upper Gumboot Lake** [SISKIYOU].

Gum Spring: see **Regan Meadow Campground** [SHASTA].

Gunbarrel Creek [TEHAMA]: *stream,* flows 4 miles to South Fork Antelope Creek 8.5 miles north of Polk Springs (lat. 40°14'25" N, long. 121°39'40" W; sec. 32, T 28 N, R 3 E). Named on Butte Meadows (1958) and Lassen Peak (1956) 15' quadrangles.

Gunsight [TEHAMA]: *relief feature,* 7 miles west of Paskenta (lat. 39°51'50" N, long. 122°40'25" W; sec. 8, T 23 N, R 7 W). Named on Hall Ridge (1967) 7.5' quadrangle.

Gunsight Peak [SISKIYOU]: *peak,* 10 miles north-northeast of Fort Jones (lat. 41°44'20" N, long. 122°46'40" W; sec. 21, T 45 N, R 8 W). Altitude 6145 feet. Named on Fort Jones (1955) 15' quadrangle.

Gurnsey Creek [TEHAMA]: *stream,* flows 7 miles to Deer Creek (2) 1 mile east-northeast of Deer Creek Station (lat. 40°16'10" N, long. 121°25'55" W; sec. 21, T 28 N, R 5 E). Named on Mount Harkness (1956) 15' quadrangle.

Gurnsey Creek Campground [TEHAMA]: *locality,* 3.25 miles north-northeast of Deer Creek Station (lat. 40°18'30" N, long. 121°25'30" W; on S line sec. 4, T 28 N, R 5 E); the place is along Gurnsey Creek. Named on Mount Harkness (1956) 15' quadrangle.

Guyre Creek [TEHAMA]: *stream,* flows 7 miles to Cold Fork (1) 6.5 miles north-northeast of Wakefield Flat (lat. 40°12'05" N, long. 122°34' W; at N line sec. 17, T 27 N, R 6 W). Named on Cold Fork (1967) and Oxbow Bridge (1967) 7.5' quadrangles. South Fork enters nearly 2 miles upstream from the mouth of the main creek and is 2.5 miles long. Middle Fork enters South Fork 1.25 miles upstream from the mouth of South Fork and is 2 miles long. Both forks are named on Oxbow Bridge (1967) 7.5' quadrangle.

Guys Gulch [SISKIYOU]: *canyon,* 4.5 miles long, opens into Shasta Valley 7.5 miles south-southwest of Yreka (lat. 41°38'10" N, long. 122°34'15" W; near NE cor. sec. 30, T 44 N, R 6 W). Named on Yreka (1954) 15' quadrangle.

– H –

Hagaman Gulch [SHASTA]: *canyon,* drained by a stream that flows 1.5 miles to South Cow Creek 3.5 miles southeast of Whitmore (lat. 40°36'10" N, long. 121°51'40" W; sec. 28, T 32 N, R 1 E). Named on Whitmore (1956) 15' quadrangle.

Hagen Flat [SHASTA]: *area,* 11 miles north-northeast of the village of Montgomery Creek along Pit River (lat. 40°59'30" N, long. 121°51'30" W; near E line sec. 9, T 36 N, R 1 E). Named on Montgomery Creek (1956) 15' quadrangle.

Haight Mountain [SISKIYOU]: *peak,* 8 miles south of Bray (lat. 41°31'50" N, long. 121°57'45" W; on W line sec. 34, T 43 N, R 1 W). Named on Bray (1950) 15' quadrangle. United States Board on Geographic Names (1967b, p. 4) approved the name "Picadilly Ridge" for a feature, 4 miles long, that trends southeast from Haight Mountain (lat. 41°30'15" N, long. 121°54'50" W at the SE end).

Haight Mountain: see **West Haight Mountain** [SISKIYOU].

Halcyon: see **Delta** [SHASTA].

Halfmoon Creek [SISKIYOU]: *stream,* flows 2 miles to Bridge Creek 15 miles north of Forks of Salmon (lat. 41°28'35" N, long. 123°21'20" W). Named on Medicine Mountain (1978), Somes Bar (1979), and Ukonom Mountain (1980) 7.5' quadrangles.

Halfmoon Meadow [SISKIYOU]: *area,* 4.5 miles south-southwest of Ukonom Lake (lat. 41°30' N, long. 123°23'10" W); the place is west of Halfmoon Creek. Named on Somes Bar (1979) and Ukonom Mountain (1980) 7.5' quadrangles.

Halfway Cove [SHASTA]: *embayment,* 13 miles south-southeast of Lamoine along Sacramento River Arm Shasta Lake (lat. 40°47'30" N, long. 122°22' W; sec. 19, T 34 N, R 4 W). Named on Lamoine (1957) 15' quadrangle.

Hall: see **Harry Hall Gulch** [SISKIYOU].

Hall Butte [SHASTA]: *crater,* 15 miles north of Lassen Peak (lat. 40°41'45" N, long. 121°33'30" W; near NE cor. sec. 30, T 33 N, R 4 E). Named on Manzanita Lake (1956) 15' quadrangle. Steger (p. 35) associated the name with Wid Hall's homestead.

Hall Creek [SHASTA]: *stream,* flows 5 miles to Roaring Creek 3.5 miles north of the village of Montgomery Creek (lat. 40°53'40" N, long. 121°56'05" W; near NE cor. sec. 14, T 35 N, R 1 W). Named on Montgomery Creek (1956) 15' quadrangle.

Hall Creek [TEHAMA]: *stream,* formed by the confluence of North Fork and South Fork, flows nearly 2 miles to Brannin Creek 3.5 miles south of Corning (lat. 39°52'35" N, long. 122°10'45" W; near E line sec. 3, T 23 N, R 3 W). Named on Corning (1951) 7.5' quadrangle. North Fork is 8.5 miles long and South Fork is nearly 7 miles long; both forks are named on Black Butte Dam (1967), Corning (1951), and Henleyville (1967) 7.5' quadrangles. Middle Fork joins North Fork nearly 3 miles south-southwest of Corning; it is 4.25 miles long and is named on Corning (1951) and Henleyville (1967) 7.5' quadrangles.

Halley Spring [TEHAMA]: *spring,* 7 miles northwest of Wakefield Flat (lat. 40°12'30" N, long. 122°42'45" W; sec. 12, T 27 N, R 8 W). Named on Cold Fork (1967) 7.5' quadrangle.

Hall Ridge [TEHAMA]: *ridge,* generally east-trending, 3.25 miles long, 8.5 miles west-southwest of Paskenta (lat. 39°50'15" N, long. 122°41'30" W). Named on Hall Ridge (1967) 7.5' quadrangle.

Halls Crossing: see **Tehama** [TEHAMA].

Halls Ranch: see **Tehama** [TEHAMA].

Halverson Creek [SISKIYOU]: *stream,* flows nearly 3 miles to Klamath River 11 miles north of Orleans, which is in Humboldt County (lat. 41°27'30" N, long. 123°30' W). Named on Bark Shanty Gulch (1974) 7.5' quadrangle.

Hambone [SISKIYOU]: *locality,* 8 miles northeast of Bartle (lat. 41°20'10" N, long. 121°41'45" W; near W line sec. 1, T 40 N, R 2 E). Named on Hambone (1961) 15' quadrangle. Bartle (1939) 30' quadrangle shows Hambone situated along McCloud River Railroad before the tracks were realigned.

Hambone Butte [SISKIYOU]: *hill,* 11 miles northeast of Bartle (lat. 41°20'45" N, long. 121°38'15" W; at W line sec. 33, T 41 N, R 3 E). Altitude 4731 feet. Named on Hambone (1961) 15' quadrangle.

Hambone Island [SISKIYOU]: *relief feature,* 12.5 miles northeast of Bartle (lat. 41°21' N, long. 121°37'10" W; on E line sec. 33, T 41 N, R 3 E); the feature is 1 mile east of Hambone Butte. Named on Hambone (1961) 15' quadrangle.

Hambone Well [SISKIYOU]: *well,* 9.5 miles northeast of Bartle (lat. 41°20'55" N, long. 121°40'15" W; sec. 31, T 41 N, R 3 E). Named on Hambone (1961) 15' quadrangle.

Hambright Creek [GLENN]: *stream,* flows 17 miles to Stony Creek [GLENN-TEHAMA] 1.5 miles east-northeast of Orland (lat. 39°45'20" N, long. 122°10'05" W; sec. 14, T 22 N, R 3 W). Named on Black Butte Dam (1967), Fruto NE (1952), Julian Rocks (1968), and Kirkwood (1949) 7.5' quadrangles. The name commemorates Robert Hambright, who settled by the stream (Gudde, 1949, p. 140).

Hamburg [SISKIYOU]: *village,* 8 miles east-southeast of the village of Seiad Valley along Klamath River (lat. 41°47' N, long. 123°03'30" W). Named on Hamburg (1980) 7.5' quadrangle. Postal authorities established Hamburgh Bar post office in 1878, changed the name to Hamburg in 1886, moved it 0.25 mile east in 1940, and discontinued it in 1954 (Salley, p. 92). Sigmund Simon founded and named the place about 1850 (Gudde, 1975, p. 149). Gudde (1975, p. 159) listed a mining place called Hoosier Hill that was located 0.5 mile west of Hamburg Bar and was worked as early as 1856.

Hamburg Gulch [SISKIYOU]: *canyon,* drained by a stream that flows 2.25 miles to Horse Creek (2) 8.5 miles east of the village of Seiad Valley (lat. 41°50'35" N, long. 123°02'05" W; sec. 8, T 46 N, R 10 W). Named on Hamburg (1980) 7.5' quadrangle.

Hamburgh Bar : see **Hamburg** [SISKIYOU].

Hamilton: see **Hamilton City** [GLENN]; **Oroville** [BUTTE].

Hamilton Bend [SHASTA]: *bend,* 6.5 miles west-southwest of Shoeinhorse Mountain along McCloud River [SHASTA-SISKIYOU] (lat. 41°02'35" N, long. 122°11'30" W). Named on Shoeinhorse Mountain (1954) 15' quadrangle.

Hamilton Camp [SISKIYOU]: *locality,* 9 miles north-northeast of Forks of Salmon (lat. 41°23' N, long. 123°15'20" W). Named on Medicine Mountain (1978) 7.5' quadrangle.

Hamilton City [GLENN]: *town,* 9.5 miles east of Orland (lat. 39°44'30" N, long. 122°00'45" W). Named on Hamilton City (1949) 7.5 quadrangle. Called Hamilton on Willows (1906) 15' quadrangle. Postal authorities established Hamilton City post office in 1906 (Frickstad, p. 40). The town began in 1905 with construction of a large sugar-beet factory; the name commemorates J.G. Hamilton, president of the sugar company (Hoover, Rensch, and Rensch, p. 98).

Hamilton Creek [GLENN-TEHAMA]: *stream,* heads in Tehama County and flows 2.5 miles to Grindstone Creek [GLENN-TEHAMA] 5.5 miles northeast of Black Butte in Glenn County (lat. 39°47' N, long. 122°47'45" W). Named on Log Spring (1967) 7.5' quadrangle.

Hamilton Glade [GLENN]: *area,* 6.5 miles northeast of Black Butte (lat. 39°47'55" N, long. 122°47'35" W; near NW cor. sec. 5, T 22 N, R 8 W); the place is near Hamilton Creek. Named on Log Spring (1967) 7.5' quadrangle.

Hamilton Glade [TEHAMA]: *area,* 1.25 miles southeast of Tomhead Mountain (lat. 40°07'30" N, long. 122°47'45" W; near NW cor. sec. 8, T 26 N, R 8 W); the place is on the north side of Hamilton Gulch. Named on Yolla Bolly (1954) 15' quadrangle.

Hamilton Gulch [TEHAMA]: *canyon,* drained by a stream that flows 2.25 miles to South Fork Cottonwood Creek [SHASTA-TEHAMA] 2.5 miles southeast of Tomhead Mountain (lat. 40°07' N, long. 122°46'30" W; sec. 9, T 26 N, R 8 W). Named on Yolla Bolly (1954) 15' quadrangle

Hamilton Slough [BUTTE]: *water feature,* diverges from Feather River 5 miles northeast of Biggs (lat. 39°27'15" N, long. 121°38'15" W), and extends to a ditch just south of Biggs. Named on Biggs (1970) 7.5' quadrangle.

Hamlin Canyon [BUTTE]: *canyon,* drained by a stream that flows 8.5 miles to lowlands 8.5 miles southwest of Paradise (lat. 39°39'30" N, long. 121°43'05" W; sec. 23, T 21 N, R 2 E). Named on Hamlin Canyon (1951) 7.5' quadrangle.

Hamlin Gulch [SISKIYOU]: *canyon,* drained by a stream that flows 4.5 miles to Scott Valley 3 miles south-southwest of Fort Jones (lat. 41°34' N, long. 122°49' W; sec. 19, T 43 N, R 8 W). Named on Fort Jones (1955) 15' quadrangle.

Hamlin Slough [BUTTE]: *stream,* flows 9 miles from the mouth of Hamlin Canyon to Butte Creek [BUTTE-GLENN] 5 miles south of Durham (lat. 39°34'30" N, long. 121°48'30" W). Named on Hamlin Canyon (1951), Nelson (1948), and Shippee (1948) 7.5' quadrangles. Called Roberts Creek on Clear Creek (1912) and Nelson (1912) 7.5' quadrangles.

Hammel Creek [SISKIYOU]: *stream,* flows 4.25 miles to Northheimer Creek 3.25 miles west-northwest of Forks of Salmon (lat. 41°17'05" N, long. 123°22'40" W). Named on Orleans Mountain (1974) 7.5' quadrangle.

Hammerhorn Mountain [TEHAMA]: *peak,* 12 miles southwest of Tomhead Mountain on Tehama-Trinity County line (lat. 40°00'10" N, long. 122°57' W; near E line sec. 22, T 25 N, R 10 W). Altitude 7567 feet. Named on Yolla Bolly (1954) 15' quadrangle.

Hammond Crossing [SISKIYOU]: *locality,* 6.5 miles east-southeast of Bartle along Bear Creek [SHASTA-SISKIYOU] (lat. 41°11'05" N, long. 121°35'20" W; sec. 26, T 39 N, R 3 E). Named on Pondosa (1961) 15' quadrangle.

Hamp Creek [SHASTA]: *stream,* flows nearly 3 miles to South Cow Creek 2.5 miles south of Whitmore (lat. 40°35'40" N, long. 121°54'45" W; near SW cor. sec. 30, T 32 N, R 1 E). Named on Whitmore (1956) 15' quadrangle.

Hampton Butte [TEHAMA]: *peak,* 2.5 miles west-northwest of Mineral (lat. 40°21'50" N, long. 121°38'15" W; near N line sec. 22, T 29 N, R 3 E). Named on Lassen Peak (1956) 15' quadrangle.

Hancock Creek [SISKIYOU]: *stream,* flows nearly 7 miles to Wooley Creek 13 miles north of Forks of Salmon (lat. 41°27'05" N, long. 123°18'30" W). Named on English Peak (1977) and Medicine Mountain (1978) 7.5' quadrangles.

Hancock Lake [SISKIYOU]: *lake,* 2100 feet long, 10 miles north-northwest of Sawyers Bar (lat. 41°25'15" N, long. 123°13'30" W); the lake is near the head of Hancock Creek. Named on English Peak (1977) 7.5' quadrangle.

Hancock Lake: see **Little Hancock Lake** [SISKIYOU].

Handy Camp [TEHAMA]: *locality,* 5.25 miles north-northwest of Tomhead Mountain (lat. 40°12'35" N, long. 122°50'35" W; near NE cor. sec. 11, T 27 N, R 9 W). Named on Yolla Bolly (1954) 15' quadrangle.

Handy Camp Gulch [TEHAMA]: *canyon,* drained by a stream that flows 3 miles to Cold Fork (1) 3.5 miles north-northwest of Tomhead Mountain (lat. 40°11'15" N, long. 122°50'05" W; sec. 13, T 27 N, R 9 W); Handy Camp is in the canyon. Named on Yolla Bolly (1954) 15' quadrangle.

Haney Mountain [SHASTA]: *peak,* 2.5 miles west of Fall River Mills (lat. 41°00'15" N, long. 121°28'55" W; near W line sec. 35, T 37 N, R 4 E). Named on Fall River Mills (1961) 15' quadrangle.

Hanland Peak [SHASTA]: *peak,* 8 miles east-southeast of Lamoine (lat. 40°56'30" N, long. 122°17'05" W; sec. 35, T 36, N, R 4 W). Altitude 4170 feet. Named on Lamoine (1957) 15' quadrangle.

Hanson Island [GLENN]: *area,* 10.5 miles east-southeast of Willows along Sacramento River (lat. 39°28'55" N, long. 122°00'25" W). Named on Butte City (1952) and Princeton (1952) 7.5' quadrangles.

Haphazard Creek [BUTTE]: *stream,* heads just inside Plumas County and flows 5 miles to West Branch French Creek 5.5 miles east-southeast of Pulga (lat. 39°45'40" N, long. 121°21'45" W; sec. 13, T 22 N, R 5 E). Named on Soapstone Hill (1979) 7.5' quadrangle.

Happy Camp [SISKIYOU]: *town,* 38 miles west of Yreka (lat. 41°47'40" N, long. 123°22'35" W; in and near sec. 11, T 16 N, R 7 E). Named on Happy Camp (1980) and Slater Butte (1980) 7.5' quadrangles. Postal authorities established Happy Camp post office in 1858 (Frickstad, p. 188). The place first was called Murderer's Bar (Gibbs, p. 155). Gudde (1975, p. 232) attributed the name "Murderers Bar" to an incident involving Indians who killed three miners at the place in 1851. Gudde (1975, p. 45) also listed a place called Brandons Bar that was situated 1 mile above Happy Camp.

Happy Camp Ridge [GLENN]: *ridge,* northwest-trending, 1.5 miles long, 11 miles west-southwest of the village of Elk Creek (lat. 39°31'50" N, long. 122°43'35" W). Named on Felkner Hill (1968) 7.5' quadrangle.

Happy Hollow Creek [BUTTE]: *stream,* flows 2 miles to West Branch French Creek 4.5 miles east-southeast of Pulga (lat. 39°46'45" N, long. 121°22' W; sec. 12, T 22 N, R 5 E). Named on Soapstone Hill (1979) 7.5' quadrangle.

Happy Hunting Grounds [SHASTA]: *area,* 2 miles west of Shoeinhorse Mountain (lat. 41°02'30" N, long. 122°04'45" W). Named on Shoeinhorse Mountain (1954) 15' quadrangle.

Happy Valley [SHASTA]: *area,* 10 miles south-southwest of Redding around Olinda (lat. 40°27'15" N, long. 122°26'15" W). Named on Olinda (1964) 7.5' quadrangle. Postal authorities established Happy Valley post office 7 miles southeast of Igo in 1881 and discontinued it in 1882 (Salley, p. 93). The place was called Oak Highlands before the 1880's (Steger, p. 35).

Harbean Slough [BUTTE]: *water feature,* 11.5 miles west-northwest of Chico in lowlands near Sacramento River (lat. 39°48'45" N, long. 120°01'15" W). Named on Foster Island (1950) 7.5' quadrangle.

Hardin Butte [SISKIYOU]: *crater,* 9 miles east-southeast of Mount Dome (lat. 41°46'05" N, long. 121°31'25" W; on W line sec. 4, T 45 N, R 4 E). Named on Mount Dome (1950) 15' quadrangle. United States Board on Geographic Names (1940, p. 20) rejected the names "Goosenest Butte" and "Goose Nest Mountain" for the feature. The Board (1975, p. 4, 5) approved several names for features near Hardin Butte. It approved the name "Clinton Draw" for a ravine (sec. 5, T 45 N, R 4 E, and sec. 32, T 46 N, R 4 E) that trends north-northeast for 2230 feet before it opens out 3270 feet northwest of Hardin Butte; the name is for Sergeant Milachi Clinton, who fought in a battle with Modoc Indians in the region in 1873. The Board approved the name "Cranston Knob" for a hill at the northwest edge of Hardin Butte (sec. 4, 5, T 45 N, R 4 E); the name honors Lieutenant Arthur Cranston, whom Modoc Indians killed at the place during a battle in 1873. The Board approved the name "Harris Knoll" for a hill situated 2580 feet west of Hardin Butte (sec. 5, T 45 N, R 4 E); the name commemorates Lieutenant George M. Harris, who died of wounds that Modoc Indians inflicted on him during a battle near the place in 1873. The Board approved the name "Howe Point" for a feature located 2060 feet west of Hardin Butte (sec. 5, T 45 N, R 4 E); the name is for Lieutenant Albion Howe, whom Modoc Indians killed near the place during a battle in 1873. The Board approved the name "Roemer Ridge" for a feature, 1330 feet long, situated 0.8 mile northwest of Hardin Butte (sec. 32, T 46 N, R 4 E); the name honors Sergeant Robert Roemer, whom Modoc Indians killed near the place during a battle in 1873. The Board approved the name "Ross Flow" for a lava flow, 0.8 mile long, located 0.8 mile northwest of Hardin Butte at Ross Chimneys. The Board approved the name "Semig Basin" for a feature located between Hardin Butte and Wright Ridge (T 45 N, R 4 E); the name commemorates Bernard Gustav Semig, a civilian doctor who was wounded in a battle with Modoc Indians at the place in 1873. The Board approved the name "The Thumb of the Glove" for a cove 2920 feet west of Hardin Butte at the southwest end of Semig Basin (sec. 5, T 45 N, R 4 E). The Board approved the name "Thomas Hill" for a feature located 0.5 mile west of Hardin Butte at the southwest end of Semig Basin (sec. 5, T 45 N, R 4 E); the name is for Captain Evan Thomas, whom Modoc Indians ambushed and killed near the hill in 1873. The Board approved the name "Wright Ridge" for a feature, 0.8 mile long, located 0.5 mile west of Hardin Butte on the west edge of Semig Basin (sec. 32, T 46 N, R 4 E, and sec. 5, T 45 N, R 4 E); the name is for Lieutenant Thomas F. Wright, whom Modoc Indians killed near the place in a battle in 1873.

Harding Spring [TEHAMA]: *spring,* 6 miles south of Tomhead Mountain (lat. 40°03'10" N, long. 122°49'10" W; sec. 1, T 25 N, R 9 W). Named on Yolla Bolly (1954) 15' quadrangle.

Hardin Hole Ridge [GLENN]: *ridge,* south-southwest- to west-trending, 3.5 miles long, 12 miles northwest of the village of Elk Creek (lat. 39°43'45" N, long. 122°41'15" W). Named on Alder Springs (1967) 7.5')quadrangle.

Hardin Hole Spring [GLENN]: *spring,* 12 miles northwest of the village of

Elk Creek (lat. 39°44'35" N, long. 122°39'55" W); the spring is on Hardin Hole Ridge. Named on Alder Springs (1967) 7.5' quadrangle.

Hardin Ridge [GLENN]: *ridge,* northeast- to east-trending, 5 miles long, 6 miles east of Black Butte (lat. 39°44'40" N, long. 122°45'45" W). Named on Alder Springs (1967) and Plaskett Meadows (1967) 7.5' quadrangles.

Hardscrabble: see **Hi-you Gulch** [SISKIYOU].

Hardscrabble Gulch [SISKIYOU]: *canyon,* drained by a stream that flows 1 mile to McAdam Creek 5.5 miles north of Fort Jones (lat. 41°41' N, long. 122°49'30" W; sec. 12, T 44 N, R 9 W). Named on Fort Jones (1955) 15' quadrangle.

Hard Spring [GLENN]: *spring,* 8.5 miles northwest of the village of Elk Creek (lat. 39°41'20" N, long. 122°39'05" W). Named on Alder Springs (1967) 7.5' quadrangle.

Harlan Davis Canyon [SISKIYOU]: *canyon,* drained by a stream that flows 1.5 miles to lowlands 10 miles south of Macdoel (lat. 41°41' N, long. 122°01'20" W; at S line sec. 1, T 44 N, R 2 W). Named on The Whaleback (1954) 15' quadrangle.

Harleson: see **Del Harleson Camp** [GLENN].

Harmes Spring [GLENN]: *spring,* 7.5 miles north of Fruto (lat. 39°41'40" N, long. 122°26'25" W; near E line sec. 8, T 21 N, R 5 W). Named on Julian Rocks (1968) 7.5' quadrangle.

Harrill's Mill: see **Millville** [SHASTA].

Harrington Mountain [SISKIYOU]: *peak,* 6 miles west-southwest of Bear Peak (lat. 41°40'25" N, long. 123°41'05" W); the peak is 1000 feet east of Harrington Lake, which is in Del Norte County. Altitude 5891 feet. Named on Prescott Mountain (1981) 7.5' quadrangle. United States Board on Geographic Names (1978b, p. 4) approved the name "Lost Spoon Lake" for a feature, 0.1 mile wide, situated 0.5 mile east-northeast of Harrington Mountain (lat. 41°40'31" N, long. 123°40'30" W); the name is from an incident that occurred during a state fish and wildlife resources survey in 1974. At the same time (p. 5), the Board approved the name "Solitaire Lake" for a feature, 0.1 mile wide, located 1.25 mile south-southeast of Harrington Mountain (lat. 41°39'25" N, long. 123°40'30" W)—the name is for Townsend's Solitaire (*Myadestes townsendi*), a bird found in the vicinity during a survey in 1974.

Harris Creek [SISKIYOU]: *stream,* flows 3.5 miles to Butte Valley 7 miles west-northwest of Macdoel (lat. 41°51'10" N, long. 122°08' W; near SE cor. sec. 6, T 46 N, R 2 W). Named on Macdoel (1954) 15' quadrangle.

Harris Knoll: see **Hardin Butte** [SISKIYOU].

Harris Mountain [SISKIYOU]: *peak,* 14 miles north-northeast of Bartle (lat. 41°27' N, long. 121°45'15" W; on E line sec. 29, T 42 N, R 2 E). Altitude 5786 feet. Named on Bartle (1961) 15' quadrangle.

Harrison Gulch [SHASTA]: *canyon,* drained by a stream that flows 5.25 miles to Middle Fork Cottonwood Creek [SHASTA-TEHAMA] 6 miles southwest of Arbuckle Mountain (lat. 40°21'05" N, long. 122°57' W; sec. 23, T 29 N, R 10 W). Named on Chanchelulla Peak (1951) 15' quadrangle. The name is for William H. Harrison, a county judge in 1850 (Steger, p. 38).

Harrison Gulch: see **Knob** [SHASTA]; **Stone Gulch** [SHASTA].

Harrison Ridge [BUTTE]: *ridge,* south-southwest-trending, less than 2 miles long in Butte County, 6.5 miles north-northeast of Clipper Mills on Butte-Plumas County line (lat. 39°36'30" N, long. 121°05'15" W). Named on Strawberry Valley (1948) 7.5' quadrangle.

Harris Spring [SISKIYOU]: *spring,* 14 miles north of Bartle (lat. 41°27'30" N, long. 121°47'05" W; on N line sec. 30, T 42 N, R 2 E); the spring is less than 2 miles west-northwest of Harris Mountain. Named on Bartle (1961) 15' quadrangle.

Harry Hall Gulch [SISKIYOU]: *canyon,* drained by a stream that flows 1 mile to Bug Gulch 12.5 miles north of Sawyers Bar (lat. 41°28'35" N, long. 123°05'25" W). Named on Yellow Dog Peak (1977) 7.5' quadrangle.

Hart [SHASTA]: *locality,* 6 miles north-northwest of Redding (lat. 40°39'45" N, long. 122°26'15" W; sec. 4, T 32 N, R 5 W). Named on Redding (1901) 30' quadrangle. Postal authorities established Hart post office in 1891 and discontinued in 1900; the name was for Richard G. Hart, Sr., a prominent citizen of the place (Salley, p. 94).

Hart Camp: see **Harts Camp** [SISKIYOU].

Hart Gulch [TEHAMA]: *canyon,* drained by a stream that flows 2 miles to Long Gulch (2) 1.5 miles southeast of Rosewood (lat. 40°15'10" N, long. 122°32' W; sec. 27, T 28 N, R 6 W). Named on Ono (1952) 15' quadrangle, and on Oxbow Bridge (1967) 7.5' quadrangle.

Hartley Island [GLENN]: *area,* 4 miles north of Butte City along Sacramento River (lat. 39°31'10" N, long. 121°59'30" W). Named on Glenn (1951) and Llano Seco (1948) 7.5' quadrangles. Called The Island on Newhard (1912) 7.5' quadrangle, which shows the feature on Butte-Glenn County line.

Harts Camp [SISKIYOU]: *locality,* 17 miles north-northeast of McCloud (lat. 41°29'30" N, long. 122°03'15" W; near NW cor. sec. 14, T 42 N, R 2 W); the place is near the west end of Harts Meadow. Named on Shasta (1954) 15' quadrangle. Dunsmuir (1935) 30' quadrangle shows Hart Camp situated about 1.5 miles farther east (sec. 13, T 42 N, R 2 W).

Harts Meadow [SISKIYOU]: *area,* 17 miles north-northeast of McCloud along Butte Creek (lat. 41°29'10" N, long. 122°01'45" W). Named on Shasta (1954) 15' quadrangle.

Harts Mill [BUTTE]: *locality,* 2.5 miles north of Bidwells Bar (lat. 39°37'20" N, long. 121°26' W). Named on Bidwell Bar (1897) 30' quadrangle. F.D. Dunn (p. 49) gave the alternate name "Virginia Mill" for Hart's Mill.

Harvey: see **Jack Harveys Crossing** [SISKIYOU].

Harvey Creek [TEHAMA]: *stream,* flows 5.25 mile to South Fork Cottonwood Creek [SHASTA-TEHAMA] 3 miles southwest of Tomhead Mountain (lat. 40°06'35" N, long. 122°51'30" W; near NE cor. sec. 15, T 26 N, R 9 W); the stream heads near Harvey Peak. Named on Yolla Bolly (1954) 15' quadrangle.

Harvey Gulch [SISKIYOU]: *canyon,* drained by a stream that flows 0.5 mile to Eddy Gulch 2 miles south of Sawyers Bar (lat. 41°16'10" N, long. 123°07'20" W). Named on Tanners Peak (1977) 7.5' quadrangle.

Harvey Peak [TEHAMA]: *peak,* 8 miles south-southwest of Tomhead Mountain (lat. 40°02'35" N, long. 122°54' W; near W line sec. 5, T 25 N, R 9 W). Altitude 7361 feet. Named on Yolla Bolly (1954) 15' quadrangle.

Harvey Ridge [TEHAMA]: *ridge,* north- to northeast-trending, 4 miles long, 6.5 miles southwest of Tomhead Mountain (lat. 40°04'10" N, long. 122°53'30" W); Harvey Peak is at the south end of the ridge. Named on Yolla Bolly (1954) 15' quadrangle.

Harvey Spring Creek [GLENN]: *stream,* flows 2 miles to Grindstone Creek [GLENN-TEHAMA] 5.5 miles north-northeast of Black Butte (lat. 39°47'30" N, long. 122°49' W; sec. 6, T 22 N, R 8 W); the stream is east of Harvey Spring Ridge. Named on Log Spring (1967) 7.5' quadrangle.

Harvey Spring Ridge [GLENN]: *ridge,* generally north-northeast-trending, 4 miles long, 3.5 miles north-northeast of Black Butte (lat. 39°46'30" N, long. 122°51' W); the ridge is west of Harvey Spring Creek. Named on Log Spring (1967) 7.5' quadrangle.

Haselbusch [BUTTE]: *locality,* 4 miles northeast of Biggs along Northern Electric Railroad (lat. 39°26'55" N, long. 121°38'55" W). Named on Biggs (1912) 7.5' quadrangle. California Division of Highways' (1934) map shows a place called Losee located along Sacramento Northern Railroad 0.5 mile south of Haselbusch.

Hatchet Creek [SHASTA]: *stream,* flows 17 miles to Pit River 2.5 miles northwest of the village of Montgomery Creek (lat. 40°52'10" N, long. 121°57'15" W; near SW cor. sec. 22, T 35 N, R 1 W). Named on Montgomery Creek (1956) 15' quadrangle. The name recalls an incident involving an Indian who stole a hatchet from an emigrant (Steger, p. 38).

Hatchet Creek: see **Little Hatchet Creek** [SHASTA].

Hatchet Creek Mountains: see **Hatchet Mountain** [SHASTA].

Hatchet Mountain [SHASTA]: *ridge,* northwest-trending, 4 miles long, 7.5 miles east-northeast of the village of Montgomery Creek (lat. 40°53'15" N, long. 121°47'30" W); branches of Hatchet Creek head near the ridge. Named on Montgomery Creek (1956) 15' quadrangle. Called Hatchet Cr. Mts. on Averill's (1939) map.

Hatchet Mountain Pass [SHASTA]: *pass,* 8.5 miles east of the village of Montgomery Creek (lat. 40°51'10" N, long. 121°45'40" W; near NW cor. sec. 33, T 35 N, R 2 E); the pass is at the southeast end of Hatchet Mountain. Named on Montgomery Creek (1956) 15' quadrangle.

Hatch Flat [TEHAMA]: *area,* 6 miles west-southwest of Paskenta (lat. 39°51'20" N, long. 122°38'50" W; near NE cor. sec. 16, T 23 N, R 7 W). Named on Hall Ridge (1967) 7.5' quadrangle.

Hat Creek [SHASTA]: *stream,* formed by the confluence of East Fork and West Fork 3.25 miles northeast of Lassen Peak, flows 44 miles to Pit River 9 miles north-northeast of Burney (lat. 40°59'20" N, long. 121°34'40" W; sec. 12, T 36 N, R 3 E). Named on Burney (1957), Jellico (1957), and Prospect Peak (1957) 15' quadrangles. Fremont called the stream Poinsett Creek in 1845 for the Secretary of War at that time; the name "Hat Creek" came after D.D. Harrell lost his hat by the stream in 1852 while he was with a party that was blazing a trail for an emigrant road (Steger, p. 38). The stream was called Canoe Creek on army maps of 1857, where the name "Hat Creek" applied only to an upper tributary, but eventually the name "Hat Creek" came to apply to the whole stream (Pease, p. 66). East Fork is 3 miles long and West Fork is 2.5 miles long; both forks are named on Mount Harkness (1956) and Prospect Peak (1957) 15' quadrangles.

Hat Creek: see **Cassel** [SHASTA]; **Hat Creek Post Office** [SHASTA]; **Old Station** [SHASTA].

Hat Creek Campground [SHASTA]: *locality,* 13 miles north-northeast of Lassen Peak (lat. 40°40'05" N, long. 121°26'45" W; at S line sec. 32, T 33 N, R 5 E); the place is along Hat Creek. Named on Prospect Peak (1957) 15' quadrangle.

Hat Creek Hill [SHASTA]: *peak,* 11.5 miles north of Lassen Peak (lat. 40°39'15" N, long. 121°28'30" W; sec. 1, T 32 N, R 4 E); the peak is west of Hat Creek. Altitude 4759 feet. Named on Prospect Peak (1957) 15' quadrangle.

Hat Creek Post Office [SHASTA]: *locality,* 10.5 miles southeast of Burney (lat. 40°47'30" N, long. 121°30'20" W; sec. 22, T 34 N, R 4 E); the place is along Hat Creek. Named on Burney (1957) 15' quadrangle. Called Hat Creek on Burney (1939) 30' quadrangle. Postal authorities established Hat Creek post office in 1884, discontinued it in 1887, reestablished it in

1909, and moved it 1.25 miles south in 1938 (Salley, p. 94).

Hat Creek Rim [SHASTA]: *escarpment,* generally north-trending, 21 miles long, center about 7 miles south-southwest of Coble Mountain (lat. 40°47'30" N, long. 121°24'30" W). Named on Jellico (1957) and Prospect Peak (1957) 15' quadrangles.

Hat Creek Valley [SHASTA]: *valley,* along Hat Creek above a point 8 miles east-northeast of Burney (lat. 40°56'30" N, long. 121°32'30" W). Named on Burney (1957) and Jellico (1957) 15' quadrangles.

Hatfield [SISKIYOU]: *locality,* 16 miles northeast of Mount Dome near California-Oregon State line (lat. 41°59'50" N, long. 121°31' W; sec. 16, T 48 N, R 4 E). Named on Mount Dome (1950) 15' quadrangle.

Hat Lake [SHASTA]: *lake,* 300 feet long, 2.5 miles northeast of Lassen Peak (lat. 40°30'30" N, long. 121°27'50" W; near E line sec. 25, T 31 N, R 4 E); the lake is along West Fork Hat Creek. Named on Prospect Peak (1957) 15' quadrangle. A mudflow from Lassen Peak formed the lake during the 1915 eruption of the peak (Davis, p. 228).

Hat Mountain [SHASTA]:

(1) *crater,* 5 miles east-northeast of Lassen Peak (lat. 40°30'30" N, long. 121°24'50" W; near NW cor. sec. 34, T 31 N, R 5 E). Named on Prospect Peak (1957) 15' quadrangle.

(2) *peak,* 7.5 miles west-southwest of Shoeinhorse Mountain (lat. 41°01'20" N, long. 122°11'55" W). Altitude 4208 feet. Named on Shoeinhorse Mountain (1954) 15' quadrangle.

Hat Mountain Creek [SHASTA]: *stream,* flows nearly 2 miles to McCloud River [SHASTA-SISKIYOU] 6.5 miles west-southwest of Shoeinhorse Mountain (lat. 41°02'30" N, long. 122°11'20" W); the stream heads at Hat Mountain (2). Named on Shoeinhorse Mountain (1954) 15' quadrangle.

Haw Creek [BUTTE]: *stream,* flows 4.25 miles to Butte Creek [BUTTE-GLENN] 6 miles north-northwest of Stirling City (lat. 39°58'45" N, long. 121°35'15" W). Named on Butte Meadows (1958) 15' quadrangle, and on Stirling City (1979) 7.5' quadrangle.

Hawk Camp [TEHAMA]: *locality,* 3.25 miles west-southwest of Tomhead Mountain (lat. 40°07'25" N, long. 122°52'30" W; near NW cor. sec. 10, T 26 N, R 9 W). Named on Yolla Bolly (1954) 15' quadrangle.

Hawk Creek [SHASTA]: *stream,* flows less than 1 mile to Pit River 10 miles north-northeast of the village of Montgomery Creek (lat. 40°57'50" N, long. 121°49'50" W). Named on Montgomery Creek (1956) 15' quadrangle.

Hawkins Camp [BUTTE]: *locality,* 4.25 miles south-southeast of Butte Meadows along West Branch Feather River (lat. 40°01'40" N, long. 121°30'55" W; sec. 15, T 25 N, R 4 E). Named on Butte Meadows (1958) 15' quadrangle.

Hawkins Creek [SHASTA]: *stream,* flows 8 miles to McCloud River [SHASTA-SISKIYOU] 3.5 miles north of Shoeinhorse Mountain (lat. 41°07' N, long. 122°03'40" W). Named on Big Bend (1961) and Shoeinhorse Mountain (1954) 15' quadrangles. J.H. Sisson named the stream about 1880 for the lost Hawkins mine, for which he was searching (Steger, p. 38).

Hawkinsville [SISKIYOU]: *village,* 11 miles south-southwest of Hornbrook along Yreka Creek (lat. 41°45'40" N, long. 122°36'15" W; sec. 11, T 45 N, R 7 W). Named on Hornbrook (1955) 15' quadrangle. Postal authorities established Hawkinsville post office in 1888, discontinued it in 1890, reestablished it in 1895, and discontinued it in 1913; the name was for Jacob Hawkins, owner of a trading post (Salley, p. 94). The place also had the names "Lower Town" and "Frogtown" (Gudde, 1975, p. 154).

Hawk Ravine [BUTTE]: *canyon,* drained by a stream that flows 2.5 miles to West Fork North Honcut Creek 8 miles north-northwest of Bangor (lat. 39°29'45" N, long. 121°27'30" W; near N line sec. 19, T 19 N, R 5 E). Named on Bangor (1947) and Oroville Dam (1970) 7.5' quadrangles. Bidwell Bar (1897) 30' quadrangle shows a locality called Hawk Ravine in the canyon.

Haycock Peak [SHASTA]: *peak,* 8 miles south-southeast of Lamoine (lat. 40°52'15" N, long. 122°22'30" W; near E line sec. 24, T 35 N, R 5 W). Altitude 2029 feet. Named on Lamoine (1957) 15' quadrangle.

Hayden Ridge: see **Callahan** [SISKIYOU].

Hayes Canyon [BUTTE]: *canyon,* drained by a stream that flows 5.5 miles to Little Dry Creek 11.5 miles northwest of Oroville (lat. 39°37'55" N, long. 121°42'10" W; sec. 36, T 21 N, R 2 E). Named on Hamlin Canyon (1951) 7.5' quadrangle.

Hayes Creek [SISKIYOU]: *stream,* flows nearly 2 miles to Kidder Creek 16 miles south of Scott Bar (lat. 41°30'25" N, long. 123°00'35" W). Named on Boulder Peak (1981) 7.5' quadrangle.

Hayes Gulch [SISKIYOU]: *canyon,* drained by a stream that flows 1.5 miles to Grouse Creek (3) 13 miles southeast of Etna (lat. 41°18'50" N, long. 122°43'05" W; sec. 19, T 40 N, R 7 W). Named on China Mountain (1955) 15' quadrangle.

Hayes Hollow Creek [GLENN]: *stream,* flows 11.5 miles to South Fork Willow Creek 11 miles east-southeast of Fruto (lat. 39°33'15" N, long. 122°15'05" W; at N line sec. 36, T 20 N, R 4 W). Named on Fruto (1968), Julian Rocks (1968), and Stone Valley (1952) 7.5' quadrangles.

Haynes Flat [SHASTA]: *area,* 3 miles west-southwest of Burney (lat. 40°52'15" N, long. 121°43'15" W; sec. 23, 26, T 35 N, R 2 E). Named on Burney (1957) 15' quadrangle. The name is for R.W. Haynes, who acquired the place in 1907 (Steger, p. 38).

Haypatch Creek [TEHAMA]: *stream,* flows 2 miles to Log Spring Creek 5.25 miles south of Ball Mountain (lat. 39°51'20" N, long. 122°47'30" W; near NE cor. sec. 18, T 23 N, R 8 W). Named on Log Spring (1967) 7.5' quadrangle.

Haypress Creek [SISKIYOU]: *stream,* flows 7.5 miles to Wooley Creek 12.5 miles north-northwest of Forks of Salmon (lat. 41°25'50" N, long. 123°22'35" W); the stream goes through Haypress Meadows. Named on Somes Bar (1979) and Ukonom Mountain (1980) 7.5' quadrangles.

Haypress Meadow [SISKIYOU]: *area,* 6.5 miles east of Cecilville (lat. 41°08'25" N, long. 123°00'45" W). Named on Grasshopper Ridge (1979) 7.5' quadrangle.

Haypress Meadows [SISKIYOU]: *area,* 6 miles south-southwest of Ukonom Lake (lat. 41°30' N, long. 123°24'30" W); the place is northwest of Haypress Creek. Named on Somes Bar (1979) and Ukonom Mountain (1980) 7.5' quadrangles.

Haystack [SISKIYOU]: *hill,* 25 miles southwest of Macdoel (lat. 41°32'05" N, long. 122°16'40" W; at NW cor. sec. 35, T 43 N, R 4 W). Altitude 4163 feet. Named on Lake Shastina (1954) 15' quadrangle. Called Haystack Butte on Averill's (1935) map.

Haystack Butte [SISKIYOU]: *peak,* 12.5 miles south-southeast of Condrey Mountain (lat. 41°47'15" N, long. 122°50'10" W; sec. 36, T 46 N, R 9 W). Altitude 4078 feet. Named on Condrey Mountain (1955) 15' quadrangle.

Haystack Butte: see **Haystack** [SISKIYOU].

Hazel Bend [BUTTE-TEHAMA]: *bend,* 15 miles northwest of Chico along Sacramento River on Butte-Tehama County line (lat. 39°52'50" N, long. 122°02'45" W). Named on Vina (1904) 15' quadrangle.

Hazel Creek [SHASTA]: *stream,* flows 7 miles to Sacramento River 6 miles south-southwest of Castella (lat. 41°03'45" N, long. 122°21'50" W; near SW cor. sec. 17, T 37 N, R 4 W). Named on Dunsmuir (1954) 15' quadrangle. North Fork enters from the north 4 miles upstream from the mouth of the main creek and is 3.5 miles long. South Fork enters 1.5 miles upstream from the mouth of the main creek and is 4.5 miles long. Both forks are named on Dunsmuir (1954) 15' quadrangle.

Hazel Creek: see **Sims** [SHASTA].

Hazel Gulch [SISKIYOU]: *canyon,* drained by a stream that flows 1 mile to East Fork of South Fork Salmon River 8 miles northeast of Cecilville (lat. 41°13'15" N, long. 123°01'10" W). Named on Grasshopper Ridge (1979) 7.5' quadrangle.

Hazen Flat [TEHAMA]: *area,* 3.5 miles northwest of Mineral (lat. 40°23'15" N, long. 121°38'30" W; mainly in sec. 10, T 29 N, R 3 E). Named on Lassen Peak (1956) 15' quadrangle.

Head: see **Tom Head Creek** [SHASTA].

Headwater Gulch [SISKIYOU]: *canyon,* 0.5 mile long, 14 miles southeast of Condrey Mountain at the head of Humbug Creek (lat. 41°46'10" N, long. 122°48'30" W; sec. 7, T 45 N, R 8 W). Named on Condrey Mountain (1955) 15' quadrangle.

Hearst: see **Vista Robles** [BUTTE].

Heart Lake [SHASTA]: *lake,* 850 feet long, 6 miles southwest of Lassen Peak (lat. 40°26'05" N, long. 121°35'40" W). Named on Lassen Peak (1956) 15' quadrangle.

Heart Lake [SISKIYOU]: *lake,* 200 feet long, nearly 6 miles west of Dunsmuir (lat. 41°13'15" N, long. 122°23' W; near SE cor. sec. 24, T 39 N, R 5 W). Named on Dunsmuir (1954) 15' quadrangle.

Heartstrand Gulch [SISKIYOU]: *canyon,* drained by a stream that flows 4 miles to Scott Valley 4 miles east-northeast of Etna (lat. 41°29' N, long. 122°49'25" W; at S line sec. 13, T 42 N, R 9 W). Named on Etna (1955) 15' quadrangle.

Heather Lake [SISKIYOU]: *lake,* 225 feet long, 13 miles north of Sawyers Bar (lat. 41°29'15" N, long. 123°08'20" W). Named on English Peak (1977) 7.5' quadrangle.

Heavey Gulch [SHASTA]: *canyon,* drained by a stream that flows 1.5 miles to Clear Creek (lat. 40°55'25" N, long. 122°35'30" W; sec. 6, T 35 N, R 6 W). Named on Schell Mountain (1950) 15' quadrangle.

Heavey Sheep Camp [SHASTA]: *locality,* 7 miles north-northwest of Schell Mountain (lat. 40°56'15" N, long. 122°36'15" W; sec. 31, T 36 N, R 6 W); the place is at the head of Heavey Gulch. Named on Schell Mountain (1950) 15' quadrangle.

Hebron Mountain: see **Mount Hebron** [SISKIYOU] (1).

Hecks Camp [GLENN]: *locality,* 10 miles west-southwest of the village of Elk Creek (lat. 39°31'50" N, long. 122°41'55" W; at E line sec. 1, T 19 N, R 8 E). Named on Felkner Hill (1968) 7.5' quadrangle.

Hedge Creek [SISKIYOU]: *stream,* flows 2 miles to Sacramento River less than 2 miles north of downtown Dunsmuir (lat. 41°14'20" N, long. 122°16'10" W; sec. 13, T 39 N, R 4 W). Named on Dunsmuir (1954) 15' quadrangle.

Heifer Camp Creek [GLENN]: *stream,* flows 10.5 miles to North Fork (2) Stony Creek [GLENN-TEHAMA] at Newville (lat. 39°47'35" N, long. 122°31'35" W; sec. 3, T 22 N, R 6 W). Named on Alder Springs (1967),

Chrome (1968), Hall Ridge (1967), and Newville (1967) 7.5' quadrangles. Called Heipher Camp Cr. on Paskenta (1920) 15' quadrangle.

Heifer Ridge [GLENN]: *ridge,* generally east-trending, nearly 5 miles long, 5.25 miles west-southwest of Newville (lat. 39°45'45" N, long. 122°37' W). Named on Hall Ridge (1967) and Newville (1967) 7.5' quadrangles.

Heine Gulch: see **Heiney Gulch** [SISKIYOU].

Heiney Bar [SISKIYOU]: *locality,* nearly 6 miles west of Sawyers Bar along North Fork Salmon River (lat. 41°17'35" N, long. 123°14'30" W); the place is near the mouth of Heiney Gulch. Named on Sawyers Bar (1979) 7.5' quadrangle.

Heiney Gulch [SISKIYOU]: *canyon,* drained by a stream that flows 1.5 miles to North Fork Salmon River nearly 6 miles west of Sawyers Bar (lat. 41°17'30" N, long. 123°14'35" W). Named on Sawyers Bar (1979) 7.5' quadrangle. United States Board on Geographic Names (1960a, p. 14) rejected the form "Heine Gulch" for the name.

Heinz Creek [BUTTE]: *stream,* flows nearly 3 miles to North Fork Feather River 1.5 miles northeast of Pulga (lat. 39°48'50" N, long. 121°25'35" W; near SW cor. sec. 28, T 23 N, R 5 E). Named on Pulga (1979) 7.5' quadrangle.

Heipher Camp Creek: see **Heifer Camp Creek** [GLENN].

Helen: see **Lake Helen** [SHASTA].

Helen Lake [SISKIYOU]: *lake,* 250 feet long, 10 miles north-northwest of McCloud (lat. 41°23'20" N, long. 122°12'35" W; at E line sec. 20, T 41 N, R 3 W). Named on Shasta (1954) 15' quadrangle.

Hell Creek [SHASTA]: *stream,* flows 1.5 miles to Clear Creek 6.5 miles north-northwest of Schell Mountain (lat. 40°56'25" N, long. 122°35'10" W; near NW cor. sec. 32, T 36 N, R 6 W). Named on Schell Mountain (1950) 15' quadrangle.

Hell Hole Creek [SISKIYOU]: *stream,* flows 2.5 miles to Wooley Creek 15 miles north of Forks of Salmon (lat. 41°28'30" N, long. 123°16'25" W); the stream heads on Hell Hole Ridge. Named on English Peak (1977) and Medicine Mountain (1978) 7.5' quadrangles.

Hell Hole Ridge [SISKIYOU]: *ridge,* generally west-trending, 5.5 miles long, 11.5 miles north-northwest of Sawyers Bar (lat. 41°27'40" N, long. 123°13'30" W). Named on English Peak (1977) and Medicine Mountain (1978) 7.5' quadrangles.

Hello Canyon [SISKIYOU]: *canyon,* drained by a stream that flows 3 miles to Butte Fork Applegate River 8.5 miles north of the village of Seiad Valley (lat. 41°57'40" N, long. 123°11'25" W). Named on Kangaroo Mountain (1980) 7.5' quadrangle.

Hello Lake [SISKIYOU]: *lake,* 450 feet long, 6.5 miles north of the village of Seiad Valley (lat. 41°56'05" N, long. 123°11'45" W); the lake is in Hello Canyon. Named on Kangaroo Mountain (1980) 7.5' quadrangle.

Hell Roaring Gulch [SHASTA]: *canyon,* drained by a stream that flows 1.5 miles to Cut-throat Gulch 4.25 miles north-northeast of Arbuckle Mountain (lat. 40°27'35" N, long. 122°50'35" W; at S line sec. 11, T 30 N, R 9 W). Named on Chanchelulla Peak (1951) 15' quadrangle.

Hells Canyon [SISKIYOU]: *canyon,* drained by a stream that flows 3 miles to Bogus Creek 17 miles west-northwest of Macdoel (lat. 41°53'10" N, long. 122°20' W; sec. 32, T 47 N, R 4 W). Named on Copco (1954) 15' quadrangle.

Hells Meadows [SISKIYOU]: *area,* nearly 4 miles south-southwest of Ukonom Lake (lat. 41°31'40" N, long. 123°22'30" W). Named on Ukonom Lake (1980) and Ukonom Mountain (1980) 7.5' quadrangles.

Helltown [BUTTE]: *locality,* 4 miles north-northwest of Paradise (lat. 39°48'45" N, long. 121°39'20" W; near NE cor. sec. 32, T 23 N, R 3 E). Site named on Paradise West (1980) 7.5' quadrangle. The place first was called Butte Creek; the name "Helltown" is thought to have been derived from the name "Hilltown" (Dunn, F.D., p. 49). Gudde (1975, p. 251) listed a place called Omit Bar that was situated along Butte Creek [BUTTE-GLENN] just below Helltown. F.D. Dunn (p. 105) noted that Sycamore Crossing was the wagon-road crossing of Butte Creek [BUTTE-GLENN] just below Helltown (sec. 32, T 23 N, R 3 E). F.D. Dunn (p. 83) also stated that a mining camp called Paradise Flat was located along Butte Creek [BUTTE-GLENN] halfway between Helltown and Whiskey Flat—the place was called Paradise before that name was taken for the post office at present Paradise.

Hemlock Lake [SHASTA]: *lake,* 700 feet long, 3.5 miles southeast of Lassen Peak (lat. 40°27'30" N, long. 121°27'20" W; near W line sec. 17, T 30 N, R 5 E). Named on Mount Harkness (1956) 15' quadrangle. Carl Swartzlow, naturalist at Lassen Volcanic National Park, suggested the name in 1937 to replace the name "Little Long Lake"—the feature was called Edwards Lake on old maps (Schulz, p. 24).

Hemlock Lake [SISKIYOU]: *lake,* 400 feet long, 16 miles north-northwest of Bartle (lat. 41°28'45" N, long. 121°55'35" W; at S line sec. 14, T 42 N, R 1 W); the lake is near the west end of Hemlock Ridge. Named on Bartle (1961) 15' quadrangle.

Hemlock Ridge [SISKIYOU]: *ridge,* generally west-trending, 2 miles long, 16 miles north-northwest of Bartle (lat. 41°29' N, long. 121°54' W). Named on Bartle (1961) 15' quadrangle.

Henderson: see **Big Bend** [SHASTA].

Henderson Canyon [TEHAMA]: *canyon,* drained by a stream that flows 4 miles to Thomes Creek 10.5 miles west of Paskenta (lat. 39°52'20" N, long. 122°44'15" W; near SE cor. sec. 3, T 23 N, R 8 W). Named on Riley Ridge (1967) 7.5' quadrangle.

Henderson Glade [TEHAMA]: *area,* 10 miles west of Paskenta (lat. 39°53' N, long. 122°44'10" W; at E line sec. 3, T 23 N, R 8 W). Named on Riley Ridge (1967) 7.5' quadrangle.

Hendrick Reservoir: see **Cannon Reservoir** [BUTTE].

Hengy: see **Oregon City** [BUTTE].

Henley [SISKIYOU]: *village,* less than 1 mile south-southwest of Hornbrook (lat. 41°54'10" N, long. 122°33'40" W; sec. 20, T 47 N, R 6 W); the village is along Cottonwood Creek (1). Named on Hornbrook (1955) 15' quadrangle. Postal authorities established Henley post office in 1856 and discontinued it in 1912 (Frickstad, p. 188). The name commemorates Colonel T.J. Henley, who commanded troops in the region in the 1850's (Hanna, p. 137). The village first was called Cottonwood (Bancroft, p. 367). Postal authorities established Virginia Ranch post office about 4 miles southwest of Henley in 1871 and discontinued it the same year (Salley, p. 232).

Henleyville [TEHAMA]: *locality,* 6.5 miles east-northeast of Flournoy (lat. 39°57'45" N, long. 122°19'35" W; at W line sec. 4, T 24 N, R 4 W). Named on Henleyville (1967) 7.5' quadrangle.

Henry Bell Creek: see **Negro Creek** [SISKIYOU] (1).

Henry Bell Gulch [SISKIYOU]: *canyon,* drained by a stream that flows 1.25 miles to North Fork Salmon River 8 miles east-northeast of Salmon Mountain (lat. 41°14'35" N, long. 123°16'55" W). Named on Forks of Salmon (1978) and Youngs Peak (1979) 7.5' quadrangles. The stream is called Niggerville Cr. on Sawyers Bar (1923) 30' quadrangle, where present Negro Creek (1) is called Henry Bell Cr.

Henrys Gulch [SISKIYOU]: *canyon,* drained by a stream that flows 2 miles to South Fork Taylor Creek (1) 4 miles east-northeast of Cecilville (lat. 41°09'30" N, long. 123°03'50" W). Named on Grasshopper Ridge (1979) 7.5' quadrangle.

Hensley Creek [TEHAMA]: *stream,* formed by the confluence of North Fork and South Fork, flows 1 mile to South Fork Cottonwood Creek [SHASTA-TEHAMA] 4.5 miles west-southwest of Wakefield Flat (lat. 40°07'15" N, long. 122°42'55" W). Named on Raglin Ridge (1967) 7.5' quadrangle. North Fork is nearly 2 miles long and South Fork is 1.5 miles long; both forks are named on Raglin Ridge (1967) 7.5' quadrangle.

Hensley Glade [TEHAMA]: *area,* 2 miles southeast of Ball Mountain (lat. 39°54'40" N, long. 122°45'35" W; sec. 28, T 24 N, R 8 W). Named on Ball Mountain (1967) 7.5' quadrangle.

Hensley's Mineral Spring: see **Hensley Springs** [TEHAMA].

Hensley Springs [TEHAMA]: *springs,* 4.5 miles west-southwest of Wakefield Flat (lat. 40°06'15" N, long. 122°43'30" W; at E line sec. 14, T 26 N, R 8 W); the springs are near South Fork Hensley Creek. Named on Raglin Ridge (1967) 7.5' quadrangle. Called Hensley's Mineral Spring on Red Bluff (1894) 1° quadrangle.

Heppe Cave [SISKIYOU]: *cave,* 8.5 miles north-northeast of Medicine Lake (lat. 41°41'55" N, long. 121°32'40" W; at E line sec. 31, T 45 N, R 4 E); the cave is near Heppe Chimney. Named on Medicine Lake (1952) 15' quadrangle. The name commemorates Ernest Heppe, who set up his camp near the cave in the 1890's (Knox, p. 57).

Heppe Chimney [SISKIYOU]: *relief feature,* 8.5 miles north-northeast of Medicine Lake (lat. 41°41'55" N, long. 121°32'40" W; at E line sec. 31, T 45 N, R 4 E); the feature is near Heppe Cave. Named on Medicine Lake (1952) 15' quadrangle.

Herd Peak [SISKIYOU]: *peak,* 18 miles southwest of Macdoel (lat. 41°37'15" N, long. 122°13'50" W; sec. 30, T 44 N, R 3 W). Altitude 7071 feet. Named on The Whaleback (1954) 15' quadrangle.

Heroult: see **Baird** [SHASTA].

Herr Creek [SISKIYOU]: *stream,* flows 1.25 miles to North Fork Salmon River 8 miles north of Sawyers Bar (lat. 41°25'20" N, long. 123°06'20" W). Named on Yellow Dog Peak (1977) 7.5' quadrangle.

Heryford [SHASTA]: *locality,* nearly 3 miles northeast of Millville (lat. 40°34'10" N, long. 122°08' W; sec. 6, T 31 N, R 2 W). Named on Redding (1901) 30' quadrangle.

Hibbard Creek [BUTTE]: *stream,* flows 2 miles to Bear Ranch Creek 4 miles northeast of Pulga (lat. 39°50'10" N, long. 121°23'05" W; sec. 23, T 23 N, R 5 E). Named on Pulga (1979) and Soapstone Hill (1979) 7.5' quadrangles.

Hibbard Gulch: see **Hubbard Gulch** [TEHAMA].

Hibbs Soda Spring: see **Lower Soda Spring**, under **Soda Spring** [SHASTA] (1).

Hickey Gulch [SISKIYOU]: *canyon,* drained by a stream that flows 1.25 miles to North Fork Salmon River 3.25 miles east of Sawyers Bar (lat. 41°18'20" N, long. 123°04'15" W); the mouth of the canyon is 0.5 mile downstream from the mouth of Applesauce Gulch.. Named on Tanners Peak (1977) 7.5' quadrangle. On Sawyers Bar (1923) 30' quadrangle, the stream in the canyon has the name "Applesauce Cr."

Hicks Gulch [SISKIYOU]: *canyon,* drained by a stream that flows 1.5 miles to Klamath River 6 miles east-southeast of the village of Seiad Valley (lat.

41°47'55" N, long. 123°05'30" W). Named on Hamburg (1980) 7.5' quadrangle.

Hidden Lake [SHASTA]: *lake,* 1300 feet long, 9.5 miles east of Lassen Peak (lat. 40°29'30" N, long. 121°19'50" W; sec. 5, T 30 N, R 6 E). Named on Mount Harkness (1956) 15' quadrangle. United States Board on Geographic Names (1933, p. 364) rejected the name "Twin Lakes" for the feature.

Hidden Lake [SISKIYOU]: *lake,* 700 feet long, 8.5 miles south of Etna (lat. 41°12'35" N, long. 122°54'20" W; sec. 28, T 39 N, R 9 W). Named on Coffee Creek (1955) 15' quadrangle. Called South Fork Lake on Etna (1934) 30' quadrangle.

High Flat [TEHAMA]: *area,* 7 miles north-northwest of Paskenta (lat. 39°58'30" N, long. 122°35'35" W; near SE cor. sec. 36, T 25 N, R 7 W). Named on Paskenta (1967) 7.5' quadrangle.

High Flat Ridge [TEHAMA]: *ridge,* south-trending, 3 miles long, 7 miles north-northwest of Paskenta (lat. 39°58'30" N, long. 122°36' W); the ridge is west of High Flat. Named on Paskenta (1967) 7.5' quadrangle.

High Hole Crater [SISKIYOU]: *crater,* 6.25 miles south-southeast of Medicine Lake (lat. 41°30'35" N, long. 121°31'45" W). Altitude 6186 feet. Named on Medicine Lake (1952) 15' quadrangle.

High Lake [SISKIYOU]: *lake,* 600 feet long, 11.5 miles south-southwest of Etna (lat. 41°17'50" N, long. 122°57'25" W; near E line sec. 25, T 40 N, R 10 W). Named on Etna (1955) 15' quadrangle.

Highland Creek [SISKIYOU]: *stream,* flows 1.5 miles to Music Creek 6.5 miles east-northeast of Sawyers Bar (lat. 41°19'25" N, long. 123°00'50" W). Named on Tanners Peak (1977) 7.5' quadrangle.

Highland Ridge [SHASTA]: *ridge,* generally east-southeast-trending, 3 miles long, 3.25 miles north-northwest of the village of French Gulch (lat. 40°44'30" N, long. 122°40'15" W). Named on Schell Mountain (1950) 15' quadrangle, and on French Gulch (1979) 7.5' quadrangle.

High Mountain [SHASTA]: *peak,* 8.5 miles east of Lamoine (lat. 40°59'30" N, long. 122°15'20" W; sec. 12, T 36 N, R 4 W). Altitude 5464 feet. Named on Lamoine (1957) 15' quadrangle.

High Peak [GLENN]: *peak,* 13 miles west-southwest of Willows (lat. 39°25'30" N, long. 122°25'15" W; sec. 9, T 18 N, R 5 W). Altitude 1894 feet. Named on Lodoga (1960) 15' quadrangle.

High Point [SISKIYOU]:
(1) *peak,* 2.25 miles east of Salmon Mountain (lat. 41°11'10" N, long. 123°22' W). Altitude 5614 feet. Named on Youngs Peak (1979) 7.5' quadrangle.
(2) *relief feature,* 6 miles north of Cecilville (lat. 41°13'40" N, long. 123°09' W). Named on Cecilville (1979) 7.5' quadrangle.

High Prairie [SISKIYOU]: *area,* 6.5 miles southwest of Cecilville on Siskiyou-Trinity County line (lat. 41°04'25" N, long. 123°12'45" W). Named on Cecil Lake (1979) 7.5' quadrangle.

High Rim [SISKIYOU]: *ridge,* south-trending, 7 miles long, 11 miles north-northeast of Mount Dome (lat. 41°56'45" N, long. 121°34'30" W). Named on Mount Dome (1950) 15' quadrangle. United States Board on Geographic Names (1986b, p. 2) rejected the name "Sheepy Ridge" for the feature.

High Rock Ravine [BUTTE]: *canyon,* drained by a stream that flows 1.5 miles to Last Chance Creek (1) 3.25 miles north of Stirling City (lat. 39°57'15" N, long. 121°31' W; sec. 10, T 24 N, R 4 E). Named on Kimshew Point (1979) and Stirling City (1979) 7.5' quadrangles.

High Rock Ravine: see **Potter Ravine** [BUTTE].

High Rocks: see **The High Rocks** [BUTTE].

Hightower Gulch [SHASTA]: *canyon,* drained by a stream that flows 4 miles to Middle Fork Cottonwood Creek [SHASTA-TEHAMA] 8.5 miles south of Ono (lat. 40°21'15" N, long. 122°36' W; sec. 24, T 29 N, R 7 W). Named on Ono (1952) 15' quadrangle.

High Trestle [TEHAMA]: *pass,* 11 miles south of Manton (lat. 40°16'40" N, long. 121°50'45" W; sec. 15, T 28 N, R 1 E). Named on Manton (1956) 15' quadrangle.

Hill: see **Jack Hill Ravine** [BUTTE].

Hillcrest [SHASTA]: *locality,* 1.5 miles north-northeast of the village of Montgomery Creek (lat. 40°51'45" N, long. 121°54'30" W; sec. 30, T 35 N, R 1 E). Named on Montgomery Creek (1956) 15' quadrangle. The place was called Back Action Flat in the early days because it was at the top of a steep grade where the first wagon of a two-wagon freight outfit was brought up and left until the second wagon could be brought up and the two reassembled to continue the journey (Steger, p. 39).

Hillhouse [TEHAMA]: *locality,* 11.5 miles south-southeast of Manton (lat. 40°17'05" N, long. 121°47'30" W; near N line sec. 18, T 28 N, R 2 E). Named on Manton (1956) 15' quadrangle.

Hilt [SISKIYOU]: *village,* 7 miles north-northwest of Hornbrook (lat. 41°59'45" N, long. 122°37'20" W; sec. 23, T 48 N, R 7 W). Named on Hornbrook (1955) 15' quadrangle. Called Hilts on Yreka (1939) 30' quadrangle, but United States Board on Geographic Names (1967b, p. 3) rejected this form of the name. Postal authorities established Coles post office in 1888; they moved it 1 mile south and changed the name to Hilts in 1903, changed the name to Hilt in 1967, and discontinued it in 1974—the name "Coles" was for Byron Coles, a rancher (Salley, p. 47, 98). The name "Hilt" commemorates John Hilt, who came to Siskiyou County in 1855 and built a sawmill; lumbermen who bought Hilt's estate named their company and the community for Mr. Hilt (Gudde, 1969, p. 141).

Hines Camp [SISKIYOU]: *locality,* 6.5 miles north-northwest of Orleans, which is in Humboldt County (lat. 41°23'40" N, long. 123°33'35" W); the place is near the head of a branch of Hines Creek. Named on Bark Shanty Gulch (1974) 7.5' quadrangle.

Hines Creek [SISKIYOU]: *stream,* flows 2 miles to Camp Creek 8 miles north-northwest of Orleans, which is in Humboldt County (lat. 41°24'45" N, long. 123°35' W). Named on Bark Shanty Gulch (1974) 7.5' quadrangle. United States Board on Geographic Names (1977b, p. 5) gave the name "Camp Creek" as a variant.

Hippo Butte [SISKIYOU]: *hill,* about 10 miles north-northeast of Medicine Lake (lat. 41°42'55" N, long. 121°31'50" W; sec. 29, T 45 N, R 4 E). Named on Medicine Lake (1952) 15' quadrangle.

Hirt Mountain: see **Hirz Mountain** [SHASTA].

Hirz Bay [SHASTA]: *embayment,* 12 miles southeast of Lamoine along McCloud River Arm Shasta Lake (lat. 40°52' N, long. 122°16' W); the feature is the inundated lower part of the canyon of Hirz Creek. Named on Lamoine (1957) 15' quadrangle.

Hirz Creek [SHASTA]: *stream,* flows 1 mile to Hirz Bay 11 miles south-southeast of Lamoine (lat. 40°52' N, long. 122°16'30" W). Named on Lamoine (1957) 15' quadrangle.

Hirz Mountain [SHASTA]: *ridge,* generally east-southeast-trending, 1.25 miles long, 11 miles southeast of Lamoine (lat. 40°53'45" N, long. 122°15'10" W). Named on Bollibokka Mountain (1957) and Lamoine (1957) 15' quadrangles. United States Board on Geographic Names (1990, p. 7) rejected the name "Hirt Mountain" for the feature, and noted that the name "Hirz" is for Christian Hirz, a pioneer who had a sawmill and gold mine in the neighborhood.

Hites Landing [BUTTE]: *locality,* 11 miles west-southwest of Durham along Sacramento River (lat. 39°37'10" N, long. 121°59'30" W). Named on Newhard (1912) 7.5' quadrangle.

Hi-you Gulch [SISKIYOU]: *canyon,* drained by a stream that flows 2 miles to McAdam Creek 7.25 miles north of Fort Jones (lat. 41°42'35" N, long. 123°48'45" W; sec. 31, T 45 N, R 8 W). Named on Fort Jones (1955) 15' quadrangle. Yreka (1939) 30' quadrangle has the form "Hiyou Gulch" for the name. A little community called Hardscrabble was situated in Hi You Gulch (Hoover, Rensch, and Rensch, p. 506).

Hoadley Peaks [SHASTA]: *peaks,* 6 miles west of the village of French Gulch on Shasta-Trinity County line (lat. 40°41'20" N, long. 122°45' W; sec. 27, T 33 N, R 8 W). Named on Weaverville (1950) 15' quadrangle, and on French Gulch (1979) 7.5' quadrangle. Called Trinity Mountain on Red Bluff (1894) 1° quadrangle, and called Hoadley Pk. on Weaverville (1913) 30' quadrangle.

Hoags Camp [SISKIYOU]: *locality,* 3.5 miles south-southeast of the village of Seiad Valley along Walker Creek (lat. 41°47'45" N, long. 123°09'55" W; near S line sec. 30, T 46 N, R 11 W). Named on Seiad Valley (1980) 7.5' quadrangle.

Hoag Slough [TEHAMA]: *stream,* flows 6.5 miles to Sacramento River 3.25 miles south of Vina (lat. 39°53'05" N, long. 122°02'50" W). Named on Vina (1950) 7.5' quadrangle.

Hobson Camp [TEHAMA]: *locality,* 17 miles south-southwest of Panther Spring along Deer Creek (2) (lat. 40°01'15" N, long. 121°53'40" W; sec. 17, T 25 N, R 1 E). Named on Panther Spring (1953) 15' quadrangle.

Hockaday Springs [SISKIYOU]: *springs,* 5 miles southwest of Etna along Etna Creek (lat. 41°24'55" N, long. 122°58'10" W; near W line sec. 11, T 41 N, R 10 W). Named on Etna (1955) 15' quadrangle.

Hodapp Creek [BUTTE]: *stream,* flows 2.5 miles to West Branch Feather River 5.25 miles southeast of Paradise (lat. 39°41'55" N, long. 121°33'35" W; near SW cor. sec. 5, T 21 N, R 4 E). Named on Cherokee (1970) 7.5' quadrangle. The name commemorates the Hodapp family (Dunn, F.D., p. 50).

Hoey: see **Grass Lake** [SISKIYOU] (2).

Hoffman: see **Little Mount Hoffman** [SISKIYOU]; **Mount Hoffman** [SISKIYOU].

Hoffman Mill [SISKIYOU]: *locality,* 8.5 miles southwest of Macdoel (lat. 41°43'35" N, long. 122°06'05" W; sec. 20, T 45 N, R 2 W). Site named on The Whaleback (1954) 15' quadrangle.

Hoffmeister Creek [SHASTA]: *stream,* flows nearly 2 miles to Squaw Creek (2) 6.25 miles east of Bollibokka Mountain (lat. 40°55'20" N, long. 122°05'45" W; sec. 4, T 35 N, R 2 W). Named on Bollibokka Mountain (1957) 15' quadrangle. Steger (p. 39) associated the name with Charles Hoffmeister and Tom Hoffmeister, whose stock range was along the creek.

Hogan Creek [SISKIYOU]: *stream,* flows 2 miles to Taylor Creek (2) 8 miles northeast of Sawyers Bar (lat. 41°21'55" N, long. 123°00'40" W); the stream heads at Hogan Lake. Named on Etna (1955) 15' quadrangle, and on Tanners Peak (1977) 7.5' quadrangle.

Hogan Lake [SISKIYOU]: *lake,* 850 feet long, 9 miles south-southwest of Etna (lat. 41°20'50" N, long. 122°59'25" W; sec. 11, T 40 N, R 10 W); the lake is at the head of Hogan Creek. Named on Etna (1955) 15' quadrangle.

Hogback: see **The Hogback** [TEHAMA].

Hogback Creek [SHASTA]: *stream,* flows 1.5 miles to Pit River 2.5 miles west-northwest of the village of Montgomery Creek (lat. 40°51'30" N, long. 121°58' W; near W line sec. 27, T 35 N, R 1 W); the stream heads at Hogback Mountain. Named on Montgomery Creek (1956) 15' quadrangle.

Hogback Mountain [SHASTA]: *ridge,* southeast-trending, 2.5 miles long, 4.25 miles west-northwest of the village of Montgomery Creek (lat. 40°52'30" N, long. 121°59'25" W). Named on Bollibokka Mountain (1957) and Montgomery Creek (1956) 15' quadrangles.

Hogback Ridge [SHASTA]: *ridge,* generally north-northwest-trending, 3.5 miles long, 8 miles northwest of Coble Mountain (lat. 40°57'15" N, long. 121°27'15" W). Named on Jellico (1957) 15' quadrangle.

Hogback Ridge [TEHAMA]: *ridge,* generally west-trending, 7.5 miles long, 12 miles south of Manton (lat. 40°16' N, long. 121°52'30" W). Named on Manton (1956) 15' quadrangle.

Hog Gulch [TEHAMA]:

(1) *canyon,* drained by a stream that flows 1.5 miles to Wells Creek 8 miles north-northeast of Tomhead Mountain (lat. 40°14'45" N, long. 122°46'25" W; near S line sec. 28, T 28 N, R 8 W). Named on Chanchelulla Peak (1951) and Yolla Bolly (1954) 15' quadrangles.

(2) *canyon,* drained by a stream that flows 3.25 miles to lowlands 8 miles east-southeast of Red Bluff (lat. 40°08'45" N, long. 122°05'25" W). Named on Tuscon Springs (1951) 7.5' quadrangle.

Hog Lake [TEHAMA]: *lake,* 1600 feet long, 3.25 miles southwest of Dales (lat. 40°17' N, long. 122°07'10" W; near W line sec. 17, T 28 N, R 2 W). Named on Dales (1965) 7.5' quadrangle.

Hog Range [SISKIYOU]: *ridge,* south-southeast-trending, 0.5 mile long, 1.5 miles north of Forks of Salmon (lat. 41°16'50" N, long. 123°19'10" W). Named on Forks of Salmon (1978) 7.5' quadrangle.

Hogs Back [TEHAMA]: *ridge,* generally east-southeast-trending, 0.5 mile long, 5 miles southeast of Manton (lat. 40°22'45" N, long. 121°49' W; on W line sec. 12, T 29 N, R 1 E). Named on Manton (1956) 15' quadrangle.

Hogs Back: see **Cohasset Ridge** [BUTTE-TEHAMA].

Hog Spring [BUTTE]: *spring,* 6 miles west of Paradise (lat. 39°45'25" N, long. 121°44'05" W; sec. 15, T 22 N, R 2 E). Named on Paradise West (1980) 7.5' quadrangle.

Hogtown [SHASTA]: *locality,* 4 miles west-northwest of Redding (lat. 40°37' N, long. 122°27'45" W). Named on Red Bluff (1894) 30' quadrangle.

Hokey Pokey Ridge [GLENN]: *ridge,* generally east-northeast-trending, 3.5 miles long, 4 miles northeast of Black Butte (lat. 39°46' N, long. 122°49'30" W). Named on Log Spring (1967) 7.5' quadrangle.

Hole in Ground Spring [SHASTA]: *spring,* 17 miles north-northeast of Lassen Peak (lat. 40°42' N, long. 121°21' W; near N line sec. 30, T 33 N, R 6 E). Named on Prospect Peak (1957) 15' quadrangle.

Hole in Rock [SISKIYOU]: *relief feature,* 16 miles south-southeast of Medicine Lake (lat. 41°22'30" N, long. 121°27'40" W; sec. 24, T 41 N, R 4 E). Named on White Horse (1962) 15' quadrangle.

Hole in the Ground [TEHAMA]:

(1) *relief feature,* wide place in the canyon of Mill Creek (3) 3 miles southeast of Mineral (lat. 40°18'45" N, long. 121°34' W). Named on Lassen Peak (1956) 15' quadrangle.

(2) *relief feature,* 4.5 miles north-northwest of Wakefield Flat along Cold Creek (1) (lat. 40°11'20" N, long. 122°40'25" W; near SE cor. sec. 17, T 27 N, R 7 W). Named on Cold Fork (1967) 7.5' quadrangle.

Hole in the Ground: see **Deep Hole** [SHASTA].

Hollenbeak Swamp [SHASTA]: *marsh,* 7.5 miles north-northeast of Fall River Mills (lat. 41°06'15" N, long. 121°23'20" W). Named on Fall River Mills (1961) 15' quadrangle. United States Board on Geographic Names (1990, p. 8) rejected the name "Hollenbeck Swamp" for the feature.

Hollenbush: see **Camp Hollenbush**, under **Fall River Valley** [SHASTA].

Hollensworth Flat: see **Brokeoff Meadows** [SHASTA].

Honcut [BUTTE]:

(1) *land grant,* mainly in Yuba County, but extends into Butte County 7 miles southwest of Bangor. Named on Loma Rica (1947) 7.5' quadrangle. Theodore Cordua received 7 leagues in 1844; Charles Covilland (should be Covillaud) claimed 31,080 acres patented in 1863 (Cowan, p. 39-40). The name "Honcut" is of Indian origin (Kroeber, p. 42).

(2) *village,* 13 miles south of Oroville (lat. 39°19'40" N, long. 121°32' W; sec. 19, T 17 N, R 4 E). Named on Honcut (1952) 7.5' quadrangle. Marysville (1895) 30' quadrangle has the name "Moores Station" for the present village of Honcut, and has the name "Honcut" for a place located 1.5 miles farther east-southeast at present Phillips Corner. Postal authorities established Honcut post office in Yuba County in 1856, moved it to a new site in Butte County in 1878, moved it back into Yuba County in 1884, discontinued it in 1892, reestablished it in Butte County in 1892, and discontinued it in 1943 (Salley, p. 99). They established Moores Station post office 4 miles northwest of the original site of Honcut post office in 1869, discontinued it in 1875, reestablished it in 1876, and discontinued it in 1892; the name was for John C. Moore, first postmaster (Salley, p. 146).

Honcut City: see **Wyandotte** [BUTTE].

Honcut Creek [BUTTE]: *stream,* formed by the confluence of North Honcut Creek and South Honcut Creek, flows 2.5 miles to Feather River 5.25 miles west-southwest of Honcut (lat. 39°17'45" N, long. 121°37'20" W). Named on Honcut (1952) 7.5' quadrangle. The stream forms part of Butte-Yuba County line. Gudde (1975, p. 359) listed a town called Veazie City, Veza City, or Charleys Ranch that was laid out in 1850 along Feather River near the mouth of Honcut Creek. The name "Veazie" was from the promoter of the place (Hoover, Rensch, and Rensch, p. 40). Postal authorities established Charleys Rancho post office in 1852, changed the name to Charley's Ranch the same year, and discontinued it in 1858; the name was for Charles Clark, first postmaster and owner of the site (Salley, p. 42). Promoters laid out a town called Fredonia on the east bank of Feather River a few miles above Veazie City (Dunn, F.D., p. 42), and another town called Yatestown along the river opposite Fredonia (Bancroft, p. 490).

Honcut Creek: see **North Honcut Creek** [BUTTE]; **South Honcut Creek** [BUTTE].

Honeybee Gulch [SHASTA]: *canyon,* about 0.5 mile long, 6.25 miles southeast of the village of French Gulch (lat. 40°38'20" N, long. 122°33'15" W). Named on French Gulch (1944) 15' quadrangle. Water of Whiskeytown Lake now floods the feature.

Honeymoon ridge [SHASTA]: *ridge,* generally south-southeast-trending, 3 miles long, 3.25 miles west-southwest of Schell Mountain (lat. 40°49'45" N, long. 122°37'30" W). Named on Schell Mountain (1950) 15' quadrangle.

Honey Run [BUTTE]: *stream,* flows 4.25 miles to Little Butte Creek [BUTTE-GLENN] 2.5 miles west-southwest of Paradise (lat. 39°45' N, long. 121°40'20" W; near W line sec. 20, T 22 N, R 3 E). Named on Hamlin Canyon (1951), Paradise East (1980), and Paradise West (1980) 7.5' quadrangles. The name is from a nest of bees found near the feature (Adams, p. 133).

Honn Creek [SHASTA]: *stream,* diverges from Hat Creek and flows 2.5 miles to rejoin Hat Creek 11 miles southeast of Burney (lat. 40°47' N, long. 121°30'10" W; at N line sec. 27, T 34 N, R 4 E). Named on Burney (1957) and Jellico (1957) 15' quadrangles.

Honn Creek Camp Ground [SHASTA]: *locality,* 11.5 miles southeast of Burney (lat. 40°46'55" N, long. 121°30'05" W; sec. 27, T 34 N, R 4 E); the place is along Honn Creek. Named on Burney (1957) 15' quadrangle.

Honolulu: see **Gottville** [SISKIYOU].

Hoodlum Chute [TEHAMA]: *relief feature,* 5.5 miles east-southeast of Kirkwood along Sacramento River (lat. 39°49'30" N, long. 122°03'45" W). Named on Vina (1904) 15' quadrangle.

Hoodoo Hills [GLENN]: *relief features,* 7.5 miles east-southeast of Fruto (lat. 39°32'05" N, long. 122°19'45" W; in and near sec. 5, T 19 N, R 4 W). Named on Stone Valley (1952) 7.5' quadrangle.

Hoodoo Island [BUTTE-GLENN]: *island,* 6.5 miles east-southeast of Butte City in Butte Creek [BUTTE-GLENN] on Butte-Glenn County line (lat. 39°24'10" N, long. 121°52'55" W). Named on Marysville (1895) 30' quadrangle.

Hooker [TEHAMA]: *locality,* 9 miles north-northwest of Red Bluff along Southern Pacific Railroad (lat. 40°18'05" N, long. 122°19'30" W; near N line sec. 9, T 28 N, R 4 W); the place is along Hooker Creek. Named on Hooker (1965) 7.5' quadrangle. Postal authorities established Hooker post office in 1885, discontinued it in 1887, reestablished it in 1889, and discontinued it in 1928 (Frickstad, p. 204). California Mining Bureau's (1917b) map shows a place called Draper located along the railroad about 4 miles north-northeast of Hooker, and a place called Ivrea located along the railroad about 2.5 miles south-southeast of Hooker.

Hooker Creek [TEHAMA]: *stream,* flows 16 miles to Cottonwood Creek [SHASTA-TEHAMA] 5 miles north of Hooker (lat. 40°22'15" N, long. 122°18'35" W; at W line sec. 15, T 29 N, R 4 W). Named on Blossom (1952), Hooker (1965), and Mitchell Gulch (1965) 7.5' quadrangles. The name is for J.M. Hooker, who settled near the mouth of the stream in 1852 (Gudde, 1969, p. 144).

Hooligan Lake [SISKIYOU]: *lake,* 800 feet long, 5 miles south-southeast of Ukonom Lake (lat. 41°31' N, long. 123°18'40" W). Named on Ukonom Lake (1980) 7.5' quadrangle.

Hooper [SISKIYOU]: *locality,* 1.5 miles northwest of McCloud (lat. 41°16'05" N, long. 122°09'40" W; sec. 35, T 40 N, R 3 W). Named on Shasta (1954) 15' quadrangle.

Hooper: see **Fort Hooper**, under **Hooperville** [SISKIYOU].

Hooper Creek [TEHAMA]: *stream,* flows nearly 5 miles to Meeker Creek 9.5 miles east-northeast of Red Bluff (lat. 40°14'15" N, long. 122°05' W; near W line sec. 34, T 28 N, R 2 W). Named on Tuscan Springs (1951) 7.5' quadrangle.

Hooperville [SISKIYOU]: *locality,* 5 miles north of Fort Jones along Indian Creek (3) (lat. 41°40'45" N, long. 122°50'45" W; sec. 11, T 44 N, R 9 W). Named on Fort Jones (1955) 15' quadrangle. The place was a mining camp named for Frank Hooper, a prospector (Gudde, 1975, p. 159). Whiting and Whiting (p. 33) listed a trading post called Fort Hooper that Frank Hooper's father built along McAdams Creek in 1852.

Hoosier Hill: see **Hamburg** [SISKIYOU].

Hooten Gulch [SHASTA]: *canyon,* drained by a stream that flows 3.5 miles to South Cow Creek 8 miles east of Millville (lat. 40°34' N, long. 122°01'40" W; near SW cor. sec. 6, T 31 N, R 1 W). Named on Millville (1953) and Whitmore (1956) 15' quadrangles.

Hoover Creek: see **Ducket Creek** [SHASTA].

Hoover Gulch [SHASTA]: *canyon,* drained by a stream that flows 0.5 mile to Winston Gulch 8.5 miles south-southeast of Bollibokka Mountain (lat. 40°49' N, long. 122°09'35" W; sec. 12, T 34 N, R 3 W). Named on Bollibokka Mountain (1957) 15' quadrangle.

Hope: see **Mount Hope** [BUTTE].

Hopper Gulch [SHASTA]: *canyon,* drained by a stream that flows 1 mile to Cline Gulch 2.5 miles east-northeast of the village of French Gulch (lat. 40°42'55" N, long. 122°35'20" W; sec. 18, T 33 N, R 6 W). Named on Whiskeytown (1979) 7.5' quadrangle.

Hornbrook [SISKIYOU]: *town,* 13 miles north-northeast of Yreka along Cottonwood Creek (1) (lat. 41°54'45" N, long. 122°33'15" W; sec. 20, 21, T 47 N, R 6 W). Named on Hornbrook (1955) 15' quadrangle. Postal authorities established Cadillac post office in 1889 and moved it 2.5 miles northwest in 1891 when they changed the name to Hornbrook (Salley, p. 31). The name "Hornbrook," given in 1886, is from a small stream that ran through the property of David Horn (Stewart, G.R., p. 211).

Horn Creek [SISKIYOU]: *stream,* flows 2.25 miles to Salmon River less than 0.5 mile west-northwest of Forks of Salmon (lat. 41°15'35" N, long. 123°19'45" W). Named on Forks of Salmon (1978) and Youngs Peak (1979) 7.5' quadrangles.

Horn Creek Gap [SISKIYOU]: *pass,* 5 miles north-northeast of Salmon Mountain (lat. 41°14'50" N, long. 123°21'50" W); the pass is at the head of a branch of Horn Creek. Named on Youngs Peak (1979) 7.5' quadrangle.

Horned Owl Gulch [SHASTA]: *canyon,* drained by a stream that flows 1 mile to Hawkins Creek 3.5 miles north-northeast of Shoeinhorse Mountain (lat. 41°06'45" N, long. 122°02'20" W). Named on Shoeinhorse Mountain (1954) 15' quadrangle.

Hornet Gulch [SHASTA]:
(1) *canyon,* drained by a stream that flows 2 miles to Lick Creek (1) 7.25 miles north-northeast of Shoeinhorse Mountain (lat. 41°10'15" N, long. 122°02'10" W). Named on Shoeinhorse Mountain (1954) 15' quadrangle.
(2) *canyon,* drained by a stream that flows 1 mile to Hawkins Creek 4 miles east-northeast of Shoeinhorse Mountain (lat. 41°05'50" N, long. 122°00'20" W). Named on Shoeinhorse Mountain (1954) 15' quadrangle.

Horn Field [SISKIYOU]: *area,* 0.5 mile northwest of Forks of Salmon (lat. 41°15'50" N, long. 123°19'45" W). Named on Forks of Salmon (1978) 7.5' quadrangle.

Horn Flat [SISKIYOU]: *area,* 0.5 mile northwest of Forks of Salmon along Salmon River (lat. 41°15'50" N, long. 123°19'55" W); the place is just downstream from the mouth of Horn Creek. Named on Forks of Salmon (1978) 7.5' quadrangle.

Horn Peak [SISKIYOU]: *peak,* 1.5 miles north-northeast of Hornbrook (lat. 41°56' N, long. 122°32'20" W; sec. 9, T 47 N, R 6 W). Altitude 3645 feet. Named on Hornbrook (1955) 15' quadrangle.

Horr Pond [SHASTA]: *lake,* 1.25 miles long, 7.25 miles north of Fall River Mills along Tule River (lat. 41°06'30" N, long. 121°26' W). Named on Fall River Mills (1961) 15' quadrangle.

Horrs Four Corners [SHASTA]: *locality,* 10 miles northeast of Burney Falls (lat. 41°07'20" N, long. 121°31'15" W; near NW cor. sec. 21, T 38 N, R 4 E). Named on Pondosa (1961) 15' quadrangle.

Horseback Ridge [TEHAMA]: *ridge,* generally northwest-trending, 2.5 miles long, 2.5 miles southwest of Panther Spring (lat. 40°13'10" N, long. 121°48' W). Named on Panther Spring (1953) 15' quadrangle.

Horsebone Ridge [SHASTA]: *ridge,* generally southwest-trending, 1 mile long, 3.5 miles north of Schell Mountain (lat. 40°54'10" N, long. 122°32'30" W; sec. 9, 10, T 35 N, R 6 W). Named on Schell Mountain (1950) 15' quadrangle.

Horse Camp [SISKIYOU]: *locality,* 8 miles north of the village of Seiad Valley (lat. 41°57'25" N, long. 123°10'20" W). Named on Kangaroo Mountain (1980) 7.5' quadrangle.

Horse Camp: see **Shasta Alpine Lodge** [SISKIYOU].

Horse Creek [SHASTA]:
(1) *stream,* flows 1 mile to Squaw Creek (2) 3 miles south-southeast of Shoeinhorse Mountain (lat. 41°01'45" N, long. 122°03'15" W). Named on Shoeinhorse Mountain (1954) 15' quadrangle.
(2) *stream,* flows 2.5 miles to Squaw Creek Arm Shasta Lake 10 miles south of Bollibokka Mountain (lat. 40°47'15" N, long. 122°12'25" W; sec. 21, T 34 N, R 3 W); the stream is east of Horse Mountain. Named on Bollibokka Mountain (1957) 15' quadrangle.

Horse Creek [SISKIYOU]:
(1) *stream,* flows 3.5 miles to Klamath River 3.25 miles east-southeast of Happy Camp (lat. 41°47' N, long. 123°18'55" W; sec. 17, T 16 N, R 8 E). Named on Slater Butte (1980) 7.5' quadrangle.
(2) *stream,* formed by the confluence of East Fork and West Fork, flows 9 miles to Klamath River 10 miles east of the village of Seiad Valley (lat. 41°49'25" N, long. 123°00'15" W; near SE cor. sec. 16, T 46 N, R 10 W). Named on Dutch Creek (1980) and Hamburg (1980) 7.5' quadrangles. East Fork is 3.5 miles long and West Fork is 3 miles long; both forks are named on Dutch Creek (1980) 7.5' quadrangle.
(3) *stream,* flows less than 1 mile to South Fork Salmon River 5.25 miles west-northwest of Cecilville (lat. 41°10'35" N, long. 123°13'15" W). Named on Cecilville (1979) 7.5' quadrangle.
(4) *village,* 10 miles east of the village of Seiad Valley near the mouth of Horse Creek (2) (lat. 41°49'30" N, long. 123°00' W; near S line sec. 15, T 46 N, R 10 W). Named on Condrey Mountain (1955) and Seiad Valley (1955) 15' quadrangles. Postal authorities established Horsecreek post office in 1907, discontinued it in 1911, and reestablished it with the name "Horse Creek" in 1930 (Salley, p. 100).

Horse Creek: see **Horse Range Creek** [SISKIYOU].

Horsefly Spring [SISKIYOU]: *spring,* 6 miles north-northwest of the village of Seiad Valley (lat. 41°55'20" N, long. 123°13'55" W). Named on Kangaroo Mountain (1980) 7.5' quadrangle.

Horse Gulch [TEHAMA]: *canyon,* drained by a stream that flows 2.5 miles to Dry Creek (1) 4 miles north-northwest of Rosewood (lat. 40°17'40" N, long. 122°37'15" W; sec. 11, T 28 N, R 7 W). Named on Ono (1952) 15' quadrangle.

Horse Heaven Buttes [SHASTA]: *peaks,* two, 19 miles north-northwest of Lassen Peak (lat. 40°44'10" N, long. 121°37'50" W). Altitude of highest peak is 5853 feet. Named on Manzanita Lake (1956) 15' quadrangle.

Horse Lake [SHASTA]: *lake,* 150 feet long, 11 miles north-northeast of the village of Big Bend (lat. 41°09'45" N, long. 121°49'15" W; sec. 11, T 38 N, R 1 E). Named on Big Bend (1961) 15' quadrangle.

Horse Mountain [SHASTA]: *peak,* 9.5 miles south of Bollibokka Mountain (lat. 40°48'10" N, long. 122°14'10" W; sec. 18, T 34 N, R 3 W). Altitude 4025 feet. Named on Bollibokka Mountain (1957) 15' quadrangle.

Horse Mountain [SISKIYOU]: *peak,* 8.5 miles east of Salmon Mountain (lat. 41°09'15" N, long. 123°15'05" W). Named on Youngs Peak (1979) 7.5' quadrangle.

Horse Peak [SISKIYOU]: *peak,* 16 miles north of Bartle (lat. 41°29'25" N, long. 121°51'30" W; sec. 16, T 42 N, R 1 E). Altitude 6525 feet. Named on Bartle (1961) 15' quadrangle.

Horse Peak: see **Little Horse Peak** [SISKIYOU].

Horse Pocket [SISKIYOU]: *area,* 4.5 miles south of Ukonom Lake (lat. 41°30'45" N, long. 123°21'20" W). Named on Ukonom Lake (1980) 7.5' quadrangle.

Horse Range Creek [SISKIYOU]: *stream,* flows 4.5 miles to French Creek (2) 7 miles south of Etna (lat. 41°21'30" N, long. 122°54'10" W; sec. 32, T 41 N, R 9 W); the stream heads at Horse Range Lakes. Named on Etna (1955) 15' quadrangle. Called Horse Cr. on Etna (1934) 30' quadrangle. United States Board on Geographic Names (1983b, p. 6) approved the name "North Fork Horse Range Creek" for a tributary, 2.5 miles long, that enters Horse Range Creek 8 miles south-southwest of Etna (lat. 41°20'52" N, long. 122°55'06" W)—the Board at the same time rejected the form "North Fork of Horse Range Creek" for the name.

Horse Range Lake [SISKIYOU]: *lake,* 450 feet long, 9.5 miles north-northwest of Sawyers Bar (lat. 41°25'35" N, long. 123°12'20" W). Named on English Peak (1977) 7.5' quadrangle.

Horse Range Lakes [SISKIYOU]: *lakes,* three, largest 400 feet long, 10.5 miles south-southwest of Etna (lat. 41°18'55" N, long. 122°57'35" W; sec. 24, T 40 N, R 10 W). Named on Etna (1955) 15' quadrangle.

Horse Ridge [SHASTA]: *ridge,* northwest-trending, 3 miles long, 4 miles northeast of Bollibokka Mountain (lat. 40°57'50" N, long. 122°09'30" W). Named on Bollibokka Mountain (1957) 15' quadrangle.

Horseshoe Bend [SISKIYOU]: *bend,* 6.5 miles southeast of Cecilville along South Fork Salmon River (lat. 41°05'05" N, long. 123°02'10" W). Named on Thompson Peak (1979) 7.5' quadrangle.

Horseshoe Gulch [SISKIYOU]: *canyon,* drained by a stream that flows 2 miles to McConaughy Gulch 6.25 miles east-southeast of Etna (lat. 41°25'40" N, long. 122°46'50" W; sec. 4, T 41 N, R 8 W). Named on Etna (1955) 15' quadrangle.

Horseshoe Gulch [TEHAMA]: *canyon,* drained by a stream that flows less than 1 mile to Sulphur Gulch (1) 6 miles east-southeast of Beegum Peak (lat. 40°16'55" N, long. 122°47' W; at E line sec. 17, T 28 N, R 8 W). Named on Chanchelulla Peak (1951) 15' quadrangle.

Horseshoe Lake [BUTTE]: *lake,* 1100 feet long, 4.25 miles northeast of downtown Chico (lat. 39°46'20" N, long. 121°46'50" W). Named on Richardson Springs (1951) 7.5' quadrangle.

Horseshoe Lake [SHASTA]: *lake,* 3300 feet long, 9 miles east of Lassen Peak (lat. 40°28'20" N, long. 121°20'15" W; sec. 8, T 30 N, R 6 E). Named on Mount Harkness (1956) 15' quadrangle. United States Board on Geographic Names (1933, p. 374) rejected the names "Grassy Lake" and "Twin Lakes" for the feature.

Horseshoe Lake [SISKIYOU]: *lake,* 800 feet long, 10 miles south-southwest of Etna (lat. 41°19'20" N, long. 122°56'45" W; at N line sec. 18, T 40 N, R 9 W). Named on Etna (1955) 15' quadrangle.

Horsetail Falls [SISKIYOU]: *waterfall,* 7 miles north-northeast of the village of Seiad Valley on a branch of East Fork Seiad Creek (lat. 41°55'45" N, long. 123°07'45" W). Named on Kangaroo Mountain (1980) 7.5' quadrangle.

Horsethief Bend: see **Bend** [TEHAMA].

Horsethief Butte [SISKIYOU]: *peak,* 10.5 miles south of Macdoel (lat. 41°40'50" N, long. 122°02'15" W; near NW cor. sec. 12, T 44 N, R 2 W). Altitude 5681 feet. Named on The Whaleback (1954) 15' quadrangle.

Horsethief Canyon [BUTTE]: *canyon,* drained by a stream that flows 4.5 miles to Dry Creek 8.5 miles south of Paradise (lat. 39°37'50" N, long. 121°37'05" W; at E line sec. 34, T 21 N, R 3 E). Named on Cherokee (1970) 7.5' quadrangle.

Horsethief Creek [SISKIYOU]: *stream,* flows 6.5 miles to lowlands 11.5 miles south-southwest of Macdoel (lat. 41°39'45" N, long. 122°02'50" W; sec. 14, T 44 N, R 2 W); the stream is west of Horsethief Butte. Named on The Whaleback (1954) 15' quadrangle.

Horsetown: see **Reading Bar** [SHASTA].

Horse Trough Creek [TEHAMA]: *stream,* flows 2.5 miles to Thomes Creek 9.5 miles west of Paskenta (lat. 39°51'35" N, long. 122°43'10" W; near SE cor. sec. 11, T 23 N, R 8 W); the stream is southeast of Horse Trough Ridge. Named on Hall Ridge (1967) 7.5' quadrangle.

Horse Trough Ridge [TEHAMA]: *ridge,* north- to northeast-trending, nearly 3 miles long, 6 miles south-southeast of Ball Mountain (lat. 39°50'50" N, long. 122°45'10" W). Named on Hall Ridge (1967) and Log Spring (1967) 7.5' quadrangles.

Hospital Rock [SISKIYOU]: *relief feature,* 8.5 miles south of Tulelake (lat. 41°50' N, long. 121°28'10" W; at N line sec. 13, T 46 N, R 4 E). Named on Tulelake (1951) 15' quadrangle.

Hospital Spring [BUTTE]: *spring,* 2.25 miles north-northwest of Oroville (lat. 39°33'15" N, long. 121°33'55" W; sec. 31, T 20 N, R 4 E). Named on Oroville (1970) 7.5' quadrangle.

Hot Creek [SISKIYOU]: *stream,* flows 3 miles to Indian Tom Lake 3 miles east-northeast of Dorris (lat. 41°59'15" N, long. 121°52'05" W; sec. 21, T 48 N, R 1 E). Named on Dorris (1950) 15' quadrangle.

Hotelling Campground [SISKIYOU]: *locality,* 8 miles east-northeast of Salmon Mountain along North Fork Salmon River (lat. 41°14'25" N, long. 123°16'30" W); the place is near the mouth of Hotelling Gulch. Named on Youngs Peak (1979) 7.5' quadrangle.

Hotelling Gulch [SISKIYOU]: *canyon,* drained by a stream that flows 1.5 miles to South Fork Salmon River 8 miles east-northeast of Salmon Mountain (lat. 41°14'20" N, long. 123°16'35" W); the feature is at the north end of Hotelling Ridge. Named on Youngs Peak (1979) 7.5' quadrangle.

Hotelling Ridge [SISKIYOU]: *ridge,* generally north-trending, 6.5 miles long, 6.25 miles east of Salmon Mountain (lat. 41°11'30" N, long. 123°17'30" W). Named on Youngs Peak (1979) 7.5' quadrangle.

Hotlum [SISKIYOU]: *locality,* 5 miles northeast of Weed along Southern Pacific Railroad (lat. 41°28'30" N, long. 122°18'50" W; sec. 21, T 42 N, R 4 W). Named on Weed (1954) 15' quadrangle.

Hotlum Glacier [SISKIYOU]: *glacier,* 11.5 miles north of McCloud on Mount Shasta (lat. 41°25'05" N, long. 122°11'10" W). Named on Shasta (1954) 15' quadrangle.

Hot Rock [SHASTA]: *relief feature,* nearly 3 miles north-northeast of Lassen Peak (lat. 40°32'05" N, long. 121°29'25" W; sec. 14, T 31 N, R 4 E). Named on Prospect Peak (1957) 15' quadrangle. The feature is a huge boulder that retained appreciable heat for many days after it came to rest at the site during the 1915 eruption of Mount Lassen (Schulz, p. 25, 28).

Hot Spot [SISKIYOU]: *locality,* 4.25 miles east-northeast of Medicine Lake (lat. 41°36'20" N, long. 121°31'20" W; near SW cor. sec. 33, T 44 N, R 4 E). Named on Medicine Lake (1952) 15' quadrangle.

Hot Springs Valley: see **Little Hot Springs Valley** [SHASTA].

Hot Spring Valley: see **Big Hot Spring Valley**, under **Morgan Hot Spring** [TEHAMA].

Houghton Creek [TEHAMA]: *stream,* flows 12.5 miles to Burch Creek 8 miles east of Flournoy (lat. 39°55'35" N, long. 122°16'55" W; sec. 23, T 24 N, R 4 W). Named on Flournoy (1967) and Henleyville (1967) 7.5' quadrangles.

Houston [SHASTA]: *locality,* 7 miles northeast of Redding (lat. 40°39' N, long. 122°18' W; near SE cor. sec. 3, T 32 N, R 4 W). Named on Redding (1901) 30' quadrangle.

Houston [SISKIYOU]: *locality,* 15 miles east-southeast of Etna (lat. 41°22'45" N, long. 122°36'55" W; near SE cor. sec. 23, T 41 N, R 7 W). Named on Etna (1934) 30' quadrangle. China Mountain (1955) 15' quadrangle shows Houston cabin at the site.

Houston Creek [SISKIYOU]: *stream,* flows 4.5 miles to East Fork Scott River 13 miles east-southeast of Etna (lat. 41°24'10" N, long. 122°38'50" W; sec. 15, T 41 N, R 7 W). Named on China Mountain (1955) 15' quadrangle.

Houston Creek: see **Little Houston Creek** [SISKIYOU].

Hovey Gulch [SISKIYOU]: *canyon,* drained by a stream that flows 2.25 miles to the valley of Little Shasta River 20 miles west-southwest of Macdoel (lat. 41°43'55" N, long. 122°22'15" W; sec. 24, T 45 N, R 5 W). Named on Copco (1954) and Lake Shastina (1954) 15' quadrangles.

Hovey Point [SISKIYOU]: *promontory,* 9 miles east of Mount Dome (lat. 41°50'15" N, long. 121°30'45" W; near SE cor. sec. 9, T 46 N, R 4 E). Named on Mount Dome (1950) 15' quadrangle.

Howard [SISKIYOU]: *locality,* less than 2 miles east of the town of Mount Shasta along Southern Pacific Railroad (lat. 41°18'45" N, long. 122°16'30" W; sec. 14, T 40 N, R 4 W). Named on Weed (1954) 15' quadrangle.

Howard Creek [GLENN]: *stream,* flows 1.5 miles to Colusa County 3 miles south of High Peak (lat. 39°23' N, long. 122°25'45" W; near W line sec. 28, T 18 N, R 5 W). Named on Lodoga (1960) 15' quadrangle.

Howard Creek [TEHAMA]: *stream,* flows 6 miles to South Fork Antelope Creek 9 miles north-northwest of Polk Springs (lat. 40°14'10" N, long. 121°43'15" W; sec. 35, T 28 N, R 2 E). Named on Butte Meadows (1958) and Lassen Peak (1956) 15' quadrangles.

Howard Meadows [TEHAMA]: *area,* 8 miles southwest of Mineral (lat. 40°15'20" N, long. 121°41' W; near NW cor. sec. 30, T 28 N, R 3 E); the place is along Howard Creek. Named on Lassen Peak (1956) 15' quadrangle.

Howards Gulch [SISKIYOU]: *canyon,* drained by a stream that flows 1.25 miles to Klamath River 9.5 miles east of the village of Seiad Valley (lat. 41°49'10" N, long. 123°00'50" W; sec. 21, T 46 N, R 10 E); the mouth of the canyon is about 1 mile upstream from the mouth of present Sambo Gulch. Named on Hamburg (1980) 7.5' quadrangle. Called Sambo Gulch on Seiad Valley (1955) 15' quadrangle, but United States Board on Geographic Names (1981b, p. 3) rejected this name for the canyon; the Board noted that the name "Howard Gulch" is for Howard Sambo, who lived at the mouth of the feature and had a placer claim there.

Howards Gulch: see **Sambo Gulch** [SISKIYOU].

Howard Slough [GLENN]: *stream,* diverges from Butte Creek [BUTTE-GLENN] and flows 5.25 miles before rejoining Butte Creek [BUTTE-GLENN] 7.5 miles southeast of Butte City (lat. 39°23'10" N, long. 121°53'20" W; sec. 29, T 18 N, R 1 E). Named on Butte City (1952) and West of Biggs (1952) 7.5' quadrangles.

Howard Springs [SHASTA]: *spring,* 21 miles northwest of Lassen Peak (lat. 40°43'30" N, long. 121°44'45" W; near SE cor. sec. 9, T 33 N, R 2 E). Named on Manzanita Lake (1956) 15' quadrangle.

Howell Ridge [TEHAMA]: *ridge,* generally west-trending, 5.5 miles long, 8 miles south of Manton (lat. 40°19'30" N, long. 121°49'30" W). Named on Manton (1956) 15' quadrangle.

Howell Saddle [TEHAMA]: *pass,* 1 mile east-northeast of Ball Mountain (lat. 39°56'15" N, long. 122°45'45" W; sec. 16, T 24 N, R 8 W). Named on Ball Mountain (1967) 7.5' quadrangle.

Howell Valley [TEHAMA]: *canyon,* about 19 miles west of Red Bluff (lat. 40°13'30" N, long. 122°34'30" W). Named on Red Bluff (1894) 1° quadrangle.

Howe Point: see **Hardin Butte** [SISKIYOU].

Howitzer Point [SISKIYOU]; *peak,* 7 miles east-northeast of Mount Dome (lat. 41°49'50" N, long. 121°33'35" W; sec. 18, T 46 N, R 4 E). Named on Mount Dome (1950) 15' quadrangle.

Hubbard Gulch [TEHAMA]: *canyon,* drained by a stream that flows 3.5 miles to lowlands 5 miles northeast of Los Molinos (lat. 40°04'20" N, long. 122°01'30" W; near S line sec. 30, T 26 N, R 1 W). Named on Panther Spring (1953) 15' quadrangle, and on Los Molinos (1952) 7.5' quadrangle. Called Hibbard Gulch on Mineral (1941) 30' quadrangle.

Hubbard Valley [GLENN]: *valley,* 5.5 miles south of Fruto (lat. 39°30'40" N, long. 122°25'50" W). Named on Fruto (1968) 7.5' quadrangle.

Huckleberry Creek [SHASTA-SISKIYOU]: *stream,* heads in Siskiyou County and flows 4 miles to McCloud River [SHASTA-SISKIYOU] 6 miles southeast of McCloud in Shasta County (lat. 41°11' N, long. 122°04'20" W; sec. 34, T 39 N, R 2 W). Named on Shoeinhorse Mountain (1954) 15' quadrangle.

Huckleberry Lake [SHASTA]: *lake,* 500 feet long, 14 miles northwest of Lassen Peak and 0.5 mile north-northwest of Manzanita Lake (lat. 40°38'45" N, long. 121°39'15" W; at SE cor. sec. 5, T 32 N, R 3 E). Named on Manzanita Lake (1956) 15' quadrangle.

Huckleberry Lake [TEHAMA]: *lake,* 850 feet long, 5 miles north-northeast of Mineral (lat. 40°24'25" N, long. 121°32'50" W; near N line sec. 4, T 29 N, R 4 E). Named on Lassen Peak (1956) 15' quadrangle.

Huckleberry Meadows [SHASTA]: *area,* 14 miles northwest of Lassen Peak (lat. 40°38'55" N, long. 121°40'05" W; near SW cor. sec. 5, T 32 N, R 3 E); the place is 1 mile northwest of Huckleberry Mountain. Named on Manzanita Lake (1956) 15' quadrangle.

Huckleberry Mountain [SHASTA]: *peak,* 13 miles northwest of Lassen Peak (lat. 40°38'20" N, long. 121°39'05" W; on W line sec. 9, T 32 N, R 3 E). Altitude 7064 feet. Named on Manzanita Lake (1956) 15' quadrangle.

Huckleberry Mountain [SISKIYOU]: *peak,* 9 miles north-northeast of Ukonom Lake (lat. 41°41'25" N, long. 123°15'40" W). Altitude 6293 feet. Named on Huckleberry Mountain (1980) 7.5' quadrangle.

Hudson Creek: see **Hutton Creek** [SISKIYOU].

Hufford Lake [SHASTA]: *lake,* 700 feet long, 15 miles north-northwest of Lassen Peak (lat. 40°42'10" N, long. 121°34'20" W; near W line sec. 19, T

33 N, R 4 E). Named on Manzanita Lake (1956) 15' quadrangle. Called Huffard Lake on Burney (1939) 30' quadrangle.

Huffs Bar: see **Nolton Creek** [BUTTE].

Huling Creek [SHASTA]: *stream,* flows nearly 6 miles to North Fork Cottonwood Creek [SHASTA-TEHAMA] (lat. 40°27'15" N, long. 122°33'35" W; sec. 17, T 30 N, R 6 W). Named on Ono (1952) 15' quadrangle, and on Igo (1979) 7.5' quadrangle. The name recalls William Huling, who settled by the stream in 1851 (Steger, p. 40).

Hull Canyon [TEHAMA]: *canyon,* 1 mile long, 4.5 miles northwest of Paskenta (lat. 39°56'10" N, long. 122°36'20" W; sec. 13, T 24 N, R 7 W). Named on Paskenta (1967) 7.5' quadrangle.

Humboldt Peak [BUTTE]: *peak,* 3.25 miles northeast of Jonesville on Butte-Plumas County line (lat. 40°09' N, long. 121°25'45" W). Altitude 7087 feet. Named on Jonesville (1958) 15' quadrangle.

Humboldt Summit [BUTTE-TEHAMA]: *pass,* 3.25 miles north-northeast of Jonesville, where Butte County, Tehama County, and Plumas County meet at a common point (lat. 40°09'10" N, long. 121°26'05" W); the pass is just west of Humboldt Peak. Named on Jonesville (1958) 15' quadrangle.

Humbug: see **Humbug Creek** [SISKIYOU].

Humbug City: see **Humbug Creek** [SISKIYOU].

Humbug Creek [SISKIYOU]: *stream,* flows 11.5 miles to Klamath River 7 miles north-northwest of Yreka (lat. 41°50'05" N, long. 122°39'50" W; sec. 16, T 46 N, R 7 W). Named on Condrey Mountain (1955) and Hornbrook (1955) 15' quadrangles. Middle Fork enters 5.5 miles upstream from the mouth of the main stream; it is nearly 4 miles long and is named on Condrey Mountain (1955), Fort Jones (1955), and Hornbrook (1955) 15' quadrangles. South Fork enters Middle Fork from the southeast near the mouth of Middle Fork; it is 2 miles long and is named on Hornbrook (1955) 15' quadrangle. Clark (p. 138) noted that a community called Humbug City was founded in 1851 in the neighborhood of Humbug Creek—the community first was called Humbug Creek, and later was called Humbug (Hanna, p. 144). Postal authorities established Humbug Creek post office 8 miles northwest of Yreka in 1861 and discontinued it in 1862 (Salley, p. 101). A mining camp called Freetown was situated 2 miles above Humbug City in the 1850's (Gudde, 1975, p. 121).

Humbug Creek: see **Little Humbug Creek** [SISKIYOU].

Humbug Gulch [SISKIYOU]: *canyon,* drained by a stream that flows 2 miles to lowlands 0.5 mile west-northwest of Yreka (lat. 41°44'15" N, long. 122°39'30" W; sec. 21, T 45 N, R 7 W). Named on Yreka (1954) 15' quadrangle.

Humbug Point [SISKIYOU]: *bend,* 8 miles southwest of Hornbrook along Klamath River (lat. 41°49'40" N, long. 122°39'30" W); the bend is just upstream from the mouth of Humbug Creek. Named on Hornbrook (1955) 15' quadrangle.

Humbug Summit [BUTTE]: *pass,* 4.5 miles east of Jonesville on Butte-Plumas County line (lat. 40°06'30" N, long. 121°22'45" W; sec. 14, T 26 N, R 5 E). Named on Jonesville (1958) 15' quadrangle.

Hume [BUTTE]: *locality,* 3.5 miles east-northeast of Biggs along Northern Electric Railroad (lat. 39°25'40" N, long. 121°38'55" W). Named on Biggs (1912) 7.5' quadrangle.

Hummingbird Creek [SISKIYOU]: *stream,* flows nearly 2 miles to Elk Creek 4.5 miles northeast of Ukonom Lake (lat. 41°37'05" N, long. 123°17'05" W). Named on Ukonom Lake (1980) 7.5' quadrangle.

Hummingbird Spring [GLENN]: *spring,* 10 miles northwest of the village of Elk Creek (lat. 39°42'25" N, long. 122°39'35" W). Named on Alder Springs (1967) 7.5' quadrangle.

Humpback Ridge [SISKIYOU]: *ridge,* north-trending, 1 mile long, 2.5 miles south of Sawyers Bar (lat. 41°15'40" N, long. 123°07'35" W). Named on Sawyers Bar (1979) 7.5' quadrangle.

Hump Hill [BUTTE]: *peak,* 7.25 miles east-southeast of Paradise (lat. 39°42'05" N, long. 121°30'30" W; near E line sec. 3, T 21 N, R 4 E). Altitude 1838 feet. Named on Cherokee (1970) 7.5' quadrangle.

Hungry Creek [SISKIYOU]: *stream,* flows 4.5 miles to Beaver Creek (1) 11 miles east of Condrey Mountain (lat. 41°58'20" N, long. 122°46'35" W; at N line sec. 33, T 48 N, R 8 W). Named on Condrey Mountain (1955) and Hornbrook (1955) 15' quadrangles. The name is attributed to the condition of the men who discovered of the stream—they were stranded by snow and had no provisions (Gudde, 1949, p. 157).

Hungry Creek: see **North Hungry Creek** [SISKIYOU].

Hungry Hollow [SISKIYOU]: *relief feature,* 3.25 miles southeast of Fort Jones (lat. 41°34'30" N, long. 122°47'30" W). Named on Fort Jones (1955) 15' quadrangle. The feature includes part of Hamlin Gulch and a branch of Hamlin Gulch.

Hungry Hollow [TEHAMA]: *canyon,* drained by a stream that flows 6.25 miles to the canyon of Red Bank Creek at Red Bank (lat. 40°05'45" N, long. 122°26'40" W; at E line sec. 20, T 26 N, R 5 W). Named on Lowery (1967) and Red Bank (1952) 7.5' quadrangles.

Hungry Hunt Peak [BUTTE]: *peak,* 2.5 miles south-southeast of Pulga (lat. 39°45'55" N, long. 121°26'10" W; sec. 17, T 22 N, R 5 E). Altitude 4041 feet. Named on Pulga (1979) 7.5' quadrangle.

Hunt: see **Dan Hunt Meadows** [SHASTA]; **Dan Hunt Mountain** [SHASTA].

Hunt Creek [SHASTA]: *stream,* flows 2.5 miles to West Hunt Creek 9 miles east-northeast of Whitmore (lat. 40°42'05" N, long. 121°46'40" W; sec. 20, T 33 N, R 2 E). Named on Whitmore (1956) 15' quadrangle.

Hunt Creek: see **West Hunt Creek** [SHASTA].

Hunter Creek [GLENN]: *stream,* flows 2.25 miles to Black Butte River 6 miles south of Black Butte (lat. 39°38'35" N, long. 122°53'15" W). Named on Plaskett Meadows (1967) and Plaskett Ridge (1967) 7.5' quadrangles.

Hunter Ridge [GLENN]: *ridge,* west-trending, 1 mile long, 4.25 miles south of Black Butte (lat. 39°39'55" N, long. 122°52' W). Named on Plaskett Meadows (1967) 7.5' quadrangle.

Hunters: see **Red Bluff** [TEHAMA].

Hunters Creek [GLENN]: *stream,* flows 14 miles to Colusa County 9.5 miles south of Willows (lat. 39°23'05" N, long. 122°13' W; sec. 29, T 18 N, R 3 W). Named on Lodoga (1960) 15' quadrangle, and on Logandale (1952) and Logan Ridge (1958) 7.5' quadrangles.

Hunters Gulch [SISKIYOU]: *canyon,* 1 mile long, opens into the canyon of Indian Creek (3) nearly 3 miles north-northwest of Fort Jones (lat. 41°38'20" N, long. 122°52'15" W; sec. 27, T 44 N, R 9 W). Named on Fort Jones (1955) 15' quadrangle.

Hunters Hill [SISKIYOU]: *ridge,* southwest-trending, 1 mile long, 10 miles northeast of Bartle (lat. 41°22' N, long. 121°41'15" W; sec. 25, T 41 N, R 2 E). Named on Hambone (1961) 15' quadrangle.

Hunt Hot Spring [SHASTA]: *spring,* 1.5 miles northwest of Big Bend (lat. 41°02' N, long. 121°55'45" W; on W line sec. 25, T 37 N, R 1 W). Named on Big Bend (1961) 15' quadrangle.

Hunt Meadows: see **Dan Hunt Meadows** [SHASTA].

Hunts Creek [SISKIYOU]: *stream,* flows 3 miles to Cottonwood Creek (1) 7 miles northwest of Hornbrook (lat. 41°59'20" N, long. 122°38'10" W; near S line sec. 22, T 48 N, R 7 W). Named on Hornbrook (1955) 15' quadrangle.

Hupp: see **De Sabla** [BUTTE].

Hupps Mill: see **De Sabla** [BUTTE].

Hurds Gulch [SISKIYOU]: *canyon,* 2 miles long, opens into Scott Valley 4.5 miles south-southeast of Fort Jones (lat. 41°32'45" N, long. 122°49' W; at W line sec. 30, T 43 N, R 8 W). Named on Fort Jones (1955) 15' quadrangle.

Hurleton [BUTTE]: *village,* 7.5 miles north of Bangor (lat. 39°29'50" N, long. 121°23'10" W; near NW cor. sec. 23, T 19 N, R 5 E). Named on Bangor (1947) 7.5' quadrangle.

Hutchins Mill [BUTTE]: *locality,* 2.5 miles north-northwest of Pulga (lat. 39°50'05" N, long. 121°27'30" W). Named on Bidwell Bar (1897) 30' quadrangle.

Hutton: see **Eileen** [SISKIYOU].

Hutton Creek [SISKIYOU]: *stream,* heads in the State of Oregon and flows 6 miles in Siskiyou County to Cottonwood Creek (1) nearly 2 miles northwest of Hornbrook (lat. 41°55'45" N, long. 122°34'50" W; at N line sec. 18, T 47 N, R 6 W). Named on Hornbrook (1955) 15' quadrangle. Called Hudson Creek on Shasta (1894) 1° quadrangle.

Hylandville: see **Bangor** [BUTTE].

— I —

I-Am-Up- Ridge [SISKIYOU]: *ridge,* generally west-southwest-trending, 4.5 miles long, 7 miles east-northeast of Cecilville (lat. 41°11'30" N, long. 123°01'10" W). Named on Coffee Creek (1955) 15' quadrangle, and on Grasshopper Ridge (1979) 7.5' quadrangle.

Ice Cave Mountain [TEHAMA]: *peak,* 6 miles north-northeast of Deer Creek Station on Tehama-Plumas County line (lat. 40°20'20" N, long. 121°23'40" W; sec. 26, T 29 N, R 5 E). Named on Mount Harkness (1956) 15' quadrangle, which shows an ice cave located 1.5 miles west of the peak.

Ice Spring [GLENN]: *spring,* 4.25 miles east of Black Butte (lat. 39°48'40" N, long. 122°47'30" W; sec. 32, T 22 N, R 8 W). Named on Plaskett Meadows (1967) 7.5' quadrangle.

Ida Creek [GLENN]: *stream,* flows 1.25 miles to North Fork (1) Stony Creek [GLENN-TEHAMA] 3 miles east of Saint John Mountain (lat. 39°26'10" N, long. 122°38'05" W). Named on Saint John Mountain (1968) 7.5' quadrangle.

Ides Cove [TEHAMA]: *relief feature,* 7.5 miles south of Tomhead Mountain (lat. 40°01'55" N, long. 122°50'35" W; near E line sec. 10, T 25 N, R 9 W). Named on Yolla Bolly (1954) 15' quadrangle.

Idlewild Campground [SISKIYOU]: *locality,* 4.25 miles east-northeast of Sawyers Bar along North Fork Salmon River (lat. 41°19'50" N, long. 123°03'30" W). Named on Tanners Peak (1977) 7.5' quadrangle.

Igerna [SISKIYOU]: *locality,* less than 2 miles south of Weed along Southern Pacific Railroad (lat. 41°24' N, long. 122°22'45" W; near W line sec. 13, T 41 N, R 5 W). Named on Weed (1954) 15' quadrangle. Postal authorities established Igerna post office in 1888 and discontinued it in 1912 (Frickstad, p. 188).

Igo [SHASTA]: *village,* 10 miles southwest of Redding (lat. 40°30'20" N, long. 122°32'25" W; at SW cor. sec. 27, T 31 N, R 6 W). Named on Igo (1979) 7.5' quadrangle. Postal authorities established Igo post office in 1873 (Frickstad, p. 180). They established Roaring River post office 12 miles south of Igo near the stream called Roaring River (SW quarter sec. 4, T 29 N, R 6 W) in 1874 and discontinued it in 1887 (Salley, p. 186).

Ike Dye Hill [TEHAMA]: *peak,* 3 miles southeast of Polk Springs (lat. 40°05'20" N, long. 121°37'15" W; sec. 22, T 26 N, R 3 E). Named on Butte Meadows (1958) 15' quadrangle.

Ikes Creek [SISKIYOU]:

(1) *stream,* flows 2.5 miles to Indian Creek (1) 2.5 miles north of Happy Camp (lat. 41°49'55" N, long. 123°22'50" W); the stream heads at Slater Butte. Named on Happy Camp (1980) and Slater Butte (1980) 7.5' quadrangles. Called Slater Creek on Happy Camp (1956) 15' quadrangle, but United States Board on Geographic Names (1981c, p. 4) rejected this name for the stream, and pointed out that the name "Ikes Creek" commemorates Ike Hendrickson, who homesteaded in the neighborhood.

(2) *stream,* flows 3.5 miles to Butte Valley 8 miles west-northwest of Macdoel (lat. 41°51'50" N, long. 123°08'10" W; near N line sec. 6, T 46 N, R 2 W). Named on Macdoel (1954) 15' quadrangle.

Ikes Flat [SISKIYOU]: *area,* 7.5 miles west-northwest of Macdoel (lat. 41°52'20" N, long. 122°08'10" W; sec. 31, T 47 N, R 2 W); the place is just east of Ikes Mountain. Named on Macdoel (1954) 15' quadrangle.

Ikes Mountain [SISKIYOU]: *peak,* 8 miles west-northwest of Macdoel (lat. 41°52'25" N, long. 122°08'50" W; near W line sec. 31, T 47 N, R 2 W); the peak is north of Ikes Creek (2). Altitude 5493 feet. Named on Macdoel (1954) 15' quadrangle.

Incline: see **The Incline** [SHASTA].

Incline Ridge [SISKIYOU]: *ridge,* northwest-trending, 1 mile long, 3 miles south-southeast of Sawyers Bar (lat. 41°15'15" N, long. 123°06'20" W). Named on Tanners Peak (1977) 7.5' quadrangle.

Inconstance Creek [SISKIYOU]: *stream,* flows 5 miles to lowlands 15 miles north of McCloud (lat. 41°28'45" N, long. 122°08' W; near NE cor. sec. 24, T 42 N, R 3 W). Named on Shasta (1954) 15' quadrangle. Called Mountainhouse Creek on Dunsmuir (1935) 30' quadrangle, but United States Board on Geographic Names (1980, p. 3) rejected the names "Mountainhouse Creek" and "Mountain House Creek" for the stream. On Dunsmuir (1935) 30' quadrangle, the name "Inconstance Creek" applies to present Whitney Creek.

Independence Creek [SISKIYOU]: *stream,* flows 9.5 miles to Klamath River 7.5 miles northwest of Ukonom Lake (lat. 41°39'30" N, long. 123°27' W); the stream heads near Independence Lake and goes through Independence Valley. Named on Clear Creek (1981), Ukonom Lake (1980), and Ukonom Mountain (1980) 7.5' quadrangles.

Independence Lake [SISKIYOU]: *lake,* 200 feet long, 0.5 mile east-northeast of Ukonom Lake (lat. 47°35'10" N, long. 123°20'35" W). Named on Ukonom Lake (1980) 7.5' quadrangle.

Independence Valley [SISKIYOU]: *valley,* 1.5 miles north-northeast of Ukonom Lake (lat. 41°36' N, long. 122°20'50" W); the valley is along upper reaches of Independence Creek. Named on Ukonom Lake (1980) 7.5' quadrangle.

Indian Bar: see **Indian Creek** [SISKIYOU] (1).

Indian Butte [SISKIYOU]: *hill,* 6 miles northeast of Medicine Lake (lat. 41°38'10" N, long. 121°30' W; on E line sec. 21, T 44 N, R 4 E). Altitude 6818 feet. Named on Medicine Lake (1952) 7.5' quadrangle.

Indian Creek [BUTTE]: *stream,* flows 2.25 miles to Middle Fork Feather River 2.5 miles east-southeast of the village of Brush Creek (lat. 39°40'30" N, long. 121°17'45" W). Named on Brush Creek (1970) 7.5' quadrangle.

Indian Creek [SHASTA]:

(1) *stream,* flows 2 miles to Castle Creek 0.5 mile north-northwest of Castella (lat. 41°08'50" N, long. 122°19'50" W; near SE cor. sec. 16, T 38 N, R 4 W). Named on Dunsmuir (1954) 15' quadrangle.

(2) *stream,* flows 2.5 miles to Nelson Creek (1) 5.5 miles northeast of Big Bend (lat. 41°04'15" N, long. 121°49'35" W; sec. 14, T 37 N, R 1 E). Named on Big Bend (1961) 15' quadrangle.

(3) *stream,* flows 2 miles to Sacramento River Arm Shasta Lake 7 miles south-southeast of Lamoine (lat. 40°53'40" N, long. 122°21'40" W; near N line sec. 18, T 35 N, R 4 W). Named on Lamoine (1957) 15' quadrangle.

Indian Creek [SISKIYOU]:

(1) *stream,* flows 18 miles to Klamath River at Happy Camp (lat. 41°47'25" N, long. 123°22'40" W; sec. 11, T 16 N, R 7 E). Named on Deadman Point (1981), Happy Camp (1980), and Polar Bear Mountain (1982) 7.5' quadrangles. East Fork heads in the State of Oregon and enters the main stream 6.25 miles north-northwest of Happy Camp; it is 10.5 miles long in Siskiyou County and is named on Happy Camp (1980) 7.5' quadrangle. South Fork enters the main stream 6.25 miles north-northwest of Happy Camp; it is 11.5 miles long and is named on Deadman Point (1981), Happy Camp (1980), and Preston Peak (1982) 7.5' quadrangles. Little South Fork enters South Fork 8 miles northwest of Happy Camp; it is 5.5 miles long and is named on Happy Camp (1980) and Preston Peak (1982) 7.5' quadrangles. West Fork of Little South Fork enters Little South Fork 1.5 miles upstream from the mouth of Little South Fork; it is 3.5 miles long and is named on Happy Camp (1980) and Preston Peak (1982) 7.5' quadrangles. West Branch Indian Creek enters the main stream from the west 11 miles north-northwest of Happy Camp; it is 4.5 miles long and is named on Deadman Point (1981) and Polar Bear Mountain (1982) 7.5' quadrangles. Gudde (1975, p. 167) listed a mining place called Indian Bar that was situated at the mouth of Indian Creek (1).

(2) *stream,* flows 4.5 miles to South Fork Salmon River nearly 7 miles northwest of Cecilville (lat. 41°12'40" N, long. 123°13'50" W). Named on Cecilville (1979) and Sawyers Bar (1979) 7.5' quadrangles.

(3) *stream,* flows 10 miles to Scott River 2 miles west-northwest of Fort Jones (lat. 41°37' N, long. 122°52'40" W; sec. 33, T 44 N, R 9 W). Named on Fort Jones (1955) 15' quadrangle. West Branch enters from the north-northwest 7.5 miles north of Fort Jones; it is 1.5 miles long and is named on Fort Jones (1955) 15' quadrangle.

(4) *stream,* flows 3 miles to Deer Creek (2) 18 miles west-northwest of Macdoel (lat. 41°58'10" N, long. 122°18'10" W; at W line sec. 34, T 48 N, R 4 W). Named on Copco (1954) 15' quadrangle.

Indian Creek [TEHAMA]: *stream,* flows 5 miles to Antelope Creek nearly 6 miles west of Panther Spring (lat. 40°14' N, long. 121°52'40" W; near E line sec. 32, T 28 N, R 1 E). Named on Panther Spring (1953) 15' quadrangle.

Indian Creek Baldy [SISKIYOU]: *peak,* 9 miles north of Fort Jones (lat. 41°44'20" N, long. 122°49'40" W; sec. 24, T 45 N, R 9 W); the peak is at the head of Indian Creek (3). Altitude 6275 feet. Named on Fort Jones (1955) 15' quadrangle.

Indian Fishery [BUTTE-GLENN]: *water feature,* cutoff meander of Sacramento River 6 miles west of Chico on Butte-Glenn County line (lat. 39°43'50" N, long. 121°56'50" W). Named on Ord Ferry (1949) 7.5' quadrangle.

Indian Gulch [SISKIYOU]:

(1) *canyon,* drained by a stream that flows 1 mile to South Fork Salmon River less than 0.5 mile west of Cecilville (lat. 41°08'30" N, long. 123°08'55" W). Named on Cecilville (1979) 7.5' quadrangle.

(2) *canyon,* drained by a stream that flows nearly 2 miles to the stream in McConaughy Gulch 5.5 miles east-southeast of Etna (lat. 41°24'55" N, long. 123°48'15" W; at W line sec. 8, T 41 N, R 8 W). Named on Etna (1955) 15' quadrangle.

Indian Lake [SHASTA]: *lake,* 800 feet long, 10 miles east-southeast of Lassen Peak (lat. 40°27'25" N, long. 121°19'40" W; near E line sec. 17, T 30 N, R 6 E). Named on Mount Harkness (1956) 15' quadrangle

Indian Point [SISKIYOU]:

(1) *relief feature,* 1.5 miles northeast of Forks of Salmon along North Fork Salmon River (lat. 41°16'25" N, long. 123°17'40" W). Named on Forks of Salmon (1978) 7.5' quadrangle.

(2) *promontory,* 7.5 miles north of Macdoel along Butte Valley (lat. 41°56' N, long. 122°01'30" W; in and near sec. 7, T 47 N, R 1 W). Named on Macdoel (1954) 15' quadrangle.

Indian Reservoir [SHASTA]: *intermittent lake,* 200 feet long, 11 miles north-northeast of Fall River Mills (lat. 41°08'40" N, long. 121°20'45" W; sec. 12, T 38 N, R 5 E). Named on Fall River Mills (1961) 15' quadrangle.

Indian Ridge [TEHAMA]: *ridge,* generally northwest-trending, 5.5 miles long, 4 miles southwest of Panther Spring (lat. 40°13' N, long. 121°50' W). Named on Panther Spring (1953) 15' quadrangle.

Indian Rocks [SISKIYOU]: *relief feature,* 1.25 miles north-northwest of Salmon Mountain on Siskiyou-Humboldt County line (lat. 41°12' N, long. 123°25'15" W). Named on Salmon Mountain (1978) 7.5' quadrangle.

Indian Scalp River: see **Klamath River** [SISKIYOU].

Indian Spring [SHASTA]:

(1) *spring,* 7.5 miles southeast of Lamoine (lat. 40°53'45" N, long. 122°20'15" W; near SE cor. sec. 8, T 35 N, R 4 W); the spring is at the head of a branch of Indian Creek (3). Named on Lamoine (1957) 15' quadrangle.

(2) *spring,* 4.5 miles east-southeast of the village of Montgomery Creek {lat. 40°48'45" N, long. 121°50'40" W; sec. 10, T 34 N, R 1 E). Named on Montgomery Creek (1956) 15' quadrangle. Called Indian Springs on Burney (1939) 30' quadrangle.

Indian Spring [SISKIYOU]: *spring,* 17 miles east-northeast of Bartle (lat. 41°21'15" N, long. 121°31'10" W; near NW cor. sec. 33, T 41 N, R 4 E). Named on Hambone (1961) 15' quadrangle.

Indian Spring Mountain [SISKIYOU]: *ridge,* south-trending, 3.5 miles long, 16 miles east-northeast of Bartle (lat. 41°18'45" N, long. 121°31' W). Named on Hambone (1961) 15' quadrangle.

Indian Tom Lake [SISKIYOU]: *lake,* 1 mile long, 3 miles northeast of Dorris (lat. 41°59'30" N, long. 121°52'35" W; in and near sec. 20, 21, T 48 N, R 1 E). Named on Dorris (1950) 15' quadrangle.

Indian Valley [GLENN]: *valley,* 9 miles east-southeast of Saint John Mountain on Glenn-Colusa County line (lat. 39°23'05" N, long. 122°33'15" W). Named on Stonyford (1968) 7.5' quadrangle.

Ingot [SHASTA]: *locality,* 14 miles north-northeast of Millville (lat. 40°43'40"

N, long. 122°04'35" W; sec. 10, T 33 N, R 2 W). Named on Millville (1953) 15' quadrangle. Postal authorities established Ingot post office in 1904 and discontinued it in 1940 (Frickstad, p. 180). The deserted mine and smelter of Afterthought Mining Company is at the site (Hanna, p. 149).

Initial Creek [SHASTA]: *stream,* flows 2.5 miles to Cedar Salt Log Creek 4.5 miles west-southwest of Big Bend (lat. 41°00'20" N, long. 121°59'30" W; near E line sec. 5, T 36 N, R 1 W). Named on Big Bend (1961) and Shoeinhorse Mountain (1954) 15' quadrangles.

Initial Gulch [TEHAMA]: *canyon,* drained by a stream that flows 3 miles to South Fork Battle Creek [SHASTA-TEHAMA] 4.25 miles southeast of Manton (lat. 40°22'30" N, long. 121°48'30" W; at S line sec. 12, T 29 N, R 1 E). Named on Manton (1956) 15' quadrangle.

Ink Lake [SHASTA]: *lake,* 150 feet long, nearly 3 miles south of Lassen Peak (lat. 40°27'05" N, long. 121°31' W; near NE cor. sec. 22, T 30 N, R 4 E). Named on Lassen Peak (1956) 15' quadrangle. M.J. Klausen, a ranger, named the lake for its dark color (Schulz, p. 28).

Inks Creek [TEHAMA]: *stream,* flows nearly 4 miles to Sacramento River 6 miles north-northeast of Bend (lat. 40°19'50" N, long. 122°09'05" W). Named on Bend (1965) and Dales (1965) 7.5' quadrangles.

Inlow Butte [SISKIYOU]: *hill,* 8 miles south of Dorris (lat. 41°51'25" N, long. 121°53'15" W; sec. 5, T 46 N, R 1 E). Altitude 4870 feet. Named on Dorris (1950) 15' quadrangle.

Inskip [BUTTE]: *locality,* nearly 6 miles north of Stirling City (lat. 39°59'25" N, long. 121°39'55" W; at E line sec. 29, T 25 N, R 4 E). Named on Stirling City (1979) 7.5' quadrangle. Postal authorities established Inskip post office in 1862, discontinued it for a time in 1873, and discontinued it finally in 1915 (Frickstad, p. 10). The place was named in 1857 for Mr. Enskeep, who discovered gold there (Gudde, 1949, p. 160). F.D. Dunn (p. 11) noted that a feature called Blowhard Ravine heads at Inskip and extends to West Branch Feather River.

Inskip Caves [TEHAMA]: *cave,* nearly 7 miles south-southeast of Manton (lat. 40°21'10" N, long. 121°56'20" W; sec. 23, T 29 N, R 1 W); the cave is less than 1 mile north-northeast of Inskip Hill. Named on Manton (1956) 15' quadrangle.

Inskip Creek [BUTTE]: *stream,* flows 3 miles to Butte Creek [BUTTE-GLENN] 6 miles north-northwest of Stirling City (lat. 39°58'45" N, long. 121°35'15" W). Named on Stirling City (1979) 7.5' quadrangle.

Inskip Hill [TEHAMA]: *peak,* 7.5 miles south-southwest of Manton (lat. 40°20'30" N, long. 121°56'35" W; sec. 26, T 29 N, R 1 W). Altitude 3100 feet. Named on Manton (1956) 15' quadrangle.

Inskip Hill: see **Little Inskip Hill** [TEHAMA].

Intake: see **Poe** [BUTTE].

Intake Spring [SISKIYOU]: *spring,* 4.5 miles north of McCloud (lat. 41°19'20" N, long. 122°08'15" W; near SE cor. sec. 12, T 40 N, R 3 W). Named on Shasta (1954) 15' quadrangle. The name is from the location of the spring at the intake to the water supply for McCloud (United States Board on Geographic Names, 1985a, p. 3).

Inwood [SHASTA]: *locality,* 7.5 miles south-southwest of Whitmore (lat. 40°31'30" N, long. 121°57'20" W; sec. 22, T 31 N, R 1 W). Named on Whitmore (1956) 15' quadrangle. Postal authorities established Inwood post office in 1887, moved it 1.5 miles west in 1937, and discontinued it in 1947 (Salley, p. 104).

Iodine Prairie [SISKIYOU]: *area,* 4.5 miles south of Medicine Lake (lat. 41°31' N, long. 121°36' W; on S line sec. 35, T 43 N, R 3 E). Named on Medicine Lake (1952) 15' quadrangle.

Irish Bridge [SISKIYOU]: *relief feature,* 11 miles north-northeast of Medicine Lake (lat. 41°43'50" N, long. 121°30'55" W; sec. 21, T 45 N, R 4 E). Named on Medicine Lake (1952) 15' quadrangle.

Irish Glade [TEHAMA]: *area,* 8.5 miles west of Ball Mountain (lat. 39°54'30" N, long. 122°56'15" W; near N line sec. 26, T 24 N, R 10 W). Named on Buck Rock (1967) 7.5' quadrangle.

Irish Ravine [BUTTE]: *canyon,* drained by a stream that flows nearly 3 miles to North Honcut Creek 4 miles north-northwest of Bangor (lat. 39°26'25" N, long. 121°26'15" W; near S line sec. 5, T 18 N, R 5 E). Named on Bangor (1947) 7.5' quadrangle.

Irish Town [BUTTE]: *settlement,* 3.5 miles north of Paradise (lat. 39°48'30" N, long. 121°37'30" W; sec. 34, T 23 N, R 3 E). Named on Paradise East (1980) and Paradise West (1980) 7.5' quadrangles.

Iron Canyon [BUTTE]: *canyon,* 2 miles long, along Cave Creek above the mouth of that stream, which is 8.5 miles north-northeast of Chico (lat. 39°50'25" N, long. 121°46'35" W; near N line sec. 20, T 23 N, R 2 E). Named on Richardson Springs (1951) 7.5' quadrangle.

Iron Canyon [SHASTA]: *canyon,* nearly 3 miles long, along Cedar Salt Log Creek (present Iron Canyon Creek) below a point 4.5 miles west of the village of Big Bend (lat. 41°01' N, long. 121°59'30" W; at S line sec. 32, T 37 N, R 1 W). Named on Big Bend (1961) and Montgomery Creek (1956) 15' quadrangles.

Iron Canyon [TEHAMA]: *canyon,* 3.5 miles long, 2 miles west of Bend along Sacramento River (lat. 40°15' N, long. 122°10'15" W). Named on Bend (1965) and Red Bluff East (1951) 7.5' quadrangles.

Iron Canyon Creek: see **Cedar Salt Log Creek** [SHASTA].

Iron Creek [SISKIYOU]: *stream,* flows 4.5 miles to Cold Creek (1) 19 miles west-northwest of Macdoel (lat. 41°56'35" N, long. 122°20'20" W; sec. 8, T 47 N, R 4 W). Named on Copco (1954) 15' quadrangle.

Iron Creek [TEHAMA]: *stream,* flows 2.5 miles to Deer Creek (2) 5 miles southwest of Polk Springs (lat. 40°04'25" N, long. 121°44'10" W; near S line sec. 27, T 26 N, R 2 E); the stream is east of Iron Mountain. Named on Butte Meadows (1958) 15' quadrangle.

Iron Gate Reservoir [SISKIYOU]: *lake,* behind Iron Gate Dam on Klamath River 23 miles west-northwest of Macdoel (lat. 41°56'05" N, long. 122°26'05" W; sec. 9, T 47 N, R 5 W). Named on Copco (1954) 15' quadrangle.

Iron Mountain [SHASTA]:

(1) *peak,* 6 miles east-southeast of the village of French Gulch (lat. 40°40'30" N, long. 122°31'50" W; sec. 34, T 33 N, R 6 W). Named on Whiskeytown (1979) 7.5' quadrangle.

(2) *locality,* nearly 6.5 miles east-southeast of the village of French Gulch (lat. 40°40'15" N, long. 122°31'25" W; sec. 34, T 33 N, R 6 W); the place is 0.5 mile southeast of Iron Mountain (1). Named on Whiskeytown (1979) 7.5' quadrangle. Postal authorities established Iron Mountain post office in 1885 and discontinued it in 1886 (Frickstad, p. 180). The community developed at iron mines (Gudde, 1949, p. 161).

Iron Mountain [TEHAMA]: *peak,* 4.25 miles west-southwest of Polk Springs (lat. 40°05'15" N, long. 121°44' W; near SE cor. sec. 22, T 26 N, R 2 E). Altitude 3274 feet. Named on Butte Meadows (1958) 15' quadrangle.

Iron Phone [SISKIYOU]: *locality,* nearly 4 miles east-northeast of Dillon Mountain (lat. 41°32'35" N, long. 123°30'05" W). Named on Dillon Mountain (1983) 7.5' quadrangle.

Iron Spring [TEHAMA]: *spring,* 1.5 miles west-northwest of Tomhead Mountain (lat. 40°08'50" N, long. 122°50'40" W; sec. 35, T 27 N, R 9 W). Named on Yolla Bolly (1954) 15' quadrangle.

Iron Spring Gulch [TEHAMA]: *canyon,* drained by a stream that flows 1 mile to Tomhead Gulch nearly 2 miles west of Tomhead Mountain (lat. 40°08' N, long. 122°51'05" W; sec. 2, T 26 N, R 9 W). Named on Yolla Bolly (1954) 15' quadrangle.

Iron Spring Ridge [TEHAMA]: *ridge,* generally south-southwest-trending, 2 miles long, 2.25 miles west of Tomhead Mountain (lat. 40°08'30" N, long. 122°51'30" W); the ridge is northwest of Iron Spring Gulch. Named on Yolla Bolly (1954) 15' quadrangle.

Irving Creek [SISKIYOU]: *stream,* flows 7 miles to Klamath River 17 miles north-northwest of Forks of Salmon (lat. 41°28'05" N, long. 123°29'55" W). Named on Somes Bar (1979) 7.5' quadrangle.

Irving Mountain [SISKIYOU]: *peak,* 17 miles north-northwest of Forks of Salmon (lat. 41°29'10" N, long. 123°26'05" W). Named on Somes Bar (1979) 7.5' quadrangle.

Isaiah [BUTTE]: *locality,* 5.5 miles north-northwest of the village of Berry Creek along Western Pacific Railroad (lat. 39°43' N, long. 121°26'25" W; sec. 32, T 22 N, R 5 E). Named on Big Bend Mountain (1948) 15' quadrangle. Postal authorities established Isaiah post office in 1919, discontinued it in 1943, reestablished it in 1947, and discontinued it in 1954 (Frickstad, p. 10).

Ishii Caves: see **Yahi Indian Camp** [TEHAMA].

Ishi Pishi Falls [SISKIYOU]: *waterfall,* 12.5 miles northwest of Forks of Salmon along Klamath River (lat. 41°23' N, long. 123°29'50" W). Named on Somes Bar (1979) 7.5' quadrangle.

Isinglass Creek [SISKIYOU]: *stream,* flows 2.5 miles to Scott River 7.25 miles south-southwest of Scott Bar (lat. 41°38'35" N, long. 123°02'50" W; near S line sec. 19, T 44 N, R 10 W); the stream heads at Isinglass Lake. Named on Boulder Peak (1981) and Scott Bar (1980) 7.5' quadrangles.

Isinglass Lake [SISKIYOU]: *lake,* 350 feet long, 10 miles south-southwest of Scott Bar (lat. 41°36'30" N, long. 123°03'05" W). Named on Boulder Peak (1981) 7.5' quadrangle.

Island: see **The Island** [SHASTA]; **The Island**, under **Hartley Island** [GLENN].

Island Bar [BUTTE]: *locality,* 4.5 miles west-northwest of the village of Berry Creek along North Fork Feather River (lat. 39°40'35" N, long. 121°28'45" W; sec. 13, T 21 N, R 4 E). Named on Big Bend Mountain (1948) 15' quadrangle. Water of Lake Oroville now covers the site

Island Bar Hill [BUTTE]: *peak,* 5.5 miles north-northwest of Forbestown (lat. 39°35'10" N, long. 121°19'30" W; on S line sec. 17, T 20 N, R 6 E). Named on Forbestown (1970) 7.5' quadrangle.

Island Butte [SISKIYOU]: *hill,* 8 miles north of Medicine Lake (lat. 41°41'45" N, long. 121°35'25" W; sec. 35, T 45 N, R 3 E). Named on Medicine Lake (1952) 15' quadrangle.

Island Number 1 [TEHAMA]: *island,* 3 miles south-southwest of Vina in Sacramento River (lat. 39°53'30" N, long. 122°04'10" W). Named on Vina (1904) 15' quadrangle.

Ives: see **Pete Ives Glade** [SISKIYOU].

Ivory Mill Saddle [GLENN]: *pass,* 9 miles west-southwest of the village of Elk Creek (lat. 39°34'25" N, long. 122°42'05" W; near E line sec. 24, T 20 N, R 8 W). Named on Felkner Hill (1968) 7.5' quadrangle.

Ivory Mill Station [GLENN]: *locality,* 9 miles west-southwest of the village of Elk Creek (lat. 39°34'30" N, long. 122°42' W; near E line sec. 24, T 20 N, R 8 W); the place is 700 feet north-northeast of Ivory Mill Saddle. Named on Felkner Hill (1968) 7.5' quadrangle.

Ivrea: see **Hooker** [TEHAMA].

— J —

Jacinto [GLENN]:

(1) *land grant*, northeast of Willows. Named on Glenn (1951), Hamilton City (1949), Llano Seco (1948), and Ord Ferry (1949) 7.5' quadrangles. Jacinto Rodriguez received 8 leagues in 1844; William H. McKee claimed 35,488 acres patented in 1859 (Cowan, p. 41). The name of the grant is from the grantee's first name (Hoover, Rensch, and Rensch, p. 97).

(2) *locality*, 11 miles east-northeast of Willows along Sacramento River (lat. 39°34'55" N, long. 122°00'20" W); the place is on Jacinto grant. Named on Glenn (1951) 7.5' quadrangle. Postal authorities established Jacinto post office in 1858 and discontinued it in 1910 (Frickstad, p. 40).

Jackass Butte [TEHAMA]: *peak*, 4.5 miles south-southwest of Manton (lat. 40°22'45" N, long. 121°55' W; near E line sec. 12, T 29 N, R 1 W). Altitude 2023 feet. Named on Manton (1956) 15' quadrangle.

Jackass Canyon [TEHAMA]: *canyon*, drained by a stream that flows 4.5 miles to North Fork Red Bank Creek 4.5 miles east of Wakefield Flat (lat. 40°08'05" N, long. 122°33'20" W; near W line sec. 4, T 26 N, R 6 W). Named on Cold Fork (1967) and Oxbow Bridge (1967) 7.5' quadrangles.

Jackass Creek [SHASTA]:

(1) *stream*, flows 1.5 miles to Squaw Creek (2) 6 miles east-northeast of Bollibokka Mountain (lat. 40°57'30" N, long. 122°06'20" W; near NW cor. sec. 28, T 36 N, R 2 W). Named on Bollibokka Mountain (1957) 15' quadrangle.

(2) *stream*, flows less than 1 mile to Backbone Creek 11 miles south of Lamoine (lat. 40°49'20" N, long. 122°27'40" W; sec. 8, T 34 N, R 5 W). Named on Lamoine (1957) 15' quadrangle.

Jackass Creek [SISKIYOU]: *stream*, flows nearly 4 miles to North Fork Dillon Creek 6.25 miles north of Dillon Mountain (lat. 41°37'10" N, long. 123°35'45" W). Named on Bear Peak (1982), Dillon Mountain (1983), and Prescott Mountain (1981) 7.5' quadrangles.

Jackass Flat [BUTTE]: *area*, 3.5 miles north of Clipper Mills (lat. 39°35' N, long. 121°09'15" W; at N line sec. 23, T 20 N, R 7 E). Named on Clipper Mills (1948) 7.5' quadrangle.

Jackass Flat Diggings: see **Reading Bar** [SHASTA].

Jackass Gulch [SISKIYOU]: *canyon*, drained by a stream that flows 4 miles to North Fork Salmon River nearly 1.5 miles west of Sawyers Bar (lat. 41°18'10" N, long. 123°09'25" W). Named on Sawyers Bar (1979) and Tanners Peak (1977) 7.5' quadrangles.

Jackass Gulch [TEHAMA]: *canyon*, drained by a stream that flows 2.25 miles to Middle Fork Antelope Creek 8.5 miles southwest of Mineral (lat. 40°16'25" N, long. 121°43'10" W; near S line sec. 14, T 28 N, R 2 E). Named on Lassen Peak (1956) 15' quadrangle.

Jackass Mountain [SHASTA]: *peak*, 10.5 miles south of Lamoine (lat. 40°49'40" N, long. 122°27' W; near SE cor. sec. 5, T 34 N, R 5 W); the peak is east of Jackass Creek (2). Altitude 2692 feet. Named on Lamoine (1957) 15' quadrangle.

Jackass Spring [SISKIYOU]; *spring*, 3.5 miles north of the village of Seiad Valley (lat. 41°53'40" N, long. 123°12'15" W). Named on Kangaroo Mountain (1980) 7.5' quadrangle.

Jack Creek [BUTTE]: *stream*, flows 1.25 miles to French Creek 5 miles north-northeast of the village of Berry Creek (lat. 39°43' N, long. 121°22'45" W; sec. 35, T 22 N, R 5 E). Named on Berry Creek (1970) 7.5' quadrangle.

Jack Harveys Crossing [SISKIYOU]: *locality*, 2.5 miles east of Salmon Mountain along West Fork Knownothing Creek (lat. 41°10'30" N, long. 123°21'35" W). Named on Salmon Mountain (1955) 15' quadrangle.

Jack Hill Ravine [BUTTE]: *canyon*, drained by a stream that flows 1 mile to Middle Fork Feather River 6.25 miles northeast of Forbestown (lat. 39°35'05" N, long. 121°21'10" W; near NE cor. sec. 24, T 20 N, R 5 E). Named on Forbestown (1970) 7.5' quadrangle.

Jackrabbit Flat [SHASTA]: *area*, 1.5 miles southwest of Burney (lat. 40°52'10" N, long. 121°41'45" W; at N line sec. 25, T 35 N, R 2 E). Named on Burney (1957) 15' quadrangle.

Jacks Backbone [SHASTA]: *ridge*, northwest-trending, 2 miles long, 16 miles northwest of Lassen Peak (lat. 40°40'30" N, long. 121°40'40" W; mainly in sec. 31, T 33 N, R 3 E). Named on Manzanita Lake (1956) 15' quadrangle. According to Steger (p. 40-41), the name came about when J.M. Simmons likened the backbone of his hired man, Jack, to the ridge.

Jackson: see **Mount Jackson**, under **Mount Shasta** [SISKIYOU] (1).

Jackson Creek [SISKIYOU]: *stream*, flows 3 miles to join Little Jackson Creek and form Scott River 14 miles south of Etna (lat. 41°15'30" N, long. 122°53'40" W; near W line sec. 10, T 39 N, R 9 W). Named on Etna (1955) 15' quadrangle.

Jackson Creek: see **Little Jackson Creek** [SISKIYOU].

Jackson Lake [SISKIYOU]: *lake*, 1850 feet long, 14 miles south of Etna (lat. 41°15'35" N, long. 122°56'30" W; sec. 7, T 39 N, R 9 W); the lake is at the head of a branch of Jackson Creek. Named on Etna (1955) 15' quadrangle.

Jackson Lake: see **Little Jackson Lake** [SISKIYOU].

Jackson Peak [SISKIYOU]: *peak*, 6.25 miles north of Happy Camp (lat. 41°53'10" N, long. 123°22'05" W). Altitude 5048 feet. Named on Figurehead Mountain (1980) 7.5' quadrangle.

Jackson Spring [TEHAMA]: *spring*, nearly 6 miles south of Flournoy (lat. 39°50'25" N, long. 122°27'05" W; near N line sec. 20, T 23 N, R 5 W). Named on Sehorn Creek (1967) 7.5' quadrangle.

Jackson Spring Creek [TEHAMA]: *stream*, flows 9 miles to join Elmore Creek and form Burch Creek 6 miles southeast of Flournoy (lat. 39°51'50" N, long. 122°21' W; sec. 7, T 23 N, R 4 W); Jackson Spring is along the stream. Named on Black Butte Dam (1967) and Sehorn Creek (1967) 7.5' quadrangles.

Jackstaff Bend [TEHAMA]: *bend*, 5.5 miles east-southeast of Kirkwood along Sacramento River (lat. 39°49'10" N, long. 122°04' W). Named on Vina (1904) 15' quadrangle.

Jacobs Ladder [SISKIYOU]: *relief feature*, 2.5 miles west-northwest of Ukonom Lake (lat. 41°36' N, long. 123°23'35" W). Named on Ukonom Mountain (1980) 7.5' quadrangle. Ukonom Lake (1955) 15' quadrangle shows a series of switchbacks along a trail at the place.

Jacobs Well [SISKIYOU]: *spring*, 2.5 miles northwest of Ukonom Lake (lat. 41°36'15" N, long. 123°23'45" W); the spring is just north of Jacobs Ladder. Named on Ukonom Mountain (1980) 7.5' quadrangle.

Jail Gulch [SISKIYOU]: *canyon*, drained by a stream that flows 1 mile to Klamath River 5.25 miles south-southwest of Hornbrook (lat. 41°50'20" N, long. 122°34'50" W; sec. 18, T 46 N, R 6 W). Named on Hornbrook (1955) 15' quadrangle.

Jake Allgood Gulch [SISKIYOU]: *canyon*, drained by a stream that flows 1.25 miles to Salmon River 6.5 miles north-northwest of Forks of Salmon (lat. 41°20'30" N, long. 123°22'55" W). Named on Orleans Mountain (1974) 7.5' quadrangle.

Jakes Gulch [SISKIYOU]: *canyon*, drained by a stream that flows 1.5 miles to Humbug Creek 15 miles southeast of Condrey Mountain (lat. 41°46'50" N, long. 122°45'50" W; sec. 3, T 45 N, R 8 W). Named on Condrey Mountain (1955) 15' quadrangle.

Jake Spring [SHASTA]: *spring*, 5 miles west of Burney Falls (lat. 41°01'20" N, long. 121°44'45" W; sec. 33, T 37 N, R 2 E). Named on Pondosa (1961) 15' quadrangle.

James:[BUTTE]: *locality*, 8 miles south-southeast of Paradise along Western Pacific Railroad (lat. 39°39'10" N, long. 121°32'50" W; at N line sec. 29, T 21 N, R 4 E). Named on Cherokee (1970) 7.5' quadrangle.

Jap Gulch [SISKIYOU]: *canyon*, drained by a stream that flows 0.5 mile to South Russian Creek 5.5 miles east of Sawyers Bar (lat. 41°19'10" N, long. 123°01'45" W; sec. 20, T 40 N, R 10 W). Named on Sawyers Bar (1955) 15' quadrangle.

Jarbo Gap [BUTTE]: *pass*, 8 miles northwest of the village of Berry Creek (lat. 39°44'15" N, long. 121°29'45" W; near N line sec. 26, T 22 N, R 4 E). Named on Berry Creek (1970) 7.5' quadrangle. The name is for Ben J. Jarboe, landowner at the place (Dunn, F.D., p. 55).

Ja She Creek: see **Squaw Creek** [SHASTA] (1).

Jawbone Camp [SISKIYOU]: *locality*, 6.25 miles south-southwest of Ukonom Lake (lat. 41°30'15" N, long. 123°25'10" W). Named on Ukonom Mountain (1980) 7.5' quadrangle.

Jaynes Canyon [SISKIYOU]: *canyon*, drained by a stream that flows 5 miles to West Fork Beaver Creek (1) 5.5 miles east-northeast of Condrey Mountain (lat. 41°57'20" N, long. 122°52'25" W; sec. 3, T 47 N, R 9 W). Named on Condrey Mountain (1955) 15' quadrangle.

Jelly: see **Jellys Ferry** [TEHAMA].

Jellys Ferry [TEHAMA]: *locality*, 4.5 miles north-northeast of Bend along Sacramento River (lat. 40°19' N, long. 122°11'15" W; at S line sec. 34, T 29 N, R 3 W). Named on Tuscan Buttes (1947) 15' quadrangle. Diller and others' (1915) map shows a place called Jelly situated on the north side of Sacramento River at or near the site of Jellys Ferry. Postal authorities established Jelly post office in 1901 and discontinued it in 1934; the name was for Frank L. Jelly, first postmaster—Andrew Jelly operated the ferry at the site (Salley, p. 107).

Jennie Creek: see **Jenny Creek** [SISKIYOU].

Jennings Gulch [SISKIYOU]: *canyon*, drained by a stream that flows 1.5 miles to South Fork Salmon River 5.5 miles northwest of Cecilville (lat. 41°11'40" N, long. 123°12'50" W). Named on Cecilville (1979) 7.5' quadrangle.

Jenny Creek [SHASTA]: *stream*, flows 1.5 miles to Sacramento River 1 mile northwest of downtown Redding (lat. 40°35'30" N, long. 122°24'40" W). Named on Redding (1957) 7.5' quadrangle.

Jenny Creek [SISKIYOU]: *stream*, heads in the State of Oregon and flows nearly 4 miles to Klamath River 23 miles west-northwest of Macdoel (lat. 41°58'15" N, long. 122°24'15" W). Named on Copco (1954) 15' quadrangle. United States Board on Geographic Names (1962, p. 20) rejected the names "Beaver Creek," "Grizzly Creek," and "Jennie Creek" for the feature.

Jenny Lind Bend [BUTTE-GLENN]: *relief feature,* cutoff meander of Sacramento River 7 miles west of Chico on Butte-Glenn County line (lat. 39°43'05" N, long. 121°57'40" W). Named on Ord Ferry (1949) 7.5' quadrangle.

Jensen Mill [SISKIYOU]: *locality,* 14 miles west-northwest of Yreka along McKinney Creek (lat. 41°48' N, long. 122°54'30" W). Named on Yreka (1939) 30' quadrangle.

Jerome [SISKIYOU]: *locality,* 6.25 miles north-northwest of Bray along Southern Pacific Railroad (lat. 41°43'55" N, long. 121°59'55" W; sec. 20, T 45 N, R 1 W). Named on Bray (1950) 15' quadrangle. Shasta (1894) 1° quadrangle shows a place called Bayes located just west of the site of present Jerome. United States Board on Geographic Names (1967b, p. 3) approved the name "Jerome Butte" for a hill, altitude 4651 feet, located less than 1 mile northwest of Jerome (lat. 41°44'30" N, long. 122°00'30" W), and approved the name "East Jerome Butte" for a hill, altitude 4480 feet, located 0.5 mile north-northeast of Jerome (lat. 41°44'30" N, long. 121°59'40" W; sec. 17, 20, T 45 N, R 1 W).

Jerome Butte: see **Jerome** [SISKIYOU].

Jerusalem Creek [SHASTA]: *stream,* flows 8 miles to North Fork Cottonwood Creek [SHASTA-TEHAMA] nearly 5 miles west-southwest of Ono (lat. 40°27'25" N, long. 122°42'15" W; near NW cor. sec. 18, T 30 N, R 7 W). Named on Ono (1952) and Weaverville (1950) 15' quadrangles, and on Shasta Bally (1978) 7.5' quadrangle. Jewish settlers named the stream (Steger, p. 41).

Jerusalem Spring [GLENN]: *spring,* 9 miles west-southwest of the village of Elk Creek (lat. 39°33'40" N, long. 122°42'05" W; sec. 25, T 20 N, R 8 W). Named on Felkner Hill (1968) 7.5' quadrangle.

Jessen Meadows: see **Devastated Area** [SHASTA].

Jessen Mountain: see **Raker Peak** [SHASTA].

Jessie Creek [SHASTA]: *stream,* flows nearly 2 miles to Squaw Creek (2) 2.25 miles east of Shoeinhorse Mountain (lat. 41°04'10" N, long. 122°01'45" W). Named on Shoeinhorse Mountain (1954) 15' quadrangle.

Jessops Gulch: see **Jessups Gulch** [SISKIYOU].

Jessups Gulch [SISKIYOU]: *canyon,* drained by a stream that flows nearly 2 miles to North Fork Salmon River opposite Sawyers Bar (lat. 41°17'50" N, long. 123°07'45" W). Named on Sawyers Bar (1979) 7.5' quadrangle. United States Board on Geographic Names (1960a, p. 14) rejected the form "Jessops Gulch" for the name.

Jesús María: see **Mount Shasta** [SISKIYOU] (1).

Jewel Lake [SISKIYOU]: *lake,* 150 feet long, 15 miles south-southwest of Scott Bar (lat. 41°32'30" N, long. 123°08' W); the feature is near Gem Lake. Named on Marble Mountain (1980) 7.5' quadrangle.

Jewell Spring [SISKIYOU]: *spring,* 10.5 miles west-northwest of Macdoel (lat. 41°53'20" N, long. 122°11'30" W; near E line sec. 27, T 47 N, R 3 W). Named on Macdoel (1954) 15' quadrangle. United States Board on Geographic Names (1986c, p. 3) approved the form "Jewel Spring" for the name.

Jewel Spring: see **Jewell Spring** [SISKIYOU].

Jewett Creek [TEHAMA]: *stream,* flows 20 miles to Sacramento River 4 miles south of Vina (lat. 39°52'40" N, long. 122°04' W; sec. 3, T 23 N, R 2 W). Named on Corning (1951), Henleyville (1967), and Vina (1950) 7.5' quadrangles.

J.F. Mountain: see **Mahogany Mountain** [SISKIYOU].

Jic Gulch [SHASTA]: *canyon,* drained by a stream that flows 1.5 miles to Cline Gulch 2.5 miles east-northeast of the village of French Gulch (lat. 40°42'50" N, long. 122°35'40" W; near W line sec. 18, T 33 N, R 6 W). Named on Whiskeytown (1979) 7.5' quadrangle.

Jillsonville: see **Cline Gulch** [SHASTA].

Jim Creek [SHASTA]: *stream,* flows 1.5 miles to Yank Creek 10 miles north of Millville (lat. 40°41'10" N, long. 122°12'45" W; sec. 28, T 33 N, R 3 W). Named on Bella Vista (1965) 7.5' quadrangle. On Millville (1953) 15' quadrangle, present Yank Creek is called Jim Creek.

Jim Creek [SISKIYOU]: *stream,* flows less than 1 mile to Klamath River 7.5 miles southeast of the village of Seiad Valley (lat. 41°46'55" N, long. 123°04'10" W); the mouth of the stream is 300 feet upstream from the mouth of Mitchell Creek. Named on Hamburg (1980) 7.5' quadrangle. On Seiad Valley (1955) 15' quadrangle, present Mitchell Creek is called Jim Creek. United States Board on Geographic Names (1981b, p. 3) rejected the name "Mitchell Creek" for present Jim Creek, and noted that the name "Jim Creek" is for James Mitchell, who had a placer claim at the mouth of the stream.

Jimmy Creek: see **Mitchell Creek** [SISKIYOU].

Jims Camp [SISKIYOU]: *locality,* 5.5 miles south-southwest of Hornbrook along Klamath River (lat. 41°50' N, long. 122°32'30" W; sec. 18, T 46 N, R 6 W). Named on Yreka (1939) 30' quadrangle. Gudde (1975, p. 56) listed a mining place called California Bar, located 9 miles southwest of Hornbrook along Klamath River; according to Brown (p. 861), California Bar mine is near the site of Jims Camp (sec. 18, T 46 N, R 6 W).

Jim Springs [SISKIYOU]: *spring,* 17 miles west-southwest of Macdoel (lat. 41°43'50" N, long. 122°19'20" W; near E line sec. 20, T 45 N, R 4 W). Named on Lake Shastina (1954) 15' quadrangle.

Joe Bar [SISKIYOU]: *locality,* 12 miles north of the village of Seiad Valley along Middle Fork Applegate River at California-Oregon State line (lat. 42°15' N, long. 123°09'15" W; sec. 17, T 48 N, R 11 W). Named on Seiad Valley (1955) 15' quadrangle.

Joe Creek [SISKIYOU]: *stream,* flows 4.25 miles to Elliot Creek 11.5 miles north-northeast of the village of Seiad Valley (lat. 41°59'55" N, long. 123°07'35" W). Named on Dutch Creek (1980) and Kangaroo Mountain (1980) 7.5' quadrangles.

Joe Flat: see **Little Joe Flat** [SHASTA].

Joe Keen Meadows [SISKIYOU]: *area,* 14 miles south of Etna (lat. 41°14'45" N, long. 122°52'40" W; near NE cor. sec. 15, T 39 N, R 9 W). Named on Coffee Creek (1955) 15' quadrangle.

Joe Miles Creek [SISKIYOU]; *stream,* flows 2 miles to Klamath River 4.5 miles east-northeast of Happy Camp (lat. 41°49'15" N, long. 123°17'55" W). Named on Slater Butte (1980) 7.5' quadrangle.

John Adams: see **Centerville** [BUTTE].

John Creek: see **Scotts John Creek** [BUTTE].

Johnny Bull Gulch [SISKIYOU]: *canyon,* drained by a stream that flows 0.5 mile to McAdam Creek 6.25 miles north of Fort Jones (lat. 41°41'45" N, long. 122°49'05" W; near NW cor. sec. 6, T 44 N, R 8 W). Named on Fort Jones (1955) 15' quadrangle.

Johnny O'Neil Ridge [SISKIYOU]: *ridge,* south- and east-trending, 6 miles long, center 5 miles east of the village of Seiad Valley (lat. 41°50' N, long. 123°16' W). Named on Seiad Valley (1955) 15' quadrangle.

Johnny Sisk Creek [SHASTA]: *stream,* flows 1.5 miles to Middle Salt Creek 5 miles southeast of Lamoine (lat. 40°55'30" N, long. 122°21'45" W; sec. 6, T 35 N, R 4 E). Named on Lamoine (1957) 15' quadrangle.

Johns Creek [SHASTA]: *stream,* flows 1.25 miles to McCloud River [SHASTA-SISKIYOU] 15 miles south-southeast of Lamoine (lat. 40°47'15" N, long. 122°17'50" W; at E line sec. 22, T 34 N, R 4 W). Named on Lamoine (1946) 15' quadrangle. Water of Shasta Lake now floods the canyon of the stream

Johns Gulch [SHASTA]: *canyon,* drained by a stream that flows 1.5 miles to Clear Creek opposite the village of French Gulch (lat. 40°42'10" N, long. 122°38' W; at W line sec. 23, T 33 N, R 7 W). Named on French Gulch (1979) and Whiskeytown (1979) 7.5' quadrangles.

Johns Meadows [SISKIYOU]: *area,* 6.25 miles east of Sawyers Bar (lat. 41°17'35" N, long. 123°00'50" W). Named on Tanners Peak (1977) 7.5' quadrangle.

Johns Meadows Creek [SISKIYOU]: *stream,* flows 2 miles to South Russian Creek 5 miles east-northeast of Sawyers Bar (lat. 41°19'05" N, long. 123°02'30" W); the stream heads near Johns Meadows. Named on Tanners Peak (1977) 7.5' quadrangle.

Johnson: see **Chico** [BUTTE].

Johnson Creek [SISKIYOU]:

(1) *stream,* flows 2.25 miles to Elk Creek 5.5 miles north-northeast of Ukonom Lake (lat. 41°39'05" N, long. 123°18'50" W). Named on Huckleberry Mountain (1980) 7.5' quadrangle.

(2) *stream,* flows nearly 1 mile to Methodist Creek 8 miles east of Salmon Mountain (lat. 41°12'15" N, long. 123°15'45" W). Named on Youngs Peak (1979) 7.5' quadrangle.

(3) *stream,* flows 3 miles to Scott Valley 0.5 mile north-northwest of Etna (lat. 41°27'45" N, long. 122°54'15" W; sec. 29, T 42 N, R 9 W). Named on Etna (1955) 15' quadrangle.

Johnsons Bar: see **Steelhead** [SISKIYOU].

Johnsons Hunting Ground: [SISKIYOU] *area,* 2.5 miles north of Ukonom Lake (lat. 41°37'15" N, long. 123°20'40" W). Named on Huckleberry Mountain (1980) and Ukonom Lake (1980) 7.5' quadrangles.

Johnson Spring [SHASTA]: *spring,* 6.5 miles east-southeast of Whitmore (lat. 40°35'30" N, long. 121°48' W; near SE cor. sec. 25, T 32 N, R 1 E). Named on Whitmore (1956) 15' quadrangle.

Jolly Camp [GLENN]: *locality,* 8 miles south-southeast of Black Butte (lat. 39°36'30" N, long. 122°50' W; at SE cor. sec. 2, T 20 N, R 9 W). Named on Hull Mountain (1952) 15' quadrangle.

Jones: see **Captain Jones Rapids** [TEHAMA]; **Fort Jones** [SISKIYOU]; **Tom Jones Reservoir** [BUTTE].

Jones Camp Creek [TEHAMA]: *stream,* flows 1.5 miles to Cold Fork (1) 5 miles northeast of Tomhead Mountain (lat. 40°11'20" N, long. 122°53' W; sec. 16, T 27 N, R 9 W). Named on Yolla Bolly (1954) 15' quadrangle.

Jones Creek [BUTTE]: *stream,* flows 4 miles to Willow Creek [BUTTE-TEHAMA] 0.5 mile west-northwest of Jonesville (lat. 40°07' N, long. 121°28'30" W; near S line sec. 12, T 26 N, R 4 E). Named on Jonesville (1958) 15' quadrangle.

Jones Gulch [SISKIYOU]: *canyon,* drained by a stream that flows 2.25 miles to North Fork Salmon River 5 miles west of Sawyers Bar (lat. 41°17'35" N, long. 123°13'40" W); the canyon heads at Jones Lake. Named on Sawyers Bar (1979) 7.5' quadrangle.

Jones Lake [SISKIYOU]: *lake,* 225 feet long, 4.25 miles west-southwest of Sawyers Bar (lat. 41°16'15" N, long. 123°12'10" W); the lake is at the head of Jones Gulch. Named on Sawyers Bar (1979) 7.5' quadrangle.

Jones Meadow [BUTTE]: *area,* 13 miles north of Pulga (lat. 39°59'20" N, long. 121°26'55" W; near SE cor. sec. 30, T 25 N, R 5 E). Named on Kimshew Point (1979) 7.5' quadrangle.

Jones Valley [SHASTA]: *valley,* 12.5 miles north-northwest of Millville on upper reaches of Dry Creek (1) (lat. 40°43'35" N, long. 122°14'10" W; near SW cor. sec. 8, T 33 N, R 3 W). Named on Bella Vista (1965) 7.5' quadrangle. The name is for Mrs. Jones, whom Indians killed at the place in 1854 (Steger, p. 41).

Jones Valley [TEHAMA]: *area,* 1.25 miles southeast of Mineral (lat. 40°19'15" N, long. 121°33'35" W). Named on Lassen Peak (1956) 15' quadrangle.

Jones Valley Campground [SHASTA]: *locality,* 13 miles north of Millville along Shasta Lake (lat. 40°43'40" N, long. 122°13'40" W; sec. 8, T 33 N, R 3 W); the place is 0.5 mile east of Jones Valley. Named on Bella Vista (1965) 7.5' quadrangle.

Jonesville [BUTTE]: *village,* 5 miles east-northeast of Butte Meadows (lat. 40°06'45" N, long. 121°27'50" W; mainly in sec. 13, T 26 N, R 4 E); the village is along Jones Creek. Named on Jonesville (1958) 15' quadrangle.

Jordan: see **Cecilville** [SISKIYOU].

Jordan Creek [BUTTE]: *stream,* flows nearly 2 miles to Marble Creek 9.5 miles east-southeast of Pulga (lat. 39°45'35" N, long. 121°16'40" W; sec. 14, T 22 N, R 6 E). Named on Soapstone Hill (1979) 7.5' quadrangle.

Jordan Hill [BUTTE]: *ridge,* south-trending, 1.25 miles long, 4 miles east of Paradise (lat. 39°44'40" N, long. 121°33' W; sec. 20, 29, T 22 N, R 4 E). Named on Cherokee (1970) 7.5' quadrangle.

Joseph [SHASTA]: *locality,* about 6 miles north-northwest of Millville (lat. 40°38' N, long. 122°12'30" W). Named on Red Bluff (1894) 1° quadrangle.

Josephine Lake [SISKIYOU]:
(1) *lake,* 300 feet long, 10 miles south-southwest of Etna (lat. 41°19' N, long. 122°57' W; sec. 18, T 40 N, R 9 W). Named on Etna (1955) 15' quadrangle.
(2) *lake,* 2000 feet long, 30 miles south of Etna (lat. 41°01'05" N, long. 122°56'40" W; on W line sec. 31, T 37 N, R 9 W). Named on Coffee Creek (1955) 15' quadrangle.

Joyland Gulch [SISKIYOU]: *canyon,* drained by a stream that flows 1.25 miles to Scott River 7.25 miles west-northwest of Fort Jones (lat. 41°38'15" N, long. 122°58'30" W; at W line sec. 26, T 44 N, R 10 W). Named on Fort Jones (1955) 15' quadrangle.

Juanita Lake [SISKIYOU]: *lake,* 0.5 mile long, 6.25 miles west of Macdoel (lat. 41°48'50" N, long. 122°07'15" W; sec. 20, T 46 N, R 2 W). Named on Macdoel (1954) 15' quadrangle.

Judd Creek [TEHAMA]: *stream,* flows 11 miles to North Fork Antelope Creek 12 miles south of Manton (lat. 40°16'10" N, long. 121°49'15" W; near NE cor. sec. 23, T 28 N, R 1 E). Named on Lassen Peak (1956) and Manton (1956) 15' quadrangles.

Julia Glover Flat [SISKIYOU]: *area,* 15 miles east-northeast of Bartle (lat. 41°20'25" N, long. 121°32'50" W; at N line sec. 6, T 40 N, R 4 E). Named on Hambone (1961) 15' quadrangle.

Julian Rocks [GLENN]: *narrows,* 8 miles north of Fruto along Stony Creek [GLENN-TEHAMA] (lat. 39°42'05" N, long. 122°28'40" W; near SE cor. sec. 1, T 21 N, R 6 W). Named on Julian Rocks (1968) 7.5' quadrangle.

Julien Creek [SISKIYOU]: *stream,* flows 8.5 miles to Shasta River 8.5 miles southeast of Yreka (lat. 41°40' N, long. 122°30'05" W; sec. 14, T 44 N, R 6 W). Named on Yreka (1954) 15' quadrangle. United States Board on Geographic Names (1985b, p. 2) rejected the form "Julian Creek" for the name.

Jumbo Spring [GLENN]: *spring,* 11 miles west of the village of Elk Creek (lat. 39°37' N, long. 122°44'25" W; sec. 3, T 20 N, R 8 W). Named on Felkner Hill (1968) 7.5' quadrangle.

Junction: see **Eagle Creek**, under **Ono** [SHASTA].

Junction Bar: see **Steelhead** [SISKIYOU].

Junction House [BUTTE]: *locality,* 4.25 miles northeast of the village of Brush Creek (lat. 39°44'25" N, long. 121°17'20" W; near S line sec. 22, T 22 N, R 6 E). Named on Brush Creek (1970) 7.5' quadrangle. A stage station called Peavine was situated about 2 miles up the road from Junction House. Postal authorities established Pea Vine post office 7 miles northeast of Brush Creek in 1856 and discontinued in it 1864 (Salley, p. 169).

Junction Spring [SISKIYOU]: *spring,* 10.5 miles north-northeast of McCloud (lat. 41°23'10" N, long. 122°02'05" W; near W line sec. 24, T 41 N, R 2 W). Named on Shasta (1954) 15' quadrangle.

Jungle Spring [TEHAMA]: *spring,* 9.5 miles south-southeast of Wakefield Flat (lat. 40°00'35" N, long. 122°33'35" W; near W line sec. 21, T 25 N, R 6 W). Named on Lowrey (1967) 7.5' quadrangle.

Juniper Flat [SISKIYOU]: *area,* 25 miles southwest of Macdoel (lat. 41°34' N, long. 122°20'30" W). Named on Lake Shastina (1954) 15' quadrangle.

Juniper Flat [TEHAMA]: *area,* 6.5 miles east of Beegum Peak (lat. 40°19'15" N, long. 122°46' W; near E line sec. 33, T 29 N, R 8 W). Named on Chanchelulla Peak (1951) 15' quadrangle.

Juniper Gulch [TEHAMA]:
(1) *canyon,* drained by a stream that flows 2 miles to North Fork Battle Creek [SHASTA-TEHAMA] 5.5 miles west of Manton (lat. 40°25'15" N, long. 121°58'30" W; sec. 28, T 30 N, R 1 W). Named on Manton (1956) 15' quadrangle.
(2) *canyon,* drained by a stream that flows 2.5 miles to lowlands 6.5 miles north-northeast of Los Molinos (lat. 40°06'50" N, long. 122°03'35" W). Named on Los Molinos (1952) 7.5' quadrangle.
(3) *canyon,* drained by a stream that flows about 6.25 miles to Deer Creek (2) 2.5 miles north-northeast of Vina (lat. 39°57'45" N, long. 122°02' W. Named on Panther Spring (1953) 15' quadrangle, and on Richardson Springs NW (1952) 7.5' quadrangle.

Juniper Knoll [SISKIYOU]: *hill,* 9.5 miles south-southwest of Dorris (lat. 41°50'10" N, long. 121°59'05" W; on S line sec. 9, T 46 N, R 1 W). Altitude 4566 feet. Named on Dorris (1950) 15' quadrangle.

Juniper Point [TEHAMA]: *ridge,* east-trending, less than 0.5 mile long, 5.25 miles north-northwest of Bend (lat. 40°19'40" N, long. 122°14' W; on W line sec. 32, T 29 N, R 3 W). Named on Bend (1965) 7.5' quadrangle.

— K —

Kabyai Creek [SHASTA]: *stream,* flows 1.5 miles to McCloud River [SHASTA-SISKIYOU] nearly 2 miles west of Bollibokka Mountain (lat. 40°56' N, long. 122°14'55" W; at S line sec. 31, T 36 N, R 3 W). Named on Lamoine (1957) 15' quadrangle.

Kabyai Creek: see **Little Kabyai Creek** [SHASTA].

Kaiser Creek: see **Keyser Creek** [BUTTE].

Kaiser Meadow [SISKIYOU]: *area,* 4.5 miles northwest of the town of Mount Shasta (lat. 41°21'15" N, long. 122°22'30" W; sec. 36, T 41 N, R 5 W). Named on Weed (1954) 15' quadrangle.

Kanaka Bar [BUTTE]: *locality,* 6.25 miles north-northwest of Forbestown along Middle Fork Feather River (lat. 39°36' N, long. 121°19' W; near SE cor. sec. 8, T 20 N, R 6 E); the place is at the mouth of Kanaka Creek (2). Named on Big Bend Mountain (1948) 15' quadrangle. Water of Lake Oroville now covers the site. F.D. Dunn (p. 102) listed a place called Big Stony Bar that was situated along Middle Fork Feather River just below Kanaka Bar.

Kanaka Bar [SISKIYOU]: *locality,* 9.5 miles west-southwest of Hornbrook at the mouth of Dutch Creek (4) (lat. 41°51'55" N, long. 122°43'30" W; sec. 1, T 46 N, R 8 W). Named on Hornbrook (1955) 15' quadrangle.

Kanaka Creek [BUTTE]:
(1) *stream,* flows 2 miles to Clear Creek (1) 3.5 miles northwest of Stirling City (lat. 39°56'35" N, long. 121°34'30" W; near NW cor. sec. 18, T 24 N, R 4 E). Named on Stirling City (1979) 7.5' quadrangle.
(2) *stream,* flows nearly 2 miles to Middle Fork Feather River 6 miles north-northwest of Forbestown (lat. 39°36'05" N, long. 121°18'50" W; near SW cor. sec. 9, T 20 N, R 6 E); the stream is north of Kanaka Peak. Named on Forbestown (1970) 7.5' quadrangle.

Kanaka Creek [SHASTA]: *stream,* flows 3.5 miles to Clear Creek 3 miles north of Igo (lat. 40°32'30" N, long. 122°31'55" W; sec. 15, T 31 N, R 6 W); the stream is south of Kanaka Peak. Named on Igo (1979) 7.5' quadrangle.

Kanaka Creek [SISKIYOU]: *stream,* flows less than 1 mile to Klamath River 11.5 miles north of Ukonom Lake (lat. 41°44'40" N, long. 123°23'55" W). Named on Clear Creek (1981) 7.5' quadrangle.

Kanaka Creek: see **Little Kanaka Creek** [SHASTA].

Kanaka Gulch [SISKIYOU]: *canyon,* drained by a stream that flows 1.5 miles to North Fork Salmon River 4.5 miles west of Sawyers Bar (lat. 41°17'55" N, long. 123°13'15" W). Named on Sawyers Bar (1979) 7.5' quadrangle. Called Boulder Gulch on Sawyers Bar (1923) 30' quadrangle, but United States Board on Geographic Names (1960a, p. 15) rejected this name for the feature.

Kanaka Peak [BUTTE]: *peak,* nearly 5 miles north-northwest of Forbestown (lat. 39°34'55" N, long. 121°18'15" W; sec. 21, T 20 N, R 6 E); the peak is south of Kanaka Creek (2). Altitude 3044 feet. Named on Forbestown (1970) 7.5' quadrangle.

Kanaka Peak [SHASTA]: *peak,* 4 miles north of Igo (lat. 40°33'55" N, long. 122°33'10" W; on N line sec 9, T 31 N, R 6 W); the peak is north of Kanaka Creek. Named on Igo (1978) 7.5' quadrangle.

Kanawha: see **Willows** [GLENN].

Kangaroo Creek [SISKIYOU]: *stream,* flows 4.5 miles to East Fork Scott River 12.5 miles southeast of Etna (lat. 41°20'10" N, long. 122°43'05" W; at N line sec. 18, T 40 N, R 7 W). Named on China Mountain (1955) 15' quadrangle.

Kangaroo Lake [SISKIYOU]: *lake,* 1800 feet long, 16 miles east-southeast of Etna (lat. 41°20' N, long. 122°38' W; sec. 14, T 40 N, R 7 W). Named on China Mountain (1955) 15' quadrangle.

Kangaroo Mountain [SISKIYOU]: *peak,* 5.5 miles north of the village of Seiad Valley (lat. 41°55'15" N, long. 123°11'55" W). Named on Kangaroo Mountain (1980) 7.5' quadrangle. Called Kangaro Mt. on Averill's

(1935) map. G.R. Stewart (p. 233) suggested that the name probably was for the kangaroo rat.

Kangaroo Spring [SISKIYOU]: *spring,* 5.25 miles north of the village of Seiad Valley (lat. 41°55' N, long. 123°11'40" W); the spring is 1800 feet southeast of Kangaroo Mountain. Named on Kangaroo Mountain (1980) 7.5' quadrangle.

Katherine: see **Lake Katherine** [SISKIYOU].

Katskill Hill [BUTTE]: *peak,* 1.25 miles northwest of Bangor (lat. 39°24'05" N, long. 121°25'10" W; sec. 21, T 18 N, R 5 E). Altitude 828 feet. Named on Bangor (1947) 7.5' quadrangle.

K.C. Mine Camp [SISKIYOU]: *locality,* 11 miles south of Condrey Mountain (lat. 41°47'10" N, long. 122°55'35" W; sec. 32, T 46 N, R 9 W). Named on Condrey Mountain (1955) 15' quadrangle.

Keefer Pinery: see **Cohasset Ridge** [BUTTE-TEHAMA].

Keefer Ridge [BUTTE]: *ridge,* southwest-trending, 5 miles long, 11 miles north-northeast of Chico (lat. 39°52'40" N, long. 121°47' W). Named on Campbell Mound (1952) and Richardson Springs (1951) 7.5' quadrangles.

Keefer Ridge: see **Cohasset Ridge** [BUTTE-TEHAMA].

Keefer Slough [BUTTE]: *stream,* flows 5.5 miles to Rock Creek [BUTTE-TEHAMA] 2.25 miles north-northeast of Nord (lat. 39°48'25" N, long. 121°56'05" W; sec. 36, T 23 N, R 1 W). Named on Nord (1951) 7.5' quadrangle.

Keefers Mill [BUTTE]: *locality,* 14 miles north-northeast of Chico (lat. 39°54'30" N, long. 121°43'35" W). Named on Chico (1895) 30' quadrangle.

Keefers Old Mill [BUTTE]: *locality,* 8 miles north of Chico (lat. 39°50'45" N, long. 121°50' W). Named on Chico (1895) 30' quadrangle.

Keefers Ridge: see **Cohasset** [BUTTE].

Keefers Station: see **Rock Creek**, under **Chico** [BUTTE].

Keeler Creek [SISKIYOU]: *stream,* flows 1 mile to Punch Creek 13 miles southwest of Hornbrook (lat. 41°45'40" N, long. 122°42'55" W; sec. 12, T 45 N, R 8 W). Named on Hornbrook (1955) 15' quadrangle.

Keen: see **Joe Keen Meadows** [SISKIYOU].

Keeran Camp [GLENN]: *locality,* 2.5 miles south-southeast of Black Butte (lat. 39°41'25" N, long. 122°51'15" W). Named on Plaskett Meadows (1967) 7.5' quadrangle.

Kegg [SISKIYOU]: *locality,* 3.25 miles north-northwest of Bray along Southern Pacific Railroad (lat. 41°41'20" N, long. 121°59'10" W; sec. 5, T 44 N, R 1 W). Named on Bray (1950) 15' quadrangle.

Keller Lake [GLENN]: *lake,* 250 feet long, 1 mile west-southwest of Black Butte (lat. 39°43'10" N, long. 122°53'20" W). Named on Plaskett Ridge (1967) 7.5' quadrangle, which shows Keller place situated less than 1 mile farther west-southwest (sec. 32, T 22 N, R 9 W).

Keller Soda Spring: see **Cinnabar Springs** [SISKIYOU].

Kelley Lake: see **Kelly Lake** [SISKIYOU].

Kelly [SHASTA]: *locality,* 5.5 miles east-southeast of present Bollibokka Mountain (lat. 40°55' N, long. 122°06'35" W; at W line sec. 4, T 35 N, R 2 W). Named on Redding (1901) 30' quadrangle.

Kelly Gulch [SISKIYOU]:

(1) *canyon,* drained by a stream that flows 2 miles to North Fork Salmon River 2 miles west-northwest of Sawyers Bar (lat. 41°18'55" N, long. 123°10'05" W). Named on Sawyers Bar (1979) 7.5' quadrangle.

(2) *canyon,* drained by a stream that flows 1 mile to Deadwood Creek 9.5 miles north of Fort Jones (lat. 41°44'45" N, long. 122°48'40" W; sec. 18, T 45 N, R 8 W). Named on Condrey Mountain (1955) and Fort Jones (1955) 15' quadrangles.

Kelly Lake [SISKIYOU]: *lake,* 1200 feet long, 7.25 miles northeast of Preston Peak (lat. 41°54'50" N, long. 123°31' W). Named on Polar Bear Mountain (1982) 7.5' quadrangle. Called Kelley Lake on Preston Peak (1956) 15' quadrangle, but United States Board on Geographic Names (1983b, p. 1) rejected this name for the feature.

Kelly Ridge [BUTTE]: *ridge,* north-northeast-trending, 1.5 miles long, less than 1 mile east of Oroville Dam (lat. 39°32'10" N, long. 121°27'55" W). Named on Oroville Dam (1970) 7.5' quadrangle.

Kelsey Camp [SISKIYOU]: *locality,* 9 miles southwest of Scott Bar (lat. 41°38'45" N, long. 123°07' W; sec. 21, T 44 N, R 11 W); the place is near the mouth of Kelsey Creek. Named on Scott Bar (1955) 15' quadrangle. Averill's (1935) map has the name "Turners Camp" at the site.

Kelsey Creek [SISKIYOU]: *stream,* flows 6 miles to Scott River 9 miles southwest of Scott Bar (lat. 41°38'45" N, long. 123°06'50" W). Named on Grider Valley (1981), Marble Mountain (1980), and Scott Bar (1980) 7.5' quadrangles. North Fork enters from the northwest 3.5 miles upstream from the mouth of the main creek; it is 1.5 miles long and is named on Grider Valley (1981) 7.5' quadrangle. South Fork enters from the southwest 1.25 miles upstream from the mouth of the main creek; it is 5.25 miles long and is named on Grider Valley (1981) and Marble Mountain (1980) 7.5' quadrangles.

Kelsey Gulch [TEHAMA]: *canyon,* 1.25 miles long, along Dry Creek (1) above a point 1.5 miles east of Beegum Peak (lat. 40°19'10" N, long. 122°51'20" W; near W line sec. 35, T 29 N, R 9 W). Named on Chanchelulla Peak (1951) 15' quadrangle.

Kelsey Range [SISKIYOU]: *ridge,* extends 5 miles west from Bear Peak (center near lat. 41°41'50" N, long. 123°37' W). Named on Bear Peak (1982) and Prescott Mountain (1981) 7.5' quadrangles.

Keluche Creek [SHASTA]: *stream,* flows 1.25 miles to McCloud River Arm Shasta Lake 12.5 miles southeast of Lamoine (lat. 40°50'25" N, long. 122°16'40" W; at W line sec. 36, T 35 N, R 4 W). Named on Lamoine (1957) 15' quadrangle. The name recalls the supervisor of an Indian orphanage (Steger, p. 41).

Kemper Gulch: see **Swearingen Gulch** [SISKIYOU].

Kemp Flat [SHASTA]: *area,* 10.5 miles north-northwest of Burney Falls along Bear Creek [SHASTA-SISKIYOU] (lat. 41°08'35" N, long. 121°44'55" W; sec. 9, T 38 N, R 2 E). Named on Pondosa (1961) 15' quadrangle.

Kendon: see **Oak Run** [SHASTA].

Kendrick Creek [TEHAMA]: *stream,* flows 8 miles to North Fork Stony Creek [GLENN-TEHAMA] 8 miles south of Flournoy (lat. 39°48'15" N, long. 122°25'45" W; sec. 33, T 23 N, R 5 W). Named on Newville (1967) and Sehorn Creek (1967) 7.5' quadrangles.

Kenebeck Creek [BUTTE]: *stream,* flows 2 miles to Fall River 9.5 miles north-northwest of Clipper Mills (lat. 39°39'50" N, long. 121°12'55" W; sec. 20, T 21 N, R 7 E). Named on Cascade (1948) 7.5' quadrangle.

Kenebeck Ridge [BUTTE]: *ridge,* south-to south-southwest-trending, 2.25 miles long, 10 miles north of Clipper Mills (lat. 39°40'30" N, long. 121°11'45" W); the ridge is east of Kenebeck Creek. Named on Cascade (1948) 7.5' quadrangle.

Kennebec Gulch [SISKIYOU]: *canyon,* drained by a stream that flows 2.25 miles to Humbug Creek 13 miles southwest of Hornbrook (lat. 41°46'30" N, long. 122°43'20" W; sec. 1, T 45 N, R 8 W). Named on Hornbrook (1955) 15' quadrangle.

Kennedy Creek [SISKIYOU]: *stream,* flows 1.5 miles to Klamath River 2.5 miles east-northeast of Dillon Mountain (lat. 41°32'25" N, long. 123°31'35" W). Named on Dillon Mountain (1983) 7.5' quadrangle, which shows Kennedy homestead near the head of the stream.

Kennedy Ravine [BUTTE]: *canyon,* drained by a stream that flows 1.5 miles to North Fork Feather River 4.25 miles north-northwest of Bidwell Bar (lat. 39°36'35" N, long. 121°29'05" W; near NE cor. sec. 11, T 20 N, R 4 E). Named on Big Bend Mountain (1948) 15' quadrangle.

Kennett [SHASTA]: *locality,* 11 miles north of Redding along Sacramento River (lat. 40°44'30" N, long. 122°24'30" W; at SW cor. sec. 2, T 33 N, R 5 W). Named on Redding (1901) 30' quadrangle. Water of Shasta Lake now covers the site. Postal authorities established Kennett post office in 1886 and discontinued it in 1942 (Frickstad, p. 180). Officials of Central Pacific Railroad named the community in 1884 for Squire Kennett, a stockholder (Gudde, 1949, p. 172). California Mining Bureau's (1909b) map shows a place called Mammoth located 4 miles by stage northwest of Kennett. Postal authorities established Mammoth post office, named for a copper mine, in 1907, discontinued it in 1921, reestablished it in 1923, and discontinued it in 1925 (Salley, p. 131).

Kenny Ridge [TEHAMA]: *ridge,* generally northeast-trending, 2.5 miles long, 5.5 miles south of Ball Mountain (lat. 39°51'15" N, long. 122°48'30" W). Named on Log Spring (1967) 7.5' quadrangle.

Kenshaw Spring [SHASTA]: *spring,* 6.5 miles west of Arbuckle Mountain (lat. 40°24'40" N, long. 122°58' W). Named on Red Bluff (1894) 1° quadrangle.

Kentuck Gulch [SISKIYOU]: *canyon,* drained by a stream that flows 1 mile to Tennessee Gulch (2) 7.5 miles north of Fort Jones (lat. 41°42'20" N, long. 122°51'35" W; sec. 34, T 45 N, R 9 W). Named on Fort Jones (1955) 15' quadrangle.

Kern Point [GLENN]: *peak,* 9.5 miles west-southwest of the village of Elk Creek (lat. 39°33'35" N, long. 122°42'30" W); the peak is at the northeast end of Kern Ridge. Altitude 5052 feet. Named on Felkner Hill (1968) 7.5' quadrangle.

Kern Ridge [GLENN]: *ridge,* west-southwest-trending, 1.25 miles long, 10 miles west-southwest of the village of Elk Creek (lat. 39°33'25" N, long. 122°43' W; sec. 25, 26, T 20 N, R 8 W). Named on Felkner Hill (1968) 7.5' quadrangle.

Keswick [SHASTA]: *locality,* 4.5 miles northwest of Redding (lat. 40°37'15" N, long. 122°27'45" W; near NW cor. sec. 20, T 32 N, R 5 W). Named on Redding (1957) 7.5' quadrangle. Redding (1901) 30' quadrangle has both the names "Keswick" and "Taylor" at or near the site, and also has the name "Keswick" for a place situated about 1 mile farther northeast along Southern Pacific Railroad. Postal authorities established Keswick post office in 1896 and discontinued it in 1923 (Frickstad, p. 180). The place was the smelter site, railroad station, and post office of Mountain Copper Company; officials of the company named the place for Lord Keswick, president of the enterprise (Steger, p. 42). The community of Taylor, located just south of Keswick, started shortly after Mountain Copper Company broke ground for its plant (Kett, p. 113). Postal authorities established Taylor post office 1.5 miles southwest of Keswick in 1897 and discontinued it in 1922 (Salley, p. 219). They established Fielding post office 12 miles northwest of Keswick in 1897 and discontinued it in 1903

(Salley, p. 74). They established Old Diggings post office 4 miles northeast of Keswick (NE quarter sec. 4, T 32 N, R 5 W) in 1918 and discontinued it in 1927 (Salley, p. 160).

Ketchum Gulch [SISKIYOU]: *canyon,* drained by a stream that flows nearly 1 mile to East Fork of South Fork Salmon River 2.25 miles east-northeast of Cecilville (lat. 41°09'30" N, long. 123°05'55" W). Named on Grasshopper Ridge (1979) 7.5' quadrangle.

Kett [SHASTA]: *locality,* 4 miles west-northwest of Redding along Southern Pacific Railroad (lat. 40°36'25" N, long. 122°27'45" W; near NW cor. sec. 29, T 32 N, R 5 W). Named on Redding (1957) 7.5' quadrangle.

Kettlebelly Ridge [SHASTA]: *ridge,* east- to southeast-trending, 1 mile long, 1.5 miles north-northeast of Castella (lat. 41°09'35" N, long. 122°18'15" W). Named on Dunsmuir (1954) 15' quadrangle.

Kettle Mountain [SHASTA]: *peak,* 11 miles east of Bollibokka Mountain (lat. 40°57' N, long. 122°00'35" W; near E line sec. 30, T 36 N, R 1 W). Named on Bollibokka Mountain (1957) 15' quadrangle.

Keyser Creek [BUTTE]: *stream,* flows 3.25 miles to Big Kimshew Creek 8.5 miles north of Pulga (lat. 39°55'25" N, long. 121°26'40" W; near W line sec. 20, T 24 N, R 5 E). Named on Kimshew Point (1979) 7.5 quadrangle. Called Kaiser Creek on Bidwell Bar (1897) 30' quadrangle.

Kid Camp [SISKIYOU]: *locality,* 11 miles south-southwest of Scott Bar (lat. 41°36'45" N, long. 123°07'30" W). Named on Seiad (1922) 30' quadrangle.

Kidd Creek [SISKIYOU]: *stream,* flows 1.5 miles to South Fork Salmon River 30 miles south of Etna (lat. 41°01'30" N, long. 122°55'40" W; near NE cor. sec. 31, T 37 N, R 9 W). Named on Coffee Creek (1955) 15' quadrangle.

Kidder Creek [SISKIYOU]: *stream,* flows 18 miles to Scott River less than 1 mile west-southwest of Fort Jones (lat. 41°36' N, long. 122°51'15" W; at NW cor. sec. 11, T 43 N, R 9 W); the stream heads at Kidder Lake. Named on Fort Jones (1955) 15' quadrangle, and on Boulder Peak (1981) 7.5' quadrangle. Babs Fork enters 17 miles south of Scott Bar; it is nearly 4 miles long and is named on Yellow Dog Peak (1977) 7.5' quadrangle. Glendenning Fork enters 17 miles south of Scott Bar; it is 2.5 miles long and is named on Yellow Dog Peak (1977) 7.5' quadrangle. Shelly Fork enters 17 miles south of Scott Bar; it is 2.25 miles long and is named on Boulder Peak (1981) and Yellow Dog Peak (1977) 7.5' quadrangles.

Kidder Lake [SISKIYOU]: *lake,* 550 feet long, 17 miles south-southwest of Scott Bar (lat. 41°30'55" N, long. 123°06'15" W); the lake is at the head of Kidder Creek. Named on Boulder Peak (1981) 7.5' quadrangle.

Kilarc Reservoir [SHASTA]: *lake,* 700 feet long, 4 miles northeast of Whitmore (lat. 40°40'10" N, long. 121°51'30" W; sec. 33, T 33 N, R 1 E). Named on Whitmore (1956) 15' quadrangle.

Kilgore Ridge [GLENN]: *ridge,* generally southwest-trending, 1.5 miles long, 8.5 miles west-southwest of Newville (lat. 39°45' N, long. 122°40'30" W). Named on Alder Springs (1967) and Hall Ridge (1967) 7.5' quadrangles.

Killanger Peak [SHASTA]: *peak,* 10 miles south of Bollibokka Mountain (lat. 40°47'10" N, long. 122°13' W; sec. 21, T 34 N, R 3 W). Altitude 1469 feet. Named on Bollibokka Mountain (1957) 15' quadrangle.

Kill Dry Creek [GLENN]: *stream,* flows 5.5 miles to Grindstone Creek [GLENN-TEHAMA] 6 miles northeast of Black Butte (lat. 39°46'35" N, long. 122°46'55" W). Named on Log Spring (1967) and Plaskett Meadows (1967) 7.5' quadrangles.

Kill Dry Ridge [GLENN]: *ridge,* north-northeast- to east-northeast-trending, 1.5 miles long, 3 miles northeast of Black Butte (lat. 39°45' N, long. 122°49'10" W); the ridge is south of Kill Dry Creek. Named on Log Spring (1967) and Plaskett Meadows (1967) 7.5' quadrangles.

Kimball Plains [TEHAMA]: *area,* 5.5 miles west-northwest of Tehama (lat. 40°03' N, long. 122°13' W). Named on Tehama (1905) 15' quadrangle.

Kimberly: see **Coram** [SHASTA].

Kimshew Creek: see **Big Kimshew Creek** [BUTTE]; **Little Kimshew Creek** [BUTTE].

Kimshew Point [BUTTE]: *ridge,* east-northeast-trending, 1.5 miles long, 7 miles north of Pulga (lat. 39°54' N, long. 121°28' W). Named on Kimshew Point (1979) 7.5' quadrangle.

Kimshew Table Mountain: see **Table Mountain** [BUTTE].

Kindig Camp [SISKIYOU]: *locality,* 9 miles southwest of Fort Jones along Kidder Creek (lat. 41°31'20" N, long. 122°58'15" W; near NW cor. sec. 2, T 42 N, R 10 W). Named on Fort Jones (1955) 15' quadrangle.

King: see **Clarence King Lake** [SISKIYOU].

King Creek [SISKIYOU]: *stream,* flows 5 miles to Klamath River 6.5 miles west-northwest of Ukonom Lake (lat. 41°37'05" N, long. 123°28'15" W). Named on Ukonom Mountain (1980) 7.5' quadrangle.

Kings Castle [SISKIYOU]: *peak,* 14 miles southwest of Scott Bar (lat. 41°36'55" N, long. 123°13'15" W). Altitude 7405 feet. Named on Marble Mountain (1980) 7.5' quadrangle.

Kings Creek [SHASTA]: *stream,* flows 8.5 miles to Plumas County 8 miles east-southeast of Lassen Peak (lat. 40°26'45" N, long. 121°21'45" W; sec. 19, T 30 N, R 6 E). Named on Mount Harkness (1956) 15' quadrangle. The name is for James M. King, who lived along the stream (Steger, p. 42).

Kings Creek Campground [SHASTA]: *locality,* 2.5 miles southeast of Lassen Peak (lat. 40°27'40" N, long. 121°28'25" W; near W line sec. 18, T 30 N, R 5 E); the place is along Kings Creek. Named on Mount Harkness (1956) 15' quadrangle.

Kings Creek Falls: see **Kings Falls** [SHASTA].

Kings Creek Meadow: see **Lower Kings Creek Meadow**, under **Lower Meadow** [SHASTA].

Kings Falls [SHASTA]: *waterfall,* 4 miles east-southeast of Lassen Peak (lat. 40°27'35" N, long. 121°26'20" W; at E line sec. 17, T 30 N, R 5 E); the feature is along Kings Creek. Named on Mount Harkness (1956) 15' quadrangle. United States Board on Geographic Names (1933, p. 428) once approved the name "Kings Creek Falls" for the feature.

King's Ford: see **Millville** [SHASTA].

Kingsley Cave [TEHAMA]: *cave,* 6.25 miles south-southwest of Panther Spring (lat. 40°10'10" N, long. 121°50'05" W). Named on Panther Spring (1953) 15' quadrangle.

Kingsley Cove [TEHAMA]: *relief feature,* 6 miles south-southwest of Panther Spring (lat. 40°10'15" N, long. 121°50'10" W). Named on Panther Spring (1953) 15' quadrangle.

Kingsley Creek [TEHAMA]: *stream,* flows about 2.5 miles to Cold Fork (1) 5 miles northwest of Wakefield Flat (lat. 40°10'10" N, long. 122°43'05" W; near S line sec. 24, T 27 N, R 8 W). Named on Cold Fork (1967) 7.5' quadrangle.

Kingsley Glade [TEHAMA]: *area,* 2.25 miles south-southeast of Ball Mountain (lat. 39°54'10" N, long. 122°45'55" W; near S line sec. 28, T 24 N, R 8 W). Named on Ball Mountain (1967) 7.5' quadrangle.

Kingsley Glades [TEHAMA]: *area,* 6.5 miles northwest of Wakefield Flat (lat. 40°11'25" N, long. 122°44'05" W; sec. 14, T 27 N, R 8 W). Named on Cold Fork (1967) 7.5' quadrangle.

Kingsley Gulch [TEHAMA]: *canyon,* drained by a stream that flows 4 miles to lowlands 7 miles north-northeast of Los Molinos (lat. 40°07'20" N, long. 122°03'55" W). Named on Los Molinos (1952) and Tuscan Springs (1951) 7.5' quadrangles.

Kingsley Lake [TEHAMA]: *dry lake,* 200 feet long, 10 miles southwest of Tomhead Mountain (lat. 40°02' N, long. 122°56'30" W; sec. 11, T 25 N, R 10 W). Named on Yolla Bolly (1954) 15' quadrangle.

Kinner Falls [SHASTA]: *waterfall,* 2 miles southeast of the village of Big Bend along Pit River (lat. 41°00'05" N, long. 121°52'50" W; sec. 5, T 36 N, R 1 E). Named on Big Bend (1961) 15' quadrangle.

Kinsman Creek [SISKIYOU]: *stream,* flows 2 miles to Klamath River 9.5 miles east-southeast of the village of Seiad Valley (lat. 41°48'25" N, long. 123°00'55" W; sec. 28, T 46 N, R 10 W). Named on Condrey Mountain (1955) 15' quadrangle, and on Hamburg (1980) 7.5' quadrangle. Called McKinsman Cr. on Seiad (1922) 30' quadrangle.

Kinyon [SISKIYOU]: *locality,* 4 miles west-southwest of Bartle (lat. 41°16'15" N, long. 121°53'35" W; sec. 31, T 40 N, R 1 E). Named on Bartle (1961) 15' quadrangle. Postal authorities established Kinyon post office in 1952 and discontinued it in 1964; the name was for the manager of the logging camp at the site (Salley, p. 112).

Kirkwood [TEHAMA]: *locality,* 5 miles south of Corning (lat. 39°51'25" N, long. 122°09'40" W; near SE cor. sec. 11, T 23 N, R 3 W). Named on Kirkwood (1949) 7.5' quadrangle. Postal authorities established Kirkwood post office in 1886 and discontinued it in 1953 (Frickstad, p. 204). The name commemorates Samuel J. Kirkwood, Secretary of the Interior in 1881 (Gudde, 1949, p. 176).

Kiska [TEHAMA]: *locality,* 1 mile north-northwest of Gerber along Southern Pacific Railroad (lat. 40°04'05" N, long. 122°09'35" W). Named on Gerber (1950) 7.5' quadrangle.

Klamath Hot Springs: see **Beswick** [SISKIYOU].

Klamath Lake: see **Lower Klamath Lake** [SISKIYOU].

Klamath Mill: see **Sawyers Bar** [SISKIYOU].

Klamathon [SISKIYOU]: *locality,* 2.5 miles east-southeast of Hornbrook (lat. 41°54' N, long. 122°30'30" W; near N line sec. 26, T 47 N, R 6 W); the place is along Klamath River. Named on Hornbrook (1955) 15' quadrangle. Postal authorities established Pokegama post office 2.5 miles southeast of Hornbrook in 1892, changed the name to Klamathon in 1897, and discontinued it in 1918 (Salley, p. 112, 175). James McLaughlin built a mill at the site in 1890 and called the place Pokagama (not the post office form "Pokegama"), an Indian name from Wisconsin; John R. Cook ran the mill in 1892 and renamed the place Klamathton (with the extra "t") (Gudde, 1949, p. 176). Postal authorities established Cataract post office 14 miles east of Klamathon in 1899 and discontinued it in 1903 (Salley, p. 40).

Klamathon Spring [SISKIYOU]: *spring,* 3 miles south-southeast of Hornbrook (lat. 41°52'10" N, long. 122°31'20" W; sec. 34, T 47 N, R 8 W); the spring is nearly 2 miles south-southwest of Klamathon. Named on Hornbrook (1955) 15' quadrangle.

Klamath River [SISKIYOU]: *stream,* heads in the State of Oregon and flows about 63 miles in Siskiyou County to Humboldt County 13 miles northwest of Forks of Salmon (lat. 41°22'50" N, long. 123°29'50" W; near N line sec. 4, T 40 N, R 6 E). Named on Weed (1963) 1°x 2° quadrangle. Called Smiths R. on Burr's (1839) map, called Too too tut na or Klamet R. on Wilkes' (1841) map, called Smith's R. on Fremont's (1845) map, called Tlamath R. on Tanner's (1849) map, and called R. del Tlamachi on Ferry's (1851) map. The feature also was known as Clamitte River and Indian Scalp River (Hoover, Rensch, and Rensch, p. 504).

Klamath River: see **Gottville** [SISKIYOU].

Klamath River Post Office [SISKIYOU]: *village,* 9.5 miles southeast of Condrey Mountain (lat. 41°51'45" N, long. 122°49'30" W; sec. 6, T 46 N, R 8 W). Named on Condrey Mountain (1955) 15' quadrangle. Called Browns Resort on Yreka (1939) 30' quadrangle. Averill's (1935) map has the name "Browns" at the site. Postal authorities established Klamath River post office in 1934 and moved it 3.5 miles west in 1942 (Salley, p. 112).

Klamet River: see **Klamath River** [SISKIYOU].

Kleaver Lake [SISKIYOU]: *lake,* 700 feet long, 18 miles south-southwest of Scott Bar (lat. 41°30'05" N, long. 123°08'10" W). Named on Marble Mountain (1980) 7.5' quadrangle.

Klotz Spur: see **Panorama Point** [SHASTA].

Kluntuchi Butte [SISKIYOU]: *hill,* 13 miles north of Bartle (lat. 41°26'20" N, long. 121°51' W; near SW cor. sec. 34, T 42 N, R 1 E). Altitude 5230 feet. Named on Bartle (1961) 15' quadrangle.

Knass Spring [TEHAMA]: *spring,* 0.5 mile southeast of Panther Spring (lat. 40°14'20" N, long. 121°46' W; sec. 32, T 28 N, R 2 E). Named on Panther Spring (1953) 15' quadrangle.

Kneecap Ridge [GLENN]: *ridge,* south-southwest- to west-trending, 4.5 miles long, 11 miles south-southeast of Black Butte on Glenn-Lake County line (lat. 39°34'20" N, long. 122°48'15" W). Named on Kneecap Ridge (1967) 7.5' quadrangle.

Knob [SHASTA]: *locality,* 6.5 miles west of Arbuckle Mountain (lat. 40°23'20" N, long. 122°59'15" W; at SW cor. sec. 3, T 29 N, R 10 W); the place is 2 miles west-southwest of Knob Mountain. Named on Chanchelulla Peak (1951) 15' quadrangle. Postal authorities established Knob post office in 1896 and discontinued it in 1944 (Frickstad, p. 180). Giles (p. 193) gave the alternate name "Harrison Gulch" for the place.

Knob Gulch [SHASTA]: *canyon,* drained by a stream that flows 5.25 miles to Middle Fork Cottonwood Creek [SHASTA-TEHAMA] 1.25 miles west-northwest of Arbuckle Mountain (lat. 40°24'25" N, long. 122°53'10" W; sec. 33, T 30 N, R 9 W); the canyon heads north of Knob Peak. Named on Chanchelulla Peak (1951) 15' quadrangle.

Knob Peak [SHASTA]: *peak,* nearly 5 miles west of Arbuckle Mountain (lat. 40°24' N, long. 122°57'20" W; near N line sec. 2, T 29 N, R 10 W). Altitude 4826 feet. Named on Chanchelulla Peak (1951) 15' quadrangle.

Knochs Reservoir [SHASTA]: *lake,* 750 feet long, 2 miles east of Fall River Mills (lat. 41°40' N, long. 121°23'50" W; sec. 28, T 37 N, R 5 E). Named on Fall River Mills (1961) 15' quadrangle United States Board on Geographic Names (1990, p. 8) approved the name "Knoch Reservoir" for the feature, and rejected the forms "Knochs Reservoir" and "Knoches Reservoir" for the name.

Know-nothing Creek [BUTTE]: *stream,* flows 3.25 miles to South Fork Feather River 3.5 miles north-northwest of Clipper Mills (lat. 39°35'10" N, long. 121°10'15" W; at S line sec. 15, T 20 N, R 7 E). Named on Clipper Mills (1948) 7.5' quadrangle. Bidwell Bar (1897) 30' quadrangle has the form "Knownothing Creek" for the name.

Knownothing Creek [SISKIYOU]: *stream,* formed by the confluence of East Fork and West Fork, flows 2.5 miles to South Salmon River 7.5 miles northeast of Salmon Mountain (lat. 41°14'35" N, long. 123°17'30" W). Named on Youngs Peak (1979) 7.5' quadrangle. East Fork is 5.5 miles long and West Fork is 5.5 miles long; both forks are named on Youngs Peak (1979) 7.5' quadrangle. The name is from Knownothing mine (Gudde, 1949, p. 177).

Knownothing Lake [SISKIYOU]: *lake,* 375 feet long, 2.25 miles southeast of Salmon Mountain (lat. 41°09'40" N, long. 123°22'20" W). Named on Youngs Peak (1979) 7.5' quadrangle.

Knox Gulch [SISKIYOU]: *canyon,* drained by a stream that flows 1.25 miles to Middle Fork Applegate River 15 miles north-northeast of Happy Camp (lat. 41°59'45" N, long. 123°15'20" W). Named on Figurehead Mountain (1980) 7.5' quadrangle.

Knudsen Bar [SISKIYOU]: *locality,* 2.25 miles northwest of Forks of Salmon along Salmon River (lat. 41°16'50" N, long. 123°21'05" W). Named on Forks of Salmon (1978) 7.5' quadrangle.

Kohl Creek [SISKIYOU]: *stream,* flows 4 miles to Klamath River 7 miles south-southeast of Condrey Mountain (lat. 41°50'20" N, long. 122°55'50" W; sec. 7, T 46 N, R 9 W). Named on Condrey Mountain (1955) 15' quadrangle. United States Board on Geographic Names (1967b, p. 3) approved the name "Chase Gulch" for a canyon, 1.5 miles long, that opens into the canyon of Klamath River about 1 mile upstream from the mouth of Kohl Creek (sec. 8, T 46 N, R 9 W).

Konwakiton Glacier [SISKIYOU]: *glacier,* 10.5 miles north-northwest of McCloud (lat. 41°24' N, long. 122°11'40" W; sec. 16, T 41 N, R 3 W); the glacier is at the head of Mud Creek (2). Named on Shasta (1954) 15' quadrangle. The feature also was known as Mud Creek Glacier or McCloud Glacier (McAllister, p. 193), but United States Board on Geographic Names (1933, p. 435) rejected the name "McCloud Glacier" for it. According to Eichorn, (p. 13), the name "Konwakiton" is of Indian origin and has the meaning "dirty" or "muddy."

Kopta Slough [TEHAMA]: *water feature,* joins Sacramento River 2.5 miles southwest of Vina (lat. 39°54'35" N, long. 122°05'35" W; sec. 28, T 24 N, R 2 W). Named on Vina (1950) 7.5' quadrangle.

Kosk [SHASTA]: *locality,* 1.5 miles northwest of the present village of Big Bend (lat. 41°02'20" N, long. 121°56'15" W); the place is along Kosk Creek. Named on Modoc Lava Bed (1892) 1° quadrangle.

Kosk Creek [SHASTA]: *stream,* flows 15 miles to Pit River 1.25 miles west-northwest of the village of Big Bend (lat. 41°01'40" N, long. 121°55'50" W; at NE cor. sec. 35, T 37 N, R 1 W). Named on Big Bend (1961) 15' quadrangle. The name commemorates John Kosk, or Kosh, a Russian who supervised Silver City mine in the 1860's (Steger, p. 43).

Kram [BUTTE]: *locality,* 3.25 miles north-northwest of Oroville along Western Pacific Railroad (lat. 39°33'10" N, long. 121°35' W; on S line sec. 25, T 20 N, R 3 E). Named on Oroville (1970) 7.5' quadrangle.

Kunkle Reservoir [BUTTE]: *lake,* 1400 feet long, 4 miles southeast of Paradise (lat. 39°42'50" N, long. 121°34'25" W; near SW cor. sec. 31, T 22 N, R 4 E). Named on Cherokee (1970) 7.5' quadrangle. The name recalls a mining place called Kunkles after a settler (Gudde, 1969, p. 168). United States Board on Geographic Names (1973, p. 3) gave the variant name "Kunckle Reservoir" for the feature. Kunkle, Kunkles, or Kunkles ranch (in NW quarter sec. 31, T 22 N, R 4 E) was a stage stop and voting precinct in the 1850's (Dunn, F.D., p. 59).

Kunkles: see **Kunkle Reservoir** [BUTTE].

Kuntz Creek [SISKIYOU]: *stream,* flows 4 miles to Klamath River nearly 7 miles east-southeast of the village of Seiad Valley (lat. 41°47'30" N, long. 123°05' W). Named on Hamburg (1980) 7.5' quadrangle.

Kurand [GLENN]: *locality,* 9.5 miles east-southeast of Fruto along Southern Pacific Railroad (lat. 39°31'50" N, long. 122°17'15" W; near E line sec. 3, T 19 N, R 4 W). Named on Fruto (1944) 15' quadrangle.

Kusal Island [GLENN]: *island,* 18 miles north of Butte City along Sacramento River (lat. 39°44'15" N, long. 121°57'50" W). Named on Chico Landing (1912) 7.5' quadrangle.

Kusal Slough [BUTTE]: *water feature,* 3 miles long, joins Mud Creek 5.5 miles west of Chico (lat. 39°43'30" N, long. 121°56'15" W). Named on Nord (1951) and Ord Ferry (1949) 7.5' quadrangles.

— L —

La Barranca Colorada [TEHAMA]: *land grant,* south of Red Bluff. Named on Gerber (1950), Red Bluff East (1951), and West of Gerber (1951) 7.5' quadrangles. Josiah Belden received 4 leagues in 1844; William B. Ide claimed 17,707 acres patented in 1860 (Cowan, p. 18).

Lack Creek [SHASTA]: *stream,* flows 12.5 miles to Bear Creek (2) nearly 5 miles north-northeast of Balls Ferry (lat. 40°28'50" N, long. 122°09'15" W; sec. 1, T 30 N, R 3 W). Named on Manton (1956) 15' quadrangle, and on Balls Ferry (1965) and Tuscan Buttes NE (1965) 7.5' quadrangles. Steger (p. 43) associated the name with De Marcus Franklin Lack, who settled 9 miles east of Balls Ferry about 1860.

Ladds Creek [SISKIYOU]: *stream,* flows nearly 2 miles to Klamath River 7.25 miles northeast of Happy Camp (lat. 41°51'35" N, long. 123°15'45" W; sec. 5, T 46 N, R 12 W). Named on Slater Butte (1980) 7.5' quadrangle.

Ladybug Butte [SHASTA]: *peak,* 1 mile west-northwest of Shoeinhorse Mountain (lat. 41°04'30" N, long. 122°05'30" W); the peak is south of Ladybug Creek. Altitude 4960 feet. Named on Shoeinhorse Mountain (1954) 15' quadrangle.

Ladybug Creek [SHASTA]: *stream,* flows 2.5 miles to Bones Gulch 2.5 miles northwest of Shoeinhorse Mountain (lat. 41°05'30" N, long. 122°06'40" W); the stream is north of Ladybug Butte. Named on Shoeinhorse Mountain (1954) 15' quadrangle.

Lafayette Point [SISKIYOU]: *relief feature,* 5 miles north of Cecilville (lat. 41°12'45" N, long. 123°08'35" W). Named on Cecilville (1979) 7.5' quadrangle.

Lagoon: see **The Lagoon** [BUTTE].

La Honda Well [SISKIYOU]: *well,* 5.5 miles east of Bray (lat. 41°38'25" N, long. 121°51'25" W; at E line sec. 21, T 44 N, R 1 E). Named on Bray (1950) 15' quadrangle.

Laird Lake [SISKIYOU]: *intermittent lake,* 1000 feet long, 3 miles north-northeast of Mount Dome (lat. 41°51'05" N, long. 121°40' W; near SE cor. sec. 6, T 46 N, R 3 E). Named on Mount Dome (1950) 15' quadrangle.

Laird Landing [SISKIYOU]: *locality,* 5 miles north-northwest of Mount Dome (lat. 41°52'30" N, long. 121°43'20" W; at W line sec. 35, T 47 N, R 2 E). Named on Mount Dome (1950) 15' quadrangle.

Lairds Camp [SISKIYOU]: *locality,* 2 miles south-southeast of Mount Dome (lat. 41°47'05" N, long. 121°40'40" W; sec. 31, T 46 N, R 3 E). Named on

Mount Dome (1950) 15' quadrangle.

Lairds Well [SISKIYOU]: *well,* 11 miles north-northwest of Medicine Lake (lat. 41°43'50" N, long. 121°40' W; sec. 19, T 45 N, R 3 E). Named on Medicine Lake (1952) 15' quadrangle.

Lake Britton [SHASTA]: *lake,* behind a dam on Pit River 1.5 miles north-west of Burney Falls (lat. 41°01'50" N, long. 121°40'30" W; at SW cor. sec. 19, T 37 N, R 3 E). Named on Burney (1957) and Pondosa (1961) 15' quadrangles. The lake was formed in 1925 and named in memory of John A. Britton, general manager of Pacific Gas and Electric Company (Gudde, 1949, p. 41).

Lake Canyon [GLENN]: *canyon,* drained by a stream that flows 1.5 miles to South Fork Willow Creek 4 miles north-northwest of High Peak (lat. 39°28'30" N, long. 122°26'25" W; sec. 29, T 19 N, R 5 W). Named on Lodoga (1960) 15' quadrangle.

Lake De Sabla [BUTTE]: *lake,* 1300 feet long, 5 miles west-southwest of Stirling City (lat. 39°07'25" N, long. 121°36'40" W; near S line sec. 2, T 23 N, R 3 E); the lake is at De Sabla. Named on Paradise East (1980) and Stirling City (1979) 7.5' quadrangles. California Division of Highways' (1934) map had the name "De Sabla Reservoir" for the feature.

Lake Dwinnell: see **Lake Shastina** [SISKIYOU].

Lake Eiler [SHASTA]: *lake,* 3500 feet long, 17 miles north of Lassen Peak (lat. 40°43'35" N, long. 121°34'05" W; at S line sec. 7, T 33 N, R 4 E); the lake is northwest of Eiler Butte. Named on Manzanita Lake (1956) 15' quadrangle. Called Lake Eiter on Lassen Peak (1894) 1° quadrangle. The name is for Lu Eiler, who discovered Thousand Lake Valley (Steger, p. 30).

Lake Ethel [SISKIYOU]: *lake,* 900 feet long, 11 miles north-northwest of Sawyers Bar (lat. 41°27'05" N, long. 123°12'20" W). Named on English Peak (1977) 7.5' quadrangle.

Lake Freanor: see **Cornaz Lake** [SHASTA].

Lakehead [SHASTA]: *locality,* nearly 6 miles south-southeast of Lamoine along Southern Pacific Railroad (lat. 40°54'15" N, long. 122°22'40" W; sec. 12, T 35 N, R 5 W); the place is near the head of Sacramento River Arm Shasta Lake. Named on Lamoine (1957) 15' quadrangle. Postal authorities established Lakehead post office in 1950 (Frickstad, p. 181). United States Board on Geographic Names (1969c, p. 4) rejected the names "Lakeshore," "Lakeside," "Loftus," and "Pollock" for the place.

Lake Helen [SHASTA]:

(1) *lake,* 450 feet long, 10 miles west-northwest of Castella (lat. 41°10'50" N, long. 122°29'40" W; sec. 1, T 38 N, R 6 W). Named on Dunsmuir (1954) 15' quadrangle.

(2) *lake,* 1200 feet long, 1.5 miles south of Mount Lassen (lat. 40°28'05" N, long. 121°30'35" W; on S line sec. 11, T 30 N, R 4 E). Named on Lassen Peak (1956) 15' quadrangle. P.B. Reading named the lake for Helen Tanner Brodt, who climbed Lassen Peak in 1864, the first woman to do so (Steger, p. 43).

Lake Hollow [TEHAMA]: *relief feature,* 7.25 miles west-southwest of Paskenta (lat. 39°51'15" N, long. 122°40'25" W; sec. 17, T 23 N, R 7 W). Named on Hall Ridge (1967) 7.5' quadrangle.

Lake Katherine [SISKIYOU]: *lake,* 750 feet long, 11.5 miles north-north-west of Sawyers Bar (lat. 41°27'10" N, long. 123°12'30" W). Named on English Peak (1977) 7.5' quadrangle.

Lake McCloud: see **Skunk Hill** [SHASTA].

Lake Mountain [SISKIYOU]: *peak,* 7 miles west of Scott Bar (lat. 41°44'55" N, long. 123°07'55" W). Altitude 6877 feet. Named on Grider Valley (1981) and Seiad Valley (1980) 7.5' quadrangles.

Lake of the Island [SISKIYOU]: *lake,* 950 feet long, 8.5 miles north of Sawyers Bar (lat. 41°25'05" N, long. 123°10'05" W). Named on English Peak (1977) 7.5' quadrangle, which shows a small island in the lake.

Lake of the Island Creek [SISKIYOU]: *stream,* flows 1.5 miles to North Fork Salmon River 10 miles north of Sawyers Bar (lat. 41°26'15" N, long. 123°09'20" W); the stream heads at Lake of the Island. Named on English Peak (1977) 7.5' quadrangle.

Lake One [SISKIYOU]: *intermittent lake,* 1100 feet long, 7 miles northeast of Mount Dome (lat. 41°53' N, long. 122°35'45" W; sec. 26, T 47 N, R 3 E). Named on Mount Dome (1950) 15' quadrangle.

Lake Oroville [BUTTE]: *lake,* behind Oroville Dam on Feather River 3.5 miles east-northeast of Oroville (lat. 39°32'15" N, long. 121°29' W; on E line sec. 2, T 19 N, R 4 E). Named on Berry Creek (1970), Brush Creek (1970), Cherokee (1970), Forbestown (1970), and Oroville Dam (1970) 7.5' quadrangles.

Lake Redding [SHASTA]: *lake,* behind a small dam on Sacramento River at Redding (lat. 40°35'35" N, long. 122°23'35" W). Named on Redding (1957) 7.5' quadrangle. Construction of a dam for an irrigation project formed the lake in 1916 (Steger, p. 43).

Lake Ridge [GLENN-TEHAMA]: *ridge,* generally north-northeast-trending, 1.25 miles long, 5 miles north-northwest of Black Butte on Glenn-Tehama County line (lat. 39°47'45" N, long. 122°54'15" W). Named on Mendocino Pass (1967) 7.5' quadrangle.

Lake Shastina [SISKIYOU]: *lake,* behind a dam on Shasta River 28 miles southwest of Macdoel (lat. 41°32'30" N, long. 122°22'30" W; sec. 25, T 43 N, R 5 W). Named on Lake Shastina (1954) 15' quadrangle. Called Dwinnell Reservoir on Dwinnell Reservoir (1954) 15' quadrangle, called Lake Dwinnell Res. on Averill's (1935) map, and called Dwinnell Lake on Williams' (1949) map. United States Board on Geographic Names (1972a, p. 4) listed the variant names "Dwinnell Reservoir" and "Lake Dwinnell" for the feature.

Lakeshore [SHASTA]: *locality,* 7.25 miles south-southeast of Lamoine along Sacramento River Arm of Shasta Lake (lat. 40°52'45" N, long. 122°23'20" W; at N line sec. 24, T 35 N, R 5 W). Named on Lamoine (1957) 15' quadrangle. Lamoine (1946) 15' quadrangle has the name "Loftus P.O." at present Lakeshore. Postal authorities established Loftus post office in 1944 and discontinued it in 1954; the name was for Charles Loftus, a pioneer resident at the site (Salley, p. 124). United States Board on Geographic Names (1950, p. 5) rejected the name "Pollock" for Loftus.

Lakeshore: see **Lakehead** [SHASTA].

Lakeside: see **Lakehead** [SHASTA].

Lake Tillman: see **Lower Twin Lake** [SHASTA] (2).

Lake Wyandotte [BUTTE]: *lake,* behind a dam on North Honcut Creek 4 miles southeast of Oroville Dam (lat. 39°30'25" N, long. 121°25'10" W; sec. 16, T 19 N, R 5 E). Named on Oroville Dam (1970) 7.5' quadrangle.

Lakin [SISKIYOU]: *locality,* 15 miles northeast of Bartle along the railroad (lat. 41°22'45" N, long. 121°33'45" W; on W line sec. 19, T 41 N, R 4 E). Named on Hambone (1961) 15' quadrangle.

Lamoine [SHASTA]: *locality,* 27 miles north of Redding along Sacramento River (lat. 40°58'40" N, long. 122°25'50" W; sec. 15, T 36 N, R 5 W). Named on Lamoine (1957) 15' quadrangle. Postal authorities established Slatonis post office in 1899, changed the name to La Moine in 1902, and discontinued it in 1955; the name "Slatonis" was from slate shingles made near the site, and the name "La Moine" was for Lamoine Lumber and Trading Company (Salley, p. 117, 206). The name Lamoine recalls Andrew La Moyne, who gave some of the early deeds for property at the site; the place first was known as Slate Creek Stage Station (Steger, p. 43). Postal authorities established Slate Creek post office—presumably at the stage station—in 1880 and discontinued it in 1885 (Salley, p. 206).

Land [BUTTE]: *locality,* 1.5 miles west-southwest of Bidwell Bar along Western Pacific Railroad (lat. 39°33'15" N, long. 121°28' W; near NE cor. sec. 36, T 20 N, R 4 E). Named on Big Bend Mountain (1948) 15' quadrangle. Water of Lake Oroville now covers the site. The name is for A.H. Land, president of Feather River Pine Mills (Dunn, F.D., p. 59).

Lane Valley [TEHAMA]: *valley,* 5.5 miles south-southwest of Manton along Morgan Creek (lat. 40°21'25" N, long. 121°53'45" W; sec. 19, 20, T 29 N, R 1 E). Named on Manton (1956) 15' quadrangle.

Laniger Lakes [TEHAMA]: *intermittent lakes,* largest 1800 feet long, nearly 3 miles north-northeast of Vina (lat. 39°58'20" N, long. 122°02'15" W; near S line sec. 36, T 25 N, R 2 W). Named on Vina (1950) 7.5' quadrangle.

Lannigan Gulch [BUTTE]: *canyon,* drained by a stream that flows less than 1 mile to Lake Oroville 5.5 miles east-northeast of Oroville Dam (lat. 39°34'15" N, long. 121°23'20" W; at SW cor. sec. 23, T 20 N, R 5 E). Named on Oroville Dam (1970) 7.5' quadrangle.

Lantz Ridge [TEHAMA]: *ridge,* northwest-trending, 1.25 miles long, 6.25 miles south of Ball Mountain (lat. 39°50'50" N, long. 122°46'10" W). Named on Log Spring (1967) 7.5' quadrangle. Anthony Peak (1952) 15' quadrangle shows the site of Lantz cabin on the ridge.

Larkin: see **Centerville** [SHASTA].

Larkins Childrens Rancho [GLENN]: *land grant,* southeast of Willows on the west side of Sacramento River on Glenn-Colusa County line. Named on Butte City (1952), Glenn (1951), Llano Seco (1948), and Princeton (1952) 7.5' quadrangles. F. Larkin and others received 10 leagues in 1844 and claimed 44,364 acres patented in 1857 (Cowan, p. 44). The three minor children of United States Council Thomas O. Larkin received the land; the children were born in California and thereby were Mexican citizens and eligible for the grant, which their father, a United States citizen, was not (Hague and Langum, p. 182).

Las Flores [TEHAMA]:

(1) *land grant,* at Gerber. Named on Gerber (1950), Los Molinos (1952), and West of Gerber (1951) 7.5' quadrangles. William Chard received 3 leagues in 1844 and claimed 13,316 acres patented in 1859 (Cowan, p. 36).

(2) *village,* 1.25 miles north-northwest of Gerber (lat. 40°04'35" N, long. 122°09'40" W); the village is on Las Flores grant. Named on Gerber (1950) 7.5' quadrangle. Postal authorities established Las Flores post office in 1921 and discontinued it in 1924 (Frickstad, p. 204). Promoters laid out the community in 1916 and named it for the grant (Gudde, 1949, p. 117).

Lashes Gulch [SISKIYOU]: *canyon,* drained by a stream that flows less than 1 mile to Humbug Creek 15 miles southeast of Condrey Mountain (lat. 41°46'45" N, long. 122°46'30" W; sec. 4, T 45 N, R 8 W). Named on Condrey Mountain (1955) 15' quadrangle.

Las Plumas [BUTTE]: *locality,* 5 miles west-northwest of the village of Berry Creek along North Fork Feather River (lat. 39°40'20" N, long. 121°29'15" W; at W line sec. 14, T 21 N, R 4 E). Named on Big Bend

Mountain (1948) 15' quadrangle. Water of Lake Oroville now covers the site. Postal authorities established Las Plumas post office in 1908, discontinued it in 1909, reestablished it in 1912, and discontinued it in 1967 (Salley, p. 118). The name is from the location of the place along Feather River (Gudde, 1969, p. 172)—*las plumas* means "the feathers" in Spanish.

Lassen: see **Camp Lassen** [BUTTE]; **Mount Lassen**, under **Brokeoff Mountain** [SHASTA]; **Tehama** [TEHAMA].

Lassen Butte: see **Lassen Peak** [SHASTA].

Lassen Camp: see **Lassen Lodge** [TEHAMA].

Lassen Lodge [TEHAMA]: *locality,* 6 miles west of Mineral (lat. 40°20'45" N, long. 121°42'30" W; on S line sec. 23, T 29 N, R 2 E). Named on Lassen Peak (1956) 15' quadrangle. Called Lassen Camp on Mineral (1941) 30' quadrangle.

Lassen Peak [SHASTA]: *crater,* 29 miles south-southeast of Burney (lat. 40°29'25" N, long. 121°30'30" W; sec. 34, T 31 N, R 4 E). Named on Lassen Peak (1956) and Mount Harkness (1956) 15' quadrangles. Called Mt. Saint Joseph on Schofield's (1851) map, called Lassen's Butte on Williamson and Abbot's (1855) map, and called Lassen Butte on Goddard's (1857) map. The feature also was called Snow Mountain and Lawson's Peak (Steger, p. 43). United States Board on Geographic Names (1933, p. 449) rejected the form "Mount Lassen" for the name, which commemorates Peter Lassen, a pioneer in the region (Hanna, p. 168). United States Board on Geographic Names (1933, p. 763) approved the name "Tophet Springs" for hot sulphur springs situated 3 miles southwest of Lassen Peak (near SW cor. sec. 15, T 30 N, R 4 E).

Lassen's: see **Tehama** [TEHAMA].

Lassen's Butte: see **Lassen Peak** [SHASTA].

Last Camp [TEHAMA]: *locality,* 11 miles southwest of Tomhead Mountain (lat. 40°01' N, long. 122°56'50" W; on W line sec. 14, T 25 N, R 10 W). Named on Yolla Bolly (1954) 15' quadrangle.

Last Chance Creek [BUTTE]:

(1) *stream,* flows 8 miles to West Branch Feather River 2.25 miles north of Stirling City (lat. 39°56'25" N, long. 121°31'55" W; sec. 16, T 24 N, R 4 E). Named on Kimshew Point (1979) and Stirling City (1979) 7.5' quadrangles. Called Fish Creek on Chico (1895) 30' quadrangle, where present Fish Creek is called Last Chance Creek. East Fork enters from the east-northeast 13 miles north of Pulga; it is 2.5 miles long and is named on Kimshew Point (1979) 7.5' quadrangle.

(2) *stream,* flows 1.5 miles to Chino Creek 6 miles north of the village of Berry Creek (lat. 39°43'45" N, long. 121°24'55" W; near SE cor. sec. 28, T 22 N, R 5 E). Named on Berry Creek (1970) 7.5' quadrangle.

Last Chance Creek [TEHAMA]: *stream,* flows 4 miles to Red Bank Creek 6.5 miles east of Wakefield Flat (lat. 40°06'15" N, long. 122°31'10" W; at W line sec. 14, T 26 N, R 6 W). Named on Lowrey (1967) 7.5' quadrangle.

Last Chance Gulch [TEHAMA]: *canyon,* drained by a stream that flows 2 miles to Wells Creek 6.5 miles southeast of Beegum Peak (lat. 40°15'20" N, long. 122°47'25" W; at N line sec. 29, T 28 N, R 8 W. Named on Chanchelulla Peak (1951) and Yolla Bolly (1954) 15' quadrangles.

Lastfeed Flat [TEHAMA]: *area,* 1 mile southwest of Wakefield Flat (lat. 40°06'55" N, long. 122°39'40" W; at S line sec. 9, T 26 N, R 7 W). Named on Raglin Ridge (1967) 7.5' quadrangle.

Latimer Bar: see **Bloomer Hill** [BUTTE].

Latona: see **Redding** [SHASTA].

Latour Butte [SHASTA]: *peak,* 13 miles northwest of Lassen Peak (lat. 40°36'30" N, long. 121°42'30" W; near E line sec. 23, T 32 N, R 2 W). Named on Manzanita Lake (1956) 15' quadrangle. Called Latur Butte on Lassen Peak (1894) 1° quadrangle. The name is for James La Tour, who settled in the region in the late 1850's and homesteaded near the peak in 1872 (Steger, p. 44).

Latson: see **Montgomery Creek** [SHASTA] (2).

Lattimores Bar: see **Bloomer Hill** [BUTTE].

Latur Butte: see **Latour Butte** [SHASTA].

Lava Beds: see **Pacific Heights** [BUTTE].

Lava Camp [SISKIYOU]: *locality,* 7.25 miles north of Medicine Lake (lat. 41°41'05" N, long. 121°37'20" W; at W line sec. 3, T 44 N, R 3 E). Named on Medicine Lake (1952) 15' quadrangle.

Lava Crack Spring [SISKIYOU]: *spring,* 12.5 miles north-northeast of Bartle (lat. 41°24'30" N, long. 121°41'05" W); sec. 12, T 41 N, R 2 E). Named on Hambone (1961) 15' quadrangle.

Lava Creek [SHASTA]: *water feature,* lakelike stream that joins Little Tule River 8 miles north-northwest of Fall River Mills (lat. 41°06'35" N, long. 121°29'30" W). Named on Fall River Mills (1961) 15' quadrangle.

Lava Park [SISKIYOU]: *area,* 6 miles northeast of Weed (lat. 41°29' N, long. 122°16'30" W). Named on Dunsmuir (1935) 30' quadrangle.

Lawrence Basin [SHASTA]: *canyon,* less than 1 mile long, 4.25 miles west-northwest of Whitmore (lat. 40°39'15" N, long. 121°59'15" W; near SW cor. sec. 4, T 32 N, R 1 W). Named on Whitmore (1956) 15' quadrangle.

Lawson Gulch [SISKIYOU]: *canyon,* drained by a stream that flows 1 mile to Humbug Creek 15 miles southeast of Condrey Mountain (lat. 41°46'50" N, long. 122°46' W; near W line sec. 3, T 45 N, R 8 W). Named on Condrey Mountain (1955) 15' quadrangle. Crawford (1896, p. 405) referred to Lawson's Gulch.

Lawson's Peak: see **Lassen Peak** [SHASTA].

Lazyman Butte [TEHAMA]: *peak,* 6.25 miles west-southwest of Tomhead Mountain (lat. 40°06'40" N, long. 122°55'45" W; at SW cor. sec. 7, T 26 N, R 9 W). Named on Yolla Bolly (1954) 15' quadrangle.

Lazyman Camp [TEHAMA]: *locality,* 5 miles west-southwest of Tomhead Mountain (lat. 40°06'15" N, long. 122°54' W; sec. 17, T 26 N, R 9 W); the place is 1.5 miles east-southeast of Lazyman Butte. Named on Yolla Bolly (1954) 15' quadrangle.

Lazyman Ridge [TEHAMA]: *ridge,* north- to east-trending, 6 miles long, 6.25 miles west-south west of Tomhead Mountain (lat. 40°06'40" N, long. 122°55'45" W); Lazyman Butte is on the ridge. Named on Yolla Bolly (1954) 15' quadrangle.

Leaf [SISKIYOU]: *locality,* 1.5 miles west of Bray along Southern Pacific Railroad (lat. 41°38'30" N, long. 121°59'50" W; on E line sec. 20, T 44 N, R 1 W). Named on Bray (1950) and The Whaleback (1954) 15' quadrangles.

Leaf Camp [SISKIYOU]: *locality,* 13 miles south of Macdoel (lat. 41°38'20" N, long. 122°01' W; at N line sec. 30, T 44 N, R 1 W); the place is less than 1 mile west-southwest of Leaf. Named on The Whaleback (1954) 15' quadrangle.

Lee Camp [TEHAMA]: *locality,* 12.5 miles south-southwest of Panther Spring (lat. 40°05'30" N, long. 121°53' W). Named on Panther Spring (1953) 15' quadrangle. Called Clough Camp on Mineral (1941) 30' quadrangle.

Lee Logan Camp [GLENN]: *locality,* 8.5 miles south of Black Butte (lat. 39°36'15" N, long. 122°52'40" W; sec. 9, T 20 N, R 9 W). Named on Hull Mountain (1967) 7.5' quadrangle.

Lee March Gulch [SHASTA]: *canyon,* 1 mile long, 16 miles northwest of Lassen Peak at the head of Atkins Creek (lat. 40°39'15" N, long. 121°43' W; sec. 2, T 32 N, R 2 E). Named on Manzanita Lake (1958) 15' quadrangle.

Lees Lodge [SISKIYOU]: *locality,* 4.5 miles west-southwest of Weed along Eddy Creek (lat. 41°23'55" N, long. 122°27'50" W; sec. 18, T 41 N, R 5 W). Named on Weed (1954) 15' quadrangle.

Lees Meadow [SISKIYOU]: *area,* 14 miles south of Etna (lat. 41°14'55" N, long. 122°55'55" W; at SW cor. sec. 8, T 39 N, R 9 W). Named on Coffee Creek (1955) 15' quadrangle.

Leighton: see **Loomis Corners** [SHASTA].

Leininger Camp [TEHAMA]: *locality,* 14 miles south-southwest of Panther Spring (lat. 40°04' N, long. 121°51'45" W). Named on Panther Spring (1953) 15' quadrangle.

Leland: see **Castella** [SHASTA].

Lena: see **Lyonsville** [TEHAMA].

Lennox Rock [SISKIYOU]: *peak,* 18 miles west-northwest of Macdoel (lat. 41°58'10" N, long. 122°17'45" W; sec. 34, T 48 N, R 4 W). Altitude 3251 feet. Named on Copco (1954) 15' quadrangle.

Leodocia: see **Red Bluff** [TEHAMA].

Leonards Mill: see **Paradise** [BUTTE].

Let-er Buck Meadow [SISKIYOU]: *area,* 17 miles north of Forks of Salmon (lat. 41°29'50" N, long. 123°23'35" W). Named on Somes Bar (1979) 7.5' quadrangle.

Lewis Creek [SISKIYOU]: *stream,* flows 3.5 miles to Salmon River 5 miles northwest of Forks of Salmon (lat. 41°18'50" N, long. 123°22'35" W). Named on Orleans Mountain (1974) 7.5' quadrangle.

Lewis Flat [BUTTE]: *area,* 4.25 miles north-northeast of Clipper Mills (lat. 39°35'20" N, long. 121°07'20" W; sec. 18, T 20 N, R 8 E). Named on Strawberry Valley (1948) 7.5' quadrangle.

Lewis Flat [TEHAMA]: *area,* 5 miles east-southeast of Wakefield Flat (lat. 40°06'30" N, long. 122°33' W; sec. 16, T 26 N, R 6 W). Named on Lowrey (1967) 7.5' quadrangle.

Lewis Ridge [BUTTE]: *ridge,* southwest-trending, 3 miles long, 5.5 miles north-northeast of Clipper Mills (lat. 39°36'15" N, long. 121°07' W). Named on Clipper Mills (1948) and Strawberry Valley (1948) 7.5' quadrangles.

Liberty Cabbage Gulch: see **Sauerkraut Gulch** [SISKIYOU].

Liberty Gulch [SHASTA]: *canyon,* drained by a stream that flows 1.5 miles to Whiskeytown Lake 5.5 miles southeast of the village of French Gulch (lat. 40°39'10" N, long. 122°33'10" W; near S line sec. 4, T 32 N, R 6 W). Named on Whiskeytown (1979) 7.5' quadrangle.

Lick Canyon [SHASTA]: *canyon,* drained by a stream that flows 1 mile to Squaw Creek Arm Shasta Lake 10 miles south-southeast of Bollibokka Mountain (lat. 40°47'55" N, long. 122°09'10" W; sec. 13, T 34 N, R 3 W). Named on Bollibokka Mountain (1957) 15' quadrangle.

Lick Creek [SHASTA]:

(1) *stream,* flows 3 miles to McCloud River [SHASTA-SISKIYOU] 6.5 miles north of Shoeinhorse Mountain (lat. 41°09'45" N, long. 122°04'25" W). Named on Shoeinhorse Mountain (1954) 15' quadrangle.

(2) *stream,* flows 0.5 mile to North Fork Backbone Creek 10 miles south-

southwest of Lamoine (lat. 40°50'20" N, long. 122°28'35" W; near S line sec. 31, T 35 N, R 5 W). Named on Lamoine (1957) 15' quadrangle.

Lick Creek [SISKIYOU]:
(1) *stream,* flows 2.5 miles to North Fork Dillon Creek nearly 3 miles southwest of Bear Peak (lat. 41°39'45" N, long. 123°36'50" W). Named on Bear Peak (1982) 7.5' quadrangle.
(2) *stream,* flows nearly 3 miles to Elk Creek 5.5 miles north-northeast of Ukonom Lake (lat. 41°39'30" N, long. 123°19'05" W). Named on Huckleberry Mountain (1980) 7.5' quadrangle.
(3) *stream,* flows 2 miles to Ukonom Creek 4.5 miles west of Ukonom Lake (lat. 41°34'50" N, long. 123°26'45" W). Named on Ukonom Mountain (1980) 7.5' quadrangle.

Lick Creek: see **Ripgut Creek** [SHASTA].

Lick Gulch [SHASTA]: *canyon,* drained by a stream that flows 1 mile to Shasta Lake 4.25 miles north of the town of Central Valley (lat. 40°44'35" N, long. 122°21'30" W; near E line sec. 6, T 33 N, R 4 W). Named on Project City (1957) 7.5' quadrangle.

Lick Gulch [SISKIYOU]: *canyon,* drained by a stream that flows 1 mile to Applegate River 10.5 miles north of the village of Seiad Valley (lat. 41°59'35" N, long. 123°09'30" W); the canyon heads near Lick Mountain. Named on Kangaroo Mountain (1980) 7.5' quadrangle.

Lick Gulch: see **Middle Lick Gulch** [SISKIYOU].

Lick Mountain [SISKIYOU]: *peak,* 10.5 miles north-northeast of the village of Seiad Valley (lat. 41°59' N, long. 123°08'05" W); the peak is near the head of Lick Gulch. Altitude 4423 feet. Named on Kangaroo Mountain (1980) 7.5' quadrangle.

Lick Springs: see **Tuscan Springs** [TEHAMA].

Lieutenants: see **The Lieutenants** [SISKIYOU].

Lightning Canyon [SHASTA]: *canyon,* drained by a stream that flows 0.5 mile to Salt Creek (6) 10 miles southeast of Lamoine (lat. 41°52'15" N, long. 122°18'35" W; sec. 22, T 35 N, R 4 W). Named on Lamoine (1957) 15' quadrangle.

Lightning Gulch [SISKIYOU]:
(1) *canyon,* drained by a stream that flows 3 miles to Salal Gulch 14 miles north of Orleans, which is in Humboldt County (lat. 41°29'50" N, long. 123°34'45" W); the canyon is southeast of Lightning Ridge. Named on Bark Shanty Gulch (1974) 7.5' quadrangle.
(2) *canyon,* drained by a stream that flows 1 mile to Seiad Creek 3 miles north-northeast of the village of Seiad Valley (lat. 41°51'50" N, long. 123°08'35" W). Named on Seiad Valley (1980) 7.5' quadrangle.

Lightning Ridge [SISKIYOU]; *ridge,* northeast-trending, 2.25 miles long, 13 miles north-northwest of Orleans, which is in Humboldt County (lat. 41°29' N, long. 123°36'30" W). Named on Bark Shanty Gulch (1974) 7.5' quadrangle.

Lightning Spring [TEHAMA]: *spring,* 8 miles southwest of Ball Mountain (lat. 39°50'55" N, long. 122°53'30" W; sec. 17, T 23 N, R 9 W). Named on Mendocino Pass (1967) 7.5' quadrangle.

Lilienthal [SHASTA]: *locality,* 9 miles northeast of Redding (lat. 40°40'55" N, long. 122°17'30" W; near SW cor. sec. 26, T 33 N, R 4 W). Named on Redding (1901) 30' quadrangle.

Lilly Mountain [SISKIYOU]: *peak,* 4.5 miles north of Condrey Mountain at California-Oregon State line (lat. 42°00'05" N, long. 122°58'55" W; on N line sec. 23, T 48 N, R 10 W). Named on Condrey Mountain (1955) 15' quadrangle.

Lily Lake [SISKIYOU]: *lake,* 600 feet long, 9 miles north-northeast of Forks of Salmon (lat. 41°22'50" N, long. 123°16'05" W). Named on Medicine Mountain (1978) 7.5' quadrangle.

Lily Mountain [SISKIYOU]: *peak,* 4.5 miles north of Condrey Mountain on California-Oregon State line (lat. 42°00'10" N, long. 122°38'55" W; at S line sec. 14, T 48 N, R 10 W). Named on Condrey Mountain (1955) 15' quadrangle.

Lily Pad Lake [SISKIYOU]:
(1) *lake,* 250 feet long, 5.5 miles north of the village of Seiad Valley (lat. 41°55'20" N, long. 123°11'05" W). Named on Kangaroo Mountain (1980) 7.5' quadrangle.
(2) *lake,* 400 feet long, 16 miles east-southeast of Etna (lat. 41°20'10" N, long. 122°38'45" W; at S line sec. 11, T 40 N, R 7 W). Named on China Mountain (1955) 15' quadrangle.

Lily Pond [SHASTA]: *lake,* 400 feet long, nearly 5 miles northwest of Lassen Peak (lat. 40°32'30" N, long. 121°33'30" W; near NE cor. sec. 18, T 31 N, R 4 E). Named on Manzanita Lake (1956) 15' quadrangle.

Lime Gulch [SISKIYOU]:
(1) *canyon,* drained by a stream that flows nearly 2 miles to Klamath River 8 miles south of Condrey Mountain (lat. 41°49'20" N, long. 122°57'50" W; near SW cor. sec. 13, T 46 N, R 10 W). Named on Condrey Mountain (1955) 15' quadrangle.
(2) *canyon,* drained by a stream that flows 1 mile to Deadwood Creek 9 miles north of Fort Jones (lat. 41°44'15" N, long. 122°48'20" W; near E line sec. 19, T 45 N, R 8 W). Named on Fort Jones (1955) 15' quadrangle.
(3) *canyon,* drained by a stream that flows 1.25 miles to Cherry Creek (2) 8.5 miles north-northeast of Fort Jones (lat. 41°43'10" N, long. 122°45'50" W; sec. 27, T 45 N, R 8 W). Named on Fort Jones (1955) 15' quadrangle.
(4) *canyon,* drained by a stream that flows 2.5 miles to Klamath River 8 miles west-southwest of Hornbrook (lat. 41°50'50" N, long. 122°41'10" W; sec. 8, T 46 N, R 7 W). Named on Hornbrook (1955) 15' quadrangle.

Limekiln Gulch [SISKIYOU]: *canyon,* drained by a stream that flows 1 mile to Scott River 9.5 miles south-southeast of Etna (lat. 41°20' N, long. 122°48'40" W; sec. 7, T 40 N, R 8 W). Named on Etna (1955) 15' quadrangle.

Limerock Gulch [SHASTA]: *canyon,* drained by a stream that flows 0.5 mile to Backbone Creek Inlet 14 miles south of Lamoine (lat. 40°46'40" N, long. 122°25'20" W; sec. 27, T 34 N, R 5 W). Named on Lamoine (1957) 15' quadrangle.

Lime Saddle [BUTTE]: *pass,* 5.5 miles southeast of Paradise (lat. 39°41'20" N, long. 121°34' W; sec. 7, T 21 N, R 4 E). Named on Cherokee (1970) 7.5' quadrangle. The place was a source of lime for making mortar in the early days (Dunn, F.D., p. 61).

Limestone Bluffs [SISKIYOU]:
(1) *relief feature,* 5.5 miles south-southwest of the village of Seiad Valley (lat. 41°46'15" N, long. 123°14'15" W). Named on Seiad Valley (1980) 7.5' quadrangle.
(2) *relief feature,* 3 miles west of Cecilville on both sides of South Fork Salmon River (lat. 41°08'45" N, long. 123°11'45" W); the feature is just downstream from the mouth of Limestone Gulch. Named on Cecilville (1979) 7.5' quadrangle.

Limestone Gulch [SISKIYOU]; *canyon,* drained by a stream that flows 1.25 miles to South Fork Salmon River nearly 3 miles west of Cecilville (lat. 41°08'40" N, long. 123°11'25" W). Named on Cecilville (1979) 7.5' quadrangle.

Limestone Valley Creek: see **Lower Limetone Valley Creek** [SHASTA]; **Upper Limestone Valley Creek** [SHASTA].

Lincoln Bend [BUTTE-GLENN]: *bend,* 7.5 miles west-southwest of Chico along Sacramento River on Butte-Glenn County line (lat. 39°41'45" N, long. 121°57'45" W). Named on Chico Landing (1912) 7.5' quadrangle.

Lind: see **Jenny Lind Bend** [GLENN].

Linden Spring [BUTTE]: *spring,* 2.25 miles west of the village of Berry Creek (lat. 39°38'55" N, long. 121°26'40" W; sec. 29, T 21 N, R 5 E). Named on Berry Creek (1970) 7.5' quadrangle.

Lindo Channel [BUTTE]: *water feature,* 8.5 miles long, diverges from Big Chico Creek [BUTTE-TEHAMA] 3.5 miles northeast of downtown Chico, and rejoins Big Chico Creek 4.25 miles west of Chico (lat. 39°43' N, long. 121°55'15" W). Named on Chico (1948) and Ord Ferry (1949) 7.5' quadrangles. The course of the feature is called Sandy Gulch on Chico (1895) 30' quadrangle.

Linn: see **Mount Linn** [TEHAMA].

Lipstick Lake [SISKIYOU]: *lake,* 200 feet long, 9.5 miles south-southwest of Etna (lat. 41°19'50" N, long. 122°57'40" W; sec. 13, T 40 N, R 10 W). Named on Etna (1955) 15' quadrangle.

Lisbon: see **Sims** [SHASTA].

Little Antelope Creek [TEHAMA]: *stream,* flows 17 miles to Antelope Creek 5.5 miles east of Red Bluff (lat. 40°09'40" N, long. 122°08' W). Named on Panther Spring (1953) 15' quadrangle, and on Red Bluff East (1951) and Tuscan Springs (1951) 7.5' quadrangles.

Little Backbone Creek [SHASTA]: *stream,* flows 2 miles to Shasta Lake 15 miles south of Lamoine (lat. 40°45'40" N, long. 122°26'05" W; sec. 33, T 34 N, R 5 W). Named on Lamoine (1957) 15' quadrangle. North Fork enters from the northwest 1 mile upstream from the mouth of the main creek; it is nearly 2 miles long and is named on Lamoine (1957) 15' quadrangle.

Little Bagley Mountain [SHASTA]: *peak,* about 5 miles south-southeast of Shoeinhorse Mountain (lat. 41°01' N, long. 122°02'35" W). Altitude 3859 feet. Named on Shoeinhorse Mountain (1954) 15' quadrangle.

Little Bald Rock [BUTTE]: *relief feature,* 2.5 miles south of the village of Brush Creek (lat. 39°38'20" N, long. 121°19'50" W; near N line sec. 29, T 21 N, R 6 E); the feature is 1 mile northeast of Big Bald Peak. Named on Brush Creek (1970) 7.5' quadrangle.

Little Baldy [SISKIYOU]; *peak,* 10.5 miles south of Condrey Mountain (lat. 41°47'05" N, long. 122°58'15" W; sec. 35, T 46 N, R 10 W); the peak is 1.25 miles west-northwest of Bald Mountain (2). Altitude 4859 feet. Named on Condrey Mountain (1955) 15' quadrangle.

Little Bally [SHASTA]: *peak,* 2.25 miles south of Shasta Bally (lat. 40°34'15" N, long. 122°38'20" W). Named on Shasta Bally (1978) 7.5' quadrangle.

Little Barkhouse Gulch [SISKIYOU]: *canyon,* drained by a stream that flows 2 miles to Barkhouse Creek 11 miles southeast of Condrey Mountain (lat. 41°48'45" N, long. 122°51'20" W; sec. 23, T 46 N, R 9 W). Named on Condrey Mountain (1955) 15' quadrangle.

Little Basin Creek [TEHAMA]: *stream,* flows nearly 1 mile to North Fork Elder Creek 7.25 miles south-southwest of Wakefield Flat (lat. 40°01'40" N, long. 122°41'55" W; at NE cor. sec. 13, T 25 N, R 8 W); the mouth of the creek is less than 1 mile upstream from the mouth of Basin Creek. Named on Raglin Ridge (1967) 7.5' quadrangle.

Little Bear Creek [TEHAMA]: *stream,* flows 1 mile to Big Chico Creek

[BUTTE-TEHAMA] 7.5 miles south of Polk Springs (lat. 40°00'30" N, long. 121°39'05" W; near W line sec. 21, T 25 N, R 3 E); the mouth of the creek is 1 mile downstream from the mouth of Big Bear Creek. Named on Butte Meadows (1958) 15' quadrangle.

Little Bear Flat [SHASTA]: *area,* 12 miles north-northwest of Burney Falls (lat. 41°10'30" N, long. 121°43'05" W; sec. 34, T 39 N, R 2 E). Named on Pondosa (1961) 15' quadrangle.

Little Bear Gulch [SHASTA]:

(1) *canyon,* drained by a stream that flows 1 mile to Bear Gulch (1) 8 miles north-northwest of Schell Mountain (lat. 40°57'45" N, long. 122°35'20" W; at E line sec. 19, T 36 N, R 6 W). Named on Schell Mountain (1950) 15' quadrangle.

(2) *canyon,* drained by a stream that flows 1.5 miles to Middle Fork Cottonwood Creek [SHASTA-TEHAMA] 1 mile north-northwest of Chanchelulla Peak (lat. 40°24'45" N, long. 122°52'30" W; near W line sec. 34, T 30 N, R 9 W). Named on Chanchelulla Peak (1951) 15' quadrangle.

Little Bear Lake [SHASTA]: *lake,* 600 feet long, nearly 6 miles east-northeast of Lassen Peak (lat. 40°31'20" N, long. 121°24'20" W; sec. 27, T 31 N, R 5 E); the lake is 0.25 mile west-southwest of Big Bear Lake. Named on Prospect Peak (1957) 15' quadrangle. The feature is one of the group called Cluster Lakes.

Little Bear Valley [SISKIYOU]: *valley,* 0.5 mile north-northwest of Bear Peak (lat. 41°42'05" N, long. 123°34'45" W). Named on Bear Peak (1982) 7.5' quadrangle.

Little Bear Valley Creek [SISKIYOU]: *stream,* flows 2.5 miles to Clear Creek (1) 2.5 miles north of Bear Peak (lat. 41°43'50" N, long. 123°34'55" W); the stream goes through Little Bear Valley. Named on Bear Peak (1982) 7.5' quadrangle.

Little Black Fox Mountain [SISKIYOU]: *peak,* 7 miles north-northwest of Bartle (lat. 41°20'50" N, long. 121°51'55" W; near NW cor. sec. 4, T 40 N, R 1 E); the peak is 1.25 miles east of Black Fox Mountain. Altitude 6187 feet. Named on Bartle (1961) 15' quadrangle.

Little Black Rock [SHASTA]: *peak,* 10 miles west-southwest of Arbuckle Mountain on Shasta-Trinity County line (lat. 40°20'55" N, long. 123°03'25" W; sec. 24, T 29 N, R 11 W). Named on Dubakella Mountain (1954) 15' quadrangle.

Little Bogus Creek [SISKIYOU]: *stream,* flows 7 miles to Klamath River 24 miles west-northwest of Macdoel (lat. 41°54'10" N, long. 122°27'50" W; at N line sec. 30, T 47 N, R 5 W); the mouth of the stream is 2.5 miles downstream from the mouth of Bogus Creek. Named on Copco (1954) 15' quadrangle. Called Little Bogue Cr. on Averill's (1935) map.

Little Bollibokka Creek [SHASTA]: *stream,* flows 1.5 miles to McCloud River [SHASTA-SISKIYOU] nearly 2 miles north of Bollibokka Mountain (lat. 40°57'35" N, long. 122°12'45" W; near N line sec. 28, T 36 N, R 3 W); the mouth of the stream is 1000 feet upstream from the mouth of Big Bollibokka Creek. Named on Bollibokka Mountain (1957) 15' quadrangle.

Little Brushy Gulch [SISKIYOU]: *canyon,* drained by a stream that flows 0.5 mile to Indian Creek (3) 7.5 miles north of Fort Jones (lat. 41°42'55" N, long. 122°51'05" W; sec. 26, T 45 N, R 9 W). Named on Fort Jones (1955) 15' quadrangle.

Little Buckeye Creek [BUTTE]: *stream,* flows less than 1 mile to Sucker Run 5.5 miles northwest of Clipper Mills (lat. 39°35' N, long. 121°14'15" W; near W line sec. 19, T 20 N, R 7 E). Named on Clipper Mills (1948) 7.5' quadrangle.

Little Buck Ridge [SISKIYOU]: *ridge,* north-trending, 1.5 miles long, 5.5 miles east of Preston Peak (lat. 41°49'35' N, long. 123°30'20" W); the feature is east of Big Buck Ridge. Named on Preston Peak (1982) 7.5' quadrangle.

Little Bunch Grass Meadow [SHASTA]: *area,* 9.5 miles north-northeast of Lassen Peak (lat. 40°36'20" N, long. 121°25'10" W; at E line sec. 28, T 32 N, R 5 E). Named on Prospect Peak (1957) 15' quadrangle. Called Little Bunch Grass Valley on Halls Flat (1939) 30' quadrangle.

Little Bunch Grass Valley: see **Little Bunch Grass Meadow** [SHASTA].

Little Butte Creek [BUTTE]: *stream,* flows 18 miles to Butte Creek [BUTTE-GLENN] 17 miles north-northwest of Oroville (lat. 39°44' N, long. 121°42' W; sec. 25, T 22 N, R 2 E). Named on Hamlin Canyon (1951), Paradise East (1980), Paradise West (1980), and Stirling City (1979) 7.5' quadrangles.

Little Butte Creek [BUTTE-GLENN]: *stream,* diverges from Angel Creek in Butte County and flows 13 miles to Butte Creek [BUTTE-GLENN] 6.5 miles east-northeast of Butte City in Glenn County (lat. 39°29'10" N, long. 121°52'15" W). Named on Butte City (1954) and Chico (1949) 15' quadrangles.

Little Caribou Lake [SISKIYOU]: *lake,* 600 feet long, 29 miles south of Etna (lat. 41°02'40" N, long. 122°58'05" W); the feature is 1.5 miles north-northeast of Caribou Lake. Named on Coffee Creek (1955) 15' quadrangle.

Little Carmen Creek [SISKIYOU]: *stream,* flows 1 mile to Big Carmen Creek 14 miles southeast of Etna (lat. 41°18'45" N, long. 122°42'15" W; near W line sec. 20, T 40 N, R 7 W). Named on China Mountain (1955) 15' quadrangle.

Little Carmen Lake [SISKIYOU]: *lake,* 400 feet long, 16 miles southeast of Etna (lat. 41°17'20" N, long. 122°41' W; near W line sec. 33, T 40 N, R 7 W); the feature is 0.25 mile southeast of Big Carmen Lake. Named on China Mountain (1955) 15' quadrangle.

Little Castle Creek [SISKIYOU]; *stream,* flows 5.5 miles to Sacramento River 2.25 miles south-southwest of Dunsmuir at Siskiyou-Shasta County line (lat. 41°11'05" N, long. 122°17' W; at W line sec. 1, T 38 N, R 4 W). Named on Dunsmuir (1954) 15' quadrangle.

Little Castle Lake [SISKIYOU]: *lake,* 300 feet long, 5.25 miles west of Dunsmuir (lat. 41°13'20" N, long. 122°22'15" W; sec. 19, T 39 N, R 4 W); the feature is 0.5 mile east-southeast of Castle Lake. Named on Dunsmuir (1954) 15' quadrangle.

Little Castle Lake Creek: see **Ney Springs Creek** [SISKIYOU].

Little Chico Creek [BUTTE]: *stream,* flows 24 miles to Angel Slough 9.5 miles southwest of Chico (lat. 39°36'55" N, long. 121°57'05" W). Named on Cohasset (1979), Hamlin Canyon (1951), Ord Ferry (1949), and Paradise West (1980) 7.5' quadrangles.

Little China Gulch [SISKIYOU]: *canyon,* drained by a stream that flows less than 1 mile to North Russian Creek 5.25 miles east-northeast of Sawyers Bar (lat. 41°20'20" N, long. 123°02'40" W); the mouth of the canyon is 3000 feet downstream along North Russian Creek from the mouth of China Gulch (2) Named on Tanners Peak (1977) 7.5' quadrangle.

Little Churn Creek [SHASTA]: *stream,* flows 1.5 miles to Churn Creek 0.25 mile south of Summit City (lat. 40°41' N, long. 122°24'05" W; sec. 26, T 33 N, R 5 W). Named on Shasta Dam (1956) 7.5' quadrangle.

Little Conrad Gulch [SISKIYOU]: *canyon,* drained by a stream that flows 0.5 mile to South Fork Salmon River 27 miles south of Etna (lat. 41°03'55" N, long. 122°57'35" W); the canyon is west of Big Conrad Gulch. Named on Coffee Creek (1955) 15' quadrangle.

Little Cottonwood Creek [BUTTE]: *stream,* flows 9 miles to Cottonwood Creek 7 miles west of Oroville (lat. 39°31'40" N, long. 121°40'55" W; sec. 6, T 19 N, R 3 E). Named on Oroville (1970) and Shippee (1948) 7.5' quadrangles.

Little Cottonwood Peak: see **Cottonwood Peak** [SISKIYOU].

Little Cow Creek [SHASTA]: *stream,* flows 36 miles to Cow Creek 3 miles west of Millville (lat. 40°33'20" N, long. 122°13'50" W; sec. 8, T 31 N, R 3 W). Named on Bollibokka Mountain (1957), Millville (1953), Montgomery Creek (1956), and Whitmore (1956) 15' quadrangles. North Fork enters from the northeast 5.25 miles south-southeast of the village of Montgomery Creek; it is 6 miles long and is named on Montgomery Creek (1956) 15' quadrangle.

Little Cow Gulch [SHASTA]: *canyon,* drained by a stream that flows 2.5 miles to Middle Fork Cottonwood Creek [SHASTA-TEHAMA] 2 miles south-southwest of Arbuckle Mountain (lat. 40°22'35" N, long. 122°53'15" W; sec. 9, T 29 N, R 9 W); the mouth of the canyon is just above the mouth of Cow Creek. Named on Chanchelulla Peak (1951) 15' quadrangle.

Little Crane Creek [TEHAMA]: *stream,* flows 4.5 miles to Big Crane Creek 2 miles east of Rosewood (lat. 40°16'20" N, long. 122°31' W; near NW cor. sec. 23, T 28 N, R 6 W). Named on Ono (1952) 15' quadrangle, and on Oxbow Bridge (1967) 7.5' quadrangle.

Little Crater Lake [SISKIYOU]: *lake,* 1400 feet long, 8 miles west of the town of Mount Shasta (lat. 41°20'15" N, long. 122°27'45" W; near SE cor. sec. 6, T 40 N, R 5 W). Named on Weed (1954) 15' quadrangle.

Little Deer Mountain [SISKIYOU]: *peak,* 12 miles south-southwest of Macdoel (lat. 41°40'45" N, long. 122°06'55" W; sec. 8, T 44 N, R 2 W); the peak is 5 miles north of Deer Mountain. Altitude 6068 feet. Named on The Whaleback (1954) 15' quadrangle.

Little Devils Canyon [SHASTA]: *canyon,* drained by a stream that flows 1.5 miles to Kosk Creek 5.5 miles north of the village of Big Bend (lat. 41°06' N, long. 121°55'15" W; near N line sec. 1, T 37 N, R 1 W); the mouth of the canyon is 0.5 mile along Kosk Creek below the mouth of Devils Canyon (1). Named on Big Bend (1961) 15' quadrangle.

Little Devils Mountain [SHASTA]: *peak,* 5.5 miles north of the village of Big Bend (lat. 41°06'10" N, long. 121°54'20" W; near S line sec. 31, T 38 N, R 1 E); the peak is 1.25 miles south-southeast of Devils Mountain. Named on Big Bend (1961) 15' quadrangle.

Little Dog Creek [SHASTA]: *stream,* flows 1.5 miles to Dog Creek 3 miles south-southeast of Lamoine (lat. 40°56'15" N, long. 122°25'15" W; near E line sec. 34, T 36 N, R 5 W). Named on Lamoine (1957) 15' quadrangle.

Little Dry Creek [BUTTE]: *stream,* flows 34 miles to a ditch about 9 miles east-southeast of Biggs (lat. 39°22'15" N, long. 121°52'15" W; sec. 33, T 18 N, R 1 E). Named on Butte City (1954) 15' quadrangle, and on Hamlin Canyon (1951), Nelson (1948), and Shippee (1948) 7.5' quadrangles. Called Dry Creek on Marysville (1895) 30' quadrangle, and called Ash Creek on Clear Creek (1912), Dry Creek (1912), and Nelson (1912) 7.5' quadrangles.

Little Dry Creek [TEHAMA]:

(1) *stream,* formed by confluence of the stream in China Gulch (1) and the stream in Packer Gulch, flows 5.25 miles to Cottonwood Creek [SHASTA-TEHAMA] 7 miles northwest of Hooker (lat. 40°22'25" N, long.

122°24'05" W; at N line sec. 14, T 29 N, R 5 W). Named on Mitchel Gulch (1965) 7.5' quadrangle. On Anderson (1947) 15' quadrangle, the name "China Gulch" applies to present Little Dry Creek (1) up to the mouth of Devils Gulch (1), and United States Board on Geographic Names (1983a, p. 3) accepted this nomenclature.

(2) *stream,* flows 11.5 miles to join Big Dry Creek and form Dry Creek (3) 18 miles southwest of Panther Spring (lat. 40°02'15" N, long. 121°58'35" W; near E line sec. 9, T 25 N, R 1 W). Named on Panther Spring (1953) 15' quadrangle.

Little Duck Lake [SISKIYOU]: *lake,* 800 feet long, 11 miles south-southwest of Etna (lat. 41°18'30" N, long. 122°57'05" W; near NW cor. sec. 19, T 40 N, R 9 W); the lake is 0.5 mile west of Big Duck Lake at the head of Duck Lake Creek. Named on Etna (1955) 15' quadrangle.

Little Dutch Creek [SISKIYOU]: *stream,* flows 1.25 miles to Dutch Creek (1) 12 miles northeast of the village of Seiad Valley (lat. 41°57'50" N, long. 123°01'45" W; sec. 32, T 48 N, R 10 W). Named on Dutch Creek (1980) 7.5' quadrangle.

Little Elk Creek [SISKIYOU]: *stream,* flows nearly 2 miles to East Fork Elk Creek 11.5 miles north of Okonom Lake (lat. 41°44'35" N, long. 123°18'55" W). Named on Huckleberry Mountain (1980) and Slater Butte (1980) 7.5' quadrangles.

Little Elk Lake [SISKIYOU]: *lake,* 700 feet long, 14 miles south-southwest of Scott Bar along Little Elk Lake Creek (lat. 41°33'50" N, long. 123°07'55" W). Named on Marble Mountain (1980) 7.5' quadrangle.

Little Elk Lake Creek [SISKIYOU]: *stream,* flows 3 miles to Canyon Creek (3) 13 miles southwest of Scott Bar (lat. 41°35'25" N, long. 123°08'30" W); the stream goes through Little Elk Lake. Named on Marble Mountain (1980) 7.5' quadrangle.

Little Elk Lake Creek: see **Deep Lake Creek** [SISKIYOU].

Little Ferry Creek [SISKIYOU]: *stream,* flows 2.5 miles to Scott River 2.5 miles south-southwest of Scott Bar (lat. 41°42'35" N, long. 123°01'05" W; sec. 32, T 45 N, R 10 W); the mouth of the stream is 1200 feet upstream from the mouth of Big Ferry Creek. Named on Scott Bar (1980) 7.5' quadrangle.

Littlefield Reservoir [BUTTE]: *intermittent lake,* 1700 feet long, 10 miles south-southeast of Paradise (lat. 39°37'45" N, long. 121°31'55" W; sec. 33, T 21 N, R 4 E). Named on Cherokee (1970) 7.5' quadrangle.

Little Frey Creek [BUTTE]: *stream,* flows 2 miles to Frey Creek 9 miles north-northwest of Clipper Mills (lat. 39°38'25" N, long. 121°14'40" W; near NE cor. sec. 36, T 21 N, R 6 E). Named on Cascade (1948) 7.5' quadrangle.

Little Gap Creek [SHASTA]: *stream,* flows 1.5 miles to Gap Creek 4.5 miles west-northwest of the village of Big Bend (lat. 41°02'45" N, long. 121°59'30" W; sec. 20, T 37 N, R 1 W). Named on Big Bend (1961) 15' quadrangle.

Little Glass Mountain [SISKIYOU]: *peak,* 4.5 miles west-southwest of Medicine Lake (lat. 41°34' N, long. 121°41' W); the peak is 10 miles west-southwest of Glass Mountain. Named on Medicine Lake (1952) 15' quadrangle.

Little Grapevine Creek [TEHAMA]: *stream,* flows 8 miles to Antelope Creek 11 miles west of Panther Spring (lat. 40°13'50" N, long. 121°58'45" W; near S line sec. 33, T 28 N, R 1 W). Named on Panther Spring (1953) 15' quadrangle. United States Board on Geographic Names (1986c, p. 3) rejected the name "Grapevine Creek" for the stream.

Little Grayback [SISKIYOU]: *peak,* 10 miles northeast of Broken Rib Mountain on Siskiyou-Del Norte County line (lat. 41°58'40" N, long. 123°32'05" W). Altitude 6161 feet. Named on Polar Bear Mountain (1982) 7.5' quadrangle.

Little Grider Creek [SISKIYOU]: *stream,* flows 5.25 miles to Klamath River 1 mile southwest of Happy Camp (lat. 41°47'05" N, long. 123°23'35" W; near N line sec. 15, T 16 N, R 7 E). Named on Happy Camp (1980) 7.5' quadrangle.

Little Grizzly Creek [SISKIYOU]: *stream,* flows 3 miles to South Fork Salmon River 7 miles southeast of Cecilville (lat. 41°04'40" N, long. 123°01'45" W); the stream heads near Grizzly Butte. Named on Thompson Peak (1979) 7.5' quadrangle.

Little Grizzly Creek [TEHAMA]: *stream,* flows 4.25 miles to Grizzly Creek 2.5 miles east-southeast of Wakefield Flat (lat. 40°06'25" N, long. 122°35'50" W; near E line sec. 13, T 26 N, R 7 W). Named on Lowrey (1967) and Raglin Ridge (1967) 7.5' quadrangles.

Little Hancock Lake [SISKIYOU]; *lake,* 425 feet long, 9.5 miles north-northwest of Sawyers Bar (lat. 41°24'55" N, long. 123°13'25" W); the lake is 750 feet south of Hancock Lake. Named on English Peak (1977) 7.5' quadrangle.

Little Hatchet Creek [SHASTA]: *stream,* flows 3.25 miles to Hatchet Creek 5.25 miles east-northeast of the village of Montgomery Creek (lat. 40°51'45" N, long. 121°49'30" W; at W line sec. 25, T 35 N, R 1 E). Named on Montgomery Creek (1956) 15' quadrangle.

Little Horse Peak [SISKIYOU]: *peak,* 8.5 miles south-southeast of Bray (lat. 41°32'15" N, long. 121°53'05" W; near S line sec. 29, T 43 N, R 1 E); the peak is 3 miles north of House Peak. Altitude 6064 feet. Named on Bray (1950) 15' quadrangle.

Little Hot Springs Valley [SHASTA]: *canyon,* 3.5 miles south-southwest of Lassen Peak along East Sulphur Creek [SHASTA-TEHAMA] (lat. 40°27'30" N, long. 121°31' W). Named on Lassen Peak (1956) 15' quadrangle.

Little Houston Creek [SISKIYOU]: *stream,* flows 1.5 miles to Houston Creek 14 miles east-southeast of Etna (lat. 41°23'40" N, long. 122°38' W; near NE cor. sec. 22, T 41 N, R 7 W). Named on China Mountain (1955) 15' quadrangle.

Little Humbug Creek [SISKIYOU]: *stream,* flows 4.5 miles to Klamath River 10 miles southeast of Condrey Mountain (lat. 41°50'15" N, long. 122°50'15" W; sec. 13, T 46 N, R 9 W); the stream joins Klamath River 12.5 miles downstream from the mouth of Humbug Creek. Named on Condrey Mountain (1955) 15' quadrangle.

Little Inskip Hill [TEHAMA]: *peak,* 7 miles southwest of Manton (lat. 40°21'50" N, long. 121°57'30" W; sec. 15, T 29 N, R 1 W); the peak is 1.5 miles north-northwest of Inskip Hill. Altitude 2382 feet. Named on Manton (1956) 15' quadrangle.

Little Jackson Creek [SISKIYOU]: *stream,* flows 2 miles to join Jackson Creek and form Scott River 14 miles south of Etna (lat. 41°15'30" N, long. 122°53'40" W; near W line sec. 10, T 39 N, R 9 W). Named on Coffee Creek (1955) and Etna (1955) 15' quadrangles.

Little Jackson Lake [SISKIYOU]: *lake,* 600 feet long, 15 miles south of Etna (lat. 41°14'25" N, long. 122°54'45" W; near W line sec. 16, T 39 N, R 9 W); the lake is at the head of a branch of Little Jackson Creek. Named on Coffee Creek (1955) 15' quadrangle.

Little Joe Flat [SHASTA]: *area,* 3 miles west-southwest of Big Bend along Pit River (lat. 41°00'20" N, long. 121°57'40" W; sec. 3, T 36 N, R 1 W). Named on Big Bend (1961) 15' quadrangle.

Little Kabyai Creek [SHASTA]: *stream,* flows 1 mile to McCloud River [SHASTA-SISKIYOU] nearly 2 miles west of Bollibokka Mountain (lat. 40°55'55" N, long. 122°14'55" W; at S line sec. 31, T 36 N, R 3 W); the mouth of the stream is just south of the mouth of Kabyai Creek. Named on Lamoine (1957) 15' quadrangle.

Little Kanaka Creek [SHASTA]: *stream,* flows less than 1 mile to Clear Creek 2.25 miles north of Igo (lat. 40°32'20" N, long. 122°32'05" W; sec. 15, T 31 N, R 6 W); the mouth of the stream is 1350 feet below the mouth of Kanaka Creek. Named on Igo (1979) 7.5' quadrangle.

Little Kimshew Creek [BUTTE]: *stream,* flows nearly 6 miles to Big Kimshew Creek 8 miles north of Pulga (lat. 39°55'05" N, long. 121°26'50" W; at W line sec. 20, T 24 N, R 5 E). Named on Kimshew Point (1979) 7.5' quadrangle.

Little Klamath Lake: see **Lower Klamath Lake** [SISKIYOU].

Little Lagoon [BUTTE]: *water feature,* 12 miles west-northwest of Chico along the east side of Wilson Island (lat. 39°48'05" N, long. 122°02'50" W). Named on McIntosh Landing (1914) 7.5' quadrangle.

Little Logan Butte [SHASTA]: *peak,* 12 miles north of Lassen Peak (lat. 40°39'30" N, long. 121°30'35" W; sec. 3, T 32 N, R 4 E). Altitude 6038 feet. Named on Manzanita Lake (1956) 15' quadrangle.

Little Long Lake: see **Hemlock Lake** [SHASTA].

Little Marble Valley [SISKIYOU]: *relief feature,* 16 miles southwest of Scott Bar (lat. 40°33'30" N, long. 123°11'50" W); the feature is 0.5 mile south of Marble Valley. Named on Marble Mountain (1980) 7.5' quadrangle.

Little Meadows [SHASTA]: *area,* 6.5 miles north-northwest of the village of Big Bend (lat. 41°06'25" N, long. 121°57'40" W). Named on Big Bend (1961) 15' quadrangle.

Little Medicine Creek [SISKIYOU]: *stream,* flows 2 miles to North Fork Wooley Creek 15 miles north of Forks of Salmon (lat. 41°28'50" N, long. 123°16'40" W); the mouth of the creek is 1500 feet downstream along North Fork Wooley Creek from the mouth of Big Medicine Creek. Named on Medicine Mountain (1978) 7.5' quadrangle.

Little Medicine Lake [SISKIYOU]: *lake,* 400 feet long, 0.25 mile northwest of Medicine Lake (lat. 41°35'20" N, long. 121°36'40" W; near N line sec. 10, T 43 N, R 3 E). Named on Medicine Lake (1952) 15' quadrangle.

Little Medicine Mountain [SISKIYOU]: *peak,* 6.25 miles northwest of Dillon Mountain (lat. 41°35'50" N, long. 123°39'05" W). Altitude 4987 feet. Named on Chimney Rock (1981) 7.5' quadrangle. Called Medicine Mtn. on Dillon Mountain (1955) 15' quadrangle.

Little Mill Creek [SISKIYOU]: *stream,* flows 4.25 miles to Big Mill Creek 13 miles south-southeast of Etna (lat. 41°17'30" N, long. 122°45'15" W; sec. 26, T 40 N, R 8 W). Named on Coffee Creek (1955) and Etna (1955) 15' quadrangles.

Little Mill Creek [TEHAMA]: *stream,* formed by the confluence of North Fork and South Fork, flows 1.25 miles to Mill Creek (3) 11 miles south-southwest of Panther Spring (lat. 40°06'35" N, long. 121°52'35" W). Named on Panther Spring (1953) 15' quadrangle. North Fork and South Fork each are 3 miles long; both forks are named on Panther Spring (1953) 15' quadrangle.

Little Mount Hoffman [SISKIYOU]: *peak,* 3 miles west of Medicine Lake (lat. 41°34'45" N, long. 121°39'25" W; sec. 8, T 43 N, R 3 E); the peak is 6 miles west-southwest of Mount Hoffman. Altitude 7309 feet. Named on

Medicine Lake (1952) 15' quadrangle.

Little North Fork Campground [SISKIYOU]: *locality,* nearly 3 miles west-northwest of Sawyers Bar (lat. 41°19'10" N, long. 123°10'40" W); the place is at the mouth of Little North Fork Salmon River. Named on Sawyers Bar (1979) 7.5' quadrangle.

Little Pilot [SISKIYOU]: *peak,* 4 miles north of Hornbrook (lat. 41°58'15" N, long. 122°32'30" W; sec. 33, T 48 N, R 6 W). Altitude 4342 feet. Named on Hornbrook (1955) 15' quadrangle.

Little Pine Creek [TEHAMA]: *stream,* flows nearly 2 miles to Deer Creek (2) 4.5 miles southwest of Polk Springs (lat. 40°04'10" N, long. 121°43'30" W; near NW cor. sec. 35, T 26 N, R 2 E). Named on Butte Meadows (1958) 15' quadrangle.

Little Potato Butte [SHASTA]: *crater,* 11.5 miles north-northeast of Lassen Peak (lat. 40°38'50" N, long. 121°26'10" W; near E line sec. 8, T 32 N, R 5 E); the feature is less than 1 mile north of Potato Butte. Named on Prospect Peak (1957) 15' quadrangle.

Little Preston [SISKIYOU]: *peak,* 0.5 mile east-northeast of Preston Peak (lat. 41°50'20" N, long. 123°35'55" W). Altitude 6421 feet. Named on Preston Peak (1982) 7.5' quadrangle.

Little Ram Creek [BUTTE]: *stream,* flows 1.25 miles to Ram Creek 2 miles north of the village of Brush Creek (lat. 39°43'15" N, long. 121°20'10" W; sec. 32, T 22 N, R 6 E). Named on Brush Creek (1970) 7.5' quadrangle.

Little Rattlesnake Gulch [SISKIYOU]: *canyon,* drained by a stream that flows 0.5 mile to North Fork Salmon River 2.25 miles east of Sawyers Bar (lat. 41°17'45" N, long. 123°06'05" W); the mouth of the canyon is 3500 feet upstream along North Fork Salmon River from the mouth of Rattlesnake Gulch (1). Named on Tanners Peak (1977) 7.5' quadrangle.

Little Red Mountain [TEHAMA]: *peak,* 4.5 miles west-southwest of Beegum Peak (lat. 40°17'20" N, long. 122°57'45" W; sec. 11, T 28 N, R 10 W). Named on Chanchelulla Peak (1951) 15' quadrangle.

Little Red Mountain Creek [TEHAMA]: *stream,* flows 1.5 miles to Beegum Creek [SHASTA-TEHAMA] 4 miles west of Beegum Peak (lat. 40°18'40" N, long. 122°57'50" W; near W line sec. 2, T 28 N, R 10 W); the stream heads west of Little Red Mountain. Named on Chanchelulla Peak (1951) 15' quadrangle.

Little Roaring Creek [SHASTA]: *stream,* flows 7.5 miles to Roaring Creek nearly 4 miles north-northwest of the village of Montgomery Creek (lat. 40°53'40" N, long. 121°56'35" W; near N line sec. 14, T 35 N, R 1 W). Named on Montgomery Creek (1956) 15' quadrangle.

Little Rock Creek [BUTTE]: *stream,* flows 5 miles to Big Kimshew Creek 6.5 miles north-northwest of Pulga (lat. 39°53'15" N, long. 121°29'45" W; near S line sec. 35, T 24 N, R 4 E). Named on Kimshew Point (1979) 7.5' quadrangle.

Little Rody Creek [BUTTE]: *stream,* flows nearly 1 mile to Rody Creek 5.25 miles east of Pulga (lat. 39°47'35" N, long. 121°20'55" W; sec. 6, T 22 N, R 5 E). Named on Soapstone Hill (1979) 7.5' quadrangle.

Little Round Mountain [SHASTA]:

(1) *peak,* 3.5 miles west-southwest of the village of Montgomery Creek (lat. 40°50' N, long. 121°59'20" W; near W line sec. 4, T 34 N, R 1 W); the peak is 2.5 miles northwest of Round Mountain (1). Named on Montgomery Creek (1956) 15' quadrangle.

(2) *peak,* 10 miles north-northeast of Millville (lat. 40°40'40" N, long. 122°05'30" W; near NE cor. sec. 33, T 33 N, R 2 W). Altitude 1294 feet. Named on Millville (1953) 15' quadrangle.

(3) *peak,* 4.5 miles southwest of Arbuckle Mountain (lat. 40°21'40" N, long. 122°55'50" W; near SE cor. sec. 13, T 29 N, R 10 W). Altitude 3460 feet. Named on Chanchelulla Peak (1951) 15' quadrangle.

Little Round Valley [TEHAMA]: *area,* 3.5 miles east of Mineral (lat. 40°21' N, long. 121°31'40" W; at N line sec. 27, T 29 N, R 4 E). Named on Lassen Peak (1956) 15' quadrangle.

Little Salt Creek [TEHAMA]:

(1) *stream,* flows 2.5 miles to Cottonwood Creek [SHASTA-TEHAMA] 11 miles west-northwest of Rosewood (lat. 40°20'55" N, long. 122°43'50" W; sec. 23, T 29 N, R 8 W); the mouth of the creek is 2.5 miles upstream along Cottonwood Creek [SHASTA-TEHAMA] from the mouth of Big Salt Creek. Named on Chanchelulla Peak (1951) and Ono (1952) 15' quadrangles.

(2) *stream,* flows nearly 6 miles to Salt Creek (2) 3.5 miles east-northeast of Red Bluff (lat. 40°11'55" N, long. 122°10'40" W; near NW cor. sec. 14, T 27 N, R 3 W). Named on Red Bluff East (1951) and Tuscan Springs (1951) 7.5' quadrangles.

Little Shasta [SISKIYOU]: *locality,* 21 miles west-southwest of Macdoel (lat. 41°42'45" N, long. 122°23'15" W; at S line sec. 26, T 45 N, R 5 W); the place is along Little Shasta River. Named on Lake Shastina (1954) 15' quadrangle. Postal authorities established Little Shasta post office in 1888, moved it 0.5 mile west the same year, moved it 0.5 mile east in 1898, and discontinued it in 1920 (Salley, p. 123). California Mining Bureau's (1909a) map shows a place called Roselawn located 5 miles east of Little Shasta at the end of a stage line. Postal authorities established Roselawn post office 3.5 miles south of Little Shasta in 1902, discontinued it in 1905, reestablished it in 1906, and discontinued it in 1918 (Salley, p. 189). They established Mayten post office 8.5 miles south of Little Shasta in 1887, moved it 3 miles northeast in 1914, and discontinued it in 1919 (Salley, p. 135).

Little Shasta Creek: see **Little Shasta River** [SISKIYOU].

Little Shasta Meadow [SISKIYOU]: *area,* 10 miles west of Macdoel (lat. 41°48'30" N, long. 122°11'50" W; sec. 22, 27, T 46 N, R 3 W); the place is near the head of Little Shasta River. Named on Macdoel (1954) 15' quadrangle.

Little Shasta River [SISKIYOU]: *stream,* flows 24 miles to Shasta River 6 miles east-southeast of Yreka (lat. 41°42'05" N, long. 122°31'50" W; sec. 34, T 45 N, R 6 W). Named on Copco (1954), Lake Shastina (1954), Macdoel (1954), and Yreka (1954) 15' quadrangles. Bancroft's (1864) map has the name "Lit. Shasta Cr." for the stream.

Little Shasta Spring [SISKIYOU]: *spring,* 11 miles west-southwest of Macdoel (lat. 41°47'45" N, long. 122°12'40" W; near SE cor. sec. 28, T 46 N, R 3 W); the spring is at the head of Little Shasta River. Named on Macdoel (1954) 15' quadrangle.

Little Shasta Valley [SISKIYOU]: *valley,* 10 miles east of Yreka on the northeast side of Shasta Valley (lat. 41°42' N, long. 122°25' W); Little Shasta River crosses the valley. Named on Shasta (1894) 1° quadrangle.

Little Shoeinhorse Mountain [SHASTA]: *peak,* 0.5 mile north-northeast of Shoeinhorse Mountain (lat. 41°04'30" N, long. 122°03'50" W). Named on Shoeinhorse Mountain (1954) 15' quadrangle.

Little Shotgun Creek [SHASTA]: *stream,* flows 1.5 miles to Kosk Creek 3.25 miles north of the village of Big Bend (lat. 41°03'55" N, long. 121°55'20" W; sec. 13, T 37 N, R 1 W); the mouth of the stream is 300 feet along Kosk Creek above the mouth of Shotgun Creek (1). Named on Big Bend (1961) 15' quadrangle.

Little Slate Creek [SHASTA]: *stream,* flows 3.5 miles to Sacramento River at Lamoine (lat. 40°58'40" N, long. 122°25'45" W; sec. 15, T 36 N, R 5 W); the mouth of the stream is 400 feet above the mouth of Slate Creek (1). Named on Dunsmuir (1954) and Lamoine (1957) 15' quadrangles.

Little Slate Creek: see **Whitlow Creek** [SHASTA].

Little Smoky Creek [SISKIYOU]: *stream,* flows less than 1 mile to Beaver Creek (1) 10 miles east of Condrey Mountain (lat. 41°58' N, long. 122°47'15" W; near E line sec. 32, T 48 N, R 8 W); the mouth of the creek is 800 feet upstream from the mouth of Smokey Creek. Named on Condrey Mountain (1955) 15' quadrangle.

Little Smoky Creek [TEHAMA]: *stream,* flows nearly 3 miles to Big Chico Creek [BUTTE-TEHAMA] 5.25 miles south-southeast of Polk Springs (lat. 40°02'45" N, long. 121°37'45" W; near N line sec. 10, T 25 N, R 3 E). Named on Butte Meadows (1958) 15' quadrangle.

Little Soda Creek [SISKIYOU]: *stream,* flows 1.25 miles to West Fork Beaver Creek (1) 7.5 miles east of Condrey Mountain (lat. 41°56'45" N, long, 122°50' W; near SE cor. sec. 1, T 47 N, R 9 W); the mouth of the stream is 2.25 miles west-southwest of the mouth of Soda Creek. Named on Condrey Mountain (1955) 15' quadrangle.

Little South Fork Lake [SISKIYOU]: *lake,* 900 feet long, 10.5 miles southeast of Cecilville (lat. 41°01'05" N, long. 123°00'50" W); the lake is at the head of Little South Fork Salmon River. Named on Thompson Peak (1979) 7.5' quadrangle. United States Board on Geographic Names (1960a, p. 15) rejected the name "Frog Lake" for the feature.

Little Spring [SISKIYOU]: *spring,* 7.5 miles north-northwest of Bartle (lat. 41°20'45" W, long. 121°54'15" W; near E line sec. 1, T 40 N, R 1 W). Named on Bartle (1961) 15' quadrangle.

Little Spring Gulch [TEHAMA]: *canyon,* drained by a stream that flows 1 mile to Dry Creek (1) 3 miles west-northwest of Rosewood (lat. 40°17'30" N, long. 122°35'35" W; near W line sec. 7, T 28 N, R 6 E); the mouth of the canyon is 4.5 miles upstream from the mouth of Spring Gulch (2). Named on Ono (1952) 15' quadrangle.

Little Springs Canyon [SISKIYOU]: *canyon,* drained by a stream that flows 2.5 miles to Bogus Creek 17 miles west-northwest of Macdoel (lat. 41°54'30" N, long. 122°20'20" W; sec. 20, T 47 N, R 4 W). Named on Copco (1954) 15' quadrangle.

Little Stony Creek [GLENN]: *stream,* heads in Colusa County and flows nearly 3 miles in Glenn County to Stony Creek [GLENN-TEHAMA] 9.5 miles east of Saint John Mountain (lat. 39°25'20" N, long. 122°31' W; near S line sec. 10, T 18 N, R 6 W). Named on Stonyford (1968) 7.5' quadrangle.

Little Sucker Run [BUTTE]: *stream,* flows 2 miles to Sucker Run 3.25 miles north-northwest of Forbestown (lat. 39°33'50" N, long. 121°17'15" W; sec. 27, T 20 N, R 6 E). Named on Forbestown (1970) 7.5' quadrangle.

Little Sugarloaf Creek [SHASTA]: *stream,* flows 1.25 miles to Sacramento River Arm Shasta Lake 10 miles south of Lamoine (lat. 40°50' N, long. 122°25'55" W; near E line sec. 4, T 34 N, R 5 W). Named on Lamoine (1957) 15' quadrangle.

Little Tableland [SISKIYOU]: *relief feature,* mesalike elevation 3.5 miles northwest of Mount Dome (lat. 41°51' N, long. 121°43'45" W; mainly in sec. 3, 10, T 46 N, R 2 E). Named on Mount Dome (1950) 15' quadrangle.

Little Tule River [SHASTA]: *water feature,* lakelike body of water that connects with Tule River 6 miles north of Fall River Mills (lat. 41°05'10" N, long. 121°27'10" W). Named on Fall River Mills (1961) 15' quadrangle. United States Board on Geographic Names (1964, p. 11) rejected the name "Eastman Lake" for the feature.

Little Twin Creek [SISKIYOU]: *stream,* flows 1.5 miles to North Fork Salmon River 6.25 miles north-northeast of Sawyers Bar (lat. 41°23'05" N, long. 123°05'15" W); the mouth of the creek is 650 feet upstream along North Fork Salmon River from the mouth of Big Twin Creek. Named on Yellow Dog Peak (1977) 7.5' quadrangle.

Little Valley [SHASTA]:
(1) *area,* 8 miles north-northwest of Whitmore (lat. 40°44'25" N, long. 121°57'20" W; near SE cor. sec. 3, T 33 N, R 1 W). Named on Whitmore (1956) 15' quadrangle.
(2) *valley,* 8 miles north-northwest of Millville (lat. 40°39'35" N, long. 122°13'50" W; sec. 5, T 32 N, R 3 W). Named on Bella Vista (1965) 7.5' quadrangle.

Little Wildcat Creek [TEHAMA]: *stream,* flows 2.5 miles to Wildcat Creek (1) 5.5 miles north-northeast of Los Molinos (lat. 40°05'20" N, long. 122°02'30" W; sec. 24, T 26 N, R 2 W). Named on Los Molinos (1952) 7.5' quadrangle.

Live Oak Canyon [SHASTA]: *canyon,* drained by a stream that flows 3.5 miles to Kosk Creek 7.25 miles north of the village of Big Bend (lat. 41°07'30" N, long. 121°53'35" W; at SE cor. sec. 19, T 38 N, R 1 E). Named on Big Bend (1961) 15' quadrangle.

Live Oak Slough [BUTTE]: *stream,* flows 6.25 miles to a ditch 4 miles south-southeast of Gridley (lat. 39°18'45" N, long. 121°39'40" W). Named on Gridley (1952) 7.5' quadrangle.

Live Yankee Gulch [SISKIYOU]: *canyon,* drained by a stream that flows 1 mile to East Fork Eddy Gulch 2.25 miles south-southeast of Sawyers Bar (lat. 41°16'05" N, long. 123°06'50" W). Named on Tanners Peak (1977) 7.5' quadrangle.

Liza Creek [TEHAMA]: *stream,* flows 11 miles to Reeds Creek 5.5 miles west-southwest of downtown Red Bluff (lat. 40°09'30" N, long. 122°20'15" W; near N line sec. 32, T 27 N, R 4 W). Named on Blossom (1952), Oxbow Bridge (1967), and Red Bluff West (1951) 7.5' quadrangles. Called North Fork Reeds Creek on Red Bank (1952) 15' quadrangle.

Lizard Creek [SHASTA]: *stream,* flows 1.5 miles to McCloud River [SHASTA-SISKIYOU] 4.5 miles north of Shoeinhorse Mountain (lat. 41°07'50" N, long. 122°04'05" W). Named on Shoeinhorse Mountain (1954) 15' quadrangle.

Llano Seco [BUTTE]: *land grant,* 12 miles south-southwest of Chico on the east side of Sacramento River. Named on Glenn (1951), Llano Seco (1948), and Ord Ferry (1949) 7.5' quadrangles. Sebastian Keyser received 4 leagues in 1844 and 1845; C.J. Brenham and others claimed 17,767 acres patented in 1860 (Cowan, p. 45).

Loafer Creek [BUTTE]: *stream,* flows 1 mile to Lake Oroville 2.5 miles east of Oroville Dam (lat. 39°31'55" N, long. 121°26'20" W; sec. 5, T 19 N, R 5 E). Named on Oroville Dam (1970) 7.5' quadrangle.

Loafer Creek Campground [BUTTE]: *locality,* 2 miles east-southeast of Oroville Dam near Lake Oroville (lat. 39°31'40" N, long. 121°26'40" W; at W line sec. 5, T 19 N, R 5 E); the place is nearly 0.5 mile west of Loafer Creek. Named on Oroville Dam (1970) 7.5' quadrangle.

Lockerman Creek [BUTTE]: *stream,* flows 2.5 miles to Camp Creek 3.5 miles north-northeast of Pulga (lat. 39°51'05" N, long. 121°25'50" W; near E line sec. 17, T 23 N, R 5 E). Named on Kimshew Point (1979) and Pulga (1979) 7.5' quadrangles.

Lockhart Creek [SHASTA]: *stream,* flows less than 1 mile to North Fork Backbone Creek 8.5 miles south-southwest of Lamoine (lat. 40°51'50" N, long. 122°29'35" W). Named on Lamoine (1957) and Schell Mountain (1950) 15' quadrangles.

Lofton: see **Dad Lofton Spring** [SHASTA].

Loftus: see **Lakehead** [SHASTA]; **Lakeshore** [SHASTA]; **Sugarloaf** [SHASTA] (4).

Logan: see **Lee Logan Camp** [GLENN].

Logan Butte: see **Little Logan Butte** [SHASTA].

Logan Creek [GLENN]: *stream,* flows 15 miles to Colusa County 10 miles south-southeast of Willows (lat. 39°23'10" N, long. 122°08'25" W; sec. 25, T 18 N, R 3 W). Named on Lodoga (1960) 15' quadrangle, and on Fruto (1968), Logandale (1952), and Logan Ridge (1958) 7.5' quadrangles. North Fork enters 9.5 miles south-southeast of Willows; it is 16 miles long and is named on Logandale (1952), Logan Ridge (1958), and Stone Valley (1952) 7.5' quadrangles.

Logandale [GLENN]: *locality,* 6 miles south of Willows along Southern Pacific Railroad (lat. 39°26'15" N, long. 122°11'30" W; at SW cor. sec. 3, T 18 N, R 3 W). Named on Logandale (1952) 7.5' quadrangle.

Logan Gulch [SHASTA]: *canyon,* 2.5 miles long, 12 miles north of Lassen Peak (lat. 40°39'30" N, long. 121°31' W); the feature heads at Logan Mountain. Named on Lassen Peak (1956) 15' quadrangle.

Logan Gulch [SISKIYOU]: *canyon,* drained by a stream that flows nearly 1 mile to Salmon River 1.25 miles northwest of Forks of Salmon (lat. 41°16'20" N, long. 123°20'25" W). Named on Forks of Salmon (1978) 7.5' quadrangle.

Logan Lake [SHASTA]: *lake,* 0.5 mile long, 12 miles north of Lassen Peak (lat. 40°39'40" N, long. 121°29' W; at E line sec. 2, T 32 N, R 4 E). Named on Prospect Peak (1957) 15' quadrangle. Griffin Logan ran sheep in the neighborhood of the lake (Steger, p. 44).

Logan Mountain [SHASTA]: *peak,* 13 miles north of Lassen Peak (lat. 40°41' N, long. 121°31'50" W; at S line sec. 28, T 33 N, R 4 E). Altitude 7245 feet. Named on Manzanita Lake (1956) 15' quadrangle.

Logan Ridge [GLENN]: *ridge,* north-trending, 2 miles long, 6 miles east-southeast of High Peak on Glenn-Colusa County line (lat. 39°23'05" N, long. 122°19'30" W). Named on Logan Ridge (1958) 7.5' quadrangle.

Logan's Ferry [SHASTA]: *locality,* 1.25 miles north-northwest of Ball's Ferry at the mouth of Bear Creek (2) (lat. 40°26'15" N, long. 122°12'15" W). Named on Red Bluff (1894) 1° quadrangle. The place was called Adam's Ferry in the 1860's; P.D. Logan bought the ferry in 1878 (Steger, p. 44).

Log Gulch [SISKIYOU]: *canyon,* drained by a stream that flows 1 mile to Moffett Creek 8.5 miles south-southwest of Yreka (lat. 41°37'45" N, long. 122°42'50" W; sec. 25, T 44 N, R 8 W). Named on Yreka (1954) 15' quadrangle.

Log Lake [SISKIYOU]: *lake,* 300 feet long, 14 miles south-southwest of Scott Bar (lat. 41°32'45" N, long. 123°05'55" W). Named on Boulder Peak (1981) 7.5' quadrangle.

Log Spring [TEHAMA]: *spring,* 8 miles south of Ball Mountain (lat. 39°49'10" N, long. 122°46'30" W; near E line sec. 29, T 23 N, R 8 W). Named on Log Spring (1967) 7.5' quadrangle.

Log Spring Creek [TEHAMA]: *stream,* flows 3.5 miles to Thomes Creek 4.5 miles south of Ball Mountain (lat. 39°52'10" N, long. 122°47' W; sec. 8, T 23 N, R 8 W); the stream heads at Log Spring Ridge. Named on Log Spring (1967) 7.5' quadrangle.

Log Spring Ridge [GLENN-TEHAMA]: *ridge,* generally southeast-trending, 10 miles long, mainly in Tehama County—only the southeasternmost end is in Glenn County; center about 7.5 miles south of Ball Mountain (lat. 39°49'45" N, long. 122°45' W); Log Spring is on the ridge. Named on Hall Ridge (1967) and Log Spring (1967) 7.5' quadrangles.

Lomo [BUTTE]: *locality,* 4.5 miles southwest of Butte Meadows (lat. 40°02'20" N, long. 121°36'55" W; near W line sec. 11, T 25 N, R 3 E). Named on Butte Meadows (1958) 15' quadrangle. Postal authorities established Lomo post office in 1878 and discontinued it in 1881 (Frickstad, p. 10). The place first was known as Wakefields Station (Dunn, F.D., p. 63).

Lone Pine Bar [SISKIYOU]: *locality,* nearly 3 miles east-northeast of Dillon Mountain along Klamath River (lat. 41°32'55" N, long. 123°31'30" W). Named on Dillon Mountain (1983) 7.5' quadrangle.

Lone Pine Camp [TEHAMA]: *locality,* 5.5 miles east of Tehama along Toomes Creek, which is present Dry Creek (3) (lat. 40°01'10" N, long. 122°01' W; sec. 18, T 25 N, R 1 W). Named on Tehama (1905) 15' quadrangle.

Lone Pine Ridge [SISKIYOU]:
(1) *ridge,* southeast-trending, 2.5 miles long, 26 miles west-northwest of Macdoel on California-Oregon State line (lat. 41°59'45" N, long. 122°27'15" W). Named on Copco (1954) 15' quadrangle.
(2) *ridge,* north-northeast-trending, 2.5 miles long, 4.5 miles south-southwest of Bartle (lat. 41°11'45" N, long. 121°51' W). Named on Big Bend (1961) 15' quadrangle.

Lone Pine Spring [TEHAMA]: *spring,* 3 miles north of Tomhead Mountain (lat. 40°10'50" N, long. 122°49'45" W; near N line sec. 24, T 27 N, R 9 W). Named on Yolla Bolly (1954) 15' quadrangle.

Lonesome Lake [SISKIYOU]: *lake,* 500 feet long, 11.5 miles north-northeast of Happy Camp (lat. 41°57' N, long. 123°17'45" W). Named on Figurehead Mountain (1980) 7.5' quadrangle. United States Board on Geographic Names (1960b, p. 8) rejected the name "Fish Lake" for the feature.

Lone Star [GLENN]: *locality,* 3.5 miles east-southeast of Black Butte (lat. 39°42'35" N, long. 122°48'30" W; sec. 6, T 21 N, R 8 E). Named on Plaskett Meadows (1967) 7.5' quadrangle. Hull Mountain (1952) 15' quadrangle shows Lone Star Campground at the site.

Lone Star Campground: see **Lone Star** [GLENN].

Longfellow Creek [SISKIYOU]: *stream,* flows 2.5 miles to Dutch Creek (4) 8 miles west-southwest of Hornbrook (lat. 40°53'15" N, long. 122°42'15" W; near S line sec. 30, T 47 N, R 7 W). Named on Hornbrook (1955) 15' quadrangle.

Long Gulch [SHASTA]: *canyon,* drained by a stream that flows 1.5 miles to Middle Fork Cottonwood Creek [SHASTA-TEHAMA] 3.5 miles east-northeast of Arbuckle Mountain (lat. 40°25'30" N, long. 122°48'35" W; sec. 30, T 30 N, R 8 W). Named on Chanchelulla Peak (1951) 15' quadrangle.

Long Gulch [SISKIYOU]:
(1) *canyon,* drained by a stream that flows 1.5 miles to South Fork Salmon River 2.5 miles east-southeast of Cecilville (lat. 41°07'50" N, long. 123°05'40" W). Named on Grasshopper Ridge (1979) 7.5' quadrangle.
(2) *canyon,* drained by a stream that flows nearly 3 miles to East Fork Scott

River 11 miles south-southeast of Etna (lat. 41°18'45" N, long. 122°48' W; near SW cor. sec. 16, T 40 N, R 8 W). Named on Etna (1955) 15' quadrangle.

(3) *canyon,* drained by a stream that flows 2 miles to East Fork of South Fork Salmon River 16 miles south of Etna (lat. 41°13'15" N, long. 122°55'30" W; sec. 20, T 39 N, R 9 W). Named on Coffee Creek (1955) 15' quadrangle. Called Trail Gulch on Etna (1934) 30' quadrangle, where present Trail Gulch (3) is called Long Gulch.

(4) *canyon,* drained by a stream that flows 3 miles to Duzel Creek 14 miles south-southwest of Yreka (lat. 41°33'10" N, long. 122°44'20" W; near N line sec. 26, T 43 N, R 8 W). Named on Fort Jones (1955) and Yreka (1954) 15' quadrangles.

(5) *canyon,* 1.5 miles long, opens into lowlands 13 miles south of Yreka (lat. 41°32'50" N, long. 122°36'10" W; sec. 25, T 43 N, R 7 W). Named on Yreka (1954) 15' quadrangle.

(6) *canyon,* drained by a stream that flows 2 miles to Klamath River 6 miles south-southwest of Hornbrook (lat. 41°50' N, long. 122°36'15' W; sec. 13, T 46 N, R 7 W). Named on Hornbrook (1955) 15' quadrangle.

(7) *canyon,* drained by a stream that flows 3 miles to Yreka Creek 11 miles south-southwest of Hornbrook (lat. 41°45'35" N, long. 122°37'20" W; sec. 11, T 45 N, R 7 W). Named on Hornbrook (1955) 15' quadrangle.

(8) *canyon,* drained by a stream that flows 2.25 miles to Klamath River 24 miles west-northwest of Macdoel (lat. 41°56'45" N, long. 122°25'55" W; near N line sec. 9, T 47 N, R 5 W). Named on Copco (1954) 15' quadrangle.

Long Gulch [TEHAMA]:

(1) *canyon,* drained by a stream that flows about 2.5 miles to Dry Creek (1) (lat. 40°18'45" N, long. 122°49'40" W; near N line sec. 1, T 28 N, R 9 W). Named on Chanchelulla Peak (1951) 15' quadrangle.

(2) *canyon,* drained by a stream that flows 12 miles to Dry Creek (1) 9 miles west of Hooker (lat. 40°16'55" N, long. 122°29'45" W; sec. 13, T 28 N, R 6 W). Named on Ono (1952) 15' quadrangle, and on Cold Fork (1967), Mitchell Gulch (1965), and Oxbow Bridge (1967) 7.5' quadrangles.

(3) *canyon,* drained by a stream that flows 3.5 miles to South Fork Cottonwood Creek [SHASTA-TEHAMA] 3.25 miles west-southwest of Tomhead Mountain (lat. 40°07'25" N, long. 122°52'30" W; near NW cor. sec. 10, T 26 N, R 9 W). Named on Yolla Bolly (1954) 15' quadrangle.

(4) *canyon,* drained by a stream that flows 4.5 miles to South Fork Cottonwood Creek [SHASTA-TEHAMA] 1.5 miles north-northwest of Wakefield Flat (lat. 40°08'45" N, long. 122°38'50" W). Named on Cold Fork (1967) and Raglin Ridge (1967) 7.5' quadrangles.

(5) *canyon,* drained by a stream that flows 10 miles to lowlands 9 miles east-southeast of Red Bluff (lat. 40°08'10" N, long. 122°04'40" W). Named on Panther Spring (1953) 15' quadrangle, and on Tuscan Springs (1951) 7.5' quadrangle.

Long Gulch: see **Blue Canyon** [SHASTA]; **Long Ravine** [BUTTE] (1).

Long Gulch Lake [SISKIYOU]: *lake,* 1200 feet long, 18 miles south of Etna (lat. 41°11'30" N, long. 122°55'05" W); the lake is at the head of Long Gulch (3). Named on Coffee Creek (1955) 15' quadrangle. Called Trail Gulch Lake on Etna (1934) 30' quadrangle, where present Trail Gulch Lake is called Long Gulch Lake, but United States Board on Geographic Names (1978c, p. 3) rejected the name "Trail Gulch Lake" for present Long Gulch Lake.

Long Hay Flat [SHASTA]: *area,* 6.5 miles east of Shingletown (lat. 40°28'55" N, long. 121°45'50" W). Named on Manton (1956) 15' quadrangle.

Long High Creek [SISKIYOU]: *stream,* flows 1.5 miles to Shackleford Creek 14 miles south-southwest of Scott Bar (lat. 41°33'05" N, long. 123°04'25" W); the stream heads near Long High Lake. Named on Boulder Peak (1981) 7.5' quadrangle.

Long High Lake [SISKIYOU]: *lake,* 500 feet long, 13 miles south-southwest of Scott Bar (lat. 41°33'55" N, long. 123°05'35" W). Named on Boulder Peak (1981) 7.5' quadrangle. On Seiad (1922) 30' quadrangle, this lake and nearby Calf Lake together are called Calf Lakes.

Long Hollow [SHASTA]: *canyon,* drained by a stream that flows nearly 2 miles to South Fork Bear Creek (2) 7.5 miles south of Whitmore (lat. 40°31'15" N, long. 121°55' W; near SW cor. sec. 19, T 31 N, R 1 E). Named on Whitmore (1956) 15' quadrangle.

Long Hollow [TEHAMA]: *canyon,* drained by a stream that flows nearly 2 miles to Grizzly Creek 4.5 miles east-southeast of Wakefield Flat (lat. 40°06'10" N, long. 122°33'45" W; sec. 17, T 26 N, R 6 W). Named on Lowrey (1967) 7.5' quadrangle.

Long Lake [TEHAMA]: *dry lake,* 400 feet long, 7 miles south-southwest of Tomhead Mountain (lat. 40°02'40" N, long. 122°51'35" W; near W line sec. 3, T 25 N, R 9 W). Named on Yolla Bolly (1954) 15' quadrangle.

Long Lake: see **Little Long Lake**, under **Hemlock Lake** [SHASTA].

Long Meadow [SISKIYOU]: *area,* 5 miles south-southwest of Ukonom Lake (lat. 41°31' N, long. 123°24'10" W). Named on Ukonom Mountain (1980) 7.5' quadrangle.

Long Pine Meadow [SISKIYOU]: *area,* 5.5 miles south-southwest of Ukonom Lake (lat. 41°30'45" N, long. 123°25'10" W). Named on Ukonom Mountain (1980) 7.5' quadrangle.

Long Point [GLENN]: *ridge,* north- to north-northeast-trending, 1.5 miles long, 11 miles west-northwest of the village of Elk Creek (lat. 39°41'20" N, long. 122°42'25" W). Named on Alder Springs (1967) 7.5' quadrangle.

Long Point [TEHAMA]: *ridge,* south-trending, nearly 2 miles long, 3.5 miles south-southeast of Panther Spring (lat. 40°12' N, long. 121°45'30" W). Named on Panther Spring (1953) 15' quadrangle.

Long Prairie [SISKIYOU]: *valley,* 7.5 miles east-northeast of Bray (lat. 41°40'15" N, long. 121°49'15" W). Named on Bray (1950) 15' quadrangle.

Long Prairie Creek [SISKIYOU]: *stream,* heads in the State of Oregon and flows 3.5 miles in Siskiyou County to Klamath River 16 miles west-northwest of Macdoel (lat. 41°57'55" N, long. 122°15'25" W; sec. 36, T 48 N, R 4 W). Named on Copco (1954) and Macdoel (1954) 15' quadrangles.

Long Ravine [BUTTE]:

(1) *canyon,* drained by a stream that flows 4.5 miles to Little West Fork [of West Fork Feather River] 2 miles southwest of Stirling City (lat. 39°53'20" N, long. 121°33'40" W; near E line sec. 31, T 24 N, R 4 E). Named on Stirling City (1979) 7.5' quadrangle. Called Long Gulch on Chico (1895) 30' quadrangle.

(2) *canyon,* drained by a stream that flows 1 mile to Oregon Gulch (2) 4.5 miles north-northeast of Oroville (lat. 39°34'45" N, long. 121°30'55" W; near N line sec. 27, T 20 N, R 4 E). Named on Oroville (1970) 7.5' quadrangle.

Long Ridge [TEHAMA]:

(1) *ridge,* southwest-trending, 2.5 miles long, 5 miles east-southeast of Manton (lat. 40°24'25" N, long. 121°47'10" W). Named on Manton (1956) 15' quadrangle.

(2) *ridge,* south- to south-southwest-trending, 1.5 miles long, 5 miles west-northwest of Tomhead Mountain (lat. 40°09'30" N, long. 122°54'30" W). Named on Yolla Bolly (1954) 15' quadrangle. United States Board on Geographic Names (1979a, p. 4) rejected the name "Sanford Ridge" for the feature.

Long Ridge: see **Sanford Ridge** [TEHAMA].

Long's Bar: see **Oroville** [BUTTE].

Long Tom Creek [SHASTA]: *stream,* flows 2 miles to Salt Creek (6) 9 miles southeast of Lamoine (lat. 40°53'15" N, long. 122°18'20" W; sec. 15, T 35 N, R 4 W). Named on Lamoine (1957) 15' quadrangle.

Long Valley [SHASTA]: *valley,* 5.5 miles north of Burney along Burney Creek (lat. 40°57'40" N, long. 121°39'30" W). Named on Burney (1957) 15' quadrangle.

Long Valley Mountain [SHASTA]: *peak,* 7.5 miles north of Burney (lat. 40°59'20" N, long. 121°40'50" W; near S line sec. 7, T 36 N, R 3 E); the peak is north of the head of Long Valley. Named on Burney (1957) 15' quadrangle.

Lookout Butte: see **Fourmile Hill** [SISKIYOU].

Lookout Mountain [SHASTA]:

(1) *peak,* 5 miles north of Burney (lat. 40°57'15" N, long. 121°40'05" W; at E line sec. 30, T 36 N, R 3 E). Altitude 4519 feet. Named on Burney (1957) 15' quadrangle.

(2) *peak,* 5.5 miles south-southeast of the village of Montgomery Creek (lat. 40°46'25" N, long. 121°52' W). Altitude 4690 feet. Named on Montgomery Creek (1956) 15' quadrangle.

(3) *peak,* 8.5 miles east of Whitmore (lat. 40°38'25" N, long. 121°45'30" W; sec. 9, T 32 N, R 2 E). Named on Whitmore (1956) 15' quadrangle.

Lookout Mountain [SISKIYOU]: *peak,* 5.25 miles east-northeast of Broken Rib Mountain on Siskiyou-Del Norte County line (lat. 41°54'25" N, long. 123°35'30" W). Altitude 6372 feet. Named on Polar Bear Mountain (1982) 7.5' quadrangle.

Lookout Mountain [TEHAMA]: *peak,* 1.25 miles north of Bend (lat. 40°16'25" N, long. 122°12'35" W; near S line sec. 16, T 28 N, R 3 W). Altitude 558 feet. Named on Bend (1965) 7.5' quadrangle.

Lookout Peak [SHASTA]: *peak,* 9.5 miles southwest of Shasta Bally (lat. 40°30'20" N, long. 122°46'55" W; near W line sec. 28, T 31 N, R 8 W). Altitude 5715 feet. Named on Weaverville (1950) 15' quadrangle.

Lookout Point [SHASTA]: *relief feature,* 5.5 miles north of Schell Mountain (lat. 40°56' N, long. 122°31' W; sec. 35, T 36 N, R 6 W). Named on Schell Mountain (1950) 15' quadrangle.

Lookout Point [SISKIYOU]: *peak,* 11 miles north of Bartle (lat. 41°25' N, long. 121°48'10" W; sec. 12, T 41 N, R 1 E). Altitude 5310 feet. Named on Bartle (1961) 15' quadrangle.

Loomis: see **Shingletown** [SHASTA]; **Viola** [SHASTA].

Loomis Corners [SHASTA]: *locality,* 4.5 miles east of Redding (lat. 40°35'20" N, long. 122°18'20" W; sec. 34, T 32 N, R 4 W). Named on Enterprise (1957) 7.5' quadrangle. The name is for H.W. Loomis, who bought the place in 1861; Leighton post office was at the site (Steger, p. 45). Postal authorities established Leighton post office in 1889 and discontinued it in 1894; the name was for the Leighton family, pioneer settlers (Salley, p. 120).

Loomis Peak [SHASTA]: *peak,* 2 miles west of Lassen Peak (lat. 40°29'15" N, long. 121°32'35" W; near SE cor. sec, 32, T 31 N, R 4 E). Altitude 8658 feet. Named on Lassen Peak (1956) 15' quadrangle. The name honors B.F. Loomis, an early settler (United States Board on Geographic Names,

1933, p. 474).

Lorraine [BUTTE]: *locality,* 5 miles northeast of Biggs along Sacramento Northern Railroad (lat. 39°28'10" N, long. 121°39' W; near SE cor. sec. 29, T 19 N, R 3 E). Named on Gridley (1952) 15' quadrangle.

Losa: see **Willows** [GLENN].

Losee: see **Haselbusch** [BUTTE].

Los Molinos [TEHAMA]: *town,* 13 miles south-southeast of Red Bluff (lat. 40°01'15" N, long. 122°05'45" W); the town is on Rio de los Molinos grant. Named on Los Molinos (1952) 7.5' quadrangle. Postal authorities established Los Molinos post office in 1905 (Frickstad, p. 204).

Lost Camp [TEHAMA]: *locality,* 5 miles north of Polk Springs (lat. 40°11'10" N, long. 121°38'50" W; near N line sec. 21, T 27 N, R 3 E). Named on Butte Meadows (1958) 15' quadrangle.

Lost Camp Ridge [BUTTE]: *ridge,* northeast-trending, 1.5 miles long, 9.5 miles southwest of the village of Elk Creek (lat. 39°31'45" N, long. 122°41'30" W; mainly in sec. 6, T 19 N, R 7 W). Named on Felkner Hill (1968) 7.5' quadrangle.

Lost Creek [BUTTE]: *stream,* heads in Plumas County and flows 7.5 miles in Butte County to South Fork Feather River nearly 3 miles northwest of Clipper Mills (lat. 39°33'50" N, long. 121°11'20" W; sec. 28, T 20 N, R 7 E). Named on Clipper Mills (1948) and Strawberry Valley (1948) 7.5' quadrangles.

Lost Creek [SHASTA]:

(1) *stream,* flows 8.5 miles to end 7.5 miles southwest of Coble Mountain (lat. 40°48'25" N, long. 121°27'25" W; sec. 7, T 34 N, R 5 E). Named on Jellico (1957) 15' quadrangle.

(2) *stream,* flows 7.25 miles to Hat Creek 8 miles north-northeast of Lassen Peak (lat. 40°37' N, long. 121°28' W; near S line sec. 13, T 32 N, R 4 E). Named on Manzanita Lake (1956) and Prospect Peak (1957) 15' quadrangles. United States Board on Geographic Names (1933, p. 475) rejected the name "Canoe Creek" for the stream.

Lost Creek [TEHAMA]: *stream,* flows 10 miles to Deer Creek (2) 3 miles east of Deer Creek Station (lat. 40°15'30" N, long. 121°23'45" W; sec. 26, T 28 N, R 5 E). Named on Mount Harkness (1956) 15' quadrangle.

Lost Creek: see **Tarantula Gulch** [SHASTA].

Lost Creek Camp [SHASTA]: *locality,* 5.25 miles north of Lassen Peak (lat. 40°33'45" N, long. 121°31' W; neat W line sec. 3, T 31 N, R 4 E). Named on Manzanita Lake (1956) 15' quadrangle.

Lost Creek Plateau [TEHAMA]: *ridge,* west-southwest- to south-trending, 6 miles long, 4 miles north-northeast of Deer Creek Station (lat. 40°19' N, long. 121°24'30" W); the ridge is southwest of Lost Creek. Named on Mount Harkness (1956) 15' quadrangle.

Lost Creek Reservoir [BUTTE]: *lake,* behind a dam on Lost Creek 3 miles north-northeast of Clipper Mills (lat. 39°34'30" N, long. 121°08'10" W; sec. 24, T 20 N, R 7 E). Named on Clipper Mills (1948) and Strawberry Valley (1948) 7.5' quadrangles.

Lost Creek Spring [TEHAMA]: *spring,* 5 miles northwest of Deer Creek Station (lat. 40°18'25" N, long. 121°22'20" W; near N line sec. 12, T 28 N, R 5 E); the spring is near Lost Creek. Named on Mount Harkness (1956) 15' quadrangle.

Lost Iron Well [SISKIYOU]: *well,* 14 miles north-northwest of Bartle (lat. 41°27'25" N, long. 121°44'55" W; at N line sec. 28, T 42 N, R 2 E). Named on Hambone (1961) 15' quadrangle.

Lost Lake [SISKIYOU]: *lake,* 800 feet long, 10 miles north-northeast of Forks of Salmon (lat. 41°23'45" N, long. 123°16'10" W). Named on Medicine Mountain (1978) 7.5' quadrangle.

Lost Lake Creek [SISKIYOU]: *stream,* flows 1.5 miles to Salt Log Creek 11.5 miles north-northeast of Forks of Salmon (lat. 41°24'55" N, long. 123°15'20" W); the stream heads at Lost Lake. Named on Medicine Mountain (1978) 7.5' quadrangle.

Lost River [SISKIYOU]: *stream,* heads in the State of Oregon and flows 4.5 miles in Siskiyou County to Tule Lake Sump 13 miles northeast of Mount Dome (lat. 41°56'30" N, long. 121°30'15" W). Named on Mount Dome (1950) 15' quadrangle.

Lost Spoon Lake: see **Harrington Mountain** [SISKIYOU].

Lost Spring [SISKIYOU]: *spring,* 13 miles southeast of Bray (lat. 41°31'15" N, long. 127°46'50" W). Named on Bray (1950) 15' quadrangle.

Louie Creek [SISKIYOU]: *stream,* flows 1 mile to Klamath River 4 miles east-southeast of the village of Seiad Valley (lat. 41°48'55" N, long. 123°07'35" W; sec. 21, T 46 N, R 11 W). Named on Seiad Valley (1980) 7.5' quadrangle.

Louse Creek [SISKIYOU]: *stream,* flows 1 mile to Indian Creek (1) 11.5 miles north-northeast of Preston Peak (lat. 41°58'55" N, long. 123°30'25" W). Named on Polar Bear Mountain (1982) 7.5' quadrangle.

Love Branch [TEHAMA]: *stream,* diverges from Digger Creek [SHASTA-TEHAMA] and flows 1.25 miles to rejoin Digger Creek 5 miles east of Manton (lat. 40°26'15" N, long. 121°46'30" W; at S line sec. 21, T 30 N, R 2 E). Named on Manton (1956) 15' quadrangle. United States Board on Geographic Names (1986c, p. 3) rejected the name "Love Branch Dry Gulch" for the feature.

Love Branch Dry Gulch: see **Love Branch** [TEHAMA].

Love Cabin Spring [TEHAMA]: *spring,* 7 miles southwest of Wakefield Flat (lat. 40°04' N, long. 122°44'40" W; near E line sec. 34, T 26 N, R 8 W). Named on Raglin Ridge (1967) 7.5' quadrangle.

Lovelady Gulch [SISKIYOU]: *canyon,* drained by a stream that flows 1 mile to McAdam Creek 6.5 miles north of Fort Jones (lat. 41°41'45" N, long. 122°49' W; near NW cor. sec. 6, T 44 N, R 8 W). Named on Fort Jones (1955) 15' quadrangle.

Lovelock [BUTTE]: *village,* 2.5 miles west-southwest of Stirling City (lat. 39°53'30" N, long. 121°34'35" W; on W line sec. 31, T 24 N, R 4 E). Named on Stirling City (1979) 7.5' quadrangle. Postal authorities established Lovelock post office in 1871 and discontinued it in 1922 (Frickstad, p. 10). The name commemorates George Lovelock, who started the community when he opened a hotel and store there in 1855 (Gudde, 1949, p. 196).

Lovelock: see **Old Lovelock**, under **Coutolenc** [BUTTE].

Lovers Camp [SISKIYOU]: *locality,* 13 miles southwest of Scott Bar (lat. 41°35'40" N, long. 123°08'30" W). Named on Scott Bar (1980) 7.5' quadrangle.

Lovers Leap [SISKIYOU]: *relief feature,* 12.5 miles east-southeast of Etna (lat. 41°21'55" N, long. 122°41'30" W; near NE cor. sec. 31, T 41 N, R 7 W). Named on China Mountaln (1955) 15' quadrangle.

Lowe: see **Camp Lowe** [SISKIYOU].

Lower Bear Lake [SISKIYOU]: *lake,* 1300 feet long, 0.5 mile north of Bear Peak (lat. 41°42'05" N, long. 123°34'45" W); the feature is in Little Bear Valley 0.25 mile downstream from Bear Lake (1). Named on Bear Peak (1982) 7.5' quadrangle.

Lower Boulder Lake [SISKIYOU]: *lake,* 700 feet long, 16 miles south-southeast of Etna (lat. 41°14'20" N, long. 122°47'35" W; sec. 16, T 39 N, R 8 W); the lake is 0.5 mile northwest of East Boulder Lake. Named on Coffee Creek (1955) 15' quadrangle.

Lower Caribou Lake [SISKIYOU]: *lake,* 1400 feet long, 30 miles south of Etna (lat. 41°01'45" N, long. 122°58'30" W); the feature is 0.25 mile north of Caribou Lake. Named on Coffee Creek (1955) 15' quadrangle.

Lower Cliff Lake [SISKIYOU]: *lake,* 500 feet long, 11.5 miles west of Dunsmuir (lat. 41°12'15" N, long. 122°29'20" W; at SW cor. sec. 30, T 39 N, R 5 W); the feature is 1000 feet downstream from Cliff Lake (2). Named on Dunsmuir (1954) 15' quadrangle.

Lower Crossing [SISKIYOU]: *locality,* 10.5 miles northwest of Macdoel along Shovel Creek (lat. 41°55'45" N, long. 122°09'30" W; sec. 12, T 47 N, R 3 W); the place is 4 miles downstream from Upper Crossing. Site named on Macdoel (1954) 15' quadrangle.

Lower Devils Peak [SISKIYOU]: *peak,* 3 miles north of the village of Seiad Valley (lat. 41°52'30" N, long. 123°12' W); the feature is 3150 feet south of Middle Devils Peak. Altitude 5081 feet. Named on Kangaroo Mountain (1980) and Seiad Valley (1980) 7.5' quadrangles. Whitney (p. 357) used the name "Three Devils" for Lower Devils Peak, Middle Devils Peak, and Upper Devils Peak together.

Lower Falls [SISKIYOU]: *waterfall,* 6 miles east of McCloud along McCloud River [SHASTA-SISKIYOU] (lat. 41°14' N, long. 122°01'25" W; sec. 12, T 39 N, R 2 W); the feature is 1 mile below Middle Falls. Named on Shoeinhorse Mountain (1954) 15' quadrangle.

Lower Foster Island [TEHAMA]: *island,* 8 miles southeast of Corning in Sacramento River (lat. 39°50'45" N, long. 122°04'05" W). Named on Foster Island (1950) 7.5' quadrangle. Called Foster Island on Vina (1904) 15' quadrangle.

Lower Kings Creek Meadow: see **Lower Meadow** [SHASTA].

Lower Klamath Lake [SISKIYOU]: *lake,* about 8 miles long, center 9 miles north of Mount Dome (lat. 41°56'30" N, long. 121°41'30" W). Named on Dorris (1950) and Mount Dome (1950) 15' quadrangles. Called Little Klamet L. on Wilkes' (1841) map, and called Little Klamath Lake on California Mining Bureau's (1917a) map, but United States Board on Geographic Names (1933, p. 477) rejected the name "Little Klamath Lake" for the feature. Mount Dome (1950) 15' quadrangle has the name "Lower Klamath Lake Sump" for the south part of the lake.

Lower Klamath Lake Sump: see **Lower Klamath Lake** [SISKIYOU].

Lower Limestone Valley Creek [SHASTA]: *stream,* flows 0.5 mile to Backbone Creek Arm Shasta Lake 13 miles south of Lamoine (lat. 40°47'40" N, long. 121°25' W; sec. 22, T 34 N, R 5 W); the stream is less than 0.5 mile south of Upper Limestone Valley Creek. Named on Lamoine (1957) 15' quadrangle.

Lower Maple Spring [SISKIYOU]: *spring,* 6.25 miles south of Hornbrook (lat. 41°49'10" N, long. 122°32'30" W; sec. 21, T 46 N, R 6 W); the spring is 350 feet north-northeast of Upper Maple Spring. Named on Hornbrook (1955) 15' quadrangle.

Lower Meadow [SHASTA]: *area,* 3.5 miles southeast of Lassen Peak along Kings Creek (lat. 40°27'30" N, long. 121°27'10" W; sec. 17, T 30 N, R 5 E); the place is less than 1 mile east-southeast of Upper Meadow. Named on Mount Harkness (1956) 15' quadrangle. United States Board on Geographic Names (1933, p. 477) once approved the name "Lower Kings Creek Meadow" for the place.

Lower Mill Lake [SISKIYOU]: *lake,* 450 feet long, 15 miles south-southeast of Etna (lat. 41°16' N, long. 122°45'20" W; near S line sec. 35, T 40 N, R 8 W); the lake is at the head of Big Mill Creek. Named on Etna (1955) 15' quadrangle.

Lower Rocky Honcut Creek [BUTTE]: *stream,* flows nearly 3 miles to join Upper Rocky Honcut Creek and form Rocky Honcut Creek 4 miles north of Bangor (lat. 39°26'50" N, long. 121°23'25" W; near E line sec. 3, T 18 N, R 5 E). Named on Bangor (1947) and Rackerby (1948) 7.5' quadrangles.

Lower Russian Lake [SISKIYOU]: *lake,* 500 feet long, 14 miles south-southwest of Etna (lat. 41°16'05" N, long. 122°58'45" W; sec. 2, T 39 N, R 10 W); the lake is 0.25 mile north-northwest of Russian Lake at the head of a branch of South Russian Creek. Named on Etna (1955) 15' quadrangle.

Lower Salt Creek Resort [SHASTA]: *locality,* 10.5 miles south-southeast of Lamoine (lat. 40°50'30" N, long. 122°20'55" W; sec. 32, T 35 N, R 4 W); the place is 1 mile south-southwest of Upper Salt Creek Resort along Salt Creek Inlet. Named on Lamoine (1957) 15' quadrangle.

Lower Seven Lake [SHASTA-SISKIYOU]: *lake,* 450 feet long, 12 miles west of Dunsmuir on Siskiyou-Shasta County line (lat. 41°11'05" N, long. 122°29'25" W; at E line sec. 1, T 38 N, R 6 W); the feature is in Seven Lakes Basin. Named on Dunsmuir (1954) 15' quadrangle.

Lower Sky High Lake [SISKIYOU]: *lake,* 1500 feet long, 16 miles south-southwest of Scott Bar (lat. 41°33' N, long. 123°10'35" W); the lake is just east of Upper Sky High Lake. Named on Marble Mountain (1980) 7.5' quadrangle. United States Board on Geographic Names (1981c, p. 4) rejected the names "Sky High Lake," "Sky High Lakes," and "Sky Lakes."

Lower Soda Spring: see **Castle Crag** [SHASTA]; **Soda Spring** [SHASTA] (1).

Lower Town: see **Hawkinsville** [SISKIYOU].

Lower Twin Lake [SHASTA]:

(1) *lake,* 400 feet long, 16 miles north-northwest of Lassen Peak (lat. 40°42'15" N, long. 121°35'40" W; near E line sec. 23, T 33 N, R 3 E); the lake is 800 feet southeast of Upper Twin Lake (1). Named on Manzanita Lake (1956) 15' quadrangle. On Burney (1939) 30' quadrangle, present Lower Twin Lake and Upper Twin Lake together are called Twin Lakes.

(2) *lake,* 0.5 mile long, 7.5 miles east of Lassen Peak (lat. 40°30'25" N, long. 121°21'45" W; at E line sec. 36, T 31 N, R 5 E). Named on Prospect Peak (1957) 15' quadrangle. Called Upper Twin Lake on Halls Flat (1939) 30' quadrangle, where present Upper Twin Lake (2) is called Lower Twin Lakes. Lassen Peak (1894) 1° quadrangle shows Lake Tillman where Prospect Peak (1957) 15' quadrangle shows Upper Twin Lake and Lower Twin Lake. United States Board on Geographic Names (1933, p. 776) rejected the names "Bee Lake" and "Tillman Lake" for the two lakes. The Board later (1937, p. 19, 31) rejected the name "Twin Lakes" for Lower Twin Lake and Upper Twin Lake together.

Lower Wright Lake [SISKIYOU]: *lake,* 1650 feet long, 12 miles south-southwest of Scott Bar (lat. 41°35' N, long. 123°05'10" W); the feature is 1500 feet west of Upper Wright Lake. Named on Boulder Peak (1981) 7.5' quadrangle.

Low Gap [SISKIYOU]: *pass,* 5.5 miles northeast of the village of Seiad Valley (lat. 41°53'30" N, long. 123°06'30" W). Named on Dutch Creek (1980) 7.5' quadrangle. United States Board on Geographic Names (1978b, p. 5) approved the name "Seiad Low Gap" for the pass.

Low Gap [TEHAMA]: *pass,* 5 miles west-northwest of Tomhead Mountain (lat. 40°10'15" N, long. 122°54' W; near SE cor. sec. 20, T 27 N, R 9 W). Named on Yolla Bolly (1954) 15' quadrangle. United States Board on Geographic Names (1979a, p. 3) approved the name "East Low Gap" for the pass.

Low Gap: see **Mendocino Pass** [GLENN].

Low Pass Creek [SHASTA]: *stream,* flows about 2 miles to Squaw Creek (2) 7.25 miles southeast of Bollibokka Mountain (lat. 40°51'30" N, long. 122°07'10" W; sec. 29, T 35 N, R 2 W). Named on Bollibokka Mountain (1957) 15' quadrangle.

Lowrey [TEHAMA]: *locality,* 9 miles south-southeast of Wakefield Flat (lat. 40°00'50" N, long. 122°33'10" W; at W line sec. 21, T 25 N, R 6 W). Named on Lowrey (1967) 7.5' quadrangle.

Luce: see **Magalia** [BUTTE].

Luce Gulch [SISKIYOU]: *canyon,* 2.5 miles long, opens into the canyon of Moffett Creek 2.5 miles northeast of Fort Jones (lat. 41°37'45" N, long. 122°48'15" W; sec. 29, T 44 N, R 8 W). Named on Fort Jones (1955) 15' quadrangle.

Lucky Spring [SISKIYOU]: *spring,* 14 miles west-northwest of Macdoel (lat. 41°55'50" N, long. 122°14'25" W; sec. 8, T 47 N, R 3 W). Named on Macdoel (1954) 15' quadrangle.

Lumgrey Creek [SISKIYOU]: *stream,* flows 5.25 miles to Klamath River 10 miles west-southwest of Hornbrook at Gottville (lat. 41°52' N, long. 122°44'15" W; sec. 2, T 46 N, R 8 W). Named on Condrey Mountain (1955) and Hornbrook (1955) 15' quadrangles. Logan (p. 450) used the form "Lum Grey Creek" for the name.

Lumpkin [BUTTE]: *locality,* 6 miles north-northwest of Clipper Mills along Feather River Railway (lat. 39°36'35" N, long. 121°12'30" W; sec. 8, T 20 N, R 7 E). Named on Clipper Mills (1948) 7.5' quadrangle. Postal authorities established Lumpkin post office in 1886 and discontinued it in 1919 (Frickstad, p. 10).

Lumpkin Ridge [BUTTE]: *ridge,* southwest- to south-southwest-trending, 13 miles long, 8 miles north of Clipper Mills on Butte-Plumas County line (lat. 39°39' N, long. 121°08'10" W). Named on Cascade (1948) 7.5 quadrangle.

Lunch Creek [SISKIYOU]:

(1) *stream,* flows 2 miles to Nordheimer Creek 2.5 miles west of Forks of Salmon (lat. 41°15' N, long. 123°23'35" W). Named on Orleans Mountain (1974) and Youngs Peak (1979) 7.5' quadrangles.

(2) *stream,* flows 0.5 mile to Etna Creek 6 miles south-southwest of Etna (lat. 41°24'15" N, long. 122°58'50" W; sec. 15, T 41 N, R 10 W). Named on Etna (1955) 15' quadrangle.

Lunch Gulch [SHASTA]: *canyon,* 0.5 mile long, 6 miles north of Schell Mountain (lat. 40°56'30" N, long. 122°31'15" W). Named on Schell Mountain (1950) 15' quadrangle.

Luther Gulch [SISKIYOU]: *canyon,* drained by a stream that flows 2.25 miles to Indian Creek (1) 4.5 miles north-northwest of Happy Camp (lat. 41°51'35" N, long. 123°24'05" W; near E line sec. 16, T 17 N, R 7 E). Named on Happy Camp (1980) and Slater Butte (1980) 7.5' quadrangles.

Lyman [GLENN]: *locality,* 3 miles north of Willows along Southern Pacific Railroad (lat. 39°34'10" N, long. 122°11'35" W). Named on Willows (1906) 15' quadrangle.

Lyman Spring [TEHAMA]: *locality,* 10.5 miles south-southeast of Manton (lat. 40°18'35" N, long. 121°45'55" W; sec. 5, T 28 N, R 2 E). Named on Manton (1956) 15' quadrangle. On Mineral (1941) 30' quadrangle, the name applies to a spring at the site.

Lynchburg: see **Oroville** [BUTTE].

Lyons Peak [SISKIYOU]: *peak,* 3.5 miles east of Medicine Lake (lat. 41°34'45" N, long. 121°30'30" W). Altitude 7903 feet. Named on Medicine Lake (1952) 15' quadrangle. The name honors George Washington Lyons, supervisor of Modoc National Forest, who died by accident while performing his duties (United States Board on Geographic Names, 1933, p. 482).

Lyons Peak [TEHAMA]: *peak,* 4 miles south-southwest of Mineral (lat. 40°18'05" N, long. 121°38'20" W; on S line sec. 4, T 28 N, R 3 E). Altitude 6651 feet. Named on Lassen Peak (1956) 15' quadrangle.

Lyonsville [TEHAMA]: *locality,* 9 miles south-southeast of Manton (lat. 40°18'30" N, long. 121°44'10" W; sec. 3, T 28 N, R 2 E). Named on Lassen Peak (1956) 15' quadrangle. Postal authorities established Lyonsville post office in 1883 and discontinued it in 1937 (Frickstad, p. 204). The name commemorates Darwin B. Lyon, a superintendent of Sierra Flume and Lumber Company (Hoover, Rensch, and Rensch, p. 551). Postal authorities established Lena post office 8 miles northwest of Lyonsville in 1896 and discontinued it in 1897 (Salley, p. 121).

Lytles Bar: see **Steelhead** [SISKIYOU].

– M –

Mabel: see **Delta** [SHASTA].

Macam Springs [TEHAMA]: *springs,* 5.5 miles southwest of Manton (lat. 40°23'25" N, long. 121°57'20" W; near S line sec. 3, T 29 N, R 1 W). Named on Manton (1956) 15' quadrangle. United States. Board on Geographic Names (1986c, p. 3) approved the name "Macon Springs" for the feature.

Macdoel [SISKIYOU]: *town,* 33 miles east of Yreka in Butte Valley (lat. 41°49'45" N, long. 122°00'15" W; in and near sec. 17, T 46 N, R 1 W). Named on Dorris (1950) and Macdoel (1954) 15' quadrangles. California Mining Bureau's (1917a) map has the form "McDoel" for the name. Postal authorities established Macdoel post office in 1907 (Frickstad, p. 188). Officials of Southern Pacific Railroad named the place in 1906 for William MacDoel, owner of land there (Gudde, 1949, p. 199).

Macks Creek [SISKIYOU]: *stream,* flows 4.5 miles to Klamath River 8 miles east-southeast of the village of Seiad Valley (lat. 41°47'05" N, long. 123°03'30" W). Named on Hamburg (1980) 7.5' quadrangle.

Macon Springs: see **Macam Springs** [TEHAMA].

Macum: see **Manton** [TEHAMA].

Mad Creek [GLENN]: *stream,* flows 5.5 miles to Briscoe Creek 4.25 miles south-southwest of the village of Elk Creek (lat. 39°32'50" N, long. 122°34'20" W; sec. 31, T 20 N, R 6 W). Named on Elk Creek (1968) and Felkner Hill (1968) 7.5' quadrangles.

Madison Canyon [SHASTA]: *canyon,* drained by a stream that flows nearly 2 miles to Squaw Creek Arm Shasta Lake 8 miles south-southeast of Bollibokka Mountain (lat. 40°49'50" N, long. 122°08'15" W; sec. 6, T 34 N, R 2 W); the mouth of the canyon is 1 mile north-northeast of the mouth of Madison Gulch. Named on Bollibokka Mountain (1957) 15' quadrangle.

Madison Gulch [SHASTA]: *canyon,* drained by a stream that flows nearly 1 mile to Squaw Creek Arm Shasta Lake 9 miles south-southeast of Bollibokka Mountain (lat. 40°49' N, long. 122°08'45" W; at W line sec. 7,

T 34 N, R 2 W); the mouth of the canyon is 1 mile south-southwest of the mouth of Madison Canyon. Named on Bollibokka Mountain (1957) 15' quadrangle.

Mad Mule Gulch [SHASTA]: *canyon,* drained by a stream that flows 1 mile to Whiskey Creek 4.25 miles east-southeast of the village of French Gulch (lat. 40°40'20" N, long. 122°33'50" W; sec. 32, T 33 N, R 6 W). Named on Whiskeytown (1979) 7.5' quadrangle.

Mad Mule Mountain [SHASTA]: *peak,* 3.25 miles southeast of the village of French Gulch (lat. 40°40'30" N, long. 122°35'15" W; sec. 31, T 33 N, R 6 W); the peak is near the head of Mad Mule Gulch. Named on Whiskeytown (1979) 7.5' quadrangle.

Mad Ox Gulch [SHASTA]: *canyon,* drained by a stream that flows 1.5 miles to Whiskey Creek 4.25 miles east-southeast of the village of French Gulch (lat. 40°40'45" N, long. 122°33'50" W; near N line sec. 32, T 33 N, R 6 W). Named on Whiskeytown (1979) 7.5' quadrangle, which shows Mad Ox mine in the canyon.

Madrone Lake [BUTTE]: *lake,* behind a dam on Berry Creek (1) less than 0.5 mile northwest of the village of Berry Creek (lat. 39°39' N, long. 121°24'30" W; sec. 27, T 21 N, R 5 E). Named on Berry Creek (1970) 7.5' quadrangle.

Magalia [BUTTE]: *village,* 4 miles northeast of Paradise (lat. 39°48'35" N, long. 121°34'40" W; at E line sec. 36, T 23 N, R 3 E). Named on Paradise East (1980) 7.5' quadrangle. Postal authorities established Butte Mills post office in 1857, changed the name to Magalia in 1861, and discontinued it for a time in 1873 (Frickstad, p. 8, 10). A man named Bassett built a cabin at the site in 1850; his wife bred and sold dogs, which gave the name "Dogtown" to the place—it also was known as Mountain View (Wells and Chambers, p. 252). Dogtown and Mill City, later called Magalia, were adjacent but separate communities that shared Butte Mills post office, but eventually Magalia took over Dogtown (Dunn, F.D., p. 33). California Division of Highways' (1934) map shows a place called Appleton located 2.5 miles north of Magalia along Southern Pacific Railroad (sec. 18, T 23 N, R 4 E), and a place called Luce situated 3 miles north-northeast of Magalia along the same railroad (at S line sec. 7, T 23 N, R 4 E). Postal authorities established Channel post office 3.5 miles north of Magalia in 1886 and discontinued it in 1890 (Salley, p. 42).

Magalia Camp [BUTTE]: *locality,* 6.5 miles north-northeast of Paradise (lat. 39°51'15" N, long. 121°35' W; sec. 13, T 23 N, R 3 E). Named on Paradise East (1980) 7.5' quadrangle.

Magalia Reservoir [BUTTE]: *lake,* behind a dam on Little Butte Creek [BUTTE-GLENN] 4.5 miles north-northeast of Paradise (lat. 39°48'55" N, long. 121°34'55" W; near SE cor. sec. 25, T 23 N, R 3 E). Named on Paradise East (1980) 7.5' quadrangle.

Magee Lake [SHASTA]: *lake,* 750 feet long, 16 miles north-northwest of Lassen Peak (lat. 40°42' N, long. 121°36'05" W; sec. 23, T 33 N, R 3 E). Named on Manzanita Lake (1956) 15' quadrangle.

Magee Peak [SHASTA]: *peak,* 15 miles north-northwest of Lassen Peak (lat. 40°41'25" N, long. 121°37'05" W; sec. 27, T 33 N, R 3 E). Altitude 8550 feet. Named on Manzanita Lake (1956) 15' quadrangle. The name commemorates William Magee, who surveyed in the region in the 1860's (Gudde, 1949, p. 201).

Magee Peak: see **Freaner Peak** [SHASTA].

Magee Ridge [BUTTE]: *ridge,* west-southwest-trending, 2 miles long, 3 miles east-northeast of Pulga (lat. 39°49'05" N, long. 121°23'45" W). Named on Pulga (1979) 7.5' quadrangle.

Mahogany Mountain [SISKIYOU]: *peak,* 7 miles south-southeast of Dorris (lat. 41°52'30" N, long. 121°51'20" W; sec. 34, T 47 N, R 1 E). Altitude 6255 feet. Named on Dorris (1950) 15' quadrangle. Wood (p. 13) used the name "Mahogany Mountain Ridge" for the elevation on which Mahogany Mountain is a high point. United States Board on Geographic Names (1986c, p. 3) approved the name "J.F. Mountain" for a peak, altitude 6208 feet, situated less than 1 mile east-northeast of present Mahogany Mountain (lat. 41°52'46" N, long. 121°50'38" W), and rejected the name "Mahogany Mountain" for it.

Mahogany Mountain Ridge: see **Mahogany Mountain** [SISKIYOU].

Maidenhair Spring [TEHAMA]: *spring,* 7 miles southwest of Mineral (lat. 40°17'15" N, long. 121°42'10" W; near SW cor. sec. 12, T 28 N, R 2 E). Named on Lassen Peak (1956) 15' quadrangle.

Malinda Gulch [SHASTA]: *canyon,* drained by a stream that flows 2 miles to Pit River 11 miles northeast of the village of Montgomery Creek (lat. 40°57'50" N, long. 121°47'20" W). Named on Montgomery Creek (1956) 15' quadrangle.

Mallethead Rock [SISKIYOU]: *relief feature,* 14 miles east of Etna (lat. 41°28'50" N, long. 122°37'20" W; at N line sec. 23, T 42 N, R 7 W). Named on China Mountain (1955) 15' quadrangle.

Malone Creek [SISKIYOU]: *stream,* flows nearly 2 miles to Elk Creek 8 miles north of Ukonom Lake (lat. 41°42' N, long. 123°21'15" W). Named on Clear Creek (1981) and Huckleberry Mountain (1980) 7.5' quadrangles.

Malton [GLENN]: *locality,* 3.5 miles north-northeast of Orland along Southern Pacific Railroad (lat. 39°02'45" N, long. 122°10'45" W; near NE cor. sec. 3, T 22 N, R 3 W). Named on Vina (1904) 15' quadrangle.

Mammoth: see **Kennett** [SHASTA].

Mammoth Butte [SHASTA]: *peak,* 15 miles south of Lamoine (lat. 40°45'50" N, long. 122°28'15" W; near E line sec. 31, T 34 N, R 5 W). Named on Lamoine (1957) 15' quadrangle.

Mammoth Crater [SISKIYOU]: *crater,* 8 miles north-northeast of Medicine Lake (lat. 41°41'35" N, long. 121°32'50" W; at SE cor. sec. 31, T 45 N, R 4 E). Named on Medicine Lake (1952) 15' quadrangle.

Man Eaten Lake [SISKIYOU]: *lake,* 1500 feet long, 18 miles south-southwest of Scott Bar (lat. 41°30'20" N, long. 123°07'40" W). Named on Marble Mountain (1980) 7.5' quadrangle.

Manhattan Island [GLENN]: *island,* 2.25 miles south-southwest of Butte City in Sacramento River (lat. 39°25'30" N, long. 121°59'55" W). Named on Marysville (1895) 30' quadrangle.

Mankinsville: see **Churntown** [SHASTA].

Mannon: see **Dunsmuir** [SISKIYOU].

Manton [TEHAMA]: *village,* 15 miles west-northwest of Mineral (lat. 40°26'15" N, long. 121°52'10" W; sec. 21, T 30 N, R 1 E). Named on Manton (1956) 15' quadrangle. Postal authorities established Manton post office in Tehama County in 1889, moved it into Shasta County in 1897, and moved it back into Tehama County in 1898 (Salley, p. 132). They established Macum post office 8 miles southwest of Manton in 1895, moved it 1.25 miles southeast in 1896, and discontinued it in 1905; the name was for a pioneer homesteader—Indians killed the man in 1850 (Salley, p. 130).

Manzanita: see **Red Bluff** [TEHAMA].

Manzanita Chute [SHASTA]: *area,* 6.5 miles west-northwest of Lassen Peak (lat. 40°32'15" N, long. 121°36'30" W). Named on Manzanita Lake (1956) 15' quadrangle.

Manzanita Creek [SHASTA]: *stream,* flows about 13 miles to Deer Creek (1) 12 miles west-northwest of Lassen Peak (lat. 40°32'05" N, long. 121°43'15" W; sec. 14, T 31 N, R 2 E). Named on Lassen Peak (1956) and Manzanita Lake (1956) 15' quadrangles.

Manzanita Flat [TEHAMA]: *area,* 8.5 miles northeast of Wakefield Flat (lat. 40°12'20" N, long. 122°30'50" W; sec. 11, T 27 N, R 6 W). Named on Oxbow Bridge (1967) 7.5' quadrangle.

Manzanita Gulch [SISKIYOU]: *canyon,* drained by a stream that flows nearly 1 mile to Joe Creek 10 miles north-northeast of the village of Seiad Valley (lat. 41°58'40" N, long. 123°07'10" W). Named on Dutch Creek (1980) 7.5' quadrangle.

Manzanita Hill [SHASTA]: *ridge,* west-trending, 1.25 miles long, 5 miles southwest of the village of Montgomery Creek (lat. 40°47'30" N, long. 121°59'10" W; near NW cor. sec. 21, T 34 N, R 1 W). Named on Montgomery Creek (1956) 15' quadrangle.

Manzanita Hill [SISKIYOU]: *peak,* 5.5 miles south of Yreka (lat. 41°39'10" N, long. 122°38'50" W; near NW cor. sec. 22, T 44 N, R 7 W). Altitude 4433 feet. Named on Yreka (1954) 15' quadrangle.

Manzanita Lake [SHASTA]:

(1) *lake,* 2400 feet long, 4.5 miles northwest of Lassen Peak (lat. 40°32' N, long. 121°34' W; sec. 18, T 31 N, R 4 E). Named on Manzanita Lake (1956) 15' quadrangle. Called Reflection Lake on Burney (1939) 30' quadrangle.

(2) *locality,* 4.25 miles northwest of Lassen Peak (lat. 40°32'10" N, long. 121°33'20" W; on W line sec. 17, T 31 N, R 4 E); the place is just east of Manzanita Lake (1). Named on Manzanita Lake (1956) 15' quadrangle. Postal authorities established Manzanita Lake post office in 1934 and discontinued it in 1974 (Salley, p. 132).

Manzanita Mountain: see **Table Mountain** [SHASTA].

Manzanita Ridge [TEHAMA]: *ridge,* generally east-trending, 1.5 miles long, 7.25 miles west-southwest of Tomhead Mountain (lat. 40°05'15" N, long. 122°56' W; on E line sec. 24, T 26 N, R 10 W). Named on Yolla Bolly (1954) 15' quadrangle.

Manzanita Spring [GLENN]: *spring,* 9 miles northwest of the village of Elk Creek (lat. 39°42'20" N, long. 122°38'25" W). Named on Alder Springs (1967) 7.5' quadrangle.

Manzanita Spring [SHASTA]: *spring,* 12 miles west-northwest of Lassen Peak (lat. 40°32'20" N, long. 121°43' W; sec. 14, T 31 N, R 2 E). Named on Manzanita Lake (1956) 15' quadrangle.

Maple Branch [BUTTE]: *stream,* flows 7.5 miles to Mud Creek 8 miles north-northeast of Chico (lat. 39°50'20" N, long. 121°47'10" W; near NW cor. sec. 20, T 23 N, R 2 E). Named on Campbell Mound (1952), Cohasset (1979), and Richardson Springs (1951) 7.5' quadrangles.

Maple Creek [TEHAMA]: *stream,* flows 6 miles to South Fork Cottonwood Creek [SHASTA-TEHAMA] 5 miles west of Wakefield Flat (lat. 40°07'35" N, long. 122°44' W). Named on Yolla Bolly (1954) 15' quadrangle, and on Cold Fork (1967) 7.5' quadrangle. United States Board on Geographic Names (1979a, p. 6) approved the name "Switzel-Baum Creek" for a stream that flows 1.5 miles to Maple Creek nearly 3 miles northeast of Tomhead Mountain (lat. 40°09'30" N, long. 122°46'18" W; sec. 28, T 27 N, R 8 W).

Maple Falls [SISKIYOU]: *waterfall,* 11.5 miles southwest of Scott Bar along Kelsey Creek (lat. 41°38'50" N, long. 123°10'45" W). Named on Grider Valley (1981) 7.5' quadrangle.

Maple Grove Spring [SISKIYOU]: *spring,* 5.5 miles west-southwest of Hornbrook (lat. 41°53'15" N, long. 122°39'30" W; near SE cor. sec. 28, T 47 N, R 7 W). Named on Hornbrook (1955) 15' quadrangle.

Maple Gulch [SISKIYOU]:

(1) *canyon,* drained by a stream that flows 1.5 miles to Horse Creek (2) 6 miles east of the village of Seiad Valley (lat. 41°51'20" N, long. 123°04'50" W; near SE cor. sec. 2, T 46 N, R 11 W). Named on Hamburg (1980) 7.5' quadrangle.

(2) *canyon,* drained by a stream that flows less than 1 mile to Ash Creek (1) 4.5 miles southwest of Hornbrook (lat. 41°52'15" N, long. 122°37'15" W; near W line sec. 1, T 46 N, R 7 W). Named on Hornbrook (1955) 15' quadrangle.

Maple Gulch [TEHAMA]: *canyon,* drained by Maple Creek, which flows 6 miles to South Fork Cottonwood Creek [SHASTA-TEHAMA] 5 miles west of Wakefield Flat (lat. 40°07'35" N, long. 122°44' W). Named on Colyear Springs (1957) 15' quadrangle.

Maple Spring [SHASTA]: *spring,* 5.25 miles south of Lamoine (lat. 40°54'15" N, long. 122°26'30" W; sec. 9, T 35 N, R 5 W). Named on Lamoine (1957) 15' quadrangle.

Maple Spring [SISKIYOU]:

(1) *spring,* 9.5 miles north-northwest of Orleans, which is in Humboldt County (lat. 41°25'55" N, long. 123°36'30" W). Named on Bark Shanty Gulch (1974) 7.5' quadrangle.

(2) *spring,* 4.5 miles north of Hornbrook (lat. 41°58'30" N, long. 122°33'15" W; on W line sec. 28, T 48 N, R 6 W). Named on Hornbrook (1955) 15' quadrangle.

(3) *spring,* 6.25 miles south of the village of Seiad Valley (lat. 41°45'05" N, long. 123°10'50" W). Named on Seiad Valley (1980) 7.5' quadrangle.

(4) *spring,* 2 miles west-southwest of Forks of Salmon (lat. 41°15'05" N, long. 123°21'40" W). Named on Forks of Salmon (1978) 7.5' quadrangle.

(5) *spring,* nearly 7 miles northeast of Cecilville (lat. 41°12'40" N, long. 123°02'40" W). Named on Grasshopper Ridge (1979) 7.5' quadrangle.

Maple Spring: see **Lower Maple Spring** [SISKIYOU]; **Upper Maple Spring** [SISKIYOU].

Maple Spring Camp [SISKIYOU]: *locality,* 6.25 miles south of the village of Seiad Valley (lat. 41°45'10" N, long. 123°10'50" W; near NE cor. sec. 14, T 45 N, R 12 W); the place is at present Maple Spring (3). Named on Seiad Valley (1955) 15' quadrangle.

Marble Creek [BUTTE]: *stream,* heads in Plumas County and flows 2 miles in Butte County to Little North Fork [of Middle Fork Feather River] 5.25 miles northeast of the village of Brush Creek (lat. 39°44'45" N, long. 121°16'10" W; sec. 23, T 22 N, R 6 E). Named on Brush Creek (1970) and Soapstone Hill (1979) 7.5' quadrangles.

Marble Creek [SHASTA]:

(1) *stream,* flows 6 miles to Pit River 4 miles northwest of the village of Montgomery Creek (lat. 40°53'25" N, long. 121°58'05" W; at W line sec. 15, T 35 N, R 1 W). Named on Montgomery Creek (1956) 15' quadrangle.

(2) *stream,* flows 0.5 mile to McCloud River Arm Shasta Lake 16 miles south-southeast of Lamoine (lat. 40°47'05" N, long. 122°17'10" W; sec. 23, T 34 N, R 4 W). Named on Lamoine (1957) 15' quadrangle.

Marble Creek [SISKIYOU]: *stream,* flows about 1.5 miles to Beaver Creek (1) 9 miles east-southeast of Condrey Mountain (lat. 41°53'05" N, long. 122°49'15" W; sec. 31, T 47 N, R 8 W). Named on Condrey Mountain (1955) 15' quadrangle.

Marble Gulch [SISKIYOU]: *canyon,* drained by a stream that flows 1.5 miles to Middle Fork Applegate River 9.5 miles north of the village of Seiad Valley (lat. 41°58'45" N, long. 123°13'15" W). Named on Kangaroo Mountain (1980) 7.5' quadrangle.

Marble Mountain [SISKIYOU]: *ridge,* south-trending, 1 mile long, 16 miles southwest of Scott Bar (lat. 41°34' N, long. 123°12'35" W); the feature is in Marble Mountains. Named on Marble Mountain (1980) 7.5' quadrangle. The ridge contains white marble and limestone (United States Board on Geographic Names, 1977a, p. 4).

Marble Mountain Range: see **Marble Mountains** [SISKIYOU].

Marble Mountains [SISKIYOU]: *range,* bounded on the north and west by Klamath River, bounded on the east by Scott River and Scott Valley, and bounded on the south by North Russian Creek, Etna Creek, Salmon River, and North Fork Salmon River. Named on Weed (1963) 1°x 2° quadrangle. United States Board on Geographic Names (1977a, p. 4) noted that the name is from Marble Mountain, and gave the names "Marble Mountain Range" and "Salmon Mountains" as variants.

Marble Valley [SISKIYOU]: *relief feature,* 16 miles southwest of Scott Bar (lat. 41°34' N, long. 123°11'50" W); the feature is about 0.5 mile east of Marble Mountain. Named on Marble Mountain (1980) 7.5' quadrangle.

Marble Valley: see **Little Marble Valley** [SISKIYOU].

March: see **Lee March Gulch** [SHASTA].

Markham Ridge [GLENN]: *ridge,* 6.5 miles south-southeast of Black Butte (lat. 39°38'15" N, long. 122°50'15" W). Named on Plaskett Meadows (1967) 7.5' quadrangle.

Marks Bar: see **Union Bar** [BUTTE].

Marley Gulch [SISKIYOU]: *canyon,* drained by a stream that flows 0.5 mile to Black Bear Creek 7.25 miles north-northwest of Cecilville (lat. 41°14'45" N, long. 123°10'25" W). Named on Cecilville (1979) 7.5' quadrangle.

Marlowe Gulch [SHASTA]: *canyon,* 0.5 mile long, opens into the canyon of Whiskey Creek 5 miles southeast of the village of French Gulch (lat. 40°39'25" N, long. 122°33'30" W). Named on French Gulch (1944) 15' quadrangle.

Marston: see **Craig** [BUTTE] (2).

Martin: see **Tom Martin Creek** [SISKIYOU]; **Tom Martin Peak** [SISKIYOU].

Martin Creek [BUTTE]: *stream,* flows 2.5 miles to Galen Creek 0.5 mile north-northeast of the village of Berry Creek (lat. 39°39'10" N, long. 121°23'50" W; sec. 27, T 21 N, R 5 E). Named on Berry Creek (1970) and Brush Creek (1970) 7.5' quadrangles.

Martin Creek [TEHAMA]: *stream,* flows 6 miles to South Fork Battle Creek [SHASTA-TEHAMA] less than 1 mile south of Mineral (lat. 40°20'15" N, long. 121°35'45" W; at N line sec. 36, T 29 N, R 3 E). Named on Lassen Peak (1956) 15' quadrangle.

Martin Gulch [SHASTA]:

(1) *canyon,* drained by a stream that flows 1.25 miles to Middle Fork Cottonwood Creek [SHASTA-TEHAMA] nearly 6 miles east of Arbuckle Mountain (lat. 40°23'40" N, long. 122°45'35" W; sec. 3, T 29 N, R 8 W). Named on Chanchelulla Peak (1951) 15' quadrangle.

(2) *canyon,* drained by a stream that flows 0.5 mile to Alder Gulch (2) 1.5 miles south-southwest of Arbuckle Mountain (lat. 40°22'40" N, long. 122°52'35" W; at W line sec. 10, T 29 N, R 9 W). Named on Chanchelulla Peak (1951) 15' quadrangle.

Martin Hill [SISKIYOU]: *hill,* 19 miles west-southwest of Macdoel (lat. 41°41'50" N, long. 122°19'15" W; at SE cor. sec. 32, T 45 N, R 4 W). Named on Lake Shastina (1954) 15' quadrangle.

Martinsburgh: see **Gridley** [BUTTE].

Martin Soda Spring: see **Table Rock** [SISKIYOU].

Mary Blaine Mountain [SISKIYOU]: *peak,* 10 miles southeast of Salmon Mountain on Siskiyou-Trinity County line (lat. 41°05'35" N, long. 123°15'25" W). Altitude 6747 feet. Named on Dees Peak (1978) 7.5' quadrangle.

Mary Fork: see **Squaw Creek** [SHASTA] (3).

Marys Peak [SISKIYOU]: *hill,* 24 miles west of Macdoel (lat. 41°49'15" N, long. 122°28'15" W; sec. 19, T 46 N, R 5 W). Altitude 3268 feet. Named on Copco (1954) 15' quadrangle.

Mason Camp [TEHAMA]: *locality,* 2 miles south-southeast of Ball Mountain (lat. 39°54'20" N, long. 122°45'50" W; sec. 28, T 24 N, R 8 W). Named on Ball Mountain (1967) 7.5' quadrangle.

Masonic Bar [SISKIYOU]: *locality,* 8 miles southwest of Hornbrook along Klamath River (lat. 41°50'05" N, long. 122°39'50" W; sec. 16, T 46 N, R 7 W). Named on Hornbrook (1955) 15' quadrangle.

Masonic Rock [SISKIYOU]: *peak,* 10.5 miles north of Bartle (lat. 41°24'20" N, long. 121°51'45" W; near N line sec. 16, T 41 N, R 1 E). Altitude 5708 feet. Named on Bartle (1961) 15' quadrangle.

Masterson Campground [GLENN]: *locality,* 1.5 miles east-northeast of Black Butte (lat. 39°44'05" N, long. 122°50'30" W; sec. 26, T 22 N, R 9 W). Named on Plaskett Meadows (1967) 7.5' quadrangle.

Masterson Hollow [GLENN]: *canyon,* drained by a stream that flows 3 miles to the canyon of North Fork (2) Stony Creek [GLENN-TEHAMA] 13 miles west-northwest of Orland (lat. 39°47'55" N, long. 122°25'50" W; at N line sec. 4, T 22 N, R 5 W). Named on Sehorn Creek (1967) 7.5' quadrangle.

Matheson [SHASTA]: *locality,* 3.5 miles west-southwest of Summit City along Southern Pacific Railroad (lat. 40°39'45" N, long. 122°27'40" W; near NW cor. sec. 5, T 32 N, R 5 W). Named on Shasta Dam (1956) 7.5' quadrangle. Postal authorities established Matheson post office in 1922 and discontinued it in 1954 (Frickstad, p. 181). Officials of Mountain Copper Company named the place in 1920 in memory of James Matheson, who founded Matheson and Company of London, parent firm of the copper company (Gudde, 1949, p. 207).

Mathews Creek: see **Matthews Creek** [SISKIYOU].

Mathles Creek [SHASTA]: *stream,* flows 2 miles to McCloud River Arm Shasta Lake 3.5 miles south of Bollibokka Mountain (lat. 40°53' N, long. 122°13'20" W; at E line sec. 17, T 35 N, R 3 W). Named on Bollibokka Mountain (1957) 15' quadrangle.

Matquaw Flat [SHASTA]: *area,* 9 miles southeast of Lamoine (lat. 41°53'25" N, long. 122°17'25" W; near E line sec. 15, R 35 N, R 4 W). Named on Lamoine (1957) 15' quadrangle.

Matthews: see **Cecilville** [SISKIYOU].

Matthews Creek [SISKIYOU]: *stream,* flows 3.5 miles to South Fork Salmon River 5 miles northwest of Cecilville (lat. 41°11'15" N, long. 123°12'50" W). Named on Cecilville (1979) 7.5' quadrangle. United States Board on Geographic Names (1960a, p. 16) rejected the form "Mathews Creek" for the name.

Matthews Creek Campground [SISKIYOU]: *locality,* 5 miles northwest of Cecilville along South Fork Salmon River (lat. 41°11'15" N, long. 123°12'45" W); the place is at the mouth of Matthews Creek. Named on Cecilville (1979) 7.5' quadrangle.

Maupin Flat [TEHAMA]: *area,* 5 miles north-northwest of Paskenta (lat. 39°57'10" N, long. 122°35'10" W; sec. 7, T 24 N, R 6 W). Named on Paskenta (1967) 7.5' quadrangle.

Mavis Lake [SISKIYOU]: *lake,* 450 feet long, 17 miles south of Etna (lat. 41°12'35" N, long. 122°50'15" W; sec. 25, T 39 N, R 9 W). Named on Coffee Creek (1955) 15' quadrangle.

May [SISKIYOU]: *locality,* 4.5 miles south-southwest of Dorris (lat. 41°54'15" N, long. 121°57'15" W). Named on Dorris (1950) 15' quadrangle. California Mining Bureau's (1917a) map shows a place called Ruby located about 6 miles west of May. Postal authorities established Ruby post office in 1891, moved it 3 miles northeast in 1901, moved it 5.5 miles southwest in 1906, moved it back to the previous site in 1907, and discontinued it in 1913 (Salley, p. 190).

Mayaro [BUTTE]: *locality,* 2 miles northeast of Pulga (lat. 39°49'30" N, long. 121°25'15" W; sec. 28, T 23 N, R 5 E). Named on Pulga (1979) 7.5' quadrangle. Postal authorities established Mayaro post office in 1930 and discontinued it in 1956 (Salley, p. 135).

Mayfield Ice Cave [SISKIYOU]: *cave,* 15 miles east-northeast of Bartle (lat. 41°19'30" N, long. 121°32'35" W; near NE cor. sec. 7, T 40 N, R 4 E). Named on Hambone (1961) 15' quadrangle.

Mayfield Spring [SISKIYOU]: *spring,* 15 miles east-northeast of Bartle (lat. 41°19'10" N, long. 121°31'40" W; sec. 8, T 40 N, R 4 E). Named on Hambone (1961) 15' quadrangle.

Mayten: see **Little Shasta** [SISKIYOU].

McAdam Creek [SISKIYOU]: *stream,* formed by the confluence of Cherry Creek (2) and Deadwood Creek, flows nearly 7 miles to Moffett Creek 1.5 miles north-northeast of Fort Jones (lat. 41°37'40" N, long. 122°49'40" W). Named on Fort Jones (1955) 15' quadrangle. Bancroft (p. 367) referred to McAdam's Creek. The name is from a Scot who mined along the stream in 1854 (Gudde, 1949, p. 198). Postal authorities established McAdams post office, named for the creek, 6 miles north of Fort Jones in 1881 and discontinued it in 1882 (Salley, p. 136).

McAdams: see **McAdam Creek** [SISKIYOU].

McArthur [SHASTA]: *village,* 3.5 miles northeast of Fall River Mills (lat. 41°03' N, long. 121°23'55" W; sec. 9, 16, T 37 N, R 5 E). Named on Fall River Mills (1961) 15' quadrangle. Postal authorities established McArthur post office in 1904 (Frickstad, p. 181) The name commemorates John McArthur, a pioneer of Fall River Valley (Steger, p. 46).

McArthur Swamp [SHASTA]: *area,* 6 miles north of Fall River Mills (lat. 41°05'35" N, long. 121°25'45" W); the place is 3.5 miles north-northwest of McArthur. Named on Fall River Mills (1961) 15' quadrangle.

McBride Springs [SISKIYOU]: *springs,* 3.25 miles north-northeast of the town of Mount Shasta (lat. 41°21'15" N, long. 122°16'50" W; sec. 35, T 41 N, R 4 W). Named on Weed (1954) 15' quadrangle.

McCabe Creek [BUTTE]: *stream,* flows 2.25 miles to Lake Oroville 4 miles west of Forbestown (lat. 39°31'15" N, long. 121°20'40" W; sec. 7, T 19 N, R 6 E). Named on Forbestown (1970) 7.5' quadrangle.

McCall Gulch [SHASTA]: *canyon,* drained by a stream that flows 1.25 miles to Dog Creek nearly 4 miles south-southwest of Lamoine (lat. 40°55'55" N, long. 122°28'15" W; near S line sec. 32, T 36 N, R 5 W). Named on Lamoine (1957) 15' quadrangle. John McCall owned mining claims along the stream and ran cattle there (Steger, p. 46).

McCandless Gulch [SHASTA]: *canyon,* drained by a stream that flows 2.5 miles to Little Cedar Gulch 16 miles southeast of Bollibokka Mountain (lat. 40°45'45" N, long. 122°00'40" W; sec. 31, T 34 N, R 1 W). Named on Bollibokka Mountain (1957) 15' quadrangle. The pioneer McCandless family lived in the canyon (Steger, p. 46).

McCardle Gulch [SHASTA]: *canyon,* drained by a stream that flows 1.25 miles to Sacramento River 1.5 miles south of Lamoine (lat. 40°57'10" N, long. 122°25'45" W; sec. 27, T 36 N, R 5 W). Named on Lamoine (1957) 15' quadrangle.

McCarthy Creek [SISKIYOU]: *stream,* flows 2.5 miles to Scott River 5 miles southwest of Scott Bar (lat. 41°41'25" N, long. 123°04'15" W). Named on Scott Bar (1980) 15' quadrangle. Called McCarty Cr. on Seiad (1922) 30' quadrangle, but United States Board on Geographic Names (1960a, p. 16) rejected this name for the feature.

McCarthy Point [TEHAMA]: *peak,* nearly 5 miles north of Polk Springs (lat. 40°11' N, long. 121°40'45" W; near N line sec. 19, T 27 N, R 3 E). Named on Butte Meadows (1958) 15' quadrangle.

McCarty Creek [TEHAMA]:

(1) *stream,* flows 5.5 miles to South Fork Antelope Creek 8.5 miles north-northwest of Polk Springs (lat. 40°14'10" N, long. 121°42' W; sec. 36, T 28 N, R 2 E). Named on Butte Meadows (1958) and Lassen Peak (1956) 15' quadrangles.

(2) *stream,* flows 10 miles to Thomes Creek 1 mile west-southwest of Flournoy (lat. 39°54'55" N, long. 122°27'15" W; at N line sec. 24, T 24 N, R 5 W). Named on Flournoy (1967) and Paskenta (1967) 7.5' quadrangles.

McCarty Creek: see **McCarthy Creek** [SISKIYOU].

McCash Fork: see **Ukonom Creek** [SISKIYOU].

McCash Lake [SISKIYOU]: *lake,* 550 feet long, 4 miles south-southwest of Ukonom Lake (lat. 41°31'25" N, long. 123°22'25" W); the lake is at the head of McCash Fork Ukonom Creek. Named on Ukonom Lake (1980) 7.5' quadrangle.

McClendon Gulch [TEHAMA]: *canyon,* drained by a stream that flows 1 mile to Beegum Creek [SHASTA-TEHAMA] 4.25 miles northeast of Beegum Peak (lat. 40°21' N, long. 122°49'30" W; sec. 24, T 29 N, R 9 W). Named on Chanchelulla Peak (1951) 15' quadrangle.

McCloud [SISKIYOU]: *town,* 17 miles southeast of Weed (lat. 41°15'15" N, long. 122°08'15" W; in and near sec. 1, T 39 N, R 3 W). Named on Shasta (1954) and Shoeinhorse Mountain (1954) 15' quadrangles. Postal authorities established McCloud post office in 1898; the name is from McCloud Lumber Company, owner of the town until the late 1960's (Salley, p. 136).

McCloud: see **Lake McCloud**, under **Skunk Hill** [SHASTA]; **Point McCloud** [SHASTA].

McCloud Dam Reservoir: see **Lake McCloud**, under **Skunk Hill** [SHASTA].

McCloud Glacier: see **Konwakiton Glacier** [SISKIYOU].

McCloud Reservoir: see **Lake McCloud**, under **Skunk Hill** [SHASTA].

McCloud River [SHASTA-SISKIYOU]: *stream,* heads in Siskiyou County and flows 57 miles to McCloud River Arm Shasta Lake 1.5 miles west-northwest of Bollibokka Mountain in Shasta County (lat. 40°56'20" N, long. 122°14'45" W; near E line sec. 31, T 36 N, R 3 W). Named on Bartle (1961), Big Bend (1961), Bollibokka Mountain (1957), and Shoeinhorse Mountain (1954) 15' quadrangles. Called McLeod's Fork on Eddy's (1854) map. The name is for A.R. McLeod of Hudson's Bay Company, who trapped in the region in 1828 and 1829 (Stewart, G.R., p. 270). Whitney (p. 329) used the form "McCloud's Fork" for the name.

McCloud River Arm [SHASTA]: *embayment,* opens into Pit River Arm Shasta Lake 16 miles south-southeast of Lamoine (lat. 40°46' N, long. 122°18' W); the feature is the flooded lower part of the canyon of McCloud River [SHASTA-SISKIYOU]. Named on Bollibokka Mountain (1957) and Lamoine (1957) 15' quadrangles.

McCloud's Fork: see **McCloud River** [SHASTA-SISKIYOU].

McClure Creek [TEHAMA]:

(1) *stream,* flows 3 miles to Thomes Creek 5 miles west-northwest of Ball Mountain (lat. 39°57'20" N, long. 122°52'20" W; sec. 4, T 24 N, R 9 W). Named on Buck Rock (1967) 7.5' quadrangle.

(2) *stream,* flows 20 miles to Sacramento River 5.25 miles northwest of Vina (lat. 39°59'40" N, long. 122°06'50" W). Named on Flournoy (1967), Gerber (1950), Henleyville (1967), Los Molinos (1952), Vina (1950), and West of Gerber (1951) 7.5' quadrangles. Called Clark Slough on Vina (1904) 15' quadrangle.

McClure Gulch [SHASTA]: *canyon,* drained by a stream that flows less than 1 mile to Squaw Creek Arm Shasta Lake 11.5 miles south of Bollibokka Mountain (lat. 40°46'15" N, long. 122°11'20" W; sec. 27, T 34 N, R 3 W). Named on Bollibokka Mountain (1957) 15' quadrangle. The name is for a copper-mine worker who lived in the canyon (Steger, p. 46).

McColl [SHASTA]: *locality,* nearly 4 miles north-northeast of the town of Central Valley along Southern Pacific Railroad (lat. 40°43'40" N, long. 122°19'40" W; sec. 9, T 33 N, R 4 W). Named on Project City (1957) 7.5' quadrangle. The name is for John McColl, state senator from Shasta and Trinity Counties from 1932 until 1938 (Steger, p. 46).

McConaughy Gulch [SISKIYOU]: *canyon,* drained by a stream that flows 7.25 miles to Scott Valley 5 miles southeast of Etna (lat. 41°24'20" N, long. 122°49'30" W; sec. 13, T 41 N, R 9 W). Named on China Mountain (1955) and Etna (1955) 15' quadrangles. Called McConnahue Gulch on Etna (1934) 30' quadrangle.

McConnahue Gulch: see **McConaughy Gulch** [SISKIYOU].

McConnell Bar [SISKIYOU]: *locality,* 8 miles southwest of Hornbrook along Klamath River (lat. 41°50' N, long. 122°39'45" W; near SE cor. sec. 16, T 46 N, R 7 W). Named on Hornbrook (1955) 15' quadrangle.

McCook: see **Oak Bar** [SISKIYOU].

McCumber: see **Camp McCumber** [SHASTA].

McCumber Flat [SHASTA]: *area,* 13 miles west-northwest of Lassen Peak (lat. 40°32'50" N, long. 121°44' W). Named on Manzanita Lake (1956) and Whitmore (1956) 15' quadrangles. George W. McCumber settled at the place in the late 1850's (Steger, p. 47).

McCumber Reservoir [SHASTA]: *lake,* 0.5 mile long, 12.5 miles west-northwest of Lassen Peak along North Fork Battle Creek [SHASTA-TEHAMA] (lat. 40°32'25" N, long. 121°43'50" W; sec. 15, T 31 N, R 2 E); the lake is at McCumber Flat. Named on Manzanita Lake (1956) 15' quadrangle. The lake formed in 1906 (Gudde, 1969, p. 187).

McDowell Camp [SISKIYOU]: *locality,* 6 miles north of Cecilville (lat. 41°13'55" N, long. 123°07'40" W). Named on Cecilville (1979) 7.5' quadrangle.

McElroy Flat [SHASTA]: *area,* 17 miles north of Lassen Peak (lat. 40°43'30" N, long. 121°29' W; at SE cor. sec. 11, T 33 N, R 4 E). Named on Prospect Peak (1957) 15' quadrangle.

McFarland Ridge: see **Regan Meadow Campground** [SHASTA].

McGavin Peak [SISKIYOU]: *peak,* 9.5 miles northwest of Macdoel (lat. 41°56' N, long. 122°07'30" W; sec. 8, T 47 N, R 2 W). Altitude 5489 feet. Named on Macdoel (1954) 15' quadrangle.

McGavis: see **Bartle** [SISKIYOU].

McGill Creek [GLENN]: *stream,* flows 4 miles to North Fork Elk Creek (1) 3 miles west of the village of Elk Creek (lat. 39°36'05" N, long. 122°35'35" W; sec. 12, T 20 N, R 7 W). Named on Elk Creek (1968) and Felkner Hill (1968) 7.5' quadrangles.

McGill Creek [SHASTA]: *stream,* flows 4 miles to Deadlun Creek 4 miles west-northwest of the village of Big Bend (lat. 41°03' N, long. 121°58'35" W; sec. 21, T 37 N, R 1 W). Named on Big Bend (1961) 15' quadrangle.

McGill Ridge [GLENN]: *ridge,* generally east-trending, 3 miles long, 5 miles west of the village of Elk Creek (lat. 39°35'45" N, long. 122°38'15" W); the feature is north of McGill Creek. Named on Elk Creek (1968) and Felkner Hill (1968) 7.5' quadrangles.

McGinnis Springs [SISKIYOU]: *springs,* 6.5 miles northwest of McCloud (lat. 41°19'45" N, long. 122°12'50" W; sec. 8, T 40 N, R 3 W). Named on Shasta (1954) 15' quadrangle.

McGowan Lake [TEHAMA]: *lake,* 1000 feet long, 4 miles north-northeast of Mineral (lat. 40°23'35" N, long. 121°33'10" W; on W line sec. 9, T 29 N, R 4 E). Named on Lassen Peak (1956) 15' quadrangle.

McGrew Spring [GLENN]: *spring,* 9 miles west-northwest of the village of Elk Creek (lat. 39°38'15" N, long. 122°41'10" W). Named on Alder Springs (1967) 7.5' quadrangle.

McGuffy Creek [SISKIYOU]: *stream,* flows 3.25 miles Scott River 2.5 miles south-southwest of Scott Bar (lat. 41°42'40" N, long. 123°00'55" W; near S line sec. 29, T 45 N, R 10 W). Named on Scott Bar (1980) 7.5' quadrangle.

McIntosh Island [GLENN]: *island,* 8.5 miles east-northeast of Orland in Sacramento River (lat. 39°47' N, long. 122°02' W); the feature is just north of McIntosh Landing. Named on Vina (1904) 15' quadrangle.

McIntosh Landing [GLENN]: *locality,* 9 miles east-northeast of Orland along Sacramento River (lat. 39°46'35" N, long. 122°01'50" W). Site named on Foster Island (1950) 7.5' quadrangle.

McIntosh Well [SISKIYOU]: *well,* 2 miles north-northeast of Bartle (lat. 41°17' N, long. 121°48'10" W; sec. 25, T 40 N, R 1 E). Named on Bartle (1961) 15' quadrangle.

McKay Creek [SISKIYOU]: *stream,* flows 4 miles to lowlands 2.5 miles north-northwest of Bartle (lat. 41°17'15" N, long. 121°50'35" W; sec. 27, T 40 N, R 1 E). Named on Bartle (1961) 15' quadrangle.

McKay Meadow: see **Powellton** [BUTTE].

McKay Ridge [BUTTE]: *ridge,* southwest-trending, 6 miles long, 3.5 miles south-southwest of Paradise (lat. 39°42' N, long 121°39' W). Named on Hamlin Canyon (1951) 7.5' quadrangle.

McKay Springs [SISKIYOU]: *spring,* 2.5 miles north-northwest of Bartle (lat. 41°17'20" N, long. 121°50'15" W; sec. 27, T 40 N, R 1 E). Named on Bartle (1961) 15' quadrangle.

McKeen Divide [SISKIYOU]: *relief feature,* 13 miles south-southeast of Etna (lat. 41°16'50" N, long. 122°48'55" W; at S line sec. 29, T 40 N, R 8 W). Named on Etna (1955) 15' quadrangle.

McKenzie Butte [SISKIYOU]: *peak,* 5 miles north-northwest of McCloud (lat. 41°19' N, long. 122°11'15" W; on E line sec. 9, T 40 N, R 3 W). Altitude 6038 feet. Named on Shasta (1954) 15' quadrangle.

McKenzie Mountain [SHASTA]: *peak,* 3 miles south-southwest of Shoeinhorse Mountain (lat. 41°02'20" N, long. 122°06'10" W). Altitude 5056 feet. Named on Shoeinhorse Mountain (1954) 15' quadrangle.

McKinley Mountain [SISKIYOU]: *peak,* 16 miles southeast of Condrey Mountain (lat. 41°45'15" N, long. 122°47'40" W). Altitude 6220 feet. Named on Condrey Mountain (1955) 15' quadrangle.

McKinney Creek [SISKIYOU]: *stream,* flows 7.5 miles to Klamath River 8 miles southeast of Condrey Mountain (lat. 41°50'35" N, long. 122°53'25" W; at E line sec. 9, T 46 N, R 9 W). Named on Condrey Mountain (1955) 15' quadrangle. West Fork enters from the southwest 4.25 miles upstream from the mouth of the main creek; it is 1.5 miles long and is named on Condrey Mountain (1955) 15' quadrangle.

McKinsey Ridge [SHASTA]: *ridge,* generally east-trending, 1 mile long, 5.25 miles north of Schell Mountain (lat. 40°55'45" N, long. 122°31' W; at N line sec. 2, T 35 N, R 6 W). Named on Schell Mountain (1950) 15' quadrangle.

McKinsman Creek: see **Kinsman Creek** [SISKIYOU].

McLeod's Fork: see **McCloud River** [SHASTA-SISKIYOU].

McMoran Flat [TEHAMA]: *area,* 6 miles north-northwest of Wakefield Flat (lat. 40°12'40" N, long. 122°40'15" W; on E line sec. 8, T 27 N, R 7 W). Named on Cold Fork (1967) 7.5' quadrangle.

McMullen Mountain [SHASTA]: *peak,* 15 miles northwest of Lassen Peak (lat. 40°38'30" N, long. 121°42' W; near NW cor. sec. 12, T 32 N, R 2 W). Altitude 6500 feet. Named on Manzanita Lake (1956) 15' quadrangle.

McNeal Creek [SISKIYOU]: *stream,* flows 3 miles to South Fork Salmon River less than 0.5 mile southeast of Forks of Salmon (lat. 41°15'15" N, long. 123°18'55" W). Named on Forks of Salmon (1978) and Youngs Peak (1979) 7.5' quadrangles. United States Board on Geographic Names (1977b, p. 5) gave the named "McNeil Creek" as a variant.

McNeil Creek [SISKIYOU]: *stream,* flows 3 miles to Rush Creek 6.5 miles east-southeast of Cecilville (lat. 41°06'35" N, long. 123°01'05" W). Named on Coffee Creek (1955) 15' quadrangle, and on Thompson Peak (1979) 7.5' quadrangle.

McNeil Creek: see **McNeal Creek** [SISKIYOU].

Meadow Gulch [SISKIYOU]: *canyon,* drained by a stream that flows 6.5 miles to East Fork Scott River 11.5 miles east-southeast of Etna (lat. 41°22'15" N, long. 122°42'35" W; near E line sec. 25, T 41 N, R 8 W). Named on China Mountain (1955) 15' quadrangle.

Meadow Gulch [TEHAMA]: *canyon,* drained by a stream that flows 5.25 miles to Salt Creek (1) 2.5 miles west-southwest of Rosewood (lat. 40°15'30" N, long. 122°36'10" W; near S line sec. 24, T 28 N, R 7 W). Named on Ono (1952) 15' quadrangle.

Meadow Gulch: see **South Meadow Gulch** [TEHAMA].

Meamber Creek [SISKIYOU]: *stream,* flows 3.5 miles to Scott River 8 miles west-northwest of Fort Jones (lat. 41°38'20" N, long. 122°59'25" W; sec. 27, T 44 N, R 10 W). Named on Fort Jones (1955) 15' quadrangle. Called Meander Cr. on Yreka (1939) 30' quadrangle.

Meamber Gulch [SISKIYOU]: *canyon,* drained by a stream that flows 2.5 miles to Scott River 8 miles west-northwest of Fort Jones (lat. 41°38'20" N, long. 122°59'30" W sec. 27, T 44 N, R 10 W). Named on Fort Jones (1955) 15' quadrangle.

Meander Creek: see **Meamber Creek** [SISKIYOU].

Mears Creek [SHASTA]: *stream,* flows nearly 6 miles to Sacramento River 5.25 miles south-southwest of Castella (lat. 41°04'15" N, long. 122°21'15" W; sec. 17, T 37 N, R 4 W). Named on Dunsmuir (1954) 15' quadrangle.

Mears Ridge [SHASTA]: *ridge,* generally east-southeast-trending, 5.5 miles long, 4.5 miles west-southwest of Castella (lat. 41°06'30" N, long. 122°23'30" W); the ridge is north of Mears Creek. Named on Dunsmuir (1954) 15' quadrangle.

Medicine Creek [SISKIYOU]: *stream,* flows 3.25 miles to Copper Creek (2) 5.25 miles northwest of Dillon Mountain (lat. 41°35'35" N, long. 123°37'50" W); the stream is south of Little Medicine Mountain. Named on Chimney Rock (1981) 7.5' quadrangle.

Medicine Creek: see **Big Medicine Creek** [SISKIYOU]; **Little Medicine Creek** [SISKIYOU].

Medicine Lake [SISKIYOU]: *lake,* nearly 1.5 miles long, 31 miles south-southwest of Dorris (lat. 41°34'55" N, long. 121°35'55" W; sec. 10, 11, T 43 N, R 3 E). Named on Medicine Lake (1952) 15' quadrangle. Called Crystal Lake on California Mining Bureau's (1917a) map.

Medicine Lake: see **Little Medicine Lake** [SISKIYOU].

Medicine Lake Glass Flow [SISKIYOU]: *relief feature,* less than 1 mile north of Medicine Lake (lat. 41°36' N, long. 121°36' W). Named on Medicine Lake (1952) 15' quadrangle.

Medicine Mountain [SISKIYOU]:

(1) *peak,* 16 miles north of Forks of Salmon (lat. 41°29'45" N, long. 123°19'05" W). Altitude 6832 feet. Named on Medicine Mountain (1978) 7.5' quadrangle.

(2) *ridge,* east-trending, 2 miles long, 1 mile south of Medicine Lake (lat. 41°33'50" N, long. 121°36' W; mainly in sec. 14, 15, T 43 N, R 3 E). Named on Medicine Lake (1952) 15' quadrangle.

Medicine Mountain: see **Little Medicine Mountain** [SISKIYOU].

Meeker Creek [TEHAMA]: *stream,* flows 6 miles to Salt Creek (2) 9 miles east-northeast of Red Bluff (lat. 40°14'05" N, long. 122°05'15" W; near E line sec. 33, T 28 N, R 2 W). Named on Manton (1956) 15' quadrangle, and on Dales (1965) and Tuscan Springs (1951) 7.5' quadrangles.

Meeks Lake: see **Meeks Meadow Lake** [SISKIYOU].

Meeks Meadow Creek [SISKIYOU]: *stream,* flows 3.25 miles to North Fork French Creek (2) nearly 6 miles south of Etna (lat. 41°22'30" N, long. 122°54'40" W; sec. 29, T 41 N, R 9 W). Named on Etna (1955) 15' quadrangle.

Meeks Meadow Lake [SISKIYOU]: *lake,* 400 feet long, 6.5 miles south-southwest of Etna (lat. 41°22'30" N, long. 122°57'30" W; sec. 26, T 41 N, R 10 W); the lake is at the head of a branch of Meeks Meadow Creek. Named on Etna (1955) 15' quadrangle. Called Meeks Lake on Etna (1934) 30' quadrangle.

Meiss Lake [SISKIYOU]: *lake,* 4.5 miles long, 4 miles northwest of Macdoel in Butte Valley (lat. 41°51'30" N, long. 122°03'30" W). Named on Macdoel (1954) 15' quadrangle, which shows Meiss ranch southwest of the lake. Called Butte Reservoir on Weed (1963) 1°x 2° quadrangle. Macdoel (1941) 30' quadrangle shows marsh at the place.

Memorial Spring [BUTTE]: *spring,* 3.5 miles south-southeast of Butte Meadows (lat. 40°02'20" N, long. 121°30'55" W; sec. 10, T 25 N, R 4 E). Named on Butte Meadows (1958) 15' quadrangle.

Mendocino Pass [GLENN]: *pass,* 6 miles northwest of Black Butte near Glenn-Mendocino County line (lat. 39°47'35" N, long. 122°56'05" W; sec. 2, T 22 N, R 10 W). Named on Mendocino Pass (1967) 7.5' quadrangle. United States Board on Geographic Names (1933, p. 513) rejected the name "Low Gap" for the feature.

Merchants Bar [BUTTE]: *locality,* 8 miles northeast of Paradise along West Branch Feather River (lat. 39°51'30" N, long. 121°32'15" W; near SW cor. sec. 9, T 23 N, R 4 E). Named on Paradise East (1980) 7.5' quadrangle.

Merrill Creek [SISKIYOU]: *stream,* flows 4 miles to Salmon River 11.5 miles northwest of Forks of Salmon (lat. 41°22'45" N, long. 123°28'20" W). Named on Somes Bar (1979) 7.5' quadrangle.

Merrill Ice Cave: see **Bearpaw Butte** [SISKIYOU].

Merrill Mountain [SISKIYOU]: *peak,* 13 miles north-northwest of Forks of Salmon (lat. 41°25'30" N, long. 123°26' W). Altitude 4500 feet. Named on Somes Bar (1979) 7.5' quadrangle. Called Merrill Pk. on Averill's (1935) map.

Merrill Peak: see **Merrill Mountain** [SISKIYOU].

Merrills Landing [BUTTE]: *locality,* 14 miles northwest of Chico on the east side of Sacramento River (lat. 39°52'40" N, long. 122°02'25" W). Named on Vina (1950) 7.5' quadrangle.

Merrimac [BUTTE]: *locality,* 8 miles east-southeast of Pulga (lat. 39°45'55" N, long. 121°18'20" W; near NE cor. sec. 16, T 22 N, R 6 E); the place is at the head of Peavine Creek. Site named on Soapstone Hill (1979) 7.5' quadrangle. Postal authorities established Merrimac post office in 1883, discontinued it in 1902, reestablished it in 1915, and discontinued it in 1934 (Frickstad, p. 11). The place first was called Peavine (Hanna, p. 191).

Merry Mountain [SHASTA]: *peak,* 2.5 miles south-southeast of the village of French Gulch (lat. 40°40'20" N, long. 122°36'45" W; on W line sec. 36, T 33 N, R 7 W). Altitude 2983 feet. Named on Whiskeytown (1979) 7.5' quadrangle.

Messilla Valley [BUTTE]: *canyon,* 6.5 miles south-southeast of Paradise along Dry Creek (lat. 39°39'30" N, long. 121°35' W). Named on Cherokee (1970) 7.5' quadrangle. Mrs. Burnham named the valley (Wells and Chambers, p. 251).

Messner Gulch [SISKIYOU]: *canyon,* drained by a stream that flows 2 miles to Scott River 8.5 miles south-southeast of Etna (lat. 41°20'40" N, long. 122°49'20" W; at W line sec. 6, T 40 N, R 8 W). Named on Etna (1955) 15' quadrangle.

Metcalf [SISKIYOU]: *locality,* 6.25 miles northwest of Weed along Southern Pacific Railroad (lat. 41°29' N, long. 122°28'50" W; sec. 13, T 42 N, R 6 W). Named on Dunsmuir (1935) 30' quadrangle.

Meteor Lake [SISKIYOU]: *lake,* 700 feet long, 3.25 miles south of Ukonom Lake (lat. 41°31'55" N, long. 123°20'40" W). Named on Ukonom Lake (1980) 7.5' quadrangle.

Methodist Creek [SISKIYOU]: *stream,* flows 8 miles to South Fork Salmon River 8 miles northwest of Cecilville (lat. 41°13'20" N, long. 123°14'55" W). Named on Youngs Peak (1979) 7.5' quadrangle.

Mexican Spring [SHASTA]: *spring,* 7.5 miles southeast of the village of French Creek (lat. 40°38'10" N, long. 122°31'25" W; at S line sec. 10, T 32 N, R 6 W). Named on Whiskeytown (1979) 7.5' quadrangle.

Mica Gulch [SHASTA]: *canyon,* drained by a stream that flows 1 mile to Hawkins Creek 7 miles north-northwest of the village of Big Bend (lat. 41°06'35" N, long. 121°58'35" W). Named on Big Bend (1961) 15' quadrangle.

Middle Boulder Lake [SISKIYOU]: *lake,* 800 feet long, 17 miles south-southeast of Etna (lat. 41°13' N, long. 122°48' W; near NE cor. sec. 29, T 39 N, R 8 W); the feature is about halfway between East Boulder Lake and West Boulder Lake at the head of a branch of West Boulder Creek. Named on Coffee Creek (1955) 15' quadrangle.

Middle Butte Creek [BUTTE]: *stream,* flows 6 miles to Little Butte Creek 2 miles north of downtown Paradise (lat. 39°47'10" N, long. 121°37'35" W; sec. 3, T 22 N, R 3 E). Named on Paradise East (1980) and Paradise West (1980) 7.5' quadrangles.

Middle Creek [GLENN]: *stream,* heads in Lake County and flows 3.5 miles to join Estell Creek and form Black Butte River 9 miles south of Black Butte (lat. 39°35'40" N, long. 122°51'25" W; at N line sec. 15, T 20 N, R 9 W); the stream is southwest of Middle Ridge (2). Named on Kneecap Ridge (1967) 7.5' quadrangle.

Middle Creek [SHASTA]:

(1) *stream,* flows 4 miles to Sacramento River 2.5 miles west-northwest of Redding (lat. 40°35'50" N, long. 122°26' W; sec. 28, T 32 N, R 5 W). Named on Redding (1957) 7.5' quadrangle

(2) *locality,* 2.25 miles west-northwest of Redding (lat. 40°35'30" N, long. 122°31'10" W). Named on Redding (1901) 30' quadrangle, which also has the name "Waugh" at the place. Postal authorities established Waugh post office in 1885 and discontinued it in 1906 (Frickstad, p. 183).

Middle Creek [SISKIYOU]:

(1) *stream,* flows 6.5 miles to Horse Creek (2) 9 miles east of the village of Seiad Valley (lat. 41°50'35" N, long. 123°01'35" W; sec. 8, T 46 N, R 10 W). Named on Dutch Creek (1980) and Hamburg (1980) 7.5' quadrangles.

(2) *stream,* flows 4.5 miles to Scott River 7.5 miles southwest of Scott Bar (lat. 41°40'05" N, long. 123°06'30" W). Named on Grider Valley (1981) and Scott Bar (1980) 7.5' quadrangles.

Middle Creek Camp [SISKIYOU]: *locality,* 7.5 miles southwest of Scott Bar (lat. 41°40'05" N, long. 123°06'35" W; near NE cor. sec. 16, T 44 N, R 11 W); the place is near the mouth of Middle Creek (2). Named on Scott Bar (1955) 15' quadrangle.

Middle Creek Meadows [SISKIYOU]: *area,* 8.5 miles west-southwest of Scott Bar (lat. 41°41' N, long. 123°08'45" W); the place is north of Middle Creek (2). Named on Grider Valley (1981) 7.5' quadrangle.

Middle Creek Ridge [SISKIYOU]: *ridge,* generally southwest-trending, 6.5 miles long, 10.5 miles east-northeast of the village of Seiad Valley (lat. 41°53'30" N, long. 123°00'10" W); the ridge is east of Middle Creek (1). Named on Condrey Mountain (1955) 15' quadrangle, and on Dutch Creek (1980) and Hamburg (1980) 7.5' quadrangles.

Middle Devils Peak [SISKIYOU]: *peak,* 3 miles north of the village of Seiad Valley (lat. 41°53'05" N, long. 123°12' W); the feature is between Upper Devils Peak and Lower Devils Peak. Altitude 5566 feet. Named on Kangaroo Mountain (1980) 7.5' quadrangle.

Middle Falls [SISKIYOU]: *waterfall,* 7 miles east of McCloud along McCloud River [SHASTA-SISKIYOU] (lat. 41°14'35" N, long. 122°00'30" W; sec. 7, T 39 N, R 1 W); the feature is 0.25 mile downstream from Upper Falls. Named on Shoeinhorse Mountain (1954) 15' quadrangle.

Middlefork: see **Cottonwood Creek** [SHASTA-TEHAMA].

Middle Gulch [SISKIYOU]: *canyon,* drained by a stream that flows less than 1 mile to Cabin Gulch 12.5 miles north of Sawyers Bar (lat. 41°28'40" N, long. 123°06'05" W). Named on Yellow Dog Peak (1977) 7.5' quadrangle.

Middle Lick Gulch [SISKIYOU]: *canyon,* drained by a stream that flows 1.5 miles to Scott River 11.5 miles south-southeast of the village of Seiad Valley (lat. 41°45'20" N, long. 123°00'35" W; near NE cor. sec. 17, T 45 N, R 10 W). Named on Condrey Mountain (1955) 15' quadrangle, and on Hamburg (1980) 7.5' quadrangle.

Middle Ridge [GLENN]:

(1) *ridge,* northeast-trending, 1.25 miles long, 8 miles southeast of Black Butte (lat. 39°38'45" N, long. 122°46' W; sec. 28, T 21 N, R 8 W). Named on Plaskett Meadows (1967) 7.5' quadrangle.

(2) *ridge,* northwest-trending, 1.5 miles long, 10.5 miles south of Black Butte on Glenn-Lake County line (lat. 39°34'50" N, long. 122°49'45" W); the ridge is northeast of Middle Creek. Named on Kneecap Ridge (1967) 7.5' quadrangle.

Middle Ridge [TEHAMA]:

(1) *ridge,* generally west-trending, 6 miles long, 13 miles south-southeast of Manton (lat. 40°15'45" N, long. 121°46'45" W). Named on Lassen Peak (1956) and Manton (1956) 15' quadrangles.

(2) *ridge,* northeast-trending, 1.5 miles long, 2.5 miles north-northwest of Tomhead Mountain (lat. 40°10'10" N, long. 122°50'20" W). Named on Yolla Bolly (1954) 15' quadrangle.

(3) *ridge,* northwest- to west-southwest-trending, 3.5 miles long, center 2 miles northwest of Ball Mountain, which is at the southeast end of the ridge (lat. 39°57' N, long. 122°48'35" W). Named on Ball Mountain (1967) 7.5' quadrangle.

Middle Ridge: see **Shotgun Creek** [SHASTA] (2).

Middle Salt Creek [SHASTA]: *stream,* flows 5.25 miles to Sacramento River Arm Shasta Lake 5 miles southeast of Lamoine (lat. 40°55'40" N, long. 122°21'45" W; sec. 6, T 35 N, R 4 W). Named on Lamoine (1957) 15' quadrangle. Present Eye Creek is called North Fork Middle Salt Creek on Redding (1901) 30' quadrangle.

Middleshell Creek: see **Dog Fork**, under **Elliot Creek** [SISKIYOU].

Middletown: see **Redding** [SHASTA].

Midway [SHASTA]: *locality,* 9 miles south-southwest of Whitmore (lat. 40°30'10" N, long. 121°57'25" W; sec. 34, T 31 N, R 1 W). Named on Whitmore (1956) 15' quadrangle.

Miles: see **Joe Miles Creek** [SISKIYOU].

Military Pass [SISKIYOU]: *pass,* 16 miles north of McCloud (lat. 41°29'45" N, long. 122°08'40" W; at S line sec. 12, T 42 N, R 3 W). Named on Shasta (1954) 15' quadrangle.

Milk Creek [SISKIYOU]: *stream,* flows 2.25 miles to Copco Lake 16 miles west-northwest of Macdoel (lat. 41°57'50" N, long. 122°16' W; near SE cor. sec. 35, T 48 N, R 4 W). Named on Copco (1954) 15' quadrangle.

Milk Ranch Meadows: see **Big Meadows** [SISKIYOU] (3).

Mill City: see **Magalia** [BUTTE].

Mill Creek [BUTTE]: *stream,* flows nearly 5 miles to North Fork Feather River 0.5 mile east-northeast of Pulga (lat. 39°48'20" N, long. 121°26'20" W; sec. 32, T 23 N, R 5 E). Named on Pulga (1979) and Soapstone Hill (1979) 7.5' quadrangles. South Branch enters from the southeast nearly 1 mile upstream from the mouth of the main creek; it is 1.5 miles long and is named on Pulga (1979) 7.5' quadrangle.

Mill Creek [GLENN]: *stream,* flows 8 miles to Grindstone Creek [GLENN-TEHAMA] 12 miles northwest of the village of Elk Creek (lat. 39°42'45" N, long. 122°42'50" W). Named on Alder Springs (1967) and Plaskett Meadows (1967) 7.5' quadrangles. Called South Fork Grindstone Creek on Elk Creek (1918) 15' quadrangle.

Mill Creek [SHASTA]:

(1) *stream,* flows 6 miles to Little Cow Creek 6.5 miles south of the village

of Montgomery Creek (lat. 40°45'10" N, long. 121°56' W; near NE cor. sec. 2, T 33 N, R 1 W). Named on Whitmore (1956) 15' quadrangle.
(2) *stream,* flows 3.5 miles to South Cow Creek 4.5 miles southwest of Whitmore (lat. 40°35'35" N, long. 121°58'55" W; at N line sec. 33, T 32 N, R 1 W). Named on Whitmore (1956) 15' quadrangle. Called Miller Creek on Averill's (1939) map.
(3) *stream,* flows nearly 3 miles to Clear Creek 2.5 miles south of the village of French Gulch (lat. 40°39'40" N, long. 122°38' W; near E line sec. 3, T 32 N, R 7 W). Named on French Gulch (1979) 7.5' quadrangle.

Mill Creek [SISKIYOU]:
(1) *stream,* flows 3.5 miles to Dillon Creek 3 miles north-northeast of Dillon Mountain (lat. 41°34'20" N, long. 123°33'35" W). Named on Dillon Mountain (1983) 7.5' quadrangle.
(2) *stream,* flows 6 miles to Indian Creek (1) 10 miles north-northwest of Happy Camp (lat. 41°55'10" N, long. 123°28'05" W; sec. 25, T 18 N, R 6 E). Named on Deadman Point (1981) 7.5' quadrangle.
(3) *stream,* flows 1.5 miles to Thompson Creek 7.25 miles north-northeast of Happy Camp (lat. 41°53'35" N, long. 123°19'50" W). Named on Figurehead Mountain (1980) 7.5' quadrangle.
(4) *stream,* flows nearly 3 miles to Klamath River 7.25 miles east-southeast of the village of Seiad Valley (lat. 41°47'20" N, long. 123°04'40" W; near E line sec. 35, T 46 N, R 11 W). Named on Hamburg (1980) 7.5' quadrangle.
(5) *stream,* flows 7.25 miles to Scott River at Scott Bar (lat. 41°44'35" N, long. 123°00'05" W; near S line sec. 16, T 45 N, R 10 W). Named on Condrey Mountain (1955) and Fort Jones (1955) 15' quadrangles. South Fork enters from the south 2.5 miles upstream from the mouth of the main creek; it is 3.5 miles long and is named on Fort Jones (1955) 15' quadrangle.
(6) *stream,* flows 9 miles to Shackleford Creek 6.25 miles west of Fort Jones (lat. 41°35'50" N, long. 122°57'40" W; sec. 11, T 43 N, R 10 W). Named on Fort Jones (1955) 15' quadrangle, and on Boulder Peak (1981) 7.5' quadrangle.
(7) *stream,* flows 5 miles to Etna Creek nearly 4 miles west-southwest of Etna (lat. 41°25'45" N, long. 122°57'20" W; sec. 2, T 41 N, R 10 W). Named on Etna (1955) 15' quadrangle, and on Yellow Dog Peak (1977) 7.5' quadrangle.
(8) *stream,* flows 2 miles to Greenhorn Creek 3 miles west-southwest of Yreka (lat. 41°43'20" N, long. 122°41'40" W; sec. 30, T 45 N, R 8 W). Named on Yreka (1954) 15' quadrangle.

Mill Creek [TEHAMA]:
(1) *stream,* flows 13 miles to Thomes Creek 4.5 miles east-northeast of Flournoy (lat. 39°57' N, long. 122°21'30" W; sec. 7, T 24 N, R 4 W). Named on Flournoy (1967) and Paskenta (1967) 7.5' quadrangles.
(2) *stream,* flows nearly 7 miles to Thomes Creek 4.25 miles west-southwest of Paskenta (lat. 39°51'35" N, long. 122°36'55" W; near S line sec. 11, T 23 N, R 7 W); Patton Mill is along the stream. Named on Hall Ridge (1967), Newville (1967), and Riley Ridge (1967) 7.5' quadrangles.
(3) *stream,* formed by the confluence of East Sulphur Creek and West Sulphur Creek, flows 52 miles to Sacramento River 1.5 miles northwest of Los Molinos (lat. 40°02'15" N, long. 122°06'55" W). Named on Butte Meadows (1958), Lassen Peak (1956), and Panther Spring (1953) 15' quadrangles, and on Los Molinos (1952, photorevised 1969) 7.5' quadrangle. Called Rio de los Molinos on a diseño made in 1844 of Rio de los Molinos grant (Becker, 1964). North Fork, which diverges from the main creek and flows 1.5 miles to Sacramento River nearly 1 mile upstream from the mouth of the main creek, is named on Los Molinos (1952) 7.5' quadrangle.
(4) *village,* 4.25 miles east-southeast of Mineral (lat. 40°19'35" N, long. 121°31'15" W; sec. 34, T 29 N, R 4 E); the village is along Mill Creek (3). Named on Lassen Peak (1956) 15' quadrangle. Called Mill Creek Homesite on Mineral (1941) 30' quadrangle. Postal authorities established Mill Creek post office in 1936 (Frickstad, p. 204). E.J. Foster and W.H. Foster suggested the post office name (Gudde, 1949, p. 215).

Mill Creek: see **Big Mill Creek** [SISKIYOU]; **Etna Creek** [SISKIYOU]; **Little Mill Creek** [SISKIYOU]; **Little Mill Creek** [TEHAMA]; **Sawmill Gulch** [SISKIYOU] (2).

Mill Creek Homesite: see **Mill Creek** [TEHAMA] (4).

Mill Creek Lake [SISKIYOU]: *lake,* 550 feet long, 15 miles south-southeast of Etna (lat. 41°14'20" N, long. 122°46'25" W; sec. 15, T 39 N, R 8 W); the lake is at the head of Little Mill Creek. Named on Coffee Creek (1955) 15' quadrangle.

Mill Creek Plateau [TEHAMA]: *ridge,* north-northwest- to northwest-trending, 6 miles long, 6.5 miles southeast of Mineral (lat. 40°17' N, long. 121°31' W); the ridge is east of Mill Creek (3). Named on Lassen Peak (1956) and Mount Harkness (1956) 15' quadrangles.

Mill Creek Ponds [SISKIYOU]: *lakes,* largest 500 feet long, 15 miles south-southwest of Scott Bar (lat. 41°31'45" N, long. 123°04'45" W); the lakes are at the head of Mill Creek (6). Named on Boulder Peak (1981) 7.5' quadrangle.

Mill Creek Ridge [SISKIYOU]: *ridge,* generally south-trending, 5 miles long, center 12.5 miles north-northwest of Happy Camp (lat. 41°58' N, long. 123°28' W); the ridge is west of Mill Creek (2). Named on Deadman Point (1981) 7.5' quadrangle.

Mill Creek Ridge: see **Mill Creek Rim** [TEHAMA].

Mill Creek Rim [TEHAMA]: *relief feature,* 6.5 miles north of Polk Springs (lat. 40°12'30" N, long. 121°40'30" W); the feature is northwest of Mill Creek (3). Named on Butte Meadows (1958) 15' quadrangle. Called Mill Cr. Ridge on O'Brien's (1946) map.

Miller Bar [BUTTE]: *locality,* nearly 2 miles east of Bidwell Bar along Middle Fork Feather River (lat. 39°33'30" N, long. 121°24'25" W; near W line sec. 27, T 20 N, R 5 E). Named on Big Bend Mountain (1948) 15' quadrangle.

Miller Buttes [SHASTA]: *peaks,* 3 miles east of the town of Central Valley (lat. 40°40'50" N, long. 122°18'40" W; on S line sec. 27, T 33 N, R 4 W). Named on Project City (1957) 7.5' quadrangle.

Miller Creek: see **Mill Creek** [SHASTA] (2).

Miller Glade [SISKIYOU]: *area,* 3.5 miles northeast of Condrey Mountain (lat. 41°58'45" N, long. 122°56'20" W; sec. 30, T 48 N, R 9 W). Named on Condrey Mountain (1955) 7.5' quadrangle.

Miller Gulch [SISKIYOU]: *canyon,* drained by a stream that flows 2.25 miles to Klamath River 10 miles east-southeast of Condrey Mountain (lat. 41°52'10" N, long. 122°48'35" W; near W line sec. 5, T 46 N, R 8 W). Named on Condrey Mountain (1955) 15' quadrangle.

Miller Hill [BUTTE]: *peak,* 2 miles northeast of Bangor (lat. 39°24'35" N, long. 121°22'35" W; on N line sec. 23, T 18 N, R 5 E). Named on Bangor (1947) and Rackerby (1948) 7.5' quadrangles.

Miller Mountain [SHASTA]: *ridge,* west-southwest-trending, 3.5 miles long, 6.5 miles east-northeast of Whitmore (lat. 40°40'40" N, long. 121°48'45" W). Named on Whitmore (1956) 15' quadrangle.

Miller Mountain [SISKIYOU]: *ridge,* north-trending, 5 miles long, 17 miles southwest of Macdoel (lat. 41°39' N, long. 122°14'45" W). Named on The Whaleback (1954) 15' quadrangle. On Macdoel (1941) 30' quadrangle, the name applies to a peak on the ridge.

Millers Ranch: see **Bangor** [BUTTE].

Miller Valley [SHASTA]: *canyon,* 0.5 mile long, 3.25 miles east-northeast of Whitmore (lat. 40°49'15" N, long. 121°51'45" W; sec. 4, T 32 N, R 1 E). Named on Whitmore (1956) 15' quadrangle.

Mill Gulch [SISKIYOU]: *canyon,* drained by a stream that flows 2.5 miles to Moffett Creek 12 miles south of Yreka (lat. 41°34' N, long. 122°41'10" W; at S line sec. 17, T 43 N, R 7 W). Named on Yreka (1954) 15' quadrangle. The feature also was known as Tannery Gulch for a tannery that operated in the canyon (Herzog, p. 67).

Mill Lake: see **Lower Mill Lake** [SISKIYOU].

Millrace Creek [TEHAMA]: *stream,* flows nearly 4 miles to Salt Creek (2) 3.5 miles east-southeast of Red Bluff (lat. 40°09'55" N, long. 122°10'20" W). Named on Red Bluff East (1951) 7.5' quadrangle.

Millsaps [SHASTA]: *locality,* 11 miles west-northwest of Ono (lat. 40°22'45" N, long. 122°43'15" W). Named on Red Bluff (1894) 1° quadrangle.

Millsaps: see **Chrome** [GLENN].

Millseat Creek [SHASTA]: *stream,* flows nearly 7 miles to North Fork Battle Creek [SHASTA-TEHAMA] 3.5 miles south of Shingletown (lat. 40°26'30" N, long. 121°52'30" W; near NW cor. sec. 21, T 30 N, R 1 E). Named on Manton (1956) and Whitmore (1956) 15' quadrangles. The stream first was known as Millsite Creek for several sawmills built along it in the early days (Steger, p. 47).

Mills Flat [SISKIYOU]: *area,* less than 0.5 mile northeast of Forks of Salmon along North Fork Salmon River (lat. 41°15'40" N, long. 123°18'55" W). Named on Forks of Salmon (1978) 7.5' quadrangle.

Millsholm [GLENN]: *locality,* 7 miles east-southeast of Fruto along Southern Pacific Railroad (lat. 39°32'25" N, long. 122°20'40" W; near SE cor. sec. 31, T 20 N, R 4 W). Named on Fruto (1944) 15' quadrangle. The name was for Edgar Mills, landowner at the site in the 1880's (Gudde, 1949, p. 216).

Millsite Creek: see **Millseat Creek** [SHASTA].

Millville [SHASTA]: *village,* 11 miles east-southeast of Redding (lat. 40°33' N, long. 122°10'30" W; on S line sec. 11, T 31 N, R 3 W). Named on Palo Cedro (1965) 7.5' quadrangle. Postal authorities established Millville post office in 1860 (Frickstad, p. 181). After D.D. Harrill built a grist mill at the site, the place was known in 1855 as Harrill's Mill, and in 1856 as Buscombe for Harrill's birthplace in North Carolina; the name was changed to Millville in 1857 (Gudde, 1949, p. 215). Giles (p. 48) referred to "King's Ford (Millville)."

Millville Plains [SHASTA]: *area,* center about 2 miles south of Millville (lat. 40°30'15" N, long. 122°10'30" W). Named on Balls Ferry (1965) and Palo Cedro (1965) 7.5' quadrangles.

Milne: see **Anthony Milne Camp** [SISKIYOU].

Milne Lake [SISKIYOU]: *lake,* 850 feet long, 14 miles north of Sawyers Bar (lat. 41°29'55" N, long. 123°07'50" W). Named on English Peak (1977) and Marble Mountain (1980) 7.5' quadrangles.

Milsap Bar [BUTTE]: *locality,* 4 miles east-northeast of the village of Brush Creek along Middle Fork Feather River (lat. 39°42'35" N, long. 121°16'15"

W). Named on Brush Creek (1970) 7.5' quadrangle.

Mineral [TEHAMA]: *village,* 35 miles east-northeast of Red Bluff (lat. 40°20'55" N, long. 121°35'45" W; sec. 25, T 29 N, R 3 E). Named on Lassen Peak (1956) 15' quadrangle. Postal authorities established Mineral post office in 1894 and moved it 6 miles west in 1902 to the present site (Salley, p. 141).

Mineral Range [SISKIYOU]: *ridge,* generally west-trending, 4.5 miles long, center 2.5 miles east of Fort Jones (lat. 41°36'30" N, long. 122°47'30" W). Named on Fort Jones (1955) 15' quadrangle.

Mineral Slide [BUTTE]: *locality,* 2.25 miles northwest of Paradise (lat. 39°47'05" N, long 121°37'30" W; at S line sec. 3, T 22 N, R 3 E). Site named on Paradise (1953) 15' quadrangle.

Mineral Spring Ravine [BUTTE]: *canyon,* drained by a stream that flows 1.25 miles to Fall River 8.5 miles north of Clipper Mills (lat. 39°39'20" N, long. 121°11'05" W; near N line sec. 27, T 21 N, R 7 E). Named on Cascade (1948) 7.5' quadrangle.

Mineral Summit [TEHAMA]: *pass,* 2 miles south-southeast of Mineral (lat. 40°19'30" N, long. 121°34'35" W; near SE cor. sec. 31, T 29 N, R 4 E). Named on Lassen Peak (1956) 15' quadrangle.

Miners Cabin Spring [TEHAMA]: *spring,* 1600 feet west-northwest of Tomhead Mountain (lat. 40°08'20" N, long. 122°49'15" W; near NE cor. sec. 1, T 26 N, R 9 W). Named on Yolla Bolly (1954) 15' quadrangle.

Miners Creek [SISKIYOU]: *stream,* flows about 3.5 miles to French Creek (2) nearly 5 miles south-southeast of Etna (lat. 41°23'20" N, long. 122°52'15" W; sec. 22, T 41 N, R 9 W). Named on Etna (1955) 15' quadrangle.

Miners Gulch [SHASTA]: *canyon,* drained by a stream that flows 1.5 miles to Dickerson Creek 5 miles southeast of Whitmore (lat. 40°35' N, long. 121°50'45" W; sec. 34, T 32 N, R 1 E). Named on Whitmore (1956) 15' quadrangle.

Miners Ranch [BUTTE]: *locality,* 3.5 miles south-southwest of Bidwell Bar (lat. 39°30'30" N, long. 121°27'50" W; at W line sec. 18, T 19 N, R 5 E). Named on Big Bend Mountain (1948) 15' quadrangle.

Miners Ranch Reservoir [BUTTE]: *lake,* 0.5 mile long, 2.5 miles southeast of Oroville Dam (lat. 39°30'30" N, long. 121°27'50" W; sec. 18, T 19 N, R 5 E). Named on Oroville (1970) 7.5' quadrangle.

Mink Creek [SHASTA]: *stream,* flows 1.5 miles to Squirrel Creek 2.5 miles north of Shoeinhorse Mountain (lat. 41°06'15" N, long. 122°03'50" W). Named on Shoeinhorse Mountain (1954) 15' quadrangle.

Minnesota [SHASTA]: *locality,* nearly 5 miles west-southwest of Summit City (lat. 40°39'45" N, long. 122°29'15" W; near NE cor. sec. 1, T 32 N, R 6 W). Named on Shasta Dam (1956) 7.5' quadrangle.

Minnesota Mountain [SHASTA]: *peak,* 6 miles south-southeast of Bollibokka Mountain (lat. 40°51' N, long. 122°11'10" W; near NE cor. sec. 34, T 35 N, R 3 W). Altitude 4293 feet. Named on Bollibokka Mountain (1957) 15' quadrangle.

Minnie Creek [BUTTE]: *stream,* flows 2.5 miles to East Fork Canyon Creek 5.5 miles northeast of Oroville Dam (lat. 39°35'40" N, long. 121°24'50" W; sec. 16, T 20 N, R 5 E). Named on Oroville Dam (1970) 7.5' quadrangle.

Minnie Glade [TEHAMA]: *area,* 9 miles west-southwest of Ball Mountain (lat. 39°53'55" N, long. 122°56'35" W; on N line sec. 35, T 24 N, R 10 W). Named on Buck Rock (1967) 7.5' quadrangle.

Minnow Creek [SHASTA]: *stream,* flows 2.25 miles to Willow Creek (2) nearly 2 miles south-southwest of the village of Montgomery Creek (lat. 40°49'15" N, long. 121°56'05" W; near NE cor. sec. 11, T 34 N, R 1 W). Named on Montgomery Creek (1956) 15' quadrangle.

Minton Creek [GLENN]: *stream,* flows 5.5 miles to Logan Creek nearly 5 miles northeast of High Peak (lat. 39°28'10" N, long. 122°21'20" W; sec. 30, T 19 N, R 4 W). Named on Lodoga (1960) 15' quadrangle.

Mirror Lake [SHASTA]: *lake,* 1400 feet long, 9 miles north-northwest of Millville (lat. 40°40'10" N, long. 122°13'40" W; sec. 32, T 33 N, R 3 W). Named on Bella Vista (1965) 7.5' quadrangle.

Missouri Bar [SISKIYOU]: *locality,* 7.25 miles northeast of Salmon Mountain along South Fork Salmon River (lat. 41°14'55" N, long. 123°18'10" W). Named on Youngs Peak (1979) 7.5' quadrangle.

Missouri Bend [BUTTE]: *bend,* 14 miles west-northwest of Chico along Sacramento River (lat. 39°50'10" N, long. 122°03'25" W). Named on McIntosh Landing (1914) 7.5' quadrangle.

Mitchell: see **Emery and Mitchell Island** [BUTTE].

Mitchell Creek [SISKIYOU]: *stream,* flows nearly 2 miles to Klamath River 7.5 miles southeast of the village of Seiad Valley (lat. 41°46'55" N, long. 123°04'15" W); the mouth of the creek is 300 feet downstream along Klamath River from the mouth of present Jim Creek. Named on Hamburg (1980) 7.5' quadrangle. Called Jim Creek on Seiad Valley (1955) 15' quadrangle, but United States Board on Geographic Names (1981b, p. 4) rejected the names "Jim Creek" and "Jimmy Creek" for the stream.

Mitchell Gulch [TEHAMA]: *canyon,* drained by a stream that flows 6.5 miles to South Fork Cottonwood Creek [SHASTA-TEHAMA] 4 miles northwest of Hooker (lat. 40°20'15" N, long. 122°22'45" W; sec. 25, T 29 N, R 5 W). Named on Mitchell Gulch (1965) 7.5' quadrangle.

Moak Cove [TEHAMA]: *relief feature,* 15 miles south of Panther Spring (lat. 40°02'20" N, long. 121°48'55" W; sec. 12, T 25 N, R 1 E). Named on Panther Spring (1953) 15' quadrangle.

Moboy Gulch [TEHAMA]: *canyon,* drained by a stream that flows 5 miles to Little Dry Creek (1) 8.5 miles west-northwest of Hooker (lat. 40°20'50" N, long. 122°28'15" W; near S line sec. 19, T 29 N, R 5 W). Named on Ono (1952) 15' quadrangle, and on Mitchel Gulch (1965) 7.5' quadrangle

Moccasin Creek [SHASTA]: *stream,* flows 1 mile to Sacramento River 2.5 miles northwest of Summit City (lat. 40°42'25" N, long. 122°26'20" W; sec. 21, T 33 N, R 5 W). Named on Shasta Dam (1956) 7.5' quadrangle.

Modesto Fork [SHASTA]: *stream,* flows 2 miles to Backbone Creek 2.25 miles south-southeast of Schell Mountain (lat. 40°49'30" N, long. 122°30'50" W; near N line sec. 11, T 34 N, R 6 W). Named on Schell Mountain (1950) 15' quadrangle.

Modesty Gulch [SHASTA]: *canyon,* drained by a stream that flows nearly 1 mile to Grizzly Gulch 3.5 miles southeast of the village of French Gulch (lat. 40°39'35" N, long. 122°35'55" W; near E line sec. 1, T 32 N, R 7 W). Named on Whiskeytown (1979) 7.5' quadrangle.

Modin Creek [SHASTA]: *stream,* flows 2.5 miles to Squaw Creek (2) 8.5 miles east-northeast of Bollibokka Mountain (lat. 40°58' N, long. 122°03'30" W; sec. 23, T 36 N, R 2 W). Named on Bollibokka Mountain (1957) 15' quadrangle. Steger (p. 47) associated the name with Jim Modin, who lived along the stream.

Modoc Crater [SISKIYOU]: *crater,* 9.5 miles north-northeast of Medicine Lake (lat. 41°43' N, long. 121°33'05" W; sec. 30, T 45 N, R 4 E). Named on Medicine Lake (1952) 15' quadrangle.

Moffett Creek [SISKIYOU]: *stream,* flows 23 miles to Scott River 1 mile west of Fort Jones (lat. 41°36'20" N, long. 122°51'35" W; sec. 3, T 43 N, R 9 W). Named on China Mountain (1955), Fort Jones (1955), and Yreka (1954) 15' quadrangles. The name commemorates a prospector who settled by the stream for a short time in 1850 (Gudde, 1949, p. 219). Called Moffat Creek on Shasta (1894) 1° quadrangle. United States Board on Geographic Names (1978b, p. 4) rejected the form "Moffet Creek" for the name. Spring Branch enters 15 miles south of Yreka; it is 2 miles long and is named on Yreka (1954) 15' quadrangle.

Monarch Mountain [SHASTA]: *peak,* 6.25 miles north-northwest of Igo (lat. 40°35'35" N, long. 122°34'10" W; near N line sec. 32, T 32 N, R 6 W). Altitude 2550 feet. Named on Igo (1979) 7.5' quadrangle.

Monday Flat [SHASTA]: *area,* 10 miles south-southeast of Bollibokka Mountain (lat. 40°47'50" N, long. 122°10'15" W; near S line sec. 14, T 34 N, R 3 W). Named on Bollibokka Mountain (1957) 15' quadrangle.

Monroeville: see **Munroeville** [GLENN].

Montague [SISKIYOU]: *town,* 6 miles east of Yreka (lat. 41°43'30" N, long. 122°31'30" W; on S line sec. 22, T 45 N, R 6 W). Named on Yreka (1954) 15' quadrangle. Postal authorities established Montague post office in 1887; the name was for S.S. Montague, chief engineer of Central Pacific Railroad (Salley, p. 144). The town incorporated in 1909.

Monte Creek [SISKIYOU]:

(1) *stream,* flows nearly 2 miles to Salmon River 10 miles northwest of Forks of Salmon (lat. 41°22'15" N, long. 123°26'40" W). Named on Orleans Mountain (1974) 7.5' quadrangle.

(2) *stream,* flows 1 mile to Grouse Creek (1) 12 miles east-northeast of Condrey Mountain (lat. 41°59'55" N, long. 122°46'05" W; near NE cor. sec. 21, T 48 N, R 8 W). Named on Condrey Mountain (1955) 15' quadrangle.

Monte de Oro [BUTTE]: *peak,* 3 miles north-northeast of Oroville (lat. 39°33'10" N, long. 121°31'30" W; near NE cor. sec. 33, T 20 N, R 4 E). Altitude 1152 feet. Named on Oroville (1970) 7.5' quadrangle.

Monterey Bar: see **Long's Bar**, under **Oroville** [BUTTE].

Monterey Point [TEHAMA]: *relief feature,* 5.25 miles south-southwest of Mineral (lat. 40°17'10" N, long. 121°38'45" W; at NW cor. sec. 16, T 28 N, R 3 E). Named on Lassen Peak (1956) 15' quadrangle.

Montgomery Bar [BUTTE]: *locality,* 2.25 miles east of Bidwell Bar along Middle Fork Feather River (lat. 39°34' N, long. 121°24' W; sec. 27, T 20 N, R 5 E). Named on Big Bend Mountain (1948) 15' quadrangle. Water of Lake Oroville now covers the site. F.D. Dunn (p. 112) listed a place called Wild Irish Bar that was located on the west side of Middle Fork Feather River just above Montgomery Bar.

Montgomery Bar Ravine [BUTTE]: *canyon,* drained by a stream that flows 0.5 mile to Lake Oroville 5.5 miles east-northeast of Oroville Dam (lat. 39°33'50" N, long. 121°23'15" W; near W line sec. 26, T 20 N, R 5 E). Named on Oroville Dam (1970) 7.5' quadrangle.

Montgomery Creek [GLENN]: *stream,* heads in Colusa County and flows 3.5 miles in Glenn County to Stony Creek [GLENN-TEHAMA] 10.5 miles east of Saint John Mountain (lat. 39°25'55" N, long. 122°30'10" W; sec. 11, T 18 N, R 6 W). Named on Stonyford (1968) 7.5' quadrangle.

Montgomery Creek [SHASTA]:

(1) *stream,* formed by the confluence of North Fork and South Fork, flows 6 miles to Pit River 2.25 miles west-northwest of the village of Montgomery Creek (lat. 40°51'15" N, long. 121°57'40" W; at S line sec. 27, T 35 N, R 1 W). Named on Montgomery Creek (1956) 15' quadrangle. The name

commemorates Zack Montgomery, who caught a large number of fish in the stream in the early 1850's (Steger, p. 48). North Fork is 7 miles long and South Fork is 5 miles long; both forks are named on Montgomery Creek (1956) 15' quadrangle.

(2) *village,* 14 miles west-southwest of Burney (lat. 40°50'40" N, long. 121°55'15" W; sec. 36, T 35 N, R 1 W); the place is along Montgomery Creek (1). Named on Montgomery Creek (1956) 15' quadrangle. Postal authorities established Montgomery Ferry post office in 1877 and changed the name to Montgomery Creek in 1878 (Frickstad, p. 181). They established Elena post office 18 miles north of Montgomery Creek post office in 1890 and discontinued it in 1906 (Salley, p. 67). According to Steger (p. 30-31), the name "Elena" was for Ellen E. Hinderlong, the postmaster; according to Gudde (1949, p. 105), the name was for Elena Haggen, one of the first women to settle in the neighborhood. Postal authorities established Burgess post office, named for a pioneer settler, 8 miles north of Montgomery Creek post office in 1891 and discontinued it in 1903 (Salley, p. 29). They established Latson post office 7 miles north of Montgomery Creek post office in 1891 and discontinued it in 1895 (Salley, p. 119). They established Pineland post office 5 miles north of Montgomery Creek post office in 1901 and discontinued it in 1917 (Salley, p. 172). Montgomery Creek (1956) 15' quadrangle shows the abandoned Pineland school situated 3.25 miles north-northeast of the village of Montgomery Creek (sec. 18, T 35 N, R 1 E).

Montgomery Creek Falls [SHASTA]: *waterfall,* 3 miles southeast of the village of Montgomery Creek (lat. 40°49'40" N, long. 121°52'45" W; at W line sec. 9, T 34 N, R 1 E); the feature is along Montgomery Creek (1). Named on Burney (1939) 30' quadrangle.

Montgomery Ferry: see **Montgomery Creek** [SHASTA] (2).

Montreal Bar: see **Big Bar** [BUTTE].

Monument Gulch [SISKIYOU]: *canyon,* drained by a stream that flows 1.5 miles to Klamath River 8 miles south of Condrey Mountain (lat. 41°49'20" N, long. 122°57'10" W; near SW cor. sec. 13, T 46 N, R 10 W); the feature heads near Monument Point. Named on Condrey Mountain (1955) 15' quadrangle.

Monument Lake [SISKIYOU]: *lake,* 475 feet long, 4 miles south of Ukonom Lake (lat. 41°31'15" N, long. 123°20'55" W). Named on Ukonom Lake (1980) 7.5' quadrangle.

Monument Point [SISKIYOU]: *peak,* 8.5 miles south-southeast of Condrey Mountain (lat. 41°49'15" N, long. 122°56'10" W; at N line sec. 19, T 46 N, R 9 W). Altitude 3957 feet. Named on Condrey Mountain (1955) 15' quadrangle.

Moody Creek [SHASTA]: *stream,* flows 5.5 miles to West Fork Stillwater Creek 3 miles southeast of the town of Central Valley (lat. 40°39'10" N, long. 122°19'45" W; near S line sec. 4, T 32 N, R 4 W). Named on Project City (1957) 7.5' quadrangle. Steger (p. 48) associated the name with M.G. Moody and Elizabeth Moody, who filed a land claim along the stream in 1852.

Moody Spring [SHASTA]: *spring,* 1.5 miles north-northeast of the village of Montgomery Creek (lat. 40°51'10" N, long. 121°53'45" W; near NW cor. sec. 32, T 35 N, R 1@ E). Named on Montgomery Creek (1956) 15' quadrangle.

Moone Bar [TEHAMA]: *locality,* 3.5 miles south-southwest of Vina on the west side of Sacramento River (lat. 39°53'15" N, long. 122°04'30" W; on S line sec. 34, T 24 N, R 2 W). Named on Vina (1904) 15' quadrangle.

Mooney Island [TEHAMA]: *island,* 3.5 miles north of Gerber along Sacramento River (lat. 40°06'25" N, long. 122°08'25" W). Named on Gerber (1950) 7.5' quadrangle.

Moon Fork: see **Cottonwood Creek** [SHASTA-TEHAMA].

Moon Springs [SHASTA]: *springs,* 1.5 miles west-southwest of Coble Mountain (lat. 40°52'20" N, long. 121°22'30" W; near NE cor. sec. 26, T 35 N, R 5 E). Named on Jellico (1957) 15' quadrangle.

Moon Springs Reservoir [SHASTA]: *lake,* 300 feet long, 3 miles west-southwest of Coble Mountain (lat. 40°51'35" N, long. 121°23'50" W; near SE cor. sec. 27, T 35 N, R 5 E); the lake is 1.5 miles southeast of Moon Springs. Named on Jellico (1957) 15' quadrangle.

Moon's Ranch: see **Tehama** [TEHAMA].

Moore Creek [SHASTA]: *stream,* flows 1 mile to McCloud River Arm Shasta Lake 3.5 miles south-southwest of Bollibokka Mountain (lat. 40°53' N, long. 122°13'45" W; near S line sec. 17, T 35 N, R 3 W). Named on Bollibokka Mountain (1957) 15' quadrangle.

Moore Creek [TEHAMA]: *stream,* flows 8.5 miles to Sour Grass Creek 1.5 miles south-southeast of Kirkwood (lat. 39°50'10" N, long. 122°09'10" W; sec. 24, T 23 N, R 3 W). Named on Black Butte Dam (1967) and Kirkwood (1949) 7.5' quadrangles. On Flournoy (1944) 15' quadrangle, present Sour Grass Creek is called Moore Creek.

Moores Gulch [SISKIYOU]: *canyon,* drained by a stream that flows 1 mile to Rattlesnake Creek 5 miles north-northwest of Fort Jones (lat. 41°40'05" N, long. 122°53' W; sec. 16, T 44 N, R 9 W). Named on Fort Jones (1955) 15' quadrangle.

Moores Station: see **Honcut** [BUTTE] (2).

Mooretown: see **Feather Falls** [BUTTE] (2).

Mooretown Ridge [BUTTE]: *ridge,* southwest-trending, 6 miles long, center 5 miles north-northwest of Forbestown between Middle Fork Feather River and South Fork Feather River (lat. 39°35' N, long. 121°18'30" W). Named on Forbestown (1970) 7.5' quadrangle.

Mooreville Ridge [BUTTE]: *ridge,* generally southwest-trending, 5.5 miles long in Butte County, 7 miles northwest of Clipper Mills on Butte-Plumas County line (lat. 39°37'49" N, long. 121°07' W). Named on American House (1948), Clipper Mills (1948), and Strawberry Valley (1948) 7.5' quadrangles.

Moose Camp [SHASTA]: *locality,* 4 miles east-northeast of the village of Montgomery Creek (lat. 40°51'30" N, long. 121°50'45" W; sec. 27, T 35 N, R 1 E). Named on Montgomery Creek (1956) 15' quadrangle.

Moosehead Creek [SHASTA-SISKIYOU]: *stream,* heads in Shasta County and flows nearly 4 miles to McCloud River [SHASTA-SISKIYOU] 3.5 miles south-southeast of Bartle in Siskiyou County (lat. 41°12'25" N, long. 121°47'45" W; sec. 24, T 39 N, R 1 E). Named on Big Bend (1961) 15' quadrangle. Steger (p. 48) associated the name with the moosehead deer.

Moraine Lake [SISKIYOU]: *lake,* 250 feet long, 11 miles southeast of Cecilville (lat. 41°01' N, long. 123°00'45" W). Named on Thompson Peak (1979) 7.5' quadrangle.

Moraine Lake: see **Elk Lake** [SISKIYOU].

Morehead [BUTTE]: *locality,* 1.5 miles west-southwest of downtown Chico along Northern Electric Railroad (lat. 39°43' N, long. 121°52'15" W). Named on Durham (1912) 7.5' quadrangle.

Morehouse Creek [SISKIYOU]: *stream,* flows 7.25 miles to Salmon River 5 miles northwest of Forks of Salmon (lat. 41°19'05" N, long. 123°22'50" W). Named on Forks of Salmon (1978) 7.5' quadrangle.

Morehouse Meadows [SISKIYOU]: *area,* 7 miles north of Forks of Salmon (lat. 41°21'35" N, long. 123°17'30" W). Named on Forks of Salmon (1978) 7.5' quadrangle.

Morgan: see **Morgan Springs** [TEHAMA].

Morgan Creek [SISKIYOU]: *stream,* flows 1.25 miles to Thompson Creek 8.5 miles north of Happy Camp (lat. 41°55'10" N, long. 123°20'50" W). Named on Figurehead Mountain (1980) 7.5' quadrangle.

Morgan Creek [TEHAMA]: *stream,* flows 13 miles to Battle Creek [SHASTA-TEHAMA] 15 miles northeast of Bend (lat. 40°25'05" N, long. 122°01'40" W; at SE cor. sec. 25, T 30 N, R 2 W). Named on Manton (1956) 15' quadrangle.

Morgan Hot Spring [TEHAMA]: *spring,* 5 miles east-northeast of Mineral along Mill Creek (3) (lat. 40°23' N, long. 121°30'45" W; near W line sec. 11, T 29 N, R 4 E). Named on Lassen Peak (1956) 15' quadrangle. According to Tucker (p. 263), 25 springs and pools are the basis of a summer resort located along Mill Creek in a meadow called Big Hot Spring Valley.

Morgan Meadows [SISKIYOU]: *area,* 6 miles west of the town of Mount Shasta (lat. 41°18'50" N, long. 122°25'15" W; near E line sec. 16, T 40 N, R 5 W). Named on Weed (1954) 15' quadrangle.

Morgan Mountain [TEHAMA]: *peak,* 4.25 miles east-northeast of Mineral (lat. 40°22'15" N, long. 121°31'20" W; sec. 15, T 29 N, R 4 E); the peak is 1 mile south-southwest of Morgan Hot Spring. Named on Lassen Peak (1956) 15' quadrangle.

Morgan Point [SISKIYOU]: *relief feature,* 2.5 miles east-southeast of Happy Camp along Klamath River (lat. 41°46'30" N, long. 123°20'15" W; mainly in sec. 18, T 16 N, R 8 E). Named on Slater Butte (1980) 7.5' quadrangle.

Morgan Ravine [BUTTE]: *canyon,* drained by a stream that flows 1.25 miles to Rocky Honcut Creek 3.25 miles north of Bangor (lat. 39°26'10" N, long. 121°24'15" W; sec. 10, T 18 N, R 5 E). Named on Bangor (1947) 7.5' quadrangle.

Morgan Reservoir [BUTTE]: *lake,* 300 feet long, 10.5 miles south-southeast of Paradise (lat. 39°37'30" N, long. 121°31'55" W; at N line sec. 4, T 20 N, R 4 E). Named on Cherokee (1970) and Oroville (1970) 7.5' quadrangles.

Morgan Ridge [BUTTE]: *ridge,* generally south-trending, 5.5 miles long, 3.25 miles south-southeast of Paradise (lat. 39°42'45" N, long. 121°35'35" W). Named on Cherokee (1970) 7.5' quadrangle.

Morgan Springs [TEHAMA]: *locality,* 4.5 miles east of Mineral along Mill Creek (3) (lat. 40°21'45" N, long. 121°30'40" W; near NW cor. sec. 23, T 29 N, R 4 E). Named on Lassen Peak (1956) 15' quadrangle. Called Morgan on Mineral (1941) 30' quadrangle.

Morgan Summit [TEHAMA]: *pass,* 3.5 miles east-northeast of Mineral (lat. 40°21'45" N, long. 121°32' W; near NE cor. sec. 21, T 29 N, R 4 E); the pass is nearly 1 mile southwest of Morgan Mountain. Named on Lassen Peak (1956) 15' quadrangle.

Morley [SHASTA]: *locality,* 14 miles south of Lamoine along Southern Pacific Railroad (lat. 40°46'40" N, long. 122°23' W; sec. 25, T 34 N, R 5 W). Named on Redding (1901) 30' quadrangle. California Division of Highways' (1934) map shows a place called Pit located 1.5 miles south of Morley along Southern Pacific Railroad (sec. 36, T 34 N, R 5 W) near the mouth of Pit River.

Morris Flat [TEHAMA]: *area,* 13 miles south-southwest of Panther Spring (lat. 40°01'45" N, long. 121°53'30" W). Named on Panther Spring (1953) 15' quadrangle.

Morrison: see **Grass Lake** [SISKIYOU] (2).

Morrison Slough [BUTTE]: *stream,* flows 4.5 miles to Sutter County 4 miles south of Gridley (lat. 39°18'15" N, long. 121°41'20" W; at S line sec. 24, T 17 N, R 2 E). Named on Gridley (1952) 7.5' quadrangle.

Morris Ravine [BUTTE]: *canyon,* drained by a stream that flows 1.5 miles to Feather River 2.5 miles north-northeast of Oroville (lat. 39°32'40" N, long. 121°32'15" W; near W line sec. 33, T 20 N, R 4 E). Named on Oroville (1970) 7.5' quadrangle. F.D. Dunn (p. 97) listed a mining place called Sebastopol that was located in Morris Ravine (sec. 29, T 20 N, R 4 E).

Morrowville: see **French Gulch** [SHASTA] (3).

Mortimer: see **Oroville** [BUTTE].

Mose Genot Glade [TEHAMA]: *area,* 9 miles south of Ball Mountain (lat. 39°48'15" N, long. 122°47'20" W; near SW cor. sec. 32, T 23 N, R 8 W). Named on Log Spring (1967) 7.5' quadrangle.

Moses: see **Camp Moses**, under **Shasta Alpine Lodge** [SISKIYOU].

Mosquito Creek [BUTTE]:

(1) *stream,* flows 1.5 miles to Paradise Lake 7 miles north-northeast of Paradise (lat. 38°51'40" N, long. 121°34'15" W; sec. 7, T 23 N, R 4 E). Named on Paradise East (1980) and Stirling City (1979) 7.5' quadrangles.

(2) *stream,* flows 2 miles to French Creek 2 miles west-northwest of the village of Brush Creek (lat. 39°41'50" N, long. 121°22'20" W; near NW cor. sec, 12, T 21 N, R 5 E); the stream is south of Mosquito Ridge. Named on Brush Creek (1970) 7.5' quadrangle.

(3) *locality,* 6.5 miles north of Paradise (lat. 39°51' N, long. 121°34'45" W); the place is near the mouth of Mosquito Creek (1). Named on Chico (1895) 30' quadrangle. Water of Magalia Reservoir now covers the site.

Mosquito Creek [SHASTA]: *stream,* flows 4.5 miles to Sacramento River 1.5 miles south of Lamoine (lat. 40°57'10" N, long. 122°25'50" W; sec. 27, T 36 N, R 5 W). Named on Lamoine (1957) and Schell Mountain (1950) 15' quadrangles.

Mosquito Creek Ridge [SHASTA]: *ridge,* east-trending, 4.5 miles long, 3 miles southwest of Lamoine (lat. 40°56'45" N, long. 122°28'30" W); the ridge is south of Mosquito Creek. Named on Lamoine (1957) and Schell Mountain (1950) 15' quadrangles.

Mosquito Gulch [BUTTE]: *canyon,* drained by a stream that flows nearly 1 mile to Forbestown Ravine 1.25 miles north-northeast of Forbestown (lat. 39°32'10" N, long. 121°15'55" W; sec. 2, T 19 N, R 6 E). Named on Forbestown (1970) 7.5' quadrangle.

Mosquito Ridge [BUTTE]: *ridge,* generally west-southwest-trending, 2 miles long, 2 miles north-northwest of the village of Brush Creek (lat. 39°42'45" N, long. 121°21'15" W); the ridge is north of Mosquito Creek (2). Named on Brush Creek (1970) 7.5' quadrangle.

Mossbrae Falls [SISKIYOU]: *waterfall,* 2 miles north of Dunsmuir along Sacramento River (lat. 41°14'30" N, long. 122°16' W; near E line sec. 13, T 39 N, R 4 W). Named on Dunsmuir (1954) 15' quadrangle. Called Crescent Falls on Shasta (1894) 1° quadrangle. Diller and others' (1915) map has the form "Moss Brae Falls" for the name.

Moss Creek [SHASTA]: *stream,* flows 0.5 mile to Salt Creek (6) 10 miles southeast of Lamoine (lat. 41°52'15" N, long. 122°18'20" W; sec. 22, T 35 N, R 4 W). Named on Lamoine (1957) 15' quadrangle.

Motion [SHASTA]: *locality,* 3 miles west of Summit City (lat. 40°40'30" N, long. 122°27'30" W; sec. 32, T 33 N, R 5 W); the place is nearly 1 mile south-southwest of the mouth of Motion Creek. Named on Shasta Dam (1956) 7.5' quadrangle. Called Copley on Redding (1901) 30' quadrangle. Postal authorities established Copley post office in 1886 and discontinued it in 1913 (Frickstad, p. 179). Copley first was known as Camp Bailey (Steger, p. 26). California Mining Bureau's (1917b) map shows a place called Cuargo located 1.5 miles south-southeast of Motion along Southern Pacific Railroad.

Motion Creek [SHASTA]: *stream,* flows 3 miles to Sacramento River 2.5 miles west of Summit City (lat. 40°41'10" N, long. 122°27' W; sec. 29, T 33 N, R 5 W). Named on Shasta Dam (1956) 7.5' quadrangle. South Fork enters 1 mile upstream from the mouth of the main creek; it is 1.25 miles long and is named on Shasta Dam (1956) 7.5' quadrangle.

Mott [SISKIYOU]: *locality,* 4 miles south-southeast of the town of Mount Shasta along Southern Pacific Railroad (lat. 41°15'45" N, long. 122°16'30" W; near S line sec. 35, T 40 N, R 4 W). Named on Weed (1954) 15' quadrangle. Postal authorities established Mott post office in 1887 and discontinued it in 1910 (Frickstad, p. 189). The name commemorates M.H. Mott, road master of the railroad (Gudde, 1949, p. 226).

Mountain Gate [SHASTA]: *village,* 3.25 miles northeast of the town of Central Valley (lat. 40°43' N, long. 122°19'50" W; sec. 16, T 33 N, R 4 W); the village is along West Fork Stillwater Creek. Named on Project City (1957) 7.5' quadrangle. The place was called Bass in 1857, and called Stillwater in 1870; DeWitt Clinton Johnson of Stillwater, New York, settled at the site in 1853 (Steger, p. 48, 61). Postal authorities established Stillwater post office in 1870, discontinued it for a time in 1880, and discontinued it finally in 1900 (Frickstad, p. 183).

Mountain Home Spring [SHASTA]: *spring,* 12 miles west-northwest of Lassen Peak (lat. 40°32'10" N, long. 121°43'15" W; sec. 14, T 31 N, R 2 E). Named on Manzanita Lake (1956) 15' quadrangle.

Mountain House [BUTTE]: *locality,* 1.5 miles north-northeast of the village of Brush Creek (lat. 39°40'25" N, long. 121°19'25" W; sec. 5, T 21 N, R 6 E). Named on Brush Creek (1970) 7.5' quadrangle. Called Brush Creek on Bidwell Bar (1897) 30' quadrangle. Brush Creek post office was at the site until the post office moved, taking the name "Brush Creek" with it, and Mountain House gained its present name—the place earlier was called Campbell Station (Dunn, F.D., p. 17, 72)

Mountain House [SISKIYOU]: *locality,* nearly 4 miles northwest of China Mountain along East Fork Scott River (lat. 41°24'45" N, long. 122°37'45" W; near W line sec. 11, T 41 N, R 7 W). Named on China Mountain (1955) 15' quadrangle.

Mountain House Creek [BUTTE]: *stream,* flows nearly 3 miles to Little North Fork [of Middle Fork Feather River] 3 miles northeast of the village of Brush Creek (lat. 39°43' N, long. 121°17'40" W; sec. 34, T 22 N, R 6 E); the stream goes past Mountain House. Named on Brush Creek (1970) 7.5' quadrangle.

Mountain House Creek [SISKIYOU]: *stream,* flows 2 miles to East Fork Scott River 4 miles north-northwest of China Mountain (lat. 41°24'50" N, long. 122°37'30" W; sec. 11, T 41 N, R 7 W); the mouth of the stream is near Mountain House. Named on China Mountain (1955) 15' quadrangle.

Mountainhouse Creek: see **Inconstance Creek** [SISKIYOU].

Mountain Lake [TEHAMA]: *intermittent lake,* 3750 feet long, 4 miles north-northeast of Bend (lat. 40°18'30" N, long. 122°10'25" W); the feature is on Table Mountain (1). Named on Bend (1965) 7.5' quadrangle. Called Table Mountain Lake on Tuscan Buttes (1944) 15' quadrangle.

Mountain Spring: see **Enterprise** [BUTTE].

Mountain Spring House Ridge [BUTTE]: *ridge,* generally west-trending, 2.25 miles long, 13 miles north-northwest of Clipper Mills (lat. 39°42'40" N, long. 121°13'30" W); Mountain Spring House, which is in Plumas County, is near the east end of the ridge. Named on Cascade (1948) 7.5' quadrangle.

Mountain View: see **Magalia** [BUTTE].

Mount Bradley [SISKIYOU]: *peak,* 2 miles west-northwest of Dunsmuir (lat. 41°13'20" N, long. 122°18'30" W; sec. 22, T 39 N, R 4 W). Altitude 5556 feet. Named on Dunsmuir (1954) 15' quadrangle. Called Dunsmuir Rock on Averill's (1935) map.

Mount Conard [TEHAMA]: *peak,* 7.5 miles northeast of Mineral (lat. 40°25'45" N, long. 121°30' W; sec. 26, T 30 N, R 4 E). Altitude 8204 feet. Named on Lassen Peak (1956) and Mount Harkness (1956) 15' quadrangles. Called Black Butte on Mineral (1941) 30' quadrangle, but United States Board on Geographic Names (1948a, p. 4-5) rejected this name for the feature, and pointed out that the name "Mount Conard" honors Arthur L. Conard of Red Bluff, who was involved in the creation of Lassen Volcanic National Park.

Mount Diller [SHASTA]: *peak,* 2.5 miles southwest of Lassen Peak (lat. 40°27'50" N, long. 121°32'10" W; near N line sec. 16, T 30 N, R 4 E). Altitude 9087 feet. Named on Lassen Peak (1956) 15' quadrangle. The name commemorates J.S. Diller, who studied the geology of the Lassen Peak neighborhood (United States Board on Geographic Names, 1933, p. 265).

Mount Dome [SISKIYOU]: *peak,* 16 miles southeast of Dorris (lat. 41°48'35" N, long. 121°41'10" W; near E line sec. 24, T 46 N, R 2 E). Altitude 6518 feet. Named on Mount Dome (1950) 15' quadrangle. Called Dome Mtn. on Modoc Lava Bed (1892) 1° quadrangle. The feature was called Van Bremer's Peak in the early days—Van Bremer's ranch was at the west base of the peak (Murray, p. 104-105). Postal authorities established Mount Dome post office 18 miles southeast of Dorris near Mount Dome in 1910 and discontinued it in 1927 (Salley, p. 148).

Mount Eddy [SISKIYOU]: *peak,* 9 miles west of the town of Mount Shasta on Siskiyou-Trinity County line (lat. 41°19'10" N, long. 122°28'40" W; at N line sec. 18, T 40 N, R 5 W). Altitude 9025 feet. Named on Weed (1954) 15' quadrangle. Called Eddy Mt. on Shasta (1894) 1° quadrangle. The name commemorates Nelson Harvey Eddy, a pioneer of Shasta Valley (Stewart, C.L., p. 65).

Mount Emily [SISKIYOU]: *peak,* 13 miles north-northeast of Happy Camp (lat. 41°58'20" N, long. 123°16'30" W). Named on Figurehead Mountain (1980) 7.5' quadrangle.

Mount Hebron [SISKIYOU]:

(1) *peak,* 8.5 miles south of Macdoel (lat. 41°42'15" N, long. 122°01' W; sec. 36, T 45 N, R 2 W). Altitude 6143 feet. Named on The Whaleback (1954) 15' quadrangle. Called Hebron Mt. on O'Brien's (1947) map, but United States Board on Geographic Names (1978b, p. 4) rejected this name for the feature.

(2) *village,* 3 miles south of Macdoel (lat. 41°47'15" N, long. 122°00'10" W; sec. 32, T 46 N, R 1 W); the village is 8 miles east of Ball Mountain. Named on Dorris (1950) and Macdoel (1954) 15' quadrangles. Postal authorities established Mount Hebron post office in 1887, moved it 1 mile north in 1894, moved it 1.5 miles north in 1906, discontinued it for a time in 1918, discontinued it again in 1919, and reestablished it in 1921 (Salley, p. 148). They established Ball post office, named for H.S. Ball, pio-

neer rancher, in 1880, discontinued it in 1881, reestablished it with the name "Ball's Ranch" in 1888, discontinued it in 1894, reestablished it with the name "Ball" in 1894, and discontinued it in 1906, when they moved the service to Mount Hebron (Salley, p. 14).

Mount Hoffman [SISKIYOU]: *peak,* 3 miles northwest of Medicine Lake (lat. 41°36'45" N, long. 121°33'10" W; sec. 31, T 44 N, R 4 E). Altitude 7913 feet. Named on Medicine Lake (1952) 15' quadrangle.

Mount Hoffman: see **Little Mount Hoffman** [SISKIYOU].

Mount Hope [BUTTE]: *peak,* 5.25 miles northeast of Oroville Dam (lat. 39°36' N, long. 121°25'30" W; near SW cor. sec. 9, T 20 N, R 5 E). Named on Oroville Dam (1970) 7.5' quadrangle.

Mount Jackson: see **Mount Shasta** [SISKIYOU] (1).

Mount Lassen: see **Brokeoff Mountain** [SHASTA]; **Lassen Peak** [SHASTA].

Mount Linn [TEHAMA]: *peak,* 7.25 miles south-southwest of Tomhead Mountain (lat. 40°02'15" N, long. 122°51'10" W; near N line sec. 10, T 25 N, R 9 W). Altitude 8092 feet. Named on Yolla Bolly (1954) 15' quadrangle. The peak is one of the group called South Yolla Bolly Mountains. Fremont gave the name "Mount Linn" to a peak to honor Lewis F. Linn, a senator from Missouri who was involved in the acquisition of Oregon (Gudde, 1949, p. 188).

Mount Ratchel [BUTTE]: *peak,* 4 miles northeast of Oroville Dam (lat. 39°35'10" N, long. 121°26'15" W; near S line sec. 17, T 20 N, R 5 E). Altitude 1442 feet. Named on Oroville Dam (1970) 7.5' quadrangle.

Mount Saint Joseph: see **Lassen Peak** [SHASTA].

Mount Shasta [SISKIYOU]:

(1) *mountain,* 11 miles north-northwest of McCloud (lat. 41°24'35" N, long. 122°11'35" W). Named on Shasta (1954) 15' quadrangle. Called Mt. Shaste on Wilkes (1841) map, called Mt. Jackson on Farnham's (1845) map, called Shasta Butte on Williamson and Abbott's (1855) map, called Mt. Tsashtl on Fremont's (1848) map, called Mt. Shaste on Tanner's (1849) map, and called Shaste Pk. on Wilkes' (1849) map. Spanish soldiers named it Jesús María in 1817 (Hall, p. 252-253). Alexander Henry called it Shatasla in 1814, and Peter Skene Ogden gave it the name "Mt. Sastise" in 1827 (Hoover, Rensch, and Rensch, p. 498). Other names include Snowy Butte and Chasta Butte; the name "Shasta" itself had many forms in the early days, including Shastl, Shaste, Saste, Shasty, and Sastean·(Eichorn, p. 23).

(2) *town,* 8.5 miles south-southeast of Weed (lat. 41°18'45" N, long. 12218'30" W; mainly in sec. 16, T 40 N, R 4 W). Named on Weed (1954) 15' quadrangle. Shasta (1894) 1° quadrangle shows a place called Berryvale situated near the site of the present town of Mount Shasta, and Diller and others' (1915) map has the name "Sisson" at the site. Berryvale, and Strawberry Valley where it was situated, both were named for the abundance of wild strawberries found there (Gudde, 1969, p. 323). Postal authorities established Berryvale post office in 1870, moved it 1 mile east to the railroad in 1888 when they changed the name to Sisson, and changed the name to Mount Shasta in 1924; the name "Sisson" was for John H. Sisson, who donated land for the town (Salley, p. 20, 205). They had established another Mount Shasta post office in 1870 and discontinued it in 1888 (Salley, p. 148). The town of Mount Shasta incorporated in 1905. Postal authorities established Forestvale post office at a resort located 14 miles east of Mount Shasta post office in 1880 and discontinued in 1881 (Salley, p. 77).

Mount Shasta Silica Camp [SHASTA]: *locality,* 4 miles west of Burney Falls (lat. 41°00'55" N, long. 121°43'30" W; on S line sec. 34, T 37 N, R 2 E). Named on Bartle (1939) 30' quadrangle.

Mount Shasta Woods [SISKIYOU]: *settlement,* 16 miles south-southwest of Macdoel (lat. 41°35'45" N, long. 122°04'05" W; near S line sec. 3, T 43 N, R 2 W). Named on The Whaleback (1954) 15' quadrangle.

Mount Tsashtl: see **Mount Shasta** [SISKIYOU] (1).

Mowry Flat: see **French Town** [SISKIYOU].

Muck-a-Muck Creek [SISKIYOU]: *stream,* flows 1.5 miles to Klamath River 9.5 miles east-southeast of the village of Seiad Valley (lat. 41°46'30" N, long. 123°01'50" W; sec. 6, T 45 N, R 10 W). Named on Hamburg (1980) 7.5' quadrangle. Crawford (1896, p. 387) referred to Muck-a-Much Gulch.

Mud Creek [BUTTE]: *stream,* formed by the confluence of East Branch and Middle Branch, flows 21 miles to Big Chico Creek [BUTTE-TEHAMA] 5.5 miles west-southwest of Chico (lat. 39°42'25" N, long. 121°56'05" W). Named on Cohasset (1979), Nord (1951), Ord Ferry (1949), Paradise West (1980), and Richardson Springs (1951) 7.5' quadrangles. East Branch is 4 miles long and Middle Branch is 3 miles long; both branches are named on Cohasset (1979) 7.5' quadrangle. On Richardson Springs (1944) 15' quadrangle, present Cave Creek is shown as the upper part of Mud Creek, and present Mud Creek is called East Branch. West Branch enters less than 0.5 mile downstream from the confluence of East Fork and Middle Fork; it is 4.5 miles long and is named on Cohasset (1979) 7.5' quadrangle.

Mud Creek [SISKIYOU]:

(1) *stream,* flows 0.5 mile to Klamath River 2.5 miles east-northeast of Dillon Mountain (lat. 41°32'35" N, long. 123°31'45" W). Named on Dillon Mountain (1983) 7.5' quadrangle.

(2) *stream,* flows 17 miles to McCloud River [SHASTA-SISKIYOU] 5 miles east-southeast of McCloud (lat. 41°12'50" N, long. 122°03'45" W; sec. 22, T 39 N, R 2 W). Named on Shasta (1954) and Shoeinhorse Mountain (1954) 15' quadrangles. On Dunsmuir (1935) 30' quadrangle, the name "Mud Creek" follows a distributary, and present Mud Creek below the head of the distributary is called Elk Creek.

Mud Creek Glacier: see **Konwakiton Glacier** [SISKIYOU].

Muddy Gulch: see **Picayune Gulch** [SISKIYOU].

Muddy Spring Creek [SHASTA]: *stream,* flows 1 mile to Squaw Creek (2) nearly 5 miles south of Shoeinhorse Mountain (lat. 41°00' N, long. 122°03'10" W). Named on Shoeinhorse Mountain (1954) 15' quadrangle.

Mud Flat Campground [TEHAMA]: *locality,* 7.25 miles southwest of Paskenta (lat. 39°49'40" N, long. 122°39'25" W; near N line sec. 28, T 23 N, R 7 W). Named on Hall Ridge (1967) 7.5' quadrangle.

Mud Lake [SHASTA]:

(1) *dry lake,* 16 miles north-northeast of Lassen Peak (lat. 40°42'10" N, long. 121°24' W; sec. 27, T 33 N, R 5 E). Named on Prospect Peak (1957) 15' quadrangle.

(2) *lake,* 500 feet long, 10 miles north-northwest of Lassen Peak (lat. 40°37'45" N, long. 121°33'40" W; near NE cor. sec. 18, T 32 N, R 4 E). Named on Manzanita Lake (1956) 15' quadrangle.

Mud Lake [SISKIYOU]:

(1) *lake,* 200 feet long, 5.5 miles west-northwest of Sawyers Bar (lat. 41°20'10" N, long. 123°13'35" W). Named on Sawyers Bar (1979) 7.5 quadrangle.

(2) *lake,* 700 feet long, 6.25 miles south-southwest of Macdoel (lat. 41°45'05" N, long. 122°04'05" W; at E line sec. 16, T 45 N, R 2 W). Named on Macdoel (1954) 15' quadrangle.

(3) *intermittent lake,* 450 feet long, 4 miles west-southwest of Sawyers Bar (lat. 41°16'35" N, long. 123°11'55" W). Named on Sawyers Bar (1979) 7.5' quadrangle.

Mud Spring [SHASTA]: *spring,* 12.5 miles northeast of the village of Montgomery Creek (lat. 40°58'10" N, long. 121°45'40" W; sec. 21, T 36 N, R 2 E). Named on Montgomery Creek (1956) 15' quadrangle.

Mud Spring [SISKIYOU]:

(1) *spring,* 2 miles northeast of Condrey Mountain (lat. 41°57'30" N, long. 122°57'10" W; near N line sec. 1, T 47 N, R 10 W). Named on Condrey Mountain (1955) 15' quadrangle.

(2) *spring,* 4.25 miles north of Hornbrook (lat. 41°58'10" N, long. 122°33'30" W; sec. 32, T 48 N, R 6 W). Named on Hornbrook (1955) 15' quadrangle.

(3) *spring,* 8 miles south of Hornbrook (lat. 41°48' N, long. 122°33'40" W; at N line sec. 32, T 46 N, R 6 W). Named on Hornbrook (1955) 15' quadrangle.

(4) *spring,* 19 miles east of Bartle (lat. 41°16'20" N, long. 121°26'50" W; near E line sec. 25, T 40 N, R 4 E). Named on White Horse (1962) 15' quadrangle.

Mud Spring [TEHAMA]: *spring,* 11.5 miles east-northeast of Red Bluff along Flume Creek (lat. 40°13'10" N, long. 122°01'45" W; near W line sec. 6, T 27 N, R 1 W). Named on Tuscan Springs (1951) 7.5' quadrangle. Called Mud Springs on Red Bluff (1952) 15' quadrangle.

Mud Springs: see **Mud Spring** [TEHAMA]; **Richardson Springs** [BUTTE].

Mud Springs Plains [TEHAMA]: *area,* 12 miles east-northeast of Red Bluff (lat. 40°13'45" N, long. 122°01'15" W); the place is north of Mud Spring. Named on Panther Spring (1953) 15' quadrangle, and on Tuscan Springs (1951) 7.5' quadrangle.

Mud Swamp [SHASTA]: *marsh,* 5.5 miles north of Fall River Mills (lat. 41°05'45" N, long. 121°24'55" W). Named on Fall River Mills (1961) 15' quadrangle.

Mud Valley [TEHAMA]: *canyon,* drained by a stream that flows 1.5 miles to South Fork Cottonwood Creek [SHASTA-TEHAMA] 4 miles northeast of Wakefield Flat (lat. 40°09'35" N, long. 122°34'40" W; near SE cor. sec. 30, T 27 N, R 6 W). Named on Oxbow Bridge (1967) 7.5' quadrangle.

Mugginsville [SISKIYOU]: *village,* 6.25 miles west-southwest of Fort Jones (lat. 41°34'25" N, long. 122°57' W; near SW cor. sec. 13, T 43 N, R 10 W); the village is near the south end of Quartz Valley. Named on Fort Jones (1955) 15' quadrangle. Bancroft (p. 367) used the designation "Mugginsville, or Quartz Valley." Postal authorities established Quartz Valley post office 12 miles west of Fort Jones in 1861 and discontinued it in 1862 (Salley, p. 179).

Mugginsville: see **Bloomer Hill** [BUTTE].

Muir Butte: see **Black Butte** [SISKIYOU] (1).

Mulberry: see **Chico** [BUTTE].

Mule Bridge Campground [SISKIYOU]: *locality,* 5 miles northeast of Sawyers Bar along North Fork Salmon River (lat. 41°21'25" N, long. 123°04'25" W). Named on Tanners Peak (1977) 7.5' quadrangle.

Mule Canyon [GLENN]: *canyon,* drained by a stream that flows 2 miles to North Fork (1) Stony Creek [GLENN-TEHAMA] 3 miles east of Saint John Mountain (lat. 39°26'35" N, long. 122°38'15" W). Named on Saint John Mountain (1968) 7.5' quadrangle.

Mule Creek [SISKIYOU]: *stream,* flows 3 miles to East Fork Scott River

12.5 miles southeast of Etna (lat. 41°18'15" N, long. 122°44'50" W; sec. 23, T 40 N, R 8 W). Named on China Mountain (1955) 15' quadrangle.

Mule Mountain [SHASTA]: *peak,* 3.5 miles north-northeast of Igo (lat. 40°33'10" N, long. 122°30'50" W; sec. 11, T 31 N, R 6 W). Altitude 2325 feet. Named on Igo (1979) 7.5' quadrangle.

Mule Pocket [SISKIYOU]: *relief feature,* 3.25 miles south-southeast of Ukonom Lake (lat. 41°32' N, long. 123°20'15" W). Named on Ukonom Lake (1980) 7.5' quadrangle.

Mule Shoe [SHASTA]: *locality,* nearly 7 miles west of Shoeinhorse Mountain (lat. 40°03'50" N, long. 122°11'50" W; sec. 15, T 37 N, R 3 W). Named on Shoeinhorse Mountain (1954) 15' quadrangle.

Muletown [SHASTA]: *locality,* 2.5 miles north-northeast of Igo (lat. 40°32'15" N, long. 122°31'30" W). Named on Red Bluff (1894) 1° quadrangle. The place originally was called One Mule Town (Gudde, 1975, p. 231).

Mullen: see **Turkey Mullen Gulch** [TEHAMA].

Mullen Gulch [TEHAMA]: *canyon,* drained by a stream that flows 2.5 miles to Cold Fork (1) 3.5 miles north of Tomhead Mountain (lat. 40°11'20" N, long. 122°49'05" W; near W line sec. 18, T 27 N, R 8 W). Named on Yolla Bolly (1954) 15' quadrangle.

Mullens Camp [SISKIYOU]: *locality,* nearly 1 mile southeast of Salmon Mountain (lat. 41°10'40" N, long. 123°23'45" W). Named on Salmon Mountain (1978) 7.5' quadrangle.

Munroeville [GLENN]: *locality,* 15 miles north of Butte City near the mouth of Stony Creek [GLENN-TEHAMA] (lat. 39°40'35" N, long. 121°59'20" W); the place is 1.5 miles west-southwest of Phelan Island. Named on Chico Landing (1912) 7.5' quadrangle, which has the name "Munroeville Island" for present Phelan Island. Postal authorities established Monroeville post office before 1853 at the mouth of Stony Creek [GLENN-TEHAMA] and discontinued it in 1862 (Salley, p. 144). U.P. Monroe had a ranch and hotel at the place after the discovery of gold in 1848; Monroeville was the county seat of Colusa County from 1851 until 1853—this was before organization of Glenn County (Hoover, Rensch, and Rensch, p. 96-97).

Munroeville Island: see **Phelan Island** [GLENN].

Munson Mill [SISKIYOU]: *locality,* 6 miles south of Etna along French Creek (2) (lat. 41°22'20" N, long. 122°53'45" W; near W line sec. 28, T 41 N, R 9 W). Named on Etna (1934) 30' quadrangle.

Murderers Bar [SISKIYOU]: *locality,* 9.5 miles north-northwest of Forks of Salmon along Salmon River (lat. 41°22'30" N, long. 123°25' W). Named on Orleans Mountain (1974) and Somes Bar (1979) 7.5' quadrangles. Indians killed three white men at the place (Gudde, 1949, p. 229).

Murderer's Bar: see **Happy Camp** [SISKIYOU].

Murderers Gulch [SHASTA]: *canyon,* drained by a stream that flows nearly 0.5 mile to Whiskeytown Lake 5.5 miles southeast of the village of French Gulch (lat. 40°38'30" N, long. 122°34'10" W; sec. 8, T 32 N, R 6 W). Named on Whiskeytown (1979) 7.5' quadrangle.

Murderers Gulch [SISKIYOU]: *canyon,* drained by a stream that flows nearly 2 miles to North Fork Salmon River 2 miles northeast of Forks of Salmon (lat. 41°16'25" N, long. 123°17'20" W). Named on Forks of Salmon (1978) 7.5' quadrangle. The name is from Murderers Bar (Gudde, 1949, p. 229).

Murken Bench [SHASTA]: *relief feature,* 6.25 miles southwest of Coble Mountain (lat. 40°49'45" N, long. 121°26'30" W). Named on Jellico (1957) 15' quadrangle.

Murken Lake [SHASTA]: *intermittent lake,* 1600 feet long, 6 miles west-southwest of Coble Mountain (lat. 40°50'50" N, long. 121°27'10" W; near SE cor. sec. 31, T 35 N, R 5 E); the feature is at the northwest end of Murken Bench. Named on Jellico (1957) 15' quadrangle.

Murphy Canyon [SHASTA]: *canyon,* drained by a stream that flows 0.5 mile to Shasta Lake 13 miles south of Bollibokka Mountain (lat. 40°45'15" N, long. 122°10' W; near SE cor. sec. 35, T 34 N, R 3 W). Named on Bollibokka Mountain (1957) 15' quadrangle.

Murphy Canyon [TEHAMA]: *canyon,* drained by a stream that flows 4 miles to Thomes Creek 4.5 miles south of Ball Mountain (lat. 39°52'10" N, long. 122°46'25" W; near NE cor. sec. 8, T 23 N, R 8 W). Named on Ball Mountain (1967) and Log Spring (1967) 7.5' quadrangles.

Murphy Glades [TEHAMA]: *area,* 7 miles west-northwest of Tomhead Mountain (lat. 40°11'15" N, long. 122°55'45" W; at W line sec. 18, T 27 N, R 9 W). Named on Yolla Bolly (1954) 15' quadrangle.

Murphy Gulch [SISKIYOU]: *canyon,* drained by a stream that flows 3.5 miles to Black Bear Creek 6.5 miles north-northwest of Cecilville (lat. 41°13'50" N, long. 123°11'10" W). Named on Cecilville (1979) 7.5' quadrangle.

Murphy Rock [SISKIYOU]: *peak,* 4.25 miles north of Cecilville (lat. 41°12'20" N, long. 123°09'10" W). Altitude 5350 feet. Named on Cecilville (1979) 7.5' quadrangle.

Murphy Slough [BUTTE]: *water feature,* abandoned bend of Sacramento River 8 miles west-southwest of Chico (lat. 39°40' N, long. 121°57'55" W). Named on Ord Ferry (1949) 7.5' quadrangle.

Murphy Well [SISKIYOU]: *well,* 11.5 miles south-southwest of Macdoel (lat. 41°40'15" N, long. 122°05'15" W; sec. 9, T 44 N, R 2 W). Named on The Whaleback (1954) 15' quadrangle.

Muse Meadow [SISKIYOU]: *area,* 12 miles south-southwest of Scott Bar (lat. 41°35'10" N, long. 123°06'20" W). Named on Boulder Peak (1981) 7.5' quadrangle.

Museum Canyon [SHASTA]: *canyon,* drained by a stream that flows 0.5 mile to Squaw Creek Arm Shasta Lake 10.5 miles south-southeast of Bollibokka Mountain (lat. 40°47'20" N, long. 122°09'45" W; near W line sec. 24, T 34 N, R 3 W). Named on Bollibokka Mountain (1957) 15' quadrangle.

Mushroom Rock [SHASTA]: *peak,* 11 miles north-northeast of the village of Big Bend (lat. 41°10'30" N, long. 121°51'05" W; near E line sec. 33, T 39 N, R 1 E). Named on Big Bend (1961) 15' quadrangle.

Music Creek [SISKIYOU]: *stream,* flows 3.25 miles to South Russian Creek 6.25 miles east-northeast of Sawyers Bar (lat. 41°19'25" N, long. 123°00'50" W). Named on Etna (1955) 15' quadrangle, and on Tanners Peak (1977) 7.5' quadrangle.

Muskgrave Creek [SISKIYOU]: *stream,* flows 3.5 miles to Butte Valley 6.5 miles west of Macdoel (lat. 41°50'40" N, long. 122°07'30" W; sec. 8, T 46 N, R 2 W). Named on Macdoel (1954) 15' quadrangle.

Musselbeck Reservoir: see **Rainbow Lake** [SHASTA] (1).

Musselmans: see **Coutolenc** [BUTTE].

Musty Buck Ridge [BUTTE]: *ridge,* south-trending, 13 miles long, center 9 miles north-northwest of Paradise (lat. 39°52' N, long. 121°43'15" W). Named on Cohasset (1979) and Paradise West (1980) 7.5' quadrangles.

Mutton Gulch [SISKIYOU]: *canyon,* drained by a stream that flows 2 miles to Shasta Valley 10 miles south of Hornbrook (lat. 41°46'15" N, long. 122°33'10" W; at SW cor. sec. 4, T 45 N, R 6 W). Named on Hornbrook (1955) 15' quadrangle.

Myer [SHASTA]: *locality,* about 8 miles north of Millville (lat. 40°39'45" N, long. 122°12' W). Named on Red Bluff (1894) 1° quadrangle.

Myrtle Gulch [SISKIYOU]: *canyon,* drained by a stream that flows less than 2 miles to Beaver Creek (1) 7.5 miles east of Condrey Mountain (lat. 41°55' N, long. 122°50'10" W; at S line sec. 13, T 47 N, R 9 W). Named on Condrey Mountain (1955) 15' quadrangle.

—N—

Nabar: see **Soda Springs** [SISKIYOU] (3).

Nabob Ridge [SISKIYOU]: *ridge,* north- to northwest-trending, 3 miles long, 10.5 miles north-northeast of the village of Seiad Valley (lat. 41°58'45" N, long. 123°05'50" W). Named on Dutch Creek (1980) 7.5' quadrangle.

Nance Canyon [BUTTE]: *canyon,* drained by a stream that flows 8 miles to lowlands 8.5 miles southwest of Paradise (lat. 39°40' N, long. 121°44'30" W). Named on Hamlin Canyon (1951) 7.5' quadrangle.

Nanny Creek [TEHAMA]: *stream,* flows 4.25 mile to join Summit Creek and form South Fork Battle Creek [SHASTA-TEHAMA] 1.5 miles east-northeast of Mineral (lat. 40°21'15" N, long. 121°34'15" W; near SW cor. sec. 20, T 29 N, R 4 E). Named on Lassen Peak (1956) 15' quadrangle.

Narrows: see **The Narrows** [BUTTE]; **The Narrows** [TEHAMA].

Natchez Creek [BUTTE]: *stream,* flows 5.5 miles, partly in Yuba County, to South Honcut Creek 4.5 miles northeast of Bangor (lat. 39°25'45" N, long. 121°20' W; near E line sec. 7, T 18 N, R 6 E); Butte-Yuba County line follows lower reaches of the stream. Named on Rackerby (1948) 7.5' quadrangle.

Natuket Creek [SISKIYOU]: *stream,* flows nearly 3 miles to Klamath River 7.25 miles north-northeast of Orleans, which is in Humboldt County (lat. 41°24'05" N, long. 123°30'10" W). Named on Bark Shanty Gulch (1974) 7.5' quadrangle.

Nawtawaket Creek [SHASTA]: *stream,* flows nearly 4 miles to McCloud River [SHASTA-SISKIYOU] nearly 2 miles north-northwest of Bollibokka Mountain (lat. 40°57' N, long. 122°14'15" W; sec. 29, T 36 N, R 3 W). Named on Bollibokka Mountain (1957) and Lamoine (1957) 15' quadrangles. The name is of Indian origin (Steger, p. 49).

Nawtawaket Mountain [SHASTA]: *peak,* 3.25 miles north-northwest of Bollibokka Mountain (lat. 40°58'40" N, long. 122°14'05" W; sec. 17, T 36 N, R 3 W). Altitude 4551 feet. Named on Bollibokka Mountain (1957) 15' quadrangle.

Neal: see **Tom Neal Creek** [SHASTA].

Neals Diggings: see **Oroville** [BUTTE].

Negro Camp [SHASTA]: *locality,* 4.5 miles south of Coble Mountain (lat. 40°44'10" N, long. 121°20'15" W; at SW cor. sec. 8, T 34 N, R 6 E). Named on Jellico (1957) 15' quadrangle. Halls Flat (1939) 30' quadrangle has the name "Nigger Cabin" at the place.

Negro Camp Gulch [SHASTA]: *canyon,* drained by a stream that heads in Lassen County and flows 3 miles to an unnamed stream 2.5 miles south of Coble Mountain in Shasta County (lat. 40°50'50" N, long. 121°21'20" W; at SW cor. sec. 31, T 35 N, R 6 E). Named on Jellico (1957) 15' quadrangle. Called Nigger Camp Gulch on Halls Flat (1939) 30' quadrangle.

Negro Creek [SISKIYOU]:

(1) *stream,* flows 3.5 miles to North Fork Salmon River 8.5 miles east-

northeast of Salmon Mountain (lat. 41°14'20" N, long. 123°16'05" W). Named on Forks of Salmon (1978), Sawyers Bar (1979), and Youngs Peak (1979) 7.5' quadrangles. Called Nigger Cr. on Averill's (1935) map, and called Henry Bell Cr. on Sawyers Bar (1923) 30' quadrangle, which shows Niggerville Creek nearby in present Henry Bell Gulch. Gudde (1975, p. 235-236) listed a mining place called Negro Flat that was located at the mouth of Negro Creek.

(2) *stream,* flows 2.5 miles to Klamath River 5.5 miles east-southeast of the village of Seiad Valley (lat. 41°48'25" N, long. 123°05'45" W). Named on Hamburg (1980) 7.5' quadrangle. Called Nigger Cr. on Seiad (1922) 30' quadrangle.

Negro Creek Canyon [SISKIYOU]: *canyon,* drained by a stream that flows 3.5 miles to Shovel Creek 13 miles northwest of Macdoel (lat. 41°58' N, long. 122°11'30" W; at N line sec. 34, T 48 N, R 3 W). Named on Macdoel (1954) 15' quadrangle. The stream in the canyon is called Nigger Cr. on Averill's (1935) map.

Negro Flat: see **Negro Creek** [SISKIYOU] (1).

Negro Gulch [BUTTE-TEHAMA]: *canyon,* drained by a stream that heads in Tehama County and flows 1.5 miles to Rock Creek [BUTTE-TEHAMA] 6.25 miles south of Campbell Mound in Butte County (lat. 39°53'05" N, long. 121°47'55" W; near N line sec. 6, T 23 N, R 2 E). Named on Campbell Mound (1952) 7.5' quadrangle. Called Nigger Gulch on Richardson Springs (1944) 15' quadrangle, and United States Board on Geographic Names (1970b, p. 2) gave this name as a variant.

Negro Gulch [SISKIYOU]: *canyon,* drained by a stream that flows nearly 2 miles to Rail Creek 13 miles east-southeast of Etna (lat. 41°22'50" N, long. 122°40'05" W; near SW cor. sec. 21, T 41 N, R 7 W). Named on China Mountain (1955) 15' quadrangle.

Negro Sam Slough [GLENN]: *water feature,* 15 miles north of Butte City in a cutoff meander of Sacramento River at the north border of Phelan Island (lat. 39°41'25" N, long. 121°57'50" W). Named on Ord Ferry (1949) 7.5' quadrangle.

Negro Spring [TEHAMA]: *spring,* nearly 5 miles south of Campbell Mound (lat. 39°54'15" N, long. 121°48'45" W; sec. 25, T 24 N, R 1 E); the feature is near the head of Negro Gulch [BUTTE-TEHAMA]. Named on Campbell Mound (1952) 7.5' quadrangle. Called Nigger Spring on Richardson Springs (1944) 15' quadrangle, and United States Board on Geographic Names (1970b, p. 2) gave this name as a variant.

Neil: see **Tom Neil Creek**, under **Slate Creek** [SHASTA] (1), **North Fork**.

Nellie Gray Gulch [SISKIYOU]: *canyon,* drained by a stream that flows 0.5 mile to McAdam Creek 7 miles north of Fort Jones (lat. 41°42'20" N, long. 122°48'50" W; sec. 31, T 45 N, R 8 W). Named on Fort Jones (1955) 15' quadrangle.

Nelson [BUTTE]: *village,* 6.5 miles south-southeast of Durham (lat. 39°33'10" N, long. 121°47'50" W). Named on Nelson (1948) 7.5' quadrangle. Postal authorities established Nelson post office in 1873 (Frickstad, p. 11). Officials of California and Oregon Railroad Company had the place laid out in 1873 and named it for A.D. Nelson, an early settler (Wells and Chambers, p. 249).

Nelson Bar [BUTTE]: *locality,* 5.25 miles southeast of Paradise along West Branch Feather River (lat. 39°41'45" N, long. 121°33'40" W; sec. 7, T 21 N, R 4 E). Named on Oroville (1942) 15' quadrangle. Water of Lake Oroville now covers the site. F.D. Dunn (p. 80) listed a place called Oregon Bar that was located along West Branch Feather River a short way below Nelson Bar.

Nelson Creek [SHASTA]:

(1) *stream,* flows 7.5 miles to Pit River at the village of Big Bend (lat. 41°01'20" N, long. 121°54'10" W; sec. 31, T 37 N, R 1 E). Named on Big Bend (1961) 15' quadrangle. East Fork enters from the east 2 miles upstream from the mouth of the main creek; it is 5.5 miles long and is named on Big Bend (1961) 15' quadrangle.

(2) *stream,* flows 1.5 miles to Salt Creek Inlet 10 miles south-southeast of Lamoine (lat. 40°51'10" N, long. 122°20'45" W; at S line sec. 29, T 35 N, R 4 W). Named on Lamoine (1957) 15' quadrangle.

(3) *stream,* flows 2.25 miles to Churn Creek 1.5 miles south-southeast of Summit City (lat. 40°39'50" N, long. 122°23'10" W; near N line sec. 1, T 32 N, R 5 W). Named on Shasta Dam (1956) 7.5' quadrangle.

Nelson Creek [TEHAMA]: *stream,* flows 2.25 miles to Dry Creek (1) about 1.5 miles east of Beegum Peak (lat. 40°19'10" N, long. 122°51'20" W; sec. 35, T 29 N, R 9 W). Named on Chanchelulla Peak (1951) 15' quadrangle.

Nelson Creek Slides [SHASTA]: *relief feature,* 6.5 miles northeast of Big Bend along upper reaches of Nelson Creek (1) (lat. 41°05'15" N, long. 121°49' W). Named on Big Bend (1961) 15' quadrangle.

Nelson Flat [SHASTA]: *area,* 4.25 miles west of the village of Big Bend along Cedar Salt Log Creek (lat. 41°01'50" N, long. 121°59'15" W; at E line sec. 29, T 37 N, R 1 W). Named on Big Bend (1961) 15' quadrangle.

Nelson Ravine [BUTTE]:

(1) *canyon,* drained by a stream that flows 3 miles to West Branch Butte Creek [BUTTE-GLENN] 14 miles north of Paradise (lat. 39°58' N, long. 121°37'55" W; sec. 3, T 24 N, R 3 E). Named on Cohasset (1979) 7.5' quadrangle. The stream in the canyon is called Campbell Creek on Chico (1895) 30' quadrangle.

(2) *canyon,* drained by a stream that flows 1.5 miles to South Honcut Creek 2.25 miles south-southeast of Bangor (lat. 39°21'50" N, long. 121°22'50" W; sec. 2, T 17 N, R 5 E). Named on Bangor (1947) and Loma Rica (1947) 7.5' quadrangle.

Nelsons Crossing [BUTTE]: *locality,* 9.5 miles north-northwest of Clipper Mills along Fall Creek (lat. 39°39'50" N, long. 121°12'55" W; sec. 20, T 21 N, R 7 E). Named on Cascade (1948) 7.5' quadrangle.

Nevada Bottom [TEHAMA]: *valley,* 3.5 miles north of Paskenta (lat. 39°56'10" N, long. 122°32'30" W; sec. 15, 16, T 24 N, R 6 W); the valley is along Nevada Creek. Named on Paskenta (1967) 7.5' quadrangle.

Nevada Creek [TEHAMA]: *stream,* flows 4.5 miles to McCarty Creek (2) 3 miles north-northeast of Paskenta (lat. 39°55'05" N, long. 122°30'40" W; near SW cor. sec. 23, T 24 N, R 6 W). Named on Paskenta (1967) 7.5' quadrangle.

Neversweat Gulch [SISKIYOU]: *canyon,* drained by a stream that flows 0.5 mile to McAdam Creek 3.5 miles north of Fort Jones (lat. 41°39'20" N, long. 122°50'05" W; near NW cor. sec. 24, T 44 N, R 9 W). Named on Fort Jones (1955) 15' quadrangle.

New Barn Gulch [SISKIYOU]: *canyon,* drained by a stream that flows 1.5 miles to Mill Creek (5) 12 miles northwest of Fort Jones (lat. 41°44'35" N, long. 122°58'30" W; at S line sec. 15, T 45 N, R 10 W). Named on Condrey Mountain (1955) and Fort Jones (1955) 15' quadrangles.

New Blinzig [BUTTE]: *locality,* 5.25 miles north of the village Berry Creek along Western Pacific Railroad (lat. 39°43'10" N, long. 121°25'10" W; sec. 33, T 22 N, R 5 E); the place is less than 1 mile northwest of Blinzig. Named on Berry Creek (1970) 7.5' quadrangle.

New Creek [TEHAMA]: *stream,* diverges from Antelope Creek and flows 3 miles to Salt Creek (2) 4 miles east-southeast of Red Bluff (lat. 40°09'25" N, long. 122°09'50" W). Named on Red Bluff East (1951) 7.5' quadrangle.

New Gulch [SHASTA]: *canyon,* drained by a stream that flows 2 miles to Beegum Creek [SHASTA-TEHAMA] 3.5 miles south of Arbuckle Mountain (lat. 40°20'50" N, long. 122°51'45"W; sec. 22, T 29 N, R 9 W). Named on Chanchelulla Peak (1951) 15' quadrangle.

Newhard Landing [BUTTE]: *locality,* 13 miles southwest of Durham along Sacramento River (lat. 39°31'50" N, long. 121°59'05" W). Named on Newhard (1912) 7.5' quadrangle. On Llano Seco (1948) 7.5' quadrangle, the site is shown on or near Butte-Glenn County line.

New Philadelphia: see **Thompson Flat** [BUTTE].

Newtown [SHASTA]: *locality,* 2 miles south of Summit City (lat. 40°39'25" N, long. 122°23'50" W; sec. 2, T 32 N, R 5 W). Named on Shasta Dam (1956) 7.5' quadrangle.

Newtown Creek [SHASTA]: *stream,* flows nearly 4 miles to Churn Creek 3 miles south of the town of Central Valley (lat. 40°38'20" N, long. 122°22' W; sec. 7, T 32 N, R 4 W); the stream goes past Newtown. Named on Project City (1957) and Shasta Dam (1956) 7.5' quadrangles.

Newville [GLENN]: *village,* 18 miles west of Orland (lat. 39°47'35" N, long. 122°31'35" W; sec. 3, T 22 N, R 6 W). Named on Newville (1967) 7.5' quadrangle. Postal authorities established Newville post office in 1868 and discontinued it in 1918 (Frickstad, p. 40).

New York Gulch [SHASTA]: *canyon,* drained by a stream that flows 1.5 miles to Whiskeytown Lake 5 miles southeast of the village of French Gulch (lat. 40°38'45" N, long. 122°34'35" W; near W line sec. 8, T 32 N, R 6 W). Named on Whiskeytown (1979) 7.5' quadrangle.

New York Gulch [SISKIYOU]: *canyon,* drained by a stream that flows about 1 mile to Indian Creek (3) 5.25 miles north of Fort Jones (lat. 41°41'05" N, long. 122°51'05" W; near N line sec. 11, T 44 N, R 9 W). Named on Fort Jones (1955) 15' quadrangle.

Ney Springs [SISKIYOU]: *locality,* 4 miles south-southwest of the town of Mount Shasta (lat. 41°15'35" N, long. 122°20' W; at N line sec. 9, T 39 N, R 4 W). Site named on Weed (1954) 15' quadrangle. John Ney discovered the springs in 1887 and established a small resort there (Waring, p. 264).

Ney Springs Creek [SISKIYOU]: *stream,* flows 5.5 miles to Sacramento River 3.25 miles south of the town of Mount Shasta (lat. 41°16' N, long. 122°18'50" W; sec. 33, T 40 N, R 4 W); the stream heads at Little Castle Lake and goes past the site of Ney Springs. Named on Dunsmuir (1954) and Weed (1954) 15' quadrangles. Waring (p. 264) called the feature Little Castle Lake Creek.

Nicklwaite Creek [SISKIYOU]: *stream,* flows 2 miles to Beaver Creek (1) 12 miles east-northeast of Condrey Mountain (lat. 41°58'30" N, long. 122°45'20" W; near S line sec. 27, T 48 N, R 8 W). Named on Condrey Mountain (1955) and Hornbrook (1955) 15' quadrangles.

Nielon Gulch [SISKIYOU]: *canyon,* drained by a stream that flows nearly 1 mile to Jackass Gulch 2.25 miles north of Sawyers Bar (lat. 41°19'55" N, long. 123°07'45" W). Named on Sawyers Bar (1979) and Tanners Peak (1977) 7.5' quadrangles.

Nigger Camp Gulch: see **Negro Camp Gulch** [SHASTA].

Nigger Creek: see **Negro Creek** [SISKIYOU] (1); **Negro Creek** [SISKIYOU] (2); **Negro Creek Canyon** [SISKIYOU].

Nigger Gulch: see **Negro Gulch** [BUTTE-TEHAMA].

Nigger Hole Butte [SISKIYOU]: *relief feature,* 7.5 miles north of Medicine Lake (lat. 41°41'25" N, long. 121°37'30" W; near NE cor. sec. 4, T 44 N, R 3 E). Named on Medicine Lake (1952) 15' quadrangle.

Nigger Spring: see **Negro Spring** [TEHAMA].

Niggerville Creek: see **Henry Bell Gulch** [SISKIYOU].

Niles Canyon [SHASTA]: *canyon,* drained by a stream that flows nearly 4 miles to lowlands along Sacramento River 4 miles north-northeast of Olinda (lat. 40°29'45" N, long. 122°22'55" W). Named on Olinda (1964) 7.5' quadrangle.

Nimshew [BUTTE]: *village,* 5.5 miles north of Paradise (lat. 39°50'30" N, long. 121°37'10" W; at N line sec. 22, T 23 N, R 3 E); the village is near the north end of Nimshew Ridge. Named on Paradise East (1980) 7.5' quadrangle. Postal authorities established Nimshew post office in 1880 and discontinued it in 1923 (Frickstad, p. 11). The name is of Indian origin (Kroeber, p. 50).

Nimshew Ridge [BUTTE]: *ridge,* south-trending, 3.5 miles long, center 4.5 miles north of Paradise (lat. 39°49'30" N, long. 121°37'20" W); Nimshew is near the north end of the ridge. Named on Paradise East (1980) and Paradise West (1980) 7.5' quadrangles.

Nine Buck Butte [SISKIYOU]: *peak,* 16 miles north of Bartle (lat. 41°29'10" N, long. 121°47'30" W; at NW cor. sec. 18, T 42 N, R 2 E). Named on Bartle (1961) 15' quadrangle.

Ninemile [TEHAMA]: *locality,* 3 miles east-southeast of Hooker (lat. 40°17'10" N, long. 122°16'35" W; near NE cor. sec. 14, T 28 N, R 4 W). Named on Anderson (1947) 15' quadrangle. Red Bluff (1894) 1° quadrangle shows Nine Mile House at the site.

Ninemile Creek [TEHAMA]: *stream,* flows 4 miles to Big Chico Creek [BUTTE-TEHAMA] 5.25 miles south-southeast of Polk Springs (lat. 40°02'45" N, long. 121°38'10" W; near NE cor. sec. 9, T 25 N, R 3 E). Named on Butte Meadows (1958) 15' quadrangle.

Nine Mile House: see **Ninemile** [TEHAMA].

Nitwit Camp [SISKIYOU]: *locality,* 5.25 miles west of Bartle (lat. 41°15'55" N, long. 121°55'05" W; near SW cor. sec. 36, T 40 N, R 1 W). Named on Bartle (1961) 15' quadrangle.

Nob Gulch [SHASTA]: *canyon,* drained by a stream that flows 0.5 mile to Mad Ox Gulch 4.25 miles east-southeast of the village of French Gulch (lat. 40°40'55" N, long. 122°33'35" W; near SE cor. sec. 29, T 33 N, R 6 W). Named on Whiskeytown (1979) 7.5' quadrangle.

Noble Pass [SHASTA]: *pass,* nearly 5 miles north-northwest of Lassen Peak (lat. 40°33' N, long. 121°32'45" W; sec. 8, T 31 N, R 4 E). Named on Manzanita Lake (1956) 15' quadrangle, which shows the pass along the old emigrant trail. United States Board on Geographic Names (1967a, p. 9) approved the form "Nobles Pass" for the name, and pointed out that the feature is named for William H. Nobles, who pioneered the road through the pass in 1852.

Noble Ridge [SHASTA]: *ridge,* generally east-trending, 7 miles long, 7 miles southwest of Arbuckle Mountain (lat. 40°20'10" N, long. 122°56'45" W). Named on Chanchelulla Peak (1951) and Dubakella Mountain (1954) 15' quadrangles.

Nobles Pass: see **Noble Pass** [SHASTA].

Noel Spring [GLENN]: *spring,* 8.5 miles southwest of the village of Elk Creek (lat. 39°31'40" N, long. 122°39'55" W; sec. 5, T 19 N, R 7 W). Named on Felkner Hill (1968) 7.5' quadrangle.

Noel Spring Ridge [GLENN]: *ridge,* east-southeast-trending, 3.5 miles long, 7.5 miles southwest of the village of Elk Creek (lat. 39°31'30" N, long. 122°38' W). Named on Elk Creek (1968) and Felkner Hill (1968) 7.5' quadrangles.

Noland Gulch [SISKIYOU]: *canyon,* 0.5 mile long, 16 miles south of Etna (lat. 41°13'35" N, long. 122°52'20" W; on W line sec. 23, T 39 N, R 9 W). Named on Coffee Creek (1955) 15' quadrangle.

Nolton [SISKIYOU]: *locality,* 6 miles northeast of Happy Camp along Klamath River at the mouth of Thompson Creek (lat. 41°51'45" N, long. 123°18'35" W). Site named on Slater Butte (1980) 7.5' quadrangle. Postal authorities established Nolton post office in 1896 and discontinued it in 1912; the name was for the operator of a trading post for nearby placer mines (Salley, p. 155).

Nolton Creek [BUTTE]: *stream,* flows 1 mile to North Fork Feather River 5.5 miles north-northwest of the village of Berry Creek (lat. 39°42'50" N, long. 121°27'40" W; near S line sec. 31, T 22 N, R 5 E). Named on Berry Creek (1970) 7.5' quadrangle. Wells and Chambers' (1882) map shows a place called Huffs Bar situated along North Fork Feather River at the mouth of present Nolton Creek.

No Mans Creek [SISKIYOU]: *stream,* flows 1.25 miles to Clear Creek (1) 3.5 miles northeast of Bear Peak (lat. 41°43'50" N, long. 123°31'55" W). Named on Bear Peak (1982) 7.5' quadrangle.

No Name Creek [SISKIYOU]: *stream,* flows 1 mile to Grider Creek 3 miles south-southwest of the village of Seiad Valley (lat. 41°48'20" N, long. 123°13'10" W; sec. 27, T 46 N, R 12 W). Named on Seiad Valley (1980) 7.5' quadrangle.

Nora Lake [SHASTA]: *lake,* 700 feet long, nearly 2 miles east-southeast of Shingletown (lat. 40°28'40" N, long. 121°51'40" W; near SE cor. sec. 4, T 30 N, R 1 E). Named on Manton (1956) 15' quadrangle. The name commemorates the daughter of H.H. Noble of Shasta County Power Company (Steger, p. 49).

Nord [BUTTE]: *village,* 7.5 miles west-northwest of Chico (lat. 39°46'45" N, long. 121°57'20" W; on E line sec. 10, T 22 N, R 1 W). Named on Nord (1951) 7.5' quadrangle. Postal authorities established Nord post office in 1871, discontinued it in 1919, reestablished it in 1920, and discontinued it in 1933 (Frickstad, p. 11). G.W. Colby moved to the site from Colby's Landing and laid out the community in 1871 (Wells and Chambers, p. 245-246). California Mining Bureau's (1917c) map shows a place called Pond located about halfway between Chico and Nord along the railroad, and California Division of Highways' (1934) map shows a place called Gimbal situated along Southern Pacific Railroad 2 miles south-southeast of Nord.

Nordheimer Creek [SISKIYOU]: *stream,* flows 11 miles to Salmon River 3.25 miles northwest of Forks of Salmon (lat. 41°17'50" N, long. 123°21'30" W); Nordheimer Flat is at the mouth of the stream. Named on Forks of Salmon (1978), Orleans Mountain (1974), Salmon Mountain (1978), and Youngs Peak (1979) 7.5' quadrangles. The name commemorates a prospector who lived in the neighborhood in the 1930's (Gudde, 1949, p. 238).

Nordheimer Flat [SISKIYOU]: *area,* 3.5 miles northwest of Forks of Salmon (lat. 41°17'55" N, long. 123°21'40" W); the feature is at the mouth of Nordheimer Creek. Named on Forks of Salmon (1978) 7.5' quadrangle. Daggett (1957a, p. 2) mentioned a place called Olivers Flat that was situated at the mouth of Nordheimer Creek.

Nordheimer Lake [SISKIYOU]: *intermittent lake,* 100 feet long, 1 mile north of Salmon Mountain (lat. 41°12' N, long. 123°24'50" W); the feature is at the head of a branch of Nordheimer Creek. Named on Salmon Mountain (1978) 7.5' quadrangle.

Norman [GLENN]: *locality,* 8 miles south of Willows along Southern Pacific Railroad (lat. 39°24'30" N, long. 122°11'30" W; at SW cor. sec. 15, T 18 N, R 3 W). Named on Logandale (1952) 7.5' quadrangle. Postal authorities established Norman post office in 1879, discontinued it in 1889, reestablished it in 1890, and discontinued it in 1914 (Frickstad, p. 40).

North Battle Creek Reservoir [SHASTA]: *lake,* 3500 feet long, behind a dam on North Fork Battle Creek [SHASTA-TEHAMA] 11 miles northwest of Lassen Peak (lat. 40°36'10" N, long. 121°39'15" W; near SE cor. sec. 20, T 32 N, R 3 E). Named on Manzanita Lake (1956) 15' quadrangle.

North Bidwell Hill [BUTTE]: *peak,* 3.25 miles east-northeast of Oroville Dam (lat. 39°33'25" N, long. 121°25'45" W; near SE cor. sec. 29, T 20 N, R 5 E); the peak is 1.25 miles north-northwest of South Bidwell Hill. Named on Oroville Dam (1970) 7.5' quadrangle.

North Fork Camp [SISKIYOU]: *locality,* 14 miles north of Forks of Salmon (lat. 41°28'15" N, long. 121°16'40" W); the place is near the mouth of North Fork Wooley Creek. Named on Forks of Salmon (1955) 15' quadrangle.

North Fork Campground: see **Little North Fork Campground** [SISKIYOU].

North Fork Creek [SISKIYOU]: *stream,* flows 5 miles to North Fork Bear Creek [SHASTA-SISKIYOU] 5 miles east-southeast of Bartle (lat. 41°12'35" N, long. 121°44'10" W; near N line sec. 21, T 39 N, R 2 E). Named on Bartle (1961), Big Bend (1961), and Pondosa (1961) 15' quadrangles. United States Board on Geographic Names (1964, p. 13) rejected the name "North Fork Bear Creek" for the stream.

North Fork Mountain [SHASTA]: *peak,* 4.25 miles south-southwest of Shoeinhorse Mountain (lat. 41°01' N, long. 122°06'30" W); the peak is near the head of East Fork of North Fork Squaw Creek (2). Altitude 5342 feet. Named on Shoeinhorse Mountain (1954) 15' quadrangle.

North Gate [SISKIYOU]: *relief feature,* 14 miles north of McCloud (lat. 41°27'40" N, long. 122°11' W; sec. 27, T 42 N, R 3 W). Named on Shasta (1954) 15' quadrangle.

North Gray Rocks [SHASTA]: *relief feature,* 15 miles southeast of Lamoine (lat. 40°48' N, long. 122°16'30" W; sec. 13, 14, T 34 N, R 4 W). Named on Lamoine (1957) 15' quadrangle.

North Honcut Creek [BUTTE]: *stream,* flows 24 miles to join South Honcut Creek and form Honcut Creek nearly 4 miles west-southwest of Honcut (lat. 39°18'50" N, long. 121°36'10" W). Named on Bangor (1947), Honcut (1952), Loma Rica (1947), and Oroville Dam (1970) 7.5' quadrangles. West Fork enters from the northwest 5 miles north-northwest of Bangor; it is 4.5 miles long and is named on Bangor (1947) and Oroville Dam (1970) 7.5' quadrangles.

North Hungry Creek [SISKIYOU]: *stream,* heads in the State of Oregon and flows 2.5 miles in Siskiyou County to Hungry Creek 11 miles west-northwest of Hornbrook (lat. 41°58'35" N, long. 122°44'45" W; sec. 26, T 48 N, R 8 W). Named on Hornbrook (1955) 15' quadrangle.

North Point: see **Cohasset** [BUTTE].

North Red Mountain [SHASTA]: *peak,* 8 miles northeast of the village of Big Bend (lat. 41°06'15" N, long. 121°48'10" W; sec. 36, T 38 N, R 1 E). Named on Big Bend (1961) 15' quadrangle.

North Russian Creek [SISKIYOU]: *stream,* flows 8 miles to North Fork Salmon River 4 miles east-northeast of Sawyers Bar (lat. 41°19'25" N, long. 123°03'35" W). Named on Tanners Peak (1977) and Yellow Dog Peak (1977) 7.5' quadrangles.

North Salt Creek [SHASTA]: *stream,* flows 7 miles to Sacramento River 2 miles northeast of Lamoine (lat. 41°00' N, long. 122°24'15" W; near N line sec. 11, T 36 N, R 5 W). Named on Dunsmuir (1954) and Lamoine (1957) 15' quadrangles. North Fork enters 2.5 miles upstream from the mouth of the main creek; it is 5.25 miles long and is named on Dunsmuir (1954) and Lamoine (1957) 15' quadrangles.

North Stover Mountain [TEHAMA]: *ridge,* south-trending, 1.5 miles long, 6 miles northeast of Deer Creek Station on Tehama-Plumas County line (lat. 40°19'45" N, long. 121°22' W; mainly in sec. 36, T 29 N, R 5 E); the ridge is northwest of Stover Mountain, which is in Plumas County. Named on Mount Harkness (1956) 15' quadrangle.

North Table Mountain [BUTTE]: *ridge,* generally south-trending, 5 miles long, center about 6 miles north of Oroville (lat. 39°36'15" N, long. 121°33' W). Named on Cherokee (1970) and Oroville (1970) 7.5' quadrangles. Called Table Mountain on Chico (1895) 30' quadrangle.

North Yolla Bolly Lake [TEHAMA]: *dry lake,* 400 feet long, 9.5 miles west-northwest of Tomhead Mountain (lat. 40°12'15" N, long. 122°58' W; at W line sec. 11, T 27 N, R 10 W); the lake is 0.5 mile north-northeast of North Yolla Bolly Mountain. Named on Yolla Bolly (1954) 15' quadrangle.

North Yolla Bolly Mountains [TEHAMA]: *peaks,* 9.5 miles west-northwest of Tomhead Mountain on Tehama-Trinity County line (lat. 40°11'45" N, long. 122°58'20" W). Named on Yolla Bolly (1954) 15' quadrangle. Called North Yallo Balley Mountain on Red Bluff (1894) 1° quadrangle. United States Board on Geographic Names (1982b, p. 2) rejected the names "North Yallo Bally," "North Yolla Bolly," "North Yolla Bolly Mountain," "Yalla Balla," "Yalla Balley," "Yalla Bally," "Yallo Bally," "Yola Bola," "Yola Buli," "Yolla Balley," "Yolla Bally," "Yollo Bolly," and "Yollo Bolly Mountains" for the feature. The name "Yallo Balley" is of Indian origin (Kroeber, p. 67). The Board (1979a, p. 4-5) approved the name "North Yolla Bolly Spring" for a feature situated south of North Yolla Bolly Mountains (sec. 22, T 27 N, R 10 W).

North Yolla Bolly Spring: see **North Yolla Bolly Mountains** [TEHAMA].

Norton Gulch [SHASTA]: *canyon,* drained by a stream that flows 3.5 miles to Little Cow Creek 12 miles north-northeast of Millville (lat. 40°42'45" N, long. 122°05' W; near SW cor. sec. 15, T 33 N, R 2 W). Named on Millville (1953) 15' quadrangle.

No-See-Em Camp [SISKIYOU]: *locality,* 8.5 miles north-northeast of the village of Seiad Valley along Cook and Green Creek (lat. 41°57'30" N, long. 123°08' W). Named on Kangaroo Mountain (1980) 7.5' quadrangle.

Nosoni Creek [SHASTA]: *stream,* flows 4.5 miles to McCloud River Arm Shasta Lake 1.5 miles south of Bollibokka Mountain (lat. 40°12'40" N, long. 122°12'40" W; near N line sec. 9, T 35 N, R 3 W). Named on Bollibokka Mountain (1957) 15' quadrangle. The name is of Indian origin (Steger, p. 49). North Fork enters from the north 1 mile upstream from the mouth of the main creek; it is 3.25 miles long and is named on Bollibokka Mountain (1957) 15' quadrangle.

Nosoni Mountain [SHASTA]: *peak,* 2.25 miles east-northeast of Bollibokka Mountain (lat. 40°56'40" N, long. 122°10'20" W; near NE cor. sec. 35, T 36 N, R 3 W); the peak is at the head of North Fork Nosoni Creek. Altitude 3632 feet. Named on Bollibokka Mountain (1957) 15' quadrangle.

Novelty: see **Forks of Salmon** [SISKIYOU].

Noyes Valley [SISKIYOU]: *canyon,* 6 miles long, 9.5 miles east-southeast of Etna (lat. 41°22'30" N, long. 122°44'45" W). Named on China Mountain (1955) and Etna (1955) 15' quadrangles.

Noza Creek: see **Battle Creek** [SHASTA-TEHAMA].

Nugen Canyon [BUTTE]: *canyon,* drained by stream that flows 3.25 miles to Hamlin Canyon 7 miles southwest of Paradise (lat. 39°40'15" N, long. 121°42'10" W; near S line sec. 13, T 21 N, R 2 E). Named on Hamlin Canyon (1951) 7.5' quadrangle.

Nuisance Ridge: see **Tomhead Mountain** [TEHAMA].

Numhebe Creek: see **Ducket Creek** [SHASTA].

Nutmeg Creek [BUTTE]: *stream,* flows 2 miles to Middle Fork Feather River 6 miles north-northwest of Forbestown (lat. 39°36'15" N, long. 121°18'05" W; sec. 9, T 20 N, R 6 E). Named on Forbestown (1970) 7.5' quadrangle.

Nye Creek [GLENN]: *stream,* flows 14 miles to South Fork Willow Creek 8.5 miles southeast of Fruto (lat. 39°31'10" N, long. 122°19' W; sec. 9, T 19 N, R 4 W). Named on Fruto (1968) and Stone Valley (1952) 7.5' quadrangles.

—O—

Oak: see **Olinda** [SHASTA].

Oak Arbor: see **Berry Creek** [BUTTE] (2).

Oak Bar [SISKIYOU]: *locality,* 7.25 miles south-southeast of Condrey Mountain along Klamath River (lat. 41°50'25" N, long. 122°56' W; near S line sec. 7, T 46 N, R 9 W). Named on Condrey Mountain (1955) 15' quadrangle. On Yreka (1939) 30' quadrangle, the name has the form "Oakbar." Postal authorities established Oak Bar post office in 1874 and discontinued it in 1928 (Frickstad, p. 189), and they established McCook post office 12 miles south of Oak Bar in 1892 and discontinued it in 1894 (Salley, p. 136).

Oak Bottom [SHASTA]:

(1) *area,* 1.5 miles north-northeast of Schell Mountain (lat. 40°52'30" N, long. 122°30'45" W). Named on Schell Mountain (1950) 15' quadrangle.

(2) *village,* 4.5 miles southeast of the village of French Gulch along Clear Creek (lat. 40°38'55" N, long. 122°34'55" W). Named on French Gulch (1944) 15' quadrangle. Water of Whiskeytown Lake now covers the site.

Oak Bottom Campground [SHASTA]: *locality,* 4.25 miles south-southeast of the village of French Gulch along Whiskeytown Lake (lat. 40°38'55" N, long. 122°35'30" W; sec. 7, T 32 N, R 6 W); the place is near the site of Oak Bottom (2). Named on Whiskeytown (1979) 7.5' quadrangle.

Oak Creek [SHASTA]: *stream,* flows 3 miles to McCloud River [SHASTA-SISKIYOU] 8 miles west-southwest of Shoeinhorse Mountain (lat. 41°01'40" N, long. 122°13'15" W). Named on Dunsmuir (1954) and Shoeinhorse Mountain (1954) 15' quadrangles.

Oak Creek [TEHAMA]: *stream,* flows 4.5 mile to Plum Creek 10 miles south-southwest of Manton (lat. 40°18'15" N, long. 121°56'40" W; at S line sec. 2, T 28 N, R 1 W). Named on Manton (1956) 15' quadrangle. United States Board on Geographic Names (1986c, p. 4) approved the name "Oat Creek" for the stream.

Oak Flat [SHASTA]:

(1) *area,* 13 miles north-northeast of Millville along Oak Run Creek (lat. 40°42' N, long. 122°01'45" W; on E line sec. 24, T 33 N, R 2 W). Named on Millville (1953) 15' quadrangle.

(2) *area,* 10 miles north-northeast of the village of Montgomery Creek along Pit River (lat. 40°58' N, long. 121°49'30" W). Named on Montgomery Creek (1956) 15' quadrangle.

Oak Flat [TEHAMA]:

(1) *area,* 5.5 miles east-northeast of Beegum Peak (lat. 40°20'30" N, long. 122°47'15" W; near NE cor. sec. 29, T 29 N, R 8 W). Named on Chanchelulla Peak (1951) 15' quadrangle.

(2) *valley,* 6.5 miles northwest of Wakefield Flat along Bone Gulch (lat. 40°12'15" N, long. 122°42'50" W; sec. 12, T 27 N, R 8 W). Named on Cold Fork (1967) 7.5' quadrangle.

Oak Flat Creek [SISKIYOU]: *stream,* flows 6.25 miles to Klamath River 11 miles north-northwest of Ukonom Lake (lat. 41°43'50" N, long. 123°26' W). Named on Clear Creek (1981) and Happy Camp (1980) 7.5' quadrangles.

Oak Flat Creek [TEHAMA]: *stream,* flows 2 miles to Big Salt Creek 7 miles east-northeast of Beegum Peak (lat. 40°20'20" N, long. 122°45'30" W; sec. 27, T 29 N, R 8 W); the stream heads at Oak Flat (1). Named on Chanchelulla Peak (1951) 15' quadrangle.

Oak Flat Gulch [TEHAMA]: *canyon,* drained by a stream that flows nearly 2 miles to Dry Creek (1) 10 miles west of Rosewood (lat. 40°16'50" N, long. 122°44'30" W; near W line sec. 14, T 28 N, R 8 W). Named on Chanchelulla Peak (1951) and Ono (1952) 15' quadrangles.

Oak Grove [BUTTE]: *village,* 3.25 miles west of Palermo (lat. 39°25'45" N, long. 121°36'15" W; sec. 11, T 18 N, R 3 E). Named on Palermo (1970) 7.5' quadrangle.

Oak Gulch [SISKIYOU]: *canyon,* drained by a stream that flows 1.5 miles to Scott Valley 7.25 miles south-southeast of Etna (lat. 41°21'50" N, long. 122°49'45" W; sec. 36, T 41 N, R 8 W). Named on Etna (1955) 15' quadrangle.

Oak Highlands: see **Happy Valley** [SHASTA].

Oak Hollow Creek [SISKIYOU]: *stream,* flows nearly 1 mile to Klamath River 3.5 miles east-northeast of Happy Camp (lat. 41°49' N, long. 123°18'35" W). Named on Slater Butte (1980) 7.5' quadrangle.

Oak Knob [SHASTA]: *peak,* 5.5 miles north-northeast of Shoeinhorse Mountain (lat. 41°08'20" N, long. 122°02' W). Altitude 5000 feet. Named on Shoeinhorse Mountain (1954) 15' quadrangle.

Oak Knoll [GLENN]: *peak,* 5.25 miles northwest of Black Butte (lat. 39°47'20" N, long. 122°55'45" W; near E line sec. 2, T 22 N, R 10 W). Named on Mendocino Pass (1967) 7.5' quadrangle.

Oak Leaf Island [BUTTE-GLENN]: *island,* 6 miles east-southeast of Butte City in Butte Creek [BUTTE-GLENN] on Butte-Glenn County line (lat. 39°25'45" N, long. 121°52'30" W). Named on Marysville (1895) 30' quadrangle.

Oak Mountain [SHASTA]: *peak,* 3 miles west of the village of Big Bend (lat. 41°01'20" N, long. 121°58'05" W; sec. 33, T 37 N, R 1 W). Altitude 3528 feet. Named on Big Bend (1961) 15' quadrangle.

Oak Opening Creek [SHASTA]: *stream,* flows 0.5 mile to Backbone Creek 11 miles south of Lamoine (lat. 40°49' N, long. 122°26'45" W; at W line sec. 9, T 34 N, R 5 W). Named on Lamoine (1957) 15' quadrangle.

Oak Point [BUTTE]: *peak,* 8.5 miles north of Pulga (lat. 39°55'35" N, long. 121°27'45" W; near NW cor. sec. 19, T 24 N, R 5 E). Named on Kimshew Point (1979) 7.5' quadrangle.

Oak Run [SHASTA]: *locality,* 12.5 miles northeast of Millville (lat. 40°41'05" N, long. 122°01'30" W; sec. 30, T 33 N, R 1 W). Named on Millville (1953) 15' quadrangle. Called Oakrun on California Division of Highways' (1934) map. Postal authorities established Oak Run post office in 1877, moved it 2.5 miles north in 1909, and moved it 3.5 miles southwest in 1941 (Salley, p. 158). They established Kendon post office 6 miles north of Oak Run in 1900 and discontinued it the same year (Salley, p. 110).

Oak Run Creek [SHASTA]: *stream,* flows 23 miles to Cow Creek 2.5 miles west-northwest of Millville (lat. 40°33'50" N, long. 122°13'05" W; at NW cor. sec. 9, T 31 N, R 3 W). Named on Millville (1953) and Whitmore (1956) 15' quadrangles. United States Board on Geographic Names (1978a, p. 7) rejected the name "Oak Run" for the stream. The feature first was called Dry Creek (Steger, p. 50).

Oat Creek [SHASTA]: *stream,* flows 4.25 miles to Little Cow Creek nearly 3 miles west-northwest of Millville (lat. 40°34'05" N, long. 122°13'30" W; sec. 5, T 31 N, R 3 W). Named on Palo Cedro (1965) 7.5' quadrangle.

Oat Creek [TEHAMA]: *stream,* flows 20 miles to Sacramento River 4 miles north-northwest of Los Molinos (lat. 40°04'25" N, long. 122°07'20" W). Named on Gerber (1950), Los Molinos (1952), Red Bank (1952), and West of Gerber (1951) 7.5' quadrangles.

Oat Creek: see **Oak Creek** [TEHAMA].

Obe Fields Spring [TEHAMA]: *spring,* nearly 3 miles west-northwest of Polk Springs (lat. 40°08' N, long. 121°42'45" W; near E line sec. 2, T 26 N, R 2 E). Named on Butte Meadows (1958) 15' quadrangle.

Obie [SHASTA]: *locality,* 11.5 miles north-northwest of Burney Falls along McCloud River Railroad (lat. 41°10'10" N, long. 121°42'15" W; near SW cor. sec. 35, T 39 N, T 2 E). Named on Pondosa (1961) 15' quadrangle.

O'Brien [SHASTA]: *locality,* 13 miles south-southeast of Lamoine (lat. 40°48'45" N, long. 122°19'25" W; sec. 9, T 34 N, R 4 W); the place is 1 mile north-northeast of O'Brien Mountain. Named on Lamoine (1957) 15' quadrangle. Postal authorities established O'Brien post office in 1945; the name is for Con O'Brien, who built a vacation resort at the place (Salley, p. 159).

O'Brien Creek [SHASTA]: *stream,* flows 3 miles to Sacramento River 12 miles south-southeast of Lamoine (lat. 40°48'25" N, long. 122°22'30" W; near NE cor. sec. 13, T 34 N, R 5 W). Named on Lamoine (1946) 15' quadrangle. Water of Shasta Lake now floods the feature.

O'Brien Creek Inlet [SHASTA]: *embayment,* 12 miles south-southeast of Lamoine along Sacramento River Arm Shasta Lake (lat. 40°49' N, long. 122°21'30" W); water of the embayment covers the canyon of O'Brien Creek. Named on Lamoine (1957) 15' quadrangle.

O'Brien Mountain [SHASTA]: *peak,* 13 miles south-southeast of Lamoine (lat. 40°48'15" N, long. 122°20'15" W; near E line sec. 17, T 34 N, R 4 W). Altitude 2109 feet. Named on Lamoine (1957) 15' quadrangle.

Ocean View [GLENN]: *peak,* 4.5 miles south-southeast of Black Butte at the south end of Brushy Mountain (lat. 39°39'50" N, long. 122°51'05" W). Altitude 6760 feet. Named on Plaskett Meadows (1967) 7.5' quadrangle.

O'Farrill Gulch [SISKIYOU]: *canyon,* drained by a stream that flows 1.5 miles to South Fork Salmon River 9 miles east-northeast of Salmon Mountain (lat. 41°13'55" N, long. 123°15'20" W). Named on Cecilville (1979) and Youngs Peak (1979) 7.5' quadrangles. Called Ferrils Gulch on Sawyers Bar (1923) 30' quadrangle.

Offield Mountain [SISKIYOU]: *ridge,* west-northwest-trending, 0.5 mile long, 14 miles northwest of Forks of Salmon (lat. 41°25'25" N, long. 123°28'10" W). Named on Somes Bar (1979) 7.5' quadrangle.

Offield Saddle [SISKIYOU]: *pass,* 14 miles north-northwest of Forks of Salmon (lat. 41°25'45" N, long. 123°27'10" W); the pass is 1 mile east-northeast of Offield Mountain. Named on Somes Bar (1979) 7.5' quadrangle.

Ogaromtoc Lake [SISKIYOU]: *lake,* 550 feet long, 13 miles north of Orleans, which is in Humboldt County (lat. 41°29'10" N, long. 123°32'25" W). Named on Bark Shanty Gulch (1974) 7.5' quadrangle.

Ogburn [SHASTA]: *locality,* 2.25 miles west-northwest of Shingletown along present Shingle Creek (lat. 40°30'10" N, long. 121°55'50" W). Named on Lassen Peak (1894) 1° quadrangle.

Ogo Station [SHASTA]: *locality,* 7.25 miles west-southwest of Ono (lat. 40°25'25" N, long. 122°44'15" W; sec. 26, T 30 N, R 8 W). Named on Ono (1952) 15' quadrangle.

Ohio City: seer **Buckeye** [SHASTA].

Oklahoma Flat [SISKIYOU]: *area,* 8 miles east-southeast of Dorris (lat. 41°54'45" N, long. 121°46'50" W; around SE cor. sec. 18, T 47 N, R 2 E). Named on Dorris (1950) 15' quadrangle.

Old Boundary Spring [SHASTA]: *spring,* nearly 3 miles north-northeast of Lassen Peak (lat. 40°31'20" N, long. 121°28'45" W; near W line sec. 24, T 31 N, R 4 E). Named on Prospect Peak (1957) 15' quadrangle. The spring is situated practically on the original north boundary of Lassen Volcanic National Park (Schulz, p. 41).

Old Cow Creek [SHASTA]: *stream,* flows 33 miles to join South Cow Creek and form Cow Creek 2.25 miles east of Millville (lat. 40°32'40" N, long. 122°07'50" W; sec. 18, T 31 N, R 2 W). Named on Manzanita Lake (1956), Millville (1953) and Whitmore (1956) 15' quadrangles.

Old Cow Creek Campground [SHASTA]: *locality,* 19 miles northwest of Lassen Peak (lat. 40°41'15" N, long. 121°44'35" W; near W line sec. 27, T 33 N, R 2 E); the place is along Old Cow Creek. Named on Manzanita Lake (1956) 15' quadrangle.

Old Cow Creek Meadows: see **Cow Creek Meadows** [SHASTA].

Old Defiance Mill [BUTTE]: *locality,* 4 miles north-northwest of present Pulga (lat. 39°51'15" N, long. 121°28'10" W). Named on Bidwell Bar (1897) 30' quadrangle.

Old Diggings: see **Keswick** [SHASTA].

Old Forbestown [BUTTE]: *locality,* 1 mile northwest of Forbestown (lat. 39°31'40" N, long. 121°16'45" W; on N line sec. 10, T 19 N, R 6 E). Named on Forbestown (1970) 7.5' quadrangle.

Old Four Corners: see **Four Corners** [SHASTA].

Old Green Burney Camp [SHASTA]: *locality,* 5.5 miles south-southwest of Burney (lat. 40°48'45" N, long. 121°43'05" W; at S line sec. 11, T 34 N, R 2 E); the place is at the mouth of Green Burney Creek. Named on Burney (1957) 15' quadrangle.

Old Lovelock: see **Coutolenc** [BUTTE].

Old Man Rock [SHASTA]: *peak,* 2 miles east-southeast of Arbuckle Mountain (lat. 40°23'05" N, long. 122°50" W; near N line sec. 12, T 29 N, R 9 W). Named on Chanchelulla Peak (1951) 15' quadrangle.

Old Man Springs Creek [TEHAMA]: *stream,* flows 2.5 miles to Squaw Hollow Creek 3.5 miles southeast of Beegum Peak (lat. 40°16'50" N, long. 122°50'10" W; sec. 13, T 28 N, R 9 W). Named on Chanchelulla Peak (1951) 15' quadrangle.

Old Station [SHASTA]: *village,* 14 miles north-northeast of Lassen Peak (lat. 40°40'30" N, long. 121°25'55" W; near W line sec. 33, T 33 N, R 5 E). Named on Prospect Peak (1957) 15' quadrangle, which has the designation "Old Station (P.O.)" at a place situated 2 miles southwest of present Old Station (lat. 40°39'10" N, long. 121°27'30" W; sec. 7, T 32 N, R 5 E). Hat Creek stage station was at the site in 1856; the place became known as Old Station after the stage station was abandoned (Steger, p. 50).

Olimpo: see **Orland** [GLENN].

Olinda [SHASTA]: *village,* 10 miles south of Redding (lat. 40°26'35" N, long. 122°24'25" W; on E line sec. 22, T 30 N, R 5 W). Named on Olinda (1964) 7.5' quadrangle. Postal authorities established Olinda post office in 1890 (Frickstad, p. 182). Samuel T. Alexander, who owned a summer home in Olinda, Hawaii, settled in Shasta County in the 1880's and assisted in starting the post office (Steger, p. 50). Diller and others' (1915) map shows a place called Oak located 4 miles west-northwest of Olinda. Postal authorities established Onward post office in 1886 and discontinued in 1889; they established Oak post office at the old site of Onward post office in 1897, moved it 0.5 mile east in 1939, and discontinued it in 1943 (Salley, p. 157, 161).

Olinda Creek [SHASTA]: *stream,* flows 7 miles to Anderson Creek 0.5 mile south-southwest of downtown Anderson (lat. 40°26'25" N, long. 122°18'05" W; sec. 22, T 30 N, R 4 W). Named on Cottonwood (1965) and Olinda (1964) 7.5' quadrangles.

Olinda Reservoir [SHASTA]: *intermittent lake,* 750 feet long, less than 0.5 mile southwest of the center of Olinda (lat. 40°26'20" N, long. 122°24'45" W; sec. 22, T 30 N, R 5 W); the feature is along Olinda Creek. Named on Olinda (1964) 7.5' quadrangle.

Oliphant Creek [SHASTA]: *stream,* flows 1.25 miles to Middle Fork Cottonwood Creek [SHASTA-TEHAMA] 8.5 miles west-southwest of Arbuckle Mountain (lat. 40°21'05" N, long. 123°00'20" W; near E line sec. 20, T 29 N, R 10 W). Named on Dubakella Mountain (1954) 15' quadrangle.

Olivers Flat: see **Nordheimer Flat** [SISKIYOU].

Olney Creek [SHASTA]: *stream,* flows 10 miles to Sacramento River 5.25 miles south-southeast of Redding (lat. 40°30'30" N, long. 122°22' W). Named on Enterprise (1957) and Redding (1957) 7.5' quadrangles. The name is for Nathan Olney, who mined along the stream before the rush of gold miners in 1849 (Steger, p. 50).

Olsen Creek [SISKIYOU]: *stream,* flows 2 miles to North Fork Salmon River 5.25 miles west of Sawyers Bar (lat. 41°17'35" N, long. 123°13'55" W). Named on Sawyers Bar (1979) 7.5' quadrangle.

Olsen Meadows [SISKIYOU]: *area,* 6 miles west-northwest of Sawyers Bar (lat. 41°19'50" N, long. 123°14'50" W); the place is near the head of Olsen Creek. Named on Sawyers Bar (1979) 7.5' quadrangle.

Omit Bar: see **Helltown** [BUTTE].

One Bee Camp [TEHAMA]: *locality,* 9 miles south-southwest of Ball Mountain (lat. 39°49'35" N, long. 122°52'15" W; sec. 28, T 23 N, R 9 W). Named on Log Spring (1967) 7.5' quadrangle.

One-Horse Town: see **Horsetown**, under **Reading Bar** [SHASTA].

O'Neil: see **Johnny O'Neil Ridge** [SISKIYOU].

O'Neil Creek [SISKIYOU]: *stream,* flows 3.25 miles to Klamath River 4.5 miles east-southeast of the village of Seiad Valley (lat. 41°48'35" N, long. 123°06'50" W). Named on Hamburg (1980) and Seiad Valley (1980) 7.5' quadrangles.

O'Neil Creek Campground [SISKIYOU]: *locality,* 4.5 miles east-southeast of the village of Seiad Valley along Klamath River (lat. 41°48'35" N, long. 123°06'50" W; near SW cor. sec. 22, T 46 N, R 11 W); the place is near the mouth of O'Neil Creek. Named on Seiad Valley (1955) 15' quadrangle.

O'Neil Glade [GLENN]: *area,* 5.5 miles east of Black Butte (lat. 39°44'25" N, long. 122°46'15" W). Named on Plaskett Meadows (1967) 7.5' quadrangle.

Onemile Creek [GLENN]: *water feature,* 11 miles southeast of Willows on Glenn-Colusa County line (lat. 39°24'50" N, long. 122°01'40" W). Named on Maxwell (1906) 15' quadrangle.

Onemile Creek [SISKIYOU]: *stream,* flows 2.5 miles to Ukonom Creek 1.25 miles west-southwest of Ukonom Lake (lat. 41°34'25" N, long. 123°22'40" W); the stream heads at Onemile Lake. Named on Ukonom Lake (1980) 7.5' quadrangle.

Onemile Lake [SISKIYOU]: *lake,* 1100 feet long, 2.5 miles south-southeast of Ukonom Lake (lat. 41°32'45" N, long. 123°20'25" W). Named on Ukonom Lake (1980) 7.5' quadrangle. Averill's (1935) map has the form "One Mile L." for the name.

One Mule Town: see **Muletown** [SHASTA].

Onion Butte [TEHAMA]: *peak,* 8 miles northeast of Polk Springs (lat. 40°12' N, long. 121°34' W). Altitude 5518 feet. Named on Butte Meadows (1958) 15' quadrangle. Called Onion Hill on Lassen Peak (1894) 1° quadrangle.

Onion Creek [SHASTA]:

(1) *stream,* flows 1 mile to Clear Creek 4.5 miles north-northwest of Schell Mountain (lat. 40°54'30" N, long. 122°34'20" W; at S line sec. 5, T 35 N, R 6 W). Named on Schell Mountain (1950) 15' quadrangle.

(2) *stream,* flows 5.5 miles to Rock Creek (3) 12.5 miles west of Lassen Peak (lat. 40°27'25" N, long. 121°44'10" W; sec. 14, T 30 N, R 2 E). Named on Lassen Peak (1956) 15' quadrangle.

Onion Creek: see **Forked Creek** [TEHAMA].

Onion Creek Ridge [SHASTA]: *ridge,* generally west-southwest-trending, 1.25 miles long, 6 miles north-northwest of Schell Mountain (lat. 40°50'25" N, long. 122°34' W); the ridge is north of Onion Creek (1). Named on Schell Mountain (1950) 15' quadrangle.

Onion Flat [SISKIYOU]: *area,* 12.5 miles northeast of the village of Seiad Valley (lat. 41°57'20" N, long. 123°00'30" W). Named on Dutch Creek (1980) 7.5' quadrangle.

Onion Hill: see **Onion Butte** [TEHAMA].

Onion Meadow [SISKIYOU]: *area,* 22 miles south of Etna (lat. 41°08'50" N, long. 122°59' W). Named on Coffee Creek (1955) 15' quadrangle.

Onion Springs [SHASTA]: *springs,* 3.5 miles west of Lassen Peak (lat. 40°29'45" N, long. 121°34'30" W; at W line sec. 31, T 31 N, R 4 E). Named on Lassen Peak (1956) 15' quadrangle.

Onion Springs [TEHAMA]: *spring,* 2.5 miles southwest of Ball Mountain (lat. 39°54'40" N, long. 122°49'20" W; near N line sec. 25, T 24 N, R 9 W). Named on Ball Mountain (1967) 7.5' quadrangle.

Ono [SHASTA]: *village,* 14 miles southwest of Redding (lat. 40°28'30" N, long. 122°37'10" W; on S line sec. 2, T 30 N, R 7 W); the village is along Eagle Creek. Named on Ono (1952) 15' quadrangle. A place called Eagle Creek, originally known as Junction, moved to the site of present Ono in the early 1860's; after postal authorities refused the request for a post office there called Oro Fino (Giles, p. 192), the Reverend W.S. Kidder submitted the biblical name "Ono" for the post office (Steger, p. 51). Postal authorities established Ono post office in 1883 (Frickstad, p. 182).

Onward: see **Olinda** [SHASTA].

Onyett [BUTTE]: *locality,* 4.5 miles northwest of Forbestown along Feather River Railroad (lat. 39°34'20" N, long. 121°19' W; near SE cor. sec. 20, T 20 N, R 6 E). Named on Big Bend Mountain (1948) 15' quadrangle.

Opdyke Hill [SHASTA]: *peak,* 9 miles southeast of Burney (lat. 40°48'30" N, long. 121°31'35" W; sec. 16, T 34 N, R 4 E). Altitude 4642 feet. Named on Burney (1957) 15' quadrangle.

Open Ridge [GLENN]: *ridge,* east-southeast-trending, 3 miles long, 3 miles northeast of Saint John Mountain (lat. 39°27'55" N, long. 122°39'20" W). Named on Saint John Mountain (1968) 7.5' quadrangle.

Ophir City: see **Oroville** [BUTTE].

Opium Glade Ridge [TEHAMA]: *ridge,* generally northeast-trending, 1.5 miles long, 7 miles west of Tomhead Mountain (lat. 40°08'45" N, long. 122°56'40" W; sec. 35, 36, T 27 N, R 10 W). Named on Yolla Bolly (1954) 15' quadrangle.

Optimo: see **Paradise** [BUTTE].

Ordbend [GLENN]: *locality,* 12.5 miles northeast of Willows along Southern Pacific Railroad (lat. 39°37'45" N, long. 122°00'15" W; at NW cor. sec. 19, T 21 N, R 1 W). Named on Hamilton City (1949) 7.5' quadrangle.

Ord Ferry [BUTTE-GLENN]: *locality,* 11 miles southwest of Chico along Sacramento River on Butte-Glenn County line (lat. 39°37'45" N, long. 121°59'30" W). Site named on Ord Ferry (1949) 7.5' quadrangle.

Ord Ranch: see **Peachton** [BUTTE].

Oregon Bar: see **Nelson Bar** [BUTTE]; **Shasta River** [SISKIYOU].

Oregon City [BUTTE]: *locality,* 5.5 miles north-northeast of Oroville (lat. 39°35'40" N, long. 121°31'40" W; sec. 16, T 20 N, R 4 E); the place is in Oregon Gulch (2). Named on Oroville (1970) 7.5' quadrangle. Postal authorities established Hengy post office, named for Jessie Hengy, first postmaster, at Oregon City in 1894, discontinued it in 1900, reestablished it in 1901, changed the name to Bloomingdale in 1902, and discontinued it in 1905 (Salley, p. 23, 96; Dunn, F.D., p. 50). Gold miners from the State of Oregon came to the place in 1849, and a town was laid out there in 1856 (Wells and Chambers, p. 250).

Oregon Gulch [BUTTE]:

(1) *canyon,* drained by a stream that flows 5 miles to Lake Oroville 5 miles east of Oroville Dam (lat. 39°32'35" N, long. 121°23'10" W; near SW cor. sec. 35, T 20 N, R 5 E). Named on Forbestown (1970) and Oroville Dam (1970) 7.5' quadrangles.

(2) *canyon,* drained by a stream that flows 6.25 miles to Feather River 3 miles northeast of Oroville (lat. 39°32'25" N, long. 121°30'40" W; at S line sec. 34, T 20 N, R 4 E); Oregon City is in the Canyon. Named on Oroville (1970) 7.5' quadrangle. F.D. Dunn (p. 111) listed a place called White Rock, White Rock Bar, or White Rock Camp—named for a large white rock in the river—that was situated just east of the mouth of Oregon Gulch; water behind Thermalito Diversion Dam now covers the site.

Oregon Gulch [SHASTA]: *canyon,* drained by a stream that flows 4 miles to lowlands along Sacramento River 2.5 miles south of Redding (lat. 40°32'35" N, long. 122°23'25" W). Named on Redding (1957) 7.5' quadrangle.

Oregon Slough [SISKIYOU]: *stream,* flows 8 miles to Shasta River 4.25 miles east of Yreka (lat. 41°44'25" N, long. 122°33'30" W; sec. 20, T 45 N, R 6 W). Named on Copco (1954), Hornbrook (1955), and Yreka (1954) 15' quadrangles.

Oriental: see **Alder Springs** [GLENN].

Orland [GLENN]: *town,* 15 miles north of Willows (lat. 39°44'50" N, long. 122°11'40" W; in and near sec. 21, 22, T 22 N, R 3 W). Named on Kirkwood (1949) and Orland (1951) 7.5' quadrangles. Postal authorities established Orland post office in 1876 (Frickstad, p. 40), and the town incorporated in 1909. The name, which was selected by lot, is from the birthplace in England of an early settler at the town (Gudde 1949, p. 245). California Mining Bureau's (1909c) map shows a place called Floyd located 10 miles west of Orland on the road from Orland to Newville. Postal authorities established Floyd post office 12 miles west of Orland in 1906 and discontinued it in 1911 (Salley, p. 76). They established Olimpo post office 6 miles northwest of Orland in 1872 and discontinued it in 1883; the name is from the Spanish version of an Indian word (Salley, p. 160).

Orland Buttes [GLENN]: *ridge,* northwest- to north-northwest-trending, 4 miles long, 8.5 miles west-northwest of Orland (lat. 39°46'45" N, long. 122°20'25" W). Named on Black Butte Dam (1967) and Fruto NE (1952) 7.5' quadrangles.

Orleans Mountain [SISKIYOU]: *peak,* nearly 5 miles east-southeast of Orleans, which is in Humboldt County, on Siskiyou-Humboldt County line (lat. 41°16'45" N, long. 123°27'10" W). Altitude 6188 feet. Named on Orleans Mountain (1974) 7.5' quadrangle.

Orloff: see **Paradise** [BUTTE].

Oro Fino [SISKIYOU]: *village,* 4.5 miles west-southwest of Fort Jones (lat. 41°34'40" N, long. 122°55'10" W; sec. 18, T 43 N, R 9 W); the village is along Oro Fino Creek. Named on Fort Jones (1955) 15' quadrangle. Postal authorities established Oro Fino post office in 1861, discontinued it for a time in 1873, and discontinued it finally in 1903 (Frickstad, p. 189).

Oro Fino: see **Ono** [SHASTA].

Oro Fino Creek [SISKIYOU]: *stream,* flows 7.5 miles to Scott River 3 miles west of Fort Jones (lat. 41°37' N, long. 122°53'50" W; near SE cor. sec. 32, T 44 N, R 9 W). Named on Fort Jones (1955) 15' quadrangle.

Orofino Gulch [SHASTA]: *canyon,* drained by a stream that flows 1.5 miles to Clear Creek 5 miles north of Igo (lat. 40°34'45" N, long. 122°32'10" W; near S line sec. 34, T 32 N, R 6 W). Named on Igo (1979) 7.5' quadrangle.

Oro Fino Mountain: see **Quartz Hill** [SISKIYOU].

Oroleve [BUTTE]: *locality,* 1.25 miles west-southwest of Clipper Mills (lat. 39°31'40" N, long. 121°10'40" W; at S line sec. 3, T 19 N, R 7 E). Named on Clipper Mills (1948) 7.5' quadrangle. Called Oroleeve on Bidwell Bar (1897) 30' quadrangle. F.D. Dunn (p. 81) gave the forms "Oroleve," "Oro Lewa," "Oro Leva," "Oroliva," and "Oroluve" for the name.

Oroleve Creek [BUTTE]: *stream,* flows 4.5 miles to South Fork Feather River 3.25 miles west-northwest of Clipper Mills (lat. 39°32'55" N, long. 121°12'55" W; sec. 32, T 20 N, R 7 E); the stream goes past Oroleve. Named on Clipper Mills (1948) 7.5' quadrangle. Called Oroleeve Creek on Bidwell Bar (1897) 30' quadrangle.

Oroville [BUTTE]: *town,* in south-central Butte County along Feather River, where the river debouches from highlands (lat. 39°30'45" N, long. 121°33'20" W). Named on Oroville (1970) 7.5' quadrangle. Postal authorities established Oroville post office in 1854 (Frickstad, p. 11), and the town incorporated in 1906. The place first was called Ophir City, but the name was changed to Oroville when the post office came—Judge J.M. Burt is credited with both names; the first store opened in the winter of 1849 and 1850 (Wells and Chambers, p. 233-234). The same winter a rival community called Lynchburg sprang up 1 mile southeast of Oroville, where George H. Lynch opened a store (Wells and Chambers, p. 238). An early community called Center Ville was between Oroville and Lynchburg, and a mining camp called Bagdad was situated on a bluff along Feather River 2 miles below Oroville (Dunn, F.D., p. 3, 20). A.G. Simpson discovered gold at Bagdad and named the site (Wells and Chambers, p. 234). A place called Long's Bar was located along Feather River about 2 miles above Oroville; the Long Brothers opened a store there in 1849 (Jackson *in* Windeler, p. 213); the place first was called Monterey Bar (Gudde, 1975, p. 198). In 1848 Sam Neal started a mining camp called Neals Diggins on the south side of Feather River across from Long's Bar (sec. 3, T 19 N, R 4 E); later the same year George Adams reestablished the place, which then was called Adamstown, Adamsville, or Adams Bar (Dunn, F.D., p. 1, 74). General Bidwell discovered placer gold along Feather River about 15 miles below Oroville in 1848, and a community called Hamilton developed there on the west side of the river (S half sec. 33, T 19 N, R 3 E); Hamilton was the county seat of Butte County before 1853 and was named for Alexander Hamilton's nephew, who helped lay it out (Dunn, F.D., p. 48; Jackson *in* Windeler, p. 214; Wells and Chambers, p. 257). Postal authorities established Hamilton post office in 1851 and discontinued it in 1865 (Frickstad, p. 10). California Mining Bureau's (1917c) map shows a place called Chardon located along the railroad between Tres Vias and Rio Bonito. Postal authorities established Chardon post office, named for Charles Langdon, a pioneer settler, 8 miles southwest of Oroville (N half sec. 9, T 18 N, R 3 E) in 1894, moved it 2 miles southwest in 1897, and discontinued it in 1907 (Dunn, F.D., p. 21; Salley, p. 42). They established Mortimer post office 25 miles northeast of Oroville in 1880 and discontinued it in 1881 (Salley, p. 147). They established Rio Seco post office 10 miles northwest of Oroville in 1857; discontinued it in 1874, reestablished it in 1880, discontinued it in 1882, reestablished it in 1885, and discontinued it in 1888; the post office was along Dry Creek (Salley, p. 186).

Oroville: see **Lake Oroville** [BUTTE]: **South Oroville** [BUTTE].

Oroville Junction [BUTTE]: *locality,* 5 miles west of Oroville along Sacramento Northern Railroad (lat. 39°30'35" N, long. 121°39' W; at SW cor. sec. 8, T 19 N, R 3 E). Named on Shippee (1948) 7.5' quadrangle. Called Tres Vias on Dry Creek (1912) 7.5' quadrangle. California Division of Highways' (1934) map shows a place called Summit located along Sacramento Northern Railroad 2 miles east of Oroville Junction (near SW cor. sec. 10, T 19 N, R 3 E).

Orr Lake [SISKIYOU]: *lake,* 3700 feet long, 1.5 miles northwest of Bray (lat. 41°39'45" N, long. 121°59'25" W; sec. 17, T 44 N, R 1 W); the lake is 1 mile west-southwest of Orr Mountain. Named on Bray (1950) 15' quadrangle.

Orr Mountain [SISKIYOU]: *mountain,* 1.5 miles north of Bray (lat. 41°40' N, long. 121°58'25" W; on S line sec. 9, T 44 N, R 1 W); the feature is 1 mile east-northeast of Orr Lake. Altitude 5823 feet. Named on Bray (1950) 15' quadrangle.

Orton Gulch [SISKIYOU]: *canyon,* drained by a stream that flows 1.5 miles to South Fork Salmon River 1 mile west of Cecilville (lat. 41°08'30" N, long. 123°09'35" W). Named on Cecilville (1979) 7.5' quadrangle.

Osborne [SHASTA]: *locality,* 14 miles north-northeast of Millville (lat. 40°43' N, long. 122°01'45" W; near W line sec. 18, T 33 N, R 1 W). Named on Redding (1901) 30' quadrangle.

Osburger Gulch [SISKIYOU]: *canyon,* drained by a stream that flows 1.5 miles to Klamath River 2.5 miles south of Hornbrook (lat. 41°52'30" N, long. 122°33'20" W; near SE cor. sec. 32, T 47 N, R 6 W). Named on Hornbrook (1955) 15' quadrangle.

Oso Butte [SISKIYOU]: *peak,* 13 miles north of Bartle (lat. 41°27'10" N, long. 121°48' W; on S line sec. 25, T 42 N, R 1 E). Altitude 5297 feet. Named on Bartle (1961) 15' quadrangle.

Osprey Lake [SISKIYOU]: *lake,* 300 feet long, 14 miles north of Sawyers Bar (lat. 41°29'45" N, long. 123°07'40" W). Named on English Peak (1977) 7.5' quadrangle.

Osterried Gulch: see **Camp Eden** [SISKIYOU].

Ostrander: see **Paradise** [BUTTE].

Otey Island [SISKIYOU]: *hill,* 4.5 miles east-northeast of Dorris (lat. 41°59'45" N, long. 121°55'15" W; on N line sec. 23, T 48 N, R 1 E). Named on Dorris (1950) 15' quadrangle.

Otey's Ranch: see **Dorris** [SISKIYOU].

Ottitiewa: see **Fort Jones** [SISKIYOU].

Ottley Gulch [SISKIYOU]: *canyon,* drained by a stream that flows nearly 1 mile to Klamath River 2.5 miles east-southeast of Happy Camp (lat. 41°46'15" N, long. 123°20'10" W; at S line sec. 18, T 16 N, R 8 E). Named on Slater Butte (1980) 7.5' quadrangle.

Oven Lid [TEHAMA]: *peak,* 7.5 miles south of Tomhead Mountain (lat. 40°01'50" N, long. 122°47'50" W; at N line sec. 18, T 25 N, R 8 W). Altitude 6602 feet. Named on Yolla Bolly (1954) 15' quadrangle.

Owens Butte [TEHAMA]: *hill,* 1.5 miles northwest of Paskenta (lat. 39°53'50" N, long. 122°34'15" W; near W line sec. 32, T 24 N, R 6 W). Altitude 1172 feet. Named on Paskenta (1967) 7.5' quadrangle.

Owens Ravine [BUTTE]: *canyon,* drained by a stream that flows 2 miles to North Honcut Creek 5.5 miles north-northwest of Bangor (lat. 39°27'50" N, long. 121°26'25" W; sec. 32, T 19 N, R 5 E). Named on Bangor (1947) 7.5' quadrangle.

Owl Creek [BUTTE]: *stream,* flows nearly 2.5 miles to Sucker Run 5 miles west-northwest of Clipper Mills (lat. 39°34'25" N, long. 121°13'55" W; near SW cor. sec. 19, T 20 N, R 7 E). Named on Clipper Mills (1948) 7.5' quadrangle.

Owl Lake [SHASTA]: *lake,* 8 miles north-northwest of Burney Falls (lat. 41°06'30" N, long. 121°43'25" W; on N line sec. 27, T 38 N, R 2 E). Named on Pondosa (1961) 15' quadrangle. On Bartle (1939) 30' quadrangle, three lakes at the place are called Owl Lakes.

Owls Head [SISKIYOU]: *peak,* 25 miles west-southwest of Macdoel (lat. 41°39'50" N, long. 122°25'25" W; sec. 16, T 44 N, R 5 W). Altitude 3437 feet. Named on Lake Shastina (1954) 15' quadrangle.

Oxone Spring: see **Shasta Springs** [SISKIYOU].

— P —

Pacheco [SHASTA]: *locality,* 5.5 miles southeast of Redding (lat. 40°30'35" N, long. 122°20' W; on W line sec. 28, T 31 N, R 4 W). Named on Redding (1901) 30' quadrangle.

Pacific Heights [BUTTE]: *locality,* 3.25 miles west-northwest of Palermo (lat. 39°27'10" N, long. 121°36'10" W). Named on Palermo (1912) 7.5' quadrangle. Marysville (1895) 30' quadrangle shows a place called Lava Beds located 2.5 miles north-northwest of Palermo at or near present Pacific Heights; it was a community of Chinese miners (Dunn, F.D., p. 60-61).

Packer Gulch [TEHAMA]: *canyon,* drained by a stream that flows nearly 5 miles to China Gulch (1) 9 miles west of Hooker (lat. 40°19'05" N, long. 122°29'10" W; near S line sec. 36, T 29 N, R 6 W). Named on Mitchell Gulch (1965) 7.5' quadrangle.

Packer Island [GLENN]: *area,* 11.5 miles east-southeast of Willows near Sacramento River (lat. 39°26'45" N, long. 122°00'25" W); the place is partly enclosed by water of Packer Lake. Named on Princeton (1952) 7.5' quadrangle.

Packer Lake [GLENN]: *lake,* 11.5 miles east-southeast of Willows in a cutoff meander of Sacramento River (lat. 39°27' N, long. 122°00'30" W). Named on Princeton (1952) 7.5' quadrangle. Called Packer Slough on Maxwell (1906) 15' quadrangle.

Packers Bay [SHASTA]: *embayment,* 15 miles south-southeast of Lamoine along Shasta Lake (lat. 40°16'10" N, long. 122°20'30" W; sec. 29, 32, T 34 N, R 4 W); the feature is the flooded lower part of Packers Gulch. Named on Lamoine (1957) 15' quadrangle.

Packers Gulch [SHASTA]: *canyon,* drained by a stream that flows 0.25 mile to Packers Bay 15 miles south-southeast of Lamoine (lat. 40°46'35" N, long. 122°20'30" W; sec. 29, T 34 N, R 4 W). Named on Lamoine (1957) 15' quadrangle. Steger (p. 51) associated the name with an old pack-train trail.

Packer Slough: see **Packer Lake** [GLENN].

Packers Peak [SISKIYOU]: *peak,* 26 miles south of Etna on Siskiyou-Trinity County line (lat. 41°05'30" N, long. 122°58'10" W). Altitude 7828 feet. Named on Coffee Creek (1955) 15' quadrangle.

Packers Valley [SISKIYOU]: *valley,* 13 miles southwest of Scott Bar (lat. 41°38'20" N, long. 123°12'20" W). Named on Grider Valley (1981) 7.5' quadrangle.

Paige Bar [SHASTA]: *locality,* 5.25 miles north of Igo along Clear Creek (lat. 40°34'55" N, long. 122°32'55" W; near SW cor. sec. 34, T 32 N, R 6 W). Named on Igo (1979) 7.5' quadrangle.

Paige Boulder Creek [SHASTA]: *stream,* flows 3.5 miles to Clear Creek 5.25 miles north of Igo (lat. 40°34'55" N, long. 122°32'25" W; near W line sec. 34, T 32 N, R 6 W); the mouth of the stream is at Paige Bar. Named on Igo (1979) 7.5' quadrangle. Called Boulder Creek on Weaverville (1913) 30' quadrangle.

Paine's Creek: see **Paynes Creek** [TEHAMA] (1).

Painter Creek [SHASTA]: *stream,* flows less than 1 mile to Shasta Lake 13 miles north of Millville (lat. 40°44'15" N, long. 122°11'05" W; near S line sec. 2, T 33 N, R 3 W). Named on Bella Vista (1965) 7.5' quadrangle.

Paint Pot Crater [SISKIYOU]: *peak,* 6 miles west-southwest of Medicine Lake (lat. 41°33' N, long. 121°42'30" W). Altitude 6318 feet. Named on Medicine Lake (1952) 15' quadrangle.

Palermo [BUTTE]: *town,* 5.5 miles south of Oroville (lat. 39°26'10" N, long. 121°32'35" W; mainly in sec. 5, 8, T 18 N, R 4 E). Named on Palermo (1970) 7.5' quadrangle. Postal authorities established Palermo post office in 1888 (Frickstad, p. 11). The town was named after Palermo in Sicily because, like Sicily, the place is suited to olive culture (Gudde, 1949, p. 249).

Palmer Gulch [TEHAMA]: *canyon,* drained by a stream that flows 2.5 miles to Paynes Creek (1) nearly 2 miles west-southwest of Dales (lat. 40°18'10" N, long. 122°06' W; near SW cor. sec. 4, T 28 N, R 2 W). Named on Dales (1965) 7.5' quadrangle.

Palo Cedro [SHASTA]: *town,* 3.5 miles north-northwest of Millville (lat. 40°33'50" N, long. 122°14'15" W; around SW cor. sec. 3, T 31 N, R 3 W).

Named on Palo Cedro (1965) 7.5' quadrangle. Called Palocedro on Redding (1901) 30' quadrangle. Postal authorities established Albertson post office 4 miles west of Millville in 1883, changed the name to Roberts in 1885, changed the name to Palocedro in 1893, and changed the name to Palo Cedro in 1906; the name "Albertson" was for William A. Albertson, first postmaster, and the name "Roberts" was for B.F. Roberts, a pioneer teacher in the neighborhood (Salley, p. 4, 166, 187).

Panhandle Hills [SISKIYOU]: *range,* 3.25 miles south-southeast of Mount Dome (lat. 41°46'10" N, long. 121°39'30" W). Named on Mount Dome (1950) 15' quadrangle.

Panhandle Lake [SISKIYOU]: *intermittent lake,* 700 feet long, 2.5 miles southeast of Mount Dome (lat. 41°46'50" N, long. 121°39'30" W; sec. 32, T 46 N, R 3 E). Named on Mount Dome (1950) 15' quadrangle.

Panorama Point [SHASTA]: *peak,* 3 miles west-southwest of Balls Ferry (lat. 40°24'15" N, long. 122°14'55" W; at N line sec. 6, T 29 N, R 3 E). Named on Balls Ferry (1965) 7.5' quadrangle. The railroad stop at Panorama Point was called Culp, for H.A. Culp, the retired assistant superintendent of Southern Pacific Railroad; Klotz Spur also was at this place (Steger, p. 27).

Panther Canyon [SISKIYOU]: *canyon,* drained by a stream that flows nearly 4 miles to Shovel Creek 12.5 miles northwest of Macdoel (lat. 41°57' N, long. 122°10'30" W; near N line sec. 2, T 47 N, R 3 W). Named on Macdoel (1954) 15' quadrangle.

Panther Cove [SISKIYOU]: *relief feature,* 6.5 miles south-southwest of Scott Bar (lat. 41°39' N, long. 123°03' W; on E line sec. 24, T 44 N, R 11 W). Named on Scott Bar (1980) 7.5' quadrangle.

Panther Creek [GLENN-TEHAMA]: *stream,* heads in Glenn County and flows 4.5 miles to Grindstone Creek [GLENN-TEHAMA] 5.5 miles north of Black Butte [GLENN] in Tehama County (lat. 39°48'20" N, long. 122°51'45" W; sec. 34, T 23 N, R 9 W). Named on Log Spring (1967) and Mendocino Pass (1967) 7.5' quadrangles.

Panther Creek [SHASTA]: *stream,* flows 2.25 miles to McCloud River [SHASTA-SISKIYOU] 4.5 miles north of Shoeinhorse Mountain (lat. 41°08'10" N, long. 122°04'30" W). Named on Shoeinhorse Mountain (1954) 15' quadrangle.

Panther Creek [SISKIYOU]:

(1) *stream,* flows 2.25 miles to Ukonom Creek 4.5 miles west of Ukonom Lake (lat. 41°34'40" N, long. 123°26'30" W). Named on Ukonom Mountain (1980) 7.5' quadrangle.

(2) *stream,* flows 7.25 miles to end just northwest of McCloud (lat. 41°15'50" N, long. 122°08'45" W; sec. 36, T 40 N, R 3 W); the stream heads near Panther Meadow. Named on Shasta (1954) 15' quadrangle.

Panther Creek [TEHAMA]:

(1) *stream,* flows 8 miles to South Fork Battle Creek [SHASTA-TEHAMA] 7 miles west of Mineral (lat. 40°21'25" N, long. 121°43'40" W; near NE cor. sec. 22, T 29 N, R 2 E). Named on Lassen Peak (1956) 15' quadrangle.

(2) *stream,* flows 3.5 miles to Deer Creek (2) 5 miles northeast of Polk Springs (lat. 40°09'50" N, long. 121°35'30" W; near W line sec. 25, T 27 N, R 3 E). Named on Butte Meadows (1958) 15' quadrangle.

Panther Gulch [SHASTA]: *canyon,* drained by a stream that flows 1.5 miles to Middle Fork Cottonwood Creek [SHASTA-TEHAMA] 2.5 miles northeast of Arbuckle Mountain (lat. 40°25'15" N, long. 122°49'40" W; sec. 25, T 30 N, R 9 W). Named on Chanchelulla Peak (1951) 15' quadrangle.

Panther Gulch [SISKIYOU]: *canyon,* drained by a stream that flows 1.5 miles to Seiad Creek 4.25 miles northeast of the village of Seiad Valley (lat. 41°52'40" N, long. 123°07'40" W). Named on Dutch Creek (1980) 7.5' quadrangle.

Panther Gulch [TEHAMA]: *canyon,* drained by a stream that flows 3.5 miles to Cold Fork (1) 4.25 miles northwest of Wakefield Flat (lat. 40°09'45" N, long. 122°42'15" W; near W line sec. 30, T 27 N, R 7 W). Named on Cold Fork (1967) 7.5' quadrangle.

Panther Meadow [SISKIYOU]: *area,* 7.5 miles north-northwest of McCloud (lat. 41°21'20" N, long. 122°12' W; sec. 33, T 41 N, R 3 W). Named on Shasta (1954) 15' quadrangle.

Panther Rock [SISKIYOU]: *relief feature,* 12.5 miles west-southwest of Macdoel (lat. 41°47'15" N, long. 122°14'15" W; sec. 32, T 46 N, R 3 W). Named on Macdoel (1954) 15' quadrangle.

Panther Rock [TEHAMA]: *relief feature,* 2.25 miles east-southeast of Wakefield Flat (lat. 40°06'50" N, long. 122°36'05" W; at N line sec. 13, T 26 N, R 7 W). Named on Lowrey (1967) 7.5 quadrangle.

Panther Spring [TEHAMA]: *spring,* 12 miles southwest of Mineral (lat. 40°14'50" N, long. 121°46'20" W; near S line sec. 29, T 28 N, R 2 E). Named on Panther Spring (1953) 15' quadrangle.

Papoose Gulch [SHASTA]: *canyon,* drained by a stream that flows less than 1 mile to Brandy Creek 7 miles north-northwest of Igo (lat. 40°36'15" N, long. 122°34'55" W; sec. 30, T 32 N, R 6 W). Named on Igo (1979) 7.5' quadrangle.

Papoose Hill [SISKIYOU]: *peak,* 5 miles south-southwest of Medicine Lake (lat. 41°29'55" N, long. 121°38'25" W). Altitude 5981 feet. Named on Hambone (1961) and Medicine Lake (1952) 15' quadrangles.

Paradise [BUTTE]: *town,* 12 miles east-northeast of Chico (lat. 39°45'35" N, long. 121°37'20" W). Named on Cherokee (1970), Hamlin Canyon (1951), Paradise East (1980), and Paradise West (1980) 7.5' quadrangles. Postal authorities established Paradise post office in 1877, discontinued it in 1911, and reestablished it the same year when they moved Orloff post office and renamed it Paradise (Frickstad, p. 11). The town incorporated in 1979. The name "Paradise" applied to Paradise Flat before the post office took the name to present Paradise, which first was called Leonards Mill, and sometimes Poverty Ridge (Dunn, F.D., p. 83). California Mining Bureau's (1909d) map shows a place called Orloff situated 14.5 miles east of Chico. Postal authorities established Orloff post office 1.5 miles southwest of Paradise in 1905 and discontinued it in 1911, when they moved it to present Paradise; the name was for Orloff Miller, an early settler (Salley, p. 163). F.D. Dunn (p. 80) listed a place called Optimo that was located about 3 miles northeast of downtown Paradise (NE quarter sec. 1, T 22 N, R 3 E). California Division of Highways' (1934) map shows a place called Wagstaff located along Southern Pacific Railroad 2 miles northeast of downtown Paradise (sec. 11, T 22 N, R 3 E); the same map shows a place called Ostrander situated along the railroad 1.5 miles northeast of downtown Paradise (at S line sec. 11, T 22 N, R 3 E).

Paradise: see **Paradise Flat,** under **Helltown** [BUTTE].

Paradise Craggy [SISKIYOU]: *peak,* nearly 7 miles south of Hornbrook (lat. 41°48'50" N, long. 122°32'45" W; at N line sec. 28, T 46 N, R 6 W). Altitude 4911 feet. Named on Hornbrook (1955) 15' quadrangle. Called Badger Peak on Shasta (1894) 1° quadrangle, and called Craggy on Averill's (1935) map, which has the name "Fools Paradise" at or near the feature.

Paradise Flat: see **Helltown** [BUTTE].

Paradise Lake [BUTTE]: *lake,* behind a dam on Little Butte Creek 6.5 miles north-northeast of Paradise (lat. 39°51'05" N, long. 121°34'40" W; near W line sec. 18, T 23 N, R 4 E). Named on Paradise East (1980) 7.5' quadrangle.

Paradise Lake [SISKIYOU]: *lake,* 650 feet long, 14 miles southwest of Scott Bar (lat. 41°36'45" N, long. 123°12'35" W). Named on Marble Mountain (1980) 7.5' quadrangle.

Paradise Peak [SHASTA]: *peak,* 6 miles southwest of Shasta Bally on Shasta-Trinity County line (lat. 40°33'15" N, long. 122°44'35" W; sec. 11, T 31 N, R 8 E). Named on Shasta Bally (1978) 7.5' quadrangle.

Paradise Pines [BUTTE]: *district,* 4.5 miles north-northeast of downtown Paradise (lat. 39°49'15" N, long. 121°36' W). Named on Paradise East (1980) 7.5' quadrangle.

Parish Camp [BUTTE]: *locality,* 6.25 miles south-southeast of Paradise (lat. 39°40'40" N, long. 121°33'50" W; sec. 18, T 21 N, R 4 E). Named on Cherokee (1970) 7.5' quadrangle.

Parker [SISKIYOU]: *locality,* 12.5 miles east-southeast of Etna along East Fork Scott River (lat. 41°23' N, long. 122°41' W). Named on Shasta (1894) 1° quadrangle.

Parker Camp [SISKIYOU]: *locality,* 13 miles west of Macdoel (lat. 41°50'10" N, long. 122°16' W; sec. 14, T 46 N, R 4 W); the place is near the head of Parker Creek. Named on Copco (1954) 15' quadrangle. Macdoel (1941) 30' quadrangle shows Parker cabin at the site.

Parker Creek [SISKIYOU]: *stream,* flows 3.5 miles to Bogus Creek 16 miles west of Macdoel (lat. 41°50'20" N, long. 122°18'45" W; sec. 16, T 46 N, R 4 W). Named on Copco (1954) 15' quadrangle.

Parker Creek [TEHAMA]: *stream,* flows 8.5 miles to Burch Creek 7.25 miles east of Flournoy (lat. 39°54'15" N, long. 122°18'15" W; sec. 27, T 24 N, R 4 W). Named on Flournoy (1967), Henleyville (1967), and Sehorn Creek (1967) 7.5' quadrangles.

Park Gulch [SISKIYOU]: *canyon,* drained by a stream that flows 1.5 miles to Elliott Creek 12 miles north-northeast of the village of Seiad Valley (lat. 41°59'55" N, long. 123°05'55" W). Named on Dutch Creek (1980) 7.5' quadrangle.

Parkhill [BUTTE]: *locality,* 7.5 miles northwest of the village of Berry Creek (lat. 39°43'20" N, long. 121°29'45" W; sec. 35, T 21 N, R 4 E). Named on Berry Creek (1970) 7.5' quadrangle.

Park Lakes: see **West Park Lakes** [SISKIYOU].

Parks Canyon [SISKIYOU]: *canyon,* drained by a stream that flows less than 1 mile to Copco Lake 17 miles west-northwest of Macdoel (lat. 41°58'10" N, long. 122°17'05" W; near E line sec. 34, T 48 N, R 4 W). Named on Copco (1954) 15' quadrangle.

Parks Creek [SISKIYOU]: *stream,* flows 20 miles to Shasta River 28 miles southwest of Macdoel (lat. 41°34'50" N, long. 122°25'45" W; at S line sec. 9, T 43 N, R 5 W). Named on China Mountain (1955), Lake Shastina (1954), and Weed (1954) 15' quadrangles. West Fork enters from the west 6 miles west of Weed; it is 5 miles long and is named on China Mountain (1955) 15' quadrangle.

Parks Hill [BUTTE]: *peak,* nearly 2 miles east-northeast of Bangor (lat. 39°23'40" N, long. 121°22'20" W; near NE cor. sec. 26, T 18 N, R 5 E). Altitude 1554 feet. Named on Rackerby (1948) 7.5' quadrangle.

Parkville: see **Balls Ferry** [SHASTA].

Parrot Mill [SISKIYOU]: *locality,* 5.5 miles south of Etna along North Fork French Creek (2) (lat. 41°22'35" N, long. 122°54'35" W; sec. 29, T 41 N,

R 9 W). Named on Etna (1934) 30' quadrangle.

Parrott Landing [BUTTE]: *locality,* 10 miles west of Durham along Sacramento River (lat. 39°37'05" N, long. 121°58'45" W). Named on Llano Seco (1948) 7.5' quadrangle.

Parsons Well [SISKIYOU]: *well,* 8 miles northeast of Bray (lat. 41°44'15" N, long. 121°52' W; near S line sec. 16, T 45 N, R 1 E). Named on Bray (1950) 15' quadrangle.

Paskenta [TEHAMA]: *village,* 20 miles west of Corning (lat. 39°53'05" N, long. 122°32'45" W; near N line sec. 4, 5, T 23 N, R 6 W). Named on Paskenta (1967) 7.5' quadrangle. Postal authorities established Paskenta post office in 1872 (Frickstad, p. 205). The name is of Indian origin (Kroeber, p. 54).

Pat Ford Creek [SISKIYOU]: *stream,* flows 3 miles to Scott River 1 mile south of Scott Bar (lat. 41°43'35" N, long. 123°00'30" W; near NW cor. sec. 28, T 45 N, R 10 W). Named on Fort Jones (1955) 15' quadrangle, and on Scott Bar (1980) 7.5' quadrangle. South Fork enters from the southeast 1400 feet upstream from the mouth of the main creek; it is less than 1 mile long and is named on Scott Bar (1980) 7.5' quadrangle.

Patricia Lake [TEHAMA]: *lake,* 300 feet long, 10 miles north of Deer Creek Station on Tehama-Plumas County line (lat. 40°24'05" N, long. 121°29' W; sec. 1, T 29 N, R 4 E). Named on Mount Harkness (1956) 15' quadrangle.

Patterson Creek [SISKIYOU]:
(1) *stream,* flows 3.5 miles to end near Scott River 6 miles west-northwest of Fort Jones (lat. 41°38'35" N, long. 122°56'45" W; near N line sec. 25, T 44 N, R 10 W). Named on Fort Jones (1955) 15' quadrangle.
(2) *stream,* flows 13 miles to Kidder Creek 3.5 miles south-southwest of Fort Jones in Scott Valley (lat. 41°33'25" N, long. 122°51'55" W; near S line sec. 22, T 43 N, R 9 W). Named on Etna (1955) and Fort Jones (1955) 15' quadrangles.

Patterson Creek [TEHAMA]: *stream,* formed by the confluence of North Fork and South Fork, flows 3.5 miles to Cottonwood Creek [SHASTA-TEHAMA] 9 miles north of Bend (lat. 40°22'55" N, long. 122°12'40" W). Named on Balls Ferry (1965), Bend (1965), and Hooker (1965) 7.5' quadrangles. North Fork is 3 miles long and South Fork is 4 miles long; both forks are named on Bend (1965) and Hooker (1965) 7.5' quadrangles.

Patton Mill [TEHAMA]: *locality,* 7.25 miles west of Paskenta (lat. 39°54'30" N, long. 122°40'40" W; sec. 29, T 24 N, R 7 W). Named on Riley Ridge (1967) 7.5' quadrangle. Paskenta (1920) 15' quadrangle shows Patton Mill House situated at or near the place.

Patton Peak [BUTTE]: *peak,* 8.5 miles southeast of Paradise (lat. 39°40'20" N, long. 121°30'45" W; sec. 15, T 21 N, R 4 E). Altitude 1458 feet. Named on Cherokee (1970) 7.5' quadrangle.

Pattymocus Butte [TEHAMA]: *peak,* 1.5 miles southeast of Beegum Peak (lat. 40°17'45" N, long. 122°52' W; sec. 10, T 28 N, R 9 W). Altitude 4020 feet. Named on Chanchelulla Peak (1951) 15' quadrangle.

Paul Gulch [SISKIYOU]: *canyon,* drained by a stream that flows 0.5 mile to Hungry Creek 10.5 miles west-northwest of Hornbrook (lat. 41°58'30" N, long. 122°44'15" W; sec. 26, T 48 N, R 8 W). Named on Hornbrook (1955) 15' quadrangle.

Pawnee: see **Whitmore** [SHASTA].

Payne: see **Tom Payne Creek** [SISKIYOU]; **Tom Payne Peak** [SISKIYOU].

Payne Creek: see **Paynes Creek** [TEHAMA] (1) and (2).

Payne Lake: see **Paynes Lakie** [SISKIYOU].

Paynes Creek [SISKIYOU]: *stream,* flows 4.25 miles to end 11 miles northeast of Bartle (lat. 41°29'30" N, long. 121°33'45" W; at W line sec. 7, T 42 N, R 4 E). Named on Medicine Lake (1952) 15' quadrangle.

Paynes Creek [TEHAMA]:
(1) *stream,* flows 32 miles to Sacramento River nearly 2 miles east of Bend (lat. 40°15'20" N, long. 122°10'25" W; sec. 26, T 28 N, R 3 W). Named on Lassen Peak (1956) and Manton (1956) 15' quadrangles, and on Bend (1965) and Dales (1965) 7.5' quadrangles. Called Payne Creek on Lassen Peak (1894) 1° quadrangle, and called Paine's Creek on Red Bluff (1894) 1° quadrangle.
(2) *village,* 7.25 miles south-southwest of Manton (lat. 40°20'05" N, long. 121°54'45" W; on E line sec. 25, T 29 N, R 1 W); the place is along Paynes Creek (1). Named on Manton (1956) 15' quadrangle. Called Payne Creek on Lassen Peak (1894) 1° quadrangle, and called Paynescreek on California Mining Bureau's (1909b) map. Postal authorities established Paynes Creek post office in 1890 (Frickstad, p. 205). Waring (p. 360) listed Tadpole Spring, located beside the stage road 3 miles east of Paynes Creek post office.

Paynes Lake [SISKIYOU]: *lake,* 1500 feet long, 8.5 miles south-southwest of Etna (lat. 41°20'30" N, long. 122°57'40" W; sec. 12, T 40 N, R 10 W). Named on Etna (1955) 15' quadrangle. Called Payne Lake on Etna (1934) 30' quadrangle.

Paynes Lake Creek [SISKIYOU]: *stream,* flows 4.25 miles to French Creek (2) 6.5 miles south of Etna (lat. 41°21'45" N, long. 122°54' W; sec. 32, T 41 N, R 9 W); the stream heads at Paynes Lake. Named on Etna (1955) 15' quadrangle.

Paynes Slough [TEHAMA]: *water feature,* joins Sacramento River 2.5 miles east-southeast of Red Bluff (lat. 40°09'15" N, long. 122°11'30" W). Named on Red Bluff East (1951) 7.5' quadrangle.

Paynes Springs [SISKIYOU]: *springs,* 2.5 miles southeast of Medicine Lake (lat. 41°33'40" N, long. 121°33'35" W); the springs are at the head of Paynes Creek. Named on Medicine Lake (1952) 15' quadrangle.

Peachton [BUTTE]: *locality,* 3.5 miles southeast of Biggs (lat. 39°22'50" N, long. 121°39'40" W). Named on Biggs (1970) 7.5' quadrangle. Biggs (1912) 7.5' quadrangle shows a place called Ord Ranch located along Northern Electric Railroad at the place.

Peacock Creek [SHASTA]: *stream,* flows 2.5 miles to Pit River 2.5 miles northeast of Fall River Mills (lat. 41°02'15" N, long. 121°24'20" W; near SW cor. sec. 16, T 37 N, R 5 E). Named on Fall River Mills (1961) 15' quadrangle.

Pear Lake [TEHAMA]: *lake,* 500 feet long, 3 miles south-southwest of Mineral (lat. 40°18'25" N, long. 121°37'15" W; sec. 3, T 28 N, R 3 E). Named on Lassen Peak (1956) 15' quadrangle.

Pea Vine: see **Junction House** [BUTTE].

Peavine: see **Junction House** [BUTTE]; **Merrimac** [BUTTE].

Peavine Creek [BUTTE]: *stream,* flows 4.25 miles to French Creek 2 miles north-northwest of the village of Brush Creek (lat. 39°43'50" N, long. 121°21'15" W; sec. 30, T 22 N, R 6 E). Named on Brush Creek (1970) and Soapstone Hill (1979) 7.5' quadrangles.

Peavine Creek [SHASTA]:
(1) *stream,* flows 1.5 miles to Rock Creek (1) 7.5 miles east-northeast of the village of Big Bend (lat. 41°04' N, long. 121°46'50" W; sec. 18, T 37 N, R 2 E). Named on Big Bend (1961) 15' quadrangle.
(2) *stream,* flows 0.5 mile to Clear Creek 5 miles northwest of Schell Mountain (lat. 40°49'45" N, long. 122°35' W; at E line sec. 6, T 35 N, R 6 W). Named on Schell Mountain (1950) 15' quadrangle.

Peavine Gulch [SHASTA]: *canyon,* 1 mile long, 16 miles northwest of Lassen Peak (lat. 40°39'35" N, long. 121°42'05" W; mainly in sec. 1, T 32 N, R 2 E). Named on Manzanita Lake (1956) 15' quadrangle.

Pebble: see **Dunsmuir** [SISKIYOU].

Peck Gulch [SISKIYOU]: *canyon,* drained by a stream that flows less than 1 mile to North Fork Salmon River 3.5 miles west of Sawyers Bar (lat. 41°18'30" N, long. 123°11'55" W). Named on Sawyers Bar (1979) 7.5' quadrangle.

Pecks [SHASTA]: *locality,* about 1.5 miles north of present Burney Falls along Pit River (lat. 41°01'45" N, long. 121°38'30" W). Named on Modoc Lava Bed (1892) 1° quadrangle.

Pelican Mound [GLENN]: *hill,* 4.5 miles south of Willows (lat. 39°27'40" N, long. 122°11'45" W; sec. 33, T 19 N, R 3 W). Named on Maxwell (1906) 15' quadrangle.

Peligreen Gulch [TEHAMA]: *canyon,* drained by a stream that flows 2 miles to Round Mountain Creek 3 miles west-southwest of Panther Spring (lat. 40°13'40" N, long. 121°49'20" W). Named on Panther Spring (1953) 15' quadrangle, which shows Peligreen place near the head of the canyon. On Mineral (1941) 30' quadrangle, the stream in present Peligreen Gulch is called South Fork Round Mountain Creek.

Peninsula Bay [SISKIYOU]: *area,* 9.5 miles east of Mount Dome (lat. 41°49'50" N, long. 121°30'10" W; sec. 10, 15, T 46 N, R 4 E). Named on Tulelake (1951) 15' quadrangle.

Penoyar [SISKIYOU]: *locality,* 11.5 miles south-southwest of Macdoel along Southern Pacific Railroad (lat. 41°40' N, long. 122°03'30" W; at NE cor. sec. 15, T 44 N, R 2 W). Named on The Whaleback (1954) 15' quadrangle.

Pentacola Field [TEHAMA]: *valley,* 8 miles west-northwest of Rosewood (lat. 40°18'50" N, long. 122°41'45" W; near N line sec. 6, T 28 N, R 7 W); the feature is at the head of Pentacola Gulch. Named on Ono (1952) 15' quadrangle.

Pentacola Gulch [TEHAMA]: *canyon,* drained by a stream that flows 2 miles to Dry Creek (1) 6.5 miles west-northwest of Rosewood (lat. 40°18' N, long. 122°40'10" W; at NW cor. sec. 9, T 28 N, R 7 W). Named on Ono (1952) 15' quadrangle.

Pentz [BUTTE]: *village,* 7 miles south-southeast of Paradise in Messilla Valley (lat. 39°39'20" N, long. 121°35' W; near SE cor. sec. 24, T 21 N, R 3 E). Named on Cherokee (1970) 7.5' quadrangle. Postal authorities established Pentz post office in 1864 and discontinued it in 1912; the misspelled name was for Manoah Pence, first postmaster (Salley, p. 169). Mr. Pence, one of several men who came to the site in 1850 and opened a store and eating place there, became sole owner of the property in 1866 (Wells and Chambers, p. 251). Postal authorities established Clear Creek post office 3 miles southwest of Pentz at the confluence of East Branch Clear Creek and West Branch Clear Creek in 1877 and discontinued it in 1906 (Salley, p. 45).

Pepperwood Spring [GLENN]: *spring,* 9.5 miles northwest of the village of Elk Creek (lat. 39°43' N, long. 122°38'10" W). Named on Alder Springs (1967) 7.5' quadrangle.

Pepperwood Spring [TEHAMA]:
(1) *spring,* 8 miles south of Wakefield Flat (lat. 40°00'35" N, long. 122°39'30" W; sec. 21, T 25 N, R 7 W). Named on Raglin Ridge (1967) 7.5' quadrangle.
(2) *spring,* 7 miles west-northwest of Paskenta (lat. 39°54'45" N, long.

122°39'50" W; near NE cor. sec. 29, T 24 N, R 7 W). Named on Paskenta (1920) 15' quadrangle.

Perch Slough [GLENN]: *water feature,* cutoff meander of Sacramento River 13 miles north of Butte City (lat. 39°39'20" N, long. 121°59'50" W). Named on Ord Ferry (1949) 7.5' quadrangle.

Perkins Gulch [SISKIYOU]: *canyon,* drained by a stream that flows 2.25 miles to Indian Creek (1) less than 1 mile north-northwest of Happy Camp (lat. 41°48'25" N, long. 123°23'05" W; sec. 3, T 16 N, R 7 E). Named on Happy Camp (1980) 7.5' quadrangle.

Perkins Lake [BUTTE]: *lake,* 1 mile long, 9.5 miles west-southwest of Durham (lat. 39°35'15" N, long. 121°57'35" W). Named on Llano Seco (1948) 7.5' quadrangle.

Perkins Ridge [BUTTE]: *ridge,* south-southwest-trending, 4 miles long, 5.5 miles south of Paradise (lat. 39°41'10" N, long. 121°38'30" W). Named on Hamlin Canyon (1951) 7.5' quadrangle.

Perks Pasture [SISKIYOU]: *area,* 4.5 miles north of Condrey Mountain (lat. 42°00' N, long. 122°57'55" W; at NW cor. sec. 24, T 48 N, R 10 W). Named on Condrey Mountain (1955) 15' quadrangle.

Persido Bar [SISKIYOU]: *locality,* 2.5 miles east-northeast of Dillon Mountain along Klamath River (lat. 41°32'35" N, long. 123°31'35" W). Named on Dillon Mountain (1983) 7.5' quadrangle. The name is the Anglicization of an Indian word {Gudde, 1949, p. 258).

Pete Ives Glade [SISKIYOU]: *relief feature,* 9 miles north-northwest of the village of Seiad Valley at the head of Marble Gulch (lat. 41°58'05" N, long. 123°14'35" W). Named on Kangaroo Mountain (1980) 7.5' quadrangle.

Petersburgh: see **Salmon River** [SISKIYOU].

Peterson Gulch [SHASTA]: *canyon,* less than 1 mile long, 15 miles south of Lamoine (lat. 40°45'45" N, long. 122°24'50" W; sec. 34, T 34 N, R 5 W). Named on Lamoine (1946) 15' quadrangle. Water of Shasta Lake now floods the feature.

Petty Butte [SHASTA]: *peak,* 1 mile west-northwest of Igo (lat. 40°30'45" N, long. 122°33'30" W; near W line sec. 28, T 31 N, R 6 W). Altitude 1768 feet. Named on Igo (1979) 7.5' quadrangle.

Phantom Meadows [SISKIYOU]: *area,* 12.5 miles north of Happy Camp (lat. 41°58'20" N, long. 123°19' W). Named on Figurehead Mountain (1980) 7.5' quadrangle.

Phelan Island [GLENN]: *area,* 15 miles north of Butte City between Sacramento River and Negro Sam Slough (lat. 39°41' N, long. 121°57'20" W). Named on Ord Ferry (1949) 7.5' quadrangle. Called Munroeville Island on Chico Landing (1912) 7.5' quadrangle.

Philadelphia: see **New Philadelphia**, under **Thompson Flat** [BUTTE].

Philbrook Creek [BUTTE]: *stream,* flows 6 miles to West Branch Feather River 4 miles south-southeast of Butte Meadows (lat. 40°01'55" N, long. 121°30'40" W; near S line sec. 10, T 25 N, R 4 E). Named on Butte Meadows (1958) and Jonesville (1958) 15' quadrangles.

Philbrook Reservoir [BUTTE]: *lake,* behind a dam 5.5 miles south of Jonesville on Philbrook Creek (lat. 40°01'50" N, long. 121°28'15" W). Named on Jonesville (1958) 15' quadrangle.

Phillips Corner [BUTTE]: *locality,* 1.5 miles east-southeast of Honcut (lat. 39°19'10" N, long. 121°30'20" W; sec. 22, T 17 N, R 4 E). Named on Honcut (1952) 7.5' quadrangle. Honcut post office was at the site until 1878 (Dunn, F.D., p. 85).

Phillips Gulch [SISKIYOU]: *canyon,* drained by a stream that flows 1.5 miles to Oak Flat Creek 4.5 miles southwest of Happy Camp (lat. 41°45'05" N, long. 123°26'40" W). Named on Happy Camp (1980) 7.5' quadrangle.

Philpot Lake [SHASTA]: *lake,* 200 feet long, 4 miles west-northwest of Arbuckle Mountain (lat. 40°24'55" N, long. 122°56'10" W; at S line sec. 25, T 30 N, R 10 W). Named on Chanchelulla Peak (1951) 15' quadrangle.

Phoenix Hill [BUTTE]: *peak,* 6.5 miles north of Bangor (lat. 39°29' N, long. 121°24'40" W; at S line sec. 21, T 19 N, R 5 E). Named on Bangor (1947) 7.5' quadrangle.

Picadilly Ridge: see **Haight Mountain** [SISKIYOU].

Picard: see **Dorris** [SISKIYOU].

Pick-Aw-Ish Campground: see **Pick-i-a-wish Campground** [SISKIYOU].

Picayune Gulch [SISKIYOU]: *canyon,* drained by a stream that flows less than 1 mile to North Fork Salmon River 3.5 miles east-northeast of Forks of Salmon (lat. 41°16'50" N, long. 123°15'20" W). Named on Forks of Salmon (1978) 7.5' quadrangle. Called Muddy Gulch on Sawyers Bar (1923) 30' quadrangle.

Picayune Lake [SISKIYOU]: *lake,* 350 feet long, 3.5 miles east of Forks of Salmon (lat. 41°15'55" N, long. 123°15'25" W); the feature is above the head of Picayune Gulch. Named on Forks of Salmon (1978) 7.5' quadrangle.

Pick-i-a-wish Campground [SISKIYOU]: *locality,* 10 miles north-northwest of Ukonom Lake near the mouth of Clear Creek (1) (lat. 41°42'20" N, long. 123°27' W; sec. 7, T 15 N, R 7 E). Named on Ukonom Lake (1955) 15' quadrangle. Called Pick-Aw-Ish Campground on Averill's (1935) map.

Pickle Camp [SISKIYOU]: *locality,* nearly 5 miles south of Ukonom Lake (lat. 41°30'40" N, long. 123°21'45" W). Named on Ukonom Lake (1980) 7.5' quadrangle.

Picnic Creek [SISKIYOU]: *stream,* flows 2 miles to Mill Creek (5) 13 miles south-southeast of Condrey Mountain (lat. 41°45'20" N, long. 122°54'05" W; sec. 17, T 45 N, R 9 W). Named on Condrey Mountain (1955) and Fort Jones (1955) 15' quadrangles.

Pierce [SISKIYOU]: *locality,* 4.5 miles west-northwest of McCloud along McCloud River Railroad (lat. 41°16'10" N, long. 122°13'15" W; sec. 32, T 40 N, R 3 W). Named on Shasta (1954) 15' quadrangle.

Pierces Draw [SISKIYOU]: *canyon,* drained by a stream that flows 1 mile to Cold Springs Creek 10 miles north of Sawyers Bar (lat. 41°26'25" N, long. 123°10'40" W). Named on English Peak (1977) 7.5' quadrangle.

Piety Hill [SHASTA]: *locality,* 0.5 mile northeast of Igo (lat. 40°30'30" N, long. 122°31'40" W). Named on Red Bluff (1894) 1° quadrangle. The name reportedly is from Piety Hill, Michigan, former home of one of the residents of the place; American families at Piety Hill gradually moved to Igo, and by 1880 only Chinese residents remained (Steger, p. 52).

Pig Creek [SISKIYOU]: *stream,* flows 2.5 miles to Squaw Valley Creek 5 miles south of McCloud (lat. 41°12'40" N, long. 122°09' W; sec. 24, T 39 N, R 3 W). Named on Shoeinhorse Mountain (1954) 15' quadrangle.

Pigeon Creek [GLENN]: *stream,* flows 3 miles to Stony Creek [GLENN-TEHAMA] 10.5 miles east of Saint John Mountain (lat. 39°26'05" N, long. 122°30'05" W; near N line sec. 11, T 18 N, R 6 W). Named on Lodoga (1960) 15' quadrangle.

Pigeon Creek [SHASTA]: *stream,* flows 1 mile to Big Basin Creek 11 miles north-northwest of the village of Big Bend (lat. 41°09'50" N, long. 121°59'25" W). Named on Big Bend (1961) 15' quadrangle.

Pigeon Hill [SHASTA]: *peak,* 10 miles north-northwest of the village of Big Bend (lat. 41°09'05" N, long. 121°57'30" W). Named on Big Bend (1961) 15' quadrangle.

Pigeon Roost [SISKIYOU]: *peak,* 4 miles east-southeast of Ukonom Lake (lat. 41°33'20" N, long. 123°17'15" W). Named on Ukonom Lake (1980) 7.5' quadrangle.

Pigpen Creek [TEHAMA]: *stream,* flows 6 miles to Red Bank Creek nearly 3 miles west of Red Bank (lat. 40°06'20" N, long. 122°29'45" W). Named on Lowrey (1967) and Red Bank (1952) 7.5' quadrangles.

Pilgrim Creek [SISKIYOU]: *stream,* flows 8.5 miles to lowlands 9 miles northeast of McCloud (lat. 41°20'10" N, long. 122°00'30" W; at S line sec. 6, T 40 N, R 1 W). Named on Shasta (1954) 15' quadrangle.

Pilot: see **Little Pilot** [SISKIYOU].

Pilot Mountain [SHASTA]: *peak,* 7.25 miles east of Lassen Peak (lat. 40°27'50" N, long. 121°22'30" W; sec. 13, T 30 N, R 5 E). Altitude 7175 feet. Named on Mount Harkness (1956) 15' quadrangle.

Pilot Pinnacle [SHASTA]: *relief feature,* 2 miles southwest of Lassen Peak (lat. 40°28' N, long. 121°32' W; at NE cor. sec. 16, T 30 N, R 4 E). Altitude 8886 feet. Named on Lassen Peak (1956) 15' quadrangle.

Pinchard Creek: see **Pinkard Creek** [BUTTE].

Pinckney: see **Gas Point** [SHASTA].

Pine Basin [SHASTA]: *relief feature,* 6.5 miles south-southwest of Whitmore (lat. 40°32'35" N, long. 121°57'30" W; sec. 15, T 31 N, R 1 W). Named on Whitmore (1956) 15' quadrangle.

Pine Creek [BUTTE-TEHAMA]: *stream,* heads in Tehama County and flows 31 miles to Sacramento River 7 miles west of Chico in Butte County (lat. 39°44'30" N, long. 121°58' W). Named on Butte Meadows (1958) 15' quadrangle, and on Campbell Mound (1952), Cohasset (1979), Foster Island (1950), Nord (1951), Ord Ferry (1949), and Richardson Springs NW (1952) 7.5' quadrangles.

Pine Creek [TEHAMA]:

(1) *stream,* flows 9 miles to South Fork Cottonwood Creek [SHASTA-TEHAMA] nearly 4 miles northwest of Hooker (lat. 40°20'25" N, long. 122°22'20" W; sec. 25, T 29 N, R 5 W). Named on Blossom (1952), Hooker (1965), and Mitchell Gulch (1965) 7.5' quadrangles.

(2) *stream,* flows 16 miles to Reeds Creek 2.5 miles west-southwest of Red Bluff (lat. 40°09'50" N, long. 122°16'45" W; sec. 26, T 27 N, R 4 W). Named on Blossom (1952), Oxbow Bridge (1967) and Red Bluff West (1951) 7.5' quadrangles.

Pine Creek: see **Little Pine Creek** [TEHAMA].

Pine Flat [SHASTA]: *area,* 8.5 miles west-southwest of Shoeinhorse Mountain along McCloud River [SHASTA-SISKIYOU] (lat. 41°01'10" N, long. 122°12'50" W). Named on Shoeinhorse Mountain (1954) 15' quadrangle.

Pine Grove [SHASTA]: *town,* 1.5 miles southeast of the town of Central Valley (lat. 40°39'50" N, long. 122°21'05" W; near NW cor. sec. 5, T 32 N, R 4 W). Named on Project City (1957) 7.5' quadrangle.

Pine Grove Mill: see **Clipper Mills** [BUTTE].

Pine Lake [SISKIYOU]: *lake,* 1350 feet long, 9 miles northwest of Sawyers Bar (lat. 41°24'10" N, long. 123°13'55" W). Named on English Peak (1977) 7.5' quadrangle.

Pineland: see **Cougar** [SISKIYOU]; **Montgomery Creek** [SHASTA] (2).

Pine Meadows: see **Badger Flat** [SHASTA].

Pines: see **The Pines** [BUTTE].

Pine Spring [TEHAMA]: *spring,* 5.5 miles south-southwest of Wakefield

Flat (lat. 40°03' N, long. 122°40'20" W; sec. 5, T 25 N, R 7 W). Named on Raglin Ridge (1967) 7.5' quadrangle.

Pine Timber Gulch [SHASTA]: *canyon,* drained by a stream that flows 5.25 miles to South Cow Creek 8 miles east of Millville (lat. 40°34' N, long. 122°01'40" W; near SW cor. sec. 6, T 31 N, R 1 W). Named on Millville (1953) and Whitmore (1956) 15' quadrangles.

Pine Tree Hollow [SISKIYOU]: *relief feature,* 6 miles east-southeast of McCloud along McCloud River [SHASTA-SISKIYOU] (lat. 41°14'15" N, long. 122°01'30" W; sec. 12, T 39 N, R 2 W). Named on Shoeinhorse Mountain (1954) 15' quadrangle.

Pine View: see **Shingletown** [SHASTA].

Pingston Ravine: see **Pinkston Canyon** [BUTTE].

Pinkard Creek [BUTTE]: *stream,* flows 3.25 miles to Lost Creek Reservoir 3.5 miles north-northeast of Clipper Mills (lat. 39°34'45" N, long. 121°08' W; sec. 24, T 20 N, R 7 E). Named on Clipper Mills (1948) and Strawberry Valley (1948) 7.5' quadrangles. F.D. Dunn (p. 86) gave the alternate names "Pinchard Creek" and "East Creek" for the stream.

Pinkston Canyon [BUTTE]: *canyon,* drained by a stream that flows 2 miles to Deadwood Creek 5.5 miles east of Cherokee (lat. 39°44'20" N, long. 121°31'40" W). Named on Cherokee (1970) 7.5' quadrangle. Called Pingston Ravine on Oroville (1942) 15' quadrangle. The name "Pinkston" is for a family that lived at the place about 1900 (United States Board on Geographic Names, 1973, p. 3).

Pinto Creek [GLENN]: *stream,* flows 1.5 miles to Mendocino County 2.5 miles west-northwest of Black Butte (lat. 39°44'40" N, long. 122°54'40" W; at W line sec. 20, T 22 N, R 9 W); the stream is on the north side of Pinto Ridge. Named on Plaskett Ridge (1967) 7.5' quadrangle.

Pinto Ridge [GLENN]: *ridge,* west-southwest-trending, 3.25 miles long, 2 miles west-northwest of Black Butte on Glenn-Mendocino County line (lat. 39°44'20" N, long. 122°54'30" W); the ridge is south of Pinto Creek. Named on Plaskett Ridge (1967) 7.5' quadrangle.

Pioneer [SISKIYOU]: *locality,* 1.25 miles south of the town of Mount Shasta along Southern Pacific Railroad (lat. 41°17'45" N, long. 122°18'30" W; sec. 21, T 40 N, R 4 W). Named on Weed (1954) 15' quadrangle.

Pismire Ridge [SHASTA]: *ridge,* southeast- to south-trending, 1.5 miles long, 2.25 miles north-northeast of Schell Mountain (lat. 40°53' N, long. 122°30'30" W). Named on Schell Mountain (1950) 15' quadrangle.

Pit: see **Morley** [SHASTA].

Pitbridge [SHASTA]: *locality,* 16 miles south-southeast of Lamoine along Southern Pacific Railroad (lat. 40°46' N, long. 122°19' W; near SE cor. sec. 28, T 34 N, R 4 W); the place is near a railroad bridge across Pit River. Named on Lamoine (1946) 15' quadrangle.

Pitch Fork [SISKIYOU]: *stream,* flows 1.25 miles to East Fork Seiad Creek 6 miles north-northeast of the village of Seiad Valley (lat. 41°54'50" N, long. 123°08'15" W). Named on Dutch Creek (1980) and Kangaroo Mountain (1980) 7.5' quadrangles.

Pit Four Reservoir [SHASTA]: *lake,* behind a dam on Pit River 13 miles northeast of the village of Montgomery Creek (lat. 40°59'20" N, long. 121°46'10" W). Named on Montgomery Creek (1956) 15' quadrangle.

Pit River [SHASTA]: *stream,* enters from Lassen County and flows 74 miles in Shasta County to Pit River Arm Shasta Lake 11.5 miles southeast of Bollibokka Mountain (lat. 40°48'40" N, long. 122°04' W; near SE cor. sec. 10, T 34 N, R 2 W). Named on Big Bend (1961), Bollibokka Mountain (1957), Burney (1957), Fall River Mills (1961), Jellico (1957), Montgomery Creek (1956), and Pondosa (1961) 15' quadrangles. United States Board on Geographic Names (1933, p. 607) rejected the form "Pitt River" for the name. Ogden mentioned the stream in his journal of 1827, and named it for pits that Indians dug near the river to trap game (Steger, p. 52). Whitney (p. 325-326) referred to Stone's Ferry, which was situated on Pit River a short distance below the mouth of McCloud River [SHASTA-SISKIYOU].

Pit River Arm [SHASTA]: *embayment,* opens into Shasta Lake 16 miles south-southeast of Lamoine (lat. 40°45'30" N, long. 122°20' W; sec. 33, T 33 N, R 4 W); the feature is the flooded lower part of the canyon of Pit River. Named on Lamoine (1957) 15' quadrangle.

Pit River Falls [SHASTA]: *waterfall,* 9.5 miles northwest of Coble Mountain (lat. 40°59'10" N, long. 121°28'15" W; at S line sec. 12, T 36 N, R 4 E); the feature is along Pit River. Named on Jellico (1957) 15' quadrangle.

Pittsburg: see **Bully Hill** [SHASTA] (2).

Pittville [SHASTA]: *village,* 6.25 miles east-northeast of Fall River Mills at Shasta-Lassen County line (lat. 41°02'55" N, long. 121°19'50" W; at E line sec. 13, T 37 N, R 5 E). Named on Fall River Mills (1961) 15' quadrangle. Postal authorities established Pittville post office in 1873, discontinued it in 1875, and reestablished it in 1878 (Frickstad, p. 182).

Plantation: see **The Plantation** [SHASTA].

Plantation Gulch [TEHAMA]: *canyon,* drained by a stream that flows 1.25 miles to Martin Creek 2.25 miles north-northeast of Mineral (lat. 40°22'50" N, long. 121°35'05" W; near N line sec. 18, T 29 N, R 4 E). Named on Lassen Peak (1956) 15' quadrangle.

Plaskett Creek [GLENN]: *stream,* flows nearly 2 miles to Cold Creek 3 miles east-southeast of Black Butte (lat. 39°42'30" N, long. 122°49'30" W); the stream heads at Plaskett Meadows. Named on Plaskett Meadows (1967) 7.5' quadrangle.

Plaskett Meadows [GLENN]: *area,* 1.5 miles east of Black Butte (lat. 39°43'35" N, long. 122°50'35" W; at S line sec. 26, T 22 N, R 9 W). Named on Plaskett Meadows (1967) 7.5' quadrangle.

Plaskett Ridge [GLENN]: *ridge,* southwest-trending, 2 miles long, on Glenn-Mendocino County line, center 1.25 miles southwest of Black Butte (lat. 39°42'45" N, long. 122°53'15" W). Named on Plaskett Ridge (1967) 7.5' quadrangle.

Plateau [SHASTA]: *locality,* 3.5 miles east-southeast of Shingletown (lat. 40°28'15" N, long. 121°49'45" W). Named on Lassen Peak (1894) 1° quadrangle. Postal authorities established Plateau post office in 1889 and discontinued it in 1909 (Salley, p. 174).

Platina [SHASTA]: *village,* 3 miles south-southwest of Arbuckle Mountain (lat. 40°21'35" N, long. 122°53'30" W; near SW cor. sec. 16, T 29 N, R 9 W); the village is at the mouth of Platinum Gulch. Named on Chanchelulla Peak (1951) 15' quadrangle. Postal authorities established Platina post office in 1921 (Frickstad, p. 182).

Platinum Gulch [SHASTA]: *canyon,* drained by a stream that flows 1 mile to Middle Fork Cottonwood Creek [SHASTA-TEHAMA] 3 miles south-southwest of Arbuckle Mountain (lat. 40°21'35" N, long. 122°53'30" W; near SW cor. sec. 16, T 29 N, R 9 W). Named on Chanchelulla Peak (1951) 15' quadrangle.

Platte Mountain [BUTTE]: *peak,* 12 miles north of Paradise (lat. 39°56'05" N, long. 121°38'40" W; sec. 16, T 24 N, R 3 E). Named on Cohasset (1979) 7.5' quadrangle.

Platte Ravine [BUTTE]: *canyon,* drained by a stream that flows 1.5 miles to West Branch Butte Creek [BUTTE-GLENN] 12 miles north of Paradise (lat. 39°56'05" N, long. 121°37'30" W; sec. 15, T 24 N, R 3 E); the canyon heads north of Platte Mountain. Named on Cohasset (1979) 7.5' quadrangle.

Platts: see **Forest Ranch** [BUTTE].

Pleasant Lake [SISKIYOU]: *lake,* 1100 feet long, 4 miles south-southeast of Ukonom Lake (lat. 41°31'50" N, long. 123°19' W); the lake is 0.5 mile west-northwest of Pleasant Valley (1). Named on Ukonom Lake (1980) 7.5' quadrangle.

Pleasant Valley [BUTTE]: *valley,* 1.5 miles east-northeast of downtown Oroville (lat. 39°31'10" N, long. 121°31'45" W; mainly in sec. 9, T 19 N, R 4 E). Named on Oroville (1970) 7.5' quadrangle.

Pleasant Valley [GLENN]: *valley,* 3.25 miles east of Saint John Mountain along North Fork (1) Stony Creek [GLENN-TEHAMA] (lat. 39°25'45" N, long. 122°37'50" W). Named on Saint John Mountain (1968) 7.5' quadrangle.

Pleasant Valley [SISKIYOU]:

(1) *canyon,* 4.25 miles southeast of Ukonom Lake (lat. 41°32' N, long. 123°17'50" W); the canyon is 0.5 mile east-northeast of Pleasant Lake. Named on Ukonom Lake (1980) 7.5' quadrangle.

(2) *valley,* 11.5 miles north of Macdoel (lat. 41°59'30" N, long. 122°01'15" W). Named on Dorris (1950) and Macdoel (1954) 15' quadrangles.

Plugtown: see **French Town** [SISKIYOU].

Plumas Rapids [TEHAMA]: *water feature,* 5 miles north-northwest of Vina (lat. 39°59'45" N, long. 122°06' W). Named on Vina (1904) 15' quadrangle.

Plumb Gulch [TEHAMA]: *canyon,* drained by a stream that flows 1.25 miles to Salt Creek (1) 8.5 miles north of Wakefield Flat (lat. 40°14'50" N, long. 122°40'10" W; near W line sec. 28, T 28 N, R 7 W). Named on Ono (1952) 15' quadrangle, and on Cold Fork (1967) 7.5' quadrangle.

Plum Creek [TEHAMA]: *stream,* flows about 12.5 miles to Paynes Creek (1) 10 miles southwest of Manton (lat. 40°18'40" N, long. 121°58'40" W; sec. 4, T 28 N, R 1 W). Named on Manton (1956) 15' quadrangle. North Fork enters from the northeast 4.5 miles upstream from the mouth of the main creek; it is 3.5 miles long and is named on Manton (1956) 15' quadrangle.

Plum Creek Ridge [TEHAMA]: *ridge,* generally west-northwest-trending, 6.5 miles long, 9 miles south of Manton (lat. 40°18'15" N, long. 121°52'30" W); the ridge is south of Plum Creek. Named on Manton (1956) 15' quadrangle.

Plum Garden [TEHAMA]: *area,* 3.25 miles west-southwest of Tomhead Mountain (lat. 40°07'20" N, long. 122°51'20" W; near W line sec. 11, T 26 N, R 9 W). Named on Yolla Bolly (1954) 15' quadrangle.

Plummer Creek [SISKIYOU]: *stream,* flows 6.5 miles to South Fork Salmon Creek nearly 4 miles west of Cecilville (lat. 41°09'05" N, long. 123°12'35" W). Named on Cecil Lake (1979) and Cecilville (1979) 7.5' quadrangles. West Fork enters from the southwest 1.5 miles upstream from the mouth of the main creek; it is 2.25 miles long and is named on Cecilville (1979) and Youngs Peak (1979) 7.5' quadrangles.

Plum Valley [SHASTA]: *area,* 17 miles north-northeast of Lassen Peak (lat. 40°43' N, long. 121°23'45" W; near W line sec 14, R 33 N, R 5 E). Named on Prospect Peak (1957) 15' quadrangle.

Pluto Cave [SISKIYOU]: *cave,* 23 miles southwest of Macdoel (lat. 41°34' N, long. 122°17' W; at SE cor. sec. 15, T 43 N, R 4 W). Named on Lake

Shastina (1954) 15' quadrangle. Called The Caves on Macdoel (1941) 30' quadrangle, and Whitney (p. 351) used the name "Pluto's Cave" for the feature.

Pocket: see **The Pocket** [GLENN].

Pocket Gulch [SHASTA]: *canyon,* 0.5 mile long, opens into the canyon of Whiskey Creek 6 miles southeast of the village of French Gulch at Whiskeytown (lat. 40°37'55" N, long. 122°33'20" W). Named on French Gulch (1944) 15' quadrangle.

Poe [BUTTE]: *locality,* 3.5 miles south-southwest of Pulga along Western Pacific Railroad (lat. 39°45'10" N, long. 121°28'10" W; at NE cor. sec. 24, T 22 N, R 4 E). Named on Pulga (1979) 7.5' quadrangle. California Mining Bureau's (1917c) map shows a place called Intake located 2.5 miles south of Poe along the railroad; it was at the intake of a tunnel to a powerhouse (Dunn, F.D., p. 54).

Poinsett Creek: see **Hat Creek** [SHASTA].

Pointers Gulch [SISKIYOU]: *canyon,* drained by a stream that flows 2 miles to Right Hand Fork of North Fork Salmon River 11 miles north-northeast of Sawyers Bar (lat. 41°27'15" N, long. 123°04'55" W). Named on Yellow Dog Peak (1977) 7.5' quadrangle.

Point McCloud [SHASTA]: *locality,* 1.5 miles west-southwest of Bollibokka Mountain along McCloud River Arm Shasta Lake (lat. 40°55'25" N, long. 122°14'30" W; near E line sec. 6, T 35 N, R 3 W). Named on Bollibokka Mountain (1957) 15' quadrangle.

Point Spring [SISKIYOU]: *spring,* 9.5 miles north of Bartle (lat. 41°23'45" N, long. 121°49'20" W; near S line sec. 14, T 41 N, R 1 E). Named on Bartle (1961) 15' quadrangle.

Poison Canyon: see **Poison Creek** [SISKIYOU].

Poison Creek [SHASTA]: *stream,* flows 2 miles to Sacramento River 8.5 miles east of the village of Big Bend (lat. 41°00'55" N, long. 121°45'05" W). Named on Big Bend (1961) 15' quadrangle.

Poison Creek [SISKIYOU]: *stream,* flows 1.5 miles to Taylor Creek (1) 20 miles south-southwest of Etna (lat. 41°10'35" N, long. 122°59'35" W); the stream heads at Poison Lake. Named on Coffee Creek (1955) 15' quadrangle. On Etna (1934) 30' quadrangle, the canyon of the stream is called Poison Canyon.

Poison Glade [TEHAMA]: *area,* 8.5 miles south of Ball Mountain (lat. 39°48'45" N, long. 122°48' W; near N line sec. 31, T 23 N, R 8 W). Named on Log Spring (1967) 7.5' quadrangle.

Poison Lake [SISKIYOU]: *lake,* 350 feet long, 19 miles south of Etna (lat. 41°10'45" N, long. 122°58'05" W). Named on Coffee Creek (1953) 15' quadrangle.

Poison Spring [SISKIYOU]: *spring,* 14 miles west-northwest of Macdoel (lat. 41°53'10" N, long. 122°16' W; sec. 35, T 47 N, R 4 W). Named on Copco (1954) 15' quadrangle.

Pokegama: see **Klamathon** [SISKIYOU].

Poker Flat [SISKIYOU]: *area,* 7.5 miles north-northeast of Preston Peak (lat. 41°55'55" N, long. 123°32'40" W). Named on Polar Bear Mountain (1982) 7.5' quadrangle.

Poker Flat [TEHAMA]: *area,* 6.25 miles west-northwest of Wakefield Flat (lat. 40°09'40" N, long. 122°44'55" W). Named on Cold Fork (1967) 7.5' quadrangle.

Polar Bear Mountain [SISKIYOU]: *peak,* 4.25 miles north of Preston Peak on Siskiyou-Del Norte County line (lat. 41°53'55" N, long. 123°35'50" W). Named on Polar Bear Mountain (1982) 7.5' quadrangle.

Pole Corral [TEHAMA]: *locality,* 8 miles south of Tomhead Mountain (lat. 40°01'15" N, long. 122°51' W; sec. 15, T 25 N, R 9 W). Named on Yolla Bolly (1954) 15' quadrangle.

Pole Corral Creek [TEHAMA]: *stream,* flows 5.25 miles to Dry Creek (1) 3.25 miles southwest of Beegum Peak (lat. 40°16'50" N, long. 122°55'35" W; sec. 18, T 28 N, R 9 W). Named on Chanchelulla Peak (1951) and Dubakella Mountain (1954) 15' quadrangles.

Pole Corral Gap [TEHAMA]: *pass,* 5 miles west-southwest of Beegum Peak (lat. 40°17'15" N, long. 122°58'20" W; near SE cor. sec. 10, T 28 N, R 10 W); the pass is north of Pole Corral Creek. Named on Chanchelulla Peak (1951) 15' quadrangle.

Pole Creek [SISKIYOU]: *stream,* flows 2 miles to Bear Creek [SHASTA-SISKIYOU] 6.5 miles southeast of Bartle (lat. 41°11'20" N, long. 121°44'05" W; near E line sec. 28, T 39 N, R 2 E). Named on Pondosa (1961) 15' quadrangle.

Polk Springs [TEHAMA]: *locality,* 16 miles south-southwest of Mineral (lat. 40°07' N, long. 121°39'55" W; near S line sec. 8, T 26 N, R 3 E). Named on Butte Meadows (1958) 15' quadrangle.

Pollack Flat: see **Pollic Flat** [SISKIYOU].

Pollard Flat [SHASTA]: *locality,* 1.5 miles north-northeast of Lamoine (lat. 40°59'40" N, long. 122°25'05" W; sec. 11, T 36 N, R 5 W). Named on Lamoine (1957) 15' quadrangle.

Pollard Gulch [SHASTA]: *canyon,* drained by a stream that flows 1 mile to Sacramento River 1.5 miles north-northeast of Lamoine (lat. 40°59'45" N, long. 122°25' W; sec. 11, T 36 N, R 5 W); Pollard Flat is at the mouth of the canyon. Named on Lamoine (1957) 15' quadrangle.

Pollic Flat [SISKIYOU]: *area,* 2.25 miles south-southeast of Bray (lat. 41°36'40" N, long. 121°57'20" W; near SW cor. sec. 34, T 44 N, R 1 W). Named on Bray (1950) 15' quadrangle. United States Board on Geographic Names (1989, p. 4) approved the name "Pollock Flat" for the place, and rejected the names "Pollack Flat" and "Pollic Flat."

Pollock [SHASTA]: *locality,* 5 miles south-southeast of Lamoine (lat. 40°55' N, long. 122°23'05" W; sec. 1, T 35 N, R 5 W). Named on Lamoine (1957) 15' quadrangle. Postal authorities established Pollock post office in 1924 and named it for George Pollock, who built a bridge over Sacramento River; they moved the post office 5 miles north in 1939, moved it another 2 miles north in 1940, and discontinued it in 1944 (Salley, p. 175).

Pollock: see **Lakehead** [SHASTA]; **Loftus**, under **Lakeshore** [SHASTA].

Pollock Flat: see **Pollic Flat** [SISKIYOU].

Pollocks Gulch [SISKIYOU]: *canyon,* drained by a stream that flows 1.5 miles to Salmon River nearly 1.5 miles northeast of Forks of Salmon (lat. 41°16'15" N, long. 123°18'05" W). Named on Forks of Salmon (1978) 7.5' quadrangle.

Polly Creek [SHASTA]: *stream,* flows less than 1 mile to North Fork Backbone Creek 9.5 miles south-southwest of Lamoine (lat. 40°51' N, long. 122°29'10" W; near NE cor. sec. 36, T 35 N, R 6 W). Named on Lamoine (1957) 15' quadrangle. United States Board on Geographic Names (1990, p. 10) rejected the name "Potly Creek" for the stream.

Polly Gulch [SISKIYOU]: *canyon,* drained by a stream that flows 1.5 miles to Beaver Creek (1) 8.5 miles east-southeast of Condrey Mountain (lat. 41°54'10" N, long. 122°49'20" W; at N line sec. 30, T 47 N, R 8 W). Named on Condrey Mountain (1955) 15' quadrangle.

Pomeroy [SISKIYOU]: *locality,* 17 miles south-southwest of Macdoel along Southern Pacific Railroad (lat. 41°37' N, long. 122°11'30" W; sec. 33, T 44 N, R 3 W). Named on Macdoel (1941) 30' quadrangle.

Pomeroy Creek [SISKIYOU]: *stream,* flows 4.5 miles to Butte Creek (lat. 41°32'50" N, long. 122°03'50" W; near N line sec. 27, T 43 N, R 2 W). Named on The Whaleback (1954) 15' quadrangle.

Pompys Creek [BUTTE]: *stream,* flows 1.25 miles to Middle Fork Feather River 3.5 miles east of the village of Brush Creek (lat. 39°41'25" N, long. 121°16'15" W); the stream is south of Pompys Point. Named on Brush Creek (1970) 7.5' quadrangle.

Pompys Point [BUTTE]: *relief feature,* 4.5 miles east of the village of Brush Creek (lat. 39°41'45" N, long. 121°15'20" W). Named on Brush Creek (1970) 7.5' quadrangle.

Pond: see **Nord** [BUTTE].

Ponderosa Reservoir [BUTTE]: *lake,* behind a dam 2.5 miles northwest of Forbestown on South Fork Feather River (lat. 39°33' N, long. 121°18'15" W; sec. 33, T 20 N, R 6 E). Named on Forbestown (1970) 7.5' quadrangle.

Pondosa [SISKIYOU]: *village,* 8 miles west-southwest of Bartle (lat. 41°11'55" N, long. 121°41'15" W; sec. 24, T 39 N, R 2 E). Named on Pondosa (1961) 15' quadrangle. Postal authorities established Pondosa post office in 1925, discontinued it in 1932, and reestablished it in 1938 (Frickstad, p. 190). Elmer E. Hall, a lumberman, named the place for the ponderosa pine (Hanna, p. 240).

Pony Peak [SISKIYOU]: *peak,* 5.5 miles north of Dillon Mountain (lat. 41°36'45" N, long. 123°34' W). Altitude 5341 feet. Named on Dillon Mountain (1983) 7.5' quadrangle.

Pony Spring [TEHAMA]: *spring,* 3.5 miles west-northwest of Paskenta (lat. 39°54'45" N, long. 122°36'10" W; near N line sec. 25, T 24 N, R 7 W). Named on Paskenta (1967) 7.5' quadrangle

Ponytail Falls [SISKIYOU]: *waterfall,* 7.25 miles north-northeast of the village of Seiad Valley along a branch of East Fork Seiad Creek (lat. 41°55'55" N, long. 123°07'45" W); the feature is 1150 feet north-northeast of Horsetail Falls, which is along another branch of East Fork Seiad Creek. Named on Kangaroo Mountain (1980) 7.5' quadrangle.

Poopoteyuk River: see **Black Butte River** [GLENN].

Poorman Flat [SHASTA]: *area,* 9 miles southeast of Whitmore (lat. 40°32'45" N, long. 121°47'30" W; on N line sec. 18, T 31 N, R 2 E). Named on Whitmore (1956) 15' quadrangle.

Poor Mans Bar: see **Scott Bar** [SISKIYOU].

Popcorn Cave [SHASTA]: *cave,* 5 miles north-northwest of Coble Mountain (lat. 40°57'10" N, long. 121°22'30" W; sec. 15, T 36 N, R 5 S). Named on Jellico (1957) 15' quadrangle. On Halls Flat (1939) 30' quadrangle, the name has the plural form "Popcorn Caves."

Porcupine Butte [SISKIYOU]: *hill,* 16 miles northeast of Bartle (lat. 41°25'30" N, long. 121°36'05" W). Altitude 5010 feet. Named on Hambone (1961) 15' quadrangle.

Porcupine Lake [SISKIYOU]:

(1) *lake,* 950 feet long, 8 miles south-southeast of China Mountain (lat. 41°16'25" N, long. 122°30'25" W; on W line sec. 1, T 39 N, R 6 W). Named on China Mountain (1955) 15' quadrangle.

(2) *intermittent lake,* 300 feet long 15 miles northeast of Bartle (lat. 41°24'25" N, long. 121°36'35" W); the feature is 1.5 miles south-southwest of Porcupine Butte. Named on Hambone (1961) 15' quadrangle.

Porcupine Reservoir [SHASTA]: *lake,* 900 feet long, 8.5 miles south of Coble Mountain (lat. 40°45'45" N, long. 121°22'30" W; near W line sec. 36, T 34 N, R 5 E). Named on Jellico (1957) 15' quadrangle. United States

Board on Geographic Names (1983b, p. 7) approved the name "Twin Ponds" for a tank located about 1 mile east-northeast of Porcupine Reservoir (lat. 40°46'06" N, long. 121°21'15" W; sec. 31, T 34 N, R 6 E). The Board (1983c, p. 4) also approved the name "Cone Reservoir" for a tank located about 0.5 mile east-northeast of Porcupine Reservoir (lat. 40°45'52" N, long. 121°21'55" W; sec. 36, T 34 N, R 5 E).

Portal Inn [SHASTA]: *locality,* 4.5 miles north-northeast of the town of Central Valley (lat. 40°44'10" N, long. 122°19'10" W; near NE cor. sec. 9, T 33 N, R 4 W). Named on Project City (1957) 7.5' quadrangle.

Portugese Gulch [SISKIYOU]: *canyon,* drained by a stream that flows 2.5 miles to Moffett Creek 12.5 miles south-southwest of Yreka (lat. 41°33'30" N, long. 122°41'05" W; sec. 20, T 43 N, R 7 W). Named on Yreka (1954) 15' quadrangle. Called Portuguese Gulch on Yreka (1939) 30' quadrangle.

Portuguese: see **Hazel Creek**, under **Sims** [SHASTA].

Portuguese Bar: see **Portuguese Creek** [SISKIYOU] (2).

Portuguese Creek [SISKIYOU]:

(1) *stream,* flows nearly 3 miles to Salmon River 6 miles north-northwest of Forks of Salmon (lat. 41°20'05"N, long. 123°22'15" W); the stream heads near Portuguese Peak. Named on Forks of Salmon (1978) 7.5' quadrangle.

(2) *stream,* flows 5 miles to Klamath River 3 miles west-northwest of the village of Seiad Valley (lat. 41°51'30" N, long. 123°14'45" W; sec. 4, T 46 N, R 12 W). Named on Kangaroo Mountain (1980) and Seiad Valley (1980) 7.5' quadrangles. East Fork enters from the east-northeast 1.25 miles upstream from the mouth of the main creek; it is 2.25 miles long and is named on Kangaroo Mountain (1980) and Seiad Valley (1980) 7.5' quadrangles. Gudde (1975, p. 273) listed a mining place called Portuguese Bar that was situated near the mouth of Portuguese Creek (2).

Portuguese Flat [SHASTA]: *area,* 5 miles east-southeast of the village of French Gulch along Whiskey Creek (lat. 40°39'50" N, long. 122°33'30" W; at NE cor. sec. 5, T 32 N, R 6 W). Named on Whiskeytown (1979) 7.5' quadrangle. Miners at the place in the early 1850's were mainly Portuguese (Hoover, Rensch, and Rensch, p. 488).

Portuguese Flat: see **Gibson** [SHASTA].

Portuguese Gulch: see **Portugese Gulch** [SISKIYOU].

Portuguese Peak [SISKIYOU]: *peak,* 7.5 miles north of Forks of Salmon (lat. 41°22'05" N, long. 123°19'55" W); the peak is near the head of Portuguese Creek (1). Altitude 5720 feet. Named on Forks of Salmon (1978) 7.5' quadrangle.

Portuguese Point [BUTTE]: *ridge,* south-trending, 2 miles long, 5.5 miles west-northwest of Stirling City (lat. 39°56'55" N, long. 121°37'15" W; sec. 10, 15, T 24 N, R 3 E). Named on Stirling City (1979) 7.5' quadrangle.

Post Creek [TEHAMA]: *stream,* flows 2.25 miles to South Fork Beegum Creek [SHASTA-TEHAMA] 9.5 miles northwest of Tomhead Mountain (lat. 40°14'25" N, long. 122°56' W; near SW cor. sec. 25, T 28 N, R 10 W). Named on Yolla Bolly (1954) 15' quadrangle.

Post Gulch [SHASTA]: *canyon,* drained by a stream that flows 3.5 miles to Dry Creek (2) 9 miles northeast of Millville (lat. 40°38'50" N, long. 122°03'50" W; near W line sec. 11, T 32 N, R 2 W). Named on Millville (1953) 15' quadrangle.

Postpile Camp [TEHAMA]: *locality,* 11 miles west-northwest of Paskenta (lat. 39°56'25" N, long. 122°44'25" W; sec. 15, T 24 N, R 8 W). Named on Riley Ridge (1967) 7.5' quadrangle.

Potato Butte [SHASTA]: *crater,* 11 miles north-northeast of Lassen Peak (lat. 40°38'15" N, long. 121°26'15" W; near E line sec. 17, T 32 N, R 5 E). Named on Prospect Peak (1957) 15' quadrangle.

Potato Butte: see **Little Potato Butte** [SHASTA].

Potato Hill [TEHAMA]: *peak,* 12.5 miles east of Red Bluff (lat. 40°11'25" N, long. 122°00'25" W; sec. 17, T 27 N, R 1 W). Altitude 1254 feet. Named on Tuscan Springs (1951) 7.5' quadrangle.

Potato Patch Campground [TEHAMA]: *locality,* 8.5 miles east-northeast of Polk Springs (lat. 40°11'20" N, long. 121°31'50" W; at N line sec. 21, T 27 N, R 4 E). Named on Butte Meadows (1958) 15' quadrangle. Mineral (1941) 30' quadrangle has the name "Potato Patch" at the site.

Potem Creek [SHASTA]: *stream,* flows 7 miles to Pit River 12 miles southeast of Bollibokka Mountain (lat. 40°20'15" N, long. 122°00'15" W; near N line sec. 6, T 34 N, R 1 W). Named on Bollibokka Mountain (1957) 15' quadrangle. According to Gudde (1949, p. 271), Indians named the stream for the first white settler along it, who befriended them.

Potem Falls [SHASTA]: *waterfall,* 12 miles southeast of Bollibokka Mountain (lat. 40°50'15" N, long. 122°01'40" W; near S line sec. 31, T 35 N, R 1 W); the feature is along Potem Creek. Named on Bollibokka Mountain (1957) 15' quadrangle.

Potly Creek: see **Polly Creek** [SHASTA].

Pot Spring [SHASTA]: *spring,* 9 miles southeast of Burney (lat. 40°46'50" N, long. 121°34'10" W; near NW cor. sec. 30, T 34 N, R 4 E). Named on Burney (1939) 30' quadrangle.

Potter Caves: see **Potter Creek** [SHASTA].

Potter Creek [SHASTA]: *stream,* flows 0.5 mile to McCloud River Arm Shasta Lake 16 miles south-southeast of Lamoine (lat. 40°46'55" N, long. 122°17' W; near S line sec. 23, T 34 N, R 4 W). Named on Lamoine (1957) 15' quadrangle. Steger (p. 53) associated the name with I.B. Potter, who bought property along the creek in 1855, and noted that Potter Caves are located near the head of the stream (sec. 22, T 34 N, R 4 W).

Potter Ravine [BUTTE]: *canyon,* drained by a stream that flows 2 miles to Lake Oroville 5 miles north-northeast of Oroville (lat. 39°34'45" N, long. 121°30' W; near W line sec. 23, T 20 N, R 4 E); the canyon is less than 1 mile east of The High Rocks. Named on Oroville (1970) 7.5' quadrangle. Called High Rock Ravine on Bidwell Bar (1897) 30' quadrangle. West Branch enters from the north-northwest less than 1 mile above the mouth of the main canyon; it is 1.25 miles long and is named on Oroville (1970) 7.5' quadrangle.

Potter's Bar: see **Bidwell Bar** [BUTTE].

Poverty Flat [SISKIYOU]: *area,* 9 miles north-northeast of Mount Dome (lat. 41°55'10" N, long. 121°36' W; around NW cor. sec. 14, T 47 N, R 3 E). Named on Mount Dome (1950) 15' quadrangle.

Poverty Gulch [SHASTA]: *canyon,* drained by a stream that flows 3.5 miles to Middle Fork Cottonwood Creek [SHASTA-TEHAMA] 8 miles south-southeast of Ono (lat. 40°22'05" N, long. 122°34'30" W; near W line sec. 17, T 29 N, R 6 W). Named on Ono (1952) 15' quadrangle.

Poverty Gulch [SISKIYOU]: *canyon,* drained by a stream that flows 1.5 miles to West Fork Knownothing Creek 4.5 miles east-northeast of Salmon Mountain (lat. 41°12'10" N, long. 123°19'40" W). Named on Youngs Peak (1979) 7.5' quadrangle.

Poverty Ridge: see **Paradise** [BUTTE].

Powder Hill [SISKIYOU]: *hill,* 18 miles north-northeast of Bartle (lat. 41°28'35" N, long. 121°37'30" W). Altitude 5729 feet. Named on Hambone (1961) 15' quadrangle.

Powder Spur [SHASTA]: *ridge,* south-trending, 0.5 mile long, 1.5 miles west of Burney Falls (lat. 41°00'40" N, long. 121°40'50" W; sec. 6, T 36 N, R 3 E). Named on Pondosa (1961) 15' quadrangle.

Powell Creek [BUTTE]: *stream,* flows 3.25 miles to Lake Oroville 5 miles west of Forbestown (lat. 39°31'30" N, long. 121°21'50" W; near N line sec. 12, T 19 N, R 5 E). Named on Forbestown (1970) and Rackerby (1948) 7.5' quadrangles.

Powellton [BUTTE]: *locality,* 2.5 miles west-northwest of Stirling City (lat. 39°55'45" N, long. 121°34'15" W; near N line sec. 19, T 24 N, R 4 E). Site named on Stirling City (1979) 7.5' quadrangle. Postal authorities established Powellton post office in 1872 and discontinued it in 1906 (Frickstad. p. 11). R.P. Powell came to the place in 1853 (Wells and Chambers, p. 259). The name "McKay Meadow," for William H. McKay, applied to a place located just north of Powellton, and the name "Powellton Meadow" applied to a place located just south of Powellton (Dunn, F.D., p. 73, 88).

Powellton Meadow: see **Powellton** [BUTTE].

Prather Creek [SISKIYOU]: *stream,* flows 5 miles to Meiss Lake 3 miles west of Macdoel (lat. 41°50' N, long. 122°03'50" W; sec. 14, T 46 N, R 2 W). Named on Macdoel (1954) 15' quadrangle, which shows Prather ranch near the stream.

Preachers Peak [SISKIYOU]: *peak,* 28 miles south of Etna on Siskiyou-Trinity County line (lat. 41°03'35" N, long. 122°55' W; sec. 17, T 37 N, R 9 W). Altitude 7180 feet. Named on Coffee Creek (1955) 15' quadrangle.

Prescott Mountain [SISKIYOU]: *peak,* 4.25 miles north of Harrington Mountain on Siskiyou-Del Norte County line (lat. 41°44'05" N, long. 123°40'20" W). Altitude 5871 feet. Named on Prescott Mountain (1981) 7.5' quadrangle.

Preston: see **Little Preston** [SISKIYOU].

Preston Creek [SISKIYOU]: *stream,* flows about 4.5 miles to Clear Creek (1) 3.25 miles south-southwest of Preston Peak (lat. 41°47'30" N, long. 123°37'40" W); the stream heads at Preston Peak. Named on Devils Punchbowl (1981) and Preston Peak (1982) 7.5' quadrangles.

Preston Peak [SISKIYOU]: *peak,* 12.5 miles west-northwest of Happy Camp (lat. 41°50'10" N, long. 123°36'40" W). Altitude 7309 feet. Named on Preston Peak (1982) 7.5' quadrangle.

Preston Spring [BUTTE]: *spring,* 2.5 miles north-northwest of Oroville (lat. 39°32'50" N, long. 121°34'15" W; sec. 31, T 20 N, R 4 E). Named on Oroville (1970) 7.5' quadrangle.

Printer Gulch [SISKIYOU]:*canyon,* drained by a stream that flows 2.5 miles to Klamath River 3.25 miles south of Hornbrook (lat. 41°52' N, long. 122°33'45" W; sec. 5, T 46 N, R 6 W). Named on Hornbrook (1955) 15' quadrangle. Hoover, Rensch, and Rensch (p. 507) referred to Printer's Gulch.

Price Hollow [SHASTA]: *canyon,* 1.5 miles long, 10 miles northeast of Millville along Dry Creek (2) (lat. 40°39'30" N, long. 122°03'15" W). Named on Millville (1953) 15' quadrangle.

Proberta [TEHAMA]: *village,* 2 miles north-northwest of Gerber (lat. 40°04'55" N, long. 122°10'15" W). Named on Gerber (1950) 7.5' quadrangle. Postal authorities established Proberta post office in 1888; the name commemorates Edward Probert, who granted right-of-way at the place to Southern Pacific Railroad (Salley, p. 178).

Procter Creek [SHASTA]: *stream,* flows nearly 7 miles to end 2.5 miles west-southwest of Coble Mountain (lat. 40°52'20" N, long. 121°23'50"

W; near NE cor. sec. 27, T 35 N, R 5 E). Named on Jellico (1957) 15' quadrangle.

Professor Gulch [SHASTA]: *canyon,* drained by a stream that flows 1 mile to Clear Creek 8 miles north-northwest of Schell Mountain (lat. 40°58' N, long. 122°34' W; near W line sec. 21, T 36 N, R 6 W). Named on Schell Mountain (1950) 15' quadrangle.

Project City [SHASTA]: *town,* just east of the town of Central Valley (lat. 40°40'55" N, long. 122°21'10" W; around SW cor. sec. 29, T 33 N, R 4 W). Named on Project City (1957) 7.5' quadrangle. Postal authorities established Project City post office in 1939 (Frickstad, p. 182). The town began in 1938 when construction began on Shasta Dam, the main unit of the Central Valley Project (Gudde, 1949, p. 62).

Promontory Point [TEHAMA]: *peak,* 4.25 miles east of Campbell Mound (lat. 39°59'15" N, long. 121°44'10" W; near E line sec. 34, T 25 N, R 2 E). Altitude 3622 feet. Named on Cohasset (1979) 7.5' quadrangle.

Prospect Creek [SHASTA]: *stream,* flows about 2 miles to Squaw Creek (2) 2.25 miles southeast of Shoeinhorse Mountain (lat. 41°02'45" N, long. 122°02'30" W). Named on Shoeinhorse Mountain (1954) 15' quadrangle.

Prospect Hill [SISKIYOU]: *ridge,* north-trending, about 2 miles long, 6.25 miles north of Orleans, which is in Humboldt County (lat. 41°23'40" N, long. 123°33' W). Named on Bark Shanty Gulch (1974) 7.5' quadrangle.

Prospect Peak [SHASTA]: *peak,* 10 miles northeast of Lassen Peak (lat. 40°34'25" N, long. 121°20'45" W; near SE cor. sec. 6, T 31 N, R 6 E). Altitude 8338 feet. Named on Prospect Peak (1957) 15' quadrangle. United States Board on Geographic Names (1933, p. 621) rejected the names "East Prospect Peak," "Sand Peak," and "Black Butte" for the feature.

Prospect Peak: see **West Prospect Peak** [SHASTA].

P-38 Crossing [TEHAMA]: *locality,* 8.5 miles southwest of Panther Spring along Little Antelope Creek (lat. 40°10'10" N, long. 121°53'45" W). Named on Panther Spring (1953) 15' quadrangle.

Pulga [BUTTE]: *village,* 9 miles east-northeast of Paradise along North Fork Feather River (lat. 39°49'10" N, long. 121°26'50" W; on E line sec. 31, T 23 N, R 5 E); the village is at the mouth of Flea Valley Creek. Named on Pulga (1979) 7.5' quadrangle. Postal authorities established Pulga post office in 1906 (Frickstad, p. 12). According to Hanna (p. 245), officials of Western Pacific Railroad probably named the station at the place for its position at the mouth of Flea Valley Creek—*pulga* means "flea" in Spanish.

Pulga Bar: see **Big Bar** [BUTTE].

Pumice Stone Mountain [SISKIYOU]: *peak,* 6.25 miles west-southwest of Medicine Lake (lat. 41°33'40" N, long. 121°42'45" W; at S line sec. 14, T 43 N, R 2 E). Altitude 6962 feet. Named on Medicine Lake (1952) 15' quadrangle.

Pumice Stone Well [SISKIYOU]: *well,* 5.5 miles west of Medicine Lake (lat. 41°34'10" N, long. 121°42'20" W; sec. 14, T 43 N, R 2 E); the well is 0.5 mile north-northeast of Pumice Stone Mountain. Named on Medicine Lake (1952) 15' quadrangle.

Pumpkinseed Lake [SISKIYOU]: *lake,* 500 feet long, 7.5 miles south-southwest of Macdoel (lat. 41°43'45" N, long. 122°04'05" W; near E line sec. 21, T 45 N, R 2 W). Named on The Whaleback (1954) 15' quadrangle.

Punch Creek [SISKIYOU]: *stream,* flows 1.5 miles to South Fork Humbug Creek 13 miles southwest of Hornbrook (lat. 41°46' N, long. 122°42'50" W). Named on Hornbrook (1955) 15' quadrangle.

Puppy Creek [SHASTA]: *stream,* flows 1 mile to Little Dog Creek 2 miles south of Lamoine (lat. 40°56'10" N, long. 122°25'15" W; near E line sec. 34, T 36 N, R 5 W). Named on Lamoine (1957) 15' quadrangle.

Pusher: see **Dunsmuir** [SISKIYOU].

Pyramid Peak [SISKIYOU]: *peak,* 13 miles north of Happy Camp (lat. 41°58'55" N, long. 123°20'30" W). Altitude 6451 feet. Named on Figurehead Mountain (1980) 7.5' quadrangle.

Pythian Cave [SISKIYOU]: *cave,* 10 miles south-southeast of Yreka (lat. 41°35'35" N, long. 122°35' W; sec. 7, T 43 N, R 6 W). Named on Yreka (1954) 15' quadrangle.

– Q –

Quail Creek: see **Elkhorn Creek** [TEHAMA] (2).

Quail Flat [SISKIYOU]: *area,* 3 miles northwest of Forks of Salmon along Salmon River (lat. 41°17'20" N, long. 123°21'50" W). Named on Forks of Salmon (1978) 7.5' quadrangle.

Quail Gulch [SHASTA]: *canyon,* drained by a stream that flows 2 miles to Lick Creek (1) 7 miles north of Shoeinhorse Mountain (lat. 41°10'05" N, long. 122°03'50" W). Named on Shoeinhorse Mountain (1954) 15' quadrangle.

Quail Gulch [TEHAMA]: *canyon,* drained by a stream that flows 0.5 mile to South Fork Cottonwood Creek [SHASTA-TEHAMA] 4.25 miles west of Wakefield Flat (lat. 40°07'10" N, long. 122°43'10" W). Named on Raglin Ridge (1967) 7.5' quadrangle.

Quail Hill [SISKIYOU]: *peak,* 0.5 mile southeast of the center of the town of Mount Shasta (lat. 41°18'20" N, long. 122°17'55" W; near S line sec. 15, T 40 N, R 4 W). Named on Weed (1954) 15' quadrangle.

Quail Spring [SISKIYOU]: *spring,* 2 miles north-northeast of the village of Seiad Valley (lat. 41°52'15" N, long. 123°10'40" W). Named on Seiad Valley (1980) 7.5' quadrangle.

Quaken Asp Glade [SISKIYOU]: *area,* 4.25 miles north of Condrey Mountain (lat. 42°00' N, long. 122°58'30" W; on N line sec. 23, T 48 N, R 10 W). Named on Condrey Mountain (1955) 7.5' quadrangle

Quartz Hill [SHASTA]: *peak,* 3.25 miles south-southwest of Summit City (lat. 40°38'20" N, long. 122°24'50" W; near SE cor. sec. 10, T 32 N, R 5 W). Named on Shasta Dam (1956) 7.5' quadrangle. The name is from a mass of quartz that was taken from the feature in 1906 and used as flux at Keswick smelter (Steger, p. 54).

Quartz Hill [SISKIYOU]: *mountain,* 5 miles west of Fort Jones (lat. 41°36' N, long. 122°56' W). Named on Fort Jones (1955) 15' quadrangle. According to Walker (p. 83), the name "Oro Fino Mountain" was an early designation for the feature.

Quartz Valley [SISKIYOU]: *valley,* 6.5 miles west of Fort Jones along Mill Creek (6) and Shackleford Creek (lat. 41°35'30" N, long. 122°58' W). Named on Fort Jones (1955) 15' quadrangle.

Quartz Valley: see **Mugginsville** [SISKIYOU].

Queens Draw [SHASTA]: *canyon,* drained by a stream that flows less than 0.5 mile to French Gulch (2) 0.5 mile west-northwest of the village of French Gulch (lat. 40°42'10" N, long. 122°38'50" W; sec. 22, T 33 N, R 7 W). Named on French Gulch (1979) 7.5' quadrangle.

Quigleys Cove [SISKIYOU]: *canyon,* drained by a stream that flows 2 miles to Klamath River 9.5 miles southeast of Condrey Mountain at the village of Klamath River (lat. 41°51'45" N, long. 122°44'30" W; sec. 6, T 46 N, R 8 W). Named on Condrey Mountain (1955) 15' quadrangle.

– R –

Rabbit Flat [SHASTA]: *area,* 5 miles southeast of Lamoine along Middle Salt Creek (lat. 40°55'55" N, long. 122°21'20" W; on N line sec. 6, T 35 N, R 4 W). Named on Lamoine (1957) 15' quadrangle.

Rabbit Hill [SISKIYOU]: *hill,* 11 miles west-southwest of Macdoel (lat. 41°40'15" N, long. 122°23'10" W; sec. 11, T 44 N, R 5 W). Named on Lake Shastina (1954) 15' quadrangle.

Raccoon Creek [SISKIYOU]: *stream,* flows 5 miles to McCloud River [SHASTA-SISKIYOU] 5 miles west of Bartle (lat. 40°15'50" N, long. 121°54'45" W; near S line sec. 36, T 40 N, R 1 W). Named on Bartle (1961) and Big Bend (1961) 15' quadrangles.

Rafter Gulch [SHASTA]: *canyon,* drained by a stream that flows 2.5 miles to Jerusalem Creek 8 miles southwest of Shasta Bally (lat. 40°30'55" N, long. 122°45'15" W; near N line sec. 27, T 31 N, R 8 W). Named on Weaverville (1950) 15' quadrangle. The stream in the canyon is called Rattlesnake Creek on Shasta Bally (1978) 7.5' quadrangle; United States Board on Geographic Names (1977b, p. 5) approved this name for the stream, and gave the name "Rafter Gulch" as a variant.

Rag Dump [BUTTE]: *locality,* 4 miles north-northwest of Pulga (lat. 39°51'25" N, long. 121°28'25" W; near N line sec. 13, T 23 N, R 4 E). Named on Pulga (1979) 7.5' quadrangle.

Ragged Gulch [SISKIYOU]: *canyon,* drained by a stream that flows 1.25 miles to Beaver Creek (1) 8 miles east of Condrey Mountain (lat. 41°55'20" N, long. 122°49'50" W; at E line sec. 13, T 47 N, R 9 W). Named on Condrey Mountain (1955) 15' quadrangle.

Raglin Ridge [TEHAMA]: *ridge,* generally east-trending, 7 miles long, 9 miles south-southwest of Wakefield Flat (lat. 40°00' N, long. 122°42' W). Named on Yolla Bolly (1954) 15' quadrangle, and on Raglin Ridge (1967) and Riley Ridge (1967) 7.5' quadrangles.

Rail Canyon [GLENN]: *canyon,* 3.25 miles southwest of High Peak at Glenn-Colusa County line (lat. 39°23'30" N, long. 122°28' W). Named on Lodoga (1960) 15' quadrangle.

Rail Canyon [SHASTA]: *canyon,* drained by a stream that heads in Lassen County and flows nearly 2 miles to Fall River Valley 11 miles north-northeast of Fall River Mills in Shasta County (lat. 41°08'45" N, long. 121°19'55" W; sec. 12, T 38 N, R 5 E). Named on Fall River Mills (1961) 15' quadrangle.

Rail Canyon: see **Badger Mountain** [SHASTA].

Rail Creek [SISKIYOU]: *stream,* flows 4.5 miles to East Fork Scott River 12.5 miles east-southeast of Etna (lat. 41°23' N, long. 122°40'35" W; sec. 20, T 41 N, R 7 W). Named on China Mountain (1955) 15' quadrangle.

Rainbow Lake [SHASTA]:

(1) *lake,* behind a dam on North Fork Cottonwood Creek [SHASTA-TEHAMA] 7.5 miles south-southwest of Shasta Bally (lat. 40°30'05" N, long. 122°41'45" W; sec. 31, T 31 N, R 7 W). Named on Shasta Bally (1978) 7.5' quadrangle. Steger (p. 47) gave the name "Rainbow Lake" as another designation for Messelbeck Reservoir, and noted that the reservoir was completed in 1875 and named for Frank Messelbeck, who owned the property.

(2) *lake,* 1500 feet long, 8.5 miles east of Lassen Peak (lat. 40°30'45" N,

long. 121°20'55" W; on S line sec. 30, T 31 N, R 6 E). Named on Prospect Peak 15' (1957) quadrangle.

Rainbow Lake [SISKIYOU]: *lake,* 500 feet long, 15 miles north-northwest of Bartle (lat. 41°27'20" N, long. 121°56'10" W; sec. 26, T 42 N, R 1 W); the lake is 1.5 miles south-southeast of Rainbow Mountain. Named on Bartle (1961) 15' quadrangle.

Rainbow Mountain [SISKIYOU]: *peak,* 17 miles north-northwest of Bartle (lat. 41°28'25" N, long. 121°57'20" W; sec. 22, T 42 N, R 1 W). Altitude 7623 feet. Named on Bartle (1961) 15' quadrangle.

Rainbow Ridge [SISKIYOU]: *ridge,* south- to southeast-trending, 4.5 miles long, 2.5 miles west of the town of Mount Shasta (lat. 41°18'20" N, long. 122°21'45" W). Named on Weed (1954) 15' quadrangle.

Rainbow Spring [SHASTA]: *locality,* 9 miles northeast of Burney Falls (lat. 41°06'50" N, long. 121°33' W; sec. 19, T 38 N, R 4 E). Named on Pondosa (1961) 15' quadrangle.

Rainbow Well [SISKIYOU]: *well,* 10 miles east of Bray (lat. 41°38'30" N, long. 121°46'15" W; sec. 20, T 44 N, R 2 E). Named on Bray (1950) 15' quadrangle.

Rainey Gulch [SHASTA]: *canyon,* drained by a stream that flows 1 mile to West Fork Crow Gulch 3 miles southeast of Arbuckle Mountain (lat. 40°22' N, long. 122°50' W; sec. 13, T 29 N, R 9 W). Named on Chanchelulla Peak (1951) 15' quadrangle.

Rainy Lake [SISKIYOU]: *lake,* 700 feet long, 18 miles southwest of Scott Bar (lat. 41°33'40" N, long. 123°14'15" W); the lake is at the head of Rainy Valley Creek. Named on Marble Mountain (1980) 7.5' quadrangle.

Rainy Valley [SISKIYOU]: *valley,* 17 miles southwest of Scott Bar (lat. 41°34'40" N, long. 123°14'15" W). Named on Marble Mountain (1980) 7.5' quadrangle.

Rainy Valley Creek [SISKIYOU]: *stream,* flows 3 miles to Elk Creek 16 miles southwest of Scott Bar (lat. 41°35'55" N, long. 123°14'55" W); Rainy Valley is on the upper reaches of the stream. Named on Marble Mountain (1980) 7.5' quadrangle.

Raker Peak [SHASTA]: *peak,* 3.5 miles north-northeast of Lassen Peak (lat. 40°32' N, long. 121°28'15" W; sec. 13, T 31 N, R 4 E). Named on Prospect Peak (1957) 15' quadrangle. The name honors John E. Raker, congressman from California who introduced the bill to create Lassen Volcanic National Park (United States Board on Geographic Names, 1933, p. 632). The feature first was called Jessen Mountain for nearby Jessen Meadows, and then after the 1915 eruption of Lassen Peak, it was called Divide Peak or Barrier Peak for its role in splitting the great mudflow that resulted from the eruption (Schulz, p. 44).

Ramada [BUTTE]: *locality,* 9 miles west-northwest of Oroville along Sacramento Northern Railroad (lat. 39°33'20" N, long. 121°42'35" W; sec. 26, T 20 N, R 2 E). Named on Shippee (1948) 7.5' quadrangle.

Ram Creek [BUTTE]: *stream,* flows nearly 3 miles to French Creek 2.5 miles north-northwest of the village of Brush Creek (lat. 39°43'20" N, long. 121°21'50" W; sec. 36, T 22 N, R 5 E). Named on Brush Creek (1970) 7.5' quadrangle.

Ram Creek: see **Little Ram Creek** [BUTTE].

Ramsey Bar [BUTTE]: *locality,* 8 miles north of Pulga along Little Kimshew Creek (lat. 39°55'05" N, long. 121°25'45" W; at W line sec. 21, T 24 N, R 5 E). Named on Kimshew Point (1979) 7.5' quadrangle.

Rancheria Camp: see **Rancheria Spring** [SISKIYOU].

Rancheria Creek [SHASTA]:

(1) *stream,* flows 2.25 miles to Moody Creek 1.25 miles northeast of the town of Central Valley (lat. 40°41'30" N, long. 122°20'50" W; near N line sec. 29, T 33 N, R 4 W). Named on Project City (1957) 7.5' quadrangle.

(2) *stream,* flows 5.25 miles to Ash Creek (2) nearly 5.5 miles east-northeast of Balls Ferry (lat. 40°27'05" N, long. 122°06'15" W; at W line sec. 16, T 30 N, R 2 W). Named on Tuscan Buttes NE (1965) 7.5' quadrangle.

Rancheria Creek [SISKIYOU]: *stream,* flows 4.25 miles to Grider Creek 11.5 miles west of Scott Bar (lat. 41°44'45" N, long. 123°13'30" W); the stream heads at Rancheria Spring. Named on Grider Valley (1981) 7.5' quadrangle. Whitney (p. 353) called the feature Rancherie Creek.

Rancheria Creek [TEHAMA]: *stream,* flows about 2 miles to Mill Creek (3) 5 miles south of Panther Spring (lat. 40°10'45" N, long. 121°47'40" W; sec. 19, T 27 N, R 2 E). Named on Panther Spring (1953) 15' quadrangle.

Rancheria Gulch [SISKIYOU]: *canyon,* drained by a stream that flows 5 miles to Cottonwood Creek (1) at Hornbrook (lat. 41°54'35" N, long. 122°33'20" W; near E line sec. 20, T 47 N, R 6 W). Named on Hornbrook (1955) 15' quadrangle.

Rancheria Spring [SISKIYOU]: *spring,* 8 miles west of Scott Bar (lat. 41°44'35" N, long. 123°09'35" W); the spring is at the head of Rancheria Creek. Named on Grider Valley (1981) 7.5' quadrangle. Scott Bar (1955) 15' quadrangle shows Rancheria Camp at the place.

Rancherie Creek: see **Rancheria Creek** [SISKIYOU].

Rancherie Island: see **Goat Island** [SHASTA].

Ranch Gulch [SISKIYOU]: *canyon,* drained by a stream that flows 2 miles to Klamath River 1 mile northeast of the center of Happy Camp (lat. 41°48'20" N, long. 123°21'45" W; near W line sec. 1, T 16 N, R 7 E). Named on Slater Butte (1980) 7.5' quadrangle.

Rancho de Farwell: see **Arroyo Chico** [BUTTE].

Raney Peak [TEHAMA]: *peak,* 7 miles north of Tomhead Mountain (lat. 40°14'05" N, long. 122°47'40" W; sec. 32, T 28 N, R 8 W). Named on Yolla Bolly (1954) 15' quadrangle.

Raney Peak Gulch [TEHAMA]: *canyon,* drained by a stream that flows 1.5 miles to Wells Creek 6.5 miles southeast of Beegum Peak (lat. 40°15'15" N, long. 122°47'15" W; near N line sec. 29, T 28 N, R 8 W); the canyon heads at Raney Peak. Named on Chanchelulla Peak (1951) and Yolla Bolly (1954) 15' quadrangles.

Rasor Lakes [GLENN]: *lakes,* 9 miles east-southeast of Willows (lat. 39°28' N, long. 122°02'45" W); the lakes are 2 miles west of Rasor Slough. Named on Maxwell (1906) 15' quadrangle.

Rasor Slough [GLENN]: *lake,* 11 miles east-southeast of Willows in a cut-off meander of Sacramento River (lat. 39°27'45" N, long. 122°00'35" W). Named on Princeton (1952) 7.5' quadrangle.

Raspberry Camp Spring [TEHAMA]: *spring,* 9.5 miles south-southwest of Wakefield Flat (lat. 40°00'40" N, long. 122°44'45" W; sec. 22, T 23 N, R 8 W). Named on Raglin Ridge (1967) 7.5' quadrangle. Colyear Springs (1957) 15' quadrangle shows Raspberry Camp at the site.

Raspberry Lake [SISKIYOU]: *lake,* 950 feet long, 1 mile north-northwest of Preston Peak (lat. 41°50'55" N, long. 123°37'10" W). Named on Preston Peak (1982) 7.5' quadrangle.

Ratchel: see **Mount Ratchel** [BUTTE].

Rattlesnake Bar [SISKIYOU]: *locality,* nearly 3.5 miles northeast of Dillon Mountain along Klamath River (lat. 41°33'45" N, long. 123°31'30" W). Named on Dillon Mountain (1983) 7.5' quadrangle.

Rattlesnake Butte [SISKIYOU]: *hill,* 14 miles south of Dorris (lat. 41°45'50" N, long. 121°58'25" W; sec. 9, T 45 N, R 1 W). Named on Dorris (1950) 15' quadrangle.

Rattlesnake Creek [BUTTE]: *stream,* flows 1.5 miles to West Branch Feather River 4.5 miles northeast of Paradise (lat. 38°48'55" N, long. 121°34'10" W; near S line sec. 30, T 23 N, R 4 E). Named on Paradise East (1980) 7.5' quadrangle.

Rattlesnake Creek [GLENN]: *stream,* flows 5.25 miles to Salt Creek (1) 5 miles northwest of the village of Elk Creek (lat. 39°38'35" N, long. 122°36'50" W); the stream is north of Rattlesnake Ridge. Named on Alder Springs (1967) and Chrome (1968) 7.5' quadrangles.

Rattlesnake Creek [SISKIYOU]: *stream,* flows 5.25 miles to the valley of Scott River 3.25 miles northwest of Fort Jones (lat. 41°38' N, long. 122°53'30" W; sec. 28, T 44 N, R 9 W). Named on Fort Jones (1955) 15' quadrangle. East Fork enters 4 miles upstream from the mouth of the main creek, and West Fork enters 3.5 miles upstream from the mouth of the main creek. Each fork is 1 mile long and is named on Fort Jones (1955) 15' quadrangle.

Rattlesnake Creek [TEHAMA]:

(1) *stream,* flows 6 miles to Deer Creek (2) 7.5 miles northeast of Polk Springs (lat. 40°10'40" N, long. 121°33' W; sec. 20, T 27 N, R 4 E). Named on Butte Meadows (1958) and Jonesville (1958) 15' quadrangles.

(2) *stream,* formed by the confluence of North Fork and South Fork, flows 6.5 miles to Singer Creek 8.5 miles west-southwest of Campbell Mound (lat. 39°54'45" N, long. 121°57'20" W; at SW cor. sec. 23, T 24 N, R 1 W). Named on Campbell Mound (1952) and Richardson Springs NW (1952) 7.5' quadrangles. North Fork is 1.5 miles long and South fork is 2 miles long; both forks are named on Campbell Mound (1952) 7.5' quadrangle.

Rattlesnake Creek: see **Rafter Gulch** [SHASTA].

Rattlesnake Gulch [SHASTA]: *canyon,* drained by a stream that flows 1.5 miles to Clear Creek 2.5 miles west-northwest of Schell Mountain (lat. 40°52'15" N, long. 122°34'30" W). Named on Schell Mountain (1950) 15' quadrangle.

Rattlesnake Gulch [SISKIYOU]:

(1) *canyon,* drained by a stream that flows less than 1 mile to North Fork Salmon River 1.5 miles east of Sawyers Bar (lat. 41°17'45" N, long. 123°06'05" W). Named on Tanners Peak (1977) 7.5' quadrangle.

(2) *canyon,* drained by a stream that flows 1.5 miles to Ash Creek (1) 4.5 miles southwest of Hornbrook (lat. 41°52'15" N, long. 122°37'30" W; near N line sec. 2, T 46 N, R 7 W). Named on Hornbrook (1955) 15' quadrangle.

Rattlesnake Gulch: see **Little Rattlesnake Gulch** [SISKIYOU].

Rattlesnake Hill [SHASTA]: *peak,* 10 miles southwest of Castella (lat. 41°03'35" N, long. 122°28'15" W; near N line sec. 20, T 37 N, R 5 W). Altitude 6154 feet. Named on Dunsmuir (1954) 15' quadrangle.

Rattlesnake Meadow [SISKIYOU]: *area,* 0.5 mile west of Preston Peak (lat. 41°50' N, long. 123°37'20" W). Named on Devils Punchbowl (1981) and Preston Peak (1982) 7.5' quadrangles.

Rattlesnake Mountain [SISKIYOU]: *peak,* 6 miles north-northwest of the village of Seiad Valley (lat. 41°55'30" N, long. 123°14'15" W). Altitude 6307 feet. Named on Kangaroo Mountain (1980) 7.5' quadrangle.

Rattlesnake Point [BUTTE]: *peak,* 5.5 miles north of Bangor (lat. 39°28'10" N, long. 121°24'30" W; at SE cor. sec. 28, T 19 N, R 5 E). Altitude 2167 feet. Named on Bangor (1947) 7.5' quadrangle.

Rattlesnake Point [TEHAMA]: *relief feature,* 8 miles southwest of Mineral (lat. 40°16'30" N, long. 121°42'35" W; sec. 14, T 28 N, R 2 E). Named on Lassen Peak (1956) 15' quadrangle.

Rattlesnake Ridge [GLENN]: *ridge,* generally east-trending, 4.25 miles long, 7 miles west-northwest of the village of Elk Creek (lat. 39°39'25" N, long. 122°39'45" W); the ridge is south of Rattlesnake Creek.. Named on Alder Springs (1967) 7.5' quadrangle.

Rattlesnake Spring [TEHAMA]: *spring,* nearly 7 miles northwest of Mineral (lat. 40°24'10" N, long. 121°41'55" W; sec. 6, T 29 N, R 3 E). Named on Lassen Peak (1956) 15' quadrangle.

Rattlesnake Valley [TEHAMA]: *valley,* 8.5 miles south-southeast of Wakefield Flat (lat. 40°00'50" N, long. 122°34'55" W; sec. 19, T 25 N, R 6 W). Named on Lowrey (1967) 7.5' quadrangle. On Colyear Springs (1957) 15' quadrangle, the name applies to the lower part of the canyon of North Fork Elder Creek.

Rat Trap Gap: see **Rat Trap Ridge** [TEHAMA].

Rat Trap Ridge [TEHAMA]: *ridge,* northwest-trending, 2 miles long, 8.5 miles northwest of Tomhead Mountain (lat. 40°13'10" N, long. 122°56'15" W). Named on Yolla Bolly (1954) 15' quadrangle. United States Board on Geographic Names (1978c, p. 3) approved the name "Rat Trap Gap" for a pass located south of Rat Trap Ridge (lat. 40°12'10" N, long. 122°55'42" W; sec. 7, T 7 N, R 9 W).

Rawson [TEHAMA]: *locality,* nearly 5 miles north-northwest of Gerber along Southern Pacific Railroad (lat. 40°07'05" N, long. 122°11'40" W). Named on Gerber (1950) 7.5' quadrangle.

Raymond Gulch [SISKIYOU]: *canyon,* drained by a stream that heads in the State of Oregon and flows 2.5 miles in Siskiyou County to Copco Lake 18 miles west-northwest of Macdoel (lat. 41°59' N, long. 122°17'50" W; sec. 27, T 48 N, R 4 W). Named on Copco (1954) 15' quadrangle.

Rays Gulch [SISKIYOU]: *canyon,* drained by a stream that flows 2.5 miles to South Fork Salmon River 4 miles southeast of Cecilville (lat. 41°06'10" N, long. 123°04'45" W). Named on Thompson Peak (1979) 7.5' quadrangle.

Rays Peak [SISKIYOU] *peak,* 5.5 miles south-southeast of Cecilville on Siskiyou-Trinity County line (lat. 41°03'55" N, long. 123°06'15" W). Altitude 7006 feet. Named on Thompson Peak (1979) 7.5' quadrangle.

Razor Ridge [SISKIYOU]: *ridge,* generally northwest-trending, 4 miles long, 9.5 miles north-northeast of Sawyers Bar (lat. 41°26' N, long. 123°03'45" W). Named on Yellow Dog Peak (1977) 7.5' quadrangle.

Reading: see **Fort Reading** [SHASTA]; **Redding** [SHASTA].

Reading Bar [SHASTA]: *locality,* 5.5 miles northwest of Olinda along Clear Creek (lat. 40°29'35" N, long. 122°29'40" W; sec. 36, T 31 N, R 5 W). Named on Olinda (1964) 7.5' quadrangle. Called Redding Bar on Anderson (1947) 15' quadrangle. United States Board on Geographic Names (1971a, p. 3) approved the name "Readings Bar" for the place, and gave the form "Reading Bar" as a variant; the Board noted that Major Pierson Barton Reading discovered gold at the site in 1848. Red Bluff (1894) 1° quadrangle has the name "Horsetown" at or near the the place. A mining camp on a flat adjoining Readings Bar was known first as Clear Creek Diggings, and later as One-Horse Town and as Horse Town (Hoover, Rensch, and Rensch, p. 487). Postal authorities established Horse Town post office in 1852 and discontinued in it 1876 (Salley, p. 100). A mining camp called Briggsville was situated about 1 mile east of Horsetown; Ben Briggs located the place a short time before Horsetown was started (Steger, p. 19). Jackass Flat Diggings, a rich gold mining place of the 1850's, was at a site between Horsetown and Centerville (Steger, p. 40).

Reading Island: see **Goat Island** [SHASTA].

Reading Peak [SHASTA]: *ridge,* east-southeast- to east-northeast-trending, 2 miles long, 3 miles east-southeast of Lassen Peak (lat. 40°28'15" N, long. 121°27'30" W; sec. 7, 8, T 30 N, R 5 E). Named on Mount Harkness (1956) 15' quadrangle. United States Board on Geographic Names (1933, p. 813) once approved the name "White Mountain" for the feature, but at the request of members of Shasta Historical Society the name was changed to honor Pierson B. Reading (Schulz, p. 45).

Readings Bar: see **Reading Bar** [SHASTA].

Reading's Springs: see **Shasta** [SHASTA].

Read's Creek: see **Reeds Creek** [TEHAMA].

Reavis Ferry: see **Chico Landing** [BUTTE].

Recer Ridge [GLENN-TEHAMA]: *ridge,* north- to north-northeast-trending, 2.5 miles long, 4.25 miles north of Black Butte on Glenn-Tehama County line, mainly in Glenn County (lat. 39°47'30" N, long. 122°53' W). Named on Mendocino Pass (1967) 7.5' quadrangle.

Rector Creek [SHASTA]: *stream,* flows 3.5 miles to North Fork Cottonwood Creek [SHASTA-TEHAMA] 0.25 mile south-southwest of Ono (lat. 40°28'15" N, long. 122°37'15" W; sec. 11, T 30 N, R 7 W); the stream heads near Rector Peak. Named on Ono (1952) 15' quadrangle.

Rector Peak [SHASTA]: *peak,* 5.25 miles south of Shasta Bally (lat. 40°31'40" N, long. 122°38'05" W; at W line sec. 23, T 31 N, R 7 W). Altitude 3534 feet. Named on Shasta Bally (1978) 7.5' quadrangle. Called Ducket Peak on French Gulch (1944) 15' quadrangle.

Red Ant Gulch [SISKIYOU]: *canyon,* drained by a stream that flows 1.5 miles to Angel Creek 6.5 miles southwest of Bartle (lat. 41°12'15" N, long. 121°55'45" W; at N line sec. 26, T 39 N, R 1 W). Named on Big Bend (1961) 15' quadrangle.

Red Bank [TEHAMA]: *locality,* 12 miles west-southwest of Red Bluff (lat. 40°05'55" N, long. 122°26'45" W; at NE cor. sec. 20, T 26 N, R 5 W). Named on Red Bank (1952) 7.5' quadrangle. Called Redbank on California Mining Bureau's (1909b) map. Postal authorities established Colyer post office 10 miles southwest of Red Bluff in 1889, moved it 5 miles west in 1894 when they changed the name to Eby, changed the name to Redbank in 1904, and discontinued it in 1918; the name "Colyer" was for John G. Colyer, a homesteader of 1862, and the name "Eby" was for Jackson Eby, a landowner (Salley, p. 48, 65, 182). They reestablished Colyer post office in 1905 with the name "Colyear," and discontinued it in 1910 (Salley, p. 48)

Red Bank Campground [SISKIYOU]: *locality,* 5 miles west of Sawyers Bar along North Fork Salmon River (lat. 41°17'55" N, long. 123°13'45" W). Named on Sawyers Bar (1979) 7.5' quadrangle.

Red Bank Creek [TEHAMA]: *stream,* flows 39 miles to Sacramento River 2.25 miles southeast of downtown Red Bluff (lat. 40°09'10" N, long. 122°12'20" W; sec. 36, T 27 N, R 3 W). Named on Lowrey (1967), Raglin Ridge (1967), Red Bank (1952), Red Bluff East (1951), Red Bluff West (1951), and West of Gerber (1951) 7.5' quadrangles. Called Redbank Creek on Tehama (1905) 15' quadrangle, but United States Board on Geographic Names (1967b, p. 4) rejected this form of the name. Called Baranca Colorada in 1844 on a diseño of Las Flores grant (Becker, 1964). North Fork enters from the northwest 1.5 miles north-northwest of Red Bank; it is 12.5 miles long and is named on Blossom (1952), Lowrey (1967), Oxbow Bridge (1967), Raglin Ridge (1967), and Red Bank (1952) 7.5' quadrangles.

Red Bank Gulch [TEHAMA]: *canyon,* drained by a stream that flows 5.25 miles to South Fork Cottonwood Creek [SHASTA-TEHAMA] 8 miles northeast of Wakefield Flat (lat. 40°12'50" N, long. 122°32'30" W). Named on Cold Fork (1967) and Oxbow Bridge (1967) 7.5' quadrangles.

Red Banks [SISKIYOU]: *relief feature,* 10.5 miles north-northwest of McCloud (lat. 41°24' N, long. 122°12' W; sec. 16, T 41 N, R 3 W). Named on Shasta (1954) 15' quadrangle.

Red Bluff [TEHAMA]: *city,* a little north of the center of Tehama County along Sacramento River (lat. 40°10'35" N, long. 122°14'05" W; mainly in sec. 19, 20, T 27 N, R 3 W). Named on Red Bluff East (1951) and Red Bluff West (1951) 7.5' quadrangles. Called Red Bluffs on Goddard's (1857) map. United States Board on Geographic Names (1933, p. 636) rejected the form "Redbluff" for the name. Postal authorities established Red Bluff post office in 1853 (Frickstad, p. 205), and the city incorporated in 1876. Mr. S. Woods laid out the community and called it Leodocia (Bancroft, p. 496). Gudde (1949, p. 282) noted that the place was known as Covertsburg in 1853. Adobe Ferry was situated on Sacramento River 1.5 miles northeast of Red Bluff and operated for more than 30 years before it was abandoned in 1876; the name was from a house known as the Ide adobe that was built on the west bank of the river in the late 1840's or early 1850's (Hoover, Rensch, and Rensch, p. 550). California Mining Bureau's (1909b) map shows a place called Hunters located 10.5 miles west of Red Bluff on the stage route. Postal authorities established Hunters post office in 1888, moved it 1 mile west in 1900, and discontinued it in 1930; the name was for the operator of a boat landing on South Fork Cottonwood Creek [SHASTA-TEHAMA] (Salley, p. 101). They established Dobson post office 6.5 miles southwest of Hunters post office in 1896 and discontinued it in 1897; the name was for Malinda Dobson, first postmaster (Salley, p. 60). They established Elder Creek post office 12 miles southwest of Red Bluff in 1878 and discontinued it in 1882 (Salley, p. 66). They established Manzanita post office 14 miles northwest of Red Bluff in 1892 and discontinued it in 1896 (Salley, p. 132). They established Whittington post office 20 miles northwest of Red Bluff in 1884 and discontinued it in 1885 (Salley, p. 240).

Red Butte [SISKIYOU]:

(1) *peak,* 6.25 miles north of the village of Seiad Valley (lat. 41°55'50" N, long. 123°11' W). Altitude 6739 feet. Named on Kangaroo Mountain (1980) 7.5' quadrangle United States Board on Geographic Names (1983c, p. 4) approved the name "Cook and Green Butte" for a feature, altitude 6270 feet, located 1.2 miles northeast of Red Butte (lat. 41°56'22" N, long. 123°09'45" W); the name commemorates Robert Cook and the two Green brothers, who prospected and mined in the neighborhood. The Board at the same time (p. 5) approved the name "Desolation Peak" for a feature, altitude 6148 feet, located 1.8 miles west of Red Butte (lat. 41°55'37" N, long. 123°13'08" W); the name is from the lack of vegetation on the peak.

(2) *peak,* 7.5 miles northwest of McCloud (lat. 41°21'40" N, long. 122°10'50" W; sec. 34, T 41 N, R 3 W). Named on Shasta (1954) 15' quadrangle.

(3) *hill,* 9 miles north-northeast of Medicine Lake (lat. 41°42'10" N, long. 121°31'40" W; near NE cor. sec. 32, T 45 N, R 4 E). Named on Medicine Lake (1952) 15' quadrangle.

Red Cap Mountain [SISKIYOU]: *peak,* 8 miles west-southwest of Medicine Lake (lat. 41°32'45" N, long. 121°44'40" W). Named on Bray (1950) and Medicine Lake (1952) 15' quadrangles.

Red Cliff [SHASTA]: *relief feature,* 15 miles north-northwest of Lassen Peak (lat. 40°41'40" N, long. 121°36' W; at N line sec. 26, T 33 N, R 3 E). Named on Manzanita Lake (1956) 15' quadrangle.

Redding [SHASTA]: *city,* along Sacramento River in the southwest part of Shasta County (lat. 40°34'55" N, long. 122°23'40" W). Named on Enterprise (1957) and Redding (1957) 7.5' quadrangles. Postal authorities established Redding post office in 1872 (Frickstad, p. 182), and the city incorporated in 1887. Major P.B. Reading had a town called Reading—or Latona, for the steamboat *Latona,* which landed near the mouth of Clear Creek in 1856—platted in 1862 on his land south of present Redding near the mouth of Clear Creek, but the place failed to develop (Steger, p. 44, 55). Present Redding was laid out in 1872 by B.B. Redding, land agent for Central Pacific Railroad, and named for him; because the residents wanted to honor the pioneer, P.B. Reading, the legislature changed the name "Redding" to "Reading" in 1874, but the railroad refused to recognize the change, and in 1880 the legislature reversed itself (Gudde, 1949, p. 282). A place called Middletown was situated about 4.5 miles south of Redding (McGregor, p. 627)—the name was for the location of the place about midway between Horsetown and Shasta (Giles, p. 193). Postal authorities established Middletown post office in 1856 and discontinued it in 1858 (Frickstad, p. 181). They established Bell's Bridge post office 5 miles south of Redding in 1870, discontinued it in 1871, reestablished it in 1873, and discontinued it in 1881; the name was for J.J. Bell, first postmaster and builder of a toll bridge across Clear Creek in 1853 (Salley, p. 18). They established Brincard post office 6 miles southwest of Redding in 1879 and discontinued it in 1881; the name was for the discoverer of gold at the site (Salley, p. 27). They established Goering post office 12 miles northeast of Redding (sec. 34, T 33 N, R 4 W) in 1879 and discontinued it the same year; the name was for John Goering, first postmaster (Salley, p. 86). They established Dolde post office 5 miles southwest of Redding in 1890 and discontinued it in 1893; the name was for Arnold C. Dolde, first postmaster (Salley, p. 60).

Redding: see **Lake Redding** [SHASTA].

Redding Bar: see **Reading Bar** [SHASTA].

Red Fir Ridge [SISKIYOU]: *ridge,* south-southeast- to east-southeast-trending, 7.25 miles north of McCloud (lat. 41°21'30" N, long. 122°09' W). Named on Shasta (1954) 15' quadrangle.

Red Flat [TEHAMA]: *area,* 3.5 miles northeast of Tomhead Mountain (lat. 40°10' N, long. 122°46' W; on N line sec. 28, T 27 N, R 8 W). Named on Yolla Bolly (1954) 15' quadrangle.

Red Gulch [SHASTA]: *canyon,* drained by a stream that flows nearly 1 mile to Whiskeytown Lake 6.5 miles southeast of the village of French Gulch (lat. 40°38'50" N, long. 122°33' W; sec. 9, T 32 N, R 6 W). Named on Whiskeytown (1979) 7.5' quadrangle.

Red Hill [BUTTE]: *ridge,* generally north-northeast-trending, less than 1 mile long; 8.5 miles southeast of Paradise (lat. 39°39'15" N, long. 121°31'40" W; on N line sec. 28, T 21 N, R 4 E). Named on Cherokee (1970) 7.5' quadrangle.

Red Hill [SISKIYOU]:

(1) *peak,* 2.25 miles west of Bear Peak (lat. 41°41'50" N, long. 123°37'10" W). Altitude 5638 feet. Named on Bear Peak (1982) 7.5' quadrangle.

(2) *peak,* 6 miles north-northwest of McCloud (lat. 41°20' N, long. 122°11'40" W; on S line sec. 4, T 40 N, R 3 W). Altitude 6866 feet. Named on Dunsmuir (1935) 30' quadrangle.

(3) *hill,* 4.5 miles west of McCloud (lat. 41°16' N, long. 122°03'15" W; near W line sec. 35, T 40 N, R 2 W). Named on Shasta (1954) 15' quadrangle.

(4) *peak,* 3.5 miles southwest of Medicine Lake (lat. 41°32'35" N, long. 121°38'35" W). Altitude 6478 feet. Named on Medicine Lake (1952) 15' quadrangle.

(5) *hill,* 17 miles northeast of Bartle (lat. 41°25'05" N, long. 121°33' W; sec. 6, T 41 N, R 4 E). Named on Hambone (1961) 15' quadrangle.

Red Hill Creek [SISKIYOU]: *stream,* flows nearly 3 miles to Clear Creek (1) 3 miles north-northwest of Bear Peak (lat. 41°43'55" N, long. 123°36' W); a branch of the stream heads near Red Hill (1). Named on Bear Peak (1982) 7.5' quadrangle.

Red Hill Gulch [SHASTA]: *canyon,* drained by a stream that flows 1 mile to Clear Creek nearly 7 miles southwest of Schell Mountain (lat. 40°46'40" N, long. 122°36'30" W; sec. 25, T 34 N, R 7 W). Named on Schell Mountain (1950) 15' quadrangle.

Red Lake [SHASTA]: *lake,* 800 feet long, 9 miles northwest of Lassen Peak (lat. 40°35'40" N, long. 121°36'15" W; sec. 26, T 32 N, R 3 E). Named on Manzanita Lake (1956) 15' quadrangle.

Red Lake Mountain [SHASTA]: *peak,* 7.5 miles northwest of Lassen Peak (lat. 40°34'15" N, long. 121°35'30" W; at NW cor. sec. 1, T 31 N, R 3 E); the peak is 1.5 miles south-southeast of Red Lake. Altitude 6680 feet. Named on Manzanita Lake (1956) 15' quadrangle.

Red Mountain [GLENN]: *peak,* 10 miles north-northwest of the village of Elk Creek (lat. 39°44'35" N, long. 122°36'30" W). Altitude 3635 feet. Named on Chrome (1968) 7.5' quadrangle.

Red Mountain [SHASTA]:

(1) *peak,* 8 miles northeast of the village of Big Bend (lat. 41°05'45" N, long. 121°48' W; near NE cor. sec. 1, T 37 N, R 1 E). Named on Big Bend (1961) 15' quadrangle.

(2) *peak,* 7 miles northwest of Lassen Peak (lat. 40°34'10" N, long. 121°35' W; sec. 1, T 31 N, R 3 E). Altitude 6432 feet. Named on Manzanita Lake (1956) 15' quadrangle.

Red Mountain [SISKIYOU]: *ridge,* southwest-trending, 5 miles long, 15 miles south-southwest of Scott Bar (lat. 41°04'30" N, long. 123°05'30" W). Named on Boulder Peak (1981) 7.5' quadrangle.

Red Mountain [TEHAMA]: *peak,* 8 miles northwest of Paskenta (lat. 39°57'50" N, long. 122°39'05" W; sec. 4, T 24 N, R 7 W). Altitude 3228 feet. Named on Riley Ridge (1967) 7.5' quadrangle.

Red Mountain: see **Boulder Peak** [SISKIYOU]; **Little Red Mountain** [TEHAMA]; **North Red Mountain** [SHASTA].

Red Mountain Creek: see **Little Red Mountain Creek** [TEHAMA].

Red Rock [GLENN]: *relief feature,* 2.5 miles northeast of Saint John Mountain (lat. 39°27'35" N, long. 122°39'20" W; near E line sec. 32, T 19 N, R 7 W). Named on Saint John Mountain (1968) 7.5' quadrangle.

Red Rock [SISKIYOU]: *ridge,* north-northwest-trending, nearly 1 mile long, 15 miles west-southwest of Scott Bar (lat. 41°37'55" N, long. 123°14'20" W). Named on Grider Valley (1981) 7.5' quadrangle.

Red Rock Creek [SISKIYOU]: *stream,* flows 3.25 miles to Little Elk Creek 13 miles south-southwest of Scott Bar (lat. 41°35'15" N, long. 123°08'25" W); the stream goes through Red Rock Valley (1). Named on Marble Mountain (1980) 7.5' quadrangle.

Red Rock Hill [SHASTA]: *peak,* 10 miles southeast of Burney (lat. 40°46'55" N, long. 121°31'55" W; near N line sec. 28, T 34 N, R 4 E). Altitude 5240 feet. Named on Burney (1957) 15' quadrangle.

Red Rock Lakes [SISKIYOU]: *lakes,* two, largest 0.5 mile long, 11 miles south-southeast of Dorris (lat. 41°49'30" N, long. 121°49'30" W; mainly in sec. 14, T 46 N, R 1 E). Named on Dorris (1950) 15' quadrangle.

Red Rock Mountain [SHASTA]: *peak,* 5.5 miles west-southwest of Lassen Peak (lat. 40°27'30" N, long. 121°36' W). Altitude 7555 feet. Named on Lassen Peak (1956) 15' quadrangle. Mineral (1941) 30' quadrangle has the form "Redrock Mountain" for the name.

Red Rock Mountain [SISKIYOU]: *peak,* 30 miles south of Etna on Siskiyou-Trinity County line (lat. 41°01'50" N, long. 122°53'50" W; near S line sec. 28, T 37 N, R 9 W). Altitude 7853 feet. Named on Coffee Creek (1955) 15' quadrangle.

Red Rock Valley [SISKIYOU]:

(1) *valley,* 14 miles south-southwest of Scott Bar (lat. 41°33'40" N, long. 123°08'40" W); the valley is along Red Rock Creek. Named on Marble Mountain (1980) 7.5' quadrangle.

(2) *valley,* 16 miles south-southeast of Dorris (lat. 41°45' N, long. 121°49' W). Named on Bray (1950) and Dorris (1950) 15' quadrangles.

Red Shale Butte [SISKIYOU]: *peak,* 4 miles east of Medicine Lake (lat. 41°34'45" N, long. 121°31'15" W). Named on Medicine Lake (1952) 15' quadrangle.

Red Tank Spring [SISKIYOU]: *spring,* 6 miles north-northeast of Bartle (lat. 41°20'25" N, long. 121°47'10" W; at E line sec. 1, T 40 N, R 1 E). Named on Bartle (1961) 15' quadrangle.

Redwoods [SHASTA]: *locality,* 2.5 miles south-southwest of Whitmore (lat. 40°35'50" N, long. 121°56' W; near W line sec. 25, T 32 N, R 1 W). Named on Whitmore (1956) 15' quadrangle

Reeds Creek [TEHAMA]: *stream,* flows 20 miles to Sacramento River 0.5 mile southeast of downtown Red Bluff (lat. 40°10'20" N, long. 122°13'35" W; at N line sec. 29, T 27 N, R 3 W). Named on Blossom (1952), Oxbow Bridge (1967), Red Bluff East (1951), and Red Bluff West (1951) 7.5' quadrangles. Called Read's Creek on Red Bluff (1894) 1° quadrangle, and called Reed Creek on Tehama (1905) 15' quadrangle. On Red Bank (1952) 15' quadrangle, present Liza Creek is called North Fork Reeds Creek.

Reese Reservoir [SHASTA]: *lake,* 1250 feet long, 5 miles southwest of Redding (lat. 40°31'50" N, long. 122°27'40" W; near NW cor. sec. 20, T 31 N, R 5 W). Named on Redding (1957, photorevised 1969) 7.5' quadrangle.

Reeves Ranch Spring [SISKIYOU]: *spring,* 12 miles northeast of the village of Seiad Valley (lat. 41°55'55" N, long. 123°00'35" W; at S line sec. 9, T 47 N, R 10 W). Named on Dutch Creek (1980) 7.5' quadrangle. Seiad Valley (1955) 15' quadrangle shows three springs with the name "Reeves Ranch Springs."

Reflection Lake [SHASTA]: *lake,* 1400 feet long, 4.5 miles northwest of Lassen Peak along Manzanita Creek (lat. 40°32'15" N, long. 122°33'50" W; sec. 18, T 31 N, R 4 E). Named on Manzanita Lake (1956) 15' quadrangle. The feature also was called Stockton Lake—it was the site of a fish farm operated by Dr. J.E. Stockton in the 1880's (Giles, p. 249, 257). On Burney (1939) 30' quadrangle, nearby Manzanita Lake (1) is called Reflection Lake.

Regan Meadow Campground [SHASTA]: *locality,* 11.5 miles southwest of Arbuckle Mountain (lat. 40°18'05" N, long. 123°02'35" W; near SW cor. sec. 6, T 28 N, R 10 W). Named on Dubakella Mountain (1954) 15' quadrangle. United States Board on Geographic Names (1978c, p. 2) approved the name "Gum Spring" for a feature located 2 miles northeast of Regan Meadow Campground (lat. 40°19'09" N, long. 123°00'50" W; sec. 32, T 29 N, R 10 W), and (1979a, p. 4) approved the name McFarland Ridge for a feature, 3 miles long, located 4.5 miles north of Regan Meadow Campground on Shasta-Trinity County line (lat. 40°22'40" N, long. 123°02'35" W).

Reilly Landing [GLENN]: *locality,* 2.5 miles north of Butte City along Sacramento River (lat. 39°29'55" N, long. 121°59'40" W; sec. 17, T 19 N, R 1 W). Named on Butte City (1912) 7.5' quadrangle.

Rend Island Campground [SHASTA]: *locality,* 14 miles north of Millville along Shasta Lake (lat. 40°45' N, long. 122°10'30" W; near N line sec. 2, T 33 N, R 3 W). Named on Bella Vista (1965) 7.5' quadrangle.

Renfro: see **Sugarloaf** [SHASTA] (4).

Reno Canyon [SHASTA]: *canyon,* drained by a stream that flows 0.5 mile to Shasta Lake 12.5 miles south of Bollibokka Mountain (lat. 40°45'15" N, long. 122°10'40" W; sec. 35, T 34 N, R 3 W). Named on Bollibokka Mountain (1957) 15' quadrangle.

Reservoir Gulch [SISKIYOU]:

(1) *canyon,* drained by a stream that flows 1 mile to Applegate River 10 miles north of the village of Seiad Valley (lat. 41°59'05" N, long. 123°10'35" W). Named on Kangaroo Mountain (1980) 7.5' quadrangle.

(2) *canyon,* drained by a stream that flows about 0.5 mile to Indian Creek (3) 6 miles north of Fort Jones (lat. 41°41'30" N, long. 122°51'20" W; at E line sec. 3, T 44 N, R 9 W). Named on Fort Jones (1955) 15' quadrangle.

Reservoir Public Camp [SHASTA]: *locality,* 11 miles northwest of Manzanita Lake (lat. 40°36'25" N, long. 121°38'50" W; sec. 21, T 32 N, R 3 E); the place is along North Battle Creek Reservoir. Named on Manzanita Lake (1956) 15' quadrangle.

Retreat: see **Shasta Retreat** [SISKIYOU].

Retson Camp [BUTTE]: *locality,* 1 mile north-northeast of Stirling City along West Branch Feather River (lat. 39°55'20" N, long. 121°31'20" W; on E line sec. 21, T 24 N, R 4 E). Named on Stirling City (1979) 7.5' quadrangle.

Reynolds Basin [SHASTA]: *relief feature,* 10.5 miles east of Bollibokka Mountain (lat. 40°54'45" N, long. 122°01'15" W; sec. 6, 7, T 35 N, R 1 W). Named on Bollibokka Mountain (1957) 15' quadrangle. The name commemorates a settler in the neighborhood (Steger, p. 55).

Reynolds Creek [SHASTA]:

(1) *stream,* flows 4.5 miles to Nelson Creek (1) 1.5 miles northeast of the village of Big Bend (lat. 41°02'10" N, long. 121°53' W; sec. 29, T 37 N, R 1 E). Named on Big Bend (1961) 15' quadrangle.

(2) *stream,* flows 1 mile to Pit River Arm Shasta Lake 12 miles south-southeast of Bollibokka Mountain (lat. 40°45'50" N, long. 122°09'15" W; sec. 36, T 34 N, R 3 W). Named on Bollibokka Mountain (1957) 15' quadrangle. The name commemorates Reynolds of Reynolds Basin (Steger, p. 55).

Reynolds Creek [SISKIYOU]: *stream,* flows nearly 3 miles to Klamath River 9 miles north of Orleans, which is in Humboldt County (lat. 41°25'45" N, long. 123°30'10" W); the stream is south of Reynolds Ridge. Named on Bark Shanty Gulch (1974) 7.5' quadrangle.

Reynolds Ridge [SISKIYOU]: *ridge,* north-northeast- to east-trending, 2 miles long, 9.5 miles north of Orleans, which is in Humboldt County (lat. 41°26'20" N, long. 123°32'45" W); the ridge is north of Reynolds Creek. Named on Bark Shanty Gulch (1974) 7.5' quadrangle.

Rhett Lake: see **Tule Lake Sump** [SISKIYOU].

Rhodonite Creek [SISKIYOU]: *stream,* flows 1.5 miles to East Fork Indian Creek (1) 7.25 miles north of Happy Camp (lat. 41°53'50" N, long. 123°24'15" W; near NE cor. sec. 4, T 17 N, R 7 W). Named on Deadman Point (1981) 7.5' quadrangle.

Rice Creek [TEHAMA]: *stream,* flows 13 miles to Burch Creek 6.5 miles south-southwest of Vina (lat. 39°50'35" N, long. 122°05'20" W). Named on Black Butte Dam (1967) and Kirkwood (1949) 7.5' quadrangles.

Rice Creek: see **Burch Creek** [TEHAMA].

Riceton [BUTTE]: *locality,* 2.5 miles north-northwest of Biggs along Southern Pacific Railroad (lat. 39°26'55" N, long. 121°43'30" W; near NE cor. sec. 3, T 18 N, R 2 E). Named on Biggs (1970) 7.5' quadrangle.

Riceville: see **Corning** [TEHAMA].

Richardson Creek [SHASTA]: *stream,* flows 4 miles to Roaring Creek 4.25 miles north of the village of Montgomery Creek (lat. 40°54'10" N, long. 121°55'10" W; sec. 12, T 35 N, R 1 E). Named on Montgomery Creek (1956) 15' quadrangle.

Richardson Springs [BUTTE]: *locality,* 8.5 miles north-northeast of Chico along Mud Creek (lat. 39°50'25" N, long. 121°46'35" W; near N line sec. 20, T 23 N, R 2 E). Named on Richardson Springs (1951) 7.5' quadrangle. Postal authorities established Richardson Springs post office in 1933 (Frickstad, p. 12). The name commemorates J.H. Richardson and Lee Richardson, who developed a resort at five medicinal springs at the site in 1898 (Hanna, p. 255). The place first was called Mud Springs (Dunn, F.D., p. 73).

Rich Bar: see **Diamondville** [BUTTE]; **Thompson Flat** [BUTTE].

Richfield [TEHAMA]: *village,* 3.25 miles north of Corning (lat. 39°58'35" N, long. 122°10'35" W). Named on Corning (1951) 7.5' quadrangle. Postal authorities established Richfield post office in 1912 and discontinued it in 1970 (Salley, p. 185).

Rich Gulch [BUTTE]: *canyon,* drained by a stream that flows nearly 3 miles to West Branch Feather River 8.5 miles southeast of Paradise (lat. 39°40' N, long. 121°31'05" W; sec. 22, T 21 N, R 4 E). Named on Cherokee (1970) 7.5' quadrangle.

Rich Gulch [SHASTA]:

(1) *canyon,* drained by a stream that flows 1.5 miles to Churn Creek at Summit City (lat. 40°41' N, long. 122°24'05" W; sec. 26, T 33 N, R 5 W). Named on Shasta Dam (1956) 7.5' quadrangle.

(2) *canyon,* drained by a stream that flows nearly 2 miles to Brandy Creek 7 miles north-northwest of Igo (lat. 40°35'40" N, long. 122°36'10" W; near S line sec. 25, T 32 N, R 7 W). Named on Igo (1979) 7.5' quadrangle.

Rich Gulch: see **Thompson Flat** [BUTTE]; **Yankee Hill** [BUTTE].

Richie Peak [SHASTA]: *peak,* nearly 3.5 miles west of Igo (lat. 40°30'50" N, long. 122°36'10" W; sec. 25, T 31 N, R 7 W). Altitude 2254 feet. Named on Igo (1979) 7.5' quadrangle.

Richland [BUTTE]: *locality,* 3.5 miles east-southeast of Biggs along Northern Electric Railroad (lat. 39°23'50" N, long. 121°39'05" W). Named on Biggs (1912) 7.5' quadrangle. On Gridley (1952) 15' quadrangle, the name applies to a place located about 0.5 mile farther west.

Richvale [BUTTE]: *village,* 6 miles north-northwest of Biggs (lat. 39°29'05" N, long. 121°44'35" W; around SE cor. sec. 16, T 19 N, R 2 E). Named on Biggs (1970) 7.5' quadrangle. Postal authorities established Richvale post office in 1911 (Frickstad, p. 12). Richvale Land Company started the place about 1911 at what was known as Selbys Switch (Hanna, p. 255).

Rider Gulch [SISKIYOU]: *canyon,* 2 miles long, opens into the canyon of Humbug Creek 16 miles southeast of Condrey Mountain (lat. 41°46'30" N, long. 122°45' W). Named on Condrey Mountain (1955) 15' quadrangle.

Riderville: see **French Town** [SISKIYOU].

Ridge Lakes [SHASTA]: *lakes,* two, largest 500 feet long, 3.25 miles southwest of Lassen Peak (lat. 40°27'20" N, long. 121°32'50" W; sec. 16, T 30 N, R 4 E). Named on Lassen (1956) 15' quadrangle.

Right Fork [SHASTA]: *canyon,* drained by a stream that flows 3.5 miles to French Gulch (2) 2 miles west-northwest of the village of French Gulch (lat. 40°42'50" N, long. 122°40'10" W; near W line sec. 16, T 33 N, R 7 W). Named on French Gulch (1979) 7.5' quadrangle.

Riley: see **Cottonwood** [SHASTA].

Riley Gulch [SHASTA]: *canyon,* drained by a stream that flows nearly 1 mile to Little Churn Creek 1 mile west-southwest of Summit City (lat. 40°40'50" N, long. 122°25'10" W; at N line sec. 34, T 33 N, R 5 W). Named on Shasta Dam (1956) 7.5' quadrangle.

Riley Ridge [TEHAMA]: *ridge,* east- to east-southeast-trending, 3.5 miles long, 9.5 miles northwest of Paskenta (lat. 39°57'45" N, long. 122°41'30" W). Named on Riley Ridge (1967) 7.5' quadrangle, which shows Riley cabin on the side of the ridge.

Rim: see **The Rim** [SHASTA].

Rinckel [SHASTA]: *locality,* 4.5 miles north of Shoeinhorse Mountain along McCloud River [SHASTA-SISKIYOU] (lat. 41°08' N, long. 122°04'30" W). Named on Shoeinhorse Mountain (1954) 15' quadrangle.

Ringeye Creek [SHASTA]: *stream,* flows 1 mile to Backbone Creek 11 miles south of Lamoine (lat. 41°44'15" N, long. 122°27'40" W; sec. 8, T 34 N, R 5 W). Named on Lamoine (1957) 15' quadrangle.

Rio Bonito: see **East Biggs** [BUTTE].

Rio de las Plumas: see **Feather River** [BUTTE].

Rio de los Berrendo: see **Dye Creek** [TEHAMA]; **El Primer Cañon or Rio de los Berrendo** [TEHAMA].

Rio de los Molinos [TEHAMA]: *land grant,* east of Sacramento River at Los Molinos. Named on Los Molinos (1952) and Vina (1950) 7.5' quadrangles. Albert G. Tomes received 5 leagues in 1844 and claimed 22,172 acres patented in 1858 (Cowan, p. 49).

Rio de los Molinos: see **Mill Creek** [TEHAMA] (3).

Rio del Plumas: see **Feather River** [BUTTE].

Rio del Tlamachi: see **Klamath River** [SISKIYOU].

Rio Sacramento: see **Sacramento River**.

Rio Seco: see **Oroville** [BUTTE].

Ripgut Creek [SHASTA]: *stream,* flows 5 miles to Pit River 11.5 miles southeast of Bollibokka Mountain (lat. 40°49' N, long. 122°03'30" W; sec. 11, T 34 N, R 2 W). Named on Bollibokka Mountain (1957) 15' quadrangle. Called Lick Creek on Redding (1901) 30' quadrangle. William Bowers named the stream after he ripped his clothes to shreds on shrubs growing along it (Steger, p. 56).

Ripley Creek [TEHAMA]: *stream,* flows 4 miles to South Fork Battle Creek [SHASTA-TEHAMA] 4.25 miles southwest of Manton (lat. 40°23'40" N, long. 121°55'55" W; sec. 1, T 29 N, R 1 W). Named on Manton (1956) 15' quadrangle.

Rippley Gulch [SHASTA]: *canyon,* drained by a stream that flows 1 mile to

Cline Gulch 2 miles east-northeast of the village of French Gulch (lat. 40°42'45" N, long. 122°36'05" W; near S line sec. 13, T 33 N, R 7 W). Named on Whiskeytown (1979) 7.5' quadrangle.

Rising River [SHASTA]: *stream,* flows 3.5 miles to Hat Creek 6.25 miles east-northeast of Burney (lat. 40°54'25" N, long. 121°33'15" W; near W line sec. 8, T 35 N, R 4 E). Named on Burney (1957) 15' quadrangle. The stream rises in a marshy meadow (Steger, p. 56).

Rising River Lake [SHASTA]: *lake,* 3300 feet long, 7.5 miles east of Burney (lat. 40°54' N, long. 121°31'30" W; sec. 9, 16, T 35 N, R 4 E); the lake is at the head of a branch of Rising River. Named on Burney (1957) 15' quadrangle.

Ritts Mill [SHASTA]: *locality,* 9.5 miles southeast of Whitmore (lat. 40°33'35" N, long. 121°45'55" W; near NE cor. sec. 8, T 31 N, R 2 E). Named on Whitmore (1956) 15' quadrangle.

Riverview [SHASTA]: *locality,* 4 miles south-southeast of Lamoine (lat. 40°55'20" N, long. 122°24' W; sec. 2, T 35 N, R 5 W); the place is along Sacramento River. Named on Lamoine (1957) 15' quadrangle.

Riverview [SISKIYOU]: *peak,* 7.5 miles south-southwest of Hornbrook (lat. 41°49' N, long. 122°36'55" W; near SW cor. sec. 24, T 46 N, R 7 W). Altitude 4547 feet. Named on Hornbrook (1955) 15' quadrangle.

Riz Siding [GLENN]: *locality,* 4 miles south of Willows along Southern Pacific Railroad (lat. 39°27'55" N, long. 122°11'30" W; at NW cor. sec. 34, T 19 N, R 3 W). Named on Logandale (1952) 7.5' quadrangle.

Roadside Spring [BUTTE]: *spring,* 2.5 miles west-southwest of Forbestown (lat. 39°30'10" N, long. 121°18'45" W; near W line sec. 16, T 19 N, R 6 E). Named on Forbestown (1970) 7.5' quadrangle.

Road Valley [TEHAMA]: *area,* 5.25 miles southwest of Paskenta (lat. 39°50' N, long. 122°37' W; sec. 23, T 23 N, R 7 W). Named on Paskenta (1920) 15' quadrangle.

Roaring Creek [SHASTA]: *stream,* flows 9.5 miles to Pit River 3 miles northwest of the village of Montgomery Creek (lat. 40°53'25" N, long. 121°58'25" W; near NE cor. sec. 22, T 35 N, R 1 W). Named on Montgomery Creek (1956) 15' quadrangle.

Roaring Creek: see **Little Roaring Creek** [SHASTA].

Roaring River [SHASTA]: *stream,* flows 11 miles to North Fork Cottonwood Creek [SHASTA-TEHAMA] 7.5 miles southeast of Ono (lat. 40°23'50" N, long. 122°31'35" W; sec. 3, T 29 N, R 6 W). Named on Ono (1952) 15' quadrangle. The name is from the noise of rapids along the stream (Steger, p. 56).

Roaring River: see **Igo** [SHASTA].

Roaring Spring [SHASTA]: *spring,* 16 miles northwest of Lassen Peak (lat. 40°37'40" N, long. 121°44'30" W; near NW cor. sec. 15, T 32 N, R 2 E). Named on Manzanita Lake (1956) 15' quadrangle.

Robbers Roost [BUTTE]: *relief feature,* 6.5 miles south-southwest of Paradise (lat. 39°39'35" N, long. 121°39'20" W; at E line sec. 20, T 21 N, R 3 E). Named on Hamlin Canyon (1951) 7.5' quadrangle.

Roberts: see **Palo Cedro** [SHASTA].

Roberts Canyon [SHASTA]: *canyon,* drained by a stream that flows 1 mile to Pit River 13 miles southeast of Bollibokka Mountain (lat. 40°48'45" N, long. 122°01'55" W; near E line sec. 12, T 34 N, R 2 W). Named on Bollibokka Mountain (1957) 15' quadrangle. The name recalls B.F. Roberts, a pioneer teacher who died in the canyon in 1897 (Steger, p. 56).

Roberts Creek: see **Hamlin Slough** [BUTTE].

Robinson Flat [SISKIYOU]:

(1) *area,* 4 miles east-northeast of Sawyers Bar (lat. 41°19' N, long. 123°03'30" W); the place is opposite the mouth of Robinson Gulch (2). Named on Tanners Peak (1977) 7.5' quadrangle.

(2) *area,* 9.5 miles northeast of Mount Dome (lat. 41°54'45" N, long. 121°34'10" W; mainly in sec. 13, T 47 N, R 3 E). Named on Mount Dome (1950) 15' quadrangle.

Robinson Gulch [SISKIYOU]:

(1) *canyon,* drained by a stream that flows nearly 1.5 miles to Horse Creek (2) 6 miles east-northeast of the village of Seiad Valley (lat. 41°51'25" N, long. 123°05'10" W; near N line sec. 2, T 46 N, R 11 W). Named on Hamburg (1980) 7.5' quadrangle.

(2) *canyon,* drained by a stream that flows 2.25 miles to North Fork Salmon River 4 miles east-northeast of Sawyers Bar (lat. 41°19' N, long. 123°03'30" W); Robinson Flat (1) is at the mouth of the canyon. Named on Tanners Peak (1977) 7.5' quadrangle.

Robinson Mills [BUTTE]: *locality,* 8.5 miles north-northeast of Bangor (lat. 39°29'40" N, long. 121°19'05" W; sec. 20, T 19 N, R 6 W). Named on Rackerby (1948) 7.5' quadrangle. Called Robinson Sawmill on Bangor (1941) 15' quadrangle.

Robinson Ravine [BUTTE]: *canyon,* 2.25 miles long, opens into the canyon of South Honcut Creek 3 miles east-northeast of Bangor (lat. 39°24'35" N, long. 121°21'25" W; at S line sec. 13, T 18 N, R 5 E). Named on Rackerby (1948) 7.5' quadrangle.

Robinsons Corner [BUTTE]: *locality,* 4.5 miles west-northwest of Honcut (lat. 39°21'50" N, long. 121°36'25" W; at N line sec. 2, T 17 N, R 3 E). Named on Honcut (1952) 7.5' quadrangle.

Roble: see **Durham** [BUTTE].

Robles: see **Durham** [BUTTE].

Roble Station: see **Durham** [BUTTE].

Robley Point [BUTTE]: *relief feature,* 9 miles northeast of Paradise (lat. 39°51'50" N, long. 121°30'55" W; sec. 10, T 23 N, R 4 E). Named on Paradise East (1980) 7.5' quadrangle.

Rock Creek [BUTTE]: *stream,* heads in Plumas County and flows 1.25 miles in Butte County to South Fork Feather River 6 miles north of Clipper Mills (lat. 39°37'15" N, long. 121°08'25" W; sec. 1, T 20 N, R 7 E). Named on Cascade (1948) and Clipper Mills (1948) 7.5' quadrangles.

Rock Creek [BUTTE-TEHAMA]: *stream,* heads just inside Tehama County and flows 25 miles, partly along Butte-Tehama County line, to Pine Creek [BUTTE-TEHAMA] 1.25 miles southwest of Nord in Butte County (lat. 39°45'50" N, long. 121°58'15" W; sec. 9, T 22 N, R 1 W). Named on Campbell Mound (1952), Cohasset (1979), Nord (1951), and Richardson Springs (1951) 7.5' quadrangles. West Fork heads in Tehama County and flows 5 miles to join the main creek 6 miles south of Campbell Mound in Butte County; it is named on Campbell Mound (1952) 7.5' quadrangle.

Rock Creek [SHASTA]:

(1) *stream,* flows 10 miles to Pit River nearly 3 miles west of Burney Falls (lat. 41°00'35" N, long. 121°42'15" W). Named on Big Bend (1961) and Pondosa (1961) 15' quadrangles. The name is from the so-called Rock Indians, who buried their dead in an upright position in graves along the creek (Steger, p. 56). North Fork enters 5.5 miles upstream from the mouth of the main creek; it is 3 miles long and is named on Big Bend (1961) and Pondosa (1961) 15' quadrangles.

(2) *stream,* flows 4.25 miles to Sacramento River 3.25 miles northwest of Redding (lat. 40°36'30" N, long. 122°26'45" W; near SW cor. sec. 21, T 32 N, R 5 W). Named on Igo (1979) and Redding (1957) 7.5' quadrangles.

(3) *stream,* flows 10 miles to Bailey Creek 3 miles southeast of Shingletown (lat. 40°27'30" N, long. 121°51'05" W; sec. 15, T 30 N, R 1 E); the feature heads at Rock Spring (2). Named on Lassen Peak (1956) and Manton (1956) 15' quadrangles. Steger (p. 56) attributed the name to ledges of rock along the lower course of the stream.

Rock Creek [SISKIYOU]:

(1) *stream,* flows 9 miles to Klamath River 2.5 miles east-southeast of Dillon Mountain (lat. 41°30'45" N, long. 123°31'45" W). Named on Bark Shanty Gulch (1974) and Dillon Mountain (1983) 7.5' quadrangles.

(2) *stream,* flows 4.5 miles to Wooley Creek 13 miles north of Forks of Salmon (lat. 41°26'35" N, long. 123°20'20" W). Named on Medicine Mountain (1978) 7.5' quadrangle.

(3) *stream,* flows 1.5 miles to Jaynes Canyon 3.5 miles east of Condrey Mountain (lat. 41°56'50" N, long. 122°54'50" W; sec. 5, T 47 N, R 9 W). Named on Condrey Mountain (1955) 15' quadrangle.

(4) *stream,* flows 1.5 miles to the State of Oregon 13 miles north-northwest of Macdoel (lat. 42°00'20" N, long. 122°06'10" W; sec. 16, T 48 N, R 2 W). Named on Macdoel (1954) 15' quadrangle.

(5) stream, flows 1.5 miles to Shovel Creek 9.5 miles west-northwest of Macdoel (lat. 41°52'45" N, long. 122°10'10" W; near NW cor. sec. 36, T 47 N, R 3 W). Named on Macdoel (1954) 15' quadrangle.

Rock Creek [TEHAMA]: *stream,* flows 1.25 miles to Deer Creek (2) 15 miles south of Panther Spring (lat. 40°02' N, long. 121°48'15" W; near NW cor. sec. 18, T 25 N, R 2 E). Named on Panther Spring (1953) 15' quadrangle.

Rock Creek: see **Chico** [BUTTE]; **China Gulch** [BUTTE]; **Little Rock Creek** [BUTTE].

Rock Creek Butte [SISKIYOU]: *peak,* 3.5 miles west of Dillon Mountain (lat. 41°32'20" N, long. 123°38'20" W); the peak is at the head of a branch of Rock Creek (1). Named on Chimney Rock (1981) 7.5' quadrangle.

Rocker Springs: see **Sims** [SHASTA].

Rock Fence Creek [SISKIYOU]: *stream,* flows 3 miles to Rail Creek 14 miles east-southeast of Etna (lat. 41°21'45" N, long. 122°38'45" W; sec. 34, T 41 N, R 7 W); the stream heads at Rock Fence Lake. Named on China Mountain (1955) 15' quadrangle.

Rock Fence Lake [SISKIYOU]: *lake,* 700 feet long, 17 miles east-southeast of Etna (lat. 41°20'05" N, long. 122°36'30" W; near NE cor. sec. 13, T 40 N, R 7 W). Named on China Mountain (1955) 15' quadrangle.

Rock Gulch Creek [TEHAMA]: *stream,* flows 2.25 miles to Mill Creek (3) 4 miles south-southeast of Mineral (lat. 40°17'35" N, long. 121°34'10" W). Named on Lassen Peak (1956) 15' quadrangle.

Rock Lake [SISKIYOU]: *lake,* 350 feet long, nearly 3 miles southeast of Salmon Mountain (lat. 41°09'10" N, long. 123°22'25" W). Named on Salmon Mountain (1978) and Youngs Peak (1979) 7.5' quadrangles.

Rock Spring [SHASTA]:

(1) *spring,* 7.5 miles east-northeast of Burney (lat. 40°55'15" N, long. 121°32' W; near W line sec. 4, T 35 N, R 4 E). Named on Burney (1957) 15' quadrangle.

(2) *spring,* 9 miles west-southwest of Lassen Peak (lat. 40°27'30" N, long. 121°40'30" W; sec. 17, T 30 N, R 3 E); the feature is at the head of Rock Creek (3). Named on Lassen Peak (1956) 15' quadrangle.

Rock Spring [TEHAMA]: *spring,* 8 miles southwest of Ball Mountain (lat. 39°50'45" N, long. 122°52'50" W; near SW cor. sec. 16, T 23 N, R 9 W).

Named on Mendocino Pass (1967) 7.5' quadrangle.

Rockwell Ridge [GLENN]: *ridge,* east-southeast- to east-trending, 2.25 miles long, 7 miles southeast of Black Butte (lat. 39°40'20" N, long. 122°45'30" W). Named on Alder Springs (1967) and Plaskett Meadows (1967) 7.5' quadrangles.

Rocky Bar [BUTTE]: *locality,* 1.5 miles east of Bidwell Bar along Middle Fork Feather River (lat. 39°33'10" N, long. 121°24'45" W; sec. 33, T 20 N, R 5 E). Named on Big Bend Mountain (1948) 15' quadrangle. Water of Lake Oroville now covers the site.

Rocky Bar Campground [SISKIYOU]: *locality,* 4 miles east-southeast of the village of Seiad Valley along Klamath River (lat. 41°48'55" N, long. 123°07'35" W; sec. 21, T 46 N, R 11 W). Named on Seiad Valley (1955) 15' quadrangle.

Rocky Basin [GLENN]: *relief feature,* 3.5 miles south of Black Butte (lat. 39°40'30" N, long. 122°52'45" W). Named on Plaskett Ridge (1967) 7.5' quadrangle.

Rocky Basin Creek [GLENN]: *stream,* flows 2.25 miles to Mendocino County 4.25 miles south-southwest of Black Butte (lat. 39°40' N, long. 122°53'25" W); the stream is south of Rocky Basin Ridge. Named on Plaskett Meadows (1967) and Plaskett Ridge (1967) 7.5' quadrangles.

Rocky Basin Ridge [GLENN]: *ridge,* west- to west-southwest-trending, 2.5 miles long, 2.5 miles south of Black Butte (lat. 39°40'30" N, long. 121°53' W); Rocky Basin is on the ridge. Named on Plaskett Meadows (1967) and Plaskett Ridge (1967) 7.5' quadrangles.

Rocky Cabin Spring [TEHAMA]: *spring,* 11.5 miles west-northwest of Paskenta (lat. 39°57'15" N, long. 122°44'20" W; near E line sec. 10, T 24 N, R 8 W). Named on Riley Ridge (1967) 7.5' quadrangle.

Rocky Campground [SHASTA]: *locality,* 17 miles north-northeast of Lassen Peak (lat. 40°43'35" N, long. 121°25'40" W; near S line sec. 9, T 33 N, R 5 E). Named on Prospect Peak (1957) 15' quadrangle.

Rocky Creek [SHASTA]: *stream,* flows 3.5 miles to Middle Fork Cottonwood Creek [SHASTA-TEHAMA] 6 miles east-southeast of Arbuckle Mountain (lat. 40°22'35" N, long. 122°45'30" W; sec. 10, T 29 N, R 8 W). Named on Chanchelulla Peak (1951) 15' quadrangle.

Rocky Gulch [SISKIYOU]:

(1) *canyon,* drained by a stream that flows about 0.5 mile to Indian Creek (3) 4.5 miles north of Fort Jones (lat. 41°40'10" N, long. 122°50'50" W; near N line sec. 14, T 44 N, R 9 W). Named on Fort Jones (1955) 15' quadrangle.

(2) *canyon,* drained by a stream that flows 2.5 miles to Yreka Creek 11 miles south-southwest of Hornbrook at Hawkinsville (lat. 41°45'40" N, long. 122°37'10" W; sec. 11, T 45 N, R 7 W). Named on Hornbrook (1955) 15' quadrangle.

(3) *canyon,* flows 3.25 miles to Cottonwood Creek (1) less than 1 mile south-southeast of Hornbrook (lat. 41°53'55" N, long. 122°32'55" W; sec. 28, T 47 N, R 6 W). Named on Hornbrook (1955) 15' quadrangle.

(4) *canyon,* drained by a stream that heads in the State of Oregon and flows 2 miles in Siskiyou County to Camp Creek 24 miles west-northwest of Macdoel (lat. 41°59'15" N, long. 122°26' W; sec. 28, T 48 N, R 5 W). Named on Copco (1954) 15' quadrangle.

(5) *canyon,* 1.5 miles long, opens into the canyon of Moffett Creek 8.5 miles southwest of Yreka (lat. 41°38' N, long. 122°44'10" W; sec. 26, T 44 N, R 8 W). Named on Yreka (1954) 15' quadrangle.

Rocky Honcut Creek [BUTTE]: *stream,* formed by the confluence of Lower Rocky Honcut Creek and Upper Rocky Honcut Creek, flows nearly 4 miles to Honcut Creek 3 miles northwest of Bangor (lat. 39°25'20" N, long. 121°26'25" W; near N line sec. 17, T 18 N, R 5 E). Named on Bangor (1947) 7.5' quadrangle.

Rocky Honcut Creek: see **Lower Rocky Honcut Creek** [BUTTE]; **Upper Rocky Honcut Creek** [BUTTE].

Rocky Knob [SISKIYOU]: *peak,* 2.5 miles southeast of Broken Rib Mountain on Siskiyou-Del Norte County line (lat. 41°51'40" N, long. 123°38'55" W). Altitude 5716 feet. Named on Devils Punchbowl (1981) 7.5' quadrangle.

Rocky Ledge [SHASTA]: *escarpment,* north-trending, 4 miles long, 3.25 miles northeast of Burney (lat. 40°54'30" N, long. 121°37' W). Named on Burney (1957) 15' quadrangle.

Rocky Ledge Butte [SHASTA]: *peak,* 3 miles southeast of Burney (lat. 40°51'05" N, long. 121°37'50" W; on W line sec. 34, T 35 N, R 3 E); the peak is at the south end of Rocky Ledge. Named on Burney (1957) 15' quadrangle.

Rocky Peak [BUTTE]: *peak,* 9.5 miles southeast of Paradise (lat. 39°39'20" N, long. 121°30'15" W; at SW cor. sec. 23, T 21 N, R 4 E). Named on Cherokee (1970) 7.5' quadrangle.

Rocky Peak [TEHAMA]:

(1) *peak,* 5.5 miles north of Mineral (lat. 40°25'35" N, long. 121°35'45" W). Altitude 7171 feet. Named on Lassen Peak (1956) 15' quadrangle.

(2) *peak,* 4.25 miles west-northwest of Wakefield Flat (lat. 40°08'50" N, long. 122°43'05" W). Altitude 2354 feet. Named on Cold Fork (1967) 7.5' quadrangle.

Rocky Point: see **Rocky Point Peak** [BUTTE].

Rocky Point Gulch [SISKIYOU]: *canyon,* drained by a stream that flows 1 mile to Empire Creek 9 miles west of Hornbrook (lat. 41°53'45" N, long. 122°43'50" W). Named on Hornbrook (1955) 15' quadrangle.

Rocky Point Peak [BUTTE]: *peak,* 5.25 miles west-northwest of Forbestown (lat. 39°33' N, long. 121°21'20" W; near E line sec. 36, T 20 N, R 5 E). Altitude 1523 feet. Named on Forbestown (1970) 7.5' quadrangle. United States Board on Geographic Names (1973, p. 3) gave the variant name "Rocky Point" for the peak.

Rocky Ridge [BUTTE]: *ridge,* south-trending, 2.25 miles long, 1.5 miles southwest of Pulga (lat. 39°47'30" N, long. 121°28'20" W). Named on Pulga (1979) 7.5' quadrangle.

Rocky Ridge [GLENN-TEHAMA]: *ridge,* generally south-trending, 10 miles long, on Glenn-Tehama County line—only the northernmost end is in Tehama County; center about 1 mile south of Newville [GLENN] (lat. 39°46'30" N, long. 122°31'30" W). Named on Chrome (1968) and Newville (1967) 7.5' quadrangles.

Rocky Ridge [TEHAMA]: *ridge,* northwest-trending, 2 miles long, 3 miles north-northeast of Wakefield Flat (lat. 40°10' N, long. 122°37'30" W). Named on Cold Fork (1967) and Oxbow Bridge (1967) 7.5' quadrangles.

Rocky Ridge Campground [SHASTA]: *locality,* 13 miles north of Millville along Shasta Lake (lat. 40°44'05" N, long. 122°13'40" W; sec. 8, T 33 N, R 3 W). Named on Bella Vista (1965) 7.5' quadrangle.

Rodeo Creek [TEHAMA]: *stream,* flows nearly 4 miles to a ditch 2.25 miles south of Gerber (lat. 40°01'35" N, long. 122°08'35" W). Named on Gerber (1950) 7.5' quadrangle.

Rodgers Gulch [SHASTA]: *canyon,* 1 mile long, 8.5 miles north-northeast of Millville (lat. 40°38'50" N, long. 122°05'10" W; near W line sec. 10, T 32 N, R 2 W). Named on Millville (1953) 15' quadrangle.

Rody Creek [BUTTE]: *stream,* flows 1.5 miles to Clear Creek (2) 5 miles east-southeast of Pulga (lat. 39°47'15" N, long. 121°21'20" W; near W line sec. 6, T 22 N, R 6 E). Named on Soapstone Hill (1979) 7.5' quadrangle.

Rody Creek: see **Little Rody Creek** [BUTTE].

Roemer Ridge: see **Hardin Butte** [SISKIYOU].

Rogers Cow Camp [BUTTE]: *locality,* 8 miles east-southeast of Pulga along Coon Creek (2) (lat. 39°46'05" N, long. 121°18'40" W; near N line sec. 16, T 22 N, R 6 E). Named on Soapstone Hill (1979) 7.5' quadrangle.

Rogers Creek [SISKIYOU]: *stream,* flows 5 miles to Klamath River 16 miles north-northwest of Forks of Salmon (lat. 41°26'40" N, long. 123°29'20" W). Named on Forks of Salmon (1978) 7.5' quadrangle.

Rogerville [BUTTE]: *locality,* 6.25 miles north-northwest of Clipper Mills (lat. 39°36'40" N, long. 121°13'20" W; at E line sec. 7, T 20 N, R 7 E). Named on Clipper Mills (1948) 7.5' quadrangle.

Rollin [SISKIYOU]: *locality,* 2.5 miles south-southeast of Sawyers Bar (lat. 41°15'45" N, long. 123°06'55" W). Named on Tanners Peak (1977) 7.5' quadrangle. Postal authorities established Rollin post office in 1898 and discontinued it in 1927; the name was for Rollin L. Fagundes, first postmaster (Salley, p. 188).

Rooster Comb [SHASTA]: *relief feature,* 14 miles northwest of Lassen Peak on N side of Latour Butte (lat. 40°37' N, long. 121°42'30" W). Named on Manzanita Lake (1956) 15' quadrangle.

Root Creek [SHASTA]:

(1) *stream,* flows 2.5 miles to Sacramento River 2 miles northeast of Castella (lat. 41°09'45" N, long. 122°17'35" W; sec. 11, T 38 N, R 4 W). Named on Dunsmuir (1954) 15' quadrangle. The name commemorates Orin Root, who diverted water from a spring to create the stream (Steger, p. 56).

(2) *stream,* flows 2 miles to Castle Creek 3.5 miles west of Castella (lat. 41°08'55" N, long. 122°22'45" W; at E line sec. 13, T 38 N, R 5 W). Named on Dunsmuir (1954) 15' quadrangle.

Root Spring [TEHAMA]: *spring,* 4 miles south-southeast of Campbell Mound (lat. 39°55'30" N, long. 122°47' W; sec. 20, T 24 N, R 2 E). Named on Campbell Mound (1952) 7.5' quadrangle.

Rosebriar Creek [SHASTA]: *stream,* flows 4.25 miles to Dry Clover Creek 11 miles northeast of Millville (lat. 40°38'40" N, long. 122°00'15" W; sec. 8, T 32 N, R 1 W). Named on Millville (1953) and Whitmore (1956) 15' quadrangles.

Roselawn: see **Little Shasta** [SISKIYOU].

Rose Spring [SISKIYOU]: *spring,* 16 miles south-southwest of Macdoel (lat. 41°35'50" N, long. 122°03'55" W; sec. 3, T 43 N, R 2 W). Named on The Whaleback (1954) 15' quadrangle.

Rosewood [TEHAMA]: *locality,* 18 miles west-northwest of Red Bluff along Dry Creek (1) (lat. 40°46'10" N, long. 122°33'20" W; at NW cor. sec. 21, T 28 N, R 6 W). Named on Ono (1952) 15' quadrangle. Postal authorities established Rosewood post office in 1898 and discontinued it in 1909 (Frickstad, p. 205).

Ross: see **Camp Ross**, under **Shasta Alpine Lodge** [SISKIYOU].

Ross Chimneys [SISKIYOU]: *relief feature,* 8 miles east-southeast of Mount Dome (lat. 41°46'35" N, long. 121°32'30" W; at S line sec. 32, T 46 N, R 4 E). Named on Mount Dome (1950) 15' quadrangle.

Ross Flow: see **Hardin Butte** [SISKIYOU].

Ross Gates Spring [TEHAMA]: *spring,* 4 miles north-northeast of Dales (lat. 40°21'50" N, long. 122°01'50" W; sec. 13, T 29 N, R 2 W). Named on Dales (1965) 7.5' quadrangle.

Ross Meadow [SISKIYOU]: *area,* 6 miles southwest of Ukonom Lake (lat. 41°30'35" N, long. 123°25'35" W). Named on Ukonom Mountain (1980) 7.5' quadrangle.

Rotavele [GLENN]: *locality,* 15 miles north of Butte City along Southern Pacific Railroad (lat. 39°41'05" N, long. 122°59'55" W). Named on Ord Ferry (1949) 7.5' quadrangle.

Rough and Ready: see **Etna** [SISKIYOU].

Rough and Ready Creek [SHASTA]: *stream,* flows 3 miles to Kosk Creek 6 miles north of the village of Big Bend (lat. 41°06'45" N, long. 121°54'50" W; at W line sec. 31, T 38 N, R 1 E). Named on Big Bend (1961) 15' quadrangle.

Rough and Ready Mills: see **Etna** [SISKIYOU].

Rough Creek [SISKIYOU]: *stream,* flows 1 mile to Copper Creek (2) 4.5 miles northwest of Dillon Mountain (lat. 41°34'20" N, long. 123°38'25" W). Named on Chimney Rock (1981) 7.5' quadrangle.

Round Bar [SISKIYOU]: *locality,* 10 miles southeast of Condrey Mountain along Klamath River (lat. 41°50'20" N, long. 122°50'15" W; sec. 13, T 46 N, R 9 W). Named on Condrey Mountain (1955) 15' quadrangle.

Round Bottom [SHASTA]: *area,* 10 miles southwest of Arbuckle Mountain (lat. 40°18'20" N, long. 123°01'10" W; sec. 5, T 28 N, R 10 W). Named on Dubakella Mountain (1954) 15' quadrangle.

Round Hill: see **Black Mountain** [SISKIYOU] (3).

Round Meadow [SISKIYOU]: *area,* 5.25 miles south of Ukonom Lake (lat. 41°30'20" N, long. 123°22'15" W). Named on Ukonom Lake (1980) 7.5' quadrangle.

Round Meadow Hill: see **Round Valley** [TEHAMA].

Round Mountain [SHASTA]:

(1) *peak,* 3.25 miles south-southwest of the village of Montgomery Creek (lat. 40°48'20" N, long. 121°57'30" W). Altitude 3419 feet. Named on Montgomery Creek (1956) 15' quadrangle.

(2) *peak,* 5 miles east-southeast of Arbuckle Mountain (lat. 40°22'50" N, long. 122°46'20" W; sec. 9, T 29 N, R 8 W). Named on Chanchelulla Peak (1951) 15' quadrangle.

(3) *village,* 2.5 miles south-southwest of the village of Montgomery Creek (lat. 40°47'40" N, long. 121°56'20" W; on N line sec. 23, T 34 N, R 1 W); the village is 1.25 miles southeast of Round Mountain (1). Named on Montgomery Creek (1956) 15' quadrangle. Postal authorities established Round Mountain post office in 1872, and moved it in 1873, 1874, 1877, 1882, and 1915 (Salley, p. 190). The post office started at a place called Bullskin, and from 1874 until 1877 was at the residence of Frank Kenyon (Steger, p. 20, 42). From 1882 until 1905, Round Mountain post office was at a place called Buzzard Roost, a stage station in the 1880's (Steger, p. 21). Postal authorities established Eilers post office, named for Lu Eiler, 6 miles southwest of Round Mountain post office in 1895 and discontinued it in 1899 (Salley, p. 66).

Round Mountain [SISKIYOU]:

(1) *peak,* 7 miles east-southeast of Condrey Mountain (lat. 41°53'35" N, long. 122°50'25" W; sec. 26, T 47 N, R 9 W). Named on Condrey Mountain (1955) 15' quadrangle.

(2) *hill,* 13 miles southeast of Medicine Lake (lat. 41°25'40" N, long. 121°27'40" W; near NW cor. sec. 1, T 41 N, R 4 E). Altitude 5258 feet. Named on White Horse (1962) 15' quadrangle.

Round Mountain [TEHAMA]:

(1) *peak,* 8 miles west-southwest of Beegum Peak (lat. 40°16'45" N, long. 123°01'40" W; near E line sec. 18, T 28 N, R 10 W). Altitude 5831 feet. Named on Dubakella Mountain (1954) 15' quadrangle.

(2) *peak,* 4 miles north-northwest of Bend (lat. 40°18'35" N, long. 122°13'50" W; sec. 5, T 28 N, R 3 W). Altitude 588 feet. Named on Bend (1965) 7.5' quadrangle.

(3) *peak,* nearly 2 miles south-southeast of Panther Spring (lat. 40°13'30" N, long. 121°45'35" W; at W line sec. 4, T 27 N, R 2 E). Altitude 4126 feet. Named on Panther Spring (1953) 15' quadrangle.

(4) *peak,* 7 miles west-northwest of Paskenta (lat. 39°55'05" N, long. 122°40'10" W; near S line sec. 20, T 24 N, R 7 W). Altitude 4287 feet. Named on Riley Ridge (1967) 7.5' quadrangle.

Round Mountain: see **Little Round Mountain** [SHASTA].

Round Mountain Creek [TEHAMA]: *stream,* flows 4.5 miles to South Fork Antelope Creek 3.25 miles west-southwest of Panther Spring (lat. 40°13'50" N, long. 121°49'50" W; at S line sec. 35, T 28 N, R 1 E); the stream heads south of Round Mountain (3). Named on Panther Spring (1953) 15' quadrangle. On Mineral (1941) 30' quadrangle, the stream in present Peligreen Gulch is called South Fork Round Mountain Creek.

Round Mountain Number 1 Camp [TEHAMA]: *locality,* 8 miles west-southwest of Beegum Peak (lat. 40°16'15" N, long. 123°01'45" W; near N line sec. 19, T 28 N, R 10 W); the place is 0.5 mile south-southwest of Round Mountain (1). Named on Dubakella Mountain (1954) 15' quadrangle.

Round Mountain Number 2 Camp [TEHAMA]: *locality,* 8.5 miles west-southwest of Beegum Peak (lat. 40°16' N, long. 123°02'25" W; near W line sec. 19, T 29 N, R 10 W); the place is 1.25 miles south-southwest of Round Mountain (1). Named on Dubakella Mountain (1954) 15' quadrangle.

Round Mountain Spring [TEHAMA]: *spring,* 2.5 miles south-southeast of Panther Spring (lat. 40°12'50" N, long. 121°45'30" W; near NW cor. sec. 9, T 27 N, R 2 E); the spring is nearly 1 mile south of Round Mountain (3). Named on Panther Spring (1953) 15' quadrangle.

Round Spring [GLENN]: *spring,* 11 miles west of Newville (lat. 39°46'20" N, long. 122°44' W). Named on Hall Ridge (1967) 7.5' quadrangle.

Round Valley [SISKIYOU]: *valley,* 2.5 miles northeast of Bray (lat. 41°41'10" N, long. 121°55'45" W; in and near sec. 2, T 44 N, R 1 W). Named on Bray (1950) 15' quadrangle.

Round Valley [TEHAMA]: *locality,* 12 miles northeast of Polk Springs (lat. 40°14'20" N, long. 121°30'20" W; near S line sec. 35, T 28 N, R 4 E). Named on Butte Meadows (1958) 15' quadrangle. Lassen Peak (1894) 1° quadrangle shows a peak called Round Meadow Hill located just west of present Round Valley (lat. 40°14'30" N, long. 121°31'45" W).

Round Valley: see **Little Round Valley** [TEHAMA].

Round Valley Creek [TEHAMA]: *stream,* flows 2.25 miles to Deer Creek (2) 4.25 miles southwest of Deer Creek Station (lat. 40°12'50" N, long. 121°29'30" W; near N line sec. 11, T 27 N, R 4 E); the stream heads at Round Valley. Named on Butte Meadows (1958) and Jonesville (1958) 15' quadrangles.

Round Valley Reservoir: see **Snag Lake** [BUTTE].

Rouse Flat [TEHAMA]: *area,* 8.5 miles south-southeast of Wakefield Flat (lat. 40°00'30" N, long. 122°36' W; sec. 24, T 25 N, R 7 W). Named on Lowrey (1967) 7.5' quadrangle.

Rouse Gardens [TEHAMA]: *area,* 8.5 miles north-northwest of Paskenta (lat. 40°00' N, long. 122°36' W; on N line sec. 25, T 25 N, R 7 W); the place is 0.5 mile south-southwest of Rouse Flat. Named on Lowrey (1967) and Paskenta (1967) 7.5' quadrangles.

Rubberboot Gap [TEHAMA]: *pass,* 4 miles east-southeast of Beegum Peak (lat. 40°18'05" N, long. 122°48'55" W; near S line sec. 6, T 28 N, R 8 W). Named on Chanchelulla Peak (1951) 15' quadrangle.

Ruby: see **May** [SISKIYOU].

Ruffey Creek [SISKIYOU]: *stream,* flows 2 miles to Etna Creek 4.5 miles southwest of Etna (lat. 41°25' N, long. 122°57'55" W; sec. 11, T 41 N, R 10 W). Named on Etna (1955) 15' quadrangle.

Ruffey Gap [SISKIYOU]: *pass,* 2.5 miles south of Etna (lat. 41°25'20" N, long. 122°54' W; near NE cor. sec. 8, T 41 N, R 9 W). Named on Etna (1955) 15' quadrangle.

Ruffey Lakes [SISKIYOU]: *lakes,* two, largest 500 feet long, 6.5 miles southwest of Etna (lat. 41°22'55" N, long. 122°58' W; sec. 23, T 41 N, R 10 W). Named on Etna (1955) 15' quadrangle. The largest of the two lakes has the designation "Upper Ruffey L." on Averill's (1935) map.

Ruling Creek [SHASTA]: *stream,* flows 1 mile to Pit River 12.5 miles northeast of village of Montgomery Creek (lat. 40°59' N, long. 121°46'45" W). Named on Montgomery Creek (1956) 15' quadrangle.

Runaway Point [SISKIYOU]: *relief feature,* 7.5 miles northwest of Happy Camp (lat. 41°51'55" N, long. 123°29'30" W). Named on Happy Camp (1980) 7.5' quadrangle.

Rusby Gulch [SISKIYOU]: *canyon,* drained by a stream that flows nearly 1 mile to Deadwood Creek 10 miles north of Fort Jones (lat. 41°45' N, long. 122°48'50" W; sec. 18, T 45 N, R 8 W). Named on Fort Jones (1955) 15' quadrangle.

Rush Creek [SISKIYOU]: *stream,* flows nearly 7 miles to South Fork Salmon River 5.5 miles southeast of Cecilville (lat. 41°05'30" N, long. 123°03'05" W). Named on Coffee Creek (1955) 15' quadrangle, and on Thompson Peak (1979) 7.5' quadrangle.

Rush Creek [TEHAMA]: *stream,* flows 1 mile to Deer Creek (2) 4.25 miles northeast of Polk Springs (lat. 40°10' N, long. 121°36'50" W; near E line sec. 27, T 27 N, R 3 E). Named on Butte Meadows (1958) 15' quadrangle.

Rush Creek Lake [SISKIYOU]: *lake,* 500 feet long, 21 miles south of Etna (lat. 41°09'05" N, long. 122°57'40" W); the lake is at the head of Rush Creek. Named on Coffee Creek (1955) 15' quadrangle.

Rush Gulch [SHASTA]: *canyon,* drained by a stream that flows 2.5 miles to Middle Fork Cottonwood Creek [SHASTA-TEHAMA] 9 miles south of Ono (lat. 40°20'50" N, long. 122°37' W; near S line sec. 23, T 29 N, R 7 W). Named on Ono (1952) 15' quadrangle.

Russell Lake [SISKIYOU]: *intermittent lake,* 1400 feet long, 8.5 miles northeast of Bray (lat. 41°44'35" N, long. 121°51'45" W; sec. 16, T 45 N, R 1 E). Named on Bray (1950) 15' quadrangle.

Russell Peak [SISKIYOU]: *peak,* 6.25 miles northwest of Fort Jones (lat. 41°40'45" N, long. 122°54'55" W; at E line sec. 7, T 44 N, R 9 W). Altitude 5538 feet. Named on Fort Jones (1955) 15' quadrangle.

Russian Creek: see **North Russian Creek** [SISKIYOU]; **South Russian Creek** [SISKIYOU].

Russian Lake [SISKIYOU]: *lake,* 950 feet long, 14 miles south-southwest of Etna (lat. 41°15'45" N, long. 122°58'25" W; on W line sec. 12, T 39 N, R 10 W); the lake is at the head of South Russian Creek. Named on Etna (1955) 15' quadrangle.

Russian Lake: see **Golden Russian Lake**, under **Russian Peak** [SISKIYOU]; **Lower Russian Lake** [SISKIYOU].

Russian Peak [SISKIYOU]: *peak*, 12.5 miles south-southwest of Etna (lat. 41°17' N, long. 122°57' W; near SW cor. sec. 30, T 40 N, R 9 W). Altitude 8196 feet. Named on Etna (1955) 15' quadrangle. United States Board on Geographic Names (1968a, p. 5) approved the name "Golden Russian Lake" for a feature, 0.1 mile long, located 2 miles west-southwest of Russian Peak (sec. 2, T 39 N, R 10 W).

Russianville: see **Little North Fork**, under **Salmon River** [SISKIYOU].

Ryan Island [BUTTE]: *island*, 10 miles west of Durham along Sacramento River (lat. 39°37'30" N, long. 121°59'05" W). Named on Llano Seco (1948) and Ord Ferry (1949) 7.5' quadrangles.

—S—

Sacramento Bar [TEHAMA]: *locality*, 3 miles north-northeast of Gerber on the east side of Sacramento River (lat. 40°05'40" N, long. 122°07'35" W). Named on Gerber (1950, photorevised 1969) and Los Molinos (1952) 7.5' quadrangles. On Tehama (1905) 15' quadrangle, the name applies to a place situated about 1 mile farther north (lat. 40°06'45" N, long. 122°07'45" W).

Sacramento House: see **Tehama** [TEHAMA].

Sacramento Mountain [SHASTA]: *peak*, 8.5 miles southeast of Lamoine (lat. 40°51'45" N, long. 122°20' W; at NW cor. sec. 21, T 35 N, R 4 W). Altitude 3354 feet. Named on Lamoine (1957) 15' quadrangle.

Sacramento River [BUTTE-GLENN-SHASTA-SISKIYOU-TEHAMA]: *stream*, formed by the confluence of Middle Fork and South Fork 5.5 miles west-southwest of the town of Mount Shasta in Siskiyou County, flows about 200 miles in Butte, Glenn, Shasta, Siskiyou, and Tehama Counties to Colusa County 12 miles east-southeast of Willows [GLENN]. Named on Chico (1958), Redding (1958), Ukiah (1957), and Weed (1963) 1°x 2° quadrangles. Called Rio Sacramento on Fremont's (1845) map. Wilkes' (1841) map has the name "Destruction River" for the upper part of present Sacramento River—Emmons gave this name to the stream in 1841 (Dillon, 1975, p. 322). Gabriel Moraga applied the name "Sacramento" to present Feather River in 1808, and present Sacramento River had the names "San Francisco" and "Buena Ventura" or "Bonaventura" before the name "Sacramento" was shifted to it—*Sacramento* means "Holy Sacrament" in Spanish (Hart, p. 364). Middle Fork is 5.5 miles long and is named on Weed (1954) 15' quadrangle. North Fork enters the main stream from the northwest 4 miles west-southwest of the town of Mount Shasta; it is 6.5 miles long and is named on Weed (1954) 15' quadrangle. South Fork is 7.25 miles long and is named on Dunsmuir (1954) and Weed (1954) 15' quadrangles.

Sacramento River Arm [SHASTA]: *water feature*, part of Shasta Lake along the canyon of Sacramento River. Named on Lamoine (1957) 15' quadrangle.

Sacramento Valley: see "Regional setting."

Saddle: see **The Saddle** [SHASTA].

Saddle Back [SHASTA]: *ridge*, 0.5 mile long, 3.5 miles north of the town of Central Valley (lat. 40°43'35" N, long. 122°21'50" W; sec. 7, T 33 N, R 4 W); two peaks give the ridge a saddle-shaped outline. Named on Project City (1957) 7.5' quadrangle.

Saddleback Mountain: see **Bass Mountain** [SHASTA].

Saddle Mountain [SHASTA]:

(1) *peak*, 3.25 miles west-northwest of Fall River Mills (lat. 41°01'10" N, long. 121°29'45" W; near N line sec. 27, T 37 N, R 4 E); the peak is 1 mile northwest of The Saddle. Altitude 4981 feet. Named on Fall River Mills (1961) 15' quadrangle.

(2) *peak*, 9 miles east-southeast of Mount Lassen (lat. 40°27'15" N, long. 121°20'45" W; at SE cor. sec. 18, T 30 N, R 6 E). Altitude 7638 feet. Named on Mount Harkness (1956) 15' quadrangle.

Sage Hen Hill [SHASTA]: *peak*, 13 miles southeast of Bollibokka Mountain (lat. 40°47'40" N, long. 122°02'15" W; on S line sec. 13, T 34 N, R 2 W). Named on Bollibokka Mountain (1957) 15' quadrangle.

Saint Bernard [TEHAMA]: *locality*, 4.5 miles east of Deer Creek Station (lat. 40°15'35" N, long. 121°22'20" W; sec. 25, T 28 N, R 5 E). Named on Mount Harkness (1956) 15' quadrangle.

Saint Clair Creek [SISKIYOU]: *stream*, flows nearly 6 miles to South Fork Salmon River 1.5 miles west of Cecilville (lat. 41°08'30" N, long. 123°10'15" W). Named on Cecil Lake (1979) and Cecilville (1979) 7.5' quadrangles.

Saint John [GLENN]: *locality*, 10.5 miles east-southeast of Orland (lat. 39°47'45" N, long. 122°00'10" W). Site named on Hamilton City (1949) 7.5' quadrangle. Postal authorities established St. John post office in 1864 and discontinued it in 1917 (Frickstad, p. 40). Aden C. St. John founded the place about 1856 (Hoover, Rensch, and Rensch, p. 98).

Saint John Mountain [GLENN]: *peak*, 14 miles south-southwest of the village of Elk Creek (lat. 39°26'05" N, long. 122°41'30" W). Altitude 6746 feet. Named on Saint John Mountain (1968) 7.5' quadrangle. Called M. St. John on Eddy's (1854) map.

Saint Joseph: see **Mount Saint Joseph**, under **Lassen Peak** [SHASTA].

Salal Gulch [SISKIYOU]: *canyon*, drained by a stream that flows 2.5 miles to Rock Creek (1) 14 miles north of Orleans, which is in Humboldt County (lat. 41°29'50" N, long. 123°34'30" W); the feature heads near Salal Spring. Named on Bark Shanty Gulch (1974) 7.5' quadrangle.

Salal Spring [SISKIYOU]: *spring*, 14 miles north-northwest of Orleans, which is in Humboldt County (lat. 41°29'15" N, long. 123°37'45" W). Named on Lonesome Ridge (1974) 7.5' quadrangle.

Salee: see **Delamar** [SHASTA].

Salmon Alps: see **Salmon Mountains** [SISKIYOU].

Salmon Creek [SHASTA]: *stream*, flows 9 miles to Stillwater Creek 5.5 miles east of Redding (lat. 40°33'50" N, long. 122°17'20" W; at S line sec. 2, T 31 N, R 4 W). Named on Enterprise (1957) and Project City (1957) 7.5' quadrangles.

Salmon Mountain [SISKIYOU]: *peak*, 7 miles southwest of Forks of Salmon where Siskiyou, Humboldt, and Trinity Counties meet (lat. 41°11' N, long. 123°24'35" W); the peak is in Salmon Mountains. Altitude 6956 feet. Named on Salmon Mountain (1978) 7.5' quadrangle.

Salmon Mountain Range: see **Salmon Mountains** [SISKIYOU].

Salmon Mountains [SISKIYOU]: *range*, in Siskiyou, Humboldt, and Trinity Counties. United States Board on Geographic Names (1977a, p. 5) defined the range as bounded on the north by Salmon River, North Fork Salmon River, North Russian Creek, and Etna Creek, bounded on the east by Scott River, South Fork Scott River, Coffee Creek, North Fork Coffee Creek, Trinity River, Clair Engle Lake, and Lewiston Lake, bounded on the south by Trinity River, and bounded on the west by Trinity River and Klamath River—the Board gave the name "Salmon Alps" as a variant. Named on Weed (1963) 1°x 2° quadrangle. Hobson (p. 655, 656) referred to Salmon Mountain Range, and to Salmon River Range.

Salmon Mountains: see **Marble Mountains** [SISKIYOU].

Salmon River [SISKIYOU]: *stream*, formed by the confluence of North Fork and South Fork at Forks of Salmon, flows 16 miles to Klamath River 12 miles northwest of Forks of Salmon near Somes Bar (lat. 41°22'40" N, long. 123°29'30" W). Named on Forks of Salmon (1978), Orleans Mountain (1974), and Somes Bar (1979) 7.5' quadrangles. North Fork is 32 miles long and is named on Weed (1963) 1°x 2° quadrangle. Right Hand Fork of North Fork enters North Fork 9 miles north of Sawyers Bar; it is 6 miles long and is named on Yellow Dog Peak (1977) 7.5' quadrangle. Little North Fork enters North Fork from the north nearly 3 miles west-northwest of Sawyers Bar; it is 9.5 miles long and is named on English Peak (1977) and Sawyers Bar (1979) 7.5' quadrangles. Gudde (1975, p. 299) listed a mining place called Russianville that was located at the mouth of of Little North Fork; a colony of Russians mined there in the 1850's. South Fork is 33 miles long and is named on Weed (1963) 1°x 2° quadrangle. East Fork of South Fork enters South Fork from the northeast 1.5 miles east-northeast of Cecilville; it is 11.5 miles long and is named on Coffee Creek (1955) 15' quadrangle, and on Grasshopper Ridge (1979) 7.5' quadrangle. On Etna (1934) 30' quadrangle, present East Fork of South Fork is called South Fork Salmon River. Gudde (1975, p. 263) listed a mining place of the 1860's and 1870's called Petersburg that was situated along South Fork above the confluence with East Fork of South Fork; postal authorities established Petersburgh (with the final "h") post office in 1869 and discontinued it in 1876; the name was for Peter S. Ogden (Salley, p. 170). Little South Fork of South Fork Salmon River enters South Fork from the south 7.5 miles southeast of Cecilville; it is 4.5 miles long and is named on Thompson Peak (1979) 7.5' quadrangle. Present Little South Fork of South Fork is called Thompson Creek on Sawyers Bar (1923) 30' quadrangle, but United States Board on Geographic Names (1960a, p. 15) rejected this name for the stream. Middle Fork of Little South Fork of South Fork Salmon River enters Little South Fork 1.25 miles upstream from the mouth of Little South Fork; it is 3.25 miles long and is named on Coffee Creek (1955) 15' quadrangle, and on Thompson Peak (1979) 7.5' quadrangle.

Salmon River Range: see **Salmon Mountains** [SISKIYOU].

Salmon Summit [SISKIYOU]: *pass*, 1.5 miles southeast of Salmon Mountain on Siskiyou-Trinity County line (lat. 41°10'05" N, long. 123°23'30" W). Named on Salmon Mountain (1978) 7.5' quadrangle.

Salmon Trinity Alps: see **Trinity Alps** [SISKIYOU].

Salt Creek [GLENN]:

(1) *stream*, flows 13 miles to Stony Creek [GLENN-TEHAMA] 2 miles north-northeast of the village of Elk Creek (lat. 39°37'55" N, long. 122°31'15" W; sec. 34, T 21 N, R 6 W). Named on Alder Springs (1967), Chrome (1968), and Elk Creek (1968) 7.5' quadrangles.

(2) *stream*, flows 5.25 miles to Stony Creek [GLENN-TEHAMA] 8.5 miles east of Saint John Mountain (lat. 39°25'10" N, long. 122°32'05" W; sec. 16, T 18 N, R 6 W). Named on Stonyford (1968) 7.5' quadrangle.

Salt Creek [GLENN-TEHAMA]: *stream*, flows 10.5 miles, in and out of Glenn and Tehama Counties, to North Fork Stony Creek [GLENN-TEHAMA] at Newville in Glenn County (lat. 39°47'35" N, long. 122°31'45" W; near W line sec. 3, T 22 N, R 6 W). Named on Hall Ridge (1967) and

Newville (1967) 7.5' quadrangles.

Salt Creek [SHASTA]:

(1) *stream,* flows 4 miles to Squaw Creek (2) 7.5 miles southeast of Bollibokka Mountain (lat. 40°50'50" N, long. 122°07'50" W; at E line sec. 31, T 35 N, R 2 W). Named on Bollibokka Mountain (1957) 15' quadrangle.

(2) *stream,* flows 5 miles to Churn Creek 3.5 miles south of the town of Central Valley (lat. 40°37'55" N, long. 122°21'25" W; near E line sec. 18, T 32 N, R 4 W). Named on Project City (1957) 7.5' quadrangle.

(3) *stream,* flows 4.25 miles to Little Cow Creek 7.25 miles north of Millville (lat. 40°39'15" N, long. 122°12'05" W; at W line sec. 3, T 32 N, R 3 W). Named on Bella Vista (1965) 7.5' quadrangle.

(4) *stream,* flows nearly 3 miles to Sacramento River 3.5 miles west-northwest of Redding (lat. 40°35'40" N, long. 122°26'05" W; near S line sec. 28, T 32 N, R 5 W). Named on Redding (1957) 7.5' quadrangle.

(5) *stream,* flows 1.5 miles to Clear Creek 4.5 miles north of Igo (lat. 40°34'20" N, long. 122°31'50" W; sec. 3, T 31 N, R 6 W). Named on Igo (1979) 7.5' quadrangle.

(6) *stream,* formed by the confluence of North Fork and West Fork, flows 6.5 miles to Salt Creek Inlet Shasta Lake 10 miles south-southeast of Lamoine (lat. 40°51' N, long. 122°19'50" W; near NW cor. sec. 33, T 35 N, R 4 W). Named on Lamoine (1957) 15' quadrangle. North Fork and West Fork both are 1.25 miles long, and both are named on Lamoine (1957) 15' quadrangle.

Salt Creek [SISKIYOU]:

(1) *stream,* flows 2.25 miles to Grider Creek 2 miles south-southwest of the village of Seiad Valley (lat. 41°49' N, long. 123°12'40" W; near W line sec. 23, T 46 N, R 12 W). Named on Seiad Valley (1980) 7.5' quadrangle.

(2) *stream,* heads in the State of Oregon and flows less than 1 mile in Siskiyou County to Camp Creek 26 miles west-northwest of Copco (lat. 42°00' N, long. 122°26'30" W; sec. 20, T 48 N, R 5 W). Named on Copco (1954) 15' quadrangle.

Salt Creek [TEHAMA]:

(1) *stream,* flows 12 miles to Dry Creek (1) near Rosewood (lat. 40°16'20" N, long. 122°33'25" W; at SE cor. sec. 17, T 28 N, R 6 W). Named on Ono (1952) 15' quadrangle, and on Cold Fork (1967) 7.5' quadrangle.

(2) *stream,* flows 18 miles to Sacramento River 4.5 miles east-southeast of Red Bluff (lat. 40°08'50" N, long. 122°09'10" W). Named on Dales (1965), Red Bluff East (1951), and Tuscan Springs (1951) 7.5' quadrangles.

(3) *stream,* flows 3 miles to an unnamed stream 8.5 miles north-northwest of Paskenta (lat. 39°59'45" N, long. 122°37'10" W; sec. 26, T 25 N, R 7 W). Named on Raglin Ridge (1967) 7.5' quadrangle.

Salt Creek: see **Big Salt Creek** [TEHAMA]; **Little Salt Creek** [TEHAMA]; **Middle Salt Creek** [SHASTA]; **North Salt Creek** [SHASTA]; **Salt Gulch** [TEHAMA].

Salt Creek Inlet [SHASTA]: *embayment,* 10 miles south-southeast of Lamoine along Sacramento River Arm Shasta Lake (lat. 40°50'30" N, long. 122°21'45" W); the feature is the flooded lower part of the canyon of Salt Creek (6). Named on Lamoine (1957) 15' quadrangle.

Salt Creek Peak [TEHAMA]: *peak,* 9.5 miles north-northwest of Wakefield Flat (lat. 40°14'10" N, long. 122°44'50" W; near E line sec. 34, T 28 N, R 8 W). Named on Cold Fork (1967) 7.5' quadrangle.

Salt Creek Resort: see **Lower Salt Creek Resort** [SHASTA]; **Upper Salt Creek Resort** [SHASTA].

Salt Creek Saddle [TEHAMA]: *pass,* 6.5 miles southwest of Paskenta (lat. 39°48'45" N, long. 122°37'35" W; near N line sec. 34, T 23 N, R 7 W); the pass is north of Salt Creek [GLENN-TEHAMA]. Named on Hall Ridge (1967) 7.5' quadrangle.

Salt Gulch [GLENN]:

(1) *canyon,* drained by a stream that flows 3.5 miles to Grindstone Creek [GLENN-TEHAMA] 11 miles northwest of the village of Elk Creek (lat. 39°42'20" N, long. 122°41'30" W). Named on Alder Springs (1967) 7.5' quadrangle.

(2) *canyon,* drained by a stream that flows 7.25 miles to French Creek (2) 8.5 miles east of Fruto (lat. 39°34'45" N, long. 122°17'10" W; near E line sec. 22, T 20 N, R 4 W). Named on Julian Rocks (1968) and Stone Valley (1952) 7.5' quadrangles.

Salt Gulch [SISKIYOU]: *canyon,* drained by a stream that flows nearly 2 miles to Horse Creek (2) 6 miles east-northeast of the village of Seiad Valley (lat. 41°52'20" N, long. 123°05'05" W; sec. 35, T 47 N, R 11 W). Named on Dutch Creek (1980) and Hamburg (1980) 7.5' quadrangles.

Salt Gulch [TEHAMA]: *canyon,* drained by a stream that flows 1.5 miles to Panther Gulch 4.25 miles northwest of Wakefield Flat (lat. 40°09'40" N, long. 122°42'15" W); Salt Lick is in the canyon. Named on Cold Fork (1967) 7.5' quadrangle. On Colyear Springs (1957) 15' quadrangle, the lower part of present Salt Gulch is considered part of Freshwater Gulch, and a stream that enters present Salt Gulch has the name "Salt Creek." United States Board on Geographic Names (1968b, p. 9) rejected the names "Freshwater Gulch" and "Salt Creek" for present Salt Gulch.

Salt Lake [SISKIYOU]: *lake,* 1100 feet long, 27 miles west-southwest of Macdoel (lat. 41°38'15" N, long. 122°27' W; near N line sec. 29, T 44 N, R 5 W). Named on Lake Shastina (1954) 15' quadrangle.

Salt Lick [TEHAMA]: *spring,* 5 miles west-northwest of Wakefield Flat (lat. 40°09'30" N, long. 122°43'25" W); the feature is in Salt Gulch. Named on Cold Fork (1967) 7.5' quadrangle.

Salt Lick Gulch [SISKIYOU]: *canyon,* drained by a stream that flows less than 1 mile to Doggett Creek 6.5 miles southeast of Condrey Mountain (lat. 41°52'15" N, long. 122°53'10" W; sec. 34, T 47 N, R 9 W). Named on Condrey Mountain (1955) 15' quadrangle.

Salt Lick Spring [TEHAMA]: *spring,* 6 miles south of Wakefield Flat (lat. 40°02'20" N, long. 122°38'15" W; sec. 10, T 25 N, R 7 W). Named on Raglin Ridge (1967) 7.5' quadrangle.

Salt Log Creek [SISKIYOU]: *stream,* flows 4 miles to Hancock Creek 12.5 miles north of Forks of Salmon (lat. 41°25'55" N, long. 123°16'35" W). Named on Medicine Mountain (1978) 7.5' quadrangle.

Salt Log Gulch [SISKIYOU]: *canyon,* drained by a stream that flows 1.5 miles to Cottonwood Creek (2) 9.5 miles south of Yreka (lat. 41°35'45" N, long. 122°40'15" W; at SW cor. sec. 4, T 43 N, R 7 W). Named on Yreka (1954) 15' quadrangle.

Salt Log Ridge [BUTTE]: *ridge,* generally east-trending, 2 miles long, 6.5 miles east-northeast of Black Butte (lat. 39°41'10" N, long. 122°45'30" W). Named on Alder Springs (1967) and Plaskett Meadows (1967) 7.5' quadrangles.

Salt Spring [GLENN]: *spring,* 8.5 miles east of Saint John Mountain (lat. 39°25'50" N, long. 122°32'10" W; sec. 9, T 18 N, R 6 W). Named on Stonyford (1968) 7.5' quadrangle. Waring (p. 299) reported that the spring yields several gallons of salty water a minute, and the crust that forms there naturally is scraped up and used as stock salt.

Salt Spring Valley [GLENN]: *valley,* 8 miles east of Saint John Mountain along Salt Creek (2) (lat. 39°26'05" N, long. 122°33'05" W); Salt Spring is at the east side of the valley. Named on Stonyford (1968) 7.5' quadrangle.

Salt Works [TEHAMA]: *locality,* 7 miles south of Wakefield Flat (lat. 40°01'40" N, long. 122°38'20" W; near NE cor. sec. 16, T 25 N, R 7 W). Named on Colyear Springs (1957) 15' quadrangle.

Sambo Gulch [SISKIYOU]: *canyon,* drained by a stream that flows 2.5 miles to Klamath River 9.5 miles east-southeast of the village of Seiad Valley (lat. 41°48'25" N, long. 123°01' W; sec. 28, T 46 N, R 10 W); the mouth of the canyon is about 1 mile downstream along Klamath River from the mouth of present Howards Gulch. Named on Hamburg (1980) 7.5' quadrangle. Called Howards Gulch on Seiad Valley (1980) 7.5' quadrangle, but United States Board on Geographic Names (1981b, p. 4) rejected this name for the feature, and noted that the name "Sambo" is for an Indian family that settled in the canyon in 1870.

Sambo Gulch: see **Howards Gulch** [SISKIYOU].

Sampson Slough [TEHAMA]: *water feature,* joins Paynes Creek Slough 2 miles east-southeast of Red Bluff (lat. 40°10' N, long. 122°11'55" W). Named on Red Bluff East (1951) 7.5' quadrangle.

Sams Neck [SISKIYOU]: *pass,* 8.5 miles northwest of Macdoel (lat. 41°55'10" N, long. 122°06'20" W; in and near sec. 16, T 47 N, R 2 W). Named on Macdoel (1954) 15' quadrangle.

Sanborn Slough [BUTTE]: *water feature,* 10.5 miles west-southwest of Biggs (lat. 39°21'10" N, long. 121°53'30" W). Named on Sanborn Slough (1952) 7.5' quadrangle.

Sand Creek: see **Wescott Creek** [GLENN].

Sander's Bend: see **Bend** [TEHAMA].

Sand Flat [SISKIYOU]: *area,* 9 miles northwest of McCloud (lat. 41°21'20" N, long. 122°14'50" W; on W line sec. 31, T 41 N, R 3 W). Named on Shasta (1954) 15' quadrangle.

Sand Flat: see **Big Sand Flat** [SISKIYOU].

Sand Flat Well [SISKIYOU]: *well,* 8.5 miles east of Bartle (lat. 41°16'50" N, long. 121°39'10" W; sec. 29, T 40 N, R 3 E). Named on Hambone (1961) 15' quadrangle.

Sand Peak: see **Prospect Peak** [SHASTA].

Sand Slough: see **East Sand Slough** [TEHAMA].

Sand Spring Canyon [TEHAMA]: *canyon,* drained by a stream that flows 4.25 miles to Soap Creek nearly 5 miles southeast of Manton (lat. 40°23'35" N, long. 121°48'10" W; near E line sec. 1, T 29 N, R 1 E). Named on Manton (1956) 15' quadrangle. Called Darling Ravine on Mineral (1941) 30' quadrangle.

Sandy Bar Creek [SISKIYOU]: *stream,* flows 6.5 miles to Klamath River 13 miles north of Orleans, which is in Humboldt County (lat. 41°29'10" N, long. 123°30'55" W). Named on Bark Shanty Gulch (1974), Somes Bar (1979), and Ukonom Mountain (1980) 7.5' quadrangles.

Sandy Gulch [BUTTE]: *gully,* 2.5 miles long, along lower reaches of Lindo Channel 3.25 miles west of Chico (lat. 39°43'50" N, long. 121°54' W). Named on Ord Ferry (1949) 7.5' quadrangle.

Sandy Gulch: see **Lindo Channel** [BUTTE].

Sandy Ridge [SISKIYOU]: *ridge,* generally east-northeast-trending, less than 1 mile long, 4.5 miles south of Ukonom Lake (lat. 41°30'55" N, long. 123°21'35" W). Named on Ukonom Lake (1980) 7.5' quadrangle.

Sanford Ridge [TEHAMA]: *ridge,* south-southeast-trending, 2.5 miles long,

4 miles west of Tomhead Mountain (lat. 40°08'30" N, long. 122°53'30" W). Named on Yolla Bolly (1954) 15' quadrangle. United States Board on Geographic Names (1979a, p. 5) rejected the name "Long Ridge" for the feature.

Sanford Ridge: see **Long Ridge** [TEHAMA] (2).

Sanhedrin Ridge [GLENN]: *ridge,* generally east-trending, 6 miles long, 6.5 miles west-northwest of the village of Elk Creek (lat. 39°37'45" N, long. 122°39'30" W). Named on Alder Springs (1967) 7.5' quadrangle.

Sarah Totten Campground [SISKIYOU]: *locality,* 8.5 miles east-southeast of the village of Seiad Valley along Klamath River (lat. 41°47'15" N, long. 123°03'05" W; sec. 31, T 46 N, R 10 W). Named on Hamburg (1980) 7.5' quadrangle. Called Totten Campground on Seiad Valley (1955) 15' quadrangle.

Sardine Flat [SISKIYOU]: *area,* 7 miles north-northeast of Mount Dome along Lower Klamath Lake (lat. 41°54'15" N, long. 121°38'45" W; sec. 20, T 47 N, R 3 E). Named on Mount Dome (1950) 15' quadrangle.

Sargents Ridge [SISKIYOU]: *ridge,* south-southeast-trending, 2.5 miles long. 9 miles north-northwest of McCloud (lat. 41°22'45" N, long. 122°11'30" W). Named on Shasta (1954) 15' quadrangle.

Saturday Camp [TEHAMA]: *locality,* 5.5 miles south-southwest of Ball Mountain (lat. 39°51'40" N, long. 122°49'55" W; sec. 11, T 23 N, R 9 W). Named on Log Spring (1967) 7.5' quadrangle.

Saucos [TEHAMA]: *land grant,* at and west of Tehama, and north of Corning. Named on Corning (1951), Gerber (1950), Los Molinos (1952), and Vina (1950) 7.5' quadrangles. Robert H. Thomes received 5 leagues in 1844 and claimed 22,212 acres patented in 1857 (Cowan, p. 96).

Sauerkraut Gulch [SISKIYOU]: *canyon,* drained by a stream that flows 1.5 miles to Salmon River 4 miles northwest of Forks of Salmon (lat. 41°18'10" N, long. 123°22'05" W); the canyon heads at Sauerkraut Peak. Named on Forks of Salmon (1978) 7.5' quadrangle. Patriots changed the name to Liberty Cabbage Gulch during the anti-German feeling of World War I (Gudde, 1975, p. 309).

Sauerkraut Peak [SISKIYOU]: *peak,* 4.5 miles north-northwest of Forks of Salmon (lat. 41°19'15" N, long. 123°20'30" W); the peak is at the head of Sauerkraut Gulch. Altitude 5102 feet. Named on Forks of Salmon (1978) 7.5' quadrangle.

Saunders Flat [TEHAMA]: *area,* 5 miles west-southwest of Rosewood along Salt Creek (1) (lat. 40°15'10" N, long. 122°38'40" W; sec. 27, T 28 N, R 7 W). Named on Ono (1952) 15' quadrangle.

Sausage Mountain [BUTTE]: *peak,* 6.5 miles south-southeast of Paradise (lat. 39°39'40" N, long. 121°35'40" W; sec. 24, T 21 N, R 3 E). Altitude 927 feet. Named on Cherokee (1970) 7.5' quadrangle.

Savage Rapids [SISKIYOU]: *water feature,* 7.5 miles northeast of Happy Camp along Klamath River (lat. 41°51'55" N, long. 123°16' W). Named on Slater Butte (1980) 7.5' quadrangle.

Savona: see **Chico** [BUTTE].

Sawmill Gulch [SISKIYOU]:

(1) *canyon,* drained by a stream that flows 0.5 mile to Seiad Creek 3.25 miles east-northeast of the village of Seiad Valley (lat. 41°52' N, long. 123°08'20" W). Named on Seiad Valley (1980) 7.5' quadrangle.

(2) *canyon,* drained by a stream that flows 2.25 miles to North Fork Salmon River 4.5 miles northeast of Sawyers Bar (lat. 41°20'35" N, long. 123°04'10" W). Named on Tanners Peak (1977) 7.5' quadrangle. The stream in the canyon has the name "Mill Creek" on Sawyers Bar (1923) 30' quadrangle.

Sawmill Peak [BUTTE]: *peak,* 5 miles northeast of Paradise (lat. 39°48'45" N, long. 121°33'30" W; near NW cor. sec. 32, T 23 N, R 4 E); the feature is 1 mile east of Magalia, which also was known as Dogtown. Altitude 3338 feet. Named on Paradise East (1980) 7.5' quadrangle. Called Dogtown Peak on a map of 1862 (Dunn, F.D., p. 96).

Sawmill Ravine [BUTTE]: *canyon,* 2 miles long, 8.5 miles south-southeast of Paradise (lat. 39°38'30" N, long. 121°32'45" W). Named on Cherokee (1970) 7.5' quadrangle. Chico 1895) 30' quadrangle has the form "Saw Mill Ravine" for the name.

Sawpit Flat [SISKIYOU]: *area,* 3 miles east-northeast of Forks of Salmon along North Fork Salmon River (lat. 41°16'40" N, long. 123°16' W). Named on Forks of Salmon (1978) 7.5' quadrangle.

Sawtooth Mountain [SISKIYOU]: *peak,* 9 miles northwest of Dillon Mountain on Del Norte-Siskiyou County line (lat. 41°36'45" N, long. 123°42'40" W). Altitude 5781 feet. Named on Chimney Rock (1981) 7.5' quadrangle.

Sawtooth Ridge [SISKIYOU]: *ridge,* generally west-trending, 3.5 miles long, 31 miles south of Etna on Siskiyou-Trinity County line (lat. 41°00'45" N, long. 122°58'30" W). Named on Coffee Creek (1955) and Trinity Dam (1950) 15' quadrangles.

Sawyers Bar [SISKIYOU]: *village,* 17 miles southwest of Etna along North Fork Salmon River (lat. 41°17'55" N, long. 123°07'35" W). Named on Sawyers Bar (1979) 7.5' quadrangle. Postal authorities established Sawyers Bar post office in 1858 (Frickstad, p. 190). The name commemorates Dan Sawyer, who lived and mined near the site (Gudde, 1949, p. 322). Bancroft (p. 370) referred to Sawyer Bar, and Hobson (p. 656) mentioned Sawyer's Bar. Postal authorities established Klamath Mill post office 3 miles south of Sawyers Bar at Eddys Gulch in 1875 and discontinued it in 1882—the name was for Klamath Quartz Mining Company, which had a mill at the site (Salley, p. 112).

Scarface Gulch: see **Swede Gulch** [SISKIYOU].

Scarface Ridge [SISKIYOU]: *ridge,* north-northwest-trending, 4.5 miles long, 14 miles south of Yreka (lat. 41°31'45" N, long. 122°38'15" W). Named on Yreka (1954) 15' quadrangle.

Schell Mountain [SHASTA]: *peak,* 20 miles north-northwest of Redding (lat. 40°51'20" N, long. 122°31'50" W). Altitude 5221 feet. Named on Schell Mountain (1950) 15' quadrangle. Called Schnell Mountain on Weaverville (1913) 30' quadrangle.

Schilling: see **Whiskeytown** [SHASTA].

Schirmer Ravine [BUTTE]: *canyon,* 2.5 miles long, along Little Cottonwood Creek 3.5 miles north-northwest of Oroville (lat. 39°33'35" N, long. 121°34'45" W; near E line sec. 25, T 20 N, R 3 E). Named on Oroville (1970) 7.5' quadrangle. Called Chambers Ravine on Chico (1895) 30' quadrangle.

Schmeider Gulch [SHASTA]: *canyon,* drained by a stream that flows nearly 1 mile to lowlands along Cottonwood Creek [SHASTA-TEHAMA] 4.25 miles southwest of Anderson (lat. 40°24'10" N, long. 122°15' W; sec. 6, T 29 N, R 3 W). Named on Cottonwood (1965) 7.5' quadrangle.

Schmitt Mill [SISKIYOU]: *locality,* 14 miles east-southeast of Etna along East Fork Scott River near present Mountain House (lat. 41°24'45" N, long. 122°37'45" W; near SW cor. sec. 11, T 41 N, R 7 W). Named on Etna (1934) 30' quadrangle.

Schneider: see **Callahan** [SISKIYOU].

Schneider Gulch [SHASTA]: *canyon,* drained by a stream that flows 1.5 miles to Middle Fork Cottonwood Creek [SHASTA-TEHAMA] 3.5 miles southwest of Arbuckle Mountain (lat. 40°21'35" N, long. 122°54'30" W; near SW cor. sec. 17, T 29 N, R 9 W). Named on Chanchelulla Peak (1951) 15' quadrangle.

Schneider Hill [SISKIYOU]: *ridge,* north-trending, 1.5 miles long, 11.5 miles southeast of Etna (lat. 41°20'20" N, long. 122°44'15" W). Named on China Mountain (1955) 15' quadrangle.

Schnell Mountain: see **Schell Mountain** [SHASTA].

Schonchin Butte [SISKIYOU]: *hill,* 11.5 miles north-northeast of Medicine Lake (lat. 41°44'15" N, long. 121°31'45" W; near SE cor. sec. 17, T 45 N, R 4 E). Altitude 5253 feet. Named on Medicine Lake (1952) 15' quadrangle.

Schonchin Spring [SISKIYOU]: *spring,* 1 mile west-northwest of Medicine Lake (lat. 41°35'35" N, long. 121°37'10" W; sec. 3, T 43 N, R 3 E). Named on Medicine Lake (1952) 15' quadrangle.

Schoolhouse Creek [SISKIYOU]: *stream,* flows 2 miles to Seiad Creek less than 0.5 mile west-northwest of the village of Seiad Valley (lat. 41°50'40" N, long. 123°12'10" W). Named on Seiad Valley (1980) 7.5' quadrangle. Seiad (1922) 30' quadrangle shows Lowden School situated at the mouth of the stream.

Schoolhouse Flat [SISKIYOU]: *area,* 3.5 miles southeast of Cecilville along South Fork Salmon River (lat. 41°06'25" N, long. 123°05'05" W). Named on Thompson Peak (1979) 7.5' quadrangle.

Schoolhouse Flat [TEHAMA]: *area,* nearly 6 miles north-northwest of Wakefield Flat (lat. 40°11'55" N, long. 122°41'35" W; near N line sec. 18, T 27 N, R 7 W). Named on Cold Fork (1967) 7.5' quadrangle.

Schoolhouse Gulch [SISKIYOU]:

(1) *canyon,* drained by a stream that flows 2 miles to a ditch along Moffett Creek 4.5 miles east-northeast of Fort Jones (lat. 41°37'50" N, long. 122°45'40" W; sec. 27, T 44 N, R 8 W). Named on Fort Jones (1955) 15' quadrangle. Yreka (1939) 30' quadrangle shows Moffett Creek school situated near the mouth of the stream.

(2) *canyon,* drained by a stream that flows nearly 1 mile to Humbug Creek 12.5 miles southwest of Hornbrook (lat. 41°46'45" N, long. 122°42'50" W; sec. 1, T 45 N, R 8 W). Named on Hornbrook (1955) 15' quadrangle.

Schoolhouse Hill [SISKIYOU]: *ridge,* north-trending, 4 miles long, 11 miles southeast of Etna (lat. 41°21' N, long. 122°44' W). Named on China Mountain (1955) 15' quadrangle.

Schuler Gulch [SISKIYOU]: *canyon,* drained by a stream that flows 1.5 miles to Scott River 3.5 miles south-southwest of Scott Bar (lat. 41°41'55" N, long. 123°02'20" W; near N line sec. 6, T 44 N, R 10 W). Named on Scott Bar (1980) 7.5' quadrangle. Called Schuller Gulch on Seiad (1922) 30' quadrangle, but United States Board on Geographic Names (1960a, p. 17) rejected this form for the name.

Schulmeyer Gulch [SISKIYOU]: *canyon,* drained by a stream that flows 5 miles to Shasta Valley 5 miles south-southeast of Yreka (lat. 41°39'35" N, long. 122°36'45" W; at W line sec. 18, T 44 N, R 6 W). Named on Yreka (1954) 15' quadrangle. Averill's (1935) map shows Shamrock Camp near the mouth of the canyon

Schultz Sheep Camp [SHASTA]: *locality,* 1.5 miles northwest of Schell Mountain (lat. 40°52'10" N, long. 122°32'45" W). Named on Schell Mountain (1950) 15' quadrangle.

Schutts Gulch [SISKIYOU]: *canyon,* drained by a stream that flows 2 miles to Klamath River 3 miles east-southeast of the village of Seiad Valley (lat.

41°49'40" N, long. 123°08'20" W; sec. 17, T 46 N, R 11 W). Named on Hamburg (1980) and Seiad Valley (1980) 7.5' quadrangles.

Schwartz Meadow [BUTTE]: *area,* 6.25 miles northeast of Clipper Mills on Butte-Plumas County line (lat. 39°36'10" N, long. 121°05'05" W; sec. 9, T 20 N, R 8 E). Named on Strawberry Valley (1948) 7.5' quadrangle.

Sciad Creek: see **Seiad Creek** [SISKIYOU].

Sciad Valley: see **Seiad Valley** [SISKIYOU] (1).

Scofield Flat [TEHAMA]: *area,* nearly 5 miles north-northeast of Wakefield Flat along Guyre Creek (lat. 40°11'35" N, long. 122°36'55" W; near E line sec. 14, T 27 N, R 7 W). Named on Oxbow Bridge (1967) 7.5' quadrangle.

Scorpion Creek: see **Scorpion Gulch** [SHASTA] (1).

Scorpion Gulch [SHASTA]:

(1) *canyon,* drained by a stream that flows 1.5 miles to Tom Dow Creek 9 miles west of Shoeinhorse Mountain (lat. 41°44' N, long. 122°14'45" W; near E line sec. 18, T 37 N, R 3 W). Named on Dunsmuir (1954) 15' quadrangle. The stream in the canyon is called Scorpion Creek on Dunsmuir (1935) 30' quadrangle.

(2) *canyon,* drained by a stream that flows 2.5 miles to French Gulch (2) 2 miles west-northwest of the village of French Gulch (lat. 40°42'50" N, long. 122°40'10" W; near W line sec. 16, T 33 N, R 7 W). Named on French Gulch (1979) 7.5' quadrangle.

Scotch Creek [SISKIYOU]: *stream,* heads in the State of Oregon and flows 4 miles in Siskiyou County to Camp Creek 24 miles west-northwest of Copco (lat. 41°58'20" N, long. 122°26'10" W; near NW cor. sec. 33, T 48 N, R 5 W). Named on Copco (1954) 15' quadrangle. On Macdoel (1941) 30' quadrangle, present Slide Creek (4) is called West Fork Scotch Creek.

Scott Bar [SISKIYOU]: *village,* 19 miles east of Happy Camp along Scott River (lat. 41°44'30" N, long. 123°00'10" W; near N line sec. 21, T 45 N, R 10 W). Named on Scott Bar (1980) 7.5' quadrangle. Called Scotts Bar on California Mining Bureau's (1917a) map. Whitney (p. 356) referred to Scott's Bar. Postal authorities established Scott River post office in 1856, changed the name to Scott Bar in 1906, discontinued it in 1944, and reestablished it in 1947 (Salley, p. 199). The name commemorates John W. Scott, leader of a group of miners who came to the site in 1850 and mined there until Indians drove them away (Hanna, p. 297, 298). The Scott Bar of 1850 was situated a few hundred yards above and across the river from present Scott Bar (Hoover, Rensch, and Rensch, p. 505). United States Board on Geographic Names (1981a, p. 1) approved the name "Bill Berry Creek" for a stream, 1.5 miles long, that enters Scott River south of Scott Bar (lat. 41°44'11" N, long. 123°00'03" W); the name is for Bill Berry, Justice of the Peace in the vicinity of Scott Bar in the nineteenth century. Gudde (1975, p. 123) listed a mining place of the 1850's called French Bar that was located below Scott Bar along Scott River near its confluence with Klamath River. Gudde (1975, p. 273) also listed a mining place called Poor Mans Bar that was located along Scott River opposite Scott Bar, and (p. 31) a mining place called Beebee Bar that was situated along Scott River below Scott Bar.

Scott Bar Mountains [SISKIYOU]: *range,* between Yreka and Scott River north of Scott Valley. Named on Weed (1963) 1°x 2° quadrangle.

Scott Bar Pond [SISKIYOU]: *lake,* 250 feet long, 2 miles west of Scott Bar (lat. 41°44'30" N, long. 123°02'35" W). Named on Scott Bar (1980) 7.5' quadrangle.

Scott Camp Creek [SISKIYOU]: *stream,* flows 7 miles to Sacramento River 2.5 miles south-southwest of the town of Mount Shasta (lat. 41°16'45" N, long. 122°20' W; sec. 29, T 40 N, R 4 W); the stream heads at Scott Lake. Named on Dunsmuir (1954) and Weed (1954) 15' quadrangles.

Scott Camp Ridge [SISKIYOU]: *ridge,* north-trending, 3 miles long, 8 miles west-northwest of Dunsmuir (lat. 41°14'30" N, long. 122°24'45" W). Named on Dunsmuir (1954) and Weed (1954) 15' quadrangles.

Scott Creek [GLENN-TEHAMA]: *stream,* heads in Tehama County and flows 4.25 miles to Grindstone Creek [GLENN-TEHAMA] 7 miles east-northeast of Black Butte in Glenn County (lat. 39°46'10" N, long. 122°45'10" W). Named on Log Spring (1967) and Hall Ridge (1967) 7.5' quadrangles. Called Scotts Creek on Paskenta (1952) 15' quadrangle. United States Board on Geographic Names (1983a, p. 4) approved the name "Scotts Glade" for a meadow located east of Scott Creek in Glenn County (lat. 39°45'45" N, long. 122°43'55" W; sec. 11, T 22 N, R 8 W); Forest Service officials proposed in 1981 to name the meadow for the creek.

Scott Creek: see **Scotts John Creek** [BUTTE].

Scott Lake [SISKIYOU]: *lake,* 400 feet long, 8 miles west of Dunsmuir (lat. 41°12'55" N, long. 122°25'05" W; near NE cor. sec. 27, T 39 N, R 5 W). Named on Dunsmuir (1954) 15' quadrangle.

Scott Mountain [SISKIYOU]: *peak,* 17 miles southeast of Etna on Siskiyou-Trinity County line (lat. 41°16'45" N, long. 122°40'35" W; sec. 33, T 40 N, R 7 W); the peak is in Scott Mountains. Altitude 6829 feet. Named on China Mountain (1955) 15' quadrangle. Called Scotts Mtn. on Miller's (1890) map, and Hobson (p. 655) called the feature Scott's Peak.

Scott Mountain: see **Craggy Peak** [SISKIYOU].

Scott Mountains [SISKIYOU]: *range,* about 20 miles southwest of Weed on Siskiyou-Trinity County line (lat. 41°17' N, long. 122°41' W); the range is 17 miles south-southeast of the center of Scott Valley. Named on Weed (1963) 1°x 2° quadrangle. Hobson (p. 655) called the feature Scott's Mountains.

Scott Mountain Summit [SISKIYOU]: *pass,* 8 miles southwest of China Mountain (lat. 41°16'35" N, long. 122°41'45" W; at N line sec. 5, T 39 N, R 7 W); the pass is at the head of Scott Mountain Creek, which is in Trinity County. Named on China Mountain (1955) 15' quadrangle.

Scott River [SISKIYOU]: *stream,* formed by the confluence of East Fork and South Fork near Callahan, flows 55 miles to Klamath River 9.5 miles east-southeast of the village of Seiad Valley (lat. 41°46'45" N, long. 123°02'05" W; near N line sec. 6, T 45 N, R 10 W). Named on Etna (1955) and Fort Jones (1955) 15' quadrangles, and on Hamburg (1980) and Scott Bar (1980) 7.5' quadrangles. United States Board on Geographic Names (1977a, p. 5) noted that the name commemorates John W. Scott, of Scott Bar, and listed the names "Beaver River," "Scotts Fork," and "Scott's River" as variants. East Fork is 16 miles long and is named on China Mountain (1955) and Etna (1955) 15' quadrangles. South Fork is 11 miles long and is named on Coffee Creek (1955) and Etna (1955) 15' quadrangles. United States Board on Geographic Names (1977b, p. 6) noted the variant name "Scott River" for South Fork.

Scott River: see **Scott Bar** [SISKIYOU].

Scott's Bar: see **Scott Bar** [SISKIYOU].

Scottsburg: see **Fort Jones** [SISKIYOU].

Scotts Creek: see **Scott Creek** [GLENN-TEHAMA].

Scotts Fork: see **Scott River** [SISKIYOU].

Scotts Glade [TEHAMA]: *area,* 12 miles west-southwest of Paskenta (lat. 39°48'15" N, long. 122°49'30" W; sec. 34, T 23 N, R 8 W). Named on Pasketna (1920) 15' quadrangle.

Scotts Glade: see **Scott Creek** [GLENN-TEHAMA].

Scotts John Creek [BUTTE]: *stream,* flows 4 miles to Butte Creek [BUTTE-GLENN] 1.5 miles east-southeast of Jonesville (lat. 40°06'10" N, long. 121°26'20" W; near SW cor. sec. 17, T 26 N, R 5 E). Named on Jonesville (1958) 15' quadrangle. United States Board on Geographic Names (1990, p. 10) rejected the names "John Creek" and "Scott Creek" for the stream.

Scotts Mountain: see **Scott Mountain** [SISKIYOU].

Scott's Mountains: see **Scott Mountains** [SISKIYOU].

Scott's Peak: see **Scott Mountain** [SISKIYOU].

Scott Springs: see **Shasta Springs** [SISKIYOU].

Scott's River: see **Scott River** [SISKIYOU].

Scott Valley [SISKIYOU]: *valley,* extends for 17 miles south along Scott River from Fort Jones past Etna (center near lat. 41°29' N, long. 122°52' W). Named on Etna (1955) and Fort Jones (1955) 7.5' quadrangles. Bancroft (p. 494) used the form "Scott's Valley" for the name, which he noted was for J.W. Scott of Scott Bar.

Scraggy Mountain [SISKIYOU]: *peak,* 13 miles northeast of the village of Seiad Valley (lat. 41°57'35" N, long. 123°00'05" W; at S line sec. 34, T 48 N, R 10 W). Altitude 6995 feet. Named on Condrey Mountain (1955) 15' quadrangle, and on Dutch Creek (1980) 7.5' quadrangle.

Screwdriver Creek [SHASTA]: *stream,* flows 4.25 miles to Pit River 9 miles north-northwest of Burney (lat. 40°59'50" N, long. 121°44'50" W). Named on Big Bend (1961) and Pondosa (1961) 15' quadrangles. The name is from the screwlike movement of the stream (Steger, p. 57).

Seaman Gulch [SHASTA]: *canyon,* drained by a stream that flows 3 miles to Little Cow Creek 12 miles north-northeast of Millville (lat. 40°42'45" N, long. 122°05'15" W; near SW cor sec. 15, T 33 N, R 2 W). Named on Millville (1953) 15' quadrangle. George Seaman located a claim at the place in the 1860's (Steger, p. 57).

Seattle Creek [SISKIYOU]: *stream,* flows nearly 1 mile to Klamath River 5.25 miles northeast of Happy Camp (lat. 41°50'35" N, long. 123°18' W). Named on Slater Butte (1980) 7.5' quadrangle.

Sebastopol: see **Morris Ravine** [BUTTE].

Second Creek [SHASTA]: *stream,* flows 2.5 mile to Squaw Creek Arm Shasta Lake 9.5 miles south-southeast of Bollibokka Mountain (lat. 40°47'55" N, long. 122°10'20" W; sec. 14, T 34 N, R 3 W); the mouth of the stream is less than 1 mile east of the mouth of First Creek. Named on Bollibokka Mountain (1957) 15' quadrangle.

Second Valley Creek [SISKIYOU]: *stream,* flows 3.5 miles to Canyon Creek (3) 11 miles south-southwest of Scott Bar (lat. 41°36'50" N, long. 123°07'05" W). Named on Boulder Peak (1981) 7.5' quadrangle. Called Deep Lake Cr. on Seiad (1922) 30' quadrangle, but United States Board on Geographic Names (1960a, p. 17) rejected this name for the stream.

Secret Creek [BUTTE]: *stream,* flows 3 miles to Bull Creek 5.5 miles south of Butte Meadows (lat. 40°10'10" N, long. 121°34'25" W; near SW cor. sec. 19, T 25 N, R 4 E). Named on Butte Meadows (1958) 15' quadrangle.

Secret Flat [TEHAMA]: *area,* 3.5 miles west of Wakefield Flat along South Fork Cottonwood Creek [SHASTA-TEHAMA] (lat. 40°07'10" N, long. 122°42'25" W). Named on Raglin Ridge (1967) 7.5' quadrangle.

Secret Lake [SISKIYOU]: *lake,* 1000 feet long, 2 miles south of Ukonom Lake (lat. 41°33' N, long. 123°21'45" W). Named on Ukonom Lake (1980) 7.5' quadrangle.

Secret Spring [SISKIYOU]: *spring,* 12.5 miles north-northwest of Macdoel (lat. 41°59'20" N, long. 122°06'45" W; near E line sec. 20, T 48 N, R 2 W). Named on Macdoel (1954) 15' quadrangle.

Secret Spring Mountain [SISKIYOU]: *peak,* 12 miles north-northwest of Macdoel (lat. 41°58'25" N, long. 122°08' W); the peak is 1.5 miles southwest of Secret Spring. Altitude 5704 feet. Named on Macdoel (1954) 15' quadrangle.

Secret Valley [SISKIYOU]: *valley,* 2 miles south of Ukonom Lake (lat. 41°33' N, long. 123°21'30" W); Secret Lake is in the valley. Named on Ukonom Lake (1955) 15' quadrangle.

Section Line Lake [SISKIYOU]: *lake,* 500 feet long, 17 miles south of Etna (lat. 41°12'10" N, long. 122°50'40" W; near N line sec. 36, T 39 N, R 9 W). Named on Coffee Creek (1955) 15' quadrangle.

Seger: see **Weed** [SISKIYOU].

Sehorn Creek [TEHAMA]: *stream,* flows 11 miles to Jackson Spring Creek 6 miles southeast of Flournoy (lat. 39°51'40" N, long. 122°21'15" W; sec. 7, T 23 N, R 4 W). Named on Black Butte Dam (1967), Newville (1967), and Sehorn Creek (1967) 7.5' quadrangles.

Seiad Creek [SISKIYOU]: *stream,* formed by the confluence of East Fork and West Fork, flows 7.5 miles to Klamath River at the village of Seiad Valley (lat. 41°50'35" N, long. 123°12'40" W). Named on Kangaroo Mountain (1980) and Seiad Valley (1980) 7.5' quadrangles. Whitney (p. 357) used the form "Sciad Creek" for the name. East Fork is 2.25 miles long and West Fork is 3 miles long; both forks are named on Kangaroo Mountain (1980) 7.5' quadrangle.

Seiad Low Gap: see **Low Gap** [SISKIYOU].

Seiad Valley [SISKIYOU]:

(1) *valley,* extends for 3.5 miles east-northeast from the village of Seiad Valley along the lower reaches of Seiad Creek (center near lat. 41°51'05" N, long. 123°10'15" W). Named on Seiad Valley (1980) 7.5' quadrangle. Whitney (p. 357) used the form "Sciad Valley" for the name.

(2) *village,* 10 miles east-northeast of Happy Camp along Klamath River (lat. 41°50'35" N, long. 123°11'40" W); the village is at the mouth of Seiad Creek. Named on Seiad Valley (1980) 7.5' quadrangle. Postal authorities established Seiad Valley post office in 1858 (Salley, p. 201). The name is of Indian origin (Gudde, 1975, p. 315).

Seikel Creek [SISKIYOU]: *stream,* flows 1.5 miles to Musgrave Creek 7 miles west of Macdoel (lat. 41°50'20" N, long. 122°07'55"W; near SE cor. sec. 7, T 46 N, R 2 W). Named on Macdoel (1954) 15' quadrangle.

Selbys Switch: see **Richvale** [BUTTE].

Self Ridge [GLENN]: *ridge,* east-trending, 2.5 miles long, nearly 6 miles west-southwest of the village of Elk Creek (lat. 39°35'05" N, long. 122°38'25" W). Named on Felkner Hill (1968) 7.5' quadrangle.

Semi Crater [SISKIYOU]: *relief feature,* 12 miles north-northeast of Medicine Lake (lat. 41°44'55" N, long. 121°32'10" W; at N line sec. 17, T 45 N, R 4 E). Named on Medicine Lake (1952) 15' quadrangle.

Semig Basin: see **Hardin Butte** [SISKIYOU].

Seminary Ridge [GLENN]: *ridge,* south-southeast-trending, 1.25 miles long, 2.5 miles south-southeast of High Peak (lat. 39°23'30" N, long. 122°24'05" W). Named on Lodoga (1960) 15' quadrangle. The south end of the ridge is in Colusa County.

Seros Spring [GLENN]: *spring,* 8.5 miles west-northwest of the village of Elk Creek (lat. 39°39'05" N, long. 122°41'05" W). Named on Alder Springs (1967) 7.5' quadrangle.

Serpentine Point [BUTTE]: *peak,* 6.5 miles southeast of Paradise (lat. 39°41'55" N, long. 121°31'50" W; at S line sec. 4, T 21 N, R 4 E). Named on Cherokee (1970) 7.5' quadrangle.

Sesma [TEHAMA]: *locality,* 1 mile east of Tehama along Southern Pacific Railroad (lat. 40°01'20" N, long. 122°06' W). Named on Tehama (1905) 15' quadrangle. On Red Bluff (1894) 1° quadrangle, the name applies to a place about 1 mile farther north, and away from the railroad.

Sevenglass Spring [TEHAMA]: *spring,* 5.25 miles northwest of Wakefield Flat (lat. 40°11'05" N, long. 122°41'55" W; near N lines sec. 19, T 27 N, R 7 W). Named on Cold Fork (1967) 7.5' quadrangle.

Seven Lake: see **Lower Seven Lake** [SHASTA-SISKIYOU]; **Upper Seven Lake** [SISKIYOU].

Seven Lakes [SHASTA]: *lakes,* 11 miles northeast of Whitmore (lat. 40°44'55" N, long. 121°46'50" W; near W line sec. 5, T 33 N, R 2 E). Named on Whitmore (1956) 15' quadrangle.

Seven Lakes Basin [SHASTA-SISKIYOU]: *relief feature,* 11.5 miles west of Dunsmuir on Shasta-Siskiyou County line (lat. 41°11' N, long. 122°29' W). Named on Dunsmuir (1954) 15' quadrangle.

Sevenmile Creek [TEHAMA]: *stream,* flows 5.25 miles to Sacramento River 5.25 miles north-northeast of Red Bluff (lat. 40°14'20" N, long. 122°10'40" W; near W line sec. 35, T 28 N, R 3 W). Named on Bend (1965), Dales (1965), and Red Bluff East (1951) 7.5' quadrangles.

17 Hill [SHASTA]: *peak,* 4 miles southwest of Redding (lat. 40°32'40" N, long. 122°27' W; near N line sec. 17, T 31 N, R 5 W). Altitude 1024 feet. Named on Redding (1957) 7.5' quadrangle.

Seven Troughs Spring [GLENN]: *spring,* nearly 5 miles north-northwest of Black Butte (lat. 39°46'55" N, long. 122°55'15" W; sec. 12, T 22 N, R 10 W). Named on Mendocino Pass (1967) 7.5' quadrangle.

Shackleford Creek [SISKIYOU]: *stream,* flows 13 miles to Scott River 6.5 miles west-northwest of Fort Jones (lat. 41°38' N, long. 122°57'40" W; sec. 26, T 44 N, R 10 W). Named on Fort Jones (1955) 15' quadrangle, and on Boulder Peak (1981) 7.5' quadrangle. The name is for John M. Shackleford, who built an eight-stamp quartz mill by the stream in 1852 (Gudde, 1949, p. 326).

Shadow Creek [SISKIYOU]: *stream,* flows 3.5 miles to East Fork of South Fork Salmon River 5.5 miles northeast of Cecilville (lat. 41°12'05" N, long. 123°04'05" W). Named on Grasshopper Ridge (1979) 7.5' quadrangle. Ball (p. 19) mentioned the old name "Shadrick Creek" for the stream. West Fork enters from the north-northwest less than 1 mile upstream from the mouth of the main creek; it is nearly 3 miles long and is named on Grasshopper Ridge (1979) 7.5' quadrangle.

Shadow Creek Campground [SISKIYOU]: *locality,* 5.5 miles northeast of Cecilville (lat. 41°12'10" N, long. 123°04'05" W). Named on Grasshopper Ridge (1979) 7.5' quadrangle. Called Shadow Creek Forest Camp on Cecilville (1955) 15' quadrangle. Gudde (1975, p. 315) noted that a mining camp of the 1880's called Shadricks was situated at the site of the present campground.

Shadow Lake [SHASTA]: *lake,* 1200 feet long, 2 miles east-southeast of Lassen Peak (lat. 40°28'45" N, long. 121°28' W; near N line sec. 7, T 30 N, R 5 E). Named on Mount Harkness (1956) 15' quadrangle.

Shadow Lake [SISKIYOU]: *lake,* 600 feet long, 16 miles south-southeast of Scott Bar (lat. 41°32'50" N, long. 123°10'25" W). Named on Marble Mountain (1980) 7.5' quadrangle.

Shadrick Creek: see **Shadow Creek** [SISKIYOU].

Shadricks: see **Shadow Creek Campground** [SISKIYOU].

Shady Gulch [SISKIYOU]: *canyon,* drained by a stream that flows 5.5 miles to McCloud River [SHASTA-SISKIYOU] 5 miles west of Bartle (lat. 41°15'50" N, long. 121°55' W; near S line sec. 36, T 40 N, R 1 W). Named on Bartle (1961) and Big Bend (1961) 15' quadrangles.

Shaft Rock [SISKIYOU]: *relief feature,* 7 miles west of Hornbrook (lat. 41°55'50" N, long. 122°41'15" W; at N line sec. 17, T 47 N, R 7 W). Altitude 5801 feet. Named on Hornbrook (1955) 15' quadrangle.

Shakecabin Flat [TEHAMA]: *area,* nearly 5 miles north of Wakefield Flat (lat. 40°11'40" N, long. 122°39'25" W; sec. 16, T 27 N, R 7 W). Named on Cold Fork (1967) 7.5' quadrangle.

Shake Camp [SISKIYOU]: *locality,* 14 miles west-northwest of Macdoel (lat. 41°54'25" N, long. 122°15'50" W; on W line sec. 24, T 47 N, R 4 W). Named on Copco (1954) 15' quadrangle. Averill's (1935) map has the form "Shakecamp" for the name.

Shake Canyon [SISKIYOU]: *canyon,* 1.5 miles long, 15 miles east of Bartle (lat. 41°17'30" N, long. 121°31'30" W; sec. 17, 20, T 40 N, R 4 E). Named on Hambone (1961) 15' quadrangle.

Shake Creek [SHASTA]: *stream,* flows about 1.25 miles to Squaw Creek (2) 9 miles east-northeast of Bollibokka Mountain (lat. 40°59'15" N, long. 122°03'25" W; near N line sec. 14, T 36 N, R 2 W). Named on Bollibokka Mountain (1957) 15' quadrangle.

Shake Gulch [SISKIYOU]: *canyon,* drained by a stream that flows 1 mile to Ash Creek (1) 5.25 miles southwest of Hornbrook (lat. 41°51'15" N, long. 122°37'15" W; at E line sec. 11, T 46 N, R 7 W). Named on Hornbrook (1955) 15' quadrangle.

Shake House [TEHAMA]: *locality,* 10 miles south-southeast of Manton (lat. 40°17'50" N, long. 121°48' W; at E line sec. 12, T 28 N, R 1 E). Named on Manton (1956) 15' quadrangle.

Shake Ravine [BUTTE]: *canyon,* drained by a stream that flows 2.25 miles to West Branch Feather River 8 miles northeast of Paradise (lat. 39°51'40" N, long. 121°32' W; sec. 9, T 23 N, R 4 E). Named on Paradise East (1980) and Stirling City (1979) 7.5' quadrangles.

Shake Tree Gulch [SHASTA]: *canyon,* drained by a stream that flows 1.25 miles to Backbone Creek 11.5 miles south of Lamoine (lat. 40°48'45" N, long. 122°26'05" W; at N line sec. 16, T 34 N, R 5 W). Named on Lamoine (1957) 15' quadrangle.

Shamrock Camp: see **Schulmeyer Gulch** [SISKIYOU].

Shannon Slough [GLENN]: *water feature,* cutoff meander of Sacramento River 18 miles north of Butte City (lat. 39°39'30" N, long. 121°58'50" W). Named on Ord Ferry (1949) 7.5' quadrangle.

Sharkey Bottom [BUTTE]: *area,* 1.5 miles southwest of Nord along Pine Creek (lat. 39°46'15" N, long. 121°59' W). Named on Richardson Springs (1944) 15' quadrangle.

Sharp Mountain [SISKIYOU]: *mountain,* 11 miles east-northeast of Bray (lat. 41°42'15" N, long. 121°46'05" W; sec. 32, T 45 N, R 2 E). Altitude 6251 feet. Named on Bray (1950) 15' quadrangle.

Sharps Gulch [SISKIYOU]: *canyon,* 2.5 miles long, opens into Scott Valley 5 miles south of Fort Jones (lat. 41°32'15" N, long. 122°49'40" W; sec. 36, T 43 N, R 9 W). Named on Fort Jones (1955) 15' quadrangle.

Shasta [SHASTA]: *town,* 5.25 miles west-northwest of Redding (lat. 40°35'55" N, long. 122°29'25" W; sec. 25, T 32 N, R 6 W). Named on Redding (1957) 7.5' quadrangle. Called Shasta City on Eddy's (1854) map. Postal authorities established Shasta post office in 1851 (Frickstad,

p. 182). The town is on land that belonged to P.B. Reading (Bancroft, p. 492-493), and. the first settlers at the place in 1849 called it Reading's Springs, but the residents changed the name to Shasta the following year (Hoover, Rensch, and Rensch, p. 486).

Shasta: see **Camp Shasta** [SHASTA]; **Little Shasta** [SISKIYOU]; **Mount Shasta** [SISKIYOU].

Shasta Alpine Lodge [SISKIYOU]: *locality,* 9.5 miles north-northwest of McCloud (lat. 41°22'20" N, long. 122°13'45" W; near E line sec. 30, T 41 N, R 3 W); the place is on the southwest flank of Mount Shasta (1). Named on Shasta (1954) 15' quadrangle, which has the alternate name "Horse Camp" for the place. Horse Camp was known in the early days as Camp Ross and as Camp Moses (Eichorn, p. 108).

Shasta Bally [SHASTA]: *peak,* 24 miles west of Redding (lat. 40°36'10" N, long. 122°39' W; near W line sec. 27, T 32 N, R 7 W). Named on Shasta Bally (1978) 7.5' quadrangle. Called Bally Mountain on Red Bluff (1894) 1° quadrangle. The term "Bally" is of Indian origin (Kroeber, p. 35).

Shasta Butte: see **Mount Shasta** [SISKIYOU] (1).

Shasta Butte City: see **Yreka** [SISKIYOU].

Shasta City: see **Shasta** [SHASTA].

Shasta Creek: see **Little Shasta Creek**, under **Little Shasta River** [SISKIYOU].

Shasta Dam [SHASTA]: *locality,* 2.25 miles north-northwest of Summit City (lat. 40°42'45" N, long. 122°25'15" W; sec. 15, T 33 N, R 5 W); the place is just below the dam of the same name. Named on Redding (1944) 15' quadrangle. Postal authorities established Shasta Dam post office in 1939 and discontinued it in 1945 (Frickstad, p. 182).

Shasta Lake [SHASTA]: *lake,* behind Shasta Dam on Sacramento River 2.5 miles north-northwest of Summit City (lat. 40°43'05" N, long. 122°25'05" W; sec. 15, T 33 N, R 5 W). Named on Lamoine (1957) 15' quadrangle, and on Bella Vista (1965), Project City (1957), and Shasta Dam (1956) 7.5' quadrangles. Called Shasta Reservoir on Lamoine (1946) 15' quadrangle, but United States Board on Geographic Names (1950, p. 6) rejected this name for the feature. Residents of a community located about 3 miles south of the lake incorporated their town of 9000 people under the name "Shasta Lake" in 1993 (*San Jose Mercury-News,* January 16, 1994).

Shasta Marina [SHASTA]: *locality,* 12.5 miles south-southeast of Lamoine at the head of O'Brien Creek Inlet (lat. 40°49' N, long. 122°19'45" W; sec. 9, T 34 N, R 4 W). Named on Lamoine (1957) 15' quadrangle.

Shasta Meadow: see **Little Shasta Meadow** [SISKIYOU].

Shasta Reservoir: see **Shasta Lake** [SHASTA].

Shasta Retreat [SISKIYOU]: *locality,* 1.25 miles north of downtown Dunsmuir (lat. 41°14' N, long. 122°16'30" W; sec. 13, 24, T 39 N, R 4 W). Named on Dunsmuir (1954) 15' quadrangle. Called Retreat on California Mining Bureau's (1909a) map. Postal authorities established Retreat post office, named for Shasta Retreat, in 1903 and discontinued it in 1931 (Salley, p. 184).

Shasta River [SISKIYOU]: *stream,* flows 50 miles to Klamath River 6 miles south-southwest of Hornbrook (lat. 41°49'50" N, long. 122°35'30" W; near SE cor. sec. 13, T 46 N, R 7 W). Named on Hornbrook (1955), Lake Shastina (1954), Weed (1954), and Yreka (1954) 15' quadrangles. Present Dale Creek is called Middle Fork Shasta River on Shasta (1894) 1° quadrangle. Gudde (1975, p. 253) listed a mining place called Oregon Bar that was situated on the north bank of Klamath River just above the mouth of Shasta River.

Shasta River: see **Little Shasta River** [SISKIYOU].

Shasta River, Middle Fork: see **Dale Creek** [SISKIYOU].

Shasta Spring: see **Little Shasta Spring** [SISKIYOU].

Shasta Springs [SISKIYOU]: *locality,* 2.5 miles north of Dunsmuir (lat. 41°14'45" N, long. 122°15'40" W; near NW cor. sec. 7, T 39 N, R 3 W). Named on Dunsmuir (1954) 15' quadrangle. Postal authorities established Shasta Springs post office in 1892 and discontinued it in 1935 (Frickstad, p. 190). Commercial development of water from springs at the site began soon after construction of the railroad past the place in 1887 (Waring, p. 220). Other named springs near Shasta Springs include Castle Springs, located about 300 yards west of Shasta Springs, Glacier Spring, located one-third of a mile by zigzag trail northeast of Shasta Springs station, and Oxone Spring, which rises nearly 1 mile east of Shasta Springs resort (Waring, p. 222, 333). Watts (p. 452) described Scott Springs, located about 0.75 mile southeast of Shasta Springs on the property of J.J. Scott and Company (sec. 7, T 39 N, R 3 E).

Shasta Valley [SISKIYOU]: *valley,* northwest of Mount Shasta (1), mainly between Yreka and Weed. (center near lat. 41°36' N, long. 122°27' W). Named on Weed (1963) 1°x 2° quadrangle.

Shasta Valley: see **Little Shasta Valley** [SISKIYOU].

Shastina [SISKIYOU]: *peak,* 11.5 miles north-northwest of McCloud on the west side of Mount Shasta (1) (lat. 41°24'35" N, long. 122°13'20" W; sec. 8, T 41 N, R 3 W). Altitude 12,330 feet. Named on Shasta (1954) 15' quadrangle. Called Shastina Crater on Russell's (1883) map.

Shastina: see **Lake Shastina** [SISKIYOU].

Shastina Crater: see **Shastina** [SISKIYOU].

Shastine Crater [SISKIYOU]: *relief feature,* 4.5 miles south-southwest of Medicine Lake (lat. 41°31'05" N, long. 121°37'40" W). Named on Medicine Lake (1952) 15' quadrangle.

Shaw Creek [TEHAMA]: *stream,* flows 2 miles to Cottonwood Creek 10 miles west-southwest of Panther Spring (lat. 40°12'40" N, long. 121°57' W; at W line sec. 11, T 27 N, R 1 W). Named on Panther Spring (1953) 15' quadrangle.

Shawmut: see **Yoakumville** [SISKIYOU].

Sheep Camp [SHASTA]:

(1) *locality,* 5.25 miles south-southwest of Shoeinhorse Mountain (lat. 41°00'15" N, long. 122°07'15" W). Named on Shoeinhorse Mountain (1954) 15' quadrangle.

(2) *locality,* 7 miles north-northwest of Igo (lat. 40°36' N, long. 122°35'35" W; sec. 30, T 32 N, R 6 W). Named on Igo (1979) 7.5' quadrangle.

Sheep Camp [SISKIYOU]: *locality,* 4.5 miles west-southwest of Happy Camp (lat. 41°46'50" N, long. 123°27'45" W). Named on Happy Camp (1956) 15' quadrangle.

Sheep Camp Butte [SISKIYOU]: *hill,* 4.5 miles east-southeast of Mount Dome (lat. 41°47'35" N, long. 121°36'05" W; near SW cor. sec. 26, T 46 N, R 3 E). Named on Mount Dome (1950) 15' quadrangle.

Sheep Camp Lake [SISKIYOU]: *intermittent lake,* 2100 feet long, 1.5 miles east of Mount Dome (lat. 41°48'40" N, long. 121°39'20" W; sec. 20, T 46 N, R 3 E). Named on Mount Dome (1950) 15' quadrangle.

Sheep Camp Spring [TEHAMA]: *spring,* 9.5 miles north-northwest of Polk Springs (lat. 40°14'50" N, long. 121°42'20" W; sec. 25, T 28 N, R 2 E). Named on Butte Meadows (1958) 15' quadrangle.

Sheep Corral Creek [GLENN]: *stream,* flows 15 miles to Wilson Creek 4.5 miles north-northwest of Willows (lat. 39°34'40" N, long. 122°14' W; sec. 19, T 20 N, R 36 W). Named on Fruto NE (1952), Julian Rocks (1968), Stone Valley (1952), and Willows (1951, photorevised 1969) 7.5' quadrangles.

Sheep Creek [GLENN]: *stream,* flows 2.5 miles to Estell Creek 8.5 miles south of Black Butte (lat. 39°35'30" N, long. 122°50'05" W; sec. 14, T 20 N, R 9 W); the stream is south of Sheep Ridge. Named on Kneecap Ridge (1967) 7.5' quadrangle.

Sheep Creek [SHASTA]: *stream,* flows 2.5 miles to Hawkins Creek 3.5 miles northeast of Shoeinhorse Mountain (lat. 41°06'35" N, long. 122°01'40" W). Named on Shoeinhorse Mountain (1954) 15' quadrangle.

Sheep Flat [SHASTA]: *area,* 13 miles northeast of Lassen Peak (lat. 40°52'35" N, long. 121°19'45" W; sec. 20, 29, T 35 N, R 6 E). Named on Jellico (1957) 15' quadrangle.

Sheep Gulch [TEHAMA]: *canyon,* drained by a stream that flows 4 miles to Paynes Creek 0.5 mile southwest of Dales (lat. 40°18'40" N, long. 122°04'35" W; sec. 4, T 28 N, R 2 W). Named on Dales (1965) 7.5' quadrangle.

Sheepheaven Butte [SISKIYOU]: *peak,* 5 miles north of Bartle (lat. 41°19'35" N, long. 121°48'40" W; near W line sec. 12, T 40 N, R 1 E). Named on Bartle (1961) 15' quadrangle. United States Board on Geographic Names (1964, p. 14) rejected the form "Sheep Heaven Butte" for the name.

Sheepheaven Spring [SISKIYOU]: *spring,* 5.25 miles north of Bartle (lat. 41°19'55" N, long. 121°49'10" W; sec. 1, T 40 N, R 1 E); the spring is 0.5 mile northwest of Sheepheaven Butte. Named on Bartle (1961) 15' quadrangle.

Sheep Hollow [BUTTE]: *canyon,* drained by a stream that flows 6.5 miles to Sycamore Creek (1) 4 miles north-northeast of Chico (lat. 39°46'45" N, long. 121°51'15" W; sec. 11, T 22 N, R 1 E). Named on Richardson Springs (1951) 7.5' quadrangle.

Sheep Mountain [SISKIYOU]: *peak,* 11.5 miles south of Dorris (lat. 41°48'10" N, long. 122°53' W; sec. 29, T 46 N, R 1 E). Altitude 6210 feet. Named on Dorris (1950) 15' quadrangle.

Sheep Pelt Camp [TEHAMA]: *locality,* 3 miles north-northwest of Polk Springs (lat. 40°09'10" N, long. 121°41'25" W; near E line sec. 36, T 27 N, R 2 E). Named on Butte Meadows (1958) 15' quadrangle.

Sheep Ridge [GLENN]: *ridge,* west-trending, 2 miles long, 10 miles south-southeast of Black Butte (lat. 39°35'35" N, long. 122°48'40" W); the ridge is north of Sheep Creek. Named on Kneecap Ridge (1967) 7.5' quadrangle.

Sheep Rock [SISKIYOU]: *ridge,* south-southeast- to east-trending, 2.5 miles long, 20 miles south-southwest of Macdoel (lat. 41°34'50" N, long. 122°13'15" W; at and near SW cor. sec. 8, T 43 N, R 3 W). Named on The Whaleback (1954) 15' quadrangle. The ridge was a favorite camping spot for trappers from Hudson's Bay Company; it was one of the few places that mountain sheep were found west of the Sierra Nevada (Dillon, 1971, p. 69).

Sheep Springs [SHASTA]: *spring,* 5 miles west-northwest of Summit City (lat. 40°42'15" N, long. 122°29'50" W; sec. 24, T 33 N, R 6 W). Named on Shasta Dam (1956) 7.5' quadrangle.

Sheep Trail Gulch [TEHAMA]: *canyon,* drained by a stream that flows 2 miles to Maple Creek 3.25 miles east-northeast of Tomhead Mountain (lat. 40°09'20" N, long. 122°45'40" W; near SW cor. sec. 27, T 27 N, R 8 W). Named on Yolla Bolly (1954) 15' quadrangle.

Sheep Trail Ridge [TEHAMA]: *ridge,* generally north-northeast-trending,

2 miles long, 1 mile north of Tomhead Mountain (lat. 40°09'10" N, long. 122°48'45" W). Named on Yolla Bolly (1954) 15' quadrangle.

Sheepy Creek [SISKIYOU]: *stream,* flows 3 miles to Sheepy Lake 5.5 miles east of Dorris (lat. 41°58'40" N, long. 121°48'30" W; sec. 25, T 48 N, R 1 E). Named on Dorris (1950) 15' quadrangle.

Sheepy Creek Island [SISKIYOU]: *ridge,* south-trending, 1.5 miles long, 5.5 miles east of Dorris (lat. 41°57'40" N, long. 121°48'30" W; mainly in sec. 36, T 48 N, R 1 E); the ridge is east of Sheepy Creek. Named on Dorris (1950) 15' quadrangle.

Sheepy Lake [SISKIYOU]: *lake,* 1.5 miles long, 7.25 miles east of Dorris (lat. 41°58'20" N, long. 121°47'40" W; in and near sec. 30, 31, T 48 N, R 2 E). Named on Dorris (1950) 15' quadrangle. The feature is connected to Lower Klamath Lake.

Sheepy Peak [SISKIYOU]: *peak,* 11.5 miles north-northeast of Mount Dome (lat. 41°57'10" N, long. 121°34'35" W; sec. 36, T 48 N, R 3 E). Named on Mount Dome (1950) 15' quadrangle.

Sheepy Ridge: see **High Rim** [SISKIYOU].

Sheetiron Spring [GLENN]: *spring,* 4.5 miles north-northwest of Saint John Mountain (lat. 39°29'50" N, long. 122°37'30" W); the feature is less than 1 mile northeast of Sheetiron Mountain, which is in Lake County. Named on Saint John Mountain (1968) 7.5' quadrangle.

Shell Butte [SISKIYOU]: *hill,* 21 miles northeast of Bartle (lat. 41°26'20" N, long. 121°30'10" W; near W line sec. 34, T 42 N, R 4 E). Named on Hambone (1961) 15' quadrangle.

Shell Gulch [SISKIYOU]: *canyon,* drained by a stream that flows 3 miles to Scott Valley 7.25 miles south of Fort Jones (lat. 41°30'10" N, long. 122°50' W; sec. 12, T 42 N, R 9 W). Named on Fort Jones (1955) 15' quadrangle.

Shelly Creek [SHASTA]: *stream,* flows 2.25 miles to Pit River 1.25 miles northeast of Fall River Mills (lat. 41°01'15" N, long. 121°25'15" W; near N line sec. 29, T 37 N, R 5 E). Named on Fall River Mills (1961) 15' quadrangle.

Shelly Fork: se **Kidder Creek** [SISKIYOU].

Shelly Gulch [SISKIYOU]: *canyon,* drained by a stream that flows 1 mile to Right Hand Fork of North Fork Salmon River 12 miles north-northeast of Sawyers Bar (lat. 41°28'15" N, long. 123°04'50" W). Named on Yellow Dog Peak (1977) 7.5' quadrangle.

Shelly Lake [SISKIYOU]: *lake,* 1000 feet long, 13 miles north-northeast of Sawyers Bar (lat. 41°28'35" N, long. 123°03'40" W); the lake is at the head of a branch of Shelly Gulch. Named on Yellow Dog Peak (1977) 7.5' quadrangle.

Shelly Meadows [SISKIYOU]: *area,* 13 miles north-northeast of Sawyers Bar (lat. 41°28'40" N, long. 123°04'05" W); the place is in a branch of Shelly Gulch. Named on Yellow Dog Peak (1977) 7.5' quadrangle.

Shelton Camp [TEHAMA]: *locality,* 9 miles southwest of Mineral (lat. 40°16'35" N, long. 121°44'20" W; sec. 15, T 28 N, R 2 E); the place is on Shelton Ridge. Named on Lassen Peak (1956) 15' quadrangle.

Shelton Creek [SISKIYOU]: *stream,* flows 2 miles to Cottonwood Creek (1) 1.5 miles northwest of Hornbrook (lat. 41°55'45" N, long. 122°34'20" W; near NW cor. sec. 17, T 47 N, R 6 W). Named on Hornbrook (1955) 15' quadrangle. Called Shetter Creek on Shasta (1894) 1° quadrangle.

Shelton Ridge [TEHAMA]: *ridge,* west-southwest- to west-trending, 5 miles long, 9 miles southwest of Mineral (lat. 40°16'30" N, long. 121°44' W). Named on Lassen Peak (1956) 15' quadrangle.

Shelton Rock: see **Bailey Hill** [SISKIYOU].

Shepard Slough [GLENN]: *water feature,* extends for 5 miles west of Sacramento River before ending 10 miles east-southeast of Willows (lat. 39°28'35" N, long. 122°01' W). Named on Glenn (1951) and Princeton (1952) 7.5' quadrangles. Called Shepards Slough on Willows (1906) 15' quadrangle.

Shepherd Creek [GLENN]: *stream,* flows 5 miles to Grindstone Creek [GLENN-TEHAMA] 13 miles northwest of the village of Elk Creek (lat. 39°43'30" N, long. 122°43'25" W). Named on Alder Springs (1967) and Plaskett Meadows (1967) 7.5' quadrangles.

Shepherd Ridge [GLENN]: *ridge,* northeast-trending, 3 miles long, 6.25 miles east-southeast of Black Butte (lat. 39°42' N, long. 122°45'30" W); the ridge is south of Shepherd Creek. Named on Alder Springs (1967) and Plaskett Meadows (1967) 7.5' quadrangles.

Sheraton Flats [SHASTA]: *area,* 19 miles northwest of Lassen Peak (lat. 40°41'50" N, long. 121°43'30" W; at SW cor. sec. 23, T 33 N, R 2 E). Named on Manzanita Lake (1956) 15' quadrangle.

Sheridan Creek [SHASTA]: *stream,* flows 4 miles to Bear Creek (2) 8.5 miles east of Millville (lat. 40°31'45" N, long. 122°01' W; sec. 19, T 31 N, R 1 W). Named on Millville (1953) and Whitmore (1956) 15' quadrangles. George W. Sheridan settled along the stream before 1859 (Steger, p. 58).

Sherman [SHASTA]: *locality,* 12 miles northeast of Redding (lat. 40°42'50" N, long. 122°14'20" W; at E line sec. 18, T 33 N, R 3 W). Named on Redding (1901) 30' quadrangle.

Shetter Creek: see **Shelton Creek** [SISKIYOU].

Shields Gulch [BUTTE]: *canyon,* drained by a stream that flows 1.5 miles to North Fork Feather River 4.5 miles west-northwest of the village of Berry Creek (lat. 39°40'45" N, long. 121°28'30" W). Named on Berry Creek (1970) 7.5' quadrangle.

Shiell Gulch [SHASTA]: *canyon,* drained by a stream that flows 1 mile to Spiers Gulch 7 miles west-southwest of Arbuckle Mountain (lat. 40°22'30" N, long. 122°59'30" W; near S line sec. 9, T 29 N, R 10 W). Named on Chanchelulla Peak (1951) 15' quadrangle.

Shiloah Mineral Springs [SHASTA]: *spring,* 7.5 miles south-southwest of Castella (lat. 41°02'45" N, long. 122°23'30" W; at S line sec. 24, T 37 N, R 5 W). Named on Dunsmuir (1954) 15' quadrangle. Mr. Dougherty, owner of the feature, named it for an ancient spring in the Holy Land (Giles, p. 245).

Shiltos Creek [SISKIYOU]: *stream,* flows 2.5 miles to North Fork Salmon River 2 miles west-northwest of Sawyers Bar (lat. 41°18'35" N, long. 123°10'10" W). Named on Sawyers Bar (1979) 7.5' quadrangle.

Shinar Creek [SISKIYOU]: *stream,* flows 1.5 miles to Klamath River 5.25 miles northeast of Happy Camp (lat. 41°51'10" N, long. 123°18'30" W). Named on Slater Butte (1980) 7.5' quadrangle. Called Shinars Cr. on Averill's (1935) map.

Shinar Saddle [SISKIYOU]: *pass,* 4.25 miles north-northeast of Happy Camp (lat. 41°50'50" N, long. 123°20' W); the pass is near the head of a branch of Shinar Creek. Named on Slater Butte (1980) 7.5' quadrangle.

Shingle Camp: see **Shingletown** [SHASTA].

Shingle Creek [SHASTA]:

(1) *stream,* flows 1 mile to Squaw Valley Creek [SHASTA-SISKIYOU] 8 miles northwest of Shoeinhorse Mountain (lat. 41°09' N, long. 122°10'05" W; sec. 11, T 38 N, R 3 W). Named on Shoeinhorse Mountain (1954) 15' quadrangle.

(2) *stream,* flows 7.5 miles to Bear Creek (2) 8.5 miles east of Millville (lat. 40°31'30" N, long. 122°01'15" W; sec. 19, T 31 N, R 1 W); the stream heads near Shingletown. Named on Manton (1956), Millville (1953), and Whitmore (1956) 15' quadrangles.

Shingle Creek [SISKIYOU]: *stream,* flows 1.5 miles to Mule Creek 10 miles southwest of China Mountain (lat. 41°17'30" N, long. 122°43'50" W; near N line sec. 25, T 40 N, R 8 W). Named on China Mountain (1955) 15' quadrangle.

Shingle Creek: see **Ash Creek** [SHASTA] (2).

Shingle Flat [SISKIYOU]: *area,* 6.5 miles northeast of Salmon Mountain (lat. 41°14'50" N, long. 123°19' W). Named on Youngs Peak (1979) 7.5' quadrangle.

Shingle Springs [SISKIYOU]: *spring,* 19 miles south-southeast of Macdoel (lat. 41°33'20" N, long. 122°05'35" W; sec. 21, T 43 N, R 2 W). Named on The Whaleback (1954) 15' quadrangle.

Shingletown [SHASTA]: *village,* 20 miles west of Lassen Peak (lat. 40°29'30" N, long. 121°53'15" W; at S line sec. 32, T 31 N, R 1 E). Named on Manton (1956) 15' quadrangle. Postal authorities established Shingletown post office in 1874, discontinued it in 1919, and reestablished it in 1945 (Frickstad, p. 183). A.F. Smith, a pioneer settler, named the community in 1872 for the fifteen shingle mills that operated there between 1870 and 1874 (Hanna, p. 304). The place first was known as Shingle Camp (Steger, p. 58). Postal authorities established Loomis post office 18 miles east of Shingletown in 1878 and discontinued it in 1879; the name was for B.F. Loomis, an early settler (Salley, p. 126). They established Pine View post office 8 miles west of Shingletown in 1885 and discontinued it in 1886 (Salley, p. 172). They established Zinn post office 10 miles northeast of Shingletown in 1889 and discontinued it in 1890; the name was for John L. Zinn, first postmaster (Salley, p. 246).

Shingletown Ridge [SHASTA]: *ridge,* generally west-southwest-trending, 5 miles long, center about 3 miles west of Shingletown (lat. 40°29' N, long. 121°56'30" W). Named on Manton (1956) 15' quadrangle.

Shippee [BUTTE]: *locality,* 7.5 miles west-northwest of Oroville along Sacramento Northern Railroad (lat. 39°32'29" N, long. 121°41'15" W; near SW cor. sec. 31, T 20 N, R 3 E); the place is at the railroad crossing of Shippee Road. Named on Shippee (1948) 7.5' quadrangle. Called Shippee Road on Dry Creek (1912) 7.5' quadrangle, which shows the place along Northern Electric Railroad.

Shippee Road: see **Shippee** [BUTTE].

Shirttail Canyon [BUTTE]: *canyon,* drained by a stream that flows nearly 1 mile to West Branch Clear Creek 5 miles south of Paradise (lat. 39°40'35" N, long. 121°37'50" W; sec. 15, T 21 N, R 3 E). Named on Hamlin Canyon (1951) 7.5' quadrangle.

Shirttail Canyon [SISKIYOU]: *canyon,* 2 miles long, 5.5 miles north-northwest of Bartle (lat. 41°20' N, long. 121°51'25" W). Named on Bartle (1961) 15' quadrangle.

Shirttail Gulch [SHASTA]: *canyon,* drained by a stream that flows 1 mile to East Fork Clear Creek 7.5 miles south-southwest of Schell Mountain (lat. 40°45'20" N, long. 122°35'30" W; sec. 31, T 34 N, R 6 W). Named on Schell Mountain (1950) 15' quadrangle, and on Whiskeytown (1979) 7.5' quadrangle. When Wilbur Dodge, Sr., and others who were mining along the stream in 1850 were swept downstream, Dodge's shirt tail caught on a snag and he was the only one of the miners saved—the name is from this incident (Steger, p. 58).

Shirttail Peak [SHASTA]: *peak,* 3.5 miles northeast of the village of French

Gulch (lat. 40°44'25" N, long. 122°35'35" W; near SW cor. sec. 6, T 33 N, R 6 W); the peak is at the head of Shirttail Gulch. Altitude 4100 feet. Named on Whiskeytown (1979) 7.5' quadrangle.

Shoeinhorse Mountain [SHASTA]: *peak,* 14 miles east-southeast of Castella (lat. 41°04'10" N, long. 122°04'15" W). Altitude 5277 feet. Named on Shoeinhorse Mountain (1954) 15' quadrangle.

Shoeinhorse Mountain: see **Little Shoeinhorse Mountain** [SHASTA].

Shoemaker Balley [SHASTA]: *peak,* 3.5 miles southwest of Shasta Balley on Shasta-Trinity County line (lat. 40°34'10" N, long. 122°41'50" W). Altitude 5955 feet. Named on Shasta Bally (1978) 7.5' quadrangle. The place was Simon Shoemaker's favorite hunting ground (Steger, p. 59).

Shoemaker Creek [SHASTA]: *stream,* flows 1.5 miles to Backbone Creek Arm Shasta Lake 12.5 miles south of Lamoine (lat. 40°48' N, long. 122°25'35" W; at SW cor. sec. 15, T 34 N, R 5 W). Named on Lamoine (1957) 15' quadrangle.

Shoemaker Gulch [SHASTA]:

(1) *canyon,* drained by a stream that flows about 2 miles to Slate Creek (1) 12 miles southwest of Castella (lat. 41°03'05" N, long. 121°00'25" W; sec. 24, T 37 N, R 6 W). Named on Bonanza King (1955) 15' quadrangle.

(2) *canyon,* drained by a stream that flows 2 miles to Shasta Lake 4.5 miles north-northwest of Summit City (lat. 40°44'30" N, long. 122°26'45" W; near SW cor. sec. 4, T 33 N, R 5 W). Named on Lamoine (1957) 15' quadrangle, and on Shasta Dam (1956) 7.5' quadrangle.

Shoemaker Spring [SHASTA]: *spring,* 15 miles south of Lamoine (lat. 41°45'35" N, long. 122°27'45" W; sec. 32, T 34 N, R 5 W). Named on Lamoine (1957) 15' quadrangle.

Short Creek [SHASTA]: *stream,* flows 1 mile to Pit River nearly 7 miles north-northwest of the village of Montgomery Creek (lat. 40°55'30" N, long. 121°59'30" W; near NE cor. sec. 5, T 35 N, R 1 W). Named on Montgomery Creek (1956) 15' quadrangle.

Short Creek [SISKIYOU]: *stream,* flows less than 1 mile to Dead Cow Creek 2.5 miles east-southeast of Condrey Mountain (lat. 41°55'30" N, long. 122°55'50" W; sec. 18, T 47 N, R 9 W). Named on Condrey Mountain (1955) 15' quadrangle.

Short Ridge [GLENN-TEHAMA]: *ridge,* 0.5 mile long, 12 miles southwest of Ball Mountain on Glenn-Tehama County line (lat. 39°48' N, long. 122°55'45" W; on S line sec. 35, T 23 N, R 10 W). Named on Mendocino Pass (1967) 7.5' quadrangle.

Short Ridge [TEHAMA]: *ridge,* southeast-trending, 1.5 miles long, 7.5 miles west-southwest of Ball Mountain (lat. 39°54'15" N, long. 122°55' W; mainly in sec. 25, T 24 N, R 10 W). Named on Buck Rock (1967) 7.5' quadrangle.

Shotgun Creek [SHASTA]:

(1) *stream,* flows 4 miles to Kosk Creek 3.25 miles north of the village of Big Bend (lat. 41°03'50" N, long. 121°55'20" W; sec. 13, T 37 N, R 1 W). Named on Big Bend (1961) 15' quadrangle. United States Board on Geographic Names (1979b, p. 8) rejected the form "Shot Gun Creek" for the name.

(2) *stream,* formed by the confluence of North Fork and South Fork, flows 1 mile to Sacramento River 7 miles south-southwest of Castella (lat. 41°03'10" N, long. 122°22'30" W; sec. 19, T 37 N, R 4 W). Named on Shasta (1894) 1° quadrangle. North Fork is 5 miles long, and South Fork is 6 miles long; both forks are named on Dunsmuir (1954) 15' quadrangle. United States Board on Geographic Names (1979b, p. 8) rejected the name "Shotgun Creek" for North Fork. The Board (1979a, p. 4) approved the name "Middle Ridge" for a feature, 4.5 miles long, that trends east and west between North Fork Shotgun Creek and South Fork Shotgun Creek.

Shotgun Creek: see **Little Shotgun Creek** [SHASTA].

Shotgun Gulch [SISKIYOU]: *canyon,* drained by a stream that flows 1.25 miles to Right Hand Fork of North Fork Salmon River 11.5 miles north-northeast of Sawyers Bar (lat. 41°27'40" N, long. 123°04'50" W). Named on Yellow Dog Peak (1977) 7.5' quadrangle.

Shotgun Peak [SISKIYOU]: *peak,* 4.5 miles southeast of Medicine Lake (lat. 41°31'50" N, long. 121°32'50" W). Altitude 6643 feet. Named on Medicine Lake (1952) 15' quadrangle.

Shovel Creek [SISKIYOU]: *stream,* flows 14 miles to Klamath River 14 miles northwest of Macdoel (lat. 41°58'20" N, long. 122°12'05" W; sec. 27, T 48 N, R 3 W). Named on Macdoel (1954) 15' quadrangle.

Shovel Creek Meadow [SISKIYOU]: *area,* 11 miles west of Macdoel (lat. 41°50'35" N, long. 122°13' W; sec. 9, T 46 N, R 3 W). Named on Macdoel (1954) 15' quadrangle.

Shovel Creek Mud Springs: see **Beswick** [SISKIYOU].

Shovel Creek Springs: see **Beswick** [SISKIYOU].

Shumway Bar: see **Shumway Flat** [SISKIYOU].

Shumway Flat [SISKIYOU]: *area,* 1 mile east-northeast of Forks of Salmon along North Fork Salmon River (lat. 41°15'55" N, long. 123°18'10" W). Named on Forks of Salmon (1978) 7.5' quadrangle. Gudde (1975, p. 318) listed a mining place called Shumway Bar that was situated along North Fork Salmon River about 1 mile from Forks of Salmon; the name was for Edward Shumway and Edwin Shumway, twin brothers who mined at the site until they sold out about 1910.

Shute Mountain [BUTTE]: *ridge,* southwest- to west-trending, 2.25 miles long, 2 miles east-northeast of the village of Brush Creek (lat. 39°41'45" N, long. 121°18'15" W). Named on Brush Creek (1970) 7.5' quadrangle.

Sick Doe Gulch [SISKIYOU]: *canyon,* drained by a stream that flows less than 1 mile to Hancock Creek 11.5 miles north-northwest of Sawyers Bar (lat. 41°26'35" N, long. 123°13'50" W). Named on English Peak (1977) 7.5' quadrangle.

Sidds Landing [GLENN]: *locality,* 10.5 miles east of Willows along Sacramento River (lat. 39°33'25" N, long. 122°00'10" W). Named on Glenn (1951) 7.5' quadrangle. Called Sidd Landing on Chico (1895) 30' quadrangle.

Side Rod Camp [TEHAMA]: *locality,* 7 miles southwest of Ball Mountain (lat. 39°51'15" N, long. 122°51'55" W; at W line sec. 15, T 23 N, R 9 W). Named on Log Spring (1967) 7.5' quadrangle.

Sierra de San Marcos: see **Sierra Nevada**, under "Regional setting."

Sifford Lakes [SHASTA]: *lakes,* 4 miles southeast of Lassen Peak (lat. 40°27' N, long. 121°26'45" W; sec. 20, T 30 N, R 5 E). Named on Mount Harkness (1956) 15' quadrangle. L.W.Collins, superintendent of Lassen Volcanic National Park, recommended the name to honor Alex Sifford, an early settler (Schulz, p. 48).

Signal Butte [SHASTA]: *peak,* 5.5 miles northeast of Bollibokka Mountain (lat. 40°58'30" N, long. 122°07'10" W; at SE cor. sec. 18, T 36 N, R 2 W). Altitude 3958 feet. Named on Bollibokka Mountain (1957) 15' quadrangle.

Signal Butte [SISKIYOU]:

(1) *peak,* 2.5 miles northwest of McCloud (lat. 41°17' N, long. 122°10'15" W; on E line sec. 27, T 40 N, R 3 W). Named on Shasta (1954) 15' quadrangle. Called Bear Butte on Diller's (1895) map.

(2) *locality,* 3 miles northwest of McCloud along McCloud River Railroad (lat. 41°16'55" N, long. 122°11' W; sec. 27, T 40 N, R 3 W); the place is 0.5 mile west of Signal Butte (1). Named on Shasta (1954) 15' quadrangle.

Sign Creek [SISKIYOU]: *stream,* flows nearly 3 miles to Methodist Creek 7.5 miles east of Salmon Mountain (lat. 41°11'50" N, long. 123°16'10" W). Named on Youngs Peak (1979) 7.5' quadrangle.

Silsby [BUTTE]: *locality,* 5.25 miles north-northwest of Biggs along Southern Pacific Railroad at present Richvale (lat. 39°29' N, long. 121°44'30" W). Named on Marysville (1895) 30' quadrangle.

Silver Creek [SHASTA]: *stream,* flows 5 miles to Clover Creek (1) nearly 6 miles north-northeast of Whitmore (lat. 40°42'20" N, long. 121°52'30" W, near NE cor. sec. 20, T 33 N, R 1 E). Named on Whitmore (1956) 15' quadrangle.

Silver Fork: see **Elliot Creek** [SISKIYOU].

Silver Lake [SHASTA]:

(1) *lake,* 0.25 mile long, 8.5 miles north-northeast of Whitmore (lat. 40°44'05" N, long. 121°50'15" W; at SW cor. sec. 2, T 33 N, R 1 E); the lake is along Silver Creek. Named on Whitmore (1956) 15' quadrangle.

(2) *lake,* 1700 feet long, 7 miles east-northeast of Lassen Peak (lat. 40°31'45" N, long. 121°23'10" W; at S line sec. 23, T 31 N, R 5 E). Named on Prospect Peak (1957) 15' quadrangle. The feature is one of a group called Cluster Lakes.

Silver Lake Buttes: see **Snow Mountain** [SHASTA].

Silverthorn [SHASTA]: *locality,* 2.5 miles south of Summit City along Southern Pacific Railroad (lat. 40°38'50" N, long. 122°23'30" W; at W line sec. 12, T 32 N, R 5 W). Named on Shasta Dam (1956) 7.5' quadrangle.

Silverthorn Bay: see **Silverthorn Creek** [SHASTA].

Silverthorn Creek [SHASTA]: *embayment,* 14 miles north of Millville (lat. 40°44'55" N, long. 122°14'05" W; sec. 5, T 33 N, R 3 W). Named on Bella Vista (1965) 7.5' quadrangle. United States Board on Geographic Names (1990, p. 10) approved the name "Silverthorn Bay" for the feature.

Sims [SHASTA]: *locality,* 5 miles south-southwest of Castella along Southern Pacific Railroad (lat. 41°04'15" N, long. 122°21'15" W; sec. 17, T 37 N, R 4 W). Named on Dunsmuir (1954) 15' quadrangle. Called Sims Station on Dunsmuir (1935) 30' quadrangle, which shows Hazel Creek post office at the site. The place first was called Rocker Springs, then Southerns, Hazel Creek, Welch, and finally Sims, for Sims Southern, whose home was a well-known resort (Steger, p. 59). On California Division on Highways' (1934) map, Hazel Creek post office is shown 0.5 mile south of Sims. Postal authorities established Portuguese post office in 1870, changed the name to Hazel Creek in 1877, discontinued it for a time in 1922, and discontinued it finally in 1954 (Frickstad, p, 180, 182). California Division of Highways' (1934) map shows a place called Flume located 1.5 miles north of Sims (at W line sec. 4, T 37 N, R 4 W). Postal authorities established Flume post office, named for Flume Creek, in 1903, discontinued it in 1904, reestablished it in 1907, and discontinued it in 1910 (Salley, p. 76). They established Lisbon post office 7 miles south of Hazel Creek post office in 1886 and discontinued it the same year (Salley, p. 123). They established Deerhaven post office 3 miles north of Hazel Creek post office in 1918 and discontinued it in 1919 (Salley, p. 56).

Sims Station: see **Sims** [SHASTA].

Singer Creek [BUTTE-TEHAMA]: *stream,* formed by the confluence of North Fork and South Fork in Tehama County, flows 11 miles to Pine

Creek 6.5 miles north-northwest of Nord in Butte County (lat. 39°52'15" N, long. 121°59'15" W; sec. 4, T 23 N, R 1 W). Named on Campbell Mound (1952), Nord (1951), and Richardson Springs NW (1952) 7.5' quadrangles. North Fork and South Fork each are 4.25 miles long; both forks are named on Panther Spring (1953) 15' quadrangle, and on Campbell Mound (1952) 7.5' quadrangle. North Fork is called Singer Creek on Mineral (1941) 30' quadrangle.

Singleton Creek [SISKIYOU]: *stream,* flows about 3.5 miles to Mill Creek (5) 11.5 miles north-northwest of Fort Jones (lat. 41°44'50" N, long. 122°57'25" W; sec. 14, T 45 N, R 10 W). Named on Fort Jones (1955) 15' quadrangle.

Siphon Lake [SISKIYOU]: *lake,* 450 feet long, 14 miles south-southwest of Etna (lat. 41°15'30" N, long. 122°58'10" W; sec. 12, T 39 N, R 10 W). Named on Etna (1955) 15' quadrangle.

Sisk: see **Johnny Sisk Creek** [SHASTA].

Siskiyou Mineral Springs: see **Cinnabar Springs** [SISKIYOU].

Siskiyou Mountains [SISKIYOU]: *range,* north and west of Klamath River in Siskiyou, Del Norte, and Humboldt Counties; extends north into the State of Oregon. Named on Weed (1963) 1°x 2° quadrangle. Trappers of Hudson's Bay Company first used the name "Siskiyou" in the region about 1828 (Gudde, 1949, p. 333).

Siskiyou Pass [SISKIYOU]: *pass,* 4.5 miles south of Broken Rib Mountain on Siskiyou-Del Norte County line (lat. 41°49'05" N, long. 123°41'50" W); the pass is in Siskiyou Mountains. Named on Devils Punchbowl (1981) 7.5' quadrangle.

Sissel Gulch [SISKIYOU]: *canyon,* drained by a stream that flows nearly 4 miles to Moffett Creek 15 miles south of Yreka (lat. 41°31'30" N, long. 122°40'15" W; near SW cor. sec. 32, T 43 N, R 7 W). Named on China Mountain (1955) and Yreka (1954) 15' quadrangles.

Sisson: see **Mount Shasta** [SISKIYOU] (2).

Sisson Lake [SISKIYOU]: *lake,* 400 feet long, 11.5 miles north-northwest of McCloud (lat. 41°24'35" N, long. 122°12'55" W; sec. 8, T 41 N, R 3 W). Named on Shasta (1954) 15' quadrangle.

Siwash Gulch [SISKIYOU]: *canyon,* drained by a stream that flows 1 mile to McAdam Creek 5.5 miles north-northeast of Fort Jones (lat. 41°41'15" N, long. 122°49' W; sec. 6, T 44 N, R 8 W). Named on Fort Jones (1955) 15' quadrangle.

Six-Bit Crossing [TEHAMA]: *locality,* 10.5 miles south-southwest of Panther Spring along Big Dry Creek (lat. 40°05'50" N, long. 121°44' W). Named on Panther Spring (1953) 15' quadrangle.

Sixmile Creek [SISKIYOU]: *stream,* flows 3.5 miles to East Fork of South Fork Salmon River 8.5 miles northeast of Cecilville (lat. 41°13'20" N, long. 123°00'55" W). Named on Coffee Creek (1955) and Etna (1955) 15' quadrangles, and on Grasshopper Ridge (1979) 7.5' quadrangle.

Sixmile Hill [SHASTA]: *ridge,* south-trending, 0.5 mile long, 6.5 miles northwest of Coble Mountain (lat. 46°55'55" N, long. 121°27'15" W; near W line sec. 30, T 36 N, R 5 E). Named on Jellico (1957) 15' quadrangle.

Six Shooter Butte [SISKIYOU]: *peak,* 5 miles south of Medicine Lake (lat. 41°30'40" N, long. 121°37' W). Altitude 6380 feet. Named on Medicine Lake (1952) 15' quadrangle.

Six Shooter Pass: see **Three Sisters** [SISKIYOU] (1).

Skeahan Bar [SISKIYOU]: *locality,* 8.5 miles west-southwest of Hornbrook along Klamath River (lat. 41°51'40" N, long. 122°42'10" W; sec. 6, T 46 N, R 7 W). Named on Hornbrook (1955) 15' quadrangle.

Skeleton Camp [TEHAMA]: *locality,* 10.5 miles south of Panther Spring along Big Dry Creek (lat. 40°06'10" N, long. 121°48'10" W; near SW cor. sec. 18, T 26 N, R 2 E). Named on Panther Spring (1953) 15' quadrangle.

Skidmore Ridge [GLENN]: *ridge,* southeast- to south-trending, 2.25 miles long, 9 miles west-southwest of Newville (lat. 39°45'35" N, long. 122°41'40" W). Named on Alder Springs (1967) and Hall Ridge (1967) 7.5' quadrangles.

Ski Heil Peak [SHASTA]: *peak,* 1.25 miles south-southwest of Lassen Peak (lat. 40°28'20" N, long. 121°31'15" W; sec. 10, T 30 N, R 4 E). Named on Lassen Peak (1956) 15' quadrangle. Chief Ranger Barton of Lassen Volcanic National Park proposed the name in 1937 from the popular German greeting used by skiers; the finest open ski slopes in the park are on the side of the peak—the feature also was called Cyclorama Peak (Schulz p. 27, 48).

Ski-Hi [GLENN]: *locality,* 10 miles west of the village of Elk Creek (lat. 39°37'20" N, long. 122°43'15" W; on W line sec. 1, T 20 N, R 8 W). Named on Felkner Hill (1968) 7.5' quadrangle.

Ski Hill [TEHAMA]: *relief feature,* 1.25 miles southeast of Mineral (lat. 40°20'05" N, long. 121°34'45" W; sec. 31, T 29 N, R 4 E). Named on Lassen Peak (1956) 15' quadrangle.

Ski Island [SHASTA]: *island,* 0.5 mile long, 18 miles south-southeast of Lamoine in Pit River Arm Shasta Lake (lat. 40°45'35" N, long. 122°15'30" W; on W line sec. 31, T 34 N, R 3 W). Named on Lamoine (1957) 15' quadrangle.

Skookum Gulch [SISKIYOU]: *canyon,* drained by a stream that flows 2.5 miles to Moffett Creek 11 miles east-northeast of Etna (lat. 41°29'40" N, long. 122°41'40" W; near N line sec. 18, T 42 N, R 7 W). Named on China Mountain (1955) 15' quadrangle. The name is from Chinook jargon, or trade language, used in the Pacific Northwest (Gudde, 1949, p. 334).

Skukum Rock: see **Duzel Rock** [SISKIYOU].

Skunk Gulch [SISKIYOU]: *canyon,* drained by a stream that flows 1.5 miles to Klamath River 8 miles southwest of Hornbrook (lat. 41°50'30" N, long. 122°40'30" W; sec. 16, T 46 N, R 7 W). Named on Hornbrook (1955) 15' quadrangle.

Skunk Hill [SHASTA]: *peak,* 4 miles north of Shoeinhorse Mountain (lat. 41°07'30" N, long. 122°04'40" W). Named on Shoeinhorse Mountain (1954) 15' quadrangle. United States Board on Geographic Names (1969d, p. 8), approved the name "Lake McCloud" for a reservoir, 4 miles long, formed by a dam on McCloud River [SHASTA-SISKIYOU] at Skunk Hill, and rejected the names "McCloud Dam Reservoir" and "McCloud Reservoir" for the feature.

Skunk Hollow [SISKIYOU]: *relief feature,* 5 miles west of Bartle along McCloud River [SHASTA-SISKIYOU] (lat. 41°16' N, long. 121°54'35" W; sec. 36, T 40 N, R 1 W). Named on Bartle (1961) 15' quadrangle.

Skunk Ridge [SHASTA]: *ridge,* west-northwest-trending, 2.5 miles long, 3 miles east of the village of Big Bend (lat. 41°01' N, long. 121°51' W). Named on Big Bend (1961) 15' quadrangle.

Sky High [BUTTE]: *peak,* 4.5 miles east-northeast of the village of Brush Creek (lat. 39°43'50" N, long. 121°16' W; on E line sec. 26, T 22 N, R 6 E). Named on Brush Creek (1970) 7.5' quadrangle.

Sky High Lake: see **Lower Sky High Lake** [SISKIYOU]; **Upper Sky High Lake** [SISKIYOU].

Sky High Valley [SISKIYOU]: *relief feature,* 16 miles south-southwest of Scott Bar (lat. 41°33'20" N, long. 123°10'40" W). Named on Marble Mountain (1980) 7.5' quadrangle. The name is from the high altitude of the place (Gudde, 1949, p. 334).

Sky Lakes: see **Lower Sky High Lake** [SISKIYOU]; **Upper Sky High Lake** [SISKIYOU].

Slagger [SISKIYOU]: *locality,* 6.5 miles northeast of Bartle along McCloud River Railroad (lat. 41°19'40" N, long. 121°43'15" W; near S line sec. 3, T 40 N, R 2 E). Named on Hambone (1961) 15' quadrangle.

Slagger Camp [SISKIYOU]: *locality,* 7.5 miles north-northeast of Bartle (lat. 41°21'45" N, long. 121°47'10" W; sec. 30, T 41 N, R 2 E). Named on Bartle (1961) 15' quadrangle. California Mining Bureau's (1917a) map shows a place called Slagger Creek located along the railroad about 11 miles north of Bartle, or about 3.5 miles north of present Slagger Camp.

Slagger Creek: see **Slagger Camp** [SISKIYOU].

Slagger Spring [SISKIYOU]: *spring,* 7 miles north of Bartle (lat. 41°21'20" N, long. 121°48'10" W; sec. 36, T 41 N, R 1 E); the spring is 1 mile west-southwest of Slagger Camp. Named on Bartle (1961) 15' quadrangle.

Slanes Flat [TEHAMA]: *area,* 7.5 miles west-northwest of Ball Mountain (lat. 39°58'30" N, long. 122°54'35" W; at E line sec. 36, T 25 N, R 10 W). Named on Buck Rock (1967) 7.5' quadrangle.

Slanes Flat Ridge [TEHAMA]: *ridge,* east-southeast-trending, nearly 2 miles long, 7 miles west-northwest of Ball Mountain (lat. 39°58'15" N, long. 122°53'30" W); Slanes Flat is at the west end of the ridge. Named on Buck Rock (1967) 7.5' quadrangle.

Slapjack Bar: see **Eddy Gulch** [SISKIYOU].

Slapjack Spring [GLENN]: *spring,* 9 miles southeast of Black Butte (lat. 39°37'55" N, long. 122°45'15" W; sec. 34, T 21 N, R 8 W). Named on Plaskett Meadows (1967) 7.5' quadrangle.

Slate Creek [SHASTA]:

(1) *stream,* flows 11 miles to Sacramento River at Lamoine (lat. 40°58'35" N, long. 122°25'45" W; near S line sec. 15, T 36 N, R 5 W). Named on Bonanza King (1955), Dunsmuir (1954), and Lamoine (1957) 15' quadrangles. North Fork enters from the north 2.5 miles upstream from the mouth of the main creek; it is 4 miles long and is named on Dunsmuir (1954) and Lamoine (1957) 15' quadrangles. Present North Fork is called Tom Neil Creek on Lamoine (1946) 15' quadrangle, where present Slate Creek above the mouth of South Fork has the name "North Fork." South Fork enters 3 miles upstream from the mouth of the main creek; it is 4 miles long and is named on Lamoine (1957) and Schell Mountain (1950) 15' quadrangles.

(2) *stream,* flows 2.5 miles to Clear Creek 3.5 miles west of Schell Mountain (lat. 40°50'45" N, long. 122°35'50" W; sec. 36, T 35 N, R 7 W). Named on Schell Mountain (1950) 15' quadrangle.

Slate Creek [TEHAMA]:

(1) *stream,* flows nearly 5 miles to Deer Creek (2) 2 miles south-southwest of Deer Creek Station (lat. 40°14'10" N, long. 121°27'30" W; near SW cor. sec. 32, T 28 N, R 5 E). Named on Jonesville (1958) and Lassen Peak (1956) 15' quadrangles.

(2) *stream,* flows 5.5 miles to Thomes Creek 5.5 miles west-southwest of Paskenta (lat. 39°51'35" N, long. 122°38'20" W; near SW cor. sec. 10, T 23 N, R 7 W). Named on Hall Ridge (1967) and Riley Ridge (1967) 7.5' quadrangles.

Slate Creek: see **Lamoine** [SHASTA]; **Little Slate Creek** [SHASTA].

Slate Creek Stage Station: see **Lamoine** [SHASTA].

Slate Gap [SISKIYOU]: *pass,* 3 miles east-southeast of Salmon Mountain on Siskiyou-Trinity County line (lat. 41°09'40" N, long. 123°21'45" W). Named on Youngs Peak (1979) 7.5' quadrangle.

Slate Gulch [SHASTA]: *canyon,* drained by a stream that flows 1 mile to Clear Creek nearly 3 miles south of the village of French Gulch (lat. 40°39'45" N, long. 122°37'40" W). Named on Whiskeytown (1979) 7.5' quadrangle.

Slate Mountain [SHASTA]: *peak,* 15 miles southwest of Castella on Shasta-Trinity County line (lat. 41°00'10" N, long. 122°32'15" W; near SE cor. sec. 3, T 36 N, R 6 W). Altitude 5520 feet. Named on Bonanza King (1955) 15' quadrangle.

Slater Butte [SISKIYOU]: *peak,* 4.5 miles north-northeast of Happy Camp (lat. 41°51'30" N, long. 123°21'10" W). Named on Slater Butte (1980) 7.5' quadrangle.

Slater Creek: see **Ikes Creek** [SISKIYOU] (1).

Slatonis: see **Lamoine** [SHASTA].

Slaughter House Flat [SISKIYOU]: *area,* 10 miles northeast of the village of Seiad Valley (lat. 41°57'20" N, long. 123°04'40" W). Named on Dutch Creek (1980) 7.5' quadrangle.

Slaughterhouse Gulch [SHASTA]: *canyon,* drained by a stream that flows less than 1 mile to the canyon of Clear Creek 1.5 miles north-northeast of the village of French Gulch (lat. 40°43'25" N, long. 122°37'35" W; at S line sec. 11, T 33 N, R 7 W). Named on French Gulch (1979) 7.5' quadrangle.

Slaughterhouse Island [SHASTA]: *island,* 0.5 mile long, 15 miles south of Lamoine in Shasta Lake (lat. 40°44'55" N, long. 122°22'50" W; sec. 36, T 34 N, R 5 W). Named on Lamoine (1957) 15' quadrangle.

Slaughterhouse Ravine [BUTTE]: *canyon,* drained by a stream that flows 1.25 miles to Middle Butte Creek [BUTTE-GLENN] 4.5 miles north of Paradise (lat. 39°49'25" N, long. 121°36'40" W; sec. 26, T 23 N, R 3 E). Named on Paradise East (1980) 7.5' quadrangle.

Slaughter Pole Creek [SHASTA]: *stream,* flows 3 miles to Dry Clover Creek 4 miles west of Whitmore (lat. 40°38'25" N, long. 121°59'25" W; near W line sec. 9, T 32 N, R 1 W). Named on Whitmore (1956) 15' quadrangle.

Sleepy Hollow [SHASTA]: *relief feature,* 5.5 miles east-northeast of Fall River Mills (lat. 41°02'25" N, long. 121°20'45" W; near SW cor. sec. 13,T 37 N, R 5 E). Named on Fall River Mills (1961) 15' quadrangle.

Slickrock Creek [SHASTA]: *stream,* flows about 7.5 miles to Spring Creek (6) 8 miles east-southeast of the village of French Gulch (lat. 40°39'20" N, long. 122°30' W; near W line sec. 1, T 32 N, R 6 W). Named on Whiskeytown (1979) 7.5' quadrangle.

Slide Creek [SISKIYOU]:

(1) *stream,* flows 2 miles to Thompson Creek 6.5 miles north-northeast of Happy Camp (lat. 41°52'40" N, long. 123°19'10" W). Named on Figurehead Mountain (1980) and Slater Butte (1980) 7.5' quadrangles.

(2) *stream,* flows 1.5 miles to Right Hand Fork of North Fork Salmon River 11 miles north of Sawyers Bar (lat. 41°27'05" N, long. 123°05'35" W). Named on Yellow Dog Creek (1977) 7.5' quadrangle.

(3) *stream,* flows 2 miles to Fox Creek 14 miles south-southeast of Etna (lat. 41°15'25" N, long. 122°50'10" W; at W line sec. 7, T 39 N, R 8 W). Named on Coffee Creek (1955) and Etna (1955) 15' quadrangles.

(4) *stream,* heads in the State of Oregon and flows 4.5 miles in Siskiyou County to Camp Creek 26 miles west-northwest of Macdoel (lat. 41°59' N, long. 122°27'30" W; at E line sec. 30, T 48 N, R 5 W); the stream is southwest of Slide Ridge. Named on Copco (1954) and Hornbrook (1955) 15' quadrangles. Called West Fork Scotch Creek on Macdoel (1941) 30' quadrangle.

Slide Creek [TEHAMA]: *stream,* flows 1.5 miles to Cedar Creek 2.5 miles north of Tomhead Mountain (lat. 40°10'20" N, long. 122°49'30" W). Named on Yolla Bolly (1954) 15' quadrangle.

Slide Ridge [SISKIYOU]: *ridge,* on California-Oregon State line; the part of the ridge in Siskiyou County is southeast-trending, 2.5 miles long, and lies 28 miles west-northwest of Macdoel (lat. 42°00' N, long. 122°29' W); the ridge is northeast of Slide Creek (4). Named on Copco (1954) 15' quadrangle.

Slides Creek [TEHAMA]: *stream,* flows 3.25 miles to South Fork Cottonwood Creek [SHASTA-TEHAMA] nearly 3 miles south of Tomhead Mountain (lat. 40°05'55" N, long. 122°49'40" W; near S line sec. 13, T 26 N, R 9 W); the stream is east of Slides Ridge. Named on Yolla Bolly (1954) 15' quadrangle.

Slides Glade [TEHAMA]: *area,* nearly 5 miles south-southeast of Tomhead Mountain (lat. 40°04'15" N, long. 122°50'10" W; at SW cor. sec. 25, T 26 N, R 9 W); the place is near Slides Creek. Named on Yolla Bolly (1954) 15' quadrangle.

Slides Ridge [TEHAMA]: *ridge,* north-trending, 4 miles long, 4.5 miles south-southwest of Tomhead Mountain (lat. 40°04'45" N, long. 122°51'15" W). Named on Yolla Bolly (1954) 15' quadrangle.

Slinkard Peak [SISKIYOU]: *peak,* 3 miles southeast of the village of Seiad Valley (lat. 41°49'05" N, long. 123°08'50" W); the peak is at the north end of Slinkard Ridge. Altitude 3871 feet. Named on Seiad Valley (1980) 7.5' quadrangle.

Slinkard Ridge [SISKIYOU]: *ridge,* north-trending, 5 miles long, center 4 miles southeast of the village of Seiad Valley (lat. 41°47'45" N, long. 123°08'45" W). Named on Seiad Valley (1980) 7.5' quadrangle.

Slippery Creek [SISKIYOU]: *stream,* flows nearly 3 miles to Clear Creek (1) 4 miles east-northeast of Bear Peak (lat. 41°43'15" N, long. 123°30'25" W). Named on Bear Peak (1982) 7.5' quadrangle.

Sloan Butte [SISKIYOU]: *peak,* 21 miles west-northwest of Macdoel (lat. 42°05' N, long. 122°20'05" W; sec. 20, T 48 N, R 4 W). Altitude 3641 feet. Name on Copco (1954) 15' quadrangle. United States Board on Geographic Names (1984c, p. 2) approved the name "Close Butte" for this feature, and (p. 3) approved the name "Sloan Butte" for a peak, altitude 3377 feet, located about 1 mile farther southwest (lat. 41°59'30" N, long. 122°20'58" W; sec. 19, 30, T 48 N, R 4 W).

Slug Gulch [SHASTA]: *canyon,* drained by a stream that flows less than 0.5 mile to Slickrock Creek 5.5 miles east-southeast of the village of French Gulch (lat. 40°40'25" N, long. 122°32'15" W; near W line sec. 34, T 33 N, R 6 W). Named on Whiskeytown (1979) 7.5' quadrangle.

Slug Gulch [SISKIYOU]:

(1) *canyon,* drained by a stream that flows 0.5 mile to Moores Gulch 5 miles north-northwest of Fort Jones (lat. 41°40'25" N, long. 122°52'45" W; sec. 9, T 44 N, R 9 W). Named on Fort Jones (1955) 15' quadrangle. United States Board on Geographic Names (1984c, p. 3) attributed the name to the coarse gold nuggets, called slugs, reportedly found in the canyon. The Board (1984c, p. 2) approved the name "Franklin Gulch" for a canyon, 0.7 mile long, that opens into Moores Gulch 0.4 mile northeast of Slug Gulch, and rejected the name "Slug Gulch" for this second feature; the name "Franklin" is for Franklin mine, located at the northeast end of Franklin Gulch.

(2) *canyon,* drained by a stream that flows less than 1 mile to Cherry Creek (2) 8 miles north-northeast of Fort Jones (lat. 41°42'50" N, long. 122°47'45" W; sec. 29, T 45 N, R 8 W). Named on Fort Jones (1955) 15' quadrangle.

Sly Creek [BUTTE]:

(1) *stream,* flows less than 1 mile to Carey Gulch 3.5 miles north-northeast of the village of Brush Creek (lat. 39°44'10" N, long. 121°18'45" W; sec. 28, T 22 N, R 6 E). Named on Brush Creek (1970) 7.5' quadrangle.

(2) *stream,* heads in Plumas County and flows 2.5 miles in Butte County to Lost Creek 4 miles north-northeast of Clipper Mills (lat. 39°35' N, long. 121°06'45" W; near NW cor. sec. 20, T 20 N, R 8 E). Named on Strawberry Valley (1948) 7.5' quadrangle.

Sly Creek Reservoir [BUTTE]: *lake,* behind a dam on Lost Creek 4 miles north-northeast of Clipper Mills (lat. 39°34'55" N, long. 121°06'50" W; near NW cor. sec. 20, T 20 N, R 8 E); the dam that forms the lake is near the mouth of Sly Creek (2). Named on Strawberry Valley (1948, photorevised 1975) 7.5' quadrangle.

Small [SISKIYOU]: *locality,* nearly 5 miles south-southeast of the town of Mount Shasta along Southern Pacific Railroad (lat. 41°15' N, long. 122°16'20" W; sec. 12, T 39 N, R 4 W). Named on Dunsmuir (1954) and Weed (1954) 15' quadrangles.

Smallwood Gulch [TEHAMA]: *canyon,* drained by a stream that flows 3.5 miles to Elder Creek 9 miles southeast of Wakefield Flat (lat. 40°00'55" N, long. 122°32'20" W; near N line sec. 21, T 25 N, R 6 W). Named on Lowrey (1967) 7.5' quadrangle.

Smiley Camp [GLENN]: *locality,* 7.25 miles west of the village of Elk Creek (lat. 39°35'10" N, long. 122°40'10" W). Named on Felkner Hill (1968) 7.5' quadrangle.

Smith: see **Al Smith Gulch** [SHASTA].

Smith Camp [GLENN]: *locality,* nearly 3 miles north-northwest of Black Butte (lat. 39°45'50" N, long. 122°53'15" W; sec. 16, T 22 N, R 9 W). Named on Mendocino Pass (1967) 7.5' quadrangle.

Smith Creek [SHASTA]: *stream,* flows 1.5 miles to Squaw Creek (2) 6.5 miles east-southeast of Bollibokka Mountain (lat. 41°53'10" N, long. 122°06'30" W; near W line sec. 16, T 35 N, R 2 W). Named on Bollibokka Mountain (1957) 15' quadrangle.

Smith Creek [SISKIYOU]: *stream,* flows 1.5 miles to South Fork Salmon River nearly 5 miles west-northwest of Cecilville (lat. 41°10'20" N, long. 123°13'10" W). Named on Cecilville (1979) 7.5' quadrangle.

Smith Flat [SHASTA]: *area,* nearly 4 miles northwest of the village of Big Bend along McGill Creek (lat. 41°03'15" N, long. 121°57'55" W; near NW cor. sec. 22, T 37 N, R 1 W). Named on Big Bend (1961) 15' quadrangle.

Smith Fork: see **Bridge Creek** [SISKIYOU].

Smith Gulch [SISKIYOU]: *canyon,* drained by a stream that flows 2 miles to Klamath River 9.5 miles southeast of Condrey Mountain (lat. 41°50'55" N, long. 122°50'10" W; sec. 12, T 46 N, R 9 W). Named on Condrey Mountain (1955) 15' quadrangle.

Smith Hill [SISKIYOU]: *peak,* 8 miles south of Etna (lat. 41°20'20" N, long. 122°52'15" W; near S line sec. 3, T 40 N, R 9 W). Named on Etna (1955) 15' quadrangle.

Smith Lake [SISKIYOU]: *lake,* 900 feet long, 7 miles south-southwest of Etna (lat. 41°22'10" N, long. 122°57'35" W; sec. 26, T 41 N, R 10 W). Named on Etna (1955) 15' quadrangle.

Smith Ridge [SISKIYOU]: *ridge,* northeast-trending, 2.5 miles long, 3 miles west of Sawyers Bar (lat. 41°18' N, long. 123°11'30" W). Named on Sawyers Bar (1979) 7.5' quadrangle.

Smiths Lake [SISKIYOU]: *lake,* 350 feet long, 7.25 miles northwest of Sawyers Bar (lat. 41°22'05" N, long. 123°14'15" W). Named on Sawyers Bar (1979) 7.5' quadrangle.

Smithson: see **Delta** [SHASTA].

Smith Spring [SISKIYOU]: *spring,* 9.5 miles west-southwest of Macdoel (lat. 41°45'35" N, long. 122°09'25" W; sec. 11, T 45 N, R 3 W). Named on Macdoel (1954) 15' quadrangle.

Smiths River: see **Klamath River** [SISKIYOU].

Smokey Lake: see **Smoky Lake** [SHASTA].

Smoky Cabin [SHASTA]: *locality,* 18 miles north-northeast of Lassen Peak (lat. 40°43'45" N, long. 121°23'20" W; sec. 11, T 33 N, R 5 E). Named on Prospect Peak (1957) 15' quadrangle.

Smoky Creek [SISKIYOU]: *stream,* flows about 1.5 miles to Beaver Creek (1) 10 miles east of Condrey Mountain (lat. 41°57'50" N, long. 122°47'20" W; sec. 32, T 48 N, R 8 W). Named on Condrey Mountain (1955) 15' quadrangle.

Smoky Creek: see **Big Smoky Creek** [TEHAMA]; **Little Smoky Creek** [SISKIYOU]; **Little Smoky Creek** [TEHAMA].

Smoky Lake [SHASTA]: *intermittent lake,* 1300 feet long, 8.5 miles north-northwest of Burney Falls (lat. 41°06'55" N, long. 121°44'20" W; sec. 21, T 38 N, R 2 E). Named on Pondosa (1961) 15' quadrangle. United States Board on Geographic Names (1964, p. 14) approved the form "Smokey Lake" for the name.

Snackenburg Creek [SISKIYOU]: *stream,* flows 3.5 miles to Copco Lake 17 miles west-northwest of Macdoel (lat. 41°58'10" N, long. 122°16'25" W; sec. 35, T 48 N, R 4 W). Named on Copco (1954) 15' quadrangle.

Snaden Island [BUTTE]: *island,* 13 miles west-northwest of Chico between Sacramento River and Snaden Slough (lat. 39°48'55" N, long. 122°03' W). Named on Foster Island (1950) 7.5' quadrangle.

Snaden Slough [BUTTE]: *water feature,* joins Sacramento River 13 miles west-northwest of Chico (lat. 39°48'15" N, long. 122°02'55" W); the feature is on the east side of Snaden Island. Named on Foster Island (1950) 7.5' quadrangle

Snag Hill [SISKIYOU]: *hill,* 17 miles north-northeast of Bartle (lat. 41°28'25" N, long. 121°38'45" W). Altitude 5610 feet. Named on Hambone (1961) 15' quadrangle.

Snag Lake [BUTTE]: *lake,* 4200 feet long, 2.5 miles south-southeast of Jonesville along West Branch Feather River (lat. 40°04'40" N, long. 121°27' W; sec. 30, T 26 N, R 5 E). Named on Jonesville (1958) 15' quadrangle. Called Round Valley Reservoir on California Division of Highways' (1934) map. F.D. Dunn (p. 99) gave the alternate name "Spring Valley Reservoir" for the feature.

Snake Creek [TEHAMA]: *stream,* flows 2.5 miles to Fish Creek 4 miles north-northwest of Ball Mountain (lat. 39°59'25" N, long. 122°48'10" W; sec. 30, T 25 N, R 8 W). Named on Yolla Bolly (1954) 15' quadrangle, and on Ball Mountain (1967) 7.5' quadrangle.

Snake Lake [SISKIYOU]: *lake,* 300 feet long, 12 miles north-northeast of Happy Camp (lat. 41°57'30" N, long. 123°17'55" W). Named on Figurehead Mountain (1980) 7.5' quadrangle.

Snake Ridge [TEHAMA]: *ridge,* south- to west-trending, 2.25 miles long, 3.5 miles north-northeast of Ball Mountain (lat. 39°59' N, long. 122°45'50" W); the ridge is southeast of Snake Creek. Named on Ball Mountain (1967) 7.5' quadrangle.

Snake River [BUTTE]: *water feature,* 5 miles southwest of Gridley on Butte-Sutter County line (lat. 39°18'15" N, long. 121°45'05" W; at S line sec. 21, T 17 N, R 2 E). Named on Pennington (1954) 7.5' quadrangle.

Snell Butte [SISKIYOU]: *hill,* 21 miles east-northeast of Bartle (lat. 41°26'20" N, long. 121°30'10" W; sec. 34, T 42 N, R 4 E). Named on Hambone (1961) 15' quadrangle.

Snicktaw Creek [SISKIYOU]: *stream,* flows 5 miles to the valley of Scott River 7 miles west of Fort Jones (lat. 41°37'30" N, long. 122°58'30" W; sec. 34, T 44 N, R 10 W). Named on Fort Jones (1955) 15' quadrangle, and on Boulder Peak (1981) 7.5' quadrangle. According to G.R. Stewart (p. 450), the name, which is the word "watkins" spelled backward, probably is for W.F. Watkins, a journalist of the 1850's who used the pseudonym "Sniktaw."

Snicktaw Meadow [SISKIYOU]: *area,* 10.5 miles south of Scott Bar (lat. 41°35'45" N, long. 123°02'40" W; near NW cor. sec. 7, T 43 N, R 10 W); the place is at the head of Sniktaw Creek. Named on Boulder Peak (1981) 7.5' quadrangle.

Snoozer Ridge [SISKIYOU]; *ridge,* generally south-trending, 5 miles long, 6.25 miles northeast of Sawyers Bar (lat. 41°22' N, long. 123°02'50" W). Named on Tanners Peak (1977) and Yellow Dog Peak (1977) 7.5' quadrangles.

Snoqualmie Gulch [TEHAMA]: *canyon,* drained by a stream that flows nearly 7 miles to Grapevine Canyon 7 miles southeast of Manton (lat. 40°22'15" N, long. 121°46'30" W; near W line sec. 17, T 29 N, R 2 E). Named on Lassen Peak (1956) and Manton (1956) 15' quadrangles.

Snow Basin [GLENN]: *relief feature,* less than 1 mile northeast of Black Butte (lat. 39°44'05" N, long. 122°51'40" W; sec. 27, T 22 N, R 9 W). Named on Plaskett Meadows (1967) 7.5' quadrangle.

Snow Basin Creek [GLENN]; *stream,* flows 1.5 miles to Cold Creek 1.5 miles southeast of Black Butte (lat. 39°42'40" N, long. 122°51'20" W); the stream heads at Snow Basin. Named on Plaskett Meadows (1967) 7.5' quadrangle.

Snow Camp [SHASTA]: *locality,* 6.5 miles east-northeast of the village of Big Bend (lat. 41°02'50" N, long. 121°47'15" W; sec. 19, T 37 N, R 2 E). Named on Bartle (1939) 30' quadrangle.

Snow Creek [SHASTA]: *stream,* flows 4.5 miles to North Fork Bear Creek (2) 5.25 miles south of Whitmore (lat. 40°33'10" N, long. 121°54'45" W; near W line sec. 7, T 31 N, R 1 E). Named on Whitmore (1956) 15' quadrangle.

Snow Creek [SISKIYOU]: *stream,* flows nearly 2 miles to Scott River 7 miles south-southwest of Scott Bar (lat. 41°38'40" N, long. 123°02'35" W; sec. 19, T 44 N, R 10 W). Named on Boulder Peak (1981) and Scott Bar (1980) 7.5' quadrangles.

Snowden [SISKIYOU]: *locality,* 6.25 miles northeast of Sawyers Bar along North Russian Creek (lat. 41°21'20" N, long. 123°02'05" W). Named on Tanners Peak (1977) 7.5' quadrangle. Postal authorities established Snowden post office in 1904, discontinued it in 1913, reestablished it in 1914, and discontinued it in 1915 (Frickstad, p. 190).

Snowden: see **Snowdon** [SISKIYOU].

Snowdon [SISKIYOU]: *locality,* 31 miles west of Macdoel along Southern Pacific Railroad (lat. 41°47'35" N, long. 122°28'40" W; at W line sec. 31, T 46 N, R 5 W). Named on Copco (1954) 15' quadrangle. United States Board on Geographic Names (1985c, p. 2) approved the name "Snowden" for the place.

Snowmans Hill [SISKIYOU]: *ridge,* east-trending, 1.5 miles long, 3.5 miles west of McCloud (lat. 41°15'50" N, long. 122°12' W). Named on Shasta (1954) 15' quadrangle.

Snow Meadow [BUTTE]: *area,* 12.5 miles north of Pulga (lat. 39°58'45" N, long. 121°24'45" W; sec. 33, T 25 N, R 5 E). Named on Kimshew Point (1979) 7.5' quadrangle.

Snow Mountain [BUTTE]: *peak,* 4 miles southeast of Jonesville (lat. 40°04' N, long. 121°25'15" W; sec. 33, T 26 N, R 5 E). Named on Jonesville (1958) 15' quadrangle.

Snow Mountain [SHASTA]: *peak,* 8.5 miles southeast of the village of Montgomery Creek (lat. 40°45'45" N, long. 121°47'45" W; near W line sec. 31, T 34 N, R 2 E). Altitude 6814 feet. Named on Montgomery Creek (1956) 15' quadrangle. Steger (p. 60) gave the name "Silver Lake Buttes" as an alternate.

Snow Mountain: see **Lassen Peak** [SHASTA].

Snowshoe Creek [SISKIYOU]: *stream,* flows 1.5 miles to Bear Creek (1) 6.5 miles northeast of Okonom Lake (lat. 41°38'55" N, long. 123°16'05" W). Named on Huckleberry Mountain (1980) 7.5' quadrangle.

Snowslide Creek [SHASTA]: *stream,* flows about 4 miles to Nelson Creek (1) 2.25 miles northeast of the village of Big Bend (lat. 41°02'30" N, long. 121°52'40" W; near N line sec. 29, T 37 N, R 1 E). Named on Big Bend (1961) 15' quadrangle.

Snowslide Gulch [SISKIYOU]:

(1) *canyon,* drained by a stream that flows nearly 1 mile to Bridge Creek 16 miles north of Forks of Salmon (lat. 41°29'30" N, long. 123°20'50" W). Named on Medicine Mountain (1978) 7.5' quadrangle.

(2) *canyon,* drained by a stream that flows 1 mile to North Fork Salmon River 10 miles north of Sawyers Bar (lat. 41°26'50" N, long. 123°08'50" W). Named on English Peak (1977) 7.5' quadrangle.

(3) *canyon,* drained by a stream that flows 1.5 miles to Little North Fork Salmon River 7 miles northwest of Sawyers Bar (lat. 41°22'40" N, long. 123°12'35" W). Named on English Peak (1977) 7.5' quadrangle.

Snowslide Lake [SISKIYOU]: *lake,* 1100 feet long, 30 miles south of Etna (lat. 41°01'45" N, long. 122°58'15" W). Named on Coffee Creek (1955) 15' quadrangle.

Snowy Butte: see **Mount Shasta** [SISKIYOU] (1).

Snowy Mountains: see **Sierra Nevada**, under "Regional setting."

Snowy Range: see **Sierra Nevada**, under "Regional setting."

Snyder Lake [SISKIYOU]: *lake,* 550 feet long, 1.5 miles east of Ukonom Lake (lat. 41°34'50" N, long. 123°19'35" W. Named on Ukonom Lake (1980) 7.5' quadrangle.

Soap Butte [TEHAMA]: *peak,* 5 miles northeast of Dales (lat. 40°22'05" N, long. 122°00'10" W; sec. 17, T 29 N, R 1 W). Altitude 1833 feet. Named on Dales (1965) 7.5' quadrangle.

Soap Creek [SISKIYOU]: *stream,* flows 5 miles to Moffett Creek 9 miles southwest of Yreka (lat. 41°38' N, long. 122°45' W; sec. 27, T 44 N, R 8 W). Named on Yreka (1954) 15' quadrangle.

Soap Creek [TEHAMA]: *stream,* flows 4 miles to a canal 4.5 miles southeast of Manton (lat. 40°23'10" N, long. 121°49' W; at W line sec. 12, T 29 N, R 1 E). Named on Manton (1956) 15' quadrangle.

Soap Creek Ridge [SISKIYOU]: *ridge,* south-southeast-trending, 1.5 miles long, 5.5 miles west-southwest of Yreka (lat. 41°42' N, long. 122°43'55" W); the ridge is east of upper reaches of Soap Creek. Named on Yreka

(1954) 15' quadrangle.

Soap Lake [SHASTA]: *lake,* 1100 feet long, 8 miles northeast of Lassen Peak (lat. 40°33'05" N, long. 121°22'45" W; on W line sec. 13, T 31 N, R 5 E). Named on Prospect Peak (1957) 15' quadrangle.

Soapstone Creek [SISKIYOU]: *stream,* flows 2.5 miles to South Fork Sacramento River 9.5 miles west of Dunsmuir (lat. 41°13'40" N, long. 122°27' W; sec. 21, T 39 N, R 5 W). Named on Dunsmuir (1954) 15' quadrangle.

Soapstone Gulch [SISKIYOU]; *canyon,* 1.25 miles long, 9.5 miles west of Dunsmuir on upper reaches of Soapstone Creek (lat. 41°12'15" N, long. 122°26'45" W; on S line sec. 28, T 39 N, R 5 W). Named on Dunsmuir (1954) 15' quadrangle.

Soapstone Lake: see **Soapstone Pond** [SISKIYOU].

Soapstone Pond [SISKIYOU]: *lake,* 350 feet long, 9.5 miles west of Dunsmuir (lat. 41°11'50" N, long. 122°26'45" W; sec. 33, T 39 N, R 5 W); the lake is near the head of Soapstone Gulch. Named on Dunsmuir (1954) 15' quadrangle. Dunsmuir (1935) 30' quadrangle shows Soapstone Lake located less than 1 mile east of present Soapstone Pond (sec. 34, T 39 N, R 5 W).

Soares Gulch: see **Big Wheel Gulch** [SISKIYOU].

Soda Creek [SHASTA-SISKIYOU]: *stream,* heads in Siskiyou County and flows 9.5 miles to Sacramento River 2 miles northeast of Castella in Shasta County (lat. 41°09'35" N, long. 122°17'30" W; at S line sec. 11, T 38 N, R 4 W); Soda Spring [SHASTA] (1) is along the stream. Named on Dunsmuir (1954) and Shoeinhorse Mountain (1954) 15' quadrangles.

Soda Creek [SISKIYOU]: *stream,* flows about 2.25 miles to Beaver Creek (1) 10 miles east of Condrey Mountain (lat. 41°57'40" N, long. 122°47'30" W; near S line sec. 32, T 48 N, R 8 W). Named on Condrey Mountain (1955) 15' quadrangle.

Soda Creek: see **Little Soda Creek** [SISKIYOU]; **South Soda Creek** [SHASTA].

Soda Creek Ridge [SHASTA-SISKIYOU]: *ridge,* south- to south-southwest-trending, about 5 miles long, 1.25 miles east of Dunsmuir on Siskiyou-Shasta County line (lat. 41°12'30" N, long. 122°15' W); the ridge is west of Soda Creek (2). Named on Dunsmuir (1954) and Shoeinhorse Mountain (1954) 15' quadrangles.

Soda Lake [SHASTA]: *lake,* 600 feet long, 2 miles south-southwest of Lassen Peak (lat. 40°28'25" N, long. 121°32'15" W; sec. 9, T 30 N, R 4 E). Named on Lassen Peak (1956) 15' quadrangle.

Soda Lake: see **Cold Boiling Lake** [SHASTA].

Soda Spring [SHASTA]:

(1) *spring,* 2.5 miles northeast of Castella (lat. 41°10'10" N, long. 122°17' W; at W line sec. 12, T 38 N, R 4 W); the feature is along Soda Creek [SHASTA-SISKIYOU]. Named on Dunsmuir (1954) 15' quadrangle. Called Lower Soda Spring on Shasta (1894) 1° quadrangle, which shows it situated 2.5 miles south-southwest of Upper Soda Spring [SISKIYOU]; this appears to be the spring that Waring (p. 224) called Castle Crag Spring—Waring gave the names "Hibbs Soda Spring" and "Lower Soda Spring" as earlier designations for his Castle Crag Spring.

(2) *spring,* 6 miles east-southeast of Whitmore (lat. 40°36'35" N, long. 121°48'15" W; sec. 24, T 32 N, R 1 E). Named on Whitmore (1956) 15' quadrangle.

Soda Spring [SISKIYOU]: *spring,* 4.5 miles northwest of Weed along Parks Creek (lat. 41°28'10" N, long. 122°27'10" W; sec. 20, T 42 N, R 5 W). Named on Weed (1954) 15' quadrangle.

Soda Spring: see **Lower Soda Spring,** under **Castle Crag** [SHASTA]; **Upper Soda Spring** [SISKIYOU]; **Soda Springs** [SISKIYOU] (3).

Soda Springs [BUTTE]: *locality,* 2 miles west-northwest of Butte Meadows (lat. 40°05'15" N, long. 121°35'10" W; near S line sec. 24, T 26 N, R 3 E). Named on Butte Meadows (1958) 15' quadrangle.

Soda Springs [SISKIYOU]:

(1) *spring,* 5.5 miles northwest of Hornbrook (lat. 41°58'20" N, long. 122°37'40" W; near N line sec. 35, T 48 N, R 7 W). Named on Hornbrook (1955) 15' quadrangle.

(2) *springs,* 20 miles west-northwest of Macdoel (lat. 41°55'10" N, long. 122°22'15" W; near S line sec. 13, T 47 N, R 5 W). Named on Copco (1954) 15' quadrangle.

(3) *springs,* nearly 2 miles south of McCloud (lat. 41°13'45" N, long. 122°08'20" W; sec. 13, T 39 N, R 3 W). Named on Shoeinhorse Mountain (1954) 15' quadrangle. Called Soda Spring on Dunsmuir (1935) 30' quadrangle. Waring (p. 223) used the name "Warmcastle Soda Springs" for the feature. Postal authorities established Warmcastle post office, named for Judge Warmcastle, in 1896 and discontinued it in 1902, when they moved the service to McCloud (Salley, p. 234). They established Elklawn post office in 1888 and discontinued it in 1897, when they moved the service to Warmcastle (Salley, p. 67). Shasta (1894) 1° quadrangle shows a place called Nabar located near present Soda Springs (3).

Soft Water Spring [SISKIYOU]: *spring,* 17 miles south-southwest of Scott Bar (lat. 41°32'35" N, long. 123°10'35" W). Named on Marble Mountain (1980) 7.5' quadrangle.

Soldier Creek [SHASTA]: *stream,* flows 5 miles to Lake Britton 4.25 miles east of Burney Falls (lat. 41°05' N, long. 121°34'20" W; at SE cor. sec. 1, T 36 N, R 3 E); the stream heads southwest of Soldier Mountain. Named on Pondosa (1961) 15' quadrangle.

Soldier Creek [SISKIYOU]: *stream,* flows less than 1 mile to Klamath River 3 miles northeast of Dillon Mountain (lat. 41°33'20" N, long. 123°31'30" W). Named on Dillon Mountain (1983) 7.5' quadrangle.

Soldier Mountain [SHASTA]: *peak,* 6.5 miles northeast of Burney Falls (lat. 41°04'30" N, long. 121°33'45" W; at E line sec. 1, T 37 N, R 3 E). Altitude 5540 feet. Named on Pondosa (1961) 15' quadrangle. Soldiers from Fort Crook sought protection from Indians at the place, and by doing so gave it the name (Giles, p. 125).

Soldier Mountain Reservoir [SHASTA]: *intermittent lake,* 700 feet long, 5 miles east-northeast of Burney Falls (lat. 41°02'30" N, long. 121°33'50" W; sec. 13, T 37 N, R 3 E); the feature is 2.25 miles south of Soldier Mountain along a branch of Soldier Creek. Named on Pondosa (1961) 15' quadrangle.

Solitaire Lake: see **Harrington Mountain** [SISKIYOU].

Solomon Gulch [TEHAMA]: *canyon,* drained by a stream that flows 2 miles to Hooker Creek 2.25 miles south-southwest of Hooker (lat. 40°16'20" N, long. 122°20'50" W; near NW cor. sec. 20, T 28 N, R 4 W). Named on Hooker (1965) and Mitchell Gulch (1965) 7.5' quadrangles.

Solomon Peak [TEHAMA]: *peak,* 11 miles southwest of Tomhead Mountain on Tehama-Trinity County line (lat. 40°01'15" N, long. 122°57'15" W; sec. 15, T 25 N, R 10 W). Altitude 7581 feet. Named on Yolla Bolly (1954) 15' quadrangle.

Solomons Temple [SISKIYOU]: *peak,* 17 miles west-southwest of Macdoel (lat. 41°44'25" N, long. 122°18'35" W; near N line sec. 21, T 45 N, R 4 W). Altitude 3907 feet. Named on Lake Shastina (1954) 15' quadrangle.

Somerset [SISKIYOU]: *locality,* 9 miles south-southwest of Dorris along Southern Pacific Railroad (lat. 41°51'10" N, long. 121°59'30" W; near SW cor. sec. 4, T 46 N, R 1 W). Named on Dorris (1950) 15' quadrangle.

Somerville: see **Summerville** [SISKIYOU].

Somes Bar [SISKIYOU]: *locality,* 12 miles northwest of Forks of Salmon along Salmon River near the its confluence with Klamath River (lat. 41°22'50" N, long. 123°29'15" W). Named on Somes Bar (1979) 7.5' quadrangle. Called Somesbar on Forks of Salmon (1955) 15' quadrangle, which shows the place situated about 1 mile farther east, but United States Board on Geographic Names (1970a, p. 1) rejected the one-word form of the name. Crawford (1894, p. 278) used the name "Somes' Bar." Postal authorities established Somes Bar post office in 1875 and changed the name to Somesbar in 1894; the name commemorates George Somes, who discovered gold at the site in 1850 (Salley, p. 208).

Somes' Bar Creek: see **Somes Creek** [SISKIYOU].

Somes Creek [SISKIYOU]: *stream,* flows nearly 4 miles to Salmon River 10.5 miles northwest of Forks of Salmon (lat. 41°22'25" N, long. 123°27'15" W). Named on Orleans Mountain (1974) 7.5' quadrangle. Crawford (1894, p. 278) referred to Somes' Bar Creek.

Somes Mountain [SISKIYOU]: *peak,* 3 miles north of Orleans Mountain on Siskiyou-Humboldt County line (lat. 41°19'10" N, long. 123°27'50" W); the peak is at the head of Somes Creek. Altitude 5305 feet. Named on Orleans Mountain (1974) 7.5' quadrangle.

Sommey Flat [BUTTE]: *area,* 8 miles north-northeast of Bangor (lat. 39°29'50" N, long. 121°20'55" W; at and near NW cor. sec. 19, T 19 N, R 6 W). Named on Rackerby (1948) 7.5' quadrangle.

Sorensen Hill [BUTTE]: *hill,* 5 miles northwest of Oroville (lat. 39°34'05" N, long. 121°37'10" W; at S line sec. 22, T 20 N, R 3 E). Altitude 517 feet. Named on Oroville (1970) 7.5' quadrangle. The name commemorates Neils Sorensen, who homesteaded at the place about 1880 (United States Board on Geographic Names, 1965a, p. 15).

Soto [BUTTE]: *locality,* 14 miles northwest of Chico along Southern Pacific Railroad (lat. 39°52'35" N, long. 122°01'10" W); the place is east of Soto Lake. Named on Vina (1904) 15' quadrangle.

Soto Lake [BUTTE]: *intermittent lake,* 2400 feet long, 14 miles northwest of Chico (lat. 39°52'15" N, long. 122°01'35" W). Named on Foster Island (1950) 7.5' quadrangle.

Soupan Springs: see **Sulphur Works** [SHASTA].

Sour Grass Creek [TEHAMA]: *stream,* flows 10.5 miles to Burch Creek 2 miles east-southeast of Kirkwood (lat. 39°50'55" N, long. 122°07'25" W). Named on Black Butte Dam (1967) and Kirkwood (1949) 7.5' quadrangles. Called Moore Creek on Flournoy (1944) 15' quadrangle.

Sour Grass Gulch [TEHAMA]: *canyon,* drained by a stream that flows 3 miles to South Fork Cottonwood Creek [SHASTA-TEHAMA] 7.25 miles northeast of Wakefield Flat (lat. 40°12'05" N, long. 122°32'40" W; at N line sec. 16, T 27 N, R 6 W). Named on Oxbow Bridge (1967) 7.5' quadrangle.

South Antelope Campground [TEHAMA]: *locality,* less than 1 mile east-northeast of Panther Spring (lat. 40°15'10" N, long. 121°45'30" W); the place is along South Fork Antelope Creek. Named on Manton (1956) 15' quadrangle.

South Bidwell Hill [BUTTE]: *peak,* 3.25 miles east of Oroville Dam (lat. 39°32'15" N, long. 121°25'15" W; sec. 4, T 19 N, R 5 E); the peak is 1.25 miles south-southeast of North Bidwell Hill. Altitude 1973 feet. Named on Oroville Dam (1970) 7.5' quadrangle.

South China Mountain [SISKIYOU]: *peak,* 17 miles east-southeast of Etna (lat. 41°21'40" N, long. 122°35'20" W; sec. 31, T 41 N, R 6 W); the peak is 1.25 miles south-southwest of China Mountain. Altitude 8206 feet. Named on China Mountain (1955) 15' quadrangle.

South Cow Creek [SHASTA]: *stream,* flows 28 miles to join Old Cow Creek and form Cow Creek 2.25 miles east of Millville (lat. 40°32'40" N, long. 122°07'50" W; sec. 18, T 31 N, R 2 W). Named on Manzanita Lake (1956), Millville (1953), and Whitmore (1956) 15' quadrangles. Called South Fork Cow Creek on Lassen Peak (1894) 1° quadrangle.

South Cow Creek Campground [SHASTA]: *locality,* 3.5 miles east-southeast of Whitmore (lat. 40°36'25" N, long. 121°51'10" W; near SW cor. sec. 22, T 32 N, R 1 E). Named on Whitmore (1956) 15' quadrangle.

South Digger Creek: see **South Fork**, under **Digger Creek** [SHASTA-TEHAMA].

Southerns: see **Sims** [SHASTA].

South Fork [BUTTE]: *locality,* 1.25 miles east-southeast of Bidwell Bar along Feather River Railway (lat. 39°33' N, long. 121°25'10" W; sec. 33, T 20 N, R 5 E); the place is near the mouth of South Fork Feather River—water of Lake Oroville now covers the site. Named on Big Bend Mountain (1948) 15' quadrangle.

South Fork Lake: see **Hidden Lake** [SISKIYOU]; **Little South Fork Lake** [SISKIYOU].

South Fork Lakes [SISKIYOU]: *lakes,* two, largest 800 feet long, 17 miles south of Etna (lat. 41°12'10" N, long. 122°54'05" W; on and near N line sec. 33, T 39 N, R 9 W); the lakes are at the head of South Fork Scott River. Named on Coffee Creek (1955) 15' quadrangle.

South Fork Mountain [SHASTA]:

(1) *ridge,* generally southeast-trending, 1 mile long, 6.5 miles east-southeast of village of French Gulch (lat. 40°39'30" N, long. 122°31'25" W); the ridge is at the head of South Fork Spring Creek (6). Named on Whiskeytown (1979) 7.5' quadrangle.

(2) *peak,* 5.5 miles northwest of Igo (lat. 40°34' N, long. 122°36'45" W; sec. 1, T 31 N, R 7 W). Altitude 5191 feet. Named on Igo (1979) 7.5' quadrangle.

South Honcut Creek [BUTTE]: *stream,* heads in Yuba County and flows 27 miles, partly in Yuba County and partly along Butte-Yuba County line, to join North Honcut Creek and form Honcut Creek nearly 4 miles west-southwest of Honcut (lat. 39°18'50" N, long. 121°36'10" W). Named on Honcut (1952), Loma Rica (1947), Oregon House (1948), and Rackerby (1948) 7.5' quadrangles. Marysville (1895) 30' quadrangle has the name "South Honcut Creek" for present Wilson Creek.

South Meadow Gulch [TEHAMA]: *canyon,* drained by a stream that flows 2.5 miles to Meadow Gulch nearly 5 miles west of Rosewood (lat. 40°16'10" N, long. 122°38'40" W; sec. 22, T 28 N, R 7 W). Named on Ono (1952) 15' quadrangle.

South Oroville [BUTTE]: *district,* 1.25 miles south-southeast of downtown Oroville (lat. 39°29'50" N, long. 121°32'45" W; sec. 17, 20, T. 19 N, R 4 E). Named on Oroville (1970) and Palermo (1970) 7.5' quadrangles.

South Ridge [TEHAMA]: *ridge,* generally southwest-trending, 3.25 miles long, center 1.5 miles southwest of Ball Mountain (lat. 39°55' N, long. 122°48'15" W). Named on Ball Mountain (1967) 7.5' quadrangle.

South Russian Creek [SISKIYOU]: *stream,* flows 7.25 miles to North Russian Creek 4.5 miles east-northeast of Sawyers Bar (lat. 41°19'35" N, long. 123°03'20" W); the stream heads at Russian Lake. Named on Etna (1955) 15' quadrangle, and on Tanners Peak (1977) 7.5' quadrangle. United States Board on Geographic Names (1968c, p. 4) approved the name "Blakes Fork" for a stream, 1.2 miles long, that joins South Russian Creek 12 miles south-southwest of Etna (sec. 26, T 40 N, R 10 W).

South Soda Creek [SHASTA]: *stream,* flows 4 miles to Soda Creek [SHASTA-SISKIYOU] 3.25 miles northeast of Castella (lat. 41°10'20" N, long. 122°16'20" W; near N line sec. 12, T 38 N, R 4 W). Named on Dunsmuir (1954) and Shoeinhorse Mountain (1954) 15' quadrangles.

South Sugar Lake [SISKIYOU]: *lake,* 700 feet long, 12.5 miles south of Etna (lat. 41°16'50" N, long. 122°56'35" W; on S line sec. 30, T 40 N, R 9 W); the lake is 1.25 miles south of Sugar Lake at the head of a branch of Sugar Creek. Named on Etna (1955) 15' quadrangle.

South Table Mountain [BUTTE]: *ridge,* generally west-trending, 1.5 miles long, 2.5 miles north of Oroville (lat. 39°33'05" N, long. 121°33'30" W). Named on Oroville (1970) 7.5' quadrangle. On Dry Creek (1912) and Oroville (1912) 7.5' quadrangles, present Campbell Hill and present Table Mountain together are called South Table Mountain.

South Yolla Bolly Mountains [TEHAMA]: *peaks,* 7.25 miles south-southwest of Tomhead Mountain (lat. 40°02'15" N, long. 122°51'10" W). Named on Yolla Bolly (1954) 15' quadrangle. United States Board on Geographic Names (1982b, p. 3) rejected the names "South Yallo Bally," "South Yolla Bolly," "South Yolla Bolly Mountain," "Yalla Balla," "Yalla Balley," "Yalla Bally," "Yallo Balley," "Yola Bola," "Yola Buli," "Yolla," "Yolla Balley," "Yolla Bally," "Yolla Bolly," "Yolla Bolly Mountain," and "Yolla Bolly Mountains" for the peaks.

Sowell Ravine [BUTTE]: *canyon,* drained by a stream that flows 1.25 miles to South Honcut Creek 2.5 miles east-northeast of Bangor (lat. 39°24'20" N, long. 121°21'40" W; sec. 24, T 18 N, R 5 E). Named on Rackerby (1948) 7.5' quadrangle.

Spalding Corner [SHASTA]: *locality,* 9 miles north-northeast of Burney Falls (lat. 41°07'45" N, long. 121°34'45" W; near W line sec. 13, T 38 N, R 3 E). Named on Pondosa (1961) 15' quadrangle. United States Board on Geographic Names (1964, p. 14) rejected the form "Spaulding Corner" for the name.

Spanish Canyon [SHASTA]: *canyon,* drained by a stream that flows 6 miles to lowlands along Sacramento River 2.25 miles west-northwest of Anderson (lat. 40°27'30" N, long. 122°20'30" W). Named on Cottonwood (1965) and Olinda (1964) 7.5' quadrangles. South Fork opens into the main canyon 1.25 miles north of Olinda; it is 2.5 miles long and is named on Olinda (1964) 7.5' quadrangle.

Spanish Creek [GLENN]: *stream,* flows 7.25 miles to Black Butte River 8.5 miles south of Black Butte (lat. 39°36'20" N, long. 122°51'55" W; at W line sec. 10, T 20 N, R 9 W). Named on Kneecap Ridge (1967) and Plaskett Meadows (1967) 7.5' quadrangles.

Spanish Gulch [SHASTA]: *canyon,* drained by a stream that flows less than 0.5 mile to Mad Ox Gulch 5 miles east of the village of French Gulch (lat. 40°41'25" N, long. 122°32'45" W; sec. 28, T 33 N, R 6 W). Named on Whiskeytown (1979) 7.5' quadrangle.

Spanish Ridge [GLENN]: *ridge,* south-trending, 3.5 miles long, 6.5 miles south of Black Butte (lat. 39°37'50" N, long. 122°51'15" W). Named on Kneecap Ridge (1967) and Plaskett Meadows (1967) 7.5' quadrangles.

Spanishtown: see **Yankee Hill** [BUTTE].

Spannaus Gulch [SISKIYOU]: *canyon,* drained by a stream that flows 1 mile to Copco Lake 17 miles west-northwest of Macdoel (lat. 41°58'20" N, long. 122°16'40" W; sec. 35, T 48 N, R 4 W). Named on Copco (1954) 15' quadrangle.

Spannus Spring [SISKIYOU]: *spring,* 13 miles west-northwest of Macdoel (lat. 41°55'40" N, long. 122°13'30" W; sec. 9, T 47 N, R 3 W). Named on Macdoel (1954) 15' quadrangle.

Spaulding Corner: see **Spalding Corner** [SHASTA].

Spaulding Creek [SISKIYOU]: *stream,* flows 4 miles to Cottonwood Creek (1) 8 miles northwest of Hornbrook (lat. 42°00'15" N, long. 122°38'45" W; sec. 15, T 48 N, R 7 W). Named on Hornbrook (1955) 15' quadrangle.

Specimen Creek [SISKIYOU]; *stream,* flows 3.5 miles to Little North Fork Salmon River nearly 4 miles northwest of Sawyers Bar (lat. 41°20'45" N, long. 123°10'20" W). Named on Sawyers Bar (1979) 7.5' quadrangle. Left Hand Fork enters 1.25 miles upstream from the mouth of the main creek; it is 2.5 miles long and is named on Sawyers Bar (1979) 7.5' quadrangle.

Specimen Gulch [SISKIYOU]: *canyon,* drained by a stream that flows less than 1 mile to South Fork Salmon River nearly 1 mile east-southeast of Cecilville (lat. 41°08'25" N, long. 123°07'25" W). Named on Grasshopper Ridge (1979) 7.5' quadrangle.

Speed: see **Chico** [BUTTE].

Speedway: see **Chico** [BUTTE].

Spees Peak [SISKIYOU]: *peak,* 15 miles north-northwest of Happy Camp (lat. 41°59'50" N, long. 123°28'15" W; near W line sec. 36, T 19 N, R 6 E). Altitude 5830 feet. Named on Deadman Point (1981) 7.5' quadrangle.

Spencer Meadow [TEHAMA]: *area,* 11 miles north of Deer Creek Station (lat. 40°25'10" N, long. 121°29'10" W; sec. 36, T 30 N, R 4 E). Named on Mount Harkness (1956) 15' quadrangle.

Spiers Gulch [SHASTA]: *canyon,* drained by a stream that flows nearly 3 miles to Harrison Gulch 6 miles west-southwest of Arbuckle Mountain (lat. 40°22'10" N, long. 122°58'25" W; sec. 15, T 29 N, R 10 W). Named on Chanchelulla Peak (1951) and Dubakella Mountain (1954) 15' quadrangles.

Spirit Lake [SISKIYOU]: *lake,* 650 feet long, 5 miles east-southeast of Ukonom Lake (lat. 41°33'35" N, long. 123°15'50" W). Named on Ukonom Lake (1980) 7.5' quadrangle.

Spoon Ravine [BUTTE]: *canyon,* drained by a stream that flows 1.5 miles to Little North Fork [of Middle Fork Feather River] 4 miles northeast of the village of Brush Creek (lat. 39°43'50" N, long. 121°17'10" W; near E line sec. 27, T 22 N, R 6 E). Named on Brush Creek (1970) 7.5' quadrangle.

Spring Branch [SHASTA]: *stream,* flows nearly 3 miles to West Fork Stillwater Creek 3 miles northeast of the town of Central Valley (lat. 40°42'35" N, long. 122°19'40" W; near S line sec. 16, T 33 N, R 4 W). Named on Project City (1957) 7.5' quadrangle.

Spring Branch [SISKIYOU]: *stream,* flows 2 miles to Moffett Creek 15 miles south of Yreka (lat. 41°31' N, long. 122°41'30" W). Named on Yreka (1954) 15' quadrangle.

Spring Branch [TEHAMA]:

(1) *stream,* flows 8 miles to Battle Creek [SHASTA-TEHAMA] 12.5 miles north-northeast of Bend (lat. 40°24'35" N, long. 122°05'40" W; sec. 33, T 30 N, R 2 W). Named on Manton (1956) 15' quadrangle, and on Tuscan Buttes NE (1965) 7.5' quadrangle.

(2) *stream,* flows less than 1 mile to Grizzly Creek 3 miles east-southeast of Wakefield Flat (lat. 40°06'15" N, long. 122°35'20" W; sec. 18, T 26 N, R

6 W). Named on Lowrey (1967) 7.5' quadrangle.

Spring Branch: see **Moffett Creek** [SISKIYOU].

Spring Creek [SHASTA]:

(1) *water feature*, lakelike stream that joins Fall River 9.5 miles northeast of Burney Falls (lat. 41°06'05" N, long. 121°30'50" W; sec. 28, T 38 N, R 4 E). Named on Pondosa (1961) 15' quadrangle.

(2) *stream*, flows 1 mile to Sacramento River 12 miles south of Lamoine (lat. 40°48'45" N, long. 122°23' W; near S line sec. 12, T 34 N, R 5 W). Named on Lamoine (1946) 15' quadrangle. Water of Shasta Lake now floods the feature.

(3) *stream*, flows 2.25 miles to Little Cow Creek (lat. 40°33'20" N, long. 122°13'45" W; sec. 8, T 31 N, R 3 W). Named on Millville (1953) 15' quadrangle.

(4) *stream*, flows 1.5 miles to Bailey Creek 4 miles east-southeast of Shingletown (lat. 40°28' N, long. 121°49'45" W; at E line sec. 11, T 30 N, R 1 E). Named on Manton (1956) 15' quadrangle.

(5) *stream*, flows 1 mile to Squaw Creek (2) 2.25 miles southeast of Shoeinhorse Mountain (lat. 41°02'30" N, long. 122°02'45" W. Named on Shoeinhorse Mountain (1954) 15' quadrangle.

(6) *stream*, flows 11 miles to Sacramento River 5 miles southwest of Summit City (lat. 40°37'50" N, long. 122°27'35" W; sec. 17, T 32 N, R 5 W). Named on Shasta Dam (1956) and Whiskeytown (1979) 7.5' quadrangles. South Fork enters less than 2 miles upstream from the mouth of the main creek; it is 2.25 miles long and is named on Shasta Dam (1956) and Whiskeytown (1979) 7.5' quadrangles.

Spring Creek [SISKIYOU]: *stream*, flows 4.5 miles to lowlands 22 miles southwest of Macdoel (lat. 41°37'30" N, long. 122°19'30" W; sec. 29, T 44 N, R 4 W). Named on Lake Shastina (1954) 15' quadrangle.

Spring Creek [TEHAMA]:

(1) *stream*, flows 4.5 miles to South Fork Battle Creek [SHASTA-TEHAMA] 4 miles southwest of Manton (lat. 40°23'45" N, long. 121°55'05" W; sec. 1, T 29 N, R 1 W). Named on Manton (1956) 15' quadrangle.

(2) *stream*, flows 4 miles to Sacramento River 1 mile northwest of Bend (lat. 40°15'50" N, long. 122°13'25" W; sec. 20, T 28 N, R 3 W). Named on Bend (1965) and Hooker (1965) 7.5' quadrangles.

Springflat: see **Spring Flat Campground** [SISKIYOU].

Spring Flat Campground [SISKIYOU]: *locality*, 9 miles southwest of Scott Bar along Scott River (lat. 41°38'25" N, long. 123°06'35" W). Named on Scott Bar (1980) 7.5' quadrangle. Averill's (1935) map has the name "Springflat" at the place.

Spring Gardens [TEHAMA]: *springs*, 3.5 miles west-southwest of Manton (lat. 40°24'50" N, long. 121°56' W; sec. 35, 36, T 30 N, R 1 W). Named on Manton (1956) 15' quadrangle.

Spring Gulch [SHASTA]:

(1) *canyon*, drained by a stream that flows 1 mile to Middle Fork Cottonwood Creek [SHASTA-TEHAMA] nearly 2 miles northeast of Arbuckle Mountain (lat. 40°24'55" N, long. 122°50'20" W; at NW cor. sec. 36, T 30 N, R 9 W). Named on Chanchelulla Peak (1951) 15' quadrangle.

(2) *canyon*, drained by a stream that flows less than 1 mile to Knob Gulch 4 miles west of Arbuckle Mountain (40°24'30" N, long. 122°56'30" W; sec. 36, T 30 N, R 10 W). Named on Chanchelulla Peak (1951) 15' quadrangle.

(3) *canyon*, drained by a stream that flows nearly 4 miles to lowlands along Sacramento River 2.25 miles west of Anderson (lat. 40°27'30" N, long. 122°20'30" W). Named on Cottonwood (1965) and Olinda (1964) 7.5' quadrangles. The canyon divides at the head into North Fork and South Fork. North Fork is 3 miles long and South Fork in 2.5 miles long; both forks are named on Olinda (1964) 7.5' quadrangle.

(4) *canyon*, drained by a stream that flows less than 0.5 mile to Mad Ox Gulch nearly 5 miles east of the village of French Gulch (lat. 40°41'25" N, long. 122°32'45" W; sec. 28, T 33 N, R 6 W). Named on Whiskeytown (1979) 7.5' quadrangle.

Spring Gulch [SISKIYOU]: *canyon*, drained by a stream that flows nearly 1 mile to East Fork of South Fork Salmon River 2 miles east-northeast of Cecilville (lat. 41°09'20" N, long. 123°06'15" W). Named on Grasshopper Ridge (1979) 7.5' quadrangle.

Spring Gulch [TEHAMA]:

(1) *canyon*, drained by a stream that flows 1 mile to Beegum Creek [SHASTA-TEHAMA] 2.5 miles north-northeast of Beegum Peak (lat. 40°20'45" N, long. 122°51'40" W; near SE cor. sec. 22, T 29 N, R 9 W). Named on Chanchelulla Peak (1951) 15' quadrangle.

(2) *canyon*, drained by a stream that flows about 2.25 miles to Dry Creek (1) 1.5 miles east-northeast of Rosewood (lat. 40°16'35" N, long. 122°31'35" W; sec. 15, T 28 N, R 6 W). Named on Ono (1952) 15' quadrangle.

Spring Gulch: see **Little Spring Gulch** [TEHAMA].

Spring Hill [SISKIYOU]: *hill*, 1.5 miles north-northwest of the town of Mount Shasta (lat. 41°20' N, long. 122°19'30" W; at NE cor. sec. 8, T 40 N, R 4 W); the hill is just north of Big Springs (1). Named on Weed (1954) 15' quadrangle.

Spring Hollow [BUTTE]: *canyon*, drained by a stream that flows less than 1 mile to Lake Oroville 4.5 miles east-northeast of Oroville Dam (lat. 39°33'20" N, long. 121°24' W; near N line sec. 34, T 20 N, R 5 E). Named on Oroville Dam (1970) 7.5' quadrangle, which shows a spring in the canyon.

Spring House: see **Elliot Spring House** [BUTTE].

Spring Ravine [BUTTE]: *canyon*, drained by a stream that flows 2 miles to North Honcut Creek nearly 4 miles north-northwest of Bangor (lat. 39°26'20" N, long. 121°26'10" W; near N line sec. 8, T 18 N, R 5 E). Named on Bangor (1947) 7.5' quadrangle.

Springs Canyon: see **Little Springs Canyon** [SISKIYOU].

Springtown: see **Callahan** [SISKIYOU].

Spring Valley Gulch [BUTTE]: *canyon*, drained by a stream that flows 3.5 miles to West Branch Feather River 9 miles southeast of Paradise (lat. 39°39'50" N, long. 121°30'35" W; sec. 22, T 21 N, R 4 E). Named on Cherokee (1970) 7.5' quadrangle.

Spring Valley Reservoir [BUTTE]: *intermittent lake*, 1150 feet long, 8 miles north-northeast of Oroville (lat. 39°37'25" N, long. 121°30'40" W; sec. 3, T 20 N, R 4 E); the feature is near the head of Spring Valley Gulch. Named on Oroville (1970) 7.5' quadrangle.

Spring Valley Reservoir: see **Concow Reservoir** [BUTTE]; **Snag Lake** [BUTTE].

Square Lake [TEHAMA]: *dry lake*, 200 feet long, nearly 7 miles south-southwest of Tomhead Mountain (lat. 40°01'45" N, long. 122°50'35" W; sec. 3, T 25 N, R 9 W). Named on Yolla Bolly (1954) 15' quadrangle.

Squaw Camp [GLENN]: *locality*, 6 miles south-southeast of Black Butte (lat. 39°39'25" N, long. 122°48'30" W; near S line sec. 19, T 21 N, R 8 W). Named on Plaskett Meadows (1967) 7.5' quadrangle.

Squaw Creek [SHASTA]:

(1) *water feature*, embaymentlike feature that joins Tule River 7 miles north of Fall River Mills (lat. 41°06'20" N, long. 121°26'40" W). Named on Fall River Mills (1961) 15' quadrangle. United States Board on Geographic Names (1988a, p. 1) approved the name "Ja She Creek" for the feature, and rejected the names "Squaw Creek" and "Ja-She Creek" (with the hyphen) for it.

(2) *stream*, flows 22 miles to Squaw Creek Arm Shasta Lake 8 miles south-southeast of Bollibokka Mountain (lat. 40°50'15" N, long. 122°08'10" W; near S line sec. 31, T 35 N, R 2 W). Named on Bollibokka Mountain (1957) and Shoeinhorse Mountain (1954) 15' quadrangles. North Fork enters from the north 6.5 miles upstream from the mouth of the main creek; it is 8 miles long and is named on Bollibokka Mountain (1957) 15' quadrangle. East Fork of North Fork enters North Fork from the east 6.5 miles upstream from the mouth of North Fork; it is 3.5 miles long and is named on Bollibokka Mountain (1957) and Shoeinhorse Mountain (1954) 15' quadrangles. East Fork enters from the east 11.5 miles upstream from the mouth of the main creek; it is 3.5 miles long and is named on Bollibokka Mountain (1957) 15' quadrangle. West Fork enters 3.5 miles south of Shoeinhorse Mountain; it is 2.25 miles long and is named on Shoeinhorse Mountain (1954) 15' quadrangle.

(3) *stream*, formed by the confluence of North Fork and South Fork, flows 1.5 miles to Shasta Lake 5 miles northwest of Summit City (lat. 40°44'25" N, long. 122°28' W; at NE cor. sec. 7, T 33 N, R 5 W). Named on Shasta Dam (1956) 7.5' quadrangle. North Fork is 3.5 miles long and is named on Lamoine (1957) 15' quadrangle, and on Shasta Dam (1956) 7.5' quadrangle. South Fork is 4 miles long and is named on Shasta Dam (1956) and Whiskeytown (1979) 7.5' quadrangles. Dry Fork enters Shasta Lake 4 miles northwest of Summit City, where it joins Squaw Creek in the lake; it is 1.25 miles long and is named on Shasta Dam (1956) 7.5' quadrangle. Mary Fork enters at the mouth of the main creek; it is 1.25 miles long and is named on Lamoine (1957) 15' quadrangle, and on Shasta Dam (1956) 7.5' quadrangle. United States Board on Geographic Names (1990, p. 9) rejected the form "Marys Fork" for the name.

(4) *stream*, flows 4.5 miles to Crow Creek 6 miles southeast of Ono (lat. 40°24'25" N, long. 122°32'55" W; sec. 33, T 30 N, R 6 W). Named on Ono (1952) 15' quadrangle.

Squaw Creek : see **Avery Creek** [TEHAMA]; **Squaw Valley Creek** [SHASTA-SISKIYOU].

Squaw Creek Arm [SHASTA]: *embayment*, opens into Pit River Arm Shasta Lake 11 miles south of Bollibokka Mountain (lat. 40°46'30" N, long. 122°13' W); the feature is the flooded lower part of the canyon of Squaw Creek (2). Named on Bollibokka Mountain (1957) 15' quadrangle.

Squaw Flat [GLENN]: *valley*, 6.5 miles south-southeast of Fruto (lat. 39°30'15" N, long. 122°22'50" W). Named on Lodoga (1960) 15' quadrangle, and on Fruto (1968) 7.5' quadrangle.

Squaw Flat [SHASTA]: *area*, 9 miles east-northeast of the village of Big Bend (lat. 41°05'10" N, long. 121°46' W; near W line sec. 32, T 38 N, R 2 E). Named on Big Bend (1961) 15' quadrangle.

Squaw Gulch [SISKIYOU]: *canyon*, drained by a stream that flows 1.25 miles to Scott Valley 8 miles southeast of Etna (lat. 41°21'05" N, long. 122°49'55" W; near N line sec. 1, T 40 N, R 9 W). Named on Etna (1955) 15' quadrangle.

Squaw Hill [TEHAMA]: *locality*, 4.5 miles east-southeast of Corning on the west bank of Sacramento River (lat. 39°54'35" N, long. 122°05'35" W; sec. 28, T 24 N, R 2 W). Named on Vina (1950) 7.5' quadrangle. Vina (1904) 15' quadrangle has the name for a topographic feature at the site, and also shows Squaw Hill Ferry on Sacramento River at the place. According to MacMullen (p. 87), the Sacramento River landing for Corning, called Squaw House for a shack occupied by two old squaws, was active in commerce on the river from 1875 until the last time a steamboat stopped there in 1910.

Squaw Hill Ferry: see **Squaw Hill** [TEHAMA].

Squaw Hollow [TEHAMA]: *canyon,* drained by a stream that flows 5.25 mile to Houghton Creek 6.5 miles east of Flournoy (lat. 39°55'25" N, long. 122°18'50" W; sec. 21, T 24 N, R 4 W). Named on Flournoy (1967) and Henleyville (1967) 7.5' quadrangles.

Squaw Hollow Creek [TEHAMA]: *stream,* flows 2.25 miles to Wells Creek 5 miles southeast of Beegum Peak (lat. 40°16'10" N, long. 122°48'55" W; sec. 19, T 28 N, R 8 W). Named on Chanchelulla Peak (1951) 15' quadrangle.

Squaw House: see **Squaw Hill** [TEHAMA].

Squaw Peak: see **Garner Mountain** [SISKIYOU].

Squaw Valley Creek [SHASTA-SISKIYOU]: *stream,* heads in Siskiyou County and flows 30 miles to McCloud River [SHASTA-SISKIYOU] 7.25 miles west-southwest of Shoeinhorse Mountain in Shasta County (lat. 41°02'25" N, long. 122°12'20" W). Named on Shasta (1954) and Shoeinhorse Mountain (1954) 15' quadrangles. Called Squaw Creek on Shasta (1894) 1° quadrangle.

Squirrel Creek [SHASTA]: *stream,* flows 2.5 miles to McCloud River [SHASTA-SISKIYOU] 3 miles north of Shoeinhorse Mountain (lat. 41°06'50" N, long. 122°03'50" W). Named on Shoeinhorse Mountain (1954) 15' quadrangle.

Squirrel Creek [SISKIYOU]: *stream,* flows nearly 1.5 miles to Klamath River 2.5 miles east-northeast of Dillon Mountain (lat. 41°32'50" N, long. 123°31'40" W). Named on Dillon Mountain (1983) 7.5' quadrangle.

Stacey Creek [SHASTA]: *stream,* flows 4 miles to Clear Creek 3.5 miles north-northwest of Schell Mountain (lat. 40°53'35" N, long. 122°34'15" W). Named on Schell Mountain (1950) 15' quadrangle. South Fork enters 1 mile upstream from the mouth of the main creek; it is 1.5 miles long and is named on Schell Mountain (1950) 15' quadrangle

Stacher Butte [SHASTA]: *peak,* 9 miles northeast of Whitmore (lat. 40°43'10" N, long. 121°47'30" W; sec. 18, T 33 N, R 2 E). Altitude 5807 feet. Named on Whitmore (1956) 15' quadrangle.

Stack Gulch [SISKIYOU]: *canyon,* drained by a stream that flows 1 mile to Duzel Creek 12.5 miles south-southwest of Yreka (lat. 41°34'05" N, long. 122°43'25" W; at S line sec. 13, T 43 N, R 8 W). Named on Yreka (1954) 15' quadrangle.

Stage Gulch [SISKIYOU]: *canyon,* drained by a stream that flows 1 mile to South Fork Salmon River 3.5 miles southeast of Cecilville (lat. 41°06'20" N, long. 120°05'05" W). Named on Thompson Peak (1979) 7.5' quadrangle.

Stanshaw Creek [SISKIYOU]: *stream,* flows 3.5 miles to Klamath River 12 miles north of Orleans, which is in Humboldt County (lat. 41°28'35" N, long. 123°30'40" W). Named on Bark Shanty Gulch (1974) and Somes Bar (1979) 7.5' quadrangles.

Stanshaw Meadows [SISKIYOU]: *area,* 17 miles north-northwest of Forks of Salmon (lat. 41°29'35" N, long. 123°25'50" W). Named on Somes Bar (1979) and Ukonom Mountain (1980) 7.5' quadrangles.

Stanwood: see **Brush Creek** [BUTTE] (2).

Stanwood Saddle [BUTTE]: *pass,* 1.25 miles west of the village of Brush Creek on Stephens Ridge (lat. 39°41'05" N, long. 121°21'40" W; near SE cor. sec. 12, T 21 N, R 5 E). Named on Brush Creek (1970) 7.5' quadrangle.

Stanza Creek [SISKIYOU]: *stream,* flows 2 miles to Elk Creek 6 miles north-northeast of Ukonom Lake (lat. 41°39'40" N, long. 123°19'10" W). Named on Huckleberry Mountain (1980) 7.5' quadrangle.

Star City Creek [SHASTA]: *stream,* flows 10.5 miles to McCloud River [SHASTA-SISKIYOU] 5.5 miles north of Shoeinhorse Mountain (lat. 41°08'55" N, long. 122°04'50" W). Named on Big Bend (1961) and Shoeinhorse Mountain (1954) 15' quadrangles. The name recalls Star City mining district, and the trading post that John B. Star had there in the late 1850's (Gudde, 1949, p. 342).

Star City Meadow: see **Stouts Meadow** [SHASTA].

Star Mountain [TEHAMA]: *peak,* 7.5 miles west-southwest of Beegum Peak on Tehama-Trinity County line (lat. 40°15'30" N, long. 123°00'30" W; on W line sec. 21, T 28 N, R 10 W). Named on Chanchelulla Peak (1951) and Dubakella Mountain (1954 15' quadrangles.

Starvation Gulch [SHASTA]: *gully,* 2 miles long, 5 miles east-northeast of Fall River Mills (lat. 41°02'15" N, long. 121°21'15" W; sec. 14, 23, T 37 N, R 5 E). Named on Fall River Mills (1961) 15' quadrangle.

Starve-Out: see **Grenada** [SISKIYOU].

Station Gulch [SHASTA]: *canyon,* 0.5 mile long, 6.25 miles north of Schell Mountain at the upper end of Damnation Creek (lat. 40°56'45" N, long. 122°32'30" W; on S line sec. 27, T 36 N, R 6 W). Named on Schell Mountain (1950) 15' quadrangle.

Station Gulch [SISKIYOU]: *canyon,* drained by a stream that flows nearly 1 mile to Crawford Creek (2) 0.5 mile northeast of Cecilville (lat. 41°09'05" N, long. 123°07'55" W). Named on Cecilville (1979) 7.5' quadrangle.

Statue Lake [SISKIYOU]: *lake,* 300 feet long, 11 miles south-southwest of Etna (lat. 41°18'35" N, long. 122°58'20" W; near SW cor. sec. 24, T 40 N, R 10 W). Named on Etna (1955) 15' quadrangle.

Steamboat Gulch [SISKIYOU]: *canyon,* drained by a stream that flows 1 mile to Clear Creek (2) 5 miles north of Fort Jones (lat. 41°40'45" N, long. 122°49'30" W; sec. 12, T 44 N, R 9 W). Named on Fort Jones (1955) 15' quadrangle.

Steamboat Mountain [SISKIYOU]: *hill,* 26 miles west-southwest of Macdoel (lat. 41°42'10" N, long. 122°27'45" W; mainly in sec. 31, T 45 N, R 5 W). Altitude 3101 feet. Named on Lake Shastina (1954) 15' quadrangle.

Steamboat Mountain [TEHAMA]: *peak,* 13 miles south of Panther Spring (lat. 40°03'30" N, long. 121°47'30" W; at S line sec. 31, T 26 N, R 2 E). Named on Mineral (1941) 30' quadrangle.

Steamboat Point [TEHAMA]: *relief feature,* 3.25 miles south of Campbell Mound (lat. 39°55'40" N, long. 121°48'15" W). Named on Campbell Mound (1952) 7.5' quadrangle.

Steamboat Rock [BUTTE]: *peak,* 6.5 miles south of Paradise (lat. 39°40'25" N, long. 121°38'20" W; near E line sec. 16, T 21 N, R 3 E). Altitude 836 feet. Named on Hamlin Canyon (1951) 7.5' quadrangle.

Steamboat Rock [TEHAMA]: *relief feature,* 15 miles south of Panther Spring (lat. 40°02'05" N, long. 121°46' W; near NW cor. sec. 16, T 25 N, R 2 E). Named on Panther Spring (1953) 15' quadrangle. The name is from the fancied resemblance of the feature to the front end of a steamboat (United States Board on Geographic Names, 1987a, p. 2).

Steelhead [SISKIYOU]: *locality,* 9.5 miles east-southeast of the village of Seiad Valley at the confluence of Klamath River and Scott River (lat. 41°46'40" N, long. 123°02' W; sec. 6, T 45 N, R 10 W). Named on Hamburg (1980) 7.5' quadrangle. Gudde (1975, p. 180) listed a mining place called Junction Bar that was situated at the confluence of Klamath River and Scotts River. Gudde (1975, p. 178, 201, 360) also listed three other mining places, Johnsons Bar, Lytles Bar, and Virginia Bar, that were located near the confluence.

Steep Hollow [SISKIYOU]: *canyon,* drained by a stream that flows 1.5 miles to Angel Creek 8 miles west-southwest of Bartle (lat. 41°12'20" N, long. 121°57'20" W; near SW cor. sec. 22, T 39 N, R 1 W). Named on Big Bend (1961) 15' quadrangle.

Steep Hollow [TEHAMA]:

(1) *canyon,* drained by a stream that flows less than 1 mile to South Fork Cottonwood Creek [SHASTA-TEHAMA] 3 miles northeast of Wakefield Flat (lat. 40°09'10" N, long. 122°35'45" W; near E line sec. 36, T 27 N, R 7 W). Named on Oxbow Bridge (1967) 7.5' quadrangle.

(2) *relief feature,* 8 miles south of Panther Spring (lat. 40°07'55" N, long. 121°45'05" W; near E line sec. 4, T 26 N, R 2 E). Named on Panther Spring (1953) 15' quadrangle.

Steep Trail Creek [SISKIYOU]: *stream,* flows 3 miles to Bogus Creek 17 miles west of Macdoel (lat. 41°52'15" N, long. 122°19'45" W; sec. 5, T 46 N, R 4 W). Named on Copco (1954) 15' quadrangle.

Steinacher Creek [SISKIYOU]: *stream,* flows 9.5 miles to Wooley Creek 10 miles north-northwest of Forks of Salmon (lat. 41°23' N, long. 123°25'05" W); the stream heads at Steinacher Lake. Named on Forks of Salmon (1978), Medicine Mountain (1978), and Somes Bar (1979) 7.5' quadrangles. Called East Fork [of Wooley Creek] on Sawyers Bar (1923) 30' quadrangle.

Steinacher Lake [SISKIYOU]: *lake,* 550 feet long, 8 miles north-northeast of Forks of Salmon (lat. 41°22'05" N, long. 123°16'50" W); the lake is at the head of Steinacher Creek. Named on Forks of Salmon (1978) 7.5' quadrangle.

Steinacher Ridge [SISKIYOU]: *ridge,* north-northeast- to east-southeast-trending, 8 miles long, center 11 miles north of Forks of Salmon (lat. 41°24'45" N, long. 123°21' W); the ridge is north of Steinacher Creek. Named on Medicine Mountain (1978) and Somes Bar (1979) 7.5' quadrangles.

Stein Creek [SHASTA]: *stream,* flows 2.25 miles to Pit River Arm Shasta Lake 11.5 miles southeast of Bollibokka Mountain (lat. 40°48'35" N, long. 122°04'15" W; near SE cor. sec. 10, T 34 N, R 2 W). Named on Bollibokka Mountain (1957) 15' quadrangle.

Stein Gulch [SISKIYOU]: *canyon,* drained by a stream that heads in the State of Oregon and flows 0.5 mile in Siskiyou County to Elliot Creek 12 miles north-northeast of the village of Seiad Valley (lat. 41°59'55" N, long. 123°06'25" W; near E line sec. 22, T 48 N, R 11 W). Named on Seiad Valley (1955) 15' quadrangle.

Stella: see **Whiskeytown** [SHASTA].

Stephens Butte [SISKIYOU]: *mountain,* 10 miles south-southeast of Bray (lat. 41°30'50" N, long. 121°52'50" W; sec. 5, T 42 N, R 1 E). Altitude 6785 feet. Named on Bray (1950) 15' quadrangle.

Stephens Pass [SISKIYOU]: *pass,* 10 miles south-southeast of Bray (lat.

41°30'30" N, long. 121°54' W; near NW cor. sec. 7, T 42 N, R 1 E); the pass is 1 mile west-southwest of Stephens Butte. Named on Bray (1950) 15' quadrangle.

Stephens Pass Camp [SISKIYOU]: *locality,* 17 miles north-northwest of Bartle (lat. 41°29'45" N, long. 121°53'10" W; on S line sec. 6, T 42 N, R 1 E); the place is about 1 mile southeast of Stephens Pass. Named on Bartle (1961) 15' quadrangle.

Stephens Ridge [BUTTE]: *ridge,* south-southwest-trending, 4.25 miles long, center about 2.5 miles north-northeast of the village of Berry Creek (lat. 39°40'50" N, long. 121°22'45" W). Named on Berry Creek (1970) and Brush Creek (1970) 7.5' quadrangles.

Sterling Mountain [SISKIYOU]: *peak,* 8.5 miles east-northeast of Condrey Mountain (lat. 41°59'45" N, long. 122°50'10" W). Named on Condrey Mountain (1955) 15' quadrangle.

Steve Fork [SISKIYOU]: *stream,* flows 1.5 miles to the State of Oregon 14 miles north of Happy Camp (lat. 42°00' N, long. 123°19'50" W). Named on Figurehead Mountain (1980) 7.5' quadrangle.

Stevenson Peak [TEHAMA]: *peak,* nearly 4 miles northwest of Wakefield Flat (lat. 40°09'50" N, long. 122°41'20" W; near E line sec. 30, T 27 N, R 7 W). Altitude 1889 feet. Named on Cold Fork (1967) 7.5' quadrangle.

Stewart Springs [SISKIYOU]: *locality,* 20 miles east of Etna along Parks Creek (lat. 41°25'10" N, long. 122°30'10" W; near N line sec. 11, T 41 N, R 6 W). Named on China Mountain (1955) 15' quadrangle.

Stillwater: see **Mountain Gate** [SHASTA].

Stillwater Butte [SISKIYOU]: *peak,* 4 miles north-northeast of Bartle (lat. 41°18'40" N, long. 121°48'10" W; sec. 13, T 40 N, R 1 E). Altitude 5141 feet. Named on Bartle (1961) 15' quadrangle.

Stillwater Creek [SHASTA]: *stream,* formed by the confluence of East Fork and West Fork, flows 12.5 miles to Sacramento River 4.25 miles north-west of Balls Ferry (lat. 40°27'55" N, long. 122°14'50" W). Named on Balls Ferry (1965) 7.5' quadrangle. DeWitt Clinton Johnson of Stillwater, New York, settled by the stream in 1853 (Steger, p. 61). East Fork in 7.5 miles long and West Fork is 11 miles long; both forks are named on Project City (1957) 7.5' quadrangle.

Stillwater Meadows [SISKIYOU]: *area,* 3.5 miles north-northeast of Bartle along Bartle Creek (lat. 41°18'10" N, long. 121°47'30" W; on E line sec. 24, T 40 N, R 1 E); the place is southeast of Stillwater Butte. Named on Bartle (1961) 15' quadrangle.

Stillwater Plains [SHASTA]: *area,* 8 miles southeast of Redding (lat. 40°30'45" N, long. 122°17' W); the place is along lower reaches of Stillwater Creek. Named on Balls Ferry (1965), Cottonwood (1965), Enterprise (1957), and Palo Cedro (1965) 7.5' quadrangles.

Stink Creek [SISKIYOU]: *stream,* flows 3 miles to Sacramento River 3.25 miles south of the town of Mount Shasta (lat. 41°15'55" N, long. 122°18'30" W; sec. 33, T 40 N, R 4 W). Named on Dunsmuir (1954) and Weed (1954) 15' quadrangles.

Stinking Canyon [SHASTA]: *canyon,* drained by a stream that flows 3 miles to Dry Creek (1) 8 miles north-northwest of Millville (lat. 40°39'15" N, long. 122°14'35" W; near SE cor. sec. 6, T 32 N, R 3 W). Named on Bella Vista (1965) and Project City (1957) 7.5' quadrangles.

Stinking Creek [TEHAMA]: *stream,* flows 8.5 miles to Salt Creek (1) 8.5 miles north-northwest of Wakefield Flat (lat. 40°14'15" N, long. 122°42'05" W; sec. 31, T 28 N, R 7 W). Named on Yolla Bolly (1954) 15' quadrangle, and on Cold Fork (1967) 7.5' quadrangle.

Stinking Springs [TEHAMA]: *spring,* 9 miles northwest of Wakefield Flat (lat. 40°13'20" N, long. 122°45' W; sec. 3, T 27 N, R 8 W); the feature is along Stinking Creek. Named on Cold Fork (1967) 7.5' quadrangle.

Stirling City [BUTTE]: *village,* 11.5 miles north-northeast of Paradise (lat. 39°54'20" N, long. 121°31'40" W; sec. 28, T 24 N, R 4 E). Named on Stirling City (1979) 7.5' quadrangle. Postal authorities established Stirling City post office in 1903 (Frickstad, p. 12). J.F. Nash, superintendent of the saw mill that Diamond Match Company built at the site in 1903, named the place after he noted that boilers for the mill were made by Stirling Boiler Works (Gudde, 1949, p. 344).

Stirling Junction [BUTTE]: *locality,* 1.5 miles southeast of downtown Chico along Sacramento Northern Railroad (lat. 39°42'35" N, long, 121°48'30" W; sec. 1, T 21 N, R 1 E); the place is at the rail junction with Southern Pacific Railroad. Named on Chico (1948) 7.5' quadrangle. Durham (1912) 7.5' quadrangle shows the intersection of Northern Pacific Railroad and Butte County Railroad at the place.

Stockton Lake: see **Reflection Lake** [SHASTA].

Stone Corral Hollow [TEHAMA]: *canyon,* drained by a stream that flows 2.5 miles to Boat Gunwale Creek 6.5 miles south-southwest of Panther Spring (lat. 40°09'30" N, long. 121°48'25" W). Named on Panther Spring (1953) 15' quadrangle.

Stone Gulch [SHASTA]: *canyon,* drained by a stream that flows less than 1 mile to Cline Gulch nearly 3 miles east-northeast of the village of French Gulch (lat. 40°42'55" N, long. 122°35'10" W; sec. 18, T 33 N, R 6 W). Named on Whiskeytown (1979) 7.5' quadrangle. Called Harrison Gulch on French Gulch (1944) 15' quadrangle.

Stone House Bar: see **Stony Creek** [BUTTE].

Stoneman Caves [SHASTA]: **Baird Caves**, under **Bard** [SHASTA].

Stoner Gulch [SISKIYOU]: *canyon,* drained by a stream that flows 2 miles to lowlands 13 miles south of Yreka (lat. 41°32'40" N, long. 122°36'10" W; sec. 25, T 43 N, R 7 W). Named on Yreka (1954) 15' quadrangle.

Stone's Ferry: see **Pit River** [SHASTA].

Stones Valley [SISKIYOU]: *canyon,* 12 miles west-southwest of Scott Bar (lat. 41°40'30" N, long. 123°13' W). Named on Grider Valley (1981) 7.5' quadrangle. Called Stone Valley on Averill's (1935) map.

Stone Valley [GLENN]: *valley,* about 5 miles long, 7 miles east of Fruto along French Creek (2) (lat. 39°36'30" N, long. 122°18'30" W). Named on Fruto NE (1952), Julian Rocks (1968), and Stone Valley (1952) 7.5' quadrangles.

Stone Valley: see **Stones Valley** [SISKIYOU].

Stoney Peak: see **Freaner Peak** [SHASTA].

Stony Bar: see **Big Stony Bar**, under **Kanaka Bar** [BUTTE].

Stony Butte: see **Freaner Peak** [SHASTA].

Stony Creek [BUTTE]: *stream,* flows 3.5 miles to North Fork Feather River 5.5 miles north-northwest of the village of Berry Creek (lat. 39°43'15" N, long. 121°25'45" W; at W line sec. 33, T 22 N, R 5 E). Named on Berry Creek (1970) and Pulga (1979) 7.5' quadrangles. Wells and Chambers (1882) map shows a place called Stone House Bar situated along North Fork Feather River opposite Stony Creek.

Stony Creek [GLENN]: *locality,* 17 miles north of Butte City along Southern Pacific Railroad (lat. 39°42'25" N, long. 121°59'55" W); the place is at the railroad crossing of Stony Creek [GLENN-TEHAMA]. Named on Ord Ferry (1949) 7.5' quadrangle.

Stony Creek [GLENN-TEHAMA]: *stream,* formed by the confluence of North Fork and South Fork in Black Butte Reservoir, flows 64 miles—mainly in Glenn County, but partly in Tehama County—to Sacramento River 15 miles north of Butte City [GLENN] (lat. 39°40'35" N, long. 121°58'20" W). Named on Black Butte Dam (1967), Chrome (1968), Elk Creek (1968), Foster Island (1950), Hamilton City (1949), Julian Rocks (1968), Kirkwood (1949), Ord Ferry (1949), Sehorn Creek (1967), and Stonyford (1968) 7.5' quadrangles. Middle Fork heads in Lake County and flows 5 miles in Glenn County to Colusa County, where it joins South Fork; it is named on Saint John Mountain (1968) 7.5' quadrangle. North Fork (1) heads in Glenn County and flows 11 miles to Colusa County, where it joins Stony Creek; North Fork (1) is named on Saint John Mountain (1968) 7.5' quadrangle. North Fork (2) enters Glenn County from Tehama County, and flows 7 miles, mainly in Glenn County, to Black Butte Reservoir 12.5 miles west-northwest of Orland in Tehama County—it joins Stony Creek in the reservoir; North Fork (2) is named on Newville (1967) and Sehorn Creek (1967) 7.5' quadrangles.

Stony Creek: see **Little Stony Creek** [GLENN]; **Wyo** [GLENN].

Stony Gorge Reservoir [GLENN]: *lake,* behind a dam on Stony Creek [GLENN-TEHAMA] 1.5 miles south-southeast of the village of Elk Creek (lat. 39°35'10" N, long. 122°31'55" W). Named on Elk Creek (1968) 7.5' quadrangle.

Stony Gulch [SHASTA]: *canyon,* drained by a stream that flows 1.25 miles to Clear Creek 2.5 miles north of Igo (lat. 40°32'25" N, long. 122°31'50" W; sec. 15, T 31 N, R 6 W). Named on Igo (1979) 7.5' quadrangle.

Stony Peak: see **Freaner Peak** [SHASTA].

Stony Point [TEHAMA]: *relief feature,* 9.5 miles northwest of Paskenta on Riley Ridge (lat. 39°57'45" N, long. 122°41'40" W; sec. 6, T 24 N, R 7 W). Named on Riley Ridge (1967) 7.5' quadrangle.

Story Flat [TEHAMA]: *area,* nearly 2 miles northwest of Wakefield Flat along South Fork Cottonwood Creek [SHASTA-TEHAMA] (lat. 40°08'30" N, long. 122°40' W; near NW cor. sec. 4, T 26 N, R 7 W). Named on Cold Fork (1967) 7.5' quadrangle.

Stottard Gulch [SHASTA]: *canyon,* drained by a stream that flows nearly 1 mile to East Fork Clear Creek 5 miles south of Schell Mountain (lat. 40°46'55" N, long. 122°32'20" W; at N line sec. 27, T 34 N, R 6 W). Named on Schell Mountain (1950) 15' quadrangle.

Stouts Meadow [SHASTA]: *area,* 10.5 miles north of the village of Big Bend (lat. 41°10'10" N, long. 121°56'10" W; sec. 11, T 38 N, R 1 W); the place is along Star City Creek. Named on Big Bend (1961) 15' quadrangle. United States Board on Geographic Names (1964, p. 14) rejected the name "Star City Meadow" for the feature.

Stover Mountain: see **North Stover Mountain** [TEHAMA].

Stove Spring Canyon [SISKIYOU]: *canyon,* drained by a stream that flows 3 miles to Bear Canyon 12.5 miles northwest of Macdoel (lat. 41°57' N, long. 122°10'40" W; sec. 2, T 47 N, R 3 W). Named on Macdoel (1954) 15' quadrangle.

Straight Arrow Camp [TEHAMA]: *locality,* 3.5 miles south of Ball Mountain (lat. 39°52'45" N, long. 122°46'30" W; near E line sec. 5, T 23 N, R 8 W). Named on Ball Mountain (1967) 7.5' quadrangle.

Strawberry Valley: see **Mount Shasta** [SISKIYOU] (2).

Strawberry Valley Creek [BUTTE]: *stream,* heads in Yuba County and flows 1.5 miles to Lost Creek Reservoir 3.5 miles north-northeast of Clipper Mills in Butte County (lat. 39°34'35" N, long. 121°07'35" W; sec. 19, T 20 N, R 8 E). Named on Strawberry Valley (1948) 7.5' quadrangle.

Stricklin Butte [SISKIYOU]: *peak,* 11 miles north of the village of Seiad Valley (lat. 42°05' N, long. 123°11'30" W; at SW cor. sec. 13, T 48 N, R 12 W). Named on Seiad Valley (1955) 15' quadrangle.

Stringtown [BUTTE]: *locality,* 2.5 miles east-southeast of Bidwell Bar along South Fork Feather River (lat. 39°31'55" N, long. 121°23'20" W). Named on Bidwell Bar (1897) 30' quadrangle. Postal authorities established Stringtown post office in 1854, discontinued it in 1855, reestablished it in 1857, and discontinued it in 1858 (Frickstad, p. 12). The name is from the way that buildings and tents at the place were strung out along the canyon like beads on a string (Hanna, p. 318).

Stringtown Bar [BUTTE]: *locality,* 3.25 miles east-southeast of Bidwell Bar along South Fork Feather River (lat. 39°32' N, long. 121°23'10" W; sec. 2, T 19 N, R 5 E); the place is about 0.25 mile west of the site of Stringtown. Named on Big Bend Mountain (1948) 15' quadrangle. Water of Lake Oroville now covers the site.

Stringtown Hill: see **Stringtown Mountain** [BUTTE].

Stringtown Mountain [BUTTE]: *peak,* 4.5 miles east of Oroville Dam (lat. 39°31'50" N, long. 121°23'50" W; sec. 3, T 19 N, R 5 E); the peak is about 1 mile west of Stringtown Bar. Altitude 2369 feet. Named on Oroville Dam (1970) 7.5' quadrangle. Called Stringtown Hill on Bidwell Bar (1897) 30' quadrangle.

Stuart Gap [TEHAMA]: *pass,* 10.5 miles northwest of Tomhead Mountain on Tehama-Trinity County line (lat. 40°13'45" N, long. 122°58'30" W; sec. 34, T 28 N, R 10 W). Named on Yolla Bolly (1954) 15' quadrangle.

Stud Hill [SISKIYOU]: *hill,* 20 miles northeast of Bartle (lat. 41°29'30" N, long. 121°35' W). Altitude 5844 feet. Named on Hambone (1961) 15' quadrangle.

Stud Horse Camp: see **Stud Horse Spring** [SISKIYOU].

Studhorse Creek [SISKIYOU]: *stream,* flows 3.25 miles to Elliot Creek 3.25 miles north of Condrey Mountain (lat. 41°59' N, long. 122°59'10" W; near E line sec. 27, T 48 N, R 10 W). Named on Condrey Mountain (1955) 15' quadrangle.

Studhorse Gulch [SHASTA]: *canyon,* drained by a stream that flows nearly 1 mile to Grizzly Gulch 3 miles southeast of the village of French Gulch (lat. 40°40'10" N, long. 122°35'55" W; near SE cor. sec. 36, T 33 N, R 7 W). Named on Whiskeytown (1979) 7.5' quadrangle.

Stud Horse Spring [SISKIYOU]: *spring,* 11 miles west-southwest of Scott Bar (lat. 41°40'05" N, long. 123°10'50" W). Named on Grider Valley (1981) 7.5' quadrangle. Scott Bar (1955) 15' quadrangle shows Stud Horse Camp at the site.

Stump Camp: see **Big Stump Camp** [TEHAMA].

Stump Creek [SHASTA]: *stream,* flows 2 miles to Kosk Creek 3.25 miles north-northwest of the village of Big Bend (lat. 41°03'55" N, long. 121°55'20" W; sec. 11, T 37 N, R 1 W). Named on Big Bend (1961) 15' quadrangle.

Stump Creek Butte [SHASTA]: *peak,* 5.25 miles north-northwest of the village of Big Bend (lat. 41°05'30" N, long. 121°56'50" W; at W line sec. 2, T 37 N, R 1 W); the peak is at the head of Stump Creek. Altitude 4121 feet. Named on Big Bend (1961) 15' quadrangle.

Subway Cave [SHASTA]: *cave,* 15 miles north-northeast of Lassen Peak (lat. 40°41'10" N, long. 121°25' W; near E line sec. 28, T 33 N, R 5 E). Named on Prospect Peak (1957) 15' quadrangle.

Sucker Creek [SISKIYOU]: *stream,* flows 2 miles to Humbug Creek 15 miles southeast of Condrey Mountain (lat. 41°46'25" N, long. 122°44'55" W; near E line sec. 3, T 45 N, R 8 W). Named on Condrey Mountain (1955) 15' quadrangle.

Sucker Run [BUTTE]: *stream,* flows 10.5 miles to South Fork Feather River 3 miles northwest of Forbestown (lat. 39°33' N, long. 121°18'35" W; sec. 33, T 20 N, R 6 E). Named on Clipper Mills (1948) and Forbestown (1970) 7.5' quadrangles.

Sucker Run: see **Little Sucker Run** [BUTTE].

Sugar Creek [SISKIYOU]: *stream,* flows 9 miles to Scott River 8.5 miles south-southeast of Etna (lat. 41°20'40" N, long. 122°49'20" W; at E line sec. 1, T 40 N, R 9 W). Named on Etna (1955) 15' quadrangle. Tiger Fork enters 2.5 miles upstream from the mouth of the main creek; it is 0.25 mile long and is named on Etna (1955) 15' quadrangle.

Sugarfoot Creek [TEHAMA]: *stream,* flows 3.5 miles to Thomes Creek 4.25 miles south of Ball Mountain (lat. 39°52'10" N, long. 122°46'25" W; near NE cor. sec. 8, T 23 N, R 8 W). Named on Ball Mountain (1967) and Log Spring (1967) 7.5' quadrangles.

Sugarfoot Glade [TEHAMA]: *area,* 3.5 miles south of Ball Mountain (lat. 39°52'55" N, long. 122°46'30" W; sec. 4, 5, T 23 N, R 8 W); the place is east of Sugarfoot Creek. Named on Ball Mountain (1967) 7.5' quadrangle.

Sugar Hill [SISKIYOU]: *peak,* 13 miles south-southeast of Etna (lat. 41°16'20" N, long. 122°50'15" W; sec. 36, T 40 N, R 9 W). Altitude 5532 feet. Named on Etna (1955) 15' quadrangle.

Sugar Lake [SISKIYOU]: *lake,* 400 feet long, 11 miles south of Etna (lat. 41°17'50" N, long. 122°56'25" W; sec. 19, T 40 N, R 9 W); the lake is along Sugar Creek. Named on Etna (1955) 15' quadrangle.

Sugar Lake: see **South Sugar Lake** [SISKIYOU].

Sugarloaf [BUTTE]: *peak,* 9 miles south-southeast of Paradise (lat. 39°38'15" N, long. 121°32'15" W; near NW cor. sec. 33, T 21 N, R 4 E). Altitude 1651 feet. Named on Cherokee (1970) 7.5' quadrangle.

Sugarloaf [SHASTA]:

(1) *peak,* 4.5 miles south of Lamoine (lat. 40°54'50" N, long. 122°26'40" W; sec. 4, T 35 N, R 5 W). Altitude 3942 feet. Named on Lamoine (1957) 15' quadrangle.

(2) *peak,* 14 miles south-southeast of Bollibokka Mountain (lat. 40°45'25" N, long. 122°06'20" W; near S line sec. 33, T 34 N, R 2 W). Named on Bollibokka Mountain (1957) 15' quadrangle.

(3) *peak,* 4 miles west-southwest of Redding (lat. 40°33'15" N, long. 122°27'35" W; sec. 8, T 31 N, R 5 W). Altitude 1210 feet. Named on Redding (1957) 7.5' quadrangle.

(4) *locality,* 8.5 miles south-southeast of Lamoine (lat. 40°51'30" N, long. 122°23'45" W; sec. 26, T 35 N, R 5 W). Named on Lamoine (1957) 15' quadrangle. United States Board on Geographic Names (1969a, p. 4) rejected the names "Loftus" and "Renfro" for the place.

Sugarloaf [SISKIYOU]:

(1) *hill,* 12.5 miles northwest of Forks of Salmon along Klamath River near Somes Bar (lat. 41°22'55" N, long. 123°29'45" W). Named on Somes Bar (1979) 7.5' quadrangle.

(2) *locality,* 12.5 miles northwest of Forks of Salmon (lat. 41°23'15" N, long. 123°09'30" W; near SE cor. sec. 33, T 41 N, R 6 E); the place is just northeast of present Sugarloaf (1). Named on Sawyers Bar (1923) 30' quadrangle.

Sugarloaf [TEHAMA]: *peak,* 3.25 miles north-northeast of Polk Springs (lat. 40°09'20" N, long. 121°37'45" W; sec. 34, T 27 N, R 3 E). Named on Butte Meadows (1958) 15' quadrangle.

Sugarloaf: see **Black Butte** [SISKIYOU] (1).

Sugarloaf Creek [SHASTA]: *stream,* flows 3.25 miles to Sacramento River Arm Shasta Lake 8.5 miles south of Lamoine (lat. 40°51'10" N, long. 122°26'30" W; near S line sec. 28, T 35 N, R 5 W). Named on Lamoine (1957) 15' quadrangle.

Sugarloaf Creek: see **Little Sugarloaf Creek** [SHASTA].

Sugarloaf Hill [GLENN]: *peak,* 7 miles east of Saint John Mountain (lat. 39°26'25" N, long. 122°33'50" W; sec. 6, T 18 N, R 6 W). Named on Stonyford (1968) 7.5' quadrangle.

Sugarloaf Mountain [SHASTA]: *peak,* 6.5 miles east of the village of French Creek (lat. 40°41'20" N, long. 122°30'35" W; sec. 26, T 33 N, R 6 W). Altitude 3913 feet. Named on Whiskeytown (1979) 7.5' quadrangle.

Sugarloaf Mountain [TEHAMA]:

(1) *peak,* 1 mile north-northeast of Beegum Peak (lat. 40°19'40" N, long. 122°52'30" W; at NW cor. sec. 34, T 29 N, R 9 W). Named on Chanchelulla Peak (1951) 15' quadrangle.

(2) *peak,* 9.5 miles southwest of Tomhead Mountain on Tehama-Trinity County line (lat. 40°02'45" N, long. 122°57'10" W; sec. 3, T 25 N, R 10 W). Altitude 7367 feet. Named on Yolla Bolly (1954) 15' quadrangle.

(3) *ridge,* generally south-southwest-trending, 3.5 miles long, 5 miles south-southeast of Campbell Mound (lat. 39°54'45" N, long. 121°45'50" W). Named on Campbell Mound (1952) 7.5' quadrangle.

Sugarloaf Peak [BUTTE]: *peak,* 3.5 miles west-northwest of Oroville (lat. 39°31'50" N, long. 121°36'55" W; near E line sec. 3, T 19 N, R 3 E). Altitude 550 feet. Named on Oroville (1970) 7.5' quadrangle.

Sugarloaf Peak [SHASTA]: *peak,* 15 miles north of Lassen Peak (lat. 40°41'45" N, long. 121°27'30" W; at NE cor. sec. 25, T 33 N, R 4 E). Named on Prospect Peak (1957) 15' quadrangle.

Sugar Pine Butte [SISKIYOU]: *hill,* 11 miles north-northeast of McCloud (lat. 41°23'20" N, long. 122°01'45" W; sec. 24, T 41 N, R 2 W). Altitude 5354 feet. Named on Shasta (1954) 15' quadrangle.

Sugar Pine Camp [SISKIYOU]: *locality,* 11 miles north-northeast of Happy Camp (lat. 41°55'25" N, long. 123°15'35" W). Named on Figurehead Mountain (1980) 7.5' quadrangle.

Sugarpine Canyon [SHASTA]: *canyon,* drained by a stream that flows 2 miles to Pit River Arm Shasta Lake 14 miles south-southeast of Bollibokka Mountain (lat. 40°45'25" N, long. 122°06'20" W; near W line sec. 33, T 34 N, R 2 W). Named on Bollibokka Mountain (1957) 15' quadrangle. Called Sugarpine Gulch on Redding (1901) 30' quadrangle.

Sugarpine Flat [TEHAMA]: *area,* 5.5 miles northwest of Mineral (lat. 40°24'15" N, long. 121°40' W). Named on Lassen Peak (1956) 15' quadrangle.

Sugar Pine Gap [BUTTE]: *pass,* 4.5 miles north of Clipper Mills (lat. 39°35'55" N, long. 121°10" W; near NE cor. sec. 15, T 20 N, R 7 E); the pass is just north of Sugar Pine Point. Named on Clipper Mills (1948) 7.5' quadrangle.

Sugarpine Gulch [SISKIYOU]: *canyon,* drained by a stream that flows 1 mile to Scott River 4 miles southwest of Scott Bar (lat. 41°41'50" N, long. 123°03' W). Named on Scott Bar (1980) 7.5' quadrangle.

Sugarpine Gulch: see **Sugarpine Canyon** [SHASTA].

Sugar Pine Mountain [SHASTA]: *peak,* 7.5 miles northeast of Whitmore (lat. 40°42'35" N, long. 121°49'15" W; near SE cor. sec. 14, T 33 N, R 1 E). Named on Whitmore (1956) 15' quadrangle.

Sugar Pine Point [BUTTE]: *peak,* 4.25 miles north of Clipper Mills (lat.

39°35'45" N, long. 121°10'10" W; near E line sec. 15, T 20 N, R 7 E); the peak is just south of Sugar Pine Gap. Named on Clipper Mills (1948) 7.5' quadrangle.

Sugar Pine Sheep Camp [SHASTA]: *locality,* 3.25 miles north-northeast of Schell Mountain (lat. 40°53'55" N, long. 122°30'50" W; sec. 11, T 35 N, R 6 W). Named on Schell Mountain (1950) 15' quadrangle.

Sugarpine Spring [TEHAMA]: *spring,* 5 miles west-northwest of Mineral (lat. 40°23' N, long. 121°40'35" W; near S line sec. 8, T 29 N, R 3 E). Named on Lassen Peak (1956) 15' quadrangle.

Sugar Spring [TEHAMA]: *spring,* 8.5 miles southwest of Ball Mountain (lat. 39°51'40" N, long. 122°54'55" W; near E line sec. 12, T 23 N, R 10 W). Named on Mendocino Pass (1967) 7.5' quadrangle.

Sulphur Creek [TEHAMA]:

(1) *stream,* flows nearly 4 miles to South Fork Cottonwood Creek [SHASTA-TEHAMA] 3 miles south-southeast of Tomhead Mountain (lat. 40°05'40" N, long. 122°47'45" W; sec. 20, T 26 N, R 8 W). Named on Yolla Bolly (1954) 15' quadrangle.

(2) *stream,* flows nearly 4 miles to Deer Creek (2) 15 miles south of Panther Spring (lat. 40°02'05" N, long. 121°48' W; near N line sec. 18, T 25 N, R 2 E); Sulphur Lick is along the stream. Named on Butte Meadows (1958) and Panther Spring (1953) 15' quadrangles.

Sulphur Creek: see **East Sulphur Creek** [SHASTA-TEHAMA]; **West Sulphur Creek** [SHASTA-TEHAMA].

Sulphur Gulch [TEHAMA]:

(1) *canyon,* drained by a stream that flows about 2.5 miles to Dry Creek (1) 6 miles east-southeast of Beegum Peak (lat. 40°17'20" N, long. 122°46'40" W; near SW cor. sec. 9, T 28 N, R 8 W). Named on Chanchelulla Peak (1951) 15' quadrangle

(2) *canyon,* drained by a stream that flows 4 miles to Cold Fork (1) 5.5 miles north-northeast of Wakefield Flat (lat. 40°12'15" N, long. 122°36'55" W; near E line sec. 11, T 27 N, R 7 W). Named on Cold Fork (1967) and Oxbow Bridge (1967) 7.5' quadrangles.

Sulphur Lick [TEHAMA]: *spring,* 16 miles south of Panther Spring (lat. 40°01'30" N, long. 121°46' W; near SW cor. sec. 16, T 25 N, R 2 E); the spring is along Sulphur Creek (2). Named on Panther Spring (1953) 15' quadrangle. United States Board on Geographic Names (1986c, p. 4) rejected the name "Sulphur Lick Spring" for the feature.

Sulphur Lick Spring: see **Sulphur Lick** [TEHAMA].

Sulphur Spring [GLENN]: *spring,* 8.5 miles east of Saint John Mountain (lat. 39°26' N, long. 122°32'20" W; near NW cor. sec. 9, T 18 N, R 6 W). Named on Stonyford (1968) 7.5' quadrangle.

Sulphur Spring [SISKIYOU]: *spring,* 12.5 miles north-northwest of Forks of Salmon (lat. 41°24' N, long. 123°27'30" W; sec. 26, T 12 N, R 6 E). Named on Forks of Salmon (1955) 15' quadrangle.

Sulphur Spring [TEHAMA]:

(1) *spring,* 5 miles north-northwest of Wakefield Flat (lat. 40°11'45" N, long. 122°39'30" W; sec. 16, T 27 N, R 7 W). Named on Cold Fork (1967) 7.5' quadrangle.

(2) *spring,* 4 miles north of Wakefield Flat (lat. 40°11' N, long. 122°39' W; on W line sec. 22, T 27 N, R 7 W); the spring is in Sulphur Gulch (2). Named on Cold Fork (1967) 7.5' quadrangle.

(3) *spring,* 4 miles north-northeast of Wakefield Flat along South Fork Guyre Creek (lat. 40°10'35" N, long. 122°36'15" W; sec. 24, T 27 N, R 7 W). Named on Oxbow Bridge (1967) 7.5' quadrangle.

(4) *spring,* 3.5 miles west-southwest of Tomhead Mountain (lat. 40°07'15" N, long. 122°52'45" W; near E line sec. 9, T 26 N, R 9 W). Named on Yolla Bolly (1954) 15' quadrangle.

(5) *spring,* nearly 4 miles west of Wakefield Flat (lat. 40°07'05" N, long. 122°42'35" W). Named on Raglin Ridge (1967) 7.5' quadrangle.

(6) *spring,* less than 1 mile east-southeast of Wakefield Flat (lat. 40°07'10" N, long. 122°37'40" W; near W line sec. 11, T 26 N, R 7 W). Named on Colyear Springs (1957) 15' quadrangle.

(7) *spring,* 5.25 miles southwest of Ball Mountain (lat. 39°07'20" N, long. 122°50'45" W; near SW cor. sec. 2, T 23 N, R 9 W). Named on Log Spring (1967) 7.5' quadrangle.

Sulphur Springs [SISKIYOU]: *spring,* 6 miles north-northeast of Ukonom Lake along Elk Creek (lat. 41°39'30" N, long. 123°19'05" W). Named on Huckleberry Mountain (1980) 7.5' quadrangle. Called Sulphur Spring on Seiad (1922) 30' quadrangle.

Sulphur Springs [TEHAMA]: *spring,* 4 miles northwest of Paskenta (lat. 39°55'55" N, long. 122°35'35" W; near SE cor. sec. 13, T 24 N, R 7 W). Named on Paskenta (1967) 7.5' quadrangle.

Sulphur Works [SHASTA]: *water feature,* 3 miles south-southeast of Lassen Peak (lat. 40°26'55" N, long. 121°32'10" W; near E line sec. 21, T 30 N, R 4 E). Named on Lassen Peak (1956) 15' quadrangle. Called Soupan Springs on Lassen Peak (1894) 1° quadrangle. The name "Sulphur Works" is from an early attempt to recover sulphur commercially at the place; Dr. Supan supervised the operation in 1865 (Schulz, p. 50-51).

Summertown [SHASTA]: *locality,* 5 miles northwest of Lassen Peak (lat. 40°32'40" N, long. 121°33'55" W; at S line sec. 7, T 31 N, R 4 E). Named on Manzanita Lake (1956) 15' quadrangle.

Summerville [SISKIYOU]: *locality,* 4.5 miles southeast of Cecilville (lat. 41°06' N, long. 123°03'45" W). Named on Thompson Peak (1979) 7.5' quadrangle. The place first was called Somerville (Ball, p. 19).

Summerville [TEHAMA]: *locality,* 11 miles south-southwest of Mineral along Mill Creek (3) (lat. 40°11'50" N, long. 121°40'45" W; sec. 18, T 27 N, R 3 E). Named on Mineral (1941) 30' quadrangle.

Summit: see **Oroville Junction** [BUTTE].

Summit City [SHASTA]: *town,* 7.5 miles north of Redding (lat. 40°41'05" N, long. 122°24' W; sec. 26, T 33 N, R 5 W). Named on Shasta Dam (1956) 7.5' quadrangle. Postal authorities established Summit City post office in 1939 (Frickstad, p. 183). Promoters laid out the town when construction began on Shasta Dam in 1938 (Steger, p. 61- 62).

Summit Creek [SHASTA]: *stream,* flows 1.5 miles to Kings Creek 5.5 miles east-southeast of Lassen Peak (lat. 40°38'10" N, long. 121°24'30" W; at S line sec. 10, T 30 N, R 5 E); the feature heads near Summit Lake (3). Named on Mount Harkness (1956) 15' quadrangle. The stream sometimes is called Duck Creek, from Duck Lake, an early name for Summit Lake (3) (Schulz, p. 51), but United States Board on Geographic Names (1933, p. 728) rejected this name for the feature.

Summit Creek [TEHAMA]: *stream,* flows 3.5 miles to join Nanny Creek and form South Fork Battle Creek [SHASTA-TEHAMA] 1.5 miles east-northeast of Mineral (lat. 40°21'15" N, long. 121°34'15" W; near SW cor. sec. 20, T 29 N, R 4 E). Named on Lassen Peak (1956) 15' quadrangle.

Summit Gulch [SHASTA]: *canyon,* drained by a stream that flows 4.25 miles to Willow Creek (4) 2.25 miles south-southwest of the village of French Gulch (lat. 40°40'15" N, long. 122°39'25" W; sec. 33, T 33 N, R 7 W). Named on French Gulch (1979) 7.5' quadrangle, which shows Summit mine located near the head of the canyon.

Summit Lake [BUTTE]: *lake,* 1100 feet long, 4 miles southeast of Jonesville (lat. 40°04'35" N, long. 121°24'45" W; sec. 28, T 26 N, R 5 E). Named on Jonesville (1958) 15' quadrangle.

Summit Lake [SHASTA]:

(1) *intermittent lake,* 400 feet long, 6 miles east of the village of Big Bend (lat. 41°01' N, long. 121°47'45" W; at SW cor. sec. 31, T 37 N, R 2 E). Named on Big Bend (1961) 15' quadrangle.

(2) *dry lake,* 15 miles north-northeast of Lassen Peak (lat. 40°40'30" N, long. 121°21'50" W; sec. 36, T 33 N, R 5 E). Named on Prospect Peak (1957) 15' quadrangle.

(3) *lake,* 0.25 mile long, 4.5 miles east of Lassen Peak (lat. 40°29'35" N, long. 121°25'20" W; at E line sec. 4, T 30 N, R 5 E). Named on Mount Harkness (1956) 15' quadrangle. United States Board on Geographic Names (1933, p. 728) rejected the name "Duck Lake" for the feature.

Summit Lake [SISKIYOU]:

(1) *lake,* 800 feet long, 16 miles south-southwest of Scott Bar (lat. 41°32'10" N, long. 123°07'40" W). Named on Marble Mountain (1980) 7.5' quadrangle.

(2) *lake,* 400 feet long, 3 miles south-southeast of Weed (lat. 41°23'15" N, long. 122°22'15" W; sec. 24, T 41 N, R 5 W). Named on Weed (1954) 15' quadrangle.

(3) *intermittent lake,* 800 feet long, nearly 5 miles north-northeast of Mount Dome (lat. 41°52'05" N, long. 121°38'15" W; sec. 33, T 47 N, R 3 E). Named on Mount Dome (1950) 15' quadrangle.

Summit Meadow Lake [SISKIYOU]: *lake,* 550 feet long, 16 miles south-southwest of Scott Bar (lat. 41°32' N, long. 123°07'30" W). Named on Boulder Peak (1981) and Marble Mountain (1980) 7.5' quadrangles.

Summit Spring: see **Buckhorn Spring** [SISKIYOU] (1).

Summit Springs [GLENN]: *spring,* 11 miles west of the village of Elk Creek (lat. 39°37'10" N, long. 122°44'10" W; near W line sec. 2, T 20 N, R 8 W). Named on Felkner Hill (1968) 7.5' quadrangle.

Summit Springs Hill [GLENN]: *peak,* 11 miles west of the village of Elk Creek (lat. 39°36'55" N, long. 122°44'05" W); the peak is 1100 feet south-southeast of Summit Springs. Altitude 5947 feet. Named on Felkner Hill (1968) 7.5' quadrangle.

Sundale: see **Wicks Corner** [BUTTE].

Sunday Gulch [SHASTA]: *canyon,* 1 mile long, opens into the canyon of Middle Fork Cottonwood Creek [SHASTA-TEHAMA] 5 miles southwest of Arbuckle Mountain (lat. 40°21'15" N, long. 122°56'25" W; sec. 24, T 29 N, R 10 W); the canyon divides at the head into East Fork and West Fork. Named on Chanchelulla Peak (1951) 15' quadrangle. Workers in nearby mines in the 1920's washed gravel in the canyon for gold on their Sunday holidays (Steger, p. 62). East Fork is 2 miles long and West Fork is 2.5 miles long; both forks are named on Chanchelulla Peak (1951) 15' quadrangle.

Sundown Gulch [SISKIYOU]: *canyon,* drained by a stream that flows 1 mile to Empire Creek 9.5 miles west-southwest of Hornbrook (lat. 41°52'50" N, long. 122°43'45" W; sec. 36, T 47 N, R 8 W). Named on Hornbrook (1955) 15' quadrangle.

Sunflower Flat [SHASTA]: *area,* 5 miles north-northwest of Lassen Peak (lat. 40°33'15" N, long. 121°32' W; near N line sec. 9, T 31 N, R 4 E). Named on Manzanita Lake (1956) 15' quadrangle.

Sunflower Flat [TEHAMA]: *area,* 3 miles south of Wakefield Flat (lat.

40°04'50" N, long. 122°38'35" W; sec. 27, T 26 N, R 7 W); the place is south of Sunflower Gulch. Named on Raglin Ridge (1967) 7.5' quadrangle.

Sunflower Gulch [TEHAMA]: *canyon,* drained by a stream that flows 5 miles to Red Bank Creek nearly 5 miles southeast of Wakefield Flat (lat. 40°04'25" N, long. 122°34'50" W; near W line sec. 30, T 26 N, R 6 W). Named on Lowrey (1967) and Raglin Ridge (1967) 7.5' quadrangles.

Sunk Gulch [SISKIYOU]: *canyon,* drained by a stream that flows 1 mile to Angel Creek 8 miles east-southeast of McCloud (lat. 41°12' N, long. 122°00'25" W; sec. 30, T 39 N, R 1 W). Named on Big Bend (1961) and Shoeinhorse Mountain (1954) 15' quadrangles.

Sunnyside [TEHAMA]: *locality,* 7.5 miles south-southwest of Ball Mountain (lat. 39°50'40" N, long. 122°51'50" W; near SW cor. sec. 15, T 23 N, R 9 W). Named on Log Spring (1967) 7.5' quadrangle.

Sunnyslope [BUTTE]: *locality,* 2 miles southwest of Bangor (lat. 39°22'05" N, long. 121°25'50" W; near SE cor. sec. 32, T 18 N, R 5 E). Named on Loma Rica (1947) 7.5' quadrangle.

Sunset Campground [SHASTA]: *locality,* 4.25 miles northwest of Lassen Peak just SE of Manzanita Lake (1) (lat. 40°31'50" N, long. 121°33'45" W; near SE cor. sec. 18, T 31 N, R 4 E). Named on Manzanita Lake (1956) 15' quadrangle.

Sunset Gulch [SHASTA]: *canyon,* drained by a stream that flows 1 mile to Atkins Creek (lat. 40°39' N, long. 121°46'05" W; sec. 5, T 32 N, R 2 E). Named on Whitmore (1956) 15' quadrangle.

Sunset Hill [BUTTE]: *peak,* 1.5 miles west of Forbestown (lat. 39°21'25" N, long. 121°17'55" W; sec. 9, T 19 N, R 6 E). Altitude 3321 feet. Named on Forbestown (1970) 7.5' quadrangle.

Supan Gulch [TEHAMA]: *canyon,* drained by a stream that flows 2.5 miles to Paynes Creek (1) 1.5 miles southwest of Dales (lat. 40°18'10" N, long. 122°05'30" W; near W line sec. 4, T 28 N, R 2 W). Named on Dales (1965) 7.5' quadrangle.

Sur Cree Creek [SISKIYOU]: *stream,* flows nearly 2 miles to Little North Fork Salmon River 4.5 miles northwest of Sawyers Bar (lat. 41°21'15" N, long. 123°11' W). Named on Sawyers Bar (1979) 7.5' quadrangle.

Surprise Lake [SISKIYOU]: *lake,* 500 feet long, 15 miles north-northeast of McCloud (lat. 41°27'55" N, long. 122°03'20" W; near NW cor. sec. 26, T 42 N, R 2 W). Named on Shasta (1954) 15' quadrangle.

Surveyor Gulch [TEHAMA]: *canyon,* drained by a stream that flows 2.25 miles to Dry Creek (1) 9.5 miles west of Rosewood (lat. 40°16'55" N, long. 122°44'10" W; sec. 14, T 28 N, R 8 W). Named on Chanchelulla Peak (1951) and Ono (1952) 15' quadrangles.

Surveyors Glade [SISKIYOU]: *area,* 14 miles west-northwest of Macdoel (lat. 41°53'50" N, long. 122°15'20" W; sec. 25, T 47 N, R 4 W). Named on Copco (1954) 15' quadrangle.

Susanville Canyon [SHASTA]: *canyon,* drained by a stream that flows 2.5 miles to Pit River Arm Shasta Lake 11.5 miles south-southeast of Bollibokka Mountain (lat. 40°47'35" N, long. 122°05'50" W; near N line sec. 21, T 34 N, R 2 W). Named on Bollibokka Mountain (1957) 15' quadrangle.

Sutcliffe Creek [SISKIYOU]: *stream,* flows 3.25 miles to West Branch Indian Creek (1) 11 miles north-northwest of Happy Camp (lat. 41°55'55" N, long. 123°29'05" W). Named on Deadman Point (1981) and Polar Bear Mountain (1982) 7.5' quadrangles.

Swain Hill [BUTTE]:

(1) *peak,* 7.25 miles northwest of Clipper Mills (lat. 39°37' N, long. 121°14'30" W; near SE cor. sec. 1, T 20 N, R 6 E). Named on Clipper Mills (1948) 7.5' quadrangle. On Bidwell Bar (1897) 30' quadrangle, the name applies to a peak located about 2 miles farther east-northeast.

(2) *peak,* 2.25 miles south of Bangor (lat. 39°21'25" N, long. 121°24'15" W; sec. 3, T 17 N, R 5 E). Altitude 903 feet. Named on Loma Rica (1947) 7.5' quadrangle.

Swain Ravine [BUTTE]: *canyon,* drained by a stream that flows 1.5 miles to South Honcut Creek 3 miles south of Bangor (lat. 39°20'40" N, long. 121°24'20" W; near W line sec. 10, T 17 N, R 5 E); the canyon is west of Swain Hill (2). Named on Loma Rica (1947) 7.5' quadrangle.

Swamp Creek [SISKIYOU]: *stream,* flows 7.25 miles to lowlands 13 miles northwest of Bartle (lat. 41°23'30" N, long. 121°59'35" W; near N line sec. 20, T 41 N, R 1 W). Named on Bartle (1961) and Shasta (1954) 15' quadrangles.

Swamp Creek [TEHAMA]: *stream,* flows about 3.5 miles to Slate Creek (1) 2 miles south-southwest of Deer Creek Station (lat. 40°14'30" N, long. 121°27'50" W; sec. 31, T 28 N, R 5 E). Named on Jonesville (1958) and Mount Harkness (1956) 15' quadrangles.

Swamp Creek Ridge [SISKIYOU]: *ridge,* south- to south-southwest-trending, 12.5 miles north-northeast of McCloud (lat. 41°24'30" N, long. 122°00'55" W; mainly in sec. 7, 18, T 41 N, R 1 W); the ridge is west of Swamp Creek. Named on Shasta (1954) 15' quadrangle.

Swan Lake [SHASTA]: *lake,* 1300 feet long, 8 miles east of Lassen Peak (lat. 40°29'50" N, long. 121°21'45" W; at NW cor. sec. 6, T 30 N, R 6 E). Named on Mount Harkness (1956) 15' quadrangle.

Swans Gulch [SISKIYOU]: *canyon,* drained by a stream that flows less than 1 mile to North Fork Salmon River 0.5 mile northeast of Forks of Salmon (lat. 41°15'45" N, long. 123°19' W). Named on Forks of Salmon (1978) 7.5' quadrangle.

Swanson Gulch [SISKIYOU]: *canyon,* drained by a stream that flows 1.25 miles to Scott River less than 1 mile south of Scott Bar (lat. 41°43'50" N, long. 123°00'20" W; sec. 21, T 45 N, R 10 W). Named on Scott Bar (1980) 7.5' quadrangle.

Swanston: see **Grass Lake** [SISKIYOU] (2).

Swasey: see **Glenburn** [SHASTA].

Swayne: see **Brush Creek** [BUTTE] (2).

Swayne Hill [BUTTE]: *ridge,* north- to northwest-trending, 1.5 miles long, 5 miles north of the village of Berry Creek (lat. 39°43' N, long. 121°23'45" W). Named on Berry Creek (1970) 7.5' quadrangle. Wells and Chambers' (1882) map shows a place called Ah Moon Bar located along North Fork Feather River just west of present Swayne Hill.

Swearingen Gulch [SISKIYOU]: *canyon,* drained by a stream that flows 1.5 miles to Indian Creek (1) 8 miles north-northwest of Happy Camp (lat. 41°54'10" N, long. 123°26'20" W). Named on Deadman Point (1981) 7.5' quadrangle. Called Kemper Gulch on Happy Camp (1956) 15' quadrangle, but United States Board on Geographic Names (1981c, p. 4) rejected this name for the feature, and noted that the name "Swearingen" is for Benoni Swearingen, who homesteaded in the neighborhood in 1892.

Sweaty Gulch [SISKIYOU]: *canyon,* drained by a stream that flows nearly 1 mile to Middle Fork Applegate River 14 miles north-northeast of Happy Camp (lat. 41°59'25" N, long. 123°17'10" W). Named on Figurehead Mountain (1980) 7.5' quadrangle.

Swede Basin [SHASTA]: *relief feature,* 8.5 miles north-northeast of Millville along present Swede Creek (lat. 40°39'30" N, long. 122°06' W; sec. 4, T 32 N, R 2 W). Named on Millville (1953) 15' quadrangle.

Swede Creek [SHASTA]: *stream,* flows 10 miles to Little Cow Creek 3.5 miles northwest of Millville (lat. 40°35'05" N, long. 122°13'30" W; sec. 32, T 32 N, R 3 W). Named on Bella Vista (1965) and Palo Cedro (1965) 7.5' quadrangles. Called French Creek on Redding (1901) 30' quadrangle, where present French Creek is called Swede Creek, but United States Board on Geographic Names (1965b, p. 13) rejected the name "French Creek" for the stream. H.O. Akerstrom of Sweden settled near the mouth of the creek in 1854 (Steger, p. 62).

Swede Creek Plains [SHASTA]: *area,* 7 miles north of Millville (lat. 40°39' N, long. 122°11' W); the place is north of Swede Creek. Named on Millville (1953) 15' quadrangle.

Swede Gulch [SISKIYOU]: *canyon,* drained by a stream that flows 2 miles to lowlands 13 miles south of Yreka (lat. 41°32'50" N, long. 122°36'15" W; sec. 25, T 43 N, R 7 W); the canyon heads on Scarface Ridge. Named on Yreka (1954) 15' quadrangle. This appears to be the feature called Scarface Gulch on Shasta (1894) 1° quadrangle.

Swedes Flat [BUTTE]: *area,* 4 miles north-northeast of Bangor (lat. 39°26'30" N, long. 121°22'30" W). Named on Bangor (1947) and Rackerby (1948) 7.5' quadrangles. Smartsville (1895) 30' quadrangle shows a locality called Swedes Flat at the site.

Sweetbriar [SHASTA]: *locality,* about 0.5 mile south of Castella along Sacramento River (lat. 41°07'50" N, long. 122°19'10" W; near NW cor. sec. 27, T 38 N, R 4 W); the place is 1.25 miles north of the mouth of Sweetbriar Creek. Named on Dunsmuir (1954) 15' quadrangle.

Sweetbrier Creek [SHASTA]: *stream,* flows 2.5 miles to Sacramento River 2 miles south of Castella (lat. 41°06'45" N, long. 122°19'30" W; near E line sec. 33, T 38 N, R 4 W); the stream is north of Sweetbrier Ridge. Named on Dunsmuir (1954) 15' quadrangle.

Sweetbrier Ridge [SHASTA]: *ridge,* generally southwest-trending, 5.5 miles long, 3.5 miles south of Castella (lat. 41°05'30" N, long. 122°19' W); the ridge is south of Sweetbriar Creek. Named on Dunsmuir (1954) 15' quadrangle.

Sweetwater Gulch [SISKIYOU]: *stream,* flows 1.25 miles to the canyon of Humbug Creek 12.5 miles southwest of Hornbrook (lat. 41°46'40" N, long. 122°44'15" W; sec. 2, T 45 N, R 8 W). Named on Hornbrook (1955) 15' quadrangle.

Swett Canyon [SHASTA]: *canyon,* drained by a stream that flows 4 miles to Middle Fork Cottonwood Creek [SHASTA-TEHAMA] nearly 1 mile north-northeast of Arbuckle Mountain (lat. 40°24'45" N, long. 122°51'40" W; sec. 34, T 30 N, R 9 W). Named on Chanchelulla Peak (1951) 15' quadrangle.

Swift Creek [SHASTA]: *stream,* flows 0.5 mile to Pit River 10.5 miles north-northeast of the village of Montgomery Creek (lat. 40°59'05" N, long. 121°50'55" W; at S line sec. 10, T 36 N, R 1 E). Named on Montgomery Creek (1956) 15' quadrangle.

Swillup Creek [SISKIYOU]: *stream,* flows 5.25 miles to Klamath River 6.5 miles north-northeast of Dillon Mountain (lat. 41°36'30" N, long. 123°30' W). Named on Bear Peak (1982) and Dillon Mountain (1983) 7.5' quadrangles.

Swiss Bar [SISKIYOU]: *locality,* 8.5 miles west-southwest of Hornbrook along Klamath River (lat. 41°51'50" N, long. 122°42'20" W; sec. 6, T 46 N, R 7 W); the place is by the mouth of Swiss Gulch. Named on Hornbrook (1955) 15' quadrangle.

Swiss Gulch [SISKIYOU]: *canyon*, drained by a stream that flows 2 miles to Klamath River 8.5 miles west-southwest of Hornbrook (lat. 41°51'50" N, long. 122°42'20" W; sec. 6, T 46 N, R 7 W). Named on Hornbrook (1955) 15' quadrangle.

Switzel-Baum Creek: see **Maple Creek** [TEHAMA].

Swobe [SISKIYOU]: *locality*, 5 miles west-northwest of Bartle (lat. 41°16'40" N, long. 121°54'50" W; at S line sec. 25, T 40 N, R 1 W). Site named on Bartle (1961) 15' quadrangle. Bartle (1939) 30' quadrangle shows the place at McCloud River Railroad.

Sycamore Creek [BUTTE]:

(1) *stream*, flows 9 miles to Mud Creek 4 miles east of Nord (lat. 39°47'05" N, long. 121°52'55" W; near SE cor. sec. 5, T 22 N, R 1 E). Named on Paradise West (1980) and Richardson Springs (1951) 7.5' quadrangles. On Chico (1895) 30' quadrangle, the canyon of the stream is called Sycamore Hollow.

(2) *stream*, flows 1.5 miles to Middle Fork Feather River 2.5 miles east-northeast of Bidwell Bar (lat. 39°34'30" N, long. 121°23'45" W; sec. 22, T 20 N, R 5 E). Named on Big Bend Mountain (1948) 15' quadrangle.

(3) *stream*, flows 0.5 mile to Lake Oroville 4.5 miles north-northeast of Oroville Dam (lat. 39°36'05" N, long. 121°28' W; near E line sec. 12, T 20 N, R 4 E). Named on Oroville Dam (1970) 7.5' quadrangle.

Sycamore Creek: see **Battle Creek** [SHASTA-TEHAMA].

Sycamore Crossing: see **Helltown** [BUTTE].

Sycamore Hill [BUTTE]: *peak*, 2.5 miles northeast of Oroville (lat. 39°32'05" N, long. 121°31'15" W; at E line sec. 4, T 19 N, R 4 E). Altitude 727 feet. Named on Oroville (1970) 7.5' quadrangle.

Sycamore Hollow: see **Sycamore Creek** [BUTTE] (1).

Sycamore Lodge [TEHAMA]: *locality*, 6 miles east of Red Bluff (lat. 40°10'15" N, long. 122°07'30" W). Named on Tehama (1905) 15' quadrangle.

Sycamore Reservoir [BUTTE]: *lake*, 450 feet long, 2 miles east-northeast of downtown Oroville (lat. 39°31'25" N, long. 121°31'10" W; near NW cor. sec. 10, T 19 N, R 4 E); the lake is less than 1 mile south of Sycamore Hill. Named on Oroville (1970) 7.5' quadrangle.

Syd Cabin Glade [TEHAMA]: *area*, 2.5 miles southwest of Tomhead Mountain (lat. 40°07' N, long. 122°51'10" W; sec. 11, T 26 N, R 9 W); the place is south of Syd Cabin Ridge. Named on Yolla Bolly (1954) 15' quadrangle.

Syd Cabin Ridge [TEHAMA]: *ridge*, generally west-southwest-trending, 2.5 miles long, 1.5 miles west-southwest of Tomhead Mountain (lat. 40°07'35" N, long. 122°50'30" W). Named on Yolla Bolly (1954) 15' quadrangle.

Symbol Bridge [SISKIYOU]: *relief feature*, 11 miles north-northeast of Medicine Lake (lat. 41°44' N, long. 121°31'30" W; near NW cor. sec. 21, T 45 N, R 4 E). Named on Medicine Lake (1952) 15' quadrangle.

— T —

Tableland: see **Big Tableland** [SISKIYOU]; **Little Tableland** [SISKIYOU].

Table Mountain [BUTTE]: *ridge*, north-northeast-trending, 1 mile long, 12 miles north of Pulga (lat. 39°58'40" N, long. 121°25'25" W; in and near sec. 33, T 25 N, R 5 E). Named on Kimshew Point (1979) 7.5' quadrangle. F.D. Dunn (p. 105) noted the name "Kimshew Table Mountain" for the feature.

Table Mountain [SHASTA]: *ridge*, north-northeast-trending, 1.5 miles long, 5.5 miles north-northwest of Lassen Peak (lat. 40°33'20" N, long. 121°33'15" W; around NE cor. sec. 7, T 31 N, R 4 E). Named on Manzanita Lake (1956) 15' quadrangle. United States Board on Geographic Names (1933, p. 736) rejected the name "Manzanita Mountain" for the feature.

Table Mountain [TEHAMA]:

(1) *relief feature*, 4 miles north-northeast of Bend (lat. 40°18'30" N, long. 122°10'25" W). Named on Bend (1965) 7.5' quadrangle.

(2) *peak*, 7.25 miles northeast of Wakefield Flat (lat. 40°11'10" N, long. 122°31'40" W; on S line sec. 15, T 27 N, R 6 W). Altitude 1106 feet. Named on Oxbow Bridge (1967) 7.5' quadrangle.

(3) *peak*, 6.25 miles south-southwest of Panther Spring (lat. 40°09'45" N, long. 121°49'15" W). Named on Panther Spring (1953) 15' quadrangle.

(4) *peak*, 5.5 miles north-northwest of Flournoy (lat. 39°59'25" N, long. 122°28'45" W; near SE cor. sec. 25, T 25 N, R 6 W). Altitude 1188 feet. Named on Flournoy (1967) 7.5' quadrangle.

Table Mountain: see **Flat Top** [SHASTA]; **North Table Mountain** [BUTTE]; **South Table Mountain** [BUTTE].

Table Mountain Creek: see **Dry Creek** [BUTTE].

Table Mountain Lake: see **Mountain Lake** [TEHAMA].

Tablemount Creek: see **Dry Creek** [BUTTE].

Table Rock [SISKIYOU]: *hill*, 18 miles west-southwest of Macdoel (lat. 41°44' N, long. 122°19'50" W; sec. 20, T 45 N, R 4 W). Altitude 3727 feet. Named on Lake Shastina (1954) 15' quadrangle. Waring (p. 219) listed Table Rock Spring, a carbonated-water feature situated at the north base of Table Rock, and Martin Soda Spring, a carbonated-water feature located near the south base of Table Rock on the property of Mrs. M.F. Martin.

Table Rock Spring: see **Table Rock** [SISKIYOU].

Tabournel Gulch [SHASTA]: *canyon*, drained by a stream that flows 1 mile to Clover Creek less than 1 mile northeast of Millville (lat. 40°33'20" N, long. 122°09'50" W; at W line sec. 12, T 31 N, R 3 W). Named on Redding (1901) 30' quadrangle.

Tadpole Creek [SHASTA]: *stream*, flows 5 miles to Olney Creek 4 miles south-southwest of Redding (lat. 40°31'45" N, long. 122°25'30" W). Named on Redding (1957) 7.5' quadrangle.

Tadpole Spring: see **Paynes Creek** [TEHAMA] (2).

Tail Holt Spring [TEHAMA]: *spring*, 1 mile southeast of Panther Spring (lat. 40°14' N, long. 121°45'40" W; at W line sec. 33, T 28 N, R 2 E). Named on Panther Spring (1953) 15' quadrangle.

Tall Cabin Creek [GLENN]: *stream*, flows 7.5 miles to Wilson Creek 9 miles northeast of Fruto (lat. 39°40'45" N, long. 122°19'45" W; sec. 17, T 21 N, R 4 W). Named on Julian Rocks (1968) 7.5' quadrangle.

Tamarack: see **Whitmore** [SHASTA].

Tamarack Flat [SISKIYOU]:

(1) *area*, 20 miles east-southeast of Etna (lat. 41°22'25" N, long. 122°31'50" W; near W line sec. 27, T 41 N, R 6 W). Named on China Mountain (1955) 15' quadrangle.

(2) *valley*, 11 miles east-southeast of Bray (lat. 41°36' N, long. 121°45'45" W; mainly in sec. 5, T 43 N, R 2 E). Named on Bray (1950) 15' quadrangle.

Tamarack Lake: see **Garner Mountain** [SISKIYOU].

Tamarack Mountain [SHASTA]: *peak*, 1 mile north-northeast of Shoeinhorse Mountain (lat. 41°05' N, long. 122°03'35" W). Named on Altitude 5221 feet. Named on Shoeinhorse Mountain (1954) 15' quadrangle.

Tamarack Mountain: see **Freaner Peak** [SHASTA].

Tamarack Peak: see **Freaner Peak** [SHASTA].

Tamarack Spring [SISKIYOU]: *spring*, 10.5 miles east-southeast of Bray (lat. 41°36'10" N, long. 121°46'30" W; near NW cor. sec. 5, T 43 N, R 2 E); the spring is just west of Tamarack Flat (2). Named on Bray (1950) 15' quadrangle.

Tamarack Spring [TEHAMA]: *spring*, 6.25 miles south of Mineral (lat. 40°15'30" N, long. 121°36'05" W). Named on Lassen Peak (1956) 15' quadrangle.

Tamarack Swale [SHASTA]: *relief feature*, 16 miles north of Lassen Peak (lat. 40°42'45" N, long. 121°31' W). Named on Manzanita Lake (1956) 15' quadrangle.

Tanner Gulch [SISKIYOU]:

(1) *canyon*, drained by a stream that flows 1.5 miles to South Fork Indian Creek (1) 7 miles northwest of Happy Camp (lat. 41°52'30" N, long. 123°27'40" W). Named on Happy Camp (1980) 7.5' quadrangle.

(2) *canyon*, drained by a stream that flows 2.25 miles to North Fork Salmon River at Sawyers Bar (lat. 41°17'50" N, long. 123°07'30" W); the canyon heads near Tanners Peak. Named on Sawyers Bar (1979) and Tanners Peak (1977) 7.5' quadrangles.

Tanners Peak [SISKIYOU]: *peak*, 2.25 miles northeast of Sawyers Bar (lat. 41°19'30" N, long. 123°06'15" W). Altitude 6615 feet. Named on Tanners Peak (1977) 7.5' quadrangle. Hobson (p. 658) referred to Tanner's Peak.

Tannery Gulch: see **Mill Gulch** [SISKIYOU].

Tapplin Gulch [SISKIYOU]: *canyon*, drained by a stream that flows 1.25 miles to Moffett Creek 13 miles south of Yreka (lat. 41°32'30" N, long. 122°40'45" W; sec. 29, T 43 N, R 7 W). Named on Yreka (1954) 15' quadrangle.

Tarantula Canyon: see **Tarantula Gulch** [SHASTA].

Tarantula Gulch [SHASTA]: *canyon*, drained by a stream that flows 2.25 miles to McCloud River [SHASTA-SISKIYOU] 6 miles north of Shoeinhorse Mountain (lat. 41°09'10" N, long. 122°04'45" W). Named on Shoeinhorse Mountain (1954) 15' quadrangle. On Dunsmuir (1935) 30' quadrangle, the stream in the lower part of the canyon is called Lost Creek, and the name "Tarantula Canyon" applies to a branch of the canyon of Lost Creek.

Tar Bully [SHASTA]: *ridge*, east-trending, 2 miles long, 7.5 miles southwest of Ono (lat. 40°23'30" N, long. 122°42'15" W; on W line sec. 6, T 29 N, R 7 W). Named on Ono (1952) 15' quadrangle.

Tar Flat [GLENN]: *area*, 10 miles south of Black Butte (lat. 39°35'05" N, long. 122°52'50" W; sec. 16, T 20 N, R 9 W). Named on Hull Mountain (1967) 7.5' quadrangle.

Tarr's Ranch: see **Wyandotte** [BUTTE].

Tate Creek [SISKIYOU]: *stream*, flows 7.25 miles to McCloud River [SHASTA-SISKIYOU] 6.25 miles west of Bartle (lat. 41°15'05" N, long. 121°56'25" W; at W line sec. 2, T 39 N, R 1 W). Named on Bartle (1961) and Big Bend (1961) 15' quadrangles.

Tater Hill [SHASTA]: *peak*, 8 miles south-southeast of Castelia (lat. 41°02' N, long. 122°15'45" W; sec. 30, T 37 N, R 3 W). Named on Dunsmuir (1954) 15' quadrangle.

Tatham Ridge [TEHAMA]: *ridge*, southeast- to south-trending, 2.25 miles long, 9 miles west-northwest of Paskenta (lat. 39°54'45" N, long. 122°42'40" W). Named on Riley Ridge (1967) 7.5' quadrangle.

Taylor: see **Keswick** [SHASTA].

Taylor Creek [SISKIYOU]:

(1) *stream*, flows 6.5 miles to East Fork of South Fork Salmon River 3 miles northeast of Cecilville (lat. 41°10'20" N, long. 123°05'35" W). Named on Coffee Creek (1955) 15' quadrangle, and on Grasshopper Ridge (1979) 7.5' quadrangle. South Fork enters from the southeast nearly 1 mile upstream from the mouth of the main creek; it is 4.5 miles long and is named on Grasshopper Ridge (1979) 7.5' quadrangle.

(2) *stream*, flows 4.5 miles to North Russian Creek 7.5 miles northeast of Sawyers Bar (lat. 41°22'10" N, long. 123°01'35" W); the stream heads at Taylor Lake. Named on Etna (1955) 15' quadrangle, and on Tanners Peak (1977) 7.5' quadrangle.

Taylor Divide [SISKIYOU]: *pass*, 8 miles southwest of Fort Jones (lat. 41°31'10" N, long. 122°56'30" W; sec. 1, T 42 N, R 10 W). Named on Fort Jones (1955) 15' quadrangle.

Taylor Gulch [SHASTA]: *canyon*, drained by a stream that flows 1.25 miles to Cottonwood Creek [SHASTA-TEHAMA] 6.5 miles south-southwest of Shasta Bally (lat. 40°31'05" N, long. 122°42'40" W; at SE cor. sec. 24, T 31 N, R 8 W). Named on Shasta Bally (1978) 7.5' quadrangle.

Taylor Lake [SISKIYOU]: *lake*, 2100 feet long, 7.5 miles south-southwest of Etna (lat. 41°21'40" N, long. 122°58' W; sec. 35, T 41 N, R 10 W). Named on Etna (1955) 15' quadrangle.

Tea Bar: see **Ti Bar** [SISKIYOU].

Tea Creek: see **Ti Creek** [SISKIYOU].

Tecnor [SISKIYOU]: *locality*, 11 miles northeast of Bray (lat. 41°44'10" N, long. 121°47'55" W; at NE cor. sec. 24, T 45 N, R 1 E). Named on Bray (1950) 15' quadrangle. Postal authorities established Tecnor post office in 1908, moved it 1 mile west the same year, discontinued it for a time in 1920, discontinued it again in 1928, reestablished it in 1930, and discontinued it finally in 1935 (Salley, p. 219).

Tedoc Gap [TEHAMA]: *pass*, 8.5 miles north-northwest of Tomhead Mountain (lat. 40°14'30" N, long. 122°54' W; near S line sec. 29, T 28 N, R 9 W); the pass is 0.5 mile southwest of Tedoc Mountain. Named on Yolla Bolly (1954) 15' quadrangle.

Tedoc Mountain [TEHAMA]: *peak*, 9 miles north-northwest of Tomhead Mountain (lat. 40°14'50" N, long. 121°53'45" W; at E line sec. 29, T 28 N, R 9 W). Named on Yolla Bolly (1954) 15' quadrangle.

Tehama [TEHAMA]: *village*, 1.5 miles west of Los Molinos on the west side of Sacramento River (lat. 40°01'40" N, long. 122°07'15" W). Named on Gerber (1950) and Los Molinos (1952) 7.5' quadrangles. Postal authorities established Tehama post office in 1851 and discontinued it for a time in 1870 (Frickstad, p. 205). The community incorporated in 1906. The place also was known as Halls Ranch and Halls Crossing (Hanna, p. 326). The name "Tehama" is of Indian origin (Kroeber, p. 61). William George Chard built a log cabin in 1846 along Sacramento River 4 miles north of present Tehama; the place was known as Sacramento House and was a popular travelers stop (Hoover, Rensch, and Rensch, p. 549). Postal authorities established Moon's Ranch post office 13 miles south of Tehama in 1851 and discontinued it in 1857 (Salley, p. 146). They established Lassen's post office 8 miles southeast of Tehama in Butte County in 1851 and discontinued it in 1860—a county boundary change in 1864 placed the site in Tehama County; they reestablished the post office with the name "Lassen" in 1870 and discontinued it in 1872 (Salley, p. 119). They established Comosa post office 7 miles west-southwest of Tehama in 1880, discontinued it in 1882, reestablished it in 1884, and discontinued it in 1885 (Salley, p. 49).

Tehama: see **Camp Tehama** [TEHAMA].

Telephone Camp [TEHAMA]: *locality*, 2 miles south of Ball Mountain (lat. 39°54'10" N, long. 122°46'30" W; near SE cor. sec. 29, T 24 N, R 8 W). Named on Ball Mountain (1967) 7.5' quadrangle.

Telephone Campground [GLENN]: *locality*, 1.5 miles north-northwest of Black Butte (lat. 39°44'55" N, long. 122°52'55" W; sec. 21, T 22 N, R 9 W). Named on Plaskett Ridge (1967) 7.5' quadrangle.

Telephone Flat [SISKIYOU]: *area*, 2 miles southeast of Medicine Lake (lat. 41°33'45" N, long. 121°34'15" W; near SE cor. sec. 13, T 43 N, R 3 E). Named on Medicine Lake (1952) 15' quadrangle.

Telephone Gulch [SHASTA]: *canyon*, drained by a stream that flows 8.5 miles to Olinda Creek 1 mile southwest of Anderson (lat. 40°26'25" N, long. 122°18'40" W; at E line sec. 21, T 30 N, R 4 W). Named on Cottonwood (1965) and Olinda (1964) 7.5' quadrangles.

Telephone Gulch [SISKIYOU]: *canyon*, drained by a stream that flows 1 mile to Duzel Creek 15 miles south-southwest of Yreka (lat. 41°32'10" N, long. 122°44'50" W; near E line sec. 34, T 43 N, R 8 W). Named on Yreka (1954) 15' quadrangle.

Telephone Lake [SISKIYOU]: *lake*, 500 feet long, 17 miles south-southeast of Etna (lat. 41°12'45" N, long. 122°48'15" W; sec. 29, T 39 N, R 8 W). Named on Coffee Creek (1955) 15' quadrangle.

Telephone Ridge [TEHAMA]: *ridge*, generally south-trending, 2.25 miles long, 2.5 miles south of Ball Mountain (lat. 39°53'40" N, long. 122°47'35" W). Named on Ball Mountain (1967) 7.5' quadrangle.

Telephone Saddle [SISKIYOU]: *pass*, 6.25 miles southeast of the village of Seiad Valley (lat. 41°46'10" N, long. 123°07'10" W). Named on Hamburg (1980) 7.5' quadrangle.

Temple Rock [SISKIYOU]: *peak*, 16 miles west-southwest of Macdoel (lat. 41°44'20" N, long. 122°18'05" W; at NE cor. sec. 21, T 45 N, R 4 W). Named on Lake Shastina (1954) 15' quadrangle.

Ten Bear Mountain [SISKIYOU]: *peak*, 4.5 miles west-southwest of Ukonom Lake (lat. 41°33'05" N, long. 123°26' W). Altitude 4822 feet. Named on Ukonom Mountain (1980) 7.5' quadrangle.

Teneyck: see **Teneyck Creek** [SISKIYOU].

Teneyck Creek [SISKIYOU]: *stream*, flows 2.5 miles to Klamath River 7.25 north-northeast of Orleans, which is in Humboldt County (lat. 41°24'10" N, long. 123°30'10" W). Named on Bark Shanty Gulch (1974) 7.5' quadrangle. Postal authorities established Teneyck post office 10 miles northwest of Orleans in 1897 and discontinued it in 1900 (Salley, p. 220).

Tenmile [TEHAMA]: *locality*, 15 miles southwest of Panther Spring (lat. 40°04'15" N, long. 121°57' W). Site named on Panther Spring (1953) 15' quadrangle.

Tenmile Creek [SISKIYOU]: *stream*, flows about 7 miles to Clear Creek (1) 3.5 miles north-northeast of Bear Peak (lat. 41°44'05" N, long. 123°32'45" W). Named on Bear Peak (1982) and Preston Peak (1982) 7.5' quadrangles. Called Ten Mile Cr. on Averill's (1935) map, but United States Board on Geographic Names (1965c, p. 12) rejected this form for the name.

Tenmile Hollow [TEHAMA]: *canyon*, drained by a stream that flows less than 1 mile to Big Dry Creek 16 miles southwest of Panther Creek (lat. 40°03'35" N, long. 121°57'20" W); the canyon heads at the site of Tenmile. Named on Panther Creek (1953) 15' quadrangle.

Tenmile House [BUTTE]: *locality*, 6 miles northwest of Paradise (lat. 39°48'20" N, long. 121°42'50" W; near E line sec. 35, T 23 N, R 2 E). Site named on Paradise (1953) 15' quadrangle. Chico (1895) 30' quadrangle has the form "10 mile House" for the name.

Tennant [SISKIYOU]: *locality*, 5 miles south-southeast of Bray (lat. 41°35'05" N, long. 121°54'40" W; sec. 12, T 43 N, R 1 W). Named on Bray (1950) 15' quadrangle. Postal authorities established Tennant post office in 1922 and discontinued it 1957; the name was for William Tennant, an official of Long Bell Lumber County (Salley, p. 220).

Tennessee Gulch [SISKIYOU]:

(1) *canyon*, drained by a stream that flows 1.25 miles to South Fork Indian Creek (1) 7.5 miles northwest of Happy Camp (lat. 41°52'35" N, long. 123°28'40" W). Named on Happy Camp (1980) 7.5' quadrangle.

(2) *canyon*, drained by a stream that flows about 2 miles to Indian Creek (3) 7 miles north of Fort Jones (lat. 41°42'15" N, long. 122°51'25" W; near E line sec. 34, T 45 N, R 9 W). Named on Fort Jones (1955) 15' quadrangle.

Tent Camp [TEHAMA]: *locality*, 5.5 miles southwest of Mineral (lat. 40°17'40" N, long. 121°40'30" W; sec. 7, T 28 N, R 3 E). Site named on Lassen Peak (1956) 15' quadrangle.

Terrace Lake [SHASTA]: *lake*, 600 feet long, 2 miles east-southeast of Lassen Peak (lat. 40°28'45" N, long. 121°28'20" W; near N line sec. 7, T 30 N, R 5 E). Named on Mount Harkness (1956) 15' quadrangle. The lake is situated on a natural terrace (Schulz, p. 55).

Terrace Lake [SISKIYOU]: *lake*, 500 feet long, 11 miles west of Dunsmuir (lat. 41°11'50" N, long. 122°28'55" W; sec. 31, T 39 N, R 5 W). Named on Dunsmuir (1954) 15' quadrangle.

Terry Lake [SHASTA]: *lake*, 1500 feet long, 9 miles east of the village of Montgomery Creek (lat. 40°49'30" N, long. 121°45'30" W; on N line sec. 9, T 34 N, R 2 E). Named on Montgomery Creek (1956) 15' quadrangle.

Terwilliger Peak [SISKIYOU]: *peak*, 22 miles west-southwest of Macdoel (lat. 41°45' N, long. 122°25'15" W; near E line sec. 16, T 45 N, R 5 W). Altitude 3468 feet. Named on Copco (1954) and Lake Shastina (1954) 15' quadrangles.

Thatcher Ridge [BUTTE]: *ridge*, south-southeast-trending, 1.5 miles long, 7 miles north-northwest of Stirling City (lat. 39°59'40" N, long. 121°35'50" W). Named on Stirling City (1979) 7.5' quadrangle.

Thatchers Meadows [SHASTA]: *area*, 13 miles west-northwest of Lassen Peak (lat. 40°34' N, long. 121°44' W; sec. 3, T 31 N, R 2 E). Named on Manzanita Lake (1956) 15' quadrangle.

The Basin [GLENN]: *relief feature*, 9 miles south of Black Butte (lat. 39°35'45" N, long. 122°51'25" W; on S line sec. 10, T 20 N, R 9 W). Named on Kneecap Ridge (1967) 7.5' quadrangle.

The Bend [SHASTA]: *bend*, 8 miles north of Shoeinhorse Mountain along McCloud River [SHASTA-SISKIYOU] (lat. 41°10'50" N, long. 122°04'05" W; sec. 34, T 39 N, R 2 W). Named on Shoeinhorse Mountain (1954) 15' quadrangle.

The Burn [TEHAMA]: *area*, 7 miles east-southeast of Manton (lat. 40°23'45" N, long. 121°45' W). Named on Lassen Peak (1956) and Manton (1956) 15' quadrangles.

The Castles [SISKIYOU]: *relief feature*, 11 miles north-northeast of Medicine Lake (lat. 41°44' N, long. 121°32'10" W; near N line sec. 20, T 45 N, R 4 E). Named on Medicine Lake (1952) 15' quadrangle.

The Caves: see **Pluto Cave** [SISKIYOU].

The Cedars [SISKIYOU]: *locality,* 6.25 miles north-northeast of Sawyers Bar (lat. 41°22'55" N, long. 123°05' W). Named on Yellow Dog Peak (1977) 7.5' quadrangle.

The Corduroy [SHASTA]: *area,* 20 miles north-northwest of Lassen Peak (lat. 40°43' N, long. 121°42'50" W; sec. 14, T 33 N, R 2 E). Named on Manzanita Lake (1956) 15' quadrangle.

The Cove [SHASTA]: *relief feature,* 2 miles north-northwest of the village of Montgomery Creek (lat. 40°53' N, long. 121°56'30" W). Named on Montgomery Creek (1956) 15' quadrangle.

The Eddys [SISKIYOU]: *area,* west of the town of Mount Shasta on Siskiyou-Trinity County line; the area is around Mount Eddy. Named on Bonanza King (1955), China Mountain (1955), Dunsmuir (1954), and Weed (1954) 15' quadrangles.

The Frog Pond [SISKIYOU]: *area,* a drained part of former Tule Lake 5.5 miles south of Tulelake on Siskiyou-Modoc County line (lat. 41°52'50" N, long. 121°27'30" W). Named on Tulelake (1951) 15' quadrangle.

The Gardens [SHASTA]: *area,* 20 miles north-northwest of Lassen Peak (lat. 40°44'25" N, long. 121°41'30" W; near SE cor. sec. 1, T 33 N, R 2 E). Named on Manzanita Lake (1956) 15' quadrangle. Called Gardens on Burney (1939) 30' quadrangle.

The Gate [SISKIYOU]: *pass,* 8 miles north-northwest of McCloud (lat. 41°21'50" N, long. 122°11' W; at S line sec. 27, T 41 N, R 3 W). Named on Shasta (1954) 15' quadrangle.

The Gorge [TEHAMA]: *narrows,* 6.5 miles west-southwest of Paskenta along Thomes Creek (lat. 39°51'25" N, long. 122°39'55" W; near E line sec. 17, T 23 N, R 7 W). Named on Hall Ridge (1967) 7.5' quadrangle.

The High Rocks [BUTTE]: *peaks,* 5.5 miles north-northeast of Oroville (lat. 39°35'25" N, long. 121°31'10" W; near W line sec. 15, T 20 N, R 4 E). Named on Oroville (1970) 7.5' quadrangle.

The Hogback [TEHAMA]: *relief feature,* 6.5 miles east-northeast of Red Bluff (lat. 40°12'35" N, long. 122°07'10" W). Named on Tuscan Springs (1951) 7.5' quadrangle

The Incline [SHASTA]: *canyon,* drained by a stream that flows 1.25 miles to Slate Creek (2) 9 miles north of Schell Mountain (lat. 40°58'50" N, long. 122°30'30" W; sec. 13, T 36 N, R 6 W). Named on Schell Mountain (1950) 15' quadrangle.

The Island [SHASTA]: *area,* 7 miles north-northwest of Fall River Mills between Spring Creek, Lava Creek, Little Tule River, Tule River, and Fall River (lat. 41°06' N, long. 121°28'30" W). Named on Fall River Mills (1961) and Pondosa (1961) 15' quadrangles.

The Island: see **Hartley Island** [GLENN].

The Lagoon [BUTTE]: *lake,* nearly 1 mile long, occupies a cutoff bend of Sacramento River 10 miles west-southwest of Durham (lat. 39°36'15" N, long. 121°58'30" W). Named on Llano Seco (1948) 7.5' quadrangle.

The Lieutenants [SISKIYOU]: *peaks,* two, 0.5 mile apart, 3 miles north of Preston Peak (lat. 41°52'40" N, long. 123°35'45" W). Altitude of highest peak is 6205 feet. Named on Polar Bear Mountain (1982) 7.5' quadrangle.

The Narrows [BUTTE]: *relief feature,* narrow place on a ridge 6 miles south-west of Paradise (lat. 39°41'25" N, long. 121°42'05" W; sec. 12, T 21 N, R 2 E). Named on Hamlin Canyon (1951) 7.5' quadrangle.

The Narrows [TEHAMA]:

(1) *relief feature,* narrow place on a ridge 4 miles north of Polk Springs (lat. 40°10'30" N, long. 121°40' W; at S line sec. 20, T 27 N, R 3 E). Named on Butte Meadows (1958) 15' quadrangle.

(2) *narrows,* 5.25 miles east-southeast of Wakefield Flat along Red Bank Creek (lat. 40°06'20" N, long. 122°32'45" W; sec. 16, T 26 N, R 6 W). Named on Lowrey (1967) 7.5' quadrangle.

(3) *relief feature,* narrow place on a ridge 14 miles south-southwest of Panther Spring (lat. 40°04'55" N, long. 121°54'45" W). Named on Panther Spring (1953) 15' quadrangle.

The Pines [BUTTE]: *locality,* 6 miles east-southeast of Paradise (lat. 39°43'35" N, long. 121°31'25" W; at NE cor. sec. 33, T 22 N, R 4 E). Named on Cherokee (1970) 7.5' quadrangle.

The Plantation [SHASTA]: *area,* 6.5 miles west-northwest of Lassen Peak (lat. 40°31'15" N, long. 121°36'50" W; on E line sec. 22, T 31 N, R 3 E). Named on Manzanita Lake (1956) 15' quadrangle.

The Pocket [GLENN]: *relief feature,* 2.25 miles north-northwest of Saint John Mountain (lat. 39°27'55" N, long. 122°42'35" W). Named on Saint John Mountain (1968) 7.5' quadrangle.

The Rim [SHASTA]: *relief feature,* steep south side of the canyon of North Fork Hatchet Creek 3.25 miles east-southeast of the village of Montgomery Creek (lat. 40°49'30" N, long. 121°51'55" W). Named on Montgomery Creek (1956) 15' quadrangle.

Thermalito [BUTTE]: *town,* 1.5 miles west of downtown Oroville (lat. 39°30'30" N, long. 121°35'15" W). Named on Oroville (1970) and Palermo (1970) 7.5' quadrangles. Postal authorities established Thermalito post office in 1895 and discontinued it in 1920 (Frickstad, p. 12).

Thermalito Afterbay [BUTTE]: *water feature,* empties into Feather River 5 miles northeast of Biggs (lat. 39°27'30" N, long. 121°38'20" W). Named on Biggs (1970) and Shippee (1948, photorevised 1969) 7.5' quadrangles.

Thermalito Diversion Pool [BUTTE]: *water feature,* behind a dam on Feather River 1.25 miles north-northeast of downtown Oroville (lat. 39°31'40" N, long. 121°12'35" W; sec. 5, T 19 N, R 4 E). Named on Oroville (1970) and Oroville Dam (1970) 7.5' quadrangles.

Thermalito Forebay [BUTTE]: *lake,* behind a dam 4 miles west of Oroville (lat. 39°30'55" N, long. 121°37'45" W; near W line sec. 10, T 19 N, R 3 E). Named on Oroville (1970) and Shippee (1948, photorevised 1969) 7.5' quadrangles.

The Saddle [SHASTA]: *pass,* 2.5 miles west of Fall River Mills (lat. 41°00'30" N, long. 121°29'15" W; at SE cor. sec. 27, T 37 N, R 4 E). Named on Fall River Mills (1961) 15' quadrangle.

The Thumb of the Glove: see **Hardin Butte** [SISKIYOU].

The Vineyard [TEHAMA]: *locality,* 6.5 miles west-southwest of Panther Spring (lat. 40°12'35" N, long. 121°53'15" W). Named on Panther Spring (1953) 15' quadrangle.

The Whaleback [SISKIYOU]: *ridge,* east-trending, 3.5 miles long, 21 miles south-southwest of Macdoel (lat. 41°31'50" N, long. 122°07'15" W). Named on The Whaleback (1954) 15' quadrangle. On Macdoel (1941) 30' quadrangle, the name applies to a peak near the west end of the ridge—Shasta (1894) 1° quadrangle has the name "Black Crater" for this same peak. Called Whaleback Mt. on O'Brien's (1947) map. United States Board on Geographic Names (1970b, p. 2) gave the names "Black Crater" and "Whaleback Mountain" as variants.

Thimbleberry Ridge [SISKIYOU]: *ridge,* south-trending, 4 miles long, center 3 miles north of McCloud (lat. 41°18' N, long. 122°09' W). Named on Shasta (1954) 15' quadrangle.

Thomas Creek [SISKIYOU]: *stream,* flows 2 miles to Klamath River 6 miles northeast of Orleans Mountain (lat. 41°36'05" N, long. 123°30'10" W). Named on Dillon Mountain (1983) and Ukonom Mountain (1980) 7.5' quadrangles.

Thomas Creek: see **Thomes Creek** [TEHAMA].

Thomas Hill: see **Hardin Butte** [SISKIYOU].

Thomas Pocket Ridge [TEHAMA]: *ridge,* south-trending, 2.5 miles long, 9.5 miles south-southwest of Tomhead Mountain (lat. 40°01' N, long. 122°53'35" W). Named on Yolla Bolly (1954) 15' quadrangle, and on Buck Rock (1967) 7.5' quadrangle.

Thomes Creek [TEHAMA]: *stream,* flows 62 miles to Sacramento River 4.5 miles north-northwest of Vina (lat. 39°59'25" N, long. 122°05'40" W). Named on Yolla Bolly (1954) 15' quadrangle, and on Ball Mountain (1967), Buck Rock (1967), Corning (1951), Flournoy (1967), Hall Ridge (1967), Henleyville (1967), Log Spring (1967), Newville (1967), Paskenta (1967), and Vina (1950) 7.5' quadrangles. Called Thoms Cr. on Paskenta (1920) 15' quadrangle, but United States Board on Geographic Names (1968b, p. 10) rejected the names "Thoms Creek," "Toms Creek," and "Thomas Creek" for the stream. The name commemorates Robert H. Thomes, who held Los Saucos grant; the stream was called Arroyo Arenoso on some early maps (Gudde, 1969, p. 13).

Thompson Creek [SISKIYOU]: *stream,* heads in the State of Oregon and flows 11.5 mile in Siskiyou County to Klamath River 6 miles north-northeast of Happy Camp (lat. 41°51'50" N, long. 123°18'25" W). Named on Deadman Point (1981), Figurehead Mountain (1980), and Slater Butte (1980) 7.5' quadrangles. East Fork enters from the northeast 10.5 miles north of Happy Camp; it is 2.5 miles long and is named on Figurehead Mountain (1980) 7.5' quadrangle.

Thompson Creek: see **Little South Fork of South Fork**, under **Salmon River** [SISKIYOU].

Thompson Dry Diggings: see **Yreka** [SISKIYOU].

Thompson Flat [BUTTE]: *area,* 1.5 miles north-northwest of Oroville (lat. 39°32'10" N, long. 121°34' W; in and near sec. 6, T 19 N, R 4 E). Named on Oroville (1970) 7.5' quadrangle. Oroville (1912) 7.5' quadrangle shows a community called Thompson Flat located just east of the area (sec. 5, T 19 N, R 4 E). Postal authorities established Thompson's Flat post office in 1857 and discontinued it in 1870 (Frickstad, p. 12). An early mining camp along Feather River was called Rich Bar or Rich Gulch; when the gold gave out, the camp was moved to present Thompson Flat and named New Philadelphia; later the place was called Thompsons Flat, for G.W. Thompson, who headed a company that brought water to the diggings in a ditch (Dunn, F.D., p. 106).

Thompson Gulch [SISKIYOU]: *canyon,* drained by a stream that flows 1.5 miles to Wildcat Creek 11 miles south-southeast of Etna (lat. 41°18'35" N, long. 122°49'25" W; near SE cor. sec. 13, T 40 N, R 9 W). Named on Etna (1955) 15' quadrangle.

Thompson Ridge [SISKIYOU]: *ridge,* generally south-trending, 7.5 miles long, center 10 miles north of Happy Camp (lat. 41°56'45" N, long. 123°23'30" W); the ridge is west of Thompson Creek. Named on Deadman Point (1981) and Figurehead Mountain (1980) 7.5' quadrangles.

Thompsons [BUTTE]: *locality,* 13 miles north of Paradise (lat. 39°56'35" N, long. 121°33'15" W). Named on Chico (1895) 30' quadrangle.

Thoms Creek: see **Thomes Creek** [TEHAMA].

Thousand Lakes Valley [SHASTA]: *valley,* 16 miles north-northwest of Lassen Peak (lat. 40°43'10" N, long. 121°34'30" W). Named on Manzanita Lake (1956) 15' quadrangle. Called Thousand Lake Valley on Burney (1939) 30' quadrangle.

Thousand Springs [SHASTA]: *locality,* 9 miles north-northeast of Burney Falls (lat. 41°07'10" N, long. 121°33'15" W; sec. 19, T 38 N, R 4 E). Named on Pondosa (1961) 15' quadrangle.

Thrall: see **Ager** [SISKIYOU].

Three Biscuit Gulch [SISKIYOU]: *canyon,* drained by a stream that flows 1.25 miles to South Fork China Creek (1) (lat. 41°47'05" N, long. 123°16'45" W). Named on Slater Butte (1980) 7.5' quadrangle.

Three Creeks [SISKIYOU]: *stream,* flows 1.5 miles to Klamath River 4 miles north-northeast of Dillon Mountain (lat. 41°34'50" N, long. 123°32'05" W). Named on Dillon Mountain (1983) 7.5' quadrangle.

Three Devils: see **Lower Devils Peak** [SISKIYOU].

Three-dollar Bar [SISKIYOU]: *locality,* 10.5 miles northwest of Forks of Salmon along Salmon River (lat. 41°22'30" N, long. 123°26'30" W). Named on Orleans Mountain (1974) and Somes Bar (1979) 7.5' quadrangles.

Three Prong Campground [TEHAMA]: *locality,* 1 mile south-southwest of Ball Mountain (lat. 39°55'15" N, long. 122°47'25" W; near W line sec. 20, T 24 N, R 8 W); the place is at Three Prong Valley. Named on Ball Mountain (1967) 7.5' quadrangle.

Three Prong Valley [TEHAMA]: *area,* 1 mile south-southwest of Ball Mountain (lat. 39°55'10" N, long. 122°47'30" W; on E line sec. 19, T 24 N, R 8 W). Named on Ball Mountain (1967) 7.5' quadrangle.

Three Sisters [SISKIYOU]:

(1) *peaks,* three, 12 miles northwest of Medicine Lake on a north-trending ridge 1.5 miles long (lat. 41°43' N, long. 121°44'20" W). Named on Medicine Lake (1952) 15' quadrangle. United States Board on Geographic Names (1967b, p. 4) approved the name "Six Shooter Pass" for a pass situated 1 mile east of the north end of Three Sisters (sec. 23, T 45 N, R 2 E).

(2) *peaks,* three, 12.5 miles north-northeast of Medicine Lake (lat. 41°44'40" N, long. 121°28'10" W; at E line sec. 14, T 45 N, R 4 E). Named on Timber Mountain (1952) 15' quadrangle.

Thumb of the Glove: see **The Thumb of the Glove,** under **Hardin Butte** [SISKIYOU].

Thumb Rock [SISKIYOU]: *relief feature,* 10.5 miles north-northwest of McCloud (lat. 41°23'50" N, long. 122°11'45" W; sec. 16, T 41 N, R 3 W). Named on Shasta (1954) 15' quadrangle.

Thunder Camp [TEHAMA]: *locality,* 3.25 miles south of Tomhead Mountain (lat. 40°05'20" N, long. 122°49'20" W; sec. 24, T 26 N, R 9 W). Named on Yolla Bolly (1954) 15' quadrangle.

Ti Bar [SISKIYOU]: *locality,* 2.5 miles east of Dillon Mountain along Klamath River (lat. 41°31'50" N, long. 123°31'35" W); the place is near the mouth of Ti Creek. Named on Dillon Mountain (1983) 7.5' quadrangle. The mining camp at the place was called both Tea Bar and Ti Bar; the name is from the designation of an Indian village (Gudde, 1975, p. 346).

Tichner Creek: see **Tickner Creek** [SISKIYOU].

Tickner Cave [SISKIYOU]: *cave,* 8 miles north-northeast of Medicine Lake (lat. 41°41'15" N, long. 121°31'50" W; sec. 5, T 44 N, R 4 E). Named on Medicine Lake (1952) 15' quadrangle.

Tickner Creek [SISKIYOU]: *stream,* flows nearly 2 miles to Granite Creek (2) 3.5 miles northeast of Ukonom Lake (lat. 41°36'25" N, long. 123°17'55" W). Named on Ukonom Lake (1980) 7.5' quadrangle. United States Board on Geographic Names (1981c, p. 4) rejected the form "Tichner Creek" for the name.

Tickner Hole [SISKIYOU]: *valley,* 1.25 miles east-northeast of Ukonom Lake (lat. 47°35'05" N, long. 123°19'50" W); the valley is along upper reaches of Tickner Creek. Named on Ukonom Lake (1980) 7.5' quadrangle.

Tickner Lake [SISKIYOU]: *lake,* 250 feet long, 1.25 miles east of Ukonom Lake (lat. 41°34'40" N, long. 123°19'50" W). Named on Ukonom Lake (1980) 7.5' quadrangle.

Ti Creek [SISKIYOU]: *stream,* flows 6 miles to Klamath River 2.5 miles east of Dillon Mountain (lat. 41°31'35" N, long. 123°31'40" W). Named on Dillon Mountain (1983) and Ukonom Mountain (1980) 7.5' quadrangles. Called Tea Creek on Preston Peak (1922) 30' quadrangle, but United States Board on Geographic Names (1960a, p. 18) rejected this form for the name.

Ti Creek Meadows [SISKIYOU]: *area,* 6 miles southwest of Ukonom Lake (lat. 41°30'35" N, long. 123°25'10" W); the place is near the head of a branch of Ti Creek. Named on Ukonom Mountain (1980) 7.5' quadrangle.

Tiger Fork: see **Sugar Creek** [SISKIYOU].

Tigus Creek [BUTTE]: *stream,* flows 1 mile to Middle Fork Feather River 3.5 miles east of the village of Brush Creek (lat. 39°42' N, long. 121°16'10" W). Named on Brush Creek (1970) 7.5' quadrangle.

Tilden: see **Brush Creek** [BUTTE] (2).

Tillman Lake: see **Lower Twin Lake** [SHASTA] (2).

Timber Camp [SISKIYOU]: *locality,* 8.5 miles north-northeast of Cecilville (lat. 41°14'50" N, long. 123°02'45" W). Site named on Grasshopper Ridge (1979) 7.5' quadrangle.

Timber Canyon: see **Bills Creek** [SHASTA].

Timbered Crater [SHASTA]: *crater,* 12 miles north of Fall River Mills (lat. 41°10'20" N, long. 121°29'30" W). Named on Fall River Mills (1961) 15' quadrangle.

Timber Gulch [SISKIYOU]:

(1) *canyon,* drained by a stream that flows nearly 1 mile to South Fork Salmon River about 1 mile west of Cecilville (lat. 41°08'30" N, long. 123°09'10" W). Named on Cecilville (1979) 7.5' quadrangle.

(2) *canyon,* drained by a stream that flows less than 1 mile to Klamath River 12.5 miles east-southeast of Condrey Mountain (lat. 41°51'20" N, long. 122°46'10" W; sec. 10, T 46 N, R 8 W). Named on Condrey Mountain (1955) 15' quadrangle.

(3) *canyon,* drained by a stream that flows 1.5 miles to Cherry Creek (2) 8.5 miles north-northeast of Fort Jones (lat. 41°43'05" N, long. 122°46'45" W; sec. 28, T 45 N, R 8 W). Named on Fort Jones (1955) 15' quadrangle.

Timber Lake [SISKIYOU]: *lake,* 600 feet long, 8 miles west of Dunsmuir (lat. 41°12'50" N, long. 122°25'40" W; sec. 27, T 39 N, R 5 W). Named on Dunsmuir (1954) 15' quadrangle. The lake is one of the group called Gray Rock Lakes on Dunsmuir (1935) 30' quadrangle.

Timber Ridge [GLENN-TEHAMA]: *ridge,* south-trending, 2 miles long, 9 miles south of Ball Mountain on Glenn-Tehama County line (lat. 39°48'15" N, long. 122°46'30" W). Named on Log Spring (1967) 7.5' quadrangle.

Timber Ridge [TEHAMA]: *ridge,* east-northeast-trending, 1.5 miles long, 10 miles southwest of Ball Mountain (lat. 39°50'45" N, long. 122°56'15" W). Named on Mendocino Pass (1967) 7.5' quadrangle. United States Board on Geographic Names (1988b, p. 3) approved the name "Derby Ridge" for the feature—the name commemorates William Flagg Derby, former assistant supervisor of Mendocino National Forest.

Timothy Gulch [SISKIYOU]: *canyon,* drained by a stream that flows 1.5 miles to Bug Gulch 13 miles north of Sawyers Bar (lat. 41°28'35" N, long. 123°05'15" W). Named on Yellow Dog Peak (1977) 7.5' quadrangle.

Tims Creek [SISKIYOU]: *stream,* flows 1.5 miles to Klamath River 6.5 miles northeast of Happy Camp (lat. 41°52'05" N, long. 123°17'55" W); the stream heads near Tims Peak. Named on Figurehead Mountain (1980) and Slater Butte (1980) 7.5' quadrangles.

Tims Peak [SISKIYOU]: *peak,* 8 miles north-northeast of Happy Camp (lat. 41°53'45" N, long. 123°18' W). Altitude 4872 feet. Named on Figurehead Mountain (1980) 7.5' quadrangle.

Tincup Gulch [SHASTA]: *canyon,* drained by a stream that flows 1 mile to Crow Gulch 2.25 miles southeast of Arbuckle Mountain (lat. 40°22'45" N, long. 122°50' W; sec. 12, T 29 N, R 9 W). Named on Chanchelulla Peak (1951) 15' quadrangle. The name is from the claim of miners that they could take a tin cup full of gold from the canyon each day (Steger, p. 63).

Tincup Gulch [SISKIYOU]: *canyon,* drained by a stream that flows less than 1 mile to Humbug Creek 13 miles southwest of Hornbrook (lat. 41°46'30" N, long. 122°43'15" W; sec. 1, T 45 N, R 8 W). Named on Hornbrook (1955) 15' quadrangle.

Tinkham Creek [SISKIYOU]: *stream,* flows 2.5 miles to Titus Creek 7.25 miles north-northwest of Ukonom Lake (lat. 41°40'10" N, long. 123°25'30" W). Named on Clear Creek (1981) 7.5' quadrangle.

Titcomb Gulch [SISKIYOU]: *canyon,* drained by a stream that flows less than 1 mile to Rattlesnake Creek 4.5 miles north-northwest of Fort Jones (lat. 41°39'55" N, long. 122°53' W; sec. 16, T 44 N, R 9 W). Named on Fort Jones (1955) 15' quadrangle.

Titmouse Gulch [SISKIYOU]: *canyon,* drained by a stream that flows 1.25 miles to Little North Fork Salmon River 4 miles northwest of Sawyers Bar (lat. 41°20'50" N, long. 123°10'50" W). Named on Sawyers Bar (1979) 7.5' quadrangle.

Titus Creek [SISKIYOU]: *stream,* flows 3.5 miles to Klamath River 7.5 miles north-northwest of Ukonom Lake (lat. 41°40'15" N, long. 123°25'45" W); the stream heads on Titus Ridge. Named on Clear Creek (1981) 7.5' quadrangle. Middle Fork enters about 0.5 mile upstream from the mouth of the main creek; it is 2.25 miles long and is named on Clear Creek (1981) 7.5' quadrangle. United States Board on Geographic Names (1985a, p. 4) approved the name "Titus Gap" for a pass situated on Titus Ridge at the head of Titus Creek (lat. 41°41'44" N, long. 123°22'38" W; sec. 14, T 15 N, R 7 E). Clear Creek (1981) 7.5' quadrangle shows the pass situated about 3.5 miles south-southwest of the location given by the Board (lat. 41°38'50" N, long. 123°24'40" W).

Titus Gap: see **Titus Creek** [SISKIYOU].

Titus Ridge [SISKIYOU]: *ridge,* generally north-northwest-trending, 15 miles long, center about 6.5 miles north of Ukonom Lake (lat. 41°40'30" N, long. 123°22'15" W). Named on Clear Creek (1981), Happy Camp (1980), Huckleberry Mountain (1980), and Ukonom Lake (1980) 7.5' quadrangles.

Tlamath River: see **Klamath River** [SISKIYOU].

Toad Lake [SISKIYOU]:

(1) *lake,* 1700 feet long, 10 miles west of the town of Mount Shasta (lat. 41°16'55" N, long. 122°30' W; sec. 36, T 40 N, R 6 W). Named on China Mountain (1955) and Weed (1954) 15' quadrangles.

(2) *intermittent lake,* 700 feet long, 11 miles north-northeast of Bartle (lat. 41°24'10" N, long. 121°45'05" W; near SW cor. sec. 9, T 41 N, R 2 E); the feature is 1 mile southeast of Toad Mountain. Named on Bartle (1961) 15' quadrangle.

Toad Mountain [SISKIYOU]: *hill,* 11 miles north-northeast of Bartle (lat. 41°24'55" N, long. 121°45'45" W; at S line sec. 5, T 41 N, R 2 E). Altitude 5292 feet. Named on Bartle (1961) 15' quadrangle.

Toadtown [BUTTE]: *locality,* 3.5 miles west-southwest of Stirling City along Little Butte Creek (lat. 39°53'15" N, long. 121°35'25" W; near S line sec. 36, T 24 N, R 3 E). Named on Stirling City (1979) 7.5' quadrangle. The place first was called Allentown; according to one account, the children of the community were tow heads, and the present name is a corruption of the term "Tow Town" (Dunn, F.D., p. 106).

Toad Well [SISKIYOU]: *well,* 10.5 mile north-northeast of Bartle (lat. 41°24'05" N, long. 121°45'25" W; near SE cor. sec. 8, T 41 N, R 2 E); the well is 1 mile south-southeast of Toad Mountain. Named on Bartle (1961) 15' quadrangle.

Tobacco Lake [SISKIYOU]: *lake,* 350 feet long, 10 miles north-northwest of Sawyers Bar (lat. 41°25'05" N, long. 123°13'55" W). Named on English Peak (1977) 7.5' quadrangle.

Todd Island [TEHAMA]: *island,* 4.25 miles north of Gerber along Sacramento River (lat. 40°06'55" N, long. 122°08'10" W). Named on Gerber (1950, photorevised 1969) 7.5' quadrangle.

Toehead Lake [SISKIYOU]: *intermittent lake,* 250 feet long, 6 miles north of the village of Seiad Valley (lat. 41°55'40" N, long. 123°11'40" W). Named on Kangaroo Mountain (1980) 7.5' quadrangle. United States Board on Geographic Names (1983c, p. 7) approved the name "Towhead Lake" for the feature.

Tolladay Peak [SHASTA]: *peak,* nearly 5 miles south-southeast of the village of Montgomery Creek (lat. 40°46'50" N, long. 121°53'05" W; near S line sec. 20, T 34 N, R 1 E). Altitude 3958 feet. Named on Montgomery Creek (1956) 15' quadrangle.

Tollgate [SHASTA]: *locality,* 12.5 miles north-northeast of Millville (lat. 40°42'55" N, long. 122°04'55" W; sec. 15, T 33 N, R 2 W). Site named on Millville (1953) 15' quadrangle.

Tollhouse [SHASTA]: *locality,* 4.25 miles north of Schell Mountain (lat. 40°55' N, long. 122°31'40" W; sec. 3, T 35 N, R 6 W). Named on Schell Mountain (1950) 15' quadrangle.

Toll's Old Diggins: see **Forbestown** [BUTTE].

Tomar: see **Cottage Grove** [SISKIYOU].

Tombstone Mountain [SHASTA]: *peak,* 7.25 miles south-southeast of Castella (lat. 41°02'50" N, long. 122°15'10" W; near S line sec. 19, T 37 N, R 3 W). Named on Dunsmuir (1954) 15' quadrangle.

Tom Dow Creek [SHASTA]: *stream,* flows 4.5 miles to Squaw Valley Creek 7 miles west of Shoeinhorse Mountain (lat. 41°03'05" N, long. 122°12' W; sec. 22, T 37 N, R 3 W). Named on Shoeinhorse Mountain (1954) 15' quadrangle.

Tom Gray Gulch [SISKIYOU]: *canyon,* drained by a stream that flows 2 miles to Indian Creek (1) 9.5 miles north-northwest of Happy Camp (lat. 41°55' N, long. 123°28' W; sec. 25, T 18 N, R 6 E). Named on Deadman Point (1981) and Polar Bear Mountain (1982) 7.5' quadrangles.

Tom Head Creek [SHASTA]: *stream,* flows 1 mile to Salt Creek (6) 9 miles southeast of Lamoine (lat. 40°53' N, long. 122°18'35" W; sec. 15, T 35 N, R 4 W). Named on Lamoine (1957) 15' quadrangle.

Tomhead Gulch [TEHAMA]: *canyon,* drained by a stream that flows 2.5 miles to Long Gulch (3) 3 miles west-southwest of Tomhead Mountain (lat. 40°07'45" N, long. 122°52'20" W; near W line sec. 3, T 26 N, R 9 W). Named on Yolla Bolly (1954) 15' quadrangle.

Tomhead Mountain [TEHAMA]: *peak,* 30 miles west of Red Bluff (lat. 40°08'10" N, long. 122°49' W; near NW cor. sec. 6, T 26 N, R 8 W). Named on Yolla Bolly (1954) 15' quadrangle. Called Tom's Head on Red Bluff (1894) 1° quadrangle, and called Toms Head on California Mining Bureau's (1917b) map. United States Board on Geographic Names (1978c, p. 3) approved the name "Nuisance Ridge" for a feature, 2.5 miles long, that extends east from Tomhead Mountain.

Tomhead Spring [TEHAMA]: *spring,* less than 1 mile west-southwest of Tomhead Mountain (lat. 40°08' N, long. 122°49'45" W; sec. 1, T 26 N, R 9 W). Named on Yolla Bolly (1954) 15' quadrangle.

Tom Jones Reservoir [BUTTE]: *lake,* 10 miles south-southeast of Paradise (lat. 39°37'35" N, long. 121°31'55" W; near S line sec. 33, T 21 N, R 4 E). Named on Cherokee (1970) 7.5' quadrangle.

Tom Martin Creek [SISKIYOU]: *stream,* flows nearly 4 miles to Klamath River 9 miles east-southeast of the village of Seiad Valley (lat. 41°47'05" N, long. 123°02'25" W; near E line sec. 31, T 46 N, R 10 W). Named on Hamburg (1980) and Scott Bar (1980) 7.5' quadrangles.

Tom Martin Peak [SISKIYOU]: *peak,* nearly 4 miles west of Scott Bar (lat. 41°44'20" N, long. 123°04'35" W); the peak is near the head of Tom Martin Creek. Altitude 7021 feet. Named on Scott Bar (1980) 7.5' quadrangle.

Tom Neal Creek [SHASTA]: *stream,* flows nearly 5 miles to Squaw Valley Creek [SHASTA-SISKIYOU] 7 miles east-northeast of Shoeinhorse Mountain (lat. 41°05'45" N, long. 122°12' W; sec. 33, T 38 N, R 3 W). Named on Dunsmuir (1954) and Shoeinhorse Mountain (1954) 15' quadrangles. North Fork enters from the north 2.5 miles upstream from the mouth of the main creek; it is 2 miles long and is named on Shoeinhorse Mountain (1954) 15' quadrangle

Tom Neil Creek: see **Slate Creek** [SHASTA] (1).

Tom Payne Creek [SISKIYOU]: *stream,* flows nearly 2 miles to Salmon River 9 miles north-northwest of Forks of Salmon (lat. 41°21'55" N, long. 123°24'45" W); the stream heads near Tom Payne Peak. Named on Orleans Mountain (1974) 7.5' quadrangle.

Tom Payne Peak [SISKIYOU]: *peak,* 8 miles north-northwest of Forks of Salmon (lat. 41°22'25" N, long. 123°21'45" W). Altitude 5098 feet. Named on Forks of Salmon (1978) 7.5' quadrangle.

Tompkins Creek [SISKIYOU]: *stream,* flows 5.25 miles to Scott River 6.5 miles southwest of Scott Bar (lat. 41°40'50" N, long. 123°05'45" W). Named on Scott Bar (1980) 7.5' quadrangle.

Toms Cabin Gulch [SISKIYOU]: *canyon,* drained by a stream that flows nearly 2 miles to Jaynes Canyon 3 miles east of Condrey Mountain (lat. 41°56'45" N, long. 122°55'15" W; near N line sec. 8, T 47 N, R 9 W). Named on Condrey Mountain (1955) 15' quadrangle.

Tom's Camp [TEHAMA]: *locality,* 11.5 miles west-northwest of Paskenta (lat. 39°56'30" N, long. 122°44'55" W; sec. 15, T 24 N, R 8 W). Named on Paskenta (1920) 15' quadrangle.

Toms Creek: see **Thomes Creek** [TEHAMA].

Toms Gulch [TEHAMA]: *canyon,* drained by a stream that flows 1 mile to Sulphur Gulch (1) 5.5 miles east-southeast of Beegum Peak (lat. 40°16'40" N, long. 122°47'35" W; sec. 17, T 28 N, R 8 W). Named on Chanchelulla Peak (1951) 15' quadrangle.

Tom's Head: see **Tomhead Mountain** [TEHAMA].

Toms Lake [SISKIYOU]:

(1) *lake,* 800 feet long, 5 miles east of Ukonom Lake (lat. 41°33'55" N, long. 123°15'50" W); the lake is at the head of Toms Valley Creek. Named on Ukonom Lake (1980) 7.5' quadrangle.

(2) *lake,* 350 feet long, 9 miles northwest of Sawyers Bar (lat. 41°24'25" N, long. 123°13'25" W). Named on English Peak (1977) 7.5' quadrangle, which shows Tom Taylor cabin located about 0.5 mile south of the lake.

Toms Valley Creek [SISKIYOU]: *stream,* flows 2.5 miles to Elk Creek 5.25 miles east-northeast of Ukonom Lake (lat. 41°36'05" N, long. 123°15'30" W); the stream heads at Toms Lake (1). Named on Ukonom Lake (1980) 7.5' quadrangle.

Tom Young Flat [SISKIYOU]: *area,* 6.5 miles east-southeast of Bartle (lat. 41°13'40" N, long. 121°41'50" W; in and near sec. 11, T 39 N, R 2 E). Named on Pondosa (1961) 15' quadrangle.

Tool Cache Ridge [GLENN]: *ridge,* northeast-trending, 1.5 miles long, 7 miles west-southwest of the village of Elk Creek (lat. 39°33' N, long. 122°39'15" W). Named on Felkner Hill (1968) 7.5' quadrangle.

Toomes Camp [TEHAMA]: *locality,* 20 miles south-southeast of Tomhead Mountain (lat. 40°00'10" N, long. 122°45'30" W; near SE cor. sec. 21, T 25 N, R 8 W). Named on Yolla Bolly (1954) 15' quadrangle.

Toomes Creek [TEHAMA]: *stream,* flows 4.5 miles to Sacramento River 2.5 miles northwest of Vina (lat. 39°57'50" N, long. 122°04'50" W). Named on Vina (1950) 7.5' quadrangle. On Vina (1904) 15' quadrangle, the name "Toomes Creek" applies also to present Dry Creek (3). The name "Toomes" commemorates Albert G. Toomes, who held Rio de los Molinos grant (Gudde, 1949, p. 365).

Too too tut na: see **Klamath River** [SISKIYOU].

Tophet Springs: see **Lassen Peak** [SHASTA].

Topnotch Ridge [SHASTA]: *ridge,* east-southeast-trending, about 1 mile long, 5 miles north of Schell Mountain (lat. 40°50'30" N, long. 122°31' W; sec. 2, T 35 N, R 6 W). Named on Schell Mountain (1950) 15' quadrangle.

Totten Campground: see **Sarah Totten Campground** [SISKIYOU].

Tower House [SHASTA]: *locality,* 2.5 miles south of the village of French Gulch (lat. 40°39'50" N, long. 122°38'10" W; near N line sec. 3, T 32 N, R 7 W). Named on French Gulch (1979) 7.5' quadrangle. Levi Tower built the three-story Tower House at the site in 1851 (Giles, p. 190).

Towhead Lake: see **Toehead Lake** [SISKIYOU].

Town Creek [SHASTA]: *stream,* flows 1 mile to Squaw Creek Arm Shasta Lake 10 miles south of Bollibokka Mountain (lat. 40°47'30" N, long. 122°11'30" W; sec. 22, T 34 N, R 3 W). Named on Bollibokka Mountain (1957) 15' quadrangle.

Town Mountain [SHASTA]: *ridge,* east-trending, 1.5 miles long, 7.5 miles south of Bollibokka Mountain (lat. 40°49'30" N, long. 122°12'45" W; sec. 4, 9, T 34 N, R 3 W). Named on Bollibokka Mountain (1957) 15' quadrangle.

Townsend Gulch [SHASTA]: *canyon,* drained by a stream that flows 5.5 miles to South Cow Creek 7.25 miles east of Millville (lat. 40°33'20" N, long. 122°02'25" W; sec. 12, T 31 N, R 2 W). Named on Millville (1953) and Whitmore (1956) 15' quadrangles.

Townsend Gulch [SISKIYOU]: *canyon,* drained by a stream that flows nearly 2 miles to Scott River 5.25 miles southwest of Scott Bay (lat. 41°41'20" N, long. 123°04'45" W). Named on Scott Bar (1980) 7.5' quadrangle.

Toyon: see **Government Camp** [SHASTA].

Tracy Creek [SHASTA]: *stream,* flows 2.5 miles to Oak Run Creek 9.5 miles north-northeast of Millville (lat. 40°39'45" N, long. 122°04'15" W; near NE cor. sec. 3, T 32 N, R 2 W). Named on Millville (1953) 15' quadrangle.

Trail Creek [SISKIYOU]: *stream,* flows 2.5 miles to East Fork of South Fork Salmon River 16 miles south-southwest of Etna (lat. 41°13'35" N, long. 122°58'30" W; sec. 23, T 39 N, R 10 W). Named on Coffee Creek (1955) and Etna (1955) 15' quadrangles. Called Trails Cr. on Averill's (1935) map.

Trail Gulch [SHASTA]: *canyon,* drained by a stream that flows 3.25 miles to Willow Creek (4) nearly 4 miles southwest of the village of French Gulch (lat. 40°40'05" N, long. 122°41'40" W; near S line sec. 31, T 33 N, R 7 W). Named on French Gulch (1979) 7.5' quadrangle.

Trail Gulch [SISKIYOU]:

(1) *canyon,* drained by a stream that flows 1.5 miles to Lumgrey Creek 12 miles east of Condrey Mountain (lat. 41°54'15" N, long. 122°45'20" W; near S line sec. 22, T 47 N, R 8 W). Named on Condrey Mountain (1955) 15' quadrangle.

(2) *canyon,* drained by a stream that flows 2.25 miles to McConaughy Gulch 4.5 miles east-southeast of Etna (lat. 41°25' N, long. 122°48' W; sec. 8, T 41 N, R 8 W). Named on Etna (1955) 15' quadrangle.

(3) *canyon,* drained by a stream that flows 3 miles to East Fork of South Fork Salmon River 16 miles south of Etna (lat. 41°13'15" N, long. 122°55'50" W; sec. 20, T 39 N, R 9 W). Named on Coffee Creek (1955) 15' quadrangle. Called Long Gulch on Etna (1934) 30' quadrangle, where present Long Gulch (3) is called Trail Gulch.

(4) *canyon,* drained by a stream that flows 2 miles to Hamburg Creek 10.5 miles southwest of Hornbrook (lat. 41°47'45" N, long. 122°41'15" W; sec. 32, T 46 N, R 7 W). Named on Hornbrook (1955) 15' quadrangle.

(5) *canyon,* drained by a stream that flows nearly 3 miles to Moffett Creek 8 miles south-southwest of Yreka (lat. 41°37'50" N, long. 122°43' W; sec. 25, T 44 N, R 8 W). Named on Yreka (1954) 15' quadrangle.

Trail Gulch Lake [SISKIYOU]: *lake,* 1300 feet long, 19 miles south of Etna (lat. 41°10'55" N, long. 122°56'10" W; sec. 6, T 38 N, R 9 W). Named on Coffee Creek (1955) 15' quadrangle. Called Long Gulch Lake on Etna (1934) 30' quadrangle, where nearby Long Gulch Lake is called Trail Gulch Lake, but United States Board on Geographic Names (1978c, p. 4) rejected the name "Long Gulch Lake" for present Trail Gulch Lake.

Trail Meadow [SISKIYOU]: *area,* 17 miles north-northwest of Forks of Salmon (lat. 41°29'50" N, long. 123°24'05" W). Named on Somes Bar (1979) 7.5' quadrangle.

Trail Mountain [SISKIYOU]: *ridge,* east-trending, 1.5 miles long, 9.5 miles north-northwest of Orleans, which is in Humboldt County (lat. 41°25'40" N, long. 122°36'45" W). Named on Bark Shanty Gulch (1974) 7.5' quadrangle.

Transfer [TEHAMA]: *locality,* nearly 5 miles east-northeast of Polk Springs (lat. 40°08'10" N, long. 121°34'45" W; sec. 1, T 26 N, R 3 E). Named on Butte Meadows (1958) 15' quadrangle.

Transfer Ridge [BUTTE]: *ridge,* generally south-trending, 4.5 miles long, 8.5 miles north-northwest of Pulga (lat. 39°55' N, long. 121°29'45" W). Named on Kimshew Point (1979) and Stirling City (1979) 7.5' quadrangles.

Trapper Creek [SISKIYOU]: *stream,* flows 2.5 miles to West Fork Beaver Creek (1) 5.5 miles east-northeast of Condrey Mountain (lat. 41°58'05" N, long. 122°52'45" W; sec. 34, T 48 N, R 9 W). Named on Condrey Mountain (1955) 15' quadrangle.

Trapper Point [SISKIYOU]: *relief feature,* 7 miles northeast of Condrey Mountain (lat. 41°59'50" N, long. 122°52'15" W); the feature is near the head of Trapper Creek. Named on Condrey Mountain (1955) 15' quadrangle.

Trapper Spring [SISKIYOU]: *spring,* 17 miles south of Macdoel (lat. 41°34'10" N, long. 122°00'15" W; near NE cor. sec. 18, T 43 N, R 1 W). Named on The Whaleback (1954) 15' quadrangle.

Tres Picos Creek: see **Butte Creek** [BUTTE-GLENN].

Tres Vias: see **Oroville Junction** [BUTTE].

Trickling Creek [BUTTE]: *stream,* flows less than 1 mile to Hodapp Creek 5.5 miles east-southeast of Paradise (lat. 39°42'50" N, long. 121°32'25" W; near SW cor. sec. 33, T 22 N, R 4 E). Named on Cherokee (1970) 7.5' quadrangle.

Tri-Forest Peak [SISKIYOU]: *peak,* 18 miles north of Weaverville, which is in Trinity County, on Siskiyou-Trinity County line (lat. 40°59'40" N, long. 122°55' W; near E line sec. 8, T 36 N, R 9 W); Klamath National Forest, Shasta National Forest, and Trinity National Forest meet at the spot. Altitude 7681 feet. Named on Trinity Dam (1950) 15' quadrangle.

Trinity Alps [SISKIYOU]: *range,* 11 miles southeast of Cecilville on Siskiyou-Trinity County line (lat. 41°00'45" N, long. 123°00' W). Named on Cecilville (1955), Coffee Creek (1955), and Trinity Lake (1950) 15' quadrangles. United States Board on Geographic Names (1960a, p. 18) rejected the name "Salmon Trinity Alps" for the feature.

Trinity Mountain: see **Hoadley Peaks** [SHASTA].

Trinity Mountains [SHASTA-SISKIYOU]: *range,* mainly along Shasta-Trinity County line between Sacramento River and Trinity River. Named on Redding (1958) 1°x 2° quadrangle. Called Bully Choop Mountains on Red Bluff (1894) 1° quadrangle.

Triplet Butte [GLENN]: *peak,* 3.5 miles northeast of Saint John Mountain (lat. 39°28'20" N, long. 122°38'45" W). Altitude 2999 feet. Named on Saint John Mountain (1968) 7.5' quadrangle.

Tripp Creek [SISKIYOU]: *stream,* flows 0.5 mile to Salmon River 5 miles northwest of Forks of Salmon (lat. 41°19'05" N, long. 123°22'45" W). Named on Orleans Mountain (1974) 7.5' quadrangle.

Tripp Point [SISKIYOU]: *relief feature,* 5.5 miles north-northwest of Forks of Salmon along Salmon River (lat. 41°20' N, long. 123°22'05" W). Named on Forks of Salmon (1978) 7.5' quadrangle.

Trooks Flat [SISKIYOU]: *locality,* nearly 3 miles east of Sawyers Bar along North Fork Salmon River (lat. 41°17'50" N, long. 123°04'45" W). Named on Tanners Peak (1977) 7.5' quadrangle. Daggett (1957a, p. 2) noted that Mr. A. Trooks had a large store at Trooks Flat in 1851.

Trough Creek [SHASTA]: *stream,* flows 3 miles to Squaw Valley Creek [SHASTA-SISKIYOU] nearly 6 miles northwest of Shoeinhorse Mountain (lat. 41°07' N, long. 122°09'45" W; sec. 27, T 38 N, R 3 W); the stream heads at Water Trough Springs. Named on Shoeinhorse Mountain (1954) 15' quadrangle.

Trough Ridge [TEHAMA]: *ridge,* generally south-trending, 2 miles long, 10.5 miles west of Paskenta (lat. 39°54'25" N, long. 122°44'30" W). Named on Riley Ridge (1967) 7.5' quadrangle.

Trough Spring Ridge [TEHAMA]: *ridge,* southeast- to east-trending, 2 miles long, 1.5 miles south-southeast of Tomhead Mountain (lat. 40°06'50" N, long. 122°48'20" W). Named on Yolla Bolly (1954) 15' quadrangle.

Trout Camp [SISKIYOU]: *locality,* 2.5 miles west-southwest of Preston Peak along Clear Creek (1) (lat. 41°49'20" N, long. 123°39'05" W). Named on Devils Punchbowl (1981) 7.5' quadrangle.

Trout Creek [SISKIYOU]: *stream,* flows 12 mile to Dry Creek (3) 10 miles northwest of Bartle (lat. 41°21'55" N, long. 121°56'40" W; at S line sec. 27, T 41 N, R 1 W). Named on Bartle (1961) 15' quadrangle.

Trout Creek Butte [SISKIYOU]: *hill,* 12.5 miles north-northwest of Bartle (lat. 41°25'05" N, long. 121°55'45" W; sec. 11, T 41 N, R 1 W); the hill is west of Trout Creek. Named on Bartle (1961) 15' quadrangle.

Truckee Creek [TEHAMA]: *stream,* flows 7 miles to McClure Creek 2.5 miles south of Gerber (lat. 40°01'20" N, long. 122°08'50" W). Named on Gerber (1950) and West of Gerber (1951) 7.5' quadrangles.

Trueblood Gulch [TEHAMA]: *canyon,* drained by a stream that flows 4.5 miles to Salt Creek (1) 3.5 miles west-southwest of Rosewood (lat. 40°15'15" N, long. 122°37' W; sec. 26, T 28 N, R 7 W). Named on Ono (1952) 15' quadrangle, and on Cold Fork (1967) and Oxbow Bridge (1967) 7.5' quadrangles.

Tsashtl: see **Mount Tsashtl**, under **Mount Shasta** [SISKIYOU].

Tucker Butte [SHASTA]: *peak,* 8.5 miles northeast of Whitmore (lat. 40°41'45" N, long. 121°47' W; at NW cor. sec. 29, T 33 N, R 2 E). Named on Whitmore (1956) 15' quadrangle.

Tuft Creek [SISKIYOU]: *stream,* flows 5.25 miles to Julia Glover Flat 15 miles east-northeast of Bartle (lat. 41°20'20" N, long. 121°32'15" W; near N line sec. 6, T 40 N, R 4 E). Named on Hambone (1961) and White Horse (1962) 15' quadrangles.

Tule Lake [SHASTA]: *lake,* 300 feet long, 3.5 miles south-southwest of Millville (lat. 40°30'10" N, long. 122°12'25" W; near N line sec. 33, T 31 N, R 3 W). Named on Palo Cedro (1965) 7.5' quadrangle.

Tule Lake: see **Tule Lake Sump** [SISKIYOU]; **Tule River** [SHASTA].

Tulelake [SISKIYOU]: *town,* 23 miles east of Dorris (lat. 41°57'30" N, long. 121°28'30" W; sec. 35, T 48 N, R 4 E). Named on Tulelake (1951) 15' quadrangle. Postal authorities established Tulelake post office in 1931 (Frickstad, p. 191), and the town incorporated in 1937.

Tule Lake Sump [SISKIYOU]: *water feature,* southwest and south of the town of Tulelake on Siskiyou-Modoc County line. Named on Mount Dome (1950) and Tulelake (1951) 15' quadrangles. The feature is the confined remnant of Tule Lake, which formerly lay on California-Oregon State line. Tule Lake itself is named on Modoc Lave Bed (1892) 1° quadrangle, and is called Rhett Lake on Fremont's (1848) map—Fremont gave the name "Rhett Lake" in 1846, apparently for his friend Barnwell Rhett (Gudde, 1949, p. 371). United States Board on Geographic Names (1986a, p. 2) approved the name "Tule Lake" for the feature, and rejected the names "Tule Lake Sump" and "Rhett Lake" for it; the Board described modern Tule Lake as a reservoir in two sections.

Tule River [SHASTA]: *water feature,* lakelike feature that joins Fall River 5 miles north-northwest of Fall River Mills (lat. 41°04'20" N, long. 121°27'45" W; at W line sec. 1, T 37 N, R 4 E). Named on Fall River Mills (1961) 15' quadrangle. The upper part of present Tule River is called Tule Lake on Alturas (1954) 1°x 2° quadrangle, but United States Board on Geographic Names (1990, p. 11) rejected this name.

Tule River: see **Little Tule River** [SHASTA].

Tumble Buttes [SHASTA]: *peaks,* two, 13 miles north of Lassen Peak (lat. 40°40'30" N, long. 121°33' W; sec. 32, T 33 N, R 4 E). Named on Manzanita Lake (1956) 15' quadrangle.

Tuna Creek [SHASTA]: *stream,* flows 3.5 miles to McCloud River [SHASTA-SISKIYOU] 4.25 miles north of Bollibokka Mountain (lat. 40°59'40" N, long. 122°12'40" W; sec. 9, T 36 N, R 3 W). Named on Bollibokka Mountain (1957) and Lamoine (1957) 15' quadrangles. According to Steger (p. 64), the stream should have the name "Tune Creek," a name of Indian origin.

Tunnel Inn [SHASTA]: *locality,* nearly 4 miles north-northeast of the town of Central Valley (lat. 40°43'30" N, long. 122°19'25" W; near S line sec. 9, T 33 N, R 4 W). Named on Project City (1957) 7.5' quadrangle.

Tunnel Reservoir [SHASTA]: *lake,* 0.5 mile long, 11 miles north of the village of Montgomery Creek (lat. 40°59'55" N, long. 121°53'20" W; at NW cor. sec. 8, T 36 N, R 1 E). Named on Montgomery Creek (1956) 15' quadrangle.

Turkey Mullen Gulch [TEHAMA]: *canyon,* drained by a stream that flows 1.5 miles to Cold Fork (1) 4.5 miles northwest of Tomhead Mountain (lat. 40°11'25" N, long. 122°52' W; sec. 15, T 27 N, R 9 W). Named on Yolla Bolly (1954) 15' quadrangle.

Turk Lake [SISKIYOU]: *lake,* 500 feet long, 13 miles southwest of Scott Bar (lat. 41°37'35" N, long. 123°12'30" W). Named on Grider Valley (1981) 7.5' quadrangle.

Turner Lake [TEHAMA]: *lake,* 400 feet long, 4 miles south-southwest of Mineral (lat. 40°17'45" N, long. 121°37'50" W; near E line sec. 9, T 28 N, R 3 E); the lake is nearly 1 mile west-southwest of Turner Mountain. Named on Lassen Peak (1956) 15' quadrangle.

Turner Mountain [TEHAMA]: *peak,* 3.5 miles south-southwest of Mineral (lat. 40°18' N, long. 121°37' W; near N line sec. 10, T 28 N, R 3 E). Altitude 6893 feet. Named on Lassen Peak (1956) 15' quadrangle.

Turners Camp: see **Kelsey Camp** [SISKIYOU].

Turners Mill [BUTTE]: *locality,* 5 miles northeast of Bidwell Bar (lat. 39°40' N, long. 121°19'05" W). Named on Bidwell Bar (1897) 30' quadrangle.

Turntable Creek [SHASTA]: *stream,* flows less than 1 mile to Pit River 16 miles south-southeast of Lamoine (lat. 40°46'30" N, long. 122°18' W; sec. 27, T 34 N, R 4 W). Named on Lamoine (1946) 15' quadrangle. Water of Shasta Lake now floods the feature.

Turtle Creek [SISKIYOU]: *stream,* flows 2 miles to Angel Creek 10 miles west-southwest of Bartle (lat. 41°11'55" N, long. 121°59'40" W; sec. 29, T 39 N, R 1 W). Named on Big Bend (1961) 15' quadrangle.

Tuscan: see **Tuscan Buttes** [TEHAMA].

Tuscan Buttes [TEHAMA]: *peaks,* about 4 miles south-southwest of Dales (lat. 40°15'45" N, long. 122°05'30" W; mainly in sec. 21, T 28 N, R 2 W). Altitude of highest 1868 feet. Named on Dales (1965) 7.5' quadrangle. Diller and others' (1915) map shows a place called Tuscan located at Tuscan Buttes. Postal authorities established Tuscan post office 1895 and discontinued it in 1919 (Frickstad, p. 205).

Tuscan Springs [TEHAMA]: *locality,* 8 miles northeast of Red Bluff along Little Salt Creek (2) (lat. 40°14'35" N, long. 122°06'35" W; sec. 32, T 28 N, R 2 W). Named on Tuscan Springs (1951) 7.5' quadrangle. Dr. John A. Veatch purchased the property in 1854 and named the springs there after similar springs in Tuscany, Italy (Hoover, Rensch, and Rensch, p. 551). The place also was called Lick Springs (Whitney, p. 206). A resort with a hotel and bathhouse made medicinal use of the spring water (Waring, p. 289).

Tuttle Gulch [SISKIYOU]: *canyon,* 1 mile long, opens into the valley of Scott River 5 miles west of Fort Jones (lat. 41°37'15" N, long. 122°56' W; at E line sec. 36, T 44 N, R 10 W). Named on Fort Jones (1955) 15' quadrangle.

Twentymile Crossing [TEHAMA]: *locality,* 7.5 miles south of Panther Spring (lat. 40°06'45" N, long. 121°48'45" W); the place is in Twentymile Hollow. Named on Panther Spring (1953) 15' quadrangle.

Twentymile Hollow [TEHAMA]: *canyon,* drained by a stream that flows 10 miles to Big Dry Creek 16 miles south-southwest of Panther Spring (lat. 40°03'40" N, long. 121°56' W). Named on Panther Spring (1953) 15' quadrangle.

Twin Bridges Campground [SHASTA]: *locality,* 9 miles north of Lassen Peak along Hat Creek (lat. 40°37' N, long. 121°28' W; near S line sec. 13, T 32 N, R 4 E). Named on Prospect Peak (1957) 15' quadrangle.

Twin Buttes [SHASTA]: *hills,* two, 0.5 mile apart, highest 8.5 miles south-southeast of Burney (lat. 40°46'35" N, long. 121°35'30" W; near W line sec. 25, T 34 N, R 3 E). Altitude of the highest hill is 5351 feet. Named on Burney (1957) 15' quadrangle.

Twin Creek: see **Big Twin Creek** [SISKIYOU]; **Little Twin Creek** [SISKIYOU].

Twin Creeks [SISKIYOU]: *streams,* two, each about 1.5 miles long, that enter Elk Creek together 10.5 miles north of Ukonom Lake (lat. 41°43'45" N, long. 123°22' W). Named on Clear Creek (1981) and Huckleberry Mountain (1980) 7.5' quadrangles.

Twin Lake: see **Lower Twin Lake** [SHASTA]; **Upper Twin Lake** [SHASTA].

Twin Lakes [SISKIYOU]:

(1) *lakes,* two, largest 250 feet long, 8.5 miles south-southwest of Etna (lat. 41°21'10" N, long. 122°58'40" W; sec. 2, T 40 N, R 10 W). Named on Etna (1955) 15' quadrangle.

(2) *lakes,* two, each about 300 feet long, 18 miles south-southwest of Etna (lat. 41°11'50" N, long. 122°58'25" W; sec. 35, T 39 N, R 10 W). Named on Coffee Creek (1955) 15' quadrangle.

Twin Lakes: see **Hidden Lake** [SHASTA]; **Horseshoe Lake** [SHASTA]; **Lower Twin Lake** [SHASTA] (1); **Lower Twin Lake** [SHASTA] (2).

Twin Meadows [TEHAMA]: *area,* 5.5 miles north of Mineral (lat. 40°25'40" N, long. 121°34'55" W; sec. 30, T 30 N, R 4 E). Named on Lassen Peak (1956) 15' quadrangle.

Twin Peaks [SISKIYOU]: *peak,* 2.5 miles south of Broken Rib Mountain on Siskiyou-Del Norte County line (lat. 41°50'15" N, long. 123°40'50" W). Altitude 5944 feet. Named on Devils Punchbowl (1981) 7.5' quadrangle. Preston Peak (1922) 30' quadrangle shows two peaks close together at the summit of the feature.

Twin Peaks [TEHAMA]: *peak,* 8.5 miles south of Tomhead Mountain (lat. 40°00'55" N, long. 122°51'05" W; sec. 15, T 25 N, R 9 W). Altitude 7407 feet. Named on Yolla Bolly (1954) 15' quadrangle.

Twin Ponds: see **Porcupine Reservoir** [SHASTA].

Twin Springs [GLENN]: *springs,* nearly 2 miles east of Saint John Mountain (lat. 39°26'10" N, long. 122°39'30" W). Named on Saint John Mountain (1968) 7.5' quadrangle.

Twin Springs [SISKIYOU]: *springs,* 2.5 miles north-northwest of Bartle (lat. 41°18'15" N, long. 121°49'10" W; near N line sec. 23, T 40 N, R 1 E). Named on Bartle (1961) 15' quadrangle.

Twin Springs [TEHAMA]: *springs,* 9 miles south-southwest of Wakefield Flat (lat. 40°00'05" N, long. 122°41'10" W; at S line sec. 19, T 25 N, R 7 W). Named on Raglin Ridge (1967) 7.5' quadrangle.

Twin Valley [SISKIYOU]: *valley,* 4.5 miles north-northeast of Preston Peak (lat. 41°53'55" N, long. 123°34'55" W). Named on Polar Bear Mountain (1982) 7.5' quadrangle.

Twin Valley Creek [SISKIYOU]: *stream,* flows 5 miles to South Fork Indian Creek (1) 5.25 miles east-northeast of Preston Peak (lat. 41°52'05" N, long. 123°31'05" W); the stream heads at Twin Valley. Named on Polar Bear Mountain (1982) and Preston Peak (1982) 7.5' quadrangles.

Two-Barrel Spring [TEHAMA]: *spring,* 1.5 miles east-southeast of Panther Spring (lat. 40°14'10" N, long. 121°45'10" W; sec. 33, T 28 N, R 2 E). Named on Panther Spring (1953) 15' quadrangle.

Two Bit Gulch [SISKIYOU]: *canyon,* drained by a stream that heads in the State of Oregon and flows less than 1 mile in Siskiyou County to Green Creek 15 miles north-northwest of Happy Camp (lat. 41°59'25" N, long. 123°29'20" W; near SW cor. sec. 35, T 19 N, R 6 E); the canyon is east of Four Bit Gulch. Named on Deadman Point (1981) 7.5' quadrangle.

Two Pine [SHASTA]: *locality,* 6.5 miles west of Shoeinhorse Mountain along Squaw Valley Creek [SHASTA-SISKIYOU] (lat. 41°03'50" N, long. 122°11'50" W; sec. 15, T 37 N, R 3 W). Named on Shoeinhorse Mountain (1954) 15' quadrangle.

Two Rock Ridge [SHASTA]: *ridge,* east-southeast- to south-southeast-trending, 1.5 miles long, 10 miles southwest of Shasta Bally (lat. 40°30' N, long. 122°47'50" W). Named on Chanchelulla Peak (1951) and Weaverville (1950) 15' quadrangles.

Two Springs [SISKIYOU]: *springs,* 4.25 miles east-southeast of Bartle (lat. 41°14' N, long. 121°44'15" W; near E line sec. 9, T 39 N, R 2 E). Named on Pondosa (1961) 15' quadrangle.

Tyler [TEHAMA]: *locality,* just south of present Gerber along Southern Pacific Railroad (lat. 40°03'05" N, long. 122°08'55" W). Named on Tehama (1905) 15' quadrangle.

Tyler Gulch [SISKIYOU]: *canyon,* drained by a stream that flows 2.5 miles to the valley of Scott River 5 miles west-northwest of Fort Jones (lat. 41°38'30" N, long. 122°55'10" W; sec. 30, T 44 N, R 9 W). Named on Fort Jones (1955) 15' quadrangle.

Tyler Meadows [SISKIYOU]: *area,* 9 miles west-southwest of Scott Bar (lat. 41°42'20" N, long. 123°09'55" W). Named on Grider Valley (1981) 7.5' quadrangle.

Typhoon Mesa: see **Garner Mountain** [SISKIYOU].

– U –

U-Fish Creek [SISKIYOU]: *stream,* flows 1.5 miles to Klamath River 12.5 miles north-northwest of Ukonom Lake (lat. 41°42'15" N, long. 123°26'45" W). Named on Clear Creek (1981) 7.5' quadrangle.

Uhl Peak [TEHAMA]: *peak,* 10 miles west-southwest of Ball Mountain on Tehama-Mendocino County line (lat. 39°51'45" N, long. 122°57'05" W; sec. 10, T 23 N, R 10 W). Named on Mendocino Pass (1967) 7.5' quadrangle.

Uhl Spring [TEHAMA]: *spring,* 4.5 miles north-northwest of Paskenta (lat. 39°56'40" N, long. 122°35' W; at S line sec. 7, T 24 N, R 6 W). Named on Paskenta (1967) 7.5' quadrangle.

Ukonom Creek [SISKIYOU]: *stream,* flows 8.5 miles to Klamath River 7 miles west-northwest of Ukonom Lake (lat. 41°37' N, long. 123°29" W); the stream heads at Ukonom Lake. Named on Ukonom Lake (1980) and

Ukonom Mountain (1980) 7.5' quadrangles. The name is of Indian origin (Gudde, 1949, p. 374). Flems Fork enters nearly 7 miles upstream from the mouth of the main creek and is 3 miles long. McCash Fork enters 5.5 miles upstream from the mouth of the main creek; it heads at McCash Lake and is 4 miles long. Both forks are named on Ukonom Lake (1980) and Ukonom Mountain (1980) 7.5' quadrangles.

Ukonom Lake [SISKIYOU]: *lake,* 2400 feet long, 15 miles south of Happy Camp (lat. 41°34'50" N, long. 123°21'20" W). Named on Ukonom Lake (1980) 7.5' quadrangle.

Ukonom Mountain [SISKIYOU]: *peak,* 6.25 miles west of Ukonom Lake (lat. 41°35'05" N, long. 123°28'30" W). Altitude 4581 feet. Named on Ukonom Mountain (1980) 7.5' quadrangle.

Umbrella Creek [GLENN]: *stream,* heads in Mendocino County and flows 0.5 mile in Glenn County to Black Butte River 7.25 miles south of Black Butte (lat. 39°37'25" N, long. 122°53'15" W; near NW cor. sec. 4, T 20 N, R 9 W); the stream is southeast of Umbrella Butte, which is in Mendocino County. Named on Hull Mountain (1967) and Plaskett Ridge (1967) 7.5' quadrangles.

Uncles Creek [SISKIYOU]: *stream,* flows 3.5 miles to Little North Fork Salmon River 6 miles north-northwest of Sawyers Bar (lat. 41°22'40" N, long. 123°10'50" W). Named on English Peak (1977) 7.5' quadrangle. Left Hand Fork enters 3000 feet upstream from the mouth of the main creek; it heads at Uncles Lake and is 2.25 miles long. Right Hand Fork enters 2000 feet upstream from the mouth of the main creek and is 2.5 miles long. Both forks are named on English Peak (1977) 7.5' quadrangle.

Uncles Lake [SISKIYOU]: *lake,* 450 feet long, 8.5 miles north-northwest of Sawyers Bar (lat. 41°24'15" N, long. 123°12'15" W). Named on English Peak (1977) 7.5' quadrangle.

Underground Creek [SHASTA]: *stream,* flows 2 miles to Pit River 8 miles east of the village of Big Bend (lat. 41°00' N, long. 121°45'20" W). Named on Big Bend (1961) 15' quadrangle.

Undertakers Camp [SISKIYOU]: *locality,* 4 miles east-southeast of Medicine Lake (lat. 41°33'25" N, long. 121°31'50" W). Named on Medicine Lake (1952) 15' quadrangle.

Union Bar [BUTTE]: *locality,* 3 miles east-northeast of Bidwell Bar along Middle Fork Feather River (lat. 39°34'35" N, long. 121°23'35" W; near E line sec. 22, T 20 N, R 5 E); the place is at the mouth of Union Creek—water of Lake Oroville now covers the site. Named on Big Bend Mountain (1948) 15' quadrangle. F.D. Dunn (p. 66) listed a place called Marks Bar that was next to and downstream from Union Bar.

Union Creek [BUTTE]: *stream,* flows less than 1 mile to Lake Oroville 5.5 miles northeast of Oroville Dam (lat. 39°35'10" N, long. 121°23'50" W; near S line sec. 15, T 20 N, R 5 E); the mouth of the stream is 1 mile west of Union Hill. Named on Oroville Dam (1970) 7.5' quadrangle.

Union Hill [BUTTE]: *peak,* 6.5 miles east-northeast of Oroville Dam (lat. 39°35'15" N, long. 121°22'45" W; sec. 14, T 20 N, R 5 E); the peak is 1 mile east of the mouth of Union Creek. Altitude 1924 feet. Named on Oroville Dam (1970) 7.5' quadrangle.

Updyke Hill [SHASTA]: *peak,* 9 miles east-southeast of Burney (lat. 40°48'30" N, long. 121°31'35" W; sec. 16, T 34 N, R 4 E). Altitude 4642 feet. Named on Burney (1957) 15' quadrangle.

Upper Albert Lake [SISKIYOU]: *lake,* 400 feet long, 9 miles south-southwest of Etna (lat. 41°20'30" N, long. 122°58'15" W; sec. 12, T 40 N, R 10 W); the lake is 700 feet upstream from Albert Lake. Named on Etna (1955) 15' quadrangle.

Upper Cliff Lake [SISKIYOU]: *lake,* 400 feet long, 12 miles west of Dunsmuir (lat. 41°11'45" N, long. 122°29'30" W; near E line sec. 36, T 39 N, R 6 W); the lake is 900 feet south-southwest of Cliff Lake (2). Named on Dunsmuir (1954) 15' quadrangle.

Upper Crossing [SISKIYOU]: *locality,* 9 miles west-northwest of Macdoel along Shovel Creek (lat. 41°52'50" N, long. 122°09'50" W; near S line sec. 25, T 47 N, R 3 W); the place is 4 miles upstream from the site of Lower Crossing. Named on Macdoel (1954) 15' quadrangle.

Upper Devils Peak [SISKIYOU]: *peak,* 3.5 miles north of the village of Seiad Valley (lat. 41°53'35" N, long. 123°12' W); the feature is 3300 feet north of Middle Devils Peak. Altitude 6004 feet. Named on Kangaroo Mountain (1980) 7.5' quadrangle. Called Devils Pk. on Seiad (1922) 30' quadrangle.

Upper English Lake [SISKIYOU]: *lake,* 450 feet long, 9 miles north-northwest of Sawyers Bar (lat. 41°24'40" N, long. 123°12'40" W); the lake is 800 feet southwest of English Lake. Named on English Peak (1977) 7.5' quadrangle.

Upper Falls [SISKIYOU]: *waterfall,* 7 miles east of McCloud along McCloud River [SHASTA-SISKIYOU] (lat. 41°14'30" N, long. 122°00'25" W; sec. 7, T 39 N, R 1 W); the feature is 0.25 mile upstream from Middle Falls. Named on Shoeinhorse Mountain (1954) 15' quadrangle.

Upper Gray Rock Lake [SISKIYOU]: *lake,* 500 feet long, 8 miles west of Dunsmuir (lat. 41°12'45" N, long. 122°25'50" W; sec. 27, T 39 N, R 5 W). Named on Dunsmuir (1954) 15' quadrangle. The feature is one of the group called Gray Rock Lakes on Dunsmuir (1935) 30' quadrangle.

Upper Gumboot Lake [SISKIYOU]: *lake,* 600 feet long, 26 miles southeast of Etna (lat. 41°12'35" N, long. 122°30'45" W; sec. 26, T 39 N, R 6 W); the lake is 0.25 mile southwest of Gumboot Lake. Named on Bonanza King (1955) 15' quadrangle.

Upper Ice Cave [SISKIYOU]: *cave,* 8 miles north of Medicine Lake (lat. 41°41'50" N, long. 121°34'15" W; sec. 36, T 45 N, R 3 E). Named on Medicine Lake (1952) 15' quadrangle.

Upper Limestone Valley Creek [SHASTA]: *stream,* flows 0.5 mile to Backbone Creek Inlet 12.5 miles south of Lamoine (lat. 40°47'55" N, long. 122°25'25" W; near N line sec. 22, T 34 N, R 5 W); the stream is less than 0.5 mile north of Lower Limestone Valley Creek. Named on Lamoine (1957) 15' quadrangle.

Upper Maple Spring [SISKIYOU]: *spring,* 6.5 miles south of Hornbrook (lat. 41°49'10" N, long. 122°33' W; sec. 21, T 46 N, R 6 W); the spring is 350 feet south-southwest of Lower Maple Spring. Named on Hornbrook (1955) 15' quadrangle.

Upper Meadow [SHASTA]: *area,* nearly 3 miles southeast of Lassen Peak along Kings Creek (lat. 40°27'40" N, long. 121°28' W; sec. 18, T 30 N, R 5 E); the place is less than 1 mile west-northwest of Lower Meadow. Named on Mount Harkness (1956) 15' quadrangle.

Upper Rocky Honcut Creek [BUTTE]: *stream,* flows 3.5 miles to join Lower Rocky Honcut Creek and form Rocky Honcut Creek 4 miles north of Bangor (lat. 39°26'50" N, long. 121°23'25" W; near E line sec. 3, T 18 N, R 5 E). Named on Bangor (1947) 7.5' quadrangle.

Upper Ruffey Lake: see **Ruffey Lakes** [SISKIYOU].

Upper Salt Creek Resort [SHASTA]: *locality,* 10 miles south-southeast of Lamoine (lat. 40°51'20" N, long. 122°20'15" W; near SE cor. sec. 29, T 35 N, R 4 W); the place is 1 mile north-northeast of Lower Salt Creek Resort near Salt Creek (6). Named on Lamoine (1957) 15' quadrangle.

Upper Seven Lake [SISKIYOU]: *lake,* 600 feet long, 12 miles west of Dunsmuir (lat. 41°11'15" N, long. 122°29'25" W; near NE cor. sec. 1, T 38 N, R 6 W); the lake is 300 feet north of Lower Seven Lake. Named on Dunsmuir (1954) 15' quadrangle.

Upper Sky High Lake [SISKIYOU]: *lake,* 650 feet long, 16 miles south-southwest of Scott Bar (lat. 41°32'55" N, long. 123°10'50" W); the lake is just west of Lower Sky High Lake. Named on Marble Mountain (1980) 7.5' quadrangle. United States Board on Geographic Names (1981c, p. 4) rejected the names "Sky High Lake," "Sky High Lakes," and "Sky Lakes" for the feature.

Upper Soda Spring [SISKIYOU]: *locality,* at present Dunsmuir along Sacramento River (lat. 41°11'50" N, long. 122°16'10" W). Named on Shasta (1894) 1° quadrangle. Ross McCloud built an inn and developed the spring at the site in 1857; the name was changed from Soda Springs to Upper Soda Springs about 1889 to distinguish the place from Lower Soda Springs, located 5 miles farther south (Gudde, 1949, p. 337). The spring also was known as Campbells Soda Spring and Freys Soda Spring (Waring, p. 223). Waring (p. 224) listed a feature called Cave Spring situated about 0.5 mile north of Upper Soda Spring; it issues from a crevice at the base of a cliff, beneath which is a small cave that gives the spring its name.

Upper Twin Lake [SHASTA]:

(1) *lake,* 400 feet long, 16 miles north-northwest of Lassen Peak (lat. 40°42'20" N, long. 121°35'50" W; sec. 23, T 33 N, R 3 E); the lake is 800 feet northwest of Lower Twin Lake (1). Named on Manzanita Lake (1956) 15' quadrangle.

(2) *lake,* 1600 feet long, 7.25 miles east of Lassen Peak (lat. 40°30'05" N, long. 121°22'15" W; sec. 36, T 31 N, R 5 E). Named on Mount Harkness (1956) and Prospect Peak (1957) 15' quadrangles. Called Lower Twin Lakes on Halls Flat (1939) 30' quadrangle, where present Lower Twin Lake (2) is called Upper Twin Lake. United States Board on Geographic Names (1937, p. 31) rejected the name "Twin Lakes" for present Upper Twin Lake.

Upper Wright Lake [SISKIYOU]: *lake,* 1000 feet long, 11.5 miles south-southwest of Scott Bar (lat. 41°35'10" N, long. 123°04'35" W); the lake is 1500 feet east of Lower Wright Lake. Named on Boulder Peak (1981) 7.5' quadrangle. Called Wright L. on Averill's (1935) map.

Upton [SISKIYOU]: *locality,* 2.5 miles northwest of the town of Mount Shasta along Southern Pacific Railroad (lat. 41°20'25" N, long. 122°20'40" W; at E line sec. 6, T 40 N, R 4 W). Named on Weed (1954) 15' quadrangle. Postal authorities established Upton post office in 1897 and discontinued it in 1907 (Frickstad, p. 191).

—V—

Vale Gulch [TEHAMA]: *canyon,* drained by a stream that flows 9 miles to Red Bank Creek 0.5 mile east-southeast of Red Bank (lat. 40°05'50" N, long. 122°26' W; sec. 21, T 26 N, R 5 W). Named on Lowrey (1967) and Red Bank (1952) 7.5' quadrangles.

Valentine Cave [SISKIYOU]: *cave,* 10.5 miles north-northeast of Medicine Lake (lat. 41°42'35" N, long. 121°28'35" W; sec. 26, T 45 N, R 4 E). Named on Timber Mountain (1952) 15' quadrangle.

Valentine Ridge [TEHAMA]: *ridge,* generally east-trending, 12.5 miles long, center about 6 miles south-southwest of Wakefield Flat (lat. 40°03'45" N, long. 122°45' W). Named on Yolla Bolly (1954) 15' quadrangle, and on Lowrey (1967) and Raglin Ridge (1967) 7.5' quadrangles.

Valentine Spring [TEHAMA]: *spring,* 6.25 miles south-southeast of Tomhead Mountain (lat. 40°03'30" N, long. 122°45'30" W; near SW cor. sec. 34, T 26 N, R 8 W); the spring is on Valentine Ridge. Named on Yolla Bolly (1954) 15' quadrangle.

Valley Blossom [TEHAMA]: *locality,* about 11 miles west of Red Bluff (lat. 40°10'45" N, long. 122°26' W). Named on Red Bluff (1894) 1° quadrangle.

Valley Creek [BUTTE]: *stream,* flows 4 miles to West Branch Butte Creek [BUTTE-GLENN] 5 miles west-northwest of Stirling City (lat. 39°55'45" N, long. 121°37' W; near NE cor. sec. 22, T 24 N, R 3 E). Named on Stirling City (1979) 7.5' quadrangle.

Valley Creek: see **East Valley Creek** [SHASTA].

Valley View Mountain: see **Valley View Spring** [GLENN].

Valley View Spring [GLENN]: *spring,* 8.5 miles west of Newville (lat. 39°46'25" N, long. 122°40'55" W). Named on Hull Mountain (1967) 7.5' quadrangle, which shows the spring situated 1100 feet north-northeast of Valley View lookout tower. In 1981 Forest Service officials proposed the name "Valley View Mountain" for the place that the tower is located, and United States Board on Geographic Names (1982b, p. 3) approved the name.

Van Bremer's Peak: see **Mount Dome** [SISKIYOU].

Van Bremmer Well [SISKIYOU]: *well,* 9 miles east of Bray (lat. 41°38'05" N, long. 121°47'30" N; near S line sec. 19, T 44 N, R 2 E). Named on Bray (1950) 15' quadrangle.

Vandergrift Lake [BUTTE]: *intermittent lake,* 14 miles northwest of Chico (lat. 39°52'45" N, long. 121°59'55" W; sec. 5, T 23 N, R 1 W). Named on Richardson Springs NW (1952) and Vina (1950) 7.5' quadrangles.

Vanderpoole Mill [SISKIYOU]: *locality,* 6 miles south of Etna (lat. 41°22'15" N, long. 122°52'20" W; sec. 27, T 41 N, R 9 W). Named on Etna (1934) 30' quadrangle.

Van Horn Flat [TEHAMA]: *area,* 4.5 miles north of Wakefield Flat along Guyre Creek (lat. 40°11'20" N, long. 122°37'30" W; near S line sec. 14, T 27 N, R 7 W). Named on Colyear Springs (1957) 15' quadrangle.

Van Horn Gulch [SISKIYOU]: *canyon,* drained by a stream that flows 1.5 miles to Cherry Creek (2) 8 miles north-northeast of Fort Jones (lat. 41°43' N, long. 122°47'30" W; sec. 29, T 45 N, R 8 W). Named on Fort Jones (1955) 15' quadrangle.

Vann Creek [SISKIYOU]: *stream,* flows 2.5 miles to North Fork Dillon Creek nearly 3 miles south-southwest of Bear Peak (lat. 41°39'05" N, long. 123°35'25" W). Named on Bear Peak (1982) 7.5' quadrangle.

Van Ridge [TEHAMA]: *ridge,* south-southwest- to south-trending, 1.5 miles long, 3.25 miles west-northwest of Tomhead Mountain (lat. 40°09'10" N, long. 122°52'15" W; on S line sec. 27, T 27 N, R 9 W). Named on Yolla Bolly (1954) 15' quadrangle.

Vans Camp [SISKIYOU]: *locality,* 10 miles north-northwest of Orleans, which is in Humboldt County (lat. 41°25'10" N, long. 123°38'35" W). Named on Orleans (1952) 15' quadrangle.

Van Sicklin Butte [SHASTA]: *peak,* 1.5 miles north-northwest of Shoeinhorse Mountain (lat. 41°05'20" N, long. 122°04'55" W). Altitude 5041 feet. Named on Shoeinhorse Mountain (1954) 15' quadrangle.

Van Spring [TEHAMA]: *spring,* 2.5 miles west-northwest of Tomhead Mountain (lat. 40°09'20" N, long. 122°51'30" W; near SE cor. sec. 27, T 27 N, R 9 W). Named on Yolla Bolly (1954) 15' quadrangle.

Van Spring Gulch [TEHAMA]: *canyon,* drained by a stream that flows 2 miles to Long Gulch (3) 3 miles west of Tomhead Mountain (lat. 40°07'55" N, long. 122°52'25" W; near W line sec. 3, T 26 N, R 9 W); Van Spring is at the head of the canyon. Named on Yolla Bolly (1954) 15' quadrangle.

Varey Creek [BUTTE]: *stream,* flows 4 miles to West Branch Butte Creek [BUTTE-GLENN] 5 miles west-northwest of Stirling City (lat. 39°55'50" N, long. 121°37' W; near NE cor. sec. 22, T 24 N, R 3 E). Named on Stirling City (1979) 7.5' quadrangle. Called East Fork Big Butte Creek on Chico (1895) 30' quadrangle.

Veazie City: see **Honcut Creek** [BUTTE].

Vesa Bluffs [SISKIYOU]: *relief feature,* 14 miles southeast of Condrey Mountain (lat. 41°49' N, long. 122°45'45" W; sec. 22, T 46 N, R 8 W); the feature is at the head of Vesa Creek. Named on Condrey Mountain (1955) and Hornbrook (1955) 15' quadrangles.

Vesa Creek [SISKIYOU]: *stream,* flows 3 miles to Klamath River 12.5 miles east-southeast of Condrey Mountain (lat. 41°51'20" N, long. 122°45'40" W). Named on Condrey Mountain (1955) 15' quadrangle.

Vestal Flat [TEHAMA]: *area,* 8 miles north of Wakefield Flat (lat. 40°14'20" N, long. 122°38'45" W; sec. 34, T 28 N, R 7 W). Named on Cold Fork (1967) 7.5' quadrangle.

Vestals Swamp [SHASTA]: *marsh,* 7 miles north-northeast of Fall River Mills (lat. 41°05'45" N, long. 121°22' W; at N line sec. 35, T 38 N, R 5 E). Named on Fall River Mills (1961) 15' quadrangle.

Villa Verona [BUTTE]: *locality,* 2.5 miles north of Palermo along Southern Pacific Railroad (lat. 39°28'15" N, long. 121°33'05" W). Named on Palermo (1912) 7.5' quadrangle.

Vina [TEHAMA]: *village,* 7 miles east of Corning (lat. 39°56' N, long. 122°03'15" W). Named on Vina (1950) 7.5' quadrangle. Postal authorities established Vina post office in 1871 (Frickstad, p. 205). Peter Lassen laid out a town in 1847 on his ranch about 1 mile north of present Vina and called it Benton City for Senator Thomas H. Benton of Missouri, but the place failed to develop (Hoover, Rensch, and Rensch, p. 548). Postal authorities established Grove City post office, named by David Rowles, first postmaster, in 1858 and discontinued it in 1864; the post office probably was situated about 6 miles southeast of present Vina (Salley, p. 90).

Vina Slough [TEHAMA]: *dry wash,* 1.5 miles west-northwest of Vina (lat. 35°56'30" N, long. 121°04'30" W). Named on Vina (1904) 15' quadrangle.

Vinegar Peak [TEHAMA]: *peak,* 9 miles west-southwest of Tomhead Mountain on Tehama-Trinity County line (lat. 40°04'15" N, long. 122°58' W; at NE cor. sec. 34, T 26 N, R 10 W). Altitude 6549 feet. Named on Yolla Bolly (1954) 15' quadrangle.

Vineyard: see **The Vineyard** [TEHAMA].

Vintin Gulch: see **Vinton Gulch** [BUTTE].

Vinton Gulch [BUTTE]: *canyon,* drained by a stream that flows 0.5 mile to Lake Oroville 8 miles south-southeast of Paradise (lat. 39°39'15" N, long. 121°32'15" W; at N line sec. 28, T 21 N, R 4 E). Named on Cherokee (1970) 7.5' quadrangle. Called Vintin Gulch on Oroville (1942) 15' quadrangle, and United States Board on Geographic Names (1973, p. 3) gave this name as a variant. On Chico (1895) 30' quadrangle, the stream in the canyon is called Cherokee Cr.

Viola [SHASTA]: *village,* 9.5 miles west-northwest of Lassen Peak (lat. 40°31'10" N, long. 121°40'35" W; sec. 19, T 31 N, R 3 E). Named on Manzanita Lake (1956) 15' quadrangle. Postal authorities established Viola post office in 1898, discontinued it in 1943, reestablished it in 1948, and discontinued it in 1953 (Salley, p. 232). B.F. Loomis homesteaded at the place and reportedly named the community for his mother; a map of 1884 has the name "Loomis" at the site (Steger, p. 64).

Virginia Bar: see **Steelhead** [SISKIYOU].

Virginia Lake [SISKIYOU]: *lake,* 400 feet long, 17 miles south of Etna (lat. 41°12'20" N, long. 122°51'25" W; near SE cor. sec. 26, T 39 N, R 9 W). Named on Coffee Creek (1955) 15' quadrangle.

Virginia Mill: see **Harts Mill** [BUTTE].

Virginia Mills: see **Berry Creek** [BUTTE] (2).

Virginia Ranch: see **Henley** [SISKIYOU].

Vista Robles [BUTTE]: *locality,* 1 mile south-southwest of Palermo (lat. 39°25'15" N, long. 121°33' W; sec. 17, T 18 N, R 4 E). Named on Palermo (1970) 7.5' quadrangle, which shows an old railroad grade at the site. On Palermo (1912) 7.5' quadrangle, a place called Hearst is situated along Southern Pacific Railroad at present Vista Robles. The name "Hearst" was for George Hearst, who had a home nearby (Dunn, F.D., p. 49).

Vollmers [SHASTA]: *locality,* 2.25 miles south of Lamoine (lat. 40°56'40" N, long. 122°26'10" W; near NW cor. sec. 34, T 36 N, R 5 W). Named on Lamoine (1957) 15' quadrangle.

Vulcans Castle [SHASTA]: *relief feature,* 1.25 miles southwest of Lassen Peak (lat. 40°28'30" N, long. 121°31'45" W; sec. 10, T 30 N, R 4 E). Named on Lassen Peak (1956) 15' quadrangle.

— W —

Wadsworth Flat [SISKIYOU]: *area,* 26 miles west-northwest of Macdoel (lat. 41°56'30" N, long. 122°28'45" W; in and near sec. 12, T 47 N, R 6 W). Named on Copco (1954) 15' quadrangle.

Wagner Gulch [SISKIYOU]: *canyon,* drained by a stream that flows 1.5 miles to Indian Creek (1) 8.5 miles north-northwest of Happy Camp (lat. 41°54'30" N, long. 123°26'40" W). Named on Deadman Point (1981) 7.5' quadrangle.

Wagners [BUTTE]: *locality,* 9 miles north-northwest of Clipper Mills (lat. 39°38'50" N, long. 121°13'50" W). Named on Bidwell Bar (1897) 30' quadrangle.

Wagners Valley [BUTTE]: *relief feature,* 5 miles southeast of the village of Brush Creek (lat. 39°38'20" N, long. 121°16'10" W). Named on Brush Creek (1970) 7.5' quadrangle.

Wagon Camp [SISKIYOU]: *locality,* 6.5 miles northwest of McCloud (lat. 41°19'30" N, long. 122°12'50" W; near E line sec. 8, T 40 N, R 3 W). Named on Shasta (1954) 15' quadrangle.

Wagon Creek [SISKIYOU]: *stream,* flows 11 miles to Sacramento River 2.5 miles south-southwest of the town of Mount Shasta (lat. 41°16'50" N, long. 122°19'50" W; sec. 29, T 40 N, R 4 W). Named on Weed (1954) 15' quadrangle. Called Wagon Valley Creek on Shasta (1894) 1° quadrangle.

Wagoner [SHASTA]: *locality,* 8 miles east of Millville (lat. 40°33'50" N, long. 122°01'40" W; near S line sec. 6, T 31 N, R 1 W). Named on Redding (1901) 30' quadrangle.

Wagoner Canyon [SHASTA]: *canyon,* 3 miles long, along South Cow Creek above a point 8 miles east of Millville (lat. 40°34'30" N, long. 122°01'35" W). Named on Millville (1953) and Whitmore (1956) 15' quadrangles.

Wagon Road Gulch [SHASTA]: *canyon,* drained by a stream that flows nearly 3 miles to Dry Creek (5) 3 miles west-southwest of Olinda (lat. 40°25'15" N, long. 122°27'10" W; sec. 29, T 30 N, R 5 W). Named on Olinda (1964) 7.5' quadrangle.

Wagon Valley Creek: see **Wagon Creek** [SISKIYOU].

Wagon Wheel Draw [TEHAMA]: *canyon,* drained by a stream that flows less than 1 mile to Vale Gulch 7.5 miles southeast of Wakefield Flat (lat. 40°03'15" N, long. 122°32' W; at E line sec. 4, T 25 N, R 6 W). Named on Lowrey (1967) 7.5' quadrangle.

Wagstaff: see **Paradise** [BUTTE].

Wakefield Flat [TEHAMA]: *area,* 22 miles west of Red Bluff (lat. 40°37'35" N, long. 122°38'20" W; sec. 10, T 26 N, R 7 W). Named on Cold Fork (1967) and Raglin Ridge (1967) 7.5' quadrangles.

Wakefields Station: see **Lomo** [BUTTE].

Walbridge Gulch [SISKIYOU]: *canyon,* drained by a stream that flows 1.5 miles to lowlands 18 miles west-southwest of Macdoel (lat. 41°42'30" N, long. 122°19'30" W; sec. 32, T 45 N, R 4 W). Named on Lake Shastina (1954) 15' quadrangle.

Walker [SISKIYOU]: *locality,* 10 miles southeast of Condrey Mountain along Klamath River (lat. 41°50' N, long. 122°50'10" W). Named on Yreka (1939) 30' quadrangle. Postal authorities established Walker post office in 1890 and discontinued it in 1942 (Frickstad, p. 191).

Walker Creek [GLENN]: *stream,* formed by the confluence of North Fork and South Fork 3.5 miles southwest of Orland, flows 16 miles to join South Fork Wilson Creek and form Willow Creek 1.5 miles east of Willows (lat. 39°31'10" N, long. 122°09'40" W; sec. 11, T 19 N, R 3 W). Named on Orland (1951) and Willows (1951) 7.5' quadrangles. Called North Fork Willow Creek on Willows (1906) 15' quadrangle. The name "Walker" commemorates Jeff Walker, a sheepherder in the early 1850's (Gudde, 1949, p. 382). North Fork in 7 miles long and is named on Black Butte Dam (1967), Fruto NE (1952), and Orland (1951) 7.5' quadrangles. South Fork is 12 miles long and is named on Fruto NE (1952), Julian Rocks (1968), and Orland (1951) 7.5' quadrangles.

Walker Creek [SISKIYOU]: *stream,* flows 6.5 miles to Klamath River 1.25 miles east-southeast of the village of Seiad Valley (lat. 41°50'10" N, long. 123°10'15" W). Named on Seiad Valley (1980) 7.5' quadrangle.

Walker Creek: see **East Walker Creek** [SISKIYOU].

Walker Gulch [SISKIYOU]: *canyon,* drained by a stream that flows 3 miles to Klamath River 2.5 miles east-southeast of the village of Seiad Valley (lat. 41°49'55" N, long. 123°09'05" W; sec. 17, T 46 N, R 11 W). Named on Hamburg (1980) and Seiad Valley (1980) 7.5' quadrangles.

Walker Point [TEHAMA]: *peak,* 1.25 miles south-southwest of Beegum Peak (lat. 40°17'50" N, long. 122°53'45" W; near NE cor. sec. 8, T 28 N, R 9 W). Named on Chanchelulla Peak (1951) 15' quadrangle.

Walker Ridge [SISKIYOU]: *ridge,* north- to north-northwest-trending, 2 miles long, 5 miles south of the village of Seiad Valley (lat. 41°46' N, long. 123°11' W); the ridge is west of Walker Creek. Named on Seiad Valley (1980) 7.5' quadrangle.

Walking Bear Camp [SHASTA]: *locality,* 12 miles north-northeast of the village of Big Bend along Moosehead Creek [SHASTA-SISKIYOU] (lat. 41°10'50" N, long. 122°48'45" W; near NE cor. sec. 35, T 39 N, R 1 E). Named on Big Bend (1961) 15' quadrangle.

Walla Walla Creek [SISKIYOU]: *stream,* flows 2 mile to Indian Creek (3) 6.5 miles north of Fort Jones (lat. 41°41'55" N, long. 122°51'30" W; near NE cor. sec. 3, T 44 N, R 9 W); the stream heads on the northeast side of Walla Walla Ridge. Named on Fort Jones (1955) 15' quadrangle.

Walla Walla Ridge [SISKIYOU]: *ridge,* southeast-trending, 1.25 miles long, 7.5 miles north-northwest of Fort Jones (lat. 41°42'20" N, long. 122°53'50" W). Named on Fort Jones (1955) 15' quadrangle.

Walters Gulch [SISKIYOU]: *canyon,* 3 miles long, opens into lowlands 2.5 miles south of Yreka (lat. 41°40'45" N, long. 122°38'30" W; sec. 10, T 44 N, R 7 W). Named on Yreka (1954) 15' quadrangle.

Walts Gulch [SHASTA]: *canyon,* drained by a stream that flows nearly 1 mile to East Fork Clear Creek 6.25 miles south-southwest of Schell Mountain (lat. 40°46' N, long. 122°33'25" W; near S line sec. 28, T 34 N, R 6 W). Named on Schell Mountain (1950) 15' quadrangle.

Ward: see **Camp Eighteen** [BUTTE].

Ward Butte [SHASTA]: *peak,* 5.5 miles southwest of Burney (lat. 40°49'20" N, long. 121°44' W; sec. 10, T 34 N, R 2 E). Named on Burney (1957) 15' quadrangle.

Ward Goat Camp: see **Goat Camp** [TEHAMA] (4).

Wards Creek: see **Wards Fork**, under **Elliot Creek** [SISKIYOU].

Wards Fork: see **Elliot Creek** [SISKIYOU].

Wards Fork Gap: see **Elliot Creek** [SISKIYOU].

Ward Spring: see **Government Well** [SHASTA].

Warmcastle: see **Soda Springs** [SISKIYOU] (3).

Warmcastle Soda Springs: see **Soda Springs** [SISKIYOU] (3).

Warner Grade Reservoir [SHASTA]: *intermittent lake,* 350 feet long, 5 miles east of Burney Falls (lat. 41°00'55" N, long. 121°33' W; near W line sec. 30, T 37 N, R 4 E). Named on Pondosa (1961) 15' quadrangle.

Washbasin Lake [SISKIYOU]: *lake,* 1000 feet long, 16 miles south-southeast of Etna (lat. 41°14'40" N, long. 122°45'40" W; near E line sec. 15, T 39 N, R 8 W). Named on Coffee Creek (1955) 15' quadrangle.

Watakma Butte [SISKIYOU]: *hill,* 13 miles north-northwest of Bartle (lat. 41°26'10" N, long. 121°53'35" W; near NE cor. sec. 6, T 41 N, R 1 E). Named on Bartle (1961) 15' quadrangle.

Water Canyon [GLENN]: *canyon,* 1.25 miles long, 3 miles west-southwest of High Peak (lat. 39°24'50" N, long. 122°28'30" W; mainly in sec. 13, T 18 N, R 6 W). Named on Lodoga (1960) 15' quadrangle.

Water Caves [SISKIYOU]: *caves,* 17 miles north-northeast of Bartle (lat. 41°27'30" N, long. 121°37'45" W). Named on Hambone (1961) 15' quadrangle.

Waterdog Lake [SISKIYOU]: *lake,* 800 feet long, 14 miles south-southwest of Etna (lat. 41°15'55" N, long. 122°58'35" W; near SE cor. sec. 2, T 39 N, R 10 W). Named on Etna (1955) 15' quadrangle.

Water Hollow [TEHAMA]: *canyon,* drained by a stream that flows 2 miles to Big Dry Creek 10 miles south of Panther Spring (lat. 40°06'25" N, long. 121°46'45" W; sec. 17, T 26 N, R 2 E). Named on Panther Spring (1953) 15' quadrangle.

Waters Gulch [SHASTA]:

(1) *canyon,* drained by a stream that flows about 2 miles to Willow Creek (4) 4 miles southwest of the village of French Gulch (lat. 40°40'05" N, long. 122°41'45" W; near S line sec. 31, T 33 N, R 7 W). Named on French Gulch (1979) 7.5' quadrangle.

(2) *canyon,* drained by a stream that flows 1.25 miles to Sacramento River Arm Shasta Lake 14 miles south-southeast of Lamoine (lat. 40°47'05" N, long. 122°20'40" W; sec. 20, T 34 N, R 4 W). Named on Lamoine (1957) 15' quadrangle.

Watertank Hill: see **Braselton Hill** [BUTTE].

Water Trough Springs [SHASTA]: *spring,* 6 miles north-northwest of Shoeinhorse Mountain (lat. 41°08'30" N, long. 122°07'20" W; at W line sec. 20, T 38 N, R 2 W). Named on Shoeinhorse Mountain (1954) 15' quadrangle.

Watson [TEHAMA]: *locality,* 5.5 miles south-southwest of Wakefield Flat (lat. 40°03'15" N, long. 122°41'10" W; near NE cor. sec. 6, T 25 N, R 7 W). Named on Colyear Springs (1957) 15' quadrangle.

Watson Creek [GLENN]: *stream,* flows 8.5 miles to Grindstone Creek [GLENN-TEHAMA] 5.25 miles north of the village of Elk Creek (lat. 39°40'45" N, long. 122°31'45" W; near W line sec. 15, T 21 N, R 6 W). Named on Alder Springs (1967) and Chrome (1968) 7.5' quadrangles. The name commemorates Henry Watson, a settler that Indians killed in 1862 (Dillon, 1971, unnumbered page 11). Chrome (1968) 7.5' quadrangle shows Watson grave located 3 miles west-northwest of the mouth of the stream.

Watson Creek: see **Watson Gulch** [SHASTA].

Watson Gulch [SHASTA]: *canyon,* drained by a stream that flows 2.5 miles to Wilson Creek nearly 6 miles southwest of Ono (lat. 40°25'50" N, long. 122°42'35" W; near NE cor. sec. 25, T 30 N, R 8 W). Named on Ono (1952) 15' quadrangle. On Averill's (1939) map, the stream in the canyon is called Watson Cr. The name "Watson Gulch" commemorates an Oregonian who mined in the canyon in 1850 (Steger, p. 65).

Watson Ridge [BUTTE]: *ridge,* west- to southwest-trending, 6 miles long, 12 miles north-northwest of Clipper Mills (lat. 39°41'30" N, long. 121°14'30" W). Named on Brush Creek (1970) and Cascade (1948) 7.5' quadrangles.

Watson Spring [GLENN]: *spring,* 4 miles east-northeast of Saint John Mountain (lat. 39°28' N, long. 122°37'45" W). Named on Saint John Mountain (1968) 7.5' quadrangle.

Watts Gulch [SHASTA]: *canyon,* drained by a stream that flows less than 1 mile to East Fork Clear Creek 6.25 miles south-southwest of Schell Mountain (lat. 40°45' N, long. 122°33'25" W; near SW cor. sec. 28, T 34 N, R 6 W). Named on Schell Mountain (1950) 15' quadrangle.

Waugh: see **Middle Creek** [SHASTA] (2).

Webb Canyon: see **Web Hollow** [BUTTE-TEHAMA].

Webb Creek: see **Web Hollow** [BUTTE-TEHAMA].

Webb Gulch [SISKIYOU]: *canyon,* drained by a stream that flows 3 miles to Shasta Valley 21 miles west-southwest of Macdoel (lat. 41°44'05" N, long. 122°24' W; sec. 22, T 45 N, R 5 W). Named on Copco (1954) and Lake Shastina (1954) 15' quadrangles.

Web Hollow [BUTTE-TEHAMA]: *canyon,* drained by a stream that heads in Tehama County and flows 6 miles to Big Chico Creek [BUTTE-TEHAMA] 15 miles north of Paradise in Butte County (lat. 39°58'30" N, long. 121°40'05" W; near N line sec. 5, T 24 N, R 3 E). Named on Butte Meadows (1958) 15' quadrangle, and on Cohasset (1979) 7.5' quadrangle. Called Webb Canyon on Chico (1895) 30' quadrangle. The stream in the canyon is called Webb Creek on Mineral (1941) 30' quadrangle.

Weed [SISKIYOU]: *town,* 24 miles southeast of Yreka (lat. 41°25'30" N, long. 122°23' W; in and near sec. 1, 2, T 41 N, R 5 W). Named on Weed (1954) 15' quadrangle. Postal authorities established Weed post office in 1901 (Frickstad, p. 191), and the town incorporated in 1961. The name commemorates Abner Weed, founder of Weed Lumber Company, and a county supervisor and state senator (Gudde, 1949, p. 386). Diller and others' (1915) map shows a place called Evans located 3 miles north-northeast of Weed along the railroad, a place called Seger located 4.5 miles north-northeast of Weed along the railroad, and an place called Delaney located 11 miles northeast of Weed along the railroad. California Mining Bureau's (1917a) map shows a place called Coggins located about 2 miles south-southeast of Weed along the railroad, and a place called Geagan located 5 miles northeast of Weed along the railroad.

Weemasoul Creek [TEHAMA]: *stream,* flows nearly 7 miles to Salt Creek (1) 8 miles north-northwest of Wakefield Flat (lat. 40°14'40" N, long. 122°40'35" W; near S line sec. 29, T 28 N, R 7 W). Named on Cold Fork (1967) 7.5' quadrangle.

Weemasoul Spring [TEHAMA]: *spring,* 6 miles north-northwest of Wakefield Flat (lat. 40°12'15" N, long. 122°41'25" W; near E line sec. 7, T 27 N, R 7 W); the spring is along Weemasoul Creek. Named on Cold Fork (1967) 7.5' quadrangle.

Welch: see **Sims** [SHASTA].

Wells Cabin Campground [TEHAMA]: *locality,* 11 miles southwest of Ball Mountain (lat. 39°50'15" N, long. 122°56'55" W; near E line sec. 22, T 23 N, R 10 W). Named on Mendocino Pass (1967) 7.5' quadrangle.

Wells Creek [TEHAMA]: *stream,* flows 13 miles to Dry Creek (1) 8.5 miles west of Rosewood (lat. 40°17'10" N, long. 122°42'55" W; at N line sec. 13, T 28 N, R 8 W). Named on Chanchelulla Peak (1951), Ono (1952), and Yolla Bolly (1954) 15' quadrangles.

Wells Creek Peaks [TEHAMA]: *peaks,* 6.5 miles north-northwest of Tomhead Mountain (lat. 40°13'15" N, long. 122°51'25" W; sec. 2, 3, T 27 N, R 9 W); the peaks are near the head of Wells Creek. Altitude of highest peak is 5064 feet. Named on Yolla Bolly (1954) 15' quadrangle.

Wengler [SHASTA]: *locality,* 5 miles north of the village of Montgomery Creek (lat. 40°54'45" N, long. 121°54'30" W; near SW cor. sec. 6, T 35 N, R 1 E). Named on Montgomery Creek (1956) 15' quadrangle. Postal authorities established Wengler post office in 1899, moved it 1.75 miles southeast in 1903, moved it 2.5 miles northwest in 1907, moved it 3 miles southwest in 1908, moved it 0.75 mile east in 1941, and discontinued it in 1942; the name was for Mathias Wengler, first postmaster (Salley, p. 236).

Wescott Creek [GLENN]: *stream,* flows 3.5 miles to Lake County 12 miles south-southeast of Black Butte (lat. 39°34'50" N, long. 122°45'45" W; at S line sec. 16, T 20 N, R 8 W). Named on Kneecap Ridge (1967) 7.5' quadrangle. United States Board on Geographic Names (1933, p. 808) rejected the name "Sand Creek" for the stream.

West Beaver Creek: see **West Fork**, under **Beaver Creek** [SISKIYOU] (1).

West Boulder Creek [SISKIYOU]: *stream,* flows 4 miles to join Wolf Creek (2) and form Boulder Creek (3) 14 miles south-southeast of Etna (lat. 41°15'40" N, long. 122°49'20" W; sec. 7, T 39 N, R 8 W). Named on Coffee Creek (1955) and Etna (1955) 15' quadrangles.

West Boulder Lake [SISKIYOU]: *lake,* 750 feet long, 17 miles south-southeast of Etna (lat. 41°12'40" N, long. 122°49' W; near E line sec. 30, T 39 N, R 8 W); the lake is near the head of West Boulder Creek, and less than 1 mile west-southwest of Middle Boulder Lake. Named on Coffee Creek (1955) 15' quadrangle.

West Branch [BUTTE]: *locality,* 15 miles north of Paradise (lat. 39°58'45" N, long. 121°38'20" W). Named on Chico (1895) 30' quadrangle. California Mining Bureau's (1909d) map has the form "Westbranch" for the name. Postal authorities established West Branch post office in 1878 and discontinued it in 1911 (Frickstad, p. 12).

West Branch Camp [BUTTE]: *locality,* 4 miles southeast of Butte Meadows (lat. 40°02'05" N, long. 121°30'25" W; sec. 10, T 25 N, R 4 E); the place is along West Branch Feather River. Named on Butte Meadows (1958) 15' quadrangle.

West China Point [BUTTE]: *ridge,* south-southwest-trending, 1 mile long, 1.5 miles south-southwest of Stirling City (lat. 39°53'05" N, long. 121°32'25" W). Named on Stirling City (1979) 7.5' quadrangle.

West Grider Creek [SISKIYOU]: *stream,* flows 3.25 miles to Klamath River less than 1 mile west of the village of Seiad Valley (lat. 41°50'35" N, long. 123°12'40" W); the mouth of the creek is 1500 feet upstream along Klamath River from the mouth of Grider Creek. Named on Seiad Valley (1980) and Slater Butte (1980) 7.5' quadrangles.

West Haight Mountain [SISKIYOU]: *peak,* 20 miles south of Macdoel (lat. 41°32'30" N, long. 122°00'05" W; near E line sec. 30, T 43 N, R 1 W); the peak is 2.25 miles west-northwest of Haight Mountain. Altitude 8002 feet. Named on Bray (1950) and The Whaleback (1954) 15' quadrangles.

West Hunt Creek [SHASTA]: *stream,* flows 2 miles to Old Cow Creek 9 miles east-northeast of Whitmore (lat. 40°41'25" N, long. 121°46'15" W; sec. 29, T 33 N, R 2 E). Named on Whitmore (1956) 15' quadrangle.

Weston Gulch [SISKIYOU]: *canyon,* drained by a stream that flows 1.25 miles to Scott Valley 4 miles east-northeast of Etna (lat. 41°28'20" N, long. 122°49' W; at W line sec. 19, T 42 N, R 8 W). Named on Etna (1955) 15' quadrangle.

West Park Lakes [SISKIYOU]: *lakes,* three, largest 400 feet long, 18 miles east-southeast of Etna (lat. 41°23' N, long. 122°33'30" W; sec. 20, 21, T 41 N, R 6 W); the lakes are at the head of a branch of Parks Creek. Named on China Mountain (1955) 15' quadrangle.

West Prospect Peak [SHASTA]: *peak,* 10 miles northeast of Lassen Peak (lat. 40°35'45" N, long. 121°22'45" W; on E line sec. 35, T 32 N, R 5 E); the peak is 2.5 miles northwest of Prospect Peak. Altitude 8172 feet. Named on Prospect Peak (1957) 15' quadrangle.

West Sulphur Creek [SHASTA-TEHAMA]: *stream,* heads in Shasta County and flows 2.5 miles to join East Sulphur Creek and form Mill Creek [TEHAMA] (3) 7 miles northeast of Mineral in Tehama County (lat. 40°25'45" N, long. 121°31'20" W; sec. 27, T 30 N, R 4 E); the stream flows through Sulphur Works [SHASTA]. Named on Lassen Peak (1956) 15' quadrangle.

Wet Weather Lake [SISKIYOU]: *intermittent lake,* 1100 feet long, 18 miles east of Bartle (lat. 41°17'50" N, long. 121°29'55" W; on S line sec. 15, T 40 N, R 4 E). Named on White Horse (1962) 15' quadrangle.

Whaleback: see **The Whaleback** [SISKIYOU].

Whaleback Mountain: see **The Whaleback** [SISKIYOU].

Wheel Gulch: see **Big Wheel Gulch** [SISKIYOU].

Wheelock: see **Fort Jones** [SISKIYOU].

Whiskey: see **Whiskeytown** [SHASTA].

Whiskey Bar: see **China Gulch** [BUTTE].

Whiskey Butte: see **Whisky Butte** [SISKIYOU].

Whiskey Creek [SHASTA]: *stream,* flows 4.5 miles to Whiskeytown Lake 5.5 miles southeast of the village of French Gulch (lat. 40°39'10" N, long. 122°33'20" W; near SW cor. sec. 4, T 32 N, R 6 W). Named on Whiskeytown (1979) 7.5' quadrangle.

Whiskey Creek [SISKIYOU]: *stream,* flows 2.5 miles to McCloud River [SHASTA-SISKIYOU] 6.5 miles west of Bartle (lat. 41°14'45" N, long. 121°56'30" W; near NW cor. sec. 11, T 39 N, R 1 W). Named on Big Bend (1961) 15' quadrangle.

Whiskey Creek: see **Whiskeytown**[SHASTA].

Whiskey Creek Diggings: see **Whiskeytown** [SHASTA].

Whiskey Flat [BUTTE]:

(1) *locality,* 5.25 miles north-northwest of Paradise along Butte Creek [BUTTE-GLENN] (lat. 39°50' N, long. 121°38'40" W; sec. 21, T 23 N, R 3 E). Named on Paradise West (1980) 7.5' quadrangle.

(2) *locality,* 5.25 miles north-northeast of Paradise along West Branch Feather River (lat. 39°49'25" N, long. 121°34'05" W; sec. 30, T 23 N, R 4 E). Named on Paradise East (1980) 7.5' quadrangle.

Whiskey Saddle [TEHAMA]: *pass,* 8.5 miles west of Paskenta (lat. 39°53'35" N, long. 122°42'20" W; sec. 36, T 24 N, R 8 W). Named on Riley Ridge (1967) 7.5' quadrangle.

Whiskeytown [SHASTA]: *locality,* 6.5 miles south of the village of French Gulch (lat. 40°37'45" N, long. 122°33'20" W); the place is at the mouth of Whiskey Creek. Named on French Gulch (1944) 15' quadrangle. Called Whiskey Town on Eddy's (1854) map, and called Whiskey on Goddard's (1857) map. Red Bluff (1894) 1° quadrangle shows Stella P.O. at the place. On Whiskeytown (1979) 7.5' quadrangle, water of Whiskeytown Lake covers the site, and the name "Whiskeytown" applies to a locality situated about 0.5 mile north of the original site (lat. 40°38'20" N, long. 122°33'30" W). The mining camp of Whiskeytown started in 1849 and was known as Whiskey Creek Diggings and as Franklin City for a short time (Steger, p. 65). Postal authorities established Whiskey Creek post office 4 miles northwest of Shasta in 1856 and discontinued it in 1864 (Salley, p. 239). They established Blair post office at Whiskeytown in 1881, changed the name to Stella in 1885, and discontinued it in 1909; the name "Blair" was for Eunice F. Blair, first postmaster, and the name "Stella" was for the postmaster's wife (Salley, p. 22, 212). They established Schilling post office at Whiskeytown in 1917, discontinued it for a time in 1931, and discontinued it finally in 1952, when they finally recognized the name "Whiskeytown" and established Whiskeytown post office; the name "Schilling" was for John F. Schilling, first postmaster (Salley, p. 199).

Whiskeytown Lake [SHASTA]: *lake,* behind a dam on Clear Creek 6.25 miles north of Igo (lat. 40°35'55" N, long. 122°32'15" W; sec. 27, T 32 N, R 6 W); the lake covers the original site of Whiskeytown. Named on French Gulch (1979), Igo (1979), and Whiskeytown (1979) 7.5' quadrangles.

Whisky Butte [SISKIYOU]: *peak,* 3.5 miles west of Etna (lat. 41°26'50" N, long. 122°57'30" W; sec. 35, T 42 N, R 10 W); the peak is near the head of Whisky Creek (2). Altitude 6889 feet. Named on Etna (1955) 15' quadrangle. United States Board on Geographic Names (1978c, p. 4) rejected the form "Whiskey Butte" for the name.

Whisky Camp [SISKIYOU]: *locality,* 18 miles southwest of Scott Bar (lat. 41°33'15" N, long. 123°13'45" W). Named on Marble Mountain (1980) 7.5' quadrangle.

Whisky Creek [SISKIYOU]:

(1) *stream,* heads in the State of Oregon and flows 3.5 miles in Siskiyou County to Applegate River 9 miles north of the village of Seiad Valley (lat. 41°58'25" N, long. 123°10'50" W). Named on Kangaroo Mountain (1980) 7.5' quadrangle.

(2) *stream,* flows 1.5 miles to Etna Creek 1.5 miles south-southwest of Etna (lat. 41°26'15" N, long. 122°54'35" W; near N line sec. 5, T 41 N, R 9 W); the stream heads near Whisky Butte. Named on Etna (1955) 15' quadrangle.

Whisky Ridge [SISKIYOU]: *ridge,* southeast-trending, 2 miles long, 10.5

miles north of the village of Seiad Valley (lat. 41°59'25" N, long. 123°13' W); the ridge is southwest of Whisky Creek (1). Named on Kangaroo Mountain (1980) 7.5' quadrangle.

Whisky Ridge [TEHAMA]: *ridge,* south- to south-southeast-trending, nearly 2 miles long, 7.25 miles southwest of Wakefield Flat (lat. 40°02'30" N, long. 122°43'20" W). Named on Raglin Ridge (1967) 7.5' quadrangle.

White Cabin Creek [GLENN]: *stream,* flows 10 miles to Sheep Corral Creek 14 miles northeast of Fruto (lat. 39°36'25" N, long. 122°15' W; near E line sec. 12, T 20 N, R 4 W). Named on Fruto NE (1952), Julian Rocks (1968), and Stone Valley (1952) 7.5' quadrangles.

White Cloud Mountain [SISKIYOU]: *peak,* 7.5 miles east-northeast of the village of Seiad Valley (lat. 41°52'15" N, long. 123°03'30" W; on W line sec. 31, T 47 N, R 10 W). Altitude 4238 feet. Named on Hamburg (1980) 7.5' quadrangle.

White Deer Lake [SISKIYOU]: *intermittent lake,* 2800 feet long, 7 miles north-northeast of Bartle (lat. 41°20'20" N, long. 121°44'25" W; on N line sec. 4, T 40 N, R 2 E). Named on Hambone (1961) 15' quadrangle.

White Deer Well [SISKIYOU]: *well,* 7 miles north-northeast of Bartle (lat. 41°20'30" N, long. 121°44'30" W; near S line sec. 33, T 41 N, R 2 E); the well is by White Deer Lake. Named on Hambone (1961) 15' quadrangle.

White Fawn Gulch [SHASTA]: *canyon,* 1 mile long, 16 miles northwest of Lassen Peak (lat. 40°39'20" N, long. 121°42'35" W; mainly in sec. 2, T 32 N, R 2 E). Named on Manzanita Lake (1956) 15' quadrangle.

Whitehall Ravine [BUTTE]: *canyon,* drained by a stream that flows 3.5 miles to Rocky Honcut Creek 2.5 miles north-northwest of Bangor (lat. 39°25'15" N, long. 121°25'35" W; at E line sec. 17, T 18 N, R 5 E). Named on Bangor (1947) 7.5' quadrangle.

White Horse Creek [GLENN]: *stream,* heads in Mendocino County and flows 2 miles to Black Butte River 8 miles south of Black Butte (lat. 39°36'35" N, long. 122°52'05" W; near SE cor. sec. 4, T 20 N, R 9 W). Named on Hull Mountain (1967) and Kneecap Ridge (1967) 7.5' quadrangles.

White Horse Mountains [SISKIYOU]: *ridge,* northwest-trending, 5 miles long, 18 miles east of Bartle on Siskiyou-Modoc County line (lat. 41°16'45" N, long. 121°28' W). Named on White Horse (1962) 15' quadrangle.

Whitehouse [SHASTA]: *locality,* 5.5 miles north-northwest of Redding (lat. 40°39'15" N, long. 122°26' W; sec. 4, T 32 N, R 5 W). Named on Redding (1901) 30' quadrangle. Postal authorities established Whitehouse post office in 1893, discontinued it in 1906, reestablished it in 1907, and discontinued it in 1913; the name was for Whitehouse & Bliss of London, operator of a mine at the place (Salley, p. 239).

White Lake [SISKIYOU]: *intermittent lake,* about 2 miles long, 13 miles north-northeast of Mount Dome on California-Oregon State line (lat. 41°59'45" N, long. 121°37'45" W). Named on Mount Dome (1950) 15' quadrangle.

Whiteman Canyon [TEHAMA]: *canyon,* drained by a stream that flows 2 miles to Beegum Creek [SHASTA-TEHAMA] 6 miles east-northeast of Beegum Peak (lat. 40°21'20" N, long. 122°47'20" W; near N line sec. 20, T 29 N, R 8 W). Named on Chanchelulla Peak (1951) 15' quadrangle.

White Mountain [SISKIYOU]: *peak,* 10.5 miles northeast of the village of Seiad Valley (lat. 41°57'15" N, long. 123°03'20" W; sec. 6, T 47 N, R 10 W); the peak is 2200 feet east of Black Mountain (2). Altitude 6460 feet. Named on Dutch Creek (1980) 7.5' quadrangle.

White Mountain: see **Reading Peak** [SHASTA].

White Ridge [SISKIYOU]: *ridge,* generally west-southwest-trending, 4 miles long, 10 miles west-southwest of the town of Mount Shasta (lat. 41°15'05" N, long. 122°29' W). Named on Bonanza King (1955), Dunsmuir (1954), and Weed (1954) 15' quadrangles.

White Rock [SHASTA]: *peak,* 6.5 miles southwest of Shoeinhorse Mountain (lat. 41°00'35" N, long. 122°10'05" W). Altitude 4114 feet. Named on Shoeinhorse Mountain (1954) 15' quadrangle.

White Rock [TEHAMA] *peak,* 7.5 miles west-southwest of Beegum Peak on Tehama-Trinity County line (lat. 40°15'50" N, long. 123°01'10" W; sec. 20, T 28 N, R 10 W). Named on Dubakella Mountain (1954) 15' quadrangle.

White Rock: see **Oregon Gulch** [BUTTE] (2).

White Rock Bar: see **Oregon Gulch** [BUTTE] (2).

White Rock Camp: see **Oregon Gulch** [BUTTE] (2).

White Rock Gulch [SHASTA]: *canyon,* drained by a stream that flows 1 mile to Whiskeytown Lake 6.5 miles southeast of the village of French Gulch (lat. 40°38'25" N, long. 122°32'35" W; sec. 9, T 32 N, R 6 W). Named on Whiskeytown (1979) 7.5' quadrangle.

Whites Gulch [SISKIYOU]:

(1) *canyon,* 1.5 miles long, opens into the canyon of North Fork Salmon River 2.5 miles east of Sawyers Bar (lat. 41°17'55" N, long. 123°04'55" W); the canyon splits at the head into East Fork and West Fork. Named on Tanners Peak (1977) 7.5' quadrangle. East Fork is 4.25 miles long and West Fork is 2.25 miles long; both forks are named on Tanners Peak (1977) 7.5' quadrangle.

(2) *canyon,* drained by a stream that flows about 1 mile to Indian Creek (3) 5 miles north of Fort Jones (lat. 41°40'45" N, long. 122°50'50" W; sec. 11, T 44 N, R 9 W). Named on Fort Jones (1955) 15' quadrangle.

(3) *canyon,* drained by a stream that flows 1.5 miles to Humbug Creek 11 miles southwest of Hornbrook (lat. 41°47'45" N, long. 122°41'15" W; sec. 32, T 46 N, R 7 W). Named on Hornbrook (1955) 15' quadrangle.

(4) *canyon,* drained by a stream that flows 1.25 miles to Duzel Creek 7.25 miles southeast of Fort Jones (lat. 41°31'45" N, long. 123°45'10" W; sec. 34, T 43 N, R 8 W). Named on Yreka (1954) 15' quadrangle.

White Spring [BUTTE]: *spring,* 3.5 miles south-southwest of Paradise (lat. 39°42'20" N, long. 121°38'20" W; sec. 4, T 21 N, R 3 E). Named on Hamlin Canyon (1951) 7.5' quadrangle.

White Spring Ridge [BUTTE]: *ridge,* generally south-southwest-trending, 3.5 miles long, 2.5 miles south of Paradise (lat. 39°43'30" N, long. 121°37'25" W); White Spring is near the southwest end of the ridge. Named on Cherokee (1970) and Hamlin Canyon (1951) 7.5' quadrangles.

Whites Stage Station [SISKIYOU]: *locality,* 8 miles south-southwest of Scott Bar along the Scott River (lat. 41°34'10" N, long. 123°02'10" W). Named on Seiad (1922) 30" quadrangle.

White Sulphur Spring [TEHAMA]: *spring,* nearly 2 miles east-northeast of Mineral (lat. 40°21'20" N, long. 121°33'45" W; sec. 20, T 29 N, R 4 E). Named on Lassen Peak (1956) 15' quadrangle.

Whiteys Peak [SISKIYOU] *peak,* 2.25 miles north-northwest of Salmon Mountain on Siskiyou-Humboldt County line (lat. 41°12'45" N, long. 123°26' W). Named on Salmon Mountain (1978) 7.5' quadrangle.

Whitlock Butte [TEHAMA]: *peak,* 3 miles northwest of Paskenta (lat. 39°54'50" N, long. 122°35'15" W; at N line sec. 30, T 24 N, R 6 W). Altitude 1405 feet. Named on Pasketna (1967) 7.5' quadrangle.

Whitlock Campground [TEHAMA]: *locality,* 8 miles west-northwest of Paskenta (lat. 39°55'10" N, long. 122°41'10" W; sec. 19, T 24 N, R 7 W). Named on Riley Ridge (1967) 7.5' quadrangle. Called Whitlock Camp on Paskenta (1952) 15' quadrangle.

Whitlow Creek [SHASTA]: *stream,* flows 2.25 miles to Sacramento River less than 0.5 mile south-southeast of Lamoine (lat. 40°58'20" N, long. 122°25'40" W; at S line sec. 15, T 36 N, R 5 W). Named on Lamoine (1957) 15' quadrangle. Called Little Slate Cr. on Redding (1901) 30' quadrangle.

Whitlow Ridge [SISKIYOU]: *ridge,* south-southeast-trending, 3.5 miles long, 8 miles east of Bartle (lat. 41°15'15" N, long. 121°40' W). Named on Hambone (1961) and Pondosa (1961) 15' quadrangles.

Whitmore [SHASTA]: *village,* 22 miles southwest of Burney (lat. 40°37'45" N, long. 121°54'45" W; at W line sec. 18, T 32 N, R 1 E). Named on Whitmore (1956) 15' quadrangle. Postal authorities established Whitmore post office in 1885, moved it 0.75 mile east in 1899, and moved it 0.75 mile west in 1896 (Salley, p. 240). The name is for Simon H. Whitmore, who aided in establishing the post office; early settlers at the place called their community Tamarack (Steger, p. 66). Postal authorities established Pawnee post office 7 miles west of Whitmore in 1894 and discontinued it in 1902; postmaster Robert Crews suggested the name (Salley, p. 168).

Whitney: see **Gregory** [SHASTA]; **Whitney Gulch** [SHASTA].

Whitney Butte [SISKIYOU]: *hill,* 11 miles north of Medicine Lake (lat. 41°44'20" N, long. 121°35'25" W; sec. 14, T 45 N, R 3 E). Altitude 5004 feet. Named on Medicine Lake (1952) 15' quadrangle.

Whitney Creek [SISKIYOU]: *stream,* flows 9.5 miles to end 25 miles southwest of Macdoel (lat. 41°32'40" N, long. 122°18' W; near W line sec. 27, T 43 N, R 4 W); the stream heads near Whitney Glacier. Named on Lake Shastina (1954), Shasta (1954), and Weed (1954) 15' quadrangles. Called Inconstance Creek on Dunsmuir (1935) 30' quadrangle.

Whitney Falls [SISKIYOU]: *waterfall,* 15 miles north-northwest of McCloud along Whitney Creek (lat. 41°27'40" N, long. 122°14'20" W; sec. 30, T 42 N, R 3 W). Named on Shasta (1954) 15' quadrangle.

Whitney Glacier [SISKIYOU]: *glacier,* about 12 miles north-northwest of McCloud on Mount Shasta (1) (lat. 41°24'45" N, long. 122°12'40" W); the feature is near the head of Whitney Creek. Named on Shasta (1954) 15' quadrangle. The name commemorates Josiah Dwight Whitney (Eichorn, p. 13), head of Geological Survey of California in the 1860's.

Whitney Gulch [SHASTA]: *canyon,* drained by a stream that flows 3 miles to Clear Creek 6.25 miles southwest of Schell Mountain (lat. 40°47'15" N, long. 122°36'30" W; sec. 24, T 34 N, R 7 W). Named on Schell Mountain (1950) 15' quadrangle. Weaverville (1913) 30' quadrangle has the name "Whitney" for a place situated less than 0.25 mile north of the mouth of Whitney Creek in present Whitney Gulch. Steger (p. 66) associated the name "Whitney" with Jack Whitney, who owned Whitney ranch and Mountain House on the stage route from Shasta to Yreka.

Whittington: see **Red Bluff** [TEHAMA]; **Whittington Place** [SHASTA].

Whittington Butte [SHASTA]: *peak,* 9 miles south of Burney (lat. 40°45'20" N, long. 121°38'30" W; near S line sec. 33, T 34 N, R 3 E). Named on Burney (1957) 15' quadrangle.

Whittington Place [SHASTA]: *locality,* 18 miles north-northwest of Lassen Peak (lat. 40°42'35" N, long. 121°40'45" W; at N line sec. 19, T 33 N, R 3 E). Site named on Manzanita Lake (1956) 15' quadrangle. Called Whittington on Burney (1939) 30' quadrangle.

Wible Spring [TEHAMA]: *spring,* 8 miles southwest of Mineral (lat.

40°15'50" N, long. 121°42' W; sec. 24, T 28 N, R 2 E). Named on Lassen Peak (1956) 15' quadrangle.

Wick: see **Wicks Corner** [BUTTE].

Wicks Corner [BUTTE]: *locality,* 6 miles northwest of Oroville (lat. 39°34'55" N, long. 121°37'15" W; near S line sec. 15, T 20 N, R 3 E). Named on Oroville (1970) 7.5' quadrangle. Called Wick on Chico (1895) 30' quadrangle. Postal authorities established Wick post office in 1884, moved it 2 miles southeast and changed the name to Sundale in 1886, and discontinued it in 1897; the name was for Moses Wick, first postmaster (Salley, p. 215, 240). Wicks Corner was called Antelope Springs before Mr. Wick came to the place (Dunn, F.D., p. 112).

Wicks Lake [SISKIYOU]: *lake,* 250 feet long, 6.25 miles southwest of Etna (lat. 41°23'35" N, long. 122°58'30" W; near E line sec. 22, T 41 N, R 10 W. Named on Etna (1955) 15' quadrangle.

Widow Spring [SISKIYOU]: *spring,* 8 miles north-northeast of McCloud (lat. 41°20'50" N, long. 122°04' W; near NE cor. sec. 3, T 40 N, R 2 W). Named on Shasta (1954) 15' quadrangle.

Widow Wilson Field [TEHAMA]: *area,* 8.5 miles north of Wakefield Flat along Salt Creek (1) (lat. 40°14'55" N, long. 122°39'55" W; sec. 28, T 28 N, R 7 W). Named on Cold Fork (1967) 7.5' quadrangle.

Wilcox Flat [TEHAMA]: *area,* 3.5 miles north-northwest of Wakefield Flat along Cold Fork (1) (lat. 40°10'05" N, long. 122°40'35" W; sec. 29, T 27 N, R 7 W). Named on Cold Fork (1967) 7.5' quadrangle.

Wilcox Peak [SHASTA]: *peak,* 14 miles north of Lassen Peak (lat. 40°41'35" N, long. 121°29'40" W; near NW cor. sec. 26, T 33 N, R 4 E). Altitude 6442 feet. Named on Prospect Peak (1957) 15' quadrangle. Steger (p. 66) associated the name with Charles W. Wilcox, who came to the Hat Creek neighborhood in 1872 and lived there until his death in 1900.

Wilcox Spring [SHASTA]: *spring,* 16 miles north of Lassen Peak (lat. 40°42'50" N, long. 121°30'40" W; sec. 15, T 33 N, R 4 E). Named on Manzanita Lake (1956) 15' quadrangle.

Wild Bill Gulch [SHASTA]: *canyon,* less than 1 mile long, 6 miles north of Schell Mountain (lat. 40°51'20" N, long. 122°31'30" W; sec. 35, T 36 N, R 6 W). Named on Schell Mountain (1950) 15' quadrangle.

Wildcat Canyon [GLENN]: *canyon,* drained by a stream that flows 1.5 miles to Mill Creek 11.5 miles west-northwest of the village of Elk Creek (lat. 39°40'50" N, long. 122°43'40" W). Named on Alder Springs (1967) 7.5' quadrangle.

Wildcat Canyon [SHASTA]: *canyon,* drained by a stream that flows 1.25 miles to Clikapudi Creek 12.5 miles north of Millville (lat. 40°43'45" N, long. 122°11'50" W; sec. 10, T 33 N, R 3 W). Named on Bella Vista (1965) 7.5' quadrangle.

Wildcat Canyon [TEHAMA]: *canyon,* 5 miles long, along Wildcat Creek (1) above a point 5.5 miles north-northeast of Los Molinos (lat. 40°05'25" N, long. 122°02'15" W; sec. 24, T 26 N, R 2 W). Named on Panther Spring (1953) 15' quadrangle, and on Los Molinos (1952) 7.5' quadrangle.

Wildcat Creek [SHASTA]: *stream,* flows 3 miles to Dry Clover Creek 2.5 miles northwest of Whitmore (lat. 40°39'30" N, long. 121°56'20" W; sec. 2, T 32 N, R 1 W). Named on Whitmore (1956) 15' quadrangle.

Wildcat Creek [SISKIYOU]: *stream,* flows 5.5 miles to Scott River 10.5 miles south-southeast of Etna (lat. 41°19'15" N, long. 122°48'35" W; near N line sec. 17, T 40 N, R 8 W); the stream heads near Wildcat Peak. Named on Etna (1955) 15' quadrangle.

Wildcat Creek [TEHAMA]:

(1) *stream,* flows nearly 7 miles to Dye Creek 5 miles northeast of Los Molinos (lat. 40°05'30" N, long. 122°04'10" W; at W line sec. 23, T 26 N, R 2 W). Named on Los Molinos (1952) 7.5' quadrangle.

(2) *stream,* flows nearly 5 miles to Deer Creek (2) 14 miles south of Panther Spring (lat. 40°02'55" N, long. 121°47'30" W; near NE cor. sec. 7, T 25 N, R 2 E). Named on Butte Meadows (1958) and Panther Spring (1953) 15' quadrangles.

Wildcat Creek: see **Little Wildcat Creek** [TEHAMA].

Wildcat Gulch [SISKIYOU]: *canyon,* drained by a stream that flows about 2.25 miles to Slide Creek (4) 28 miles west-northwest of Macdoel (lat. 41°59' N, long. 122°28' W; sec. 30, T 48 N, R 5 W). Named on Copco (1954) 15' quadrangle.

Wildcat Gulch [TEHAMA]: *canyon,* drained by a stream that flows 2.5 miles to Stinking Creek (lat. 40°12'50" N, long. 122°44'30" W; sec. 2, T 27 N, R 8 W). Named on Cold Fork (1967) 15' quadrangle.

Wildcat Peak [SISKIYOU]: *peak,* 12.5 miles south of Etna (lat. 41°16'45" N, long. 122°55'20" W; near NE cor. sec. 31, T 40 N, R 9 W); the peak is near the head of Wildcat Creek. Altitude 7893 feet. Named on Etna (1955) 15' quadrangle.

Wildcat Point [TEHAMA]: *ridge,* east- to northeast-trending, less than 0.5 mile long, 5.5 miles north of Bend (lat. 40°20'15" N, long. 122°13' W; on E line sec. 29, T 29 N, R 3 W). Named on Bend (1965) 7.5' quadrangle.

Wild Cattle Mountain [TEHAMA]: *ridge,* south- to east-trending, 5.5 miles long, 7 miles north of Deer Creek Station on Tehama-Plumas County line (lat. 40°21'30" N, long. 121°28'30" W). Named on Mount Harkness (1956) 15' quadrangle.

Wild Cow Mountain [SHASTA]: *peak,* 1.5 miles south-southwest of Schell Mountain (lat. 40°50'05" N, long. 122°32'15" W; sec. 3, T 34 N, R 6 W). Altitude 4769 feet. Named on Schell Mountain (1950) 15' quadrangle.

Wilderness Falls [SISKIYOU]: *waterfall,* 3.25 miles south-southwest of Preston Peak along Clear Creek (1) (lat. 41°47'25" N, long. 123°37'40" W). Named on Devils Punchbowl (1981) 7.5' quadrangle.

Wild Gulch [SISKIYOU]: *canyon,* drained by a stream that flows 1.25 miles to North Fork Salmon Creek 8.5 miles north of Sawyers Bar (lat. 41°25'05" N, long. 123°06' W). Named on Yellow Dog Peak (1977) 7.5' quadrangle.

Wildhide Gulch [TEHAMA]: *canyon,* drained by a stream that flows nearly 5 miles to South Fork Cottonwood Creek [SHASTA-TEHAMA] 9 miles northeast of Wakefield Flat (lat. 40°13'25" N, long. 122°31'45" W; sec. 3, T 27 N, R 6 W). Named on Oxbow Bridge (1967) 7.5' quadrangle.

Wild Horse Mountain [SISKIYOU]: *peak,* 9.5 miles east of Bray (lat. 41°40'15" N, long. 121°47'15" W; sec. 7, T 44 N, R 2 E). Altitude 6048 feet. Named on Bray (1950) 15' quadrangle. O'Brien's (1947) map has the form "Wildhorse Mt." for the name.

Wild Horse Ridge [TEHAMA]: *ridge,* generally north-trending, 2 miles long, 7.25 miles southeast of Beegum Peak (lat. 40°45'20" N, long. 122°46'30" W). Named on Chanchelulla Peak (1951) and Yolla Bolly (1954) 15' quadrangles.

Wild Irish Bar: see **Montgomery Bar** [BUTTE].

Wild Lake [SISKIYOU]: *lake,* 650 feet long, 11.5 miles north of Sawyers Bar (lat. 41°27'30" N, long. 123°11' W). Named on English Peak (1977) 7.5' quadrangle.

Wild Yankee: see **Wild Yankee Creek** [BUTTE].

Wild Yankee Creek [BUTTE]: *stream,* flows 2.5 mile to Berry Creek (1) 1 mile northwest of the village of Berry Creek (lat. 39°39'25" N, long. 121°24'50" W; near SE cor. sec. 21, T 21 N, R 5 E). Named on Berry Creek (1970) 7.5' quadrangle. The name recalls a mining camp called Wild Yankee that was located north of the village of Berry Creek (Gudde, 1975, p. 372).

Wild Yankee Hill [BUTTE]: *peak,* 1.5 miles north-northwest of the village of Berry Creek (lat. 39°40'05" N, long. 121°24'50" W; near NE cor. sec. 21, T 21 N, R 5 E); the peak is northwest of Wild Yankee Creek. Altitude 2685 feet. Named on Berry Creek (1970) 7.5' quadrangle.

Wiley Flat [SHASTA]: *area,* 8 miles south-southwest of Ono (lat. 40°22'05" N, long. 122°41' W; mainly in sec. 17, T 29 N, R 7 W). Named on Ono (1952) 15' quadrangle.

Wiley Flat Gulch [SHASTA]: *canyon,* drained by a stream that flows 4 miles to Middle Fork Cottonwood Creek [SHASTA-TEHAMA] 10 miles south of Ono (lat. 40°20' N, long. 122°38'35" W; sec. 27, T 29 N, R 7 W); Wiley Flat is at the head of the canyon. Named on Ono (1952) 15' quadrangle.

Wilk Gulch [SHASTA]: *canyon,* drained by a stream that flows 1.5 miles to South Cow Creek 6.5 miles east of Millville (lat. 40°33'10" N, long. 122°03'10" W; near S line sec. 11, T 31 N, R 2 W). Named on Millville (1953) 15' quadrangle.

Wilkinson [SHASTA]: *locality,* 8.5 miles northeast of Millville (lat. 40°38'35" N, long. 122°04'35" W; sec. 10, T 32 N, R 2 W). Named on Redding (1901) 30' quadrangle.

Willards Camp [TEHAMA]: *locality,* 7.25 miles west of Panther Spring (lat. 40°14'50" N, long. 121°54'50" W; near S line sec. 30, T 28 N, R 1 E). Named on Panther Spring (1953) 15' quadrangle.

Williams: see **Copper City** [SHASTA]; **George Williams Gulch** [SHASTA].

Williams Butte [TEHAMA]: *peak,* 2 miles west-southwest of Paskenta (lat. 39°52'10" N, long. 122°34'40" W; sec. 7, T 23 N, R 6 W). Altitude 1610 feet. Named on Newville (1967) 7.5' quadrangle. Paskenta (1920) 15' quadrangle shows Williams Buttes.

Williams Camp [TEHAMA]: *locality,* 11 miles west-northwest of Paskenta (lat. 39°56'20" N, long. 122°44'05" W; near W line sec. 14, T 24 N, R 8 W). Named on Riley Ridge (1967) 7.5' quadrangle.

Williams Creek [SISKIYOU]: *stream,* flows 3 miles to Klamath River 4 miles south-southwest of Hornbrook (lat. 41°51'20" N, long. 122°34'15" W; near NW cor. sec. 8, T 46 N, R 6 W). Named on Hornbrook (1955) 15' quadrangle.

Williams Gulch [SISKIYOU]: *canyon,* drained by a stream that flows 1.5 miles to Seiad Creek 3.5 miles northeast of the village of Seiad Valley (lat. 41°52'10" N, long. 123°08'10" W). Named on Hamburg (1980) and Seiad Valley (1980) 7.5' quadrangles.

Williams Point [SISKIYOU]: *relief feature,* 3 miles east of Happy Camp along Klamath River (lat. 41°47'20" N, long. 123°19' W; sec. 8, T 16 N, R 8 E). Named on Slater Butte (1980) 7.5' quadrangle.

Willis Hole [SISKIYOU]: *marsh,* 5 miles west of Bear Peak (lat. 41°41'20" N, long. 123°39'55" W). Named on Prescott Mountain (1981) 7.5' quadrangle. United States Board on Geographic Names (1965c, p. 12) rejected the name "Willis Jepson Hole" for the feature, but pointed out that the name "Willis Hole" commemorates Willis Jepson, an authority on plants of California.

Willis Jepson Hole: see **Willis Hole** [SISKIYOU].

Willow: see **Willows** [GLENN].

Willow Campground [TEHAMA]: *locality,* 5 miles northeast of Deer Creek Station along Lost Creek (lat. 40°18'20" N, long. 121°22'30" W; near N line sec. 12, T 28 N, R 5 E). Named on Mount Harkness (1956) 15' quadrangle.

Willow Creek [BUTTE-TEHAMA]: *stream,* heads in Tehama County and flows 3.5 miles to Colby Creek 1 mile west of Jonesville in Butte County (lat. 40°06'45" N, long. 121°29' W; sec. 14, T 26 N, R 4 E). Named on Jonesville (1958) 15' quadrangle.

Willow Creek [GLENN]: *stream,* formed by the confluence of Walker Creek—which is called North Fork Willow Creek on Willows (1906) 15' quadrangle—and South Fork Willow Creek, flows 10 miles to Colusa County 9.5 miles southeast of Willows (lat. 39°24'50" N, long. 122°04'45" W). Named on Glenn (1951), Princeton (1952), and Willows (1951) 7.5' quadrangles. South Fork is 35 miles long and is named on Lodoga (1960) 15' quadrangle, and on Fruto (1968), Stone Valley (1952), and Willows (1951, photorevised 1969) 7.5' quadrangles.

Willow Creek [SHASTA]:

(1) *stream,* flows nearly 2 miles to Squaw Valley Creek [SHASTA-SISKIYOU] 8 miles north-northwest of Shoeinhorse Mountain (lat. 41°09'50" N, long. 122°09'15" W; at E line sec. 2, T 38 N, R 3 W). Named on Shoeinhorse Mountain (1954) 15' quadrangle.

(2) *stream,* flows 5 miles to Montgomery Creek (1) 1 mile southwest of the village of Montgomery Creek (lat. 40°50'10" N, long. 121°56'15" W; near NE cor. sec. 2, T 34 N, R 1 W). Named on Montgomery Creek (1956) 15' quadrangle.

(3) *stream,* flows 2.5 miles to Bacon Creek 9 miles north of Millville (lat. 40°40'50" N, long. 122°11'15" W; at S line sec. 27, T 33 N, R 3 W). Named on Bella Vista (1965) 7.5' quadrangle. United States Board on Geographic Names (1966, p. 7) rejected the name "Bacon Creek" for the stream.

(4) *stream,* flows 6.5 miles to Clear Creek 2.5 miles south of the village of French Gulch (lat. 40°39'50" N, long. 122°38'05" W; near NE cor. sec. 3, T 32 N, R 7 W). Named on French Gulch (1979) 7.5' quadrangle.

Willow Creek [SISKIYOU]:

(1) *stream,* flows 7 miles to Julien Creek 8.5 miles southwest of Yreka (lat. 41°39'45" N, long. 122°30'20" W; sec. 14, T 44 N, R 6 W). Named on Yreka (1954) 15' quadrangle. On Yreka (1939) 30' quadrangle, Willow Creek (1) and Willow Creek (2) are shown connected.

(2) *stream,* flows 13 miles to end 14 miles south-southeast of Yreka in Shasta Valley (lat. 41°33'15" N, long. 122°31' W; sec. 27, T 43 N, R 6 W). Named on China Mountain (1955) and Yreka (1954) 15' quadrangles. South Fork enters from the south 16 miles east of Etna; it is 4.5 miles long and is named on China Mountain (1955) 15' quadrangle.

(3) *stream,* flows 17 miles to Klamath River 26 miles west of Macdoel (lat. 41°53'55" N, long. 123°29'30" W; sec. 25, T 47 N, R 6 W). Named on Copco (1954) 15' quadrangle.

(4) *stream,* flows 14 miles to Oklahoma Flat 8.5 miles east-southeast of Dorris (lat. 41°54'25" N, long. 121°46'20" W; sec. 20, T 47 N, R 2 E). Named on Dorris (1950) and Mount Dome (1950) 15' quadrangles.

Willow Creek [TEHAMA]:

(1) *stream,* flows 1.25 miles to South Fork Cottonwood Creek [SHASTA-TEHAMA] 6 miles west-northwest of Tomhead Mountain (lat. 40°09'10" N, long. 122°55'35" W; near SW cor. sec. 30, T 27 N, R 9 W). Named on Yolla Bolly (1954) 15' quadrangle.

(2) *stream,* flows 6.5 miles to Thomes Creek nearly 5 miles south-southwest of Ball Mountain (lat. 39°52'25" N, long. 122°49'45" W; near SE cor. sec. 2, T 23 N, R 9 W). Named on Buck Rock (1967), Log Spring (1967), and Mendocino Pass (1967) 7.5' quadrangles.

(3) *stream,* flows 13 miles to Oat Creek 3 miles northwest of Gerber (lat. 40°04'20" N, long. 122°11'55" W). Named on Gerber (1950), Red Bank (1952), and West of Gerber (1951) 7.5' quadrangles.

Willow Creek: see **Ager** [SISKIYOU]; **Angel Creek** [SISKIYOU]; **Bacon Creek** [SHASTA].

Willow Creek Mountain [SISKIYOU]: *peak,* 12.5 miles west of Macdoel (lat. 41°48'55" N, long. 122°14'30" W; sec. 20, T 46 N, R 3 W). Altitude 7830 feet. Named on Macdoel (1954) 15' quadrangle.

Willow Flat [SISKIYOU]: *area,* 13 miles northeast of Dutch Creek (lat. 41°58'10" N, long. 123°01' W; sec. 33, T 48 N, R 10 W). Named on Dutch Creek (1980) 7.5' quadrangle.

Willows [GLENN]: *town,* at about the center of the southeast part of Glenn County (lat. 39°31'15" N, long. 122°11'45" W; around NE cor. sec. 9, T 19 N, R 3 W). Named on Willows (1951) 7.5' quadrangle. United States Board on Geographic Names (1933, p. 820) rejected the form "Willow" for the name. Postal authorities established Willow post office in 1876 and changed the name to Willows in 1916 (Frickstad, p. 40). The town name is from a clump of willow trees that bordered a large spring-fed watering place that was situated 1 mile east of the present community (Hoover, Rensch, and Rensch, p. 97). Postal authorities established Belvedere post office 12 miles southeast of present Willows in Colusa County in 1879 and discontinued it the same year—the site now is in Glenn County (Salley, p. 18). They established Kanawha post office 4 miles west of present Willows in 1871 and discontinued it in 1879 (Salley, p. 109). California Mining Bureau's (1917d) map shows a place called Losa located along the railroad just west of Willows.

Willow Spring [SHASTA]: *spring,* 3.5 miles west-northwest of the village of Big Bend (lat. 41°02'05" N, long. 121°58' W; at W line sec. 27, T 37 N, R 1 W). Named on Big Bend (1961) 15' quadrangle.

Willow Spring [TEHAMA]:

(1) *spring,* nearly 5 miles north-northwest of Mineral (lat. 40°24'40" N, long. 121°37'20" W; near SE cor. sec. 34, T 30 N, R 3 E). Named on Lassen Peak (1956) 15' quadrangle.

(2) *spring,* 7.25 miles west of Ball Mountain (lat. 39°54'50" N, long. 122°55'05" W; near S line sec. 24, T 24 N, R 10 W). Named on Buck Rock (1967) 7.5' quadrangle.

Willow Spring Gulch [SHASTA]: *canyon,* drained by a stream that flows 2 miles to Middle Fork Cottonwood Creek [SHASTA-TEHAMA] 8 miles south-southeast of Ono (lat. 40°21'50" N, long. 122°34'50" W; sec. 18, T 29 N, R 6 W). Named on Ono (1952) 15' quadrangle.

Willow Springs [TEHAMA]: *spring,* 9 miles southwest of Paskenta (lat. 39°48'50" N, long. 122°41' W; near N line sec. 31, T 23 N, R 7 W). Named on Paskenta (1920) 15' quadrangle.

Wilson: see **Widow Wilson Field** [TEHAMA].

Wilson Cove [TEHAMA]: *relief feature,* 4 miles north-northeast of Polk Springs (lat. 40°10'20" N, long. 121°38'10" W; near NE cor. sec. 28, T 27 N, R 3 E). Named on Butte Meadows (1958) 15' quadrangle.

Wilson Creek [BUTTE]: *stream,* flows 15 miles, partly along Butte-Yuba County line, to North Honcut Creek 2.25 miles west-southwest of Honcut (lat. 39°18'35" N, long, 121°34'15" W). Named on Bangor (1947), Honcut (1952), and Loma Rica (1947) 7.5' quadrangles. Marysville (1895) 30' quadrangle has the names "Date Creek" and "South Honcut Creek" for present Wilson Creek.

Wilson Creek [GLENN]: *stream,* flows 22 miles to Willow Creek 1.5 miles north-northeast of Willows (lat. 39°32'50" N, long. 122°11'05" W; sec. 34, T 20 N, R 3 W). Named on Fruto NE (1952), Julian Rocks (1968), Stone Valley (1952), and Willows (1951, photorevised 1969) 7.5' quadrangles.

Wilson Creek [SHASTA]: *stream,* flows 10 miles to Roaring River 4.5 miles south-southwest of Ono (lat. 40°24'35" N, long. 122°38'20" W; sec. 34, T 30 N, R 7 W). Named on Ono (1952) 15' quadrangle.

Wilson Creek [SISKIYOU]: *stream,* flows nearly 2 miles to Klamath River 11 miles north-northwest of Ukonom Lake (lat. 41°44'10" N, long. 123°24'45" W). Named on Clear Creek (1981) 7.5' quadrangle.

Wilson Field [TEHAMA]: *area,* 7 miles west of Rosewood (lat. 40°16'30" N, long. 122°41'15" W). Named on Ono (1952) 15' quadrangle.

Wilson Flat [TEHAMA]: *area,* 8 miles west of Rosewood (lat. 40°15'30" N, long. 122°42'30" W; at SE cor. sec. 24, T 28 N, R 8 W). Named on Ono (1952) 15' quadrangle.

Wilson Gulch [SISKIYOU]: *canyon,* drained by a stream that flows 1.25 miles to Salmon River 8 miles north-northwest of Forks of Salmon (lat. 41°21'05" N, long. 123°24'05" W). Named on Orleans Mountain (1974) 7.5' quadrangle.

Wilson Island [BUTTE]: *island,* 12 miles west-northwest of Chico between Little Lagoon and Sacramento River (lat. 39°48'10" N, long. 122°02'50" W). Named on McIntosh Landing (1914) 7.5' quadrangle.

Wilson Lake [TEHAMA]: *lake,* 3200 feet long, 5.25 miles north of Deer Creek Station (lat. 40°20'20" N, long. 121°25'55" W; mainly in sec. 28, T 29 N, R 5 E). Named on Mount Harkness (1956) 15' quadrangle.

Wilson Landing [BUTTE]: *locality,* 11 miles west-northwest of Chico on the east side of Sacramento River (lat. 39°47'50" N, long. 122°01'15" W). Site named on Foster Island (1950) 7.5' quadrangle. McIntosh Landing (1914) 7.5' quadrangle shows the place situated about 0.5 mile farther upstream. Colonel C.L. Wilson ran the landing (Dunn, F.D., p. 114).

Wilson Meadow [TEHAMA]: *area,* 3.5 miles northeast of Mineral (lat. 40°22'35" N, long. 121°33'40" W; sec. 17, T 29 N, R 4 E). Named on Lassen Peak (1956) 15' quadrangle.

Wilson Mill [SISKIYOU]: *locality,* 4 miles west-northwest of Yreka (lat. 41°45'35" N, long. 122°42'15" W; sec. 12, T 45 N, R 7 W). Named on Yreka (1939) 30' quadrangle.

Wilson Reservoir [BUTTE]: *lake,* 700 feet long, 10.5 miles south-southeast of Paradise (lat. 39°37'35" N, long. 121°31'35" W; near NE cor. sec. 4, T 20 N, R 4 E). Named on Cherokee (1970) and Oroville (1970) 7.5' quadrangles.

Windler Gulch [SISKIYOU]: *canyon,* drained by a stream that flows 0.5 mile to North Fork Salmon River 3.5 miles west of Sawyers Bar (lat. 41°18'35" N, long. 123°11'45" W). Named on Sawyers Bar (1979) 7.5' quadrangle.

Windy Camp [SISKIYOU]: *locality,* 2 miles southeast of Condrey Mountain (lat. 41°55' N, long. 122°57' W; near NE cor. sec. 24, T 47 N, R 10 W). Named on Condrey Mountain (1955) 15' quadrangle, which shows a spring at the site; United States Board on Geographic Names (1978b, p. 5) approved the name "Windy Spring" for this spring.

Windy Cut [TEHAMA]: *locality,* 13 miles south of Mineral (lat. 40°09'40" N, long. 121°34'30" W; near SW cor. sec. 30, T 27 N, R 4 E). Named on Mineral (1941) 30' quadrangle.

Windy Gap [SISKIYOU]: *pass,* 4 miles north of Cecilville (lat. 41°11'55" N, long. 123°09'05" W). Named on Cecilville (1979) 7.5' quadrangle.

Windy Mountain: see **Windy Peak** [SISKIYOU].

Windy Peak [SISKIYOU]: *peak,* 10 miles north-northeast of the village of Seiad Valley (lat. 41°58'30" N, long. 123°08'05" W). Altitude 4934 feet. Named on Kangaroo Mountain (1980) 7.5' quadrangle. Called Windy Mt. on Averill's (1935) map.

Windy Point [SHASTA]: *relief feature,* 3 miles southeast of the village of Montgomery Creek (lat. 40°49'05" N, long. 121°53' W; sec. 8, T 34 N, R 1 E). Named on Montgomery Creek (1956) 15' quadrangle.

Windy Spring: see **Windy Camp** [SISKIYOU].

Wingate Bar [SISKIYOU]: *locality,* 11 miles north-northwest of Ukonom Lake along Klamath River (lat. 41°43'20" N, long. 123°26'10" W); the place is just upstream from the mouth of Wingate Creek. Named on Clear Creek (1981) 7.5' quadrangle.

Wingate Creek [SISKIYOU]: *stream,* flows 2 miles to Klamath River 11 miles north-northwest of Ukonom Lake (lat. 41°43'20" N, long. 123°26'30" W); the mouth of the creek is just downstream from Wingate Bar. Named on Clear Creek (1981) 7.5' quadrangle.

Winnibulli Creek [SHASTA]: *stream,* flows about 2.25 miles to Salt Creek (1) 6.5 miles southeast of Bollibokka Mountain (lat. 40°51'30" N, long. 122°08'30" W; sec. 30, T 35 N, R 2 W). Named on Bollibokka Mountain (1957) 15' quadrangle.

Winnibulli Mountain [SHASTA]: *peak,* 7 miles south-southeast of Bollibokka Mountain (lat. 40°50'55" N, long. 122°08'40" W; near NW cor. sec. 31, T 35 N, R 2 W). Altitude 2697 feet. Named on Bollibokka Mountain (1957) 15' quadrangle. The name is of Indian origin (Steger, p. 66).

Winslow: see **Elk Creek** [GLENN] (2).

Winston Gulch [SHASTA]: *canyon,* drained by a stream that flows 0.5 mile to Squaw Creek Arm Shasta Lake 8.5 miles south-southeast of Bollibokka Mountain (lat. 40°49' N, long. 122°09'30" W; sec. 12, T 34 N, R 3 W). Named on Bollibokka Mountain (1957) 15' quadrangle.

Winters Creek [BUTTE]: *stream,* flows 2 miles to Sucker Run 5.25 miles northwest of Clipper Mills (lat. 39°35'10" N, long. 121°13'35" W; near SE cor.sec. 18, T 20 N, R 7 E). Named on Clipper Mills (1948) 7.5' quadrangle.

Winters Creek [BUTTE]: see **Big Winters Creek** [BUTTE].

Winters Gulch [SISKIYOU]: *canyon,* drained by a stream that flows 2 miles to lowlands 14 miles south of Yreka (lat. 41°32'15" N, long. 122°35'45" W; at N line sec. 36, T 43 N, R 7 W). Named on Yreka (1954) 15' quadrangle.

Winthrop: see **Delamar** [SHASTA].

Winton Canyon [SHASTA]: *canyon,* drained by a stream that flows 1 mile to Indian Creek (1) 1.5 miles north-northwest of Castella (lat. 41°09'30" N, long. 122°19'50" W; sec. 16, T 38 N, R 4 W). Named on Dunsmuir (1954) 15' quadrangle.

Wintoon Butte: see **Black Butte** [SISKIYOU] (1).

Wintoon Glacier: see **Wintun Glacier** [SISKIYOU].

Wintun Falls: see **Wintun Glacier** [SISKIYOU].

Wintun Glacier [SISKIYOU]: *glacier,* about 11 miles north-northwest of McCloud on Mount Shasta (1) (lat. 41°24'20" N, long. 122°10'45" W). Named on Shasta (1954) 15' quadrangle. The name is from an Indian tribe (Eichorn, p. 13). McAllister (p. 193) used the form "Wintoon Glacier" for the name. Russell's (1883) map shows Wintun Falls located below the glacier.

Wintun Lodge [SHASTA]: *locality,* 14 miles south of Lamoine (lat. 40°46'30" N, long. 122°23' W; sec. 25, T 34 N, R 5 W). Named on Redding (1901) 30' quadrangle.

Wittawaket Creek [SHASTA]: *stream,* flows 1.5 miles to McCloud River [SHASTA-SISKIYOU] nearly 2 miles northwest of Bollibokka Mountain (lat. 40°57'10" N, long 122°14'10" W; sec. 29, T 36 N, R 3 W). Named on Bollibokka Mountain (1957) 15' quadrangle. United States Board on Geographic Names (1991, p. 7) rejected the names "Weitawaket Creek" and "Willawaket Creek" for the stream. The name is of Indian origin (Steger, p. 66).

Wolf Creek [SISKIYOU]:

(1) *stream,* flows 2.5 miles to China Creek (1) nearly 5 miles west of Happy Camp (lat. 41°47'50" N, long. 123°17' W; sec. 20, T 46 N, R 12 W). Named on Seiad Valley (1980) and Slater Butte (1980) 7.5' quadrangles.

(2) *stream,* flows nearly 2 miles to join West Boulder Creek and form Boulder Creek (3) 14 miles south-southeast of Etna (lat. 41°15'40" N, long. 122°49'20" W; sec. 7, T 39 N, R 8 W). Named on Coffee Creek (1955) and Etna (1955) 15' quadrangles.

Wolverine Lake [SISKIYOU]: *lake,* 300 feet long, 14 miles south-southwest of Scott Bar (lat. 41°33'50" N, long. 123°06'55" W). Named on Boulder Peak (1981) 7.5' quadrangle.

Woodall Creek: see **Baldwin Creek** [SHASTA].

Woodchopper Gulch [SISKIYOU]: *canyon,* drained by a stream that flows nearly 2 miles to Lumgrey Creek 10 miles west-southwest of Hornbrook (lat. 41°52'40" N, long. 122°44'20" W; sec. 35, T 47 N, R 8 W). Named on Condrey Mountain (1955) and Hornbrook (1955) 15' quadrangles.

Wood Creek: see **Woods Creek** [SISKIYOU].

Wood Gulch [SHASTA]: *canyon,* drained by a stream that flows 1.5 miles to North Fork Squaw Creek (3) 16 miles south-southwest of Lamoine (lat. 40°45'10" N, long. 122°29'30" W; near N line sec. 1, T 33 N, R 6 W). Named on Lamoine (1957) and Schell Mountain (1950) 15' quadrangles.

Wood Gulch [SISKIYOU]:

(1) *canyon,* drained by a stream that flows 1 mile to Walla Walla Creek 6.5 miles north-northwest of Fort Jones (lat. 41°42' N, long. 122°52'05" W; at S line sec 34, T 45 N, R 9 W). Named on Fort Jones (1955) 15' quadrangle.

(2) *canyon,* drained by a stream that flows 1.25 miles to Williams Creek 5 miles south of Hornbrook (lat. 41°50'15" N, long. 122°32'50" W; sec. 16, T 46 N, R 6 W). Named on Hornbrook (1955) 15' quadrangle.

Woodhall Creek: see **Baldwin Creek** [SHASTA].

Woodleaf Creek [BUTTE]: *stream,* flows 2 miles, partly in Yuba County, to Oroleve Creek nearly 3 miles west-northwest of Clipper Mills (lat. 39°32'40" N, long. 121°12'20" W; near E line sec. 32, T 20 N, R 7 E). Named on Clipper Mills (1948) 7.5' quadrangle.

Woodman [SHASTA]: *locality,* about 8 miles north of Millville (lat. 40°40'15" N, long. 122°10'45" W). Named on Red Bluff (1894) 1° quadrangle.

Woodman Creek [SHASTA]: *stream,* flows 7.5 miles to Little Cow Creek 8 miles north of Millville (lat. 40°39'50" N, long. 122°10'40" W; near N line sec. 2, T 32 N, R 3 W); the stream goes past Woodman Hill. Named on Millville (1953) 15' quadrangle. Steger (p. 66) associated the name with L.C. Woodman and George Woodman, who settled along Cow Creek in 1852.

Woodman Hill [SHASTA]: *peak,* 10 miles north of Millville (lat. 40°41'10" N, long. 122°08'35" W; at E line sec. 30, T 33 N, R 2 W). Named on Bella Vista (1965) 7.5' quadrangle.

Woodman Ravine [BUTTE]: *canyon,* drained by a stream that flows 2.5 miles to Lake Oroville 4 miles east of Oroville Dam (lat. 39°32'05" N, long. 121°24'45" W; sec. 4, T 19 N, R 5 E). Named on Oroville Dam (1970) 7.5' quadrangle.

Woodrat Bar [SISKIYOU]: *locality,* 7.5 miles southwest of Hornbrook along Klamath River (lat. 41°49'40" N, long. 122°38'35" W; sec. 22, T 46 N, R 7 W). Named on Hornbrook (1955) 15' quadrangle.

Woods Bar [SISKIYOU]: *locality,* 2 miles east of Happy Camp along Klamath River (lat. 41°47'20" N, long. 123°20'20" W; sec. 7, T 16 N, R 8 E); the place is just downstream from the mouth of Woods Creek. Named on Slater Butte (1980) 7.5' quadrangle.

Woods Creek [SISKIYOU]: *stream,* flows 1.25 miles to Klamath River 2 miles east-southeast of Happy Camp (lat. 41°46'55" N, long. 123°20'25" W; sec. 18, T 16 N, R 8 E); the mouth of the stream is just upstream from Woods Bar. Named on Slater Butte (1980) 7.5' quadrangle. Called Wood Creek on Happy Camp (1956) 15' quadrangle, but United States Board on Geographic Names (1981c, p. 4) rejected this name for the stream.

Woodyard Flat [TEHAMA]:

(1) *area,* 3 miles north-northwest of Wakefield Flat (lat. 40°10' N, long. 122°39'50" W; sec. 28, T 27 N, R 7 W). Named on Cold Fork (1967) 7.5' quadrangle.

(2) *area,* 6.5 miles southeast of Wakefield Flat (lat. 40°02'55" N, long. 122°33'40" W; near S line sec. 5, T 25 N, R 6 W). Named on Lowrey (1967) 7.5' quadrangle.

Wooley Camp [SISKIYOU]: *locality,* 12 miles north-northwest of Forks of Salmon (lat. 41°25'35" N, long. 123°22'55" W); the place is along Wooley Creek. Named on Somes Bar (1979) 7.5' quadrangle.

Wooley Creek [SISKIYOU]: *stream,* flows 22 miles to Salmon River 10 miles north-northwest of Forks of Salmon (lat. 41°22'40" N, long. 123°25'15" W). Named on English Peak (1977), Marble Mountain (1980), Medicine Mountain (1978), and Somes Bar (1979) 7.5' quadrangles. Big Elk Fork enters 18 miles south-southwest of Scott Bar; it heads at Big Elk Lake, is 4.25 miles long, and is named on Marble Mountain (1980) 7.5' quadrangle. North Fork enters from the north 15 miles north of Forks of Salmon; it is 7.25 miles long and is named on Medicine Mountain (1978) and Ukonom Lake (1980) 7.5' quadrangles. Cuddihy Fork enters North Fork 6.5 miles southeast of Ukonom Lake; it heads at Cuddihy Lakes, is 5 miles long, and is named on Ukonom Lake (1980) 7.5' quadrangle. South Fork enters from the southeast 15 miles north-northwest of Sawyers Bar; it heads at Wooley Lake, is 5 miles long, and is named on English Peak (1977) 7.5' quadrangle. Present Steinacher Creek is called East Fork [of Wooley Creek] on Sawyers Bar (1923) 30' quadrangle.

Wooley Creek Pocket [SISKIYOU]: *relief feature,* 18 miles southwest of Scott Bar (lat. 41°32'05" N, long. 123°13' W; sec. 34, T 43 N, R 12 W); the feature is at the head of a branch of Big Elk Fork Wooley Creek. Named on Grider Valley (1981) 15' quadrangle.

Wooley Lake [SISKIYOU]: *lake,* 950 feet long, 13 miles north of Sawyers Bar (lat. 41°29'35" N, long. 123°08' W); the lake is at the head of South Fork Wooley Creek. Named on English Peak (1977) 7.5' quadrangle.

Wooliver Creek [SISKIYOU]: *stream,* flows 2 miles to Scott River 0.5 mile south of Scott Bar (lat. 41°44'05" N, long. 123°00'10" W; sec. 21, T 45 N,

R 10 W). Named on Fort Jones (1955) 15' quadrangle.

Wright Lake: see **Lower Wright Lake** [SISKIYOU]; **Upper Wright Lake** [SISKIYOU].

Wright Ridge: see **Hardin Butte** [SISKIYOU].

Wyandotte [BUTTE]: *village,* nearly 6 miles northwest of Bangor (lat. 39°27'25" N, long. 121°28' W; near SE cor. sec. 36, T 19 N, R 4 E). Named on Bangor (1947) 7.5' quadrangle. Postal authorities established Tarr's Ranch post office 6.5 miles southeast of Oroville in 1856, and moved it when they changed the name to Wyandotte in 1859; the first name was for the ranch owned by Joseph L.Tarr, first postmaster (Salley, p. 218). They discontinued Wyandotte post office in 1867, reestablished it in 1880, and discontinued it in 1915 (Frickstad, p. 13). A party of Wyandotte Indians came to the site prospecting for gold in 1850 (Wells and Chambers, p. 266.). A place called Honcut City was situated southeast of Wyandotte near North Honcut Creek (Gudde, 1975, p. 159).

Wyandotte: see **Lake Wyandotte** [BUTTE].

Wyandotte Creek [BUTTE]: *stream,* flows 16 miles to North Honcut Creek 2.5 miles west-southwest of Honcut (lat. 39°18'50" N, long. 121°34'35" W); the stream heads near Wyandotte. Named on Bangor (1947), Honcut (1952), and Palermo (1970) 7.5' quadrangles.

Wyman Ravine [BUTTE]: *canyon,* drained by a stream that flows 18 miles to North Honcut Creek nearly 3 miles west-southwest of Honcut (lat. 39°18'50" N, long. 121°35' W; sec. 24, T 17 N, R 3 E). Named on Honcut (1952) and Palermo (1970) 7.5' quadrangles.

Wyman Spring [BUTTE]: *spring,* 2.5 miles southeast of Pulga (lat. 39°46'20" N, long. 121°25'20" W; sec. 9, T 22 N, R 5 E). Named on Pulga (1979) 7.5' quadrangle.

Wyndham: see **Baird** [SHASTA].

Wyntoon [SISKIYOU]: *locality,* 6 miles southeast of McCloud along McCloud River [SHASTA-SISKIYOU] (lat. 41°11'30" N, long. 122°03'40" W; near SE cor. sec. 27, T 39 N, R 2 W). Named on Shoeinhorse Mountain (1954) 15' quadrangle.

Wyo [GLENN]: *locality,* 1.5 miles north of downtown Orland along Southern Pacific Railroad (lat. 39°46'10" N, long. 122°11'25" W; near S line sec. 10, T 22 N, R 3 W). Named on Kirkwood (1949) 7.5' quadrangle. Called Stony Creek on Vina (1904) 15' quadrangle. A spur line from the place serviced Stony Creek gravel pit (Bradley, p. 200).

Wyreka: see **Yreka** [SISKIYOU].

—X - Y—

Yahi Indian Camp [TEHAMA]: *locality,* 16 miles south of Panther Spring (lat. 40°01'45" N, long. 121°49'30" W; at S line sec. 11, T 25 N, R 1 E). Named on Panther Spring (1953) 15' quadrangle, which has the alternate name "Ishii Caves" at the place.

Yank Creek [SHASTA]: *stream,* flows 5.25 miles to Dry Creek (1) 7 miles north-northwest of Millville (lat. 40°38'10" N, long. 122°14'05" W; near NW cor. sec. 17, T 32 N, R 3 W). Named on Bella Vista (1965) 7.5' quadrangle. Called Jim Creek on Millville (1953) 15' quadrangle.

Yankee Billy Ridge [SHASTA]: *ridge,* south-southeast- to south-trending, 2 miles long, 2 miles northwest of the village of French Gulch (lat. 40°43'25" N, long. 122°39'45" W). Named on French Gulch (1979) 7.5' quadrangle.

Yankee Flat: see **Enterprise** [BUTTE].

Yankee Gulch [SHASTA]: *canyon,* drained by a stream that flows nearly 2 miles to Summit Gulch 1.5 miles southwest of the village of French Gulch (lat. 40°41'05" N, long. 122°39'35" W; sec. 28, T 33 N, R 7 W). Named on French Gulch (1979) 7.5' quadrangle.

Yankee Hill [BUTTE]: *locality,* 6.5 miles east-southeast of Paradise (lat. 39°42'15" N, long. 121°31'15" W; near W line sec. 3, T 21 N, R 4 E); the place is at the head of Rich Gulch. Named on Cherokee (1970) 7.5' quadrangle. Oroville (1942) 15' quadrangle shows Yankee Hill post office situated 1.5 miles northwest of present Yankee Hill (near W line sec. 33, T 22 N, R 4 E). Postal authorities established Yankee Hill post office in 1858 and discontinued it in 1951 (Frickstad, p. 13). According to Hanna (p. 360), Yankee Hill first was settled in 1850 and was known as Rich Gulch; with the arrival of Spanish and Chilean miners in the middle 1850's, the name became Spanishtown; the present name came after New Englanders succeeded the Latins. According to Gudde (1975, p. 291), Rich Gulch was a separate mining camp that declined as nearby Yankee Hill grew. Postal authorities established Evans post office 3 miles north of Yankee Hill in 1899 and discontinued it in 1902; the name was for Valeria A. Evans, first postmaster (Salley, p. 71).

Yatestown: see **Honcut Creek** [BUTTE].

Ycotti Creek [SHASTA]: *stream,* flows 1 mile to McCloud River Arm Shasta Lake 12.5 miles southeast of Lamoine (lat. 40°49'35" N, long. 122°17'45" W; at W line sec. 2, T 34 N, R 4 W). Named on Lamoine (1957) 15' quadrangle. The name is for an Indian medicine man (Steger, p. 67).

Ydalpom: see **Copper City** [SHASTA].

Yellow Butte [SISKIYOU]:

(1) *ridge,* north-northwest-trending, 1 mile long, 24 miles south-southwest of Macdoel (lat. 41°32'30" N, long. 122°15'30" W; near W line sec. 25, T 43 N, R 4 W). Named on Lake Shastina (1954) 15' quadrangle. On Macdoel (1941) 30' quadrangle, the name applies to a peak at the north end of the ridge.

(2) *hill,* 4.5 miles southeast of Mount Dome (lat. 41°45'30" N, long. 121°38'10" W; sec. 9, T 45 N, R 3 E). Named on Mount Dome (1950) 15' quadrangle.

Yellow Dog Creek [SISKIYOU]: *stream,* flows 2.25 miles to North Fork Salmon River 5.5 miles north-northeast of Sawyers Bar (lat. 41°22'10" N, long. 123°04'40" W); the stream heads near Yellow Dog Peak. Named on Tanners Peak (1977) and Yellow Dog Peak (1977) 7.5' quadrangles.

Yellow Dog Peak [SISKIYOU]: *peak,* 7.5 miles north-northeast of Sawyers Bar (lat. 41°23'20" N, long. 123°03'25" W). Altitude 7044 feet. Named on Yellow Dog Peak (1977) 7.5' quadrangle.

Yellowjacket [TEHAMA]: *locality,* 8.5 miles north of Polk Springs (lat. 40°14'30" N, long. 121°41'30" W; near NE cor. sec. 36, T 28 N, R 2 E). Named on Butte Meadows (1958) 15' quadrangle.

Yellow Jacket Basin [SISKIYOU]: *relief feature,* 3 miles south-southeast of Cecilville (lat. 41°05'50" N, long. 123°07' W). Named on Thompson Peak (1979) 7.5' quadrangle.

Yellowjacket Butte [SISKIYOU]: *peak,* 5.25 miles south-southeast of Medicine Lake (lat. 41°30'50" N, long. 121°33' W; sec. 6, T 42 N, R 4 E). Named on Medicine Lake (1952) 15' quadrangle.

Yellowjacket Camp: see **Yellowjacket Spring** [SISKIYOU].

Yellow Jacket Creek [SISKIYOU]: *stream,* flows 2 miles to Bridge Creek 15 miles north of Forks of Salmon (lat. 41°27'40" N, long. 123°21'25" W). Named on Medicine Mountain (1978) 7.5' quadrangle.

Yellow Jacket Glade [GLENN]: *area,* 0.5 mile south-southeast of Black Butte (lat. 39°43'05" N, long. 122°51'55" W). Named on Plaskett Meadows (1967) 7.5' quadrangle.

Yellowjacket Ice Cave [SISKIYOU]: *cave,* 5.5 miles south-southeast of Medicine Lake (lat. 41°30'50" N, long. 121°32'45" W; near E line sec. 6, T 42 N, R 4 E); the cave is just east of Yellowjacket Butte. Named on Medicine Lake (1952) 15' quadrangle.

Yellowjacket Mountain [SHASTA]: *peak,* 9 miles west of Shoeinhorse Mountain (lat. 41°05' N, long. 122°14'20" W; sec. 8, T 37 N, R 3 W). Altitude 5016 feet. Named on Shoeinhorse Mountain (1954) 15' quadrangle.

Yellow Jacket Ridge [SISKIYOU]: *ridge,* generally southwest-trending, 7.5 miles long, center 3.5 miles north-northeast of Forks of Salmon (lat. 41°19'15" N, long. 123°15'45" W); Crapo Mountain is at the northeast end of the ridge. Named on Forks of Salmon (1978) and Sawyers Bar (1979) 7.5' quadrangles. On Sawyers Bar (1923) 30' quadrangle, the name "Crapo Mountain" applies to the entire ridge.

Yellowjacket Spring [SISKIYOU]: *spring,* 8 miles west of Scott Bar (lat. 41°43'50" N, long. 123°09'20" W). Named on Grider Valley (1981) 7.5' quadrangle. Scott Bar (1955) 15' quadrangle shows Yellowjacket Camp at the site.

Yellow Slides [SHASTA]: *relief feature,* 3.5 miles east of the village of Big Bend (lat. 41°00'40" N, long. 121°50'20" W). Named on Big Bend (1961) 15' quadrangle.

Yoakumville [SISKIYOU]: *locality,* 8 miles northwest of Cecilville (lat. 41°13'25" N, long. 123°14'55" W). Site named on Cecilville (1979) 7.5' quadrangle. Postal authorities established Yocumville post office in 1869 and discontinued it in 1891 (Frickstad, p. 191)—J.B. Yocum founded the place (Daggett, 1957a, p. 2). They established Shawmut post office 5 miles north of Yocumville post office in 1881 and discontinued it the same year (Salley, p. 202).

Yocumville: see **Yoakumville** [SISKIYOU].

Yolla Bolly Lake: see **North Yolla Bolly Lake** [TEHAMA].

Yolla Bolly Mountains: see **North Yolla Bolly Mountains** [TEHAMA]; **South Yolla Bolly Mountains** [TEHAMA].

Yonka Gulch [SISKIYOU]: *canyon,* drained by a stream that flows 0.5 mile to Empire Creek 9 miles west of Hornbrook (lat. 41°53'15" N, long. 122°43'40" W; at S line sec. 25, T 47 N, R 8 W). Named on Hornbrook (1955) 15' quadrangle.

Young: see **Tom Young Flat** [SISKIYOU].

Youngs Peak [SISKIYOU]:

(1) *peak,* 2.5 miles east of Broken Rib Mountain on Siskiyou-Del Norte County line (lat. 41°53'25" N, long. 123°38'20" W). Altitude 6308 feet. Named on Broken Rib Mountain (1982) 7.5' quadrangle. Called Broken Rib Peak on Weed (1963) 1°x 2° quadrangle.

(2) *peak,* 4 miles east-southeast of Salmon Mountain on Siskiyou-Trinity County line (lat. 41°09'25" N, long. 123°20'25" W). Altitude 6329 feet. Named on Youngs Peak (1979) 7.5' quadrangle.

Youngs Valley [SISKIYOU]: *valley,* 3.25 miles north-northwest of Preston Peak (lat. 47°52'30" N, long. 123°37'45" W); the valley is less than 1 mile southeast of Youngs Peak. Named on Broken Rib Mountain (1982) 7.5' quadrangle.

Yreka [SISKIYOU]: *city,* on the west side of Shasta Valley near the geographic center of Siskiyou County (lat. 41°44' N, long. 122°38'15" W; in and near sec. 22, T 45 N, R 7 W). Named on Yreka (1954) 15' quadrangle. Called Wyreka on Gibbes' (1852) map. Postal authorities established Yreka post office in 1853 (Frickstad, p. 191), and the city incorporated in 1857. Gold mining began in 1851 at the place, which first was known as Thompson Dry Diggings for Abraham Thompson, a pioneer miner; the town that grew at the gold diggings originally was called Shasta Butte City, but the name was changed to Wyreka, and finally to Yreka, from the Indian designation of Mount Shasta (1) (Hanna, p. 363).

Yreka Creek [SISKIYOU]: *stream,* flows 12 miles to Shasta River 9.5 miles south of Hornbrook (lat. 41°46'35" N, long. 122°35'35" W; near E line sec. 1, T 45 N, R 7 W); the stream goes through Yreka. Named on Hornbrook (1955) and Yreka (1954) 15 quadrangles.

Yuka Gulch [TEHAMA]: *canyon,* drained by a stream that flows 2.25 miles to Cottonwood Creek [SHASTA-TEHAMA] 7 miles northwest of Rosewood (lat. 40°20'20" N, long. 122°37'30" W; sec. 26, T 29 N, R 7 W). Named on Ono (1952) 15' quadrangle.

– Z –

Zachary Gulch [SHASTA]: *canyon,* drained by a stream that flows 1.5 miles to Beegum Creek [SHASTA-TEHAMA] 7 miles south-southwest of Arbuckle Mountain (lat. 40°18'40" N, long. 122°55'45" W; at W line sec. 6, T 28 N, R 9 W). Named on Chanchelulla Peak (1951) 15' quadrangle.

Zerr Gulch [SHASTA]: *canyon,* drained by a stream that flows 1 mile to Middle Fork Cottonwood Creek [SHASTA-TEHAMA] 5 miles southwest of Arbuckle Mountain (lat. 40°21'10" N, long. 122°55'55" W; near E line sec. 24, T 29 N, R 10 W). Named on Chanchelulla Peak (1951) 15' quadrangle.

Zimmershed Creek [TEHAMA]: *stream,* flows 11 miles to Pine Creek [BUTTE-TEHAMA] 8 miles southwest of Campbell Mound (lat. 39°53'45" N, long. 121°55'35" W; near N line sec. 36, T 24 N, R 1 W). Named on Campbell Mound (1952) and Richardson Springs NW (1952) 7.5' quadrangles.

Zinc Creek [SHASTA]: *stream,* flows 0.5 mile to Squaw Creek Arm Shasta Lake 10 miles south of Bollibokka Mountain (lat. 40°47'20" N, long. 122°12'50" W; sec. 21, T 34 N, R 3 W). Named on Bollibokka Mountain (1957) 15' quadrangle.

Zinn: see **Shingletown** [SHASTA].

Zuleka: see **Cole** [SISKIYOU].

Zumwalt Creek [GLENN-TEHAMA]: *stream,* heads in Tehama County and flows 2.5 miles to Scott Creek 12 miles west of Newville in Glenn County (lat. 39°47'25" N, long. 122°44'40" W; sec. 3, T 22 N, R 8 W). Named on Hall Ridge (1967) and Log Spring (1967) 7.5' quadrangles.

North Sacramento Valley Region
Butte, Glenn, Shasta, Siskiyou and Tehama Counties

References Cited

BOOKS AND ARTICLES

Adams, Kramer A. 1963. *Covered bridges of the West.* Berkeley, California: Howell-North, 146 p.

Amesbury, Robert. 1967. *Nobles' emigrant trail.* (Author), 37 p.

Averill, Chas. Volney. 1935. "Redding field district (Mines and mineral resources of Siskiyou County)." *California Journal of Mines and Geology,* v. 31, no. 3, p. 255-338.

_____1939. "Redding field district (Mineral resources of Shasta County)." *California Journal of Mines and Geology,* v. 35, no. 2, p. 108-191.

Ball, Lottie A. 1957. "Four men from Petersburg." *Siskiyou Pioneer,* v. 2, no. 10, p. 19-23.

Bancroft, Hubert Howe. 1888. *History of California, Volume VI, 1848-1859.* San Francisco: The History Company, Publishers, 787 p.

Becker, Robert H. 1964. *Diseños of California ranchos.* San Francisco: The Book Club of California, (no pagination).

_____1969. *Designs on the land.* San Francisco: The Book Club of California, (no pagination).

Beckwith, E.G. 1854. "Reports of explorations for a route for the Pacific railroad, on the line of the forty-first parallel of north latitude." *Reports of explorations and surveys, to ascertain the most practicable and economical route for a railroad from the Mississippi River to the Pacific Ocean.* Volume II. (33d Cong., 2nd Sess., House Ex. Doc. No. 91.) Washington: A.O.P. Nicholson, Printer, 132 p.

Boyd, William Harland. 1972. *A California middle border, The Kern River country, 1772-1880.* Richardson, Texas: The Havilah Press, 226 p.

Bradley, Walter W. 1915. "The counties of Colusa, Glenn, Lake, Marin, Napa, Solano, Sonoma, Yolo." *Report XIV of the State Mineralogist.* Sacramento: California State Mining Bureau, p. 173-370.

Brown, G. Chester. 1915. "The counties of Shasta, Siskiyou, Trinity." *Report XIV of the State Mineralogist.* Sacramento: California State Mining Bureau, p. 745-925.

California Division of Highways. 1934. *California highway transportation survey, 1934.* Sacramento: Department of Public Works, Division of Highways, 130 p. + appendices.

Clark, William B. 1970. *Gold districts of California.* (California Division of Mines and Geology Bulletin 193.) San Francisco: California Division of Mines and Geology, 186 p.

Cowan, Robert G. 1956. *Ranchos of California.* Fresno, California: Academy Library Guild, 151 p.

Coy, Owen C. 1923. *California county boundaries.* Berkeley: California Historical Survey Commission, 335 p.

Crawford, J.J. 1894. "Report of the State Mineralogist." *Twelfth report of the State Mineralogist, (Second Biennial,) two years ending September 15, 1894.* Sacramento: California State Mining Bureau, p. 8-412.

_____1896. "Report of the State Mineralogist." *Thirteenth report (Third Biennial) of the State Mineralogist for the two years ending September 15, 1896.* Sacramento: California State Mining Bureau, p. 10-646.

Daggett, Hallie M. 1957a. "Early day mining camps of the Salmon River." *Siskiyou Pioneer,* v. 2, no. 10, p. 2.

_____1957b. "Placer mines of the Salmon River." *Siskiyou Pioneer,* v. 2, no. 10, p. 7-9.

Davis, William Morris. 1948. "The lakes of California." *California Journal of Mines and Geology,* v. 44, no. 2, p. 201-242.

Delano, A. 1854. *Life on the plains and among the diggins; being scenes and adventures of an overland journey to California.* Auburn and Buffalo: Miller, Orton & Mulligan, 384 p.

Denny, Karl V. 1957. "Callahan mines." *Siskiyou Pioneer,* v. 2, no. 10, p. 41-44.

Diller, J.S. 1889. "Geology of the Lassen Peak district." *Eighth Annual Report of the United States Geological Survey, 1886-87.* Washington: Government Printing Office, p. 395-432.

_____1895. "Mount Shasta, A typical volcano." *The physiography of the United States.* New York: American Book Company, p. 237-268.

Diller, J.S., and others. 1915. *Guidebook of the Western United States, Part D. The Shasta Route and Coast Line.* (United States Geological Survey Bulletin 614.) Washington: Government Printing Office, 142 p.

Dillon, Richard (editor). 1971. *A long road to Stony Creek.* Ashland: Lewis Osborne, 71 p.

_____1975. *Siskiyou trail.* New York: McGraw-Hill Book Company, 381 p.

Dunn, Forrest D. 1977. *Butte County place names.* (Occasional Publication Number 3.) Chico, California: Association for Northern California Records and Research, 121 p.

Dunn, R.L. 1893. "Siskiyou County." *Eleventh Report of the State Mineralogist, (First Biennial,) two years ending September 15, 1892.* Sacramento: California State Mining Bureau, p. 420-449.

Eichorn, Arthur Francis, Sr. 1957. *The Mount Shasta story.* Mount Shasta, California: Mount Shasta Herald, 125 p.

Farnham, Thomas Jefferson. 1947. *Travels in California.* Oakland, California: Biobooks, 166 p.

Frazer, Robert W. 1965. *Forts of the West.* Norman: University of Oklahoma Press, 246 p.

Frickstad, Walter N. 1955. *A century of California post offices, 1848 to 1954.* Oakland, California: Philatelic Research Society, 395 p.

Gibbs, George. 1972. *George Gibb's journal of Redick McKee's expedition through northwestern California in 1851.* Berkeley: University of California, Department of Anthropology, Archeological Research Facility, 88 p.

Giles, Rosena A. 1949. *Shasta County, California.* Oakland, California: Biobooks, 301 p.

Goodyear, W.A. 1890. "Lake County." *Tenth annual report of the State Mineralogist, for the year ending December 1, 1890.* Sacramento: California State Mining Bureau, p. 227-271.

Gudde, Erwin G. 1949. *California place names.* Berkeley and Los Angeles: University of California Press, 431 p.

_____1969. *California place names.* Berkeley and Los Angeles: University of California Press, 416 p.

_____1975. *California gold camps.* Berkeley, Los Angeles, London: University of California Press, 467 p.

Hague, Harlan, and Lanum, David J. 1990. *Thomas O. Larkin.* Norman and London: University of Oklahoma Press, 304 p.

Hall, Ansel F. 1926. "Mount Shasta." *Sierra Club Bulletin,* v. 12, no. 3, p. 252-267.

Hanna, Phil Townsend. 1951. *The dictionary of California land names.* Los Angeles: The Automobile Club of Southern California, 392 p.

Hart, James D. 1978. *A companion to California.* New York: Oxford University Press, 504 p.

Herzog, Frank. 1957. "Greenhorn Creek gold mining." *Siskiyou Pioneer,* v. 2, no. 10, p. 66-69

Hobson, J.B. 1890. "Siskiyou County." *Tenth annual report of the State Mineralogist, for the year ending December 1, 1890.* Sacramento: California State Mining Bureau, p. 655-658.

Hoover, Mildred Brooke, Rensch, Hero Eugene, and Rensch, Ethel Grace. 1966. *Historic spots in California.* (Third edition, revised by William N. Abeloe.) Stanford, California: Stanford University Press, 642 p.

Irelan, William, Jr. 1888. "Report of the State Mineralogist." *Eighth annual report of the State Mineralogist. for the year ending October 1, 1888.* Sacramento: California State Mining Bureau, p. 12-695.

Kett, William F. 1947. "Fifty years of operation by The Mountain Copper Company, Ltd., in Shasta County, California." *California Journal of Mines and Geology,* v. 43, no. 2, p. 105-162.

Kip, Leonard. 1946. *California sketches, with recollections of the gold mines.* Los Angeles: N.A. Kovach, 58 p.

Knox, Raymond G. 1959. "The land of the burnt out fires, Lava Beds National Monument, California." *National Speleological Society Bulletin,* v. 21, pt. 2, p. 55-61.

Kroeber, A.L. 1916. "California place names of Indian origin." *University of California Publications in American Archæology and Ethnology,* v. 12, no. 2, p. 31-69.

Logan, C.A. 1925. "Sacramento field division (Siskiyou County)." *Mining in California,* v. 21, no. 4, p. 413-498.

Lyman, C.S. 1849. "Observations on California." *American Journal of Science and Arts* (series 2), v. 7, no. 20, p. 290-292, 305-309.
MacMullen, Jerry. 1944. *Paddle-wheel days in California.* Stanford, California: Stanford University Press, 157 p.
McAllister, M. Hall. 1925. "Notes on Mount Shasta." *Sierra Club Bulletin,* v. 12, no. 2, p. 193-194.
McArthur, Lewis A. 1974. *Oregon geographic names.* (Fourth edition, revised and enlarged by Lewis L. McArthur.) Portland, Oregon: Oregon Historical Society, 835 p.
McGregor, Alex. 1890. "Shasta County." *Tenth annual report of the State Mineralogist, for the year ending December 1, 1890.* Sacramento: California State Mining Bureau, p. 627-641.
Miller, Wm. P. 1890. "Trinity County." *Tenth annual report of the State Mineralogist, for the year ending December 1, 1890.* Sacramento: California State Mining Bureau, p. 695-727.
Murray, Keith A. 1959. *The Modocs and their war.* Norman: University of Oklahoma Press, 346 p.
O'Brien, J.C. 1946. "Mines and mining in Tehama County, California." *California Journal of Mines and Geology,* v. 42, no. 3, p. 183-195.
_____1947. "Mines and mineral resources of Siskiyou County." *California Journal of Mines and Geology,* v. 43, no. 4, p. 413-462.
Pease, Robert W. *Modoc County, A geographic time continuum on the California volcanic tableland.* (University of California Publications in Geography, Volume 17.) Berkeley and Los Angeles: University of California Press, 304 p.
Perez, Crisostomo N. 1996. *Land grants in Alta California.* Rancho Cordova, California: Landmark Enterprises, 264 p.
Russell, Israel C. 1885. "Existing glaciers of the United States." *Fifth Annual Report of the United States Geological Survey.* Washington: Government Printing Office, p. 303-355.
Salley, H.E. 1977. *History of California post offices, 1849-1976.* La Mesa, California: Postal History Associates, Inc., 300 p.
Schulz, Paul E. 1949. *Stories of Lassen's place names.* Mineral, California: Loomis Museum Association, 57 p.
Steger, Gertrude A. 1966. *Place names of Shasta County.* (Revised by Helen Hinckley Jones.) Glendale, California: La Siesta Press, 71 p.
Stewart, Charles L. 1934. "Early ascents of Mount Shasta." *Sierra Club Bulletin,* v. 19, no. 3, p. 58-70.
Stewart, George R. 1970. *American place-names., A concise and selective dictionary for the continental United States of America.* New York: Oxford University Press, 550 p.
Thompson, Erwin N. 1971. *Modoc war, Its military history and topography.* Sacramento: Argus Books, 188 p.
Tucker, W. Burling. 1919. "Tehama County." *Report XV of the State Mineralogist.* Sacramento: California State Mining Bureau, p. 258-266.
United States Board on Geographic Names (under name "United States Geographic Board"). 1933. *Sixth report of the United States Geographic Board, 1890 to 1932.* Washington: Government Printing Office, 834 p.
_____(under name "United States Board on Geographical Names"). 1936. *Decisions of the United States Board on Geographical Names, Decisions rendered between July 1, 1934, and June 30, 1935.* Washington: Government Printing Office, 26 p.
_____(under name "United States Board on Geographical Names"). 1937. *Decisions of the United States Board on Geographical Names, Decisions rendered between July 1, 1936, and June 30, 1937.* Washington: Government Printing Office, 33 p.
_____(under name "United States Board on Geographical Names"). 1940. *Decisions of the United States Board on Geographical Names, Decisions rendered between July 1, 1939, and June 30, 1940.* Washington: Government Printing Office, 46 p.
_____(under name "Board on Geographical Names"). 1943. *Decisions rendered between July 1, 1941, and June 30, 1943.* Washington: Department of the Interior, 104 p.
_____(under name "United States Board on Geographical Names"). 1947. *Decision lists nos. 4701, 4702, 4703.* Washington: Department of the Interior, 14 p.
_____1948a. *Decision lists nos. 4801-4806, January-June, 1948.* Washington: Department of the Interior, 25 p.
_____1948b. *Decision lists nos. 4807, 4808, 4809, July, August, September 1948.* Washington: Department of the Interior, 16 p.
_____1949. *Decision lists nos. 4810, 4811, 4812, October, November, December, 1948* Washington: Department of the Interior, 25 p.
_____1950. *Decisions on names in the United States and Alaska rendered during April, May, and June 1950.* (Decision list no. 5006.) Washington: Department of the Interior, 47 p.
_____1959. *Decisions on names in the United States, Decisions rendered from January, 1959 through April, 1959.* (Decision list no. 5902.) Washington: Department of the Interior, 49 p.
_____1960a. *Decisions on names in the Unites States and Puerto Rico, Decisions rendered in May, June, July, and August, 1959.* (Decision list no. 5903.) Washington: Department of the Interior, 79 p.
_____1960b. *Decisions on names in the United States, Decisions rendered from September 1959 through December 1959.* (Decision list no. 5904.) Washington: Department of the Interior, 68 p.
_____1961. *Decisions on names in the United States, Decisions rendered from September through December 1960.* (Decision list no. 6003.) Washington: Department of the Interior, 73 p.
_____1962. *Decisions on names in the United States, Decisions rendered from May through August 1962.* (Decision list no. 6202.) Washington: Department of the Interior, 81 p.
_____1964. *Decisions on geographic names in the United States, September through December 1963.* (Decision list no. 6303.) Washington: Department of the Interior, 66 p.
_____1965a. *Decisions on geographic names in the United States, January through March 1963.* (Decision list no. 6501.) Washington: Department of the Interior, 85 p.
_____1965b. *Decisions on geographic names in the United States, April through June 1965.* (Decision list no. 6502.) Washington: Department of the Interior, 39 p.
_____1965c. *Decisions on geographic names in the United States, July through September 1965.* (Decision list no. 6503.) Washington: Department of the Interior, 74 p.
_____1966. *Decisions on geographic names in the United States, January through March 1966.* (Decision list no. 6601.) Washington: Department of the Interior, 44 p.
_____1967a. *Decisions on geographic names in the United States, July through September 1966.* (Decision list no. 6603.) Washington: Department of the Interior, 38 p.
_____1967b. *Decisions on geographic names in the United States, April through June 1967.* (Decision list no. 6702.) Washington: Department of the Interior, 26 p.
_____1968a. *Decisions on geographic names in the United States, October through December 1967.* (Decision list no. 6704.) Washington: Department of the Interior, 46 p.
_____1968b. *Decisions on geographic names in the United States, January through March 1968.* (Decision list no. 6801.) Washington: Department of the Interior, 51 p.
_____1968c. *Decisions on geographic names in the United States, April through June 1968.* (Decision list no. 6802.) Washington: Department of the Interior, 42 p.
_____1969a. *Decisions on geographic names in the United States, October through December 1968.* (Decision list no. 6804.) Washington: Department of the Interior, 33 p.
_____1969b. *Decisions on geographic names in the United States, January through March 1969.* (Decision list no. 6901.) Washington: Department of the Interior, 31 p.
_____1969c. *Decisions on geographic names in the United States, April through June 1969.* (Decision list no. 6902.) Washington: Department of the Interior, 28 p.
_____1969d. *Decisions on geographic names in the United States, July through September 1969.* (Decision list no. 6903.) Washington: Department of the Interior, 36 p.
_____1970a. *Decisions on geographic names in the United States, October through December 1969.* (Decision list no. 6904.) Washington: Department of the Interior, 35 p.
_____1970b. *Decisions on geographic names in the United States, July through September 1970.* (Decision list no. 7003.) Washington: Department of the Interior, 15 p.
_____1971a. *Decisions on geographic names in the United States, October through December 1970.* (Decision list no. 7004.) Washington: Department of the Interior, 28 p.
_____1971b. *Decisions on geographic names in the United States, January through March 1971.* (Decision list no. 7101.) Washington: Department of the Interior, 19 p.
_____1972a. *Decisions on geographic names in the United States, January through March 1972.* (Decision list no. 7201.) Washington: Department of the Interior, 32 p.
_____1972b. *Decisions on geographic names in the United States, April through June 1972.* (Decision list no. 7202.) Washington: Department of the Interior, 30 p.
_____1972c. *Decisions on geographic names in the United States, July through September 1972.* (Decision list no. 7203.) Washington: Department of the Interior, 17 p.
_____1973. *Decisions on geographic names in the United States, April through June 1973.* (Decision list no. 7302.) Washington: Department of the Interior, 16 p.
_____1975. *Decisions on geographic names in the United States, July through September 1975.* (Decision list no. 7503.) Washington: Department of the Interior, 33 p.
_____1977a. *Decisions on geographic names in the United States, January through March 1977.* (Decision list no. 7701.) Washington: Department of the Interior, 32 p.

_____1977b. *Decisions on geographic names in the United States, April through June 1977.* (Decision list no. 7702.) Washington: Department of the Interior, 40 p.

_____1978a. *Decisions on geographic names in the United States, October through December 1977.* (Decision list no. 7704.) Washington: Department of the Interior, 29 p.

_____1978b. *Decisions on geographic names in the United States, July through September 1978.* (Decision list no. 7803.) Washington: Department of the Interior, 32 p.

_____1978c. *Decisions on geographic names in the United States, October through December 1978.* (Decision list no. 7804.) Washington: Department of the Interior, 48 p.

_____1979a. *Decisions on geographic names in the United States, January through March 1979.* (Decision list no. 7901.) Washington: Department of the Interior, 27 p.

_____1979b. *Decisions on geographic names in the United States, April through June 1979.* (Decision list no. 7902.) Washington: Department of the Interior, 33 p.

_____1980. *Decisions on geographic names in the United States, October through December 1979.* (Decision list no. 7904.) Washington: Department of the Interior, 26 p.

_____1981a. *Decisions on geographic names in the United States, October through December 1980.* (Decision list no. 8004.) Washington: Department of the Interior, 21 p.

_____1981b. *Decisions on geographic names in the United States, January through March 1981.* (Decision list no. 8101.) Washington: Department of the Interior, 23 p.

_____1981c. *Decisions on geographic names in the United States, April through June 1981.* (Decision list no. 8102.) Washington: Department of the Interior, 28 p.

_____1982a. *Decisions on geographic names in the United States, January through March 1982.* (Decision list no. 8201.) Washington: Department of the Interior, 17 p.

_____1982b. *Decisions on geographic names in the United States, April through June 1982.* (Decision list no. 8202.) Washington: Department of the Interior, 21 p.

_____1983a. *Decisions on geographic names in the United States, July through September 1982.* (Decision list no. 8203.) Washington: Department of the Interior, 25 p.

_____1983b. *Decisions on geographic names in the United States, January through March 1983.* (Decision list no. 8301.) Washington: Department of the Interior, 33 p.

_____1983c. *Decisions on geographic names in the United States, April through June 1983.* (Decision list no. 8302.) Washington: Department of the Interior, 29 p.

_____1984a. *Decisions on geographic names in the United States, January through March 1984.* (Decision list no. 8401.) Washington: Department of the Interior, 29 p.

_____1984b. *Decisions on geographic names in the United States, April through June 1984.* (Decision list no. 8402.) Washington: Department of the Interior, 22 p.

_____1984c. *Decisions on geographic names in the United States, October through December 1984.* (Decision list no. 8404.) Washington: Department of the Interior, 18 p.

_____1985a. *Decisions on geographic names in the United States, January through March 1985.* (Decision list no. 8501.) Washington: Department of the Interior, 18 p.

_____1985b. *Decisions on geographic names in the United States, April through June 1985.* (Decision list no. 8502.) Washington: Department of the Interior, 12 p.

_____1985c. *Decisions on geographic names in the United States, October through December 1985.* (Decision list no. 8504.) Washington: Department of the Interior, p. 12 p.

_____1986a. *Decisions on geographic names in the United States, April through June 1986.* (Decision list no. 8602.) Washington: Department of the Interior, 10 p.

_____1986b. *Decisions on geographic names in the United States, July through September 1986.* (Decision list no. 8603.) Washington: Department of the Interior, 11 p.

_____1986c. *Decisions on geographic names in the United States, October through December 1986.* (Decision list no. 8604.) Washington: Department of the Interior, 22 p.

_____1987a. *Decisions on geographic names in the United States, January through March 1987.* (Decision list no. 8701.) Washington: Department of the Interior, 22 p,

_____1987b. *Decisions on geographic names in the United States, April through June 1987.* (Decision list no. 8702.) Washington: Department of the Interior, 17 p.

_____1987c. *Decisions on geographic names in the United States, October through December 1987.* (Decision list no. 8704.) Washington: Department of the Interior, 15 p.

_____1988a. *Decisions on geographic names in the United States, April through June 1988.* (Decision list no. 8802.) Washington: Department of the Interior, 19 p.

_____1988b. *Decisions on geographic names in the United States, July through September 1988.* (Decision list no. 8803.) Washington: Department of the Interior, 19 p.

_____1989. *Decisions on geographic names in the United States, January through March 1989.* (Decision list no. 8901.) Washington: Department of the Interior, 9 p.

_____1990. *Decisions on geographic names in the United States.* (Decision list 1990.) Washington: Department of the Interior, 35 p.

_____1991. *Decisions on geographic names in the United States.* (Decision list 1991.) Washington: Department of the Interior, 40 p.

Walker, Dorothy Reichman. 1957. "Oro Fino district, Morrison-Carlock mine." *Siskiyou Pioneer,* v. 2, no. 10, p. 83-86,

Waring, Gerald A. 1915. *Springs of California.* (United States Geological Survey Water-Supply Paper 338.) Washington: Government Printing Office, 410 p.

Watts, W.L. 1893. "Mineral springs in Siskiyou County." *Eleventh report of the State Mineralogist, (First Biennial,) two years ending September 15, 1892.* Sacramento: California State Mining Bureau, p. 449-452.

Wells, Harry L., and Chambers, W.L. 1882. *History of Butte County, California.* San Francisco: Harry L.Wells, 305 p.

Whiting, J.S., and Whiting, Richard J. 1960. *Forts of the State of California.* (Authors), 90 p.

Whitney, J.D. 1865. *Report of progress and synopsis of the field-work, from 1860 to 1864.* (Geological Survey of California, Geology, Volume I.) Published by authority of the Legislature of California, 498 p.

Wilkes, Charles. 1958. *Columbia River to the Sacramento.* Oakland, California: Biobooks, 140 p.

Williams, Howell. 1949. *Geology of the Macdoel quadrangle.* (Division of Mines Bulletin 151.) San Francisco: California Division of Mines, p. 7-60.

Windeler, Adolphus. 1969. *The California gold rush diary of a German sailor.* (Edited by W. Turrentine Jackson.) Berkeley, California: Howell-North Books, 236 p.

Wood, P.R. 1960. *Geology and ground-water features of the Butte Valley region, Siskiyou County, California.* (United States Geological Survey Water-Supply Paper 1491.) Washington: Government Printing Office, 150 p.

QUADRANGLE MAPS

(All maps published by United States Geological Survey, except as noted. Dates identify the editions of the maps. If a reprinted or revised map was used, the year of reprinting or revision is given in parentheses, unless the reprinted or revised map is cited specifically in the text.)

Alder Springs 7.5'—1967.
Alturas 1°x 2°—1954 (limited revision 1962).
American House 7.5'—1948.
Anderson 15'—1947.
Anthony Peak 15'—1952.
Ball Mountain 7.5'—1967.
Balls Ferry 7.5'—1965.
Bangor 15'—1941.
7.5'—1947 (photorevised 1969).
Bark Shanty Gulch 7.5'—1974.
Bartle 30'—1939.
15'—1961.
Bear Peak 7.5'—1982.
Bella Vista 7.5'—1965.
Bend 7.5'—1965.
Berry Creek 7.5'—1970.
Bidwell Bar 30'—1897 (reprinted 1928).
Big Bend 15'—1961.
Big Bend Mountain 15'—1948.
Biggs 7.5'—1912; 1970.
Black Butte Dam 7.5'—1967.
Blossom 7.5'—1952 (photorevised 1969).
Bollibokka Mountain 15'—1957.
Bonanza King 15'—1955.
Boulder Peak 7.5'—1981.
Bray 15'—1950 (minor corrections 1965).
Broken Rib Mountain 7.5'—1982.
Brush Creek 7.5'—1970.
Buck Rock 7.5'—1967.
Burney 30'—1939 (reprinted 1947).
15'—1957.
Butte City 15' (same area as Butte Sink 15')—1954.
7.5'—1912; 1952; 1952 (photorevised 1973).
Butte Meadows 15'—1958.

Campbell Mound 7.5'—1952 (photorevised 1969).
Cascade 7.5'—1948.
Cecil Lake 7.5'—1979.
Cecilville 15'—1955.
7.5'—1979.
Chanchelulla Peak 15'—1951.
Cherokee 7.5'—1970.
Chico 1°x 2°—1958 (limited revision 1966).
30'—1895 (reprinted 1944).
15'—1949.
7.5' (same area as Durham 7.5')—1948 (photorevised 1969).
Chico Landing 7.5' (same area as Ord Ferry 7.5')—1912 (reprinted 1931).
Chimney Rock 7.5'—1981.
China Mountain 15'—1955.
Chrome 7.5'—1968.
Clear Creek 7.5' (same area as Hamlin Canyon 7.5')—1912; 1981.
Clipper Mills 7.5'—1948.
Coffee Creek 15'—1955.
Cohasset 7.5'—1979.
Cold Fork 7.5'—1967.
Colyear Springs 15'—1957.
Condrey Mountain 15'—1955.
Copco 15'—1954.
Corning 15' (same area as Vina 15')—1951.
7.5'—1951 (photorevised 1969).
Cottonwood 7.5'—1965.
Dales 7.5'—1965.
Deadman Point 7.5'—1981.
Dees Peak 7.5'—1978.
Devils Punchbowl 7.5'—1981.
Dillon Mountain 15'—1955.
7.5'—1983.
Dorris 15'—1950.
Dry Creek 7.5' (same area as Shippee 7.5')—1912.
Dubakella Mountain 15'—1954.
Dunsmuir 30'—1935 (reprinted 1943).
15'—1954.
Durham 7.5' (same area as Chico 7.5')—1912.
Dutch Creek 7.5'—1980.
Dwinnell Reservoir 15' (same area as Lake Shastina 15')—1954.
Elk Creek 15'—1918 (reprinted 1939; Army advance sheet).
7.5'—1968.
English Peak 7.5'—1977.
Enterprise 7.5'—1957 (photorevised 1969).
Etna 30'—1934.
15'—1955.
Fall River Mills 15'—1961.
Felkner Hill 7.5'—1968.
Figurehead Mountain 7.5'—1980.
Flournoy 15'—1944; 1958.
7.5'—1967.
Forbestown 7.5'—1970.
Forks of Salmon 15'—1955.
7.5'—1978.
Fort Jones 15'—1955.
Foster Island 7.5' (same area as McIntosh Landing 7.5')—1950 (photorevised 1969).
French Gulch 15'—1944.
7.5'—1979.
Fruto 15'—1944.
7.5'—1968.
Fruto NE 7.5' (same area as Walker Creek 7.5')—1952 (photorevised 1969).
Gerber 7.5'—1950; 1950, photorevised 1969.
Glenn 7.5' (same area as Jacinto 7.5')—1951 (photorevised 1969).
Grasshopper Ridge 7.5'—1979.
Grider Valley 7.5'—1981.
Gridley 15'—1952.
7.5'—1912; 1952 (photorevised 1973).
Hall Ridge 7.5'—1967.
Halls Flat 30'—1939 (reprinted 1948).
Hambone 15'—1961.
Hamburg 7.5'—1980.
Hamilton City 7.5' (same area as Hamilton 7.5')—1949 (photorevised 1969).
Hamlin Canyon 7.5' (same area as Clear Creek 7.5')—1951 (photorevised 1969).
Happy Camp 15'—1956.
7.5'—1980.
Henleyville 7.5—1967.
Hoaglin 30'—1935 (reprinted 1944).
Honcut 7.5'—1912; 1952 (photorevised 1973).
Hooker 7.5'—1965.
Hornbrook 15'—1955.
Huckleberry Mountain 7.5'—1980.
Hull Mountain 15'—1952.
7.5'—1967.
Igo 7.5'—1979.
Jellico 15'—1957.
Jonesville 15'—1958.
Julian Rocks 7.5'—1968.
Kangaroo Mountain 7.5'—1980.
Kimshew Point 7.5'—1979.
Kirkwood 7.5'—1949 (photorevised 1969).
Kneecap Ridge 7.5'—1967.
Lake Shastina 15' (same area as Dwinnell Reservoir 15')—1954.
Lamoine 15'—1946; 1957.
Lassen Peak 1°—1894.
15'—1956.
Llano Seco 7.5' (same area as Newhard 7.5')—1948.
Lodoga 15'—1960.
Logandale 7.5'—1952.
Logan Ridge 7.5' (same area as Logan Creek 7.5')—1958.
Log Spring 7.5'—1967.
Loma Rica 7.5' (same area as Prairie Creek 7.5')—1947 (photorevised 1969).
Lonesome Ridge 7.5'—1974.
Los Molinos 7.5'—1952; 1952, photorevised 1969.
Lowrey 7.5'—1967.
Macdoel 30'—1941.
15'—1954.
Manton 15'—1956.
Manzanita Lake 15'—1956.
Marble Mountain 7.5'—1980.
Marysville 30'—1895 (reprinted 1911).
Maxwell 15'—1906 (reprinted 1936).
McIntosh Landing 7.5' (same area as Foster Island 7.5')—1914.
Medicine Lake 15'—1952.
Medicine Mountain 7.5'—1978.
Mendocino Pass 7.5'—1967.
Millville 15'—1953.
Mineral 30'—1941 (reprinted 1948).
Mitchell Gulch 7.5'—1965.
Modoc Lava Bed 1°—1892 (reprinted 1908).
Montgomery Creek 15'—1956.
Mount Dome 15'—1950.
Mount Harkness 15'—1956.
Nelson 7.5'—1912 (reprinted 1947); 1948 (photorevised 1969).
Newhard 7.5' (same area as Llano Seco 7.5')—1912.
Newville 7.5'—1967.
Nord 7.5'—1951 (photorevised 1969).
Olinda 7.5'—1964.
Ono 15'—1952.
Ord Ferry 7.5' (same area as Chico Landing 7.5')—1949 (photorevised 1969).
Oregon House 7.5'—1948 (photorevised 1969).
Orland 7.5'—1951 (photorevised 1969).
Orleans 15'—1952.
Orleans Mountain 7.5'—1974.
Oroville 15'—1942.
7.5'—1912 (reprinted 1922); 1970.
Oroville Dam 7.5'—1970.
Oxbow Bridge 7.5'—1967.
Palermo 7.5'—1912 (reprinted 1947); 1970.
Palo Cedro 7.5'—1965.
Panther Spring 15'—1953.
Paradise 15'—1953.
Paradise East 7.5'—1980.
Paradise West 7.5'—1980.
Paskenta 15'—1920 (reprinted 1938; Army); 1952.
7.5'—1967.
Pennington 7.5'—1954 (photorevised 1973).
Plaskett Meadows 7.5'—1967.
Plaskett Ridge 7.5'—1967.
Polar Bear Mountain 7.5'—1982.
Pondosa 15'—1961.
Prescott Mountain 7.5'—1981.
Preston Peak 30'—1922 (reprinted 1944).
15'—1956.
7.5'—1982.
Princeton 7.5'—1952 (photorevised 1973).
Project City 7.5'—1957 (photorevised 1969).
Prospect Peak 15'—1957.
Pulga 15'—1957.
7.5'—1979.
Rackerby 7.5'—1948 (photorevised 1969).

Raglin Ridge 7.5'—1967.
Red Bank 15'—1952.
7.5'—1952 (photorevised 1969).
Red Bluff 1°—1894.
15'—1952.
Red Bluff East 7.5'—1951 (photorevised 1969).
Red Bluff West 7.5'—1951 (photorevised 1969).
Redding 1°x 2°—1958.
30'—1901.
15'—1944.
7.5'—1957; 1957, photorevised 1969.
Richardson Springs 15'—1944; 1952.
7.5' (same area as Keefers 7.5')—1951 (photorevised 1969).
Richardson Springs NW 7.5' (same area as Singer Creek 7.5')—1952 (photorevised 1969).
Riley Ridge 7.5'—1967.
Saint John Mountain 7.5'—1968.
Salmon Mountain 15'—1955.
7.5'—1978.
Sanborn Slough 7.5'—1952 (photorevised 1973).
Sawyers Bar 30'—1923 (reprinted 1945).
15'—1955.
7.5'—1979.
Schell Mountain 15'—1950.
Scott Bar 15'—1980.
Sehorn Creek 7.5'—1967.
Seiad 30'—1922.
Seiad Valley 15'—1955.
7.5'—1980.
Shasta 1°—1894 (reprinted 1934).
15'—1954.
Shasta Bally 7.5'—1978.
Shasta Dam 7.5'—1956 (photorevised 1969).
Shippee 7.5' (same area as Dry Creek 7.5')—1948; 1948, photorevised 1969.
Shoeinhorse Mountain 15'—1954.
Slater Butte 7.5'—1980.
Smartsville 30'—1895 (reprinted 1912).
Soapstone Hill 7.5'—1979.
Somes Bar 7.5'—1979.
Stirling City 7.5'—1979.
Stone Valley 7.5' (same area as Kurand 7.5')—1952; 1952, photorevised 1969.
Stonyford 7.5'—1968.
Strawberry Valley 7.5'—1948; 1948, photorevised 1975.
Susanville 1°x 2°—1962.
Tanners Peak 7.5'—1977.
Tehama 15' (same area as Red Bluff 15')—1905 (reprinted 1947).
The Whaleback 15'—1954.
Thompson Peak 7.5'—1979.
Timber Mountain 15'—1952.
Trinity Dam 15' (same area as Trinity Lake 15')—1950 (minor corrections 1964, 1968).
Trinity Lake 15' (same area as Trinity Dam 15')—1950 (minor revisions 1962).
Tulelake 15'—1951.
Tuscan Buttes 15'—1944; 1947
Tuscan Buttes NE 7.5'—1965.
Tuscan Springs 7.5'—1951 (photorevised 1969).
Ukiah 1°x 2°—1957
Ukonom Lake 15'—1955.
7.5'—1980.
Ukonom Mountain 7.5'—1980.
Vina 15' (same area as Corning 15')—1904 (reprinted 1947).
7.5'—1950 (photorevised 1969).
Weaverville 30'—1913 (reprinted 1947).
15'—1950.
Weed 1°x 2°—1963.
15'—1954.
West of Biggs 7.5' (same area as Landlow 7.5')—1952 (photorevised 1973).
West of Gerber 7.5'—1951 (photorevised 1969).
Whiskeytown 7.5'—1979.
White Horse 15'—1962.
Whitmore 15'—1956.
Wilbur Springs 15' (same area as Venado 15')—1961.
Willows 15'—(1906 (reprinted 1914).
7.5' (same area as Lyman 7.5')—1951; 1951, photorevised 1969).
Yellow Dog Peak 7.5'—1977.
Yolla Bolly 15'—1954.
Youngs Peak 7.5'—1979.
Yreka 30'—1939 (reprinted 1947).
15'—1954.

MISCELLANEOUS MAPS

Averill. 1935. "Map of western portion Siskiyou County showing locations of principal gold mines." (Plate IV *in* Averill, 1935.)

_____1939. "Map of Shasta County showing locations of principal mineral deposits." (Plate II *in* Averill, 1939.)

Baker. 1855. "Map of the mining region, of California." Drawn by Geo. A. Baker.

Bancroft. 1864. "Bancroft's map of the Pacific States." Compiled by Wm. H. Knight. Published by H.H. Bancroft & Co., Booksellers and Stationers, San Francisco, Cal.

Burr. 1839. "Map of the United States of North America with parts of the adjacent countries." By David N. Burr. (Late Topographer to the Post Office.) Geographer to the House of Representatives of the U.S.

California Division of Highways. 1934. (Appendix "A" *of* California Division of Highways.)

California Mining Bureau. 1909a. "Del Norte and Siskiyou Counties." (*In* California State Mining Bureau Bulletin 56.)

_____1909b. "Shasta and Tehama Counties." (*In* California State Mining Bureau Bulletin 56.)

_____1909c. "Mendocino, Glenn, Lake, and Colusa Counties." (*In* California State Mining Bureau Bulletin 56.)

_____1909d. "Butte and Plumas Counties." (*In* California State Mining Bureau Bulletin 56).

_____1917a. (Untitled map *in* California State Mining Bureau Bulletin 74, p. 158.)

_____1917b. (Untitled map *in* California State Mining Bureau Bulletin 74, p. 160.)

_____1917c. (Untitled map *in* California State Mining Bureau Bulletin 74, p. 161.)

_____1917d. (Untitled map *in* California State Mining Bureau Bulletin 74, p. 162.)

Diller. 1895. "Map of Mount Shasta." (*In* Diller, 1895, p. 246.)

Diller and others. 1915. "Geologic and topographic map of the Shasta route from Seattle, Washington, to San Francisco, California." (*In* Diller and others.)

Eddy. 1854. "Approved and declared to the the official map of the State of California by an act of the Legislature passed March 25th 1853." Compiled by W.M. Eddy, State Surveyor General. Published for R.A. Eddy, Marysville, California, by J.H. Colton, New York.

Farnham. 1845. "Map of the Californias." (*Accompanies* Farnham.)

Ferry. 1851. "Nuova California." By Hypolite Ferry.

Fremont. 1845: "Map of an exploring expedition to the Rocky Mountains in the year 1842 and to Oregon & North California in the years 1843-44." By Brevet Capt. J.C. Frémont.

_____1848. "Map of Oregon and Upper California from the surveys of John Charles Frémont, and other authorities." Drawn by Charles Preuss. Washington City.

Gibbes. 1852. "A new map of California." By Charles Drayton Gibbes, from his own and other recent surveys and explorations. Published by C.D. Gibbes, Stockton, Cal.

Goddard. 1857. "Britton & Rey's map of the State of California." By George H. Goddard.

Miller. 1890. "Geological map of Trinity County, Cal." (*In* Miller.)

O'Brien. 1946. "Map of Tehama County, California, showing locations of principal mineral deposits." (Plate 28 *in* O'Brien, 1946.)

_____1947. "Map of eastern portion of Siskiyou County, California, showing locations of mineral deposits." (Plate 43 *in* O'Brien, 1947.)

Russell. 1883. "Topographical sketch of Mt. Shasta, California." (Plate XLIV *in* Russell.)

Sage. 1846. "Map of Oregon, California, New Mexico, N.W. Texas, & the proposed territory of Ne-Bras-ka." By Rufus B. Sage.

Scholfield. 1851. "Map of southern Oregon and northern California." Compiled from the best authorities, and from personal surveys and explorations, by N. Scholfield, Civil Engineer. Published by Marvin & Hitchcock, San Francisco.

Tanner. 1849. "Map of California, New Mexico, Texas, &c." Published by H.S.Tanner.

Wells and Chambers. 1882. (Untitled map *in* Wells and Chambers, opposite p. 209.)

Wilkes. 1841. "Map of Upper California." By the U.S. Ex. Ex. and best authorities.

_____1849. "Map of Upper California." By the best authorities.

Williams. 1949. "Geologic map of the Macdoel quadrangle, California." (Plate 1 *in* Williams.)

Williamson and Abbott. 1855. "Map No. 1, from San Francisco Bay to the northern boundary of California." (In *Reports of explorations and surveys, to ascertain the most practicable and economical route for a railroad from the Mississippi River to the Pacific Ocean.* Volume XI. 1861.)

Part Three
Northeast Region
Lassen, Modoc and Plumas Counties

Part Three–Northeast Region

Northeast Region
Lassen, Modoc and Plumas Counties

Regional Setting

General.—This section concerns geographic features in three counties—Lassen, Modoc, and Plumas—in the northeast part of the State of California. Townships (T) and Ranges (R) refer to Mount Diablo Base and Meridian. Trappers and explorers came to the region before the middle of the nineteenth century, but permanent settlement came only after American acquisition of the land. Lumbering, ranching, recreation, and farming support the present-day population. The map on the facing page shows the location of the Northeast Region and the counties in it.

Lassen County.—Lassen County was organized in 1864 from parts of previously formed Plumas and Shasta Counties—only minor changes have been made in the original county boundaries (Coy, p. 133-139). Susanville is and always has been the county seat; the county name commemorates Peter Lassen, a pioneer of the region (Hoover, Rensch, and Rensch, p. 145).

Modoc County.—Modoc County occupies the northeast corner of California, where volcanic features dominate the landscape. The county was created in 1874 from part of Siskiyou County, and the county boundaries remain as originally defined (Coy, p. 181). Alturas is the original and only county seat; the county name is from Modoc Indians (Hoover, Rensch, and Rensch, p. 207).

Plumas County.—Plumas County lies in the northern Sierra Nevada on upper reaches of the forks and branches of Feather River. The county was organized in 1854, largely from part of previously established Butte County; the county boundaries are about as originally defined (Coy, p. 203-206). Quincy has been the county seat from the beginning; the county name is from the Spanish designation of Feather River—*El Rio de las Plumas* (Hoover, Rensch, and Rensch, p. 278).

Northeast Region
Lassen, Modoc and Plumas Counties

—A—

Abbott Spring [LASSEN]: *spring,* 6 miles north-northeast of Lava Peak (lat. 40°54'30" N, long. 120°51'05" W; sec. 32, T 36 N, R 10 E). Named on Hayden Hill (1956) 15' quadrangle.

Accomodation Spring [LASSEN]: *spring,* 8 miles northeast of Observation Peak (lat. 40°50'10" N, long. 120°02'50" W; at W line sec. 3, T 34 N, R 17 E). Named on Observation Peak (1954) 15' quadrangle.

Adams Neck [PLUMAS]: *area,* 3 miles north-northwest of Chilcoot (lat. 39°50'20" N, long. 120°09' W; sec. 14, 23, T 23 N, R 16 E). Named on Chilcoot (1979) 7.5' quadrangle.

Adams Peak [LASSEN-PLUMAS]: *peak,* 4.25 miles south of Constantia [LASSEN] on Lassen-Plumas County line (lat. 39°54'40" N, long. 120°06' W; on S line sec. 20, T 24 N, R 17 E). Altitude 8197 feet. Named on Constantia (1977) 7.5' quadrangle.

Addington: see **Hayden Hill** [LASSEN] (2).

Adin [MODOC]: *town,* 29 miles southwest of Alturas (lat. 41°11'45" N, long. 120°56'35" W; sec. 21, 28, T 39 N, R 9 E). Named on Adin (1962) 15' quadrangle. Postal authorities established Aidenville post office in 1871 and changed the name to Adin in 1876 (Frickstad, p. 102). The name commemorates Adin G. McDowell, who settled at the place in 1869 (Hanna, p. 2). According to Pease (p. 93), McDowell's first name had the form "Aiden." Postal authorities established Hot Springs post office 20 miles north of Adin (SE quarter of sec. 12, T 41 N, R 9 E) in 1871, changed the name to Clover Swale in 1876, and discontinued it in 1878 (Salley, p. 46, 100). California Division of Highways' (1934) map shows a place called Mattes located 2 miles northeast of Alturas along Nevada-California-Oregon Railroad.

Adin Pass [MODOC]: *pass,* 7.25 miles south-southwest of Canby (lat. 41°20'45" N, long. 120°55'10" W; sec. 34, T 41 N, R 9 E). Named on Canby (1961) 15' quadrangle.

Adin Summit Pond [MODOC]: *water feature,* 8 miles south-southwest of Canby (lat. 41°20'15" N, long. 120°56' W; near E line sec. 4, T 40 N, R 9 E). Named on Canby (1961) 15' quadrangle.

Aidenville: see **Adin** [MODOC].

Ainshea Butte [MODOC]: *locality,* 4 miles north-northwest of Timber Mountain along Great Northern Railroad (lat. 41°40'35" N, long. 121°20' W; near NE cor. sec. 12, T 44 N, R 5 E). Named on Timber Mountain (1952) 15' quadrangle.

Ake Reservoir [MODOC]: *intermittent lake,* 8.5 miles west-southwest of Willow Ranch (lat. 41°50'15" N, long. 120°29'30" W; near SE cor. sec. 8, T 46 N, R 13 E). Named on Willow Ranch (1962) 15' quadrangle.

Alaska Canyon [LASSEN]: *canyon,* 6 miles long, drained by Red Rock Creek above a point 16 miles east of Madeline (lat. 41°02'30" N, long. 120°09'35" W; sec. 28, T 37 N, R 16 E). Named on Boot Lake (1962) 7.5' quadrangle.

Alderman Ridge [MODOC]: ridge, north-trending, 2 miles long, 4 miles west of Lookout (lat. 41°11'55" N, long. 121°13'45" W; sec. 24, 25, T 39 N, R 6 E). Named on Bieber (1961) 15' quadrangle.

Alexander: see **Camp Wallace Alexander** [PLUMAS].

Alkali Lake [MODOC]: *dry lake,* 17 miles south of Alturas (lat. 41°15'10" N, long. 120°36'15" W; on S line sec. 33, T 40 N, R 12 E). Named on Alturas (1961) 15' quadrangle.

Alkali Lake: see **Lower Alkali Lake**, under **Lower Lake** [MODOC]; **Middle Alkali Lake** [MODOC]; **Upper Alkali Lake**, under **Upper Lake** [MODOC].

Alkali Lakes: see **Middle Alkali Lake** [MODOC].

Allen Butte [MODOC]: *peak,* 3.5 miles southeast of Crank Mountain (lat. 41°21'40" N, long. 121°05'15" W; sec. 30, T 41 N, R 8 E). Altitude 4682 feet. Named on Crank Mountain (1962) 15' quadrangle.

Allen Camp [MODOC]: *locality,* 3.25 miles east-southeast of Crank Mountain along Pit River (lat. 41°22'10" N, long. 121°05'05" W; near N line sec. 30, T 41 N, R 8 E); the place is 0.5 mile north of Allen Butte. Named on Crank Mountain (1962) 15' quadrangle.

Almanor [PLUMAS]:

(1) *village,* 7 miles south-southeast of Chester (lat. 40°13' N, long. 121°10'15" W; sec. 10, 11, T 27 N, R 7 E); the place is along Lake Almanor. Named on Almanor (1979) 7.5' quadrangle. Postal authorities established Almanor post office in 1932; the name was coined from the words "Alice," "Martha," and "Elinor," the names of daughters of Guy C. Earl, president of Great Western Power Company—the place also was known as Plumas Pines (Salley, p. 5).

(2) *locality,* 6.25 miles east-southeast of the village of Almanor along Western Pacific Railroad near Canyondam (lat. 40°10'30" N, long. 121°04'15" W; sec. 27, T 27 N, R 8 E). Named on Canyondam (1979) 7.5' quadrangle.

Almanor: see **Camp Almanor** [PLUMAS]; **Lake Almanor** [PLUMAS].

Almanor Peninsula [PLUMAS]: *peninsula,* 6 miles southeast of Chester along Lake Almanor (lat. 40°15' N, long. 121°08'45" W). Named on Almanor (1979) and Chester (1979) 7.5' quadrangles.

Al Shinn Canyon [LASSEN]: *canyon,* 4.5 miles long, opens into lowlands along Smoke Creek 10 miles southeast of Observation Peak (lat. 40°40'30" N, long. 120°03'55" W; near SW cor. sec. 33, T 33 N, R 17 E). Named on Shinn Mountain (1954) 15' quadrangle.

Alturas [MODOC]: *town,* situated a little east of the center of Modoc County along Pit River (lat. 41°29'30" N, long. 120°32'30" W; around SW cor. sec. 12, T 42 N, R 12 E). Named on Alturas (1961) and Big Sage Reservoir (1962) 15' quadrangles. Postal authorities established Dorris Bridge post office in 1871 and changed the name to Alturas in 1876 (Frickstad, p. 102). The town incorporated in 1901. Pressley A. Dorris and his nephew, Jim Dorris, started a cattle ranch and built a bridge across Pit River at the site in 1870 (Laird, p. 121-122). The community at the bridge first was called Dorris' Bridge, and the place is called Dorrisville on a map of 1874; the state legislature changed the name to Alturas in 1876 (Gudde, 1949, p. 9). Pease (p. 97) noted that a place called Centerville was located just west of Alturas. Wheeler's (1877) map shows a feature called Alturas Hill situated just west of the town.

Alturas Hill: see **Alturas** [MODOC].

Ambrose [MODOC]: *locality,* 11 miles southwest of Jacks Butte along Southern Pacific Railroad (lat. 41°30'10" N, long. 120°58'45" W; at S line sec. 6, T 42 N, R 9 E). Named on Jacks Butte (1962) 15' quadrangle.

Ambrose Canyon [LASSEN]: *canyon,* drained by a stream that flows nearly 2 miles to Ambrose Valley 6.5 miles east of Adin (lat. 41° 10'40" N, long. 120°49'15" W; near E line sec. 33, T 39 N, R 10 E). Named on Adin (1962) 15' quadrangle.

Ambrose Reservoir [LASSEN]: *lake,* 400 feet long, 8 miles north-northeast of Lava Peak (lat. 40°56'05" N, long. 120°49'10" W; near NE cor. sec. 28, T 36 N, R 10 E). Named on Hayden Hill (1956) 15' quadrangle.

Ambrose Valley [LASSEN-MODOC]: *area,* 6.25 miles east-southeast of Adin [MODOC] on Lassen-Modoc County line, mainly in Lassen County (lat. 41°10'30" N, long. 120°49'30" W). Named on Adin (1962) 15' quadrangle.

Amedee [LASSEN]: *locality,* 27 miles east-southeast of Susanville along Nevada-California-Oregon Railroad (lat. 40°16'10" N, long. 120°10'30" W). Named on Honey Lake (1893) 1° quadrangle. Postal authorities established Amedee post office in 1890 and discontinued it in 1924 (Frickstad, p. 66). The place first was known as Lower Hot Springs, for a group of hot springs there, to distinguish it from Upper Hot Springs at Wendel; after arrival of the railroad in 1890, the site was called Heriot's place for a former manager of the railroad, but soon it was renamed Amedee to honor Amedee Depau Moran, part owner and developer of the railroad (Purdy, 1983, p. 1, 4).

Amedee Canyon [LASSEN]: *canyon,* drained by a stream that flows 3.5 miles to Honey Lake Valley 3.25 miles southeast of Wendel (lat. 40°19'15" N, long. 120°11' W); the canyon is in Amedee Mountains. Named on Wendel (1954) 15' quadrangle.

Amedee Hot Springs [LASSEN]: *springs,* 4 miles south-southeast of Wendel (lat. 40°18'10" N, long. 120°11'40" W; sec. 8, T 28 N, R 16 E). Named on Wendel (1954) 15' quadrangle. Scalding hot water forms several groups of shallow pools; in 1909 a small bathhouse was situated near one of the largest groups of springs (Waring, p. 127).

Amedee Mountains [LASSEN]: *ridge,* south-southeast- to east-trending, 6 miles long, 6 miles east of Wendel (lat. 40°20' N, long. 120°08' W). Named on Wendel (1954) 15' quadrangle.

American Grass Valley: see **Little Grass Valley** [PLUMAS].

American House [PLUMAS]: *locality,* 20 miles south of Quincy (lat. 39°39'10" N, long. 121°01'20" W; near W line sec. 30, T 21 N, R 9 E). Named on American House (1948) 7.5' quadrangle.

American House Ravine [PLUMAS]: *canyon,* drained by a stream that flows 1 mile to Slate Creek (3) 1 mile south-southeast of American House (lat. 39°38'25" N, long. 121°00'40" W; sec. 31, T 21 N, R 9 E). Named on American House (1948) 7.5' quadrangle.

American Ranch: see **Quincy** [PLUMAS].

American Valley [PLUMAS]: *valley,* at and east of Quincy (lat. 39° 57' N, long. 120°55'30" W). Named on Quincy (1950) and Spring Garden (1950) 7.5' quadrangles. The name is from American Ranch at present Quincy (Gudde, 1969, p. 10).

Ampa Lake: see **Clear Lake Reservoir** [MODOC].

Anderson Canyon [LASSEN]: *canyon,* 2.5 miles long, 11.5 miles north-northwest of Termo (lat. 41°00' N, long. 120°35'10" W); the canyon is east of Anderson Mountain. Named on Grasshopper Valley (1954) and Likely (1962) 15' quadrangles.

Anderson Mountain [LASSEN]: *peak,* 11.5 miles northwest of Termo (lat. 40°59'30" N, long. 120°36'15" W; at SW cor. sec. 33, T 37 N, R 12 E). Altitude 6742 feet. Named on Grasshopper Valley (1954) and Likely (1962) 15' quadrangles. The name commemorates Albert Anderson and his family, who came to the region in 1888 or 1889 (Garate, p. 82).

Andrews Spring [MODOC]: *spring,* nearly 7 miles south-southeast of Crank Mountain in Howell Canyon (lat. 41°17'50" N, long. 121° 05' W; at W line sec. 20, T 40 N, R 8 E). Named on Crank Mountain (1962) 15' quadrangle.

Anna Lake: see **Long Lake** [LASSEN] (2); **Snag Lake** [LASSEN].

Annie: see **Lake Annie** [MODOC].

Antelope: see **Horse Lake** [LASSEN] (2).

Antelope Creek [PLUMAS]: *stream,* flows 4 miles to Antelope Lake 9 miles east-northeast of Kettle Rock (lat. 40°11'20" N, long. 120° 34'10" W; near E line sec. 24, T 27 N, R 12 E). Named on Antelope Lake (1972) 7.5' quadrangle.

Antelope Creek: see **Little Antelope Creek** [PLUMAS]; **Lost River** [MODOC].

Antelope Hill: see **Antelope Mountain** [LASSEN] (2).

Antelope House [PLUMAS]: *locality,* 2.25 miles southeast of Wash (present Clio) (lat. 39°43' N, long. 120°33'20" W). Named on Downieville (1897) 30' quadrangle.

Antelope Lake [PLUMAS]: *lake,* behind a dam on Indian Creek (2) 7 miles east-northeast of Kettle Rock (lat. 40°10'50" N, long. 120° 36'25" W; near E line sec. 22, T 27 N, R 12 E); water of the lake covers much of Antelope Valley. Named on Antelope Lake (1972) 7.5' quadrangle. United States Board on Geographic Names (1965b, p. 13) rejected the names "Antelope Reservoir" and "Antelope Valley Reservoir" for the feature.

Antelope Mountain [LASSEN]:

(1) *ridge,* generally east-trending, 3 miles long, 9 miles west-southwest of Pelican Point (lat. 40°35'30" N, long. 120°54' W). Named on Antelope Mountain (1956) 15' quadrangle.

(2) *ridge,* east-southeast-trending, 3 miles long, 6 miles east-northeast of Susanville (lat. 40°27' N, long. 120°33' W). Named on Susanville (1954) 15' quadrangle. Preston (1890a, p. 275) called the feature Antelope Hill.

Antelope Plains [MODOC]: *area,* 3 miles north-northeast of Jacks Butte (lat. 41°37'30" N, long. 120°47' W). Named on Jacks Butte (1962) 15' quadrangle. Alturas (1954) 1°x 2° quadrangle shows an intermittent lake at the place.

Antelope Reservoir [MODOC]: *intermittent lake,* 1.25 miles long, 1 mile east-southeast of Jacks Butte (lat. 41°34'50" N, long. 120°46'45" W; sec. 11, T 43 N, R 10 E). Named on Jacks Butte (1962) 15' quadrangle.

Antelope Reservoir: see **Antelope Lake** [PLUMAS].

Antelope Spring [LASSEN]: *spring,* 8.5 miles northeast of Wendel (lat. 40°26'05" N, long. 120°07'15" W; sec. 25, T 30 N, R 16 E). Named on Wendel (1954) 15' quadrangle.

Antelope Spring [MODOC]: *spring,* 12.5 miles south-southwest of Canby (lat. 41°16' N, long. 120°55'30" W; sec. 34, T 40 N, R 9 E). Named on Canby (1961) 15' quadrangle.

Antelope Valley [LASSEN]: *valley,* 8.5 miles west-northwest of Pelican Point (lat. 40°40'20" N, long. 120°54' W; at SW cor. sec. 31, T 33 N, R 10 E). Named on Antelope Mountain (1956) 15' quadrangle.

Antelope Valley [PLUMAS]: *valley,* 8 miles east-northeast of Kettle Rock (lat. 40°10'45" N, long. 120°34'45" W); the valley is along Antelope Creek and Little Antelope Creek. Named on Kettle Rock (1950) 15' quadrangle.

Antelope Valley: see **Little Antelope Valley** [LASSEN].

Antelope Valley Reservoir: see **Antelope Lake** [PLUMAS].

Antelope Well: see **Little Antelope Well** [LASSEN].

Ant Spring [LASSEN]: *spring,* 22 miles east-northeast of Madeline (lat. 41°07'20" N, long. 120°03'05" W; at N line sec. 33, T 38 N, R 17 E). Named on Little Hat Mountain (1962) 7.5' quadrangle.

Ararat: see **Mount Ararat** [PLUMAS].

Argentine [PLUMAS]: *locality,* 9 miles east of Quincy (lat. 39°55'30" N, long. 120°46'30" W). Named on Downieville (1897) 30' quadrangle. The site first was called Greenhorn Diggings; the name "Argentine" came after discovery of silver at the place (Gudde, 1975, p. 21).

Argentine Rock [PLUMAS]: *peak,* 4 miles north-northeast of Spring Garden (lat. 39°57'10" N, long. 120°45'45" W; near N line sec. 17, T 24 N, R 11 E). Altitude 7209 feet. Named on Spring Garden (1950) 7.5' quadrangle.

Argusville: see **Bieber** [LASSEN].

Arkansas Ravine [PLUMAS]: *canyon,* drained by a stream that flows nearly 1 mile to Coldwater Creek (2) 6 miles south-southwest of Bucks Lodge (lat. 30°47'35" N, long. 121°12'45" W; near E line sec. 5, T 22 N, R 7 E). Named on Haskins Valley (1980) 7.5' quadrangle. Bidwell Bar (1897) 30' quadrangle shows an inhabited place called Gravel Range located at the head of Arkansas Ravine.

Arlington Heights [PLUMAS]: *area,* 3 miles south-southeast of Crescent Mills (lat. 40°03'15" N, long. 120°53'05" W; sec. 5, T 25 N, R 10 E). Named on Crescent Mills (1980) 7.5' quadrangle.

Arlington Springs: see **Crescent Mills** [PLUMAS].

Armentrout Flat [MODOC]: *area,* 6.25 miles south-southwest of Crank Mountain (lat. 41°18'25" N, long. 121°12'15" W; in and near sec. 18, T 40 N, R 7 E). Named on Crank Mountain (1962) 15' quadrangle.

Armentrout Spring [MODOC]: *spring,* 6.5 miles south-southwest of Crank Mountain (lat. 41°18' N, long. 121°11'40" W; near S line sec. 17, T 40 N, R 7 E); the spring is at Armentrout Flat. Named on Crank Mountain (1962) 15' quadrangle.

Armstrong: see **Termo** [LASSEN].

Arnett Spring [MODOC]: *spring,* 14 miles south-southwest of Alturas (lat. 41°18'15" N, long. 120°38'05" W; sec. 18, T 40 N, R 12 E). Named on Alturas (1961) 15' quadrangle.

Artray Creek [PLUMAS]: *stream,* flows 2.5 miles to Last Chance Creek (2) 8 miles east-northeast of Squaw Valley Peak (lat. 40° 03'40" N, long. 120°15'25" W; sec. 35, T 26 N, R 15 E). Named on Ferris Creek (1977) 7.5' quadrangle. The name is from the given names of Forest Service employees Arthur Barrett and Raymond Orr (Stewart, p. 24).

Ash Butte [LASSEN]: *peak,* 11.5 miles south-southwest of Cal Mountain (lat. 40°31'25" N, long. 121°16' W; near NE cor. sec. 26, T 31 N, R 6 E). Named on Prospect Peak (1957) 15' quadrangle. The name is from volcanic cinders that form the feature (Schulz, p. 1).

Ash Creek [LASSEN-MODOC]: *stream,* heads in Lassen County and flows 35 miles to Big Swamp 3.5 miles east-southeast of Lookout in Modoc County (lat. 41°11'10" N, long. 121°05'25" W; sec. 30, T 39 N, R 8 E). Named on Adin (1962), Bieber (1961), and Likely (1962) 15' quadrangles.

Ash Creek Campground [LASSEN]: *locality,* 6.5 miles east-southeast of Adin [MODOC] along Ash Creek [LASSEN-MODOC] (lat. 41°09'40" N, long. 120°49'45" W; sec, 4, T 38 N, R 10 E). Named on Adin (1962) 15' quadrangle.

Ash Creek Valley: see **Ash Valley** [LASSEN].

Ashton: see **Madeline** [LASSEN].

Ashurst Lake [LASSEN]: *lake,* 3600 feet long, marsh separates the lake into two parts, 14 miles northwest of Pelican Point (lat. 40° 45' N, long. 120°57'30" W; sec. 4, T 33 N, R 9 E); the lake is 1.25 miles northeast of Ashurst Mountain. Named on Antelope Mountain (1956) and Hayden Hill (1956) 15' quadrangles.

Ashurst Mountain [LASSEN]: *peak,* 14 miles west-northwest of Pelican Point (lat. 40°44'20" N, long. 120°58'45" W; near E line sec. 8, T 33 N, R 9 E). Altitude 7089 feet. Named on Antelope Mountain (1956) 15' quadrangle.

Ashurst Well [LASSEN]: *well,* 7.25 miles southwest of Lava Peak (lat. 40°45'20" N, long. 120°59'05" W; sec. 5, T 33 N, R 9 E). Named on Hayden Hill (1956) 15' quadrangle.

Ash Valley [LASSEN]: *valley,* 15 miles southwest of Likely [MODOC] (lat. 41°05' N, long. 120°43' W); the valley is along Ash Creek. Named on Aden (1962) and Likely (1962) 15' quadrangles. Called Ash Creek Valley on Alturas 1° quadrangle.

Ash Valley: see **Little Valley** [LASSEN] (1).

Aspen Flat [LASSEN]:

(1) *area,* 6 miles north-northeast of Cal Mountain (lat. 40°44'15" N, long. 121°06' W; sec. 8, T 33 N, R 8 E). Named on Harvey Mountain (1956) 15' quadrangle.

(2) *area,* 8 miles south of Susanville (lat. 40°18'15" N, long. 120° 38'35" W; at NE cor. sec. 8, T 28 N, R 12 E). Named on Diamond Mountain (1972) 7.5' quadrangle.

Aspen Well [LASSEN]: *well,* 5.25 miles east-northeast of Cal Mountain (lat. 41°42'25" N, long. 121°04'40" W; near E line sec. 21, T 33 N, R 8 E). Named on Harvey Mountain (1956) 15' quadrangle.

Atola: see **Wendel** [LASSEN].

Auto Camp: see **Layman Bar** [PLUMAS].

Avanzino Reservoir [MODOC]: *lake,* behind a dam on Fletcher Creek 5 miles southeast of Blue Mountain (lat. 41°46'50" N, long. 120°47'45" W; near SW cor. sec. 35, T 46 N, R 10 E). Named on Steele Swamp (1962) 15' quadrangle.

Avilla: see **Ben Avilla Water Hole**, under **Ben Eberli Waterhole** [MODOC].

Axford Creek: see **Oxford Creek** [PLUMAS].

Axford Ravine: see **Oxford Creek** [PLUMAS].

— B —

Babcock Crossing [PLUMAS]: *locality,* 5.25 miles east of Kettle Rock along Indian Creek (2) (lat. 40°07'35" N, long. 120°37'35" W). Named on Kettle Rock (1972) 7.5' quadrangle.

Babcock Meadows [PLUMAS]: *area,* 8.5 miles southeast of Kettle Rock (lat. 40°04'25" N, long. 120°35'45" W; sec. 35, T 26 N, R 12 E); the place is 1.25 miles south of Babcock Peak. Named on Babcock Peak (1972) 7.5' quadrangle. Called Babcock Meadow on Kettle Rock (1950) 15' quadrangle; United States Board on Geographic Names (1974a, p. 2) gave this name as a variation.

Babcock Peak [PLUMAS]: *peak,* 7.5 miles east-southeast of Kettle Peak (lat. 40°05'35" N, long. 120°35'55" W; near S line sec. 23, T 26 N, R 12 E). Altitude 7015 feet. Named on Babcock Peak (1972) 7.5' quadrangle.

Bachs Creek [PLUMAS]: *stream,* flows 2.5 miles to Middle Fork Feather River 6.25 miles south-southeast of Quincy (lat. 39°51'10" N, long. 120°54'10" W; sec. 18, T 23 N, R 10 E). Named on Onion Valley (1950) and Quincy (1950) 7.5' quadrangles.

Bachs Creek Ridge [PLUMAS]: *ridge,* southeast-trending, 2 miles long, 4.5 miles south-southeast of Quincy (lat. 39°52'30" N, long. 120°54'25" W); the ridge is northeast of Bachs Creek. Named on Onion Valley (1950) and Quincy (1950) 7.5' quadrangles.

Bach Springs: see **Crescent Mills** [PLUMAS].

Badger Canyon [MODOC]: *canyon,* drained by a stream that flows 2.5 miles to lowlands along Goose Lake (1) 5.5 miles north-northeast of Willow Ranch (lat. 41°58'05" N, long. 120°18' W; sec. 25, T 48 N, R 14 E). Named on Willow Ranch (1962) 15' quadrangle.

Badger Well [MODOC]: *well,* 7.25 miles north-northeast of Hackamore (lat. 41°39' N, long. 121°03'55" W). Named on Hackamore (1952) 15' quadrangle.

Baggett Gulch [MODOC]: *canyon,* drained by a stream that flows 5 miles to Warm Spring Valley 3.25 miles south of Canby (lat. 41° 23'45" N, long. 120°53' W; sec. 13, T 41 N, R 9 E). Named on Canby (1961) 15' quadrangle.

Bagley Pass [PLUMAS]: *pass,* 6 miles east-southeast of Mount Ingalls (lat. 39°56'50" N, long. 120°31'40" W; near W line sec. 16, T 24 N, R 13 E). Named on Grizzly Valley (1972) 7.5' quadrangle.

Bagwell Reservoir [LASSEN]: *water feature,* nearly 6 miles west-southwest of Bieber (lat. 41°04'55" N, long. 121°14'25" W; near SE cor. sec. 35, T 38 N, R 6 E). Named on Bieber (1961) 15' quadrangle.

Bailey Creek [LASSEN]: *stream,* flows 3.25 miles to Madeline Plains 8 miles west-southwest of Termo (lat. 40°49'25" N, long. 120°35'45" W; at E line sec. 10, T 34 N, R 12 E). Named on Grasshopper Valley (1954) 15' quadrangle.

Bailey Creek [PLUMAS]: *stream,* flows 16 miles to Lake Almanor 4 miles east-southeast of Chester (lat. 40°17'10" N, long. 121°09'20" W; near E line sec. 14, T 28 N, R 7 E). Named on Chester (1979) and Red Cinder (1979) 7.5' quadrangles.

Bailey Reservoir [LASSEN]: *lake,* 800 feet long, 9 miles west-southwest of Termo (lat. 40°48'15" N, long. 120°36'40" W; near SW cor. sec. 15, T 34 N, R 12 E); the lake is along Bailey Creek. Named on Grasshopper Valley (1954) 15' quadrangle.

Baker Reservoir [MODOC]: *intermittent lake,* 1000 feet long, 12 miles north-northwest of Double Head Mountain (lat. 41°55'20" N, long. 121°14'40" W; on S line sec. 11, T 47 N, R 6 E). Named on Clear Lake Reservoir (1951) 15' quadrangle.

Bald Eagle Lake [PLUMAS]: *lake,* 300 feet long, 6 miles northwest of Bucks Lodge (lat. 39°56'30" N, long. 121°14'45" W; at W line sec. 18, T 24 N, R 7 E); the lake is 0.5 mile west-northwest of Bald Eagle Mountain. Named on Bucks Lake (1979) 7.5' quadrangle.

Bald Eagle Mountain [PLUMAS]: *peak,* 5.5 miles northwest of Bucks Lodge (lat. 39°56'20" N, long. 121°14'05" W; sec. 18, T 24 N, R 7 E). Altitude 7183 feet. Named on Bucks Lake (1979) 7.5' quadrangle.

Bald Hill [LASSEN]: *peak,* 8 miles north-northeast of Westwood (lat. 40°24'30" N, long. 120°56'30" W; near N line sec. 2, T 29 N, R 9 E). Named on Pegleg Mountain (1980) 7.5' quadrangle.

Bald Hills [LASSEN]: *range,* center 6.5 miles north of Pelican Point (lat. 40°43'30" N, long. 120°45' W). Named on Antelope Mountain (1956), Fredonyer Peak (1954), and Hayden Hill (1956) 15' quadrangles. The name is from the scarcity of trees in the range (Purdy, 1988, p. 117).

Bald Mountain [LASSEN]:

(1) *ridge,* east-trending, 1.5 miles long, 5 miles east-northeast of the village of Little Valley (lat. 40°55' N, long. 121°05'30" W). Named on Little Valley (1957) 15' quadrangle.

(2) *peak,* 5 miles southwest of Litchfield (lat. 40°20'20" N, long. 120°27'25" W; near SE cor. sec. 25, T 29 N, R 13 E). Altitude 5219 feet. Named on Standish (1972) 7.5' quadrangle.

Bald Mountain [MODOC]:

(1) *peak,* 10 miles south-southeast of the village of Davis Creek (lat. 41°36'40" N, long. 120°16'10" W; sec. 9, T 43 N, R 15 E). Altitude 8270 feet. Named on Davis Creek (1962) 15' quadrangle. Called Cedar Peak on Alturas 1° quadrangle, where nearby present Cedar Mountain is unnamed.

(2) *ridge,* generally north-northeast-trending, 1.25 miles long, 7.5 miles southwest of Eagleville (lat. 41°14'55" N, long. 120°13'50" W; near NE cor. sec. 2, T 39 N, R 15 E). Named on Eagle Peak (1963) and Emerson Peak (1962) 7.5' quadrangles.

Bald Mountain: see **La Porte Bald Mountain** [PLUMAS].

Bald Mountain Flat [LASSEN]: *area,* 5.25 miles northeast of the village of Little Valley (lat. 46°56'50" N, long. 121°06'30" W; on S line sec. 13, T 36 N, R 7 E); the place is 2.25 miles north-northwest of Bald Mountain (1). Named on Little Valley (1957) 15' quadrangle.

Bald Mountain Reservoir [LASSEN]: *intermittent lake,* 400 feet long, 4.25 miles east-northeast of the village of Little Valley (lat. 40°55'30" N, long. 121°06'35" W; sec. 25, T 36 N, R 7 E); the feature is 1 mile west-northwest of Bald Mountain (1). Named on Little Valley (1957) 15' quadrangle.

Bald Mountain Sink [LASSEN]: *area,* 6 miles east-northeast of the village of Little Valley (lat. 40°55'50" N, long. 121°04'25" W; sec. 29, T 36 N, R 8 E); the place is 1.25 miles northeast of Bald Mountain (1). Named on Little Valley (1957) 15' quadrangle.

Bald Mountain Spring [LASSEN]: *spring,* 6 miles west-southwest of Litchfield (lat. 40°20'35" N, long. 120°29'15" W; sec. 26, T 29 N, R 13 E); the spring is 1.5 miles west of Bald Mountain (2). Named on Standish (1972) 7.5' quadrangle.

Bald Ridges [LASSEN]: *ridge,* south-trending, 1.5 miles long, 7.5 miles north-northwest of Lava Peak (lat. 40°56' N, long. 120° 57' W). Named on Hayden Hill (1956) 15' quadrangle.

Bald Rock [PLUMAS]: *peak,* 11.5 miles east-northeast of Portola (lat. 39°52'10" N, long. 120°16' W; near S line sec. 2, T 23 N, R 15 E). Altitude 7166 feet. Named on Reconnaissance Peak (1972) 7.5' quadrangle.

Baldy: see **Little Baldy** [MODOC].

Baldy Mountain: see **Little Baldy Mountain** [LASSEN].

Baldy Reservoir [LASSEN]: *water feature,* 9.5 miles west of Bieber (lat. 41°08'05" N, long. 121°19'20" W; sec. 7, T 38 N, R 6 E); the feature is 1 mile south-southwest of Little Baldy Mountain. Named on Fall River Mills (1961) 15' quadrangle.

Ballard Reservoir [MODOC]: *lake,* behind a dam on Toms Creek 4 miles southeast of Canby (lat. 41°23'35" N, long. 120°49'15" W; sec. 16, T 41 N, R 10 E). Named on Canby (1961) 15' quadrangle. United States Board on Geographic Names (1964a, p. 8) rejected the name "Toreson Reservoir" for the feature.

Ballard Reservoir [LASSEN]: *lake,* 850 feet long, 8.5 miles northwest of Cal Mountain (lat. 46°44'45" N, long. 121°17'25" W; on S line sec. 3, T 33 N, R 6 E). Named on Prospect Peak (1957) 15' quadrangle. Halls Flat (1939) 30' quadrangle shows Ballard Spring at the place.

Ballard Ridge [MODOC]: *ridge,* northwest-trending, 3.5 miles long, 5 miles south of Canby (lat. 41°22'30" N, long. 120°51' W). Named on Canby (1961) 15' quadrangle.

Ballard Spring: see **Ballard Reservoir** [LASSEN].

Balls Canyon [LASSEN]: *canyon,* drained by a stream that flows 10 miles to Willow Creek 4 miles northwest of Litchfield (lat. 40°24'55" N, long. 120°26'30" W; sec. 31, T 30 N, R 14 E). Named on Karlo (1954) and Litchfield (1954) 15' quadrangles.

Bankhead Creek [LASSEN]: *stream,* flows 5.5 miles to Baxter Creek 7.5 miles southwest of Litchfield (lat. 40°18'35" N, long. 120°29'45" W; sec. 3, T 28 N, R 13 E). Named on Janesville (1972) 7.5' quadrangle.

Barber Canyon [MODOC]: *canyon,* drained by a stream that flows nearly 7 miles to Ash Creek 1.25 miles north-northeast of Adin (lat. 41°12'35" N, long. 120°55'50" W; near NW cor. sec. 22, T 39 N, R 9 E); the canyon is northeast of Barber Ridge. Named on Adin (1962), Canby (1961), and Crank Mountain (1962) 15' quadrangles.

Barber Creek: see **North Barber Creek** [MODOC]; **South Barber Creek** [MODOC].

Barber Ridge [MODOC]: *ridge,* southeast-trending, 7.5 miles long, center 4 miles northwest of Adin (lat. 41°14'30" N, long. 120°59'30" W); the feature is southwest of Barber Canyon. Named on Adin (1962), Bieber (1961), and Crank Mountain (1962) 15' quadrangles.

Bare Creek [LASSEN]: *stream,* flows 9.5 miles to Surprise Valley 24 miles east-northeast of Madeline (lat. 41°09'50" N, long. 120° 02' W; sec. 15, T 38 N, R 17 E). Named on Little Hat Mountain (1962) and Snake Lake (1962) 7.5' quadrangles. Called Bare's Creek on Alturas 1° quadrangle. The name commemorates Thomas Bare, who built a cabin by the creek; the stream first was called Wood Creek (Laird, p. 51).

Barker Gulch [PLUMAS]: *canyon,* drained by a stream that flows nearly 1 mile to Owl Creek 6.5 miles north-northwest of Twain (lat. 40°06'35" N, long. 121°06'50" W; near W line sec. 17, T 26 N, R 8 E). Named on Twain (1980) 7.5' quadrangle.

Bark Spring [MODOC]: *spring,* 7.5 miles north-northeast of Crank Mountain (lat. 41°28'30" N, long. 121°03'40" W; near SW cor. sec. 16, T 42 N, R 8 E). Named on Crank Mountain (1962) 15' quadrangle.

Barnards Diggins [PLUMAS]: *locality,* 1.5 miles south of La Porte (lat. 39°39'35" N, long. 120°59'20" W; near SE cor. sec. 20, T 21 N, R 9 E). Named on La Porte (1951) 7.5' quadrangle. Gudde (1975, p. 27) noted that the place also was called Bernard Diggings.

Barnes Creek [MODOC]: *stream,* flows 2.5 miles to lowlands along Goose Lake (1) 2.5 miles east-northeast of Willow Ranch (lat. 41° 54'50" N, long. 120°18'30" W; sec. 13, T 47 N, R 14 E). Named on Willow Ranch (1962) 15' quadrangle.

Barnes Flat [LASSEN]: *area,* 12 miles north-northwest of Westwood (lat. 40°28' N, long. 121°05'30" W). Named on Swain Mountain (1979) 7.5' quadrangle.

Barrell Pit Reservoir [LASSEN]: *lake,* 300 feet long, 9.5 miles east-northeast of Cal Mountain (lat. 40°44'30" N, long. 121°00'30" W; sec. 7, T 33 N, R 9 E). Named on Harvey Mountain (1956) 15' quadrangle.

Barrel Spring [LASSEN]: *spring,* 5.5 miles north-northwest of Westwood (lat. 40°23' N, long. 121°02' W; sec. 12, T 29 N, R 8 E). Named on Swain Mountain (1979) 7.5' quadrangle.

Barrington Creek [MODOC]: *stream,* flows 0.5 mile to the State of Oregon 10.5 miles north of South Mountain (lat. 41°59'35" N, long. 120°38' W; at N line sec. 19, T 48 N, R 12 E). Named on South Mountain (1962) 15' quadrangle.

Berry Creek [PLUMAS]: *stream,* flows 4.25 miles, partly in Sierra County, to Sulphur Creek 3.5 miles southeast of Clio (lat. 39°42'30" N, long. 120°31'55" W; at E line sec. 5, T 21 N, R 13 E). Named on Calpine (1981) and Clio (1981) 7.5' quadrangles.

Barry Tank [MODOC]: *water feature,* 9 miles northeast of Double Head Mountain (lat. 41°51'50" N, long. 121°02'50" W; at SW cor. sec. 34, T 47 N, R 8 E). Named on Clear Lake Reservoir (1951) 15' quadrangle.

Baseball Reservoir [MODOC]: *intermittent lake,* 4000 feet long, 7.5 miles north-northwest of Blue Mountain (lat. 41°55'15" N, long. 120°46'45" W; on E line sec. 14, T 47 N, R 10 E); the feature is 1.5 miles south of Kellogg Mountain. Named on Steele Swamp (1962) 15' quadrangle. United States Board on Geographic Names (1970, p. 1) approved the name "Diamond Reservoir" for a lake, 0.7 mile long, situated 1.6 miles south-southwest of Kellogg Mountain (sec. 14, T 47 N, R 10 E)—the name is from the shape of the lake.

Bassett Hot Springs [LASSEN]: *spring,* 2.25 miles northeast of Bieber (lat. 41°08'45" N, long. 121°06'35" W; sec. 12, T 38 N, R 7 E). Named on Bieber (1961) 15' quadrangle. The name is from a former owner of the feature (Waring, p. 117). Waring (p. 117-118) listed Stonebreaker Hot Springs, located 3.5 miles southeast of Bassett Hot Springs and named for a former owner.

Bass Hill [LASSEN]: *ridge,* northwest- to west-trending, 4 miles long, 9.5 miles southeast of Susanville (lat. 40°20'15" N, long. 120°30'45" W). Named on Janesville (1972) and Standish (1972) 7.5' quadrangles.

Bath Spring [LASSEN]: *spring,* 16 miles northwest of Termo (lat. 40°59'10" N, long. 120°42'40" W; sec. 4, T 36 N, R 11 E). Named on Grasshopper Valley (1954) 15' quadrangle.

Bathtub Lake [LASSEN]: *lake,* 400 feet long, 10 miles southwest of Cal Mountain (lat. 40°34'15" N, long. 121°17'45" W; on S line sec. 3, T 31 N, R 6 E). Named on Prospect Peak (1957) 15' quadrangle. Harlan Lee, a park ranger, proposed the name, which was adopted in 1936 at the recommendation of Superintendent Collins of Lassen Volcanic National Park; this lake and a nearby lake were known at one time as Twin Lakes (Schulz, p. 2-3).

Baxter Creek [LASSEN]: *stream,* flows 8.5 miles to Honey Lake Valley 9 miles southeast of Susanville (lat. 40°19'25" N, long. 120° 31'40" W; near SW cor. sec. 33, T 29 N, R 13 E). Named on Diamond Mountain (1972), Janesville (1972), and Standish (1972) 7.5' quadrangles.

Bayley [MODOC]: *locality,* 14 miles south of Alturas along Southern Pacific Railroad (lat. 40°17'20" N, long. 120°32'15" W). Named on Alturas (1961) 15' quadrangle. California Division of Highways' (1934) map has the name "Bayley" at a place located about 0.5 mile farther north, and has the name "Widgeon" along the railroad at or near present Bayley.

Bayley Reservoir [MODOC]: *lake,* 16 miles south-southwest of Alturas (lat. 41°16' N, long. 120°38' W; on S line sec. 30, T 40 N, R 12 E). Named on Alturas (1961) 15' quadrangle.

Bayley Tank [MODOC]: *lake,* 0.5 mile long, 5.5 miles west-southwest of South Mountain (lat. 41°48' N, long. 120°43'40" W; sec. 29, T 46 N, R 11 E). Named on South Mountain (1962) 15' quadrangle.

Bean Creek [PLUMAS]: *stream,* flows about 2.25 miles to Spanish Creek (1) nearly 3 miles north-northwest of the village of Meadow Valley (lat. 39°58' N, long. 121°05'05" W; near E line sec. 4, T 24 N, R 8 E). Named on Meadow Valley (1980) 7.5' quadrangle.

Bean Hill [PLUMAS]: *relief feature,* 3 miles north-northwest of the village of Meadow Valley (lat. 39°58'25" N, long. 121°05' W; on E line sec. 4, T 24 N, R 8 E); the feature is east of Bean Creek. Named on Meadow Valley (1980) 7.5' quadrangle.

Bearcamp Flat [MODOC]: *area,* 7 miles south-southwest of Eagleville (lat. 41°13'10" N, long. 120°09'15" W; sec. 27, 28, T 39 N, R 16 E); the place is less than 1 mile southeast of Bearcamp Mountain. Named on Emerson Peak (1962) 7.5' quadrangle.

Bearcamp Mountain [MODOC]: *peak,* 7 miles south-southwest of Eagleville (lat. 41°13'25" N, long. 120°10' W; near N line sec. 28, T 39 N, R 16 E). Named on Emerson Peak (1962) 7.5' quadrangle.

Bear Creek [MODOC]: *stream,* flows 2 miles to Thoms Creek 13 miles south-southeast of the village of Davis Creek (lat. 41°33'35" N, long. 120°17'15" W; near SW cor. sec. 29, T 43 N, R 15 E). Named on Davis Creek (1962) 15' quadrangle.

Bear Creek [PLUMAS]:

(1) *stream,* flows 0.5 mile to Kirkham Ravine 6.25 miles north of Twain (lat. 40°06'40" N, long. 121°04'15" W; sec. 15, T 26 N, R 8 E). Named on Twain (1980) 7.5' quadrangle.

(2) *stream,* formed by the confluence of Marrow Creek and Third Water Creek, flows 4.5 miles to Middle Fork Feather River 1.5 miles north of Dogwood Peak (lat. 39°48'20" N, long. 121°03'35" W; near SW cor. sec. 35, T 23 N, R 8 E). Named on Dogwood Peak (1979) 7.5' quadrangle.

(3) *stream,* flows 3.5 miles to Eureka Creek 4 miles west-northwest of Blairsden (lat. 39°48' N, long. 120°41'15" W; sec. 1, T 22 N, R 11 E). Named on Johnsville (1972) 7.5' quadrangle.

(4) *stream,* flows 1.25 miles to South Fork Feather River 3.5 miles northwest of American House (lat. 39°41'35" N, long. 121°03'40" W; at W line sec. 11, T 21 N, R 8 E). Named on American House (1948) 7.5' quadrangle.

Bear Creek: see **Little Bear Creek** [PLUMAS].

Bear Flat [LASSEN]: *area,* 9 miles south-southeast of Susanville (lat. 40°17'35" N, long. 120°36'25" W; on S line sec. 10, T 28 N, R 12 E). Named on Janesville (1972) 7.5' quadrangle.

Bear Flat [MODOC]: *area,* 17 miles southeast of Alturas (lat. 41° 18' N, long. 120°18'50" W; mainly in sec. 13, T 40 N, R 14 E). Named on Soup Creek (1963) 7.5' quadrangle.

Bear Gulch [PLUMAS]: *canyon,* drained by a stream that flows 3.5 miles to Butte County 5 miles northwest of Cascade (lat. 39°44'55" N, long. 121°14'55" W; at W line sec. 19, T 22 N, R 7 E). Named on Cascade (1948) and Haskins Valley (1980) 7.5' quadrangles.

Bear Lake [LASSEN]: *intermittent lake,* 1300 feet long, 10 miles south-southeast of the village of Little Valley (lat. 40°46'05" N, long. 121°06'10" W; sec. 32, T 34 N, R 8 W). Named on Little Valley (1957) 15' quadrangle.

Bear Lake [PLUMAS]: *lake,* 900 feet long, 6.5 miles northwest of Storrie (lat. 39°59'35" N, long. 121°23'35" W; near E line sec. 27, T 25 N, R 5 E). Named on Kimshew Point (1979) 7.5' quadrangle.

Bear Lake: see **Big Bear Lake** [PLUMAS]; **Little Bear Lake** [PLUMAS].

Bear Lakes [PLUMAS]: *lakes,* 6 miles southwest of Wash (present Clio) (lat. 39°41' N, long. 120°40'15" W). Named on Downieville (1897) 30' quadrangle. The group includes present Big Bear Lake, Little Bear Lake, Cub Lake, Silver Lake, and Round Lake

Bear Mountain [MODOC]: *peak,* 13 miles south-southeast of the village of Davis Creek (lat. 41°34'15" N, long. 120°15'30" W; near NE cor. sec. 28, T 43 N, R 15 E). Altitude 7431 feet. Named on Davis Creek (1962) 15' quadrangle.

Bear Ravine [PLUMAS]: *canyon,* drained by a stream that flows 2.25 miles to Bucks Creek 4.25 miles northwest of Bucks Lodge (lat. 39°54'50" N, long. 121°14'10" W; at N line sec. 30, T 24 N, R 7 E). Named on Bucks Lake (1979) 7.5' quadrangle.

Bear Spring [LASSEN]: *spring,* 9 miles west-northwest of Bieber (lat. 41°10'05" N, long. 121°17'50" W; at NE cor. sec. 5, T 38 N, R 6 E). Named on Fall River Mills (1961) 15' quadrangle.

Bear Spring [MODOC]: *spring,* 9 miles east of Adin (lat. 41°11'15" N, long. 120°46'15" W; sec. 25, T 39 N, R 10 E). Named on Adin (1962) 15' quadrangle.

Beartrap Mountain [PLUMAS]: *peak,* 10 miles east-northeast of La Porte on Plumas-Sierra County line (lat. 39°43'15" N, long. 120° 48'30" W; sec. 36, T 22 N, R 10 E). Altitude 7232 feet. Named on Mount Fillmore (1951) 7.5' quadrangle.

Beartrap Spring [LASSEN]: *spring,* 15 miles north-northeast of Westwood (lat. 40°29'30" N, long. 120°50'55" W; sec. 3, T 30 N, R 10 E). Named on Roop Mountain (1980) 7.5' quadrangle.

Bear Valley [MODOC]: *valley,* 7 miles southwest of Fort Bidwell (lat. 41°47'10" N, long, 120°15' W; sec. 10, T 45 N, R 15 E). Named on Fort Bidwell (1962) and Willow Ranch (1962) 15' quadrangles.

Bear Valley [PLUMAS]: *relief feature,* 3 miles southwest of Diamond Mountain [LASSEN] (lat. 40°17' N, long. 120°43'45" W; sec. 15, T 28 N, R 11 E); the feature is along Bear Valley Creek. Named on Diamond Mountain (1972) 7.5' quadrangle.

Bear Valley: see **Bear Valley Reservoir** [LASSEN]; **Lower Bear Valley** [MODOC].

Bear Valley Creek [PLUMAS]: *stream,* flows 4 miles to Lights Creek 4.5 miles east-northeast of Moonlight Peak (lat. 40°15'15" N, long. 120°45'20" W; near E line sec. 29, T 28 N, R 11 E). Named on Diamond Mountain (1972) and Fredonyer Pass (1980) 7.5' quadrangles.

Bear Valley Reservoir [LASSEN]: *intermittent lake,* 1.5 miles long, 8.5 miles south-southeast of the village of Little Valley (lat. 40° 46'50" N, long. 121°07'25" W; mainly in sec. 30, T 34 N, R 8 E). Named on Little Valley (1957) 15' quadrangle. Halls Flat (1939) 30' quadrangle shows Bear Valley at the place.

Bear Wallow [PLUMAS]: *water feature,* 2.5 miles south-southwest of Clio (lat. 39°42'30" N, long. 120°36'10" W; sec. 2, T 21 N, R 12 E). Named on Clio (1981) 7.5' quadrangle.

Beauty Lake [LASSEN]: *lake,* 1450 feet long, 15 miles northwest of Westwood (lat. 40°27'10" N, long. 121°12'35" W; on N line sec. 21, T 30 N, R 7 E). Named on Red Cinder (1979) 7.5' quadrangle.

Beaver Creek [LASSEN]: *stream,* flows 19 miles to Shasta County 12 miles southwest of Bieber (lat. 41°01' N, long. 121°19'50" W; at W line sec. 30, T 37 N, R 6 E); the stream heads at Beaver Spring. Named on Fall River Mills (1961), Jellico (1957), and Little Valley (1957) 15' quadrangles. United States Board on Geographic Names (1983b, p. 4) approved the name Beaver Creek Reservoir for a tank located in the course of Beaver Creek (lat. 40°48'55" N, long. 121°15'15" W; sec. 13, T 34 N, R 6 E).

Beaver Creek [MODOC]: *stream,* flows 1.5 miles to Fletcher Creek 5.25 miles southeast of Blue Mountain (lat. 41°46'10" N, long. 120°48'10" W; sec. 3, T 45 N, R 10 E). Named on Steele Swamp (1962) 15' quadrangle.

Beaver Creek Pasture [LASSEN]: *area,* 5.5 miles south-southwest of the village of Little Valley (lat. 40°49'45" N, long. 121°14' W; sec. 7, T 34 N, R 7 E); the place is along Beaver Creek. Named on Little Valley (1957) 15' quadrangle.

Beaver Creek Reservoir: see **Beaver Creek** [LASSEN].

Beaver Creek Rim [LASSEN]: *escarpment,* north-trending, 6 miles long, 8 miles northwest of the village of Little Valley (lat. 40°57'30" N, long. 121°18' W); the feature is along part of Beaver Creek. Named on Jellico (1957) 15' quadrangle.

Beaver Mountain [MODOC]: *peak,* 8 miles north-northwest of South Mountain (lat. 41°57'20" N, long. 120°42'20" W; near SE cor. sec. 33, T 48 N, R 11 E). Named on South Mountain (1962) 15' quadrangle.

Beaver Mountain Reservoir [MODOC]: *lake,* 400 feet long, 9 miles north-northwest of South Mountain (lat. 41°57' N, long. 120°43'25" W; near NE cor. sec. 5, T 47 N, R 41 E); the lake is 1 mile west-southwest of Beaver Mountain. Named on South Mountain (1962) 15' quadrangle.

Beaver Ponds: see **The Beaver Ponds** [PLUMAS].

Beaver Spring [LASSEN]: *spring,* 5.5 miles south-southwest of the village of Little Valley (lat. 40°49'25" N, long. 121°13'25" W; sec. 8, T 34 N, R 7 E); the spring is at the head of Beaver Creek. Named on Little Valley (1957) 15' quadrangle.

Beckwith: see **Beckwourth** [PLUMAS].

Beckwith Butte: see **Beckwourth Peak** [PLUMAS].

Beckwith Pass: see **Beckwourth Pass** [LASSEN-PLUMAS].

Beckwith Peak: see **Beckwourth Peak** [PLUMAS].

Beckworth Pass: see **Beckwourth Pass** [LASSEN-PLUMAS].

Beckwourth [PLUMAS]: *village,* 5 miles east of Portola (lat. 39°49'15" N, long. 120°22'35" W; sec. 26, T 23 N, R 14 E); the village is 14 miles west of Beckwourth Pass. Named on Portola (1972) and Reconnaissance Peak (1972) 7.5' quadrangles. Called Beckwith on Sierraville (1894) 30' quadrangle, but United States Board on Geographic Names (1950, p. 4) rejected this name for the place. Postal authorities established Beckwith post office in 1870 and changed the name to Beckwourth in 1932 (Salley, p. 17). Tillman (p. 1255) referred to Beckworth's Post Office. California Mining Bureau's (1909b) map shows a place called Kettle located 6 miles by stage line southeast of Beckwith (present Beckwourth). Postal authorities established Kettle post office in 1899, moved it 1 mile southeast in 1906, and discontinued it in 1910; the name was from the Kettle family, pioneers of the neighborhood (Salley, p. 111). United States Board on Geographic Names (1975, p. 12) approved the name "Turner Ridge" for a feature that extends for 26 miles from Beckwourth to Genesee Valley; the name honors Henry Ward Turner, a United States Geological Survey employee who worked in the region.

Beckwourth Butte: see **Beckwourth Peak** [PLUMAS].

Beckwourth Pass [LASSEN-PLUMAS]: *pass,* nearly 2 miles east of Chilcoot [PLUMAS] on Lassen-Plumas County line (lat. 39°47'25" N, long. 120°06'30" W; on W line sec. 5, T 22 N, R 17 E). Named on Beckwourth Pass (1975) 7.5' quadrangle. Called Beckwourths Pass on Goddard's (1857) map, and called Beckwith Pass on Sierraville (1894) 30' quadrangle. Tillman (p. 1255) referred to Beckworth's Pass. United States Board on Geographic Names (1950, p. 4) rejected the names "Beckwith Pass" and "Beckworth Pass" for the feature. The name is for James Beckwourth, who discovered the feature in 1851 (Hoover, Rensch, and Rensch, p. 278).

Beckwourth Peak [PLUMAS]: *peak,* 3 miles southeast of Portola (lat. 39°46'25" N, long. 120°25'50" W; sec. 8, T 22 N, R 14 E); the peak is 4.25 miles southwest of Beckwourth. Altitude 7252 feet. Named on Portola (1972) 7.5' quadrangle. Called Beckwith Butte on Sierraville (1894) 30' quadrangle. United States Board on Geographic Names (1950, p. 4) rejected the names "Beckwith Butte," "Beckwith Buttes," "Beckwith Peak," "Beckwourth Butte," and "Bogue Mountain" for the feature.

Beebe: see **Dan Beebe Campground** [PLUMAS].

Belden [PLUMAS]: *village,* 7 miles southwest of Caribou along North Fork Feather River (lat. 40°00'20" N, long. 121°14'55" W; near E line sec. 24, T 25 N, R 6 E). Named on Jonesville (1958) 15' quadrangle, and on Caribou (1979) 7.5' quadrangle. Postal authorities established Belden post office in 1909; Robert Belden was the first postmaster (Salley, p. 17).

Belden Forebay [PLUMAS]: *lake,* behind a dam on North Fork Feather River 0.5 mile southwest of Caribou (lat. 40°04'35" N, long. 121°09'35" W; sec. 26, T 26 N, R 7 E). Named on Caribou (1979) 7.5' quadrangle.

Belden Ravine [PLUMAS]: *canyon,* drained by a stream that flows 1.5 miles to North Fork Feather River 7 miles southwest of Caribou (lat. 40°00'25" N, long. 121°14'55" W; sec. 24, T 25 N, R 6 E); Belden is at the mouth of the canyon. Named on Bucks Lake (1979) and Caribou (1979) 7.5' quadrangles.

Beldens Bar: see **Rock Creek** [PLUMAS] (4).

Belfast [LASSEN]: *locality,* 5.5 miles northwest of Litchfield (lat. 40°26'35" N, long. 120°27' W; sec. 19, T 30 N, R 14 E). Named on Litchfield (1954) 15' quadrangle. Captain Charles A. Merrill started a community at the place in 1880 and named it for his birthplace in Maine (Purdy, 1988, p. 29-30).

Bellas Creek [PLUMAS]: *stream,* flows 2.5 miles to Round Valley Reservoir 2.5 miles west of Crescent Mills (lat. 40°06' N, long. 120°57'15" W; sec. 22, T 26 N, R 9 E). Named on Crescent Mills (1980) 7.5' quadrangle.

Bellas Flat [PLUMAS]: *area,* 2.5 miles west of Crescent Mills at the mouth of Bellas Creek (lat. 40°06' N, long. 120°57'30" W; sec. 22, T 26 N, R 9 E). Named on Crescent Mills (1980) 7.5' quadrangle.

Bell Bar [PLUMAS]: *locality,* 11.5 miles east-southeast of Quincy along Middle Fork Feather River (lat. 39°51'55" N, long. 120°45'10" W; at S line sec. 9, T 23 N, R 11 E). Named on Blue Nose Mountain (1951) 7.5' quadrangle. Called Bells Bar on Downieville (1897) 30' quadrangle.

Bell Bar Creek [PLUMAS]: *stream,* flows 1.5 miles to Middle Fork Feather River 11 miles east-southeast of Quincy (lat. 39°51'50" N, long. 120°45'35" W; near NE cor. sec. 17, T 23 N, R 11 E); the mouth of the stream is 0.5 mile downstream from Bell Bar. Named on Blue Nose Mountain (1951) 7.5' quadrangle.

Bells Bar: see **Bell Bar** [PLUMAS].

Ben Avilla Water Hole: see **Ben Eberli Waterhole** [MODOC].

Ben Eberli Waterhole [MODOC]: *intermittent lake,* 1400 feet long, 7.5 miles east-northeast of White Horse (lat. 41°21'40" N, long. 121°16'25" W; near SE cor. sec. 28, T 41 N, R 6 E). Named on White Horse (1962) 15' quadrangle. United States Board on Geographic Names (1965c, p. 10) rejected the name "Ben Avilla Water Hole" for the feature, and noted that the name commemorates Benedict Eberli, a local resident.

Ben Lomond [PLUMAS]: *peak,* 17 miles south-southwest of the village of Almanor (lat. 40°00'10" N, long. 121°18'20" W; near SE cor. sec. 21, T 25 N, R 6 E). Altitude 6453 feet. Named on Jonesville (1958) 15' quadrangle.

Benner Creek [PLUMAS]:

(1) *stream,* flows 8 miles to Lake Almanor 1.25 miles north-northeast of Chester (lat. 40°19'35" N, long. 121°12'55" W; sec. 32, T 29 N, R 7 E); the stream heads at Benner Springs. Named on Mount Harkness (1956) 15' quadrangle, and on Chester (1979) 7.5' quadrangle.

(2) *stream,* flows 1.5 miles to Butt Creek 2.5 miles north of Caribou (lat. 40°06'50" N, long. 121°08'35" W; near N line sec. 13, T 26 N, R 7 E). Named on Caribou (1979) 7.5' quadrangle.

Benner Creek Campground [PLUMAS]: *locality,* 3 miles southeast of Mount Harkness (lat. 40°23'45" N, long. 121°16'05" W; at SW cor. sec. 1, T 29 N, R 6 E); the place is along Benner Creek (1). Named on Mount Harkness (1956) 15' quadrangle.

Benner Springs [PLUMAS]: *springs,* 2 miles south-southeast of Mount Harkness (lat. 40°24'30" N, long. 121°17'10" W; near NW cor. sec. 2, T 29 N, R 6 E); the springs are at the head of Benner Creek (1). Named on Mount Harkness (1956) 15' quadrangle.

Bennett Canyon [MODOC]: *canyon,* drained by a stream that flows 3 miles to Round Valley (2) 13 miles south of Canby (lat. 41°15'15" N, long. 120°52'30" W; near NW cor. sec. 1, T 39 N, R 9 E). Named on Canby (1961) 15' quadrangle.

Bennett Knoll [LASSEN]: *hill,* 13 miles north of Westwood (lat. 40° 29'40" N, long. 121°03'05" W; sec. 2, T 30 N, R 8 E). Altitude 6089 feet. Named on Swain Mountain (1979) 7.5' quadrangle

Benton Meadow [MODOC]: *area,* 5 miles southeast of the village of Davis Creek (lat. 41°41'05" N, long. 120°18' W; sec. 1, T 44 N, R 14 E). Named on Davis Creek (1962) 15' quadrangle.

Bernard Diggings: see **Barnards Diggins** [PLUMAS].

Berry Creek [PLUMAS]:

(1) *stream,* flows 1.5 miles to Middle Branch of North Fork Feather River

1.25 miles west-southwest of Twain (lat. 40°00'55" N, long. 121°05'35" W; sec. 21, T 25 N, R 8 E). Named on Meadow Valley (1980) and Twain (1980) 7.5' quadrangles.

(2) *stream,* flows 2 miles to the canyon of Spanish Creek (1) 3.5 miles northeast of Quincy (lat. 39°58'40" N, long. 120°54'05" W; near N line sec. 6, T 24 N, R 10 E). Named on Quincy (1950) and Spring Garden (1950) 7.5' quadrangles.

Bert Bath Spring [LASSEN]: *spring,* 10.5 miles southeast of Adin [MODOC] (lat. 41°04'15" N, long. 120°49'25" W; sec. 4, T 37 N, R 10 E). Named on Adin (1962) 15' quadrangle.

Besler Reservoir [MODOC]: *intermittent lake,* 5800 feet long, 3.25 miles south-southeast of Hackamore (lat. 41°30'35" N, long. 121° 06'15" W; in and near sec. 1, T 42 N, R 7 E). Named on Hackamore (1952) 15' quadrangle.

Betsyburg: see **Elizabethtown**, under **Elizabethtown Flat** [PLUMAS].

Betterton Creek [PLUMAS]: *stream,* flows 2.5 miles to Willow Creek (7) nearly 3 miles east-southeast of Blairsden (lat. 39°45'40" N, long. 120°34'05" W; near NW cor. sec. 19, T 22 N, R 13 E). Named on Blairsden (1972) 7.5' quadrangle.

Betty Lake [LASSEN]: *lake,* 950 feet long, 15 miles north-northwest of Westwood (lat. 40°29'15" N, long. 121°08'50" W; sec. 1, T 30 N, R 7 E). Named on Red Cinder (1979) 7.5' quadrangle.

Bidwell: see **Fort Bidwell** [MODOC]; **Mount Bidwell** [MODOC].

Bidwell Creek [MODOC]: *stream,* flows 12 miles to Upper Lake 2.5 miles south-southeast of Fort Bidwell (lat. 41°49'25" N, long. 120° 08'15" W; sec. 28, T 46 N, R 16 E). Named on Fort Bidwell (1962) 15' quadrangle. The stream first was called Willow Creek (Laird, p. 54). On Hill's (1915) map, a branch of Bidwell Creek that heads in present North Star Basin is called Sunset Creek, and another branch that heads east of Yellow Mountain is called Evening Star Creek; the map also shows mining claims with the names "Sunset" and "Evening Star."

Bidwell Lake: see **Butte Lake** [LASSEN].

Bidwell Mountain [MODOC]: *peak,* 6.25 miles north of Fort Bidwell (lat. 41°56'50" N, long. 120°08'10" W; near NE cor. sec. 16, T 47 N, R 16 E); the peak is 2 miles southeast of Mount Bidwell. Named on Fort Bidwell (1962) 15' quadrangle. Called Bidwell Peak on Alturas 1° quadrangle.

Bidwell Mountain: see **Mount Bidwell** [MODOC].

Bidwell Peak: see **Bidwell Mountain** [MODOC]; **Mount Bidwell** [MODOC].

Bidwell Spring [LASSEN]: *spring,* nearly 7 miles west-southwest of Cal Mountain (lat. 40°37'40" N, long. 121°16'45" W; at N line sec. 23, T 32 N, R 6 E). Named on Prospect Peak (1957) 15' quadrangle.

Bieber [LASSEN]: *village,* 55 miles north-northwest of Susanville along Pit River (lat. 41°07'20" N, long. 121°08'30" W; on W line sec. 23, T 38 N, R 7 E); the village is in Big Valley. Named on Bieber (1961) 15' quadrangle. Postal authorities established Bieber post office in 1877; the name was for Nathan Bieber, first postmaster (Salley, p. 20). The crossing of Pit River at the site was called Chalk Ford before Mr. Bieber built the first house and opened a store at the place in 1877—the name "Chalk Ford" was from the chalky appearance of the ground at the crossing (Hanna, p. 32). Postal authorities established Big Valley post office 3 miles northeast of present Bieber in 1873, discontinued it in 1875, reestablished it in 1876, and discontinued it in 1877 (Salley, p. 21). They established Argusville post office about 3 miles north of present Bieber in 1873 and discontinued it in 1878 (Salley, p. 9). They established Juniper post office 10 miles southwest of Bieber (NW quarter SE quarter sec. 29, T 38 N, R 6 E) in 1888, discontinued it in 1903, reestablished it in 1924, and discontinued it in 1934; the place also was called Fairview (Salley, p. 109).

Bieber Station [LASSEN]: *locality,* 2.5 miles southwest of Bieber along Western Pacific Railroad (lat. 41°05'40" N, long. 121°10'20" W; at N line sec. 33, T 38 N, R 7 E); the place is 0.25 mile east of Nubieber. Named on Bieber (1961) 15' quadrangle.

Big Bear Lake [PLUMAS]: *lake,* 1750 feet long, 6 miles southwest of Clio (lat. 39°41'25" N, long. 120°40'05" W; on S line sec. 7, T 21 N, R 12 E). Named on Gold Lake (1981) 7.5' quadrangle. The lake is one of the group called Bear Lakes on Downieville (1897) 30' quadrangle

Big Blackhawk Creek [PLUMAS]: *stream,* flows nearly 3 miles to Spanish Creek (1) 4.5 miles north of Quincy (lat. 40°00'10" N, long. 120°57'15" W; near NE cor. sec. 27, T 25 N, R 9 E). Named on Quincy (1950) 7.5' quadrangle.

Big Boulder Creek [PLUMAS]: *stream,* heads in Sierra County and flows nearly 1 mile in Plumas County to Sulphur Creek 2.5 miles southeast of Clio (lat. 38°43' N, long. 120°32'55" W; near NW cor. sec. 5, T 21 N, R 13 E). Named on Clio (1981) 7.5' quadrangle.

Big Canyon [MODOC]: *canyon,* drained by a stream that flows 3 miles to Pit River 5.25 miles east of Crank Mountain (lat. 41°23' N, long. 121°02'30" W; near NW cor. sec. 22, T 41 N, R 8 E). Named on Crank Mountain (1962) 15' quadrangle.

Big Cove [PLUMAS]: *embayment,* 5.25 miles east-southeast of Chester along Lake Almanor (lat. 40°16'25" N, long. 121°07'25" W; sec. 19, T 28 N, R 8 E). Named on Chester (1979) and Westwood West (1980) 7.5' quadrangles.

Big Cove Campground [PLUMAS]: *locality,* 7.5 miles north-northwest of Chilcoot by Frenchman Lake (lat. 39°54'10" N, long. 120° 10'20" W; sec. 27, T 24 N, R 16 E). Named on Frenchman Lake (1979) 7.5' quadrangle.

Big Creek [PLUMAS]: *stream,* flows 5 miles to join Clear Creek (4) and form Meadow Valley Creek 1.5 miles west-southwest of the village of Meadow Valley (lat. 39°55'25" N, long. 121°05' W; at E line sec. 21, T 24 N, R 8 E). Named on Meadow Valley (1980) 7.5' quadrangle. East Branch enters from the southeast 2 miles upstream from the mouth of the main creek; it is 1.5 miles long and is named on Meadow Valley (1980) 7.5' quadrangle.

Big Dry Lake [LASSEN]: *intermittent lake,* 3600 feet long, 5.5 miles south-east of Pelican Point (lat. 40°35' N, long. 120°39'30" W; on NW cor. sec. 5, T 31 N, R 12 E). Named on Fredonyer Peak (1954) 15' quadrangle.

Big Flat [PLUMAS]: *area,* 5 miles west-southwest of Milford [LASSEN] along Cottonwood Creek (2) (lat. 40°09' N, long. 120° 27'30" W; near SE cor. sec. 36, T 27 N, R 13 E). Named on Stony Ridge (1978) 7.5' quadrangle.

Big Flat Spring [PLUMAS]: *spring,* 5 miles west-southwest of Milford [LASSEN] (lat. 40°08'50" N, long. 120°27'35" W; at N line sec. 1, T 26 N, R 13 E); the spring is at the south end of Big Flat. Named on Stony Ridge (1978) 7.5' quadrangle.

Big Grizzly Creek [PLUMAS]: *stream,* flows 18 miles to Middle Fork Feather River 2.25 miles east-northeast of Portola (lat. 39°49'05" N, long. 120°25'35" W; near E line sec. 29, T 23 N, R 14 E). Named on Crocker Mountain (1972), Grizzly Valley (1972), and Portola (1972) 7.5' quadrangles. Called Grizzly Creek on Sierraville (1894) 30' quadrangle.

Big Hill [PLUMAS]: *ridge,* east-northeast-trending, 1.5 miles long, 6.5 miles northwest of Blairsden (lat. 39°50'05" N, long. 120°42'50" W). Named on Johnsville (1972) 7.5' quadrangle.

Big Hill: see **The Big Hill** [PLUMAS].

Big Jack Lake [LASSEN]: *intermittent lake,* 4300 feet long, 5.5 miles west-southwest of Lava Peak in Jess Valley (lat. 40°48'15" N, long. 120°59'10" W; on S line sec. 17, T 34 N, R 9 E). Named on Hayden Hill (1956) 15' quadrangle, which shows a small permanent lake in the feature.

Big John Spring [MODOC]: *spring,* 8.5 miles west-southwest of Likely (lat. 41°12' N, long. 120°39'25" W; near S line sec. 24, T 39 N, R 11 E). Named on Likely (1962) 15' quadrangle.

Big Juniper Creek [MODOC]: *stream,* flows 8.5 miles to lowlands along South Fork Pit River 12 miles south of Alturas (lat. 41°20'20" N, long. 120°30'40" W; sec. 8, T 40 N, R 13 E); the stream is 1.5 miles south of Little Juniper Creek. Named on Alturas (1961) 15' quadrangle, and on Little Juniper Reservoir (1963) and Soup Creek (1963) 7.5' quadrangles.

Big Meadows [PLUMAS]: *valley,* 14 miles south-southeast of Harkness Peak (present Mount Harkness) (lat. 40°15' N, long. 121° 10' W). Named on Lassen Peak (1894) 1° quadrangle, which shows marsh in much of the valley—water of Lake Almanor now covers most of it.

Big Meadows: see **Chester** [PLUMAS]; **Prattville** [PLUMAS].

Big Meadows Reservoir [LASSEN]: *lake,* 1000 feet long, 7.5 miles east-southeast of Madeline (lat. 41°01'45" N, long. 120°20'05" W; sec. 36, T 37 N, R 14 E). Named on Cold Spring Mountain (1962) 7.5' quadrangle.

Big Meadows Reservoir: see **Lake Almanor** [PLUMAS].

Big Merrill Flat [LASSEN]: *area,* about 12 miles southwest of Pelican Point (lat. 40°30'30" N, long. 120°53'30" W); the place is 2.5 miles southwest of Little Merrill Flat. Named on Antelope Mountain (1956) 15' quadrangle.

Big Mud Lake [MODOC]: *intermittent lake,* 2 miles long, 7.5 miles east of Fort Bidwell (lat. 41°52'30" N, long. 120°00'35" W). Named on Fort Bidwell (1962) 15' quadrangle. United States Board on Geographic Names (1964b, p. 11) rejected the name "Mud Lake" for the feature.

Big Peak [PLUMAS]: *peak,* 7 miles northwest of American House (lat. 39°43'55" N, long. 121°06'05" W; near SE cor. sec. 29, T 22 N, R 8 E); the peak is 0.5 mile east-northeast of Little Peak. Named on American House (1948) 7.5' quadrangle.

Big Peak Ravine [PLUMAS]: *canyon,* drained by a stream that flows 1.5 miles to South Branch of Middle Fork Feather River 7.5 miles northwest of American House (lat. 39°44'25" N, long. 121°06'35" W; sec. 29, T 22 N, R 8 E); the canyon is north of Big Peak. Named on American House (1948) 7.5' quadrangle.

Big Pine Spring [MODOC]: *spring,* 7 miles east-northeast of Adin (lat. 41°14'05" N, long. 120°49'15" W; at E line sec. 9, T 39 N, R 10 E). Named on Adin (1962) 15' quadrangle.

Big Pine Spring [PLUMAS]: *spring,* 14 miles southeast of Kettle Rock (lat. 40°01'35" N, long. 120°31'15" W; near NW cor. sec. 15, T 25 N, R 13 E). Named on Babcock Peak (1972) 7.5' quadrangle.

Big Ravine [PLUMAS]: *canyon,* drained by a stream that flows 2.25 miles to Grizzly Creek (2) 4 miles south of Storrie (lat. 39°51'45" N, long. 121°19'30" W; near E line sec. 8, T 23 N, R 6 E). Named on Soapstone Hill (1979) and Storrie (1979) 7.5' quadrangles.

Big Sage Campground [MODOC]: *locality,* 8 miles north-northwest of Alturas (lat. 41°34'50" N, long. 120°37'45" W; sec. 7, T 43 N, R 12 E); the place is by Big Sage Reservoir. Named on Big Sage Reservoir (1962) 15'

quadrangle.

Big Sage Reservoir [MODOC]: *lake,* behind a dam on Rattlesnake Creek 7 miles north-northwest of Alturas (lat. 41°34'45" N, long. 120°37'30" W; sec. 7, T 43 N, R 12 E). Named on Big Sage Reservoir (1962) 15' quadrangle.

Big Sand Butte [MODOC]: *hill,* 8 miles northwest of Timber Mountain (lat. 41°41'30" N, long. 121°25' W; on S line sec. 32, T 45 N, R 5 E); the hill is 1.5 miles north of Little Sand Butte. Named on Timber Mountain (1952) 15' quadrangle.

Big Spring [LASSEN]:
(1) *spring,* nearly 3 miles east-southeast of Observation Peak (lat. 40°45'25" N, long. 120°07'25" W; at W line sec. 1, T 33 N, R 16 E). Named on Observation Peak (1954) 15' quadrangle.
(2) *spring,* 13 miles northeast of Westwood (lat. 40°26'15" N, long. 120°50'10" W; near NE cor. sec. 27, T 30 N, R 10 E). Named on Roop Mountain (1980) 7.5' quadrangle.

Big Spring [MODOC]: *spring,* 6.5 miles northwest of South Mountain (lat. 41°54'45" N, long. 120°43' W; near SW cor. sec. 16, T 47 N, R 11 E). Named on South Mountain (1962) 15' quadrangle.

Big Springs [LASSEN]: *springs,* 7.25 miles north of Termo (lat. 40° 58' N, long. 120°25'45" W; sec. 12, T 36 N, R 13 E). Named on Ravendale (1954) 15' quadrangle.

Big Springs [PLUMAS]:
(1) *springs,* 7.5 miles east-southeast of Chester at the edge of Lake Almanor (lat. 40°16'20" N, long. 121°05'40" W; sec. 21, T 28 N, R 8 E). Named on Westwood West (1980) 7.5' quadrangle.
(2) *springs,* 13 miles southwest of the village of Almanor (lat. 40° 05'50" N, long. 121°21'35" W; sec. 19, T 26 N, R 6 E). Named on Jonesville (1958) 7.5' quadrangle.
(3) *springs,* 7.5 miles southwest of the village of Almanor in Humbug Valley (1) (lat. 40°08'10" N, long. 121°15'55" W; near W line sec. 1, T 26 N, R 6 E). Named on Jonesville (1958) 15' quadrangle.

Big Swamp [LASSEN-MODOC]: *marsh,* 4.5 miles north-northeast of Bieber [LASSEN] on Lassen-Modoc County line, mainly in Lassen County (lat. 41°10'30" N, long. 121°06' W). Named on Bieber (1961) 15' quadrangle.

Big Valley [LASSEN-MODOC]: *valley,* along Pit River on Lassen-Modoc County line around and north of Bieber. Named on Adin (1962), Bieber (1961), and Crank Mountain (1962) 15' quadrangles. Called Round Valley on Goddard's (1857) map—Fremont gave this name, which remained in use until after settlement of the valley in 1869 (Pease, p. 93).

Big Valley: see **Bieber** [LASSEN].

Big Valley Mountains [LASSEN-MODOC]: *range,* west of Big Valley [LASSEN-MODOC] on Lassen-Modoc County line; center 7.5 miles west-northwest of Bieber (lat. 41°09'30" N, long. 121° 16'45" W). Named on Bieber (1961), Fall River Mills (1961), and White House (1962) 15' quadrangles. United States Board on Geographic Names (1990, p. 5) rejected the name "Big Valley Mountain" for the feature.

Big Waterholes [MODOC]: *water feature,* 13 miles north-northeast of White Horse (lat. 41°29'40" N, long. 121°19'15" W). Named on White Horse (1962) 15' quadrangle.

Bills Cabin Spring [LASSEN]: *spring,* 6 miles south of Observation Peak (lat. 40°41'15" N, long. 120°11'10" W; near S line sec. 29, T 33 N, R 16 E). Named on Shinn Mountain (1954) 15' quadrangle.

Billy Packwood Spring [LASSEN]: *spring,* 8.5 miles southeast of Bieber (lat. 41°02' N, long. 121°01'40" W; near E line sec. 22, T 37 N, R 8 E); the spring is 1.5 miles northwest of Jim Packwood Spring. Named on Bieber (1961) 15' quadrangle.

Bird Canyon [LASSEN-PLUMAS]: *canyon,* drained by a stream that heads in Plumas County and flows 1.5 miles to Honey Lake Valley 7.5 miles northwest of Doyle in Lassen County (lat. 40°06' N, long. 120°12'10" W; at N line sec. 20, T 26 N, R 16 E). Named on McKesick Peak (1978) 7.5' quadrangle.

Bird Creek [PLUMAS]:
(1) *stream,* flows 3 miles to the canyon of Last Chance Creek (2) 8 miles east-northeast of Squaw Valley Peak (lat. 40°04'05" N, long. 120°15'20" W; sec. 35, T 26 N, R 15 E). Named on Ferris Creek (1977) and McKesick Peak (1978) 7.5' quadrangles.
(2) *stream,* flows 2.25 miles to Onion Valley Creek 10 miles south of Quincy (lat. 39°47'40" N, long. 120°55'55" W; near W line sec. 1, T 22 N, R 9 E). Named on Onion Valley (1950) 7.5' quadrangle.

Bird Hills [LASSEN]: *relief feature,* 6 miles northwest of Doyle (lat. 40°05'15" N, long. 120°11'15" W); the feature is east of Bird Canyon. Named on McKesick Peak (1978) 7.5' quadrangle.

Bird Island [MODOC]: *island,* 1600 feet long, 6.5 miles north of Double Head Mountain in Clear Lake Reservoir (lat. 41°51'20" N, long. 121°09'05" W). Named on Clear Lake Reservoir (1951) 15' quadrangle.

Bird Spring [MODOC]: *spring,* 2 miles northwest of Blue Mountain (lat. 41°50'45" N, long. 120°53'30" W; near W line sec. 12, T 46 N, R 9 E). Named on Steele Swamp (1962) 15' quadrangle.

Bird Spring Ridge [MODOC]: *ridge,* north-trending, 2.5 miles long, 4 miles northwest of Blue Mountain (lat. 41°52'40" N, long. 120° 54'15" W; mainly in sec. 26, 35, T 47 N, R 9 E). Named on Steele Swamp (1962) 15' quadrangle. United States Board on Geographic Names (1968b, p. 5-6) rejected the names "Bird Springs Ridge" and "Timbered Ridge" for the feature.

Black Butte [LASSEN]: *crater,* 9.5 miles south-southwest of Cal Mountain (lat. 40°32'30" N, long. 121°13'45" W; at SE cor. sec. 18, T 31 N, R 7 E). Named on Harvey Mountain (1956) 15' quadrangle.

Black Butte [MODOC]: *peak,* 5 miles southeast of Crank Mountain (lat. 41°19'45" N, long. 121°05' W; on N line sec. 8, T 40 N, R 8 E). Named on Crank Mountain (1962) 15' quadrangle.

Black Butte: see **Blacks Mountain** [LASSEN]; **Cinder Cone** [LASSEN].

Black Cinder Rock [LASSEN]: *peak,* 16 miles northwest of Westwood (lat. 40°27'10" N, long. 121°14'10" W; near NE cor. sec. 19, T 30 N, R 7 E). Altitude 7758 feet. Named on Red Cinder (1979) 7.5' quadrangle.

Black Cone [LASSEN]: *peak,* 20 miles east-northeast of Madeline (lat. 41°10'35" N, long. 120°08'30" W; sec. 10, T 38 N, R 16 E). Named on Emerson Peak (1962) 7.5' quadrangle.

Black Diamond Ridge [PLUMAS]: *ridge,* north-trending, 1.25 miles long, 14 miles south-southeast of Quincy (lat. 39°45'30" N, long. 120°49'30" W). Named on Blue Nose Mountain (1951) 7.5' quadrangle.

Black Gulch [PLUMAS]: *canyon,* drained by a stream that flows 2 miles to Clear Creek (4) 1.5 miles west-southwest of the village of Meadow Valley (lat. 39°55'35" N, long. 121°05'20" W; sec. 21, T 24 N, R 8 E). Named on Meadow Valley (1980) 7.5' quadrangle.

Black Gulch: see **Blacks Gulch** [LASSEN].

Blackhawk Creek: see **Big Blackhawk Creek** [PLUMAS]; **Little Blackhawk Creek** [PLUMAS].

Black Hole [LASSEN]: *canyon,* drained by a stream that flows 4 miles to Indian Creek nearly 6 miles west-northwest of Lava Peak (lat. 40°52'05" N, long. 120°59'10" W; sec. 29, T 35 N, R 9 E). Named on Hayden Hill (1956) 15' quadrangle.

Black Lake [LASSEN]: *lake,* 1000 feet long, 11.5 miles south-southwest of Cal Mountain (lat. 40°30'25" N, long. 121°12'35" W; near E line sec. 32, T 31 N, R 7 E). Named on Harvey Mountain (1956) 15' quadrangle.

Black Lake: see **Blacks Lake** [LASSEN].

Black Mountain [LASSEN]:
(1) *peak,* 3 miles south-southeast of Pelican Point (lat. 40°35'35" N, long. 120°43'40" W; near W line sec. 34, T 32 N, R 11 E). Altitude 6297 feet. Named on Fredonyer Peak (1954) 15' quadrangle.
(2) *mountain,* 9 miles west-northwest of Karlo (lat. 40°36'20" N, long. 120°27'55" W). Altitude 6100 feet. Named on Karlo (1954) 15' quadrangle.
(3) *peak,* 5 miles southeast of Milford near Lassen-Plumas County line (lat. 40°07' N, long. 120°19' W; near S line sec. 8, T 26 N, R 15 E). Altitude 7161 feet. Named on Ferris Creek (1977) 7.5' quadrangle.

Black Mountain: see **Blacks Mountain** [LASSEN].

Black Mountain Spring [PLUMAS]: *spring,* 5.5 miles south-southeast of Milford [LASSEN] (lat. 40°06'20" N, long. 120°18'50" W; sec. 17, T 26 N, R 15 E); the spring is less than 1 mile south of Black Mountain [LASSEN]. Named on Ferris Creek (1977) 7.5' quadrangle.

Black Reservoir [MODOC]: *intermittent lake,* 1500 feet long, 8.5 miles north-northeast of South Mountain (lat. 41°56'40" N, long. 120°33' W; near E line sec. 2, T 47 N, R 12 E). Named on South Mountain (1962) 15' quadrangle.

Black Rock: see **Walker Plains** [PLUMAS].

Black Rock Creek [PLUMAS]: *stream,* flows 4.5 miles to South Fork Feather River 5 miles north of American House (lat. 39° 43'30" N, long. 121°00'20" W; at W line sec. 32, T 22 N, R 9 E). Named on American House (1948) and Onion Valley (1950) 7.5' quadrangles.

Black Rock Reservoir: see **West Black Rock Reservoir** [MODOC].

Blacks Canyon [MODOC]: *canyon,* drained by a stream that flows 6 miles to Warm Springs Valley 2 miles north of Canby (lat. 41°28'30" N, long. 120°52'15" W; near NW cor. sec. 19, T 42 N, R 10 E). Named on Canby (1961) and Jacks Butte (1962) 15' quadrangles. Called Black's Cañon on Alturas 1° quadrangle.

Blacks Gulch [LASSEN]: *canyon,* drained by a stream that flows 8.5 miles to Beaver Creek 4 miles west-northwest of the village of Little Valley (lat. 40°54'30" N, long. 121°15'20" W; near SE cor. sec. 34, T 36 N, R 6 E); the canyon heads near Blacks Ridge. Named on Little Valley (1957) 15' quadrangle. Called Black Gulch on Halls Flat (1939) 30' quadrangle.

Blacks Lake [LASSEN]: *lake,* 450 feet long, 5.5 miles south of the village of Little Valley (lat. 40°49'05" N, long. 121°11'55" W; on S line sec. 9, T 34 N, R 7 E). Named on Little Valley (1957) 15' quadrangle. Called Black Lake on Halls Flat (1939) 30' quadrangle.

Blacks Mountain [LASSEN]: *peak,* 8 miles south of the village of Little Valley (lat. 40°46'30" N, long. 121°11'25" W; near SE cor. sec. 28, T 34 N, R 7 E). Altitude 7286 feet. Named on Little Valley (1957) 15' quadrangle. Called Black Butte on Lassen Peak (1894) 1° quadrangle, and called Black Mountain on Halls Flat (1939) 30' quadrangle.

Blacks Ridge [LASSEN]: *ridge,* north-northwest-trending, 3 miles long, 4.25 miles south of the village of Little Valley (lat. 40°50' N, long. 121°10'15"

W); the ridge is near the head of Blacks Gulch. Named on Little Valley (1957) 15' quadrangle.

Blairsden [PLUMAS]: *village,* 20 miles east-southeast of Quincy (lat. 39°46'50" N, long. 120°36'55" W; near S line sec. 10, T 22 N, R 12 E). Named on Blairsden (1972) 7.5' quadrangle. Postal authorities established Blairsden post office in 1913 (Frickstad, p. 123). The name is from the country home of James A. Blair, who was prominent in the financing of Western Pacific Railroad (Gudde, 1949, p. 33).

Blakeless Creek [PLUMAS]: *stream,* flows 3.5 miles to Little Grizzly Creek nearly 4 miles south-southwest of Mount Ingalls (lat. 39°56'35" N, long. 120°39'20" W; sec. 17, T 24 N, R 12 E). Named on Grizzly Valley (1972) and Mount Ingalls (1972) 7.5' quadrangles. United States Board on Geographic Names (1974a, p. 2) gave the name "Little Grizzly Creek" as a variant.

Bloody Point [MODOC]: *promontory,* 4.5 miles north of Newell (lat. 41°57'15" N, long. 121°21'15" W; near SW cor. sec. 36, T 48 N, R 5 E). Named on Tulelake (1951) 15' quadrangle. Modoc Indians killed all but one of a band of more than 90 emigrants at the place in 1850 (Hoover, Rensch, and Rensch, p. 208). On Modoc Lava-Bed (1892) 1° quadrangle, the name applies to a hill situated 4 miles south-southwest of present Newell at or near present Prisoners Rock (lat. 41°49'45" N, long. 121°23'30" W).

Bloomer Lake [PLUMAS]: *lake,* 400 feet long, 13 miles north of Chilcoot (lat. 39°58'55" N, long. 120°11'15" W; near N line sec. 33, T 25 N, R 16 E). Named on Frenchman Lake (1979) 7.5' quadrangle.

Blough: see **Dan Blough Cove** [PLUMAS]; **Dan Blough Creek** [PLUMAS].

Blue Brush Spring [MODOC]: *spring,* 2 miles north of Day (lat. 41° 14'15" N, long. 121°22'55"W; near N line sec. 10, T 39 N, R 5 E). Named on Fall River Mills (1961) 15' quadrangle.

Blue Door Flat [LASSEN]: *valley,* 6.5 miles east of Madeline (lat. 41°03'20" N, long. 120°20'35" W; on E line sec. 23, T 37 N, R 14 E). Named on Cold Spring Mountain (1962) 7.5' quadrangle.

Blue Lake [LASSEN]: *lake,* 3900 feet long, 12 miles northeast of Madeline (lat. 41°08'40" N, long. 120°17'05" W; sec. 20, 21, T 38 N, R 15 E). Named on Jess Valley (1962) 7.5' quadrangle.

Blue Lake [PLUMAS]:

(1) *lake,* 1300 feet long, 9 miles west-southwest of Mount Harkness (lat. 40°24'10" N, long. 121°27'55" W; sec. 6, T 29 N, R 5 E). Named on Mount Harkness (1956) 15' quadrangle.

(2) *lake,* 1400 feet long, 3 miles south of Mount Harkness (lat. 40° 23'20" N, long. 121°17'55" W; sec. 10, T 29 N, R 6 E). Named on Mount Harkness (1956) 15' quadrangle, which shows Fleischmann Boy Scout Camp near the lake. United States Board on Geographic Names (1954, p. 3) approved the name "Fleischmann Lake" for the feature; the name honors Max C. Fleischmann, a supporter of Boy Scouts of America.

(3) *lake,* 400 feet long, nearly 5 miles north-northwest of Bucks Lodge (lat. 39°56'15" N, long. 121°12'50" W; near E line sec. 17, T 24 N, R 7 E). Named on Bucks Lake (1979) 7.5' quadrangle. United States Board on Geographic Names (1979, p. 2) rejected the name "Mud Lake" for the feature.

Blue Lead Gulch [PLUMAS]: *canyon,* drained by a stream that flows 1.5 miles to Cottonwood Creek (1) 10 miles south-southwest of the village of Almanor (lat. 40°04'10" N, long. 121°15'05" W; sec. 36, T 26 N, R 6 E). Named on Almanor (1955) and Jonesville (1958) 15' quadrangles.

Blue Mountain [MODOC]: *peak,* 29 miles north-northwest of Alturas (lat. 41°49'45" N, long. 120°51'45" W; sec. 18, T 46 N, R 10 E). Altitude 5740 feet. Named on Steele Swamp (1962) 15' quadrangle. California Mining Bureau's (1917a) map shows a place called Triangle located about 6 miles south of Blue Mountain. Postal authorities established Triangle post office 23 miles northwest of Alturas in 1912 and discontinued it in 1919; the name was from a triangle formed by roads at the site (Salley, p. 224).

Blue Mountain Meadows Tank [MODOC]: *intermittent lake,* 400 feet long, 2 miles east of Blue Mountain (lat. 41°49'40" N, long. 120°49'30" W; sec. 16, T 46 N, R 10 E). Named on Steele Swamp (1962) 15' quadrangle.

Blue Mountain Spring [MODOC]: *spring,* 2 miles northeast of Blue Mountain (lat. 41°50'45" N, long. 120°50" W; sec. 9, T 46 N, R 10 E). Named on Steele Swamp (1962) 15' quadrangle.

Blue Nose Mountain [PLUMAS]: *peak,* 13 miles south-southeast of Quincy (lat. 39°46'25" N, long. 120°48'35" W); the peak is at the north end of Blue Nose Ridge. Altitude 7290 feet. Named on Blue Nose Mountain (1951) 7.5' quadrangle.

Blue Nose Ravine [PLUMAS]: *canyon,* drained by a stream that flows 0.5 mile to East Branch Hopkins Creek 13 miles south-southeast of Quincy (lat. 39°46'05" N, long. 120°49'20" W); the canyon heads on Blue Nose Ridge. Named on Blue Nose Mountain (1951) 7.5' quadrangle.

Blue Nose Ridge [PLUMAS]: *ridge,* south-trending, 1.5 miles long, 14 miles south-southeast of Quincy (lat. 39°45'35" N, long. 120° 48'35" W); Blue Nose Mountain is at the north end of the ridge. Named on Blue Nose Mountain (1951) 7.5' quadrangle.

Blue Spring [MODOC]: *spring,* about 7.5 miles southeast of Willow Creek (3) (lat. 41°48'50" N, long. 120°16'05" W; near E line sec. 32, T 46 N, R 15 E). Named on Willow Ranch (1962) 15' quadrangle.

Blue Water [LASSEN]: *water feature,* 1.5 miles west of Lava Peak (lat. 40°50' N, long. 120°55'10" W; near SW cor. sec. 1, T 34 N, R 9 E). Named on Hayden Hill (1956) 15' quadrangle.

Board Cabin Spring [LASSEN]: *spring,* 3.25 miles north-northeast of Lava Peak (lat. 40°52'30" N, long. 120°52'15" W; near N line sec. 29, T 35 N, R 10 E). Named on Hayden Hill (1956) 15' quadrangle.

Bob Creek [LASSEN]: *stream,* flows 2 miles to Pit River 6 miles northwest of the village of Little Valley (lat. 40°57'40" N, long. 121°15'05" W; sec. 14, T 36 N, R 6 E). Named on Jellico (1957) and Little Valley (1957) 15' quadrangles.

Bob Creek Spring [LASSEN]: *spring,* 5 miles northwest of the village of Little Valley (lat. 40°56'15" N, long. 121°15' W; near S line sec. 23, T 36 N, R 6 E); the spring is at the head of Bob Creek. Named on Little Valley (1957) 15' quadrangle. Halls Flat (1939) 30' quadrangle has the name "Bob Creek Springs" for two springs at the site.

Bob Young Flat [MODOC]: *area,* 11 miles north-northwest of Hackamore (lat. 41°41'15" N, long. 121°13'45" W; sec. 1, T 44 N, R 6 E). Named on Hackamore (1952) 15' quadrangle.

Bogard Buttes [LASSEN]: *peaks,* highest 5.5 miles south of Cal Mountain (lat. 40°35'05" N, long. 121°09'05" W; sec. 35, T 32 N, R 7 E). Altitude of highest 7574 feet. Named on Harvey Mountain (1956) 15' quadrangle.

Bogard Campground [LASSEN]: *locality,* 7.5 miles south-southeast of Cal Mountain (lat. 40°34'35" N, long. 121°05'50" W; near E line sec. 5, T 31 N, R 8 E); the place is 3 miles east-southeast of Bogard Buttes. Named on Harvey Mountain (1956) 15' quadrangle.

Bogue Mountain: see **Beckwourth Peak** [PLUMAS].

Boiling Springs Lake [PLUMAS]: *lake,* 600 feet long, 5 miles west of Mount Harkness (lat. 40°26'10" N, long. 121°23'50" W; on E line sec. 27, T 30 N, R 5 E). Named on Mount Harkness (1956) 15' quadrangle. Called Tartarus Lake on Lassen Peak (1894) 1° quadrangle. United States Board on Geographic Names (1933, p. 154) rejected the names "Hot Lake" and "Lake Tartarus" for the feature. Submerged hot springs give a boiling appearance to water of the lake—the feature also was called Hot Springs Lake (Schulz, p. 5).

Bolan Creek [MODOC]: *stream,* flows 3 miles to Thoms Creek 12.5 miles south-southeast of the village of Davis Creek (lat. 41°33'40" N, long. 120°19'10" W; sec. 14, T 43 N, R 14 E). Named on Davis Creek (1962) 15' quadrangle.

Boles [MODOC]: *locality,* 3.25 miles east-southeast of Hackamore along Southern Pacific Railroad (lat. 41°32'20" N, long. 121°03'30" W; sec. 28, T 43 N, R 8 E). Named on Hackamore (1952) 15' quadrangle.

Boles Creek [MODOC]: *stream,* flows 16 miles to join North Fork Willow Creek (1) and form Willow Creek (1) 13 miles northeast of Double Head Mountain (lat. 41°54'35" N, long. 121°00'20" W; sec. 13, T 47 N, R 8 E); the stream heads at Boles Meadows. Named on Clear Lake Reservoir (1951), Jacks Butte (1962), and Steele Swamp (1962) 15' quadrangles.

Boles Meadows [MODOC]: *area,* 11 miles north-northwest of Jacks Butte (lat. 41°42'45" N, long. 120°52'45" W). Named on Jacks Butte (1962) 15' quadrangle. Alturas 1° quadrangle has the singular form "Boles Meadow" for the name, and United States Board on Geographic Names (1990, p. 6) approved this form. Alturas (1954) 1°x 2° quadrangle shows an intermittent lake at the place.

Boles Spring [MODOC]: *spring,* 6.5 miles south-southeast of Blue Mountain (lat. 41°45'15" N, long. 120°47'25" W; sec. 11, T 45 N, R 10 E). Named on Steele Swamp (1962) 15' quadrangle.

Bond Valley [PLUMAS]: *relief feature,* 10 miles north-northeast of Chester (lat. 40°25'55" N, long. 121°08'15" W). Named on Red Cinder (1979) 7.5' quadrangle.

Bonta Creek [PLUMAS]:

(1) *stream,* flows 4 miles to Middle Fork Feather River 1 mile west of Blairsden (lat. 39°46'55" N, long. 120°37'55" W; sec. 9, T 22 N, R 12 E); the stream is east of Bonta Ridge. Named on Blairden (1972) and Johnsville (1972) 7.5' quadrangles. Downieville (1897) 30' quadrangle has the name "Bontes" for a place situated near the mouth of present Bonta Creek (1).

(2) *stream,* flows 2.5 miles to Sierra Valley 8.5 miles east-northeast of Portola (lat. 39°50'15" N, long. 120°18'45" W; near NW cor. sec. 21, T 23 N, R 15 E). Named on Reconnaissance Peak (1972) 7.5' quadrangle.

Bonta Ridge [PLUMAS]: *ridge,* south-southwest- to west-trending, 3 miles long, 3 miles north of Blairsden (lat. 39°49'20" N, long. 120° 37'15" W). Named on Blairsden (1972) and Johnsville (1972) 7.5' quadrangles.

Bonte Peak [PLUMAS]: *peak,* 2 miles east-northeast of Mount Harkness (lat. 40°26'30" N, long. 121°16' W; near SW cor. sec. 24, T 30 N, R 6 E). Altitude 7777 feet. Named on Mount Harkness (1956) 15' quadrangle. United States Board on Geographic Names (1933, p. 157) rejected the name "Bontes Peak" for the feature. The name commemorates Dr. J.H.C. Bonte, rector of St. Paul's Episcopal Church in Sacramento and a frequent visitor to the region (Hanna, p. 37-38).

Bontes: see **Bonta Creek** [PLUMAS].

Boomer Creek [PLUMAS]: *stream,* flows 1.5 miles to Butte County 2.25 miles south-southeast of Cascade (lat. 39°40'15" N, long. 121° 09'45" W; near N line sec. 23, T 21 N, R 7 E). Named on Cascade (1948) 7.5'

quadrangle.

Boot Lake [LASSEN]: *intermittent lake,* nearly 2 miles long, 18 miles east of Madeline (lat. 41°04'30" N, long. 120°08'15" W). Named on Boot Lake (1962) and Little Hat Mountain (1962) 7.5' quadrangles.

Boot Lake Creek [LASSEN]: *stream,* flows nearly 3 miles from Boot Lake to Red Rock Creek 17 miles east of Madeline (lat. 41°01'40" N, long. 120°09' W; near W line sec. 34, T 37 N, R 16 E). Named on Boot Lake (1962) 7.5' quadrangle.

Bootleg Reservoir [LASSEN]: *lake,* 700 feet long, 12 miles south-southwest of the village of Little Valley (lat. 40°45'15" N, long. 121°18'15" W; sec. 4, T 33 N, R 6 E). Named on Jellico (1957) 15' quadrangle.

Bootsole Creek [PLUMAS]: *stream,* flows 1.25 miles to Clarks Creek 12.5 miles east-northeast of Kettle Rock (lat. 40°14' N, long. 120°31'20" W; near N line sec. 4, T 27 N, R 13 E). Named on Antelope Lake (1972) 7.5' quadrangle.

Boring Mill Ravine [PLUMAS]: *canyon,* drained by a stream that flows 1.5 miles to Clear Creek (4) 3 miles west-southwest of the village of Meadow Valley (lat. 39°55'10" N, long. 121°06'35" W; sec. 29, T 24 N, R 8 E). Named on Meadow Valley (1980) 7.5' quadrangle.

Bottle Creek [MODOC]: *stream,* flows 3 miles to Fletcher Creek 11 miles north of Jacks Butte (lat. 41°44'30" N, long. 120°49'55" W; at W line sec. 16, T 45 N, R 10 E); the stream heads at Bottle Spring. Named on Jacks Butte (1962) 15' quadrangle.

Bottle Spring [MODOC]: *spring,* 9 miles north of Jacks Butte (lat. 41°43' N, long. 120°47'40" W; near NE cor. sec. 27, T 45 N, R 10 E). Named on Jacks Butte (1962) 15' quadrangle.

Bottle Springs [PLUMAS]: *spring,* 6 miles south-southwest of Quincy (lat. 39°51'50" N, long. 121°00' W; near S line sec. 8, T 23 N, R 9 E). Named on Onion Valley (1950) 7.5' quadrangle.

Boulder Creek [PLUMAS]:

(1) *stream,* flows 7.25 miles to Antelope Lake 7.25 miles northeast of Kettle Rock (lat. 40°11'45" N, long. 120°36'40" W; sec. 15, T 27 N, R 12 E). Named on Antelope Lake (1972) and Janesville (1972) 7.5' quadrangles.

(2) *stream,* flows 2 miles to Little North Fork of Middle Fork Feather River 7 miles south-southeast of Storrie (lat. 39°49'45" N, long. 121°15'40" W; near SW cor. sec. 24, T 23 N, R 6 E). Named on Soapstone Hill (1979) 7.5' quadrangle.

Boulder Creek: see **Big Boulder Creek** [PLUMAS].

Boulder Creek Campground [PLUMAS]: *locality,* 7 miles northeast of Kettle Rock along Antelope Lake (lat. 40°11'30" N, long. 120° 36'45" W; on S line sec. 15, T 27 N, R 12 E); the place is at the mouth of Boulder Creek (1). Named on Antelope Lake (1972) 7.5' quadrangle.

Boulder Creek Meadow [PLUMAS]: *area,* nearly 3 miles south-southeast of Clio (lat. 39°42'35" N, long. 120°33'10" W; near E line sec. 6, T 21 N, R 13 E); the place is along Big Boulder Creek. Named on Clio (1981) 7.5' quadrangle.

Bowers Spring [MODOC]: *spring,* 8 miles south-southwest of the village of Davis Creek (lat. 41°37'45" N, long. 120°26'15" W; sec. 26, T 44 N, R 13 E). Named on Davis Creek (1962) 15' quadrangle.

Bowman Spring [MODOC]: *spring,* 3 miles south of White Horse (lat. 41°16'15" N, long. 121°23'35" W; near S line sec. 28, T 40 N, R 5 E). Named on White Horse (1962) 15' quadrangle.

Bowman Springs [MODOC]: *spring,* 4 miles south-southwest of White Horse (lat. 41°15'45" N, long. 121°26'30" W; near W line sec. 31, T 40 N, R 5 E). Named on White Horse (1962) 15' quadrangle.

Box: see **Letter Box** [PLUMAS].

Box Spring [LASSEN]:

(1) *spring,* 7.5 miles east of Madeline (lat. 41°03' N, long. 120°19'30" W; at NE cor. sec. 25, T 37 N, R 14 E). Named on Cold Spring Mountain (1962) 7.5' quadrangle.

(2) *spring,* 8.5 miles north-northeast of Lava Peak (lat. 40°56'15" N, long. 120°48'30" W; sec. 22, T 36 N, R 10 E). Named on Hayden Hill (1956) 15' quadrangle.

Box Springs [LASSEN]: *springs,* 6 miles southwest of Likely [MODOC] (lat. 41°11' N, long. 120°36'10" W; sec. 28, T 39 N, R 12 E). Named on Likely (1962) 15' quadrangle.

Boyd Creek [MODOC]: *stream,* flows 2.5 miles to Upper Lake 11 miles north of Cedarville (lat. 41°41'30" N, long. 120°11'50" W; near SW cor. sec. 7, T 44 N, R 16 E). Named on Cedarville (1962) 15' quadrangle.

Boyd Hill [LASSEN]: *peak,* 9 miles northeast of the village of Little Valley (lat. 40°59'10" N, long. 121°03'30" W; sec. 4, T 36 N, R 8 E). Altitude 5933 feet. Named on Little Valley (1957) 15' quadrangle.

Boyd Hot Spring [MODOC]: *spring,* 14 miles north-northeast of Cedarville (lat. 41°43'30" N, long. 120°05" W; near W line sec. 31, T 45 N, R 17 E). Named on Cedarville (1962) 15' quadrangle. Called Boyd's Hot Spring on Alturas 1° quadrangle. Waring (p. 124) preferred the name "Boyd Spring" for the feature because the temperature of the water in 1909 was only 67° Fahrenheit—United States Board on Geographic Names (1990, p. 6) approved this name.

Boyd Spring [LASSEN]: *spring,* 9 miles northeast of the village of Little Valley (lat. 40°58'20" N, long. 121°02'50" W; on E line sec. 9, T 36 N, R 8 E); the spring is 1 mile southeast of Boyd Hill. Named on Little Valley (1957) 15' quadrangle.

Boyd Spring: see **Boyd Hot Spring** [MODOC].

Boyle Ravine [PLUMAS]: *canyon,* drained by a stream that flows 1 mile to American Valley at Quincy (lat. 39°55'45" N, long. 120° 56'40" W; sec. 23, T 24 N, R 9 E). Named on Quincy (1950) 7.5' quadrangle.

Bradys Camp [PLUMAS]: *locality,* 4.5 miles north-northeast of Spring Garden (lat. 39°57'30" N, long. 120°45'25" W; near W line sec. 9, T 24 N, R 11 E). Named on Spring Garden (1950) 7.5' quadrangle.

Brandy Spring [LASSEN]: *spring,* 6.5 miles west-northwest of Bieber (lat. 41°09'05" N, long. 121°15'30" W; near NE cor. sec. 10, T 38 N, R 6 E). Named on Fall River Mills (1961) 15' quadrangle.

Branham Reservoir [LASSEN]: *intermittent lake,* 0.5 mile long, 14 miles east-northeast of Pelican Point (lat. 40°43'45" N, long. 120° 31'05" W; sec. 9, T 33 N, R 13 E). Named on Fredonyer Peak (1954) 15' quadrangle.

Branley: see **Lily Lake** [MODOC].

Bray Creek [PLUMAS]: *stream,* flows 2 miles to Middle Fork Feather River 7.5 miles southeast of Quincy (lat. 39°51'40" N, long. 120°50'45" W; sec. 15, T 23 N, R 10 E). Named on Blue Nose Mountain (1951) 7.5' quadrangle.

Bridge Creek [LASSEN]: *stream,* flows nearly 5 miles to McCoy Flat Reservoir 12 miles north of Westwood (lat. 40°28'55" N, long. 120°57'25" W; near N line sec. 10, T 30 N, R 9 E). Named on Antelope Mountain (1956) 15' quadrangle, and on Pegleg Mountain (1980) 7.5' quadrangle.

Briggs Canyon [MODOC]: *canyon,* drained by a stream that flows 2.5 miles to Long Canyon 5 miles east-northeast of Fort Bidwell (lat. 41°52'55" N, long. 120°03'45" W; sec. 6, T 46 N, R 17 E). Named on Fort Bidwell (1962) 15' quadrangle.

Briles Reservoir [MODOC]: *lake,* 1500 feet long, 9.5 miles south of Willow Ranch (lat. 41°46' N, long. 120°21' W; on E line sec. 4, T 45 N, R 14 E). Named on Willow Ranch (1962) 15' quadrangle.

Briles Spring [MODOC]: *spring,* 7.25 miles south of Willow Ranch (lat. 41°48' N, long. 120°20'25" W; sec. 27, T 46 N, R 14 E). Named on Willow Ranch (1962) 15' quadrangle.

Brine Spring [LASSEN]: *spring,* 17 miles north-northeast of Observation Peak (lat. 40°59' N, long. 120°01'10" W; near E line sec. 15, T 36 N, R 17 E). Named on Observation Peak (1954) 15' quadrangle.

Brisco Butte [LASSEN]: *peak,* 3.5 miles south-southeast of Adin [MODOC] (lat. 41°09'05" N, long. 120°54'20" W; sec. 11, T 38 N, R 9 E). Altitude 5053 feet. Named on Adin (1962) 15' quadrangle.

Brockman [LASSEN]: *locality,* 7 miles north-northwest of Termo along Southern Pacific Railroad (lat. 40°57'50" N, long. 120°29'50" W; near S line sec. 8 , T 36 N, R 13 E). Named on Ravendale (1954) 15' quadrangle. Postal authorities established Brockman post office in 1911 and discontinued it in 1919 (Frickstad, p. 66).

Brockman Canyon [LASSEN]: *canyon,* drained by a stream that flows 1.25 miles to Honey Lake Valley 3 miles northwest of Milford (lat. 40°11'55" N, long. 120°24'55" W; at E line sec. 17, T 27 N, R 14 E). Named on Stony Ridge (1978) 7.5' quadrangle.

Brockman Flat Lava Beds [LASSEN]: *relief feature,* 3.5 miles west of Pelican Point (lat. 40°38' N, long. 120°48'30" W). Named on Antelope Mountain (1956) 15' quadrangle. William Brockman had a horse-herding camp at the place (Purdy, 1988, p. 117).

Brockmans Horse Camp [LASSEN]: *locality,* 8.5 miles north-northeast of Termo (lat. 40°58'55" N, long. 120°25'45" W; sec. 1, T 36 N, R 13 E). Named on Ravendale (1954) 15' quadrangle.

Brockman Slough [LASSEN]: *water feature,* 2 miles east-southeast of Susanville (lat. 40°24'20" N, long. 120°37' W; sec. 3, T 29 N, R 12 E). Named on Susanville (1954) 15' quadrangle.

Brooks Mill [MODOC]: *locality,* 19 miles southeast of Alturas along Soup Creek (lat. 41°16'45" N, long. 120°18'35" W; near N line sec. 25, T 40 N, R 14 E). Named on Soup Creek (1963) 7.5' quadrangle.

Brown Canyon [LASSEN]: *canyon,* 4.5 miles long, drained by Cedar Run Creek, which enters Big Valley 3.5 miles west-northwest of Bieber (lat. 41°09' N, long. 121°12' W; sec. 7, T 38 N, R 7 E). Named on Bieber (1961) and Fall River Mills (1961) 15' quadrangles. Fall River Mills (1961) 15' quadrangle shows Brown cabin in the canyon.

Brown Creek [MODOC]: *stream,* flows 2 miles to Surprise Valley 7.25 miles north-northwest of Cedarville (lat. 41°37'45" N, long. 120°12'50" W; near N line sec. 1, T 43 N, R 15 E). Named on Cedarville (1962) 15' quadrangle.

Brownell Creek [LASSEN]: *stream,* flows 1.5 miles to Honey Lake Valley 7 miles northwest of Milford (lat. 40°14'45" N, long. 120° 27'50" W; sec. 36, T 28 N, R 13 E). Named on Stony Ridge (1978) 7.5' quadrangle.

Browns Bar: see **Feather River** [PLUMAS].

Browns Hill: see **Browns Hill Ridge** [PLUMAS].

Browns Hill Ridge [PLUMAS]: *ridge,* west-southwest- to west-trending, 2.5 miles long, 2.25 miles northeast of Cascade (lat. 39° 43'10" N, long. 121°08'45" W). Named on Cascade (1948) 7.5' quadrangle. Bidwell Bar (1897) 30' quadrangle shows an inhabited place called Browns Hill located near the northeast end of present Browns Hill Ridge.

Browns Well [MODOC]: *well,* 5.5 miles northeast of Hackamore (lat. 41°36'40" N, long. 121°02'50" W). Named on Hackamore (1952) 15' quadrangle. Alturas (1954) 1°x 2° quadrangle shows Browns Well Camp at the place.

Browns Well Camp: see **Browns Well** [MODOC].

Brubeck Spring: see **Bruebeck Spring** [LASSEN].

Bruebeck Spring [LASSEN]: *spring,* 6 miles northeast of Wendel (lat. 40°24'55" N, long. 120°19'40" W; sec. 34, T 30 N, R 16 E). Named on Wendel (1954) 15' quadrangle. United States Board on Geographic Names (1989b, p. 2) approved the name "Brubeck Spring" for the feature, and pointed out that the name is for Lewis W. Brubeck, who owned the feature.

Brush Hill [PLUMAS]: *peak,* 9.5 miles east-northeast of Chester (lat. 40°22'35" N, long. 121°04'25" W; sec. 15, T 29 N, R 8 E). Named on Swain Mountain (1979) and Westwood West (1980) 7.5' quadrangles.

Brush Spring [PLUMAS]: *spring,* 9 miles east-northeast of Chester (lat. 40°22'15" N, long. 121°05' W; sec. 16, T 29 N, R 8 E); the spring is 0.5 mile west-southwest of Brush Hill. Named on Westwood West (1980) 15' quadrangle.

Buchanan Flat [MODOC]: *area,* 10 miles north of Blue Mountain (lat. 41°58'15" N, long. 120°50'10" W; on W line sec. 28, T 48 N, R 10 E). Named on Steele Swamp (1962) 15' quadrangle.

Bucher Creek [MODOC]: *stream,* flows 3 miles to Surprise Valley 12 miles north of Cedarville (lat. 41°41'50" N, long. 120°12'45" W; sec. 12, T 44 N, R 15 E). Named on Cedarville (1962) 15' quadrangle.

Bucher Swamp [MODOC]: *area,* 6 miles west of Jacks Butte (lat. 41°34'35" N, long. 120°55' W). Named on Jacks Butte (1962) 15' quadrangleAlturas (1954) 1°x 2° quadrangle shows a lake at the place.

Buck: see **Bucks Lake** [PLUMAS].

Buck Bay [LASSEN]: *embayment,* 3 miles north of Pelican Point along Eagle Lake (lat. 40°40'45" N, long. 120°44'15" W); the feature is west of Buck Point. Named on Fredonyer Peak (1954) 15' quadrangle.

Buck Creek [MODOC]: *stream,* flows 3.5 miles to Willow Creek (3) 3.5 miles southeast of Willow Ranch (lat. 41°52'20" N, long. 120° 18' W; sec. 36, T 46 N, R 14 E). Named on Willow Ranch (1962) 15' quadrangle.

Buckeye [PLUMAS]: *locality,* 8.5 miles south of Storrie (lat. 39°47'40" N, long. 121°18'10" W; near NW cor. sec. 3, T 22 N, R 6 E). Site named on Soapstone Hill (1979) 7.5' quadrangle.

Buckeye Creek [PLUMAS]: *stream,* flows 0.5 mile to Yuba County 4.5 miles south-southwest of American House (lat. 39°36'05" N, long. 121°04'05" W; near S line sec. 10, T 20 N, R 8 E). Named on Strawberry Valley (1948) 7.5' quadrangle.

Buckeye Ranch: see **Bucks Lake** [PLUMAS].

Buckhorn Canyon [LASSEN]: *canyon,* 6 miles long, opens into Madeline Plains 5 miles north-northeast of Observation Peak (lat. 40°50'20" N, long. 120°07'50" W; sec. 2, T 34 N, R 16 E). Named on Observation Peak (1954) 15' quadrangle.

Buckhorn Creek [PLUMAS]: *stream,* flows 1.5 miles to Frazier Creek (1) 5 miles southwest of Bucks Lodge (lat. 39°49'30" N, long. 121°14'15" W; near N line sec. 30, T 23 N, R 7 E). Named on Haskins Valley (1980) 7.5' quadrangle.

Buckhorn Lake [LASSEN]: *lake,* 1400 feet long, 12.5 miles northeast of Observation Peak (lat. 40°55' N, long. 120°01'30" W; near NW cor. sec. 11, T 35 N, R 17 E). Named on Observation Peak (1954) 15' quadrangle.

Buckhorn Reservoir [LASSEN]: *lake,* 3700 feet long, 7 miles northeast of Observation Peak (lat. 40°51'10" N, long. 120°05'15" W; on E line sec. 31, T 35 N, R 17 E); the lake is in Buckhorn Canyon. Named on Observation Peak (1954) 15' quadrangle.

Buckhorn Waterhole [LASSEN]: *lake,* 1000 feet long, 7 miles north-northwest of Lava Peak (lat. 40°55'40" N, long. 120°56'10" W; sec. 28, T 36 N, R 9 E). Named on Hayden Hill (1956) 15' quadrangle.

Buck Mountain [LASSEN]: *peak,* 16 miles east-northeast of Madeline (lat. 41°08'20" N, long. 120°11' W; near S line sec. 20, T 38 N, R 16 E). Altitude 8634 feet. Named on Emerson Peak (1962) 7.5' quadrangle.

Buck Mountain [MODOC]: *peak,* 5 miles east-southeast of the village of Davis Creek (lat. 41°43' N, long. 120°16'40" W; near NE cor. sec. 5, T 44 N, R 15 E). Altitude 7932 feet. Named on Davis Creek (1962) 15' quadrangle.

Buck Pasture Ridge [MODOC]: *ridge,* south-southeast-trending, 1.5 miles long, 2.5 miles west of Lookout (lat. 41°12'30" N, long. 121° 11'45" W; on N line sec. 20, T 39 N, R 7 E). Named on Bieber (1961) 15' quadrangle.

Buck Point [LASSEN]: *promontory,* 2.5 miles north-northeast of Pelican Point on the west side of Eagle Lake (lat. 40°39'50" N, long. 120°43' W); the feature is east of Buck Bay. Named on Fredonyer Peak (1954) 15' quadrangle.

Bucks Creek [PLUMAS]: *stream,* flows 15 miles to North Fork Feather River 0.5 mile south-southwest of Storrie (lat. 39°54'40" N, long. 121°19'35" W). Named on Bucks Lake (1979), Meadow Valley (1980), and Storrie (1979) 7.5' quadrangles.

Bucks Lake [PLUMAS]: *lake,* behind a dam on Bucks Creek 2 miles northwest of Bucks Lodge (lat. 39°53'45" N, long. 121°12'10" W; sec. 33, T 24 N, R 7 E). Named on Bucks Lake (1979) and Haskins Valley (1980) 7.5' quadrangles. Bidwell Bar (1897) 30' quadrangle shows Bucks Valley at the site, and shows a place called Bucks Ranch situated on the south side of the valley (lat. 39°52'45" N, long. 121°10'30" W). Postal authorities established Buck's Ranch post office in 1861, moved it 10 miles southwest in 1868 when they changed the name to Buckeye Ranch, changed the name to Buck in 1894, discontinued it in 1909, reestablished it in 1910, discontinued it in 1913, reestablished it in 1927, and discontinued it the same year (Frickstad, p. 123; Salley, p. 28). Horace "Buck" Bucklin and Francis Walker started Bucks ranch at the site in 1850, and eventually it became an important trading center for nearby mining camps—water of Bucks Lake now covers the site (Hanna, p. 43). Bidwell Bar (1897) 30' quadrangle shows a place called Rutherfords located 1.25 miles northwest of Bucks Ranch.

Bucks Lake: see **Bucks Lodge** [PLUMAS]; **Lower Bucks Lake** [PLUMAS].

Bucks Lodge [PLUMAS]: *locality,* 13 miles west-southwest of Quincy along the south side of Bucks Lake (lat. 39°52'35" N, long. 121°10'25" W; sec. 2, 3, T 23 N, R 7 E). Named on Bucks Lake (1979) 7.5' quadrangle. Called Bucks Lake on Chico (1958) 1°x 2° quadrangle. Postal authorities established Bucks Lake post office in 1940 and discontinued it in 1942 (Frickstad, p. 123).

Bucks Mountain [PLUMAS]: *peak,* 3.5 miles north-northwest of Bucks Lodge (lat. 39°55'10" N, long. 121°12'25" W; sec. 21, T 24 N, R 7 E). Altitude 6819 feet. Named on Bucks Lake (1979) 7.5' quadrangle.

Buck's Ranch: see **Bucks Lake** [PLUMAS].

Bucks Summit [PLUMAS]: *pass,* 3 miles southwest of the village of Meadow Valley (lat. 39°54' N, long. 121°07'10" W; near W line sec. 32, T 24 N, R 8 E). Named on Meadow Valley (1980) 7.5' quadrangle.

Bucks Valley: see **Bucks Lake** [PLUMAS].

Bull: see **Bull Flat Camp** [LASSEN].

Bullard Lake [LASSEN]: *lake,* 3200 feet long, nearly 4 miles south of Lava Peak (lat. 40°46'30" N, long. 120°54' W; on E line sec. 31, T 34 N, R 10 E). Named on Hayden Hill (1956) 15' quadrangle.

Bull Creek [LASSEN]: *stream,* flows 7.5 miles to Deep Creek 12 miles northeast of Wendel in Bull Valley (lat. 40°29' N, long. 120° 05' W; at N line sec. 8, T 30 N, R 17 E). Named on Wendel (1954) 15' quadrangle.

Bull Creek [MODOC]: *stream,* heads in the State of Nevada and flows 2 miles in Modoc County to lowlands along Middle Alkali Lake 9 miles east-southeast of Cedarville (lat. 41°27'20" N, long. 120°01'25" W; at E line sec. 33, T 42 N, R 17 E). Named on Hansen Island (1963) 7.5' quadrangle.

Bull Flat [LASSEN]: *valley,* 12 miles northeast of Wendel (lat. 40°29'15" N, long. 120°05'50" W); the feature is at the mouth of Bull Creek. Named on Wendel (1954) 15' quadrangle.

Bull Flat [PLUMAS]: *area,* 5 miles south of Bucks Lodge (lat. 39°48'10" N, long. 121°11' W; sec. 34, T 23 N, R 7 E). Named on Haskins Valley (1980) 7.5' quadrangle.

Bull Flat Camp [LASSEN]: *locality,* 12 miles northeast of Wendel (lat. 40°28'20" N, long. 120°04'45" W; near SE cor. sec. 8, T 30 N, R 17 E). Named on Wendel (1954) 15' quadrangle. Honey Lake (1893) 1° quadrangle has the name "Bull" at the site.

Bullfrog Ravine [PLUMAS]: *canyon,* drained by a stream that flows 1.5 miles to Rush Creek 4.5 miles north-northeast of Twain (lat. 40°04'55" N, long. 121°02'10" W; sec. 25, T 26 N, R 8 E). Named on Twain (1980) 7.5' quadrangle.

Bull Run Creek [PLUMAS]: *stream,* flows 2.25 miles to Long Valley Creek 8.5 miles south of Mount Ingalls (lat. 39°52'30" N, long. 120°39'15" W; sec. 8, T 23 N, R 12 E). Named on Mount Ingalls (1972) 7.5' quadrangle.

Bull Run Slough [LASSEN]: *water feature,* joins Pit River 5.25 miles south of Bieber (lat. 41°02'40" N, long. 121°08'20" W; near W line sec. 14, T 37 N, R 7 E). Named on Bieber (1961) 15' quadrangle.

Bull Spring [LASSEN]: *spring,* 11.5 miles northeast of Wendel (lat. 40°28'45" N, long. 120°05'45" W; on E line sec. 7, T 30 N, R 17 E). Named on Wendel (1954) 15' quadrangle. Honey Lake (1893) 1° quadrangle shows Mud Springs at or near the site. According to Amesbury (p. 24), Mud Springs was an important stop for emigrants, and later had a stage station.

Bull Spring [MODOC]: *spring,* 7.5 miles north-northeast of Newell (lat. 41°59'15" N, long. 121°18'45" W; sec. 20, T 48 N, R 6 E). Named on Tulelake (1951) 15' quadrangle.

Bull Spring [PLUMAS]: *spring,* 3.25 miles southwest of Milford [LASSEN] (lat. 40°08'05" N, long. 120°24'30" W; sec. 4, T 26 N, R 14 E). Named on Stop Ridge (1978) 7.5' quadrangle.

Bump Heads [MODOC]: *relief feature,* 6.5 miles northeast of Double Head Mountain (lat. 41°49'10" N, long. 121°03'45" W; sec. 16, 21, T 46 N, R 8 E). Named on Clear Lake Reservoir (1951) 15' quadrangle.

Bunchgrass Creek [PLUMAS]: *stream,* flows 2.25 miles to South Arm Rice Creek 9.5 miles west-southwest of Mount Harkness (lat. 40°22'50" N, long. 121°27'45" W; at S line sec. 7, T 29 N, R 5 E). Named on Mount Harkness (1956) 15' quadrangle.

Bunker Hill: see **Mount Washington** [PLUMAS].

Bunker Hill Creek [PLUMAS]: *stream,* flows 1.5 miles to West Branch Hopkins Creek 12.5 miles south-southeast of Quincy (lat. 39°46'45" N, long. 120°50'15" W); the stream heads at Bunker Hill Ridge. Named on Blue Nose Mountain (1951) 7.5' quadrangle.

Bunker Hill Ridge [PLUMAS]: *ridge,* southeast-trending, 1.25 miles long, 13 miles south-southeast of Quincy on Plumas-Sierra County line (lat. 39°46' N, long. 120°51'30" W). Named on Blue Nose Mountain (1951) 7.5' quadrangle.

Bunnel: see **Goumaz** [LASSEN].

Bunnel Point [PLUMAS]: *promontory,* 2 miles east of the village of Almanor along Lake Almanor at the south end of Almanor Peninsula (lat. 40°13'20" N, long. 121°08'10" W; near E line sec. 1, T 27 N, R 7 E). Named on Almanor (1979) 7.5' quadrangle.

Bunselmeier Spring [LASSEN]: *spring,* 11 miles north-northwest of Lava Peak (lat. 40°59' N, long. 120°56'30" W; sec. 4, T 36 N, R 9 E). Named on Hayden Hill (1956) 15' quadrangle.

Buntingville [LASSEN]: *village,* 8.5 miles southwest of Litchfield (lat. 40°17'10" N, long. 120°29'05" W; sec. 14, T 28 N, R 13 E). Named on Standish (1972) 7.5' quadrangle. Postal authorities established Buntingville post office in 1883, discontinued it in 1884, reestablished it in 1899, discontinued it in 1907, reestablished it in 1915, and discontinued it in 1920 (Frickstad, p. 66). The name commemorates A.J. Bunting, who opened a general store at the place in 1878 (Hanna, p. 45).

Burgess Meadows [LASSEN]: *valley,* 7.25 miles east-northeast of Cal Mountain (lat. 40°41'35" N, long. 121°02' W; at W line sec. 25, T 33 N, R 8 E). Named on Harvey Mountain (1956) 15' quadrangle.

Burgess Springs [LASSEN]: *springs,* 7.25 miles east-northeast of Cal Mountain (lat. 40°42'10" N, long. 121°02'10" W; at SE cor. sec. 23, T 33 N, R 8 E); the springs are at the north end of Burgess Meadows. Named on Harvey Mountain (1956) 15' quadrangle. Halls Flat (1939) 30' quadrangle has the singular form "Burgess Spring" for the name.

Burnham Meadow [PLUMAS]: *area,* 4 miles north-northeast of Portola (lat. 39°51'40" N, long. 120°26'35" W; sec. 7, 8, T 23 N, R 14 E). Named on Portola (1972) 7.5' quadrangle.

Burton Gulch [PLUMAS]: *canyon,* drained by a stream that flows 2 miles to Spanish Creek (1) 2 miles northwest of the village of Meadow Valley (lat. 39°57'10" N, long. 121°04'50" W; near W line sec. 10, T 24 N, R 8 E). Named on Meadow Valley (1980) 7.5' quadrangle.

Burton Ridge [PLUMAS]: *ridge,* southeast-trending, 1 mile long, 3 miles northwest of the village of Meadow Valley (lat. 39°57'25" N, long. 121°06'10" W; on E line sec. 8, T 24 N, R 8 E). Named on Meadow Valley (1980) 7.5' quadrangle.

Busters Reservoir [LASSEN]: *intermittent lake,* 600 feet long, nearly 6 miles south-southeast of the village of Little Valley (lat. 40°48'40" N, long. 121°09'15" W; sec. 14, T 34 N, R 7 E). Named on Little Valley (1957) 15' quadrangle.

Butt Creek [PLUMAS]: *stream,* flows 24 miles to North Fork Feather River 1.5 miles east-northeast of Caribou (lat. 40°05'35" N, long. 121°07'50" W). Named on Jonesville (1958) 15' quadrangle, and on Almanor (1979) and Caribou (1979) 7.5' quadrangles.

Butte Bar [PLUMAS]: *locality,* 1.5 miles north-northeast of Dogwood Peak along Middle Fork Feather River (lat. 39°48'25" N, long. 121°02'50" W; near E line sec. 35, T 23 N, R 8 E). Named on Dogwood Peak (1979) 7.5' quadrangle.

Butte Camp [LASSEN]: *locality,* 9.5 miles southwest of the village of Little Valley (lat. 40°48' N, long. 121°18'30" W; sec. 21, T 34 N, R 6 E); the place is less than 1 mile south of Ladder Butte. Named on Jellico (1957) 15' quadrangle.

Butte Creek [LASSEN]: *stream,* flows 12 miles to Shasta County 9 miles west-northwest of Cal Mountain (lat. 40°42'45" N, long. 121°19'15" W; at W line sec. 20, T 33 N, R 6 E); the stream heads at Butte Lake. Named on Prospect Peak (1957) 15' quadrangle.

Butte Creek [LASSEN-MODOC]: *stream,* heads in Lassen County and flows 14 miles to Ash Creek less than 1 mile west of Adin in Modoc County (lat. 41°11'40" N, long. 120°57'30" W; sec. 29, T 39 N, R 9 E). Named on Adin (1962) 15' quadrangle.

Butte Creek Campground [LASSEN]: *locality,* 8 miles west-southwest of Cal Mountain along Butte Creek (lat. 40°36'45" N, long. 121°17'45" W; near N line sec. 27, T 32 N, R 6 E). Named on Prospect Peak (1957) 15' quadrangle.

Butte Creek Rim [LASSEN]: *escarpment,* mainly in Shasta County, but extends south-southeast into Lassen County 9.5 miles west-northwest of Cal Mountain (lat. 40°44'30" N, long. 121°19'15" W); the feature is near Butte Creek. Named on Prospect Peak (1957) 15' quadrangle.

Butte Lake [LASSEN]: *lake,* 1.25 miles long, 10 miles southwest of Cal Mountain (lat. 40°33'30" N, long. 121°17'15" W; mainly in sec. 10, T 31 N, R 6 E). Named on Prospect Peak (1957) 15' quadrangle. Called Lake Bidwell on Lassen Peak (1894) 1° quadrangle. United States Board on Geographic Names (1933, p. 178) rejected the names "Bidwell Lake," "Feather Lake," and "General Bidwell Lake" for the feature. The name "Butte Lake" apparently is from nearby Cinder Cone, which had the names "Black Butte" and "Cinder Butte" (Schulz, p. 8).

Butterfly Creek [PLUMAS]: *stream,* flows nearly 2 miles to Spanish Creek (1) 6.5 miles south-southwest of Crescent Mills (lat. 40°00'25" N, long. 120°57'40" W; at N line sec. 27, T 25 N, R 9 E). Named on Crescent Mills (1980) and Quincy (1950) 7.5' quadrangles.

Butterfly Valley [PLUMAS]: *valley,* 4.5 miles north-northwest of Quincy (lat. 40°00' N, long. 120°58'40" W; sec. 28, T 25 N, R 9 E); the valley is along Butterfly Creek. Named on Crescent Mills (1980) and Quincy (1950) 7.5' quadrangles.

Buttes: see **The Buttes** [PLUMAS].

Butte Valley: see **Butt Valley Reservoir** [PLUMAS].

Button Mountain [LASSEN]: *ridge,* generally southwest-trending, 1.25 miles long, 10 miles northeast of Observation Peak (lat. 40° 51'20" N, long. 120°00'50" W; sec. 35, 36, T 35 N, R 17 E). Named on Observation Peak (1954) 15' quadrangle.

Butt Valley: see **Butt Valley Reservoir** [PLUMAS].

Butt Valley Reservoir [PLUMAS]: *lake,* behind a dam on Butt Creek 2.5 miles north-northeast of Caribou (lat. 40°06'55" N, long. 121° 08'30" W; near N line sec. 13, T 26 N, R 7 E). Named on Almanor (1979) and Caribou (1979) 7.5' quadrangles. Lassen Peak (1894) 1° quadrangle has the name "Butt Valley" at the site of the lake. The name "Butt" commemorates Horace Butts, who settled in the lower part of the valley (Gudde, 1949, p. 47). Lassen Peak (1894) 1° quadrangle also shows an inhabited place called Butte Valley situated near the south end of Butt Valley. Postal authorities established Butte Valley post office 9 miles southeast of Prattville post office in 1887 and discontinued it in 1912 (Salley, p. 30).

Buzzard Springs [PLUMAS]: *springs,* 7 miles southwest of Mount Harkness (lat. 40°22'15" N, long. 121°24'15" W; sec. 15, T 29 N, R 5 E). Named on Mount Harkness (1956) 15' quadrangle.

Buzzards Roost Ridge [PLUMAS]: *ridge,* north-trending, 2 miles long, 9.5 miles south-southeast of Quincy (lat. 39°48'30" N, long. 120°52' W). Named on Blue Nose Mountain (1951) 7.5' quadrangle.

Byers Pass [LASSEN]: *pass,* 6 miles west-southwest of Litchfield (lat. 40°20'20" N, long. 120°29'05" W; sec. 26, T 29 N, R 13 E). Named on Standish (1972) 7.5' quadrangle.

— C —

Cache Valley: see **Indian Valley** [PLUMAS].

Cairn Butte [PLUMAS]: *peak,* 1.5 miles north-northeast of Moonlight Peak (lat. 40°15'35" N, long. 121°49'45" W; near NW cor. sec. 26, T 28 N, R 10 E). Altitude 7296 feet. Named on Fredonyer Pass (1980) 7.5' quadrangle.

Calfpasture Creek [PLUMAS]: *stream,* flows 4.25 miles to Sulphur Creek 1 mile southeast of Clio (lat. 39°43'50" N, long. 120°33'50" W; sec. 31, T 22 N, R 13 E). Named on Blairsden (1972) and Clio (1981) 7.5' quadrangles.

California Pines Lake: see **Donavan Reservoir** [MODOC].

Cal Mountain [LASSEN]: *mountain,* 32 miles northwest of Susanville (lat. 40°40'10" N, long. 121°09'50" W; near NW cor. sec. 2, T 32 N, R 7 E). Named on Harvey Mountain (1956) 15' quadrangle.

Calneva [LASSEN]: *locality,* 10 miles north-northeast of Doyle along Western Pacific Railroad (lat. 40°09'10" N, long. 120°00'15" W; sec. 36, T 27 N, R 17 E). Named on Doyle (1954) 15' quadrangle. Postal authorities established Calneva post office in 1911, discontinued it in 1919, reestablished it in 1920, and discontinued it in 1933 (Frickstad, p. 66). The name is from the location of the place at California-Nevada State line (Hanna, p. 52).

Calneva Lake [LASSEN]: *intermittent lake,* 10.5 miles north-northeast of Doyle (lat. 40°09'50" N, long. 120°00'45" W; on E line sec. 26, T 27 N, R 17 E); the feature is less than 1 mile north-northwest of Calneva. Named on Doyle (1954) 15' quadrangle.

Cambron Lake [MODOC]: *intermittent lake,* 4500 feet long, 2.5 miles east-northeast of Eagleville between Middle Alkali Lake and Lower Lake (lat. 41°19'50" N, long. 120°04'10" W; sec. 17, T 40 N, R 17 E). Named on Eagleville (1963) 7.5' quadrangle.

Camel Peak [PLUMAS]: *peak,* 6.25 miles northwest of American House (lat. 39°43'15" N, long. 121°06' W; at E line sec. 32, T 22 N, R 8 E). Altitude 5723 feet. Named on American House (1948) 7.5' quadrangle. Called Cammel Peak on Bidwell Bar (1897) 30' quadrangle.

Camero: see **Scotts** [LASSEN].

Cameron Meadow [LASSEN]: *area,* 4 miles north of Mount Harkness [PLUMAS] (lat. 40°29'20" N, long. 121°18' W; sec . 3, T 30 N, R 6 E). Named on Mount Harkness (1956) 15' quadrangle, which shows marsh in the area. The name is for Jeff Cameron, who homesteaded at the place in the 1880's (Schulz, p. 9).

Cammel Peak: see **Camel Peak** [PLUMAS].

Camp Almanor [PLUMAS]: *locality,* less than 1 mile west of Canyondam (lat. 40°10'20" N, long. 121°05'10" W; sec. 28, T 27 N, R 8 E); the place is just south of the dam that forms Lake Almanor. Named on Canyondam (1979) 7.5' quadrangle.

Campbell Cow Camp [PLUMAS]: *locality,* 3.25 miles west-northwest of Storrie (lat. 39°56'10" N, long. 121°22'50" W; sec. 14, T 24 N, R 5 E). Named on Kimshew Point (1979) 7.5' quadrangle.

Campbell Lake [PLUMAS]: *lake,* 8500 feet long, nearly 6 miles north-northwest of Storrie (lat. 39°59'50" N, long. 121°21'35" W; sec. 30, T 25 N, R 6 E). Named on Storrie (1979) 7.5' quadrangle. On Bidwell Bar (1897) 30' quadrangle, the name "Campbells Lakes" applies to present Long Lake (1) and present Campbell Lake together, but United States Board on Geographic Names (1960b, p. 6) rejected this name for the pair of lakes.

Campbell Mountain [LASSEN]: *mountain,* 13 miles west-southwest of Pelican Point (lat. 40°33'30" N, long. 120°58'20" W; near SW cor. sec. 9, T 31 N, R 9 E). Altitude 6762 feet. Named on Antelope Mountain (1956) and Harvey Mountain (1958) 15' quadrangles

Campbells Lakes: see **Campbell Lake** [PLUMAS].

Camp Bidwell: see **Fort Bidwell** [MODOC].

Camp Creek [PLUMAS]: *stream,* flows 1.5 miles to Poplar Creek 12.5 miles southeast of Quincy (lat. 39°49'50" N, long. 120°45'10" W; sec. 28, T 23 N, R 11 E). Named on Blue Nose Mountain (1951) 7.5' quadrangle.

Camp 8: see **Summit Camp** [LASSEN].

Camp Harvey [LASSEN]: *locality,* 10.5 miles south-southeast of the village of Little Valley (lat. 40°46'30" N, long. 121°03'50" W; near S line sec. 27, T 34 N, R 8 E). Named on Little Valley (1957) 15' quadrangle..

Camp One: see **Old Camp One** [MODOC].

Camp One Spring [LASSEN]: *spring,* 19 miles east-northeast of Madeline (lat. 41°09'55" N, long. 120°08'30" W; near N line sec. 15, T 38 N, R 16 E). Named on Emerson Peak (1962) 7.5' quadrangle.

Camp Rodgers: see **Rodgers Flat** [PLUMAS].

Camp Rodgers Saddle [PLUMAS]: *pass,* 3.5 miles east-northeast of Storrie (lat. 39°56'30" N, long. 121°15'50" W; at SW cor. sec. 12, T 24 N, R 6 E). Named on Storrie (1979) 7.5' quadrangle.

Camp Stanford [LASSEN]: *locality,* 2.5 miles southwest of Lava Peak (lat. 40°48'30" N, long. 120°55'35" W; sec. 14, T 34 N, R 9 E). Named on Hayden Hill (1956) 15' quadrangle.

Camp Ten [LASSEN]: *locality,* 12 miles west of Pelican Point (lat. 40°38'05" N, long. 120°58'10" W; sec. 16, T 32 N, R 9 E). Site named on Antelope Mountain (1956) 15' quadrangle.

Camp 13 [PLUMAS]: *locality,* 3.5 miles west of Squaw Valley Peak in Squaw Valley (lat. 40°01'45" N, long. 120°28' W; near SE cor. sec. 12, T 25 N, R 13 E). Named on Squaw Valley Peak (1977) 7.5' quadrangle.

Camp Wallace Alexander [PLUMAS]: *locality,* 5.5 miles south-southwest of Crescent Mills along Spanish Creek (1) (lat. 40°01'40" N, long. 120°57'50" W; sec. 15, T 25 N, R 9 E). Named on Greenville (1950) 15' quadrangle.

Camp Wieland: see **Mohawk Boys Camp** [PLUMAS].

Canby [MODOC]: *village,* 17 miles west of Alturas (lat. 41°26'40" N, long. 120°52'15" W; around SE cor. sec. 26, T 42 N, R 9 E). Named on Canby (1961) 15' quadrangle. Postal authorities established Canby post office in 1874 (Frickstad, p. 102). The name commemorates General Canby, whom Modoc Indians murdered at about the time that the village was founded (Pease, p. 93). Bancroft's (1864) map shows a place called 9 Mile Gap situated along Pit River at or near the site of present Canby; the gap is in a range called Pitt River Mts. on the map, which shows the range extending south-southeast for about 100 miles from north of California-Oregon State line. California Division of Highways' (1934) map shows a place called Ghent located 2 miles northwest of Canby along Southern Pacific Railroad. Postal authorities established Lillian post office 6 miles southwest of Canby in 1881 and discontinued it in 1882 (Salley, p. 122). Anderson (p. 119) listed Coal Valley Boiling Springs, located about 8 miles west of Canby, that produce water with a temperature of 214° Fahrenheit.

Cannon Field [LASSEN]: *area,* 3 miles west-southwest of Doyle (lat. 40°01'05" N, long. 120°09'25" W; sec. 14, T 25 N, R 16 E). Named on McKesick Peak (1978) 7.5' quadrangle.

Cannon Tank [MODOC]: *water feature,* 2 miles west-southwest of Hackamore (lat. 41°32'30" N, long. 121°09'20" W; near W line sec. 27, T 43 N, R 7 E). Named on Hackamore (1952) 15' quadrangle.

Cantebury Gulch [PLUMAS]: *canyon,* drained by a stream that flows 1 mile to Butt Valley Reservoir 6 miles south of the village of Almanor (lat. 40°07'50" N, long. 121°10'25" W; near NE cor. sec. 10, T 26 N, R 7 E). Named on Almanor (1979) and Caribou (1979) 7.5' quadrangles.

Cantrall Creek [MODOC]: *stream,* flows 3 miles to Thoms Creek 12.5 miles south of the village of Davis Creek (lat. 41°33'25" N, long. 120°20'05" W; near NE cor. sec. 22, T 43 N, R 14 E). Named on Davis Creek (1962) 15' quadrangle.

Cantrall Mill [MODOC]: *locality,* 16 miles southeast of Alturas near the mouth of Cherry Creek (1) (lat. 41°19'10" N, long. 120°19'35" W; sec. 11, T 40 N, R 14 E). Named on Soup Creek (1963) 7.5' quadrangle.

Canyon Creek [MODOC]: *stream,* flows 13 miles to Pit River 11 miles west-southwest of Alturas (lat. 41°25'40" N, long. 120°43'55" W; near NW cor. sec. 5, T 41 N, R 11 E). Named on Alturas (1961) and Canby (1961) 15' quadrangles. South Fork enters from the south 17 miles south-southwest of Alturas; it is 4.25 miles long and is named on Alturas (1961) and Canby (1961) 15' quadrangles.

Canyondam [PLUMAS]: *village,* 6.25 miles east-southeast of the village of Almanor (lat. 40°10'20" N, long. 121°04'20" W; sec. 27, T 27 N, R 8 E); the village is less than 1 mile east of the dam that forms Lake Almanor. Named on Canyondam (1979) 7.5' quadrangle. Postal authorities established Canyondam post office in 1940, discontinued it in 1944, and reestablished it in 1952 (Frickstad, p. 123).

Cape Horne [MODOC]: *ridge,* northwest-trending, 4000 feet long, 15 miles north of Double Head Mountain (lat. 41°58'35" N, long. 121°11'10" W; near NE cor. sec. 29, T 48 N, R 7 E). Named on Clear Lake Reservoir (1951) 15' quadrangle.

Cape Lake [PLUMAS]: *lake,* 1300 feet long, 4 miles north-northwest of Bucks Lodge (lat. 39°55'40" N, long. 121°12'35" W; near NW cor. sec. 21, T 24 N, R 7 E). Named on Bucks Lake (1979) 7.5' quadrangle.

Cariboo: see **Caribou** [PLUMAS].

Caribou [PLUMAS]: *locality,* 9.5 miles south of the village of Almanor along North Fork Feather River (lat. 40°04'50" N, long. 121°09'15" W; on E line sec. 26, T 26 N, R 7 E). Named on Caribou (1979) 7.5' quadrangle. Lassen Peak (1894) 1° quadrangle shows Caribou bridge at or near the site. Postal authorities established Caribou post office in 1922 and discontinued it in 1976 (Salley, p. 37). The place was a placer-mining camp of 1850 named for Johnny Caribou, an Indian miner (Hanna, p. 55). Present Caribou is 2 miles above the old mining camp of Caribou; the name also had the form "Cariboo" (Gudde, 1975, p. 61).

Caribou: see **North Caribou** [LASSEN]; **South Caribou** [LASSEN].

Caribou Lake [LASSEN]: *lake,* 3100 feet long, 11.5 miles south of Cal Mountain (lat. 40°30'10" N, long. 121°10'05" W; on W line sec. 35, T 31 N, R 7 E). Named on Harvey Mountain (1956) 15' quadrangle. On Lassen Peak (1894) 1° quadrangle, the name "Lake Caribou" applies to a feature south of present Carbou Lake.

Caribou Peak [LASSEN]: *peak,* 9.5 miles south of Cal Mountain (lat. 40°32'05" N, long. 121°11'20" W; at W line sec. 22, T 31 N, R 7 E). Named on Harvey Mountain (1956) 15' quadrangle.

Carman Creek, East Fork [PLUMAS]: *stream,* flows 4.5 miles to Sierra County 7 miles south of Portola (lat. 39°42'25" N, long. 120°27'40" W; at S line sec. 1, T 21 N, R 13 E). Named on Calpine (1981) and Portola (1972) 7.5' quadrangles. The stream joins West Fork in Sierra County to form Carman Creek. United States Board on Geographic Names (1974a, p. 2) gave the name "East Fork Carmen Creek" as a variant.

Carman Creek, West Fork [PLUMAS]: *stream,* flows 4.25 miles to Sierra County 7 miles south of Portola (lat. 39°42'25" N, long. 120°28'15" W; at S line sec. 1, T 21 N, R 13 E). Named on Calpine (1981) and Portola (1972) 7.5' quadrangles. The stream joins East Fork in Sierra County to form Carman Creek. United States Board on Geographic Names (1973a, p. 3) gave the name "West Fork Carmen Creek" as a variant.

Carman Saddle [PLUMAS]: *pass,* 3 miles south of Portola (lat. 39° 45'50" N, long. 120°28'10" W; near S line sec. 13, T 22 N, R 13 E); the pass is at the head of West Fork Carman Creek. Named on Portola (1972) 7.5' quadrangle.

Carman Valley [PLUMAS]: *valley,* 6 miles south of Portola (lat. 39° 43'40" N, long. 120°28'20" W; sec. 35, 36, T 22 N, R 13 E); the valley is along West Fork Carman Creek. Named on Calpine (1981) 7.5' quadrangle.

Carpenter Bar [PLUMAS]: *locality,* 2 miles west-northwest of Dogwood Peak along Middle Fork Feather River (lat. 39°47'40" N, long. 121°05'25" W; sec. 4, T 22 N, R 8 E); the place is at the mouth of Carpenter Creek. Named on Dogwood Peak (1979) 7.5' quadrangle.

Carpenter Creek [PLUMAS]: *stream,* flows 1.25 miles to Middle Fork Feather River 2 miles west-northwest of Dogwood Peak (lat. 39°47'40" N, long. 121°05'30" W; sec. 4, T 22 N, R 8 E). Named on Dogwood Peak (1979) 7.5' quadrangle.

Carr Butte [MODOC]: *hill,* 13 miles north of Double Head Mountain (lat. 41°57'25" N, long. 121°10' W; near E line sec. 33, T 48 N, R 7 E). Altitude 5482 feet. Named on Clear Lake Reservoir (1951) 15' quadrangle.

Cary Reservoir [LASSEN]: *lake,* 250 feet long, 7 miles south-southwest of Adin [MODOC] (lat. 41°06'20" N, long. 120°59'50" W; sec. 25, T 38 N, R 8 E). Named on Adin (1962) 15' quadrangle.

Cary Spring [LASSEN]: *spring,* 7.5 miles east of Bieber (lat. 41° 06' N, long. 121°00'10" W; sec. 25, T 38 N, R 8 E). Named on Bieber (1961) 15' quadrangle.

Cascade [PLUMAS]: *locality,* 20 miles southwest of Quincy (lat. 39° 42' N, long. 121°10'40" W; at S line sec. 3, T 21 N, R 7 E); the place is along Cascade Creek (1). Named on Cascade (1948) 7.5' quadrangle.

Cascade Creek [PLUMAS]:

(1) *stream,* flows 5 miles to Butte County 1.25 miles west of Cascade (lat. 39°42' N, long. 121°12'05" W; at S line sec. 4, T 21 N, R 7 E). Named on American House (1948) and Cascade (1948) 7.5' quadrangles.

(2) *stream,* flows 2 miles to Little Grizzly Creek 4.5 miles west-southwest of Mount Ingalls (lat. 39°57'40" N, long. 120°41'45" W; sec. 12, T 24 N, R 11 E). Named on Mount Ingalls (1972) 7.5' quadrangle.

Cashman Creek [PLUMAS]: *stream,* flows 3.5 miles to Spanish Creek (1) 6.5 miles south-southwest of Crescent Mills (lat. 40°00'15" N, long.

120°56'25" W; near N line sec. 26, T 25 N, R 9 E). Named on Crescent Mills (1980) 7.5' quadrangle.

Cassaway Reservoir: see **Gassaway Reservoir** [MODOC].

Castle Rocks [PLUMAS]: *peak,* 13 miles southwest of the village of Almanor (lat. 40°05' N, long. 121°20'50" W; sec. 30, T 26 N, R 6 E). Altitude 6440 feet. Named on Jonesville (1958) 15' quadrangle.

Casuse Mountain [MODOC]: *peak,* 6.25 miles south-southeast of Newell (lat. 41°48'05" N, long. 121°20' W; sec. 30, T 46 N, R 6 E). Altitude 4508 feet. Named on Tulelake (1951) 15' quadrangle.

Cate Place [PLUMAS]: *locality,* 7 miles south-southeast of Mount Ingalls (lat. 30°55'45" N, long. 120°34'35" W; sec. 24, T 24 N, R 12 E). Site named on Grizzly Valley (1972) 7.5' quadrangle. Downieville (1897) 30' quadrangle has the name "Cates" at the site.

Cates: see **Cate Place** [PLUMAS].

Catfish Beach [PLUMAS]: *beach,* 2.5 miles east of Chester along Lake Almanor (lat. 40°18'40" N, long. 121°10'30" W; on E line sec. 3, T 28 N, R 7 E). Named on Chester (1979) 7.5' quadrangle.

Catfish Reservoir [LASSEN]:

(1) *lake,* 900 feet long, 6.5 miles north-northeast of Lava Peak (lat. 40°54'50" N, long. 120°49'35" W; sec. 33, T 36 N, R 10 E). Named on Hayden Hill (1956) 15' quadrangle.

(2) *lake,* 1200 feet long, 6 miles east-southeast of the village of Little Valley (lat. 40°52'05" N, long. 121°04'20" W; near W line sec. 27, T 35 N, R 8 E). Named on Little Valley (1957) 15' quadrangle.

Cat Hill [MODOC]: *peak,* 4 miles east-southeast of Crank Mountain (lat. 41°22'15" N, long. 121°04'10" W; at N line sec. 29, T 41 N, R 8 E). Named on Crank Mountain (1962) 15' quadrangle.

Catrell Creek [PLUMAS]: *stream,* flows about 2.25 miles to Willow Creek (5) 6.5 miles south of Bucks Lodge (lat. 39°46'55" N, long. 121°09'25" W; near SE cor. sec. 2, T 22 N, R 7 E). Named on Haskins Valley (1980) 7.5' quadrangle.

Cave Lake [MODOC]: *lake,* 600 feet long, 9 miles north-northwest of Fort Bidwell (lat. 41°58'50" N, long. 120°12'30" W; at SW cor. sec. 36, T 48 N, R 15 E). Named on Fort Bidwell (1962) 15' quadrangle. Hill's (1915) map shows a mining camp called High Grade situated 4000 feet east of Cave Lake. High Grade first had the name "Hoag" for the army scout who first discovered gold at the site (Cook, p. 96). Postal authorities established Hoag post office 7 miles northwest of Fort Bidwell in 1909 and discontinued it in 1911 (Salley, p. 98). They established High Grade post office in 1912, discontinued it in 1913, reestablished it in 1914, and discontinued it in 1918 (Salley, p. 97).

Cave Mountain [LASSEN]: *peak,* 8 miles northwest of Pelican Point (lat. 40°42'05" N, long. 120°51'20" W; on S line sec. 21, T 33 N, R 10 E). Altitude 6578 feet. Named on Antelope Mountain (1956) 15' quadrangle. A large cave is near the summit of the feature (Purdy, 1988, p. 117).

Cedar Creek [LASSEN]: *stream,* flows 19 miles to West Valley Reservoir 10 miles north-northeast of Madeline (lat. 41°10'50" N, long. 120°23'10" W; at N line sec. 32, T 39 N, R 14 E). Named on Boot Lake (1962), Cold Spring Mountain (1962), Emerson Peak (1962), Jess Valley (1962), and Tule Mountain (1967) 7.5' quadrangles.

Cedar Creek [MODOC]: *stream,* flows 7.5 miles to Middle Alkali Lake nearly 3 miles northeast of Cedarville (lat. 41°33'30" N, long. 120°08' W; at N line sec. 34, T 43 N, R 16 E). Named on Cedarville (1962) and Davis Creek (1962) 15' quadrangles.

Cedar Creek [PLUMAS]:

(1) *stream,* flows 1 mile to North Fork Feather River 3.25 miles southwest of Storrie (lat. 39°53'05" N, long. 121°22'05" W). Named on Kimshew Point (1979) and Storrie (1979) 7.5' quadrangles

(2) *stream,* flows 0.5 mile to Butte County 5.5 miles southwest of Storrie (lat. 39°52'15" N, long. 121°24'25" W; at S line sec. 3, T 23 N, R 5 E). Named on Kimshew Point (1979) and Pulga (1979) 7.5' quadrangles.

(3) *stream,* flows 2.5 miles to Middle Fork Feather River 4.5 miles northwest of Blairsden (lat. 39°49'50" N, long. 120°40'20" W; sec. 30, T 23 N, R 12 E). Named on Johnsville (1972) 7.5' quadrangle.

Cedar Flat [PLUMAS]: *area,* nearly 2 miles south-southwest of Bucks Lodge (lat. 39°51'10" N, long. 121°11'10" W; near N line sec. 15, T 23 N, R 7 E). Named on Haskins Valley (1980) 7.5' quadrangle.

Cedar Glen: see **Tobin** [PLUMAS].

Cedar Mountain [MODOC]: *peak,* 11.5 miles south-southeast of the village of Davis Creek (lat. 41°35'20" N, long. 120°16'20" W; near SW cor. sec. 16, T 43 N, R 15 E). Altitude 8152 feet. Named on Davis Creek (1962) 15' quadrangle.

Cedar Pass [MODOC]: *pass,* 13 miles south-southeast of the village of Davis Creek (lat. 41°33'50" N, long. 120°16'05" W; sec. 28, T 43 N, R 15 E). Named on Davis Creek (1962) 15' quadrangle. Preston (1890b, p. 334) used the name "Cedarville Pass" for the feature.

Cedar Pass Campground [MODOC]: *locality,* 13 miles south-southeast of the village of Davis Creek (lat. 41°33'35" N, long. 120°17'35" W; near SE cor. sec. 13, T 43 N, R 14 E); the place is 1.25 miles west of Cedar Pass. Named on Davis Creek (1962) 15' quadrangle.

Cedar Peak: see **Bald Mountain** [MODOC] (1).

Cedar Run Creek [LASSEN]: *stream,* flows 4.5 miles to Big Valley 3.5 miles west-northwest of Bieber (lat. 41°09' N, long. 121°12' W; sec. 7, T 38 N, R 7 E). Named on Bieber (1961) and Fall River Mills (1961) 15' quadrangles. The stream drains Brown Canyon.

Cedar Spring [MODOC]: *spring,* 5 miles northeast of Crank Mountain (lat. 41°25'30" N, long. 121°03'45" W; near E line sec. 5, T 41 N, R 8 E). Named on Crank Mountain (1962) 15' quadrangle.

Cedar Spring [PLUMAS]: *spring,* 6.5 miles west of Milford [LASSEN] (lat. 40°09'15" N, long. 120°29'40" W; near E line sec. 34, T 27 N, R 13 E). Named on Stony Ridge (1978) 7.5' quadrangle.

Cedarville [MODOC]: *town,* 20 miles east of Alturas (lat. 41°31'45" N, long. 120°10'15" W; mainly in sec. 5, 8, T 42 N, R 16 E). Named on Cedarville (1962) 15' quadrangle. Postal authorities established Cedarville post office in 1869 (Frickstad, p. 102). The community first was called Surprise Valley (Pease, p. 75) and Deep Creek (Laird, p. 48). Then in 1867 J.H. Bonner named the town for his former home in Ohio (Gudde, 1949, p. 62).

Cedarville Pass: see **Cedar Pass** [MODOC].

Centerville: see **Alturas** [MODOC].

Centerville Butte: see **Rattlesnake Butte** [MODOC] (2).

Chalk Bluff Reservoir [LASSEN]: *intermittent lake,* 500 feet long, 10 miles north of Wendel (lat. 40°29'20" N, long. 120°13'30" W; sec. 6, T 30 N, R 16 E). Named on Wendel (1954) 15' quadrangle.

Chalk Ford: see **Bieber** [LASSEN].

Chalk Spring [MODOC]: *spring,* 12.5 miles south of Canby (lat. 41° 15'50" N, long. 120°50' W; sec. 33, T 40 N, R 10 E). Named on Canby (1961) 15' quadrangle.

Chambers Creek [PLUMAS]: *stream,* flows nearly 5 miles to North Fork Feather River 3 miles north-northeast of Storrie (lat. 39°57'25" N, long. 121°17'30" W; near S line sec. 3, T 24 N, R 6 E). Named on Storrie (1979) 7.5' quadrangle.

Chambers Peak [PLUMAS]: *peak,* 3.25 miles north of Storrie (lat. 39°57'50" N, long. 121°19'30" W; sec. 5, T 24 N, R 6 E); the peak is 0.5 mile southwest of Chambers Creek. Altitude 6115 feet. Named on Storrie (1979) 7.5' quadrangle.

Champ's [LASSEN]: *locality,* 25 miles northwest of Susanville along Pine Creek (1) (lat. 40°42'30" N, long. 120°57' W). Named on Honey Lake (1893) 1° quadrangle. Called Champ on California Mining Bureau's (1917b) map.

Champs Flat [LASSEN]: *valley,* 10.5 miles west-northwest of Pelican Point (lat. 40°42'30" N, long. 120°55' W). Named on Antelope Mountain (1956) 15' quadrangle. The name is for Mr. Champlin, who grazed sheep at the place in the 1880's (Purdy, 1988, p. 118).

Chandler Creek [PLUMAS]: *stream,* flows 2.5 miles to Greenhorn Creek 3.5 miles east-northeast of Quincy (lat. 39°57'10" N, long. 120°53'10" W; near S line sec. 8, T 24 N, R 10 E). Named on Quincy (1950) and Spring Garden (1950) 7.5' quadrangles.

Chaparral Hill [LASSEN]: *ridge,* west-northwest-trending, 1.5 miles long, 8 miles northeast of Westwood (lat. 40°23'05" N, long. 120° 53'20" W). Named on Pegleg Mountain (1980) 7.5' quadrangle.

Chaparral Hill [PLUMAS]: *peak,* 6 miles northwest of the village of Meadow Valley (lat. 39°59'55" N, long. 121°07'55" W). Named on Bidwell Bar (1897) 30' quadrangle.

Charles Creek [PLUMAS]: *stream,* flows 3.5 miles to Last Chance Creek (2) 3.5 miles south of McKesick Peak (lat. 40°02'50" N, long. 120°14'20" W; near E line sec. 1, T 25 N, R 15 E). Named on Ferris Creek (1977) and McKesick Peak (1978) 7.5' quadrangles.

Charles Valley [PLUMAS]: *valley,* 1.5 miles northwest of Portola (lat. 39°49'35" N, long. 120°29'15" W; mainly in sec. 26, T 23 N, R 13 E). Named on Portola (1972) 7.5' quadrangle. Called Charlies Valley on Sierraville (1894) 30' quadrangle.

Charles Valley Creek [PLUMAS]: *stream,* flows 4.25 miles to Humbug Creek (2) 2 miles northwest of Portola (lat. 39°49'35" N, long. 120°29'50" W; near E line sec. 27, T 23 N, R 13 E); the stream goes through Charles Valley. Named on Portola (1972) 7.5' quadrangle.

Charlie Spring [LASSEN]: *spring,* 5 miles southwest of Litchfield (lat. 40°20'20" N, long. 120°27'35" W; sec. 25, T 29 N, R 13 E). Named on Standish (1972) 7.5' quadrangle.

Charlies Valley: see **Charles Valley** [PLUMAS].

Chase Canyon [LASSEN]: *canyon,* drained by a stream that flows 3.5 miles to Madeline Plains 7 miles west-southwest of Termo (lat. 40°49'10" N, long. 120°34'30" W; near W line sec. 12, T 34 N, R 12 E). Named on Grasshopper Valley (1954) 15' quadrangle.

Chases [PLUMAS]: *locality,* 6 miles east-southeast of Mount Ingalls in Red Clover Valley (lat. 39°58' N, long. 120°31'10" W). Named on Downieville (1897) 30' quadrangle.

Chase Valley [LASSEN]: *valley,* 4.5 miles southeast of Adin [MODOC] (lat. 41°09' N, long. 120°53' W; in and near sec. 1, 12, T 38 N, R 9 E). Named on Adin (1962) 15' quadrangle.

Chat: see **Chats** [LASSEN].

Chats [LASSEN]: *locality,* 2 miles east-southeast of Beckwith Pass (present

Beckwourth Pass) along Nevada-California-Oregon Railroad (lat. 39°46'30" N, long. 120°04'30" W). Named on Sierraville (1894) 30' quadrangle. Postal authorities established Chat post office 3.5 miles southeast of Summit [PLUMAS] post office in 1885, discontinued it in 1894, reestablished it in 1896, and discontinued it in 1900; the name is from an abbreviation of an Indian word for the digger pine (Salley, p. 42). They established Gest post office 8 miles north of Chat post office in 1893, moved it 0.5 mile north in 1894, and discontinued it in 1895; the name was for Erasmus Gest, manager of Nevada-California-Oregon Railroad (Salley, p. 84). California Mining Bureau's (1910) map shows a place called Cuba located about 2 miles south of Chat; California Mining Bureau's (1917a) map has the name "Plumas Jc." at the same place. Postal authorities established Cuba post office 5.5 miles south of Summit [PLUMAS] post office in 1897 and discontinued it in 1907 (Salley p. 53). They established Plumas Junction post office at the junction of Nevada-California-Oregon Railroad and Sierra and Mohawk Railway in 1908, discontinued it in 1909, reestablished it in 1913, and discontinued it in 1918 (Salley, p. 174). They established Junction House post office 6 miles southeast of Summit [PLUMAS] post office in 1869, discontinued it for a time in 1874, discontinued it in 1876, reestablished it with the name "Junction" in 1879, discontinued it for a time in 1881, and discontinued it finally in 1882; the place was at the junction of the trail that ran from Reno, Nevada, to Oregon with the trail that went over Beckwourth Pass—later the place was at the junction of Nevada-California-Oregon Railroad with Sierra and Mohawk Railway (Salley, p. 108-109).

Cheney Creek [LASSEN]: *stream,* flows 6.5 miles to Susan River 5 miles west of Susanville (lat. 40°24'10" N, long. 120°44'55" W; sec. 4, T 29 N, R 11 E). Named on Susanville (1954) 15' quadrangle, and on Fredonyer Pass (1980) 7.5' quadrangle.

Cherry Creek [LASSEN]: *stream,* flows 4.25 miles to Secret Creek nearly 7 miles north-northeast of Karlo (lat. 40°38'15" N, long. 120°15'25" W; at E line sec. 15, T 32 N, R 15 E). Named on Karlo (1954) and Shinn Mountain (1954) 15' quadrangles.

Cherry Creek [MODOC]:

(1) *stream,* flows 2 miles to South Fork Fitzhugh Creek 16 miles southeast of Alturas (lat. 41°19'10" N, long. 120°19'40" W; sec. 11, T 40 N, R 14 E). Named on Soup Creek (1963) 7.5' quadrangle.

(2) *stream,* flows 2 miles to Surprise Valley 2.5 miles south-southwest of Cedarville (lat. 41°29'55" N, long. 120°11'30" W; sec. 19, T 42 N, R 16 E). Named on Warren Peak (1963) 7.5' quadrangle.

Cherry Hill [PLUMAS]: *peak,* 1.5 miles southeast of Caribou (lat. 40°03'40" N, long. 121°08'10" W; near E line sec. 36, T 26 N, R 7 E). Altitude 5764 feet. Named on Caribou (1979) 7.5' quadrangle.

Cherry Mountain [LASSEN]: *ridge,* generally south-southeast-trending, 3 miles long, 13 miles southeast of Observation Peak (lat. 40°37' N, long. 120°03'15" W). Named on Shinn Mountain (1954) 15' quadrangle.

Cherry Spring [LASSEN]:

(1) *spring,* 16 miles south-southeast of Observation Peak (lat. 40° 33'25" N, long. 120°05'10" W; near SE cor. sec. 7, T 31 N, R 17 E). Named on Shinn Mountain (1954) 15' quadrangle.

(2) *spring,* 10 miles east-northeast of Wendel (lat. 40°23'30" N, long. 120°03'25" W; near W line sec. 10, T 29 N, R 17 E). Named on Wendel (1954) 15' quadrangle.

Cherry Spring [MODOC]: *spring,* 10 miles south of Canby (lat. 41° 17'55" N, long. 120°51'50" W; at N line sec. 19, T 40 N, R 10 E). Named on Canby (1961) 15' quadrangle.

Chester [PLUMAS]: *town,* 30 miles north-northwest of Quincy along Lake Almanor (lat. 40°18'40" N, long. 121°13'30" W; in and near sec. 5, 8, T 28 N, R 7 E). Named on Chester (1979) 7.5' quadrangle. Postal authorities established Chester post office in 1894 and moved it 1.5 miles west in 1908 (Salley, p. 42). The place first was called Big Meadows; two early settlers, Bert Johnson from Chester, Missouri, and Oscar Martin, from Chester, Vermont, gave the name "Chester" to the place (Hanna, p. 62). Postal authorities established Wonderland post office at a vacation resort located 12 miles northwest of Chester in 1924 and discontinued it in 1946 (Salley, p. 242).

Chicago Ravine [PLUMAS]: *canyon,* drained by a stream that flows nearly 2 miles to Onion Valley Creek 10 miles south of Quincy (lat. 39°47'45" N, long. 120°56'30" W; sec. 2, T 22 N, R 9 E). Named on Onion Valley (1950) 7.5' quadrangle.

Chicken Spring [LASSEN]: *spring,* 12.5 miles north-northeast of Lava Peak (lat. 40°58'40" N, long. 120°45'35" W; at SE cor. sec. 1, T 36 N, R 10 E). Named on Hayden Hill (1956) 15' quadrangle.

Chico Flat [LASSEN]: *area,* 5.5 miles east-southeast of the village of Little Valley (lat. 40°51'10" N, long. 121°05'25" W; sec. 32, 33, T 35 N, R 8 E). Named on Little Valley (1957) 15' quadrangle.

Chilcoot [PLUMAS]: *village,* 17 miles east of Portola (lat. 39°47'50" N, long. 120°08'20" W; sec. 36, T 23 N, R 16 E). Named on Chilcoot (1979) 7.5' quadrangle. Postal authorities established Chilcoot post office in 1898, moved it 1.5 miles east into Lassen County in 1909, and returned it to Plumas County in 1910 (Salley, p. 42). The name is from Chilcoot Pass of Alaskan gold-rush fame (Hanna, p. 62). California Mining Bureau's (1909b) map shows a place called Hindu located about 7 miles west of Chilcoot along Western Pacific Railroad. California Division of Highways' (1934) map has the form "Hindoo" for the name.

Chilcoot Campground [PLUMAS]: *locality,* 5 miles north-northwest of Chilcoot along Little Last Chance Creek (lat. 39°51'55" N, long. 120°09'55" W; near NE cor. sec. 10, T 23 N, R 16 E). Named on Chilcoot (1979) 7.5' quadrangle.

Chimney Canyon [LASSEN]: *canyon,* drained by a stream that flows 2.25 miles to Honey Lake Valley 6 miles northwest of McKesick Peak (lat. 40°05'15" N, long. 120°11' W; near S line sec. 21, T 26 N, R 16 E). Named on McKesick Peak (1978) 7.5' quadrangle.

Chimney Rock [PLUMAS]: *relief feature,* 11.5 miles south of Quincy (lat. 39°46'20" N, long. 120°57'40" W; near N line sec. 15, T 22 N, R 9 E). Named on Onion Valley (1950) 7.5' quadrangle.

China Bar [PLUMAS]:

(1) *locality,* nearly 6 miles north-northwest of Twain along North Fork Feather River (lat. 40°05'45" N, long. 121°07'20" W; sec. 19, T 26 N, R 8 E). Named on Twain (1980) 7.5' quadrangle.

(2) *locality,* less than 1 mile east of Twain along East Branch of North Fork Feather River (lat. 40°01'10" N, long. 121°03'25" W; sec. 23, T 25 N, R 8 E). Named on Twain (1980) 7.5' quadrangle.

(3) *locality,* 2.25 miles south of La Porte along Slate Creek (3) on Plumas-Sierra County line (lat. 39°38'55" N, long. 120°59' W; sec. 28, T 21 N, R 9 E). Named on La Porte (1951) 7.5' quadrangle.

China Creek [PLUMAS]: *stream,* flows about 1.25 miles to Rock Creek (4) 1.5 miles west-northwest of Storrie (lat. 39°55'40" N, long. 121°21'05" W). Named on Storrie (1979) 7.5' quadrangle.

China Gulch [PLUMAS]:

(1) *canyon,* drained by a stream that flows nearly 2 miles to Lights Creek 4.5 miles east-southeast of Moonlight Peak (lat. 40°12'40" N, long. 120°45'55" W; sec. 8, T 27 N, R 11 E). Named on Kettle Rock (1972) and Moonlight Peak (1980) 7.5' quadrangles.

(2) *canyon,* drained by a stream that flows about 2 miles to Willow Creek (5) 5.5 miles south of Bucks Lodge (lat. 39°47'50" N, long. 121°09'40" W; near S line sec. 35, T 23 N, R 7 E). Named on Haskins Valley (1980) 7.5' quadrangle. On Bidwell Bar (1897) 30' quadrangle, an inhabited place in the canyon has the name "China Gulch."

China Ravine [PLUMAS]: *canyon,* drained by a stream that flows less than 1 mile to Mosquito Creek 3.5 miles west of Caribou (lat. 40°04'55" N, long. 121°13'05" W; near S line sec. 20, T 26 N, R 7 E). Named on Caribou (1979) 7.5' quadrangle.

Chip Creek: see **Chips Creek** [PLUMAS].

Chipmunk Creek [PLUMAS]: *stream,* flows 3.25 miles to North Valley Creek 4.5 miles west of Storrie (lat. 39°55'40" N, long. 121°24'10" W; near N line sec. 22, T 24 N, R 5 E). Named on Kimshew Point (1979) 7.5' quadrangle.

Chipmunk Spring [PLUMAS]: *spring,* 9.5 miles east of Kettle Rock (lat. 40°09'25" N, long. 120°32'55" W; near W line sec. 32, T 27 N, R 13 E). Named on Antelope Lake (1972) 7.5' quadrangle.

Chips Creek [PLUMAS]: *stream,* flows 8 miles to North Fork Feather River 16 miles south-southwest of the village of Almanor (lat. 40°00' N, long. 121°16'10" W; near N line sec. 26, T 25 N, R 6 E). Named on Jonesville (1958) 15' quadrangle. Called Chip Creek on Lassen Peak (1894) 1° quadrangle.

Chips Lake [PLUMAS]: *lake,* 700 feet long, 17 miles south-southwest of the village of Almanor (lat. 40°00'30" N, long. 121°19'30" W; near E line sec. 20, T 25 N, R 6 E). Named on Jonesville (1958) 15' quadrangle.

Chris Creek [PLUMAS]: *stream,* flows 2.5 miles to Poplar Creek nearly 7 miles west-northwest of Blairsden (lat. 39°48'55" N, long. 120°44'05" W; sec. 34, T 23 N, R 11 E). Named on Johnsville (1972) 7.5' quadrangle. Called Little Poplar Creek on Dowieville (1897) 30' quadrangle.

Chucks Rock [PLUMAS]: *relief feature,* 3.5 miles north of Bucks Lodge (lat. 39°55'30" N, long. 121°11'10" W; sec. 22, T 24 N, R 7 E). Named on Bucks Lake (1979) 7.5' quadrangle.

Cinder Butte: see **Cinder Cone** [LASSEN].

Cinder Cone [LASSEN]: *crater,* 12 miles southwest of Cal Mountain (lat. 40°32'50" N, long. 121°19'10" W; near W line sec. 16, T 31 N, R 6 E). Named on Prospect Peak (1957) 15' quadrangle. The feature was called Black Butte as early as 1845 (Diller, p. 19), and it also was called Cinder Butte (Schulz, p. 11).

Cinder Spring [PLUMAS]: *spring,* 12.5 miles southeast of Kettle Rock (lat. 40°01'30" N, long. 120°33'10" W; sec. 17, T 25 N, R 13 E). Named on Babcock Peak (1972) 7.5' quadrangle.

City Rock [MODOC]: *relief feature,* 3.5 miles west-southwest of Canby (lat. 41°25'20" N, long. 120°56' W; sec. 4, T 41 N, R 9 E). Named on Canby (1961) 15' quadrangle.

Claim Creek [PLUMAS]: *stream,* flows 3.5 miles to Smith Creek (2) 2.5 miles southwest of Blairsden (lat. 39°46' N, long. 120°38'45" W; near E line sec. 17, T 22 N, R 12 E). Named on Gold Lake (1981) 7.5' quadrangle. The name is from a mining claim situated on the west side of the canyon of the stream (United States Board on Geographic Names, 1982b, p. 1).

Claremont [PLUMAS]: *peak,* 3.5 miles south of Quincy (lat. 39° 53' N, long. 120°56'40" W; sec. 2, T 23 N, R 9 E). Altitude 6994 feet. Named on Quincy (1950) 7.5' quadrangle. Called Clermont Hill on Downieville (1897) 30' quadrangle.

Claremont: see **East Claremont** [PLUMAS].

Claremont Creek [PLUMAS]: *stream,* flows 2 miles to Middle Fork Feather River 6 miles south of Quincy (lat. 39°51'15" N, long. 120° 57'10" W; near E line sec. 15, T 23 N, R 9 E); the stream heads near Claremont and East Claremont. Named on Onion Valley (1950) 7.5' quadrangle.

Claireville Flat [PLUMAS]: *area,* 4 miles east of Blairsden (lat. 39° 46'35" N, long. 120°32'35" W; at N line sec. 17, T 22 N, R 13 E). Named on Blairsden (1972) 7.5' quadrangle.

Clark [LASSEN]: *locality,* 5 miles northwest of Milford (lat. 40° 14' N, long. 120°26'30" W). Named on Honey Lake (1893) 1° quadrangle. Stony Ridge (1978) 7.5' quadrangle shows Clark ranch near the site.

Clark Canyon [MODOC]: *canyon,* drained by a stream that flows 3.25 miles to the stream in Messenger Canyon 4.25 miles east-northeast of Adin (lat. 41°13' N, long. 120°52'10" W; sec. 18, T 39 N, R 10 E). Named on Adin (1962) 15' quadrangle.

Clark Reservoir [LASSEN]: *water feature,* 10 miles west of Bieber (lat. 41°07'40" N, long. 121°19'50" W; at W line sec. 18, T 38 N, R 6 E). Named on Fall River Mills (1961) 15' quadrangle.

Clarks Creek [PLUMAS]: *stream,* flows 12 miles to Last Chance Creek (2) 12 miles east of Kettle Peak (lat. 40°07' N, long. 120° 30'15" W; near S line sec. 10, T 26 N, R 13 E). Named on Antelope Lake (1972), Babcock Peak (1972), Janesville (1972), and Stony Ridge (1978) 7.5' quadrangles. Called Thompson Creek on Kettle Rock (1950), Milford (1950) and Susanville (1954) 15' quadrangles; United States Board on Geographic Names (1974b, p. 2) gave this name as a variant, and noted that the name "Clarks" is for an early ranch family.

Clarks Creek: see **Thompson Creek** [PLUMAS] (1).

Clarks Peak [PLUMAS]: *peak,* 12 miles east-northeast of Kettle Rock (lat. 40°12'25" N, long. 120°30'50" W; at S line sec. 9, T 27 N, R 13 E). Altitude 7179 feet. Named on Antelope Lake (1972) 7.5' quadrangle.

Clark Spring [MODOC]: *spring,* 7 miles east-northeast of Adin (lat. 41°13'50" N, long. 120°48'45" W; sec. 15, T 39 N, R 10 E). Named on Adin (1962) 15' quadrangle.

Clarks Ravine [PLUMAS]: *canyon,* drained by a stream that flows 1.5 miles to Slate Creek (3) 2.25 miles south of La Porte (lat. 39° 38'55" N, long. 120°59' W; sec. 28, T 21 N, R 9 E). Named on La Porte (1951) 7.5' quadrangle.

Clarks Reservoir [MODOC]: *intermittent lake,* 0.5 mile long, 17 miles south-southwest of Alturas (lat. 41°15'50" N, long. 120°41'20" W; on E line sec. 34, T 40 N, R 11 E). Named on Alturas (1961) 15' quadrangle.

Clarks Valley [LASSEN]: *valley,* 11 miles east of Madeline (lat. 41° 04'05" N, long. 120°15'10" W). Named on Boot Lake (1962) and Cold Spring Mountain (1962) 15' quadrangles.

Clarks Valley: see **Clark Valley** [LASSEN].

Clark Valley [LASSEN]: *valley,* 2.25 miles north of the village of Little Valley (lat. 40°55'40" N, long. 121°10'20" W; sec. 28, T 36 N, R 7 E). Named on Little Valley (1957) 15' quadrangle. Called Clarks Valley on Lassen Peak (1894) 1° quadrangle, and United States Board on Geographic Names (1983d, p. 4) approved this name.

Clear Creek [LASSEN]:

(1) *stream,* flows 1 mile to Hamilton Branch [LASSEN-PLUMAS] 3 miles west-southwest of Westwood (lat. 40°17'30" N, long. 121° 03'10" W; near N line sec. 14, T 25 N, R 8 E). Named on Westwood West (1980) 7.5' quadrangle.

(2) *village,* 2.5 miles west-southwest of Westwood (lat. 40°17'45" N, long. 121°02'55" W; sec. 11, T 28 N, R 8 E); the village is along Clear Creek (1). Named on Westwood West (1980) 7.5' quadrangle.

Clear Creek [PLUMAS]:

(1) *stream,* flows 3.25 miles to North Fork Feather River nearly 6 miles north-northwest of Twain (lat. 40°05'45" N, long. 121°07'20" W; sec. 19, T 26 N, R 8 E). Named on Almanor (1979), Caribou (1979), and Twain (1980) 7.5' quadrangles.

(2) *stream,* flows 3.5 miles to Spanish Creek (1) 5.5 miles south-southeast of Crescent Mills (lat. 40°01'35" N, long. 120°57'40" W; sec. 15, T 25 N, R 9 E). Named on Crescent Mills (1980) 7.5' quadrangle.

(3) *stream,* flows nearly 4 miles to Mill Creek (1) 5.5 miles south-southwest of Caribou (lat. 40°00'10" N, long. 121°10'45" W; near S line sec. 22, T 25 N, R 7 E). Named on Bucks Lake (1979) 7.5' quadrangle.

(4) *stream,* flows 3.25 miles to join Big Creek and form Meadow Valley Creek 1.5 miles west-southwest of the village of Meadow Valley (lat. 39°55'25" N, long. 121°05' W; at E line sec. 21, T 24 N, R 8 E). Named on Bucks Lake (1979) and Meadow Valley (1980) 7.5' quadrangles.

(5) *stream,* flows 2.5 miles to Wolf Creek 2.25 miles east of Canyondam (lat. 40°10'05" N, long. 121°01'40" W; sec. 25, T 27 N, R 8 E). Named on Canyondam (1979) 7.5' quadrangle.

Clear Creek Junction [PLUMAS]: *locality,* 8.5 miles east of Chester along Western Pacific Railroad at the junction with Almanor Railroad (lat. 40°17'40" N, long. 121°03'50" W; near S line sec. 10, T 28 N, R 8 E); the place is less than 1 mile west-southwest of the village of Clear Creek [LASSEN]. Named on Westwood West (1980) 7.5' quadrangle.

Clear Lake [MODOC]: *lake,* 0.5 mile long, 20 miles southeast of Alturas along Mill Creek (1) (lat. 41°16'30" N, long. 120°16'35" W; sec. 28, T 40 N, R 15 E). Named on Soup Creek (1963) 7.5' quadrangle.

Clear Lake: see **Clear Lake Reservoir** [MODOC].

Clear Lake Hills [MODOC]: *ridge,* south- to southeast-trending, 4 miles long, 6 miles northwest of Double Head Mountain (lat. 41° 49'45" N, long. 121°14' W); the ridge is southwest of Clear Lake Reservoir. Named on Clear Lake Reservoir (1951) 15' quadrangle.

Clear Lake Reservoir [MODOC]: *lake,* behind a dam on Lost River 12 miles north-northeast of Double Head Mountain (lat. 41°55'35" N, long. 121°04'30" W; sec. 8, T 47 N, R 8 E). Named on Clear Lake Reservoir (1951) 15' quadrangle. Williamson and Abbott's (1855) map shows Wright Lake at the place, and Steptoe's (1855) map shows Ampa Lake there. Modoc Lava-Bed (1892) 1° quadrangle shows a natural lake, called Clear Lake, in what now is the west part of present Clear Lake Reservoir, and shows an inhabited place called Clear Lake situated just north of the natural lake (lat. 41°54' N, long. 121°11' W). Postal authorities established Clear Lake post office 12 miles northeast of Cornell in 1875, discontinued it in 1886, reestablished it in 1887, moved it 13 miles west in 1893, and discontinued it the same year (Salley, p. 45).

Clear Stream [PLUMAS]: *water feature,* joins Spanish Creek (1) 1.5 miles north-northeast of Quincy (lat. 39°57'20" N, long. 120°55'50" W; near W line sec. 12, T 24 N, R 9 E). Named on Quincy (1950) 7.5' quadrangle.

Clearwater Creek [PLUMAS]: *stream,* flows 2.25 miles to Red Clover Creek 8 miles south-southeast of Kettle Rock (lat. 40°02'25" N, long. 120°39' W; sec. 8, T 25 N, R 12 E). Named on Genesee Valley (1972) 7.5' quadrangle.

Cleghorn Bar [PLUMAS]: *locality,* 3.5 miles northeast of Dogwood Peak along Middle Fork Feather River (lat. 39°49'05" N, long. 121°00'30" W). Named on Dogwood Peak (1979) 7.5' quadrangle.

Cleghorn Bar Campground [PLUMAS]: *locality,* 3.25 miles northeast of Dogwood Peak along Middle Fork Feather River (lat. 39° 49'10" N, long. 121°00'50" W); the place is less than 0.5 mile west-northwest of Cleghorn Bar. Named on Dogwood Peak (1979) 7.5' quadrangle.

Cleghorn Creek [LASSEN]: *stream,* flows nearly 6 miles to Eagle Lake 6.25 miles north-northeast of Pelican Point (lat. 40°43'20" N, long. 120°43'05" W; sec. 15, T 33 N, R 11 E). Named on Antelope Mountain (1956), Fredonyer Peak (1954), and Hayden Hill (1956) 15' quadrangles.

Cleghorn Flat [LASSEN]: *area,* 9.5 miles southwest of Termo (lat. 40°46'20" N, long. 120°35'35" W; around NW cor. sec. 35, T 34 N, R 12 E). Named on Grasshopper Valley (1954) 15' quadrangle. The name commemorates Peter Morrison Cleghorn, who ran sheep at the place in the 1870's and 1880's (Purdy, 1988, p. 118).

Cleghorn Reservoir [LASSEN]: *lake,* 3700 feet long, 6 miles southeast of Lava Peak (lat. 40°46'35" N, long. 120°48'15" W; around SW cor. sec. 25, T 34 N, R 10 E). Named on Hayden Hill (1956) 15' quadrangle.

Cleghorn Reservoir: see **Little Cleghorn Reservoir** [LASSEN].

Clermont Hill: see **Claremont** [PLUMAS].

Cliffs: see **The Cliffs** [MODOC].

Clinton: see **Susanville** [LASSEN].

Clio [PLUMAS]: *village,* 23 miles southeast of Quincy (lat. 39°44'35" N, long. 120°34'50" W; sec. 25, T 22 N, R 12 E). Named on Clio (1981) 7.5' quadrangle. Called Wash on Downieville (1897) 30' quadrangle. Postal authorities established Wash post office in 1875, moved it from the home of the postmaster to the railroad depot and changed the name to Clio in 1904 (Salley, p. 235). The name "Wash" was for a pioneer; according to local legend, the name "Clio" was from the brand name of a heating stove (Gudde, 1949, p. 70-71).

Cloud Canyon [MODOC]: *canyon,* drained by a stream that flows 1.5 miles to lowlands along Goose Lake (1) 5 miles northeast of Willow Ranch (lat. 41°57'40" N, long. 120°17'45" W; sec. 36, T 48 N, R 14 E). Named on Willow Ranch (1962) 15' quadrangle.

Clover Butte [LASSEN]: *hill,* 12.5 miles north of Westwood (lat. 40° 28'55" N, long. 121°02'50" W; at N line sec. 11, T 30 N, R 8 E); the hill is east of Clover Valley (2). Altitude 6190 feet. Named on Swain Mountain (1979) 7.5' quadrangle.

Clover Swale [MODOC]: *area,* 5 miles east-northeast of Canby (lat. 41°28'30" N, long. 120°46'45" W; mainly in sec. 14, 23, T 42 N, R 10 E). Named on Canby (1961) 15' quadrangle.

Clover Swale: see **Adin** [MODOC].

Clover Swale Creek [MODOC]: *stream,* flows 12.5 miles to Pit River 5 miles east-southeast of Canby (lat. 41°25'25" N, long. 120° 47' W; sec. 2, T 41 N, R 10 E); the stream goes through Clover Swale. Named on Canby (1961) 15' quadrangle.

Clover Valley [LASSEN]:

(1) *valley,* 3 miles south-southeast of Lava Peak (lat. 40°47'15" N, long.

120°52'20" W; on S line sec. 20, T 34 N, R 10 E). Named on Hayden Hill (1956) 15' quadrangle.

(2) *valley,* 13 miles north-northwest of Westwood (lat. 40°29' N, long. 121°03'45" W). Named on Swain Mountain (1979) 7.5' quadrangle.

Clover Valley: see **Red Clover Valley** [PLUMAS].

Coalpit Canyon [MODOC]: *canyon,* drained by a stream that flows 1.5 miles to Cottonwood Creek (1) 5 miles northeast of Willow Ranch (lat. 41°56'45" N, long. 120°17'05" W; sec. 17, T 47 N, R 15 E). Named on Willow Ranch (1962) 15' quadrangle.

Coal Valley Boiling Springs: see **Canby** [MODOC].

Cochran Hill [LASSEN]: *peak,* 2.25 miles south of Madeline (lat. 41°01'10" N, long. 120°28'25" W; at NE cor. sec. 28, T 37 N, R 13 E). Altitude 5907 feet. Named on Madeline (1962) 7.5' quadrangle.

Coffee Mill Gulch [MODOC]: *canyon,* drained by a stream that flows 2.5 miles to Washington Creek 8.5 miles northeast of Crank Mountain (lat. 41°27'15" N, long. 121°00'45" W; sec. 26, T 42 N, R 8 E). Named on Crank Mountain (1962) 15' quadrangle.

Coffee Mill Spring [MODOC]: *spring,* 4 miles north of South Mountain (lat. 41°53'45" N, long. 120°37'40" W; near SE cor. sec. 19, T 47 N, R 12 E). Named on South Mountain (1962) 15' quadrangle.

Cogswell Creek: see **Cogswell Ravine** [PLUMAS].

Cogswell Ravine [PLUMAS]: *canyon,* drained by a stream that flows 2.5 miles to Jackson Creek 6.25 miles northwest of Blairsden (lat. 39°51'05" N, long. 120°41'20" W; at S line sec. 13, T 23 N, R 11 E). Named on Johnsville (1972) 7.5' quadrangle. Downieville (1897) 30' quadrangle has the name "Cogswell Creek." for the stream in the canyon.

Cold Brook Creek [PLUMAS]: *stream,* flows 2 miles to North Fork Feather River 0.25 mile south-southwest of Caribou (lat. 40°04'35" N, long. 121°09'25" W; sec. 26, T 26 N, R 7 E). Named on Caribou (1979) 7.5' quadrangle.

Cold Creek [MODOC]: *stream,* flows about 3.25 miles to Willow Creek (3) 6.25 miles south-southeast of Willow Ranch (lat. 41°49'30" N, long. 120°17'40" W; near E line sec. 13, T 46 N, R 14 E). Named on Willow Ranch (1962) 15' quadrangle.

Cold Spring Creek [LASSEN]: *stream,* flows 2 miles to the upper end of Cold Spring Valley 15 miles north of Observation Peak (lat. 40°59'30" N, long. 120°14'35" W; near N line sec. 14, T 36 N, R 15 E); the stream heads at Cold Spring Mountain. Named on Observation Peak (1954) 15' quadrangle, and on Cold Spring Mountain (1962) 7.5' quadrangle. A second stream that heads in the lower part of Cold Spring Valley and flows into Madeline Plains also has the name "Cold Spring Creek," but is unconnected on the surface to the first Cold Spring Creek. This second Cold Spring Creek and present Dry Creek (1) together are called Red Rock Creek on Honey Lake (1893) 1° quadrangle.

Cold Spring Hill [PLUMAS]: *peak,* 6.5 miles north-northeast of Twain (lat. 40°06'55" N, long. 121°02'30" W; near NE cor. sec. 14, T 26 N, R 8 E). Altitude 6260 feet. Named on Twain (1980) 7.5' quadrangle.

Cold Spring Mountain [LASSEN]: *ridge,* generally west-northwest-trending, 1 mile long, 11.5 miles east of Madeline (lat. 41°01'45" N, long. 120°15'35" W; mainly in sec. 34, T 37 N, R 15 E). Named on Cold Spring Mountain (1962) 7.5' quadrangle.

Cold Spring Ravine [PLUMAS]: *canyon,* drained by a stream that flows nearly 1 mile to East Branch of North Fork Feather River 6 miles south-southwest of Caribou (lat. 40°00'35" N, long. 121°13'05" W; sec. 20, T 25 N, R 7 E). Named on Caribou (1979) 7.5' quadrangle.

Cold Spring Valley [LASSEN]: *valley,* 13 miles north of Observation Peak (lat. 40°57'30" N, long. 120°13' W). Named on Observation Peak (1954) 15' quadrangle.

Cold Stream [PLUMAS]: *stream,* flows 2.5 miles to Indian Creek (2) 5.5 miles east of Kettle Rock (lat. 40°09'45" N, long. 120°37'20" W; at S line sec. 27, T 27 N, R 12 E). Named on Antelope Lake (1972) and Kettle Rock (1972) 7.5' quadrangles.

Cold Water Creek [PLUMAS]: *stream,* flows 3 miles to Nelson Creek 9.5 miles southeast of Quincy (lat. 39°49'40" N, long. 120° 49'55" W). Named on Blue Nose Mountain (1951) 7.5' quadrangle.

Coldwater Creek [PLUMAS]:

(1) *stream,* flows nearly 3 miles to Red Clover Creek 3 miles east of Mount Ingalls (lat. 39°59'20" N, long. 120°34'10" W; near SE cor. sec. 25, T 25 N, R 12 E). Named on Grizzly Valley (1972) 7.5' quadrangle.

(2) *stream,* formed by the confluence of East Branch and West Branch, flows 4.5 miles to Little North Fork of Middle Fork Feather River 6.5 miles south-southwest of Bucks Lodge (lat. 39° 47'50" N, long. 121°14'50" W; at SW cor. sec. 31, T 23 N, R 7 E). Named on Haskins Valley (1980) 7.5' quadrangle. East Branch is 1 mile long and West Branch is 1.5 miles long; both branches are named on Haskins Valley (1980) 7.5' quadrangle.

Coldwater Spring [PLUMAS]: *spring,* 1.5 miles southeast of Mount Ingalls (lat. 49°58'40" N, long. 120°36'30" W; near E line sec. 34, T 25 N, R 12 E); the spring is near the head of Coldwater Creek (1). Named on Grizzly Valley (1972) 7.5' quadrangle.

Cole Creek [MODOC]: *stream,* flows 2 miles to Emerson Creek 2.5 miles south of Eagleville (lat. 41°16'35" N, long. 120°07'15" W; sec. 2, T 39 N, R 16 E). Named on Eagle Peak (1963) and Eagleville (1963) 7.5' quadrangles.

Cole Peak [MODOC]: *peak,* nearly 4 miles southwest of Eagleville (lat. 41°16'40" N, long. 120°10' W; sec. 4, T 39 N, R 16 E); the peak is near the head of Cole Creek. Named on Eagle Peak (1963) 7.5' quadrangle. Preston (1890b, p. 332) used the name "Cole's Peak" for the feature.

Colman Lake [LASSEN]: *lake,* 1900 feet long, 8.5 miles south of Pelican Point (lat. 40°30'50" N, long. 120°42'55" W; near S line sec. 27, T 31 N, R 11 E). Named on Fredonyer Peak (1954) 15' quadrangle.

Comfort Cabin Springs [MODOC]: *spring,* 12 miles west of Likely (lat. 41°11'10" N, long. 120°43'45" W; sec. 29, T 39 N, R 11 W). Named on Likely (1962) 15' quadrangle.

Compton Spring [LASSEN]: *spring,* 8 miles west-northwest of the village of Little Valley (lat. 40°57'05" N, long. 121°18'35" W; near SW cor. sec. 17, T 36 N, R 6 E). Named on Jellico (1957) 15' quadrangle.

Con Camp Spring [PLUMAS]: *spring,* 1.5 miles south-southeast of Squaw Valley Peak (lat. 40°00'25" N, long. 120°25'15" W; near W line sec. 23, T 25 N, R 14 E). Named on Squaw Valley Peak (1977) 7.5' quadrangle.

Cone Lake [LASSEN]: *lake,* 400 feet long, 8.5 miles west-southwest of Cal Mountain (lat. 40°33'10" N, long. 121°12'15" W; sec. 16, T 31 N, R 7 E). Named on Harvey Mountain (1956) 15' quadrangle.

Cone Mountain [LASSEN]: *peak,* 3 miles northeast of Cal Mountain (lat. 40°41'50" N, long. 121°07' W; sec. 30, T 33 N, R 8 E). Altitude 6647 feet. Named on Harvey Mountain (1956) 15' quadrangle.

Conklin Canyon [MODOC]: *canyon,* drained by a stream that flows 1 mile to Surprise Valley 6 miles south of Cedarville (lat. 41°26'35" N, long. 120°10' W; at N line sec. 8, T 41 N, R 16 E). Named on Warren Peak (1963) 7.5' quadrangle.

Conklin Park Campground [PLUMAS]: *locality,* 2.25 miles northeast of Squaw Valley Peak along Willow Creek (3) (lat. 40° 02'50" N, long. 120°22' W; near W line sec. 1, T 25 N, R 14 E). Named on Ferris Creek (1977) 7.5' quadrangle.

Conklin Spring [MODOC]: *spring,* 12 miles south of Canby (lat. 41° 16'10" N, long. 120°55'10" W; near N line sec. 34, T 40 N, R 9 E). Named on Canby (1961) 15' quadrangle.

Conlan Spring [MODOC]: *spring,* 6.5 miles east of Fort Bidwell (lat. 41°51'55" N, long. 120°01'35" W; at S line sec. 9, T 46 N, R 17 E). Named on Fort Bidwell (1962) 15' quadrangle.

Conman: see **Westwood** [LASSEN].

Consignee Creek [PLUMAS]: *stream,* flows 3.25 miles to Middle Fork Feather River 4 miles northwest of Blairsden (lat. 39°49'30" N, long. 120°39'55" W; near SE cor. sec. 30, T 23 N, R 12 E). Named on Blairsden (1972) and Johnsville (1972) 7.5' quadrangles.

Constantia [LASSEN]: *locality,* 45 miles southeast of Susanville (lat. 39°57' N, long. 120°02'15" W; sec. 11, T 24 N, R 17 E); the place is near the south end of Long Valley (2). Named on Constantia (1977) 7.5' quadrangle. Postal authorities established Long Valley post office in 1869, moved it 5 miles southeast in 1898, moved it in 1912 when they changed the name to Constantia, and discontinued it in 1927 (Salley; p. 49, 126). They established Lake Greeno post office 7 miles north of Long Valley post office in 1892, moved it 3 miles west in 1896, and discontinued it in 1903; the name was for George Greeno, who built a reservoir along Long Valley Creek (Salley, p. 115).

Continental Ravine [PLUMAS]: *canyon,* drained by a stream that flows 0.5 mile to Porter Ravine 15 miles south-southeast of Quincy (lat. 39°45'20" N, long. 120°47'15" W; sec. 19, T 22 N, R 11 E). Named on Blue Nose Mountain (1951) 7.5' quadrangle.

Cooks Canyon [MODOC]: *canyon,* drained by a stream that flows 4.5 miles to Surprise Valley 2.5 miles north-northwest of Cedarville (lat. 41°33'50" N, long. 120°11' W; near E line sec. 30, T 43 N, R 16 E). Named on Cedarville (1962) 15' quadrangle.

Cooks Canyon: see **Cooks Creek** [PLUMAS].

Cooks Creek [PLUMAS]: *stream,* flows 10.5 miles to Lights Creek 2 miles north-northeast of Taylorsville (lat. 40°06'15" N, long. 120° 49'35" W; sec. 14, T 26 N, R 10 E). Named on Moonlight Peak (1980) and Taylorsville (1980) 7.5' quadrangles. On Honey Lake (1893) 1° quadrangle, the canyon of present Cooks Creek above North Arm Indian Valley is called Cooks Canyon.

Cooley Gulch [MODOC]: *canyon,* drained by a stream that flows 4 miles to Warm Springs Valley nearly 2 miles south of Canby (lat. 41°25'10" N, long. 120°52' W; near W line sec. 6, T 41 N, R 10 E). Named on Canby (1961) 15' quadrangle.

Cool Springs Campground [PLUMAS]: *locality,* 5 miles south of the village of Almanor along Butt Valley Reservoir (lat. 40°08'40" N, long. 121°09'55" W; near N line sec. 2, T 26 N, R 7 E). Named on Almanor (1979) 7.5' quadrangle.

Coon Camp [LASSEN]: *locality,* 15 miles northwest of Karlo (lat. 40°43'25" N, long. 120°28'35" W; near NE cor. sec. 14, T 33 N, R 13 E). Named on Karlo (1954) 15' quadrangle.

Coon Camp Springs [LASSEN]: *springs,* 6.25 miles east-northeast of Lava Peak (lat. 40°52'45" N, long. 120°47'30" W; sec. 24, T 35 N, R 10 E).

Named on Hayden Hill (1956) 15' quadrangle.

Cooper Meadow [LASSEN]: *area,* 15 miles north-northwest of Westwood (lat. 40°29'35" N, long. 121°09'05" W; sec. 1, T 30 N, R 7 E). Named on Chester (1956) 15' quadrangle, which shows marsh in the area. Called Cooper Swamp on Red Cinder (1979) 7.5' quadrangle, which also shows marsh in the area. United States Board on Geographic Names (1977a, p. 5) approved the name "Cooper Swamp" for the feature, and gave the names "Cooper Meadow" and "Cooper Meadows" as variants.

Cooper Swamp [LASSEN]: *marsh,* 11.5 miles south of Cal Mountain (lat. 40°30'15" N, long. 121°08' W; on W line sec. 31, T 31 N, R 8 E). Named on Harvey Mountain (1956) 15' quadrangle.

Cooper Swamp: see **Cooper Meadow** [LASSEN].

Copco [MODOC]: *locality,* 0.5 mile north-northeast of downtown Alturas along Southern Pacific Railroad (lat. 41°29'55" N, long. 120°32' W; sec. 12, T 42 N, R 12 E). Named on Alturas (1961) 15' quadrangle.

Copic [MODOC]: *locality,* 2 miles southeast of Newell along Southern Pacific Railroad (lat. 41°52' N, long. 121°20'30" W; at SE cor. sec. 36, T 47 N, R 5 E); the place is in Copic Bay. Named on Tulelake (1951) 15' quadrangle.

Copic Bay [MODOC]: *area,* part of the drained bed of old Tule Lake; center 2.5 miles south-southeast of Newell (lat. 41°51' N, long. 121°21'30" W). Named on Tulelake (1951) 15' quadrangle. Called Coppack Bay on Alturas (1954) 1°x 2° quadrangle.

Coppack Bay: see **Copic Bay** [MODOC].

Coppersmith Hills [LASSEN]: *range,* 23 miles east of Madeline (lat. 41°05'30" N, long. 120°01'30" W). Named on Little Hat Mountain (1962) 7.5' quadrangle.

Coppervale [LASSEN]: *locality,* nearly 6 miles east-northeast of Westwood (lat. 40°20'50" N, long. 120°54'15" W; sec. 30, T 29 N, R 10 E). Named on Westwood East (1980) 7.5' quadrangle. Postal authorities established Copper Vale post office in 1864, discontinued it in 1867, reestablished it in 1868, discontinued it in 1886, reestablished it in 1890, changed the name to Coppervale in 1894, moved it 2 miles northeast in 1901, and discontinued it in 1914—the name was from nearby copper mines (Salley, p. 50).

Coquette Creek [PLUMAS]: *stream,* flows 3.25 miles to Coldwater Creek (2) 6.5 miles south-southwest of Bucks Lodge (lat. 39°47'45" N, long. 121°14'15" W; near N line sec. 6, T 22 N, R 7 E). Named on Haskins Valley (1980) 7.5' quadrangle.

Corall Creek: see **Corral Creek** [MODOC].

Corders Reservoir [LASSEN]: *intermittent lake,* 2100 feet long, nearly 6 miles south-southeast of the village of Little Valley (lat. 40°49' N, long. 121°08'10" W; on S line sec. 12, T 34 N, R 7 E). Named on Little Valley (1957) 15' quadrangle.

Cornell [MODOC]: *locality,* 6.5 miles south-southeast of Newell along Southern Pacific Railroad (lat. 41°48' N, long. 121°19' W; sec. 29, T 46 N, R 6 E). Named on Tulelake (1951) 15' quadrangle. On Modoc Lava-Bed (1892) 1° quadrangle, the name applies to a place nearly 4 miles farther north. Postal authorities established Cornell post office, named for a pioneer family, in 1884, discontinued it for a time in 1890, and discontinued it finally in 1904 (Salley, p. 50).

Corporation Meadow [LASSEN]: *area,* 16 miles east-northeast of Madeline (lat. 41°10'05" N, long. 120°12'45" W; near SE cor. sec. 36, T 39 N, R 15 E). Named on Emerson Peak (1962) 7.5' quadrangle.

Corral Creek [MODOC]: *stream,* flows 5.5 mile to Goose Lake (1) 8.5 miles northeast of South Mountain (lat. 41°55' N, long. 120°30'45" W; sec. 18, T 47 N, R 13 E). Named on South Mountain (1962) 15' quadrangle. United States Board on Geographic Names (1964c, p. 14) rejected the form "Corall Creek" for the name.

Corral Hollow [LASSEN]: *canyon,* 3 miles long, center 2.5 miles north-northeast of Lava Peak (lat. 40°51'45" N, long. 120°52'45" W). Named on Hayden Hill (1956) 15' quadrangle.

Corral Spring [MODOC]: *spring,* 12 miles north-northwest of Alturas (lat. 41°39' N, long. 120°37'45" W; near S line sec. 18, T 44 N, R 12 E). Named on Big Sage Reservoir (1962) 15' quadrangle. United States Board on Geographic Names (1990, p. 6) rejected the name "Goose Lake Corral Spring" for the feature.

Corral Valley [LASSEN]: *valley,* 3.5 miles north of Lava Peak (lat. 40°52'45" N, long. 120°53'20" W; sec. 19, T 35 N, R 10 E); the feature is at the mouth of Corral Hollow. Named on Hayden Hill (1956) 15' quadrangle.

Correca Canyon [PLUMAS]: *canyon,* drained by a stream that flows 3.5 miles to Sierra Valley 5 miles southwest of Chilcoot (lat. 39° 44'45" N, long. 120°12'15" W; at E line sec. 20, T 22 N, R 16 E). Named on Loyalton (1981) 7.5' quadrangle. Called Correco Canyon on Loyalton (1955) 15' quadrangle.

Cottonwood Canyon [LASSEN]:

(1) *canyon,* 2.5 miles long, 13 miles west-southwest of Likely [MODOC] (lat. 41°08'45" N, long. 120°44' W); the canyon is along Cottonwood Creek [LASSEN-MODOC]. Named on Likely (1962) 15' quadrangle.

(2) *canyon,* drained by a stream that flows 7 miles to lowlands 12 miles east of Pelican Point (lat. 40°38'20" N, long. 120°31'15" W; at N line sec. 16, T 32 N, R 13 E). Named on Fredonyer Peak (1954) 15' quadrangle. United States Board on Geographic Names (1989c, p. 1) approved the name "Long Canyon" for this feature, and at the same time approved the name "Cottonwood Canyon" for a branch of the canyon, 2.5 miles long, that enters 2.5 miles west-southwest of Horse Lake (1) (lat. 40°38'37" N, long. 120°34'05" W; sec. 12, T 32 N, R 12 E)—Cottonwood Spring (4) is in this Cottonwood Canyon.

Cottonwood Creek [LASSEN]: *stream,* flows 3.5 miles to Mountain Meadows 5.25 miles east-southeast of Westwood (lat. 40°16'25" N, long. 120°54'30" W; at E line sec. 24, T 28 N, R 9 E). Named on Fredonyer Pass (1980) and Westwood East (1980) 7.5' quadrangles.

Cottonwood Creek [LASSEN-MODOC]: *stream,* heads in Modoc County and flows 12.5 miles to Ash Creek 11 miles east-southeast of Adin [MODOC] in Lassen County (lat. 41°07'25" N, long. 120° 45'20" W; sec. 19, T 38 N, R 11 E). Named on Adin (1962), Canby (1961), and Likely (1962) 15' quadrangles.

Cottonwood Creek [MODOC]:

(1) *stream,* formed by the confluence of North Fork and South Fork, flows 3.5 miles to Goose Lake (1) 3.5 miles north-northeast of Willow Ranch (lat. 41°56'55" N, long. 120°20' W; near E line sec. 3, T 47 N, R 14 E). Named on Willow Ranch (1962) 15' quadrangle. North Fork in nearly 3 miles long and is named on Fort Bidwell (1962) and Willow Ranch (1962) 15' quadrangles. South Fork is 1.5 miles long and is named on Willow Ranch (1962) 15' quadrangle.

(2) *stream,* flows 8.5 miles to Middle Alkali Lake 8.5 miles south-southeast of Cedarville (lat. 41°25'20" N, long. 120°04'50" W). Named on Hansen Island (1963) and Warren Peak (1963) 7.5' quadrangles.

Cottonwood Creek [PLUMAS]:

(1) *stream,* flows 2.25 miles to Yellow Creek 10.5 miles south-southwest of the village of Almanor (lat. 40°04'50" N, long. 121° 14'50" W; near W line sec. 30, T 26 N, R 7 E). Named on Jonesville (1958) 15' quadrangle.

(2) *stream,* flows 6.25 miles to Last Chance Creek 6.5 miles southwest of Milford [LASSEN] (lat. 40°07'05" N, long. 120°28'15" W; near SW cor. sec. 12, T 26 N, R 13 E). Named on Squaw Valley Peak (1977) and Stony Ridge (1978) 7.5' quadrangles.

Cottonwood Creek: see **Little Cottonwood Creek** [MODOC].

Cottonwood Flat [MODOC]:

(1) *area,* 5.5 miles northwest of Crank Mountain (lat. 41°25'50" N, long. 121°03'40" W; near SW cor. sec. 33, T 42 N, R 8 E). Named on Crank Mountain (1962) 15' quadrangle

(2) *area,* 9 miles south-southeast of Willow Ranch (lat. 41°46'40" N, long. 120°17'45" W). Named on Willow Ranch (1962) 15' quadrangle.

Cottonwood Lake [MODOC]: *lake,* 400 feet long, 10 miles south-southwest of Cedarville (lat. 41°23'25" N, long. 120°13'20" W; sec. 15, T 41 N, R 15 E); the lake is near the head of Cottonwood Creek (2). Named on Warren Peak (1963) 7.5' quadrangle.

Cottonwood Meadow [PLUMAS]: *area,* 10 miles south-southwest of the village of Almanor along Cottonwood Creek (1) (lat. 40°05'45" N, long. 121°15'30" W; sec. 24, T 26 N, R 6 E). Named on Jonesville (1958) 15' quadrangle.

Cottonwood Mountain [PLUMAS]: *peak,* 4.25 miles west of Milford [LASSEN] (lat. 40°10'10" N, long. 120°27'05" W; near W line sec. 30, T 27 N, R 14 E); the peak is east of Cottonwood Creek (2). Altitude 6396 feet. Named on Stony Ridge (1978) 7.5' quadrangle.

Cottonwood Mountains [LASSEN]: *ridge,* generally south-trending, 5 miles long, 15 miles north-northeast of Observation Peak (lat. 40°58' N, long. 120°04' W). Named on Observation Peak (1954) 15' quadrangle, and on Little Hat Mountain (1962) 7.5' quadrangle.

Cottonwood Peak [LASSEN-PLUMAS]: *peak,* 3.5 miles west of Milford on Lassen-Plumas County line (lat. 40°10'40" N, long. 120° 26'10" W; at SE cor. sec. 19, T 27 N, R 14 E); the peak is 1 mile northeast of Cottonwood Mountain [PLUMAS]. Altitude 6639 feet. Named on Stony Ridge (1978) 7.5' quadrangle.

Cottonwood Spring [LASSEN]:

(1) *spring,* 8.5 miles east of Adin [MODOC] (lat. 41°10'45" N, long. 120°47' W; sec. 35, T 39 N, R 10 E). Named on Adin (1962) 15' quadrangle.

(2) *spring,* 6 miles east of Lava Peak (lat. 40°49'35" N, long. 120° 46'30" W; sec. 7, T 34 N, R 11 E). Named on Hayden Hill (1956) 15' quadrangle.

(3) *spring,* 6 miles south of Observation Peak (lat. 40°41'20" N, long. 120°12'10" W; near E line sec. 30, T 33 N, R 16 E). Named on Shinn Mountain (1954) 15' quadrangle.

(4) *spring,* 9 miles east of Pelican Point (lat. 40°39'20" N, long. 120°34'50" W; near NW cor. sec. 12, T 32 N, R 12 E). Named on Fredonyer Peak (1954) 15' quadrangle.

Cottonwood Spring: see **Little Cottonwood Spring** [LASSEN].

Cottonwood Spring Campground [PLUMAS]: *locality,* 7.5 miles north-northwest of Chilcoot near Frenchman Lake (lat. 39°53'25" N, long. 120°12'30" W; sec. 32, T 24 N, R 16 E). Named on Frenchman Lake (1979) 7.5' quadrangle.

Cottonwood Springs [MODOC]: *springs,* 4.25 miles west-southwest of Likely (lat. 41°11'50" N, long. 120°34'40" W; sec. 22, T 39 N, R 12 E).

Named on Likely (1962) 15' quadrangle.

Couch Creek [MODOC]: *stream,* flows 3 miles to Joseph Creek 8.5 miles south of the village of Davis Creek (lat. 41°36'35" N, long. 120°20'35" W; sec. 34, T 44 N, R 14 E). Named on Davis Creek (1962) 15' quadrangle.

Cougar Pass Tank [MODOC]: *water feature,* nearly 7 miles south-southwest of South Mountain (lat. 41°45'10" N, long. 120°41'30" W; sec. 10, T 45 N, R 11 E). Named on South Mountain (1962) 15' quadrangle.

Cou Head Spring: see **Cow Head Spring** [MODOC].

Coulee Canyon [LASSEN]: *canyon,* drained by a stream that flows 4 miles to Upper Long Valley 4.5 miles south of Beckwourth Pass (lat. 39°43'35" N, long. 120°05'45" W). Named on Evans Canyon (1978) 7.5' quadrangle.

Coulthurst Flat [LASSEN]: *valley,* 5 miles southeast of Lava Peak (lat. 40°46'30" N, long. 120°50' W; on S line sec. 27, T 34 N, R 10 E). Named on Hayden Hill (1956) 15' quadrangle.

Courtright Reservoir [MODOC]: *intermittent lake,* 700 feet long, 6.25 miles north of Crank Mountain (lat. 41°28'25" N, long. 121° 09'10" W; at S line sec. 15, T 42 N, R 7 E). Named on Crank Mountain (1962) 15' quadrangle.

Cove Spring [MODOC]: *spring,* 6 miles southeast of Crank Mountain (lat. 41°19'10" N, long. 121°04' W; near E line sec. 8, T 40 N, R 8 E). Named on Crank Mountain (1962) 15' quadrangle.

Cowboy Lake [LASSEN]: *lake,* 1000 feet long, 12 miles south of Cal Mountain (lat. 40°30'05" N, long. 121°10'35" W; sec. 34, T 31 N, R 7 E). Named on Harvey Mountain (1956) 15' quadrangle.

Cow Creek [PLUMAS]:

(1) *stream,* flows 1.25 miles to Rush Creek 6.25 miles north-northeast of Twain (lat. 40°06'20" N, long. 121°01'40" W; near S line sec. 13, T 26 N, R 8 E). Named on Twain (1980) 7.5' quadrangle.

(2) *stream,* flows 4 miles to Lake Davis 7.25 miles southeast of Mount Ingalls (lat. 39°54'50" N, long. 120°32'10" W; sec. 29, T 24 N, R 13 E). Named on Grizzly Valley (1972) 7.5' quadrangle.

Cow Head Lake [MODOC]: *area,* 7.5 miles northeast of Fort Bidwell (lat. 41°55'10" N, long. 120°01'45" W). Named on Fort Bidwell (1962) 15' quadrangle. Alturas 1° quadrangle shows a lake in the area. Called Pelican Lake on California Division of Highways' (1934) map. United States Board on Geographic Names (1964b, p. 12) rejected the forms "Cowhead Lake," "Cowhead Lake Basin," and "Cow Head Lake Basin," for the name.

Cow Head Lake Basin: see **Cow Head Lake** [MODOC].

Cow Head Slough [MODOC]: *stream,* flows 5.5 miles to the State of Oregon 12 miles northwest of Fort Bidwell (lat. 41°59'40" N, long. 120°00'45" W; near SW cor. sec. 27, T 48 N, R 17 E). Named on Fort Bidwell (1962) 15' quadrangle.

Cow Head Spring [MODOC]: *spring,* 18 miles north-northwest of Alturas (lat. 41°44'20" N, long. 120°38' W; sec. 18, T 45 N, R 12 E). Named on Big Sage Reservoir (1962) 15' quadrangle. United States Board on Geographic Names (1983b, p. 4) rejected the name "Cou Head Spring" for the feature.

Cow Head Tank [MODOC]: *water feature,* 6 miles south of South Mountain (lat. 41°45'15" N, long. 120°38'30" W; sec. 12, T 45 N, R 11 E). Named on South Mountain (1962) 15' quadrangle.

Cow Lake [LASSEN]: *lake,* 1800 feet long, 5.5 miles northwest of Lava Peak (lat. 40°53'10" N, long. 120°57'40" W; near NE cor. sec. 21, T 35 N, R 9 E). Named on Hayden Hill (1956) 15' quadrangle.

Cox Canyon [MODOC]: *canyon,* drained by a stream that flows 2 miles to Round Valley (2) 12.5 miles south of Canby (lat. 41° 16' N, long. 120°54'30" W; sec. 35, T 40 N, R 9 E). Named on Canby (1961) 15' quadrangle.

Coyote Butte [MODOC]: *peak,* 6.5 miles southeast of Newell (lat. 41°49'15" N, long. 121°16'30" W;near S line sec. 15, T 46 N, R 6 E). Altitude 4775 feet. Named on Tulelake (1951) 15' quadrangle.

Coyote Canyon [LASSEN]: *canyon,* drained by a stream that flows 1.5 miles to Indian Creek 7 miles northwest of Lava Peak (lat. 40° 53'15" N, long. 121°00' W; near NE cor. sec. 19, T 35 N, R 9 E). Named on Hayden Hill (1956) 15' quadrangle.

Coyote Creek [MODOC]: *stream,* flows 4 miles to Jess Valley 21 miles southeast of Alturas (lat. 41°13'45" N, long. 120°18' W; near E line sec. 12, T 39 N, R 15 E). Named on Jess Valley (1962) 7.5' quadrangle.

Coyote Creek [PLUMAS]: *stream,* flows less than 1 mile to Fall River 3 miles southeast of Cascade (lat. 39°40'25" N, long. 121°07'50" W; sec. 18, T 21 N, R 8 E). Named on American House (1948) and Cascade (1948) 7.5' quadrangles.

Coyote Flat [LASSEN]:

(1) *area,* 13 miles southeast of Adin [MODOC] (lat. 41°02'40" N, long. 120°46'45" W; on W line sec. 13, T 37 N, R 10 E). Named on Adin (1962) 15' quadrangle.

(2) *area,* 8.5 miles east of Termo (lat. 40°53'15" N, long. 120°17'45" W). Named on Ravendale (1954) 15' quadrangle.

(3) *area,* 8.5 miles northwest of Pelican Point (lat. 40°43'10" N, long. 120°51'25" W; near SW cor. sec. 16, T 33 N, R 10 E). Named on Antelope Mountain (1956) 15' quadrangle.

Coyote Flat [MODOC]: *area,* 3.5 miles north-northwest of Fort Bidwell (lat. 41°54'15" N, long. 120°11' W; near N line sec. 31, T 47 N, R 16 E). Named on Fort Bidwell (1962) 15' quadrangle.

Coyote Flat [PLUMAS]: *area,* 7 miles west-northwest of the village of Almanor (lat. 40°14'55" N, long. 121°17'45" W; on N line sec. 34, T 28 N, R 6 E). Named on Jonesville (1958) and Mount Harkness (1956) 15' quadrangles.

Coyote Flat Draw [LASSEN]: *canyon,* about 2 miles long, 14 miles southeast of Adin [MODOC] (lat. 41°02'15" N, long. 120°47'15" W; sec. 14, 23, T 37 N, R 10 E); the canyon is southwest of Coyote Flat (1). Named on Adin (1962) 15' quadrangle.

Coyote Hills [PLUMAS]: *range,* 12.5 miles north of Portola (lat. 39° 58'45" N, long. 120°26'15" W). Named on Crocker Mountain (1972) 7.5' quadrangle.

Coyote Hole [LASSEN]: *relief feature,* 5 miles southeast of Lava Peak (lat. 40°47'20" N, long. 120°49'05" W; at S line sec. 23, T 34 N, R 10 E). Named on Hayden Hill (1956) 15' quadrangle.

Coyote Meadow [MODOC]: *area,* 10 miles north of Blue Mountain (lat. 41°58'30" N, long. 120°52'10" W; sec. 30, T 48 N, R 10 E). Named on Steele Swamp (1962) 15' quadrangle.

Coyote Peak [LASSEN]: *peak,* 9 miles east of Westwood (lat. 40°17'25" N, long. 120°49'50" W; near NW cor. sec. 14, T 28 N, R 10 E). Altitude 7650 feet. Named on Fredonyer Pass (1980) 7.5' quadrangle.

Coyote Reservoir [LASSEN]: *lake,* 6200 feet long, 7 miles northwest of Lava Peak (lat. 40°54'15" N, long. 120°58'30" W; on S line sec. 31, T 36 N, R 9 E); the lake is at the head of Coyote Canyon. Named on Hayden Hill (1956) 15' quadrangle.

Coyote Springs [MODOC]: *springs,* 8.5 miles north-northwest of Jacks Butte (lat. 41°42'10" N, long. 120°50'20" W; near N line sec. 32, T 45 N, R 10 E). Named on Jacks Butte (1962) 15' quadrangle.

Crablouse Ravine [PLUMAS]: *canyon,* drained by a stream that flows 1.5 miles to North Fork Feather River 1.5 miles southwest of Caribou (lat. 40°04' N, long. 121°10'45" W; sec. 34, T 26 N, R 7 E). Named on Caribou (1979) 7.5' quadrangle.

Cradle Valley [PLUMAS]: *valley,* 13 miles east-northeast of Kettle Rock along Clarks Creek (lat. 40°13'55" N, long. 120°30'30" W; sec. 3, 4, T 27 N, R 13 E). Named on Antelope Lake (1972) 7.5' quadrangle.

Craemer Reservoir [LASSEN]: *intermittent lake,* 1.5 miles long, 12.5 miles east of Pelican Point (lat. 40°38'10" N, long. 120°30'20" W). Named on Fredonyer Peak (1954) and Karlo (1954) 15' quadrangles.

Craemer Springs [LASSEN]: *spring,* 11 miles east-northeast of Pelican Point (lat. 40°41'15" N, long. 120°32'50" W; near E line sec. 30, T 33 N, R 13 E). Named on Fredonyer Peak (1954) 15' quadrangle.

Craig: see **Lookout** [MODOC].

Craig Spring [MODOC]: *spring,* 6.5 miles north-northeast of Crank Mountain (lat. 41°28'10" N, long. 121°06' W; near NE cor. sec. 24, T 42 N, R 7 E). Named on Crank Mountain (1962) 15' quadrangle.

Crank Mountain [MODOC]: *peak,* 17 miles northwest of Adin (lat. 41°23'05" N, long. 121°08'35" W; sec. 22, T 41 N, R 7 E). Altitude 5243 feet. Named on Crank Mountain (1962) 15' quadrangle.

Crank Spring [MODOC]: *spring,* 2 miles southwest of Crank Mountain (lat. 41°22'10" N, long. 121°10'35" W; on W line sec. 28, T 41 N, R 7 E). Named on Crank Mountain (1962) 15' quadrangle.

Crater Lake [LASSEN]: *lake,* 1500 feet long, 7 miles east-southeast of Cal Mountain (lat. 40°37'35" N, long. 121°02'50" W; near N line sec. 23, T 32 N, R 8 E); the lake is in a crater. Named on Harvey Mountain (1956) 15' quadrangle.

Crater Lake Mountain [LASSEN]: *mountain,* 8 miles east-southeast of Cal Mountain (lat. 40°37'30" N, long. 121°01'50" W; in and around sec. 24, T 32 N, R 8 E); Crater Lake is on the mountain. Named on Harvey Mountain (1956) 15' quadrangle. Called Crater Mountain on Halls Flat (1939) 30' quadrangle, and United States Board on Geographic Names (1965c, p. 11) approved this name for the feature.

Crater Mountain: see **Crater Lake Mountain** [LASSEN].

Crazy Harry Gulch [LASSEN]: *canyon,* drained by a stream that flows 3.5 miles to Susan River 11.5 miles northeast of Westwood (lat. 40°25'15" N, long. 120°50'30" W; sec. 34, T 30 N, R 10 E). Named on Roop Mountain (1980) 7.5' quadrangle.

Creed Ravine [PLUMAS]: *canyon,* drained by a stream that flows nearly 1 mile to Kenzie Ravine 4 miles north-northeast of La Porte (lat. 39°44'10" N, long. 120°57'40" W; sec. 27, T 22 N, R 9 E). Named on La Porte (1951) 7.5' quadrangle.

Crescent: see **Crescent Mills** [PLUMAS].

Crescent City: see **Crescent Mills** [PLUMAS].

Crescent Hill [PLUMAS]: *peak,* 5 miles south of Quincy (lat. 39° 52' N, long. 120°56' W; at E line sec. 11, T 23 N, R 9 E). Altitude 6544 feet. Named on Onion Valley (1950) 7.5' quadrangle.

Crescent Mills [PLUMAS]: *village,* 3.5 miles southeast of Greenville (lat. 40°05'50" N, long. 120°54'35" W; on E line sec. 24, T 26 N, R 9 E). Named on Crescent Mills (1980) 7.5' quadrangle. Called Crescent on Honey Lake (1893) 1° quadrangle. Wheeler (1879, p. 145) referred to Crescent City. Postal authorities established Crescent Mills post office in

1870 (Frickstad, p. 123). Crescent Mills (1980) 7.5' quadrangle shows Arlington bridge over Indian Creek (2) less than 10 miles south-southwest of Crescent Mills (sec. 25, T 26 N, R 9 E). Waring (p. 229) used the name "Arlington Springs" for two springs of carbonated water located near Arlington bridge, and gave the name "Bach Springs" as an alternate.

Crest [LASSEN]: *locality,* 12 miles north-northwest of Karlo along Southern Pacific Railroad (lat. 40°43'25" N, long. 120°22'10" W; on E line sec. 15, T 33 N, R 14 E). Named on Karlo (1954) 15' quadrangle.

Crocker Creek [PLUMAS]: *stream,* flows 4.25 miles to Red Clover Valley 8.5 miles north-northeast of Portola (lat. 39°55'15" N, long. 120°24'45" W; sec. 21, T 24 N, R 14 E); the stream is east of Crocker Mountain. Named on Crocker Mountain (1972) 7.5' quadrangle.

Crocker Meadow [PLUMAS]: *area,* 6 miles north-northeast of Portola (lat. 39°53' N, long. 120°25'15" W; on S line sec. 33, T 24 N, R 14 E); the place is along Crocker Creek. Named on Crocker Mountain (1972) and Portola (1972) 7.5' quadrangles.

Crocker Mountain [PLUMAS]: *ridge,* north- to northwest-trending, 4 miles long, 7.5 miles north of Portola (lat. 39°54'30" N, long. 120°27' W). Named on Crocker Mountain (1972) and Portola (1972) 7.5' quadrangles.

Cromberg [PLUMAS]:

(1) *village,* 6.5 miles northwest of Blairsden (lat. 39°51'35" N, long. 120°41'20" W; sec. 13, T 23 N, R 11 E). Named on Johnsville (1972) 7.5' quadrangle. Called Cromberg P.O. on Blairsden (1956) 15' quadrangle. Downieville (1897) 30' quadrangle has the name "Teft" at the site. Postal authorities established Cromberg post office in 1880, discontinued it in 1912, reestablished it in 1919, discontinued it in 1931, and reestablished it in 1950 (Frickstad, p. 123). Gerhard A. Langhorst, first postmaster, chose the name, which is the Americanized form of his mother's family name "Krumberg" (Gudde, 1949, p. 84; Salley, p, 53).

(2) *locality,* 6.5 miles northwest of Blairsden along Western Pacific Railroad (lat. 39°51'05" N, long. 120°41'35" W; on S line sec. 13, T 23 N, R 11 E); the place is less than 1 mile south-southwest of present Cromberg (1). Named on Blairsden (1956) 15' quadrangle. Johnsville (1972) 7.5' quadrangle has name "Twentymile House" at the site, which is 21 miles from Quincy along the road to Reno, Nevada (Gudde, 1949, p. 84).

Cromberg Spring [PLUMAS]: *spring,* 6 miles north-northwest of Blairsden (lat. 39°51'05" N, long. 120°40'50" W; near SW cor. sec. 18, T 23 N, R 12 E); the spring is less than 1 mile southeast of Cromberg (1). Named on Johnsville (1972) 7.5' quadrangle.

Cromwell: see **Doyle** [LASSEN].

Crooks Canyon [MODOC]: *canyon,* 3.5 miles long, drained by Hilton Creek above a point 15 miles south of Alturas (lat. 41°16'25" N, long. 120°34'30" W; sec. 27, T 40 N, R 12 E). Named on Alturas (1961) 15' quadrangle.

Crossing: see **The Crossing** [LASSEN].

Crowder Mountain [MODOC]: *ridge,* north-trending, 2 miles long, 7.25 miles south-southeast of South Mountain (lat. 41°45'15" N, long. 120°33'25" W; in and near sec. 11, T 45 N, R 12 E). Named on Big Sage Reservoir (1962) and South Mountain (1962) 15' quadrangles.

Crowder Mountain Reservoir [MODOC]: *intermittent lake,* 5900 feet long, 5.25 miles southeast of South Mountain (lat. 41°47'10" N, long. 120°34'15" W; on W line sec. 35, T 46 N, R 12 E); the feature is north of Crowder Mountain. Named on South Mountain (1962) 15' quadrangle.

Crowder Mountain Spring [MODOC]: *spring,* 16 miles north of Alturas (lat. 41°43'15" N, long. 120°33'30" W; at S line sec. 23, T 45 N, R 12 E); the spring is 2.5 miles south of Crowder Mountain. Named on Big Sage Reservoir (1962) 15' quadrangle.

Crum Reservoir [LASSEN]: *lake,* 1900 feet long, 9 miles west of Bieber along Frazier Creek (lat. 41°06'20" N, long. 121°18'45" W; on W line sec. 29, T 38 N, R 6 E). Named on Fall River Mills (1961) 15' quadrangle.

Crystal Cliffs [LASSEN]: *relief feature,* 2.5 miles north-northeast of Mount Harkness [PLUMAS] (lat. 40°27'50" N, long. 121°17'40" W; sec. 15, T 30 N, R 6 E). Named on Mount Harkness (1956) 15' quadrangle. The name is from nearby Crystal Lake (Schulz, p. 14).

Crystal Creek [PLUMAS]: *stream,* flows 1.5 miles to Red Clover Creek 3 miles east of Mount Ingalls (lat. 39°59'35" N, long. 120° 34'10" W; at E line sec. 25, T 25 N, R 12 E). Named on Grizzly Valley (1972) 7.5' quadrangle.

Crystal Lake [LASSEN]: *lake,* 800 feet long, 2 miles north-northeast of Mount Harkness [PLUMAS] (lat. 40°27'30" N, long. 121°17'25" W; near E line sec. 15, T 30 N, R 6 E). Named on Mount Harkness (1956) 15' quadrangle. The name is from the crystal clarity of the water in the lake (Schulz, p. 14).

Crystal Lake [PLUMAS]: *lake,* 950 feet long, 3.5 miles south-southeast of Crescent Mills (lat. 40°02'55" N, long. 120°53' W; sec. 8, T 25 N, R 10 E). Named on Crescent Mills (1980) 7.5' quadrangle.

Crystal Peak [LASSEN-PLUMAS]: *peak,* 4.5 miles west of Constantia at Lassen-Plumas County line (lat. 39°56'35" N, long. 120° 07'25" W; near SW cor. sec. 7, T 24 N, R 17 E). Named on Constantia (1977) 7.5' quadrangle.

Crystal Waterholes [MODOC]: *water feature,* 12.5 miles north-northeast of White Horse (lat. 41°29'05" N, long. 121°20'15" W; near N line sec. 13, T 42 N, R 5 E). Named on White Horse (1962) 15' quadrangle.

Cuba: see **Chats** [LASSEN].

Cub Creek [PLUMAS]: *stream,* flows about 1.25 miles to Squirrel Creek (1) 12 miles south-southeast of the village of Almanor (lat. 40°03'55" N, long. 121°16'30" W; sec. 35, T 26 N, R 6 E). Named on Jonesville (1958) 15' quadrangle.

Cub Lake [PLUMAS]: *lake,* 500 feet long, 6.25 miles southwest of Clio (lat. 39°41'30" N, long. 120°40'25" W; near S line sec. 7, T 21 N, R 12 E). Named on Gold Lake (1981) 7.5' quadrangle. The lake is one of the group called Bear Lakes on Downieville (1897) 30' quadrangle

Cub Valley [PLUMAS]: *valley,* 5.5 miles northwest of Blairsden (lat. 39°50'15" N, long. 120°41'15" W; at and near SE cor. sec. 24, T 23 N, R 11 E). Named on Johnsville (1972) 7.5' quadrangle.

Cummings Reservoir: see **Lower Cummings Reservoir** [MODOC]; **Upper Cummings Reservoir** [MODOC].

Cummings Spring [LASSEN]: *spring,* 13 miles north-northwest of Westwood (lat. 40°27'35" N, long. 121°08'50" W; sec. 13, T 30 N, R 7 E). Named on Red Cinder (1979) 7.5' quadrangle.

Cummins Lake [MODOC]: *intermittent lake,* 1200 feet long, 12.5 miles north-northwest of Hackamore (lat. 41°42'20" N, long. 121° 14'40" W; on S line sec. 26, T 45 N, R 6 E). Named on Hackamore (1952) 15' quadrangle.

Cuppy Butte [MODOC]: *peak,* 4.25 miles east-northeast of Crank Mountain (lat. 41°24'45" N, long. 121°04'05" W; near line sec. 8, T 41 N, R 8 E); the peak is near the head of Cuppy Gulch. Named on Crank Mountain (1962) 15' quadrangle.

Cuppy Gulch [MODOC]: *canyon,* drained by a stream that flows 2 miles to Pit River 6.5 miles west of Crank Mountain (lat. 41°24'10" N, long. 121°01'15" W; near SW cor. sec. 11, T 41 N, R 8 E); the feature heads near Cuppy Butte. Named on Crank Mountain (1962) 15' quadrangle.

Curtis Ravine [PLUMAS]: *canyon,* drained by a stream that flows 2 miles to Indian Creek (2) 3.5 miles southwest of Crescent Mills (lat. 40°03'35" N, long. 120°57'40" W; near N line sec. 3, T 25 N, R 9 E). Named on Crescent Mills (1980) 7.5' quadrangle.

Curtis Waterhole [MODOC]: *water feature,* 5.25 miles northeast of White Horse (lat. 41°21'40" N, long. 121°19'35" W; near W line sec. 30, T 41 N, R 6 E). Named on White Horse (1962) 15' quadrangle.

Cutler Meadow [PLUMAS]: *area,* nearly 4 miles west of Spring Garden (lat. 39°53'20" N, long. 120°51'20" W; near NW cor. sec. 3, T 23 N, R 10 E). Named on Spring Garden (1950) 7.5' quadrangle.

Cypress Lake [LASSEN]: *lake,* 650 feet long, 16 miles northwest of Westwood (lat. 40°29'10" N, long. 121°11'15" W; sec. 3, T 30 N, R 7 E). Named on Red Cinder (1979) 7.5' quadrangle.

—D—

Dago Spring [LASSEN]: *spring,* 10 miles north-northeast of Lava Peak (lat. 40°58' N, long. 120°50'05" W; on W line sec. 9, T 36 N, R 10 E). Named on Hayden Hill (1956) 15' quadrangle.

Dairy Spring [LASSEN]:

(1) *spring,* nearly 3 miles south of Lava Peak (lat. 40°47'30" N, long. 120°53'20" W; sec. 19, T 34 N, R 10 E). Named on Hayden Hill (1956) 15' quadrangle.

(2) *spring,* 15 miles west of Termo (lat. 40°50' N, long. 120°44'05" W; near S line sec. 4, T 34 N, R 11 E). Named on Grasshopper Valley (1954) 15' quadrangle.

Daisy Dean Spring [LASSEN]: *spring,* 11 miles north of Lava Peak (lat. 40°59'10" N long. 120°51'15" W; on E line sec. 6, T 36 N, R 10 E); the spring is 1.25 miles southeast of Hayden Hill (1). Named on Hayden Hill (1956) 15' quadrangle. Tucker (p. 231) listed Daisy Dean mine, located 1 mile southeast of Hayden Hill

Dale Spring [MODOC]: *spring,* nearly 3 miles east-northeast of Crank Mountain (lat. 41°24'10" N, long. 121°05'45" W; at S line sec. 7, T 41 N, R 8 E). Named on Crank Mountain (1962) 15' quadrangle.

Dalton [MODOC]: *locality,* 4.5 miles northwest of Newell along Great Northern Railroad (lat. 41°56'15" N, long. 121°25' W; at SW cor. sec. 4, T 47 N, R 5 E). Named on Tulelake (1951) 15' quadrangle.

Dalton Reservoir [MODOC]: *intermittent lake,* 2600 feet long, 13 miles north-northeast of Hackamore along Mowitz Creek (lat. 41° 43'50" N, long. 121°01'50" W; sec. 22, T 45 N, R 8 E). Named on Hackamore (1952) 15' quadrangle.

Damons Butte [MODOC]: *peak,* 4.5 miles west-southwest of Hackamore (lat. 41°31'20" N, long. 121°11'40" W; near W line sec. 32, T 43 N, R 7 E). Altitude 4817 feet. Named on Hackamore (1952) 15' quadrangle.

Damons Cave [MODOC]: *cave,* 4 miles southwest of Hackamore (lat. 41°31'10" N, long. 121°10'40" W; near SE cor. sec. 32, T 43 N, R 7 E); the cave is less than 1 mile east-southeast of Damons Butte. Named on Hackamore (1952) 15' quadrangle.

Dan Beebe Campground [PLUMAS]: *locality,* nearly 7 miles south of Bucks Lodge along Middle Fork Feather River (lat. 39°46'40" N, long. 121°09'35"

W; near NE cor. sec. 11, T 22 N, R 7 E). Named on Haskins Valley (1980) 7.5' quadrangle.

Dan Blough Cove [PLUMAS]: *embayment,* 6.25 miles north-northwest of Portola along Lake Davis (lat. 39°53'40" N, long. 120°29'50" W; on S line sec. 34, T 24 N, R 13 E); the feature is at the mouth of Dan Blough Creek. Named on Grizzly Valley (1972) 7.5' quadrangle.

Dan Blough Creek [PLUMAS]: *stream,* flows 2 miles to Lake Davis 9.5 miles southeast of Mount Ingalls (lat. 39°53'35" N, long. 120° 30'10" W; at N line sec. 3, T 23 N, R 13 E). Named on Grizzly Valley (1972) 7.5' quadrangle.

Danhauser Reservoir: see **Dannhauser Reservoir** [MODOC].

Daniels Creek [MODOC]: *stream,* flows 1.5 miles to Surprise Valley 6.25 miles north-northwest of Cedarville (lat. 41°37' N, long. 120° 12'30" W; near N line sec. 12, T 43 N, R 15 E). Named on Cedarville (1962) 15' quadrangle.

Daniels Creek [PLUMAS]: *stream,* flows nearly 1 mile to Haskins Creek 1 mile east-southeast of Bucks Lodge (lat. 39°52'05" N, long. 121°09'20" W; near NE cor. sec. 11, T 23 N, R 7 E). Named on Haskins Valley (1980) 7.5' quadrangle.

Daniel Zink Campground [PLUMAS]: *locality,* 6 miles southeast of Storrie (lat. 39°50'35" N, long. 121°15'45" W; near SW cor. sec. 13, T 23 N, R 6 E). Named on Soapstone Hill (1979) 7.5' quadrangle.

Dannhauser Reservoir [MODOC]: *lake,* nearly 1 mile long, 6 miles south-southeast of Alturas (lat. 41°24'25" N, long. 120°29' W; sec. 8, 9, T 41 N, R 13 E). Named on Dorris Reservoir (1963) 7.5' quadrangle. United States Board on Geographic Names (1965b, p. 13) rejected the form "Danhauser Reservoir" for the name.

Daphnedale Park [MODOC]: *district,* 1.5 miles north of downtown Alturas (lat. 41°30'40" N, long. 120°32'40" W; at E line sec. 2, T 42 N, R 12 E). Named on Big Sage Reservoir (1962) 15' quadrangle.

Darby Meadow [PLUMAS]: *area,* 2 miles west-southwest of Bucks Lodge (lat. 39°51'55" N, long. 121°12'25" W; near NW cor. sec. 9, T 23 N, R 7 E). Named on Haskins Valley (1980) 7.5' quadrangle.

Dark Ravine [PLUMAS]:

(1) *canyon,* drained by a stream that flows 1.5 miles to Rush Creek 5.5 miles north-northeast of Twain (lat. 40°05'35" N, long. 121° 02' W; near S line sec. 24, T 26 N, R 8 E). Named on Twain (1980) 7.5' quadrangle.

(2) *canyon,* drained by a stream that flows 1 mile to Slate Creek (3) nearly 2 miles east-southeast of La Porte (lat. 39°40'35" N, long. 120°57'05" W; sec. 22, T 21 N, R 9 E). Named on La Porte (1951) 7.5' quadrangle.

Datura: see **Standish** [LASSEN].

Davies Mill: see **Graeagle** [PLUMAS].

Davis: see **Lake Davis** [PLUMAS].

Davis Creek [LASSEN]: *stream,* flows 8 miles to Horse Creek 3.5 miles east of the village of Little Valley (lat. 40°53' N, long. 121° 06'30" W; sec. 20, T 35 N, R 8 E). Named on Little Valley (1957) 15' quadrangle.

Davis Creek [MODOC]:

(1) *stream,* formed by the confluence of Middle Fork and South Fork, flows 7 miles to end 10 miles south-southwest of Willow Ranch near Goose Lake (1) (lat. 41°46'10" N, long. 120°25'20" W). Named on Davis Creek (1962) and Willow Ranch (1962) 15' quadrangles. The name, given about 1868, commemorates a prospector who worked in the neighborhood (Hanna, p. 83). Middle Fork is 3 miles long and South Fork in 4.5 miles long; both forks are named on Davis Creek (1962) 15' quadrangle. North Fork enters from the northeast 1.25 miles downstream from the confluence of Middle Fork and South Fork; it is 5 miles long and is named on Davis Creek (1962) and Willow Ranch (1962) 15' quadrangles.

(2) *stream,* diverges from Davis Creek (1) near the village of Davis Creek and flows 4 miles before ending 9 miles south-southwest of Willow Ranch near Goose Lake (1) (lat. 41°46'40" N, long. 120° 24' W). Named on Davis Creek (1962) and Willow Ranch (1962) 15' quadrangles.

(3) *village,* 19 miles north-northeast of Alturas (lat. 41°44' N, long. 120°22'25" W; at SW cor. sec. 16, T 45 N, R 14 E); the place is along Davis Creek (1). Named on Davis Creek (1962) 15' quadrangle. Postal authorities established Davis's Creek post office in 1877 and changed the name to Davis Creek before April of 1879 (Salley, p. 56).

Davis Creek [PLUMAS]:

(1) *stream,* flows 1.5 miles to North Fork Feather River 7 miles north of Twain (lat. 40°07'25" N, long. 121°05'10" W; sec. 9, T 26 N, R 8 E). Named on Canyondam (1979) and Twain (1980) 7.5' quadrangles.

(2) *stream,* flows 2.5 miles to Hosselkus Creek 2.25 miles south-southeast of Kettle Rock (lat. 40°06'40" N, long. 120°42'35" W; sec. 14, T 26 N, R 11 E). Named on Genesee Valley (1972) and Kettle Rock (1972) 7.5' quadrangles.

(3) *stream,* flows 1.25 miles to Fall River 5.25 miles northwest of American House (lat. 39°42'05" N, long. 121°05'45" W; at S line sec. 4, T 21 N, R 8 E). Named on American House (1948) 7.5' quadrangle.

Davis Creek: see **Little Davis Creek** [LASSEN].

Davis Spring [MODOC]: *spring,* 12 miles north of Hackamore (lat. 41°43'45" N, long. 121°05'35" W). Named on Hackamore (1952) 15' quadrangle.

Day [MODOC]: *village,* 22 miles west of Adin (lat. 41°12'45" N, long. 121°22'20" W; near SE cor. sec. 15, T 39 N, R 5 E). Named on Fall River Mills (1961) 15' quadrangle. Postal authorities established Day post office in 1888, discontinued it in 1925, reestablished it in 1926, and discontinued it in 1953 (Frickstad, p. 102). The name is for the first settler in the neighborhood (Laird, p. 45).

Day Rock [MODOC]: *relief feature,* 4 miles northwest of Day (lat. 41°14'55" N , long. 121°25'30" W; at W line sec. 5, T 39 N, R 5 E). Named on Fall River Mills (1961) 15' quadrangle.

Dayton: see **Susanville** [LASSEN].

Dead Horse Canyon [MODOC]: *canyon,* 0.5 mile long, 9.5 miles south-southeast of Newell (lat. 41°45'35" N, long. 121°17'30" W; sec. 8, 9, T 45 N, R 6 E). Named on Tulelake (1951) 15' quadrangle.

Deadhorse Canyon [LASSEN]: *canyon,* 1.5 miles long, 4 miles northeast of the village of Little Valley (lat. 40°56'25" N, long. 121°07'45" W; sec. 23, 24, T 36 N, R 7 E). Named on Little Valley (1957) 15' quadrangle.

Deadhorse Flat Reservoir [MODOC]: *intermittent lake,* 1.5 miles long, 10 miles northwest of Jacks Butte (lat. 41°41' N, long. 120° 56'45" W; mainly in sec. 4, 5, T 44 N, R 9 E). Named on Jacks Butte (1962) 15' quadrangle. Alturas (1954) 1°x 2° quadrangle has the form "Dead Horse Flat" for the name.

Dead Horse Reservoir [MODOC]: *intermittent lake,* 1.5 miles long, 15 miles north of Alturas (lat. 41°42'15" N, long. 120°35'26" W). Named on Big Sage Reservoir (1962) 15' quadrangle.

Deadman Gulch [PLUMAS]: *canyon,* drained by a stream that flows nearly 1 mile to Middle Fork Feather River 3.25 miles north-northwest of Cascade (lat. 39°44'25" N, long. 121°12'25" W; at S line sec. 21, T 22 N, R 7 E). Named on Cascade (1948) 7.5' quadrangle.

Deadman Spring [PLUMAS]: *spring,* 1.5 miles north of Dogwood Peak (lat. 39°48'35" N, long. 121°03'20" W; sec. 35, T 23 N, R 8 E). Named on Dogwood Peak (1979) 7.5' quadrangle.

Deadwood: see **Deadwood Creek** [PLUMAS].

Deadwood Canyon [PLUMAS]: *canyon,* drained by a stream that flows 2.25 miles to North Fork Feather River 1 mile southwest of Caribou (lat. 40°04'20" N, long. 121°10'15" W; near NW cor. sec. 35, T 26 N, R 7 E). Named on Caribou (1979) 7.5' quadrangle.

Deadwood Creek [PLUMAS]: *stream,* flows 2 miles to Big Creek nearly 2 miles west-southwest of the village of Meadow Valley (lat. 39°55'15" N, long. 121°05'25" W; at S line sec. 21, T 24 N, R 8 E). Named on Meadow Valley (1980) 7.5' quadrangle, which shows the stream situated about 2 miles southeast of Spanish Peak. Gudde (1975, p. 92) listed a mining place called Deadwood that was located about 1.5 miles southeast of Spanish Peak.

Deadwood Saddle [PLUMAS]: *pass,* 2 miles south of Caribou (lat. 40°03' N, long. 121°09'20" W; at E line sec. 2, T 25 N, R 7 E); the pass is at the head of Deadwood Canyon. Named on Caribou (1979) 7.5' quadrangle.

Dean: see **Daisy Dean Spring** [LASSEN].

Deanes Valley [PLUMAS]: *valley,* 4 miles south-southeast of the village of Meadow Valley along South Fork Rock Creek (5) (lat. 39°53'05" N, long. 121°01'10" W; sec. 6, T 23 N, R 9 E). Named on Meadow Valley (1980) 7.5' quadrangle. Bidwell Bar (1897) 30' quadrangle shows a lake called Dean Valley Reservoir in the valley.

Deans Meadow [LASSEN]: *area,* 5.5 miles south-southeast of Pelican Point (lat. 40°33'25" N, long. 120°43'15" W; sec. 10, T 31 N, R 11 E). Named on Fredonyer Peak (1954) 15' quadrangle.

Deans Ridge [LASSEN]: *ridge,* southeast-trending, 2 miles long, 5 miles south-southeast of Pelican Point (lat. 40°33'45" N, long. 120° 43'10" W; mainly in sec. 10, T 31 N, R 11 E). Named on Fredonyer Peak (1954) 15' quadrangle.

Dean Valley Reservoir: see **Deanes Valley** [PLUMAS].

De Camp Tank [MODOC]: *water feature,* 18 miles northwest of Alturas (lat. 41°42'25" N, long. 120°44'40" W). Named on Big Sage Reservoir (1962) 15' quadrangle.

Dedication Island [PLUMAS]: *island,* 350 feet long, 7 miles east-northeast of Kettle Rock in Antelope Lake (lat. 40°11'05" N, long. 120°36'15" W; near W line sec. 23, T 27 N, R 12 E). Named on Antelope Lake (1972) 7.5' quadrangle.

Deep Canyon [LASSEN]: *canyon,* drained by a stream that flows 2.25 miles to Cedar Creek 8 miles northeast of Madeline (lat. 41° 07'45" N, long. 120°21'55" W; sec. 16, T 38 N, R 14 E). Named on Cold Spring Mountain (1962) and Jess Valley (1962) 7.5' quadrangles.

Deep Creek [LASSEN]: *stream,* flows 19 miles to Secret Creek 3 miles south of Karlo (lat. 40°30'30" N, long. 120°18'35" W; near W line sec. 32, T 31 N, R 15 E). Named on Karlo (1954), Shinn Mountain (1954), and Wendel (1954) 15' quadrangles.

Deep Creek: see **Cedarville** [MODOC]; **Dismal Creek** [MODOC]; **North Deep Creek** [MODOC]; **South Deep Creek** [MODOC].

Deep Cut [LASSEN]: *canyon,* about 1 mile long, 17 miles south of Observation Peak (lat. 40°01'45" N, long. 120°10' W; on N line sec. 28, T 31 N, R 16 E); the canyon is along Deep Creek. Named on Shinn Mountain (1954) 15' quadrangle.

Deep Cut Spring [MODOC]: *spring,* 7.25 miles southeast of Crank Mountain (lat. 41°18'35" N, long. 121°03' W; near E line sec. 16, T 40 N, R 8 E). Named on Crank Mountain (1962) 15' quadrangle.

Deep Waterhole [MODOC]: *water feature,* 5 miles north of White Horse (lat. 41°23'20" N, long. 121°22'40" W). Named on White Horse (1962) 15' quadrangle.

Deer Creek [PLUMAS]:

(1) *stream,* flows 1.5 miles to French Creek (1) less than 0.5 mile north-northeast of Caribou (lat. 40°05'05" N, long. 121°09'05" W; near NW cor. sec. 25, T 26 N, R 7 E). Named on Caribou (1979) 7.5' quadrangle.

(2) *stream,* flows 2.5 miles to Rock Creek (5) 2.25 miles east-southeast of the village of Meadow Valley (lat. 39°55'05" N, long. 121°01'15" W; sec. 30, T 24 N, R 9 E). Named on Meadow Valley (1980) and Quincy (1950) 7.5' quadrangles.

(3) *stream,* flows 3 miles to Eureka Creek 4.25 miles west of Blairsden (lat. 39°46'35" N, long. 120°41'50" W; near N line sec. 13, T 22 N, R 11 E). Named on Johnsville (1972) 7.5' quadrangle.

Deerheart Creek [LASSEN]: *stream,* flows 3.5 miles to Mountain Meadows Reservoir 3.5 miles south-southeast of Westwood (lat. 40°15'45" N, long. 120°58'10" W; near N line sec. 28, T 28 N, R 9 E); the stream heads at Deerheart Lake. Named on Greenville (1979) and Westwood East (1980) 7.5' quadrangles.

Deerheart Lake [LASSEN]: *lake,* 850 feet long, 5 miles south of Westwood (lat. 40°14'10" N, long. 120°59'10" W; near SE cor. sec. 32, T 28 N, R 9 E). Named on Greenville (1979) 7.5' quadrangle.

Deer Hill [MODOC]:

(1) *peak,* nearly 4 miles north-northwest of Hackamore (lat. 41°36'20" N, long. 121°08'40" W; near SE cor. sec. 34, T 44 N, R 7 E). Named on Hackamore (1952) 15' quadrangle.

(2) *peak,* 3.5 miles west of South Mountain (lat. 41°50'25" N, long. 120°42'20" W; near SE cor. sec. 9, T 46 N, R 11 E). Named on South Mountain (1962) 15' quadrangle.

Deer Hill Tank [MODOC]: *water feature,* 3.5 miles west-southwest of South Mountain (lat. 41°49'30" N, long. 120°41'50" W; near SW cor. sec. 15, T 46 N, R 11 E); the feature is 1.25 miles south-southeast of Deer Hill (2). Named on South Mountain (1962) 15' quadrangle.

Deer Park [PLUMAS]: *area,* 11 miles south-southeast of Storrie (lat. 30°46'05" N, long. 121°15'55" W; on SW cor. sec. 12, T 22 N, R 6 E). Named on Soapstone Hill (1979) 7.5' quadrangle.

Deer Spring [LASSEN]:

(1) *spring,* 9 miles south-southwest of Adin [MODOC] (lat. 41°04'20" N, long. 120°59'25" W; near E line sec. 1, T 37 N, R 8 E). Named on Adin (1962) 15' quadrangle.

(2) *spring,* 8 miles north-northeast of Termo (lat. 40°58'30" N, long. 120°24'35" W; near N line sec. 20, T 36 N, R 14 E). Named on Ravendale (1954) 15' quadrangle.

Deer Spring [MODOC]:

(1) *spring,* 1 mile east-southeast of Hackamore (lat. 41°33' N, long. 121°06' W; at W line sec. 19, T 43 N, R 8 E). Named on Hackamore (1952) 15' quadrangle.

(2) *spring,* 8 miles east of Adin (lat. 40°11'30" N, long. 120°47'40" W; sec. 26, T 39 N, R 10 E). Named on Adin (1962) 15' quadrangle.

Deer Spring Ridge [MODOC]: *ridge,* south-southeast-trending, 4 miles long, 8 miles east of Adin (lat. 41°12'45" N, long. 120°48'15" W); Deer Spring (2) is near the south end of the ridge. Named on Adin (1962) 15' quadrangle.

Dejonah Creek [PLUMAS]: *stream,* flows 2.5 miles to Middle Fork Feather River 1.5 miles west-northwest of Dogwood Peak (lat. 39° 47'35" N, long. 121°04'50" W; near W line sec. 3, T 22 N, R 8 E). Named on Dogwood Peak (1979) 7.5' quadrangle.

Delleker [PLUMAS]: *locality,* 1.5 miles west of Portola (lat. 39°48'30" N, long. 120°29'45" W; sec. 34, 35, T 23 N, R 13 E). Named on Blairsden (1972) and Portola (1972) 7.5' quadrangles. Sierraville (1894) 30' quadrangle has the name "Hawks" at the place. Postal authorities established Delleker post office in 1927 and discontinued it in 1954 (Frickstad, p. 123). The name commemorates W.H. Delleker, a lumberman (Gudde, 1949, p. 92).

Del Prat Spring [MODOC]: *springs,* 4.5 miles east of Willow Ranch (lat. 41°53'50" N, long. 120°16'10" W; sec. 32, T 47 N, R 15 E). Named on Willow Ranch (1962) 15' quadrangle.

Delta Lake [MODOC]: *lake,* 6000 feet long, 6.5 miles west-northwest of Likely (lat. 41°14'45" N, long. 120°36'45" W; sec. 4, 5, T 39 N, R 12 E). Named on Alturas (1961) and Likely (1962) 15' quadrangles.

Demuth [MODOC]: *locality,* 7.25 miles east-northeast of White Horse along Great Northern Railroad (lat. 41°20'15" N, long. 121° 15'55" W; sec. 3, T 40 N, R 6 E). Named on White Horse (1962) 15' quadrangle.

Denten Creek [PLUMAS]: *stream,* flows 2.5 miles to Middle Fork Feather River 1 mile south-southeast of Blairsden (lat. 39°46' N, long. 120°36'15" W; near W line sec. 14, T 22 N, R 12 E). Named on Blairsden (1972) 7.5' quadrangle. Downieville (1897) 30' quadrangle has the name "Dentens" for a place situated near the mouth of present Denten Creek.

Dentens: see **Denten Creek** [PLUMAS].

Derby Lake: see **Honey Lake** [LASSEN].

Devil Canyon [PLUMAS]: *canyon,* 3 miles northwest of Cascade along Middle Fork Feather River on Plumas-Butte County line (lat. 39°43'30" N, long. 121°13'30" W). Named on Cascade (1948) 7.5' quadrangle.

Devils Corral [LASSEN]: *relief feature,* 13 miles east-northeast of Westwood (lat. 40°23'45" N, long. 120°46'40" W; at NE cor. sec. 7, T 29 N, R 11 E). Named on Roop Mountain (1980) 7.5' quadrangle.

Devils Gap [PLUMAS]: *pass,* 2.5 miles north-northwest of American House (lat. 39°41'10" N, long. 121°02'55" W; at N line sec. 14, T 21 N, R 8 E). Named on American House (1948) 7.5' quadrangle.

Devils Kitchen [PLUMAS]: *area,* 7 miles west of Mount Harkness (lat. 40°26'30" N, long. 121°26' W; near SW cor. sec. 21, T 30 N, R 5 E). Named on Mount Harkness (1956) 15' quadrangle. Bubbling pools, steam vents, and clouds of vapor occur at the place (Waring, p. 141).

Devils Punch Bowl [PLUMAS]: *crater,* 4.5 miles south-southeast of Taylorsville (lat. 40°01'05" N, long. 120°48'05" W; near W line sec. 19, T 25 N, R 11 E). Named on Taylorsville (1980) 7.5' quadrangle.

Dewitt: see **Wendel** [LASSEN].

Diamond Mountain [LASSEN]: *peak,* 7.5 miles south-southwest of Susanville (lat. 40°18'45" N, long. 120°41'30" W; sec. 1, T 28 N, R 11 E); the peak is near the northwest end of Diamond Mountains. Altitude 7738 feet. Named on Diamond Mountain (1972) 7.5' quadrangle.

Diamond Mountains [LASSEN-PLUMAS]: *range,* on southwest side of Honey Lake Valley on Lassen-Plumas County line. Named on Susanville (1962) 1°x 2° quadrangle.

Diamond Ravine [PLUMAS]: *canyon,* drained by a stream that flows 0.5 mile to Onion Creek 2 miles south-southwest of American House (lat. 39°37'35" N, long. 121°02'30" W; near NE cor. sec. 2, T 20 N, R 8 E); the canyon heads near Diamond Springs. Named on American House (1948) 7.5' quadrangle.

Diamond Reservoir: see **Baseball Reservoir** [MODOC].

Diamond Springs [PLUMAS]: *springs,* 2.25 miles southwest of American House (lat. 39°37'55" N, long. 121°03'15" W; sec. 35, T 21 N, R 8 E). Named on American House (1948) 7.5' quadrangle.

Diamond Springs Hill [PLUMAS]: *ridge,* northeast-trending, less than 1 mile long, 1.5 miles southwest of American House (lat. 39° 38'15" N, long. 121°02'45" W; mainly in sec. 35, T 21 N, R 8 E); the ridge extends northeast from Diamond Springs. Named on American House (1948) 7.5' quadrangle.

Diaz Flat [LASSEN]: *area,* 17 miles west-northwest of Termo (lat. 40°59'35" N, long. 120°44'35" W; at SE cor. sec. 31, T 37 N, R 11 E). Named on Grasshopper Valley (1954) 15' quadrangle.

Diaz Spring [LASSEN]: *spring,* 20 miles southwest of Likely [MODOC] (lat. 41°00'40" N, long. 120°44'30" W; near SE cor. sec. 30, T 37 N, R 11 E). Named on Likely (1962) 15' quadrangle.

Digger Creek [PLUMAS]: *stream,* flows 1.5 miles to North Fork Feather River 1 mile southwest of Caribou (lat. 40°04'15" N, long. 121°10'10" W; near NW cor. sec. 35, T 26 N, R 7 E). Named on Caribou (1979) 7.5' quadrangle.

Digger Ravine [PLUMAS]: *canyon,* drained by a stream that flows 1.25 miles to East Branch of North Fork Feather River 0.5 mile west-southwest of Twain (lat. 40°01'05" N, long 121°04'45" W; sec. 22, T 25 N, R 8 E). Named on Twain (1980) 7.5' quadrangle.

Dill Butte [LASSEN]: *hill,* 9 miles east-southeast of Termo (lat. 40°49'25" N, long. 120°18'15" W; sec. 8, T 34 N, R 15 E). Altitude 5741 feet. Named on Ravendale (1954) 15' quadrangle. Called Rocky Butte on Honey Lake (1893) 1° quadrangle.

Dill Field [LASSEN]: *area,* 9.5 miles east-southeast of Madeline (lat. 41°00'10" N, long. 120°18'35" W; in and near sec. 7, T 36 N, R 15 E). Named on Cold Spring Mountain (1962) 7.5' quadrangle.

Dillon Creek [PLUMAS]: *stream,* flows 4.25 miles to Bailey Creek 5.5 miles north-northeast of Chester (lat. 40°22'50" N, long. 121° 10'20" W; near SW cor. sec. 11, T 29 N, R 7 E). Named on Red Cinder (1979) 7.5' quadrangle.

Dillon Lake [LASSEN]: *lake,* 9 miles north of Lava Peak (lat. 40°57'30" N, long. 120°53'15" W; on W line sec. 13, T 36 N, R 9 E). Named on Hayden Hill (1956) 15' quadrangle.

Dill Slough [LASSEN]: *water feature,* 3 miles south-southeast of Litchfield in Honey Lake Valley (lat. 40°20'50" N, long. 120° 22' W. Named on Litchfield (1954) 15' quadrangle.

Dinky Spring [PLUMAS]: *spring,* 5.25 miles west of Milford [LASSEN] (lat. 40°10'45" N, long. 120°28'15" W; near SW cor. sec. 24, T 27 N, R 13 E). Named on Stony Ridge (1978) 7.5' quadrangle.

Dinwiddie Arm [LASSEN]: *relief feature,* 3 miles south-southeast of Beckwourth Pass (lat. 39°45' N, long. 120°05'15" W). Named on Beckwourth Pass (1975) and Evans Canyon (1978) 7.5' quadrangles.

Dip Spring [MODOC]: *spring,* 11.5 miles north of Blue Mountain at California-Oregon State line (lat. 41°59'35" N, long. 120°49'40" W; near N line sec. 21, T 48 N, R 10 E). Named on Steele Swamp (1962) 15' quadrangle.

Dismal Creek [MODOC]: *stream,* flows 1.5 miles to the State of Oregon 9.5

miles north of Fort Bidwell (lat. 41°59'40" N, long. 120°10' W); the stream goes through Dismal Swamp. Named on Fort Bidwell (1962) 15' quadrangle. Called Deep Creek on Hill's (1915) map. United States Board on Geographic Names (1964c, p. 14) rejected the name "East Fork Dismal Creek" for the stream.

Dismal Swamp [MODOC]: *water feature,* 9 miles north of Fort Bidwell (lat. 41°59'10" N, long. 120°10'15" W). Named on Fort Bidwell (1962) 15' quadrangle.

Ditch Camp [LASSEN]: *locality,* 7 miles east-southeast of Bieber (lat. 41°04'55" N, long. 121°01'25" W; at S line sec. 35, T 38 N, R 8 E). Named on Bieber (1961) 15' quadrangle.

Divide Lake: see **North Divide Lake** [LASSEN]; **South Divide Lake** [LASSEN].

Dixie [LASSEN]: *locality,* 3.5 miles north of the village of Little Valley along Western Pacific Railroad (lat. 40°56'40" N, long. 121°10'10" W; sec. 21, T 36 N, R 7 E). Named on LittleValley (1957) 15' quadrangle. Postal authorities established Dixie post office in 1907 and discontinued it in 1912 (Frickstad, p. 67).

Dixie Camp [PLUMAS]: *locality,* 13 miles north-northwest of Chilcoot along Lookout Creek (lat. 39°58'15" N, long. 120°13'55" W; near S line sec. 31, T 25 N, R 16 E); the place is 0.25 mile south of Dixie Spring. Named on Frenchman Lake (1979) 7.5' quadrangle.

Dixie Creek [PLUMAS]:

(1) *stream,* flows 1.5 miles to Indian Creek (2) 2 miles southwest of Crescent Mills (lat. 40°04'35" N, long. 120°56'05" W; near N line sec. 35, T 26 N, R 9 E). Named on Crescent Mills (1980) 7.5' quadrangle.

(2) *stream,* flows 12.5 miles to Red Clover Creek 10 miles north of Portola (lat. 39°57'10" N, long. 120°26'40" W; near W line sec. 8, T 24 N, R 14 E). Named on Crocker Mountain (1972) and Dixie Mountain (1972) 7.5' quadrangles.

Dixie Crossing [LASSEN]: *locality,* 3.25 miles east of the village of Little Valley along Horse Creek (lat. 40°53'15" N, long. 121°06'55" W; sec. 19, T 35 N, R 8 E); the place is near the west end of Dixie Valley. Named on Little Valley (1957) 15' quadrangle.

Dixie Mountain [PLUMAS]: *peak,* 14 miles northeast of Portola (lat. 39°56'20" N, long. 120°17'05" W; near N line sec. 15, T 24 N, R 15 E). Altitude 8327 feet. Named on Dixie Mountain (1972) 7.5' quadrangle. Called Dixie Pk. on California Mining Bureau's (1917b) map.

Dixie Peak [LASSEN]: *peak,* 5 miles east-northeast of the village of Little Valley on Bald Mountain (1) (lat. 40°55' N, long. 121°05'30" W). Altitude 6067 feet. Named on LittleValley (1957) 15' quadrangle.

Dixie Peak: see **Dixie Mountain** [PLUMAS];

Dixie Spring [LASSEN]: *spring,* 8 miles southeast of the village of Little Valley (lat. 40°48'15" N, long. 120°05'15" W; near S line sec. 16, T 34 N, R 8 E). Named on LittleValley (1957) 15' quadrangle.

Dixie Spring [PLUMAS]: *spring,* 13 miles north-northwest of Chilcoot (lat. 39°58'30" N, long. 120°13'55" W; sec. 31, T 25 N, R 16 E). Named on Frenchman Lake (1979) 7.5' quadrangle.

Dixie Springs [LASSEN]: *springs,* 6 miles east-northeast of Cal Mountain (lat. 40°42'20" N, long. 121°03'45" W; sec. 22, T 33 N, R 8 E). Named on Harvey Mountain (1956) 15' quadrangle. Called Dixie Spring on Halls Flat (1939) 30' quadrangle.

Dixie Valley [LASSEN]: *valley,* 6 miles east of the village of Little Valley (lat. 40°52'45" N, long. 121°03'45" W). Named on Little Valley (1957) 15' quadrangle.

Dixie Valley [PLUMAS]: *canyon,* along Dixie Creek (2) above a point about 13 miles north-northeast of Portola (lat. 39°58'50" N, long. 120°24' W). Named on Crocker Mountain (1972) and Dixie Mountain (1972) 7.5' quadrangles.

Dixon Creek [PLUMAS]: *stream,* flows 3.25 miles to Nelson Creek 9 miles southeast of Quincy (lat. 39°50'15" N, long. 120°50'50" W). Named on Blue Nose Mountain (1951) and Onion Valley (1950) 7.5' quadrangles.

Dixon Flat [LASSEN]: *area,* 9 miles southwest of Bieber (lat. 41°01'45" N, long. 121°15'50" W; mainly in sec. 22, T 37 N, R 6 E). Named on Fall River Mills (1961) 15' quadrangle.

Dixon Flat [MODOC]: *area,* 8 miles southeast of Canby (lat. 41°21'30" N, long. 120°45'30" W; near SE cor. sec. 25, T 41 N, R 10 E). Named on Canby (1961) 15' quadrangle.

Dixon Hill [LASSEN]: *peak,* 8.5 miles southwest of Bieber (lat. 41° 01'45" N, long. 121°14'35" W; sec. 23, T 37 N, R 6 E); the peak is east of Dixon Flat. Altitude 4723 feet. Named on Bieber (1961) 15' quadrangle.

Dobe Swale [MODOC]: *marsh,* 3.25 miles south-southwest of Jacks Butte (lat. 41°32'50" N, long. 120°50' W; on S line sec. 20, T 43 N, R 10 E). Named on Jacks Butte (1962) 15' quadrangle.

Dobie Flat [MODOC]: *area,* 8.5 miles south-southeast of Newell (lat. 41°46'15" N, long. 121°19'15" W; sec. 6, T 45 N, R 6 E). Named on Tulelake (1951) 15' quadrangle.

Doc Smith Flat [PLUMAS]: *area,* 11 miles east-northeast of Kettle Peak (lat. 40°12'15" N; long. 120°32'10" W; near N line sec. 17, T 27 N, R 13 E). Named on Antelope Lake (1972) 7.5' quadrangle.

Dodge Reservoir [LASSEN]: *lake,* 1.5 miles long, 14 miles north of Observation Peak along Red Rock Creek (lat. 40°58'40" N, long. 120°08'15" W). Named on Observation Peak (1954) 15' quadrangle.

Dodge Spring [LASSEN]: *spring,* 11.5 miles northeast of Termo (lat. 40°59'15" N, long. 120°18'30" W; near E line sec. 18, T 36 N, R 15 E). Named on Ravendale (1954) 15' quadrangle.

Doe Spring [MODOC]: *spring,* 13 miles south-southeast of Canby (lat. 41°15'30" N, long. 120°48' W; near SW cor. sec. 35, T 40 N, R 10 E). Named on Canby (1961) 15' quadrangle.

Dogwood Creek [PLUMAS]: *stream,* flows 4.25 miles to Middle Fork Feather River 1.25 miles north of Dogwood Peak (lat. 39°48'10" N, long. 121°03'15" W; near N line sec. 2, T 22 N, R 8 E). Named on Dogwood Peak (1979) 7.5' quadrangle.

Dogwood Peak [PLUMAS]: *peak,* 12 miles south-southwest of Quincy (lat. 39°47'05" N, long. 121°03'20" W; sec. 11, T 22 N, R 8 E). Altitude 6108 feet. Named on Dogwood Peak (1979) 7.5' quadrangle.

Doles: see **Hackamore** [MODOC].

Dolly Creek [PLUMAS]: *stream,* flows 1.5 miles to Little Grizzly Creek 4 miles southwest of Mount Ingalls (lat. 39°57'20" N, long. 120°41' W; near SE cor. sec. 12, T 24 N, R 11 E). Named on Mount Ingalls (1972) 7.5' quadrangle.

Domingo Creek [PLUMAS]: *stream,* flows 1.5 miles to North Fork Feather River 6 miles south-southwest of Mount Harkness (lat. 40° 20'50" N, long. 121°19'50" W; sec. 29, T 29 N, R 6 E); the stream heads at Domingo Spring. Named on Mount Harkness (1956) 15' quadrangle.

Domingo Spring [PLUMAS]: *spring,* 5.5 miles south-southwest of Mount Harkness (lat. 40°21'40" N, long. 121°20'50" W; near E line sec. 19, T 29 N, R 6 E); the spring is at the head of Domingo Creek. Named on Mount Harkness (1956) 15' quadrangle.

Donavan Reservoir [MODOC]: *lake,* about 1 mile long, 9.5 miles southwest of Alturas (lat. 41°24'15" N, long. 120°41'15" W; sec. 10, T 41 N, R 11 E). Named on Alturas (1961) 15' quadrangle. United States Board on Geographic Names (1988, p. 1) approved the name "Donovan Reservoir" for the lake, and rejected the names "Donavan Reservoir" and "California Pines Lake" for it.

Donica Mountain [MODOC]: *peak,* 3.5 miles south-southwest of Crank Mountain (lat. 41°20' N, long. 121°09'45" W; on E line sec. 4, T 40 N, R 7 E). Altitude 4956 feet. Named on Crank Mountain (1962) 15' quadrangle.

Donovan Reservoir : see **Donavan Reservoir** [MODOC].

Dooley Canyon [PLUMAS]: *canyon,* drained by Little Dooley Creek, which flows 5 miles to Little Last Chance Creek 12.5 miles north-northwest of Chilcoot (lat. 39°58'10" N, long. 120°12'25" W; near N line sec. 5, T 24 N, R 16 E). Named on Frenchman Lake (1979) 7.5' quadrangle.

Dooley Canyon Spring [PLUMAS]: *spring,* 11 miles north of Chilcoot (lat. 39°57'25" N, long. 120°09'55" W; near SE cor. sec. 3, T 24 N, R 16 E); the spring is in a branch of Dooley Canyon. Named on Frenchman Lake (1979) 7.5' quadrangle.

Dooley Creek [PLUMAS]: *stream,* flows 4 miles to Last Chance Creek (2) 5.5 miles northeast of Squaw Valley Peak (lat. 40°04'30" N, long. 126°18'45" W; sec. 29, T 26 N, R 15 E). Named on Ferris Creek (1977) 7.5' quadrangle.

Dooley Creek: see **Little Dooley Creek** [PLUMAS].

Dorris' Bridge: see **Alturas** [MODOC].

Dorris Brothers Reservoir [MODOC]: *intermittent lake,* 1 mile long, 17 miles north-northwest of Alturas (lat. 41°43' N, long. 120° 41' W; sec. 22, 27, T 45 N, R 11 E). Named on Big Sage Reservoir (1962) 15' quadrangle.

Dorris Reservoir [MODOC]: *lake,* 2 miles long, 3.5 miles east of Alturas (lat. 41°29' N, long. 120°28'30" W). Named on Dorris Reservoir (1963) 7.5' quadrangle. Called Stockdill Slough Reservoir on California Division of Highways' (1934) map.

Dorrisville: see **Alturas** [MODOC].

Dorsey Butte [LASSEN]: *peak,* 12 miles east-northeast of Termo (lat. 40°57' N, long. 120°15'30" W; on N line sec. 34, T 36 N, R 15 E). Named on Ravendale (1954) 15' quadrangle.

Dotta Canyon [PLUMAS]: *canyon,* drained by a stream that flows 5.5 miles to Red Clover Valley 9 miles north-northeast of Portola (lat. 39°55'30" N, long. 120°24'20" W; near NW cor. sec. 22, T 24 N, R 14 E). Named on Crocker Mountain (1972) and Dixie Mountain (1972) 7.5' quadrangles.

Dotta Neck [PLUMAS]: *area,* 8 miles northeast of Portola (lat. 39° 53'40" N, long. 120°22' W; near NW cor. sec. 36, T 24 N, R 14 E); the place is in Dotta Canyon. Named on Dixie Mountain (1972) 7.5' quadrangle.

Dotta Saddle [PLUMAS]: *pass,* 8 miles northeast of Portola (lat. 39° 52'15" N, long. 120°20'50" W; near SW cor. sec. 6, T 23 N, R 15 E); the pass is at the head of Dotta Canyon. Named on Reconnaissance Peak (1972) 7.5' quadrangle.

Dotta Spring [PLUMAS]: *spring,* 8.5 miles northwest of Chilcoot (lat. 39°53'45" N, long. 120°13'35" W; near N line sec. 31, T 24 N, R 16 E). Named on Frenchman Lake (1979) 7.5' quadrangle.

Double Head: see **Double Head Mountain** [MODOC].

Double Head Lake [MODOC]: *intermittent lake,* 2800 feet long, 2.5 miles southeast of Double Head Mountain (lat. 41°45'10" N, long. 121°08'15" W; mainly in sec. 11, T 45 N, R 7 E). Named on Clear Lake Reservoir (1951) and Hackamore (1952) 15' quadrangles.

Double Head Mountain [MODOC]: *mountain,* 37 miles west-northwest of Alturas (lat. 41°45'50" N, long. 121°10' W; around NE cor. sec. 9, T 45 N, R 7 E). Altitude 5582 feet. Named on Clear Lake Reservoir (1951) 15' quadrangle. Called Double Head on Modoc Lava-Bed (1892) 1° quadrangle. Ray (p. 209) used the designation "Double Head (Saddle Mountain)."

Dow Butte [LASSEN]: *peak,* 9 miles north-northwest of Pelican Point (lat. 40°44'55" N, long. 120°49'35" W; at E line sec. 3, T 33 N, R 10 E). Named on Antelope Mountain (1956) and Hayden Hill (1956) 15' quadrangles. The name commemorates William Dow, who settled in the vicinity in 1875 (Purdy, 1988, p. 118).

Dow Flat [LASSEN]: *area,* 7 miles north-northwest of Pelican Point (lat. 40°43'15" N, long. 120°48'30" W; at E line sec. 14, T 33 N, R 10 E). Named on Antelope Mountain (1956) 15' quadrangle.

Downing Cabin Spring [PLUMAS]: *spring,* 7.5 miles southeast of Milford [LASSEN] (lat. 40°05'45" N, long. 120°16' W; near E line sec. 22, T 26 N, R 15 E). Named on Ferris Creek (1977) 7.5' quadrangle, which shows Downing cabin near the spring.

Downing Canyon [LASSEN]: *canyon,* drained by a stream that flows 2 miles to Honey Lake Valley 3.5 miles west-northwest of Doyle (lat. 40°02'50" N, long. 120°09'45" W; at W line sec. 2, T 25 N, R 16 E). Named on McKesick Peak (1978) 7.5' quadrangle.

Dow Wells [LASSEN]: *wells,* nearly 7 miles north-northwest of Pelican Point (lat. 40°43' N, long. 120°48'35" W; near SE cor. sec. 14, T 33 N, R 10 E); the wells are at the south end of Dow Flat. Named on Antelope Mountain (1956) 15' quadrangle.

Doyle [LASSEN]: *village,* 40 miles southeast of Susanville (lat. 40° 01'45" N, long. 120°06'10" W; sec. 8, 17, T 25 N, R 17 E). Named on Doyle (1954) 15' quadrangle. Postal authorities established Doyle post office in 1908 (Frickstad, p. 67). The name is for Oscar Doyle, who settled at the place in the 1870's and donated land for the townsite (Hanna, p. 90). Postal authorities established Cromwell post office 9 miles north of Doyle in 1912 and discontinued it in 1913; the name was for F.T. Cromwell, who laid out a townsite at the place (Salley, p. 53).

Doyle Crossing [PLUMAS]: *locality,* 7.25 miles northwest of Squaw Valley Peak along Last Chance Creek (2) (lat. 40°06'45" N, long. 120°29' W; near N line sec. 14, T 26 N, R 13 E). Named on Squaw Valley Peak (1977) 7.5' quadrangle.

Doyle Reservoir [PLUMAS]: *intermittent lake,* 1500 feet long, 2.5 miles southwest of Milford (lat. 40°08'40" N, long. 120°24'20" W; near N line sec. 4, T 26 N, R 14 E). Named on Stony Ridge (1978) 7.5' quadrangle.

Drake: see **Drakesbad** [PLUMAS].

Drake Lake [PLUMAS]: *lake,* 900 feet long, 6.5 miles west of Mount Harkness (lat. 40°25'45" N, long. 121°25'35" W; sec. 28, T 30 N, R 5 E); the lake is 1.5 miles southwest of Drakesbad. Named on Mount Harkness (1956) 15' quadrangle.

Drakesbad [PLUMAS]: *locality,* 5.5 miles west of Mount Harkness along Hot Springs Creek (lat. 40°26'40" N, long. 121°24'15" W; sec. 22, T 30 N, R 5 E). Named on Mount Harkness (1956) 15' quadrangle. Postal authorities established Drake post office at present Drakesbad in 1901 and discontinued it in 1902 (Salley, p. 62). The place first was called Hot Spring Valley and then it was called Drake's place or Drake's Hot Springs for the owner, E.R. Drake, who settled there in the 1860's and sold the property to the Sifford family in 1900; the new owners added the German term *bad* to the former owner's name to give the place the new name "Drakesbad" (Gudde, 1949, p. 99). Schulz (p. 17) noted that hot baths at the site about 1880 were called Malgin's Hot Springs.

Drake's Hot Springs: see **Drakesbad** [PLUMAS].

Dream Lake [PLUMAS]: *lake,* 500 feet long, 5.5 miles west of Mount Harkness (lat. 40°26'30" N, long. 121°24'20" W; near S line sec. 22, T 30 N, R 5 E). Named on Mount Harkness (1956) 15' quadrangle.

Drift Fence Tank [MODOC]: *water feature,* 3 miles east-northeast of South Mountain (lat. 41°51' N, long. 120°34'35" W; near N line sec. 10, T 46 N, R 12 E). Named on South Mountain (1962) 15' quadrangle.

Dry Creek [LASSEN]:

(1) *stream,* flows 7.5 miles to Cold Spring Valley about 15 miles north-northwest of Observation Peak (lat. 40°58'45" N, long. 120° 14'30" W; sec. 14, T 36 N, R 15 E). Named on Observation Peak (1954) and Ravendale (1954) 15' quadrangles, and on Cold Spring Mountain (1962) 7.5' quadrangle.

(2) *stream,* flows nearly 5 miles to Clear Creek (1) 2.5 miles west of Westwood (lat. 40°18'10" W; long. 121°02'50" W; sec. 11, T 28 N, R 8 E). Named on Westwood West (1980) 7.5' quadrangle.

Dry Creek [LASSEN-MODOC]: *stream,* heads in Lassen County and flows 11.5 miles to lowlands near South Fork Pit River at Likely in Modoc County (lat. 41°14'05" N, long. 120°30' W; sec. 8, T 39 N, R 13 E). Named on Likely (1962) 15' quadrangle.

Dry Creek [MODOC]: *stream,* flows 5.5 miles to Parker Creek 11.5 miles east of Alturas (lat. 41°27'15" N, long. 120°19'35" W). Named on Davis Creek (1962) 15' quadrangle, and on Shields Creek (1963) 7.5' quadrangle.

Dry Creek [PLUMAS]: *stream,* flows nearly 1 mile to Nelson Creek 9 miles southeast of Quincy (lat. 39°50'05" N, long. 120°50'35" W). Named on Blue Nose Mountain (1951) 7.5' quadrangle.

Dry Creek: see **East Dry Creek** [MODOC]; **Granger Creek** [MODOC].

Dry Creek Basin [MODOC]: *valley,* 11 miles east of Alturas (lat. 41° 30' N, long. 120°20' W); the place is along Dry Creek. Named on Davis Creek (1962) 15' quadrangle, and on Shields Creek (1963) 7.5' quadrangle.

Dry Creek Rim [MODOC]: *escarpment,* generally east-trending, 10 miles long, center 9 miles north-northeast of South Mountain (lat. 41°58' N, long. 120°35' W); the feature is at and just south of California-Oregon State line. Named on South Mountain (1962) 15' quadrangle.

Dry Flat [PLUMAS]: *area,* 10 miles east of Kettle Rock (lat. 40°08'15" N, long. 120°32'25" W; mainly in sec. 5, T 26 N, R 13 E). Named on Antelope Lake (1972) 7.5' quadrangle.

Dry Lake [LASSEN]:

(1) *intermittent lake,* 1600 feet long, 10 miles northeast of the village of Little Valley (lat. 40°59'50" N, long. 121°02'45" W; at W line sec. 34, T 37 N, R 8 E). Named on Little Valley (1957) 15' quadrangle.

(2) *intermittent lake,* 4000 feet long, 10 miles northeast of Observation Peak (lat. 40°52' N, long. 120°01'15" W; sec. 26, T 35 N, R 17 E). Named on Observation Peak (1954) 15' quadrangle.

(3) *marsh,* 4.25 miles west-southwest of Lava Peak (lat. 40°49'05" N, long. 120°58'10" W; on S line sec. 9, T 34 N, R 9 E). Named on Hayden Hill (1956) 15' quadrangle.

Dry Lake [MODOC]:

(1) *intermittent lake,* 1.25 miles long, 4 miles north of Timber Mountain (lat. 41°41' N, long. 121°17'15" W; mainly in sec. 4, T 44 N, R 6 E). Named on Timber Mountain (1952) 15' quadrangle. The feature was called Sorass Lake before 1873, when soldiers who expected to find water there renamed the lake when they found it dry (Gudde, 1949, p. 99).

(2) *locality,* about 6.5 miles southwest of Double Head (present Double Head Mountain) (lat. 41°42'10" N, long. 121°16'45" W). Named on Modoc Lava-Bed (1892) 1° quadrangle. Timber Mountain (1952) 15' quadrangle shows Dry Lake guard station at or near the place.

Dry Lake [PLUMAS]: *intermittent lake,* 200 feet long, 4.25 miles north-northwest of Bucks Lodge (lat. 39°55'55" N, long. 121°12'15" W; near S line sec. 16, T 24 N, R 7 E). Named on Bucks Lake (1979) 7.5' quadrangle.

Dry Lake: see **Big Dry Lake** [LASSEN]; **Lower Day Lake** [LASSEN].

Dry Taylor Creek [PLUMAS]: *stream,* flows 3.25 miles to Taylor Creek 5.5 miles northwest of Spring Garden (lat. 39°57'15" N, long. 120°51'35" W; near E line sec. 9, T 24 N, R 10 E). Named on Spring Garden (1950) 7.5' quadrangle.

Dry Valley [LASSEN]:

(1) *valley,* 11 miles west of Termo (lat. 40°52'15" N, long. 120°40'15" W). Named on Grasshopper Valley (1954) 15' quadrangle.

(2) *canyon,* along Dry Valley Creek above a point 2 miles northeast of Constantia (lat. 39°58' N, long. 120°00'45" W; at NW cor. sec. 7, T 24 N, R 18 E); the canyon extends southeast into the State of Nevada. Named on Constantia (1977) 7.5' quadrangle.

Dry Valley Creek [LASSEN]: *stream,* heads in the State of Nevada and flows 8.5 miles in Lassen County to Long Valley Creek near Doyle (lat. 40°01'55" N, long. 120°05'50" W; sec. 8, T 25 N, R 17 E). Named on Doyle (1954) 15' quadrangle, and on Constantia (1977) 7.5' quadrangle.

Dry Valley Creek: see **Long Valley Creek** [LASSEN].

Dry Valley Gap [LASSEN]: *pass,* 9 miles west of Termo (lat. 40°50'35" N, long. 120°37'30" W; near N line sec. 4, T 34 N, R 12 E). Named on Grasshopper Valley (1954) 15' quadrangle.

Dry Valley Reservoir [MODOC]: *intermittent lake,* 5 miles east of Blue Mountain (lat. 41°50'30" N, long. 120°45'45" W; near SE cor. sec. 12, T 46 N, R 10 E). Named on Steele Swamp (1962) 15' quadrangle. Alturas 1° quadrangle has the name "Willow Creek Meadow" at or near present Dry Valley Reservoir.

Dry Valley Ridge [LASSEN]: *ridge,* south-southeast-trending, 5 miles long, 10.5 miles west of Termo (lat. 40°53'30" N, long. 120° 39'30" W); the ridge is east of Dry Valley (1). Named on Grasshopper Valley (1954) 15' quadrangle.

Dublin Jack Ravine [PLUMAS]: *canyon,* drained by a stream that flows 1.25 miles to American Valley 1.5 miles west of Quincy (lat. 39°56'25" N, long. 120°58'15" W; near E line sec. 16, T 24 N, R 9 E). Named on Quincy (1950) 7.5' quadrangle.

Ducasse Reservoir [LASSEN]: *lake,* 1000 feet long, 2.5 miles south-southwest of Termo (lat. 40°50'05" N, long. 120°28'55" W; at E line sec. 3, T 34 N, R 13 E). Named on Ravendale (1954) 15' quadrangle.

Duck Lake [LASSEN]:

(1) *lake,* 700 feet long, 9 miles southwest of Cal Mountain (lat. 40° 34'35" N, long. 121°16'50" W; near W line sec. 2, T 31 N, R 6 E). Named on Prospect Peak (1957) 15' quadrangle.

(2) *lake,* 500 feet long, 3.5 miles north of Westwood (lat. 40°21'25" N,

long. 120°59'45" W; sec. 20, T 29 N, R 9 E). Named on Westwood East (1980) 7.5' quadrangle.

(3) *intermittent lake,* 1 mile long, 11.5 miles northeast of Doyle (lat. 40°11'15" N, long. 120°02'45" W; sec. 15, 22, T 27 N, R 17 E). Named on Doyle (1954) 15' quadrangle.

Duck Lake [PLUMAS]: *lake,* 400 feet long, 9 miles west-southwest of Mount Harkness (lat. 40°23'55" N, long. 121°28' W; sec. 6, T 29 N, R 5 E). Named on Mount Harkness (1956) 15' quadrangle.

Duffey Dome [PLUMAS]: *peak,* nearly 5 miles south of Storrie (lat. 39°51' N, long. 121°18'40" W; sec. 16, T 23 N, R 6 E). Altitude 5532 feet. Named on Soapstone Hill (1979) 7.5' quadrangle.

Duffy Creek [LASSEN]: *stream,* flows 4 miles to Mountain Meadows 4.5 miles east-southeast of Westwood (lat. 40°17'20" N, long. 120°54'50" W; sec. 13, T 28 N, R 9 E). Named on Fredonyer Pass (1980) and Westwood East (1980) 7.5' quadrangles.

Duncan Reservoir [MODOC]: *lake,* 7200 feet long, 9 miles southwest of Jacks Butte (lat. 41°31'15" N, long. 120°56'35" W; in and near sec. 33, T 43 N, R 9 E). Named on Jacks Butte (1962) 15' quadrangle. The name commemorates Charles Duncan, a pioneer settler in Modoc County, who built the reservoir (Gudde, 1969, p. 95).

Dunn Reservoir [LASSEN]: *lake,* 4000 feet long, 10 miles north of Observation Peak (lat. 40°55'10" N, long. 120°10'40" W; at SW cor. sec. 4, T 35 N, R 16 E). Named on Observation Peak (1954) 15' quadrangle.

Dusenbery Peak [MODOC]: *peak,* 4.5 miles west-northwest of Eagleville (lat. 41°20'40" N, long. 120°11'15" W; sec. 8, T 40 N, R 16 E). Altitude 9097 feet. Named on Eagle Peak (1963) 7.5' quadrangle. United States Board on Geographic Names (1973b, p. 2) approved the form "Dusenbury Peak" for the name, and gave the forms "Dusenbery Peak" and "Duzenberry Peak" as variants; the Board pointed out that the name commemorates James Dusenbury, a local resident who climbed the peak in 1887.

Dusenbury Peak: see **Dusenbery Peak** [MODOC].

Dustys Waterhole [MODOC]: *water feature,* 11.5 miles north-northeast of White Horse (lat. 41°28'10" N, long. 121°19'40" W). Named on White Horse (1962) 15' quadrangle.

Dutch Creek [PLUMAS]: *stream,* flows nearly 2 miles to East Branch of North Fork Feather River 2.25 miles east of Twain (lat. 40°01'25" N, long. 121°01'40" W; near SE cor. sec. 13, T 25 N, R 8 E). Named on Twain (1980) 7.5' quadrangle.

Dutch Diggins: see **Upper Dutch Diggins** [PLUMAS].

Dutch Flat [MODOC]:

(1) *area,* 10 miles southeast of Crank Mountain (lat. 41°17'10" N, long. 121°00'30" W; at SW cor. sec. 24, T 40 N, R 8 E). Named on Crank Mountain (1962) 15' quadrangle.

(2) *area,* 6 miles north of Jacks Butte (lat. 41°40'20" N, long. 120° 47'15" W; sec. 11, T 44 N, R 10 E). Named on Jacks Butte (1962) 15' quadrangle.

Dutch Flat Canyon [MODOC]: *canyon,* 6 miles long, drained by Dutch Flat Creek above a point 13 miles south-southwest of Canby (lat. 41°15'45" N, long. 120°58' W; sec. 31, T 40 N, R 9 E). Named on Canby (1961) and Crank Mountain (1962) 15' quadrangles.

Dutch Flat Creek [MODOC]: *stream,* flows 11 miles to Ash Creek 1.5 miles north-northeast of Adin (lat. 41°12'55" N, long. 120°55'45" W; near W line sec. 15, T 39 N, R 9 E). Named on Adin (1962), Canby (1961), and Crank Mountain (1962) 15' quadrangles.

Dutch Hill: see **Seneca** [PLUMAS].

Duzenberry Peak: see **Dusenbery Peak** [MODOC].

Dyer Mountain [LASSEN]: *peak,* 4 miles southwest of Westwood (lat. 40°14'20" N, long. 121°01'55" W; sec. 36, T 28 N, R 8 E). Altitude 7476 feet. Named on Canyondam (1979) 7.5' quadrangle. Called Dyer Peak on Lassen Peak (1894) 1° quadrangle. California Mining Bureau's (1917a) map shows Mt. Dyer.

Dyer Mountain: see **Little Dyer Mountain** [LASSEN].

Dyer Peak: see **Dyer Mountain** [LASSEN].

Dyson Slough [PLUMAS]: *water feature,* diverges from North Channel of Little Last Chance Creek 6 miles west-southwest of Chilcoot (lat. 39°46'25" N, long. 120°14'40" W; sec. 12, T 22 N, R 15 E). Named on Antelope Valley (1981), Chilcoot (1979), and Reconnaissance Peak (1972) 7.5' quadrangles.

— E —

Eades Spring [MODOC]: *spring,* nearly 5 miles southeast of Crank Mountain (lat. 41°20'05" N, long. 121°05' W; near W line sec. 5, T 40 N, R 8 E). Named on Crank Mountain (1962) 15' quadrangle.

Eagle Campground [LASSEN]: *locality,* 6.25 miles south-southwest of Pelican Point near the southwest end of Eagle Lake (lat. 40° 32'50" N, long. 120°46'50" W; sec. 18, T 31 N, R 11 E). Named on Antelope Mountain (1956) 15' quadrangle.

Eagle Creek [MODOC]: *stream,* flows 9 miles to Lower Lake 3 miles southeast of Eagleville (lat. 41°18'15" N, long. 120°03'30" W); the stream heads near Eagle Peak. Named on Eagle Peak (1963) and Eagleville (1963) 7.5' quadrangles. North Fork enters from the northwest 3 miles southwest of Eagleville; it is 2 miles long and is named on Eagle Peak (1963) 7.5' quadrangle.

Eagle Gulch [PLUMAS]: *canyon,* drained by a stream that flows nearly 2 miles to Big Creek 2.25 miles southeast of the village of Meadow Valley (lat. 39°54'30" N, long. 121°05'30" W; near S line sec. 28, T 24 N, R 8 E). Named on Meadow Valley (1980) 7.5' quadrangle.

Eagle Lake [LASSEN]: *lake,* 13 miles long, 16 miles north-northwest of Susanville (lat. 40°38' N, long. 120°44'15" W). Named on Antelope Mountain (1956) and Fredonyer Peak (1954) 15' quadrangles. Lieutenant E.G. Beckwith discovered and named the lake in 1854 when he was seeking a pass in the region (Purdy, 1988, p. 68). United States Board on Geographic Names (1983b, p. 5) approved the name "Eagles Nest" for a locality on the southeast side of Eagle Lake (lat. 40°35'03" N, long. 120°44'52" W), and rejected the names "Eagle Nest" and "Eagle Nest Homesites" for the place.

Eagle Lake Resort [LASSEN]: *locality,* 6.5 miles southwest of Pelican Point (lat. 40°34'20" N, long. 120°50'15" W; sec. 3, T 31 N, R 10 E); the place is near the southwest end of Eagle Lake. Named on Antelope Mountain (1956) 15' quadrangle.

Eagle Lodge [LASSEN]: *locality,* 7 miles south-southwest of Pelican Point (lat. 40°33' N, long. 120°48'50" W; sec. 14, T 31 N, R 10 E); the place is at the southwest end of Eagle Lake. Named on Antelope Mountain (1956) 15' quadrangle.

Eagle Nest: see **Eagle Lake** [LASSEN].

Eagle Nest Homesites: see **Eagles Nest**, under **Eagle Lake** [LASSEN].

Eagle Peak [MODOC]: *peak,* 5 miles west-southwest of Eagleville (lat. 41°17' N, long. 120°12' W; near S line sec. 31, T 40 N, R 16 E). Altitude 9892 feet. Named on Eagle Peak (1963) 7.5' quadrangle. The name is from eagles seen flying about the peak (Laird, p. 51).

Eagle Rock [PLUMAS]: *peak,* 4 miles northwest of Twain (lat. 40° 03'25" N, long. 121°07'10" W; sec. 6, T 25 N, R 8 E). Altitude 6277 feet. Named on Twain (1980) 7.5' quadrangle.

Eagle Rocks [PLUMAS]: *relief feature,* 13 miles west-southwest of the village of Almanor (lat. 40°09'45" N, long. 121°24'30" W). Named on Jonesville (1958) 15' quadrangle.

Eagles Nest: see **Eagle Lake** [LASSEN].

Eagleville [MODOC]: *village,* 25 miles east-southeast of Alturas (lat. 41°18'55" N, long. 120°06'55" W; at W line sec. 24, T 40 N, R 16 E). Named on Eagleville (1963) 7.5' quadrangle. Postal authorities established Eagleville post office in 1868 (Frickstad, p. 102). The name is from Eagle Peak (Pease, p. 93). Postal authorities established Hausen post office 12 miles south of Eagleville in Lassen County in 1885, discontinued it in 1887, reestablished it in 1890, and discontinued it in 1898 (Salley, p. 94).

East Canyon [LASSEN]: *canyon,* drained by a stream that flows 2.5 miles to the canyon of McDermott Creek 2 miles south-southeast of Milford (lat. 40°09' N, long. 120°20'55" W; sec. 36, T 27 N, R 14 E). Named on Ferris Creek (1977) and Milford (1977) 7.5' quadrangles.

East Claremont [PLUMAS]: *peak,* 3.5 miles south-southeast of Quincy (lat. 39°53'10" N, long. 120°55'50" W; near W line sec. 1, T 23 N, R 9 E); the peak is less than 1 mile east of Claremont. Altitude 6902 feet. Named on Quincy (1950) 7.5' quadrangle

East Creek [LASSEN-MODOC]: *stream,* flows 13 miles, mostly in Modoc County but partly in Lassen County, to Jess Valley [MODOC] 21 miles southeast of Alturas [MODOC] (lat. 41°14'25" N, long. 120°18' W; near SE cor. sec. 1, T 39 N, R 14 E). Named on Emerson Peak (1962) and Jess Valley (1962) 7.5' quadrangles. North Fork enters from the north 8.5 miles southwest of Eagleville; it is 3.5 miles long and is named on Eagle Peak (1963) and Emerson Peak (1962) 7.5' quadrangles. South Fork heads in Lassen County and enters the main stream from the south 9 miles south-southwest of Eagleville in Modoc County; it is 3.5 miles long and is named on Emerson Peak (1962) 7.5' quadrangle. Little North Fork enters North Fork 0.5 mile upstream from the mouth of North Fork; it is 2.5 miles long and is named on Emerson Peak (1962) 7.5' quadrangle.

East Dry Creek [MODOC]: *stream,* flows nearly 3 miles to Dry Creek 11.5 miles east of Alturas (lat. 41°27'45" N, long. 120°19'20" W). Named on Shields Creek (1963) 7.5' quadrangle.

East Lake [LASSEN]: *lake,* 750 feet long, 3 miles east-northeast of Mount Harkness [PLUMAS] (lat. 40°27' N, long. 121°15'20" W; near N line sec. 24, T 30 N, R 6 E). Named on Mount Harkness (1956) 15' quadrangle.

East Nelson Creek [PLUMAS]: *stream,* flows 5.5 miles to join West Branch Nelson Creek and form Nelson Creek 12 miles southeast of Quincy (lat. 39°48'05" N, long. 120°48'30" W). Named on Blue Nose Mountain (1951) and Mount Fillmore (1951) 7.5' quadrangles. Called East Branch Nelson Creek on Downieville (1897) 30' quadrangle.

East Point [MODOC]: *peak,* 0.5 mile east of Blue Mountain (lat. 41° 49'45" N, long. 120°51' W; sec. 17, T 46 N, R 10 E). Altitude 5750 feet. Named on Steele Swamp (1962) 15' quadrangle.

East Quincy [PLUMAS]: *district,* 2.5 miles east of downtown Quincy (lat.

39°56' N, long. 120°53'45" W). Named on Quincy (1950) 7.5' quadrangle.

East Sand Butte [MODOC]: *hill,* 6 miles northwest of Timber Mountain (lat. 41°40'55" N, long. 121°22'30" W; sec. 3, T 44 N, R 5 E); the hill is 2 miles east-southeast of Big Sand Butte. Named on Timber Mountain (1952) 15' quadrangle.

East Side Reservoir [LASSEN]: *lake,* 300 feet long, 12 miles east of Wendel (lat. 40°20'25" N, long. 120°00'45" W; sec. 25, T 29 N, R 17 E). Named on Wendel (1954) 15' quadrangle.

Eberli: see **Ben Eberli Waterhole** [MODOC].

Ebey Lake [LASSEN]: *lake,* 1050 feet long, 3.5 miles northwest of Cal Mountain (lat. 40°41'45" N, long. 121°13'15" W; sec. 29, T 33 N, R 7 E). Named on Harvey Mountain (1956) 15' quadrangle.

Echo Lake [PLUMAS]: *lake,* 1700 feet long. 9 miles north-northeast of Chester (lat. 40°25'55" N, long. 121°09'40" W; sec. 26, T 30 N, R 7 E). Named on Red Cinder (1979) 7.5' quadrangle.

Eclipse: see **Onion Valley** [PLUMAS].

Edgemont [LASSEN]: *locality,* 5.5 miles south-southwest of Litchfield (lat. 40°18'45" N, long. 120°26'15" W; sec. 6, T 28 N, R 14 E). Named on Litchfield (1954) 15' quadrangle Postal authorities established Spoonville post office in 1903, changed the name to Edgemont in 1913, and discontinued it in 1918; the name "Spoonville" was for Florella A. Spoon, and the name "Edgemont" was for the location of the place near the edge of Bald Mountain (2) (Salley, p. 65, 210).

Edler Spring [MODOC]: *spring,* 14 miles north-northeast of Double Head Mountain (lat. 41°56'55" N, long. 121°04'30" W; near N line sec. 5, T 47 N, R 8 E). Named on Clear Lake Reservoir (1951) 15' quadrangle. United States Board on Geographic Names (1989b, p. 2) approved the name "Elder Spring" for the feature.

Edmanton [PLUMAS]: *locality,* 2.5 miles southwest of the village of Meadow Valley along Big Creek (lat. 39°54' N, long. 121°06'05" W). Named on Bidwell Bar (1897) 30' quadrangle.

Egg Flat: see **Egg Lake** [MODOC].

Egg Lake [MODOC]: *marsh,* 5.5 miles east of White Horse (lat. 41°19'15" N, long. 121°17'15" W; in and near sec. 9, T 40 N, R 6 E). Named on White Horse (1962) 15' quadrangle. Modoc Lava-Bed (1892) 1° quadrangle has the name "Egg Flat" at the place, and Alturas (1954) 1°x 2° quadrangle shows a lake there. The nesting of waterfowl at the site suggested the name (Gudde, 1969, p. 98).

Egg Lake: see **Little Egg Lake** [MODOC].

Egg Lake Butte [MODOC]: *peak,* 5.25 miles east of White Horse (lat. 41°17'50" N, long. 121°18'05" W; at N line sec. 20, T 40 N, R 6 E); the peak is 1.5 miles south-southwest of Egg Lake. Named on White Horse (1962) 15' quadrangle.

Egg Lake Slough [LASSEN]: *water feature,* joins Bull Run Slough 3.5 miles south-southwest of Bieber (lat. 41°04'15" N, long. 121° 09'30" W; near W line sec. 3, T 37 N, R 7 E). Named on Bieber (1961) 15' quadrangle.

Eightmile Creek [MODOC]: *stream,* flows 5.5 miles to Cow Head Lake 7.25 miles northeast of Fort Bidwell (lat. 41°56'15" N, long. 120°03'30" W; at S line sec. 18, T 47 N, R 17 E). Named on Fort Bidwell (1962) 15' quadrangle. Alturas 1° quadrangle has the form "Eight Mile Creek" for the name.

Eisenheimer Peak [PLUMAS]: *peak,* 2 miles north of Kettle Rock (lat. 40°10'15" N, long. 120°43'25" W; sec. 27, T 27 N, R 11 E). Altitude 7500 feet. Named on Kettle Rock (1972) 7.5' quadrangle.

Elder Spring: see **Edler Spring** [MODOC].

Eleanor Lake [LASSEN]: *lake,* 900 feet long, 11 miles south of Cal Mountain (lat. 40°30'30" N, long. 121°11'25" W; at E line sec. 33, T 31 N, R 7 E). Named on Harvey Mountain (1956) 15' quadrangle.

Elephant Butte [PLUMAS]: *relief feature,* 4 miles southwest of Storrie (lat. 39°52'30" N, long. 121°22' W; sec. 1, T 23 N, T 5 E). Named on Soapstone Hill (1979) and Storrie (1979) 7.5' quadrangles.

Elephants Playground [PLUMAS]: *valley,* 6.5 miles southeast of Kettle Rock (lat. 40°04'45" N, long. 120°37'50" W; sec. 28, 33, T 26 N, R 12 E). Named on Genesee Valley (1972) 7.5' quadrangle.

Elevenmile Creek [MODOC]: *stream,* flows 2.5 miles to Cow Head Slough 10.5 miles northeast of Fort Bidwell (lat. 41°58'30" N, long. 120°01' W; near E line sec. 4, T 47 N, R 17 E). Named on Fort Bidwell (1962) 15' quadrangle.

Elizabeth Lake [PLUMAS]: *lake,* 200 feet long, 10 miles west of Mount Harkness (lat. 40°24'10" N, long. 121°28'50" W; near E line sec. 1, T 29 N, R 4 E). Named on Mount Harkness (1956) 15' quadrangle.

Elizabethtown: see **Elizabethtown Flat** [PLUMAS].

Elizabethtown Flat [PLUMAS]: *area,* 1.5 miles north-northwest of Quincy (lat. 39°57'30" N, long. 120°57'15" W; near E line sec. 10, T 24 N, R 9 E). Named on Quincy (1950) 7.5' quadrangle. The name recalls the mining camp of Elizabethtown; miners named the camp to honor Elizabeth Stark, the only unmarried woman there (Hoover, Rensch, and Rensch, p. 283). The place also was called Betsyburg (Bancroft, p. 363). Postal authorities established Elizabethtown post office in 1855 and discontinued it the same year (Frickstad, p. 124).

Elwell: see **Mount Elwell** [PLUMAS].

Elwell Lodge [PLUMAS]: *locality,* 5.5 miles southwest of Clio (lat. 39°41'50" N, long. 120°39'50" W; at E line sec. 7, T 21 N, R 12 E). Named on Gold Lake (1981) 7.5' quadrangle.

Elysian Creek [LASSEN]: *stream,* flows nearly 6 miles to Baxter Creek 9 miles southeast of Susanville (lat. 40°19'35" N, long. 120° 32'35" W; sec. 32, T 29 N, R 13 E); the stream goes through Elysian Valley. Named on Janesville (1972) 7.5' quadrangle.

Elysian Valley [LASSEN]: *valley,* 9 miles south-southeast of Susanville (lat. 40°18'30" N, long. 120°34'20" W). Named on Janesville (1972) 7.5' quadrangle. Daney H. Keatley and L.N. Breed named the place to suggest its beauty when they settled there in 1856 (Gudde, 1949, p. 107).

Emerald Lake [LASSEN]: *lake,* 750 feet long, 16 miles northwest of Westwood (lat. 40°29'45" N, long. 121°11'05" W; near N line sec. 3, T 30 N, R 7 E). Named on Red Cinder (1979) 7.5' quadrangle.

Emerald Lake: see **Gem Lake** [LASSEN].

Emerson Creek [MODOC]: *stream,* formed by the confluence of North Fork and South Fork, flows 5.5 miles to Lower Lake 3.5 miles southeast of Eagleville (lat. 41°17'35" N, long. 120°04'05" W; sec. 32, T 40 N, R 17 E). Named on Eagle Peak (1963) and Eagleville (1963) 7.5' quadrangles. North Fork heads at North Emerson Lake and South Fork heads at South Emerson Lake; each fork is 1.5 miles long and is named on Eagle Peak (1963) 7.5' quadrangle.

Emerson Lake [LASSEN]: *lake,* 1800 feet long, 3.5 miles south of Susanville (lat. 40°22' N, long. 120°38'35" W; at SW cor. sec. 16, T 29 N, R 12 E). Named on Diamond Mountain (1972) 7.5' quadrangle.

Emerson Lake: see **North Emerson Lake** [MODOC]; **South Emerson Lake** [MODOC].

Emerson Peak [MODOC]: *peak,* 6 miles south-southwest of Eagleville (lat. 41°14'15" N, long. 120°09'45" W; near N line sec. 21, T 39 N, R 16 E). Altitude 8989 feet. Named on Emerson Peak (1962) 7.5' quadrangle.

Emerson Spring [LASSEN]: *spring,* 3.25 miles south of Susanville (lat. 40°22'15" N, long. 120°38'35" W; near W line sec. 16, T 29 N, R 12 E). Named on Diamond Mountain (1972) 7.5' quadrangle.

Emigrant Creek [PLUMAS]: *stream,* flows nearly 2 miles to Little Grizzly Creek 4 miles south-southwest of Mount Ingalls (lat. 39° 56'50" N, long. 120°40' W; sec. 18, T 24 N, R 12 E). Named on Mount Ingalls (1972) 7.5' quadrangle.

Emigrant Spring [MODOC]: *spring,* 8 miles north of Alturas (lat. 41°36' N, long. 120°32'35" W; near NW cor. sec. 1, T 43 N, R 12 E). Named on Big Sage Reservoir (1962) 15' quadrangle.

Empire Ravine [PLUMAS]: *canyon,* drained by a stream that flows 1.5 miles to Dry Taylor Creek 5.5 miles northwest of Spring Garden (lat. 39°57'25" N, long. 120°51'10" W; sec. 10, T 24 N, R 10 E). Named on Spring Garden (1950) 7.5' quadrangle.

Enchantment: see **Lake Enchantment**, under **Snag Lake** [LASSEN].

Engelmine: see **Superior Ravine** [PLUMAS].

English Bar [PLUMAS]: *locality,* 8 miles southeast of Quincy along Middle Fork Feather River (lat. 39°52'25" N, long. 120°49'30" W; sec. 11, T 23 N, R 10 E). Named on Blue Nose Mountain (1951) 7.5' quadrangle.

Enquist Reservoir [MODOC]: *intermittent lake,* 0.5 mile long, 7 miles northeast of South Mountain (lat. 41°54'30" N, long. 120°32'10" W; on N line sec. 24, T 47 N, R 12 E). Named on South Mountain (1962) 15' quadrangle.

Ericksons Spring [LASSEN]: *spring,* 9.5 miles southwest of the village of Little Valley (lat. 40°47'15" N, long. 121°17'10" W; near NE cor. sec. 27, T 34 N, R 6 E). Named on Jellico (1957) 15' quadrangle.

Essex Reservoir [MODOC]: *intermittent lake,* 1.25 miles long, 10.5 miles west-northwest of Alturas (lat. 41°31'15" N, long. 120°44'30" W). Named on Big Sage Reservoir (1962) and Jacks Butte (1962) 15' quadrangles.

Essex Spring [MODOC]: *spring,* 3 miles southeast of Jacks Butte (lat. 41°33'10" N, long. 120°46' W; sec. 24, T 43 N, R 10 E). Named on Jacks Butte (1962) 15' quadrangle.

Essex Tank [MODOC]: *intermittent lake,* 1300 feet long, 4.5 miles southwest of Jacks Butte (lat. 41°32'30" N, long. 120°52' W; near NW cor. sec. 30, T 43 N, R 10 E). Named on Jacks Butte (1962) 15' quadrangle.

Estray Creek [PLUMAS]: *stream,* flows 7.25 miles to Greenhorn Creek 1.5 miles northwest of Spring Garden (lat. 39°54'35" N, long. 120°48'30" W; sec. 25, T 24 N, R 10 E). Named on Mount Ingalls (1972) and Spring Garden (1950) 7.5' quadrangles. On Downieville (1897) 30' quadrangle, the lower part of present Estray Creek is called Spring Garden Creek.

Etchecopar Spring [LASSEN]: *spring,* 9.5 miles north-northeast of Termo (lat. 40°59' N, long. 120°21'45" W; on E line sec. 15, T 36 N, R 14 E). Named on Ravendale (1954) 15' quadrangle.

Etna: see **Mount Etna** [PLUMAS].

Eureka Creek [PLUMAS]: *stream,* flows 5 miles to Jamison Creek 4 miles west-northwest of Blairsden (lat. 39°48'20" N, long. 120°41'05" W; near NE cor. sec. 1, T 22 N, R 11 E); the stream heads near Eureka Peak. Named on Johnsville (1972) 7.5' quadrangle.

Eureka Lake [PLUMAS]: *lake,* 1900 feet long, 5.25 miles west-southwest of Blairsden (lat. 39°45'40" N, long. 120°42'40" W; sec. 14, 23, T 22 N, R 11 E); the lake is along Eureka Creek. Named on Johnsville (1972) 7.5'

quadrangle.

Eureka Mills: see **Johnsville** [PLUMAS].

Eureka Peak [PLUMAS]: *peak,* 7.5 miles west of Clio (lat. 39°44'50" N, long. 120°43'15" W; at NW cor. sec. 26, T 22 N, R 11 E). Altitude 7447 feet. Named on Gold Lake (1981) 7.5' quadrangle. The feature first was called Gold Mountain (Plumas County Historical Society, p. 1).

Eureka Ridge [PLUMAS]: *ridge,* south-southeast- to south-trending, 9 miles long, center 13 miles southeast of Quincy (lat. 39°48'30" N, long. 120°46' W). Named on Blue Nose Mountain (1951) and Johnsville (1972) 7.5' quadrangles.

Evans Canyon [LASSEN]: *canyon,* drained by a stream that heads in Sierra County and flows 1.5 miles in Lassen County to Long Valley Creek 5.5 miles southeast of Beckwourth Pass (lat. 39°43'40" N, long. 120°02'30" W; sec. 26, T 22 N, R 17 E). Named on Evans Canyon (1978) 7.5' quadrangle.

Evans Peak [PLUMAS]: *peak,* 4.25 miles south of Moonlight Peak (lat. 40°10'40" N, long. 120°50'50" W; at N line sec. 27, T 27 N, R 10 E). Altitude 5308 feet. Named on Moonlight Peak (1980) 7.5' quadrangle.

Evan's Ranch: see **Milford** [LASSEN].

Evelyn Lake [LASSEN]: *lake,* 400 feet long, 15 miles northwest of Westwood (lat. 40°26'50" N, long. 120°12'50" W; at E line sec. 20, T 30 N, R 7 E). Named on Red Cinder (1979) 7.5' quadrangle.

Evening Star Creek: see **Bidwell Creek** [MODOC].

Everly Reservoir [MODOC]: *intermittent lake,* 5 miles northeast of South Mountain (lat. 41°53'30" N, long. 120°33'55" W; at NE cor. sec. 27, T 47 N, R 12 E). Named on South Mountain (1962) 15' quadrangle.

Express Canyon [LASSEN]: *canyon,* drained by a stream that heads in the State of Nevada and flows 1.25 miles to reenter Nevada 25 miles east of Madeline (lat. 41°00'55" N, long. 119°59'50" W; at E line sec. 2, T 36 N, R 17 E). Named on Little Hat Mountain (1962) 7.5' quadrangle.

— F —

Facht: see **Mason Station** [LASSEN].

Faggs Debris Pond [PLUMAS]: *lake,* 850 feet long, 2.5 miles south-southeast of Bucks Lodge along Willow Creek (5) (lat. 39°50'25" N, long. 121°09'40" W; near S line sec. 14, T 23 N, R 7 E). Named on Haskins Valley (1980) 7.5' quadrangle, which shows Faggs ranch situated less than 1 mile north-northwest of the lake.

Faggs Reservoir [PLUMAS]: *lake,* 600 feet long, 2.5 miles south-southwest of Bucks Lodge (lat. 39°50'30" N, long. 121°11'05" W; near S line sec. 15, T 23 N, R 7 E). Named on Haskins Valley (1980) 7.5' quadrangle, which shows Faggs ranch 1 mile northeast of the lake.

Fairchild's Meadow: see **Fairchild Swamp** [MODOC].

Fairchild Swamp [MODOC]: *area,* 3 miles northwest of Jacks Butte (lat. 41°37' N, long. 120°51' W). Named on Jacks Butte (1962) 15' quadrangle. Called Fairchild's Meadow on Alturas 1° quadrangle.

Fairport: see **New Pine Creek** [MODOC].

Fairview: see **Juniper**, under **Bieber** [LASSEN].

Fales Basin [PLUMAS]: *relief feature,* 5.5 miles south of Caribou (lat. 40°00'10" N, long. 121°09' W); the feature is 4.5 miles north-northwest of Spanish Peak. Named on Bucks Lake (1979) and Caribou (1979) 7.5' quadrangles. Gudde (1975, p. 113) listed a mining place called Fales Hill that was located about 4.5 miles north of Spanish Peak.

Fales Creek [PLUMAS]: *stream,* flows 2 miles to Mill Creek (1) 8 miles north of Bucks Lodge (lat. 39°59'40" N, long. 121°10'15" W; near W line sec. 26, T 25 N, R 7 E). Named on Bucks Lake (1979) 7.5' quadrangle.

Fales Hill: see **Fales Basin** [PLUMAS].

Fall River [PLUMAS]: *stream,* flows 9 miles to Butte County 3.5 miles south-southeast of Cascade (lat. 39°39'25" N, long. 121°08'25" W; at S line sec. 24, T 21 N, R 7 E). Named on American House (1948) and Cascade (1948) 7.5' quadrangles.

Fanani Meadow [PLUMAS]: *area,* 6 miles west-southwest of the village of Almanor along Butt Creek (lat. 40°11'45" N, long. 121° 17' W; sec. 14, 15, T 27 N, R 6 E). Named on Jonesville (1958) 15' quadrangle.

Fandango Creek: see **Willow Creek** [MODOC] (3).

Fandango Pass [MODOC]: *pass,* nearly 5 miles southwest of Fort Bidwell (lat. 41°48'05" N, long. 120°12'20" W; sec. 1, T 45 N, R 15 E); the pass is near the southeast end of Fandango Valley. Named on Fort Bidwell (1962) 15' quadrangle. Called Lassen's Pass on Goddard's (1857) map, and called Lassen Pass on Bancroft's (1864) map. Gold seekers of 1849 following the route explored by Peter Lassen the previous year named the pass for Lassen; the modern name is derived from Fandango Valley and apparently came into use in the 1870's (Pease, p. 66-67). The feature also was called Lassen Horn (Gudde, 1949, p. 53).

Fandango Peak [MODOC]: *peak,* 4.5 miles west of Fort Bidwell (lat. 41°51'45" N, long. 120°14'10" W); the peak is north of Fandango Valley. Altitude 7792 feet. Named on Fort Bidwell (1962) 15' quadrangle.

Fandango Valley [MODOC]: *valley,* 5.5 miles west-southwest of Fort Bidwell (lat. 41°49' N, long. 120°14'30" W. Named on Fort Bidwell (1962) and Willow Ranch (1962) 15' quadrangles. The name reportedly is from a dance, or fandango, that emigrants held at the place in 1849 (Pease, p. 67).

Fantastic Lava Beds [LASSEN]: *relief feature,* 11.5 miles southwest of Cal Mountain (lat. 40°32'45" N, long. 121°18' W). Named on Prospect Peak (1957) 15' quadrangle.

Fant Creek [PLUMAS]: *stream,* flows 2 miles to Smith Creek (1) 7 miles north of Kettle Rock (lat. 40°14'20" N, long. 120°43'25" W; sec. 34, T 28 N, R 11 E). Named on Kettle Rock (1972) 7.5' quadrangle.

Feather Lake [LASSEN]: *intermittent lake,* 6000 feet long, 12 miles southeast of Cal Mountain (lat. 40°32'10" N, long. 121°01'10" W; on and near E line sec. 24, T 31 N, R 8 E). Named on Harvey Mountain (1956) 15' quadrangle.

Feather Lake: see **Butte Lake** [LASSEN]; **Snag Lake** [LASSEN].

Feather River [PLUMAS]: *stream.* North Fork Feather River flows 62 miles in Plumas County to Butte County 5 miles southwest of Storrie; it is named on Jonesville (1958) and Mount Harkness (1956) 15' quadrangles, and on Canyondam (1979), Caribou (1979), Chester (1979), Pulga (1979), Soapstone Hill (1979), Storrie (1979), and Twain (1980) 7.5' quadrangles. East Branch of North Fork, which is formed by the confluence of Indian Creek (2) and Spanish Creek (1), enters North Fork from the east 6 miles southwest of Caribou; it is 17 miles long and is named on Caribou (1979), Crescent Mills (1980), and Twain (1980) 7.5' quadrangles—East Branch of North Fork is called Indian Creek on Lassen Peak (1894) 1° quadrangle. Middle Fork Feather River heads at Sierra Valley and flows 55 miles in Plumas County to Butte County nearly 3 miles northwest of Cascade; it is named on Blairsden (1972), Blue Nose Mountain (1951), Cascade (1948), Clio (1981), Haskins Valley (1980), Johnsville (1972), Onion Valley (1950), and Portola (1972) 7.5' quadrangles. United States Board on Geographic Names (1974b, p. 3) gave the name "Middle Fork Feather River" as a variant name for Little Last Chance Creek, and for North Channel Last Chance Creek. Little North Fork of Middle Fork flows 9 miles in Plumas County to Butte County 12 miles south-southeast of Storrie; it is named on Soapstone Hill (1979) 7.5' quadrangle. South Branch of Middle Fork flows 12 miles in Plumas County to Butte County 1.5 miles west-northwest of Cascade; it is named on American House (1948), Cascade (1948), and Dogwood Peak (1979) 7.5' quadrangles—United States Board on Geographic Names (1977b, p. 5) gave the name "South Branch Feather River" as a variant name for South Branch of Middle Fork Feather River. South Fork Feather River flows 21 miles in Plumas County to Butte County 5.5 miles south-southeast of Cascade; it is named on American House (1948), Cascade (1948), La Porte (1951), and Onion Valley (1950) 7.5' quadrangles. Feather River is called Rio de las Plumas on Fremont's (1845) map, and called Rio del Plumas on Sage's (1846) map. Luís Argüello is said to have given the name "El Rio de las Plumas" to the stream in 1817 because he saw bird feathers on the water there (Hart, p. 135)—*las plumas* means "the feathers" in Spanish. Gudde (1975, p. 47) listed a mining place called Browns Bar that was located along North Fork Feather River near the junction with East Fork Feather River; and (p. 180) listed a mining place called Junction Bar that was located at the junction of North Fork Feather River with its East Branch.

Feather River Homesite [PLUMAS]: *locality,* 6 miles south-southwest of Mount Harkness along North Fork Feather River (lat. 40° 20'50" N, long. 121°19'45" W; mainly in sec. 29, T 29 N, R 6 E). Named on Mount Harkness (1956) 15' quadrangle.

Feather River Inn [PLUMAS]: *locality,* 1 mile northwest of Blairsden (lat. 39°47'25" N, long. 120°37'45" W; near NE cor. sec. 9, T 22 N, R 12 E). Named on Blairsden (1956) 15' quadrangle.

Feather River Lodge: see **Sierra Lodge** [PLUMAS].

Feather River Meadows [PLUMAS]: *valley,* 9 miles southwest of Mount Harkness (lat. 40°21'30" N, long. 121°26'15" W); the valley is along North Fork Feather River. Named on Mount Harkness (1956) 15' quadrangle.

Feather River Park [PLUMAS]: *locality,* less than 1 mile west of Blairsden (lat. 39°46'45" N, long. 120°37'45" W; near SE cor. sec. 9, T 22 N, R 12 E); the place is along Middle Fork Feather River. Named on Johnsville (1972) 7.5' quadrangle.

Fee Reservoir [MODOC]: *lake,* 9500 feet long, 7 miles east-southeast of Fort Bidwell (lat. 41°49'45" N, long. 120°01'15" W; on N line sec. 28, T 46 N, R 17 E). Named on Fort Bidwell (1962) 15' quadrangle.

Fells Creek [PLUMAS]: *stream,* flows 2 miles to Middle Fork Feather River 7.5 miles southeast of Quincy (lat. 39°52'25" N, long. 120°49'40" W; sec. 11, T 23 N, R 10 E). Named on Spring Garden (1950) 7.5' quadrangle.

Fells Flat [PLUMAS]: *area,* 7.5 miles southeast of Quincy at the mouth of Fells Creek (lat. 39°52'30" N, long. 120°49'35" W; sec. 11, T 23 N, R 10 E). Named on Blue Nose Mountain (1951) and Spring Garden (1950) 7.5' quadrangles.

Fender Flat [MODOC]: *area,* 10 miles south of Willow Ranch (lat. 41°45'30" N, long. 120°20' W; on E line sec. 10, T 45 N, R 14 E). Named on Willow Ranch (1962) 15' quadrangle.

Fender Flat Spring [MODOC]: *spring,* 10 miles south-southeast of Willow Ranch (lat. 41°45'40" N, long. 120°18'45" W; near NE cor. sec. 11, T 45

N, R 14 E); the spring is 1 mile east-northeast of Fender Flat. Named on Willow Ranch (1962) 15' quadrangle.

Feney Ravine [PLUMAS]: *canyon,* drained by a stream that flows less than 1 mile to Slate Creek (3) 3.25 miles south-southwest of American House (lat. 39°36'45" N, long. 121°03'15" W; near N line sec. 11, T 20 N, R 8 E). Named on Strawberry Valley (1948) 7.5' quadrangle.

Fern Canyon [PLUMAS]: *canyon,* drained by a stream that flows 2 miles to North Fork Feather River 7 miles southwest of Caribou (lat. 40°00'20" N, long. 121°14'35" W; near W line sec. 19, T 25 N, R 7 E). Named on Bucks Lake (1979) and Caribou (1979) 7.5' quadrangles.

Fern Cave [MODOC]: *cave,* nearly 7 miles southwest of Newell (lat. 41°48'45" N, long. 121°27'15" W; near W line sec. 19, T 46 N, R 5 E). Named on Tulelake (1951) 15' quadrangle.

Fern Falls [PLUMAS]: *waterfall,* 5 miles west-southwest of Clio (lat. 39°42'30" N, long. 120°40'10" W; near E line sec. 6, T 21 N, R 12 E). Named on Gold Lake (1981) 7.5' quadrangle.

Fern Spring [MODOC]: *spring,* 10 miles east of Alturas (lat. 41°28'15" N, long. 120°20'40" W). Named on Shields Creek (1963) 7.5' quadrangle.

Fern Spring Canyon [MODOC]: *canyon,* drained by a stream that flows 1 mile to Payne Canyon 10 miles east of Alturas (lat. 41°27'50" N, long. 120°21'10" W); Fern Spring is in the canyon. Named on Shields Creek (1963) 7.5' quadrangle.

Ferris Creek [PLUMAS]: *stream,* flows 6 miles to Last Chance Creek (2) 5.5 miles northeast of Squaw Valley Peak (lat. 40°04'40" N, long. 120°19'15" W; at W line sec. 29, T 26 N, R 15 E). Named on Ferris Creek (1977) 7.5' quadrangle.

Ferris Flat [PLUMAS]: *area,* 2.25 miles northeast of Squaw Valley Peak (lat. 40°04'30" N, long. 120°19'30" W; mainly in sec. 30, T 26 N, R 15 E); the place is at the mouth of Ferris Creek. Named on Ferris Creek (1977) 7.5' quadrangle.

Fiddlers Green [MODOC]: *area,* 10 miles north of Double Head Mountain (lat. 41°54'30" N, long. 121°11'45" W; sec. 17, T 47 N, R 7 E). Named on Clear Lake Reservoir (1951) 15' quadrangle.

Finger Board [PLUMAS]: *peak,* 9 miles south-southeast of Quincy (lat. 39°49' N, long. 120°53'35" W; near NW cor. sec. 32, T 23 N, R 10 E). Altitude 6874 feet. Named on Onion Valley (1950) 7.5' quadrangle.

First Butte [LASSEN]: *hill,* 6 miles north of the village of Little Valley (lat. 40°58'55" N, long. 121°10'35" W; near W line sec. 4, T 36 N, R 7 E); the hill is less than 1 mile east of Second Butte. Altitude 4539 feet. Named on Little Valley (1957) 15' quadrangle.

First Creek [MODOC]: *stream,* flows 6 miles to lowlands along Upper Lake 8 miles south-southeast of Fort Bidwell (lat. 41°45'35" N, long. 120°05' W; sec. 19, T 45 N, R 17 E). Named on Cedarville (1962) and Fort Bidwell (1962) 15' quadrangles. United States Board on Geographic Names (1964b, p. 12) rejected the name "West Creek" for the stream.

Firstwater Creek [PLUMAS]: *stream,* flows 1.25 miles to Soda Creek (1) 14 miles southwest of the village of Almanor (lat. 40°03'55" N, long. 121°20'40" W; near E line sec. 31, T 26 N, R 6 E). Named on Jonesville (1958) 15' quadrangle.

First Water Trough Creek [PLUMAS]: *stream,* flows nearly 3 miles to Wolf Creek 2.5 miles north-northwest of Greenville (lat. 40°10'15" N, long. 120°58'15" W; sec. 28, T 27 N, R 9 E). Named on Greenville (1979) 7.5' quadrangle.

Fish Cabin [LASSEN]: *locality,* 4 miles north-northwest of Pelican Point at the north end of Eagle Lake (lat. 40°41'10" N, long. 120° 46' W). Named on Antelope Mountain (1956) 15' quadrangle.

Fish Creek [PLUMAS]:

(1) *stream,* flows nearly 2 miles to Onion Valley Creek 10.5 miles south-southwest of Quincy (lat. 39°47'30" N, long. 120°59' W; near S line sec. 4, T 22 N, R 9 E). Named on Onion Valley (1950) 7.5' quadrangle.

(2) *stream,* flows nearly 2 miles to Nelson Creek 11 miles southeast of Quincy (lat. 39°48'35" N, long. 120°49' W). Named on Blue Nose Mountain (1951) 7.5' quadrangle.

Fish Slough [LASSEN]: *water feature,* 1.25 miles southwest of Litchfield in Honey Lake Valley (lat. 40°22'05" N, long. 120°24'10" W). Named on Standish (1972) 7.5' quadrangle.

Fitch Canyon [PLUMAS]: *canyon,* drained by a stream that flows 2.5 miles to Cottonwood Canyon (2) 4.5 miles west-southwest of Milford [LASSEN] (lat. 40°09'10" N, long. 120°27'15" W; at W line sec. 31, T 27 N, R 14 E). Named on Stony Ridge (1978) 7.5' quadrangle.

Fitzhugh Creek [MODOC]:

(1) *stream,* flows 4.25 miles to South Fork Canyon Creek 15 miles southwest of Alturas (lat. 41°19'20" N, long. 120°43'35" W; at E line sec. 8, T 40 N, R 11 E). Named on Alturas (1961) and Canby (1961) 15' quadrangles.

(2) *stream,* formed by the confluence of North Fork and South Fork, flows 9.5 miles to lowlands along South Fork Pit River 9 miles south of Alturas (lat. 41°21'30" N, long. 120°31'15" W; near SW cor. sec. 30, T 41 N, R 13 E). Named on Alturas (1961) 15' quadrangle, and on Dorris Reservoir (1963) and Little Juniper Reservoir (1963) 7.5' quadrangles. North Fork is 15 miles long and is named on Eagle Peak (1963), Little Juniper Reservoir (1963), and Soup Creek (1963) 7.5' quadrangles. South Fork is 10.5 miles long and is named on Little Juniper Reservoir (1963) and Soup Creek (1963) 7.5' quadrangles.

Fitzhugh Springs [MODOC]: *springs,* 8.5 miles east-southeast of Alturas (lat. 41°25'30" N, long. 120°20'35" W). Named on Shields Creek (1963) 7.5 quadrangle.

Five Points [PLUMAS]: *locality,* 6.5 miles north-northeast of Blairsden (lat. 39°52'15" N, long. 120°34'20" W; near E line sec. 12, T 23 N, R 12 E). Named on Blairsden (1972) 7.5' quadrangle.

Five Springs [LASSEN]: *springs,* 17 miles south of Observation Peak (lat. 40°32'30" N, long. 120°07'40" W; on S line sec. 14, T 31 N, R 16 E). Named on Shinn Mountain (1954) 15' quadrangle.

Five Springs Mountain [LASSEN]: *ridge,* generally east-southeast-trending, 7 miles long, 15 miles south-southeast of Observation Peak (lat. 40°34' N, long. 120°07'30" W); the feature called Five Springs is on the south side of the ridge. Named on Shinn Mountain (1954) 15' quadrangle.

Five Troughs [LASSEN]: *water feature,* less than 1 mile south-southeast of Lava Peak (lat. 40°49'10" N, long. 120°53'10" W; near SE cor. sec. 7, T 34 N, R 10 E). Named on Hayden Hill (1956) 15' quadrangle.

Flatiron Ridge [PLUMAS]: *ridge,* east-southeast-trending, 2.5 miles long, 4.5 miles west-northwest of Mount Harkness (lat. 40°27' N, long. 121°23'15" W). Named on Mount Harkness (1956) 15' quadrangle. The name is from the shape of the ridge (Schulz, p. 20). The feature is mainly in Shasta County—only the southeast end is in Plumas County

Fleener: see **Lookout** [MODOC].

Fleener Butte [MODOC]: *peak,* 6 miles north of Crank Mountain (lat. 41°27'50" N, long. 121°08'15" W; at W line sec. 23, T 42 N, R 7 E). Altitude 5167 feet. Named on Crank Mountain (1962) 15' quadrangle.

Fleischmann Lake: see **Blue Lake** [PLUMAS] (2).

Fleming Sheep Camp [LASSEN]: *locality,* 12 miles south-southwest of Likely [MODOC] (lat. 41°04'55" N, long. 120°37'40" W; near E line sec. 31, T 38 N, R 12 E). Named on Likely (1962) 15' quadrangle.

Fleming Spring [LASSEN]:

(1) *spring,* 13 miles southwest of Likely [MODOC] (lat. 41°07' N, long. 120°41'45" W; sec. 22, T 38 N, R 11 E). Named on Likely (1962) 15' quadrangle.

(2) *spring,* 9 miles south-southeast of Termo (lat. 40°45'05" N, long. 120°22'35" W; sec. 3, T 33 N, R 14 E). Named on Ravendale (1954) 15' quadrangle.

Flemings Sheep Camp [PLUMAS]: *locality,* nearly 6 miles northeast of Moonlight Peak along Lights Creek (lat. 40°17'20" N, long. 120°45'10" W; near W line sec. 16, T 28 N, R 11 E). Site named on Fredonyer Pass (1980) 7.5' quadrangle.

Fleming Well [LASSEN]: *well,* 12 miles west-northwest of Pelican Point (lat. 40°43'15" N, long. 120°56'15" W; sec. 14, T 33 N, R 9 E). Named on Antelope Mountain (1956) 15' quadrangle.

Fletcher [MODOC]: *locality,* 11 miles west-southwest of Alturas along Southern Pacific Railroad (lat. 41°26'45" N, long. 120°44'40" W; sec. 30, T 42 N, R 11 E). Named on Alturas (1961) 15' quadrangle.

Fletcher Creek [MODOC]: *stream,* flows 28 miles to Boles Meadows 10 miles north-northwest of Jacks Butte (lat. 41°43'30" N, long. 120°51' W; sec. 20, T 45 N, R 10 E). Named on Jacks Butte (1962), South Mountain (1962), and Steele Swamp (1962) 15' quadrangles.

Florentine Canyon [PLUMAS]: *canyon,* drained by a stream that flows 1.5 miles to Jamison Creek 8 miles west of Clio (lat. 39° 44' N, long. 120°43'25" W; near NE cor. sec. 34, T 22 N, R 11 E). Named on Gold Lake (1981) 7.5' quadrangle.

Flournoy [PLUMAS]: *locality,* 6 miles south-southeast of Kettle Rock near the mouth of Red Clover Creek (lat. 40°03'45" N, long. 120°40'30" W). Named on Honey Lake (1893) 1° quadrangle. Genesee Valley (1972) 7.5' quadrangle shows Flournoy bridge near the site.

Flournoy Reservoir [MODOC]: *intermittent lake,* 0.5 mile long, 16 miles south-southeast of Alturas (lat. 41°15'15" N, long. 120°28'25" W; at SW cor. sec. 34, T 40 N, R 13 E). Named on Little Juniper Reservoir (1963) 7.5' quadrangle.

Flournoy Swale [MODOC]: *relief feature,* 17 miles southeast of Alturas (lat. 41°17'25" N, long. 120°21' W; in and near sec. 22, T 40 N, R 14 E). Named on Soup Creek (1963) 7.5' quadrangle.

Flukey Well [MODOC]: *well,* 9.5 miles northwest of Hackamore (lat. 41°39'20" N, long. 121°14'20" W; near E line sec. 14, T 44 N, R 6 E). Named on Hackamore (1952) 15' quadrangle.

Folchi Meadows [PLUMAS]: *area,* 7 miles south-southeast of Portola on Plumas-Sierra County line (lat. 39°43'10" N, long. 120°25'15" W). Named on Calpine (1981) 7.5' quadrangle.

Forebay Reservoir: see **Pine Creek Reservoir** [MODOC].

Foreman: see **Foreman Ravine** [PLUMAS].

Foreman Creek [PLUMAS]: *stream,* flows 1.25 miles to Grizzly Creek (2) 3 miles south-southeast of Storrie (lat. 39°52'35" N, long. 121°18'15" W; near E line sec. 4, T 23 N, R 6 E). Named on Soapstone Hill (1979) and Storrie (1979) 7.5' quadrangles.

Foreman Ravine [PLUMAS]: *canyon,* drained by a stream that flows 0.5

mile to Lights Creek 2.25 miles north-northeast of Taylorsville (lat. 40°06'20" N, long. 120°49'20" W; at N line sec. 23, T 26 N, R 10 E). Named on Taylorsville (1980) 7.5' quadrangle. The canyon divides at the head into North Fork and South Fork. North Fork is 2.5 miles long and South Fork is 3 miles long; both forks are named on Taylorsville (1980) 7.5' quadrangle. United States Geological Survey's (1893b) map has the name "Forman" for an inhabited place located near the mouth of the canyon.

Forgay Point [PLUMAS]: *relief feature,* 2 miles north-northeast of Crescent Mills (lat. 40°07'30" N, long. 120°53'45" W; mainly in sec. 7, T 26 N, R 10 E). Named on Crescent Mills (1980) and Greenville (1979) 7.5' quadrangles.

Fork Spring [MODOC]: *spring,* 11.5 miles south-southwest of Canby (lat. 41°18' N, long. 120°58' W; at NW cor. sec. 20, T 40 N, R 9 E). Named on Canby (1961) 15' quadrangle.

Fort Bidwell [MODOC]: *village,* 32 miles northwest of Alturas (lat. 41°51'30" N, long. 120°09' W; sec. 16, 17, T 46 N, R 16 E). Named on Fort Bidwell (1962) 15' quadrangle. Postal authorities established Fort Bidwell post office in 1868 (Frickstad, p. 102). A military post called Camp Bidwell, named for California pioneer John Bidwell, was established in 1863 to control Indians in the vicinity; the post was abandoned in 1865, reestablished later the same year, and the name was changed to Fort Bidwell in 1879—the troops left in 1893, when the place became an Indian school and headquarters for an Indian reservation (Frazer, p. 20, 22).

Fort Sage Mountains [LASSEN]: *range,* 4.5 miles east-northeast of Doyle (lat. 40°03'30" N, long. 120°02' W). Named on Doyle (1954) 15' quadrangle, and on Constantia (1977) 7.5' quadrangle.

Fortynine Creek [MODOC]: *stream,* heads in the State of Nevada and flows 6.25 miles to Middle Alkali Lake 5 miles east-southeast of Cedarville (lat. 41°29'50" N, long. 120°04'55" W). Named on Cedarville (1962) 15' quadrangle, and on Hansen Island (1963) 7.5' quadrangle.

Fossett Spring [MODOC]: *spring,* nearly 6 miles southwest of Fort Bidwell (lat. 41°47'35" N, long. 120°13'05" W; near SW cor. sec. 1, T 45 N, R 15 E). Named on Fort Bidwell (1962) 15' quadrangle.

Foster Draw [LASSEN]: *canyon,* 3 miles long, along Butte Creek above a point 9 miles south-southeast of Adin [MODOC] (lat. 41° 04'50" N, long. 120°51'15" W). Named on Adin (1962) 15' quadrangle.

Foster Spring [LASSEN]: *spring,* 11 miles south-southeast of Adin [MODOC] (lat. 41°03'45" N, long. 120°49'55" W; sec. 9, T 37 N, R 10 E); the spring is in Foster Draw. Named on Adin (1962) 15' quadrangle.

Four Bits Creek [PLUMAS]: *stream,* flows nearly 2 miles to West Branch Nelson Creek 14 miles southeast of Quincy (lat. 39°46'50" N, long. 120°47'15" W; sec. 7, T 22 N, R 11 E). Named on Blue Nose Mountain (1951) 7.5' quadrangle.

Four Corners [LASSEN]: *locality,* 2.5 miles west of Bieber (lat. 41° 07'30" N, long. 121°11'20" W; on S line sec. 17, T 38 N, R 7 E). Named on Bieber (1961) 15' quadrangle.

Fourmile Creek [MODOC]: *stream,* heads in the State of Oregon and flows 6.5 miles in Modoc County to North Fork Willow Creek (1) 6 miles north of Blue Mountain (lat. 41°55'05" N, long. 120°52'40" W; sec. 13, T 47 N, R 9 E). Named on Steele Swamp (1962) 15' quadrangle. United States Board on Geographic Names (1990, p. 7) rejected the names "Four Mile Creek" and "Fourmile Valley Creek" for the stream.

Fourmile Reservoir [MODOC]: *lake,* 400 feet long, 10.5 miles north-northwest of Blue Mountain (lat. 41°58'30" N, long. 120°54'30" W; sec. 26, T 48 N, R 9 E); the lake is along Fourmile Creek. Named on Steele Swamp (1962) 15' quadrangle.

Fourmile Valley [MODOC]: *valley,* 9 miles north of Blue Mountain (lat. 41°57'30" N, long. 120°53'30" W; on W line sec. 30, T 48 N, R 9 E); the feature is along Fourmile Creek. Named on Steele Swmp (1962) 15' quadrangle.

Fourmile Valley Creek: see **Fourmile Creek** [MODOC].

Four Pine Spring [LASSEN]: *spring,* 9 miles north-northeast of Lava Peak (lat. 40°57'15" N, long. 120°49'30" W; sec. 16, T 36 N, R 10 E). Named on Hayden Hill (1956) 15' quadrangle.

Fourth Butte [LASSEN]: *hill,* 7 miles north-northwest of the village of Little Valley (lat. 40°59'20" N, long. 121°13'50" W; sec. 1, T 36 N, R 6 E); the hill is less than 1 mile west-northwest of Third Butte. Altitude 4750 feet. Named on Little Valley (1957) 15' quadrangle.

Fourth Water Creek [PLUMAS]: *stream,* flows 3.5 miles to Third Water Creek 5.25 miles north-northwest of Dogwood Peak (lat. 39°51'30" N, long. 121°05'15" W; sec. 16, T 23 N, R 8 E). Named on Dogwood Peak (1979) 7.5' quadrangle.

Four Trees [PLUMAS]: *locality,* 7.25 miles south of Storrie (lat. 39° 48'50" N, long. 121°19'10" W; near SW cor. sec. 28, T 23 N, R 6 E). Named on Soapstone Hill (1979) 7.5' quadrangle.

Fowler Creek [PLUMAS]: *stream,* flows nearly 2 miles to Dogwood Creek 1.5 miles east of Dogwood Peak (lat. 39°47' N, long. 121° 01'50" W; sec. 12, T 22 N, R 8 E); the stream heads at Fowler Lake. Named on Dogwood Peak (1979) 7.5' quadrangle. Called Slate Creek on Bucks Lake (1950) 15' quadrangle, but United States Board on Geographic Names (1979, p. 3) rejected this name for the stream.

Fowler Lake [PLUMAS]: *lake,* 800 feet long, 3 miles east-southeast of Dogwood Peak (lat. 39°46'25" N, long. 121°00'15" W; near NW cor. sec. 17, T 22 N, R 9 E). Named on Dogwood Peak (1979) 7.5' quadrangle.

Fowler Peak [PLUMAS]: *peak,* 12 miles south-southwest of Quincy (lat. 39°46'15" N, long. 120°59'50" W; sec. 17, T 22 N, R 9 E). Altitude 6065 feet. Named on Onion Valley (1950) 7.5' quadrangle.

Fox Draw [MODOC]: *canyon,* drained by a stream that flows 4 miles to lowlands along Pit River 8 miles south-southeast of Crank Mountain (lat. 41°16'20" N, long. 121°06'10" W; at W line sec. 30, T 40 N, R 8 E); the canyon heads near Fox Mountain. Named on Crank Mountain (1962) 15' quadrangle.

Fox Farm Campground [PLUMAS]: *locality,* nearly 3 miles northwest of Canyondam along Lake Almanor (lat. 40°11'45" N, long. 121°06'45" W; sec. 17, T 27 N, R 8 E). Named on Canyondam (1979) 7.5' quadrangle.

Fox Flat [MODOC]: *area,* 8.5 miles south-southeast of Crank Mountain (lat. 41°16'45" N, long. 121°03'15" W; sec. 28, T 40 N, R 8 E). Named on Crank Mountain (1962) 15' quadrangle.

Fox Mountain [LASSEN]: *peak,* 9 miles west-southwest of Pelican Point (lat. 40°34'10" N, long. 120°53'10" W; near N line sec. 7, T 31 N, R 10 E). Named on Antelope Mountain (1956) 15' quadrangle.

Fox Mountain [MODOC]: *peak,* 10 miles south-southeast of Crank Mountain (lat. 41°16' N, long. 121°02'10" W; on N line sec. 34, T 40 N, R 8 E). Altitude 6394 feet. Named on Crank Mountain (1962) 15' quadrangle.

Fox Mountain Spring [MODOC]: *spring,* 10 miles southeast of Crank Mountain (lat. 41°16'10" N, long. 121°01'15" W; near N line sec. 35, T 40 N, R 8 E); the spring is less than 1 mile east-northeast of Fox Mountain. Named on Crank Mountain (1962) 15' quadrangle.

Frank Canyon Spring [MODOC]: *spring,* 8 miles south-southeast of Canby along Toms Creek (lat. 41°20'20" N, long. 120°48'25" W; sec. 3, T 40 N, R 10 E). Named on Canby (1961) 15' quadrangle.

Franklin Canyon [PLUMAS]: *canyon,* 1.5 miles west-northwest of Dogwood Peak along Middle Fork Feather River (lat. 39°47'35" N, long. 121°04'40" W; sec. 3, 4, T 22 N, R 8 E). Named on Dogwood Peak (1979) 7.5' quadrangle.

Franklin Creek [MODOC]: *stream,* flows 4.5 miles to lowlands nearly 5 miles south of the village of Davis Creek (lat. 41°39'55" N, long. 120°22'55" W; sec. 8, T 44 N, R 14 E). Named on Davis Creek (1962) 15' quadrangle. Called Swedrengen Creek on Alturas 1° quadrangle.

Franks Valley [PLUMAS]: *valley,* 2.25 miles east-southeast of Kettle Rock along Hosselkus Creek (lat. 40°07'30" N, long. 120°41'10" W; sec. 12, 13, T 26 N, R 11 E). Named on Genesee Valley (1972) and Kettle Rock (1972) 7.5' quadrangles. Called Hosselkus Valley on Honey Lake (1893) 1° quadrangle.

Fraxier Creek: see **Frazier Creek** [PLUMAS] (2).

Frazier Creek [LASSEN]: *stream,* flows 4.25 miles to Shasta County 10 miles west of Bieber (lat. 41°06'50" N, long. 121°19'50" W; at W line sec. 19, T 38 N, R 6 E). Named on Fall River Mills (1961) 15' quadrangle. The stream ends after flowing less than 1 mile in Shasta County.

Frazier Creek [PLUMAS]:

(1) *stream,* flows nearly 5 miles to Little North Fork of Middle Fork Feather River 6.5 miles south-southwest of Bucks Lodge (lat. 39°47'50" N, long. 121°14'55" W; at SE cor. sec. 36, T 23 N, R 6 E). Named on Haskins Valley (1980) 7.5' quadrangle.

(2) *stream,* heads in Sierras County and flows 6.25 miles to Middle Fork Feather River nearly 2 miles south-southeast of Blairsden (lat. 39°45'25" N, long. 120°35'50" W; sec. 23, T 22 N, R 12 E). Named on Blairsden (1972), Clio (1981), and Gold Lake (1981) 7.5' quadrangles. Called Fraxier Creek on Downieville (1897) 30' quadrangle, and on Blairsden (1943) 15' quadrangle.

Frazier Falls [PLUMAS]: *waterfall,* 4 miles southwest of Clio along Frazier Creek (2) (lat. 39°42'25" N, long. 120°32'30" W; near SW cor. sec. 4, T 21 N, R 12 E). Named on Gold Lak (1981) 7.5' quadrangle.

Fredonia: see **Susanville** [LASSEN].

Fredonia Pass: see **Fredonyer Pass** [LASSEN].

Fredonyer: see **Little Fredonyer** [LASSEN].

Fredonyer Butte [LASSEN]: *peak,* 10 miles northeast of Westwood (lat. 40°23' N, long. 120°50'45" W; near S line sec. 10, T 29 N, R 10 E). Altitude 6454 feet. Named on Roop Mountain (1980) 7.5' quadrangle.

Fredonyer Campground [LASSEN]: *locality,* 10 miles east-northeast of Westwood (lat. 40°22'30" N, long. 120°49'55" W; at W line sec. 14, T 29 N, R 10 E); the place is 1 mile southeast of Fredonyer Butte. Named on Westwood (1955) 15' quadrangle.

Fredonyer Pass [LASSEN]: *pass,* 8 miles east-northeast of Westwood (lat. 40°21'40" N, long. 120°51'45" W; sec. 21, T 29 N, R 10 E). Named on Fredonyer Pass (1980) 7.5' quadrangle. United States Board on Geographic Names (1933, p. 311) rejected the name "Fredonia Pass" for the feature. Dr. Atlas Fredonyer, discovered the pass in 1852 (Gudde, 1949, p. 121).

Fredonyer Peak [LASSEN]: *peak,* 8.5 miles east-northeast of Pelican Point (lat. 40°41'15" N; long. 120°35'50" W; near W line sec. 26, T 33 N, R 12 E). Altitude 7943 feet. Named on Fredonyer Peak (1954) 15' quadrangle.

Fredonyer Reservoir [LASSEN]: *lake,* 700 feet long, 12 miles east-northeast of Pelican Point (lat. 40°41'55" N, long. 120°32'05" W; at S line sec. 20, T 33 N, R 13 E); the lake is 3.5 miles east of Fredonyer Peak. Named on Fredonyer Peak (1954) 15' quadrangle.

Freds Creek [PLUMAS]: *stream,* flows nearly 3 miles to Lights Creek 6 miles south-southeast of Moonlight Peak (lat. 40°09'45" N, long. 120°47'30" W; near N line sec. 31, T 27 N, R 11 E). Named on Moonlight Peak (1980) 7.5' quadrangle.

Freebe Reservoir: see **Ladder Butte** [LASSEN].

Freeman Creek [PLUMAS]: *stream,* flows 5.5 miles to Lake Davis 6.25 miles southeast of Mount Ingalls (lat. 39°55'20" N, long. 120° 33' W; near NW cor. sec. 29, T 24 N, R 13 E). Named on Blairsden (1972) and Grizzly Valley (1972) 7.5' quadrangles.

French Bar [PLUMAS]: *locality,* 5.5 miles south-southwest of Caribou along East Branch of North Fork Feather River (lat. 40°00'55" N, long. 121°12'50" W; at N line sec. 20, T 25 N, R 7 E). Named on Caribou (1979) 7.5' quadrangle. This apparently is the place that Gudde (1975, p. 125) called Frenchmans Bar.

French Camp [PLUMAS]: *locality,* 2 miles east of La Porte along Slate Creek (3) (lat. 39°40'50" N, long. 120°56'55" W; near W line sec. 14, T 21 N, R 9 E). Named on La Porte (1951) 7.5' quadrangle.

French Creek [PLUMAS]:

(1) *stream,* flows 2 miles to North Fork Feather River less than 0.5 mile north-northeast of Caribou (lat. 40°05'05" N, long. 121° 09' W; near NW cor. sec. 25, T 26 N, R 7 E). Named on Caribou (1979) 7.5' quadrangle.

(2) *stream,* flows 2 miles to Lost Creek (2) 4.5 miles southwest of American House (lat. 39°37' N, long. 121°05'40" W; near W line sec. 4, T 20 N, R 8 E). Named on American House (1948) and Strawberry Valley (1948) 7.5' quadrangles.

French Creek: see **French Ravine** [PLUMAS].

French Hotel Creek [PLUMAS]: *stream,* flows 2.25 miles to Grizzly Creek (2) 4 miles south of Storrie (lat. 39°51'50" N, long. 121°18'45" W; sec. 9, T 23 N, R 6 E). Named on Soapstone Hill (1979) 7.5' quadrangle.

Frenchman Campground [PLUMAS]: *locality,* 7.5 miles north-northwest of Chilcoot (lat. 39°54' N, long. 120°11'15" W; sec. 28, T 24 N, R 16 E); the place is along Frenchman Lake. Named on Frenchman Lake (1979) 7.5' quadrangle.

Frenchman Cove [PLUMAS]: *canyon,* 1.5 miles long, opens into the canyon of Frenchman Creek 12.5 miles east-northeast of Portola (lat. 39°53'40" N, long. 120°16' W; sec. 35, T 24 N, R 15 E). Named on Dixie Mountain (1972) 7.5' quadrangle.

Frenchman Creek [PLUMAS]: *stream,* flows 6 miles to Frenchman Lake 8 miles north-northwest of Chilcoot (lat. 39°54'05" N, long. 120°13'05" W; near W line sec. 29, T 24 N, R 16 E). Named on Dixie Mountain (1972) and Frenchman Lake (1979) 7.5' quadrangles. (Gudde, 1975, p. 125) associated the name with two Frenchmen who came to Sierra Valley in 1858.

Frenchman Hill [PLUMAS]: *peak,* nearly 4 miles west-southwest of Bucks Lodge (lat. 39°51'15" N, long. 121°14'20" W; on S line sec. 7, T 23 N, R 7 E). Altitude 5940 feet. Named on Haskins Valley (1980) 7.5' quadrangle.

Frenchman Lake [PLUMAS]: *lake,* behind a dam 7.25 miles north-northwest of Chilcoot along Little Last Chance Creek (lat. 39°53'35" N, long. 120°11'20" W; sec. 33, T 24 N, R 16 E). Named on Frenchman Lake (1979) 7.5' quadrangle. United States Board on Geographic Names (1965b, p. 14) rejected the name "Frenchman Reservoir" for the feature.

Frenchman Ravine [PLUMAS]: *canyon,* drained by a stream that flows 1.5 miles to West Branch Nelson Creek 14 miles southeast of Quincy (lat. 39°46'30" N, long. 120°47'15" W; near N line sec. 18, T 22 N, R 11 E). Named on Blue Nose Mountain (1951) 7.5' quadrangle.

Frenchman Reservoir: see **Frenchman Lake** [PLUMAS].

Frenchmans Bar: see **French Bar** [PLUMAS].

French Ravine [PLUMAS]: *canyon,* drained by a stream that flows 1.25 miles to East Branch of North Fork Feather River 5.25 miles south-southwest of Caribou (lat. 40°00'30" N, long. 121°11'20" W; sec. 22, T 25 N, R 7 E). Named on Bucks Lake (1979) and Caribou (1979) 7.5' quadrangles. The stream in the canyon is called French Creek on Almanor (1955) and Bucks Lake (1950) 15' quadrangles.

French Reservoir [MODOC]: *lake,* 1400 feet long, 8 miles south-southeast of Alturas (lat. 41°23' N, long. 120°28'35" W; sec. 21, T 41 N, R 13 E). Named on Dorris Reservoir (1963) 7.5' quadrangle.

Frog Lake [PLUMAS]: *lake,* 300 feet long, 16 miles southwest of the village of Almanor (lat. 40°03'10" N, long. 121°22'05" W; sec. 1, T 25 N, R 5 E). Named on Jonesville (1958) 15' quadrangle.

Frog Pond: see **The Frog Pond** [MODOC].

Frog Waterhole [MODOC]: *water feature,* 5 miles north of White Horse (lat. 41°22'50" N, long. 121°23'25" W). Named on White Horse (1962) 15' quadrangle.

Frying Pan Creek [PLUMAS]: *stream,* flows about 2 miles to Rock Creek (4) 6 miles northwest of Storrie (lat. 39°58'55" N, long. 121° 23'40" W; sec. 34, T 25 N, R 5 E). Named on Kimshew Point (1979) 7.5' quadrangle.

Fulstone Spring [LASSEN]: *spring,* 20 miles southwest of Likely [MODOC] (lat. 41°00'25" N, long. 120°43'55" W). Named on Likely (1962) 15' quadrangle.

— G —

Galeppi Creek [PLUMAS]: *stream,* flows 4.25 miles to Frenchman Lake 7.5 miles north-northwest of Chilcoot (lat. 39°54'05" N, long. 120°10'30" W; sec. 27, T 24 N, R 16 E). Named on Frenchman Lake (1979) 7.5' quadrangle.

Gallatin [LASSEN]: *locality,* 19 miles north-northwest of Susanville on the west side of Eagle Lake near the mouth of Pine Creek (1) (lat. 40°40' N, long. 120°46'45" W). Named on Honey Lake (1893) 1° quadrangle.

Gallatin Beach [LASSEN]: *beach,* 5.5 miles south-southwest of Pelican Point along Eagle Lake (lat. 40°33'30" N, long. 120°46' W; sec. 7, 8, T 31 N, R 11 E). Named on Antelope Mountain (1956) 15' quadrangle.

Gallatin Peak [LASSEN]: *peak,* 5 miles south of Pelican Peak (lat. 40°33'50" N, long. 120°44'25" W; sec. 9, T 31 N, R 11 E). Altitude 6948 feet. Named on Fredonyer Peak (1954) 15' quadrangle. The name honors members of the Albert Gallatin family who began acquiring property in the neighborhood of Eagle Lake in the 1880's (Purdy, 1988, p. 118).

Gansner Bar Campground [PLUMAS]: *locality,* 5.5 miles southwest of Caribou along North Fork Feather River (lat. 40°01'10" N, long. 121°13'20" W; sec. 17, T 25 N, R 7 E). Named on Caribou (1979) 7.5' quadrangle.

Gansner Creek [PLUMAS]: *stream,* flows 3 miles to American Valley 0.5 mile west of Quincy (lat. 39°56'15" N, long. 120°57'35" W; sec. 15, T 24 N, R 9 E). Named on Quincy (1950) 7.5' quadrangle.

Garabini Ravine [PLUMAS]: *canyon,* drained by a stream that flows 2 miles to East Nelson Creek 12.5 miles southeast of Quincy (lat. 39°47'20" N, long. 120°47'50" W; near W line sec. 6, T 22 N, R 11 E). Named on Blue Nose Mountain (1951) 7.5' quadrangle.

Garden Gulch [MODOC]: *canyon,* drained by a stream that flows 2.5 miles to Turner Creek (1) 7 miles west-southwest of Canby (lat. 41°25'10" N, long. 120°59'50" W; sec. 1, T 41 N, R 8 E). Named on Canby (1961) 15' quadrangle.

Garden Spring: see **Orchard Spring** [LASSEN].

Gas Drum Flat [MODOC]: *area,* 10 miles west-northwest of Jacks Butte (lat. 41°37'50" N, long. 120°58'50" W; at NW cor. sec. 30, T 44 N, R 9 E). Named on Jacks Butte (1962) 15' quadrangle.

Gasper Meadow [MODOC]: *area,* 4.5 miles southeast of White Horse (lat. 41°16' N, long. 121°20' W; at NE cor. sec. 35, T 40 N, R 5 E). Named on White Horse (1962) 15' quadrangle.

Gas Point: see **Janesville** [LASSEN].

Gassaway Reservoir [MODOC]: *intermittent lake,* 700 feet long, 4 miles west-northwest of Day (lat. 41°14' N, long. 121°26'30" W; sec. 7, T 39 N, R 5 E). Named on Fall River Mills (1961) 15' quadrangle. United States Board on Geographic Names (1964a, p. 10) rejected the name "Cassaway Reservoir" for the feature.

Gaston Spring [MODOC]: *spring,* 7 miles south of Willow Ranch (lat. 41°48'15" N, long. 120°19'40" W; near NW cor. sec. 26, T 46 N, R 14 E). Named on Willow Ranch (1962) 15' quadrangle.

Gem Lake [LASSEN]: *lake,* 1100 feet long, 12 miles south of Cal Mountain (lat. 40°30'05" N, long. 121°11'35" W; sec. 33, T 31 N, R 7 E). Named on Harvey Mountain (1956) 15' quadrangle, and on Red Cinder (1979) 7.5' quadrangle. Called Emerald Lake on Halls Flat (1939) 30' quadrangle.

General Bidwell Lake: see **Butte Lake** [LASSEN].

Genesee [PLUMAS]: *locality,* 5 miles east-southeast of Taylorsville (lat. 40°02'35" N, long. 120°45'10" W; sec. 9, T 25, R 11 E); the place is near the west end of Genesee Valley. Named on Genesee Valley (1972) and Taylorsville (1980) 7.5' quadrangles. Postal authorities established Geneseo post office in 1865, discontinued it in 1868, reestablished it with the name "Genesee" in 1880, and discontinued it in 1940 (Salley, p. 83).

Genesee Valley [PLUMAS]: *valley,* along Indian Valley Creek above a point about 3 miles east-southeast of Taylorsville (lat. 40°02'55" N, long. 120°47'30" W). Named on Genesee Valley (1972) and Taylorsville (1980) 7.5' quadrangles.

Geneseo: see **Genesee** [PLUMAS].

Gerig Camp [MODOC]: *locality,* 2.25 miles east-northeast of Crank Mountain (lat. 41°23'30" N, long. 121°06' W; near E line sec. 13, T 41 N, R 7 E). Named on Crank Mountain (1962) 15' quadrangle.

Gerig Spring [LASSEN]: *spring,* 9 miles north-northeast of the village of Little Valley (lat. 40°59'50" N, long. 121°04'45" W; sec. 32, T 37 N, R 8 E). Named on Little Valley (1957) 15' quadrangle.

Gerlach Spring [LASSEN]: *spring,* 16 miles north-northeast of Observation Peak (lat. 40°59'15" N, long. 120°04'55" W; sec. 18, T 36 N, R 17 E). Named on Observation Peak (1954) 15' quadrangle.

Gest: see **Chats** [LASSEN].

Geyser: see **The Geyser**, under **Terminal Geyser** [PLUMAS].

Ghent: see **Canby** [MODOC].

Gibbs Spring [LASSEN]: *spring,* 4.5 miles south-southwest of village of Little Valley (lat. 40°50'30" N, long. 121°13'40" W; near E line sec. 6, T 34 N, R 7 E). Named on Little Valley (1957) 15' quadrangle.

Gibralter [PLUMAS]: *peak,* 11 miles east of La Porte on Plumas-Sierra County line (lat. 39°42'45" N, long. 120°46'30" W; near W line sec. 5, T 21 N, R 11 E). Altitude 7343 feet. Named on Mount Fillmore (1951) 7.5' quadrangle.

Gibsonville Ridge [PLUMAS]: *ridge,* generally southwest-trending, 8 miles long, partly on Plumas-Sierra County line, center about 13 miles south of Quincy (lat. 39°45' N, long. 120°55'20" W). Named on Blue Nose Mountain (1951), La Porte (1951), and Onion Valley (1950) 7.5' quadrangles.

Gilhooley Slough [LASSEN]: *water feature,* 1.5 miles southeast of Litchfield (lat. 40°22'05" N, long. 120°22'40" W). Named on Standish (1972) 7.5' quadrangle.

Gillium Creek [MODOC]: *stream,* flows 1 mile to Renner Lake 11 miles north of South Mountain at California-Oregon State line (lat. 41°59'35" N, long. 120°37' W; sec. 20, T 48 N, R 12 E). Named on South Mountain (1962) 15' quadrangle.

Gilman Basin [LASSEN]: *relief feature,* 8 miles south-southwest of Susanville (lat. 40°18'40" N, long. 120°42'50" W; near SW cor. sec. 2, T 28 N, R 11 E). Named on Diamond Mountain (1972) 7.5' quadrangle.

Gilman Spring [LASSEN]:
(1) *spring,* 7.25 miles north-northeast of Litchfield (lat. 40°28'05" N, long. 120°19'10" W; near S line sec. 8, T 30 N, R 15 E). Named on Litchfield (1954) 15' quadrangle.
(2) *spring,* 14 miles east-southeast of Wendel (lat. 40°27'20" N, long. 120°00'30" W; near S line sec. 13, T 30 N, R 17 E). Named on Wendel (1954) 15' quadrangle.

Gilson Creek [PLUMAS]: *stream,* flows about 1.5 miles to Spanish Creek (1) 4 miles north-northeast of Quincy (lat. 39°59'35" N, long. 120°55'05" W; near N line sec. 36, T 25 N, R 9 E). Named on Crescent Mills (1980) and Quincy (1950) 7.5' quadrangles.

Glade: see **Ravendale** [LASSEN].

Glass Mountain: see **Meares** [MODOC].

Glazer Creek [PLUMAS]: *stream,* flows 1.25 miles to Little North Fork of Middle Fork Feather River 11 miles south-southeast of Storrie (lat. 39°46'05" N, long. 121°15'25" W); the stream is northwest of Glazer Ridge. Named on Haskins Valley (1980) and Soapstone Hill (1979) 7.5' quadrangles.

Glazer Point [PLUMAS]: *peak,* 7 miles south-southwest of Bucks Lodge (lat. 39°47'10" N, long. 121°14'05" W; sec. 6, T 22 N, R 7 E); the peak is at the north end of Glazer Ridge. Altitude 5426 feet. Named on Haskins Valley (1980) 7.5' quadrangle.

Glazer Ridge [PLUMAS]: *ridge,* generally southwest-trending, 2.25 miles long, 8 miles south-southwest of Bucks Lodge (lat. 39°46'15" N, long. 121°14'30" W). Named on Haskins Valley (1980) and Soapstone Hill (1979) 7.5' quadrangles.

Glazer Ridge: see **Little Glazer Ridge** [PLUMAS].

Gleason Creek [MODOC]: *stream,* flows 7.5 miles to Parker Creek 16 miles south-southwest of the village of Davis Creek (lat. 41° 31'10" N, long. 120°28'15" W; near SE cor. sec. 33, T 43 N, R 13 E). Named on Davis Creek (1962) 15' quadrangle.

Glen Lake [LASSEN]: *lake,* 800 feet long, 2 miles north-northeast of Mount Harkness [PLUMAS] (lat. 40°27'15" N, long. 121°16'50" W; on S line sec. 14, T 30 N, R 6 E). Named on Mount Harkness (1956) 15' quadrangle.

Goat Mountain [LASSEN]: *peak,* 12.5 miles northeast of Westwood (lat. 40°25'15" N, long. 120°49'20" W; near N line sec. 35, T 30 N, R 10 E). Altitude 5792 feet. Named on Roop Mountain (1980) 7.5' quadrangle.

Goat Mountain [PLUMAS]: *peak,* 2.5 miles north-northeast of La Porte (lat. 39°43'05" N, long. 120°57'35" W; at S line sec. 34, T 22 N, R 9 E). Altitude 5696 feet. Named on La Porte (1951) 7.5' quadrangle.

Gobel Slough [LASSEN]: *water feature,* joins Pit River 4 miles south of Bieber (lat. 41°03'55" N, long. 121°07'50" W; at N line sec. 11, T 37 N, R 7 E). Named on Bieber (1961) 15' quadrangle.

Golden Creek [PLUMAS]: *stream,* flows 1 mile to Cold Water Creek 10 miles southeast of Quincy (lat. 39°49'45" N, long. 120°49'25" W). Named on Blue Nose Mountain (1951) 7.5' quadrangle.

Gold Hill: see **Little Gold Hill** [LASSEN].

Gold Lake [PLUMAS]: *lake,* 950 feet long, 5 miles north-northeast of Bucks Lodge (lat. 39°56'30" N, long. 121°08'05" W; on W line sec. 18, T 24 N, R 8 E). Named on Bucks Lake (1979) 7.5' quadrangle.

Gold Lake Lodge [PLUMAS]: *locality,* 5.5 miles southwest of Clio (lat. 39°41'35" N, long. 120°39'25" W; sec. 8, T 21 N, R 12 E); the place is 0.5 mile northwest of the Gold Lake that is in Sierra County. Named on Gold Lake (1981) 7.5' quadrangle.

Gold Mountain: see **Eureka Peak** [PLUMAS].

Gold Run: see **Gold Run Creek** [LASSEN].

Gold Run Creek [LASSEN]: *stream,* flows 7.5 miles to lowlands 3 miles south of Susanville (lat. 40°22'30" N, long. 120°39' W; sec. 17, T 29 N, R 12 E). Named on Susanville (1954) 15' quadrangle. Called Gold Run on Honey Lake (1893) 1° quadrangle.

Gooch Camp [LASSEN]: *locality,* 4 miles south-southeast of Lava Peak (lat. 40°46'50" N, long. 120°51'15" W; sec. 28, T 34 N, R 10 E); the place is on the east side of Lower Gooch Valley. Named on Hayden Hill (1956) 15' quadrangle.

Gooch Mountain [LASSEN]: *peak,* 3.5 miles southeast of Lava Peak (lat. 40°47'40" N, long. 120°50'45" W; near E line sec. 21, T 34 N, R 10 E); the peak is east of Lower Gooch Valley. Named on Hayden Hill (1956) 15' quadrangle.

Gooch Valley: see **Lower Gooch Valley** [LASSEN]; **Upper Gooch Valley** [LASSEN].

Goodrich Creek [LASSEN]: *stream,* flows 9.5 miles to Mountain Meadows Reservoir 2.5 miles east-southeast of Westwood (lat. 40° 17'10" N, long. 120°57'35" W; sec. 15, T 28 N, R 9 E). Named on Westwood East (1980) 7.5' quadrangle.

Goodrich Mountain [LASSEN]: *ridge,* east-trending, 2.5 miles long, nearly 3 miles northeast of Westwood (lat. 40°19'50" N, long. 120° 57'30" W). Named on Westwood East (1980) 7.5' quadrangle.

Goose Creek [MODOC]: *stream,* flows 5 miles to Upper Lake 12 miles north of Cedarville (lat. 41°42'15" N, long. 120°11'35" W; near N line sec 7, T 44 N, R 16 E). Named on Cedarville (1962) and Davis Creek (1962) 15' quadrangles. The name is from a German settler whose surname had the spelling "Goos" (Stewart, p. 184).

Goose Lake [MODOC]:
(1) *lake,* about 20 miles long (16 miles long in California), 7 miles north-northwest of Willow Ranch on California-Oregon State line (lat. 41°59'35" N, long. 120°24'30" W). Named on South Mountain (1962) and Willow Ranch (1962) 15' quadrangles. Rogers and Johnston's (1857) map has the designation "Goose or Pitt's L." for the feature. United States Board on Geographic Names (1965d, p. 9) rejected the name "Upper Goose Lake" for it.
(2) *intermittent lake,* 1200 feet long, 12.5 miles north-northwest of Alturas (lat. 41°38'50" N, long. 120°37'50" W; at S line sec. 18, T 44 N, R 12 E). Named on Big Sage Reservoir (1962) 15' quadrangle.

Goose Lake Corral Spring: see **Corral Spring** [MODOC].

Gopher Hill [PLUMAS]: *relief feature,* 2.25 miles northeast of the village of Meadow Valley (lat. 39°57'15" N, long. 121°01'35" W; on E line sec. 12, T 24 N, R 8 E). Named on Meadow Valley (1980) 7.5' quadrangle.

Gordon Lake [LASSEN]: *lake,* 3500 feet long, 4.5 miles south of Lava Peak (lat. 40°46'05" N, long. 120°52'55" W; on E line sec. 31, T 34 N, R 10 E); the lake is 1.25 miles northwest of Gordon Valley. Named on Hayden Hill (1956) 15' quadrangle.

Gordon Valley [LASSEN]: *valley,* 5.5 miles south-southeast of Lava Peak (lat. 40°45'15" N, long. 120°51'50" W; mainly in sec. 4, 5, T 33 N, R 10 E). Named on Hayden Hill (1956) 15' quadrangle.

Gordon Well [LASSEN]: *well,* 10 miles northwest of Pelican Point (lat. 40°44'15" N, long. 120°52'15" W; sec. 8, T 33 N, R 10 E); the well is 1.25 miles south of Gordon Valley. Named on Antelope Mountain (1956) 15' quadrangle.

Gosch Spring [MODOC]: *spring,* 5 miles west of Canby (lat. 41°26'55" N, long. 120°58' W; at E line sec. 30, T 42 N, R 9 E). Named on Canby (1961) 15' quadrangle.

Gould Swamp [PLUMAS]: *water feature,* 2.5 miles east-southeast of Chester (lat. 40°18'10" N, long. 121°11' W); the feature is part of Lake Almanor. Named on Chester (1979) 7.5' quadrangle. Chester (1956) 15' quadrangle shows marsh at the place.

Goumaz [LASSEN]: *locality,* 10.5 miles northeast of Westwood along Southern Pacific Railroad (lat. 40°24'50" N, long. 120°51'30" W; sec. 33, T 30 N, R 10 E). Named on Westwood (1955) 15' quadrangle. Called Goumez on California Mining Bureau's (1917a) map, which shows a place called Wheaton situated 2 miles west of Goumez along the railroad. California Division of Highways' (1934) map shows a place called Bunnel located along the railroad 3.5 miles east of Goumaz.

Government Reservoir [MODOC]: *intermittent lake,* 2200 feet long, 18 miles north of Alturas (lat. 41°44'50" N, long. 120°35'35" W; on N line sec. 16, T 45 N, R 12 E). Named on Big Sage Reservoir (1962) and South Mountain (1962) 15' quadrangles.

Graeagle [PLUMAS]: *village,* 1 mile south of Blairsden (lat. 39°45'50" N, long. 120°36'55" W; sec. 15, 22, T 22 N, R 12 E); the village is near the mouth of Gray Eagle Creek. Named on Blairsden (1972) and Johnsville (1972) 7.5' quadrangles. Postal authorities established Davies Mill post office in 1918 and changed the name to Graeagle 1920; the name "Graeagle" is a contraction of the words "Gray Eagle" (Salley, p. 56, 87).

Granger Creek [MODOC]: *stream,* flows nearly 5 miles to Surprise Valley 4 miles south of Cedarville (lat. 41°28'40" N, long. 120°10'45" W; near W line sec. 29, T 42 N, R 16 E). Named on Warren Peak (1963) 7.5' quadrangle. Called Dry Creek on Alturas 1° quadrangle.

Granite Basin [PLUMAS]: *area,* 6.5 miles south-southeast of Storrie (lat. 30°49'45" N, long. 121°15' W). Named on Haskins Valley (1980) and Soapstone Hill (1979) 7.5' quadrangles. On Pulga (1957) 15' quadrangle, the name applies to an area 1.5 miles farther west.

Granite Creek [PLUMAS]: *stream,* flows 1.5 miles to North Fork Feather River 2.5 miles north-northeast of Storrie (lat. 39°57'05" N, long. 121°18' W; near W line sec. 10, T 24 N, R 6 E). Named on Storrie (1979) 7.5'

quadrangle.

Granite Spring [PLUMAS]: *spring,* 4.5 miles south-southeast of Milford [LASSEN] (lat. 40°06'30" N, long. 120°20'45" W; sec. 13, T 26 N, R 15 E). Named on Ferris Creek (1977) 7.5' quadrangle.

Grasshopper Flat Campground [PLUMAS]: *locality,* 6 miles north of Portola along Lake Davis (lat. 39°53'30" N, long. 120°28'40" W; near NE cor. sec. 2, T 23 N, R 13 E). Named on Crocker Mountain (1972) 7.5' quadrangle.

Grasshopper Ridge [LASSEN]: *ridge,* south- to south-southeast-trending, 4 miles long, 11.5 miles west of Termo (lat. 40°50'30" N, long. 120°40'30" W); the ridge is east of Grasshopper Valley. Named on Grasshopper Valley (1954) 15' quadrangle.

Grasshopper Valley [LASSEN]: *valley,* 13 miles west of Termo (lat. 40°51' N, long. 120°42'30" W). Named on Grasshopper Valley (1954) and Hayden Hill (1956) 15' quadrangles. Preston (1890a, p. 275) used the name "Meadow Valley" for the feature.

Grass Lake [PLUMAS]:

(1) *lake,* 1700 feet long, 6.5 miles west of Clio along Little Jamison Creek (lat. 39°43'35" N, long. 120°41'50" W; near W line sec. 36, T 22 N, R 11 E). Named on Gold Lake (1981) 7.5' quadrangle.

(2) *lake,* 400 feet long, 4.25 miles west-southwest of Clio (lat. 39° 42'10" N, long. 120°39'45" W; on W line sec. 8, T 21 N, R 12 E). Named on Gold Lake (1981) 7.5' quadrangle.

Grass Valley: see **Little Grass Valley** [PLUMAS].

Grass Valley Bald Mountain [PLUMAS]: *peak,* 13 miles south of Quincy (lat. 39°45'20" N, long. 120°58'55" W; sec. 21, T 22 N, R 9 E); the peak is 1 mile north of Little Grass Valley. Altitude 6255 feet. Named on Onion Valley (1950) 7.5' quadrangle. Called Grass Valley Hill on Downieville (1897) 30' quadrangle.

Grass Valley Hill: see **Grass Valley Bald Mountain** [PLUMAS].

Grassy Creek [LASSEN]: *stream,* flows 2.5 miles from Snag Lake to Shasta County 3.25 miles north-northwest of Mount Harkness [PLUMAS] (lat. 40°28'30" N, long. 121°19'35" W; at W line sec. 9, T 30 N, R 6 E). Named on Mount Harkness (1956) 15' quadrangle.

Grassy Flat [PLUMAS]: *area,* 18 miles southwest of the village of Almanor (lat. 40°00'10" N, long. 121°23' W; on S line sec. 23, T 25 N, R 5 E). Named on Jonesville (1958) 15' quadrangle.

Grassy Lake [PLUMAS]: *lake,* 1000 feet long, 4.5 miles north-northwest of Storrie (lat. 39°58'55" N, long. 121°21'10" W; sec. 31, T 25 N, R 6 E). Named on Storrie (1979) 7.5' quadrangle.

Grassy Lakes [PLUMAS]: *lakes,* two, largest 750 feet long, 7 miles north-northwest of Bucks Lodge (lat. 39°58'25" N, long. 121°12'50" W; near S line sec. 32, T 25 N, R 7 E). Named on Bucks Lake (1979) 7.5' quadrangle.

Grassy Ravine [MODOC]: *canyon,* drained by a stream that flows 5.25 miles to Fletcher Creek nearly 4 miles west-northwest of South Mountain (lat. 41°51'50" N, long. 121°41'45" W; near N line sec. 3, T 46 N, R 11 E). Named on South Mountain (1962) 15' quadrangle.

Gravel Range: see **Arkansas Ravine** [PLUMAS].

Gravel Range Creek: see **Hunters Ravine** [PLUMAS]; **Scotch Creek** [PLUMAS].

Graven Reservoir [MODOC]: *lake,* 1 mile long, 15 miles southwest of Alturas (lat. 41°17' N, long. 120°40' W; around SW cor. sec. 24, T 40 N, R 11 E). Named on Alturas (1961) 15' quadrangle.

Graven Ridge [MODOC]: *ridge,* northwest-trending, 5 miles long, 14 miles south-southwest of Alturas (lat. 41°18'30" N, long. 120° 40' W). Named on Alturas (1961) 15' quadrangle.

Graves Reservoir [MODOC]: *lake,* 6000 feet long, 10.5 miles south-southwest of Alturas (lat. 41°21'35" N, long. 120°38'30" W; at SE cor. sec. 25, T 41 N, R 11 E). Named on Alturas (1961) 15' quadrangle.

Graves Valley [MODOC]: *valley,* 15 miles northwest of Alturas (lat. 41°39' N, long. 120°44'30" W; in and near sec. 18, T 44 N, R 11 E). Named on Big Sage Reservoir (1962) 15' quadrangle.

Gray Eagle Creek [PLUMAS]: *stream,* flows 6.25 miles to Middle Fork Feather River less than 1 mile south-southeast of Blairsden (lat. 39°46'05" N, long. 120°36'40" W; near E line sec. 15, T 22 N, R 12 E). Named on Blairsden (1972), Gold Lake (1981), and Johnsville (1972) 7.5' quadrangles. Downieville (1897) 30' quadrangle has the name "Gray Eagle Valley" along upper reaches of Gray Eagle Creek.

Gray Eagle Lodge [PLUMAS]: *locality,* 3.5 miles west-southwest of Clio (lat. 39°43'20" N, long. 120°39'40" W; near SW cor. sec. 32, T 22 N, R 12 E); the place is along Gray Eagle Creek. Named on Gold Lake (1981) 7.5' quadrangle..

Gray Eagle Valley: see **Gray Eagle Creek** [PLUMAS].

Grays Flat [LASSEN]: *area,* 4.5 miles south-southwest of Cal Mountain (lat. 40°36'30" N, long. 121°12' W; sec. 28, T 32 N, R 7 E); the place is 4 miles west-southwest of Grays Valley. Named on Harvey Mountain (1956) 15' quadrangle.

Grays Flat [PLUMAS]: *locality,* 0.25 mile east of, and across East Branch of North Fork Feather River from Twain (lat. 40°01'15" N, long. 121°03'50" W; at NW cor. sec. 23, T 25 N, R 8 E). Named on Twain (1980) 7.5' quadrangle.

Grays Flat: see **Twain** [PLUMAS].

Grays Valley [LASSEN]: *valley,* 3 miles southeast of Cal Mountain (lat. 40°38'15" N, long. 121°07'45" W). Named on Harvey Mountain (1956) 15' quadrangle.

Grays Valley Well [LASSEN]: *well,* 3 miles south-southeast of Cal Mountain (lat. 40°37'50" N, long. 121°08'10" W; near SE cor. sec. 13, T 32 N, R 7 E); the well is in Grays Valley. Named on Harvey Mountain (1956) 15' quadrangle.

Green Flat [PLUMAS]: *area,* 1.5 miles south-southwest of Kettle Rock (lat. 40°07'05" N, long. 120°43'55" W; near N line sec. 15, T 26 N, R 11 E). Named on Genesee Valley (1972) 7.5' quadrangle.

Greenhorn Creek [PLUMAS]: *stream,* flows 14 miles to Spanish Creek (1) nearly 3 miles northeast of Quincy (lat. 39°58'05" N, long. 120°54'50" W; at E line sec. 1, T 24 N, R 9 E). Named on Mount Ingalls (1972), Quincy (1950), and Spring Garden (1950) 7.5' quadrangles. On Dowieville (1897) 30' quadrangle, present Estray Creek and present Greenhorn Creek below Estray Creek are called Spring Garden Creek.

Greenhorn Diggings: see **Argentine** [PLUMAS].

Green Island Lake [PLUMAS]: *lake,* 1400 feet long, 15 miles southwest of the village of Almanor (lat. 40°03' N, long. 121°21'45" W; on W line sec. 6, T 25 N, R 6 E). Named on Jonesville (1958) 15' quadrangle.

Greeno: see **Lake Greeno**, under **Constantia** [LASSEN].

Greens Canyon [MODOC]: *canyon,* drained by a stream that flows nearly 2 miles to North Deep Creek 3 miles west-southwest of Cedarville (lat. 41°30'45" N, long. 120°13'30" W). Named on Cedarville (1962) 15' quadrangle.

Greens Flat [PLUMAS]:

(1) *area,* 5 miles south of Bucks Lodge (lat. 39°48'10" N, long. 121°11'20" W; near W line sec. 34, T 23 N, R 7 E). Named on Haskins Valley (1980) 7.5' quadrangle.

(2) *area,* 2 miles north-northwest of the village of Meadow Valley (lat. 39°57'30" N, long. 121°04'45" W; near W line sec. 10, T 24 N, R 8 E). Named on Meadow Valley (1980) 7.5' quadrangle.

Greens Peak [LASSEN]: *peak,* 9 miles south-southeast of Pelican Point (lat. 40°30'25" N, long. 120°42'15" W; sec. 35, T 31 N, R 11 E). Altitude 7145 feet. Named on Fredonyer Peak (1954) 15' quadrangle.

Green Spring [MODOC]: *spring,* 2.5 miles east-northeast of South Mountain (lat. 41°51'30" N, long. 120°35'30" W; sec. 4, T 46 N, R 12 E). Named on South Mountain (1962) 15' quadrangle.

Green Tank [MODOC]: *water feature,* less than 1 mile east of South Mountain (lat. 41°50'30" N, long. 120°37' W). Named on South Mountain (1962) 15' quadrangle.

Green Valley [LASSEN]: *valley,* 2.5 miles north-northwest of Cal Mountain (lat. 40°42' N, long. 121°11' W). Named on Harvey Mountain (1956) 15' quadrangle.

Greenville [PLUMAS]: *town,* 19 miles southeast of Chester (lat. 40° 08'25" N, long. 120°57' W; sec. 2, 3, T 26 N, R 9 E). Named on Greenville (1979) 7.5' quadrangle. Postal authorities established Greenville post office in 1867 and named it for Mr. Green, who settled at the site in 1852 and operated a tavern (Salley, p. 89). California Division of Highways' (1934) map shows a place called Mohala located about 2.5 miles north-northwest of Greenville along the railroad (sec. 28, T 27 N, R 9 E).

Greenville Campground [PLUMAS]: *locality,* 1.25 miles north of Greenville (lat. 40°09'25" N, long. 120°57'15" W; sec. 34, T 27 N, R 9 E). Named on Greenville (1979) 7.5' quadrangle.

Greenville Creek [LASSEN]: *stream,* flows nearly 4 miles to Mountain Meadows Reservoir 6 miles southeast of Westwood (lat. 40° 14'30" N, long. 120°54'50" W; sec. 36, T 28 N, R 9 E). Named on Greenville (1979) 7.5' quadrangle.

Griener Reservoir [MODOC]: *intermittent lake,* 2300 feet long, 13 miles south-southwest of the village of Davis Creek (lat. 41°33'40" N, long. 120°29'10" W; at SE cor. sec. 17, T 43 N, R 13 E). Named on Davis Creek (1962) 15' quadrangle.

Griffith Hill [LASSEN]: *ridge,* east-northeast-trending, 1.25 miles long, 13 miles north-northwest of Westwood (lat. 40°28'55" N, long. 121°06' W). Named on Swain Mountain (1979) 7.5' quadrangle.

Grigsby Camp [PLUMAS]: *locality,* 11.5 miles north-northwest of Chilcoot (lat. 39°56'45" N, long. 120°13'30" W; sec. 7, T 24 N, R 16 E); the place is along Grigsby Creek. Named on Frenchman Lake (1979) 7.5' quadrangle.

Grigsby Creek [PLUMAS]: *stream,* flows 4 miles to Frenchman Lake 10.5 miles north-northwest of Chilcoot (lat. 39°56'25" N, long. 120°12'35" W; near N line sec. 17, T 24 N, R 16 E). Named on Dixie Mountain (1972) and Frenchman Lake (1979) 7.5' quadrangles. The name commemorates Challan Grigsby of the Forest Service (Gudde, 1949, p. 136).

Grizzlie Spring: see **Little Grizzlie Spring** [MODOC].

Grizzly Campground [PLUMAS]: *locality,* 5.5 miles north of Portola along Lake Davis (lat. 39°53'15" N, long. 120°28'25" W; near W line sec. 1, T 23 N, R 13 E). Named on Crocker Mountain (1972) 7.5' quadrangle.

Grizzly Creek [PLUMAS]:

(1) *stream,* flows 8 miles to Yellow Creek 11.5 miles south-southwest of the village of Almanor (lat. 40°04'10" N, long. 121°15'05" W; sec. 36, T 26 N, R 6 E). Named on Jonesville (1958) 15' quadrangle.
(2) *stream,* flows 12.5 miles to North Fork Feather River 4.25 miles south-west of Storrie (lat. 39°52'05" N, long. 121°22'20" W; near N line sec. 12, T 23 N, R 5 E). Named on Bucks Lake (1979), Haskins Valley (1980), Soapstone Hill (1979), and Storrie (1979) 7.5' quadrangles.
(3) *stream,* flows 1.5 miles to Middle Fork Feather River 7.5 miles south-southwest of Quincy (lat. 39°50'10" N, long. 120°59'20" W; near SW cor. sec. 21, T 23 N, R 9 E). Named on Dogwood Peak (1979) and Onion Valley (1950) 7.5' quadrangles.

Grizzly Creek: see **Big Grizzly Creek** [PLUMAS]; **Little Grizzly Creek** [PLUMAS]; **Little Grizzly Creek**, under **Blakeless Creek** [PLUMAS].

Grizzly Creek Campground [PLUMAS]: *locality,* nearly 3 miles west-south-west of Bucks Lodge (lat. 39°52' N, long. 121°12'20" W; near NW cor. sec. 9, T 23 N, R 7 E); the place is along a branch of Grizzly Creek (2). Named on Haskins Valley (1980) 7.5' quadrangle.

Grizzly Dome [PLUMAS]: *peak,* 3.25 miles south-southwest of Storrie (lat. 39°52'20" N, long. 121°20'35" W; near E line sec. 6, T 23 N, R 6 E). Altitude 4940 feet. Named on Soapstone Hill (1979) 7.5' quadrangle.

Grizzly Forebay [PLUMAS]: *lake,* behind a dam on Grizzly Creek (2) 2.5 miles southeast of Storrie (lat. 39°53'30" N, long. 121°17'25" W; sec. 34, T 24 N, R 6 E). Named on Storrie (1979) 7.5' quadrangle.

Grizzly Gulch [PLUMAS]: *canyon,* drained by a stream that flows 1 mile to North Fork Feather River 3.25 miles south-southwest of Canyondam (lat. 40°07'35" N, long. 121°05'25" W; sec. 9, T 26 N, R 8 E). Named on Canyondam (1979) 7.5' quadrangle.

Grizzly Hill: see **Red Mountain** [PLUMAS] (2).

Grizzly Ice Pond [PLUMAS]: *lake,* 1050 feet long, 3 miles northeast of Portola (lat. 39°50'20" N, long. 120°25'45" W; on N line sec. 20, T 23 N, R 14 E); the lake is along Big Grizzly Creek. Named on Portola (1972) 7.5' quadrangle.

Grizzly Lake [PLUMAS]: *lake,* 600 feet long, 2.5 miles west-southwest of Bucks Lodge (lat. 39°51'25" N, long. 121°13'05" W; on S line sec. 8, T 23 N, R 7 E); the lake is along a branch of Grizzly Creek (2). Named on Haskins Valley (1980) 7.5' quadrangle.

Grizzly Mountain [PLUMAS]: *ridge,* 3.25 miles long, about 5 miles south-southeast of Taylorsville (lat. 40°00'30" N, long. 120°47'50" W). Named on Spring Garden (1950) and Taylorsville (1980) 7.5' quadrangles. Called Grizzly Mountains on United States Geological Survey's (1907) map.

Grizzly Mountain: see **Red Mountain** [PLUMAS] (2).

Grizzly Mountains: see **Grizzly Mountain** [PLUMAS].

Grizzly Peak [PLUMAS]: *peak,* 4.5 miles south-southeast of Taylorsville (lat. 40°00'55" N, long. 120°47'55" W; near W line sec. 19, T 25 N, R 11 E). Altitude 7711 feet. Named on Taylorsville (1980) 7.5' quadrangle.

Grizzly Peak: see **Smith Peak** [PLUMAS].

Grizzly Ridge [PLUMAS]: *ridge,* generally southeast-trending, 13 miles long, center 5.5 miles south-southwest of Mount Ingalls (lat. 39°55'25" N, long. 120°40'15" W). Named on Grizzly Valley (1972), Mount Ingalls (1972), and Spring Garden (1950) 7.5' quadrangles.

Grizzly Springs Camp: see **Little Grizzlie Spring** [MODOC].

Grizzly Summit [PLUMAS]: *pass,* 5 miles south-southeast of Storrie (lat. 39°51'30" N, long. 121°16'25" W; sec. 11, T 23 N, R 6 E). Named on Soapstone Hill (1979) 7.5' quadrangle.

Grizzly Valley [PLUMAS]: *valley,* along Big Grizzly Creek above a point 5.5 miles north of Portola (lat. 39°53' N, long. 120°28'30" W). Named on Portola (1950) 15' quadrangle, and on Grizzly Valley (1972) and Mount Ingalls (1972) 7.5' quadrangles. Water of Lake Davis covers part of the valley.

Grizzly Valley: see **Little Grizzly Valley** [PLUMAS].

Grouse Hollow [PLUMAS]: *canyon,* drained by a stream that flows 2.5 miles to Milk Ranch Creek 5 miles northeast of Storrie (lat. 39° 57'55" N, long. 121°15'05" W; sec. 1, T 24 N, R 6 E). Named on Bucks Lake (1979) 7.5' quadrangle.

Grouse Hollow Creek [PLUMAS]: *stream,* flows 1.5 miles to Middle Fork Feather River 3.5 miles north-northwest of Cascade (lat. 39° 44'45" N, long. 121°12' W; sec. 21, T 22 N, R 7 E). Named on Haskins Valley (1980) 7.5' quadrangle. Called Hunters Ravine on Bucks Lake (1950) 15' quadrangle, and on Cascade (1948) 7.5' quadrangle, but United States Board on Geographic Names (1979, p. 3) rejected this name for the stream.

Grouse Mountain [MODOC]: *peak,* 8 miles south of Canby (lat. 41° 19'40" N, long. 120°50'55" W; on S line sec. 5, T 40 N, R 10 E). Altitude 6931 feet. Named on Canby (1961) 15' quadrangle.

Grouse Spring [MODOC]:
(1) *spring,* 4 miles north-northeast of Crank Mountain (lat. 41°26'05" N, long. 121°06'30" W). Named on Crank Mountain (1962) 15' quadrangle.
(2) *spring,* 8 miles south of Canby (lat. 41°19'45" N, long. 120°50'30" W; near SE cor. sec. 5, T 40 N, R 10 E); the spring is 0.5 mile east of Grouse Mountain. Named on Canby (1961) 15' quadrangle.

Grubbs Cow Camp [PLUMAS]: *locality,* 2.5 miles west-southwest of Bucks Lodge (lat. 39°51'45" N, long. 121°13'25" W; sec. 8, T 23 N, R 7 E). Named on Haskins Valley (1980) 7.5' quadrangle.

Grub Flat [PLUMAS]: *area,* northwest of the village of Meadow Valley (lat. 39°56' N, long. 121°04' W); the place is part of present Meadow Valley (1). Named on Bidwell Bar (1897) 30' quadrangle.

– H –

Hackamore [MODOC]: *locality,* 30 miles west of Alturas along Southern Pacific Railroad (lat. 41°33'10" N, long. 121°07'15" W; at E line sec. 23, T 43 N, R 7 E). Named on Hackamore (1952) 15' quadrangle. Postal authorities established Hackamore post office in 1903 and discontinued it in 1904 (Frickstad, p. 102). Alturas (1954) 1°x 2° quadrangle has the name "Hackamore" at a site 0.25 mile southwest of the railroad, and has the name "Hackamore Siding" 1.5 miles farther west-northwest along the railroad. California Division of Highways' (1934) map shows a place called Doles located nearly 4 miles east-southeast of Hackamore along the railroad. Postal authorities established Stobie post office in 1897, moved it 3 miles northeast in 1902, and moved it 2.5 miles north in 1903 when they changed the name to Hackmore; they reestablished Stobie post office in 1910 and discontinued it in 1912—the name "Stobie" was for Violet Stobie, first postmaster (Salley, p. 213).

Hackamore Reservoir [MODOC]: *intermittent lake,* 4200 feet long, 0.5 mile west-northwest of Hackamore (lat. 41°33'20" N, long. 121°07'50" W; sec. 14, 23, T 43 N, R 7 E). Named on Hackamore (1952) 15' quadrangle.

Hackamore Siding: see **Hackamore** [MODOC].

Hacker Flat [MODOC]: *area,* 18 miles southeast of Alturas (lat. 41° 16'20" N, long. 120°19'35" W; sec. 26, T 40 N, R 14 E). Named on Soup Creek (1963) 7.5' quadrangle.

Hackstaff: see **Rayl**, under **Herlong** [LASSEN] (1).

Hagata Canyon [LASSEN]: *canyon,* drained by a stream that flows 6.5 miles to end 10.5 miles southeast of Pelican Point in Willow Creek Valley (lat. 40°33'05" N, long. 120°34'25" W; near N line sec. 13, T 31 N, R 12 E). Named on Fredonyer Peak (1954) 15' quadrangle.

Hagata Reservoir [LASSEN]: *lake,* 950 feet long, 11 miles east-southeast of Pelican Point near the mouth of Hagata Canyon (lat. 40°33'50" N, long. 120°33'50" W; near W line sec. 7, T 31 N, R 13 E). Named on Fredonyer Peak (1954) 15' quadrangle.

Hager Basin [MODOC]: *area,* 5.5 miles east-southeast of Blue Mountain (lat. 41°47'50" N, long. 120°46' W; sec. 25, 36, T 46 N, R 10 E). Named on Steele Swamp (1962) 15' quadrangle.

Hager Basin Reservoir [MODOC]: *intermittent lake,* 1400 feet long, 6.5 miles southeast of Blue Mountain (lat. 41°46'20" N, long. 120° 45'40" W; sec. 1, T 45 N, R 10 E). Named on Steele Swamp (1962) 15' quadrangle.

Half Cabin Reservoir [LASSEN]: *lake,* 800 feet long, nearly 5 miles west-northwest of Cal Mountain (lat. 40°41' N, long. 121°13'55" W; sec. 31, T 33 N, R 7 E). Named on Harvey Mountain (1956) 15' quadrangle.

Halfmoon Beach [LASSEN]: *beach,* 4 miles northwest of Pelican Point at northwest end of Eagle Lake (lat. 40°40'45" N, long. 120° 47'15" W). Named on Antelope Mountain (1956) 15' quadrangle.

Hall Cabin Spring [PLUMAS]: *spring,* 6.5 miles south-southeast of McKesick Peak (lat. 40°00' N, long. 120°12'55" W; near S line sec. 20, T 25 N, R 16 E). Named on McKesick Peak (1978) 7.5' quadrangle.

Hallelujah Junction [LASSEN]: *locality,* nearly 4 miles east-southeast of Beckwourth Pass (lat. 39°46'30" N, long. 120°02'15" W; sec. 11, T 22 N, R 17 E). Named on Beckwourth Pass (1975) 7.5' quadrangle.

Hallett Meadow [PLUMAS]: *area,* 9 miles northeast of Kettle Rock along Boulder Creek (1) (lat. 40°13'25" N, long. 120°35'45" W; sec. 2, T 27 N, R 12 E). Named on Antelope Lake (1972) 7.5' quadrangle.

Halls [LASSEN]: *locality,* 10 miles northwest of Susanville near the south end of Eagle Lake (lat. 40°32' N, long. 120°46' W). Named on Honey Lake (1893) 1° quadrangle.

Halls Canyon [MODOC]: *canyon,* drained by a stream that flows 4.5 miles to lowlands along Pit River nearly 6.5 miles south-southeast of Crank Mountain (lat. 41°17'45" N, long. 121°06'40" W; sec. 24, T 40 N, R 7 E). Named on Crank Mountain (1962) 15' quadrangle.

Halls Flat [LASSEN]:
(1) *area,* 7.5 miles west-northwest of Cal Mountain (lat. 40°43'45" N, long. 121°17' W; around NW cor. sec. 14, T 33 N, R 6 E). Named on Prospect Peak (1957) 15' quadrangle. Forest Service officials named the feature for William G. Hall and his sons, who had a summer cattle camp at the place about 1880 (Gudde, 1949, p. 140).
(2) *locality,* 10.5 miles south-southwest of the village of Little Valley along Western Pacific Railroad (lat. 40°45'20" N, long. 121°15'30" W; near NW cor. sec. 1, T 33 N, R 6 E); the place is 2.5 miles north-northeast of Halls Flat (1). Named on Jellico (1957) 15' quadrangle.

Halls Meadows [MODOC]: *area,* 7.5 miles south-southeast of the village of Davis Creek (lat. 41°38'50" N, long. 120°19'10" W; on S line sec. 14, T 44 N, R 14 E). Named on Davis Creek (1962) 15' quadrangle. United States Board on Geographic Names (1991, p. 4) rejected the singular form

"Halls Meadow" for the name. The Board (1991, p. 5) approved the designation "Halls Meadows Reservoir" for a lake, 0.4 mile long, located at Halls Meadows (lat. 41°38'40" N, long. 120°19'17" W; sec. 15, 22, 23, T 44 N, R 14 E), and rejected the name "Scammon Reservoir" for the feature.

Halls Meadows Reservoir: see **Halls Meadows** [MODOC].

Hall Springs [LASSEN]: *spring,* 9.5 miles south of Observation Peak (lat. 40°38'20" N, long. 120°10'20" W; sec. 16, T 32 N, R 16 E). Named on Shinn Mountain (1954) 15' quadrangle.

Halls Springs [MODOC]: *springs,* 6.5 miles southeast of Crank Mountain (lat. 40°18'30" N, long. 121°04'20" W; sec. 17, T 40 N, R 8 E); the springs are on the south side of Halls Canyon. Named on Crank Mountain (1962) 15' quadrangle.

Hallsted Flat [PLUMAS]: *area,* 0.25 mile southwest of Twain along East Branch of North Fork Feather River (lat. 40°01'05" N, long. 121°04'30" W; sec. 22, T 25 N, R 8 E). Named on Twain (1980) 7.5' quadrangle. Called Halsted Flat on Almanor (1955) 15' quadrangle, but United States Board on Geographic Names (1981, p. 2) rejected the forms "Halsted Flat" and "Halstead Flat" for the name.

Halsted Flat: see **Hallsted Flat** [PLUMAS]: **Twain** [PLUMAS].

Hambly Ravine [PLUMAS]: *canyon,* drained by a stream that flows 2 miles to Mill Creek (2) 1 mile south of Twain (lat. 40°00'20" N, long. 121°04'15" W; near N line sec. 27, T 25 N, R 8 E). Named on Twain (1980) 7.5' quadrangle.

Hamilton Branch [LASSEN-PLUMAS]: *stream,* heads at Mountain Meadows Reservoir in Lassen County and flows 5 miles to Lake Almanor 8 miles east-southeast of Chester in Plumas County (lat. 40°16'10" N, long. 121°05'15" W; sec. 21, T 28 N, R 8 E). Named on Westwood West (1980) 7.5' quadrangle.

Hamilton Branch [PLUMAS]: *locality,* 8 miles east-southeast of Chester (lat. 40°16'30" N, long. 121°05'15" W; sec. 21, T 28 N, R 8 E); the place is near the mouth of Hamilton Branch [LASSEN-PLUMAS]. Named on Westwood West (1980) 7.5' quadrangle.

Hamilton Mountain [LASSEN]: *peak,* 8 miles east of Westwood (lat. 40°19' N, long. 120°51' W; at W line sec. 3, T 28 N, R 10 E). Altitude 7387 feet. Named on Fredonyer Pass (1980) 7.5' quadrangle.

Hamlin Springs [LASSEN]: *springs,* 8.5 miles west-northwest of Bieber (lat. 41°10'50" N, long. 121°17' W; sec. 33, T 39 N, R 6 E). Named on Fall River Mills (1961) 15' quadrangle.

Hanging Rock [MODOC]: *relief feature,* 5.5 miles east of Crank Mountain (lat. 41°23' N, long. 121°02'20" W; near NW cor. sec. 22, T 41 N, R 8 E). Named on Crank Mountain (1962) 15' quadrangle.

Hansen Island [MODOC]: *ridge,* generally west-trending, 1.5 miles long, 8 miles southeast of Cedarville along the east shore of Middle Alkali Lake (lat. 41°26'15" N, long. 120°04'15" W). Named on Hansen Island (1963) 7.5' quadrangle.

Hansons Bar [PLUMAS]: *locality,* 2.5 miles north-northwest of Cascade along Middle Fork Feather River (lat. 39°44' N, long. 121°12'15" W; sec. 28, T 22 N, R 7 E). Named on Cascade (1948) 7.5' quadrangle.

Happy Camp: see **Happy Camp Spring** [MODOC].

Happy Camp Mountain [MODOC]: *ridge,* northwest-trending, 2.5 miles long, 3 miles northeast of Crank Mountain (lat. 41°25' N, long. 121°06'30" W); the ridge is 2.5 miles southeast of Happy Camp Spring. Named on Crank Mountain (1962) 15' quadrangle. Modoc Lava-Bed (1892) 1° quadrangle has the name "Turret" for a peak on the ridge.

Happy Camp Spring [MODOC]: *spring,* 4.5 miles north of Crank Mountain (lat. 41°27' N, long. 121°08'15" W; near E line sec. 27, T 42 N, R 7 E). Named on Crank Mountain (1962) 15' quadrangle. Modoc Lava-Bed (1892) 1° quadrangle shows Happy Camp at the site.

Happy Valley [PLUMAS]: *valley,* 7.5 miles south of Mount Ingalls along Long Valley Creek (lat. 39°53' N, long. 120°37' W; sec. 3, T 23 N, R 12 E). Named on Grizzly Valley (1972) 7.5' quadrangle.

Hardin Reservoir [LASSEN]: *intermittent lake,* 250 feet long, 5.5 miles west of Bieber (lat. 41°06'40" N, long. 121°14'55" W; at S line sec. 23, T 38 N, R 6 E). Named on Bieber (1961) 15' quadrangle.

Harkness: see **Mount Harkness** [PLUMAS].

Harkness Peak: see **Mount Harkness** [PLUMAS].

Harper Hill [MODOC]: *ridge,* southeast-trending, 2.5 miles long, 3.25 miles north of Adin (lat. 41°14'15" N, long. 120°57'10" W). Named on Adin (1962) 15' quadrangle.

Harper Spring [MODOC]: *spring,* 12.5 miles south-southwest of Canby (lat. 41°17'30" N, long. 120°59'30" W; near E line sec. 24, T 40 N, R 8 E). Named on Canby (1961) 15' quadrangle.

Harrington Spring [LASSEN]: *spring,* 8 miles north-northeast of Termo (lat. 40°58'30" N, long. 120°24'30" W; near N line sec. 20, T 36 N, R 14 E). Named on Ravendale (1954) 15' quadrangle.

Harris Flat [MODOC]: *area,* 10.5 miles south-southeast of Willow Ranch (lat. 41°46' N, long. 120°16'10" W; sec. 16, T 45 N, R 15 E). Named on Willow Ranch (1962) 15' quadrangle.

Harrison Flat [PLUMAS]: *area,* 11.5 miles southeast of Quincy (lat. 39°48'10" N, long. 120°49'05" W). Named on Blue Nose Mountain (1951) 7.5' quadrangle.

Harrison Ridge [PLUMAS]: *ridge,* west-southwest- to south-southwest-trending, 6 miles long, center 3.5 miles west-southwest of American House (lat. 39°37'30" N, long. 121°05' W). Named on American House (1948) and Strawberry Valley (1948) 7.5' quadrangles. The southwest end of the ridge is in Butte County.

Harrison Spring [LASSEN]: *spring,* 6.25 miles east of Observation Peak (lat. 40°47'30" N, long. 120°03'20" W; sec. 21, T 34 N, R 17 E). Named on Observation Peak (1954) 15' quadrangle.

Harris Spring [MODOC]: *spring,* 7.25 miles south-southwest of Canby (lat. 41°21' N, long. 120°55'45" W; near E line sec. 33, T 41 N, R 9 E). Named on Canby (1961) 15' quadrangle.

Harter Spring: see **Nelson Spring** [LASSEN].

Hartman Bar [PLUMAS]: *locality,* nearly 7 miles south of Bucks Lodge along Middle Fork Feather River (lat. 39°46'40" N, long. 121°09'35" W; neat NE cor. sec. 11, T 22 N, R 7 E). Named on Haskins Valley (1980) 7.5' quadrangle.

Hartman Bar Ridge [PLUMAS]: *ridge,* west- to southwest-trending, 7.5 miles long, center 8.5 miles south of Bucks Lodge (lat. 39°45'30" N, long. 121°08'45" W); the ridge is south of Hartman Bar. Named on Cascade (1948), Dogwood Peak (1979), and Haskins Valley (1980) 7.5' quadrangles.

Hartson Lake [LASSEN]: *lake,* 6500 feet long, 6.25 miles south of Litchfield (lat. 40°17'35" N, long. 120°22'45" W; around SE cor. sec. 10, T 28 N, R 14 E). Named on Litchfield (1954) 15' quadrangle.

Hartson Sand Ridge [LASSEN]: *relief feature,* 7 miles south of Litchfield along Honey Lake (lat. 40°17'05" N, long. 120°24'35" W). Named on Standish (1972) 7.5' quadrangle.

Hartson Slough [LASSEN]: *water feature,* 3.5 miles south-southeast of Litchfield in Honey Lake Valley (lat. 40°20' N, long. 120°22'20" W). Named on Litchfield (1954) 15' quadrangle.

Hartwell: see **Quincy Junction** [PLUMAS].

Harvel Canyon [MODOC]: *canyon,* 1 mile long, 4.5 miles west-northwest of Lookout (lat. 41°14'15" N, long. 121°14' W; mainly in sec. 12, T 39 N, R 6 E). Named on Bieber (1961) 15' quadrangle.

Harvey: see **Camp Harvey** [LASSEN].

Harvey Creek [LASSEN-MODOC]: *stream,* heads in Lassen County and flows 3.25 miles to Jess Valley 24 miles south-southeast of Alturas in Modoc County (lat. 41°11'40" N, long. 120°18'50" W; near S line sec. 24, T 39 N, R 14 E). Named on Jess Valley (1962) 7.5' quadrangle.

Harvey Jones Butte [MODOC]: *peak,* 11 miles south-southeast of Newell (lat. 41°45'10" N, long. 121°15'15" W; on W line sec. 11, T 45 N, R 6 E). Altitude 5178 feet. Named on Tulelake (1951) 15' quadrangle.

Harvey Lake [MODOC]: *intermittent lake,* 10 miles southeast of Newell (lat. 41°46'15" N, long. 121°15' W; sec. 2, T 45 N, R 6 E). Named on Clear Lake Reservoir (1951) and Tulelake (1951) 15' quadrangles.

Harvey Mountain [LASSEN]: *peak,* 8.5 miles northeast of Cal Mountain (lat. 40°44'30" N, long. 121°02' W; near NW cor. sec. 12, T 33 N, R 8 E). Altitude 7354 feet. Named on Harvey Mountain (1956) and Little Valley (1957) 15' quadrangles.

Harvey Mountain: see **Little Harvey Mountain** [LASSEN].

Harvey Valley [LASSEN]: *valley,* 6 miles east of Cal Mountain (lat. 40°41'15" N, long. 121°03'15" W); the valley is 4 miles south-southwest of Harvey Mountain. Named on Harvey Mountain (1956) 15' quadrangle.

Harvey Valley: see **Little Harvey Valley** [LASSEN].

Haskell Peak [LASSEN]: *peak,* 5.5 miles south of Beckwourth Pass (lat. 39°42'40" N, long. 120°05'35" W; near SE cor. sec. 32, T 22 N, R 17 E). Altitude 7136 feet. Named on Evans Canyon (1978) 7.5' quadrangle.

Haskell Peak: see **Little Haskell Peak** [LASSEN].

Haskins Bay [PLUMAS]: *embayment,* 0.5 mile southwest of Bucks Lodge along Bucks Lake (lat. 39°52'15" N, long. 121°10'25" W; mainly in sec. 3, T 23 N, R 7 E); the feature is at the mouth of Haskins Creek. Named on Haskins Valley (1980) 7.5' quadrangle.

Haskins Creek [PLUMAS]: *stream,* flows 2.5 miles to Bucks Lake 0.5 mile south of Bucks Lodge (lat. 39°52'10" N, long. 121°10'25" W; near SW cor. sec. 2, T 23 N, R 7 E). Named on Haskins Valley (1980) 7.5' quadrangle. South Fork enters from the south 1.5 miles upstream from the mouth of the main creek; it is 1 mile long and is named on Haskins Valley (1980) 7.5' quadrangle.

Haskins Valley [PLUMAS]: *valley,* 0.5 mile south-southeast of Bucks Lodge (lat. 39°52'05" N, long. 121°10' W); the valley is along Haskins Creek. Named on Haskins Valley (1980) 7.5' quadrangle.

Hat: see **The Hat** [MODOC].

Hatfield Reservoir [LASSEN]: *lake,* 200 feet long, 8 miles north-northeast of Lava Peak (lat. 40°56'45" N, long. 120°51'15" W; at W line sec. 20, T 36 N, R 10 E). Named on Hayden Hill (1956) 15' quadrangle.

Hat Mountain [LASSEN]: *peak,* 19 miles east-northeast of Madeline (lat. 41°08'55" N, long. 120°07'35" W; sec. 23, T 38 N, R 16 E). Named on Emerson Peak (1962) and Snake Lake (1962) 7.5' quadrangles. Called Hat Peak on California Mining Bureau's (1917a) map.

Hat Mountain: see **Little Hat Mountain** [LASSEN].

Hat Peak: see **Hat Mountain** [LASSEN]; **Little Hat Mountain** [LASSEN].

Hauns Creek [PLUMAS]: *stream,* flows 3 miles to Wolf Creek 3.5 miles northwest of Greenville (lat. 40°10'30" N, long. 120°59'50" W; near N line sec. 29, T 27 N, R 9 E). Named on Canyondam (1979) and Greenville (1979) 7.5' quadrangles.
Hauns Meadow [PLUMAS]: *area,* 4 miles east-northeast of Canyondam (lat. 40°12'05" N, long. 121°00'10" W; at E line sec. 18, T 27 N, R 9 E). Named on Canyondam (1979) 7.5' quadrangle.
Hausen: see **Eagleville** [MODOC].
Hawk Reservoir [MODOC]: *water feature,* 17 miles north-northeast of Cedarville (lat. 41°34' N, long. 120°00'20" W; near SW cor. sec. 26, T 45 N, R 17 E). Named on Cedarville (1962) 15' quadrangle.
Hawks: see **Delleker** [PLUMAS].
Hawley [PLUMAS]: *locality,* 6.25 miles east of Portola along Western Pacific Railroad (lat. 39°48'40" N, long. 120°21'15" W; near SE cor. sec. 25, T 23 N, R 14 E). Named on Reconnaissance Peak (1972) 7.5' quadrangle.
Haw Spring [MODOC]: *spring,* 13 miles south of Canby (lat. 41°15'15" N, long. 120°52'30" W; near NE cor. sec. 1, T 39 N, R 9 E). Named on Canby (1961) 15' quadrangle.
Hayden: see **Hayden Hill** [LASSEN] (2)
Hayden City: see **Hayden Hill** [LASSEN] (2).
Hayden Hill [LASSEN]:
(1) *hill,* 11.5 miles north of Lava Peak (lat. 40°59'55" N, long. 120° 52'10" W; near W line sec. 31, T 37 N, R 10 E). Altitude 6300 feet. Named on Hayden Hill (1956) 15' quadrangle. The name is for J.W. Hayden, who located mines on the hill about 1870 (Gudde, 1949, p. 144).
(2) *locality,* 11.5 miles north of Lava Peak (lat. 40°59'45" N, long. 120°53' W; near S line sec. 36, T 37 N, R 9 E); the place is just west of Hayden Hill (1). Named on Hayden Hill (1956) 15' quadrangle. Called Hayden City on Alturas 1° quadrangle, and called Haydenhill on California Mining Bureau's (1909a) map. Postal authorities established Hayden post office in 1871, discontinued it in 1875, reestablished it with the name "Hayden Hill" in 1878, discontinued it in 1887, reestablished it in 1888, changed the name to Haydenhill in 1895, discontinued it in 1912, reestablished it in 1915, and discontinued it in 1919 (Salley, p. 96). The place first was known as Providence City—Providence mine was nearby (Hanna, p. 135). It also was called Mount Hope (Gudde, 1975, p. 154). Postal authorities established Addington post office 15 miles southeast of Hayden Hill in 1890, discontinued it in 1894, reestablished it in 1908, and discontinued it in 1910; the name was for Joseph Addington and Jess L. Addington, farmers in the neighborhood in the 1870's and 1880's (Salley, p. 1).
Hay Meadow [PLUMAS]: *marsh,* 8.5 miles north-northwest of Chester (lat. 40°26' N, long. 121°11'20" W; sec. 27, T 30 N, R 7 E). Named on Red Cinder (1979) 7.5' quadrangle. On Chester (1956) 15' quadrangle, the name applies to a dry area.
Hays Canyon [MODOC]: *canyon,* drained by a stream that flows 3 miles to lowlands 5.5 miles east-northeast of Lookout (lat. 41°13'50" N, long. 121°04'30" W; sec. 8, T 39 N, R 8 E). Named on Bieber (1961) 15' quadrangle.
Hays Springs [MODOC]: *springs,* 10.5 miles south-southeast of Crank Mountain (lat. 41°15'10" N, long. 121°02'40" W; sec. 3, T 39 N, R 8 E). Named on Crank Mountain (1962) 15' quadrangle.
Hazelton Reservoir [LASSEN]: *lake,* 500 feet long, 9.5 miles north of Lava Peak (lat. 40°57'50" N, long. 120°51'35" W; at S line sec. 7, T 36 N, R 10 E). Named on Hayden Hill (1956) 15' quadrangle.
Hazelton Spring [MODOC]: *spring,* nearly 3 miles east of White Horse (lat. 41°19' N, long. 121°20'45" W; near W line sec. 12, T 40 N, R 5 E). Named on White Horse (1962) 15' quadrangle.
Head of Rush Creek Campground [MODOC]: *locality,* 11 miles south-southeast of Canby (lat. 41°17'40" N, long. 120°49'05" W; near W line sec. 22, T 40 N, R 10 E); the place is at the head of Rush Creek. Named on Canby (1961) 15' quadrangle.
Headquarters: see **Portola** [PLUMAS].
Heath Creek [MODOC]: *stream,* flows 2.5 miles to Surprise Valley 14 miles north of Cedarville (lat. 41°43'45" N, long. 120°11'55" W; at W line sec. 31, T 45 N, R 16 E). Named on Cedarville (1962) 15' quadrangle.
Heavey Mountain [LASSEN]: *mountain,* 7.5 miles east-southeast of Lava Peak (lat. 40°47'15" N, long. 120°45'50" W; on N line sec. 29, T 34 N, R 11 E). Altitude 6564 feet. Named on Hayden Hill (1956) 15' quadrangle. Purdy (1988, p. 118) used the form "Heavy Mountain" for the name, and noted that it is from John Heavy, a sheepman who patented land in the neighborhood in 1875.
Hellgramite Lake [PLUMAS]: *lake,* 200 feet long, 6.5 miles southwest of Clio (lat. 39°41'30" N, long. 120°41' W; at E line sec. 12, T 21 N, R 11 E). Named on Gold Lake (1981) 7.5' quadrangle. United States Board on Geographic Names (1982a, p. 3) approved the name "Hellgrammite Lake" for the feature, and noted that the name is from the hellgrammite, a carnivorous aquatic larva of an insect (*Corydalus cornutus*) used as fish bait. On Sierra City (1955) 15' quadrangle, the name "Helgramite Lake" applies to a lake located nearly 0.5 mile north of present Hellgrammite Lake.
Hencratt Camp [LASSEN]: *locality,* 7.5 miles north-northeast of Lava Peak (lat. 40°55'20" N, long. 120°48'50" W; near SW cor. sec. 27, T 36 N, R 10 E). Named on Hayden Hill (1956) 15' quadrangle.
Henderson Meadow [MODOC]: *area,* 18 miles south-southeast of Alturas (lat. 41°15'30" N, long. 120°20'45" W; sec. 34, T 40 N, R 14 E). Named on Soup Creek (1963) 7.5' quadrangle.
Henpeck Camp: see **Nelson Point** [PLUMAS].
Henrys Flat [PLUMAS]: *area,* 19 miles southwest of the village of Almanor (lat. 40°00'50" N, long. 121°23'50" W; near N line sec. 22, T 25 N, R 5 E). Named on Jonesville (1958) 15' quadrangle.
Henry Valley: see **Willow Creek** [MODOC] (2).
Heriot's Place: see **Amedee** [LASSEN].
Herlong [LASSEN]:
(1) *town,* 8 miles north of Doyle (lat. 40°08'30" N, long. 120°08' W; sec. 1, 2, T 26 N, R 16 E). Named on Doyle (1954) 15' quadrangle. Postal authorities established Herlong post office in 1942 (Frickstad, p. 67). The army established an ordnance depot at the place and named the community for Captain Henry W. Herlong, the first American ordnance officer killed in World War II (Gudde, 1949, p. 147). California Mining Bureau's (1917a) map shows a place called Rayl located along the railroad at or near present Herlong (1), and has the alternate name "Liegan" for the place. Postal authorities established Rayl post office 9 miles north of Doyle in 1915, changed the name to Hackstaff in 1922, and discontinued it that same year; the name "Rayl" was for David Rayl, hotel and store owner (Salley, p. 91, 181). California Division of Highways' (1934) map shows a place called Hackstaff situated 7.5 miles north of Doyle along Western Pacific Railroad (sec. 1, T 26 N, R 16 E) near present Herlong (1).
(2) *locality,* 8.5 miles southeast of Wendel along Southern Pacific Railroad (lat. 40°16'15" N, long. 120°06'45" W; near E line sec. 24, T 28 N, R 16 E). Named on Wendel (1954) 15' quadrangle.
Herlong Junction [LASSEN]: *locality,* 10 miles northwest of Doyle (lat. 40°07'30" N, long. 120°14'45" W; at W line sec. 12, T 26 N, R 15 E); the place is 6 miles west-southwest of Herlong (1). Named on Doyle (1954) 15' quadrangle.
Hermit Butte [MODOC]: *peak,* 9 miles south-southeast of Canby (lat. 41°19'55" N, long. 120°46'50" W; at W line sec. 1, T 40 N, R 10 E). Altitude 6399 feet. Named on Canby (1961) 15' quadrangle.
Hess Flat [MODOC]: *area,* 2 miles north-northwest of Crank Mountain (lat. 41°24'40" N, long. 121°09'10" W; sec. 10, T 41 N, R 7 E); the place is 0.5 mile southwest of Hess Spring. Named on Crank Mountain (1962) 15' quadrangle.
Hess Flat: see **Keeney Flat** [MODOC].
Hess Spring [MODOC]: *spring,* 2.25 miles north of Crank Mountain (lat. 41°25'05" N, long. 121°08'30" W; near SE cor. sec. 3, T 41 N, R 7 E); the spring is 0.5 mile northeast of Hess Flat. Named on Crank Mountain (1962) 15' quadrangle.
Hidden Basin Tank [MODOC]: *water feature,* 8.5 miles west-northwest of Jacks Butte (lat. 41°36'40" N, long. 120°57'50" W; near W line sec. 32, T 44 N, R 9 E). Named on Jacks Butte (1962) 15' quadrangle.
Hidden Lake [LASSEN]: *lake,* 500 feet long, 5.5 miles south-southeast of Westwood (lat. 40°13'50" N, long. 120°58'45" W). Named on Greenville (1979) 7.5' quadrangle.
Hidden Lake [PLUMAS]: *lake,* 500 feet long, 5.5 miles west-southwest of Clio (lat. 39°43' N, long. 120°40'45" W; near NW cor. sec. 6, T 21 N, R 12 E). Named on Gold Lake (1981) 7.5' quadrangle.
Hidden Lakes [LASSEN]: *lakes,* 15 miles northwest of Westwood (lat. 40°27'10" N, long. 121°11'40" W; around NE cor. sec. 21, T 30 N, R 7 E). Named on Red Cinder (1979) 7.5' quadrangle.
Hidden Valley [LASSEN]: *area,* 3.5 miles northeast of Susanville (lat. 40°27' N, long. 120°36'15" W). Named on Susanville (1954) 15' quadrangle.
Hidden Valley [MODOC]: *valley,* 7.5 miles north of Blue Mountain along North Fork Willow Creek (1) (lat. 41°56'15" N, long. 120° 51'30" W). Named on Steele Swamp (1962) 15' quadrangle. Called Weed Valley on Alturas (1954) 1°x 2° quadrangle.
Higgens Spring: see **Higgins Spring** [MODOC].
Higgins Canyon [MODOC]: *canyon,* drained by a stream that flows 2 miles to Rush Creek 11.5 miles south of Canby (lat. 41°16'40" N, long. 120°53'45" W; near E line sec. 26, T 40 N, R 9 E). Named on Canby (1961) 15' quadrangle.
Higgins Flat [MODOC]: *area,* 10 miles south-southwest of Canby (lat. 41°18'25" N, long. 120°55' W; sec. 15, T 40 N, R 9 E). Named on Canby (1961) 15' quadrangle.
Higgins Spring [MODOC]: *spring,* 14 miles south-southwest of Alturas (lat. 41°18'05" N, long. 120°38'45" W; near W line sec. 18, T 40 N, R 12 E). Named on Alturas (1961) 15' quadrangle. United States Board on Geographic Names (1990, p. 7) rejected the form "Higgens Spring" for the name.
High Bridge Campground [PLUMAS]: *locality,* 6.5 miles south of Mount Harkness near the mouth of Warner Creek (lat. 40°20'15" N, long. 121°18'20" W; near SW cor. sec. 27, T 29 N, R 6 E). Named on Mount Harkness (1956) 15' quadrangle, which shows High Bridge near the place.
High Grade: see **Cave Lake** [MODOC].

Highgrade Spring [MODOC]: *spring,* 7.25 miles northwest of Fort Bidwell (lat. 41°56'35" N, long. 120°13'45" W; near E line sec. 15, T 47 N, R 15 E). Named on Fort Bidwell (1962) 15' quadrangle.

High Reefs [MODOC]: *relief feature,* 10.5 miles north-northeast of White Horse (lat. 41°26'30" N, long. 121°18'30" W). Named on White Horse (1962) 15' quadrangle.

Highrock Creek [MODOC]: *stream,* flows nearly 3 miles to Surprise Valley 1 mile west-southwest of Eagleville (lat. 41°18'40" N, long. 120°08'10" W; at SW cor. sec. 23, T 40 N, R 16 E). Named on Eagle Peak (1963) and Eagleville (1963) 7.5' quadrangles.

Hills Creek [LASSEN]: *stream,* flows 3.5 miles to Gold Run Creek 3.5 miles south of Susanville (lat. 40°22' N, long. 120°39'40" W; near SW cor. sec. 17, T 29 N, R 12 E). Named on Diamond Mountain (1972) 7.5' quadrangle.

Hillside: see **Lookout** [MODOC].

Hilton Creek [MODOC]: *stream,* flows 14 miles to lowlands along South Fork Pit River 15 miles south of Alturas (lat. 41°16'25" N, long. 120°34'30" W; sec. 27, T 40 N, R 12 E). Named on Alturas (1961) and Likely (1962) 15' quadrangles.

Hinchman Ravine [PLUMAS]: *canyon,* drained by a stream that flows 2.25 miles to Indian Creek (2) 3.25 miles southeast of Taylorsville (lat. 40°02'50" N, long. 120°47'10" W; sec. 7, T 25 N, R 11 E). Named on Taylorsville (1980) 7.5' quadrangle.

Hindoo: see **Chilcoot** [PLUMAS].

Hindu: see **Chilcoot** [PLUMAS].

Hines Reservoir [MODOC]: *lake,* 2400 feet long, 8 miles south of Crank Mountain (lat. 41°16'10" N, long. 121°09' W; on N line sec. 34, T 40 N, R 7 E). Named on Crank Mountain (1962) 15' quadrangle.

Hoag: see **High Grade**, under **Cave Lake** [MODOC].

Hoffman: see **Mount Hoffman** [LASSEN].

Hogback: see **The Hogback** [PLUMAS].

Hog Flat Reservoir [LASSEN]: *intermittent lake,* 2 miles long, 11 miles north-northeast of Westwood (lat. 40°26'25" N, long. 120°53'30" W). Named on Pegleg Mountain (1980) and Roop Mountain (1980) 7.5' quadrangles.

Hog Gulch [MODOC]: *canyon,* drained by a stream that flows 3 miles to Parker Creek 8.5 miles east of Alturas (lat. 41°28'05" N, long. 120°23'15" W). Named on Dorris Reservoir (1963) and Shields Creek (1963) 7.5' quadrangles.

Hog Lake [MODOC]: *intermittent lake,* 3800 feet long, 5 miles east of Hackamore (lat. 41°33' N, long. 121°01'05" W; sec. 22, T 43 N, R 8 E). Named on Hackamore (1952) 15' quadrangle.

Hog Ridge [MODOC]: *ridge,* north-northeast-trending, 1.5 miles long, 8 miles north-northwest of Alturas (lat. 41°35'15" N, long. 120°36'15" W; on N line sec. 8, T 43 N, R 12 E). Named on Big Sage Reservoir (1962) 15' quadrangle.

Hog Spring [LASSEN]: *spring,* 8 miles east-northeast of Observation Peak (lat. 40°48'50" N, long. 120°01'50" W; near NE cor. sec. 15, T 34 N, R 17 E). Named on Observation Peak (1954) 15' quadrangle.

Hog Valley [LASSEN]: *valley,* 7 miles southeast of Bieber along South Fork Juniper Creek (lat. 41°03'40" N, long. 121°02'15" W; sec. 10, T 37 N, R 8 E). Named on Bieber (1961) 15' quadrangle.

Hog Valley Reservoir [LASSEN]: *water feature,* 9 miles southeast of Bieber (lat. 41°02'20" N, long. 121°00'40" W; near SE cor. sec. 14, T 37 N, R 8 E); the feature is 2 miles southeast of Hog Valley. Named on Bieber (1961) 15' quadrangle.

Holbrook Canyon [LASSEN]: *canyon,* extends for 7 miles from Ash Valley to Madeline Plains 13 miles south of Likely [MODOC] (lat. 41°03' N, long. 121°32'30" W). Named on Likely (1962) 15' quadrangle.

Hole: see **The Hole** [PLUMAS].

Hole in Ground: see **The Hole** [PLUMAS].

Hollenbeck [MODOC]: *locality,* 12 miles north-northeast of White Horse along Great Northern Railroad (lat. 41°27'45" N, long. 121° 17' W); the place is 1 mile south of Hollenbeck Flat. Named on White Horse (1962) 15' quadrangle.

Hollenbeck Butte [MODOC]: *peak,* 12.5 miles north-northeast of White Horse (lat. 41°28' N, long. 121°16'25" W; on W line sec. 22, T 42 N, R 6 E). Named on White Horse (1962) 15' quadrangle. The name commemorates Asa Hollenbeck, who ran cattle in the region from the 1880's until the 1920's (Gudde, 1949, p. 150).

Hollenbeck Flat [MODOC]: *area,* 13 miles north-northeast of White Horse (lat. 41°28'45" N, long. 121°17'10" W); the place is 1 mile northwest of Hollenbeck Butte. Named on White Horse (1962) 15' quadrangle.

Homer Lake [LASSEN-PLUMAS]: *lake,* 1600 feet long, 5.5 miles north of Greenville on Lassen-Plumas County line (lat. 40°13'15" N, long. 120°57'55" W; on SW cor. sec. 3, T 27 N, R 9 E). Named on Greenville (1979) 7.5' quadrangle.

Homestead [MODOC]: *locality,* 3 miles northwest of Newell along Southern Pacific Railroad (lat. 41°54'45" N, long. 121°25'15" W; near E line sec. 17, T 47 N, R 5 E). Named on Tulelake (1951) 15' quadrangle.

Homestead Flat [MODOC]: *area,* 8.5 miles south-southwest of Eagleville (lat. 41°11'50" N, long. 120°09'50" W; on S line sec. 33, T 39 N, R 16 E). Named on Emerson Peak (1962) 7.5' quadrangle.

Homestead Well [MODOC]: *well,* 10 miles north-northwest of South Mountain (lat. 41°57'25" N, long. 120°44'40" W; near E line sec. 31, T 48 N, R 11 E). Named on South Mountain (1962) 15' quadrangle.

Honey Lake [LASSEN]: *intermittent lake,* about 15 miles long, 20 miles southeast of Susanville (lat. 40°16' N, long. 120°20' W). Named on Susanville (1962) 1°x 2° quadrangle. J. Goldsborough Bruff (p. 871) named the feature Derby Lake for his friend Captain Derby of the Topographical Engineers; Bruff (p. 907) also used the designation "Honey or Hot Spring Basin & Lake," and (p. 925) noted that the name "Honey Lake," in use locally, was from a sweet substance that exudes from the heads of wild oats.

Honey Lake Valley [LASSEN]: *valley,* at and southeast of Honey Lake; extends east into the State of Nevada. Named on Susanville (1962) 1°x 2° quadrangle.

Hoover Flat: see **Hoover Flat Reservoir** [LASSEN].

Hoover Flat Reservoir [LASSEN]: *intermittent lake,* 3600 feet long, 7.5 miles northeast of the village of Little Valley (lat. 40°58'50" N, long. 121°05' W; on W line sec. 5, T 36 N, R 8 E). Named on Little Valley (1957) 15' quadrangle. Halls Flat (1939) 30' quadrangle shows Hoover Flat at the site.

Hope: see **Mount Hope**, under **Hayden Hill** [LASSEN] (2); **Mount Hope** [PLUMAS].

Hopeless Pass [MODOC]: *pass,* 15 miles north of Double Head Mountain (lat. 41°59' N, long. 121°12' W; on E line sec. 19, T 48 N, R 7 E). Named on Clear Lake Reservoir (1951) 15' quadrangle.

Hopkins Creek [PLUMAS]: *stream,* flows 4.25 miles to Poorman Creek 11 miles south-southeast of Quincy (lat. 39°48'30" N, long. 120°49'30" W). Named on Blue Nose Mountain (1951) 7.5' quadrangle. East Branch, which enters from the southeast nearly 3 miles upstream from the mouth of the main creek, is 1.5 miles long. West Branch, which enters from the west 2 miles upstream from the mouth of the main creek, is 2 miles long. Both branches are named on Blue Nose Mountain (1951) 7.5' quadrangle. Gudde (1975, p. 159) listed a mining place called Hopkinsville that was located near the confluence of Hopkins Creek and Poorman Creek.

Hopkinsville: see **Hopkins Creek** [PLUMAS].

Hornback Creek [MODOC]: *stream,* flows nearly 3 miles to Surprise Valley 2 miles north-northwest of Eagleville (lat. 41°20'35" N, long. 120°07'50" W; near S line sec. 11, T 40 N, R 16 E). Named on Eagle Peak (1963) 7.5' quadrangle.

Hornfels Point: see **Wheeler Peak** [PLUMAS].

Horns [LASSEN]: *locality,* 4.5 miles north-northeast of Observation Peak (lat. 40°49'40" N, long. 120°07'55" W). Named on Honey Lake (1893) 1° quadrangle. Observation Peak (1954) 15' quadrangle shows Horne ranch at or near the site.

Horn Springs [LASSEN]: *spring,* 6.5 miles east-southeast of Observation Peak (lat. 40°43'40" N, long. 120°05'10" W; near NE cor. sec. 18, T 33 N, R 17 E). Named on Shinn Mountain (1954) 15' quadrangle.

Horse Camp [MODOC]: *locality,* 6.5 miles north-northwest of Hackamore (lat. 41°38'35" N, long. 121°09'15" W; sec. 22, T 44 N, R 7 E). Named on Hackamore (1952) 15' quadrangle.

Horsecamp Reservoir [LASSEN]: *lake,* 300 feet long, 7 miles north-northeast of Wendel (lat. 40°25'50" N, long. 120°09'45" W; sec. 27, T 30 N, R 16 E). Named on Wendel (1954) 15' quadrangle.

Horse Camp Spring [LASSEN]: *spring,* nearly 6 miles east of Lava Peak (lat. 40°49'15" N, long. 120°47' W; near W line sec. 7, T 34 N, R 11 E). Named on Hayden Hill (1956) 15' quadrangle.

Horse Canyon [MODOC]: *canyon,* drained by a stream that flows 1.5 miles to South Deep Creek 3.5 miles southwest of Cedarville (lat. 41°30'05" N, long. 120°13'45" W). Named on Cedarville (1962) 15' quadrangle.

Horse Creek [LASSEN]: *stream,* flows 11.5 miles to Pit River 3.25 miles northwest of the village of Little Valley (lat. 40°56' N, long. 121°13' W; near NE cor. sec. 25, T 36 N, R 6 E). Named on Little Valley (1957) 15' quadrangle.

Horsehead Mountain [MODOC]: *peak,* 9 miles south of Canby (lat. 41°19'05" N, long. 120°51'20" W; near W line sec. 8, T 40 N, R 10 E). Altitude 6531 feet. Named on Canby (1961) 15' quadrangle.

Horsehead Spring [MODOC]: *spring,* 9 miles south of Canby (lat. 41°18'50" N, long. 120°51'30" W; near SE cor. sec. 7, T 40 N, R 10 E); the spring is 2000 feet south-southwest of Horsehead Mountain. Named on Canby (1961) 15' quadrangle.

Horse Lake [LASSEN]:

(1) *intermittent lake,* 4 miles long, 13 miles east of Pelican Point (lat. 40°40' N, long. 120°30' W). Named on Fredonyer Peak (1954) and Karlo (1954) 15' quadrangles.

(2) *locality,* 10 miles north-northwest of Karlo along Southern Pacific Railroad (lat. 40°40'30" N, long. 120°24'10" W; near S line sec. 33, T 33 N, R 14 E); the place is about 5 miles east of Horse Lake (1). Named on Karlo (1954) 15' quadrangle. California Mining Bureau's (1917a) map has the form "Horselake" for the name; the same map shows a place called Ante-

lope located along the railroad about halfway from Horselake to Karlo, and a place called Waverly situated along the railroad 7 miles north of Horselake.

Horse Lake Mountain [LASSEN]: *ridge,* south-southeast- to southeast-trending, 11 miles east-southeast of Pelican Point (lat. 40°35'30" N, long. 120°32'45" W). Named on Fredonyer Peak (1954) and Karlo (1954) 15' quadrangles.

Horse Mountain [MODOC]:

(1) *peak,* 3.5 miles east of Newell (lat. 41°53'35" N, long. 121°17'45" W; at SW cor. sec. 21, T 47 N, R 6 E). Altitude 5095 feet. Named on Tulelake (1951) 15' quadrangle.

(2) *ridge,* generally south-trending, 2.25 miles long, 7 miles south of Eagleville (lat. 41°12'40" N, long. 120°07'55" W). Named on Emerson Peak (1962) 7.5' quadrangle.

Horse Mountain: see **Little Horse Mountain** [MODOC].

Horseshoe Bend [PLUMAS]: *bend,* 7.5 miles south-southwest of Quincy along Middle Fork Feather River (lat. 39°49'50" N, long. 120°59'25" W; at E line sec. 29, T 23 N, R 9 E). Named on Onion Valley (1950) 7.5' quadrangle.

Horseshoe Spring [PLUMAS]: *spring,* 8 miles southeast of Milford [LASSEN] (lat. 40°05'15" N, long. 120°15'55" W; near SE cor. sec. 22, T 26 N, R 15 E). Named on Ferris Creek (1977) 7.5' quadrangle.

Horse Springs [MODOC]: *springs,* 7 miles south of Canby (lat. 41° 20'30" N, long. 120°52'55" W; at S line sec. 36, T 41 N, R 9 E). Named on Canby (1961) 15' quadrangle.

Horton Canyon [PLUMAS]: *canyon,* drained by a stream that flows 2 miles to Red Clover Valley 9.5 miles north-northeast of Portola (lat. 39°56'10" N, long. 120°23'30" W; near E line sec. 15, T 24 N, R 14 E); the canyon heads on Horton Ridge. Named on Crocker Mountain (1972) and Dixie Mountain (1972) 7.5' quadrangles.

Horton Ridge [PLUMAS]: *ridge,* generally south-southeast-trending, 7.5 miles long, 10 miles northeast of Portola (lat. 39°55'30" N, long. 120°21' W). Named on Crocker Mountain (1972) and Dixie Mountain (1972) 7.5' quadrangles.

Hoskins Spring [MODOC]: *spring,* 9.5 miles south-southwest of Canby (lat. 41°19'45" N, long. 120°57'30" W; near S line sec. 5, T 40 N, R 9 E). Named on Canby (1961) 15' quadrangle.

Hosselkus Creek [PLUMAS]: *stream,* flows 8.5 miles to Indian Creek (2) nearly 5 miles east-southeast of Taylorsville (lat. 40°02'30" N, long. 120°45'35" W; at E line sec. 8, T 25 N, R 11 E). Named on Genesee Valley (1972), Kettle Rock (1972), and Taylorsville (1980) 7.5' quadrangles. The name commemorates a family who settled in the neighborhood in the 1850's (Gudde, 1969, p. 146).

Hosselkus Valley: see **Franks Valley** [PLUMAS].

Hostetter and Johnson Spring [LASSEN]: *spring,* 15 miles southeast of Observation Peak (lat. 40°37' N, long. 120°00' W; sec. 24, T 32 N, R 17 E). Named on Shinn Mountain (1954) 15' quadrangle.

Hostetters [LASSEN]: *locality,* 13 miles southeast of Susanville (lat. 40°18'20" N, long. 120°27' W). Named on Honey Lake (1893) 1° quadrangle.

Hot Creek [MODOC]: *stream,* flows 3.25 miles to Pit River 7.5 miles west of Alturas (lat. 41°29'10" N, long. 120°41'10" W; at N line sec. 15, T 42 N, R 11 E). Named on Alturas (1961) and Big Sage Reservoir (1962) 15' quadrangles. Water from numerous thermal springs forms the creek (Waring, p. 119).

Hot Lake: see **Boiling Springs Lake** [PLUMAS].

Hot Spring: see **Little Hot Spring** [MODOC].

Hot Springs [PLUMAS]: *locality,* 2 miles east of Twain (lat. 40°01'10" N, long. 121°02' W; sec. 24, T 25 N, R 8 E); the place is at the mouth of Hot Springs Ravine. Named on Twain (1980) 7.5' quadrangle. Called Twain on Almanor (1955) 15' quadrangle, but United States Board on Geographic Names (1981, p. 2) rejected this name for the place.

Hot Springs: see **Adin** [MODOC].

Hot Springs Creek [PLUMAS]: *stream,* heads just inside Shasta County and flows 7.5 miles to join Kings Creek and form Warner Creek 2.25 miles west-southwest of Mount Harkness (lat. 40°25'15" N, long. 121°20'30" W; sec. 32, T 30 N, R 6 E). Named on Mount Harkness (1956) 15' quadrangle. The valley of the creek is called Hot Spring Valley on Lassen Peak (1894) 1° quadrangle.

Hot Springs Lake: see **Boiling Springs Lake** [PLUMAS].

Hot Springs Peak [LASSEN]: *peak,* 6.25 miles east-northeast of Wendel (lat. 40°22'30" N, long. 120°07'15" W; sec. 13, T 29 N, R 16 E). Altitude 7680 feet. Named on Wendel (1954) 15' quadrangle.

Hot Springs Ravine [PLUMAS]: *canyon,* drained by a stream that flows nearly 1 mile to East Branch of North Fork Feather River 2 miles east of Twain (lat. 40°01'10" N, long. 121°02'05" W; sec. 24, T 25 N, R 8 E). Named on Twain (1980) 7.5' quadrangle.

Hot Springs Slough [LASSEN]: *water feature,* 5.5 miles east of Bieber (lat. 41°08'15" N, long. 121°02'30" W). Named on Bieber (1961) 15' quadrangle.

Hot Springs Valley: see **Warm Springs Valley** [MODOC].

Hot Spring Valley: see **Drakesbad** [PLUMAS]; **Hot Springs Creek** [PLUMAS].

Hottentot Creek [PLUMAS]: *stream,* flows nearly 2 miles to Middle Fork Feather River 7 miles south-southeast of Quincy (lat. 39°50'55" N, long. 120°53'25" W; near S line sec. 17, T 23 N, R 10 E). Named on Onion Valley (1950) 7.5' quadrangle.

Hough Creek [PLUMAS]: *stream,* flows 3 miles to Indian Valley 1.5 miles southeast of Crescent Mills (lat. 40°04'50" N, long. 120°53'10" W). Named on Crescent Mills (1980) and Taylorsville (1980) 7.5' quadrangles. Called Houghs Creek on United States Geological Survey's (1907) map.

Houghs Peak: see **Mount Hough** [PLUMAS].

Householder Reservoir [MODOC]: *lake,* 300 feet long, 5.5 miles northeast of South Mountain (lat. 41°53'40" N, long. 120°33'20" W; at N line sec. 26, T 47 N, R 12 E). Named on South Mountain (1962) 15' quadrangle.

Houseman Camp Reservoir [LASSEN]: *water feature,* 8 miles northwest of Pelican Point (lat. 40°43'20" N, long. 120°50'15" W; sec. 15, T 33 N, R 10 E). Named on Antelope Mountain (1956) 15' quadrangle. R.P. Houseman homesteaded at the place in 1884 (Purdy, 1988, p. 118).

Howard Flat [MODOC]: *area,* 6 miles east-southeast of Willow Ranch (lat. 41°52' N, long. 120°15'15" W). Named on Willow Ranch (1962) 15' quadrangle.

Howards Gulch [MODOC]: *canyon,* drained by a stream that flows 4.5 miles to Warm Springs Valley 2 miles northwest of Canby (lat. 41°27'30" N, long. 120°54'30" W; near SW cor. sec. 23, T 42 N, R 9 E). Named on Canby (1961) 15' quadrangle.

Howell Canyon [MODOC]: *canyon,* drained by a stream that flows 2 miles to lowlands along Pit River 7 miles south-southeast of Crank Mountain (lat. 41°16'45" N, long. 121°06'10" W; sec. 24, T 40 N, R 7 E). Named on Crank Mountain (1962) 15' quadrangle.

Huffman Butte [MODOC]: *peak,* 5.25 miles northeast of Blue Mountain (lat. 41°52'15" N, long. 120°46'30" W; sec. 36, T 47 N, R 11 E). Named on Steele Swamp (1962) 15' quadrangle.

Huffman Butte Tank [MODOC]: *intermittent lake,* 1600 feet long, 4.25 miles northeast of Blue Mountain (lat. 41°52'20" N, long. 120°48'15" W; sec. 34, T 47 N, R 10 E); the feature is 1.5 miles west of Huffman Butte. Named on Steele Swamp (1962) 15' quadrangle.

Hulbert Creek [MODOC]: *stream,* flows about 4.25 miles to Turner Creek (1) 7.5 miles east-northeast of Crank Mountain (lat. 41° 26'10" N, long. 121°01'15" W; near W line sec. 35, T 42 N, R 8 E). Named on Crank Mountain (1962) 15' quadrangle, which shows the old Hulbert place along the stream.

Humboldt: see **Prattville** [PLUMAS].

Humboldt Peak [PLUMAS]: *peak,* 15 miles west-southwest of the village of Almanor on Plumas-Butte County line (lat. 40°09' N, long. 121°25'45" W). Altitude 7087 feet. Named on Jonesville (1958) 15' quadrangle.

Humboldt Summit [PLUMAS]: *pass,* 15 miles west-southwest of the village of Almanor, where Plumas, Butte, and Tehama Counties meet (lat. 40°09'10" N, long. 121°26'05" W); the pass is just west of Humboldt Peak. Named on Jonesville (1958) 15' quadrangle.

Humbug Creek [PLUMAS]:

(1) *stream,* flows 4 miles to Yellow Creek 7.25 miles south-southwest of the village of Almanor (lat. 40°07'50" N, long. 121°14'55" W; near NE cor. sec. 12, T 26 N, R 6 E). Named on Almanor (1979) 7.5' quadrangle.

(2) *stream,* flows 5.5 miles to Middle Fork Feather River 6 miles east-northeast of Blairsden (lat. 39°48' N, long. 120°30'10" W; sec. 3, T 22 N, R 13 E). Named on Blairsden (1972) and Portola (1972) 7.5' quadrangles. West Branch enters from the northwest 1 mile upstream from the mouth of the main creek; it is nearly 3 miles long and is named on Blairsden (1972) 7.5' quadrangle.

Humbug Summit [PLUMAS]: *pass,* 13 miles southwest of the village of Almanor on Plumas-Butte County line (lat. 40°06'30" N, long. 121°22'45" W; sec. 14, T 26 N, R 5 E). Named on Jonesville (1958) 15' quadrangle.

Humbug Valley [PLUMAS]:

(1) *valley,* 7 miles southwest of the village of Almanor along Yellow Creek (lat. 40°08'45" N, long. 121°15'30" W); the valley is at the mouth of Humbug Creek (1). Named on Almanor (1955) and Jonesville (1958) 15' quadrangles.

(2) *valley,* 1.5 miles west of Portola along Middle Fork Feather River (lat. 39°48'10" N, long. 120°30' W; sec. 2, 3, T 22 N, R 13 E); the valley is at the mouth of Humbug Creek (2). Named on Blairsden (1972) and Portola (1972) 7.5' quadrangles.

Hungry Creek [PLUMAS]: *stream,* flows 8 miles to Indian Creek (2) 5 miles east-southeast of Kettle Rock (lat. 40°06'40" N, long. 120° 38'20" W; sec. 16, T 26 N, R 12 E). Named on Genesee Valley (1972) and Kettle Rock (1972) 7.5' quadrangles.

Hunsinger Draw [LASSEN]: *canyon,* 4 miles long, opens into the canyon of Ash Creek 7.25 miles east-southeast of Adin [MODOC] (lat. 41°09' N, long. 120°49' W; near W line sec. 10, T 38 N, R 10 E). Named on Adin (1962) 15' quadrangle.

Hunsinger Flat [LASSEN]: *area,* 11 miles southeast of Adin [MODOC] (lat. 41°05' N, long. 120°46'50" W; at NE cor. sec. 2, T 37 N, R 10 E).

Named on Adin (1962) 15' quadrangle.

Hunt Canyon [PLUMAS]: *canyon,* drained by a stream that flows 1.25 miles to Indian Valley 7 miles south of Moonlight Peak (lat. 40°08'30" N, long. 120°51'50" W; sec. 4, T 26 N, R 10 E). Named on Moonlight Peak (1980) 7.5' quadrangle.

Hunter Spring [LASSEN]: *spring,* 4 miles north-northeast of the village of Little Valley (lat. 40°51'55" N, long. 121°09'10" W; at N line sec. 22, T 35 N, R 7 E). Named on Little Valley (1957) 15' quadrangle.

Hunter Spring [MODOC]: *spring,* 12 miles west of Likely (lat. 41° 11'30" N, long. 120°43'30" W; near E line sec. 29, T 39 N, R 11 E). Named on Likely (1962) 15' quadrangle.

Hunters Ravine [PLUMAS]: *canyon,* drained by a stream that flows 2.25 miles to Middle Fork Feather River 8.5 miles south of Bucks Lodge (lat. 39°45'05" N, long. 121°11'10" W; near N line sec. 22, T 22 N, R 7 E). Named on Haskins Valley (1980) 7.5' quadrangle. The stream in the canyon is called Scotch Creek on Bucks Lake (1950) 15' quadrangle, but United States Board on Geographic Names (1979, p. 4) rejected the names "Scotch Creek" and "Gravel Range Creek" for the feature.

Hunters Ravine: see **Grouse Hollow Creek** [PLUMAS].

Hunters Ridge [MODOC]: *ridge,* generally west-northwest-trending, 3.5 miles long, 12 miles south of Canby (lat. 41°16'30" N, long. 120°49'45" W). Named on Canby (1961) 15' quadrangle.

— I —

Ice Cave Mountain [PLUMAS]: *peak,* 8 miles south-southwest of Mount Harkness on Plumas-Tehama County line (lat. 40°20'20" N, long. 121°23'40" W; sec. 26, T 29 N, R 5 E). Named on Mount Harkness (1956) 15' quadrangle, which shows an ice cave located 1.5 miles west of the peak in Tehama County.

Ice Cave Ridge [LASSEN]: *ridge,* generally south-southeast-trending, 1 mile long, 5.5 miles northwest of Pelican Point (lat. 40° 40'20" N, long. 120°49'40" W; sec. 34, T 33 N, R 10 E). Named on Antelope Mountain (1956) 15' quadrangle. The name is from ice caves in the vicinity (Purdy, 1988, p. 118).

Ice Creek [PLUMAS]: *stream,* flows less than 1 mile to South Fork Feather River 5 miles north of American House (lat. 39°43'25" N, long. 121°00'35" W; near E line sec. 31, T 22 N, R 9 E). Named on American House (1948) 7.5' quadrangle.

Illinois Ridge [PLUMAS]: *ridge,* south-trending, 1.5 miles long, 1.5 miles south-southeast of La Porte (lat. 39°39'40" N, long. 120°58'30" W; sec. 21, 28, T 21 N, R 9 E). Named on La Porte (1951) 7.5' quadrangle.

Independence Bar: see **Nelson Creek** [PLUMAS].

Indian Bar [PLUMAS]: *locality,* 5.25 miles south-southwest of Caribou along East Branch of North Fork Feather River (lat. 40°00'40" N, long. 121°12'05" W; sec. 21, T 25 N, R 7 E). Named on Caribou (1979) 7.5' quadrangle.

Indian Bar: see **Lower Indian Bar**, under **Yellow Creek** [PLUMAS].

Indian Camp: see **Likely** [MODOC].

Indian Creek [LASSEN]: *stream,* flows 8.5 miles to end 7.5 miles east of the village of Little Valley in Dixie Valley (lat. 40°52'35" N, long. 121°02'30" W; at S line sec. 23, T 35 N, R 8 E). Named on Hayden Hill (1956) and Little Valley (1957) 15' quadrangles.

Indian Creek [PLUMAS]:

(1) *stream,* flows 5 miles to North Fork Feather River 16 miles south-southwest of the village of Almanor (lat. 40°00'15" N, long. 121°15'45" W; sec. 24, T 25 N, R 6 E). Named on Jonesville (1958) 15' quadrangle.

(2) *stream,* flows 47 miles to join Spanish Creek (1) and form East Branch of North Fork Feather River 5.5 miles southwest of Crescent Mills (lat. 40°02'20" N, long. 120°58'55" W; near S line sec. 9, T 25 N, R 9 E). Named on Antelope Lake (1972), Crescent Mills (1980), Diamond Mountain (1972), Genesee Valley (1972), Kettle Rock (1972), and Taylorsville (1980) 7.5' quadrangles.

Indian Creek: see **East Branch of North Fork**, under **Feather River** [PLUMAS].

Indian Falls [PLUMAS]:

(1) *waterfall,* 3.5 miles southwest of Crescent Mills along Indian Creek (2) (lat. 40°03'40" N, long. 120°57'35" W; near N line sec. 3, T 25 N, R 9 E). Named on Crescent Mills (1980) 7.5' quadrangle.

(2) *village,* 4 miles southwest of Crescent Mills (lat. 40°03'25" N, long. 120°57'50" W; sec. 3, T 25 N, R 9 E); the village is 0.25 mile southwest of Indian Falls (1). Named on Crescent Mills (1980) 7.5' quadrangle. Called Shoofly on Honey Lake (1893) 1° quadrangle, and called Shoo Fly on United States Geological Survey's (1907) map. Postal authorities established Indian Falls post office in 1909 and discontinued it in 1916 (Frickstad, p. 124).

Indian Falls Ridge [PLUMAS]: *ridge,* northwest- to west-trending, 3.5 miles long, 2.5 miles south of Crescent Mills (lat. 40°03'35" N, long. 120°54'45" W); the feature is east of Indian Falls (1). Named on Crescent Mills (1980) 7.5' quadrangle.

Indian Meadow [PLUMAS]: *marsh,* 9 miles north-northeast of Chester (lat. 40°26'20" N, long. 121°11'25" W; near NW cor. sec. 27, T 30 N, R 7 E). Named on Red Cinder (1979) 7.5' quadrangle. Called Indian Meadows on Chester (1956) 15' quadrangle, which has the name for an area containing marsh and lakes.

Indian Mountain [LASSEN]: *peak,* 6.5 miles northwest of Lassen Peak (lat. 40°53'35" N, long. 120°58'45" W; near SE cor. sec. 17, T 35 N, R 9 E). Altitude 5618 feet. Named on Hayden Hill (1956) 15' quadrangle.

Indian Peak [LASSEN]: *relief feature,* 6 miles east of Bieber (lat. 41°06'50" N, long. 121°01'50" W; near SE cor. sec. 22, T 38 N, R 8 E). Named on Bieber (1961) 15' quadrangle.

Indian Spring [LASSEN]:

(1) *spring,* 12 miles north of Lava Peak (lat. 40°59'55" N, long. 120°50'55" W; sec. 32, T 37 N, R 10 E). Named on Hayden Hill (1956) 15' quadrangle.

(2) *spring,* 3 miles northeast of Doyle (lat. 40°03'20" N, long. 120° 03'30" W; on N line sec. 3, T 25 N, R 17 E). Named on Doyle (1954) 15' quadrangle.

Indian Spring [MODOC]: *spring,* 5 miles northwest of Alturas along Rock Creek (3) (lat. 41°32' N, long. 120°36'35" W; sec. 29, T 43 N, R 12 E). Named on Big Sage Reservoir (1962) 15' quadrangle. United States Board on Geographic Names (1990, p. 8) rejected the plural form "Indian Springs" for the name. United States Board on Geographic Names (1970, p. 2) approved the name "Indian Spring Reservoir" for a lake formed by a dam on Rock Creek (3) 4.5 miles northwest of Alturas; the name is from Indian Spring, which feeds the reservoir. The Board (1990, p. 8) rejected the form "Indian Springs Reservoir" for the name.

Indian Spring Reservoir: see **Indian Spring** [MODOC].

Indian Springs [LASSEN]: *spring,* 14 miles west-southwest of Likely [MODOC] (lat. 41°08'30" N, long. 120°44'50" W; at N line sec. 18, T 38 N, R 11 E). Named on Likely (1962) 15' quadrangle.

Indian Springs [MODOC]: *locality,* 7 miles west-southwest of Likely (lat. 41°12'10" N, long. 120°37'50" W; near E line sec. 19, T 39 N, R 12 E). Named on Likely (1962) 15' quadrangle.

Indian Springs [PLUMAS]: *spring,* 13 miles south-southwest of the village of Almanor (lat. 40°03'10" N, long. 121°18'10" W; near W line sec. 3, T 25 N, R 6 E); the spring is at the head of a branch of Indian Creek (1). Named on Jonesville (1958) 15' quadrangle.

Indian Springs: see **Indian Spring** [MODOC].

Indian Springs Reservoir: see **Indian Spring Reservoir**, under **Indian Spring** [MODOC].

Indian Valley [PLUMAS]: *valley,* mainly between Greenville and Taylorsville along Indian Creek (2) and its tributaries (center near lat. 40°07' N, long. 120°52'30" W). Named on Crescent Mills (1980), Greenville (1979), Moonlight Peak (1980), and Taylorsville (1980) 7.5' quadrangles. Peter Lassen, the first settler there, called the place Cache Valley in 1850 (Hoover, Rensch, and Rensch, p. 285). The northeast extension of Indian Valley along Lights Creek is called North Arm Indian Valley; it is named on Moonlight Peak (1980) and Taylorsville (1980) 7.5' quadrangles.

Indian Valley Hot Springs [PLUMAS]: *water feature,* less than 1 mile east of Greenville (lat. 40°08'30" N, long. 120°56'05" W; sec. 2, T 26 N, R 9 E); the feature is in Indian Valley. Named on Greenville (1979) 7.5' quadrangle. Waring (p. 128) used the name "Kruger Spring" for the feature, and noted that it was a popular bathing spot during the prosperous mining days.

Indian Well [LASSEN]: *locality,* 6.5 miles southeast of Lava Peak (lat. 40°45'10" N, long. 120°48'55" W; sec. 2, T 33 N, R 10 E). Named on Hayden Hill (1956) 15' quadrangle.

Indicator Peak [LASSEN]: *peak,* 10.5 miles east of Westwood (lat. 40°16'15" N, long. 120°48'20" W; near S line sec. 13, T 28 N, R 10 E). Altitude 7500 feet. Named on Fredonyer Pass (1980) 7.5' quadrangle.

Infernal Caverns [MODOC]: *cave,* 16 miles south of Alturas (lat. 41°15'50" N, long. 120°35' W; sec. 27, T 40 N, R 12 E). Named on Alturas (1961) 15' quadrangle.

Ingalls: see **Mount Ingalls** [PLUMAS].

Ingalls Lake: see **Ingalls Swamp** [MODOC].

Ingalls Swamp [MODOC]: *area,* 16 miles north-northwest of Alturas (lat. 41°41' N, long. 120°41'20" W). Named on Big Sage Reservoir (1962) 15' quadrangle. United States Board on Geographic Names (1990, p. 8) rejected the form "Ingall Swamp" for the name. Alturas 1° quadrangle has the name "Ingalls Valley" at the place, and Alturas (1954) 1°x 2° quadrangle shows marsh there. Steptoe's (1855) map shows Ingalls Lake situated north of the site of present Ingalls Swamp near California-Oregon State line along a trail that has the designation "Capt. Ingalls Route."

Ingalls Valley: see **Ingalls Swamp** [MODOC].

Injun Jim Campground [PLUMAS]: *locality,* 2.5 miles north-northeast of Pulga along North Fork Feather River (lat. 39°57' N, long. 121°18' W; near NW cor. sec. 10, T 24 N, R 6 E). Named on Pulga (1957) 15' quadrangle.

Inspiration Point [LASSEN]: *relief feature,* 3 miles north of Mount Harkness [PLUMAS] (lat. 40°28'25" N, long. 121°18'10" W; sec. 10, T 30 N, R 6

E). Named on Mount Harkness (1956) 15' quadrangle. C.P. Snell, owner of Juniper Lake Resort, named the feature for the inspirational view from the place (Schulz, p. 29).

International: see **Walkermine** [PLUMAS].

Iron Mountain [MODOC]: *peak,* 5.5 miles southeast of Crank Mountain (lat. 41°19'45" N, long. 121°04' W; at SW cor. sec. 4, T 40 N, R 8 E). Named on Crank Mountain (1962) 15' quadrangle.

Island: see **The Island** [LASSEN]; **The Island** [PLUMAS].

Island Lake [LASSEN]: *lake,* 1000 feet long, 2.25 miles east-northeast of Mount Harkness [PLUMAS] (lat. 40°27' N, long. 121°15'50" W; near NW cor. sec. 24, T 30 N, R 6 E). Named on Mount Harkness (1956) 15' quadrangle, which shows an island in the lake.

Island Meadow [MODOC]: *area,* nearly 5 miles north-northwest of South Mountain (lat. 41°54'20" N, long. 120°39'30" W; sec. 24, T 47 N, R 11 E). Named on South Mountain (1962) 15' quadrangle.

Ivy: see **Likely** [MODOC].

—J—

Jackass Creek [PLUMAS]: *stream,* flows nearly 4 miles to North Fork Feather River 1.25 miles north-northeast of Storrie (lat. 39° 56'05" N, long. 121°18'55" W). Named on Storrie (1979) 7.5' quadrangle.

Jack Lake: see **Big Jack Lake** [LASSEN].

Jacks Butte [MODOC]: *peak,* 15 miles west-northwest of Alturas (lat. 41°35'10" N, long. 120°48'05" W; near N line sec. 10, T 43 N, R 10 E). Altitude 5168 feet. Named on Jacks Butte (1962) 15' quadrangle.

Jacks Butte Tank [MODOC]: *intermittent lake,* 0.5 mile long, nearly 2 miles west of Jacks Butte (lat. 41°35'20" N, long. 120°50'10" W; on S line sec. 5, T 43 N, R 10 E). Named on Jacks Butte (1962) 15' quadrangle.

Jacks Lake [LASSEN]: *intermittent lake,* 0.5 mile long, 10 miles southeast of the village of Little Valley (lat. 40°48'35" N, long. 121°01'30" W; sec. 13, T 34 N, R 8 E). Named on Little Valley (1957) 15' quadrangle.

Jacks Lake: see **Little Jacks Lake** [LASSEN].

Jacks Meadow Creek [PLUMAS]: *stream,* flows 1.25 miles to Silver Creek (1) 3.5 miles west-northwest of the village of Meadow Valley (lat. 39°57'15" N, long. 121°07' W; sec. 8, T 24 N, R 8 E). Named on Bucks Lake (1979) and Meadow Valley (1980) 7.5' quadrangles.

Jacks Meadow Pond [PLUMAS]: *lake,* 1050 feet long, 5.5 miles north-northeast of Bucks Lodge (lat. 39°56'55" N, long. 121°07'50" W; at N line sec. 18, T 24 N, R 8 E); the lake is along Jacks Meadow Creek. Named on Bucks Lake (1979) 7.5' quadrangle, which shows areas of marsh in the lake.

Jackson: see **Mount Jackson** [PLUMAS].

Jackson Cabin Spring [MODOC]: *spring,* 10 miles south-southeast of Canby (lat. 41°18'40" N, long. 120°47' W; near N line sec. 14, T 40 N, R 10 E). Named on Canby (1961) 15' quadrangle.

Jackson Canyon [MODOC]: *canyon,* drained by a stream that flows 1 mile to Surprise Valley 7.5 miles south of Cedarville (lat. 41°25'05" N, long. 120°09'10" W; sec. 16, T 41 N, R 16 E). Named on Warren Peak (1963) 7.5' quadrangle.

Jackson Canyon: see **Little Jackson Canyon** [MODOC].

Jackson Creek [PLUMAS]: *stream,* flows 6 miles to Middle Fork Feather River 6.5 miles northwest of Blairsden (lat. 39°51'05" N, long. 120°41'40" W; near N line sec. 24, T 23 N, R 11 E). Named on Blairsden (1972) and Johnsville (1972) 7.5' quadrangles.

Jackson Creek Campground [PLUMAS]: *locality,* 5.5 miles northwest of Blairsden (lat. 39°50'50" N, long. 120°40'35" W; sec. 19, T 23 N, R 12 E); the place is along Jackson Creek. Named on Johnsville (1972) 7.5' quadrangle.

Jacks Swamp [MODOC]: *area,* 1.25 miles south-southwest of Jacks Butte (lat. 41°34'10" N, long. 120°48'35" W; on E line sec. 16, T 43 N, R 10 E). Named on Jacks Butte (1962) 15' quadrangle.

Jakey Lake [LASSEN]: *lake,* 1100 feet long, 3.5 miles north-northeast of Mount Harkness [PLUMAS] (lat. 40°28'40" N, long. 121°16'35" W; sec. 11, T 30 N, R 6 E). Named on Mount Harkness (1956) 15' quadrangle. The name commemorates Jakey Olson, who homesteaded at the place (Schulz, p. 29).

James Canyon [LASSEN]: *canyon,* drained by a stream that flows 2 miles to Honey Lake Valley 3 miles east-southeast of Wendel (lat. 40°19'35" N, long. 120°11' W; sec. 33, T 29 N, R 16 E). Named on Wendel (1954) 15' quadrangle.

James Reservoir [MODOC]: *lake,* 1 mile long, 6.25 miles northeast of Blue Mountain (lat. 41°53' N, long. 120°46'10" W; mainly in sec. 25, T 47 N, R 10 E). Named on Steele Swamp (1962) 15' quadrangle.

Jamieson City: see **Jamison** [PLUMAS].

Jamison [PLUMAS]: *locality,* 1.25 miles north-northeast of Johnsville (lat. 39°46'30" N, long. 120°41' W); the place is along Jamison Creek. Named on Downieville (1897) 30' quadrangle. Postal authorities established Jamison post office in 1871, discontinued it in 1877, reestablished it in 1880, and discontinued it in 1882 (Frickstad, p. 124). Bancroft (p. 363) referred to Jamieson City.

Jamison: see **Little Jamison** [PLUMAS].

Jamison Creek [PLUMAS]: *stream,* flows 11 miles to Middle Fork Feather River 4 miles northwest of Blairsden (lat. 39°49'20" N, long. 120°39'55" W; near SE cor. sec. 30, T 23 N, R 12 E). Named on Gold Lake (1981), Johnsville (1972), and Mount Fillmore (1951) 7.5' quadrangles.

Jamison Creek: see **Little Jamison Creek** [PLUMAS].

Jamison Lake [PLUMAS]: *lake,* 2000 feet long, nearly 7 miles west-southwest of Clio (lat. 39°42'35" N, long. 120°41'55" W; near W line sec. 1, T 21 N, R 11 E); the lake is along Little Jamison Creek. Named on Gold Lake (1981) 7.5' quadrangle. On Downieville (1897) 30' quadrangle, present Jamison Lake and present Rock Lake (3) are called Jamison Lakes.

Jamison Lakes: see **Jamison Lake** [PLUMAS].

Janesville [LASSEN]: *village,* 11 miles southeast of Susanville (lat. 40°17'50" N, long. 120°31'20" W; sec. 9, T 28 N, R 13 E). Named on Janesville (1972) 7.5' quadrangle. Postal authorities established Janesville post office in 1861, discontinued it for a time in 1864, changed the name to Lassen in 1914, and changed the name back to Janesville in 1923 (Salley, p. 106). The name "Janesville" is for Jane Bankhead, wife of Malcolm Bankhead; Mr. Bankhead arrived at the site in 1857 and built a log hotel (Hanna, p. 153). Gudde (1975, p. 175) gave the name "Gas Point" an an early designation for the place.

Jauriga Spring [LASSEN]: *spring,* 8.5 miles northeast of Pelican Point (lat. 40°43'30" N, long. 120°38' W; sec. 16, T 33 N, R 12 E). Named on Fredonyer Peak (1954) 15' quadrangle.

Jellico [LASSEN]: *locality,* 7 miles west-southwest of the village of Little Valley along Western Pacific Railroad (lat. 40°50'45" N, long. 121°17'30" W; at N line sec. 3, T 34 N, R 6 E). Named on Jellico (1957) 15' quadrangle.

Jelly Camp [LASSEN]: *locality,* 9 miles south-southwest of the village of Little Valley (lat. 40°46'50" N, long. 121°15'50" W; near E line sec. 26, T 34 N, R 6 E); the place is 800 feet northwest of Jelly Spring. Named on Jellico (1957) 15' quadrangle.

Jelly Spring [LASSEN]: *spring,* 9 miles south-southeast of the village of Little Valley (lat. 40°46'45" N, long. 121°15'45" W; near W line sec. 25, T 34 N, R 6 E). Named on Jellico (1957) 15' quadrangle.

Jenkins Cove [PLUMAS]: *embayment,* 9 miles southeast of Mount Ingalls along Lake Davis (lat. 39°53'55" N, long. 120°30'20" W; sec. 34, T 24 N, R 13 E); the feature is near the mouth of Jenkins Creek. Named on Grizzly Valley (1972) 7.5' quadrangle.

Jenkins Creek [PLUMAS]: *stream,* flows 0.5 mile to Lake Davis 9 miles southeast of Mount Ingalls (lat. 39°53'55" N, long. 120°30'45" W; near W line sec. 34, T 24 N, R 13 E). Named on Grizzly Valley (1972) 7.5' quadrangle.

Jenkins Sheep Camp [PLUMAS]: *locality,* 4.25 miles west-northwest of Squaw Valley Peak (lat. 40°02'35" N, long. 120°28'35" W; near N line sec. 12, T 25 N, R 13 E). Named on Squaw Valley Peak (1977) 7.5' quadrangle.

Jenkins Spring [LASSEN]:

(1) *spring,* 14 miles east-northeast of Madeline (lat. 41°07'45" N, long. 120°14' W; sec. 26, T 38 N, R 15 E). Named on Emerson Peak (1962) 7.5' quadrangle.

(2) *spring,* 9 miles northeast of Wendel (lat. 40°26'10" N, long. 120°06'26" W; sec. 30, T 30 N, R 17 E). Named on Wendel (1954) 15' quadrangle.

Jenkins Springs [PLUMAS]: *springs,* 3.5 miles west-northwest of Squaw Valley Peak (lat. 40°03'05" N, long. 120°27'45" W; near W line sec. 6, T 25 N, R 14 E); the springs are 1 mile northeast of Jenkins Sheep Camp. Named on Squaw Valley Peak (1977) 7.5' quadrangle.

Jennie Creek [PLUMAS]: *stream,* flows about 6.25 miles to Rock Creek (1) 7 miles east-northeast of Chester (lat. 40°20'20" N, long. 121°06'10" W; sec. 29, T 29 N, R 8 E); the stream heads at Jennie Spring. Named on Swain Mountain (1979) and Westwood West (1980) 7.5' quadrangles.

Jennie Mountain [PLUMAS]: *peak,* 11 miles northeast of Chester (lat. 40°24'40" N, long. 121°04'15" W; near S line sec. 34, T 30 N, R 8 E); the spring is at the head of Jennie Creek. Named on Swain Mountain (1979) 7.5' quadrangle.

Jennie Spring [PLUMAS]: *spring,* 10.5 miles northwest of Chester (lat. 40°24'25" N, long. 121°04'30" W; near NW cor. sec. 3, T 29 N, R 8 E); the spring is 0.25 mile southwest of Jennie Mountain. Named on Swain Mountain (1979) 7.5' quadrangle.

Jensen Slough [LASSEN]: *water feature,* diverges from Susan River 1.5 miles east-southeast of Susanville (lat. 40°24'25" N, long. 120° 37'50" W; near N line sec. 4, T 29 N, R 12 E). Named on Susanville (1954) 15' quadrangle.

Jessen Valley [LASSEN]: *valley,* 5.5 miles west-southwest of Lava Peak (lat. 40°48' N, long. 120°59'15" W; sec. 17, 20, T 34 N, R 9 E). Named on Hayden Hill (1956) 15' quadrangle.

Jess Valley [MODOC]: *valley,* 21 miles southeast of Alturas (lat. 41° 13'45" N, long. 120°19' W). Named on Jess Valley (1962) and Soup Creek (1963) 7.5' quadrangles. Symons (p. 116) used the form "Jess's Valley" for the name, which commemorates John Jess and Archie Jess, early settlers in the valley (Laird, p. 63).

Jesus Spring [LASSEN]: *spring,* 3.5 miles east of Doyle (lat. 40°02'15" N, long. 120°01' W; at E line sec. 12, T 25 N, R 17 E). Named on Doyle (1954) 15' quadrangle.

Jewell Lake [LASSEN]: *lake,* 750 feet long, 11.5 miles south of Cal Mountain (lat. 40°30'20" N, long. 121°11'25" W; on E line sec. 33, T 31 N, R 7 E). Named on Harvey Mountain (1956) 15' quadrangle.

Jim Creek [MODOC]: *stream,* diverges from North Fork Fitzhugh Creek and flows 9 miles to the valley of South Fork Pit River 4.5 miles south-southeast of Alturas (lat. 41°25'30" N, long. 120° 31' W; sec. 6, T 41 N, R 13 E). Named on Dorris Reservoir (1963), Shields Creek (1963), and Soup Creek (1963) 7.5' quadrangles. Shields Creek (1963) 7.5' quadrangle shows Yankee Jim ranch situated along the stream.

Jimmerson Mountain [MODOC]: *peak,* 6.25 miles east-northeast of Day (lat. 41°14'05" N, long. 121°15'35" W; at E line sec. 10, T 39 N, R 6 E). Altitude 5275 feet. Named on Bieber (1961), Crank Mountain (1962), Fall River Mills (1961), and White Horse (1962) 15' quadrangles.

Jimmerson Spring [MODOC]: *spring,* 4.5 miles east-northeast of Day (lat. 41°14'45" N, long. 121°17'45" W; at E line sec. 5, T 39 N, R 6 E); the spring is 2 miles west-northwest of Jimmerson Mountain. Named on Fall River Mills (1961) 15' quadrangle.

Jimmerson Spring: see **Little Jimmerson Spring** [LASSEN].

Jim Packwood Spring [LASSEN]: *spring,* 10.5 miles southeast of Bieber (lat. 41°00'55" N, long. 121°00'30" W; at E line sec. 26, T 37 N, R 8 E); the spring is 1.5 miles southeast of Billy Packwood Spring. Named on Bieber (1961) 15' quadrangle.

Jim Peterson Hill [LASSEN]: *hill,* 9 miles southeast of Susanville (lat. 40°19'15" N, long. 120°32'05" W; at N line sec. 5, T 28 N, R 13 E). Named on Janesville (1972) 7.5' quadrangle.

Jims Flat [MODOC]: *area,* 12 miles north-northeast of Blue Mountain (lat. 41°58'55" N, long. 120°45'20" W; on N line sec. 30, T 48 N, R 11 E). Named on Steele Swamp (1962) 15' quadrangle.

Joffre: see **New Pine Creek** [MODOC].

Johnson: see **Hostetter and Johnson Spring** [LASSEN].

Johnson Camp [LASSEN]: *locality,* 6.5 miles north-northeast of Lava Peak (lat. 40°54'40" N, long. 120°49'45" W; sec. 33, T 36 N, R 10 E). Named on Hayden Hill (1956) 15' quadrangle.

Johnson Creek [MODOC]: *stream,* flows 6 miles to Rush Creek 11 miles south of Canby (lat. 41°17'15" N, long. 120°53'30" W; near SW cor. sec. 24, T 40 N, R 9 E). Named on Canby (1961) 15' quadrangle.

Johnson Creek [PLUMAS]: *stream,* extends for 1.5 miles from North Fork Feather River to Lake Almanor less than 1 mile northeast of Chester (lat. 40°19'10" N, long. 121°12'50" W; near NE cor. sec. 5, T 28 N, R 7 E). Named on Chester (1979) 7.5' quadrangle.

Johnson Fields [PLUMAS]: *locality,* less than 0.5 mile east of the center of Chester (lat. 40°18'40" N, long. 121°13'05" W; sec. 5, T 28 N, R 7 E). Named on Chester (1979) 7.5' quadrangle.

Johnson Gulch [MODOC]: *canyon,* drained by a stream that flows 2.5 miles to Toms Creek 7.5 miles south-southeast of Canby (lat. 41°20'55" N, long. 120°48'15" W; sec. 34, T 41 N, R 10 E). Named on Canby (1961) 15' quadrangle.

Johnson Hill [PLUMAS]:

(1) *peak,* nearly 5 miles south of Milford [LASSEN] (lat. 40°06'05" N, long. 120°22'25" W; at S line sec. 14, T 26 N, R 14 E). Altitude 6555 feet. Named on Ferris Creek (1977) and Squaw Valley Peak (1977) 7.5' quadrangles.

(2) *peak,* 5.25 miles northwest of Spring Garden (lat. 39°56'50" N, long. 120°51'25" W; on W line sec. 15, T 24 N, R 10 E). Altitude 4502 feet. Named on Spring Garden (1950) 7.5' quadrangle.

Johnson Mill Spring [PLUMAS]: *spring,* 4 miles south of Milford (lat. 40°06'50" N, long. 120°22'10" W; near N line sec. 14, T 26 N, R 14 E). Named on Ferris Creek (1977) 7.5' quadrangle.

Johnson Ravine [PLUMAS]: *canyon,* drained by a stream that flows nearly 3 miles to Rush Creek 1.5 miles north-northwest of Twain (lat. 40°02'35" N, long. 121°05' W; near W line sec. 10, T 25 N, R 8 E). Named on Twain (1980) 7.5' quadrangle.

Johnson Spring [LASSEN]: *spring,* 7 miles east-northeast of the village of Little Valley (lat. 40°55' N, long. 121°03' W; near E line sec. 33, T 36 N, R 8 E). Named on Little Valley (1957) 15' quadrangle.

John Spring [MODOC]: *spring,* 7.5 miles east of Adin (lat. 40°12'25" N, long. 120°48'10" W; near E line sec. 22, T 39 N, R 10 E). Named on Adin (1962) 15' quadrangle.

John Spring: see **Big John Spring** [MODOC].

Johnstonville [LASSEN]: *village,* 4.5 miles east-southeast of Susanville (lat. 40°23'05" N, long. 120°35'10" W; at and near SW cor. sec. 12, T 29 N, R 12 E). Named on Susanville (1954) 15' quadrangle. Postal authorities established Johnstonville post office in 1902 and discontinued it in 1943 (Frickstad, p. 67). Settlers came to the site in 1857 and called it Toadtown for the abundance of toads there after heavy rains; later the place was named for Robert Johnston, who was active in development of the village (Hanna, p. 155).

Johnstown: see **Johnsville** [PLUMAS].

Johns Valley [LASSEN]: *valley,* 7 miles south-southwest of Bieber (lat. 41°01'45" N, long. 121°11'20" W; mainly in sec. 20, T 37 N, R 7 E). Named on Bieber (1961) 15' quadrangle.

Johnsville [PLUMAS]: *locality,* 4.25 miles west-southwest of Blairsden (lat. 39°45'40" N, long. 120°41'35" W; at N line sec. 24, T 22 N, R 11 E). Named on Johnsville (1972) 7.5' quadrangle. Postal authorities established Johnstown post office in 1882, moved it and changed the name to Johnsville the same year, and discontinued it in 1953 (Salley, p. 108). William Johns, general manager of Plumas Eureka mine, started a community, which by popular agreement was called Johnstown and then Johnsville for the general manager (Plumas County Historical Society, p. 30). Postal authorities established Eureka Mills post office 1 mile south of Johnsville in 1875 and discontinued it in 1895 (Salley, p. 71).

Joiner Reservoir [MODOC]: *lake,* 1300 feet long, 7.5 miles south-southwest of Crank Mountain (lat. 41°17'40" N, long. 121°13'20" W; near NE cor. sec. 21, T 40 N, R 6 E). Named on Crank Mountain (1962) 15' quadrangle.

Jones [LASSEN]: *locality,* 12 miles north of Observation Peak (lat. 40°56'45" N, long. 120°12'55" W). Named on Honey Lake (1893) 1° quadrangle.

Jones: see **Harvey Jones Butte** [MODOC].

Jordan Creek [PLUMAS]: *stream,* flows nearly 2 miles to Last Chance Creek (2) 6.25 miles east-northeast of Squaw Valley Peak (lat. 40°04'10" N, long. 120°17'45" W; near N line sec. 33, T 26 N, R 15 E). Named on Ferris Creek (1977) 7.5' quadrangle.

Jordan Flat [PLUMAS]: *area,* 6.25 miles east-northeast of Squaw Valley Peak at the mouth of Jordan Creek (lat. 40°04' N, long. 120° 17'45" W; sec. 33, T 26 N, R 15 E). Named on Ferris Creek (1977) 7.5' quadrangle.

Joseph Creek [MODOC]: *stream,* flows 8.5 miles to North Fork Pit River 8.5 miles south-southwest of the village of Davis Creek (lat. 41°36'50" N, long. 120°25'10" W; sec. 36, T 44 N, R 13 E). Named on Davis Creek (1962) 15' quadrangle. Wheeler (1878, p. 56) used the form "Joseph's Creek" for the name.

Joseph Creek [PLUMAS]: *stream,* flows 1.5 miles to Little Grizzly Creek 4.5 miles west-southwest of Mount Ingalls (lat. 39°58'05" N, long. 120°42'35" W; near S line sec. 2, T 24 N, R 11 E). Named on Mount Ingalls (1972) 7.5' quadrangle.

Joseph Creek Basin [MODOC]: *relief feature,* 8.5 miles south of the village of Davis Creek (lat. 41°36'45" N, long. 120°20' W; sec. 34, T 44 N, R 14 E); the feature is along Joseph Creek. Named on Davis Creek (1962) 15' quadrangle.

Junction: see **Junction House**, under **Chats** [LASSEN].

Junction Bar: see **Feather River, East Branch of North Fork** [PLUMAS].

Junction House: see **Chats** [LASSEN].

Juniper [MODOC]: *locality,* nearly 2 miles west-southwest of downtown Alturas along Southern Pacific Railroad (lat. 41°28'50" N, long. 120°34'20" W; sec. 15, T 42 N, R 12 E). Named on Alturas (1961) 15' quadrangle. California Division of Highways' (1934) map has the name at a place located 3.5 miles west of Alturas along Southern Pacific Railroad.

Juniper: see **Bieber** [LASSEN].

Juniper Butte [MODOC]: *peak,* 8 miles south-southwest of Newell (lat. 41°47'30" N, long. 121°27' W; on S line sec. 30, T 46 N, R 4 E). Named on Tulelake (1951) 15' quadrangle.

Juniper Creek [LASSEN]: *stream,* formed by the confluence of East Fork and South Fork, flows 3.5 miles to Pit River 3 miles southeast of Bieber (lat. 41°05'15" N, long. 121°06'40" W; sec. 36, T 38 N, R 7 E). Named on Bieber (1961) 15' quadrangle. East Fork is 14 miles long, and South Fork is 9 miles long; both forks are named on Adin (1962), Bieber (1961), and Hayden Hill (1956) 15' quadrangles.

Juniper Creek: see **Big Juniper Creek** [MODOC]; **Little Juniper Creek** [MODOC].

Juniper Jim Spring [LASSEN]: *spring,* 2.5 miles south of Observation Peak (lat. 40°43'30" N, long. 120°11'15" W; sec. 17, T 33 N, R 16 E). Named on Shinn Mountain (1954) 15' quadrangle.

Juniper Lake [LASSEN]: *lake,* 2800 feet long, 8 miles north of Lava Peak (lat. 40°56'50" N, long. 120°55' W; on N line sec. 22, T 36 N, R 9 E). Named on Hayden Hill (1956) 15' quadrangle.

Juniper Lake [LASSEN-PLUMAS]: *lake,* 9000 feet long, 1.5 miles north-northwest of Mount Harkness [PLUMAS] on Lassen-Plumas County line (lat. 40°27'15" N, long. 121°18'30" W). Named on Mount Harkness (1956) 15' quadrangle. The name is from Mount Juniper, an early designation of present Mount Harkness [PLUMAS] (Gudde, 1949, p. 169). The feature also was called Louisa Lake (Schulz, p. 30).

Juniper Mountain: see **Mount Harkness** [PLUMAS].

Juniper Reservoir: see **Little Juniper Reservoir** [MODOC].

Juniper Ridge [LASSEN]: *ridge,* south-southeast-trending, 5.5 miles east of Termo (lat. 40°52'45" N, long. 120°21' W). Named on Ravendale (1954) 15' quadrangle.

Juniper Ridge [MODOC]: *ridge,* southwest- to south-trending, 2 miles long, 3 miles south-southwest of South Mountain (lat. 41° 48' N, long. 120°39'55" W). Named on South Mountain (1962) 15' quadrangle.

Juniper Spring [LASSEN]:
(1) *spring,* about 9 miles east-northeast of the village of Little Valley (lat. 40°56'10" N, long. 121°01' W; at S line sec. 23, T 36 N, R 8 E). Named on Little Valley (1957) 15' quadrangle.
(2) *spring,* 6.25 miles north-northeast of Lava Peak (lat. 40°54'20" N, long. 120°49'30" W; on S line sec. 33, T 36 N, R 10 E). Named on Hayden Hill (1956) 15' quadrangle.
(3) *spring,* 23 miles east of Madeline (lat. 41°00'35" N, long. 120° 02'50" W; near S line sec. 4, T 36 N, R 17 E). Named on Little Hat Mountain (1962) 7.5' quadrangle.

Juniper Spring [MODOC]: *spring,* 9 miles northeast of Blue Mountain (lat. 41°55'55" N, long. 120°45'30" W; at W line sec. 7, T 47 N, R 11 E). Named on Steele Swamp (1962) 15' quadrangle.

Juniper Spring [PLUMAS]:
(1) *spring,* 6 miles west-southwest of Milford [LASSEN] (lat. 40°08'45" N, long. 120°28'50" W; near N line sec. 2, T 26 N, R 13 E). Named on Stony Ridge (1978) 7.5' quadrangle.
(2) *spring,* 7 miles southeast of Milford [LASSEN] (lat. 40°06'10" N, long. 120°16'30" W; near S line sec. 15, T 26 N, R 15 E). Named on Ferris Creek (1977) 7.5' quadrangle.

Jura: see **Mount Jura** [PLUMAS].

– K –

Kaiser Canyon [MODOC]: *canyon,* drained by a stream that flows 2 miles to Surprise Valley 5.25 miles south of Cedarville (lat. 41° 27'25" N, long. 120°10'40" W; at NW cor. sec. 5, T 41 N, R 16 E). Named on Warren Peak (1963) 7.5' quadrangle.

Kalina [MODOC]: *locality,* 8 miles north-northwest of Newell along Great Northern Railroad (lat. 41°59'40" N, long. 121°25' W; near SE cor. sec. 17, T 48 N, R 5 E). Named on Tulelake (1951) 15' quadrangle.

Kandra [MODOC]: *locality,* 4.5 miles south-southwest of Newell along Great Northern Railroad (lat. 41°49'35" N, long. 121°23'50" W; at W line sec. 15, T 46 N, R 5 E). Named on Tulelake (1951) 15' quadrangle.

Karlo [LASSEN]: *locality,* 20 miles east-northeast of Susanville along Southern Pacific Railroad (lat. 40°33' N, long. 120°18'50" W; at E line sec. 18, T 31 N, R 15 E). Named on Karlo (1954) 15' quadrangle. Postal authorities established Secret post office in Secret Valley in 1892, discontinued it in 1895, reestablished it in 1896, changed the name to Karlo in 1911, and discontinued it in 1934—the name "Karlo" was from Frank De Carlow, a pioneer of 1886 in the neighborhood (Salley, p. 109, 200). California Mining Bureau's (1917a) map shows a place called Murray located along the railroad 7.5 miles south of Karlo. California Division of Highways' (1934) map shows a place called Molitor situated 5.25 miles south of Karlo along Nevada-California-Oregon Railroad (sec. 9, T 30 N, R 15 E). Waring (p. 324-325) listed several places in the vicinity: Tiptons Springs, located at Secret post office; Sheep Springs, located 4.5 miles northeast of Tiptons Springs; Secret Springs, located about 4 miles east of Tiptons Springs at the south border of Secret Valley; and Sellicks Springs, situated at the north edge of Secret Valley about 1.25 miles northwest of Karlo.

Keddie [PLUMAS]: *village,* 6.25 miles south-southwest of Crescent Mills (lat. 40°00'55" N, long. 120°57'40" W; sec. 22, T 25 N, R 9 E). Named on Crescent Mills (1980) 7.5' quadrangle. Postal authorities established Keddie post office in 1910 (Frickstad, p. 124). The name commemorates Arthur W. Keddie, surveyor of Plumas County in the 1870's, and later surveyor of the route for Western Pacific Railroad (Hanna, p. 159).

Keddie Peak [PLUMAS]: *peak,* 5.25 miles north of Greenville (lat. 40°13' N, long. 120°58'05" W; sec. 9, T 27 N, R 9 E); the peak is on Keddie Ridge. Altitude 7499 feet. Named on Greenville (1979) 7.5' quadrangle. On Honey Lake (1893) 1° quadrangle, the name applies to a peak located 4 miles farther east-southeast.

Keddie Point [PLUMAS]: *relief feature,* 2.5 miles north of Taylorsville (lat. 40°06'45" N, long. 120°49'55" W; near W line sec. 14, T 26 N, R 10 E); the feature is at the south end of Keddie Ridge. Named on Taylorsville (1980) 7.5' quadrangle.

Keddie Ridge [LASSEN-PLUMAS]: *ridge,* generally northwest-trending, 14 miles long, on Lassen-Plumas County line, center about 4 miles northeast of Greenville [PLUMAS] (lat. 40°11'30" N, long. 120°53'45" W) Named on Canyondam (1979), Greenville (1979), Moonlight Peak (1980), and Taylorsville (1980) 7.5' quadrangles.

Keefer [LASSEN]: *locality,* 28 miles north-northeast of Susanville (lat. 40°48'15" N, long. 120°28'45" W). Named on Honey Lake (1893) 1° quadrangle.

Keeney Flat [MODOC]: *area,* 1.25 miles west-northwest of Crank Mountain (lat. 41°23'30" N, long. 121°09'45" W; mainly in sec. 16, T 41 N, R 7 E). Named on Crank Mountain (1962) 15' quadrangle. Called Hess Flat on Alturas (1954) 1°x 2° quadrangle.

Keep: see **Spanish Ranch** [PLUMAS].

Kelley Hot Spring: see **Kelly Hot Spring** [MODOC].

Kelley Reservoir [MODOC]: *intermittent lake,* 1.5 miles long, 8 miles west-northwest of Alturas (lat. 41°31'40" N, long. 120°41'30" W; mainly in sec. 27, 34, T 43 N, R 11 E). Named on Big Sage Reservoir (1962) 15' quadrangle.

Kellogg Lake: see **Kellog Lake** [PLUMAS].

Kellogg Mountain [MODOC]: *peak,* 8.5 miles north-northeast of Blue Mountain (lat. 41°56'35" N, long. 120°47' W; sec. 2, T 47 N, R 10 E). Named on Steele Swamp (1962) 15' quadrangle.

Kellogg Tank [MODOC]: *water feature,* 7.5 miles north-northeast of Blue Mountain (lat. 41°55'55" N, long. 120°48'50" W; sec. 10, T 47 N, R 10 E); the feature is 1.25 miles southwest of Kellogg Mountain. Named on Steele Swamp (1962) 15' quadrangle.

Kellog Hot Springs [LASSEN]: *springs,* 6 miles east of Bieber (lat. 41°07'35" N, long. 121°01'30" W; near SW cor. sec. 14, T 38 N, R 8 E). Named on Bieber (1961) 15' quadrangle.

Kellog Lake [PLUMAS]: *lake,* 450 feet long, 7.5 miles north-northwest of Bucks Lodge (lat. 39°58'55" N, long. 121°12'45" W; near E line sec. 32, T 25 N, R 7 E); the lake is at the head of Kellog Ravine (1). Named on Bucks Lake (1979) 7.5' quadrangle. United States Board on Geographic Names (1977b, p. 4) approved the name "Kellogg Lake" for the feature, and gave the form "Kellog Lake" as a variant.

Kellog Ravine [PLUMAS]:
(1) *canyon,* drained by a stream that flows 2.25 miles to East Branch of North Fork Feather River 5.25 miles south-southwest of Caribou (lat. 40°00'35" N, long. 121°11'35" W); the canyon heads at Kellog Lake. Named on Bucks Lake (1979) and Caribou (1979) 7.5' quadrangles. United States Board on Geographic Names (1977b, p. 4) approved the name "Kellogg Ravine" for the feature, and gave the form "Kellog Ravine" as a variant
(2) *canyon,* drained by a stream that flows 2 miles to Middle Fork Feather River 3 miles northwest of Cascade (lat. 39°43'55" N, long. 121°12'45" W; sec. 29, T 22 N, R 7 E). Named on Cascade (1948) and Haskins Valley (1980) 7.5' quadrangles.

Kelly [PLUMAS]: *locality,* 5.5 miles east of Chester along Almanor Railroad (lat. 40°17'55" N, long. 121°07'25" W; sec. 7, T 28 N, R 8 E). Named on Westwood West (1980) 7.5' quadrangle.

Kelly Camp [PLUMAS]: *locality,* 3 miles west of Mount Harkness (lat. 40°25'55" N, long. 121°21'20" W; sec. 30, T 30 N, R 6 E); the place is less than 2 miles north-northwest of Kelly Mountain. Named on Mount Harkness (1956) 15' quadrangle. Jim Kelly homesteaded at the site (Schulz, p. 30).

Kelly Draw [MODOC]: *canyon,* drained by a stream that flows 4.5 miles to Ash Creek 2.5 miles northeast of Adin (lat. 41°13'40" N, long. 120°54'45" W; at SW cor. sec. 11, T 39 N, R 9 E). Named on Adin (1962) and Canby (1961) 15' quadrangles.

Kelly Hot Spring [MODOC]: *spring,* 2 miles east-northeast of Canby (lat. 41°27'15" N, long. 120°50' W; sec. 29, T 42 N, R 10 E). Named on Canby (1961) 15' quadrangle. United States Board on Geographic Names (1990, p. 8) approved the form "Kelley Hot Spring" for the name. John Kelley came to Modoc County in 1872 and founded a ranch at the spring, where the effect of the hot water on the local climate permitted the growth of vegetables not normally produced in the region (Brown, p. 157-158).

Kelly Mountain [PLUMAS]: *ridge,* generally northwest-trending, 4.5 miles long, 3 miles southwest of Mount Harkness (lat. 40°24'30" N, long. 121°20'45" W). Named on Mount Harkness (1956) 15' quadrangle. The name commemorates the head of the Kelly family, first settlers in the neighborhood (United States Board on Geographic Names, 1933, p. 421).

Kelly Reservoir [MODOC]: *intermittent lake,* 4200 feet long, 12 miles west-southwest of Alturas (lat. 41°24'30" N, long. 120°44'20" W; mainly in sec. 7, T 41 N, R 11 E). Named on Alturas (1961) 15' quadrangle.

Kelly Spring [MODOC]:
(1) *spring,* 12 miles south of Canby (lat. 41°16'10" N, long. 120°51'30" W; at NW cor. sec. 32, T 40 N, R 10 E). Named on Canby (1961) 15' quadrangle.
(2) *spring,* 7.5 miles north-northwest of Alturas (lat. 41°35'20" N, long. 120°35'20" W; near SE cor. sec. 4, T 43 N, R 12 E). Named on Big Sage Reservoir (1962) 15' quadrangle.

Kennedy Butte [PLUMAS]: *peak,* 2.5 miles north-northwest of Cascade (lat. 39°44'10" N, long. 121°11'40" W; sec. 28, T 22 N, R 7 E). Named on Cascade (1948) 7.5' quadrangle, which shows Kennedy cabin situated 0.5 mile north of the peak.

Kenzie Ravine [PLUMAS]: *canyon,* drained by a stream that flows 3.25 miles to South Fork Feather River nearly 4 miles north of La Porte (lat. 39°44'10" N, long. 120°59' W; sec. 28, T 22 N, R 9 E). Named on La Porte (1951) 7.5' quadrangle.

Kephart [MODOC]: *locally,* 3 miles south-southwest of Timber Mountain along Great Northern Railroad (lat. 41°35'20" N, long. 121°18'45" W; near NW cor. sec. 8, T 43 N, R 6 E). Named on Timber Mountain (1952) 15' quadrangle.

Kessler Peak [PLUMAS]: *peak,* 2.25 miles south-southwest of Kettle Rock (lat. 40°06'30" N, long. 120°44'20" W; near SW cor. sec. 15, T 26 N, R 11 E). Named on Genesee Valley (1972) 7.5' quadrangle.

Kettle: see **Beckwourth** [PLUMAS].

Kettle Rock [PLUMAS]: *peak*, 11.5 miles east of Greenville (lat. 40° 08'25" N, long. 120°43'30" W; near E line sec. 3, T 26 N, R 11 E). Altitude 7820 feet. Named on Kettle Rock (1972) 7.5' quadrangle.

Kettle Rock Creek: see **Peters Creek** [PLUMAS].

Kettle Rock Lake [PLUMAS]: *lake*, 100 feet long, 3500 feet northeast of Kettle Rock (lat. 40°08'50" N, long. 120°43' W; near N line sec. 2, T 26 N, R 11 E). Named on Kettle Rock (1972) 7.5' quadrangle.

Kettle Rock Spring [PLUMAS]: *spring*, less than 0.5 mile east-northeast of Kettle Rock (lat. 40°08'35" N, long. 120°43' W; near W line sec. 2, T 26 N, R 11 E). Named on Kettle Rock (1972) 7.5' quadrangle.

Kilby Creek [LASSEN]: *stream*, flows 3 miles to Madeline Plains nearly 3 miles northeast of Termo (lat. 40°53'45" N, long. 120°25'25" W; near E line sec. 18, T 35 N, R 14 E). Named on Ravendale (1954) 15' quadrangle.

Kingsbury Ravine [PLUMAS]: *canyon*, drained by a stream that flows 2 miles to East Branch of North Fork Feather River 0.25 mile south-southwest of Twain (lat. 40°01' N, long. 121°04'25" W; sec. 22, T 25 N, R 8 E). Named on Twain (1980) 7.5' quadrangle.

Kings Creek [PLUMAS]: *stream*, heads in Shasta County and flows 2.25 miles in Plumas County to join Hot Springs Creek and form Warner Creek 2.25 miles west-southwest of Mount Harkness (lat. 40°25'15" N, long. 121°20'30" W; sec. 32, T 30 N, R 6 E). Named on Mount Harkness (1956) 15' quadrangle. Schulz (p. 31) associated the name with James M. King, who lived near the stream and ran horses and mules along it in the summertime.

Kinyon: see **White Horse** [MODOC].

Kirkham Ravine [PLUMAS]: *canyon*, drained by a stream that flows 2.5 miles to North Fork Feather River 6 miles north of Twain (lat. 40°06'25" N, long. 121°04'45" W; near E line sec. 16, T 26 N, R 8 E). Named on Canyondam (1979) and Twain (1980) 7.5' quadrangles.

Knickrem Hill [PLUMAS]: *locality*, 5.5 miles west-northwest of Blairsden (lat. 39°48'35" N, long. 120°42'45" W; near S line sec. 35, T 23 N, R 11 E). Site named on Johnsville (1972) 7.5' quadrangle.

Knobcone Butte [MODOC]: *peak*, 3.5 miles north-northeast of Hackamore (lat. 41°35'50" N, long. 121°04'45" W; at W line sec. 6, T 43 N, R 8 E). Altitude 5063 feet. Named on Hackamore (1952) 15' quadrangle.

Knox Flat [LASSEN-MODOC]: *area*, 12 miles west of Likely [MODOC] along Cottonwood Creek [LASSEN-MODOC] on Lassen-Modoc County line (lat. 41°11'05" N, long. 120°43'50" W; on S line sec. 29, T 39 N, R 11 E). Named on Likely (1962) 15' quadrangle.

Knox Mountain [LASSEN-MODOC]: *ridge*, southeast- to south-trending, 8.5 miles long, 11 miles west-southwest of Likely [MODOC] on Lassen-Modoc County line (lat. 41°10'45" N, long. 120°41'45" W). Named on Likely (1962) 15' quadrangle. The name commemorates Robert Knox, who built a sawmill at the place in 1874 (Gudde, 1969, p. 167).

Knox Spring [LASSEN]: *spring*, 4.25 miles west of Bieber (lat. 41° 07'30" N, long. 121°13'30" W; near S line sec. 13, T 38 N, R 6 E). Named on Bieber (1961) 15' quadrangle.

Kramer Reservoir [MODOC]:
(1) *lake*, 3300 feet long, 7 miles east-southeast of White Horse (lat. 41°17'15" N, long. 121°16'20" W; near W line sec. 22, T 40 N, R 6 E). Named on White Horse (1962) 15' quadrangle.
(2) *lake*, 1700 feet long, 3.5 miles west-southwest of Lookout (lat. 41°11'10" N, long. 121°12'35" W; sec. 30, T 39 N, R 7 E). Named on Bieber (1961) 15' quadrangle.

Kresge Spring [MODOC]: *spring*, 11.5 miles south of Canby (lat. 41°16'50" N, long. 120°50'50" W; sec. 29, T 40 N, R 10 E). Named on Canby (1961) 15' quadrangle.

Kruger Spring: see **Indian Valley Hot Springs** [PLUMAS].

— L —

Ladder Butte [LASSEN]: *peak*, 9 miles southwest of the village of Little Valley (lat. 40°48'40" N, long. 121°18'20" W; sec. 16, T 34 N, R 6 E). Altitude 5742 feet. Named on Jellico (1957) 15' quadrangle. Officials of the Forest Service named the feature about 1929 (Gudde, 1949, p. 178). United States Board on Geographic Names (1983b, p. 5) approved the name "Freebe Reservoir" for a tank located 3.5 miles south-southwest of Ladder Butte (lat. 40°45'45" N, long. 121°18'45" W; sec. 33, T 34 N, R 6 E).

Lake Almanor [PLUMAS]: *lake*, behind a dam on North Fork Feather River less than 1 mile west of Canyondam (lat. 40°10'30" N, long. 121°05'15" W; sec. 28, T 27 N, R 8 E); water of the lake covers Big Meadows. Named on Almanor (1979), Canyondam (1979), Chester (1979), and Westwood West (1980) 7.5' quadrangles. The dam that forms the lake was completed in 1917; the lake first was called Big Meadows Reservoir, but Julius M. Howells, who was in charge of constructing the dam, coined the name "Almanor" from the names "Alice," "Martha," and "Elinor," daughters of Guy C. Earl, president of Great Western Power Company (Gudde, 1949, p. 8).

Lake Annie [MODOC]: *lake*, 1900 feet long, 4.25 miles north-northeast of Fort Bidwell (lat. 41°54'35" N, long. 120°06'20" W; at S line sec. 26, T 47 N, R 16 E). Named on Fort Bidwell (1962) 15' quadrangle.

Lake Annie Mountain [MODOC]: *peak*, 4.5 miles northeast of Fort Bidwell (lat. 41°54'30" N, long. 120°05'40" W; near SE cor. sec. 26, T 47 N, R 16 E); the peak is 0.5 mile east of Lake Annie. Altitude 6007 feet. Named on Fort Bidwell (1962) 15' quadrangle.

Lake Bidwell: see **Butte Lake** [LASSEN].

Lake Caribou: see **Caribou Lake** [LASSEN].

Lake City [MODOC]: *village*, 8.5 miles north-northwest of Cedarville (lat. 41°38'30" N, long. 120°12'45" W; sec. 36, T 44 N, R 15 E). Named on Cedarville (1962) 15' quadrangle. Postal authorities established Lake City post office in 1868; the place first was called Tri-Lake City, but postal authorities shortened the name (Salley, p. 115).

Lake City Canyon [MODOC]: *canyon*, 4.25 miles long, drained by Mill Creek (3) and a branch of that creek; opens into Surprise Valley 8 miles north-northwest of Cedarville (lat. 41°38'30" N, long. 120°13' W; near W line sec. 36, T 44 N, R 15 E); the mouth of the canyon is at Lake City. Named on Cedarville (1962) and Davis Creek (1962) 15' quadrangles.

Lake Davis [PLUMAS]: *lake*, behind a dam on Big Grizzly Creek 5.5 miles north of Portola (lat. 39°53' N, long. 120°28'30" W; on E line sec. 2, T 23 N, R 13 E). Named on Crocker Mountain (1972) and Grizzly Valley (1972) 7.5' quadrangles. The name commemorates Lester T. Davis, who promoted creation of the lake (United States Board on Geographic Names, 1965b, p. 13).

Lake Enchantment: see **Snag Lake** [LASSEN].

Lake Greeno: see **Constantia** [LASSEN].

Lake Lapilli: see **Snag Lake** [LASSEN].

Lake Leavitt [LASSEN]: *lake*, 1.5 miles long, 8.5 miles east-southeast of Susanville (lat. 40°22' N, long. 120°30'40" W; around SW cor. sec. 15, T 29 N, R 13 E). Named on Litchfield (1954) and Susanville (1954) 15' quadrangles.

Lake Nokopen: see **Westwood** [LASSEN].

Lake Norvell [LASSEN]: *intermittent lake*, 950 feet long, 13 miles north of Westwood (lat. 40°29'35" N, long. 121°00'10" W; at W line sec. 5, T 30 N, R 9 E); the feature is at Norvell Flat. Named on Swain Mountain (1979) 7.5' quadrangle.

Lake of the Woods [LASSEN]: *locality*, 2.25 miles southwest of Pelican Point (lat. 40°36'55" N, long. 120°47' W; near S line sec. 19, T 32 N, R 11 E). Named on Antelope Mountain (1956) 15' quadrangle.

Lakes Basin [PLUMAS]: *relief feature*, 6 miles southwest of Clio (lat. 39°41'45" N, long. 120°40'30" W). Named on Gold Lake (1981) 7.5' quadrangle.

Lakes Basin Campground [PLUMAS]: *locality*, 5.25 miles southwest of Clio (lat. 39°42'05" N, long. 120°39'40" W; near NW cor sec. 8, T 21 N, R 12 E); the place is in Lakes Basin. Named on Sierra City (1955) 15' quadrangle.

Lakeshore Reservoir [MODOC]: *intermittent lake*, 2200 feet long, 4.5 miles east-southeast of South Mountain (lat. 41°48'25" N, long. 120°33'35" W; on N line sec. 26, T 46 N, R 12 E). Named on South Mountain (1962) 15' quadrangle.

Lake Tartarus: see **Boiling Springs Lake** [PLUMAS].

Lakeview Junction [MODOC]: *locality*, 1 mile south-southeast of downtown Alturas along Southern Pacific Railroad (lat. 41°28'30" N, long. 120°32'05" W; near S line sec. 13, T 42 N, R 12 E). Named on Alturas (1961) 15' quadrangle.

Lands Island [MODOC]: *hill*, 3 miles southeast of Newell in the Copic Bay part of the drained bed of Tule Lake (lat. 41°51'10" N, long. 121°19'40" W; sec. 6, T 46 N, R 6 E). Named on Tulelake (1951) 15' quadrangle.

Lane Reservoir [LASSEN]: *lake*, 0.5 mile long, 12.5 miles southeast of Adin [MODOC] (lat. 41°04'50" N, long. 120°45'20" W; near NW cor. sec. 6, T 37 N, R 11 E). Named on Adin (1962) 15' quadrangle.

Lanning Spring [LASSEN]: *spring*, 9.5 miles north-northeast of Termo (lat. 40°49'20" N, long. 120°23'20" W; near NE cor. sec. 16, T 36 N, R 14 E). Named on Ravendale (1954) 15' quadrangle.

Lansford Spring [MODOC]: *spring*, 18 miles southwest of Alturas (lat. 41°16'55" N, long. 120°44'40" W; at NW cor. sec. 29, T 40 N, R 11 E). Named on Alturas (1961) 15' quadrangle.

Lapilli: see **Lake Lapilli**, under **Snag Lake** [LASSEN].

La Porte [PLUMAS]: *village*, 18 miles south of Quincy (lat. 39°40'55" N, long. 120°59' W; sec. 16, T 21 N, R 9 E); the village is along Rabbit Creek. Named on La Porte (1951) 7.5' quadrangle. Postal authorities established Rabbit Town post office, named from Rabbit Creek, in 1855 and changed the name to La Porte in 1857 (Salley, p. 180). The community was called Rabbit Creek and Rabbit Town before it was renamed for La Porte, Indiana, birthplace of Frank Everts, a local banker (Gudde, 1949, p. 182, 277).

La Porte Bald Mountain [PLUMAS]: *peak*, 1 mile north of La Porte (lat. 39°41'50" N, long. 120°58'45" W; sec. 9, T 21 N, R 9 E). Altitude 5906 feet. Named on La Porte (1951) 7.5' quadrangle. Called Bald Mt. on

Downieville (1897) 30' quadrangle.

Large: see **Tom Large Flat** [MODOC].

Larkspur Hills [MODOC]: *ridge,* north-northwest-trending, 4.5 miles long, 5.5 miles east-southeast of Fort Bidwell (lat. 41°49'30" N, long. 120°03'15" W). Named on Fort Bidwell (1962) 15' quadrangle.

Larry Flat Campground [MODOC]: *locality,* 6 miles north-northwest of Fort Bidwell (lat. 41°56'15" N, long. 120°11'15" W; at SW cor. sec. 18, T 47 N, R 16 E). Named on Fort Bidwell (1962) 15' quadrangle. United States Board on Geographic Names (1990, p. 9) approved the name "O' Leary Flat" for the the site, and noted that the name is for John O' Leary, who cut wood at the place.

Lasco [LASSEN]: *locality,* 8 miles north of Westwood along Southern Pacific Railroad (lat. 40°25'25" N, long. 120°58'15" W; near N line sec. 33, T 30 N, R 9 E). Named on Westwood (1955) 15' quadrangle.

Lassen: see **Janesville** [LASSEN].

Lassen Creek [LASSEN]: *stream,* flows 5.5 miles to lowlands 4.5 miles south-southeast of Susanville (lat. 40°22'15" N, long. 120°36'20" W; near W line sec. 14, T 29 N, R 2 E). Named on Susanville (1954) 15' quadrangle.

Lassen Creek [MODOC]: *stream,* flows 15 miles to Goose Lake (1) less than 1 mile south-southwest of Willow Ranch (lat. 41°53'30" N, long. 120°21'50" W; sec. 28, T 47 N, R 14 E). Named on Davis Creek (1962) and Willow Ranch (1962) 15' quadrangles. Wheeler (1878, p. 56) used the form "Lassen's Creek" for the name.

Lassen Horn: see **Fandango Pass** [MODOC].

Lassen's Pass: see **Fandango Pass** [MODOC].

Lassen View [PLUMAS]: *locality,* 8.5 miles east-southeast of Chester along Western Pacific Railroad (lat. 40°15'45" N, long. 121°04'45" W; near NE cor. sec. 28, T 28 N, R 8 E). Named on Chester (1956) 15' quadrangle. Postal authorities established Lassen View post office in 1937 and discontinued it in 1941 (Frickstad, p. 124).

Last Chance [PLUMAS]: *locality,* 9.5 miles south-southwest of Quincy (lat. 39°48'15" N, long. 120°59'15" W; at SW cor. sec. 33, T 23 N, R 9 E); the place is along Last Chance Creek (3). Site named on Onion Valley (1950) 7.5' quadrangle.

Last Chance Campground [PLUMAS]: *locality,* 3 miles north of Chester (lat. 40°21'15" N, long. 121°13'20" W; sec. 20, T 29 N, R 7 E); the place is along Last Chance Creek (1). Named on Chester (1979) 7.5' quadrangle.

Last Chance Creek [PLUMAS]:

(1) *stream,* flows 2.5 miles to marsh along Lake Almanor 2.5 miles north of Chester (lat. 40°21'05" N, long. 121°13'10" W; at S line sec. 20, T 29 N, R 7 E). Named on Chester (1979) and Red Cinder (1979) 7.5' quadrangles.

(2) *stream,* flows 38 miles to Red Clover Creek 6.5 miles south-southeast of Kettle Rock (lat. 40°03'25" N, long. 120°40' W; sec. 6, T 25 N, R 12 E). Named on Babcock Peak (1972), Ferris Creek (1977), Genesee Valley (1972), and McKesick Peak (1978) 7.5' quadrangles. On Honey Lake (1893) 1° quadrangle, the part of present Last Chance Creek (2) below the junction with present Squaw Queen Creek is called Squaw Creek.

(3) *stream,* flows 2.25 miles to Middle Fork Feather River nearly 4 miles northeast of Dogwood Peak (lat. 39°49'25" N, long. 121°00'20" W). Named on Dogwood Peak (1979) and Onion Valley (1950) 7.5' quadrangles.

Last Chance Creek: see **Little Last Chance Creek** [PLUMAS].

Last Chance Lake: see **Little Last Chance Lake** [PLUMAS].

Last Chance Spring [MODOC]: *spring,* 4 miles southwest of Crank Mountain (lat. 41°20'45" N, long. 121°12'15" W; sec. 31, T 41 N, R 7 E). Named on Crank Mountain (1962) 15' quadrangle.

Last Chance Valley: see **Little Last Chance Valley** [PLUMAS].

Lauer Reservoir [MODOC]: *intermittent lake,* 7000 feet long, 7.25 miles southwest of the village of Davis Creek (lat. 41°39'45" N, long. 120°28'20" W; on S line sec. 9, T 44 N, R 13 E). Named on Davis Creek (1962) 15' quadrangle. Called Lauers Reservoir on California Division of Highways (1934) map.

Laufman Campground [LASSEN]: *locality,* 2.25 miles south-southeast of Milford (lat. 40°08'10" N, long. 120°20'50" W; sec. 1, T 26 N, R 14 E). Named on Milford (1977) 7.5' quadrangle.

Lava Campground [MODOC]: *locality,* 7 miles north-northeast of White Horse (lat. 41°24'10" N, long. 121°20'15" W). Named on White Horse (1962) 15' quadrangle.

Lava Creek [PLUMAS]: *stream,* flows 2.5 miles to Pinchard Creek 1.5 miles east-northeast of Cascade (lat. 39°42'20" N, long. 121°09'05" W; near SW cor. sec. 36, T 22 N, R 7 E). Named on American House (1948) and Cascade (1948) 7.5' quadrangles.

Lava Lake [MODOC]: *water feature,* 12 miles north-northeast of White Horse (lat. 41°27'30" N, long. 121°17'25" W). Named on White Horse (1962) 15' quadrangle.

Lava Peak [LASSEN]: *peak,* 26 miles north-northwest of Susanville (lat. 40°49'55" N, long. 120°53'30" W; at N line sec. 7, T 34 N, R 10 E). Altitude 6613 feet. Named on Hayden Hill (1956) 15' quadrangle.

Lava Peak [PLUMAS]: *peak,* 7.25 miles north-northwest of Blairsden (lat. 39°52'25" N, long. 120°40'45" W; sec. 7, T 23 N, R 12 E). Altitude 5889 feet. Named on Johnsville (1972) 7.5' quadrangle.

Lava Rock Reservoir [LASSEN]: *lake,* 200 feet long, 8 miles north of Wendel (lat. 40°28' N, long. 120°13' W; near N line sec. 18, T 30 N, R 16 E). Named on Wendel (1954) 15' quadrangle.

Lava Slides [LASSEN]: *relief feature,* 20 miles east-northeast of Madeline (lat. 41°06'30" N, long. 120°05'45" W; at NE cor. sec. 1, T 37 N, R 16 E). Named on Little Hat Mountain (1962) 7.5' quadrangle.

Lava Spring [PLUMAS]: *spring,* 11 miles north-northeast of Portola (lat. 39°57'10" N, long. 120°23'40" W; sec. 10, T 24 N, R 14 E). Named on Crocker Mountain (1972) 7.5' quadrangle.

Lavassi Creek [PLUMAS]: *stream,* flows nearly 2 miles to Mill Creek (3) 3.25 miles north of Bucks Lodge (lat. 39°55'25" N, long. 121°11' W; sec. 22, T 24 N, R 7 E). Named on Bucks Lake (1979) 7.5' quadrangle.

Lava Top [PLUMAS]: *ridge,* northwest-trending, less than 1 mile long, nearly 1 mile south-southeast of Cascade (lat. 39°41'20" N, long. 121°10'10" W; sec. 10, 11, T 21 N, R 7 E). Named on Cascade (1948) 7.5' quadrangle.

Lawton Meadow [PLUMAS]: *area,* 3.25 miles north of Portola (lat. 39°51'15" N, long. 120°28'20" W; at W line sec. 13, T 23 N, R 13 E). Named on Portola (1972) 7.5' quadrangle.

Layman Bar [PLUMAS]: *locality,* 5 miles northwest of Blairsden along Middle Fork Feather River (lat. 39°50'10" N, long. 120°40'35" W; on N line sec. 30, T 23 N, R 12 E). Named on Johnsville (1972) 7.5' quadrangle. Blairsden (1943) 15' quadrangle has the name "Auto Camp" at the place, and Blairsden (1956) 15' quadrangle has the name "Layman Camp" there.

Layman Camp: see **Layman Bar** [PLUMAS].

Layton Spring [MODOC]: *spring,* 13 miles north-northwest of Alturas (lat. 41°40'10" N, long. 120°38' W; sec. 7, T 44 N, R 12 E). Named on Big Sage Reservoir (1962) 15' quadrangle.

Leavitt [LASSEN]: *locality,* 7 miles east of Susanville along Southern Pacific Railroad (lat. 40°23'45" N, long. 120°31'20" W; near S line sec. 4, T 29 N, R 13 E). Named on Susanville (1954) 15' quadrangle. Leavitt post office was established in 1914 and discontinued in 1920; the name was for May L. Leavitt, first postmaster (Salley, p. 120).

Leavitt: see **Lake Leavitt** [LASSEN].

Lee: see **Tom Lee Meadows** [MODOC].

Lee Camp [PLUMAS]: *locality,* 1.5 miles west-southwest of Mount Harkness in Warner Valley (lat. 40°25'10" N, long. 121°19'35" W; on E line sec. 32, T 30 N, R 6 E). Named on Mount Harkness (1956) 15' quadrangle.

Lee Summit [PLUMAS]: *pass,* 10.5 miles east-southeast of Quincy (lat. 39°52'45" N, long. 120°45'30" W; at NE cor. sec. 8, T 23 N, R 11 E). Named on Spring Garden (1950) 7.5' quadrangle.

Left Hand Canyon [PLUMAS]: *canyon,* drained by a stream that flows 1 mile to Fitch Canyon 4 miles west-southwest of Milford [LASSEN] (lat. 40°09'20" N, long. 120°26'40" W; sec. 31, T 27 N, R 14 E). Named on Stony Ridge (1978) 7.5' quadrangle.

Leonards Hot Springs [MODOC]: *spring,* 6.25 miles northeast of Cedarville (lat. 41°36' N, long. 120°05'30" W; sec. 13, T 43 N, R 16 E). Named on Cedarville (1962) 15' quadrangle.

Leonard Spring [MODOC]: *spring,* 9.5 miles south-southwest of the village of Davis Creek (lat. 41°36'40" N, long. 120°26'30" W; sec. 35, T 44 N, R 13 E). Named on Davis Creek (1962) 15' quadrangle.

Letter Box [PLUMAS]: *locality,* 5.25 miles southeast of Storrie (lat. 39°51'30" N, long. 121°15'40" W; sec. 12, T 23 N, R 6 E). Named on Soapstone Hill (1979) 7.5' quadrangle. Postal authorities established Box post office at the site in 1896 and discontinued it in 1901 (Salley, p. 25).

Letterbox Canyon [LASSEN]: *canyon,* drained by a stream that flows 1.25 miles to Preston Canyon 13 miles south-southeast of Adin [MODOC] (lat. 41°00'45" N, long. 120°53' W; sec. 25, T 37 N, R 9 E); the canyon is south of Letterbox Hill. Named on Adin (1962) 15' quadrangle.

Letterbox Creek [PLUMAS]: *stream,* flows nearly 2 miles to Grizzly Creek (2) 4.5 miles southeast of Storrie (lat. 39°52'40" N, long. 121°15'15" W; sec. 1, T 23 N, R 6 E); the stream heads near Letter Box. Named on Soapstone Hill (1979) and Storrie (1979) 7.5' quadrangles.

Letterbox Hill [LASSEN]: *peak,* 12.5 miles south-southeast of Adin [MODOC] (lat. 41°01'10" N, long. 120°52'50" W; near N line sec. 25, T 37 N, R 9 E); the peak is north of Letterbox Canyon. Named on Adin (1962) 15' quadrangle.

Level Reservoir [MODOC]: *intermittent lake,* 700 feet long, 15 miles north-northeast of Cedarville (lat. 41°42'45" N, long. 120°01'45" W; at E line sec. 4, T 44 N, R 17 E). Named on Cedarville (1962) 15' quadrangle.

Lexington Hill [PLUMAS]: *ridge,* north-trending, 1.25 miles long, 2 miles north-northeast of American House (lat. 39°40'50" N, long. 121°00'30" W; near E line sec. 18, T 21 N, R 9 E). Named on American House (1948) 7.5' quadrangle.

Lieberman Canyon [MODOC]: *canyon,* drained by a stream that flows 6.5 miles to Surprise Valley 6 miles southeast of Fort Bidwell (lat. 41°48'15" N, long. 120°03'40" W; near N line sec. 5, T 45 N, R 17 E). Named on Cedarville (1962) and Fort Bidwell (1962) 15' quadrangles.

Liegan: see **Rayl**, under **Herlong** [LASSEN] (1).

Lightning Tree Point [PLUMAS]: *promontory,* 7.5 miles southeast of Mount Ingalls along Lake Davis (lat. 39°55'30" N, long. 120°30'40" W; near SW cor. sec. 22, T 24 N, R 13 E). Named on Grizzly Valley (1972) 7.5' quadrangle.

Lights Creek [PLUMAS]: *stream,* flows 19 miles to Indian Creek (2) nearly 2 miles north-northwest of Taylorsville (lat. 40°06' N, long. 120°50'55" W; sec. 22, T 26 N, R 10 E). Named on Diamond Mountain (1972), Fredonyer Pass (1980), Moonlight Peak (1980), and Taylorsville (1980) 7.5' quadrangles. Preston (1890c, p. 467) referred to Light's Creek. The name commemorates Ephraim Light, a pioneer rancher (Gudde, 1949, p. 187). East Branch enters from the east 4.5 miles east of Moonlight Peak; it is nearly 6 miles long and is named on Kettle Rock (1972) 7.5' quadrangle. West Branch enters from the west 4.5 miles east of Moonlight Peak; it is 3.5 miles long and is named on Fredonyer Pass (1980) and Moonlight Peak (1980) 7.5' quadrangles.

Likely [MODOC]: *village,* 18 miles south of Alturas (lat. 41°13'50" N, long. 120°30'10" W; sec. 8, T 39 N, R 13 E); the village is near South Fork Pit River. Named on Likely (1962) 15' quadrangle. The place first was called South Fork (Laird, p. 62). Postal authorities established South Fork post office 18 miles south of Alturas along South Fork Pit River in 1878 and discontinued it in 1882; they established Likely post office in 1886 (Salley, p. 209, 122). According to local legend, the name "Likely" was chosen for the post office after the name "South Fork" was rejected by postal authorities, and residents of the community thought that it was not likely that the post office ever would receive a name (Pease, p. 93). California Mining Bureau's (1909a) map shows a place called Ivy located on the stage line about half way between Likely and Eagleville. Postal authorities established Ivy post office 16 miles east of Likely in 1899, discontinued it in 1920, reestablished it in 1921, and discontinued it in 1922 (Salley, p. 106). The name was from a huge pot of ivy at the post office (Laird, p. 64). California Division of Highways (1934) map shows a place called Indian Camp located 2.5 miles southeast of Likely along Nevada-California-Oregon Railroad.

Likely Mill: see **Old Likely Mill** [MODOC].

Likely Mountain: see **South Fork Mountain** [LASSEN].

Lillian: see **Canby** [MODOC].

Lily Lake [MODOC]: *lake,* 800 feet long, 9 miles north-northwest of Fort Bidwell (lat. 41°58'35" N, long. 120°12'30" W; on W line sec. 1, T 47 N, R 15 E). Named on Fort Bidwell (1962) 15' quadrangle. Hill's (1915) map shows a mining camp called Branley situated 5000 feet south-southeast of Lily Lake.

Lily Lake [PLUMAS]: *lake,* 550 feet long, 4.5 miles west-southwest of Clio (lat. 39°43' N, long. 120°39'30" W; near N line sec. 5, T 21 N, R 12 E). Named on Gold Lake (1981) 7.5' quadrangle.

Lily Lake: see **Little Lily Lake** [MODOC].

Limestone Point [PLUMAS]: *relief feature,* 6.25 miles south-southeast of Quincy (lat. 39°51'25" N, long. 120°53'35" W; near W line sec. 17, T 23 N, R 10 E). Named on Onion Valley (1950) 7.5' quadrangle.

Linaman Lake: see **Linderman Lake** [MODOC].

Lindale: see **Linnville Creek** [MODOC].

Lindemenn Lake: see **Linderman Lake** [MODOC].

Linderman Lake [MODOC]: *lake,* 600 feet long, 10.5 miles south of Cedarville (lat. 41°22'50" N, long. 120°11'45" W; near W line sec. 31, T 41 N, R 16 E). Named on Warren Peak (1963) 7.5' quadrangle. United States Board on Geographic Names (1965a, p. 9-10) approved the name "Lindemenn Lake" for the feature, and rejected the names "Linderman Lake," "Linaman Lake," and "Lineman Lake." According to Gudde (1969, p. 178), the name is for J.B. Lindemann, a resident of Eagleville in the 1870's.

Lineman Lake: see **Linderman Lake** [MODOC].

Linnville Creek [MODOC]: *stream,* flows 4 miles to lowlands 3.5 miles south of the village of Davis Creek (lat. 41°40'55" N, long. 120°22'30" W; sec. 5, T 44 N, R 14 E). Named on Davis Creek (1962) 15' quadrangle. Postal authorities established Lindale post office 7 miles south of Davis Creek post office in 1876 and discontinued it in 1884; the name was for L.G. Linville, a pioneer settler—the place also was known as Linville (Salley, p. 122).

Liskey [MODOC]: *locality,* 3.25 miles southwest of Newell along Great Northern Railroad (lat. 41°50'55" N, long. 121°24'30" W; at N line sec. 9, T 46 N, R 5 E). Named on Tulelake (1951) 15' quadrangle.

Litchfield [LASSEN]: *village,* 15 miles east of Susanville (lat. 40°22'55" N, long. 120°23' W; near S line sec. 10, T 29 N, R 14 E). Named on Litchfield (1954) 15' quadrangle. Postal authorities established Litchfield post office in 1914 and moved it about 0.5 mile north in 1941 (Salley, p. 123). Mrs. B.F. Gibson named the place around 1910 to honor her father, Thomas Litch, a pioneer settler (Hanna, p. 172). California Division of Highways' (1934) map shows a place called Mapes located 2.5 miles east-southeast of Litchfield along Southern Pacific Railroad (sec. 13, T 29 N, R 14 E).

Little Antelope Creek [PLUMAS]: *stream,* flows 2.5 miles to Antelope Lake 8 miles east-northeast of Kettle Rock (lat. 40°10'20" N, long. 120°34'45" W; sec. 25, T 27 N, R 12 E). Named on Antelope Lake (1972) 7.5' quadrangle.

Little Antelope Valley [LASSEN]: *valley,* 7.5 miles west of Pelican Point (lat. 40°38'35" N, long. 120°53'20" W; sec. 18, T 32 N, R 10 E); the valley is 2 miles south-southeast of Antelope Valley. Named on Antelope Mountain (1956) 15' quadrangle.

Little Antelope Well [LASSEN]: *well,* 7.5 miles west of Pelican Point (lat. 40°38'15" N, long. 120°53'15" W; sec. 18, T 32 N, R 10 E); the well is near the south end of Little Antelope Valley. Named on Antelope Mountain (1956) 15' quadrangle.

Little Baldy [MODOC]: *peak,* 10 miles south-southeast of the village of Davis Creek (lat. 41°38'30" N, long. 120°16' W; sec. 33, T 44 N, R 15 E); the peak is 2 miles north of Bald Mountain (1). Altitude 8270 feet. Named on Davis Creek (1962) 15' quadrangle.

Little Baldy Mountain [LASSEN]: *peak,* 9.5 miles west-northwest of Bieber (lat. 41°09'20" N, long. 121°18'50" W; near SW cor. sec. 5, T 38 N, R 6 E). Altitude 5885 feet. Named on Fall River Mills (1961) 15' quadrangle.

Little Bear Creek [PLUMAS]: *stream,* flows 2.5 miles to Middle Fork Feather River 3.25 miles west of Dogwood Peak (lat. 39°47'25" N, long. 121°07' W). Named on Dogwood Peak (1979) 7.5' quadrangle.

Little Bear Lake [PLUMAS]: *lake,* 1000 feet long, 6 miles southwest of Clio (lat. 39°41'30" N, long. 120°40'15" W; at S line sec. 7, T 21 N, R 12 E). Named on Gold Lake (1981) 7.5' quadrangle. The feature is one of the group called Bear Lakes on Downieville (1897) 30' quadrangle

Little Blackhawk Creek [PLUMAS]: *stream,* flows 3.5 miles to Big Blackhawk Creek 4 miles north of Quincy (lat. 39°59'50" N, long. 120°57'20" W; near E line sec. 27, T 25 N, R 9 E). Named on Quincy (1950) 7.5' quadrangle. Called Blackhawk Creek on Quincy (1951) 15' quadrangle.

Little Canyon [MODOC]: *canyon,* drained by a stream that flows 2.25 miles to Surprise Valley 5.5 miles south of Cedarville (lat. 41° 27'15" N, long. 120°10'30" W; near N line sec. 5, T 41 N, R 16 E). Named on Warren Peak (1963) 7.5' quadrangle.

Little Cleghorn Reservoir [LASSEN]: *lake,* 3400 feet long, 6 miles east-southeast of Lava Peak (lat. 40°47'15" N, long. 120°47'40" W; on N line sec. 25, T 34 N, R 10 E); the lake is less than 1 mile northeast of Cleghorn Reservoir. Named on Hayden Hill (1956) 15' quadrangle.

Little Cottonwood Creek [MODOC]: *stream,* flows 2.5 miles to Surprise Valley 8.5 miles south of Cedarville (lat. 41°24'10" N, long. 120°09'05" W; sec. 21, T 41 N, R 16 E); the stream joins Cottonwood Creek (2) in Surprise Valley. Named on Warren Peak (1963) 7.5' quadrangle. United States Board on Geographic Names (1965a, p. 10) rejected the name "Mosquito Creek" for the stream.

Little Cottonwood Spring [LASSEN]: *spring,* 8 miles east of Wendel (lat. 40°22'20" N, long. 120°05'20" W; sec. 17, T 29 N, R 17 E). Named on Wendel (1954) 15' quadrangle.

Little Davis Creek [LASSEN]: *stream,* flows 4.25 miles to Dixie Valley 3.5 miles southeast of the village of Little Valley (lat. 40° 51'30" N, long. 121°07'40" W; near W line sec. 31, T 35 N, R 8 E); the stream enters Dixie Valley 0.5 mile west of the mouth of Davis Creek. Named on Little Valley (1957) 15' quadrangle.

Little Dooley Creek [PLUMAS]: *stream,* flows nearly 5 miles to Little Last Chance Creek 12.5 miles north-northwest of Chilcoot (lat. 39°58'10" N, long. 120°12'25" W; near N line sec. 5, T 24 N, R 16 E). Named on Frenchman Lake (1979) 7.5' quadrangle.

Little Dyer Mountain [LASSEN]: *peak,* 4 miles southwest of Westwood at Lassen-Plumas County line (lat. 40°16'05" N, long. 121° 03'30" W; sec. 23, T 28 N, R 8 E); the peak is 2.5 miles northwest of Dyer Mountain. Altitude 6367 feet. Named on Westwood West (1980) 7.5' quadrangle. Chester (1956) 15' quadrangle has the name "Little Dyer Mountain" for a feature located 2 miles farther east (sec. 19, T 28 N, R 9 E).

Little Egg Lake [MODOC]: *intermittent lake,* 0.5 mile long, 7.5 miles southwest of Crank Mountain (lat. 41°18'45" N, long. 121° 14'50" W; sec. 11, 14, T 40 N, R 6 E). Named on Crank Mountain (1962) and White Horse (1962) 15' quadrangles.

Little Fredonyer [LASSEN]:

(1) *peak,* 12 miles east-northeast of Pelican Point (lat. 40°41'20" N, long. 120°31'50" W; sec. 29, T 33 N, R 13 E); the peak is 3.5 miles east of Fredonyer Peak. Altitude 5847 feet. Named on Fedonyer Peak (1954) 15' quadrangle.

(2) *peak,* 11.5 miles northeast of Westwood (lat. 40°23'35" N, long. 120°49'20" W; sec. 11, T 29 N, R 10 E); the peak is 1.25 miles east-northeast of Fredonyer Butte. Altitude 5891 feet. Named on Roop Mountain (1980) 7.5' quadrangle.

Little Glazer Ridge [PLUMAS]: *ridge,* south-southwest-trending, 1 mile long, 10.5 miles south-southeast of Storrie (lat. 39°46'45" N, long. 121°15'10" W; mainly in sec. 12, T 22 N, R 6 E). Named on Soapstone Hill (1979) 7.5' quadrangle. Called Glazer Ridge on Pulga (1957) 15' quadrangle, but United States Board on Geographic Names (1979, p. 4) rejected this name.

Little Gold Hill [LASSEN]: *relief feature,* 5.5 miles south-southeast of Adin [MODOC] (lat. 41°07' N, long. 120°55' W; sec. 22, T 38 N, R 9 E). Named on Adin (1962) 15' quadrangle.

Little Grass Valley [PLUMAS]: *valley,* 4 miles north of La Porte along South Fork Feather River (lat. 39°44'15" N, long. 120°58'30" W). Named on La Porte (1951) and Onion Valley (1950) 7.5' quadrangles. The feature also was called Grass Valley and American Grass Valley (Gudde, 1975, p. 141, 195).

Little Grizzlie Spring [MODOC]: *spring,* nearly 4 miles north of South Mountain (lat. 41°53'30" N, long. 120°38'30" W; near NW cor. sec. 30, T 47 N, R 12 E). Named on South Mountain (1962) 15' quadrangle. Alturas (1954) 1°x 2° quadrangle shows Grizzly Springs Camp at the place.

Little Grizzly Creek [PLUMAS]:

(1) *stream,* flows 11.5 miles to Indian Creek (2) 4.25 miles east-southeast of Taylorsville (lat. 40°02'30" N, long. 120°46'05" W; sec. 8, T 25 N, R 11 E); the stream heads near Grizzly Valley. Named on Genesee Valley (1972), Mount Ingalls (1972), and Taylorsville (1980) 7.5' quadrangles. Preston (1890c, p. 476) called the stream Grizzly Creek, and noted that small copper-hearth furnaces were operated at a village called Wardtown that was situated near the mouth of present Little Grizzly Creek (1).

(2) *stream,* flows 1.25 miles to Grizzly Creek (2) 2.5 miles west-southwest of Bucks Lodge (lat. 39°51'55" N, long. 121°13'25" W; sec. 8, T 23 N, R 7 E). Named on Haskins Valley (1980) 7.5' quadrangle.

Little Grizzly Creek: see **Blakeless Creek** [PLUMAS].

Little Grizzly Valley [PLUMAS]: *area,* 10.5 miles southwest of the village of Almanor (lat. 40°07'35" N, long. 121°19'45" W; sec. 8, T 26 N, R 6 E); the place is along Grizzly Creek (1). Named on Jonesville (1958) 15' quadrangle.

Little Harvey Mountain [LASSEN]: *peak,* 12.5 miles west-northwest of Pelican Point (lat. 40°40'35" N, long. 120°58'20" W; sec. 33, T 33 N, R 9 E); the peak is 5.5 miles southeast of Harvey Mountain. Named on Antelope Mountain (1956) 15' quadrangle.

Little Harvey Valley [LASSEN]: *valley,* 13 miles west of Pelican Point (lat. 40°40'15" N, long. 120°59'30" W; around NW cor. sec. 5, T 32 N, R 9 E); the valley is 3 miles east-southeast of Harvey Valley. Named on Antelope Mountain (1956) and Harvey Mountain (1956) 15' quadrangles.

Little Haskell Peak [LASSEN]: *peak,* 4.5 miles south-southeast of Beckwourth Pass (lat. 39°43'45" N, long. 120°05' W; sec. 28, T 22 N, R 17 E); the peak is 1.25 miles north-northeast of Haskell Peak. Named on Evans Canyon (1978) 7.5' quadrangle.

Little Hat Mountain [LASSEN]: *peak,* 20 miles east of Madeline (lat. 41°04'05" N, long, 120°06'10" W; near S line sec. 13, T 37 N, R 16 E); the peak is 6 miles south of Hat Mountain. Altitude 7759 feet. Named on Little Hat Mountain (1962) 7.5' quadrangle. Called Hat Peak on Alturas 1° quadrangle.

Little Horse Mountain [MODOC] *hill,* 2 miles east-northeast of Newell (lat. 41°53'50" N, long. 121°19'45" W; sec. 19, T 47 N, R 6 E); the hill is 2 miles west of Horse Mountain (1). Altitude 4287 feet. Named on Tulelake (1951) 15' quadrangle.

Little Hot Spring [MODOC]: *spring,* 2 miles northwest of Day (lat. 41°13'50" N, long. 121°24'15" W; near W line sec. 9, T 39 N, R 5 E). Named on Fall River Mills (1961) 15' quadrangle. United States Board on Geographic Names (1990, p. 9) rejected the form "Little Hot Springs" for the name.

Little Hot Spring Valley [MODOC]: *valley,* center 1 mile west of Day (lat. 41°12'40" N, long. 121°23'45" W); Little Hot Spring is in the valley. Named on Fall River Mills (1961) 15' quadrangle. United States Board on Geographic Names (1964a, p. 11) rejected the form "Little Hot Springs Valley" for the name.

Little Jacks Lake [LASSEN]: *intermittent lake,* 1300 feet long, 10.5 miles southeast of the village of Little Valley (lat. 40°48'20" N, long. 121°01'05" W; near SE cor. sec. 13, T 34 N, R 8 E); the feature is southeast of Jacks Lake. Named on Little Valley (1957) 15' quadrangle.

Little Jackson Canyon [MODOC]: *canyon,* drained by a stream that flows 1 mile to Surprise Valley 7.5 miles south of Cedarville (lat. 41°24'55" N, long. 120°09'15" W; sec. 16, T 41 N, R 16 E); the mouth of the canyon is 650 feet south of the mouth of Jackson Canyon. Named on Warren Peak (1963) 7.5' quadrangle.

Little Jamison [PLUMAS]: *locality,* 6 miles west of Wash (present Clio) (lat. 39°44'25" N, long. 120°42' W); the place is along Little Jamison Creek. Named on Downieville (1897) 30' quadrangle.

Little Jamison Creek [PLUMAS]: *stream,* flows nearly 2 miles to Jamison Creek 6.5 miles west of Clio (lat. 39°44'45" N, long. 120° 42' W; near NW cor. sec. 25, T 22 N, R 11 E). Named on Gold Lake (1981) 7.5' quadrangle.

Little Jimmerson Spring [LASSEN]: *spring,* 5.5 miles west-northwest of Bieber (lat. 41°09'05" N, long. 121°14'15" W; on E line sec. 11, T 38 N, R 6 E). Named on Bieber (1961) 15' quadrangle.

Little Juniper Creek [MODOC]: *stream,* flows 9.5 miles to lowlands along South Fork Pit River 10.5 miles south of Alturas (lat. 41°20'20" N, long. 120°30'40" W; near NW cor. sec. 5, T 40 N, R 13 E); the stream is 1.5 miles north of Big Juniper Creek. Named on Alturas (1961) 15' quadrangle, and on Little Juniper Reservoir (1963) and Soup Creek (1963) 7.5' quadrangles.

Little Juniper Reservoir [MODOC]: *lake,* behind a dam on Little Juniper Creek 10.5 miles south-southeast of Alturas (lat. 41°20'25" N, long. 120°28'55" W; near N line sec. 4, T 40 N, R 13 E). Named on Little Juniper Reservoir (1963) 7.5' quadrangle.

Little Last Chance Creek [PLUMAS]: *stream,* flows 17 miles to a point 2 miles northwest of Chilcoot (lat. 39°49'25" N, long. 120° 09'40" W; near NW cor. sec. 26, T 23 N, R 16 E), where it divides to form North Channel Little Last Chance Creek and East Channel Little Last Chance Creek. Named on Chilcoot (1979), Frenchman Lake (1979), and McKesick Peak (1978) 7.5' quadrangles. Called Last Chance Creek on Sierraville (1894) 30' quadrangle. United States Board on Geographic Names (1974b, p. 3) gave the variant name "Middle Fork Feather River" for Little Last Chance Creek and for North Channel Little Last Chance Creek.

Little Last Chance Lake [PLUMAS]: *lake,* about 1 mile long, 9 miles east-southeast of Portola (lat. 39°46'35" N, long. 120°18'15" W; sec. 9, T 22 N, R 15 E). Named on Reconnaissance Peak (1972) 7.5' quadrangle.

Little Last Chance Valley [PLUMAS]: *valley,* along Little Last Chance Creek above a point 8.5 miles north-northwest of Chilcoot (lat. 39°54'50" N, long. 120°12'10" W). Named on Chilcoot (1950) 15' quadrangle. Called Last Chance Valley on Sierraville (1894) 30' quadrangle. Water of Frenchman Lake now floods most of the valley.

Little Lavas [MODOC]: *relief feature,* 8 miles northwest of Crank Mountain (lat. 41°28'30" N, long. 121°14' W). Named on Crank Mountain (1962) 15' quadrangle.

Little Lily Lake [MODOC]: *lake,* 250 feet long, 8 miles north-northwest of Fort Bidwell (lat. 41°57'25" N, long. 120°13'15" W; sec. 11, T 47 N, R 15 E). Named on Fort Bidwell (1962) 15' quadrangle. Called Lily Lake on Hill's (1915) map.

Little Long Valley Creek [PLUMAS]: *stream,* flows 4.5 miles to Long Valley Creek 7.5 miles northwest of Blairsden in Long Valley (lat. 39°51'55" N, long. 120°42'30" W; near N line sec. 14, T 23 N, R 11 E). Named on Johnsville (1972) and Mount Ingalls (1972) 7.5' quadrangles.

Little Marble Cone [PLUMAS]: *peak,* 4.25 miles northwest of Cascade (lat. 39°44'55" N, long. 121°13'25" W; sec. 20, T 22 N, R 7 E). Named on Cascade (1948) 7.5' quadrangle.

Little Meadows Campground [MODOC]: *locality,* 20 miles south-southeast of Alturas along South Fork Pit River (lat. 41°13'55" N, long. 120°21'50" W; sec. 9, T 39 N, R 14 E). Named on Jess Valley (1962) 7.5' quadrangle.

Little Merrill Flat [LASSEN]: *valley,* 8.5 miles southwest of Pelican Point (lat. 40°02'10" N, long. 120°50'20" W); the valley is 2.5 miles northeast of Big Merrill Flat. Named on Antelope Mountain (1956) 15' quadrangle.

Little Mud Flat [LASSEN]: *dry lake,* 1.5 miles long, 6.5 miles north of Wendel (lat. 40°26'30" N, long. 120°13'15" W; sec. 19, 30, T 30 N, R 16 E); the feature is 3 miles southeast of Mud Flat. Named on Wendel (1954) 15' quadrangle.

Little Mud Lake [MODOC]: *lake,* 2900 feet long, 7.5 miles east-southeast of Fort Bidwell (lat. 41°48'10" N, long. 120°01'35" W; at NE cor. sec. 4, T 45 N, R 17 E). Named on Fort Bidwell (1962) 15' quadrangle.

Little North Fork Campground [PLUMAS]: *locality,* 10 miles south-southeast of Storrie along Little North Fork of Middle Fork Feather River (lat. 39°46'55" N, long. 121°15'30" W; near N line sec. 12, T 22 N, R 6 E). Named on Soapstone Hill (1979) 7.5' quadrangle.

Little North Valley Creek [PLUMAS]: *stream,* flows 2.5 miles to North Valley Creek 3.5 miles west-northwest of Storrie (lat. 39°55'45" N, long. 121°23' W; at S line sec. 14, T 24 N, R 5 E). Named on Kimshew Point (1979) 7.5' quadrangle.

Little Owl Creek [MODOC]: *stream,* flows 2 miles to Owl Creek 5 miles northwest of Eagleville (lat. 41°21'55" N, long. 120°10'35" W; at E line sec. 5, T 40 N, R 16 E). Named on Eagle Peak (1963) 7.5' quadrangle.

Little Parsnip Creek [LASSEN]: *stream,* flows 3.5 miles to Parsnip Creek 10 miles northeast of Madeline (lat. 41°09'45" N, long. 120° 20'55" W; sec. 3, T 38 N, R 14 E). Named on Jess Valley (1962) 7.5' quadrangle.

Little Peak [PLUMAS]: *peak,* 7 miles northwest of American House (lat. 39°43'45" N, long. 121°06'30" W; on N line sec. 32, T 22 N, R 8 E); the peak is 0.5 mile west-southwest of Big Peak. Named on American House (1948) 7.5' quadrangle.

Little Poplar Creek: see **Chris Creek** [PLUMAS].

Little Poplar Valley: see **Poplar Creek** [PLUMAS].

Little Porcupine Tank [MODOC]: *water feature,* nearly 3 miles southeast of Jacks Butte (lat. 41°33'35" N, long. 120°45'35" W; at S line sec. 13, T 43 N, R 10 E). Named on Jacks Butte (1962) 15' quadrangle.

Little Quaking Asp Spring [MODOC]: *spring,* 8.5 miles south of Timber Mountain (lat. 41°30'35" N, long. 121°19'10" W; sec. 6, T 42 N, R 6 E); the spring is 1 mile east of Quaking Asp Spring. Named on Timber Mountain (1952) 15' quadrangle.

Little Round Valley [LASSEN]: *area,* 9.5 miles south-southeast of Cal Mountain (lat. 40°32'45" N, long. 121°05'15" W; sec. 16, T 31 N, R 8 E). Named on Harvey Mountain (1956) 15' quadrangle, which shows marsh in the area.

Little Sand Butte [MODOC]: *hill,* 7 miles west-northwest of Timber Mountain (lat. 41°40'15" N, long. 121°25' W; sec. 8, T 44 N, R 5 E); the hill is

1.5 miles south of Big Sand Butte. Named on Timber Mountain (1952) 15' quadrangle.

Little Schneider Creek [PLUMAS]: *stream,* flows 3.25 miles to Meadow Valley Creek less than 1 mile east-southeast of the village of Meadow Valley (lat. 39°55'50" N, long. 121°02'35" W; near W line sec. 24, T 24 N, R 8 E); the mouth of the stream is 1 mile downstream from the mouth of Schneider Creek. Named on Meadow Valley (1980) 7.5' quadrangle.

Little Spring [PLUMAS]: *spring,* 12 miles east-southeast of Kettle Rock (lat. 40°06' N, long. 120°30'25" W; near N line sec. 22, T 26 N, R 13 E). Named on Babcock Peak (1972) 7.5' quadrangle.

Little Stony Creek [PLUMAS]: *stream,* flows nearly 4 miles to Last Chance Creek (2) 4 miles north-northeast of Squaw Valley Peak (lat. 40°05'15" N, long. 120°22'55" W; near S line sec. 22, T 26 N, R 14 E). Named on Squaw Valley Peak (1977) 7.5' quadrangle. Called Stony Creek on Milford (1950) 15' quadrangle, but United States Board on Geographic Names (1978a, p. 6) rejected this name for the stream.

Little Summit Lake [PLUMAS]: *lake,* 1450 feet long, 4 miles south-southwest of Mount Ingalls (lat. 39°56'20" N, long. 120°38'45" W; at NE cor. sec. 20, T 24 N, R 12 E); the lake is 1 mile west-northwest of Summit Lake (present Summit Marsh). Named on Mount Ingalls (1972) 7.5' quadrangle.

Little Troxel Point [LASSEN]: *promontory,* 2.25 miles northeast of Pelican Point on the east side of Eagle Lake (lat. 40°39'20" N, long. 120°42'40" W); the feature is 1.5 miles south of Troxel Point. Named on Fredonyer Peak (1954) 15' quadrangle.

Little Tuledad Canyon [LASSEN]: *canyon,* drained by a stream that flows 2 miles to Tuledad Valley 23 miles east of Madeline (lat. 41° 01'25" N, long. 120°01'30" W; at S line sec. 34, T 37 N, R 17 E). Named on Little Hat Mountain (1962) 7.5' quadrangle.

Little Tule Lake [LASSEN]: *lake,* 900 feet long, 11 miles south of Cal Mountain (lat. 40°30'30" N, long. 121°09'50" W; near N line sec. 35, T 31 N, R 7 E). Named on Harvey Mountain (1956) 15' quadrangle.

Little Valley [LASSEN]:
(1) *valley,* center about 1 mile southeast of the village of Little Valley (lat. 40°52'50" N, long. 121°10' W). Named on Little Valley (1957) 15' quadrangle. Called Ash Valley on Lassen Peak (1894) 1° quadrangle.
(2) *village,* 43 miles northwest of Susanville (lat. 40°53'35" N, long. 121°10'45" W; sec. 15, T 35 N, R 7 E); the place is in Little Valley (1). Named on Little Valley (1957) 15' quadrangle.

Little Valley [MODOC]: *valley,* nearly 3 miles southeast of the village of Davis Creek (lat. 41°42'35" N, long. 120°19'45" W; on W line sec. 26, T 45 N, R 14 E). Named on Davis Creek (1962) 15' quadrangle.

Little Volcano [PLUMAS]: *peak,* 6.25 miles south-southeast of Quincy (lat. 39°51'30" N, long. 120°53'35" W; near W line sec. 17, T 23 N, R 10 E). Altitude 5801 feet. Named on Onion Valley (1950) 7.5' quadrangle.

Little Willow Lake [PLUMAS]: *lake,* 750 feet long, 5 miles west-southwest of Mount Harkness (lat. 40°24'40" N, long. 121°23'20" W; near S line sec. 35, T 30 N, R 5 E); the lake is 1.5 miles west-northwest of Willow Lake at the head of Willow Creek (1). Named on Mount Harkness (1956) 15' quadrangle.

Locherman Canyon [PLUMAS]: *canyon,* drained by a stream that flows 3.5 miles to North Fork Feather River 8 miles south of Mount Harkness (lat. 40°19'15" N, long. 121°18'10" W; near N line sec. 3, T 28 N, R 6 E). Named on Mount Harkness (1956) 15' quadrangle.

Lodgepole [LASSEN]: *locality,* 5 miles southeast of Cal Mountain along Western Pacific Railroad (lat. 40°36'50" N, long. 121°06'20" W; on N line sec. 29, T 32 N, R 8 E). Named on Harvey Mountain (1956) 15' quadrangle.

Logan Mountain [LASSEN]: *mountain,* 10 miles west of Pelican Point (lat. 40°38'35" N, long. 120°55'35" W; on N line sec. 14, T 32 N, R 9 E). Named on Antelope Mountain (1956) 15' quadrangle. The name commemorates Griffin Logan, a sheepherder who was murdered on the mountain in 1885 (Purdy, 1888, p. 120).

Logan Slough [MODOC]: *stream,* flows 8.5 miles to Big Sage Reservoir 13 miles north-northwest of Alturas (lat. 41°39'25" N, long. 120°39'25" W; near W line sec. 13, T 44 N, R 11 E). Named on Big Sage Reservoir (1962) 15' quadrangle.

Logan Spring [LASSEN]: *spring,* 12.5 miles west of Pelican Point (lat. 40°39'10" N, long. 120°58'35" W; at E line sec. 8, T 32 N, R 9 E); the spring is 2.5 miles west-northwest of Logan Mountain. Named on Antelope Mountain (1956) 15' quadrangle.

Logan Spring [MODOC]: *spring,* 14 miles north-northwest of Alturas (lat. 41°40'10" N, long. 120°38'40" W; sec. 12, T 44 N, R 11 E); the spring is near Logan Slough. Named on Big Sage Reservoir (1962) 15' quadrangle.

Log Corral Spring [MODOC]: *spring,* nearly 6 miles northeast of Crank Mountain (lat. 41°26'45" N, long 121°04' W; on S line sec. 29, T 42 N, R 8 E). Named on Crank Mountain (1962) 15' quadrangle.

Logue Meadows [PLUMAS]: *area,* nearly 5 miles west-southwest of Storrie (lat. 39°53'35" N, long. 121°24'25" W; near W line sec. 34, T 24 N, R 5 E). Named on Kimshew Point (1979) 7.5' quadrangle.

Lone Pine Butte [MODOC]: *peak,* 8.5 miles north of Hackamore (lat. 41°40'35" N, long. 121°05'45" W). Altitude 4965 feet. Named on Hackamore (1952) 15' quadrangle.

Lone Pine Lake [MODOC]: *intermittent lake,* 4700 feet long, 12 miles north of Hackamore (lat. 41°43'45" N, long. 121°07' W; sec. 23, 24, T 45 N, R 7 E). Named on Hackamore (1952) 15' quadrangle.

Lone Rock [PLUMAS]: *peak,* 7.25 miles north of Kettle Rock (lat. 40°14'40" N, long. 120°42'30" W; sec. 35, T 28 N, R 11 E). Altitude 5998 feet. Named on Kettle Rock (1972) 7.5' quadrangle.

Lone Rock Campground [PLUMAS]: *locality,* 7.25 miles northeast of Kettle Rock (lat. 40°11'45" N, long. 120°37' W; sec. 15, T 27 N, R 12 E); the place is at the mouth of Lone Rock Creek. Named on Antelope Lake (1972) 7.5' quadrangle.

Lone Rock Creek [PLUMAS]: *stream,* flows 7.25 miles to Antelope Lake 7 miles northeast of Kettle Rock (lat. 40°11'45" N, long. 120° 37'15" W; near W line sec. 15, T 27 N, R 12 E); the stream heads near Lone Rock. Named on Antelope Lake (1972) and Kettle Rock (1972) 7.5' quadrangles.

Lone Rock Valley [PLUMAS]: *valley,* along Lone Rock Creek above a point 6.25 miles north-northeast of Kettle Rock (lat. 40°13'45" N, long. 120°40'45" W; near W line sec. 6, T 27 N, R 12 E). Named on Kettle Rock (1972) 7.5' quadrangle.

Lone Rock Valley: see **Lower Lone Rock Valley** [PLUMAS].

Lonesome Canyon [PLUMAS]: *canyon,* drained by a stream that flows 1.5 miles to Lone Rock Creek 5.5 miles north-northeast of Kettle Rock (lat. 40°12'50" N, long. 120°40'15" W; sec. 7, T 27 N, R 12 E). Named on Kettle Rock (1972) 7.5' quadrangle.

Lone Spring [PLUMAS]: *spring,* 4 miles southwest of Milford [LASSEN] (lat. 40°07'55" N, long. 120°25'25" W; near S line sec. 5, T 26 N, R 14 E). Named on Stony Ridge (1978) 7.5' quadrangle.

Lone Spring Mountain [PLUMAS]: *ridge,* generally northwest-trending, 1.25 miles long, 3.5 miles southwest of Milford [LASSEN] (lat. 40°08' N, long. 120°25'15" W); the ridge is northeast of Lone Spring. Named on Stony Ridge (1978) 7.5' quadrangle.

Long Bell Station [MODOC]: *locality,* 11 miles north of White Horse (lat. 41°28'15" N, long. 121°24'45" W; near N line sec. 20, T 42 N, R 5 E). Named on White Horse (1962) 15' quadrangle.

Long Billy Spring [MODOC]: *spring,* 5.5 miles east-northeast of Lookout (lat. 41°14'30" N, long. 121°03'15" W; on N line sec. 9, T 39 N, R 8 E). Named on Bieber (1961) 15' quadrangle.

Long Branch [MODOC]: *stream,* flows 5.25 miles to Goose Lake (1) 7.5 miles east-northeast of South Mountain (lat. 41°52'45" N, long. 120°30'10" W; sec. 32, T 47 N, R 13 E). Named on South Mountain (1962) 15' quadrangle.

Long Canyon [LASSEN]:
(1) *canyon,* drained by a stream that flows about 4 miles to Coyote Flat (2) 7 miles east-northeast of Termo (lat. 40°53'50" N, long. 120°20'20" W; sec. 13, T 35 N, R 14 E). Named on Ravendale (1954) 15' quadrangle.
(2) *canyon,* drained by a stream that flows 4 miles to Petes Valley 8.5 miles west of Karlo (lat. 40°32'05" N, long. 120°28'30" W; sec. 23, T 31 N, R 13 E). Named on Fredonyer Peak (1954) and Karlo (1954) 15' quadrangles.

Long Canyon [MODOC]: *canyon,* drained by a stream that flows 5 miles to Surprise Valley 4 miles east of Fort Bidwell (lat. 41°52'05" N, long. 120°04'40" W; near E line sec. 12, T 46 N, R 16 E). Named on Fort Bidwell (1962) 15' quadrangle.

Long Canyon [PLUMAS]: *canyon,* drained by a stream that flows 2 miles to Red Clover Valley 9 miles north of Portola (lat. 39°56'30" N, long. 120°27'25" W; near E line sec. 13, T 24 N, R 13 E). Named on Crocker Mountain (1972) 7.5' quadrangle.

Long Canyon: see **Cottonwood Canyon** [LASSEN] (2).

Long Flat [LASSEN]: *area,* 7 miles north-northeast of Lava Peak (lat. 40°55'20" N, long. 120°50'40" W; in and near sec. 29, T 36 N, R 10 E). Named on Hayden Hill (1956) 15' quadrangle.

Long Hill [LASSEN]: *ridge,* northwest-trending, 3 miles long, 7 miles southeast of Adin [MODOC] (lat. 41°08'20" N, long. 120° 50' W). Named on Adin (1962) 15' quadrangle.

Long Lake [LASSEN]:
(1) *intermittent lake,* 3000 feet long, 9 miles southeast of the village of Little Valley (lat. 40°47'50" N, long. 121°03'35" W; sec. 22, T 34 N, R 8 E); the feature is in Long Valley (1). Named on Little Valley (1957) 15' quadrangle.
(2) *intermittent lake,* 1 mile long, 13 miles southeast of Harvey Mountain (lat. 40°30'50" N, long. 121°01'15" W; at and near SE cor. sec. 25, T 31 N, R 8 E). Named on Harvey Mountain (1956) 15' quadrangle. Called Anna L. on Halls Flat (1939) 30' quadrangle.
(3) *lake,* 2400 feet long, 15 miles northwest of Westwood (lat. 40° 27'50" N, long. 121°12'20" W; sec. 16, T 30 N, R 7 E). Named on Red Cinder (1979) 7.5' quadrangle.

Long Lake [PLUMAS]:
(1) *lake,* 1800 feet long, 5.5 miles north-northwest of Storrie (lat. 39°59'30" N, long. 121°21'40" W; sec. 30, T 25 N, R 6 E). Named on Storrie (1979) 7.5' quadrangle. On Bidwell Bar (1897) 30' quadrangle, present Long Lake (1) and nearby Campbell Lake together are called Campbells Lakes, but

United States Board on Geographic Names (1960b, p. 9) rejected this name.

(2) *lake,* 4500 feet long, 6 miles west-southwest of Clio along Gray Eagle Creek (lat. 39°42' N, long. 120°40'50" W). Named on Gold Lake (1981) 7.5' quadrangle.

Long Meadow [MODOC]: *area,* 7.5 miles north of South Mountain (lat. 41°56'50" N, long. 120°38'45" W; on W line sec. 6, T 47 N, R 12 E). Named on South Mountain (1962) 15' quadrangle.

Long Point [PLUMAS]: *peninsula,* 8.5 miles east-northeast of Kettle Rock along Antelope Lake (lat. 40°10'45" N, long. 120°35' W; near S line sec. 24, T 27 N, R 12 E). Named on Antelope Lake (1972) 7.5' quadrangle.

Long Ravine [PLUMAS]: *canyon,* drained by a stream that flows 1.5 miles to Swamp Creek 5 miles southwest of Storrie (lat. 39°53'15" N, long. 121°23'35" W; near SE cor. sec. 34, T 24 N, R 5 E). Named on Kimshew Point (1979) 7.5' quadrangle.

Long Reservoir [LASSEN]: *lake,* 900 feet long, 5.25 miles north-northeast of Lava Peak (lat. 40°53'55" N, long. 120°50'15" W; sec. 15, T 35 N, R 10 E). Named on Hayden Hill (1956) 15' quadrangle.

Long Spring [LASSEN]: *spring,* 10 miles northeast of Termo (lat. 40°57'35" N, long. 120°19'20" W; near W line sec. 30, T 36 N, R 15 E). Named on Ravendale (1954) 15' quadrangle.

Long Valley [LASSEN]:

(1) *valley,* 10 miles southeast of the village of Little Valley (lat. 40° 47'45" N, long. 121°03' W; sec. 22, 23, T 34 N, R 8 E). Named on Little Valley (1957) 15' quadrangle.

(2) *valley,* along Long Valley Creek at Doyle and southeast to Constantia. Named on Doyle (1954) 15' quadrangle, and on Constantia (1977) 7.5' quadrangle. The north part of the feature is called Upper Long Valley on Honey Lake (1893) 1° quadrangle.

Long Valley [LASSEN-MODOC]: *valley,* 4 miles long, 15 miles east-northeast of Madeline on Lassen-Modoc County line, mainly in Lassen County (lat. 41°10' N, long. 120°14' W). Named on Emerson Peak (1962) 7.5' quadrangle.

Long Valley [PLUMAS]:

(1) *canyon,* 1.5 miles long, along Rush Creek above a point about 6.5 miles north-northeast of Twain (lat. 40°06'40" N, long. 121° 01'30" W). Named on Canyondam (1979) and Twain (1980) 7.5' quadrangles.

(2) *valley,* 8 miles northwest of Blairsden (lat. 39°52' N, long. 120° 42'30" W). Named on Johnsville (1972) 7.5' quadrangle.

Long Valley: see **Constantia** [LASSEN]; **Upper Long Valley** [LASSEN].

Long Valley Creek [LASSEN]: *stream,* heads in Sierra County and flows 44 miles in Lassen County to Honey Lake 11.5 miles northwest of Doyle (lat. 40°09'10" N, long. 120°15' W). Named on Doyle (1954) 15' quadrangle, and on Beckwourth Pass (1975), Constantia (1977), and Evans Canyon (1978) 7.5' quadrangles. United States Board on Geographic Names (1978a, p. 6) rejected the name "Dry Valley Creek" for the stream.

Long Valley Creek [PLUMAS]: *stream,* flows 9.5 miles to Middle Fork Feather River 8.5 miles northwest of Blairsden (lat. 39°51'55" N, long. 120°43'55" W; near N line sec. 15, T 23 N, R 11 E); the stream goes through Long Valley (2). Named on Blairsden (1972), Grizzly Valley (1972), Johnsville (1972), and Mount Ingalls (1972) 7.5' quadrangles. South Fork enters from the south 6.5 miles north of Blairsden; it is nearly 3 miles long and is named on Blairsden (1972) and Johnsville (1972) 7.5' quadrangles.

Long Valley Creek: see **Little Long Valley Creek** [PLUMAS].

Longville [PLUMAS]: *locality,* about 6 miles southwest of the village of Almanor (lat. 40°08'55" N, long. 121°14'35" W; near S line sec. 31, T 27 N, R 7 E). Named on Almanor (1979) 7.5' quadrangle. Longville post office was established in 1861 and discontinued in 1918; the name was for W.B. Long, who built a hotel and sawmill at the place (Salley, p. 126).

Lonkey Hill [LASSEN]: *ridge,* north-northwest-trending, 2.5 miles long, 9.5 miles south-southeast of Adin [MODOC] (lat. 41°03'45" N, long. 120°54' W). Named on Adin (1962) 15' quadrangle.

Loody Springs [MODOC]: *springs,* 5.5 miles south of Crank Mountain (lat. 41°18'25" N, long. 121°09'30" W; near W line sec. 15, T 40 N, R 7 E). Named on Crank Mountain (1962) 15' quadrangle.

Lookout [MODOC]: *village,* 11 miles west of Adin (lat. 41°12'30" N, long. 121°09' W; sec. 22, T 39 N, R 7 E). Named on Bieber (1961) 15' quadrangle. The community received the name "Lookout" about 1860 because Indians had kept lookout for their enemies on a hill above the place (Gudde, 1949, p. 193). Postal authorities established Whitley's Ford post office 12 miles west of Adin in 1874 and discontinued it in 1875; they established Lookout post office at the site in 1880; the name "Whitley's Ford" was for James W. Whitley, pioneer hotel and livery-stable keeper at the ford of Pit River (Salley, p. 126, 239). They established Wade post office 12 miles north of Lookout in 1880 and discontinued it in 1881; the name was for Pinkston Wade, first postmaster (Salley, p. 233). They established Hillside post office in Lassen County 12 miles south of Lookout in 1880 and discontinued it in 1881 (Salley, p. 98). They established Craig post office 10 miles north of Lookout in 1886 and discontinued it in 1903; the name was for Robert A. Craig, first postmaster (Salley, p. 52). They established Mud Lake post office 20 miles north of Lookout in 1886, discontinued it in 1888, and reestablished it in 1889; they changed the post office name to Fleener in 1889, and discontinued it in 1893—the name "Fleener" was for Sam Fleener, a pioneer homesteader in the neighborhood (Salley, p. 75). They established Potter post office 12 miles northwest of Lookout in 1889 and discontinued it in 1896; the name was for Richard R. Potter, first postmaster (Salley, p. 177).

Lookout Creek [PLUMAS]: *stream,* flows 5.5 miles to Little Last Chance Creek 12 miles north-northwest of Chilcoot (lat. 39°57'50" N, long. 120°12'30" W; sec. 5, T 24 N, R 16 E). Named on Dixie Mountain (1972) and Frenchman Lake (1979) 7.5' quadrangles.

Lookout Junction [MODOC]: *locality,* 10 miles south-southwest of Crank Mountain along Great Northern Railroad (lat. 41°15'30" N, long. 121°14' W; sec. 36, T 40 N, R 6 E). Named on Crank Mountain (1962) 15' quadrangle.

Lookout Rock [PLUMAS]: *relief feature,* 4.5 miles northwest of Dogwood Peak (lat. 39°50' N, long. 121°06'45" W; near S line sec. 20, T 23 N, R 8 E). Named on Dogwood Peak (1979) 7.5' quadrangle.

Lookout Siding [MODOC]: *locality,* 5 miles northwest of Lookout along Great Northern Railroad (lat. 41°14'40" N, long. 121°13'35" W; sec. 1, T 39 N, R 6 E). Named on Bieber (1961) 15' quadrangle. Called Modoc on Alturas (1954) 1°x 2° quadrangle.

Loomis Reservoir [LASSEN]: *intermittent lake,* 300 feet long, 5 miles north-northeast of the village of Little Valley (lat. 40°57'40" N, long. 121°08'30"W; near E line sec. 15, T 36 N, R 7 E). Named on Little Valley (1957) 15' quadrangle.

Lost Cabin Spring [PLUMAS]: *spring,* 6.5 miles south-southeast of Quincy (lat. 39°51'25" N, long. 121°52'40" W; near E line sec. 17, T 23 N, R 10 E). Named on Onion Valley (1950) 7.5' quadrangle.

Lost Creek [PLUMAS]:

(1) *stream,* flows 1.5 miles to Antelope Lake 7.5 miles east-northeast of Kettle Rock (lat. 40°11'35" N, long. 120°35'35" W; near S line sec. 14, T 27 N, R 12 E). Named on Antelope Lake (1972) 7.5' quadrangle.

(2) *stream,* flows 10 miles to Butte County 5 miles southwest of American House (lat. 39°36'50" N, long. 121°05'45" W; near SW cor. sec. 4, T 20 N, R 8 E). Named on American House (1948) and Strawberry Valley (1948) 7.5' quadrangles.

Lost Hill [MODOC]: *peak,* 15 miles north of Alturas (lat. 41°42'30" N, long. 120°33'25" W; sec. 26, T 45 N, R 12 E). Named on Big Sage Reservoir (1962) 15' quadrangle.

Lost Lake [LASSEN]: *lake,* 850 feet long, 19 miles east-northeast of Madeline (lat. 41°09'20" N, long. 120°08'20" W; near S line sec. 15, T 38 N, R 16 E); the lake is at the head of Silver Creek.. Named on Emerson Peak (1962) 7.5' quadrangle. Called Silver Lake on California Mining Bureau's (1917a) map

Lost Lake [PLUMAS]:

(1) *lake,* 500 feet long, 13 miles west-southwest of the village of Almanor (lat. 40°08'10" N, long. 121°23'50" W; sec. 3, T 26 N, R 5 E). Named on Jonesville (1958) 15' quadrangle.

(2) *lake,* 700 feet long, 6.5 miles north of Bucks Lodge (lat. 39°58'15" N, long. 121°10'30" W; near NE cor. sec. 3, T 24 N, R 7 E). Named on Bucks Lake (1979) 7.5' quadrangle.

Lost Meadows [LASSEN]: *area,* 5 miles south of Susanville (lat. 40° 20'55" N, long. 120°38'40" W; at NE cor. sec. 29, T 29 N, R 12 E). Named on Diamond Mountain (1972) 7.5' quadrangle.

Lost Reservoir [MODOC]: *lake,* 1600 feet long, nearly 6 miles east-southeast of White Horse (lat. 41°17'15" N, long. 121°17'30" W; near SW cor. sec. 21, T 40 N, R 6 E). Named on White Horse (1962) 15' quadrangle.

Lost River [MODOC]: *stream,* heads in Clear Lake Reservoir and flows 11.5 miles to the State of Oregon 16 miles north of Double Head Mountain (lat. 41°59'50" N, long. 121°12'30" W; sec. 18, T 48 N, R 7 E). Named on Clear Lake Reservoir (1951) 15' quadrangle. Fremont discovered the stream in 1846 and called it McCrady River for a boyhood friend of his (McArthur, p. 454). The name "Lost River" is from disappearance of the stream between Clear Lake Reservoir and Tule Lake (Gudde, 1949, p. 195). East Branch heads in the State of Oregon and enters the main stream from the east 2 miles upstream from the California-Oregon State line; it is 1.5 miles long in Modoc County and is named on Clear Lake Reservoir (1951) 15' quadrangle. United States Board on Geographic Names (1963, p. 14) rejected the names "Antelope Creek" and "East Fork Lost River" for East Branch.

Lost Spring [LASSEN]:

(1) *spring,* nearly 4 miles northeast of Cal Mountain (lat. 40°42'15" N, long. 121°06'25" W; hear S line sec. 20, T 33 N, R 8 E). Named on Harvey Mountain (1956) 15' quadrangle.

(2) *spring,* 8 miles southwest of Cal Mountain (lat. 40°35'05" N, long. 121°16'15" W; on S line sec. 35, T 32 N, R 6 E). Named on Prospect Peak (1957) 15' quadrangle.

Lost Valley [MODOC]: *area,* 6.5 miles west-northwest of Jacks Butte (lat. 41°37'30" N, long. 120°55' W; in and near sec. 27, T 44 N, R 9 E). Named on Jacks Butte (1962) 15' quadrangle.

Lost Valley Reservoir [LASSEN]: *lake,* 1100 feet long, 9 miles north-northwest of Lava Peak (lat. 40°56'25" N, long. 120°58'40" W; sec. 19, T 36 N, R 9 E). Named on Hayden Hill (1956) 15' quadrangle.

Lotts Lake [PLUMAS]: *lake,* 1900 feet long, 18 miles southwest of the village of Almanor (lat. 40°01'25" N, long. 121°23'40" W; sec. 15, T 25 N, R 5 E). Named on Jonesville (1958) 15' quadrangle.

Louisa Lake: see **Juniper Lake** [LASSEN-PLUMAS].

Louse Creek [PLUMAS]: *stream,* flows nearly 3 miles to North Fork Feather River 9 miles south of Mount Harkness (lat. 40°18'25" N, long. 121°16'10" W; at NW cor. sec. 12, T 28 N, R 6 E). Named on Mount Harkness (1956) 15' quadrangle.

Louse Spring [PLUMAS]: *spring,* 4 miles south of Mount Harkness (lat. 40°22'20" N, long. 121°17'20" W; near E line sec. 15, T 29 N, R 6 E); the spring is along Louse Creek. Named on Mount Harkness (1956) 15' quadrangle.

Lovejoy [PLUMAS]: *locality,* nearly 4 miles south-southwest of Mount Ingalls (lat. 39°56'40" N, long. 120°39'20" W; sec. 17, T 24 N, R 12 E). Site named on Mount Ingalls (1972) 7.5' quadrangle. Called Lovejoys on Downieville (1897) 30' quadrangle.

Lovejoy Creek [PLUMAS]: *stream,* flows 1 mile to Little Grizzly Creek 5 miles south-southwest of Mount Ingalls (lat. 39°56'40" N, long. 120°39'35" W; near W line sec. 17, T 24 N, R 12 E); the site of Lovejoy is at the mouth of the stream. Named on Mount Ingalls (1972) 7.5' quadrangle.

Loveland Gulch [LASSEN]: *canyon,* drained by a stream that flows nearly 2 miles to Lower Gooch Valley 2.5 miles south-southeast of Lava Peak (lat. 40°48' N, long. 120°52' W; near E line sec. 20, T 34 N, R 10 E). Named on Hayden Hill (1956) 15' quadrangle.

Lowe Flat [PLUMAS]: *area,* 5 miles southwest of Janesville [LASSEN] along Boulder Creek (1) (lat. 40°15'10" N, long. 120°36'10" W; near W line sec. 26, T 28 N, R 12 E). Named on Janesville (1972) 7.5' quadrangle.

Lower Alkali Lake: see **Lower Lake** [MODOC].

Lower Bear Valley [MODOC]: *valley,* 9 miles south-southeast of Willow Ranch (lat. 41°47'30" N, long. 120°16' W; on S line sec. 4, T 45 N, R 15 E); the valley is 1 mile west-northwest of Bear Valley. Named on Willow Ranch (1962) 15' quadrangle.

Lower Bucks Lake [PLUMAS]: *lake,* behind a dam on Bucks Creek 3.25 miles west-northwest of Bucks Lodge (lat. 39°54'05" N, long. 121°13'40" W; near SW cor. sec. 29, T 24 N, R 7 E); the dam that forms the lake is 1.5 miles downstream from the dam that forms Bucks Lake. Named on Bucks Lake (1979) 7.5' quadrangle.

Lower Cummings Reservoir [MODOC]: *intermittent lake,* 1700 feet long, nearly 6 miles west-northwest of Alturas (lat. 41°30'55" N, long. 120°38'50" W; on S line sec. 36, T 43 N, R 11 E); the feature is 2 miles south of Upper Cummings Reservoir. Named on Big Sage Reservoir (1962) 15' quadrangle.

Lower Dry Lake [LASSEN]: *intermittent lake,* 1900 feet long, 4 miles east-southeast of Pelican Point (lat. 40°36'50" N, long. 120° 40'20" W; at NE cor. sec. 25, T 32 N, R 11 E). Named on Fredonyer Peak (1954) 15' quadrangle.

Lower Gooch Valley [LASSEN]: *valley,* 3.5 miles south-southeast of Lava Peak (lat. 40°47'15" N, long. 120°51'30" W); the valley is 3 miles south-southeast of Upper Gooch Valley. Named on Hayden Hill (1956) 15' quadrangle.

Lower Hot Springs: see **Amedee** [LASSEN].

Lower Indian Bar: see **Yellow Creek** [PLUMAS].

Lower Lake [MODOC]: *intermittent lake,* 7.5 miles long, center about 6 miles southeast of Cedarville (lat. 41°15' N, long. 120°02'30" W); the feature is at the south end of Surprise Valley, and the southeast end is in the State of Nevada. Named on Eagleville (1963) and Snake Lake (1962) 7.5' quadrangles. Called Lower Alkali Lake on Wheeler's (1877) map.

Lower Lone Rock Valley [PLUMAS]: *valley,* 5 miles northeast of Kettle Rock (lat. 40°12' N, long. 120°39'30" W; sec. 17, 18, T 27 N, R 12 E); the valley is along Lone Rock Creek about 2 miles downstream from Lone Rock Valley. Named on Kettle Rock (1972) 7.5' quadrangle.

Lower McBride Springs [LASSEN]: *springs,* 14 miles south-southeast of Adin [MODOC] (lat. 41°01' N, long. 120°50' W; at W line sec. 28, T 37 N, R 10 E). Named on Adin (1962) 15' quadrangle.

Lower Muldoon Tank [MODOC]: *water feature,* 10.5 miles north-northwest of South Mountain (lat. 41°59'05" N, long. 120°41'30" W; near S line sec. 22, T 48 N, R 11 E); the feature is 1 mile southeast of Upper Muldoon Tank. Named on South Mountain (1962) 15' quadrangle.

Lower Roberts Reservoir [MODOC]: *lake,* nearly 2 miles long, 2 miles north of Lookout (lat. 41°14'15" N, long. 121°09' W); the lake is 4 miles southeast of Upper Roberts Reservoir. Named on Bieber (1961) 15' quadrangle. Called Roberts Lower Reservoir on California Division of Highways' (1934) map.

Lower Rush Creek Campground [MODOC]: *locality,* 10.5 miles south of Canby (lat. 41°17'35" N, long. 120°52'40" W; near E line sec. 24, T 40 N, R 9 E); the place is along Rush Creek 1.5 miles downstream from Upper Rush Creek Campground. Named on Canby (1961) 15' quadrangle.

Lower Signal Butte [LASSEN]: *peak,* 5.5 miles north-northwest of Pelican Point (lat. 40°42'30" N, long. 120°46'45" W; sec. 19, T 33 N, R 10 E); the peak is 1.5 miles south-southeast of Signal Butte. Altitude 5907 feet. Named on Antelope Mountain (1956) 15' quadrangle.

Lower Taylor [PLUMAS]: *peak,* 6 miles north of Spring Garden (lat. 39°58'55" N, long. 120°48'10" W; near SW cor. sec. 31, T 25 N, R 11 E); the peak is nearly 1.5 miles south-southeast of Taylor Rock. Altitude 7024 feet. Named on Spring Garden (1950) 7.5' quadrangle.

L-T Creek [PLUMAS]: *stream,* flows 3 miles to Soda Creek (1) 12.5 miles southwest of the village of Almanor (lat. 40°04'55" N, long. 121°19'25" W; near W line sec. 28, T 26 N, R 6 E). Named on Jonesville (1958) 15' quadrangle.

Lumpkin Ridge [PLUMAS]: *ridge,* southwest-trending, 9 miles long, center 4 miles northwest of American House (lat. 39°41'15" N, long. 121°05'10" W). Named on American House (1948) and Cascade (1948) 7.5' quadrangles. The southwest end of the ridge is in Butte County.

Lunsford Spring [MODOC]: *spring,* 18 miles south-southwest of Alturas (lat. 41°17' N, long. 120°44'40" W; at NW cor. sec. 29, T 40 N, R 11 E). Named on Alturas (1961) 15' quadrangle.

Lynch Meadows [PLUMAS]: *area,* 4.25 miles west of Storrie (lat. 39°54'30" N, long. 121°24' W; sec. 27, T 24 N, R 5 E). Named on Kimshew Point (1979) 7.5' quadrangle.

—M—

Mabie [PLUMAS]: *locality,* 5 miles east of Blairsden along Western Pacific Railroad (lat. 39°47'35" N, long. 120°31'15" W; near S line sec. 4, T 22 N, R 13 E). Named on Blairsden (1972) 7.5' quadrangle.

Mac Afee Flat [MODOC]: *area,* 4.25 miles southeast of White Horse (lat. 41°15'50" N, long. 121°20'40" W; sec. 36, T 40 N, R 5 E). Named on White Horse (1962) 15' quadrangle.

Madeline [LASSEN]: *village,* 45 miles north-northeast of Susanville (lat. 41°03'05" N, long. 120°28'25" W; near E line sec. 9, T 37 N, R 13 E); the village is in Madeline Plains. Named on Madeline (1962) 7.5' quadrangle. Honey Lake (1893) 1° quadrangle has the name "Madeline" for an inhabited place located 26 miles north of Susanville near the south end of Grasshopper Valley (lat. 40° 47'45" N, long. 120°42'50" W). Postal authorities established Madeline post office in 1875, discontinued it in 1878, reestablished it in 1879, discontinued it in 1882, reestablished it in 1887, and moved it 4 miles north in 1902 (Salley, p. 130). California Mining Bureau's (1909a) map shows a stage stop called Moll Ranch located 17 miles northwest of Madeline. California Mining Bureau's (1917a) map shows a place called Prockmans located 7 miles south of Madeline along the railroad. Postal authorities established Ashton post office 13 miles west of Madeline in 1889, moved it 1 mile northeast in 1897, and discontinued it in 1900; the name was from the location of the place along Ash Creek (Salley, p. 11). They established Roscoe post office 21 miles east of Madeline in 1903 and discontinued it in 1905 (Salley, p. 188).

Madeline Plains [LASSEN]: *valley,* extends south from Madeline to Termo, and east nearly to the State of Nevada. Named on Grasshopper Valley (1954), Likely (1962), Observation Peak (1954), and Ravendale (1954) 15' quadrangles, and on Madeline (1962) 7.5' quadrangle. Indians killed a little girl at the place in the 1850's, and the name commemorates the child (Gudde, 1949, p. 201).

Madora Lake [PLUMAS]: *lake,* 1900 feet long, 3 miles west of Blairsden (lat. 39°47' N, long. 120°40'20" W; sec. 7, T 22 N, R 12 E). Named on Johnsville (1972) 7.5' quadrangle.

Magpie Flat [PLUMAS]: *area,* 5 miles northwest of the village of Meadow Valley (lat. 39°59'05" N, long. 121°07'25" W; sec. 31, T 25 N, R 8 E). Named on Meadow Valley (1980) 7.5' quadrangle.

Mahogany Lake [LASSEN]: *lake,* 1000 feet long, 7 miles south of Pelican Point (lat. 40°32' N, long. 120°43'55" W; near E line sec. 21, T 31 N, R 11 E). Named on Fredonyer Peak (1954) 15' quadrangle.

Mahogany Mountain [LASSEN]: *ridge,* generally north-trending, 2 miles long, 23 miles east-northeast of Madeline (lat. 41°06'30" N, long. 120°02'35" W; on S line sec. 33, T 38 N, R 17 E). Named on Little Hat Mountain (1962) 7.5' quadrangle. United States Board on Geographic Names (1983b, p. 6) rejected the form "Mahagony Mountain" for the name.

Mahogany Peak [LASSEN]: *peak,* 7 miles south of Pelican Point (lat. 40°32'45" N, long. 120°44'05" W; sec. 16, T 31 N, R 11 E). Altitude 7294 feet. Named on Fredonyer Peak (1954) 15' quadrangle. The name is from mountain mahogany growing near the top of the peak (Purdy, 1988, p. 120).

Mahogany Ridge [LASSEN-MODOC]: *ridge,* generally north-trending, 2 miles long, 26 miles southeast of Alturas [MODOC] on Lassen-Modoc County line (lat. 41°11'05" N, long. 120°15'35" W). Named on Jess Valley (1962) 7.5' quadrangle.

Mahogany Ridge [MODOC]: *ridge,* generally northwest-trending, 3 miles long, 5.5 miles northwest of Alturas (lat. 41°33' N, long. 120°36'15" W). Named on Big Sage Reservoir (1962) 15' quadrangle.

Mahogany Springs [LASSEN]: *spring,* 23 miles east of Madeline (lat. 41°07'05" N, long. 120°02'10" W; near W line sec. 34, T 38 N, R 17 E). Named on Little Hat Mountain (1962) 7.5' quadrangle. United States Board on Geographic Names (1983b, p. 6) rejected the form "Mahagony Springs" for the name.

Maiden Flat [LASSEN]: *valley,* 8.5 miles northeast of Termo (lat. 40°57'15" N, long. 120°20'45" W; sec. 25, 26, T 36 N, R 14 E). Named on Ravendale (1954) 15' quadrangle.

Major Canyon [MODOC]: *canyon,* drained by a stream that flows 2.5 miles to lowlands along Ash Creek 7.5 miles east of Lookout (lat. 41°12'30" N, long. 121°00'20" W; near W line sec. 24, T 39 N, R 8 E). Named on Bieber (1961) 15' quadrangle.

Malgin's Hot Springs: see **Drakesbad** [PLUMAS].

Maloy: see **Pat Maloy Ravine** [PLUMAS].

Mammoth [MODOC]: *locality,* 8 miles north-northwest of Timber Mountain along Great Northern Railroad (lat. 41°43'50" N, long. 121°21'05" W; at E line sec. 23, T 45 N, R 5 E). Named on Timber Mountain (1952) 15' quadrangle.

Mammoth Cave [MODOC]: *cave,* 3.5 miles north-northwest of Timber Mountain (lat. 41°40'30" N, long. 121°20' W; at E line sec. 12, T 44 N, R 5 E). Named on Timber Mountain (1952) 15' quadrangle.

Mammoth Springs [MODOC]: *springs,* 10.5 miles north-northeast of Double Head Mountain (lat. 41°53'30" N, long. 121°04' W; at NW cor. sec. 28, T 47 N, R 8 E). Named on Clear Lake Reservoir (1951) 15' quadrangle.

Manzanita Hill [LASSEN]: *ridge,* south-southeast-trending, 2 miles long, 9.5 miles south of Adin [MODOC] (lat. 41°03'35" N, long. 120°56' W). Named on Adin (1962) 15' quadrangle.

Manzanita Mountain [MODOC]: *peak,* 12 miles south-southeast of Canby (lat. 41°16'45" N, long. 120°48' W; on W line sec. 26, T 40 N, R 10 E); the peak is on Manzanita Ridge. Altitude 7036 feet. Named on Canby (1961) 15' quadrangle.

Manzanita Mountain [PLUMAS]: *peak,* 3 miles east-northeast of Chester (lat. 40°20' N, long. 121°10'25" W; near NE cor. sec. 34, T 29 N, R 7 E). Altitude 5878 feet. Named on Chester (1979) 7.5' quadrangle.

Manzanita Ridge [MODOC]: *ridge,* north- to northwest-trending, 3.5 miles long, 12 miles south-southeast of Canby (lat. 41°16'45" N, long. 120°48' W). Named on Canby (1961) 15' quadrangle.

Mapes: see **Litchfield** [LASSEN].

Mapes Canyon [PLUMAS]: *canyon,* 2.5 miles long, opens into Sierra Valley 6 miles northeast of Portola (lat. 39°50'55" N, long. 120°22'05" W; at W line sec. 13, T 23 N, R 14 E). Named on Portola (1972) and Reconnaissance Peak (1972) 7.5' quadrangles.

Mapes Cow Camp [LASSEN]: *locality,* 12 miles west-southwest of Pelican Point (lat. 40°35'15" N, long. 120°57'40" W; near SE cor. sec. 33, T 32 N, R 9 E). Named on Antelope Mountain (1956) 15' quadrangle.

Mapes Reservoir [MODOC]: *intermittent lake,* 3600 feet long, 2.5 miles east-northeast of Jacks Butte (lat. 41°36'10" N, long. 120°45'40" W; on N line sec. 1, T 43 N, R 10 E). Named on Jacks Butte (1962) 15' quadrangle.

Mapes Spring [LASSEN]: *spring,* 8.5 miles west of Karlo (lat. 40°33'35" N, long. 120°28'30" W; sec. 11, T 31 N, R 13 E). Named on Karlo (1954) 15' quadrangle.

Maple Flat [PLUMAS]: *area,* 8 miles north-northeast of Bucks Lodge (lat. 39°59'10" N, long. 121°07'35" W; sec. 31, T 25 N, R 8 E). Named on Bucks Lake (1979) 7.5' quadrangle.

Marble Cone [PLUMAS]: *relief feature,* nearly 7 miles south-southeast of Bucks Lodge (lat. 39°46'55" N, long. 121°08'10" W; at SE cor. sec. 1, T 22 N, R 7 E). Named on Haskins Valley (1980) 7.5' quadrangle.

Marble Cone: see **Little Marble Cone** [PLUMAS].

Marble Creek [PLUMAS]: *stream,* flows 5 miles to Butte County 10.5 miles south-southeast of Storrie (lat. 39°46'05" N, long. 121° 16'25" W; at S line sec. 11, T 22 N, R 6 E). Named on Soapstone Hill (1979) 7.5' quadrangle.

Marble Hot Springs [PLUMAS]: *spring,* 7 miles east-southeast of Portola (lat. 39°45'20" N, long. 120°21'30" W; near S line sec. 13, T 22 N, R 14 E). Named on Reconnaissance Peak (1972) 7.5' quadrangle.

Marian Creek [PLUMAS]: *stream,* flows 3.5 miles to lowlands 12 miles south of Mount Harkness (lat. 40°15'35" N, long. 121°18'20" W; near W line sec. 27, T 28 N, R 6 E). Named on Mount Harkness (1956) 15' quadrangle.

Marion Ravine [PLUMAS]: *canyon,* drained by a stream that flows 2 miles to North Fork Feather River 6 miles north of Twain (lat. 40° 06'15" N, long. 121°05'30" W; at N line sec. 21, T 26 N, R 8 E). Named on Twain (1980) 7.5' quadrangle.

Marrow Creek: see **Morrow Creek** [PLUMAS].

Marshall Spring [MODOC]: *spring,* 3 miles east-southeast of White Horse (lat. 41°17'40" N, long. 121°20'30" W; sec. 24, T 40 N, R 5 E). Named on White Horse (1962) 15' quadrangle.

Marston: see **Quincy Junction** [PLUMAS].

Martin Creek [LASSEN]: *stream,* flows 5 miles to lowlands 12.5 miles west-southwest of Pelican Point (lat. 40°35' N, long. 120° 58' W; at N line sec. 4, T 31 N, R 9 E). Named on Antelope Mountain (1956) 15' quadrangle.

Martineck Canyon: see **Martin Neck Canyon** [PLUMAS].

Martin Neck Canyon [PLUMAS]: *canyon,* 2.25 miles long, 3.25 miles south of Chilcoot (lat. 39°45' N, long. 120°08'35" W). Named on Chilcoot (1979) and Loyalton (1981) 7.5' quadrangles. Called Martineck Canyon on Chilcoot (1950) and Loyalton (1955) 15' quadrangles, but United States Board on Geographic Names (1977c, p. 5) rejected this name for the feature; the Board pointed out that the name "Martin" is for R. Martin, a merchant at the community of Summit.

Martin Springs [LASSEN]: *springs,* 11 miles west-southwest of Pelican Point (lat. 40°33'05" N, long. 120°55'30" W; near NE cor. sec. 14, T 31 N, R 9 E); the springs are along Martin Creek. Named on Antelope Mountain (1956) 15' quadrangle.

Mary Pete Spring [MODOC]: *spring,* 11 miles southwest of Alturas (lat. 41°22'40" N, long. 120°41'20" W; sec. 22, T 41 N, R 11 E). Named on Alturas (1961) 15' quadrangle.

Mason Creek [MODOC]: *stream,* flows about 1.5 miles to Willow Creek (3) 5.5 miles southeast of Willow Ranch (lat. 41°51'10" N, long. 120°16'30" W; sec. 17, T 46 N, R 15 E). Named on Willow Ranch (1962) 15' quadrangle.

Mason Reservoir [MODOC]: *water feature,* 4 miles east of Newell (lat. 41°52'20" N, long. 121°17'30" W; sec. 33, T 47 N, R 6 E). Named on Tulelake (1951) 15' quadrangle.

Mason Station [LASSEN]: *locality,* 4 miles north of Westwood along Western Pacific Railroad (lat. 40°21'55" N, long. 121°00'05" W; at NW cor. sec. 20, T 29 N, R 9 E). Named on Chester (1956) 15' quadrangle. California Mining Bureau's (1917a) map shows a place called Facht located at or near present Mason Station.

Massack [PLUMAS]: *locality,* 3.5 miles northwest of Spring Garden along Western Pacific Railroad (lat. 39°55'35" N, long. 120°49'55" W; sec. 23, T 24 N, R 10 E); the place is near the mouth of Massack Creek. Named on Spring Garden (1950) 7.5' quadrangle. Postal authorities established Massack post office in 1917, moved it 0.5 mile north in 1937, and discontinued it in 1939; the name was from Massack Creek (Salley, p. 134).

Massack Creek [PLUMAS]: *stream,* flows nearly 4 miles to Greenhorn Creek 3.5 miles northwest of Spring Garden (lat. 39°55'40" N, long. 120°50'20" W). Named on Spring Garden (1950) 7.5' quadrangle. Miners named the stream for Massaic County, Illinois (Salley, p. 134).

Mattes: see **Adin** [MODOC].

Maxwell [PLUMAS]: *locality,* 7 miles south-southwest of Crescent (present Crescent Mills) along Spanish Creek (1) (lat. 40°01' N, long. 120°58'15" W). Named on Honey Lake (1893) 1° quadrangle.

McArthur [MODOC]: *locality,* 11 miles south of Alturas along Southern Pacific Railroad (lat. 41°19'55" N, long. 120°32'10" W; near E line sec. 1, T 40 N, R 12 E). Named on Alturas (1961) 15' quadrangle.

McArthur Cow Camp [MODOC]: *locality,* 3 miles south of White Horse (lat. 40°16'15" N, long. 121°23'40" W; sec. 28, T 40 N, R 5 E). Named on White Horse (1962) 15' quadrangle.

McBride Springs: see **Lower McBride Springs** [LASSEN]; **Upper McBride Springs** [LASSEN].

McCarthy Bar [PLUMAS]: *locality,* 6 miles south of Quincy (lat. 39°51'15" N, long. 120°57'10" W; at E line sec. 15, T 23 N, R 9 E). Named on Onion Valley (1950) 7.5' quadrangle.

McCarthy Creek [PLUMAS]: *stream,* flows nearly 3 miles to Middle Fork Feather River 7.5 miles south-southwest of Quincy (lat. 39° 49'50" N, long. 120°59'25" W; at E line sec. 29, T 23 N, R 9 E). Named on Onion Valley (1950) 7.5' quadrangle.

McClellan Canyon [PLUMAS]: *canyon,* drained by a stream that flows 4.5 miles to Last Chance Creek (2) 7.25 miles northwest of Squaw Valley Peak (lat. 46°06'40" N, long. 120°29'05" W; sec. 14, T 26 N, R 13 E). Named on Squaw Valley Peak (1977) 7.5' quadrangle. On Milford (1950) 15' quadrangle, the stream in present McClellan Canyon is called Rogers Creek, but United States Board on Geographic Names (1978a, p. 6) rejected this name.

McClellan Canyon: see **Ross Canyon** [PLUMAS] (1).

McClellan Ravine: see **North Canyon** [PLUMAS].

McClelland Reservoir [LASSEN]: *intermittent lake,* 1000 feet long, 8.5 miles south of Adin [MODOC] (lat. 41°04'30" N, long. 120°57'45" W; sec. 5, T 37 N, R 9 E). Named on Adin (1962) 15' quadrangle. United States Board on Geographic Names (1968a, p. 5) rejected the form "McClellan Reservoir" for the name.

McClure Spring [MODOC]: *spring,* 12.5 miles south-southwest of Canby (lat. 41°16'45" N, long. 120°57'10" W; near E line sec. 29, T 40 N, R 9 E). Named on Canby (1961) 15' quadrangle.

McCoy Flat [LASSEN]:

(1) *valley,* 9.5 miles west-southwest of Termo (lat. 40°48'20" N, long. 120°37'30" W; mainly in sec. 16, T 34 N, R 12 E). Named on Grasshopper Valley (1954) 15' quadrangle.

(2) *area,* 7.25 miles west-northwest of Pelican Point (lat. 40°40'50" N, long. 120°51'45" W; sec. 32, 33, T 33 N, R 10 E). Named on Antelope Mountain (1956) 15' quadrangle. Leo S. McCoy claimed land at the place in 1874 (Purdy, 1988, p. 120).

McCoy Flat Reservoir [LASSEN]: *intermittent lake,* 2.5 miles long, 12 miles north-northeast of Westwood (lat. 40°28'10" N, long. 120°59'10" W). Named on Pegleg Mountain (1980) 7.5' quadrangle.

McCoy Water Pit [LASSEN]: *water feature,* 8 miles west-northwest of Pelican Point (lat. 40°40'35" N, long. 120°52'40" W; sec. 32, T 33 N, R 10 E); the feature is at McCoy Flat (2). Named on Antelope Mountain (1956) 15' quadrangle.

McCrady River: see **Lost River** [MODOC].

McDermott Creek [LASSEN]: *stream,* flows 2.25 miles to Honey Lake Valley 1.5 miles southeast of Milford (lat. 40°09'25" N, long. 120°21'20" W; sec. 36, T 27 N, R 14 E). Named on Milford (1977) 7.5' quadrangle.

McDermott Ravine [PLUMAS]: *canyon,* drained by a stream that flows 1 mile to lowlands 8.5 miles south-southwest of Mount Ingalls (lat. 39°53' N, long. 120°42'15" W; near SE cor. sec. 2, T 23 N, R 11 E). Named on Mount Ingalls (1972) 7.5' quadrangle.

McDonald Peak [LASSEN]: *peak,* nearly 6 miles north-northeast of Termo (lat. 40°56'30" N, long. 120°24'40" W; near W line sec. 32, T 36 N, R 14 E). Altitude 7931 feet. Named on Ravendale (1954) 15' quadrangle. Symons (p. 116) referred to McDonald's Peak.

McElroy Hill [PLUMAS]: *peak,* 7 miles south-southeast of Portola (lat. 39°42'45" N, long. 120°24'30" W; on W line sec. 34, T 22 N, R 14 E). Altitude 5526 feet. Named on Calpine (1981) 7.5' quadrangle.

McFarland Ravine [PLUMAS]: *canyon,* drained by a stream that flows 2 miles to Morrow Creek 5.5 miles north-northwest of Dogwood Peak (lat. 39°51'30" N, long. 121°05'45" W; sec. 16, T 23 N, R 8 E). Named on Dogwood Peak (1979) 7.5' quadrangle.

McFarlane Ravine [PLUMAS]: *canyon,* drained by a stream that flows less than 1 mile to Mosquito Creek 3.5 miles west-northwest of Caribou (lat. 40°05'35" N, long. 121°13' W; sec. 20, T 26 N, R 7 E). Named on Caribou (1979) 7.5' quadrangle.

McGarva Reservoir [MODOC]: *water feature,* 12.5 miles south of Alturas (lat. 41°18'45" N, long. 120°34'40" W; near S line sec. 10, T 40 N, R 12 E). Named on Alturas (1961) 15' quadrangle.

McGarva Reservoir 2 [MODOC]: *water feature,* 13 miles south of Alturas (lat. 41°18'10" N, long. 120°34'50" W; sec. 15, T 40 N, R 12 E); the feature is less than 1 mile south-southwest of McGarva Reservoir. Named on Alturas (1961) 15' quadrangle.

McGinty Point [MODOC]: *promontory,* 9.5 miles south-southwest of Willow Ranch near the south end of Goose Lake (1) (lat. 41°47'20" N, long. 120°27'40" W; sec. 34, T 46 N, R 13 E). Named on Willow Ranch (1962) 15' quadrangle.

McGinty Reservoir [MODOC]: *lake,* 3700 feet long, 6.5 miles east-southeast of South Mountain (lat. 41°48'15" N, long. 120°31'10" W; sec. 30, T 46 N, R 13 E). Named on South Mountain (1962) 15' quadrangle.

McKabe Flat [LASSEN]: *area,* 7.25 miles northeast of Madeline (lat. 41°07'30" N, long. 120°22'30" W). Named on Jess Valley (1962), Madeline (1962), and Tule Mountain (1967) 7.5' quadrangles.

McKay Butte [MODOC]: *peak,* 5.25 miles north-northeast of Crank Mountain (lat. 41°27'30" N, long. 121°07' W; at SW cor. sec. 24, T 42 N, R 7 E). Named on Crank Mountain (1962) 15' quadrangle.

McKay Flat [MODOC]: *area,* 7 miles north-northeast of Crank Mountain (lat. 41°29' N, long. 121°06'30" W; mainly in sec. 13, T 42 N, R 7 E). Named on Crank Mountain (1962) 15' quadrangle.

McKenzie Cow Camp [LASSEN]: *locality,* 7.5 miles south-southeast of Cal Mountain (lat. 40°34'35" N, long. 121°05'20" W; sec. 4, T 31 N, R 8 E). Named on Harvey Mountain (1956) 15' quadrangle.

McKenzie Meadows [LASSEN]: *valley,* 4.25 miles northeast of Westwood (lat. 40°20'30" N, long. 120°55'50" W). Named on Westwood East (1980) 7.5' quadrangle.

McKesick Peak [PLUMAS]: *peak,* 8.5 miles southeast of Milford [LASSEN] near Lassen-Plumas County line (lat. 40°05'25" N, long. 120°14'50" W; near E line sec. 23, T 26 N, R 15 E). Altitude 7096 feet. Named on McKesick Peak (1978) 7.5' quadrangle.

McKissick Spring [LASSEN]: *spring,* 9.5 miles south of Observation Peak (lat. 40°38'15" N, long. 120°12' W; near E line sec. 18, T 32 N, R 16 E). Named on Shinn Mountain (1954) 15' quadrangle.

McKissick Stage Station: see **Secret Valley** [LASSEN].

McLain Spring [MODOC]: *spring,* 6.5 miles east-northeast of South Mountain (lat. 41°51'50" N, long. 120°30'40" W; near NE cor. sec. 6, T 46 N, R 13 E). Named on South Mountain (1962) 15' quadrangle.

McNair Saddle [PLUMAS]: *pass,* 4.5 miles northwest of American House (lat. 39°42'30" N, long. 121°04'20" W; sec. 3, T 21 N, R 8 E). Named on American House (1948) 7.5' quadrangle.

McRae Meadow [PLUMAS]: *canyon,* 4 miles long, along East Nelson Creek above a point 14 miles southeast of Quincy (lat. 39° 47'15" N, long. 120°46'15" W), and along upper reaches of Jamison Creek. Named on Blue Nose Mountain (1951) and Mount Fillmore (1951) 7.5' quadrangles.

McRae Ridge [PLUMAS]: *ridge,* north-tending, 4 miles long, 16 miles southeast of Quincy (lat. 39°45' N, long. 120°46' W); the ridge is west of McRae Meadow. Named on Blue Nose Mountain (1951) and Mount Fillmore (1951) 7.5' quadrangles.

McReynolds Valley [PLUMAS]: *valley,* 13 miles north of Portola (lat. 39°39'50" N, long. 120°27' W). Named on Crocker Mountain (1972) and Squaw Valley Peak (1977) 7.5' quadrangles.

Meadow Creek [PLUMAS]: *stream,* flows 3.25 miles to Red Clover Creek 12.5 miles southeast of Kettle Rock (lat. 40°00'25" N, long. 120°34'25" W; sec. 24, T 25 N, R 12 E). Named on Babcock Peak (1972) and Grizzly Valley (1972) 7.5' quadrangles.

Meadow Valley [PLUMAS]:

(1) *valley,* around the village of Meadow Valley (lat. 39°56'15" N, long. 121°03'30" W). Named on Meadow Valley (1980) 7.5' quadrangle.

(2) *village,* 6.5 miles west of Quincy (lat. 39°55'55" N, long. 121° 03'35" W); the place is in Meadow Valley (1). Named on Meadow Valley (1980) 7.5' quadrangle. Postal authorities established Meadow Valley post office in 1855, discontinued it in 1861, and reestablished it in 1864 (Salley, p. 137).

Meadow Valley: see **Grasshopper Valley** [LASSEN].

Meadow Valley Creek [PLUMAS]: *stream,* formed by the confluence of Big Creek and Clear Creek (4), flows 3 miles to Rock Creek (5) 1.5 miles east of the village of Meadow Valley (lat. 39° 56' N, long. 121°02' W; sec. 24, T 24 N, R 8 E); the stream goes through part of Meadow Valley (1). Named on Meadow Valley (1980) 7.5' quadrangle.

Meadow View Peak [LASSEN-PLUMAS]: *peak,* 6 miles west-northwest of Doyle [LASSEN] on Lassen-Plumas County line (lat. 40°02'50" N, long. 120°12'35" W; sec. 5, T 25 N, R 16 E). Altitude 6965 feet. Named on McKessick Peak (1978) 7.5' quadrangle.

Meares [MODOC]: *locality,* 6.25 miles northwest of Hackamore (lat. 41°37'15" N, long. 121°11'50" W; on E line sec. 30, T 44 N, R 7 E). Named on Hackamore (1952) 15' quadrangle. California Division of Highways' (1934) map shows a place called Glass Mountain located 6 miles west-southwest of Meares along Great Northern Railroad.

Meeker Bar [PLUMAS]: *locality,* 6 miles north-northwest of Twain along North Fork Feather River (lat. 40°05'55" N, long. 121°06'55" W; on W line sec. 20, T 26 N, R 8 E). Named on Twain (1980) 7.5' quadrangle.

Mendiboure Reservoir [LASSEN]: *lake,* 2400 feet long, 9.5 miles north-northeast of Termo (lat. 40°59'55" N, long. 120°24'15" W; sec. 8, T 36 N, R 14 E). Named on Ravendale (1954) 15' quadrangle, and on Madeline (1962) 7.5' quadrangle.

Menlo Baths [MODOC]: *locality,* nearly 4 miles south-southeast of Eagleville (lat. 41°16' N, long. 120°04'50" W; near NE cor. sec. 7, T 39 N, R 17 E). Named on Eagleville (1963) 7.5' quadrangle.

Merlin [PLUMAS]: *locality,* 3 miles southwest of Storrie along Western Pacific Railroad (lat. 39°53'15" N, long. 121°22' W). Named on Storrie (1979) 7.5' quadrangle.

Merrill Creek [LASSEN]: *stream,* flows 2.5 miles to Eagle Lake 6.5 miles south-southwest of Pelican Point (lat. 40°33'10" N, long. 120°48'20" W; sec. 14, T 31 N, R 10 E); the stream heads at Little Merrill Flat. Named on Antelope Mountain (1956) 15' quadrangle.

Merrill Flat: see **Big Merrill Flat** [LASSEN]; **Little Merrill Flat** [LASSEN].

Merrill Mountain [LASSEN]: *hill,* 7.5 miles southwest of Pelican Point (lat. 40°32'50" N, long. 120°49'50" W; sec. 15, T 31 N, R 10 E); the hill is less than 1 mile north-northeast of Little Merrill Flat. Altitude 5768 feet. Named on Antelope Mountain (1956) 15' quadrangle.

Merrillville [LASSEN]: *locality,* 11 miles north of Susanville near the northwest end of present Willow Creek Valley (lat. 40°34' N, long. 120°41'45" W). Named on Honey Lake (1893) 1° quadrangle. Postal authorities established Merrillville post office in 1875, moved it 1 mile southeast in 1906, moved it 1.25 miles northwest in 1907, moved it 6 miles southeast in 1909, discontinued it in 1912, reestablished it in 1913, and discontinued it in 1928 (Salley, p. 138). The name commemorates Captain Charles A. Merrill, who promoted use of water from Eagle Lake (Purdy, 1988, p. 120).

Messenger Gulch [MODOC]: *canyon,* drained by a stream that flows 4.5 miles to Ash Creek 4 miles east-southeast of Adin (lat. 41° 13' N, long. 120°52'10" W; sec. 18, T 39 N, R 10 E). Named on Adin (1962) and Canby (1961) 15' quadrangles.

Meteorite Tank [MODOC]: *water feature,* 10.5 miles north-northeast of South Mountain (lat. 41°58'30" N, long. 120°32'45" W; at W line sec. 25, T 48 N, R 12 E). Named on South Mountain (1962) 15' quadrangle. The name recalls a meteorite discovered near the site in 1938 (Butler, p. 296-297).

Meyers Flat: see **Myer Flat** [LASSEN].

Meyer Spring: see **Myer Spring** [LASSEN].

Middle Alkali Lake [MODOC]: *intermittent lake,* 18 miles long, in Surprise Valley between Upper Lake and Lower Lake (lat. 41° 28' N, long. 120°06' W). Named on Cedarville (1962) 15' quadrangle, and on Eagleville (1963), Hansen Island (1963), and Warren Peak (1963) 7.5' quadrangles. Present Upper Lake, Middle Alkali Lake, and Lower Lake together have had the name "Alkali Lakes," evidently a name descriptive of the water; present Middle Alkali Lake also has been called simply Middle Lake (Pease, p. 78).

Middle Bar: see **Smith Point** [PLUMAS].

Middle Campsite [PLUMAS]: *locality,* 5 miles west of Caribou (lat. 40°03'55" N, long. 121°14'50" W; near W line sec. 31, T 26 N, R 7 E). Named on Caribou (1979) 7.5' quadrangle. Called Middle Campground on Almanor (1955) 15' quadrangle.

Middle Creek [LASSEN]: *stream,* flows 1.5 miles to lowlands along Horse Lake (1) 11.5 miles east of Pelican Point (lat. 40°39'45" N, long. 120°31'50" W; sec. 5, T 32 N, R 13 E). Named on Fredonyer Peak (1954) 15' quadrangle.

Middle Creek [PLUMAS]:
(1) *stream,* flows 4.25 miles to Hungry Creek nearly 5 miles east-southeast of Kettle Rock (lat. 40°07'05" N, long. 120°38'30" W; near NW cor. sec. 16, T 26 N, R 12 E). Named on Genesee Valley (1972) and Kettle Rock (1972) 7.5' quadrangles.
(2) *stream,* flows 1.5 miles to Peoria Creek 10 miles southeast of Quincy (lat. 39°51'25" N, long. 120°47'10" W; sec. 18, T 23 N, R 11 E). Named on Blue Nose Mountain (1951) 7.5' quadrangle.

Middle Fork Spring [MODOC]: *spring,* 9 miles south of Eagleville (lat. 41°11'25" N, long. 120°09'05" W; at W line sec. 3, T 38 N, R 16 E). Named on Emerson Peak (1962) 7.5' quadrangle.

Middle Hollow [PLUMAS]: *canyon,* drained by a stream that flows 1.5 miles to Humbug Valley (1) 8 miles southwest of the village of Almanor (lat. 40°08'15" N, long. 121°16'20" W; sec. 2, T 26 N, R 6 E). Named on Jonesville (1958) 15' quadrangle.

Middle Lake: see **Middle Alkali Lake** [MODOC].

Middle Ravine [PLUMAS]: *canyon,* drained by a stream that flows 2 miles to West Branch Soda Creek (2) 3.25 miles northeast of Twain (lat. 40°02'45" N, long. 121°01'05" W; sec. 7, T 25 N, R 9 E). Named on Twain (1980) 7.5' quadrangle.

Middle Ridge [MODOC]: *ridge,* north-northwest-trending, 1.5 miles long, 9 miles east of Adin (lat. 41°11'55" N, long. 120°46'30" W; on N line sec. 25, T 39 N, R 10 E). Named on Adin (1962) 15' quadrangle.

Midway House [PLUMAS]: *locality,* 4.5 miles south-southeast of Mount Ingalls (lat. 39°55'50" N, long. 120°35'50" W; sec. 23, T 24 N, R 12 E). Site named on Grizzly Valley (1972) 7.5' quadrangle.

Mile Creek [MODOC]: *stream,* flows 3.5 miles to Thoms Creek 12.5 miles south of the village of Davis Creek (lat. 41°33'20" N, long. 120°20'45" W; near W line sec. 22, T 43 N, R 14 E). Named on Davis Creek (1962) 15' quadrangle. United States Board on Geographic Names (1991, p. 5) rejected the name "Mill Creek" for the stream.

Milford [LASSEN]: *village,* 15 miles south of Litchfield (lat. 40° 10'15" N, long. 120°22'15" W; sec. 26, T 27 N, R 14 E); the village is along Mill Creek [LASSEN-PLUMAS]. Named on Milford (1977) 7.5' quadrangle. Postal authorities established Milford post office in 1864 and discontinued it for a short time in 1879 (Frickstad, p. 68). J.C. Wemple, who with Judson Dakin built a gristmill at the place, named the village in 1861 (Hanna, p. 192). Postal authorities established Evan's Ranch post office 25 miles southeast of Milford in 1866 and discontinued it in 1868; the name was for Alvira Evans, first postmaster (Salley, p. 71).

Milk Creek [MODOC]: *stream,* flows 4.5 miles to Surprise Valley 5 miles south of Cedarville (lat. 41°27'20" N, long. 120°09'45" W; at NW cor. sec. 4, T 41 N, R 16 E). Named on Warren Peak (1963) 7.5' quadrangle.

Milkhouse Flat [PLUMAS]: *area,* 14 miles southwest of the village of Almanor (lat. 40°05'25" N, long. 121°21'50" W; near SW cor sec. 19, T 26 N, R 6 E). Named on Jonesville (1958) 15' quadrangle.

Milk Ranch Creek [PLUMAS]: *stream,* flows 4.5 miles to North Fork Feather River 4 miles northeast of Storrie (lat. 39°57'45" N, long. 121°16'25" W; sec. 2, T 24 N, R 6 E). Named on Bucks Lake (1979) and Storrie (1979) 7.5' quadrangles.

Milk Spring [MODOC]: *spring,* 6.25 miles south-southeast of Willow Ranch (lat. 41°49' N, long. 120°19'20" W; sec. 23, T 46 N, R 14 E). Named on Willow Ranch (1962) 15' quadrangle.

Mill Creek [LASSEN-PLUMAS]: *stream,* heads in Plumas County and flows 2.5 miles to Honey Lake Valley 0.5 mile south of Milford (lat. 40°09'45" N, long. 120°22'25" W; near S line sec. 26, T 27 N, R 14 E). Named on Milford (1977) and Stony Ridge (1978) 7.5' quadrangles.

Mill Creek [MODOC]:
(1) *stream,* flows 13 miles to South Fork Pit River 20 miles south-southeast of Alturas (lat. 41°14'05" N, long. 120°20'20" W; near E line sec. 10, T 39 N, R 14 E). Named on Eagle Peak (1963), Jess Valley (1962), and Soup Creek (1963) 7.5' quadrangles.
(2) *stream,* flows 4.25 miles to Bidwell Creek 3 miles northwest of Fort Bidwell (lat. 41°53'35" N, long. 120°10'55" W; at S line sec. 31, T 47 N, R 16 E). Named on Fort Bidwell (1962) 15' quadrangle.
(3) *stream,* flows nearly 5 miles to Surprise Valley 8 miles north-northeast of Cedarville (lat. 41°38'30" N, long. 120°13' W; near W line sec. 36, T 44 N, R 15 E). Named on Cedarville (1962) and Davis Creek (1962) 15' quadrangles. South Fork enters from the southwest 1.5 miles upstream from the entrance of the main creek into Surprise Valley; it is nearly 3 miles long and is named on Cedarville (1962) and Davis Creek (1962) 15' quadrangles.

Mill Creek [PLUMAS]:
(1) *stream,* flows 4.5 miles to East Branch of North Fork Feather River 5 miles south-southwest of Caribou (lat. 40°00'45" N, long. 121°11'05" W; sec. 22, T 25 N, R 7 E). Named on Bucks Lake (1979) and Caribou (1979) 7.5' quadrangles.
(2) *stream,* flows 1.5 miles to East Branch of North Fork Feather River 0.5 mile west-southwest of Twain (lat. 40°01' N, long. 121° 04'40" W; sec. 22, T 25 N, R 8 E). Named on Meadow Valley (1980) and Twain (1980) 7.5' quadrangles.
(3) *stream,* flows 4.5 miles to Bucks Lake 3 miles north of Bucks Lodge (lat. 39°55' N, long. 121°11'05" W; near S line sec. 22, T 24 N, R 7 E). Named on Bucks Lake (1979) 7.5' quadrangle. Middle Fork Mill Creek (3) enters Bucks Lake 2 miles north of Bucks Lodge; it is 1.5 miles long and is named on Bucks Lake (1979) 7.5' quadrangle. Right Hand Branch Mill Creek (3) enters Bucks Lake 1.5 miles north of Bucks Lodge; it is 3.5 miles long and is named on Bucks Lake (1979) 7.5' quadrangle. Right Hand Branch is called Left Hand Branch on Bucks Lake (1950) 15' quadrangle, but United States Board on Geographic Names (1979, p. 5) rejected the names "Left Hand Branch Mill Creek" and "Right Hand Creek" for the stream
(4) *stream,* formed by the confluence of Middle Branch and West Branch, flows 3.5 miles to Spanish Creek (1) 2 miles northeast of Quincy (lat. 39°57'10" N, long. 120°55'35" W; sec. 12, T 24 N, R 9 E). Named on Quincy (1950) 7.5' quadrangle. Middle Branch is 2.5 miles long, and West Branch is 3 miles long. East Branch, which enters 850 feet downstream from the confluence of Middle Branch and West Branch, is 1.5 miles long. All three branches are named on Quincy (1950) 7.5' quadrangle.

Mill Creek: see **Mile Creek** [MODOC].

Mill Creek Falls [MODOC]: *waterfall,* 20 miles southeast of Alturas along Mill Creek (1) (lat. 41°16'45" N, long. 120°17'05" W; at E line sec. 29, T 40 N, R 15 E). Named on Soup Creek (1963) 7.5' quadrangle.

Mill Creek Falls Campground [MODOC]: *locality,* 20 miles southeast of Alturas (lat. 41°16'35" N, long. 120°17'15" W; sec. 29, T 40 N, R 15 E); the place is 1100 feet southwest of Mill Creek Falls. Named on Soup Creek (1963) 7.5' quadrangle.

Mill Creek Meadows [MODOC]: *area,* 6.5 miles west of Eagleville (lat. 41°20' N, long. 120°14'10" W); the place is along upper reaches of Mill Creek (1). Named on Eagle Peak (1963) 7.5' quadrangle.

Miller Creek [PLUMAS]:
(1) *stream,* flows 1.5 miles to Humbug Creek (1) 6 miles southwest of the village of Almanor (lat. 40°08'50" N, long. 121°14'20" W; near S line sec. 31, T 27 N, R 7 E). Named on Almanor (1979) 7.5' quadrangle.
(2) *stream,* flows 1.5 miles to Poplar Creek 12.5 miles southeast of Quincy (lat. 39°49'55" N, long. 120°45'05" W; sec. 28, T 23 N, R 11 E). Named on Blue Nose Mountain (1951) 7.5' quadrangle.

Miller Flat [MODOC]: *area,* 7.5 miles southeast of Crank Mountain (lat. 41°19'30" N, long. 121°01'40" W; on W line sec. 11, T 40 N, R 8 E). Named on Crank Mountain (1962) 15' quadrangle.

Miller Fork: see **Third Water Creek** [PLUMAS].

Miller Gulch [MODOC]: *canyon,* drained by a stream that flows 2.5 miles to Pit River 5.5 miles east-southeast of Crank Mountain (lat. 41°21'30" N, long. 121°02'45" W; near SE cor. sec. 28, T 41 N, R 8 E). Named on Crank Mountain (1962) 15' quadrangle.

Miller Ravine [PLUMAS]: *canyon,* drained by a stream that flows about 3.25 miles to Humbug Valley (1) 8 miles southwest of the village of Almanor (lat. 40°07'50" N, long. 121°15'40" W; at N line sec. 12, T 26 N, R 6 E). Named on Jonesville (1958) 15' quadrangle.

Miller Spring [MODOC]: *spring,* 7 miles southeast of Crank Mountain (lat. 40°19'45" N, long. 121°01'55" W; near SE cor. sec. 3, T 40 N, R 8 E); the spring is less than 0.5 mile north-northwest of Miller Flat. Named on Crank Mountain (1962) 15' quadrangle.

Mill Spring [MODOC]: *spring,* 12 miles northwest of Alturas (lat. 41°37'05" N, long. 120°41'15" W; at S line sec. 27, T 44 N, R 11 E). Named on Big Sage Reservoir (1962) 15' quadrangle. United States Board on Geographic Names (1990, p. 9) rejected the plural form "Mill Springs" for the name.

Mineral Spring [MODOC]: *spring,* 8 miles north-northwest of Fort Bidwell (lat. 41°58'05" N, long. 120°11'55" W; near SW cor. sec. 1, T 47 N, R 15 E). Named on Fort Bidwell (1962) 15' quadrangle.

Miners Bay [LASSEN]: *embayment,* 3.25 miles south of Pelican Point along Eagle Lake (lat. 40°35'15" N, long. 120°44'55" W). Named on Fredonyer Peak (1954) 15' quadrangle.

Miners Point [LASSEN]: *promontory,* 1.25 miles south-southeast of Pelican Point on the east side of Eagle Lake (lat. 40°36'50" N, long. 120°44'20" W). Named on Fredonyer Peak (1954) 15' quadrangle.

Minerva Bar [PLUMAS]: *locality,* 6.25 miles south of Quincy along Middle Fork Feather River (lat. 39°50'55" N, long. 120°55'30" W; on N line sec. 24, T 23 N, R 9 E). Named on Onion Valley (1950) 7.5' quadrangle.

Missouri Bar [PLUMAS]: *locality,* 5.25 miles south-southwest of Caribou along East Branch of North Fork Feather River (lat. 40°00'30" N, long. 121°12'20" W; sec. 21, T 25 N, R 7 E). Named on Caribou (1979) 7.5' quadrangle.

Missouri Gulch [PLUMAS]: *canyon,* drained by a stream that flows 1.25

miles to Long Valley Creek 8 miles south of Mount Ingalls (lat. 39°52'35" N, long. 120°37'50" W; sec. 9, T 23 N, R 12 E). Named on Mount Ingalls (1972) 7.5' quadrangle.

Mitchell Field [LASSEN]: *valley,* 3 miles east of Madeline (lat. 41° 03'15" N, long. 120°25' W); the feature is just east of Mitchell Hill. Named on Madeline (1962) 7.5' quadrangle, which shows an intermittent lake in the valley.

Mitchell Hill [LASSEN]: *peak,* 2.5 miles east of Madeline (lat. 41° 03' N, long. 120°25'40" W; at S line sec. 12, T 37 N, R 13 E). Altitude 6172 feet. Named on Madeline (1962) 7.5' quadrangle.

Moccasin [PLUMAS]: *locality,* 2.25 miles southwest of Crescent Mills along Western Pacific Railroad (lat. 40°04'25" N, long. 120° 56'15" W; near N line sec. 35, T 26 N, R 9 E); the place is 0.5 mile west-southwest of the mouth of Moccasin Creek. Named on Crescent Mills (1980) 7.5' quadrangle.

Moccasin Creek [PLUMAS]: *stream,* flows about 1 mile to Indian Creek (2) 1.5 miles southwest of Crescent Mills (lat. 40°04'35" N, long. 120°55'40" W; at NW cor. sec. 36, T 26 N, R 9 E). Named on Crescent Mills (1980) 7.5' quadrangle.

Modoc: see **Lookout Siding** [MODOC].

Mohala: see **Greenville** [PLUMAS].

Mohawk [PLUMAS]: *village,* 1 mile west of Blairsden (lat. 39°46'40" N, long. 120°38' W; on S line sec. 9, T 22 N, R 12 E); the village is in Mohawk Valley. Named on Johnsville (1972) 7.5' quadrangle. Postal authorities established Mohawk Valley post office in 1870, moved it 1.5 miles southeast in 1881 when they changed the name to Mohawk, and discontinued it in 1926 (Salley, p. 143).

Mohawk Boys Camp [PLUMAS]: *locality,* 2.25 miles west-northwest of Blairsden (lat. 39°47'50" N, long. 120°39' W; sec. 5, T 22 N, R 12 E). Named on Blairsden (1956) 15' quadrangle. Called Camp Wieland on Blairsden (1943) 15' quadrangle.

Mohawk Creek [PLUMAS]: *stream,* heads in Sierra County and flows 4 miles to Middle Fork Feather River 0.5 mile west-northwest of Clio in Plumas County (lat. 39°44'45" N, long. 120°35'20" W; on E line sec. 26, T 22 N, R 12 E). Named on Clio (1981) 7.5' quadrangle.

Mohawk Creek: see **Sulphur Creek** [PLUMAS].

Mohawk Valley [PLUMAS]: *valley,* extends for about 8 miles along Middle Fork Feather River; center 1.25 miles south-southeast of Blairsden (lat. 39°45'45" N, long. 120°36'30" W). Named on Blairsden (1972), Clio (1981), and Johnsville (1972) 7.5' quadrangles.

Mohawk Valley: see **Mohawk** [PLUMAS].

Molitor: see **Karlo** [LASSEN].

Moll Ranch: see **Madeline** [LASSEN].

Moll Reservoir [LASSEN]: *intermittent lake,* 2400 feet long, 11 miles southeast of Adin [MODOC] (lat. 41°06'15" N, long. 120°46'30" W; sec. 25, T 38 N, R 10 E). Named on Adin (1962) 15' quadrangle.

Monitor Flat [PLUMAS]: *area,* 9 miles south-southeast of Quincy (lat. 39°48'40" N, long. 120°54'20" W; sec. 31, T 23 N, R 10 E). Named on Onion Valley (1950) 7.5' quadrangle.

Montgomery Creek [PLUMAS]: *stream,* flows 3.25 miles to Indian Creek (2) 2 miles south-southeast of Taylorsville (lat. 40°02'55" N, long. 120°49'15" W; near W line sec. 12, T 25 N, R 10 E). Named on Taylorsville (1980) 7.5' quadrangle.

Moody Meadows [PLUMAS]: *area,* 12 miles south of Mount Harkness (lat. 40°15'30" N, long. 121°16'30" W; mainly in sec. 26, T 28 N, R 6 E). Named on Mount Harkness (1956) 15' quadrangle.

Moon Lake [LASSEN]: see: **Tule Lake Reservoir** [LASSEN].

Moonlight: see **Moonlight Valley** [PLUMAS].

Moonlight Creek [PLUMAS]: *stream,* flows nearly 7 miles to Lights Creek 5.5 miles south-southeast of Moonlight Peak (lat. 40°10'20" N, long. 120°47'25" W; sec. 30, T 27 N, R 11 E); the stream goes through Moonlight Valley. Named on Moonlight Peak (1980) 7.5' quadrangle. Called Surprise Creek on United States Geological Survey's (1907) map.

Moonlight Pass [PLUMAS]: *pass,* 1.25 miles west of Moonlight Peak (lat. 40°14'20" N, long. 120°51'55" W; sec. 33, T 28 N, R 10 E). Named on Moonlight Peak (1980) 7.5' quadrangle.

Moonlight Peak [PLUMAS]: *peak,* 9 miles northeast of Greenville (lat. 40°14'25" N, long. 120°50'20" W; sec. 34, T 28 N, R 10 E). Altitude 6828 feet. Named on Moonlight Peak (1980) 7.5' quadrangle.

Moonlight Valley [PLUMAS]: *valley,* 1.5 miles east-southeast of Moonlight Peak (lat. 40°13'45" N, long. 120°48'45" W; on W line sec. 1, T 27 N, R 10 E); the valley is along Moonlight Creek. Named on Moonlight Peak (1980) 7.5' quadrangle. Honey Lake (1893) 1° quadrangle has the name "Moonlight" for a place in the valley.

Mooreville Ridge [PLUMAS]: *ridge,* generally southwest-trending, 9 miles long, center 3 miles west-northwest of American House (lat. 39°39'45" N, long. 121°04'45" W); the southwest end of the ridge is in Butte County. Named on American House (1948) 7.5' quadrangle.

Moran [LASSEN]: *locality,* 3 miles north-northwest of Termo along Southern Pacific Railroad (lat. 40°54'05" W; long. 120°29'20" W; near N line sec. 15, T 35 N, R 13 E). Named on Ravendale (1954) 15' quadrangle.

Morgan Bar [PLUMAS]: *locality,* nearly 3 miles northeast of Cascade along South Branch of Middle Fork Feather River (lat. 39°43'45" N, long. 121°08'40" W; sec. 25, T 22 N, R 7 E). Named on Cascade (1948) 7.5' quadrangle.

Morgan Spring [LASSEN]: *spring,* 10 miles northeast of Wendel (lat. 40°26' N, long. 120°04'30" W; at W line sec. 28, T 30 N, R 17 E). Named on Wendel (1954) 15' quadrangle.

Mormon: see **Portola** [PLUMAS].

Morris: see **Pat Morris Camp** [LASSEN]; **Pat Morris Spring** [LASSEN].

Morris Lake [PLUMAS]: *lake,* 2000 feet long, 18 miles south-southwest of the village of Almanor (lat. 40°00'30" N, long. 121°21'10" W; sec. 19, T 25 N, R 6 E). Named on Jonesville (1958) 15' quadrangle.

Morrow Creek [PLUMAS]: *stream,* flows 2.25 miles to join Third Water Creek and form Bear Creek (2) 5.25 miles north-northwest of Dogwood Peak (lat. 39°51'20" N, long. 121°05'30" W; sec. 16, T 23 N, R 8 E). Named on Dogwood Peak (1979) and Meadow Valley (1980) 7.5' quadrangles. United States Board on Geographic Names (1977c, p. 5) gave the name "Marrow Creek" as a variant.

Morton Creek [PLUMAS]: *stream,* flows 4.25 miles to East Branch Lights Creek nearly 7 miles north of Kettle Rock (lat. 40°14'15" N, long. 120°44'50" W; near S line sec. 33, T 28 N, R 11 E). Named on Diamond Mountain (1972) and Kettle Rock (1972) 7.5' quadrangles.

Mosquito Creek [LASSEN]: *stream,* flows nearly 3 miles to East Creek [LASSEN-MODOC] 16 miles east-northeast of Madeline (lat. 41°10'20" N, long. 120°12'30" W; at W line sec. 7, T 38 N, R 16 E). Named on Emerson Peak (1962) 7.5' quadrangle.

Mosquito Creek [MODOC]: *stream,* flows 6.5 miles to Willow Creek (2) 6 miles west-northwest of South Mountain (lat. 41°52'10" N, long. 120°44'30" W; at E line sec. 31, T 47 N, R 11 E). Named on South Mountain (1962) and Steele Swamp (1962) 15' quadrangle.

Mosquito Creek [PLUMAS]:

(1) *stream,* formed by the confluence of North Branch and South Branch, flows nearly 5.5 miles to North Fork Feather River 2.5 miles west-southwest of Caribou (lat. 40°03'40" N, long. 121°11'55" W; sec. 33, T 26 N, R 7 E). Named on Caribou (1979) 7.5' quadrangle. North Branch is 2 miles long and is named on Almanor (1979) and Caribou (1979) 7.5' quadrangles. South Branch is 1.25 miles long and is named on Caribou (1979) 7.5' quadrangle. Middle Branch enters South Branch less than 0.25 mile upstream from the confluence of North Branch and South Branch; it is 1.5 miles long and is named on Caribou (1979) 7.5' quadrangle. Middle Branch and South Branch both head on Mosquito Ridge. According to United States Board on Geographic Names (1977b, p. 5), Mosquito Creek is formed by the confluence of its Middle Branch and South Branch.

(2) *stream,* flows less than 1 mile to Willow Creek (5) 2.25 miles south of Bucks Lodge (lat. 38°50'35" N, long. 121°10'05" W; near S line sec. 14, T 23 N, R 7 E). Named on Haskins Valley (1980) 7.5' quadrangle.

Mosquito Creek: see **Little Cottonwood Creek** [MODOC].

Mosquito Flat [LASSEN]: *valley,* 5.25 miles southwest of Lava Peak (lat. 40°46' N, long. 120°56'40" W; sec. 34, T 34 N, R 9 E). Named on Hayden Hill (1956) 15' quadrangle.

Mosquito Flat [PLUMAS]: *area,* 2.5 miles south of Bucks Lodge (lat. 39°50'25" N, long. 121°10'15" W; near SW cor. sec. 14, T 23 N, R 7 E); the place is along Mosquito Creek (2). Named on Haskins Valley (1980) 7.5' quadrangle.

Mosquito Lake [MODOC]:

(1) *lake,* 1 mile long, 2.25 miles west-northwest of White Horse (lat. 41°19'30" N, long. 121°26' W; sec. 6, 7, T 40 N, R 5 E). Named on White Horse (1962) 15' quadrangle.

(2) *lake,* 300 feet long, 9 miles south of Cedarville (lat. 41°24'05" N, long. 120°11'45" W; near SW cor. sec. 19, T 41 N, R 16 E). Named on Warren Peak (1963) 7.5' quadrangle.

Mosquito Ridge [PLUMAS]: *ridge,* east- to northeast-trending, 3 miles long, center 1.5 miles northwest of Caribou (lat. 40°05'50" W; long. 121°10'45" W). Named on Caribou (1979) 7.5' quadrangle.

Mosquito Springs [PLUMAS]: *springs,* 5 miles south-southwest of Mount Harkness (lat. 40°21'50" N, long. 121°20'10" W; near N line sec. 20, T 29 N, R 6 E). Named on Mount Harkness (1956) 15' quadrangle.

Moultons [LASSEN]: *locality,* 9 miles north of Observation Peak (lat. 40°54'05" N, long. 120°11'30" W). Named on Honey Lake (1893) 1° quadrangle. Postal authorities established Redrock post office 13 miles northeast of Ravendale (NE quarter sec. 14, T 35 N, R 15 E) in 1891, moved it 6 miles west and changed the name to Red Rock in 1907, and discontinued it in 1933 (Salley, p. 183). Moulton stage station was located at Red Rock (Garate, p. 123).

Moulton Stage Station: see **Moultons** [LASSEN].

Mountain Home [LASSEN]: *locality,* 8 miles west-northwest of Cal Mountain (lat. 40°41'50" N, long. 121°18'40" W; sec. 28, T 33 N, R 6 E). Named on Prospect Peak (1957) 15' quadrangle.

Mountain House: see **Spanish Peak** [PLUMAS].

Mountain Meadows [LASSEN]: *valley,* 3.5 miles east-southeast of Westwood (lat. 40°16'45" N, long. 120°56'15" W). Named on Greenville (1979) and

Westwood East (1980) 7.5' quadrangles. Water of present Mountain Meadows Reservoir covers part of the valley.

Mountain Meadows Creek [LASSEN]: *stream,* flows nearly 7 miles to Mountain Meadows Reservoir 5 miles southeast of Westwood (lat. 40°15'40" N, long. 120°55'35" W; at W line sec. 25, T 28 N, R 9 E). Named on Fredonyer Pass (1980) and Westwood East (1980) 7.5' quadrangles.

Mountain Meadows Reservoir [LASSEN]: *lake,* behind a dam on Hamilton Branch 2 miles southwest of Westwood (lat. 40°17' N, long. 121°01'25" W; near E line sec. 13, T 28 N, R 8 E); the lake is in Mountain Meadows. Named on Greenville (1979), Westwood East (1980), and Westwood West (1980) 7.5' quadrangles.

Mountain Spring House [PLUMAS]: *locality,* 2 miles west-northwest of Cascade (lat. 39°42'50" N, long. 121°12'35" W; near SW cor. sec. 33, T 22 N, R 7 E). Named on Cascade (1948) 7.5' quadrangle.

Mountain View Campground [PLUMAS]: *locality,* 2.5 miles west-northwest of Canyondam along Lake Almanor (lat. 40°11'35" N, long. 121°06'35" W; near S line sec. 17, T 27 N, R 8 E). Named on Canyondam (1979) 7.5' quadrangle.

Mount Ararat [PLUMAS]: *peak,* 4.25 miles south-southeast of Bucks Lodge (lat. 39°49'25" N, long. 121°08' W; near W line sec. 30, T 23 N, R 8 E). Named on Haskins Valley (1980) 7.5' quadrangle.

Mount Ararat Creek [PLUMAS]: *stream,* flows 2 miles to Willow Creek (5) nearly 6 miles south of Bucks Lodge (lat. 39°47'35" N, long. 121°09'15" W; near W line sec. 1, T 22 N, R 7 E); the stream heads at Mount Ararat. Named on Haskins Valley (1980) 7.5' quadrangle.

Mount Bidwell [MODOC]: *peak,* 7.5 miles north of Fort Bidwell (lat. 41°57'55" N, long. 120°09'55" W; on S line sec. 5, T 47 N, R 16 E); the peak is 2 miles northwest of Bidwell Mountain. Named on Fort Bidwell (1962) 15' quadrangle. United States Board on Geographic Names (1964c, p. 13) rejected the names "Bidwell Mountain," "Bidwell Mountains," and "Bidwell Peak" for the feature.

Mount Dyer: see **Dyer Mountain** [LASSEN].

Mount Elwell [PLUMAS]: *peak,* 6.25 miles west-southwest of Clio (lat. 39°42'30" N, long. 120°41'15" W; sec. 1, T 21 N, R 11 E). Altitude 7818 feet. Named on Gold Lake (1981) 7.5' quadrangle.

Mount Etna [PLUMAS]: *peak,* 9 miles east-northeast of La Porte on Plumas-Sierra County line (lat. 39°44'45" N, long. 120°50'15" W; at NW cor. sec. 26, T 22 N, R 10 E). Altitude 7163 feet. Named on Mount Fillmore (1951) 7.5' quadrangle.

Mount Harkness [PLUMAS]: *peak,* 9 miles north-northwest of Chester (lat. 40°25'50" N, long. 121°18' W; sec. 27, T 30 N, R 6 E). Altitude 8045 feet. Named on Mount Harkness (1956) 15' quadrangle. Called Harkness Peak on Lassen Peak (1894) 1° quadrangle. The name commemorates Harvey W. Harkness, president of California Academy of Sciences from 1887 until 1895; the feature also was called Juniper Mountain (Schulz, p. 21).

Mount Hoffman [LASSEN]: *peak,* 4.5 miles north of Mount Harkness [PLUMAS] (lat. 40°29'50" N, long. 121°17'15" W; at NW cor. sec. 2, T 30 N, R 6 E). Altitude 7833 feet. Named on Mount Harkness (1956) 15' quadrangle.

Mount Hope [PLUMAS]: *peak,* 17 miles south-southwest of the village of Almanor (lat. 40°00'55" N, long. 121°20'40" W; near NE cor. sec. 19, T 25 N, R 6 E). Altitude 6610 feet. Named on Jonesville (1958) 15' quadrangle.

Mount Hope: see **Hayden Hill** [LASSEN] (2).

Mount Hough [PLUMAS]: *peak,* nearly 4 miles south-southeast of Crescent Mills (lat. 40°02'40" N, long. 120°53'05" W; sec. 8, T 25 N, R 10 E). Altitude 7232 feet. Named on Crescent Mills (1980) 7.5' quadrangle. Called Houghs Peak on Honey Lake (1893) 1° quadrangle, and called Hough Peak on United States Geological Survey's (1893b) map.

Mount Ingalls [PLUMAS]: *ridge,* north-trending, 1 mile long, 15 miles north of Blairsden (lat. 39°59'40" N, long. 120°37'35" W). Named on Grizzly Valley (1972) and Mount Ingalls (1972) 7.5' quadrangles. On Blairsden (1956) 15' quadrangle, the name "Mount Ingalls" applies to the high point on the ridge. The name commemorates the Ingalls family, settlers in Genesee Valley before 1870 (Gudde, 1949, p. 160).

Mount Jackson [PLUMAS]: *peak,* 4.5 miles north-northwest of Blairsden (lat. 39°50'30" N, long. 120°39'05" W; sec. 20, T 23 N, R 12 E); the peak is north of Jackson Creek. Altitude 6583 feet. Named on Johnsville (1972) 7.5' quadrangle.

Mount Jura [PLUMAS]: *peak,* 2 miles east of Taylorsville (lat. 40° 04'20" N, long. 120°47'50" W; at E line sec. 36, T 26 N, R 10 E). Altitude 6274 feet. Named on Taylorsville (1980) 7.5' quadrangle.

Mount Observation: see **Observation Peak** [LASSEN].

Mount Pleasant [PLUMAS]: *ridge,* southeast- to east-trending, 1.5 miles long, 6 miles north of Bucks Lake (lat. 39°37'45" N, long. 121°10'20" W; sec. 2, 3, T 24 N, R 7 E). Named on Bucks Lake (1979) 7.5' quadrangle.

Mount Saddleback: see **Saddleback** [MODOC].

Mount Stover: see **Stover Mountain** [PLUMAS].

Mount Vernon Gulch [MODOC]: *canyon,* drained by a stream that flows 1.5 miles to Washington Creek 9.5 miles northeast of Crank Mountain (lat. 41°28'30" N, long. 121°00'25" W; near SE cor. sec. 14, T 42 N, R 8 E). Named on Crank Mountain (1962) 15' quadrangle.

Mount Vida [MODOC]: *peak,* 6.5 miles northwest of Fort Bidwell (lat. 41°56'05" N, long. 120°13'25" W; near NW cor. sec. 23, T 47 N, R 15 E). Altitude 8224 feet. Named on Fort Bidwell (1962) 15' quadrangle.

Mount Washington [PLUMAS]: *peak,* 7.25 miles west of Clio (lat. 39°43'30" N, long. 120°42'45" W; sec. 35, T 22 N, R 11 E). Altitude 7369 feet. Named on Gold Lake (1981) 7.5' quadrangle. Called Bunker Hill on Downieville (1897) 30' quadrangle, but United States Board on Geographic Names (1960a, p. 18) rejected this name for the feature.

Mouse Spring [MODOC]: *spring,* 4.5 miles northwest of South Mountain (lat. 41°53'10" N, long. 120°41'45" W; sec. 27, T 47 N, R 11 E). Named on South Mountain (1962) 15' quadrangle.

Mowitz Butte [MODOC]: *peak,* 12.5 miles northwest of Jacks Butte (lat. 41°41'35" N, long. 120°59'25" W; near SE cor. sec. 36, T 45 N, R 8 E). Altitude 5128 feet. Named on Jacks Butte (1962) 15' quadrangle.

Mowitz Butte Tank [MODOC]: *intermittent lake,* 400 feet long, 11.5 miles northwest of Jacks Butte (lat. 41°40'25" N, long. 120°59'05" W); the feature is 1.25 miles south of Mowitz Butte along Mowitz Creek. Named on Jacks Butte (1962) 15' quadrangle.

Mowitz Creek [MODOC]: *stream,* flows 10.5 miles to Clear Lake Reservoir 7 miles northeast of Double Head Mountain (lat. 41°50'20" N, long. 121°04'45" W; sec. 8, T 46 N, R 8 E). Named on Clear Lake Reservoir (1951), Hackamore (1952), and Jacks Butte (1962) 15' quadrangles.

Muck Valley [LASSEN]: *valley,* 7 miles north of the village of Little Valley (lat. 40°59'45" N, long. 121°10'45" W). Named on Bieber (1961) and Little Valley (1957) 15' quadrangles.

Mud Creek [PLUMAS]: *stream,* flows nearly 6 miles to marsh along Lake Almanor 2.25 miles north-northeast of Chester (lat. 40°20'25" N, long. 121°12'25" W; sec. 28, T 29 N, R 7 E). Named on Chester (1979) and Red Cinder (1979) 7.5' quadrangles.

Mud Creek Butte [PLUMAS]: *peak,* 4.25 miles north of Chester (lat. 40°22'20" N, long. 121°12'45" W; at E line sec. 17, T 29 N, R 7 E); the peak is less than 1 mile west of Mud Creek. Named on Chester (1979) 7.5' quadrangle.

Mud Creek Rim [PLUMAS]: *escarpment*, generally northwest-trending, 6 miles long, center 3.5 mile north of Chester (lat. 40°21'45" N, long. 121°13'30" W); Mud Creek passes through the escarpment. Named on Chester (1979) and Red Cinder (1979) 7.5' quadrangles.

Mud Flat [LASSEN]: *area,* 9 miles northeast of Litchfield (lat. 40° 28'30" N, long. 120°16' W). Named on Litchfield (1954) and Wendel (1954) 15' quadrangles.

Mud Flat: see **Little Mud Flat** [LASSEN].

Mud Flat Reservoir [LASSEN]: *lake,* 300 feet long, 8 miles north-northeast of Wendel (lat. 40°26'20" N, long. 120°10'15" W; near NW cor. sec. 27, T 30 N, R 16 E); the lake is 2.5 miles east of Little Mud Flat. Named on Wendel (1954) 15' quadrangle.

Mudhole Hollow [PLUMAS]: *canyon,* drained by a stream that flows 1 mile to Humbug Valley (1) 8 miles southwest of the village of Almanor (lat. 40°08'10" N, long. 121°16' W; at W line sec. 1, T 26 N, R 6 E). Named on Jonesville (1958) 15' quadrangle.

Mud Lake [LASSEN]: *lake,* 2200 feet long, 12.5 miles west-southwest of Pelican Point (lat. 40°30'45" N, long. 120°59'25" W; on S line sec. 29, T 31 N, R 9 E). Named on Antelope Mountain (1956) 15' quadrangle.

Mud Lake [MODOC]:

(1) *intermittent lake,* 2500 feet long, 9.5 miles north-northwest of Double Head (lat. 41°53' N, long. 121°14'50" W; sec. 26, T 47 N, R 6 E). Named on Clear Lake Reservoir (1951) and Tulelake (1951) 15' quadrangles.

(2) *intermittent lake,* 7.5 miles north-northwest of Crank Mountain (lat. 41°29'30" N, long. 121°10'55" W; sec. 8, T 42 N, R 7 E). Named on Crank Mountain (1962) 15' quadrangle.

(3) *intermittent lake,* 1700 feet long, 2.5 miles east-southeast of South Mountain (lat. 41°49'30" N, long. 120°35'30" W; near S line sec. 16, T 46 N, T 12 E). Named on South Mountain (1962) 15' quadrangle.

(4) *lake,* 0.5 mile long, 20 miles south-southeast of Alturas (lat. 41° 12'10" N, long. 120°25'25" W; sec. 24, T 39 N, R 13 E). Named on Tule Mountain (1967) 7.5' quadrangle.

(5) *dry lake,* 0.5 mile long, 11 miles north-northeast of Cedarville (lat. 41°3940" N, long. 120°02'45" W; on SE cor. sec. 20, T 44 N, R 17 E). Named on Cedarville (1962) 15' quadrangle.

Mud Lake [PLUMAS]:

(1) *intermittent lake,* 3400 feet long, 4.25 miles west-northwest of the village of Almanor (lat. 40°14' N, long. 121°15' W; at SE cor. sec. 36, T 28 N, R 6 E). Named on Almanor (1955) and Jonesville (1958) 15' quadrangles.

(2) *lake,* 300 feet long, 2.5 miles north of Kettle Rock (lat. 40°10'35" N, long. 120°42'50" W; near N line sec. 26, T 27 N, R 11 E). Named on Kettle Rock (1972) 7.5' quadrangle.

(3) *lake,* 350 feet long, 5.5 miles north of Storrie (lat. 39°59'45" N, long. 121°20'05" W; sec. 29, T 25 N, R 6 E). Named on Storrie (1979) 7.5' quadrangle.

(4) *lake,* 550 feet long, 5 miles north-northeast of Bucks Lodge (lat. 39°56'45" N, long. 121°08'35" W; near S line sec. 12, T 24 N, R 7 E). Named on Bucks Lake (1979) 7.5' quadrangle.
(5) *lake,* 400 feet long, 4.5 miles north-northwest of Bucks Lodge (lat. 39°56'10" N, long. 121°12'25" W; near W line sec. 16, T 24 N, R 7 E). Named on Bucks Lake (1979) 7.5' quadrangle.
(6) *lake,* 1300 feet long, 6.5 miles west-southwest of Clio (lat. 39° 41'50" N, long. 120°41'15" W; sec. 12, T 21 N, R 11 E). Named on Gold Lake (1981) 7.5' quadrangle.

Mud Lake: see **Big Mud Lake** [MODOC]; **Blue Lake** [PLUMAS] (3); **Little Mud Lake** [MODOC]; **Lookout** [MODOC]; **Mud Lake Reservoir** [MODOC]; **Upper Mud Lake** [MODOC]; **Upper Mud Lake** [PLUMAS].

Mud Lake Reservoir [MODOC]: *lake,* 4400 feet long, 14 miles south-southwest of the village of Davis Creek (lat. 41°33'15" N, long. 120°29'40" W; mainly in sec. 20, T 43 N, R 13 E). Named on Davis Creek (1962) 15' quadrangle. Called Mud Lake on Alturas (1954) 1°x 2° quadrangle, but United States Board on Geographic Names (1983b, p. 6) rejected this name for the feature.

Mud Spring [LASSEN]:
(1) *spring,* 9 miles southwest of Likely [MODOC] (lat. 41°09'10" N, long. 120°38'35" W; near SW cor. sec. 6, T 38 N, R 12 E). Named on Likely (1962) 15' quadrangle.
(2) *spring,* 3.25 miles southwest of the village of Little Valley (lat. 40°51'40" N, long. 121°13'30" W; at SW cor. sec. 29, T 35 N, R 7 E). Named on Little Valley (1957) 15' quadrangle.
(3) *spring,* 3.5 miles north-northwest of Lava Peak (lat. 40°52'50" N, long. 120°54'35" W; sec. 24, T 35 N, R 9 E). Named on Hayden Hill (1956) 15' quadrangle.

Mud Spring [MODOC]:
(1) *spring,* 7.5 miles southeast of Crank Mountain (lat. 41°17'45" N, long. 121°03'30" W; sec. 21, T 40 N, R 8 E). Named on Crank Mountain (1962) 15' quadrangle.
(2) *spring,* 12.5 miles south of Canby (lat. 41°16' N, long. 120° 49'35" W; sec. 33, T 40 N, R 10 E). Named on Canby (1961) 15' quadrangle.

Mud Spring Gulch [MODOC]: *canyon,* drained by a stream that flows 1 mile to Shields Creek 11.5 miles east-southeast of Alturas (lat. 41°26'05" N, long. 120°19'30" W). Named on Shields Creek (1963) 7.5' quadrangle.

Mud Springs [MODOC]: *water feature,* 14 miles north-northeast of White Horse (lat. 41°29'45" N, long. 121°17' W; sec. 9, T 42 N, R 6 E). Named on White Horse (1962) 15' quadrangle.

Mud Springs: see **Bull Spring** [LASSEN].

Muggins Creek [PLUMAS]: *stream,* flows 3 miles to North Fork Feather River 6 miles north-northwest of Twain (lat. 40°06' N, long. 121°06'35" W; sec. 20, T 26 N, R 8 E). Named on Twain (1980) 7.5' quadrangle.

Muldoon Mountain [MODOC]: *peak,* 11 miles north-northwest of South Mountain on California-Oregon State line (lat. 41°59'35" N, long. 120°41'30" W; at N line sec. 22, T 48 N, R 11 E). Named on South Mountain (1962) 15' quadrangle.

Muldoon Tank: see **Lower Muldoon Tank** [MODOC]; **Upper Muldoon Tank** [MODOC].

Mule Tail Spring [LASSEN]: *spring,* 2.25 miles east-southeast of Lava Peak (lat. 40°49'20" N, long. 120°51' W; sec. 9, T 34 N, R 10 E). Named on Hayden Hill (1956) 15' quadrangle.

Mulkey Canyon [MODOC]: *canyon,* drained by a stream that flows nearly 2 miles to lowlands along Goose Lake (1) 8.5 miles south of Willow Ranch (lat. 41°47' N, long. 120°22'10" W; at E line sec. 32, T 46 N, R 14 E). Named on Willow Ranch (1962) 15' quadrangle

Mullens Spring [LASSEN]: *spring,* 7.25 miles south-southwest of Bieber (lat. 41°02'20" N, long. 121°13'30" W; near S line sec. 13, T 37 N, R 6 E). Named on Bieber (1961) 15' quadrangle.

Mulligan Slide [PLUMAS]: *relief feature,* 5 miles northwest of the village of Meadow Valley (lat. 39°59'10" N, long. 121°07' W; near W line sec. 32, T 25 N, R 8 E). Named on Meadow Valley (1980) 7.5' quadrangle.

Mumfords Hill: see **Spanish Peak** [PLUMAS].

Murdock Crossing [PLUMAS]: *locality,* 10.5 miles east of Kettle Rock along Last Chance Creek (2) (lat. 40°07'05" N, long. 120° 32' W; near SE cor. sec. 8, T 26 N, R 13 E). Named on Babcock Peak (1972) 7.5' quadrangle.

Murdock Crossing Spring [PLUMAS]: *spring,* 10.5 miles east of Kettle Rock (lat. 40°07'20" N, long. 120°32'05" W; near E line sec. 8, T 26 N, R 13 E); the spring is 1600 feet north-northwest of Murdock Crossing. Named on Babcock Peak (1972) 7.5' quadrangle.

Murphy Creek [PLUMAS]: *stream,* flows 1.5 miles to North Fork Feather River 5.5 miles north-northeast of Storrie (lat. 39°59'30" N, long. 121°16'45" W; sec. 26, T 25 N, R 6 E). Named on Storrie (1979) 7.5' quadrangle.

Murphy Flat [PLUMAS]: *area,* 5.5 miles north of Storrie (lat. 39°59'55" N, long. 121°18'55" W; sec. 28, T 25 N, R 6 E); the place is 0.5 mile north-northeast of Murphy Lake. Named on Jonesville (1958) 15' quadrangle, and on Storrie (1979) 7.5' quadrangle.

Murphy Lake [PLUMAS]: *lake,* 550 feet long, 5 miles north of Storrie (lat. 39°59'25" N, long. 121°19'05" W; near SW cor. sec. 28, T 25 N, R 6 E); the lake is 0.5 mile south-southwest of Murphy Flat. Named on Storrie (1979) 7.5' quadrangle.

Murray: see **Karlo** [LASSEN].

Murrers Upper Meadow [LASSEN]: *area,* 3 miles southeast of Pelican Point (lat. 40°36'15" N, long. 120°42' W; sec. 26, T 32 N, R 11 E). Named on Fredonyer Peak (1954) 15' quadrangle.

Myer Flat [LASSEN]: *area,* 12.5 miles south-southwest of Adin [MODOC] (lat. 41°01'15" N, long. 120°59'40" W; on S line sec. 24, T 37 N, R 8 E). Named on Adin (1962) 15' quadrangle. United States Board on Geographic Names (1968a, p. 6) rejected the form "Meyers Flat" for the name.

Myer Spring [LASSEN]: *spring,* 12.5 miles south-southwest of Adin [MODOC] (lat. 41°01' N, long. 120°59'40" W; sec. 25, T 37 N, R 8 E); the spring is at Myer Flat. Named on Adin (1962) 15' quadrangle. United States Board on Geographic Names (1968a, p. 6) rejected the form "Meyer Spring" for the name.

Myers Reservoir [LASSEN]: *lake,* 2400 feet long, 5 miles south-southwest of Adin [MODOC] (lat. 41°07'30" N, long. 120°58'10" W; at NW cor. sec. 20, T 38 N, R 9 E). Named on Adin (1962) 15' quadrangle.

Myrtle Creek: see **Pleasants Canyon** [MODOC].

— N —

Nagel Reservoir [LASSEN]: *intermittent lake,* 850 feet long, 4 miles south-southwest of Susanville (lat. 40°21'40" N, long. 120°40'10" W; sec. 19, T 29 N, R 12 E). Named on Diamond Mountain (1972) 7.5' quadrangle.

Nanney [LASSEN]: *locality,* 14 miles west-southwest of Susanville (lat. 40°20'30" N, long. 120°54'15" W). Named on Honey Lake (1893) 1° quadrangle.

Nasham Creek: see **Nesham Creek** [MODOC].

Neasham Creek: see **Nesham Creek** [MODOC].

Needle Grass Spring [MODOC]: *spring,* 5.5 miles east-northeast of the village of Davis Creek (lat. 41°44'55" N, long. 120°16'05" W; on S line sec. 21, T 45 N, R 15 E). Named on Davis Creek (1962) 15' quadrangle.

Negro Bend Spring [MODOC]: *spring,* 7 miles northeast of Double Head Mountain (lat. 41°49'50" N, long. 121°04'05" W; near NE cor. sec. 17, T 46 N, R 8 E). Named on Clear Lake Reservoir (1951) 15' quadrangle. United States Board on Geographic Names (1964a, p. 12) rejected the name "Nigger Bend Spring" for the feature.

Negro Ben Spring: see **Tionesta** [MODOC].

Negro Camp Gulch [LASSEN]: *canyon,* 3.5 miles long, mainly in Shasta County, but extends east into Lassen County 8.5 miles west-southwest of the village of Little Valley (lat. 40°50' N, long. 121°19'10" W; at SW cor. sec. 4, T 34 N, R 6 E); the feature is south of Negro Camp Mountain. Named on Jellico (1957) 15' quadrangle. Called Nigger Camp Gulch on Halls Flat (1939) 30' quadrangle.

Negro Camp Mountain [LASSEN]: *peak,* 7.5 miles southwest of the village of Little Valley (lat. 40°50'25" N, long. 121°18'05" W; on E line sec. 4, T 34 N, R 6 E). Named on Jellico (1957) 15' quadrangle. Called Niggercamp Mountain on Halls Flat (1939) 30' quadrangle. United States Board on Geographic Names (1964a, p. 12) rejected the name "Nigger Camp Mountain" for the feature.

Negro Camp Spring [LASSEN]: *spring,* 8.5 miles west-southwest of the village of Little Valley (lat. 40°49'45" N, long. 121°18'55" W; sec. 9, T 34 N, R 6 E); the spring is north of Negro Camp Mountain. Named on Jellico (1957) 15' quadrangle. Halls Flat (1939) 30' quadrangle has the name "Nigger Camp" at the site.

Negro Creek [MODOC]: *stream,* flows 4.5 miles to Parker Creek 16 miles south of the village of Davis Creek (lat. 41°30'35" N, long. 120°25'55" W; sec. 2, T 42 N, R 3 E). Named on Davis Creek (1962) 15' quadrangle, and on Dorris Reservoir (1963) 7.5' quadrangle.

Negro Gulch: see **Nigger Gulch** [MODOC].

Nelson Corral Reservoir [LASSEN]: *area,* 9 miles south-southwest of Likely [MODOC] along Dry Creek [LASSEN-MODOC] (lat. 41° 06'30" N, long. 120°33'30" W; sec. 23, 26, T 38 N, R 12 E). Named on Likely (1962) 15' quadrangle. United States Board on Geographic Names (1964b, p. 13) rejected the name "Nelson Reservoir" for the feature.

Nelson Creek [PLUMAS]: *stream,* formed by the confluence of West Branch Nelson Creek and East Nelson Creek, flows 6 miles to Middle Fork Feather River 7 miles southeast of Quincy (lat. 39°51'30" N, long. 120°51'55" W; sec. 16, T 23 N, R 10 E). Named on Blue Nose Mountain (1951) 7.5' quadrangle. The name commemorates one of the men who discovered gold along the creek (Hoover, Rensch, and Rensch, p. 281), and who had a store at the mouth of the stream (Gudde, 1949, p. 233). West Branch is 7.5 miles long and is named on Blue Nose Mountain (1951) and Mount Fillmore (1951) 7.5' quadrangles. Present East Nelson Creek is called East Branch Nelson Creek on Downieville (1897) 30' quadrangle. Postal authorities established Nelson's Creek post office 17 miles south of Quincy in 1855 and discontinued it in 1859 (Salley, p. 153). McKevitt (p. 495) mentioned a mining place of 1850 called Independence Bar that was located 4 miles up Nelson Creek.

Nelson Creek: see **East Nelson Creek** [PLUMAS].

Nelson Point [PLUMAS]: *locality,* 1.5 miles southeast of Quincy along Middle Fork Feather River (lat. 39°51'30" N, long. 120° 51' W; sec. 15, T 23 N, R 10 E); the place is nearly 1 mile east of the mouth of Nelson Creek. Site named on Blue Nose Mountain (1951) 7.5' quadrangle. Called Nelsonpoint on California Mining Bureau's (1909b) map. Whitney (p. 307) used the form "Nelson's Point" for the name. The community of Nelson's Point began at the mouth of Nelson Creek soon after discovery of gold in the creek in 1850; later it moved about a mile up Middle Fork Feather River to the stage road; a forest fire destroyed the place in 1924 (Hoover, Rensch, and Rensch, p. 281). Gudde (1975, p. 155) listed a mining site called Henpeck Camp that was along Nelson Creek less than a mile from Nelson Point.

Nelson Reservoir: see **Nelson Corral Reservoir** [LASSEN].

Nelson's Creek: see **Nelson Creek** [PLUMAS].

Nelson Spring [LASSEN]: *spring,* 8 miles south of Likely [MODOC] (lat. 41°07'05" N, long. 120°31'25" W; sec. 19, T 38 N, R 13 E). Named on Likely (1962) 15' quadrangle. United States Board on Geographic Names (1990, p. 9) rejected the name "Harter Spring" for the feature.

Nelson Springs [MODOC]: *springs,* 16 miles south-southeast of Alturas (lat. 41°16'05" N, long. 120°26'30" W; near S line sec. 26, T 40 N, R 13 E). Named on Little Juniper Reservoir (1963) 7.5' quadrangle.

Nesham Creek [MODOC]: *stream,* flows 2.5 miles to Upper Lake 6.5 miles south-southwest of Fort Bidwell (lat. 41°46'05" N, long. 120°10'40" W; sec. 17, T 45 N, R 16 E). Named on Fort Bidwell (1962) 15' quadrangle. United States Board on Geographic Names (1991, p. 5) approved the name "Neasham Creek" for the stream, and rejected the forms "Nesham Creek" and "Nasham Creek" for the name, which is for Ralph Neasham, a homesteader by the creek.

Newell [MODOC]: *village,* 50 miles west-northwest of Alturas (lat. 41°53'10" N, long. 121°22' W; sec. 26, T 47 N, R 5 E). Named on Tulelake (1951) 15' quadrangle. The name commemorates Frederick H. Newell, first chief engineer of the Reclamation Service; a Japanese relocation center was at the place during World War II (Gudde, 1949, p. 235).

Newland Meadows [LASSEN]: *valley,* 21 miles east of Madeline along Bare Creek (lat. 41°06'40" N, long. 120°04'50" W; sec. 31, T 38 N, R 17 E). Named on Little Hat Mountain (1962) 7.5' quadrangle.

Newland Reservoir [LASSEN]: *lake,* 2400 feet long, 20 miles east of Madeline along Bare Creek (lat. 41°05'40" N, long. 120°05' W; on S line sec. 6, T 37 N, R 17 E); the lake is 1.25 miles south of Newland Meadows. Named on Little Hat Mountain (1962) 7.5' quadrangle.

Newland Springs [LASSEN]: *springs,* 20 miles east of Madeline along Bare Creek (lat. 41°04'50" N, long. 120°06'05" W; on N line sec. 13, T 37 N, R 16 E); the springs are 2.5 miles south-southwest of Newland Meadows. Named on Little Hat Mountain (1962) 7.5' quadrangle.

New Pine Creek [MODOC]: *village,* 7 miles north-northeast of Willow Ranch on California-Oregon State line (lat. 41°59'35" N, long. 120°17'50" W; at NE cor. sec. 24, T 48 N, R 14 E); the village is along Pine Creek (2). Named on Willow Ranch (1962) 15' quadrangle. Postal authorities established Fairport post office 2 miles southwest of New Pine Creek in 1912, discontinued it for a time in 1924, and discontinued it finally in 1932; cattle and timber were ferried across Goose Lake (1) to the railroad at the place (Salley, p. 72). California Division of Highways' (1934) map shows a place called Joffre located along Nevada-California-Oregon Railroad 4.5 miles south-southwest of Pine Creek (present New Pine Creek).

Newton Flat: see **Newtown Flat** [PLUMAS].

Newtown Flat [PLUMAS]: *area,* 3 miles north-northwest of Quincy (lat. 39°58'30" N, long. 120°57'35" W; sec. 3, T 24 N, R 9 E). Named on Quincy (1950) 7.5' quadrangle. Called Newton Flat on Quincy (1951) 15' quadrangle.

Nichols Spring [MODOC]: *spring,* nearly 7 miles southeast of Crank Mountain (lat. 40°18'30" N, long. 121°03'50" W; near W line sec. 16, T 40 N, R 8 E). Named on Crank Mountain (1962) 15' quadrangle.

Nigger Bend Spring: see **Negro Bend Spring** [MODOC].

Nigger Ben Spring: see **Negro Bend Spring**, under **Tionesta** [MODOC].

Nigger Camp: see **Negro Camp Spring** [LASSEN].

Nigger Camp Gulch: see **Negro Camp Gulch** [LASSEN].

Niggercamp Mountain: see **Negro Camp Mountain** [LASSEN].

Nigger Gulch [MODOC]: *canyon,* drained by a stream that flows 3 miles to Turner Creek (1) 8 miles east-northeast of Crank Mountain (lat. 41°25'30" N, long. 121°00'10" W; near W line sec. 1, T 41 N, R 8 E). Named on Canby (1961) 15' quadrangle. United States Board on Geographic Names (1968a, p. 6) approved the name "Negro Gulch" for the canyon.

Nigger Mountain [LASSEN]: *peak,* 4 miles northwest of Lava Peak (lat. 40°52'45" N, long. 120°56'15" W; near SW cor. sec. 23, T 35 N, R 9 E). Named on Hayden Hill (1956) 15' quadrangle.

Nigger Run Ravine [PLUMAS]: *canyon,* drained by a stream that flows 2.25 miles to South Branch of Middle Fork Feather River nearly 2 miles north-northeast of Cascade (lat. 39°43'30" N, long. 121°09'40" W; near N line sec. 35, T 22 N, R 7 E). Named on Cascade (1948) 7.5' quadrangle.

Niles Canyon [MODOC]: *canyon,* drained by a stream that flows 1 mile to Higgins Flat (lat. 41°18'25" N, long. 120°55'05" W; sec. 15, T 40 N, R 9 E). Named on Canby (1961) 15' quadrangle.

Niles Flat [MODOC]: *area,* 11 miles south-southwest of Canby (lat. 41°18' N, long. 120°56'40" W; on S line sec. 16, T 40 N, R 9 E); the place is 1 mile west of Niles Canyon. Named on Canby (1961) 15' quadrangle.

Niles Spring [MODOC]: *spring,* 11 miles south-southwest of Canby (lat. 41°17'40" N, long. 120°56'30" W; sec. 21, T 40 N, R 9 E); the spring is near the south end of Niles Flat. Named on Canby (1961) 15' quadrangle.

Ninemile Creek [MODOC]: *stream,* flows 3 miles to Cow Head Lake 8 miles northeast of Fort Bidwell (lat. 41°56'40" N, long. 120°03'15" W; at E line sec. 18, T 47 N, R 17 E). Named on Fort Bidwell (1962) 15' quadrangle.

9 Mile Gap: see **Canby** [MODOC].

Ninemile Point [LASSEN]: *promontory,* 9 miles west-northwest of Termo along Madeline Plains (lat. 40°56' N, long. 120°36'30" W; around NE cor. sec. 29, T 36 N, R 12 E). Named on Grasshopper Valley (1954) 15' quadrangle.

Nine Springs Reservoir [LASSEN]: *lake,* 1700 feet long, 3.25 miles west of Bieber (lat. 41°07'30" N, long. 120°12'20" W; on N line sec. 19, T 38 N, R 7 E). Named on Bieber (1961) 15' quadrangle.

Noble Bluff [MODOC]: *relief feature,* 3.5 miles east-northeast of Crank Mountain (lat. 41°24'10" N, long. 121°04'50" W). Named on Crank Mountain (1962) 15' quadrangle.

Noble Creek [MODOC]: *stream,* flows 4.5 miles to Pit River 4.25 miles west of Alturas (lat. 41°29'05" N, long. 120°37'40" W; sec. 18, T 42 N, R 12 E). Named on Alturas (1961) and Big Sage Reservoir (1962) 15' quadrangles.

No Ear Bar [PLUMAS]: *locality,* 6.5 miles south of Quincy along Middle Fork Feather River (lat. 39°50'45" N, long. 120°58'05" W; near NW cor. sec. 22, T 23 N, R 9 E). Named on Onion Valley (1950) 7.5' quadrangle.

Nokopen: see **Lake Nokopen**, under **Westwood** [LASSEN].

Noonas Spring [MODOC]: *spring,* 3.5 miles east-southeast of White Horse (lat. 41°17'05" N, long. 121°20'30" W; near S line sec. 24, T 40 N, R 5 E). Named on White Horse (1962) 15' quadrangle.

North Arm Indian Valley: see **Indian Valley** [PLUMAS].

North Arm Rice Creek [PLUMAS]: *stream,* flows 9.5 miles to North Fork Feather River 8 miles southwest of Mount Harkness (lat. 40° 21'15" N, long. 121°24'45" W; near S line sec. 22, T 29 N, R 5 E). Named on Mount Harkness (1956) 15' quadrangle.

North Barber Creek [MODOC]: *stream,* flows 3.25 miles to Surprise Valley 6 miles south-southeast of Eagleville (lat. 41°14'15" N, long. 120°04'40" W; near NE cor. sec. 19, T 39 N, R 17 E). Named on Emerson Peak (1962) and Snake Lake (1962) 7.5' quadrangles.

North Canyon [PLUMAS]: *canyon,* drained by a stream that flows 1.5 miles to Wolf Creek at Greenville (lat. 40°08'15" N, long. 120° 57'05" W; sec. 3, T 26 N, R 9 E). Named on Crescent Mills (1980) and Greenville (1979) 7.5' quadrangles. The name is from the location of the feature north of Round Valley Reservoir (Gudde, 1975, p. 245). United States Geological Survey's (1907) map has the name "McClellan Ravine" for a canyon situated about 1 mile east of North Canyon.

North Caribou [LASSEN]: *peak,* 15 miles northwest of Westwood (lat. 40°28'35" N, long. 121°11'05" W; sec. 10, T 30 N, R 7 E); the peak is 1 mile north-northwest of South Caribou. Altitude 7793 feet. Named on Red Cinder (1979) 7.5' quadrangle.

North Creek [LASSEN]: *stream,* flows 3.25 miles to Bare Creek 22 miles east-northeast of Madeline (lat. 41°08'30" N, long. 120°04'35" W; at W line sec. 20, T 38 N, R 17 E). Named on Snake Lake (1962) 7.5' quadrangle.

North Deep Creek [MODOC]: *stream,* flows 4.5 miles to Surprise Valley 2 miles southwest of Cedarville (lat. 41°30'30" N, long. 120°11'55" W; at W line sec. 18, T 42 N, R 16 E). Named on Cedarville (1962) and Davis Creek (1962) 15' quadrangles.

North Divide Lake [LASSEN]: *lake,* 1800 feet long, 17 miles northwest of Westwood (lat. 40°29'45" N, long. 121°12'15" W; near N line sec. 4, T 30 N, R 7 E); the lake is 1700 feet northeast of South Divide Lake. Named on Red Cinder (1979) 7.5' quadrangle.

North Emerson Lake [MODOC]: *lake,* 750 feet long, 4.5 miles southwest of Eagleville (lat. 41°16'05" N, long. 120°10'35" W; near NE cor. sec. 8, T 39 N, R 16 E); the lake is at the head of North Fork Emerson Creek. Named on Eagle Peak (1963) 7.5' quadrangle.

North Fork: see **Seneca** [PLUMAS].

Northfork: see **Rush Creek** [PLUMAS].

North Fork Campground [PLUMAS]: *locality,* 4.5 miles southwest of Caribou (lat. 40°02'25" N, long. 121°13'10" W; sec. 8, T 25 N, R 7 E); the place is along North Fork Feather River. Named on Caribou (1979) 7.5' quadrangle.

North Fork Campground: see **Little North Fork Campground** [PLUMAS].

North Fork Creek: see **Twelvemile Creek** [MODOC].

North Gulch [LASSEN]: *canyon,* drained by a stream that flows 1.5 miles to Pit River 7.25 miles north of the village of Little Valley (lat. 40°59'40"

N, long. 121°09'10" W; at S line sec. 34, T 37 N, R 7 E). Named on Little Valley (1957) 15' quadrangle.

North Mountain [MODOC]: *peak,* 13 miles north of Alturas (lat. 41° 40'20" N, long. 120°30'40" W; sec. 7, T 44 N, R 13 E). Altitude 5152 feet. Named on Big Sage Reservoir (1962) 15' quadrangle.

North Spring [MODOC]: *spring,* 2.25 miles east-northeast of Hackamore (lat. 41°33'50" N, long. 121°04'45" W; near SW cor. sec. 17, T 43 N, R 8 E). Named on Hackamore (1952) 15' quadrangle.

North Star Basin [MODOC]: *relief feature,* 7 miles north-northwest of Fort Bidwell (lat. 41°56'45" N, long. 120°13' W; sec. 14, T 47 N, R 15 E). Named on Fort Bidwell (1962) 15' quadrangle.

North Stover Mountain [PLUMAS]: *ridge,* northwest-trending, 2.5 miles long, 7.5 miles south-southwest of Mount Harkness (lat. 40° 19'50" N, long. 121°21' W); the ridge is northwest of Stover Mountain. Named on Mount Harkness (1956) 15' quadrangle.

North Valley [PLUMAS]: *valley,* 3.25 miles west-northwest of Storrie (lat. 39°56' N, long. 121°22'50" W; sec. 14, T 24 N, R 5 E). Named on Kimshew Point (1979) 7.5' quadrangle.

North Valley Creek [PLUMAS]: *stream,* flows about 5.5 miles to Rock Creek (4) 2.5 miles northwest of Storrie (lat. 39°56'15" N, long. 121°21'40" W); the stream goes through North Valley. Named on Kimshew Point (1979) and Storrie (1979) 7.5' quadrangles.

North Valley Creek: see **Little North Valley Creek** [PLUMAS].

Norvell [LASSEN]: *locality,* 12.5 miles north of Westwood along Western Pacific Railroad (lat. 40°29'10" N, long. 121°00'15" W; near SE cor. sec. 6, T 30 N, R 9 E). Named on Chester (1956) 15' quadrangle.

Norvell: see **Lake Norvell** [LASSEN].

Norvell Flat [LASSEN]: *area,* 12.5 miles north of Westwood (lat. 40°29'15" N, long. 121°00'30" W). Named on Harvey Mountain (1956) 15' quadrangle, and on Swain Mountain (1979) 7.5' quadrangle.

Nubieber [LASSEN]: *village,* nearly 3 miles southwest of Bieber (lat. 41°05'45" N, long. 121°10'50" W; around SE cor. sec. 29, T 38 N, R 7 E). Named on Bieber (1961) 15' quadrangle. Postal authorities established Nubieber post office in 1931; the name is from the term "New Bieber" (Salley, p. 157). L.H. Martin of Bieber Chamber of Commerce named the place when Great Northern Railroad and Western Pacific Railroad were extended to meet at the site in 1931 (Gudde, 1949, p. 239).

Nye Creek [PLUMAS]: *stream,* flows 3 miles to South Branch Ward Creek 10 miles south of Kettle Rock (lat. 40°00'05" N, long. 120° 42'05" W; at E line sec. 26, T 25 N, R 11 E); the stream heads at Nye Meadows. Named on Genesee Valley (1972) and Mount Ingalls (1972) 7.5' quadrangles.

Nye Meadows [PLUMAS]: *area,* 1.25 miles west-southwest of Mount Ingalls (lat. 39°59'20" N, long. 120°39' W; sec. 29, T 25 N, R 12 E). Named on Mount Inglls (1972) 7.5' quadrangle.

Nye Spring [LASSEN]: *spring,* 5.25 miles southwest of Observation Peak (lat. 40°42'10" N, long. 120°13'30" W; near S line sec. 24, T 33 N, R 15 E). Named on Shinn Mountain (1954) 15' quadrangle.

—O—

Oak Flat [PLUMAS]:

(1) *area,* less than 0.5 mile northwest of Caribou (lat. 40°05'05" N, long. 121°09'30" W; at N line sec. 26, T 26 N, R 7 E). Named on Caribou (1979) 7.5' quadrangle.

(2) *area,* 8.5 miles south-southeast of Kettle Rock along Red Clover Creek (lat. 40°02'20" N, long. 120°38'30" W; near W line sec. 9, T 25 N, R 12 E). Named on Genesee Valley (1972) 7.5' quadrangle. On Kettle Rock (1950) 15' quadrangle, the name applies to an area located nearly 0.5 mile farther east.

Oak Ravine [PLUMAS]: *canyon,* drained by a stream that flows 2.25 miles to East Branch of North Fork Feather River 6 miles southwest of Caribou (lat. 40°00'50" N, long. 121°13'20" W; near N line sec. 20, T 25 N, R 7 E). Named on Bucks Lake (1979) and Caribou (1979) 7.5' quadrangles.

Oak Ridge [MODOC]: *ridge,* south-southwest-tending, 2.5 miles long, 8.5 miles northeast or Crank Mountain (41°28'45" N, long. 121°02'15" W). Named on Crank Mountain (1962) 15' quadrangle.

Oak Ridge [PLUMAS]: *ridge,* west-trending, 2.25 miles long, 4.25 miles south-southeast of Storrie (lat. 39°52' N, long. 121°17' W). Named on Soapstone Hill (1979) 7.5' quadrangle.

Oats Meadow [PLUMAS]: *area,* 3.5 miles north of La Porte in Pancake Ravine (lat. 39°43'20" N, long. 120°58'25" W; sec. 33, T 22 N, R 9 E). Named on La Porte (1951) 7.5' quadrangle.

Observation Peak [LASSEN]: *peak,* 35 miles northeast of Susanville (lat. 40°46'30" N, long. 120°10'15" W). Altitude 7964 feet. Named on Observation Peak (1954) 15' quadrangle. United States Board on Geographic Names (1978b, p. 4) rejected the name "Mount Observation" for the peak.

O' Connors Flat [MODOC]: *area,* 6.25 miles north-northwest of Fort Bidwell (lat. 41°56'50" N, long. 120°11' W; sec. 18, T 47 N, R 16 E). Named on Fort Bidwell (1962) 15' quadrangle.

Oddie Bar [PLUMAS]: *locality,* 7.5 miles south-southwest of Quincy (lat. 39°50'10" N, long. 120°59'25" W; near SE cor. sec. 20, T 23 N, R 9 E). Named on Onion Valley (1950) 7.5' quadrangle.

Ohio Creek [PLUMAS]: *stream,* flows 3.5 miles to North Fork Feather River 2.5 miles south-southwest of Canyondam (lat. 40°08'35" N, long. 121°06' W; near E line sec. 5, T 26 N, R 8 E). Named on Almanor (1979) and Canyondam (1979) 7.5' quadrangles.

Ohio Ravine [PLUMAS]: *canyon,* drained by a stream that flows 0.5 mile to Coldwater Creek (2) 5.25 miles south-southwest of Bucks Lodge (lat. 39°48'20" N, long. 121°12'25" W; near W line sec. 33, T 23 N, R 7 E). Named on Haskins Valley (1980) 7.5' quadrangle.

Ohio Valley [PLUMAS]: *relief feature,* 3.5 miles southwest of Canyondam (lat. 40°08'45" N, long. 121°07'30" W; sec. 6, T 26 N, R 8 E); the feature is along Ohio Creek. Named on Almanor (1979) and Canyondam (1979) 7.5' quadrangles.

Old Camp One [MODOC]: *locality,* 7.5 miles west-southwest of Timber Mountain (lat. 41°34'45" N, long. 121°25'15" W; sec. 8, T 43 N, R 5 E). Named on Timber Mountain (1952) 15' quadrangle.

Oldhouse Creek [PLUMAS]: *stream,* flows 2 miles to Big Grizzly Creek 5.25 miles south-southeast of Mount Ingalls (lat. 39°55'40" N, long. 120°34'35" W; near S line sec. 24, T 24 N, R 12 E). Named on Grizzly Valley (1972) 7.5' quadrangle. Downieville (1897) 30' quadrangle has the form "Old House Cr." for the name.

Old Likely Mill [MODOC]: *locality,* 9.5 miles west of Likely (lat. 41°13'15" N, long. 120°40'45" W; sec. 14, T 39 N, R 11 E). Named on Likely (1962) 15' quadrangle.

O' Leary Flat: see **Larry Flat Campground** [MODOC].

Oliver Creek [PLUMAS]:

(1) *stream,* flows 1.5 miles to Little Grizzly Creek 5 miles west of Mount Ingalls (lat. 39°59'05" N, long. 120°42'55" W; sec. 35, T 25 N, R 11 E). Named on Mount Ingalls (1972) 7.5' quadrangle.

(2) *stream,* flows 2 miles to Middle Fork Feather River 9 miles east-southeast of Quincy (lat. 39°52' N, long. 120°48'10" W; near E line sec. 12, T 23 N, R 10 E). Named on Blue Nose Mountain (1951) 7.5' quadrangle.

Oliver Flat [PLUMAS]: *area,* 4.5 miles north of Storrie (lat. 39°59'05" N, long. 121°19'40" W; near N line sec. 32, T 25 N, R 6 E); the place is 0.25 mile north of Oliver Lake. Named on Storrie (1979) 7.5' quadrangle.

Oliver Lake [PLUMAS]: *lake,* 450 feet long, 4.25 miles north of Storrie (lat. 39°58'50" N, long. 121°19'45" W; sec. 32, T 25 N, R 6 E). Named on Storrie (1979) 7.5' quadrangle.

Ollie Rivis Spring [LASSEN]: *spring,* 5 miles north-northwest of Lava Peak in Sheep Valley (lat. 40°53'35" N, long. 120°56'05" W; sec. 14, T 35 N, R 9 E). Named on Hayden Hill (1956) 15' quadrangle.

Olson Mountain [LASSEN]: *peak,* nearly 4 miles south-southeast of Madeline (lat. 41°00'20" N, long. 120°26' W; at SW cor. sec. 25, T 37 N, R 13 E). Altitude 6807 feet. Named on Madeline (1962) 7.5' quadrangle.

Omira [LASSEN]: *locality,* 2.25 miles west-northwest of Constantia along Western Pacific Railroad (lat. 39°57'55" N, long. 120°04'35" W; sec. 4, T 24 N, R 17 E). Named on Constantia (1977) 7.5' quadrangle. Postal authorities established Omira post office in 1910, discontinued it in 1911, reestablished it in 1915, and discontinued it in 1918; officials of Western Pacific Railroad named the place for a woman who promised to build a church at the site if they would name the place for her (Salley, p. 161).

O' Neals Springs [MODOC]: *springs,* 5.25 miles east-northeast of Lookout (lat. 41°13'45" N, long. 121°03'15" W; near S line sec. 9, T 39 N, R 8 E). Named on Bieber (1961) 15' quadrangle.

Onion Creek [PLUMAS]: *stream,* flows 2.5 miles to Slate Creek (3) 2.5 miles south-southwest of American House (lat. 39°37'05" N, long. 121°02'45" W; sec. 2, T 20 N, R 8 E). Named on American House (1948) and Strawberry Valley (1948) 7.5' quadrangles.

Onion Flat [PLUMAS]: *area,* 4.5 miles north-northeast of Twain (lat. 40°04'35" N, long. 121°01'40" W; on S line sec. 25, T 26 N, R 8 E). Named on Twain (1980) 7.5' quadrangle.

Onion Valley [PLUMAS]: *locality,* 10.5 miles south-southeast of Quincy (lat. 39°47'40" N, long. 120°52'55" W; sec. 5, T 22 N, R 10 E). Site named on Onion Valley (1950) 7.5' quadrangle. Postal authorities established Onion Valley post office in 1855, discontinued it in 1870, reestablished it in 1918, and discontinued it in 1923 (Salley, p. 161). A party of prospectors gave the name "Onion Valley" to the spot in 1850 because of wild onions there (Hoover, Rensch, and Rensch, p. 280-281). According to Gudde (1975, p. 106), the name "Eclipse" was an alternate designation for Onion Valley. Postal authorities established Eclipse post office 9 miles south of Nelson Point in 1897 and discontinued it in 1912; the name was from Eclipse mining claim (Salley, p. 65).

Onion Valley Creek [PLUMAS]: *stream,* flows 11.5 miles to Middle Fork Feather River 1.5 miles north-northeast of Dogwood Peak (lat. 39°48'30" N, long. 121°02'35" W; at W line sec. 36, T 23 N, R 8 E); the stream goes past the site of the old community of Onion Valley. Named on Blue Nose Mountain (1951), Dogwood Peak (1979), and Onion Valley (1950) 7.5' quadrangles.

Onion Valley Reservoir [PLUMAS]: *lake,* 450 feet long, 10.5 miles south-southeast of Quincy (lat. 39°47'35" N, long. 120°52'40" W; near E line sec. 5, T 22 N, R 10 E); the lake is along Onion Valley Creek at the site of the old community of Onion Valley. Named on Onion Valley (1950) 7.5' quadrangle.

Opahwah Butte [MODOC]: see **Rattlesnake Butte** [MODOC] (2).

Opapee Creek [PLUMAS]: *stream*, flows 1.5 miles to North Fork Feather River 5 miles north-northeast of Storrie (lat. 39°59'10" N, long. 121°16'50" W; near NW cor. sec. 35, T 25 N, R 6 E). Named on Storrie (1979) 7.5' quadrangle.

Opdyke Cow Camp [LASSEN]: *locality*, 10 miles west-northwest of Pelican Point (lat. 40°42'25" N, long. 120°54'45" W; sec. 24, T 33 N, R 9 E). Named on Antelope Mountain (1956) 15' quadrangle.

Orchard: see **The Orchard**, under **Orchard Spring** [LASSEN].

Orchard Spring [LASSEN]: *spring*, 23 miles east of Madeline (lat. 41°01'55" N, long. 120°01'55" W; sec. 34, T 37 N, R 17 E). Named on Little Hat Mountain (1962) 7.5' quadrangle United States Board on Geographic Names (1964b, p. 13) rejected the names "Garden Spring," "Reeders Garden," and "The Orchard" for the feature; the Board pointed out that the name "Orchard Spring" is from an abandoned apple orchard near the spring.

Oregon Rim Reservoir [MODOC]: *lake*, 200 feet long, 9 miles north of South Mountain (lat. 41°58'20" N, long. 120°18'05" W; sec. 30, T 48 N, R 12 E). Named on South Mountain (1962) 15' quadrangle.

Ostrom Point [MODOC]: *relief feature*, 2 miles southeast of Crank Mountain along Pit River (lat. 41°21'45" N, long. 121°07' W; at W line sec. 25, T 41 N, R 7 E). Named on Crank Mountain (1962) 15' quadrangle.

Otis Canyon [LASSEN]: *canyon*, drained by a stream that flows nearly 2 miles to Honey Lake Valley 5.5 miles east-southeast of Milford (lat. 40°08'10" N, long. 120°16'15" W; sec. 3, T 26 N, R 15 E). Named on Ferris Creek (1977) and Milford (1977) 7.5' quadrangles.

Owl Creek [MODOC]: *stream*, flows 8 miles to marsh along Middle Alkali Lake 3.5 miles north-northeast of Eagleville (lat. 41°22' N, long. 120°05'30" W; sec. 6, T 40 N, R 17 E). Named on Eagle Peak (1963), Eagleville (1963), Hansen Island (1963), and Warren Peak (1963) 7.5' quadrangles. The name is from a large rock outcrop that has the appearance a huge owl (Payne, p. 6).

Owl Creek [PLUMAS]: *stream*, flows 2 miles to Clear Creek (1) 6.5 miles north-northwest of Twain (lat. 40°06'30" N, long. 121°07'25" W; sec. 18, T 26 N, R 8 E). Named on Twain (1980) 7.5' quadrangle.

Owl Creek: see **Little Owl Creek** [MODOC].

Oxendine Draw [LASSEN]: *canyon*, 1.5 miles long, 14 miles southeast of Adin [MODOC] (lat. 41°02'55" N, long. 120°45'30" W). Named on Adin (1962) 15' quadrangle.

Oxendine Spring [LASSEN]: *spring*, 18 miles southwest of Likely [MODOC] (lat. 41°03'30" N, long. 120°44'55" W; sec. 7, T 37 N, R 11 E); the spring is near the mouth of Oxendine Draw. Named on Likely (1962) 15' quadrangle.

Oxford Creek [PLUMAS]: *stream*, flows nearly 1 mile to Frazier Creek (1) 6 miles southwest of Bucks Lodge (lat. 39°48'25" N, long. 121°14'25" W; sec. 31, T 23 N, R 7 E). Named on Haskins Valley (1980) 7.5' quadrangle. On Bidwell Bar (1897) 30' quadrangle, the canyon of the stream is called Axford Ravine, but United States Board on Geographic Names (1979, p. 5) rejected both the names "Axford Ravine" and "Axford Creek" for the feature

—P—

Packwood: see **Billy Packwood Spring** [LASSEN]; **Jim Packwood Spring** [LASSEN].

Packwood Flat [LASSEN]: *area*, 13 miles south of Adin [MODOC] along East Fork Juniper Creek (lat. 41°00'30" N, long. 120°58'30" W). Named on Adin (1962) and Hayden Hill (1956) 15' quadrangles.

Painted Dunes [LASSEN]: *relief feature*, 12 miles southwest of Cal Mountain on Lassen-Shasta County line (lat. 40°32'30" N, long. 121°19' W; at S line sec. 16, T 31 N, R 6 E); the feature is on the south side of Cinder Cone. Named on Prospect Peak (1957) 15 quadrangle. The colorful feature is composed of debris from Cinder Cone (Schulz, p. 41).

Painters Creek [LASSEN]: *stream*, flows 7 miles to Madeline Plains 4.25 miles north-northeast of Observation Peak (lat. 40°50' N, long. 120°08'30" W; near SW cor. sec. 2, T 34 N, R 16 E). Named on Observation Peak (1954) 15' quadrangle.

Painters Flat [LASSEN]: *area*, 8 miles east of Observation Peak (lat. 40°46' N, long. 120°01' W). Named on Observation Peak (1954) and Shinn Mountain (1954) 15' quadrangles. Symons (p. 116) referred to Painter's Flat. The feature extends east into the State of Nevada.

Palmetto [PLUMAS]: *locality*, 6.5 miles south of Storrie (lat. 39°49'20" N, long. 121°19'10" W; near NW cor. sec. 28, T 23 N, R 6 E). Named on Soapstone Hill (1979) 7.5' quadrangle.

Palmetto Creek [PLUMAS]: *stream*, flows 1.5 miles to Wildcat Creek 6 miles south of Storrie (lat. 39°49'55" N, long. 121°20'35" W; near E line sec. 19, T 23 N, R 6 E); the stream heads near Palmetto. Named on Soapstone Hill (1979) 7.5' quadrangle.

Pancake Ravine [PLUMAS]: *canyon*, drained by a stream that flows 3.25 miles to South Fork Feather River 3.25 miles north of La Porte (lat. 39°43'45" N, long. 120°59'35" W; sec. 32, T 22 N, R 9 E). Named on La Porte (1951) 7.5' quadrangle.

Panhandle: see **The Panhandle** [MODOC].

Panhandle Creek [PLUMAS]: *stream*, flows 1.5 miles to L-T Creek 13 miles southwest of the village of Almanor (lat. 40°05'30" N, long. 121°20'35" W; near W line sec. 20, T 26 N, R 6 E). Named on Jonesville (1958) 15' quadrangle.

Panther Creek [PLUMAS]: *stream*, flows 2.25 miles to North Arm Rice Creek 8 miles west of Mount Harkness (lat. 40°24'40" N, long. 121°26'35" W; near SE cor. sec. 32, T 30 N, R 6 E). Named on Mount Harkness (1956) 15' quadrangle.

Panther Spring [LASSEN]: *spring*, 13 miles southwest of Cal Mountain (lat. 40°31'40" N, long. 121°18'45" W; at N line sec. 28, T 31 N, R 6 E). Named on Prospect Peak (1957) 15' quadrangle.

Paola [MODOC]: *locality*, 2.5 miles south-southeast of Alturas along Southern Pacific Railroad (lat. 41°27'20" N, long. 120°31'35" W; near NE cor. sec. 25, T 42 N, R 12 E). Named on Alturas (1961) 15' quadrangle.

Papoose Creek [LASSEN]: *stream*, flows 2 miles to Eagle Lake 5.25 miles south of Pelican Point (lat. 40°33'10" N, long. 120°45'50" W; sec. 8, T 31 N, R 11 E). Named on Antelope Mountain (1956) 15' quadrangle. The name is from an Indian baby found after a conflict between Indians and settlers in 1866 (Purdy, 1988, p. 120).

Papoose Meadows [LASSEN]: *valley*, 8 miles south of Pelican Point (lat. 40°31'30" N, long. 120°45'30" W; sec. 20, 29, T 31 N, R 11 E); the valley is at the head of Papoose Creek. Named on Antelope Mountain (1956) 15' quadrangle, which shows marsh in part of the valley.

Papoose Peak [PLUMAS]: *peak*, 12.5 miles east-southeast of Kettle Rock (lat. 40°04'25" N, long. 120°30'15" W; near S line sec. 27, T 26 N, R 13 E). Altitude 6705 feet. Named on Babcock Peak (1972) 7.5' quadrangle.

Paradise Creek [PLUMAS]: *stream*, flows 1.5 miles to Little Grizzly Creek 4 miles south-southwest of Mount Ingalls (lat. 39°56'25" N, long. 120°39'05" W; near S line sec. 17, T 24 N, R 12 E). Named on Mount Ingalls (1972) 7.5' quadrangle.

Parker Creek [LASSEN]: *stream*, flows 3.5 miles to Honey Lake Valley 9 miles southwest of Litchfield (lat. 40°17'15" N, long. 120°29'45" W; sec. 15, T 28 N, R 13 E). Named on Janesville (1972) and Standish (1972) 7.5' quadrangles.

Parker Creek [MODOC]: *stream*, formed by the confluence of Middle Fork and North Fork, flows 12.5 miles to North Fork Pit River 16 miles south-southwest of the village of Davis Creek (lat. 41°31'15" N, long. 120°28'30" W; sec. 33, T 43 N, R 13 E). Named on Davis Creek (1962) 15' quadrangle, and on Dorris Reservoir (1963) and Shields Creek (1963) 7.5' quadrangles. The name recalls R.L. Parker and his family, who settled by the stream in 1870 (Laird, p. 36-37). Middle Fork is 5 miles long and North Fork is 3 miles long; both forks are named on Shields Creek (1963) and Warren Peak (1963) 7.5' quadrangles. South Fork enters from the south nearly 0.5 mile downstream from the confluence of Middle Fork and North Fork; it is 5.5 miles long and is named on Sheilds Creek (1963) and Warren Peak (1963) 7.5' quadrangles. Little North Fork enters from the north nearly 0.5 mile downstream from the confluence of Middle Fork and North Fork; it is 2.5 miles long and is named on Shields Creek (1963) 7.5' quadrangle.

Parsnip Creek [LASSEN]: *stream*, flows 8 miles to Cedar Creek 8.5 miles northeast of Madeline (lat. 41°09'05" N, long. 120°22'15" W; near S line sec. 4, T 38 N, R 14 E). Named on Jess Valley (1962) 7.5' quadrangle.

Parsnip Creek: see **Little Parsnip Creek** [LASSEN].

Parsnip Springs [LASSEN]: *locality*, 13 miles east-northeast of Madeline (lat. 41°09'30" N, long. 120°15'45" W; sec. 15, T 38 N, R 15 E); the place is along a branch of Parsnip Creek. Named on Jess Valley (1962) 7.5' quadrangle.

Pat Maloy Ravine [PLUMAS]: *canyon*, drained by a stream that flows 2 miles to Lower Bucks Lake 2.5 miles northwest of Bucks Lodge (lat. 39°53'55" N, long. 121°12'25" W; near N line sec. 33, T 24 N, R 7 E). Named on Bucks Lake (1979) 7.5' quadrangle.

Pat Morris Camp [LASSEN]: *locality*, 1.25 miles northwest of Lava Peak (lat. 40°50'30" N, long. 120°54'45" W; sec. 1, T 34 N, R 9 E); the place is 3500 feet southwest of Pat Morris Spring. Named on Hayden Hill (1956) 15' quadrangle.

Pat Morris Spring [LASSEN]: *spring*, 1.25 miles north-northwest of Lava Peak (lat. 40°50'50" N, long. 120°54' W; at SW cor. sec. 31, T 35 N, R 10 E). Named on Hayden Hill (1956) 15' quadrangle.

Patricia Lake [PLUMAS]: *lake*, 300 feet long, 10 miles west-southwest of Mount Harkness on Plumas-Tehama County line (lat. 40° 24'05" N, long. 121°29' W; sec. 1, T 29 N, R 4 E). Named on Mount Harkness (1956) 15' quadrangle.

Pat Spring [MODOC]: *spring*, 13 miles south of Alturas (lat. 41°18'10" N, long. 120°30'20" W; sec. 17, T 40 N, R 13 E). Named on Alturas (1961) 15' quadrangle.

Patterson Flat [LASSEN]: *area,* 4 miles north of Cal Mountain (lat. 40°44'35" N, long. 121°09'40" W; on N line sec. 11, T 33 N, R 7 E). Named on Harvey Mountain (1956) 15' quadrangle.

Patterson Lake [MODOC]: *lake,* 0.25 mile long, 10 miles south-southwest of Cedarville (lat. 41°22'55" N, long. 120°13'10" W; near NE cor. sec. 22, T 41 N, R 15 E). Named on Warren Peak (1963) 7.5' quadrangle.

Patterson Meadow [MODOC]: *valley,* 9.5 miles south-southwest of Eagleville (lat. 41°11'30" N, long. 120°11'35" W; sec. 5, 6, T 38 N, R 16 E). Named on Emerson Peak (1962) 7.5' quadrangle.

Patterson Mountain [LASSEN]: *peak,* 10.5 miles south-southeast of Little Valley (lat. 40°45'10" N, long. 121°07' W; sec. 6, T 33 N, R 8 E). Altitude 6882 feet. Named on Harvey Mountain (1956) and Little Valley (1957) 15' quadrangles.

Patterson Well [LASSEN]: *well,* 5 miles north of Cal Mountain (lat. 40°44'30" N, long. 121°09'20" W; sec. 11, T 33 N, R 7 E); the well is at Patterson Flat. Named on Harvey Mountain (1956) 15' quadrangle.

Pauls Creek [PLUMAS]: *stream,* flows 1.5 miles to North Fork Feather River 6 miles north-northeast of Storrie (lat. 39°59'55" N, long. 121°16'25" W; sec. 26, T 25 N, R 6 E). Named on Jonesville (1958) 15' quadrangle, and on Storrie (1979) 7.5' quadrangle.

Paxton [PLUMAS]: *village,* 6 miles southwest of Crescent Mills along East Branch of North Fork Feather River (lat. 40°02'20" N, long. 120°59'40" W; at S line sec. 8, T 25 N, R 9 E). Named on Crescent Mills (1980) 7.5' quadrangle. Postal authorities established Paxton post office in 1917, moved it 0.5 mile south in 1939, and discontinued it in 1952 (Salley, p. 168). United States Geological Survey's (1907) map shows a place called Soda Bar at the site. The name "Paxton" commemorates Elmer E. Paxton, general manager of Indian Valley Railroad and of Engel Mining Company (Gudde, 1949, p. 256). The name "Soda Bar" was from mineral springs at the place (Hanna, p. 231).

Paxton Siding [PLUMAS]: *locality,* 4 miles east-northeast of Twain along Western Pacific Railroad (lat. 40°02' N, long. 121°00' W; sec. 17, T 25 N, R 9 E); the place is 0.5 mile southwest of Paxton. Named on Twain (1980) 7.5' quadrangle.

Payne Canyon [MODOC]: *canyon,* 2.25 miles long, 10 miles east of Alturas (lat. 41°28' N, long. 120°21'10" W). Named on Shields Creek (1963) 7.5' quadrangle

Payne Peak [MODOC]: *peak,* 14 miles south-southeast of the village of Davis Creek (lat. 41°32'30" N, long. 120°16'30" W). Altitude 7618 feet. Named on Davis Creek (1962) 15' quadrangle.

Payne Reservoir [MODOC]: *lake,* 1.25 miles long, 7.25 miles southeast of Alturas (lat. 41°23'45" N, long. 120°27'45" W; sec. 10, 15, 16, T 41 N, R 13 E). Named on Dorris Reservoir (1963) 7.5' quadrangle.

Peacock Point [PLUMAS]: *peak,* 11 miles southwest of the village of Almanor (lat. 40°05'40" N, long. 121°19'05" W; sec. 21, T 26 N, R 6 E). Named on Jonesville (1958) 15' quadrangle.

Pea Creek [LASSEN]: *stream,* flows 7.5 miles to Deep Creek 12 miles northeast of Wendel (lat. 40°29'15" N, long. 120°06' W; sec. 6, T 30 N, R 17 E). Named on Wendel (1954) 15' quadrangle.

Pease Flat [MODOC]: *area,* 4.5 miles north-northeast of South Mountain (lat. 40°54' N, long. 120°35'30" W; in and near sec. 21, T 47 N, R 12 E). Named on South Mountain (1962) 15' quadrangle.

Pea Soup Bar [PLUMAS]: *locality,* 5.25 miles south-southwest of Caribou along East Branch of North Fork Feather River (lat. 40°00'45" N, long. 121°11'50" W; sec. 21, T 25 N, R 7 E). Named on Caribou (1979) 7.5' quadrangle.

Pecks Valley [PLUMAS]: *relief feature,* 2.5 miles northeast of Greenville (lat. 40°10'05" N, long. 120°55'10" W; sec. 25, T 27 N, R 9 E). Named on Greenville (1979) 7.5' quadrangle.

Pecks Valley Creek [PLUMAS]: *stream,* flows nearly 3 miles to Williams Creek 1.25 miles north-northeast of Greenville (lat. 40° 09'25" N, long. 120°56'25" W; sec. 35, T 27 N, R 9 E); the stream goes through Pecks Valley. Named on Greenville (1979) 7.5' quadrangle.

Peel Ridge [PLUMAS]: *ridge,* northwest-trending, 1.25 miles long, 8 miles south of Kettle Rock (lat. 40°01'20" N, long. 120°44'30" W). Named on Genesee Valley (1972) 7.5' quadrangle.

Pegleg Mountain [LASSEN]: *ridge,* generally east-northeast-trending, 1 mile long, 7.5 miles north-northeast of Westwood (lat. 40° 24'30" N, long. 120°56'45" W). Named on Pegleg Mountain (1980) 7.5' quadrangle. The name is for J.J. "Pegleg" Johnson, who had a homestead near the ridge in the 1850's (Gudde, 1949, p. 257).

Pelican Lake: see **Cow Head Lake** [MODOC].

Pelican Point [LASSEN]: *promontory,* 16 miles north-northwest of Susanville on the west side of Eagle Lake (lat. 40°38' N, long. 120° 44'35" W). Named on Antelope Mountain (1956) and Fredonyer Peak (1954) 15' quadrangles. Pelicans nest at the place (Purdy, 1988, p. 120).

Peninsula: see **The Peninsula** [MODOC].

Peninsula Village [PLUMAS]: *locality,* about 6 miles east-southeast of Chester along Lake Almanor (lat. 40°16'25" N, long. 121°07'45" W; sec. 19, T 28 N, R 8 E); the place is on Almanor Peninsula. Named on Chester (1979) and Westwood West (1980) 7.5' quadrangles.

Penitentiary Flat [LASSEN]: *valley,* 5.5 miles west-northwest of Pelican Point (lat. 40°39'30" N, long. 120°50'45" W; mainly in sec. 4, 9, T 32 N, R 10 E). Named on Antelope Mountain (1956) 15' quadrangle.

Penman Peak [PLUMAS]: *peak,* 3 miles north-northeast of Blairsden (lat. 39°49'15" N, long. 120°35'50" W; on N line sec. 35, T 23 N, R 12 E). Altitude 7180 feet. Named on Blairsden (1972) 7.5' quadrangle.

Penman Saddle [PLUMAS]: *pass,* 3.5 miles north of Blairsden (lat. 39°50' N, long. 120°36'10" W; near NW cor. sec. 26, T 23 N, R 12 E); the pass is 1 mile north-northwest of Penman Peak. Named on Blairsden (1972) 7.5' quadrangle.

Penning's Stage Station: see **Spanish Springs** [LASSEN].

Peoria Creek [PLUMAS]: *stream,* flows nearly 2 miles to Middle Fork Feather River 10 miles east-southeast of Quincy (lat. 39°51'50" N, long. 120°46'50" W; near N line sec. 18, T 23 N, R 11 E). Named on Blue Nose Mountain (1951) 7.5' quadrangle.

Peppard Flat [PLUMAS]: *area,* nearly 4 miles east-southeast of Quincy (lat. 39°54'25" N, long. 120°53'15" W; on S line sec. 29, T 24 N, R 10 E). Named on Quincy (1950) 7.5' quadrangle.

Pepperdine Camp [MODOC]: *locality,* 6.5 miles southwest of Cedarville (lat. 41°27'15" N, long. 120°14'45" W; sec. 28, T 42 N, R 15 E). Named on Warren Peak (1963) 7.5' quadrangle.

Perez [MODOC]: *locality,* 4 miles north-northeast of Timber Mountain along Southern Pacific Railroad (lat. 41°40'20" N, long. 121° 15'15" W; at NW cor. sec. 11, T 44 N, R 6 E). Named on Timber Mountain (1952) 15' quadrangle. California Mining Bureau's (1917a) map shows a place called Straw near present Perez. Postal authorities established Straw post office in 1902 and discontinued it in 1928; the name was for Isaac J. Straw, first postmaster (Salley, p. 214).

Pete: see **Mary Pete Spring** [MODOC].

Peters Creek [PLUMAS]: *stream,* flows 6.5 miles to Lights Creek 3 miles north-northeast of Taylorsville (lat. 40°06'45" N, long. 120° 48'50" W; near W line sec. 13, T 26 N, R 10 E). Named on Kettle Rock (1972), Moonlight Peak (1980), and Taylorsville (1980) 7.5' quadrangles. Called Peter Creek on United States Geological Survey's (1893a) map. United States Geological Survey's (1907) map has the name "Kettle Rock Creek" for a branch of Peters Creek that heads near Kettle Rock.

Peterson: see **Jim Peterson Hill** [LASSEN].

Petes Creek [LASSEN]: *stream,* heads at Horse Lake (1) and flows 15 miles to Willow Creek 9 miles north-northwest of Litchfield (lat. 40°29'25" N, long. 120°28'30" W; near E line sec. 2, T 30 N, R 13 E); the stream goes through Petes Valley. Named on Karlo (1954) and Litchfield (1954) 15' quadrangles.

Pete Spring [MODOC]: *spring,* 2.25 miles north-northeast of Day (lat. 41°14'30" N, long. 121°21'25" W; near S line sec. 2, T 39 N, R 5 E). Named on Fall River Mills (1961) 15' quadrangle.

Petes Spring [LASSEN]: *spring,* 9.5 miles east-southeast of Observation Peak (lat. 40°44'10" N, long. 120°01'20" W; sec. 11, T 33 N, R 17 E). Named on Shinn Mountain (1954) 15' quadrangle.

Petes Valley [LASSEN]: *valley,* 8 miles west-southwest of Karlo (lat. 40°31'30" N, long. 120°27'45" W); the valley is along Petes Creek. Named on Karlo (1954) 15' quadrangle.

Picnic Grove Reservoir [MODOC]: *intermittent lake,* 0.5 mile long, 6.25 miles north-northeast of Blue Mountain (lat. 41°55'10" N, long. 120°50'05" W; near NW cor. sec. 16, T 47 N, R 10 E). Named on Steele Swamp (1962) 15' quadrangle.

Pidgeon Roost Creek [PLUMAS]: *stream,* flows 1.5 miles to Middle Fork Feather River 4 miles northeast of Dogwood Peak (lat. 39°49'30" N, long. 121°00'15" W; sec. 29, T 23 N, R 9 E). Named on Dogwood Peak (1979) 7.5' quadrangle. Called Pigeon Roost Cr. on Bucks Lake (1950) 15' quadrangle.

Pierce Creek [PLUMAS]: *stream,* flows 4 miles to Indian Creek (2) 7.5 miles north-northeast of Kettle Rock (lat. 40°14'15" N, long. 120°39'10" W; sec. 32, T 28 N, R 12 E). Named on Diamond Mountain (1972) and Kettle Rock (1972) 7.5' quadrangles.

Pigeon Roost Creek: see **Pidgeon Roost Creek** [PLUMAS].

Pigtail Ravine [PLUMAS]: *canyon,* drained by a stream that flows 1 mile to Scotch Creek 6.5 miles south of Bucks Lodge (lat. 39°46'50" N, long. 121°11' W; near N line sec. 10, T 22 N, R 7 E). Named on Haskins Valley (1980) 7.5' quadrangle.

Pikes Point [LASSEN]: *promontory,* 5.5 miles south-southwest of Pelican Point near the south end of Eagle Lake (lat. 40°33'30" N, long. 120°47' W; sec. 7, T 31 N, R 11 E). Named on Antelope Mountain (1956) 15' quadrangle.

Pilot Butte [MODOC]: *hill,* 2.5 miles east of Lookout (lat. 41°12'30" N, long. 121°06'20" W; on E line sec. 24, T 39 N, R 7 E). Named on Bieber (1961) 15' quadrangle.

Pilot Peak [PLUMAS]: *peak,* 11.5 miles south-southeast of Quincy (lat. 30°47' N, long. 120°52'05" W; sec. 9, T 22 N, R 10 E). Altitude 7457 feet. Named on Blue Nose Mountain (1951) 7.5' quadrangle.

Pinchard Creek [PLUMAS]: *stream,* flows 5.5 miles to South Branch of Middle Fork Feather River 1 mile northwest of Cascade (lat. 39°42'35" N, long. 121°11'35" W; near NE cor. sec. 4, T 21 N, R 7 E). Named on American House (1948) and Cascade (1948) 7.5' quadrangles. Called Pinkard Creek on Bidwell Bar (1897) 30' quadrangle.

Pine Creek [LASSEN]:

(1) *stream,* flows 33 miles to Eagle Lake 3.5 miles north-northwest of Pelican Point (lat. 40°40'45" N, long. 120°47' W). Named on Antelope Mountain (1956) and Harvey Mountain (1956) 15' quadrangles.

(2) *stream,* flows 8 miles to Horse Lake (1) 11.5 miles east-northeast of Pelican Point (lat. 40°41'10" N, long. 120°31' W; near S line sec. 28, T 33 N, R 13 E). Named on Fredonyer Peak (1954) 15' quadrangle.

Pine Creek [MODOC]:

(1) *stream,* formed by the confluence of Middle Fork and North Fork, flows 12 miles to the valley of South Fork Pit River 3 miles south of Alturas (lat. 41°27' N, long. 120°31'25" W; at W line sec. 25, T 42 N, R 12 E). Named on Alturas (1961) 15' quadrangle, and on Dorris Reservoir (1963) and Shields Creek (1963) 7.5' quadrangles. Middle Fork is 5.5 miles long and is named on Shields Creek (1963) and Soup Creek (1963) 7.5' quadrangles. North Fork is 5.5 miles long and is named on Shields Creek (1963) and Warren Peak (1963) 7.5' quadrangles. South Fork enters Middle Fork from the southeast 2 miles upstream from the confluence of Middle Fork and North Fork; it is 3.5 miles long and is named on Eagle Peak (1963) and Soup Creek (1963) 7.5' quadrangles.

(2) *stream,* flows 7 miles to Goose Lake (1) 6.5 miles north-northeast of Willow Ranch near California-Oregon State line (lat. 41°59'30" N, long. 120°19'35" W; near N line sec. 23, T 46 N, R 14 E). Named on Fort Bidwell (1962) and Willow Ranch (1962) 15' quadrangles.

Pine Creek [PLUMAS]:

(1) *stream,* flows 3.5 miles to Rock Creek (4) 2.25 miles west-northwest of Storrie (lat. 39°56'05" N, long. 121°21'30" W). Named on Storrie (1979) 7.5' quadrangle.

(2) *stream,* flows 5 miles to Greenhorn Creek 1.5 miles north-northeast of Spring Garden (lat. 39°55' N, long. 120°46'30" W; near W line sec. 29, T 24 N, R 11 E). Named on Spring Garden (1950) 7.5' quadrangle. On Downieville (1897) 30' quadrangle, the name "Pine Creek" applies to present Greenhorn Creek below the junction of Greenhorn Creek and Pine Creek (2).

Pine Creek Basin [MODOC]: *relief feature,* 8 miles west-northwest of Eagleville (lat. 41°21'45" N, long. 120°14'15" W; sec. 26, 27, T 41 N, R 15 E); the feature is at the head of South Fork Pine Creek (1). Named on Eagle Peak (1963) 7.5' quadrangle.

Pine Creek Reservoir [MODOC]: *lake,* 1100 feet long, 7.5 miles southeast of Alturas (lat. 41°25'25" N, long. 120°25'20" W; sec. 1, T 41 N, R 13 E); the lake is near Pine Creek (1). Named on Dorris Reservoir (1963) 7.5' quadrangle. United States Board on Geographic Names (1965b, p. 14) rejected the name "Forebay Reservoir" for the feature.

Pine Creek Valley [LASSEN]: *valley,* 9.5 miles southeast of Cal Mountain (lat. 40°34'15" N, long. 121°02'30" W); the valley is along Pine Creek (1). Named on Harvey Mountain (1956) 15' quadrangle.

Pine Creek Valley [PLUMAS]: *valley,* 5.5 miles north-northeast of Spring Garden (lat. 39°58'15" N, long. 120°45'45" W); the valley is on upper reaches of Pine Creek (2). Named on Spring Garden (1950) 7.5' quadrangle.

Pine Lake [LASSEN]: *lake,* 1600 feet long, 11 miles south of Cal Mountain (lat. 40°30'50" N, long. 121°09'50" W; on S line sec. 26, T 31 N, R 7 E); the lake is near the head of Pine Creek (1). Named on Harvey Mountain (1956) 15' quadrangle.

Pineleaf Creek [PLUMAS]: *stream,* flows nearly 1 mile to Spanish Creek (1) 1 mile north-northeast of the village of Meadow Valley (lat. 39°56'50" N, long. 121°02'55" W; near NE cor. sec. 14, T 24 N, R 8 E). Named on Meadow Valley (1980) 7.5' quadrangle.

Pine Spring [MODOC]:

(1) *spring,* 5 miles southeast of Crank Mountain (lat. 41°20'45" N, long. 121°04' W; sec. 32, T 41 N, R 8 E). Named on Crank Mountain (1962) 15' quadrangle.

(2) *spring,* 4.5 miles south-southwest of Jacks Butte (lat. 41°31'30" N, long. 120°50' W; at E line sec. 32, T 43 N, R 10 E). Named on Jacks Butte (1962) 15' quadrangle.

(3) *spring,* 5.25 miles south of South Mountain (lat. 41°46' N, long. 120°36'50" W; sec. 5, T 45 N, R 12 E). Named on South Mountain (1962) 15' quadrangle.

(4) *spring,* 13 miles east-southeast of Alturas (lat. 41°24'05" N, long. 120°18'55" W). Named on Shields Creek (1963) 7.5' quadrangle.

Pine Spring: see **Big Pine Spring** [MODOC]; **Big Pine Spring** [PLUMAS].

Pine Town [LASSEN]: *locality,* 0.5 mile east-southeast of Westwood (lat. 40°18'15" N, long. 120°59'20" W; sec. 8, T 28 N, R 9 E). Named on Westwood East (1980) 7.5' quadrangle.

Pinkard Creek: see **Pinchard Creek** [PLUMAS].

Pinnacle Lake [MODOC]: *intermittent lake,* 4500 feet long, 5.25 miles east of Double Head Mountain (lat. 41°45'50" N, long. 121° 02'45" W; sec. 4, 9, T 45 N, R 8 E). Named on Clear Lake Reservoir (1951) 15' quadrangle.

Pinnio [LASSEN]: *locality,* 1.5 miles north of Madeline along Southern Pacific Railroad (lat. 41°04'25" N, long. 120°25'05" W; sec. 3, T 37 N, R 13 E). Named on Madeline (1962) 7.5' quadrangle.

Pit River [LASSEN]: *locality,* 5.25 miles south of Bieber along Western Pacific Railroad (lat. 41°02'50" N, long. 121°08'40" W; near E line sec. 15, T 37 N, R 7 E); the place is near Pit River [LASSEN-MODOC]. Named on Bieber (1961) 15' quadrangle.

Pit River [LASSEN-MODOC]: *stream,* formed by the confluence of North Fork and South Fork in Modoc County, flows 96 miles to Shasta County 11 miles west-southwest of Bieber (lat. 41°02'45" N, long. 121°19'50" W; at W line sec. 18, T 37 N, R 6 E). Named on Alturas (1961), Bieber (1961), Canby (1961), Crank Mountain (1962), Fall River Mills (1961), Jellico (1957), and Little Valley (1957) 15' quadrangles. Goddard's (1857) map has the designation "Upper Sacramento or Pitt River" for present Pit River and its North Fork. United States Board on Geographic Names (1933, p. 607) rejected the form "Pitt" for the name. The name "Pit" generally is attributed to Hudson's Bay trappers, who found pits dug by Indians along the river to trap wild animals; the form "Pitt" for the name may stem from confusion with the name of the prominent English statesman (Pease, p. 65). North Fork is 21 miles long and is named on Alturas (1961) and Davis Creek (1962) 15' quadrangles, and on Dorris Reservoir (1963) 7.5' quadrangle. On Colton's (1855) map, present North Fork is called North Pitt R. South Fork is 28 miles long and is named on Alturas (1961) and Likely (1962) 15' quadrangles, and on Jess Valley (1962) and Tule Mountain (1967) 7.5' quadrangles. Present South Fork is called South Br. on Colton's (1855) map, and is called South Pit River on Alturas 1° quadrangle

Pitt River: see **Pit River** [LASSEN-MODOC].

Pitt River Butte: see **Rattlesnake Butte** [MODOC] (2).

Pitt River Mountains: see **Canby** [MODOC].

Pitt's Lake: see **Goose Lake** [MODOC] (1).

Pittville [LASSEN]: *village,* 11 miles west-southwest of Bieber on Lassen-Shasta County line, mainly in Shasta County (lat. 41°02'55" N, long. 121°19'50" W; at W line sec. 18, T 37 N, R 6 E); the village is along Pit River. Named on Fall River Mills (1961) 15' quadrangle. Postal authorities established Pittville post office in 1873, discontinued it in 1875, reestablished it in 1878, and discontinued it in 1961; they moved the post office back and fourth several times between Shasta County and Lassen County (Salley, p. 173).

Piute Creek [LASSEN]: *stream,* flows 10 miles to Susan River in Susanville (lat. 40°24'50" N, long. 120°39'10" W; sec. 32, T 30 N, R 12 E). Named on Susanville (1954) 15' quadrangle.

Pleasant: see **Mount Pleasant** [PLUMAS].

Pleasants Canyon [MODOC]: *canyon,* drained by a stream that flows 2 miles to lowlands along Goose Lake (1) 2.5 miles east of Willow Ranch (lat. 41°54'20" N, long. 120°18'30" W; near NW cor. sec. 24, T 47 N, R 14 E). Named on Willow Ranch (1962) 15' quadrangle. Alturas 1° quadrangle has the name "Myrtle Creek" for the stream that heads in the canyon.

Plinco Sheep Troughs Spring [PLUMAS]: *spring,* 8 miles east-northeast of Squaw Valley Peak along Dooley Creek (lat. 40°05'10" N, long. 120°16'35" W; near N line sec. 27, T 26 N, R 15 E). Named on Ferris Creek (1977) 7.5' quadrangle.

Pliocene Creek [PLUMAS]: *stream,* flows nearly 2 miles to North Fork Feather River 3.25 miles south-southwest of Canyondam (lat. 40°07'40" N, long. 121°05'30" W; sec. 9, T 26 N, R 8 E). Named on Canyondam (1979) 7.5' quadrangle.

Plumas [LASSEN]: *locality,* 2.25 miles southeast of Beckwourth Pass along Western Pacific Railroad (lat. 39°45'20" N, long. 120°03'55" W; sec. 15, T 22 N, R 17 E). Named on Chilcoot (1950) 15' quadrangle.

Plumas Junction: see **Chats** [LASSEN].

Plumas Pines: see **Almanor** [PLUMAS] (1).

Plum Creek [MODOC]: *stream,* flows 6.5 mile to Parker Creek 6 miles east of Alturas (lat. 41°29'30" N, long. 120°25'20" W; sec. 12, T 42 N, R 13 E). Named on Dorris Reservoir (1963) 7.5' quadrangle.

Plum Ridge [MODOC]: *peak,* 3 miles northwest of Hackamore (lat. 41°34'50" N, long. 121°10' W; sec. 9, T 43 N, R 7 E). Named on Hackamore (1952) 15' quadrangle.

Plum Spring [MODOC]:

(1) *spring,* 14 miles north of Double Head (lat. 41°57'30" N, long. 121°07'10" W; sec. 36, T 48 N, R 7 E). Named on Clear Lake Reservoir (1951) 15' quadrangle.

(2) *spring,* 12.5 miles south-southwest of Canby (lat. 41°16'55" N, long. 120°58'30" W; sec. 30, T 40 N, R 9 E). Named on Canby (1961) 15' quadrangle.

Plum Valley Campground [MODOC]: *locality,* 3 miles east-southeast of the village of Davis Creek (lat. 41°42'45" N, long. 120°19'30" W; sec. 26, T 45 N, R 14 E); the place is along South Fork Davis Creek (1). Named on Davis Creek (1962) 15' quadrangle.

Poindexter Reservoir [MODOC]: *intermittent lake,* 1600 feet long, 5.5 miles east of South Mountain (lat. 41°51'10" N, long. 120°31'40" W; on SW cor. sec. 6, T 46 N, R 13 E). Named on South Mountain (1962) 15' quadrangle.

Poison Creek [MODOC]: *stream,* flows 1.5 miles to Mill Creek (1) 21 miles southeast of Alturas (lat. 41°16'20" N, long. 120°15'10" W). Named on Eagle Peak (1963) and Soup Creek (1963) 7.5' quadrangles.

Poison Creek [PLUMAS]: *stream,* flows 3.25 miles to Last Chance Creek (2) 9.5 miles east-southeast of Kettle Rock (lat. 40°06'15" N, long. 120°33'10" W; near E line sec. 18, T 26 N, R 13 E). Named on Babcock Peak (1972) 7.5' quadrangle.

Poison Creek Spring [PLUMAS]: *spring,* 11.5 miles east-southeast of Kettle Rock (lat. 40°05'40" N, long. 120°31'15" W; sec. 21, T 26 N, R 13 E); the spring is 950 feet east of Poison Creek. Named on Babcock Peak (1972) 7.5' quadrangle.

Poison Flat [MODOC]: *area,* 22 miles southeast of Alturas (lat. 41° 15'15" N, long. 120°15'15" W). Named on Eagle Peak (1963) and Soup Creek (1963) 7.5' quadrangles.

Poison Lake [LASSEN]: *lake,* 4100 feet long, 2 miles west-southwest of Cal Mountain (lat. 40°39'40" N, long. 121°11'55" W; sec. 4, T 32 N, R 7 E). Named on Harvey Mountain (1956) 15' quadrangle.

Poison Lake [MODOC]: *lake,* 100 feet long, 8.5 miles northwest of Fort Bidwell (lat. 41°57'20" N, long. 120°14'45" W; near W line sec. 10, T 47 N, R 15 E). Named on Fort Bidwell (1962) 15' quadrangle.

Poison Spring [MODOC]: *spring,* 8.5 miles north-northeast of South Mountain (lat. 41°56'55" N, long. 120°33'15" W; sec. 2, T 47 N, R 12 E). Named on South Mountain (1962) 15' quadrangle.

Poison Spring [PLUMAS]: *spring,* 17 miles southwest of the village of Almanor (lat. 40°02'45" N, long. 121°23'35" W; near SE cor. sec. 3, T 25 N, R 5 E). Named on Jonesville (1958) 15' quadrangle.

Poison Springs [MODOC]: *springs,* 9 miles east-southeast of Fort Bidwell (lat. 41°47'40" N, long. 120°00'20" W; near SW cor. sec. 2, T 45 N, R 17 E). Named on Fort Bidwell (1962) 15' quadrangle.

Poison Springs Canyon [MODOC]: *canyon,* drained by a stream that heads in the State of Nevada and flows 9.5 miles in Modoc County to Surprise Valley 4 miles east of Fort Bidwell (lat. 41°51'30" N, long. 120°05' W; sec. 13, T 46 N, R 16 E); Poison Springs are in the canyon. Named on Fort Bidwell (1962) 15' quadrangle. United States Board on Geographic Names (1964b, p. 14) rejected the form "Poison Spring Canyon" for the name.

Poison Station [LASSEN]: *locality,* 1.5 miles west-northwest of Cal Mountain along Western Pacific Railroad (lat. 40°40'45" N, long. 121°11'35" W; sec. 33, T 33 N, R 7 E); the place is 1 mile north of Poison Lake. Named on Harvey Mountain (1956) 15' quadrangle.

Pole Spring [LASSEN]: *spring,* 8.5 miles southwest of Cal Mountain (lat. 40°34'50" N, long. 121°16'30" W; sec. 2, T 31 N, R 6 E). Named on Prospect Peak (1957) 15' quadrangle.

Ponderosa Flat Campground [PLUMAS]: *locality,* 3.5 miles south of the village of Almanor along Butt Valley Reservoir (lat. 40° 10' N, long. 121°11' W; sec. 27, T 27 N, R 7 E). Named on Almanor (1979) 7.5' quadrangle.

Poorman Creek [PLUMAS]: *stream,* flows 3 miles to Nelson Creek 11 miles south-southeast of Quincy (lat. 39°48'40" N, long. 120° 49'15" W). Named on Blue Nose Mountain (1951) 7.5' quadrangle. The name also had the forms "Poor Man's Creek" and "Poor Men's Creek" (Gudde, 1975, p. 273). South Fork enters from the southwest nearly 2 miles upstream from the mouth of the main stream; it is 1.25 miles long and is named on Blue Nose Mountain (1951) 7.5' quadrangle.

Poplar Creek [PLUMAS]: *stream,* flows 6.5 miles to Middle Fork Feather River 11.5 miles east-southeast of Quincy (lat. 39°51'55" N, long. 120°45'05" W; at N line sec. 16, T 23 N, R 11 E). Named on Blue Nose Mountain (1951) and Johnsville (1972) 7.5' quadrangles. Downieville (1897) 30' quadrangle has the name "Poplar Valley" along Poplar Creek north of the mouth of Camp Creek, and has the name "Little Poplar Val." along Poplar Creek south of the mouth of Camp Creek.

Poplar Creek: see **Little Poplar Creek**, under **Chris Creek** [PLUMAS].

Poplar Valley: see **Poplar Creek** [PLUMAS].

Porcupine Rim [MODOC]: *relief feature,* center 12.5 miles northwest of Alturas (lat. 41°36' N, long. 120°44' W); the feature is east of Porcupine Valley. Named on Big Sage Reservoir (1962) 15' quadrangle.

Porcupine Tank: see **Little Porcupine Tank** [MODOC].

Porcupine Valley [MODOC]: *valley,* 2.5 miles east of Jacks Butte (lat. 41°35'20" N, long. 120°45'20" W). Named on Big Sage Reservoir (1962) and Jacks Butte (1962) 15' quadrangles.

Porter Canyon [LASSEN]: *canyon,* drained by a stream that flows 1.5 miles to Honey Lake Valley 8.5 miles northwest of Doyle (lat. 40°06'20" N, long. 120°13'30" W; near W line sec. 18, T 26 N, R 16 E). Named on McKesick Peak (1978) 7.5' quadrangle.

Porter Ravine [PLUMAS]: *canyon,* drained by a stream that flows 1.25 miles to West Branch Nelson Creek 15 miles south-southeast of Quincy (lat. 39°45'35" N, long. 120°47'35" W; sec. 19, T 22 N, R 11 E). Named on Blue Nose Mountain (1951) 7.5' quadrangle.

Porter Reservoir [MODOC]:

(1) *lake,* 1100 feet long, 16 miles south of the village of Davis Creek (lat. 41°30'30" N, long. 120°25'10" W; sec. 1, T 42 N, R 13 E). Named on Davis Creek (1962) 15' quadrangle.

(2) *intermittent lake,* 1850 feet long, 9 miles east-southeast of Alturas (lat. 41°26'30" N, long. 120°22'25" W). Named on Dorris Reservoir (1963) and Shields Creek (1963) 7.5' quadrangles.

(3) *lake,* 700 feet long, 6.5 miles southwest of Cedarville (lat. 41° 27'20" N, long. 120°14'50" W; sec. 28, T 42 N, R 15 E). Named on Warren Peak (1963) 7.5' quadrangle.

Portola [PLUMAS]: *town,* 27 miles east-southeast of Quincy (lat. 39° 48'25" N, long. 120°28'05" W; sec. 36, T 23 N, R 13 E, and sec. 1, T 22 N, R 13 E). Named on Portola (1972) 7.5' quadrangle. Postal authorities established Portola post office in 1909; the site also was known as Headquarters, Mormon, and Reposa (Salley, p. 176). The town incorporated in 1946.

Portuguese Ridge [MODOC]: *ridge,* northwest-trending, 5 miles long, 6.5 miles southeast of Canby (lat. 41°23' N, long. 120°46'30" W). Named on Alturas (1961) and Canby (1961) 15' quadrangles.

Portuguese Sheep Camp [LASSEN]: *locality,* 9.5 miles west-southwest of Likely [MODOC] (lat. 41°09'30" N, long. 120°39'25" W; sec. 1, T 38 N, R 11 E). Named on Likely (1962) 15' quadrangle.

Portuguese Spring [MODOC]: *spring,* 13 miles southwest of Alturas (lat. 41°22'50" N, long. 120°45' W; sec. 19, T 41 N, R 11 E). Named on Alturas (1961) 15' quadrangle.

Posey Lake [LASSEN]: *lake,* 1150 feet long, 16 miles northwest of Westwood (lat. 40°27'25" N, long. 121°12'55" W; near E line sec. 17, T 30 N, R 7 E). Named on Red Cinder (1979) 7.5' quadrangle.

Post Camp [LASSEN]: *locality,* 2.5 miles south-southeast of Observation Peak (lat. 40°44'20" N, long. 120°10'45" W; sec. 9, T 33 N, R 16 E). Named on Shinn Mountain (1954) 15' quadrangle.

Post Canyon [LASSEN]: *canyon,* drained by a stream that flows 5.5 miles to Tuledad Canyon 22 miles east of Madeline (lat. 41°01'15" N, long. 120°04' W; at S line sec. 32, T 37 N, R 17 E). Named on Little Hat Mountain (1962) 7.5' quadrangle.

Post Canyon [MODOC]:

(1) *canyon,* drained by a stream that flows 2 miles to Pit River 5 miles east-southeast of Crank Mountain (lat. 41°21'40" N, long. 121°03'10" W; sec. 28, T 41 N, R 8 E). Named on Crank Mountain (1962) 15' quadrangle.

(2) *canyon,* drained by a stream that flows 1.5 miles to Rush Creek 12 miles south of Canby (lat. 41°16'10" N, long. 120°53'40" W; at SW cor. sec. 25, T 40 N, R 9 E). Named on Canby (1961) 15' quadrangle.

Post Creek [PLUMAS]: *stream,* flows 2.25 miles to South Fork Feather River 3.5 miles north-northwest of American House (lat. 39°41'55" N, long. 121°03'25" W; near NW cor. sec. 11, T 21 N, R 8 E). Named on American House (1948) 7.5' quadrangle.

Pothole Gulch [MODOC]: *canyon,* drained by a stream that flows 2.5 miles to Pit River 5 miles east-southeast of Crank Mountain (lat. 41°21'40" N, long. 121°03'15" W; near S line sec. 28, T 41 N, R 8 E). Named on Crank Mountain (1962) 15' quadrangle.

Pot Hole Meadow: see **Pothole Valley** [MODOC].

Pothole Spring [LASSEN]: *spring,* 4 miles northwest of Observation Peak (lat. 40°48'55" N, long. 120°13'20" W; at N line sec. 13, T 34 N, R 15 E). Named on Observation Peak (1954) 15' quadrangle.

Pot Hole Spring [MODOC]: *spring,* 8 miles east of Adin (lat. 41°12'45" N, long. 120°47'30" W; at S line sec. 14, T 39 N, R 10 E). Named on Adin (1962) 15' quadrangle.

Pothole Spring [MODOC]: *spring,* nearly 3 miles west of Blue Mountain (lat. 41°49'30" N, long. 120°55' W; at E line sec. 15, T 46 N, R 9 E). Named on Steele Swamp (1962) 15' quadrangle. Alturas 1° quadrangle has the form "Pot Hole Spring" for the name.

Pothole Valley [MODOC]: *valley,* 6.5 miles west of Blue Mountain (lat. 41°48'45" N, long. 120°59' W; in and near sec. 19, T 46 N, R 9 E). Named on Steele Swamp (1962) 15' quadrangle. Called Pot Hole Meadow on Alturas 1° quadrangle.

Potter: see **Lookout** [MODOC].

Potters Well [MODOC]: *well,* 7.25 miles north-northwest of Hackamore (lat. 41°38'55" N, long. 121°10'30" W; near SW cor. sec. 16, T 44 N, R 7 E). Named on Hackamore (1952) 15' quadrangle.

Poulsen Spring [LASSEN]: *spring,* 10 miles north-northeast of Termo (lat. 40°59'50" N, long. 120°22'30" W; sec. 10, T 36 N, R 14 E). Named on Ravendale (1954) 15' quadrangle.

Poverty Bar: see **Rich Bar** [PLUMAS] (1).

Powell Reservoir [LASSEN]: *intermittent lake,* 3200 feet long, 14 miles northeast of Observation Peak (lat. 40°55'50" N, long. 120° 00'30" W; on W line sec. 1, T 35 N, R 17 E). Named on Observation Peak (1954) 15' quadrangle.

Powley Creek [MODOC]: *stream,* flows 2.5 miles to Surprise Valley 10 miles north-northwest of Cedarville (lat. 41°40'20" N, long. 120°13'05" W; at E line sec. 23, T 44 N, R 15 E). Named on Cedarville (1962) 15' quadrangle.

Prat: see **Del Prat Spring** [MODOC].

Prattville [PLUMAS]: *village,* 1 mile southeast of the village of Almanor along Lake Almanor (lat. 40°12'30" N, long. 121°09'20" W; sec. 11, 12, T 27 N, R 7 E). Named on Almanor (1979) 7.5' quadrangle. Postal authorities established Big Meadows post office in 1868, changed the name to Prattville in 1874, and discontinued it in 1914; the name "Prattville" was for Dr. Willard Pratt, first postmaster (Salley, p. 21, 177). United States Board on Geographic Names (1977b, p. 5) gave the form "Pratville" as a variant. Postal authorities established Humboldt post office 9 miles west of Prattville in 1900 and discontinued it the same year (Salley, p. 101).

Prescott Canyon: see **Preston Canyon** [LASSEN].

Preston Canyon [LASSEN]: *canyon,* drained by a stream that flows 4 miles to Willow Creek [LASSEN-MODOC] 10 miles south-southeast of Adin [MODOC] (lat. 41°03'15" N, long. 120°52'50" W; sec. 12, T 37 N, R 9 E). Named on Adin (1962) 15' quadrangle. United States Board on Geographic Names (1968a, p. 7) rejected the name "Prescott Canyon" for the feature.

Pretty Tree Reservoir [MODOC]: *intermittent lake,* 7.5 miles north of Alturas (lat. 41°36'35" N, long. 120°30'30" W; sec. 31, T 44 N, R 13 E). Named on Big Sage Reservoir (1962) 15' quadrangle.

Prisoners Rock [MODOC]: *hill,* 3 miles south-southwest of Newell (lat. 41°50'45" N, long. 121°23'15" W; sec. 10, T 46 N, R 5 E). Named on Tulelake (1951) 15' quadrangle. Modoc Lava-Bed (1892) 1° quadrangle has the name "Bloody Point" at or near the place.

Prison Spring [LASSEN]: *spring,* 6 miles west-southwest of Pelican Point (lat. 40°40" N, long. 120°51' W; sec. 4, T 32 N, R 10 E); the spring is at the north end of Penitentiary Flat. Named on Antelope Mountain (1956) 15' quadrangle.

Pritchard Creek [PLUMAS]: *stream,* flows 5.25 miles to South Branch of Middle Fork Feather River 1 mile northwest of Cascade (lat. 39°42'35" N, long. 121°11'35" W; near NE cor. sec. 4, T 21 N, R 7 E). Named on American House (1948) and Cascade (1948) 7.5' quadrangles.

Prockmans: see **Madeline** [LASSEN].

Providence City: see **Hayden Hill** [LASSEN] (2).

Puls Camp [LASSEN]: *locality,* 10 miles south-southeast of the village of Little Valley (lat. 40°46'05" N, long. 121°05'15" W; sec. 33, T 34 N, R 8 E). Named on Little Valley (1957) 15' quadrangle.

Pumpkin Center [LASSEN]: *locality,* 2.25 miles east-southeast of Bieber (lat. 41°06'40" N, long. 121°06'15" W; at SE cor. sec. 24, T 38 N, R 7 E). Named on Bieber (1961) 15' quadrangle.

Purser: see **Wendel** [LASSEN].

—Q—

Quail Spring [MODOC]: *spring,* 9 miles south of Canby (lat. 41°18'50" N, long. 120°53' W; near S line sec. 12, T 40 N, R 9 E). Named on Canby (1961) 15' quadrangle.

Quaking Asp Creek [LASSEN]: *stream,* flows 2.5 miles to Alaska Canyon 16 miles east of Madeline (lat. 41°03'35" N, long. 120° 10' W; sec. 21, T 37 N, R 16 E). Named on Boot Lake (1962) 7.5' quadrangle.

Quaking Aspen Spring [MODOC]:

(1) *spring,* 7.5 miles east-southeast of Crank Mountain (lat. 41°19'40" N, long. 121°01'15" W; at N line sec. 11, T 40 N, R 8 E). Named on Crank Mountain (1962) 15' quadrangle.

(2) *spring,* 2.25 miles west-northwest of Blue Mountain (lat. 41°50'30" N, long. 120°54'10" W; sec. 11, T 46 N, R 9 E). Named on Steele Swamp (1962) 15' quadrangle.

Quaking Asp Spring [MODOC]: *spring,* 8.5 miles south-southwest of Timber Mountain (lat. 41°30'30" N, long. 121°20'15" W; sec. 1, T 42 N, R 5 E). Named on Timber Mountain (1952) 15' quadrangle.

Quaking Asp Spring: see **Little Quaking Asp Spring** [MODOC].

Quartz Point [PLUMAS]: *relief feature,* 7.5 miles south-southeast of Quincy (lat. 39°50'30" N, long. 120°52'55" W; sec. 20, T 23 N, R 10 E). Named on Onion Valley (1950) 7.5' quadrangle.

Queen Lily Campground [PLUMAS]: *locality,* 4 miles southwest of Caribou along North Fork Feather River (lat. 40°02'45" N, long. 121°13' W; near S line sec. 5, T 25 N, R 7 E). Named on Caribou (1979) 7.5' quadrangle.

Quincy [PLUMAS]: *town,* in the central part of Plumas County in American Valley (lat. 39°56'10" N, long. 120°56'45" W; on S line sec. 14, T 24 N, R 9 E). Named on Quincy (1950) 7.5' quadrangle. Called Quinsy on Goddard's (1857) map. Postal authorities established Quincy post office in 1855 (Frickstad, p. 125). James H. Bradley, owner of American Ranch and one of the commissioners who organized Plumas County, had the county seat placed at the hotel on his ranch; Bradley then laid out the town and named it for his home in Illinois (Hoover, Rensch, and Rensch, p. 284). Gudde (1975, p. 292) listed a mining place called Richmond Hill that was located 10 miles southeast of Quincy.

Quincy: see **East Quincy** [PLUMAS].

Quincy Junction [PLUMAS]: *locality,* 3.25 miles east-northeast of Quincy along Western Pacific Railroad (lat. 39°57'50" N, long. 120°53'50" W; near NE cor. sec. 7, T 24 N, R 10 E). Named on Quincy (1950) 7.5' quadrangle. Postal authorities established Marston post office at present Quincy Junction in 1913 and discontinued it the same year—the name was for the man who financed the building of the railroad to the site (Salley, p. 134). They had established Hartwell post office nearby at a station along the railroad on Hartwell ranch in 1910 and discontinued it in 1911 (NW quarter sec. 8, T 24 N, R 10 E) (Salley, p. 94).

—R—

Rabbit Creek [PLUMAS]: *stream,* flows 3.5 miles to Slate Creek (3) nearly 2 miles southeast of La Porte (lat. 39°39'40" N, long. 120° 57'50" W; near S line sec. 22, T 21 N, R 9 E). Named on La Porte (1951) 7.5' quadrangle. East Branch enters from the northeast 2.25 miles upstream from the mouth of the main creek; it is 2.25 miles long and is named on La Porte (1951) 7.5' quadrangle.

Rabbit Creek: see **La Porte** [PLUMAS].

Rabbit Town: see **La Porte** [PLUMAS].

Radio Hill [PLUMAS]: *hill,* 1 mile east-northeast of the center of Quincy (lat. 39°56'25" N, long. 120°55'40" W; sec. 13, T 24 N, R 9 E). Altitude 3939 feet. Named on Quincy (1950) 7.5' quadrangle. The name came into use after the Forest Service began operating a radio station on top of the hill about 1945 (Gudde, 1949, p. 278).

Rager Reservoir [LASSEN]: *lake,* 600 feet long, 14 miles north of Observation Peak (lat. 40°58'30" N, long. 120°12'45" W; near NE cor. sec. 24, T 36 N, R 15 E). Named on Observation Peak (1954) 15' quadrangle.

Raider Creek [MODOC]: *stream,* flows 6.5 miles to end near Middle Alkali Lake 2.25 miles northeast of Eagleville (lat. 41°20'20" N, long. 120°05' W; near N line sec. 18, T 40 N, R 17 E). Named on Eagle Peak (1963) and Eagleville (1963) 7.5' quadrangles. South Fork enters from the southwest 3 miles west-northwest of Eagleville; it is 1.5 miles long and is named on Eagle Peak (1963) 7.5' quadrangle.

Rail Canyon [LASSEN]: *canyon,* drained by a stream that flows 1.5 miles to Shasta County 10 miles west of Bieber (lat. 41°08'45" N, long. 121°19'50" W; at W line sec. 7, T 38 N, R 6 E). Named on Fall River Mills (1961) 15' quadrangle.

Rail Canyon [LASSEN-MODOC]: *canyon,* drained by a stream that heads just inside Modoc County and flows 5 miles to Ash Creek 10.5 miles east-southeast of Adin [MODOC] in Lassen County (lat. 41°07'50" N, long. 120°45'30" W; near W line sec. 18, T 38 N, R 11 E). Named on Adin (1962) 15' quadrangle.

Rail Meadow [MODOC]: *area,* 5 miles north-northwest of South Mountain (lat. 41°54'10" N, long. 120°40'15" W; sec. 23, T 47 N, R 11 E). Named on South Mountain (1962) 15' quadrangle.

Rail Mountain [MODOC]: *peak,* 9 miles west-southwest of Jacks Butte (lat. 41°33' N, long. 120°57'35" W; sec. 20, T 43 N, R 9 E). Altitude 5415 feet. Named on Jacks Butte (1962) 15' quadrangle.

Rail Spring [MODOC]: *spring,* 4.5 miles north-northwest of South Mountain (lat. 41°54' N, long. 120°40'05" W; sec. 23, T 47 N, R 11 E); the spring is at Rail Meadow. Named on South Mountain (1962) 15' quadrangle.

Rainbow Point [PLUMAS]: *peninsula,* 1.25 miles north-northwest of Bucks Lodge along Bucks Lake (lat. 39°53'35" N, long. 121°10'55" W; sec. 34, T 24 N, R 7 E). Named on Bucks Lake (1979) 7.5' quadrangle.

Raker and Thomas Reservoirs [MODOC]: *intermittent lake,* 3 miles long, 10 miles north of Alturas (lat. 41°38'15" N, long. 120°33' W). Named on Big Sage Reservoir (1962) 15' quadrangle.

Ralston Gulch [MODOC]: *canyon,* 4 miles long, opens into Warm Springs Valley 4.25 miles southeast of Canby (lat. 41°24'30" N, long. 120°48'30" W; sec. 10, T 41 N, R 10 E). Named on Canby (1961) 15' quadrangle.

Ramelli Creek [PLUMAS]: *stream,* formed by the confluence of North Fork and South Fork, flows 2 miles to Little Last Chance Creek 14 miles north-northwest of Chilcoot (lat. 39°59'15" N, long. 120°12'45" W; near S line sec. 29, T 25 N, R 16 E). Named on Frenchman Lake (1979) 7.5' quadrangle. North Fork and South Fork each are 2.5 miles long; both forks are named on Dixie Mountain (1972) and Frenchman Lake (1979) 7.5' quadrangles.

Rankin Flat [LASSEN]: *area,* 3 miles northwest of Pelican Point (lat. 40°39'35" N, long. 120°47'35" W; near SE cor. sec. 1, T 32 N, R 10 E). Named on Antelope Mountain (1956) 15' quadrangle. The name commemorates Oscar Rankin, who lived in the neighborhood of Eagle Lake from 1907 until 1917 (Purdy, 1988, p. 122).

Rattlesnake Butte [MODOC]:

(1) *peak,* 4.5 miles southeast of Crank Mountain (lat. 41°20' N, long. 121°05'15" W; near E line sec. 6, T 40 N, R 8 E). Altitude 5780 feet. Named on Crank Mountain (1962) 15' quadrangle.

(2) *hill,* 10.5 miles west-southwest of Alturas (lat. 41°26'30" N, long. 120°43'55" W; near NW cor. sec. 32, T 42 N, R 11 E). Altitude 4862 feet. Named on Alturas (1961) 15' quadrangle. United States Board on Geographic Names (1933, p. 573) approved the name "Opahwah Butte" for the feature, but later (1968a, p. 7) approved the name "Rattlesnake Butte" and rejected the names "Opahwah Butte" and "Centerville Butte"—the name "Opahwah" is of Indian origin. Pease (p. 78) used the name "Pitt River Butte" for the hill.

Rattlesnake Creek [MODOC]: *stream,* flows 10 miles from Big Sage Reservoir to Pit River 3.5 miles west of Alturas (lat. 41°29'30" N, long.

120°36'20" W). Named on Alturas (1961) and Big Sage Reservoir (1962) 15' quadrangles.

Rattlesnake Creek [PLUMAS]: *stream,* flows nearly 4 miles to Middle Fork Feather River 8.5 miles northwest of Blairsden (lat. 39°52' N, long. 120°44'05" W; near S line sec. 10, T 23 N, R 11 E). Named on Johnsville (1972) and Mount Ingalls (1972) 7.5' quadrangles.

Rattlesnake Gulch [PLUMAS]: *canyon,* drained by a stream that flows 1.5 miles to East Branch of North Fork Feather River 4 miles south of Caribou (lat. 40°01'25" N, long. 121°08'45" W; sec. 13, T 25 N, R 7 E). Named on Caribou (1979) 7.5' quadrangle.

Rattlesnake Hill [PLUMAS]: *peak,* 3 miles south of Canyondam (lat. 40°07'40" N, long. 121°03'40" W; near E line sec. 10, T 26 N, R 8 E). Altitude 6190 feet. Named on Canyondam (1979) 7.5' quadrangle.

Rattlesnake Peak [PLUMAS]: *peak,* 2 miles northwest of Kettle Rock (lat. 40°10'20" N, long. 120°44'30" W; sec. 28, T 27 N, R 11 E). Altitude 7431 feet. Named on Kettle Rock (1972) 7.5' quadrangle.

Rattlesnake Ravine [PLUMAS]: *canyon,* drained by a stream that flows 0.5 mile to Indian Creek (2) 5.5 miles southeast of Kettle Rock (lat. 40°04'50" N, long. 120°39'30" W; sec. 29, T 26 N, R 12 E). Named on Genesee Valley (1972) 7.5' quadrangle.

Ravendale [LASSEN]: *village,* 7 miles southeast of Termo (lat. 40° 47'55" N, long. 120°21'50" W; at NE cor. sec. 22, T 34 N, R 14 E). Named on Ravendale (1954) 15' quadrangle. Postal authorities established Ravendale post office in 1910, discontinued it in 1920, and reestablished it in 1921 (Frickstad, p. 68). They established Glade post office 17 miles northeast of Ravendale in 1908, moved it 3 miles north in 1910, and discontinued it in 1918 (Salley, p. 85).

Rawl Canyon [LASSEN]: *canyon,* drained by a stream that flows 1.5 miles to Big Valley 4 miles west-northwest of Bieber (lat. 41°08'10" N, long. 121°13' W; near W line sec. 18, T 38 N, R 7 E). Named on Bieber (1961) 15' quadrangle.

Rayl: see **Herlong** [LASSEN] (1).

Reconnaissance Peak [PLUMAS]: *peak,* 10 miles northeast of Portola (lat. 39°52'20" N, long. 120°18'30" W; sec. 4, T 23 N, R 15 E). Altitude 7629 feet. Named on Reconnaissance Peak (1972) 7.5' quadrangle. The name is from reconnaissance work on timber carried out at the peak in 1914 and 1915 (Gudde, 1949, p. 280).

Red Camp: see **Scotts** [LASSEN].

Red Cinder [LASSEN]: *peak,* 19 miles northwest of Westwood (lat. 40°29'45" N, long. 121°14'45" W; near N line sec. 6, T 30 N, R 7 E). Altitude 8375 feet. Named on Harvey Mountain (1956) 15' quadrangle, and on Red Cinder (1979) 7.5' quadrangle.

Red Cinder Cone [LASSEN]: *peak,* 5.25 miles north-northeast of Mount Harkness [PLUMAS] (lat. 40°29'50" N, long. 121°15'20" W; on N line sec. 1, T 30 N, R 6 E). Altitude 8008 feet. Named on Mount Harkness (1956) and Prospect Peak (1957) 15' quadrangles.

Red Clover: see **Red Clover Valley** [PLUMAS].

Red Clover Creek [PLUMAS]: *stream,* flows 24 miles to Indian Creek (2) 6 miles south-southeast of Kettle Rock (lat. 40°03'55" N, long. 120°40'30" W; sec. 31, T 26 N, R 12 E); the stream goes through Red Clover Valley. Named on Babcock Peak (1972), Crocker Mountain (1972), Genesee Valley (1972), and Grizzly Valley (1972) 7.5' quadrangles.

Red Clover Valley [PLUMAS]: *valley,* center 10.5 miles north of Portola (lat. 39°57'30" N, long. 120°28' W); the valley is along Red Clover Creek. Named on Crocker Mountain (1972) and Grizzly Valley (1972) 7.5' quadrangles. Called Clover Valley on Portola (1950) 15' quadrangle, and United States Board on Geographic Names (1974a, p. 3) gave this name as a variant. Postal authorities established Red Clover post office 16 miles north of Beckwith (present Beckwourth) in Red Clover Valley in 1879, discontinued it in 1882, reestablished it in 1887, and discontinued it in 1899 (Salley, p. 182).

Red Hill [PLUMAS]: *ridge,* generally northeast-trending, 2 miles long, 3 miles south-southwest of Caribou (lat. 40°02'35" N, long. 121°10'45" W). Named on Caribou (1979) 7.5' quadrangle.

Red Lake [MODOC]: *intermittent lake,* 3000 feet long, 5.25 miles east-northeast of Double Head Mountain (lat. 41°47'45" N, long. 120°04'30" W; sec. 29, T 46 N, R 8 E). Named on Clear Lake Reservoir (1951) 15' quadrangle.

Red Mountain [PLUMAS]:

(1) *peak,* 6 miles west of Mount Harkness (lat. 40°25'10" N, long. 121°24'45" W; sec. 34, T 30 N, R 5 E). Altitude 7408 feet. Named on Mount Harkness (1956) 15' quadrangle. United States Board on Geographic Names (1973a, p. 3) approved the name "Sifford Mountain" for the feature, and gave the name "Red Mountain" as a variant; the name "Sifford" commemorates Alexander Sifford, an early scientific investigator and explorer in the region.

(2) *ridge,* east-southeast-trending, 2.5 miles long, 3 miles south-southwest of Bucks Lodge (lat. 39°50'35" N, long. 121°12'30" W). Named on Haskins Valley (1980) 7.5' quadrangle. The peak at the southeast end of the ridge is called Grizzly Hill on Bidwell Bar (1897) 30' quadrangle, and is called Grizzly Mountain on Bucks Lake (1950) 15' quadrangle, but United States Board on Geographic Names (1979, p. 5) rejected both of these names.

Red Ridge [PLUMAS]: *ridge,* north- to east-trending, 1.25 miles long, 5.5 miles north-northwest of Dogwood Peak (lat. 39°51'15" N, long. 121°06'25" W; sec. 16, 17, T 23 N, R 8 E). Named on Dogwood Peak (1979) 7.5' quadrangle.

Red Rock [LASSEN]: *locality,* nearly 3 miles south-southeast of Constantia along Western Pacific Railroad (lat. 39°54'40" N, long. 120°01'15" W; sec. 24, T 24 N, R 17 E). Named on Constantia (1977) 7.5' quadrangle.

Red Rock [PLUMAS]: *peak,* 1.25 miles southwest of Diamond Mountain [LASSEN] (lat. 40°17'50" N, long. 120°42'30" W; sec. 11, T 28 N, R 11 E). Altitude 7596 feet. Named on Diamond Mountain (1972) 7.5' quadrangle.

Red Rock: see **Moultons** [LASSEN].

Red Rock Canyon [LASSEN]: *canyon,* drained by a stream that heads in the State of Nevada and flows 1 mile in Lassen County to Long Valley Creek 5 miles south-southeast of Constantia (lat. 39° 54'30" N, long. 120°00'50" W). Named on Constantia (1977) 7.5' quadrangle.

Red Rock Creek [LASSEN]: *stream,* flows 17 miles to Madeline Plains 9 miles north of Observation Peak (lat. 40°54'15" N, long. 120°09'15" W; at N line sec. 15, T 35 N, R 16 E). Named on Observation Peak (1954) 15' quadrangle, and on Boot Lake (1962) 7.5' quadrangle.

Red Rock Creek: see **Cold Spring Creek** [LASSEN].

Red Rock Lake [LASSEN]: *intermittent lake,* 9300 feet long, 14 miles east of Madeline (lat. 41°03' N, long. 120°12'45" W; around NW cor. sec. 30, T 37 N, R 16 E); the feature is in Red Rock Valley. Named on Boot Lake (1962) 7.5' quadrangle.

Red Rock Mountain [LASSEN]: *ridge,* south-southwest-trending, 11 miles long, 18 miles east-northeast of Madeline (lat. 41°07'30" N, long. 120°08'20" W). Named on Boot Lake (1962) and Emerson Peak (1962) 7.5' quadrangles

Red Rock Spring [PLUMAS]: *spring,* 1.5 miles south of Diamond Mountain [LASSEN] (lat. 40°17'35" N, long. 120°41'50" W; near NE cor sec. 14, T 28 N, R 11 E); the spring is less than 1 mile east-southeast of Red Rock. Named on Diamond Mountain (1972) 7.5' quadrangle.

Red Rock Valley [LASSEN]: *valley,* 14 miles east of Madeline (lat. 41°02'30" N, long. 120°11'30" W). Named on Boot Lake (1962) 7.5' quadrangle.

Reed Draw: see **Reid Draw** [MODOC].

Reeders Garden: see **Orchard Spring** [LASSEN].

Reese Flat [PLUMAS]: *area,* 3.25 miles north-northwest of Storrie (lat. 39°57'35" N, long. 121°20'50" W; sec. 6, T 24 N, R 6 E). Named on Storrie (1979) 7.5' quadrangle.

Reid Draw [MODOC]: *canyon,* drained by a stream that flows 1.5 miles to Ambrose Valley [LASSEN-MODOC] 6 miles east of Adin (lat. 41°11'20" N, long. 120°50' W; sec. 28, T 39 N, R 10 E). Named on Adin (1962) 15' quadrangle. United States Board on Geographic Names (1968a, p. 7) rejected the names "Reed Draw" and "Wayman Draw" for the feature.

Releford Creek [MODOC]: *stream,* flows 4.5 miles to end near Upper Lake 8.5 miles north of Cedarville (lat. 41°39'30" N, long. 120°10'50" W; near NE cor. sec. 30, T 44 N, R 16 E). Named on Cedarville (1962) 15' quadrangle.

Renfro Canyon [MODOC]: *canyon,* drained by a stream that flows 2.5 miles to lowlands along Parker Creek 6.25 miles east of Alturas (lat. 41°29'30" N, long. 120°25'10" W; sec. 12, T 42 N, R 13 E). Named on Dorris Reservoir (1963) 7.5' quadrangle.

Renner Lake [MODOC]: *lake,* mainly in the State of Oregon, but extends south into Modoc County 10.5 miles north of South Mountain (lat. 41°59'35" N, long. 121°37'10" W; at N line sec. 20, T 48 N, R 12 E). Named on South Mountain (1962) 15' quadrangle.

Reno Junction [LASSEN]: *locality,* 0.5 mile east of Beckwourth Pass along Western Pacific Railroad (lat. 39°47'30" N, long. 120° 06' W; sec. 5, T 22 N, R 17 E). Named on Beckwourth Pass (1975) 7.5' quadrangle.

Reposa: see **Portola** [PLUMAS].

Reservoir C [MODOC]: *intermittent lake,* 1400 feet long, 5.5 miles north-northeast of Jacks Butte (lat. 41°39'40" N, long. 120°46'15" W; at NW cor. sec. 13, T 44 N, R 10 E). Named on Jacks Butte (1962) 15' quadrangle.

Reservoir F [MODOC]: *intermittent lake,* 2.5 miles long, 5 miles west-southwest of Jacks Butte (lat. 41°34'15" N, long. 120°52'45" W; sec. 12, 13, 24, T 43 N, R 9 E). Named on Jacks Butte (1962) 15' quadrangle.

Reservoir G [MODOC]: *lake,* 1000 feet long, 9 miles north of Jacks Butte (lat. 41°43'10" N, long. 120°48'35" W; at NW cor. sec. 27, T 45 N, R 10 E). Named on Jacks Butte (1962) 15' quadrangle.

Reservoir M [MODOC]: *intermittent lake,* 1.5 miles long, 6 miles northwest of Jacks Butte (lat. 41°39' N, long. 120°52'30" W; sec. 13, 24, T 44 N, R 9 E). Named on Jacks Butte (1962) 15' quadrangle.

Reservoir N [MODOC]: *intermittent lake,* 1.25 miles long, 5.25 miles northwest of Jacks Butte (lat. 41°37'45" N, long. 120°53' W; sec. 24, 25, T 44 N, R 9 E). Named on Jacks Butte (1962) 15' quadrangle.

Rhett Lake: see **Tule Lake Sump** [MODOC].

Rhinehart Meadow [PLUMAS]: *area,* 4.5 miles south-southwest of

Taylorsville along Tollgate Creek (lat. 40°00'50" N, long. 120°51'35" W; at W line sec. 22, T 25 N, R 10 E). Named on Taylorsville (1980) 7.5' quadrangle, which shows ruins of Rhinehart cabin at the place.

Rhodes Creek [LASSEN]: *stream,* flows nearly 3 miles to Long Valley (2) 2 miles west of Constantia (lat. 39°57' N, long. 120°04'25" W; sec. 9, T 24 N, R 17 E). Named on Constantia (1977) 7.5' quadrangle.

Rhodes Meadow [PLUMAS]: *area,* 9 miles west of Mount Harkness (lat. 40°25' N, long. 121°28'15" W; sec. 31, T 30 N, R 5 E). Named on Mount Harkness (1956) 15' quadrangle.

Rice Creek: see **North Arm Rice Creek** [PLUMAS]; **South Arm Rice Creek** [PLUMAS].

Rice Creek Campground [PLUMAS]: *locality,* 6.5 miles south of Mount Harkness along North Fork Feather River (lat. 40°20'20" N, long. 121°18'30" W; near SE cor. sec. 28, T 29 N, R 6 E). Named on Mount Harkness (1956) 15' quadrangle.

Rice Flat [MODOC]: *area,* 8.5 miles south-southwest of Canby (lat. 41°19' N, long. 120°54'45" W; on W line sec. 11, T 40 N, R 9 E); the place is 1.5 miles southeast of Rice Spring. Named on Canby (1961) 15' quadrangle.

Rice Lake [LASSEN]: *intermittent lake,* 1150 feet long, 2.5 miles north of Westwood (lat. 40°20'40" N, long. 120°59'35" W; near E line sec. 29, T 29 N, R 9 E). Named on Westwood East (1980) 7.5' quadrangle.

Rices Canyon [LASSEN]: *canyon,* drained by a stream that flows 7.25 miles to Susan River 7 miles east-southeast of Susanville (lat. 40°23'15" N, long. 120°32' W; sec. 8, T 29 N, R 13 E). Named on Susanville (1954) 15' quadrangle.

Rice Spring [MODOC]: *spring,* 8.5 miles south-southwest of Canby (lat. 41°20' N, long. 120°56' W; near E line sec. 4, T 40 N, R 9 E). Named on Canby (1961) 15' quadrangle.

Rice Springs [MODOC]: *springs,* 13 miles south of Canby (lat. 41° 15'25" N, long. 120°53' W; on S line sec. 36, T 40 N, R 9 E). Named on Canby (1961) 15' quadrangle.

Rich: see **Rich Bar** [PLUMAS] (1).

Rich Bar [PLUMAS]:

(1) *locality,* 5.25 miles south-southwest of Caribou along East Branch of North Fork Feather River (lat. 40°00'35" N, long. 121° 11'30" W; on E line sec. 21, T 25 N, R 7 E). Named on Caribou (1979) 7.5' quadrangle. Postal authorities established Rich Bar post office in 1862, discontinued it in 1863, reestablished it with the name "Rich" in 1913, changed the name back to Rich Bar in 1935, and discontinued it in 1942 (Salley, p. 185). A mining camp called Poverty Bar was situated across the river from Rich Bar (Hoover, Rensch, and Rensch, p. 282).

(2) *locality,* 6.5 miles south-southeast of Quincy along Middle Fork Feather River (lat. 39°50'55" N, long. 120°53'40" W; at SW cor. sec. 17, T 23 N, R 10 E). Named on Onion Valley (1950) 7.5' quadrangle.

Rich Gulch [PLUMAS]: *canyon,* drained by a stream that flows 2.25 miles to Rush Creek 2.5 miles west-northwest of Twain (lat. 40° 02' N, long. 121°07'05" W; near W line sec. 17, T 25 N, R 8 E). Named on Caribou (1979) and Twain (1980) 7.5' quadrangles.

Richman Spring [LASSEN]: *spring,* 6.5 miles east of Bieber (lat. 41° 07' N, long. 121°01' W; sec. 23, T 38 N, R 8 E). Named on Bieber (1961) 15' quadrangle.

Richmond Hill: see **Quincy** [PLUMAS].

Ricketts Hill [LASSEN]: *peak,* 4 miles south-southwest of Bieber (lat. 41°04'15" N, long. 121°10'15" W; sec. 4, T 37 N, R 7 E). Altitude 4581 feet. Named on Bieber (1961) 15' quadrangle.

Ridenoure Reservoir [LASSEN]: *lake,* 1300 feet long, 3.5 miles south of Susanville (lat. 40°22'05" N, long. 120°39'05" W; near S line sec. 17, T 29 N, R 12 E). Named on Diamond Mountain (1972) 7.5' quadrangle.

Ridge Lake [PLUMAS]: *lake,* 1100 feet long, 9 miles west of Mount Harkness (lat. 40°24'50" N, long. 121°27'45" W; sec. 31, T 30 N, R 5 E). Named on Mount Harkness (1956) 15' quadrangle.

Right Hand Canyon [PLUMAS]: *canyon,* drained by a stream that flows 1 mile to Fitch Canyon 4.25 miles west-southwest of Milford [LASSEN] (lat. 40°09'15" N, long. 120°26'50" W; sec. 31, T 27 N, R 14 E). Named on Stony Ridge (1978) 7.5' quadrangle.

Right Hand Creek: see **Right Hand Branch**, under **Mill Creek** [PLUMAS] (3).

Right Hand Salt Rock [PLUMAS]: *stream,* flows 2.5 miles to Mill Creek (3) 4 miles north of Bucks Lodge (lat. 39°55'55" N, long. 121°11'20" W; near SW cor. sec. 15, T 24 N, R 7 E). Named on Bucks Lake (1979) 7.5' quadrangle.

Rim Lake [LASSEN]: *lake,* 600 feet long, 16 miles northwest of Westwood (lat. 40°29'35" N, long. 121°11'10" W; sec. 3, T 30 N, R 7 E). Named on Red Cinder (1979) 15' quadrangle.

Rimrock Lake [MODOC]: *intermittent lake,* 1800 feet long, 11.5 miles north-northwest of Hackamore (lat. 41°42'25" N, long. 121° 11'55" W; near SE cor. sec. 30, T 45 N, R 7 E). Named on Hackamore (1952) 15' quadrangle.

Rimrock Spring [MODOC]: *spring,* 15 miles north-northeast of Double Head Mountain (lat. 41°56'50" N, long. 121°01'30" W; near W line sec. 2, T 47 N, R 8 E). Named on Clear Lake Reservoir (1951) 15' quadrangle.

Rimrock Valley [MODOC]: *canyon,* 2 miles long, 3.5 miles southeast of South Mountain (lat. 41°48' N, long. 120°35'30" W). Named on South Mountain (1962) 15' quadrangle.

Rimrock Valley Reservoir [MODOC]: *intermittent lake,* 900 feet long, 3 miles southeast of South Mountain (lat. 41°48'45" N, long. 120°35'35" W; sec. 21, T 46 N, R 12 E); the feature is at the north end of Rimrock Valley. Named on South Mountain (1962) 15' quadrangle.

Rio de los Plumas: see **Feather River** [PLUMAS].

Rivalier Canyon [MODOC]: *canyon,* drained by a stream that flows 4 miles to the stream in Clark Canyon 4.25 miles east-southeast of Adin (lat. 41°13'10" N, long. 120°51'45" W; sec. 18, T 39 N, R 10 E). Named on Adin (1962) 15' quadrangle.

Rivis: see **Ollie Rivis Spring** [LASSEN].

Robbers Creek [LASSEN]: *locality,* 4.25 miles north of Westwood along Western Pacific Railroad (lat. 40°22'15" N, long. 121°00'15" W; near E line sec. 18, T 29 N, R 9 E); the place is near Robbers Creek [LASSEN-PLUMAS]. Named on Westwood West (1980) 7.5' quadrangle.

Robbers Creek [LASSEN-PLUMAS]: *stream,* heads in Plumas County and flows 19 miles to Mountain Meadows Reservoir 1.25 miles south of the center of Westwood in Lassen County (lat. 40° 17'25" N, long. 121°00'15" W; near NE cor. sec. 18, T 28 N, R 9 E). Named on Swain Mountain (1979), Westwood East (1980), and Westwood West (1980) 7.5' quadrangles. The name came into use after James Doyle was robbed near the stream in 1865 or 1866 (Gudde, 1949, p. 288).

Robbers Roost [PLUMAS]: *relief feature,* 15 miles west-southwest of the village of Almanor (lat. 40°09'30" N, long. 121°26'15" W). Named on Jonesville (1958) 15' quadrangle.

Robbers Spring [LASSEN]:

(1) *spring,* 1.5 miles south-southwest of Cal Mountain (lat. 40°38'50" N, long. 121°10'15" W; near E line sec. 10, T 32 N, R 7 E). Named on Harvey Mountain (1956) 15' quadrangle. United States Board on Geographic Names (1983d, p. 5) approved this name for a spring located about 1.5 miles farther southeast (lat. 40°37'55" N, long. 121°08'52" W; sec. 13, T 32 N, R 7 E).

(2) *spring,* 12.5 miles north-northwest of Westwood (lat. 40°27'20" N, long. 121°07'15" W; near SE cor. sec. 18, T 30 N, R 8 E); the spring is along Robbers Creek [LASSEN-PLUMAS]. Named on Swain Mountain (1979) 7.5' quadrangle.

Roberts Butte [MODOC]: *ridge,* northeast-trending, 1 mile long, 2 miles northeast of Lookout (lat. 41°13'40" N, long. 121°07'20" W; on NW cor. sec. 13, T 39 N, R 7 E); the ridge is southeast of Lower Roberts Reservoir. Named on Bieber (1961) 15' quadrangle.

Roberts Camp [MODOC]: *locality,* 8.5 miles south of Crank Mountain (lat. 41°15'45" N, long. 121°10' W; sec. 33, T 40 N, R 7 E). Named on Crank Mountain (1962) 15' quadrangle.

Roberts Canyon [LASSEN]: *canyon,* drained by a stream that flows 2.5 miles to Upper Long Valley 4 miles south of Beckwouth Pass (lat. 39°44' N, long. 120°06'25" W; sec. 29, T 22 N, R 17 E). Named on Evans Canyon (1978) and Loyalton (1981) 7.5' quadrangles.

Roberts Creek [MODOC]: *stream,* flows 5.5 miles to lowlands along Goose Lake (1) 1.25 miles south-southeast of the village of Davis Creek (lat. 41°42'50" N, long. 120°22' W). Named on Davis Creek (1962) 15' quadrangle.

Roberts Lower Reservoir: see **Lower Roberts Reservoir** [MODOC].

Roberts Reservoir: see **Lower Roberts Reservoir** [MODOC]; **Upper Roberts Reservoir** [MODOC].

Robinson Canyon [LASSEN]: *canyon,* drained by a stream that flows nearly 3 miles to Willow Ranch Creek 1.5 miles west-southwest of Doyle (lat. 40°00'50" N, long. 120°07'45" W; near S line sec. 13, T 25 N, R 16 E). Named on Frenchman Lake (1979) and McKesick Peak (1978) 7.5' quadrangles.

Robinson Creek [PLUMAS]: *stream,* flows 1 mile to Last Chance Creek (2) 8 miles east of Squaw Valley Peak (lat. 40°03'10" N, long. 120°15'05" W; sec. 1, T 25 N, R 15 E). Named on Ferris Creek (1977) 7.5' quadrangle.

Rock Cabin Well [LASSEN]: *well,* 2.5 miles east-southeast of Cal Mountain (lat. 40°39'20" N, long. 121°07' W; sec. 7, T 32 N, R 8 E). Named on Harvey Mountain (1956) 15' quadrangle

Rock Canyon [LASSEN]: *canyon,* 2.25 miles long, 8 miles west-northwest of Bieber (lat. 41°08'25" N, long. 121°17'45" W). Named on Fall River Mills (1961) 15' quadrangle.

Rock Creek [MODOC]:

(1) *stream,* flows 10 miles to Lost River 14 miles north-northeast of Double Head Mountain (lat. 41°58'10" N, long. 121°05'50" W; sec. 30, T 48 N, R 8 E). Named on Clear Lake Reservoir (1951) and Steele Swamp (1962) 15' quadrangles.

(2) *stream,* flows 6 miles to North Fork Willow Creek nearly 6 miles north-northwest of Blue Mountain (lat. 41°54'40" N, long. 120°53'30" W; near S line sec. 13, T 47 N, R 9 E). Named on Steele Swamp (1962) 15' quadrangle.

(3) *stream,* flows 3.5 miles to Pit River 3.5 miles north of Alturas (lat. 41°29'35" N, long. 120°36'25" W; sec. 8, T 42 N, R 12 E). Named on Alturas (1961) and Big Sage Reservoir (1962) 15' quadrangles.

Rock Creek [PLUMAS]:
(1) *stream,* flows 12 miles to Hamilton Branch 8 miles east-southeast of Chester (lat. 40°16'55" N, long. 121°05'05" W; sec. 16, T 28 N, R 8 E). Named on Red Cinder (1979) and Westwood West (1980) 7.5' quadrangles.
(2) *stream,* flows 2.25 miles to Grizzly Creek (1) 10.5 miles southwest of the village of Almanor (lat. 40°07'20" N, long. 121°19'40" W; near E line sec. 8, T 26 N, R 6 E). Named on Jonesville (1958) 15' quadrangle.
(3) *stream,* flows 1.25 miles to Red Clover Creek 7.5 miles south-southeast of Kettle Rock (lat. 40°02'55" N, long. 120°39'50" W; at E line sec. 6, T 25 N, R 12 E). Named on Genesee Valley (1972) 7.5' quadrangle.
(4) *stream,* flows 10 miles to North Fork Feather River 2.25 miles west-southwest of Storrie (lat. 39°54' N, long. 121°21'30" W). Named on Jonesville (1958) 15' quadrangle, and on Kimshew Point (1979) and Storrie (1979) 7.5' quadrangles. Gudde (1975, p. 31) listed a mining place called Beldens Bar that was along North Fork Feather River above the mouth of Rock Creek (4).
(5) *stream,* formed by the confluence of East Branch and South Fork, flows 4.25 miles to Spanish Creek (1) 2.25 miles east-northeast of the village of Meadow Valley (lat. 39°56'35" N, long. 121° 01' W; near N line sec. 18, T 24 N, R 9 E). Named on Meadow Valley (1980) 7.5' quadrangle. East Branch is 4 miles long and is named on Meadow Valley (1980) and Quincy (1950) 7.5' quadrangles; it is called North Fork on Bidwell Bar (1897) and Downieville (1897) 30' quadrangles. South Fork is 7 miles long and is named on Dogwood Peak (1979), Meadow Valley (1980), and Onion Valley (1950) 7.5' quadrangles.
(6) *stream,* flows 1.5 miles to Estray Creek 8.5 miles southwest of Mount Ingalls (lat. 39°54'15" N, long. 120°44'30" W; near E line sec. 33, T 24 N, R 11 E). Named on Mount Ingalls (1972) 7.5' quadrangle.
(7) *stream,* flows nearly 5 miles to Butte County 5 miles south-southeast of Cascade (lat. 39°38'10" N, long. 121°08'10" W; at W line sec. 31, T 21 N, R 8 E). Named on American House (1948) and Cascade (1948) 7.5' quadrangles.
(8) *stream,* flows 0.5 mile to China Gulch (2) 5.25 miles south of Bucks Lodge (lat. 39°48' N, long. 121°09'55" W; sec. 35, T 23 N, R 7 E). Named on Haskins Valley (1980) 7.5' quadrangle.
(9) *locality,* 2 miles west-southwest of Storrie along Western Pacific Railroad (lat. 39°54'10" N, long. 121°21'05" W); the place is near the mouth of Rock Creek (4). Named on Storrie (1979) 7.5' quadrangle.

Rock Creek: see **West Rock Creek** [MODOC].

Rock Creek Camp: see **Rock Crest** [PLUMAS].

Rock Creek Campground [PLUMAS]: *locality,* 3 miles southeast of the village of Meadow Valley (lat. 39°54'05" N, long. 121°01'20" W; near W line sec. 31, T 24 N, R 9 E); the place is near the head of Rock Creek (5). Named on Meadow Valley (1980) 7.5' quadrangle.

Rock Creek Reservoir [MODOC]: *intermittent lake,* 300 feet long, 4 miles north-northeast of Blue Mountain (lat. 41°53'05" N, long. 120°50'10" W; near W line sec. 28, T 47 N, R 10 E); the feature is along Rock Creek (2). Named on Steele Swamp (1962) 15' quadrangle.

Rock Creek Reservoir [PLUMAS]: *lake,* behind a dam on North Fork Feather River 5.25 miles north-northeast of Storrie (lat. 39°59'10" N, long. 121°16'55" W; at NW cor. sec. 35, T 25 N, R 6 E). Named on Storrie (1979) 7.5' quadrangle.

Rock Crest [PLUMAS]: *locality,* less than 1 mile north-northeast of Storrie (lat. 39°55'35" N, long. 121°18'55" W). Named on Storrie (1979) 7.5' quadrangle. Pulga (1957) 15' quadrangle shows Rock Creek Camp at the site.

Rock Island Ridge [PLUMAS]: *ridge,* southeast-trending, 2 miles long, 7.5 miles south-southeast of Storrie (lat. 39°48'45" N, long. 121°17'15" W). Named on Soapstone Hill (1979) 7.5' quadrangle.

Rock Lake [MODOC]: *lake,* 100 feet long, 10 miles north-northwest of Fort Bidwell (lat. 41°59' N, long. 120°13'45" W; near E line sec. 34, T 48 N, R 15 E). Named on Fort Bidwell (1962) 15' quadrangle.

Rock Lake [PLUMAS]:
(1) *lake,* 1900 feet long, 1.5 miles west-northwest of the village of Almanor (lat. 40°14'05" N, long. 121°14'15" W; on S line sec. 31, T 28 N, R 7 E). Named on Almanor (1979) 7.5' quadrangle.
(2) *lake,* 400 feet long, nearly 5 miles north-northeast of Bucks Lodge (lat. 39°56'30" N, long. 121°08'30" W; sec. 13, T 24 N, R 7 E). Named on Bucks Lake (1979) 7.5' quadrangle.
(3) *lake,* 1300 feet long, 6.5 miles west-southwest of Clio (lat. 39° 42'55" N, long. 120°41'50" W; near NW cor. sec. 1, T 21 N, R 11 E). Named on Gold Lake (1981) 7.5' quadrangle. On Downieville (1897) 30' quadrangle, present Rock Lake (3) and present Jamison Lake together are called Jamison Lakes.

Rock Spring [LASSEN]: *spring,* 14 miles east of Madeline (lat. 41° 02'40" N, long. 120°12'30" W; at E line sec. 25, T 37 N, R 15 E). Named on Boot Lake (1962) 7.5' quadrangle.

Rock Spring [MODOC]:
(1) *spring,* 5.5 miles west-northwest of Alturas (lat. 41°31'40" N, long. 120°38'10" W; near NW cor. sec. 31, T 43 N, R 12 E); the feature is at the head of a branch of West Rock Creek. Named on Big Sage Reservoir (1962) 15' quadrangle. United States Board on Geographic Names (1990, p. 10) rejected the plural form "Rock Springs" for the name.
(2) *spring,* 14 miles southeast of Alturas (lat. 41°19'25" N, long. 120°22'15" W; sec. 9, T 40 N, R 14 E). Named on Soup Creek (1963) 7.5' quadrangle.

Rock Springs [MODOC]: *springs,* 5.5 miles west-southwest of Likely (lat. 41°12'40" N, long. 120°36'10" W; sec. 16, T 39 N, R 12 E). Named on Likely (1962) 15' quadrangle.

Rocky Butte: see **Dill Butte** [LASSEN].

Rocky Creek [PLUMAS]: *stream,* flows 1.25 miles to Lost Creek (2) 3.5 miles west-southwest of American House (lat. 39°38'25" N, long. 121°05'10" W; sec. 33, T 21 N, R 8 E). Named on American House (1948) 7.5' quadrangle.

Rocky Flat Tank [MODOC]: *water feature,* 10 miles north-northwest of South Mountain (lat. 41°58'10" N, long. 120°43' W; sec. 28, T 48 N, R 11 E). Named on South Mountain (1962) 15' quadrangle.

Rocky Knoll Campground [LASSEN]: *locality,* 16 miles north-northwest of Westwood (lat. 40°29'55" N, long. 121°09'20" W; near S line sec. 35, T 31 N, R 7 E). Named on Red Cinder (1979) 7.5' quadrangle.

Rocky Point [LASSEN]: *promontory,* 2 miles north of Pelican Point along the west side of Eagle Lake (lat. 40°39'50" N, long. 120°44'25" W). Named on Antelope Mountain (1956) and Fredonyer Peak (1954) 15' quadrangles.

Rocky Point [PLUMAS]:
(1) *promontory,* 2 miles northwest of Canyondam along Lake Almanor (lat. 40°11'25" N, long. 121°05'55" W; near SE cor. sec. 17, T 27 N, R 8 E). Named on Canyondam (1979) 7.5' quadrangle.
(2) *relief feature,* 6.5 miles south-southwest of Quincy (lat. 39°50'50" N, long. 120°58'30" W; near NE cor. sec. 21, T 23 N, R 9 E). Named on Onion Valley (1950) 7.5' quadrangle.
(3) *hill,* 2.5 miles east-northeast of Portola (lat. 39°49'15" N, long. 120°25'30" W; on W line sec. 28, T 23 N, R 14 E). Named on Portola (1972) 7.5' quadrangle.

Rocky Point Campground [PLUMAS]: *locality,* 2.25 miles northwest of Canyondam (lat. 40°11'25" N, long. 121°06'15" W; at S line sec. 17, T 27 N, R 8 E); the place is 0.25 mile west of Rocky Point (1). Named on Canyondam (1979) 7.5' quadrangle.

Rocky Point Spring [PLUMAS]: *spring,* 14 miles southeast of Kettle Rock (lat. 40°00'55" N, long. 120°30'45" W; at S line sec. 15, T 25 N, R 13 E). Named on Babcock Peak (1972) 7.5' quadrangle.

Rocky Prairie [MODOC]: *area,* 16 miles south-southwest of Alturas (lat. 41°16'45" N, long. 120°40'30" W). Named on Alturas (1961) and Likely (1962) 15' quadrangles.

Rodeo Flat [LASSEN]: *valley,* 10.5 miles northeast of Observation Peak (lat. 40°53'15" N, long. 120°02'30" W; sec. 15, 22, T 35 N, R 17 E). Named on Observation Peak (1954) 15' quadrangle.

Rodgers: see **Camp Rodgers**, under **Rodgers Flat** [PLUMAS].

Rodgers Flat [PLUMAS]: *locality,* 3.5 miles northeast of Storrie along Western Pacific Railroad (lat. 39°57'35" N, long. 121°16'40" W; sec. 2, T 24 N, R 6 E). Named on Storrie (1979) 7.5' quadrangle. Pulga (1957) 15' quadrangle shows Camp Rodgers at the site. Postal authorities established Camp Rodgers post office in 1916 and discontinued it in 1936; the name was for the operator of a vacation resort at the place (Salley, p. 35).

Rogers Creek: see **McClellan Canyon** [PLUMAS].

Rogers Lake [PLUMAS]: *lake,* 500 feet long, 3 miles west-southwest of Bucks Lodge (lat. 39°51'15" N, long. 121°13'15" W; on S line sec. 8, T 23 N, R 7 E). Named on Haskins Valley (1980) 7.5' quadrangle.

Romero Creek [MODOC]: *stream,* flows 10 miles to lowlands along South Fork Pit River 14 miles south of Alturas (lat. 40°17'15" N, long. 120°31'30" W; sec. 19, T 40 N, R 13 E). Named on Alturas (1961) 15' quadrangle, and on Little Juniper Reservoir (1963) 7.5' quadrangle.

Romstock Canyon [LASSEN]: *canyon,* drained by a stream that flows 3 miles to Willow Creek Valley 7.25 miles south-southeast of Pelican Point (lat. 40°32'45" N, long. 120°40'30" W; near E line sec. 13, T 31 N, R 11 E). Named on Fredonyer Peak (1954) 15' quadrangle.

Roney Corral [LASSEN]: *locality,* 10.5 miles southwest of Pelican Point (lat. 40°30'45" N, long. 120°51'15" W; near S line sec. 28, T 31 N, R 10 E). Named on Antelope Mountain (1956) 15' quadrangle.

Roney Flat [MODOC]: *area,* 10 miles south-southwest of Canby (lat. 41°18'30" N, long. 120°56'10" W; sec. 16, T 40 N, R 9 E). Named on Canby (1961) 15' quadrangle.

Roop Mountain [LASSEN]: *ridge,* south-trending, 2 miles long, 15 miles northeast of Westwood (lat. 40°28'15" N, long. 120°48'35" W). Named on Roop Mountain (1980) 7.5' quadrangle. The feature first was called Worley Mountain, for Jess Worley, who had a ranch near it; the name "Roop" was given in 1922 to honor Isaac N. Roop of Susanville (Purdy, 1988, p. 122).

Rooptown: see **Susanville** [LASSEN].

Roscoe: see **Madeline** [LASSEN].

Rose Canyon [MODOC]: *canyon,* drained by a stream that flows 5.5 miles to Pit River 2.5 miles south of Crank Mountain (lat. 41°20'50" N, long. 121°08'10" W; near W line sec. 35, T 41 N, R 7 E). Named on Crank Mountain (1962) 15' quadrangle.

Ross Campground [PLUMAS]: *locality,* 9 miles west of Clio along Jamison Creek (lat. 39°44'05" N, long. 120°44'55" W; at S line sec. 28, T 22 N, R 11 E). Named on Gold Lake (1981) 7.5' quadrangle.

Ross Canyon [PLUMAS]:

(1) *canyon,* drained by a stream that flows 6 miles to Last Chance Creek (2) 7.25 miles northwest of Squaw Valley Peak (lat. 40° 06'50" N, long. 120°28'50" W; at N line sec. 14, T 26 N, R 13 E). Named on Squaw Valley Peak (1977) 7.5' quadrangle. Called McClellan Canyon on Milford (1950) 15' quadrangle, but United States Board on Geographic Names (1978a, p. 7) rejected this name for the feature.

(2) *canyon,* drained by a stream that flows about 3.5 miles to Dixie Creek (2) 12.5 miles north-northeast of Portola (lat. 39°58'05" N, long. 120°21'25" W; near N line sec. 1, T 24 N, R 14 E). Named on Dixie Mountain (1972) 7.5' quadrangle.

Ross Creek [MODOC]: *stream,* flows 2.5 miles to lowlands along Goose Lake (1) 8 miles south of Willow Ranch (lat. 41°47'30" N, long. 120°22' W; near NW cor. sec. 33, T 46 N, R 14 E). Named on Willow Ranch (1962) 15' quadrangle.

Ross Ranch Meadow [PLUMAS]: *canyon,* 1.5 miles long, opens into the canyon of Middle Fork Feather River 3.25 miles east of Portola (lat. 39°48'55" N, long. 120°24'35" N; near E line sec. 28, T 23 N, R 14 E). Named on Portola (1972) 7.5' quadrangle.

Round Lake [PLUMAS]: *lake,* 1100 feet long, 6.5 miles southwest of Clio (lat. 39°41'10" N, long. 120°40'40" W; near N line sec. 18, T 21 N, R 12 E). Named on Gold Lake (1981) 7.5' quadrangle. The feature is one of the group called Bear Lakes on Downieville (1897) 30' quadrangle

Round Mountain [LASSEN]: *hill,* 4 miles east-southeast of Westwood (lat. 40°17'05" N, long. 120°55'50" W; sec. 14, T 28 N, R 9 E). Altitude 5199 feet. Named on Westwood East (1980) 7.5' quadrangle.

Round Mountain [MODOC]: *peak,* 9 miles southwest of the village of Davis Creek (lat. 41°37'50" N, long. 120°28'10" W; near NE cor. sec. 28, T 44 N, R 13 E). Altitude 5381 feet. Named on Davis Creek (1962) 15' quadrangle.

Round Mountain [PLUMAS]: *peak,* 7.5 miles west-southwest of Milford [LASSEN] (lat. 40°08'50" N, long. 120°29'35" W; at SE cor. sec. 34, T 27 N, R 13 E). Altitude 6395 feet. Named on Stony Ridge (1978) 7.5' quadrangle.

Round Mountain Spring [PLUMAS]: *spring,* 6.5 miles west-southwest of Milford [LASSEN] (lat. 40°08'40" N, long. 120°29'20" W; near NW cor. sec. 2, T 26 N, R 13 E); the spring is 1600 feet southeast of Round Mountain. Named on Stony Ridge (1978) 7.5' quadrangle.

Round Valley [LASSEN]: *valley,* 9 miles south-southeast of Pelican Point (lat. 40°30'45" N, long. 120°40'15" W; around SE cor. sec. 25, T 31 N, R 11 E). Named on Fredonyer Peak (1954) 15' quadrangle.

Round Valley [MODOC]:

(1) *area,* 6.5 miles north-northwest of Jacks Butte (lat. 41°40'30" N, long. 120°50'45" W; around SW cor. sec. 5, T 44 N, R 10 E). Named on Jacks Butte (1962) 15' quadrangle.

(2) *valley,* 4 miles north-northeast of Adin (lat. 41°15' N, long. 120° 54'15" W). Named on Adin (1962) and Canby (1961) 15' quadrangles. The name is from the shape of the valley (Preston, 1890b, p. 333).

Round Valley [PLUMAS]: *locality,* 3.5 miles west-northwest of Crescent Mills (lat. 40°06'55" N, long. 120°58' W; near E line sec. 16, T 26 N, R 9 E); the place is just northwest of Round Valley Reservoir. Site named on Crescent Mills (1980) 7.5' quadrangle. Postal authorities established Round Valley post office in 1863, discontinued it in 1870, reestablished it the same year, and discontinued it in 1873 (Frickstad, p. 125).

Round Valley: see **Big Valley** [LASSEN-MODOC]; **Little Round Valley** [LASSEN].

Round Valley Butte [LASSEN]: *hill,* 10.5 miles south-southeast of Cal Mountain (lat. 40°31'55" N, long. 121°04'30" W; on E line sec. 21, T 31 N, R 8 E); the hill is 1 mile south-southeast of Little Round Valley. Altitude 6610 feet. Named on Harvey Mountain (1956) 15' quadrangle.

Round Valley Campground [PLUMAS]: *locality,* 2.5 miles west-northwest of Crescent Mills along Round Valley Reservoir (lat. 40° 06'40" N, long. 120°57'10" W; sec. 15, T 26 N, R 9 E). Named on Crescent Mills (1980) 7.5' quadrangle.

Round Valley Reservoir [LASSEN]: *lake,* 3100 feet long, 9.5 miles south-southeast of Pelican Point (lat. 40°30'50" N, long. 120°39'45" W; near SE cor. sec. 30, T 31 N, R 12 E). Named on Fredonyer Peak (1954) 15' quadrangle.

Round Valley Reservoir [PLUMAS]: *lake,* 1.25 miles long, 2.5 miles west-northwest of Crescent Mills (lat. 40°06'30" N, long. 120°57'30" W). Named on Crescent Mills (1980) 7.5' quadrangle.

Round Willows [MODOC]: *area,* 6.25 miles north of South Mountain (lat. 41°55'45" N, long. 120°39' W; sec. 12, T 47 N, R 11 E). Named on South Mountain (1962) 15' quadrangle.

Rowland Creek [PLUMAS]: *stream,* flows 3.25 mile to Little Last Chance Creek 5 miles south of McKesick Peak (lat. 40°01'05" N, long. 120°13'50" W; sec. 18, T 25 N, R 16 E). Named on Ferris Creek (1977) and McKesick Peak (1978) 7.5' quadrangles.

Rucker Hill [MODOC]: *peak,* nearly 7 miles southwest of Canby (lat. 41°23'35" N, long. 120°58'50" W; sec. 18, T 41 N, R 9 E). Altitude 5073 feet. Named on Canby (1961) 15' quadrangle.

Rucker Hill Tank [MODOC]: *water feature,* 7 miles southwest of Canby (lat. 41°22'45" N, long. 120°58'30" W; sec. 19, T 41 N, R 9 E); the feature is 1 mile south of Rucker Hill. Named on Canby (1961) 15' quadrangle.

Ruffa Ridge [PLUMAS]: *ridge,* east-trending, 2.5 miles long, 10.5 miles west of the village of Almanor (lat. 40°11'15" N, long. 121° 21'45" W). Named on Jonesville (1958) 15' quadrangle, which shows Ruffa ranch west and south of the ridge.

Runyon Springs [LASSEN]: *springs,* 19 miles east of Madeline (lat. 41°02'15" N, long. 120°07'20" W; at S line sec. 26, T 37 N, R 16 E). Named on Little Hat Mountain (1962) 7.5' quadrangle.

Rush Creek [LASSEN]: *stream,* flows 8 miles to the State of Nevada 19 miles south-southeast of Observation Peak (lat. 40°33'15" N, long. 119°59'40" W; near N line sec. 13, T 31 N, R 17 E). Named on Shinn Mountain (1954) 15' quadrangle.

Rush Creek [MODOC]: *stream,* flows 9 miles to Ash Creek 2.5 miles northeast of Adin (lat. 41°13'40" N, long. 120°54'45" W; at SW cor. sec. 11, T 39 N, R 9 E). Named on Adin (1962) and Canby (1961) 15' quadrangles.

Rush Creek [PLUMAS]: *stream,* flows 11.5 miles to East Branch of North Fork Feather River 2.5 miles west of Twain (lat. 40°01'25" N, long. 121°07'20" W; near SE cor. sec. 18, T 25 N, R 8 E). Named on Twain (1980) 7.5' quadrangle. The stream also is called Northfork (Jackson *in* Windeler, p. 217).

Rush Creek Campground: see **Lower Rush Creek Campground** [MODOC]; **Upper Rush Creek Campground** [MODOC].

Rush Creek Hill [PLUMAS]: *peak,* 4 miles northwest of Twain (lat. 40°04' N, long. 121°07' W; at E line sec. 31, T 26 N, R 8 E); the peak is 3 miles north of the mouth of Rush Creek. Altitude 6339 feet. Named on Twain (1980) 7.5' quadrangle.

Rush Creek Mountain [LASSEN]: *ridge,* west-northwest-trending, 4 miles long, 10.5 miles south-southeast of Observation Peak (lat. 40°37'50" N, long. 120°07'45" W); the ridge is at the head of Rush Creek. Named on Shinn Mountain (1954) 15' quadrangle.

Rush Creek Spring [LASSEN]: *spring,* 14 miles south-southeast of Observation Peak (lat. 40°35'40" N, long. 120°05'15" W; near E line sec. 31, T 32 N, R 17 E); the spring is along Rush Creek. Named on Shinn Mountain (1954) 15' quadrangle.

Rush Hill [PLUMAS]: *ridge,* generally north-northeast-trending, 1.25 miles long, 5 miles north of Twain (lat. 40°05'40" N, long. 121°03'05" W); the ridge is west of Rush Creek. Named on Twain (1980) 7.5' quadrangle.

Russell Canyon [MODOC]: *canyon,* drained by a stream that flows 1 mile to the State of Oregon 8.5 miles north-northeast of Newell (lat. 41°59'50" N, long. 121°17'45" W; near W line sec. 16, T 48 N, R 6 E). Named on Tulelake (1951) 15' quadrangle.

Russell Dairy Spring [LASSEN]: *spring,* 9.5 miles east-southeast of the village of Little Valley (lat. 40°49'35" N, long. 121°01'30" W; sec. 12, T 34 N, R 8 E). Named on Little Valley (1957) 15' quadrangle.

Russell Slough [MODOC]: *stream,* flows 4.25 miles to North Fork Pit River 6 miles south-southwest of village of Davis Creek (lat. 41°39'20" N, long. 120°25'40" W; at E line sec. 14, T 44 N, R 13 E). Named on Davis Creek (1962) 15' quadrangle.

Rutherfords: see **Bucks Lake** [PLUMAS].

Ryan Canyon [MODOC]: *canyon,* drained by a stream that flows 2 miles to Barber Canyon 3 miles north-northwest of Adin (lat. 41° 14'05" N, long. 120°57'45" W; sec. 8, T 39 N, R 9 E). Named on Adin (1962) and Canby (1961) 15' quadrangles.

Ryan Ridge [MODOC]: *ridge,* generally southeast-trending, 5 miles long, center 11 miles southeast of Crank Mountain (lat. 41°16'10" N, long. 121°00'25" W). Named on Adin (1962), Canby (1961), and Crank Mountain (1962) 15' quadrangles.

Rye Grass Swale [MODOC]: *area,* 10 miles southwest of Alturas (lat. 41°22'30" N, long. 120°40' W). Named on Alturas (1961) 15' quadrangle.

Rye Patch Canyon [LASSEN]: *canyon,* 6 miles long, opens into lowlands 10 miles north-northeast of Karlo (lat. 40°41'10" N, long. 120°16'30" W; near NE cor. sec. 33, T 33 N, R 15 E). Named on Karlo (1954) and Shinn Mountain (1954) 15' quadrangles.

Rye Patch Spring [LASSEN]: *spring,* 10 miles north-northeast of Karlo (lat. 40°41'25" N, long. 120°16'25" W; near SW cor. sec. 27, T 33 N, R 15 E); the spring is near the mouth of Rye Patch Canyon. Named on Karlo (1954) 15' quadrangle.

—S—

Saddleback [MODOC]: *ridge,* north-trending, 2 miles long, 4.5 miles west-southwest of Eagleville (lat. 41°17'30" N, long. 120°12' W). Named on Eagle Peak (1963) 7.5' quadrangle. Preston (1890b, p. 332) referred to Mount Saddleback.

Saddle Blanket Flat [MODOC]: *area,* 8.5 miles southeast of Newell (lat.

41°47'10" N, long. 121°16'45" W). Named on Tulelake (1951) 15' quadrangle.

Saddle Lake [PLUMAS]: *lake,* 800 feet long, 5 miles north-northwest of Storrie (lat. 39°59'10" N, long. 121°20'55" W; on S line sec. 30, T 25 N, R 6 E). Named on Storrie (1979) 7.5' quadrangle.

Saddle Mountain: see **Double Head Mountain** [MODOC].

Saddle Rock [LASSEN]: *peak,* 5 miles north-northeast of Karlo (lat. 40°36'45" N, long. 120°16'25" W; at NW cor. sec. 27, T 32 N, R 15 E). Altitude 5470 feet. Named on Karlo (1954) 15' quadrangle.

Sagebrush Butte [MODOC]: *peak,* 12 miles northeast of Double Head Mountain (lat. 41°54'25" N, long. 121°02' W; on S line sec. 15, T 47 N, R 8 E). Altitude 4733 feet. Named on Clear Lake Reservoir (1951) 15' quadrangle.

Sagebrush Flat [LASSEN]: *valley,* 16 miles south-southwest of Likely [MODOC] (lat. 41°01'10" N, long. 120°36'45" W). Named on Likely (1962) 15' quadrangle.

Sage Campground: see **Big Sage Campground** [MODOC].

Sage Creek [PLUMAS]: *stream,* flows nearly 1 mile to Middle Creek 4 miles east of Kettle Rock (lat. 40°08'55" N, long. 120°38'50" W; near S line sec. 32, T 27 N, R 12 E). Named on Kettle Rock (1972) 7.5' quadrangle.

Sage Hen [LASSEN]: *locality,* 4 miles north of Madeline along Southern Pacific Railroad (lat. 41°06'40" N, long. 120°28'35" W; sec. 21, T 38 N, R 13 E); the place is near the northwest end of Sage Hen Flat (1). Named on Madeline (1962) 7.5' quadrangle.

Sage Hen Flat [LASSEN]:

(1) *valley,* 3.5 miles north of Madeline (lat. 41°06' N, long. 120°28'05" W; mainly in sec. 27, T 38 N, R 13 E). Named on Madeline (1962) 7.5' quadrangle. Smith stage station was at the edge of Sage Hen Flat (Garate, p. 121).

(2) *area,* 10.5 miles east-northeast of the village of Little Valley (lat. 40°57'45" N, long. 121°00'10" W; sec. 12, 13, T 36 N, R 8 E). Named on Little Valley (1957) 15' quadrangle.

Sage Hen Spring [LASSEN]: *spring,* 8 miles south-southeast of Observation Peak (lat. 40°41'10" N, long. 120°07'25" W; at SE cor. sec. 26, T 33 N, R 16 E). Named on Shinn Mountain (1954) 15' quadrangle.

Sage Lake [MODOC]: *intermittent lake,* 4200 feet long, 6 miles east of Newell (lat. 41°54'10" N, long. 121°15'15" W; sec. 23, T 47 N, R 6 E). Named on Clear Lake Reservoir (1951) and Tulelake (1951) 15' quadrangles.

Sager Canyon [MODOC]: *canyon,* drained by a stream that flows 2 miles to Messenger Gulch 6 miles northeast of Adin (lat. 41°14'05" N, long. 120°50'45" W; sec. 8, T 39 N, R 10 E). Named on Adin (1962) 15' quadrangle.

Sage Reservoir: see **Big Sage Reservoir** [MODOC].

Said Valley [LASSEN]: *valley,* 9.5 miles northeast of Lava Peak (lat. 40°55'30" N, long. 120°45'30" W). Named on Hayden Hill (1956) 15' quadrangle. Preston (1890a, p. 275) used the form "Sed Valley" for the name.

Said Valley Reservoir [LASSEN]: *lake,* 3500 feet long, 9.5 miles northeast of Lava Peak (lat. 40°55'10" N, long. 120°45'10" W; on S line sec. 30, T 36 N, R 11 E); the lake is at the southeast end of Said Valley. Named on Grasshopper Valley (1954) and Hayden Hill (1956) 15' quadrangles.

Salisbury Gulch: see **Salsbury Gulch** [MODOC].

Salmon Creek [PLUMAS]: *stream,* flows 2 miles to North Fork Feather River nearly 3 miles south-southwest of Canyondam (lat. 40°08'05" N, long. 121°05'40" W; near SW cor. sec. 4, T 26 N, R 8 E). Named on Canyondam (1979) 7.5' quadrangle.

Salsbury Gulch [MODOC]: *canyon,* drained by a stream that flows 5.5 miles from Essex Reservoir to Big Sage Reservoir 10.5 miles northwest of Alturas (lat. 41°35'05" N, long. 120°41'25" W; sec. 10, T 43 N, R 11 E). Named on Big Sage Reservoir (1962) 15' quadrangle. United States Board on Geographic Names (1983c, p. 7) approved the name "Salisbury Gulch" for the feature.

Salt Cabin [LASSEN]: *locality,* 12.5 miles west-northwest of Pelican Point (lat. 40°43'30" N, long. 120°56'35" W; sec. 15, T 33 N, R 9 E). Site named on Antelope Mountain (1956) 15' quadrangle.

Salt Log Spring [MODOC]: *spring,* 12.5 miles west of Likely (lat. 41°12'30" N, long. 120°44'35" W; on W line sec. 20, T 39 N, R 11 E). Named on Likely (1962) 15' quadrangle.

Sand Butte: see **Big Sand Butte** [MODOC]; **East Sand Butte** [MODOC]; **Little Sand Butte** [MODOC].

Sand Creek [MODOC]: *stream,* heads in the State of Nevada and flows 9 miles in Modoc County to Surprise Valley 7.5 miles east-northeast of Cedarville (lat. 41°34'45" N, long. 120°02'30" W; sec. 21, T 43 N, R 17 E). Named on Cedarville (1962) 15' quadrangle.

Sand Flat [MODOC]: *area,* 6 miles northwest of Crank Mountain (lat. 41°26'40" N, long. 121°13'15" W). Named on Crank Mountain (1962) 15' quadrangle.

Sand Slough [LASSEN]: *stream,* flows 3.5 miles to Honey Lake Valley 4.5 miles southeast of Susanville (lat. 40°22'15" N, long. 120°35'30" W). Named on Janesville (1972) 7.5' quadrangle.

Sandy Beach [LASSEN]: *beach,* 4 miles north-northwest of Pelican Point along the north end of Eagle Lake (lat. 40°41'15" N, long. 120°46'15" W). Named on Antelope Mountain (1956) 15' quadrangle.

Saucer Lake [PLUMAS]: *lake,* 700 feet long, 15 miles southwest of the village of Almanor (lat. 40°03' N, long. 121°20'50" W; sec. 6, T 25 N, R 6 E). Named on Jonesville (1958) 15' quadrangle.

Saw Logs Creek [PLUMAS]: *stream,* flows nearly 2 miles to Mill Creek (3) 3.5 miles north of Bucks Lodge (lat. 39°55'35" N, long. 121°10'50" W; near N line sec. 22, T 24 N, R 7 E). Named on Bucks Lake (1979) 7.5' quadrangle.

Sawmill Flat [PLUMAS]: *area,* 8.5 mile south of Quincy (lat. 39° 49' N, long. 120°57'45" W; sec. 34, T 23 N, R 9 E). Named on Onion Valley (1950) 7.5' quadrangle.

Sawmill Tom Creek [PLUMAS]:

(1) *stream,* flows 3.5 miles to Grizzly Creek (1) 11 miles southwest of the village of Almanor (lat. 40°07' N, long. 121°19'30" W; near SE cor. sec. 8, T 26 N, R 6 E). Named on Jonesville (1958) 15' quadrangle.

(2) *stream,* flows 3 miles to Last Chance Creek (3) 8.5 miles south-southwest of Quincy (lat. 39°49'25" N, long. 120°59'45" W; sec. 29, T 23 N, R 9 E). Named on Onion Valley (1950) 7.5' quadrangle.

Sawpit: see **Sawpit Flat** [PLUMAS].

Sawpit Flat [PLUMAS]: *area,* 9.5 miles south-southeast of Quincy (lat. 39°48'20" N, long. 120°54' W; on S line sec. 31, T 23 N, R 10 E). Named on Onion Valley (1950) 7.5' quadrangle. Downieville (1897) 30' quadrangle has the name "Sawpit" at the place. Postal authorities established Sawpit post office in 1870 and discontinued it in 1873 (Frickstad, p. 125).

Scad Point: see **Spanish Peak** [PLUMAS].

Scammon Reservoir: see **Halls Meadows Reservoir**, under **Halls Meadows** [MODOC].

Scarface [MODOC]: *locality,* 9 miles northeast of White Horse along Great Northern Railroad (lat. 41°24'40" N, long. 121°17'35" W; near E line sec. 8, T 41 N, R 6 E). Named on White Horse (1962) 15' quadrangle. The name is for Scarface Charlie, an Indian of Captain Jack's band in the Modoc War of 1873 (Gudde, 1949, p. 322).

Schaffer Mountain [MODOC]: *ridge,* west-northwest-trending, 3 miles long, 6 miles south-southwest of Canby (lat. 41°21'40" N, long. 120°54'30" W). Named on Canby (1961) 15' quadrangle. Called Scheffer Mt. on Alturas 1° quadrangle, but United States Board on Geographic Names (1964a, p. 14) rejected the names "Scheffer Mountain" and "Shaeffer Mountain" for the ridge.

Schaffer Spring [MODOC]: *spring,* 6.5 miles southwest of Canby (lat. 41°21'20" N, long. 120°54'40" W; near NE cor. sec. 34, T 41 N, R 9 E); the spring is on the south side of Schaffer Mountain. Named on Canby (1961) 15' quadrangle.

Schamp Creek [MODOC]: *stream,* flows 2.5 miles to Poison Springs Canyon 5 miles east of Fort Bidwell (lat. 41°51'10" N, long. 120° 02'45" W; near SE cor. sec. 18, T 46 N, R 17 E). Named on Fort Bidwell (1962) 15' quadrangle.

Scheffer Mountain: see **Schaffer Mountain** [MODOC].

Schneider Creek [PLUMAS]: *stream,* flows 3 miles to Meadow Valley Creek 0.5 mile south of the village of Meadow Creek (lat. 39°55'35" N, long. 121°03'35" W; near W line sec. 23, T 24 N, R 8 E). Named on Meadow Valley (1980) 7.5' quadrangle. East Branch enters from the southeast 1.25 miles upstream from the mouth of the main creek; it is 1.25 miles long and is named on Meadow Valley (1980) 7.5' quadrangle.

Schneider Creek: see **Little Schneider Creek** [PLUMAS].

Schneider Ravine [PLUMAS]: *canyon,* drained by a stream that flows 2 miles to Rush Creek nearly 3 miles north-northeast of Twain (lat. 40°03'35" N, long. 121°03'30" W; sec. 2, T 25 N, R 8 E). Named on Twain (1980) 7.5' quadrangle.

Schoonamaker Lake [LASSEN]: *intermittent lake,* 600 feet long. 10.5 miles southeast of Little Valley (lat. 40°46'50" N, long. 121° 02'35" W; sec. 26, T 34 N, R 8 E). Named on Little Valley (1957) 15' quadrangle.

Schott Canyon [LASSEN]: *canyon,* 2.5 miles long, opens into Madeline Plains 3.25 miles south of Termo (lat. 40°49' N, long. 120°27'25" W; sec. 12, T 34 N, R 13 E). Named on Ravendale (1954) 15' quadrangle.

Schroder Lake [LASSEN]: *intermittent lake,* 3600 feet long, 7.25 miles south-southeast of the village of Little Valley (lat. 40°48' N, long. 121°07'05" W; on N line sec. 19, T 34 N, R 8 E). Named on Little Valley (1957) 15' quadrangle.

Schumacher Spring [PLUMAS]: *spring,* 7.5 miles east of Chester (lat. 40°17'35" N, long. 121°05'15" W; at N line sec. 16, T 28 N, R 8 E). Named on Westwood West (1980) 7.5' quadrangle.

Schwartz Meadow [PLUMAS]: *area,* 5 miles southwest of American House on Plumas-Butte County line (lat. 39°36'10" N, long. 121° 05'05" W; sec. 9, T 20 N, R 8 E). Named on Strawberry Valley (1948) 7.5' quadrangle.

Scorpion Point [MODOC]: *ridge,* north-trending, 5.5 miles south of Newell (lat. 41°48'20" N, long. 121°22' W). Named on Tulelake (1951) 15' quadrangle.

Scotch Creek [PLUMAS]: *stream,* flows 2.25 miles to Middle Fork Feather River 7.25 miles south of Bucks Lodge (lat. 39°46'10" N, long. 121°10'15"

W; near SW cor. sec. 11, T 22 N, R 7 E). Named on Haskins Valley (1980) 7.5' quadrangle. On Bucks Lake (1950) 15' quadrangle, the upper part of present Scotch Creek above the mouth of Pigtail Ravine is called Gravel Range Creek.

Scotch Creek: see **Hunters Ravine** [PLUMAS].

Scotts [LASSEN]: *locality,* 4 miles north-northeast of Beckwourth Pass along Western Pacific Railroad (lat. 39°50'45" N, long. 120° 05'30" W; near E line sec. 17, T 23 N, R 17 E). Named on Beckwourth Pass (1975) 7.5' quadrangle. Postal authorities established Scotts post office in 1912 and discontinued it in 1916; the name was for Charles A. Scott, first postmaster (Salley, p. 199). California Mining Bureau's (1917a) shows a place called Red Camp situated along Nevada-California-Oregon Railroad about 3 miles east of Scotts, and a place called Camero located along the railroad about 3 miles south of Scotts.

Sears Flat [LASSEN-MODOC]: *area,* 7 miles west-southwest of Likely [MODOC] at Lassen-Modoc County line (lat. 41°10'45" N, long. 120°37' W; sec. 29, 32, R 39 N, R 12 E). Named on Likely (1962) 15' quadrangle.

Sears Flat Spring [LASSEN]: *spring,* 7 miles west-southwest of Likely [MODOC] (lat. 41°11' N, long. 120°37'05" W; sec. 29, T 39 N, R 12 E); the spring is in Sears Flat. Named on Likely (1962) 15' quadrangle.

Second Butte [LASSEN]: *hill,* 6 miles north of the village of Little Valley (lat. 40°59'05" N, long. 121°11'25" W; sec. 5, T 36 N, R 7 E); the hill is between First Butte and Third Butte. Altitude 4664 feet. Named on Little Valley (1957) 15' quadrangle.

Second Creek [MODOC]: *stream,* flows 8 miles to Upper Lake 6 miles south-southeast of Fort Bidwell (lat. 41°46'45" N, long. 120° 06' W). Named on Cedarville (1962) and Fort Bidwell (1962) 15' quadrangles.

Second Water Trough Creek [PLUMAS]: *stream,* flows 3.5 miles to Wolf Creek 3.5 miles east of Canyondam (lat. 40°10'25" N, long. 121°00'30" W; sec. 30, T 27 N, R 9 E). Named on Canyondam (1979) 7.5' quadrangle.

Secret [LASSEN]: *locality,* 7.5 miles northwest of Karlo along Southern Pacific Railroad (lat. 40°37'15" N, long. 120°25'25" W; sec. 20, T 32 N, R 14 E). Named on Karlo (1954) 15' quadrangle. California Division of Highways' (1934) map shows a place called Secret located about 1 mile farther south along Nevada-California-Oregon Railroad (sec. 32, T 32 N, R 14 E).

Secret: see **Karlo** [LASSEN].

Secret Creek [LASSEN]: *stream,* flows 17 miles to the stream in Balls Canyon 3.5 miles south of Karlo (lat. 40°30' N, long. 120°19'25" W; near S line sec. 31, T 31 N, R 15 E); the stream goes through Secret Valley. Named on Karlo (1954) and Shinn Mountain (1954) 15' quadrangles.

Secret Diggins [PLUMAS]: *locality,* 1.25 miles south-southeast of La Porte (lat. 39°39'50" N, long. 120°58'40" W; sec. 21, T 21 N, R 9 E). Named on La Porte (1951) 7.5' quadrangle.

Secret Springs: see **Karlo** [LASSEN].

Secret Valley [LASSEN]: *valley,* at and near Karlo (lat. 40°32'30" N, long. 120°16'30" W). Named on Karlo (1954) 15' quadrangle. According to Garate (p. 12), McKissick stage station was in Secret Valley.

Section 15 Spring [PLUMAS]: *spring,* 14 miles southeast of Kettle Rock (lat. 40°01'15" N, long. 120°31'05" W; near W line sec. 15, T 25 N, R 13 E). Named on Babcock Peak (1972) 7.5' quadrangle.

Sed Valley: see **Said Valley** [LASSEN].

Selic Canyon [LASSEN]: *canyon,* drained by a stream that flows 5 miles to Clarks Valley 12 miles east of Madeline (lat. 41°04'20" N, long. 120°14'50" W; near E line sec. 15, T 37 N, R 15 E). Named on Boot Lake (1962) 7.5' quadrangle.

Sellicks Springs: see **Karlo** [LASSEN].

Seneca [PLUMAS]: *village,* 6.25 miles north of Twain along North Fork Feather River (lat. 40°06'40" N, long. 121°04'55" W; sec. 16, T 26 N, R 8 E). Named on Twain (1980) 7.5' quadrangle. Postal authorities established Seneca post office in 1902, discontinued it in 1918, reestablished it in 1923, moved it 0.5 mile north in 1941, and discontinued it in 1943 (Salley, p. 201). R.K. Dunn, a pioneer settler, named the village for the township there (Gudde, 1949, p. 325). Postal authorities established Dutch Hill post office near present Seneca (NW quarter of sec. 17, T 26 N, R 8 E) in 1874 and discontinued it in 1887 (Salley, p. 63). Twain (1980) 7.5' quadrangle shows Dutch Hill tunnel located 1.5 miles west-northwest of Seneca (NW quarter sec. 17, T 26 N, R 8 E). Gudde (1975, p. 245) listed a mining place called North Fork that was at the site of present Seneca.

Serpentine Canyon [PLUMAS]: *canyon,* 4 miles south of Caribou along East Branch of North Fork Feather River (lat. 40°01'20" N, long. 121°09'45" W). Named on Caribou (1979) 7.5' quadrangle.

Service Flat [MODOC]: *area,* 4.25 miles west of Crank Mountain (lat. 41°23' N, long. 121°13'40" W; on N line sec. 24, T 41 N, R 6 E); the place is in Service Gulch. Named on Crank Mountain (1962) 15' quadrangle.

Service Gulch [MODOC]: *canyon,* drained by a stream that flows 8 miles to a marsh 6.5 miles east-northeast of White Horse (lat. 41° 20'55" N, long. 121°17' W; sec. 33, T 41 N, R 6 E). Named on Crank Mountain (1962) and White Horse (1962) 15' quadrangles.

Service Spring [MODOC]: *spring,* 6 miles east-northeast of Lookout (lat. 41°15' N, long. 121°03'10" W; sec. 4, T 39 N, R 8 E). Named on Bieber (1961) 15' quadrangle.

Seven Lakes Hill: see **Seven Lakes Mountain** [LASSEN].

Seven Lakes Mountain [LASSEN]: *mountain,* mainly in the State of Nevada, but extends northwest into Lassen County 2.5 miles southeast of Constantia (lat. 39°55'15" N, long. 120°00' W). Named on Constantia (1977) 7.5' quadrangle. United States Board on Geographic Names (1960c, p. 20) rejected the name "Seven Lakes Hill" for the feature, and pointed out that the mountain has seven lakes on its crest.

Sevenmile Flat [MODOC]: *area,* 10.5 miles west-southwest of Jacks Butte (lat. 41°32'55" N, long. 120°59'45" W; sec. 24, T 43 N, R 8 E). Named on Jacks Butte (1962) 15' quadrangle.

Shafer's Station: see **Shaffer** [LASSEN].

Shaffer [LASSEN]: *locality,* 18 miles east of Susanville (lat. 40°22'30" N, long. 120°19'15" W); the place is south of Shaffer Peak (present Shaffer Mountain). Named on Honey Lake (1893) 1° quadrangle. Wheeler (1878, p. 58) referred to Shafer's Station.

Shaffer Mountain [LASSEN]: *mountain,* 5 miles north-northeast of Litchfield (lat. 40°26'50" N, long. 120°21'25" W). Altitude 6735 feet. Named on Litchfield (1954) 15' quadrangle. Called Shaffer Peak on Honey Lake (1893) 1° quadrangle.

Shaffer Mountain [MODOC]: *ridge,* generally west-northwest-trending, 2.5 miles long, 6 miles south-southwest of Canby (lat. 41°21'45" N, long. 120°54'30" W). Named on Canby (1961) 15' quadrangle.

Shaffer Peak: see **Shaffer Mountain** [LASSEN].

Shaffer Well [LASSEN]: *well,* 3 miles south-southwest of Karlo (lat. 40°31'10" N, long. 120°20'45" W; sec. 25, T 31 N, R 14 E). Named on Karlo (1954) 15' quadrangle.

Shake Cabin Ravine [PLUMAS]: *canyon,* drained by a stream that flows 1 mile to West Branch Nelson Creek 14 miles southeast of Quincy (lat. 39°47' N, long. 120°47'25" W; sec. 7, T 22 N, R 11 E). Named on Blue Nose Mountain (1951) 7.5' quadrangle.

Shake Canyon [MODOC]: *canyon,* drained by a stream that flows 2 miles to Pit River 4.5 miles southwest of Canby (lat. 41°23'55" N, long. 120°56'20" W; near N line sec. 16, T 41 N, R 9 E); the canyon heads near Shake Spring. Named on Canby (1961) 15' quadrangle. United States Board on Geographic Names (1964a, p. 14) rejected the name "Snake Canyon" for the feature.

Shake Spring [MODOC]: *spring,* 6 miles south-southwest of Canby (lat. 41°22'20" N, long. 120°55'45" W; near SE cor. sec. 21, T 41 N, R 9 E). Named on Canby (1961) 15' quadrangle.

Shanghai Creek [PLUMAS]: *stream,* flows nearly 4 miles to Butt Creek 9 miles west-southwest of the village of Almanor (lat. 40° 11'10" N, long. 121°19'45" W; sec. 20, T 27 N, R 6 E). Named on Jonesville (1958) 15' quadrangle.

Shartell Canyon [MODOC]: *canyon,* drained by a stream that flows 2 miles to Surprise Valley 14 miles north of Cedarville (lat. 41°44'10" N, long. 120°11'55" W; near W line sec. 30, T 45 N, R 16 E). Named on Cedarville (1962) 15' quadrangle.

Shays Hole Reservoir [LASSEN]: *water feature,* 11.5 miles northwest of Pelican Point (lat. 40°44'35" N, long. 120°54'15" W; near NE cor. sec. 12, T 33 N, R 9 E). Named onAntelope Mountain (1956) 15' quadrangle.

Sheepcamp Creek [PLUMAS]: *stream,* flows 5.25 miles to Wolf Creek 2.25 miles east of Canyondam (lat. 40°10'20" N, long. 121° 01'45" W; sec. 25, T 27 N, R 8 E). Named on Canyondam (1979) 7.5' quadrangle.

Sheep Camp Meadow [LASSEN]: *area,* 11.5 miles southwest of Pelican Point (lat. 40°31'30" N, long. 120°54'15" W). Named on Antelope Mountain (1956) 15' quadrangle.

Sheep Gulch [MODOC]: *canyon,* flows 2 miles to Canyon Creek 14 miles southwest of Alturas (lat. 41°20'10" N, long. 120°43'40" W; near E line sec. 5, T 40 N, R 11 E). Named on Alturas (1961) 15' quadrangle.

Sheephead Valley: see **Sheepshead Valley** [LASSEN].

Sheep Rock [MODOC]: *peak,* 15 miles south of the village of Davis Creek (lat. 41°31'25" N, long. 120°19'50" W; at E line sec. 34, T 43 N, R 14 E). Altitude 7164 feet. Named on Davis Creek (1962) 15' quadrangle.

Sheepshead [LASSEN]: *locality,* 4 miles east-northeast of Lava Peak (lat. 40°51'20" N, long. 120°49'20" W; near W line sec. 35, T 35 N, R 10 E); the place is east of Sheepshead Mountain at the north end of Sheepshead Valley. Named on Hayden Hill (1956) 15' quadrangle.

Sheepshead Mountain [LASSEN]: *ridge,* north-northwest-trending, 3 miles long, 3.25 miles east-northeast of Lava Peak (lat. 40°50'45" N, long. 120°50' W; on S line sec. 34, T 35 N, R 10 E); the ridge is west of Sheepshead Valley. Named on Hayden Hill (1956) 15' quadrangle.

Sheepshead Valley [LASSEN]: *valley,* 4.25 miles west of Lava Peak (lat. 40°50'30" N, long. 120°48'45" W); the valley is east of Sheepshead Mountain. Named on Hayden Hill (1956) 15' quadrangle. Called Sheephead Valley on Honey Lake (1893) 1° quadrangle.

Sheep Springs: see **Karlo** [LASSEN].

Sheep Valley [LASSEN]: *canyon,* 1.5 miles long, 5.25 miles north-northwest of Lava Peak (lat. 40°53'45" N, long. 120°56'15" W; on W line sec. 14, T 35 N, R 9 E). Named on Hayden Hill (1956) 15' quadrangle.

Sherer Spring [MODOC]: *spring,* nearly 4 miles north-northeast of Crank Mountain (lat. 41°25'40" N, long. 121°06'05" W; near NE cor. sec. 1, T 41 N, R 7 E). Named on Crank Mountain (1962) 15' quadrangle.

Sherlock Spring [MODOC]: *spring,* 9 miles south-southwest of Alturas (lat. 41°22' N, long. 120°36'05" W; at E line sec. 29, T 41 N, R 12 E). Named on Alturas (1961) 15' quadrangle.

Sherman Bar [PLUMAS]: *locality,* 2.25 miles north-northeast of Dogwood Peak along Middle Fork Feather River (lat. 39°48'50" N, long. 121°02'10" W; sec. 36, T 23 N, R 8 E). Named on Dogwood Peak (1979) 7.5' quadrangle.

Sherman Creek [PLUMAS]:

(1) *stream,* flows 1.5 miles to Middle Fork Feather River 2.25 miles north-northeast of Dogwood Peak (lat. 39°48'50" N, long. 121°02'10" W; sec. 36, T 23 N, R 8 E). Named on Dogwood Peak (1979) 7.5' quadrangle.

(2) *stream,* flows 0.5 mile to Hopkins Creek 14 miles south-southeast of Quincy (lat. 39°45'20" N, long. 120°49'55" W). Named on Blue Nose Mountain (1951) 7.5' quadrangle.

Sherwin Ravine [PLUMAS]: *canyon,* drained by a stream that flows 1.25 miles to Claremont Creek 5.25 miles south of Quincy (lat. 39° 51'40" N, long. 120°57' W; near NW cor. sec. 14, T 23 N, R 9 E). Named on Onion Valley (1950) and Quincy (1950) 7.5' quadrangles.

Shields Creek [MODOC]: *stream,* formed by the confluence of North Fork and South Fork, flows 6.25 mile to Parker Creek 8.5 miles east of Alturas (lat. 41°28'15" N, long. 120°23'35" W). Named on Dorris Reservoir (1963) and Shields Creek (1963) 7.5' quadrangles. North Fork is 3.25 miles long and South Fork is 1.5 miles long; both forks are named on Shields Creek (1963) 7.5' quadrangle.

Shingle Canyon [MODOC]: *canyon,* drained by a stream that flows 1 mile to Cedar Creek 3.25 miles west of Cedarville (lat. 41°32'05" N, long. 120°13'50" W). Named on Cedarville (1962) 15' quadrangle.

Shingle Mill Spring [LASSEN]: *spring,* 10.5 miles southeast of Adin [MODOC] (lat. 41°04'50" N, long. 120°48'50" W; near NW cor. sec. 3, T 37 N, R 10 E). Named on Adin (1962) 15' quadrangle.

Shinn: see **Al Shinn Canyon** [LASSEN].

Shinn Mountain [LASSEN]: *ridge,* generally northeast-trending, 6 miles long, 6 miles south of Observation Peak (lat. 40°41'30" N, long. 120°12'30" W). Named on Shinn Mountain (1954) 15' quadrangle.

Shinn Peaks [LASSEN]: *peaks,* 6 miles south-southwest of Observation Peak (lat. 40°41'30" N, long. 120°12'45" W; near SW cor. sec. 30, T 33 N, R 16 E); the peaks are on Shinn Mountain. Altitude of highest 7562 feet. Named on Shinn Mountain (1954) 15' quadrangle. Honey Lake (1893) 1° quadrangle shows Shinns Peak.

Shoals Creek [LASSEN]: *stream,* flows 4.25 miles to lowlands near Horse Lake 11 miles east of Pelican Point (lat. 40°39' N, long. 120° 32' W; sec. 8, T 32 N, R 13 E). Named on Fredonyer Peak (1954) 15' quadrangle.

Shoestring Draw [LASSEN]: *canyon,* 1.25 miles long, 7 miles east of Cal Mountain (lat. 40°41' N, long. 121°00'45" W; sec. 30, 31, T 33 N, R 8 E). Named on Harvey Mountain (1956) 15' quadrangle.

Shoofly: see **Indian Falls** [PLUMAS] (2).

Shores Gap [PLUMAS]: *pass,* 17 miles south-southwest of the village of Almanor (lat. 40°00'05" N, long. 121°19' W; at S line sec. 21, T 25 N, R 6 E). Named on Jonesville (1958) 15' quadrangle.

Shotoverin Lake [LASSEN]: *lake,* 1150 feet long, 14 miles north-northwest of Westwood (lat. 40°28'55" N, long. 121°08'40" W; near N line sec. 12, T 30 N, R 7 E). Named on Red Cinder (1979) 7.5' quadrangle.

Shugru Hill [LASSEN]: *peak,* 6 miles southeast of Susanville (lat. 40°21' N, long. 120°35'10" W; at SW cor. sec. 24, T 29 N, R 12 E). Altitude 4626 feet. Named on Janesville (1972) 7.5' quadrangle.

Shugru Reservoir [LASSEN]: *intermittent lake,* 1650 feet long, 7 miles southeast of Susanville (lat. 40°21'05" N, long. 120°33'10" W; on S line sec. 19, T 29 N, R 13 E. Named on Janesville (1972) 7.5' quadrangle.

Shumway [LASSEN]: *locality,* 14 miles northwest of Karlo (lat. 40° 41'50" N, long. 120°29'25" W; at NE cor. sec. 27, T 33 N, R 13 E). Named on Karlo (1954) 15' quadrangle. Postal authorities established Shumway post office in 1887 and discontinued it in 1913; the name was for Susie Shumway, first postmaster (Salley, p. 204).

Sibley Draw [MODOC]: *canyon,* 11 miles north-northwest of South Mountain on California-Oregon State line (lat. 41°59'35" N, long. 120°35'25" W; on N line sec. 21, T 48 N, R 12 E). Named on South Mountain (1962) 15' quadrangle.

Siegfried Canyon [PLUMAS]: *canyon,* drained by a stream that flows 3.25 miles to Squaw Valley 3 miles west of Squaw Valley Peak (lat. 40°01'40" N, long. 120°27'15" W; near N line sec. 18, T 25 N, R 14 E). Named on Squaw Valley Peak (1977) 7.5' quadrangle.

Sierra [PLUMAS]: *locality,* 4.25 miles north-northeast of Quincy along Western Pacific Railroad (lat. 39°59'30" N, long 120°55' W; at NE cor. sec. 36, T 25 N, R 9 E). Named on Quincy (1951) 15' quadrangle. Postal authorities established Sierra post office in 1925 and discontinued it in 1942; the post office served a vacation resort situated along Spanish Creek (1) (Salley, p. 204).

Sierra Lodge [PLUMAS]: *locality,* 2 miles west-northwest of Blairsden (lat. 39°47'30" N, long. 120°39' W; at S line sec. 5, T 22 N, R 12 E). Named on Blairsden (1956) 15' quadrangle. Called Feather River Lodge on Blairsden (1943) 15' quadrangle.

Sierra Valley [PLUMAS]: *valley,* at the head of Middle Fork Feather River between Beckwourth and Vinton in Plumas County, and extends south into Sierra County. Named on Antelope Valley (1981), Loyalton (1981), Portola (1972), and Reconnaissance Peak (1972) 7.5' quadrangles.

Sierra Valley Channels [PLUMAS]: *water feature*; according to United States Board on Geographic Names (1974b, p. 3), the name applies to a network of ditches and drains that head at the south end of Sierra Valley in Sierra County and flow north to converge at the head of Middle Fork Feather River 0.5 mile south of Beckwourth in Plumas County. Named on Antelope Valley (1981), Portola (1972), and Reconnaissance Peak (1972) 7.5' quadrangles.

Sifford Mountain: see **Red Mountain** [PLUMAS] (1).

Signal Butte [LASSEN]: *peak,* 7 miles north-northwest of Pelican Point (lat. 40°43'50" N, long. 120°47'15" W; at SE cor. sec. 12, T 33 N, R 10 E). Altitude 6364 feet. Named on Antelope Mountain (1956) 15' quadrangle.

Signal Butte [MODOC]: *peak,* 7 miles south of Alturas (lat. 41°23'15" N, long. 120°32'15" W; at S line sec. 13, T 41 N, R 12 E). Altitude 4647 feet. Named on Alturas (1961) 15' quadrangle.

Signal Butte: see **Lower Signal Butte** [LASSEN].

Signal Butte Reservoir [LASSEN]: *lake,* 200 feet long, 8.5 miles north-northwest of Pelican Point (lat. 40°44'55" N, long. 120°47'40" W; sec. 1, T 33 N, R 10 E); the lake is 1.25 miles north-northwest of Signal Butte. Named on Antelope Mountain (1956) 15' quadrangle.

Signal Reservoir [MODOC]: *lake,* 300 feet long, 9.5 miles southwest of Alturas (lat. 41°22'50" N, long. 120°38'50" W; sec. 24, T 41 N, R 11 E). Named on Alturas (1961) 15' quadrangle. United States Board on Geographic Names (1990, p. 10) rejected the name "Signal Spring" for the feature

Signal Rock [MODOC]: *peak,* 4.5 miles east of Crank Mountain (lat. 41°22'50" N, long. 121°03'30" W; near W line sec. 21, T 41 N, R 8 E). Named on Crank Mountain (1962) 15' quadrangle.

Signal Spring: see **Signal Reservoir** [MODOC].

Silva Flat Reservoir [LASSEN]: *lake,* 2 miles long, 9 miles north of Lava Peak (lat. 41°57'30" N, long. 120°54'30" W). Named on Hayden Hill (1956) 15' quadrangle. The lake is at Silva's Flat, which is named for a sheepman who pastured his animals at the place—the reservoir was built in the 1920's and named for the flat (Gudde, 1969, p. 310).

Silva Ravine [PLUMAS]: *canyon,* drained by a stream that flows less than 1 mile to Mosquito Creek 3.5 miles west of Caribou (lat. 40° 04'55" N, long. 121°13' W; sec. 29, T 26 N, R 7 E). Named on Caribou (1979) 7.5' quadrangle.

Silva's Flat: see **Silva Flat Reservoir** [LASSEN].

Silver Bowl Campground [LASSEN]: *locality,* 16 miles north-northwest of Westwood (lat. 40°29'55" N, long. 121°09'50" W; near S line sec. 35, T 31 N, R 7 E); the place is just north of Silver Lake. Named on Red Cinder (1979) 7.5' quadrangle.

Silver Creek [LASSEN]: *stream,* flows 6 miles to Bare Creek 22 miles east-northeast of Madeline (lat. 41°08'50" N, long. 120°04'05" W; sec. 20, T 38 N, R 17 E). Named on Emerson Peak (1962) and Snake Lake (1967) 7.5' quadrangles.

Silver Creek [PLUMAS]:

(1) *stream,* flows 5 miles to Spanish Creek (1) 1 mile northwest of village of Meadow Valley (lat. 39°56'35" N, long. 121°04'10" W; sec. 15, T 24 N, R 8 E); the stream heads at Silver Lake (1). Named on Bucks Lake (1979) and Meadow Valley (1980) 7.5' quadrangles.

(2) *stream,* flows 1 mile to Nelson Creek 10.5 miles southeast of Quincy (lat. 39°49'05" N, long. 120°49'30" W). Named on Blue Nose Mountain (1951) 7.5' quadrangle.

(3) *locality,* 1.25 miles north-northwest of the village of Meadow Valley (lat. 39°56'40" N, long. 121°04'20" W); the place is near the mouth of Silver Creek (1). Named on Bidwell Bar (1897) 30' quadrangle.

Silver Lake [LASSEN]: *lake,* 3500 feet long, 16 miles north-northwest of Westwood (lat. 40°29'40" N, long. 121°09'45" W). Named on Red Cinder (1979) 7.5' quadrangle.

Silver Lake [PLUMAS]:

(1) *lake,* 4200 feet long, nearly 6 miles north-northeast of Bucks Lodge (lat. 39°57'20" N, long. 121°08'20" W; mainly in sec. 12, T 24 N, R 7 E). Named on Bucks Lake (1979) 7.5' quadrangle.

(2) *lake,* 850 feet long, 6.5 miles southwest of Clio (lat. 39°41'25" N, long. 120°40'45" W; near SW cor. sec. 7, T 21 N, R 12 E). Named on Gold Lake (1981) 7.5' quadrangle. The feature is one of the group called Bear Lakes on Downieville (1897) 30' quadrangle.

Silver Lake: see **Lost Lake** [LASSEN].

Simpson Canyon [MODOC]: *canyon,* drained by a stream that flows 1.5 mile to Surprise Valley nearly 6 miles north-northwest of Cedarville (lat. 41°36'30" N, long. 120°12'30" W; sec. 12, T 43 N, R 15 E). Named on Cedarville (1962) 15' quadrangle.

Six-Shooter Tank [MODOC]: *intermittent lake,* nearly 1 mile long, 6.5 miles west-southwest of Jacks Butte (lat. 41°32'40" N, long. 120°54'45" W; on N line sec. 27, T 43 N, R 9 E). Named on Jacks Butte (1962) 15' quadrangle.

Skedaddle Creek [LASSEN]: *stream,* flows about 18 miles, partly in the State of Nevada, to Honey Lake Valley 12.5 miles east-southeast of Wendel (lat. 40°16'15" N, long. 120°01'30" W; sec. 23, T 28 N, R 17 E); the stream heads in Skedaddle Mountains. Named on Doyle (1954) and Wendel (1954) 15' quadrangles. The name "Skedaddle" originated when surveyors marking California-Nevada State line met some Indians, and both parties "skedaddled" to avoid conflict (Uzes, p. 79-80).

Skedaddle Mountains [LASSEN]: *ridge,* east-southeast-trending, 13 miles long, center 6 miles east-northeast of Wendel (lat. 40°22'30" N, long. 120°17' W). Named on Wendel (1954) 15' quadrangle.

Skedaddle Spring [LASSEN]: *spring,* 10.5 miles east-northeast of Wendel (lat. 40°24'20" N, long. 120°02'55" W; sec. 3, T 29 N, R 17 E); the spring is along Skedaddle Creek. Named on Wendel (1954) 15' quadrangle.

Skeleton Flat [LASSEN]: *valley,* 8 miles north-northeast of Termo (lat. 40°58' N, long. 120°23'35" W; sec. 21, T 36 N, R 14 E). Named on Ravendale (1954) 15' quadrangle.

Skinner Flat [PLUMAS]: *area,* 1 mile west-southwest of Canyondam (lat. 40°09'50" N, long. 121°05'15" W; near S line sec. 28, T 27 N, R 8 E). Named on Canyondam (1979) 7.5' quadrangle.

Skunk Cabbage Creek [LASSEN]: *stream,* flows 2.25 miles to Lost Lake 19 miles east-northeast of Madeline (lat. 41°09'15" N, long. 120°08'25" W; near S line sec. 15, T 38 N, R 16 E). Named on Emerson Peak (1962) 7.5' quadrangle.

Slate Creek [LASSEN]: *stream,* flows 10.5 miles to Grasshopper Valley 7.25 miles east of Lava Peak (lat. 40°51' N, long. 120°45'20" W; sec. 32, T 35 N, R 11 E). Named on Hayden Hill (1956) 15' quadrangle.

Slate Creek [PLUMAS]:

(1) *stream,* flows 1.5 miles to Rock Creek (2) 1.5 miles west-southwest of the village of Almanor (lat. 40°07'40" N, long. 121°21'15" W; sec. 7, T 26 N, R 6 E). Named on Jonesville (1958) 15' quadrangle.

(2) *stream,* flows 3.25 miles to Spanish Creek (1) 2.5 miles east-northeast of the village of Meadow Valley (lat. 39°56'35" N, long. 121°01' W; sec. 18, T 24 N, R 9 E). Named on Meadow Valley (1980) and Quincy (1950) 7.5' quadrangles.

(3) *stream,* heads in Sierra County and flows 11.5 miles along Plumas-Sierra County line, and in Plumas County and Yuba County, to finally enter Yuba County 3.25 miles southwest of American House (lat. 39°36'40" N, long. 121°03'15" W; sec. 11, T 20 N, R 8 E). Named on American House (1948), La Porte (1951), and Strawberry Valley (1948) 7.5' quadrangles.

Slate Creek: see **Fowler Creek** [PLUMAS]; **Stag Creek** [PLUMAS].

Slate Creek Springs [LASSEN]: *springs,* 4.25 miles east-southeast of Lava Peak (lat. 40°48'50" N, long. 120°48'40" W; near N line sec. 14, T 34 N, R 10 E); the springs are along Slate Creek. Named on Hayden Hill (1956) 15' quadrangle.

Slate Mountain [LASSEN]: *ridge,* south-trending, 2.5 miles long, 2.25 miles east-southeast of Lava Peak (lat. 40°49'10" N, long. 120°51'15" W). Named on Hayden Hill (1956) 15' quadrangle.

Slate Spring [LASSEN]: *spring,* 8 miles east-southeast of Adin [MODOC] (lat. 41°09'45" N, long. 120°47'45" W; sec. 2, T 38 N, R 10 E). Named on Adin (1962) 15' quadrangle.

Slate Spring Ridge [LASSEN]: *ridge,* south-southeast-trending, 3 miles long, 8.5 miles east-southeast of Adin [MODOC] (lat. 41°09'30" N, long. 120°46'50" W); the ridge is east of Slate Spring. Named on Adin (1962) 15' quadrangle.

Slide Creek [MODOC]: *stream,* flows 2.25 miles to Mill Creek (1) 7.25 miles west-southwest of Eagleville (lat. 41°17'40" N, long. 120°15' W). Named on Eagle Peak (1963) 7.5' quadrangle.

Slide Ravine [PLUMAS]: *canyon,* drained by a stream that flows 1.25 miles to Bucks Creek 4.5 miles northwest of Bucks Lodge (lat. 39°55' N, long. 121°14'35" W; near S line sec. 19, T 24 N, R 7 E). Named on Bucks Lake (1979) 7.5' quadrangle.

Sloat [PLUMAS]: *village,* 8.5 miles northwest of Blairsden (lat. 39° 52' N, long. 120°43'30" W; at S line sec. 10, T 23 N, R 11 E). Named on Johnsville (1972) 7.5' quadrangle. Postal authorities established Sloat post office in 1914 (Frickstad, p. 125). Officials of Western Pacific Railroad named the place in 1910 to honor Commodore John Drake Sloat, who took possession of California for the United States in 1846 (Gudde, 1949, p. 334-335).

Sloss Creek [LASSEN]: *stream,* flows 4.5 miles to Bankhead Creek 11 miles southeast of Susanville (lat. 40°18'30" N, long. 120°30'25" W; sec. 3, T 28 N, R 13 E). Named on Janesville (1972) 7.5' quadrangle.

Slough Point [LASSEN]: *promontory,* 2 miles southwest of Pelican Point along the west side of Eagle Lake (lat. 40°36'45" N, long. 120°46'05" W). Named on Antelope Mountain (1956) 15' quadrangle.

Sly Creek [PLUMAS]: *stream,* flows 4 miles to Butte County 5 miles southwest of American House (lat. 39°36'15" N, long. 121°05'10" W; sec. 9, T 20 N, R 8 E). Named on American House (1948) and Strawberry Valley (1948) 7.5' quadrangles.

Small Butte [PLUMAS]: *peak,* 8 miles west-southwest of Mount Harkness (lat. 40°22'30" N, long. 121°26'15" W; near W line sec. 16, T 29 N, R 5 E). Altitude 6114 feet. Named on Mount Harkness (1956) 15' quadrangle.

Smalls Canyon [MODOC]: *canyon,* drained by a stream that flows nearly 2 miles to Cedar Creek 3.5 miles west-northwest of Cedarville (lat. 41°32'30" N, long. 120°14'30" W). Named on Cedarville (1962) and Davis Creek (1962) 15' quadrangles.

Smith: see **Doc Smith Flat** [PLUMAS].

Smith Bar: see **Smith Point** [PLUMAS].

Smith Cow Camp [LASSEN]: *locality,* 11 miles west-northwest of Pelican Point (lat. 40°42'30" N, long. 120°55'25" W; sec. 23, T 33 N, R 9 E). Named on Antelope Mountain (1956) 15' quadrangle.

Smith Creek [PLUMAS]:

(1) *stream,* flows 3.5 miles to East Branch Lights Creek nearly 7 miles north of Kettle Rock (lat. 40°14'20" N, long. 120°44'35" W; near S line sec. 33, T 28 N, R 11 E). Named on Diamond Mountain (1972) and Kettle Rock (1972) 7.5' quadrangles.

(2) *stream,* flows 4.5 miles to Middle Fork Feather River nearly 1 mile west of Blairsden (lat. 39°46'55" N, long. 120°37'55" W; sec. 9, T 22 N, R 12 E); the stream heads near Smith Lake (2). Named on Gold Lake (1981) and Johnsville (1972) 7.5' quadrangles.

Smith Flat [LASSEN]:

(1) *valley,* 7 miles east-northeast of Madeline along Cedar Creek (lat. 41°04'55" N, long. 120°20'35" W; sec. 34, 35, T 38 N, R 14 E). Named on Cold Spring Mountain (1962) 7.5' quadrangle.

(2) *area,* 14 miles south-southeast of Adin [MODOC] (lat. 41°01'15" N, long. 120°48'35" W; on S line sec. 22, T 37 N, R 10 E). Named on Adin (1962) 15' quadrangle.

Smith Lake [PLUMAS]:

(1) *lake,* 2100 feet long, 4.25 miles north-northeast of the village of Meadow Valley (lat. 39°59'10" N, long. 121°01' W; sec. 31, T 25 N, R 9 E). Named on Meadow Valley (1980) 7.5' quadrangle.

(2) *lake,* 1650 feet long, 5 miles west of Clio (lat. 39°43'55" N, long. 120°40'20" W; at N line sec. 31, T 22 N, R 12 E); the lake is near the head of Smith Creek (2). Named on Gold Lake (1981) 7.5' quadrangle.

Smith Peak [PLUMAS]: *peak,* 7.5 miles northeast of Blairsden (lat. 39°52'05" N, long. 120°31'45" W; near SW cor. sec. 9, T 23 N, R 13 E). Altitude 7693 feet. Named on Blairsden (1972) 7.5' quadrangle. Called Grizzly Pk. on Downieville (1897) 30' quadrangle, and called Smiths Pk. on California Mining Bureau's (1917b) map.

Smith Point [PLUMAS]: *area,* 5.5 miles south-southwest of Caribou along East Branch of North Fork Feather River (lat. 40°00'50" N, long. 121°12'30" W; near NW cor. sec. 21, T 25 N, R 7 E). Named on Caribou (1979) 7.5' quadrangle. Gudde (1975, p. 324) listed a mining place called Smith Bar that was located at or near present Smith Point. Gudde (1975, p. 215) also listed a mining place called Middle Bar that was located along East Fork of North Fork Feather River between Smith Bar and Frenchmans Bar (present French Bar).

Smith Reservoir [LASSEN]: *intermittent lake,* 300 feet long, 5 miles north of Madeline (lat. 41°07'30" N, long. 120°29'20" W; near W line sec. 16, T 38 N, R 13 E). Named on Madeline (1962) and Tule Mountain (1967) 7.5' quadrangles.

Smith Stage Station: see **Sage Hen Flat** [LASSEN] (1).

Smoke Creek [LASSEN]: *stream,* flows 14 miles to Smoke Creek Reservoir 14 miles southeast of Observation Peak (lat. 40°38'15" N, long. 120°00'20" W; sec. 13, T 32 N, R 17 E). Named on Observation Peak (1954) and Shinn Mountain (1954) 15' quadrangles.

Smoke Creek Reservoir [LASSEN]: *lake,* 4700 feet long, behind a dam on Smoke Creek 15 miles southeast of Observation Peak at California-Nevada State line (lat. 40°37'35" N, long. 119°59'50" W; near N line sec. 24, T 32 N, R 17 E). Named on Shinn Mountain (1954) 15' quadrangle.

Smolloron Spring [MODOC]: *spring,* 2.5 miles east-northeast of Crank Mountain (lat. 41°23'50" N, long. 121°06' W; at E line sec. 13, T 41 N, R 7 E). Named on Crank Mountain (1962) 15' quadrangle.

Snag Hill [LASSEN]: *ridge,* north-trending, 1.5 miles long, 10.5 miles northeast of the village of Little Valley (lat. 40°58'20" N, long. 121°00'40" W; near E line sec. 11, T 36 N, R 8 E). Named on Little Valley (1957) 15' quadrangle.

Snag Lake [LASSEN]: *lake,* 1.5 miles long, 13 miles south-southwest of Cal Mountain (lat. 40°30'50" N, long. 121°18'30" W; sec. 27, 28, 33, T 31 N, R 6 E). Named on Prospect Peak (1957) 15' quadrangle. United States Board on Geographic Names (1933, p. 702) rejected the name "Feather Lake" for the feature. The name "Snag Lake" is from the dead trees in the lake that were killed when a lava flow formed the lake and flooded the forest; the feature also had the names "Lake Enchantment," "Lake Lapilli," and "Anna Lake" (Schulz, p. 48-49).

Snake Canyon: see **Shake Canyon** [MODOC].

Snake Island [MODOC]: *hill,* 2 miles southeast of Newell in the drained bed of Tule Lake (lat. 41°52'10" N, long. 121°20'25" W; at E line sec. 36, T 47 N, R 5 E). Named on Tulelake (1951) 15' quadrangle.

Snake Lake [MODOC]: *intermittent lake,* nearly 1 mile long, 8 miles south-southeast of Eagleville (lat. 41°12'15" N, long. 120°04'30" W; on W line sec. 32, T 39 N, R 17 E). Named on Snake Lake (1962) 7.5' quadrangle.

Snake Lake [PLUMAS]: *lake,* behind a dam on Wapaunise Creek 3.5 miles northeast of the village of Meadow Valley (lat. 39°58'25" N, long. 121°00'55" W; sec. 6, T 24 N, R 9 E). Named on Meadow Valley (1980) 7.5' quadrangle.

Snake Lake: see **Widow Lake** [LASSEN].

Snake Lake Valley [PLUMAS]: *valley,* 4 miles northwest of Quincy (lat. 39°58'05" N, long. 121°00' W); water of Snake Lake now covers much of the valley. Named on Quincy (1951) 15' quadrangle.

Snell Spring [MODOC]: *spring,* 9 miles east of Adin (lat. 40°11'50" N, long. 120°46' W; near N line sec. 25, T 39 N, R 10 E). Named on Adin (1962) 15' quadrangle.

Snider Lake [LASSEN]: *intermittent lake,* 12 miles south of Adin (lat. 41°01'05" N, long. 120°15'25" W; sec. 27, T 37 N, R 9 E). Named on Adin (1962) 15' quadrangle.

Snider Waterhole: see **Snyder Waterhole** [LASSEN].

Snoring Spring [PLUMAS]: *spring,* 2 miles west of Diamond Mountain [LASSEN] (lat. 40°18'30" N, long. 129°43'50" W; at N line sec. 10, T 28 N, R 11 E). Named on Diamond Mountain (1972) 7.5' quadrangle.

Snow Lake [PLUMAS]: *lake,* 500 feet long, 5.25 miles north of Chilcoot (lat. 39°52'15" N, long. 120°07'15" W; sec. 6, T 23 N, R 17 E). Named on Beckwourth Pass (1975) 7.5' quadrangle.

Snowslide Canyon [MODOC]: *canyon,* 0.5 mile long, 8 miles south of Eagleville (lat. 41°12'30" N, long. 120°07'20" W; sec. 35, T 39 N, R 16 E). Named on Emerson Peak (1962) and Snake Lake (1962) 7.5' quadrangles.

Snowstorm: see **Termo** [LASSEN].

Snowstorm Creek [LASSEN]: *stream,* flows 21 miles to Secret Creek nearly 3 miles south of Karlo (lat. 40°30'45" N, long. 120° 18'25" W; at S line sec. 29, T 31 N, R 15 E). Named on Karlo (1954) 15' quadrangle.

Snowstorm Mountain [LASSEN]: *mountain,* 6.5 miles north-northwest of Karlo (lat. 40°38'25" N, long. 120°21'30" W). Altitude 6561 feet. Named on Karlo (1954) 15' quadrangle.

Snyder Waterhole [LASSEN]: *lake,* 900 feet long, 11 miles north of Lava Peak (lat. 40°59'30" N, long. 120°54'25" W; near NW cor. sec. 2, T 36 N, R 9 E). Named on Hayden Hill (1956) 15' quadrangle. United States Board on Geographic Names (1983d, p. 5) approved the form "Snider Waterhole" for the name.

Soapstone Creek [PLUMAS]: *stream,* flows 2.5 miles to Wildcat Creek 5 miles south of Storrie (lat. 39°50'45" N, long. 121°20' W; sec. 17, T 23 N, R 6 E); the stream heads near Soapstone Hill. Named on Soapstone Hill (1979) 7.5' quadrangle.

Soapstone Hill [PLUMAS]: *peak,* 6 miles south of Storrie (lat. 39° 50' N, long. 121°18' W; near W line sec. 22, T 23 N, R 6 E). Altitude 5495 feet. Named on Soapstone Hill (1979) 7.5' quadrangle.

Sockum Creek [PLUMAS]: *stream,* flows 3 miles to Greenhorn Creek 4.25 miles northwest of Spring Garden (lat. 39°55'55" N, long. 120°51'05" W; sec. 22, T 24 N, R 10 E). Named on Spring Garden (1950) 7.5' quadrangle.

Soda Bar: see **Paxton** [PLUMAS].

Soda Creek [PLUMAS]:

(1) *stream,* flows 7.5 miles to Yellow Creek 11.5 miles south-southwest of the village of Almanor (lat. 40°03'50" N, long. 121° 15'10" W; sec. 36, T 26 N, R 6 E). Named on Jonesville (1958) 15' quadrangle.

(2) *stream,* flows 5.5 miles to East Branch of North Fork Feather River 6 miles southwest of Crescent Mills (lat. 40°02'20" N, long. 120°59'55" W; near S line sec. 8, T 25 N, R 9 E). Named on Crescent Mills (1980) and Twain (1980) 7.5' quadrangles. East Branch enters from the northeast 0.25 mile upstream from the mouth of the main creek; it is 2 miles long and is named on Crescent Mills (1980) 7.5' quadrangle. West Branch enters from the west less than 1 mile upstream from the mouth of the main creek; it is 2.5 miles long and is named on Twain (1980) 7.5' quadrangle.

Soda Ravine [PLUMAS]: *canyon,* drained by a stream that flows 1 mile to Mosquito Creek 4 miles west-northwest of Caribou (lat. 40°06'20" N, long. 121°13'15" W; sec. 17, T 26 N, R 7 E); Soda Spring (3) is in the canyon. Named on Caribou (1979) 7.5' quadrangle.

Soda Ridge [PLUMAS]: *ridge,* northeast- to east-trending, 2 miles long, 12.5 miles southwest of the village of Almanor (lat. 40°04'30" N, long. 121°19' W); the ridge is south of Soda Creek (1). Named on Jonesville (1958) 15' quadrangle.

Soda Spring [PLUMAS]:

(1) *spring,* 14 miles southwest of Almanor (lat. 40°04'05" N, long. 121°20'35" W; at W line sec. 32, T 26 N, R 6 E); the spring is along Soda Creek (1). Named on Jonesville (1958) 15' quadrangle.

(2) *spring,* 6.5 miles south-southwest of the village of Almanor (lat. 40°08'30" N, long. 121°14'35" W; sec. 6, T 26 N, R 7 E). Named on Almanor (1979) 7.5' quadrangle

(3) *spring,* 4.5 miles west-northwest of Caribou (lat. 40°06'40" N, long. 121°13'40" W; near W line sec. 17, T 26 N, R 7 E); the spring is on the side of Soda Ravine. Named on Caribou (1979) 7.5' quadrangle.

Soldier Creek [MODOC]:

(1) *stream,* flows 2 miles to Surprise Valley at Fort Bidwell (lat. 41°51'40" N, long. 120°09'20" W; sec. 17, T 46 N, R 16 E). Named on Fort Bidwell (1962) 15' quadrangle. The name recalls a story about a drunken soldier who fell from his horse and froze to death (Barry, p. 5).

(2) *stream,* flows 8 miles to Upper Lake 8.5 miles north of Cedarville (lat. 41°39' N, long. 120°10'30" W; sec. 29, T 44 N, R 16 E). Named on Cedarville (1962) and Davis Creek (1962) 15' quadrangles.

Soldier Creek [PLUMAS]: *stream,* flows 7.5 miles to Butt Creek 5.5 miles west-southwest of the village of Almanor (lat. 40°11'55" N, long. 121°16'10" W; near E line sec. 14, T 27 N, R 6 E). Named on Jonesville (1958) 15' quadrangle. United States Board on Geographic Names (1990, p. 10) rejected the names "Soldier Meadows Creek" and "Soldiers Meadow Creek" for the feature.

Soldier Meadows [PLUMAS]: *valley,* 8 miles west-northwest of the village of Almanor (lat. 40°14'30" N, long. 121°19' W); the valley is along Soldier Creek. Named on Jonesville (1958) and Mount Harkness (1956) 15' quadrangles.

Soldier Meadows Creek: see **Soldier Creek** [PLUMAS].

Soldier's Bridge: see **Susanville** [LASSEN].

Soldiers Meadow Creek: see **Soldier Creek** [PLUMAS].

Sorass Lake: see **Dry Lake** [MODOC] (1).

Sorholus Tank [MODOC]: *water feature,* 4.5 miles north-northeast of Hackamore (lat. 41°36'55" N, long. 121°05' W). Named on Hackamore (1952) 15' quadrangle.

Soup Creek [MODOC]: *stream,* flows 5.25 miles to Mill Creek (1) 20 miles southeast of Alturas (lat. 41°15'25" N, long. 120°18'15" W; sec. 36, T 40 N, R 14 E); the stream heads at Soup Spring. Named on Soup Creek (1963) 7.5' quadrangle.

Soup Spring [MODOC]: *spring,* 18 miles southeast of Alturas (lat. 41°18'35" N, long. 120°16'35" W; at N line sec. 16, T 40 N, R 15 E). Named on Soup Creek (1963) 7.5' quadrangle.

South Arm Rice Creek [PLUMAS]: *stream,* flows nearly 5 miles to North Fork Feather River 9.5 miles southwest of Mount Harkness (lat. 40°21'20" N, long. 121°27' W; sec. 20, T 29 N, R 5 E). Named on Mount Harkness (1956) 15' quadrangle.

South Barber Creek [MODOC]: *stream,* flows nearly 2 miles to North Barber Creek 5.25 miles south of Eagle Creek (lat. 41°14'25" N, long. 120°06'15" W; at S line sec. 13, T 39 N, R 16 E). Named on Emerson Peak (1962) and Snake Lake (1962) 7.5' quadrangles.

South Caribou [LASSEN]: *peak,* 14 miles northwest of Westwood (lat. 40°27'50" N, long. 121°10'45" W; near E line sec. 15, T 30 N, R 7 E); the peak is 1 mile south-southeast of North Caribou. Altitude 7767 feet. Named on Red Cinder (1979) 7.5' quadrangle.

South Deep Creek [MODOC]: *stream,* flows 5.25 miles to Surprise Valley 1.25 miles south-southwest of Cedarville (lat. 41°30'10" N, long. 120°12' W; sec. 18, T 42 N, R 16 E). Named on Cedarville (1962) and Davis Creek (1962) 15' quadrangles, and on Warren Peak (1963) 7.5' quadrangle. United States Board on Geographic Names (1965c, p. 12) rejected the name "Deep Creek" for the stream.

South Divide Lake [LASSEN]: *lake,* 650 feet long, 17 miles northwest of Westwood (lat. 40°29'30" N, long. 121°12'30" W; sec. 4, T 30 N, R 7 E); the lake is 1700 feet southwest of North Divide Lake. Named on Red Cinder (1979) 7.5' quadrangle.

South Emerson Lake [MODOC]: *lake,* 300 feet long, 5.5 miles southwest of Eagleville (lat. 41°15'05" N, long. 120°10'40" W; near NE cor. sec. 17, T 39 N, R 16 E); the lake is 1 mile south of North Emerson Lake at the head of South Fork Emerson Creek. Named on Eagle Peak (1963) 7.5' quadrangle.

South Fork: see **Likely** [MODOC].

South Fork Mountain [LASSEN]: *peak,* 6 miles south-southwest of Likely [MODOC] (lat. 41°09'20" N, long. 120°33'45" W; sec. 2, T 38 N, R 12 E). Altitude 7376 feet. Named on Likely (1962) 15' quadrangle. Called South Fork Peak on Alturas 1° quadrangle. The name "South Fork Mountain" is from the proximity of the peak to South Fork Pit River (Gudde, 1949, p. 340). United States Board on Geographic Names (1965d, p. 10) approved the name "Likely Mountain" for the feature.

South Fork Peak: see **South Fork Mountain** [LASSEN].

South Fork Reservoir [LASSEN]: *lake,* 350 feet long, 9.5 miles east of Wendel (lat. 40°19'30" N, long 120°03'20" W; near SW cor. sec. 34, T 29 N, R 17 E). Named on Wendel (1954) 15' quadrangle.

South Knob [LASSEN]: *peak,* 16 miles west-northwest of Termo (lat. 40°57'10" N, long. 120°44'40" W; sec. 18, T 36 N, R 11 E). Altitude 6874 feet. Named on Grasshopper Valley (1954) 15' quadrangle.

South Mountain [MODOC]: *peak,* 25 miles north of Alturas (lat. 41° 50'25" N, long. 120°38' W; near S line sec. 7, T 46 N, R 12 E). Named on South Mountain (1962) 15' quadrangle.

South Mountain Reservoir [MODOC]: *intermittent lake,* 6000 feet long, 2.5 miles southwest of South Mountain (lat. 41°48'15" N, long. 120°38'45" W). Named on South Mountain (1962) 15' quadrangle.

South Mountain Springs [MODOC]: *springs,* 1 mile west of South Mountain (lat. 41°50'25" N, long. 120°39'15" W; near S line sec. 12, T 46 N, R 11 E). Named on South Mountain (1962) 15' quadrangle.

South Pit River: see **South Fork**, under **Pit River** [LASSEN-MODOC].

Spalding Tract: see **Spaulding Tract** [LASSEN].

Spanish Creek [PLUMAS]:

(1) *stream,* flows 28 miles to join Indian Creek (2) and form East Branch of North Fork Feather River 5.5 miles southwest of Crescent Mills (lat. 40°02'20" N, long. 120°58'55" W; near S line sec. 9, T 25 N, R 9 E). Named on Bucks Lake (1979), Crescent Mills (1980), Meadow Valley (1980), and Quincy (1950) 7.5' quadrangles.

(2) *locality,* 4 miles north-northeast of Quincy along Western Pacific Railroad (lat. 39°59'10" N, long. 120°54'15" W; sec. 31, T 25 N, R 10 E); the place is near Spanish Creek (1). Named on Quincy (1950) 7.5' quadrangle. Postal authorities established Spanish Creek post office in 1942, discontinued it in 1945, reestablished it in 1947, and discontinued it in 1955; the post office served a vacation resort situated along Spanish Creek (1) (Salley, p. 210).

Spanish Flat [PLUMAS]: *area,* less than 1 mile southeast of La Porte (lat. 39°40'30" N, long. 120°58'15" W; near SE cor. sec. 16, T 21 N, R 9 E); the area is at the head of Spanish Ravine. Named on La Porte (1951) 7.5' quadrangle.

Spanish Peak [PLUMAS]: *peak,* nearly 5 miles north-northeast of Bucks Lodge (lat. 39°56'05" N, long. 121°07'30" W; at N line sec. 19, T 24 N, R 8 E); the peak is 5 miles west-southwest of Spanish Ranch.. Altitude 7020 feet. Named on Bucks Lake (1979) and Meadow Valley (1980) 7.5' quadrangles. The name is from the proximity of the peaks to Spanish Ranch (Hoover, Rensch, and Rensch, p. 282). Gudde (1975, p. 231) listed a mining place called Mumfords Hill that was located about 3 miles southeast of Spanish Peak, and (p. 310) a mining place called Scad Point that was situated about one-third of a mile north of Mumfords Hill. Gudde (1975, p. 227) also listed a place called Mountain House that was located about 3.5 miles north of Spanish Peak.

Spanish Ranch [PLUMAS]: *locality,* 1.25 miles north-northeast of the village of Meadow Valley (lat. 39°57' N, long. 121°03' W; on N line sec. 14, T 24 N, R 8 E); the place is near Spanish Creek (1). Named on Meadow Valley (1980) 7.5' quadrangle. Postal authorities established Spanish Ranch post office in 1861 and discontinued it in 1913 (Frickstad, p. 126). The name came after two Mexicans set up a camp at the site in July 1850; the place soon became a distribution center for surrounding mining camps (Hoover, Rensch, and Rensch, p. 282). Postal authorities established Keep post office 14 miles west of Spanish Ranch in 1901 and discontinued it in 1902; the name was for the Keep brothers' trading post, where the post office was situated (Salley, p. 110).

Spanish Ravine [PLUMAS]: *canyon,* drained by a stream that flows less than 1 mile to Slate Creek (3) 1.5 miles southeast of La Porte (lat. 39°39'55" N, long. 120°57'45" W; sec. 22, T 21 N, R 9 E); the canyon heads at Spanish Flat. Named on La Porte (1951) 7.5' quadrangle.

Spanish Springs [LASSEN]: *springs,* 12 miles north of Karlo (lat. 40°43'25" N, long. 120°18'35" W; near W line sec. 17, T 33 N, R 15 E). Named on Karlo (1954) 15' quadrangle. Penning's stage station was situated at Spanish Springs about 1900 (Garate, p. 121).

Spanish Springs Peak [LASSEN]: *peak,* 3 miles southwest of Observation Peak (lat. 40°44'45" N, long. 120°14'25" W; near SE cor. sec. 2, T 33 N, R 15 E). Altitude 7626 feet. Named on Shinn Mountain (1954) 15' quadrangle.

Spaulding: see **Spaulding Tract** [LASSEN].

Spaulding Butte [MODOC]: *peak,* 1 mile southwest of Hackamore (lat. 41°32'40" N, long. 121°07'55" W; near N line sec. 26, T 43 N, R 7 E). Named on Hackamore (1952) 15' quadrangle.

Spaulding Reservoir [MODOC]: *intermittent lake,* 2000 feet long, 3 miles south of Hackamore (lat. 41°30'40" N, long. 121°07'35" W; sec. 2, T 42 N, R 7 E). Named on Hackamore (1952) 15' quadrangle.

Spaulding Tract [LASSEN]: *locality,* 2 miles northwest of Pelican Point near Eagle Lake (lat. 40°39'10" N, long. 120°46'15" W; sec. 7, T 32 N, R 11 E). Named on Antelope Mountain (1956) 15' quadrangle. United States Board on Geographic Names (1983b, p. 7) approved the name "Spalding Tract" for the place, and rejected the names "Spaulding" and "Spaulding Tract." The place was subdivided in 1924 and named for John S. Spalding, who first laid out a town at the site in 1914 (Purdy, 1988, p. 122).

Spencer Basin [LASSEN]: *relief feature,* 6 miles east of Wendel (lat. 40°20'35" N, long. 120°07'30" W; sec. 25, T 29 N, R 16 E); the feature is near the head of Spencer Creek. Named on Wendel (1954) 15' quadrangle.

Spencer Creek [LASSEN]: *stream,* flows 8.5 miles to Honey Lake Valley 10.5 miles east-southeast of Wendel (lat. 40°16'15" N, long. 120°03'50" W; sec. 21, T 28 N, R 17 E). Named on Wendel (1954) 15' quadrangle.

Splawn Mountain [MODOC]: *peak,* 6.25 miles south of Crank Mountain (lat. 41°17'40" N, long. 121°09'15" W; sec. 22, T 40 N, R 7 E). Altitude 4859 feet. Named on Crank Mountain (1962) 15' quadrangle.

Spooner Reservoir [LASSEN]: *intermittent lake,* 3800 feet long, 16 miles south-southwest of Likely (lat. 41°01' N, long. 120°37'30" W; sec. 29, 30, T 37 N, R 12 E). Named on Likely (1962) 15' quadrangle.

Spooner Trough Canyon [LASSEN]: *canyon,* 4.5 miles long, 14 miles west-northwest of Termo (lat. 40°58'30" N, long. 120°41'15" W). Named on Grasshopper Valley (1954) and Likely (1962) 15' quadrangles.

Spoonville: see **Edgemont** [LASSEN].

Spring Branch [MODOC]: *stream,* flows 1 mile before ending near Willow Creek (3) 5 miles southeast of Willow Ranch (lat. 41°51'50" N, long. 120°16'30" W; at N line sec. 17, T 46 N, R 15 E). Named on Willow Ranch (1962) 15' quadrangle.

Spring Branch: see **Taylor Creek** [LASSEN-MODOC].

Spring Creek [LASSEN]: *stream,* flows 0.5 mile to Clear Creek (1) 3 miles west-southwest of Westwood (lat. 40°17'35" N, long. 121° 03'05" W; near N line sec. 14, T 28 N, R 8 E). Named on Westwood West (1980) 7.5' quadrangle.

Spring Creek [PLUMAS]: *stream,* flows 5.25 miles to Frenchman Lake 7.25 miles north-northwest of Chilcoot (lat. 39°53'50" N, long. 120°10'30" W; at S line sec. 27, T 24 N, R 16 E). Named on Frenchman Lake (1979) 7.5' quadrangle.

Spring Creek Campground [PLUMAS]: *locality,* 7.25 miles north-northwest of Chilcoot along Frenchman Lake (lat. 39°53'45" N, long. 120°10'35" W; at N line sec. 34, T 24 N, R 16 E); the place is near the mouth of Spring Creek. Named on Frenchman Lake (1979) 7.5' quadrangle.

Spring Garden [PLUMAS]: *village,* 9 miles east-southeast of Quincy (lat. 39°53'40" N, long. 120°47'05" W; on S line sec. 31, T 24 N, R 11 E). Named on Spring Garden (1950) 7.5' quadrangle. Postal authorities established Spring Garden post office, named for Spring Garden ranch, in 1910 (Salley, p. 210). On Downieville (1897) 30' quadrangle, Spring Garden ranch is shown situated less than 1 mile north-northwest of present Spring Garden.

Spring Garden Creek: see **Greenhorn Creek** [PLUMAS].

Spring Gulch [LASSEN]: *canyon,* drained by a stream that flows 4.25 miles to Pit River 5.5 miles north of the village of Little Valley (lat. 40°59' N, long. 121°09'30" W; near W line sec. 3, T 36 N, R 7 E). Named on Little Valley (1957) 15' quadrangle.

Spring Hill [LASSEN]: *peak,* 11 miles north-northeast of Lava Peak (lat. 40°58'45" N, long. 120°49'55" W; near SW cor. sec. 4, T 36 N, R 10 E). Altitude 6452 feet. Named on Hayden Hill (1956) 15' quadrangle.

Spring Hill Spring [LASSEN]: *spring,* 10.5 miles north-northeast of Lava Peak (lat. 40°58'15" N, long. 120°48'45" W; near W line sec. 10, T 36 N, R 10 E). Named on Hayden Hill (1956) 15' quadrangle.

Spring Valley Lake [PLUMAS]: *lake,* 1500 feet long, 18 miles southwest of the village of Almanor (lat. 40°00'50" N, long. 121° 23'15" W; near NW cor. sec. 23, T 25 N, R 5 E). Named on Jonesville (1958) 15' quadrangle.

Spring Valley Mountain [PLUMAS]: *peak,* 15 miles southwest of Almanor (lat. 40°01'05" N, long. 121°22'45" W; near S line sec. 14, T 25 N, R 5 E); the peak is 0.5 mile northeast of Spring Valley Lake. Altitude 6862 feet. Named on Jonesville (1958) 15' quadrangle.

Squatty [MODOC]: *hill,* 9 miles north-northwest of Double Head Mountain (lat. 41°52'50" N, long. 121°13'10" W; near SW cor. sec. 30, T 47 N, R 7 E). Named on Clear Lake Reservoir (1951) 15' quadrangle. United States Board on Geographic Names (1989a, p. 4) approved the name "Squatty Butte" for the feature.

Squatty Butte: see **Squatty** [MODOC].

Squaw Canyon [PLUMAS]: *canyon,* drained by a stream that flows 4.5 miles to Last Chance Creek (2) 7.25 miles northwest of Squaw Valley Peak (lat. 40°06'40" N, long. 120°29'15" W; sec. 14, T 26 N, R 13 E). Named on Squaw Valley Peak (1977) 7.5' quadrangle.

Squaw Canyon Springs [PLUMAS]: *spring,* 5.5 miles northwest of Squaw Valley Peak (lat. 40°04'55" N, long. 120°28'50" W; sec. 26, T 26 N, R 13 E); the feature is in Squaw Canyon. Named on Squaw Valley Peak (1977) 7.5' quadrangle.

Squaw Creek: see **Last Chance Creek** [PLUMAS] (2); **Squaw Queen Creek** [PLUMAS].

Squaw Peak [MODOC]: *peak,* 8 miles south-southwest of Cedarville (lat. 41°25'10" N, long. 120°13'05" W; near E line sec. 3, T 41 N, R 15 E). Altitude 8646 feet. Named on Warren Peak (1963) 7.5' quadrangle.

Squaw Peak [PLUMAS]: *peak,* 2 miles west-northwest of Squaw Valley Peak (lat. 40°02'25" N, long. 120°26'05" W; sec. 8, T 25 N, R 14 E); the peak is 1.5 miles north of Squaw Valley. Named on Squaw Valley Peak (1977) 7.5' quadrangle.

Squaw Queen Creek [PLUMAS]: *stream,* flows 12.5 miles to Last Chance Creek (2) 10 miles southwest of Kettle Rock (lat. 40°03'25" N, long. 120°34'15" W; near E line sec. 1, T 25 N, R 12 E); the stream goes through Squaw Valley. Named on Babcock Peak (1972), Crocker Mountain (1972), and Squaw Valley Peak (1977) 7.5' quadrangles. Squaw Queen Creek and present Last Chance Creek (2) below its junction with Squaw Queen Creek are called Squaw Creek on Honey Lake (1893) 1° quadrangle.

Squaw Valley [LASSEN]: *valley,* 14 miles west-northwest of Pelican Point (lat. 40°42'25" N, long. 120°59'05" W; sec. 20, T 33 N, R 9 E). Named on Antelope Mountain (1956) 15' quadrangle.

Squaw Valley [PLUMAS]: *valley,* along Squaw Queen Creek above a point about 11 miles southeast of Kettle Rock (lat. 40°02'50" N, long. 120°33' W). Named on Babcock Peak (1972), Crocker Mountain (1972), and Squaw Valley Peak (1977) 7.5' quadrangles.

Squaw Valley Peak [PLUMAS]: *peak,* 10 miles south of Milford [LASSEN] (lat. 40°01'45" N, long. 120°24' W; on N line sec. 15, T 25 N, R 14 E); the peak is 1.5 miles northeast of Squaw Valley. Altitude 6849 feet. Named on Squaw Valley Peak (1977) 7.5' quadrangle.

Squaw Valley Peak Springs [PLUMAS]: *springs,* 0.5 mile north-northwest of Squaw Valley Peak (lat. 40°02'10" N, long. 120°24'20" W; near W line sec. 10, T 25 N, R 14 E). Named on Squaw Valley Peak (1977) 7.5' quadrangle.

Squaw Valley Spring [PLUMAS]: *spring,* 4.5 miles west-southwest of Squaw Valley Peak (lat. 40°00'45" N, long. 120°28'50" W; near NW cor. sec. 24, T 25 N, R 13 E). Named on Squaw Valley Peak (1977) 7.5' quadrangle.

Squirrel Creek [PLUMAS]:

(1) *stream,* flows 4.5 miles to Yellow Creek 13 miles south-southwest of the village of Almanor (lat. 40°02'35" N, long. 121°14'55" W; near NE cor. sec. 12, T 25 N, R 6 E). Named on Jonesville (1958) 15' quadrangle.

(2) *stream,* flows 8 miles to Greenhorn Creek 1.5 miles northwest of Spring Garden (lat. 39°54'35" N, long. 120°48'30" W; sec. 25, T 24 N, R 10 E). Named on Spring Garden (1950) and Taylorsville (1980) 7.5' quadrangles.

(3) *stream,* flows 3.5 miles to Jamison Creek 4.25 miles west-northwest of Blairsden (lat. 39°48'45" N, long. 120°40'55" W; near W line sec. 31, T 23 N, R 12 E). Named on Johnsville (1972) 7.5' quadrangle.

(4) *locality,* 8 miles west-northwest of Wash (present Clio) (lat. 39° 47'30" N, long. 120°43'30" W); the place is near Squirrel Creek (3). Named on Downieville (1897) 30' quadrangle.

Stacy [LASSEN]: *locality,* 15 miles north-northeast of Doyle (lat. 40° 13'45" N, long. 120°01'15" W; at S line sec. 35, T 28 N, R 17 E). Named on Doyle (1954) 15' quadrangle. Postal authorities established Stacy post office in 1912 and discontinued it in 1951 (Frickstad, p. 69). The name commemorates Mrs. Stacy Spoon (Gudde, 1949, p. 341).

Stafford Mountain [PLUMAS]: *peak,* 9.5 miles east-northeast of La Porte on Plumas-Sierra County line (lat. 39°44'30" N, long. 120° 49'30" W; sec. 26, T 22 N, R 10 E). Altitude 7019 feet. Named on Mount Fillmore (1951) 7.5' quadrangle.

Stag Creek [PLUMAS]: *stream,* flows 2.25 miles to Middle Fork Feather River 1.5 miles west-northwest of Dogwood Peak (lat. 39° 47'35" N, long. 121°04'40" W; near W line sec. 3, T 22 N, R 8 E). Named on Dogwood Peak (1979) 7.5' quadrangle. Called Slate Creek on Bucks Lake (1950) 15' quadrangle, but United States Board on Geographic Names (1979, p. 6) rejected this name for the feature.

Stag Point [PLUMAS]: *relief feature,* 1.5 miles west-northwest of Dogwood Peak along Middle Fork Feather River (lat. 39°47'35" N, long. 121°04'45" W; near W line sec. 3, T 22 N, R 8 E); the feature is at the mouth of Stag Creek. Named on Dogwood Peak (1979) 7.5' quadrangle.

Standish [LASSEN]: *village,* 2.25 miles southwest of Litchfield (lat. 40°21'55" N, long. 120°25'15" W; near NE cor. sec. 20, T 29 N, R 14 E). Named on Standish (1972) 7.5' quadrangle. Postal authorities established Datura post office, named for a common weed, in 1895 and moved it 0.75 mile west in 1899, when they changed the name to Standish (Salley, p. 55). Promoters laid out the community in 1897; H.R.T. Coffin settled there in 1899 and named the community for Miles Standish of *Mayflower* fame (Gudde, 1969, p. 319).

Stanford: see **Camp Stanford** [LASSEN].

Stanford Spring [LASSEN]: *spring,* 14 miles west-northwest of Pelican Point (lat. 40°43'35" N, long. 120°59'15" W; sec. 17, T 33 N, R 9 E). Named on Antelope Mountain (1956) 15' quadrangle.

Stanford Trough [LASSEN]: *water feature,* nearly 2 miles north of Lava Peak (lat. 40°51'20" N, long. 120°53'50" W; sec. 31, T 35 N, R 10 E). Named on Hayden Hill (1956) 15' quadrangle.

Star Butte [PLUMAS]: *peak,* 9 miles north-northeast of Chester (lat. 40°25'10" N, long. 121°08'40" W; sec. 36, T 30 N, R 7 E). Altitude 6696 feet. Named on Red Cinder (1979) 7.5' quadrangle.

Star Lake [PLUMAS]: *lake,* 1050 feet long, 8.5 miles north-northeast of Chester (lat. 40°25'05" N, long. 121°09'20" W; on E line sec. 35, T 30 N, R 7 E); the lake is 0.5 mile west-southwest of Star Butte. Named on Red Cinder (1979) 7.5' quadrangle.

Steamboat Canyon [MODOC]: *canyon,* 2.5 miles long, along Steamboat Creek above a point 7 miles south of Cedarville (lat. 41° 25'40" N, long. 120°09'20" W; near S line sec. 9, T 41 N, R 16 E). Named on Warren Peak (1963) 7.5' quadrangle.

Steamboat Creek [MODOC]: *stream,* flows 4.5 miles to end 7 miles south-southeast of Cedarville (lat. 41°26'10" N, long. 120°07'25" W; at E line sec. 10, T 41 N, R 16 E); the stream drains Steamboat Canyon. Named on Warren Peak (1963) 7.5' quadrangle.

Steamboat Springs: see **Terminal Geyser** [PLUMAS].

Steele's Meadow: see **Steele Swamp** [MODOC].

Steele Swamp [MODOC]: *area,* 7 miles northwest of Blue Mountain (lat. 41°53'15" N, long. 120°58'15" W). Named on Steele Swamp (1962) 15' quadrangle, which shows some marsh in the area. Called Steele's Meadow on Alturas 1° quadrangle. Postal authorities established Steele Swamp post office 14.5 miles east of Clear Lake post office in 1888, changed the name to Steeleswamp in 1894, discontinued it in 1912, reestablished it in 1916, and discontinued it in 1926 (Salley, p. 212). The name commemorates Mr. E. Steele, a pioneer sportsman (Hanna, p. 315).

Stephens Campground [LASSEN]: *locality,* 8 miles south of Cal Mountain (lat. 40°32'30" N, long. 121°09' W; at SE cor. sec. 14, T 31 N, R 7 E); the place is 1 mile north-northwest of Upper Stephens Meadow. Named on Harvey Mountain (1956) 15' quadrangle.

Stevens Meadow: see **Upper Stevens Meadow** [LASSEN].

Steward Ravine [PLUMAS]: *canyon,* drained by a stream that flows 1.25 miles to Fall River 5.25 miles north-northwest of American House (lat. 39°43'05" N, long. 121°04'40" W; near SW cor. sec. 34, T 22 N, R 8 E). Named on American House (1948) 7.5' quadrangle.

Stiles Canyon [LASSEN]: *canyon,* drained by a stream that flows 3.5 miles to Honey Lake Valley 3.5 miles east-southeast of Milford (lat. 40°08'55" N, long. 120°18'30" W; sec. 32, T 27 N, R 15 E). Named on Milford (1977) 7.5' quadrangle.

Stobie: see **Hackamore** [MODOC].

Stockdill Slough Reservoir: see **Dorris Reservoir** [MODOC].

Stocktons [LASSEN]: *locality,* 7 miles west of Susanville (lat. 40°24'30" N, long. 120°47'30" W). Named on Honey Lake (1893) 1° quadrangle.

Stonebreaker Crossing [LASSEN]: *locality,* 9 miles south-southwest of Adin [MODOC] (lat. 41°04'05" N, long. 120°58'30" W; near SE cor. sec. 6, T 37 N, R 9 E). Named on Adin (1962) 15' quadrangle.

Stonebreaker Hot Springs: see **Bassett Hot Springs** [LASSEN].

Stone Coal Creek [MODOC]: *stream,* flows nearly 4 miles to Pit River 6 miles east of Crank Mountain (lat. 41°22'10" N, long. 121° 01'45" W; sec. 27, T 41 N, R 8 E). Named on Canby (1961) and Crank Mountain (1962) 15' quadrangles. The name is from a deposit of impure coal found along a branch of the stream (Hill, p. 51).

Stone Coal Mountain [MODOC]: *ridge,* 7.5 miles east of Crank Mountain (lat. 41°23' N, long. 121°00'10" W; near NW cor. sec. 24, T 41 N, R 8 E); the ridge is 1.5 miles north of Stone Coal Creek. Named on Canby (1961) and Crank Mountain (1962) 15' quadrangles.

Stone Coal Valley [MODOC]: *valley,* 7.5 miles east-southeast of Crank Mountain (lat. 41°21'30" N, long. 121°00'30" W); the valley is along Stone Coal Creek. Named on Canby (1961) and Crank Mountain (1962) 15' quadrangles.

Stone Island [MODOC]: *hill,* 4.25 miles south of Newell in the drained bed of Tule Lake (lat. 41°49'30" N, long. 121°22' W; sec. 14, T 46 N, R 5 E). Named on Tulelake (1951) 15' quadrangle.

Stone Reservoir: see **Stowe Reservoir** [MODOC].

Stones Canyon [MODOC]: *canyon,* 4.5 miles long, opens into lowlands along South Fork Pit River 3 miles west-southwest of Likely (lat. 41°12'35" N, long. 120°33' W; near SE cor. sec. 14, T 39 N, R 12 E). Named on Likely (1962) 15' quadrangle. The name is for Joe N. Stone, a rancher and sheepman who came to the region in the early 1870's (Laird, p. 62).

Stony Creek [LASSEN]: *stream,* flows 8.5 miles to Deep Creek 15 miles south of Observation Peak (lat. 40°33'15" N, long. 120°13'20" W; near N line sec. 13, T 31 N, R 15 E). Named on Shinn Mountain (1954) 15' quadrangle.

Stony Creek [PLUMAS]: *stream,* flows 4.25 miles to Cottonwood Creek (2) 5.25 miles west-southwest of Milford [LASSEN] (lat. 40° 08'35" N, long. 120°27'40" W; sec. 1, T 26 N, R 13 E); the stream is east of Stony Ridge. Named on Stony Ridge (1978) 7.5' quadrangle.

Stony Creek: see **Little Stony Creek** [PLUMAS].

Stony Creek Spring [LASSEN]: *spring,* 13 miles south of Observation Peak (lat. 40°35'45" N, long. 120°08'30" W; near E line sec. 34, T 32 N, R 16 E); the spring is along Stony Creek. Named on Shinn Mountain (1954) 15' quadrangle.

Stony Ridge [PLUMAS]: *ridge,* north-trending, 2.5 miles long, 6 miles west of Milford [LASSEN] (lat. 40°10'30" N, long. 120°29'15" W); the ridge is west of Stony Creek (2). Named on Stony Ridge (1978) 7.5' quadrangle.

Storrie [PLUMAS]: *village,* 20 miles west of Quincy along North Fork Feather River (lat. 39°55'05" N, long. 121°19'20" W; on E line sec. 20, T 24 N, R 6 E). Named on Storrie (1979) 7.5' quadrangle. Postal authorities established Storrie post office in 1926; the name was for R.C. Storrie, first postmaster and builder of a dam and power plant at the place (Salley, p. 213).

Stough Reservoir: see **Stowe Reservoir** [MODOC].

Stovepipe Flat Reservoir: see **Stovepipe Flat Tank** [MODOC].

Stovepipe Flat Tank [MODOC]: *intermittent lake,* 2500 feet long, 6.25 miles east-northeast of Hackamore (lat. 41°34'50" N, long. 121°00'15" W; on E line sec. 11 T 43 N, R 8 E). Named on Hackamore (1952) 15' quadrangle. Called Stovepipe Flat Reservoir on Alturas (1954) 1°x 2° quadrangle.

Stover Camp [PLUMAS]: *locality,* 9.5 miles south-southwest of Mount Harkness (lat. 40°17'50" N, long. 121°20'30" W; sec. 8, T 28 N, R 6 E); the place is west of Stover Mountain. Named on Mount Harkness (1956) 15' quadrangle.

Stove Reservoir: see **Stowe Reservoir** [MODOC].

Stover Mountain [PLUMAS]: *ridge,* northwest-trending, 4.5 miles long, 9.5 miles south of Mount Harkness (lat. 40°17'45" N, long. 121°18'45" W). Named on Mount Harkness (1956) 15' quadrangle. Called Mt. Stover on Lassen Peak (1894) 1° quadrangle.

Stover Mountain: see **North Stover Mountain** [PLUMAS].

Stove Spring [LASSEN]: *spring,* 5.5 miles east-southeast of Observation Peak (lat. 40°44'05" N, long. 120°06'05" W; sec. 7, T 33 N, R 17 E). Named on Shinn Mountain (1954) 15' quadrangle.

Stowe Reservoir [MODOC]: *water feature,* 14 miles south-southeast of the village of Davis Creek (lat. 41°33'45" N, long. 120°15'15" W; sec. 27, T 43 N, R 15 E). Named on Davis Creek (1962) 15' quadrangle. Called Stough Reservoir on Alturas (1954) 1°x 2° quadrangle, and United States Board on Geographic Names (1965c, p. 12) approved this name for the feature—at the same time the Board rejected the names "Stone Reservoir," "Stove Reservoir," and "Stowe Reservoir" for it.

Stratton Spring [LASSEN]: *spring,* 9.5 miles northeast of Lava Peak (lat. 40°56'15" N, long. 120°47' W; sec. 23, T 36 N, R 10 E). Named on Hayden Hill (1956) 15' quadrangle.

Straw: see **Perez** [MODOC].

Straylor Lake [LASSEN]: *lake,* 3200 feet long, 7.5 miles southeast of the village of Little Valley (lat. 40°48'50" N, long. 121°04'55" W; on N line sec. 16, T 34 N, R 8 E). Named on Little Valley (1957) 15' quadrangle.

Streshley Reservoir [LASSEN]: *intermittent lake,* 1400 feet long, 11 miles southeast of Pelican Point (lat. 40°31'55" N, long. 120°35'30" W; sec. 23, T 31 N, R 12 E). Named on Fredonyer Peak (1954) 15' quadrangle.

Stronghold [MODOC]: *locality,* 3 miles northwest of Newell along Southern Pacific Railroad (lat. 41°54'15" N, long. 121°24'15" W; near E line sec. 21, T 47 N, R 5 E). Named on Tulelake (1951) 15' quadrangle. The name is from Captain Jack's Stronghold, held by Indians in 1872 and 1873 during the Modoc War (Gudde, 1949, p. 345).

Studley Spring [MODOC]: *spring,* 8 miles southeast of Crank Mountain (lat. 41°18'20" N, long. 121°01'55" W; near E line sec. 15, T 40 N, R 8 E). Named on Crank Mountain (1962) 15' quadrangle.

Stump Ranch [PLUMAS]: *marsh,* 6 miles southwest of Mount Harkness (lat. 40°21'40" N, long. 121°22'15" W; sec. 24, T 29 N, R 5 E). Named on Mount Harkness (1956) 15' quadrangle.

Stump Spring [MODOC]: *spring,* 7.5 miles east of Adin (lat. 40°11'45" N, long. 120°48'15" W; sec. 27, T 39 N, R 10 E). Named on Adin (1962) 15' quadrangle.

Sugar Hill [MODOC]: *peak,* 7 miles south-southeast of Willow Ranch (lat. 4148'15" N, long. 120°19'30" W; near N line sec. 26, T 46 N, R 14 E). Altitude 7267 feet. Named on Willow Ranch (1962) 15' quadrangle. According to Gudde (1949, p. 346), the name is from sugar scattered on the hillside when a wagon broke down there in the early 1870's.

Sugar Loaf [PLUMAS]: *peak,* 8 miles east-northeast of Portola (lat. 39°50'25" N, long. 120°19'45" W; near SW cor. sec. 17, T 23 N, R 15 E). Altitude 6396 feet. Named on Reconnaissance Peak (1972) 7.5' quadrangle. Called Sugarloaf Peak on Sierraville (1894) 30' quadrangle.

Sugarloaf [LASSEN]: *peak,* 12 miles north of Observation Peak (lat. 40°57'05" N, long. 120°10'20" W; near SE cor. sec. 29, T 36 N, R 16 E). Altitude 6267 feet. Named on Observation Peak (1954) 15' quadrangle.

Sugarloaf [PLUMAS]: *peak,* nearly 5 miles south-southeast of McKesick Peak (lat. 40°01'30" N, long. 120°13'10" W; on E line sec. 18, T 25 N, R 16 E). Altitude 6631 feet. Named on McKesick Peak (1978) 7.5' quadrangle.

Sugar Loaf Mountain [PLUMAS]: *peak,* 3 miles west-southwest of Storrie (lat. 39°53'45" N, long. 121°22'15" W). Altitude 3553 feet. Named on Storrie (1979) 7.5' quadrangle.

Sugarloaf Peak: see **Sugar Loaf** [PLUMAS].

Sugar Pine Basin [LASSEN]: *relief feature,* 7.5 miles west of Bieber at the head of Rock Canyon (lat. 41°08'40" N, long. 121°17' W; sec. 9, T 38 N, R 6 E). Named on Fall River Mills (1961) 15' quadrangle.

Sugar Pine Ridge [MODOC]: *ridge,* north-trending, 2 miles long, 6.5 miles north-northeast of White Horse (lat. 41°23'20" N, long. 121°19'55" W). Named on White Horse (1962) 15' quadrangle.

Sugar Pine Spring [LASSEN]: *spring,* 7.25 miles west-northwest of Bieber (lat. 41°08'50" N, long. 121°16'40" W; near E line sec. 9, T 38 N, R 6 E); the spring is near Sugar Pine Basin. Named on Fall River Mills (1961) 15' quadrangle.

Sulphur Creek [PLUMAS]: *stream,* heads in Sierra County and flows 4 miles in Plumas County to Middle Fork Feather River at Clio (lat. 39°44'25" N, long. 120°34'45" W; sec. 25, T 22 N, R 12 E). Named on Clio (1981) 7.5' quadrangle. Called Mohawk Creek on Downieville (1897) 30' quadrangle, but United States Board on Geographic Names (1960a, p. 17) rejected this name for the stream.

Sulphur Spring House [PLUMAS]: *locality,* 2 miles east-southeast of Wash (present Clio) (lat. 39°43'45" N, long. 120°33'10" W). Named on Downieville (1897) 30' quadrangle.

Summit [PLUMAS]: *locality,* 1 mile east-southeast of Chilcoot (lat. 39°47'35" N, long. 120°07'15" W; near N line sec. 6, T 22 N, R 17 E). Site named on Beckwourth Pass (1975) 7.5' quadrangle. Postal authorities established Summit post office at the summit of Beckwourth Pass in 1864 and discontinued it in 1897 (Salley, p. 215).

Summit Camp [LASSEN]: *locality,* 9 miles west of Pelican Point (lat. 40°37'15" N, long. 120°54'45" W; sec. 24, T 32 N, R 9 E). Named on Antelope Mountain (1956) 15' quadrangle. A logging camp called Camp 8 was at the place in the 1920's (Purdy, 1988, p. 122).

Summit Canyon [MODOC]:

(1) *canyon,* less than 1 mile long, 5 miles west-northwest of Lookout (lat. 41°14'25" N, long. 121°14' W; at NW cor. sec. 12, T 39 N, R 6 E). Named on Bieber (1961) 15' quadrangle.

(2) *canyon,* 1.5 miles long, along Thoms Creek above a point 13 miles south-southeast of the village of Davis Creek (lat. 41°33'45" N, long. 120°16'10" W; sec. 28, T 43 N, R 15 E). Named on Davis Creek (1962) 15' quadrangle.

Summit Lake [LASSEN]:

(1) *lake,* 3200 feet long, 5.25 miles south-southeast of Lava Peak (lat. 40°45'55" N, long. 120°50'20" W; sec. 34, T 34 N, R 10 E). Named on Hayden Hill (1956) 15' quadrangle.

(2) *intermittent lake,* 900 feet long, 6 miles southeast of Pelican Point (lat. 40°34'30" N, long. 120°39'35" W; on E line sec. 6, T 31 N, R 12 E). Named on Fredonyer Peak (1954) 15' quadrangle.

Summit Lake [PLUMAS]: *marsh,* 4 miles south of Mount Ingalls at the west end of Grizzly Valley (lat. 39°56' N, long. 120°37'45" W; sec. 21, T 24 N, R 12 E). Named on Mount Ingalls (1972) 7.5' quadrangle. Blairsden (1943) 15' quadrangle shows an intermittent lake at the place. United States Board on Geographic Names (1983a, p. 2) approved the name "Summit Marsh" for the feature.

Summit Lake: see **Little Summit Lake** [PLUMAS].

Summit Marsh: see **Summit Lake** [PLUMAS].

Summit Spring [LASSEN]: *spring,* 11 miles north-northwest of Lava Peak (lat. 40°58'30" N, long. 120°59'15" W; on W line sec. 7, T 36 N, R 9 E). Named on Hayden Hill (1956) 15' quadrangle.

Summit Troughs [LASSEN]: *spring,* 3.5 miles south-southwest of Observation Peak (lat. 40°43'40" N, long. 120°13' W; near E line sec. 13, T 33 N, R 15 E). Named on Shinn Mountain (1954) 15' quadrangle.

Sunflower Flat [LASSEN]: *area,* 2 miles east-northeast of the village of Little Valley (lat. 40°54'15" N, long. 121°08'45" W). Named on Little Valley (1957) 15' quadrangle.

Sunflower Flat [PLUMAS]:

(1) *area,* 7.5 miles south of Mount Harkness (lat. 40°19'35" N, long. 121°17'10" W; on W line sec. 35, T 29 N, R 6 E). Named on Mount Harkness (1956) 15' quadrangle.

(2) *area,* 15 miles southwest of the village of Almanor (lat. 40°04'05" N, long. 121°21'45" W; on W line sec. 31, T 26 N, R 6 E). Named on Jonesville (1958) 15' quadrangle.

Sunflower Knob [MODOC]: *peak,* 10 miles southwest of Eagleville (lat. 41°12'30" N, long. 120°14'10" W; on S line sec. 14, T 39 N, R 15 E). Altitude 7361 feet. Named on Emerson Peak (1962) 7.5' quadrangle.

Sunflower Spring [LASSEN]: *spring,* 9 miles east of Adin [MODOC] (lat. 41°10'45" N, long. 120°46'40" W; at W line sec. 36, T 39 N, R 10 E). Named on Adin (1962) 15' quadrangle.

Sunrise Peak [LASSEN]: *peak,* 10 miles southwest of Cal Mountain (lat. 40°33'20" N, long. 121°16'35" W; at S line sec. 11, T 31 N, R 6 E). Altitude 7139 feet. Named on Prospect Peak (1957) 15' quadrangle.

Sunset Creek: see **Bidwell Creek** [MODOC].

Superior Ravine [PLUMAS]: *canyon,* drained by a stream that flows nearly 2 miles to Lights Creek 4.25 miles east-southeast of Moonlight Peak (lat. 40°12'25" N, long. 120°46'10" W; at N line sec. 17, T 27 N, R 11 E). Named on Kettle Rock (1972) 7.5' quadrangle, and on Moonlight Peak (1980) 7.5' quadrangle, which shows Engel mine located 1900 feet south-southwest of the mouth of Superior Ravine along Lights Creek. Postal authorities established Engelmine post office in 1916 and discontinued it in 1930 (Frickstad, p. 124).

Surprise [MODOC]: *locality,* 11.5 miles south-southwest of the village of Davis Creek along Southern Pacific Railroad (lat. 41°34'30" N, long. 120°26'05" W; at S line sec. 11, T 43 N, R 13 E). Named on Davis Creek (1962) 15' quadrangle. United States Board on Geographic Names (1991, p. 6) approved the name "Surprise Station" for the place, and rejected the names "Surprise" and "Surprise Siding."

Surprise Creek: see **Moonlight Creek** [PLUMAS].

Surprise Siding: see **Surprise** [MODOC].

Surprise Station: see **Surprise** [MODOC].

Surprise Valley [LASSEN-MODOC]: *valley,* east of Warner Mountains near California-Nevada State line; mainly in Modoc County, but the southernmost end extends into Lassen County and into the State of Nevada. Named on Alturas (1954) 1°x 2° quadrangle. The coining of the name has been attributed both to a group of settlers who entered the valley in 1860 and to surveyors marking the eastern boundary of California at about the same time (Pease, p. 77).

Surprise Valley: see **Cedarville** [MODOC].

Surprise Valley Mineral Wells [MODOC]: *locality,* 5 miles east of Cedarville (lat. 41°32' N, long. 120°04'40" W; sec. 6, T 42 N, R 17 E); the place is in Surprise Valley. Named on Cedarville (1962) 15' quadrangle.

Surveyors Valley: see **Surveyors Valley Reservoir** [MODOC].

Surveyors Valley Reservoir [MODOC]: *intermittent lake*, 1.25 miles long, 8.5 miles northwest of Jacks Butte (lat. 41°40'45" N, long. 120°54'30" W; around SE cor. sec. 3, T 44 N, R 9 E). Named on Jacks Butte (1962) 15' quadrangle. Alturas (1954) 1°x 2° quadrangle shows Surveyors Valley at the place.

Susan River [LASSEN]: *stream*, flows 54 miles to marsh near Honey Lake less than 0.5 mile south of Litchfield (lat. 40°22'30" N, long. 120°23'15" W; sec. 15, T 29 N, R 14 E); the stream goes past Susanville. Named on Harvey Mountain (1956), Litchfield (1954), and Susanville (1954) 15' quadrangles, and on Pegleg Mountain (1980), Red Cinder (1979), Roop Mountain (1980), and Swain Mountain (1979) 7.5' quadrangles. Isaac Roop named the stream for his daughter (Gudde, 1949, p. 348).

Susan River Campground [LASSEN]: *locality*, 14 miles north-northwest of Westwood (lat. 40°29'35" N, long. 121°05'30" W; sec. 4, T 30 N, R 8 E); the place is along Susan River. Named on Chester (1956) 15' quadrangle.

Susanville [LASSEN]: *town*, in the south-central part of Lassen County (lat. 40°25' N, long. 120°39'15" W; in and near sec. 32, T 30 N, R 12 E); the town is along Susan River. Named on Susanville (1954) 15' quadrangle. Postal authorities established Susanville post office in 1860 (Frickstad, p. 69), and the town incorporated in 1900. Isaac Roop named the place for his daughter, Susan; the community was called Rooptown until 1857 (Gudde, 1949, p. 348). California Mining Bureau's (1917a) map shows a place called Fredonia located about 7.5 miles west-southwest of Susanville along Southern Pacific Railroad. Postal authorities established Soldier's Bridge post office 16 miles southeast of Susanville (SE quarter sec. 15, T 29 N, R 14 E) in 1864 and discontinued it in 1867; a company of soldiers built a bridge at the place (Salley, p. 207). They established Dayton post office 20 miles east of Susanville (NE quarter sec. 18, T 29 N, R 15 E) in 1873 and discontinued it in 1875; the name was from the postmaster's former home in the State of Nevada (Salley, p. 56). They established Clinton post office 8 miles east of Susanville in 1896 and discontinued it in 1915; B.H. Leavitt, a pioneer rancher, named the post office for his hometown in Maine (Salley, p. 46).

Susanville Peak [LASSEN]: *peak*, 3.5 miles north of Susanville (lat. 40°28'15" N, long. 120°39'15" W; sec. 8, T 30 N, R 12 E). Altitude 6576 feet. Named on Susanville (1954) 15' quadrangle.

Suty [MODOC]: *locality*, 2.5 miles west-southwest of Newell along Great Northern Railroad (lat. 41°52'20" N, long. 121°25' W; on E line sec. 32, T 47 N, R 5 E). Named on Tulelake (1951) 15' quadrangle.

Swain Meadow [PLUMAS]: *valley*, 12 miles northeast of Chester along Robbers Creek (lat. 40°26' N, long. 121°04'10" W; mainly in sec. 27, T 30 N, R 8 E); the feature is 2 miles east-northeast of Swain Mountain. Named on Swain Mountain (1979) 7.5' quadrangle.

Swain Mountain [PLUMAS]: *mountain*, 10 miles northwest of Chester (lat. 40°25'20" N, long. 121°06'25" W). Named on Swain Mountain (1979) 7.5' quadrangle.

Swains Hole [LASSEN]: *water feature*, 5.5 miles west of Cal Mountain (lat. 40°40'55" N, long. 121°16'05" W; near E line sec. 35, T 33 N, R 6 E). Named on Prospect Peak (1957) 15' quadrangle.

Swamp Creek [PLUMAS]: *stream*, flows 3.5 miles to North Fork Feather River 3.5 miles southwest of Storrie (lat. 39°52'45" N, long. 121°22'20" W; sec. 1, T 23 N, R 5 E). Named on Kimshew Point (1979) and Storrie (1979) 7.5' quadrangles.

Swanberger Reservoir [LASSEN]: *lake*, 0.5 mile long, 4.5 miles east-northeast of Lava Peak (lat. 40°51'35" N, long. 120°48'35" W; on S line sec. 26, T 35 N, R 10 E). Named on Hayden Hill (1956) 15' quadrangle.

Sweagert Flat [MODOC]: *area*, 9 miles east-northeast of Adin along Cottonwood Creek [LASSEN-MODOC] (lat. 41°14' N, long. 120°46'45" W). Named on Adin (1962) 15' quadrangle.

Swedrengen Creek: see **Franklin Creek** [MODOC].

Sworinger Reservoir [LASSEN-MODOC]: *lake*, 9 miles south of Eagleville [MODOC] on Lassen-Modoc County line (lat. 41°11'35" N, long. 120°05'55" W; mainly in sec. 1, T 38 N, R 16 E). Named on Snake Lake (1962) 7.5' quadrangle.

— T —

Table Mountain [PLUMAS]: *peak*, 1.5 miles southwest of Dogwood Peak (lat. 39°46'20" N, long. 121°04'35" W; near N line sec. 15, T 22 N, R 8 E). Altitude 6088 feet. Named on Dogwood Peak (1979) 7.5' quadrangle.

Table Rock [PLUMAS]: *peak*, 8 miles east-northeast of Portola (lat. 39°51'20" N, long. 120°19'55" W; near SW cor. sec. 8, T 23 N, R 15 E). Altitude 6103 feet. Named on Reconnaissance Peak (1972) 7.5' quadrangle.

Tamarack Flat [PLUMAS]: *area*, 6.5 miles north of American House (lat. 39°44'50" N, long. 121°02'45" W; near SE cor. sec. 23, T 22 N, R 8 E). Named on American House (1948) and Meadow Valley (1980) 7.5' quadrangles.

Tamarack Springs [LASSEN]: *springs*, 4 miles north-northwest of Westwood (lat. 40°21"50" N, long. 120°01' W; near N line sec. 19, T 29 N, R 9 E). Named on Westwood West (1980) 7.5' quadrangle.

Tanner Slough [LASSEN]: *water feature*, 1 mile south-southeast of Litchfield in Honey Lake Valley (lat. 40°22'25" N, long. 120°22'40" W). Named on Standish (1972) 7.5' quadrangle.

Tanners Rock [PLUMAS]: *peak*, 1.25 miles north-northwest of Kettle Rock (lat. 40°09'20" N, long. 120°44'10" W; near W line sec. 34, T 27 N, R 11 E). Altitude 7209 feet. Named on Kettle Rock (1972) 7.5' quadrangle.

Tar Flat: see **Wagontire Flat** [LASSEN].

Tartarus Lake: see **Boiling Springs Lake** [PLUMAS].

Taylor: see **Lower Taylor** [PLUMAS].

Taylor Creek [LASSEN-MODOC]: *stream*, heads in Modoc County and flows 20 miles, partly in Lassen County, to Egg Lake Slough 3.25 miles north of Bieber (lat. 41°10'10" N, long. 121°09'25" W; at S line sec. 34, T 39 N, R 7 E). Named on Bieber (1961), Crank Mountain (1962), and White Horse (1962) 15' quadrangles. Called Spring Branch on Williamson and Abbotts (1855) map.

Taylor Creek [PLUMAS]: *stream*, flows 7.25 miles to Greenhorn Creek nearly 4 miles east of Quincy (lat. 39°56'40" N, long. 120° 52'35" W; at W line sec. 16, T 24 N, R 10 E). Named on Spring Garden (1950) and Taylorsville (1980) 7.5' quadrangles.

Taylor Creek: see **Dry Taylor Creek** [PLUMAS].

Taylor Diggings [PLUMAS]: *locality*, 4 miles east of Taylorsville (lat. 40°05'05" N, long. 120°46' W; sec. 29, T 26 N, R 11 E). Named on Taylorsville (1980) 7.5' quadrangle.

Taylor Gulch [PLUMAS]: *canyon*, drained by a stream that flows 2 miles to Meadow Valley Creek 1.25 miles southwest of the village of Meadow Valley (lat. 39°55'15" N, long. 121°04'45" W; at S line sec. 22, T 24 N, R 8 E). Named on Meadow Valley (1980) 7.5' quadrangle.

Taylor Knob [LASSEN]: *hill*, 9.5 miles southwest of Bieber (lat. 41° 01'55" N, long. 121°16'20" W; at E line sec. 21, T 37 N, R 6 E). Altitude 3924 feet. Named on Fall River Mills (1961) 15' quadrangle.

Taylor Lake [PLUMAS]: *lake*, 2000 feet long, 1 mile north-northeast of Kettle Rock (lat. 40°09'15" N, long. 120°43'05" W; on W line sec. 35, T 27 N, R 11 E). Named on Kettle Rock (1972) 7.5' quadrangle.

Taylor Mountain [MODOC]: *ridge*, generally south-southwest-trending, 2 miles long, 3 miles southeast of White Horse (lat. 41° 17'05" N, long. 121°21' W); the ridge is north of upper reaches of Taylor Creek. Named on White Horse (1962) 15' quadrangle.

Taylor Reservoir [MODOC]: *lake*, 3600 feet long, 2.5 miles west-northwest of Lookout (lat. 41°13'45" N, long. 121°11'35" W; mainly in sec. 8, T 39 N, R 7 E). Named on Bieber (1961) 15' quadrangle. Called Whaley Reservoir on Alturas (1954) 1°x 2° quadrangle.

Taylor Rock [PLUMAS]: *peak*, 5.25 miles south-southeast of Taylorsville (lat. 40°00' N, long. 120°19' W; sec. 25, T 25 N, R 10 E). Altitude 7338 feet. Named on Spring Garden (1950) and Taylorsville (1980) 7.5' quadrangles.

Taylors Creek [PLUMAS]: *stream*, flows 1.25 miles to Indian Valley at Taylorsville (lat. 40°04'25" N, long. 120°50'15" W; near NE cor. sec. 34, T 26 N, R 10 E). Named on Taylorsville (1980) 7.5' quadrangles.

Taylor's Ranch: see **Taylorsville** [PLUMAS].

Taylorsville [PLUMAS]: *village*, 7.5 miles southeast of Greenville (lat. 40°04'30" N, long. 120°50'15" W; sec. 27, 34, T 26 N, R 10 E). Named on Taylorsville (1980) 7.5' quadrangle. Postal authorities established Taylor's Ranch post office in 1861 and changed the name to Taylorsville in 1864 (Frickstad, p. 126). Wheeler (1879, p. 145) used the name "Taylorville." Jobe T. Taylor settled at the place in 1852 (Hoover, Rensch, and Rensch, p. 285).

Teal Lake [LASSEN]: *lake*, 900 feet long, 12.5 miles south-southwest of Cal Mountain (lat. 40°30'45" N, long. 121°17'15" W; at S line sec. 27, T 31 N, R 6 E). Named on Prospect Peak (1957) 15' quadrangle.

Teft: see **Cromberg** [PLUMAS] (1).

Telephone Flat Reservoir [MODOC]: *intermittent lake*, 7500 feet long, 5 miles south-southwest of South Mountain (lat. 41°46'25" N, long. 120°40'15" W; in and near sec. 2, T 45 N, R 11 E). Named on South Mountain (1962) 15' quadrangle. Telephone Flat was named in 1917 when the Forest Service built a telephone line across the feature (Gudde, 1949, p. 356).

Tenmile Creek [MODOC]: *stream*, flows 3 miles to Twelvemile Creek 10.5 miles north-northeast of Fort Bidwell (lat. 41°59'40" N, long. 120°04'15" W; at NW cor. sec. 31, T 48 N, R 17 E). Named on Fort Bidwell (1962) 15' quadrangle.

Terminal Geyser [PLUMAS]: *spring*, 4 miles west of Mount Harkness (lat. 40°25'15" N, long. 121°22'35" W; sec. 36, T 30 N, R 5 E). Named on Mount Harkness (1956) 15' quadrangle. According to Schulz (p. 55), this is the feature that Brewer called Steamboat Springs in 1862. Waring (p. 143) used the name "The Geyser" for the spring.

Termo [LASSEN]: *locality*, 32 miles north-northeast of Susanville along Southern Pacific Railroad (lat. 40°51'55" N, long. 120°27'30" W). Named on Ravendale (1954) 15' quadrangle. Postal authorities established Termo post office in 1908, discontinued it in 1914, and reestablished it in 1915 (Salley, p. 220). The place was the terminus of Nevada-California-Oregon Railroad in 1900; it also had the names "Armstrong" and "Snowstorm" (Garate, p. 108, 119).

Termo Buttes [LASSEN]: *hills,* less than 2 miles west of Termo (lat. 40°51'45" N, long. 120°29'30" W; sec. 27, 34, T 35 N, R 13 E). Named on Ravendale (1954) 15' quadrangle.

The Beaver Ponds [PLUMAS]: *lakes,* two, largest 300 feet long, nearly 2 miles south of Diamond Mountain [LASSEN] (lat. 40°17'15" N, long. 120°41'35" W; sec. 13, T 28 N, R 11 E). Named on Diamond Mountain (1972) 7.5' quadrangle.

The Big Hill [PLUMAS]: *peak,* 5.25 miles west of Storrie (lat. 39° 54'45" N, long. 121°24'55" W; near N line sec. 28, T 24 N, R 5 E). Altitude 4879 feet. Named on Kimshew Point (1979) 7.5' quadrangle.

The Buttes [PLUMAS]: *hill,* 9 miles east of Portola in Sierra Valley (lat. 39°48'45" N, long. 120°18' W; mainly in sec. 28, T 23 N, R 15 E). Named on Reconnaissance Peak (1972) 7.5' quadrangle.

The Cliffs [MODOC]: *relief feature,* 12 miles south-southwest of Canby (lat. 41°16'35" N, long. 120°56' W; near E line sec. 28, T 40 N, R 9 E). Named on Canby (1961) 15' quadrangle.

The Crossing [LASSEN]: *locality,* 8.5 miles north-northwest of Litchfield along Willow Creek (lat. 40°29'15" N, long. 120°28'30" W; at E line sec. 2, T 30 N, R 13 E). Named on Litchfield (1954) 15' quadrangle.

The Frog Pond [MODOC]: *area,* a drained part of old Tule Lake 5 miles west of Newell on Modoc-Siskiyou County line (lat. 41°52'50" N, long. 121°27'30" W). Named on Tulelake (1951) 15' quadrangle.

The Geyser: see **Terminal Geyser** [PLUMAS].

The Hat [MODOC]: *relief feature,* 3.5 miles west-southwest of Alturas (lat. 41°28'30" N, long. 120°36'35" W; sec. 17, T 42 N, R 12 E). Named on Alturas (1961) 15' quadrangle.

The Hogback [PLUMAS]: *ridge,* generally north-northeast-trending, 1.5 miles long, 8 miles south-southeast of Quincy (lat. 39°49'40" N, long. 120°52'45" W; mainly in sec. 29, T 23 N, R 10 E). Named on Onion Valley (1950) 7.5' quadrangle.

The Hole [PLUMAS]: *relief feature,* 9.5 miles north-northeast of Chester (lat. 40°25'45" N, long. 121°07'50" W; sec. 30, T 30 N, R 8 E). Named on Red Cinder (1979) 7.5' quadrangle. On Chester (1956) 15' quadrangle, the name applies to a canyon situated south of the position of the present feature called The Hole. United States Board on Geographic Names (1977a, p. 6) classified The Hole as a swamp, and gave the names "Hole in Ground" and "The Hole in the Ground" as variants.

The Hole in the Ground: see **The Hole** [PLUMAS].

The Island [LASSEN]: *peninsula,* 7 miles east-northeast of Milford at the southeast end of Honey Lake (lat. 40°12' N, long. 120° 15' W). Named on Doyle (1954) and Milford (1950) 15' quadrangles.

The Island [PLUMAS]: *peak,* 2 miles west-northwest of Storrie (lat. 39°55'35" N, long. 121°21'25" W). Named on Storrie (1979) 7.5' quadrangle.

The Orchard: see **Orchard Spring** [LASSEN].

The Panhandle [MODOC]: *area,* part of the drained bed of Tule Lake 5.5 miles south-southwest of Newell (lat. 41°49' N, long. 121°24'30" W). Named on Tulelake (1951) 15' quadrangle.

The Peninsula [MODOC]: *ridge,* north-northeast-trending, 2 miles long, center 1.25 miles southwest of Newell at the edge of the drained Tule Lake (lat. 41°52'30" N, long. 121°23'15" W; mainly in sec. 27, 34, T 47 N, R 5 E). Named on Tulelake (1951) 15' quadrangle.

The Three Sisters [MODOC]: *peaks,* three, 4 miles southwest of Alturas (lat. 41°27'10" N, long. 120°36'10" W; near E line sec. 29, T 42 N, R 12 E). Named on Alturas (1961) 15' quadrangle.

The "U" [MODOC]: *peninsula,* 7 miles north-northeast of Double Head Mountain along Clear Lake Reservoir (lat. 41°51'30" N, long. 121°07' W). Named on Clear Lake Reservoir (1951) 15' quadrangle.

Third Butte [LASSEN]: *hill,* 8.5 miles north-northwest of the village of Little Valley (lat. 40°59'10" N, long. 121°13' W; at E line sec. 1, T 36 N, R 6 E); the hill is between Second Butte and Fourth Butte. Altitude 4681 feet. Named on Little Valley (1957) 15' quadrangle.

Third Water Creek [PLUMAS]: *stream,* flows 4.5 miles to join Morrow Creek and form Bear Creek (2) 5.25 miles north-northwest of Dogwood Peak (lat. 39°51'20" N, long. 121°05'30" W; sec. 16, T 23 N, R 8 E). Named on Dogwood Peak (1979) 7.5' quadrangle. Miller Fork enters less than 1 mile upstream from the mouth of the main creek; it is 2.25 miles long and is named on Dogwood Peak (1979) and Meadow Valley (1980) 7.5' quadrangles.

Thomas: see **Raker and Thomas Reservoir** [MODOC].

Thompson Creek [PLUMAS]:

(1) *stream,* flows 3.5 miles to Boulder Creek (1) 9 miles northeast of Kettle Rock (lat. 40°13'40" N, long. 120°35'50" W); the stream heads near Thompson Peak. Named on Antelope Lake (1972) 7.5' quadrangle. Called Clarks Creek on Kettle Rock (1950) 15' quadrangle, and United States Board on Geographic Names (1974b, p. 3) gave this name as a variant.

(2) *stream,* flows 7 miles to Greenhorn Creek 5.5 miles northwest of Spring Garden (lat. 39°56'30" N, long. 120°52'20" W; sec. 16, T 24 N, R 10 E). Named on Quincy (1950) and Spring Garden (1950) 7.5' quadrangles.

Thompson Creek: see **Clarks Creek** [PLUMAS].

Thompson Lake [PLUMAS]: *lake,* 650 feet long, 1.5 miles west of Bucks Lodge (lat. 39°52'40" N, long. 121°12' W; sec. 4, T 23 N, R 7 E). Named on Bucks Lake (1979) 7.5' quadrangle.

Thompson Peak [PLUMAS]: *peak,* 3 miles southwest of Janesville [LASSEN] (lat. 40°15'40" N, long. 120°33'25" W; near N line sec. 30, T 28 N, R 13 E). Altitude 7795 feet. Named on Janesville (1972) 7.5' quadrangle.

Thompson Reservoir [LASSEN]: *lake,* 450 feet long, 5.25 miles south-southwest of Bieber (lat. 41°02'50" N, long. 121°09'50" W; near E line sec. 16, T 37 N, R 7 E). Named on Bieber (1961) 15' quadrangle.

Thompson Valley [PLUMAS]:

(1) *valley,* 5.25 miles west-northwest of Spring Garden (lat. 39°55'35" N, long. 120°52'30" W; sec. 20, 21, T 24 N, R 10 E); the valley is along Thompson Creek (2). Named on Quincy (1950) and Spring Garden (1950) 7.5' quadrangles.

(2) *valley,* 12.5 miles north of Portola (lat. 39°59'20" N, long. 120° 28'05" W; mainly in sec. 25, T 25 N, R 13 E). Named on Crocker Mountain (1972) 7.5' quadrangle.

Thoms Creek [MODOC]: *stream,* flows 11 miles to North Fork Pit River 10 miles south-southwest of the village of Davis Creek (lat. 41°35'40" N, long. 120°25'20" W; sec. 1, T 43 N, R 13 E). Named on Davis Creek (1962) 15' quadrangle. Called Tom Creek on Alturas 1° quadrangle.

Thousand Spring Canyon [LASSEN]: *canyon,* drained by a stream that flows 2.5 miles to Honey Lake Valley 7.5 miles east-southeast of Wendel (lat. 40°17'35" N, long. 120°06'30" W; near W line sec. 7, T 28 N, R 17 E). Named on Wendel (1954) 15' quadrangle.

Three Corner Slough [MODOC]: *water feature,* diverges from Pit River less than 1 mile east of Lookout (lat. 41°12'30" N, long. 121° 08'10" W; sec. 23, T 39 N, R 7 E). Named on Bieber (1961) 15' quadrangle.

Three Lakes [PLUMAS]: *lakes,* three, largest 1800 feet long, 7 miles north-northwest of Bucks Lodge (lat. 39°58'10" N, long. 121° 13' W; mainly in sec. 5, T 24 N, R 7 E). Named on Bucks Lake (1979) 7.5' quadrangle.

Threemile Canyon [LASSEN]: *canyon,* 2.5 miles long, opens into Madeline Plains 7 miles north-northwest of Termo (lat. 40°57'30" N, long. 120°30' W; sec. 17, T 36 N, R 13 E). Named on Ravendale (1954) 15' quadrangle.

Threemile Reservoir [LASSEN]: *lake,* 500 feet long, 6 miles north of Termo (lat. 40°57' N, long. 120°27'45" W; near S line sec. 15, T 36 N, R 13 E); the lake is in Threemile Canyon. Named on Ravendale (1954) 15' quadrangle.

Threemile Rock [PLUMAS]: *peak,* 8 miles south-southeast of Mount Ingalls (lat. 39°53'20" N, long. 120°33'35" W; sec. 6, T 23 N, R 13 E); the peak is east of Threemile Valley. Altitude 6442 feet. Named on Grizzly Valley (1972) 7.5' quadrangle.

Threemile Valley [PLUMAS]: *canyon,* 3 miles long, along Freeman Creek above a point 7.25 miles south-southeast of Mount Ingalls (lat. 39°53'45" N, long. 120°34'25" W). Named on Blairsden (1972) and Grizzly Valley (1972) 7.5' quadrangles. Downieville (1897) 30' quadrangle has the form "Three Mile Valley" for the name.

Three Peaks [LASSEN]: *peaks,* three, 5 miles north of Termo (lat. 40°56'15" N, long. 120°27'30" W; sec. 22, T 36 N, R 13 E). Altitude of highest 7001 feet. Named on Ravendale (1954) 15' quadrangle.

Three Sisters: see **The Three Sisters** [MODOC].

Three Springs [LASSEN]:

(1) *spring,* 6 miles east of the village of Little Valley (lat. 40°54'25" N, long. 121°04'05" W; near SE cor. sec. 32, T 36 N, R 8 E). Named on Little Valley (1957) 15' quadrangle.

(2) *springs,* 17 miles south-southeast of Observation Peak (lat. 40° 31'50" N, long. 120°06'40" W; sec. 24, T 31 N, R 16 E). Named on Shinn Mountain (1954) 15' quadrangle.

Timbered Mountain [MODOC]: *ridge,* northeast-trending, 3 miles long, 20 miles north-northwest of Alturas (lat. 41°44' N, long. 120° 44' W). Named on Big Sage Reservoir (1962) 15' quadrangle.

Timbered Mountain Tank [MODOC]: *water feature,* 20 miles north-northwest of Alturas (lat. 41°44' N, long. 120°43'55" W; near SW cor. sec. 17, T 45 N, R 11 E); the feature is on Timbered Mountain. Named on Big Sage Reservoir (1962) 15' quadrangle

Timbered Ridge [MODOC]: *ridge,* northwest-trending, 4 miles long, 4.5 miles south-southwest of Blue Mountain (lat. 41°46'45" N, long. 120°53'15" W). Named on Steele Swamp (1962) 15' quadrangle.

Timbered Ridge: see **Bird Spring Ridge** [MODOC].

Timbered Ridge Reservoir [MODOC]: *water feature,* 2.25 miles south-southwest of Blue Mountain (lat. 41°48' N, long. 120°52'40" W; near E line sec. 25, T 46 N, R 9 E); the feature is 1.5 miles northeast of Timbered Ridge. Named on Steele Swamp (1962) 15' quadrangle.

Timber Mountain [MODOC]: *mountain,* 40 miles west-northwest of Alturas (lat. 41°07'45" N, long. 121°17'40" W; near NE cor. sec. 29, T 44 N, R 6 E). Altitude 5086 feet. Named on Timber Mountain (1952) 15' quadrangle.

Tin House Spring [LASSEN]: *spring,* 8 miles north-northeast of Wendel (lat. 40°23'45" N, long. 120°05'40" W; at NW cor. sec. 8, T 29 N, R 17 E). Named on Wendel (1954) 15' quadrangle.

Tionesta [MODOC]: *locality,* 2 miles northwest of Timber Mountain along Great Northern Railroad (lat. 41°38'45" N, long. 121°19'30" W; near N line sec. 19, T 44 N, R 6 E). Named on Timber Mountain (1952) 15' quadrangle. J.R. Shaw of Shaw Lumber Company named the place for Tionesta Forest in Pennsylvania (Cook, p. 98). United States Board on Geographic Names (1964a, p. 12) approved the name "Negro Ben Spring" for a feature situated 4 miles north-northeast of Tionesta (NE quarter sec. 32, T 45 N, R 6 E), and rejected the name "Nigger Ben Spring" for it.

Tionesta Post Office [MODOC]: *locality,* 1.5 miles north-northeast of Timber Mountain (lat. 41°38'50" N, long. 121°17'20" W; at S line sec. 16, T 44 N, R 6 E); the place is 2 miles east of Tionesta. Named on Timber Mountain (1952) 15' quadrangle. Postal authorities established Tionesta post office in 1939 and discontinued it in 1955 (Salley, p. 222).

Tiptons Springs: see **Karlo** [LASSEN].

Toadtown: see **Johnstonville** [LASSEN].

Tobin [PLUMAS]: *locality,* 1.25 miles north-northeast of Storrie (lat. 39°56' N, long. 121°18'50" W). Named on Storrie (1979) 7.5' quadrangle. On Pulga (1957) 15' quadrangle, the name applies to a place located 0.5 mile northeast of present Tobin along Western Pacific Railroad. Postal authorities established Cedar Glen post office in 1914, changed the name to Tobin in 1921, and discontinued it in 1931; the name "Tobin" was for the operator of a summer vacation resort (Salley, p. 40, 222).

Tobin Ridge [PLUMAS]: *ridge,* south-trending, 1.5 miles long, 1.25 miles northwest of Storrie (lat. 39°56' N, long. 121°20'10" W); the ridge is about 1 mile west of Tobin. Named on Storrie (1979) 7.5' quadrangle.

Toland Creek [PLUMAS]: *stream,* flows nearly 3 miles to Little North Fork of Middle Fork Feather River 8 miles south-southeast of Storrie (lat. 39°48'50" N, long. 121°16' W; near SW cor. sec. 25, T 23 N, R 6 E); the stream is west of Toland Ridge. Named on Soapstone Hill (1979) 7.5' quadrangle.

Toland Ridge [PLUMAS]: *ridge,* generally south-trending, 1.5 miles long, 6.5 miles south-southeast of Storrie (lat. 39°49'55" N, long. 121°16'15" W). Named on Soapstone Hill (1979) 7.5' quadrangle.

Toll Gate [PLUMAS]: *locality,* 2.5 miles west-southwest of the village of Meadow Valley (lat. 39°55'05" N, long. 121°06'20" W; near NE cor. sec. 29, T 24 N, R 8 E). Site named on Meadow Valley (1980) 7.5' quadrangle.

Tollgate Creek [PLUMAS]: *stream,* flows about 6 miles to Spanish Creek (1) nearly 4 miles north-northeast of Quincy (lat. 39°58'55" N, long. 120°54'20" W; sec. 31, T 25 N, R 10 E). Named on Crescent Mills (1980), Quincy (1950), Spring Garden (1950), and Taylorsville (1980) 7.5' quadrangles. Downieville (1897) 30' quadrangle has the form "Toll Gate Creek" for the name.

Toll House Reservoir [LASSEN]: *intermittent lake,* 500 feet long, 6.5 miles west of Bieber (lat. 41°06'30" N, long. 121°16' W; near N line sec. 27, T 38 N, R 6 E). Named on Fall River Mills (1961) 15' quadrangle.

Tom Creek: see **Thoms Creek** [MODOC].

Tom Large Flat [MODOC]: *area,* 4 miles east of White Horse (lat. 41°18'45" N, long. 121°19'10" W; near N line sec. 18, T 40 N, R 6 E). Named on White Horse (1962) 15' quadrangle.

Tom Lee Meadows [MODOC]: *area,* 6.5 miles south-southwest of Cedarville (lat. 41°26'40" N, long. 120°13'15" W; at S line sec. 27, T 42 N, R 15 E). Named on Warren Peak (1963) 7.5' quadrangle.

Toms Cabin Spring [LASSEN]: *spring,* 5 miles south-southeast of Observation Peak (lat. 40°42'30" N, long. 120°10'05" W; sec. 21, T 33 N, R 16 E). Named on Shinn Mountain (1954) 15' quadrangle.

Toms Creek [MODOC]: *stream,* flows 11 miles to Pit River 2.5 miles east-southeast of Canby (lat. 41°25'50" N, long. 120°49'30" W; at S line sec. 33, T 42 N, R 10 E). Named on Canby (1961) 15' quadrangle.

Tooms Creek [PLUMAS]: *stream,* flows 2 miles to South Fork Feather River 3.25 miles north of La Porte (lat. 39°43'40" N, long. 120°59'45" W; sec. 32, T 22 N, R 9 E). Named on La Porte (1951) 7.5' quadrangle.

Toreson Reservoir: see **Ballard Reservoir** [MODOC].

Totten Camp [LASSEN]: *locality,* 12.5 miles northeast of Lava Peak (lat. 40°58'30" N, long. 120°45'15" W; near N line sec. 7, T 36 N, R 11 E). Named on Hayden Hill (1956) 15' quadrangle.

Tournquist Spring [MODOC]: *spring,* 6 miles northwest of South Mountain (lat. 41°54'35" N, long. 120°42' W; at SW cor. sec. 15, T 47 N, R 11 E). Named on South Mountain (1962) 15' quadrangle.

Tower Rock [PLUMAS]: *peak,* 7 miles north of Spring Garden (lat. 39°59'45" N, long. 120°46'35" W; at SW cor. sec. 29, T 25 N, R 11 E). Altitude 7779 feet. Named on Spring Garden (1950) 7.5' quadrangle.

Trail Lake [LASSEN]: *lake,* 1050 feet long, 14 miles north-northwest of Westwood (lat. 40°28'40" N, long. 121°09'05" W; sec. 12, T 30 N, R 7 E). Named on Red Cinder (1979) 7.5' quadrangle.

Tramp Spring [MODOC]: *spring,* 1.5 miles north-northeast of Blue Mountain (lat. 41°51' N, long. 120°51' W; near N line sec. 8, T 46 N, R 10 E). Named on Steele Swamp (1962) 15' quadrangle.

Traverse Creek [MODOC]: *stream,* flows 0.5 mile to the State of Oregon 11 miles north of South Mountain (lat. 41°59'35" N, long. 120°39' W; at N line sec. 24, T 48 N, R 11 E). Named on South Mountain (1962) 15' quadrangle.

Triangle: see **Blue Mountain** [MODOC].

Triangle Lake [LASSEN]: *lake,* 3300 feet long, 10.5 miles south-southwest of Cal Mountain (lat. 40°31'40" N, long. 121°13' W; on S line sec. 20, T 31 N, R 7 E). Named on Harvey Mountain (1956) 15' quadrangle.

Tri-Lake City: see **Lake City** [MODOC].

Trosi Canyon [PLUMAS]: *canyon,* drained by a stream that flows 2 miles to Sierra Valley 5.5 miles northwest of Chilcoot (lat. 39°51'15" N, long. 120°12'45" W; at S line sec. 8, T 23 N, R 16 E). Named on Chilcoot (1979) 7.5' quadrangle.

Trosi Spring [PLUMAS]: *spring,* 11 miles northwest of Chilcoot (lat. 39°56'35" N, long. 120°13'35" W; near S line sec. 7, T 24 N, R 16 E). Named on Frenchman Lake (1979) 7.5' quadrangle.

Troxel Point [LASSEN]: *promontory,* 4 miles north-northeast of Pelican Point on the east side of Eagle Lake (lat. 40°40'50" N, long. 120°42'30" W). Named on Fredonyer Peak (1954) 15' quadrangle. The name recalls the Troxel family, who ran a ranch and stage stop from 1888 until 1918 (Purdy, 1988, p. 122).

Troxel Point: see **Little Troxel Point** [LASSEN].

Truck Ravine [PLUMAS]: *canyon,* drained by a stream that flows nearly 2 miles to Marble Creek 10 miles south of Storrie (lat. 39° 46'30" N, long. 121°16'45" W; sec. 11, T 22 N, R 6 E). Named on Soapstone Hill (1979) 7.5' quadrangle.

Tuber [MODOC]: *locality,* 5.5 miles northwest of Newell along Southern Pacific Railroad (lat. 41°56'10" N, long. 121°26'55" W; near N line sec. 7, T 47 N, R 5 E). Named on Tulelake (1951) 15' quadrangle.

Tucker Butte [MODOC]: *peak,* 8.5 miles southeast of Newell (lat. 41°47'45" N, long. 121°15'30" W; sec. 26, T 46 N, R 6 E). Altitude 5187 feet. Named on Tulelake (1951) 15' quadrangle.

Tuilla Lake: see **Tule Lake Sump** [MODOC].

Tuledad Canyon [LASSEN]: *canyon,* 4.5 miles long, 21 miles east of Madeline (lat. 41°01'40" N, long. 120°05' W). Named on Little Hat Mountain (1962) 7.5' quadrangle. The name is for Tuledad Matney, who ran cattle and horses at the place (Gudde, 1949, p. 371).

Tuledad Canyon: see **Little Tuledad Canyon** [LASSEN].

Tuledad Valley [LASSEN]: *valley,* 24 miles east of Madeline on California-Nevada State line (lat. 41°01'10" N, long. 120°01' W). Named on Little Hat Mountain (1962) 7.5' quadrangle.

Tuledad Valley: see **Upper Tuledad Valley** [LASSEN].

Tule Lake: see **Little Tule Lake** [LASSEN]; **Tule Lake Sump** [MODOC].

Tule Lake Reservoir [LASSEN]: *lake,* 3.5 miles long, 5 miles northeast of Madeline (lat. 41°05'45" N, long. 120°24' W). Named on Cold Spring Mountain (1962) and Madeline (1962) 7.5' quadrangles. United States Board on Geographic Names (1969, p. 3) approved the name "Moon Lake" for the feature, and rejected the names "Tule Lake Reservoir" and "Tulelake Reservoir." Alturas 1° quadrangle shows Tule Marsh at the place.

Tule Lake Sump [MODOC]: *water feature,* 5 miles southwest of Newell on Modoc-Siskiyou County line. Named on Tulelake (1951) 15' quadrangle. The feature is the confined remnant of Tule Lake, which formerly lay on California-Oregon State line. Tule Lake itself is named on Modoc Lava-Bed (1892) 1° quadrangle, and is called Rhett Lake on Fremont's (1848) map—Fremont gave the name "Rhett Lake" in 1846 to honor his friend Barnwell Rhett (Gudde, 1949, p. 371). Steptoe's (1855) map has the designation "Rhett (Tuilla) Lake" for the feature. United States Board on Geographic Names (1986, p. 2) approved the name "Tule Lake" for it, and rejected the names "Tule Lake Sump" and "Rhett Lake"—the Board described Tule Lake as a reservoir in two sections.

Tule Marsh: see **Tule Lake Reservoir** [LASSEN].

Tule Mountain [LASSEN]: *mountain,* 6 miles north of Madeline (lat. 41°08'20" N, long. 120°27'05" W). Named on Madeline (1962) and Tule Mountain (1967) 7.5' quadrangles

Tule Patch Spring [LASSEN]: *spring,* 7.25 miles north-northeast of Karlo (lat. 40°38'45" N, long. 120°15'35" W; near SE cor. sec. 10, T 32 N, R 15 E). Named on Karlo (1954) 15' quadrangle.

Tunnel Spring [LASSEN]: *spring,* 5 miles south-southeast of Termo (lat. 40°48'05" N, long. 120°25'45" W; at S line sec. 18, T 34 N, R 14 E). Named on Ravendale (1954) 15' quadrangle.

Tunnison Mountain [LASSEN]: *ridge,* south- to southeast-trending, 5 miles long, 14 miles southeast of Pelican Point (lat. 40°31'20" N, long. 120°32' W. Named on Fredonyer Peak (1954), Karlo (1954), and Litchfield (1954) 15' quadrangles.

Turkeytown Diggins [PLUMAS]: *locality,* 12 miles south-southeast of Quincy along Hopkins Creek (lat. 39°46'45" N, long. 120°49'45" W). Named on Blue Nose Mountain (1951) 7.5' quadrangle.

Turnaround Lake [LASSEN]: *lake,* 1800 feet long, 11 miles south-southwest of Cal Mountain (lat. 40°30'45" N, long. 121°12'45" W; on S line sec. 29, T 31 N, R 7 E). Named on Harvey Mountain (1956) 15' quadrangle.

Turner Canyon [MODOC]: *canyon,* 1.5 miles long, drained by Turner Creek (1) above a point 10 miles south-southeast of Crank Mountain (lat.

41°15'05" N, long. 121°04'30" W; sec. 5, T 39 N, R 8 E). Named on Crank Mountain (1962) 15' quadrangle,

Turner Creek [MODOC]:

(1) *stream,* flows 10 miles to Pit River nearly 7 miles west-southwest of Canby (lat. 41°24'55" N, long. 120°59'40" W; near S line sec. 1, T 41 N, R 8 E). Named on Canby (1961) and Crank Mountain (1962) 15' quadrangles.

(2) *stream,* flows 5 miles to Pit River 2 miles northeast of Lookout (lat. 41°13'55" N, long. 121°07'40" W; near E line sec. 11, T 39 N, R 7 E). Named on Bieber (1961) 15' quadrangle.

Turner Ridge: see **Beckwourth** [PLUMAS].

Turner Spring [MODOC]: *spring,* 11 miles north-northwest of South Mountain (lat. 41°59' N, long. 120°44' W; at S line sec. 20, T 48 N, R 11 E). Named on South Mountain (1962) 15' quadrangle.

Turret: see **Happy Camp Mountain** [MODOC].

Turtle Mountain [LASSEN]: *peak,* 5.5 miles north of Doyle (lat. 40° 06'35" N, long. 120°05' W; sec. 17, T 26 N, R 17 E). Altitude 4818 feet. Named on Doyle (1954) 15' quadrangle.

Twain [PLUMAS]: *village,* 15 miles south-southeast of the village of Almanor (lat. 40°01'15" N, long. 121°04'15" W; near N line sec. 22, T 25 N, R 8 E). Named on Twain (1980) 7.5' quadrangle. Called Halsted Flat on Almanor (1955) 15' quadrangle, which has the name "Twain" for present Hot Springs. United States Board on Geographic Names (1981, p. 3) rejected the names "Halsted Flat," "Halstead Flat," and "Grays Flat" for the place. Postal authorities established Twain post office in 1910 and moved it 1 mile west in 1940 (Salley, p. 226). According to local tradition, the name commemorates Mark Twain (Gudde, 1949, p. 373).

Twain: see **Hot Springs** [PLUMAS].

Twain Siding [PLUMAS]: *locality,* 1.25 miles east-southeast of Twain along Western Pacific Railroad (lat. 40°01' N, long. 121°02'50" W; on E line sec. 23, T 25 N, R 8 E). Named on Twain (1980) 7.5' quadrangle.

12 Mile Bar [PLUMAS]: *locality,* 4 miles south-southeast of Caribou along East Branch of North Fork Feather River (lat. 40°01'40" N, long. 121°07'35" W; sec. 18, T 25 N, R 8 E); the place is near the mouth of Twelvemile Ravine. Named on Caribou (1979) 7.5' quadrangle.

Twelvemile Creek [MODOC]: *stream,* flows 4 miles to the State of Oregon 10 miles north-northeast of Fort Bidwell (lat. 41°59'40" N, long. 120°05'25" W), and then flows eastward in and out of Oregon for 4.5 miles before it finally enters Oregon to stay. Named on Fort Bidwell (1962) 15' quadrangle. United States Board on Geographic Names (1964c, p. 16) rejected the names "North Fork Creek," "South Fork Twelvemile Creek," "Twelve Mile Creek," "Twelve Mile North Fork Creek," and "Twentymile Creek" for the stream. South Fork enters from the southwest 8 miles north of Fort Bidwell; it is 2 miles long and is named on Fort Bidwell (1962) 15' quadrangle. United States Board on Geographic Names (1964c, p. 16) rejected the names "Twelve Mile Creek" and "Twelvemile Creek" for present South Fork.

Twelve Mile North Fork Creek: see **Twelvemile Creek** [MODOC].

Twelvemile Ravine [PLUMAS]: *canyon,* drained by a stream that flows 0.5 mile to East Branch of North Fork Feather River nearly 3 miles west of Twain (lat. 40°01'30" N, long. 121°07'25" W; sec. 18, T 25 N, R 8 E). Named on Caribou (1979) 7.5' quadrangle.

Twentymile Creek: see **Twelvemile Creek** [MODOC].

Twentymile House: see **Cromberg** [PLUMAS] (2).

Twin Bridges [LASSEN]: *locality,* 4.25 miles north of Bieber along Pit River at Lassen-Modoc County line (lat. 41°11' N, long. 121° 09'15" W; near N line sec. 34, T 39 N, R 7 E). Named on Bieber (1961) 15' quadrangle.

Twin Buttes [LASSEN]: *peaks,* two, 10 miles southeast of Ravendale (lat. 40°46'50" N, long. 120°18'20" W; around NW cor. sec. 29, T 34 N, R 15 E). Altitude of highest is 6113 feet. Named on Ravendale (1954) 15' quadrangle.

Twin Lakes [LASSEN]:

(1) *intermittent lake,* 10 miles south of Adin [MODOC] (lat. 41°02'55" N, long. 120°55'15" W; sec. 15, T 37 N, R 9 E). Named on Adin (1962) 15' quadrangle.

(2) *marsh,* 3.5 miles west-southwest of Lava Peak (lat. 40°48'20" N, long. 120°57'05" W; sec. 15, 22, T 34 N, R 9 E). Named on Hayden Hill (1956) 15' quadrangle.

(3) *lakes,* largest 700 feet long, 11 miles south-southwest of Cal Mountain (lat. 40°31'15" N, long. 121°13' W; sec. 29, T 31 N, R 7 E). Named on Harvey Mountain (1956) 15' quadrangle.

Twin Lakes [MODOC]:

(1) *lakes,* two, largest 200 feet long, 4 miles southeast of Crank Mountain (lat. 41°20'15" N, long. 121°05'45" W; sec. 6, T 40 N, R 8 E). Named on Crank Mountain (1962) 15' quadrangle.

(2) *lakes,* two, largest 3500 feet long, 11.5 miles northeast of Fort Bidwell (lat. 41°58'45" N, long. 120°00'05" W); the east edge of the largest lake extends into the State of Nevada. Named on Fort Bidwell (1962) 15' quadrangle.

Twin Lakes: see **Bathtub Lake** [LASSEN].

Twin Meadows [PLUMAS]: *areas,* 9 miles west of Mount Harkness (lat. 40°25'50" N, long. 121°28'20" W; near W line sec. 30, T 30 N, R 5 E). Named on Mount Harkness (1956) 15' quadrangle.

Twin Sister [MODOC]: *peak,* 9.5 miles south of Newell (lat. 41°45'05" N, long. 121°22'50" W; sec. 10, T 45 N, R 5 E). Named on Tulelake (1951) 15' quadrangle.

Twin Springs [LASSEN]: *springs,* 2 miles north-northeast of Lava Peak (lat. 40°51'40" N, long. 120°52'40" W; on N line sec. 32, T 35 N, R 10 E). Named on Hayden Hill (1956) 15' quadrangle.

Twin Springs [MODOC]: *springs,* two, nearly 7 miles northwest of South Mountain (lat. 41°53'45" N, long. 120°44'30" W; at SE cor. sec. 19, T 47 N, R 11 E). Named on South Mountain (1962) 15' quadrangle.

Two Buttes [MODOC]: *peaks,* two, 9 miles north-northeast of Fort Bidwell (lat. 40°57'55" N, long. 120°03'30" W; at NE cor. sec. 7, T 47 N, R 17 E). Altitude of highest 6123 feet. Named on Fort Bidwell (1962) 15' quadrangle.

Two Rivers [PLUMAS]: *locality,* 4 miles northwest of Blairsden (lat. 39°49'25" N, long. 120°40' W; near SE cor. sec. 30, T 23 N, R 12 E); the place is near the confluence of Jamison Creek and Middle Fork Feather River. Named on Johnsville (1972) 7.5' quadrangle.

Two Spring [MODOC]: *spring,* 9 miles south of Canby (lat. 41°18'50" N, long. 120°51'50" W; at N line sec. 18, T 40 N, R 10 E). Named on Canby (1961) 15' quadrangle.

—U—

"U": see **The "U"** [MODOC].

Union Creek [PLUMAS]: *stream,* flows 2.25 miles to Nelson Creek 9 miles southeast of Quincy (lat. 39°50'10" N, long. 120°50'35" W). Named on Blue Nose Mountain (1951) 7.5' quadrangle.

Union Reservoir [LASSEN]: *lake,* 1100 feet long, 9.5 miles north of Observation Peak (lat. 40°54'40" N, long. 120°09' W; sec. 10, T 35 N, R 16 E). Named on Observation Peak (1954) 15' quadrangle.

Upper Alkali Lake: see **Upper Lake** [MODOC].

Upper Cummings Reservoir [MODOC]: *intermittent lake,* 3300 feet long, 6.5 miles northwest of Alturas (lat. 41°32'45" N, long. 120° 38'40" W; on S line sec. 24, T 43 N, R 11 E); the feature is 2 miles north of Lower Cummings Reservoir. Named on Big Sage Reservoir (1962) 15' quadrangle.

Upper Dutch Diggins [PLUMAS]: *locality,* 0.5 mile north-northwest of La Porte (lat. 39°41'30" N, long. 120°59'15" W; sec. 8, 9, T 21 N, R 9 E). Named on La Porte (1951) 7.5' quadrangle.

Upper Gooch Valley [LASSEN]: *valley,* 0.5 mile south-southeast of Lava Peak (lat. 40°49'30" N, long. 120°52'45" W); the valley is 3 miles west-northwest of Lower Gooch Valley. Named on Hayden Hill (1956) 15' quadrangle.

Upper Goose Lake: see **Goose Lake** [MODOC] (1).

Upper Lake [MODOC]: *intermittent lake,* 17 miles long, south of Fort Bidwell in Surprise Valley (lat. 41°44' N, long. 120°09' W). Named on Cedarville (1962) and Fort Bidwell (1962) 15' quadrangles. United States Board on Geographic Names (1965c, p. 13) rejected the name "Upper Alkali Lake" for the feature.

Upper Long Valley [LASSEN]: *valley,* along Long Valley Creek from Scotts south into Sierra County. Named on Beckwourth Pass (1975) and Evans Canyon (1978) 7.5' quadrangles. On Honey Lake (1893) 1° quadrangle, the name "Upper Long Valley": applies to the north part of present Long Valley (2).

Upper McBride Springs [LASSEN]: *springs,* 12 miles north-northeast of Lava Peak along Willow Creek [LASSEN-MODOC] (lat. 40° 59'25" N, long. 120°48' W; near NE cor. sec. 3, T 36 N, R 10 E). Named on Hayden Hill (1956) 15' quadrangle.

Upper Mud Lake [MODOC]: *intermittent lake,* 4.5 miles south-southwest of Hackamore (lat. 41°30' N, long. 121°10' W); the feature is connected at the south end to Mud Lake (2). Named on Crank Mountain (1962) and Hackamore (1952) 15' quadrangles.

Upper Mud Lake [PLUMAS]: *lake,* 350 feet long, 5 miles north-northwest of Bucks Lodge (lat. 39°56'30" N, long. 121°12'35" W; at W line sec. 16, T 24 N, R 7 E); the lake is 1800 feet north-northwest of Mud Lake (5). Named on Bucks Lake (1979) 7.5' quadrangle.

Upper Muldoon Tank [MODOC]: *water feature,* 11.5 miles north-northwest of South Mountain at California-Oregon State line (lat. 41°59'35" N, long. 120°42'15" W; at N line sec. 21, T 48 N, R 11 E); the feature is 1 mile northwest of Lower Muldoon Tank.. Named on South Mountain (1962) 15' quadrangle.

Upper Roberts Reservoir [MODOC]: *intermittent lake,* 0.5 mile long, 7.5 miles south-southwest of Crank Mountain (lat. 41°16'50" N, long. 121°11'50" W; sec. 29, 30, T 40 N, R 7 E); the lake is 4 miles northwest of Lower Roberts Reservoir. Named on Crank Mountain (1962) 15' quadrangle. Called Roberts Reservoir on California Division of Highways' (1934) map.

Upper Rush Creek Campground [MODOC]: *locality,* 10 miles south of Canby (lat. 41°18'05" N, long. 120°51' W; sec. 17, T 40 N, R 10 E); the place is along Rush Creek 1.5 miles upstream from Lower Rush Creek Campground. Named on Canby (1961) 15' quadrangle.

Upper Sacramento River: see **Pit River** [MODOC].

Upper Stevens Meadow [LASSEN]: *area,* 10 miles south of Cal Mountain (lat. 40°31'30" N, long. 121°08'30" W; on S line sec. 24, T 31 N, R 7 E). Named on Harvey Mountain (1956) 15' quadrangle, which shows marsh in the area.

Upper Tuledad Valley [LASSEN]: *valley,* 21 miles east of Madeline (lat. 41°01'30" N, long. 120°04'45" W; mainly in sec. 31, 32, T 37 N, R 17 E); the valley is in Tuledad Canyon. Named on Little Hat Mountain (1962) 7.5' quadrangle.

— V —

Valley Creek [PLUMAS]: *stream,* flows 3.5 miles to Lost Creek (2) 1.5 miles west-northwest of American House (lat. 39°39'30" N, long. 121°03'10" W; at N line sec. 26, T 21 N, R 8 E). Named on American House (1948) 7.5' quadrangle.

Van Loan Creek [LASSEN]: *stream,* flows 6 miles to Madeline Plains 8.5 miles north of Termo (lat. 40°59'10" N, long. 120°28'30" W; at E line sec. 4, T 36 N, R 13 E). Named on Ravendale (1954) 15' quadrangle, and on Madeline (1962) 7.5' quadrangle.

Van Loan Reservoir [LASSEN]: *lake,* 1100 feet long, 8 miles north of Termo (lat. 40°58'50" N, long. 120°27'35" W; near S line sec. 3, T 36 N, R 13 E); the lake is along Van Loan Creek. Named on Ravendale (1954) 15' quadrangle.

Van Lone [LASSEN]: *locality,* 41 miles north-northeast of Susanville (lat. 40°59'50" N, long. 120°28' W); the place is near the mouth of present Van Loan Creek. Named on Honey Lake (1893) 1° quadrangle. Elmer Van Loan ran a stage station at Van Loan ranch (Garate, p. 60).

Van Riper Spring [MODOC]: *spring,* 7 miles south of Eagleville (lat. 41°13'15" N, long. 120°06'35" W; sec. 25, T 39 N, R 16 E). Named on Snake Lake (1962) 7.5' quadrangle.

Van Sickle Lake [LASSEN]: *lake,* 2200 feet long, 5.25 miles north of Lava Peak (lat. 40°54'20" N, long. 120°53'20" W; on S line sec. 36, T 36 N, R 9 E). Named on Hayden Hill (1956) 15' quadrangle.

Vaughn Canyon [MODOC]: *canyon,* drained by a stream that flows 1.25 miles to Surprise Valley 7.25 miles south-southwest of Fort Bidwell (lat. 41°45'30" N, long. 120°11'30" W; sec. 19, T 45 N, R 16 E). Named on Fort Bidwell (1962) 15' quadrangle.

Venning Creek [MODOC]: *stream,* flows 5.25 mile to Upper Lake about 2 miles south of Fort Bidwell (lat. 41°49'50" N, long. 120° 09'20" W; sec. 29, T 46 N, R 16 E). Named on Fort Bidwell (1962) 15' quadrangle.

Vicker Springs [MODOC]: *springs,* 3.5 miles west-southwest of Lookout (lat. 41°11'30" N, long. 121°12'55" W; sec. 30, T 39 N, R 7 E). Named on Bieber (1961) 15' quadrangle.

Vida: see **Mount Vida** [MODOC].

Viewland [LASSEN]: *locality,* 6.5 miles east-northeast of Litchfield along Southern Pacific Railroad (lat. 40°25'50" N, long. 120°16'45" W; sec. 27, T 30 N, R 15 E). Named on Litchfield (1954) 15' quadrangle. Amesbury (p. 27) used the form "View Land" for the name.

Vinton [PLUMAS]: *village,* 2 miles west of Chilcoot (lat. 39°48'15" N, long. 120°10'30" W; sec. 34, T 23 N, R 16 E). Named on Chilcoot (1979) 7.5' quadrangle. Postal authorities established Vinton post office in 1897 and named it for Vinton Bowen, daughter of an official of Sierra Valley Railway (Salley, p. 232).

Virgilia [PLUMAS]: *locality,* 2 miles west of Twain (lat. 40°01'10" N, long. 121°06'25" W; near NE cor. sec. 20, T 25 N, R 8 E). Named on Twain (1980) 7.5' quadrangle. Postal authorities established Virgilia post office in 1929 and discontinued it in 1965 (Salley, p. 232). The name is for Virgilia Bogue, daughter of Virgil G. Bogue (Gudde, 1949, p. 380).

Volcano: see **Little Volcano** [PLUMAS].

— W —

Wade: see **Lookout** [MODOC].

Wades Lake [PLUMAS]: *lake,* 1200 feet long, 7.5 miles west-southwest of Clio (lat. 39°42'40" N, long. 120°42'40" W; sec. 2, T 21 N, R 11 E). Named on Gold Lake (1981) 7.5' quadrangle.

Wade Williams Spring [MODOC]: *spring,* 11 miles south-southwest of Alturas (lat. 41°20'15" N, long. 120°37'10" W; sec. 5, T 40 N, R 12 E). Named on Alturas (1961) 15' quadrangle.

Wagner Canyon [LASSEN]: *canyon,* drained by a stream that flows 1 mile to Honey Lake Valley 8 miles northwest of Doyle (lat. 40° 06' N, long. 120°12'50" W; at N line sec. 19, T 26 N, R 16 E). Named on McKesick Peak (1978) 7.5' quadrangle.

Wagontire Creek [LASSEN]: *stream,* flows 7.25 miles to Dixie Valley 7.25 miles east of the village of Little Valley (lat. 40°53'30" N, long. 121°02'30" W; near S line sec. 14, T 35 N, R 8 E). Named on Little Valley (1957) 15' quadrangle.

Wagontire Flat [LASSEN]: *area,* 7 miles northeast of the village of Little Valley (lat. 40°57'10" N, long. 121°04'15" W; mainly in sec. 17, T 36 N, R 8 E). Named on Little Valley (1957) 15' quadrangle. Called Tar Flat on Halls Flat (1939) 30' quadrangle, but United States Board on Geographic Names (1960a, p. 18) rejected this name for the feature.

Wagontire Reservoir [LASSEN]: *intermittent lake,* 400 feet long, 7 miles northeast of the village of Little Valley (lat. 40°57'05" N, long. 121°04'05" W; near SE cor. sec. 17, T 36 N, R 8 E); the feature is in Wagontire Flat. Named on Little Valley (1957) 15' quadrangle.

Wagontire Spring [LASSEN]: *spring,* 5 miles east-southeast of Observation Peak (lat. 40°44'40" N, long. 120°06'45" W; near N line sec. 12, T 33 N, R 16 E). Named on Shinn Mountain (1954) 15' quadrangle.

Wales Canyon [LASSEN]: *canyon,* drained by a stream that flows 2.25 miles to Honey Lake Valley 5.5 miles northwest of Milford (lat. 40°13'40" N, long. 120°26'55" W; sec. 6, T 27 N, R 14 E). Named on Stony Ridge (1978) 7.5' quadrangle.

Walker Draw [LASSEN]: *canyon,* 2 miles long, 9.5 miles southeast of Adin [MODOC] (lat. 41°05'20" N, long. 120°49'25" W; sec. 33, T 38 N, R 10 E, and sec. 4, T 37 N, R 10 E). Named on Adin (1962) 15' quadrangle.

Walkermine [PLUMAS]: *locality,* 3 miles southwest of Mount Ingalls (lat. 39°57'50" N, long. 120°40' W; near NE cor. sec. 7, T 24 N, R 12 E). Site named on Blairsden (1943) 15' quadrangle. Mount Ingalls (1972) 7.5' quadrangle shows Walker mine at the place. Postal authorities established International post office, named for a mine, at the site in 1918 and discontinued it in 1923; they established Walkermine post office there in 1930 and discontinued it in 1941 (Salley, p. 104, 234).

Walker Plains [PLUMAS]: *area,* 8 miles south of Storrie at Plumas-Butte County line (lat. 39°47'55" N, long. 121°18'30" W; on S line sec. 33, T 23 N, R 6 E). Named on Soapstone Hill (1979) 7.5' quadrangle. United States Board on Geographic Names (1979, p. 6) rejected the singular form "Walker Plain" for the name. Hoover, Rensch, and Rensch (p. 283) noted that Walker's Plains or lava beds provided rough going for stagecoach wheels in pioneer days. Gudde (1975, p. 39) listed a mining place of the early 1860's called Black Rock that was situated adjacent to Walkers Plains.

Walker Spring [LASSEN]:

(1) *spring,* 10 miles southeast of Bieber (lat. 41°00'50" N, long. 121°01'05" W; sec. 26, T 37 N, R 8 E). Named on Bieber (1961) 15' quadrangle.

(2) *spring,* 2.5 miles west-southwest of Westwood (lat. 40°17'40" N, long. 121°02'30" W; near SE cor. sec. 11, T 28 N, R 8 E). Named on Westwood West (1980) 7.5' quadrangle.

Walker Spring: see **Walker Springs** [LASSEN].

Walker Springs [LASSEN]: *springs,* 9 miles southeast of Adin [MODOC] (lat. 41°06' N, long. 120°49'15" W; near SE cor. sec. 28, T 38 N, R 10 E). Named on Adin (1962) 15' quadrangle. United States Board on Geographic Names (1990, p. 11) approved the singular form "Walker Spring" for the name.

Wallace Alexander: see **Camp Wallace Alexander** [PLUMAS].

Wallace Creek [PLUMAS]: *stream,* heads in Sierra County and flows 2.5 miles, partly in Plumas County, to Slate Creek (3) 3.5 miles east-northeast of La Porte in Sierra County (lat. 39°42'35" N, long. 120°55'40" W; near W line sec. 1, T 21 N, R 9 E). Named on La Porte (1951) 7.5' quadrangle.

Wallace Hollow: see **Wallack Hollow** [PLUMAS].

Wallack Hollow [PLUMAS]: *canyon,* drained by a stream that flows 2.5 miles to Humbug Valley (1) 7.5 miles south-southwest of the village of Almanor (lat. 40°07'30" N, long. 121°15'05" W; sec. 12, T 26 N, R 6 E). Named on Jonesville (1958) 15' quadrangle. United States Board on Geographic Names (1990, p. 11) rejected the name "Wallace Hollow" for the feature, and noted that the name "Wallack" is for Eli Wallack, a pioneer who lived at the mouth of the canyon.

Waller Creek [PLUMAS]: *stream,* flows 1.5 miles to North Fork Feather River 5 miles southwest of Caribou (lat. 40°01'20" N, long. 121°13' W; sec. 17, T 25 N, R 7 E). Named on Caribou (1979) 7.5' quadrangle.

Wall Spring [MODOC]: *spring,* 5.5 miles northwest of South Mountain (lat. 41°54'05" N, long. 120°42'05" W; at E line sec. 21, T 47 N, R 11 E). Named on South Mountain (1962) 15' quadrangle.

Wall Springs [MODOC]: *spring,* 14 miles southeast of Alturas (lat. 41°19'20" N, long. 120°23'05" W; near N line sec. 8, T 40 N, R 14 E). Named on Little Juniper Reservoir (1963) 7.5' quadrangle.

Walter Flat [MODOC]: *area,* 16 miles north of Double Head Mountain along Lost Creek (lat. 41°59'30" N, long. 121°10' W; mainly in sec. 21, T 48 N, R 7 E). Named on Clear Lake Reservoir (1951) 15' quadrangle.

Wapaunsie Creek [PLUMAS]: *stream,* flows 2.25 miles to Spanish Creek (1) 1.5 miles northeast of the village of Meadow Valley (lat. 39°57' N, long. 121°02'15" W; at S line sec. 12, T 24 N, R 8 E). Named on Meadow Valley (1980) 7.5' quadrangle.

Ward Creek [PLUMAS]: *stream,* formed by the confluence of North Branch and South Branch, flows 2 miles to Indian Creek (2) 7 miles south of Kettle Rock (lat. 40°02'20" N, long. 120°43'55" W; near S line sec. 10, T 25 N, R 11 E). Named on Genesee Valley (1972) 7.5' quadrangle. Called Wards Creek on United States Geological Survey's (1907) map. North

Branch is 3.25 miles long and is named on Genesee Valley (1972) 7.5' quadrangle. South Branch is 4 miles long and is named on Genesee Valley (1972) and Mount Ingalls (1972) 7.5' quadrangles. Middle Branch enters South Branch 1.5 miles above the confluence of North Branch and South Branch; it is 1 mile long and in named on Mount Ingalls (1972) 7.5' quadrangle.

Wards Lake [LASSEN]: *lake,* 0.5 mile long, nearly 3 miles northwest of Litchfield (lat. 40°24'20" N, long. 120°25'50" W; at N line sec. 5, T 29 N, R 14 E). Named on Litchfield (1954) 15' quadrangle.

Wardtown: see **Little Grizzly Creek** [PLUMAS] (1).

Warm Creek [MODOC]: *stream,* flows 3.25 miles to end near South Fork Pit River 18 miles south of Alturas (lat. 41°13'50" N, long. 120°29' W; sec. 9, T 39 N, R 13 E). Named on Tule Mountain (1967) 7.5' quadrangle.

Warm Springs Valley [MODOC]: *valley,* at and east of Canby along Pit River (lat. 41°27' N, long. 120°45' W). Named on Alturas (1961) and Canby (1961) 15' quadrangles. Preston (1890b, p. 333) called the place Hot Springs Valley, and noted that this name is from hot springs that occur in the valley.

Warner Creek [PLUMAS]: *stream,* formed by the confluence of Hot Springs Creek and Kings Creek, flows 7 miles to North Fork Feather River nearly 7 miles south of Mount Harkness (lat. 40° 20' N, long. 121°18'20" W; near NW cor. sec. 34, T 29 N, R 6 E). Named on Mount Harkness (1956) 15' quadrangle.

Warner Creek Campground [PLUMAS]: *locality,* nearly 5 miles south of Mount Harkness (lat. 40°21'45" N, long. 121°18'25" W; near E line sec. 21, T 29 N, R 6 E); the place is along Warner Creek. Named on Mount Harkness (1956) 15' quadrangle.

Warner Mountains [MODOC]: *range,* between Goose Lake (1) and Surprise Valley. Named on Alturas (1954) 1°x 2° quadrangle. Preston (1890b, p. 332) used the names "Warner's Range" and "Warner Range" for the feature. The name commemorates Captain W.H. Warner—Indians killed the captain near the west base of the range in 1849 (Pease, p. 77).

Warner Range: see **Warner Mountains** [MODOC].

Warner Valley [PLUMAS]: *valley,* center 2 miles southwest of Mount Harkness (lat. 40°24'30" N, long. 121°19'15" W); the valley is along Warner Creek. Named on Mount Harkness (1956) 15' quadrangle.

Warner Valley Campground [PLUMAS]: *locality,* 5 miles west of Mount Harkness along Hot Springs Creek (lat. 40°26'30" N, long. 121°23'35" W; near SW cor. sec. 23, T 30 N, R 5 E). Named on Mount Harkness (1956) 15' quadrangle.

Warner Valley Rim [PLUMAS]: *escarpment,* 3 miles south-southwest of Mount Harkness (lat. 40°23'30" N, long. 121°19' W); the feature is west of Warner Valley. Named on Mount Harkness (1956) 15' quadrangle.

Warren Creek [PLUMAS]: *stream,* flows 1.5 miles to Lights Creek 4.5 miles southeast of Moonlight Peak (lat. 40°11'30" N, long. 120°47'05" W; near N line sec. 19, T 27 N, R 11 E). Named on Moonlight Peak (1980) 7.5' quadrangle.

Warren Peak [MODOC]: *peak,* 11 miles south-southwest of Cedarville (lat. 41°22'45" N, long. 120°13'10" W; near E line sec. 22, T 41 N, R 15 E). Altitude 9710 feet. Named on Warren Peak (1963) 7.5' quadrangle.

Wart on Tree Tank [MODOC]: *intermittent lake,* 6 miles northeast of Hackamore (lat. 41°35'50" N, long. 121°01'20" W; on W line sec. 2, T 43 N, R 8 E). Named on Hackamore (1952) 15' quadrangle.

Wash: see **Clio** [PLUMAS].

Washington: see **Mount Washington** [PLUMAS].

Washington Creek [MODOC]: *stream,* flows 5 miles to Turner Creek (1) 7.5 miles east-northeast of Crank Mountain (lat. 41°26'10" N, long. 121°01'15" W; near W line sec. 35, T 42 N, R 8 E). Named on Crank Mountain (1962) 15' quadrangle.

Washington Creek [PLUMAS]: *stream,* flows 2.25 miles to Middle Fork Feather River 6.25 miles south of Quincy (lat. 39°50'55" N, long. 120°55'25" W; at N line sec. 24, T 23 N, R 9 E). Named on Onion Valley (1950) 7.5' quadrangle.

Washington Hill [PLUMAS]: *ridge,* generally south-trending, 1.5 miles long, 9.5 miles south-southeast of Quincy (lat. 39°48'30" N, long. 120°53'25" W; on S line sec. 32, T 23 N, R 10 E). Named on Onion Valley (1950) 7.5' quadrangle.

Washington Mountain [MODOC]: *peak,* 5 miles west-northwest of Canby (lat. 41°27'50" N, long. 120°57'30" W; sec. 20, T 42 N, R 9 E). Altitude 5318 feet. Named on Canby (1961) 15' quadrangle.

Waterbox Canyon [MODOC]: *canyon,* 1 mile long, 7 miles south of Eagleville (lat. 41°13' N, long. 120°07'10" W; sec. 25, 26, T 39 N, R 16 E). Named on Emerson Peak (1962) and Snake Lake (1962) 7.5' quadrangles.

Water Canyon [LASSEN]: *canyon,* 4 miles long, 8 miles southwest of Likely [MODOC] (lat. 41°08'50" N, long. 120°36'10" W). Named on Likely (1962) 15' quadrangle.

Water Canyon Spring [LASSEN]: *spring,* 8 miles southwest of Likely [MODOC] (lat. 41°08'30" N, long. 120°35'30" W; near E line sec. 9, T 38 N, R 12 E); the spring is in Water Canyon. Named on Likely (1962) 15' quadrangle.

Water Creek [PLUMAS]: *stream,* flows about 2.5 miles to Humbug Valley (1) 7.5 miles southwest of the village of Almanor (lat. 40° 08'20" N, long. 121°16'25" W; sec. 2, T 26 N, R 6 E). Named on Jonesville (1958) 15' quadrangle.

Waterholes: see **Big Waterholes** [MODOC].

Waverly: see **Horse Lake** [LASSEN] (2).

Wayman Draw: see **Reid Draw** [MODOC].

Wayman Spring [LASSEN]: *spring,* 14 miles southeast of Adin [MODOC] (lat. 41°02'20" N, long. 120°46' W; sec. 13, T 37 N, R 10 E). Named on Adin (1962) 15' quadrangle.

Webb Butte [MODOC]: *peak,* 5 miles west-northwest of Crank Mountain (lat. 41°25' N, long. 121°13'35" W; at S line sec. 1, T 41 N, R 6 E). Named on Crank Mountain (1962) 15' quadrangle.

Webb Flat [MODOC]: *area,* 3.25 miles northwest of Crank Mountain (lat. 41°25' N, long. 121°11'15" W; sec. 5, 8, T 41 N, R 7 E); the place is 2.25 miles east of Webb Butte. Named on Crank Mountain (1962) 15' quadrangle.

Webb Flat Reservoir [MODOC]: *intermittent lake,* 1400 feet long, 3.25 miles northwest of Crank Mountain (lat. 41°24'50" N, long. 121°11'25" W; on N line sec. 8, T 41 N, R 7 E); the feature is in Webb Flat. Named on Crank Mountain (1962) 15' quadrangle.

Weed Valley [MODOC]: *valley,* 9.5 miles north-northeast of Blue Mountain (lat. 41°57'45" N, long. 120°48'50" W). Named on Steele Swamp (1962) 15' quadrangle.

Weed Valley: see **Hidden Valley** [MODOC].

Wendel [LASSEN]: *village,* 23 miles east-southeast of Susanville (lat. 40°21' N, long. 120°14' W; near NE cor. sec. 25, T 29 N, R 15 E). Named on Wendel (1954) 15' quadrangle. Postal authorities established Purser post office in 1902, discontinued it in 1903, reestablished it in 1908, moved it 3 miles east in 1915 when they and changed the name to Wendel, discontinued it in 1920, and reestablished it in 1921; the name "Purser" was for Edward T. Purser, a rancher who developed an irrigation system for Honey Lake Valley (Salley, p. 179, 236). Thomas Moran, president of Nevada-California-Oregon Railroad, named the village for a friend with the given name "Wendel" (Gudde, 1949, p. 386). California Mining Bureau's (1917a) map shows a place called Atola located about 4 miles west-northwest of Wendel along Southern Pacific Railroad. Postal authorities established Dewitt post office 5 miles west of Purser post office in 1903 and discontinued it in 1927; the name was for Walter B. Dewitt, first postmaster (Salley, p. 58).

Wendel Canyon [LASSEN]: *canyon,* 3 miles long, opens into Honey Lake Valley 2 miles east-northeast of Wendel (lat. 40°21'45" N, long. 120°11'45" W; sec. 20, T 29 N, R 16 E). Named on Wendel (1954) 15' quadrangle.

Wendel Hot Springs [LASSEN]: *spring,* 7.25 miles east of Litchfield (lat. 40°21'25" N, long. 120°15'20" W; sec. 23, T 29 N, R 15 E). Named on Litchfield (1954) 15' quadrangle.

Wendt Spring [MODOC]: *spring,* 3.5 miles east of Day (lat. 41°13'15" N, long. 121°18'20" W; sec. 17, T 39 N, R 6 E). Named on Fall River Mills (1961) 15' quadrangle.

West Black Rock Reservoir [MODOC]: *intermittent lake,* 400 feet long, 9.5 miles north-northeast of Jacks Butte (lat. 41°43'15" N, long. 120°45'40" W; near S line sec. 24, T 45 N, R 10 E). Named on Jacks Butte (1962) 15' quadrangle.

West Creek: see **First Creek** [MODOC].

Westlake Butte [MODOC]: *peak,* 4.5 miles west of Canby (lat. 41° 26' N, long. 120°57'10" W; sec. 32, T 42 N, R 9 E). Altitude 5279 feet. Named on Canby (1961) 15' quadrangle.

Westlake Creek [MODOC]: *stream,* flows 4 miles to Pit River 1 mile southwest of Canby (lat. 41°26' N, long. 120°52'55" W; sec. 36, T 42 N, R 9 E); the stream heads at Westlake Butte. Named on Canby (1961) 15' quadrangle.

West Rock Creek [MODOC]: *stream,* flows 3.25 miles to Rock Creek (3) 4 miles west-northwest of Alturas (lat. 41°30'40" N, long. 120°36'50" W; sec. 5, T 42 N, R 12 E). Named on Big Sage Reservoir (1962) 15' quadrangle.

West Valley Cañon: see **West Valley Creek** [MODOC].

West Valley Creek [MODOC]: *stream,* flows 0.5 mile from West Valley Reservoir to South Fork Pit River 19 miles south-southeast of Alturas (lat. 41°13'50" N, long. 120°24'55" W; near W line sec. 7, T 39 N, R 14 E). Named on Tule Mountain (1967) 7.5' quadrangle. The canyon of the stream is called West Valley Cañon on Alturas 1° quadrangle—water of West Valley Reservoir now floods most of the canyon.

West Valley Reservoir [LASSEN-MODOC]: *lake,* 3.5 miles long, behind a dam on West Valley Creek 20 miles south-southeast of Alturas (lat. 41°13'25" N, long. 120°24'40" W; near N line sec. 18, T 39 N, R 14 E). Named on Tule Mountain (1967) 7.5' quadrangle. The south end of the lake is in Lassen County

West Valley Spring [MODOC]: *spring,* 22 miles south-southeast of Alturas (lat. 41°12'05" N, long. 120°21'25" W; sec. 22, T 39 N, R 14 E). Named on Jess Valley (1962) 7.5' quadrangle.

Westwood [LASSEN]: *town,* 20 miles west-southwest of Susanville (lat.

40°18'25" N, long. 121°00' W; sec. 5, 6, 7, 8, T 28 N, R 9 E). Named on Westwood East (1980) and Westwood West (1980) 7.5' quadrangles. Postal authorities established Westwood post office in 1913 (Frickstad, p. 69). Officials of Red River Lumber Company of Minnesota named the place in 1913, when it became the center for the company's lumber operations in the West (Hanna, p. 352). California Division of Highways' (1934) map shows a place called Conman located less than 1 mile north of Westwood along Southern Pacific Railroad (near W line sec. 5, T 28 N, R 9 W). Postal authorities established Lake Nokopen post office in 1938 at a summer resort located 21 miles northwest of Westwood and discontinued it in 1940 (Salley, p. 116).

Westwood Junction [LASSEN]: *locality,* 9.5 miles north-northeast of Westwood along Southern Pacific Railroad (lat. 40°26' N, long. 120°56'45" W; on E line sec. 27, T 30 N, R 9 E). Named on Westwood (1955) 15' quadrangle.

Whaleback Mountain [LASSEN]: *peak,* 6.5 miles west of Pelican Point (lat. 40°38' N, long. 120°52' W; near SE cor. sec. 17, T 32 N, R 10 E). Altitude 6924 feet. Named on Antelope Mountain (1956) 15' quadrangle.

Whalen Spring [MODOC]: *spring,* 3.5 miles south-southwest of Crank Mountain (lat. 41°20'30" N, long. 121°11' W; near NE cor. sec. 5, T 40 N, R 7 E). Named on Crank Mountain (1962) 15' quadrangle.

Whaley Reservoir: see **Taylor Reservoir** [MODOC].

Wheaton: see **Goumaz** [LASSEN].

Wheeler Peak [PLUMAS]: *peak,* 3.5 miles southeast of Kettle Rock (lat. 40°06'10" N, long. 120°41' W; on W line sec. 19, T 26 N, R 12 E). Named on Genesee Valley (1972) 7.5' quadrangle. On Honey Lake (1893) 1° quadrangle, the name "Hornfels Point" applies to the ridge that extends for about 5 miles generally southwest from present Wheeler Peak.

Whipple Springs [MODOC]: *spring,* 3 miles south of White Horse (lat. 41°15'55" N, long. 121°23'50" W; sec. 33, T 40 N, R 5 E). Named on White Horse (1962) 15' quadrangle.

Whiskey Canyon [LASSEN]: *canyon,* drained by a stream that flows 5 miles to Madeline Plains 7.25 miles west-southwest of Termo (lat. 40°49'10" N, long. 120°35' W; sec. 11, T 34 N, R 12 E). Named on Grasshopper Valley (1954) 15' quadrangle.

Whiskey Canyon [PLUMAS]: *canyon,* drained by a stream that flows 2.5 miles to Sierra Valley 5.5 miles northwest of Chilcoot (lat. 39° 51'10" N, long. 120°13'10" W; near NW cor. sec. 17, T 23 N, R 16 E). Named on Chilcoot (1979) and Frenchman Lake (1979) 7.5' quadrangles.

Whiskey Hill [PLUMAS]: *peak,* 1.5 miles northwest of Cascade (lat. 39°43'05" N, long. 121°11'50" W; sec. 33, T 22 N, R 7 E). Named on Cascade (1948) 7.5' quadrangle.

White Cap [PLUMAS]: *peak,* 11 miles southeast of Quincy (lat. 39° 50'05" N, long. 120°47'05" W; at N line sec. 30, T 23 N, R 11 E). Altitude 6458 feet. Named on Blue Nose Mountain (1951) 7.5' quadrangle.

White Creek [PLUMAS]: *stream,* flows 1 mile to American Valley 1.5 miles west-northwest of Quincy (lat. 39°56'35" N, long. 120° 58'35" W; sec. 16, T 24 N, R 9 E). Named on Quincy (1950) 7.5' quadrangle.

Whitehead Slough [LASSEN]: *water feature,* enters Honey Lake 6 miles south-southeast of Litchfield (lat. 40°18'40" N, long. 120°19'30" W). Named on Litchfield (1954) 15' quadrangle.

White Horse [MODOC]: *locality,* 25 miles west-northwest of Adin along Great Northern Railroad (lat. 41°18'10" N, long. 121°23'50" W; near N line sec. 16, T 40 N, R 5 E). Named on White Horse (1962) 15' quadrangle. United States Board on Geographic Names (1965c, p. 13) rejected the form "Whitehorse" for the name. Postal authorities established White Horse post office in 1930, changed the name to Kinyon in 1952, and discontinued it in 1964; the name "Kinyon" was for the manager of the logging camp at the site (Salley, p. 113, 239).

White Horse Canyon [MODOC]: *canyon,* drained by a stream that flows 3.25 miles to lowlands along Parker Creek 7.5 miles east of Alturas (lat. 41°29'05" N, long. 120°24'15" W). Named on Dorris Reservoir (1963) and Shields Creek (1963) 7.5' quadrangles.

Whitehorse Creek [PLUMAS]: *stream,* flows nearly 2 miles to Bucks Creek 2 miles east-northeast of Bucks Lodge (lat. 39°53'15" N, long. 121°08'30" W; near S line sec. 36, T 24 N, R 7 E). Named on Bucks Lake (1979) 7.5' quadrangle.

White Horse Flat Reservoir [MODOC]: *intermittent lake,* 4 miles long, center 1.5 miles west-southwest of White Horse (lat. 41°18'05" N, long. 121°25'30" W). Named on White Horse (1962) 15' quadrangle. Called White Horse Res. on California Division of Highways' (1934) map. United States Board on Geographic Names (1965c, p. 13) approved the form "Whitehorse Flat Reservoir" for the name. Modoc Lava-Bed (1892) 1° quadrangle shows White Horse Valley at the place.

White Horse Mountains [MODOC]: *ridge,* mainly in Siskiyou County, but extends southeast into Modoc County 4 miles southwest of White Horse (lat. 41°16'10" N, long. 121°26'40" W). Named on White Horse (1962) 15' quadrangle.

White Horse Reservoir [LASSEN]: *lake,* 1000 feet long, 4.5 miles east of Cal Mountain (lat. 40°40'05" N, long. 121°04'40" W; near NE cor. sec. 4, T 32 N, R 8 E). Named on Harvey Mountain (1956) 15' quadrangle.

White Horse Reservoir: see **White Horse Flat Reservoir** [MODOC].

White Horse Valley: see **White Horse Flat Reservoir** [MODOC].

White Reservoir [MODOC]: *intermittent lake,* 0.5 mile long, 7 miles southeast of Canby (lat. 41°22'20" N, long. 120°46'40" W; near SE cor. sec. 23, T 41 N, R 10 E). Named on Canby (1961) 15' quadrangle.

Whit Flat [LASSEN]: *area,* 8 miles south of Adin [MODOC] (lat. 41° 04'50" N, long. 120°56'35" W; on N line sec. 4, T 37 N, R 9 E). Named on Adin (1962) 15' quadrangle.

Whitinger Mountain [LASSEN]: *peak,* 12 miles northwest of Termo (lat. 40°57'45" N, long. 120°39'05" W; at N line sec. 13, T 36 N, R 11 E). Altitude 7072 feet. Named on Grasshopper Valley (1954) 15' quadrangle.

Whitley's Ford: see **Lookout** [MODOC].

Whitlock Ravine [PLUMAS]: *canyon,* drained by a stream that flows 1.5 miles to Spanish Creek (1) 2.5 miles east-northeast of the village of Meadow Valley (lat. 39°57' N, long. 121°01' W; near N line sec. 18, T 24 N, R 9 E). Named on Meadow Valley (1980) and Quincy (1950) 7.5' quadrangles.

Whitney Reservoir [MODOC]: *intermittent lake,* 6000 feet long, 1.5 miles north-northwest of Hackamore (lat. 41°34'35" N, long. 121° 07'45" W; in and near sec. 11, T 43 N, R 7 E). Named on Hackamore (1952) 15' quadrangle.

Whittemore Ridge [MODOC]: *ridge,* north-trending, 3 miles long, 13 miles northwest of Alturas (lat. 41°38'20" N, long. 120°41'45" W). Named on Big Sage Reservoir (1962) 15' quadrangle.

Whittemore Spring [MODOC]: *spring,* 14 miles northwest of Alturas (lat. 41°39' N, long. 120°42' W; near E line sec. 16, T 44 N, R 11 E); the spring is near the north end of Whittemore Ridge. Named on Big Sage Reservoir (1962) 15' quadrangle.

Widgeon: see **Bayley** [MODOC].

Widow Lake [LASSEN]: *lake,* 1800 feet long, 10.5 miles south-southwest of Cal Mountain (lat. 40°32'15" N, long. 121°15'40" W; sec. 24, T 31 N, R 6 E). Named on Prospect Peak (1957) 15' quadrangle. United States Board on Geographic Names (1933, p. 817) rejected the name "Snake Lake" for the feature.

Widow Mountain [LASSEN]: *peak,* 8.5 miles west-northwest of Bieber (lat. 41°09'35" N, ong. 121°17'45" W; on E line sec. 5, T 38 N, R 6 E); the peak is 4 miles southwest of Widow Valley [MODOC]. Altitude 6321 feet. Named on Fall River Mills (1961) 15' quadrangle.

Widow Valley [MODOC]:

(1) *canyon,* 5.5 miles long, drained by Widow Valley Creek above a point 4 miles west of Lookout (lat. 41°12'45" N, long. 121°13'10" W; at S line sec. 13, T 39 N, R 6 E). Named on Bieber (1961) and Fall River Mills (1961) 15' quadrangles.

(2) *valley,* 8.5 miles west of Jacks Butte (lat. 41°34'30" N, long. 120°58' W). Named on Jacks Butte (1962) 15' quadrangle.

Widow Valley Creek [MODOC]: *stream,* flows 9.5 miles to Kramer Reservoir 3.5 miles west-southwest of Lookout (lat. 41°11'20" N, long. 121°12'45" W; sec. 30, T 39 N, R 7 E); the stream drains Widow Valley (1). Named on Bieber (1961) and Fall River Mills (1961) 15' quadrangles.

Widow Valley Mountains [LASSEN-MODOC]: *range,* 6.5 miles northwest of Bieber (lat. 41°10'45" N, long. 121°14' W); the range is south of Widow Valley [MODOC] (1) on Lassen-Modoc County line, mainly in Lassen County. Named on Bieber (1961) and Fall River Mills (1961) 15' quadrangles.

Wieland: see **Camp Wieland**, under **Mohawk Boys Camp** [PLUMAS].

Wiggle Tail [PLUMAS]: *creek,* flows 0.25 mile to Bucks Lake 2.5 miles north-northwest of Bucks Lodge (lat. 39°54'35" N, long. 121°11'10" W; sec. 27, T 24 N, R 7 E). Named on Bucks Lake (1979) 7.5' quadrangle.

Wilcox Spring [MODOC]: *spring,* 6.25 miles north of Blue Mountain (lat. 41°55'10" N, long. 120°52'15" W; sec. 18, T 47 N, R 10 E). Named on Steele Swamp (1962) 15' quadrangle.

Wilcox Valley [PLUMAS]: *valley,* 3.5 miles north of Kettle Rock at the head of Hungry Creek (lat. 40°11'25" N, long. 120°42'40" W; sec. 23, T 27 N, R 11 E). Named on Kettle Rock (1972) 7.5' quadrangle.

Wildcat Creek [PLUMAS]: *stream,* flows nearly 4 miles to Grizzly Creek (2) 4.25 miles south of Storrie (lat. 39°51'20" N, long. 121° 20'05" W; near S line sec. 8, T 23 N, R 6 E). Named on Soapstone Hill (1979) 7.5' quadrangle.

Wildcat Point [LASSEN]: *promontory,* 5 miles southwest of Pelican Point along the west side of Eagle Lake (lat. 40°34'40" N, long. 120°48'20" W; sec. 2, T 31 N, R 10 E). Named on Antelope Mountain (1956) 15' quadrangle.

Wildcat Ridge [PLUMAS]: *ridge,* generally south-trending, 4 miles long, 9 miles northeast of Kettle Rock (lat. 40°14'15" N, long. 120° 37'05" W). Named on Antelope Lake (1972), Diamond Mountain (1972), and Janesville (1972) 7.5' quadrangles.

Wild Cattle Mountain [PLUMAS]: *ridge,* south- to southeast-trending, 5.5 miles long, 10.5 miles south-southwest of Mount Harkness on Plumas-Tehama County line (lat. 40°21'30" N, long. 121°28'30" W). Named on Mount Harkness (1956) 15' quadrangle.

Wild Horse Creek [MODOC]: *stream,* heads in the State of Oregon and flows 4.5 miles in Modoc County to Fourmile Creek 7.5 miles north of Blue Mountain (lat. 46°56'15" N, long. 120°52'45" W; at S line sec. 1, T 47 N, R 9 E). Named on Steele Swamp (1962) 15' quadrangle.

Wild Horse Reservoir [LASSEN]: *lake,* 400 feet long, 12.5 miles east-northeast of Wendel (lat. 40°26'50" N, long. 120°02'20" W; near E line sec. 22, T 30 N, R 17 E). Named on Wendel (1954) 15' quadrangle.

Wild Horse Reservoir [MODOC]: *intermittent lake,* 2200 feet long, 8.5 miles north of Blue Mountain (lat. 41°57' N, long. 120°51'30" W; at NE cor. sec. 6, T 47 N, R 10 E); the feature is along Wild Horse Creek in Wild Horse Valley. Named on Steele Swamp (1962) 15' quadrangle.

Wild Horse Valley [MODOC]: *valley,* 8.5 miles north of Blue Mountain (lat. 41°56'10" N, long. 120°51'30" W); the valley is along Wild Horse Creek. Named on Steele Swamp (1962) 15' quadrangle.

Wilkinson Creek [MODOC]: *stream,* flows 3.5 miles to Surprise Valley 9.5 miles north-northwest of Cedarville (lat. 41°39'30" N, long. 120°13'30" W; near NE cor. sec. 26, T 44 N, R 15 E). Named on Cedarville (1962) and Davis Creek (1962) 15' quadrangles.

Willard Creek [LASSEN]: *stream,* flows 9 miles to Susan River 13 miles east-northeast of Westwood (lat. 40°23'40" N, long. 120°46'35" W; near NE cor. sec. 7, T 29 N, R 11 E). Named on Fredonyer Pass (1980) and Roop Mountain (1980) 7.5' quadrangles. Called Willard's Cr. on Honey Lake (1893) 1° quadrangle. Roop Mountain (1980) 7.5' quadrangle shows Willard ranch along the stream. East Fork enters from the southeast 2.5 miles upstream from the mouth of the main stream; it is nearly 4 miles long and is named on Fredonyer Pass (1980) 7.5' quadrangle. West Fork enters from the southwest 1.5 miles upstream from the mouth of the main stream; it is 4 miles long and is named on Fredonyer Pass (1980) and Roop Mountain (1980) 7.5' quadrangles.

Williams: see **Wade Williams Spring** [MODOC].

Williams Creek [LASSEN]: *stream,* flows nearly 4 miles to Susan River 13 miles east-northeast of Westwood (lat. 40°23'40" N, long. 120°46'30" W; at E line sec. 7, T 29 N, R 11 E). Named on Fredonyer Pass (1980) and Roop Mountain (1980) 7.5' quadrangles.

Williams Creek [PLUMAS]: *stream,* flows 6 miles to Wolf Creek 2 miles east of Greenville (lat. 40°08'20" N, long. 120°54'30" W; at W line sec. 6, T 26 N, R 10 E). Named on Greenville (1979) 7.5' quadrangle.

Williams Loop [PLUMAS]: *locality,* 1.5 miles northwest of Spring Garden along Western Pacific Railroad, where the line makes a 360° turn to gain elevation (lat. 39°54'35" N, long. 120°48'25" W; sec. 25, T 24 N, R 10 E). Named on Spring Garden (1950) 7.5' quadrangle.

Williams Ravine [PLUMAS]: *canyon,* drained by a stream that flows less than 1 mile to Lava Creek 2 miles east-northeast of Cascade (lat. 39°42'35" N, long. 121°08'35" W). Named on Cascade (1948) 7.5' quadrangle.

Williams Reservoir [LASSEN]: *water feature,* 15 miles southeast of Adin [MODOC] (lat. 41°01'15" N, long. 120°46'50" W; at S line sec. 23, T 37 N, R 10 E). Named on Adin (1962) 15' quadrangle.

Williams Reservoir [MODOC]: *intermittent lake,* 1.5 miles long, 8 miles west-southwest of Jacks Butte (lat. 41°32'45" N, long. 120° 56'45" W). Named on Jacks Butte (1962) 15' quadrangle.

Williams Valley [MODOC]: *valley,* 6.25 miles north-northeast of Jacks Butte (lat. 41°40'15" N, long. 120°45'10" W; in and near sec. 6, 7, T 44 N, R 11 E). Named on Big Sage Reservoir (1962) and Jacks Butte (1962) 15' quadrangles.

Williams Valley [PLUMAS]: *valley,* 2.25 miles north of Greenville along Williams Creek (lat. 40°10'20" N, long. 120°56'25" W; sec. 26, T 27 N, R 9 E). Named on Greenville (1979) 7.5' quadrangle.

Williams Valley Tank [MODOC]: *water feature,* 16 miles northwest of Alturas (lat. 41°40' N, long. 120°43'30" W; sec. 8, T 44 N, R 11 E); the feature is 1.5 miles east of Williams Valley. Named on Big Sage Reservoir (1962) 15' quadrangle.

Willow Creek [LASSEN]: *stream,* flows 16 miles from Willow Creek Valley to Susan River 2.5 miles west of Litchfield (lat. 40° 22'50" N, long. 120°26' W; near SW cor. sec. 8, T 29 N, R 14 E). Named on Litchfield (1954) and Susanville (1954) 15' quadrangles.

Willow Creek [LASSEN-MODOC]: *stream,* heads in Lassen County and flows 20 miles to Ash Creek 2.5 miles west of Adin in Modoc County [MODOC] (lat. 41°11'45" N, long. 120°59'40" W; sec. 25, T 39 N, R 8 E). Named on Adin (1962) and Hayden Hill (1956) 15' quadrangles. West Fork enters 12 miles north-northeast of Lava Peak; it is 3 miles long, lies entirely in Lassen County, and is named on Hayden Hill (1956) 15' quadrangle.

Willow Creek [MODOC]:

(1) *stream,* formed by the confluence of North Fork and Boles Creek, flows 4.5 miles to Clear Lake Reservoir 10.5 miles north-northeast of Double Head Mountain (lat. 41°54'05" N, long. 121° 04'25" W; sec. 20, T 47 N, R 8 E). Named on Clear Lake Reservoir (1951) 15' quadrangle. North Fork heads in the State of Oregon and is 18 miles long in Modoc County; it is named on Clear Lake Reservoir (1951) and Steele Swamp (1962) 15' quadrangles. On Alturas 1° quadrangle, present Boles Creek, part of present Fletcher Creek, and present Willow Creek (2) are called South Fork Willow Creek (1).

(2) *stream,* flows 11.5 miles to Fletcher Creek 6 miles west of South Mountain (lat. 41°50'10" N, long. 120°44'50" W; near N line sec. 18, T 46 N, R 11 E). Named on South Mountain (1962) 15' quadrangle. Alturas 1° quadrangle has the name "Henry Valley" along present Willow Creek (2) (lat. 41°53'30" N, long. 120° 44' W).

(3) *stream,* flows 12 miles to Goose Lake (1) 0.5 mile northwest of Willow Ranch (lat. 41°54'25" N, long. 120°21'50" W; at N line sec. 21, T 47 N, R 14 E). Named on Fort Bidwell (1962) and Willow Ranch (1962) 15' quadrangles. The stream, which goes through Fandango Valley, is called Fandango Creek on Alturas 1° quadrangle.

Willow Creek [PLUMAS]:

(1) *stream,* flows 6.5 miles to North Fork Feather River 6 miles south of Mount Harkness (lat. 40°20'50" N, long. 121°19'30" W; at E line sec. 29, T 29 N, R 6 E); the stream heads at Little Willow Lake and goes through Willow Lake. Named on Mount Harkness (1956) 15' quadrangle.

(2) *stream,* flows nearly 3 miles to Indian Creek (2) 7 miles northeast of Kettle Rock (lat. 40°13'05" N, long. 120°38'20" W; near NW cor. sec. 9, T 27 N, R 12 E). Named on Diamond Mountain (1972) and Kettle Rock (1972) 7.5' quadrangles.

(3) *stream,* flows 6 miles to Last Chance Creek (2) 4 miles north-northeast of Squaw Valley Peak (lat. 40°05'10" N, long. 120°22'35" W; near NW cor. sec. 26, T 26 N, R 14 E). Named on Ferris Creek (1977) and Squaw Valley Peak (1977) 7.5' quadrangles.

(4) *stream,* flows 4.5 miles to Middle Fork Feather River 7.5 miles southeast of Quincy (lat. 39°51'35" N, long. 120°50'50" W; sec. 15, T 23 N, R 10 E). Named on Blue Nose Mountain (1951), Onion Valley (1950), and Quincy (1950) 7.5' quadrangles.

(5) *stream,* flows 9 miles to Middle Fork Feather River 7 miles south of Bucks Lodge (lat. 39°46'40" N, long. 121°09'25" W; near E line sec. 11, T 22 N, R 7 E). Named on Haskins Valley (1980) 7.5' quadrangle.

(6) *stream,* flows nearly 2 miles to South Branch of Middle Fork Feather River 7.5 miles north-northwest of American House (lat. 39°44'50" N, long. 121°05'25" W; sec. 21, T 22 N, R 8 E). Named on American House (1948) and Dogwood Peak (1979) 7.5' quadrangles.

(7) *stream,* flows 10 miles to Middle Fork Feather River less than 0.5 mile east of Clio (lat. 39°44'40" N, long. 120°34'25" W; sec. 25, T 22 N, R 12 E). Named on Blairsden (1972) 7.5' quadrangle.

Willow Creek: see **Bidwell Creek** [MODOC]; **Willow Creek Valley** [LASSEN].

Willow Creek Homesite [PLUMAS]: *locality,* 5 miles south-southwest of Mount Harkness (lat. 40°21'35" N, long. 121°19'25" W; near W line sec. 21, T 29 N, R 6 E); the place is along Willow Creek (1). Named on Mount Harkness (1956) 15' quadrangle.

Willow Creek Meadow: see **Dry Valley Reservoir** [MODOC].

Willow Creek Valley [LASSEN]: *valley,* 9 miles southeast of Pelican Point (lat. 40°32'45" N, long. 120°37'45" W). Named on Fredonyer Peak (1954) 15' quadrangle. Honey Lake (1893) 1° quadrangle shows Willow Creek in the valley.

Willow Lake [LASSEN]: *intermittent lake,* 3400 feet long, 13 miles northeast of Observation Peak at California-Nevada State line (lat. 40°54'55" N, long. 120°00'05" W; sec. 12, T 35 N, R 17 E). Named on Observation Peak (1954) 15' quadrangle.

Willow Lake [PLUMAS]: *lake,* 2300 feet long, 3.5 miles west-southwest of Mount Harkness (lat. 40°24'15" N, long. 121°21'35" W; mainly in sec. 6, T 29 N, R 6 E); the lake is along Willow Creek (1). Named on Mount Harkness (1956) 15' quadrangle.

Willow Lake: see **Little Willow Lake** [PLUMAS].

Willow Ranch [MODOC]: *village,* 7.5 miles north-northeast of Alturas (lat. 41°54'10" N, long. 120°21'25" W; sec. 21, T 47 N, R 14 E). Named on Willow Ranch (1962) 15' quadrangle. Postal authorities established Willow Ranch post office in 1871, discontinued it in 1882, reestablished it in 1883, changed the name to Willowranch in 1896, moved it 1 mile north in 1900, and changed the name back to Willow Ranch in 1950 (Salley, p. 241). The name is from a nearby ranch (Cook, p. 96-97). The original service center with the name "Willow Ranch" was abandoned when a new narrow-gauge railroad took traffic from the old wagon road, but the name "Willow Ranch" was moved 2 miles and applied to a place on the railroad (Pease, p. 97).

Willow Ranch Creek [LASSEN]: *stream,* flows 5 miles to Long Valley (2) 0.5 mile west of Doyle (lat. 40°01'40" N, long. 120°06'45" W; near N line sec. 18, T 25 N, R 17 E). Named on Doyle (1954) 15' quadrangle. Honey Lake (1893) 1° quadrangle shows Willow Ranch situated at the mouth of present Willow Ranch Creek.

Willow Spring [LASSEN]:

(1) *spring,* 8.5 miles east-northeast of the village of Little Valley (lat. 40°56'30" N, long. 121°02'35" W; near W line sec. 22, T 36 N, R 8 E). Named on Little Valley (1957) 15' quadrangle.

(2) *spring,* 5 miles west of the village of Little Valley (lat. 40°53'10" N, long. 121°16'20" W; sec. 23, T 35 N, R 6 E). Named on Jellico (1957) 15' quadrangle.

(3) *spring,* 5 miles northeast of Lava Peak (lat. 40°53' N, long. 120° 49'40"

W; near E line sec. 22, T 35 N, R 10 E). Named on Hayden Hill (1956) 15' quadrangle.
(4) *spring,* 14 miles west-southwest of Pelican Point (lat. 40°31'45" N, long. 120°58'45" W; on E line sec. 20, T 31 N, R 9 E). Named on Antelope Mountain (1956) 15' quadrangle.
(5) *spring,* 10 miles northeast of Wendel (lat. 40°26'10" N, long. 120°05'10" W; sec. 29, T 30 N, R 17 E). Named on Wendel (1954) 15' quadrangle.

Willow Spring [PLUMAS]: *spring,* 5 miles north of Portola (lat. 39° 52' N, long. 120°28'05" W; near S line sec. 12, T 23 N, R 13 E). Named on Portola (1972) 7.5' quadrangle.

Willow Spring Canyon [MODOC]: *canyon,* drained by a stream that flows 3 miles to North Fork Parker Creek 13 miles east of Alturas (lat. 41°27'50" N, long. 120°17'05" W; sec. 19, T 42 N, R 15 E). Named on Shields Creek (1963) 7.5' quadrangle.

Willow Springs [LASSEN]: *spring,* 3.25 miles west-southwest of the village of Little Valley (lat. 40°52'40" N, long. 121°14'40" W; near SW cor. sec. 19, T 35 N, R 7 E). Named on Little Valley (1957) 15' quadrangle. United States Board on Geographic Names (1983b p. 7) approved the name "Wilson Spring" for the feature, and rejected the names "Willow Springs" and "Wilson Springs."

Wilson Reservoir [MODOC]: *lake,* 1200 feet long, 1.5 miles south of Canby (lat. 41°25'15" N, long. 120°52'15" W; on E line sec. 1, T 41 N, R 9 E). Named on Canby (1961) 15' quadrangle.

Wilson Spring: see **Willow Springs** [LASSEN].

Wilson Valley [MODOC]: *valley,* 16 miles north-northeast of Double Head Mountain along Rock Creek (1) (lat. 41°58'15" N, long. 121° 00'45" W). Named on Clear Lake Reservoir (1951) and Steele Swamp (1962) 15' quadrangles.

Windmill Flat [LASSEN]:
(1) *area,* 11.5 miles south of Adin [MODOC] (lat. 41°01'45" N, long. 120°56'30" W; in and near sec. 21, T 37 N, R 9 E). Named on Adin (1962) 15' quadrangle.
(2) *area,* 11.5 miles north-northwest of Lava Peak (lat. 40°59'20" N, long. 120°56'30" W; sec. 4, T 36 N, R 9 E). Named on Hayden Hill (1956) 15' quadrangle.

Windy Flat [LASSEN]: *area,* 18 miles east of Madeline (lat. 41°02'10" N, long. 120°08'10" W; near NE cor. sec. 34, T 37 N, R 16 E). Named on Boot Lake (1962) 7.5' quadrangle.

Windy Gap Well [LASSEN]: *well,* 2.25 miles east of Cal Mountain (lat. 40°39'40" N, long. 121°07'20" W; sec. 6, T 32 N, R 8 E). Named on Harvey Mountain (1956) 15' quadrangle.

Windy Hollow [LASSEN]: *area,* 10.5 miles southeast of Cal Mountain (lat. 40°32'40" N, long. 121°03'15" W; at and near SW cor. sec. 14, T 31 N, R 8 E). Named on Harvey Mountain (1956) 15' quadrangle.

Wing Reservoir [LASSEN]: *lake,* 200 feet long, 10.5 miles north-northeast of Lava Peak (lat. 40°57'15" N, long. 120°46'35" W; near W line sec. 13, T 36 N, R 10 E). Named on Hayden Hill (1956) 15' quadrangle.

Winters Creek [PLUMAS]: *stream,* flows 2.25 miles to Middle Fork Feather River 6.5 miles south-southeast of Quincy (lat. 39°51' N, long. 120°53'50" W; near SE cor. sec. 18, T 23 N, R 10 E). Named on Onion Valley (1950) 7.5' quadrangle.

Winthrop House [PLUMAS]: *locality,* 3.25 miles southwest of American House (lat. 39°37' N, long. 121°03'45" W). Named on Bidwell Bar (1897) 30' quadrangle.

Wire Corral Spring [LASSEN]: *spring,* 8.5 miles east-northeast of Observation Peak (lat. 40°50'10" N, long. 120°00'30" W; near W line sec. 1, T 34 N, R 17 E). Named on Observation Peak (1954) 15' quadrangle.

Wire Lake [LASSEN]: *dry lake,* 4700 feet long, 24 miles east of Madeline (lat. 41°04'25" N, long. 120°01'20" W; sec. 14, 15, T 37 N, R 17 E). Named on Little Hat Mountain (1962) 7.5' quadrangle.

Wire Spring [LASSEN]:
(1) *spring,* 7 miles north of Termo (lat. 40°57'55" N, long. 120°26'10" W; near SE cor. sec. 11, T 36 N, R 13 E). Named on Ravendale (1954) 15' quadrangle.
(2) *spring,* 10 miles west-northwest of Karlo (lat. 40°36' N, long. 120°29'30" W; near E line sec. 27, T 32 N, R 13 E). Named on Karlo (1954) 15' quadrangle.

Wisconsin Ravine [PLUMAS]: *canyon,* drained by a stream that flows 1.5 miles to Slate Creek (3) 1.5 miles east-southeast of La Porte (lat. 39°40'10" N, long. 120°57'25" W; sec. 22, T 21 N, R 9 E). Named on La Porte (1951) 7.5' quadrangle.

Witcher Creek [MODOC]: *stream,* flows 7.25 miles to Clover Swale Creek 5 miles east-northeast of Canby (lat. 41°28'45" N, long. 120° 47' W; sec. 14, T 42 N, R 10 E). Named on Canby (1961) and Jacks Butte (1962) 15' quadrangles.

Wolf Creek [PLUMAS]: *stream,* flows 15 miles to Indian Creek (2) 2 miles northeast of Crescent Mills (lat. 40°07'10" N, long. 120°53'10" W). Named on Canyondam (1979), Crescent Mills (1980), and Greenville (1979) 7.5' quadrangles.

Wonderland: see **Chester** [PLUMAS].

Wood Creek: see **Bare Creek** [LASSEN].

Wood Flat Reservoir [MODOC]: *lake,* 3700 feet long, 7.25 miles north of Big Sage Reservoir (lat. 41°35'20" N, long. 120°31'10" W; on S line sec. 6, T 43 N, R 13 E). Named on Big Sage Reservoir (1962) 15' quadrangle.

Workmans Bar [PLUMAS]: *locality,* 4 miles northeast of Storrie along North Fork Feather River (lat. 39°57'45" N, long. 121°16'40" W; sec. 2, T 24 N, R 6 E). Named on Pulga (1957) 15' quadrangle.

Worley Mountain: see **Roop Mountain** [LASSEN].

Wright Lake: see **Clear Lake Reservoir** [MODOC].

– X - Y –

Yankee Hill [PLUMAS]: *relief feature,* 2 miles east of La Porte (lat. 39°41'15" N, long. 120°56'40" W; on S line sec. 11, T 21 N, R 9 E). Named on La Porte (1951) 7.5' quadrangle.

Yard House [PLUMAS]: *locality,* 1 mile north of Cascade (lat. 39° 42'50" N, long. 121°10'30" W; near SE cor. sec. 34, T 22 N, R 7 E). Named on Cascade (1948) 7.5' quadrangle.

Yellow Creek [PLUMAS]: *stream,* flows 22 miles to North Fork Feather River 7 miles southwest of Caribou at Belden (lat. 40°00'25" N, long. 121°14'55" W; near E line sec. 24, T 25 N, R 6 E). Named on Jonesville (1958) 15' quadrangle, and on Almanor (1979) and Caribou (1979) 7.5' quadrangles. Gudde (1975, p. 200) listed a mining place called Lower Indian Bar that was located along North Fork Feather River 2 miles below the mouth of Yellow Creek.

Yellow Jacket Spring [MODOC]: *spring,* 10 miles east of Adin (lat. 41°11'35" N, long. 120°45'20" W; sec. 30, T 39 N, R 11 E). Named on Adin (1962) 15' quadrangle.

Yellowjacket Spring [MODOC]:
(1) *spring,* 6.25 miles east-northeast of Crank Mountain (lat. 41°24'55" N, long. 121°01'55" W; on N line sec. 10, T 41 N, R 8 E). Named on Crank Mountain (1962) 15' quadrangle.
(2) *spring,* 11 miles west of Likely (lat. 41°13'20" N, long. 120°42'30" W; sec. 16, T 39 N, R 11 E). Named on Likely (1962) 15' quadrangle.

Yellow Mountain [MODOC]: *peak,* 8 miles north-northwest of Fort Bidwell (lat. 41°58' N, long. 120°12'25" W; near SW cor. sec. 1, T 47 N, R 15 E). Named on Fort Bidwell (1962) 15' quadrangle.

York Creek [PLUMAS]: *stream,* flows 1.5 miles to East Branch of North Fork Feather River 2 miles west of Twain (lat. 40°01'20" N, long. 121°06'20" W; at N line sec. 20, T 25 N, R 8 E). Named on Twain (1980) 7.5' quadrangle.

Young: see **Bob Young Flat** [MODOC].

Young Falls [LASSEN]: *waterfall,* 10.5 miles west-southwest of Bieber along Pit River (lat. 41°02'35" N, long. 121°19' W; sec. 18, T 37 N, R 6 E). Named on Fall River Mills (1961) 15' quadrangle.

– Z –

Zamboni Hot Springs [LASSEN]: *spring,* 2 miles south-southeast of Constantia (lat. 39°55'20" N, long. 120°01'25" W; sec. 24, T 24 N, R 17 E). Named on Constantia (1977) 7.5' quadrangle.

Zink: see **Daniel Zink Campground** [PLUMAS].

Zumwalt Flat [PLUMAS]: *area,* 11 miles southeast of Quincy along Nelson Creek (lat. 39°48'45" N, long. 120°49' W). Named on Blue Nose Mountain (1951) 7.5' quadrangle.

NORTHEAST REGION
LASSEN, MODOC AND PLUMAS COUNTIES

REFERENCES CITED

BOOKS AND ARTICLES

Amesbury, Robert. 1967. *Nobles' emigrant trail.* (Author), 37 p.

Anderson, Winslow. 1892. *Mineral springs and health resorts of California.* San Francisco: The Bancroft Company, 347 p.

Bancroft, Hubert Howe. 1888. *History of California, Volume VI, 1848-1859.* San Francisco: The History Company, Publishers, 787 p.

Barry, Pat. 1988. "Pro pelle cutem." *Journal of the Modoc County Historical Society,* No. 10, p. 5-9.

Brown, William S. 1951. *California northeast, The bloody ground.* Oakland, California: Biobooks, 207 p.

Bruff, J. Goldsborough. 1944. *Gold rush, The journals, drawings, and other papers of J. Goldsborough Bruff.* (Edited by Georgia Willis Reed and Ruth Gains.) New York: Columbia University Press, (2 volumes) 1400 p.

Butler, C.P. 1963. "The Goose Lake fragments." *Proceedings of the California Academy of Sciences* (series 4), v. 32, no. 9, p. 291-313.

California Division of Highways. 1934. *California highway transportation survey, 1934.* Sacramento: Department of Public Works, Division of Highways, 130 p. + appendices.

Cook, Fred S. *History of Modoc County.* Volcano, California: California Traveler, Inc., 104 p.

Coy, Owen C. 1923. *California county boundaries.* Berkeley: California Historical Survey Commission, 335 p.

Diller, Joseph Silas. 1891. *Late volcanic eruption in northern California, and its peculiar lava.* (United States Geological Survey Bulletin No. 79.) Washington: Government Printing Office, 33 p.

Frazer, Robert W. 1965. *Forts of the West.* Norman: University of Oklahoma Press, 246 p.

Frickstad, Walter N. 1955. *A century of California post offices, 1848 to 1954.* Oakland, California: Philatelic Research Society, 395 p.

Garate, Donald T. 1982. *Termo to Madeline.* Ravendale, California: (Author), 436 p.

Gudde, Erwin G. 1949. *California place names.* Berkeley and Los Angeles: University of California Press, 431 p.

_____1969. *California place names.* Berkeley and Los Angeles: University of California Press, 416 p.

_____1975. *California gold camps.* Berkeley, Los Angeles, London: University of California Press, 467 p,

Hanna, Phil Townsend. 1951. *The dictionary of California land names.* Los Angeles: The Automobile Club of Southern California, 392 p.

Hart, James D. 1978. *A companion to California.* New York: Oxford University Press, 504 p.

Hill, James M. 1915. *Some mining districts in northeastern California and northwestern Nevada.* (United States Geological Survey Bulletin 594.) Washington: Government Printing Office, 200 p.

Hoover, Mildred Brooke, Rensch, Hero Eugene, and Rensch, Ethel Grace. 1966. *Historic spots in California.* (Third edition, revised by William N. Abeloe.) Stanford, California: Stanford University Press, 642 p.

Laird, Irma W. 1971. *The Modoc country.* Alturas, California: (Author), 147 p.

McArthur, Lewis A. 1974. *Oregon geographic names.* (Fourth edition, revised and enlarged by Lewis L. McArthur.) Portland, Oregon: Oregon Historical Society, 835 p.

McKevitt, Jerry. 1964. "Gold Lake myth brought civilization to Plumas County." *Journal of the West,* v. 3, no. 4, p. 489-500.

Payne, Robert W. 1975. *Holden Dick—The lost mine in the Warner Mountains of California.* Mountain View, California: Bob the Globetrotter, 41 p.

Pease, Robert W. 1965. "Modoc County, A geographic time continuum on the California volcanic tableland." *University of California Publications in Geography,* v. 17, 304 p.

Plumas County Historical Society. 1961. *The history of mining in the Plumas Eureka State Park..* (Plumas County Historical Society Publication no. 3.) (No place), 43 p.

Preston, E.B. 1890a. "Lassen County." *Tenth annual report of the State Mineralogist, for the year ending December 1, 1890.* Sacramento: California State Mining Bureau, p. 272-276.

_____1890b. "Modoc County." *Tenth annual report of the State Mineralogist, for the year ending December 1, 1890.* Sacramento: California State Mining Bureau, p. 332-335.

_____1890c. "Plumas County." *Tenth annual report of the State Mineralogist, for the year ending December 1, 1890.* Sacramento: California State Mining Bureau, p. 466-495.

Purdy, Tim I. 1983. *Sagebrush reflections, The history of Amedee and Honey Lake.* Susanville, California: Sagebrush Reflections, 62 p.

_____1988. *Purdy's Eagle Lake.* Susanville, California: Lahontan Images, 136 p.

Ray, Verne F. 1963. *Primitive pragmatists, The Modoc Indians of northern California.* Seattle: University of Washington Press, 237 p.

Salley, H.E. 1977. *History of California post offices, 1849-1976.* La Mesa, California: Postal History Associates, Inc., 300 p.

Schulz, Paul E. 1949. *Stories of Lassen's place names.* Mineral, California: Loomis Museum Association, 57 p.

Stewart, George R. 1970. *American place-names, A concise and selective dictionary for the continental United States of America.* New York: Oxford University Press, 550 p.

Symons, Thomas W. 1878. "Executive and descriptive report of Lieutenant Thomas W. Symons, Corps of Engineers, on the operations of Party No. 1, California section, Field season of 1877." *Annual report upon the geographical surveys of the territory of the United States west of the 100th meridian, in the states and territories of California, Colorado, Kansas, Nebraska, Nevada, Oregon, Texas, Arizona, Idaho, Montana, New Mexico, Utah, Washington, and Wyoming.* (Appendix NN of *The Annual Report of the Chief of Engineers for 1878.*) Washington: Government Printing Office, p. 113-120.

Tillman, S.E. 1877. "Executive and descriptive report of Lieutenant Saml. E. Tillman, Corps of Engineers, on the operations of Party No. 1, California section, Field season of 1876." *Annual report upon the geographical surveys west of the one-hundredth meridian in the states and territories of California, Oregon, Nevada, Texas, Arizona, Colorado, Idaho, Montana, New Mexico, Utah, and Wyoming.* (Appendix NN of *The Annual Report of the Chief of Engineers for 1877.*) Washington: Government Printing Office, p. 1253-1256.

Tucker, W. Burling. 1919. "Lassen County." *Report XV of the State Mineralogist.* Sacramento: California State Mining Bureau, p. 226-238

United States Board on Geographic Names (under name "United States Geographic Board"). 1933. *Sixth report of the United States Geographic Board, 1890 to 1932.* Washington: Government Printing Office, 834 p.

_____1950. *Decisions on names in the United States and Alaska* rendered *during April, May, and June 1950.* (Decision list no. 5006.) Washington: Department of the Interior, 47 p.

_____1954. *Decisions on names in the United States, Alaska and Puerto Rico, Decisions rendered from July 1950 to May 1954.* (Decision list no. 5401.) Washington: Department of the Interior, 115 p.

_____1960a. *Decisions on names in the United States and Puerto Rico, Decisions rendered in May, June, July, and August, 1959.* (Decision list no. 5903.) Washington: Department of the Interior, 79 p.

_____1960b. *Decisions on names in the United States, Decisions rendered from September 1959 through December 1959.* (Decision list no. 5904.) Washington: Department of the Interior, 68 p.

_____1960c. *Decisions on names in the United States and The Virgin Islands, Decisions rendered from May 1960 through August 1960.* (Decision list no. 6002.) Washington: Department of the Interior, 77 p.

_____1963. *Decisions on geographic names in the United States, May through August 1963.* (Decision list no. 6302.) Washington: Department of the Interior, 81 p.

_____1964a. *Decisions on geographic names in the United States, September through December 1963.* (Decision list no. 6303.) Washington: Department of the Interior, 66 p.

_____1964b. *Decisions on geographic names in the United States, January through April 1964.* (Decision list no. 6401.) Washington: Department of the Interior, 74 p.

_____1964c. *Decisions on geographic names in the United States, May through August 1964.* (Decision list no. 6402.) Washington: Department of the Interior, 85 p.

_____1965a. *Decisions on geographic names in the United States, September through December 1964.* (Decision list no. 6403.) Washington: Department of the Interior, 66 p.

_____1965b. *Decisions on geographic names in the United States, January through March 1965.* (Decision list no. 6501.) Washington: Department of the Interior, 85 p.

_____1965c. *Decisions on geographic names in the United States, April through June 1965.* (Decision list no. 6502.) Washington: Department of the Interior, 39 p.

_____1965d. *Decisions on geographic names in the United States, July through September 1965.* (Decision list no. 6503.) Washington: Department of the Interior, 74 p.

_____1968a. *Decisions on geographic names in the United States, October through December 1967.* (Decision list no. 6704.) Washington: Department of the Interior, 46 p.

_____1968b. *Decisions on geographic names in the United States, January through March 1968.* (Decision list no. 6801.) Washington: Department of the Interior, 51 p.

_____1969. *Decisions on geographic names in the United States, October through December 1968.* (Decision list no. 6804.) Washington: Department of the Interior, 33 p.

_____1970. *Decisions on geographic names in the United States, July through September 1970.* (Decision list no. 7003.) Washington: Department of the Interior, 15 p.

_____1973a. *Decisions on geographic names in the United States, October through December 1972.* (Decision list no. 7204.) Washington: Department of the Interior, 15 p.

_____1973b. *Decisions on geographic names in the United States, April through June 1973.* (Decision list no. 7302.) Washington: Department of the Interior, 16 p.

_____1974a. *Decisions on geographic names in the United States, October through December 1973.* (Decision list no. 7304.) Washington: Department of the Interior, 15 p.

_____1974b. *Decisions on geographic names in the United States, January through March 1974.* (Decision list no. 7401.) Washington: Department of the Interior, 27 p.

_____1975. *Decisions on geographic names in the United States, January through March 1975.* (Decision list no. 7501.) Washington: Department of the Interior, 36 p.

_____1977a. *Decisions on geographic names in the United States, October through December 1976.* (Decision list no. 7604.) Washington: Department of the Interior, 34 p.

_____1977b. *Decisions on geographic names in the United States, January through March 1977.* (Decision list no. 7701.) Washington: Department of the Interior, 32 p.

_____1977c. *Decisions on geographic names in the United States, April through June 1977.* (Decision list no. 7702.) Washington: Department of the Interior, 40 p.

_____1978a. *Decisions on geographic names in the United States, October through December 1977.* (Decision list no. 7704.) Washington: Department of the Interior, 29 p.

_____1978b. *Decisions on geographic names in the United States, April through June 1978.* (Decision list no. 7802.) Washington: Department of the Interior, 30 p.

_____1979. *Decisions on geographic names in the United States, January through March 1979.* (Decision list no. 7901.) Washington: Department of the Interior, 27 p.

_____1981. *Decisions on geographic names in the United States, October through December, 1980.* (Decision list no. 8004.) Washington: Department of the Interior, 21 p.

_____1982a. *Decisions on geographic names in the United States, October through December 1981.* (Decision list no. 8104.) Washington: Department of the Interior, 26 p.

_____1982b. *Decisions on geographic names in the United States, April through June 1982.* (Decision list no. 8202.) Washington: Department of the Interior, 21 p.

_____1983a. *Decisions on geographic names in the United States, October through December 1982.* (Decision list no. 8204.) Washington: Department of the Interior, 26 p.

_____1983b. *Decisions on geographic names in the United States, January through March 1983.* (Decision list no. 8301.) Washington: Department of the Interior, 33 p.

_____1983c. *Decisions on geographic names in the United States, April through June 1983.* (Decision list no. 8302.) Washington: Department of the Interior, 29 p.

_____1983d. *Decisions on geographic names in the United States, July through September 1983.* (Decision list no. 8303.) Washington: Department of the Interior, 26 p.

_____1986. *Decisions on geographic names in the United States, April through June 1986.* (Decision list no. 8602.) Washington: Department of the Interior, 10 p.

_____1988. *Decisions on geographic names in the United States, April through June 1988.* (Decision list no. 8802.) Washington: Department of the Interior, 19 p.

_____1989a. *Decisions on geographic names in the United States, January through March 1989.* (Decision list no. 8901.) Washington: Department of the Interior. 9 p.

_____1989b. *Decisions on geographic names in the United States, April through June 1989.* (Decision list no. 8902.)Washington: Department of the Interior, 11 p.

_____1989c. *Decisions on geographic names in the United States, October through December 1989.* (Decision list no. 8904.) Washington: Department of the Interior, 9 p.

_____1990. *Decisions on geographic names in the United States.* (Decision list 1990.) Washington: Department of the Interior, 35 p.

_____1991. *Decisions on geographic names in the United States.* (Decision list 1991.) Washington: Department of the Interior, 40 p.

Uzes, Francois D. *Chaining the land, A history of surveying in California.* Sacramento, California: Landmark Enterprises, 315 p.

Waring, Gerald A. 1915. *Springs of California.* (United States Geological Survey Water-Supply Paper 338.) Washington: Government Printing Office, 410 p.

Wheeler, George M. 1878. *Annual report upon the geographical surveys of the territory of the United States west of the 100th meridian, in the states and territories of California, Colorado, Kansas, Nebraska, Nevada, Oregon, Texas, Arizona, Idaho, Montana, New Mexico, Utah, Washington, and Wyoming.* (Appendix NN of *The Annual Report of the Chief of Engineers for 1878.*) Washington: Government Printing Office, 234 p.

_____1879. *Annual report upon the geographical surveys of the territory of the United States west of the 100th meridian, in the states and territories of California, Colorado, Kansas, Nebraska, Nevada, Oregon, Texas, Arizona, Idaho, Montana, New Mexico, Utah, Washington, and Wyoming.* (Appendix OO of *The Annual Report of the Chief of Engineers for 1879.*) Washington: Government Printing Office, 340 p.

Whitney, J.D. 1865. *Report of progress and synopsis of the field-work, from 1860 to 1864.* (Geological Survey of California, Geology, Volume I.) Published by authority of the Legislature of California, 498 p.

Windeler, Adolphus. 1969. *The California gold rush diary of a German sailor.* (Edited by W. Turrentine Jackson.) Berkeley, California: Howell-North Books, 236 p.

QUADRANGLE MAPS

(All maps published by United States Geological Survey. Dates identify the editions of the maps. If a reprinted or revised map was used, the year of reprinting or revision is given in parentheses, unless the reprinted or revised map is cited specifically in the text.)

Adin 15'—1962.
Almanor 15'—1955.
7.5'—1979.
Alturas 1°x 2°—1954 (limited revision 1962).
1°—(No date.)
15'—1961.
American House 7.5'—1948.
Antelope Lake 7.5'—1972.
Antelope Mountain 15'—1956.
Antelope Valley 7.5'—1981.
Babcock Peak 7.5'—1972.
Beckwourth Pass 7.5'—1975.
Bidwell Bar 30'—1897 (reprinted 1928).
Bieber 15'—1961.
Big Sage Reservoir 15'—1962.
Blairsden 15'—1943 (reprinted 1948); 1956.
7.5'—1972.
Blue Nose Mountain 7.5'—1951.
Boot Lake 7.5'—1962.
Bucks Lake 15'—1950.
7.5'—1979.
Calpine 7.5'—1981.
Canby 15'—1961.
Canyondam 7.5'—1979.
Caribou 7.5'—1979.
Cascade 7.5'—1948.
Cedarville 15'—1962.
Chester 15'—1956.
7.5'—1979.
Chico 1°x 2°—1958 (limited revision 1966).
Chilcoot 15'—1950.

7.5'—1979.
Clear Lake Reservoir 15'—1951.
Clio 7.5'—1981.
Cold Spring Mountain 7.5'—1962.
Constantia 7.5'—1977.
Crank Mountain 15'—1962.
Crescent Mills 7.5'—1980.
Crocker Mountain 7.5'—1972.
Davis Creek 15'—1962.
Diamond Mountain 7.5'—1972.
Dixie Mountain 7.5'—1972.
Dogwood Peak 7.5'—1979.
Dorris Reservoir 7.5'—1963.
Downieville 30'—1897 (reprinted 1946).
Doyle 15'—1954.
Eagle Peak 7.5'—1963.
Eagleville 7.5'—1963.
Emerson Peak 7.5'—1962.
Evans Canyon 7.5'—1978.
Fall River Mills 15'—1961.
Ferris Creek 7.5'— 1977.
Fort Bidwell 15'—1962.
Fredonyer Pass 7.5'—1980.
Fredonyer Peak 15'—1954.
Frenchman Lake 7.5'—1979.
Genesee Valley 7.5'—1972.
Gold Lake 7.5'—1981.
Grasshopper Valley 15'—1954.
Greenville 15'—1950.
7.5'—1979.
Grizzly Valley 7.5'—1972.
Hackamore 15'—1952.
Halls Flat 30'—1939 (reprinted 1948).
Hansen Island 7.5'—1963.
Harvey Mountain 15'—1956.
Haskins Valley 7.5'—1980.
Hayden Hill 15'—1956.
Honey Lake 1°—1893 (reprinted 1930).
Jacks Butte 15'—1962.
Janesville 7.5'—1972.
Jellico 15'—1957.
Jess Valley 7.5'—1962.
Johnsville 7.5'—1972.
Jonesville 15'—1958.
Karlo 15'—1954.
Kettle Rock 15'— 1950.
7.5'—1972.
Kimshew Point 7.5'—1979.
La Porte 7.5'—1951.
Lassen Peak 1°—1894 (reprinted 1905).
Likely 15'—1962.
Litchfield 15'—1954.
Little Hat Mountain 7.5'—1962.
Little Juniper Reservoir 7.5'—1963.
Little Valley 15'—1957.
Loyalton 15'—1955.
7.5'—1981.
Madeline 7.5'—1962.
McKesick Peak 7.5'—1978.
Meadow Valley 7.5'—1980.
Milford 15'—1950.
7.5'—1977.
Modoc Lava-Bed 1°—1892.
Moonlight Peak 7.5'—1980.
Mount Fillmore 7.5'—1951.
Mount Harkness 15'—1956.
Mount Ingalls 7.5'—1972.
Observation Peak 15'—1954.
Onion Valley 7.5'—1950.
Pegleg Mountain 7.5'—1980.
Portola 15'—1950.
7.5'—1972.
Prospect Peak 15'—1957.
Pulga 15'—1957.
7.5'—1979.
Quincy 15'—1951.
7.5'—1950 (photorevised 1975).
Ravendale 15'—1954.
Reconnaissance Peak 7.5'—1972.
Red Cinder 7.5'—1979.
Roop Mountain 7.5'—1980.
Shields Creek 7.5'—1963.
Shinn Mountain 15'—1954.
Sierra City 15'—1955.
Sierraville 30'—1894 (reprinted 1903).
Snake Lake 7.5'—1962.
Soapstone Hill 7.5'—1979.
Soup Creek 7.5'—1963.
South Mountain 15'—1962.
Spring Garden 7.5'—1950 (photorevised 1975).
Squaw Valley Peak 7.5'—1977.
Standish 7.5'—1972.
Steele Swamp 15'—1962.
Stony Ridge 7.5'—1978.
Storrie 7.5'—1979.
Strawberry Valley 7.5'—1948.
Susanville 1°x 2°—1962.
15'—1954.
Swain Mountain 7.5'—1979.
Taylorsville 7.5'—1980.
Timber Mountain 15'—1952.
Tulelake 15'—1951.
Tule Mountain 7.5'—1967.
Twain 7.5'—1980.
Warren Peak 7.5'—1963.
Wendel 15'—1954.
Westwood 15'—1955.
Westwood East 7.5'—1980.
Westwood West 7.5'—1980.
White Horse 15'—1962.
Willow Ranch 15'—1962.

MISCELLANEOUS MAPS

Bancroft. 1864. "Bancroft's map of the Pacific States." Compiled by Wm. H. Knight. Published by H.H. Bancroft & Co., Booksellers and Stationers, San Francisco, Cal.
California Division of Highways. 1934. (Appendix "A" *of* California Division of Highways.)
California Mining Bureau. 1909a. "Modoc and Lassen Counties." (*In* California State Mining Bureau Bulletin 56.)
_____1909b. "Butte and Plumas Counties." (*In* California State Mining Bureau Bulletin 56.)
_____1910. "Map of California showing the approximate location of the principal mineral deposits." Compiled by the State Mining Bureau.
_____1917a. (Untitled map *in* California State Mining Bureau Bulletin 74, p. 159.)
_____1917b. (Untitled map *in* California State Mining Bureau Bulletin 74, p. 161.)
Colton. 1855. "California." J.H. Colton & Co., New York.
Fremont. 1845. "Map of an exploring expedition to the Rocky Mountains in the year 1842 and to Oregon & North California in the years 1843-44." By Brevet Capt. J.C. Frémont.
_____1848. "Map of Oregon and Upper California from the surveys of John Charles Frémont, and other authorities." Drawn by Charles Preuss. Washington City.
Goddard. 1857. "Britton & Rey's map of the State of California." By George H. Goddard.
Hill. 1915. "Sketch map of High Grade mining district, Modoc County, Cal." (Plate V *in* Hill.)
Rogers and Johnston. 1857. "State of California." By Prof. H.D. Rodgers & A. Keith Johnston.
Sage. 1846. "Map of Oregon, California, New Mexico, N.W. Texas, & the proposed territory of Ne-Bras-ka." By Rufus B. Sage.
Steptoe. 1855. "Map showing the different routes travelled over by the detachments of the overland command in the spring of 1855 from Salt Lake City to the Bay of San Francisco."
United States Geological Survey. 1893a. "Genesee map." (Reprinted 1927.)
_____1893b. "Taylorsville map." (Reprinted 1940.)
_____1907. "Indian Valley map."
Wheeler. 1877. "Parts of N.E. California & N.W. Nevada." (Atlas Sheet No. 38 (D).)
Williamson and Abbott. 1855. "Map No. 1, from San Francisco Bay to the northern boundary of California." (In *Reports of explorations and surveys, to ascertain the most practicable and economical route for a railroad from the Mississippi River to the Pacific Ocean.* Volume XI. 1861.)

Part Four
South Sacramento Valley Region

Amador, Colusa, El Dorado, Nevada, Placer, Sacramento, Sierra, Sutter, Yolo and Yuba Counties

Part Four—South Sacramento Valley Region

South Sacramento Valley Region Amador, Colusa, El Dorado, Nevada, Placer, Sacramento, Sierra, Sutter, Yolo and Yuba Counties

Regional Setting

General.—This section concerns geographic features in ten counties—Amador, Colusa, El Dorado, Nevada, Placer, Sacramento, Sierra, Sutter, Yolo, and Yuba—that lie in and near the south part of Sacramento Valley. Townships (T) and Ranges (R) refer to Mount Diablo Base and Meridian. Sacramento Valley is the north part of the Central Valley, or Great Valley, of California, and takes its name from Sacramento River, which drains it. The whole Central Valley is called Buena Ventura Valley on Wilkes' (1841) map. The Sierra Nevada is on the east side of Sacramento Valley, and other ranges separate the valley from the coast. Garces gave the name "Sierra de San Marcos" to the present Sierra Nevada in 1776 (Boyd, p. 3), Wilkes (p. 44) called the feature California Range in 1841, Lyman (p. 307) called it "Sierra Nevada, or Snowy Mountains" in 1849, and Kip (p. 46) called it Snowy Range in 1850. United States Board on Geographic Names (1933, p. 692) ruled against the form "Sierra Nevadas" for the name of the range. Whitney (1865, p. 2) pointed out that the feature long was known to the Spaniards as Sierra Nevada, or Snowy Range, because "the most distant and loftiest elevations are never entirely bare of snow, and for a large portion of the year are extensively covered with it." The map on the facing page shows the location of the South Sacramento Valley Region and the counties in it.

Amador County.—Amador County extends westward from near the crest of the Sierra Nevada into the Central Valley, generally between Cosumnes River and Mokelumne River. The state legislature created the county in 1854 from that part of previously established Calaveras County that lay north of Mokelumne River; later additions to the territory of the county came from El Dorado County in 1855, 1857, and 1863, before the east part of Amador County was lost to newly formed Alpine County in 1864 (Coy, p. 66-67). Jackson has been the county seat from the beginning. The name "Amador" commemorates Jose Maria Amador, for whom Amador City and Amador Creek were named (Hoover, Rensch, and Rensch, p. 29).

Colusa County.—Colusa County extends westward from lowlands along Sacramento River into the ranges that separate Sacramento Valley from the coast. Colusi County (as it then was called) was created in 1850, but it was not organized until 1851, when the county seat was placed at Monroeville; Monroeville now is in Glenn County, and nearly all of the present territory of Colusa County lies south of the land included in the original county boundaries (Coy, p. 83-91). The county name is from an Indian village that was situated at the site of the modern town of Colusa (Kroeber, p. 39). The county name "Colusi" was changed to "Colusa" in 1854, the same year that the county seat was moved to the town of Colusa (Hart, J.D., p. 90).

El Dorado County.—El Dorado County is between the State of Nevada and the foothills of the Sierra Nevada east of Sacramento Valley. The first state legislature created the county in 1850; some of the original territory of El Dorado County was lost to Amador County and Alpine County in the 1850's and 1860's, and El Dorado-Placer County line was adjusted in 1863 and 1913 (Coy, p. 97-100). The county seat first was at Coloma, but it moved to Placerville in 1857; the Spanish term *El Dorado* has the connotation of "the gilded one" from a legend of golden wealth in South America—the name is appropriate for the county that has the site of the gold discovery that resulted in the California gold rush of 1849 (Hoover, Rensch, and Rensch, p. 73).

Nevada County.—Nevada County extends westward from the State of Nevada across the crest of the Sierra Nevada into the foothills of that range. The county was created in 1851 from part of Yuba County; additions to the north part of Nevada County came in 1852 and 1856 (Coy, p. 194). Nevada City is and always as been the county seat (Hoover, Rensch, and Rensch, p. 247). The county took its name from Nevada City (Gudde, 1949, p. 233-234).

Placer County.—Placer County extends from the State of Nevada at Lake Tahoe westward across the crest of the Sierra Nevada into Sacramento Valley. It was created in 1851 from territory of the older Sutter County and Yuba County; only minor changes have been made in the original borders of Placer County (Coy, p. 200-202). Auburn has been the county seat from the beginning; the county name is from the Spanish term for surface mining (Hoover, Rensch, and Rensch, p. 265).

Sacramento County.—Sacramento County lies at the south end of Sacramento Valley. It is one of the original counties that the first state legislature created in 1850; except for minor modifications caused by changing river courses, the country boundaries are the same as those first defined (Coy, p. 210-212). Sacramento always has been the county seat; the county name is from Sacramento River (Hoover, Rensch, and Rensch, p. 297).

Sierra County.—Sierra County is in the Sierra Nevada between the State of Nevada and the lower elevations of the range near Sacramento Valley. It was formed in 1852 from the east part of Yuba County, and Downieville was made the county seat; the present boundaries of Sierra County are little changed from the original ones (Coy, p. 253-255). The county name obviously is from the location of the place in the Sierra Nevada.

Sutter County.—Sutter County is in Sacramento Valley between Sacramento River and Feather River, and on both sides of the lower part of Feather River. The first state legislature created the county in 1850; about one-third of the original county territory was lost to Placer County in 1851—some of this land was regained in 1866—and some additional territory was lost by boundary changes with Butte County in the 1850's (Coy, p. 272-274). The county seat first was at Oro, then it moved to Nicolaus, to Auburn (before Auburn was included in Placer county), and to Vernon before it finally settled at Yuba City (Hoover, Rensch, and Rensch, p. 543). The county name honors John A. Sutter (Bancroft, 1890, p. 439).

Yolo County.—Yolo County, originally called Yola County, extends from Sacramento River to the crest of the first range of mountains west of Sacramento Valley. It is one of the counties that the first state legislature created in 1850; nearly half of the original territory of Yolo County was lost to Colusa County in 1851, and some land was gained from Solano County in 1857 (Coy, 295-296). The county seat first was at the now vanished town of Fremont; it moved to Washington (present Broderick) in 1851, moved to Cacheville (present Yolo) in 1857, moved back to Washington in 1861, and moved to Woodland in 1862, where it remains (Hoover, Rensch, and Rensch, p. 582). The name "Yolo" is from an Indian village that stood at present Knights Landing (Kroeber, p. 67).

Yuba County.—Yuba County extends from Feather River northeastward across lowlands of Sacramento Valley into the lower parts of the Sierra Nevada. It is one of the original counties that the first state legislature created in 1850; the county lost about half of its territory when Placer County and Nevada County were organized in 1851, and lost much of its remaining territory when Sierra County was formed in 1852, but since that time the county boundaries have had only minor adjustments (Coy, p. 298-303). Marysville is and always has been the county seat (Hoover, Rensch, and Rensch, p. 587). The name "Yuba" is from an Indian village that was situated near the mouth of Yuba River (Kroeber, p. 68).

South Sacramento Valley Region
Amador, Colusa, El Dorado, Nevada, Placer, Sacramento, Sierra, Sutter, Yolo and Yuba Counties

— A —

Abbott [SUTTER]: *locality,* 8 miles south of Yuba City along Southern Pacific Railroad (lat. 39°01'15" N, long. 121°37'25" W). Named on Olivehurst (1952) 7.5' quadrangle.

Abbott House: see **Oak Grove** [YUBA].

Abbott Lake [SUTTER]: *lake,* 8 miles south of Yuba City near Feather River (lat. 39°01'10" N, long. 121°36'35" W); the lake is less than 1 mile east of Abbott. Named on Olivehurst (1952) 7.5' quadrangle.

Abrams Ravine [PLACER]: *canyon,* drained by a stream that flows 0.5 mile to Pine Nut Canyon 6 miles south-southwest of Duncan Peak (lat. 39°04'20" N, long. 120°32'20" W; near SW cor. sec. 9, T 14 N, R 13 E). Named on Greek Store (1952) 7.5' quadrangle.

Acid Flat [NEVADA]: *area,* 9.5 miles northeast of Truckee (lat. 39° 23'55" N, long. 120°01'50" W; at E line sec. 24, T 18 N, R 17 E). Named on Boca (1955) 7.5' quadrangle.

Ackerman: see **Westville** [PLACER].

Acorn Creek [EL DORADO]: *stream,* flows 2 miles to Skunk Canyon nearly 3.5 miles south of the village of Pilot Hill (lat. 38°46'55" N, long. 121°01'30" W; near NE cor. sec. 25, T 11 N, R 8 E). Named on Pilot Hill (1954) 7.5' quadrangle.

Adobe Spring [COLUSA]: *spring,* 11 miles north of Wilbur Springs (lat. 39°11'45" N, long. 122°24'40" W; sec. 34, T 16 N, R 5 W). Named on Wilbur Springs (1961) 15' quadrangle.

Adobe Spring [YOLO]: *spring,* 11.5 miles south of Esparto (lat. 38° 31'45" N, long. 122°02'05" W; sec. 24, T 8 N, R 2 W). Named on Monticello Dam (1959) 7.5' quadrangle.

African Bar [EL DORADO-PLACER]: *locality,* 4 miles north-northwest of Georgetown along Middle Fork American River on El Dorado-Placer County line (lat. 38°57'55" N, long. 121°51'10" W; at N line sec. 22, T 13 N, R 10 E). Site named on Georgetown (1949) 7.5' quadrangle.

Agassiz Camp: see **Fallen Leaf** [EL DORADO].

Agate Bay [PLACER]: *embayment,* at and west of Kings Beach along Lake Tahoe between Stateline Point and Flick Point (lat. 39°14' N, long. 120°02'15" W). Named on Kings Beach (1955) 7.5' quadrangle. The name, given in 1863, is for the large number of agates on the beach at the place (Lekisch, p. 1).

Ahart Camp [SIERRA]: *locality,* 8 miles southwest of Sierraville (lat. 39°30'05" N, long. 120°28' W; sec. 24, T 19 N, R 13 E). Named on Sattley (1981) 7.5' quadrangle.

Ahart Campground [PLACER]: *locality,* 7.5 miles west-southwest of Granite Chief along Middle Fork American River in French Meadows (lat. 39°08'45" N, long. 120°24'25" W; near SE cor. sec. 16, T 15 N, R 14 E). Named on Royal Gorge (1953) 7.5' quadrangle.

Ahart Sheep Camp [SIERRA]: *locality,* 3.5 miles southeast of Sierra City (lat. 39°32' N, long. 120°35'10" W; near NE cor. sec. 11, T 19 N, R 12 E). Named on Sierra City (1955) 15' quadrangle.

Aigare: see **Mount Aigare** [EL DORADO].

Alabama Bar [PLACER]: *locality,* 2.5 miles south of Michigan Bluff along Middle Fork American River (lat. 39°00'10" N, long. 120° 44'30" W; sec. 3, T 13 N, R 11 E). Named on Duncan Peak (1952) 15' quadrangle.

Alabama Bar [YUBA]: *locality,* 3 miles south-southwest of Strawberry Valley along North Yuba River (lat. 39°31'35" N, long. 121° 07'20" W; sec. 7, T 19 N, R 8 E). Named on Strawberry Valley (1948) 7.5' quadrangle.

Alabama Flat: see **Johntown Creek** [EL DORADO].

Alabama House [AMADOR]: *locality,* less than 1 mile south-southeast of present Carbondale (lat. 38°23'50" N, long. 121°00'15" W). Named on Carbondale (1909) 7.5' quadrangle.

Alamos: see **Catlett** [SUTTER].

Alaska Hill [SIERRA]: *peak,* less than 1 mile north-northwest of Pike (lat. 39°26'55" N, long. 121°00'15" W; on N line sec. 7, T 18 N, R 9 E). Altitude 4027 feet. Named on Camptonville (1948) 7.5' quadrangle. United States Board on Geographic Names (1991, p. 2) approved the name "Alaska Peak" for the feature.

Alaska Peak: see **Alaska Hill** [SIERRA].

Alberts Lake: see **Little Alberts Lake**, under **Elbert Lake** [EL DORADO].

Albion Ravine [YUBA]: *canyon,* drained by a stream that flows 1.25 miles to Dry Creek (2) 9.5 miles northeast of Wheatland at Waldo Junction (lat. 39°06'40" N, long. 121°18'30" W; sec. 33, T 15 N, R 6 E). Named on Camp Far West (1949) 7.5' quadrangle.

Al Brass Creek [EL DORADO]: *stream,* flows 2 miles to Rock Creek 12.5 miles northwest of Pollock Pines (lat. 38°53'25" N, long. 120° 44'30" W; sec. 15, T 12 N, R 11 E). Named on Tunnel Hill (1950) 7.5' quadrangle.

Alden: see **Manlove** [SACRAMENTO].

Alder Creek [EL DORADO]: *stream,* flows 12.5 miles to South Fork American River nearly 4 miles east of Riverton (lat. 38°46' N, long. 120°22'45" W; sec. 26, T 11 N, R 14 E). Named on Kyburz (1952), Leek Spring Hill (1951), Riverton (1950), and Tragedy Spring (1979) 7.5' quadrangles.

Alder Creek [NEVADA]:

(1) *stream,* flows 1.5 miles to Fall Creek 6.5 miles southeast of Graniteville (lat. 39°22'40" N, long. 120°38'40" W; sec. 32, T 18 N, R 12 E). Named on Graniteville (1982) 7.5' quadrangle.

(2) *stream,* flows 7 miles to Prosser Creek Reservoir 3.25 miles north of Truckee (lat. 39°22'30" N, long. 120°10'25" W; near S line sec. 26, T 18 N, R 16 E). Named on Norden (1955) and Truckee (1955) 7.5' quadrangles.

Alder Creek [SACRAMENTO]:

(1) *stream,* flows 6.25 miles to Lake Natoma 3 miles south-southwest of Folsom (lat. 38°38'20" N, long. 121°11'55" W). Named on Clarksville (1953), Folsom (1967), and Folsom SE (1954) 7.5' quadrangles.

(2) *locality,* 3 miles south-southwest of Folsom along Southern Pacific Railroad (lat. 38°38'05" N, long. 121°12' W); the place is near the mouth of Alder Creek (1). Named on Folsom (1967) 7.5' quadrangle. Called Alders on Sacramento (1892) 30' quadrangle.

Alder Creek [SIERRA]: *stream,* flows nearly 3 miles to Smithneck Creek 7 miles southeast of Loyalton (lat. 39°35'50" N, long. 120° 10'05" W; sec. 11, T 20 N, R 16 E). Named on Sardine Peak (1981) 7.5' quadrangle.

Alder Creek Camp Ground [EL DORADO]: *locality,* nearly 4 miles east of Riverton along South Fork American River (lat. 38°46' N, long. 120°22'40" W; sec. 26, T 11 N, R 14 E); the place is opposite the mouth of Alder Creek. Named on Riverton (1950) 7.5' quadrangle.

Alder Grove: see **Illinoistown** [PLACER].

Alder Hill [EL DORADO]: *peak,* 10.5 miles west-southwest of Kirkwood at the east end of Plummer Ridge (lat. 38°37'45" N, long. 120°14'15" W; near W line sec. 17, T 9 N, R 16 E). Named on Tragedy Spring (1979) 7.5' quadrangle.

Alder Hill [NEVADA]: *peak,* nearly 2 miles north-northwest of Truckee (lat. 39°21'10" N, long. 120°11'40" W; near W line sec. 3, T 17 N, R 16 E); the peak is south of Alder Creek (2). Altitude 6733 feet. Named on Truckee (1955) 7.5' quadrangle.

Alderman Creek [PLACER]: *stream,* flows 2 miles to Bear River 11 miles northwest of Auburn (lat. 39°00'45" N, long. 121°13'05" W; near N line sec. 5, T 13 N, R 7 E). Named on Gold Hill (1954) and Wolf (1949) 7'5' quadrangles.

Alder Ridge [EL DORADO]: *ridge,* generally northwest-trending, 10 miles long, center 6 miles north of Leek Spring Hill (lat. 38°43'20" N, long. 120°16'15" W). Named on Kyburz (1952), Leek Spring Hill (1951), and Tragedy Spring (1979) 7.5' quadrangles.

Alders: see **Alder Creek** [SACRAMENTO] (2).

Alder Spring [YOLO]: *spring,* 2.25 miles north of Berryessa Peak (lat. 38°41'45" N, long. 122°11'15" W). Named on Brooks (1959) 7.5' quadrangle.

Alemandra [SUTTER]: *locality,* nearly 4 miles west of Yuba City along Sacramento Northern Railroad (lat. 39°08'55" N, long. 121° 41'15" W; at W line sec. 18, T 15 N, R 3 E). Named on Sutter (1952) 7.5' quadrangle.

Algodon [YUBA]: *locality,* 7 miles south of Olivehurst along Northern Electric Railroad (lat. 38°59'25" N, long. 121°32'35" W; at E line sec. 8, T 13 N, R 4 E). Named on Nicolaus (1910) 7.5' quadrangle.

Algodon Slough [YUBA]: *water feature,* 5.5 miles south of Olivehurst in lowlands east of Feather River (lat. 39°01' N, long. 121°32'40" W). Named on Olivehurst (1952) 7.5' quadrangle.

Alicia [YUBA]: *locality,* 1.5 miles west-northwest of Olivehurst (lat. 39°06'20" N, long. 121°34'45" W). Named on Olivehurst (1952) 7.5' quadrangle.

Alleghany [SIERRA]: *village,* 6.5 miles south of Downieville (lat. 39°28'20" N, long. 120°50'35" W; sec. 34, T 19 N, R 10 E). Named on Alleghany (1949) 7.5' quadrangle. Postal authorities established Alleghany post office in 1857 (Frickstad, p. 184). The name is from Alleghany tunnel, said to have been built in 1855 by gold miners from Alleghany, Pennsylvania (Hanna, p. 7).

Allegheny Creek [EL DORADO]: *stream,* flows 2 miles to Green Spring Creek nearly 4 miles north-northwest of Clarksville (lat. 38° 42'30" N, long. 121°04'05" W; sec. 23, T 10 N, R 8 E). Named on Clarksville (1953) 7.5' quadrangle.

Allen [AMADOR]: *locality,* 5.5 miles north of Mokelumne Peak along Bear River (lat. 38°37' N, long. 120°06'35" W; sec. 21, T 9 N, R 17 E). Named on Mokelumne Peak (1979) 7.5' quadrangle.

Allen Camp [EL DORADO]: *locality,* 10 miles southwest of Kirkwood at Corral Flat (lat. 38°37'50" N, long. 120°13'15" W; near NW cor. sec. 21, T 9 N, R 16 E). Named on Bear River Reservoir (1979) 7.5' quadrangle.

Allenwood Hill [NEVADA]: *peak,* 5 miles west of Pilot Peak (lat. 39°09'50" N, long. 121°06'20" W; sec. 11, T 15 N, R 6 E). Altitude 1320 feet. Named on Smartville (1951) 7.5' quadrangle.

Alma: see **Mount Alma** [SIERRA].

Aloha: see **Lake Aloha** [EL DORADO].

Alpha [NEVADA]: *locality,* 2 miles south-southeast of Washington (lat. 39°19'45" N, long. 120°47' W). Named on Colfax (1898) 30' quadrangle. Postal authorities established Alpha post office in 1855 and discontinued it in 1862 (Frickstad, p. 112). Prospectors discovered gold at the site in 1850 and settlers arrived in 1852; the place had the nickname "Hell Out for High Noon City" in the early days (Slyter and Slyter, p. 8).

Alpha Diggings [NEVADA]: *locality,* 2 miles south-southeast of Washington (lat. 39°20'10" N, long. 120°47' W; sec. 18, T 17 N, R 11 E); the place is at or near the site of Alpha. Named on Washington (1950) 7.5' quadrangle.

Alpine Campground [EL DORADO]: *locality,* 1.5 miles south-southeast of Echo Summit along Upper Truckee River (lat. 38°47'45" N, long. 120°01'10" W; near SW cor. sec. 17, T 11 N, R 18 E). Named on Echo Lake (1955) 7.5' quadrangle.

Alpine Meadows [PLACER]: *settlement,* 5 miles west of Tahoe City along Bear Creek (lat. 39°10'30" N, long. 120°13'50" W). Named on Tahoe City (1955, photorevised 1969) 7.5' quadrangle.

Alta [PLACER]: *village,* 1.5 miles east of Dutch Flat (lat. 39°12'25" N, long. 120°48'40" W; near W line sec. 36, T 16 N, R 10 E). Named on Dutch Flat (1950) 7.5' quadrangle. Postal authorities established Alta post office in 1871 (Frickstad, p. 118). Officials of Central Pacific Railroad are said to have named the place in 1866 for the San Francisco newspaper *Alta California,* which favored the railroad (Gudde, 1949, p. 9).

Alta: see **Lake Alta** [PLACER].

Alta Hill [NEVADA]: *town,* 1 mile northwest of downtown Grass Valley (lat. 39°13'55" N, long. 121°04'30" W; near SE cor. sec. 21, T 16 N, R 8 E). Named on Grass Valley (1949) 7.5' quadrangle.

Alta Hill Reservoir [NEVADA]: *lakes,* 1 mile north of downtown Grass Valley (lat. 39°13'55" N, long. 121°03'55" W; sec. 22, T 16 N, R 8 E); the lakes are at the east edge of Alta Hill. Named on Grass Valley (1949) 7.5' quadrangle.

Al Tahoe [EL DORADO]: *district,* 7.5 miles northwest of Freel Peak in the town of South Lake Tahoe (lat. 38°56'30" N, long. 119° 59' W). Named on South Lake Tahoe (1955, photorevised 1969 and 1974) 7.5' quadrangle. Sinclair's (1901) map has the name "Rowlands" at the place. Lake House, the first lake-front hotel along Lake Tahoe, was located just west of present Al Tahoe; after Lake House burned, Tom Rowland rebuilt it and constructed a long pier that was a shipping point for lumber from Lake Valley—eventually Al Sprague replaced Rowland's establishment with a family hotel that he named Al Tahoe (Zauner, p. 8-9, 15). Postal authorities established Rowland post office in 1874 and discontinued it in 1888; they established Al Tahoe post office in 1908 (Salley, p. 5, 190). Sinclair (p. 272) noted a place called Goddard's Station that was situated 1.5 miles east of Lake House in the 1860's.

Alta Morris Lake [EL DORADO]: *lake,* 700 feet long, 4.25 miles south of Phipps Peak (lat. 38°53'35" N, long. 120°08'20" W). Named on Rockbound Valley (1955) 7.5' quadrangle.

Alta Vista [SACRAMENTO]: *locality,* 10 miles north-northeast of Galt (lat. 38°23'15" N, long. 121°13'25" W). Named on Sacramento (1957) 1°x 2° quadrangle.

Amador: see **Amador City** [AMADOR].

Amador City [AMADOR]: *village,* 4.5 miles south-southeast of Plymouth (lat. 38°25'10" N, long. 120°49'25" W; sec. 36, T 7 N, R 10 E); the place is along Amador Creek. Named on Amador City (1962) 7.5' quadrangle. Called Amador on Jackson (1902) 30' quadrangle. Postal authorities established Amador City post office in 1863 (Frickstad, p. 5), and the community incorporated in 1915. The place first was situated about 0.5 mile upstream from the present site, but was moved when placer mining for gold threatened to destroy the original buildings (McKinstry, p. 317). The village grew around the camp of Jose Maria Amador, who came to the neighborhood seeking gold in 1848 (Gudde, 1975, p. 17). A place called Amador Crossing was east of Amador City where the stage road from Jackson to Dry Creek crossed Amador Creek; Amador Crossing also was known as Upper Crossing (Gudde, 1975, p. 17).

Amador Creek [AMADOR]: *stream,* flows 10.5 miles to Dry Creek nearly 4 miles south-southwest of Plymouth (lat. 38°25'45" N, long. 120°52'30" W; near E line sec. 28, T 7 N, R 10 E); the stream goes through and is named for Amador City (Hanna, p. 10). Named on Amador City (1962) and Pine Grove (1948) 7.5' quadrangles.

Amador Crossing: see **Amador City** [AMADOR].

Amador Reservoir: see **Icehouse Pond** [AMADOR].

Amaranth [YOLO]: *locality,* nearly 1.5 miles south-southeast of Guinda along Southern Pacific Railroad in Capay Valley (lat. 38° 48'40" N, long. 122°11'10" W). Named on Rumsey (1921) 15' quadrangle.

Amelia Landing [SACRAMENTO]: *locality,* 12 miles southwest of Isleton along San Joaquin River on Sherman Island (lat. 38°01'50" N, long. 121°45'05" W). Named on Antioch North (1953) 7.5' quadrangle.

American [PLACER]: *locality,* 4 miles east of Dutch Flat along Southern Pacific Railroad (lat. 39°12'05" N, long. 120°46' W; near N line sec. 5, T 15 N, R 11 E). Named on Colfax (1938) 30' quadrangle.

American Bar [PLACER]: *locality,* 3.5 miles east-southeast of Foresthill along Middle Fork American River (lat. 39°00'20" N, long. 120°45'10" W; near N line sec. 4, T 13 N, R 11 E). Named on Foresthill (1949) 7.5' quadrangle.

American Bar: see **Buckeye Bar** [EL DORADO-PLACER].

American Basin [SACRAMENTO-SUTTER]: *area,* east of Sacramento River and north of American River on Sacramento-Sutter County line. Named on Knights Landing (1952), Pleasant Grove (1967), Rio Linda (1967), Sacramento East (1967), Sacramento West (1967), Taylor Monument (1967), and Verona (1967) 7.5' quadrangles.

American Canyon [EL DORADO]: *canyon,* drained by a stream that flows 3.25 miles to Middle Fork American River 3 miles north-northwest of Greenwood at Poverty Bar (lat. 38°56'05" N, long. 120°56'30" W; sec. 35, T 13 N, R 9 E). Named on Greenwood (1949) 7.5' quadrangle.

American Flat [EL DORADO]: *locality*, 4.5 miles north of Chili Bar (lat. 38°50'05" N, long. 120°48'50" W; sec. 1, T 11 N, R 10 E). Named on Garden Valley (1949) 7.5' quadrangle. The name is from the term "American Company," the designation that the first group of miners at the place gave to themselves (Gernes, p. 45).

American Flat [SIERRA]: *area,* 1.25 miles northwest of Alleghany (lat. 39°29'05" N, long. 120°51'35" W; sec. 28, T 19 N, R 10 E). Named on Alleghany (1949) 7.5' quadrangle.

American Fork: see **American River** [EL DORADO-PLACER-SACRAMENTO].

American Hill [PLACER]: *ridge,* south-southwest-trending, 1.5 miles long, 4.25 miles west-southwest of Duncan Peak (lat. 39°08'10" N, long. 120°35'20" W). Named on Duncan Peak (1952) 7.5' quadrangle.

American Hill [SIERRA]:

(1) *ridge,* south-southeast-trending, less than 0.5 mile long, 4.5 miles east-northeast of Alleghany (lat. 39°29'05" N, long. 120°45'35" W; sec. 29, T 19 N, R 11 E). Named on Alleghany (1949) 7.5' quadrangle.

(2) *locality,* nearly 5 miles east-northeast of Alleghany (lat. 39° 28'50" N, long. 120°45'30" W); the place is on present American Hill (1). Named on Colfax (1898) 30' quadrangle.

American Hill: see **Nevada City** [NEVADA].

American Hill Cabin [SIERRA]: *locality,* 4.25 miles east-northeast of Alleghany (lat. 39°29'45" N, long. 120°46' W; sec. 20, T 19 N, R 11 E); the place is 1 mile north-northwest of American Hill (1). Named on Alleghany (1949) 7.5' quadrangle.

American Lake [EL DORADO]: *lake,* 2200 feet long, 1.5 miles east-northeast of Pyramid Peak (lat. 38°51'20" N, long. 120°08'05" W). Named on Pyramid Peak (1955) 7.5' quadrangle.

American Ranch Hill [NEVADA]: *ridge,* 2 miles long, 4.5 miles southwest of Grass Valley (lat. 39°10'05" N, long. 121°06'45" W). Named on Grass Valley (1949) and Rough and Ready (1949) 7.5' quadrangles.

American River [EL DORADO-PLACER-SACRAMENTO]: *stream,* formed by the confluence of North Fork and South Fork in Folsom Lake, flows 30 miles to Sacramento River 1.5 miles north-northwest of downtown Sacramento (lat. 38°35'50" N, long. 121°30'25" W). Named on Carmichael (1967), Citrus Heights (1967), Folsom (1967), Sacramento East (1967), and Sacramento West (1967) 7.5' quadrangles. Called Rio de los Americanos on Fremont's (1845) map, and called American Fork on Williamson's (1849) map. The name "American River" is from a place called El Paso de los Americanos, where Canadian trappers, who were called Americanos by Spanish-speaking Indians, crossed the stream in the early days (Gudde, 1949, p. 10). North Fork heads near Granite Chief and flows 85 miles to join South Fork in Folsom Lake; it forms El Dorado-

Placer County line below its junction with Middle Fork. North Fork is named on Auburn (1953), Colfax (1949), Duncan Peak (1952), Dutch Flat (1950), Folsom (1967), Foresthill (1949), Granite Chief (1953), Greenwood (1949), Norden (1955), Pilot Hill (1954, photorevised 1973), Rocklin (1967), Royal Gorge (1953), Soda Springs (1955), and Westville (1952) 7.5' quadrangles. North Fork of North Fork American River joins North Fork 4.5 miles east-southeast of Dutch Flat; it is 18 miles long and is named on Blue Canyon (1955), Cisco Grove (1955), Dutch Flat (1950), and Westville (1952) 7.5' quadrangles. On Whitney's (1873) map, the upper part, at least, of present North Fork of North Fork is called Little North Fork. East Fork of North Fork of North Fork American River joins North Fork of North Fork 4.5 miles north-northwest of Westville; it is 7.5 miles long and is named on Blue Canyon (1955), Cisco Grove (1955), Duncan Peak (1952), and Westville (1952) 7.5' quadrangles. Middle Fork American River joins North Fork 2.25 miles east-northeast of Auburn; it is 62 miles long and is named on Auburn (1953), Bunker Hill (1953), Foresthill (1949), Georgetown (1949), Granite Chief (1953), Greek Store (1952), Greenwood (1949), Michigan Bluff (1952), and Royal Gorge (1953) 7.5' quadrangles. Middle Fork forms El Dorado-Placer County line downstream from the mouth of Rubicon River to the junction with North Fork. North Fork of Middle Fork joins Middle Fork 2.25 miles south of Michigan Bluff; it is 17 miles long and is named on Duncan Peak (1952), Greek Store (1952), and Michigan Bluff (1952) 7.5' quadrangles. South Fork, which forms part of El Dorado-Sacramento County line, heads at Echo Summit and flows for 82 miles to join North Fork in Folsom Lake. South Fork is named on Clarksville (1953), Coloma (1949), Echo Lake (1955), Folsom (1967), Garden Valley (1949), Kyburz (1952), Leek Spring Hill (1951), Pilot Hill (1954, photorevised 1973), Pollock Pines (1950), Pyramid Peak (1955), and Slate Mountain (1950) 7.5' quadrangles. Silver Fork heads at Silver Lake and flows 14 miles to South Fork 1 mile west-southwest of Kyburz, it is named on Caples Lake (1979), Kyburz (1952), Leek Spring Hill (1951), and Tragedy Spring (1979) 7.5' quadrangles. Gudde (1975) listed the several mining places situated along North Fork American River in Placer County: Calf Bar, located near the junction with Middle Fork (p. 56); Grizzly Bar, located 1 mile above the junction with Middle Fork (p. 146); Kellys Bar, located above Calf Bar (p. 183); Niggerhead Bar, located 2 miles below the mouth of Middle Fork (p. 243); and Portuguese Bar, located near Calf Bar (p. 273).

Anderson Canyon [EL DORADO]: *canyon,* drained by a stream that flows 4 miles to Middle Fork Cosumnes River 8 miles east of Caldor (lat. 38°35'25" N, long. 120°16'50" W; sec. 35, T 9 N, R 15 E). Named on Bear River Reservoir (1979) and Peddler Hill (1951) 7.5' quadrangles.

Anderson Creek [EL DORADO]: *stream,* flows 1 mile to Folsom Lake 6.25 miles southwest of the village of Pilot Hill (lat. 38°46'35" N, long. 121°06'05" W; sec. 29, T 11 N, R 8 E). Named on Pilot Hill (1954, photorevised 1973) 7.5' quadrangle.

Anderson Creek: see **Deep Ravine** [EL DORADO].

Anderson Meadow [SIERRA]: *area,* 8.5 miles south-southeast of Sierraville (lat. 39°28'40" N, long. 120°17'30" W; near SE cor. sec. 22, T 19 N, R 15 E). Named on Independence Lake (1981) 7.5' quadrangle.

Anderson Mountain [COLUSA]: *ridge,* 1.5 miles long, 8.5 miles southeast of Wilbur Springs (lat. 38°58'05" N, long. 122°17'45" W; sec. 15, 22, T 13 N, R 4 W). Named on Glascock Mountain (1958) 7.5' quadrangle.

Anderson Peak [PLACER]: *peak,* 4.25 miles south-southeast of Donner Pass (lat. 39°15'30" N, long. 120°17'45" W; near S line sec. 3, T 16 N, R 15 E). Altitude 8683 feet. Named on Norden (1955) 7.5' quadrangle.

Anderson Ridge [EL DORADO]: *ridge,* west-southwest-trending, 2 miles long, 11.5 miles southwest of Kirkwood (lat. 38°36'30" N, long. 120°14'15" W); the ridge is southeast of Anderson Canyon. Named on Bear River Reservoir (1979) 7.5' quadrangle.

Andesite Peak [NEVADA]: *peak,* 3.25 miles northwest of Donner Pass (lat. 39°21'05" N, long. 120°21'55" W; sec. 11, T 17 N, R 14 E). Altitude 8219 feet. Named on Norden (1955) 7.5' quadrangle. The name is from the kind of rock exposed at the peak (United States Board on Geographic Names, 1949b, p. 3).

Andesite Ridge [NEVADA]: *ridge,* southeast-trending, 1 mile long, 2.5 miles northwest of Donner Pass (lat. 39°20'45" N, long. 120° 21'25" W); Andesite Peak is at the northwest end of the ridge. Named on Norden (1955) 7.5' quadrangle. The name is from the kind of rock exposed on the ridge (United States Board on Geographic Names, 1949b, p. 3).

Andover [PLACER]: *locality,* 11.5 miles west of Martis Peak along Southern Pacific Railroad (lat. 39°18'35" N, long. 120°14'45" W; sec. 19, T 17 N, R 16 E). Named on Truckee (1955) 7.5' quadrangle. A division superintendent of Southern Pacific Railroad named the place for his hometown in Massachusetts (Gudde, 1949, p. 11).

Andreason Mill [EL DORADO]: *locality,* 3.5 miles south of Omo Ranch (lat. 38°31'45" N, long. 120°34'35" W; sec. 19, T 8 N, R 13 E). Site named on Omo Ranch (1952) 7.5' quadrangle.

Andrew Gray Creek [PLACER]: *stream,* flows nearly 2 miles to North Fork American River 6 miles northwest of Duncan Peak (lat. 39°12'45" N, long. 120°35'45" W; sec. 35, T 16 N, R 12 E). Named on Duncan Peak (1952) 7.5' quadrangle. The name is for Andrew Wheaton Gray, who came to the region in 1850 (United States Board on Geographic Names, 1967, p. 2).

Andrus Island [SACRAMENTO]: *island,* 28 miles south of downtown Sacramento between Sacramento River, Georgiana Slough, Mokelumne River, San Joaquin River, and Jackson Slough (lat. 38°10' N, long. 121°35' W). Named on Bouldin Island (1978) and Isleton (1978) 7.5' quadrangles. The name commemorates George Andrus, who settled at the place in 1852 (Gudde, 1949, p. 11).

Andys Canyon [COLUSA]: *canyon,* 1 mile long, 5 miles southwest of Sites along upper reaches of Grapevine Creek (lat. 39°15'15" N, long. 122°24'30" W; sec. 9, 10, T 16 N, R 5 W). Named on Lodoga (1960) 15' quadrangle.

Angela: see **Lake Angela** [NEVADA].

Angel Creek [EL DORADO]: *stream,* flows 3 miles to Gerle Creek 3 miles north of Robbs Peak (lat. 38°58'05" N, long. 120°23'35" W; sec. 15, T 13 N, R 14 E). Named on Loon Lake (1952) and Robbs Peak (1950) 7.5' quadrangles.

Angel Slough [COLUSA]: *stream,* heads in Glenn County and flows 3.5 miles in Colusa County to Butte Creek 10 miles north-northeast of Colusa (lat. 39°20'15" N, long. 121°53'45" W; sec. 7, T 17 N, R 1 E). Named on Butte City (1952) and Sanborn Slough (1952) 7.5' quadrangles.

Angora Creek [EL DORADO]: *stream,* flows 4 miles to Upper Truckee River 4.25 miles north of Echo Summit (lat. 38°52'25" N, long. 120°00'45" W; sec. 20, T 12 N, R 18 E); the stream heads at Angora Lakes. Named on Echo Lake (1955) and Emerald Bay (1955) 7.5' quadrangles.

Angora Lakes [EL DORADO]: *lakes,* largest 1000 feet long, 4 miles north-northwest of Echo Summit (lat. 38°51'50" N, long. 120°03'55" W); the lakes are 0.25 mile east-southeast of Angora Peak at the head of Angora Creek. Named on Echo Lake (1955) 7.5' quadrangle. The name "Angora" is from the herd of Angora goats that Nathan Gilmore pastured in the neighborhood (Lekisch, p. 4).

Angora Peak [EL DORADO]: *peak,* 4.5 miles north-northwest of Echo Summit (lat. 38°52' N, long. 120°04'20" W). Altitude 8588 feet. Named on Echo Lake (1955) 7.5' quadrangle.

Angus Canyon [YOLO]: *canyon,* drained by a stream that flows 2 miles to Capay Valley nearly 2 miles south-southwest of Guinda (lat. 38°48'15" N, long. 122°12' W; sec. 16, T 11 N, R 3 W). Named on Guinda (1959) 7.5' quadrangle.

Ann: see **Fort Ann**, under **Volcano** [AMADOR].

Antelope [SACRAMENTO]: *locality,* 6.25 miles north of downtown Carmichael along Southern Pacific Railroad (lat. 38°42'30" N, long. 121°19'45" W; sec. 21, T 10 N, R 6 E). Named on Citrus Heights (1967) 7.5' quadrangle. Postal authorities established Antelope post office in 1877 and discontinued it in 1973 (Salley, p. 8).

Antelope [SIERRA]: *locality,* 12 miles east of Loyalton in Upper Long Valley (lat. 39°41'25" N, long. 120°00'55" W; at W line sec. 18, T 21 N, R 18 E). Named on Loyalton (1955) 15' quadrangle.

Antelope: see **Dunnigan** [YOLO].

Antelope Creek [AMADOR]: *stream,* flows 5.5 miles to Mill Creek 9 miles east-northeast of Pine Grove (lat. 38°27'15" N, long. 120° 30'30" W; near N line sec. 23, T 7 N, R 13 E). Named on Caldor (1951), Devils Nose (1979), and West Point (1948) 7.5' quadrangles. On Mokelumne Hill (1948) 15' quadrangle, the name "Antelope Creek" seems to apply to present Mill Creek below the confluence of Antelope Creek and Mill Creek.

Antelope Creek [COLUSA]: *stream,* flows 9 miles to Stone Corral Creek 0.25 mile northwest of Sites (lat. 39°18'45" N, long. 122°20'30" W; sec. 19, T 17 N, R 4 W); the stream is in Antelope Valley. Named on Lodoga (1960) and Wilbur Springs (1961) 15' quadrangles.

Antelope Creek [PLACER]: *stream,* flows 9.5 miles to join the stream in Miners Ravine and form Dry Creek (2) 1 mile east-northeast of downtown Roseville (lat. 38°45'20" N, long. 121° 16' W; near E line sec. 35, T 11 N, R 6 E). Named on Rocklin (1967) and Roseville (1967) 7.5' quadrangles. The canyon of the stream is called Antelope Rav. on Hobson's (1890b) map.

Antelope Creek: see **Dry Creek** [PLACER-SACRAMENTO].

Antelope Ravine: see **Antelope Creek** [PLACER].

Antelope Springs [AMADOR]: *locality,* 6 miles west-southwest of present Hams Station (lat. 38°30'50" N, long. 120°38'40" W); the place is near Antelope Creek. Named on Pyramid Peak (1896) 30' quadrangle.

Antelope Valley [COLUSA]: *valley,* north-trending, 14 miles long, Antelope Creek drains much of the feature; Sites is in the valley 5.5 miles from the north end. Named on Lodoga (1960) and Wilbur Springs (1961) 15' quadrangles.

Antelope Valley [SIERRA]: *canyon,* drained by a stream that flows 5.5 miles to Sierra Valley nearly 7 miles north-northeast of Sierraville (lat. 39°40'45" N, long. 120°18'50" W; near NW cor. sec. 16, T 21 N, R 15 E). Named on Antelope Valley (1981) and Sierraville (1981) 7.5' quadrangles.

Anthony House [NEVADA]: *locality,* 5 miles north-northwest of Pilot Peak along Deer Creek (lat. 39°14'20" N, long. 120°12'45" W; at S line sec. 17, T 16 N, R 7 E). Named on Grass Valley (1949) 15' quadrangle. Water of a reservoir now covers the site. Postal authorities established Anthony House post office in 1862, discontinued it in 1866, reestablished it in 1867, discontinued it for a time in 1877, and discontinued it finally in 1906 (Frickstad, p. 113). The place was a stage station on the old turnpike that ran up San Juan Ridge (Hoover, Rensch, and Rensch, p. 250). Whitney's (1873) map shows a place called Texas Fl. [Flat] located 2 miles east of Anthony House along Deer Creek, and a relief feature called Beckman Hill located 2.25 miles northeast of Anthony House. Gudde (1975, p. 261) listed a place called Pearls Hill that was situated about 1 mile northwest of Anthony House near Deer Creek.

Antoine Canyon [PLACER]: *canyon,* drained by a stream that flows 3.25 miles to Screwauger Canyon 4 miles west-southwest of Duncan Peak (lat. 39°08'20" N, long. 120°35' W; near N line sec. 24, T 15 N, R 12 E). Named on Duncan Peak (1952) 7.5' quadrangle. Called Antone Canyon on Colfax (1898) 30' quadrangle. The name is for a half-breed Crow Indian who in 1850 was the first miner in the canyon (Hoover, Rensch, and Rensch, p. 277).

Antone Canyon: see **Antoine Canyon** [PLACER].

Antone Meadows [PLACER]: *area,* 2.25 miles north-northwest of Tahoe City (lat. 39°12'05" N, long. 120°09'10" W; near S line sec. 25, T 16 N, R 16 E). Named on Tahoe City (1955) 7.5' quadrangle. The name is for Antone Russi, who pastured cows at the place (Lekisch, p. 4).

Antwine Gulch [EL DORADO]: *canyon,* drained by a stream that flows 0.5 mile to Canyon Creek (1) 2.5 miles north-northeast of Georgetown (lat. 38°56'20" N, long. 120°49'10" W; near NE cor. sec. 35, T 13 N, R 10 E). Named on Georgetown (1949) 7.5' quadrangle.

Apex [EL DORADO]: *locality,* 1.25 miles west of downtown Placerville along Southern Pacific Railroad (lat. 38°43'40" N, long. 120° 49'20" W; near N line sec. 13, T 10 N, R 10 E). Named on Placerville (1949) 7.5' quadrangle.

Applegate [PLACER]: *town,* 7.25 miles south-southwest of Colfax (lat. 39°00'05" N, long. 120°59'25" W; near SE cor. sec. 5, T 13 N, R 9 E). Named on Colfax (1949) and Greenwood (1949) 7.5' quadrangles. California Division of Highways' (1934) map shows places called East Applegate and West Applegate located near Applegate. The name "Applegate" commemorates Lisbon Applegate and his son George; Lisbon settled at what was known as Bear River House in 1849—the place then was called Lisbon before the name was changed to Applegate (Hanna, p. 14). Postal authorities established Lisbon post office in 1855 and discontinued it in 1866; they established Applegate post office in 1875 (Salley, p. 8, 123).

Aqueduct [AMADOR]: *locality,* nearly 2 miles southwest of Pine Grove (lat. 38°23'50" N, long. 120°37'55" W). Named on Jackson (1902) 30' quadrangle. Postal authorities established Aqueduct City post office in 1855 and discontinued it the same year (Frickstad, p. 5). The name is from a flume near the place (Andrews, p. 85).

Aqueduct City: see **Aqueduct** [AMADOR].

Ararat: see **Mount Ararat** [EL DORADO].

Arbee [COLUSA]: *locality,* less than 1 mile east-southeast of downtown Colusa along Sacramento Northern Railroad (lat. 39°12'40" N, long. 121°59'40" W). Named on Meridian (1952) 7.5' quadrangle.

Arboga [YUBA]: *locality,* 3 miles south of Olivehurst along an abandoned grade of Sacramento Northern Railroad (lat. 39°03'10" N, long. 121°33'30" W; near NW cor. sec. 20, T 14 N, R 4 E). Named on Olivehurst (1952, photorevised 1973) 7.5' quadrangle. Postal authorities established Arboga post office in 1912 and discontinued it in 1926 (Frickstad, p. 222). N.M. Nelsien, pastor of Swedish Mission Church, named the place in 1911 for his former home in Sweden (Gudde, 1949, p. 13). California Division of Highways' (1934) map shows a place called Reed Jct. located 1 mile north-northwest of Arboga along Sacramento Northern Railroad, a place called Plumas situated 1.25 miles south-southeast of Arboga along the railroad, and a place called Lewis located 2.5 miles south-southeast of Arboga along the railroad. Postal authorities established Huntington post office 5 miles south of Arboga in 1912 and discontinued it the same year; the name was from Huntington subdivision (Salley, p. 102).

Arboga: see **East Arboga** [YUBA].

Arbuckle [COLUSA]: *town,* 14 miles south of Colusa (lat. 39°01' N, long. 122°03'15" W; mainly in sec. 34, 35, T 14 N, R 2 W). Named on Arbuckle (1952) 7.5' quadrangle. Postal authorities established Arbuckle post office in 1876 (Frickstad, p. 17). Railroad surveyors named the place for Tacitus R. Arbuckle, owner of the ranch where the town was founded in 1875; Mr. Arbuckle came to the spot in 1866 (Gudde, 1949, p. 13; Hanna, p. 15). Postal authorities established Cortina post office 16 miles west of Arbuckle in 1898 and discontinued it in 1901 (Salley, p. 51).

Arcade [SACRAMENTO]: *locality,* 4.25 miles south-southeast of present Rio Linda along Southern Pacific Railroad (lat. 38°38'10" N, long. 121°24'30" W); the place is near Arcade Creek. Named on Arcade (1911) 7.5' quadrangle.

Arcade [YOLO]: *locality,* nearly 5 miles northwest of Clarksburg along Sacramento Northern Railroad (lat. 38°28'30" N, long. 121° 34'45" W). Named on Clarksburg (1967) 7.5' quadrangle. Called Lisbon on Babel Slough (1916) 7.5' quadrangle. California Division of Highways' (1934) map has the name "Lisbon Island" for the area southeast of Lisbon.

Arcade Creek [SACRAMENTO]: *stream,* flows 16 miles to a drainage canal 3.25 miles north-northeast of downtown Sacramento (lat. 38°37'10" N, long. 121°28' W). Named on Citrus Heights (1967), Folsom (1967), Rio Linda (1967), and Sacramento East (1967) 7.5' quadrangles.

Arctic: see **Donner** [PLACER].

Argenta [YOLO]: *locality,* 3 miles north-northwest of Clarksburg along Sacramento Northern Railroad (lat. 38°27'30" N, long. 121° 32'40" W). Named on Courtland (1952) 15' quadrangle.

Arkansas Bar: see **Upper Arkansas Bar**, under **Green Valley** [PLACER].

Arkansas Creek [AMADOR-SACRAMENTO]: *stream,* heads in Amador County and flows 9 miles to Cosumnes River 22 miles east-southeast of downtown Sacramento in Sacramento County (lat. 38°28'50" N, long. 121°06'20" W; near N line sec. 9, T 7 N, R 8 E). Named on Carbondale (1968) and Irish Hill (1962) 7.5' quadrangles.

Arkansas Ferry: see **Lancha Plana** [AMADOR].

Armstrong Hill [EL DORADO]: *peak,* 5 miles south-southeast of Caldor (lat. 38°32'30" N, long. 120°23' W; near SW cor. sec. 13, T 8 N, R 14 E). Altitude 5701 feet. Named on Caldor (1951) 7.5' quadrangle.

Armstrong Pass [EL DORADO]: *pass,* nearly 2 miles south-southwest of Freel Peak on El Dorado-Alpine County line (lat. 38°49'55" N, long. 119°54'40" W; near E line sec. 1, T 11 N, R 18 E). Named on Freel Peak (1955) 7.5' quadrangle.

Armstrong's Mill: see **Pine Grove** [AMADOR].

Arno [SACRAMENTO]: *locality,* 5.5 miles north-northwest of Galt along Southern Pacific Railroad (lat. 38°20' N, long. 121°20'05" W). Named on Galt (1910) 7.5' quadrangle. Postal authorities established Arno post office in 1889 and discontinued it in 1927 (Frickstad, p. 131). The name is from Arno River in Italy (Gudde, 1949, p. 15).

Arnold Bend [COLUSA]: *bend,* along Sacramento River at Colusa (lat. 39°13'10" N, long. 122°00'45" W). Named on Colusa (1952) 7.5' quadrangle.

Arroyo de los Osos: see **Bear River** [NEVADA-PLACER-SUTTER-YUBA].

Arroyo de los Putos: see **Putah Creek** [YOLO].

Arroyo Seco [AMADOR-SACRAMENTO]: *land grant,* west of Ione in Amador, Sacramento, and San Joaquin Counties. Named on Carbondale (1968), Goose Creek (1968), Ione (1962), and Irish Hill (1962) 7.5' quadrangles. Teodosio Yorba received 11 leagues in 1840; Andres Pico claimed 48,858 acres patented in 1863 (Cowan, p. 17).

Arroz [YOLO]: *locality,* 4 miles south of Madison along Southern Pacific Railroad (lat. 38°37'20" N, long. 121°58'15" W; at SW cor. sec. 15, T 9 N, R 1 W). Named on Winters (1953) 7.5' quadrangle.

Arthur: see **Lake Arthur** [PLACER].

Ashland [SACRAMENTO]: *locality,* less than 1 mile north-northwest of Folsom (lat. 38°41'10" N, long. 121°10'35" W). Named on Sacramento (1892) 30' quadrangle. Called Russville on Arrowsmith's (1860) map. The place was known as Big Gulch before it was renamed Russville to honor Colonel Russ, a promoter whose schemes failed; with the decline of the fortunes of Colonel Russ, the place was called Bowlesville until it was renamed Ashland in 1860 (Hoover, Rensch, and Rensch, p. 301). Postal authorities established Russville post office in 1857 and discontinued it in 1858 (Frickstad, p. 134). A place called Rocky Bar was situated on the south side of American River opposite present Ashland (Gudde, 1975, p. 295).

Ashland: see **Ashland Creek** [AMADOR].

Ashland Creek [AMADOR]: *stream,* flows about 7 miles to Sutter Creek (1) 4 miles northeast of Pine Grove (lat. 38°27'20" N, long. 120°36'25" W; sec. 13, T 7 N, R 12 E). Named on Omo Ranch (1952) and West Point (1948) 7.5' quadrangles. Camp's (1962) map shows an inhabited place called Ashland located along Ashland Creek 2.25 miles east-northeast of Volcano.

Aspen Campgrounds [SIERRA]: *locality,* 6.5 miles southeast of Sierra City along Jackson Meadows Reservoir (lat. 39°30'20" N, long. 120°32'10" W; near N line sec. 20, T 19 N, R 13 E). Named on Haypress Valley (1981) 7.5' quadrangle.

Aspen Creek [EL DORADO]: *stream,* flows 1.25 miles to South Fork American River 3 miles west of Echo Summit (lat. 38°48'45" N, long. 120°05'05" W; sec. 10, T 11 N, R 17 E). Named on Echo Lake (1955) 7.5' quadrangle.

Atchisons Bar: see **Mill Creek** [YUBA].

Atherton Flat [EL DORADO]: *area,* 2.25 miles northeast of Kyburz (lat. 38°48'05" N, long. 120°16' W; on W line sec. 18, T 11 N, R 16 E). Named on Kyburz (1952) 7.5' quadrangle.

Atlanta: see **Fordyce Lake** [NEVADA].

Auburn [PLACER]: *town,* in the center of the west half of Placer County (lat. 38°53'55" N, long. 121°04'25" W); the town is near the head of Auburn Ravine. Named on Auburn (1953) 7.5' quadrangle. Postal authorities established Auburn post office in 1853 (Frickstad, p. 119). The town incorporated in 1860, disincorporated about 1866, and incorporated again in 1888 (Hoover, Rensch, and Rensch, p. 269). Claude Chana discovered gold in Auburn Ravine in 1848; the mining camp that grew at the site later that same year was known as Wood's Dry Diggings, for John S. Wood, before it was named Auburn in the fall of 1849 (Davis, p. 5-7). The place also was called Rich Dry Diggin's (Jackson, J.H., p. 387). Postal authorities established East Auburn post office 1 mile east of Auburn post office in 1902 and discontinued it in 1919 (Salley, p. 63). They established Lone Star post office 6 miles north of Auburn in 1861 and discontinued it in 1863; the name was from Lone Star mine (Salley, p. 125). California Mining Bureau's (1917c) map shows a place called Leta located along the railroad about 3 miles west-southwest of Auburn. Gudde (1975, p. 195) listed a mining place called Little Rattlesnake Bar that was situated 1 mile southeast of Auburn along North Fork American River.

Auburn Ravine [PLACER-SUTTER]: *relief feature,* drained by a stream that heads near Auburn and flows 28 miles to end in American Basin 7.25 miles northeast of Verona in Sutter County (lat. 38°51'10" N, long. 121°30'40" W; at S line sec. 27, T 12 N, R 4 E). Named on Auburn (1953), Gold Hill (1954), Lincoln (1953), Pleasant Grove (1967), Roseville (1967), and Verona (1967) 7.5' quadrangles.

Auburn Station: see **Newcastle** [PLACER].

Audrian Lake: see **Lake Audrian** [EL DORADO].

Aukum [EL DORADO]: *locality,* 13 miles south-southwest of Camino (lat. 38°33'25" N, long. 120°43'30" W; near SE cor. sec. 11, T 8 N, R 11 E); the place is 1.25 miles south of Mount Aukum. Named on Aukum (1952) 7.5' quadrangle. United States Board on Geographic Names (1976, p. 5) gave the names "Aukum Fork" and "Mount Aukum" as variants. Postal authorities established Aukum post office in 1895, discontinued it in 1914, reestablished it in 1920, and changed the name to Mt. Aukum in 1961 (Salley, p. 148). California Mining Bureau's (1909a) map shows a place called Uno located nearly 3 miles east of Aukum by stage line. Postal authorities established Uno post office in 1892 and discontinued it in 1920 (Frickstad, p. 30).

Aukum: see **Mount Aukum** [EL DORADO].

Aukum Fork: see **Aukum** [EL DORADO].

Aurum City: see **El Dorado** [EL DORADO].

Austin Flat [NEVADA]: *area,* 6 miles west of Wolf (lat. 39°02'50" N, long. 121°14'50" W; near SE cor. sec. 24, T 14 N, R 6 E). Named on Wolf (1949) 7.5' quadrangle.

Austin Meadow [NEVADA]: *area,* 4 miles north-northwest of English Mountain (lat. 39°29'40" N, long. 120°35'20" W; near SE cor. sec. 23, T 19 N, R 12 E). Named on English Mountain (1983) 7.5' quadrangle.

Austin Ravine [NEVADA]: *canyon,* drained by a stream that flows 1 mile to Rock Creek (2) 8.5 miles south-southwest of Pilot Peak (lat. 39°03'50" N, long. 121°15'40" W; sec. 13, T 14 N, R 6 E). Named on Camp Far West (1949) 7.5' quadrangle.

Avalanche Lake [EL DORADO]: *lake,* 650 feet long, 5.25 miles west-northwest of Echo Summit (lat. 38°50' N, long. 120°07'20" W). Named on Echo Lake (1955) 7.5' quadrangle.

Avalanche Ravine: see **Big Avalanche Ravine** [SIERRA].

Avinsino Corner [EL DORADO]: *locality,* 3 miles south of Camino (lat. 38°41'35" N, long. 120°40'30" W; sec. 29, T 10 N, R 12 E). Named on Camino (1952) 7.5' quadrangle. The name should have the form "Avansino" (Beverly Cola, personal communication, 1985).

Ayrshire: see **Eldorado Bend** [SUTTER-YOLO].

Azalea Lake [NEVADA]: *lake,* 950 feet long, 1.25 miles north of Donner Pass (lat. 39°20'05" N, long. 120°19'40" W; on E line sec. 8, T 17 N, R 15 E). Named on Norden (1955) 7.5' quadrangle.

Azure Lake [EL DORADO]: *lake,* 2300 feet long, 1.5 miles northwest of Mount Tallac (lat. 38°55'15" N, long. 120°07'25" W; on S line sec. 32, T 13 N, R 17 E). Named on Emerald Bay (1955) and Rockbound Valley (1955) 7.5' quadrangles.

— B —

Babbitt Peak [SIERRA]: *peak,* 3.25 miles north-northwest of Crystal Peak (lat. 39°36'10" N, long. 120°06'15" W; near E line sec. 8, T 20 N, R 17 E). Named on Dog Valley (1981) 7.5' quadrangle.

Babel Slough [YOLO]: *water feature,* extends for nearly 4 miles from Sacramento River to near Sacramento River Deep Water Ship Channel about 4 miles west-northwest of Clarksburg (lat. 38°26'45" N, long. 121°35'35" W). Named on Clarksburg (1967) 7.5' quadrangle. The name commemorates Frederick Babel, who settled in the vicinity in 1849 (Gudde, 1949, p. 19).

Bacchis [EL DORADO]: *locality,* 11 miles east of Georgetown (lat. 38°54'50" N, long. 120°37'30" W). Named on Placerville (1893) 30' quadrangle.

Backbone House [NEVADA]: *locality,* 2 miles north of North Bloomfield (lat. 39°23'30" N, long. 120°54'35" W). Named on Colfax (1898) 30' quadrangle. Lindgren's (1911b) map shows a lake called Waldron Reservoir located about 650 feet southeast of Backbone House.

Bacon Canyon [EL DORADO]: *canyon,* drained by a stream that flows 1.5 miles to Pilot Creek (1) 12 miles north-northwest of Pollock Pines (lat. 38°55'40" N, long. 120°38'45" W). Named on Tunnel Hill (1950) 7.5' quadrangle.

Badenaugh Canyon [SIERRA]: *canyon,* drained by a stream that flows 5.5 miles to Smithneck Creek 4 miles southeast of Loyalton (lat. 39°37'50" N, long. 120°11'55" W; sec. 33, T 21 N, R 16 E). Named on Loyalton (1981) and Sardine Peak (1981) 7.5' quadrangles.

Badger Creek [SACRAMENTO]: *stream,* flows 14 miles to Cosumnes River 6 miles northwest of Galt (lat. 38°19'25" N, long. 121° 22' W). Named on Clay (1968), Galt (1968), and Sloughhouse (1968) 7.5' quadrangles. North Fork enters from the northeast 6.25 miles north-northwest of Galt. It is 9.5 miles long and is named on Elk Grove (1968), Galt (1968), and Sloughhouse (1968) 7.5' quadrangles.

Badger Hill [EL DORADO]: *peak,* 2.5 miles west-northwest of Pollock Pines (lat. 38°46'15" N, long. 120°37'55" W; sec. 27, T 11 N, R 12 E). Named on Slate Mountain (1950) 7.5' quadrangle.

Badger Hill [NEVADA]: *locality,* 4 miles east of North San Juan at present Badger Hill Diggings (lat. 39°22'50" N, long. 121°01'50" W). Named on Smartsville (1895) 30' quadrangle.

Badger Hill Diggings [NEVADA]: *locality,* 4 miles east-northeast of North San Juan (lat. 39°22'50" N, long. 121°01'50" W; sec. 36, T 18 N, R 8 E). Named on Camptonville (1948) 7.5' quadrangle.

Baileys [EL DORADO]: *locality,* 10.5 miles south-southeast of Placerville along Spanish Creek near the mouth of Grizzly Gulch (lat. 38°34'40" N, long. 120°45'30" W). Named on Placerville (1893) 30' quadrangle.

Baileys: see **Bayley House** [EL DORADO].

Bake Oven [PLACER]: *locality,* nearly 3 miles east of Michigan Bluff along North Fork of Middle Fork American River (lat. 39°02'40" N, long. 120°41' W; near W line sec. 19, T 14 N, R 12 E). Named on Michigan Bluff (1952) 7.5' quadrangle.

Baker Divide [PLACER]: *ridge,* west-northwest-trending, 1.25 miles long, 3.5 miles north-northeast of Foresthill (lat. 39°03'40" N, long. 120°46'40" W); the ridge is north-northwest of Baker Ranch. Named on Foresthill (1949) 7.5' quadrangle. Colfax (1898) 30' quadrangle has the name "Baker Divide" for a locality on the ridge.

Baker Ranch [PLACER]: *locality,* 4 miles northeast of Foresthill (lat. 39°03'20" N, long. 120°45'40" W; sec. 17, T 14 N, R 11 E). Named on Foresthill (1949) 7.5' quadrangle. J. Hull Baker operated a travelers stop at the place in the 1850's (Gudde, 1975, p. 25).

Bakers Ford [EL DORADO]: *locality,* 9 miles southeast of Placerville along Middle Fork Cosumnes River (lat. 38°37'30" N, long. 120°41'50" W). Named on Placerville (1893) 30' quadrangle.

Balaklava: see **Quaker Hill** [NEVADA] (2).

Bald Eagle: see **Remington Hill** [NEVADA] (2).

Balderson Station [EL DORADO]: *locality,* 5 miles east-northeast of Georgetown (lat. 38°56'05" N, long. 120°45'10" W; sec. 33, T 13 N, R 11 E). Named on Georgetown (1949) 7.5' quadrangle. Allen Balderston lived at the place (Yohalem, p. 198). California Division of Highways' (1934) map has the name "Virner" at or near present Balderson Station. Postal authorities established Virner post office in 1897 and discontinued it in 1913; the name was from Camp Virner, a vacation resort (Salley, p. 232).

Bald Hill [COLUSA]: *peak,* 7.25 miles north-northeast of Wilbur Springs (lat. 39°08'20" N, long. 122°22'50" W; at N line sec. 23, T 15 N, R 5 W). Altitude 1275 feet. Named on Wilbur Springs (1961) 15' quadrangle.

Bald Hill [EL DORADO]: *peak,* 2.25 miles south-southwest of Georgetown (lat. 38°52'35" N, long. 120°51'05" W; sec. 22, T 12 N, R 10 E). Altitude 2463 feet. Named on Georgetown (1949) 7.5' quadrangle.

Bald Hill [PLACER]: *ridge,* northwest-trending, 1 mile long, 2.25 miles west-northwest of Auburn (lat. 38°54'25" N, long. 121°06'45" W; sec. 7, 8, T 12 N, R 8 E). Named on Auburn (1953) 7.5' quadrangle.

Bald Mountain [EL DORADO]:

(1) *peak,* 12 miles northwest of Pollock Pines (lat. 38°54'15" N, long. 120°42'15" W; sec. 12, T 12 N, R 11 E). Altitude 4592 feet. Named on Tunnel Hill (1950) 7.5' quadrangle.

(2) *peak,* 6.5 miles south-southwest of Pyramid Peak (lat. 38°46' N, long. 120°13'15" W; near S line sec. 28, T 11 N, R 16 E). Altitude 6980 feet. Named on Pyramid Peak (1955) 7.5' quadrangle.

Bald Mountain [NEVADA]:

(1) *peak,* 5 miles north of Nevada City (lat. 39°20'05" N, long. 121° 00'45" W; sec. 18, T 17 N, R 9 E). Altitude 3125 feet. Named on Nevada City (1948) 7.5' quadrangle.

(2) *peak,* 4.5 miles north-northwest of Wolf (lat. 39°07'05" N, long. 121°10'30" W; near SE cor. sec. 27, T 15 N, R 7 E). Named on Wolf (1949) 7.5' quadrangle.

Bald Mountain [PLACER]: *peak,* 8 miles west of Martis Peak (lat. 39°17'50" N, long. 120°10'55" W; near E line sec. 27, T 17 N, R 16 E). Altitude 6760 feet. Named on Truckee (1955) 7.5' quadrangle.

Bald Mountain [SIERRA]:

(1) *peak,* 2.5 miles north-northwest of Goodyears Bar (lat. 39° 34'30" N, long. 120°53'50" W; near N line sec. 30, T 20 N, R 10 E). Altitude 5534 feet. Named on Goodyears Bar (1951) 7.5' quadrangle.

(2) *ridge,* southwest-trending, 1 mile long, 4 miles south of Downieville (lat. 39°30'15" N, long. 120°50' W). Named on Alleghany (1949) and Downieville (1951) 7.5' quadrangles.

Bald Mountain [YOLO]: *peak,* 5 miles southeast of Guinda in Capay Hills (lat. 38°47'15" N, long. 122°07'20" W; sec. 19, T 11 N, R 2 W). Altitude 1820 feet. Named on Bird Valley (1959) 7.5' quadrangle.

Bald Mountain: see **Browns Valley** [YUBA]; **Little Bald Mountain** [EL DORADO]; **Little Bald Mountain** [PLACER]; **Verdi Peak** [SIERRA].

Bald Mountain Canyon [EL DORADO]: *canyon,* drained by a stream that heads near Bald Mountain (1) and flows nearly 4 miles to Rock Creek 11.5 miles northwest of Pollock Pines (lat. 38°52'20" N, long. 120°44'35" W; sec. 22, T 12 N, R 11 E). Named on Slate Mountain (1950) and Tunnel Hill (1950) 7.5' quadrangles.

Bald Mountain Range [SIERRA]: *ridge,* generally south-southeast-trending, 8 miles long, center 8.5 miles east-southeast of Loyalton (lat. 39°36'15" N, long. 120°06'20" W). Named on Dog Valley (1981), Evans Canyon (1978), Loyalton (1981), and Sardine Peak (1981) 7.5' quadrangles.

Bald Ridge [SIERRA]: *ridge,* generally northwest-trending, 3.5 miles long, 5.5 miles east-southeast of Sierra City (lat. 39°31'45" N, long. 120°31'40" W). Named on Haypress Valley (1981) and Sattley (1981) 7.5' quadrangles.

Bald Rock Mountain [PLACER]: *peak,* 9 miles north-northwest of Auburn (lat. 39°01'20" N, long. 121°08'35" W; sec. 36, T 14 N, R 7 E). Altitude 1695 feet. Named on Wolf (1949) 7.5' quadrangle.

Bald Top [SIERRA]: *peak,* 4.25 miles northwest of Goodyears Bar (lat. 39°34'45" N, long. 120°56'50" W; near SE cor. sec. 22, T 20 N, R 9 E). Named on Goodyears Bar (1951) 7.5' quadrangle.

Baldwin Beach [EL DORADO]: *beach,* 3 miles north-northeast of Mount Tallac along Lake Tahoe (lat. 38°56'35" N, long. 120° 04' W; sec. 26, T 13 N, R 17 E). Named on Emerald Bay (1955) 7.5' quadrangle. E.J. "Lucky" Baldwin owned the beach (Lekisch, p. 6).

Baldwin Reservoir [PLACER-SACRAMENTO]: *lake,* 1500 feet long, 2.5 miles north of Folsom on Placer-Sacramento County line (lat. 38°42'50" N, long. 121°10'45" W; on S line sec. 14, T 10 N, R 7 E). Named on Folsom (1967) 7.5' quadrangle.

Ballarat Canyon [EL DORADO]: *canyon,* drained by a stream that flows 1.5 miles to Whaler Creek 9 miles northwest of Pollock Pines (lat. 38°51' N, long. 120°42'35" W; near NW cor. sec. 36, T 12 N, R 11 E). Named on Slate Mountain (1950) 7.5' quadrangle.

Ballard Ravine [EL DORADO]: *canyon,* drained by a stream that flows nearly 2 miles to Pilot Creek (1) 10.5 miles north-northwest of Pollock Pines (lat. 38°54'30" N, long. 120°37'35" W; sec. 10, T 12 N, R 12 E). Named on Devil Peak (1950) 7.5' quadrangle.

Ballards Humbug: see **Volcano** [AMADOR].

Balls [AMADOR]: *locality,* 9 miles west of present Fiddletown on the south side of Cosumnes River near the mouth of present Grapevine Ravine (lat. 38°30'45" N, long. 120°55'30" W). Named on Placerville (1893) 30' quadrangle.

Balls Canyon [SIERRA]: *canyon,* drained by a stream that flows 3.5 miles to Upper Long Valley 10 miles east of Loyalton (lat. 39°39'25" N, long. 120°03'05" W; near W line sec. 23, T 21 N, R 17 E). Named on Evans Canyon (1978) 7.5' quadrangle, which shows Balls ranch in the canyon.

Balls Creek [SIERRA]: *stream,* flows 5.5 miles to Long Valley Creek 12 miles east of Loyalton (lat. 39°41' N, long. 120°00'55" W; at W line sec. 18, T 21 N, R 18 E); the stream drains Balls Canyon. Named on Loyalton (1955) 15' quadrangle.

Baloon Ridge [PLACER]: *ridge,* west-southwest-trending, 0.5 mile long, 4.25 miles east-northeast of Michigan Bluff (lat. 39°03'55" N, long. 120°39'45" W; sec. 17, T 14 N, R 12 E). Named on Michigan Bluff (1952) 7.5' quadrangle.

Balsam Flat [SIERRA]: *area,* 1 mile east-southeast of Alleghany (lat. 39°27'50" N, long. 120°49'35" W; on N line sec. 2, T 18 N, R 10 E). Named on Alleghany (1949) 7.5' quadrangle.

Baltic Creek [EL DORADO]: *stream,* flows nearly 3 miles to Camp Creek 8.5 miles east of Camino (lat. 38°43'20" N, long. 120°31'10" W; near N line sec. 15, T 10 N, R 13 E); the stream is north of Baltic Peak. Named on Sly Park (1952) 7.5' quadrangle.

Baltic Creek [NEVADA]: *stream,* flows 1 mile to Little Canyon Creek 4 miles south of Graniteville (lat. 39°22'55" N, long. 120° 44' W; near W line sec. 34, T 18 N, R 11 E). Named on Graniteville (1982) 7.5' quadrangle, which shows Baltic mine near the stream.

Baltic Peak [EL DORADO]: *peak,* 9 miles east-southeast of Camino (lat. 38°41'40" N, long. 120°30'50" W; near N line sec. 26, T 10 N, R 13 E); the peak is at the northwest end of Baltic Ridge. Altitude 5078 feet. Named on Sly Park (1952) 7.5' quadrangle. Forest Service officials named the feature for Baltic mine, located north of the peak (Gudde, 1969, p. 21).

Baltic Ridge [EL DORADO]: *ridge,* generally west-trending, 16 miles long, center 6 miles west-northwest of Leek Spring Hill (lat. 38°40'10" N, long. 120°22'15" W); Baltic Peak is at the northwest end of the ridge. Named on Leek Spring Hill (1951), Sly Park (1952), and Stump Spring (1951) 7.5' quadrangles.

Baltimore [PLACER]: *locality,* less than 1 mile southwest of Foresthill (lat. 39°00'50" N, long. 120°49'40" W; sec. 35, T 14 N, R 10 E). Named on Colfax (1938) 30' quadrangle.

Baltimore: see **Knights Landing** [YOLO].

Baltimore Lake [NEVADA]: *lake,* 1100 feet long, 4 miles south-southeast of English Mountain (lat. 39°23'30" N, long. 120°31'50" W; near SE cor. sec. 29, T 18 N, R 13 E); the lake is 0.25 mile north of the site of Baltimore Town. Named on English Mountain (1983) 7.5' quadrangle.

Baltimore Ravine [PLACER]: *canyon,* drained by a stream that flows less than 1 mile to Auburn Ravine 1.25 miles west-southwest of downtown Auburn (lat. 38°53'25" N, long. 121°05'35" W; sec. 16, T 12 N, R 8 E). Named on Auburn (1953) 7.5' quadrangle.

Baltimore Ravine: see **Scotchman Creek** [NEVADA].

Baltimore Town [NEVADA]: *locality,* 4.25 miles south-southeast of English Mountain (lat. 39°23'10" N, long. 120°31'50" W; near E line sec. 32, T 18 N, R 13 E). Site named on English Mountain (1983) 7.5' quadrangle. The place first was called Wightman's Camp (Fatout, p. 37).

Banjo: see **Missouri Canyon** [NEVADA] (1).

Banner Hill: see **Banner Mountain** [NEVADA].

Banner Mountain [NEVADA]: *peak,* 7 miles north of Chicago Park (lat. 39°14'45" N, long. 120°57'55" W; near SE cor. sec. 16, T 16 N, R 9 E). Altitude 3899 feet. Named on Chicago Park (1949) 7.5' quadrangle. Called Banner Hill on Colfax (1898) 30' quadrangle.

Banner Reservoir [NEVADA]: *lake,* 750 feet long, 2.5 miles east-northeast of Grass Valley (lat. 39°14'15" N, long. 121°01' W; near W line sec. 19, T 16 N, R 9 E). Named on Grass Valley (1949) 7.5' quadrangle, which shows Banner Mtn. mine near the feature.

Bannon Slough: see **First Bannon Slough** [SACRAMENTO]; **Second Bannon Slough** [SACRAMENTO].

Barker Creek [PLACER]: *stream,* flows nearly 7 miles to Rubicon River 3.5 miles east-northeast of Bunker Hill (lat. 39°03'50" N, long. 120°18'55" W; sec. 17, T 14 N, R 15 E); the stream goes through Barker Meadow. Named on Homewood (1955) and Wentworth Springs (1953) 7.5' quadrangles.

Barker House: see **Woodleaf** [YUBA].

Barker Meadow [PLACER]: *area,* 5 miles west-southwest of Homewood (lat. 39°04' N, long. 120°14'45" W); the place is on upper reaches of Barker Creek. Named on Homewood (1955) and Wentworth Springs (1953) 7.5' quadrangles.

Barker Pass [PLACER]: *pass,* 4 miles west-southwest of Homewood (lat. 39°04'35" N, long. 120°13'55" W; sec. 8, T 14 N, R 16 E); the pass is at the head of Barker Creek. Named on Homewood (1955) 7.5' quadrangle.

Barker Peak [PLACER]: *peak,* 4.25 miles west of Homewood (lat. 39°04'45" N, long. 120°14'15" W; sec. 8, T 14 N, R 16 E); the peak is 0.25 mile west-northwest of Barker Pass. Altitude 8166 feet. Named on Homewood (1955) 7.5' quadrangle.

Barker's Ranch: see **Woodleaf** [YUBA].

Bark Shanty Canyon [EL DORADO]: *canyon,* drained by a stream that flows 4.25 miles to Silver Fork American River 8 miles west of Kirkwood (lat. 38°42'40" N, long. 120°13'15" W; near SE cor. sec. 17, T 10 N, R 16 E). Named on Tragedy Spring (1979) 7.5' quadrangle.

Barley Flat [EL DORADO]: *area,* 5.5 miles north-northeast of Chili Bar (lat. 38°50'25" N, long. 120°47'20" W; near S line sec. 31, T 12 N, R 11 E). Named on Garden Valley (1949) 7.5' quadrangle.

Barney Cavanah Ridge [PLACER]: *ridge,* generally southwest-trending, 5.5 miles long, 2.5 miles southwest of Duncan Peak (lat. 39°07'30" N, long. 120°32'30" W). Named on Duncan Peak (1952) and Greek Store (1952) 7.5' quadrangles. Logan's (1925) map shows Barney Kavanaugh cabin at or near the ridge.

Barney Meadow [EL DORADO]: *area,* 4.25 miles south-southwest of Caldor along Sopiago Creek (lat. 38°33' N, long. 120°27'50" W; on E line sec. 18, T 8 N, R 14 E); the place is north of the east end of Barney Ridge. Named on Caldor (1951) 7.5' quadrangle.

Barney Mound [SUTTER]: *hill,* 2.25 miles east of Verona in American Basin (lat. 38°47'05" N, long. 121°34'35" W; sec. 19, T 11 N, R 4 E). Altitude 32 feet. Named on Verona (1967) 7.5' quadrangle.

Barney Ridge [EL DORADO]: *ridge,* generally west-trending, 6.5 miles long, center 5.5 miles southwest of Caldor (lat. 38°32'40" N, long. 120°29'30" W). Named on Caldor (1951) and Omo Ranch (1952) 7.5' quadrangles. Pyramid Peak (1896) 30' quadrangle has the name "Barneys" for a place on the ridge.

Barneys: see **Barney Ridge** [EL DORADO].

Barnham's Crossing: see **Oro**, under **Nicolaus** [SUTTER].

Barrett Lake [EL DORADO]: *lake,* 800 feet long, 5.5 miles southwest of Phipps Peak (lat. 38°54'15" N, long. 120°13'45" W; at W line sec. 9, T 12 N, R 16 E). Named on Rockbound Valley (1955) 7.5' quadrangle.

Barry Creek [SIERRA]: *stream,* heads in Plumas County and flows 2.5 miles in Sierra County before reentering Plumas County 11 miles north-northeast of Sierra City (lat. 39°42'25" N, long. 120° 31'35" W; near S line sec. 4, T 21 N, R 13 E). Named on Calpine (1981) and Clio (1981) 7.5' quadrangles.

Barton [AMADOR]: *locality,* 8 miles east-northeast of Pine Grove (lat. 38°27'20" N, long. 120°31'45" W; near S line sec. 15, T 7 N, R 13 E). Named on West Point (1948) 7.5' quadrangle.

Barton Hill [YUBA]: *ridge,* west-trending, less than 1 mile long, 1.5 miles west-southwest of Strawberry Valley (lat. 39°33'05" N, long. 121°08'05"

W; mainly in sec. 36, T 20 N, R 7 E). Named on Clipper Mills (1948) 7.5' quadrangle.

Bartons Bar: see **Parks Bar** [YUBA].

Bartons House: see **Strawberry Valley** [YUBA].

Barts Creek [EL DORADO-PLACER]: *stream,* heads in Placer County and flows 5 miles to Gerle Creek 2 miles west of Wentworth Springs at Gerle Meadow in El Dorado County (lat. 39°00'50" N, long. 120°22'35" W; sec. 35, T 14 N, R 14 E); the stream goes through Barts Valley. Named on Bunker Hill (1953) and Wentworth Springs (1953) 7.5' quadrangles.

Barts Valley [PLACER]: *canyon,* 1 mile long, 1 mile east-southeast of Bunker Hill (lat. 39°02'30" N, long. 120°21'40" W; mainly in sec. 24, T 14 N, R 14 E); the canyon is along upper reaches of Barts Creek. Named on Wentworth Springs (1953) 7.5' quadrangle.

Basin Peak [NEVADA]: *peak,* 5 miles north-northwest of Donner Pass (lat. 39°22'55" N, long. 120°21'45" W; near E line sec. 35, T 18 N, R 14 E). Altitude 9017 feet. Named on Independence Lake (1981) 7.5' quadrangle.

Bassetts [SIERRA]: *locality,* 4.25 miles north-northeast of Sierra City along North Yuba River (lat. 39°37' N, long. 120°35'25" W; sec. 11, R 20 N, R 12 E); the place is at the mouth of Howard Creek. Named on Haypress Valley (1981) 7.5' quadrangle. An inn called Hancock House opened at the site in the early 1860's; about 1865 the name of the place was changed to Howard Ranch for Howard Chris Tegerman, the owner; the name was changed again in the 1870's to Bassett's Station for Jacob Bassett and Mary Bassett (Gudde, 1975, p. 28).

Bassett's Station: see **Bassetts** [SIERRA].

Bassi [EL DORADO]: *locality,* 5.25 miles east of Robbs Peak (lat. 38° 55' N, long. 120°18'30" W). Named on Pyramid Peak (1896) 30' quadrangle.

Bassi Falls [EL DORADO]: *waterfall,* 4.5 miles east-southeast of Robbs Peak (lat. 38°53'35" N, long. 120°19'45" W; near NW cor. sec. 17, T 12 N, R 15 E); the feature is along Bassi Fork. Named on Loon Lake (1952) 7.5' quadrangle.

Bassi Fork [EL DORADO]: *stream,* flows 8 miles to Big Silver Creek 4.25 miles southeast of Robbs Peak (lat. 38°52'50" N, long. 120° 20'45" W; near SW cor. sec. 18, T 12 N, R 15 E). Named on Loon Lake (1952) 7.5' quadrangle.

Bass Lake [EL DORADO]: *lake,* 3550 feet long, 2.25 miles northeast of Clarksville (lat. 38°40'45" N, long. 121°01'15" W; on E line sec. 31, T 10 N, R 9 E). Named on Clarksville (1953, photorevised 1980) 7.5' quadrangle. Logan's (1938) map has the name "Bass Lake Reservoir" for the feature.

Bass Lake Reservoir: see **Bass Lake** [EL DORADO].

Bates Canyon: see **Batiste Canyon** [COLUSA].

Bath [PLACER]: *locality,* 1.5 miles northeast of Foresthill (lat. 39° 02' N, long. 120°47'55" W). Named on Colfax (1898) 30' quadrangle. Postal authorities established Bath post office in 1858, discontinued it in 1859, reestablished it in 1861, discontinued it in 1890, reestablished it in 1891, and discontinued it in 1899 (Frickstad, p. 119). After prospectors discovered gold at the site in 1850, the mining camp there was called Volcano for nearby Volcano Canyon; the name of the camp was changed to Sarahsville to honor the first woman at the place, and then changed to Bath when the post office was established (Hoover, Rensch, and Rensch, p. 274). Whitney's (1873) map shows a place called Forest Shades located about halfway between Bath and Foresthill.

Bathhouse Ravine [NEVADA]: *canyon,* drained by a stream that flows 1.25 miles to Middle Yuba River 5.5 miles north-northeast of North Bloomfield (lat. 39°26'10" N, long. 120°50'45" W; near SW cor. sec. 10, T 18 N, R 10 E). Named on Alleghany (1949) 7.5' quadrangle.

Batiste Canyon [COLUSA]: *canyon,* 1 mile long, 12.5 miles north of Wilbur Springs (lat. 39°14' N, long. 122°26'25" W; sec. 17, 20, T 16 N, R 5 W). Named on Wilbur Springs (1961) 15' quadrangle. Called Bates Canyon on Wilbur Springs (1944) 15' quadrangle.

Baville: see **Cooks Station** [AMADOR].

Baxter [PLACER]: *village,* 3 miles east of Dutch Flat (lat. 39°12'50" N, long. 120°46'50" W; sec. 31, T 16 N, R 11 E). Named on Dutch Flat (1950) 7.5' quadrangle. Postal authorities established Baxter post office in 1935 (Frickstad, p. 119). The name originated with a travelers stop at the place (Stewart, p. 90).

Bayley House [EL DORADO]: *locality,* 1.25 miles north of the village of Pilot Hill (lat. 38°51'15" N, long. 121°00'50" W; sec. 31, T 12 N, R 9 E). Named on Auburn (1954) 15' quadrangle. Called Baileys on Sacramento (1892) 30' quadrangle.

Beach Lake [SACRAMENTO]: *lake,* 7 miles west-northwest of Elk Grove (lat. 38°26'20" N, long. 121°29'30" W). Named on Florin (1909) 7.5' quadrangle. The name commemorates Julius C. Beach, an early settler (Dillon, p. 68).

Beacon Creek [SACRAMENTO]: *stream,* flows 6.5 miles to Morrison Creek 8 miles south-southeast of downtown Sacramento (lat. 38°27'40" N, long. 121°27'35" W). Named on Elk Grove (1968) and Florin (1968) 7.5' quadrangles.

Beacon Point [SIERRA]: *peak,* 2.5 miles southeast of Crystal Peak (lat. 39°32' N, long. 120°02'55" W; near NE cor. sec. 2, T 19 N, R 17 E). Altitude 7501 feet. Named on Dog Valley (1981) 7.5' quadrangle.

Beal Air Force Base [NEVADA-YUBA]: *military installation,* east of Marysville between Yuba River and Bear River on Nevada-Yuba County line, mainly in Yuba County. Named on Browns Valley (1947), Camp Far West (1949), Rough and Ready (1949), Smartville (1951), Wheatland (1947), and Wolf (1949) 7.5' quadrangles. Called Camp Beal Military Reservation on Grass Valley (1949) and Wheatland (1949) 15' quadrangles. War Department officials established Camp Beal in 1942 and named it for Edward Fitzgerald Beal (Hoover, Rensch, and Rensch, p. 589).

Beals Bar: see **Beals Point** [PLACER].

Beals Point [PLACER]: *promontory,* 6 miles southeast of Rocklin along Folsom Lake (lat. 38°43'15" N, long. 120°10'10" W; at W line sec. 13, T 10 N, R 7 E). Named on Folsom (1967) 7.5' quadrangle. Arrowsmith's (1860) map shows Beals Bar situated east of present Beals Point on the west side of North Fork American River just above the junction with South Fork; water of Folsom Lake now covers the site of this old mining camp. Gudde (1975, p. 347) listed a mining place called Texas Bar that was located along North Fork near Beals Bar.

Beanville Creek [EL DORADO]: *stream,* flows 3.25 miles to Silver Fork American River 1 mile south-southwest of Kyburz (lat. 38° 45'50" N, long. 120°18'05" W). Named on Kyburz (1952) and Leek Spring Hill (1951) 7.5' quadrangles.

Bear Canyon [YOLO]: *canyon,* drained by a stream that flows 1.5 miles to Fiske Creek 4 miles west of Rumsey (lat. 38°53'55" N, long. 122°18'40" W; sec. 9, T 12 N, R 4 W). Named on Glascock Mountain (1958) 7.5' quadrangle.

Bear Creek [EL DORADO]:

(1) *stream,* flows 2 miles to Silver Creek 7 miles north-northeast of Pollock Pines (lat. 38°50'50" N, long. 120°30'20" W; sec. 34, T 12 N, R 13 E). Named on Pollock Pines (1950) and Riverton (1950) 7.5' quadrangles.

(2) *stream,* flows 7.25 miles to Rock Creek 4 miles north-northeast of Chili Bar (lat. 38°49' N, long. 120°46'50" W; near W line sec. 8, T 11 N, R 11 E). Named on Garden Valley (1949) and Georgetown (1949) 7.5' quadrangles. Called West Fork Rock Creek on Placerville (1893) 30' quadrangle.

Bear Creek [COLUSA]: *stream,* flows 26 miles to Cache Creek 9 miles south-southeast of Wilbur Springs (lat. 38°55'35" N, long. 122°19'55" W; sec. 32, T 13 N, R 4 W). Named on Morgan Valley (1958) and Wilbur Springs (1961) 15' quadrangles.

Bear Creek [PLACER]: *stream,* flows 3 miles to Truckee River 3.25 miles west-northwest of Tahoe City (lat. 39°11'25" N, long. 120° 11'50" W; at W line sec. 34, T 16 N, R 16 E). Named on Tahoe City (1955) 7.5' quadrangle.

Bear Creek [SIERRA]: *stream,* flows 3.5 miles to Middle Yuba River 8 miles southeast of Downieville (lat. 39°28' N, long. 120° 44'35" W; sec. 33, T 19 N, R 11 E). Named on Alleghany (1949), Graniteville (1982), and Sierra City (1981) 7.5' quadrangles.

Bear Creek: see **Bear River** [NEVADA-PLACER-SUTTER-YUBA]; **Little Bear Creek** [PLACER].

Bear Creek Campground [PLACER]: *locality,* 3.5 miles west-northwest of Tahoe City (lat. 39°10'55" N, long. 120°12'25" W; near NW cor. sec. 3, T 15 N, R 16 E); the place is along Bear Creek. Named on Tahoe City (1955, photorevised 1969) 7.5' quadrangle.

Bear Den Canyon: see **Bear Pen Creek** [PLACER].

Bear Flat [EL DORADO]: *area,* 2.5 miles north of Georgetown (lat. 38°56'40" N, long. 120°49'50" W; sec. 26, T 13 N, R 10 E). Named on Georgetown (1949) 7.5' quadrangle.

Bear Flat [SIERRA]: *area,* 5.5 miles east-northeast of Sierraville (lat. 39°36'30" N, long. 120°15'45" W; near SW cor. sec. 1, T 20 N, R 15 E). Named on Sierraville (1981) 7.5' quadrangle.

Bear Lake [PLACER]: *lake,* 700 feet long, 4.5 miles southwest of Homewood (lat. 39°02'55" N, long. 120°13'40" W; sec. 20, T 14 N, R 16 E). Named on Homewood (1955) 7.5' quadrangle.

Bear Lake [SACRAMENTO]: *lake,* 10 miles south-southwest of Elk Grove (lat. 38°17' N, long. 121°28'15" W). Named on Bruceville (1910) 7.5' quadrangle.

Bear Meadow [EL DORADO]: *area,* 5 miles southwest of Old Iron Mountain (lat. 38°39'55" N, long. 120°28'05" W; sec. 6, T 9 N, R 14 E). Named on Stump Spring (1951) 7.5' quadrangle.

Bear Meadow Creek [EL DORADO]: *stream,* flows 1.25 miles to North Fork Cosumnes River 5 miles west-southwest of Old Iron Mountain (lat. 38°40'45" N, long. 120°28'35" W; near W line sec. 31, T 10 N, R 14 E); the stream heads near Bear Meadow. Named on Stump Spring (1951) 7.5' quadrangle.

Bear Pen Creek [PLACER]: *stream,* flows 2.5 miles to Five Lakes Creek nearly 7 miles northeast of Bunker Hill (lat. 39°06'45" N, long. 120°17'15" W; near S line sec. 27, T 15 N, R 15 E). Named on Homewood (1955) and Wentworth Springs (1953) 7.5' quadrangles. On Truckee (1940) 30' quadrangle, the canyon of the stream is called Bear Den Canyon.

Bear River [AMADOR]: *stream,* flows 19 miles to North Fork Mokelumne River 6.5 miles southeast of Hams Station (lat. 38°28'35" N, long.

120°17'45" W; sec. 11, T 7 N, R 15 E). Named on Bear River Reservoir (1979), Garnet Hill (1979), Mokelumne Peak (1979), and Peddler Hill (1951) 7.5' quadrangles. United States Board on Geographic Names (1981, p. 3) rejected the names "South Branch Bear River" and "Tragedy Creek" for any part of the stream.

Bear River [NEVADA-PLACER-SUTTER-YUBA]: *stream,* flows 63 miles along Nevada-Placer County line and along and near Sutter-Yuba County line to Feather River 2.5 miles north of Nicolaus in Yuba County (lat. 38°56'20" N, long. 121°34'45" W); the river heads at Bear Valley [NEVADA-PLACER]. Named on Blue Canyon (1955), Camp Far West (1949), Chicago Park (1949), Colfax (1949), Dutch Flat (1950), Lake Combie (1949), Nicolaus (1952), Sheridan (1953), Washington (1950), Wheatland (1947), and Wolf (1949) 7.5' quadrangles. Called Arroyo de los Osos on a diseño of 1844 (Becker). Called Bear Creek on Ord's (1848) map.

Bear River [YUBA]: *locality,* 8 miles south of Olivehurst along Northern Electric Railroad (lat. 38°58'35" N, long. 121°32'35" W; at E line sec. 17, T 13 N, R 4 E); the place is just north of Bear River. Named on Nicolaus (1910) 7.5' quadrangle.

Bear River: see **Chicago Park** [NEVADA]; **Little Bear River** [AMADOR].

Bear River Campground: see **Lower Bear River Campground** [AMADOR].

Bear River Group Campground [AMADOR]: *locality,* 7.25 miles west of Mokelumne Peak (lat. 38°32'05" N, long. 120°13'45" W; sec. 20, T 8 N, R 16 E). Named on Bear River Reservoir (1979) 7.5' quadrangle.

Bear River House: see **Applegate** [PLACER].

Bear River Lake: see **Bear River Reservoir** [AMADOR].

Bear River Pines [NEVADA]: *settlement,* 1.5 miles north of Chicago Park (lat. 39°10'10" N, long. 120°58' W; near NE cor. sec. 9, T 15 N, R 9 E). Named on Chicago Park (1949) 7.5' quadrangle.

Bear River Reservoir [AMADOR]: *lake,* 1 mile long, behind a dam on Bear River nearly 7 miles west-northwest of Mokelumne Peak (lat. 38°33'25" N, long. 120°12'55" W; sec. 9, T 8 N, R 16 E). Named on Bear River Reservoir (1979) 7.5' quadrangle. Postal authorities established Bear River Lake post office in 1967 to serve a vacation resort by the lake (Salley, p. 17).

Bear River Reservoir: see **Lower Bear River Reservoir** [AMADOR].

Bear Slough [SACRAMENTO]: *water feature,* 5 miles west of Galt (lat. 38°14'45" N, long. 121°23'25" W). Named on Thornton (1978) 7.5' quadrangle.

Bear Spring [PLACER]: *spring,* nearly 7 miles south-southwest of Duncan Peak (lat. 39°04'05" N, long. 120°34'05" W; sec. 18, T 14 N, R 13 E). Named on Greek Store (1952) 7.5' quadrangle.

Bear Spring [YOLO]: *spring,* nearly 3 miles north-northwest of Berryessa Peak on Blue Ridge (lat. 38°42' N, long. 122°12'50" W; sec. 20, T 10 N, R 3 W). Named on Brooks (1959) 7.5' quadrangle.

Bear Springs [PLACER]: *spring,* 6.25 miles west-southwest of Bunker Hill (lat. 39°00'55" N, long. 120°29'10" W; sec. 35, T 14 N, R 13 E). Named on Bunker Hill (1953) 7.5' quadrangle.

Beartrap: see **The Beartrap** [NEVADA].

Bear Trap Creek [PLACER]: *stream,* flows 2 miles to Deep Canyon nearly 5 miles southwest of Duncan Peak (lat. 39°06'40" N, long. 120°34'40" W; near NW cor. sec. 31, T 15 N, R 13 E). Named on Greek Store (1952) 7.5' quadrangle. Logan's (1925) map has the name "Bear Trap Ravine" for the canyon of the stream.

Beartrap Meadow [SIERRA]: *area,* 9 miles northeast of Sierra City (lat. 39°38'30" N, long. 120°30'15" W; sec. 34, T 21 N, R 13 E). Named on Calpine (1981) and Clio (1981) 7.5' quadrangles.

Beartrap Mountain [SIERRA]: *peak,* 2.5 miles east-southeast of Mount Fillmore on Sierra-Plumas County line (lat. 39°43'15" N, long. 120°48'30" W; sec. 36, T 22 N, R 10 E). Altitude 7232 feet. Named on Mount Fillmore (1951) 7.5' quadrangle.

Bear Trap Ravine: see **Bear Trap Creek** [PLACER].

Bear Trap Spring [NEVADA]: *spring,* 2.25 miles northwest of North Bloomfield (lat. 39°23'45" N, long. 120°55'25" W; near W line sec. 25, T 18 N, R 9 E). Named on Pike (1949) 7.5' quadrangle.

Bear Valley [COLUSA]: *valley,* 12 miles long, along Bear Creek above a point 2.25 miles north of Wilbur Springs (lat. 39°04'15" N, long. 122°24'30" W). Named on Wilbur Springs (1961) 15' quadrangle.

Bear Valley [NEVADA]: *valley,* 9.5 miles northwest of Donner Pass (lat. 39°25'45" N, long. 120°25'40" W; sec. 17, T 18 N, R 14 E). Named on Webber Peak (1981) 7.5' quadrangle.

Bear Valley [NEVADA-PLACER]: *valley,* 1 mile west-northwest of Emigrant Gap [PLACER] (1) on Nevada-Placer County line (lat. 39°18'25" N, long. 120°41' W); the valley is along Bear River. Named on Blue Canyon (1955) 7.5' quadrangle.

Bear Valley [SIERRA]:

(1) *valley,* 8 miles south of Loyalton (lat. 39°33'45" N, long. 120° 13'30" W; at N line sec. 29, T 20 N, R 16 E). Named on Sardine Peak (1981) 7.5' quadrangle.

(2) *valley,* 5.25 miles southeast of Sierra City (lat. 39°31'15" N, long. 120°33'15" W; on S line sec. 7, T 19 N, R 13 E). Named on Haypress Valley (1981) 7.5' quadrangle.

Bear Valley Buttes [COLUSA]: *ridge,* south-trending, 4.5 miles long, 11 miles north of Wilbur Springs (lat. 39°12' N, long. 122°26'30" W); the ridge is east of the north part of Bear Valley. Named on Wilbur Springs (1961) 15' quadrangle. Called Gravelly Buttes on Wilbur Springs (1944) 15' quadrangle.

Bear Valley Campground [SIERRA]: *locality,* 8 miles south of Loyalton (lat. 39°33'25" N, long. 120°14'10" W; near E line sec. 30, T 20 N, R 16 E); the place is less than 1 mile southwest of Bear Valley (1). Named on Sardine Peak (1981) 7.5' quadrangle.

Bear Valley Creek [SIERRA]: *stream,* flows 8 miles to Smithneck Creek 2 miles south-southeast of Loyalton (lat. 39°38'55" N, long. 120°13'20" W; near NE cor. sec. 30, T 21 N, R 16 E); the stream goes through Bear Valley (1). Named on Loyalton (1981) and Sardine Peak (1981) 7.5' quadrangles.

Bear Valley House [NEVADA]: *locality,* 8.5 miles south-southeast of Graniteville (lat. 39°18'30" N, long. 120°41'15" W); the place is in Bear Valley [NEVADA-PLACER] (1). Named on Colfax (1898) 30' quadrangle.

Bear Wallow [PLACER]: *relief feature,* 5.5 miles northeast of Michigan Bluff (lat. 39°06'05" N, long. 120°39'45" W; sec. 32, T 15 N, R 12 E). Named on Michigan Bluff (1952) 7.5' quadrangle.

Bear Wallows [PLACER]: *canyon,* drained by a stream that flows 1 mile to Grouse Creek 6.5 miles east-northeast of Michigan Bluff (lat. 39°05'30" N, long. 120°37'50" W; sec. 3, T 14 N, R 12 E). Named on Greek Store (1952) and Michigan Bluff (1952) 7.5' quadrangles.

Bear Wallow Spring [COLUSA]: *spring,* 0.5 mile northeast of Pacific Point (lat. 39°13'10" N, long. 122°35'20" W; sec. 24, T 16 N, R 7 W). Named on Clearlake Oaks (1960) 15' quadrangle.

Beatrice [YOLO]: *locality,* 10.5 miles northeast of Davis along Sacramento Northern Railroad (lat. 38°38'35" N, long. 121°35'40" W). Named on Taylor Monument (1967) 7.5' quadrangle.

Beauty Lake [EL DORADO]: *lake,* 650 feet long, 4.25 miles west of Pyramid Peak (lat. 38°51'20" N, long. 120°14'05" W; sec. 29, T 12 N, R 16 E). Named on Pyramid Peak (1955) 7.5' quadrangle. Shown as one of the group called Wrights Lakes on Pyramid Peak (1896) 30' quadrangle.

Beaver Bar: see **Rattlesnake Bar** [PLACER].

Beaver Creek [AMADOR]: *stream,* flows 3.5 miles to Bear River 6.25 miles southeast of Hams Station (lat. 38°29'05" N, long. 120° 17'45" W; sec. 2, T 7 N, R 15 E); the stream is east of Beaver Ridge. Named on Garnet Hill (1979) and Peddler Hill (1951) 7.5' quadrangles

Beaver Creek: see **Brandy Creek** [YUBA].

Beaver Lake [SACRAMENTO]: *marsh,* 6.25 miles north-northeast of Isleton on Grand Island (lat. 38°14'45" N, long. 121°33'40" W). Named on Isleton (1978) 7.5' quadrangle.

Beaver Lake [YOLO]: *lake,* 650 feet long, 8.5 miles east of Dunnigan near Sacramento River (lat. 38°53'20" N, long. 121°48'40" W; sec. 13, T 12 N, R 1 E). Named on Kirkville (1952) 7.5' quadrangle.

Beaver Ridge [AMADOR]: *ridge,* south-southwest-trending, 5 miles long, 3.5 miles southeast of Hams Station (lat. 38°30'45" N, long. 120°19'20" W); the ridge is west of Beaver Creek. Named on Garnet Hill (1979) and Peddler Hill (1951) 7.5' quadrangles.

Becker Flat [COLUSA]: *area,* 4.5 miles east of Wilbur Springs (lat. 39°01'40" N, long. 122°20'15" W). Named on Wilbur Springs (1961) 15' quadrangle.

Becker Peak [EL DORADO]: *peak,* 2 miles northwest of Echo Summit (lat. 38°49'55" N, long. 120°03'30" W; sec. 1, T 11 N, R 17 E). Named on Echo Lake (1955) 7.5' quadrangle. The name commemorates John S. Becker, who built a cabin in the region in 1886 and homesteaded in section 1 in 1904 (Lekisch, p. 7-8).

Beckman Hill: see **Anthony House** [NEVADA].

Beckmans Flat: see **Newtown** [NEVADA].

Bedbug: see **Ione** [AMADOR].

Beeks Bight [PLACER]: *embayment,* 6 miles east-southeast of Rocklin along Folsom Lake (lat. 38°46'15" N, long. 121°07'45" W; near S line sec 30, T 11 N, R 8 E). Named on Rocklin (1967) 7.5' quadrangle.

Beet Spur: see **Meridian** [SUTTER].

Bella Union Ravine [SIERRA]: *canyon,* drained by a stream that flows nearly 1 mile to Canyon Creek 9 miles southwest of Mount Fillmore (lat. 39°37'30" N, long. 120°56'45" W; sec. 3, T 20 N, R 9 E). Named on La Porte (1951) 7.5' quadrangle.

Bellevue [EL DORADO]: *locality,* 1.25 miles northeast of the present town of Meeks Bay along Lake Tahoe (lat. 39°03'05" N, long. 120° 06'45" W). Named on Truckee (1895) 30' quadrangle.

Bell Point [SIERRA]: *relief feature,* 3.5 miles east of Alleghany (lat. 39°28'20" N, long. 120°46'25" W; at E line sec. 31, T 19 N, E 11 E). Named on Alleghany (1949) 7.5' quadrangle.

Bells Diggings: see **Missouri Canyon** [EL DORADO].

Ben Ali [SACRAMENTO]: *locality,* 5 miles northeast of downtown Sacramento along Southern Pacific Railroad (lat. 38°37'20" N, long. 121°25'20" W). Named on Sacramento East (1967) 7.5' quadrangle. The name commemorates James Ben Ali Haggin, part owner of Del Paso grant in the 1860's (Hanna, p. 29).

Ben Bolt [EL DORADO]: *peak,* 5 miles south-southeast of Clarksville (lat.

38°35'05" N, long. 121°01'10" W; near SW cor. sec. 32, T 9 N, R 9 E); the feature is the high point on present Ben Bolt Ridge. Altitude 1139 feet. Named on Folsom (1941) 15' quadrangle.

Ben Bolt Ridge [EL DORADO]: *ridge*, northwest-trending, 3.5 miles long, 6 miles south-southeast of Clarksville (lat. 38°34'45" N, long. 121°00'45" W). Named on Folsom SE (1954) and Latrobe (1949) 7.5' quadrangles.

Bendorf Spring [EL DORADO]: *spring*, 6 miles southwest of Old Iron Mountain (lat. 38°39'10" N, long. 120°28'45" W; at W line sec. 7, T 9 N, R 14 E). Named on Stump Spring (1951) 7.5' quadrangle.

Benjamin Canyon [YOLO]: *canyon*, drained by a stream that flows 1.5 miles to Capay Valley nearly 1 mile north of Rumsey (lat. 38° 54' N, long. 122°14'05" W; near S line sec. 7, T 12 N, R 3 W). Named on Rumsey (1959) 7.5' quadrangle.

Bennett: see **Shingle Springs** [EL DORADO].

Bennett Flat [NEVADA]: *area*, 2 miles northwest of Truckee (lat. 39°20'45" N, long. 120°12'40" W; on S line sec. 4, T 17 N, R 16 E). Named on Truckee (1955) 7.5' quadrangle.

Benwood Meadow [EL DORADO]: *marsh*, less than 1 mile south of Echo Summit (lat. 38°48'05" N, long. 120°01'50" W; sec. 18, T 11 N, R 18 E). Named on Echo Lake (1955) 7.5' quadrangle.

Berg [SUTTER]: *locality*, nearly 3 miles north of downtown Yuba City along Southern Pacific Railroad (lat. 39°10'50" N, long. 121° 37'35" W). Named on Sutter (1952) 7.5' quadrangle. Officials of Central Pacific Railroad named the place in the 1870's for the property owner there (Gudde, 1949, p. 29).

Berger Campground [SIERRA]: *locality*, 4.25 miles north of Sierra City (lat. 39°37'40" N, long. 120°38'35" W; near NE cor. sec. 5, T 20 N, R 12 E). Named on Gold Lake (1981) 7.5' quadrangle.

Berkeley Soda Springs: see **Soda Springs** [PLACER].

Berlin: see **Genevra** [COLUSA].

Bermuda [YOLO]: *locality*, 2.25 miles north-northwest of Clarksburg along Sacramento Northern Railroad (lat. 38°26'40" N, long. 121°32'45" W). Named on Courtland (1952) 15' quadrangle.

Berry Creek [SIERRA]: *stream*, flows 5.5 miles to Sierra Valley 3.25 miles west-northwest of Sierraville (lat. 39°36'15" N, long. 120°25'25" W; near N line sec. 9, T 20 N, R 14 E). Named on Sattley (1981) 7.5' quadrangle. Sierraville (1955) 15' quadrangle shows Berry Creek extending up present Wild Bill Canyon.

Berryessa Peak [YOLO]: *peak*, 9.5 miles west-southwest of Esparto near the southeast end of Blue Ridge on Yolo-Napa County line (lat. 38°39'50" N, long. 122°11'20" W). Altitude 3057 feet. Named on Brooks (1959) 7.5' quadrangle. The name recalls the grantees in 1843 of Las Putas grant in present Napa County (Cowan, p. 65).

Berry Patch: see **The Berry Patch** [SUTTER].

Berts Lake [EL DORADO]: *lake*, 500 feet long, 5.25 miles northeast of Robbs Peak (lat. 38°58'35" N, long. 120°19'45" W; near E line sec. 18, T 13 N, R 15 E). Named on Loon Lake (1952, photorevised 1973) 7.5' quadrangle.

Berwick [YOLO]: *locality*, nearly 2.5 miles south-southeast of Guinda along Southern Pacific Railroad in Capay Valley (lat. 38° 47'45" N, long. 122°10'50" W). Named on Rumsey (1921) 15' quadrangle. Durst's (1916) map shows a place called Surrey located along the railroad at or near the site of Berwick.

Best Slough [YUBA]: *stream*, diverges from Dry Creek (2) and flows 17 miles to Algodon Slough 6 miles south of Olivehurst (lat. 39°00'20" N, long. 121°32'35" W; near E line sec. 5, T 13 N, R 4 E). Named on Camp Far West (1949), Olivehurst (1952), and Wheatland (1947, photorevised 1973) 7.5' quadrangles. Called Dry Slough on Marysville (1895) 30' quadrangle, and called Dry Creek on Ostrom (1911) 7.5' quadrangle.

Bethel: see **Camp Bethel**, under **Sutter** [SUTTER].

Beyers Lakes [NEVADA]: *lakes*, largest 1800 feet long, 4.25 miles south of English Mountain (lat. 39°23'05" N, long. 120°33'15" W; sec. 31, T 18 N, R 13 E). Named on English Mountain (1983) 7.5' quadrangle.

Big Avalanche Ravine [SIERRA]: *canyon*, drained by a stream that flows nearly 2 miles to North Yuba River 1.5 miles west-southwest of Sierra City (lat. 39°33'45" N, long. 120°39'30" W; near NW cor. sec. 32, T 20 N, R 12 E). Named on Sierra City (1981) 7.5' quadrangle. Called Avalanche Ravine on Downieville (1897) 30' quadrangle, but United States Board on Geographic Names (1960a, p. 12) rejected this name for the feature.

Big Bar [PLACER]: *locality*, 5.5 miles south of Duncan Peak in Duncan Canyon at the mouth of Spanish Ravine (lat. 39°04'30" N, long. 120°32' W; sec. 9, T 14 N, R 13 E). Named on Greek Store (1952) 7.5' quadrangle.

Big Bar: see **Grapevine Ravine** [AMADOR].

Big Bend [EL DORADO]: *bend*, 7 miles north-northeast of Pollock Pines along Silver Creek (lat. 38°51' N, long. 120°32' W). Named on Pollock Pines (1950) 7.5' quadrangle.

Big Bend [PLACER]:

(1) *bend*, 6.25 miles south-southeast of Colfax along North Fork American River (lat. 39°00'45" N, long. 120°55'05" W; at N line sec. 1, T 13 N, R 9 E). Named on Colfax (1949) 7.5' quadrangle.

(2) *settlement*, 1 mile east-southeast of Cisco Grove along South Yuba River (lat. 39°18'20" N, long. 120°31'10" W; sec. 28, T 17 N, R 13 E). Named on Cisco Grove (1955) 7.5' quadrangle.

Big Boulder Creek [SIERRA]: *stream*, flows 2.25 miles to Plumas County 10.5 miles north-northeast of Sierra City (lat. 39°42'35" N, long. 120°33'20" W; near S line sec. 6, T 21 N, R 13 E). Named on Clio (1981) 7.5' quadrangle.

Big Bowman Lake: see **Bowman Lake** [NEVADA].

Big Butte [EL DORADO]: *peak*, 7.5 miles southeast of Camino (lat. 38°40'35" N, long. 120°33'30" W; sec. 32, T 10 N, R 13 E); the peak is nearly 1 mile north-northwest of Little Butte. Altitude 4359 feet. Named on Sly Park (1952) 7.5' quadrangle. Big Butte, Middle Butte, and Little Butte together have the label "Buttes" on Placerville (1893) 30' quadrangle.

Big Canyon [COLUSA]: *canyon*, 1 mile long, 12.5 miles north of Wilbur Springs (lat. 39°13' N, long. 122°24'30" W; mainly in sec. 27, T 16 N, R 5 W). Named on Wilbur Springs (1961) 15' quadrangle.

Big Canyon [EL DORADO]:

(1) *canyon*, 2.25 miles long, opens into the canyon of South Fork American River at Chili Bar (lat. 38°45'55" N, long. 120°49'15" W; near NW cor. sec. 36, T 11 N, R 10 E). Named on Garden Valley (1949) and Placerville (1949) 7.5' quadrangles. Gudde (1975, p. 276) listed a mining place called Poverty Point that was located on the east side of Big Canyon 2 miles north of Placerville.

(2) *canyon*, drained by a stream that flows 5 miles to North Fork Cosumnes River 10 miles east-southeast of Camino (lat. 38°39'55" N, long. 120°31'05" W; sec. 3, T 9 N, R 13 E). Named on Sly Park (1952) and Stump Spring (1951) 7.5' quadrangles.

Big Canyon [SIERRA]: *canyon*, drained by a stream that flows 2 miles to Turner Canyon (1) 5.5 miles west-northwest of Sierraville (lat. 39°37'20" N, long. 120°27'40" W; near SW cor. sec. 31, T 21 N, R 14 E). Named on Calpine (1981) and Sattley (1981) 7.5' quadrangles.

Big Canyon [YOLO]: *canyon*, 1.25 miles long, 4.5 miles southwest of Guinda (lat. 38°46'25" N, long. 122°14'35" W; near W line sec. 30, T 11 N, R 3 W). Named on Guinda (1959) 7.5' quadrangle.

Big Canyon Creek [EL DORADO]: *stream*, flows 12 miles to Cosumnes River 3 miles southeast of Latrobe (lat. 38°31'40" N, long. 120°56'35" W; at S line sec. 24, T 8 N, R 9 E). Named on Latrobe (1949) and Shingle Springs (1949) 7.5' quadrangles.

Big Canyon Creek: see **East Big Canyon Creek** [EL DORADO].

Big Chief [PLACER]: *peak*, 5.5 miles north-northwest of Tahoe City (lat. 39°14'30" N, long. 120°11'45" W; near NW cor. sec. 15, T 16 N, R 16 E); the peak is 0.5 mile southeast of Little Chief. Altitude 7332 feet. Named on Tahoe City (1955) 7.5' quadrangle. California Division of Highways' (1934) map shows a place called Big Chief located along Southern Pacific Railroad less than 1 mile west of present Big Chief (near S line sec. 9, T 16 N, R 16 E), a place called McPhetres located along the railroad 1 mile farther north (sec. 4, T 16 N, R 16 E), and a place called Denvale situated along the railroad just north of McPhetres.

Big Crater [PLACER]: *relief feature*, 11 miles south-southwest of Duncan Peak (lat. 39°00'45" N, long. 120°36'15" W; on N line sec. 2, T 13 N, R 12 E); the feature is 2.5 miles west-southwest of Little Crater. Named on Greek Store (1952) 7.5' quadrangle.

Big Granite Creek [PLACER]: *stream*, flows 6.5 miles to North Fork American River 5 miles north of Duncan Peak (lat. 39°13'25" N, long. 120°31'45" W; near W line sec. 28, T 16 N, R 13 E). Named on Cisco Grove (1955), Duncan Peak (1952), and Soda Springs (1955) 7.5' quadrangles. Called Granite Creek on Truckee (1895) 30' quadrangle. The canyon of the stream is called Granite Canyon on Colfax (1898) 30' quadrangle.

Big Grizzly Canyon [PLACER]: *canyon*, drained by a stream that flows 8 miles to Rubicon River 4.25 miles west-southwest of Devil Peak (lat. 38°56'40" N, long. 120°37'20" W; sec. 27, T 13 N, R 12 E). Named on Devil Peak (1950) 7.5' quadrangle. On Placerville (1893) 30' quadrangle, the stream in the canyon is called Grizzly Creek.

Big Grizzly Creek [SIERRA]: *stream*, flows 2.25 miles to Canyon Creek 2.5 miles south of Mount Fillmore at Poker Flat (lat. 39°41'35" N, long. 120°50'35" W). Named on Mount Fillmore (1951) 7.5' quadrangle. Called Grizzly Ck. on Downieville (1897) 30' quadrangle.

Big Gulch: see **Ashland** [SACRAMENTO].

Big Hill [EL DORADO]: *peak*, 5.5 miles north-northeast of Riverton (lat. 38°50'35" N, long. 120°24'25" W; near E line sec. 33, T 12 N, R 14 E). Altitude 6155 feet. Named on Riverton (1950) 7.5' quadrangle.

Big Hill [PLACER]: *peak*, 7.5 miles northwest of Auburn (lat. 38°59'15" N, long. 121°09'30" W; near S line sec. 11, T 13 N, R 7 E). Altitude 1613 feet. Named on Gold Hill (1954) 7.5' quadrangle.

Big Hill [YUBA]: *peak*, 4.5 miles east-northeast of Challenge (lat. 39°31'25" N, long. 121°08'55" W; on E line sec. 11, T 19 N, T 7 E). Named on Clipper Mills (1948) 7.5' quadrangle.

Big Hill Canyon [EL DORADO]: *canyon*, drained by a stream that flows 1.5 miles to South Fork Silver Creek 4 miles north of Riverton (lat. 38°49'55" N, long. 120°26'20" W; near W line sec. 5, T 11 N, R 14 E); the canyon is southwest of Big Hill. Named on Riverton (1950) 7.5' quadrangle.

Big Hill Ridge [EL DORADO]: *ridge,* south- to west-trending, 3 miles long, 4.25 miles north-northeast of Riverton (lat. 38°49'25" N, long. 120°24'30" W); Big Hill is at the north end of the ridge. Named on Riverton (1950) 7.5' quadrangle.

Big House: see **Mosquito Valley**, under **Mosquito Creek** [EL DORADO].

Big Indian Creek [AMADOR]: *stream,* flows 17 miles to Cosumnes River 6 miles west-northwest of Fiddletown (lat. 38°33'05" N, long. 120°50'55" W; sec. 14, T 8 N, R 10 E). Named on Amador City (1962), Aukum (1952), and Fiddletown (1949) 7.5' quadrangles. Camp's (1962) map shows a canyon called Music Dale that opens into the canyon of Cosumnes River from the south nearly 3 miles southwest of the mouth of Big Indian Creek.

Big Indian Valley: see **Indian Valley** [COLUSA].

Big Iowa Canyon: see **Iowa Canyon** [EL DORADO].

Big John Hill [PLACER]: *peak,* 5 miles south-southeast of Colfax (lat. 39°02' N, long. 120°55'25" W; sec. 25, T 14 N, R 9 E); the peak is near the east end of Big John Ridge. Altitude 2252 feet. Named on Colfax (1949) 7.5' quadrangle.

Big John Ridge [PLACER]: *ridge,* generally west-trending, 2.5 miles long, 4.5 miles south of Colfax (lat. 39°02'05" N, long. 120°56'25" W); Big John Hill is near the east end of the ridge. Named on Colfax (1949) 7.5' quadrangle.

Big Lake [YOLO]: *lake,* 1.5 miles long, 2.5 miles southwest of Clarksburg at the edge of Yolo Basin (lat. 38°23'30" N, long. 121° 33'15" W). Named on Babel Slough (1916) 7.5' quadrangle. The lake now is drained.

Bigler: see **Lake Bigler**, under **Lake Tahoe** [EL DORADO-PLACER].

Bigler Lake Valley: see **Lake Valley** [EL DORADO].

Big Lick Spring [NEVADA]: *spring,* 2.5 miles north-northeast of Washington (lat. 39°23'25" N, long. 120°49'30" W; near SW cor. sec. 26, T 18 N, R 10 E). Named on Alleghany (1949) 7.5' quadrangle.

Big Meadow [EL DORADO]: *area,* 7.5 miles southwest of Freel Peak (lat. 38°46'45" N, long. 120°00' W; on S line sec. 21, T 11 N, R 18 E). Named on Echo Lake (1955) and Freel Peak (1955) 7.5' quadrangles.

Big Meadow [PLACER]: *area,* 3 miles west-northwest of Bunker Hill (lat. 39°04'20" N, long. 120°25'35" W; on N line sec. 17, T 14 N, R 14 E). Named on Bunker Hill (1953) 7.5' quadrangle.

Big Meadow Creek [EL DORADO]: *stream,* flows 3.5 miles to Upper Truckee River 1 mile southeast of Echo Summit (lat. 38°48'05" N, long. 120°00'55" W; sec. 17, T 11 N, R 18 E); the stream goes through Big Meadow. Named on Echo Lake (1955) and Freel Peak (1955) 7.5' quadrangles.

Big Meadow Creek: see **Rubicon River** [EL DORADO-PLACER].

Big Mosquito Creek [PLACER]: *stream,* flows 4.25 miles to Middle Fork American River 5.5 miles east of Michigan Bluff (lat. 39°02'25" N, long. 120°37'45" W; at S line sec. 22, T 14 N, R 12 E); the stream is south of Mosquito Ridge. Named on Greek Store (1952) and Michigan Bluff (1952) 7.5' quadrangles.

Big Mountain [EL DORADO]: *peak,* 3.5 miles east of Omo Ranch (lat. 38°34'35" N, long. 120°30'15" W; sec. 2, T 8 N, R 13 E). Altitude 4597 feet. Named on Omo Ranch (1952) 7.5' quadrangle.

Big Mountain Ridge [EL DORADO]: *ridge,* generally west-trending, 10 miles long, center 2 miles south-southwest of Caldor (lat. 38°34'50" N, long. 120°26'45" W); Big Mountain is near the west end of the ridge. Named on Caldor (1951), Omo Ranch (1952), and Peddler Hill (1951) 7.5' quadrangles.

Big Oak Flat [PLACER]: *area,* 5 miles east-northeast of Michigan Bluff (lat. 39°03'30" N, long. 120°39' W; sec. 16, 17, T 14 N, R 12 E). Named on Michigan Bluff (1952) 7.5' quadrangle.

Big Pebble Canyon [EL DORADO]: *canyon,* drained by a stream that flows 2 miles to Snow Creek 3 miles west-southwest of Old Iron Mountain (lat. 38°41'50" N, long. 120°26'50" W; sec. 29, T 10 N, R 14 E). Named on Stump Spring (1951) 7.5' quadrangle.

Big Ravine [EL DORADO]: *canyon,* 1 mile long, opens into the canyon of South Fork American River 5 miles south-southwest of the village of Pilot Hill (lat. 38°46'15" N, long. 121°03'10" W; sec. 26, T 11 N, R 8 E). Named on Pilot Hill (1954) 7.5' quadrangle.

Big Ravine [YUBA]: *canyon,* 3.5 miles long, opens into the canyon of Yuba River 2 miles northwest of Smartville (lat. 39°13'20" N, long. 121°19'30" W; at N line sec. 29, T 16 N, R 6 E); Timbuctoo is on the north side of the canyon. Named on Smartville (1951) 7.5' quadrangle. Called Timbuctoo Ravine on Wescoatt's (1861) map.

Big Reservoir [EL DORADO]: *intermittent lake,* 500 feet long, 2.5 miles south-southeast of Omo Ranch (lat. 38°32'50" N, long. 120° 33'20" W; near W line sec. 16, T 8 N, R 13 E); the feature is 1.5 miles east-southeast of Little Reservoir. Named on Omo Ranch (1952) 7.5' quadrangle.

Big Reservoir [PLACER]: *lake,* behind a dam on a tributary of Forbes Creek 6.25 miles southeast of Dutch Flat (lat. 39°08'35" N, long. 120°45'20" W; sec. 17, T 15 N, R 11 E). Named on Dutch Flat (1950, photorevised 1973) and Westville (1952, photorevised 1973) 7.5' quadrangles. United States Board on Geographic Names (1986, p. 1) rejected the names "Morning Star Lake" and "Morning Star Reservoir" for the feature.

Big Rock [YOLO]: *peak,* 4.5 miles south of Guinda (lat. 38°45'45" N, long. 122°12'20" W; sec. 33, T 11 N, R 3 W). Altitude 1521 feet. Named on Guinda (1959) 7.5' quadrangle.

Big Sailor Creek [EL DORADO]: *stream,* flows 2.5 miles to Slate Creek (1) 3.5 miles north-northwest of Chili Bar (lat. 38°48'30" N, long. 120°51'25" W; near SW cor. sec. 10, T 11 N, R 10 E). Named on Garden Valley (1949) 7.5' quadrangle.

Big Shady Creek: see **Shady Creek** [NEVADA].

Big Silver Campground [EL DORADO]: *locality,* 3 miles south-southeast of Robbs Peak along Big Silver Creek (lat. 38°52'55" N, long. 120°23'20" W; sec. 15, T 12 N, R 14 E). Named on Robbs Peak (1952) 15' quadrangle. Water of Union Valley Reservoir now covers the site.

Big Silver Creek [EL DORADO]: *stream,* flows 7.5 miles to Union Valley Reservoir 3.5 miles south-southeast of Robbs Peak (lat. 38° 52'45" N, long. 120°22' W; near SE cor. sec. 14, T 12 N, R 14 E). Named on Kyburz (1952) and Loon Lake (1952, photorevised 1973) 7.5' quadrangles. The lower part of present Big Silver Creek and all of present Bassi Fork above the confluence of the two streams are called North Fork Silver Creek on Pyramid Peak (1896) 30' quadrangle.

Big Sluice Box [EL DORADO]: *relief feature,* 4 miles east of Wentworth Springs (lat. 39°00'30" N, long. 120°15'45" W; at N line sec. 2, T 13 N, R 15 E); the feature is 1 mile southeast of Little Sluice Box. Named on Wentworth Springs (1953) 7.5' quadrangle.

Big Snyder Gulch [PLACER]: *canyon,* drained by a stream that flows 1 mile to Middle Fork American River 10.5 miles east-northeast of Auburn (lat. 38°57'35" N, long. 120°53'25" W; sec. 19, T 13 N, R 10 E). Named on Greenwood (1949) 7.5' quadrangle.

Big Spanish Hill: see **Spanish Ravine** [EL DORADO].

Big Spring [PLACER]: *spring,* 3.5 miles south-southeast of Granite Chief (lat. 39°08'55" N, long. 120°16'05" W; sec. 14, T 15 N, R 15 E). Named on Granite Chief (1953) 7.5' quadrangle.

Big Spring [YOLO]: *spring,* 3.25 miles east-northeast of Berryessa Peak (lat. 38°41'05" N, long. 122°08'10" W). Named on Brooks (1959) 7.5' quadrangle.

Big Springs [SIERRA]: *springs,* 2.5 miles north-northeast of Sierra City (lat. 39°35'55" N, long. 120°36'40" W; sec. 15, T 20 N, R 12 E). Named on Haypress Valley (1981) 7.5' quadrangle.

Big Sugar Loaf: see **China Mountain** [EL DORADO].

Big Tunnel Spring [NEVADA]: *spring,* 4 miles south-southeast of Washington (lat. 39°18'05" N, long. 120°46'25" W; at NE cor. sec. 31, T 17 N, R 11 E); the spring is near a tunnel on South Yuba canal. Named on Washington (1950) 7.5' quadrangle.

Big Valley [PLACER]: *valley,* 3.25 miles south of Cisco Grove (lat. 39°15'50" N, long. 120°33' W; in and near sec. 7, T 16 N, R 13 E). Named on Cisco Grove (1955) 7.5' quadrangle.

Big Valley Bluff [PLACER]: *ridge,* southeast-trending, 1 mile long, 6.5 miles northwest of Duncan Peak (lat 39°14' N, long. 120°34'55" W; mainly in sec. 24, T 16 N, R 12 W); the ridge is west of Big Valley Canyon. Named on Duncan Peak (1952) 7.5' quadrangle.

Big Valley Canyon [PLACER]: *canyon,* 3 miles long, opens into the canyon of North Fork American River 5 miles north-northwest of Duncan Peak (lat. 39°13'10" N, long. 120°33'20" W; sec. 30, T 16 N, R 13 E); the feature heads at Big Valley. Named on Duncan Peak (1952) 7.5' quadrangle.

Big Valley Creek [YUBA]: *stream,* flows 2.5 miles to Dry Creek (1) 5.5 miles southeast of Rackerby (lat. 39°23'15" N, long. 121°15'35" W; near E line sec. 26, T 18 N, R 6 E). Named on Rackerby (1948) 7.5' quadrangle.

Big X Mountain [EL DORADO]: *peak,* 6 miles north-northwest of Pollock Pines (lat. 38°50'10" N, long. 120°38'10" W; near NE cor. sec. 4, T 11 N, R 12 E). Named on Slate Mountain (1950) 7.5' quadrangle.

Bihlman [SUTTER]: *locality,* less than 1 mile south of Live Oak along Northern Electric Railroad (lat. 39°15'50" N, long. 121°39'40" W). Named on Gridley (1912) 7.5' quadrangle.

Bijou [EL DORADO]: *district,* 7 miles north-northwest of Freel Peak in the town of South Lake Tahoe (lat. 38°56'45" N, long. 119° 58' W; sec. 33, T 13 N, R 18 E). Named on South Lake Tahoe (1955, photorevised 1969 and 1974) 7.5' quadrangle. Postal authorities established Bijou post office in 1888 and discontinued it in 1967 (Salley, p. 21). The name is from the French word for "jewel" (Hanna, p. 33). Almon M. Taylor patented land in section 33 in 1864, and Taylor's Landing there was a shipping point for lumber; the place took the name "Bijou" when the post office was established (Lekisch, p. 8).

Bijou Park [EL DORADO]: *district,* 7 miles north-northwest of Freel Peak in the town of South Lake Tahoe (lat. 38°56'55" N, long. 119°57'15" W); the feature is east of Bijou. Named on South Lake Tahoe (1955, photorevised 1969 and 1974) 7.5' quadrangle.

Billy Hill [NEVADA]: *peak,* 2 miles north of Hobart Mills (lat. 39° 25'25" N, long. 120°10'50" W; near NE cor. sec. 10, T 18 N, R 16 E). Altitude 6694 feet. Named on Hobart Mills (1981) 7.5' quadrangle.

Billy Mack Canyon [NEVADA]: *canyon,* 1.5 miles long, opens into the valley of Donner Lake 1.5 miles east-northeast of Donner Pass (lat. 39°19'30" N, long. 120°18'10" W; sec. 15, T 17 N, R 15 E). Named on

Norden (1955) 7.5' quadrangle.

Billy Mack Flat [NEVADA]: *area,* 1.5 miles north-northeast of Donner Pass (lat. 39°20'10" N, long. 120°18'40" W; at E line sec. 9, T 17 N, R 15 E); the place is in Billy Mack Canyon. Named on Norden (1955) 7.5' quadrangle.

Billys Hill [COLUSA]: *peak,* 7.5 miles south-southeast of Wilbur Springs (lat. 38°56'55" N, long. 122°20'15" W; near E line sec. 30, T 13 N, R 4 W). Altitude 1768 feet. Named on Glascock Mountain (1958) 7.5' quadrangle.

Billys Peak: see **Granite Chief** [PLACER].

Binney Junction [YUBA]: *locality,* nearly 1 mile north of downtown Marysville, where Western Pacific Railroad and Southern Pacific Railroad intersect (lat. 39°09'25" N, long. 121°35'25" W). Named on Yuba City (1952) 7.5' quadrangle.

Birchville [NEVADA]: *locality,* nearly 2 miles north-northeast of French Corral (lat. 39°19'40" N, long. 121°08'35" W; at S line sec. 13, T 17 N, R 7 E). Named on French Corral (1948) 7.5' quadrangle. Called Birchy on California Mining Bureau's (1917c) map. The name commemorates L. Birch Adsit; until 1853 the place was called Johnson's Diggings for David Johnson, the first prospector there (Gudde, 1975, p. 38).

Birchy: see **Birchville** [NEVADA].

Bird Creek [YOLO]: *stream,* formed by the confluence of Middle Fork and South Fork, flows 3.5 miles to lowlands 2.5 miles south of Dunnigan (lat. 38°50'50" N, long. 121°57'30" W; sec. 34, T 12 N, R 1 W). Named on Bird Valley (1959) and Zamora (1953) 7.5' quadrangles. Middle Fork, which goes through Bird Valley, is 4.5 miles long, and South Fork is 1.5 miles long. North Fork, which joins the main stream just below the confluence of Middle Fork and South Fork, it is 6 miles long. All three forks are named on Bird Valley (1959) 7.5' quadrangle.

Bird Valley [YOLO]: *valley,* 9.5 miles east of Guinda in Dunnigan Hills (lat. 38°50'45" N, long. 122°01' W). Named on Bird Valley (1959) 7.5' quadrangle.

Bisbee Lake: see **Loon Lake** [EL DORADO].

Bisbee Peak [AMADOR]: *peak,* 2.5 miles west-northwest of Plymouth (lat. 38°29'30" N, long. 120°53'20" W; near W line sec. 4, T 7 N, R 10 E). Altitude 1207 feet. Named on Irish Hill (1962) 7.5' quadrangle. Camp's (1962) map has the name "Finn's Sugarloaf" as an alternate.

Bitney Corner [NEVADA]: *locality,* 2.5 miles west-northwest of Grass Valley (lat. 39°13'55" N, long. 121°06'30" W; near W line sec. 20, T 16 N, R 8 E). Named on Grass Valley (1949) 7.5' quadrangle.

Blackbird Camp Ground [EL DORADO]: *locality,* 0.5 mile west-northwest of Riverton along South Fork American River (lat. 38° 46'30" N, long. 120°27'30" W; sec. 30, T 11 N, R 14 E). Named on Riverton (1950) 7.5' quadrangle.

Black Buttes [NEVADA]: *relief feature,* 3.5 miles south of English Mountain (lat. 39°23'40" N, long. 120°33'25" W). Named on English Mountain (1983) 7.5' quadrangle. Called Black Mountains on Colfax (1898) 30' quadrangle.

Black Camp [NEVADA]: *locality,* 4.25 miles east-southeast of Graniteville (lat. 39°24'45" N, long. 120°39'45" W; near E line sec. 19, T 18 N, R 12 E). Named on Graniteville (1982) 7.5' quadrangle.

Black Canyon [PLACER]: *canyon,* drained by a stream that flows nearly 3 miles to Secret Canyon 5.5 miles west of Duncan Peak (lat. 39°09'10" N, long. 120°37' W; at N line sec. 15, T 15 N, R 12 E). Named on Duncan Peak (1952) 7.5' quadrangle.

Black Canyon [SIERRA]: *canyon,* drained by a stream that flows 1 mile to Ladies Canyon 3.25 miles west-northwest of Sierra City (lat. 39°34'55" N, long. 120°41'25" W; sec. 24, T 20 N, R 11 E). Named on Sierra City (1981) 7.5' quadrangle. United States Board on Geographic Names (1960a, p. 12) rejected the name "Ladies Canyon" for the feature.

Black Cut Ravine [NEVADA]: *canyon,* drained by a stream that flows 0.5 mile to Middle Yuba River nearly 7 miles northeast of North Bloomfield (lat. 39°26'10" N, long. 120°48'35" W; near W line sec. 12, T 18 N, R 10 E). Named on Alleghany (1949) 7.5' quadrangle.

Black Gulch [AMADOR]: *canyon,* drained by a stream that flows 1.5 miles to Mokelumne River 4 miles south of Jackson (lat. 38°17'25" N, long. 120°45'40" W; sec. 16, T 5 N, R 11 E). Named on Jackson (1962) 7.5' quadrangle.

Blackhawk Canyon [PLACER]: *canyon,* drained by a stream that flows 2 miles to the head of Third Brushy Canyon 2.5 miles north of Foresthill (lat. 39°03'20" N, long. 120°49'25" W; sec. 14, T 14 N, R 10 E). Named on Foresthill (1949) 7.5' quadrangle.

Black Jack [SIERRA]: *locality,* 5.25 miles southeast of Downieville (lat. 39°30'30" N, long. 120°45' W). Named on Downieville (1897) 30' quadrangle.

Black Jack Ravine [SIERRA]: *canyon,* drained by a stream that flows 2.5 miles to Jim Crow Creek 4.5 miles southeast of Downieville (lat. 39°31'05" N, long. 120°45'45" W; sec. 17, T 19 N, R 11 E). Named on Downieville (1951) and Sierra City (1981) 7.5' quadrangles. On Downieville (1897) 30' quadrangle, the name "Jim Crow Ravine" appears to apply to present Black Jack Ravine together with the canyon of present Jim Crow Creek. United States Board on Geographic Names (1960a, p. 12) rejected the names "Jim Crow Ravine" and "Blackjack Ravine" for present Black Jack Ravine.

Black Mountain [COLUSA]: *peak,* 4 miles west-northwest of Sites (lat. 39°19'50" N, long. 122°24'25" W; sec. 15, T 17 N, R 5 W). Altitude 1512 feet. Named on Lodoga (1960) 15' quadrangle.

Black Mountain [PLACER]: *peak,* 4 miles west-southwest of Cisco Grove on Monumental Ridge (lat. 39°17' N, long. 120°36'20" W; near E line sec. 3, T 16 N, R 12 E). Altitude 6986 feet. Named on Cisco Grove (1955) 7.5' quadrangle.

Black Mountain [YOLO]: *ridge,* south-southeast-trending, 0.5 mile long, 3 miles west-southwest of Guinda (lat. 38°48'25" N, long. 122°14'25" W; near NW cor. sec. 18, T 11 N, R 3 W). Named on Guinda (1959) 7.5' quadrangle.

Black Mountains: see **Black Buttes** [NEVADA].

Black Oak Campground [COLUSA]: *locality,* 6 miles south-southwest of Fouts Springs (lat. 39°16'40" N, long. 122°43'20" W; near SE cor. sec. 35, T 17 N, R 8 W). Named on Fouts Springs (1968) 7.5' quadrangle.

Black Oak Spring [NEVADA]: *spring,* 2.5 miles northwest of Yuba Gap (lat. 39°20'05" N, long. 120°39'15" W; sec. 17, T 17 N, R 12 E). Named on Blue Canyon (1955) 7.5' quadrangle.

Black Rock Creek [EL DORADO]: *stream,* flows nearly 6 miles to join Blue Tent Creek and form Hastings Creek 5 miles west-northwest of Coloma (lat. 38°49'50" N, long. 120°58'35" W; sec. 4, T 11 N, R 9 E). Named on Coloma (1949) and Greenwood (1949) 7.5' quadrangles. Shown as part of Hastings Creek on Placerville (1893) 30' quadrangle.

Black Rock Lake [AMADOR]: *lake,* 650 feet long, 4 miles north-northeast of Mokelumne Peak on Amador-Alpine County line (lat. 38°35'30" N, long. 120°04'20" W). Named on Mokelumne Peak (1979) 7.5' quadrangle.

Blacks: see **Zamora** [YOLO].

Black's Bridge: see **Edwards Crossing** [NEVADA].

Blacksmith Flat [PLACER]: *area,* 3 miles northwest of Devil Peak (lat. 38°59'20" N, long. 120°35'15" W; sec. 12, T 13 N, R 12 E). Named on Devil Peak (1950) 7.5' quadrangle.

Black's Station: see **Zamora** [YOLO].

Blackwood Creek [PLACER]: *stream,* flows 5.5 miles to Lake Tahoe 1.5 miles north of Homewood (lat. 39°06'25" N, long. 120° 09'30" W; sec. 36, T 15 N, R 16 E); the stream is west and north of Blackwood Ridge. Named on Homewood (1955) 7.5' quadrangle. The name commemorates Hampton Craig Blackwood, who settled at the mouth of the stream after July 1866 (Lekisch, p. 9). Middle Fork enters 4 miles above the mouth of the main stream and is 1.5 miles long. North Fork enters 3.5 miles above the mouth of the main stream and is 2 miles long. Both forks are named on Homewood (1955) 7.5' quadrangle.

Blackwood Ridge [PLACER]: *ridge,* northeast-trending, 1.5 miles long, center 1.5 miles west of Homewood (lat. 39°05'30" N, long. 120°11'15" W). Named on Homewood (1955) 7.5' quadrangle.

Blair Saw Mill [EL DORADO]: *locality,* 11.5 miles east-northeast of Placerville (lat. 38°46'30" N, long. 120°36'05" W). Named on Placerville (1893) 30' quadrangle.

Blakeley [AMADOR]: *locality,* 6.5 miles southwest of present Hams Station (lat. 38°28'05" N, long. 120°26'40" W). Named on Big Trees (1891) 30' quadrangle.

Blakeley [EL DORADO]: *locality,* 4 miles west of Pyramid Peak (lat. 38°50'30" N, long. 120°14' W). Named on Pyramid Peak (1896) 30' quadrangle.

Blakeley Reservoir [EL DORADO]: *lake,* 1000 feet long, 1.5 miles west of Camino (lat. 38°44'25" N, long. 120°42'20" W; near NE cor. sec. 12, T 10 N, R 11 E). Named on Camino (1952) 7.5' quadrangle.

Blanchard Valley [COLUSA]: *valley,* 10.5 miles north of Wilbur Springs along Calvins Creek (lat. 39°11'10" N, long. 122°22'30" W). Named on Wilbur Springs (1961) 15' quadrangle.

Blancks Hot Springs: see **Blank Spring** [COLUSA].

Blanck's Hot Sulphur Springs: see **Blank Spring** [COLUSA].

Blank Spring [COLUSA]: *spring,* less than 1 mile southwest of Wilbur Springs (lat. 39°01'50" N, long. 122°25'55" W; sec. 29, T 14 N, R 5 W). Named on Wilbur Springs (1961) 15' quadrangle. Crawford (1896, p. 509) called the spring, or the resort there, Blank's Sulphur Springs, G.A. Waring (p. 104) called it Blancks Hot Springs, and Logan (1929b, p. 291) called it Blanck's Hot Sulphur Springs. The small resort that used the water was closed after a mining shaft was sunk nearby and water ceased to flow from the spring (Waring, G.A., p. 104).

Blank's Sulphur Springs: see **Blank Spring** [COLUSA].

Blatchley Canyon [SIERRA]: *canyon,* drained by a stream that flows 4 miles to Cold Stream (1) 3.25 miles southeast of Sierraville (lat. 39°32'50" N, long. 120°20' W; near N line sec. 32, T 20 N, R 15 E). Named on Sierraville (1981) 7.5' quadrangle.

Blind Canyon [PLACER]: *canyon,* drained by a stream that flows nearly 1 mile to Middle Fork American River 1.5 miles southeast of Foresthill (lat. 39°00'05" N, long. 120°48' W; sec. 1, T 13 N, R 10 E). Named on Foresthill (1949) 7.5' quadrangle.

Blind Shady: see **Blind Shady Creek** [NEVADA].

Blind Shady Creek [NEVADA]: *stream,* flows 2.25 miles to Shady Creek 2.5 miles east-southeast of North San Juan (lat. 39°20'55" N, long. 121°03'40" W; sec. 10, T 17 N, R 8 E). Named on Nevada City (1948) 7.5' quadrangle. Called Little Shady Creek on Whitney's (1873) map. The name "Blind Shady" was used for the canyon of the stream in 1852 (Canfield, p. 230).

Blodgett Reservoir [SACRAMENTO]: *lake,* behind a dam on Laguna Creek 11.5 miles south of Folsom (lat. 38°31'10" N, long. 121°12'45" W; sec. 28, T 8 N, R 7 E). Named on Buffalo Creek (1967) 7.5' quadrangle.

Blood Gulch [AMADOR]: *canyon,* less than 1 mile long, 3 miles northwest of present Fiddletown and 1 mile west-southwest of Prospect Hill (lat. 38°31'40" N, long. 120°48'15" W). Named on Placerville (1893) 30' quadrangle.

Bloodsucker Lake [EL DORADO]: *lake,* 800 feet long, 3 miles west-southwest of Pyramid Peak (lat. 38°50'10" N, long. 120°12'35" W; near NW cor. sec. 3, T 11 N, R 16 E). Named on Pyramid Peak (1955) 7.5' quadrangle.

Bloody Gulch: see **Enterprise** [AMADOR].

Bloody Ravine [PLACER]: *canyon,* drained by a stream that flows 1 mile to Duncan Creek (lat. 39°06'10" N, long. 120°31' W; sec. 34, T 15 N, R 13 E). Named on Greek Store (1952) 7.5' quadrangle.

Bloody Run [NEVADA]: *stream,* flows 7.5 miles to Middle Yuba River 3.5 miles north of North Bloomfield (lat. 39°29'15" N, long. 120°54'45" W; sec. 13, T 18 N, R 9 E). Named on Alleghany (1949) and Pike (1949) 7.5' quadrangles.

Bloomfield: see **North Bloomfield** [NEVADA].

Blue Bluffs: see **Blue Cliffs** [YOLO]; **Midas** [PLACER].

Blue Canyon [PLACER]:

(1) *canyon,* drained by a stream that flows 7.25 miles to North Fork of North Fork American River 5.5 miles west-northwest of Westville (lat. 39°12'05" N, long. 120°44'45" W; at S line sec. 33, T 16 N, R 11 E). Named on Blue Canyon (1955) and Westville (1952) 7.5' quadrangles. The name is from blue smoke that hung over the canyon during the days of extensive lumbering, although according to one account the name is from Old Jim Blue, a miner of the 1850's (Gudde, 1969, p. 32).

(2) *village,* nearly 4 miles southwest of Emigrant Gap (1) (lat. 39° 15'20" N, long. 120°42'35" W; sec. 14, T 16 N, R 11 E); the village is on the east side of Blue Canyon (1). Named on Blue Canyon (1955) 7.5' quadrangle, which shows Blue Canon P.O. at the place. Postal authorities established Blue Canyon post office in 1867, discontinued it in 1927, reestablished it with the name "Blue Cañon" in 1936, discontinued it in 1942, reestablished it in 1948, and discontinued it in 1964 (Salley, p. 23). Whitney's (1873) map shows a place called Gilsons Station situated 1.25 miles north-northwest of the present village of Blue Canyon along Donner Road, and shows a place called Lost Camp located 1 mile south-southeast of the present village. California Division of Highways' (1934) map shows a place called Knapp located less than 1 mile west-southwest of the village of Blue Canyon along Southern Pacific Railroad (at E line sec. 15, T 16 N, R 11 E).

Blue Cliffs [YOLO]: *relief feature,* 1.5 miles east-southeast of Rumsey (lat. 38°53' N, long. 122°12'25" W; near NE cor. sec. 20, T 12 N, R 3 W). Named on Rumsey (1959) 7.5' quadrangle. Called Blue Slides on Rumsey (1945) 15' quadrangle, but United States Board on Geographic Names (1962b, p. 14) rejected the names "Blue Slides" and "Blue Bluffs" for the feature

Blue Creek: see **Little Blue Creek** [SUTTER].

Blue Cut [PLACER]: *locality,* 3 miles south-southwest of Colfax along Southern Pacific Railroad (lat. 39°03'35" N, long. 120°58'20" W; near SE cor. sec. 16, T 14 N, R 9 E). Named on Colfax (1949) 7.5' quadrangle.

Blue Eyes Canyon [PLACER]: *canyon,* drained by a stream that flows less than 1 mile to Duncan Canyon 4.5 miles south-southwest of Duncan Peak (lat. 39°05'20" N, long. 120°32' W; sec. 4, T 14 N, R 13 E). Named on Greek Store (1952) 7.5' quadrangle. Logan's (1925) map shows Old Blue Eyes cabin near the head of the canyon.

Blue Gates: see **Cache Creek** [COLUSA-YOLO].

Blue Lake [NEVADA]: *lake,* 2350 feet long, 3 miles north-northwest of Yuba Gap (lat. 39°21'35" N, long. 120°37'55" W; near N line sec. 9, T 17 N, R 12 E). Named on Blue Canyon (1955) 7.5' quadrangle.

Blue Mountain [EL DORADO]: *peak,* 2.25 miles west of Pyramid Peak (lat. 38°50'55" N, long. 120°11'50" W; sec. 34, T 12 N, R 16 E). Altitude 8772 feet. Named on Pyramid Peak (1955) 7.5' quadrangle.

Blue Ravine [NEVADA]: *canyon,* drained by a stream that flows 1.5 miles to Squirrel Creek 4.5 miles north-northeast of Pilot Peak (lat. 39°13'30" N, long. 121°08'15" W; near N line sec. 25, T 16 N, T 7 E). Named on Rough and Ready (1949) 7.5' quadrangle.

Blue Ravine [SACRAMENTO]: *valley,* 3.5 miles east-northeast of Folsom (lat. 38°41'35" N, long. 121°06'50" W). Named on Clarksville (1953) 7.5' quadrangle. California Mining Bureau's (1909b) map shows a locality called Blue Ravine located 4 miles northeast of Folsom by stage line. Postal authorities established Blue Ravine post office 5 miles northeast of Folsom in 1902 and discontinued it in 1910 (Salley, p. 23).

Blue Ravine [SIERRA]: *canyon,* drained by a stream that flows 1.5 miles to Kanaka Creek nearly 4 miles west-southwest of Alleghany (lat. 39°26'20" N, long. 120°54'05" W; sec. 7, T 18 N, R 10 E). Named on Pike (1949) 7.5' quadrangle.

Blue Ridge [COLUSA]: *ridge,* south-trending, 4.25 miles long, center 3 miles southeast of Wilbur Springs (lat. 39°00'30" N, long. 122°03'15" W). Named on Morgan Valley (1958) and Wilbur Springs (1961) 15' quadrangles.

Blue Ridge [YOLO]: *ridge,* extends north-northwest for 20 miles, mainly on Yolo-Napa County line, from near Berryessa Peak to Cache Creek. Named on Brooks (1959), Glascock Mountain (1958), Guinda (1959), and Knoxville (1958) 7.5' quadrangles. Durst's (1916) map has the name "Rumsey Range" for the feature.

Blue Slides: see **Blue Cliffs** [YOLO].

Blue Tent [NEVADA]: *locality,* 6 miles southwest of North Bloomfield (lat. 39°18'25" N, long. 120°59'10" W). Named on Colfax (1898) 30' quadrangle. Postal authorities established Blue Tent post office in 1878 and discontinued it in 1889; the name was for the first habitation at the place (Salley, p. 23). Whitney's (1873) map shows Sailor Flat Cañon opening into the canyon of South Yuba River from the south-southeast 1.5 miles north-northeast of Blue Tent, shows a place called Mt. Vernon Ho. [House] situated 1.25 miles northwest of Blue Tent, and shows a feature called Gopher Hill located 1.25 miles north-northeast of Blue Tent.

Blue Tent Creek [EL DORADO]: *stream,* flows nearly 5 miles to join Black Rock Creek and form Hastings Creek 5 miles west-northwest of Coloma (lat. 38°49'50" N, long. 120°58'35" W; sec. 4, T 11 N, R 9 E). Named on Auburn (1953), Coloma (1949), and Pilot Hill (1954) 7.5' quadrangles.

Blumenberg [SACRAMENTO]: *locality,* 9.5 miles south-southwest of Isleton along San Joaquin River on Sherman Island (lat. 38°02'50" N, long. 121°42'30" W). Named on Jersey (1910) 7.5' quadrangle. Postal authorities established Blumenburg (with the ending "burg" instead of "berg") post office in 1908 and discontinued it in 1910 (Frickstad, p. 132).

Board Camp Ridge [COLUSA]: *ridge,* southeast-trending, 2.25 miles long, 5.25 miles southwest of Fouts Springs (lat. 39°18'05" N, long. 122°44'05" W). Named on Fouts Springs (1968) and Potato Hill (1967) 7.5' quadrangles.

Board Camp Spring [COLUSA]: *spring,* 5 miles southwest of Fouts Springs (lat. 39°18'35" N, long. 122°44'25" W; sec. 22, T 17 N, R 8 W); the spring is on Board Camp Ridge. Named on Fouts Springs (1968) 7.5' quadrangle.

Bob Walker Canyon [YOLO]: *canyon,* 1.5 miles long, along South Fork Oat Creek above a point 4.5 miles east-southeast of Guinda (lat. 38°48'50" N, long. 122°06'40" W; sec. 8, T 11 N, R 2 W). Named on Bird Valley (1959) and Guinda (1959) 7.5' quadrangles.

Boca [NEVADA]: *locality,* 6.5 miles northeast of Truckee along Southern Pacific Railroad (lat. 39°23'10" N, long. 120°05'35" W; sec. 28, T 18 N, R 17 E). Named on Boca (1955) 7.5' quadrangle. Postal authorities established Boca post office in 1872 and discontinued it in 1945 (Frickstad, p. 113). Officials of Central Pacific Railroad named the place in 1867 for its location near the mouth of Little Truckee River—*boca* means "mouth" in Spanish (Gudde, 1949, p. 35). Postal authorities established Burckhalter post office 2 miles southeast of Boca in 1891 and discontinued it in 1896; the name, which also had the form "Burkhalter," was for Walter Burckhalter, first postmaster (Salley, p. 29). Wheeler's (1876-1877b) map shows a place called Virginia Ho. [House] located about 5 miles northwest of Boca. California Division of Highways' (1934) map shows an inhabited place called Prosser Creek situated about 1 mile southwest of Boca along the railroad (sec. 29, T 18 N, R 17 E).

Boca Canyon: see **East Boca Canyon** [NEVADA].

Boca Hill [NEVADA]: *peak,* 5 miles northeast of Truckee (lat. 39°22'50" N, long. 120°07' W; sec. 29, T 18 N, R 17 E); the peak is 1.5 miles west-southwest of Boca. Altitude 6669 feet. Named on Boca (1955) 7.5' quadrangle.

Boca Reservoir [NEVADA]: *lake,* behind a dam on Little Truckee River 6.5 miles northeast of Truckee (lat. 39°23'25" N, long. 120° 05'35" W; near S line sec. 21, T 18 N, R 17 E); the lake is north of Boca. Named on Boca (1955) 7.5' quadrangle.

Boca Ridge [NEVADA]: *ridge,* generally south-trending, 3.5 miles long, 10 miles northeast of Truckee (lat. 39°25'30" N, long. 120° 03'05" W); the center of the ridge is 3.5 miles northeast of Boca. Named on Boca (1955) 7.5' quadrangle.

Boca Spring [NEVADA]: *spring,* 9 miles northeast of Truckee (lat. 39°25'45" N, long. 120°04'30" W; sec. 10, T 18 N, R 17 E); the spring is 3 miles north-northeast of Boca. Named on Boca (1955) 7.5' quadrangle.

Boca Spring: see **East Boca Spring** [NEVADA].

Boga [SUTTER]: *land grant,* at and near Live Oak on Sutter-Butte County line. Named on Gridley (1952), Honcut (1952), Sutter (1952), and Yuba City (1952) 7.5' quadrangles. Charles W. Flügge received 5 leagues in 1844 and Thomas O. Larkin claimed 22,185 acres patented in 1865 (Cowan, p. 19; Cowan gave the name "Flügge" as an alternate).

Bogardus' Ranch: see **Junction House** [YUBA].

Boggs Bend [COLUSA]: *bend,* nearly 2 miles south of Princeton along Sacramento River (lat. 39°22'40" N, long. 122°00'20" W). Named on Princeton (1918) 7.5' quadrangle. Butte City (1952) and Princeton (1952) 7.5' quadrangles show the bend cut off from the present course of the river.

Boggs Landing [COLUSA]: *locality,* 2 miles south of Princeton on the west side of Sacramento River (lat. 39°22'25" N, long. 122°00'40" W); the place is south of Boggs Bend. Named on Compton Landing (1917) 7.5' quadrangle. The name commemorates John Boggs, landowner in the neighborhood (Hanna, p. 36).

Bogue [SUTTER]: *locality,* 3 miles south of Yuba City along Southern Pacific Railroad (lat. 39°05'55" N, long. 121°37'25" W). Named on Olivehurst (1952) 7.5' quadrangle. The name is for Virgil G. Bogue, who was chief engineer of Western Pacific Railroad (Gudde, 1949, p. 36).

Bogus Point [PLACER]: *peak,* nearly 3 miles south of Dutch Flat (lat. 39°09'55" N, long. 120°49'45" W; near E line sec. 10, T 15 N, R 10 E). Named on Dutch Flat (1950) 7.5' quadrangle.

Bogus Thunder [PLACER]: *locality,* 3.5 miles east-northeast of Michigan Bluff along North Fork of Middle Fork American River (lat. 39°04'05" N, long. 120°40'55" W; near NW cor. sec. 18, T 14 N, R 12 E). Named on Michigan Bluff (1952) 7.5' quadrangle. The name is from the thunderlike sound of a nearby waterfall (Hoover, Rensch, and Rensch, p. 277).

Boles Gap [EL DORADO]: *pass,* 5.5 miles south-southeast of Camino (lat. 38°40'05" N, long. 120°37'15" W; at N line sec. 2, T 9 N, R 12 E). Named on Sly Park (1952) 7.5' quadrangle. Called Boulder Pass on Placerville (1893) 30' quadrangle.

Bombay [SACRAMENTO]: *locality,* 1.5 miles west-southwest of Rio Linda along Western Pacific Railroad (lat. 38°41'15" N, long. 121° 28'45" W; near S line sec. 30, T 10 N, R 5 E). Named on Rio Linda (1967) 7.5' quadrangle.

Bonetti [EL DORADO]: *locality,* 4 miles southwest of Old Iron Mountain (lat. 38°40'30" N, long. 120°27'10" W; sec. 32, T 10 N, R 14 E). Named on Stump Spring (1951) 7.5' quadrangle.

Bonnefoy [AMADOR]: *settlement,* 1.5 miles northeast of Jackson (lat. 38°21'40" N, long. 120°45' W; sec. 22, T 6 N, R 11 E). Named on Jackson (1962) and Mokelumne Hill (1948) 7.5' quadrangles.

Bonnie View [COLUSA]: *locality,* 2.5 miles northwest of Fouts Springs (lat. 39°22'55" N, long. 122°41' W; sec. 30, T 18 N, R 7 W). Named on John Mountain (1968) 7.5' quadrangle.

Bonny Nook [PLACER]: *locality,* 2.25 miles east of Dutch Flat (lat. 39°12'35" N, long. 120°47'35" W; at E line sec. 36, T 16 N, R 10 E). Named on Dutch Flat (1950) 7.5' quadrangle.

Bonpland: see **Lake Bonpland,** under **Lake Tahoe** [EL DORADO-PLACER].

Bonta Creek [SIERRA]: *stream,* flows about 6 miles to join Cold Stream (1) and form Sierraville Creek 1.5 miles south of Sierraville (lat. 39°34' N, long. 120°21'45" W; near E line sec. 24, T 20 N, R 14 E). Named on Sattley (1981) and Sierraville (1981) 7.5' quadrangles.

Bonta Saddle [SIERRA]: *pass,* 6 miles southwest of Sierraville (lat. 39°31'15" N, long. 120°25'55" W; sec. 8, T 19 N, R 14 E); the pass is at the head of Bonta Creek. Named on Sattley (1981) 7.5' quadrangle.

Bon Ton Ravine [SIERRA]: *canyon,* drained by a stream that flows 1 mile to Canyon Creek 8 miles southwest of Mount Fillmore (lat. 39°37'55" N, long. 120°56'25" W; sec. 35, T 21 N, R 9 E). Named on La Porte (1951) 7.5' quadrangle.

Boomerang Lake [EL DORADO]: *lake,* 325 feet long, nearly 3 miles northwest of Pyramid Peak (lat. 38°52'20" N, long. 120°11'35" W). Named on Pyramid Peak (1955) 7.5' quadrangle, where the outline of the lake has the shape of a boomerang.

Boomville: see **Butte City** [AMADOR].

Boonville: see **Butte City** [AMADOR].

Booth Point [NEVADA]: *relief feature,* 1.5 miles north-northeast of Graniteville (lat. 39°27'45" N, long. 120°43'35" W; at S line sec. 34, T 19 N, R 11 E). Named on Graniteville (1982) 7.5' quadrangle.

Bope Ravine [SIERRA]: *canyon,* drained by a stream that flows 1.25 miles to Indian Creek (2) 2.25 miles east-southeast of Pike (lat. 39° 25'35" N, long. 120°57'40" W; near W line sec. 15, T 18 N, R 9 E); the feature heads near Plum Valley, where John Bope built Plum Valley House in 1854 (Hoover, Rensch, and Rensch, p. 496). Named on Pike (1949) 7.5' quadrangle.

Boreal Ridge [NEVADA]: *ridge,* west-southwest-trending, 2 miles long, 1.25 miles northwest of Donner Pass (lat. 39°19'50" N, long. 120°20'40" W). Named on Norden (1955) 7.5' quadrangle. The name, from *borealis,* the Latin word for "northern," was given because the ridge is north of Donner Pass and the railroad crossing of the Sierra Nevada (Gudde, 1969, p. 35).

Boston: see **Sacramento** [SACRAMENTO].

Boston House [AMADOR]: *locality,* 6.5 miles south-southeast of Ione (lat. 38°16'15" N, long. 120°52'35" W). Named on Jackson (1902) 30' quadrangle. The place was a combination store and inn (Hoover, Rensch, and Rensch, p. 30). It also was called Boston Store (Gudde, 1975, p. 43).

Boston Ravine [NEVADA]: *locality,* less than 1 mile south-southwest of downtown Grass Valley along Wolf Creek (lat. 39°12'30" N, long. 121°04'10" W; sec. 34, T 16 N, R 8 E). Named on Grass Valley (1949) 7.5' quadrangle. Postal authorities established Boston Ravine post office in 1889 and discontinued it in 1890 (Frickstad, p. 113). On United States Geological Survey's (1901) map, the name "Boston Ravine" applies to a canyon that opens into Wolf Creek from the west at the site of the locality called Boston Ravine. Men from Boston mined at the place in 1849 (Gudde, 1975, p. 43).

Boston Store: see **Boston House** [AMADOR].

Bosworth Meadow [EL DORADO]: *area,* 6.25 miles northwest of Kyburz (lat. 38°51'05" N, long. 120°21'45" W; near S line sec. 25, T 12 N, R 14 E). Named on Kyburz (1952) 7.5' quadrangle.

Botellas: see **Jackson** [AMADOR].

Botilleas Spring: see **Jackson** [AMADOR].

Bottle Hill [EL DORADO]: *peak,* 2.5 miles north-northwest of Georgetown (lat. 38°56'40" N, long. 120°51' W; sec. 27, T 13 N, R 10 E). Named on Georgetown (1949) 7.5' quadrangle. Postal authorities established Bottle Hill post office in 1855 and discontinued it in 1859 (Frickstad, p. 25). Gudde (1975, p. 44) listed a mining camp called Bottle Hill Diggings that was located 3 miles north of Georgetown and named in 1851 for the profusion of bottles at the site.

Bottle Hill Diggings: see **Bottle Hill** [EL DORADO].

Boughmans Mill [EL DORADO]: *locality,* 2 miles west-southwest of Omo Ranch (lat. 38°34'15" N, long. 120°36'45" W). Named on Placerville (1893) 30' quadrangle.

Boulder Bar: see **Scotchman Creek** [NEVADA].

Boulder Canyon [COLUSA]: *canyon,* drained by a stream that flows 1.5 miles to Strode Canyon nearly 7 miles east-southeast of Wilbur Springs (lat. 39°01'10" N, long. 122°18' W; sec. 33, T 14 N, R 4 W). Named on Wilbur Springs (1961) 15' quadrangle.

Boulder Creek: see **Big Boulder Creek** [SIERRA]; **Little Boulder Creek** [SIERRA].

Boulder Pass: see **Boles Gap** [EL DORADO].

Boulder Ridge [PLACER]: *ridge,* west-southwest-trending, 1.25 miles long, 6.25 miles north-northeast of Rocklin (lat. 38°52'20" N, long. 121°10'45" W). Named on Rocklin (1967) 7.5' quadrangle.

Bounde Creek [COLUSA]: *stream,* heads in Glenn County and flows 4 miles in Colusa County to Colusa Drain 9 miles northeast of Maxwell (lat. 39°22'05" N, long. 122°04'30" W). Named on Moulton Weir (1952) and Princeton (1952) 7.5' quadrangles.

Bow Creek [SIERRA]: *stream,* flows 1.5 miles to Fiddle Creek 3 miles west of Goodyears Bar (lat. 39°32'25" N, long. 120°56'15" W; sec. 2, T 19 N, R 9 E). Named on Goodyears Bar (1951) 7.5' quadrangle.

Bowlesville: see **Ashland** [SACRAMENTO].

Bowman [PLACER]: *locality,* 3.25 miles north-northeast of Auburn along Southern Pacific Railroad (lat. 38°56'30" N, long. 121°02'45" W; near N line sec. 35, T 13 N, R 8 E). Named on Auburn (1953) 7.5' quadrangle. Postal authorities established Bowman post office in 1893 (Frickstad, p. 119). The name commemorates Harry Hoisington Bowman, a pioneer fruit grower of the neighborhood (Hanna, p. 39).

Bowman Campground [NEVADA]: *locality,* 3.5 miles west-northwest of English Mountain (lat. 39°27'35" N, long. 120°36'40" W; sec. 3, T 18 N, R 12 E); the place is on the north side of the east end of Bowman Lake. Named on English Mountain (1983) 7.5' quadrangle.

Bowman House [NEVADA]: *locality,* 4.5 miles east of Graniteville (lat. 39°26'50" N, long. 120°39'20" W; at NW cor. sec. 8, T 18 N, E 12 E). Named on Graniteville (1982) 7.5' quadrangle.

Bowman Lake [NEVADA]: *lake,* behind a dam on Canyon Creek 4.5 miles east of Graniteville (lat. 39°26'55" N, long. 120°39'05" W; at S line sec. 5, T 18 N, R 12 E). Named on English Mountain (1983) and Graniteville (1982) 7.5' quadrangles. Called Bowman Reservoir on Logan's (1940) map. The name commemorates James F. Bowman, who settled in the early 1860's by what became known as Little Bowman Lake; this lake and nearby Big Bowman Lake were consolidated in 1873 into a single lake to provide water for hydraulic mining (Gudde, 1949, p. 38).

Bowman Mountain [NEVADA]: *peak,* 6 miles east of Graniteville (lat. 39°26' N, long. 120°37'45" W; at N line sec. 16, T 18 N, R 12 E); the peak is about 1 mile south of Bowman Lake. Altitude 7386 feet. Named on Graniteville (1982) 7.5' quadrangle.

Bowman Reservoir: see **Bowman Lake** [NEVADA].

Box Canyon [AMADOR]: *narrows,* 6 miles south-southwest of Jackson along Mokelumne River on Amador-Calaveras County line (lat. 38°16'25" N, long. 120°49'35" W; sec. 24, T 5 N, R 10 E). Named on Jackson (1962) 7.5' quadrangle.

Box Canyon Number 1 [NEVADA-SIERRA]: *canyon,* 4 miles south-southeast of Sierra City along Middle Yuba River on Nevada-Sierra County line (lat. 39°31'10" N, long. 120°40'20" W; near N line sec. 18, T 19 N, E 12 E); the feature is 3 miles upstream from Box Canyon Number 2. Named on Sierra City (1981) 7.5' quadrangle.

Box Canyon Number 3 [NEVADA-SIERRA]: *canyon,* 2 miles north of Graniteville [NEVADA] along Middle Yuba River on Nevada-Sierra County line (lat. 39°28'05" N, long. 120°44'20" W; near E line sec. 33, T 19 N, R 11 E); the feature is 2.5 miles downstream from Box Canyon

Number 2. Named on Graniteville (1982) 7.5' quadrangle.

Box Canyon Number 2 [NEVADA-SIERRA]: *canyon,* 4 miles north-northeast of Graniteville along Middle Yuba River on Nevada-Sierra County line (lat. 39°29'30" N, long. 120°42'30" W; on N line sec. 26, T 19 N, R 11 E); the feature is about halfway between Box Canyon Number 1 and Box Canyon Number 3. Named on Graniteville (1982) 7.5' quadrangle.

Boxer Valley [COLUSA]: *valley,* 12 miles north-northeast of Wilbur Springs (lat. 39°12'20" N, long. 122°22'10" W). Named on Wilbur Springs (1961) 15' quadrangle. Called Boxley Valley on Wilbur Springs (1944) 15' quadrangle, but United States Board on Geographic Names (1962a, p. 6) rejected this name for the feature.

Boxley Valley: see **Boxer Valley** [COLUSA].

Box Spring [COLUSA]: *spring,* 3 miles northwest of Fouts Springs (lat. 39°22'50" N, long. 122°42'15" W). Named on St. John Mountain (1968) 7.5' quadrangle.

Boyce Ravine [SIERRA]: *canyon,* drained by a stream that flows nearly 2 miles to Cherokee Creek 7.5 miles west of Goodyears Bar (lat. 39°31'10" N, long. 121°01'55" W; sec. 13, T 19 N, R 8 E). Named on Strawberry Valley (1948) 7.5' quadrangle.

Boyd [SACRAMENTO]: *locality,* 9 miles east of downtown Sacramento along Southern Pacific Railroad (lat. 38°34'35" N, long. 121°19'40" W). Named on Fair Oaks (1954) 15' quadrangle. California Division of Highways' (1934) map shows a place called Bradshaw located 0.5 mile west-southwest of Boyd along the railroad.

Boyers Bend [COLUSA-SUTTER]: *bend,* 0.25 mile north of Boyers Landing along Sacramento River on Colusa-Sutter County line (lat. 38°57'20" N, long. 121°50'20" W; near SE cor. sec. 22, T 13 N, R 1 E). Named on Kirkville (1952) 7.5' quadrangle.

Boyers Landing [COLUSA]: *locality,* 9 miles south-southeast of Grimes along Sacramento River (lat. 38°57'05" N, long. 121°50'15" W; on E line sec. 27, T 13 N, R 1 E); the place is 0.25 mile south of Boyers Bend. Named on Kirkville (1952) 7.5' quadrangle. Called Boyer's Landing on Kirkville (1915) 7.5' quadrangle.

Bradshaw: see **Boyd** [SACRAMENTO].

Brady Mountain [NEVADA]: *peak,* nearly 3 miles north-northeast of Yuba Gap (lat. 39°21'15" N, long. 120°36'10" W; near W line sec. 11, T 17 N, R 12 E). Altitude 5956 feet. Named on Cisco Grove (1955) 7.5' quadrangle.

Braggs Canyon [SUTTER]: *canyon,* drained by a stream that flows 2.5 miles to lowlands 7.5 miles northwest of Sutter (lat. 39°14'10" N, long. 121°51'15" W; near E line sec. 16, T 16 N, R 1 E). Named on Sutter Buttes (1954) 7.5' quadrangle.

Brandon Canyon [EL DORADO]: *canyon,* drained by a stream that flows 1 mile to Camp Creek 1.5 miles south-southeast of Old Iron Mountain (lat. 38°40'55" N, long. 120°23'05" W; near NE cor. sec. 35, T 10 N, R 14 E). Named on Stump Spring (1951) 7.5' quadrangle.

Brandon Corner [EL DORADO]: *locality,* 3 miles northeast of Latrobe (lat. 38°35'10" N, long. 120°55'55" W; near SE cor. sec. 36, T 9 N, R 9 E). Named on Latrobe (1949) 7.5' quadrangle. Called Brandons on Placerville (1893) 30' quadrangle.

Brandons: see **Brandon Corner** [EL DORADO].

Brandy City [SIERRA]: *locality,* 7.5 miles west of Goodyears Bar (lat. 39°32'15" N, long. 121°01'30" W; near SE cor. sec. 1, T 19 N, R 8 E). Named on Strawberry Valley (1948) 7.5' quadrangle. The place first was called Strychnine City (Gudde, 1975, p. 45).

Brandy Creek [YUBA]: *stream,* flows 3.5 miles to Willow Creek [SIERRA-YUBA] less than 1 mile northwest of Camptonville (lat. 39°27'30" N, long. 121°03'35" W; at E line sec. 3, T 18 N, R 8 E). Named on Camptonville (1948) 7.5' quadrangle. Called Beaver Creek on Smartsville (1895) 30' quadrangle.

Brandy Flat: see **Poorman Creek** [NEVADA] (1).

Brannan Island [SACRAMENTO]: *island,* 31 miles south-southwest of downtown Sacramento (lat. 38°08'30" N, long. 121°30' W). Named on Bouldin Island (1978), Isleton (1978), Jersey Island (1978), and Rio Vista (1978) 7.5' quadrangles. The name commemorates Samuel Brannan (Gudde, 1949, p. 39).

Brant Lake: see **Crystal Lake** [NEVADA] (1).

Brass Wire Bar: see **Washington** [NEVADA].

Bray Canyon [YOLO]: *canyon,* drained by a stream that flows 4 miles to Putah Creek 13 miles south-southwest of Esparto (lat. 38° 30'55" N, long. 122°04'50" W; near NE cor. sec. 28, T 8 N, R 2 W). Named on Monticello Dam (1959) 7.5' quadrangle.

Brela [EL DORADO]: *locality,* 1.5 miles northeast of Latrobe along Southern Pacific Railroad (lat. 38°34'30" N, long. 120°57'50" W; near W line sec. 2, T 8 N, R 9 E). Named on Latrobe (1949) 7.5' quadrangle.

Bretona [YOLO]: *locality,* 2.5 miles northwest of Zamora along Southern Pacific Railroad (lat. 38°49'30" N, long. 121°54'30" W; near S line sec. 6, T 11 N, R 1 E). Named on Zamora (1916) 7.5' quadrangle. Called Britona on Dunnigan (1907) 15' quadrangle.

Bretona Creek [YOLO]: *stream,* flows 5.5 miles to lowlands 2.25 miles west-northwest of Zamora and 1 mile south-southwest of the site of Bretona (lat. 38°48'40" N, long. 121°55'05" W; near S line sec. 12, T 11 N, R 1 W). Named on Zamora (1953) 7.5' quadrangle. Called Britona Creek on Dunnigan (1907) 15' quadrangle.

Brick: see **Freeport** [SACRAMENTO] (1).

Brick Chimney Canyon [YOLO]: *canyon,* drained by a stream that flows nearly 4 miles to Capay Valley 4 miles north-northeast of Berryessa Peak (lat. 38°42'55" N, long. 122°09'25" W); sec. 14, T 10 N, R 3 W). Named on Brooks (1959) 7.5' quadrangle.

Bridge House [SACRAMENTO]: *locality,* 23 miles east-southeast of downtown Sacramento along Cosumnes River (lat. 38°29'30" N, long. 121°05'25" W; sec. 3, T 7 N, R 8 E). Named on Carbondale (1968) 7.5' quadrangle. Called Bridgehouse on California Mining Bureau's (1909b) map. Postal authorities established Bridgehouse post office in 1901 and discontinued it in 1918 (Frickstad, p. 132).

Bridge House: see **Cosumne** [SACRAMENTO].

Bridgeport [AMADOR]: *locality,* 3.25 miles north-northeast of present Fiddletown on the south side of South Fork Cosumnes River (lat. 38°32'35" N, long. 120°43'30" W). Named on Placerville (1893) 30' quadrangle.

Bridgeport [NEVADA]: *locality,* 2 miles west-southwest of French Corral along South Yuba River (lat. 39°17'30" N, long. 121°11'40" W; sec. 33, T 17 N, R 7 E). Named on French Corral (1948) 7.5' quadrangle. The name is from a wooden bridge across the river; the place also was known as Nyes Landing, for Urias Nye and Manuel Nye, who built a trading post there in 1849 (Gudde, 1975, p. 46), and as Nye's Crossing (Hoover, Rensch, and Rensch, p. 250).

Bridger Creek [YUBA]: *stream,* flows 4 miles to New Bullards Bar Reservoir 2.5 miles west of Camptonville (lat. 39°27'25" N, long. 121°05'35" W; sec. 4, T 18 N, R 8 E). Named on Camptonville (1948, photorevised 1969), and Strawberry Valley (1948) 7.5' quadrangles. Called Clear Creek on Smartsville (1895) 30' quadrangle.

Brighton [SACRAMENTO]: *locality,* 4.5 miles east-southeast of downtown Sacramento along Southern Pacific Railroad (lat. 38° 33' N, long. 121°25' W; sec. 15, T 8 N, R 5 E). Named on Sacramento East (1967) 7.5' quadrangle. The name recalls a town called Brighton that speculators laid out in 1849 about 0.5 mile north of present Brighton—Mormons employed by Sutter built a flour mill there in 1847; the first Brighton was abandoned in 1852, but its hostelry, Five Mile House, operated for several years more (Hoover, Rensch, and Rensch, p. 302-303). The name "Brighton" for the first place was taken from Brighton, England (Gudde, 1949, p. 40). Postal authorities established Brighton post office in 1864 and discontinued it in 1886 (Frickstad, p. 132). A place called Norristown was founded in 1850 along American River north or west of the first site of Brighton, and a community called Hoboken was situated near Norristown (Hoover, Rensch, and Rensch, p. 303).

Brighton House: see **Grass Valley** [NEVADA].

Brimstone Creek [PLACER]: *stream,* flows 2 miles to the head of Shirttail Canyon 5 miles northeast of Foresthill (lat. 39°04'35" N, long. 120°45'45" W; sec. 8, T 14 N, R 11 E). Named on Foresthill (1949) 7.5' quadrangle. Hobson's (1890b) map has the name "Brimstone Plains" for the area at the head of present Brimstone Creek.

Brimstone Plains: see **Brimstone Creek** [PLACER].

Britona: see **Bretona** [YOLO].

Britona Creek: see **Bretona Creek** [YOLO].

Britton Spring [COLUSA]: *spring,* nearly 6 miles east of Wilbur Springs (lat. 39°01'30" N, long. 122°19' W; near NE cor. sec. 32, T 14 N, R 4 W). Named on Wilbur Springs (1961) 15' quadrangle.

Broad Slough [SACRAMENTO]:

(1) *water feature,* joins North Mokelumne River 3 miles east-southeast of Isleton on Tyler Island (lat. 38°08'45" N, long. 121°13'25" W). Named on Isleton (1978) 7.5' quadrangle.

(2) *water feature,* 15 miles southwest of Isleton along the lowermost part of San Joaquin River (lat. 38°02'45" N, long. 121° 50'20" W). Named on Antioch North (1978) 7.5' quadrangle.

Brock [PLACER]: *locality,* 5 miles northwest of Lincoln along Southern Pacific Railroad (lat. 38°56'35" N, long. 121°21'15" W; near SW cor. sec. 30, T 13 N, R 6 E). Named on Lincoln (1953) 7.5' quadrangle.

Brockliss Canyon [EL DORADO]: *canyon,* drained by a stream that flows 1.5 miles to South Fork American River 2.5 miles west of Riverton (lat. 38°46'05" N, long. 120°29'45" W; sec. 23, T 11 N, R 13 E). Named on Riverton (1950) 7.5' quadrangle.

Brockman Canyon [SUTTER]: *canyon,* drained by a stream that flows 2.25 miles to an unnamed canyon 5.5 miles west-northwest of Sutter (lat. 39°11'30" N, long. 121°50'20" W; sec. 34, T 16 N, R 1 E). Named on Sutter Buttes (1954) 7.5' quadrangle.

Brockway [PLACER]: *settlement,* 1 mile south-southeast of Kings Beach along Lake Tahoe just west of Stateline Point (lat. 39°13'35" N, long. 120°00'30" W; sec. 30, T 16 N, R 18 E). Named on Kings Beach (1955) 7.5' quadrangle. Postal authorities established Brockway post office in 1901 and discontinued it in 1966; the name commemorates Nathaniel Brockway (Salley, p. 27), who was the uncle of Frank Brockway Alverson, first postmaster (Lekisch, p. 10). Truckee (1895) 30' quadrangle has the designation "Hot Springs" at the place. G.A. Waring (p. 131) described

Brockway Hot Springs that rise in Lake Tahoe a few feet offshore from Brockway resort. The springs also were called Campbell's Hot Springs (Zauner, p. 32).

Brockway Hot Springs: see **Brockway** [PLACER].

Brockway Spring [PLACER]: *spring,* 1 mile north-northeast of Kings Beach (lat. 39°14'55" N, long. 120°00'45" W; sec. 18, T 16 N, R 18 E); the spring is 1.5 miles north of Brockway. Named on Kings Beach (1955) 7.5' quadrangle.

Brockway Summit [PLACER]: *pass,* 3 miles southwest of Martis Peak (lat. 39°15'40" N, long. 120°04'15" W; sec. 3, T 16 N, R 17 E). Named on Martis Peak (1955) 7.5' quadrangle.

Broderick [YOLO]: *town,* 1.5 miles north-northeast of downtown West Sacramento (lat. 38°35'30" N, long. 121°31'15" W). Named on Sacramento West (1967) 7.5' quadrangle. Gibbes' (1852) map has the name "Washington" at the place, and Lovdal (1916) 7.5' quadrangle has both the names "Washington" and "Broderick P.O." there. James McDowell acquired land at the site in 1846, and after McDowell's death in 1849, his widow had a town called Washington laid out at the place in 1850 (Hoover, Rensch, and Rensch, p. 584). Postal authorities established Washington post office in 1854 and discontinued it in 1856; they established Broderick post office at the site in 1893, discontinued it in 1895, reestablished it in 1896, discontinued it in 1909, and reestablished it the same year; the name "Broderick" was for David C. Broderick, senator from California in the late 1850's (Salley, p. 27, 235).

Broncho: see **Bronco** [NEVADA].

Broncho Creek: see **Bronco Creek** [NEVADA].

Bronco [NEVADA]: *locality,* 9.5 miles east-northeast of Truckee along Southern Pacific Railroad (lat. 39°23'10" N, long. 120°01'20" W); the place is north of the mouth of Bronco Creek. Named on Truckee (1895) 30' quadrangle. Postal authorities established Bronco post office in 1872 and discontinued it in 1891 (Frickstad, p. 113). United States Board on Geographic Names (1933, p. 166) rejected the form "Broncho" for the name.

Bronco Creek [NEVADA]: *stream,* heads in the State of Nevada and flows 1 mile in Nevada County to Truckee River 9.5 miles east-northeast of Truckee (lat. 39°23' N, long. 120°01'10" W; sec. 31, T 18 N, R 18 E). Named on Boca (1955) 7.5' quadrangle. United States Board on Geographic Names (1933, p. 166) rejected the form "Broncho Creek" for the name.

Brooklin: see **Red Dog** [NEVADA].

Brooklyn: see **Red Dog** [NEVADA].

Brooks [YOLO]: *locality,* 6 miles north-northeast of Berryessa Peak in Capay Valley (lat. 38°44'30" N, long. 122°08'50" W). Named on Brooks (1959) 7.5' quadrangle. Durst's (1916) map has the name "Brook's P.O." at the site. Postal authorities established Brooks post office in 1884 (Frickstad, p. 220). According to Gudde (1949, p. 41), the name is from a brook that flows past the place.

Brooks Creek [YUBA]: *stream,* flows 1.5 miles to Yuba River 2.5 miles west-northwest of Smartville (lat. 39°13'10" N, long. 121°20'40" W; sec. 30, T 16 N, R 6 E). Named on Smartville (1951) 7.5' quadrangle.

Brooks Creek: see **Palmer Canyon** [YOLO].

Brophy Canyon [COLUSA]: *canyon,* drained by a stream that flows 3.5 miles to Bear Creek 7.5 miles south-southeast of Wilbur Springs (lat. 38°56'50" N, long. 122°20'50" W; sec. 30, T 13 N, R 4 W). Named on Glascock Mountain (1958) and Wilson Valley (1958) 7.5' quadrangles.

Brown: see **Jimmy Brown Bar**, under **Scotchman Creek** [NEVADA]; **John Brown Flat** [PLACER]; **Manlove** [SACRAMENTO].

Brown Bear Creek: see **Little Brown Bear Creek** [NEVADA].

Brownell [EL DORADO]: *locality,* 10.5 miles south-southeast of Robbs Peak (lat. 38°46'15" N, long. 120°21' W). Named on Pyramid Peak (1896) 30' quadrangle.

Brown Mountain [EL DORADO]: *peak,* 7.5 miles northeast of Robbs Peak (lat. 38°59'20" N, long. 120°17'15" W; sec. 10, T 13 N, R 15 E). Altitude 7144 feet. Named on Loon Lake (1952) 7.5' quadrangle.

Brown Ravine [YUBA]: *canyon,* drained by a stream that flows 1.5 miles to Natchez Creek 0.5 mile north-northwest of Rackerby (lat. 39°26'55" N, long. 121°20'40" W; sec. 6, T 18 N, R 6 E). Named on Rackerby (1948) 7.5' quadrangle.

Brown Rock [EL DORADO]: *relief feature,* 2.5 miles north-northeast of Leek Spring Hill (lat. 38°39'40" N, long. 120°15'20" W; near E line sec. 1, T 9 N, R 15 E). Named on Leek Spring Hill (1951) 7.5' quadrangle.

Browns Bar [EL DORADO]: *locality,* 4.5 miles west-northwest of Greenwood along Middle Fork American River (lat. 38°55'30" N, long. 120°59'25" W; near NE cor. sec. 5, T 12 N, R 9 E). Named on Greenwood (1949) 7.5' quadrangle.

Browns Bar Canyon [EL DORADO]: *canyon,* drained by a stream that flows 2.25 miles to Middle Fork American River 4.5 miles west-northwest of Greenwood (lat. 38°55'40" N, long. 120°59'15" W; near SW cor. sec. 33, T 13 N, R 9 E); Browns Bar is near the mouth of the canyon. Named on Greenwood (1949) 7.5' quadrangle.

Browns Corner [YOLO]: *locality,* 1.5 miles west of downtown Woodland (lat. 38°40'40" N, long. 121°48'05" W; at SW cor. sec. 30, T 10 N, R 2 E). Named on Woodland (1952) 7.5' quadrangle. Called Browns Corners on Yolo (1915) 7.5' quadrangle.

Browns Creek [SACRAMENTO]: *stream,* flows 8 miles to Laguna 9 miles northeast of Galt (lat. 38°20'55" N, long. 121°10'40" W; near N line sec. 26, T 6 N, R 7 E). Named on Carbondale (1968), Clay (1968), and Goose Creek (1968) 7.5' quadrangles.

Browns Hill: see **You Bet** [NEVADA].

Browns Ravine [EL DORADO]: *canyon,* drained by a stream that flows nearly 3 miles to South Fork American River 5.5 miles northwest of Clarksville (lat. 38°43'05" N, long. 121°06'55" W; near E line sec. 17, T 10 N, R 8 E). Named on Clarksville (1953) 7.5' quadrangle. Water of Folsom Lake now covers the lower part of the canyon.

Browns Valley [YUBA]: *town,* 12 miles northeast of Marysville (lat. 39°14'30" N, long. 121°24'30" W; at E line sec. 16, T 16 N, R 5 E). Named on Browns Valley (1947) 7.5' quadrangle. Postal authorities established Browns Valley post office in 1864 (Frickstad, p. 222). The name commemorates a settler who came to the place in 1850 and discovered gold there (Hoover, Rensch, and Rensch, p. 592). Wescoatt's (1861) map shows a place called Empire House located 2.5 miles north of Browns Valley along Little Dry Creek, a place called Prairie Ho. [House] situated 2.25 miles north of Browns Valley, a place called Prairie Diggings located almost 3 miles north-northwest of Browns Valley near the head of Prairie Creek, a place called Galena House located nearly 4 miles north-northeast of Browns Valley, and a peak called Bald Mt. located nearly 2 miles east-northeast of Browns Valley. Prairie Diggings was a mining camp started in 1854; it also was known as Hole in the Wall (Gudde, 1975, p. 276). A stage stop called Sweet Vengeance was located 1 mile southeast of Prairie Diggings (Gudde, 1975, p. 343)—Loma Rica (1947) 7.5' quadrangle shows Sweet Vengeance mine situated 3.25 miles south of Loma Rica (sec. 9, T 16 N, R 5 E).

Browns Valley Ridge [YUBA]: *ridge,* northeast- to northwest-trending, 5.5 miles long, center 3.5 miles south of Loma Rica (lat. 39° 15' N, long. 121°25'45" W); the south end of the ridge is west of Browns Valley. Named on Browns Valley (1947) and Loma Rica (1947) 7.5' quadrangles.

Brownsville [EL DORADO]: *locality,* 1 mile south-southeast of Omo Ranch (lat. 38°34'05" N, long. 120°33'30" W; near NE cor. sec. 8, T 8 N, R 13 E). Site named on Omo Ranch (1952) 7.5' quadrangle. Called Mendon on Placerville (1893) 30' quadrangle. The name "Brownsville" is for Henry Brown, one of the discoverers of gold at the locality (Hoover, Rensch, and Rensch, p. 84). Postal authorities established Mendon post office at the place in 1867, discontinued it for a time in 1869, and discontinued it finally in 1888; the name "Mendon" was coined from letters in the name of the first postmaster, J. Edmondson (Salley, p. 138).

Brownsville [YUBA]: *town,* 4.5 miles east-northeast of Rackerby (lat. 39°28'20" N, long. 121°16'05" W; sec. 26, T 19 N, R 6 E). Named on Rackerby (1948) 7.5' quadrangle. Postal authorities established Brownsville post office in 1862 (Frickstad, p. 222). The name is from I.E. Brown, who built a sawmill near the site in 1851 (Hoover, Rensch, and Rensch, p. 593). Wescoatt's (1861) map shows a place called Union Hotel located 1.5 miles southeast of Brownsville.

Brownsville: see **Forest** [SIERRA].

Brownsville Creek [EL DORADO]: *stream,* flows 5 miles to Cedar Creek 5.5 miles east-northeast of Aukum (lat. 38°34'35" N, long. 120°32'40" W; sec. 2, T 8 N, R 12 E); the stream heads near the site of Brownsville. Named on Aukum (1952) and Omo Ranch (1952) 7.5' quadrangles.

Bruce Crossing [AMADOR]: *locality,* 5.5 miles south of Hams Station along North Fork Mokelumne River on Amador-Calaveras County line (lat. 38°27'40" N, long. 120°22'35" W; sec. 13, T 7 N, R 14 E). Named on Devils Nose (1979) 7.5' quadrangle.

Bruceville [SACRAMENTO]: *settlement,* 7 miles south-southwest of Elk Grove (lat. 38°20'05" N, long. 121°25' W; at N line sec. 34, T 6 N, R 5 E). Named on Bruceville (1968) 7.5' quadrangle. Postal authorities established Bruceville post office in 1896 and discontinued it in 1916 (Frickstad, p. 132).

Brummel Ravine [SIERRA]: *canyon,* drained by a stream that flows 1.25 miles to North Yuba River 9 miles west of Goodyears Bar (lat. 39°31'05" N, long. 121°02'55" W; sec. 14, T 19 N, R 8 E). Named on Strawberry Valley (1948) 7.5' quadrangle.

Brunt Flat [PLACER]: *valley,* 1 mile east-northeast of Colfax (lat. 39°06'20" N, long. 120°55'50" W; at E line sec. 35, T 15 N, R 9 E). Named on Colfax (1949) 7.5' quadrangle.

Brush Canyon [EL DORADO]: *canyon,* drained by a stream that flows 1 mile to Soldier Creek 2.5 miles northeast of Pollock Pines (lat. 38°47'10" N, long. 120°33'10" W; sec. 17, T 11 N, R 13 E). Named on Pollock Pines (1950) 7.5' quadrangle.

Brush Creek [COLUSA]: *stream,* flows 5 miles to Elk Creek nearly 6 miles west of Harrington (lat. 38°58'10" N, long. 122°07'20" W). Named on Rumsey (1959) and Wildwood School (1959) 7.5' quadrangles. On Harrington (1916) 7.5' quadrangle, the name applies to a stream that intersects the rail line 1.25 miles north-northwest of Harrington.

Brush Creek [EL DORADO]:

(1) *stream,* flows 6.5 miles to South Fork American River 4.25 miles west-

northwest of Pollock Pines (lat. 38°47'40" N, long. 120° 39' W; near SW cor. sec. 16, T 11 N, R 12 E). Named on Pollock Pines (1950) and Slate Mountain (1950) 7.5' quadrangles.

(2) *stream,* flows 1.5 miles to South Fork American River 2.25 miles west-northwest of Coloma (lat. 38°49' N, long. 120°55'40" W; sec. 12, T 11 N, R 9 E). Named on Coloma (1949) 7.5' quadrangle.

Brush Creek [NEVADA]: *stream,* flows 2 miles to Rock Creek (1) 2.5 miles north of Nevada City in Lake Vera (lat. 39°18'05" N, long. 121°01'25" W; near S line sec. 25, T 17 N, R 8 E). Named on Nevada City (1948) 7.5' quadrangle.

Brush Creek [PLACER]: *stream,* flows 1 mile to Truckee River 9.5 miles west of Martis Peak (lat. 39°16'20" N, long. 120°12'20" W; at N line sec. 4, T 16 N, R 16 E). Named on Truckee (1955) 7.5' quadrangle.

Brush Creek [SIERRA]: *stream,* flows 1.5 miles to Oregon Creek nearly 3 miles west of Alleghany (lat. 39°28'40" N, long. 120°53'30" W; near NE cor. sec. 31, T 19 N, R 10 E). Named on Pike (1949) 7.5' quadrangle.

Brush Creek: see **Meyers Ravine** [NEVADA].

Brush Creek Ridge [SIERRA]: *ridge,* southeast- to south-trending, 1.25 miles long, 3.5 miles west-northwest of Alleghany (lat. 39°29'15" N, long. 120°54'10" W); the ridge is west of Brush Creek. Named on Pike (1949) 7.5' quadrangle.

Brushy Canyon [EL DORADO]:

(1) *canyon,* drained by a stream that flows 2.5 miles to Iowa Canyon 4 miles west of Pollock Pines (lat. 38°45'50" N, long. 120° 39'30" W; near N line sec. 32, T 11 N, R 12 E). Named on Pollock Pines (1950) and Slate Mountain (1950) 7.5' quadrangles. This appears to be the feature called Little Iowa Canyon on Placerville (1893) 30' quadrangle.

(2) *canyon,* drained by a stream that flows nearly 3 miles to Cedar Creek 3.5 miles east of Aukum (lat. 38°33'35" N, long. 120°39'25" W; sec. 9, T 8 N, R 12 E). Named on Aukum (1952) 7.5' quadrangle. Called Cold Canyon on Placerville (1893) 30' quadrangle.

Brushy Canyon [PLACER]:

(1) *canyon,* 2.25 miles long, opens into Shirttail Canyon 3.5 miles northwest of Foresthill (lat. 39°03'30" N, long. 120°51'45" W). Named on Foresthill (1949) 7.5' quadrangle. The canyon divides at the head into First Brushy Canyon and Second Brushy Canyon. The stream in Brushy Canyon (1) and in Third Brushy Canyon is called Brushy Creek on Colfax (1898) 30' quadrangle.

(2) *canyon,* 2 miles long, opens into the canyon of Middle Fork American River 4.25 miles east-southeast of Michigan Bluff (lat. 39°01'10" N, long. 120°39'40" W; sec. 32, T 14 N, R 12 E); the canyon divides at the head into Middle Branch and South Branch. Named on Michigan Bluff (1952) 7.5' quadrangle. The stream in the canyon is called Brushy Creek on Colfax (1898) 30' quadrangle. Middle Branch is 1.5 miles long and is named on Greek Store (1952) and Michigan Bluff (1952) 7.5' quadrangles. South Branch is 3.5 miles long and is named on Devil Peak (1950), Greek Store (1952), Michigan Bluff (1952), and Tunnel Hill (1950) 7.5' quadrangles. North Branch enters less than 1 mile from the mouth of the main canyon; it is 2.5 miles long and is named on Greek Store (1952) and Michigan Bluff (1952) 7.5' quadrangles.

Brushy Canyon: see **First Brushy Canyon** [PLACER]; **Second Brushy Canyon** [PLACER]; **Third Brushy Canyon** [PLACER].

Brushy Creek [PLACER]: *stream,* flows 3.5 miles to North Fork American River 5.5 miles south-southeast of Colfax (lat. 39°01'25" N, long. 120°55' W; sec. 36, T 14 N, R 9 E). Named on Colfax (1949) 7.5' quadrangle.

Brushy Creek [YUBA]: *stream,* flows 3.5 miles to Slate Creek 2.5 miles east of Strawberry Valley (lat. 39°33'55" N, long. 121°03'40" W; near E line sec. 27, T 20 N, R 8 E). Named on Strawberry Valley (1948) 7.5' quadrangle.

Brushy Creek: see **Brushy Canyon** [PLACER] (1) and (2).

Brushy Mountain [NEVADA]: *peak,* 4.25 miles west of Wolf (lat. 39°04'05" N, long. 121°13'05" W; near N line sec. 17, T 14 N, R 7 E). Named on Wolf (1949) 7.5' quadrangle.

Brushy Mountain Canyon [PLACER]: *canyon,* drained by a stream that flows 1.25 miles to Middle Fork American River 6.5 miles east-northeast of Auburn (lat. 38°56'10" N, long. 120°57'35" W; sec. 34, T 13 N, R 9 E). Named on Greenwood (1949) 7.5' quadrangle.

Brushy Spring [PLACER]: *spring,* 11 miles south-southwest of Duncan Peak (lat. 39°00'20" N, long. 120°34'55" W; sec. 1, T 13 N, R 12 E); the spring is at the head of Brushy Creek (present South Branch Brushy Canyon). Named on Colfax (1938) 30' quadrangle.

Bryan: see **Bryan Meadow** [EL DORADO].

Bryan Creek [EL DORADO]: *stream,* flows 1 mile to South Fork American River nearly 4 miles west of Echo Summit (lat. 38°48'10" N, long. 120°05'55" W; at E line sec. 16, T 11 N, R 17 E). Named on Echo Lake (1955) 7.5' quadrangle.

Bryan Meadow [EL DORADO]: *area,* 2.5 miles south-southwest of Echo Summit (lat. 38°46'50" N, long. 120°03'20" W; near S line sec. 24, T 11 N, R 17 E). Named on Echo Lake (1955) 7.5' quadrangle. Pyramid Peak (1896) 30' quadrangle has the name "Bryan" at the place.

Bryant Creek: see **Stonebreaker Creek** [EL DORADO].

Bryants [EL DORADO]: *locality,* 4.5 miles west of Old Iron Mountain (lat. 38°43'05" N, long. 120°28'30" W; near W line sec. 18, T 10 N, R 14 E). Named on Stump Spring (1951) 7.5' quadrangle.

Bryants Spring [EL DORADO]: *spring,* 3.5 miles north of Riverton (lat. 38°49'30" N, long. 120°27'20" W; sec. 6, T 11 N, R 14 E). Named on Riverton (1950) 7.5' quadrangle.

Bryte [YOLO]: *district,* 1.5 miles north-northwest of West Sacramento along Sacramento River (lat. 38°35'40" N, long. 121°32'20" W). Named on Sacramento West (1967) 7.5' quadrangle. Postal authorities established Bryte post office in 1915 and moved it 2.5 miles west in 1937 (Salley, p. 28). The name is for George Bryte, a local dairyman; the place was called Riverbank before the name was changed to satisfy postal authorities (Gudde, 1949, p. 42).

Brytes Bend [SACRAMENTO-YOLO]: *bend,* 3.25 miles west-northwest of downtown Sacramento along Sacramento River on Sacramento-Yolo County line (lat. 38°35'55" N, long. 121°32'40" W); the feature is at present Bryte. Named on Lovdal (1916) 7.5' quadrangle.

Buckeye [EL DORADO]: *locality,* 2.5 miles east-northeast of Georgetown (lat. 38°55'25" N, long. 120°47'45" W; near N line sec. 6, T 12 N, R 11 E). Named on Georgetown (1949) 7.5' quadrangle.

Buckeye [YUBA]: *locality,* 3 miles northeast of Strawberry Valley (lat. 39°35'45" N, long. 121°04'25" W; sec. 15, T 20 N, R 8 E). Site named on Strawberry Valley (1948) 7.5' quadrangle. Bidwell Bar (1897) 30' quadrangle shows Buckeye House at the place.

Buckeye: see **Carbondale** [AMADOR]; **Winters** [YOLO].

Buckeye Bar [EL DORADO-PLACER]: *locality,* 4 miles northwest of Greenwood along Middle Fork American River on El Dorado-Placer County line (lat. 38°56' N, long. 120°58'05" W; near W line sec. 34, T 13 N, R 7 E); the place is at the mouth of Buckeye Canyon. Named on Greenwood (1949) 7.5' quadrangle. Bancroft (1888, p. 354) listed a place called American Bar that was on the north side of Middle Fork between Buckeye Bar and Sardine Bar.

Buckeye Canyon [EL DORADO]: *canyon,* drained by a stream that flows 1 mile to Middle Fork American River nearly 4 miles northwest of Greenwood at Buckeye Bar (lat. 38°55'55" N, long. 120°57'55" W; sec. 34, T 13 N, R 9 E). Named on Greenwood (1949) 7.5' quadrangle.

Buckeye Creek [YOLO]: *stream,* flows 17 miles to an artificial watercourse 1.25 miles north-northeast of Dunnigan (lat. 38°54'15" N, long. 121°57'40" W; sec. 10, T 12 N, R 1 W). Named on Dunnigan (1953), Rumsey (1959), and Wildwood School (1959) 7.5' quadrangles. South Fork enters from the southwest 12 miles east of Rumsey; it is 11.5 miles long and is named on Bird Valley (1959) and Wildwood School (1959) 7.5' quadrangles.

Buckeye Creek [YUBA]: *stream,* heads in Plumas County and flows 1.5 miles to Slate Creek 3.25 miles northeast of Strawberry Valley in Yuba County (lat. 39°35'35" N, long. 121°03'30" W; at W line sec. 14, T 20 N, R 8 E); one branch of the stream heads near the site of Buckeye. Named on Strawberry Valley (1948) 7.5' quadrangle.

Buckeye Creek: see **Little Buckeye Creek** [YOLO].

Buckeye Diggings [NEVADA]: *locality,* 8 miles north-northeast of Chicago Park (lat. 39°14'35" N, long. 120°53'25" W); the place is near the southwest end of Buckeye Ridge. Named on Chicago Park (1949) 7.5' quadrangle.

Buckeye Flat [PLACER]: *area,* 8.5 miles west-northwest of Devil Peak (lat. 38°59'15" N, long. 120°41'40" W; near S line sec. 12, T 13 N, R 11 E). Named on Tunnel Hill (1950) 7.5' quadrangle.

Buckeye House: see **Buckeye** [YUBA].

Buckeye Point [EL DORADO]: *relief feature,* 5.5 miles north of Georgetown (lat. 38°59'05" N, long. 120°48'55" W; sec. 12, T 13 N, R 10 E). Named on Georgetown (1949) 7.5' quadrangle.

Buckeye Ravine [SIERRA]: *canyon,* drained by a stream that flows 1.5 miles to Wolf Creek nearly 3 miles southeast of Alleghany (lat. 39°26'40" N, long. 120°48'15" W; near N line sec. 12, T 18 N, R 10 E). Named on Alleghany (1949) 7.5' quadrangle.

Buckeye Ridge [NEVADA]: *ridge,* southwest-trending, 3 miles long, 8 miles north-northeast of Chicago Park (lat. 39°14'45" N, long. 120°53' W). Named on Chicago Park (1949), Dutch Flat (1950), North Bloomfield (1949), and Washington (1950) 7.5' quadrangles.

Buckeye Spring [NEVADA]: *spring,* 8 miles south-southwest of Washington (lat. 39°15'10" N, long. 120°51'50" W; sec. 16, T 16 N, R 10 E); the spring is on Buckeye Ridge. Named on Washington (1950) 7.5' quadrangle.

Buck Flat [COLUSA]: *area,* 7.5 miles north-northwest of Wilbur Springs (lat. 39°07'45" N, long. 122°29'35" W; sec. 23, T 15 N, R 6 W). Named on Wilbur Springs (1961) 15' quadrangle.

Buckhorn Camp [YOLO]: *locality,* nearly 6 miles east-northeast of Guinda in Wood Canyon (lat. 38°50'55" N, long. 122°05'20" W; sec. 33, T 12 N, R 2 W). Named on Bird Valley (1959) 7.5' quadrangle.

Buckhorn Lodge [AMADOR]: *locality,* 7.25 miles east-northeast of Pine Grove (lat. 38°26'40" N, long. 120°31'50" W; sec. 22, T 7 N, R 13 E). Named on West Point (1948) 7.5' quadrangle.

Buckhorn Spring [YOLO]: *spring,* 11 miles south of Esparto (lat. 38°32'10"

N, long. 122°02'50" W; sec. 14, T 8 N, R 2 W). Named on Monticello Dam (1959) 7.5' quadrangle.

Buckingham Ridge [SIERRA]: *ridge,* west- to northwest-trending, 1.25 miles long, 3.5 miles east-southeast of Downieville (lat. 39° 32'35" N, long. 120°45'50" W; sec. 5, T 19 N, R 11 E). Named on Downieville (1951) 7.5' quadrangle.

Buck Island Lake [EL DORADO]: *lake,* 4.5 miles west of Wentworth Springs (lat. 39°00'05" N, long. 120°15'05" W). Named on Homewood (1955), Loon Lake (1952, photorevised 1973), and Wentworth Springs (1953, photorevised 1973) 7.5' quadrangles.

Buck Lake [PLACER]: *lake,* 1150 feet long, 3 miles south-southwest of Homewood (lat. 39°03' N, long. 120°11'25" W; sec. 22, T 14 N, R 16 E). Named on Homewood (1955) 7.5' quadrangle.

Buck Meadow [PLACER]: *area,* 2 miles north-northeast of Bunker Hill (lat. 39°04'30" N, long. 120°22'05" W; at E line sec. 11, T 14 N, R 14 E). Named on Wentworth Springs (1953) 7.5' quadrangle. Truckee (1940) 30' quadrangle has the name for an area located 1 mile farther northeast (sec. 1, T 14 N, R 14 E).

Buck Meadows [NEVADA]: *area,* 6 miles east of Truckee (lat. 39°20'25" N, long. 120°04'25" W; sec. 10, T 17 N, R 17 E); the place is northwest of Buck Ridge. Named on Martis Peak (1955) 7.5' quadrangle.

Buck Mountain [NEVADA]:

(1) *peak,* 1 mile southwest of North Bloomfield (lat. 39°21'35" N, long. 120°54'45" W; at S line sec. 1, T 17 N, R 9 E). Named on North Bloomfield (1949) 7.5' quadrangle.

(2) *peak,* 5 miles northeast of Higgins Corner (lat. 39°05'40" N, long. 121°01'45" W; near E line sec. 1, T 14 N, R 8 E). Altitude 2278 feet. Named on Lake Combie (1949) 7.5' quadrangle.

Buckner: see **Elk Grove** [SACRAMENTO].

Buck Pasture [EL DORADO]: *area,* nearly 3 miles northwest of Kirkwood (lat. 38°44' N, long. 120°06'15" W; sec. 8, T 10 N, R 17 E). Named on Caples Lake (1979) 7.5' quadrangle.

Buck Ridge [NEVADA]: *ridge,* south- to west-trending, 2.5 miles long, 6.25 miles east of Truckee (lat. 39°20'15" N, long. 120°03'50" W). Named on Martis Peak (1955) 7.5' quadrangle.

Bucks Bar [EL DORADO]: *locality,* 6 miles south-southwest of Camino along North Fork Cosumnes River (lat. 38°39'20" N, long. 120°42' W; near SW cor. sec. 6, T 9 N, R 12 E). Named on Camino (1952) 7.5' quadrangle. Gudde (1975, p. 374) listed a place called Wisconsin Bar that was located along North Fork Cosumnes River above Bucks Bar.

Buckskin Creek [PLACER]: *stream,* flows 2 miles to Five Lakes Creek 5 miles northeast of Bunker Hill (lat. 39°05'50" N, long. 120°18'55" W; near N line sec. 5, T 14 N, R 15 E). Named on Wentworth Springs (1953) 7.5' quadrangle.

Buckskin Joe Spring [EL DORADO]: *spring,* 1.25 miles west of Leek Spring Hill (lat. 38°37'35" N, long. 120°17'50" W; sec. 15, T 9 N, R 15 E). Named on Leek Spring Hill (1951) 7.5' quadrangle.

Buck Spring [NEVADA]: *spring,* 5.5 miles east-northeast of Truckee (lat. 39°20'40" N, long. 120°04'50" W; at N line sec. 10, T 17 N, R 17 E); the spring is 1 mile northwest of Buck Ridge. Named on Martis Peak (1955) 7.5' quadrangle.

Buenaventura River: see **Sacramento River** [COLUSA-SACRAMENTO-SUTTER-YOLO].

Buena Ventura Valley: see "Regional setting."

Buena Vista [AMADOR]: *locality,* 4 miles south-southeast of Ione in Jackson Valley (lat. 38°17'40" N, long. 120°54'45" W); the place is 1.5 miles north of Buena Vista Peaks. Named on Ione (1962) 7.5' quadrangle. Postal authorities established Buena Vista post office in 1866 and discontinued it in 1878 (Frickstad, p. 5). The place also was called the Corners (Sargent, p. 90).

Buena Vista [NEVADA]: *locality,* 3 miles north of present Chicago Park along Nevada County Narrow Gauge Railroad (lat. 39°11'15" N, long. 120°58'15" W). Named on Colfax (1898) 30' quadrangle.

Buena Vista Peaks [AMADOR]: *peaks,* nearly 6 miles south of Ione (lat. 38°16'05" N, long. 120°54'50" W; sec. 19, T 5 N, R 10 E); the peaks are 1.5 miles south of Buena Vista. Named on Ione (1962) 7.5' quadrangle. Jackson (1902) 30' quadrangle has the singular form "Buena Vista Peak" for the name.

Buffalo Creek [SACRAMENTO]: *stream,* flows 7 miles to American River 3.5 miles east-northeast of downtown Carmichael (lat. 38° 38' N, long. 121°16'05" W). Named on Buffalo Creek (1967), Carmichael (1967), and Citrus Heights (1967) 7.5' quadrangles.

Buffalo Hill [EL DORADO]: *locality,* 0.5 mile west-northwest of Georgetown (lat. 38°54'30" N, long. 120°50'45" W; sec. 10, T 12 N, R 10 E). Named on Georgetown (1949) 7.5' quadrangle.

Bugle Lake [EL DORADO-PLACER]: *lake,* 1050 feet long, 1 mile northeast of Wentworth Springs on El Dorado-Placer County line (lat. 39°01'20" N, long. 120°19'25" W; on N line sec. 32, T 14 N, R 15 E). Named on Wentworth Springs (1953) 7.5' quadrangle.

Bullard [EL DORADO]: *locality,* 3.5 miles north-northeast of Latrobe along Southern Pacific Railroad (lat. 38°36'35" N, long. 120°57'35" W; sec. 26, T 9 N, R 9 E). Named on Latrobe (1949) 7.5' quadrangle.

Bullards Bar [YUBA]: *locality,* 6 miles southeast of Challenge along North Fork Yuba River (present North Yuba River) (lat. 39°25'15" N, long. 121°08'30" W); water of New Bullards Bar Reservoir now covers the site. Named on Smartsville (1895) 30' quadrangle. Postal authorities established Bullard's Bar post office in 1866 and discontinued it in 1914 (Salley, p. 29). The name commemorates Dr. Bullard, an early miner at the site (Hoover, Rensch, and Rensch, p. 595). A mining place called English Bar was situated on the north side of the river 2 miles below Bullards Bar; two English miners worked there in 1851 (Gudde, 1975, p. 110).

Bullards Bar Reservoir: see **New Bullards Bar Reservoir** [YUBA].

Bull Creek [EL DORADO]: *stream,* flows 1.5 miles to South Fork American River 1 mile east of Riverton (lat. 38°46'10" N, long. 120°25'55" W; sec. 29, T 11 N, R 14 E). Named on Riverton (1950) 7.5' quadrangle.

Bull Diggings: see **Mameluke Hill** [EL DORADO].

Bullet Ravine [EL DORADO]: *canyon,* less than 1 mile long, opens into the canyon of Camp Creek 11 miles east-southeast of Placerville (lat. 38°41' N, long. 120°36'10" W). Named on Placerville (1893) 30' quadrangle.

Bull Flat [NEVADA]: *area,* 7.5 miles northwest of Donner Pass (lat. 39°23'50" N, long. 120°25' W; on E line sec. 29, T 18 N, R 14 E). Named on Webber Peak (1981) 7.5' quadrangle.

Bulliard Basin [YOLO]: *canyon,* nearly 1 mile long, opens into Cottonwood Canyon 7.25 miles southwest of Esparto (lat. 38°38'45" N, long. 122°07'20" W; sec. 18, T 9 N, R 2 W). Named on Esparto (1959) 7.5' quadrangle.

Bullion: see **Michigan Bluff** [PLACER].

Bullion Bend [EL DORADO]: *bend,* 17 miles west-southwest of Pyramid Peak along South Fork American River (lat. 38°46'30" N, long. 120°28' W). Named on Pyramid Peak (1896) 30' quadrangle. Robbers held up a stage at the place and their loot supposedly is buried there (Paden, p. 453).

Bullion Creek: see **West Branch**, under **El Dorado Canyon** [PLACER].

Bullock Bend [SUTTER-YOLO]: *bend,* less than 1 mile west-northwest of Kirkville along Sacramento River on Sutter-Yolo County line (lat. 38°54'50" N, long. 121°47'25" W; sec. 1, T 12 N, R 1 E). Named on Kirkville (1952) 7.5' quadrangle, which also has the name "Racetrack Bend" for the feature.

Bullpen Lake [NEVADA]: *lake,* 750 feet long, 5.5 miles east of Graniteville (lat. 39°25'20" N, long. 120°38'05" W; sec. 16, T 18 N, R 12 E). Named on Graniteville (1982) 7.5' quadrangle. Logan's (1940) map has the form "Bull Pen Lake" for the name.

Bullshead [PLACER]: *relief feature,* 5.5 miles northwest of Tahoe City (lat. 39°14'05" N, long. 120°12'05" W; sec. 16, T 16 N, R 16 E). Named on Tahoe City (1955) 7.5' quadrangle. California Division of Highways' (1934) map shows a place called Bulls Head located along Southern Pacific Railroad 0.5 mile south of Bullshead (near S line sec. 16, T 16 N, R 16 E).

Bullshead Canyon [COLUSA]: *canyon,* drained by a stream that flows 3.25 miles to Cortina Creek 10 miles southeast of Wilbur Springs (lat. 38°57'35" N, long. 122°16'05" W; sec. 23, T 13 N, R 4 W). Named on Glascock Mountain (1958) 7.5' quadrangle.

Bull Spring [YOLO]: *spring,* 9 miles south-southwest of Esparto (lat. 38°35'25" N, long. 122°06'40" W; sec. 32, T 9 N, R 2 W). Named on Monticello Dam (1959) 7.5' quadrangle.

Bumpus Cañon: see **Iowa Hill** [PLACER].

Bunch Canyon [PLACER]: *canyon,* drained by a stream that flows 5.5 miles to North Fork American River 5 miles south-southeast of Colfax (lat. 39°02'10" N, long. 120°54'30" W; sec. 30, T 14 N, R 10 E). Named on Colfax (1949) 7.5' quadrangle.

Bunker Hill [AMADOR]:

(1) *peak,* 4 miles south-southeast of Plymouth (lat. 38°25'25" N, long. 120°49'05" W; near SE cor. sec. 25, T 7 N, R 10 E). Altitude 1344 feet. Named on Amador City (1962) 7.5' quadrangle.

(2) *locality,* nearly 4 miles south-southeast of Plymouth (lat. 38°25'35" N, long. 120°49'40" W; sec. 25, T 7 N, R 10 E); the place is 0.5 mile west-northwest of Bunker Hill (1). Named on Amador City (1962) 7.5' quadrangle. Called New Philadelphia on Sutter Creek (1944) 15' quadrangle. New Philadelphia also was known as Dog Town (Gudde, 1975, p. 97).

Bunker Hill [COLUSA]: *hill,* 9 miles east-northeast of Wilbur Springs (lat. 39°05'45" N, long. 122°15'55" W; sec. 2, T 14 N, R 4 W). Named on Wilbur Springs (1961) 15' quadrangle.

Bunker Hill [NEVADA]: *ridge,* southwest- to south-trending, 1 mile long, 5 miles northwest of Nevada City (lat. 39°18'40" N, long. 121°05'30" W; sec. 28, T 17 N, R 8 E). Named on Nevada City (1948) 7.5' quadrangle.

Bunker Hill [PLACER]: *peak,* 11.5 miles south-southeast of Granite Chief (lat. 39°03' N, long. 120°22'45" W; sec. 23, T 14 N, R 14 E). Altitude 7524 feet. Named on Bunker Hill (1953) 7.5' quadrangle.

Bunker Hill [SIERRA]: *peak,* 4.5 miles south-southeast of Mount Fillmore (lat. 39°40' N, long. 120°50' W). Altitude 6967 feet. Named on Mount Fillmore (1951) 7.5' quadrangle.

Bunker Hill Ridge [SIERRA]: *ridge,* southeast-trending, 2.25 miles long, 2.5 miles north of Mount Fillmore on Sierra-Plumas County line (lat.

39°45'50" N, long. 120°51'20" W). Named on Blue Nose Mountain (1951) 7.5' quadrangle.

Bunker Lake [PLACER]: *lake,* 950 feet long, less than 0.5 mile northwest of Bunker Hill (lat. 39°03'15" N, long. 120°23'10" W; at NE cor. sec. 22, T 14 N, R 14 E). Named on Bunker Hill (1953) 7.5' quadrangle.

Bunker Meadow [PLACER]: *area,* 0.5 mile south-southeast of Bunker Hill (lat. 39°02'25" N, long. 120°22'35" W; on S line sec. 23, T 14 N, R 14 E). Named on Bunker Hill (1953) 7.5' quadrangle.

Bunkerville: see **Little Deer Creek** [NEVADA].

Bunkham Slough [SUTTER]: *stream,* diverges from Coon Creek and flows 9 miles to end in American Basin 5 miles north-northeast of Verona (lat. 38°50'55" N, long. 121°34'05" W; sec. 31, T 12 N, R 4 E). Named on Nicolaus (1952), Sheridan (1953, photorevised 1973), and Verona (1967) 7.5' quadrangles.

Burckhalter: see **Boca** [NEVADA].

Burger Canyon [YOLO]: *canyon,* 1.25 miles long, along North Fork Oat Creek above a point 6 miles east of Guinda (lat. 38°49'10" N, long. 122°05'15" W; sec. 9, T 11 N, R 2 W). Named on Bird Valley (1959) 7.5' quadrangle.

Burgoyne Creek [SACRAMENTO]: *stream,* flows 2 miles to Cosumnes River 14 miles southeast of Folsom (lat. 38°30'25" N, long. 121°01'55" W; sec. 31, T 8 N, R 9 E). Named on Folsom SE (1954) 7.5' quadrangle.

Burks Bar: see **Relief** [NEVADA].

Burlington Ridge [NEVADA]: *ridge,* west-trending, 6 miles long, between North Fork and South Fork Deer Creek; center 4 miles south-southwest of Washington (lat. 39°18'30" N, long. 120° 50' W). Named on North Bloomfield (1949) and Washington (1950) 7.5' quadrangles.

Burma Summit [SIERRA]: *peak,* 7 miles east-southeast of Loyalton (lat. 39°38'25" N, long. 120°07'05" W; sec. 30, T 21 N, R 17 E). Altitude 8062 feet. Named on Evans Canyon (1978) 7.5' quadrangle.

Burned Hill [NEVADA]: *peak,* 8.5 miles east of Truckee (lat. 39°19'15" N, long. 120°01'20" W; sec. 19, T 17 N, R 18 E). Altitude 7925 feet. Named on Martis Peak (1955) 7.5' quadrangle.

Burnett: see **Point Burnett**, under **Wood Island** [SACRAMENTO].

Burnett Canyon [PLACER]: *canyon,* drained by a stream that flows 5 miles to East Fork of North Fork of North Fork American River 4.25 miles north-northwest of Westville (lat. 39°13'55" N, long. 120°41' W; sec. 24, T 16 N, R 11 E). Named on Duncan Peak (1952) and Westville (1952) 7.5' quadrangles.

Burnett Island: see **Montezuma Island** [SACRAMENTO].

Burnt Bridge Creek [YUBA]: *stream,* flows 2.5 miles to New Bullards Bar Reservoir 4.25 miles northeast of Dobbins (lat. 39°25'20" N, long. 121°09'25" W; sec. 14, T 18 N, R 7 E). Named on Challenge (1948, photorevised 1969) 7.5' quadrangle.

Burnt Flat [NEVADA]: *area,* 6.5 miles northwest of Donner Pass (lat. 39°23'25" N, long. 120°23'45" W; near SW cor. sec. 27, T 18 N, R 14 E). Named on Webber Peak (1981) 7.5' quadrangle.

Burnt Flat [PLACER]: *area,* 1.25 miles east-northeast of Colfax (lat. 39°06'15" N, long. 120°55'50" W; near SE cor. sec. 35, T 15 N, R 9 E). Named on Colfax (1949) 7.5' quadrangle.

Burnt Shanty Creek [EL DORADO]: *stream,* flows 3 miles to South Fork American River nearly 5 miles west of Coloma (lat. 38°47'45" N, long. 120°58'45" W; sec. 21, T 11 N, R 9 E). Named on Coloma (1949) 7.5' quadrangle. Called Widow Creek on Placerville (1893) 30' quadrangle.

Burtis House: see **Camp Far West** [YUBA].

Burton Creek [PLACER]: *stream,* flows 4 miles to Lake Tahoe 6.5 miles southwest of Kings Beach (lat. 39°10'55" N, long. 120°07'20" W; sec. 5, T 15 N, R 17 E). Named on Kings Beach (1955) and Tahoe City (1955) 7.5' quadrangles. The name commemorates Captain Homer D. Burton, who homesteaded in the region in 1871 (Lekisch, p. 12).

Bush Lake [SACRAMENTO]: *intermittent lake,* 3.5 miles north-northwest of downtown Sacramento in American Basin (lat. 38°37'30" N, long. 121°31' W). Named on Arcade (1911), Brighton (1911), Elkhorn Weir (1915), and Lovdal (1916) 7.5' quadrangles.

Bushy Lake [SACRAMENTO]: *lake,* 3150 feet long, 3.25 miles east-northeast of downtown Sacramento (lat. 38°35'15" N, long. 121° 26'05" W). Named on Brighton (1911) 7.5' quadrangle.

Butcher Corral [EL DORADO]: *locality,* 9.5 miles north-northwest of Pollock Pines (lat. 38°53'35" N, long. 120°37'15" W; sec. 15, T 12 N, R 12 E). Named on Devil Peak (1950) 7.5' quadrangle.

Butcher Flat [PLACER]: *area,* 6.5 miles south-southwest of Duncan Peak (lat. 39°03'50" N, long. 120°32'30" W; near E line sec. 17, T 14 N, R 13 E). Named on Greek Store (1952) 7.5' quadrangle.

Butcher Ranch [PLACER]: *locality,* 11.5 miles east-northeast of Auburn (lat. 38°57'10" N, long. 120°57'15" W). Named on Greenwood (1949) 7.5' quadrangle. Called Butchers on Placerville (1893) 30' quadrangle. Postal authorities established Butcher Ranch post office in 1871 and discontinued it in 1935 (Frickstad, p. 119). They established McKeon post office 5.5 miles northeast of Butcher Ranch post office (SW quarter sec. 6, T 13 N, R 10 E) in 1920 and discontinued it in 1953 (Salley, p. 136).

Butcher Ranch Creek [SIERRA]: *stream,* flows 3.5 miles to Pauley Creek 6.25 miles northwest of Sierra City (lat. 39°37'25" N, long. 120°43'25" W; near S line sec. 3, T 20 N, R 11 E). Named on Gold Lake (1981) and Sierra City (1981) 7.5' quadrangles.

Butcher Ranch Meadow [SIERRA]: *area,* 5 miles northwest of Sierra City (lat. 39°37'50" N, long. 120°41'25" W; near S line sec. 1, T 20 N, R 11 E); the place is along Butcher Ranch Creek. Named on Sierra City (1981) 7.5' quadrangle.

Butchers: see **Butcher Ranch** [PLACER].

Bute Mountains: see **Sutter Buttes** [SUTTER].

Butler Spring [YOLO]: *spring,* 4.25 miles southwest of Guinda (lat. 38°47'05" N, long. 122°14'45" W; near E line sec. 24, T 11 N, R 4 W). Named on Guinda (1959) 7.5' quadrangle.

Butte Canyon [AMADOR]: *canyon,* 1.25 miles long, opens into the canyon of Mokelumne River nearly 2 miles south of Jackson Butte (lat. 38°18'45" N, long. 120°43'10" W; sec. 1, T 5 N, R 11 E). Named on Mokelumne Hill (1948) 7.5' quadrangle.

Butte City [AMADOR]: *locality,* 1.25 miles southwest of Jackson Butte (lat. 38°19'35" N, long. 120°44'05" W; sec. 35, T 6 N, R 11 E); the site is near the head of Butte Canyon. Ruins of the place are named on Mokelumne Hill (1948) 7.5' quadrangle. Postal authorities established Butte City post office in 1857 and discontinued it in 1858 (Frickstad, p. 5). Gudde (1975, p. 54) listed the possible early names "Boomville," "Boonville," "Greasertown," and "Greaserville" for the place.

Butte Creek [COLUSA-SUTTER]: *stream,* flows 16 miles along Colusa-Butte County line and along Colusa-Sutter County line to Sacramento River 4 miles east-southeast of Colusa at Moons Bend (lat. 39°11'40" N, long. 121°56'10" W; sec. 35, T 16 N, R 1 W). Named on Butte City (1952), Meridian (1952), and Sanborn Slough (1952) 7.5' quadrangles.

Butte Creek [EL DORADO]: *stream,* flows 4 miles to North Fork Cosumnes River 6.25 miles south-southeast of Camino (lat. 38°39'10" N, long. 120°37'40" W; near NW cor. sec. 11, T 9 N, R 12 E). Named on Camino (1952) and Sly Park (1952) 7.5' quadrangles.

Butte House [SUTTER]: *locality,* less than 1 mile northeast of Sutter (lat. 39°09'50" N, long. 121°44'15" W). Named on Marysville (1895) 30' quadrangle.

Butte Mountain: see **Jackson Butte** [AMADOR].

Butte Mountains: see **Sutter Buttes** [SUTTER].

Buttermilk Bend [NEVADA]: *bend,* 1.25 miles southwest of French Corral along South Yuba River (lat. 39°17'40" N, long. 121°10'50" W; sec. 34, T 17 N, R 7 E). Named on French Corral (1948) 7.5' quadrangle.

Buttes Area Camp [NEVADA]: *locality,* 9 miles west-northwest of Donner Pass on the south shore of Lake Sterling (lat. 39°21'05" N, long. 120°29'30" W; at W line sec. 11, T 17 N, R 13 E). Named on Soda Springs (1955) 7.5' quadrangle.

Buttes Flat: see **Sierra City** [SIERRA].

Butte Sink [SUTTER]: *marsh,* along and east of Butte Creek at the northwest corner of Sutter County near the junction of Sutter County, Butte County, and Colusa County. Named on Meridian (1952) and Sanborn Slough (1952) 7.5' quadrangles.

Butte Slough [COLUSA-SUTTER]: *water feature,* diverges from Sacramento River 3.5 miles north-northwest of Meridian (lat. 39° 11'40" N, long. 121°56'10" W) and extends 8 miles to Sutter Bypass 5 miles west of Sutter; the westernmost part forms Colusa-Sutter County line. Named on Meridian (1952) and Sutter Buttes (1954) 7.5' quadrangles.

Buttes Mountains: see **Sutter Buttes** [SUTTER].

Buzzard Peak [YUBA]: *peak,* 2 miles north of Smartville (lat. 39° 14'05" N, long. 121°18' W; near NE cor. sec. 21, T 16 N, R 6 E). Altitude 1288 feet. Named on Smartville (1951) 7.5' quadrangle.

Buzzard Roost [NEVADA]: *ridge,* west-southwest-trending, 0.5 long, 6.5 miles northwest of Donner Pass (lat. 39°22'20" N, long. 120°25'35" W; at N line sec. 5, T 17 N, R 14 E). Named on Soda Springs (1955) 7.5' quadrangle.

Buzzard Roost Lake [NEVADA]: *lake,* 850 feet long, 6.25 miles northwest of Donner Pass (lat. 39°22'45" N, long. 120°24'25" W; sec. 33, T 18 N, R 14 E); the lake is 1.25 miles east-northeast of Buzzard Roost. Named on Webber Peak (1981) 7.5' quadrangle.

Byers Slough [COLUSA]: *water feature,* 2.25 miles south of Grimes (lat. 39°02'25" N, long. 121°54'05" W). Named on Grimes (1954) 7.5' quadrangle.

Bypass: see **Marchant** [SUTTER].

Byrds Valley [PLACER]: *area,* 0.5 mile west of Michigan Bluff (lat. 39°02'25" N, long. 120°44'50" W; sec. 21, T 14 N, R 11 E). Named on Michigan Bluff (1952) 7.5' quadrangle. Whitney's (1873) map has the name for an inhabited place.

— C —

Cabbage Patch: see **Waldo Junction** [YUBA].

Cabin Creek [EL DORADO]: *stream,* flows 1.5 miles to Oat Creek 6.5 miles east of Caldor (lat. 38°35'45" N, long. 120°18'50" W; near SE cor.

sec. 28, T 9 N, R 15 E). Named on Peddler Hill (1951) 7.5' quadrangle.

Cabin Creek [PLACER]: *stream,* flows nearly 2 miles to Truckee River 9.5 miles west of Martis Peak (lat. 39°16'40" N, long. 120° 12'20" W; sec. 33, T 17 N, R 16 E). Named on Truckee (1955) 7.5' quadrangle. California Division of Highways' (1934) map shows a place called Headland located along Southern Pacific Railroad about 0.5 mile north of the mouth of present Cabin Creek (at N line sec. 33, T 17 N, R 16 E).

Cabin Slough [SACRAMENTO]: *water feature,* 14 miles southwest of Isleton between Sherman Island and Kimball Island (lat. 38°01'45" N, long. 121°48'50" W). Named on Antioch North (1978) 7.5' quadrangle

Cable Point [EL DORADO]: *peak,* 5.5 miles west-northwest of Pollock Pines (lat. 38°47'30" N, long. 120°40'35" W; near NE cor. sec. 19, T 11 N, R 12 E). Altitude 2879 feet. Named on Slate Mountain (1950) 7.5' quadrangle.

Cache Creek [COLUSA-YOLO]: *stream,* enters Yolo County from Lake County 7.5 miles west-northwest of Rumsey, and flows 58 miles to Cache Creek Settling Basin 10 miles north-northeast of Davis (lat. 38°41'15" N, long. 121°42' W; sec. 25, T 10 N, R 2 E). Named on Brooks (1959), Esparto (1959), Glascock Mountain (1958), Grays Bend (1953), Guinda (1959), Madison (1953, photorevised 1968), Rumsey (1959), and Woodland (1952, photorevised 1968 and 1975) 7.5' quadrangles. Called Rio de Jesus Maria on a diseño of Guesesosi grant made in 1844 and 1845 (Becker). Two bends of the stream cross Yolo-Colusa County line into Colusa County. Trappers of Hudson's Bay Company called the stream Riviere la Cache before 1832 because they had a cache or hiding place there (Gudde, 1949, p. 47-48). Tyson (p. 21) called the stream Cash Creek. Durst's (1916) map has the name "Cache Creek Cañon" along Cache Creek above Rumsey. Durst (p. 336) noted in describing the canyon that "The bluish color of the shales and the two pillars of rocks on the wagon road give rise to the name Blue Gates so frequently used in this vicinity."

Cache Creek: see **Madison** [YOLO].

Cache Creek Cañon: see **Cache Creek** [COLUSA-YOLO].

Cache Creek Ridge [COLUSA]: *ridge,* south- to southeast-trending, 8 miles long, center 5.5 miles south of Wilbur Springs on Colusa-Lake County line (lat. 38°57'30" N, long. 122°24'15" W); the ridge is north of Cache Creek. Named on Morgan Valley (1958) and Wilbur Springs (1961) 15' quadrangles.

Cache Creek Settling Basin [YOLO]: *area,* 10.5 miles north-northeast of Davis (lat. 38°41'25" N, long. 121°41'25" W; around NE cor. sec. 25, T 10 N, R 2 E); the place is at the lower end of Cache Creek. Named on Grays Bend (1953) 7.5' quadrangle. Called Cache Creek Sink on Grays Bend (1916) 7.5' quadrangle. Chandler (p. 12) used the name "Tule Basin" for the feature.

Cache Creek Sink: see **Cache Creek Settling Basin** [YOLO].

Cache Creek Slough [YOLO]: *stream,* diverges from Cache Creek at Yolo and flows 9.5 miles to Sacramento River at Knights Landing (lat. 38°48'10" N, long. 121°43'15" W). Named on Knights Landing (1910) and Ronda (1915) 7.5' quadrangles.

Cacheville: see **Yolo** [YOLO].

Cadanassa: see **Cadenasso** [YOLO].

Cadenasso [YOLO]: *settlement,* 4.5 miles northeast of Berryessa Peak in Capay Valley (lat. 38°42'50" N, long. 122°07'45" W). Named on Brooks (1959) 7.5' quadrangle. Called Cadanassa on Capay (1945) 15' quadrangle, but United States Board on Geographic Names (1962a, p. 6) rejected this form for the name, which commemorates Nicolo Cadenasso, a rancher in the neighborhood in the late nineteenth century. Postal authorities established Cadanassa post office in 1894, discontinued it in 1895, reestablished it in 1915, and discontinued it in 1918 (Salley, p. 31).

Cagwin Lake [EL DORADO]: *lake,* 600 feet long, 4 miles west-northwest of Echo Summit (lat. 38°50'35" N, long. 120°05'40" W; sec. 34, T 12 N, R 17 E). Named on Echo Lake (1955) 7.5' quadrangle. The name commemorates Hamden El Dorado Cagwin, who settled at Lower Echo Lake in 1896 (Lekisch, p. 12).

Cain: see **Tommy Cain Ravine** [PLACER].

Cain Valley [COLUSA]: *valley,* 2 miles northeast of Wilbur Springs (lat. 39°03'40" N, long. 122°23'45" W; in and near sec. 15, T 14 N, R 5 W). Named on Wilbur Springs (1961) 15' quadrangle.

Cairns: see **Lincoln** [PLACER].

Caldor [EL DORADO]: *locality,* 8.5 miles west-southwest of Leek Spring Hill (lat. 38°36'20" N, long. 120°25'50" W; sec. 28, T 9 N, R 14 E). Named on Caldor (1951) 7.5' quadrangle

Caldwell's Upper Store: see **Nevada City** [NEVADA].

Calf Bar: see **American River** [EL DORADO-PLACER-SACRAMENTO].

Cal-Ida [SIERRA]: *locality,* 7 miles west of Goodyears Bar (lat. 39° 31'35" N, long. 121°00'55" W; sec. 7, T 19 N, R 9 E). Named on Strawberry Valley (1948) 7.5' quadrangle.

California House: see **Dobbins** [YUBA].

California Range: see "Regional setting."

Calpine [SIERRA]: *village,* 6.5 miles northwest of Sierraville (lat. 39°39'55" N, long. 120°26'20" W; on S line sec. 17, T 21 N, R 14 E). Named on Calpine (1981) 7.5' quadrangle. Postal authorities established Calpine post office in 1921 and discontinued it in 1942 (Frickstad, p. 184). The place, which began in 1919 in connection with a lumber mill, first was called McAlpine; postal authorities rejected this name, but accepted the abbreviated form "Calpine" (Gudde, 1949, p. 52). California Division of Highways' (1934) map shows a place called Davis Jct. located along Western Pacific Railroad nearly 2 miles north of Calpine (sec. 8, T 21 N, R 14 E).

Calpine Reservoir [SIERRA]: *lake,* behind a dam on Fletcher Creek 1.25 miles west of Calpine (lat. 39°39'50" N, long. 120°27'40" W; near SW cor. sec. 18, T 21 N, R 14 E). Named on Calpine (1981) 7.5' quadrangle.

Calvada [SIERRA]: *locality,* 7.5 miles southeast of Crystal Peak along Southern Pacific Railroad (lat. 39°27'45" N, long. 120°00'15" W; near S line sec. 31, T 19 N, R 18 E). Named on Truckee (1940) 30' quadrangle.

Calvins Creek [COLUSA]: *stream,* flows 3.5 miles to Antelope Valley 10 miles north-northeast of Wilbur Springs (lat. 39°10'30" N, long. 122°22'05" W; sec. 1, T 15 N, R 5 W); the stream drains Blanchard Valley. Named on Wilbur Springs (1961) 15' quadrangle.

Camanche Reservoir [AMADOR]: *lake,* extends up Mokelumne River on Amador-Calaveras County line from a dam in San Joaquin County. Named on Clements (1968), Ione (1962), Jackson (1962), Valley Springs (1962), and Wallace (1962) 7.5' quadrangles. The name is from the village of Camanche, which was in Calaveras County; water of the lake now covers the site of the village. A miner named the village in 1849 for his hometown in Iowa (Cook, F.S., a, p. 3).

Camel Hump [NEVADA]: *peak,* 8 miles northeast of present Chicago Park (lat. 39°13' N, long. 120°51' W). Named on Colfax (1898) 30' quadrangle. Dutch Flat (1950) 7.5' quadrangle shows Camels Hump L.O. [Lookout] at the place.

Camels Hump [PLACER]: *peak,* 4 miles south-southeast of Colfax at the south end of Gillis Hill (lat. 39°03'05" N, long. 120°54'45" W; on E line sec. 24, T 14 N, R 9 E). Altitude 2131 feet. Named on Colfax (1949) 7.5' quadrangle.

Caminettis: see **Silver Lake** [AMADOR].

Camino [EL DORADO]: *town,* 7 miles east of Placerville (lat. 38°44'20" N, long. 120°40'25" W; sec. 8, T 10 N, R 12 E). Named on Camino (1952) 7.5' quadrangle. Postal authorities established Camino post office in 1904; a travelers stop called Seven Mile House was at the site in the early days (Salley, p. 33).

Camino Reservoir [EL DORADO]: *lake,* behind a dam on Silver Creek 5.25 miles north-northeast of Pollock Pines (lat. 38°49'40" N, long. 120°32'10" W; sec. 4, T 11 N, R 13 E). Named on Pollock Pines (1950, photorevised 1973) 7.5' quadrangle.

Campana [EL DORADO]: *locality,* 9 miles north-northeast of Pollock Pines (lat. 38°53'05" N, long. 120°31'10" W; sec. 16, T 12 N, R 13 E). Named on Devil Peak (1950) 7.5' quadrangle.

Camp Beal Military Reservation: see **Beal Air Force Base** [NEVADA-YUBA].

Campbell Creek [PLACER]: *stream,* flows 2 miles to Bear River 2.25 miles west-southwest of Colfax (lat. 39°05'05" N, long. 120° 59'15" W; near NE cor. sec. 8, T 14 N, R 9 E). Named on Colfax (1949) 7.5' quadrangle.

Campbell Gulch [SIERRA-YUBA]: *canyon,* drained by a stream that heads in Sierra County and flows 3 miles to Willow Creek 0.5 mile north-northwest of Camptonville in Yuba County (lat. 39°27'40" N, long. 121°03'10" W; sec. 2, T 18 N, R 8 E). Named on Camptonville (1948) 7.5' quadrangle.

Campbell Hot Springs [SIERRA]: *locality,* 1.5 miles southeast of Sierraville (lat. 39°34'30" N, long. 120°20'50" W; near NE cor. sec. 19, T 20 N, R 15 E). Named on Sierraville (1981) 7.5' quadrangle. Called Sulphur Spring on Sierraville (1894) 30' quadrangle. Eight thermal springs at the site are the basis of a resort started in the 1880's (Waring, G.A., p. 129).

Campbell Sheep Camp [SIERRA]: *locality,* 7.25 miles north of Sierra City (lat. 39°40'05" N, long. 120°37' W; sec. 22, T 21 N, R 12 E). Named on Sierra City (1955) 15' quadrangle.

Campbell's Hot Springs: see **Brockway** [PLACER].

Camp Bethel: see **Sutter** [SUTTER].

Camp Cody [EL DORADO]: *locality,* 6 miles south of Pyramid Peak (lat. 38°45'30" N, long. 120°08'30" W; sec. 1, T 10 N, R 16 E); the place is at Cody Lake. Named on Pyramid Peak (1955) 7.5' quadrangle.

Camp Contreras: see **Pioneer** [AMADOR].

Camp Creek [AMADOR]: *stream,* flows 3 miles to North Fork Mokelumne River 5.5 miles south-southeast of Hams Station (lat. 38°27'55" N, long. 120°21'20" W; near NE cor. sec. 18, T 7 N, R 15 E). Named on Garnet Hill (1979) 7.5' quadrangle.

Camp Creek [EL DORADO]: *stream,* formed by the confluence of Middle Fork and North Fork, flows 29 miles to North Fork Cosumnes River 5.5 miles south of Camino (lat. 38°39'20" N, long. 120°39'55" W; near SW cor. sec. 4, T 9 N, R 12 E). Named on Camino (1952), Leek Spring Hill (1951), Sly Park (1952), and Stump Spring (1951) 7.5' quadrangles. A group of Mormons on the way across the Sierra Nevada to Salt Lake City in 1848 camped by the stream and named it (Ricketts, 1983, p. 19). Middle Fork is 1 mile long and North Fork is 1.25 miles long; both forks are named on Leek Spring Hill (1951) 7.5' quadrangle. South Fork enters the main creek from the southeast less than 1 mile downstream from the junction of North Fork and Middle Fork; it is 1 mile long and is named on Leek Spring Hill (1951) 7.5' quadrangle.

Camp Eldorado: see **Camp Silverado** [AMADOR].

Camper Flat [EL DORADO]: *locality,* 2 miles west-southwest of Phipps Peak along Rubicon River in Rockbound Valley (lat. 38°56'30" N, long. 120°11' W; near SW cor. sec. 26, T 13 N, R 16 E). Named on Rockbound Valley (1955) 7.5' quadrangle.

Camp Far West [YUBA]: *locality,* 5 miles east-northeast of Wheatville on the north side of Bear River (1) (lat. 39°02'20" N, long. 121°20'30" W). Site named on Camp Far West (1949) 7.5' quadrangle. Army officials set up an installation—known variously as camp, fort, and cantonment—at the site in 1849 to protect wagon roads and emigrant trails in the vicinity; the installation functioned for three years (Hart, H.M., p. 138-139). Goddard's (1857) map shows a place called Johnsons located 2.5 miles southwest of Camp Far West on the north side of Bear River (1); Eddy's (1851) map has the name "Johnson Ranche" at the place, and Jefferson's (1849) map has the notation "Johnson's house; first settlement" there. Postal authorities established Johnson's Ranche post office in 1853 and changed the name to Johnsons Ranch in 1866 before they discontinued it and moved the service 4.5 miles east to Wheatland that same year; the name was for William Johnson, owner of Johnson Rancho grant, who operated a stage station along Bear River (1) at what was known as Johnsons Crossing (Salley, p. 107). Gibbes' (1852) map shows a place called Kearney situated on the north side of Bear River (1); this was a town laid out by the proprietors of Johnson Rancho grant near Johnsons Crossing, but the town failed to develop (Gudde, 1975, p. 182). Wescoatt's (1861) map shows a place called Kemptons Crossing located 6 miles west-southwest of Camp Far West along Bear River (1) on Sutter-Yuba County line—the place first was called Robinsons Crossing for a settler of 1849 (Gudde, 1975, p. 293). Whitney's (1873) map has both the names "Johnson" and "Burtis Ho." [House] on the north side of Bear River (1) 1 mile west-southwest of Camp Far West.

Camp Far West Reservoir [PLACER-YUBA]: *lake,* behind a dam on Bear River [NEVADA-PLACER-SUTTER-YUBA] 5.5 miles north-northeast of Sheridan on Placer-Yuba County line (lat. 39°03' N, long. 121°18'55" W; sec. 21, T 14 N, R 6 E); the lake is 1.5 miles east-northeast of the site of Camp Far West. Named on Wheatland (1949) 15' quadrangle. Camp Far West (1949, photorevised 1973) 7.5' quadrangle shows a larger lake formed by a high dam that backs up water into Nevada County.

Camp Forward [EL DORADO]: *locality,* 12 miles north-northwest of Pollock Pines (lat. 38°55'05" N, long. 120°41'25" W; at W line sec. 6, T 12 N, R 12 E). Named on Tunnel Hill (1950) 7.5' quadrangle.

Camp Gleason [SIERRA]: *locality,* 4 miles north-northwest of Alleghany (lat. 39°29'40" N, long. 120°54'15" W; near SW cor. sec. 19, T 19 N, R 10 E). Named on Pike (1949) 7.5' quadrangle.

Camp Harvey West [EL DORADO]: *locality,* 3.5 miles northwest of Echo Summit at the west end of Upper Echo Lake (lat. 38°50'45" N, long. 120°04'50" W; at W line sec. 35, T 12 N, R 17 E). Named on Echo Lake (1955) 7.5' quadrangle. The name commemorates Harvey West, a lumberman who gave money to Boy Scouts for a camp that was dedicated in 1950 (Lekisch, p. 13).

Camp Haswell [YOLO]: *locality,* 2 miles northwest of Rumsey along Cache Creek (lat. 38°54'30" N, long. 122°15'50" W; near NE cor. sec. 11, T 12 N, R 4 W). Named on Glascock Mountain (1958) 7.5' quadrangle.

Camp Kohler [SACRAMENTO]: *military installation,* 10 miles northeast of downtown Sacramento (lat. 38°40'20" N, long. 121° 21'30" W). Named on Fair Oaks (1954) 15' quadrangle. War Department officials named the place in 1942 for Lieutenant Frederick Kohler, the first Signal Corps officer killed in World War II (Gudde, 1949, p. 177).

Camp Lundeen [NEVADA]: *locality,* 5.25 miles east-southeast of Graniteville along Lindsey Creek (lat. 39°24'40" N, long. 120°38'50" W; sec. 20, T 18 N, R 12 E). Named on Graniteville (1982) 7.5' quadrangle.

Camp Minkalo [AMADOR]: *locality,* 8 miles north of Mokelumne Peak on the east side of Silver Lake (lat. 38°39'25" N, long. 120° 06'35" W; sec. 4, T 9 N, R 17 E). Named on Caples Lake (1979) 7.5' quadrangle.

Camp 19 [NEVADA]: *locality,* 5 miles northwest of Yuba Gap (lat. 39°22'05" N, long. 120°40'50" W; at E line sec. 1, T 17 N, R 11 E). Named on Blue Canyon (1955) 7.5' quadrangle.

Camp O' pera: see **Lancha Plana**[AMADOR].

Camp Pahatsi [NEVADA]: *locality,* 5 miles west of Donner Pass (lat. 39°19'10" N, long. 120°24'55" W; near SW cor. sec. 21, T 17 N, R 14 E). Named on Soda Springs (1955) 7.5' quadrangle.

Camp Pendola: see **Camptonville** [YUBA].

Camp Richardson [EL DORADO]: *village,* 4 miles northeast of Mount Tallac near Lake Tahoe (lat. 38°56'05" N, long. 120°02'20" W; at W line sec. 6, T 12 N, R 18 E). Named on Emerald Bay (1955) 7.5' quadrangle. Postal authorities established Camp Richardson post office in 1927, discontinued it in 1964, reestablished it in 1965, and discontinued it in 1973; the name was for Alonzo L. Richardson, first postmaster (Salley, p. 35), who had a resort at the place (Lekisch, p. 14).

Camp Sacramento [EL DORADO]: *locality,* 4.5 miles west of Echo Summit along South Fork American River (lat. 38°48'10" N, long. 120°06'55" W; near W line sec. 16, T 11 N, R 17 E). Named on Echo Lake (1955) 7.5' quadrangle. Postal authorities established Camp Sacramento post office in 1929 and discontinued it in 1940 (Frickstad, p. 25).

Camp Seven [EL DORADO]: *locality,* 5 miles north of Pollock Pines (lat. 38°49'55" N, long. 120°34'20" W; sec. 6, T 11 N, R 13 E). Named on Pollock Pines (1950) 7.5' quadrangle. The place was a logging camp of Michigan California Lumber Company (Beverly Cola, personal communication, 1985).

Camp Silverado [AMADOR]: *locality,* 9 miles north of Mokelumne Peak (lat. 38°40' N, long. 120°06'20" W; near S line sec. 33, T 10 N, R 17 E); the place is east of Silver Lake. Named on Caples Lake (1979) 7.5' quadrangle. Called Camp Eldorado on Silver Lake (1956) 15' quadrangle.

Camp Spaulding [NEVADA]: *locality,* 1 mile west of Yuba Gap (lat. 39°19'05" N, long. 120°38'15" W; near S line sec. 21, T 17 N, R 12 E); the place is 0.5 mile south of Lake Spaulding. Named on Blue Canyon (1955) 7.5' quadrangle. Postal authorities established Ohm post office in 1913 at a power-plant construction camp called Spaulding (SW quarter sec. 21, T 17 N, R 12 E) and discontinued it the same year—thc name "Ohm" is from a technical term for a unit of electrical resistance (Salley, p. 160).

Camp Springs [EL DORADO]: *locality,* 6.5 miles northwest of Leek Spring Hill (lat. 38°41'40" N, long. 120°21'30" W); the place is north of Camp Creek. Named on Pyramid Peak (1896) 30' quadrangle.

Camp Ten [EL DORADO]: *locality,* 9 miles north-northeast of Pollock Pines (lat. 38°53'20" N, long. 120°32'10" W; sec. 17, T 12 N, R 13 E). Named on Devil Peak (1950) 7.5' quadrangle. The place was a logging camp of Michigan California Lumber Company (Beverly Cola, personal communication, 1985).

Camptonville [YUBA]: *town,* 36 miles northeast of Marysville (lat. 39°27'05" N, long. 121°02'55" W; sec. 2, T 18 N, R 8 E). Named on Camptonville (1948) 7.5' quadrangle. Postal authorities established Camptonville post office in 1854 (Frickstad, p. 222). United States Board on Geographic Names (1933, p. 189) rejected the form "Comptonville" for the name. Gold was discovered in 1850 and 1851 at the place, which first was known as Gold Ridge (Hanna, p. 53). A hotel built at the site was called Nevada House, but the community that developed around the hotel was named for Robert Campton, a blacksmith there (Gudde, 1975, p. 58-59). Wescoatt's (1861) map shows a community called Rail Road Hill located 1 mile northeast of Camptonville near the mouth of a canyon called Rail Road Gulch. The name "Rail Road" was from the iron rails used to carry dirt to sluice boxes (Hoover, Rensch, and Rensch, p. 596). Gudde (1975, p. 95) listed a place called Depot Hill that was situated 2 miles north of Camptonville. United States Board on Geographic Names (1991, p. 3) approved the name "Camp Pendola" for a place situated 3.5 miles northwest of Camptonville (lat. 39°29'25" N, long. 121°05'03" W; sec. 21, 28, T 19 N, R 8 E), and rejected the name "Pendola Ranch" for the locality.

Camp Two Sentinels [EL DORADO]: *locality,* 0.5 mile west of Kirkwood (lat. 38°42'15" N, long. 120°04'55" W; on W line sec. 22, T 10 N, R 17 E); the place is 0.5 mile north-northeast of the peaks called Two Sentinels [AMADOR]. Named on Caples Lake (1979) 7.5' quadrangle.

Camp Union: see **Lancha Plana** [AMADOR]; **Sutterville** [SACRAMENTO].

Camp Virner: see **Balderson Station** [EL DORADO].

Camp Wasiu [EL DORADO]: *locality,* 1.5 miles southwest of the town of Meeks Bay near Meeks Creek (lat. 39°01'20" N, long. 120°08'45" W; near N line sec. 31, T 14 N, R 17 E). Named on Homewood (1955, photorevised 1969) 7.5' quadrangle.

Camp Winton [AMADOR]: *locality,* 7.5 miles west of Mokelumne Peak on the southeast side of Lower Bear River Reservoir (lat. 38°32'35" N, long. 120°13'35" W; sec. 17, T 8 N, R 16 E). Named on Bear River Reservoir (1979) 7.5' quadrangle.

Camp Yuba [SIERRA]: *locality,* 6.25 miles west of Sierra City along North Yuba River (lat. 39°33'35" N, long. 120°44'55" W; near W line sec. 33, T 20 N, R 11 E). Named on Sierra City (1981) 7.5' quadrangle.

Canaan: see **Colusa** [COLUSA].

Cañada de Capay [YOLO]: *land grant,* covers Capay Valley. Named on Brooks (1959), Esparto (1959), Glascock Mountain (1958), Guinda (1959), Madison (1953), and Rumsey (1959) 7.5' quadrangles. Francisco Berryessa received 9 leagues in 1846; Jasper O' Farrell and others claimed 40,079 acres patented in 1865 (Cowan, p. 23).

Canada Hill [PLACER]: *ridge,* generally west-trending, 1.5 miles long, 1.5 miles north-northwest of Duncan Peak (lat. 39°10'40" N, long. 120°31'15" W; on E line sec. 4, T 15 N, R 13 E). Named on Duncan Peak (1952) 7.5' quadrangle. Whitney's (1880) map shows an inhabited place called Canada Hill on or near the ridge.

Canal Bar: see **Canyon Creek** [NEVADA].

Candy Bucket Spring [COLUSA]: *spring,* 1.5 miles northeast of Fouts Springs (lat. 37°22'05" N, long. 122°38'25" W). Named on Fouts Springs (1968) 7.5' quadrangle. According to G.A. Waring (p. 370), "Candybucket Spring is thus locally known because a candy bucket was for some time kept near it for the use of teamsters in watering their teams and of automobilists in replenishing their radiators."

Canterbury Mountain [YOLO]: *peak,* 6.5 miles southwest of Esparto (lat. 38°38'35" N, long. 122°07' W; near E line sec. 7, T 9 N, R 2 W). Altitude 2474 feet. Named on Esparto (1959) 7.5' quadrangle.

Canyon: see **Shingle Springs** [EL DORADO].

Canyon Creek [EL DORADO]:

(1) *stream,* flows 9 miles to Middle Fork American River 4 miles north of Greenwood (lat. 38°57'10" N, long. 120°54'05" W; near N line sec. 30, T 13 N, R 10 E). Named on Georgetown (1949) and Greenwood (1949) 7.5' quadrangles. Whitney's (1880) map has the name "Jones Cr." for the next tributary—which enters from the south—to Middle Fork American River upstream from Canyon Creek (1), and shows a settlement called Jones Hill near the head of Jones Creek.

(2) *stream,* flows 2.5 miles to Rock Creek 13 miles northwest of Pollock Pines (lat. 38°55'05" N, long. 120°44'10" W; sec. 3, T 12 N, R 11 E). Named on Tunnel Hill (1950) 7.5' quadrangle.

Canyon Creek [NEVADA]: *stream,* flows 17 miles to South Yuba River 8 miles west-northwest of Yuba Gap (lat. 39°21'40" N, long. 120°44'55" W; at S line sec. 4, T 17 N, R 11 E). Named on Blue Canyon (1955), English Mountain (1983), and Graniteville (1982) 7.5' quadrangles. South Fork joins Canyon Creek in Sawmill Lake; it is 3.5 miles long and is named on English Mountain (1983) 7.5' quadrangle. A mining place called Canal Bar was located along South Yuba River at the mouth of Canyon Creek (Hoover, Rensch, and Rensch, p. 255). Early in 1850 miners started a settlement called Canyonville that was situated at the mouth of Canyon Creek, but by the end of the year the place was deserted (Slyter and Slyter, p. 9).

Canyon Creek [PLACER]: *stream,* flows 10.5 miles to North Fork American River 3.5 miles south of Dutch Flat (lat. 39°09'05" N, long. 120°50'05" W; sec. 15, T 15 N, R 10 E). Named on Blue Canyon (1955), Dutch Flat (1950), and Westville (1952) 7.5' quadrangles.

Canyon Creek [SIERRA-YUBA]: *stream,* formed by the confluence of East Fork and North Fork in Sierra County, flows 22 miles to North Yuba River 9 miles west of Goodyears Bar (lat. 39°31'20" N, long. 121°03'10" W; at S line sec. 11, T 19 N, R 8 E). Named on Goodyears Bar (1951), La Porte (1951), Mount Fillmore (1951), and Strawberry Valley (1948) 7.5' quadrangles. The stream forms part of Sierra-Yuba County line. Marlette (p. 202) noted that the creek was correctly named, "for we had to send our pack mules some fifteen miles off our course to find a crossing." East Fork is 2 miles long and North Fork is nearly 1.5 miles long. South Fork, which enters the main stream just below the confluence of North Fork and East Fork, is 1.5 miles long. West Branch, which enters the main stream 2.25 miles southwest of Mount Fillmore, is 3.5 miles long. All four tributaries are named on Mount Fillmore (1951) 7.5' quadrangle.

Canyon Creek: see **Big Canyon Creek** [EL DORADO]; **Little Canyon Creek** [NEVADA]; **Little Canyon Creek** [SIERRA].

Canyon Creek Campground [NEVADA]: *locality,* 1.5 miles west-southwest of English Mountain (lat. 39°26'15" N, long. 120°34'45" W; sec. 12, T 18 N, R 12 E); the place is along Canyon Creek. Named on English Mountain (1983) 7.5' quadrangle.

Canyon 4 [SIERRA]: *canyon,* drained by a stream that flows 3.25 miles to Little Truckee River 6 miles south of Crystal Peak (lat. 39°27'55" N, long. 120°06'10" W; at E line sec. 29, T 19 N, R 17 E); the canyon is north of Canyon 3. Named on Boca (1955) 7.5' quadrangle.

Canyon 3 [SIERRA]: *canyon,* drained by a stream that flows 2 miles to Little Truckee River 7 miles south of Crystal Peak (lat. 39° 27' N, long. 120°06'10" W; near SW cor. sec. 33, T 19 N, R 17 E); the feature is between Canyon 2 and Canyon 4. Named on Boca (1955) 7.5' quadrangle.

Canyon 24 [NEVADA]: *canyon,* drained by a stream that flows 1.5 miles to Truckee River 11 miles northeast of Truckee (lat. 39°25'55" N, long. 120°01'45" W; near NE cor. sec. 12, T 18 N, R 17 E). Named on Boca (1955) 7.5' quadrangle.

Canyon 23 [NEVADA-SIERRA]: *canyon,* drained by a stream that heads in Sierra County and flows 2.5 miles to Truckee River 11.5 miles northeast of Truckee in Nevada County (lat. 39°26'05" N, long. 120°01'30" W; near SW cor sec. 7, T 18 N, R 18 E). Named on Boca (1955) 7.5' quadrangle.

Canyon 22 [NEVADA-SIERRA]: *canyon,* drained by a stream that heads in Sierra County and flows 2 miles to Truckee River 12 miles northeast of Truckee in Nevada County (lat. 39°26'30" N, long. 120°00'55" W; sec. 7, T 18 N, R 18 E); the canyon is northeast of Canyon 23. Named on Boca (1955) 7.5' quadrangle.

Canyon 2 [NEVADA-SIERRA]: *canyon,* drained by a stream that heads in Sierra County and flows nearly 3 miles to Little Truckee River 9 miles north-northeast of Truckee in Nevada County (lat. 39°26'15" N, long. 120°05'20" W; sec. 4, T 18 N, R 17 E). Named on Boca (1955) 7.5' quadrangle.

Canyonville: see **Canyon Creek** [NEVADA].

Canzatti Spring [AMADOR]: *spring,* 7.5 miles east-northeast of Pine Grove (lat. 38°26'35" N, long. 120°31'40" W; sec. 22, T 7 N, R 13 E). Named on West Point (1948) 7.5' quadrangle.

Capay [YOLO]: *village,* 2 miles west-northwest of Esparto along Cache Creek (lat. 38°42'30" N, long. 122°02'50" W); the place is at the lower end of Capay Valley. Named on Esparto (1959) 7.5' quadrangle. Postal authorities established Capay post office in 1868 (Frickstad, p. 220). The place first was called Munchville and then Langville, both names from early settlers (Gudde, 1949, p. 55). Postal authorities established Oat Valley post office 10 miles southwest of Antelope (present Dunnigan) in 1869, moved it to a site 7 miles northeast of Capay (SW quarter sec. 24, T 11 N, R 2 W) in 1873, and discontinued it in 1875 (Salley, p. 159).

Capay Hills [YOLO]: *range,* northeast of the south part of Capay Valley; center 4.5 miles southeast of Guinda (lat. 38°47'15" N, long. 122°07'30" W). Named on Bird Valley (1959) and Guinda (1959) 7.5' quadrangles. Kirby (p. 601) used the name "Rumsey Hills" for the entire range located northeast of Capay Valley.

Capay Valley [YOLO]: *valley,* along Cache Creek from near Rumsey to Capay. Named on Brooks (1959), Esparto (1959), Guinda (1959), and Rumsey (1959) 7.5' quadrangles. The name "Capay" is from an Indian word that has the meaning "stream" (Kroeber, p. 37).

Cape Cod Bar: see **Enterprise** [AMADOR].

Cape Horn [PLACER]:

(1) *ridge,* south-trending, 1 mile long, 1.5 miles northeast of Colfax (lat. 39°07'10" N, long. 120°56' W). Named on Colfax (1949) 7.5' quadrangle. Builders of Central Pacific Railroad named the feature, which was a great obstacle during construction of the rail line (Stewart, p. 45).

(2) *locality,* 2.5 miles northeast of Colfax along Southern Pacific Railroad (lat. 39°07'45" N, long. 120°55'25" W; near N line sec. 25, T 15 N, R 9 E); the place is 1 mile northeast of Cape Horn (1). Named on Chicago Park (1949) 7.5' quadrangle.

Cape Horn [YUBA]: *relief feature,* 1 mile west-northwest of Camptonville (lat. 39°27'25" N, long. 121°04' W; sec. 3, T 18 N, R 8 E). Named on Camptonville (1948) 7.5' quadrangle.

Cape Horn Bar: see **Timbuctoo** [YUBA].

Caperton Reservoir [PLACER]: *lake,* 450 feet long, 5 miles north of Rocklin (lat. 38°51'45" N, long. 121°13'10" W; sec. 29, T 12 N, R 7 E). Named on Rocklin (1967) 7.5' quadrangle.

Caples Creek [EL DORADO]: *stream,* heads at Caples Lake in Alpine County and flows 7.5 miles to Silver Fork American River 6.25 miles west of Kirkwood in El Dorado County (lat. 38°41'30" N, long. 120°11'05" W). Named on Caples Lake (1979) and Tragedy Spring (1979) 7.5' quadrangles. The name commemorates Dr. James Caples, who built a station near Caples Lake in the 1850's; the place became a regular stop on a wagon road into California (United States Board on Geographic Names, 1968b, p. 4).

Caple Spring [EL DORADO]: *spring,* 9.5 miles west-northwest of Leek Spring Hill (lat. 38°42'20" N, long. 120°24'40" W). Named on Pyramid Peak (1896) 30' quadrangle.

Capps Crossing [EL DORADO]: *locality,* 4 miles south of Old Iron Mountain along North Fork Cosumnes River (lat. 38°38'50" N, long. 120°23'40" W; sec. 11, T 9 N, R 14 E). Named on Stump Spring (1951) 7.5' quadrangle.

Caps Ravine [PLACER]: *canyon,* drained by a stream that flows 4 miles to Doty Ravine 8 miles west-northwest of Auburn (lat. 38° 55'55" N, long. 121°13' W; sec. 32, T 13 N, R 7 E). Named on Gold Hill (1954) 7.5' quadrangle.

Carbondale [AMADOR]: *locality,* nearly 6 miles northwest of Ione along Southern Pacific Railroad (lat. 38°24'30" N, long. 121°00'30" W). Named on Carbondale (1968) 7.5' quadrangle. Carbondale (1909) 7.5' quadrangle shows the place situated 0.25 mile north of the railroad, and north of present Willow Creek. Postal authorities established Carbondale post office in 1922 and discontinued it in 1955 (Frickstad, p. 5). Carbondale also had the name "Buckeye" (Sargent, p. 49). The place was a shipping point for coal after 1877 (Mosier, p. 4). Carbondale (1909) 7.5' quadrangle shows a place called May located less than 1 mile north of present Carbondale. Postal authorities established May post office in 1881 and discontinued it in 1920 (Frickstad, p. 6). California Division of Highways' (1934) map shows a place called Lignite situated about 0.5 mile southeast of Carbondale along Southern Pacific Railroad.

Carey Canyon [YOLO]: *canyon,* drained by a stream that flows nearly 3 miles to Capay Valley 4.5 miles north-northeast of Berryessa Peak (lat. 38°43'45" N, long. 122°09'45" W). Named on Brooks (1959) 7.5' quadrangle.

Carlysle: see **Old Man Mountain** [NEVADA].

Carman Creek [SIERRA]: *stream,* formed by the confluence of East Fork and West Fork, flows 3.5 miles to Sierra Valley 2.5 miles northeast of Calpine (lat. 39°41'40" N, long. 120°24'30" W; near SE cor. sec. 4, T 21 N, R 14 E). Named on Calpine (1981) 7.5' quadrangle. United States Board on Geographic Names (1974a, p. 2) gave the form "Carmen Creek" as a variant. East Fork and West Fork both head in Plumas County. Each fork is 5 miles long and each is named on Calpine (1981) 7.5' quadrangle.

Carmichael [SACRAMENTO]: *city,* 9.5 miles east-northeast of downtown Sacramento (lat. 38°37' N, long. 121°19'40" W). Named on Carmichael (1967) and Citrus Heights (1967) 7.5' quadrangles. The owner of land at the place named the community for himself in 1910 (Gudde, 1949, p. 57).

Postal authorities established Carmichael post office in 1921 (Salley, p. 38). Arrowsmith's (1860) map shows a place called Fords Bar situated along American River 1 mile east-southeast of present downtown Carmichael (lat. 38°36'35" N, long. 121°18'40" W).

Carnelian Bay [PLACER]:

(1) *embayment,* 4 miles southwest of Kings Beach along Lake Tahoe between Flick Point and Dollar Point (lat. 39°12'30" N, long. 120°05' W). Named on Kings Beach (1955) 7.5' quadrangle. Members of the Whitney survey named the embayment for the occurrence there of a variety of chalcedony called carnelian (Gudde, 1949, p. 57).

(2) *village,* 3.25 miles west-southwest of Kings Beach (lat. 39°13'40" N, long. 120°04'45" W; sec. 22, T 16 N, R 17 E); the village is at the north end of Carnelian Bay (1). Named on Kings Beach (1955) 7.5' quadrangle. Postal authorities established Cornelian post office in 1883, discontinued in 1887, reestablished it in 1891, discontinued it in 1893, and reestablished it with the name "Carnelian Bay" in 1908 (Salley, p. 38).

Carnelian Canyon [PLACER]: *canyon,* drained by a stream that flows 1.25 miles to Lake Tahoe 3.25 miles west-southwest of Kings Beach (lat. 39°13'35" N, long. 120°04'50" W; sec. 22, T 16 N, R 17 E); the mouth of the canyon is at the village of Carnelian Bay. Named on Kings Beach (1955) 7.5' quadrangle.

Carney Creek [SIERRA]: *stream,* flows 1.5 miles to Jim Crow Creek 4 miles east-southeast of Downieville (lat. 39°31'40" N, long. 120°46'05" W; sec. 8, T 19 N, R 11 E). Named on Downieville (1951) and Sierra City (1981) 7.5' quadrangles.

Caroline Diggings: see **Last Chance** [PLACER].

Carpenter [EL DORADO]: *locality,* 13 miles east of Placerville (lat. 38°44'30" N, long. 120°33'05" W). Named on Placerville (1893) 30' quadrangle.

Carpenter Creek [EL DORADO]: *stream,* flows 2.5 miles to South Fork American River 2 miles west-southwest of Kyburz (lat. 38° 45'50" N, long. 120°19'35" W; near S line sec. 29, T 11 N, R 15 E). Named on Kyburz (1952) and Leek Spring Hill (1951) 7.5' quadrangles.

Carpenter Flat [PLACER]: *valley,* about 1.25 miles east of Emigrant Gap (1) along upper reaches of Fulda Creek (lat. 39°18'15" N, long. 121°38'40" W). Named on Blue Canyon (1955) 7.5' quadrangle. Called Wilson Valley on Colfax (1898) 30' quadrangle.

Carpenter Ridge [NEVADA]: *ridge,* east-trending, 2 miles long, 6.5 miles north of Donner Pass (lat. 39°24'50" N, long. 120°19' W); the ridge is northwest of Carpenter Valley. Named on Independence Lake (1981) 7.5' quadrangle.

Carpenters Bar: see **Green Valley** [PLACER].

Carpenter Valley [NEVADA]: *valley,* 6.25 miles north-northeast of Donner Pass along North Fork Prosser Creek (lat. 39°24' N, long. 120°16'45" W); the valley is southeast of Carpenter Ridge. Named on Independence Lake (1981) 7.5' quadrangle. Called Twin Valley on Truckee (1895) 30' quadrangle.

Carrier Canyon [COLUSA]: *canyon,* drained by a stream that flows 2.5 miles to Grapevine Creek 4.25 miles east-northeast of Lodoga (lat. 39°19'45" N, long. 122°25'10" W; sec. 16, T 17 N, R 5 W). Named on Lodoga (1960) 15' quadrangle.

Carr Lake [NEVADA]: *lake,* 950 feet long, 6 miles east-southeast of Graniteville (lat. 39°24' N, long. 120°38'25" W; at W line sec. 28, T 18 N, R 12 E). Named on Graniteville (1982) 7.5' quadrangle. Colfax (1938) 30' quadrangle has the name "Feeley Lakes" for present Carr Lake and nearby Feeley Lake together.

Cars Creek [SIERRA]: *stream,* flows 2 miles to Canyon Creek 5.5 miles northwest of Goodyears Bar (lat. 39°35'50" N, long. 120°57'30" W). Named on Downieville (1897) 30' quadrangle.

Carson [EL DORADO]: *locality,* 6.25 miles north of Omo Ranch (lat. 38°40'15" N, long. 120°34'25" W). Named on Placerville (1893) 30' quadrangle.

Carson Creek [AMADOR]: *stream,* flows 1.5 miles to Jackson Creek 4 miles southeast of Ione (lat. 38°18'15" N, long. 120°52'55" W; sec. 9, T 5 N, R 10 E). Named on Ione (1962) and Jackson (1962) 7.5' quadrangles.

Carson Creek [EL DORADO-SACRAMENTO]: *stream,* heads in El Dorado County and flows 13 miles to Deer Creek 10 miles south of Folsom in Sacramento County (lat. 38°32' N, long. 121°08'25" W; sec. 19, T 8 N, R 8 E). Named on Buffalo Creek (1967), Clarksville (1953), and Folsom SE (1954) 7.5' quadrangles.

Carson Range [EL DORADO]: *range,* extends for 17 miles, largely on El Dorado-Alpine County line, north-northeast from Carson Pass in Alpine County to the State of Nevada. Named on Freel Peak (1955) and South Lake Tahoe (1955) 7.5' quadrangles. United States Board on Geographic Names (1939, p. 9) rejected the name "Rose Mountain Range" for the feature. Brewer (p. 437) used the name "Carson Spur" for the range in 1863.

Carson Spur [AMADOR]: *peak,* 11.5 miles north of Mokelumne Peak (lat. 38°42'10" N, long. 120°06' W; sec. 21, T 10 N, R 17 E). Altitude 8290 feet. Named on Caples Lake (1979) 7.5' quadrangle.

Carson Spur: see **Carson Range** [EL DORADO].

Cart Wheel Valley: see **White Oak Flat** [EL DORADO].

Carvin Campground [SIERRA]: *locality,* 5 miles north-northeast of Sierra City along North Yuba River (lat. 39°37'20" N, long. 120° 34'55" W; near SW cor. sec. 1, T 20 N, R 12 E); the place is 0.5 mile downstream from the mouth of Carvin Creek. Named on Sierra City (1981) 7.5' quadrangle.

Carvin Creek [SIERRA]: *stream,* flows 1 mile to North Yuba River 5.25 miles northeast of Sierra City (lat. 39°37'35" N, long. 120° 34'30" W; sec. 1, T 20 N, R 12 E). Named on Clio (1981) 7.5' quadrangle.

Carvin Creek Homesites [SIERRA]: *locality,* 5.25 miles north-northeast of Sierra City (lat. 39°37'40" N, long. 120°34'40" W; sec. 1, T 20 N, R 12 E); the place is near the mouth of Carvin Creek. Named on Clio (1981) 7.5' quadrangle.

Casa Loma [PLACER]: *locality,* 3.25 miles east of Dutch Flat (lat. 39°12' N, long. 120°46'30" W; at N line sec. 6, T 15 N, R 11 E). Named on Dutch Flat (1950) 7.5' quadrangle.

Cascade Creek [EL DORADO]: *stream,* flows 4 miles to Lake Tahoe 3.25 miles north-northeast of Mount Tallac (lat. 38°57'05" N, long. 120°04'35" W). Named on Emerald Bay (1955) 7.5' quadrangle.

Cascade Diggings: see **Quaker Hill** [NEVADA] (2).

Cascade Lake [EL DORADO]: *lake,* 1 mile long, 2.5 miles north of Mount Tallac (lat. 38°56'25" N, long. 120°05'25" W; mainly in sec. 27, T 13 N, R 17 E); the lake is along Cascade Creek. Named on Emerald Bay (1955) 7.5' quadrangle.

Cascade Lakes [PLACER]: *lakes,* two connected, largest 3500 feet long, 6 miles west-southwest of Donner Pass (lat. 39°18' N, long. 120°25'50" W; around NW cor. sec. 32, T 17 N, R 14 E). Named on Soda Springs (1955) 7.5' quadrangle. Hobson's (1890b) map shows a place called Cascade Station located north of present Cascade Lakes along Central Pacific Railroad.

Cascade Station: see **Cascade Lakes** [PLACER].

Casey [EL DORADO]: *locality,* 12 miles east of Placerville (lat. 38° 43'15" N, long. 120°34'40" W). Named on Placerville (1893) 30' quadrangle.

Casey Canyon [NEVADA]: *canyon,* drained by a stream that flows 2 miles to Truckee River 8 miles east-northeast of Truckee (lat. 39°22'05" N, long. 120°02'20" W; sec. 36, T 18 N, R 17 E). Named on Martis Peak (1955) 7.5' quadrangle.

Casey Corner [NEVADA]: *locality,* 2 miles north of Pilot Peak in Penn Valley (lat. 39°11'50" N, long. 121°10'35" W; near S line sec. 34, T 16 N, R 7 E). Named on Rough and Ready (1949) 7.5' quadrangle.

Casey Flats [YOLO]: *areas,* 3.5 miles southwest of Guinda (lat. 38°47'30" N, long. 122°14'30" W). Named on Guinda (1959) 7.5' quadrangle. The southernmost area is called Casey Flat on Rumsey (1945) 15' quadrangle, but United States Board on Geographic Names (1962b, p. 15) rejected the singular form of the name.

Cash Creek: see **Cache Creek** [COLUSA-YOLO].

Cashmere [YOLO]: *locality,* 2.5 miles north-northwest of Guinda along Southern Pacific Railroad in Capay Valley (lat. 38°51'30" N, long. 122°12'45" W). Named on Rumsey (1921) 15' quadrangle.

Cassidy Ravine [YUBA]: *canyon,* drained by a stream that flows less than 1 mile to North Yuba River nearly 4 miles southeast of Strawberry Valley (lat. 39°31'10" N, long. 121°03'45" W; near NE cor. sec. 15, T 19 N, R 8 E). Named on Strawberry Valley (1948) 7.5' quadrangle.

Castle Creek: see **Lower Castle Creek** [NEVADA]; **Upper Castle Creek** [NEVADA].

Castle Pass [NEVADA]: *pass,* 3.5 miles northwest of Donner Pass (lat. 39°21'30" N, long. 120°21'55" W; near NE cor. sec. 11, T 17 N, R 14 E); the pass is 1 mile west-southwest of Castle Peak. Named on Norden (1955) 7.5' quadrangle. United States Board on Geographic Names (1949b, p. 3) rejected the name "Castle Peak Pass" for the feature.

Castle Peak [NEVADA]: *peak,* 3.5 miles north-northwest of Donner Pass (lat. 39°21'55" N, long. 120°20'55" W; sec. 1, T 17 N, R 14 E). Altitude 9103 feet. Named on Norden (1955) 7.5' quadrangle.

Castle Peak Pass: see **Castle Pass** [NEVADA].

Castle Point [EL DORADO]: *peak,* 2.5 miles west of Kirkwood (lat. 38°42'15" N, long. 120°07'10" W; sec. 20, T 10 N, R 17 E). Altitude 8041 feet. Named on Caples Lake (1979) 7.5' quadrangle.

Castle Valley [NEVADA]: *valley,* 2.5 miles north-northwest of Donner Pass (lat. 39°20'55" N, long. 120°21'10" W; mainly in sec. 12, T 17 N, R 14 E); the valley is 1 mile south-southwest of Castle Peak at the head of Upper Castle Creek. Named on Norden (1955) 7.5' quadrangle. United States Board on Geographic Names (1949c, p. 4) rejected the name "Willow Valley" for the feature.

Cat Canyon [SIERRA]: *canyon,* drained by a stream that flows nearly 3 miles to Balls Canyon 8.5 miles east of Loyalton (lat. 39° 39'20" N, long. 120°05'10" W; sec. 21, T 21 N, R 17 E). Named on Dog Valley (1981) and Evans Canyon (1978) 7.5' quadrangles.

Cat Creek [EL DORADO]: *stream,* flows 5.5 miles to Middle Fork Cosumnes River nearly 5 miles east-southeast of Caldor (lat. 38°34'20" N, long. 120°21'25" W; sec. 6, T 8 N, R 15 E). Named on Peddler Hill (1951) 7.5' quadrangle.

Cat Creek Ridge [EL DORADO]: *ridge,* west-southwest-trending, 4.5 miles long, 6 miles east of Caldor (lat. 38°35'30" N, long. 120° 19' W); the ridge is south of Cat Creek. Named on Peddler Hill (1951) 7.5' quadrangle.

Catfish Lake [NEVADA]:
(1) *lake,* 1000 feet long, 1.5 miles north of English Mountain (lat. 39°28'15" N, long. 120°33'15" W; sec. 31, T 19 N, R 13 E). Named on English Mountain (1983) 7.5' quadrangle.
(2) *lake,* 850 feet long, 7.5 miles west of Donner Pass (lat. 39° 20'05" N, long. 120°27'50" W; sec. 13, T 17 N, R 13 E). Named on Soda Springs (1955) 7.5' quadrangle.

Catfish Lake: see **Little Catfish Lake**, under **Tollhouse Lake** [NEVADA].

Cathedral Creek [EL DORADO]: *stream,* flows 1 mile to Fallen Leaf Lake 1.5 miles east-southeast of Mount Tallac (lat. 38°53'55" N, long. 120°04'10" W; sec. 11, T 12 N, R 17 E); the stream heads 0.5 mile north of Cathedral Peak. Named on Emerald Bay (1955) 7.5' quadrangle.

Cathedral Lake [EL DORADO]: *lake,* 400 feet long, 1.25 miles southeast of Mount Tallac (lat. 38°53'35" N, long. 120°04'50" W); the lake is 0.5 mile north-northeast of Cathedral Peak. Named on Emerald Bay (1955) 7.5' quadrangle.

Cathedral Peak [EL DORADO]: *relief feature,* 1.5 miles south-southeast of Mount Tallac (lat. 38°53'15" N, long. 120°05' W; sec. 15, T 12 N, R 17 E). Named on Emerald Bay (1955) 7.5' quadrangle.

Catlett [SUTTER]: *locality,* 6 miles northeast of Verona along an abandoned railroad grade (lat. 38°50'45" N, long. 121°32'15" W; sec. 33, T 12 N, R 4 E). Named on Verona (1967) 7.5' quadrangle. Knights Landing (1952) 15' quadrangle shows the place along Sacramento Northern Railroad. Vernon (1910) 7.5' quadrangle shows a place called Alamos located along Northern Electric Railroad at or near present Catlett.

Cavanah: see **Barney Cavanah Ridge** [PLACER].

Cave Gulch [AMADOR]: *canyon,* less than 1 mile long, opens into the canyon of Mokelumne River 5.25 miles south-southwest of Jackson (lat. 38°16'50" N, long. 120°49'10" W; near S line sec. 13, T 5 N, R 10 E). Named on Jackson (1962) 7.5' quadrangle. Water of Pardee Reservoir now covers the lower part of the canyon.

Cecil Lake [COLUSA]: *lake,* 1000 feet long, 1.25 miles north-northwest of Grimes near Sacramento River (lat. 39°05'40" N, long. 121°54' W; sec. 6, T 14 N, R 1 E). Named on Grimes (1954) 7.5' quadrangle.

Cedar Basin [YOLO]: *relief feature,* 3 miles southwest of Rumsey at the head of Johnson Canyon (lat. 38°51'15" N, long. 121°16'40" W). Named on Knoxville (1958) 7.5' quadrangle.

Cedar Camp [COLUSA]: *locality,* 6.5 miles south-southwest of Fouts Springs (lat. 39°15'50" N, long. 122°42' W; sec. 1, T 16 N, R 8 W). Named on Fouts Springs (1968) 7.5' quadrangle.

Cedar Canyon [EL DORADO]: *canyon,* drained by a stream that flows 2.5 miles to String Canyon 9 miles southeast of Camino (lat. 38°38'15" N, long. 120°33'50" W; sec. 17, T 9 N, R 13 E). Named on Sly Park (1952) 7.5' quadrangle.

Cedar Creek [EL DORADO]: *stream,* flows 6.5 miles to Scott Creek 1.5 miles east-southeast of Aukum (lat. 38°32'45" N, long. 120°42'10" W; near W line sec. 18, T 8 N, R 12 E). Named on Aukum (1952) and Omo Ranch (1952) 7.5' quadrangles.

Cedar Creek [PLACER]: *stream,* flows 4.25 miles to North Fork American River nearly 5 miles south-southwest of Donner Pass (lat. 39°15'15" N, long. 120°22'10" W; sec. 14, T 16 N, R 14 E). Named on Norden (1955) 7.5' quadrangle

Cedar Creek Camp: see **Coyoteville** [EL DORADO].

Cedar Flat [PLACER]: *area,* 4 miles west-northwest of Kings Beach (lat. 39°12'55" N, long. 120°05'35" W; sec. 21, T 16 N, R 17 E). Named on Kings Beach (1955) 7.5' quadrangle.

Cedar Grove Ravine [SIERRA]: *canyon,* drained by a stream that flows 3.25 miles to Slate Creek 5.5 miles west-southwest of Mount Fillmore (lat. 39°41'25" N, long. 120°56'15" W; near S line sec. 11, T 21 N, R 9 E). Named on La Porte (1951) 7.5' quadrangle.

Cedar Kress: see **Union Hill** [NEVADA].

Cedar Ravine [EL DORADO]: *canyon,* drained by a stream that flows nearly 2 miles to Hangtown Creek in downtown Placerville (lat. 38°43'45" N, long. 120°47'45" W; at W line sec. 8, T 10 N, R 11 E). Named on Placerville (1949) 7.5' quadrangle.

Cedar Ravine [NEVADA]: *canyon,* drained by a stream that flows 2.5 miles to South Wolf Creek 5 miles north-northeast of Higgins Corner (lat. 39°06'05" N, long. 121°02'40" W; near NW cor. sec. 1, T 14 N, R 8 E). Named on Lake Combie (1949) 7.5' quadrangle.

Cedar Ridge [NEVADA]: *village,* 2.5 miles east-southeast of Grass Valley (lat. 39°12' N, long. 121°01'10" W; near SE cor. sec. 36, T 16 N, R 8 E). Named on Grass Valley (1949) 7.5' quadrangle. Postal authorities established Cedar Ridge post office in 1948 (Frickstad, p. 113).

Cedars: see **The Cedars** [PLACER].

Cedar Spring [EL DORADO]: *spring,* nearly 3 miles north-northwest of Riverton (lat. 38°48'35" N, long. 120°27'55" W; sec. 12, T 11 N, R 13 E). Named on Riverton (1950) 7.5' quadrangle.

Cedarville [EL DORADO]: *locality,* 4.25 miles east-northeast of Aukum (lat. 38°34'05" N, long. 120°38'50" W; near SW cor. sec. 3, T 8 N, R 12 E); the place is along Cedar Creek. Site named on Aukum (1952) 7.5' quadrangle. Postal authorities established Cedarville post office in 1853 and discontinued it in 1863 (Frickstad, p. 25).

Celestial Valley [YUBA]: *valley,* 2.5 miles south-southwest of Camptonville along Oregon Creek (lat. 39°25'15" N, long. 121°03'55" W; sec. 15, 22, T 18 N, R 8 E). Named on Camptonville (1948) 7.5' quadrangle. Numerous Chinese miners—who were called Celestials—worked at the place (Hoover, Rensch, and Rensch, p. 596).

Celina Ridge [NEVADA]: *ridge,* south-trending, 2.25 miles long, 2.5 miles southeast of Graniteville (lat. 39°24'45" N, long. 120°42'20" W). Named on Graniteville (1982) 7.5' quadrangle.

Cement Hill [EL DORADO]:
(1) *peak,* 2.5 miles north-northwest of Georgetown (lat. 38°56'30" N, long. 120°51'10" W; near SW cor. sec. 27, T 13 N, R 10 E). Named on Georgetown (1949) 7.5' quadrangle.
(2) *peak,* 2.5 miles west-southwest of Omo Ranch (lat. 38°33'40" N, long. 120°36'40" W; near W line sec. 12, T 8 N, R 12 E). Named on Omo Ranch (1952) 7.5' quadrangle.

Cement Hill [NEVADA]: *ridge,* east-southeast-trending, 2.5 miles long, center 1.5 miles northwest of downtown Nevada City (lat. 39°16'50" N, long. 121°02'30" W). Named on Nevada City (1948) 7.5' quadrangle. California Division of Highways' (1934) map shows a lake called Cement Hill Res. located 3.25 miles west-northwest of Nevada City near the west end of present Cement Hill (near S line sec. 34, T 17 N, R 8 E).

Cement Hill Reservoir: see **Cement Hill** [NEVADA].

Cement Ravine [EL DORADO]: *canyon,* drained by a stream that flows 1.5 miles to Slab Creek 8 miles north of Pollock Pines (lat. 38°52'25" N, long. 120°36'20" W; sec. 23, T 12 N, R 12 E). Named on Devil Peak (1950) 7.5' quadrangle.

Cement Spring [YOLO]: *spring,* 2.25 miles northeast of Berryessa Peak (lat. 38°41' N, long. 122°09'15" W). Named on Brooks (1959) 7.5' quadrangle.

Centennial Ravine [SIERRA]: *canyon,* drained by a stream that flows 1 mile to Buckeye Ravine 2 miles southeast of Alleghany (lat. 39°27'15" N, long. 120°48'40" W; sec. 1, T 18 N, R 10 E). Named on Alleghany (1949) 7.5' quadrangle.

Centerville: see **Pilot Hill** [EL DORADO] (2).

Central [YOLO]: *locality,* 3 miles southwest of Clarksburg along Sacramento Northern Railroad (lat. 38°23'40" N, long. 121°34'20" W). Named on Clarksburg (1967) 7.5' quadrangle.

Central: see **Williams** [COLUSA].

Central Drain [COLUSA]: *water feature,* enters Colusa County from Glenn County 6 miles west of Princeton (lat. 39°24'50" N, long. 122°07'15" W; sec. 18, T 18 N, R 2 W). Named on Moulton Weir (1952) and Princeton (1952) 7.5' quadrangles.

Central House [AMADOR]: *locality,* 2 miles south-southwest of Plymouth (lat. 38°27'20" N, long. 120°52' W; near S line sec. 15, T 7 N, R 10 E). Named on Sutter Creek (1944) 15' quadrangle.

Central House [NEVADA]: *locality,* 3.25 miles south-southeast of North Bloomfield (lat. 39°19'25" N, long. 120°52'45" W; sec. 20, T 17 N, R 10 E). Named on North Bloomfield (1949) 7.5' quadrangle. Called Galbraith on Colfax (1898) 30' quadrangle. Postal authorities established Galbraith post office in 1896 and discontinued it in 1899; the name was for Christopher Galbraith, first postmaster (Salley, p. 82).

Centralia [SACRAMENTO]: *locality,* 5.5 miles northeast of Galt along Central California Traction Railroad (lat. 38°19'10" N, long. 121°14'35" W; near NW cor. sec. 5, T 5 N, R 7 E). Named on Clay (1968) 7.5' quadrangle. Called Centralia Siding on Clay (1953) 7.5' quadrangle. California Division of Highways' (1934) map shows a place called Valensin located along the railroad 2 miles north of Centralia.

Centralia Siding: see **Centralia** [SACRAMENTO].

Central Valley: see "Regional setting."

Centreville: see **Grass Valley** [NEVADA].

Chain Island [SACRAMENTO]: *island,* 1600 feet long, 14 miles west-southwest of Isleton near the mouth of Sacramento River (lat. 38°04'10" N, long. 121°51'10" W). Named on Antioch North (1978) 7.5' quadrangle. Called Chain Islets on Ringgold's (1850a) map, which shows Tongue Shoal just south of Chain Islets, where Sacramento River and San Joaquin River join. Ringgold (p. 28) named the shoal from its shape and its location at the mouths of the rivers.

Chaix Mountain [EL DORADO]: *peak,* 5 miles north of Pollock Pines (lat. 38°50'10" N, long. 120°34'30" W; near NW cor. sec. 6, T 11 N, R 13 E). Altitude 4935 feet. Named on Pollock Pines (1950) 7.5' quadrangle.

Chalk Bluff [NEVADA]: *relief feature,* 6.5 miles northeast of Chicago Park (lat. 39°13' N, long. 120°52'50" W; near S line sec. 29, T 16 N, R 10 E). Named on Chicago Park (1949) 7.5' quadrangle.

Chalk Bluff [PLACER]: *relief feature,* 8 miles west-southwest of Granite Chief (lat. 39°08'25" N, long. 120°24'45" W; sec. 21, T 15 N, R 14 E). Named on Royal Gorge (1953) 7.5' quadrangle.

Chalk Bluff Ridge [NEVADA]: *ridge,* generally southwest-trending, 8.5 miles long, center 7 miles south-southwest of Washington (lat. 39°15'45" N, long. 120°50'15" W); Chalk Bluff is near the southwest end of the ridge. Named on Chicago Park (1949), Dutch Flat (1950), and Washington (1950) 7.5' quadrangles.

Chalk Bluffs: see **Red Dog** [NEVADA].

Chalk Flat [SIERRA]: *area*, 1.5 miles north-northeast of Pike (lat. 39°27'30" N, long. 120°59'20" W; sec. 5, T 18 N, R 9 E); the place is north of Chalk Ridge. Named on Pike (1949) 7.5' quadrangle.

Chalk Ridge [SIERRA]: *ridge*, east-trending, 1.25 miles long, 1 mile north-northeast of Pike (lat. 39°27'15" N, long. 120°59'20" W). Named on Pike (1949) 7.5' quadrangle.

Challenge [YUBA]: *town*, 30 miles northeast of Marysville along Dry Creek (1) (lat. 39°29'10" N, long. 121°13'20" W; on E line sec. 19, T 19 N, R 7 E). Named on Challenge (1948) 7.5' quadrangle. Postal authorities established Challenge post office in 1895 (Frickstad, p. 222). Wescoatt's (1861) map shows Challenge Mills at the site. The same map also shows a place called New York Ranch located 3 miles west of Challenge Mills, and a place called New York House situated 1.5 miles south-southwest of Challenge Mills. Crawford (1894, p. 322) referred to hydraulic mining activity at New York House Flat, 1.5 miles west of Challenge.

Challenge: see **Saint Louis** [SIERRA].

Challenge Mills: see **Challenge** [YUBA].

Chambers Lodge [PLACER]: *locality*, 1.25 miles southeast of Homewood along Lake Tahoe at the mouth of McKinney Creek (lat. 39°04'25" N, long. 120°08'30" W; sec. 7, T 14 N, R 17 E). Named on Homewood (1955) 7.5' quadrangle. Called McKinney on Truckee (1940) 30' quadrangle, which shows Chambers Lodge at present Tahoma. Postal authorities established McKinney post office in 1884, changed the name to Chambers Lodge in 1928, and discontinued it in 1959 (Salley, p. 41, 136). The name "McKinney" was for John McKinney, who settled at the place in 1864; the name was changed in 1928 when David H. Chambers opened his lodge at the site (Hanna, p. 61).

Chamisal Creek [COLUSA]: *stream*, flows 4.5 miles to lowlands 8 miles south of Williams (lat. 39°02'15" N, long. 122°09'45" W; sec. 26, T 14 N, R 3 W). Named on Cortina Creek (1953) 7.5' quadrangle. Called Chemisal Creek on Colusa (1942) 15' quadrangle.

Champagne Spring [COLUSA]: *spring*, 0.5 mile south-southeast of Fouts Springs (lat. 39°20'50" N, long. 122°39'55" W; near N line sec. 8, T 17 N, R 7 W). Named on Fouts Springs (1968) 7.5' quadrangle.

Champion [NEVADA]: *locality*, 1.25 miles west-southwest of Nevada City on the north side of Deer Creek [NEVADA-YUBA] (lat. 39°15'30" N, long. 121°02'20" W). Named on Smartsville (1895) 30' quadrangle. Grass Valley (1949) 7.5' quadrangle shows Champion mine situated across Deer Creek from the site.

Chandler [SUTTER]: *locality*, 2.5 miles west-northwest of Nicolaus along Southern Pacific Railroad (lat. 38°54'55" N, long. 121°37'15" W; sec. 3, T 12 N, R 3 E). Named on Nicolaus (1910) 7.5' quadrangle. California Division of Highways' (1934) map shows a place called Lee located along Southern Pacific Railroad 2.25 miles south-southeast of Chandler, and a place called Coulter located along the railroad 3 mile south of Chandler.

Chandler Canyon [YOLO]: *canyon*, drained by a stream that flows 1.25 miles to Cottonwood Canyon 3 miles southeast of Berryessa Peak (lat. 38°38' N, long. 122°08'55" W). Named on Brooks (1959) and Lake Berryessa (1959) 7.5' quadrangles.

Channel Arm: see **Pardee Reservoir** [AMADOR].

Channel Lake [EL DORADO]: *lake*, 750 feet long, 1.5 miles east-northeast of Pyramid Peak (lat. 38°51'10" N, long. 120°07'50" W). Named on Pyramid Peak (1955) 7.5' quadrangle.

Chaparral Hill [YUBA]: *peak*, 2 miles south of Oregon House (lat. 39°19'40" N, long. 121°17'05" W; sec. 15, T 17 N, R 6 E). Altitude 2150 feet. Named on Oregon House (1948) 7.5' quadrangle.

Chaparral Hill: see **Lancha Plana** [AMADOR].

Chapman Creek [SIERRA]: *stream*, flows 3.5 miles to North Yuba River 6.5 miles northeast of Sierra City (lat. 39°37'55" N, long. 120°32'50" W; near SW cor. sec. 32, T 21 N, R 13 E). Named on Clio (1981) 7.5' quadrangle.

Chapman Saddle [NEVADA]: *pass*, 9 miles northeast of Sierra City (lat. 39°39'25" N, long. 120°31'15" W; sec. 28, T 21 N, R 13 E); the pass is near the head of Chapman Creek. Named on Clio (1981) 7.5' quadrangle.

Charcoal Flat: see **Charcoal Ravine** [SIERRA].

Charcoal Ravine [SIERRA]: *canyon*, drained by a stream that flows 1.5 miles to North Yuba River 3.5 miles west of Sierra City (lat. 39°33'50" N, long. 120°42'05" W; near NE cor. sec. 35, T 20 N, R 11 E). Named on Sierra City (1981) 7.5' quadrangle. Gudde (1975, p. 68) listed a place called Charcoal Flat that was located at the mouth of Charcoal Ravine.

Charles: see **Freeport** [SACRAMENTO] (1).

Charles Creek [EL DORADO]: *stream*, flows 1.5 miles to Deer Creek (1) 5 miles west of Wentworth Springs (lat. 39°00'10" N, long. 120°25'50" W; sec. 5, T 13 N, R 14 E). Named on Bunker Hill (1953) 7.5' quadrangle.

Charleston: see **Fremont Landing** [YOLO].

Charley's Flat: see **Dutch Flat** [PLACER].

Chase Canyon [YOLO]: *canyon*, drained by a stream that flows 1 mile to Cross Canyon 2.25 miles west-northwest of Guinda (lat. 38°50'35" N, long. 122°13'50" W; sec. 31, T 12 N, R 3 W). Named on Guinda (1959) 7.5' quadrangle.

Cheese Camp Creek [EL DORADO]: *stream*, flows 4 miles to Tells Creek 2.25 miles east-southeast of Robbs Peak (lat. 38°54'35" N, long. 120°21'50" W; near SW cor. sec. 1, T 12 N, R 14 E). Named on Loon Lake (1952) 7.5' quadrangle.

Chelalian Bar: see **Chili Bar** [EL DORADO].

Chemisal: see **The Chemisal** [AMADOR].

Chemisal Creek: see **Chamisal Creek** [COLUSA].

Cherokee [NEVADA]: *settlement*, 3.5 miles east of North San Juan (lat. 39°22'10" N, long. 121°02'30" W; on E line sec. 2, T 17 N, R 8 E). Named on Nevada City (1948) 7.5' quadrangle. Called Paterson on Smartsville (1895) 30' quadrangle. Postal authorities established Patterson post office at present Cherokee in 1855, discontinued it in 1895, reestablished it in 1905, discontinued it in 1909, reestablished it with the name "Melrose" in 1910, changed the name to Tyler the same year, and discontinued it in 1924 (Salley, p. 137, 168, 226). The name "Patterson," the middle name of Eugene P. Turney, first postmaster, was given to the post office because the name "Cherokee" was already in use for a post office in California; the name "Melrose" was for the hometown in Massachusetts of postmaster James L. Morgan (Salley, p. 137, 168). The name "Cherokee" recalls Cherokee Indians who prospected at the site in 1850 (Gudde, 1975, p. 68). Whitney's (1873) map shows Cherokee Ravine extending from Cherokee to Grizzly Cañon 1 mile northeast of Cherokee.

Cherokee Bar [EL DORADO-PLACER]: *locality*, 4.25 miles north-northwest of Greenwood along Middle Fork American River on El Dorado-Placer County line (lat. 38°57'15" N, long. 120°56'15" W; on S line sec. 23, T 13 N, R 9 E); the place is west of Cherokee Flat. Named on Greenwood (1949) 7.5' quadrangle.

Cherokee Creek [SIERRA]: *stream*, flows 7 miles to North Yuba River 8 miles west of Goodyears Bar (lat. 39°30'50" N, long. 121° 02'05" W; sec. 13, T 19 N, R 8 E). Named on Goodyears Bar (1951) and Strawberry Valley (1948) 7.5' quadrangles.

Cherokee Diggings [NEVADA]: *locality*, 4 miles east of North San Juan (lat. 39°22'10" N, long. 121°01'55" W; sec. 1, T 17 N, R 8 E); the place is just east of Cherokee. Named on Nevada City (1948) 7.5' quadrangle.

Cherokee Flat [EL DORADO]: *area*, 4 miles north-northwest of Greenwood (lat. 38°57'20" N, long. 120°55'50" W; at NW cor. sec. 25, T 13 N, T 9 E); the area is east of Cherokee Bar. Named on Greenwood (1949) 7.5' quadrangle.

Cherokee Ravine: see **Cherokee** [NEVADA].

Cherry Creek Acres [NEVADA]: *settlement*, 4.25 miles north of Higgins Corner (lat. 39°06'20" N, long. 121°05'05" W; on and near W line sec. 34, T 15 N, R 8 E). Named on Lake Combie (1949) 7.5' quadrangle.

Cherry Hill [NEVADA]: *peak*, 6.5 miles east-northeast of North Bloomfield (lat. 39°25' N, long. 120°47'45" W; near NE cor. sec. 24, T 18 N, R 10 E). Altitude 5224 feet. Named on Alleghany (1949) 7.5' quadrangle.

Cherry Island [SACRAMENTO]: *island*, 4 miles long, between Dry Creek (1) and an artificial watercourse that diverges from, and then rejoins Dry Creek (1); center 1 mile east of Rio Linda (lat. 38°41'45" N, long. 121°25'45" W). Named on Rio Linda (1967) 7.5' quadrangle.

Cherry Point [PLACER]: *peak*, nearly 4 miles south-southeast of Cisco Grove (lat. 39°15'35" N, long. 120°30'45" W; at SE cor. sec. 9, T 16 N, R 13 E). Altitude 6728 feet. Named on Cisco Grove (1955) 7.5' quadrangle.

Cherry Spring [COLUSA]: *spring*, 2 miles west-northwest of Wilbur Springs (lat. 39°03'10" N, long. 122°26'55" W; near NE cor. sec. 19, T 14 N, R 5 W). Named on Wilbur Springs (1961) 15' quadrangle.

Chicago: see **New Chicago** [AMADOR].

Chicago Park [NEVADA]: *settlement*, 7 miles southeast of Grass Valley (lat. 39°08'45" N, long. 120°57'55" W; around SW cor. sec. 15, T 15 N, R 9 E). Named on Chicago Park (1949) 7.5' quadrangle. On Colfax (1898) 30' quadrangle, the name applies to a place 1.5 miles farther north along Nevada County Narrow Gauge Railroad. Postal authorities established Chicago Park post office in 1888 and moved it 1 mile southeast in 1898 (Salley, p. 42). The name is from a real-estate promotion involving investors from Chicago, Illinois, who planned to develop a townsite near Storms' Station on the narrow-gauge railroad (Browne, J.K., p. 117). California Division of Highways' (1934) map shows a locality called Bear River located 1.5 miles south-southeast of Chicago Park along Nevada County Narrow Gauge Railroad near the stream called Bear River (sec. 22, T 15 N, R 9 E).

Chicago Park: see **Colfax** [PLACER].

Chickahominy Slough [YOLO]: *stream*, flows 8 miles to lowlands 4 miles north-northwest of Winters (lat. 38°34'45" N, long. 121°59'15" W; near SW cor. sec. 33, T 9 N, R 1 W). Named on Monticello Dam (1959) and Winters (1953) 7.5' quadrangles. The name is from a fight that two ranchers had by the stream at about the time of the Civil War battle of Chickahominy in Virginia (Gudde, 1949, p. 65).

Chickemasee Flat: see **Grizzly Flat** [EL DORADO].

Chicken Flat: see **Spanish Flat** [EL DORADO].

Chicken Grove [COLUSA]: *locality*, 2 miles south-southwest of Boyers

Landing (lat. 38°55'35" N, long. 121°51'05" W; at S line sec. 34, T 13 N, R 1 E). Named on Kirkville (1952) 7.5' quadrangle.

Chicken Hawk Campground [PLACER]: *locality,* 4 miles north of Michigan Bluff (lat. 39°05'55" N, long. 120°43'20" W; sec. 34, T 15 N, R 11 E); the place is near the north end of Chicken Hawk Ridge. Named on Michigan Bluff (1952) 7.5' quadrangle.

Chicken Hawk Ridge [PLACER]: *ridge,* generally south-trending, 4 miles long, center 2 miles north-northeast of Michigan Bluff (lat. 39°04'15" N, long. 120°43'35" W). Named on Michigan Bluff (1952) 7.5' quadrangle.

Chicken Hawk Spring [EL DORADO]: *spring,* 2 miles north-northeast of Riverton (lat. 38°48' N, long. 120°25'50" W; sec. 17, T 11 N, R 14 E). Named on Riverton (1950) 7.5' quadrangle.

Chicken Ranch Slough [SACRAMENTO]: *stream,* flows 6 miles to an artificial watercourse 4.5 miles east-northeast of downtown Sacramento (lat. 38°36'10" N, long. 121°24'45" W). Named on Carmichael (1967), Citrus Heights (1967), and Sacramento East (1967) 7.5' quadrangles. Brighton (1911) 7.5' quadrangle shows Chicken Ranch Slough extending to Nigger Slough 4 miles northeast of downtown Sacramento.

Chicory Bend [SACRAMENTO-YOLO]: *bend,* 3 miles south of West Sacramento along Sacramento River on Sacramento-Yolo County line (lat. 38°31'45" N, long. 121°31'45" W). Named on Sacramento West (1967) 7.5' quadrangle.

Chief: see **Big Chief** [PLACER]; **Little Chief** [PLACER].

Chief Creek [PLACER]: *stream,* flows 2.25 miles to North Fork American River 2 miles north of Granite Chief (lat. 39°13'35" N, long. 120°17' W; near N line sec. 23, T 16 N, R 15 E). Named on Granite Chief (1953) 7.5' quadrangle.

Chilean Bar: see **Chili Bar** [EL DORADO].

Chiles [YOLO]: *locality,* nearly 2 miles east of downtown Davis along Southern Pacific Railroad (lat. 38°33' N, long. 121°42'30" W; near W line sec. 12, T 8 N, R 2 E). Named on Davis (1952) 7.5' quadrangle.

Chili Bar [EL DORADO]: *locality,* 4.5 miles east-southeast of Coloma along South Fork American River (lat. 38°46' N, long. 120°49'15" W; at SW cor. sec. 25, T 11 N, R 10 E). Named on Garden Valley (1949) 7.5' quadrangle. Chilean miners worked at the place for a time after they were run out of Johntown (Gernes, p. 54). Gudde (1975, p. 70) gave the names "Chilean Bar," "Chelalian Bar," and "Chillean Bar" as alternates, and listed (p. 347) a place called Texas Bar that was located 0.5 mile upstream from present Chili Bar.

Chillean Bar: see **Chili Bar** [EL DORADO].

Chimney Flat [EL DORADO]: *area,* 5.25 miles southwest of Pyramid Peak (lat. 38°48'10" N, long. 120°14'20" W; sec. 17, T 11 N, R 16 E). Named on Pyramid Peak (1955) 7.5' quadrangle.

Chimney Hill: see **Parks Bar** [YUBA]; **Sugarloaf Peak** [NEVADA].

Chimney Rock [SIERRA]: *relief feature,* 4 miles south-southeast of Mount Fillmore (lat. 39°40'50" N, long. 120°48'55" W). Altitude 6698 feet. Named on Mount Fillmore (1951) 7.5' quadrangle.

Chimney Rock [YOLO]: *peak,* 2.25 miles north-northeast of Berryessa Peak (lat. 38°41'40" N, long. 122°10'15" W). Named on Brooks (1959) 7.5' quadrangle.

China Bar [PLACER]: *locality,* nearly 6 miles south of Duncan Peak in Duncan Canyon (lat. 39°04'20" N, long. 120°32' W; sec. 9, T 14 N, R 13 E). Named on Greek Store (1952) 7.5' quadrangle.

China Bar [SIERRA]: *locality,* 9 miles southwest of Mount Fillmore along Slate Creek on Sierra-Plumas County line (lat. 39°38'55" N, long. 120°59' W; sec. 28, T 21 N, R 9 E). Named on La Porte (1951) 7.5' quadrangle.

China Bend [SUTTER-YOLO]: *bend,* at Kirkville along Sacramento River on Sutter-Yolo County line (lat. 38°54'15" N, long. 121°47'25" W; sec. 7, T 12 N, R 2 E). Named on Kirkville (1952) 7.5' quadrangle, which also has the name "Ministerial Bend" for the feature.

China City: see **Electra** [AMADOR].

China Cove [NEVADA]: *embayment,* 4 miles east of Donner Pass along the south shore of Donner Lake (lat. 39°19'10" N, long. 120° 15'10" W; at W line sec. 18, T 17 N, R 16 E). Named on Norden (1955) 7.5' quadrangle.

China Creek [EL DORADO]: *stream,* flows 2.5 miles to Weber Creek 2.5 miles west-southwest of Camino (lat. 38°43'05" N, long. 120°43' W; sec. 13, T 10 N, R 11 E). Named on Camino (1952) 7.5' quadrangle. Called Chunk Creek on Placerville (1893) 30' quadrangle.

China Flat [EL DORADO]:

(1) *area,* 3.25 miles south-southwest of Phipps Peak along upper reaches of Rubicon River in Rockbound Valley (lat. 38°54'15" N, long. 120°10'30" W). Named on Rockbound Valley (1955) 7.5' quadrangle.

(2) *area,* 2 miles southeast of Kyburz along Silver Fork American River (lat. 38°45'15" N, long. 120°16' W; at E line sec. 35, T 11 N, R 15 E). Named on Kyburz (1952) 7.5' quadrangle.

China Flat [NEVADA]: *area,* 3.25 miles east of Higgins Corner (lat. 39°02'30" N, long. 121°02' W; near N line sec. 25, T 14 N, R 8 E). Named on Lake Combie (1949) 7.5' quadrangle.

China Flat [SIERRA]: *area,* 6 miles west of Sierra City along North Yuba River (lat. 39°33'45" N, long. 120°44'50" W; sec. 33, T 20 N, R 11 E). Named on Sierra City (1981) 7.5' quadrangle. The place also was called Chinese Flat (Gudde, 1975, p. 71).

China Gulch [AMADOR]:

(1) *canyon,* 2.5 miles long, opens into the canyon of Mokelumne River 8.5 miles south of Ione (lat. 38°13'50" N, long. 120°54'50" W). Named on Ione (1962) and Wallace (1962) 7.5' quadrangles. Water of Camanche Reservoir.now covers the lower part of the canyon. Camp's (1962) map shows a place called Putts Bar located 1 mile west-southwest of the mouth of China Gulch along Mokelumne River. Andrews (p. 96) noted that a man named Putnam discovered gold at Put's Bar.

(2) *canyon,* 1 mile long, less than 1 mile west of Jackson Butte (lat. 38°20'20" N, long. 120°44' W; sec. 26, 35, T 6 N, R 11 E). Named on Mokelumne Hill (1948) 7.5' quadrangle.

China Gulch: see **Little China Gulch** [AMADOR].

China Mountain [EL DORADO]: *peak,* 6 miles east-northeast of Latrobe (lat. 38°35'35" N, long. 120°52'45" W; sec. 33, T 9 N, R 10 E). Altitude 1734 feet. Named on Latrobe (1949) 7.5' quadrangle. Called Big Sugar Loaf on Placerville (1893) 30' quadrangle.

China Peak [YOLO]: *peak,* 2.25 miles north of Guinda (lat. 38°51'45" N, long. 122°11'20" W; near E line sec. 28, T 12 N, R 3 W). Named on Guinda (1959) 7.5' quadrangle.

China Ravine [SIERRA]: *canyon,* drained by a stream that flows less than 1 mile to Big Grizzly Creek 2.5 miles south of Mount Fillmore (lat. 39°41'30" N, long. 120°50'30" W). Named on Mount Fillmore (1951) 7.5' quadrangle.

Chinatown: see **Dutch Flat Station** [PLACER].

Chinese Bar [NEVADA-SIERRA]: *locality,* 4 miles east-southeast of Alleghany along Middle Yuba River on Nevada-Sierra County line (lat. 39°27' N, long. 120°46'25" W; near SE cor. sec. 6, T 18 N, R 11 E). Named on Alleghany (1949) 7.5' quadrangle.

Chinese Camp Ridge [EL DORADO]: *ridge,* generally west-trending 2.25 miles long, 7 miles north-northwest of Kyburz (lat. 38°52'25" N, long. 120°20'15" W). Named on Kyburz (1952) 7.5' quadrangle.

Chinese Flat: see **China Flat** [SIERRA].

Chinkapin Point: see **Dollar Point** [PLACER].

Chipmunk Bluff [EL DORADO]: *relief feature,* 4.5 miles northeast of Robbs Peak (lat. 38°58'05" N, long. 120°20'10" W; near S line sec. 18, T 13 N, R 15 E). Named on Loon Lake (1952) 7.5' quadrangle.

Chipmunk Creek [PLACER]: *stream,* flows 3.5 miles to Middle Fork American River nearly 6.5 miles south of Duncan Peak (lat. 39°03'45" N, long. 120°30'55" W; sec. 15, T 14 N, R 13 E); the stream heads on Chipmunk Ridge. Named on Bunker Hill (1953) and Greek Store (1952) 7.5' quadrangles.

Chipmunk Ridge [PLACER]: *ridge,* extends for 13 miles southwest from Mount Mildred between Middle Fork American River and South Fork Long Canyon. Named on Bunker Hill (1953), Granite Chief (1953), Greek Store (1952), and Royal Gorge (1953) 7.5' quadrangles.

Chips Flat [SIERRA]: *locality,* 1 mile south-southeast of Alleghany (lat. 39°27'35" N, long. 120°50' W; sec. 3, T 18 N, R 10 E). Named on Alleghany (1949) 7.5' quadrangle. Postal authorities established Chip's Flat post office in 1857 and discontinued it the same year (Salley, p. 43). The name is for the English sailor who discovered gold at the place; the sailor had the nickname "Chips" because he had been a ship's carpenter (Hoover, Rensch, and Rensch, p. 495). Gudde (1975, p. 261, 352) mentioned mining places called Peavine Flat and Tolpekocking Flat that were located near Chips Flat.

Chiquita: see **Chiquita Lake** [EL DORADO].

Chiquita Lake [EL DORADO]: *lake,* 850 feet long, 14 miles north-northwest of Pollock Pines (lat. 38°56'20" N, long. 120°43'40" W; near NE cor. sec. 34, T 13 N, R 11 E). Named on Tunnel Hill (1950) 7.5' quadrangle. Logan's (1938) map has the name "Chiquita" at the place.

Chittenden Ridge [YUBA]: *ridge,* north-trending, 1.5 miles long, 3.5 miles east-southeast of Rackerby (lat. 39°25'10" N, long. 121° 16'45" W). Named on Rackerby (1948) 7.5' quadrangle.

Christian Valley [PLACER]: *valley,* 5.5 miles north-northeast of Auburn (lat. 38°58'30" N, long. 121°02'30" W; sec. 13, 14, T 13 N, R 8 E). Named on Auburn (1953) 7.5' quadrangle.

Christmas Hill Diggings [NEVADA]: *locality,* 6.5 miles northeast of Chicago Park (lat. 39°12' N, long. 120°52' W). Named on Dutch Flat (1950) 7.5' quadrangle.

Christopher: see **Lake Christopher** [EL DORADO].

Chrome Creek: see **Granite Ravine** [EL DORADO].

Chrome Mountain [AMADOR]: *peak,* 5.25 miles southwest of Jackson (lat. 38°17'15" N, long. 120°50'05" W; near E line sec. 14, T 5 N, R 10 E). Altitude 1202 feet. Named on Jackson (1962) 7.5' quadrangle.

Chubb Lake [NEVADA]: *lake,* 1300 feet long, 0.5 mile north of Yuba Gap (lat. 39°19'25" N, long. 120°36'50" W; sec. 22, T 17 N, R 12 E). Named on Cisco Grove (1955) 7.5' quadrangle.

Chuck Ravine [EL DORADO]: *canyon,* drained by a stream that flows 1 mile to South Fork American River less than 1 mile southeast of Coloma (lat. 38°47'30" N, long. 120°52'40" W; near E line sec. 20, T 11 N, R 10 E). Named on Coloma (1949) 7.5' quadrangle.

Chunk Creek: see **China Creek** [EL DORADO].

Church Bell Hill [AMADOR]: *ridge,* generally west-trending, less than 1 mile long, 2 miles northeast of Ione (lat. 38°22'25" N, long. 120°54'30" W; sec;. 17, 18, T 6 N, R 10 E). Named on Ione (1962) 7.5' quadrangle. Sutter Creek (1944) 15' quadrangle shows the feature located about 1 mile farther north. United States Board on Geographic Names (1964, p. 9) rejected the form "Churchbell Hill" for the name.

Church Camp [SIERRA]: *locality,* nearly 7 miles southwest of Sierraville along Haypress Creek (lat. 39°31'50" N, long. 120° 28' W; sec. 12, T 19 N, R 13 E). Named on Sierraville (1955) 15' quadrangle.

Church Creek [SIERRA]: *stream,* flows 4.5 miles to Salmon Creek nearly 6 miles north of Sierra City (lat. 39°38'55" N, long. 120°37'55" W; sec. 28, T 21 N, R 12 E). Named on Clio (1981) 7.5' quadrangle.

Churchman Bar: see **North Yuba River** [SIERRA-YUBA].

Church Meadows [SIERRA]: *area,* 7.5 miles north of Sierra City (lat. 39°40'40" N, long. 120°37'05" W; at S line sec. 15, T 21 N, R 12 E); the place is along Church Creek. Named on Clio (1981) 7.5' quadrangle.

Churchs Camp [NEVADA]: *locality,* 1.5 miles north-northeast of English Mountain (lat. 39°27'55" N, long. 120°32'25" W; sec. 32, T 19 N, R 13 E). Named on English Mountain (1983) 7.5' quadrangle.

Churchs Corners: see **Sattley** [SIERRA].

Chute Ravine [YUBA]: *canyon,* drained by a stream that flows 3 miles to Yuba River 3.25 miles east-southeast of Dobbins (lat. 39° 21' N, long. 121°09'05" W; sec. 11, T 17 N, R 7 E). Named on Challenge (1948) and French Corral (1948) 7.5' quadrangles.

Cicero [SACRAMENTO]: *locality,* 8 miles northeast of Galt along Southern Pacific Railroad (lat. 38°19'40" N, long. 121°11'05" W; near W line sec. 35, T 6 N, R 7 E). Named on Clay (1909) 7.5' quadrangle. Sacramento (1957) 1°x 2° quadrangle has the word "Stockyards" at or near the site of present Cicero. Postal authorities established Cicero post office in 1878 and discontinued it the same year (Frickstad, p. 132).

Cincinnati: see **Kelsey** [EL DORADO].

Cirby Creek [PLACER]: *stream,* flows 3.5 miles to Dry Creek [PLACER-SACRAMENTO] 1 mile south-southwest of downtown Roseville (lat. 38°44' N, long. 121°17'20" W; sec. 11, T 10 N, R 6 E). Named on Citrus Heights (1967) and Folsom (1967) 7.5' quadrangles. The canyon of the stream is called Walkers Ravine on Sacramento (1892) 30' quadrangle.

Cirby Creek: see **Linda Creek** [PLACER-SACRAMENTO].

Cisco [PLACER]: *locality,* 0.5 mile south-southwest of Cisco Grove along Southern Pacific Railroad (lat. 39°18'05" N, long. 120°32'45" W; at N line sec. 32, T 17 N, R 13 E). Named on Cisco Grove (1955) 7.5' quadrangle. Officials of Central Pacific Railroad named the place in 1865 to honor John J. Cisco, treasurer of the railroad; it first was called Heaton Station (Gudde, 1949, p. 69). Postal authorities established Cisco post office in 1866 and discontinued it in 1941 (Frickstad, p. 119).

Cisco Butte [PLACER]: *peak,* 1.25 miles west of Cisco Grove (lat. 39°18'30" N, long. 120°33'40" W; sec. 30, T 17 N, R 13 E). Altitude 6639 feet. Named on Cisco Grove (1955) 7.5' quadrangle.

Cisco Grove [PLACER]: *village,* 7 miles east of Emigrant Gap (1) (lat. 39°18'35" N, long. 120°32'20" W; sec. 29, T 17 N, R 13 E); the village is 0.5 mile north-northeast of Cisco. Named on Cisco Grove (1955) 7.5' quadrangle.

Citrona [YOLO]: *locality,* 3 miles south of Madison along Southern Pacific Railroad (lat. 38°38'05" N, long. 121°58'15" W; at NW cor. sec. 15, T 9 N, R 1 W). Named on Madison (1953) 7.5' quadrangle.

Citrus [SACRAMENTO]: *locality,* 3.5 miles east of downtown Carmichael along Southern Pacific Railroad (lat. 38°36'25" N, long. 121°15'55" W). Named on Carmichael (1967) 7.5' quadrangle. Called Jura on Mills (1911) 7.5' quadrangle, and called Junction on California Mining Bureau's (1909b) map.

Citrus Heights [SACRAMENTO]: *city,* 6.5 miles north-northeast of downtown Carmichael (lat. 38°42'30" N, long. 121°16'50" W). Named on Citrus Heights (1967) 7.5' quadrangle. Postal authorities established Citrus Heights post office in 1947 (Frickstad, p. 132).

City of Six Diggings: see **Slug Canyon** [SIERRA].

City of Six Ridge [SIERRA]: *ridge,* north-trending, 1 mile long, 1.25 miles south-southwest of Downieville (lat. 39°32'40" N, long. 120° 50'20" W). Named on Downieville (1951) 7.5' quadrangle, which shows City of Six mine near the south end of the ridge, which was named for a mining town of the 1850's (Gudde, 1969, p. 66).

Clamper Flat [SIERRA]: *area,* 7.5 miles south-southwest of Mount Fillmore (lat. 39°37'50" N, long. 120°54'25" W; near SW cor. sec. 31, T 21 N, R 10 E). Named on La Porte (1951) 7.5' quadrangle.

Clapboard Gulch: see **Volcano** [AMADOR].

Clapp Spring [YOLO]: *spring,* 3.5 miles west of Guinda (lat. 38°49'20" N, long. 122°15'40" W; near NW cor. sec. 12, T 11 N, R 4 W). Named on Knoxville (1958) 7.5' quadrangle.

Claraville: see **Squaw Creek** [PLACER].

Clark [EL DORADO]: *locality,* 2.25 miles southwest of Robbs Peak (lat. 38°54' N, long. 120°25'55" W). Named on Pyramid Peak (1896) 30' quadrangle.

Clark: see **Wash Clark Well** [YOLO].

Clark Creek [EL DORADO]:

(1) *stream,* flows 1 mile to South Fork American River 3.25 miles west-northwest of Coloma (lat. 38°49'05" N, long. 121°56'50" W; sec. 11, T 11 N, R 9 E); the stream is east of Clark Mountain. Named on Coloma (1949) 7.5' quadrangle.

(2) *stream,* flows 3.5 miles to Cosumnes River 3 miles south-southeast of Latrobe (lat. 38°31'20" N, long. 120°57'15" W; sec. 26, T 8 N, R 9 E). Named on Latrobe (1949) 7.5' quadrangle.

Clark Hill [YUBA]: *peak,* 2.5 miles northwest of Dobbins (lat. 39° 23'55" N, long. 121°14'05" W; near SW cor. sec. 19, T 18 N, R 7 E). Altitude 2346 feet. Named on Challenge (1948) 7.5' quadrangle.

Clark Mountain [EL DORADO]: *peak,* 3.5 miles west-northwest of Coloma (lat. 38°48'45" N, long. 120°57'25" W; on N line sec. 15, T 11 N, R 9 E); the peak is west of Clark Creek (1). Altitude 1585 feet. Named on Coloma (1949) 7.5' quadrangle.

Clark Ridge [COLUSA]: *ridge,* south-trending, 8.5 miles long, center 5 miles north of Lodoga (lat. 39°21'45" N, long. 122°28'30" W). Named on Lodoga (1960) 15' quadrangle. The ridge is at Colusa-Glenn County line.

Clarksburg [YOLO]: *town,* 11 miles south of West Sacramento along Sacramento River (lat. 38°25'05" N, long. 121°31'35" W). Named on Clarksburg (1967) 7.5' quadrangle. Postal authorities established Clarksburgh post office in 1876 and changed the name to Clarksburg in 1893; the name is for Robert C. Clark, who settled at the place in 1849 (Salley, p. 45).

Clarks Canyon [SIERRA]: *canyon,* drained by a stream that flows 1.5 miles to Rattlesnake Creek 5.5 miles south-southeast of Mount Fillmore (lat. 39°39'10" N, long. 120°48'50" W). Named on Mount Fillmore (1951) 7.5' quadrangle.

Clark Slough [YUBA]: *water feature,* joins Algodon Slough 4.5 miles south of Olivehurst (lat. 39°01'50" N, long. 121°33' W; sec. 29, T 14 N, R 4 E). Named on Olivehurst (1952, photorevised 1973) 7.5' quadrangle.

Clarkson: see **Clarksona** [AMADOR].

Clarksona [AMADOR]: *locality,* 3 miles west-northwest of Ione along Southern Pacific Railroad (lat. 38°22'25" N, long. 120° 59' W). Named on Ione (1962) 7.5' quadrangle. California Mining Bureau's (1917e) map has the name "Clarkson" for the place.

Clark's Springs: see **Wilbur Springs** [COLUSA].

Clark Station Homesites [SIERRA]: *locality,* 7.25 miles northeast of Sierra City (lat. 39°37'20" N, long. 120°31'20" W; near S line sec. 4, T 20 N, R 13 E). Named on Sierra City (1955) 15' quadrangle.

Clarksville [EL DORADO]: *locality,* 14 miles west-southwest of Placerville (lat. 38°39'20" N, long. 121°03' W; at N line sec. 12, T 9 N, R 8 E). Named on Clarksville (1953) 7.5' quadrangle. Postal authorities established Clarksville post office in 1855, discontinued it in 1924, reestablished it in 1927, and discontinued it in 1934 (Frickstad, p. 25). A travelers stop called Mormon Tavern was located 0.5 mile west of Clarksville along the emigrant road; it opened in 1849 and was a Pony Express stop in 1860 and 1861 (Hoover, Rensch, and Rensch, p. 83).

Claussenius [EL DORADO]: *locality,* 6 miles north-northwest of Pollock Pines (lat. 38°50'50" N, long. 120°36'45" W; near W line sec. 35, T 12 N, R 12 E). Named on Pollock Pines (1950) 7.5' quadrangle. The name should have the form "Clausenius" (Beverly Cola, personal communication, 1985).

Clay [SACRAMENTO]: *settlement,* 9.5 miles northeast of Galt (lat. 38°20'10" N, long. 121°09'30" W; near N line sec. 36, T 6 N, R 7 E). Named on Clay (1968) 7.5' quadrangle. Postal authorities established Clay post office in 1878 and discontinued it in 1954 (Frickstad, p. 132).

Clay Bank Bend [SACRAMENTO-YOLO]: *bend,* 4.25 miles south-southwest of West Sacramento along Sacramento River on Sacramento-Yolo County line (lat. 38°30'45" N, long. 121°33'05" W). Named on Sacramento West (1967) 7.5' quadrangle.

Clayton [EL DORADO]: *locality,* 12 miles east of Placerville (lat. 38° 44'25" N, long. 120°35'05" W). Named on Placerville (1893) 30' quadrangle.

Clayton [PLACER]: *locality,* 1.5 miles northwest of Lincoln along Southern Pacific Railroad (lat. 38°54'30" N, long. 121°18'40" W; sec. 9, T 12 N, R 6 E). Named on Lincoln (1953) 7.5' quadrangle, which shows clay pits near the place.

Clear Creek [EL DORADO]:

(1) *stream,* flows 8 miles to North Fork Cosumnes River 5.25 miles south of Camino (lat. 38°39'45" N, long. 120°41'10" W; near E line sec. 6, T 9 N, R 12 E). Named on Camino (1952) and Sly Park (1952) 7.5' quadrangles. North Fork enters from the northeast 6.5 miles above the mouth of the main stream; it is 2.5 miles long and is named on Sly Park (1952) 7.5' quadrangle.

(2) *stream,* flows 5.25 miles to Steely Fork Cosumnes River 2.5 miles north-northeast of Omo Ranch (lat. 38°36'50" N, long. 120° 33'35" W; near N line sec. 29, T 9 N, R 13 E). Named on Omo Ranch (1952) 7.5' quadrangle.

Clear Creek [NEVADA]:

(1) *stream,* flows 2 miles to Middle Yuba River nearly 1 mile north-northeast of North San Juan (lat. 39°22'55" N, long. 120°06' W; sec. 32, T 18 N,

R 8 E). Named on Camptonville (1948) and Nevada City (1948) 7.5' quadrangles.
(2) *stream,* flows 3 miles to Fall Creek 5.25 miles northwest of Yuba Gap (lat. 39°22'10" N, long. 120°41' W; sec. 1, T 17 N, R 11 E). Named on Blue Canyon (1955) and Graniteville (1982) 7.5' quadrangles.
(3) *stream,* flows 5.5 miles to Squirrel Creek 2.25 miles north of Pilot Peak in Penn Valley (lat. 39°02'05" N, long. 121°10'30" W; sec. 34, T 16 N, R 7 E). Named on Grass Valley (1949) and Rough and Ready (1949) 7.5' quadrangles.

Clear Creek: see **Bridger Creek** [YUBA].

Cleghorn Ravine [SIERRA]: *canyon,* drained by a stream that flows less than 1 mile to Canyon Creek 2.5 miles south of Mount Fillmore (lat. 39°41'30" N, long. 120°50'55" W). Named on Mount Fillmore (1951) 7.5' quadrangle.

Clementine: see **Lake Clementine**, under **North Fork Lake** [PLACER].

Cliff Canyon [PLACER]: *canyon,* drained by a stream that flows 1.5 miles to Screwauger Canyon less than 1 mile west of Duncan Peak (lat. 39°09'10" N, long. 120°31'35" W; near N line sec. 16, T 15 N, R 13 E). Named on Duncan Peak (1952) 7.5' quadrangle. This appears to be the feature called Van Cliffe Cañ. on Whitney's (1880) map.

Cliff Lake [EL DORADO]: *lake,* 750 feet long, 2.5 miles north of Phipps Peak (lat. 38°58'35" N, long. 120°08'50" W; sec. 18, T 13 N, R 17 E). Named on Rockbound Valley (1955) 7.5' quadrangle.

Clifton: see **Last Chance** [PLACER].

Clincmans Point: see **Rolleys Point** [YUBA].

Clinton [AMADOR]: *locality,* 2.5 miles south of Pine Grove (lat. 38° 22'35" N, long. 120°40' W; near W line sec. 16, T 6 N, R 12 E). Named on Pine Grove (1948) 7.5' quadrangle. The place also was called Sarahville or Sarahsville (Gudde, 1975, p. 75). Postal authorities established Sarahville post office in 1856 and discontinued it in 1859 (Frickstad, p. 6). Camp's (1962) map shows the alternate name "Lincoln" for the place. Doble (p. 76) mentioned a mining camp called Secreta that was situated along present South Fork Jackson Creek downstream from Clinton.

Clinton: see **Moores Flat** [NEVADA].

Clinton Peak [AMADOR]: *peak,* 2.5 miles south-southwest of Pine Grove (lat. 38°22'50" N, long. 120°40'30" W; near N line sec. 17, T 6 N, R 12 E); the peak is 0.5 mile northwest of Clinton. Altitude 2447 feet. Named on Pine Grove (1948) 7.5' quadrangle.

Clipper Creek [NEVADA]: *stream,* flows 5 miles to Little Greenhorn Creek 4 miles north of Chicago Park (lat. 39°12'10" N, long. 120°58'05" W; sec. 33, T 16 N, R 9 E). Named on Chicago Park (1949) and North Bloomfield (1949) 7.5' quadrangles.

Clipper Creek [PLACER]: *stream,* flows 6 miles to North Fork American River 3.25 miles northeast of Auburn (lat. 38°56' N, long. 121°02' W; sec. 36, T 13 N, R 8 E). Named on Auburn (1953) and Greenwood (1949) 7.5' quadrangles. The canyon of the stream is called Clipper Ravine on Placerville (1893) 30' quadrangle.

Clipper Creek: see **Little Clipper Creek** [NEVADA].

Clipper Gap [PLACER]: *locality,* 6 miles north-northeast of Auburn (lat. 38°58'10" N, long. 121°01'05" W; near N line sec. 19, T 13 N, R 9 E). Named on Auburn (1953) 7.5' quadrangle. Postal authorities established Clipper Gap post office in 1866, changed the name to Clippergap in 1894, moved it 2.5 miles southwest in 1881, changed the name back to Clipper Gap in 1950, and discontinued it in 1960 (Salley, p. 46).

Clipper Ravine: see **Clipper Creek** [PLACER].

Cloud Splitter [SIERRA]: *peak,* 4 miles south-southeast of Mount Fillmore (lat. 39°40'30" N, long. 120°50'10" W). Altitude 6491 feet. Named on Mount Fillmore (1951) 7.5' quadrangle.

Clover Valley [PLACER]: *valley,* 2.5 miles north of Rocklin (lat. 38° 49'45" N, long. 121°13'30" W). Named on Rocklin (1967) 7.5' quadrangle.

Clover Valley Creek [PLACER]: *stream,* flows 6.25 miles to Antelope Creek 0.5 mile north-northwest of downtown Rocklin (lat. 38°47'50" N, long. 121°14'20" W; sec. 18, T 11 N, R 7 E); the stream goes through Clover Valley. Named on Rocklin (1967) 7.5' quadrangle.

Clover Valley Reservoir [PLACER]: *lake,* 625 feet long, behind a dam on Clover Valley Creek 5.5 miles north-northeast of Rocklin (lat. 38°52'05" N, long. 121°11'45" W; at N line sec. 28, T 12 N, R 7 E). Named on Rocklin (1967) 7.5' quadrangle.

Clyde Lake [EL DORADO]: *lake,* 1300 feet long, 5.5 miles south of Phipps Peak (lat. 38°52'35" N, long. 120°10'05" W). Named on Pyramid Peak (1955) and Rockbound Valley (1955) 7.5' quadrangles.

Clyde Mountain [NEVADA]: *peak,* 3 miles northwest of Yuba Gap (lat. 39°20'35" N, long. 120°39'35" W; at W line sec. 17, T 17 N, R 12 E). Altitude 6052 feet. Named on Blue Canyon (1955) 7.5' quadrangle. Called Clydes Mt. on Colfax (1898) 30' quadrangle.

Cobbs Bend [COLUSA]: *bend,* 1.5 miles north-northeast of Colusa along Sacramento River (lat. 39°14' N, long. 122°00' W). Named on Colusa (1952) and Meridian (1952) 7.5' quadrangles.

Cobby Canyon [YOLO]: *canyon,* drained by a stream that flows 1.5 miles to Capay Valley 3 miles south of Guinda (lat. 38°47'15" N, long. 122°11'30" W; sec. 21, T 11 N, R 3 W). Named on Guinda (1959) 7.5' quadrangle.

Coburn Lake [SIERRA]: *lake,* 600 feet long, 5 miles west-southwest of Sierraville at the head of Berry Creek (lat. 39°33'35" N, long. 120°27'10" W; near W line sec. 29, T 20 N, R 14 E). Named on Sattley (1981) 7.5' quadrangle.

Coburn Station: see **Truckee** [NEVADA].

Cochrans Crossing: see **Yolo** [YOLO].

Cock Robin Point [EL DORADO]: *peak,* 4 miles north of Georgetown (lat. 38°57'55" N, long. 120°50'30" W; near NE cor. sec. 22, T 13 N, R 10 E). Altitude 2479 feet. Named on Georgetown (1949) 7.5' quadrangle.

Codfish Creek [PLACER]: *stream,* flows 3.25 miles to North Fork American River 9 miles northeast of Auburn (lat. 38°59'30" N, long. 120°57'15" W; sec. 10, T 13 N, R 9 E). Named on Colfax (1949) and Greenwood (1949) 7.5' quadrangles.

Codfish Creek: see **Little Codfish Creek** [PLACER].

Codfish Falls [PLACER]: *waterfall,* 9 miles northeast of Auburn along Codfish Creek (lat. 38°59'50" N, long. 120°57'15" W; sec. 10, T 13 N, R 9 E). Named on Greeenwood (1949) 7.5' quadrangle.

Codfish Point [PLACER]: *ridge,* south-southwest- to south-trending, 3 miles long, center 3.25 miles north-northeast of Michigan Bluff (lat. 39°05' N, long. 120°42'15" W). Named on Michigan Bluff (1952) 7.5' quadrangle.

Cody: see **Camp Cody** [EL DORADO].

Cody Creek [EL DORADO]: *stream,* flows 4 miles to Strawberry Creek 4.25 miles south of Pyramid Peak (lat. 38°47'05" N, long. 120°08'55" W; sec. 19, T 11 N, R 17 E). Named on Pyramid Peak (1955) and Tragedy Spring (1979) 7.5' quadrangles.

Cody Creek [PLACER]: *stream,* flows 1 mile to Andrew Gray Creek 7 miles northwest of Duncan Peak (lat. 39°13'35" N, long. 120°35'50" W; sec. 26, T 16 N, R 12 E). Named on Duncan Peak (1952) 7.5' quadrangle. The name commemorates George Milo Cody, pioneer rancher and fruit grower in the vicinity (United States Board on Geographic Names, 1967, p. 2).

Cody Lake [EL DORADO]: *lake,* 950 feet long, 6 miles south of Pyramid Peak (lat. 38°45'35" N, long. 120°08'30" W; sec. 1, T 10 N, R 16 E); the lake is at the head of a branch of Cody Creek. Named on Pyramid Peak (1955) 7.5' quadrangle.

Cody Meadows [EL DORADO]: *area,* 4.5 miles northwest of Kirkwood (lat. 38°44'35" N, long. 120°07'55" W; sec. 6, T 10 N, R 17 E); the place is along Cody Creek. Named on Tragedy Spring (1979) 7.5' quadrangle.

Coffing: see **Sheldon** [SACRAMENTO].

Cold Canyon [EL DORADO]: *canyon,* 1.25 miles long, on upper reaches of Park Canyon (present Sly Park Canyon) above a point 1.5 miles northwest of Old Iron Mountain (lat. 38°43'05" N, long. 120°24'35" W; sec. 18, T 10 N, R 14 E). Named on Stump Spring (1951) 7.5' quadrangle.

Cold Canyon: see **Brushy Canyon** [EL DORADO] (2).

Cold Creek [COLUSA]: *stream,* flows 1.25 miles to Trout Creek 2.5 miles northwest of Pacific Point (lat. 39°14'10" N, long. 122°37'55" W; sec. 16, T 16 N, R 7 W). Named on Clearlake Oaks (1960) 15' quadrangle.

Cold Creek [EL DORADO]: *stream,* heads at Star Lake and flows 6.5 miles to Trout Creek 5.5 miles northwest of Freel Peak (lat. 38°54'40" N, long. 119°58'10" W; sec. 3, T 12 N, R 18 E). Named on South Lake Tahoe (1955) 7.5' quadrangle.

Cold Creek [NEVADA-PLACER]: *stream,* heads in Placer County and flows 6.5 miles to Donner Creek 2.25 miles west of downtown Truckee in Nevada County (lat. 39°19'25" N, long. 120°13'20" W; sec. 17, T 17 N, R 16 E). Named on Norden (1955) and Truckee (1955) 7.5' quadrangles. Morgan (p. 425) identified present Cold Creek as the stream called Summit Creek on Jefferson's (1849) map. South Fork enters from the south 3.5 miles east-southeast of Donner Pass in Coldstream Valley; it is 3 miles long and is named on Norden (1955) 7.5' quadrangle.

Cold Creek Campground [SIERRA]: *locality,* 4.25 miles southeast of Sierraville (lat. 39°32'30" N, long. 120°18'55" W; sec. 33, T 20 N, R 15 E); the place is along Cold Stream (1). Named on Sierraville (1981) 7.5' quadrangle.

Cold Spring [SIERRA]: *locality,* 3.5 miles east-northeast of Pike (lat. 39°27'50" N, long. 120°56' W). Named on Colfax (1898) 30' quadrangle.

Cold Spring Hill [PLACER]: *peak,* 3 miles south-southwest of Dutch Flat (lat. 39°10'05" N, long. 120°51'50" W; at E line sec. 8, T 15 N, R 10 E). Altitude 3685 feet. Named on Dutch Flat (1950) 7.5' quadrangle. United States Board on Geographic Names (1933, p. 228) rejected the name "Gold Spring Hill" for the feature.

Cold Spring Mountain [COLUSA]: *peak,* 5.5 miles northwest of Wilbur Springs on Colusa-Lake County line (lat. 39°05'50" N, long. 122°29'15" W; sec. 35, T 15 N, R 6 W). Altitude 3587 feet. Named on Wilbur Springs (1961) 15' quadrangle.

Cold Springs [EL DORADO]: *locality,* 4 miles west of Placerville (lat. 38°44'30" N, long. 120°52'15" W; near NW cor. sec. 10, T 10 N, R 10 E). Site named on Placerville (1949) 7.5' quadrangle. Postal authorities established Cold Spring post office in or before 1852 and discontinued it in 1874 (Salley, p. 47).

Cold Springs Creek [EL DORADO]: *stream,* flows 2.5 miles to Weber Creek 4 miles west of Placerville (lat. 38°44'25" N, long. 120°52'15" W; near W line sec. 10, T 10 N, R 10 E); Cold Springs is near the mouth of the stream.

Named on Placerville (1949) 7.5' quadrangle.

Cold Stream [NEVADA-SIERRA]: *stream,* heads in Nevada County and flows 4.5 miles to Little Truckee River 7 miles south of Sierraville in Sierra County (lat. 39°29'35" N, long. 120°20'55" W; near SE cor. sec. 24, T 19 N, R 14 E). Named on Independence Lake (1981) 7.5' quadrangle.

Cold Stream [SIERRA]: *stream,* flows 7 miles to join Bonta Creek and form Sierraville Creek 1.5 miles south of Sierraville (lat. 39° 34' N, long. 120°21'45" W; near E line sec. 24, T 20 N, R 14 E). Named on Sierraville (1981) 7.5' quadrangle.

Cold Stream Meadow [SIERRA]: *area,* 9.5 miles south of Sierraville (lat. 39°27'10" N, long. 120°20'45" W; near E line sec. 1, T 18 N, R 14 E); the place is along Cold Stream [NEVADA-SIERRA]. Named on Independence Lake (1981) 7.5' quadrangle.

Coldstream Valley [PLACER]: *valley,* along Cold Creek [NEVADA-PLACER] above a point 11 miles west of Martis Peak (lat. 39° 19' N, long. 120°13'40" W). Named on Norden (1955) and Truckee (1955) 7.5' quadrangles.

Cole Creek [AMADOR]: *stream,* flows 14 miles to North Fork Mokelumne River 8.5 miles west-southwest of Mokelumne Peak (lat. 38°29'10" N, long. 120°14'20" W; sec. 5, T 7 N, R 16 E). Named on Bear River Reservoir (1979), Calaveras Dome (1979), and Mokelumne Peak (1979) 7.5' quadrangles.

Cole Creek Lakes [AMADOR]: *lakes,* largest 700 feet long, 3 miles north of Mokelumne Peak (lat. 38°35' N, long. 120°05'30" W); the lakes are along a branch of Cole Creek. Named on Mokelumne Peak (1979) 7.5' quadrangle

Cole Grove Point: see **Cole Point** [SUTTER].

Colegrove Point: see **Kirkville** [SUTTER].

Cole Hill [NEVADA]: *peak,* 1.5 miles north-northwest of Wolf (lat. 39°04'45" N, long. 121°09'20" W; near E line sec. 11, T 14 N, R 7 E). Altitude 1827 feet. Named on Wolf (1949) 7.5' quadrangle.

Coleman [NEVADA]: *locality,* 2 miles north of Chicago Park along Nevada County Narrow Gauge Railroad (lat. 39°10'30" N, long. 120°58'30" W; near S line sec. 4, T 15 N, R 9 E). Named on Colfax (1938) 30' quadrangle.

Coleman Spring [NEVADA]: *spring,* nearly 2 miles east-northeast of North Bloomfield (lat. 39°22'35" N, long. 120°52'05" W; on E line sec. 32, T 18 N, R 10 E). Named on Alleghany (1949) 7.5' quadrangle.

Cole Point [SUTTER]: *ridge,* extends 2.25 miles northeast from Kirkville into Sutter Basin (lat. 38°55'15" N, long. 121°46'15" W). Named on Kirkville (1952) 7.5' quadrangle. Called Cole Grove Point on Kirkville (1915) 7.5' quadrangle. The name commemorates G.S. Colegrove, who settled in the region in 1851 (Gudde, 1949, p. 74).

Coles: see **Coles Station** [EL DORADO].

Coles Station [EL DORADO]: *locality,* 3 miles north-northwest of Omo Ranch (lat. 38°37'15" N, long. 120°35'30" W; near W line sec. 19, T 9 N, R 13 E). Named on Omo Ranch (1952) 7.5' quadrangle. Called Coles on Placerville (1893) 30' quadrangle.

Colfax [PLACER]: *town,* 15 miles north-northeast of Auburn (lat. 39°06'05" N, long. 120°57'10" W; around NE cor. sec. 3, T 14 N, R 9 E). Named on Colfax (1949) 7.5' quadrangle. The name commemorates Schuyler Colfax, Speaker of the House of Representatives, who inspected the new railroad through the place in the summer of 1865 (Stewart, p. 45). Postal authorities established Colfax post office in 1866 (Frickstad, p. 119), and the town incorporated in 1910. Whitney's (1873) map shows a place called Mineral Bar located due east of Colfax along North Fork American River. California Division of Highways' (1934) map shows a place called Chicago Park located along a narrow-gauge railroad about 1 mile north-northeast of Colfax (near N line sec. 35, T 15 N, R 9 E), a place called Smiths situated about 0.5 mile farther north (sec. 26, T 15 N, R 9 E), and a place called Oilville located 0.5 mile beyond Smiths along the railroad (sec. 26, T 15 N, R 9 E); the railroad goes to and beyond Chicago Park [NEVADA].

Colfax Hill [PLACER]: *ridge,* south-trending, 1 mile long, just north of downtown Colfax (lat. 39°06'30" N, long. 120°57'10" W; near E line sec. 34, T 15 N, R 9 E). Named on Colfax (1949) 7.5' quadrangle.

Colgate: see **Dobbins Creek** [YUBA].

College City [COLUSA]: *village,* 2.5 miles east-southeast of Arbuckle (lat. 39°00'20" N, long. 122°00'25" W; sec. 5, 6, T 13 N, R 1 W). Named on Arbuckle (1952) 7.5' quadrangle. Postal authorities established College City post office in 1873 (Frickstad, p. 18). The board of trustees of Pierce Christian College founded the school in 1876 on land left to the college by Andrew Pierce, and laid out a town around it; the local high school district took over the college facilities in 1896 (Hoover, Rensch, and Rensch, p. 49).

Collins Eddy [SUTTER-YOLO]: *water feature,* cutoff meander of Sacramento River 1.5 miles south-southwest of Kirkville on Sutter-Yolo County line (lat. 38°53'20" N, long. 121°48'05" W; on E line sec. 13, T 12 N, R 1 E). Named on Kirkville (1952) 7.5' quadrangle.

Collins Eddy Cutoff [YOLO]: *water feature,* extends across the neck of a former bend, called Collins Eddy, in Sacramento River 9 miles east of Dunnigan (lat. 38°53'25" N, long. 121°48'20" W; sec. 13, T 12 N, R 1 E). Named on Kirkville (1952) 7.5' quadrangle.

Collins Ravine [SIERRA]: *canyon,* drained by a stream that flows 2 miles to Goodyears Creek 2 miles north of Goodyears Bar (lat. 39°34'15" N, long. 120°52'30" W; sec. 29, T 20 N, R 10 E). Named on Goodyears Bar (1951) 7.5' quadrangle.

Colluma: see **Coloma** [EL DORADO].

Coloma [EL DORADO]: *village,* 7 miles northwest of Placerville along South Fork American River (lat. 38°48' N, long. 120°53'25" W; sec. 17, T 11 N, R 10 E). Named on Coloma (1949) 7.5' quadrangle. Called Colluma on Derby's (1849a) map. Postal authorities established Culloma post office at the place in 1849 and changed the name to Coloma in 1851 (Frickstad, p. 26). The community grew at the site of Sutter's sawmill, where James Marshall made the gold discovery in 1848 that started the great California gold rush of 1849. In 1848 Marshall discovered and named a mining place called Live Oak Bar that was located 3 miles upstream from the sawmill (Bancroft, 1888, p. 47). A mining place called Stony Bar was situated about 5 miles upstream from Coloma, a mining place called Pleasant Flat was on the north side of South Fork American River 1 mile above Coloma, and a mining place called Snyders Bar was along South Fork 3 miles below Coloma (Gudde, 1975, p. 271, 326, 337).

Coloma Canyon [EL DORADO]: *canyon,* drained by a stream that flows 3.5 miles to Greenwood Creek less than 1 mile south of Greenwood (lat. 38°53'15" N, long. 120°54'35" W; sec. 18, T 12 N, R 10 E). Named on Coloma (1949), Garden Valley (1949), and Greenwood (1949) 7.5' quadrangles.

Columbia: see **North Columbia** [NEVADA].

Columbia Bar: see **Grapevine Gulch** [AMADOR] (2).

Columbia Flat: see **Kelsey** [EL DORADO].

Columbia Hill [NEVADA]: *relief feature,* 4 miles west-northwest of North Bloomfield (lat. 39°23'25" N, long. 121°58' W; near SE cor. sec. 28, T 18 N, R 9 E). Named on Pike (1949) 7.5' quadrangle. Colfax (1898) 30' quadrangle has the name for a feature located about 3 miles farther east. N.L. Tisdale and others gave the name to the feature in 1853 for Columbia Consolidated Mining Company (Gudde, 1949, p. 75).

Columbia Hill: see **North Columbia** [NEVADA].

Columbia House: see **Kelsey** [EL DORADO].

Colus [COLUSA]: *land grant,* near Colusa. Named on Colusa (1953) and Maxwell (1952) 15' quadrangles. John Bidwell received 2 leagues in 1845 and Charles D. Semple claimed 8876 acres patented in 1869 (Cowan, p. 29).

Colusa [COLUSA]: *town,* on the west side of Sacramento River in the east-central part of Colusa County (lat. 39°12'50" N, long. 122° 00'30" W). Named on Colusa (1952) and Meridian (1952) 7.5' quadrangles. Called Colusi, and shown in Colusi County, on Goddard's (1857) map. Postal authorities established Colusi post office in 1851 and changed the name to Colusa after the state legislature changed the name of the town to that form in 1854 (Salley, p. 48). Charles D. Semple purchased land at the site in 1849 and founded the town the following year (Hoover, Rensch, and Rensch, p. 48). The place first was called Salmon Bend (Gudde, 1949, p. 76). The name "Colusa" has an Indian origin (Kroeber, p. 39-40). California Division of Highways' (1934) map shows a place called Denco located 4 miles north of Colusa along Southern Pacific Railroad, a place called Dolan located 3 miles south-southeast of Colusa along the same railroad, and a place called Tuttle located nearly 4 miles southeast of Colusa along Sacramento Northern Railroad. Postal authorities established Hopewell post office 15 miles south of Colusa (NW quarter sec. 29, T 14 N, R 1 W) in 1864 and discontinued it in 1865; they established Spring Valley post office 22 miles southwest of Colusa (NW quarter sec. 11, T 14 N, R 4 W) in 1869 and discontinued it in 1875; they established Canaan post office 18 miles northwest of Colusa in 1871 and discontinued it in 1872 (Salley, 36, 100, 210). A number of travelers stops were named for their distance by road north of Colusa: Five Mile House, Seven Mile House, Nine Mile House, Ten Mile House, Eleven Mile House, Fourteen Mile House—also called Sterling Ranch, Sixteen Mile House at present Princeton, and Seventeen Mile House; the town of Colusa was started by mistake in 1850 at the later site of Seven Mile House, and then moved seven miles south (Hoover, Rensch, and Rensch, p. 48-49).

Colusa Basin [COLUSA-YOLO]: *area,* lowlands west of Sacramento River from near Maxwell [COLUSA] south to Knights Landing [YOLO]. Named on Colusa (1953), Dunnigan (1953), Maxwell (1952), and Sutter Buttes (1954) 15' quadrangles.

Colusa Drain [COLUSA]: *stream,* heads in Glenn County and flows 4.5 miles in Colusa County to Willow Creek 8 miles northeast of Maxwell (lat. 39°21'25" N, long. 122°04'55" W). Named on Moulton Wier (1952) and Princeton (1952) 7.5' quadrangles.

Colusa Junction [SUTTER]: *locality,* 2.25 miles west of downtown Yuba City along Sacramento Northern Railroad (lat. 39°08'55" N, long. 121°39'35" W). Named on Sutter (1952) 7.5' quadrangle. California Division of Highways' (1934) map shows a place called Harter located 0.25 mile east-southeast of Colusa Junction (near E line sec. 17, T 15 N, R 3 E) along Sacramento Northern Railroad. Clyde B. Harter, owner of the site, named the place for his father, George Harter, a pioneer; officials of Northern Electric Railroad gave the name "Las Uvas" to the site in 1906 because the rail line crossed a vineyard there—*las uvas* means "the grapes" in Spanish (Gudde, 1949, p. 143).

Colusa Junction: see **Cortena** [COLUSA].

Colusa Sulphur Springs: see **Wilbur Springs** [COLUSA].

Colusi: see **Colusa** [COLUSA].

Combie: see **Lake Combie** [NEVADA-PLACER].

Combie Crossing [NEVADA-PLACER]: *locality,* 7 miles southwest of Colfax along Bear River on Nevada-Placer County line (lat. 39° 00'50" N, long. 121°02'15" W). Named on Smartsville (1895) 30' quadrangle. Water of Lake Combie now covers the site.

Compton Landing [COLUSA]: *locality,* nearly 5 miles south-southwest of Princeton on the west side of Sacramento River (lat. 39°20'10" N, long. 122°01'50" W). Named on Moulton Weir (1952) 7.5' quadrangle.

Comptonville: see **Camptonville** [YUBA].

Conaway [YOLO]: *locality,* 10 miles north-northeast of Davis along Sacramento Northern Railroad (lat. 38°40'35" N, long. 121°40'20" W; at NE cor. sec. 31, T 9 N, R 3 E); a branch rail line extends from Conaway to Conaway ranch. Named on Grays Bend (1953) 7.5' quadrangle. Called Conway Junction on Davis (1954) 15' quadrangle.

Concord: see **Orleans Flat** [NEVADA].

Condemned Bar [YUBA]: *locality,* 3 miles south-southeast of Dobbins along Yuba River at the mouth of Dobbins Creek (lat. 39° 19'45" N, long. 121°11'40" W; sec. 16, T 17 N, R 7 E). Named on French Corral (1948) 7.5' quadrangle.

Condemned Bar: see **Folsom Lake** [EL DORADO-PLACER-SACRAMENTO].

Condon Gulch [AMADOR]: *canyon,* less than 1 mile long, opens into the canyon of Mokelumne River 5.5 miles south-southwest of Jackson (lat. 38°16'35" N, long. 120°49'20" W; sec. 24, T 5 N, R 10 E). Named on Jackson (1962) 7.5' quadrangle. Water of Pardee Reservoir now covers the lower part of the canyon.

Condon Mill: see **Old Condon Mill** [NEVADA].

Coniston [YOLO]: *locality,* 2 miles west of Clarksburg along Sacramento Northern Railroad (lat. 38°24'50" N, long. 121°33'40" W). Named on Courtland (1952) 15' quadrangle.

Conley [SACRAMENTO]: *locality,* 5 miles northeast of Galt along Southern Pacific Railroad (lat. 38°18'10" N, long. 121°14' W; sec. 8, T 5 N, R 7 E). Named on Clay (1909) 7.5' quadrangle. Postal authorities established Conley post office in 1881, discontinued it for a time in 1886, and discontinued it finally in 1910; the name was for Charles Conley, first postmaster (Salley, p. 49).

Connor Cabin [EL DORADO]: *locality,* 10 miles north-northwest of Pollock Pines (lat. 38°53'15" N, long. 120°40'45" W; sec. 18, T 12 N, R 12 E). Named on Tunnel Hill (1950) 7.5' quadrangle.

Connor Hill: see **Nevada City** [NEVADA].

Contreras: see **Camp Contreras**, under **Pioneer** [AMADOR].

Contrero Creek: see **Cortina Creek** [COLUSA].

Convict Meadow [EL DORADO]: *area,* 3.5 miles west of Kirkwood (lat. 38°42'35" N, long. 120°07'55" W). Named on Tragedy Spring (1979) 7.5' quadrangle.

Convicts Bar: see **Ramshorn Creek** [SIERRA].

Conway Junction: see **Conaway** [YOLO].

Cooks [EL DORADO]: *locality,* 5.25 miles east-southeast of Placerville (lat. 38°41'20" N, long. 120°43' W). Named on Placerville (1893) 30' quadrangle.

Cook's Bar: see **Michigan Bar** [SACRAMENTO].

Cooks Mountain [COLUSA]: *peak,* 15 miles north-northwest of Wilbur Springs (lat. 39°14'30" N, long. 122°29'45" W; sec. 14, T 16 N, R 6 W). Altitude 2212 feet. Named on Wilbur Springs (1961) 15' quadrangle.

Cooks Springs [COLUSA]: *spring,* 8 miles south of Stonyford along Indian Creek (lat. 39°15'20" N, long. 122°31'40" W; sec. 9, T 16 N, R 6 W). Named on Gilmore Peak (1968) 7.5' quadrangle. John Cooks obtained the spring about 1870 (Bradley, p. 182). The spring water was the basis of a resort that by 1910 had accommodations for 150 people (Waring, G.A., p. 204). Postal authorities established Cook Springs post office in 1879 and discontinued it in 1880 (Frickstad, p. 18).

Cooks Station [AMADOR]: *locality,* 3.25 miles west-southwest of Hams Station (lat. 38°31'35" N, long. 120°25'55" W; near S line sec. 21, T 8 N, R 14 E). Named on Caldor (1951) 7.5' quadrangle. Called Wiley on Pyramid Peak (1896) 30' quadrangle. Sargent (p. 13) referred to Cook's, formerly Wiley's Station. Postal authorities established Wiley post office in 1883 and discontinued it in 1887; the name was for Edward Wiley, first postmaster (Salley, p. 240). Pyramid Peak (1896) 30' quadrangle also shows a place called Hewett located 2 miles south-southwest of Wiley. Salley (p. 16) noted that postal authorities established Baville post office 6 miles west of Wiley in 1886, moved it 5 miles east in 1892, and discontinued it in 1894.

Cooks Station Ridge [AMADOR]: *ridge,* south-southwest-trending, 4 miles long, 5 miles southwest of Hams Station (lat. 38°30'15" N, long. 120°27' W); Cooks Station is at the north end of the ridge. Named on Caldor (1951) and Devils Nose (1979) 7.5' quadrangles.

Cool [EL DORADO]: *village,* 16 miles northwest of Placerville (lat. 38°53'15" N, long. 121°00'55" W; sec. 18, T 12 N, R 9 E). Named on Auburn (1953) 7.5' quadrangle. Postal authorities established Cool post office in 1885 (Frickstad, p. 26).

Coolbrith: see **Mount Ina Coolbrith** [SIERRA].

Coombs [YUBA]: *locality,* 11 miles north-northeast of Marysville along Southern Pacific Railroad (lat. 39°17'45" N, long. 121°31'55" W). Named on Honcut (1912) 7.5' quadrangle.

Coon Canyon [NEVADA]: *canyon,* 1.5 miles long, along North Fork Prosser Creek above a point 4.5 miles north of Donner Pass (lat. 39°23'15" N, long. 120°19'45" W; near NE cor. sec. 29, T 18 N, R 15 E). Named on Independence Lake (1981) and Norden (1955) 7.5' quadrangles.

Coon Creek [PLACER-SUTTER]: *stream,* formed in Placer County by the confluence of Dry Creek (1) and Orr Creek, flows 35 miles to end at American Basin 4.5 miles north-northeast of Verona in Sutter County (lat. 38°50'45" N, long. 121°34'25" W). Named on Gold Hill (1954), Lincoln (1953), Nicolaus (1952), Sheridan (1953), and Verona (1967) 7.5' quadrangles.

Coon Creek: see **Ophir** [PLACER].

Coon Hollow [EL DORADO]: *area,* 1 mile southwest of downtown Placerville (lat. 38°43'05" N, long. 120°48'30" W; sec. 18, T 10 N, R 11 E). Named on Placerville (1949) 7.5' quadrangle.

Coon Lake [YOLO]: *lake,* 1000 feet long, nearly 4 miles southeast of Knights Landing (lat. 38°45'10" N, long. 121°40'50" W). Named on Knights Landing (1952) 7.5' quadrangle.

Cooper: see **John Cooper Canyon** [COLUSA].

Cooper Canyon [EL DORADO]: *canyon,* drained by a stream that flows 2.5 miles to Pilot Creek (2) 2.25 miles west of the village of Pilot Hill (lat. 38°50'30" N, long. 121°03'15" W; near S line sec. 35, T 12 N, R 8 E). Named on Pilot Hill (1954) 7.5' quadrangle.

Copper Center: see **Copper Mine Gulch** [AMADOR].

Copper Creek [AMADOR]: *stream,* flows 2.5 miles to Sutter Creek 1.25 miles east of Ione (lat. 38°21'05" N, long. 120°54'30" W; at W line sec. 29, T 6 N, R 10 E). Named on Ione (1962) 7.5' quadrangle. Called Mountain Spring Creek on Jackson (1902) 30' quadrangle, but United States Board on Geographic Names (1964, p. 9) rejected the names "Mountain Spring Creek" and "Copperwater" for the stream.

Copper Gulch: see **Copper Mine Gulch** [AMADOR].

Copper Hill: see **Forest Home** [AMADOR].

Copper Lead [EL DORADO]: *locality,* 2 miles northwest of Omo Ranch along Middle Fork Cosumnes River (lat. 38°36'15" N, long. 120°36'20" W). Named on Placerville (1893) 30' quadrangle.

Copper Mine Gulch [AMADOR]: *canyon,* less than 1 mile long, opens into the canyon of Mokelumne River nearly 7 miles south-southwest of Jackson (lat. 38°15'55" N, long. 120°50'25" W; near S line sec. 23, T 5 N, R 10 E). Named on Jackson (1962) 7.5' quadrangle. Water of Pardee Reservoir now covers most of the feature. Copper Center, a copper mining camp in the lower part of the canyon, boomed during the Civil War, but vanished when the price of copper fell after the war; water of Pardee Reservoir now covers the site (Andrews, p. 125-126; Andrews called the canyon Copper Gulch). Water of Pardee Reservoir also covers the site of a place called Townerville, named for a man who came to invest in copper mines and founded the community in the 1860's (Cook, F.S., a, p. 5).

Copperwater: see **Copper Creek** [AMADOR].

Coppins Meadow [SIERRA]: *area,* 7.5 miles south-southwest of Sierraville (lat. 39°29'50" N, long. 120°25'20" W). Named on Sattley (1981) and Webber Peak (1981) 7.5' quadrangles.

Corbiere Slough [COLUSA]: *water feature,* dry watercourse that joins Dry Slough 3.25 miles northwest of Grimes (lat. 39°06'30" N, long. 121°56'15" W). Named on Grimes (1911) 7.5' quadrangle.

Cordova [SACRAMENTO]: *locality,* 4.5 miles south-southeast of downtown Sacramento along Western Pacific Railroad (lat. 38°30'35" N, long. 121°28'25" W). Named on Sacramento East (1967) 7.5' quadrangle.

Cordua Bar: see **Timbuctoo** [YUBA].

Cordua's Ranch: see **Marysville** [YUBA].

Cornelian: see **Carnelian Bay** [PLACER] (2).

Cornelius [SUTTER]: *locality,* 3 miles northeast of Nicolaus along Northern Electric Railroad (lat. 38°56'25" N, long. 121°32'35" W; at NE cor. sec. 32, T 13 N, R 4 E). Named on Nicolaus (1910) 7.5' quadrangle.

Cornell: see **Soudan** [SACRAMENTO].

Cornish Flat [SIERRA]: *area,* 4.25 miles southeast of Downieville (lat. 39°30'35" N, long. 120°46'50" W; sec. 18, T 19 N, R 11 E). Named on Downieville (1951) 7.5' quadrangle.

Cornish House [SIERRA]: *locality,* 4.5 miles southeast of Downieville (lat. 39°30'20" N, long. 120°47' W; near N line sec. 19, T 19 N, R 11 E); the place is south of Cornish Flat. Site named on Downieville (1951) 7.5' quadrangle. The place also was called Nebraska Diggings, Nebraska City, and Nebraska Flat (Gudde, 1975, p. 235).

Corral Creek: see **Latrobe Creek** [EL DORADO].

Corral Flat [AMADOR-EL DORADO]: *area,* 9 miles northwest of Mokelumne Peak on Amador-El Dorado County line (lat. 38°37'15" N, long. 120°13'10" W; near NW cor. sec. 21, T 9 N, R 16 E). Named on Bear River Reservoir (1979) 7.5' quadrangle.

Corral Flat [EL DORADO]: *area,* 10 miles southwest of Kirkwood (lat. 38°37'25" N, long. 120°13'15" W; at NW cor. sec. 21, T 9 N, R 16 E). Named on Bear River Reservoir (1979) and Tragedy Spring (1979) 7.5' quadrangles.

Corral Lake [SACRAMENTO]: *lake,* 2350 feet long, 4 miles east-northeast of downtown Sacramento at the site of present California State Exposition (lat. 38°35'25" N, long. 121°25'10" W). Named on Brighton (1911) 7.5' quadrangle.

Corral Valley [COLUSA]: *area,* 4.25 miles east-northeast of Pacific Point (lat. 39°14'45" N, long. 122°31'40" W; on S line sec. 9, T 16 N, R 6 W). Named on Clearlake Oaks (1960) 15' quadrangle.

Cortena [COLUSA]: *locality,* 5 miles north-northwest of Williams along Southern Pacific Railroad (lat. 39°13'10" N, long. 122°11'10" W; at S line sec. 22, T 16 N, R 3 W). Named on Williams (1952) 7.5' quadrangle. Called Colusa Junction of Williams (1918) 7.5' quadrangle, which shows Southern Pacific Railroad intersecting Colusa and Lake Railroad at the place. Postal authorities established Colusa Junction post office in 1886 and discontinued it in 1914 (Frickstad, p. 18).

Cortina: see **Arbuckle** [COLUSA].

Cortina Creek [COLUSA]: *stream,* flows 15 miles to lowlands 6.25 miles south-southwest of Williams (lat. 39°04'20" N, long. 122°11'30" W; at S line sec. 10, T 14 N, R 3 W). Named on Colusa (1953), Morgan Valley (1958), and Wilbur Springs (1961) 15' quadrangles. This apparently is the stream called Contrero C. on Goddard's (1857) map. The name "Cortina" evidently is from an Indian chief (Kroeber, p. 40). South Fork joins the main stream in lowlands 5.5 miles south of Williams; it is 4.5 miles long and is named on Colusa (1953) 15' quadrangle. Spring Valley (1918) 7.5' quadrangle shows Old Cortina Creek branching north from Cortina Creek about 1.25 miles downstream from where Cortina Creek enters lowlands (near center sec. 10, T 14 N, R 3 W). Powell Slough (1918) and Williams (1918) 7.5' quadrangles also name Old Cortina Creek.

Cortina Ridge [COLUSA]: *ridge,* north-trending, 13 miles long, center 6 miles east-southeast of Wilbur Springs (lat. 39°00'45" N, long. 122°19'15" W); the ridge is about 3 miles west of Cortina Creek and parallel to that stream. Named on Morgan Valley (1958) and Wilbur Springs (1961) 15' quadrangles.

Costa Creek [YUBA]: *stream,* flows 4.25 miles to Dry Creek (1) 1 mile west-southwest of Challenge (lat. 39°29' N, long. 121°14'35" W; near SE cor. sec. 24, T 19 N, R 6 E). Named on Challenge (1948) and Clipper Mills (1948) 7.5' quadrangles.

Cosumne [SACRAMENTO]: *locality,* 18 miles east-southeast of downtown Sacramento (lat. 38°29'35" N, long. 121°10'20" W); the place is on Cosumnes grant. Named on Sloughhouse (1968) 7.5' quadrangle. United States Board on Geographic Names (1933, p. 238) rejected the names "Bridge House," "Cosumnes," "Howells," and "McCosumne" for the place. Postal authorities established Cosumne post office in 1852 and discontinued it in 1915 (Frickstad,p. 132). The post office was at a place called Daylors, or Daylors Ranch, for William Daylor, who with Jared Sheldon held Omochumnes grant (Gudde, 1975, p. 91-92). Daylor's Store at the site was a stop for miners on their way to the southern mines (Ricketts, 1978, p. 17).

Cosumnes [SACRAMENTO]: *land grant,* 20 miles southeast of downtown Sacramento. Named on Clay (1968), Elk Grove (1968), Galt (1968), and Sloughhouse (1968) 7.5' quadrangles. William E.P. Hartnell received 11 leagues in 1844, and his heirs claimed 26,605 acres patented in 1869 (Cowan, p. 30; Perez, p. 64).

Cosumnes: see **Cosumne** [SACRAMENTO].

Cosumnes River [AMADOR-EL DORADO-SACRAMENTO]: *stream,* formed by the confluence of Middle Fork and North Fork, flows 50 miles to Mokelumne River 11.5 miles south-southwest of Elk Grove in Sacramento County (lat. 38°15'20" N, long. 121°26'20" W). Amador-El Dorado County line follows Cosumnes River, its Middle Fork, and its South Fork. Named on Bruceville (1968), Carbondale (1968), Elk Grove (1968), Fiddletown (1949), Folsom SE (1954), Galt (1968), Latrobe (1949), and Sloughhouse (1968) 7.5' quadrangles. Called R. de los Cosumnes on Fremont's (1845) map, and called Cosumes River on Jackson's (1850) map. Wilkes (p. 137) referred to Rio Cosmenes, and Tyson (p. 12) mentioned Cosumes River. United States Board on Geographic Names (1933, p. 238) rejected the forms "Cosumne," "Cosumni," "Mokesumne," and "Mokosumne" for the name, which evidently is from the designation of an Indian village or tribe (Kroeber, p. 40). Middle Fork is 44 miles long and is named on Aukum (1952), Bear River Reservoir (1979), Caldor (1951), Camino (1952), Fiddletown (1949), Omo Ranch (1952), and Peddler Hill (1951) 7.5' quadrangles. On Pyramid Peak (1896) 30' quadrangle, present Dogtown Creek [EL DORADO] is called North Fork of Middle Fork Cosumnes River. South Fork enters Middle Fork 2 miles upstream from the confluence of Middle Fork and North Fork; it is 25 miles long and is named on Aukum (1952), Caldor (1951), Fiddletown (1949), and Omo Ranch (1952) 7.5' quadrangles. On Placerville (1893) 30' quadrangle, South Fork above the junction of present South Fork with Scott Creek [EL DORADO] is called South Fork of South Fork Cosumnes River. North Fork heads at Leek Spring Valley and is 48 miles long; it is named on Camino (1952), Fiddletown (1949), Leek Spring Hill (1951), Placerville (1949), Sly Park (1952), Stump Spring (1951), and Tragedy Spring (1979) 7.5' quadrangles. Steely Fork, formed by the confluence of North Steely Creek and South Steely Creek, flows 9 miles to North Fork Cosumnes River 8.5 miles southeast of Camino; is is named on Caldor (1951), Omo Ranch (1952), Sly Park (1952), and Stump Spring (1951) 7.5' quadrangles. Pyramid Peak (1896) 30' quadrangle has the form "Steeley Fork" for the name, which commemorates Dr. J.W. Steely, who found gold near the stream in 1852 and built two mills there (Gudde, 1949, p. 343; Gudde used the form "Steelys Fork" for the name).

Cosumni River: see **Cosumnes River** [AMADOR-EL DORADO-SACRAMENTO].

Cothrin [EL DORADO]: *locality,* 4.25 miles south-southeast of Clarksville along Southern Pacific Railroad (lat. 38°35'50" N, long. 121°01'10" W; near N line sec. 32, T 9 N, R 9 E). Named on Folsom (1941) 15' quadrangle. Called Cothrins on Sacramento (1892) 30' quadrangle.

Cothrin Cove [PLACER]: *relief feature,* 4.5 miles west-southwest of Homewood (lat. 39°03'20" N, long. 120°14'05" W; mainly in sec. 17, T 14 N, R 16 E). Named on Homewood (1955) 7.5' quadrangle.

Cottage Creek [YUBA]: *stream,* flows 1.5 miles to New Bullards Bar Reservoir 3.5 miles east-northeast of Dobbins (lat. 39°23'40" N, long. 121°08'40" W; near W line sec. 25, T 18 N, R 7 E). Named on Challenge (1948, photorevised 1969) 7.5' quadrangle.

Cottage Hill [NEVADA]: *peak,* nearly 2 miles north-northeast of Higgins Corner (lat. 39°03'55" N, long. 121°04'35" W; sec. 15, T 14 N, R 8 E). Altitude 1728 feet. Named on Lake Combie (1949) 7.5' quadrangle. Whitney's (1873) map shows Cottage Hill Ho. [House] located 10.5 miles south of Grass Valley near present Cottage Hill.

Cottage Hill House: see **Cottage Hill** [NEVADA].

Cottage Home Creek [PLACER]: *stream,* flows 1 mile to Shirttail Canyon 4.5 miles north-northeast of Foresthill (lat. 39°04'50" N, long. 120°46'50" W; near S line sec. 6, T 14 N, R 11 E); the stream heads east of Cottage Home Hill. Named on Foresthill (1949) 7.5' quadrangle.

Cottage Home Hill [PLACER]: *peak,* 5.5 miles north-northeast of Foresthill (lat. 39°05'45" N, long. 120°47'20" W; near SW cor. sec. 31, T 15 N, R 11 E). Altitude 4100 feet. Named on Foresthill (1949) 7.5' quadrangle.

Cotton Hill: see **Relief** [NEVADA].

Cottonwood [YOLO]: *settlement,* 1.5 miles south of Madison (lat. 38°39'30" N, long. 121°58'15" W; on W line sec. 3, T 9 N, R 1 W). Named on Jacobs Corner (1916) 7.5' quadrangle.

Cottonwood Campground [SIERRA]: *locality,* nearly 4 miles southeast of Sierraville (lat. 39°33' N, long. 120°19' W; at S line sec. 28, T 20 N, R 15 E); the place is along Cottonwood Creek. Named on Sierraville (1981) 7.5' quadrangle

Cottonwood Canyon [YOLO]: *canyon,* 7 miles long, opens into lowlands 4 miles southwest of Esparto (lat. 38°38'55" N, long. 122°03'45" W). Named on Brooks (1959) and Esparto (1959) 7.5' quadrangles.

Cottonwood Creek [PLACER]: *stream,* flows 3 miles to Hell Hole Reservoir 2.5 miles north of Bunker Hill (lat. 39°05'15" N, long. 120°22'50" W; sec. 2, T 14 N, R 14 E). Named on Bunker Hill (1953) and Wentworth Springs (1953) 7.5' quadrangles.

Cottonwood Creek [SIERRA]: *stream,* flows 5.5 miles to Cold Stream 4 miles southeast of Sierraville (lat. 39°32'50" N, long. 120°19'05" W; near N line sec. 33, T 20 N, R 15 E). Named on Sardine Peak (1981) and Sierraville (1981) 7.5' quadrangles.

Cottonwood Flat [YOLO]: *area,* 7 miles southwest of Esparto (lat. 38°37'30" N, long. 122°06'45" W; near SW cor. sec. 17, T 9 N, R 2 W); the place is in Cottonwood Canyon. Named on Esparto (1959) and Monticello Dam (1959) 7.5' quadrangles.

Cottonwood Slough [YOLO]: *stream,* extends 8 miles from the mouth of Cottonwood Canyon to South Fork Willow Creek 2.25 miles east-southeast of Madison (lat. 38°40'05" N, long. 121°55'50" W; sec. 36, T 10 N, R 1 W). Named on Esparto (1959) and Madison (1953) 7.5' quadrangles. South Fork of the slough extends for 7.25 miles to an artificial watercourse 2.25 miles south of Madison (lat. 38°38'50" N, long. 121°58'15" W; at E line sec. 9, T 9 N, R 1 W). It is named on Esparto (1959) and Madison (1953) 7.5' quadrangles.

Cottonwood Spring [COLUSA]: *spring,* 6 miles east of Wilbur Springs (lat. 39°03'15" N, long. 122°19' W; at NW cor. sec. 21, T 14 N, R 4 W). Named on Wilbur Springs (1961) 15' quadrangle.

Cottonwood Spring [YOLO]: *spring,* 4.25 miles southeast of Guinda (lat. 38°47'10" N, long. 122°08'15" W; sec. 24, T 11 N, R 3 W). Named on Guinda (1959) 7.5' quadrangle.

Coulter: see **Chandler** [SUTTER].

Council Hill: see **Scales** [SIERRA].

Counsman [SUTTER]: *locality,* about 5.25 miles south of Pleasant Grove

(1) along Western Pacific Railroad (lat. 38°44'45" N, long. 121°29'25" W; sec. 1, T 10 N, R 4 E). Named on Rio Linda (1967) 7.5' quadrangle.

County Line Ridge [COLUSA]: *ridge,* generally east-southeast-trending, 3 miles long, center 1.25 miles south-southwest of Wilbur Springs (lat. 39°01'20" N, long. 122°25'40" W); the ridge is on Colusa-Lake County line. Named on Wilbur Springs (1961) 15' quadrangle.

Courtland [SACRAMENTO]: *village,* 17 miles south-southwest of downtown Sacramento along Sacramento River (lat. 38°19'55" N, long. 121°34' W). Named on Courtland (1978) 7.5' quadrangle. Postal authorities established Courtland post office in 1872 (Frickstad, p. 132). The name is for Courtland Sims, son of James V. Sims, landowner at the site, who started a steamer landing there in 1870 (Gudde, 1949, p. 81; Hanna, p. 75). A place called Onisbo was located a mile or two south of Courtland; Armstead Runyon named it for a local Indian chief who died at Runyon's ranch in 1862 (Dillon, p. 103). Postal authorities established Onisbo post office in 1854 and discontinued it in 1872 (Frickstad, p. 134). They established Walker post office 11 miles south of Courtland in 1874 and discontinued it in 1881; the name was for William C. Walker, who applied for the post office (Salley, p. 234). A Chinese community called Elliott Village was situated just north of Courtland along Sacramento River; the place burned in 1885 (Arreola, p. 9).

Cox Bar: see **Downieville** [SIERRA].

Cox Canyon [EL DORADO]: *canyon,* drained by a stream that flows 1.5 miles to join South Fork American River 1.5 miles east of Riverton (lat. 38°46'30" N, long. 120°25' W). Named on Riverton (1950) 7.5' quadrangle.

Cox Creek [YUBA]: *stream,* formed by the confluence of Daugherty Creek and Dempsey Creek, flows 3.5 miles to Dry Creek [NEVADA-YUBA] 9.5 miles northeast of Wheatland (lat. 39°06'45" N, long. 121°18'20" W; sec. 33, T 15 N, R 6 E). Named on Camp Far West (1949) and Smartville (1951) 7.5' quadrangles.

Cox-Delaney Flat [NEVADA]: *area,* 8 miles east-northeast of Truckee (lat. 39°22'30" N, long. 120°02'40" W; near SW cor. sec. 25, T 18 N, R 17 E). Named on Boca (1955) and Martis Peak (1955) 7.5' quadrangles.

Coyote Creek [PLACER]: *stream,* flows nearly 3 miles to Wooley Creek 6.5 miles south-southwest of Colfax (lat. 39°00'55" N, long. 121°00'10" W; near S line sec. 32, T 14 N, R 9 E); the stream heads east of Coyote Hill. Named on Colfax (1949) and Lake Combie (1949) 7.5' quadrangles.

Coyote Creek [SACRAMENTO]: *stream,* flows 6 miles to Carson Creek 8.5 miles south-southeast of Folsom (lat. 38°33'15" N, long. 121°08'15" W; near S line sec. 7, T 8 N, R 8 E). Named on Buffalo Creek (1967) and Folsom SE (1954) 7.5' quadrangles.

Coyote Creek: see **Wooley Creek** [PLACER].

Coyote Hill [PLACER]: *ridge,* south-southwest-trending, 1 mile long, nearly 5 miles south-southwest of Colfax (lat. 39°02'15" N, long. 120°59'25" W; on and near E line sec. 29, T 14 N, R 9 E). Named on Colfax (1949) 7.5' quadrangle.

Coyote Peak [COLUSA]: *peak,* less than 1 mile north of Wilbur Springs (lat. 39°02'55" N, long. 122°25' W; sec. 21, T 14 N, R 5 W). Altitude 1929 feet. Named on Wilbur Springs (1961) 15' quadrangle.

Coyote Ravine [SIERRA]: *canyon,* drained by a stream that flows nearly 2 miles to North Yuba River 0.5 mile west of Downieville (lat. 39°33'35" N, long. 120°50'20" W; sec. 34, T 20 N, R 10 E). Named on Downieville (1951) 7.5' quadrangle.

Coyote Ridge [EL DORADO]: *ridge,* southwest- to west-trending, 2.5 miles long, 3 miles east-northeast of Aukum (lat. 38°33'50" N, long. 120°40'30" W). Named on Aukum (1952) 7.5' quadrangle.

Coyote Spring [PLACER]: *spring,* 7.5 miles southwest of Granite Chief in French Meadows (lat. 39°08'30" N, long. 120°24'05" W; sec. 22, T 15 N, R 14 E). Named on Royal Gorge (1953) 7.5' quadrangle.

Coyoteville [EL DORADO]: *locality,* 2 miles east of Aukum (lat. 38° 33'05" N, long. 120°41'51" W; near NE cor. sec. 18, T 8 N, R 12 E); the place is south of Coyote Ridge. Named on Aukum (1952) 7.5' quadrangle. Logan's (1938) map shows a place called Cedar Creek Camp located about 0.5 mile east of Coyteville along Cedar Creek (at N line sec. 17, T 8 N, R 12 E).

Coyoteville: see **Downieville** [SIERRA]; **Nevada City** [NEVADA].

Crabtree Canyon [NEVADA]: *canyon,* drained by a stream that flows nearly 2 miles to South Fork Prosser Creek 5.5 miles northeast of Donner Pass (lat. 39°22'35" N, long. 120°15'35" W; sec. 25, T 18 N, R 15 E). Named on Independence Lake (1981) 7.5' quadrangle.

Cracked Crag [EL DORADO]: *peak,* 2.25 miles northeast of Pyramid Peak (lat. 38°52'10" N, long. 120°07'40" W). Named on Pyramid Peak (1955) 7.5' quadrangle.

Crackerbox Ridge [COLUSA]: *ridge,* east- to south-trending, 2.25 miles long, 5.5 miles south-southwest of Stonyford (lat. 39°18'40" N, long. 122°36'10" W). Named on Gilmore Peak (1968) 7.5' quadrangle.

Crag Lake [EL DORADO]: *lake,* 2200 feet long, 2.5 miles north of Phipps Peak (lat. 38°59'30" N, long. 120°09'20" W; sec. 12, T 13 N, R 16 E). Named on Rockbound Valley (1955) 7.5' quadrangle.

Craig Canyon [COLUSA]: *canyon,* drained by a stream that flows 2 miles to Bear Creek 5.5 miles southeast of Wilbur Springs (lat. 38° 58'55" N, long. 122°20'55" W; near SW cor. sec. 7, T 13 N, R 4 W). Named on Glascock Mountain (1958) and Wilson Valley (1958) 7.5' quadrangles.

Craigs Flat [SIERRA]: *area,* 7.25 miles south-southwest of Mount Fillmore (lat. 39°38'15" N, long. 120°54'45" W; on W line sec. 31, T 21 N, R 10 E). Named on La Porte (1951) 7.5' quadrangle. Bancroft (1888, p. 362) used the form "Craig's flat" for the name. Gudde (1975, p. 248) listed a mining camp called Oahu that was located at Craigs Flat, and (p. 226) a mining place called Morrisons Flat that was situated 1 mile from Craigs Flat.

Crane Ridge [YOLO]: *ridge,* east-trending, 1.25 miles long, 9.5 miles south-southwest of Esparto (lat. 38°34'15" N, long. 122° 06' W; sec. 4, 5, T 8 N, R 2 W). Named on Monticello Dam (1959) 7.5' quadrangle.

Crane's Gulch: see **Georgetown** [EL DORADO].

Cranmore [SUTTER]: *locality,* 5.5 miles north of Kirkville (lat. 38° 59'15" N, long. 121°48' W; on W line sec. 7, T 13 N, R 2 E). Named on Kirkville (1952) 7.5' quadrangle. Postal authorities established Cranmore post office in 1886, moved it 1 mile north in 1908, and discontinued it in 1928; the name is for St. Clair Cranmore, a pioneer settler (Salley, p. 52).

Cranmore Landing [SUTTER]: *locality,* 5.5 miles north of Kirkville along Sacramento River (lat. 38°59'25" N, long. 121°48'05" W); the place is 0.25 mile north of Cranmore. Named on Kirkville (1915) 7.5' quadrangle.

Crater Lake [NEVADA]: *lake,* 150 feet long, 1.5 miles west-northwest of Donner Pass (lat. 39°19'30" N, long. 120°20'20" W; sec. 24, T 17 N, R 14 E). Named on Norden (1955) 7.5' quadrangle.

Craycroft Diggings [SIERRA]: *locality,* 3.5 miles north-northeast of Downieville (lat. 39°36'50" N, long. 120°48'35" W; sec. 12, T 20 N, R 10 E); the place is on Craycroft Ridge. Named on Downieville (1951) 7.5' quadrangle.

Craycroft Ridge [SIERRA]: *ridge,* south- to south-southwest-trending, 6.5 miles long, center 7 miles south-southeast of Mount Fillmore (lat. 39°38' N, long. 120°47'35" W). Named on Downieville (1951) and Mount Fillmore (1951) 7.5' quadrangles.

Crees Flat: see **Ophir** [PLACER].

Crevis Creek [SACRAMENTO]: *stream,* flows 7 miles to Deer Creek 12 miles south of Folsom (lat. 38°30'15" N, long. 121°09'15" W; sec. 36, T 8 N, R 7 E). Named on Buffalo Creek (1967) and Folsom SE (1954) 7.5' quadrangles.

Cripple Creek [SACRAMENTO]: *stream,* flows 8.5 miles to Arcade Creek 4.5 miles north of downtown Carmichael (lat. 38°41' N, long. 121°19'25" W). Named on Citrus Heights (1967) and Folsom (1967) 7.5' quadrangles.

Critter Creek: see **Grass Valley** [NEVADA].

Crocker Creek [EL DORADO]: *stream,* flows 2.5 miles to Sweetwater Creek 5.5 miles north of Clarksville (lat. 38°44'15" N, long. 121°02'20" W; near W line sec. 7, T 10 N, R 9 E). Named on Clarksville (1953) 7.5' quadrangle.

Crocker Spring [YOLO]: *spring,* 8 miles south-southwest of Esparto (lat. 38°35'50" N, long. 122°06'15" W; sec. 29, T 9 N, R 2 W). Named on Monticello Dam (1959) 7.5' quadrangle.

Croft [EL DORADO]: *locality,* 1.5 miles south of Caldor (lat. 38°34'55" N, long. 120°26' W; near S line sec. 33, T 9 N, R 14 E). Named on Caldor (1951) 7.5' quadrangle.

Crooked Lake: see **Crooked Lakes** [NEVADA].

Crooked Lakes [NEVADA]: *lakes,* 4 miles southwest of English Mountain (lat. 39°24'30" N, long. 120°36'30" W). Named on English Mountain (1983) 7.5' quadrangle. Colfax (1938) 30' quadrangle has the name "Crooked Lake" for one of the lakes.

Cross Canyon [YOLO]: *canyon,* drained by a stream that flows nearly 3.5 miles to Capay Valley 2 miles west-northwest of Guinda (lat. 38°50'35" N, long. 122°13'30" W; near W line sec. 32, T 12 N, R 3 W). Named on Guinda (1959) and Knoxville (1958) 7.5' quadrangles.

Cross Delta Channel: see **Delta Cross Channel** [SACRAMENTO].

Crossman: see **Mount Crossman** [AMADOR].

Crows Nest [PLACER]: *peak,* 2 miles southwest of Donner Pass (lat. 39°17'50" N, long. 120°21' W; sec. 36, T 17 N, R 14 E). Altitude 7896 feet. Named on Norden (1955) 7.5' quadrangle.

Crumbecker Ravine: see **Krumbacher's Ravine**, under **Scotchman Creek** [NEVADA].

Crystal Lake [NEVADA]:

(1) *lake,* 1500 feet long, 2.25 miles east of Yuba Gap (lat. 39°19'10" N, long. 120°34'25" W; near S line sec. 24, T 17 N, R 12 E). Named on Cisco Grove (1955) 7.5' quadrangle. Morgan (p. 377) identified present Crystal Lake (1) as the feature called Brant Lake on Jefferson's (1849) map.

(2) *locality,* 2.5 miles east of Yuba Gap along Southern Pacific Railroad (lat. 39°19'20" N, long. 120°34'10" W; near E line sec. 24, T 17 N, R 12 E); the place is 0.25 mile northeast of Crystal Lake (1). Named on Cisco Grove (1955) 7.5' quadrangle.

Crystal Peak [SIERRA]: *peak,* 11.5 miles southeast of Loyalton (lat. 39°33'30" N, long. 120°05'15" W; near E line sec. 28, T 20 N, R 17 E). Altitude 8103 feet. Named on Dog Valley (1981) 7.5' quadrangle.

Crystal Peak: see **Mount Tallac** [EL DORADO]; **Verdi Peak** [SIERRA].

Crystal Peak Campground [SIERRA]: *locality,* 2.25 miles north-northeast of Crystal Peak (lat. 39°35'20" N, long. 120°04'20" W; sec. 15, T 20 N, R 17 E). Named on Dog Valley (1981) 7.5' quadrangle.

Crystal Range [EL DORADO]: *ridge,* extends for 9 miles north-northwest and northwest from Pyramid Peak; center 4.5 miles southwest of Phipps Peak (lat. 38°54' N, long. 120°11'45" W). Named on Pyramid Peak (1955) and Rockbound Valley (1955) 7.5' quadrangles.

Crystal Springs [NEVADA]: *locality,* 8 miles south-southwest of North Bloomfield (lat. 39°15'25" N, long. 120°58'35" W). Named on Colfax (1898) 30' quadrangle.

Cuba: see **Iceland** [NEVADA].

Cub Canyon [PLACER]: *canyon,* drained by a stream that flows 0.5 mile to New York Canyon (2) 4.5 miles north-northwest of Foresthill (lat. 39°05'05" N, long. 120°50'35" W; at W line sec. 3, T 14 N, R 10 E). Named on Foresthill (1949) 7.5' quadrangle.

Cuckoo Ridge [PLACER]: *ridge,* west- to southwest-trending, 3 miles long, 6 miles east-northeast of Michigan Bluff (lat. 39°04'50" N, long. 120°38'15" W). Named on Greek Store (1952) and Michigan Bluff (1952) 7.5' quadrangles.

Culbertson Lake [NEVADA]: *lake,* behind a dam 4.5 miles west-southwest of English Mountain on a tributary of Texas Creek (lat. 39°25'15" N, long. 120°37'20" W; near SW cor. sec. 16, T 18 N, R 12 E). Named on English Mountain (1983) 7.5' quadrangle.

Culloma: see **Coloma** [EL DORADO].

Cultivator Canyon [COLUSA]: *canyon,* 1 mile long, 13 miles north of Wilbur Springs (lat. 39°13'45" N, long. 122°25' W; sec. 21, T 16 N, R 5 W). Named on Wilbur Springs (1961) 15' quadrangle.

Cummings: see **El Dorado** [EL DORADO].

Cunnard [SUTTER]: *locality,* 4 miles south-southeast of Robbins along Southern Pacific Railroad in Sutter Basin (lat. 38°48'50" N, long. 121°41' W; sec. 7, T 11 N, R 3 E). Named on Knights Landing (1952) 7.5' quadrangle. California Division of Highways' (1934) map shows a place called Grace located along the railroad 0.25 mile east-northeast of Cunnard.

Cup Lake [EL DORADO]: *lake,* 450 feet long, 3.5 miles west-northwest of Echo Summit (lat. 38°49'40" N, long. 120°05'35" W; sec. 3, T 11 N, R 17 E); the lake is 1 mile west-southwest of Saucer Lake. Named on Echo Lake (1955) 7.5' quadrangle.

Cups: see **The Cups** [SIERRA].

Curry Creek [PLACER-SUTTER]: *stream,* heads in Placer County and flows 13 miles to end at American Basin 4.5 miles east of Verona in Sutter County (lat. 38°47'05" N, long. 121°31'55" W; sec. 21, T 11 N, R 4 E). Named on Pleasant Grove (1967), Roseville (1967), and Verona (1967) 7.5' quadrangles. Called Sciata Creek on Sacramento (1892) 30' quadrangle.

Curtis [YOLO]: *locality,* 14 miles north of Davis along Southern Pacific Railroad (lat. 38°44'55" N, long. 121°44'35" W). Named on Grays Bend (1916) 7.5' quadrangle. California Division of Highways' (1934) map shows a place called Saccarus located along the railroad 0.25 mile south-southwest of Curtis.

Curtis: see **Wood-Curtis Landing** [SACRAMENTO].

Cut Eye Fosters Bar [SIERRA]: *locality,* 8 miles west of Goodyears Bar along North Yuba River at the mouth of Cherokee Creek (lat. 39°30'55" N, long. 121°02'05" W; sec. 13, T 19 N, R 8 E). Named on Strawberry Valley (1948) 7.5' quadrangle. The name reportedly commemorates a professional horse thief (Gudde, 1975, p. 89). The name also had the form "Cut Eye Foster's Bar" (Marlette, p. 202).

— D —

Dads Gulch [YUBA]: *canyon,* 1 mile long, opens into the canyon of Brandy Creek nearly 3 miles north-northwest of Camptonville (lat. 29°29'25" N, long. 121°03'35" W; near NE cor. sec. 27, T 19 N, R 8 E). Named on Camptonville (1948) and Strawberry Valley (1948) 7.5' quadrangles.

Dad Youngs Spring [PLACER]: *spring,* 6.5 miles west of Devil Peak (lat. 38°58'25" N, long. 120°39'55" W; sec. 17, T 13 N, R 12 E). Named on Tunnel Hill (1950) 7.5' quadrangle.

Dagon [AMADOR]: *locality,* 1.5 miles west-southwest of Ione along Southern Pacific Railroad (lat. 38°20'40" N, long. 120°57'30" W). Named on Ione (1962) 7.5' quadrangle.

Daguerra Point [YUBA]: *hill,* 3 miles south-southwest of Browns Valley on the south side of Yuba River (lat. 39°12'25" N, long. 121°26'30" W; near NW cor. sec. 32, T 16 N, R 5 E). Named on Browns Valley (1947) 7.5' quadrangle.

Daken Flat [YUBA]: *valley,* 3.25 miles east-northeast of Rackerby (lat. 39°27'25" N, long. 121°17' W; on S line sec. 34, T 19 N, R 6 E). Named on Rackerby (1948) 7.5' quadrangle.

Damascus [PLACER]: *locality,* 4.25 miles west-southwest of Westville (lat. 39°08'50" N, long. 120°43' W; sec. 15, T 15 N, R 11 E). Site named on Westville (1952) 7.5' quadrangle. Postal authorities established Damascus post office in 1856, discontinued it in 1860, reestablished it in 1861, discontinued it in 1867, reestablished it in 1888, moved it 1 mile east in 1892, moved it 1 mile east again in 1904, and discontinued it in 1908 (Salley, p. 55). The place first was known as Damascus Diggings or Strong Diggings (Hanna, p. 81).

Damascus Diggings: see **Damascus** [PLACER].

Damfine Spring [NEVADA]: *spring,* 2.25 miles north-northwest of English Mountain (lat. 39°28'40" N, long. 120°33'45" W; near SW cor. sec. 30, T 19 N, R 13 E). Named on English Mountain (1983) 7.5' quadrangle.

Danaher: see **Mount Danaher** [EL DORADO].

Dantoni [YUBA]: *locality,* 4.25 miles east-northeast of Marysville (lat. 39°09'55" N, long. 121°30'55" W). Named on Yuba City (1952, photorevised 1973) 7.5' quadrangle.

Dantoni Junction [YUBA]: *locality,* 1.25 miles southeast of downtown Marysville along Southern Pacific Railroad, where a branch rail line to Dantoni leaves the main line (lat. 39°07'50" N, long. 121°34'30" W). Named on Marysville (1952) 15' quadrangle.

Dardanelles Creek [PLACER]: *stream,* flows 1.5 miles to Middle Fork American River 15 miles east-northeast of Auburn (lat. 38° 59'35" N, long. 120°49'20" W; near NE cor. sec. 11, T 13 N, R 10 E). Named on Foresthill (1949) and Georgetown (1949) 7.5' quadrangles.

Dardanelles Lake [EL DORADO]: *lake,* 1400 feet long, 3.5 miles south of Echo Summit (lat. 38°45'35" N, long. 120°01'15" W; sec. 5, T 10 N, R 18 E). Named on Echo Lake (1955) 7.5' quadrangle.

Dark Canyon [EL DORADO]:

(1) *canyon,* drained by a stream that flows nearly 2 miles to Canyon Creek (1) 2 miles north of Georgetown (lat. 38°56' N, long. 120° 50'15" W; near W line sec. 35, T 13 N, R 10 E). Named on Georgetown (1949) 7.5' quadrangle.

(2) *canyon,* drained by a stream that flows 1 mile to Otter Creek 5 miles northeast of Georgetown (lat. 38°57'10" N, long. 120°45'55" W; near NE cor. sec. 29, T 13 N, R 11 E). Named on Georgetown (1949) 7.5' quadrangle.

(3) *canyon,* drained by a stream that flows 1.25 miles to Slab Creek 5.5 miles northwest of Pollock Pines (lat. 38°48'40" N, long. 120° 39'35" W; sec. 8, T 11 N, R 12 E). Named on Slate Mountain (1950) 7.5' quadrangle.

(4) *canyon,* drained by a stream that flows 1.5 miles to South Fork American River 1.25 miles east of Chili Bar (lat. 38°46'10" N, long. 120°47'55" W; near W line sec. 30, T 11 N, R 11 E); the feature is 0.5 mile west of Light Canyon (1). Named on Garden Valley (1949) 7.5' quadrangle.

(5) *canyon,* drained by a stream that flows 1.25 miles to Camp Creek 6 miles northwest of Leek Spring Hill (lat. 38°01' N, long. 120°21'35" W; near S line sec 30, T 10 N, R 15 E). Named on Leek Spring Hill (1951) 7.5' quadrangle.

(6) *canyon,* drained by a stream that flows 2.25 miles to Cat Creek nearly 5 miles east of Caldor (lat. 38°35'20" N, long. 120°20'45" W; near W line sec. 32, T 9 N, R 15 E). Named on Peddler Hill (1951) 7.5' quadrangle.

Dark Canyon [PLACER]: *canyon,* drained by a stream that flows 1.5 miles to Secret Canyon 6 miles west of Duncan Peak (lat. 39° 09' N, long. 120°37'15" W; sec. 15, T 15 N, R 12 E). Named on Duncan Peak (1952) and Westville (1952) 7.5' quadrangles. On Colfax (1898) 30' quadrangle, the name applies to a nearby canyon.

Dark Canyon [SIERRA]:

(1) *canyon,* drained by a stream that flows 3.5 miles to Sierra Valley 2.25 miles west-southwest of Sierraville (lat. 39°34'40" N, long. 120°24'15" W; near N line sec. 22, T 20 N, R 14 E). Named on Sattley (1981) 7.5' quadrangle.

(2) *canyon,* drained by a stream that flows 3 miles to Lemon Canyon 3.5 miles east of Sierraville (lat. 39°34'50" N, long. 120° 18'05" W; sec. 15, T 20 N, R 15 E). Named on Sierraville (1981) 7.5' quadrangle.

(3) *canyon,* drained by a stream that flows 2.5 miles to Evans Canyon 7.25 miles east of Loyalton (lat. 39°41' N, long. 120°06'25" W; near SW cor. sec. 8, T 21 N, R 17 E). Named on Evans Canyon (1978) and Loyalton (1981) 7.5' quadrangles.

Dark Canyon Creek [EL DORADO]: *stream,* flows 2 miles to Brownsville Creek 1 mile south-southwest of Omo Ranch (lat. 38° 34' N, long. 120°34'30" W; at NW cor. sec. 8, T 8 N, R 13 E). Named on Omo Ranch (1952) 7.5' quadrangle.

Dark Day Canyon [YUBA]: *canyon,* drained by a stream that flows 0.5 mile to New Bullards Bar Reservoir 3.5 miles west-southwest of Camptonville (lat. 39°25'35" N, long. 121°06'25" W; sec. 17, T 18 N, R 8 E). Named on Camptonville (1948, photorevised 1969) 7.5' quadrangle.

Dark Hollow Creek [COLUSA]: *stream,* flows 2.5 miles to Glenn County 3.5 miles west-northwest of Fouts Springs (lat. 39°23' N, long. 122°43' W). Named on Saint John Mountain (1968) 7.5' quadrangle. The stream joins Middle Fork Stony Creek in Glenn County.

Dark Lake [EL DORADO]: *lake,* 1500 feet long, 4.5 miles west of Pyramid Peak (lat. 38°51'05" N, long. 120°14'25" W; at N line sec. 32, T 12 N, R 16 E). Named on Pyramid Peak (1955) 7.5' quadrangle. Shown as one of the group with the name "Wrights Lakes" on Pyramid Peak (1896) 30' quadrangle.

Darling Ridge [EL DORADO]: *ridge,* south-trending, 5.5 miles long, center 4.5 miles east-southeast of Georgetown (lat. 38°52'30" N, long. 120°45'40" W). Named on Garden Valley (1949) and Georgetown (1949)

7.5' quadrangles.

Darlings [EL DORADO]: *locality,* 5.25 miles southeast of Georgetown (lat. 38°51' N, long. 120°45'45" W); the place is on present Darling Ridge. Named on Placerville (1893) 30' quadrangle.

Darlington [EL DORADO]: *locality,* about 1.5 miles north-northwest of Old Iron Mountain along Plum Creek (2) (lat. 38°43'45" N, long. 120°24' W; near SE cor. sec. 10, T 10 N, R 14 E). Named on Stump Spring (1951) 7.5' quadrangle.

Darlington Flat [EL DORADO]: *area,* less than 0.25 mile east-southeast of Old Iron Mountain (lat. 38°42'15" N, long. 120°23'10" W; sec. 23, T 10 N, R 14 E). Named on Stump Spring (1951) 7.5' quadrangle.

Datey's Ferry [SACRAMENTO-YOLO]: *locality,* 7 miles northwest of downtown Sacramento along Sacramento River on Sacramento-Yolo County line (lat. 38°38'40" N, long. 121°35' W). Named on Elkhorn Weir (1915) 7.5' quadrangle.

Daugherty Creek [YUBA]: *stream,* flows 2 miles to join Dempsey Creek and form Cox Creek 3.5 miles south of Smartville (lat. 39° 09'20" N, long. 121°17'35" W; sec. 15, T 15 N, R 6 E). Named on Smartville (1951) 7.5' quadrangle.

Daugherty Hill [YUBA]: *peak,* 4.5 miles south-southwest of Oregon House (lat. 39°17'50" N, long. 121°19'10" W; near S line sec. 29, T 17 N, R 6 E). Altitude 1803 feet. Named on Oregon House (1948) 7.5' quadrangle.

Daves Ravine [SIERRA]: *canyon,* drained by a stream that flows 2.5 miles to Downie River 4.25 miles north of Downieville (lat. 37°37'20" N, long. 120°49'20" W; near S line sec. 2, T 20 N, R 10 E). Named on Downieville (1951) and Mount Fillmore (1951) 7.5' quadrangles.

Davies: see **Davis** [YOLO].

Davies Creek [SIERRA]: *stream,* flows 11.5 miles to Little Truckee River 5.5 miles south of Crystal Peak (lat. 39°28'35" N, long. 120° 06'10" W; near NW cor. sec. 28, T 19 N, R 17 E). Named on Boca (1955), Dog Valley (1981), and Sardine Peak (1981) 7.5' quadrangles. The stream now enters Stampede Reservoir.

Davies Creek Campground [SIERRA]: *locality,* 3.5 miles south of Crystal Peak (lat. 39°30'20" N, long. 120°05'55" W; at N line sec. 16, T 19 N, R 17 E); the place is along Davies Creek. Named on Dog Valley (1981) 7.5' quadrangle.

Davis [YOLO]: *city,* 9 miles south of Woodland (lat. 38°32'45" N, long. 121°44'35" W; in and near sec. 10, 15, T 8 N, R 2 E). Named on Davis (1952) and Merritt (1952) 7.5' quadrangles. Called Davies on Goddard's (1857) map, and called Davisville on Davisville (1907) 15' quadrangle. Postal authorities established Davisville post office in 1868 and changed the name to Davis in 1907 (Frickstad, p. 221). The city incorporated in 1917. The name commemorates Jerome C. Davis, who settled at the place in the early 1850's; William Dresbach leased the Davis home in 1867 for use as a hotel that he called Yolo House, and gave the name "Davisville" to the community that grew there (Hoover, Rensch, and Rensch, p. 586).

Davis Canyon [COLUSA]: *canyon,* drained by a stream that flows 1.5 miles to Mill Creek (2) 5.25 miles east of Pacific Point (lat. 39°12'55" N, long. 122°30' W; near N line sec. 26, T 16 N, R 6 W); the canyon heads near Davis Flat (2). Named on Clearlake Oaks (1960) 15' quadrangle.

Davis Canyon [YOLO]: *canyon,* along lower reaches of Davis Creek 8 miles west-northwest of Rumsey on Yolo-Lake County line (lat. 38°55'15" N, long. 122°22'40" W). Named on Wilson Valley (1958) 7.5' quadrangle.

Davis Creek [EL DORADO]: *stream,* flows 1.5 miles to Silver Creek 7 miles north-northeast of Pollock Pines (lat. 38°51'10" N, long. 120°31'35" W; sec. 28, T 12 N, R 13 E). Named on Devil Peak (1950) and Pollock Pines (1950) 7.5' quadrangles.

Davis Creek [YOLO]: *stream,* flows 10.5 miles to Lake County 8 miles west-northwest of Rumsey (lat. 38°55'30" N, long. 122°22'40" W). Named on Glascock Mountain (1958), Jericho Valley (1958), Knoxville (1958), and Wilson Valley (1958) 7.5' quadrangles. Knoxville (1958) 7.5' quadrangle shows Reid mine situated along Davis Creek near the south end of Little Blue Ridge (sec. 25, T 12 N, R 5 W). The mine began producing quicksilver in 1873 (O' Brien, p. 433; O' Brien used the form "Reed" for the name). Postal authorities established Quicksilver post office at a quicksilver operation—presumably Reid mine—in 1877 and discontinued in 1881 (Salley, p. 180).

Davis Flat [COLUSA]:

(1) *area,* 1 mile northeast of Fouts Springs along South Fork Stony Creek (lat. 39°21'45" N, long. 122°39'15" W; near NW cor. sec. 4, T 17 N, R 7 W). Named on Fouts Springs (1968) 7.5' quadrangle.

(2) *area,* about 14 miles north-northwest of Wilbur Springs (lat. 39° 13'45" N, long. 122°29'55" W). Named on Clearlake Oaks (1960) and Wilbur Springs (1961) 15' quadrangles.

Davis Junction: see **Calpine** [SIERRA].

Davisville: see **Davis** [YOLO].

Dawson Spring [PLACER]: *spring,* 7 miles northwest of Duncan Peak (lat. 39°13'30" N, long. 120°36'20" W; near E line sec. 27, T 16 N, R 12 E). Named on Duncan Peak (1952) 7.5' quadrangle.

Daylors: see **Cosumne** [SACRAMENTO].

Daylor's Store: see **Cosumne** [SACRAMENTO].

Day Meadow [YUBA]: *area,* 5 miles north-northeast of Rackerby along New York Creek (lat. 39°30' N, long. 121°17'05" W; sec. 15, 22, T 19 N, R 6 E). Named on Forbestown (1970) and Rackerby (1948) 7.5' quadrangles.

Deacon Long Ravine [SIERRA]: *canyon,* 2 miles long, opens into the canyon of Slate Creek 6 miles southwest of Mount Fillmore (lat. 39°40'55" N, long. 120°56'35" W; sec. 14, T 21 N, R 9 E). Named on La Porte (1951) 7.5' quadrangle.

Dead Horse Canyon [SIERRA]: *canyon,* drained by a stream that flows 1.5 miles to Haypress Creek 5 miles east of Sierra City (lat. 39°33'35" N, long. 120°32'30" W; sec. 32, T 20 N, R 13 E). Named on Haypress (1981) 7.5' quadrangle. Downieville (1897) 30' quadrangle has the name "Long Valley Ck." for the stream in the canyon.

Dead Horse Cut [SACRAMENTO]: *water feature,* extends from Snodgrass Slough to North Mokelumne River 7.5 miles northeast of Isleton (lat. 38°13'40" N, long. 121°29'35" W). Named on Thornton (1978) 7.5' quadrangle.

Dead Horse Island [SACRAMENTO]: *island,* nearly 1 mile long, 1 mile south-southeast of Walnut Grove between Snodgrass Slough, Dead Horse Cut, and North Mokelumne River (lat. 38°13'50" N, long. 121°30'05" W). Named on Isleton (1978) and Thornton (1978) 7.5' quadrangles. On Isleton (1910) 7.5' quadrangle, the name has the form "Deadhorse Island."

Deadman Canyon [PLACER]: *canyon,* drained by a stream that flows 4.25 miles to Coon Creek 7.25 miles northwest of Auburn (lat. 38°58' N, long. 121°10'40" W; sec. 22, T 13 N, R 7 E). Named on Gold Hill (1954) 7.5' quadrangle.

Deadman Creek [EL DORADO]: *stream,* flows 2.5 miles to Martinez Creek 5.5 miles south-southwest of Placerville (lat. 38°39'05" N, long. 120°49'30" W; sec. 12, T 9 N, R 10 E). Named on Placerville (1949) 7.5' quadrangle.

Deadman Creek [NEVADA]: *stream,* flows 2.25 miles to Poorman Creek (1) 1 mile north of Washington (lat. 39°22'20" N, long. 120° 48' W; near N line sec. 1, T 17 N, R 10 E). Named on Alleghany (1949) and Washington (1950) 7.5' quadrangles. Called Rob Roy Cr. on Colfax (1938) 30' quadrangle.

Deadman Flat [PLACER]: *area,* 5 miles west-southwest of Granite Chief along Middle Fork American River (lat. 39°11' N, long. 120° 22'30" W; sec. 2, T 15 N, R 14 E). Named on Truckee (1940) 30" quadrangle.

Deadman Fork [AMADOR]: *stream,* flows 6.5 miles to South Fork Dry Creek 4.5 miles east of Plymouth (lat. 38°28'15" N, long. 120° 45'50" W; sec. 9, T 7 N, R 11 E). Named on Amador City (1962) and Pine Grove (1948) 7.5' quadrangles. Jackson (1902) 30' quadrangle has the form "Dead Man Fork" for the name.

Deadman Gulch [SACRAMENTO]: *canyon,* 4 miles long, 1.5 miles north-northwest of Galt (lat. 38°16'30" N, long. 121°18'30" W). Named on Galt (1968) 7.5' quadrangle.

Deadman Lake [SIERRA]: *lake,* 650 feet long, 6 miles northeast of Sierra City (lat. 39°37'15" N, long. 120°33'05" W; on N line sec. 7, T 20 N, R 13 E); the lake is 0.25 mile north-northeast of Deadman Peak. Named on Haypress Valley (1981) 7.5' quadrangle. Called Deadmans Lake on Downieville (1897) 30' quadrangle.

Deadman Peak [SIERRA]: *peak,* 5.5 miles northeast of Sierra City (lat. 39°37' N, long. 120°33'10" W; sec. 7, T 20 N, R 13 E); the peak is 0.25 mile south-southwest of Deadman Lake. Altitude 7498 feet. Named on Haypress Valley (1981) 7.5' quadrangle. Called Deadmans Pk. on Downieville (1897) 30' quadrangle, and called Deadman's Pk. on Logan's (1929) map.

Deadmans Flat [NEVADA]:

(1) *area,* 3 miles west-southwest of Grass Valley at the head of Clear Creek (3) (lat. 39°12'05" N, long. 121°06'50" W; near E line sec. 31, T 16 N, R 8 E). Named on Grass Valley (1949) 7.5' quadrangle. United States Board on Geographic Names (1991, p. 6) approved the name "Osceola Ridge" for a ridge, 0.5 mile long, located 1 mile north of Deadmans Flat (lat. 39°12'58" N, long. 121°06'55" W; sec. 30, T 16 N, R 8 E).

(2) *area,* 7 miles south of Washington (lat. 39°15'35" N, long. 120° 47'10" W; on S line sec. 7, T 16 N, R 11 E). Named on Washington (1950) 7.5' quadrangle.

Deadmans Lake [SACRAMENTO]: *marsh,* 2.5 miles northeast of downtown Sacramento (lat. 38°36' N, long. 121°27'05" W). Named on Brighton (1911) 7.5' quadrangle.

Deadmans Lake: see **Deadman Lake** [SIERRA].

Deadmans Peak: see **Deadman Peak** [SIERRA].

Deadman Spring [EL DORADO]: *spring,* 0.5 mile north-northwest of Pollock Pines (lat. 38°46'15" N, long. 120°35'15" W; sec. 25, T 11 N, R 12 E). Named on Pollock Pines (1950) 7.5' quadrangle.

Deadshot Canyon [COLUSA]: *canyon,* drained by a stream that flows 2 miles to Bear Valley 4 miles north-northwest of Wilbur Springs (lat. 39°05'45" N, long. 122°26'40" W; near NE cor. sec. 6, T 14 N, R 5 W). Named on Wilbur Springs (1961) 15' quadrangle.

Dead Shot Creek [COLUSA]: *stream,* flows 1 mile to Indian Creek 4.5 miles northeast of Pacific Point (lat. 39°14'55" N, long. 122° 31'35" W; near E line sec. 9, T 16 N, R 6 W). Named on Clearlake Oaks (1960) 15' quadrangle.

Deadshot Flat [COLUSA]: *area,* 4 miles north-northwest of Wilbur Springs (lat. 39°05'05" N, long. 122°27'35" W; mainly in sec. 6, T 14 N, R 5 W). Named on Wilbur Springs (1961) 15' quadrangle, which shows Rathburn mine on the ridge east of Deadshot Flat. Crawford (1894, p. 359) noted that "the Rathburn Mines are on 'Dead Shot' ridge, which forms the western side of Bear Valley."

Dead Shot Ridge: see **Dead Shot Flat** [COLUSA].

Dead Shot Spring [COLUSA]:

(1) *spring,* 4.5 miles northeast of Pacific Point (lat. 39°14'55" N, long. 122°31'35" W; near E line sec. 9, T 16 N, R 6 W); the spring is at the mouth of Dead Shot Creek. Named on Clearlake Oaks (1960) 15' quadrangle.

(2) *spring,* 4 miles north-northwest of Wilbur Springs (lat. 39°05'10" N, long. 122°27'40" W; sec. 6, T 14 N, R 5 W); the spring is at Deadshot Flat. Named on Wilbur Springs (1961) 15' quadrangle.

Deadwood [PLACER]: *locality,* 3.5 miles northeast of Michigan Bluff (lat. 39°04'50" N, long. 120°41'15" W; sec. 12, T 14 N, R 11 E). Site named on Michigan Bluff (1952) 7.5' quadrangle. Colfax (1938) 30' quadrangle shows Deadwood House at the place. The name "Deadwood" is from a slang expression that has the meaning "a sure thing" (Hoover, Rensch, and Rensch, p. 276-277).

Deadwood [SIERRA]: *locality,* 3.5 miles south of Mount Fillmore (lat. 39°40'30" N, long. 120°51'15" W); the place is along present Deadwood Creek. Named on Downieville (1897) 30' quadrangle.

Deadwood Creek [SIERRA]: *stream,* flows 1.25 miles to Canyon Creek 3 miles south-southwest of Mount Fillmore (lat. 39°41'15" N, long. 120°51'55" W; at N line sec. 16, T 21 N, R 10 E); the stream is northeast of Deadwood Peak. Named on Mount Fillmore (1951) 7.5' quadrangle.

Deadwood Creek [YUBA]: *stream,* flows 4 miles to North Yuba River 2.5 miles south-southeast of Strawberry Valley (lat. 39°31'45" N, long. 121°05'40" W; near W line sec. 9, T 19 N, R 8 E). Named on Strawberry Valley (1948) 7.5' quadrangle. Wescoatt's (1861) map shows a place called Deadwood Mill located nearly 1 mile east-northeast of Strawberry Valley near the head of Deadwood Creek.

Deadwood Diggings [SIERRA]: *locality,* 3.5 miles south of Mount Fillmore (lat. 39°40'50" N, long. 120°51'20" W); the place is along Deadwood Creek. Named on Mount Fillmore (1951) 7.5' quadrangle.

Deadwood House: see **Deadwood** [PLACER].

Deadwood Mill: see **Deadwood Creek** [YUBA].

Deadwood Peak [SIERRA]: *peak,* 4 miles south-southwest of Mount Fillmore (lat. 39°40'25" N, long. 120°52'25" W; near NW cor. sec. 21, T 21 N, R 10 E). Altitude 6477 feet. Named on La Porte (1951) and Mount Fillmore (1951) 7.5' quadrangles.

Deadwood Ravine [SIERRA]: *canyon,* drained by a stream that flows less than 1 mile to Canyon Creek 4.25 miles south-southwest of Mount Fillmore (lat. 39°40'40" N, long. 120°53'25" W; sec. 17, T 21 N, R 10 E); the canyon is north of Deadwood Peak. Named on La Porte (1951) 7.5' quadrangle.

Deadwood Ridge [PLACER]: *ridge,* south-southwest- to south-trending, 11 miles long, extends from Foresthill Divide 1 mile east of Westville to the junction of El Dorado Canyon and North Fork of Middle Fork American River; the site of Deadwood is on the ridge. Named on Michigan Bluff (1952) and Westville (1952) 7.5' quadrangles.

Deafy Glade [COLUSA]: *area,* 3.5 miles west-southwest of Fouts Springs (lat. 39°20'20" N, long. 122°43'40" W; sec. 11, T 17 N, R 8 W). Named on Fouts Springs (1968) 7.5' quadrangle.

Deans Ravine [SIERRA]: *canyon,* drained by a stream that flows 1.25 miles to East Fork Canyon Creek 3.5 miles southeast of Mount Fillmore (lat. 39°41'50" N, long. 120°48'10" W). Named on Mount Fillmore (1951) 7.5' quadrangle.

Deep Canyon [EL DORADO]: *canyon,* drained by a stream that flows 1.5 miles to Pilot Creek (1) 13 miles north-northwest of Pollock Pines (lat. 38°56'20" N, long. 120°40'20" W). Named on Tunnel Hill (1950) 7.5' quadrangle.

Deep Canyon [PLACER]: *canyon,* drained by a stream that flows 7.5 miles to North Fork of Middle Fork American River 5 miles west-southwest of Duncan Peak (lat. 39°07'20" N, long. 120°35'35" W; sec. 25, T 15 N, R 12 E). Named on Duncan Peak (1952) and Greek Store (1952) 7.5' quadrangles.

Deep Canyon [SIERRA]: *canyon,* drained by a stream that heads in the State of Nevada and flows less than 0.5 mile in Sierra County to Truckee River 8 miles southeast of Crystal Peak (lat. 39°27'25" N, long. 120°00'25" W; sec. 6, T 18 N, R 18 E). Named on Boca (1955) 7.5' quadrangle.

Deep Creek [PLACER]: *stream,* flows 4.5 miles to Truckee River 10 miles west-southwest of Martis Peak (lat. 39°15'30" N, long. 120° 12'30" W; near S line sec. 4, T 16 N, R 16 E). Named on Granite Chief (1953), Norden (1955), and Truckee (1955) 7.5' quadrangles.

Deep Ravine [EL DORADO]: *canyon,* drained by a stream that flows 2 miles to South Fork American River 6.5 miles north-northwest of Clarksville (lat. 38°44'40" N, long. 121°05'25" W; near S line sec. 3, T 10 N, R 8 E). Named on Clarksville (1953) and Pilot Hill (1954) 7.5' quadrangles. Water of Folsom Lake now covers the lower part of the canyon. Auburn (1944) 15' quadrangle shows Anderson Creek in the canyon.

Deep Water Ship Channel: see **Sacramento River Deep Water Ship Channel** [SACRAMENTO-YOLO].

Deer Creek [AMADOR]: *stream,* flows nearly 2 miles to North Fork Mokelumne River 6 miles south-southeast of Hams Station (lat. 38°28'15" N, long. 120°25'35" W; near W line sec. 10, T 7 N, R 14 E). Named on Devils Nose (1979) 7.5' quadrangle.

Deer Creek [EL DORADO]:

(1) *stream,* flows 3.5 miles to Rubicon River 5.25 miles north-northwest of Robbs Peak (lat. 38°59'30" N, long. 120°27'05" W; sec. 7, T 13 N, R 14 E). Named on Bunker Hill (1953) and Robbs Peak (1950) 7.5' quadrangles.

(2) *locality,* 3.5 miles west of Shingle Springs along Deer Creek [EL DORADO-SACRAMENTO] (lat. 38°39'30" N, long. 120°59'30" W). Named on Placerville (1893) 30' quadrangle.

Deer Creek [EL DORADO-SACRAMENTO]: *stream,* heads in El Dorado County and flows 42 miles to Cosumnes River 7.5 miles north-northwest of Galt in Sacramento County (lat. 38°21'40" N, long. 121°20'25" W). Named on Buffalo Creek (1967), Clarksville (1953), Elk Grove (1968), Folsom SE (1954), Galt (1968), Latrobe (1949), Shingle Springs (1949), and Sloughhouse (1968) 7.5' quadrangles.

Deer Creek [NEVADA-YUBA]: *stream,* formed in Nevada County by the confluence of North Fork and South Fork, flows 26 miles to Yuba River 6.5 miles northwest of Pilot Peak just inside of Yuba County (lat. 39°13'50" N, long. 121°16'50" W; near E line sec. 22, T 16 N, R 6 E). Named on Grass Valley (1949), Nevada City (1948), North Bloomfield (1949), Rough and Ready (1949), and Smartville (1951) 7.5' quadrangles. Some hunters named the stream in 1849 when they had to abandon a freshly killed deer there (Gudde, 1975, p. 93). North Fork is 6.5 miles long and South Fork is 7.25 miles long; both forks are named on North Bloomfield (1949) and Washington (1950) 7.5' quadrangles. Eddy's (1851) map shows a place called Deer Creek Crossing situated along Deer Creek 4 or 5 miles above the mouth, and a place called Matheus located along a southern tributary to Deer Creek southwest of Deer Creek Crossing. Gudde (1975, p. 115) listed a place called Fienes Crossing that was located along Deer Creek about 1 mile above the mouth of the stream.

Deer Creek [PLACER]: *stream,* flows 2.5 miles to Truckee River nearly 5 miles northwest of Tahoe City (lat. 39°13'20" N, long. 120°11'55" W; near E line sec. 21, T 16 N, R 16 E). Named on Tahoe City (1955) 7.5' quadrangle. Called Silver Creek on Hobson's (1890b) map.

Deer Creek [SIERRA]: *stream.* flows 4.5 miles to North Yuba River 4 miles north-northeast of Sierra City (lat. 39°36'50" N, long. 120° 35'30" W; sec. 11, T 20 N, R 12 E). Named on Haypress Valley (1981) 7.5' quadrangle. The lower part of the stream is called Williams Creek on Sierra City (1955) 15' quadrangle.

Deer Creek: see **Little Deer Creek** [EL DORADO]; **Little Deer Creek** [NEVADA]; **Little Deer Creek** [SACRAMENTO].

Deer Creek Crossing: see **Deer Creek** [NEVADA-YUBA].

Deer Creek Dry Diggings: see **Nevada City** [NEVADA].

Deer Creek Reservoir [NEVADA]: *lake,* behind a dam on Deer Creek 7.5 miles south-southwest of North Bloomfield (lat. 39°16'10" N, long. 120°57'10" W; sec. 10, T 16 N, R 9 E). Named on North Bloomfield (1949) 7.5' quadrangle.

Deer Flat [COLUSA]: *area,* 3.5 miles east-northeast of Lodoga (lat. 39°18'55" N, long. 122°26'35" W; sec. 20, T 17 N, R 5 W). Named on Lodoga (1960) 15' quadrangle.

Deer Knob [EL DORADO]: *peak,* 3 miles south-southwest of Robbs Peak (lat. 38°53'25" N, long. 120°25'55" W; sec. 17, T 12 N, R 14 E). Altitude 5621 feet. Named on Robbs Peak (1950) 7.5' quadrangle.

Deer Lake [SIERRA]: *lake,* 1850 feet long, 5.5 miles north-northwest of Sierra City (lat. 39°38'40" N, long. 120°39'55" W; near NE cor. sec. 31, T 21 N, R 12 E). Named on Gold Lake (1981) 7.5' quadrangle.

Deer Lake: see **Little Deer Lake** [SIERRA].

Deer Park [PLACER]: *locality,* 4.5 miles west of Tahoe City along Bear Creek at present Alpine Meadows (lat. 39°10'45" N, long. 120°13'35" W; at W line sec. 4, T 15 N, R 16 E); the place is 1.5 miles north of Scott Peak. Named on Truckee (1940) 30' quadrangle. Called Scotts Springs on Truckee (1895) 30' quadrangle. G.A. Waring (p. 232-233) noted that four springs, called Deer Park Springs, were the basis of a resort at the place as early as the 1880's. California Division of Highways' (1934) map shows a place called Deer Park located along Southern Pacific Railroad near the mouth of Bear Creek (at SW cor. sec. 34, T 16 N, R 16 E).

Deer Park Springs: see **Deer Park** [PLACER].

Deer Valley [AMADOR]: *area,* 6 miles west of Mokelumne Peak (lat. 38°32'55" N, long. 120°12'15" W; near NW cor. sec. 15, T 8 N, R 16 E). Named on Bear River Reservoir (1979) 7.5' quadrangle.

Deer View [EL DORADO]: *locality,* 7.25 miles northwest of Pollock Pines (lat. 38°50'35" N, long. 120°40' W; sec. 32, T 12 N, R 12 E). Named on Slate Mountain (1950) 7.5' quadrangle.

Defender: see **Pine Grove** [AMADOR].

Defiance: see **Point Defiance** [NEVADA].

De Krusse Canyon [PLACER]: *canyon,* drained by a stream that flows 1.5 miles to Indian Creek (2) 6 miles north-northwest of Foresthill (lat. 39°05'55" N, long. 120°51'55" W; at N line sec. 4, T 14 N, R 10 E). Named on Colfax (1950) 15' quadrangle. On Foresthill (1949) 7.5' quadrangle, the name has the misspelling "DeKrruse Canyon."

Delahunty Lake [SIERRA]: *lake,* 750 feet long, 2.5 miles northwest of Mount Fillmore (lat. 39°45'05" N, long. 120°53'10" W; sec. 20, T 22 N, R 10 E). Named on Onion Valley (1950) 7.5' quadrangle.

Delaney: see **Cox-Delaney Flat** [NEVADA].

Delaney's Bridge: see **Chaparral Hill**, under **Lancha Plana** [AMADOR].

Delavan [COLUSA]: *locality,* 5.25 miles north of Maxwell (lat. 39° 21'15" N, long. 122°11'25" W; near W line sec. 3, T 17 N, R 3 W). Named on Maxwell (1952) 7.5' quadrangle, which has the additional designation "Delevan P.O." at the place. Called Delevan on Maxwell (1906) 15' quadrangle. United States Board on Geographic Names (1933, p. 260) approved the name "Delevan" and rejected the names "Delavan" and "Del Evan." Postal authorities established Delevan post office in 1902, discontinued it in 1917, and reestablished it in 1922 (Frickstad, p. 18).

Delevan: see **Delavan** [COLUSA].

Delirium Tremens: see **Omega** [NEVADA].

Deller Creek [EL DORADO-PLACER]: *stream,* heads in Placer County and flows 5 miles to Gerle Creek 2.5 miles west of Wentworth Springs in El Dorado County (lat. 39°00'35" N, long. 120° 22'55" W; near NW cor. sec. 2, T 13 N, R 14 E). Named on Bunker Hill (1953) and Wentworth Springs (1953) 7.5' quadrangles.

Deller Meadow [PLACER]: *area,* 0.5 mile east of Bunker Hill (lat. 39°03'05" N, long. 120°22'10" W; near NE cor. sec. 23, T 14 N, R 14 E); the place is at the head of Deller Creek. Named on Wentworth Springs (1953) 7.5' quadrangle.

Deller Spring [PLACER]: *spring,* 9 miles southwest of Duncan Peak (lat. 39°03'05" N, long. 120°36'20" W; sec. 23, T 14 N, R 12 E). Named on Greek Store (1952) 7.5' quadrangle.

Del Paso [SACRAMENTO]:

(1) *land grant,* 6.5 miles northeast of downtown Sacramento. Named on Carmichael (1967), Citrus Heights (1967), Rio Linda (1967), and Sacramento East (1967) 7.5' quadrangles. Elias Grimes received 10 leagues in 1844; Samuel Norris claimed 44,371 acres patented in 1858 (Cowan, p. 58; Perez, p. 64). The name is from a ford on American River that had the name "El paso de los Americanos" in Spanish days (Gudde, 1949, p. 92).

(2) *locality,* 8 miles east of downtown Sacramento (lat. 38°35'20" N, long. 121°20'45" W). Named on Fairoaks (1902) 15' quadrangle.

(3) *locality,* 3 miles south-southwest of Rio Linda along Western Pacific Railroad (lat. 38°39'15" N, long. 121°28'20" W). Named on Rio Linda (1967) 7.5' quadrangle.

(4) *locality,* 4.5 miles south of present Rio Linda along Northern Electric Railroad (lat. 38°37'30" N, long. 121°26'50" W); the place is on Del Paso grant. Named on Arcade (1911) 7.5' quadrangle.

Del Paso: see **Del Paso Heights** [SACRAMENTO].

Del Paso Heights [SACRAMENTO]: *district,* 6 miles northeast of downtown Sacramento (lat. 38°38'15" N, long. 121°25'20" W). Named on Rio Linda (1967) 7.5' quadrangle. Postal authorities established Del Paso post office in 1898, discontinued it in 1906, and reestablished it with the name "Del Paso Heights" in 1911 (Salley, p. 57).

Delphos [COLUSA]: *locality,* 2.5 miles north-northwest of Williams along Southern Pacific Railroad (lat. 39°11'25" N, long. 122°10'10" W; near SW cor. sec. 35, T 16 N, R 3 W). Named on Williams (1952) 7.5' quadrangle.

Del Rio: see **Freeport** [SACRAMENTO] (1).

Delta Cross Channel [SACRAMENTO]: *water feature,* extends from Snodgrass Slough to Sacramento River near Walnut Grove (lat. 38°14'50" N, long. 121°30'35" W). Named on Isleton (1978) and Thornton (1978) 7.5' quadrangles. United States Board on Geographic Names (1978b, p. 2) rejected the name "Cross Delta Channel" for the feature.

Democrat [NEVADA]: *locality,* 5.25 miles south of Washington (lat. 39°16'45" N, long. 120°46'45" W). Named on Colfax (1898) 30' quadrangle.

Democrat Peak [SIERRA]: *peak,* 4.25 miles south of Mount Fillmore (lat. 39°40'05" N, long. 120°50'40" W). Altitude 6779 feet. Named on Mount Fillmore (1951) 7.5' quadrangle.

Demory Spring [NEVADA]: *spring,* 3.25 miles west-northwest of Washington (lat. 39°22'20" N, long. 120°51'35" W; near N line sec. 4, T 17 N, R 10 E). Named on Washington (1950) 7.5' quadrangle.

Dempsey Creek [YUBA]: *stream,* flows 2.5 miles to join Daugherty Creek and form Cox Creek 3.5 miles south of Smartville (lat. 39°09'20" N, long. 121°17'35" W; sec. 15, T 15 N, R 6 E). Named on Smartville (1951) 7.5' quadrangle.

Dempsey Spring [NEVADA]: *spring,* 2.5 miles northwest of Washington (lat. 39°23'05" N, long. 121°50' W; near NE cor. sec. 34, T 18 N, R 10 E). Named on Alleghany (1949) 7.5' quadrangle.

Denco: see **Colusa** [COLUSA].

Dennis Canyon [EL DORADO]: *canyon,* drained by a stream that flows 1 mile to Camp Creek 6.25 miles northwest of Leek Spring Hill (lat. 38°41'05" N, long. 120°22'10" W; near S line sec. 25, T 10 N, R 14 E). Named on Leek Spring Hill (1951) 7.5' quadrangle.

Dennis Spring [EL DORADO]: *spring,* 6.5 miles northwest of Leek Spring Hill (lat. 38°41'40" N, long. 120°22'05" W; sec. 25, T 10 N, R 14 E); the spring is in Dennis Canyon. Named on Leek Spring Hill (1951) 7.5' quadrangle.

Denniston: see **Olivehurst** [YUBA].

Denvale: see **Big Chief** [PLACER].

Depot Hill: see **Camptonville** [YUBA].

Derbec Spring [NEVADA]: *spring,* 2 miles north-northeast of North Bloomfield (lat. 39°23'30" N, long. 121°52'45" W; sec. 29, T 18 N, R 10 E). Named on Pike (1949) 7.5' quadrangle.

Derbec Spring: see **Upper Derbec Spring** [NEVADA].

Derby Camp [YOLO]: *locality,* 11 miles east of Dunnigan along Sacramento River (lat. 38°51'50" N, long. 121°45'50" W). Named on Ronda (1915) 7.5' quadrangle.

Desert Cold Spring [PLACER]: *spring,* 4 miles northeast of Devil Peak (lat. 38°59'55" N, long. 120°29'55" W; at S line sec. 2, T 13 N, R 13 E). Named on Robbs Peak (1950) 7.5' quadrangle.

Desolation Lake [EL DORADO]: *lake,* 750 feet long, 1.5 miles east of Pyramid Peak (lat. 38°50'50" N, long. 120°07'30" W); the lake is in Desolation Valley. Named on Pyramid Peak (1955) 7.5' quadrangle.

Desolation Valley [EL DORADO]: *valley,* 1.5 miles east-northeast of Pyramid Peak (lat. 38°51' N, long. 120°08' W). Named on Echo Lake (1955) and Pyramid Peak (1955) 7.5' quadrangles. The feature was known as Devil's Valley and Devil's Basin before it received the present name (Lekisch, p. 28).

Destanella Flat [COLUSA]: *area,* 2.5 miles south-southeast of Wilbur Springs (lat. 39°00'20" N, long. 122°24'15" W; sec. 3, T 13 N, R 5 W). Named on Wilbur Springs (1961) 15' quadrangle.

Devil Peak [PLACER]: *peak,* 29 miles east of Auburn (lat. 38°57'30" N, long. 120°32'45" W; near S line sec. 20, T 13 N, R 13 E). Altitude 5302 feet. Named on Devil Peak (1950) 7.5' quadrangle.

Devil Peak: see **Devils Peak** [PLACER] (1).

Devils Basin [PLACER]: *relief feature,* 5.25 miles northeast of Michigan Bluff (lat. 39°05'35" N, long. 120°39'35" W; near N line sec. 5, T 14 N, R 12 E). Named on Michigan Bluff (1952) 7.5' quadrangle.

Devil's Basin: see **Desolation Valley** [EL DORADO].

Devils Canyon [NEVADA]: *canyon,* drained by a stream that flows 3 miles to Poorman Creek (1) 1 mile north of Washington (lat. 39° 22'25" N, long. 120°47'50" W; near N line sec. 1, T 17 N, R 10 E). Named on Alleghany (1949) and Washington (1950) 7.5' quadrangles.

Devils Canyon [PLACER]: *canyon,* drained by a stream that flows 5.5 miles to Shirttail Canyon 5.25 miles southeast of Colfax (lat. 39°02'20" N, long. 120°53'40" W; at S line sec. 19, T 14 N, R 10 E). Named on Colfax (1949) and Foresthill (1949) 7.5' quadrangles. Bancroft (1888, p. 355) used the form "Devil's cañon" for the name.

Devils Canyon [SIERRA]: *canyon,* drained by a stream that flows 1.5 miles to North Yuba River 1.5 miles west of Goodyears Bar (lat. 39°32'10" N, long. 120°54'50" W; sec. 1, T 19 N, R 9 E). Named on Goodyears Bar (1951) 7.5' quadrangle.

Devils Gate [AMADOR]: *narrows,* 6 miles west-southwest of Jackson along Jackson Creek (lat. 38°18'25" N, long. 120°52'20" W; near NE cor. sec. 9, T 5 N, R 10 E). Named on Jackson (1962) 7.5' quadrangle.

Devils Gate [PLACER]: *narrows,* 4 miles east-northeast of Michigan Bluff along North Fork of Middle Fork American River (lat. 39°04'15" N, long. 120°40'10" W; near SE cor. sec. 7, T 14 N, R 12 E). Named on Michigan Bluff (1952) 7.5' quadrangle.

Devils Gate [SIERRA]: *narrows,* 3.25 miles south-southwest of Mount Fillmore along Canyon Creek (lat. 39°41'10" N, long. 120° 52'40" W; near N line sec. 17, T 21 N, R 10 E). Named on La Porte (1951) 7.5' quadrangle.

Devils Gate [YOLO]: *narrows,* 11.5 miles south-southeast of Berryessa Peak along Putah Creek on Yolo-Solano County line (lat. 38° 30'45" N, long. 122°06' W; sec. 29, T 8 N, R 2 W). Named on Capay (1945) 15' quadrangle. O' Brien (p. 425) used the name "Devil's Gate."

Devils Hole Lake [AMADOR]: *lake,* 500 feet long, 6.5 miles north of Mokelumne Peak (lat. 38°37'55" N, long. 120°04'35" W; sec. 15, T 9 N, R 17 E). Named on Caples Lake (1979) 7.5' quadrangle.

Devil's Horn: see **Devils Thumb** [PLACER].

Devils Lake [AMADOR]: *lake,* 1400 feet long, 6 miles west-northwest of Mokelumne Peak (lat. 38°34'55" N, long. 120°11'10" W; sec. 35, T 9 N, R 16 E). Named on Silver Lake (1956) 15' quadrangle.

Devils Oven: see **Devils Oven Lake** [NEVADA].

Devils Oven Lake [NEVADA]: *lake,* 700 feet long, 5.25 miles north-northwest of Donner Pass (lat. 39°23'35" N, long. 120°21'25" W; near SW cor. sec. 25, T 18 N, R 14 E). Named on Independence Lake (1981) 7.5' quadrangle. Donner Pass (1955) 15' quadrangle has the name "Devils Oven" at the place.

Devils Peak [PLACER]:

(1) *peak*, 6.5 miles west-southwest of Donner Pass (lat. 39°16'55" N, long. 120°26'25" W; sec. 6, T 16 N, R 14 E). Altitude 7704 feet. Named on Soda Springs (1955) 7.5' quadrangle. Called Devil Peak on Truckee (1895) 30' quadrangle.
(2) *peak*, 5 miles east-southeast of Bunker Hill (lat. 39°01'45" N, long. 120°17'25" W; at E line sec. 28, T 14 N, R 15 E). Altitude 7541 feet. Named on Wentworth Springs (1953) 7.5' quadrangle.

Devils Post Pile [SIERRA]: *relief feature*, 4.25 miles south-southwest of Mount Fillmore (lat. 39°40'20" N, long. 120°52'50" W; near N line sec. 20, T 21 N, R 10 E). Named on La Porte (1951) 7.5' quadrangle.

Devils Punch Bowl: see **The Punchbowl** [NEVADA].

Devils Slide [NEVADA]: *relief feature*, 4 miles northwest of Nevada City on the southeast side of South Yuba River (lat. 39°18'25" N, long. 121°04' W; sec. 27, T 17 N, R 8 E). Named on Nevada City (1948) 7.5' quadrangle.

Devils Thumb [PLACER]: *relief feature*, 5.5 miles northeast of Michigan Bluff (lat. 39°05'45" N, long. 120°39'35" W; near S line sec. 32, T 15 N, R 12 E). Named on Michigan Bluff (1952) 7.5' quadrangle. C.A. Waring (p. 356) used the name "Devil's Horn" for the feature.

Devil's Valley: see **Desolation Valley** [EL DORADO].

Devine Gulch: see **Georgia Slide** [EL DORADO].

Dew Drop [NEVADA]: *locality*, 3 miles north of Higgins Corner (lat. 39°05'10" N, long. 121°05'05" W; near NW cor. sec. 10, T 14 N, R 8 E). Named on Lake Combie (1949) 7.5' quadrangle.

Dewey Campground [PLACER]: *locality*, 6.25 miles northwest of Bunker Hill along Middle Fork American River (lat. 39°06'45" N, long. 120°27'45" W; near NE cor. sec. 36, T 15 N, R 13 E). Named on Granite Chief (1953) 15' quadrangle. Water of French Meadows Reservoir now covers the site.

Diablo Campground [SIERRA]: *locality*, 4.5 miles north of Sierra City along Packer Creek (lat. 39°37'50" N, long. 120°38'20" W; at S line sec. 33, T 21 N, R 12 E). Named on Gold Lake (1981) 7.5' quadrangle.

Diamond: see **Diamond Springs** [EL DORADO].

Diamond Bar: see **French Bar** [AMADOR].

Diamond Creek [EL DORADO]: *stream*, flows 3.25 miles to Camp Creek 9.5 miles east of Camino (lat. 38°43'10" N, long. 120°30'05" W; sec. 14, T 10 N, R 13 E). Named on Sly Park (1952) and Stump Spring (1951) 7.5' quadrangles.

Diamond Creek [NEVADA]: *stream*, flows 4.25 miles to South Yuba River 7.25 miles west-northwest of Yuba Gap (lat. 39°21'15" N, long. 120°44'20" W; sec. 9, T 17 N, R 11 E). Named on Blue Canyon (1955) 7.5' quadrangle.

Diamond Creek: see **Omega** [NEVADA].

Diamond Crossing [PLACER]: *locality*, 6.5 miles northeast of Bunker Hill along Five Lakes Creek (lat. 39°06'35" N, long. 120° 17'25" W; near NW cor. sec. 34, T 15 N, R 15 E). Named on Wentworth Springs (1953) 7.5' quadrangle.

Diamond Ravine [YUBA]: *canyon*, drained by a stream that flows less than 1 mile to Brushy Creek 3 miles east of Strawberry Valley (lat. 39°34'20" N, long. 121°02'55" W; near S line sec. 23, T 20 N, R 8 E). Named on Strawberry Valley (1948) 7.5' quadrangle.

Diamond Springs [EL DORADO]: *town*, 2.5 miles south-southwest of Placerville (lat. 38°41'40" N, long. 120°48'50" W; on W line sec. 30, T 10 N, R 11 E). Named on Placerville (1949) 7.5' quadrangle. Called Diamond Spring on Placerville (1893) 30' quadrangle, and called Diamond on California Mining Bureau's (1909a) map. Postal authorities established Diamond Spring post office in 1853 and changed the name to Diamond Springs in 1950 (Salley, p. 59). According to Hanna (p. 86), the name is from some crystal-clear springs. According to Paden (p. 455-456), the name is from the location of springs at the corners of a diamond-shaped area.

Dicks Lake [EL DORADO]: *lake*, 0.5 mile long, 3 miles south of Phipps Peak (lat. 38°54'45" N, long. 120°08'30" W; sec. 6, R 12 N, R 17 E); the lake is less than 1 mile north-northeast of Dicks Peak. Named on Rockbound Valley (1955) 7.5' quadrangle.

Dicks Pass [EL DORADO]: *pass*, 3.5 miles south-southeast of Phipps Peak (lat. 38°54'20" N, long. 120°08'05" W; sec. 7, T 12 N, R 17 E); the pass is 1 mile east-northeast of Dicks Peak. Named on Rockbound Valley (1955) 7.5' quadrangle.

Dicks Peak [EL DORADO]: *peak*, 3.5 miles south of Phipps Peak (lat. 38°54' N, long. 120°09' W). Altitude 9974 feet. Named on Rockbound Valley (1955) 7.5' quadrangle. The name commemorates Captain Richard Barter, an eccentric English sailor who lived a lonely life at Emerald Bay in the 1860's and 1870's (Lekisch, p. 29-30).

Digger Pine Campground [COLUSA]: *locality*, 6.25 miles south-southwest of Stonyford (lat. 39°17'10" N, long. 122°34'35" W; sec. 31, T 17 N, R 6 W). Named on Gilmore Peak (1968) 7.5' quadrangle.

Diggers Bar: see **Relief** [NEVADA].

Dillard [SACRAMENTO]: *locality*, 6 miles east of Elk Grove along Central California Traction Railroad (lat. 38°24'05" N, long. 121° 15'20" W; sec. 6, T 6 N, R 7 E). Named on Elk Grove (1968) 7.5' quadrangle. Postal authorities established Dillard post office in 1914 and discontinued it the same year (Frickstad, p. 132).

Dillon [NEVADA]: *locality*, 6.5 miles east of North Bloomfield at the confluence of Poorman Creek (1) and its South Fork (lat. 39°23'05" N, long. 120°46'40" W; sec. 31, T 18 N, R 11 E). Named on Colfax (1938) 30' quadrangle.

Disney: see **Mount Disney** [PLACER].

Ditch Camp [EL DORADO]: *locality*, nearly 2 miles north-northeast of Robbs Peak (lat. 38°57' N, long. 120°23'55" W; sec. 27, T 13 N, R 14 E). Named on Robbs Peak (1950) 7.5' quadrangle.

Ditch Camp [PLACER]: *locality*, 4 miles east of Michigan Bluff (lat. 39°02'45" N, long. 120°39'35" W; sec. 20, T 14 N, R 12 E). Site named on Michigan Bluff (1952) 7.5' quadrangle.

Ditch Camp Five [EL DORADO]: *locality*, 2 miles east of Pollock Pines (lat. 38°45'55" N, long. 120°32'50" W; at S line sec. 29, T 11 N, R 13 E). Named on Pollock Pines (1950) 7.5' quadrangle.

Ditch Camp Four [EL DORADO]: *locality*, 2.5 miles west-southwest of Riverton (lat. 38°45'20" N, long. 120°29'35" W; sec. 35, T 11 N, R 13 E). Named on Riverton (1950) 7.5' quadrangle.

Ditch Camp One [EL DORADO]: *locality*, 4.5 miles west of Kyburz (lat. 38°45'50" N, long. 120°22'30" W; at S line sec. 26, T 11 N, R 14 E). Named on Kyburz (1952) 7.5' quadrangle.

Ditch Camp Point [EL DORADO]: *ridge*, north-northeast- to north-trending, 1.5 miles long, 13 miles north-northwest of Pollock Pines (lat. 38°55'45" N, long. 120°41'05" W). Named on Tunnel Hill (1950) 7.5' quadrangle.

Ditch Camp Seven [EL DORADO]: *locality*, 1.25 miles southeast of Moores (present Riverton) (lat. 38°45'30" N, long. 120°25'45" W). Named on Pyramid Peak (1896) 30' quadrangle.

Ditch Camp Ten [EL DORADO]: *locality*, 4.25 miles west-southwest of Slippery Ford (present Kyburz) (lat. 38°45'15" N, long. 120°22'30" W). Named on Pyramid Peak (1896) 30' quadrangle.

Ditch Camp Three [EL DORADO]: *locality*, 1.25 miles west-southwest of Riverton (lat. 38°45'50" N, long. 120°28'10" W; sec. 36, T 11 N, R 13 E). Named on Riverton (1950) 7.5' quadrangle.

Ditch Camp Two [EL DORADO]: *locality*, less than 1 mile east-southeast of Riverton (lat. 38°45'55" N, long. 120°26'05" W; at N line sec. 32, T 11 N, R 14 E). Named on Riverton (1950) 7.5' quadrangle.

Dixon Hill [YUBA]: *ridge*, generally south-southwest-trending, 1.25 miles long, 3.25 miles south-southwest of Dobbins (lat. 39°19'55" N, long. 121°14' W; mainly in sec. 18, T 17 N, R 7 E). Named on French Corral (1948) 7.5' quadrangle.

Doaks Ridge [AMADOR]: *ridge*, southwest-trending, 6 miles long, 3 miles south-southwest of Hams Station (lat. 38°30'15" N, long. 120°24'20" W). Named on Caldor (1951) and Devils Nose (1979) 7.5' quadrangles. Called Doak Ridge on Pyramid Peak (1896) 30' quadrangle.

Dobbas Cow Camp [PLACER]: *locality*, 6 miles northwest of Bunker Hill along Middle Fork American River (lat. 39°06'35" N, long. 120°27'35" W; sec. 36, T 15 N, R 13 E). Named on Granite Chief (1953) 15' quadrangle. Water of French Meadows Reservoir now covers the site.

Dobbins [YUBA]: *town*, 26 miles northeast of Marysville (lat. 39°22'15" N, long. 121°12'20" W; sec. 32, T 18 N, R 7 E). Named on French Corral (1948) 7.5' quadrangle. Called Dobbin on Smartsville (1895) 30' quadrangle, and called Dobbins Ranch on Wescoatt's (1861) map. Postal authorities established Dobbin's Ranche post office in 1851 and discontinued it in 1854; they established Dobbins post office in 1887 (Salley, p. 59). The name commemorates William M. Dobbins and Mark D. Dobbins, who settled at the place in 1849 (Hoover, Rensch, and Rensch, p. 594). Wescoatt's (1861) map shows a place called Kentucky R. [Ranch] located 1.5 miles southwest of Dobbins Ranch; it was an early mining camp (Hanna, p. 160). Wescoatt's (1861) map also shows a place called California House located 1.5 miles west-northwest of Dobbins Ranch. Postal authorities established Egan post office 3 miles north of Dobbins in 1896 and discontinued it in 1898 (Salley, p. 66).

Dobbins Creek [YUBA]: *stream*, flows 6 miles to Yuba River 3 miles south-southeast of Dobbins (lat. 39°19'45" N, long. 121°11'40" W; sec. 16, T 17 N, R 7 E); the stream goes past Dobbins. Named on Challenge (1948) and French Corral (1948) 7.5' quadrangles. West Branch enters from the northwest 1 mile from the mouth of the main stream. It is 2.5 miles long and is named on French Corral (1948) 7.5' quadrangle. United States Geological Survey's (1922) map shows a place called Colgate located along Middle Fork Yuba River (present Middle Yuba River) 0.25 mile east of the mouth of Dobbins Creek, where French Corral (1948) 7.5' quadrangle shows Colgate powerhouse.

Dobbin's Ranche: see **Dobbins** [YUBA].

Doby Ranch: see **Franklin** [SACRAMENTO].

Dodge Canyon [SIERRA]: *canyon*, drained by a stream that flows 3 miles to Badenaugh Canyon 4.5 miles southeast of Loyalton (lat. 39°37'45" N, long. 120°11'05" W; at W line sec. 34, T 21 N, R 16 E). Named on Loyalton (1981) 7.5' quadrangle.

Dodges [PLACER]: *locality*, 10 miles northeast of Auburn (lat. 38° 59'40" N, long. 120°55'30" W). Named on Placerville (1893) 30' quadrangle.

Doe Flat [COLUSA]: *area*, 4 miles east of Wilbur Springs (lat. 39° 03' N, long. 122°21'05" W; near W line sec. 19, T 14 N, R 4 W). Named on Wilbur Springs (1961) 15' quadrangle.

Dog Creek [SIERRA]: *stream,* flows 7 miles to the State of Nevada 5 miles east-southeast of Crystal Peak (lat. 39°31'40" N, long. 120° 00'05" W; at E line sec. 7, T 19 N, R 18 E); the stream goes through Dog Valley. Named on Dog Valley (1981) 7.5' quadrangle. North Branch enters from the north 3 miles east of Crystal Peak and is nearly 4 miles long. South Branch enters at California-Nevada State line and is 2.5 miles long. Both branches are named on Dog Valley (1981) 7.5' quadrangle.

Dog Town: see **Bunker Hill** [AMADOR] (2).

Dogtown [EL DORADO]: *locality,* 8 miles west-southwest of Leek Spring Hill (lat. 38°36'10" N, long. 120°25'30" W). Named on Pyramid Peak (1896) 30' quadrangle.

Dogtown: see **Newtown** [EL DORADO].

Dogtown Creek [EL DORADO]: *stream,* flows 10.5 miles to Middle Fork Cosumnes River 1 mile northeast of Omo Ranch (lat. 38° 35'30" N, long. 120°33'15" W; near W line sec. 33, T 9 N, R 13 E). Named on Caldor (1951), Omo Ranch (1952), and Stump Spring (1951) 7.5' quadrangles. Called North Fork of Middle Fork Cosumnes River on Pyramid Peak (1896) 30' quadrangle, which shows Dogtown situated along the stream.

Dog Valley [SIERRA]: *valley,* 2.5 miles east of Crystal Peak (lat. 39° 33'30" N, long. 120°02'30" W); the valley is along Dog Creek. Named on Dog Valley (1981) 7.5' quadrangle.

Dog Valley Campground [SIERRA]: *locality,* 1.25 miles east-northeast of Crystal Peak (lat. 39°33'55" N, long. 120°03'55" W; near SW cor. sec. 23, T 20 N, R 17 E); the place is 1.25 miles west-northwest of Dog Valley. Named on Dog Valley (1981) 7.5' quadrangle.

Dolan: see **Colusa** [COLUSA].

Dollar Creek [PLACER]: *stream,* flows 2.5 miles to Lake Tahoe nearly 5 miles southwest of Kings Beach (lat. 39°11'50" N, long. 120°05'40" W; near N line sec. 33, T 16 N, R 17 E); the stream is north of Dollar Point. Named on Kings Beach (1955) 7.5' quadrangle.

Dollar Point [PLACER]: *promontory,* 5.25 miles southwest of Kings Beach along Lake Tahoe (lat. 39°11'10" N, long. 120°05'30" W; sec. 33, T 16 N, R 17 E). Named on Kings Beach (1955) 7.5' quadrangle. Called Observatory Point on Truckee (1895) 30' quadrangle, but United States Board on Geographic Names (1963, p. 6) rejected this name for the feature. The name "Dollar Point" is for Stanley Dollar, the millionaire who owned the promontory; the name "Observatory Point" came from James Lick's offer to finance an astronomical observatory at the place, a project that never materialized—earlier the feature had the name "Lousy Point" because the sole inhabitant of the place had lice (Zauner, p. 34). The feature was called Chinkapin Point on a map of 1863 (Lekisch, p. 31).

Dollar Reservoir [PLACER]: *lake,* 300 feet long, behind a dam on Dollar Creek 5.25 miles west-southwest of Kings Beach (lat. 39°12'05" N, long. 120°06'30" W; sec. 29, T 16 N, R 17 E). Named on Kings Beach (1955) 7.5' quadrangle.

Dolly Creek [PLACER]: *stream,* flows 3.5 miles to Middle Fork American River 7.25 miles west-southwest of Granite Chief (lat. 39°08'45" N, long. 120°24'10" W; sec. 15, T 15 N, R 14 E). Named on Granite Chief (1953) and Royal Gorge (1953) 7.5' quadrangles.

Donkey Canyon [SIERRA]: *canyon,* drained by a stream that flows 2 miles to Balls Canyon 7.5 miles east of Loyalton (lat. 39°39'25" N, long. 120°05'50" W; sec. 20, T 21 N, R 17 E). Named on Evans Canyon (1978) 7.5' quadrangle.

Donlon Island [SACRAMENTO]: *island,* 12.5 miles southwest of Isleton between Mayberry Cut, Mayberry Slough, and San Joaquin River (lat. 38°01'55" N, long. 121°46'40" W). Named on Antioch North (1978) 7.5' quadrangle. Called Donlan Island on Antioch North (1953) 7.5' quadrangle. Water covers most of the feature.

Donner [PLACER]: *locality,* nearly 2 miles east-southeast of Donner Pass along Southern Pacific Railroad (lat. 39°18'30" N, long. 120° 17'40" W; sec. 22, T 17 N, R 15 E). Named on Truckee (1940) 30' quadrangle. Truckee (1895) 30' quadrangle has the name "Donner" for a place along the railroad at Donner Pass. Postal authorities established Donner post office in 1882 and discontinued it in 1926 (Frickstad, p. 120). California Mining Bureau's (1917c) map shows a place called Arctic located along the railroad about 0.5 mile east of the site of Donner.

Donner Creek [NEVADA]: *stream,* flows 2.5 miles to Truckee River 1.25 miles southwest of Truckee (lat. 39°19' N, long. 120°12' W; near SE cor. sec. 16, T 17 N, R 16 E); the stream heads at Donner Lake. Named on Truckee (1955, photorevised 1969) 7.5' quadrangle.

Donner Lake [NEVADA]: *lake,* 2.5 miles long, center 3.25 miles east of Donner Pass (lat. 39°19'20" N, long. 120°15'50" W). Named on Norden (1955) and Truckee 1955) 7.5' quadrangles. Called Truckee Lake on Goddard's (1857) map. *Californian* newspaper for August 22, 1846, mentioned Trucky's Lake. The name "Donner Lake" commemorates the tragic Donner party of emigrants, who suffered near the lake in the winter of 1846 and 1847 (Gudde, 1949, p. 97). United States Board on Geographic Names (1994, p. 5) approved the name "Mount Stephens" for a peak located 1.9 miles west of Donner Lake (lat. 39°19'12" N, long. 120°19'19" W; sec. 16, T 17 N, R 15 E); the name is for Elisha Stephens, captain of the first party to cross the Sierra Nevada with a wagon.

Donner Lake: see **Truckee** [NEVADA].

Donner Pass [NEVADA-PLACER]: *pass,* 7.5 miles west of Truckee on Nevada-Placer County line (lat. 39°19' N, long. 120°19'30" W; near SW cor. sec. 16, T 17 N, R 15 E); the pass is 2 miles west of Donner Lake. Named on Norden (1955) 7.5' quadrangle. Jefferson's (1849) map has the designation "Truckey Pass of California Mountains" for the feature. Hobson's (1890b) map shows a place called Summit Station situated along the railroad in Placer County about 0.5 mile east-southeast of Donner Pass. United States Board on Geographic Names (1984b, p. 2) approved the name "George R. Stewart Peak" for a feature situated 0.5 mile northeast of Donner Pass (lat. 39°19'26" N, long. 120°19'07" W; sec. 16, T 17 N, R 15 E; altitude 7389 feet); the name commemorates George R. Stewart, place-name scholar, historian, and novelist, whose works include a study of the Donner party. United States Board on Geographic Names (1986, p. 1) also approved the name "McGlashan Point" for a peak 6920 feet east of Donner Pass (lat. 39°19'07" N, long. 120°19'06" W; sec. 16, T 17 N, R 15 E); the name commemorates Charles Fayette McGlashan, another historian of the Donner tragedy.

Donner Peak [PLACER]: *peak,* 1 mile southeast of Donner Pass (lat. 39°18'30" N, long. 120°18'40" W; near E line sec. 21, T 17 N, R 15 E). Altitude 8019 feet. Named on Norden (1955) 7.5' quadrangle. United States Board on Geographic Names (1942, p. 27) rejected the name "Donner Peak" for nearby Mount Judah.

Donner Ridge [NEVADA]: *ridge,* northeast- to southeast-trending, 2.5 miles long, 3 miles northeast of Donner Pass (lat. 39°21'10" N, long. 120°17'20" W). Named on Norden (1955) 7.5' quadrangle.

Donovan Hill [YUBA]: *peak,* 4 miles west-southwest of Oregon House (lat. 39°20'35" N, long. 121°21' W; near W line sec. 7, T 17 N, R 6 E). Named on Oregon House (1948) 7.5' quadrangle.

Doris: see **Lake Doris** [EL DORADO].

Dormodys [EL DORADO]: *locality,* 3.25 miles north-northeast of Clarksville (lat. 38°42' N, long. 121°02' W). Named on Sacramento (1892) 30' quadrangle.

Dorsey Creek [SIERRA]: *stream,* flows 1.25 miles to North Yuba River 7.5 miles east-northeast of Sierra City (lat. 39°36'55" N, long. 120°30'20" W; sec. 10, T 20 N, R 13 E). Named on Haypress Valley (1981) and Sattley (1981) 7.5' quadrangles.

Doschville: see **Indian Hill** [AMADOR] (1).

Dotons Bar [PLACER]: *locality,* 6.5 miles east of Rocklin along North Fork American River (lat. 38°46'25" N, long. 121°06'50" W; near W line sec. 29, T 11 N, R 8 E). Site named on Auburn (1954) 15' quadrangle. Water of Folsom Lake now covers the site.

Dotons Point [PLACER]: *peninsula,* 6 miles east-southeast of Rocklin along Folsom Lake (lat. 38°45'35" N, long. 121°07'40" W; sec. 31, T 11 N, R 8 E). Named on Rocklin (1967) 7.5' quadrangle.

Doty Creek: see **Doty Ravine** [PLACER].

Doty Flat [PLACER]: *area,* 4.25 miles west of Auburn (lat. 38°54'30" N, long. 121°09' W; sec. 11, 12, T 12 N, R 7 E); the place is in Doty Ravine. Named on Gold Hill (1954) 7.5' quadrangle. Myrick (p. 115) referred to a mining camp called Doty's Flat in 1852.

Doty Ravine [PLACER]: *canyon,* drained by a stream that flows 13 miles to Coon Creek 4 miles northwest of Lincoln (lat. 38°56'20" N, long. 121°20'20" W; near W line sec. 32, T 13 N, R 6 E). Named on Gold Hill (1954) and Lincoln (1953) 7.5' quadrangles. The stream in the canyon is called Doty Creek on Markham Ravine (1942) 15' quadrangle.

Doubtful Gulch: see **Willow Glen Creek** [YUBA].

Dover [EL DORADO]: *locality,* 6 miles north of Omo Ranch (lat. 38° 40' N, long. 120°34'25" W). Named on Placerville (1893) 30' quadrangle.

Downerville: see **Downieville** [SIERRA].

Downey Lake [NEVADA]: *lake,* 1450 feet long, 4.25 miles south-southwest of English Mountain (lat. 39°23'40" N, long. 120°35'45" W; sec. 26, T 18 N, R 12 E). Named on English Mountain (1983) 7.5' quadrangle.

Downeyville: see **Downieville** [SIERRA].

Downie River [SIERRA]: *stream,* flows 8 miles to North Yuba River at Downieville (lat. 39°33'35" N, long. 120°49'40" W; sec. 35, T 20 N, R 10 E). Named on Downieville (1951) and Mount Fillmore (1951) 7.5' quadrangles. Called N. Fork of N. Fork Yuba River on Downieville (1897) 30' quadrangle, but United States Board on Geographic Names (1950, p. 5) rejected the names "North Fork of North Fork," "North Fork of North Fork of Yuba River," and "North Fork of North Fork Yuba River" for the stream. The name "Downie River" commemorates William Downie of Dowieville (Hanna, p. 90). West Branch enters from the northwest 6.5 miles south of Mount Fillmore; it is nearly 3 miles long and is named on Mount Fillmore (1951) 7.5' quadrangle.

Downieville [SIERRA]: *village,* in the west-central part of Sierra County along North Yuba River (lat. 39°33'35" N, long. 120°49'35" W; sec. 35, T 20 N, R 10 E); the village is at the mouth of Downie River. Named on Downieville (1951) 7.5' quadrangle. Called Downeyville on Eddy's (1851) map. Postal authorities established Downerville post office before October 1851 and changed the name to Downieville in 1852 (Salley, p. 61). William Downie came to the place late in 1849 and wintered just above present Downieville at Jersey Flat; the site at the mouth of present Downie River was called The Forks before the community there was named Downieville (Hoover, Rensch, and Rensch, p. 491-492). Jersey Flat was called Murraysville before Jersey Company acquired it in 1850 (Gudde, 1975, p. 176). The part of present Downieville south of North Yuba River was called Durgans Flat; it was known as Washingtonville before James Durgan built a sawmill there in 1850 (Gudde, 1975, p. 103). The following mining places were in the vicinity of present Downieville: Zumwalt Flat, located at the northeast end of the village, where William Downie mined in 1849 before Joseph Zumwalt arrived in 1850 (Gudde, 1975, p. 381); Tin Cup Diggings, where three men filled a tin cup with gold each day (Clark, p. 44); New York Flat, located about 1.5 miles east of Downieville (Gudde, 1975, p. 242); O' Donnells Flat, situated 2 miles east of Downieville, also called McCarty Flat and McDonald Flat (Gudde, 1975, p. 248); Coyoteville, located 1 mile west of Downieville (Gudde, 1975, p. 87); and Cox Bar, located 2 miles west of Downieville on the north side of North Yuba River (Gudde, 1975, p. 85).

Doyle Canyon [COLUSA]: *canyon,* drained by a stream that flows 2.5 miles to Bear Valley 7 miles north-northwest of Wilbur Springs (lat. 39°17'20" N, long. 122°27' W; sec. 19, T 15 N, R 5 W). Named on Wilbur Springs (1961) 15' quadrangle.

Dredgertown: see **Hammonton** [YUBA].

Dredgerville: see **Hammonton** [YUBA].

Drivers Flat [PLACER]: *area,* 8 miles northeast of Auburn (lat. 38° 58'20" N, long. 120°57'10" W; near SE cor. sec. 15, T 13 N, R 9 E). Named on Greenwood (1949) 7.5' quadrangle.

Drum [PLACER]: *locality,* 5 miles east-northeast of Dutch Flat (lat. 39°14'55" N, long. 120°45'15" W; sec. 16, T 16 N, R 11 E). Named on Colfax (1938) 30' quadrangle. Postal authorities established Drum post office in 1913 and discontinued it in 1915 (Frickstad, p. 120).

Drum: see **Lang Crossing** [NEVADA].

Drum Forebay [PLACER]: *lake,* 5.5 miles east-northeast of Dutch Flat (lat. 39°15' N, long. 120°45' W). Named on Blue Canyon (1955, photorevised 1973), Dutch Flat (1950, photorevised 1973), Washington (1950, photorevised 1979), and Westville (1952, photorevised 1973) 7.5' quadrangles. The name "Drum Forebay" recalls Frank G. Drum, president of Pacific Gas and Electric Company (Gudde, 1969, p. 94).

Drumheller Slough [COLUSA]: *stream,* heads in Glenn County and flows 7.5 miles to Butte Creek 7 miles northeast of Colusa in Colusa County (lat. 39°02'20" N, long. 121°55'15" W). Named on Butte City (1952) and Sanborn Slough (1952) 7.5' quadrangles.

Drummond Gulch [EL DORADO]: *canyon,* drained by a stream that flows less than 0.25 mile to Indian Creek (5) 2.5 miles south-southwest of Omo Ranch (lat. 38°32'35" N, long. 120°34'55" W). Named on Omo Ranch (1952) 7.5' quadrangle.

Dry Creek [AMADOR-SACRAMENTO]: *stream,* formed by the confluence of North Fork and South Fork in Amador County, flows 46 miles, including along Sacramento-San Joaquin County line, to Mokelumne River 6 miles west-southwest of Galt (lat. 38° 13'55" N, long. 121°24'35" W). Named on Amador City (1962), Clay (1968), Galt (1968), Goose Creek (1968), Ione (1962), Irish Hill (1962), Lockeford (1968), Lodi North (1968), and Thornton (1978) 7.5' quadrangles. North Fork is 10 miles long and is named on Amador City (1962), Aukum (1952), Fiddletown (1949), and Pine Grove (1948) 7.5' quadrangles. South Fork is 12.5 miles long and is named on Amador City (1962), Pine Grove (1948), and West Point (1948) 7.5' quadrangles; present South Fork is called Dry Creek on Jackson (1902) and Placerville (1893) 30' quadrangles. Camp's (1962) map shows a stream called Slate Creek that joins North Fork Dry Creek from the east 2.5 miles east of Plymouth, and a place called Suckertown located on the north side of Slate Creek nearly 5 miles east of Plymouth.

Dry Creek [EL DORADO]: *stream,* flows 8 miles to Weber Creek 5 miles north-northwest of Shingle Springs (lat. 38°44'10" N, long. 120°57' W; sec. 11, T 10 N, R 9 E). Named on Placerville (1949) and Shingle Springs (1949) 7.5' quadrangles.

Dry Creek [NEVADA-YUBA]: *stream,* heads in Nevada County and flows 19 miles to Bear River 8 miles south of Olivehurst in Yuba County (lat. 38°58'25" N, long. 121°31'25" W; near E line sec. 16, T 13 N, R 4 E). Named on Camp Far West (1949), Nicolaus (1952), Rough and Ready (1949), Sheridan (1953), Wheatland (1947, photorevised 1973), and Wolf (1949) 7.5' quadrangles.

Dry Creek [PLACER]: *stream,* flows 8 miles to join Orr Creek and form Coon Creek 6.25 miles north-northwest of Auburn (lat. 38° 58'30" N, long. 121°08'15" W; sec. 13, T 13 N, R 7 E). Named on Auburn (1953) and Gold Hill (1954) 7.5' quadrangles. Called South Fork Dry Creek on Sacramento (1892) 30' quadrangle. On Sacramento (1892) 30' quadrangle, present Orr Creek is called North Fork Dry Creek.

Dry Creek [PLACER-SACRAMENTO]: *stream,* formed in Placer County by the confluence of Antelope Creek and the stream in Miners Ravine, flows 15 miles to a drainage canal 2.25 miles southwest of Rio Linda in Sacramento County (lat. 38°39'50" N, long. 121°28'35" W; sec. 6, T 9 N, R 5 E). Named on Citrus Heights (1967), Rio Linda (1967), and Roseville (1967) 7.5' quadrangles. Called Linda Creek on Antelope (1911) and Arcade (1911) 7.5' quadrangles, and called Antelope Creek above the junction with present Cirby Creek on Antelope (1911) 7.5' quadrangle. United States Board on Geographic Names (1968a, p. 6) rejected the names "Linda Creek" and "Rio Linda Creek" for the stream.

Dry Creek [SACRAMENTO]: *locality,* at present Rio Linda along Northern Electric Railroad (lat. 38°41'30" N, long. 121°26'55" W); the place is near Linda Creek—present Dry Creek [PLACER-SACRAMENTO]. Named on Arcade (1911) 7.5' quadrangle.

Dry Creek [SIERRA-NEVADA]: *stream,* heads in Sierra County and flows 3.5 miles to Boca Reservoir 8 miles north-northeast of Truckee in Nevada County (lat. 39°25'35" N, long. 120°06' W; sec. 9, T 18 N, R 17 E). Named on Boca (1955) and Hobart Mills (1981) 7.5' quadrangles.

Dry Creek [YOLO]: *stream,* flows 9.5 miles to Putah Creek 0.5 mile south-southwest of Winters (lat. 38°30'55" N, long. 121°58'25" W). Named on Monticello Dam (1959) and Winters (1953) 7.5' quadrangles.

Dry Creek [YUBA]: *stream,* flows 29 miles to Yuba River 1.5 miles south of Browns Valley (lat. 39°13'15" N, long. 121°24'25" W; near SW cor. sec. 22, T 16 N, R 5 E). Named on Browns Valley (1947, photorevised 1973), Challenge (1948), Oregon House (1948), Rackerby (1948), and Smartville (1951) 7.5' quadrangles. Wescoatt's (1861) map shows a place called Ousleys Bar situated on the south side of Yuba River opposite the mouth of Dry Creek. Postal authorities established Owsley's Bar post office in 1855 and discontinued it in 1865 (Frickstad, p. 223). The name was for Dr. Ousley (or Owsley) of Missouri (Gudde, 1975, p. 257). Wescoatt's (1861) map also shows a community called Sand Flat situated on the southeast side of Yuba River just below Ousleys Bar.

Dry Creek: see **Best Slough** [YUBA]; **Linda Creek** [PLACER-SACRAMENTO]; **Little Dry Creek** [NEVADA]; **Little Dry Creek** [YUBA]; **Long Bar** [YUBA] (2).

Dry Diggings: see **Placerville** [EL DORADO].

Dry Flat [SIERRA]: *area,* 6 miles south-southeast of Loyalton (lat. 39°36' N, long. 120°11'45" W; near W line sec. 10, T 20 N, R 16 E). Named on Sardine Peak (1981) 7.5' quadrangle.

Dry Gulch [EL DORADO]: *canyon,* drained by a stream that flows 2 miles to Clear Creek (1) 9.5 miles east-southeast of Placerville (lat. 38°41'45" N, long. 120°37'45" W). Named on Placerville (1893) 30' quadrangle.

Dry Lake [EL DORADO]: *intermittent lake,* 1500 feet long, 4.5 miles west-southwest of Pyramid Peak (lat. 38°49'05" N, long. 120°14'15" W; sec. 8, T 11 N, R 16 E). Named on Pyramid Peak (1955) 7.5' quadrangle.

Dry Lake [NEVADA]: *intermittent lake,* 0.5 mile long, 5.25 miles east of Truckee (lat. 39°19'40" N, long. 120°05'10" W; on E line sec. 16, T 17 N, R 17 E). Named on Martis Peak (1955) 7.5' quadrangle.

Dry Lakes [EL DORADO]: *intermittent lakes,* 4.5 miles north of Robbs Peak (lat. 38°59'30" N, long. 120°24'30" W; sec. 9, T 13 N, R 14 E). Named on Robbs Peak (1950) 7.5' quadrangle.

Dry Meadow [SIERRA]: *area,* 8.5 miles south-southeast of Sierraville (lat. 39°28'30" N, long. 120°19'40" W; at SE cor. sec. 20, T 19 N, R 15 E). Named on Independence Lake (1981) 7.5' quadrangle.

Dry Slough [COLUSA]: *water feature,* 7.5 miles long; a mostly dry watercourse that joins Sycamore Slough 5 miles northwest of Grimes (lat. 39°07'55" N, long. 122°56'55" W). Named on Grimes (1954) 7.5' quadrangle.

Dry Slough [YOLO]: *stream,* flows 15 miles from near Winters to Willow Slough 4.25 miles north-northwest of Davis (lat. 38°36'10" N, long. 121°46' W; at E line sec. 29, T 9 N, R 2 E). Named on Merritt (1952) and Winters (1953) 7.5' quadrangles.

Dry Slough: see **Best Slough** [YUBA].

Drytown [AMADOR]: *village,* 2.5 miles south of Plymouth (lat. 38°26'25" N, long. 120°51'15" W; near SW cor. sec. 23, T 7 N, R 10 E); the village is along Dry Creek. Named on Amador City (1962) 7.5' quadrangle. Eddy's (1854) map has the form "Dry Town" for the name. Postal authorities established Drytown post office before January 21, 1852 (Salley, p. 62). Camp's (1962) map shows a place called Snake Flat located 1.5 miles east of Drytown, a place called Old Rancheria situated about 1 mile south-southeast of Drytown, and a place called Lower Rancheria located 2 miles east-southeast of Drytown along Rancheria Creek. Placer mining began at Lower Rancheria in 1848 (Hoover, Rensch, and Rensch, p. 31).

Dry Valley Creek: see **Long Valley Creek** [SIERRA] (1).

Du Bois Spring [YOLO]: *spring,* 3 miles northeast of Guinda (lat. 38°51'40" N, long. 122°09'20" W; sec. 26, T 12 N, R 3 W); the spring is 0.5 mile west of Indian Mike Spring. Named on Guinda (1959) 7.5' quadrangle. Called Indian Mike Spring on Rumsey (1945) 15' quadrangle, but United States Board on Geographic Names (1962b, p. 16) rejected this name for it.

Duck Island [SACRAMENTO]: *island,* 4400 feet long, 4.25 miles west-southwest of Isleton along Sacramento River (lat. 38°08'45" N, long. 121°41' W). Named on Rio Vista (1910) 7.5' quadrangle.

Duck Lake [EL DORADO]: *lake,* 1000 feet long, 3.5 miles southwest of the town of Meeks Bay (lat. 39°00'35" N, long. 120°10'45" W; on S line sec. 35, T 14 N, R 16 E). Named on Homewood (1955) 7.5' quadrangle.

Duck Slough [YOLO]: *water feature,* extends for 6 miles southwesterly from a canal 3 miles southwest of Clarksburg to Solano County 9 miles south-southwest of Clarksburg (lat. 38°18'50" N, long. 121°36'55" W). Named on Clarksburg (1967) and Courtland (1978) 7.5' quadrangles.

Dufftown: see **Kelsey** [EL DORADO].

Dufour [YOLO]: *locality,* 11 miles southeast of Dunnigan along Southern Pacific Railroad (lat. 38°45'45" N, long. 121°50'30" W; near E line sec. 34, T 11 N, R 1 E). Named on Eldorado Bend (1952) 7.5' quadrangle.

Dufrene Camp [AMADOR]: *locality,* 8 miles west-northwest of Mokelumne Peak (lat. 38°34'40" N, long. 120°14'05" W; sec. 5, T 8 N, R 16 E). Named on Bear River Reservoir (1979) 7.5' quadrangle.

Dufresne Gulch [AMADOR]: *canyon,* less than 1 mile long, opens into the canyon of Mokelumne River 5 miles south-southwest of Jackson (lat. 38°17' N, long. 120°49'05" W; sec. 13, T 5 N, R 10 E). Named on Jackson (1962) 7.5' quadrangle. Water of Pardee Reservoir now floods the lower part of the canyon.

Dugan [EL DORADO]: *locality,* 3.25 miles north-northeast of Latrobe along Southern Pacific Railroad (lat. 38°36'20" N, long. 120°57'25" W; sec. 26, T 9 N, R 9 E). Named on Latrobe (1949) 7.5' quadrangle.

Dugan Pond [SIERRA]: *lake,* 400 feet long, nearly 4 miles north of Sierra City (lat. 39°37'10" N, long. 120°38'45" W; near N line sec. 8, T 20 N, R 12 E). Named on Sierra City (1981) 7.5' quadrangle.

Dulzura Lake: see **Ice Lakes** [PLACER].

Duncan Canyon [PLACER]: *canyon,* drained by a stream that flows 13 miles to Middle Fork American River 8 miles south of Duncan Peak (lat. 39°02'20" N, long. 120°32'40" W; sec. 29, T 14 N, R 13 E). Named on Bunker Hill (1953), Greek Store (1952), and Royal Gorge (1953) 7.5' quadrangles. The name commemorates Thomas Duncan, who came to California in 1848 and led an expedition to the canyon in 1850 in a futile search for gold (Hoover, Rensch, and Rensch, p. 277). Colfax (1938) 30' quadrangle shows Duncan Creek in the canyon.

Duncan Canyon: see **Little Duncan Canyon** [PLACER].

Duncan Corral [EL DORADO]: *locality,* 4.5 miles south-southwest of Old Iron Mountain (lat. 38°38'45" N, long. 120°25'15" W; at W line sec. 10, T 9 N, R 14 E). Named on Stump Spring (1951) 7.5' quadrangle.

Duncan Creek: see **Duncan Canyon** [PLACER].

Duncan Hill [PLACER]: *peak,* 1.5 miles west of downtown Auburn (lat. 38°53'55" N, long. 121°05'45" W; at NW cor. sec. 16, T 12 N, R 8 E). Named on Auburn (1953) 7.5' quadrangle.

Duncan Peak [PLACER]: *peak,* 7.5 miles east of Westville (lat. 39° 09'15" N, long. 120°30'45" W; at S line sec. 10, T 15 N, R 13 E). Altitude 7116 feet. Named on Duncan Peak (1952) 7.5' quadrangle.

Duncan Spring [YOLO]: *spring,* 3.5 miles southwest of Guinda (lat. 38°47'55" N, long. 122°14'55" W; near SE cor. sec. 13, T 11 N, R 4 W). Named on Guinda (1959) 7.5' quadrangle.

Dunfield Spring [COLUSA]: *spring,* 5 miles south of Wilbur Springs (lat. 38°58'20" N, long. 122°24'10" W; sec. 15, T 13 N, R 5 W). Named on Wilson Valley (1958) 7.5' quadrangle.

Dunnigan [YOLO]: *village,* 18 miles northwest of Woodland (lat. 38°53'05" N, long. 121°58'05" W; near SW cor. sec. 15, T 12 N, R 1 W). Named on Dunnigan (1953) 7.5' quadrangle. Postal authorities established Antelope post office in 1856 and changed the name to Dunnigan in 1876 (Frickstad, p. 220). The name commemorates A.W. Dunnigan, who settled at the place in 1853 (Gudde, 1949, p. 101).

Dunnigan Creek [YOLO]: *stream,* flows 2.25 miles to an artificial watercourse 1 mile west-northwest of Dunnigan (lat. 38°53'15" N, long. 121°59'05" W; sec. 13, T 12 N, R 1 W); the stream heads in Dunnigan Hills. Named on Dunnigan (1953) and Wildwood School (1959) 7.5' quadrangles.

Dunnigan Hills [YOLO]: *range,* extends southwest from a place west of Dunnigan to Cache Creek 5 miles west-northwest of Woodland. Named on Bird Valley (1959), Dunnigan (1953), Eldorado Bend (1952), Madison (1953), Wildwood School (1959), Woodland (1952), and Zamora (1953) 7.5' quadrangles.

Dunns Ferry [COLUSA-SUTTER]:

(1) *locality,* 4 miles north-northwest of Grimes Landing (present Grimes) along Sacramento River on Colusa-Sutter County line (lat. 39°07'50" N, long. 121°55'25" W). Named on Marysville (1895) 30' quadrangle.

(2) *locality,* 1.25 miles east-northeast of present Grimes along Sacramento River on Colusa-Sutter County line (lat. 39°04'05" N, long. 121°52'15" W). Named on Tisdale Weir (1912) 7.5' quadrangle.

Durgans Flat: see **Downieville** [SIERRA].

Du Rock [EL DORADO]: *locality,* 2.5 miles west-southwest of Shingle Springs (lat. 38°39'05" N, long. 120°58'10" W). Named on Placerville (1893) 30' quadrangle. Postal authorities established El Dorado Ranch post office 8 miles west of El Dorado in 1857, changed the name to Duroc in 1858, and discontinued it in 1864 (Salley, p. 63, 66).

Dutch Canyon [EL DORADO]: *canyon,* drained by a stream that flows 2.25 miles to Rock Creek 11 miles northwest of Pollock Pines (lat. 38°51'10" N, long. 120°44'50" W; near NE cor. sec. 33, T 12 N, R 11 E). Named on Garden Valley (1949), Georgetown (1949), and Slate Mountain (1950) 7.5' quadrangles.

Dutch Charlie's Flat: see **Dutch Flat** [PLACER].

Dutch Creek [EL DORADO]: *stream,* flows 5 miles to South Fork American River 0.5 mile east of Coloma (lat. 38°47'55" N, long. 120°52'50" W; near S line sec. 17, T 11 N, R 10 E). Named on Coloma (1949) and Garden Valley (1949) 7.5' quadrangles. Two mining camps, each called Dutch Creek, were located at the headwaters of the stream (Gernes, p. 34).

Dutch Flat [PLACER]: *village,* 9.5 miles northeast of Colfax (lat. 39°12'20" N, long. 120°50'15" W; sec. 34, T 16 N, R 10 E). Named on Dutch Flat (1950) 7.5' quadrangle. Postal authorities established Dutch Flat post office in 1856 (Frickstad, p. 120). Charles Dornbach and Joseph Dornbach settled at the site in 1851; the place was known as Dutch Charlie's Flat, or Charley's Flat, before the post office opened (Gudde, 1975, p. 104).

Dutch Flat Canyon [PLACER]: *canyon,* drained by a stream that flows 1 mile to Bear River 1 mile west of Dutch Flat (lat. 39°12'15" N, long. 120°51'20" W; sec. 33, T 16 N, R 10 E); the canyon heads near Dutch Flat. Named on Dutch Flat (1950) 7.5' quadrangle.

Dutch Flat Station [PLACER]: *locality,* 1 mile south-southeast of Dutch Flat along Southern Pacific Railroad (lat. 39°11'30" N, long. 120°49'55" W; sec. 3, T 15 N, R 10 E). Named on Dutch Flat (1950) 7.5' quadrangle. Whitney's (1873) map has the designation "Station" for the locality. Colfax (1898) 30' quadrangle shows a place called Chinatown at or near present Dutch Flat Station.

Dutchmans Ranch: see **Ramms Ranch** [YUBA].

Dutch Ravine [EL DORADO]: *canyon,* drained by a stream that flows less than 1 mile to Green Spring Creek 4 miles north-northwest of Clarksville (lat. 38°42'35" N, long. 121°04'10" W; sec. 23, T 10 N, R 8 E). Named on Clarksville (1953) 7.5' quadrangle.

Dutch Ravine [PLACER]: *canyon,* drained by a stream that flows nearly 7 miles to Auburn Ravine 6 miles west of Auburn (lat. 38° 54' N, long. 121°11'05" W; sec. 10, T 12 N, R 7 E). Named on Auburn (1953) and Gold Hill (1954) 7.5' quadrangles.

Dutchtown: see **Spanish Dry Diggings** [EL DORADO].

Dutschke Hill [AMADOR]: *hill,* 3.5 miles west-northwest of Ione (lat. 38°22' N, long 120°59'35" W). Altitude 648 feet. Named on Ione (1962) 7.5' quadrangle. Called Jones Butte on Jackson (1902) 30' quadrangle, but United States Board on Geographic Names (1964, p. 9) rejected the name "Jones Butte" and pointed out that the name "Dutschke Hill" commemorates the pioneer family of Charles Dutschke.

Dyers Mill [EL DORADO]: *locality,* 5.5 miles north-northeast of Omo Ranch (lat. 38°39'30" N, long. 120°33'20" W). Named on Placerville (1893) 30' quadrangle.

— E —

Eagle Bay: see **Emerald Bay** [EL DORADO] (1).

Eagle Bird [NEVADA]: *locality,* 6.25 miles south-southeast of Graniteville along South Fork Yuba River (present South Yuba River) (lat. 39°20'40" N, long. 120°41'40" W). Named on Colfax (1898) 30' quadrangle. Colfax (1938) 30' quadrangle shows Eagle Bird mine at the place.

Eagle Cliff: see **Eagle Rock** [PLACER].

Eagle Falls [EL DORADO]: *waterfall,* 3.25 miles north-northwest of Mount Tallac (lat. 38°57'05" N, long. 120°06'35" W; near S line sec. 21, T 13 N, R 17 E). Named on Emerald Bay (1955) 7.5' quadrangle. The feature also was called Emerald Bay Falls—present Emerald Bay (1) had the name "Eagle Bay" in the early days (Lekisch, p. 32).

Eagle Falls Campground [EL DORADO]: *locality,* 3.25 miles north-northwest of Mount Tallac (lat. 38°57'10" N, long. 120°06'45" W; near SW cor. sec. 21, T 13 N, R 17 E); the place is near Eagle Falls. Named on Emerald Bay (1955) 7.5' quadrangle.

Eagle Gulch [YUBA]: *canyon,* drained by a stream that flows 0.5 mile to Butte County 1 mile west of Strawberry Valley (lat. 39° 33'50" N, long. 121°07'40" W; near W line sec. 30, T 20 N, R 8 E). Named on Clipper Mills (1948) and Strawberry Valley (1948) 7.5' quadrangles.

Eagle Lake [EL DORADO]: *lake,* 1350 feet long, nearly 3 miles north-northwest of Mount Tallac (lat. 38°56'30" N, long. 120°07'15" W; sec. 29, T 13 N, R 17 E). Named on Emerald Bay (1955) 7.5' quadrangle.

Eagle Lakes [NEVADA]: *lakes,* largest 2350 feet long, 3.5 miles northeast of Yuba Gap (lat. 39°21'15" N, long. 120°34'35" W; sec. 12, T 17 N, R 12 E). Named on Cisco Grove (1955) 7.5' quadrangle. Colfax (1938) 30' quadrangle has the name "Eagle Lake" for one of the lakes, but United States Board on Geographic Names (1962c, p. 18) rejected this name.

Eagle Point [EL DORADO]: *promontory,* 4.25 miles north-northeast of Mount Tallac along Lake Tahoe (lat. 38°57'55" N, long. 120°04'40" W). Named on Emerald Bay (1955) 7.5' quadrangle.

Eagle Ravine [NEVADA]: *canyon,* drained by a stream that flows less than 1 mile to Deer Creek 1 mile east-northeast of downtown Nevada City (lat. 39°16'05" N, long. 121°00'10" W; near E line sec. 7, T 16 N, R 9 E).

Named on Nevada City (1948) 7.5' quadrangle.

Eagle Rock [COLUSA]: *relief feature,* 3.5 miles northwest of Wilbur Springs (lat. 39°03'45" N, long. 122°27'15" W; sec. 18, T 14 N, R 5 W). Named on Wilbur Springs (1961) 15' quadrangle.

Eagle Rock [EL DORADO]: *peak,* 1.5 miles east-southeast of Kyburz (lat. 38°46'05" N, long. 120°16'05" W; near E line sec. 26, T 11 N, R 15 E). Altitude 6270 feet. Named on Kyburz (1952) 7.5' quadrangle.

Eagle Rock [PLACER]: *hill,* 1.5 miles north of Homewood (lat. 39° 06'35" N, long. 120°09'40" W; near N line sec. 36, T 15 N, R 16 E). Named on Homewood (1955) 7.5' quadrangle. The feature also was called Eagle Cliff (Lekisch, p. 32).

Eagleville [YUBA]: *locality,* 1.25 miles north-northeast of Strawberry Valley (lat. 39°34'45" N, long. 121°05'45" W; near W line sec. 21, T 20 N, R 8 E). Named on Strawberry Valley (1948) 7.5' quadrangle. The place was settled about 1851 and named for nearby Eagle mine (Gudde, 1975, p. 105). Wescoatt's (1861) map shows Union Hotel located south-southwest of Eagleville about halfway to Strawberry Valley. A travelers stop called Seneca House was between Union Hotel and Strawberry Valley (Hoover, Rensch, and Rensch, p. 594).

Early Creek [YUBA]: *stream,* flows 2.25 miles to Tennessee Creek 2.25 miles northeast of Loma Rica (lat. 39°20'05" N, long. 121°23'15" W; near W line sec. 14, T 17 N, R 5 E). Named on Loma Rica (1947) and Oregon House (1948) 7.5' quadrangles.

East Applegate: see **Applegate** [PLACER].

East Arboga [YUBA]: *locality,* 2.5 miles south of Olivehurst along Western Pacific Railroad (lat. 39°03'25" N, long. 121°33' W; near S line sec. 17, T 14 N, R 4 E); the place is 0.5 mile east-northeast of Arboga. Named on Olivehurst (1952) 7.5' quadrangle. Called Arboga on California Mining Bureau's (1917c) map, which shows a place called Oso located 1.5 miles south of Arboga (present East Arboga) along the railroad.

East Auburn: see **Auburn** [PLACER].

East Big Canyon Creek [EL DORADO]: *stream,* flows nearly 5 miles to North Fork Cosumnes River 12 miles south of Placerville (lat. 38°33'40" N, long. 120°50'40" W; sec. 11, T 8 N, R 10 E). Named on Fiddletown (1949) 7.5' quadrangle. Called Big Canyon Creek on Placerville (1893) 30' quadrangle.

East Boca Canyon [NEVADA]: *canyon,* drained by a stream that flows 3 miles to Boca Reservoir 7.5 miles northeast of Truckee (lat. 39°24'20" N, long. 120°05'05" W; near SW cor. sec. 15, T 18 N, R 17 E). Named on Boca (1955) 7.5' quadrangle.

East Boca Spring [NEVADA]: *spring,* 9 miles northeast of Truckee (lat. 39°24'55" N, long. 120°03'50" W; near NW cor. sec. 14, T 18 N, R 17 E); the spring is in East Boca Canyon. Named on Boca (1955) 7.5' quadrangle.

Eastern Canyon [NEVADA]: *canyon,* drained by a stream that flows 3 miles to South Yuba River 2 miles southeast of North Bloomfield (lat. 39°20'50" N, long. 120°52'35" W; near S line sec. 8, T 17 N, R 10 E). Named on Alleghany (1949), North Bloomfield (1949), and Washington (1950) 7.5' quadrangles.

East Fork Creek [NEVADA]: *stream,* flows 8 miles to Middle Yuba River 3 miles north-northeast of Graniteville (lat. 39°29' N, long. 120°42'45" W; sec. 26, T 19 N, R 11 E). Named on English Mountain (1983) and Graniteville (1982) 7.5' quadrangles. Called South Fork [of Middle Fork Yuba River] on Colfax (1898) 30' quadrangle.

Eastham: see **Knights Landing** [YOLO].

East Indian Creek: see **Indian Creek** [EL DORADO] (5).

East Martis Creek [PLACER]: *stream,* flows 5.25 miles to join Martis Creek near Nevada-Placer County line almost 5 miles west-northwest of Martis Peak (lat. 39°19'05" N, long. 120°06'50" W; near S line sec. 17, T 17 N, R 17 E). Named on Martis Peak (1955) 7.5' quadrangle.

East Meadow Campground [SIERRA]: *locality,* 7 miles southeast of Sierra City (lat. 39°30'05" N, long. 120°31'55" W; near E line sec. 20, T 19 N, R 13 E). Named on Haypress Valley (1981) 7.5' quadrangle.

East Nicolaus [SUTTER]: *settlement,* nearly 2 miles east-northeast of Nicolaus (lat. 38°54'35" N, long. 121°32'35" W; at NE cor. sec. 8, T 12 N, R 4 E). Named on Nicolaus (1952) 7.5' quadrangle. Called Nicolaus Sta. on Nicolaus (1910) 7.5' quadrangle, which shows the place along Northern Electric Railroad. Postal authorities established East Nicolaus post office in 1915 (Frickstad, p. 202). California Division of Highways' (1934) map shows a place called Stolp located less than 1 mile north of East Nicolaus along Sacramento Northern Railroad.

East Panther Creek [AMADOR]: *stream,* flows 7.5 miles to join West Panther Creek and form Panther Creek 4.5 miles south-southwest of Hams Station (lat. 38°29'10" N, long. 120°24'05" W; sec. 2, T 7 N, R 14 E); the stream is east of Panther Ridge. Named on Devils Nose (1979), Garnet Hill (1979), and Peddler Hill (1951) 7.5' quadrangles.

East Park Reservoir [COLUSA]: *lake,* behind a dam on Little Stony Creek 2 miles east-southeast of Stonyford (lat. 39°21'40" N, long. 122°30'45" W; sec. 3, T 17 N, R 6 W). Named on Lodoga (1960) and Stonyford (1951) 15' quadrangles.

East Scotties Canyon [COLUSA]: *canyon,* drained by a stream that flows 1 mile to Grapevine Creek 3.5 miles east of Lodoga (lat. 39° 18'20" N, long. 122°25'15" W; sec. 21, T 17 N, R 5 W); the mouth of the canyon is 400 feet north of the mouth of Scotties Canyon. Named on Lodoga (1960) 15' quadrangle.

East Slope [YOLO]: *area,* 5 miles west-southwest of Esparto (lat. 38°39'30" N, long. 122°06' W). Named on Esparto (1959) 7.5' quadrangle.

Eastwoods [EL DORADO]: *locality,* 14 miles east of Placerville along Sly Park Creek (lat. 38°43'50" N, long. 120°32'15" W). Named on Placerville (1893) 30' quadrangle.

Eaton Springs [COLUSA]: *springs,* 3.5 miles north-northwest of Wilbur Springs (lat. 39°04'50" N, long. 122°27'25" W; near N line sec. 7, T 14 N, R 5 W). Named on Wilbur Springs (1961) 15' quadrangle.

Echo [EL DORADO]: *locality,* 3.25 miles south-southeast of Pyramid Peak in Strawberry Valley at present Strawberry (lat. 38°47'55" N, long. 120°08'35" W). Named on Pyramid Peak (1896) 30' quadrangle.

Echo: see **Echo Lake** [EL DORADO].

Echo Lake [EL DORADO]: *locality,* 1.5 miles north-northwest of Echo Summit (lat. 38°50' N, long. 120°02'25" W; sec. 6, T 11 N, R 18 E); the place is near the east end of Lower Echo Lake. Named on Echo Lake (1955) 7.5' quadrangle. Postal authorities established Echo post office in 1888, discontinued it in 1910, reestablished it in 1911, discontinued it in 1913, reestablished it with the name "Echo Lake" in 1926, and discontinued it in 1973 (Salley, p. 65).

Echo Lake [NEVADA]: *lake,* 700 feet long, 900 feet east-northeast of English Mountain (lat. 39°26'50" N, long. 120°32'50" W; at NW cor. sec. 8, T 18 N, R 13 E). Named on English Mountain (1983) 7.5' quadrangle.

Echo Lake: see **Lower Echo Lake** [EL DORADO]; **Upper Echo Lake** [EL DORADO].

Echo Peak [EL DORADO]: *peak,* 4 miles northwest of Echo Summit (lat. 38°51'25" N, long. 120°04'20" W; sec. 26, T 12 N, R 17 E). Altitude 8895 feet. Named on Echo Lake (1955) 7.5' quadrangle.

Echo Summit [EL DORADO]: *pass,* 7.25 miles east-southeast of Pyramid Peak (lat. 38°48'45" N, long. 120°01'45" W; sec. 7, T 11 N, R 18 E). Named on Echo Lake (1955) 7.5' quadrangle. The feature was called Johnson Pass in the early days (Zauner, p. 7).

Eddys Ferry [COLUSA-SUTTER]: *locality,* about 1.5 miles east-southeast of Grimes along Sacramento River on Colusa-Sutter County line (lat. 39°04' N, long. 121°52'10" W; sec. 16, T 14 N, R 1 E). Site named on Tisdale Weir (1952) 7.5' quadrangle. F.S. Cook (b, p. 29) referred to Eddy's Landing located about a mile below Grimes. Tisdale Weir (1912) 7.5' quadrangle shows Dunns Ferry (2) near the site.

Eddy's Landing: see **Eddys Ferry** [COLUSA-SUTTER].

Eden Valley [PLACER]: *canyon,* 1.5 miles long, 3.25 miles south-southwest of Colfax (lat. 39°03'35" N, long. 120°59' W). Named on Colfax (1949) 7.5' quadrangle.

Eder [PLACER]: *locality,* 2 miles southeast of Donner Pass along Southern Pacific Railroad (lat. 38°18' N, long. 120°17'30" W; at NE cor. sec. 27, T 17 N, R 15 E). Named on Norden (1955) 7.5' quadrangle.

Edgar Peak [YOLO]: *peak,* 7 miles southwest of Esparto (lat. 38°36'55" N, long. 122°05'45" W; sec. 21, T 9 N, R 2 W). Altitude 2256 feet. Named on Monticello Dam (1959) 7.5' quadrangle.

Edison Cabin [EL DORADO]: *locality,* 16 miles north-northwest of Pollock Pines (lat. 38°58'15" N, long. 120°42'10" W; near SW cor. sec. 13, T 13 N, R 11 E). Named on Tunnel Hill (1950) 7.5' quadrangle. Called Edson Cabin on Saddle Mountain (1950) 15' quadrangle.

Edson: see **Lake Edson** and **Mark Edson Reservoir**, under **Stumpy Meadows Lake** [EL DORADO].

Edson Cabin: see **Edison Cabin** [EL DORADO].

Edwards Break [SACRAMENTO]: *locality,* 3 miles south-southwest of downtown Sacramento along Sacramento River (lat. 38°32'05" N, long. 121°31' W). Named on Lovdal (1916) 7.5' quadrangle.

Edward's Bridge: see **Edwards Crossing** [NEVADA].

Edwards Crossing [NEVADA]: *locality,* 5.25 miles west-southwest of North Bloomfield along South Yuba River (lat. 39°19'50" N, long. 120°59' W; near SE cor. sec. 17, T 17 N, R 9 E). Named on North Bloomfield (1949) 7.5' quadrangle. Called Edwards Bridge on Colfax (1898) 30' quadrangle. The place also was known as Edward's Bridge, Robinson's Crossing, and Black's Bridge (Hoover, Rensch, and Rensch, p. 249).

Edwin [AMADOR]: *locality,* 1.5 miles west-northwest of Ione along Southern Pacific Railroad (lat. 38°22'40" N, long. 120°59'10" W). Named on Irish Hill (1962) 7.5' quadrangle.

Egan: see **Dobbins** [YUBA].

Egbert Hill [NEVADA]: *peak,* 1.5 miles northeast of Higgins Corner (lat. 39°03'20" N, long. 121°04'15" W; near N line sec. 22, T 14 N, R 8 E). Altitude 1741 feet. Named on Lake Combie (1949) 7.5' quadrangle.

Eggers [EL DORADO]: *locality,* 3.5 miles north of Shingle Springs (lat. 38°42'50" N, long. 120°56'25" W). Named on Placerville (1893) 30' quadrangle.

Eggman Canyon [COLUSA]: *canyon,* drained by a stream that flows 3.5 miles to Grapevine Creek 4 miles west-southwest of Sites (lat. 39°17'10" N, long. 122°24'20" W; sec. 34, T 17 N, R 5 W). Named on Lodoga (1960)

15' quadrangle.

Eight Mile House [EL DORADO]: *locality,* 1 mile east-northeast of Camino (lat. 38°44'30" N, long. 120°39'35" W; near S line sec. 4, T 10 N, R 12 E). Named on Camino (1952) 15' quadrangle. Wheeler (1878, p. 60) called the place Painter's Station.

Elbert Lake [EL DORADO]: *lake,* 1100 feet long, 2.5 miles south of Echo Summit (lat. 38°46'30" N, long. 120°02' W; sec. 30, T 11 N, R 18 E). Named on Echo Lake (1955) 7.5' quadrangle. The feature also was called Little Alberts Lake (Lekisch, p. 38).

Elbow Bar [YUBA]: *locality,* 4.25 miles east of Challenge along North Yuba River (lat. 39°29'15" N, long. 121°08'35" W; sec. 24, T 19 N, R 7 E). Named on Nevada City (1948) 15' quadrangle. Water of New Bullards Bar Reservoir now covers the site. Prospectors found gold at the place in 1850; the name was given for the shape of the river bar (Gudde, 1975, p. 107).

Elder Creek [SACRAMENTO]: *stream,* flows 13 miles to Morrison Creek 7 miles south-southeast of downtown Sacramento (lat. 38° 28'40" N, long. 121°27'35" W; sec. 8, T 7 N, R 5 E). Named on Carmichael (1967), Elk Grove (1968), and Florin (1968) 7.5' quadrangles.

Elders Corner [PLACER]: *locality,* 4.25 miles north-northwest of downtown Auburn (lat. 38°57'25" N, long. 121°06' W; on S line sec. 20, T 13 N, R 8 E). Named on Auburn (1953) 7.5' quadrangle.

El Dorado [EL DORADO]: *town,* 4 miles southwest of Placerville (lat. 38°40'55" N, long. 120°50'45" W; sec. 35, T 10 N, R 10 E). Named on Placerville (1949) 7.5' quadrangle. Called Mud Springs on Placerville (1893) 30' quadrangle. California Mining Bureau's (1909a) map has the form "Eldorado" for the name. Postal authorities established Mud Spring post office in 1851 and changed the name to El Dorado in 1855 (Frickstad, p. 28). The town incorporated in 1855 and disincorporated in 1857 (Bancroft, 1888, p. 482). The name "Mud Springs" was from the muddy ground around springs that emigrants used to water their stock (Hoover, Rensch, and Rensch, p. 82). California Division of Highways' (1934) map shows a place called Cummings located about 2 miles west of El Dorado along Southern Pacific Railroad (sec. 33, T 10 N, R 10 E). Postal authorities established Aurum City post office 2 miles southeast of El Dorado in 1852 and discontinued it in 1853 (Salley, p. 12). A place called Uniontown was situated about 2 miles southeast of El Dorado along Martinez Creek; the name was from Union mine (Gudde, 1975, p. 356), which Placerville (1949) 7.5' quadrangle shows 2.5 miles south-southeast of El Dorado near Martinez Creek (sec. 12, T 9 N, R 10 E).

Eldorado: see **Camp Eldorado**, under **Camp Silverado** [AMADOR]; **Eliza Bend** [SUTTER-YUBA].

El Dorado Beach [EL DORADO]: *beach,* 7.25 miles north-northwest of Freel Peak along Lake Tahoe (lat. 38°56'45" N, long. 119°58'25" W). Named on South Lake Tahoe (1955) 7.5' quadrangle.

Eldorado Bend [SUTTER-YOLO]: *bend,* 3.5 miles south of Kirkville along Sacramento River on Sutter-Yolo County line (lat. 38°51'25" N, long. 121°47' W; at W line sec. 29, T 12 N, R 2 E). Named on Eldorado Bend (1952) 7.5' quadrangle. California Division of Highways' (1934) map shows a place called Ayrshire located less than 1 mile southeast of Eldorado Bend along Southern Pacific Railroad in Yolo County.

El Dorado Canyon [PLACER]: *canyon,* 2.25 miles long, opens into the canyon of North Fork of Middle Fork American River 1.5 miles east-southeast of Michigan Bluff (lat. 39°02' N, long. 120°42'30" W; sec. 26, T 14 N, R 11 E). Named on Michigan Bluff (1952) 7.5' quadrangle. The feature divides at the head into East Branch and West Branch. East Branch is 11 miles long and is named on Michigan Bluff (1952) and Westville (1952) 7.5' quadrangles. The stream in East Branch is called Indian Creek on Colfax (1898) 30' quadrangle. West Branch is 6.5 miles long and is named on Michigan Bluff (1952) and Westville (1952) 7.5' quadrangles. The upper part of West Branch is called Forks House Ravine on Colfax (1898) 30' quadrangle. The stream in West Branch is called El Dorado Creek on Colfax (1898) 30' quadrangle, and is called Bullion Creek on Colfax (1938) 30' quadrangle. Middle Branch opens into West Branch 4.25 miles north-northeast of Michigan Bluff; it is 1.5 miles long and is named on Michigan Bluff (1952) 7.5' quadrangle.

El Dorado Creek: see **El Dorado Canyon** [PLACER].

El Dorado Hills [EL DORADO]: *town,* 1.5 miles west-northwest of Clarksville (lat. 38°39'45" N, long. 121°04'30" W). Named on Clarksville (1953, photorevised 1980) 7.5' quadrangle.

El Dorado Ranch: see **Du Rock** [EL DORADO].

Electra [AMADOR]: *locality,* nearly 3 miles east-southeast of Jackson Butte on the north side of Mokelumne River (lat. 38°19'55" N, long. 120°40'10" W; near E line sec. 32, T 6 N, R 12 E). Named on Mokelumne Hill (1948) 7.5' quadrangle. Postal authorities established Electra post office in 1900 and discontinued it in 1923; the name is from a generating plant for electricity located along the river (Salley, p. 67). Camp's (1962) map has the name "Whites Bar" at present Electra. The same map shows a place called China City located 1.5 miles east of present Electra on the north side of Mokelumne River, and a place called Watkins Bar situated 2 miles east-northeast of present Electra on the north side of the river.

Elephants Head [SIERRA]: *peak,* 2.5 miles northeast of Loyalton (lat. 39°41'50" N, long. 120°11'55" W; near W line sec. 4, T 21 N, R 16 E). Altitude 6608 feet. Named on Loyalton (1981) 7.5' quadrangle.

Eleven Mile House: see **Colusa** [COLUSA].

Eleven Pines [EL DORADO]: *locality,* 10.5 miles north-northeast of Pollock Pines (lat. 38°54'20" N, long. 120°31'10" W; sec. 9, T 12 N, R 13 E). Named on Devil Peak (1950) 7.5' quadrangle.

Elgin Mine Hot Springs: see **Wilbur Springs** [COLUSA].

Elida: see **Rough and Ready** [NEVADA].

Eliza: see **Eliza Bend** [SUTTER-YUBA].

Eliza Bend [SUTTER-YUBA]: *bend,* 3 miles south-southeast of Yuba City along a cutoff part of Feather River on Sutter-Yuba County line (lat. 39°06'10" N, long. 121°35'20" W). Named on Olivehurst (1952) 7.5' quadrangle. Ostrom (1911) 7.5' quadrangle has the name "Eliza Bend" for present Shanghai Bend, and has the name "Shanghai Bend" for present Eliza Bend, which it has along the main course of Feather River. Gibbes' (1852) map shows a community called Eliza located in Yuba County near the bend, and a community called Eldorado situated in Yuba County just south of Eliza. Members of Kennebec Company from Massachusetts arranged with John A. Sutter to start a town on the east side of Feather River 4 miles below Marysville, and named the place Eliza for Sutter's daughter, Anna Eliza, but the project failed (Gudde, 1975, p. 108).

Elizabeth Hill: see **Refuge Canyon** [PLACER].

Elizabeth Town: see **Middle Martis Creek** [PLACER].

Elizaville: see **Forest** [SIERRA].

Elk Creek [COLUSA]: *stream,* flows 11.5 miles to Salt Creek (3) less than 1 mile west-northwest of Arbuckle (lat. 39°01'20" N, long. 122°04'05" W; sec. 34, T 14 N, R 2 W). Named on Arbuckle (1952), Rumsey (1959), and Wildwood School (1959) 7.5' quadrangles. North Fork enters 2.25 miles west-southwest of Arbuckle; it is 5 miles long and is named on Arbuckle (1952), Rumsey (1959), and Wildwood School (1959) 7.5' quadrangles. United States Board on Geographic Names (1962b, p. 19) rejected the name "Elk Creek" for North Fork.

Elk Grove [SACRAMENTO]: *town,* 13 miles south-southeast of downtown Sacramento (lat. 38°24'35" N, long. 121°22' W). Named on Elk Grove (1968) 7.5' quadrangle. Postal authorities established Elk Grove post office in 1854, discontinued it the same year, and reestablished it in 1857 (Salley, p. 67). James Hall named the place for his home in Missouri; Hall came to California in 1850 and opened a hotel at the site of the present town (Hanna, p. 96). Postal authorities established Buckner post office 21 miles south of Sacramento in 1853 and discontinued it in 1857, when they moved it to Elk Grove; the name was for James Buckner, first postmaster (Salley, p. 28).

Elk Grove Creek [SACRAMENTO]: *stream,* flows 6.5 miles to Laguna Creek 3 miles west-northwest of Elk Grove (lat. 38°25'55" N, long. 121°24'40" W; sec. 27, T 7 N, R 5 E). Named on Elk Grove (1968) and Florin (1968) 7.5' quadrangles.

Elkhorn: see **Fremont** [YOLO].

Elkhorn Ferry [SACRAMENTO-YOLO]: *locality,* 10 miles northwest of downtown Sacramento along Sacramento River on Sacramento-Yolo County line (lat. 38°40'35" N, long. 121°37'40" W; sec. 35, T 10 N, R 3 E). Named on Grays Bend (1953) 7.5' quadrangle.

Elkhorn Slough: see **Elk Slough** [YOLO].

Elkins Flat [EL DORADO]: *area,* 1.5 miles south-southwest of Caldor along Middle Dry Creek (lat. 38°35'10" N, long. 120°26'30" W; on E line sec. 32, T 9 N, R 14 E). Named on Caldor (1951) 7.5' quadrangle.

Elk Slough [YOLO]: *water feature,* extends for 9 miles from Sacramento River at Clarksburg to Sutter Slough 6.5 miles south-southwest of Clarksburg (lat. 38°19'55" N, long. 121°35' W). Named on Clarksburg (1967) and Courtland (1978) 7.5' quadrangles. Called Elkhorn Slough on Babel Slough (1916) 7.5' quadrangle, but United States Board on Geographic Names (1962a, p. 10) rejected this name for the feature.

Ellens Creek: see **Grass Valley** [NEVADA].

Ellen Spring [COLUSA]: *spring,* 4 miles west-northwest of Pacific Point (lat. 39°14'40" N, long. 122°39'40" W; near S line sec. 8, T 16 N, R 7 W). Named on Clearlake Oaks (1960) 15' quadrangle.

Ellicott [PLACER]: *locality,* 4 miles east of Devil Peak (lat. 38°57'45" N, long. 120°29' W). Named on Pyramid Peak (1896) 30' quadrangle. Robbs Peak (1950) 7.5' quadrangle shows Ellicott bridge on Rubicon River just east of the place.

Elliott Village: see **Courtland** [SACRAMENTO].

Ellis: see **Point Ellis**, under **Grand Island** [SACRAMENTO].

Ellis Creek [EL DORADO-PLACER]: *stream,* heads in Placer County and flows 2.5 miles to Pleasant Lake 2.5 miles east of Wentworth Springs in El Dorado County (lat. 39°00'45" N, long. 120°17'50" W; sec. 33, T 14 N, R 15 E). Named on Granite Chief (1953) 15' quadrangle. Wentworth Springs (1953, photorevised 1973) 7.5' quadrangle shows the stream entering a larger Pleasant Lake.

Ellis Lake [PLACER]: *lake,* 550 feet long, 2.5 miles southwest of Homewood (lat. 39°04'05" N, long. 120°12'05" W; near NW cor. sec. 15, T 14 N, R 16 E); the lake is less than 0.25 mile west-southwest of Ellis Peak. Named on

Homewood (1955) 7.5' quadrangle.

Ellis Lake [YUBA]: *lake,* 3000 feet long, in Marysville (lat. 39°08'55" N, long. 121°35'15" W). Named on Yuba City (1952) 7.5' quadrangle. The name commemorates W.T. Ellis, originator of the Marysville levee system (Hoover, Rensch, and Rensch, p. 588).

Ellis Peak [PLACER]: *peak,* 2.5 miles southwest of Homewood (lat. 39°04'05" N, long. 120°11'50" W; near S line sec. 10, T 14 N, R 16 E). Altitude 8740 feet. Named on Homewood (1955) 7.5' quadrangle. The name is for Jock Ellis, a dairyman and sheep rancher (Lekisch, p. 38).

El Macero [YOLO]: *locality,* 3 miles east of downtown Davis (lat. 38°32'55" N, long. 121°41'15" W; in and near sec. 7, T 8 N, R 3 E). Named on Davis (1952, photorevised 1968 and 1975) 7.5' quadrangle.

El Rio Villa [YOLO]: *village,* 1.5 miles east-northeast of Winters near Putah Creek (lat. 38°32' N, long. 121°56'40" W). Named on Winters (1953) 7.5' quadrangle.

Elston Spur [YOLO]: *locality,* 5.25 miles north-northeast of Davis along Southern Pacific Railroad (lat. 38°37'15" N, long. 121°45'40" W; near S line sec. 16, T 9 N, R 2 E). Named on Merritt (1952) 7.5' quadrangle.

Elvas [SACRAMENTO]: *locality,* 2.5 miles east-northeast of downtown Sacramento along Southern Pacific Railroad (lat. 38°35' N, long. 121°27' W). Named on Sacramento East (1967) 7.5' quadrangle.

Elvation [YOLO]: *locality,* 3.5 miles north-northeast of Woodland along Southern Pacific Railroad (lat. 38°43'40" N, long. 121°48'20" W). Named on Yolo (1915) 7.5' quadrangle.

Elverta [SACRAMENTO]: *settlement,* 1.5 miles north-northwest of Rio Linda (lat. 38°42'50" N, long. 121°27'40" W; near N line sec. 20, T 10 N, R 5 E). Named on Rio Linda (1967) 7.5' quadrangle. Arcade (1911) 7.5' quadrangle shows the place along Northern Electric Railroad. Postal authorities established Elverta post office in 1908 (Frickstad, p. 132). The name is for Elverta Dike, whose husband gave land for a community church (Gudde, 1949, p. 107).

Ely: see **Norton** [YOLO].

Emerald Bay [EL DORADO]:

(1) *bay,* 3.5 miles north of Mount Tallac off Lake Tahoe (lat. 38°57'25" N, long. 120°05'35" W). Named on Emerald Bay (1955) 7.5' quadrangle. The feature also was called Eagle Bay (Lekisch, p. 32).

(2) *village,* 3.5 miles north of Mount Tallac (lat. 38°57'35" N, long. 120°05'50" W; on W line sec. 22, T 13 N, R 17 E); the village is on the northwest side of Emerald Bay (1). Named on Emerald Bay (1955) 7.5' quadrangle. Pyramid Peak (1896) 30' quadrangle has the name at a site farther southwest near the end of Emerald Bay (1). California Mining Bureau's (1917c) map shows a place called Rubicon located north of the village of Emerald Bay along Lake Tahoe about halfway from the village to Placer County. Postal authorities established Rubicon post office 4.5 miles north of Emerald Bay post office in 1901, discontinued it in 1906, reestablished it in 1909, and discontinued it in 1913 (Salley, p. 190).

Emerald Bay Falls: see **Eagle Falls** [EL DORADO].

Emerald Point [EL DORADO]: *promontory,* 4.25 miles north of Mount Tallac along Lake Tahoe (lat. 38°58' N, long. 120°05' W); the feature is on the north side of the entrance to Emerald Bay (1). Named on Emerald Bay (1955) 7.5' quadrangle.

Emigrant Canyon [PLACER]: *canyon,* drained by a stream that flows 2.5 miles to Cold Creek 3.5 miles east-southeast of Donner Pass (lat. 39°17'35" N, long. 120°16'10" W; near W line sec. 25, T 17 N, R 15 E). Named on Norden (1955) 7.5' quadrangle.

Emigrant Gap [PLACER]:

(1) *pass,* 35 miles northeast of Auburn (lat. 39°18' N, long. 120° 40' W; sec. 31, T 17 N, R 12 E). Named on Blue Canyon (1955) 7.5' quadrangle. The name is from the early days, when emigrants lowered their wagons through a gap in the ridge at the place (Stewart, p. 89).

(2) *village,* 0.25 mile southwest of Emigrant Gap (1) (lat. 39°17'50" N, long. 120°40'15" W; sec. 31, T 17 N, R 12 E). Named on Blue Canyon (1955) 7.5' quadrangle. Postal authorities established Wilsons Ranch post office in 1865; they moved it and changed the name to Emigrant Gap in 1868—the name "Wilsons Ranch" was for the operator of a stage stop on the emigrant trail (Salley, p. 241). California Mining Bureau's (1909a) map shows a place called Fulda located 2 miles southwest of the village of Emigrant Gap along the railroad. Postal authorities established Fulda post office in 1906 and discontinued it in 1912 (Frickstad, p. 120).

Emmaton [SACRAMENTO]: *locality,* 9 miles southwest of Isleton on Sherman Island (lat. 38°04'50" N, long. 121°43'45" W). Named on Jersey Island (1978) 7.5' quadrangle. Postal authorities established Emmaton post office in 1871, discontinued it in 1883, reestablished it in 1905, and discontinued it in 1918 (Frickstad, p. 132).

Emory Ford: see **Emory Island** [NEVADA-YUBA].

Emory Island [NEVADA-YUBA]: *island,* 3.5 miles northeast of North San Juan in Middle Yuba River on Nevada-Yuba County line (lat. 39°23'45" N, long. 121°02'55" W; sec. 26, T 18 N, R 8 E). Named on Camptonville (1948) 7.5' quadrangle. Smartsville (1895) 30' quadrangle shows Emory Ford at or near the place, and Wescoatt's (1861) map has Emorys Crossing there.

Emorys Crossing: see **Emory Island** [NEVADA-YUBA].

Empire Creek [EL DORADO]: *stream,* flows 4 miles to join Manhattan Creek and form Johntown Creek 6.5 miles north-northwest of Chili Bar (lat. 38°51'30" N, long. 120°51' W; sec. 27, T 12 N, R 10 E). Named on Garden Valley (1949) and Georgetown (1949) 7.5' quadrangles. Miners from New York, the Empire State, named the stream in 1849 (Gernes, p. 51).

Empire Creek [SIERRA]: *stream,* flows 5.5 miles to Lavezzola Creek 4 miles northeast of Downieville (lat. 39°36'10" N, long. 120°46'50" W; sec. 18, T 20 N, R 11 E). Named on Downieville (1951) and Mount Fillmore (1951) 7.5' quadrangles. Downieville (1951) 7.5' quadrangle shows Empire ranch located near the mouth of the stream. United States Board on Geographic Names (1950, p. 5) rejected the names "Little North Fork" and "Little North Fork of Middle Fork of North Fork Yuba River" for the stream, and noted that the name "Empire Creek" is from Empire ranch.

Empire Creek [YUBA]: *stream,* flows 3.5 miles to New Bullards Bar Reservoir 3.5 miles east of Challenge (lat. 39°28'45" N, long. 121°09'35" W; sec. 26, T 19 N, R 7 E); the stream is west of Empire Ridge. Named on Challenge (1948, photorevised 1969) and Clipper Mills (1948) 7.5' quadrangles. Called Scott Bar Creek on Wescoatt's (1861) map.

Empire Creek: see **Sly Park Creek** [EL DORADO].

Empire House: see **Browns Valley** [YUBA].

Empire Ranch [YUBA]: *locality,* less than 1 mile southeast of Smartville (lat. 39°12'05" N, long. 121°17'10" W; sec. 34, T 16 N, R 6 E). Named on Smartville (1951) 7.5' quadrangle. Postal authorities established Empire Ranch post office in 1855 and discontinued it in 1865 (Frickstad, p. 223). Thomas Mooney and Michael Riley set up a trading post and hotel at the site in 1851; the place was a station of California Stage Company (Hoover, Rensch, and Rensch, p. 591).

Empire Reservoir [NEVADA]: *lake,* 900 feet long, nearly 6 miles north-northwest of Chicago Park (lat. 39°13'25" N, long. 120°59'45" W; near NW cor. sec. 29, T 16 N, R 9 E). Named on Colfax (1950) 15' quadrangle.

Empire Ridge [YUBA]: *ridge,* generally south-trending, 3.5 miles long, 4.5 miles east-northeast of Challenge (lat. 39°30'25" N, long. 121°08'40" W); the feature is east of Empire Creek. Named on Challenge (1948) and Clipper Mills (1948) 7.5' quadrangles.

Encinal [SUTTER]: *locality,* 5.5 miles north-northwest of Yuba City along Sacramento Northern Railroad (lat. 39°12'55" N, long. 121° 39'40" W; near N line sec. 29, T 16 N, R 3 E). Named on Sutter (1952) 7.5' quadrangle.

End of the World [PLACER]: *ridge,* south-southeast-trending, 0.5 mile long, 9.5 miles south-southwest of Duncan Peak (lat. 39°01'55" N, long. 120°35'50" W; at E line sec. 26, T 14 N, R 12 E). Named on Greek Store (1952) 7.5' quadrangle.

Englebright Lake [NEVADA-YUBA]: *lake,* behind a dam on Yuba River 2.5 miles north-northeast of Smartville on Nevada-Yuba County line (lat. 39°14'25" N, long. 121°16'05" W; sec. 14, T 16 N, R 6 E). Named on Smartville (1951, photorevised 1973) 7.5' quadrangle. Called Englebright Reservoir on Oregon House (1948) 7.5' quadrangle, called Harry L. Englebright Lake on French Corral (1948) 7.5' quadrangle, and called Upper Narrows Reservoir on Bangor (1941) 15' quadrangle. United States Board on Geographic Names (1972, p. 4) gave the names "Englebright Reservoir," "Harry L. Englebright Lake," "Harry L. Englebright Reservoir," and "Upper Narrows Reservoir" as variants. Officials of California Hydraulic Miners Association named the dam that forms the lake in 1945 in memory of Harry L. Englebright of Nevada City, a congressman from 1926 until 1943 (Gudde, 1949, p. 108).

Englebright Reservoir: see **Englebright Lake** [NEVADA-YUBA].

English Bar: see **Bullards Bar** [YUBA].

English Meadow [NEVADA-SIERRA]: *area,* 1.5 miles northeast of English Mountain along Middle Yuba River on Nevada-Sierra County line (lat. 39°27'35" N, long. 120°31'30" W). Named on English Mountain (1983) 7.5' quadrangle.

English Meadow: see **Moscove Meadow** [NEVADA-SIERRA].

English Mountain [NEVADA]: *peak,* 21 miles west-northwest of Truckee (lat. 39°26'50" N, long. 120°33' W; near NE cor. sec. 7, T 18 N, R 13 E); the peak is 1.25 miles south-southeast of Jackson Lake. Altitude 8373 feet. Named on English Mountain (1983) 7.5' quadrangle. Called Jackson Peak on Hobson's (1890a) map, and called English Pk. on California Mining Bureau's (1917c) map. On Emigrant Gap (1955) 15' quadrangle, the name "English Mountain" applies to the ridge on which present English Mountain is the high point.

English Peak: see **English Mountain** [NEVADA].

Enos Creek [YOLO]: *stream,* flows 7 miles to Dry Creek 10 miles south of Esparto (lat. 38°33'10" N, long. 122°01'50" W; sec. 12, T 8 N, R 2 W). Named on Monticello Dam (1959) 7.5' quadrangle.

Ensley [SUTTER]: *locality,* 4.5 miles south-southeast of Robbins in Sutter Basin at the end of a spur of Southern Pacific Railroad (lat. 38°48'25" N, long. 121°40'15" W; near SW cor. sec. 8, T 11 N, R 3 E). Named on Knights Landing (1952) 7.5' quadrangle.

Enterprise [AMADOR]: *locality,* 5.5 miles west-northwest of Fiddletown along Big Indian Creek (lat. 38°32'25" N, long. 120°50'45" W; near S line sec. 14, T 8 N, R 10 E). Named on Fiddletown (1949) 7.5' quadrangle. The old mining town of Yeomet was situated less than 1 mile north of Enterprise at the confluence of Middle Fork Cosumnes River and North Fork Cosumnes River; the name "Yeonet" reportedly is from an Indian word that has the meaning "rocky falls" and refers to some rapids upstream from the site of Yeomet (Andrews, p. 120-121). Postal authorities established Yornet post office at Yeomet in 1854 and discontinued it in 1861 (Salley, p. 245). Bancroft (1888, p. 372) gave the alternate name "Saratoga" for Yeomet, and Gudde (1975, p. 379) noted that the place also was known as Forks of the Cosumnes. Camp's (1962) map shows a place called Cape Cod Bar located 3 miles west-southwest of Enterprise on the south side of Cosumnes River, and a canyon called Bloody Gulch that opens into the canyon of Big Indian Creek from the east nearly 2.5 miles south of Enterprise.

Epperson: see **Leesville** [COLUSA].

Erie Point [NEVADA]: *ridge,* south- to southwest-trending, 2.5 miles long, 3.25 miles northeast of Washington (lat. 39°23'45" N, long. 120°45'30" W). Named on Alleghany (1949) 7.5' quadrangle.

Erle [YUBA]: *locality,* 6.25 miles north-northeast of Wheatland (lat. 39°06'05" N, long. 121°23'40" W; at NW cor. sec. 2, T 14 N, R 5 E). Named on Wheatland (1910) 7.5' quadrangle. Postal authorities established Erle post office in 1892 and discontinued it in 1909; the name commemorates a pioneer family in the region (Salley, p. 70).

Erle Siding [YUBA]: *locality,* 3 miles northwest of Wheatland along Southern Pacific Railroad (lat. 39°02'20" N, long. 121°27'55" W; near W line sec. 30, T 14 N, R 5 E). Named on Wheatland (1947) 7.5' quadrangle.

Esmeralda Creek [EL DORADO]: *stream,* flows 2 miles to South Fork American River 2.25 miles west of Riverton (lat. 38°46'05" N, long. 120°29'20" W; sec. 26, T 11 N, R 13 E). Named on Riverton (1950) and Stump Spring (1951) 7.5' quadrangles.

Esparto [YOLO]: *town,* 13 miles west of Woodland (lat. 38°41'35" N, long. 122°00'55" W). Named on Esparto (1959) 7.5' quadrangle. Postal authorities established Esparto post office in 1890 (Frickstad, p. 221). Officials of Vaca Valley Railroad gave the name "Esperanza" to their station at the place in 1875, but when a post office was established there the name was changed because California already had an Esperanza post office in Tulare County—*esparto* has the meaning "feather grass" in Spanish (Gudde, 1949, p. 109).

Esperanza: see **Esparto** [YOLO].

Estelle: see **Lake Estelle** [PLACER].

Etna: see **Mount Etna** [SIERRA].

Etta: see **Randolph** [SIERRA].

Eucher Bar [PLACER]: *locality,* 4.5 miles east-southeast of Dutch Flat along North Fork American River (lat. 39°11'15" N, long. 120°45'35" W; sec. 5, T 15 N, R 11 E). Named on Dutch Flat (1950) 7.5' quadrangle. Gudde (1975, p. 237) noted that a place called Neutral Bar was located along North Fork just below Euchre Bar.

Eucher Diggings: see **Shngle Springs** [EL DORADO].

Euer Saddle [NEVADA]: *pass,* nearly 2 miles north-northwest of Donner Pass (lat. 39°20'30" N, long. 120°20'15" W; sec. 8, T 17 N, R 15 E). Named on Norden (1955) 7.5' quadrangle. United States Board on Geographic Names (1949b, p. 3) rejected the form "Euer's Saddle" for the name.

Euer Valley [NEVADA]: *valley,* 4.5 miles north-northeast of Donner Pass along South Fork Prosser Creek (lat. 39°22'20" N, long. 120° 16'50" W). Named on Independence Lake (1981) and Norden (1955) 7.5' quadrangles. Called Euers Valley on Truckee (1940) 30' quadrangle, but United States Board on Geographic Names (1949a, p. 3) rejected the forms "Euers Valley," "Euer's Valley," and "Evers Valley" for the name.

Eula Canyon [COLUSA]: *canyon,* drained by a stream that flows 1.25 mile to Bear Creek 5 miles southeast of Wilbur Springs (lat. 38°59'25" N, long. 122°21'10" W; near E line sec. 12, T 13 N, R 5 W). Named on Glascock Mountain (1958) 7.5' quadrangle.

Eureka [SIERRA]: *locality,* 5 miles north of Goodyears Bar (lat. 39° 36'45" N, long. 120°53'35" W); the place is at present Eureka Diggings. Named on Downieville (1897) 30' quadrangle. Postal authorities established Eureka North post office in 1857 and discontinued it in 1861; the word "North" was added to the name to avoid confusion with Eureka South, which is in Nevada County (Salley, p. 71).

Eureka: see **Snow Point** [NEVADA].

Eureka Creek [SIERRA]: *stream,* flows 4 miles to Goodyears Creek 3 miles north of Goodyears Bar (lat. 39°35' N, long. 120°52'35" W; sec. 20, T 20 N, R 10 E). Named on Goodyears Bar (1951) 7.5' quadrangle.

Eureka Diggings [SIERRA]: *locality,* 5 miles north of Goodyears Bar (lat. 39°36'45" N, long. 120°53'40" W; sec. 7, T 20 N, R 10 E); the place is near Eureka Creek. Named on Goodyears Bar (1951) 7.5' quadrangle.

Eureka Gulch [YOLO]: *canyon,* drained by a stream that flows 1.25 miles to Mushoak Creek nearly 4 miles east-northeast of Guinda (lat. 38°51'10" N, long. 122°07'40" W; near N line sec. 31, T 12 N, R 2 W). Named on Guinda (1959) 7.5' quadrangle.

Eureka House: see **Long Bar** [YUBA] (2).

Eureka North: see **Eureka** [SIERRA].

Eureka South: see **Graniteville** [NEVADA].

Evans Canyon [SIERRA]: *canyon,* drained by a stream that flows 5 miles to Lassen County 10 miles east-northeast of Loyalton (lat. 39°42'30" N, long. 120°03'25" W; at N line sec. 3, T 21 N, R 17 E). Named on Evans Canyon (1978) and Loyalton (1981) 7.5' quadrangles.

Everett Flat [YOLO]: *area,* 1.5 miles east-southeast of Guinda (lat. 38°49'15" N, long. 122°09'55" W; sec. 11, T 11 N, R 3 W). Named on Guinda (1959) 7.5' quadrangle.

Everglade [SUTTER]: *locality,* 5.25 miles north-northeast of Kirkville along Southern Pacific Railroad in Sutter Basin (lat. 38°59' N, long. 121°46' W; at S line sec 8, T 13 N, R 2 E). Named on Kirkville (1952) 7.5' quadrangle. California Division of Highways' (1934) map shows a place called Pelger located along Southern Pacific Railroad 2 miles south-southeast of Everglade.

Evers Valley: see **Euer Valley** [NEVADA].

Ewing [PLACER]: *locality,* 4 miles northwest of Lincoln along Southern Pacific Railroad (lat. 38°55'55" N, long. 121°20'35" W; sec. 31, T 13 N, R 6 E). Named on Lincoln (1953) 7.5' quadrangle.

Excelsior: see **Monte Cristo** [SIERRA]; **Remington Hill** [NEVADA] (2); **Summit City** [NEVADA].

Excelsior Point [NEVADA]: *relief feature,* 5.5 miles south-southeast of Washington (lat. 39°17' N, long. 120°46'15" W; near W line sec. 5, T 16 N, R 11 E). Named on Washington (1950) 7.5' quadrangle.

Excelsior Ravine [SIERRA]: *canyon,* drained by a stream that flows 1 mile to Downie River 3 miles north of Downieville (lat. 39°36'10" N, long. 120°49'55" W; near W line sec. 14, T 20 N, R 10 E). Named on Downieville (1951) 7.5' quadrangle, which shows Excelsior mine at the head of the canyon.

— F —

Fagan: see **Kirkwood** [AMADOR-EL DORADO].

Fairbanks [EL DORADO]: *locality,* 8.5 miles north-northwest of Pollock Pines (lat. 38°51'55" N, long. 120°40'05" W; at NE cor. sec. 30, T 12 N, R 12 E). Named on Slate Mountain (1950) 7.5' quadrangle.

Fair Oaks [SACRAMENTO]: *town,* 3.5 miles northeast of downtown Carmichael (lat. 38°38'40" N, long. 121°16'15" W). Named on Citrus Heights (1967) 7.5' quadrangle. Called Fairoaks on Antelope (1911) 7.5' quadrangle. Postal authorities established Fairoaks post office in 1896 and changed the name to Fair Oaks in 1931 (Salley, p. 72). They established Pomelo post office 3 miles northeast of Fairoaks post office in 1899 and discontinued it in 1901 (Salley, p. 175). Arrowsmith's (1860) map shows a place called Sacramento Bar located on the north side of American River 1.25 miles south-southwest of present downtown Fair Oaks, and a place called Farmers Diggings situated on the south side of American River 2 miles southwest of present downtown Fair Oaks.

Fairoaks: see **Fairoaks Bridge** [SACRAMENTO].

Fairoaks Bridge [SACRAMENTO]: *locality,* 3.5 miles east-northeast of present downtown Carmichael along Southern Pacific Railroad (lat. 38°38' N, long. 121°15'45" W); the place is at the south end of a bridge across American River near Fairoaks (present Fair Oaks). Named on Antelope (1911) 7.5' quadrangle. Called Fairoaks on Fairoaks (1902) 15' quadrangle.

Fair Play [EL DORADO]: *locality,* 4.5 miles northeast of Aukum (lat. 38°35'40" N, long. 120°39'30" W; sec. 33, T 9 N, R 12 E). Named on Aukum (1952) 7.5' quadrangle. Called Fairplay on California Mining Bureau's (1909b) map. Postal authorities established Fair Play post office in 1860 and discontinued it in 1944 (Frickstad, p. 26).

Fairview [COLUSA]: *locality,* 8.5 miles northwest of Williams along Colusa and Lake Railroad (lat. 39°14'50" N, long. 122°15'50" W; at NW cor. sec. 13, T 16 N, R 4 W). Named on Fairview (1918) 7.5' quadrangle.

Fall Creek [NEVADA]: *stream,* flows 5 miles to South Yuba River 5.25 miles west-northwest of Yuba Gap (lat. 39°21'15" N, long. 120°41'55" W; at W line sec. 12, T 17 N, R 11 E). Named on Blue Canyon (1955), English Mountain (1983), and Graniteville (1982) 7.5' quadrangles

Fall Creek Mountain [NEVADA]: *peak,* 6.5 miles east-southeast of Graniteville (lat. 39°24'20" N, long. 120°37'40" W; at S line sec. 21, T 18 N, R 12 E). Altitude 7490 feet. Named on Graniteville (1982) 7.5' quadrangle.

Fallen Leaf [EL DORADO]: *town,* 2 miles southeast of Mount Tallac (lat. 38°52'55" N, long. 120°04'20" W; near SW cor. sec. 14, T 12 N, R 17 E); the town is at the south end of Fallen Leaf Lake. Named on Emerald Bay (1955) 7.5' quadrangle. Postal authorities established Fallen Leaf post office in 1908 (Frickstad, p. 26). William W. Price opened a resort called Fallen Leaf Lodge at the site in 1908; Price previously had operated Agassiz Camp there in connection with his Agassiz School for Boys at Auburn in Placer County (Hanna, p. 103).

Fallen Leaf Lake [EL DORADO]: *lake,* 3 miles long, 2 miles east of Mount Tallac (lat. 38°54' N, long. 120°03'45" W). Named on Emerald Bay (1955) 7.5' quadrangle. The name is from an Indian legend (Hanna, p. 103).

Fallen Leaf Lodge: see **Fallen Leaf** [EL DORADO].

Falls: see **The Falls** [SUTTER].

Fannette Island [EL DORADO]: *island,* 550 feet long, 3.25 miles north of Mount Tallac in Emerald Bay (1) (lat. 38°57'15" N, long. 120°06' W). Named on Emerald Bay (1955) 7.5' quadrangle.

Fanny Creek [EL DORADO]: *stream,* flows about 2 miles to Slate Creek (2) 5 miles east-northeast of Latrobe (lat. 38°35'05" N, long. 120°53'45" W; near S line sec. 32, T 9 N, R 10 E). Named on Fiddletown (1949) and Latrobe (1949) 7.5' quadrangles.

Farad: see **Mystic** [NEVADA].

Farmers Diggings: see **Fair Oaks** [SACRAMENTO].

Farnam Mill [EL DORADO]: *locality,* 4.5 miles south-southwest of Omo Ranch (lat. 38°31'20" N, long. 120°37' W); the place is along present Farnham Creek. Named on Placerville (1893) 30' quadrangle. The name should have the form "Farnham" (Beverly Cola, personal communication, 1985).

Farnham Creek [EL DORADO]: *stream,* flows nearly 5 miles to Scott Creek 4.5 miles east-southeast of Aukum (lat. 38°32'10" N, long. 120°38'40" W; sec. 22, T 8 N, R 12 E); the stream is south of Farnham Ridge. Named on Aukum (1952) and Omo Ranch (1952) 7.5' quadrangles.

Farnham Mill: see **Farnam Mill** [EL DORADO].

Farnham Ridge [EL DORADO]: *ridge,* generally west-trending, 10.5 miles long, center 4 miles south-southeast of Omo Ranch (lat. 38° 31'20" N, long. 120°32'45" W). Named on Aukum (1952), Caldor (1951), and Omo Ranch (1952) 7.5' quadrangles.

Far West: see **Camp Far West** [YUBA].

Fast Creek [YUBA]: *stream,* flows less than 1 mile to Studhorse Canyon 3.5 miles south of Camptonville (lat. 39°24'05" N, long. 121°02'20" W; near N line sec. 25, T 18 N, R 8 E). Named on Camptonville (1948) 7.5' quadrangle. This appears to be the stream called Mosquito Creek on Wescoatt's (1861) map.

Fattebort Hill [NEVADA]: *peak,* 1.5 miles southeast of Higgins Corner (lat. 39°01'30" N, long. 121°04'30" W; near NW cor. sec. 34, T 14 N, R 8 E). Altitude 1931 feet. Named on Lake Combie (1949) 7.5' quadrangle. Called Flatbort Hill on Smartsville (1895) 30' quadrangle.

Faucherie Campground [NEVADA]: *locality,* 1.5 miles southwest of English Mountain (lat. 39°25'40" N, long. 120°34'10" W; near E line sec. 13, T 18 N, R 12 E); the place is on the north shore of Faucherie Lake. Named on English Mountain (1983) 7.5' quadrangle.

Faucherie Lake [NEVADA]: *lake,* behind a dam on Canyon Creek 1.5 miles southwest of English Mountain (lat. 39°25'45" N, long. 120°34'05" W; near E line sec. 13, T 18 N, R 12 E). Named on English Mountain (1983) 7.5' quadrangle. The name is for Mr. B. Faucherie, a pioneer hydraulic engineer (Gudde, 1949, p. 114).

Fawn Lake [EL DORADO]: *lake,* 1000 feet long, nearly 5 miles east of Wentworth Springs (lat. 39°00'35" N, long. 120°15' W; sec. 6, T 13 N, R 16 E). Named on Homewood (1955) and Wentworth Springs (1953, photorevised 1973) 7.5' quadrangles.

Feather River [SUTTER-YUBA]: *stream,* enters from Butte County and flows 40 miles along Sutter-Butte County line, Sutter-Yuba County line, and in Sutter County to Sacramento River at Verona (lat. 38°47'10" N, long. 121°37'15" W; sec. 22, T 11 N, R 3 E). Named on Gridley (1952), Honcut (1952), Knights Landing (1952), Nicolaus (1952), Olivehurst (1952, photorevised 1973), Sutter (1952, photorevised 1973), Verona (1967), and Yuba City (1952, photorevised 1973) 7.5' quadrangles. Called Rio de las Plumas on Fremont's (1845) map, and called Rio del Plumas on Sage's (1846) map. Sutter-Yuba County line follows an abandoned course of Feather River for nearly 4 miles south of Shanghai Bend, placing present Feather River there in Sutter County—Ostrom (1911) 7.5' quadrangle shows the river in the old course. Luis Arguello is said to have given the name "El Rio de las Plumas" to the stream in 1817 because he saw bird feathers on the water (Hart, J.D., p. 135)—*las plumas* means "the feathers" in Spanish. United States Board on Geographic Names (1974b, p. 3) gave the variant name "Middle Fork Feather River" for present Sierra Valley Channels.

Featherton: see **Honcut Creek** [YUBA].

Feeley Lake [NEVADA]: *lake,* 3000 feet long, 6.25 miles east-southeast of Graniteville (lat. 39°24' N, long. 120°37'55" W; sec. 28, T 18 N, R 12 E). Named on Graniteville (1982) 7.5' quadrangle. Present Feeley Lake and nearby Carr Lake together are called Feeley Lakes on Colfax (1938) 30' quadrangle.

Feeley Lakes: see **Feeley Lake** [NEVADA].

Fenton Ravine [PLACER]: *canyon,* drained by a stream that flows 2.5 miles to Bear River 7 miles northeast of Sheridan (lat. 39°01'55" N, long. 121°16'10" W; sec. 26, T 14 N, R 6 E). Named on Camp Far West (1949) 7.5' quadrangle.

Ferguson Point [AMADOR]: *promontory,* 9 miles north of Mokelumne Peak on the north shore of Silver Lake (lat. 38°40'05" N, long. 120°07'05" W). Named on Caples Lake (1979) 7.5' quadrangle.

Fern Lake [PLACER]: *lake,* 650 feet long, 6.5 miles east of Bunker Hill (lat. 39°02' N, long. 120°15'30" W; at W line sec. 30, T 14 N, R 16 E). Named on Wentworth Springs (1953, photorevised 1973) 7.5' quadrangle.

Fernley: see **Rough and Ready** [NEVADA].

Fiddle Creek [SIERRA]: *stream,* flows 9 miles to North Yuba River 6.25 miles west-southwest of Goodyears Bar (lat. 39°31'05" N, long. 120°59'45" W; sec. 17, T 19 N, R 9 E). Named on Goodyears Bar (1951) 7.5' quadrangle.

Fiddle Creek: see **Little Fiddle Creek** [SIERRA].

Fiddle Creek Camp Ground [SIERRA]: *locality,* 6.25 miles west-southwest of Goodyears Bar along North Yuba River (lat. 39°31'05" N, long. 120°59'50" W; sec. 17, T 19 N, R 9 E); the place is at the mouth of Fiddle Creek. Named on Goodyears Bar (1951) 7.5' quadrangle. Called Fiddle Cr. Camp on Downieville (1951) 15' quadrangle.

Fiddle Creek Ridge [SIERRA]: *ridge,* south- to west-trending, 5 miles long, center 3.5 miles west of Goodyears Bar (lat. 39°31'55" N, long. 120°56'55" W); the ridge is between Fiddle Creek and North Yuba River. Named on Goodyears Bar (1951) 7.5' quadrangle.

Fiddlers Spring [EL DORADO]: *spring,* 1 mile southwest of Old Iron Mountain (lat. 38°41'35" N, long. 120°24'10" W; sec. 27, T 10 N, R 14 E). Named on Stump Spring (1951) 7.5' quadrangle.

Fiddletown [AMADOR]: *village,* 10.5 miles north of Jackson along North Fork Dry Creek (lat. 38°30'15" N, long. 120°45'20" W; near W line sec. 34, T 8 N, R 11 E). Named on Fiddletown (1949) 7.5' quadrangle. Called Oleta on Placerville (1893) 30' quadrangle. Eddy's (1854) map has the form "Fiddle Town" for the name. Postal authorities established Fiddletown post office in 1853, changed the name to Oleta in 1878, and changed it back to Fiddletown in 1932 (Frickstad, p. 5). A group of Missourians who settled at the place in 1849 were "always fiddling," hence the designation; the name was changed to Oleta in 1878 to make it more respectable, but the Committee on Historic Landmarks of California Historical Society led a successful effort in 1932 to restore the old name (Hoover, Rensch, and Rensch, p. 32). Camp's (1962) map shows a canyon called Loafer Gulch that opens into the canyon of North Fork Dry Creek from the east nearly 2 miles west-southwest of Fiddletown.

Fienes Crossing: see **Deer Creek** [NEVADA-YUBA].

Figtree: see **Plymouth** [AMADOR].

Fig Tree Gulch [SIERRA]: *canyon,* 0.25 mile long, 7.25 miles west-northwest of Sutter (lat. 39°12'25" N, long. 121°52'05" W; sec. 28, T 16 N, R 1 E). Named on Sutter Buttes (1954) 7.5' quadrangle.

Filipinis [EL DORADO]: *locality,* 4.5 miles east of Robbs Peak (lat. 38°56' N, long. 120°19'30" W). Named on Pyramid Peak (1896) 30' quadrangle.

Fillmore: see **Mount Fillmore** [SIERRA].

Fillmore Hill [SIERRA]: *ridge,* southwest-trending, less than 1 mile long, 4.5 miles east of Alleghany (lat. 39°28'20" N, long. 120°45'35" W; sec. 32, T 19 N, R 11 E). Named on Alleghany (1949) 7.5' quadrangle.

Findley Mountain: see **Findley Peak** [NEVADA].

Findley Peak [NEVADA]: *peak,* 3 miles north-northwest of English Mountain (lat. 39°29'05" N, long. 120°34'25" W; sec. 25, T 19 N, R 12 E). Altitude 7424 feet. Named on English Mountain (1983) 7.5' quadrangle. Called Findley Mtn. on Logan's (1940) map.

Finleys: see **Slate Range Bar** [YUBA].

Finnon Reservoir [EL DORADO]: *lake,* 1700 feet long, behind a dam on Jaybird Creek 4.25 miles east-northeast of Chili Bar (lat. 38°47'50" N, long. 120°45'05" W; sec. 16, T 11 N, R 11 E). Named on Garden Valley (1949) and Slate Mountain (1950) 7.5' quadrangles.

Finn's Sugarloaf: see **Bisbee Peak** [AMADOR].

Fir Cap [SIERRA]: *peak,* 4.25 miles north-northwest of Downieville (lat. 39°37'10" N, long. 120°51'15" W; at NE cor. sec. 9, T 20 N, R 10 E). Named on Downieville (1951) 7.5' quadrangle. Called Fir Top Mt. on Downieville (1897) 30' quadrangle, and called Firtop Pk. on California Mining Bureau's (1917a) map.

Fir Cap: see **Monte Cristo** [SIERRA].

Fir Cap Diggings: see **Monte Cristo** [SIERRA].

Fir Crags [PLACER]: *relief feature,* nearly 3 miles west of Tahoe City near Truckee River (lat. 38°10'35" N, long. 120°11'30" W; near E line sec. 3, T 15 N, R 16 E). Named on Tahoe City (1955) 7.5' quadrangle.

Firebrick [AMADOR]: *locality,* 1.25 miles south-southeast of Ione along Amador Central Railroad (lat. 38°20'05" N, long. 120°55'25" W; sec. 31, T 6 N, R 10 E). Named on Ione (1962) 7.5' quadrangle.

Fir Hill [NEVADA]: *peak,* 3.25 miles northwest of English Mountain (lat. 39°28'40" N, long. 120°35'45" W; on S line sec. 26, T 19 N, R 12 E). Altitude 6926 feet. Named on English Mountain (1983) 7.5' quadrangle.

Firs Campground [EL DORADO]: *locality,* less than 1 mile north-northwest of Echo Summit (lat. 38°49'30" N, long. 120°02'10" W; near S line sec. 6, T 11 N, R 18 E). Named on Echo Lake (1955) 7.5' quadrangle.

First Bannon Slough [SACRAMENTO]: *water feature,* joins Sacramento River 2 miles north-northwest of downtown Sacramento (lat. 38°36'05" N, long. 121°30'30" W); the feature is in American Basin 1 mile east of Second Bannon Slough. Named on Lovedal (1916) 7.5' quadrangle. Sacramento West (1967) 7.5' quadrangle shows only a remnant of the feature.

First Brushy Canyon [PLACER]: *canyon,* 2.5 miles long, opens into the head of Brushy Canyon (1) 2.25 miles west-northwest of Foresthill (lat.

39°02'15" N, long. 120°51'15" W; near N line sec. 28, T 14 N, R 10 E). Named on Foresthill (1949) 7.5' quadrangle.

First Divide [SIERRA]: *pass,* 2 miles north-northeast of Dowieville on the ridge between Larezzola Creek and Pauley Creek (lat. 39° 35'10" N, long. 120°48'35" W; sec. 24, T 20 N, R 10 E); the pass is 1 mile southwest of Second Divide. Named on Downieville (1951) 7.5' quadrangle.

First Sugarloaf [PLACER]: *peak,* 6.25 miles north-northwest of Foresthill (lat. 39°06'10" N, long. 120°52'05" W; sec. 32, T 15 N, R 10 E); the peak is less than 0.5 mile northeast of Second Sugarloaf. Altitude 3082 feet. Named on Foresthill (1949) 7.5' quadrangle. First Sugarloaf and Second Sugarloaf together are called Sugar Loaves on Colfax (1898) 30' quadrangle.

Fir Top Mountain: see **Fir Cap** [SIERRA].

Firtop Peak: see **Fir Cap** [SIERRA].

Fish Creek [NEVADA]: *stream,* flows 1.5 miles to South Yuba River 2.5 miles west-southwest of Washington (lat. 39°20'40" N, long. 120°50'45" W; near N line sec. 15, T 17 N, R 10 E). Named on Washington (1950) 7.5' quadrangle.

Fish Creek: see **Fiske Creek** [YOLO].

Fisher Lake [PLACER]: *lake,* 600 feet long, 8.5 miles west-southwest of Donner Pass (lat. 39°17'05" N, long. 120°28'40" W; sec. 2, T 16 N, R 13 E). Named on Soda Springs (1955) 7.5' quadrangle.

Fishermans Lake [SACRAMENTO]: *lake,* 6 miles northwest of downtown Sacramento in American Basin (lat. 38°39'05" N, long. 121°33'20" W; on W line sec. 9, T 9 N, R 4 E). Named on Taylor Monument (1967) 7.5' quadrangle.

Fishers Bar: see **Mississippi Bar** [SACRAMENTO].

Fish Ponds [EL DORADO]: *lakes,* largest 200 feet long, 3.5 miles south of Pyramid Peak at Strawberry (lat. 38°47'50" N, long. 120° 08'30" W; sec. 18, T 11 N, R 17 E). Named on Fallen Leaf Lake (1955) 15' quadrangle.

Fiske Canyon [YOLO]: *canyon,* drained by a stream that flows 2 miles to Salt Arroyo nearly 3 miles east of Berryessa Peak (lat. 38° 39'50" N, long. 122°08'10" W). Named on Brooks (1959) 7.5' quadrangle.

Fiske Creek [YOLO]: *stream,* flows 5.5 miles to Cache Creek 4 miles west-northwest of Rumsey (lat. 38°54'30" N, long. 122°18'30" W; near S line sec. 4, T 12 N, R 4 W). Named on Glascock Mountain (1958) and Knoxville (1958) 7.5' quadrangles. Called Fish Creek on Durst's (1916) map.

Five Corners [EL DORADO]: *locality,* 3.5 miles south-southwest of Caldor (lat. 38°33'25" N, long. 120°27'20" W; sec. 8, T 8 N, R 14 E). Named on Caldor (1951) 7.5' quadrangle.

Five Lakes [PLACER]: *lakes,* largest 850 feet long, 6 miles west of Tahoe City (lat. 39°10'30" N, long. 120°15' W; sec. 6, T 15 N, R 16 E). Named on Granite Chief (1953) and Tahoe City (1955) 7.5' quadrangles.

Five Lakes Basin [NEVADA]: *relief feature,* 2.5 miles south of English Mountain (lat. 39°24'30" N, long. 120°33'25" W; mainly in sec. 19, T 18 N, R 13 E). Named on English Mountain (1983) 7.5' quadrangle.

Five Lakes Creek [PLACER]: *stream,* flows 10 miles to Rubicon River nearly 3 miles northeast of Bunker Hill (lat. 39°04'50" N, long. 120°20'50" W; near NE cor. sec. 12, T 14 N, R 14 E); the stream heads at Five Lakes. Named on Granite Chief (1953) and Wentworth Springs (1953) 7.5' quadrangles.

Five Mile House: see **Brighton** [SACRAMENTO]; **Colusa** [COLUSA].

Fivemile House [NEVADA]: *locality,* 6 miles south-southwest of North Bloomfield (lat. 39°17'10" N, long. 120°56'40" W; at NW cor. sec. 2, T 16 N, R 9 E). Named on North Bloomfield (1949) 7.5' quadrangle.

Five Mile Terrace [EL DORADO]: *locality,* 2 miles west of Camino (lat. 38°44'15" N, long. 120°42'45" W; sec. 12, T 10 N, R 11 E). Named on Camino (1952) 7.5' quadrangle.

Flagpole Peak [EL DORADO]: *peak,* 2.5 miles north-northwest of Echo Summit (lat. 38°50'45" N, long. 120°03'20" W; sec. 36, T 12 N, R 17 E). Altitude 8363 feet. Named on Echo Lake (1955) 7.5' quadrangle.

Flagstaff Hill [EL DORADO]: *peak,* 6 miles southwest of the village of Pilot Hill (lat. 38°46'05" N, long. 121°05' W; near NW cor. sec. 33, T 11 N, R 8 E). Altitude 1421 feet. Named on Pilot Hill (1954) 7.5' quadrangle.

Flanly Peak [YUBA]: *peak,* 1 mile west-southwest of Oregon House (lat. 39°21' N, long. 121°17'45" W; at W line sec. 10, T 17 N, R 6 E). Altitude 2099 feet. Named on Oregon House (1948) 7.5' quadrangle.

Flatbort Hill: see **Fattebort Hill** [NEVADA].

Flat Creek [EL DORADO]: *stream,* flows 4.25 miles to Spanish Creek 11 miles south-southeast of Placerville (lat. 38°34'40" N, long. 120°45'20" W; sec. 3, T 8 N, R 11 E). Named on Aukum (1952) and Fiddletown (1949) 7.5' quadrangles.

Flat Ravine [PLACER]: *canyon,* drained by a stream that flows 1 mile to Deep Canyon 1.5 miles south-southwest of Duncan Peak (lat. 39°07'55" N, long. 120°31'20" W; near E line sec. 21, T 15 N, R 13 E). Named on Duncan Peak (1952) 7.5' quadrangle. Colfax (1898) 30' quadrangle has the name for an inhabited place in the canyon.

Fleetfoot Peak: see **Maggies Peaks** [EL DORADO].

Fleming Meadow [EL DORADO]: *locality,* 7 miles east-southeast of Camino (lat. 38°42'10" N, long. 120°33'10" W; on W line sec. 21, T 10 N, R 13 E). Named on Sly Park (1952) 7.5' quadrangle.

Fletcher Creek [SIERRA]: *stream,* flows 3 miles to Sierra Valley 0.5 mile south-southwest of Calpine (lat. 39°3930" N, long. 120°26'45" W; at W line sec. 20, T 21 N, R 14 E). Named on Calpine (1981) 7.5' quadrangle.

Flick Point [PLACER]: *promontory,* 2.5 miles west-southwest of Kings Beach along Lake Tahoe between Carnelian Bay (1) and Agate Bay (lat. 39°13'45" N, long. 120°04' W; at S line sec. 15, T 16 N, R 17 E). Named on Kings Beach (1955) 7.5' quadrangle. The name is for the Flick brothers, William, Joseph, and Nicholas, who settled along Carnelian Bay (Lekisch, p. 44).

Flint: see **Lake Flint** [AMADOR].

Floating Island Lake [EL DORADO]: *lake,* 450 feet long, 1 mile east-southeast of Mount Tallac (lat. 38°54'10" N, long. 120°04'40" W). Named on Emerald Bay (1955) 7.5' quadrangle.

Flonellis [EL DORADO]: *locality,* 1 mile northeast of Latrobe along Southern Pacific Railroad (lat. 38°34'10" N, long. 120°57'45" W; near NW cor. sec. 11, T 8 N, R 9 E). Named on Latrobe (1949) 7.5' quadrangle. California Division of Highways' (1934) map shows a place called Swift located along the railroad just north of Flonellis.

Flood: see **Grass Valley** [NEVADA].

Flora Lake [NEVADA]: *lake,* 950 feet long, 1 mile north of Donner Pass (lat. 39°19'55" N, long. 120°19'30" W; near SW cor. sec. 9, T 17 N, R 15 E). Named on Norden (1955) 7.5' quadrangle. Called Lytton Lake on Truckee (1940) 30' quadrangle.

Flora's: see **Volcanoville** [EL DORADO].

Florence Spring: see **Soda Springs** [PLACER].

Florin [SACRAMENTO]: *town,* 8 miles southeast of downtown Sacramento (lat. 38°29'45" N, long. 121°24' W). Named on Florin (1968) 7.5' quadrangle. Postal authorities established Florin post office in 1869 (Frickstad, p. 133). E.B. Crocker of Central Pacific Railroad named the place in 1864 for the profusion of wild flowers in the neighborhood (Hanna, p. 107).

Florin Creek [SACRAMENTO]: *stream,* flows 5.25 miles to Elder Creek 7 miles south-southeast of downtown Sacramento (lat. 38° 28'35" N, long. 121°27'05" W; sec. 8, T 7 N, R 5 E). Named on Florin (1968) 7.5' quadrangle.

Florin Road [SACRAMENTO]: *locality,* 8 miles south of downtown Carmichael along Central California Traction Railroad (lat. 38° 30' N, long. 121°21'40" W; sec. 31, T 8 N, R 6 E). Named on Carmichael (1967) and Elk Grove (1968) 7.5' quadrangles. Called Pioneer on Fair Oaks (1954) 15' quadrangle.

Floriston [NEVADA]: *village,* 10 miles east-northeast of Truckee on the east side of Truckee River (lat. 39°23'40" N, long. 120°01'15" W; sec. 30, T 18 N, R 18 E). Named on Boca (1955) 7.5' quadrangle. Postal authorities established Floriston post office in 1891 (Salley, p. 76). The name is from the abundant spring flowers at the place (Hanna, p. 107). California Division of Highways' (1934) map shows a place called Wickes located nearly 1 mile south of Floriston along Southern Pacific Railroad (sec. 31, T 18 N, R 18 E).

Flügge: see **Boga** [SUTTER].

Flume Camp [SIERRA]: *locality,* 6 miles southwest of Mount Fillmore (lat. 39°39'45" N, long. 120°55'10" W; sec. 24, T 21 N, R 9 E). Named on La Porte (1951) 7.5' quadrangle.

Flume Creek [SIERRA]: *stream,* flows 2 miles to North Yuba River 2 miles northeast of Sierra City (lat. 39°35'25" N, long. 120°36'35" W; sec. 22, T 20 N, R 12 E). Named on Haypress Valley (1981) and Sierra City (1981) 7.5' quadrangles. The name is from a flume for irrigation water that crosses the stream (United States Board on Geographic Names, 1982, p. 2).

Folsom [SACRAMENTO]: *town,* 18 miles east-northeast of downtown Sacramento along American River (lat. 38°40'30" N, long. 121°10'20" W). Named on Folsom (1967) 7.5' quadrangle. Postal authorities established Folsom City post office in 1856 and changed the name to Folsom in 1938 (Salley, p. 76). The town incorporated in 1946. Theodore D. Judah laid out the place in 1855 at the terminus of the first railroad in California; Judah named it for Joseph L. Folsom, owner of Rio de los Americanos grant, where the town lies (Gudde, 1975, p. 117). Arrowsmith's (1860) map shows Negro Bar located along American River at Folsom, and shows Texas Hill Diggings located just south of Folsom on the east side of the river. Negro miners established the mining camp called Negro Bar at the site of present Folsom shortly after the discovery of gold in California in 1848 (Winterstein, p. 1). Flood waters washed away Negro Bar, but the camp was rebuilt and named Granite City (Blenkle, p. 5); granite quarries were near the place (Bancroft, 1888, p. 485). A short-lived mining camp called Texas Hill, active in 1849, was located no more than 1 mile below present Folsom on the south bank of American River; later the place was the source of cobblestones for San Francisco streets (Winterstein, p. 27). Postal authorities established Texas Hill post office in 1851 and discontinued it in 1856; most of the miners at the place were from Texas (Salley, p. 220). A mining camp called Slate Bar was situated along American River opposite present Folsom state prison (Hoover, Rensch, and Rensch, p. 300). Postal authorities established Viola post office 3 miles south of Folsom City (present Folsom) in 1861 and discontinued it in 1866 (Salley, p. 232).

Folsom City: see **Folsom** [SACRAMENTO].

Folsom Junction [SACRAMENTO]: *locality,* 0.5 mile southwest of Folsom along Southern Pacific Railroad (lat. 38°40'05" N, long. 121°10'55" W). Named on Folsom (1967) 7.5' quadrangle.

Folsom Lake [EL DORADO-PLACER-SACRAMENTO]: *lake,* behind a dam on American River 7 miles west-northwest of Clarksville in Sacramento County (lat. 38°42'25" N, long. 121°09'25" W; sec. 24, T 10 N, R 7 E), and less than 1 mile downstream from the confluence of North Fork and South Fork; the lake extends from Sacramento County into El Dorado and Placer Counties. Named on Clarksville (1953, photorevised 1980), Folsom (1967), and Pilot Hill (1954, photorevised 1973) 7.5' quadrangles. United States Board on Geographic Names (1960b, p. 8) rejected the name "Folsom Reservoir" for the feature. Arrowsmith's (1860) map shows a place called Negro Hill located less than 1 mile east of the confluence of North Fork and South Fork American River on the ridge north of South Fork; water of Folsom Lake now covers the site. The name "Negro Hill" was from the negro miners at the place in 1849 (Bancroft, 1888, p. 352). Arrowsmith's (1860) map also shows a place called McDowell Hill located on the south side of South Fork American River 2.5 miles northeast of the confluence of North Fork and South Fork—the place also was called McDowellsville (Gudde, 1975, p. 202). The same map shows a mining camp called Condemned Bar situated along North Fork American River 2.5 miles north-northeast of the confluence of North Fork and South Fork—water of Folsom Lake now covers the site.

Folsom Reservoir: see **Folsom Lake** [EL DORADO-PLACER-SACRAMENTO].

Fontanillis Lake [EL DORADO]: *lake,* 0.5 mile long, 2.25 miles south of Phipps Peak (lat. 38°55'15" N, long. 120°09'05" W). Named on Rockbound Valley (1955) 7.5' quadrangle. The name should have the form "Fontanellis" (Beverly Cola, personal communication, 1985).

Foote Crossing [NEVADA-SIERRA]: *locality,* 4.25 miles northwest of North Bloomfield along Middle Yuba River on Nevada-Sierra County line (lat. 39°25' N, long. 120°57'05" W; near S line sec. 15, T 18 N, R 9 E). Named on Pike (1949) 7.5' quadrangle.

Foothill Farms [SACRAMENTO]: *town,* 4 miles north of downtown Carmichael (lat. 38°40'35" N, long. 121°20'25" W). Named on Citrus Heights (1967) 7.5' quadrangle.

Forbes Campground [PLACER]: *locality,* 5.5 miles south-southeast of Dutch Flat (lat. 39°07'55" N, long. 120°47'10" W; near W line sec. 19, T 15 N, R 11 E); the place is along Forbes Creek. Named on Dutch Flat (1950) 7.5' quadrangle.

Forbes Creek [PLACER]: *stream,* flows 5 miles to North Shirttail Canyon 5.5 miles south-southeast of Dutch Flat (lat. 39°07'50" N, long. 120°47'40" W; sec. 24, T 15 N, R 10 E). Named on Dutch Flat (1950) and Westville (1952) 7.5' quadrangles.

Fordice Reservoir: see **Fordyce Lake** [NEVADA].

Ford Point [PLACER]: *ridge,* west-southwest-trending, 1.25 miles long, 3.5 miles northwest of Duncan Peak (lat. 39°11'05" N, long. 120°34'05" W; sec. 6, T 15 N, R 13 E). Named on Duncan Peak (1952) 7.5' quadrangle.

Ford Ravine [PLACER]: *canyon,* drained by a stream that flows 2 miles to North Fork American River 4.25 miles east-southeast of Dutch Flat near Euchre Bar (lat. 39°11'10" N, long. 120°45'45" W). Named on Colfax (1898) 30' quadrangle.

Fords Bar [EL DORADO]: *locality,* 3.5 miles north-northwest of Georgetown along Middle Fork American River at the mouth of Otter Creek (lat. 38°57'25" N, long. 120°51'20" W; near W line sec. 22, T 13 N, R 10 E). Named on Georgetown (1949) 7.5' quadrangle. Wierzbicki (p. 51-52) called the place Ford's, or Middle Bar.

Fords Bar: see **Carmichael** [SACRAMENTO].

Ford Spring [COLUSA]: *spring,* 2.25 miles north-northwest of Pacific Point (lat. 39°14'40" N, long. 122°36'40" W; near N line sec. 14, T 16 N, R 7 W). Named on Clearlake Oaks (1960) 15' quadrangle.

Fordyce Creek [NEVADA]: *stream,* flows 9.5 miles to Lake Spaulding 2.5 miles north of Yuba Gap (lat. 39°21'05" N, long. 120°37' W; sec. 10, T 17 N, R 12 E); the stream heads at Fordyce Lake. Named on Cisco Grove (1955), English Mountain (1983), and Webber Peak (1981) 7.5' quadrangles.

Fordyce Lake [NEVADA]: *lake,* behind a dam on Fordyce Creek 10 miles west-northwest of Donner Pass (lat. 39°22'50" N, long. 120° 29'45" W; sec. 34, T 18 N, R 13 E). Named on Soda Springs (1955) and Webber Peak (1981) 7.5' quadrangles. Officials of South Yuba Canal Company had the dam built that formed the lake in the 1870's, and named the lake for the engineer who began building flumes and canals in the vicinity in 1853 (Gudde, 1949, p. 118). Called Fordice Res. on Hobson's (1890a) map. Water of the lake covers Fordyce Valley and the site of a mining camp called Atlanta, where Jerome Fordyce lived (Fatout, p. 48-49).

Fordyce Summit [NEVADA]: *pass,* 6.25 miles east-northeast of Yuba Gap (lat. 39°20'35" N, long. 120°30'15" W; near N line sec. 15, T 17 N, R 13 E). Named on Cisco Grove (1955) 7.5' quadrangle.

Fordyce Valley: see **Fordyce Lake** [NEVADA].

Forebay [PLACER]: *locality,* 6.5 miles northwest of Westville along Southern Pacific Railroad (lat. 39°14'10" N, long. 120°44'10" W; on W line sec. 22, T 16 N, R 11 E); the place is 1 mile southeast of Drum Forebay. Named on Westville (1952) 7.5' quadrangle.

Forest [SIERRA]: *village,* 1.5 miles north-northwest of Alleghany at the confluence of North Fork and South Fork Oregon Creek (lat. 39°29'25" N, long. 120°51'05" W; on W line sec. 27, T 19 N, R 10 E). Named on Alleghany (1949) 7.5' quadrangle. Postal authorities established Forest City post office in 1854, changed the name to Forest in 1895, and discontinued it in 1947 (Salley, p. 77). The place had a number of names, including: Brownsville, for I.E. Brown, who reportedly built a sawmill there in 1851; Forks of Oregon Creek, after gold was discovered there in 1853; Yomana, an Indian designation of a nearby bluff; Marietta and Elizaville, for Mary Davis, also called Eliza, the first woman at the place; and finally Forest City and Forest, after Mrs. Forest Mooney began contributing articles with the dateline "Forest City" to Marysville newspapers (Hanna, p. 108-109).

Forest: see **Lake Forest** [PLACER].

Forest City: see **Forest** [SIERRA].

Foresthill [PLACER]: *town,* 9 miles southeast of Colfax (lat. 39° 01'10" N, long. 120°49' W; mainly in sec. 35, T 14 N, R 10 E). Named on Foresthill (1949) 7.5' quadrangle. Postal authorities established Forest Hill post office in 1859 and changed the post office name to Foresthill in 1895 (Salley, p. 77). The place had a trading post in 1850 and a hotel called Forest House in 1858 (Hoover, Rensch, and Rensch, p. 274).

Forest Hill Divide [PLACER]: *ridge,* extends generally southwest for 48 miles between North Fork American River and Middle Fork American River from near Granite Chief to the confluence of the two forks; Foresthill is on the ridge. Named on Auburn (1953), Colfax (1949), Duncan Peak (1952), Foresthill (1949), Granite Chief (1953), Greenwood (1949), Michigan Bluff (1952), Royal Gorge (1953), and Westville (1952) 7.5' quadrangles.

Forest Home [AMADOR]: *locality,* 6.25 miles west of Plymouth (lat. 38°27'55" N, long. 120°57'45" W; near W line sec. 14, T 7 N, R 9 E). Named on Sutter Creek (1944) 15' quadrangle. Postal authorities established Forest Home post office in 1862, moved it 4 miles south in 1886, and discontinued it in 1905; the name was from a hostelry (Salley, p. 77). Camp's (1962) map shows a place called Copper Hill located 3.5 miles north-northwest of Forest Home between Cosumnes River and Little Indian Creek.

Forest House: see **Foresthill** [PLACER].

Forest Shades: see **Bath** [PLACER].

Forest Spring [NEVADA]: *locality,* 3.5 miles south of Grass Valley along Wolf Creek (lat. 39°09'55" N, long. 121°03'55" W). Named on Smartsville (1895) 30' quadrangle.

Forgotten Flat [EL DORADO]: *area,* 5.5 miles west-southwest of Kirkwood along Silver Fork American River (lat. 38°41'10" N, long. 120°10'25" W). Named on Tragedy Spring (1979) 7.5' quadrangle.

Forks: see **The Forks**, under **Downieville** [SIERRA].

Forks House [PLACER]: *locality,* nearly 4 miles southwest of Westville on Forest Hill Divide (lat. 39°08'10" N, long. 120°41'55" W; near NE cor. sec. 23, T 15 N, R 11 E). Site named on Westville (1952) 7.5' quadrangle. Postal authorities established Forks House post office in 1860 and discontinued it in 1861; the place was a hotel and stage stop (Salley, p. 77).

Forks House Ravine: see **West Branch**, under **El Dorado Canyon** [PLACER].

Forks of Oregon Creek: see **Forest** [SIERRA].

Forks of the Cosumnes: see **Yeomet**, under **Enterprise** [AMADOR].

Forni [EL DORADO]: *locality,* 3.5 miles northeast of Robbs Peak (lat. 38°57'30" N, long. 120°21' W). Named on Pyramid Peak (1896) 30' quadrangle.

Forni: see **Lower Forni** [EL DORADO]; **Upper Forni** [EL DORADO].

Forni Creek [EL DORADO]: *stream,* flows 2.5 miles to South Fork American River 4 miles south of Pyramid Peak (lat. 38°47'15" N, long. 120°10'05" W; sec. 24, T 11 N, R 16 E). Named on Pyramid Peak (1955) 7.5' quadrangle.

Forni Lake [EL DORADO]:

(1) *lake,* 800 feet long, 8 miles east-northeast of Robbs Peak (lat. 38°57'20" N, long. 120°15'40" W; sec. 23, T 13 N, R 15 E). Named on Loon Lake (1952, photorevised 1973) 7.5' quadrangle.

(2) *lake,* 1000 feet long, 2.25 miles south of Pyramid Peak (lat. 38° 48'50" N, long. 120°09'50" W; sec. 12, T 11 N, R 16 E); the lake is near Forni Creek. Named on Pyramid Peak (1955) 7.5' quadrangle.

Fornis [EL DORADO]:

(1) *locality,* 1.5 miles southwest of Georgetown (lat. 38°53'30" N, long. 120°51'35" W; near E line sec. 16, T 12 N, R 10 E). Named on Georgetown (1949) 7.5' quadrangle.

(2) *locality,* 13 miles east of Georgetown (lat. 38°53'30" N, long. 120°35' W). Named on Placerville (1893) 30' quadrangle.

Fort Ann: see **Volcano** [AMADOR].

Fort Grizzly [EL DORADO]: *locality,* 6 miles south-southwest of Caldor near South Fork Cosumnes River (lat. 38°31'25" N, long. 120°28'40" W;

near NW cor. sec. 30, T 8 N, R 14 E). Site named on Caldor (1951) 7.5' quadrangle.

Fort Jim: see **Old Fort Jim** [EL DORADO].

Fort John: see **Volcano** [AMADOR].

Fort Sacramento: see **Sacramento** [SACRAMENTO].

Fort Sutter: see **Sacramento** [SACRAMENTO].

Fort Trojan: see **Virginiatown** [PLACER].

45 Mile Campground [EL DORADO]: *locality,* 4.25 miles west of Echo Summit along South Fork American River (lat. 38°48'15" N, long. 120°06'30" W; sec. 16, T 11 N, R 17 E). Named on Echo Lake (1955) 7.5' quadrangle.

Fortytwo Mile Campground [EL DORADO]: *locality,* nearly 4 miles south of Pyramid Peak along South Fork American River (lat. 38° 47'25" N, long. 120°09'05" W; sec. 19, T 11 N, R 17 E). Named on Pyramid Peak (1955) 7.5' quadrangle.

Forward: see **Camp Forward** [EL DORADO].

Foster: see **Cut Eye Fosters Bar** [SIERRA].

Foster Bar [YUBA]: *locality,* 5.5 miles southeast of Challenge along North Fork Yuba River (present North Yuba River) (lat. 39°26'10" N, long. 121°08'15" W). Named on Smartsville (1895) 30' quadrangle. Called Fosters Bar on Wescoatt's (1861) map. Water of New Bullards Bar Reservoir now covers the site. Postal authorities established Foster's Bar post office before March 5, 1852, and discontinued it in 1866 (Salley, p. 79). The name is for William M. Foster, who mined and opened a store along North Yuba River in 1849 (Hoover, Rensch, and Rensch, p. 595).

Foster Meadow [EL DORADO]: *area,* 10 miles east of Caldor along Middle Fork Cosumnes River (lat. 38°35'25" N, long. 120°14'55" W; sec. 31, T 9 N, R 16 E). Named on Bear River Reservoir (1979) and Peddler Hill (1951) 7.5' quadrangles.

Foster Mountain [EL DORADO]: *peak,* 4.25 miles north of Chili Bar (lat. 38°49'40" N, long. 120°49'35" W; sec. 2, T 11 N, R 10 E). Altitude 2292 feet. Named on Garden Valley (1949) 7.5' quadrangle. The name commemorates William H. Foster, who bought land in the vicinity in 1854 (Gernes, p. 91).

Fosters: see **Lockwood** [AMADOR].

Foster's Bar: see **Foster Bar** [YUBA].

Foster's Lower Bar: see **Parks Bar** [YUBA].

Foster's Station: see **Lockwood** [AMADOR].

Fouch Camp: see **Fouts Camp** [COLUSA].

Fountain House: see **Fountain House Hill** [YUBA].

Fountain House Hill [YUBA]: *peak,* 2.5 miles north of Dobbins (lat. 39°24'35" N, long. 121°11'50" W; at N line sec. 21, T 18 N, R 7 E). Named on Challenge (1948) 7.5' quadrangle. Wescoatt's (1861) map shows Fountain Ho. [House] located 2 miles north of Dobbins Ranch (present Dobbins). Robert Johnston opened Fountain House in 1860 (Hoover, Rensch, and Rensch, p. 593).

Four Acres [PLACER]: *locality,* nearly 2 miles east-southeast of Foresthill (lat. 39°00'20" N, long. 120°47'15" W; near S line sec. 31, T 14 N, R 11 E). Named on Colfax (1938) 30' quadrangle.

Four Cornered Peak [EL DORADO]: *peak,* nearly 6 miles north of Kyburz (lat. 38°51'30" N, long. 120°17'15" W; sec. 27, T 12 N, R 15 E). Altitude 6858 feet. Named on Kyburz (1952) 7.5' quadrangle.

Four Corners [AMADOR]: *locality,* 4.5 miles west of Plymouth (lat. 38°28'50" N, long. 120°55'50" W; sec. 12, T 7 N, R 9 E). Named on Irish Hill (1962) 7.5' quadrangle.

Four Corners [EL DORADO]: *locality,* nearly 3 miles southwest of Coloma (lat. 38°46'05" N, long. 120°55'25" W; at N line sec. 36, T 11 N, R 9 E). Named on Coloma (1949) 7.5' quadrangle.

Four Corners: see **The Four Corners** [COLUSA].

Four Horse Flat [PLACER]: *area,* 3.25 miles south-southeast of Cisco Grove along Little Granite Creek (lat. 39°15'50" N, long. 120°31'30" W; sec. 9, T 16 N, R 13 E). Named on Cisco Grove (1955) 7.5' quadrangle.

Four Lakes [EL DORADO]: *lakes,* largest 850 feet long, 4 miles northeast of Kirkwood (lat. 38°44'35" N, long. 120°01' W; sec. 4, 5, T 10 N, R 18 E). Named on Caples Lake (1979) 7.5' quadrangle.

Fourmile Bend [SUTTER-YOLO]: *bend,* 3 miles north of Knights Landing along Sacramento River on Sutter-Yolo County line (lat. 38°50'30" N, long. 121°43'30" W; sec. 35, T 12 N, R 2 E). Named on Knights Landing (1952) 7.5' quadrangle.

Fourness: see **Marty** [YOLO].

4-Q Lakes [EL DORADO]: *lakes,* 3 miles west-northwest of Phipps Peak (lat. 38°56'35" N, long. 120°12'05" W; sec. 27, 28, T 13 N, R 16 E). Named on Rockbound Valley (1955) 7.5' quadrangle.

Fourteen Mile House [EL DORADO]: *locality,* 12 miles east-northeast of Placerville near present Pollock Pines (lat. 38°45'45" N, long. 120°34'40" W). Named on Placerville (1893) 30' quadrangle.

Fourteen Mile House: see **Colusa** [COLUSA].

Fourth of July Canyon [AMADOR]: *canyon,* 2 miles long, 1.5 miles east-northeast of Mokelumne Peak on Amador-Alpine County line (lat. 38°32'40" N, long. 120°04'20" W). Named on Mokelumne Peak (1979) 7.5' quadrangle.

Fourth of July Flat [EL DORADO]: *area,* 4.25 miles west-northwest of Pyramid Peak (lat. 38°52'15" N, long. 120°13'40" W; near W line sec. 21, T 12 N, R 16 E). Named on Pyramid Peak (1955) 7.5' quadrangle.

Foutch Camp: see **Fouts Camp** [COLUSA].

Fouts Camp [COLUSA]: *locality,* nearly 4 miles west of Fouts Springs (lat. 39°21'35" N, long. 122°44'05" W; sec. 2, T 17 N, R 8 E). Named on Fouts Springs (1968) 7.5' quadrangle. United States Board on Geographic Names (1969, p. 4) rejected the forms "Fouch Camp" and "Foutch Camp" for the name.

Fouts Springs [COLUSA]: *locality,* 6.25 miles west-southwest of Stonyford (lat. 39°21'15" N, long. 122°39'45" W; sec. 5, T 17 N, R 7 W). Named on Fouts Springs (1968) 7.5' quadrangle. Postal authorities established Fouts Springs post office in 1882, discontinued it in 1913, reestablished it in 1945, discontinued it in 1947, reestablished it in 1950, and discontinued it in 1956 (Salley, p. 79). The name commemorates John F. Fouts, who found springs at the place in 1873 (Gudde, 1949, p. 120). Four principal springs provided water for a resort that in 1910 had accommodations for 150 guests (Waring, G.A., p. 205-206).

Fowler Spring [NEVADA]: *spring,* 6 miles south of North Bloomfield (lat. 39°17' N, long. 120°53'10" W; sec. 5, T 16 N, R 10 E). Named on North Bloomfield (1949) 7.5' quadrangle.

Fox Canyon [COLUSA]: *canyon,* drained by a stream that flows 1 mile to Salt Creek (2) 4.5 miles northeast of Wilbur Springs (lat. 39°04'35" N, long. 122°20'45" W; sec 7, T 14 N, R 4 W). Named on Wilbur Springs (1961) 15' quadrangle.

Fox Canyon [YOLO]: *canyon,* drained by a stream that flows 2 miles to Hungry Hollow 7 miles east-southeast of Guinda (lat. 38°47'40" N, long. 122°04'15" W; near N line sec. 22, T 11 N, R 2 W). Named on Bird Valley (1959) 7.5' quadrangle.

Fox Lake [EL DORADO]: *lake,* 800 feet long, 5 miles west-northwest of Phipps Peak (lat. 38°59'35" N, long. 120°13'35" W; sec. 8, T 13 N, R 16 E). Named on Rockbound Valley (1955) 7.5' quadrangle.

Francis: see **Lake Francis** [YUBA].

Francis Cow Camp [EL DORADO]: *locality,* 5 miles north-northeast of Robbs Peak (lat. 38°59'25" N, long. 120°22'15" W; sec. 11, T 13 N, R 14 E). Named on Loon Lake (1952) 7.5' quadrangle.

Francis Lake [EL DORADO]: *lake,* 700 feet long, 6 miles north-northeast of Robbs Peak (lat. 38°59'35" N, long. 120°20'20" W; sec. 7, T 13 N, R 15 E). Named on Loon Lake (1952, photorevised 1973) 7.5' quadrangle.

Franklin [SACRAMENTO]: *village,* 5 miles west-southwest of Elk Grove (lat. 38°22'40" N, long. 121°27'15" W; on N line sec. 17, T 6 N, R 5 E). Named on Florin (1968) 7.5' quadrangle. Postal authorities established Franklin post office in 1856, discontinued it in 1858, reestablished it in 1862, and discontinued it in 1943 (Frickstad, p. 133). The name is from Franklin House that Andrew George built in 1856; the village also was known as Georgetown until 1857 (Gudde, 1949, p. 120). Postal authorities established Doby Ranch post office 6 miles southeast of Franklin (NE quarter sec. 3, T 5 N, R 5 E) in 1874 and discontinued in 1876 (Salley, p. 60). California Division of Highways' (1934) map shows a place called Runyon located along Western Pacific Railroad 4 miles north of Franklin, and a place called Glanvale situated 6 miles south of Franklin along the railroad. Runyon is called Sims on California Mining Bureau's (1917e) map. The name "Runyon" was given to honor sports writer Damon Runyon; the name "Sims" was for an old settler (Gudde, 1949, p. 292).

Franklin House: see **Franklin** [SACRAMENTO].

Fraser's Bar: see **Wambo Bar** [YUBA].

Fraser Shoal [SACRAMENTO]: *shoal,* 14 miles west-southwest of Isleton in San Joaquin River (lat. 38°03'25" N, long. 121°50'25" W). Named on Antioch North (1978) 7.5' quadrangle.

Frata Lake [EL DORADO]: *lake,* 500 feet long, 5.5 miles west-northwest of Echo Summit (lat. 38°50'45" N, long. 120°07'15" W; sec. 32, T 12 N, R 17 E). Named on Echo Lake (1955) 7.5' quadrangle.

Frazier Creek [PLACER-SIERRA]: *stream,* heads at Gold Lake in Sierra County and flows 4.5 miles to Grouse Creek nearly 6 miles southwest of Duncan Peak in Placer County (lat. 39°05'45" N, long. 120°35'05" W; near N line sec. 1, T 14 N, R 12 E). Named on Gold Lake (1981) and Greek Store (1952) 7.5' quadrangles. Logan's (1925) map has the name "Frazier Ravine" for the canyon of the stream.

Frazier Ravine: see **Frazier Creek** [PLACER-SIERRA].

Fraziers Landing [COLUSA]: *locality,* 6.25 miles southeast of Grimes (lat. 39°00'20" N, long. 121°49'05" W; near W line sec. 1, T 13 N, R 1 E). Named on Sutter Buttes (1954) 15' quadrangle.

Fredericks Spring [YOLO]: *spring,* 3 miles south-southwest of Guinda (lat. 38°47'10" N, long. 122°12'45" W; sec. 20, T 11 N, R 3 W). Named on Guinda (1959) 7.5' quadrangle.

Freds Place [EL DORADO]: *locality,* 6 miles southwest of Pyramid Peak (lat. 38°47'10" N, long. 120°14'10" W; sec. 20. T 11 N, R 16 E). Named on Fallen Leaf Lake (1955) 15' quadrangle.

Freel Meadows [EL DORADO]: *area,* 4 miles southwest of Freel Peak (lat. 38°48'40" N, long. 119°56'50" W; on E line sec. 11, T 11 N, R 18 E). Named on Freel Peak (1955) 7.5' quadrangle.

Freel Peak [EL DORADO]: *peak,* 13 miles east of Pyramid Peak on El Dorado-Alpine County line (lat. 38°51'25" N, long. 119°53'55" W; on W line sec. 31, T 12 N, R 19 E). Altitude 10, 881 feet. Named on Freel Peak (1955) 7.5' quadrangle. The name commemorates James Freel, who lived at the foot of the peak; William Eimbeck of United States Coast Survey gave the name in 1874 to the highest of the peaks then known as Jobs Peaks (Gudde, 1969, p. 114). The feature also was called Sand Mountain because of its sandy summit (Lekisch, p. 48). United States Board on Geographic Names (1991, p. 7) approved the name "Trimmer Peak" for a peak, altitude 9915 feet, located 1.5 miles northwest of Freel Peak (lat. 38°52'18" N, long. 121°55'19" W; sec. 24, T 12 N, R 18 E); the name commemorates Arnold Robert Trimmer, rancher and former owner of the last working farm near Lake Tahoe.

Freeman Meadow [SIERRA]: *area,* 8 miles north of Sierra City along Church Creek (lat. 39°40'30" N, long. 120°36'15" W; near NW cor. sec. 23, T 21 N, R 12 E). Named on Clio (1981) 7.5' quadrangle.

Freemans Bridge: see **Freemans Crossing** [NEVADA-YUBA].

Freemans Crossing [NEVADA-YUBA]: *locality,* nearly 2 miles northeast of North San Juan along Middle Yuba River on Nevada-Yuba County line (lat. 39°23'20" N, long. 121°05'05" W; near N line sec. 33, T 18 N, R 8 E). Named on Camptonville (1948) 7.5' quadrangle. Called Freemans Bridge on Smartsville (1895) 30' quadrangle. A ferry at the site in 1850 was called Nyes Crossing; after Thomas Hesse built a bridge there in 1851 the place was called Hesse's Crossing until Thomas Freeman bought the bridge in 1854 (Gudde, 1975, p. 121).

Freeport [SACRAMENTO]:

(1) *village,* 8 miles south of downtown Sacramento along Sacramento River (lat. 38°27'45" N, long. 121°30' W). Named on Clarksburg (1967) and Florin (1968) 7.5' quadrangles. The place was started to provide a spot where river boats could unload their goods for shipment by rail without paying the fees usually charged at Sacramento (Gwinn, p. 4). Postal authorities established Freeport post office in 1864 and discontinued it in 1920 (Frickstad, p. 133). California Division of Highways' (1934) map shows a place called Pocket located 1 mile north of the village of Freeport along Southern Pacific Railroad, and has the name "Pocket Tract" northwest of Pocket at a bend of Sacramento River. Postal authorities established Pocket post office in 1900 and discontinued it in 1902 (Frickstad, p. 134). California Division of Highways' (1934) map also shows a place called Del Rio located 3 miles north of the village of Freeport along Southern Pacific Railroad, a place called Charles situated 1.5 miles north of Del Rio along the railroad, and a place called Mosher located 3.25 miles south of the village of Freeport along the railroad. Postal authorities established Brick post office in 1856 3.5 miles from the village of Freeport at the home of the postmaster and discontinued it in 1858; the postmaster made bricks and built his house with them in 1854 (Salley, p. 26).

(2) *locality,* 5.5 miles east-southeast of downtown Sacramento along Sacramento and Placerville Railroad (lat. 38°32'55" N, long. 121° 23'30" W). Named on Sacramento (1892) 30' quadrangle.

Freeport Bend [SACRAMENTO-YOLO]: *bend,* nearly 4 miles north-northwest of Clarksburg along Sacramento River on Sacramento-Yolo County line (lat. 38°28'15" N, long. 121°30'15" W); the bend is just upstream from the village of Freeport. Named on Clarksburg (1967) 7.5' quadrangle. Ringgold's (1850b) map shows a place called Webster or Russian Embarcadero on the north side of Sacramento River just north of present Freeport Bend.

Freezeout: see **Ione** [AMADOR].

Fremont [YOLO]: *locality,* 11 miles northeast of Davis along Sacramento Northern Railroad (lat. 38°40'35" N, long. 121°38' W); the place is 0.5 mile west of Elkhorn Ferry. Named on Grays Bend (1953) 7.5' quadrangle. Called Elkhorn on Grays Bend (1916) 7.5' quadrangle, which shows the place along Sacramento and Woodland Railroad.

Fremont: see **Fremont Landing** [YOLO].

Fremont Landing [YOLO]: *locality,* 5.5 miles east-southeast of Knights Landing along Sacramento River opposite the mouth of Feather River (lat. 38°47' N, long. 121°37'05" W; at E line sec. 22, T 11 N, R 3 E). Site named on Verona (1967) 7.5' quadrangle. The name recalls the old town of Fremont that Jonas Spect founded in March 1849 on the west side of Sacramento River 0.5 mile below the mouth of Feather River (Hoover, Rensch, and Rensch, p. 585). Postal authorities established Fremont post office in 1850 and discontinued it in 1864 (Frickstad, p. 221). Goddard's (1857) map has the name "Fremonts" at the place. Postal authorities established Charleston post office along Sacramento River 5 miles southwest of Fremont (sec. 5, T 10 N, R 3 E) in 1858 and discontinued it in 1871; the name was for Charles H. Gray, first postmaster (Salley, p. 42).

French Bar [AMADOR]: *locality,* 4.5 miles south-southwest of Jackson along Mokelumne River (lat. 38°17'10" N, long. 120°47'45" W; near W line sec. 17, T 5 N, R 11 E). Named on Jackson (1962) 7.5' quadrangle. Water of Pardee Reservoir now covers the site. The place also was called Frenchmans Bar (Gudde, 1975, p. 122). Camp's (1962) map shows a place called Diamond Bar located 3.25 miles west-southwest of French Bar on the north side of Mokelumne River.

French Bar [NEVADA-YUBA]: *locality,* 2.5 miles west-northwest of French Corral along Yuba River on Nevada-Yuba County line (lat. 39°19'10" N, long. 121°12'10" W; near W line sec. 21, T 17 N, R 7 E). Named on French Corral (1948) 7.5' quadrangle. Called Frenchmans Bar on Wescoatt's (1861) map, and called French Corral Bar on Logan's (1940) map.

French Camp: see **Jackson Butte** [AMADOR]; **Lancha Plana** [AMADOR]; **Yolo** [YOLO].

French Corral [NEVADA]: *village,* 8 miles west-northwest of Nevada City (lat. 39°18'25" N, long. 121°09'40" W; sec. 26, T 17 N, R 7 E). Named on French Corral (1948) 7.5' quadrangle. Postal authorities established French Corral post office in 1859 and discontinued it in 1945 (Frickstad, p. 113). A Frenchman built a corral for his mules at the place in 1849 and a town developed there after the discovery of gold at the site (Hoover, Rensch, and Rensch, p. 256).

French Corral Bar: see **French Bar** [NEVADA-YUBA].

French Corral Creek [NEVADA]: *stream,* flows 3 miles to South Yuba River 1.5 miles southwest of French Corral (lat. 39°17'40" N, long. 121°10'55" W; sec. 34, T 17 N, R 7 E); the stream goes past French Corral. Named on French Corral (1948) 7.5' quadrangle.

French Creek [EL DORADO]: *stream,* flows 7 miles to Big Canyon Creek 4.25 miles east-northeast of Latrobe (lat. 38°35'10" N, long. 120°54'40" W; near SE cor. sec. 31, T 9 N, R 10 E); the stream goes past Frenchtown. Named on Latrobe (1949) and Shingle Springs (1949) 7.5' quadrangles.

French Creek [NEVADA]: *stream,* flows 1.5 miles to Middle Yuba River 1.5 miles northeast of English Mountain (lat. 39°27'50" N, long. 120°31'55" W; near SE cor. sec. 32, T 19 N, R 13 E). Named on English Mountain (1983) 7.5' quadrangle.

French Creek [SIERRA-YUBA]: *stream,* heads in Sierra County and flows 2 miles to Willow Creek 1.25 miles north of Camptonville in Yuba County (lat. 39°28'15" N, long. 121°02'45" W; sec. 35, T 19 N, R 8 E). Named on Camptonville (1948) 7.5' quadrangle.

French Creek: see **Frenchtown** [EL DORADO].

French Crossing [COLUSA]: *locality,* 10.5 miles north-northeast of Colusa along Butte Creek on Colusa-Butte County line (lat. 39°20'05" N, long. 121°53'30" W). Named on Marysville (1895) 30' quadrangle.

Frenches Ravine [YUBA]: *locality,* 3.5 miles south-southeast of Dobbin (present Dobbins) near the mouth of present French Ravine (lat. 39°18'50" N, long. 121°12'10" W). Named on Smartsville (1895) 30' quadrangle.

French Hill [EL DORADO]: *peak,* 3 miles north-northwest of Greenwood (lat. 38°56'20" N, long. 120°55'30" W; near N line sec. 36, T 13 N, R 9 E). Altitude 2146 feet. Named on Greenwood (1949) 7.5' quadrangle.

French House [PLACER]: *locality,* 7 miles south of Duncan Peak (lat. 39°03'05" N, long. 120°30'45" W; sec. 22, T 14 N, R 13 E). Site named on Greek Store (1952) 7.5' quadrangle.

French Lake [NEVADA]: *lake,* behind a dam on Canyon Creek nearly 2 miles south-southeast of English Mountain (lat. 39°25' N, long. 120°32' W). Named on English Mountain (1983) 7.5' quadrangle.

Frenchmans Bar: see **French Bar** [AMADOR]; **French Bar** [NEVADA-YUBA]; **Washngton** [NEVADA].

French Meadow [SIERRA]: *area,* 8.5 miles southwest of Sierraville (lat. 39°29'55" N, long. 120°27'45" W; sec. 24, T 19 N, R 13 E). Named on Webber Peak (1981) 7.5' quadrangle.

French Meadows [PLACER]: *valley,* along Middle Fork American River above a point 12 miles west-southwest of Granite Chief (lat. 39°06'45" N, long. 120°28'25" W). Named on Granite Chief (1953) 15' quadrangle. Called French Meadow on Truckee (1940) 30' quadrangle. Water of French Meadows Reservoir now partly covers the place.

French Meadows Reservoir [PLACER]: *lake,* behind a dam on Middle Fork American River 12 miles west-southwest of Granite Chief (lat. 39°06'45" N, long. 120°28'15" W; sec. 36, T 15 N, R 13 E). Named on Bunker Hill (1953, photorevised 1973) and Royal Gorge (1953, photorevised 1973) 7.5' quadrangles.

French Ravine [NEVADA]:

(1) *canyon,* drained by a stream that flows 0.5 mile to Wolf Creek 0.5 mile south-southwest of downtown Grass Valley (lat. 39°12'35" N, long. 121°04'05" W; sec. 34, T 16 N, R 8 E). Named on Grass Valley (1949) 7.5' quadrangle.

(2) *canyon,* drained by a stream that flows 4.5 miles to Wolf Creek 4.5 miles south of Grass Valley (lat. 39°09'15" N, long. 121°04'40" W; sec. 15, T 15 N, R 8 E). Named on Grass Valley (1949) 7.5' quadrangle.

French Ravine [SIERRA]: *canyon,* drained by a stream that flows 1 mile to Kanaka Creek 1.25 miles southwest of Alleghany (lat. 39° 27'30" N, long. 120°51'30" W; sec. 4, T 18 N, R 10 E). Named on Alleghany (1949) 7.5' quadrangle.

French Ravine [YUBA]: *canyon,* drained by a stream that flows 1 mile to Yuba River 3.5 miles south of Dobbins at French Bar (lat. 39°19'15" N, long. 121°12'10" W; near W line sec. 21, T 17 N, R 7 E). Named on French Corral (1948) 7.5' quadrangle.

Frenchtown [EL DORADO]: *locality,* nearly 2 miles south-southeast of Shingle Springs (lat. 38°38'30" N, long. 120°54'40" W; near NE cor. sec.

18, T 9 N, R 10 E); the site is along French Creek. Named on Shingle Springs (1949) 7.5' quadrangle. The place, which was an early mining camp settled largely by Frenchmen and French Canadians, also had the name "French Creek" (Hoover, Rensch, and Rensch, p. 83).

Frenchtown [YUBA]: *locality,* nearly 6 miles southeast of Rackerby along Dry Creek (lat. 39°23'15" N, long. 121°15'15" W; sec. 25, T 18 N, R 6 E). Named on Rackerby (1948) 7.5' quadrangle. A man named Vavasseur started the place (Bancroft, 1888, p. 487). Wescoatt's (1861) map shows Jefferson House situated less than 1 mile north-northwest of Frenchtown. James Evans built Jefferson House in 1852 (Hoover, Rensch, and Rensch, p. 593).

Frenchy Point [YUBA]: *relief feature,* 4.25 miles east-southeast of Challenge on the east side of North Yuba River (lat. 39°27'20" N, long. 121°09'15" W; at S line sec. 35, T 19 N, R 7 E). Named on Challenge (1948) 7.5' quadrangle.

Frenzel Creek [COLUSA]: *stream,* flows 1.5 miles to Little Stony Creek 6 miles south of Stonyford (lat. 39°17'25" N, long. 122°33'35" W; at S line sec. 29, T 17 N, R 6 W). Named on Gilmore Peak (1968) 7.5' quadrangle.

Fresh Pond [EL DORADO]: *locality,* 3 miles east of Pollock Pines (lat. 38°45'40" N, long. 120°31'45" W; sec. 33, T 11 N, R 13 E). Named on Pollock Pines (1950) 7.5' quadrangle.

Fresh Pond Ravine [EL DORADO]: *canyon,* drained by a stream that flows 1 mile to South Fork American River 3 miles east of Pollock Pines (lat. 38°45'55" N, long. 120°31'45" W; near S line sec. 28, T 11 N, R 13 E); the mouth of the canyon is near French Pond. Named on Pollock Pines (1950) 7.5' quadrangle.

Freshwater: see **Williams** [COLUSA].

Freshwater Branch [COLUSA]: *stream,* flows 2.25 miles to East Fork Sulphur Creek 2.5 miles northwest of Wilbur Springs (lat. 39° 04' N, long. 122°27'15" W; sec. 18, T 14 N, R 5 W). Named on Wilbur Springs (1961) 15' quadrangle.

Fresh-water Cañon: see **Freshwater Creek** [COLUSA].

Freshwater Creek [COLUSA]: *stream,* flows 32 miles to end in Colusa Basin 5 miles northeast of Williams (lat. 39°12'10" N, long. 122°04'05" W; near N line sec. 34, T 16 N, R 2 W). Named on Colusa (1953) and Wilbur Springs (1961) 15' quadrangles. Browne and Taylor (p. 180) mentioned use of the name "Fresh-water cañon" as early as 1857.

Frog Lake [NEVADA]: *lake,* 1850 feet long, 3.5 miles north of Donner Pass (lat. 39°22'05" N, long. 120°19'20" W; sec. 33, T 18 N, R 15 E). Named on Norden (1955) 7.5' quadrangle.

Frog Lake Cliff [NEVADA]: *relief feature,* 3.5 miles north of Donner Pass (lat. 39°22'05" N, long. 120°19'35" W; on W line sec. 33, T 18 N, R 15 E); the feature is west of Frog Lake. Named on Norden (1955) 7.5' quadrangle.

Frost Hill [PLACER]: *peak,* 1 mile southeast of Dutch Flat (lat. 39° 11'45" N, long. 120°49'15" W; near NW cor. sec. 2, T 15 N, R 10 E). Named on Dutch Flat (1950) 7.5' quadrangle.

Frosts [EL DORADO]: *locality*, nearly 3 miles south-southeast of the present town of Meeks Bay (lat. 39°00'05" N, long. 120°06'05" W). Named on Truckee (1895) 30' quadrangle.

Frosty Hollow [YUBA]: *relief feature,* 2 miles northeast of Strawberry Valley (lat. 39°34'55" N, long. 121°04'30" W; sec. 22, T 20 N, R 8 E). Named on Strawberry Valley (1948) 7.5' quadrangle.

Fruit Ridge [EL DORADO]: *ridge,* generally west-trending, 1 mile long, 3 miles west of Camino (lat. 38°44'35" N, long. 120°43'45" W). Named on Camino (1952) 7.5' quadrangle.

Fruitridge Manor [SACRAMENTO]: *district,* 4.5 miles southeast of downtown Sacramento (lat. 38°31'30" N, long. 121°26'15" W). Named on Sacramento East (1967) 7.5' quadrangle.

Fry Creek [EL DORADO]: *stream,* flows 1.5 miles to South Fork American River 4.25 miles west of Kyburz (lat. 38°46'05" N, long. 120°22'20" W; sec. 26, T 11 N, R 14 E). Named on Kyburz (1952) 7.5' quadrangle.

Frye Creek [SACRAMENTO]: *stream,* flows 3.5 miles to Laguna Creek 7.25 miles northeast of Elk Grove (lat. 38°29'10" N, long. 121°16'30" W; sec. 1, T 7 N, R 6 E). Named on Buffalo Creek (1967), Carmichael (1967), and Elk Grove (1968) 7.5' quadrangles.

Frytown: see **Ophir** [PLACER].

Fulda: see **Emigrant Gap** [PLACER] (2).

Fulda Creek [PLACER]: *stream,* flows 8 miles to North Fork of North Fork American River 4.5 miles north-northwest of Westville (lat. 39°14' N, long. 120°41'20" W; sec. 24, T 16 N, R 11 E). Named on Blue Canyon (1955) and Westville (1952) 7.5' quadrangles.

Fuller Lake [NEVADA]: *lake,* 0.5 mile long, 3 miles northwest of Yuba Gap (lat. 39°20'55" N, long. 120°39' W; on S line sec. 8, T 17 N, R 12 E). Named on Blue Canyon (1955) 7.5' quadrangle.

Funks Creek [COLUSA]: *stream,* heads in Glenn County and flows 10 miles to lowlands 2.5 miles northeast of Sites in Colusa County (lat. 39°19'50" N, long. 122°17'45" W; sec. 15, T 17 N, R 4 W). Named on Lodoga (1960) and Maxwell (1952) 15' quadrangles. The name commemorates John Funk, who owned land in the region in the 1850's (Gudde, 1949, p. 123).

Furnace Flat [NEVADA]: *area,* 6.5 miles east-northeast of Yuba Gap (lat. 39°21'15" N, long. 120°30'10" W; sec. 10, T 17 N, R 13 E). Named on Cisco Grove (1955) 7.5' quadrangle.

Fyffe [EL DORADO]: *locality,* 10.5 miles east of Placerville (lat. 38° 45' N, long. 120°36'20" W). Named on Placerville (1893) 30' quadrangle. Postal authorities established Fyffe post office in 1882 and discontinued it in 1913; the name is from the operator of a summer resort (Salley, p. 82).

— G —

Gaddis Creek [EL DORADO]: *stream,* flows 2.5 miles to Slab Creek 7.5 miles north-northwest of Pollock Pines (lat. 38°51'40" N, long. 120°38'10" W; sec. 28, T 12 N, R 12 E). Named on Slate Mountain (1950) and Tunnel Hill (1950) 7.5' quadrangles.

Gaddis Spring [EL DORADO]: *spring,* 9 miles north-northwest of Pollock Pines (lat. 38°52'55" N, long. 120°39'20" W; at S line sec. 17, T 12 N, R 12 E); the spring is west of the upper part of Gaddis Creek. Named on Tunnel Hill (1950) 7.5' quadrangle.

Gaither Canyon [COLUSA]: *canyon,* drained by a stream that flows 3 miles to Bear Valley nearly 6 miles north-northwest of Wilbur Springs (lat. 39°07'10" N, long. 122°26'45" W; at W line sec. 29, T 15 N, R 5 W). Named on Wilbur Springs (1961) 15' quadrangle.

Galbraith: see **Central House** [NEVADA].

Gale Creek [SIERRA]: *stream,* flows 1.5 miles to Oregon Creek 3 miles northeast of Pike (lat. 39°28' N, long. 120°57'15" W; sec. 34, T 19 N, R 9 E). Named on Pike (1949) 7.5' quadrangle.

Galena Hill [YUBA]:

(1) *peak,* 1.5 miles north of Camptonville (lat. 39°28'20" N, long. 121°03'10" W; sec. 35, T 19 N, R 8 E). Named on Camptonville (1948) 7.5' quadrangle.

(2) *locality,* 1.5 miles north of Camptonville (lat. 39°28'30" N, long. 121°03'05" W). Named on Smartsville (1895) 30' quadrangle. Miners from Galena, Illinois, found gold at the place in 1852, and the mining camp there was called Galena Hill (Hoover, Rensch, and Rensch, p. 596).

Galena House: see **Browns Valley** [YUBA].

Gales Orchard [SIERRA]: *locality,* 4 miles northeast of Pike (lat. 39°29' N, long. 120°57' W; sec. 27, T 19 N, R 9 E); the place is near the head of Gale Creek. Named on Pike (1949) 7.5' quadrangle.

Gallagher Slough [SACRAMENTO]: *water feature,* 9 miles south-southwest of Isleton along the southeast side of Sherman Island (lat. 38°03'15" N, long. 121°41'40" W). Named on Jersey Island (1978) 7.5' quadrangle.

Galloway Ridge: see **Old Galloway Ridge** [SIERRA].

Galt [SACRAMENTO]: *town,* 25 miles south-southeast of downtown Sacramento (lat. 38°15'10" N, long. 121°18' W). Named on Galt (1968) and Lodi North (1968) 7.5' quadrangles. Postal authorities established Galt post office in 1869 (Frickstad, p. 133), and the town incorporated in 1946. John McFarland named the place for his former home in Ontario, Canada (Gudde, 1949, p. 124).

Gambler Creek [EL DORADO]: *stream,* flows nearly 1.5 miles to South Fork American River less than 1 mile north-northwest of Coloma (lat. 38°48'35" N, long. 120°53'45" W; near NE cor. sec. 18, T 11 N, R 10 E). Named on Coloma (1949) 7.5' quadrangle.

Gambler Creek: see **Little Gambler Creek** [EL DORADO].

Garcia Bend [SACRAMENTO-YOLO]: *bend,* 6.25 miles south-southwest of downtown Sacramento along Sacramento River on Sacramento-Yolo County line (lat. 38°30' N, long. 121°33'30" W). Named on Clarksburg (1967) and Sacramento West (1967) 7.5' quadrangles.

Garden Bar [PLACER]: *locality,* 11 miles northwest of Auburn along Bear River near the mouth of Alderman Creek (lat. 39°00'40" N, long. 121°13' W); sec. 5, T 13 N, R 7 E). Named on Wolf (1949) 7.5' quadrangle.

Gardeners Point [SIERRA]: *relief feature,* 5.5 miles southwest of Mount Fillmore (lat. 39°40'55" N, long. 120°55'45" W; sec. 13, T 21 N, R 9 E). Named on La Porte (1951) 7.5' quadrangle.

Gardenland [SACRAMENTO]: *district,* 2.5 miles north-northeast of downtown Sacramento (lat. 38°36'35" N, long. 121°28'15" W). Named on Sacramento East (1967) 7.5' quadrangle.

Garden Valley [EL DORADO]: *settlement,* 6.25 miles north-northwest of Chili Bar (lat. 38°51'15" N, long. 120°51'30" W; around NE cor. sec. 33, T 12 N, R 10 E); the place is along Johntown Creek. Named on Garden Valley (1949) 7.5' quadrangle. Postal authorities established Garden Valley post office in 1852, discontinued it in 1853, reestablished it in 1854, discontinued it in 1862, reestablished it in 1872, discontinued it in 1895, reestablished it in 1896, and moved it 0.5 mile northwest in 1940 (Salley, p. 82). The place first was called Johntown for the sailor who discovered gold there; the name was changed to Garden Valley when raising vegetables became more profitable than mining gold (Hoover, Rensch, and Rensch, p. 88). A mining camp called Sailors Flat because it was founded by a group of sailors was located about 2 miles south and east of Garden Valley; a mining camp called Peru because it was founded by miners from Peru, Indiana, was situated close to Sailors Flat on the south side of Irish Creek near the head of that stream (Gernes, p. 58, 59).

Garden Valley [YUBA]:
(1) *valley,* 2.5 miles west-southwest of Camptonville along Willow Creek (lat. 39°26'35" N, long. 121°05'35" W). Named on Nevada City (1948) 15' quadrangle. Water of New Bullards Bar Reservoir now covers the valley.
(2) *locality,* 3.25 miles west-southwest of Camptonville (lat. 39° 26' N, long. 121°06'15" W). Named on Smartsville (1895) 30' quadrangle.

Gardner Mountain [EL DORADO]: *relief feature,* 4.5 miles east of Mount Tallac (lat. 38°54'40" N, long. 120°00'50" W; near S line sec. 5, T 12 N, R 18 E). Named on Emerald Bay (1955, photorevised 1969) 7.5' quadrangle.

Gardners [PLACER]: *locality,* less than 1 mile east-southeast of Devil Peak (lat. 38°57'10" N, long. 120°32'10" W). Named on Placerville (1893) 30' quadrangle.

Garlic: see **Peart** [YOLO].

Gas Canyon [NEVADA]: *canyon,* 1.25 miles long, opens into the canyon of Greenhorn Creek 7.5 miles north-northeast of Chicago Park (lat. 39'14'35" N, long. 120°54'10" W; near NW cor. sec. 19, T 16 N, R 10 E). Named on Chicago Park (1949) and North Bloomfield (1949) 7.5' quadrangles.

Gas Canyon [PLACER]: *canyon,* drained by a stream that flows 3.5 miles to Middle Fork American River 8.5 miles east-northeast of Auburn (lat. 38°57'50" N, long. 120°56' W; at W line sec. 24, T 13 N, R 9 E). Named on Colfax (1949) and Greenwood (1949) 7.5' quadrangles.

Gasoline Alley [PLACER]: *locality,* 2 miles north-northwest of downtown Auburn (lat. 38°55'30" N, long. 121°05' W; sec. 4, T 12 N, R 8 E). Named on Auburn (1953) 7.5' quadrangle.

Gaston [NEVADA]: *locality,* 3.25 miles south of Graniteville (lat. 39°23'40" N, long. 120°44'30" W; sec. 28, T 18 N, R 11 E). Site named on Graniteville (1982) 7.5' quadrangle. Postal authorities established Gaston post office in 1899 and discontinued it in 1913 (Frickstad, p. 113).

Gaston Ridge [NEVADA]: *ridge,* south-southwest-trending, 2 miles long, 3.25 miles south of Graniteville (lat. 39°23'35" N, long. 120° 44'25" W); the site of Gaston is on the ridge. Named on Graniteville (1982) 7.5' quadrangle.

Gate: see **The Gate**, under **Jackson Gate** [AMADOR].

Gates Camp [PLACER]: *locality,* 7.5 miles west-southwest of Granite Chief (lat. 39°08'20" N, long. 120°24'10" W; sec. 22, T 15 N, R 14 E). Named on Truckee (1940) 30' quadrangle. Royal Gorge (1953) 7.5' quadrangle shows Gates cabin at the place.

Gates of the Antipodes [NEVADA-SIERRA]: *narrows,* 3 miles south-southwest of Sierra City along Middle Yuba River on Nevada-Sierra County line (lat. 39°31'35" N, long. 120°39'25" W; sec. 8, T 19 N, R 12 E). Named on Sierra City (1981) 7.5' quadrangle.

Gatesville: see **Sucker Flat** [YUBA].

Gateway [NEVADA]: *locality,* 1 mile west of downtown Truckee (lat. 39°19'30" N, long. 120°12'10" W; sec. 16, T 17 N, R 16 E). Named on Truckee (1955) 7.5' quadrangle.

Gefo Lake [EL DORADO]: *lake,* 950 feet long, 1 mile east-southeast of Pyramid Peak (lat. 38°50'30" N, long. 120°08'25" W). Named on Pyramid Peak (1955) 7.5' quadrangle. The word "Gefo" was coined from letters in the name "George Foss" (Lekisch, p. 65).

Gelatt [NEVADA]: *settlement,* 2 miles east of Donner Pass at the west end of Donner Lake (lat. 39°19'10" N, long. 120°17'10" W; near SW cor. sec. 14, T 17 N, R 15 E). Named on Truckee (1940) 30' quadrangle. Postal authorities established Gelatt post office in 1923 and discontinued it in 1935; the name was for Ethel M. Gelatt, first postmaster (Salley, p. 83).

General Creek [EL DORADO]: *stream,* flows 9 mile to Lake Tahoe 1.25 miles north-northeast of the town of Meeks Bay (lat. 39°03'20" N, long. 120°06'45" W; sec. 16, T 14 N, R 17 E); the stream heads 2 miles north-northwest of Phipps Peak. Named on Homewood (1955), Meeks Bay (1955), and Rockbound Valley (1955) 7.5' quadrangle. The name commemorates General William Phipps, for whom Phipps Peak was named (Gudde, 1949, p. 125).

Genevieve: see **Lake Genevieve** [EL DORADO].

Genevra [COLUSA]: *locality,* 4 miles north-northwest of Arbuckle along Southern Pacific Railroad (lat. 39°04'10" N, long. 122°05'25" W; sec. 16, T 14 N, R 2 W). Named on Arbuckle (1952) 7.5' quadrangle. Arbuckle (1918) 7.5' quadrangle has both the names "Berlin" and "Genevra Sta" at the place, and Colusa (1942) 15' quadrangle has the designation "Genevra (Berlin)" there. Postal authorities established Berlin post office in 1876 and discontinued it in 1934 (Frickstad, p. 17). Railroad officials gave the name "Berlin" to the place in the 1870's, but postal officials changed the name of the post office to Genevra during World War I (Gudde, 1949, p. 126).

Gent Creek [NEVADA]: *stream,* flows 1.25 miles to Squirrel Creek 5 miles west of Grass Valley (lat. 39°13'10" N, long. 121°09'30" W). Named on Smartsville (1895) 30' quadrangle.

George R. Stewart Peak: see **Donner Pass** [NEVADA-PLACER].

Georges Ravine [PLACER]: *canyon,* drained by a stream that flows 1 mile to Auburn Ravine 5 miles west of Auburn (lat. 38°54'05" N, long. 121°10'55" W; sec. 11, T 12 N, R 7 E). Named on Gold Hill (1954) 7.5' quadrangle.

Georgetown [EL DORADO]: *town,* 12.5 miles north of Placerville (lat. 38°54'25" N, long. 120°50'15" W; on W line sec. 11, T 12 N, R 10 E). Named on Georgetown (1949) 7.5' quadrangle. Postal authorities established Georgetown post office in 1851 (Frickstad, p. 26). According to Hoover, Rensch, and Rensch (p. 87), the first mining camp at the place was known as Growlersburg; after this community was destroyed by fire in 1852, the residents rebuilt the town on higher ground and renamed it Georgetown for George Phipps, who had led a company of sailors to the place. Bancroft (1888, p. 482), on the other hand, related the name to George Ehrenhaft, founder of the town. Whitney (1880, p. 85) mentioned a place called Crane's Gulch that was situated between Georgetown and Johntown.

Georgetown: see **Franklin** [SACRAMENTO].

Georgetown Creek [EL DORADO]: *stream,* flows 3.5 miles to Greenwood Creek 0.5 mile south-southeast of Greenwood (lat. 38° 53'20" N, long. 120°54'30" W; sec. 18, T 12 N, R 10 E); the stream heads near Georgetown. Named on Georgetown (1949) and Greenwood (1949) 7.5' quadrangles.

Georgetown Divide [EL DORADO]: *ridge,* generally west-trending, 9 miles long (center near lat. 38°55'30" N, long. 120°46'45" W); Georgetown is near the west end of the ridge. Named on Georgetown (1949) and Tunnel Hill (1950) 7.5' quadrangles.

Georgetown Junction [EL DORADO]: *locality,* 5 miles southwest of Pyramid Peak (lat. 38°47'10" N, long. 120°12'55" W). Named on Pyramid Peak (1896) 30' quadrangle.

George Washington Hill [NEVADA]: *ridge,* generally south-southwest-trending, 1 mile long, 5.5 miles north-northwest of Pilot Peak (lat. 39°14'30" N, long. 121°13'20" W; on W line sec. 17, T 16 N, R 7 E). Named on Rough and Ready (1949) 7.5' quadrangle.

Georgia Flat: see **Georgia Slide** [EL DORADO].

Georgia Gulch [YUBA]: *canyon,* drained by a stream that flows 1 mile to Owl Gulch 1.25 miles south of Strawberry Valley (lat. 39° 32'45" N, long. 121°06'20" W; sec. 32, T 20 N, R 8 E). Named on Strawberry Valley (1948) 7.5' quadrangle.

Georgiana Slough [SACRAMENTO]: *water feature,* diverges from Sacramento River near Walnut Grove and joins Mokelumne River 3 miles south-east of Isleton (lat. 38°07'50" N, long. 121°34'35" W). Named on Isleton (1978) 7.5' quadrangle. The name is for the river steamer *Georgiana,* which was lost in the slough when its boiler exploded (Brotherton, p. 14).

Georgia Slide [EL DORADO]: *locality,* 1.5 miles north-northwest of Georgetown (lat. 38°55'35" N, long. 120°50'50" W; near N line sec. 3, T 12 N, R 10 E). Named on Georgetown (1949) 7.5' quadrangle. Miners from the State of Georgia started a mining camp called Georgia Flat at the place in 1849; the name was changed to Georgia Slide after a landslide occurred (Hoover, Rensch, and Rensch, p. 88). Gudde (1975, p. 95) listed a place called Devine Gulch that was located between Georgia Slide and Georgetown; the name was for Caleb Devine, who discovered gold at the site in 1850.

Gerber: see **Polk** [SACRAMENTO].

Gerle [EL DORADO]: *locality,* 2.25 miles west-northwest of Wentworth Springs (lat. 39°01'30" N, long. 120°22'45" W); the place is at present Gerle Meadow. Named on Truckee (1940) 30' quadrangle. United States Board on Geographic Names (1933, p. 321) rejected the form "Gurley" for the name.

Gerle Creek [EL DORADO]: *stream,* flows 9.5 miles to South Fork Rubicon River 2 miles north of Robbs Peak (lat. 38°57'15" N, long. 120°23'55" W). Named on Bunker Hill (1953), Loon Lake (1952), Robbs Peak (1950), and Wentworth Springs (1953, photorevised 1973) 7.5' quadrangles. United States Board on Geographic Names (1933, p. 321) rejected the form "Gurley Creek" for the name.

Gerle Meadow [EL DORADO]: *area,* 2 miles west of Wentworth Springs (lat. 39°00'50" N, long. 120°22'30" W); the place is along Gerle Creek. Named on Bunker Hill (1953) and Wentworth Springs (1953) 7.5' quadrangles.

Gertrude Lake [EL DORADO]: *lake,* 700 feet long, 5.5 miles south-southwest of Phipps Peak (lat. 38°53'05" N, long. 120°12' W). Named on Rockbound Valley (1955) 7.5' quadrangle.

Giant Gap [PLACER]: *narrows,* 3 miles southeast of Dutch Flat along North Fork American River (lat. 39°10'10" N, long. 120°48'15" W; near SW cor. sec. 1, T 15 N, R 10 E). Named on Dutch Flat (1950) 7.5' quadrangle. Called Grants Gap on Whitney's (1873) map.

Giant Gap Gulch [PLACER]: *canyon,* drained by a stream that flows nearly 2 miles to North Fork American River 3.25 miles southeast of Dutch Flat (lat. 39°10'20" N, long. 120°47'40" W; sec. 1, T 15 N, R 10 E); the mouth of the canyon is just upstream from Giant Gap. Named on Dutch Flat (1950) 7.5' quadrangle.

Giant Gap Ridge [PLACER]: *ridge,* north-northwest-trending, 1.25 miles long, 4 miles south-southeast of Dutch Flat (lat. 39°09'10" N, long. 120°48' W); the ridge is south of Giant Gap. Named on Dutch Flat (1950) 7.5' quadrangle.

Gibbes Spring [YOLO]: *spring,* 2.25 miles east-southeast of Guinda (lat.

38°49' N, long. 122°09'15" W; sec. 11, T 11 N, R 3 W). Named on Guinda (1959) 7.5' quadrangle.

Gibralter [SIERRA]: *peak,* 4.25 miles east-southeast of Mount Fillmore on Sierra-Plumas County line (lat. 39°42'45" N, long. 120° 46'35" W; near E line sec. 5, T 21 N, R 11 E). Altitude 7343 feet. Named on Mount Fillmore (1951) 7.5' quadrangle. Called Gibralta Pk. on Logan's (1929) map.

Gibson Creek [SIERRA]: *stream,* flows 1.5 miles to Slate Creek 3 miles west of Mount Fillmore and less than 0.5 mile south of Gibsonville (lat. 39°44'05" N, long. 120°54'20" W; sec. 30, T 22 N, R 10 E). Named on La Porte (1951) 7.5' quadrangle.

Gibsons New Diggings: see **Gibsonville** [SIERRA].

Gibsonville [SIERRA]: *locality,* 3 miles west-northwest of Mount Fillmore (lat. 39°44'30" N, long. 120°54'25" W; sec. 30, T 22 N, R 10 E). Named on La Porte (1951) 7.5' quadrangle. Postal authorities established Gibsonville post office in 1855, discontinued it for a time in 1869, and discontinued it finally in 1910 (Frickstad, p. 184). The name commemorates a prospector named Gibson, who discovered gold at the site (Hoover, Rensch, and Rensch, p. 496). The place also was called Gibsons New Diggings (Gudde, 1969 p. 120).

Gibsonville Ridge [SIERRA]: *ridge,* generally southwest-trending, 8.5 miles long, 4.25 miles west of Mount Fillmore on Sierra-Plumas County line (lat. 39°44'30" N, long. 120°55'45" W). Named on Blue Nose Mountain (1951), La Porte (1951), and Onion Valley (1950) 7.5' quadrangles.

Gilberts [EL DORADO]: *locality,* 7.25 miles southwest of Old Iron Mountain (lat. 38°38'10" N, long 120°29'35" W; sec. 13, T 9 N, R 13 E). Named on Stump Spring (1951) 7.5' quadrangle.

Gillespie Island: see **Wood Island** [SACRAMENTO].

Gillis Hill [PLACER]: *ridge,* south-southeast-trending, 3.5 miles long, 3 miles southeast of Colfax (lat. 39°04' N, long. 120°55'25" W). Named on Colfax (1949) 7.5' quadrangle.

Gilmore: see **Wilbur Springs** [COLUSA].

Gilmore Creek [EL DORADO]: *stream,* flows 1.5 miles to Big Canyon Creek 2.5 miles east-southeast of Shingle Springs (lat. 38° 39'25" N, long. 120°52'55" W; at S line sec. 4, T 9 N, R 10 E). Named on Placerville (1949) and Shingle Springs (1949) 7.5' quadrangles.

Gilmore Lake [EL DORADO]: *lake,* 2250 feet long, 1 mile south-southwest of Mount Tallac (lat. 38°53'45" N, long. 120°06'55" W; near SE cor. sec. 8, T 12 N, R 17 E). Named on Emerald Bay (1955) 7.5' quadrangle. The name commemorates Nathan Gilmore, who pastured cattle in the summer on the shore of Fallen Leaf Lake in the 1860's (Patricia Loomis in *San Jose* [California] *Mercury*, October 6, 1980).

Gilmore Peak [COLUSA]: *peak,* 4.5 miles south of Stonyford (lat. 39°18'30" N, long. 122°32'55" W; sec. 20, T 17 N, R 6 W); the peak is near the east end of Gilmore Ridge. Altitude 2524 feet. Named on Gilmore Peak (1968) 7.5' quadrangle.

Gilmore Ridge [COLUSA]: *ridge,* generally east-trending, 3.5 miles long, 4.5 miles south-southwest of Stonyford (lat. 39°18'55" N, long. 122°34'10" W); Gilmore Peak is near at the east end of the ridge. Named on Gilmore Peak (1968) 7.5' quadrangle.

Gilmores Glen Alpine Springs: see **Glen Alpine Spring** [EL DORADO].

Gilsizer Slough [SUTTER]: *stream,* heads at Yuba City and flows 16 miles to Sutter Basin 9.5 miles west-northwest of Nicolaus (lat. 38° 57'45" N, long. 121°44'05" W; sec. 22, T 13 N, R 2 E). Named on Gilsizer Slough (1952), Olivehurst (1952), Sutter Causeway (1952), and Yuba City (1952) 7.5' quadrangles.

Gilsons Station: see **Blue Canyon** [PLACER] (2).

Girard Creek [EL DORADO]: *stream,* flows nearly 3 miles to Silver Fork American River 9 miles west of Kirkwood (lat. 38°43'30" N, long. 120°14'10" W; near SW cor. sec. 8, T 10 N, R 16 E). Named on Leek Spring Hill (1951) and Tragedy Spring (1979) 7.5' quadrangles.

Girard Mill [EL DORADO]: *locality,* 12 miles northwest of Leek Spring Hill (lat. 38°44'35" N, long. 120°26'10" W; near SE cor. sec. 5, T 10 N, R 14 E). Site named on Stump Spring (1951) 7.5' quadrangle.

Girdner Bend [COLUSA-SUTTER]: *bend,* 0.5 mile north-northeast of Grimes along Sacramento River on Colusa-Sutter County line (lat. 39°04'55" N, long. 121°53'25" W; sec. 8, T 14 N, R 1 E). Named on Grimes (1954) 7.5' quadrangle.

Girot Ridge [YUBA]: *ridge,* north-northwest-trending, 1.25 miles long, 4.5 miles northeast of Dobbins (lat. 39°24'30" N, long. 121° 08'05" W; sec. 19, 24, T 18 N, R 7 E). Named on Challenge (1948) 7.5' quadrangle.

Glacier Lake [NEVADA]: *lake,* 700 feet long, 3.25 miles south of English Mountain (lat. 39°23'55" N, long. 120°33'25" W; sec. 30, T 18 N, R 13 E). Named on English Mountain (1983) 7.5' quadrangle.

Glann: see **Lambert** [SACRAMENTO].

Glanvale: see **Franklin** [SACRAMENTO].

Glascock Canyon [COLUSA]: *canyon,* drained by a stream that flows 2.5 miles to Manzanita Creek 8.5 miles east-southeast of Wilbur Springs (lat. 38°59'05" N, long. 122°17' W; near SW cor. sec. 11, T 13 N, R 4 W); the canyon heads at Glascock Spring. Named on Glascock Mountain (1958) 7.5' quadrangle.

Glascock Mountain [YOLO]: *peak,* 4 miles northwest of Rumsey (lat. 38°55'10" N, long. 122°18'05" W; near NE cor. sec. 4, T 12 N, R 4 W). Altitude 2540 feet. Named on Glascock Mountain (1958) 7.5' quadrangle.

Glascock Spring [COLUSA]: *spring,* 8 miles southeast of Wilbur Springs (lat. 38°57'45" N, long. 122°18'25" W; sec. 21, T 13 N, R 4 W); the spring is 3 miles north of Glascock Mountain [YOLO] at the head of a branch of Glascock Canyon. Named on Glascock Mountain (1958) 7.5' quadrangle.

Gleason: see **Camp Gleason** [SIERRA].

Glen Alpine: see **Glen Alpine Spring** [EL DORADO].

Glen Alpine Creek [EL DORADO]: *stream,* flows 4 miles to Fallen Leaf Lake 2.25 miles southeast of Mount Tallac (lat. 38°52'50" N, long. 120°04'05" W; near S line sec. 14, T 12 N, R 17 E). Named on Echo Lake (1955) and Emerald Bay (1955) 7.5' quadrangles.

Glen Alpine Spring [EL DORADO]: *spring,* 2 miles south of Mount Tallac (lat. 38°52'30" N, long. 120°05'45" W); the spring is near Glen Alpine Creek. Named on Emerald Bay (1955) 7.5' quadrangle. Pyramid Peak (1896) 30' quadrangle has the name "Glen Alpine Springs" for buildings at the site. Nathan Gilmore discovered the spring in the 1850's and established a resort at the place (Hanna, p. 121). The resort also was known as Gilmores Glen Alpine Springs (Waring, G.A., p. 236). Gilmore's wife chose the name "Glen Alpine" from Walter Scott's romantic poem *Lady of the Lake* (Lekisch, p. 51). Postal authorities established Glen Alpine post office in 1904, discontinued it in 1918, reestablished it in 1929, and discontinued it in 1947 (Frickstad, p. 26).

Glenbrook [NEVADA]: *settlement,* 2 miles northeast of Grass Valley (lat. 39°14'30" N, long. 121°02'15" W; around northeast cor. sec. 23, T 16 N, R 8 E). Named on Grass Valley (1949) 7.5' quadrangle.

Glenn Valley Slough [COLUSA]: *stream,* flows 9 miles to an artificial watercourse 5 miles northwest of Williams (lat. 39°12'15" N, long. 122°13' W; at N line sec. 32, T 16 N, R 3 W). Named on Manor Slough (1958) and Williams (1952) 7.5' quadrangles.

Glide Landing: see **Riverview** [YOLO].

Glide Tract: see **Riverview** [YOLO].

Globe: see **Sacramento** [SACRAMENTO].

Goat Hill [AMADOR]: *peak,* 3.5 miles south of Jackson (lat. 38°17'40" N, long. 120°46'45" W; at SE cor. sec. 8, T 5 N, R 11 E). Altitude 1516 feet. Named on Jackson (1962) 7.5' quadrangle.

Goat Mountain [COLUSA]: *peak,* 7 miles south-southwest of Fouts Springs (lat. 39°15'35" N, long. 122°42'50" W; near SE cor. sec. 2, T 16 N, R 8 W). Altitude 6121 feet. Named on Fouts Springs (1968) 7.5' quadrangle.

Goat Rock [COLUSA]: *peak,* 5.5 miles west-northwest of Pacific Point on Colusa-Lake County line (lat. 39°14'50" N, long. 122°41'20" W). Named on Bartlett Springs (1944) 15' quadrangle.

Goat Rock [NEVADA]: *peak,* 1.5 miles west of Chicago Park (lat. 39°08'35" N, long. 120°59'35" W; near N line sec. 20, T 15 N, R 9 E). Named on Chicago Park (1949) 7.5' quadrangle.

Goat Spring [PLACER]: *spring,* 4.5 miles southwest of Westville (lat. 39°07'40" N, long. 120°42'35" W; sec. 23, T 15 N, R 11 E). Named on Westville (1952) 7.5' quadrangle.

Goddard's Station: see **Al Tahoe** [EL DORADO].

Goffinet Reservoir [AMADOR]: *lake,* 1800 feet long, behind a dam on Jackass Creek 3.25 miles east-northeast of Ione (lat. 38°22'40" N, long. 120°52'55" W; sec. 16, T 6 N, R 10 E). Named on Irish Hill (1962) 7.5' quadrangle.

Goffs Ravine [SIERRA]: *canyon,* drained by a stream that flows 2 miles to Downie River 2.25 miles north of Downieville (lat. 39° 35'35" N, long. 120°49'35" W; near S line sec. 14, T 20 N, R 10 E). Named on Downieville (1951) 7.5' quadrangle.

Goggins [PLACER]: *locality,* 8 miles south of Duncan Peak (lat. 39° 02'30" N, long. 120°30'30" W; near S line sec. 22, T 14 N, R 13 E). Named on Colfax (1938) 30' quadrangle. Greek Store (1952) 7.5' quadrangle shows Goggins mine at the place.

Golconda Ravine [NEVADA]: *canyon,* drained by a stream that flows less than 1 mile to Middle Yuba River nearly 7 miles northeast of North Bloomfield (lat. 39°26'10" N, long. 120°48'30" W; sec. 12, T 18 N, R 10 E). Named on Alleghany (1949) 7.5' quadrangle.

Gold Canyon [NEVADA-SIERRA]: *canyon,* 2.5 miles southeast of Alleghany along Middle Yuba River on Nevada-Sierra County line (lat. 39°26'15" N, long. 120°48'40" W; sec. 11, 12, T 18 N, R 10 E). Named on Alleghany (1949) 7.5' quadrangle.

Gold Canyon [SIERRA]: *canyon,* drained by a stream that flows 1 mile to Canyon Creek 2.25 miles south-southeast of Mount Fillmore (lat. 39°41'50" N, long. 120°50'20" W). Named on Mount Fillmore (1951) 7.5' quadrangle

Gold Canyon: see **Potosi Creek** [SIERRA].

Golden: see **Soapweed** [EL DORADO].

Golden Ball: see **Oregon House** [YUBA].

Golden Gate [COLUSA]: *narrows,* 2.5 miles north-northeast of Sites along Funks Creek (lat. 39°20'35" N, long. 122°19'05" W; sec. 9, T 17 N, R 4 W). Named on Sites (1958) 7.5' quadrangle.

Golden Gate Creek [AMADOR]: *stream,* flows 4.5 miles to Sutter Creek (1) 4.5 miles northeast of Pine Grove (lat. 38°27'50" N, long. 120°36'15"

W; sec. 13, T 7 N, R 12 E). Named on West Point (1948) 7.5' quadrangle.

Golden Gate Ravine [YUBA]: *canyon,* drained by a stream that flows 2.25 miles to Costa Creek 1.25 miles northwest of Challenge (lat. 39°30'05" N, long. 121°14'15" W; near W line sec. 18, T 19 N, R 7 E). Named on Clipper Mills (1948) 7.5' quadrangle.

Gold Flat [NEVADA]: *locality,* 2.5 miles northeast of Grass Valley (lat. 39°14'45" N, long. 121°01'30" W; sec. 13, T 16 N, R 8 E). Named on Grass Valley (1949) 7.5' quadrangle.

Gold Hill [EL DORADO]: *settlement,* 2.5 miles south of Coloma (lat. 38°45'45" N, long. 120°53' W; sec. 32, T 11 N, R 10 E). Named on Coloma (1949) 7.5' quadrangle. Called Granite Hill on Placerville (1893) 30' quadrangle. Postal authorities established Granite Hill post office in 1874 and discontinued it in 1908 (Frickstad, p. 27).

Gold Hill [NEVADA]: *peak,* 0.5 mile southwest of downtown Grass Valley (lat. 39°12'45" N, long. 121°04'10" W; near NW cor. sec. 34, T 16 N, R 8 E). Named on Grass Valley (1949) 7.5' quadrangle.

Gold Hill [PLACER]: *locality,* 6 miles west of Auburn along Auburn Ravine (lat. 38°54'10" N, long. 121°10'50" W; sec. 10, T 12 N, R 7 E). Named on Gold Hill (1954) 7.5' quadrangle. Gudde (1975, p. 135) noted that the place was called Orr City in 1855. Gudde (1975, p. 230, 237) also mentioned a mining place called Mugginsville, located 0.5 mile below Gold Hill, and a mining place called Nesbits Bar, situated in Auburn Ravine near Gold Hill.

Gold Hill: see **Washington** [NEVADA].

Gold Lake [SIERRA]: *lake,* 8500 feet long, 8 miles north of Sierra City (lat. 39°40'45" N, long. 120°39'15" W). Named on Gold Lake (1981) 7.5' quadrangle. The name is from the false report that gold was found at the lake in 1850 (Hanna, p. 123).

Gold Lake: see **Little Gold Lake** [SIERRA].

Gold Note Ridge [EL DORADO]: *ridge,* generally west-trending, 9 miles long, center 3.5 miles south-southwest of Caldor (lat. 38°33'45" N, long. 120°28'05" W). Named on Caldor (1951) and Omo Ranch (1952) 7.5' quadrangles.

Gold Point Ravine [SIERRA]: *canyon,* drained by a stream that flows 1.25 miles to North Yuba River 5.5 miles west of Sierra City (lat. 39°34'10" N, long. 120°44'15" W; near SE cor. sec. 28, T 20 N, R 11 E). Named on Sierra City (1981) 7.5' quadrangle, which shows Gold Point mine in the canyon.

Gold Ridge: see **Camptonville** [YUBA].

Gold Run [NEVADA]: *stream,* flows 2 miles to Deer Creek in downtown Nevada City (lat. 39°15'40" N, long. 121°01'05" W; near W line sec. 7, T 16 N, R 9 E). Named on Grass Valley (1949) and Nevada City (1948) 7.5' quadrangles.

Gold Run [PLACER]: *village,* 2 miles south-southwest of Dutch Flat (lat. 39°10'55" N, long. 120°51'15" W; sec. 4, T 15 N, R 10 E). Named on Dutch Flat (1950) 7.5' quadrangle. Postal authorities established Mountain Springs post office in 1854; they moved it 1 mile north and changed the name to Gold Run in 1863—the name "Mountain Springs" was from Mountain Springs Hotel (Salley, p. 147). Whitney's (1873) map shows a mining camp called Indiana Hill located about 1 mile south of Gold Run, and a relief feature of the same name located less than 1 mile farther east-southeast.

Gold Run [SIERRA-YUBA]: *stream,* heads in Sierra County and flows 4 miles to Slate Creek 5.5 miles northeast of Strawberry Valley in Yuba County (lat. 39°36'55" N, long. 121°01'50" W; near S line sec. 1, T 20 N, R 8 E). Named on Goodyears Bar (1951) and Strawberry Valley (1948) 7.5' quadrangles. Called Gold Run Cr. on La Porte (1951) 7.5' quadrangle.

Gold Run Creek: see **Gold Run** [SIERRA-YUBA].

Gold Spring Hill: see **Cold Spring Hill** [PLACER].

Gold Valley [SIERRA]: *valley,* 7.5 miles north-northwest of Sierra City along Pauley Creek (lat. 39°39' N, long. 120°42'35" W). Named on Gold Lake (1981) 7.5' quadrangle.

Gonelson Canyon [NEVADA]: *canyon,* drained by a stream that flows 1 mile to Lake Spaulding 1.25 miles north of Yuba Gap (lat. 39°20'05" N, long. 120°37' W; sec. 15, T 17 N, R 12 E). Named on Cisco Grove (1955) 7.5' quadrangle.

Goodnow Slough [YOLO]: *stream,* southwest of Dunnigan Hills and north of Cache Creek in Hungry Hollow. Named on Bird Valley (1959), Madison (1953), and Zamora (1953) 7.5' quadrangles.

Goodyears Bar [SIERRA]: *village,* 3.25 miles west-southwest of Downieville along North Yuba River (lat. 39°32'25" N, long. 120° 53' W; sec. 5, T 19 N, R 10 E). Named on Goodyears Bar (1951) 7.5' quadrangle. Postal authorities established Goodyears Bar post office in 1851 and discontinued it briefly in 1888 (Frickstad, p. 184). The place first was called Slaughter's Bar, but in 1851 it took the name of the river bar opposite the community, where Miles Goodyear and Andrew Goodyear found gold in 1849 (Gudde, 1949, p. 131). Borthwick (p. 252) used the form "Goodyear's Bar" for the name. A mining place called Texas Bar was located 0.25 mile below Goodyears Bar opposite Hoodoo Bar (Gudde, 1975, p. 347), and a place called Rantedodler Bar was situated 0.5 mile below Goodyears Bar (Gudde, 1975, p 284). The name "Rantedodler Bar" also had the forms "Ranty Doddler Bar" (Bancroft, 1888, p. 361) and "Ranse Doddler Bar" (Hoover, Rensch, and Rensch, p. 491).

Goodyears Creek [SIERRA]: *stream,* flows nearly 7 miles to North Yuba River 0.25 mile west of Goodyears Bar (lat. 39°32'25" N, long. 120°53'15" W; sec. 5, T 19 N, R 10 E). Named on Downieville (1951) and Goodyears Bar (1951) 7.5' quadrangles.

Goose Flat [EL DORADO]: *locality,* 4.25 miles west-southwest of the village of Pilot Hill (lat. 38°48'40" N, long. 120°05'35" W; on N line sec. 16, T 11 N, R 8 E). Site named on Pilot Hill (1954) 7.5' quadrangle. Called Wild Goose Flat on Arrowsmith's (1860) map.

Goose Lake [SIERRA]: *lake,* 2300 feet long, 7.5 miles north of Sierra City (lat. 39°40'25" N, long. 120°38'10" W; at N line sec. 21, T 21 N, R 12 E). Named on Gold Lake (1981) 7.5' quadrangle.

Gooseneck Flat [PLACER]: *area,* 6.5 miles west of Martis Peak (lat. 39°17'40" N, long. 120°09'20" W; sec. 25, T 17 N, R 16 E). Named on Truckee (1955) 7.5' quadrangle.

Gopher Gulch [AMADOR]: *canyon,* 1.5 miles long, opens into the canyon of Sutter Creek (1) 6.5 miles south-southeast of Plymouth at the town of Sutter Creek (lat. 38°23'40" N, long. 120°48' W). Named on Amador City (1962) 7.5' quadrangle.

Gopher Hill [EL DORADO]: *peak,* 3 miles north of Chili Bar (lat. 38° 48'35" N, long. 120°49'35" W; near S line sec. 11, T 11 N, R 10 E). Named on Garden Valley (1949) 7.5' quadrangle.

Gopher Hill: see **Blue Tent** [NEVADA]; **Nevada City** [NEVADA].

Gophner Ravine [YUBA]: *canyon,* drained by a stream that flows nearly 1 mile to North Yuba River 2.5 miles south of Strawberry Valley (lat. 39°31'45" N, long. 121°05'55" W; sec. 8, T 19 N, R 8 E). Named on Strawberry Valley (1948) 7.5' quadrangle.

Gordons: see **Guesisosi** [YOLO].

Gorge: see **Towle** [PLACER].

Gouge Eye: see **Hunts Hill** [NEVADA]; **Pleasant Grove** [SUTTER] (1).

Government Meadow [EL DORADO]: *area,* 4.25 miles west of Kirkwood (lat. 38°42'35" N, long. 120°09'05" W; near SE cor. sec. 13, T 10 N, R 16 E). Named on Tragedy Spring (1979) 7.5' quadrangle.

Government Ridge [EL DORADO]: *ridge,* south- to south-southwest-trending, 2.5 miles long, 6.5 miles north-northwest of Riverton (lat. 38°51'30" N, long. 120°29'25" W). Named on Pollock Pines (1950) and Riverton (1950) 7.5' quadrangles.

Government Spring [PLACER]: *spring,* 2.5 miles north of Westwille (lat. 39°12'50" N, long. 120°38'10" W; near N line sec. 33, T 16 N, R 12 E). Named on Westville (1952) 7.5' quadrangle. Called Manimoth Spring on Colfax (1938) 30' quadrangle.

Grace: see **Cunard** [SUTTER].

Grafton: see **Knights Landing** [YOLO].

Graham [SACRAMENTO]: *locality,* nearly 3 miles north-northwest of Elk Grove along Southern Pacific Railroad (lat. 38°26'55" N, long. 121°22'40" W; sec. 24, T 7 N, R 5 E). Named on Florin (1909) 7.5' quadrangle.

Graino [COLUSA]: *locality,* 4.5 miles southwest of Grimes along Southern Pacific Railroad (lat. 39°02'10" N, long. 121°57'35" W). Named on Grimes (1954) 7.5' quadrangle.

Grand Island [COLUSA]:

(1) *locality,* 3.5 miles north-northwest of Grimes Landing (present Grimes) on the west side of Sacramento River (lat. 39°07'30" N, long. 121°55'30" W). Named on Marysville (1895) 30' quadrangle.

(2) *locality,* 1.5 miles east-southeast of Grimes on the south side of Sacramento River (lat. 39°04' N, long. 121°52' W; sec. 16, T 14 N, R 1 E). Named on Tisdale Weir (1952) 7.5' quadrangle. Postal authorities established Grand Island post office in 1854 and discontinued it in 1919 (Frickstad, p. 18). The term "Grand Island" designates the land lying between Sycamore Slough and Sacramento River (Cook, F.S., b, p. 28).

Grand Island [SACRAMENTO]: *island,* 10 miles long, 24 miles south of downtown Sacramento between Sacramento River and Steamboat Slough (lat. 38°14' N, long. 121°35' W). Named on Courtland (1978), Isleton (1978), and Rio Vista (1978) 7.5' quadrangles. Called Taylor I. on Ringgold's (1850b) map, which has the name "Pt. Larkin" at the extreme west tip of the island, where present Steamboat Slough and Sacramento River join; the same map has the name "Pt. Ellis" across Sacramento River from Pt. Larkin at the northwest corner of Brannan Island. Arguello in 1817 gave present Grand Island the name "La Isla de los Quenensias" for Indians who lived there (Dillon, p. 32-33).

Grand Island [YOLO]: *area,* north-northeast of Knights Landing between Sacramento River and Sycamore Slough (lat. 38°51' N, long. 121°45' W). Named on Dunnigan (1907) 15' quadrangle, and on Knights Landing (1910) 7.5' quadrangle.

Grand Point [EL DORADO]: *ridge,* west-southwest-trending, 1.5 miles long, 5.5 miles south-southeast of Camino (lat. 38°39'35" N, long. 120°39' W). Named on Camino (1952) 7.5' quadrangle.

Granite Bay [PLACER]: *embayment,* 6 miles east-southeast of Rocklin along Folsom Lake (lat. 38°45'15" N, long. 121°08'15" W). Named on Folsom (1967) and Rocklin (1967) 7.5' quadrangles.

Granite Canyon [EL DORADO]: *canyon,* 2 miles long, opens into the canyon of South Fork American River 1.25 miles west of Coloma (lat. 38°48' N, long. 120°54'45" W; near W line sec. 18, T 11 N, R 10 E). Named on Coloma (1949) 7.5' quadrangle.

Granite Canyon: see **Big Granite Creek** [PLACER]; **Little Granite Canyon**, under **Little Granite Creek** [PLACER].

Granite Chief [PLACER]: *peak,* 8.5 miles south-southeast of Donner Pass (lat. 39°11'55" N, long. 120°17'10" W; sec. 35, T 16 N, R 15 E). Altitude 9006 feet. Named on Granite Chief (1953) 7.5' quadrangle. United States Board on Geographic Names (1992, p. 4) approved the name "Billys Peak" for a feature, altitude 8617 feet, located 2.8 miles north of Granite Chief (lat. 39°14'15" N, long, 120°16'23" W; sec. 14, T 16 N, R 15 E); the name is for William Albert Dutton, a deceased member of Tahoe Nordic Search and Rescue Team.

Granite City: see **Folsom** [SACRAMENTO].

Granite Creek [EL DORADO]: *stream,* flows 2.5 miles to Granite Canyon nearly 2 miles southwest of Coloma (lat. 38°47'05" N, long. 120°54'55" W; near SE cor. sec. 24, T 11 N, R 9 E). Named on Coloma (1949) 7.5' quadrangle.

Granite Creek [NEVADA]: *stream,* flows 4.5 miles to Fordyce Creek 3.5 miles north-northeast of Yuba Gap (lat. 39°21'45" N, long. 120°35'20" W; near SE cor. sec. 2, T 17 N, R 12 E). Named on Cisco Grove (1955) and English Mountain (1983) 7.5' quadrangles.

Granite Creek: see **Big Granite Creek** [PLACER]; **Little Granite Creek** [PLACER].

Granite Hill [NEVADA]: *peak,* 1 mile south-southwest of downtown Grass Valley (lat. 39°12'20" N, long. 121°03'55" W; sec. 34, T 16 N, R 8 E). Named on Grass Valley (1949) 7.5' quadrangle.

Granite Hill: see **Gold Hill** [EL DORADO].

Granite Lake [AMADOR]: *lake,* 750 feet long, 8 miles north of Mokelumne Peak (lat. 38°39' N, long. 120°06'30" W; on S line sec. 4, T 9 N, R 17 E). Named on Caples Lake (1979) 7.5' quadrangle.

Granite Lake [EL DORADO]: *lake,* 950 feet long, 2.25 miles north-northwest of Mount Tallac (lat. 38°56'15" N, long. 120°06'30" W; near S line sec. 28, T 13 N, R 17 E). Named on Emerald Bay (1955) 7.5' quadrangle.

Granite Mountain [SIERRA]: *peak,* 6.25 miles west-southwest of Sierra City (lat. 39°31'35" N, long. 120°44'15" W; near E line sec. 9, T 19 N, R 11 E). Altitude 6482 feet. Named on Sierra City (1981) 7.5' quadrangle.

Granite Peak [SIERRA]: *peak,* 5.25 miles south-southeast of Crystal Peak (lat. 39°29'25" N, long. 120°02'30" W; near N line sec. 24, T 19 N, R 17 E). Altitude 8291 feet. Named on Boca (1955) 7.5' quadrangle.

Granite Point [YUBA]: *relief feature,* 5.5 miles south-southwest of Camptonville on the north side of Middle Yuba River (lat. 39°22'55" N, long. 121°06'10" W; sec. 32, T 18 N, R 8 E). Named on Camptonville (1948) 7.5' quadrangle.

Granite Ravine [EL DORADO]: *canyon,* drained by a stream that flows less than 1 mile to Folsom Lake 5.5 miles southwest of the village of Pilot Hill (lat. 38°47'10" N, long. 121°05'35" W; sec. 21, T 11 N, R 8 E). Named on Pilot Hill (1954, photorevised 1973) 7.5' quadrangle. The stream in the canyon is called Chrome Creek on Auburn (1944) 15' quadrangle.

Granite Spring [EL DORADO]: *spring,* 2.5 miles west-northwest of Kyburz (lat. 38°47'20" N, long. 120°20'30" W; sec. 19, T 11 N, R 15 E). Named on Kyburz (1952) 7.5' quadrangle.

Graniteville [NEVADA]: *village,* 23 miles northeast of Grass Valley along Poorman Creek (1) (lat. 39°26'30" N, long. 120°44'15" W; on E line sec. 9, T 18 N, R 11 E). Named on Graniteville (1982) 7.5' quadrangle. Postal authorities established Graniteville post office in 1867 and discontinued it in 1959 (Salley, p. 88). The place also was called Eureka South (Hanna, p. 125).

Grant Ravine [SIERRA]:

(1) *canyon,* drained by a stream that flows 1 mile to Downie River 3 miles north of Downieville (lat. 39°36'20" N, long. 120°49'45" W; near NW cor. sec. 14, T 20 N, R 10 E). Named on Downieville (1951) 7.5' quadrangle.

(2) *canyon,* drained by a stream that flows 1.25 miles to Indian Creek (1) 6.25 miles west-southwest of Goodyears Bar (lat. 39°30'05" N, long. 120°59'20" W; sec. 20, T 19 N, R 9 E). Named on Pike (1949) 7.5' quadrangle.

Grants Gap: see **Giant Gap** [PLACER].

Grapevine Creek [COLUSA]: *stream,* flows 13 miles to Funks Creek 8 miles north of Sites (lat. 39°23' N, long. 122°21'25" W; near W line sec. 30, T 18 N, R 4 W). Named on Lodoga (1960) 15' quadrangle.

Grapevine Flat [COLUSA]: *area,* 8 miles north-northwest of Wilbur Springs on Colusa-Lake County line (lat. 39°08'20" N, long. 122° 29'25" W; at N line sec. 23, T 15 N, R 6 W). Named on Wilbur Springs (1961) 15' quadrangle.

Grapevine Gulch [AMADOR]:

(1) *canyon,* drained by a stream that flows 3.5 miles to Camanche Reservoir 7 miles south-southwest of Ione (lat. 38°15'10" N, long. 120°57'50" W; near SW cor. sec. 26, T 5 N, R 9 E). Named on Ione (1962) and Wallace (1962) 7.5' quadrangles.

(2) *canyon,* 2 miles long, opens into the canyon of Mokelumne River 4.5 miles south-southwest of Jackson (lat. 38°17'20" N, long. 120°48'20" W; sec. 18, T 5 N, R 11 E). Named on Jackson (1962) 7.5' quadrangle. Water of Pardee Reservoir now covers the lower part of the canyon. Camp's (1962) map shows a place called Columbia Bar located on the north side of Mokelumne River just west of the mouth of Grapevine Gulch, and a place called Italian Bar situated on the same side of the river less than 0.5 mile downstream from Columbia Bar; water of Pardee Reservoir now covers both sites.

Grapevine Pass [COLUSA]: *pass,* 4 miles north-northeast of Lodoga (lat. 39°21'20" N, long. 122°27'35" W; sec. 6, T 17 N, R 5 W). Named on Lodoga (1960) 15' quadrangle.

Grapevine Ravine [AMADOR]: *canyon,* drained by a stream that flows 1.5 miles to Cosumnes River 9 miles west of Fiddletown (lat. 38°30'55" N, long. 120°55'25" W; near SW cor. sec. 30, T 8 N, R 10 E). Named on Latrobe (1949) 7.5' quadrangle. Camp's (1962) map shows a place called Rich Bar located on the south side of Cosumnes River less than 1 mile west-northwest of the mouth of Grapevine Ravine, a place called Possum Bar situated on the south side of the river 1.25 miles northwest of the mouth of the ravine, a place called Big Bar located on the south side of the river 1.5 miles west-northwest of the mouth of the ravine, and a place called Wisconsin Bar positioned on the south side of the river 2 miles west-northwest of the mouth of the ravine.

Grapevine Spring [YOLO]: *spring,* 11 miles south of Esparto (lat. 38°32' N, long. 122°02'15" W; near S line sec. 13, T 8 N, R 2 W). Named on Monticello Dam (1959) 7.5' quadrangle.

Grassey Canyon [COLUSA]: *canyon,* drained by a stream that flows 1 mile to Mill Creek (2) 11.5 miles north-northwest of Wilbur Springs (lat. 39°11'50" N, long. 122°29'25" W; sec. 35, T 16 N, R 6 W). Named on Wilbur Springs (1961) 15' quadrangle.

Grass Flat [SIERRA]: *locality,* 5.5 miles southwest of Mount Fillmore (lat. 39°40'35" N, long. 120°56' W; near SE cor. sec. 14, T 21 N, R 9 E). Named on La Porte (1951) 7.5' quadrangle.

Grasshopper Slough [YUBA]: *stream,* flows 13 miles to end 7.5 miles south-southeast of Olivehurst (lat. 38°59'05" N, long. 121° 30'20" W); the stream is located between Dry Creek (2) and Bear River (1). Named on Camp Far West (1949), Sheridan (1953), and Wheatland (1947) 7.5' quadrangles.

Grass Lake [EL DORADO]:

(1) *lake,* 1900 feet long, 6 miles northwest of Echo Summit (lat. 38° 52'20" N, long. 120°06'40" W). Named on Echo Lake (1955) 7.5' quadrangle.

(2) *lake,* 1650 feet long, 5.5 miles southwest of Freel Peak (lat. 38° 47'40" N, long. 119°57'50" W; near S line sec. 14, T 11 N, R 18 E). Named on Freel Peak (1955) 7.5' quadrangle.

Grass Lake [SIERRA]: *lake,* 400 feet long, 5.25 miles north-northwest of Sierra City (lat. 39°38'25" N, long. 120°39'20" W; sec. 32, T 21 N, R 12 E). Named on Gold Lake (1981) 7.5' quadrangle. On Sierra City (1955) 15' quadrangle, the name "Grass Lake" applies to a lake situated 0.5 mile south-southwest of present Grass Lake.

Grass Lake Creek [EL DORADO]: *stream,* flows 4.25 miles to Upper Truckee River 1 mile southeast of Echo Summit (lat. 38°48'05" N, long. 120°00'55" W; sec. 17, T 11 N, R 18 E); Grass Lake (2) is along the stream. Named on Echo Lake (1955) and Freel Peak (1955) 7.5' quadrangles.

Grass Valley [NEVADA]: *town,* near the center of the west half of Nevada County along Wolf Creek (lat. 39°13'05" N, long. 121°03'40" W; in and near sec. 27, T 16 N, R 8 E). Named on Grass Valley (1949) 7.5' quadrangle. Postal authorities established Centreville post office in 1851; they moved it and changed the name to Grass Valley in 1852 (Salley, p. 41). The town incorporated in 1861. The name "Grass Valley" is from the designation given by early emigrants to the valley where the town lies; the name "Centreville" was for the location of the place about halfway between the village of Rough and Ready and the town of Nevada City (Browne, p. 12). Doble (p. 76) referred to Grass Valley in 1852 as a beautiful flat some 1.5 miles long and 200 or 300 yards wide where the owners had a house that was a store and tavern. Whitney's (1873) map shows a place called Rays Flat located 2.5 miles southwest of Grass Valley, and a lake called Pine Tree Reservoir situated less than 1 mile southwest of downtown Grass Valley. United States Geological Survey's (1901) map shows a place called Brighton House located 1 mile southwest of downtown Grass Valley (at E line sec. 33, T 16 N, R 8 E). California Division of Highways' (1934) map shows a place called Pittsburg situated along Nevada County Narrow Gauge Railroad 1.25 miles south of Grass Valley (near SE cor. sec. 13, T 16 N, R 8 E), and a place called Mt. View along the railroad 0.5 mile farther west (near S line sec. 13, T 16 N, R 8 E). Postal authorities established Flood post office 3 miles south of Grass Valley in 1900 and discontinued in 1903; the name was for developer James L. Flood (Salley, p. 76). Gudde (1975, p. 190) listed a mining place called Lafayette Hill located 2 miles south of Grass Valley, and (p. 219) a mining place called Missouri Flat situated 1 mile south of Grass Valley. United States Board on Geographic Names (1992, p. 4) approved the name "Critter Creek" for a stream that flows 1.2 miles to Wolf Creek 2 miles south of Grass Valley (lat. 39°11'06" N, long. 121°03'33" W; sec. 2, T 15 N, R 8 E). The Board

(1995, p. 5) approved the name "Ellens Creek" for a stream that flows 1 mile to join Wolf Creek 2 miles south of Grass Valley (lat. 39°11'06" N, long. 121°03'32" W; sec. 2, T 15 N, R 8 E); the name commemorates Ellen Bergman, who helped settle the region.

Grass Valley: see **Grass Valley Creek** [AMADOR].

Grass Valley Creek [AMADOR]: *stream,* flows 5.5 miles to Sutter Creek (1) nearly 2 miles north-northwest of Pine Grove (lat. 38°26'10" N, long. 120°40'20" W; sec. 29, T 7 N, R 12 E). Named on Pine Grove (1948) 7.5' quadrangle.

Grass Valley Reservoir [NEVADA]: *lakes,* 0.5 mile north-northwest of downtown Grass Valley (lat. 39°13'40" N, long. 121°04' W; near S line sec. 22, T 16 N, R 8 E). Named on Grass Valley (1949) 7.5' quadrangle.

Gravelly Buttes [COLUSA]: *ridge,* south-southeast- to south-trending, 4 miles long, 13 miles north of Wilbur Springs (lat. 39°13'30" N, long. 122°28' W). Named on Wilbur Springs (1961) 15' quadrangle.

Gravelly Buttes: see **Bear Valley Buttes** [COLUSA].

Gravelly Flat [COLUSA]: *valley,* 11 miles north of Wilbur Springs (lat. 39°11'45" N, long. 122°27'05" W; mainly in sec. 31, 32, T 16 N, R 5 W); the valley is east of the south end of Gravelly Buttes. Named on Wilbur Springs (1961) 15' quadrangle.

Gravelly Ridge [COLUSA]: *ridge,* south-trending, 4 miles long, mainly in Glenn County, but extends south into Colusa County 2 miles east-northeast of Stonyford (lat. 39°23'05" N, long. 122°30'40" W). Named on Gilmore Peak (1968) and Stonyford (1968) 7.5' quadrangles.

Gravel Point [COLUSA]: *bend,* 3 miles north-northwest of Grimes along Sacramento River (lat. 39°06'50" N, long. 121°54'20" W; at N line sec. 31, T 15 N, R 1 E). Named on Grimes (1954) 7.5' quadrangle.

Gravel Point [YUBA]: *relief feature,* 4 miles south-southwest of Camptonville on the north side of Middle Yuba River (lat. 39°23'35" N, long. 121°03'45" W; sec. 27, T 18 N, R 8 E). Named on Camptonville (1948) 7.5' quadrangle.

Gray: see **Andrew Gray Creek** [PLACER]; **Harvey Gray Creek** [PLACER].

Gray Creek [NEVADA]: *stream,* formed by the confluence of North Fork and South Fork, flows 2.25 miles to Truckee River 9 miles east-northeast of Truckee (lat. 39°22'20" W; long. 120°01'50" W; near NE cor. sec. 36, T 18 N, R 17 E). Named on Martis Peak (1955) 7.5' quadrangle. North Fork heads in the State of Nevada and flows less than 0.25 mile in Nevada County to join South Fork. South Fork also heads in the State of Nevada and flows nearly 1.5 miles to join North Fork. Both forks are named on Martis Peak (1955) 7.5' quadrangle.

Gray Eagle Bar [EL DORADO]: *locality,* 2.25 miles north-northeast of Volcanoville along Middle Fork American River (lat. 39°00'35" N, long. 120°45'55" W). Named on Foresthill (1949) 7.5' quadrangle. Gudde (1975, p. 204) listed a mining place called Malcomb Bar that was located along Middle Fork below Gray Eagle Bar.

Gray Eagle Canyon [PLACER]: *canyon,* drained by a stream that flows 1 mile to Duncan Canyon 3.5 miles south of Duncan Peak (lat. 39°06'10" N, long. 120°30'55" W; sec. 34, T 15 N, R 13 E). Named on Greek Store (1952) 7.5' quadrangle.

Gray Eagle Hill: see **Grey Eagle Hill** [EL DORADO].

Gray Horse Creek [EL DORADO]: *stream,* flows 1.25 miles to Silver Creek 5.5 miles north-northwest of Riverton (lat. 38°50'45" N, long. 120°28'45" W; at W line sec. 36, T 12 N, R 13 E). Named on Riverton (1950) 7.5' quadrangle.

Grayhorse Creek [PLACER]: *stream,* flows 5 miles to Hell Hole Reservoir nearly 3 miles north-northeast of Bunker Hill (lat. 39°05'15" N, long. 120°21'50" W; near W line sec. 1, T 14 N, R 14 E). Named on Wentworth Springs (1953, photorevised 1973) 7.5' quadrangle.

Grayhorse Valley [PLACER]: *valley,* along Grayhorse Creek above a point 4 miles north-northeast of Bunker Hill (lat. 39°06'30" N, long. 120°21'45" W). Named on Granite Chief (1953) and Wentworth Springs (1953) 7.5' quadrangles.

Grays Bend [SUTTER-YOLO]: *bend,* 4 miles southwest of Verona along Old River on Sutter-Yolo County line (lat. 38°44'35" N, long. 121°40'20" W). Named on Grays Bend (1953) 7.5' quadrangle. Jackson's (1850) map has the name "Springfield" for a place situated on the north side of the river at or near present Grays Bend.

Grays Canyon [EL DORADO]: *canyon,* drained by a stream that flows 1.5 miles to South Fork American River 2.25 miles east-northeast of Pollock Pines (lat. 38°46'25" N, long. 120°32'35" W; sec. 20, T 11 N, R 13 E). Named on Pollock Pines (1950) 7.5' quadrangle.

Greasertown: see **Butte City** [AMADOR].

Greaserville: see **Butte City** [AMADOR].

Greasewood Mountain [COLUSA]: *peak,* 3.25 miles west-southwest of Sites (lat. 39°17'50" N, long. 122°23'45" W; on W line sec. 26, T 17 N, R 5 W). Named on Lodoga (1960) 15' quadrangle.

Great Eastern Ravine [SIERRA]: *canyon,* drained by a stream that flows 1.5 miles to Haypress Creek 3 miles east of Sierra City (lat. 39°34'05" N, long. 120°34'40" W; sec. 25, T 20 N, R 12 E). Named on Haypress Valley (1981) 7.5' quadrangle.

Great Valley: see "Regional setting."

Greek Store: see **Spruce Creek** [PLACER].

Green Creek [AMADOR]: *stream,* flows 2 miles to North Fork Mokelumne River 5.5 miles south-southeast of Hams Station (lat. 38°28' N, long. 120°20'45" W; near S line sec. 8, T 7 N, R 15 E). Named on Garnet Hill (1979) 7.5' quadrangle.

Greendale [YOLO]: *locality,* 4.5 miles southwest of Clarksburg along Sacramento Northern Railroad (lat. 38°22'25" N, long. 121° 35'10" W). Named on Courtland (1978) 7.5' quadrangle.

Green Flat Camp [COLUSA]: *locality,* 4 miles west-northwest of Pacific Point (lat. 39°14'20" N, long. 122°39'45" W; sec. 17, T 16 N, R 7 W). Named on Clearlake Oaks (1960) 15' quadrangle.

Greenhaven: see **Lake Greenhaven** [SACRAMENTO].

Greenhorn Bar: see **Wheatland** [YUBA].

Greenhorn Creek [NEVADA]: *stream,* flows 12.5 miles to Rollins Reservoir 2.5 miles north-northeast of Chicago Park (lat. 39°10'35" N, long. 120°56'30" W; near SW cor. sec. 2, T 15 N, R 9 E). Named on Chicago Park (1949, photorevised 1973), North Bloomfield (1949), and Washington (1950) 7.5' quadrangles. South Fork enters nearly 7 miles north-northeast of Chicago Park. It is 4 miles long and is named on Chicago Park (1949), Dutch Flat (1950), and Washington (1950) 7.5' quadrangles.

Greenhorn Creek: see **Little Greenhorn Creek** [NEVADA].

Green Mountain Bar: see **Maine Bar** [EL DORADO].

Greens Lake [YOLO]: *lake,* 3.5 miles west-southwest of West Sacramento in Yolo Bypass (lat. 38°33'40" N, long. 121°35'45" W). Named on Sacramento West (1967) 7.5' quadrangle.

Green Spring Creek [EL DORADO]: *stream,* flows 4.5 miles to New York Creek 4.25 miles north-northwest of Clarksville (lat. 38°42'50" N, long. 121°04'30" W; near NW cor. sec. 23, T 10 N, R 8 E). Named on Clarksville (1953) 7.5' quadrangle.

Green Springs: see **Rescue** [EL DORADO].

Green Valley [EL DORADO]: *locality,* 3.25 miles north-northwest of Shingle Springs (lat. 38°42'30" N, long. 120°56'40" W). Named on Placerville (1893) 30' quadrangle. Postal authorities established Green Valley post office in 1854 and discontinued it in 1855; they established Hitchcock Ranch post office 7 miles southeast of Salmon Falls in 1860, changed the name to Green Valley in 1865, moved it 1.5 miles east in 1908, and discontinued it in 1911 (Salley, p. 89, 98).

Green Valley [PLACER]: *valley,* 3.5 miles east-southeast of Dutch Flat along North Fork American River (lat. 39°10'50" N, long. 120°46'55" W; sec. 6, T 15 N, R 11 E). Named on Dutch Flat (1950) 7.5' quadrangle. Gudde (1975, p. 62, 251, 357) noted mining places called Carpenters Bar, One Horse Bar, and Upper Arkansas Bar that were situated along North Fork in Green Valley.

Green Valley: see **Greenwood** [EL DORADO].

Green Valley Cañon: see **McIntyre Gulch** [PLACER].

Greenville [YUBA]: *locality,* 4.25 miles southeast of Challenge along Little Oregon Creek (lat. 39°26'10" N, long. 121°10'30" W; sec. 10, T 18 N, R 7 E). Named on Challenge (1948) 7.5' quadrangle. Postal authorities established Greenville post office in 1857 and discontinued it in 1860 (Frickstad, p. 223). The place also was known as Oregon Hill (Bancroft, 1888, p. 360).

Greenwood [EL DORADO]: *village,* 4 miles west of Georgetown (lat. 38°53'50" N, long. 120°54'45" W; near SW cor. sec. 7, T 12 N, R 10 E). Named on Greenwood (1949) 7.5' quadrangle. The place first was called Long Valley, then Green Valley and Lewisville before it was renamed Greenwood (Bancroft, 1888, p. 354)—John Greenwood had a trading post at the site in 1848 (Hoover, Rensch, and Rensch, p. 87). Postal authorities established Louisville post office before July 28, 1851, and moved it in 1852 when they changed the name to Greenwood (Salley, p. 128). The name "Lewisville" or "Louisville" was for Lewis B. Meyers' son, the first child born near the site (Gudde, 1975, p. 145). Logan's (1938) map shows a place called Greenwood Camp about 2 miles north of Greenwood (near W line sec. 6, T 12 N, R 10 E).

Greenwood: see **John Greenwood's Creek**, under **Prosser Creek** [NEVADA].

Greenwood Camp: see **Greenwood** [EL DORADO].

Greenwood Creek [EL DORADO]: *stream,* flows 9 miles to South Fork American River 3.5 miles west-northwest of Coloma (lat. 38° 49'30" N, long. 120°56'55" W; sec. 11, T 11 N, R 9 E); the stream goes past Greenwood. Named on Coloma (1949) and Greenwood (1949) 7.5' quadrangles.

Greenwood's Camp: see **Jefferson**, under **Jefferson Creek** [NEVADA].

Gregory [EL DORADO]: *locality,* 9 miles northwest of Leek Spring Hill (lat. 38°43'10" N, long. 120°23'30" W). Named on Pyramid Peak (1896) 30' quadrangle.

Gregory: see **Mount Gregory** [EL DORADO].

Greilich Camp [EL DORADO]: *locality,* 5 miles east-southeast of Caldor (lat. 38°34'05" N, long. 120°21' W; near SE cor. sec. 6, T 8 N, R 15 E). Named on Peddler Hill (1951) 7.5' quadrangle.

Grey Eagle Hill [EL DORADO]: *peak,* 3.25 miles east of Georgetown (lat. 38°54'40" N, long. 120°46'30" W; at S line sec. 5, T 12 N, R 11 E). Named on Georgetown (1949) 7.5' quadrangle. Logan's (1938) map has the form

"Gray" for the name.

Griders: see **Roseville** [PLACER].

Griff Creek [PLACER]: *stream,* flows 4 miles to Lake Tahoe at Kings Beach (lat. 39°14'15" N, long. 120°01'45" W; near E line sec. 13, T 16 N, R 17 E). Named on Kings Beach (1955) and Martis Peak (1955) 7.5' quadrangles.

Griffith Creek [SACRAMENTO]: *stream,* flows 3 miles to Laguna 6 miles northeast of Galt (lat. 38°18'50" N, long. 121°13' W; sec. 4, T 5 N, T 7 E). Named on Clay (1968) 7.5' quadrangle.

Grimes [COLUSA]: *village,* 11.5 miles southeast of Colusa on the west side of Sacramento River (lat. 39°04'25" N, long. 121°53'35" W; around SW cor. sec. 8, T 14 N, R 1 E). Named on Grimes (1954) 7.5' quadrangle. Marysville (1895) 30' quadrangle shows Grimes Landing at the place. Postal authorities established Grimes post office in 1883 (Frickstad, p. 18). The name commemorates Cleaton Grimes, who received the land at the present village site in 1844 (Hanna, p. 127). California Division of Highways' (1934) map shows a place called Oak Flat located 4.5 miles north-northwest of Grimes along Southern Pacific Railroad.

Grimes Landing: see **Grimes** [COLUSA].

Griminger [EL DORADO]: *locality,* 1.5 miles northwest of Old Iron Mountain (lat. 38°43'10" N, long. 120°24'30" W; sec. 15, T 10 N, R 14 E). Named on Stump Spring (1951) 7.5' quadrangle.

Grissly Slough: see **Grizzly Slough** [SACRAMENTO].

Grizzly: see **Fort Grizzly** [EL DORADO].

Grizzly Bar: see **American River** [EL DORADO-PLACER-SACRAMENTO].

Grizzly Bear House [PLACER]: *locality,* 6 miles northeast of Auburn (lat. 38°56'35" N, long. 120°58'45" W; near S line sec. 28, T 13 N, R 9 E). Named on Greenwood (1949) 7.5' quadrangle. Postal authorities established Grizzly Bear House post office in 1858 and discontinued it in 1871 (Salley, p. 90).

Grizzly Canyon [EL DORADO]: *canyon,* drained by a stream that flows 1.25 miles to Missouri Canyon 5.5 miles northeast of Georgetown (lat. 38°58' N, long. 120°46'10" W; sec. 20, T 13 N, R 11 E). Named on Georgetown (1949) 7.5' quadrangle.

Grizzly Canyon [PLACER]: *canyon,* drained by a stream that flows 3.5 miles to Shirttail Canyon 3.5 miles north-northwest of Foresthill (lat. 39°04' N, long. 120°51'10" W; near N line sec. 16, T 14 N, R 10 E). Named on Foresthill (1949) 7.5' quadrangle.

Grizzly Canyon: see **Big Grizzly Canyon** [PLACER]; **Little Grizzly Canyon** [PLACER]; **Grizzly Creek** [NEVADA].

Grizzly Creek [EL DORADO]: *stream,* flows 1.5 miles to Steely Fork Cosumnes River 11 miles southeast of Camino (lat. 38°37'50" N, long. 120°31'40" W; near S line sec. 15, T 9 N, R 13 E); the stream flows past Grizzly Flat. Named on Camino (1952) 15' quadrangle.

Grizzly Creek [NEVADA]: *stream,* flows 7.25 miles to Middle Yuba River 4.5 miles east-northeast of North San Juan (lat. 39°23'20" N, long. 121°01'25" W; near NE cor. sec. 36, T 18 N, R 8 E). Named on Camptonville (1948) and Pike (1949) 7.5' quadrangles. Whitney's (1873) map has the name "Grizzly Cañon" along the stream.

Grizzly Creek [YUBA]: *stream,* flows 1 mile to Butte County 5.5 miles northeast of Challenge (lat. 39°32'45" N, long. 121°08'55" W; at W line sec. 36, T 20 N, R 7 E). Named on Clipper Mills (1948) 7.5' quadrangle.

Grizzly Creek: see **Big Grizzly Canyon** [PLACER]; **Big Grizzly Creek** [SIERRA]; **Grizzly Gulch** [SIERRA-YUBA]; **Little Grizzly Creek** [PLACER]; **Little Grizzly Creek** [SIERRA].

Grizzly Flat [EL DORADO]: *village,* 11 miles southeast of Camino (lat. 38°38'10" N, long. 120°31'35" W; sec. 15, T 9 N, R 13 E). Named on Sly Park (1952) 7.5' quadrangle. California Mining Bureau's (1909a) map has the form "Grizzly Flats" for the name. Postal authorities established Grizzly Flats post office in 1855 (Frickstad, p. 27). Miners who were surprised by a grizzly bear at the place named the community in 1850 (Hoover, Rensch, and Rensch, p. 84). Doble (p. 79) referred to Chickemasee or Grizzly Flat in 1852.

Grizzly Flat [PLACER]: *area,* 4.5 miles north of Foresthill (lat. 39° 05'20" N, long. 120°49'40" W; at E line sec. 3, T 14 N, R 10 E); the place is in the upper part of Grizzly Canyon. Named on Foresthill (1949) 7.5' quadrangle. On Whitney's (1873) map, the name applies to an inhabited place at the site.

Grizzly Flats: see **Grizzly Flat** [EL DORADO].

Grizzly Gulch [EL DORADO]: *canyon,* drained by a stream that flows 1.25 miles to Spanish Creek 11 miles south-southeast of Placerville (lat. 38°34'40" N, long. 120°45'15" W; sec. 3, T 8 N, R 11 E). Named on Fiddletown (1949) 7.5' quadrangle.

Grizzly Gulch [SIERRA]: *locality,* 1.5 miles northeast of Pike (lat. 39°27' N, long. 120°58' W); the place is at the head of Grizzly Creek, which is in present Grizzly Gulch [SIERRA-YUBA]. Named on Colfax (1898) 30' quadrangle.

Grizzly Gulch [SIERRA-YUBA]: *canyon,* drained by a stream that heads in Sierra County and flows 6 miles to Oregon Creek 1 mile south-southwest of Camptonville in Yuba County (lat. 39°26'25" N, long. 121°03'20" W; sec. 11, T 18 N, R 8 E). Named on Camptonville (1948) and Pike (1949) 7.5' quadrangles. On Colfax (1898) and Smartsville (1895) 30' quadrangles, the stream in the canyon has the name "Grizzly Creek."

Grizzly Hill: see **Relief** [NEVADA].

Grizzly Peak [SIERRA]: *peak,* 2.25 miles west of Downieville (lat. 39°33'20" N, long. 120°52'05" W; near W line sec. 33, T 20 N, R 10 E). Altitude 4638 feet. Named on Downieville (1951) 7.5' quadrangle.

Grizzly Ridge [NEVADA]: *ridge,* west-trending, 4 miles long, 4 miles northwest of North Bloomfield (lat. 39°24'30" N, long. 120° 57'30" W); the ridge is north of Grizzly Creek. Named on Colfax (1938) 30' quadrangle.

Grizzly Slough [SACRAMENTO]: *water feature,* joins Cosumnes River 11 miles south of Elk Grove (lat. 38°15'10" N, long. 121°24'20" W). Named on Thornton (1978) 7.5' quadrangle. Called Grissly Slough on Bruceville (1968) 7.5' quadrangle, but United States Board on Geographic Names (1977c, p. 3) rejected this form of the name.

Groundhog Rock [SIERRA]: *relief feature,* 12 miles south-southeast of Loyalton (lat. 39°30'40" N, long. 120°10'55" W; sec. 10, T 19 N, R 16 E). Named on Sardine Peak (1981) 7.5' quadrangle.

Grouse Canyon [PLACER]: *canyon,* drained by a stream that flows 2 miles to the canyon of Five Lakes Creek 4.5 miles south of Granite Chief (lat. 39°07'50" N, long. 120°16'15" W; sec. 23, T 15 N, R 15 E). Named on Granite Chief (1953) and Tahoe City (1955) 7.5' quadrangles.

Grouse Creek [PLACER]: *stream,* flows 5.5 miles to North Fork of Middle Fork American River 6 miles northeast of Michigan Bluff (lat. 39°05'20" N, long. 120°38'40" W; sec. 4, T 14 N, R 12 E). Named on Greek Store (1952) and Michigan Bluff (1952) 7.5' quadrangles. South Branch enters from the east 1 mile from the mouth of the main stream; it is 2 miles long and is named on Greek Store (1952) and Michigan Bluff (1952) 7.5' quadrangles.

Grouse Creek [SIERRA]: *stream,* flows 2 miles to Indian Creek (2) 3 miles east of Pike (lat. 39°25'55" N, long. 120°56'35" W; near NW cor. sec. 14, T 18 N, R 9 E). Named on Pike (1949) 7.5' quadrangle.

Grouse Lake [EL DORADO]: *lake,* 750 feet long, 2.5 miles west-northwest of Pyramid Peak (lat. 38°51'25" N, long. 120°11'55" W). Named on Pyramid Peak (1955) 7.5' quadrangle.

Grouse Lakes [EL DORADO]: *lakes,* largest 550 feet long, less than 1 mile east-northeast of Phipps Peak (lat. 38°57'40" N, long. 120°08'05" W; sec. 19, T 13 N, E 17 E). Named on Rockbound Valley (1955) 7.5' quadrangle.

Grouse Ridge [NEVADA]: *ridge,* south- to southwest-trending, 2 miles long, 4 miles north of Yuba Gap (lat. 39°22'30" N, long. 120°37'10" W). Named on Blue Canyon (1955), Cisco Grove (1955), and English Mountain (1983) 7.5' quadrangles.

Growlersburg: see **Georgetown** [EL DORADO].

Grubb: see **Peter Grubb Hut** [NEVADA].

Grubb Creek [NEVADA]: *stream,* flows 3 miles to Squirrel Creek 3 miles north-northeast of Pilot Peak (lat. 39°12'30" N, long. 121° 10' W; near NW cor. sec. 35, T 16 N, R 7 E). Named on Grass Valley (1949) and Rough and Ready (1949) 7.5' quadrangles.

Grub Gulch [PLACER]: *canyon,* drained by a stream that flows 1 mile to Grouse Creek 6.25 miles west-southwest of Duncan Peak (lat. 39°06'30" N, long. 120°36'35" W; sec. 35, T 15 N, R 12 E). Named on Greek Store (1952) 7.5' quadrangle.

Guesisosi [YOLO]: *land grant,* east-northeast of Madison along Cache Creek. Named on Madison (1953) and Woodland (1952) 7.5' quadrangles. William Gordon received 2 leagues in 1843 and claimed 8894 acres patented in 1860 (Cowan, p. 66; Cowan gave the form "Quesisosi" for the name). Derby's (1849b) map shows Gordon's Rancho, and Goddard's (1857) map has the name "Gordons" at a place along Cache Creek. William Gordon came to California with the Workman-Rowland party in 1841, and became the first white settler in present Yolo County in 1842 (Hoover, Rensch, and Rensch, p. 583).

Guide Peak [PLACER]: *peak,* nearly 4 miles east-southeast of Bunker Hill (lat. 39°02'15" N, long. 120°18'45" W; on S line sec. 20, T 14 N, R 15 E). Altitude 7741 feet. Named on Wentworth Springs (1953) 7.5' quadrangle.

Guinda [YOLO]: *village,* 13 miles northwest of Esparto in Capay Valley (lat. 38°49'45" N, long. 122°11'30" W). Named on Guinda (1959) 7.5' quadrangle. Postal authorities established Guinda post office in 1889 (Frickstad, p. 221). Officials of Southern Pacific Railroad named the place for an old cherry tree at the site—*guinda* means "cherry" in Spanish (Gudde, 1949, p. 138-139).

Gurley: see **Gerle** [EL DORADO].

Gurley Creek: see **Gerle Creek** [EL DORADO].

Gutman Landing [SACRAMENTO]: *locality,* 11 miles southwest of Isleton along San Joaquin River on Sherman Island (lat. 38°02' N, long. 121°44'10" W). Named on Jersey (1910) 7.5' quadrangle.

— H —

Hackett Creek [NEVADA]: *stream,* flows nearly 3 miles to Little Dry Creek 4 miles west-southwest of Pilot Peak (lat. 39°08'45" N, long. 121°15'15"

W; near S line sec. 13, T 15 N, R 6 E). Named on Smartville (1951) 7.5' quadrangle.

Hackmans Falls [SIERRA]: *waterfall,* 0.5 mile southeast of Sierra City (lat. 39°33'30" N, long. 120°37'35" W; sec. 33, T 20 N, R 12 E); the feature is in Hackmans Ravine. Named on Sierra City (1981) 7.5' quadrangle.

Hackmans Ravine [SIERRA]: *canyon,* drained by a stream that flows 2 miles to North Yuba River at Sierra City (lat. 39°33'55" N, long. 120°37'40" W; at N line sec. 33, T 20 N, R 12 E). Named on Sierra City (1981) 7.5' quadrangle.

Hadselville Creek [AMADOR-SACRAMENTO]: *stream,* heads in Amador County and flows 12 miles to Laguna Creek 8.5 miles northeast of Galt in Sacramento County (lat. 38°20'05" N, long. 121°11' W; near NW cor. sec. 35, T 6 N, R 7 E). Named on Clay (1968) and Goose Creek (1968) 7.5' quadrangles.

Hageman: see **Meridian** [SUTTER].

Haggin: see **Sacramento** [SACRAMENTO].

Hagginwood [SACRAMENTO]: *district,* 5 miles northeast of downtown Sacramento (lat. 38°07'35" N, long. 121°25'45" W). Named on Rio Linda (1967) 7.5' quadrangle.

Half Moon Lake [EL DORADO]: *lake,* 2100 feet long, 4 miles south of Phipps Peak (lat. 38°53'50" N, long. 120°08'10" W; sec. 7, T 12 N, R 17 E). Named on Rockbound Valley (1955) 7.5' quadrangle. The name is from the shape of the lake (Gudde, 1949, p. 140).

Halsey Afterbay [PLACER]: *lake,* 1100 feet long, 4.5 miles north-northeast of Auburn (lat. 38°57'25" N, long. 121°02'25" W; at NW cor. sec. 25, T 13 N, R 8 E). Named on Auburn (1953) 7.5' quadrangle.

Halsey Forebay [PLACER]: *lake,* 1100 feet long, 5.5 miles north-northeast of Auburn (lat. 38°58'20" N, long. 121°02'10" W; on S line sec. 13, T 13 N, R 8 E). Named on Auburn (1953) 7.5' quadrangle.

Hamilton Bend [COLUSA]: *bend,* 9.5 miles south of Princeton along Sacramento River (lat. 39°16' N, long. 122°01' W). Named on Moulton Weir (1952) 7.5' quadrangle.

Hamilton Canyon [COLUSA]: *canyon,* drained by a stream that flows 2 miles to Sulphur Creek 1 mile northeast of Wilbur Springs (lat. 39°03'05" N, long. 122°24'30" W; at W line sec. 22, T 14 N, R 5 W). Named on Wilbur Springs (1961) 15' quadrangle.

Hamilton Canyon [YOLO]: *canyon,* drained by a stream that flows 3.5 miles to Capay Valley 1 mile west of Guinda (lat. 38°49'50" N, long. 122°12'50" W; sec. 5, T 11 N, R 3 W). Named on Guinda (1959) and Knoxville (1958) 7.5' quadrangles. The stream in the canyon is called Hamilton Creek on Rumsey (1945) 15' quadrangle.

Hamilton Creek: see **Hamilton Canyon** [YOLO].

Hamilton Flat [COLUSA]: *area,* 2.5 miles east of Wilbur Springs (lat. 39°02'30" N, long. 122°22'30" W). Named on Wilbur Springs (1961) 15' quadrangle.

Hamlin Creek [SIERRA]: *stream,* flows 2.5 miles to Sierra Valley 2 miles west-southwest of Sierraville (lat. 39°34'40" N, long. 120°24'10" W; at S line sec. 15, T 20 N, R 14 E). Named on Sattley (1981) 7.5' quadrangle.

Hammel Point [PLACER]: *ridge,* west-southwest-trending, 0.5 mile long, 4 miles north-northwest of Foresthill (lat. 39°04'20" N, long. 120°51' W; sec. 9, T 14 N, R 10 E). Named on Foresthill (1949) 7.5' quadrangle.

Hammond Island: see **Kimball Island** [SACRAMENTO].

Hammonton [YUBA]: *locality,* 3.5 miles south of Browns Valley (lat. 39°11'40" N, long. 121°25'10" W; at S line sec. 33, T 16 N, R 5 E). Named on Browns Valley (1947, photorevised 1973) 7.5' quadrangle. Postal authorities established Hammonton post office in 1906 and discontinued it in 1957 (Salley, p. 92). The name commemorates W.P. Hammond, an official of a gold-dredging company; the place first was known as Dredgertown or Dredgerville (Gudde, 1975, p. 150).

Hampshire Creek [YUBA]: *stream,* flows nearly 2 miles to New Bullards Bar Reservoir 3 miles south-southwest of Strawberry Valley (lat. 39°31'20" N, long. 121°07'15" W; sec. 7, T 19 N, R 8 E). Named on Clipper Mills (1948) and Strawberry Valley (1948, photorevised 1975) 7.5' quadrangles. Wescoatt's (1861) map shows a place called Hampshire Stores situated along Hampshire Creek 0.5 mile above the mouth.

Hampshire Rocks Campground [PLACER]: *locality,* 9 miles west of Donner Pass (lat. 39°18'40" N, long. 120°29'50" W; sec. 27, T 17 N, R 13 E). Named on Soda Springs (1955) 7.5' quadrangle.

Hampshire Stores: see **Hampshire Creek** [YUBA].

Hams: see **Hams Station** [AMADOR].

Ham Spring [AMADOR]: *spring,* nearly 6 miles west-northwest of Mokelumne Peak (lat. 38°33'25" N, long. 120°11'45" W; sec. 10, T 8 N, R 16 E). Named on Bear River Reservoir (1979) 7.5' quadrangle.

Hams Station [AMADOR]: *locality,* 25 miles east-northeast of Jackson (lat. 38°32'40" N, long. 120°22'30" W; sec. 13, T 8 N, R 14 E). Named on Caldor (1951) and Peddler Hill (1951) 7.5' quadrangles. Called Hams on Pyramid Peak (1896) 30' quadrangle. Wheeler (1879, p. 177) called Ham's Station a public house.

Hancock Creek [EL DORADO]: *stream,* flows nearly 4 miles to Folsom Lake 6 miles south-southwest of the village of Pilot Hill (lat. 38°45'45" N, long. 121°04'25" W; sec. 34, T 11 N, R 8 E). Named on Pilot Hill (1954, photorevised 1973) 7.5' quadrangle.

Hancock House: see **Bassetts** [SIERRA].

Handy Camp [PLACER]: *locality,* nearly 6 miles west-southwest of Granite Chief near Middle Fork American River (lat. 39°10'35" N, long. 120°23'10" W; near SW cor. sec. 2, T 15 N, R 14 E). Named on Royal Gorge (1953) 7.5' quadrangle.

Haney Mountain [NEVADA]: *peak,* 2.5 miles south of Pilot Peak (lat. 39°07'50" N, long. 121°11' W; near S line sec. 22, T 15 N, R 7 E). Altitude 1813 feet. Named on Rough and Ready (1949) 7.5' quadrangle. Called Haney Pk. on California Mining Bureau's (1917c) map.

Haney Peak: see **Haney Mountain** [NEVADA].

Hangtown: see **Placerville** [EL DORADO].

Hangtown Creek [EL DORADO]: *stream,* flows nearly 7 miles to Weber Creek 3.5 miles west of Placerville (lat. 38°44'15" N, long. 120°51'50" W; sec. 10, T 10 N, R 10 E); the stream flows through Placerville, which had the nickname "Hangtown." Named on Placerville (1949) 7.5' quadrangle.

Hangtown Crossing: see **Mills** [SACRAMENTO].

Hangtown Hill: see **Placerville** [EL DORADO].

Hanks Exchange [EL DORADO]: *locality,* 4.5 miles southeast of Placerville (lat. 38°40'35" N, long. 120°45'05" W; sec. 34, T 10 N, R 11 E). Named on Placerville (1949) 7.5' quadrangle.

Hansonville [YUBA]: *locality,* 1 mile east of the site of present Rackerby (lat. 39°26'15" N, long. 121°19'15" W). Named on Smartsville (1895) 30' quadrangle. Rackerby (1948) 7.5' quadrangle shows Hansonville Sch. near the site. Postal authorities established Hansonville post office, named for James Hanson, first postmaster, in 1856 and discontinued it in 1862; they established Paulinville post office, named for Paulin Rouze, first postmaster, in 1866, changed the name to Hansonville in 1873, and discontinued it in 1892 (Salley, p. 93, 168).

Hansonville Branch: see **South Honcut Creek** [YUBA].

Hansonville Hill [YUBA]: *peak,* 2.5 miles east of Rackerby (lat. 39° 26'25" N, long. 121°17'30" W; on S line sec. 3, T 18 N, R 6 E); the peak is less than 2 miles east of the site of Hansonville. Named on Rackerby (1948) 7.5' quadrangle.

Happy Camp [COLUSA]: *locality,* 2 miles north-northwest of Fouts Springs along Paradise Creek (lat. 39°22'45" N, long. 122°40'40" W). Named on Saint John Mountain (1968) 7.5' quadrangle.

Happy Hol Ravine [SIERRA]: *canyon,* drained by a stream that flows less than 0.5 mile to Canyon Creek nearly 6 miles southwest of Mount Fillmore (lat. 39°39'50" N, long. 120°54'55" W; sec. 24, T 21 N, R 9 E). Named on La Porte (1951) 7.5' quadrangle.

Happy Valley [EL DORADO]:

(1) *valley,* 13 miles east-southeast of Placerville (lat. 38°40'50" N, long. 120°33'45" W). Named on Placerville (1893) 30' quadrangle.

(2) *locality,* 7.25 miles east-southeast of Camino (lat. 38°40'55" N, long. 120°33'40" W); the place is in Happy Valley (1). Named on Sly Park (1952) 7.5' quadrangle.

Hardenburg: see **Jackson** [AMADOR].

Harding Point [SIERRA]: *ridge,* northwest-trending, less than 1 mile long, 2.25 miles northeast of Sierraville (lat. 39°36'45" N, long. 120°20'10" W; sec. 5, T 20 N, R 15 E). Named on Sierraville (1981) 7.5' quadrangle.

Hardscrabble: see **Ione** [AMADOR].

Harmony Ridge [NEVADA]: *ridge,* southwest- to west-trending, 6 miles long, between Deer Creek and Rock Creek (1); center 6.5 miles south-southwest of North Bloomfield (lat. 39°17'10" N, long. 120°57'30" W). Named on Nevada City (1948) and North Bloomfield (1949) 7.5' quadrangles.

Harricks Ravine [EL DORADO]: *canyon,* drained by a stream that flows 1.25 miles to Rock Creek 5.25 miles northeast of Chili Bar (lat. 38°49'30" N, long. 120°45'25" W; sec. 4, T 11 N, R 11 E). Named on Garden Valley (1949) 7.5' quadrangle.

Harrington [COLUSA]: *locality,* 4.5 miles south-southeast of Arbuckle along Southern Pacific Railroad (lat. 38°57'30" N, long. 122°01' W; sec. 19, T 13 N, R 1 W). Named on Wildwood School (1959) 7.5' quadrangle.

Harris Meadow [SIERRA]: *area,* 6 miles southwest of Sierra City (lat. 39°31'05" N, long. 120°43'45" W; sec. 15, T 19 N, R 11 E). Named on Sierra City (1981) 7.5' quadrangle.

Harry L. Englebright Lake: see **Englebright Lake** [NEVADA-YUBA].

Harry L. Englebright Reservoir: see **Englebright Lake** [NEVADA-YUBA].

Harter: see **Colusa Junction** [SUTTER].

Hartless [EL DORADO]: *locality,* 2 miles west-northwest of Robbs Peak (lat. 38°56'15" N, long. 120°26'20" W). Named on Pyramid Peak (1896) 30' quadrangle.

Hartley Butte [NEVADA]: *peak,* 4 miles southeast of English Mountain (lat. 39°24'05" N, long. 120°30'10" W; sec. 27, T 18 N, R 13 E). Altitude 7450 feet. Named on English Mountain (1983) 7.5' quadrangle. The name commemorates Henry Hartley, who discovered gold in the vicinity of Meadow Lake in 1863 (Gudde, 1975, p. 211-212).

Harvey: see **Malby Crossing** [EL DORADO].

Harvey Gray Creek [PLACER]: *stream,* flows nearly 1 mile to Andrew

Gray Greek 6.5 miles northwest of Duncan Peak (lat. 39° 13'25" N, long. 120°35'45" W; sec. 26, T 16 N, R 12 E). Named on Duncan Peak (1952) 7.5' quadrangle. The name is for Harvey Purdy Gray, a pioneer of the dried-fruit industry in California (United States Board on Geographic Names, 1967, p. 2).

Harvey West: see **Camp Harvey West** [EL DORADO].

Haskell Creek [SIERRA]: *stream,* flows 2.25 miles to North Yuba River 6.25 miles northeast of Sierra City (lat. 39°37'55" N, long. 120°33'20" W; at N line sec. 6, T 20 N, R 13 E); the stream heads near Haskell Peak. Named on Clio (1981) 7.5' quadrangle.

Haskell Creek Homesites [SIERRA]: *locality,* 6.5 miles northeast of Sierra City (lat. 39°38'05" N, long. 120°33'10" W; near SE cor. sec. 31, T 21 N, R 13 E); the place is near the mouth of Haskell Creek. Named on Clio (1981) 7.5' quadrangle.

Haskell Peak [SIERRA]: *peak,* 8 miles north-northeast of Sierra City (lat. 39°39'45" N, long. 120°33'05" W; near SE cor. sec. 19, T 21 N, R 13 E). Altitude 8107 feet. Named on Clio (1981) 7.5' quadrangle. Called Mt. Haskells on California Division of Highways' (1934) map, and called Haskells Pk. on Logan's (1929) map. The name commemorates Edward W. Haskell, who had a ranch at the base of the peak (Gudde, 1969, p. 135).

Haskell Ravine [SIERRA]: *canyon,* drained by a stream that flows 3.25 miles to Plumas County 11 miles north-northeast of Sierra City (lat. 39°42'25" N, long. 120°32'25" W; near S line sec. 5, T 21 N, R 13 E); the canyon heads near Haskell Peak. Named on Clio (1981) 7.5' quadrangle.

Hastings Creek [EL DORADO]: *stream,* formed by the confluence of Blue Tent Creek and Black Rock Creek, flows 1.5 miles to South Fork American River 4.25 miles west-northwest of Coloma (lat. 38°49'05" N, long. 120°57'45" W; sec. 10, T 11 N, R 9 E). Named on Coloma (1949) 7.5' quadrangle. On Placerville (1893) 30' quadrangle, the name also applies to present Black Rock Creek.

Haswell: see **Camp Haswell** [YOLO]

Haven Lake [SIERRA]: *lake,* 2050 feet long, 7.25 miles north of Sierra City (lat. 39°40'15" N, long. 120°38' W; sec. 21, T 21 N, R 12 E). Named on Gold Lake (1981) 7.5' quadrangle.

Hawkins Canyon [NEVADA]: *canyon,* drained by a stream that flows 1 mile to an unnamed canyon nearly 5 miles northeast of Chicago Park (lat. 39°11'20" N, long. 120°53'50" W; sec. 6, T 15 N, R 10 E). Named on Chicago Park (1949) 7.5' quadrangle.

Hawley Lake [SIERRA]: *lake,* 700 feet long, 9 miles north-northwest of Sierra City (lat. 39°41' N, long. 120°42'35" W; sec. 14, T 21 N, R 11 E); the lake is northeast of Hawley Meadow. Named on Gold Lake (1981) 7.5' quadrangle. Called Lake Hawley on Downieville (1897) 30' quadrangle.

Hawley Meadow [SIERRA]: *area,* 9 miles north-northwest of Sierra City (lat. 39°40'45" N, long. 120°42'50" W; sec. 14, T 21 N, R 11 E); the place is southwest of Hawley Lake. Named on Gold Lake (1981) 7.5' quadrangle.

Haycock Shoals [SACRAMENTO-YOLO]: *shoals,* 4.5 miles north-northwest of Clarksburg in Sacramento River on Sacramento-Yolo County line (lat. 38°29' N, long. 121°32'50" W). Named on Clarksburg (1967) 7.5' quadrangle.

Hayden Hill [PLACER]: *peak,* 4.25 miles southeast of Dutch Flat (lat. 39°10'08" N, long. 120°45'30" W; near S line sec. 6, T 15 N, R 11 E). Named on Dutch Flat (1950) 7.5' quadrangle.

Hayes Canyon [COLUSA]: *canyon,* drained by a stream that flows 1.5 miles to Grapevine Creek 4.5 miles southwest of Sites (lat. 39° 16' N, long. 122°24'05" W; sec. 3, T 16 N, R 5 W). Named on Lodoga (1960) 15' quadrangle.

Hay Flat [EL DORADO]: *area,* 4.25 miles west-northwest of Kirkwood (lat. 38°43'25" N, long. 120°08'25" W). Named on Tragedy Spring (1979) 7.5' quadrangle.

Hayford Hill [PLACER]: *peak,* 4 miles northeast of Colfax (lat. 39°08'35" N, long. 120°54'05" W; near N line sec. 19, T 15 N, R 10 E). Altitude 3219 feet. Named on Chicago Park (1949) 7.5' quadrangle.

Haypress Creek [SIERRA]: *stream,* flows 12 miles to North Yuba River 1 mile east of Sierra City (lat. 39°34'05" N, long. 120°36'55" W; sec. 27, T 20 N, R 12 E); the stream goes through Haypress Valley. Named on Haypress Valley (1981) and Sattley (1981) 7.5' quadrangles. Called South Fork of North Fork Yuba River on Downieville (1897) 30' quadrangle, but United States Board on Geographic Names (1950, p. 5) rejected this name for the stream.

Haypress Creek: see **Long Valley Creek** [SIERRA] (2).

Haypress Meadows [EL DORADO]: *area,* 5 miles northwest of Echo Summit (lat. 38°51'15" N, long. 120°06'30" W; at S line sec. 28, T 12 N, R 17 E). Named on Echo Lake (1955) 7.5' quadrangle.

Haypress Valley [SIERRA]: *valley,* 6.25 miles east-southeast of Sierra City (lat. 39°32'30" N, long. 120°30'45" W); the valley is along Haypress Creek. Named on Haypress Valley (1981) 7.5' quadrangle. Called Tehuantepec Val. on Downieville (1897) 30' quadrangle, which has the name "Hay Press Valley" for the canyon of present Long Valley Creek (2).

Hays Ravine [SIERRA]: *canyon,* drained by a stream that flows 0.5 mile to Canyon Creek 2.5 miles south of Mount Fillmore (lat. 39° 41'30" N, long. 120°51' W). Named on Mount Fillmore (1951) 7.5' quadrangle.

Hays Spring [YOLO]: *spring,* 3 miles southeast of Berryessa Peak in Chandler Canyon (lat. 38°37'55" N, long. 122°09'05" W). Named on Brooks (1959) 7.5' quadrangle.

Haystack Mountain [NEVADA]: *peak,* 2.5 miles southwest of English Mountain (lat. 39°25'10" N, long. 120°35' W; at SW cor. sec. 13, T 18 N, R 12 E). Altitude 7391 feet. Named on English Mountain (1983) 7.5' quadrangle.

Hazel Creek [EL DORADO]: *stream,* flows 4 miles to Jenkinson Lake 8 miles east of Camino (lat. 38°44'15" N, long. 120°31'50" W; near NW cor. sec. 10, T 10 N, R 13 E). Named on Riverton (1950), Sly Park (1952, photorevised 1973), and Stump Spring (1951) 7.5' quadrangles. On Placerville (1893) 30' quadrangle, present Hazel Creek is shown as the upper part of Sly Park Creek.

Hazel Creek: see **Sly Park Creek** [EL DORADO].

Hazel Valley [EL DORADO]: *valley,* 7.5 miles east of Camino where Hazel Creek joined Sly Park Creek before creation of Jenkinson Lake (lat. 38°44' N, long. 120°32' W). Named on Camino (1952) 15' quadrangle.

Head Dam [SIERRA]: *locality,* 6 miles north-northwest of Goodyears Bar along Little Canyon Creek (lat. 39°36'55" N, long. 120° 56'35" W; near W line sec. 11, T 20 N, R 9 E). Site named on Goodyears Bar (1951) 7.5' quadrangle.

Headland: see **Cabin Creek** [PLACER].

Heather Glen [PLACER]: *area,* 6 miles south-southwest of Colfax (lat. 39°01'05" N, long. 120°58'55" W; sec. 33, T 14 N, R 9 E). Named on Colfax (1949) 7.5' quadrangle.

Heather Lake [EL DORADO]: *lake,* 2200 feet long, 5.5 miles south of Phipps Peak (lat. 38°52'40" N, long. 120°08'15" W; sec. 19, T 12 N, R 17 E). Named on Pyramid Peak (1955) and Rockbound Valley (1955) 7.5' quadrangles.

Heath Springs [PLACER]: *springs,* 7.5 miles west-northwest of Granite Chief (lat. 39°15' N, long. 120°16'50" W; sec. 16, T 16 N, R 14 E). Named on Royal Gorge (1953) 7.5' quadrangle.

Heaton Station: see **Cisco** [PLACER].

Heavenly Valley [EL DORADO]: *valley,* nearly 5 miles north of Freel Peak (lat. 38°55'25" N, long. 119°54'50" W; sec. 1, T 12 N, R 18 E). Named on South Lake Tahoe (1955) 7.5' quadrangle.

Heavenly Valley Creek [EL DORADO]: *stream,* flows 4.25 miles to Trout Creek 6 miles northwest of Freel Peak (lat. 38°55'15" N, long. 119°58'15" W; sec. 3, T 12 N, R 18 E); the creek goes through Heavenly Valley. Named on South Lake Tahoe (1955) 7.5' quadrangle. The stream first was called Miller Creek for John G. Miller, who built Miller House beside the creek in 1862 and ran a dairy (Lekisch, p. 61).

Heavens Gate [PLACER]: *pass,* 4 miles southwest of Granite Chief (lat. 39°08'55" N, long. 120°19'50" W; at E line sec. 18, T 15 N, R 15 E). Named on Granite Chief (1953) 7.5' quadrangle.

Hebron [YOLO]: *locality,* 9 miles north of Davis along Sacramento Northern Railroad (lat. 38°40'40" N, long. 121°43'50" W; near SE cor. sec. 27, T 10 N, R 2 E). Named on Grays Bend (1953) 7.5' quadrangle.

Hedge Hill [YUBA]: *ridge,* west-trending, 1 mile long, 2 miles southeast of Rackerby (lat. 39°25' N, long. 121°18'45" W; on W line sec. 16, T 18 N, R 6 E). Named on Rackerby (1948) 7.5' quadrangle.

Helester Point [PLACER]: *peak,* 3.5 miles northwest of Westville (lat. 39°12'50" N, long. 120°41'35" W; near N line sec. 36, T 16 N, R 11 E). Altitude 4930 feet. Named on Westville (1952) 7.5' quadrangle.

Helgeson Flat: see **Holbrook Flat** [NEVADA].

Hell Hole [EL DORADO]: *valley,* 3.25 miles southwest of Freel Peak (lat. 38°49'40" N, long. 119°56'35" W; near W line sec. 1, T 11 N, R 19 E). Named on Freel Peak (1955) 7.5' quadrangle.

Hell Hole: see **Lower Hell Hole** [PLACER]; **Upper Hell Hole** [PLACER].

Hell Hole Reservoir [PLACER]: *lake,* behind a dam on Rubicon River 1.5 miles west-northwest of Bunker Hill (lat. 39°03'30" N, long. 120°24'30" W; near S line sec. 16, T 14 N, R 14 E); water of the lake covers Lower Hell Hole and Upper Hell Hole. Named on Bunker Hill (1953, photorevised 1973) and Wentworth Springs (1953, photorevised 1973) 7.5' quadrangles.

Hell Out for High Noon City: see **Alpha** [NEVADA].

Hells Delight Creek [EL DORADO]: *stream,* flows 2.5 miles to Silver Fork American River 8 miles west of Kirkwood (lat. 38°42'45" N, long. 120°13'20" W; sec. 17, T 10 N, R 16 E); the stream goes through Hells Delight Valley. Named on Tragedy Spring (1979) 7.5' quadrangle.

Hells Delight Valley [EL DORADO]: *valley,* 9 miles west of Kirkwood (lat. 38°42'05" N, long. 120°14' W; near W line sec. 20, T 10 N, R 16 E). Named on Tragedy Spring (1979) 7.5' quadrangle.

Hells Half Acre [PLACER]: *relief feature,* 2 miles northeast of Bunker Hill (lat. 39°03'40" N, long. 120°21'10" W; sec. 13, T 14 N, R 14 E). Named on Wentworth Springs (1953) 7.5' quadrangle.

Helmer Hill [COLUSA]: *peak,* 4.25 miles east-southeast of Wilbur Springs (lat. 39°01' N, long. 122°20'50" W; sec. 31, T 14 N, R 4 W). Named on Wilbur Springs (1961) 15' quadrangle.

Helvetia: see **New Helvetia** [SACRAMENTO-SUTTER-YUBA].

Hemlock Lake [EL DORADO]: *lake,* 325 feet long, 2.25 miles west-northwest of Pyramid Peak (lat. 38°51'40" N, long. 120°11'35" W). Named on Pyramid Peak (1955) 7.5' quadrangle.

Henderson Reservoir [AMADOR]: *lake,* 1600 feet long, behind a dam on Jackass Creek nearly 4 miles northeast of Ione (lat. 38°23'05" N, long. 120°52'30" W; sec. 9, T 6 N, R 10 E). Named on Amador City (1962) and Irish Hill (1962) 7.5' quadrangles. Called Preston Res. on Sutter Creek (1944) 15' quadrangle, but United States Board on Geographic Names (1964, p. 10) rejected this name for the feature.

Henly Canyon [AMADOR]: *canyon,* drained by a stream that flows 2.5 miles to Bear River 6 miles east-southeast of Hams Station (lat. 38°30'25" N, long. 120°16'30" W; sec. 36, T 8 N, R 15 E). Named on Peddler Hill (1951) 7.5' quadrangle.

Henness Pass [SIERRA]: *pass,* 7.25 miles south-southwest of Sierraville (lat. 39°30'05" N, long. 120°26'15" W; at E line sec. 19, T 19 N, R 14 E). Named on Sattley (1981) 7.5' quadrangle.

Henrys Diggings [EL DORADO]: *locality,* 1.5 miles north-northeast of Omo Ranch (lat. 38°36'10" N, long. 120°33'20" W). Named on Omo Ranch (1952) 7.5' quadrangle. Called Henry Diggings on Placerville (1893) 30' quadrangle.

Hensley: see **Point Hensley**, under **Sevenmile Slough** [SACRAMENTO].

Hensley Island: see **Randall Island** [SACRAMENTO].

Hensley Slough: see **Sevenmile Slough** [SACRAMENTO].

Herald [SACRAMENTO]: *settlement,* 4.5 miles northeast of Galt (lat. 38°17'45" N, long. 121°14'35" W; near W line sec. 8, T 5 N, R 7 E). Named on Clay (1968) 7.5' quadrangle. The name was coined from the names of Herbert Fleischacker and Alden Anderson, builders in 1910 of Central California Traction Railroad from Sacramento to Stockton, which is in San Joaquin County; the community was founded along the railroad in 1911 (Hanna, p. 137). Postal authorities established Herald post office in 1913 (Frickstad, p. 133).

Herleys [EL DORADO]: *locality,* 9 miles south-southeast of Placerville (lat. 38°36'10" N, long. 120°44'25" W). Named on Placerville (1893) 30' quadrangle.

Herring Reservoir [NEVADA]: *lake,* 350 feet long, 3 miles east-northeast of Grass Valley (lat. 39°14'15" N, long. 121°00'30" W; sec. 19, T 16 N, R 9 E). Named on Grass Valley (1949) 7.5' quadrangle.

Hershey [COLUSA-YOLO]: *locality,* 3.25 miles north-northwest of Dunnigan along Southern Pacific Railroad on Colusa-Yolo County line (lat. 38°55'30" N, long. 121°59'45" W; on N line sec. 5, T 12 N, R 1 W). Named on Dunnigan (1953) 7.5' quadrangle. The name commemorates David N. Hershey, who was Yolo County's first assemblyman (Hanna, p. 137).

Hesse's Crossing: see **Freemans Crossing** [NEVADA-YUBA].

Hewett: see **Cooks Station** [AMADOR].

Hiatt Lake [SUTTER]: *lake,* less than 1 mile south of Kirkville in a cutoff meander of Sacramento River (lat. 38°53'45" N, long. 121° 47'20" W; on S line sec. 7, T 12 N, R 2 E). Named on Kirkville (1952) 7.5' quadrangle. Called Kirk Lake on Kirkville (1915) 7.5' quadrangle. The name "Kirk" was for T.D. Kirk (Gudde, 1949, p. 175).

Hicks Gulch [AMADOR]: *canyon,* drained by a stream that flows 1 mile to Sutter Creek (1) nearly 2 miles east-northeast of Ione (lat. 38°21'30" N, long. 120°54' W; sec. 20, T 6 N, R 10 E). Named on Ione (1962) 7.5' quadrangle. Camp's (1962) map shows a feature called Hicks Hill located near present Hicks Gulch.

Hicks Hill: see **Hicks Gulch** [AMADOR].

Hicksville [SACRAMENTO]: *locality,* 5.25 miles north-northwest of Galt (lat. 38°19'40" N, long. 121°19'30" W). Named on Galt (1910) 7.5' quadrangle. Postal authorities established Hicksville post office in 1860 and discontinued it in 1889; the name commemorates William Hicks, who settled in the neighborhood in 1847 (Salley, p. 97).

Hidden Gold Camp [PLACER]: *locality,* 3.25 miles south-southwest of Dutch Flat (lat. 39°09'55" N, long. 120°51'30" W; sec. 9, T 15 N, R 19 E). Named on Dutch Flat (1950) 7.5' quadrangle.

Hidden Lake [AMADOR]: *lake,* 650 feet long, 6.25 miles north of Mokelumne Peak (lat. 38°37'40" N, long. 120°06'30" W; sec. 16, T 9 N, R 17 E). Named on Caples Lake (1979) 7.5' quadrangle.

Hidden Lake [EL DORADO]:

(1) *lake,* 450 feet long, 3.25 miles east of Wentworth Springs (lat. 39°00'15" N, long. 120°16'45" W; sec. 3, T 13 N, R 15 E). Named on Wentworth Springs (1953, photorevised 1973) 7.5' quadrangle.

(2) *lake,* 750 feet long, 2.25 miles north of Phipps Peak (lat. 38° 59'10" N, long. 120°09'05" W; near SE cor. sec. 12, T 13 N, R 16 E). Named on Rockbound Valley (1955) 7.5' quadrangle.

Hidden Lake [NEVADA]: *lake,* 450 feet long, 5 miles southwest of English Mountain (lat. 39°24'05" N, long. 120°37'20" W; on E line sec. 28, T 18 N, R 12 E). Named on English Mountain (1983) 7.5' quadrangle.

Hidden Valley [PLACER]:

(1) *canyon,* drained by a stream that flows 1 mile to Campbell Creek 2 miles southwest of Colfax (lat. 39°05'10" N, long. 120° 59' W; near N line sec. 9, T 14 N, R 9 E). Named on Colfax (1949) 7.5' quadrangle.

(2) *locality,* 4.25 miles east-southeast of Rocklin (lat. 38°45'50" N, long. 121°09'45" W; near N line sec. 35, T 11 N, R 7 E). Named on Rocklin (1967) 7.5' quadrangle. Arrowsmith's (1860) map shows a place called Union House located at or near present Hidden Valley (2), and a place called Wildwood located about 0.5 mile farther north-northeast.

Higgins Corner [NEVADA]: *locality,* 12.5 miles south of Grass Valley (lat. 39°02'35" N, long. 121°05'40" W; at S line sec. 21, T 14 N, R 8 E). Named on Lake Combie (1949) 7.5' quadrangle.

Higgins Point: see **Salmon Falls** [EL DORADO] (2).

High Commission [SIERRA]: *peak,* less than 1 mile east-northeast of Downieville (lat. 39°34' N, long. 120°48'50" W; near SW cor. sec. 25, T 20 N, R 10 E). Altitude 4225 feet. Named on Downieville (1951) 7.5' quadrangle.

Highland Lake [EL DORADO]: *lake,* 1250 feet long, 5 miles west of Phipps Peak (lat. 38°57'25" N, long. 120°14'25" W; on W line sec. 20, T 13 N, R 16 E). Named on Rockbound Valley (1955) 7.5' quadrangle.

Highland Park [SACRAMENTO]: *district,* 1.5 miles south-southeast of downtown Sacramento (lat. 38°33'25" N, long. 121°28'50" W). Named on Brighton (1911) 7.5' quadrangle.

Highlands: see **North Highlands** [SACRAMENTO].

High Loch Lake [PLACER]: *lake,* 850 feet long, 9.5 miles west-southwest of Donner Pass (lat. 39°17'10" N, long. 120°29'45" W; near NE cor. sec. 3, T 16 N, R 13 E). Named on Soda Springs (1955) 7.5' quadrangle. Truckee (1940) 30' quadrangle shows the lake as one of the group called Lac Leven Lakes. United States Board on Geographic Names (1962c, p. 19) rejected the name "High Loch Leven" for the feature.

High Loch Leven: see **High Loch Lake** [PLACER].

High Meadows [EL DORADO]: *area,* 2.5 miles north of Freel Peak along Cold Creek (lat. 38°53'45" N, long. 119°54'15" W; near SE cor. sec. 12, T 12 N, R 18 E). Named on South Lake Tahoe (1955) 7.5' quadrangle. Called High Meadow on Markleeville (1889) 30' quadrangle.

High Point Ravine [YUBA]: *canyon,* drained by a stream that flows 1.25 miles to Oregon Creek 1 mile south-southwest of Camptonville (lat. 39°26'15" N, long. 121°03'30" W; near SW cor. sec. 11, T 18 N, R 8 E). Named on Camptonville (1948) 7.5' quadrangle.

High Prairie [YUBA]: *ridge,* south-trending, 1.5 miles long, 5.5 miles south of Oregon House (lat. 39°16'40" N, long. 121°17'20" W). Named on Oregon House (1948) 7.5' quadrangle.

High Rock [COLUSA]: *relief feature,* 4 miles west of Fouts Springs (lat. 39°21'35" N, long. 122°44'15" W; on W line sec. 2, T 17 N, R 8 W). Named on Fouts Springs (1968) 7.5' quadrangle.

High Spring Ridge [YUBA]: *ridge,* north- to north-northeast-trending, 2 miles long, 3.25 miles southeast of Rackerby (lat. 39°24'20" N, long. 121°17'55" W). Named on Rackerby (1948) 7.5' quadrangle

High Valley [COLUSA]: *valley,* 7 miles long, center 12 miles north of Wilbur Springs (lat. 39°12'40" N, long. 122°25'20" W). Named on Lodoga (1960) and Wilbur Springs (1961) 15' quadrangles.

Hill Crest [NEVADA]: *locality,* nearly 6 miles west-northwest of Pilot Peak (lat. 39°12'20" N, long. 121°16'40" W; at E line sec. 34, T 16 N, R 6 E). Named on Smartville (1951) 7.5' quadrangle.

Hills Flat [NEVADA]: *locality,* 0.5 mile northeast of downtown Grass Valley (lat. 39°13'25" N, long. 121°03'10" W; near NW cor. sec. 26, T 16 N, R 8 E). Named on Grass Valley (1949) 7.5' quadrangle.

Hinkle Reservoir [PLACER-SACRAMENTO]: *lake,* 1400 feet long, 2.5 miles north of Folsom on Placer-Sacramento County line (lat. 38°42'50" N, long. 121°10'20" W; on N line sec. 23, T 10 N, R 7 E). Named on Folsom (1967) 7.5' quadrangle.

Hinsdale [SUTTER]: *locality,* 10 miles south of Sutter along Southern Pacific Railroad in Sutter Basin (lat. 39°00'55" N, long. 121° 46'40" W; sec. 32, T 14 N, R 2 E). Named on Tisdale Weir (1952) 7.5' quadrangle. California Division of Highways' (1934) map shows a place called Sheffield located 0.5 mile west-northwest of Hinsdale at the end of a railroad spur.

Hinton [NEVADA]: *locality,* 7 miles east-northeast of Truckee along Southern Pacific Railroad (lat. 39°22'30" N, long. 120°04'20" W; near S line sec. 27, T 18 N, R 17 E). Named on Boca (1955) 7.5' quadrangle.

Hirschdale [NEVADA]: *locality,* 6.25 miles east-northeast of Truckee (lat. 39°22'05" N, long. 120°04'35" W; sec. 34, T 18 N, R 17 E). Named on Martis Peak (1955) 7.5' quadrangle.

Hitchcock Ranch: see **Green Valley** [EL DORADO].

Hobart Mills [NEVADA]: *locality,* 5 miles north of Truckee (lat. 39° 24'05" N, long. 120°11' W; near NE cor. sec. 22, T 18 N, R 16 E). Named on Hobart Mills (1981) 7.5' quadrangle. Postal authorities established Hobart Mills post office in 1900 and discontinued it in 1938 (Frickstad, p. 113). The name "Hobart" commemorates Walter Scott Hobart (Hanna, p. 139).

Hobart Reservoir [NEVADA]: *lake,* 400 feet long, 1.25 miles northwest of Hobart Mills (lat. 39°25' N, long. 120°11'50" W; near NW cor. sec. 15, T 18 N, R 16 E). Named on Hobart Mills (1981) 7.5' quadrangle.

Hoboken: see **Brighton** [SACRAMENTO].

Hoboken Canyon [EL DORADO]: *canyon,* drained by a stream that flows

1.5 miles to American Canyon 2.5 miles north-northwest of Greenwood (lat. 38°55'55" N, long. 120°56' W; near E line sec. 35, T 13 N, R 9 E). Named on Greenwood (1949) 7.5' quadrangle. On Placerville (1893) 30' quadrangle, the stream in the canyon has the name "Hoboken Creek."

Hoboken Creek: see **Hoboken Canyon** [EL DORADO].

Hock Farm [SUTTER]: *locality,* 6 miles south of Yuba City near Feather River (lat. 39°02'50" N, long. 121°36'45" W). Named on Marysville (1895) 30' quadrangle. John A. Sutter retired and built a mansion at the site in 1850; the name is from *hoch,* which means "upper" in German (Hoover, Rensch, and Rensch, p. 544).

Hogback [PLACER]: *ridge,* west-southwest-trending, 1 mile long, 5.25 miles west-northwest of Duncan Peak (lat. 39°11'10" N, long. 120°36'05" W; sec. 2, T 15 N, R 12 E). Named on Duncan Peak (1952) 7.5' quadrangle.

Hogback Ravine [YUBA]: *canyon,* 1 mile long, opens into the canyon of Yuba River nearly 3 miles north-northeast of Smartville (lat. 39°14'50" N, long. 121°16'10" W; sec. 14, T 16 N, R 6 E). Named on Oregon House (1948) and Smartville (1951) 7.5' quadrangles. Water of Englebright Lake floods the lower part of the canyon.

Hog Canyon [EL DORADO]: *canyon,* drained by a stream that flows 1.5 miles to Bear Creek (2) 7 miles north-northeast of Chili Bar (lat. 38°52' N, long. 120°46'45" W; sec. 29, T 12 N, R 11 E). Named on Garden Valley (1949) and Georgetown (1949) 7.5' quadrangles.

Hog Canyon [SIERRA]: *canyon,* drained by a stream that flows 4 miles to Pauley Creek 5 miles northeast of Downieville (lat. 39°36'05" N, long. 120°45'10" W; near W line sec. 16, T 20 N, R 11 E). Named on Sierra City (1981) 7.5' quadrangle.

Hog Canyon [YOLO]: *canyon,* drained by a stream that flows 2.25 miles to Taylor Canyon 2.5 miles northeast of Berryessa Peak (lat. 38°41'25" N, long. 122°09'20" W). Named on Brooks (1959) 7.5' quadrangle.

Hog Gulch [SIERRA]: *canyon,* drained by a stream that flows 1.5 miles to West Branch Canyon Creek 1.5 miles east-southeast of Mount Fillmore (lat. 39°43' N, long. 120°49'30" W; at S line sec. 35, T 22 N, R 10 E). Named on Mount Fillmore (1951) 7.5' quadrangle.

Hog Hill [NEVADA]: *peak,* 2 miles north of Wolf (lat. 39°05'20" N, long. 121°08'40" W; near S line sec. 1, T 14 N, R 7 E). Altitude 1652 feet. Named on Wolf (1949) 7.5' quadrangle.

Hog Lake [SUTTER]: *intermittent lake,* 1850 feet long, 4 miles north of Kirkville in Sutter Basin (lat. 38°58'05" N, long. 121°46'45" W; on S line sec. 17, T 13 N, R 2 E). Named on Dunnigan (1953) 15' quadrangle.

Hog Spring [COLUSA]: *spring,* 2.25 miles east of Wilbur Springs (lat. 39°02' N, long. 122°22'40" W; sec. 26, T 14 N, R 5 W). Named on Wilbur Springs (1961) 15' quadrangle.

Hoke Valley [SIERRA]: *valley,* 4 miles south of Crystal Peak (lat. 39°30' N, long. 120°05'25" W). Named on Boca (1955) and Dog Valley (1981) 7.5' quadrangles.

Holbrook Flat [NEVADA]: *area,* 2.5 miles east of Washington along South Yuba River (lat. 39°21'40" N, long. 120°45'05" W; near SW cor. sec. 4, T 17 N, R 11 E). Named on Blue Canyon (1955) and Washington (1950) 7.5' quadrangles. The place first was called Helgeson Flat in the 1880's for Charlie Helgeson, who had a store there (Slyter and Slyter, p. 7).

Holden Spring [NEVADA]: *spring,* 2.5 miles northwest of North Bloomfield (lat. 39°23'25" N, long. 120°56'25" W; near SW cor. sec. 26, T 18 N, R 9 E). Named on Pike (1949) 7.5' quadrangle.

Holdridge [EL DORADO]: *locality,* 4 miles northeast of Leek Spring Hill (lat. 38°39'45" N, long. 120°13'15" W). Named on Pyramid Peak (1896) 30' quadrangle.

Hole-in-Ground [NEVADA]: *lake,* 225 feet long, nearly 6 miles west-northwest of Donner Pass (lat. 39°21'20" N, long. 120°25'05" W; near E line sec. 8, T 17 N, R 14 E). Named on Soda Springs (1955) 7.5' quadrangle. Called Hole in Ground Reservoir on California Division of Highways' (1934) map. United States Board on Geographic Names (1994, p. 5) approved the name "Mount Marliave" for a peak situated 1 mile southeast of Hole-in-Ground (lat. 39°20'54" N, long. 120°24'02" W); the name commemorates Elmer C. Marliave and Burton H. Marliave, engineering geologists.

Hole in Ground Reservoir: see **Hole-in-Ground** [NEVADA].

Hole in the Wall: see **Prairie Diggings**, under **Browns Valley** [YUBA].

Holland Tract: see **Little Holland Tract** [YOLO].

Holley Ravine [NEVADA]: *canyon,* drained by a stream that flows 1 mile to Bloody Run 3.5 miles north-northeast of North Bloomfield (lat. 39°25' N, long. 120°54'45" W; at S line sec. 13, T 18 N, R 9 E). Named on Pike (1949) 7.5' quadrangle.

Hollow Log: see **Negro Tent** [SIERRA].

Holman Hill [YUBA]: *peak,* nearly 7 miles south-southwest of Oregon House (lat. 39°16'15" N, long. 121°20'35" W; sec. 6, T 16 N, R 6 E). Altitude 925 feet. Named on Oregon House (1948) 7.5' quadrangle.

Holsten Canyon [COLUSA]: *canyon,* drained by a stream that flows 1.25 miles to Bear Creek 7 miles southeast of Wilbur Springs (lat. 38°57'50" N, long. 122°20'25" W; sec. 19, T 13 N, R 4 W). Named on Glascock Mountain (1958) 7.5' quadrangle.

Holsten Chimney Canyon [COLUSA]: *canyon,* drained by a stream that flows 1.5 miles to Bear Creek 7 miles southeast of Wilbur Springs (lat. 38°37'30" N, long. 122°20'30" W; sec. 19, T 13 N, R 4 W); the canyon is parallel to and less than 1 mile south of Holsten Canyon. Named on Glascock Mountain (1958) 7.5' quadrangle.

Homestead [SACRAMENTO]: *locality,* nearly 2 miles east-southeast of downtown Sacramento along Sacramento and Placerville Railroad (lat. 38°33'50" N, long. 121°28' W). Named on Sacramento (1892) 30' quadrangle.

Homewood [PLACER]: *village,* 5.5 miles south of Tahoe City along Lake Tahoe (lat. 39°05'15" N, long. 120°09'40" W; sec. 1, T 14 N, R 16 E). Named on Homewood (1955) 7.5' quadrangle.

Homewood Canyon [PLACER]: *canyon,* drained by a stream that flows 2 miles to Lake Tahoe near the south end of Homewood (lat. 39°04'50" N, long. 120°09'20" W; sec. 12, T 14 N, R 16 E). Named on Homewood (1955) 7.5' quadrangle.

Honcut [YUBA]: *land grant,* east of Feather River and north of Marysville. Named on Browns Valley (1947), Gridley (1952), Honcut (1952), Loma Rica (1947), Sutter (1952), and Yuba City (1952) 7.5' quadrangles. Theodore Cordua received 7 leagues in 1844; Charles Covilland (should be Covillaud) claimed 31,080 acres patented in 1863 (Cowan, p. 39-40). The name is from an Indian village that was situated near the mouth of present Honcut Creek (Kroeber, p. 42).

Honcut Creek [YUBA]: *stream,* formed by the confluence of South Honcut Creek and North Honcut Creek (North Honcut Creek is in Butte County); flows 2.5 miles along Yuba-Butte County line to Feather River 10.5 miles north of Marysville (lat. 39°17'45" N, long. 121°37'20" W). Named on Honcut (1952) 7.5' quadrangle. Charles Covillaud, who owned Honcut grant, founded a town called Featherton along Feather River at the mouth of Honcut Creek, but the venture failed (Gudde, 1975, p. 114).

Honcut Creek: see **South Honcut Creek** [YUBA].

Honey Creek [EL DORADO]: *stream,* flows 1.25 miles to Plum Creek (1) 5 miles west-southwest of Robbs Peak (lat. 38°54'45" N, long. 120°29'35" W; near W line sec. 2, T 12 N, R 13 E). Named on Robbs Peak (1950) 7.5' quadrangle.

Hood [SACRAMENTO]: *village,* 3.5 miles northeast of Courtland along Sacramento River (lat. 38°22'05" N, long. 121°31' W). Named on Courtland (1978) 7.5' quadrangle. Called Richland on Vorden (1916) 7.5' quadrangle. Postal authorities established Richland post office in 1860 and discontinued it in 1888; they established Hood post office in 1912 (Salley, p. 99, 185). Madison P. Barnes named the place in 1910 to honor William Hood, chief engineer of Southern Pacific Railroad (Gudde, 1949, p. 152).

Hood: see **Hood Junction** [SACRAMENTO].

Hood Junction [SACRAMENTO]: *locality,* 4 miles northeast of Courtland along Southern Pacific Railroad (lat. 38°21'55" N, long. 121°30'30" W); the place is 0.5 mile east-southeast of Hood. Named on Courtland (1978) 7.5' quadrangle. Called Hood on Vorden (1916) 7.5' quadrangle, where present Hood is called Richland.

Hoodoo Bar: see **Goodyears Bar** [SIERRA].

Hoodsville: see **Slabtown**, under **Jackson Butte** [AMADOR].

Hoosier Bar [EL DORADO-PLACER]: *locality,* 4.25 miles west-northwest of Greenwood along Middle Fork American River on El Dorado-Placer County line (lat. 38°55'45" N, long. 120°58'45" W; near S line sec. 33, T 13 N, R 9 E). Named on Greenwood (1949) 7.5' quadrangle. Gudde (1975, p. 371, 372) listed a mining place called Wild Cat Bar that was located on the south side of Middle Fork between Kennebec Bar and Hoosier Bar, and a mining place called Willow Bar that was situated along Middle Fork between Hoosier Bar and Wildcat Bar.

Hope: see **Mount Hope** [EL DORADO]; **Mount Hope** [YUBA].

Hope Ravine [SIERRA]: *canyon,* drained by a stream that flows less than 1 mile to Jackass Ravine 2 miles southeast of Alleghany (lat. 39°26'55" N, long. 120°49'25" W; sec. 11, T 18 N, R 10 E). Named on Alleghany (1949) 7.5' quadrangle.

Hopewell: see **Colusa** [COLUSA].

Hopkins: see **Soda Springs** [NEVADA].

Hopkins Slough [COLUSA]: *water feature,* 3 miles west of Colusa (lat. 39°13'30" N, long. 122°03'45" W); the feature is in Colusa Basin. Named on Colusa (1952) and Moulton Weir (1952) 7.5' quadrangles.

Hopkins Springs: see **Soda Springs** [NEVADA].

Hornblende Mountains [EL DORADO]: *ridge,* south- to west-southwest-trending, 5 miles long, center 3.5 miles north-northeast of Georgetown (lat. 38°57'10" N, long. 120°48'30" W). Named on Georgetown (1949) 7.5' quadrangle.

Hornet Nest Hill [COLUSA]: *peak,* 3.5 miles south-southwest of Stonyford (lat. 39°19'50" N, long. 122°35' W); the peak is at the east end of Hornet Nest Ridge. Altitude 3077 feet. Named on Gilmore Peak (1968) 7.5' quadrangle.

Hornet Nest Ridge [COLUSA]: *ridge,* east-northeast- to east-trending, 2.5 miles long, 4.5 miles southwest of Stonyford (lat. 39°19'40" N, long. 122°36'20" W). Named on Gilmore Peak (1968) 7.5' quadrangle.

Hornet Nest Spring [COLUSA]: *spring,* nearly 4 miles southwest of Stonyford (lat. 39°20'05" N, long. 122°35'35" W); the spring is on the north side of Hornet Nest Ridge. Named on Gilmore Peak (1968) 7.5' quadrangle.

Hornswoggle Creek [YUBA]: *stream,* flows 1 mile to Moonshine Creek 4.25 miles southwest of Camptonville (lat. 39°24'25" N, long. 121°06'10" W; sec. 20, T 18 N, R 8 E). Named on Camptonville (1948) 7.5' quadrangle.

Horse Bar: see **Rice Crossing** [NEVADA-YUBA].

Horse Canyon [EL DORADO]: *canyon,* drained by a stream that flows 2.25 miles to Middle Fork Cosumnes River 7.25 miles east-southeast of Caldor (lat. 38°35' N, long. 120°18'10" W; sec. 34, T 9 N, R 15 E). Named on Peddler Hill (1951) 7.5' quadrangle

Horse Creek [AMADOR]: *stream,* flows 5.25 miles to Dry Creek 4.5 miles north-northeast of Ione (lat. 38°24'55" N, long. 120°54'45" W; sec. 31, T 7 N, R 10 E). Named on Amador City (1962) and Irish Hill (1962) 7.5' quadrangles.

Horse Hollow [COLUSA]: *area,* 3 miles west of Pacific Point (lat. 39°13'05" N, long. 122°38'50" W; sec. 21, T 16 N, R 7 W); the place is 1.25 miles east-southeast of Horse Rock. Named on Clearlake Oaks (1960) 15' quadrangle.

Horse Lake [SIERRA]: *lake,* 550 feet long, 6.25 miles north of Sierra City (lat. 39°39'10" N, long. 120°39'25" W; sec. 29, T 21 N, R 12 E). Named on Gold Lake (1981) 7.5' quadrangle.

Horse Range [NEVADA]: *valley,* 2.5 miles north-northeast of Donner Pass (lat. 39°21'05" N, long. 120°18'35" W; on E line sec. 4, T 17 N, R 15 E). Named on Norden (1955) 7.5' quadrangle.

Horse Rock [COLUSA]: *peak,* 4 miles west of Pacific Point on Colusa-Lake County line (lat. 39°13'25" N, long. 122°40'15" W). Named on Clearlake Oaks (1960) 15' quadrangle.

Horseshoe Bar [EL DORADO-PLACER]:
(1) *locality,* 2 miles northeast of Volcanoville along Middle Fork American River on El Dorado-Placer County line (lat. 39°00'10" N, long. 120°45'30" W; sec. 4, T 13 N, R 11 E). Named on Foresthill (1949) 7.5' quadrangle.
(2) *locality,* 5 miles west-southwest of the village of Pilot Hill along North Fork American River on El Dorado-Placer County line (lat. 38°48'30" N, long. 121°05'55" W; near W line sec. 16, T 11 N, R 8 E). Named on Auburn (1944) 15' quadrangle. Water of Folsom Lake now covers the site. Mormons mined for gold at the place in 1848; a mining spot called Little Horseshoe Bar was along North Fork below Horseshoe Bar (2) (Gudde, 1975, p. 160, 195).

Horseshoe Bend [PLACER]: *locality,* 3.25 miles east-southeast of Donner Pass along Southern Pacific Railroad in Coldstream Valley (lat. 39°17'35" N, long. 120°16'15" W; near W line sec. 25, T 17 N, R 15 E). Named on Norden (1955) 7.5' quadrangle.

Horseshoe Bend [SACRAMENTO]: *bend,* 7.5 miles southwest of Isleton along Sacramento River on Sacramento-Solano County line (lat. 38°05' N, long. 121°42'45" W). Named on Jersey Island (1978) 7.5' quadrangle.

Horseshoe Flat [NEVADA-YUBA]: *area,* nearly 5 miles south of Smartville on Nevada-Yuba County line (lat. 39°08'15" N, long. 121°16'50" W; at W line sec. 23, T 15 N, R 6 E). Named on Smartville (1951) 7.5' quadrangle.

Horseshoe Lake [EL DORADO]: *lake,* 1000 feet long, nearly 4 miles west of Phipps Peak (lat. 38°57'15" N, long. 120°13'15" W; on S line sec. 21, T 13 N, R 16 E). Named on Rockbound Valley (1955) 7.5' quadrangle.

Horseshoe Lake [SUTTER]:
(1) *lake,* nearly 2 miles south-southwest of Kirkville in a cutoff meander of Sacramento River (lat. 38°53'05" N, long. 121°48'20" W; sec. 13, T 12 N, R 1 E). Named on Kirkville (1952) 7.5' quadrangle.
(2) *lake,* 7 miles south of Robbins near the Sacramento River (lat. 38°46'15" N, long. 121°40'40" W; sec. 30, T 11 N, R 3 E). Named on Knights Landing (1952) 7.5' quadrangle.

Horse Spring [PLACER]: *spring,* 2.25 miles north-northeast of Devil Peak (lat. 38°59'25" N, long. 120°31'50" W; sec. 9, T 13 N, R 13 E). Named on Devil Peak (1950) 7.5' quadrangle.

Horsetail Falls [EL DORADO]: *waterfall,* 5 miles west-northwest of Echo Summit along Pyramid Creek (lat. 38°49'50" N, long. 120° 07'20" W). Named on Echo Lake (1955) 7.5' quadrangle.

Horse Thief Spring [AMADOR]: *spring,* 5 miles north of Mokelumne Peak (lat. 38°36'45" N, long. 120°05'20" W; sec. 22, T 9 N, R 18 E). Named on Mokelumne Peak (1979) 7.5' quadrangle.

Horse Valley: see **Horse Valley Creek** [YUBA].

Horse Valley Creek [YUBA]: *stream,* flows 1.5 miles to Brandy Creek 1.5 miles north-northwest of Camptonville (lat. 39°28'15" N, long. 121°03'45" W; near E line sec. 34, T 19 N, R 8 E). Named on Camptonville (1948) 7.5' quadrangle. Wescoatt's (1861) map has name "Horse Valley" for a canyon situated 1 mile north-northeast of Camptonville.

Horstville [YUBA]: *locality,* 2 miles northeast of Wheatland (lat. 39° 01'40" N, long. 121°23'25" W). Named on Wheatland (1947) 7.5' quadrangle. Postal authorities established Horstville post office in 1898 and discontinued it in 1901; the name was for E. Clemons Horst, who had his ranching headquarters at the place (Salley, p. 100).

Horton Ridge [NEVADA]: *ridge,* south-trending, 1 mile long, 2.25 miles north-northwest of Pilot Peak (lat. 39°11'50" N, long. 121° 12'15" W). Named on Rough and Ready (1949) 7.5' quadrangle.

Hotaling [PLACER]: *locality,* 6.25 miles north of Auburn (lat. 38° 59'20" N, long. 121°04'30" W; near SW cor. sec. 10, T 13 N, R 8 E). Site named on Auburn (1953) 7.5' quadrangle. Postal authorities established Hotaling post office in 1881 and discontinued it in 1886; the name was for Richard M. Hotaling, owner of Iron Mountain Company smelting works (Salley, p. 100).

Hotchkiss Hill [EL DORADO]: *peak,* 1.5 miles east-northeast of Georgetown (lat. 38°54'50" N, long. 120°48'45" W; sec. 1, T 12 N, R 10 E). Altitude 3245 feet. Named on Georgetown (1949) 7.5' quadrangle.

Hotchkiss Hill [PLACER]: *peak,* 6.5 miles south of Colfax (lat. 39° 00'25" N, long. 120°58'35" W; sec. 4, T 13 N, R 9 E). Altitude 2337 feet. Named on Colfax (1949) 7.5' quadrangle.

Hour House: see **Our House** [SIERRA].

Howard: see **Peart** [YOLO].

Howard Creek [COLUSA]: *stream,* heads in Glenn County and flows 5 miles to Grapevine Creek 5.5 miles northeast of Lodoga in Colusa County (lat. 39°21'05" N, long. 122°24'15" W; sec. 3, T 17 N, R 5 W). Named on Lodoga (1960) 15' quadrangle. Lodoga (1943) 15' quadrangle has the name along a tributary of present Howard Creek that heads near Grapevine Pass.

Howard Creek [SIERRA]: *stream,* flows 5.5 miles to North Yuba River 4.25 miles north-northeast of Sierra City (lat. 39°36'50" N, long. 120°35'30" W; sec. 11, T 20 N, R 12 E). Named on Clio (1981) and Haypress Valley (1981) 7.5' quadrangles.

Howard Creek Meadows [SIERRA]: *marsh,* 7.5 miles north-northeast of Sierra City (lat. 39°40'15" N, long. 120°35'30" W; sec. 23, T 21 N, R 12 E); the feature is along Howard Creek. Named on Clio (1981) 7.5' quadrangle. Sierra City (1955) 15' quadrangle has the name for a dry area.

Howard Hill [YUBA]: *ridge,* northwest-trending, about 1 mile long, 3 miles northwest of Smartville (lat. 39°14'30" N, long. 121°19'50" W; on E line sec. 18, T 16 N, R 6 E). Named on Smartville (1951) 7.5' quadrangle.

Howard Landing [SACRAMENTO]: *locality,* 4.5 miles north of Isleton along Steamboat Slough on Grand Island (lat. 38°13'45" N, long. 121°35'55" W). Named on Isleton (1978) 7.5' quadrangle.

Howard Landing Ferry [SACRAMENTO]: *locality,* 5 miles north of Isleton along Steamboat Slough on Sacramento-Solano County line (lat. 38°14'10" N, long. 121°36'10" W); the place is 0.5 mile north of Howard Landing. Named on Isleton (1978) 7.5' quadrangle.

Howard Ranch: see **Bassetts** [SIERRA].

Howell Hill [PLACER]: *peak,* 2.5 miles south-southwest of Colfax (lat. 39°04'05" N, long. 120°58'15" W; near E line sec. 16, T 14 N, R 9 E). Altitude 2607 feet. Named on Colfax (1949) 7.5' quadrangle.

Howells: see **Cosumne** [SACRAMENTO].

Howells Landing [COLUSA]: *locality,* 1.5 miles south of Boyers Landing along Sacramento River (lat. 38°55'50" N, long. 121°50'10" W; near W line sec. 35, T 13 N, R 1 E). Named on Kirkville (1952) 7.5' quadrangle. Called Howell's Landing on Kirkville (1915) 7.5' quadrangle.

Howells Point: see **Howells Point Ridge** [COLUSA-YOLO].

Howells Point Ridge [COLUSA-YOLO]: *ridge,* extends west-southwest from near Boyers Landing (center near lat. 38°56'10" N, long. 121°51'45" W); the feature is on Colusa-Yolo County line, mainly in Colusa County. Named on Dunnigan (1953) and Kirkville (1952) 7.5' quadrangles. Called Howells Point on Dunnigan (1907) 15' quadrangle, and on Kirkville (1915) 7.5' quadrangle.

Howland Flat [SIERRA]: *settlement,* 2.25 miles west-southwest of Mount Fillmore (lat. 39°42'55" N, long. 120°53'10" W; near N line sec. 5, T 21 N, R 10 E); the place is less than 1 mile north-northwest of Table Rock. Named on La Porte (1951) 7.5' quadrangle. The post office at the site was called Table Rock (Hoover, Rensch, and Rensch, p. 496). Postal authorities established Table Rock post office in 1857 and discontinued it in 1922 (Frickstad, p. 185).

Hoyt Crossing [NEVADA]: *locality,* 4.25 miles northwest of Grass Valley along South Yuba River (lat. 39°18'15" N, long. 120°04'40" W; near SE cor. sec. 28, T 17 N, R 8 E). Named on Nevada City (1948) 7.5' quadrangle. Called Hoyt's Crossing on Logan's (1940) map. M.F. Hoyt built a bridge at the site about 1854 (Gudde, 1975, p. 162).

Hubers [EL DORADO]: *locality,* 4.25 miles east-northeast of Georgetown (lat. 38°55'45" N, long. 120°45'45" W). Named on Placerville (1893) 30' quadrangle.

Huckleberry Flat [EL DORADO]: *area,* 1.5 miles west of Echo Summit (lat. 38°48'50" N, long. 120°03'25" W; sec. 12, T 11 N, R 17 E). Named on Echo Lake (1955) 7.5' quadrangle.

Hudsons Gulch [EL DORADO]: *canyon,* drained by a stream that flows less than 0.5 mile to Oregon Canyon 1.25 miles north-northwest of Georgetown (lat. 38°55'25" N, long. 120°50'55" W; near N line sec. 3, T 12 N, R 10 E). Named on Georgetown (1949) 7.5' quadrangle.

Hudsonville: see **Summit City** [NEVADA].

Huff Canyon [SUTTER]: *valley,* 5 miles north-northwest of Sutter (lat. 39°13'40" N, long. 121°47'20" W; near N line sec. 19, T 16 N, R 2 E). Named on Sutter Buttes (1954) 7.5' quadrangle.

Hughes Mill [PLACER]: *locality,* 5.25 miles north-northeast of Foresthill (lat. 39°05'30" N, long. 120°46'40" W; sec. 6, T 14 N, R 11 E). Named on Foresthill (1949) 7.5' quadrangle.

Humbug: see **North Bloomfield** [NEVADA].

Humbug Bar [PLACER]: *locality,* 4.25 miles west of Westville at the mouth of Humbug Canyon (lat. 39°10'45" N, long. 120°43'35" W; sec. 3, T 15 N, R 11 E). Named on Westville (1952) 7.5' quadrangle.

Humbug Canyon [PLACER]: *canyon,* drained by a stream that flows 5 miles to North Fork American River 4.25 miles west of Westville (lat. 39°10'45" N, long. 120°43'35" W; sec. 3, T 15 N, R 11 E). Named on Westville (1952) 7.5' quadrangle. The feature was called Mississippi Canyon before early in 1850; miners renamed it because of poor luck that they had finding gold there (Hoover, Rensch, and Rensch, p. 269). On Colfax (1898) 30' quadrangle, the stream in the canyon is called Humbug Creek.

Humbug Creek [NEVADA]: *stream,* flows 7.5 miles to South Yuba River 2.5 miles southwest of North Bloomfield (lat. 39°20'20" N, long. 120°55'50" W; sec. 14, T 17 N, R 9 E). Named on Alleghany (1949), North Bloomfield (1949), and Pike (1949) 7.5' quadrangles. Miners named the stream in 1851 after they failed to find gold there (Browne, p. 17).

Humbug Creek [SACRAMENTO]: *stream,* flows 2.5 miles to Willow Creek (1) 1.25 miles southeast of Folsom (lat. 38°39'40" N, long. 121°09'25" W). Named on Folsom (1967) 7.5' quadrangle.

Humbug Creek [SIERRA]: *stream,* flows 4 miles to North Yuba River nearly 5 miles west-southwest of Goodyears Bar (lat. 39°30'40" N, long. 120°57'55" W; near E line sec. 16, T 19 N, R 9 E). Named on Goodyears Bar (1951) 7.5' quadrangle.

Humbug Creek: see **Humbug Canyon** [PLACER]; **Little Humbug Creek** [SIERRA].

Humbug Ridge [PLACER]: *ridge,* generally west-trending, 3 miles long, center 1.25 miles west-northwest of Westville (lat. 39°10'45" N, long. 120°40'20" W); the ridge is north of Humbug Canyon. Named on Westville (1952) 7.5' quadrangle.

Hundred Ounce Gulch [AMADOR]: *canyon,* drained by a stream that flows 1 mile to Mokelumne River nearly 2 miles southeast of Jackson Butte (lat. 38°19'05" N, long. 120°42' W; sec. 6, T 5 N, R 12 E). Named on Mokelumne Hill (1948) 7.5' quadrangle.

Hungry Hollow [EL DORADO]: *relief feature,* 2.25 miles east of Latrobe (lat. 38°33'55" N, long. 120°56'20" W; sec. 12, T 8 N, R 9 E). Named on Latrobe (1949) 7.5' quadrangle.

Hungry Hollow [YOLO]: *valley,* southwest of Dunnigan Hills and north of Cache Creek. Named on Bird Valley (1959), Esparto (1959), Madison (1953), and Zamora (1953) 7.5' quadrangles.

Hungry Mouth Canyon [SIERRA]: *canyon,* drained by a stream that flows 2 miles to North Yuba River 0.5 mile east of Downieville (lat. 39°33'30" N, long. 120°49' W; near E line sec. 35, T 20 N, R 10 E). Named on Downieville (1951) 7.5' quadrangle.

Hunters Creek [COLUSA]: *stream,* heads in Glenn County and flows 8 miles in Colusa County to Logan Creek 7.5 miles north-northeast of Maxwell (lat. 39°21'45" N, long. 122°06'35" W). Named on Logandale (1952), Maxwell (1952), and Moulton Weir (1952) 7.5' quadrangles.

Hunters Creek: see **Hunters Valley** [EL DORADO].

Hunters Spring [PLACER]: *spring,* 4 miles northeast of Bunker Hill (lat. 39°05'50" N, long. 120°20'15" W; near N line sec. 6, T 14 N, R 15 E). Named on Wentworth Springs (1953) 7.5' quadrangle.

Hunters Valley [EL DORADO]: *canyon,* drained by a stream that flows 2 miles to Little Silver Creek (2) 4.5 miles southwest of Robbs Peak (lat. 38°52'35" N, long. 120°27'15" W; sec. 19, T 12 N, R 14 E). Named on Robbs Peak (1950) 7.5' quadrangle. The stream in the canyon is called Hunters Creek on Pyramid Peak (1896) 30' quadrangle.

Hunt Gulch [AMADOR]: *canyon,* 1.25 miles long. 2.25 miles south-southeast of Jackson (lat. 38°19'10" N, long. 120°45'05" W; mainly in sec. 3, T 5 N, R 11 E). Named on Jackson (1962) 7.5' quadrangle.

Huntington: see **Arboga** [YUBA].

Huntley Mill Lake [PLACER]: *lake,* 700 feet long, 7.5 miles west-southwest of Donner Pass (lat. 39°16'05" N, long. 120°27'05" W; near W line sec. 7, T 16 N, R 14 E). Named on Soda Springs (1955) 7.5' quadrangle.

Hunts Hill [NEVADA]: *locality,* 6.5 miles north-northeast of present Chicago Park (lat. 39°14'10" N, long. 120°55'10" W). Named on Colfax (1898) 30' quadrangle. The place also was called Gouge Eye because a French miner lost an eye in a fight there in 1855 (Browne, p. 21).

Huse Bridge [AMADOR]: *locality,* less than 1 mile north of Enterprise along Cosumnes River (lat. 38°33' N, long. 120°51' W). Named on Placerville (1893) 30' quadrangle.

Hutchins: see **Marysville** [YUBA].

Hutchinson Creek [YUBA]: *stream,* flows 18 miles to Reeds Creek 2.5 miles south-southeast of Olivehurst (lat. 39°03'45" N, long. 121°32'05" W; sec. 16, T 14 N, R 4 E). Named on Browns Valley (1947), Olivehurst (1952), Smartville (1951), and Wheatland (1947) 7.5' quadrangles.

Huttons Ranch: see **Yolo** [YOLO].

Huysink Lake [PLACER]: *lake,* 550 feet long, 1.5 miles south of Cisco Grove (lat. 39°17'15" N, long. 120°32'05" W; on S line sec. 32, T 17 N, R 13 E). Named on Cisco Grove (1955) 7.5' quadrangle. Called Huysinck Lake on Colfax (1898) 30' quadrangle.

Hyphus Creek [COLUSA]: *stream,* flows 5.5 miles to Little Stony Creek nearly 4 miles south-southeast of Stonyford (lat. 39°19'25" N, long. 122°31'25" W; near W line sec. 15, T 17 N, R 6 W). Named on Gilmore Peak (1968) 7.5' quadrangle.

— I —

Icehouse Pond [AMADOR]: *lake,* 400 feet long, 5.25 miles south-southeast of Plymouth (lat. 38°24'30" N, long. 120°48'20" W; near N line sec. 6, T 6 N, R 11 N). Named on Amador City (1962) 7.5' quadrangle. Called Amador Reservoir on California Division of Highways' (1934) map.

Ice House Reservoir [EL DORADO]: *lake,* behind a dam on South Fork Silver Creek 5 miles northwest of Kyburz (lat. 38°49'25" N, long. 120°21'35" W; sec. 1, T 11 N, R 14 E). Named on Kyburz (1952, photorevised 1973) 7.5' quadrangle, which has the name "Ice House" for a building located 1 mile southwest of the dam.

Ice Lakes [PLACER]: *lakes,* two connected, each about 2000 feet long, 3.5 miles west-southwest of Donner Pass (lat. 39°18' N, long. 120°23' W). Named on Soda Springs (1955) 7.5' quadrangle. On Truckee (1940) 30' quadrangle, the southernmost lake is called Dulzura Lake, and the other is called Serena Lake, but United States Board on Geographic Names (1962c, p. 19) rejected these names. The lakes are called Sereno Lake on Truckee (1895) 15' quadrangle.

Iceland [NEVADA]: *locality,* 9 miles east-northeast of Truckee along Southern Pacific Railroad (lat. 39°22'30" N, long. 120°01'30" W; near SW cor. sec. 31, T 18 N, R 18 E). Named on Boca (1955) 7.5' quadrangle. Postal authorities established Iceland post office in 1897 and discontinued it in 1923 (Frickstad, p. 114). The name is from the cutting and storage of ice near the site; the place first was called Cuba (Hanna, p. 147).

Idaho-Maryland Reservoir [NEVADA]: *lake,* 250 feet long, nearly 3 miles east of Grass Valley (lat. 39°13'25" N, long. 121°00'30" W; sec. 30, T 16 N, R 9 E). Named on Grass Valley (1949) 7.5' quadrangle, which shows Idaho-Maryland mine 1.5 miles west of the lake.

Ida Island [SACRAMENTO]: *island,* 4000 feet long, 1.5 miles west-northwest of Isleton in Sacramento River (lat. 38°10'10" N, long. 121°38'05" W). Named on Rio Vista (1978) 7.5' quadrangle. Called Ida's Isle on Ringgold's (1850b) map.

Ida's Isle: see **Ida Island** [SACRAMENTO].

Idlewild [PLACER]: *settlement,* 1.5 miles north of Homewood along Lake Tahoe (lat. 39°06'30" N, long. 120°09'30" W; sec. 36, T 15 N, R 16 E). Named on Homewood (1955) 7.5' quadrangle.

Illinois Canyon [EL DORADO]: *canyon,* drained by a stream that flows 2.25 miles to Canyon Creek (1) 2 miles northwest of Georgetown (lat. 38°55'50" N, long. 120°51'25" W; near E line sec. 33, T 13 N, R 10 E). Named on Georgetown (1949) 7.5' quadrangle. Gudde (1975, p. 165) gave the names "Illinois Ravine," "South Canyon," and "Thousand Dollar Canyon" as other designations for the feature, and noted that a gold nugget worth one thousand dollars was found in the canyon in 1849.

Illinois Creek [SIERRA]: *stream,* flows 2 miles to Canyon Creek 2.25 miles south-southeast of Mount Fillmore (lat. 39°41'55" N, long. 120°50'10" W). Named on Mount Fillmore (1951) 7.5' quadrangle.

Illinois Ravine: see **Illinois Canyon** [EL DORADO]; **Newtown** [NEVADA].

Illinoistown [PLACER]: *locality,* less than 1 mile south of downtown Colfax (lat. 39°05'20" N, long. 120°57'20" W; sec. 3, T 14 N, R 9 E). Site named on Colfax (1949) 7.5' quadrangle. Postal authorities established Illinoistown post office in 1853 and discontinued it in 1866 (Salley, p. 103). The place first was called Alder Grove or Upper Corral (Bancroft, 1888, p. 483).

Ina Coolbrith: see **Mount Ina Coolbrith** [SIERRA].

Ina Coolbrith Summit: see **Mount Ina Coolbrith** [SIERRA].

Independence Creek [SIERRA]: *stream,* flows 5 miles to Little Truckee River 8 miles southeast of Sierraville (lat. 39°30' N, long. 120°15'40" W; sec. 13, T 19 N, R 15 E); the stream heads at Independence Lake. Named on Independence Lake (1981) and Sierraville (1981) 7.5' quadrangles.

Independence Creek: see **Upper Independence Creek** [NEVADA].

Independence Hill: see **Monona Flat** [PLACER].

Independence Lake [NEVADA-SIERRA]: *lake,* 2.5 miles long, 9 miles north of Donner Pass on Nevada-Sierra County line (lat. 39° 26'35" N, long. 120°18'30" W). Named on Independence Lake (1981) 7.5' quadrangle. Actress Lola Montez named the lake when she picnicked there on Independence Day in 1853 (Hanna, p. 148).

Independence Point [EL DORADO]: *ridge,* west-trending, 1.5 miles long, 3.5 miles west-northwest of Pollock Pines (lat. 38°47' N, long. 120°38'30" W). Named on Slate Mountain (1950) 7.5' quadrangle.

Independence Point [SIERRA]: *ridge,* south-southeast- to south-trending, 1 mile long, 2 miles east-southeast of Alleghany (lat. 39° 27'45" N, long. 120°48'15" W; on N line sec. 1, T 18 N, R 10 E). Named on Alleghany (1949) 7.5' quadrangle.

Indiana Camp: see **Washington** [NEVADA].

Indiana Creek [YUBA]: *stream,* flows 3.5 miles to Dry Creek (1) 3.5 miles northwest of Dobbins (lat. 39°24'35" N, long. 121°14'50" W; near N line sec. 24, T 18 N, R 6 E). Named on Challenge (1948) 7.5' quadrangle.

Indiana Creek: see **Indiana Ranch** [YUBA].

Indiana Hill: see **Gold Run** [PLACER].

Indiana Ranch [YUBA]: *locality*, 2.25 miles north-northwest of Dobbins along Keystone Creek (lat. 39°24' N, long. 121°13'35" W; sec. 19, T 18 N, R 7 E). Named on Challenge (1948) 7.5' quadrangle. The Page brothers from Indiana, along with Peter Labadie and John Tolles, settled at the place in 1851; the community that formed there was called Indiana Creek or Tolles' New Diggings (Hoover, Rensch, and Rensch, p. 593). Eddy's (1851) map shows a place called Keystone R. [Ranch] located just south of Indiana R. Keystone Ranch was a stage station in the early days (Gudde, 1975, p. 186). Maple Springs House was built 1.5 miles northeast of Indiana Ranch in 1852; after Peter Labadie bought the place it also was known as Labadie's (Hoover, Rensch, and Rensch, p. 593).

Indiana Ravine [PLACER]: *canyon*, drained by a stream that flows less than 1 mile to North Fork American River 4 miles south of Dutch Flat (lat. 39°08'55" N, long. 120°50'25" W; sec. 15, T 15 N, R 10 E); the canyon heads near Indiana Hill, which is shown on Whitney's (1873) map. Named on Dutch Flat (1950) 7.5' quadrangle.

Indian Bar [PLACER]: *locality*, 2.5 miles south-southwest of Michigan Bluff along Middle Fork American River (lat. 39°00'20" N, long. 120°44'50" W; near NE cor. sec. 4, T 13 N, R 11 E). Named on Michigan Bluff (1952) 7.5' quadrangle.

Indian Cañon: see **Indian Creek** [PLACER] (2).

Indian Creek [COLUSA]: *stream*, flows nearly 7 miles to East Park Reservoir 0.5 mile north of Lodoga (lat. 39°18'30" N, long. 122° 29'20" W; at E line sec. 23, T 17 N, R 6 W). Named on Clearlake Oaks (1960), Lodoga (1960), and Stonyford (1951) 15' quadrangles.

Indian Creek [EL DORADO]:

(1) *stream*, flows 3 miles to South Fork American River 1.25 miles northwest of Coloma (lat. 38°48'50" N, long. 120°54'10" W; sec. 7, T 11 N, R 10 E). Named on Coloma (1949) 7.5' quadrangle. Called North Indian Creek on Georgetown (1949) 15' quadrangle.

(2) *stream*, flows 2 miles to South Fork American River 1 mile southeast of Coloma (lat. 38°47'30" N, long. 120°52'35" W; near W line sec. 21, T 11 N, R 10 E). Named on Coloma (1949) and Garden Valley (1949) 7.5' quadrangles.

(3) *stream*, flows 7.5 miles to Weber Creek nearly 5 miles north of Shingle Springs (lat. 38°44'05" N, long. 120°56'25" W; sec. 12, T 10 N, R 9 E). Named on Placerville (1949) and Shingle Springs (1949) 7.5' quadrangles.

(4) *stream*, flows 2.5 miles to Cosumnes River 10 miles south-southeast of Clarksville (lat. 38°30'45" N, long. 121°00'40" W; near N line sec. 32, T 8 N, R 9 E). Named on Folsom SE (1954) 7.5' quadrangle.

(5) *stream*, flows 2 miles to Scott Creek nearly 4 miles south-southwest of Omo Ranch (lat. 38°31'50" N, long. 120°36' W; sec. 24, T 8 N, R 12 E); the stream heads at the site of Indian Diggins. Named on Omo Ranch (1952) 7.5' quadrangle. Logan's (1938) map has the name "East Indian Creek" for the feature, and has the name "Oregon Cr." for the next large tributary of Scott Creek to the east (mouth near E line sec. 20, T 8 N, R 13 E).

Indian Creek [PLACER]:

(1) *stream*, flows 1.25 miles to East Branch El Dorado Canyon 1.25 miles south of Westville (lat. 39°09'20" N, long. 120°38'40" W; sec. 9, T 15 N, R 12 E). Named on Westville (1952) 7.5' quadrangle. On Colfax (1898) 30' quadrangle, the canyon of the stream is called Indian Springs Ravine.

(2) *stream*, flows 10 miles to North Fork American River 4 miles southeast of Colfax (lat. 39°03'25" N, long. 120°54'25" W; near SW cor. sec. 18, T 14 N, R 10 E). Named on Colfax (1949), Dutch Flat (1950), and Foresthill (1949) 7.5' quadrangles. The canyon of the stream is called Indian Cañon on Whitney's (1873) map.

Indian Creek [SIERRA]:

(1) *stream*, flows 4.25 miles to North Yuba River 8 miles west-southwest of Goodyears Bar (lat. 39°30'20" N, long. 121°01'25" W; near NE cor. sec. 24, T 19 N, R 8 E); the stream is 1 mile west-southwest of Indian Hill (1). Named on Goodyears Bar (1951), Pike (1949), and Strawberry Valley (1948) 7.5' quadrangles.

(2) *stream*, flows 3.5 miles to Middle Yuba River 2 miles southeast of Pike (lat. 39°25'10" N, long. 120°58'20" W; near S line sec. 16, T 18 N, R 9 E). Named on Pike (1949) 7.5' quadrangle.

Indian Creek [YUBA]: *stream*, flows 4 miles to New Bullards Bar Reservoir 3 miles east-southeast of Challenge (lat. 39°28'40" N, long. 121°09'55" W; near E line sec. 27, T 19 N, R 7 E); the stream heads near Woodleaf (formerly Woodville). Named on Challenge (1948, photorevised 1969) and Clipper Mills (1948) 7.5' quadrangles.. Called Woodville Creek on Smartsville (1895) 30' quadrangle.

Indian Creek: see **Big Indian Creek** [AMADOR]; **East Branch**, under **El Dorado Canyon** [PLACER]; **Little Indian Creek** [AMADOR]; **Little Indian Creek** [COLUSA]; **Little Indian Creek** [EL DORADO]; **Little Indian Creek** [PLACER].

Indian Diggings: see **Indian Diggins** [EL DORADO].

Indian Diggins [EL DORADO]: *locality*, 2.25 miles south-southeast of Omo Ranch (lat. 38°32'50" N, long. 120°34'30" W); the place is near the head of Indian Creek (5). Named on Placerville (1893) 30' quadrangle. Postal authorities established Indian Diggings post office in 1853, discontinued it in 1869, reestablished it with the name "Indian Diggins" in 1888, and discontinued it in 1935 (Salley, p. 103). The name was given after a group of white prospectors discovered some Indians panning for gold at the site in 1850; the place had the nickname "Whore House Gulch" in the early days (Yohalem, p. 27, 29).

Indian Flat [NEVADA]: *valley*, 2 miles west of Nevada City along upper reaches of Rush Creek (lat. 39°16'05" N, long. 121°03'20" W; around NE cor. sec. 10, T 16 N, R 8 E). Named on Nevada City (1948) 7.5' quadrangle.

Indian Flat [PLACER]: *area*, 3.5 mile south-southwest of Colfax (lat. 39°03' N, long. 120°58'10" W; on W line sec. 22, T 14 N, R 9 E). Named on Colfax (1949) 7.5' quadrangle.

Indian Gulch [AMADOR]: *canyon*, 1.25 miles long, 4.5 miles south-southeast of Plymouth (lat. 38°25'10" N, long. 120°48' W; sec. 31, 32, T 7 N, R 11 E). Named on Amador City (1962) 7.5' quadrangle.

Indian Hatties [EL DORADO]: *locality*, 3 miles east-northeast of Pollock Pines (lat. 38°47' N, long. 120°32'15" W; near SW cor. sec. 16, T 11 N, R 13 E). Named on Pollock Pines (1950) 7.5' quadrangle.

Indian Hill [AMADOR]:

(1) *hill*, 3.25 miles northwest of Ione (lat. 38°22'45" N, long. 120° 58'50" W). Named on Irish Hill (1962) 7.5' quadrangle. A man named Dosch opened the first commercial clay pit in the Ione area at Indian Hill in 1854; a town called Doschville was near the pit (Andrews, p. 58).

(2) *locality*, 3.25 miles northwest of Ione along Southern Pacific Railroad (lat. 38°22'55" N, long. 120°59'20" W); the place is 0.25 mile northwest of Indian Hill (1). Named on Irish Hill (1962) 7.5' quadrangle.

Indian Hill [SIERRA]:

(1) *ridge*, west-trending, 0.5 mile long, 7 miles west-southwest of Goodyears Bar (lat. 39°30'35" N, long. 121°00'15" W; at S line sec. 18, T 19 N, R 9 E); the ridge is 1 mile east-northeast of the mouth of Indian Creek (1). Named on Goodyears Bar (1951) and Strawberry Valley (1948) 7.5' quadrangles.

(2) *locality*, 6 miles west-southwest of Goodyears Bar (lat. 39°30'30" N, long. 120°59'20" W); the place is east of present Indian Hill (1). Named on Downieville (1897) 30' quadrangle.

Indian Knoll [PLACER]: *relief feature*, 3.25 miles east of Colfax (lat. 39°05'55" N, long. 120°53'35" W; near N line sec. 6, T 14 N, R 10 E). Named on Colfax (1949) 7.5' quadrangle.

Indian Mike Spring [YOLO]: *spring*, 3.25 miles northeast of Guinda (lat. 38°51'35" N, long. 122°08'45" W; sec. 25, T 12 N, R 3 W). Named on Guinda (1959) 7.5' quadrangle. On Rumsey (1945) 15' quadrangle, the name applies to present Du Bois Spring.

Indian Mound [SACRAMENTO]: *hill*, 2.5 miles east-northeast of Courtland (lat. 38°20'15" N, long. 121°31'20" W). Named on Vorden (1916) 7.5' quadrangle.

Indian Mound [YOLO]:

(1) *hill*, 10 miles east of Dunnigan near Sacramento River at Eldorado Bend (lat. 38°51'25" N, long. 121°47'10" W). Named on Ronda (1915) 7.5' quadrangle.

(2) *hill*, 2.5 miles south-southwest of Clarksburg near Elkhorn Slough (present Elk Slough) (lat. 38°23'05" N, long. 121°32'45" W). Named on Babel Slough (1916) 7.5' quadrangle.

Indian Mound: see **Tyndall Mound** [YOLO].

Indian Rock [EL DORADO]: *peak*, 4.25 miles northwest of Echo Summit (lat. 38°51'50" N, long. 120°04'30" W). Named on Echo Lake (1955) 7.5' quadrangle.

Indian Spring [NEVADA]: *spring*, 4 miles south-southwest of Washington (lat. 39°18'25" N, long. 120°50' W; near E line sec. 27, T 17 N, R 10 E). Named on Washington (1950) 7.5' quadrangle.

Indian Springs [NEVADA]: *locality*, 1 mile northwest of Pilot Peak (lat. 39°10'45" N, long. 121°11'30" W; at E line sec. 4, T 15 N, R 7 E). Named on Rough and Ready (1949) 7.5' quadrangle. Postal authorities established Indian Springs post office in 1858, discontinued it in 1871, reestablished it in 1892, and discontinued it in 1893 (Frickstad, p. 114). They established Painsville post office 6 miles west of Indian Springs in 1864 and discontinued it in 1869; the name was for Philander Paine, rancher and hotel owner (Salley, p. 165).

Indian Springs Creek [EL DORADO]: *stream*, flows 2 miles to Folsom Lake 4.25 miles south-southwest of the village of Pilot Hill (lat. 38°46'35" N, long. 121°02'45" W). Named on Pilot Hill (1954, photorevised 1973) 7.5' quadrangle.

Indian Springs Creek [NEVADA]: *stream*, flows 5.5 miles to Dry Creek (2) 5 miles northwest of Wolf (lat. 39°06'50" N, long. 121° 12'10" W; near N line sec. 33, T 15 N, R 7 E); the stream heads near Indian Springs. Named on Rough and Ready (1949) and Wolf (1949) 7.5' quadrangles.

Indian Springs Hill: see **Pilot Peak** [NEVADA].

Indian Springs Ravine: see **Indian Creek** [PLACER] (1).

Indian Valley [COLUSA]: *valley,* extends for 18 miles south-southeast from Glenn County near Stonyford past Lodoga. Named on Lodoga (1960), Stonyford (1951), and Wilbur Springs (1961) 15' quadrangles. The place also was called Big Indian Valley (Goodyear, p. 153).

Indian Valley [SIERRA]: *valley,* 5.5 miles west-southwest of Goodyears Bar along North Yuba River (lat. 39°30'55" N, long. 120° 59' W; sec. 16, 17, T 19 N, R 9 E). Named on Goodyears Bar (1951) 7.5' quadrangle.

Indian Valley Camp Ground [SIERRA]: *locality,* 5.5 miles west-southwest of Goodyears Bar along North Yuba River (lat. 39°30'45" N, long. 120°58'50" W; at W line sec. 16, T 19 N, R 9 E); the place is in Indian Valley. Named on Goodyears Bar (1951) 7.5' quadrangle. Called Indian Valley Camp on Downieville (1951) 15' quadrangle.

Ingram Slough [PLACER]: *stream,* flows 2.5 miles to Orchard Creek 8 miles north-northwest of Roseville (lat. 38°51'15" N, long. 121°20'15" W; near SW cor. sec. 29, T 12 N, R 6 E). Named on Roseville (1967) 7.5' quadrangle.

Injun Creek [YUBA]: *stream,* flows 2.25 miles to Woods Creek 4.5 miles south of Oregon House (lat. 39°17'20" N, long. 121°15'45" W; sec. 35, T 17 N, R 6 E). Named on Oregon House (1948) 7.5' quadrangle.

Inspiration Lodge [AMADOR]: *locality,* 9 miles east-northeast of Pine Grove (lat. 38°29' N, long. 120°31'10" W; near SW cor. sec. 2, T 7 N, R 13 E); the place is less than 1 mile north-northeast of Inspiration Point. Named on West Point (1948) 7.5' quadrangle.

Inspiration Point [AMADOR]: *locality,* 8 miles east-northeast of Pine Grove (lat. 38°28'15" N, long. 120°31'35" W; sec. 10, T 7 N, R 13 E). Named on West Point (1948) 7.5' quadrangle.

Inspiration Point [EL DORADO]: *relief feature,* nearly 3 miles north of Mount Tallac (lat. 38°56'50" N, long. 120°06' W; sec. 28, T 13 N, R 17 E). Named on Emerald Bay (1955) 7.5' quadrangle.

Ione [AMADOR]: *town,* 9 miles west of Jackson (lat. 38°21'05" N, long. 120°55'50" W); the town is at the east end of Ione Valley. Named on Ione (1962) 7.5' quadrangle. The name is from Ione Valley (Sargent, p. 49). Early names for the place include Bedbug, Freezeout (Hanna, p. 150), Rickeyville, Hardscrabble, and Woosterville (Gudde, 1949, p. 161). Postal authorities established Jone Valley post office in 1852, changed the name to Jone City in 1857, to Ione City almost immediately, to Ione Valley in 1861, and to Ione in 1880 (Salley, p. 105). The town incorporated in 1953. California Mining Bureau's (1909b) map shows a place called Ritchey located 5 miles south of Ione by stage line. Postal authorities established Ritchey post office in 1900 and discontinued it in 1914 (Frickstad, p. 6). A hostelry of the 1850's and 1860's called Q Ranch was located about 2 miles northwest of Ione; a group of men, one of whom had been in Company Q of the Ohio Volunteers during the Mexican War, started and named the hostelry in 1850 (Hoover, Rensch, and Rensch, p. 35).

Ione City: see **Ione** [AMADOR].

Ione Valley [AMADOR]: *valley,* mainly west of Ione along Sutter Creek (1) (lat. 38°21'15" N, long. 120°58' W). Named on Ione (1962) 7.5' quadrangle. Eddy's (1854) map has the name "Lone Valley" for the feature. The name "Ione" is from the heroine of Edward Bulwer-Lytton's novel *The Last Days of Pompeii,* published in London in 1834 (Hanna, p. 150).

Ione Valley: see **Ione** [AMADOR].

Iowa Canyon [EL DORADO]: *canyon,* drained by a stream that flows 6 miles to South Fork American River 6.5 miles west of Pollock Pines (lat. 38°46'20" N, long. 120°42'05" W; sec. 25, T 11 N, R 11 E). Named on Pollock Pines (1950) and Slate Mountain (1950) 7.5' quadrangles. Called Big Iowa Canyon on Placerville (1893) 30' quadrangle, which has the name "Little Iowa Canyon" for a tributary of Iowa Canyon that probably is present Brushy Canyon (1).

Iowa City [YUBA]: *locality,* 3.5 miles west-southwest of Loma Rica (lat. 39°17'30" N, long. 121°28'35" W; sec. 36, T 17 N, R 4 E). Named on Loma Rica (1947) 7.5' quadrangle.

Iowa City: see **Iowa Hill** [PLACER].

Iowa Hill [EL DORADO]: *peak,* 5.5 miles west of Pollock Pines (lat. 38°46'20" N, long. 120°41' W; sec. 30, T 11 N, R 12 E); the peak is north of the lower part of Iowa Canyon. Named on Slate Mountain (1950) 7.5' quadrangle.

Iowa Hill [PLACER]: *village,* 6.5 miles north-northwest of Foresthill (lat. 39°06'30" N, long. 120°51'30" W; sec. 33, T 15 N, R 10 E). Named on Foresthill (1949) 7.5' quadrangle. Miners from Iowa discovered gold at the place in 1853 (Hanna, p. 150). Postal authorities established Iowa City post office in 1854 and changed the name to Iowa Hill in 1901 (Frickstad, p. 120). United States Board on Geographic Names (1933, p. 390) rejected the name "Iowa City" for the village, and (1977b, p. 5) approved the name "Iowa Hill Divide" for the ridge on which the village stands; the ridge is 14 miles long and extends southwest from Forest Hill Divide to North Fork American River 5 miles east of Colfax. Whitney's (1873) map has the name "Bumpus Cañ." along present Indian Creek (2) just east of Iowa Hill.

Iowa Hill Divide: see **Iowa Hill** [PLACER].

Irish Creek [EL DORADO]: *stream,* flows nearly 3 miles to Big Sailor Creek 4.25 miles north-northwest of Chili Bar (lat. 38°49'30" N, long. 120°50'45" W; sec. 3, T 11 N, R 10 E). Named on Garden Valley (1949) 7.5' quadrangle. Dredge tailings cover the lower part of the stream.

Irish Gulch [EL DORADO]: *canyon,* drained by a stream that flows 0.5 mile to String Canyon 9.5 miles southeast of Camino (lat. 38° 38'40" N, long. 120°32'35" W; sec. 9, T 9 N, R 13 E). Named on Sly Park (1952) 7.5' quadrangle.

Irish Hill [AMADOR]: *ridge,* west-northwest-trending, less than 1 mile long, 3.5 miles north-northwest of Ione (lat. 38°24' N, long. 120°58' W). Named on Irish Hill (1962) 7.5' quadrangle. Hydraulic mining destroyed a mining camp called Irish Hill that was situated on or near the ridge (Andrews, p. 65).

Irish Town: see **Pine Grove** [AMADOR].

Iron Mountain [EL DORADO]:

(1) *peak,* 6 miles north-northwest of Clarksville (lat. 38°44'25" N, long. 121°04'35" W; at W line sec. 11, T 10 N, R 8 E). Altitude 911 feet. Named on Clarksville (1953) 7.5' quadrangle.

(2) *peak,* 6.5 miles northwest of Leek Spring Hill (lat. 38°42'15" N, long. 120°21'15" W; sec. 19, T 10 N, R 15 E); the peak is on Iron Mountain Ridge 2 miles east of Old Iron Mountain. Altitude 6242 feet. Named on Leek Spring Hill (1951) 7.5' quadrangle.

Iron Mountain [NEVADA]:

(1) *peak,* 1.5 miles northwest of Pilot Peak (lat. 39°10'55" N, long. 121°12'25" W; near W line sec. 4, T 15 N, R 7 E). Altitude 1921 feet. Named on Rough and Ready (1949) 7.5' quadrangle.

(2) *peak,* 4 miles northwest of Wolf (lat. 39°06'05" N, long. 121°11'15" W; on S line sec. 34, T 15 N, R 7 E). Altitude 1628 feet. Named on Wolf (1949) 7.5' quadrangle.

Iron Mountain: see **Old Iron Mountain** [EL DORADO].

Iron Mountain Ridge [EL DORADO]: *ridge,* generally northwest-trending, 14 miles long, center 6.5 miles northwest of Leek Spring Hill near Iron Mountain (2) (lat. 38°42'15" N, long. 120°21'15" W). Named on Leek Spring Hill (1951) and Stump Spring (1951) 7.5' quadrangles.

Iron Point [PLACER]: *ridge,* south-trending, 0.5 mile long, 4 miles east-southeast of Dutch Flat (lat. 39°11'30" N, long. 120°46'05" W; near W line sec. 5, T 15 N, R 11 E). Named on Dutch Flat (1950) 7.5' quadrangle.

Island Lake [EL DORADO]: *lake,* 2000 feet long, 5.5 miles south-southwest of Phipps Peak (lat. 38°52'35" N, long. 120°11'10" W). Named on Pyramid Peak (1955) and Rockbound Valley (1955) 7.5' quadrangles.

Island Lake [NEVADA]: *lake,* 2250 feet long, 5 miles southwest of English Mountain (lat. 39°23'55" N, long. 120°37'10" W; near W line sec. 27, T 18 N, R 12 E); the lake has three islands. Named on English Mountain (1983) 7.5' quadrangle.

Isleton [SACRAMENTO]: *town,* 30 miles south of downtown Sacramento along Sacramento River on Andrus Island (lat. 38°09'40" N, long. 121°36'30" W). Named on Isleton (1978) 7.5' quadrangle. Postal authorities established Isleton post office in 1875 (Frickstad, p. 133) and the town incorporated in 1923. Joseph Poole founded the community in 1874, when he built a drugstore, smithy, and harness shop there (Dillon, p. 106). Postal authorities established Turner post office 7 miles north of Isleton in 1892 and discontinued it in 1895; they established Roseneath post office 5 miles south of Isleton in 1905 and discontinued it in 1907 (Salley, p. 189, 226).

Italian Bar [PLACER]: *locality,* 2 miles north-northwest of Westville along North Fork American River (lat. 39°12'10" N, long. 120°39'55" W; near SE cor. sec. 31, T 16 N, R 12 E). Named on Westville (1952) 7.5' quadrangle.

Italian Bar: see Grapevine Gulch [AMADOR] (2).

— J —

Jabu Lake [EL DORADO]: *lake,* 450 feet long, 6 miles northwest of Echo Summit (lat. 38°51'55" N, long. 120°07'15" W). Named on Echo Lake (1955) 7.5' quadrangle. The word "Jabu" was coined from letters in the name "Jack Butler" (Lekisch, p. 65).

Jackass Canyon [EL DORADO]: *canyon,* drained by a stream that flows 3 miles to North Fork Cosumnes River 6.25 miles south-southeast of Camino (lat. 38°39'10" N, long. 120°37'55" W; near NE cor. sec. 10, T 9 N, R 12 E). Named on Camino (1952), Omo Ranch (1952), and Sly Park (1952) 7.5' quadrangles.

Jackass Creek [AMADOR]: *stream,* flows 5 miles to Mule Creek 2.5 miles north-northeast of Ione (lat. 38°23'10" N, long. 120°54'50" W; sec. 7, T 6 N, R 10 E). Named on Amador City (1962), Ione (1962), and Irish Hill (1962) 7.5' quadrangles.

Jackass Creek [YUBA]: *stream,* flows 0.5 mile to Deadwood Creek nearly 1.5 miles south-southeast of Strawberry Valley (lat. 39°32'50" N, long. 121°05'35" W; near SW cor. sec. 33, T 20 N, R 8 E). Named on Strawberry Valley (1948) 7.5' quadrangle.

Jackass Gulch [AMADOR]: *canyon,* drained by a stream that flows 3.5 miles to Jackson Creek 3 miles southwest of Jackson (lat. 38° 19'20" N, long. 120°49' W; near NW cor. sec. 6, T 5 N, R 11 E). Named on Jackson (1962) 7.5' quadrangle.

Jackass Gulch [PLACER]: *canyon,* drained by a stream that flows less than 1 mile to Middle Fork American River 2.25 miles south-southwest of Michigan Bluff (lat. 39°00'35" N, long. 120°44'55" W; near S line sec. 33, T 33 N, R 11 E). Named on Foresthill (1949) and Michigan Bluff (1952) 7.5' quadrangles.

Jackass Gulch: see **Volcano** [AMADOR].

Jackass Point [PLACER]: *peak,* 10.5 miles west of Martis Peak (lat. 39°18'40" N, long. 120°13'45" W; sec. 20, T 17 N, R 16 E). Named on Truckee (1955) 7.5' quadrangle.

Jackass Ravine [SIERRA]: *canyon,* drained by a stream that flows 1.5 miles to Middle Yuba River 2.5 miles south-southeast of Alleghany (lat. 39°26'15" N, long. 120°49' W; sec. 11, T 18 N, R 10 E). Named on Alleghany (1949) 7.5' quadrangle.

Jackassville: see **City of Six Diggings**, under **Slug Canyon** [SIERRA].

Jackies Orchard Spring [NEVADA]: *spring,* 3.5 miles west-northwest of North Bloomfield (lat. 39°23'25" N, long. 120°57'35" W; near SW cor. sec. 27, T 18 N, R 9 E). Named on Pike (1949) 7.5' quadrangle.

Jack Robinson Ravine [PLACER]: *canyon,* drained by a stream that flows less than 1 mile to Duncan Canyon 7 miles south of Duncan Peak (lat. 39°03'20" N, long. 120°32'15" W; near SW cor. sec. 16, T 14 N, R 13 E). Named on Greek Store (1952) 7.5' quadrangle.

Jack Slough [YUBA]: *stream,* flows 16 miles to Feather River 1.25 miles northwest of downtown Marysville (lat. 39°09'30" N, long. 121°36'30" W). Named on Loma Rica (1947, photorevised 1969) and Yuba City (1952) 7.5' quadrangles. Called Nigger Jack Slough on Yuba City (1911) and Browns Valley (1911) 7.5' quadrangles. Wescoatt's (1861) map has the name "N. Jacks" for a house located along the stream 6 miles north-northwest of Marysville (at SE cor. sec. 20, T 16 N, R 4 E).

Jackson [AMADOR]: *town,* along Jackson Creek where both North Fork and South Fork enter the main stream (lat. 38°21' N, long. 120°46'20" W; on N line sec. 28, T 6 N, R 11 E). Named on Jackson (1962) 7.5' quadrangle. Postal authorities established Jackson post office before July 10, 1851 (Salley, p. 106), and the town incorporated in 1905. The name commemorates Colonel Jackson, an early leader of the town; the site first was called Botilleas Spring (Bottle Spring) for the large number of bottles that campers had discarded at a spring there (Hoover, Rensch, and Rensch, p. 33). Mexican miners called the place Botellas in 1848 (Bancroft, 1888, p. 512). Jackson (1962) 7.5' quadrangle shows Hardenbergh mine situated 3.5 miles south-southeast of Jackson near Mokelumne River. Postal authorities established Hardenburg post office in 1893 and discontinued it in 1896; the post office served the mine (Frickstad, p. 5; Gudde, 1975, p. 151). California Division of Highways' (1934) map shows a lake called New York Reservoir located 4.5 miles northeast of Jackson (sec. 1, T 6 N, R 11 E) near where Pine Grove (1948) 7.5' quadrangle indicates New York Ranch school.

Jackson [EL DORADO]: *locality,* 14 miles east of Georgetown (lat. 38°52'25" N, long. 120°34' W). Named on Placerville (1893) 30' quadrangle.

Jackson Bluffs [YOLO]: *relief feature,* north-northwest-trending, 2.25 miles long, 6.5 miles west-southwest of Esparto (lat. 38°39'25" N, long. 122°07'30" W). Named on Brooks (1959) and Esparto (1959) 7.5' quadrangles.

Jackson Butte [AMADOR]: *peak,* 3 miles east-southeast of Jackson (lat. 38°20'25" N, long. 120°43'15" W; near S line sec. 25, T 6 N, R 11 E). Altitude 2310 feet. Named on Mokelumne Hill (1948) 7.5' quadrangle. Camp (*in* Doble, p. 75) identified Jackson Butte as the feature that Doble called Butte Mountain in 1852. Camp's (1962) map shows a place called French Camp located 1 mile east-northeast of Jackson Butte, a canyon called Soldiers Gulch that opens into the canyon of South Fork Jackson Creek 1 mile north-northeast of Jackson Butte, a canyon called Sailors Gulch that opens into the canyon of South Fork Jackson Creek 1.5 miles northeast of Jackson Butte, and a place called Slabtown situated 1.5 miles east-northeast of Jackson Butte—the same map gives the alternate name "Hoodsville" for Slabtown. The first settlers of Slabtown were too poor to use anything better for building than rough slabs of wood with the bark left on (Hoover, Rensch, and Rensch, p. 34).

Jackson Canyon [COLUSA]: *canyon,* drained by a stream that flows 1.5 miles to Bear Creek 4 miles east-southeast of Wilbur Springs (lat. 39°00'30" N, long. 122°21'25" W; near NE cor. sec. 1, T 13 N, R 5 W). Named on Wilbur Springs (1961) 15' quadrangle.

Jackson Canyon: see **South Jackson Canyon** [COLUSA].

Jackson Creek [AMADOR]: *stream,* flows 26 miles to Dry Creek [AMADOR-SACRAMENTO] 5 miles southwest of Ione (lat. 38°17'55" N, long. 121°00'45" W). Named on Ione (1962), Jackson (1962), Mokelumne Hill (1948) and Pine Grove (1948) 7.5' quadrangles. North Fork enters the main stream from the north in Jackson; it is 4 miles long and is named on Amador City (1962) and Jackson (1962) 7.5' quadrangles. South Fork enters the main stream from the southeast in Jackson; it is 10 miles long and is named on Jackson (1962), Mokelumne Hill (1948), and Pine Grove (1948) 7.5' quadrangles.

Jackson Creek [NEVADA]: *stream,* flows 3.5 miles to Bowman Lake 3 miles west-northwest of English Mountain (lat. 39°27'25" N, long. 120°36'25" W; near E line sec. 3, T 18 N, R 12 E); Jackson Lake is along the stream. Named on English Mountain (1983) 7.5' quadrangle.

Jackson Creek Campground [NEVADA]: *locality,* nearly 3 miles west-northwest of English Mountain (lat. 39°27'30" N, long. 120° 36' W; near W line sec. 2, T 18 N, R 12 E); the place is along Jackson Creek. Named on English Mountain (1983) 7.5' quadrangle.

Jackson Gate [AMADOR]: *locality,* 1 mile north of Jackson along North Fork Jackson Creek (lat. 38°21'55" N, long. 120°46'25" W; near N line sec. 21, T 6 N, R 11 E). Named on Jackson (1962) 7.5' quadrangle. The name is from a deep narrow chasm along the creek; the place also was called The Gate (Sargent, p. 91).

Jackson Lake [NEVADA]: *lake,* 2350 feet long, 1.25 miles north-northwest of English Mountain (lat. 39°27'45" N, long. 120°33'40" W; on S line sec. 31, T 19 N, R 13 E). Named on English Mountain (1983) 7.5' quadrangle.

Jackson Meadow [NEVADA-SIERRA]: *area,* 3.5 miles north of English Mountain on Nevada-Sierra County line (lat. 39°29'45" N, long. 120°33' W). Named on Emigrant Gap (1955) and Sierra City (1955) 15' quadrangles. Water of Jackson Meadows Reservoir now covers the place.

Jackson Meadows Reservoir [NEVADA-SIERRA]: *lake,* behind a dam on Middle Yuba River 4 miles north of English Mountain on Nevada-Sierra County line (lat. 39°30'30" N, long. 120°33'20" W; near S line sec. 18, T 19 N, R 13 E); water of the lake covers Jackson Meadow. Named on English Mountain (1983) and Haypress Valley (1981) 7.5' quadrangles.

Jackson Meadows Station [NEVADA]: *locality,* 2.5 miles north of English Mountain (lat. 39°28'55" N, long. 120°33'25" W; sec. 30, T 19 N, R 13 E); the place is southwest of Jackson Meadows Reservoir. Named on English Mountain (1983) 7.5' quadrangle.

Jackson Mountain [COLUSA]: *peak,* 6 miles east-southeast of Wilbur Springs (lat. 39°00'05" N, long. 122°19'15" W; sec. 5, T 13 N, R 4 W). Altitude 2790 feet. Named on Wilbur Springs (1961) 15' quadrangle.

Jackson Peak: see **English Mountain** [NEVADA].

Jackson Point Campground [SIERRA]: *locality,* 7 miles southeast of Sierra City along Jackson Meadows Reservoir (lat. 39°29'55" N, long. 120°32'55" W; sec. 20, T 19 N, R 13 E). Named on English Mountain (1983) 7.5' quadrangle.

Jackson Slough [SACRAMENTO]: *water feature,* joins Sevenmile Slough 3.25 miles south-southwest of Isleton (lat. 38°07'05" N, long. 121°37'40" W); the feature is between Andrus Island and Brannan Island. Named on Isleton (1978) and Jersey Island (1978) 7.5' quadrangles.

Jackson Spring [EL DORADO]: *spring,* 8 miles north of Pollock Pines (lat. 38°52'35" N, long. 120°34'05" W; sec. 19, T 12 N, R 13 E). Named on Devil Peak (1950) 7.5' quadrangle.

Jackson Valley [AMADOR]: *valley,* 4 miles south of Ione along Jackson Creek (lat. 38°17'30" N, long. 120°56' W). Named on Ione (1962) 7.5' quadrangle.

Jacks Peak [EL DORADO]: *peak,* 4.5 miles south of Phipps Peak (lat. 38°53'25" N, long. 120°09'10" W). Altitude 9856 feet. Named on Rockbound Valley (1955) 7.5' quadrangle.

Jacobs: see **Jacobs Corner** [YOLO].

Jacobs Corner [YOLO]: *locality,* 4 miles east of Madison (lat. 38° 40'15" N, long. 121°53'35" W; on W line sec. 32, T 10 N, R 1 E). Named on Madison (1953) 7.5' quadrangle. Postal authorities established Jacobs post office at the place in 1909 and discontinued it in 1910; the name was for Mattie Jacobs, first postmaster (Salley, p. 106).

Jacobs Creek [EL DORADO]: *stream,* flows 2 miles to South Fork American River 2.5 miles west-northwest of Coloma (lat. 38°49'05" N, long. 120°56'05" W; sec. 11, T 11 N, R 9 E). Named on Coloma (1949) 7.5' quadrangle.

Jacobsen [EL DORADO]: *locality,* 2.5 miles west-southwest of Wentworth Springs at present Jacobsen Meadow (lat. 39°00'15" N, long. 120°23'05" W). Named on Truckee (1940) 30' quadrangle. Called Jacobsens on Truckee (1895) 30' quadrangle.

Jacobsen Meadow [EL DORADO]: *area,* 2.5 miles west-southwest of Wentworth Springs (lat. 39°00'15" N, long. 120°23'05" W; on E line sec. 3, T 13 N, R 14 E). Named on Bunker Hill (1953) 7.5' quadrangle.

Jake Schneider Meadow [EL DORADO]: *area,* 5.25 miles west of Kirkwood (lat. 38°42'10" N, long. 120°10'05" W). Named on Tragedy Spring (1979) 7.5' quadrangle.

Jakes Hill: see **Jakeys Hill** [EL DORADO].

Jakes Peak: see **South Lake Tahoe** [EL DORADO].

Jakeys Hill [EL DORADO]: *ridge,* north-trending, about 1 mile long, 5.25 miles north-northeast of Georgetown (lat. 38°58'35" N, long. 120°47'40" W; sec. 7, 18, T 13 N, R 11 E). Named on Georgetown (1949) 7.5' quadrangle. Called Jakes Hill on Logan's (1938) map.

Jamesons [EL DORADO]: *locality,* 11.5 miles south of Placerville (lat. 38°33'40" N, long. 120°47'40" W). Named on Placerville (1893) 30' quadrangle.

James Ranch: see **Junction House** [YUBA].

Jamison Ravine [PLACER]: *canyon,* drained by a stream that flows 0.5 mile to Duncan Canyon 6.25 miles south of Duncan Peak (lat. 39°03'50" N, long. 120°32' W; sec. 16, T 14 N, R 13 E). Named on Greek Store

(1952) 7.5' quadrangle.

Jammer Chair Flat [SIERRA]: *area,* 2.5 miles southwest of Crystal Peak (lat. 39°32' N, long. 120°07'30" W). Named on Dog Valley (1981) and Sardine Peak (1981) 7.5' quadrangles.

Jay Bird Canyon [EL DORADO]: *canyon,* drained by a stream that flows 4 miles to Silver Creek 5.5 miles north-northeast of Pollock Pines (lat. 38°50' N, long. 120°31'50" W; near N line sec. 4, T 11 N, R 13 E). Named on Pollock Pines (1950) and Riverton (1950) 7.5' quadrangles.

Jaybird Creek [EL DORADO]: *stream,* flows 1.5 miles to South Fork American River 3 miles east-northeast of Chili Bar (lat. 38° 47' N, long. 120°46'15" W; sec. 20, T 11 N, R 11 E). Named on Garden Valley (1949) 7.5' quadrangle.

Jaybird Creek [YUBA]: *stream,* drained by a stream that flows nearly 1 mile to Brandy Creek 2 miles north-northwest of Camptonville (lat. 39°28'30" N, long. 121°04'05" W; near N line sec. 34, T 19 N, R 8 E). Named on Camptonville (1948) 7.5' quadrangle.

Jay Bird Spring [EL DORADO]: *spring,* 6 miles northeast of Pollock Pines (lat. 38°49'55" N, long. 120°30'50" W; near NW cor. sec. 3, T 11 N, R 13 E); the spring is north of Jay Bird Canyon. Named on Pollock Pines (1950) 7.5' quadrangle.

Jayhawk [EL DORADO]: *locality,* 6.5 miles southwest of Coloma (lat. 38°44'10" N, long. 120°58'40" W). Named on Placerville (1893) 30' quadrangle. Postal authorities established Jay Hawk post office in 1860 and discontinued it in 1863 (Frickstad, p. 27).

Jayhawk Creek [EL DORADO]: *stream,* flows 1.5 miles to Weber Creek 5.5 miles north-northwest of Shingle Springs (lat. 38°44'25" N, long. 120°57'30" W; sec. 11, T 10 N, R 9 E). Named on Shingle Springs (1949) 7.5' quadrangle.

Jefferson [YOLO]: *locality,* 2.5 miles south of West Sacramento along Sacramento Northern Railroad (lat. 38°32' N, long. 121°32'40" W). Named on Davis (1954) 15' quadrangle.

Jefferson: see **Jefferson Creek** [NEVADA].

Jefferson Canyon [PLACER]: *canyon,* drained by a stream that flows 1.5 miles to North Fork American River 6.5 miles south of Colfax (lat. 39°00'10" N, long. 120°56'15" W; sec. 2, T 13 N, R 9 E). Named on Colfax (1949) 7.5' quadrangle.

Jefferson Creek [NEVADA]: *stream,* flows 2.5 miles to South Yuba River 1 mile west-southwest of Washington (lat. 39°21'05" N, long. 120°49'05" W; sec. 11, T 17 N, R 10 E). Named on Washington (1950) 7.5' quadrangle. Whitney's (1873) map shows a place called Jefferson located west of the mouth of Jefferson Creek, and a feature called Jefferson Hill situated less than 1 mile south of the mouth of the stream. Jefferson first was known as Greenwood's Camp for the leader of a group of miners that came to the place from the State of Oregon in 1849 (Slyter and Slyter, p. 2). Gudde (1975, p. 196) noted that a mining place called Lizard Flat was located opposite Jefferson at the mouth of Jefferson Creek.

Jefferson Hill: see **Jefferson Creek** [NEVADA].

Jefferson House: see **Frenchtown** [YUBA].

Jenkinson Lake [EL DORADO]: *lake,* behind a dam on Sly Park Creek 6.25 miles east-southeast of Camino (lat. 38°42'55" N, long. 120°33'35" W); water of the lake covers Sly Park. Named on Sly Park (1952, photorevised 1973) 7.5' quadrangle. United States Board on Geographic Names (1957, p. 2) rejected the name "Sly Park Reservoir" for the lake, and noted that the name "Jenkinson" commemorates Walter E. Jenkinson, who was chiefly responsible for creation of the feature.

Jericho: see **Moores Flat** [NEVADA].

Jerrett Creek [EL DORADO-PLACER]: *stream,* heads in Placer County and flows 2.5 miles to Gerle Creek 0.5 mile west of Wentworth Springs in El Dorado County (lat. 39°00'45" N, long. 120° 20'50" W; near E line sec. 36, T 14 N, R 14 E). Named on Wentworth Springs (1953) 7.5' quadrangle.

Jerrett Peak [PLACER]: *peak,* 3 miles east-southeast of Bunker Hill (lat. 39°01'50" N, long. 120°19'50" W; sec. 30, T 14 N, R 15 E). Altitude 7504 feet. Named on Wentworth Springs (1953) 7.5' quadrangle.

Jerry Canyon [PLACER]: *canyon,* drained by a stream that flows 2 miles to Long Canyon 2.5 miles north-northwest of Devil Peak (lat. 38°59'50" N, long. 120°33'30" W; near NW cor. sec. 8, T 13 N, R 13 E). Named on Greek Store (1952) 7.5' quadrangle.

Jerry Lake [NEVADA]: *lake,* 800 feet long, 8 miles west-northwest of Donner Pass (lat. 39°21'55" N, long. 120°27'20" W; at E line sec. 1, T 17 N, R 13 E). Named on Soda Springs (1955, photorevised 1973) 7.5' quadrangle.

Jersey Flat: see **Downieville** [SIERRA].

Jersey Ravine [SIERRA]: *canyon,* drained by a stream that flows 1.25 miles to Oregon Creek 2.25 miles west-northwest of Alleghany (lat. 39°28'50" N, long. 120°52'45" W; near S line sec. 29, T 19 N, R 10 E). Named on Alleghany (1949) and Pike (1949) 7.5' quadrangles.

Jesse Canyon [EL DORADO]: *canyon,* drained by a stream that flows 2 miles to Middle Fork American River 4.5 miles north of Georgetown (lat. 38°58'30" N, long. 120°49'55" W; sec. 14, T 13 N, R 10 E). Named on Georgetown (1949) 7.5' quadrangle. Called Republican Cañon on Whitney's (1880) map.

Jim Crow Cañon: see **Jim Crow Creek** [SIERRA].

Jim Crow Creek [SIERRA]: *stream,* flows 4 miles to San Juan Canyon 2.5 miles east-southeast of Downieville (lat. 39°32'55" N, long. 120°46'55" W; sec. 6, T 19 N, R 11 E). Named on Downieville (1951) 7.5' quadrangle. On Downieville (1897) 30' quadrangle, the name "Jim Crow Ravine" appears to apply to the canyon of present Jim Crow Creek and to present Black Jack Ravine, but United States Board on Geographic Names (1960a, p. 15) rejected the name "Jim Crow Ravine." Logan's (1929) map shows Jim Crow Cañon. The name is for Jim Crow, a Kanaka who came to present Downieville with William Downie in 1849 (Hoover, Rensch, and Rensch, p. 491-492).

Jim Crow Ravine: see **Black Jack Ravine** [SIERRA]; **Jim Crow Creek** [SIERRA].

Jimeno [COLUSA-YOLO]: *land grant,* west of Sacramento River at Grimes and Colusa; on Colusa-Yolo County line, mainly in Colusa County. Named on Colusa (1953), Dunnigan (1953), Maxwell (1952), and Sutter Buttes (1954) 15' quadrangles, and on Eldorado Bend (1952), Kirkville (1952), Knights Landing (1952), and Sanborn Slough (1952) 7.5' quadrangles. Manuel Jimeno Casarin received 11 leagues in 1844; Thomas O. Larkin and John S. Misroon claimed 48,854 acres patented in 1862 (Cowan, p. 42).

Jimmy Brown Bar: see **Scotchman Creek** [NEVADA].

Jim Quinn Spring [EL DORADO]: *spring,* 10 miles west-southwest of Kirkwood (lat. 38°39'25" N, long. 120°14'30" W; sec. 6, T 9 N, R 16 E). Named on Tragedy Spring (1979) 7.5' quadrangle.

Joaquin River: see **San Joaquin River** [SACRAMENTO].

Job's Peaks: see **Jobs Sister** [EL DORADO].

Jobs Sister [EL DORADO]: *peak,* 1 mile east-northeast of Freel Peak on El Dorado-Alpine County line (lat. 38°51'45" N, long. 119° 53' W; sec. 31, T 12 N, R 19 E). Altitude 10,823 feet. Named on Freel Peak (1955) 7.5' quadrangle. Present Jobs Sister, Freel Peak, and Jobs Peak (Jobs Peak is in Alpine County) together were known as Job's Peaks; the name "Job" was for Moses Job, who had a store in the vicinity in the early 1850's (Gudde, 1949, p. 166-167).

Joe Miller Ravine [NEVADA]: *canyon,* drained by a stream that flows 1 mile to Englebright Lake 7 miles north-northwest of Pilot Peak (lat. 39°14'25" N, long. 121°15'35" W; near SE cor. sec. 14, T 16 N, R 6 E). Named on Rough and Ready (1949) and Smartville (1951) 7.5' quadrangles.

Joes Landing [SUTTER]: *locality,* 1 mile east-southeast of Verona along Sacramento River (lat. 38°46'50" N, long. 121°36'10" W; sec. 23, T 11 N, R 3 E). Named on Verona (1967) 7.5' quadrangle.

Joes Spring [PLACER]: *spring,* less than 0.5 mile east-southeast of Bunker Hill (lat. 39°02'45" N, long. 120°22'20" W; sec. 23, T 14 N, R 14 E). Named on Wentworth Springs (1953) 7.5' quadrangle.

John: see **Fort John**, under **Volcano** [AMADOR].

John Brown Flat [PLACER]: *area,* nearly 5 miles south of Colfax (lat. 39°01'55" N, long. 120°57'45" W; sec. 27, T 14 N, R 9 E). Named on Colfax (1949) 7.5' quadrangle.

John Cooper Canyon [COLUSA]: *canyon,* drained by a stream that flows 0.25 mile to High Valley 11 miles north of Wilbur Springs (lat. 39°11'50" N, long. 122°25'10" W; sec. 33, T 16 N, R 5 W). Named on Wilbur Springs (1961) 15' quadrangle.

John Greenwood's Creek: see **Prosser Creek** [NEVADA].

Johnnys Hill [EL DORADO]: *peak,* 2 miles west-southwest of Wentworth Springs (lat. 39°00'20" N, long. 120°22'35" W; sec. 2, T 13 N, R 14 E). Altitude 6559 feet. Named on Bunker Hill (1953) and Wentworth Springs (1953) 7.5' quadrangles.

Johns Creek: see **Prosser Creek** [NEVADA].

Johnson Canyon [EL DORADO]: *canyon,* 1.5 miles long, opens into North Canyon (2) 5.5 miles east-northeast of Placerville (lat. 38° 45'50" N, long. 120°43'50" W). Named on Placerville (1893) 30' quadrangle.

Johnson Canyon [YOLO]: *canyon,* drained by a stream that flows 3.5 miles to Capay Valley 2.5 miles northwest of Guinda (lat. 38° 51'25" N, long. 122°13'30" W; at E line sec. 30, T 12 N, R 3 W). Named on Guinda (1959) and Knoxville (1958) 7.5' quadrangles.

Johnson Pass [EL DORADO]: *pass,* less than 1 mile north of Echo Summit (lat. 38°49'25" N, long. 120°01'50" W; near S line sec. 6, T 11 N, R 18 E). Named on Echo Lake (1955) 7.5' quadrangle. The name recalls John C. "Cock Eye" Johnson, who in 1848 blazed the first trail over present Echo Summit from Placerville to the south end of Lake Tahoe (Yohalem, p. 150). Echo Summit was called Johnson Pass in the early days (Zauner, p. 7).

Johnson Peak [YUBA]: *peak,* 2 miles east-northeast of Loma Rica (lat. 39°19'15" N, long. 121°22'50" W; near N line sec. 23, T 17 N, R 5 E). Named on Loma Rica (1947) 7.5' quadrangle.

Johnson Ranche: see **Camp Far West** [YUBA].

Johnson Rancho [YUBA]: *land grant,* north of Bear River (1) at and near Wheatland. Named on Camp Far West (1949), Nicolaus (1952), Olivehurst (1952), Sheridan (1953), and Wheatland (1947) 7.5' quadrangles. Pablo Gutierrez received 5 leagues in 1844; William Johnson claimed 22,197 acres patented in 1857 (Cowan, p. 42; Cowan listed the grant under the name "Johnson's").

Johnson Ravine [SIERRA]: *canyon,* drained by a stream that flows less than 1 mile to Canyon Creek 8 miles southwest of Mount Fillmore (lat. 39°38'15" N, long. 120°56'05" W; sec. 35, T 21 N, R 9 E). Named on La Porte (1951) 7.5' quadrangle.

Johnson's: see **Johnson Rancho** [YUBA].

Johnsons: see **Camp Far West** [YUBA].

Johnsons Bluff [YUBA]: *relief feature,* 6 miles south of Challenge on the north side of Yuba River (lat. 39°17'05" N, long. 121°13'30" W; on E line sec. 31, T 17 N, R 7 E). Named on French Corral (1948) 7.5' quadrangle.

Johnsons Crossing: see **Camp Far West** [YUBA].

Johnson's Diggings: see **Birchville** [NEVADA].

Johnsons Ranch: see **Camp Far West** [YUBA].

Johnson's Ranche: see **Camp Far West** [YUBA].

Johntown: see **Garden Valley** [EL DORADO].

Johntown Creek [EL DORADO]: *stream,* formed by the confluence of Empire Creek and Manhattan Creek, flows 4.5 miles to Dutch Creek nearly 4 miles northwest of Chili Bar (lat. 38°48'20" N, long. 120°52'15" W; sec. 16, T 11 N, R 10 E). Named on Coloma (1949) and Garden Valley (1949) 7.5' quadrangles. The name recalls the old mining camp of Johntown (Gudde, 1975, p. 178). Whitney (1880, p. 85) mentioned a place called Alabama Flat that was located along Johntown Creek.

Jone City: see **Ione** [AMADOR].

Jones [EL DORADO]: *locality,* 5.25 miles south-southeast of Robbs Peak (lat. 38°51' N, long. 120°22' W). Named on Pyramid Peak (1896) 30' quadrangle. Kyburz (1952) 7.5' quadrangle shows Jones place at the site.

Jones: see **Til Jones Spring** [COLUSA].

Jones Bar [NEVADA]: *locality,* 5.25 miles west-northwest of Nevada City along South Yuba River (lat. 39°17'40" N, long. 121° 06'35" W; sec. 32, T 17 N, R 8 E); the place is 0.5 mile upstream from the mouth of Jones Ravine. Named on Nevada City (1948) 7.5' quadrangle.

Jones Butte: see **Dutschke Hill** [AMADOR].

Jones Creek: see **Canyon Creek** [EL DORADO] (1).

Jones Flat [YOLO]: *area,* 2.5 miles east of Guinda (lat. 38°49'30" N, long. 122°08'40" W; at N line sec. 12, T 11 N, R 3 W). Named on Guinda (1959) 7.5' quadrangle.

Jones Fork: see **Silver Creek** [EL DORADO].

Jones Hill: see **Canyon Creek** [EL DORADO] (1).

Jones Hot Springs: see **Jones Springs** [COLUSA].

Jones Ravine [NEVADA]: *canyon,* drained by a stream that flows 1.25 miles to South Yuba River 5.5 miles west-northwest of Nevada City (lat. 39'17'45" N, long. 121°06'55" W; sec. 31, T 17 N, R 8 E); the mouth of the canyon is nearly 0.5 mile downstream from Jones Bar. Named on Nevada City (1948) 7.5' quadrangle.

Jones Ridge [NEVADA]: *ridge,* south-southwest- to south-trending, 2 miles long, 6.25 miles north-northeast of Chicago Park (lat. 39° 14' N, long. 120°56'05" W). Named on Chicago Park (1949) 7.5' quadrangle.

Jones Springs [COLUSA]: *locality,* 0.5 mile southwest of Wilbur Springs (lat. 39°02' N, long. 122°25'35" W). Named on Venado (1920) 15' quadrangle. A resort called Jones Hot Springs used hot sulphureted salty water from a well (Waring, G.A., p. 103).

Jones Valley [NEVADA]: *valley,* 7 miles west-northwest of Donner Pass along Rattlesnake Creek (2) (lat. 39°20'25" N, long. 120°27'15" W; on W line sec. 18, T 17 N, R 14 E). Named on Soda Springs (1955) 7.5' quadrangle.

Jones Valley [SIERRA]:

(1) *valley,* 1.25 miles west of Crystal Peak (lat. 39°33'35" N, long. 120°06'45" W). Named on Dog Valley (1981) 7.5' quadrangle, which shows marsh in much of the valley.

(2) *valley,* 9.5 miles south-southwest of Sierraville along Pass Creek (lat. 39°28'35" N, long. 120°27'30" W; on N line sec. 36, T 19 N, R 13 E). Named on Webber Peak (1981) 7.5' quadrangle.

Jones Valley: see **Upper Jones Valley** [NEVADA].

Jone Valley: see **Ione** [AMADOR].

Jordan Creek [NEVADA]: *stream,* flows 1.5 miles to South Yuba River 2.25 miles west of Yuba Gap (lat. 39°19'15" N, long. 120°39'15" W; sec. 20, T 17 N, R 12 E). Named on Blue Canyon (1955) 7.5' quadrangle.

Josephine [SUTTER]: *locality,* 5.5 miles south-southwest of Sutter at the end of a branch of Southern Pacific Railroad in Sutter Basin (lat. 39°05'40" N, long. 121°47'55" W). Named on Tisdale Weir (1952) 7.5' quadrangle.

Josephine: see **Josephine Canyon** [EL DORADO].

Josephine Canyon [EL DORADO]: *canyon,* drained by a stream that flows nearly 1 mile to Middle Fork American River 7 miles north-northeast of Georgetown (lat. 39°00' N, long. 120°47'15" W; sec. 6, T 13 N, R 11 E). Named on Georgetown (1949) 7.5' quadrangle, which shows Josephine mine near the head of the canyon. Postal authorities established Josephine post office, named for the mine, in 1895, discontinued it in 1915, reestablished it in 1916, and discontinued it in 1917 (Salley, p. 108).

Joubert Diggins [SIERRA]: *locality,* 4 miles north-northwest of Pike along Willow Creek (lat. 39°29'40" N, long. 121°01'35" W; on S line sec. 24, T 19 N, R 8 E). Named on Camptonville (1948) 7.5' quadrangle. J. Joubert discovered gold at the place in 1852 (Gudde, 1975, p. 179).

Juba Creek: see **Yuba River** [NEVADA-YUBA].

Judah: see **Mount Judah** [PLACER].

Judge Palmer's Bridge: see **Chaparral Hill**, under **Lancha Plana** [AMADOR].

Junction: see **Citrus** [SACRAMENTO]; **Roseville** [PLACER].

Junction Bar [EL DORADO-PLACER]: *locality,* 3 miles northeast of Volcanoville along Middle Fork American River on El Dorado-Placer County line (lat. 39°00'35" N, long. 120°44'50" W; on N line sec. 4, T 13 N, R 11 E). Named on Michigan Bluff (1952) 7.5' quadrangle.

Junction House [NEVADA]: *locality,* 3 miles south-southwest of Washington (lat. 39°19' N, long. 120°48'40" W; near NW cor. sec. 25, T 17 N, R 10 E). Site named on Washington (1950) 7.5' quadrangle.

Junction House [YUBA]: *locality,* 2 miles west-southwest of Camptonville (lat. 39°26'30" N, long. 121°05' W). Named on Smartsville (1895) 30' quadrangle. The place also was known as Bogardus' Ranch, and later as James Ranch (Hoover, Rensch, and Rensch, p. 596). Wescoatt's (1861) map shows a place called Wisconsin Ho. [House] located less than 1 mile west-southwest of Junction House.

Juniper Creek [NEVADA-PLACER]: *stream,* heads in the State of Nevada and flows 7 miles through Placer County to Truckee River 6.5 miles east-northeast of Truckee in Nevada County (lat. 39° 21'55" N, long. 120°04'20" W; sec. 34, T 18 N, R 17 E). Named on Martis Peak (1955) 7.5' quadrangle.

Juniper Creek: see **West Juniper Creek** [NEVADA].

Juniper Flat [NEVADA]: *area,* 5.5 miles east-northeast of Truckee (lat. 39°22' N, long. 120°05'40" W; mainly in sec. 33, T 18 N, R 17 E). Named on Boca (1955) and Martis Peak (1955) 7.5' quadrangles.

Juniper Hill [NEVADA]: *peak,* 9 miles east of Truckee (lat. 39°20'45" N, long. 120°01'20" W; near SW cor. sec. 7, T 17 N, R 18 E). Altitude 7939 feet. Named on Martis Peak (1955) 7.5' quadrangle.

Juniper Ridge Spring [NEVADA]: *spring,* 8.5 miles east of Truckee (lat. 39°20'15" N, long. 120°01'20" W; sec. 18, T 17 N, R 18 E). Named on Martis Peak (1955) 7.5' quadrangle.

Jura: see **Citrus** [SACRAMENTO].

Jurgens: see **Rescue** [EL DORADO].

—K—

Kalmeia Lake: see **Kalmia Lake** [EL DORADO].

Kalmia Lake [EL DORADO]: *lake,* 700 feet long, 1.5 miles west-northwest of Mount Tallac (lat. 38°54'40" N, long. 120°07'25" W; sec. 5, T 12 N, R 17 E). Named on Emerald Bay (1955) and Rockbound Valley (1955) 7.5' quadrangles. The name is from *Kalmia polifoia,* the botanical name for alpine laurel; the earlier form "Kalmeia Lake" was changed to conform with the botanical name (Lekisch, p. 68).

Kanaka Creek [SIERRA]: *stream,* formed by the confluence of Middle Fork and South Fork, flows 9 miles to Middle Yuba River 3.25 miles east-southeast of Pike (lat. 39°25'10" N, long. 120°56'35" W; at W line sec. 14, T 18 N, R 9 E). Named on Alleghany (1949) 7.5' quadrangle. A party of Kanaka (Hawaiian) prospectors discovered gold along the stream in 1850 (Hoover, Rensch, and Rensch, p. 494-495). Middle Fork is 3.25 miles long and is named on Alleghany (1949) and Downieville (1951) 7.5' quadrangles. South Fork is 3 miles long and is named on Alleghany (1949) 7.5' quadrangle. North Fork, which enters from the north 0.5 mile south-southwest of Alleghany, is 2.5 miles long and is named on Alleghany (1949) 7.5' quadrangle. Present North Fork is called Little Kanaka Creek on Colfax (1898) 30' quadrangle.

Kanaka Cutoff [YOLO]: *water feature,* part of Sacramento River that cuts off a meander 5 miles east-southeast of Knights Landing (lat. 38°46'05" N, long. 121°38'15" W). Named on Knights Landing (1952) 7.5' quadrangle.

Kanaka Gulch [AMADOR]: *canyon,* 1.5 miles long, 5.25 miles south-southeast of Plymouth (lat. 38°24'50" N, long. 120°47'50" W; sec. 31, 32, T 7 N, R 11 E). Named on Amador City (1962) 7.'5 quadrangle.

Kanaka Gulch [EL DORADO]: *canyon,* drained by a stream that flows 1.5 miles to Middle Fork American River 6.5 miles north-northeast of Georgetown (lat. 38°59'45" N, long. 120°47'50" W; near W line sec. 6, T 13 N, R 11 E). Named on Georgetown (1949) 7.5' quadrangle.

Kane Flat: see **Sierra City** [SIERRA].

Kanes [EL DORADO]: *locality,* 10 miles south-southeast of Placerville (lat. 38°35'50" N, long. 120°42'45" W). Named on Placerville (1893) 30' quadrangle.

Karnak [SUTTER]: *locality,* 6.5 miles south-southeast of Robbins in Sutter Basin (lat. 38°47'05" N, long. 121°39'20" W; sec. 20, T 11 N, R 3 E). Named on Knights Landing (1952) 7.5' quadrangle.

Kaseberg Creek [PLACER]: *stream,* flows 6 miles to Pleasant Grove Creek 5.25 miles northwest of Roseville (lat. 38°47'35" N, long. 121°21'45" W; sec. 24, T 11 N, R 5 E). Named on Roseville (1967) 7.5' quadrangle. The name commemorates James W. Kaseberg, a rancher in the neighborhood (Gudde, 1949, p. 170).

Katesville: see **Michigan Bar** [SACRAMENTO].

Katrine Lake: see **Snow Lake** [EL DORADO].

Kearney: see **Camp Far West** [YUBA].

Keiths Dome [EL DORADO]: *peak,* 5.25 miles northwest of Echo Summit (lat. 38°51'35" N, long. 120°06'20" W; sec. 28, T 12 N, R 17 E). Altitude 8646 feet. Named on Echo Lake (1955) 7.5' quadrangle. The name commemorates W.F. Keith, a pioneer (Lekisch, p. 68).

Kelley Lake: see **Kelly Lake** [PLACER].

Kelly Bar [YUBA]: *locality,* 4 miles southeast of Strawberry Valley along North Yuba River at the mouth of Canyon Creek (lat. 39° 31'20" N, long. 121°03'10" W; near S line sec. 11, T 19 N, R 8 E). Named on Strawberry Valley (1948) 7.5' quadrangle.

Kelly Creek [EL DORADO]: *stream,* flows 4 miles to Dry Creek 4.5 miles north-northwest of Shingle Springs (lat. 38°43'35" N, long. 120°56'50" W; near NE cor. sec. 14, T 10 N, R 9 E). Named on Shingle Springs (1949) 7.5' quadrangle.

Kelly Lake [PLACER]: *lake,* 1800 feet long, 2 miles west of Cisco Grove (lat. 39°18'35" N, long. 120°34'40" W; sec. 25, T 17 N, R 12 E). Named on Cisco Grove (1955) 7.5' quadrangle. Called Kelley Lake on Emigrant Gap (1955) 15' quadrangle.

Kelly Ravine [EL DORADO]: *canyon,* drained by a stream that flows about 1 mile to Folsom Lake 4 miles west-southwest of the village of Pilot Hill (lat. 38°48'55" N, long. 121°04'50" W; at E line sec. 9, T 11 N, R 8 E). Named on Pilot Hill (1954, photorevised 1973) 7.5' quadrangle.

Kellys Bar: see **American River** [EL DORADO-PLACER-SACRAMENTO].

Kelsey [EL DORADO]: *village,* 2 miles north of Chili Bar (lat. 38°47'45" N, long. 120°49'05" W; near SW cor. sec. 13, T 11 N, R 10 E). Named on Garden Valley (1949) 7.5' quadrangle, which shows Kelsey P.O. located nearly 1 mile north of Kelsey. Postal authorities established Kelsey post office in 1856, discontinued it in 1872, reestablished it in 1875, moved it 0.5 mile west in 1895, moved it 0.5 mile southeast in 1896, discontinued it in 1903, and reestablished it in 1920 (Salley, p. 110). Benjamin Kelsey, who came to California in 1841 with the Bidwell-Bartleson party, discovered gold in 1848 at the place, which became known as Kelsey's Diggings (Hoover, Rensch, and Rensch, p. 86). A mining camp called Dufftown was close to Kelsey; the place was named by sailors who lived there and had a concoction called plum duff each Sunday for dinner (Gernes, p. 33). Postal authorities established Saint Lawrenceburgh post office 4 miles north of Kelsey in 1872, discontinued it in 1875, reestablished it with the name "Saint Lawrence" in 1880, and discontinued it in 1882; the name was from Saint Lawrence mine (Salley, p. 191). They established Slatington post office in 1903, discontinued it in 1912, reestablished it in 1916, and discontinued it in 1920, when they moved it 1.5 miles northeast and changed the name to Kelsey; the name "Slatington" was from the hand-split slate shingles made at the place (Salley, p. 206). Gudde (1975, p. 80) listed a place called Lawrenceberg, also known as Columbia Flat, that was located near Kelsey. David Martin and his family moved to Columbia Flat in 1851 and built a travelers stop there called Columbia House; a mining camp called Cincinnati was situated near Kelsey between Columbia Flat and Irish Creek (Gernes, p. 34-35).

Kelsey Canyon [EL DORADO]: *canyon,* 2 miles long, opens into the canyon of South Fork American River less than 1 mile west-northwest of Chili Bar (lat. 38°46'15" N, long. 120°49'55" W; sec. 26, T 11 N, R 10 E). Named on Garden Valley (1949) 7.5' quadrangle.

Kelsey's Diggings: see **Kelsey** [EL DORADO].

Kemptons Crossing: see **Camp Far West** [YUBA].

Kenebec Creek [NEVADA]: *stream,* flows 2 miles to South Yuba River 4.25 miles southwest of North Bloomfield (lat. 39°20'05" N, long. 120°58'05" W; sec. 16, T 17 N, R 9 E). Named on North Bloomfield (1949) 7.5' quadrangle. Whitney's (1873) map has the name "Kennebec Ravine" for the canyon of the stream.

Kenebec House: see **Long Bar** [YUBA] (2).

Kennebec Hill: see **Kennebec House** [NEVADA].

Kennebec House [NEVADA]: *locality,* 3.5 miles west-southwest of North Bloomfield (lat. 39°21' N, long. 120°58' W); the place is west of present Kenebec Creek. Named on Colfax (1898) 30' quadrangle. Whitney's (1873) map shows Kennebec Hill located 0.5 mile north of Kennebec Ho.

Kennebeck Bar [EL DORADO-PLACER]: *locality,* 4.5 miles west-northwest of Greenwood along Middle Fork American River on El Dorado-Placer County line (lat. 38°55'40" N, long. 120°59'10" W; near SW cor. sec. 33, T 13 N, R 9 E). Named on Greenwood (1949) 7.5' quadrangle.

Kennebec Ravine: see **Kenebec Creek** [NEVADA].

Kennedy Reservoir [AMADOR]: *lake,* 350 feet long, 1.5 miles north-northwest of Jackson (lat. 38°22'05" N, long. 120°47'10" W; sec. 17, T 6 N, R 11 E). Named on Jackson (1962) 7.5' quadrangle.

Kent: see **West Butte** [SUTTER] (2).

Kent Creek [PLACER]: *stream,* flows 1.5 miles to Shirttail Canyon 3.5 miles north-northeast of Foresthill (lat. 39°04'10" N, long. 120° 47'40" W; sec. 12, T 14 N, R 10 E). Named on Foresthill (1949) 7.5' quadrangle.

Kent Ravine: see **North San Juan** [NEVADA].

Kentucky Creek [YUBA]: *stream,* flows 1 mile to Deadwood Creek nearly 1 mile southeast of Strawberry Valley (lat. 39°33'20" N, long. 121°05'40" W; near NW cor. sec. 33, T 20 N, R 8 E). Named on Strawberry Valley (1948) 7.5' quadrangle.

Kentucky Flat [EL DORADO]: *area,* 16 miles north-northwest of Pollock Pines (lat. 38°57'55" N, long. 120°44'20" W; sec. 22, T 13 N, R 11 E). Named on Tunnel Hill (1950) 7.5' quadrangle. Placerville (1893) 30' quadrangle has the name for a locality.

Kentucky Ranch: see **Dobbins** [YUBA].

Kentucky Ravine [NEVADA]: *canyon,* drained by a stream that flows 5.5 miles to South Yuba River 2.25 miles west-southwest of French Corral (lat. 39°17'25" N, long. 121°11'50" W; sec. 33, T 17 N, R 7 E). Named on French Corral (1948) 7.5' quadrangle.

Kentucky Ridge [NEVADA]: *ridge,* west-trending, less than 1 mile long, 4.25 miles south-southeast of French Corral (lat. 39°15' N, long. 121°08' W); the ridge is south of upper Kentucky Ravine. Named on French Corral (1948) and Rough and Ready (1949) 7.5' quadrangles.

Keystone Creek [YUBA]: *stream,* flows 1.5 miles to Indiana Creek nearly 3 miles north-northwest of Dobbins (lat. 39°24'30" N, long. 121°13'45" W; sec. 19, T 18 N, R 7 E). Named on Challenge (1948) 7.5' quadrangle.

Keystone Gap [SIERRA]: *pass,* 2.5 miles southwest of Sierra City (lat. 39°32'15" N, long. 120°39'50" W; at S line sec. 6, T 19 N, R 12 E); the pass is at the head of Keystone Ravine. Named on Sierra City (1981) 7.5' quadrangle.

Keystone Mountain [SIERRA]: *peak,* nearly 3 miles southwest of Sierra City (lat. 39°32'20" N, long. 120°40'20" W; sec. 6, T 19 N, R 12 E); the peak is near the head of Keystone Ravine. Altitude 6912 feet. Named on Sierra City (1981) 7.5' quadrangle.

Keystone Ranch: see **Indiana Ranch** [YUBA].

Keystone Ravine [NEVADA]: *canyon,* drained by a stream that flows 1.5 miles to Englebright Reservoir (present Englebright Lake) 6 miles southwest of French Corral (lat. 39°15'15" N, long. 121°15'05" W; near S line sec. 12, T 16 N, R 6 E). Named on French Corral (1948), Oregon House (1948), and Rough and Ready (1949) 7.5' quadrangles.

Keystone Ravine [SIERRA]: *canyon,* drained by a stream that flows 2 miles to North Yuba River 2.5 miles west of Sierra City (lat. 39°34'05" N, long. 120°40'35" W; near SW cor. sec. 30, T 20 N, R 12 E); the canyon heads near Keystone Mountain. Named on Sierra City (1981) 7.5' quadrangle, which shows Keystone mine in the canyon. The mine was developed before 1857 (Gudde, 1949, p. 174).

Kidd Lake [PLACER]: *lake,* 2950 feet long, 5.5 miles west of Donner Pass (lat. 39°18'35" N, long. 120°25'35" W; sec. 29, T 17 N, R 14 E). Named on Soda Springs (1955) 7.5' quadrangle. On Hobson's (1890b) map, the name "Kidds Lakes" applies to a group of lakes that includes present Kidd Lake.

Kidds Lakes: see **Kidd Lake** [PLACER].

Kiesel [YOLO]: *locality,* 10.5 miles northeast of Davis along Sacramento Northern Railroad (lat. 38°39'50" N, long. 121°36'50" W). Named on Taylor Monument (1967) 7.5' quadrangle.

Kilaga Springs [PLACER]: *locality,* 10.5 miles west-northwest of Auburn (lat. 38°58'15" N, long. 121°14'50" W; at SE cor. sec. 13, T 13 N, R 6 E). Named on Gold Hill (1954) 7.5' quadrangle.

Kilborn Lake [NEVADA]: *lake,* 1000 feet long, nearly 5 miles west of Donner Pass (lat. 39°19'05" N, long. 120°24'55" W; near SW cor. sec. 21, T 17 N, R 14 E). Named on Soda Springs (1955) 7.5' quadrangle.

Kimball Island [SACRAMENTO]: *island,* 1.25 miles long, 14 miles southwest of Isleton in San Joaquin River (lat. 38°01'35" N, long. 121°49' W). Named on Antioch North (1978) 7.5' quadrangle. Called Hammond I. on Ringgold's (1850a) map. The name "Kimball" commemorates George W. Kimball, who came to California in 1850 and later bought the island (Gudde, 1949, p. 174).

Kimberley Creek [SIERRA]: *stream,* flows 1.5 miles to Kanaka Creek 2.5 miles southwest of Alleghany (lat. 39°26'50" N, long. 120°52'50" W; near N line sec. 8, T 18 N, R 19 E). Named on Pike (1949) 7.5' quadrangle.

Kinch Canyon [SUTTER]: *valley,* about 3.5 miles north-northwest of Sutter (lat. 39°12'30" N, long. 121°46' W; sec. 29, T 16 N, R 2 E). Named on Sutter Buttes (1954) 7.5' quadrangle.

Kinders Diggs: see **Lowell Hill** [NEVADA].

King Canyon [YOLO]: *canyon,* 1.25 miles long, along upper reaches of Mushoak Creek above a point 3.5 miles northeast of Guinda (lat. 38°51'15" N, long. 122°08' W). Named on Guinda (1959) 7.5' quadrangle.

King Flat [YOLO]: *valley,* 2.25 miles northeast of Guinda (lat. 38° 50'55" N, long. 122°09'35" W; sec. 35, T 12 N, R 3 W); the valley is at the head of King Canyon. Named on Guinda (1959) 7.5' quadrangle.

Kings Beach [PLACER]: *town,* 8 miles northeast of Tahoe City along Lake Tahoe (lat. 39°14'10" N, long. 120°01'15" W; mainly in sec. 19, T 16 N, R 18 E). Named on Kings Beach (1955) 7.5' quadrangle. Hobson's (1890b) map shows a place called Pine Grove located at the site of present Kings Beach. Postal authorities established Kings Beach post office in 1937, discontinued it in 1942, and reestablished it in 1945; the name is for Joe King, first postmaster (Salley, p. 112).

Kings Hill [PLACER]: *ridge,* west-southwest-trending, 1.5 miles long, 4.25 miles east-southeast of Colfax (lat. 39°04'40" N, long. 120°52'50" W). Named on Colfax (1949) and Foresthill (1949) 7.5' quadrangles. Gudde (1975, p. 187) gave the name "Parks Hill" as an apparent alternate.

King's Hill: see **Kings Hill Point** [PLACER].

Kings Hill Point [PLACER]: *ridge,* south-southwest-trending, 2 miles long, 4.5 miles southeast of Colfax (lat. 39°03'30" N, long. 120°53' W); the ridge extends south-southwest from Kings Hill. Named on Colfax (1949) 7.5' quadrangle. Whitney's (1873) map shows an inhabited place called King's Hill located on or near present Kings Hill Point.

King Slough [PLACER-SUTTER]: *stream,* heads in Placer County and flows 7 miles to American Basin 7 miles east-northeast of Verona in Sutter County (lat. 38°50'30" N, long. 121°30'35" W; sec. 34, T 12 N, R 4 E). Named on Pleasant Grove (1967) and Verona (1967) 7.5' quadrangles.

Kings Meadow [EL DORADO]: *area,* 7.25 miles north of Pollock Pines (lat. 38°52' N, long. 120°34'40" W; near SE cor. sec. 24, T 12 N, R 12 E). Named on Pollock Pines (1950) 7.5' quadrangle. Called Kings Meadows on Placerville (1893) 30' quadrangle.

King Spring [YOLO]: *spring,* 2.25 miles northeast of Guinda (lat. 38°51' N, long. 122°09'30" W; sec. 35, T 12 N, R 3 W); the spring is at King Flat. Named on Guinda (1959) 7.5' quadrangle.

Kings Store [EL DORADO]: *locality,* 8.5 miles east-northeast of Latrobe near North Fork Cosumnes River (lat. 38°36'40" N, long. 120°50'30" W). Named on Placerville (1893) 30' quadrangle.

Kingsville [EL DORADO]: *locality,* 5 miles southwest of Placerville (lat. 38°40'35" N, long. 120°52'30" W; sec. 33, T 10 N, R 10 E). Named on Placerville (1949) 7.5' quadrangle. Called Kingville on Placerville (1893) 30' quadrangle.

Kingvale [NEVADA]: *settlement,* 5.5 miles west of Donner Pass (lat. 39°19'15" N, long. 120°25'50" W; sec. 20, T 17 N, R 14 E). Named on Soda Springs (1955) 7.5' quadrangle.

Kingville: see **Kingsville** [EL DORADO].

King Woolford Mill [NEVADA]: *locality,* 7 miles south-southwest of Washington (lat. 39°15'45" N, long. 120°50'10" W; near SE cor. sec. 10, T 16 N, R 10 E). Site named on Washington (1950) 7.5' quadrangle.

Kirk: see **Kirkwood** [AMADOR-EL DORADO].

Kirk Lake: see **Hiatt Lake** [SUTTER].

Kirksville: see **Kirkville** [SUTTER].

Kirkville [SUTTER]: *locality,* 18 miles south-southwest of Yuba City along Sacramento River (lat. 38°54'30" N, long. 121°47'30" W; near N line sec. 7, T 12 N, R 8 E); the place is at the southwest end of Cole Point, which formerly was called Cole Grove Point. Named on Kirkville (1952) 7.5' quadrangle. The name commemorates T.D. Kirk, who laid out a town at the site in 1874 and called it Kirksville (Gudde, 1949. p. 175). The land once belonged to O.S. Colegrove of Cole Point, who called the place Colegrove Point (Hendrix, p. 123). Postal authorities established Colgrove Point post office there in 1866, and discontinued it in 1871; they established Kirksville post office in 1874 and discontinued it in 1878 (Salley, p. 47, 112).

Kirkwood [AMADOR-EL DORADO]: *locality,* 11.5 miles north of Mokelumne Peak at the junction of Amador County, El Dorado County, and Alpine County (lat. 38°42'10" N, long. 120°04'15" W; sec. 22, T 10 N, R 17 E). Named on Caples Lake (1979) 7.5' quadrangle. Called Kirk on Wheeler's (1876-1877a) map, but Wheeler (1878, p. 61) also referred to Kirkwood's. Zack Kirkwood built a stage station and inn at the place in 1864; Amador, El Dorado, and Alpine Counties met in the barroom of the inn, which housed Roundtop post office (Hoover, Rensch, and Rensch, p. 29). Postal authorities established Roundtop post office in 1887 and discontinued it in 1907; the name was from a nearby peak in Alpine County (Salley, p. 190). They established Fagan post office 5 miles west of Roundtop post office in 1891 and discontinued it in 1895; the name was for Maggie Fagan, first postmaster (Salley, p. 71).

Kirkwood Creek [AMADOR]: *stream,* heads in Alpine County and flows less than 1 mile in Amador County before reentering Alpine County 11.5 miles north of Mokelumne Peak at Kirkwood (lat. 38° 42'10" N, long. 120°04'15" W; sec. 22, T 10 N, R 17 E); the stream goes through Kirkwood Valley. Named on Caples Lake (1979) 7.5' quadrangle.

Kirkwood Lake [EL DORADO]: *lake,* 2100 feet long. 0.5 mile west-northwest of Kirkwood (lat. 38°42'20" N, long. 120°04'55" W; on W line sec. 22, T 10 N, R 17 E). Named on Caples Lake (1979) 7.5' quadrangle. Postal authorities established Lake Kirkwood post office at a resort in 1940 (Salley, p. 115).

Kirkwood Meadows [AMADOR]: *valley,* 10.5 miles north of Mokelumne Peak on Amador-Alpine County line (lat. 38°41'30" N, long. 120°04'15" W); the valley is south of Kirkwood along Kirkwood Creek. Named on Caples Lake (1979) 7.5' quadrangle.

Kirkwood Ridge [AMADOR]: *ridge,* southwest-trending, 1.25 miles long, 2.5 miles south of Jackson (lat. 38°18'45" N, long. 120° 46' W). Named on Jackson (1962) 7.5' quadrangle.

Kirkwood's: see **Kirkwood** [AMADOR-EL DORADO].

Kit Carson [AMADOR]: *settlement,* 9 miles north of Mokelumne Peak at the north end of Silver Lake (lat. 38°40'10" N, long. 120° 06'50" W; near E line sec. 32, T 10 N, R 17 E). Named on Caples Lake (1979) 7.5' quadrangle. Postal authorities established Kit Carson post office in 1951 (Frickstad, p. 5).

Kiva Beach [EL DORADO]: *beach,* 3.5 miles northeast of Mount Tallac along Lake Tahoe (lat. 38°56'25" N, long. 120°02'50" W; sec. 25, T 13 N, R 17 E). Named on Emerald Bay (1955, photorevised 1969) 7.5' quadrangle.

Klensendorf Point [YUBA]: *relief feature,* nearly 4 miles east of Dobbins and north of the confluence of North Yuba River and Middle Yuba River (lat. 39°22'20" N, long. 121°08'10" W; at N line sec. 1, T 17 N, R 7 E). Named on French Corral (1948) 7.5' quadrangle.

Klondike Meadow [PLACER]: *area,* 1.5 miles northwest of Martis Peak (lat. 39°18'20" N, long. 120°03' W; sec. 23, T 17 N, R 17 E). Named on Martis Peak (1955) 7.5' quadrangle.

Knapp: see **Blue Canyon** [PLACER] (2).

Knapp Creek: see **Spring Creek** [NEVADA].

Knee Ridge [PLACER]: *ridge,* east-trending, 1.25 miles long, about 2 miles southwest of Homewood (lat. 39°03'45" N, long. 120°11'05" W; sec. 14, 15, T 14 N, R 16 E). Named on Homewood (1955) 7.5' quadrangle.

Knickerbocker Canyon [EL DORADO]: *canyon,* 0.5 mile long, opens into the canyon of North Fork American River 3.25 miles northwest of the village of Pilot Hill (lat. 38°52'10" N, long. 121° 03'10" W; at S line sec. 23, T 12 N, R 8 E); the canyon is along lower reaches of Knickerbocker Creek. Named on Pilot Hill (1954) 7.5' quadrangle.

Knickerbocker Creek [EL DORADO]: *stream,* flows 5.5 miles to North Fork American River 3.25 miles northwest of the village of Pilot Hill (lat. 38°52'10" N, long. 121°03'10" W; at S line sec. 23, T 12 N, R 8 E). Named on Auburn (1953), Greenwood (1949), and Pilot Hill (1954) 7.5' quadrangles.

Knights Landing [YOLO]: *town,* 9 miles north-northeast of Woodland along Sacramento River at the mouth of Sycamore Slough (lat. 38°47'55" N, long. 121°43'10" W; sec. 14, T 11 N, R 2 E). Named on Knights Landing (1952) 7.5' quadrangle. Knights Landing (1910) 7.5' quadrangle shows both Knights Landing and Grafton P.O. at the place. Postal authorities established Grafton post office in 1854, changed the name to Knights Landing in 1892, changed it back to Grafton in 1893, and changed it again to Knights Landing in 1925; the name "Grafton" was for a man who started a mail route from Benicia in Solano County (Salley, p. 87). The name "Knight" commemorates William Knight, who came to California with the Workman-Rowland party in 1841 and settled in 1843 at present Knights Landing, where he built his home on an Indian mound at the junction of Sycamore Slough and Sacramento River; after failure of an attempt in 1849 to found a town called Baltimore at the place, Charles F. Reed laid out another townsite and named it Knights Landing (Hoover, Rensch, and Rensch, p. 583-584). California Division of Highways' (1934) map shows a place called Eastham located along Southern Pacific Railroad 2.5 miles north-northwest of Knights Landing, and a place called Knights Landing Jct. located along the railroad 1.5 miles south-southwest of Knights Landing.

Knights Landing Junction: see **Knights Landing** [YOLO].

Knights Landing Ridge Cut [YOLO]: *water feature,* artificial watercourse that extends for 6.5 miles from Sycamore Slough near Knights Landing to Yolo Bypass 13 miles north-northeast of Davis (lat. 38°43'20" N, long. 121°39'45" W). Named on Grays Bend (1953) and Knights Landing (1952) 7.5' quadrangles. Knights Landing (1910) 7.5' quadrangle shows a natural water feature called Roseberry Slough that occupies the north part of the course of present Knights Landing Ridge Cut.

Knoxville: see **Squaw Creek** [PLACER].

Knuthson Meadow [SIERRA]: *area,* 2.25 miles north of Calpine along Carman Creek (lat. 39°41'50" N, long. 120°26'35" W). Named on Calpine (1981) 7.5' quadrangle.

Knuts Spring [SIERRA]: *spring,* 3.25 miles west-southwest of Mount Fillmore (lat. 39°42'20" N, long. 120°54'15" W; sec. 6, T 21 N, R 10 E). Named on La Porte (1951) 7.5' quadrangle.

Kobe [YOLO]: *locality,* 3.25 miles west of West Sacramento along Southern Pacific Railroad (lat. 38°34'35" N, long. 121°35'30" W). Named on Lovdal (1916) 7.5' quadrangle.

Kohler: see **Camp Kohler** [SACRAMENTO].

Kosova: see **Sheldon** [SACRAMENTO].

Kres [NEVADA]: *locality,* 3 miles east-southeast of Grass Valley along Nevada County Narrow Gauge Railroad (lat. 39°11'45" N, long. 121°00'30" W). Named on Smartsville (1895) 30' quadrangle.

Krumbacker's Ravine: see **Scotchman Creek** [NEVADA].

KT-22 [PLACER]: *peak,* 5.5 miles west of Tahoe City (lat. 39°11' N, long. 120°14'30" W; near NW cor. sec. 5, T 15 N, R 16 E). Altitude 8070 feet. Named on Tahoe City (1955) 7.5' quadrangle.

Kyburz [EL DORADO]: *village,* 9 miles west-southwest of Pyramid Peak (lat. 38°46'30" N, long. 120°17'40" W; at NW cor. sec. 27, T 11 N, R 15

E). Named on Kyburz (1952) 7.5' quadrangle. Pyramid Peak (1896) 30' quadrangle shows Slippery Ford at the place. Postal authorities established Slippery Ford post office in 1861, changed the name to Slipperyford in 1896, and changed it to Kyburz in 1911; Albert Kyburz, son of 1846 pioneer S.E. Kyburz, was the first postmaster of Kyburz post office (Salley, p. 113, 206). Another place called Slippery Ford was located northeast of Strawberry (Beverly Cola, personal communication, 1988).

Kyburz Flat [SIERRA]: *valley,* 12 miles south of Loyalton (lat. 39° 30'15" N, long. 120°14'05" W). Named on Hobart Mills (1981) and Sardine Peak (1981) 7.5' quadrangles.

— L —

Labadie's: see **Maple Springs House**, under **Indiana Ranch** [YUBA].

La Barr Meadows [NEVADA]: *settlement,* 3 miles south-southeast of Grass Valley (lat. 39°10'30" N, long. 121°02'40" W; around SW cor. sec. 1, T 15 N, R 8 E). Named on Grass Valley (1949) 7.5' quadrangle.

Lacey Creek [NEVADA-SIERRA]: *stream,* heads in Nevada County and flows 4.5 miles to Webber Lake 8 miles south-southwest of Sierraville in Sierra County (lat. 39°28'55" N, long. 120°24'45" W; sec. 28, T 19 N, R 14 E). Named on Webber Peak (1981) 7.5' quadrangle.

Lacey Valley [SIERRA]: *valley,* 9 miles south-southwest of Sierraville (lat. 39°28'30" N, long. 120°25' W); the valley is along Lacey Creek. Named on Webber Peak (1981) 7.5' quadrangle.

Lac Leven Lakes: see **High Loch Lake** [PLACER]; **Loch Leven Lakes** [PLACER].

La Coma Tallac [COLUSA]: *peak,* 6.25 miles east of Wilbur Springs on Cortina Ridge (lat. 39°03'20" N, long. 122°19'35" W; near S line sec. 17, T 14 N, R 4 W). Altitude 2601 feet. Named on Wilbur Springs (1961) 15' quadrangle.

Laddies Cove [PLACER]: *relief feature,* 5.25 miles east-northeast of Bunker Hill (lat. 39°05'10" N, long. 120°17'40" W; near SE cor. sec. 4, T 14 N, R 15 E). Named on Wentworth Springs (1953) 7.5' quadrangle.

Ladeux: see **Ladeux Meadow** [AMADOR].

Ladeux Meadow [AMADOR]: *area,* 5 miles north of Mokelumne Peak (lat. 38°36'45" N, long. 120°04'45" W; sec. 22, T 9 N, R 17 E). Named on Mokelumne Peak (1979) 7.5' quadrangle. Pyramid Peak (1896) 30' quadrangle has the name "Ladeux" at the place.

Ladies Canyon [EL DORADO]: *canyon,* drained by a stream that flows 0.5 mile to South Fork American River 0.25 mile east-northeast of Chili Bar (lat. 38°46'45" N, long. 120°49' W; sec. 25, T 11 N, R 10 E). Named on Garden Valley (1949) 7.5' quadrangle.

Ladies Canyon [SIERRA]: *canyon,* drained by a stream that flows 4.5 miles to North Yuba River 4.5 miles west of Sierra City (lat. 39°34'10" N, long. 120°43'15" W; near SE cor. sec. 27, T 20 N, R 11 E). Named on Sierra City (1981) 7.5' quadrangle. Called Lady's Canyon on Logan's (1929) map.

Ladies Canyon: see **Black Canyon** [SIERRA]; **Ladys Canyon** [PLACER]; **Little Ladies Canyon** [SIERRA].

Ladies Paradise: see **Squaw Valley** [PLACER].

Ladybug Peak [SIERRA]: *peak,* 5.5 miles south-southeast of Crystal Peak (lat. 39°29'10" N, long. 120°02'40" W; near W line sec. 24, T 19 N, R 17 E). Altitude 8380 feet. Named on Boca (1955) 7.5' quadrangle. Called Lady Bug Peak on Truckee (1895) 30' quadrangle.

Lady Canyon: see **Ladys Canyon** [PLACER].

Ladys Canyon [PLACER]: *canyon,* drained by a stream that flows nearly 2 miles to Middle Fork American River 2.5 miles east-southeast of Foresthill (lat. 39°00'25" N, long. 120°46'20" W; at S line sec. 32, T 14 N, R 11 E). Named on Foresthill (1949) 7.5' quadrangle. Called Lady Canyon on Colfax (1898) 30' quadrangle, and Ladies Cañon on Whitney's (1873) map.

Lady's Canyon: see **Ladies Canyon** [SIERRA].

Lafayette Hill: see **Grass Valley** [NEVADA].

Lafayette Ridge [SIERRA]: *ridge,* generally west-southwest-trending, 11 miles long, center 1.25 miles south of Alleghany (lat. 39°27'15" N, long. 120°50'30" W). Named on Alleghany (1949) and Pike (1949) 7.5' quadrangles.

Lafferty Peak [YUBA]: *peak,* 1.5 miles east-northeast of Loma Rica (lat. 39°19'15" N, long. 121°23'15" W; near NW cor. sec. 23, T 17 N, R 5 E). Altitude 911 feet. Named on Loma Rica (1947) 7.5' quadrangle.

Lagoon Lake [PLACER]: *lake,* 300 feet long, 3 miles north of Bunker Hill (lat. 39°05'25" N, long. 120°22'40" W; sec. 2, T 14 N, R 14 E). Named on Bunker Hill (1953) 7.5' quadrangle.

Laguna [AMADOR-SACRAMENTO]: *stream,* heads in Amador County and flows 32 miles to Cosumnes River 8.5 miles south of Elk Grove in Sacramento County (lat. 38°17'05" N, long. 121°22'40" W). Named on Bruceville (1968), Carbondale (1968), Clay (1968), Galt (1968), and Sloughhouse (1968) 7.5' quadrangles. United States Board on Geographic Names (1964, p. 10) rejected the names "Laguna Creek," "The Laguna," and "Willow Creek" for the stream.

Laguna: see **Willow Creek** [AMADOR-SACRAMENTO].

Laguna Creek [SACRAMENTO]: *stream,* flows 26 miles to Morrison Creek 8.5 miles south of downtown Sacramento (lat. 38°27'35" N, long. 121°28'05" W). Named on Buffalo Creek (1967), Elk Grove (1968), Florin (1968), and Sloughhouse (1968) 7.5' quadrangles.

Laguna Creek: see **Laguna** [AMADOR-SACRAMENTO].

Laguna West: see **Sacramento** [SACRAMENTO].

La Isla de los Quenensias: see **Grand Island** [SACRAMENTO].

Lake Aloha [EL DORADO]: *lake,* nearly 2 miles long, 1.5 miles north-northeast of Pyramid Peak (lat. 38°52' N, long. 120°08'25" W). Named on Pyramid Peak (1955) and Rockbound Valley (1955) 7.5' quadrangles.

Lake Alta [PLACER]: *lake,* 1250 feet long, 1 mile east of Dutch Flat (lat. 39°12'15" N, long. 120°48'55" W; sec. 35, T 16 N, R 10 E); the lake is 0.25 mile southwest of Alta. Named on Dutch Flat (1950) 7.5' quadrangle.

Lake Angela [NEVADA]: *lake,* 1350 feet long, 0.5 mile north of Donner Pass (lat. 39°19'25" N, long. 120°19'35" W; near W line sec. 16, T 17 N, R 15 E). Named on Norden (1955) 7.5' quadrangle. Surveyors working for Union Pacific Railroad named the lake in 1865 for Angela King, sister of Thomas Starr King (Gudde, 1949, p. 11).

Lake Arthur [PLACER]: *lake,* 950 feet long, 5.25 miles north-northeast of Auburn (lat. 38°57'55" N, long. 121°01'25" W; near W line sec. 19, T 13 N, R 9 E). Named on Auburn (1953) 7.5' quadrangle. The name commemorates W.R. Arthur, assistant manager of a water district (Gudde, 1949, p. 16).

Lake Audrian [EL DORADO]: *lake,* 1250 feet long, less than 1 mile west-northwest of Echo Summit (lat. 38°49'10" N, long. 120°02'35" W; on W line sec. 7, T 11 N, R 18 E). Named on Echo Lake (1955) 7.5' quadrangle. Called Audrian Lake on Pyramid Peak (1896) 30' quadrangle. The misspelled name commemorates Thomas Audrain, who had a station at Echo Summit in the 1860's (Gudde, 1969, p. 17).

Lake Bigler: see **Lake Tahoe** [EL DORADO-PLACER].

Lake Bonpland: see **Lake Tahoe** [EL DORADO-PLACER].

Lake Christopher [EL DORADO]: *lake,* 1500 feet long, behind a dam on Cold Creek 5 miles northwest of Freel Peak (lat. 38°54'40" N, long. 120°58' W; near SE cor. sec. 3, T 12 N, R 18 E). Named on South Lake Tahoe (1955, photorevised 1969 and 1974) 7.5' quadrangle.

Lake City [NEVADA]: *locality,* 2.5 miles west-southwest of North Bloomfield (lat. 39°21'30" N, long. 120°56'30" W; near NW cor. sec. 11, T 17 N, R 9 E). Named on North Bloomfield (1949) 7.5' quadrangle. The Bell brothers built a hotel at the site in 1855; the name "Lake City," given in 1857, is from a lake at the place (Hanna, p. 166).

Lake Clementine: see **North Fork Lake** [PLACER].

Lake Combie [NEVADA-PLACER]: *lake,* behind a dam on Bear River 3 miles southeast of Higgins Corner on Nevada-Placer County line (lat. 39°00'35" N, long. 121°03'25" W; near W line sec. 2, T 13 N, R 8 E). Named on Lake Combie (1949) 7.5' quadrangle, which has the name "Van Geisen Dam" for the dam that forms the lake; the lake itself is called Vangeisen Combie Diversion Reservoir on Smartsville (1942) 30' quadrangle. The name "Combie" is for a Frenchman who had a ranch at a site now covered by water of the lake (Gudde, 1949, p. 76).

Lake Creek [NEVADA]: *stream,* flows 2.5 miles to Fall Creek 6 miles southeast of Graniteville (lat. 39°23' N, long. 120°30'30" W; near W line sec. 32, T 18 N, R 12 E); the stream heads at Carr Lake and Feely Lake. Named on Graniteville (1982) 7.5' quadrangle.

Lake Doris [EL DORADO]: *lake,* 450 feet long, 4.25 miles southwest of Phipps Peak (lat. 38°54'20" N, long. 120°11'40" W). Named on Rockbound Valley (1955) 7.5' quadrangle.

Lake Edson: see **Stumpy Meadows Lake** [EL DORADO].

Lake Estelle [PLACER]: *lake,* 500 feet long, nearly 6 miles west of Tahoe City (lat. 39°09'50" N, long. 120°14'55" W; sec. 7, T 15 N, R 16 E). Named on Tahoe City (1955) 7.5' quadrangle.

Lake Flint [AMADOR]: *lake,* 1250 feet long, 1.5 miles south-southwest of Ione (lat. 38°19'55" N, long. 120°56'20" W). Named on Ione (1962) 7.5' quadrangle.

Lake Forest [PLACER]: *village,* 6.25 miles southwest of Kings Beach along Lake Tahoe (lat. 39°11'05" N, long. 120°06'45" W; on S line sec. 32, T 16 N, R 17 E). Named on Kings Beach (1955) 7.5' quadrangle. Postal authorities established Lake Forest post office in 1947 and discontinued it in 1953 (Frickstad, p. 120).

Lake Francis [YUBA]: *lake,* behind a dam on Dobbins Creek less than 1 mile south of Dobbins (lat. 39°21'35" N, long. 121°12'15" W; near E line sec. 5, T 17 N, R 7 E). Named on French Corral (1948) 7.5' quadrangle.

Lake Genevieve [EL DORADO]: *lake,* 850 feet long, 3 miles north of Phipps Peak (lat. 38°59'50" N, long. 120°09'35" W; at N line sec. 12, T 13 N, R 16 E). Named on Rockbound Valley (1955) 7.5' quadrangle.

Lake Greenhaven [SACRAMENTO]: *lake,* 0.5 mile long, 5 miles south-southwest of downtown Sacramento (lat. 38°30'30" N, long. 121°32' W). Named on Sacramento West (1967) 7.5' quadrangle.

Lake Hawley: see **Hawley Lake** [SIERRA].

Lake House [NEVADA]: *locality,* 2.5 miles west of Truckee (lat. 39° 19'30" N, long. 120°13'50" W); the place is at the east end of Donner Lake. Named on Truckee (1895) 30' quadrangle.

Lake House: see **Al Tahoe** [EL DORADO].

Lake Kirkwood: see **Kirkwood Lake** [EL DORADO].

Lake LeConte [EL DORADO]: *lake,* 1050 feet long, 2 miles north-northeast of Pyramid Peak (lat. 38°52'15" N, long. 120°08'10" W). Named on Pyramid Peak (1955) 7.5' quadrangle. The name honors Professor Joseph LeConte of University of California (Lekisch, p. 72).

Lake Lois [EL DORADO]: *lake,* 1550 feet long, nearly 4 miles southwest of Phipps Peak (lat. 38°55' N, long. 120°12' W). Named on Rockbound Valley (1955) 7.5' quadrangle.

Lake Louise [PLACER]: *lake,* 800 feet long, 1.5 miles southwest of Homewood (lat. 39°04'30" N, long. 120°11'10" W; on E line sec. 10, T 14 N, R 16 E). Named on Homewood (1955, photorevised 1969) 7.5' quadrangle.

Lake Lucille [EL DORADO]: *lake,* 900 feet long, 5.5 miles northwest of Echo Summit (lat. 38°51'40" N, long. 120°06'40" W; sec. 28, T 12 N, R 17 E). Named on Echo Lake (1955) 7.5' quadrangle. The name is for Lucille Meredith, wife of a banker in Oakland, California (Lekisch, p. 76).

Lake Margaret [EL DORADO]: *lake,* 900 feet long, 1.5 miles north-northwest of Kirkwood (lat. 38°43'25" N, long. 120°05'10" W). Named on Caples Lake (1979) 7.5' quadrangle.

Lake Margery [EL DORADO]: *lake,* 800 feet long, 5.5 miles northwest of Echo Summit (lat. 38°51'30" N, long. 120°06'55" W; sec. 28, T 12 N, R 17 E). Named on Echo Lake (1955) 7.5' quadrangle.

Lake Mary [PLACER]: *lake,* 1500 feet long, 0.25 mile south-southwest of Donner Pass (lat. 39°18'45" N, long. 120°19'45" W; near NE cor. sec. 20, T 17 N, R 15 E). Named on Norden (1955) 7.5' quadrangle.

Lake Mildred [YUBA]: *lake,* behind a dam on Dry Creek (1) nearly 1 mile north-northwest of Oregon House (lat. 39°22'05" N, long. 121°17' W; near S line sec. 34, T 18 N, R 6 E). Named on Oregon House (1948) and Rackerby (1948) 7.5' quadrangles.

Lake Natoma [SACRAMENTO]: *lake,* behind a dam on American River 3.5 miles southwest of Folsom (lat. 38°38'10" N, long. 121° 13'10" W). Named on Folsom (1967) 7.5' quadrangle.

Lake Number 5 [EL DORADO]: *lake,* 750 feet long, 5.25 miles southwest of Phipps Peak (lat. 38°54'55" N, long. 120°13'50" W; at E line sec. 5, T 12 N, R 16 E). Named on Rockbound Valley (1955) 7.5' quadrangle.

Lake Number 9 [EL DORADO]: *lake,* 400 feet long, nearly 5 miles southwest of Phipps Peak (lat. 38°54'30" N, long. 120°13' W; sec. 9, T 12 N, R 16 E). Named on Rockbound Valley (1955) 7.5' quadrangle.

Lake Number 3 [EL DORADO]: *lake,* 750 feet long, nearly 5 miles west-southwest of Phipps Peak (lat. 38°55'30" N, long. 120°13'45" W; at NE cor. sec. 5, T 12 N, R 16 E). Named on Rockbound Valley (1955) 7.5' quadrangle.

Lake of the Woods [EL DORADO]: *lake,* 0.5 mile long, 5.5 miles west-northwest of Echo Summit (lat. 38°51' N, long. 120°07'05" W; at NE cor. sec. 32, T 12 N, R 17 E). Named on Echo Lake (1955) 7.5' quadrangle.

Lake of the Woods [YUBA]: *marsh,* 10 miles south of Olivehurst near Feather River (lat. 38°56'50" N, long. 121°34'25" W). Named on Nicolaus (1952) 7.5' quadrangle.

Lake of the Woods [SIERRA]: *lake,* 1200 feet long, 6 miles south-southwest of Sierraville (lat. 39°30'15" N, long. 120°23'25" W; on N line sec. 22, T 19 N, R 14 E). Named on Sattley (1981) 7.5' quadrangle.

Lake Putt [PLACER]: *lake,* 1850 feet long, 1.25 miles southwest of Emigrant Gap (1) at the head of Blue Canyon (1) (lat. 38°17'25" N, long. 120°41'10" W; at S line sec. 36, T 17 N, R 11 E). Named on Blue Canyon (1955) 7.5' quadrangle.

Lake Schmidell [EL DORADO]: *lake,* 1600 feet long, 3.5 miles west-southwest of Phipps Peak (lat. 38°55'45" N, long. 120°12'30" W; sec. 33, T 13 N, R 16 E). Named on Rockbound Valley (1955) 7.5' quadrangle.

Lakeside: see **Stateline** [EL DORADO].

Lakeside Campground [NEVADA]: *locality,* 1.25 miles south-southeast of Hobart Mills (lat. 39°23'05" N, long. 120°10'15" W; sec. 26, T 18 N, R 16 E); the place is along Prosser Creek Reservoir. Named on Hobart Mills (1981) 7.5' quadrangle.

Lake Spaulding [NEVADA]: *lake,* behind a dam on South Yuba River 1.5 miles west-northwest of Yuba Gap (lat. 39°19'35" N, long. 120°38'30" W; at E line sec. 20, T 17 N, R 12 E). Named on Blue Canyon (1955) and Cisco Grove (1955) 7.5' quadrangles. The name commemorates John Spaulding, a water-company official (Stewart, p. 89).

Lake Sterling [NEVADA]: *lake,* 2850 feet long, 9 miles west-northwest of Donner Pass (lat. 39°21'20" N, long. 120°29'15" W; mainly in sec. 11, T 17 N, R 13 E). Named on Soda Springs (1955) 7.5' quadrangle.

Lake Sylvia [EL DORADO]: *lake,* 500 feet long, less than 1 mile west of Pyramid Peak (lat. 38°50'35" N, long. 120°10'20" W). Named on Pyramid Peak (1955) 7.5' quadrangle.

Lake Tabeaud [AMADOR]: *lake,* 0.5 mile long, 2 miles east of Jackson Butte (lat. 38°20'55" N, long. 120°39'45" W; sec. 28, T 6 N, R 12 E). Named on Mokelumne Hill (1948) 7.5' quadrangle. Called Tabeaud Reservoir on California Division of Highways' (1934) map, which also shows a smaller lake, called Petty Reservoir, in section 28.

Lake Tahoe [EL DORADO-PLACER]: *lake,* 21 miles long, 47 miles northeast of Placerville on California-Nevada State line in El Dorado County and Placer County of California (lat. 39°06' N, long. 120°30' W). Named on Emerald Bay (1955), Homewood (1955), Kings Beach (1955), Meeks Bay (1955), South Lake Tahoe (1955), and Tahoe City (1955) 7.5' quadrangles. Called L. Bonpland on Fremont's (1848) map, Mountain Lake on Gibbes' (1852) map, and Lake Bigler on Goddard's (1857) map. Fremont gave the feature the name "Bonpland" to honor Baron von Humbold's botanical associate, Aime Jacques Alexandre Bonpland (Farquhar, 1930, p. 87). Fremont (map following p. 246) also used the name "Mountain Lake" for the feature. The name "Bigler" was for John Bigler, governor of California in the 1850's (Gudde, 1949, p. 351). William H. Knight prepared a new map for H.H. Bancroft & Co. in 1863 and used the name "Lake Tahoe"—Knight reported that Henry DeGroot suggested the name "Tahoe" as one used by Indians to express the meaning "big water" or "high water" (Wheat, p. 71-72). DeGroot's (1853) map has the designation "Lake Tahoe or Bigler" for the feature.

Lake Tahoe: see **South Lake Tahoe** [EL DORADO[.

Lake Theodore [PLACER]: *lake,* 1550 feet long, 6.25 miles north-northeast of Auburn (lat. 38°58'30" N, long. 121°00'35" W; near SE cor. sec. 18, T 13 N, R 9 E). Named on Auburn (1953) 7.5' quadrangle.

Lake Valley [EL DORADO]: *valley,* extends for 8 miles south from Lake Tahoe along Upper Truckee River to Meyers; center 5.5 miles west-northwest of Freel Peak (lat. 38°53' N, long. 119°59'45" W). Named on Echo Lake (1955), Emerald Bay (1955), Freel Peak (1955), and South Lake Tahoe (1955) 7.5' quadrangles. The name was used as early as 1853 (Lekisch, p. 71). Day (p. 80) referred to Bigler Lake Valley in 1855.

Lake Valley: see **Lake Valley Reservoir** [PLACER]; **Tallac** [EL DORADO].

Lake Valley Reservoir [PLACER]: *lake,* behind a dam on North Fork of North Fork American River 3.25 miles west-southwest of Cisco Grove (lat. 39°18' N, long. 120°35'50" W; sec. 35, T 17 N, R 12 E). Named on Cisco Grove (1955) 7.5' quadrangle. Colfax (1898) 30' quadrangle shows Lake Valley at the site of the lake.

Lake Van Norden [NEVADA-PLACER]: *lake,* behind a dam on South Yuba River 2.5 miles west of Donner Pass on Nevada-Placer County line (lat. 39°19'15" N, long. 120°22'35" W; sec. 23, T 17 N, R 14 E). Named on Norden (1955) and Soda Springs (1955) 7.5' quadrangles. Truckee (1895) 30' quadrangle has the name "Summit Valley" for the valley now partly covered by the lake. The name "Van Norden" commemorates Charles Van Norden, who was a water-company official (Stewart, p. 89).

Lake Vera [NEVADA]: *lake,* 1100 feet long, 2.5 miles north of Nevada City along Rock Creek (1) (lat. 39°18'05" N, long. 121°01'35" W; at S line sec. 25, T 17 N, R 8 E). Named on Nevada City (1948) 7.5' quadrangle.

Lakeview: see **Lakeview Canyon** [PLACER].

Lakeview Canyon [PLACER]: *canyon,* 1 mile long, 2 miles east-northeast of Donner Pass (lat. 39°18'30" N, long. 120°17'15" W); the canyon opens into the valley of Donner Lake. Named on Norden (1955) 7.5' quadrangle. California Division of Highways' (1934) map shows a place called Lakeview located along Southern Pacific Railroad on the northwest side of present Lakeview Canyon (sec. 22, T 17 N, R 15 E—the section is misnumbered "21" on the map).

Lake Washington [YOLO]: *lake,* 1.5 miles southwest of downtown West Sacramento (lat. 38°33'20" N, long. 121°32'45" W). Named on Sacramento West (1967) 7.5' quadrangle. The lake is a remnant of a larger feature, called Washington Lake on Lovdal (1916) 7.5' quadrangle, that now is part of the turning basin at Port of Sacramento.

Lake Winifred [EL DORADO]: *lake,* 1100 feet long, 4 miles east of Wentworth Springs (lat. 39°00'05" N, long. 120°16'10" W; sec. 2, T 13 N, R 15 E). Named on Wentworth Springs (1953, photorevised 1973) 7.5' quadrangle.

Lake Zitella [EL DORADO]: *lake,* 800 feet long, 4 miles west of Phipps Peak (lat. 38°57'35" N, long. 120°13'30" W; near E line sec. 20, T 13 N, R 16 E). Named on Rockbound Valley (1955) 7.5' quadrangle.

La Mar Flat [NEVADA]: *area,* 2 miles east-southeast of Higgins Corner (lat. 39°01'40" N, long. 121°03'45" W; at NW cor. sec. 35, T 14 N, R 8 E). Named on Lake Combie (1949) 7.5' quadrangle.

Lambert [SACRAMENTO]: *locality,* 3.5 miles east of Courtland along Southern Pacific Railroad (lat. 38°19'15" N, long. 121°30'05" W). Named on Courtland (1952) 7.5' quadrangle. Called Glann on Vorden (1916) 7.5' quadrangle.

Lambert Hill [COLUSA]: *peak,* 13 miles north of Wilbur Springs (lat. 39°13'30" N, long. 122°26'15" W; sec. 20, T 16 N, R 5 W). Named on Wilbur Springs (1961) 15' quadrangle.

Lamb Hill [YUBA]: *ridge,* west-northwest-trending, 0.5 mile long, 4.5 miles south-southeast of Rackerby (lat. 39°22'45" N, long. 121° 17'45" W; on W line sec. 34, T 18 N, R 6 E). Named on Rackerby (1948) 7.5' quadrangle.

Lamb Valley [YOLO]: *valley,* 2.25 miles west-southwest of Esparto (lat. 38°41'15" N, long. 122°03'15" W). Named on Esparto (1959) 7.5' quadrangle.

Lamb Valley Slough [YOLO]: *stream,* flows nearly 4 miles to an artificial watercourse 1 mile west of Esparto (lat. 38°41'40" N, long. 122°02' W);

the stream goes through Lamb Valley. Named on Esparto (1959) 7.5' quadrangle.

Lancha Plana [AMADOR]: *locality,* 9 miles south-southeast of Ione on the north side of Mokeumne River (lat. 38°13'25" N, long. 120° 54'05" W; sec. 5, T 4 N, R 10 E). Named on Wallace (1962) 7.5' quadrangle. Water of Camanche Reservoir now covers the site. Messers. Kaiser and Winter came to the place in 1849 or 1850 and constructed a ferry made of empty whiskey barrels lashed to a timber frame; Mexicans referred to the ferry as *la lanche plana*—which means "the flat boat" in Spanish—and this term became the name of the community that grew at the ferry site (Andrews, p. 6). The place first was called Sonora Bar (Gudde, 1975, p. 190). Postal authorities established Lancha Plana post office in 1859, discontinued it in 1912, reestablished it in 1913, and discontinued it in 1919 (Frickstad, p. 5). Camp's (1962) map shows a place called Arkansas Ferry located about 1.5 miles northwest of Lancha Plana on Mokelumne River, a place called French Camp situated 2.25 miles northeast of Lancha Plana in a canyon north of Mokelumne River, and a place called Camp Union located nearly 2 miles northeast of Lancha Plana and just west of French Camp. The first settlers at French Camp were mainly of Gallic origin (Andrews, p. 24). A mining place called Camp O'pera was started near French Camp in the summer of 1849, when miners from Sonora dry washed gold there (Cook, F.S., a, p. 5; Andrews, p. 25). A mining camp of the 1850's called Chaparral Hill was located near Lancha Plana upstream along Mokelumne River; Chaparral Hill was the site of a river crossings called Judge Palmer's Bridge, Delaney's Bridge, Westmoreland's Ferry, and Westmoreland Bridge (Andrews, p. 115). Postal authorities established Pomegranate post office in 1888 and discontinued it in 1890; the name was from a pomegranate-growing project at the site (Salley, p. 175), which was about 4 miles west-northwest of Lancha Plana.

Lander: see **Lander Crossing** [PLACER].

Lander Crossing [PLACER]: *locality,* 2.5 miles south-southwest of Colfax along Southern Pacific Railroad (lat. 39°04'10" N, long. 120°58'40" W; sec. 16, T 14 N, R 9 E). Named on Colfax (1949) 7.5' quadrangle. Called Lander on Colfax (1938) 30' quadrangle. The name commemorates Frederick West Lander, who was chief engineer and superintendent for the overland wagon road in 1858 (Hanna, p. 167).

Landers Bar: see **Smartville** [YUBA].

Land Peak [SIERRA]: *peak,* 9 miles south-southeast of Loyalton (lat. 39°33'25" N, long. 120°11'20" W; sec. 27, T 20 N, R 16 E). Altitude 8030 feet. Named on Sardine Peak (1981) 7.5' quadrangle.

Lanes [AMADOR]: *locality,* 1.5 miles southeast of Ione along Amador Central Railroad (lat. 38°20'25" N, long. 120°54'50" W; near S line sec. 30, T 6 N, R 10 E). Named on Ione (1962) 7.5' quadrangle.

Lang Crossing [NEVADA]: *locality,* 2.25 miles west of Yuba Gap along South Yuba River (lat. 39°19'05" N, long. 120°39'25" W; near S line sec. 20, T 17 N, R 12 E). Named on Blue Canyon (1955) 7.5' quadrangle. Called Langs on Colfax (1898) 30' quadrangle. California Mining Bureau's (1917c) map shows a place called Drum located near present Lang Crossing.

Langenour [YOLO]: *locality,* 13 miles north of Davis along Southern Pacific Railroad (lat. 38°44'20" N, long. 121°44'50" W). Named on Grays Bend (1916) 7.5' quadrangle.

Langs: see **Lang Crossing** [NEVADA].

Langs Peak [YOLO]: *peak,* 6.25 miles west of Rumsey (lat. 38°54'05" N, long. 122°21'10" W). Named on Glascock Mountain (1958) 7.5' quadrangle.

Langville: see **Capay** [YOLO].

Laphams: see **State Line** [EL DORADO].

Larkin: see **Point Larkin**, under **Grand Island** [SACRAMENTO].

Larkins Childrens Rancho [COLUSA]: *land grant,* on the west side of Sacramento River on Colusa-Glenn County line. Named on Moulton Weir (1952) and Princeton (1952) 7.5' quadrangles. The three minor children of Thomas O. Larkin received 10 leagues in 1844 and claimed 44,364 acres patented in 1857 (Cowan, p. 44; Gudde, 1949, p. 182).

Larsen Landing [SACRAMENTO]: *locality,* 5.25 miles southwest of Isleton along San Joaquin River on Twitchell Island (lat. 38°05'55" N, long. 121°40'05" W). Named on Jersey (1910) 7.5' quadrangle.

Larsen Reservoir [EL DORADO]: *lake,* 925 feet long, 6 miles west of Pollock Pines in North Canyon (2) (lat. 38°45'25" N, long. 120° 41'40" W; sec. 36, T 11 N, R 11 E). Named on Slate Mountain (1950) 7.5' quadrangle.

Lasslys [YUBA]: *locality,* nearly 3 miles west of Woodville (present Woodleaf) (lat. 39°31'05" N, long. 121°14'40" W). Named on Bidwell Bar (1897) 30' quadrangle.

Last Chance [PLACER]: *locality,* 7.5 miles northeast of Michigan Bluff (lat. 39°06'35" N, long. 120°37'30" W; at S line sec. 27, T 15 N, R 12 E). Named on Greek Store (1952) and Michigan Bluff (1952) 7.5' quadrangles. Postal authorities established Last Chance post office in 1865, discontinued it in 1869, reestablished it in 1909, and discontinued it in 1919; the place also was known as Clifton (Salley, p. 119) and as Caroline Diggings (Gudde, 1975, p. 192).

Las Uvas: see **Harter**, under **Colusa Junction** [SUTTER].

Latrobe [EL DORADO]: *village,* 15 miles southwest of Placerville (lat. 38°33'35" N, long. 120°58'50" W; near SW cor. sec. 10, T 8 N, R 9 E). Named on Latrobe (1949) 7.5' quadrangle. California Mining Bureau's (1917c) map has the form "La Trobe" for the name. Postal authorities established Latrobe post office in 1864 and discontinued it in 1921 (Frickstad, p. 27). The village began as the terminus of Placerville and Sacramento Railroad; F.A. Bishop, chief engineer of the railroad, named the place to honor Benjamin H. Latrobe, chief engineer of Baltimore and Ohio Railroad, the first railroad in the United States (Gudde, 1949, p. 184).

Latrobe Creek [EL DORADO]: *stream,* flows 3.5 miles to Deer Creek (2) 4 miles south-southeast of Clarksville (lat. 38°36' N, long. 121°01'15" W; near SE cor. sec. 30, T 9 N, R 9 E); the stream heads near Latrobe. Named on Folsom SE (1954) and Latrobe (1949) 7.5' quadrangles. Called Corral Creek on Placerville (1893) 30' quadrangle.

Laumann Ridge [EL DORADO]: *ridge,* northwest-trending, 2 miles long, 3 mile north-northeast of Chili Bar (lat. 38°48'20" N, long. 120°48' W). Named on Garden Valley (1949) 7.5' quadrangle.

Lava: see **Volcanoville** [EL DORADO].

Lava Cap Reservoir [NEVADA]: *lake,* 6.25 miles north of Chicago Park (lat. 39°14'15" N, long. 120°58'15" W; sec. 21, T 16 N, R 9 E). Named on Chicago Park (1949) 7.5' quadrangle, which shows Lava Cap mine 0.5 mile south of the lake.

Lavezzola Creek [SIERRA]: *stream,* flows 13 miles to Downie River 1.5 miles north-northeast of Downieville (lat. 39°35' N, long. 120° 49'10" W; sec. 23, T 20 N, R 10 E). Named on Downieville (1951), Gold Lake (1981), and Mount Fillmore (1951) 7.5' quadrangles. Downieville (1951) 7.5' quadrangle shows Lavezzola ranch near the stream. Called Middle Fork of North Fork Yuba River on Downieville (1897) 30' quadrangle, but United States Board on Geographic Names (1950, p. 5) rejected this name for the stream, and also rejected the name "North Fork of North Fork" for the upper part of the stream.

Lawrenceberg: see **Kelsey** [EL DORADO].

Lawrence Lake [EL DORADO]: *lake,* 750 feet long, 5 miles southwest of Phipps Peak (lat. 38°54'35" N, long. 120°13'30" W; near NW cor. sec. 9, T 12 N, R 16 E). Named on Rockbound Valley (1955) 7.5' quadrangle.

Lawrence Mill [EL DORADO]: *locality,* 5 miles east-southeast of Aukum (lat. 38°32'05" N, long. 120°38'20" W; sec. 22, T 8 N, R 12 E). Site named on Aukum (1952) 7.5' quadrangle.

Lawson Canyon [COLUSA]: *canyon,* drained by a stream that flows 1 mile to the stream in South Jackson Canyon 6.25 miles southeast of Wilbur Springs (lat. 38°58'45" N, long. 122°20'15" W; near E line sec. 18, T 13 N, R 4 W). Named on Glascock Mountain (1958) 7.5' quadrangle.

Lawson Spring [YOLO]: *spring,* 3.25 miles south-southwest of Guinda (lat. 38°47'10" N, long. 122°12'55" W; sec. 20, T 11 N, R 3 W). Named on Guinda (1959) 7.5' quadrangle.

Lawyer Cow Camp [EL DORADO]: *locality,* 2.5 miles west of Wentworth Springs in Gerle Meadow (lat. 39°10' N, long. 120° 23' W; near W line sec. 35, T 14 N, R 14 E). Named on Bunker Hill (1953) 7.5' quadrangle.

LeConte: see **Lake LeConte** [EL DORADO].

Lee: see **Chandler** [SUTTER].

Lee Hill [YUBA]: *ridge,* north-northwest-trending, about 1 mile long, 1.25 miles west of Smartville (lat. 39°12'20" N, long. 121°19'10" W; sec. 29, 32, T 16 N, R 6 E). Named on Smartville (1951) 7.5' quadrangle.

Leek Spring [EL DORADO]: *spring,* nearly 2 miles east-northeast of Leek Spring Hill (lat. 38°38' N, long. 120°14'45" W). Named on Pyramid Peak (1896) 30' quadrangle. Some Mormon men on their way over the Sierra Nevada to Salt Lake City in 1848 named the spring for the wild onions there (Dillon *in* Burrows and Hall, p. 67).

Leek Spring Hill [EL DORADO]: *peak,* 16 miles south-southwest of Pyramid Peak (lat. 38°37'45" N, long. 120°16'35" W; near E line sec. 14, T 9 N, R 15 E); the peak is nearly 2 miles west-southwest of Leek Spring. Altitude 7621 feet. Named on Leek Spring Hill (1951) 7.5' quadrangle.

Leek Spring Valley [EL DORADO]: *valley,* 1.5 miles east of Leek Spring Hill on upper reaches of North Fork Cosumnes River (lat. 38°38' N, long. 120°15' W). Named on Leek Spring Hill (1951) and Tragedy Spring (1979) 7.5' quadrangles.

Leesville [COLUSA]: *locality,* 10.5 miles north of Wilbur Springs (lat. 39°11'20" N, long. 122°25'20" W; at N line sec. 4, T 15 N, R 5 W). Named on Wilbur Springs (1961) 15' quadrangle. Postal authorities established Leesville post office in 1874 and discontinued it in 1920; the name was for Lee Harl, pioneer landowner (Salley, p. 120). They established Epperson post office 4 miles south of Leesville in 1878 and discontinued it in 1899; the misspelled name was for Brutus E. Eperson, first postmaster (Salley, p. 70).

Leesville Gap [COLUSA]: *pass,* 10.5 miles north of Wilbur Springs (lat. 39°11'20" N, long. 122°25'20" W; at N line sec. 4, T 15 N, R 5 W); the feature is at Leesville. Named on Wilbur Springs (1961) 15' quadrangle.

Leland Lakes [EL DORADO]: *lakes,* largest 1000 feet long, 4 miles west-southwest of Phipps Peak (lat. 38°56'05" N, long. 120°13'05" W; sec. 33,

T 13 N, R 16 E). Named on Rockbound Valley (1955) 7.5' quadrangle.

Lemon Canyon [SIERRA]: *canyon,* drained by a stream that flows nearly 6 miles to Sierra Valley 1.5 miles east-southeast of Sierraville (lat 39°35' N, long. 120°20' W). Named on Sardine Peak (1981) and Sierraville (1981) 7.5' quadrangles.

Leonardi [EL DORADO]: *locality,* 9 miles north-northeast of Pollock Pines (lat. 38°52'55" N, long. 120°32'05" W; near SE cor. sec. 17, T 12 N, R 13 E). Named on Devil Peak (1950) 7.5' quadrangle.

Leonardi Spring [EL DORADO]: *spring,* 10.5 miles north of Pollock Pines (lat. 38°54'35" N, long. 120°32'45" W; at S line sec. 5, T 12 N, R 13 E). Named on Devil Peak (1950) 7.5' quadrangle.

Leoni Meadow [EL DORADO]: *area,* 4 miles east-northeast of Omo Ranch (lat. 38°36'30" N, long. 120°30'15" W; sec. 26, T 9 N, R 13 E). Named on Omo Ranch (1952) 7.5' quadrangle. Logan's (1938) map shows a place called Leonis Station located about 1 mile southwest of present Leoni Meadow along Diamond Caldor Railroad (at SE cor. sec. 27, T 9 N, R 13 E).

Leonis Station: see **Leoni Meadow** [EL DORADO].

Leta: see **Auburn** [PLACER].

Letts Creek [COLUSA]: *stream,* flows 2.5 miles to South Fork Stony Creek 4.25 miles west-southwest of Fouts Springs (lat. 39°19'30" N, long. 122°44'05" W; sec. 14, T 17 N, R 8 W). Named on Fouts Springs (1968) 7.5' quadrangle.

Letts Lake: see **Upper Letts Lake** [COLUSA].

Letts Ridge [COLUSA]: *ridge,* generally east-trending, 3 miles long, 3 miles south-southwest of Fouts Springs (lat. 39°19' N, long. 122° 41' W); the ridge is north and east of Lower Letts Valley. Named on Fouts Springs (1968) 7.5' quadrangle.

Letts Valley: see **Lower Letts Valley** [COLUSA]; **Upper Letts Valley** [COLUSA].

Levey Ditch Camp [NEVADA]: *locality,* 7 miles west-southwest of Yuba Gap (lat. 39°17'05" N, long. 120°44'25" W; sec. 4, T 16 N, R 11 E). Named on Blue Canyon (1955) 7.5' quadrangle.

Lewis: see **Arboga** [YUBA].

Lewis Campground [PLACER]: *locality,* 8 miles southwest of Granite Chief along Middle Fork American River in French Meadows (lat. 39°08'20" N, long. 120°24'30" W; near E line sec. 21, T 15 N, R 14 E). Named on Royal Gorge (1953) 7.5' quadrangle.

Lewisville: see **Greenwood** [EL DORADO].

Liars Flat: see **Rice Crossing** [NEVADA-YUBA].

Liases Flat: see **Rice Crossing** [NEVADA-YUBA].

Liberty Hill: see **Liberty Hill Diggings** [NEVADA].

Liberty Hill Diggings [NEVADA]: *locality,* 10 miles northeast of Chicago Park (lat. 39°14'05" N, long. 120°49'10" W; sec. 23, T 16 N, R 10 E). Named on Dutch Flat (1950) 7.5' quadrangle. Whitney's (1873) map shows a community called Liberty Hill at or near the site of present Liberty Hill Diggings, and a peak called Maguires Mt. located nearly 2 miles northeast of Liberty Hill.

Lichen Creek [EL DORADO]: *stream,* flows 3.5 miles to Greenwood Creek 3.5 miles northwest of Coloma (lat. 38°49'50" N, long. 120° 56'45" W; sec. 2, T 11 N, R 9 E). Named on Coloma (1949) 7.5' quadrangle.

Light Canyon [EL DORADO]:

(1) *canyon,* drained by a stream that flows 1.25 miles to South Fork American River 1.5 miles east of Chili Bar (lat. 38°46'10" N, long. 120°47'30" W; sec. 30, T 11 N, R 11 E); the canyon is 0.5 mile east of Dark Canyon (4). Named on Garden Valley (1949) 7.5' quadrangle.

(2) *canyon,* drained by a stream that flows 1.5 miles to Alder Creek 7.25 miles north-northwest of Leek Spring Hill (lat. 38°43'30" N, long. 120°20'15" W; near N line sec. 17, T 10 N, R 15 E). Named on Leek Spring Hill (1951) 7.5' quadrangle.

Lignite: see **Carbondale** [AMADOR].

Lily Lake [EL DORADO]: *lake,* 850 feet long, 2.25 miles south-southeast of Mount Tallac (lat. 38°52'30" N, long. 120°04'50" W). Named on Echo Lake (1955) and Emerald Bay (1955) 7.5' quadrangles.

Lily Lake [PLACER]: *lake,* 2000 feet long, nearly 4 miles south-southwest of Homewood (lat. 39°02'20" N, long. 120°11'20" W; on S line sec. 22, T 14 N, R 16 E). Named on Homewood (1955) 7.5' quadrangle.

Lily Pond [COLUSA]: *lake,* nearly 4 miles southwest of Fouts Springs in Lower Letts Valley (lat. 39°18'50" N, long. 122°42'35" W; sec. 24, T 17 N, R 8 W). Named on Fouts Springs (1968) 7.5' quadrangle.

Lily Pond [NEVADA]: *lake,* 300 feet long, 6.5 miles west-northwest of Donner Pass (lat. 39°21'55" N, long. 120°25'50" W; sec. 5, T 17 N, R 14 E). Named on Soda Springs (1955) 7.5' quadrangle.

Limekiln [EL DORADO]: *locality,* 1.25 miles north of Cool (lat. 38° 54'15" N, long. 121°00'50" W). Named on Sacramento (1892) 30' quadrangle.

Lime Rock [PLACER]: *relief feature,* 5 miles northeast of Auburn (lat. 38°56'55" N, long. 121°00'30" W; sec. 30, T 13 N, R 9 E). Named on Auburn (1953) 7.5' quadrangle.

Lincoln [PLACER]: *town,* 12 miles west of Auburn (lat. 38°53'30" N, long. 121°17'30" W; sec. 15, T 12 N, R 6 E). Named on Lincoln (1953) 7.5' quadrangle. Postal authorities established Lincoln post office in 1862 (Frickstad, p. 120), and the town incorporated in 1890. The name commemorates Charles Lincoln Wilson, head of the construction company that officials of California Central Railroad hired in 1858 to build a rail line from Sacramento to Marysville (Hanna, p. 171). California Mining Bureau's (1909a) map shows a place called Vantrent located 10 miles north of Lincoln by stage line. Postal authorities established Vantrent post office in 1904 and discontinued it in 1918 (Salley, p. 230). They established Cairns post office 11 miles northeast of Lincoln in 1906 and discontinued it in 1907 (Salley, p. 31).

Lincoln: see **Clinton** [AMADOR]; **Mount Lincoln** [PLACER].

Lincoln Creek [SIERRA]: *stream,* flows 5 miles to North Yuba River 7 miles northeast of Sierra City (lat. 39°37'10" N, long. 120° 31'20" W; near N line sec. 9, T 20 N, R 13 E); the stream goes through Lincoln Valley. Named on Haypress Valley (1981) and Sattley (1981) 7.5' quadrangles.

Lincoln Creek Campground [SIERRA]: *locality,* 7 miles northeast of Sierra City along North Yuba River (lat. 39°37'15" N, long. 120°31'25" W; at N line sec. 9, T 20 N, R 13 E); the place is near the mouth of Lincoln Creek. Named on Sierra City (1955) 15' quadrangle.

Lincoln Hill [EL DORADO]: *peak,* 10.5 miles east-southeast of Camino (lat. 38°39'45" N, long. 120°30'05" W; sec. 2, T 9 N, R 13 E). Named on Sly Park (1952) 7.5' quadrangle.

Lincoln Peak: see **Mount Lincoln** [PLACER].

Lincoln Valley [SIERRA]: *valley,* 7.5 miles east-northeast of Sierra City (lat. 39°35'30" N, long. 120°30' W); the valley is along Lincoln Creek. Named on Haypress Valley (1981) and Sattley (1981) 7.5' quadrangles.

Linda [YUBA]: *town,* 2 miles north-northwest of Olivehurst (lat. 39° 07'20" N, long. 121°33'50" W). Named on Olivehurst (1952) and Yuba City (1952) 7.5' quadrangles. The name recalls an early town called Linda, for the little steamboat *Linda,* that John Rose laid out in 1850 at the supposed head of navigation on Yuba River (Gudde, 1975, p. 194). Gibbes' (1852) map shows the original Linda on the south bank of the river above Marysville. The early town lasted about two years; the site now is buried beneath tailings from hydraulic-mining operations (Hoover, Rensch, and Rensch, p. 590).

Linda Creek [PLACER-SACRAMENTO]: *stream,* heads in Placer County and flows 9.5 miles, partly in Sacramento County, to Cirby Creek 1 mile south-southeast of downtown Roseville in Placer County (lat. 38°44'05" N, long. 121°16'30" W; sec. 12, T 10 N, R 6 E). Named on Citrus Heights (1967) and Folsom (1967) 7.5' quadrangles. The upper part of the stream is called Rock Creek on Sacramento (1892) 30' quadrangle. United States Board on Geographic Names (1933, p. 461) rejected the name "Dry Creek" for the stream, and later (1968a, p. 8) rejected the name "Cirby Creek" for it.

Linda Creek: see **Dry Creek** [PLACER-SACRAMENTO].

Lindsey Creek [NEVADA]: *stream,* flows 2.5 miles to Texas Creek 4.5 miles east-southeast of Graniteville (lat. 39°24'35" N, long. 120°40' W; sec. 19, T 18 N, R 12 E); the stream heads at Lindsey Lakes. Named on Graniteville (1982) 7.5' quadrangle.

Lindsey Lakes [NEVADA]: *lakes,* largest 1900 feet long, 6 miles east-southeast of Graniteville (lat. 39°24'45" N, long. 120°38' W; mainly in sec. 21, T 18 N, R 12 E). Named on Graniteville (1982) 7.5' quadrangle.

Lira [SUTTER]: *locality,* 6.5 miles west of Sutter along Sacramento Northern Railroad (lat. 39°08'40" N, long. 121°52' W). Named on Sutter Buttes (1954) 7.5' quadrangle.

Lisbon: see **Applegate** [PLACER]; **Arcade** [YOLO].

Lisbon Island: see **Arcade** [YOLO].

Little Alberts Lake: see **Elbert Lake** [EL DORADO].

Little Bald Mountain [EL DORADO]: *peak,* 3.5 miles north-northeast of Georgetown (lat. 38°57'10" N, long. 120°48'25" W; near N line sec. 25, T 13 N, R 10 E). Altitude 3083 feet. Named on Georgetown (1949) 7.5' quadrangle.

Little Bald Mountain [PLACER]: *ridge,* west-trending, 1.5 miles long, 1 mile southeast of Duncan Peak (lat. 39°08'45" N, long. 120°29'50" W). Named on Duncan Peak (1952) and Royal Gorge (1953) 7.5' quadrangles.

Little Bear Creek [PLACER]: *stream,* flows 4 miles to Bear River less than 1 mile north of Dutch Flat (lat. 39°12'55" N, long. 120° 50'25" W). Named on Colfax (1898) 30' quadrangle.

Little Bear River [AMADOR]: *stream,* flows 2.25 miles to Lower Bear Reservoir 6.5 miles east of Hams Station (lat. 38°33'15" N, long. 120°15'05" W; sec. 7, T 8 N, R 16 E). Named on Bear River Reservoir (1979) and Peddler Hill (1951) 7.5' quadrangles.

Little Blue Creek [SUTTER]: *stream,* heads east of Sutter Buttes and flows 9 miles to Sutter Basin 4 miles south of Sutter (lat. 39°05'45" N, long. 121°45'15" W; sec. 4, T 14 N, R 2 E). Named on Gilsizer Slough (1911) and Sutter (1911) 7.5' quadrangles.

Little Boulder Creek [SIERRA]: *stream,* flows 1 mile to Big Boulder Creek 10 miles north-northeast of Sierra City (lat. 39°41'50" N, long. 120°33'45" W; sec. 7, T 21 N, R 13 E). Named on Clio (1981) 7.5' quadrangle.

Little Bowman Lake: see **Bowman Lake** [NEVADA].

Little Brown Bear Creek [NEVADA]: *stream,* flows 1 mile to South Yuba River 3.5 miles west-southwest of Washington (lat. 39°20'35" N, long.

120°52' W; near NW cor. sec. 16, T 17 N, R 10 E). Named on Washington (1950) 7.5' quadrangle.

Little Buckeye Creek [YOLO]: *stream,* flows 12 miles to Buckeye Creek 13 miles east of Rumsey (lat. 38°55'15" N, long. 122°00'15" W; sec. 5, T 12 N, R 1 W). Named on Rumsey (1959) and Wildwood School (1959) 7.5' quadrangles.

Little Butte [EL DORADO]: *peak,* 8.5 miles southeast of Camino (lat. 38°39'55" N, long. 120°33'05" W; near NW cor. sec. 4, T 9 N, R 13 E). Altitude 3835 feet. Named on Sly Park (1952) 7.5' quadrangle. Little Butte, Middle Butte, and Big Butte together have the label "Buttes" on Placerville (1893) 30' quadrangle.

Little Canyon Creek [NEVADA]: *stream,* flows 3.5 miles to Canyon Creek 7.5 miles west-northwest of Yuba Gap (lat. 39°22'15" N, long. 120°44'15" W; near E line sec. 4, T 17 N, R 11 E). Named on Blue Canyon (1955) and Graniteville (1982) 7.5' quadrangles.

Little Canyon Creek [SIERRA]: *stream,* flows 7.5 miles to Canyon Creek 6 miles northwest of Goodyears Bar (lat. 39°36'50" N, long. 120°56'55" W; sec. 10, T 20 N, R 9 E). Named on Goodyears Bar (1951) and La Port (1951) 7.5' quadrangles. East Branch enters from the east 7 miles south-southwest of Mount Fillmore; it is 2 miles long and is named on La Porte (1951) 7.5' quadrangle.

Little Catfish Lake: see **Tollhouse Lake** [NEVADA].

Little Chief [PLACER]: *peak,* 6 miles north-northwest of Tahoe City (lat. 39°14'40" N, long. 120°12'05" W; near SE cor. sec. 9, T 16 N, R 16 E); the peak is 0.5 mile northwest of Big Chief. Altitude 7255 feet. Named on Tahoe City (1955) 7.5' quadrangle.

Little China Gulch [AMADOR]: *canyon,* nearly 2 miles long, opens into China Gulch (1) 8 miles south of Ione (lat. 38°13'55" N, long. 120°54'50" W; sec. 6, T 4 N, R 10 E). Named on Wallace (1962) 7.5' quadrangle. Water of Camanche Reservoir covers the lower part of the canyon.

Little Clipper Creek [NEVADA]: *stream,* flows nearly 2 miles to Clipper Creek 4.5 miles north of Chicago Park (lat. 39°12'35" N, long. 120°58' W; sec. 33, T 16 N, R 9 E). Named on Chicago Park (1949) 7.5' quadrangle.

Little Codfish Creek [PLACER]: *stream,* flows nearly 2 miles to Codfish Creek 6.5 miles south of Colfax (lat. 39°00'10" N, long. 120°57'15" W; sec. 3, T 13 N, R 9 E). Named on Colfax (1949) 7.5' quadrangle.

Little Crater [PLACER]: *relief feature,* 10 miles south-southwest of Duncan Peak (lat. 39°01'10" N, long. 120°33'30" W; near W line sec. 32, T 14 N, R 13 E); the feature is 2.5 miles east-northeast of Big Crater. Named on Greek Store (1952) 7.5' quadrangle.

Little Deer Creek [EL DORADO]: *stream,* flows 2.5 miles to Deer Creek (1) 5 miles west of Wentworth Springs (lat. 39°00'10" N, long. 120°25'50" W; sec. 5, T 13 N, R 14 E). Named on Bunker Hill (1953) 7.5' quadrangle.

Little Deer Creek [NEVADA]: *stream,* flows 4.25 miles to Deer Creek in downtown Nevada City (lat. 39°15'45" N, long. 121°00'55" W; near W line sec. 7, T 16 N, R 9 E). Named on Chicago Park (1949), Nevada City (1948), and North Bloomfield (1949) 7.5' quadrangles. Gudde (1975, p. 53) listed a place called Bunkerville that was located 0.5 mile south of Nevada City along Little Deer Creek.

Little Deer Creek [SACRAMENTO]: *stream,* flows 4.5 miles to Deer Creek 9.5 miles south-southeast of Folsom (lat. 38°32'50" N, long. 121°06'50" W; near E line sec. 17, T 8 N, R 8 E). Named on Folsom SE (1954) 7.5' quadrangle.

Little Deer Lake [SIERRA]: *lake,* 900 feet long, 8 miles north-northwest of Sierra City (lat. 39°40'15" N, long. 120°41'20" W; sec. 24, T 21 N, R 11 E). Named on Gold Lake (1981) 7.5' quadrangle.

Little Dry Creek [NEVADA]: *stream,* flows nearly 6 miles to Dry Creek (2) 6 miles southwest of Pilot Peak (lat. 39°06'50" N, long. 121°16'05" W; near NE cor. sec. 35, T 15 N, R 6 E). Named on Camp Far West (1949), Rough and Ready (1949), and Smartville (1951) 7.5' quadrangles.

Little Dry Creek [YUBA]: *stream,* flows 6 miles to Dry Creek (1) nearly 1 mile east of Browns Valley (lat. 39°14'35" N, long. 121° 23'30" W; sec. 15, T 16 N, R 5 E). Named on Browns Valley (1947) and Loma Rica (1947) 7.5' quadrangles.

Little Duncan Canyon [PLACER]: *canyon,* drained by a stream that flows 2.5 miles to Duncan Canyon 11 miles west-southwest of Granite Chief (lat. 39°08'30" N, long. 120°28'15" W; at S line sec. 13, T 15 N, R 13 E). Named on Royal Gorge (1953, photorevised 1973) 7.5' quadrangle. Called Little Duncan on Granite Chief (1953) 15' quadrangle. On Truckee (1940) 30' quadrangle, the stream in the canyon is called Little Duncan Creek.

Little Duncan Creek: see **Little Duncan Canyon** [PLACER].

Little Fiddle Creek [SIERRA]: *stream,* flows nearly 3 miles to Fiddle Creek 3.5 miles west of Goodyears Bar (lat. 39°32'05" N, long. 120°57'05" W; at N line sec. 10, T 19 N, R 9 E). Named on Goodyears Bar (1951) 7.5' quadrangle.

Little Gambler Creek [EL DORADO]: *stream,* flows 0.5 mile to Gambler Creek less than 1 mile north of Coloma (lat. 38°48'40" N, long. 120°53'30" W; at N line sec. 17, T 11 N, R 10 E). Named on Coloma (1949) 7.5' quadrangle.

Little Gold Lake [SIERRA]: *lake,* 750 feet long, 7 miles north-northwest of Sierra City (lat. 39°40' N, long. 120°39'55" W; near E line sec. 19, T 21 N, R 12 E); the lake is 700 feet south of Gold Lake. Named on Gold Lake (1981) 7.5' quadrangle.

Little Granite Canyon: see **Little Granite Creek** [PLACER].

Little Granite Creek [PLACER]: *stream,* flows 5 miles to Big Granite Creek 5 miles north of Duncan Peak (lat. 39°13'40" N, long. 120°31'20" W; near N line sec. 28, T 16 N, R 13 E). Named on Cisco Grove (1955) and Duncan Peak (1952) 7.5' quadrangles. On Colfax (1898) 30' quadrangle, the canyon of the stream is called Little Granite Canyon.

Little Greenhorn Creek [NEVADA]: *stream,* flows 4.5 miles to Greenhorn Creek 3.25 miles north-northeast of Chicago Park (lat. 39°11'20" N, long. 120°56'25" W; sec. 2, T 15 N, R 9 E). Named on Chicago Park (1949) 7.5' quadrangle.

Little Grizzly Canyon [PLACER]: *canyon,* drained by a stream that flows 2 miles to Rubicon River 3 miles west-southwest of Devil Peak (lat. 38°56'10" N, long. 120°35'35" W; near W line sec. 36, T 13 N, R 12 E). Named on Devil Peak (1950) 7.5' quadrangle. On Placerville (1893) 30' quadrangle, the name applies to a branch of present Big Grizzly Canyon.

Little Grizzly Creek [PLACER]: *stream,* flows 1.5 miles to Deep Canyon 5.25 miles southwest of Duncan Peak (lat. 39°06'35" N, long. 120°35'15" W; sec. 36, T 15 N, R 12 E). Named on Greek Store (1952) 7.5' quadrangle.

Little Grizzly Creek [SIERRA]: *stream,* flows nearly 2 miles to Big Grizzly Creek 2.5 miles south of Mount Fillmore (lat. 39°41'35" N, long. 120°50'30" W). Named on Mount Fillmore (1951) 7.5' quadrangle.

Little Holland Tract [YOLO]: *area,* 10 miles southwest of Clarksburg in Yolo Bypass on Yolo-Solano County line (lat. 38°18'50" N, long. 121°39'15" W). Named on Liberty Island (1978) 7.5' quadrangle.

Little Horseshoe Bar: see **Horseshoe Bar** [EL DORADO-PLACER] (2).

Little Humbug Creek [SIERRA]: *stream,* flows nearly 2 miles to Humbug Creek 4.25 miles southwest of Goodyears Bar (lat. 39°30'30" N, long. 120°57' W; sec. 15, T 19 N, R 9 E). Named on Goodyears Bar (1951) and Pike (1949) 7.5' quadrangles.

Little Indian Creek [AMADOR]: *stream,* flows 12.5 miles to Cosumnes River 12 miles north-northwest of Ione (lat. 38°30'40" N, long. 121°00'50" W; sec. 32, T 8 N, R 9 E). Named on Amador City (1962), Carbondale (1968), and Irish Hill (1962) 7.5' quadrangles. Called Indian Creek on Jackson (1902) 30' quadrangle, and called South Indian Creek on Folsom SE (1954) 7.5' quadrangle, but United States Board on Geographic Names (1964, p. 11) rejected both names for the stream.

Little Indian Creek [COLUSA]: *stream,* flows 6.25 miles to Indian Creek less than 1 mile south of Lodoga (lat. 39°17'20" N, long. 122°29'20" W; at NE cor. sec. 35, T 17 N, R 6 W). Named on Lodoga (1960) and Wilbur Springs (1961) 15' quadrangles.

Little Indian Creek [EL DORADO]: *stream,* flows nearly 6 miles to Big Canyon Creek 3 miles east-southeast of Latrobe (lat. 38°33' N, long. 120°55'50" W; sec. 13, T 8 N, R 9 E). Named on Latrobe (1949) 7.5' quadrangle.

Little Indian Creek [PLACER]: *stream,* flows 1.25 miles to Indian Creek (2) 6.5 miles north of Foresthill (lat. 39°07'05" N, long. 120° 49'55" W; sec. 27, T 15 N, R 10 E). Named on Foresthill (1949) 7.5' quadrangle.

Little Iowa Canyon: see **Brushy Canyon** [EL DORADO] (1).

Little Kanaka Creek: see **North Fork**, under **Kanaka Creek** [SIERRA].

Little Ladies Canyon [SIERRA]: *canyon,* drained by a stream that flows 1.5 miles to Ladies Canyon 4.5 miles west of Sierra City (lat. 39°34'10" N, long. 120°43'05" W; near E line sec. 27, T 20 N, R 11 E). Named on Sierra City (1981) 7.5' quadrangle.

Little Mad Canyon [PLACER]: *canyon,* drained by a stream that flows 1 mile to Mad Canyon 3 miles east of Foresthill (lat. 39°00'50" N, long. 120°45'55" W; sec. 32, T 14 N, R 11 E). Named on Foresthill (1949) 7.5' quadrangle.

Little McKinstry Meadow [PLACER]: *area,* 3.5 miles east of Bunker Hill (lat. 39°02'55" N, long. 120°18'45" W; near NE cor. sec. 20, T 14 N, R 15 E); the place is 1.5 miles east-northeast of McKinstry Meadow. Named on Wentworth Springs (1953) 7.5' quadrangle.

Little Mill Creek [AMADOR]: *stream,* flows 2.25 miles to Mill Creek 9 miles east-northeast of Pine Grove (lat. 38°27'45" N, long. 120°30'20" W; sec. 14, T 7 N, R 13 E). Named on Devils Nose (1979) 7.5' quadrangle.

Little Mosquito Creek [PLACER]: *stream,* flows 1.25 miles to Big Mosquito Creek 9 miles south-southwest of Duncan Peak (lat. 39° 02'45" N, long. 120°36'05" W; sec. 23, T 14 N, R 12 E). Named on Greek Store (1952) 7.5' quadrangle.

Little Mountain [EL DORADO]: *peak,* 1.5 miles east-northeast of Omo Ranch (lat. 38°35'30" N, long. 120°32'30" W; sec. 33, T 9 N, R 13 E). Named on Omo Ranch (1952) 7.5' quadrangle.

Little Mountain Meadow [PLACER]: *area,* 1 mile north-northwest of Bunker Hill (lat. 39°03'45" N, long. 120°23'05" W; on W line sec. 14, T 14 N, R 14 E). Named on Bunker Hill (1953) 7.5' quadrangle.

Little Needle Lake [PLACER]: *lake,* 450 feet long, 1.25 miles south-southwest of Granite Chief (lat. 39°10'50" N, long. 120°17'55" W; sec. 4, T 15 N, R 15 E); the lake is 1.25 miles south of Needle Lake. Named on Granite Chief (1953) 7.5' quadrangle.

Little New York: see **Little York** [NEVADA].
Little North Fork: see **North Fork of North Fork**, under **Sacramento River** [EL DORADO-PLACER-SACRAMENTO].
Little Norway: see **Meyers** [EL DORADO].
Little Oak Flat [PLACER]: *area,* 3.5 miles east of Michigan Bluff on Mosquito Ridge (lat. 39°02' N, long. 120°40'15" W; on W line sec. 29, T 14 N, R 12 E); the place is 2 miles south-southwest of Big Oak Flat. Named on Michigan Bluff (1952) 7.5' quadrangle. Colfax (1938) 30' quadrangle shows the place situated 1 mile farther northeast (sec. 20, T 14 N, R 12 E) at the site of present Ditch Camp.
Little Oregon Creek [YUBA]: *stream,* flows 4 miles to New Bullards Bar Reservoir 5.25 miles southeast of Challenge (lat. 39° 25'40" N, long. 121°09'35" W; near S line sec. 11, T 18 N, R 7 E). Named on Challenge (1948, photorevised 1969) 7.5' quadrangle. On Smartsville (1895) 30' quadrangle, the canyon of the stream is called Rich Gulch.
Little Pebble Canyon [EL DORADO]: *canyon,* drained by a stream that flows 1 mile to Big Pebble Canyon 2.25 miles west-southwest of Old Iron Mountain (lat. 38°41'40" N, long. 120°25'50" W; sec. 28, T 10 N, R 14 E). Named on Stump Spring (1951) 7.5' quadrangle.
Little Poker Bend [SUTTER-YOLO]: *bend,* less than 1 mile southwest of Kirkville along Sacramento River on Sutter-Yolo County line (lat. 38°54'05" N, long. 121°48'05" W; near E line sec. 12, T 12 N, R 1 E); the feature is 2.5 miles downstream from Poker Bend. Named on Kirkville (1952) 7.5' quadrangle.
Little Powderhorn Creek [PLACER]: *stream,* flows 1.5 miles to Five Lakes Creek 5.5 miles northeast of Bunker Hill (lat. 39°06' N, long. 120°18'10" W; sec. 33, T 15 N, R 15 E); the mouth of the stream is less than 1 mile southwest of the mouth of Powderhorn Creek. Named on Wentworth Springs (1953) 7.5' quadrangle.
Little Rattlesnake Bar: see **Auburn** [PLACER].
Little Reservoir [EL DORADO]: *lake,* 350 feet long, 2 miles south-southwest of Omo Ranch (lat. 38°33'15" N, long. 120°34'55" W; near S line sec. 7, T 8 N, R 13 E); the lake is 1.5 miles west-northwest of Big Reservoir. Named on Omo Ranch (1952) 7.5' quadrangle.
Little Robertson Valley: see **Little Robinsons Valley** [PLACER].
Little Robinsons Valley [PLACER]: *valley,* 11.5 miles west-southwest of Granite Chief (lat. 39°09'10" N, long. 120°29'35" W; near N line sec. 14, T 15 N, R 13 E); the valley is 0.5 mile southeast of Robinsons Flat. Named on Royal Gorge (1953) 7.5' quadrangle. United States Board on Geographic Names (1961, p. 11) rejected the name "Little Robertson Valley" for the feature.
Little Rock Creek [SIERRA]: *stream,* flows 1.25 miles to Rock Creek (1) 7.25 miles west-northwest of Goodyears Bar (lat. 39°35'10" N, long. 121°00'30" W; sec. 19, T 20 N, R 9 E). Named on Strawberry Valley (1948) 7.5' quadrangle.
Little Round Top [EL DORADO]: *peak,* nearly 3 miles north-northeast of Kirkwood (lat. 38°44'25" N, long. 120°03' W; near W line sec. 6, T 10 N, R 18 E). Altitude 9590 feet. Named on Caples Lake (1979) 7.5' quadrangle.
Little Sage Hill [PLACER]: *ridge,* west-trending, less that 1 mile long, 4.5 miles south-southwest of Colfax (lat. 39°02'45" N, long. 121°00'10" W; mainly in sec. 20, T 14 N, R 9 E). Named on Colfax (1949) and Lake Combie (1949) 7.5' quadrangles.
Little Sailor Creek [EL DORADO]: *stream,* flows 0.5 mile to Big Sailor Creek 4.5 miles north-northwest of Chili Bar (lat. 38°49'35" N, long. 120°50'45" W; sec. 3, T 11 N, R 10 E). Named on Garden Valley (1949) 7.5' quadrangle.
Little Salt Canyon [YOLO]: *canyon,* drained by a stream that flows 1.5 miles to Salt Canyon 4.25 miles east of Guinda (lat. 38°50' N, long. 122°06'55" W; near W line sec. 5, T 11 N, R 2 W). Named on Bird Valley (1959) and Guinda (1959) 7.5' quadrangles.
Little Secret Canyon [PLACER]: *canyon,* drained by a stream that flows 2.25 miles to Secret Canyon 4 miles west-northwest of Duncan Peak (lat. 39°10'35" N, long. 120°34'55" W; sec. 1, T 15 N, R 12 E). Named on Duncan Peak (1952) 7.5' quadrangle.
Little Shady Creek [NEVADA]: *stream,* flows 2.5 miles to South Yuba River 1.5 miles east-southeast of French Corral (lat. 39°17'40" N, long. 121°08'15" W; sec. 36, T 17 N, R 7 E). Named on French Corral (1948) and Nevada City (1948) 7.5' quadrangles.
Little Shady Creek: see **Blind Shady Creek** [NEVADA].
Little Silver Creek [EL DORADO]:
(1) *stream,* flows 2.5 miles to Rock Creek 12.5 miles northwest of Pollock Pines (lat. 38°53'10" N, long. 120°44'40" W; near W line sec. 15, T 12 N, R 11 E). Named on Georgetown (1949) and Tunnel Hill (1950) 7.5' quadrangles.
(2) *stream,* flows 6 miles to Silver Creek 6.5 miles north of Riverton (lat. 38°51'55" N, long. 120°26'55" W; near N line sec. 30, T 12 N, R 14 E). Named on Riverton (1950, photorevised 1973) and Robbs Peak (1950) 7.5' quadrangles.
Little Slate Creek: see **Slate Creek** [SIERRA-YUBA].
Little Sluice Box [EL DORADO]: *relief feature,* 3.5 miles east of Wentworth Springs (lat. 39°01'10" N, long. 120°16'25" W; near NE cor. sec. 34, T 14 N, R 15 E); the feature is 1 mile northwest of Big Sluice Box. Named on Wentworth Springs (1953) 7.5' quadrangle.
Little Soldier Creek [EL DORADO]: *stream,* flows 1.25 miles to Soldier Creek 3.5 miles northeast of Pollock Pines (lat. 38°47'40" N, long. 120°32' W; sec. 16, T 11 N, R 13 E). Named on Pollock Pines (1950) 7.5' quadrangle.
Little South Fork Rubicon River: see **South Fork**, under **Rubicon River** [EL DORADO].
Little Steamboat Mountain [PLACER]: *peak,* 4 miles north-northeast of Bunker Hill (lat. 39°05'55" N, long. 120°20'55" W; near SE cor. sec. 36, T 15 N, R 14 E); the peak is 1 mile south-southeast of Steamboat Mountain. Named on Wentworth Springs (1953) 7.5' quadrangle.
Little Stony: see **Stonyford** [COLUSA].
Little Stony Creek [COLUSA]: *stream,* flows 20 miles to Glenn County 1.5 miles east-northeast of Stonyford (lat. 39°23'05" N, long. 122°31' W; sec. 27, T 18 N, R 6 W); the stream joins Stony Creek in Glenn County. Named on Fouts Springs (1968), Gilmore Peak (1968), and Stonyford (1968) 7.5' quadrangles.
Little Sugar Pine Mountain [EL DORADO]: *peak,* 7 miles north of Pollock Pines (lat. 38°51'45" N, long. 120°35'55" W; sec. 26, T 12 N, R 12 E). Altitude 4914 feet. Named on Pollock Pines (1950) 7.5' quadrangle.
Little Sullivan Creek [COLUSA]: *stream,* flows 2.5 miles to Sullivan Creek 7 miles south-southwest of Stonyford (lat. 39°17'15" N, long. 122°36'50" W). Named on Fouts Springs (1968) and Gilmore Peak (1968) 7.5' quadrangles.
Little Sullivan Ridge [COLUSA]: *ridge,* east-southeast- to east-trending, 1.5 miles long, 4.5 miles south-southeast of Fouts Springs (lat. 39°17'35" N, long. 122°38'20" W); the ridge is south of Little Sullivan Creek. Named on Fouts Springs (1968) 7.5' quadrangle.
Little Sulphur Canyon [COLUSA]: *canyon,* drained by a stream that flows nearly 2 miles to Pocket Canyon 10 miles southeast of Wilbur Springs (lat. 38°56'35" N, long. 122°17'05" W; near E line sec. 27, T 13 N, R 4 W); Little Sulphur Spring is in the canyon. Named on Glascock Mountain (1958) 7.5' quadrangle.
Little Sulphur Spring [COLUSA]: *spring,* 9 miles southeast of Wilbur Springs (lat. 38°56'30" N, long. 122°18'10" W; near E line sec. 28, T 13 N, R 4 W). Named on Glascock Mountain (1958) 7.5' quadrangle.
Little Table Rock [SIERRA]: *peak,* 3.5 miles southwest of Mount Fillmore (lat. 39°42' N, long. 120°54'30" W; near NW cor. sec. 7, T 21 N, R 10 E); the peak is 1.5 miles west of Table Rock. Named on La Porte (1951) 7.5' quadrangle.
Little Tiger Creek [AMADOR]: *stream,* flows nearly 3 miles to Tiger Creek 4.25 miles southwest of Hames Station (lat. 38°29'55" N, long. 120°25'50" W; sec. 33, T 8 N, R 14 E). Named on Caldor (1951) 7.5' quadrangle.
Little Truckee Lake: see **Webber Lake** [SIERRA].
Little Truckee River [NEVADA-SIERRA]: *stream,* heads in Sierra County and flows 28 miles to Truckee River 6.25 miles northeast of Truckee in Nevada County (lat. 39°23'05" N, long. 120°05'35" W; sec. 28, T 18 N, R 17 E); the stream heads at Webber Lake, which first was called Little Truckee Lake (Gudde, 1949, p. 385). Named on Boca (1955), Hobart Mills (1981), Independence Lake (1981), Sierraville (1981), and Webber Peak (1981) 7.5' quadrangles. According to Morgan (p. 377), James Clyman called the stream the Wind River in 1846.
Little Truckee Summit [SIERRA]: *pass,* 7.25 miles southeast of Sierraville at the head of Cold Stream (1) (lat. 39°30'20" N, long. 120°16'55" W; at S line sec. 11, T 19 N, R 15 E). Named on Sierraville (1981) 7.5' quadrangle.
Little Valley [COLUSA]: *valley,* 5 miles long, along Freshwater Creek above a point 3.25 miles north-northeast of Wilbur Springs (lat. 39°04'55" N, long. 122°23'30" W). Named on Wilbur Springs (1961) 15' quadrangle.
Little Valley: see **McNair Meadow** [SIERRA].
Little Wallace Canyon [PLACER]: *canyon,* drained by a stream that flows 2.5 miles to Wallace Canyon 1.25 miles north of Devil Peak (lat. 38°58'40" N, long. 120°33' W; sec. 17, T 13 N, R 13 E). Named on Devil Peak (1950) 7.5' quadrangle.
Little Willow Creek [YUBA]: *stream,* flows 2.25 miles to Moonshine Creek nearly 5 miles southwest of Camptonville (lat. 39°23'55" N, long. 121°05'55" W; near E line sec. 29, T 18 N, R 8 E). Named on Camptonville (1948) 7.5' quadrangle.
Little Wolf Creek [NEVADA]:
(1) *stream,* flows 2.5 miles to Wolf Creek 1 mile south-southwest of downtown Grass Valley (lat. 39°12'15" N, long. 121°04' W; sec. 34, T 16 N, R 8 E). Named on Grass Valley (1949) 7.5' quadrangle.
(2) *stream,* flows 9.5 miles to Bear River 5.5 miles west-southwest of Wolf (lat. 39°01'30" N, long. 121°13'55" W; sec. 31, T 14 N, R 7 E). Named on Wolf (1949) 7.5' quadrangle.
Little Wolf Creek [SIERRA]: *stream,* flows 2.25 miles to Wolf Creek 3.5 miles east of Alleghany (lat. 39°27'55" N, long. 120°46'35" W; near SE cor. sec. 31, T 19 N, R 11 E). Named on Alleghany (1949) 7.5' quadrangle.
Little York [NEVADA]: *locality,* 6 miles northeast of present Chicago Park

(lat. 39°11'35" N, long. 120°52'25" W). Named on Colfax (1898) 30' quadrangle. Postal authorities established Little York post office in 1855, discontinued it the same year, reestablished it in 1856, and discontinued it in 1886; the place first was called Little New York, but postal authorities shortened the name (Salley, p. 123).

Little York Diggings [NEVADA]: *locality,* 5.5 miles northeast of Chicago Park (lat. 39°12' N, long. 120°52'35" W; sec. 5, T 15 N, R 10 E). Named on Chicago Park (1949) and Dutch Flat (1950) 7.5' quadrangles.

Live Oak [SACRAMENTO]: *locality,* 24 miles east-southeast of downtown Sacramento (lat. 38°29' N, long. 121°04'25" W; near SW cor. sec. 2, T 7 N, R 8 E). Named on Carbondale (1968) 7.5' quadrangle. Carbondale (1909) 7.5' quadrangle has the form "Liveoak" for the name.

Live Oak [SUTTER]: *town,* 9.5 miles north-northwest of Yuba City (lat. 39°16'35" N, long. 121°39'30" W). Named on Gridley (1952) 7.5' quadrangle. Postal authorities established Live Oak post office in 1874 (Frickstad, p. 202), and the town incorporated in 1947. California Division of Highways' (1934) map shows a place called Walton located 1.5 miles south of Live Oak along Sacramento Northern Railroad.

Live Oak Bar: see **Coloma** [EL DORADO].

Live Oak Ravine [PLACER]: *canyon,* drained by a stream that flows 2 miles to Bunch Canyon 3.5 miles south-southeast of Colfax (lat. 39°03' N, long. 120°56'05" W; sec. 23, T 14 N, R 9 E). Named on Colfax (1949) 7.5' quadrangle. Colfax (1898) 30' quadrangle has the form "Liveoak Ravine" for the name.

Live Oak Slough [SUTTER]: *stream,* enters from Butte County 2 miles north of Live Oak and flows 7.5 miles in Sutter County past Live Oak to a canal 5 miles north-northwest of Yuba City (lat. 39° 12'30" N, long. 121°39'35" W; sec. 29, T 16 N, R 3 E). Named on Gridley (1952) and Sutter (1952) 7.5' quadrangles.

Lizard Flat: see **Jefferson Creek** [NEVADA].

Loafer Gulch: see **Fiddletown** [AMADOR].

Loch Lane [AMADOR]: *lake,* 3350 feet long, nearly 4 miles west of Ione (lat. 38°21'40" N, long. 121°00'10" W). Named on Goose Creek (1968) and Ione (1962) 7.5' quadrangles.

Loch Leven Lakes [PLACER]: *lakes,* largest 1750 feet long, 2.5 miles southeast of Cisco Grove (lat. 39°17'10" N, long. 120°30'10" W; sec. 34, T 17 N, R 13 E, and sec. 3, T 16 N, R 13 E). Named on Cisco Grove (1955) 7.5' quadrangle. Called Lac Leven Lakes on Colfax (1938) 30' quadrangle, but United States Board on Geographic Names (1962c, p. 20) rejected this name.

Locke [SACRAMENTO]: *town,* 0.5 mile north-northeast of Walnut Grove along Sacramento River (lat. 38°15' N, long. 121°30'30" W). Named on Courtland (1978) and Isleton (1978) 7.5' quadrangles. Chinese people moved to the place after their homes in Walnut Grove burned in 1915; Locke was the only all-Chinese town in California (Dillon, p. 109-110). California Division of Highways' (1934) map shows a place called Mofuba located about 1 mile north-northeast of Locke along Southern Pacific Railroad.

Lockwood [AMADOR]: *locality,* 7 miles northeast of Pine Grove (lat. 38°29'40" N, long. 120°34'45" W). Named on Jackson (1902) 30' quadrangle. Camp's (1962) map shows Lockwood Station, and gives the name "Fosters" as an alternate designation for the place. Wheeler (1879, p. 177) listed Foster's Station and called it a public house. Salley (p. 202) noted that postal authorities established Shake Ridge post office at the site in 1875 and discontinued it in 1878; the post office name was from the manufacture of shakes in the neighborhood.

Lockwood Station: see **Lockwood** [AMADOR].

Lodgepole Campground [SIERRA]: *locality,* 5.5 miles northeast of Sierra City along North Yuba River (lat. 39°37'45" N, long. 120° 34'10" W; sec. 1, T 20 N, R 12 E). Named on Clio (1981) 7.5' quadrangle.

Lodoga [COLUSA]: *village,* 16 miles west of Maxwell (lat. 39°18'05" N, long. 122°29'20" W; on W line sec. 25, T 17 N, R 6 W). Named on Lodoga (1960) 15' quadrangle. Postal authorities established Lodoga post office in 1898, discontinued it in 1913, reestablished it the same year, discontinued it in 1917, reestablished it in 1924, and discontinued it in 1951 (Frickstad, p. 19). California Mining Bureau's (1910) map shows a place called Zachary located about 4 miles north-northwest of Lodoga (about sec. 3, T 17 N, R 6 W). Postal authorities established Zachary post office in 1900 and discontinued it in 1906 (Frickstad, p. 20).

Lodoga Peak [COLUSA]: *peak,* 4.5 miles southeast of Lodoga (lat. 39°15'25" N, long. 122°25'20" W; sec. 9, T 16 N, R 5 W). Altitude 2441 feet. Named on Lodoga (1960) 15' quadrangle.

Logan Canyon [NEVADA]: *canyon,* drained by a stream that flows 3.25 miles to South Yuba River 3 miles west-southwest of Washington (lat. 39°20'50" N, long. 120°51'10" W; near SE cor. sec. 9, T 17 N, R 10 E). Named on Alleghany (1949) and Washington 1950) 7.5' quadrangles.

Logan Creek [COLUSA]: *stream,* heads in Glenn County and flows 5 miles in Colusa County to a ditch 7 miles northeast of Maxwell (lat. 39°20'30" N, long. 122°05'45" W). Named on Logandale (1952), Maxwell (1952), and Moulton Weir (1952) 7.5' quadrangles.

Logan Ridge [COLUSA]: *ridge,* south-trending, 2 miles long, 5.25 miles north of Sites on Colusa-Glenn County line (lat. 39°23' N, long. 122°19'30" W). Named on Logan Ridge (1958) and Sites (1958) 7.5' quadrangles.

Loganville [SIERRA]: *locality,* nearly 2 miles west of Sierra City (lat. 39°34'05" N, long. 120°40' W; sec. 30, T 20 N, R 12 E). Named on Sierra City (1981) 7.5' quadrangle. Preston (p. 403) called it Logansville. A place called Missouri Flat was located about 1 mile west of Loganville (Gudde, 1975, p. 219).

Log Cabin [YUBA]: *locality,* 1.25 miles southwest of Camptonville (lat. 39°26'30" N, long. 121°04' W; sec. 10, T 18 N, R 8 E). Named on Camptonville (1948) 7.5' quadrangle. Postal authorities established Log Cabin post office, named for its location in a log cabin, in 1926 and discontinued it in 1944 (Salley, p. 124).

Loggers Delight Canyon [EL DORADO]: *canyon,* drained by a stream that flows 1.5 miles to Cat Creek 5.25 miles east of Caldor (lat. 38°35'30" N, long. 120°20'05" W; sec. 32, T 9 N, R 15 E). Named on Peddler Hill (1951) 7.5' quadrangle.

Logtown [EL DORADO]: *locality,* 6.5 miles south-southwest of Placerville (lat. 38°38'40" N, long. 120°51' W; near SW cor. sec. 11, T 9 N, R 10 E). Site named on Placerville (1949) 7.5' quadrangle.

Logtown Ravine [EL DORADO]: *canyon,* drained by a stream that flows 2.5 miles to Slate Creek (3) 4.5 miles southwest of Placerville (lat. 38°40'35" N, long. 120°51'20" W); the canyon heads near Logtown. Named on Placerville (1893) 30' quadrangle.

Logtown Ridge [EL DORADO]: *ridge,* south-trending, 10 miles long, center 9 miles south-southwest of Placerville (lat. 38°36'30" N, long. 120°51'30" W); Logtown was on the ridge. Named on Fiddletown (1949) and Placerville (1949) 7.5' quadrangles

Lohman Ridge [SIERRA-YUBA]: *ridge,* generally west-trending, 2.5 miles long, 2 miles south-southeast of Camptonville on Sierra-Yuba County line, mainly in Yuba County (lat. 39°25'30" N, long. 121°02'15" W). Named on Camptonville (1948) 7.5' quadrangle, which shows Lohman ranch on the ridge.

Lois: see **Lake Lois** [EL DORADO].

Lola: see **Mount Lola** [NEVADA].

Lola Montez Lake: see **Lower Lola Montez Lake** [NEVADA]; **Upper Lola Montez Lake** [NEVADA].

Loma Rica [YUBA]: *town,* 15 miles northeast of Marysville (lat. 39° 18'40" N, long. 121°25' W; sec. 21, T 17 N, R 5 E). Named on Loma Rica (1947) 7.5' quadrangle.

Lombardi Point [SIERRA]: *promontory,* 8 miles north-northeast of Sierraville at the edge of Sierra Valley (lat. 39°41' N, long. 120°16'50" W; sec. 10, T 21 N, R 15 E). Named on Antelope Valley (1981) 7.5' quadrangle.

Lomo [SUTTER]: *locality,* 5.5 miles north-northwest of Yuba City along Southern Pacific Railroad (lat. 39°13'15" N, long. 121°38'25" W; near S line sec. 21, T 16 N, R 3 E). Named on Sutter (1952) 7.5' quadrangle.

Lonely Gulch [EL DORADO]: *canyon,* drained by a stream that flows 2 miles to Lake Tahoe 1.25 miles south-southeast of the town of Meeks Bay (lat. 39°01'10" N, long. 120°07' W; sec. 32, T 14 N, R 17 E). Named on Homewood (1955) and Meeks Bay (1955) 7.5' quadrangles.

Lone Star: see **Auburn** [PLACER].

Lone Tree [YUBA]: *locality,* 5 miles south-southwest of Smartville (lat. 39°08'40" N, long. 121°20'20" W; near SW cor. sec. 17, T 15 N, T 6 E). Named on Smartville (1951) 7.5' quadrangle.

Lonetree Island [SACRAMENTO]: *hill,* 5.25 miles north-northwest of downtown Sacramento in American Basin (lat. 38°39'05" N, long. 121°31'10" W). Named on Elkhorn Weir (1915) 7.5' quadrangle.

Lone Valley: see **Ione Valley** [AMADOR].

Loney Lake [NEVADA]: *lake,* 800 feet long, 5 miles south-southwest of English Mountain (lat. 39°23'10" N, long. 120°35'40" W; sec. 35, T 18 N, R 12 E). Named on English Mountain (1983) 7.5' quadrangle.

Loney Meadow [NEVADA]: *area,* 4.5 miles east of Graniteville (lat. 39°25'30" N, long. 120°39'15" W; sec. 17, T 18 N, R 12 E). Named on Graniteville (1982) 7.5' quadrangle.

Long: see **Deacon Long Ravine** [SIERRA].

Long Bar [YUBA]:

(1) *locality,* 4.5 miles east-southeast of Challenge along North Yuba River (lat. 39°27'15" N, long. 121°09'05" W; near N line sec. 2, T 18 N, R 7 E). Named on Nevada City (1948) 15' quadrangle. Water of New Bullards Bar Reservoir now covers the site. Wescoatt's (1861) map shows Long Bar on the southwest side of the river, and Texas B. [Bar] directly across the river. The same map shows Oregon B. on the west side of the river 0.5 mile northwest of Long Bar, and Pittsburg B. on the west side of the river 0.25 mile north-northeast of Oregon B.

(2) *locality,* 4 miles west of Smartville (lat. 39°13'05" N, long. 121° 22'10" W; on W line sec. 25, T 16 N, R 5 E). Named on Smartville (1951) 7.5' quadrangle. Wescoatt's (1861) map shows a community called Long Bar situated 5 miles west of Smartsville on the north side of Yuba River about 1 mile east of the mouth of Dry Creek (1). Postal authorities established Dry Creek post office in 1854, moved it 1 mile south and changed the name to Long Bar in 1858, and discontinued it in 1864 (Salley, p. 62,

125). Long Bar was named for Dr. Long (Bancroft, 1888, p. 72). Wescoatt's (1861) map shows places called Kenebec Ho. [House] and Eureka H. [House] located on the south side of Yuba River across from Long Bar. Wescoatt's (1861) map also shows a place called Swiss Bar located 3 miles west-southwest of Long Bar on the south side of Yuba River. Gudde (1975, p. 275) noted that a place called Poverty Bar was located along Yuba River opposite Swiss Bar.

Long Bar: see **Scotchman Creek** [NEVADA].

Long Canyon [COLUSA]: *canyon*, drained by a stream that flows 2.5 miles to Antelope Creek 15 miles north-northeast of Wilbur Springs (lat. 39°14'45" N, long. 122°21'30" W; near NE cor. sec. 13, T 16 S, R 5 W). Named on Lodoga (1960) and Wilbur Springs (1961) 15' quadrangles.

Long Canyon [EL DORADO]:

(1) *canyon*, 3.25 miles long, opens into the canyon of South Fork American River nearly 5 miles west-northwest of Pollock Pines (lat. 38°47'05" N, long. 120°39'55" W; sec. 20, T 11 N, R 12 E). Named on Pollock Pines (1950) and Slate Mountain (1950) 7.5' quadrangles. The canyon splits at the head into North Fork and South Fork—each fork is 1.25 miles long and is named on Pollock Pines (1950) 7.5' quadrangle.

(2) *canyon*, drained by a stream that flows 6.25 miles to Silver Fork American River 8 miles north of Leek Spring Hill (lat. 38°44'35" N, long. 120°15'25" W). Named on Leek Spring Hill (1951), Pyramid Peak (1955), and Tragedy Spring (1979) 7.5' quadrangles.

(3) *canyon*, drained by a stream that flows about 2.5 miles to Big Canyon (2) 7 miles southwest of Old Iron Mountain (lat. 38°38'20" N, long. 120°29'05" W; sec. 13, T 9 N, R 13 E). Named on Stump Spring (1951) 7.5' quadrangle.

Long Canyon [PLACER]: *canyon*, drained by a stream that flows 11 miles to Rubicon River 8 miles west-northwest of Devil Peak (lat. 38°59'25" N, long. 120°41'10" W; sec. 7, T 13 N, R 12 E). Named on Devil Peak (1950), Greek Store (1952), and Tunnel Hill (1950) 7.5' quadrangles. The canyon divides at the head into North Fork and South Fork. North Fork is nearly 7 miles long and is named on Bunker Hill (1953) and Greek Store (1952) 7.5' quadrangles—it is shown as part of Long Canyon on Truckee (1895) 30' quadrangle. South Fork is 10.5 miles long and is named on Bunker Hill (1953) and Greek Store (1952) 7.5' quadrangles.

Long Gulch [EL DORADO]: *canyon*, drained by a stream that flows 1.5 miles to One Eye Creek 5 miles northeast of Chili Bar (lat. 38° 49'05" N, long. 120°45'20" W; sec. 9, T 11 N, R 11 E). Named on Garden Valley (1949) 7.5' quadrangle.

Long Hollow [NEVADA]: *canyon*, drained by a stream that flows 2.25 miles to Wolf Creek 1 mile northwest of Higgins Corner (lat. 39°03'10" N, long. 121°06'25" W; sec. 20, T 14 N, R 8 E). Named on Lake Combie (1949) 7.5' quadrangle.

Long Island [SACRAMENTO]: *island*, 3000 feet long, less than 1 mile west-northwest of Isleton in Sacramento River (lat. 38°10' N, long. 121°37'25" W). Named on Isleton (1978) and Rio Vista (1978) 7.5' quadrangles.

Long John Creek [AMADOR]: *stream*, flows 1.25 miles to Mill Creek 6.25 miles southwest of Hams Station (lat. 38°29'45" N, long. 120°28'15" W; at S line sec. 31, T 8 N, R 14 E). Named on Caldor (1951) and Devils Nose (1979) 7.5' quadrangles.

Long John Creek [PLACER]: *stream*, flows 1.5 miles to Rubicon River 4 miles west-southwest of Bunker Hill (lat. 39°01'15" N, long. 120°26'30" W; near E line sec. 31, T 14 N, R 14 E). Named on Bunker Hill (1953) 7.5' quadrangle.

Long Lake [AMADOR]: *lake*, 1050 feet long, 2.5 miles north-northeast of Mokelumne Peak (lat. 38°34'30" N, long. 120°04'50" W). Named on Mokelumne Peak (1979) 7.5' quadrangle.

Long Lake [NEVADA]: *lake*, 1200 feet long, 4.5 miles southwest of English Mountain (lat. 39°23'55" N, long. 120°36'50" W; sec. 27, T 18 N, R 12 E). Named on English Mountain (1983) 7.5' quadrangle.

Long Lake [PLACER]:

(1) *lake*, 2350 feet long, 6 miles west-southwest of Donner Pass (lat. 39°17'35" N, long. 120°25'50" W; sec. 32, T 17 N, R 14 E). Named on Soda Springs (1955) 7.5' quadrangle.

(2) *lake*, 2150 feet long, 6.25 miles east of Bunker Hill (lat. 39° 02'20" N, long. 120°15'55" W; on S line sec. 23, T 14 N, R 15 E). Named on Wentworth Springs (1953) 7.5' quadrangle.

Long Lake [SUTTER]: *lake*, 2 miles long, 4.5 miles east-southeast of Meridian in Sutter Basin (lat. 39°06'30" N, long. 121°50'40" W). Named on Tisdale Weir (1952) 7.5' quadrangle.

Long Meadow [EL DORADO]: *area*, 3.5 miles north-northeast of Robbs Peak (lat. 38°58'15" N, long. 120°22'15" W; sec. 14, T 13 N, R 14 E). Named on Loon Lake (1952) 7.5' quadrangle.

Long Point [NEVADA]: *ridge*, south-trending, 1.5 miles long, 9 miles northeast of Chicago Park (lat. 39°14'05" N, long. 120°50'35" W; mainly in sec. 22, T 16 N, R 10 E). Named on Dutch Flat (1950) 7.5' quadrangle.

Long Point [PLACER]:

(1) *ridge*, southwest- to west-trending, 2 miles long, 3.5 miles north-northwest of Foresthill (lat. 39°04'15" N, long. 120°50' W). Named on Foresthill (1949) 7.5' quadrangle.

(2) *ridge*, east-trending, nearly 1 mile long, 7.5 miles northeast of Auburn (lat. 38°58'15" N, long. 120°58'15" W; at NE cor. sec. 21, T 13 N, R 9 E). Named on Greenwood (1949) 7.5' quadrangle.

Long Point [YUBA]: *relief feature*, 3.5 miles east-southeast of Challenge on the east side of North Yuba River (lat. 39°28'25" N, long. 121°09'30" W; sec. 26, T 19 N, R 7 E). Named on Challenge (1948) 7.5' quadrangle.

Long Point: see **South Long Point** [PLACER].

Long Ravine [EL DORADO]: *canyon*, drained by a stream that flows 1.5 miles to North Fork Cosumnes River 6.5 miles south-southwest of Camino (lat. 38°39'05" N, long. 120°43'55" W; sec. 11, T 9 N, R 11 E). Named on Camino (1952) 7.5' quadrangle.

Long Ravine [NEVADA]: *canyon*, drained by a stream that flows 1.25 miles to South Wolf Creek 2 miles north-northeast of Higgins Corner (lat. 39°04'05" N, long. 121°04'20" W; sec. 15, T 14 N, R 8 E). Named on Lake Combie (1949) 7.5' quadrangle.

Long Ravine [PLACER]: *canyon*, drained by a stream that flows 1 mile to Bear River 2.5 miles north of Colfax (lat. 39°08'15" N, long. 120°56'55" W; at E line sec. 22, T 15 N, R 9 E). Named on Colfax (1950) 15' quadrangle. The stream in the canyon now enters Rollins Reservoir.

Long Ravine [YUBA]: *canyon*, drained by a stream that flows 1 mile to Camp Far West Reservoir 8 miles east-northeast of Wheatland (lat. 39°03'10" N, long. 121°17'40" W). Named on Camp Far West (1949, photorevised 1973) 7.5' quadrangle.

Long Valley [AMADOR]: *valley*, 4.25 miles northwest of Mokelumne Peak (lat. 38°35'05" N, long. 120°08'30" W; sec. 31, T 9 N, R 17 E). Named on Bear River Reservoir (1979) 7.5' quadrangle.

Long Valley [PLACER]: *valley*, 7.25 miles southwest of Donner Pass (lat. 39°15'20" N, long. 120°26' W; sec 17, 18, T 16 N, R 14 E). Named on Soda Springs (1955) 7.5' quadrangle.

Long Valley: see **Greenwood** [EL DORADO]; **Upper Long Valley** [SIERRA].

Long Valley Creek [SIERRA]:

(1) *stream*, flows 10.5 miles to Lassen County 11 miles east of Loyalton (lat. 39°42'30" N, long. 120°02'20" W; at N line sec. 2, T 21 N, R 17 E); the stream goes through Upper Long Valley. Named on Evans Canyon (1978) 7.5' quadrangle. United States Board on Geographic Names (1978a, p. 6) rejected the name "Dry Valley Creek" for the feature.

(2) *stream*, flows 3.25 miles to Haypress Creek 6 miles east of Sierra City (lat. 39°33'10" N, long. 120°31'35" W; near SW cor. sec. 33, T 20 N, R 13 E). Named on Haypress Valley (1981) and Sattley (1981) 7.5' quadrangles. Downieville (1897) 30' quadrangle has the name "Hay Press Valley" for the canyon of the stream, and has the name "Long Valley Creek" for a stream situated about 1 mile farther northwest. United States Board on Geographic Names (1960a, p. 15) rejected the name "Haypress Creek" for present Long Valley Creek (2).

Long Valley Creek [YUBA]: *stream*, flows 1.5 miles to Big Valley Creek 4.5 miles southeast of Rackerby (lat. 39°23'40" N, long. 121°16'35" W; at W line sec. 26, T 18 N, R 6 E). Named on Rackerby (1948) 7.5' quadrangle.

Long Valley Creek: see **Dead Horse Canyon** [SIERRA].

Lookout Mountain [EL DORADO]: *peak*, 8.5 miles north of Pollock Pines (lat. 38°53' N, long. 120°33'35" W; sec. 18, T 12 N, R 13 E). Altitude 5159 feet. Named on Devil Peak (1950) 7.5' quadrangle.

Lookout Mountain [PLACER]: *peak*, 6.5 miles west-southwest of Martis Peak (lat. 39°15'45" N, long. 120°08'45" W; sec. 1, T 16 N, R 16 E). Altitude 8104 feet. Named on Truckee (1955) 7.5' quadrangle.

Loomis [PLACER]: *town*, 3 miles northeast of Rocklin (lat. 38°49'15" N, long. 121°11'35" W; near E line sec. 9, T 11 N, R 7 E). Named on Rocklin (1967) 7.5' quadrangle. Postal authorities established Placer post office in 1861, changed the name to Smithville in 1862, to Pino in 1869, and to Loomis in 1890 (Frickstad, p. 121, 122). The name "Smithville" recalls L.G. Smith, who kept a store at the place; the name "Pino" was from the old mining camp called Pine Grove, which was in Secret Ravine (2) about 1.5 miles from present Loomis (Hoover, Rensch, and Rensch, p. 272). Railroad officials named the town in 1884 for Jim Loomis, the local railroad agent, postmaster, and saloonkeeper (Gudde, 1949, p. 193).

Loon Lake [EL DORADO]: *lake*, behind a dam on Gerle Creek 1.5 miles east-southeast of Wentworth Springs (lat. 39°00'10" N, long. 120°18'35" W; on W line sec. 4, T 13 N, R 15 E). Named on Granite Chief (1953) and Robbs Peak (1952) 15' quadrangles. Loon Lake (1952, photorevised 1973) and Wentworth Springs (1953, photorevised 1973) 7.5' quadrangles show an enlarged lake. United States Board on Geographic Names (1978a, p. 6) rejected the names "Loon Lake Reservoir" and "Pleasant Lake" for the feature. California Division of Highways' (1934) map has the name "Bisbee Lake" for a southwest arm of Loon Lake (on W line sec. 8, T 13 N, R 15 E) that is shown as an unnamed part of Loon Lake on Robbs Peak (1952) 15' quadrangle.

Loon Lake Reservoir: see **Loon Lake** [EL DORADO].

Lorenz Bar: see **Rattlesnake Bar** [EL DORADO-PLACER].

Los Picos de Sutter: see **Sutter Buttes** [SUTTER].

Lost Camp: see **Blue Canyon** [PLACER] (2).

Lost Canyon [PLACER]: *canyon,* drained by a stream that flows 1.25 miles to North Fork of Middle Fork American River 5.5 miles west-southwest of Duncan Peak (lat. 39°07'35" N, long. 120°36'25" W; at S line sec. 23, T 15 N, R 12 E). Named on Duncan Peak (1952) 7.5' quadrangle.

Lost Canyon Creek [EL DORADO]: *stream,* flows 1.25 miles to Slab Creek 7 miles north-northwest of Pollock Pines (lat. 38°51'10" N, long. 120°38'35" W; near S line sec. 28, T 12 N, R 12 E). Named on Slate Mountain (1950) 7.5' quadrangle.

Lost Corner Mountain [EL DORADO]: *peak,* 4.5 miles west-southwest of the town of Meeks Bay (lat. 39°00'50" N, long. 120°12'10" W; at W line sec. 34, T 14 N, R 16 E). Altitude 8261 feet. Named on Homewood (1955) 7.5' quadrangle.

Lost Creek [YUBA]: *stream,* flows 1.5 miles to North Yuba River nearly 4 miles south-southwest of Strawberry Valley (lat. 39°30'40" N, long. 121°07'40" W; sec. 18, T 19 N, R 8 E). Named on Clipper Mills (1948) and Strawberry Valley (1948) 7.5' quadrangles.

Lost Lake [EL DORADO]:
(1) *lake,* 1000 feet long, 3.5 miles west-southwest of the town of Meeks Bay (lat. 39°00'50" N, long. 120°10'50" W; sec. 35, T 14 N, R 16 E). Named on Homewood (1955) 7.5' quadrangle.
(2) *lake,* 800 feet long, 5.5 miles southwest of Phipps Peak (lat. 38° 54'30" N, long. 120°14' W; near NE cor. sec. 8, T 12 N, R 16 E). Named on Rockbound Valley (1955) 7.5' quadrangle.
(3) *lake,* 450 feet long, 5 miles northwest of Echo Summit (lat. 38° 51'40" N, long. 120°05'45" W). Named on Echo Lake (1955) 7.5' quadrangle.

Lost Lake [SIERRA]: *lake,* 200 feet long, 5.5 miles north of Sierra City (lat. 39°38'35" N, long. 120°39'05" W; sec. 32, T 21 N, R 12 E). Named on Gold Lake (1981) 7.5' quadrangle.

Los Tres Picos: see **Sutter Buttes** [SUTTER].

Lotus [EL DORADO]: *village,* 1 mile west of Coloma (lat. 38°48' N, long. 120°54'30" W; sec. 18, T 11 N, R 10 E). Named on Coloma (1949) 7.5' quadrangle, which shows Uniontown cemetery near the site. In 1849 the community was called Marshall, for James W. Marshall, but in 1850 the name was changed to Uniontown in honor of the admission of California to the Union that year; the name was changed to Lotus when postal authorities established Lotus post office at the place in 1881 (Frickstad, p. 27; Hoover, Rensch, and Rensch, p. 86). A mining camp called Michigan Flat was situated near present Lotus (Yohalem, p. 87).

Louisa: see **Relief** [NEVADA].

Louise: see **Lake Louise** [PLACER].

Louisiana Bar [EL DORADO] *locality,* 2 miles north-northwest of Cool along Middle Fork American River 0.25 mile above the mouth of Middle Fork (lat. 38°54'45" N, long. 121°01'55" W; near N line sec. 12, T 12 N, R 8 E). Named on Auburn (1953) 7.5' quadrangle.

Louisville [EL DORADO]: *locality,* 3.25 miles north of present Chili Bar (lat. 38°48'45" N, long. 120°49'15" W). Named on Placerville (1893) 30' quadrangle.

Louisville: see **Greenwood** [EL DORADO].

Lousey Level: see **Rice Crossing** [NEVADA-YUBA].

Lousy Point: see **Dollar Point** [PLACER].

Lovdal [YOLO]:
(1) *locality,* 2.25 miles north-northwest of West Sacramento along Sacramento Northern Railroad (lat. 39°36' N, long. 121°33'05" W). Named on Sacramento West (1967) 7.5' quadrangle.
(2) *locality,* 2 miles west-northwest of West Sacramento along Southern Pacific Railroad (lat. 38°34'55" N, long. 121°34' W). Named on Lovdal (1916) 7.5' quadrangle.

Lovejoy Camp [EL DORADO]: *locality,* 6.5 miles north of Pollock Pines (lat. 38°51'30" N, long. 120°34'20" W; near W line sec. 30, T 12 N, R 13 E). Named on Pollock Pines (1950) 7.5' quadrangle.

Lovelady Ridge [COLUSA]: *ridge,* extends for 6 miles in a generally north direction from Pacific Point (center near lat. 39°15' N, long. 122°34' W). Named on Bartlett Springs (1944) and Stonyford (1951) 15' quadrangles. Clearlake Oaks (1960) 15' quadrangle has the form "Love Lady Ridge" for the name.

Loveless Dredgings [EL DORADO]: *locality,* 2.25 miles west-southwest of Omo Ranch along Brownsville Creek (lat. 38°34' N, long. 120°36'25" W; at N line sec. 12, T 8 N, R 12 E). Named on Omo Ranch (1952) 7.5' quadrangle.

Lovers Leap [EL DORADO]: *relief feature,* 3.5 miles south-southeast of Pyramid Peak (lat. 38°48' N, long. 120°08' W; near W line sec. 17, T 11 N, R 17 E). Named on Pyramid Peak (1955) 7.5' quadrangle. Postal authorities established Lovers Leap post office, named for the relief feature, 1 mile southwest of Camp Sacramento post office in 1919 and discontinued it in 1929 (Salley, p. 128).

Lovers Leap [PLACER]: *relief feature,* 2.5 miles southeast of Dutch Flat above Giant Gap (lat. 39°10'25" N, long. 120°48'25" W; on E line sec. 2, T 15 N, R 10 E). Named on Dutch Flat (1950) 7.5' quadrangle.

Loves Falls [SIERRA]: *waterfall,* 2 miles northeast of Sierra City along North Yuba River (lat. 39°34'40" N, long. 120°36'25" W; near NE cor. sec. 27, T 20 N, R 12 E). Named on Haypress Valley (1981) 7.5' quadrangle.

Lowell Hill [NEVADA]: *locality,* 6.5 miles south of Washington (lat. 39°15'55" N, long. 120°47'35" W; at E line sec. 12, T 16 N, R 10 E). Site named on Washington (1950) 7.5' quadrangle. Postal authorities established Lowell Hill post office in 1878 and discontinued it in 1918 (Frickstad, p. 114). Whitney's (1873) map shows a place called Mammoth Spring 1 mile east-southeast of Lowell Hill, and a place called Kinders Diggs 1.5 miles east of Lowell Hill.

Lowell Hill Ridge [NEVADA]: *ridge,* southwest-trending, 5.5 miles long, 7 miles west-southwest of Yuba Gap (lat. 39°17'10" N, long. 120°44'30" W); Lowell Hill is about 1 mile west of the southwest end of the ridge. Named on Blue Canyon (1955) and Washington (1950) 7.5' quadrangles.

Lower Bear River Campground [AMADOR]: *locality,* 8.5 miles west of Mokelumne Peak on the north side of Lower Bear River Reservoir (lat. 38°33'10" N, long. 120°15' W; near S line sec. 7, T 8 N, R 16 E). Named on Bear River Reservoir (1979) 7.5' quadrangle.

Lower Bear River Reservoir [AMADOR]: *lake,* behind a dam on Bear River 6.5 miles east of Hams Station (lat. 38°32'15" N, long. 120°15'15" W; at S line sec. 18, T 8 N, R 16 E); the feature is below Bear River Reservoir. Named on Bear River Reservoir (1979) and Peddler Hill (1951, photorevised 1973) 7.5' quadrangles.

Lower Castle Creek [NEVADA]: *stream,* flows 4 miles to South Yuba River 4.25 miles west-northwest of Donner Pass (lat. 39°20'05" N, long. 120°24'05" W; near E line sec. 16, T 17 N, R 14 E); the stream heads west of Castle Peak. Named on Norden (1955) and Soda Springs (1955) 7.5' quadrangles.

Lower Echo Lake [EL DORADO]: *lake,* nearly 1.5 miles long, 2.25 miles northwest of Echo Summit (lat. 38°50'20" N, long. 120°03'20" W); the feature is east of Upper Echo Lake. Named on Echo Lake (1955) 7.5' quadrangle. Called Echo Lake on Pyramid Peak (1896) 30' quadrangle.

Lower Forni [EL DORADO]: *locality,* nearly 5 miles southwest of Pyramid Peak (lat. 38°48'10" N, long. 120°13'40" W; near W line sec. 16, T 11 N, R 16 E); the place is 3.25 miles west-southwest of Upper Forni. Named on Pyramid Peak (1955) 7.5' quadrangle.

Lower Hell Hole [PLACER]: *valley,* 2.25 miles north-northwest of Bunker Hill along Rubicon River (lat. 39°05' N, long. 120°23'30" W). Named on Granite Chief (1953) 15' quadrangle. Truckee (1940) 30' quadrangle has the form "Lower Hellhole" for the name. Water of Hell Hole Reservoir now floods the valley.

Lower Letts Valley [COLUSA]: *valley,* nearly 4 miles southwest of Fouts Springs (lat. 39°18'45" N, long. 122°42'30" W; sec. 24, T 17 N, R 8 W); the valley is 0.5 mile north-northeast of Upper Letts Valley. Named on Fouts Springs (1968) 7.5' quadrangle.

Lower Lola Montez Lake [NEVADA]: *lake,* 1050 feet long, nearly 6 miles west-northwest of Donner Pass (lat. 39°20'55" N, long. 120° 25'25" W; sec. 8, T 17 N, R 14 E); the feature is 0.25 mile east-southeast of Upper Lola Montez Lake. Named on Soda Springs (1955) 7.5' quadrangle.

Lower Meadow [PLACER]: *area,* 5.25 miles west of Bunker Hill in South Fork Long Canyon (lat. 39°02'30" N, long. 120°28'45" W; at SW cor. sec. 24, T 14 N, R 13 E). Named on Bunker Hill (1953) 7.5' quadrangle.

Lower Mines: see **Mormon Island** [SACRAMENTO].

Lower Rancheria: see **Drytown** [AMADOR]; **Rancheria** [AMADOR[.

Lower Rock Lake [NEVADA]: *lake,* 900 feet long, 4 miles west-southwest of English Mountain along Texas Creek (lat. 39°25'45" N, long. 120°37'15" W; near W line sec. 15, T 18 N, R 12 E); the feature is 600 feet downstream from Rock Lake. Named on English Mountain (1983) 7.5' quadrangle.

Lower Salmon Lake [SIERRA]: *lake,* 2500 feet long, 6 miles north of Sierra City (lat. 39°39' N, long. 120°38'30" W; at W line sec. 28, T 21 N, R 12 E); the feature is along Salmon Creek 0.5 mile downstream from Upper Salmon Lake. Named on Gold Lake (1981) 7.5' quadrangle.

Lower Sardine Lake [SIERRA]: *lake,* 2200 feet long, 3.5 miles north of Sierra City (lat. 39°36'55" N, long. 120°37'35" W; mainly in sec. 9, T 20 N, R 12 E); the feature is along upper reaches of Sardine Creek less than 0.25 mile downstream from Upper Sardine Lake. Named on Haypress Valley (1981) and Sierra City (1981) 7.5' quadrangles.

Lower Town: see **Mosquito Creek** [EL DORADO].

Lower Velma Lake [EL DORADO]: *lake,* 2400 feet long, 1.25 miles south-southeast of Phipps Peak (lat. 38°56'20" N, long. 120°08'25" W; near S line sec. 30, T 13 N, R 17 E); the lake is less than 1 mile north-northeast of Upper Velma Lake. Named on Rockbound Valley (1955) 7.5' quadrangle. A Forest Service crew—at the father's request—named Lower Velma Lake, Middle Velma Lake, and Upper Velma Lake in 1900 for the baby daughter of Harry Oswald Comstock (Lekisch, p. 145).

Loyalton [SIERRA]: *town,* 32 miles east-northeast of Downieville in Sierra Valley (lat. 39°40'35" N, long. 120°14'30" W; around NE cor. sec. 13, T 21 N, R 15 E); the town is along Smithneck Creek. Named on Loyalton (1981) 7.5' quadrangle. Postal authorities established Loyalton post office in 1864 (Frickstad, p. 184), and the town incorporated in 1901. The name is from Union sympathies among the townsfolk during the Civil War; the place first was called Smith's Neck (Gudde, 1949, p. 196). Postal Route (1884) map shows a place called Oneida located about 10 miles east of

Loyalton. Postal authorities established Oneida post office in 1882 and discontinued it in 1885; the name was from a place in New York State (Salley, p. 161).

Lucas Hill [NEVADA]: *peak,* 3 miles southwest of Wolf (lat. 39°01'35" N, long. 121°10'35" W; sec. 34, T 14 N, R 7 E). Altitude 1490 feet. Named on Wolf (1949) 7.5' quadrangle.

Lucille: see **Lake Lucille** [EL DORADO].

Lucky Dog Creek [SIERRA]: *stream,* flows nearly 2.5 miles to Oregon Creek 2 miles west-northwest of Alleghany (lat. 39°29' N, long. 120°52'30" W; sec. 29, T 19 N, R 10 E). Named on Alleghany (1949), Downieville (1951), and Pike (1949) 7.5' quadrangles.

Lucky Hill Ravine [SIERRA]: *canyon,* drained by a stream that flows 1 mile to Slate Creek 9 miles southwest of Mount Fillmore (lat. 39°38'55" N, long. 120°58'40" W; sec. 28, T 21 N, R 9 E). Named on La Porte (1951) 7.5' quadrangle, which shows Lucky Hill mine near the head of the canyon.

Lunch Creek [SIERRA]: *stream,* flows 1.5 miles to North Yuba River 7.5 miles east-northeast of Sierra City (lat. 39°37' N, long. 120°30'25" W; sec. 10, T 20 N, R 13 E). Named on Calpine (1981), Clio (1981), and Haypress Valley (1981) 7.5' quadrangles.

Lundeen: see **Camp Lundeen** [NEVADA].

Lupine Point [NEVADA]: *relief feature,* 3.25 miles southwest of Washington (lat. 39°20' N, long. 120°51'10" W; at SW cor. sec. 15, T 17 N, R 10 E). Named on Washington (1950) 7.5' quadrangle.

Lurline [COLUSA]: *locality,* nearly 7 miles northwest of Williams along Colusa and Lake Railroad (lat. 39°13'10" N, long. 122°14'40" W; near SW cor. sec. 19, T 16 N, R 3 W). Named on Williams (1918) 7.5' quadrangle.

Lurline Creek [COLUSA]: *stream,* flows 15 miles to an artificial watercourse in Colusa Basin 5.25 miles north-northeast of Williams (lat. 39°13'30" N, long. 122°07'35" W). Named on Lodoga (1960) and Wilbur Springs (1961) 15' quadrangles.

Lusk Meadows [SIERRA]: *area,* 6.25 miles north of Sierra City (lat. 39°39'25" N, long. 120°37'55" W; sec. 28, T 21 N, R 12 E). Named on Gold Lake (1981) 7.5' quadrangle.

Luther Pass [EL DORADO]: *pass,* 5.5 miles south-southwest of Freel Peak on El Dorado-Alpine County line (lat. 38°47'15" N, long. 119°56'40" W; sec. 24, T 11 N, R 18 E). Named on Freel Peak (1955) 7.5' quadrangle. Called Luther's Pass on Wheeler's (1876-1877a) map. According to one account, the pass was named for Lieutenant Luther, who selected a route there for an army convoy in 1857; according to another account, the name is for Ira M. Luther, who crossed the pass in 1854 in a wagon (Gudde, 1969, p. 186; Long, p. 12).

Lynchburg Hill [PLACER]: *peak,* 4.5 miles west-northwest of Devil Peak on Ralston Ridge (lat. 38°59'40" N, long. 120°37'15" W; sec. 10, T 13 N, R 12 E). Named on Devil Peak (1950) and Tunnel Hill (1950) 7.5' quadrangles.

Lynch Canyon [COLUSA]: *canyon,* drained by a stream that flows 1.25 miles to Bear Creek 2.5 miles southeast of Wilbur Springs (lat. 39°00'55" N, long. 122°23'15" W). Named on Wilbur Springs (1961) 15' quadrangle.

Lyon Peak [PLACER]: *peak,* 1.5 miles west-northwest of Granite Chief (lat. 39°12'25" N, long. 120°18'50" W; sec. 28, T 16 N, R 15 E). Altitude 8891 feet. Named on Granite Chief (1953) 7.5' quadrangle.

Lyons [EL DORADO]: *locality,* 3.25 miles west-southwest of Pyramid Peak (lat. 38°49'15" N, long. 120°12'40" W; near NE cor. sec. 9, T 11 N, R 16 E). Site named on Pyramid Peak (1955) 7.5' quadrangle.

Lyons Creek [EL DORADO]: *stream,* flows 7 miles to South Fork Silver Creek 3.25 miles north-northeast of Kyburz (lat. 38°48'55" N, long. 120°15'40" W; sec. 7, T 11 N, R 16 E); Lyons was along the stream. Named on Kyburz (1952) and Pyramid Peak (1955) 7.5' quadrangles.

Lyons Lake [EL DORADO]: *lake,* 1150 feet long. 1.25 miles west-northwest of Pyramid Peak (lat. 38°51' N, long. 120°10'50" W). Named on Pyramid Peak (1955) 7.5' quadrangle.

Lytle Mountain [COLUSA]: *peak,* 9.5 miles southeast of Wilbur Springs (lat. 38°56'50" N, long. 122°17'35" W; sec. 27, T 13 N, R 4 W). Altitude 2144 feet. Named on Glascock Mountain (1958) 7.5' quadrangle.

Lytton Lake [NEVADA]: *lake,* 400 feet long, 1 mile northwest of Donner Pass (lat. 39°19'30" N, long. 120°20'20" W; sec. 17, T 17 N, R 15 E). Named on Norden (1955) 7.5' quadrangle. On Truckee (1940) 30' quadrangle, present Flora Lake is called Lytton Lake.

—M—

Macedon Canyon [PLACER]: *canyon,* drained by a stream that flows 0.5 mile to Secret Canyon 4.5 miles west of Duncan Peak (lat. 39°09'55" N, long. 120°35'40" W; near W line sec. 12, T 15 N, R 12 E). Named on Duncan Peak (1952) 7.5' quadrangle.

Macedon Ridge [PLACER]: *ridge,* southwest-trending, 2.5 miles long, 5 miles west-northwest of Duncan Peak (lat. 39°10'15" N, long. 120°36'05" W). Named on Duncan Peak (1952) 7.5' quadrangle.

Mack: see **Billy Mack Canyon** [NEVADA]; **Billy Mack Flat** [NEVADA].

Mackert: see **Marchant** [SUTTER].

Mack House [SIERRA]: *locality,* 1.5 miles southwest of Alleghany (lat. 39°27'25" N, long. 120°52' W; on W line sec. 5, T 18 N, R 10 E). Named on Alleghany (1949) 7.5' quadrangle.

Macklin Creek [NEVADA]: *stream,* flows 2 miles to Middle Yuba River 7.5 miles northeast of Graniteville (lat. 39°31'10" N, long. 120°37'30" W; near NE cor. sec. 16, T 19 N, R 12 E). Named on Haypress Valley (1981) 7.5' quadrangle. The name commemorates Robert M. Macklin, fisheries management supervisor for California Department of Fish and Game from 1940 until 1970 (United States Board on Geographic Names, 1971, p. 3).

Macy [COLUSA]: *locality,* 5 miles north-northwest of Arbuckle along the Southern Pacific Railroad (lat. 39°04'50" N, long. 122° 05'50" W; near E line sec. 8, T 14 N, R 2 W). Named on Arbuckle (1918) 7.5' quadrangle.

Mad Canyon [PLACER]: *canyon,* drained by a stream that flows 2.5 miles to Middle Fork American River 2.5 miles east-southeast of Foresthill (lat. 39°00'25" N, long. 120°46'20" W; at S line sec. 32, T 14 N, R 11 E). Named on Foresthill (1949) 7.5' quadrangle.

Mad Canyon: see **Little Mad Canyon** [PLACER].

Madden Creek [PLACER]: *stream,* flows nearly 3 miles to Lake Tahoe at Homewood (lat. 39°05'25" N, long. 120°09'40" W; sec. 1, T 14 N, R 16 E). Named on Homewood (1955) 7.5' quadrangle. The name is for Dick Madden, who settled by the stream (Lekisch, p. 83).

Madison [YOLO]: *village,* 10.5 miles west of Woodland (lat. 38°40'45" N, long. 121°58'10" W). Named on Madison (1953) 7.5' quadrangle. Postal authorities established Cache Creek post office before March 24, 1852; they moved it 0.5 mile south and changed the name to Madison in 1877 (Salley, p. 31). Daniel Bradley Hulbert of Madison, Wisconsin, named the place (Gudde, 1969, p. 190).

Madox: see **Robbins** [SUTTER].

Maggie's Mountains: see **Maggies Peaks** [EL DORADO].

Maggies Peaks [EL DORADO]: *peaks,* two, 2 miles north-northwest of Mount Tallac (lat. 38°55'50" N, long. 120°06'45" W). Altitudes 8699 feet and 8499 feet. Named on Emerald Bay (1955) 7.5' quadrangle. Mary McConnell climbed the southernmost of the two features and called it Fleetfoot Peak; the two peaks also were known as Round Buttons and as Maggie's Mountains (Lekisch, p. 83-84).

Magnolia [EL DORADO]: *locality,* nearly 4 miles west-northwest of Coloma (lat. 38°49'35" N, long. 120°56'40" W). Named on Placerville (1893) 30' quadrangle.

Magnolia Creek [NEVADA]: *stream,* flows 6 miles to Bear River 2 miles southwest of Higgins Corner (lat. 39°01'25" N, long. 121°07'10" W; near NE cor. sec. 31, T 14 N, R 8 E). Named on Lake Combie (1949) 7.5' quadrangle.

Magonigal Camp [NEVADA]: *locality,* 8 miles west-northwest of Donner Pass (lat. 39°22'30" N, long. 120°27' W; at N line sec. 6, T 17 N, R 14 E); the place is nearly 1.5 miles north-northeast of Magonigal Summit. Named on Soda Springs (1955) 7.5' quadrangle.

Magonigal Summit [NEVADA]: *pass,* 8 miles west-northwest of Donner Pass (lat. 39°21'25" N, long. 120°27'50" W; sec. 12, T 17 N, R 13 E). Named on Soda Springs (1955) 7.5' quadrangle.

Magpie Creek [SACRAMENTO]: *stream,* flows 8.5 miles to an artificial watercourse 3.5 miles south of Rio Linda (lat. 38°38'30" N, long. 121°27'15" W). Named on Citrus Heights (1967) and Rio Linda (1967) 7.5' quadrangles.

Magra [PLACER]: *locality,* 4.5 miles northeast of Colfax along Southern Pacific Railroad (lat. 39°08'55" N, long. 120°53'45" W; sec. 18, T 15 N, R 10 E). Named on Chicago Park (1949) 7.5' quadrangle.

Maguires Mountain: see **Liberty Hill Diggings** [NEVADA].

Mahala Flat: see **Volcano** [AMADOR].

Mahon Camp [EL DORADO]: *locality,* 8 miles west-southwest of Kirkwood (lat. 38°40'05" N, long. 120°12'55" W; near SW cor. sec. 33, T 10 N, R 16 E). Named on Tragedy Spring (1979) 7.5' quadrangle.

Maiden Valley [SIERRA]: *valley,* 5 miles west-southwest of Sierraville at the head of Dark Canyon (1) (lat. 39°33'05" N, long. 120° 26'35" W; at S line sec. 29, T 20 N, R 14 E). Named on Sattley (1981) 7.5' quadrangle.

Maine Bar [EL DORADO]: *locality,* 3.5 miles northwest of Greenwood along Middle Fork American River (lat. 38°56'20" N, long. 120°57'25" W; sec. 34, T 13 N, R 9 E). Named on Greenwood (1949) 7.5' quadrangle. Bancroft (1888, p. 354) listed a place called Green Mountain Bar that was located on the south side of Middle Fork between Maine Bar and Hoosier Bar.

Maine Bar Canyon [EL DORADO]: *canyon,* drained by a stream that flows nearly 2 miles to Middle Fork American River 3.5 miles northwest of Greenwood at Maine Bar (lat. 38°56'15" N, long. 120°57'30" W; sec. 34, T 13 N, R 9 E). Named on Greenwood (1949) 7.5' quadrangle.

Maintop [PLACER]: *locality,* 4.5 miles north of Michigan Bluff (lat. 39°06'35" N, long. 120°43'05" W; near SE cor. sec. 27, T 15 N, R 11 E). Site named on Michigan Bluff (1952) 7.5' quadrangle.

Malakoff [NEVADA]: *locality,* 1.25 miles west of North Bloomfield (lat. 39°22'10" N, long. 120°55'30" W); the site is at present Malakoff Diggings. Named on Colfax (1898) 30' quadrangle.

Malakoff Diggings [NEVADA]: *locality,* less than 1 mile west of North Bloomfield (lat. 39°22'15" N, long. 120°54'45" W; on and near N line sec. 1, T 17 N, R 9 E). Named on North Bloomfield (1949) and Pike (1949) 7.5' quadrangles. The name was given at the time of the Crimean War for Malakoff Tower near Sebastopol in Russia (Gudde, 1975, p. 204).

Malaney Flat [COLUSA]: *area,* nearly 2 miles north-northwest of Wilbur Springs (lat. 39°03'40" N, long. 120°26'05" W; sec. 17, T 14 N, R 5 W). Named on Wilbur Springs (1961) 15' quadrangle.

Malay Camp: see **Smartville** [YUBA].

Malby: see **Malby Crossing** [EL DORADO].

Malby Crossing [EL DORADO]: *locality,* 3 miles south-southwest of Clarksville along Southern Pacific Railroad at the rail crossing of Carson Creek (lat. 38°36'45" N, long. 121°04'05" W; on S line sec. 23, T 9 N, R 8 E). Named on Folsom SE (1954) 7.5' quadrangle. Called Malby on Folsom (1941) 15' quadrangle. California Division of Highways' (1934) map shows a place called Harvey 2 miles southeast of Malby along the railroad (at E line sec. 36, T 9 N, R 8 E).

Malcomb Bar: see **Gray Eagle Bar** [EL DORADO].

Males Station Campground [SIERRA]: *locality,* 3.25 miles east-southeast of Crystal Peak along South Branch Dog Creek (lat. 39° 32'30" N, long. 120°01'45" W; at W line sec. 6, T 19 N, R 18 E). Named on Dog Valley (1981) 7.5' quadrangle.

Mameluke Hill [EL DORADO]: *peak,* 0.5 mile north-northwest of Georgetown (lat. 38°54'55" N, long. 120°50'25" W; near SE cor. sec. 3, T 12 N, R 10 E). Named on Georgetown (1949) 7.5' quadrangle. Gudde (1975, p. 52) listed a mining place called Bull Diggings that was located north of Mameluke Hill on the ridge between Illinois Canyon and Oregon Canyon; the name was from bulls used to haul gravel to be washed. Gudde (1975, p. 224) also listed a mining place called Mormon Gulch that was situated on Mameluke Hill.

Mammoth Bar [PLACER]: *locality,* 4 miles east-northeast of Auburn along Middle Fork American River (lat. 38°55'05" N, long. 121°00' W; sec. 5, T 12 N, R 9 E). Named on Auburn (1953) and Greenwood (1949) 7.5' quadrangles.

Mammoth Spring [SIERRA]: *spring,* 2 miles northeast of Alleghany (lat. 39°29'25" N, long. 120°48'55" W; near NE cor. sec. 26, T 19 N, R 10 E). Named on Alleghany (1949) 7.5' quadrangle. Called Mammoth Springs on Colfax (1938) 30' quadrangle.

Mammoth Spring: see **Lowell Hill** [NEVADA].

Manhattan Bar: see **Rattlesnake Bar** [PLACER].

Manhattan Creek [EL DORADO]: *stream,* flows nearly 3 miles to join Empire Creek and form Johntown Creek 6.5 miles north-northwest of Chili Bar (lat. 38°51'30" N, long. 120°51' W; sec. 27, T 12 N, R 10 E). Named on Garden Valley (1949) and Georgetown (1949) 7.5' quadrangles. Miners from New York named the stream in 1849 (Gernes, p. 51).

Manila Canyon [PLACER]: *canyon,* drained by a stream that flows 2.5 miles to Screwauger Canyon 3.25 miles west-southwest of Duncan Peak (lat. 39°08'40" N, long. 120°34'20" W; sec. 18, T 15 N, R 13 E). Named on Duncan Peak (1952) 7.5' quadrangle.

Manimoth Spring: see **Government Spring** [PLACER].

Manlove [SACRAMENTO]: *locality,* 5 miles south-southwest of downtown Carmichael along Southern Pacific Railroad (lat. 38°33'15" N, long. 121°22'20" W; at NE cor. sec. 13, T 8 N, R 5 E). Named on Carmichael (1967) 7.5' quadrangle. California Division of Highways' (1934) map shows a place called Brown located 0.5 mile west-southwest of Manlove, and a place called Alden located 0.5 mile east-northeast of Manlove, both places along the railroad.

Manor Slough [COLUSA]: *stream,* flows 4.5 miles to Glenn Valley Slough 13 miles northeast of Wilbur Springs (lat. 39°11'10" N, long. 122°16'15" W; sec. 2, T 15 N, R 4 W). Named on Manor Slough (1958) 7.5' quadrangle.

Manzanita Creek [COLUSA]: *stream,* flows 5.25 miles to Cortina Creek 9 miles east-southeast of Wilbur Springs (lat. 39°00'10" N, long. 122°15'30" W; sec. 1, T 13 N, R 4 W). Named on Morgan Valley (1958) and Wilbur Springs (1961) 15' quadrangles.

Maple Grove Camp Ground [EL DORADO]: *locality,* less than 0.5 mile west of Riverton along South Fork American River (lat. 38° 46'20" N, long. 120°27'20" W; sec. 30, T 11 N, R 14 E). Named on Riverton (1950, photorevised 1973) 7.5' quadrangle.

Maple Grove Creek [YUBA]: *stream,* flows 1 mile to Keystone Creek 2 miles north-northwest of Dobbins (lat. 39°23'45" N, long. 121°13'20" W; at NE cor. sec. 30, T 18 N, R 7 E). Named on Challenge (1948) 7.5' quadrangle.

Maple Springs House: see **Indiana Ranch** [YUBA].

Marble Creek [EL DORADO]: *stream,* flows 3 miles to Deer Creek (2) 4.25 miles north-northwest of Latrobe (lat. 38°37'15" N, long. 120°59'50" W; sec. 21, T 9 N, R 9 E). Named on Clarksville (1953), Folsom SE (1954), and Latrobe (1949) 7.5' quadrangles.

Marble Point: see **Mokelumne River** [AMADOR-SACRAMENTO].

Marble Spring [EL DORADO]: *locality,* 3 miles south of Omo Ranch near Indian Creek (5) (lat. 38°32'20" N, long. 120°35'30" W). Named on Placerville (1893) 30' quadrangle.

Marble Springs [EL DORADO]: *spring,* 2.25 miles south-southwest of Omo Ranch (lat. 38°32'50" N, long. 120°34'45" W; sec. 18, T 8 N, R 13 E). Named on Omo Ranch (1952) 7.5' quadrangle, which shows a marble quarry near the spring.

Marble Valley [EL DORADO]: *valley,* 2.25 miles east-southeast of Clarksville on the upper reaches of Marble Creek (lat. 38°38'40" N, long. 121°00'40" W; on S line sec. 8, T 9 N, R 9 E). Named on Clarksville (1953) 7.5' quadrangle.

Marchant [SUTTER]: *locality,* 3.5 miles south-southeast of Robbins along Southern Pacific Railroad in Sutter Basin (lat. 38°49'20" N, long. 121°40'40" W; near S line sec. 6, T 11 N, R 3 E). Named on Knights Landing (1952) 7.5' quadrangle. California Division of Highways' (1934) map shows a place called Mackert located 1.25 miles north-northwest of Marchant, a place called Bypass located less than 1 mile east of Marchant, and a place called Vernon located 2 miles east-northeast of Marchant—all situated along Southern Pacific Railroad.

Marcuse [SUTTER]: *locality,* 4 miles northwest of Nicolaus along Southern Pacific Railroad (lat. 38°57'10" N, long. 121°37'30" W). Named on Marcuse (1910) and Nicolaus (1910) 7.5' quadrangles. Postal authorities established Marcuse post office in 1891, discontinued it in 1902, reestablished it in 1910, and discontinued it in 1913; the name commemorates Jonas Marcuse, a pioneer of 1869 (Salley, p. 132).

Maredith Mill [SIERRA]: *locality,* 6.5 miles south-southwest of Mount Fillmore (lat. 39°38'25" N, long. 120°52'40" W; sec. 32, T 21 N, R 10 E). Named on La Porte (1951) 7.5' quadrangle.

Margaret: see **Lake Margaret** [EL DORADO].

Margery: see **Lake Margery** [EL DORADO].

Marietta: see **Forest** [SIERRA].

Marigold [YUBA]: *village,* 5 miles south-southwest of Browns Valley (lat. 39°10'45" N, long. 121°27'25" W; sec. 6, T 15 N, R 5 E). Named on Wheatland (1949) 15' quadrangle. Postal authorities established Marigold post office in 1911 and discontinued it in 1929 (Frickstad, p. 223). The name is a contraction of the term "Marysville Gold Mining Company" (Salley, p. 133). The place was connected with gold-dredging activity early in the twentieth century, and was at the site of an earlier community called Martins (Gudde, 1975, p. 207).

Marion Creek [SIERRA]: *stream,* flows 1.5 miles to Oregon Creek 1.5 miles north-northeast of Pike (lat. 39°27'50" N, long. 120°59'30" W; near N line sec. 5, T 18 N, R 9 E). Named on Pike (1949) 7.5' quadrangle.

Mark Edson Reservoir: see **Stumpy Meadows Lake** [EL DORADO].

Markham Ravine [PLACER-SUTTER]: *canyon,* drained by a stream that heads in Placer County and flows 16 miles to a canal 8 miles northeast of Verona in Sutter County (lat. 38°52' N, long. 121°30'50" W; near N line sec. 27, T 12 N, R 4 E). Named on Lincoln (1953), Nicolaus (1952), Sheridan (1953, photorevised 1973), and Verona (1967) 7.5' quadrangles. Hobson's (1890b) map has the name "Markham Slough" for the feature.

Markham Slough: see **Markham Ravine** [PLACER].

Marliave: see **Mount Marliave**, under **Hole-in-Ground** [NEVADA].

Mars: see **Outingdale** [EL DORADO].

Marshall: see **Lotus** [EL DORADO].

Marsh Diggings: see **Parks Bar** [YUBA].

Marsh Mill [NEVADA]: *locality,* 2 miles east of Graniteville (lat. 39°26'40" N, long. 120°42'10" W; sec. 11, T 18 N, R 11 E). Site named on Graniteville (1982) 7.5' quadrangle.

Martel Creek [EL DORADO]: *stream,* flows 2.5 miles to Sweetwater Creek 5.25 miles north of Clarksville (lat. 38°43'55" N, long. 121° 02'10" W; sec. 7, T 10 N, R 9 E). Named on Clarksville (1953) 7.5' quadrangle.

Martell [AMADOR]: *village,* 1.5 miles northwest of Jackson (lat. 38° 22' N, long. 120°47'45" W; near NW cor. sec. 20, T 6 N, R 11 E). Named on Jackson (1962) 7.5' quadrangle. Postal authorities established Martell post office in 1905; the name commemorates Louis Martell, who settled in the region in the 1860's (Salley, p. 134). Camp's (1962) map gives the name "Oneida" as an alternate designation for the place.

Martin Creek [EL DORADO]: *stream,* flows 2.5 miles to Silver Fork American River 8 miles west of Krikwood (lat. 38°42'20" N, long. 120°12'55" W). Named on Tragedy Spring (1979) 7.5' quadrangle.

Martinez Creek [EL DORADO]: *stream,* flows nearly 7 miles to North Fork Cosumnes River 7.5 miles south of Placerville (lat. 38°37'05" N, long. 120°48'40" W; sec. 19, T 9 N, R 11 E). Named on Fiddletown (1949) and Placerville (1949) 7.5' quadrangles.

Martin Flat [YOLO]: *area,* 3.25 miles south-southwest of Rumsey (lat. 38°50'45" N, long. 122°15'50" W). Named on Knoxville (1958) 7.5' quadrangle.

Martin Meadow [EL DORADO]: *area,* 2.5 miles west of Kirkwood near Amador-El Dorado County line (lat. 38°41'50" N, long. 120° 07'10" W; sec. 20, T 10 N, T 17 E). Named on Caples Lake (1979) 7.5' quadrangle.

Martin Point [AMADOR]: *peak,* 10.5 miles north of Mokelumne Peak (lat. 38°41'20" N, long. 120°05'30" W; sec. 28, T 10 N, R 17 E). Altitude 9250 feet. Named on Caples Lake (1979) 7.5' quadrangle.

Martins: see **Marigold** [YUBA].

Martins House: see **Oregon House** [YUBA].

Martis Creek [NEVADA-PLACER]: *stream*, heads in Placer County and flows 12 miles to Truckee River 3.5 miles east-northeast of Truckee in Nevada County (lat. 39°21' N, long. 120°07' W; sec. 5, T 17 N, R 17 E); the stream goes through Martis Valley. Named on Martis Peak (1955), Tahoe City (1955), and Truckee (1955) 7.5' quadrangles. United States Board on Geographic Names (1972, p. 4) approved the name "Martis Creek Lake" for a lake on Nevada-Placer County line that is formed by a dam on Martis Creek 3.5 miles east of Truckee (lat. 39°19'45" N, long. 120° 07' W; sec. 17, T 17 N, R 17 E), and gave the name "Martis Creek Reservoir" as a variant.

Martis Creek: see **East Martis Creek** [PLACER]; **Middle Martis Creek** [PLACER]; **West Martis Creek** [PLACER].

Martis Creek Lake: see **Martis Creek** [NEVADA-PLACER].

Martis Creek Reservoir: see **Martis Creek** [NEVADA-PLACER].

Martis Peak [PLACER]: *peak*, 15 miles east of Donner Pass (lat. 39° 17'30" N, long. 120°01'55" W; sec. 25, T 17 N, R 17 E). Altitude 8742 feet. Named on Martis Peak (1955) 7.5' quadrangle.

Martis Valley [NEVADA-PLACER]: *valley*, 2.25 miles east-southeast of Truckee on Nevada-Placer County line (lat. 39°19' N, long. 120° 08'30" W); the valley is 6 miles west-northwest of Martis Peak along lower reaches of Martis Creek. Named on Martis Peak (1955) and Truckee (1955) 7.5' quadrangles.

Marty [YOLO]: *locality*, 10.5 miles northeast of Davis along Sacramento and Woodland Railroad (lat. 38°37'50" N, long. 121°34'55" W). Named on Elkhorn Weir (1915) 7.5' quadrangle. California Division of Highways' (1934) map shows a place called Fourness located along the railroad less than 1 mile southeast of Marty.

Mary: see **Lake Mary** [PLACER].

Mary Lake [SUTTER]: *lake*, nearly 6 miles south of Robbins in a cutoff meander of Sacramento River (lat. 38°47'20" N, long. 121° 41'05" W; sec. 19, T 11 N, R 3 E). Named on Knights Landing (1952) 7.5' quadrangle.

Marys Lake [EL DORADO]: *lake*, 800 feet long, 6.5 miles northeast of Robbs Peak (lat. 38°59'40" N, long. 120°19'20" W; on S line sec. 5, T 13 N, R 15 E). Named on Robbs Peak (1952) 15' quadrangle. The feature now is part of an enlarged Loon Lake.

Marys Ravine [YUBA]: *canyon*, drained by a stream that flows 1.5 miles to Middle Yuba River 4.25 miles east of Dobbins (lat. 39°22'50" N, long. 121°07'35" W; sec. 31, T 18 N, R 8 E). Named on Challenge (1948) 7.5' quadrangle.

Marysville [YUBA]: *town*, near the center of the west line of Yuba County on the east side of Feather River above the junction with Yuba River (lat. 39°08'45" N, long. 121°35'25" W). Named on Yuba City (1952) 7.5' quadrangle. Postal authorities established Marysville post office in 1851 (Frickstad, p. 223), and the town incorporated the same year. Theodore Cordua leased land at the site from Sutter in 1842 and set up a trading post there—he called the place New Mecklenburg for his native land, but it generally was known as Cordua's Ranch; Charles Covillaud bought a half share of the property in 1848, and the following year Michael C. Nye and William Foster acquired the other half, after which the place was known as Nye's Ranch; Manuel Ramirez, John Sampson, and Theodore Sicard acquired a three-quarters interest in the property in 1849, and in 1850 had a town laid out that was named Marysville for Covillaud's wife, the former Mary Murphy of Donner-party fame (Hoover, Rensch and Rensch, p. 587-588). Postal authorities established Newbert post office 9 miles east of Marysville in 1881 and discontinued it in 1898—the name was for Leander Newbert, first postmaster; they established Hutchins post office 10 miles north of Marysville in 1902 and discontinued it in 1903—the name was for T.B. Hutchins, who had large agricultural holdings in Yuba County and Butte County (Salley, p. 102, 153). Wescoatt's (1861) map shows a place called Prairie House located 8 miles north-northeast of Marysville. Gudde (1975, p. 248) listed a place called Oakland that was situated along Feather River 11 miles north of Marysville; it was a speculative town that John Monet laid out on his ranch in 1850, but the enterprise failed.

Marysville Buttes: see **Sutter Buttes** [SUTTER].

Marysville Lake: see **McCartie Hill** [YUBA].

Marysville Reservoir: see **McCartie Hill** [YUBA].

Mather: see **Mather Air Force Base** [SACRAMENTO]; **Soudan** [SACRAMENTO].

Mather Air Force Base [SACRAMENTO]: *military installation*, 5 miles south-southeast of downtown Carmichael (lat. 38°33'15" N, long. 121°16'30"). Named on Buffalo Creek (1967) and Carmichael (1967) 7.5' quadrangles. Carmichael (1967) 7.5' quadrangle also has the name "Mather Field" at the place. Postal authorities established Mather post office in 1918 and discontinued it in 1919; they established Mather Field post office in 1941 and changed the name to Mather Air Force Base in 1956—the name "Mather" commemorates Lieutenant Carl S. Mather, who was killed in an airplane crash in 1918 (Salley, p. 135).

Mather Field: see **Mather Air Force Base** [SACRAMENTO].

Mather Lake [SACRAMENTO]: *lake*, 6 miles southeast of downtown Carmichael (lat. 38°33'20" N, long. 121°15'05" W; sec. 7, 18, T 8 N, R 7 E); the lake is on Mather Air Force Base. Named on Buffalo Creek (1967) and Carmichael (1967) 7.5' quadrangles.

Matheus: see **Deer Creek** [NEVADA-YUBA].

Matulich Meadow [EL DORADO]: *area*, 5 miles west of Old Iron Mountain (lat. 38°41'50" N, long. 120°29' W; near N line sec. 25, T 10 N, R 13 E). Named on Stump Spring (1951) 7.5' quadrangle.

Maud Lake [EL DORADO]: *lake*, 1000 feet long, 5.5 miles southwest of Phipps Peak (lat. 38°53'30" N, long. 120°12'30" W; on E line sec. 16, T 12 N, R 16 E). Named on Rockbound Valley (1955) 7.5' quadrangle.

Maxwell [COLUSA]: *town*, 10 miles west-northwest of Colusa (lat. 39°16'35" N, long. 122°11'30" W; around SE cor. sec. 33, T 17 N, R 3 W). Named on Maxwell (1952) 7.5' quadrangle. Postal authorities established Maxwell post office in 1877 and named it for George Maxwell, an early settler; the place also was known as Occident (Salley, p. 135).

May: see **Carbondale** [AMADOR].

Mayberry Cut [SACRAMENTO]: *water feature*, on Sherman Island, extends from Mayberry Slough to San Joaquin River 13 miles southwest of Isleton (lat. 38°01'35" N, long. 121°47' W). Named on Antioch North (1978) 7.5' quadrangle.

Mayberry Slough [SACRAMENTO]: *water feature*, on Sherman Island, joins San Joaquin River 12.5 miles southwest of Isleton (lat. 38°01'50" N, long. 121°45'45" W). Named on Antioch North (1978) and Jersey Island (1978) 7.5' quadrangles.

Maybert [NEVADA]: *locality*, 5.5 miles south-southeast of Graniteville along South Fork Yuba River (present South Yuba River) (lat. 39°21' N, long. 120°42'05" W). Named on Colfax (1898) 30' quadrangle. Postal authorities established Maybert post office in 1886, moved it 0.5 mile east in 1897, discontinued it in 1905, reestablished it in 1907, and discontinued it in 1910; the name is from a gold mine at the site (Salley, p. 135).

Mayers Ravine: see **Meyers Ravine** [NEVADA].

Mayflower [PLACER]: *locality*, 1.25 miles north of Foresthill (lat. 39°02'10" N, long. 120°49'30" W). Named on Colfax (1898) 30' quadrangle. Foresthill (1949) 7.5' quadrangle shows Mayflower mine at the place.

Mayhew [SACRAMENTO]: *locality*, 4 miles south-southwest of downtown Carmichael along Southern Pacific Railroad (lat. 38°33'50" N, long. 121°21'10" W; at W line sec. 8, T 8 N, R 6 E). Named on Carmichael (1967) 7.5' quadrangle. Called Mayhews on Mills (1911) 7.5' quadrangle. Postal authorities established Mayhew's Station post office in 1870 and discontinued it in 1873; they established Russell post office in 1889, changed the name to Mayhews in 1891, and discontinued it in 1922—the name "Mayhews" was for Mr. L. Mayhew, station agent for Sacramento Valley Railroad (Salley, p. 135, 190).

Mayhew's Station: see **Mayhew** [SACRAMENTO].

Mays: see **Tahoe Valley** [EL DORADO].

Mays Flat [YOLO]: *area*, 6.5 miles north-northwest of Berryessa Peak along Blue Ridge on Yolo-Napa County line (lat. 38°45' N, long. 122°14'30" W; near NE cor. sec. 1, T 10 N, R 4 W). Named on Brooks (1959) and Guinda (1959) 7.5' quadrangles.

McAlpine: see **Calpine** [SIERRA].

McBride Creek [PLACER]: *stream*, flows 1.5 miles to the head of Shirttail Canyon 5 miles northeast of Foresthill (lat. 39°04'35" N, long. 120°45'45" W; sec. 8, T 14 N, R 11 E). Named on Foresthill (1949) and Michigan Bluff (1952) 7.5' quadrangles.

McCartie Hill [YUBA]: *peak*, 3 miles south of Browns Valley (lat. 39°11'50" N, long. 121°24'35" W; near SE cor. sec. 33, T 16 N, R 5 E). Named on Browns Valley (1947) 7.5' quadrangle. United States Board on Geographic Names (1972, p. 4) approved the name "Marysville Lake" for a lake formed by damming Yuba River 11 miles northeast of Marysville near McCartie Hill (lat. 39°12'52" N, long. 121°24'55" W; sec. 28, T 16 N, R 5 E), and gave the name "Marysville Reservoir" as a variant.

McCarty Flat [NEVADA]: *area*, 2.25 miles south-southeast of Higgins Corner (lat. 39°00'45" N, long. 121°04'20" W; at N line sec. 3, T 13 N, R 8 E). Named on Lake Combie (1949) 7.5' quadrangle.

McCarty Flat: see **O' Donnells Flat**, under **Downieville** [SIERRA].

McClellan: see **McClellan Air Force Base** [SACRAMENTO].

McClellan Air Force Base [SACRAMENTO]: *military installation*, 7.5 miles northeast of downtown Sacramento (lat. 38°39'45" N, long. 121°24' W). Named on Rio Linda (1967) 7.5' quadrangle. Called McClellan Field on Fair Oaks (1954) 15' quadrangle. Postal authorities established McClellan Field post office in 1940, changed the name to McClellan in 1949, and changed it to McClellan Air Force Base in 1956; the place also was known as Sacramento Air Depot during World War II (Salley, p. 136). War Department officials named the place in 1939 to honor Army Air Corps Major Hez McClelland (Gudde, 1949, p. 198).

McClellan Field: see **McClellan Air Force Base** [SACRAMENTO].

McConnel [SACRAMENTO]: *locality*, 8 miles north-northwest of Galt along Southern Pacific Railroad (lat. 38°21'50" N, long. 121° 20'45" W). Named on Galt (1968) 7.5' quadrangle. Called McConnell on Galt (1910) 7.5' quadrangle. Central Pacific Railroad officials named the place in the 1870's for Thomas McConnell, who came to Sacramento County in 1855 and raised sheep (Gudde, 1949, p. 199).

McConnell Lake [EL DORADO]: *lake,* 750 feet long, 4.25 miles west-southwest of Phipps Peak (lat. 38°56'35" N, long. 120°13'30" W; sec. 29, T 13 N, R 16 E); the lake 1 mile east-southeast of McConnell Peak. Named on Rockbound Valley (1955) 7.5' quadrangle.

McConnell Peak [EL DORADO]: *peak,* 5 miles west of Phipps Peak (lat. 38°56'55" N, long. 120°14'30" W; at E line sec. 30, T 13 N, R 16 E). Altitude 9099 feet. Named on Rockbound Valley (1955) 7.5' quadrangle.

McCosumne: see **Cosumne** [SACRAMENTO].

McCourtney Crossing [PLACER-YUBA]: *locality,* 6 miles northeast of Sheridan along Bear River on Placer-Yuba County line (lat. 39° 02'40" N, long. 121°17'35" W; at N line sec. 27, T 14 N, R 6 E); water of Camp Far West Reservoir now covers the site. Named on Wheatland (1949) 15' quadrangle.

McCulloh [PLACER]: *locality,* 1.25 miles east-southeast of Devil Peak in Big Grizzly Canyon (lat. 38°57'15" N, long. 120°31'30" W; near N line sec. 28, T 13 N, R 13 E). Named on Devil Peak (1950) 7.5' quadrangle.

McCulloh Spring [PLACER]: *spring,* 0.5 mile north of Devil Peak (lat. 38°58'05" N, long. 120°32'50" W; sec. 20, T 13 N, R 13 E). Named on Devil Peak (1950) 7.5' quadrangle.

McDonald Flat: see **O' Donnells Flat**, under **Downieville** [SIERRA].

McDowell Canyon [COLUSA]: *canyon,* drained by a stream that flows 1.5 miles to an unnamed canyon 2.25 miles west of Sites (lat. 39°18'55" N, long. 122°22'45" W; near E line sec. 23, T 17 N, R 5 W). Named on Lodoga (1960) 15' quadrangle.

McDowell Hill: see **Folsom Lake** [EL DORADO-PLACER-SACRAMENTO].

McDowellsville: see **McDowell Hill**, under **Folsom Lake** [EL DORADO-PLACER-SACRAMENTO].

McGinn Creek [YUBA]: *stream,* flows 2.5 miles to Tennessee Creek 5 miles southwest of Oregon House (lat. 39°19' N, long. 121°21'30" W; sec. 24, T 17 N, R 5 E); the stream is south of McGinn Hill. Named on Oregon House (1948) 7.5' quadrangle.

McGinn Hill [YUBA]: *peak,* 4.5 miles southwest of Oregon House (lat. 39°18'50" N, long. 121°20'35" W; sec. 19, T 17 N, R 6 E); the peak is north of McGinn Creek. Altitude 1232 feet. Named on Oregon House (1948) 7.5' quadrangle.

McGinnis Ravine [SIERRA]: *canyon,* drained by a stream that flows less than 1 mile to Middle Yuba River 3 miles south-southwest of Alleghany (lat. 39°25'55" N, long. 120°52'05" W; near NE cor. sec. 17, T 18 N, R 19 E). Named on Alleghany (1949) 7.5' quadrangle.

McGlashan Point: see **Donner Pass** [NEVADA-PLACER].

McGriff Lakes [SUTTER]: *lakes,* largest 2200 feet long, 4.5 miles south of Robbins near Sacramento River (lat. 38°48'10" N, long. 121°41'30" W; in and near sec. 13, T 11 N, R 2 E). Named on Knights Landing (1952) 7.5' quadrangle.

McGuire Campground [PLACER]: *locality,* 6 miles northwest of Bunker Hill along Middle Fork American River (lat. 39°06'45" N, long. 120°27'35" W; near NE cor. sec. 36, T 15 N, R 13 E). Named on Granite Chief (1953) 15' quadrangle. Water of French Meadows Reservoir now covers the site.

McGuire Mountain [NEVADA]: *peak,* 7.25 miles south of Washington (lat. 39°15'10" N, long. 120°47'40" W; near E line sec. 13, T 16 N, R 10 E). Named on Washington (1950) 7.5' quadrangle.

McIntosh Hill [PLACER]: *peak,* 1.25 miles south of Cisco Grove at the east end of Monumental Ridge (lat. 39°17'20" N, long. 120°32'20" W; near S line sec. 32, T 17 N, R 13 E). Altitude 6762 feet. Named on Cisco Grove (1955) 7.5' quadrangle.

McIntyre Gulch [PLACER]: *canyon,* drained by a stream that flows 1.25 miles to North Fork American River 3.5 miles southeast of Dutch Flat (lat. 39°10'25" N, long. 120°47'15" W; near W line sec. 6, T 15 N, R 11 E); the mouth of the canyon is just below Green Valley. Named on Dutch Flat (1950) 7.5' quadrangle. Called Green Valley Cañon on Whitney's (1873) map.

McIntyre Lake: see **Purdue Lake** [SUTTER].

McKay Spring [NEVADA]: *spring,* 5.25 miles east-northeast of Truckee (lat. 39°20'50" N, long. 120°05'20" W; sec. 4, T 17 N, R 17 E). Named on Martis Peak (1955) 7.5' quadrangle.

McKeon: see **Butchers** [PLACER].

McKilligan Creek [NEVADA]: *stream,* flows 2.25 miles to South Yuba River 1 mile west-southwest of Washington (lat. 39°21'10" N, long. 120°49'05" W; sec. 11, T 17 N, R 10 E). Named on Alleghany (1949) and Washington (1950) 7.5' quadrangles. Called McKillican Creek on Colfax (1938) 30' quadrangle.

McKinney: see **Chambers Lodge** [PLACER].

McKinney Bay [PLACER]: *embayment,* along Lake Tahoe at Homewood (lat. 39°05' N, long. 120°09' W). Named on Homewood (1955) 7.5' quadrangle. The name commemorates John McKinney, who came to the neighborhood in the early 1850's, and later opened a resort near the south end of the embayment (Gudde, 1949, p. 199).

McKinney Canyon [YOLO]: *canyon,* drained by a stream that flows 3.5 miles to Capay Valley nearly 4 miles south of Guinda (lat. 38° 46'25" N, long. 122°11'20" W; sec. 27, T 11 N, R 3 W). Named on Guinda (1959) 7.5' quadrangle.

McKinney Creek [EL DORADO]: *stream,* flows 4.5 miles to Dogtown Creek at Caldor (lat. 38°36'20" N, long. 120°26' W; sec. 28, T 9 N, R 14 E). Named on Caldor (1951) and Peddler Hill (1951) 7.5' quadrangles.

McKinney Creek [PLACER]: *stream,* flows 4 miles to Lake Tahoe 1.5 miles southeast of Homewood (lat. 39°04'25" N, long. 120°08'25" W; sec. 7, T 14 N, R 17 E); the stream enters the lake near the south end of McKinney Bay. Named on Homewood (1955) 7.5' quadrangle. The name commemorates John McKinney of McKinney Bay (Gudde, 1949, p. 199).

McKinney Lake [PLACER]: *lake,* 1650 feet long, 3.25 miles south-southwest of Homewood (lat. 39°02'25" N, long. 120°10'35" W; sec. 23, T 14 N, R 16 E); the lake is along McKinney Creek. Named on Homewood (1955) 7.5' quadrangle.

McKinstry Lake [PLACER]: *lake,* 950 feet long, 2.5 miles east of Bunker Hill (lat. 39°02'30" N, long. 120°19'50" W; sec. 19, T 14 N, R 15 E); the lake is 1 mile southeast of McKinstry Peak in McKinstry Meadow. Named on Wentworth Springs (1953) 7.5' quadrangle.

McKinstry Meadow [PLACER]: *valley,* 2.5 miles east-southeast of Bunker Hill along Jerrett Creek (lat. 39°02'20" N, long. 120°20'10" W; sec. 19, 30, T 14 N, R 15 E); the valley is 1 mile south-southeast of McKinstry Peak. Named on Wentworth Springs (1953) 7.5' quadrangle.

McKinstry Meadow: see **Little McKinstry Meadow** [PLACER].

McKinstry Peak [PLACER]: *peak,* nearly 2 miles east of Bunker Hill (lat. 39°03'05" N, long. 120°20'45" W; at NW cor. sec. 19, T 14 N, R 15 E). Named on Wentworth Springs (1953) 7.5' quadrangle. The name commemorates George McKinstry, Jr., who came to California in 1846 (Hanna, p. 181).

McMahons [SIERRA]: *locality,* 5.25 miles northwest of Goodyears Bar (lat. 39°36' N, long. 120°56'40" W). Named on Downieville (1897) 30' quadrangle.

McManus [EL DORADO]: *locality,* nearly 4 miles northeast of Pollock Pines (lat. 38°47'55" N, long. 120°32' W; sec. 9, T 11 N, R 13 E). Named on Pollock Pines (1950) 7.5' quadrangle.

McMurray Lake [NEVADA]: *lake,* 5 miles east-northeast of Graniteville (lat. 39°27'40" N, long. 120°38'50" W; near N line sec. 5, T 18 N, R 12 E). Named on Graniteville (1982) 7.5' quadrangle.

McNair Meadow [SIERRA]: *area,* 2.5 miles west-northwest of Calpine (lat. 39°40'50" N, long. 120°29'05" W; sec. 14, T 21 N, R 13 E). Named on Calpine (1981) 7.5' quadrangle. Called Little Valley on Sierraville (1894) 30' quadrangle.

McPherrin Camp [SIERRA]: *locality,* 2 miles north of Calpine (lat. 39°41'35" N, long. 120°26'35" W; near NW cor. sec. 8, T 21 N, R 14 E). Named on Calpine (1981) 7.5' quadrangle.

McPhetres: see **Big Chief** [PLACER].

Mead Hill [YUBA]: *peak,* 0.5 mile east-southeast of Smartville (lat. 39°12'20" N, long. 121°17'20" W; sec. 34, T 16 N, R 6 E). Altitude 1023 feet. Named on Smartville (1951) 7.5' quadrangle.

Meadow Brook [EL DORADO]: *locality,* 6.5 miles north of Chili Bar (lat. 38°51'35" N, long. 120°19'55" W; sec. 26, T 12 N, R 10 E). Named on Garden Valley (1949) 7.5' quadrangle.

Meadow Creek: see **West Meadow Creek** [PLACER].

Meadow Lake [NEVADA]: *lake,* 1.25 miles long, 11 miles northwest of Donner Pass (lat. 39°24'45" N, long. 120°29'45" W). Named on English Mountain (1983) and Webber Peak (1981) 7.5' quadrangles.

Meadow Lake: see **Summit City** [NEVADA].

Meadow Lake Hill [NEVADA]: *peak,* 10 miles northwest of Donner Pass (lat. 39°24'55" N, long. 120°28'50" W; sec. 23, T 18 N, R 13 E); the peak is east of Meadow Lake. Altitude 7821 feet. Named on Webber Peak (1981) 7.5' quadrangle.

Meadows [SACRAMENTO]: *locality,* 2 miles north of Elk Grove along Southern Pacific Railroad (lat. 38°26'20" N, long. 121°22'30" W; near S line sec. 24, T 7 N, R 5 E). Named on Elk Grove (1968) 75' quadrangle.

Meadow Spring [PLACER]: *spring,* 3.5 miles southwest of Cisco Grove (lat. 39°16'25" N, long. 120°35'05" W; at NW cor. sec. 12, T 16 N, R 12 E); the spring is in Mears Meadow. Named on Cisco Grove (1955) 7.5' quadrangle.

Meadows Slough: see **The Meadows Slough** [SACRAMENTO].

Meadow-Vale: see **Summit Valley** [NEVADA-PLACER].

Meadow Vista [PLACER]: *locality,* 7.5 miles south-southwest of Colfax (lat. 39°00'10" N, long. 121°01'15" W; near S line sec. 6, T 13 N, R 9 E). Named on Auburn (1953) and Lake Combie (1949) 7.5' quadrangles.

Mears Meadow [PLACER]: *area,* 3.5 miles southwest of Cisco (lat. 39°16'20" N, long. 120°35' W; at NW cor. sec. 12, T 16 N, R 12 E). Named on Cisco Grove (1955) 7.5' quadrangle.

Meathouse Meadow [SIERRA]: *area,* 8 miles south-southeast of Sierraville (lat. 39°28'35" N, long. 120°18'50" W; near S line sec. 21, T 19 N, R 15 E). Named on Independence Lake (1981) 7.5' quadrangle.

Mecklenberg: see **New Mecklenberg**, under **Marysville** [YUBA].

Medical Spring [YOLO]: *spring,* 3.25 miles east of Berryessa Peak (lat. 38°39'55" N, long. 122°07'45" W; near S line sec. 31, T 10 N, R 2 W).

Named on Brooks (1959) 7.5' quadrangle.

Meeks Bay [EL DORADO]:

(1) *embayment,* along Lake Tahoe at the town of Meeks Bay (lat. 38°02'25" N, long. 120°07' W). Named on Meeks Bay (1955) 7.5' quadrangle. United States Board on Geographic Names (1936, p. 30) rejected the name "Meigs Bay" for the feature. The name is for the Meeks brothers, who bailed 25 tons of wild hay at the place in 1862 (Zauner, p. 43).

(2) *town,* 13 miles north of Pyramid Peak (lat. 39°02'20" N, long. 120°07'20" W); the town is at the embayment of the same name. Named on Homewood (1955) and Meeks Bay (1955) 7.5' quadrangles. United States Board on Geographic Names (1936, p. 30) rejected the name "Meigs Bay" for the town. Postal authorities established Meeks Bay post office in 1929 and discontinued it in 1972 (Salley, p. 137). They established Rubicon Lodge post office at a summer resort situated 2.5 miles south of Meeks Bay post office in 1921, discontinued it in 1924, reestablished it in 1925, and discontinued it in 1931 (Salley, p. 190). Truckee (1895) 30' quadrangle has the name "Murphys" at the site of the present town of Meeks Bay.

Meeks Creek [EL DORADO]: *stream,* heads at Rubicon Lake and flows 7 miles to Lake Tahoe at Meeks Bay (1) (lat. 39°02'15" N, long. 120°07'15" W; sec. 29, T 14 N, R 17 E). Named on Homewood (1955) 7.5' quadrangle. United States Board on Geographic Names (1936, p. 30) rejected the name "Meigs Creek" for the stream

Mehrten Creek [EL DORADO]: *stream,* flows 1.5 miles to Middle Fork Cosumnes River 7 miles east-southeast of Caldor (lat. 38° 35' N, long. 120°18'30" W; sec. 34, T 9 N, R 15 E). Named on Peddler Hill (1951) 7.5' quadrangle.

Mehrten Spring [EL DORADO]: *spring,* 7 miles east-southeast of Caldor (lat. 38°34'45" N, long. 120°18'35" W; near NW cor. sec. 3, T 8 N, R 15 E). Named on Peddler Hill (1951) 7.5' quadrangle.

Meigs Bay: see **Meeks Bay** [EL DORADO].

Meigs Creek: see **Meeks Creek** [EL DORADO].

Meiss [EL DORADO]: *locality,* 3.25 miles west of Leek Spring Hill (lat. 38°38'20" N, long. 120°20'05" W; at S line sec. 8, T 9 N, R 15 E). Named on Leek Spring Hill (1951) 7.5' quadrangle.

Melburn Hill: see **Remington Hill** [NEVADA] (2).

Mello [YUBA]: *locality,* 4.5 miles north-northeast of Marysville along Southern Pacific Railroad (lat. 39°12'25" N, long. 121°33'45" W). Named on Yuba City (1952) 7.5' quadrangle.

Mello Canyon [SIERRA]: *canyon,* drained by a stream that flows 2 miles to Sierra Valley 4.5 miles north of Sierraville (lat. 39°39'05" N, long. 120°21'15" W; near SE cor. sec. 24, T 21 N, R 14 E). Named on Antelope Valley (1981) 7.5' quadrangle.

Melrose: see **Cherokee** [NEVADA].

Melsons Corner [EL DORADO]: *locality,* 4 miles north-northeast of Aukum (lat. 38°36'35" N, long. 120°42'10" W; near NW cor. sec. 30, T 9 N, R 12 E). Named on Aukum (1952) 7.5' quadrangle.

Mendon: see **Brownsville** [EL DORADO].

Mendoza [SUTTER]: *locality,* 7 miles north-northwest of Yuba City along Northern Electric Railroad (lat. 39°14'05" N, long. 121°39'40" W). Named on Sutter (1911) 7.5' quadrangle.

Meridian [SUTTER]: *village,* 9 miles west of Sutter along Sacramento River (lat. 39°08'40" N, long. 121°54'50" W; at NE cor. sec. 24, T 15 N, R 1 W); the village is on Mount Diablo Meridian. Named on Meridian (1952) 7.5' quadrangle. Postal authorities established Meridian post office in 1863 (Frickstad, p. 202). California Division of Highways' (1934) map shows a place called Beet Spur located 1 mile east of Meridian along Sacramento Northern Railroad, and a place called Hageman located 2.25 miles east of Meridian along the same railroad.

Meritt: see **Merritt** [YOLO].

Merril Creek [SIERRA]: *stream,* flows nearly 7 miles to Davies Creek 3.5 miles south of Crystal Peak (lat. 39°30'20" N, long. 120° 05'50" W; at N line sec. 16, T 19 N, R 17 E); the stream goes through Merril Valley. Named on Dog Valley (1981) 7.5' quadrangle.

Merril Valley [SIERRA]: *valley,* 2 miles south-southwest of Crystal Peak (lat. 39°31'55" N, long. 120°05'50" W; mainly in sec. 4, T 19 N, R 17 E); the valley is along Merril Creek. Named on Dog Valley (1981) 7.5' quadrangle.

Merritt [YOLO]: *locality,* 5 miles north-northwest of Davis along Southern Pacific Railroad (lat. 38°36'50" N, long. 121°45'35" W; sec. 21, T 9 N, R 2 E). Named on Merritt (1952) 7.5' quadrangle. Postal authorities established Meritt post office in 1859, discontinued it in 1860, reestablished it with the name "Merritt" in 1870, and discontinued it in 1873 (Salley, p. 138). The name is for Hiram P. Merritt, who came to the county before 1866 (Gudde, 1949, p. 211).

Merritt Island [YOLO]: *island,* 6.5 miles long, south of Clarksburg between Sacramento River and Elk Slough (center near lat. 38° 22' N, long. 121°32'30" W). Named on Clarksburg (1967) and Courtland (1978) 7.5' quadrangles.

Merritt's Slough: see **Steamboat Slough** [SACRAMENTO].

Mesick: see **Messick Lake** [YUBA].

Messick: see **Oswald** [SUTTER].

Messick Lake [YUBA]: *intermittent lake,* 1550 feet long, 4.5 miles southwest of Olivehurst (lat. 39°02'15" N, long. 121°35'30" W). Named on Olivehurst (1952) 7.5' quadrangle. Ostrom (1911) 7.5' quadrangle has the name for a much larger permanent lake. Whitney's (1873) map shows a place called Mesick located 6.25 miles south of Marysville.

Mexican Gulch [PLACER]: *canyon,* drained by a stream that flows 1.5 miles to Shirttail Canyon 5.25 miles southeast of Colfax (lat. 39°02'30" N, long. 120°53'15" W; near SE cor. sec. 19, T 14 N, R 10 E); the canyon heads near Yankee Jims. Named on Colfax (1949) and Foresthill (1949) 7.5' quadrangles. Called Yankee Jims Cañon on Whitney's (1873) map.

Meyer Ravine [NEVADA]: *canyon,* drained by a stream that flows 1.5 miles to Wolf Creek 1.5 miles west of Higgins Corner (lat. 39° 02'40" N, long. 121°07'20" W; near SE cor. sec. 19, T 14 N, R 8 E). Named on Lake Combie (1949) and Wolf (1949) 7.5' quadrangles.

Meyers [EL DORADO]: *village,* 3 miles north-northeast of Echo Summit in Lake Valley (lat. 38°51'20" N, long. 120°00'45" W; sec. 29, T 12 N, R 18 E). Named on Echo Lake (1955) 7.5' quadrangle. Called Yanks on Bancroft's (1864) map. Postal authorities established Meyers post office in 1904, discontinued it in 1957, reestablished it in 1958, and changed the name to Tahoe Paradise in 1962 (Salley, p. 139, 218). Martin Smith operated a trading post and travelers stop at the site in the early 1850's; Ephraim Clement, who had the nickname "Yank," took over the place from Smith, and it was known by the name "Yank's Station" before George Henry Dudly Meyers bought out Clement in 1873 (Farquhar, 1965, p. 96, 104). Postal authorities established Little Norway post office 9 miles west of Meyers in 1961 (Salley, p. 123).

Meyers Flat: see **Myers Flat** [YOLO].

Meyers Ravine [NEVADA]: *canyon,* drained by a stream that flows 2 miles to South Yuba River 3.5 miles north-northwest of Nevada City (lat. 39°18'40" N, long. 121°03' W; sec. 26, T 17 N, R 8 E). Named on Nevada City (1948) 7.5' quadrangle. Called Mayers Rav. on Whitney's (1873) map, and called Myers Ravine on Logan's (1940) map. On Smartsville (1895) 30' quadrangle, the stream in the canyon has the name "Brush Creek."

Michigan Bar [SACRAMENTO]: *locality,* 25 miles east-southeast of downtown Sacramento along Cosumnes River (lat. 38°30' N, long. 121°02'40" W; sec. 36, T 8 N, R 8 E). Named on Carbondale (1968) 7.5' quadrangle. Carbondale (1909) 7.5' quadrangle has the name "Michigan Bar" for a settlement located about 1 mile farther south along Cosumnes River (near SE cor. sec. 1, T 7 N, R 8 E). Postal authorities established Michigan Bar post office in 1855 and discontinued it in 1935 (Frickstad, p. 133). The place began when two men from Michigan discovered gold along Cosumnes River there (Ricketts, 1978, p. 16). Dennis Cook found a good-sized gold nugget on the south side of Cosumnes River about 2 miles downstream from Michigan Bar, and by doing so he started a mining camp called Cook's Bar (Ricketts, 1978, p. 16). The community of Cook's Bar had vanished by 1860; a mining camp called Katesville was situated near Cook's Bar (Hoover, Rensch, and Rensch, p. 301).

Michigan Bluff [PLACER]: *village,* 12.5 miles east-southeast of Colfax (lat. 39°02'30" N, long. 120°44'05" W; at W line sec. 22, T 14 N, R 11 E). Named on Michigan Bluff (1952) 7.5' quadrangle. Called Michigan Bluffs on Whitney's (1873) map. Postal authorities established Michigan Bluff post office in 1854 and discontinued it in 1943 (Frickstad, p. 121). The first community near the place was called Michigan City; when it threatened to slide away, the inhabitants moved higher up the slope and started a new community that they called Michigan Bluff (Hanna, p. 191-192). Lindgren's (1911a) map shows a place called Bullion located 4 miles north of Michigan Bluff. Postal authorities established Bullion post office in 1904 and discontinued it in 1915 (Frickstad, p. 119). They established Webster post office 6 miles northeast of Michigan Bluff in 1865 and discontinued it in 1867 (Salley, p. 236).

Michigan City: see **Michigan Bluff** [PLACER].

Michigan Flat: see **Lotus** [EL DORADO].

Midas [PLACER]: *locality,* 4.5 miles east of Dutch Flat along Southern Pacific Railroad (lat. 29°13' N, long. 120°45'25" W; near SE cor. sec. 29, T 16 N, R 11 E). Named on Dutch Flat (1950) 7.5' quadrangle. Hobson's (1890b) map shows a place called Shady Run located at or near present Midas. Postal authorities established Shady Run post office in 1872, discontinued it in 1879, reestablished it in 1903, and discontinued it in 1904 (Frickstad, p. 121). On Colfax (1898) 30' quadrangle, the name "Shady Run" applies to a stream near present Midas. Whitney's (1873) map shows a place called Blue Bluffs situated 0.5 mile north of Shady Run.

Middle Bar: see **Fords Bar** [EL DORADO].

Middle Butte [EL DORADO]: *peak,* 8 miles southeast of Camino (lat. 38°40'15" N, long. 120°33'15" W; near W line sec. 33, T 10 N, R 13 E); the peak is between Big Butte and Little Butte. Altitude 4219 feet. Named on Sly Park (1952) 7.5' quadrangle. Middle Butte, Big Butte, and Little Butte together have the label "Buttes" on Placerville (1893) 30' quadrangle.

Middle Creek [EL DORADO]: *stream,* flows 3 miles to Silver Fork American River 2.25 miles southeast of Kyburz (lat. 38°45'05" N, long. 120°15'50" W; near W line sec. 1, T 10 N, R 15 E). Named on Kyburz

(1952) and Pyramid Peak (1955) 7.5' quadrangles.

Middle Dry Creek [EL DORADO]: *stream,* flows 5.5 miles to Dogtown Creek 3 miles west-southwest of Caldor (lat. 38°35'35" N, long. 120°29'10" W; sec. 36, T 9 N, R 13 E). Named on Caldor (1951) 7.5' quadrangle.

Middle Lake [NEVADA]: *lake,* 1450 feet long, 3.5 miles southwest of English Mountain along South Fork Canyon Creek (lat. 39°24'45" N, long. 120°36'10" W; on W line sec. 23, T 18 N, R 12 E). Named on English Mountain (1983) 7.5' quadrangle.

Middle Martis Creek [PLACER]: *stream,* flows 5.25 miles to Martis Creek nearly 5 miles west of Martis Peak (lat. 39°18'05" N, long. 120°07'15" W; near SW cor. sec. 20, T 17 N, R 17 E). Named on Martis Peak (1955) 7.5' quadrangle. Hobson's (1890b) map shows a place called Elizabeth Town located along present Middle Martis Creek about 1.25 miles above the mouth of the stream (near W line sec. 28, T 17 N, R 17 E).

Middle Mountain [EL DORADO]: *peak,* 1.5 miles west of Phipps Peak (lat. 38°57'25" N, long. 120°10'50" W; sec. 23, T 13 N, R 16 E). Altitude 8333 feet. Named on Rockbound Valley (1955) 7.5' quadrangle.

Middletown: see **Placerville** [EL DORADO].

Middle Velma Lake [EL DORADO]: *lake,* 2750 feet long, 1.25 miles south of Phipps Peak (lat. 38°56'10" N, long. 120°08'55" W; at SW cor. sec. 30, T 13 N, R 17 E); the lake is between Upper Velma Lake and Lower Velma Lake. Named on Rockbound Valley (1955) 7.5' quadrangle.

Middle Wallace Canyon: see **South Wallace Canyon** [PLACER].

Middle Waters Campground [SIERRA]: *locality,* 4 miles southwest of Sierra City (lat. 39°31'30" N, long. 120°41' W; near SE cor. sec. 12, T 19 N, R 11 E). Named on Sierra City (1981) 7.5' quadrangle.

Middle Yuba River [NEVADA-SIERRA-YUBA]: *stream,* forms part of Nevada-Sierra County line and Nevada-Yuba County line, heads in Nevada County and flows 55 miles to join North Yuba River [YUBA] and form Yuba River nearly 4 miles east of Dobbins in Yuba County (lat. 39°22'05" N, long. 121°08'10" W; sec. 1, T 17 N, R 7 E). Named on Alleghany (1949), Camptonville (1948), Challenge (1948), English Mountain (1983), French Corral (1948), Graniteville (1982), Haypress Valley (1981), Pike (1949), Sierra City (1981), and Webber Peak (1981) 7.5' quadrangles. Called Middle Fork Yuba River on Downieville (1897), Smartsville (1895), and Truckee (1940) 30' quadrangles, but United States Board on Geographic Names (1950, p. 5-6) rejected this name and the name "Middle Fork" for the stream. On Smartsville (1895) 30' quadrangle, present Yuba River from the mouth of present Middle Yuba River downstream to the mouth of present South Yuba River is called Middle Fork Yuba River.

Mikon [YOLO]: *locality,* 1.25 miles north-northwest of downtown West Sacramento at the intersection of Sacramento Northern Railroad and Southern Pacific Railroad (lat. 38°35'20" N, long. 121°32'10" W). Named on Sacramento West (1967) 7.5' quadrangle. California Division of Highways' (1934) map shows a place called Rose Garden located 0.5 mile northwest of Mikon along the railroad.

Mildred: see **Lake Mildred** [YUBA]; **Mount Mildred** [PLACER].

Mildred Lakes [PLACER]: *lakes,* largest 500 feet long, 3.5 miles southwest of Granite Chief (lat. 39°09'40" N, long. 120°19'40" W; near W line sec. 8, T 15 N, R 15 E); the lakes are 1 mile north of Mount Mildred. Named on Granite Chief (1953) 7.5' quadrangle.

Mildred Ridge [PLACER]: *ridge,* north-trending, 1.5 miles long, nearly 4 miles southwest of Granite Chief (lat. 39°09'25" N, long. 120°19'50" W); Mount Mildred is at the south end of the ridge. Named on Granite Chief (1953) 7.5' quadrangle.

Mile Hill Creek [PLACER]: *stream,* flows 1.5 miles to Middle Fork American River 8 miles east-northeast of Auburn (lat. 38°57'20" N, long. 120°56'15" W; near N line sec. 26, T 13 N, R 9 E). Named on Greenwood (1949) 7.5' quadrangle.

Mile Hill Toll House [PLACER]: *locality,* 9 miles northeast of Auburn (lat. 38°59' N, long. 120°56'20" W). Named on Placerville (1893) 30' quadrangle.

Milk Lake [NEVADA]: *lake,* 1100 feet long, 4.5 miles southwest of English Mountain (lat. 39°23'40" N, long. 120°36'25" W; near E line sec. 27, T 18 N, R 12 E). Named on English Mountain (1983) 7.5' quadrangle.

Milk Ranch [YUBA]: *locality,* 4 miles southeast of Challenge (lat. 39°26'50" N, long. 121°09'50" W; near W line sec. 2, T 18 N, R 7 E). Site named on Challenge (1948) 7.5' quadrangle. The place was a popular travelers stop that also was known as Stroud's (Hoover, Rensch, and Rensch, p. 593).

Mill Campground: see **Old Mill Campground** [COLUSA].

Mill Creek [AMADOR]: *stream,* flows 7.25 miles to Tiger Creek Reservoir 9 miles east-northeast of Pine Grove (lat. 38°26'55" N, long. 120°30' W; sec. 24, T 7 N, R 13 E). Named on Caldor (1951), Devils Nose (1979), and West Point (1948) 7.5' quadrangles. On Mokelumne Hill (1948) 15' quadrangle, the name "Antelope Creek" seems to apply to present Mill Creek below the present junction of Antelope Creek and Mill Creek.

Mill Creek [COLUSA]:

(1) *stream,* flows 8.5 miles to South Fork Stony Creek less than 1 mile northeast of Fouts Springs (lat. 39°21'45" N, long. 122°39'10" W; near NW cor. sec. 4, T 17 N, R 7 W). Named on Fouts Springs (1968) 7.5' quadrangle.

(2) *stream,* formed by the confluence of Middle Fork and North Fork, flows 9 miles to Bear Creek 8 miles north of Wilbur Springs (lat. 39°09'20" N, long. 122°26'30" W; at S line sec. 8, T 15 N, R 5 W). Named on Clearlake Oaks (1960) and Wilbur Springs (1961) 15' quadrangles. Middle Fork is 2 miles long and North Fork is 1.5 miles long; both forks are named on Clearlake Oaks (1960) 15' quadrangle. South Fork joins the main creek from the southwest 1.5 miles downstream from the confluence of North Fork and Middle Fork; it is 5 miles long and is named on Clearlake Oaks (1960) 15' quadrangle. South Fork is called Mill Creek on Bartlett Springs (1944) 15' quadrangle.

Mill Creek [EL DORADO]:

(1) *stream,* flows nearly 1 mile to Slab Creek 8 miles north-northwest of Pollock Pines (lat. 38°52'10" N, long. 120°37'30" W; sec. 22, T 12 N, R 12 E). Named on Devil Peak (1950) and Slate Mountain (1950) 7.5' quadrangles.

(2) *stream,* flows 5.25 miles to South Fork American River 3 miles east of Riverton (lat. 38°46'25" N, long. 120°23'40" W; sec. 27, T 11 N, R 14 E). Named on Leek Spring Hill (1951), Riverton (1950), and Stump Spring (1951) 7.5' quadrangles. Called Wolf Creek on Pyramid Peak (1896) 30' quadrangle.

Mill Creek [PLACER]: *stream,* flows 2 miles to Shirttail Canyon nearly 4 miles north-northeast of Foresthill (lat. 39°04'15" N, long. 120°47'20" W; near W line sec. 7, T 14 N, R 11 E). Named on Foresthill (1949) 7.5' quadrangle.

Mill Creek [YUBA]: *stream,* flows nearly 5 miles to New Bullards Bar Reservoir 5.5 miles east-southeast of Challenge (lat. 39°27' N, long. 121°07'40" W; sec. 6, T 18 N, R 8 E). Named on Camptonville (1948), Challenge (1948, photorevised 1969), and Strawberry Valley (1948) 7.5' quadrangles. Wescoatt's (1861) map shows a place called Atchisons Bar located along Mill Creek near the mouth.

Mill Creek: see **Little Mill Creek** [AMADOR]; **Old Mill Creek** [SIERRA].

Mill Creek Ridge [EL DORADO]: *ridge,* north- to northwest-trending, 4 miles long, center 8 miles north-northwest of Leek Spring Hill (lat. 38°43'45" N, long. 120°21'40" W); the feature is northeast of Mill Creek (2). Named on Leek Spring Hill (1951) and Stump Spring (1951) 7.5' quadrangles.

Miller: see **Joe Miller Ravine** [NEVADA].

Miller Creek [PLACER]: *stream,* flows nearly 4 miles to the canyon of Rubicon River 6.25 miles southwest of Homewood (lat. 39°01'40" N, long. 120°14'55" W; sec. 36, T 14 N, R 16 E). Named on Homewood (1955) 7.5' quadrangle.

Miller Creek [SIERRA]: *stream,* flows 1.5 miles to Oregon Creek 4.25 miles west of Alleghany (lat. 39°28'15" N, long. 120°55'15" W; sec. 36, T 19 N, R 9 E). Named on Pike (1949) 7.5' quadrangle, which shows Miller ranch near the stream.

Miller Creek: see **Heavenly Valley Creek** [EL DORADO]; **North Miller Creek** [PLACER].

Miller House: see **Heavenly Valley Creek** [EL DORADO].

Miller Lake [PLACER]: *lake,* 2850 feet long, 4 miles south-southwest of Homewood (lat. 39°02'05" N, long. 120°12' W; at W line sec. 27, T 14 N, R 16 E); the lake is along Miller Creek. Named on Homewood (1955) 7.5' quadrangle.

Miller Meadows [PLACER]: *areas,* nearly 5 miles southwest of Homewood (lat. 39°02'05" N, long. 120°13' W; sec. 28, 29, T 14 N, R 16 E); the place is along Miller Creek. Named on Homewood (1955) 7.5' quadrangle.

Millers Defeat Cañon: see **Starr Ravine** [PLACER].

Millers Landing [COLUSA]: *locality,* 0.5 mile north of Boyer Landing along Sacramento River (lat. 38°57'25" N, long. 121°50'15" W; on E line sec. 22, T 13 N, R 1 E). Named on Kirkville (1952) 7.5' quadrangle. On Kirkville (1915) 7.5' quadrangle, the name "Miller's Landing" applies to a place located 0.5 mile farther northeast.

Miller Spring [SIERRA]: *spring,* 4 miles west-northwest of Alleghany (lat. 39°29'10" N, long. 120°55' W; sec. 25, T 19 N, R 9 E). Named on Colfax (1938) 30' quadrangle. Pike (1949) 7.5' quadrangle shows the site of Miller ranch at the place.

Millertown [PLACER]: *locality,* 1.25 miles northwest of downtown Auburn (lat. 38°54'40" N, long. 121°05'30" W; near N line sec. 9, T 12 N, R 8 E). Site named on Auburn (1953) 7.5' quadrangle. Myrick (p. 115) used the form "Miller Town" for the name.

Millionaire Camp [EL DORADO]: *locality,* 4 miles southeast of Robbs Peak (lat. 38°53'05" N, long. 120°21'15" W; sec. 13, T 12 N, R 14 E). Named on Loon Lake (1952) 7.5' quadrangle.

Million Dollar Creek [NEVADA]: *stream,* flows 1.5 miles to Steephollow Creek 7.5 miles northeast of Chicago Park (lat. 39°13'10" N, long. 120°51'35" W; sec. 28, T 16 N, R 10 E). Named on Dutch Flat (1950) 7.5' quadrangle.

Mill Pond [EL DORADO]: *lakes,* two connected, each 500 feet long, 7 miles west of Pollock Pines in South Canyon (lat. 38°45'15" N, long. 120°42'40" W; sec. 35, T 11 N, R 11 E). Named on Slate Mountain (1950, photorevised 1973) 7.5' quadrangle.

Mills [COLUSA]: *locality,* 4 miles east-southeast of Sites along Colusa and

Lake Railroad (lat. 39°16'25" N, long. 122°16'25" W; sec. 2, T 16 N, R 4 W); the place is near present Mills Orchards. Named on Sites (1904) 7.5' quadrangle. California Mining Bureau's (1917b) map has the name "Quarry" for a place situated along the railroad between Mills and Sites.

Mills [SACRAMENTO]: *locality,* 2.5 miles south-southeast of downtown Carmichael along Southern Pacific Railroad (lat. 38°35'10" N, long. 121°18'30" W). Named on Carmichael (1967) 7.5' quadrangle. Postal authorities established Mills post office in 1898 and discontinued it in 1943 (Salley, p. 140). The place also was known as Mills Station and as Hangtown Crossing; the name "Mills" came from a gristmill at the place (Hanna, p. 193).

Mills Creek [EL DORADO]: *stream,* flows 2 miles to Squaw Hollow Creek 6 miles southwest of Camino (lat. 38°40'15" N, long. 120° 44'30" W; near SE cor. sec. 34, T 10 N, R 11 E). Named on Camino (1952) 7.5' quadrangle.

Mills Orchards [COLUSA]: *locality,* 4 miles east-southeast of Sites (lat. 39°16'45" N, long. 122°16'30" W; sec. 35, T 17 N, R 4 W). Named on Sites (1958) 7.5' quadrangle.

Mills Peak [SIERRA]: *peak,* 9.5 miles north of Sierra City (lat. 39° 42'20" N, long. 120°37'20" W; at N line sec. 10, T 21 N, R 12 E). Named on Clio (1981) 7.5' quadrangle.

Mill Spur [YOLO]: *locality,* 1.25 miles south-southeast of downtown Woodland along Southern Pacific Railroad (lat. 38°39'40" N, long. 121°45'55" W; at NE cor. sec. 5, T 9 N, R 2 E). Named on Woodland (1952) 7.5' quadrangle.

Mills Spring [NEVADA]: *spring,* 7.5 miles northeast of Truckee (lat. 39°23'40" N, long. 120°04'30" W; sec. 22, T 18 N, R 17 E). Named on Boca (1955) 7.5' quadrangle.

Mills Station: see **Mills** [SACRAMENTO].

Mill Valley [COLUSA]: *valley,* 3.5 miles southwest of Fouts Springs (lat. 39°19' N, long. 122°42'25" W; sec. 24, T 17 N, R 8 W). Named on Stonyford (1951) 15' quadrangle.

Mill Valley Campground [COLUSA]: *locality,* 3.5 miles southwest of Fouts Springs (lat. 39°19'05" N, long. 122°42'25" W; near N line sec. 24, T 17 N, R 8 W); the place is in Mill Valley. Named on Fouts Springs (1968) 7.5' quadrangle.

Milton [SIERRA]: *locality,* 3.5 miles southeast of Sierra City near Middle Fork Yuba River (present Middle Yuba River) (lat. 39°31'30" N, long. 120°35'30" W). Named on Downieville (1897) 30' quadrangle.

Milton Creek [SIERRA]: *stream,* flows nearly 5 miles to Haypress Creek 2.5 miles east of Sierra City (lat. 39°33'55" N, long. 120°35'05" W; near SW cor. sec. 25, T 20 N, R 12 E). Named on Haypress Valley (1981) 7.5' quadrangle.

Milton Reservoir [NEVADA]: *lake,* behind a dam on Middle Yuba River 5.5 miles north-northwest of English Mountain (lat. 39°31'20" N, long. 120°34'55" W; near SW cor. sec. 12, T 19 N, R 12 E). Named on Haypress Valley (1981) 7.5' quadrangle. Downieville (1897) 30' quadrangle shows Milton [SIERRA] near the lake.

Mineral Bar: see **Colfax** [PLACER].

Mineral Point [PLACER]: *ridge,* south- to west-southwest-trending, 1 mile long, 7 miles northeast of Michigan Bluff (lat. 39°06' N, long. 120°37'30" W; sec. 34, T 15 N, R 12 E). Named on Greek Store (1952) and Michigan Bluff (1952) 7.5' quadrangles.

Miner Creek [COLUSA]: *stream,* flows 3.5 miles to Mill Creek (1) 3 miles south of Fouts Springs (lat. 39°18'40" N, long. 122°39'35" W; sec. 20, T 17 N, R 7 W); the stream is north of Miner Ridge. Named on Fouts Springs (1968) 7.5' quadrangle.

Miner Ridge [COLUSA]: *ridge,* generally east-trending, 3 miles long, 4 miles south-southwest of Fouts Springs (lat. 39°17'55" N, long. 122°41'15" W); the ridge is south of Miner Creek. Named on Fouts Springs (1968) 7.5' quadrangle.

Miners Ravine [PLACER]: *canyon,* drained by a stream that flows 15 miles to join Antelope Creek and form Dry Creek (2) 1 mile east-northeast of downtown Roseville (lat. 38°45'20" N, long. 121° 16' W; near E line sec. 35, T 11 N, R 6 E). Named on Pilot Hill (1954), Rocklin (1967), and Roseville (1967) 7.5' quadrangles.

Minister Gulch [AMADOR]: *canyon,* drained by a stream that flows less than 1 mile to Hunt Gulch 2.25 miles south-southeast of Jackson (lat. 38°19'10" N, long. 120°45'05" W; sec. 3, T 5 N, R 11 E). Named on Mokelumne Hill (1948) 7.5' quadrangle. The name is for Peter Y. Cool and three other ministers who mined gold in the canyon (Watson, p. 206-207).

Ministerial Bend: see **China Bend** [SUTTER-YOLO].

Minkalo: see **Camp Minkalo** [AMADOR].

Minnesota: see **Minnesota Flat** [SIERRA].

Minnesota Flat [SIERRA]: *locality,* 1.5 miles south-southeast of Alleghany (lat. 39°27' N, long. 120°49'50" W; near NW cor. sec. 11, T 18 N, R 10 E). Site named on Alleghany (1949) 7.5' quadrangle. Colfax (1898) 30' quadrangle has the name "Minnesota" at the place.

Misery Creek [AMADOR]: *stream,* flows 4.25 miles to Pioneer Creek 4.25 miles northeast of Pine Grove (lat. 38°26'50" N, long. 120°35'50" W; near E line sec. 24, T 7 N, R 12 E). Named on West Point (1948) 7.5' quadrangle.

Mission: see **Ramirez** [YUBA].

Mississippi Bar [SACRAMENTO]: *locality,* 2.5 miles southwest of Folsom on the northwest side of American River (lat. 38°39' N, long. 121°12'10" W). Named on Folsom (1967) 7.5' quadrangle. Men from Mississippi named the place, which also was called Fishers Bar (Gudde, 1975, p. 218).

Mississippi Bar: see **Mississippi Creek** [YUBA].

Mississippi Canyon: see **Humbug Canyon** [PLACER].

Mississippi Creek [YUBA]: *stream,* flows 1 mile to New Bullards Bar Reservoir 2.5 miles south of Strawberry Valley (lat. 39°31'35" N, long. 121°06'30" W; sec. 8, T 19 N, R 8 E). Named on Strawberry Valley (1948, photorevised 1975) 7.5' quadrangle. Before construction of the reservoir, the stream entered North Yuba River 2.5 miles downstream from Slate Range Bar. Borthwick (p. 262) reported that he traveled 2 or 3 miles down North Yuba River from Slate Range Bar to visit a place called Mississippi Bar, which must have been near the mouth of present Mississippi Creek.

Missouri Bar [NEVADA]: *locality,* 1.5 miles south-southeast of North Bloomfield along South Yuba River (lat. 39°20'40" N, long. 120°53'05" W; at N line sec. 17, T 17 N, R 10 E); the place is at the mouth of Missouri Canyon (1). Named on North Bloomfield (1949) 7.5' quadrangle.

Missouri Bar [YUBA]: *locality,* 4.5 miles east of Challenge along North Yuba River (lat. 39°29'25" N, long. 121°08'20" W). Named on Nevada City (1948) 15' quadrangle. Water of New Bullards Bar Reservoir now covers the site.

Missouri Bend [SUTTER-YOLO]: *bend,* 3.5 miles south-southeast of Kirkville along Sacramento River on Sutter-Yolo County line (lat. 38°51'50" N, long. 121°45'25" W; sec. 28, T 12 N, R 2 E). Named on Eldorado Bend (1952) 7.5' quadrangle.

Missouri Canyon [EL DORADO]: *canyon,* drained by a stream that flows 3.5 miles to Otter Creek 5 miles northeast of Georgetown (lat. 38°57'35" N, long. 121°46'40" W; sec. 20, T 13 N, R 11 E). Named on Georgetown (1949) and Tunnel Hill (1950) 7.5' quadrangles. Gudde (1975, p. 31) listed a mining place called Bells Diggings that was located at the head of Missouri Canyon.

Missouri Canyon [NEVADA]:

(1) *canyon,* drained by a stream that flows 3.25 miles to South Yuba River 1.5 miles south-southeast of North Bloomfield at Missouri Bar (lat. 39°20'45" N, long. 120°53'05" W; at N line sec. 17, T 17 N, R 10 E). Named on Alleghany (1949), North Bloomfield (1949), and Washington (1950) 7.5' quadrangles. Whitney's (1873) map shows a place called Banjo located near the mouth of Missouri Cañon.

(2) *canyon,* drained by a stream that flows 2.25 miles to Greenhorn Creek 5.25 miles north-northeast of Chicago Park (lat. 39°12'50" N, long. 120°55'20" W; near NW cor. sec. 36, T 16 N, R 9 E). Named on Chicago Park (1949) 7.5' quadrangle.

Missouri Creek [YUBA]: *stream,* flows 0.5 mile to New Bullards Bar Reservoir 2.5 miles south-southwest of Strawberry Valley (lat. 39°11'35" N, long. 121°07' W; near E line sec. 7, T 19 N, R 8 E). Named on Strawberry Valley (1948, photorevised 1975) 7.5' quadrangle.

Missouri Flat [EL DORADO]: *locality,* 2.5 miles west-southwest of downtown Placerville (lat. 38°43' N, long. 120°50'45" W; sec. 14, T 10 N, R 10 E). Named on Placerville (1949) 7.5' quadrangle.

Missouri Flat: see **Grass Valley** [NEVADA]; **Loganville** [SIERRA]

Missouri House: see **Placerville** [EL DORADO].

Mitchell Canyon [SIERRA]: *canyon,* drained by a stream that heads in the State of Nevada and flows 2 miles in Sierra County to North Branch Dog Creek 3 miles east-northeast of Crystal Peak (lat. 39° 34'05" N, long. 120°01'55" W; near E line sec. 24, T 20 N, R 17 E). Named on Dog Valley (1981) 7.5' quadrangle.

Mobile Flat: see **Mobile Ravine** [SIERRA].

Mobile Ravine [SIERRA]: *canyon,* drained by a stream that flows 1.25 miles to North Yuba River 3.5 miles east of Downieville, and 0.5 mile downstream from the mouth of Shaughnessy Ravine (lat. 39°33'35" N, long. 120°45'35" W; sec. 32, T 20 N, R 11 E). Named on Downieville (1951) 7.5' quadrangle. A place called Mobile Flat was located along North Yuba River 4 miles east of Downieville—it also was called Newhouse Place and Shaughnessy Place (Gudde, 1975, p. 219). A place called Shady Flat was situated 0.5 mile west of Mobile Flat (Gudde, 1975, p. 315).

Mobley Spring [NEVADA]: *spring,* 3.25 miles north-northeast of North Bloomfield (lat. 39°24'55" N, long. 120°53'05" W; near NW cor. sec. 20, T 18 N, R 10 E). Named on Pike (1949) 7.5' quadrangle.

Moco Canyon [EL DORADO]: *canyon,* drained by a stream that flows 2.5 miles to Middle Fork Cosumnes River nearly 4 miles north-northwest of Aukum (lat. 38°36'30" N, long. 120°44'45" W; sec. 27, T 9 N, R 11 E). Named on Aukum (1952) 7.5' quadrangle.

Mofuba: see **Locke** [SACRAMENTO].

Mohawk Creek [SIERRA]: *stream,* flows nearly 1 mile to Plumas County 10 miles north of Sierra City (lat. 39°42'25" N, long. 120° 36'10" W; near S line sec. 2, T 21 N, R 12 E). Named on Clio (1981) 7.5' quadrangle.

Mohawk Creek: see **Sulphur Creek** [SIERRA].

Mohawk Gap [SIERRA]: *pass,* 8.5 miles north-northeast of Sierra City (lat. 39°41'15" N, long. 120°35'45" W; sec. 14, T 21 N, R 12 E). Named on Clio (1981) 7.5' quadrangle.

Mohawk Ravine [NEVADA]: *canyon,* 7.25 miles northeast of North Bloomfield (lat. 39°26'15" N, long. 120°48'05" W; sec. 12, T 18 N, R 10 E). Named on Alleghany (1949) 7.5' quadrangle.

Mokelumne Peak [AMADOR]: *peak,* 38 miles east-northeast of Jackson (lat. 38°32'20" N, long. 120°05'35" W). Altitude 9334 feet. Named on Mokelumne Peak (1979) 7.5' quadrangle.

Mokelumne River [AMADOR-SACRAMENTO]: *stream,* formed by the confluence of North Fork and Middle Fork (Middle Fork is in Calaveras County), flows 62 miles along Amador-Calaveras and Sacramento-San Joaquin County lines to San Joaquin River 5 miles south-southeast of Isleton (lat. 38°05'50" N, long. 121°34'10" W). Named on Bouldin Island (1978), Bruceville (1968), Isleton (1978), Jackson (1962), Mokelumne Hill (1948), Rail Road Flat (1948), Thornton (1978), Valley Springs (1962), and Wallace (1962) 7.5' quadrangles. Called R. de las Mukelemnes on Fremont's (1845) map, Mokelome River on Jackson's (1850) map, and Mokelomies R. on Scholfield's (1851) map. Early writers gave the name a variety of forms: "Mogueles" by Wilkes (p. 137) in 1841; "Mocalimo" by Ingersoll (p. 44) in 1847; "Mo-kel-um-ne" by Kelly (p. 6) in 1849; and "Mokelemy" by Tyson (p. 13) in 1850. The name "Mokelumne" is from an Indian expression meaning "people of Mokel"—Mokel was an Indian village near the stream (Kroeber, p. 48). North Fork heads in Alpine County, flows for 23 miles along Amador-Calaveras County line, and is named on Calaveras Dome (1979), Devils Nose (1979), Garnet Hill (1979), Mokelumne Peak (1979), Rail Road Flat (1948), Tamarack (1979), and West Point (1948) 7.5' quadrangles. Camp's (1962) map shows a feature called Marble Point located at the intersection of North Fork and Middle Fork Mokelumne River. Mokelumne River splits 7.5 miles northeast of Isleton to form North Mokelumne River and South Mokelumne River (which is in San Joaquin County); the two streams rejoin 3 miles southeast of Isleton to reform Mokelumne River. North Mokelumne River is 10 miles long and is named on Isleton (1978) and Thornton (1978) 7.5' quadrangles; it is called North Fork Mokelumne River on Isleton (1910) and New Hope (1910) 7.5' quadrangles.

Mokelumne River Campground [AMADOR]: *locality,* 7.5 miles southeast of Hams Station (lat. 38°28'40" N, long. 120°16'10" W; sec. 12, T 7 N, R 15 E); the place is along North Fork Mokelumne River. Named on Garnet Hill (1979) 7.5' quadrangle.

Mokelumne Tetons [AMADOR]: *peaks,* 1.25 miles south of Mokelumne Peak on a southeast-trending ridge (lat. 38°31'15" N, long. 120°05'45" W). Named on Mokelumne Peak (1979) 7.5' quadrangle.

Mokesumne River: see **Cosumnes River** [AMADOR-EL DORADO-SACRAMENTO].

Mokosumne River: see **Cosumnes River** [AMADOR-EL DORADO-SACRAMENTO].

Monnona Town: see **Monona Flat** [PLACER].

Monona Flat [PLACER]: *area,* 7 miles north of Foresthill (lat. 38° 07'15" N, long. 120°49'55" W; sec. 27, T 15 N, R 10 E). Named on Foresthill (1949) 7.5' quadrangles. Whitney's (1873) map shows an inhabited place called Monnona Town at or near present Monona Flat, an inhabited place called Independence Hill located about halfway from Monnona Town to Iowa Hill, and an inhabited place called Wolverine located about 0.25 mile northwest of Monnona Town.

Monte Carlo Creek [PLACER]: *stream,* flows 2.25 miles to East Martis Creek 2.5 miles west-northwest of Martis Peak (lat. 39°18'20" N, long. 120°04'20" W; sec. 22, T 17 N, R 17 E); the stream goes through Monte Carlo Meadows. Named on Martis Peak (1955) 7.5' quadrangle.

Monte Carlo Meadows [PLACER]: *area,* 2.5 miles west of Martis Peak (lat. 39°17'50" N, long. 120°04'40" W; sec. 27, T 17 N, R 17 E); the place is along Monte Carlo Creek. Named on Martis Peak (1955) 7.5' quadrangle.

Monte Cristo [SIERRA]: *locality,* 3 miles northwest of Downieville (lat. 39°35'55" N, long. 120°51'30" W). Named on Downieville (1897) 30' quadrangle. Downieville (1951) 7.5' quadrangle shows Monte Cristo mine at or near the site. A place called Fir Cap Diggings was located about 4 miles northwest of Downieville, and a place called Excelsior was situated along Goodyears Creek near Monte Cristo (Gudde, 1975, p. 113, 115). Postal authorities established Fir Cap post office in 1869 and discontinued it in 1886 (Frickstad, p. 184).

Monte Vista [PLACER]: *locality,* 1.25 miles south-southeast of Dutch Flat (lat. 39°11'25" N, long. 120°49'50" W; sec. 3, T 15 N, R 10 E). Named on Dutch Flat (1950) 7.5' quadrangle.

Montez: see **Lower Lola Montez Lake** [NEVADA]; **Upper Lola Montez Lake** [NEVADA].

Montezuma Hill [NEVADA]:

(1) *peak,* 5 miles north-northwest of Nevada City (lat. 39°19'30" N, long. 121°03'50" W; sec. 22, T 17 N, R 8 E); the peak is 2.5 miles southwest of Montezuma Ridge. Named on Nevada City (1948) 7.5' quadrangle. Whitney's (1873) map has the name "Robinson Rav." for a canyon that heads at Montezuma Hill (1) and extends west-northwest 1 mile to Shady Creek.

(2) *locality,* 5 miles north-northwest of Nevada City (lat. 39°19'40" N, long. 121°03'35" W); the place is at Montezuma Hill (1). Named on Smartsville (1895) 30' quadrangle.

Montezuma Island [SACRAMENTO]: *island,* 0.5 mile long, 14 miles west-southwest of Isleton near the mouth of Sacramento River (lat. 38°04'25" N, long. 121°50'20" W). Named on Antioch North (1978) 7.5' quadrangle. Collinsville (1918) 7.5' quadrangle shows the island in Solano County. Called Burnett Isl. on Ringgold's (1850a) map, which has the name "Pt. Rogers" at the east end of the feature.

Montezuma Ridge [NEVADA]: *ridge,* west-northwest- to west-southwest-trending, 1.5 miles long, 5.5 miles north of Nevada City (lat. 39°20'45" N, long. 121°01'30" W); the ridge is 2.5 miles northeast of Montezuma Hill (1). Named on Nevada City (1948) 7.5' quadrangle.

Montgomery Creek [COLUSA]: *stream,* flows 1 mile to Glenn County 5.5 miles north of Lodoga (lat. 39°23'05" N, long. 122° 30' W; sec. 26, T 18 N, R 6 W). Named on Lodoga (1960) 15' quadrangle.

Monumental Creek [PLACER]: *stream,* flows 5 miles to East Fork of North Fork of North Fork American River 5 miles north of Westville (lat. 39°14'55" N, long. 120°38'30" W; at E line sec. 17, T 16 N, R 12 E); the stream heads on Monumental Ridge. Named on Blue Canyon (1955) and Cisco Grove (1955) 7.5' quadrangles.

Monumental Hill: see **Monumental Ridge** [PLACER].

Monumental Ridge [PLACER]: *ridge,* southwest- to west-trending, 5 miles long, center 3 miles southwest of Cisco Grove (lat. 39°16'45" N, long. 120°34'30" W). Named on Cisco Grove (1955) 7.5' quadrangle. Called Monumental Hill on Colfax (1898) 30' quadrangle.

Monument Hill [YOLO]: *peak,* 4.5 miles west of Woodland (lat. 38° 40'45" N, long. 121°51'30" W). Altitude 156 feet. Named on Woodland (1952) 7.5' quadrangle.

Monument Peak [EL DORADO]: *peak,* 4.5 miles north of Freel Peak on El Dorado-Alpine County line (lat. 38°55'25" N, long. 119°53'50" W; near NW cor. sec. 7, T 12 N, R 19 E); the peak is on the Von Schmidt California-Nevada State line of 1873. Altitude 10,067 feet. Named on South Lake Tahoe (1955) 7.5' quadrangle.

Moody Ridge [PLACER]: *ridge,* southwest-trending, 3 miles long, 2 miles southeast of Dutch Flat (lat. 39°11' N, long. 120°48'45" W). Named on Dutch Flat (1950) 7.5' quadrangle.

Mooney Creek [NEVADA]: *stream,* flows about 1.5 miles to Fall Creek 6 miles southeast of Graniteville (lat. 39°22'55" N, long. 120°39'10" W; sec. 32, T 18 N, R 12 E). Named on Graniteville (1982) 7.5' quadrangle.

Mooney Flat [NEVADA]: *locality,* 6 miles northwest of Pilot Peak in Slacks Ravine (lat. 39°12'55" N, long. 121°16'20" W; sec. 26, T 16 N, R 6 E). Named on Smartville (1951) 7.5' quadrangle. Called Mooneys Fl. on Whitney's (1873) map, which shows a place called Zinc Ho. [House] located 6.5 miles south of Mooneys Flat near Dry Creek (2), and a peak called Pet Hill situated 2 miles east-southeast of Mooneys Flat. The name "Mooney" commemorates Thomas Mooney, who started a hotel and trading post near the site in 1851 (Gudde, 1949, p. 224).

Mooney Ridge [PLACER]: *ridge,* west-southwest-trending, 1 mile long, 6 miles southeast of Rocklin (lat. 38°44'25" N, long. 121°09'20" W). Named on Folsom (1967) 7.5' quadrangle.

Moon Glade [COLUSA]: *area,* 0.25 mile west of Fouts Springs (lat. 39°21'15" N, long. 122°40'15" W; near SW cor. sec. 5, T 17 N, R 7 W). Named on Fouts Springs (1968) 7.5' quadrangle.

Moons Bend [COLUSA-SUTTER]: *bend,* 3.5 miles north-northwest of Meridian along Sacramento River on Colusa-Sutter County line (lat. 39°11'30" N, long. 121°56' W; sec. 35, T 16 N, R 1 W); the feature is near Moons Ferry. Named on Meridian (1952) 7.5' quadrangle.

Moons Ferry [COLUSA-SUTTER]: *locality,* 3.25 miles north-northwest of Meridian along Sacramento River on Colusa-Sutter County line (lat. 39°11'15" N, long. 121°56' W). Named on Marysville (1895) 30' quadrangle.

Moonshine Creek [YUBA]: *stream,* flows 3.5 miles to Middle Yuba River 5 miles south-southwest of Camptonville (lat. 39°23'15" N, long. 121°05'45" W; near NW cor. sec. 33, T 18 N, R 8 E). Named on Camptonville (1948) 7.5' quadrangle.

Moorc Canyon [SUTTER]: *canyon,* drained by a stream that flows nearly 2 miles to an unnamed valley 3.5 miles northwest of Sutter (lat. 39°11'55" N, long. 121°47'35" W; near NW cor. sec. 31, T 16 N, R 2 E). Named on Sutter Buttes (1954) 7.5' quadrangle.

Moores: see **Riverton** [EL DORADO].

Moores Flat [NEVADA]: *locality,* 4.25 miles north-northeast of North Bloomfield (lat. 39°25'10" N, long. 120°51' W; near SE cor. sec. 16, T 18 N, R 10 E). Site named on Alleghany (1949) 7.5' quadrangle. Postal authorities established Clinton post office in 1854, changed the name to Moores Flat in 1857, discontinued it for a time in 1903, and discontinued it finally in 1914 (Frickstad, p. 113, 114). The name "Moores" is for H.M. Moore, who built the first house and store at the place in 1851 (Gudde, 1949, p. 224). Whitney's (1873) map shows a place called Jericho situated less than 0.5 mile south of Moores Flat.

Moores Flat Creek [NEVADA]: *stream,* flows 1.5 miles to Middle Yuba River 4.5 miles north-northeast of North Bloomfield (lat. 39° 25'50" N, long. 120°51'55" W; near NW cor. sec. 16, T 18 N, R 10 E); the stream heads near Moores Flat. Named on Alleghany (1949) 7.5' quadrangle.

Moore's Station: see **Riverton** [EL DORADO].

Morattini [EL DORADO]: *locality,* nearly 7 miles east-southeast of Robbs Peak (lat. 38°53'50" N, long. 120°17' W). Named on Pyramid Peak (1896) 30' quadrangle.

Morattini Flat [EL DORADO]: *area,* 7.5 miles east-southeast of Robbs Peak (lat. 38°53'45" N, long. 120°16'20" W; at SE cor. sec. 10, T 12 N, R 15 E). Named on Loon Lake (1952) 7.5' quadrangle.

Morgan [EL DORADO]: *locality,* 9 miles west-southwest of Leek Spring Hill (lat. 38°34' N, long. 120°25'15" W). Named on Pyramid Peak (1896) 30' quadrangle.

Morgans Landing [SACRAMENTO]: *locality,* 0.25 mile southwest of Courtland along Sacramento River (lat. 38°19'40" N, long. 121° 34'20" W). Named on Courtland (1978) 7.5' quadrangle.

Mormon Basin [COLUSA]: *area,* lowlands 4.25 miles northwest of Grimes between Sycamore Slough and Dry Slough (lat. 39°06'30" N, long. 121°57'30" W). Named on Grimes (1954) and Meridian (1912) 7.5' quadrangles.

Mormon Diggings: see **Mormon Island** [SACRAMENTO].

Mormon Gulch: see **Mameluke Hill** [EL DORADO].

Mormon Hill [EL DORADO]: *peak,* 6.5 miles north-northeast of Clarksville (lat. 38°44'45" N, long. 121°00'25" W; sec. 5, T 10 N, R 9 E). Altitude 1533 feet. Named on Clarksville (1953) 7.5' quadrangle.

Mormon Island [SACRAMENTO]: *locality,* nearly 3 miles northeast of Folsom on the south side of South Fork American River (lat. 38° 42'15" N, long. 121°07'55" W). Named on Sacramento (1892) 30' quadrangle. Water of Folsom Lake now covers the site. Jackson's (1850) map has the name "Natoma" as well as the name "Mormon I." at the place. Mormons employed by Sutter discovered gold at the site soon after the discovery of gold at Sutter's Mill; the mining camp that grew there first was called Lower Mines and Mormon Diggings (Gudde, 1975, p. 225); a canal cut across the gravel bar at the place formed an island (Blenkle, p. 15)—the community called Mormon Island was on the bluff above the bar (Grimshaw, p. 28). Postal authorities established Mormon Island post office in 1851 and discontinued it in 1890 (Frickstad, p. 133). Arrowsmith's (1860) map shows places called Richmond Hill and Red Bank situated on the east side of South Fork American River northeast of Mormon Island at the extreme north tip of Sacramento County.

Mormon Ravine [EL DORADO]: *canyon,* drained by a stream that flows 1.5 miles to Pinchem Creek 6 miles north-northwest of Shingle Springs (lat. 38°44'35" N, long. 120°58'35" W; near S line sec. 3, T 10 N, R 9 E); the canyon heads southeast of Mormon Hill. Named on Clarksville (1953) and Shingle Springs (1949) 7.5' quadrangles.

Mormon Ravine [PLACER]: *canyon,* drained by a stream that flows nearly 3 miles to Folsom Lake 8 miles east-northeast of Rocklin (lat. 38°50'10" N, long. 121°05'35" W; sec. 4, T 11 N, R 8 E). Named on Pilot Hill (1954, photorevised 1973) 7.5' quadrangle.

Mormon Tavern: see **Clarsksville** [EL DORADO].

Morning Star Lake: see **Big Reservoir** [PLACER].

Morning Star Reservoir: see **Big Reservoir** [PLACER].

Morrison [EL DORADO]: *locality,* 6 miles north-northwest of Leek Spring Hill (lat. 38°42'35" N, long. 120°19'20" W; near NW cor. sec. 21, T 10 N, R 15 E). Named on Leek Spring Hill (1951) 7.5' quadrangle.

Morrison Creek [SACRAMENTO]: *stream,* flows 26 miles before coming to an end near Sacramento River 10 miles south of downtown Sacramento (lat. 38°26'20" N, long. 121°29'55" W). Named on Carmichael (1967), Florin (1968), and Sacramento East (1967) 7.5' quadrangles.

Morrisons Flat: see **Craigs Flat** [SIERRA].

Morrison Slough [SUTTER]: *stream,* enters from Butte County and flows 5 miles to Snake River 6.5 miles northwest of Yuba City (lat. 39°12'30" N, long. 121°42'20" W; near E line sec. 26, T 16 N, R 2 E). Named on Gridley (1952) and Sutter (1952) 7.5' quadrangles.

Morris Reservoir [NEVADA]: *lake,* 450 feet long, 1 mile southwest of North San Juan (lat. 39°21'30" N, long. 121°07' W; near SE cor. sec. 6, T 17 N, R 8 E). Named on Nevada City (1948) 7.5' quadrangle.

Morris Spring [YOLO]: *spring,* 8 miles southwest of Esparto (lat. 38°36'05" N, long. 122°06'40" W; sec. 29, T 9 N, R 2 W). Named on Monticello Dam (1959) 7.5' quadrangle.

Morristown [SIERRA]: *locality,* 6 miles south-southwest of Mount Fillmore (lat. 39°39'10" N, long. 120°54'15" W; sec. 30, T 21 N, R 10 E). Named on La Porte (1951) 7.5' quadrangle.

Morristown Ravine [SIERRA]: *canyon,* drained by a stream that flows 0.5 mile to Canyon Creek 6.5 miles southwest of Mount Fillmore (lat. 39°39'15" N, long. 120°55'10" W; sec. 25, T 21 N, R 9 E); the canyon is west of Morristown. Named on La Porte (1951) 7.5' quadrangle.

Morristown Ridge [SIERRA]: *ridge,* southwest-trending, 5 miles long, center 7 miles south-southwest of Mount Fillmore (lat. 39°38'35" N, long. 120°54'35" W); Morristown is on the ridge. Named on Goodyears Bar (1951) and La Port (1951) 7.5' quadrangles.

Morrs Ravine [SIERRA]: *canyon,* drained by a stream that flows 1.5 miles to Canyon Creek 7.5 miles southwest of Mount Fillmore (lat. 39°38'20" N, long. 120°55'50" W; near W line sec. 36, T 21 N, R 9 E). Named on La Porte (1951) 7.5' quadrangle.

Mortimer Flat [EL DORADO]: *area,* 5 miles west-northwest of Pyramid Peak (lat. 38°52'25" N, long. 120°14'45" W; sec. 20, T 12 N, R 16 E). Named on Pyramid Peak (1955) 7.5' quadrangle.

Moscove Meadow [NEVADA-SIERRA]: *area,* 13 miles northwest of Donner Pass on Nevada-Sierra County line (lat. 39°26'45" N, long. 120°29'35" W; near NE cor. sec. 10, T 18 N, R 13 E). Named on Webber Peak (1981) 7.5' quadrangle. Called English Meadow on Truckee (1940) 30' quadrangle.

Mosher: see **Freeport** [SACRAMENTO] (1).

Mosquito [EL DORADO]: *locality,* 6.25 miles northeast of Placerville (lat. 38°47'40" N, long. 120°43'45" W). Named on Placerville (1893) 30' quadrangle. Postal authorities established Mosquito post office in 1880, discontinued it in 1881, reestablished it in 1892, and discontinued it in 1895; the name was from Mosquito Creek (Salley, p. 147).

Mosquito Camp [EL DORADO]: *locality,* 4 miles east-northeast of Chili Bar (lat. 38°47'45" N, long. 120°45'10" W; sec. 16, T 11 N, R 11 E). Named on Garden Valley (1949) 7.5' quadrangle.

Mosquito Creek [EL DORADO]: *stream,* flows 3.25 miles to South Fork American River 3.5 miles east-northeast of Chili Bar (lat. 38° 46'50" N, long. 120°45'25" W; at S line sec. 21, T 11 N, R 11 E). Named on Garden Valley (1949) and Slate Mountain (1950) 7.5' quadrangles. Gudde (1975, p. 227) listed a mining place called Mosquito Valley that apparently was located along or near present Mosquito Creek, and mentioned two mining camps in the valley—Lower Town or Big House, and Nelsonville.

Mosquito Creek [NEVADA]: *stream,* flows 2 miles to Deer Creek 8.5 miles southwest of North Bloomfield (lat. 39°16'05" N, long. 120°59'55" W; near W line sec. 8, T 16 N, R 9 E). Named on North Bloomfield (1949) 7.5' quadrangle.

Mosquito Creek [YUBA]:

(1) *stream,* flows about 1.5 miles to Deadwood Creek 1.25 miles southeast of Strawberry Valley (lat. 39°33' N, long. 121°05'35" W; sec. 33, T 20 N, R 8 E). Named on Strawberry Valley (1948) 7.5' quadrangle.

(2) *stream,* flows 2 miles to Oregon Creek 3 miles south-southwest of Camptonville (lat. 39°24'50" N, long. 121°04'05" W; sec. 22, T 18 N, R 8 E). Named on Camptonville (1948) 7.5' quadrangle.

Mosquito Creek: see **Big Mosquito Creek** [PLACER]; **Fast Creek** [YUBA]; **Little Mosquito Creek** [PLACER].

Mosquito Lake [AMADOR]: *lake,* 1050 feet long, 3 miles north-northwest of Mokelumne Peak (lat. 38°34'35" N, long. 120°07' W). Named on Mokelumne Peak (1979) 7.5' quadrangle.

Mosquito Narrows [PLACER]: *pass,* 5.25 miles east of Michigan Bluff (lat. 39°03'05" N, long. 120°38'15" W; near NE cor. sec. 21, T 14 N, R 12 E); the pass is on Mosquito Ridge. Named on Michigan Bluff (1952) 7.5' quadrangle.

Mosquito Pass [EL DORADO]: *pass,* 5.25 miles south of Phipps Peak (lat. 38°52'40" N, long. 120°09'35" W). Named on Rockbound Valley (1955) 7.5' quadrangle.

Mosquito Ridge [PLACER]: *ridge,* generally southwest-trending, 17 miles long, lies between Middle Fork American River and North Fork of Middle Fork American River from near Little Bald Mountain to the junction of the two streams. Named on Duncan Peak (1952), Greek Store (1952), and Michigan Bluff (1952) 7.5' quadrangles.

Mosquito Valley: see **Mosquito Creek** [EL DORADO].

Moss Hills: see **Rampart** [PLACER].

Mossy Pond [NEVADA]: *intermittent lake,* 9 miles west-northwest of Donner Pass (lat. 39°22'40" N, long. 120°28'10" W; sec. 36, T 18 N, R 13 E). Named on Webber Peak (1981) 7.5' quadrangle. Donner Pass (1955) 15' quadrangle shows a permanent lake.

Motor City [EL DORADO]: *locality,* 3.5 miles west of Camino (lat. 38°44' N, long. 120°44'20" W; at W line sec. 11, T 10 N, R 11 E). Named on Camino (1952) 7.5' quadrangle.

Moulton: see **Princeton** [COLUSA].

Mounds: see **The Mounds** [SIERRA].

Mound Springs Creek [EL DORADO]: *stream,* flows nearly 3 miles to Indian Creek (3) 4.5 miles north-northeast of Shingle Springs (lat. 38°43'15" N, long. 120°53'05" W; sec. 16, T 10 N, R 10 E). Named on Placerville (1949) and Shingle Springs (1949) 7.5' quadrangles.

Mount Aigare [EL DORADO]: *peak,* 4.5 miles northeast of Latrobe (lat. 38°36'20" N, long. 120°55'05" W; sec. 30, T 9 N, R 10 E). Altitude 1564 feet. Named on Latrobe (1949) 7.5' quadrangle.

Mountain Chief Creek [PLACER]: *stream,* flows 2 miles to Sugar Pine Canyon 6.5 miles north-northeast of Foresthill (lat. 39°06' N, long. 120°45'10" W; near E line sec. 32, T 15 N, R 11 E). Named on Foresthill (1949) and Michigan Bluff (1952) 7.5' quadrangles.

Mountain Cottage [EL DORADO]: *locality,* nearly 3 miles south of the village of Pilot Hill (lat. 38°47'40" N, long. 121°01' W). Named on Sacramento (1892) 30' quadrangle.

Mountain Cottage: see **Summit House** [YUBA].

Mountain House [COLUSA]: *locality,* 8 miles north-northeast of Wilbur Springs (lat. 39°08'25" N, long. 122°20'30" W; near N line sec. 19, T 15 N, R 4 W). Named on Manor Slough (1958) 7.5' quadrangle. Venado (1920) 15' quadrangle has the designation "Mountain House (Venado)" at the site. Postal authorities established Venado post office in 1874, discontinued it in 1877, reestablished it in 1881, and discontinued it in 1914 (Frickstad, p. 20).

Mountain House: see **Old Mountain House** [SIERRA].

Mountain Lake: see **Lake Tahoe** [EL DORADO-PLACER].

Mountain Meadow [PLACER]: *area,* less than 1 mile northeast of Bunker Hill (lat. 39°03'25" N, long. 120°22'10" W; sec. 14, T 14 N, R 14 E). Named on Wentworth Springs (1953) 7.5' quadrangle.

Mountain Meadow: see **Little Mountain Meadow** [PLACER].

Mountain Meadow Lake [PLACER]: *lake,* 450 feet long, 1.5 miles north-northeast of Granite Chief at the head of North Fork American River (lat. 39°13' N, long. 120°16'25" W; sec. 23, T 16 N, R 15 E). Named on Granite Chief (1953) 7.5' quadrangle.

Mountain of the Breathing Spirit: see **The Mountain of the Breathing Spirit**, under **Sutter Buttes** [SUTTER].

Mountain Spring Creek [AMADOR]: *stream,* flows 4.25 miles to Jackson Creek 4 miles southeast of Ione (lat. 38°18'25" N, long. 120°52'45" W; sec. 9, T 5 N, R 10 E). Named on Ione (1962) and Jackson (1962) 7.5' quadrangles.

Mountain Spring Creek: see **Copper Creek** [AMADOR].

Mountain Spring House: see **Sunnybrook** [AMADOR].

Mountain Springs [AMADOR]: *locality,* 4 miles east of Ione (lat. 38°20'35" N, long. 120°51'45" W); the place is along Mountain Spring Creek. Named on Jackson (1902) 30' quadrangle.

Mountain Springs: see **Gold Run** [PLACER].

Mountain Well: see **North Bloomfield** [NEVADA].

Mount Alma [SIERRA]: *peak,* 5.25 miles south of Mount Fillmore (lat. 39°39'10" N, long. 120°51'20" W). Altitude 6477 feet. Named on Mount Fillmore (1951) 7.5' quadrangle.

Mount Ararat [EL DORADO]: *peak,* 4.5 miles northwest of Coloma (lat. 38°51'10" N, long. 120°56'20" W; sec. 35, T 12 N, R 9 E). Altitude 2012 feet. Named on Coloma (1949) 7.5' quadrangle.

Mount Aukum [EL DORADO]: *peak,* 1.25 miles north of Aukum (lat. 38°34'25" N, long. 120°43'30" W; sec. 2, T 8 N, R 11 E). Altitude 2615 feet. Named on Aukum (1952) 7.5' quadrangle. Called Mt. Orcum on Placerville (1893) 30' quadrangle.

Mount Aukum: see **Aukum** [EL DORADO].

Mount Crossman [AMADOR]: *peak,* 8 miles east-northeast of Pine Grove (lat. 38°27'25" N, long. 120°31'55" W; sec. 15, T 7 N, R 13 E). Named on West Point (1948) 7.5' quadrangle.

Mount Danaher [EL DORADO]: *peak,* 0.5 mile northeast of Camino (lat. 38°44'40" N, long. 120°40' W; near SE cor. sec. 5, T 10 N, R 12 E). Named on Camino (1952) 7.5' quadrangle.

Mount Disney [PLACER]: *peak,* 1.5 miles south-southeast of Donner Pass (lat. 39°17'40" N, long. 120°20'25" W; sec. 29, T 17 N, R 15 E). Altitude 7953 feet. Named on Norden (1955) 7.5' quadrangle. The name is for Walt Disney, who bought the first stock issued in Sugar Bowl Ski Corporation for operations near Donner Summit (Jackson, L.A., p. 145).

Mount Etna [SIERRA]: *peak,* 1.25 miles northeast of Mount Fillmore on Sierra-Plumas County line (lat. 39°44'45" N, long. 120° 50'15" W; at NW cor. sec. 26, T 22 N, R 10 E). Altitude 7163 feet. Named on Mount Fillmore (1951) 7.5' quadrangle.

Mount Fillmore [SIERRA]: *peak,* 12 miles north of Downieville (lat. 39°43'50" N, long. 120°51'05" W; near NW cor. sec. 34, T 22 N, R 10 E). Altitude 7715 feet. Named on Mount Fillmore (1951) 7.5' quadrangle.

Mount Gregory [EL DORADO]: *locality,* 7.25 miles northeast of Georgetown (lat. 38°59'05" N, long. 120°44'55" W). Named on Placerville (1893) 30' quadrangle.

Mount Haskells: see **Haskell Peak** [SIERRA].

Mount Hope [EL DORADO]: *locality,* nearly 7 miles north-northeast of Georgetown (lat. 38°59'30" N, long. 120°46'20" W; sec. 8, T 13 N, R 11 E). Named on Georgetown (1949) 7.5' quadrangle.

Mount Hope [YUBA]: *ridge,* north-northwest-trending, 1.5 miles long, 2.5 miles north-northeast of Challenge at Yuba-Butte County line (lat. 39°31'15" N, long. 121°12'20" W). Named on Clipper Mills (1948) 7.5' quadrangle.

Mount Hope House [YUBA]: *locality,* 2 miles west of Woodville (present Woodleaf) (lat. 39°31' N, long. 121°13'35" W); the place is near the west end of Mount Hope. Named on Bidwell Bar (1897) 30' quadrangle.

Mount Ina Coolbrith [SIERRA]: *ridge,* northwest-trending, 1 mile long, 5.5 miles east-northeast of Loyalton (lat. 39°42'10" N, long. 120°08'30" W). Named on Loyalton (1981) 7.5' quadrangle. United States Board on Geographic Names (1933, p. 386) rejected the name "Ina Coolbrith Summit" for the feature, and noted that California State Geographic Board named the ridge for Ina Donna Coolbrith, former poet laureate of California.

Mount Judah [PLACER]: *peak,* 1.25 miles south-southeast of Donner Pass (lat. 39°17'55" N, long. 120°18'55" W; near N line sec. 28, T 17 N, R 15 E). Altitude 8243 feet. Named on Norden (1955) 7.5' quadrangle. United States Board on Geographic Names (1942, p. 27) rejected the name "Donner Peak" for the feature, and noted that the name "Judah" commemorates Theodore Judah.

Mount Lincoln [PLACER]: *peak,* 2 miles south of Donner Pass (lat. 39°17'15" N, long. 120°19'40" W; near SW cor. sec. 28, T 17 N, R 15 E). Named on Norden (1955) 7.5' quadrangle. Called Lincoln Pk. on Hobson's (1890b) map.

Mount Lola [NEVADA]: *peak,* 8.5 miles north-northwest of Donner Pass (lat. 39°26' N, long. 120°21'50" W; near SE cor. sec. 11, T 18 N, R 14 E). Altitude 9148 feet. Named on Independence Lake (1981) 7.5' quadrangle. The name is for actress Lola Montez (Gudde, 1949, p. 191).

Mount Marliave: see **Hole-in-Ground** [NEVADA].

Mount Mildred [PLACER]: *peak,* 4.25 miles south-southwest of Granite Chief (lat. 39°08'45" N, long. 120°19'45" W; near W line sec. 17, T 15 N, R 15 E). Altitude 8398 feet. Named on Granite Chief (1953) 7.5' quadrangle.

Mount Olive [NEVADA]: *peak,* 1.5 miles west-southwest of Chicago Park (lat. 39°08'05" N, long. 120°59'35" W; sec. 20, T 15 N, R 9 E). Altitude 2569 feet. Named on Chicago Park (1949) 7.5' quadrangle.

Mount Orcum: see **Mount Aukum** [EL DORADO].

Mount Pleasant [EL DORADO]: *locality,* 4.5 miles north-northeast of Omo Ranch (lat. 38°38'05" N, long. 120°32'40" W). Named on Placerville (1893) 30' quadrangle.

Mount Pleasant [SIERRA]: *locality,* 7 miles northwest of Goodyears Bar (lat. 39°36'35" N, long. 120°58'30" W). Named on Downieville (1897) 30' quadrangle. The place first was called Mount Pleasant Ranch (Gudde, 1975, p. 229).

Mount Pleasant Canyon [PLACER]: *canyon,* drained by a stream that flows 1 mile to Third Brushy Canyon 3 miles north-northwest of Foresthill (lat. 39°03'30" N, long. 120°50'40" W; sec. 15, T 14 N, R 10 E). Named on Foresthill (1949) 7.5' quadrangle.

Mount Pleasant Ranch: see **Mount Pleasant** [SIERRA].

Mount Pluto [PLACER]: *peak,* 5 miles north of Tahoe City (lat. 39° 14'30" N, long. 120°08'20" W; near NW cor. sec. 18, T 16 N, R 17 E). Named on Tahoe City (1955) 7.5' quadrangle. Called Pluto Pk. on Wheeler's (1876-1877b) map. The name "Pluto" is for plutonic rock at the peak (Lekisch, p. 97).

Mount Price [EL DORADO]: *peak,* 1.5 miles northwest of Pyramid Peak (lat. 38°51'50" N, long. 120°10'25" W). Altitude 9975 feet. Named on Pyramid Peak (1955) 7.5' quadrangle.

Mount Stephens: see **Donner Lake** [NEVADA]

Mount Tallac [EL DORADO]: *peak,* 5.25 miles northwest of Pyramid Peak (lat. 38°54'20" N, long. 120°05'50" W; near NE cor. sec. 9, T 12 N, R 17 E). Altitude 9735 feet. Named on Emerald Bay (1955) 7.5' quadrangle. Called Crystal Peak on early maps (Lekisch, p. 134).

Mount Vernon [SUTTER]: *locality,* 1 mile north of Sutter (lat. 39° 10'20" N, long. 121°45'10" W). Named on Marysville (1895) 30' quadrangle.

Mount Vernon House: see **Blue Tent** [NEVADA].

Mount View: see **Grass Valley** [NEVADA].

Mount Watson [PLACER]: *peak,* 3.5 miles north of Tahoe City (lat. 39°13'15" N, long. 120°08'45" W; sec. 24, T 16 N, R 16 E). Altitude 8424 feet. Named on Tahoe City (1955) 7.5' quadrangle.

Mount Zion [AMADOR]: *peak,* 1.5 miles south-southeast of Pine Grove (lat. 38°23'25" N, long. 120°39'05" W; near E line sec. 9, T 6 N, R 12 E). Altitude 2968 feet. Named on Pine Grove (1948) 7.5' quadrangle.

Mount Zion: see **Snow Tent** [NEVADA].

Mud Lake [AMADOR]: *lake,* 1250 feet long, nearly 6 miles north-northeast of Mokelumne Peak (lat. 38°36'35" N, long. 120°08'55" W; near SW cor. sec. 19, T 9 N, R 17 E). Named on Bear River Reservoir (1979) 7.5' quadrangle. Pyramid Peak (1896) 30' quadrangle has the name "Mud Lakes" for three lakes in a marsh at the site of present Mud Lake.

Mud Lake [EL DORADO]: *lake,* 200 feet long, 3.5 miles east of Wentworth Springs (lat. 39°01'10" N, long. 120°16'15" W; near W line sec. 35, T 14 N, R 15 E). Named on Wentworth Springs (1953) 7.5' quadrangle.

Mud Lake [NEVADA]: *lake,* 750 feet long, 3 miles northwest of English Mountain (lat. 39°28'40" N, long. 120°35'10" W; near SE cor. sec. 26, T 19 N, R 12 E). Named on English Mountain (1983) 7.5' quadrangle.

Mud Lake [PLACER]: *lake,* 550 feet long, 6.5 miles east of Bunker Hill (lat. 39°03'05" N, long. 120°15'25" W; near NW cor. sec. 19, T 14 N, R 16 E). Named on Wentworth Springs (1953) 7.5' quadrangle.

Mud Lake [SIERRA]: *lake,* 350 feet long, 4 miles north of Sierra City (lat. 39°37'20" N, long. 120°38'35" W; near SE cor. sec. 5, T 20 N, R 12 E). Named on Sierra City (1981) 7.5' quadrangle.

Mud Lakes [EL DORADO]: *lakes,* largest 500 feet long, 3 miles east of Wentworth Springs (lat. 39°01'10" N, long. 120°16'55" W; sec. 34, T 14 N, R 15 E). Named on Wentworth Springs (1953, photorevised 1973) 7.5'

quadrangle.

Mud Lakes: see **Mud Lake** [AMADOR].

Mud Spring [AMADOR]: *spring,* nearly 2 miles east of Hams Station (lat. 38°32'45" N, long. 120°20'30" W; sec. 17, T 8 N, R 15 E). Named on Peddler Hill (1951) 7.5' quadrangle.

Mud Spring: see **El Dorado** [EL DORADO]; **Upper Mud Spring** [EL DORADO].

Mud Springs: see **El Dorado** [EL DORADO].

Mugginsville: see **Gold Hill** [PLACER].

Mule Canyon [EL DORADO]: *canyon,* drained by a stream that flows 5 miles to Silver Fork American River 8 miles west of Kirkwood (lat. 38°42'20" N, long. 120°12'50" W; near W line sec. 21, T 10 N, R 16 E). Named on Tragedy Spring (1979) 7.5' quadrangle.

Mule Creek [AMADOR]: *stream,* flows 10 miles to Dry Creek nearly 3 miles west-northwest of Ione (lat. 38°21'40" N, long. 120° 58'55" W). Named on Amador City (1962), Ione (1962), and Irish Hill (1962) 7.5' quadrangles. Camp's (1962) map shows a place called Muletown located 2 miles north-northwest of Ione along Mule Creek. Muletown was a lively camp in the 1850's (Hoover, Rensch, and Rensch, p. 34).

Mule Spring [NEVADA]: *spring,* 11.5 miles northeast of Chicago Park (lat. 39°14'40" N, long. 120°48' W; near S line sec. 13, T 16 N, R 10 E). Named on Dutch Flat (1950) 7.5' quadrangle.

Muletown: see **Mule Creek** [AMADOR].

Mullen [YOLO]: *locality,* 2 miles south-southeast of downtown Woodland along Southern Pacific Railroad (lat. 38°39'05" N, long. 121°45'55" W; on W line sec. 4, T 9 N, R 2 E). Named on Yolo (1915) 7.5' quadrangle.

Mumford Bar [PLACER]: *locality,* 6.5 miles west-northwest of Duncan Peak along North Fork American River (lat. 39°12'10" N, long. 120°37' W; near S line sec. 34, T 16 N, R 12 E). Named on Duncan Peak (1952) 7.5' quadrangle.

Mumma's Landing [COLUSA]: *locality,* 2.5 miles north-northeast of Boyer's Landing along Sacramento River (lat. 38°59'20" N, long. 121°49'15" W). Named on Kirkville (1915) 7.5' quadrangle.

Munchville: see **Capay** [YOLO].

Mundys [EL DORADO]: *locality,* 16 miles east-southeast of Georgetown (lat. 38°50'30" N, long. 120°33'15" W). Named on Placerville (1893) 30' quadrangle.

Mungers Lake [SACRAMENTO]: *intermittent lake,* 0.5 mile long, 4.5 miles south-southwest of downtown Sacramento (lat. 38°30'50" N, long. 121°30'55" W). Named on Sacramento West (1967) 7.5' quadrangle. Called Sutterville Lake on Lovedal (1916) 7.5' quadrangle.

Munson Basin [COLUSA]: *area,* 2 miles northwest of Grimes (lat. 39°05'35" N, long. 121°55'20" W). Named on Grimes (1954) and Meridian (1912) 7.5' quadrangles. The feature occupies lowlands between Dry Slough and Sacramento River.

Munson Meadow [AMADOR]: *area,* 1.5 miles north-northeast of Mokelumne Peak (lat. 38°33'35" N, long. 120°04'05" W). Named on Mokelumne Peak (1979) 7.5' quadrangle.

Murderers Bar [EL DORADO]: *locality,* 2 miles north of Cool along Middle Fork American River (lat. 38°55' N, long. 121°00'35" W; sec. 6, T 12 N, R 9 E). Named on Auburn (1953) 7.5' quadrangle. Indians massacred five miners at the place (Bancroft, 1888, p. 354).

Murderers Gulch [PLACER]: *canyon,* drained by a stream that flows 1 mile to Middle Fork American River 4 miles east-northeast of Auburn (lat. 38°55'15" N, long. 121°00'15" W; at W line sec. 5, T 12 N, R 9 E). Named on Auburn (1953) 7.5' quadrangle.

Murphy Canyon [YOLO]: *canyon,* 5 miles east of Rumsey along Buckeye Creek (lat. 38°52'35" N, long. 122°08'45" W). Named on Guinda (1959) and Rumsey (1959) 7.5' quadrangles.

Murphy Creek [AMADOR]: *stream,* flows 2.25 miles to San Joaquin County 7.5 miles southwest of Ione (lat. 38°15'40" N, long. 120° 00'35" W; sec. 29, T 5 N, R 9 E). Named on Goose Creek (1968) and Ione (1962) 7.5' quadrangles.

Murphy Flat [NEVADA]: *locality,* 2 miles east-southeast of Graniteville (lat. 39°25'35" N, long. 120°42'20" W; sec. 14, T 18 N, R 11 E). Named on Graniteville (1982) 7.5' quadrangle.

Murphy Flat: see **Myers Flat** [YOLO].

Murphy Gulch [AMADOR]: *canyon,* 1.25 miles long, 2.5 miles south-southeast of Jackson (lat. 38°19' N, long. 120°45'25" W; mainly in sec. 3, T 5 N, R 11 E). Named on Jackson (1962) 7.5' quadrangle. The name "Murphy's Gulch" was used for the feature as early as 1851 (McKinstry, p. 351).

Murphy Lake [SUTTER]: *lake,* 3 miles long, 2.5 miles northeast of Verona in American Basin (center near lat. 38°48'45" N, long. 121°35'15" W). Named on Vernon (1910) 7.5' quadrangle.

Murphy Meadows [PLACER]: *area,* 2 miles north-northeast of Martis Peak (lat. 39°18'50" N, long. 120°00'40" W; near N line sec. 30, T 17 N, R 18 E). Named on Martis Peak (1955) 7.5' quadrangle.

Murphy Mountain [EL DORADO]: *peak,* 1 mile northeast of Coloma (lat. 38°48'30" N, long. 120°52'40" W; near NE cor. sec. 17, T 11 N, R 10 E). Named on Coloma (1949) and Garden Valley (1949) 7.5' quadrangles. The name commemorates Patrick O' Brien Murphy, a stone mason who soon after discovery of gold at Sutter's Mill built a stone fort on top of the peak for protection from Indian attack (Gernes, p. 8).

Murphys: see **Meeks Bay** [EL DORADO] (2).

Murraysville: see **Jersey Flat**, under **Downieville** [SIERRA].

Murry Camp [PLACER]: *locality,* about 1.5 miles south of Bunker Hill (lat. 39°01'40" N, long. 120°22'30" W; sec. 26, T 14 N, R 14 E). Named on Bunker Hill (1953) and Wentworth Springs (1953) 7.5' quadrangles.

Mushoak Creek [YOLO]: *stream,* flows 8.5 miles to South Fork Buckeye Creek 9.5 miles east of Rumsey (lat. 38°52'55" N, long. 122°03'35" W; near NW cor. sec. 23, T 12 N, R 2 W). Named on Bird Valley (1959), Guinda (1959), and Wildwood School (1959) 7.5' quadrangles.

Music Dale: see **Big Indian Creek** [AMADOR].

Mutton Canyon [EL DORADO]: *canyon,* drained by a stream that flows 1.25 miles to Pilot Creek (1) 12 miles north-northwest of Pollock Pines (lat. 38°55'20" N, long. 120°38'25" W). Named on Tunnel Hill (1950) 7.5' quadrangle.

Myers Flat [YOLO]: *area,* 3.5 miles northwest of Guinda (lat. 38° 51'50" N, long. 122°14'40" W; at NW cor. sec. 30, T 12 N, R 3 W). Named on Guinda (1959) 7.5' quadrangle. Called Meyers Flat on Guinda (1959) 15' quadrangle, and called Murphy Flat on Rumsey (1945) 15' quadrangle. United States Board on Geographic Names (1962b, p. 19) rejected the name "Murphy Flat" for the feature.

Myers Ravine: see **Meyers Ravine** [NEVADA].

Mystic [NEVADA]: *locality,* 11.5 miles northeast of Truckee along Southern Pacific Railroad (lat. 39°26'15" N, long. 120°01'10" W; sec. 7, T 18 N, R 18 E). Named on Boca (1955) 7.5' quadrangle. California Division of Highways' (1934) map shows a place called Farad located along the railroad less than 1 mile south-southwest of Mystic (near E line sec. 12, T 18 N, R 17 E). Boca (1955) 7.5' quadrangle shows Farad powerhouse near the site—the word "farad" is from a measure of electrical capacity.

Mystic Canyon [NEVADA]: *canyon,* drained by a stream that flows 1.5 miles to Truckee River 11 miles northeast of Truckee (lat. 39° 25'55" N, long. 120°01'30" W); near SW cor. sec. 7, T 18 N, R 18 E); the mouth of the canyon is 0.5 mile southwest of Mystic. Named on Boca (1955) 7.5' quadrangle.

Mystic Lake [SUTTER]: *lake,* 2 miles south-southwest of Kirkville in a cutoff meander of Sacramento River (lat. 38°52'50" N, long. 121° 48'30" W; on S line sec. 13, T 12 N, R 1 E). Named on Kirkville (1952) 7.5' quadrangle.

— N —

Nancy Lake [PLACER]: *lake,* 750 feet long, 7.5 miles west-southwest of Donner Pass (lat. 39°17'25" N, long. 120°27'40" W; near S line sec. 36, T 17 N, R 13 E). Named on Soda Springs (1955, photorevised 1973) 7.5' quadrangle.

Narrows: see **The Narrows** [YUBA].

Nashville [EL DORADO]: *locality,* 10.5 miles south of Placerville along North Fork Cosumnes River (lat. 38°34'45" N, long. 120°50'35" W; sec. 2, T 8 N, R 10 E). Named on Fiddletown (1949) 7.5' quadrangle. Postal authorities established Nashville post office in 1852, discontinued it in 1854, reestablished it in 1870, and discontinued it in 1907 (Frickstad, p. 28). The place first was known as Nashville Bar (Hanna, p. 207). It also was called Quartzville and Quartzburg; the name "Nashville" is from the city in Tennessee (Gudde, 1975, p. 234).

Nashville Bar: see **Nashville** [EL DORADO].

Natchez: see **Natchez Creek** [YUBA].

Natchez Creek [YUBA]: *stream,* heads in Yuba County and flows 5.5 miles, first back and forth across Yuba-Butte County line, and then along that line to South Honcut Creek less than 1 mile south-southeast of Rackerby (lat. 39°25'45" N, long. 121°20' W; near E line sec. 7, T 18 N, R 6 E). Named on Rackerby (1948) 7.5' quadrangle. A mining camp along the stream was called Natchez because of a supposed resemblance of the place to Natchez, Mississippi (Hoover, Rensch, and Rensch, p. 591).

National Gulch [NEVADA]: *canyon,* drained by a stream that flows 1.25 miles to Middle Yuba River 9 miles northeast of North Bloomfield (lat. 39°26'55" N, long. 121°46'20" W; at SW cor. sec. 5, T 18 N, R 11 E). Named on Alleghany (1949) 7.5' quadrangle.

Natoma [SACRAMENTO]: *locality,* 1.5 miles south-southwest of Folsom along Southern Pacific Railroad (lat. 38°39'20" N, long. 121°10'50" W). Named on Folsom (1967) 7.5' quadrangle. On Sacramento (1892) 30' quadrangle, the name applies to a place situated 4 miles southwest of Folsom along Sacramento and Placerville Railroad (lat. 38°37'35" N, long. 121°13'05" W). Postal authorities established Natoma post office in 1884, discontinued it in 1902, reestablished it in 1907, moved it 2.5 miles northeast in 1909, and discontinued it in 1864; the post office originally was located 4 miles southwest of Folsom City (Salley, p. 150). The name presumably is from an Indian village (Kroeber, p. 50).

Natoma: see **Lake Natoma** [SACRAMENTO]; **Mormon Island**

[SACRAMENTO].

Nebenhorn [EL DORADO]: *locality,* less than 0.25 mile west-southwest of Echo Summit (lat. 38°48'40" N, long. 120°02' W; sec. 7, T 11 N, R 18 E). Named on Echo Lake (1955) 7.5' quadrangle.

Nebraska City: see **Cornish House** [SIERRA].

Nebraska Diggings: see **Cornish House** [SIERRA].

Nebraska Flat: see **Cornish House** [SIERRA].

Neck Meadow [EL DORADO]: *area,* 1 mile west of Wentworth Springs along Gerle Creek (lat. 39°00'50" N, long. 120°21'25" W; sec. 36, T 14 N, R 14 E). Named on Wentworth Springs (1953) 7.5' quadrangle.

Need [SACRAMENTO]: *locality,* 3.5 miles north-northwest of Galt along Southern Pacific Railroad (lat. 38°18'05" N, long. 121°19'25" W). Named on Galt (1968) 7.5' quadrangle.

Needle: see **Needle Peak** [PLACER].

Needle Lake [PLACER]: *lake,* 450 feet long, 0.5 mile west-northwest of Granite Chief (lat. 39°12'05" N, long. 120°17'45" W; at N line sec. 34, T 16 N, R 15 E); the lake is 1000 feet east of Needle Peak. Named on Granite Chief (1953) 7.5' quadrangle.

Needle Lake: see **Little Needle Lake** [PLACER].

Needle Peak [PLACER]: *peak,* less than 1 mile west-northwest of Granite Chief (lat. 39°12'05" N, long. 120°18' W; at N line sec. 34, T 16 N, R 15 E). Altitude 8971 feet. Named on Granite Chief (1953) 7.5' quadrangle. Called Needle on Wheeler's (1876-1877b) map.

Needle Point [SIERRA]: *peak,* nearly 5 miles southeast of Mount Fillmore (lat. 39°40'35" N, long. 120°47'35" W; near SW cor. sec. 18, T 21 N, R 11 E). Altitude 7129 feet. Named on Mount Fillmore (1951) 7.5' quadrangle.

Negro Bar [SACRAMENTO]: *locality,* 0.5 mile west-northwest of Folsom on the north side of American River (lat. 38°40'50" N, long. 121°11' W). Named on Folsom (1967) 7.5' quadrangle. Called Nigger Bar on Folsom (1941) 15' quadrangle.

Negro Bar: see **Folsom** [SACRAMENTO]; **Negro Bar Creek** [YUBA]; **Secret Canyon** [SIERRA].

Negro Bar Creek [YUBA]: *stream,* flows 1.25 miles to Englebright Reservoir (present Englebright Lake) 5.25 miles south of Oregon House (lat. 39°16'55" N, long. 121°15'50" W; near S line sec. 35, T 17 N, R 6 E). Named on Oregon House (1948) 7.5' quadrangle. United States Geological Survey's (1922) map shows a place called Nigger Bar located along Yuba River near the mouth of present Negro Bar Creek (lat. 39°16'35" N, long. 121°15'40" W); Eddy's (1851) map has the name "Negro Bar" for the same place—water of Englebright Lake now covers the site.

Negro Canyon [EL DORADO]: *canyon,* drained by a stream that flows 2.25 miles to Mule Canyon 5.5 miles west-northwest of Kirkwood (lat. 38°43'10" N, long. 120°10'15" W; sec. 14, T 10 N, R 16 E). Named on Tregedy Spring (1979) 7.5' quadrangle.

Negro Canyon [NEVADA]: *canyon,* drained by a stream that flows 1 mile to Donner Lake 2.25 miles east-northeast of Donner Pass (lat. 39°19'30" N, long. 120°17'05" W; sec. 14, T 17 N, R 15 E). Named on Norden (1955) 7.5' quadrangle.

Negro Canyon [SIERRA]: *canyon,* drained by a stream that flows 6 miles to North Yuba River 4.5 miles west of Sierra City (lat. 39° 33'50" N, long. 120°43'05" W; near NE cor. sec. 34, T 20 N, R 11 E). Named on Sierra City (1981) 7.5' quadrangle.

Negro Creek [NEVADA]: *stream,* flows 4 miles to Deer Creek 5 miles north-northwest of Pilot Peak (lat. 39°14'10" N, long. 121° 12'50" W; sec. 20, T 16 N, R 7 E). Named on Grass Valley (1949) 15' quadrangle.

Negro Flat [EL DORADO]: *area,* nearly 5 miles west-northwest of Kirkwood (lat. 38°43'35" N, long. 120°09'10" W; sec. 12, T 10 N, R 16 E); the place is in Negro Canyon. Named on Tragedy Spring (1979) 7.5' quadrangle.

Negro Flat: see **Remington Hill** [NEVADA] (2).

Negro Hill: see **Folsom Lake** [EL DORADO-PLACER-SACRAMENTO].

Negro Jack Hill [NEVADA]: *peak,* 6.5 miles south-southeast of Washington (lat. 39°15'55" N, long. 120°46'30" W; at E line sec. 7, T 16 N, R 11 E). Altitude 4635 feet. Named on Washington (1950) 7.5' quadrangle. Called Nigger Jack Hill on Colfax (1938) 30' quadrangle.

Negro Slough [SACRAMENTO]: *water feature,* 3.5 miles east-northeast of downtown Sacramento (lat. 38°36' N, long. 121°26' W). Named on Fair Oaks (1954) 15' quadrangle. Called Nigger Slough on Brighton (1911) 7.5' quadrangle. The place is at the site of present California State Exposition.

Negro Tent [SIERRA]: *locality,* 4.25 miles northeast of Pike (lat. 39° 29'20" N, long. 120°57' W; sec. 27, T 19 N, R 9 E). Named on Alleghany (1950) 15' quadrangle. Called Nigger Tent on Colfax (1898) 30' quadrangle, and called Niger Tent on Trask's (1853) map. A black man erected a tent at the site for the accommodation of travelers, and although eventually a cabin replaced the tent, the place retained the original designation "Nigger Tent" (Borthwick, p. 215). The place also was known as Hollow Log in 1850 (Gudde, 1975, p. 244). Eddy's (1851) map shows Hollow Log situated 6 miles by trail south of Goodyears Bar.

Neilsburg: see **Nielsburg** [PLACER].

Nelson Canyon [EL DORADO]: *canyon,* drained by a stream that flows 1.5 miles to Rock Creek 2.5 miles northeast of Chili Bar (lat. 38°47'30" N, long. 120°46'50" W; near W line sec. 20, T 11 N, R 11 E). Named on Garden Valley (1949) 7.5' quadrangle.

Nelson Mill [SIERRA]: *locality,* 0.5 mile south-southeast of Pike (lat. 39°26' N, long. 120°59'30" W). Named on Colfax (1898) 7.5' quadrangle.

Nelson Slough [SUTTER]: *water feature,* 2.5 miles west-southwest of Nicolaus in Sutter Bypass (lat. 38°53'35" N, long. 121°37'30" W; near N line sec. 15, T 12 N, R 3 E). Named on Nicolaus (1952) and Sutter Causeway (1952) 7.5' quadrangles.

Nelsonville: see **Mosquito Valley**, under **Mosquito Creek** [EL DORADO].

Nesbits Bar: see **Gold Hill** [PLACER].

Neutral Bar: see **Euchre Bar** [PLACER].

Nevada: see **Nevada City** [NEVADA].

Nevada City [NEVADA]: *town,* 4 miles northeast of Grass Valley along Deer Creek (lat. 39°15'50" N, long. 121°01'05" W; on W line sec. 7, T 16 N, R 9 E). Named on Nevada City (1948) 7.5' quadrangle. Called Nevada on Eddy's (1854) map. Postal authorities established Nevada City post office in 1850 (Frickstad, p. 114), and the town incorporated in 1856. Dr. A.B. Caldwell built a log cabin and store at the site in 1849, and for a time the place was known as Caldwell's Upper Store or Deer Creek Dry Diggings; the inhabitants changed the name of the community to Nevada in 1850, and to Nevada City ten years later to avoid confusion with the newly created State of Nevada (Hoover, Rensch, and Rensch, p. 253). After discovery of gold in the hills of the northwest part of present Nevada City, a community called Coyoteville grew there (Lindgren, 1897, p. 18). The name "Coyoteville" was from the fancied resemblance of holes dug for gold at the place to the burrows of coyotes (Gudde, 1975, p. 86). Whitney's (1873) map shows features called American Hill and Gopher Hill located just north of Nevada City and south of Sugar Loaf (present Sugarloaf Mountain). Whitney (1880, p. 190) described a feature called Connor Hill that was located about four miles west of Nevada City.

Nevada Creek [YUBA]: *stream,* flows 2 miles to Middle Yuba River 4 miles south of Camptonville (lat. 39°23'45" N, long. 121° 03'05" W; sec. 26, T 18 N, R 8 E). Named on Camptonville (1948) 7.5' quadrangle.

Nevada House: see **Camptonville** [YUBA].

Nevada Point [PLACER]: *ridge,* west-northwest-trending, 3.25 miles long, 6.25 miles west of Devil Peak (lat. 38°58'20" N, long. 120° 39'15" W); the ridge is at the west end of Nevada Point Ridge. Named on Tunnel Hill (1950) 7.5' quadrangle.

Nevada Point Ridge [PLACER]: *ridge,* extends generally southwest for 20 miles between Rubicon River and Long Canyon—as well as South Fork Long Canyon—from near Hell Hole Reservoir to the junction of Rubicon River and Long Canyon; Nevada Point is at the west end. Named on Bunker Hill (1953), Devil Peak (1950), Robbs Peak (1950), and Tunnel Hill (1950) 7.5' quadrangles.

Newark: see **Whiskey Diggings** [SIERRA].

Newbert: see **Marysville** [YUBA].

New Bullards Bar Reservoir [YUBA]: *lake,* behind a dam on North Yuba River nearly 4 miles east-northeast of Dobbins (lat. 39°23'35" N, long. 121°08'35" W; sec. 25, T 18 N, R 7 E). Named on Camptonville (1948, photorevised 1969), Challenge (1948, photorevised 1969), Clipper Mills (1948, photorevised 1975), and Strawberry Valley (1948, photorevised 1975) 7.5' quadrangles. Nevada City (1948) 15' quadrangle shows Bullards Bar Reservoir behind a dam located along the river 1.5 miles farther upstream (lat. 39°24'35" N, long. 121°08'35" W; sec. 24, T 18 N, R 7 E).

Newcastle [PLACER]: *town,* 8 miles northeast of Rocklin (lat. 38°52'25" N, long. 121°07'55" W; mainly in sec. 19, T 12 N, R 8 E). Named on Gold Hill (1954) and Rocklin (1967) 7.5' quadrangles. Postal authorities established Newcastle post office in 1864 (Frickstad, p. 121). They established Secret Ravine post office 3 miles southwest of Newcastle in 1854, changed the name to Auburn Station in 1863, changed it back to Secret Ravine the same year, and discontinued it in 1868 (Salley, p. 12, 200).

New Chicago [AMADOR]: *locality,* 3 miles south of Plymouth (lat. 38°26'15" N, long. 120°50'15" W; near NE cor. sec. 26, T 7 N, R 10 E). Named on Amador City (1962) 7.5' quadrangle. Called Chicago on Jackson (1902) 30' quadrangle.

New England Mills [PLACER]: *locality,* 4 miles south-southwest of Colfax (lat. 39°02'35" N, long. 120°58'20" W; near SE cor. sec. 21, T 14 N, R 9 E). Named on Colfax (1949) 7.5' quadrangle.

New Helvetia [SACRAMENTO-SUTTER-YUBA]: *land grant,* at Sacramento and along Feather River from Nicolaus north to Yuba City. Named on Nicolaus (1952), Olivehurst (1952), Sacramento East (1967), Sacramento West (1967), Sutter (1952), and Yuba City (1952) 7.5' quadrangles. John Augustus Sutter received 11 leagues in 1841 and claimed 48,839 acres patented in 1866; 2 leagues were at Sacramento and 9 leagues were along Feather River (Cowan, p. 53-54; Cowan listed the grant under the name "Nueva Helvecia"). According to Perez (p. 78), the grant was made in 1845. The name "Helvetia" is from the Roman designation of Switzerland, Sutter's ancestral homeland (Gudde, 1949, p. 235).

Newhouse Place: see **Mobile Flat**, under **Mobile Ravine** [SIERRA].

Newman Hill [AMADOR]: *peak,* 3 miles west of Ione (lat. 38°21'10" N, long. 120°59'15" W). Altitude 474 feet. Named on Ione (1962) 7.5'

quadrangle.

New Mecklenburg: see **Marysville** [YUBA].

New Orleans Gulch [EL DORADO]: *canyon,* drained by a stream that flows 1.25 miles to Middle Fork American River 4.5 miles north-northeast of Greenwood (lat. 38°57'25" N, long. 120°52'35" W; sec. 20, T 13 N, R 10 E). Named on Georgetown (1949) and Greenwood (1949) 7.5' quadrangles.

New Philadelphia: see **Bunker Hill** [AMADOR] (2).

Newton: see **Newtown** [EL DORADO]; **Newtown** [NEVADA].

Newtown [EL DORADO]: *locality,* 2.25 miles south of Camino (lat. 38°42'15" N, long. 120°40'40" W; sec. 20, T 10 N, R 12 E). Named on Camino (1952) 7.5' quadrangle. Called Newton on California Mining Bureau's (1917c) map. Logan's (1938) map has the form "New town" for the name. Postal authorities established Newtown post office in 1854, discontinued it for a time in 1875, and discontinued it finally in 1912 (Frickstad, p. 28). A mining camp called Dogtown was situated 0.5 mile northeast of Newtown (Hoover, Rensch, and Rensch, p. 84).

Newtown [NEVADA]: *locality,* 4.5 miles west of Nevada City (lat. 39°15'10" N, long. 121°06'10" W; near N line sec. 17, T 16 N, R 8 E). Named on Nevada City (1948) 7.5' quadrangle. A group of sailors made the first discovery of gold at the place, which for a time was called Sailors Flat; it also was called Newton (Gudde, 1975, p. 241). Whitney's (1873) map shows a place called Beckmans Fl. [Flat] located along Deer Creek about 1 mile southeast of Newtown, a place called Pleasant Fl. located along Deer Creek about 1 mile east-southeast of Newtown, and a place called Stockings Fl. located along Deer Creek 2.5 miles east of Newtown. Whitney (1880, p. 190) noted that a canyon called Illinois Ravine heads near Newtown and extends north to Rush Creek.

Newtown [YOLO]: *locality,* 2 miles west-southwest of Clarksburg along Sacramento Northern Railroad (lat. 38°24'10" N, long. 121° 34'05" W). Named on Courtland (1952) 15' quadrangle.

New York: see **Little New York**, under **Little York** [NEVADA].

New York Bar [EL DORADO-PLACER]: *locality,* 3 miles east-northeast of Auburn along Middle Fork American River on El Dorado-Placer County line nearly 1 mile above the mouth of Middle Fork (lat. 38°54'55" N, long. 121°01'25" W; near SW cor. sec. 6, T 12 N, R 9 E). Named on Auburn (1953) 7.5' quadrangle.

New York Bar: see **Sucker Bar** [YUBA].

New York Canyon [NEVADA]: *canyon,* drained by a stream that flows 1 mile to South Yuba River 2.25 miles south of North Bloomfield (lat. 39°20'05" N, long. 120°54'10" W; sec. 18, T 17 N, R 10 E). Named on North Bloomfield (1949) 7.5' quadrangle.

New York Canyon [PLACER]:

(1) *canyon,* drained by a stream that flows 3 miles to North Fork American River 4.5 miles north of Duncan Peak (lat. 39°13'10" N, long. 120°30'30" W; sec. 27, T 16 N, R 13 E). Named on Duncan Peak (1952) 7.5' quadrangle.

(2) *canyon,* drained by a stream that flows 2 miles to Shirttail Canyon 4 miles northwest of Foresthill (lat. 39°04'10" N, long. 120°51'30" W; at S line sec. 9, T 14 N, R 10 E). Named on Foresthill (1949) 7.5' quadrangle.

New York Creek [EL DORADO]: *stream,* drained by a stream that flows 3.25 miles to Folsom Lake 5 miles north of Clarksville (lat. 38°43'35" N, long. 121°04'10" W; sec. 14, T 10 N, R 8 E). Named on Clarksville (1953, photorevised 1980) 7.5' quadrangle.

New York Creek [YUBA]: *stream,* flows 4 miles to Dry Creek (1) 5.5 miles east-northeast of Rackerby (lat. 39°28'45" N, long. 121° 15'10" W; sec. 25, T 19 N, R 6 E). Named on Forbestown (1970) and Rackerby (1948) 7.5' quadrangles.

New York Flat [YUBA]:

(1) *valley,* 5 miles northeast of Rackerby (lat. 39°29'15" N, long. 121°16'15" W; in and near sec. 22, 23, T 19 N, R 6 E); the valley is along New York Creek. Named on Rackerby (1948) 7.5' quadrangle.

(2) *locality,* 3.25 miles west-northwest of Challenge (lat. 39°29'50" N, long. 121°16'50" W); the place is near the northwest end of New York Flat (1). Named on Smartsville (1895) 30' quadrangle.

New York Flat: see **Downieville** [SIERRA]; **New York Gulch** [AMADOR].

New York Gulch [AMADOR]: *canyon,* drained by a stream that flows 1 mile to Dry Creek 4 miles south-southwest of Plymouth (lat. 38°25'35" N, long. 120°52'55" W; near S line sec. 28, T 7 N, R 10 E). Named on Irish Hill (1962) 7.5' quadrangle. Camp's (1962) map has the designation "New York Gulch & Flat" for the place.

New York House: see **Challenge** [YUBA].

New York House Flat: see **Challenge** [YUBA].

New York Ranch: see **Challenge** [YUBA].

New York Ranch Gulch [AMADOR]: *canyon,* 3 miles long, opens into the canyon of Jackson Creek nearly 2 miles north-northwest of Jackson Butte (lat. 38°21'45" N, long. 120°44'10" W; sec. 23, T 6 N, R 11 E). Named on Mokelumne Hill (1948) and Pine Grove (1948) 7.5' quadrangles.

New York Ravine [NEVADA]: *canyon,* drained by a stream that flows nearly 1.5 miles to Middle Yuba River 6 miles northeast of North Bloomfield (lat. 39°26'05" N, long. 120°49'30" W; sec. 11, T 18 N, R 10 E). Named on Alleghany (1949) 7.5' quadrangle.

New York Ravine [SIERRA]: *canyon,* drained by a stream that flows 2.25 miles to North Yuba River 2 miles east of Downieville (lat. 39°33'20" N, long. 120°47'20" W; sec. 31, T 20 N, R 11 E). Named on Downieville (1951) 7.5' quadrangle.

New York Reservoir: see **Jackson** [AMADOR].

Nichols: see **Nicolaus** [SUTTER].

Nichols Mill [SIERRA]: *locality,* nearly 3 miles south-southwest of Sierraville along Bonta Creek (lat. 39°33'05" N, long. 120°23'15" W; sec. 26, T 20 N, R 14 E). Site named on Sattley (1981) 7.5' quadrangle.

Nick Welsh Spring [PLACER]: *spring,* 1.5 miles north-northeast of Foresthill (lat. 39°02'25" N, long. 120°48'10" W; sec. 24, T 14 N, R 10 E). Named on Foresthill (1949) 7.5' quadrangle.

Nicolaus [SUTTER]: *village,* 16 miles south of Yuba City near Feather River (lat. 38°54'15" N, long. 121°34'35" W). Named on Nicolaus (1952) 7.5' quadrangle. Called Nichols on Jefferson's (1849) map, and called Nicholaus on Scholfield's (1851) map. Derby's (1849b) map has the name "Nicholas Alleger" at the place. Postal authorities established Nicolaus post office in 1851 (Frickstad, p. 202). Nicolaus Allgeier, a Hudson's Bay Company trapper, received land at the place from John A. Sutter as compensation for helping to build an adobe house at Sutter's Hock Farm; Allgeier operated a ferry across Feather River in 1843, put up an adobe house in 1847, erected a hotel in 1849, and sold over 300 town lots in 1850 (Hoover, Rensch, and Rensch, p. 544). Gibbes' (1852) map shows a place called Oro located at the mouth of Bear River about 2.25 miles north of Nicholas (present Nicolaus) at or near present Placer-Sutter County line. Thomas Jefferson Green bought land from Sutter along the south side of Bear River and laid out a townsite that he called Oro; Green, a state senator, then used his influence to have Oro declared the county seat when the state legislature created Sutter County in 1850, but the place failed to develop (Hoover, Rensch, and Rensch, p. 545). Barham's Crossing later was at this site; a settler named Barham built a bridge there in 1850 (Hendrix, p. 107).

Nicolaus: see **East Nicolaus** [SUTTER].

Nicolaus Station: see **East Nicolaus** [SUTTER].

Nielsburg [PLACER]: *locality,* 4.5 miles north-northeast of Auburn (lat. 38°57'25" N, long. 121°01'50" W; at S line sec. 24, T 13 N, R 8 E). Site named on Auburn (1953) 7.5' quadrangle. According to Salley (p. 152), postal authorities established Neilsburgh post office in 1855 and discontinued it in 1866; the name, which also had the form "Neillsburgh," was for Arthur C. Neill, first postmaster (Salley, p. 152).

Nigger Bar: see **Negro Bar** [SACRAMENTO]; **Negro Bar Creek** [YUBA].

Nigger George Ravine [PLACER]: *canyon,* drained by a stream that flows 2.5 miles to North Fork American River 2.25 miles east-southeast of Colfax (lat. 39°05' N, long. 120°55' W; sec. 12, T 14 N, R 9 E). Named on Colfax (1949) 7.5' quadrangle.

Niggerhead Bar: see **American River** [EL DORADO-PLACER-SACRAMENTO].

Nigger Heaven [YOLO]: *ridge,* north-northwest-trending, 7 miles long, center 2.5 miles north-northeast of Guinda (lat. 38°51'45" N, long. 122°10'20" W). Named on Guinda (1959) 15' quadrangle. Durst 's (1916) map has the name "Summit Valley" along the ridge.

Nigger Jack Hill: see **Negro Jack Hill** [NEVADA].

Nigger Jack Slough: see **Jack Slough** [YUBA].

Nigger Slide: see **Ramshorn Creek** [SIERRA].

Nigger Slough: see **Negro Slough** [SACRAMENTO].

Niggers Ravine [PLACER]: *canyon,* drained by a stream that flows 1 mile to Bunch Canyon 4 miles south-southeast of Colfax (lat. 39° 02'55" N, long. 120°55'45" W; sec. 24, T 13 N, R 9 E). Named on Colfax (1949) 7.5' quadrangle.

Nigger Tent: see **Negro Tent** [SIERRA].

Nimbus [SACRAMENTO]: *locality,* 4 miles southwest of Folsom along Southern Pacific Railroad (lat. 38°37'45" N, long. 121°12'50" W). Named on Folsom (1967) 7.5' quadrangle.

Nine Mile House: see **Colusa** [COLUSA].

Norden [NEVADA]: *village,* 1.5 miles west of Donner Pass (lat. 39° 19'05" N, long. 120°21'15" W; near S line sec. 24, T 17 N, R 14 E). Named on Norden (1955) 7.5' quadrangle. Postal authorities established Norden post office in 1926, discontinued it in 1943, and reestablished it in 1947 (Frickstad, p. 114). The name is for Charles Van Norden, a water-company official (Stewart, p. 89).

Norristown: see **Brighton** [SACRAMENTO].

North Arm: see **Pardee Reservoir** [AMADOR].

North Bloomfield [NEVADA]: *village,* 13 miles northeast of Grass Valley along Humbug Creek (lat. 39°22'05" N, long. 120°53'55" W; sec. 6, T 17 N, R 10 E). Named on North Bloomfield (1949) 7.5' quadrangle. Postal authorities established North Bloomfield post office in 1857, moved it to a new site in 1875, and discontinued it in 1942; the word "North" was added to the name "Bloomfield" to distinguish the place from Bloomfield in Sonoma County (Salley, p. 155). The place originally was called Humbug (Hanna, p. 34). Whitney's (1873) map shows a place called Mountain Wells situated 3.5 miles south of North Bloomfield. Postal authorities established Mountain Well post office in 1858 and discontinued it in 1866 (Frickstad, p. 114).

North Butte [SUTTER]: *peak,* 5.5 miles north-northwest of Sutter in Sutter Buttes (lat. 39°14'10" N, long. 121°47'10" W; sec. 18, T 16 N, R 2 E). Altitude 1863 feet. Named on Sutter Buttes (1954) 7.5' quadrangle.

North Butte: see **Pennington** [SUTTER].

North Canyon [EL DORADO]:

(1) *canyon,* drained by a stream that flows 1.25 miles to Canyon Creek (1) 1.5 miles north-northwest of Georgetown (lat. 38°55'50" N, long. 120°50'40" W; sec. 34, T 13 N, R 10 E). Named on Georgetown (1949) 7.5' quadrangle.

(2) *canyon,* drained by a stream that flows 2.5 miles to South Fork American River 7 miles west of Pollock Pines (lat. 38°46'20" N, long. 120°42'30" W; sec. 26, T 11 N, R 11 E); the canyon is east of South Canyon. Named on Slate Mountain (1950) 7.5' quadrangle.

(3) *canyon,* drained by a stream that flows about 2 miles to Big Canyon (2) 11 miles east-southeast of Camino (lat. 38°39'15" N, long. 120°30'15" W; sec. 11, T 9 N, R 13 E). Named on Sly Park (1952) and Stump Spring (1951) 7.5' quadrangles.

North Canyon [NEVADA]: *canyon,* drained by a stream that flows nearly 1 mile to South Yuba River 3.25 miles southwest of North Bloomfield (lat. 39°20'35" N, long. 120°56'55" W; near N line sec. 15, T 17 N, R 9 E). Named on North Bloomfield (1949) 7.5' quadrangle.

North Columbia [NEVADA]: *settlement,* 4.5 miles west of North Bloomfield (lat. 39°22'20" N, long. 120°59'10" W; on S line sec. 32, T 18 N, R 9 E). Named on North Bloomfield (1949) and Pike (1949) 7.5' quadrangles. Postal authorities established North Columbia post office in 1860 and discontinued it in 1931; the word "North" was added to the name "Columbia" to distinguish the place from Columbia post office in Tuolumne County (Salley, p. 155). The community originally was called Columbia Hill (Hanna, p. 70).

North Creek [EL DORADO]: *stream,* flows 3.5 miles to Alder Creek 6.5 miles north-northwest of Leek Spring Hill (lat. 38°42'45" N, long. 120°19'50" W; sec. 17, T 10 N, R 15 E). Named on Leek Spring Hill (1951) 7.5' quadrangle.

North Creek [NEVADA]: *stream,* flows 5.5 miles to Fordyce Lake 9 miles northwest of Donner Pass (lat. 39°23'40" N, long. 120°27'20" W; near E line sec. 25, T 18 N, R 13 E). Named on Independence Lake (1981) and Webber Peak (1981) 7.5' quadrangles.

North Fork Campground [COLUSA]: *locality,* 2 miles north-northwest of Fouts Springs (lat. 39°22'45" N, long. 122°38'50" W); the place is near the mouth of North Fork Stony Creek. Named on Saint John Mountain (1968) 7.5' quadrangle.

North Fork Lake [PLACER]: *lake,* behind a dam on North Fork American River 3.5 miles northeast of Auburn (lat. 38°56'10" N, long. 121°01'25" W; near W line sec. 31, T 13 N, R 9 E). Named on Auburn (1953) 7.5' quadrangle. Called Lake Clementine on Greenwood (1949) 7.5' quadrangle. United States Board on Geographic Names (1972, p. 4) gave the names "Lake Clementine" and "North Fork Reservoir" as variants.

North Fork Reservoir [PLACER-SACRAMENTO]: *lake,* 1200 feet long, 2.5 miles north of Folsom on Placer-Sacramento County line (lat. 38°42'45" N, long. 121°10" W). Named on Folsom (1941) 15' quadrangle.

North Fork Reservoir: see **North Fork Lake** [PLACER].

North Highlands [SACRAMENTO]: *city,* 5.5 miles north-northwest of downtown Carmichael (lat. 38°41'15" N, long. 121°22'15" W). Named on Citrus Heights (1967) and Rio Linda (1967) 7.5' quadrangles. Postal authorities established North Highlands post office in 1951 (Frickstad, p. 134).

North Indian Creek: see **Indian Creek** [EL DORADO] (1).

North Miller Creek [PLACER]: *stream,* flows nearly 2 miles to Miller Creek 4.5 miles southwest of Homewood at Miller Meadows (lat. 39°02'05" N, long. 120°13' W; sec. 28, T 14 N, R 16 E). Named on Homewood (1955) 7.5' quadrangle.

North Mokelumne River: see **Mokelumne River** [AMADOR-SACRAMENTO].

North Park Creek: see **North Sly Park Creek** [EL DORADO].

North Ravine [PLACER]: *canyon,* drained by a stream that flows 3.25 miles to Auburn Ravine 1.5 miles west-southwest of downtown Auburn (lat. 38°53'25" N, long. 121°06'10" W; sec. 17, T 12 N, R 8 E). Named on Auburn (1953) 7.5' quadrangle.

North Sacramento [SACRAMENTO]: *district,* 3 miles northeast of downtown Sacramento (lat. 38°36'30" N, long. 121°27' W). Named on Sacramento East (1967) 7.5' quadrangle. Postal authorities established North Sacramento post office in 1915 and discontinued it in 1966 (Salley, p. 156).

North San Juan [NEVADA]: *village,* 10.5 miles north of Grass Valley (lat. 39°22'10" N, long. 121°06'15" W; sec. 5, T 17 N, R 8 E); the village is on San Juan Ridge. Named on Nevada City (1948) 7.5' quadrangle. Postal authorities established North San Juan post office in 1857; the word "North" was added to the name to avoid confusion with San Juan in San Benito County (Salley, p. 156). Christian Kientz, a veteran of the Mexican War, settled at the site in 1853 and gave it the name "San Juan" because he thought he saw a resemblance between a bluff there and the Castle of San Juan de Ulloa at Vera Cruz, Mexico (Hanna, p. 279). Whitney's (1873) map has the name "Kent Rav." for a canyon just southwest of North San Juan.

North Shirttail Canyon [PLACER]: *canyon,* drained by a stream that flows 9 miles to Shirttail Canyon 3.5 miles north of Foresthill (lat. 39°04'15" N, long. 120°48'40" W; near E line sec. 11, T 14 N, R 10 E). Named on Dutch Flat (1950), Foresthill (1949), and Westville (1952) 7.5' quadrangles. Present North Shirttail Canyon is shown as the upper part of Shirttail Canyon on Colfax (1938) 30' quadrangle.

North Slate Creek: see **Slate Creek** [EL DORADO] (3).

North Sly Park Creek [EL DORADO]: *stream,* flows 2.5 miles to Sly Park Creek 4.5 miles west-northwest of Old Iron Mountain (lat. 38°43'50" N, long. 120°28'20" W; sec. 7, T 10 N, R 14 E). Named on Leek Spring Hill (1951) 15' quadrangle. Called North Park Creek on Stump Spring (1951) 7.5' quadrangle, which has the name "Park Creek" for present Sly Park Creek. United States Board on Geographic Names (1978a, p. 7) rejected the names "North Fork Park Creek" and "North Park Creek" for the stream.

North Star [YUBA]: *locality,* 2 miles northeast of Strawberry Valley (lat. 39°35'10" N, long. 121°04'35" W; near SW cor. sec. 15, T 20 N, R 8 E). Named on Strawberry Valley (1948) 7.5' quadrangle. Bidwell Bar (1897) 30' quadrangle shows North Star House there.

North Star House: see **North Star** [YUBA].

North Steely Creek [EL DORADO]: *stream,* flows 4.5 miles to join South Steely Creek and form Steely Fork Cosumnes River 2 miles west-northwest of Caldor (lat. 38°37' N, long. 120°28' W; sec. 19, T 9 N, R 14 E). Named on Caldor (1951) and Stump Spring (1951) 7.5' quadrangles.

North Tragedy Creek [EL DORADO]: *stream,* flows 5.5 miles to Sherman Canyon 7 miles west of Kirkwood (lat. 38°41'20" N, long. 120°11'55" W); the stream heads near Tragedy Spring. Named on Tragedy Spring (1979) 7.5' quadrangle.

North Wallace Canyon [PLACER]: *canyon,* drained by a stream that flows 3.25 miles to Wallace Canyon 2 miles north-northeast of Devil Peak (lat. 38°59' N, long. 120°31'35" W; near N line sec. 16, T 13 N, R 13 E). Named on Bunker Hill (1953), Devil Peak (1950), and Greek Store (1952) 7.5' quadrangles. Present North Wallace Canyon is shown as part of Wallace Canyon on Placerville (1893) 30' quadrangle.

North Yuba River [SIERRA-YUBA]: *stream,* flows 41 miles—the last mile along Sierra-Yuba County line—to join Middle Yuba River and form Yuba River nearly 4 miles east of Dobbins in Yuba County (lat. 39°22'05" N, long. 121°08'10" W; sec. 1, T 17 N, R 7 E); the stream heads at Yuba Pass. Named on Challenge (1948), Clipper Mills (1948), Clio (1981), Downieville (1951), French Corral (1948), Goodyears Bar (1951), Haypress Valley (1981), Sierra City (1981), and Strawberry Valley (1948) 7.5' quadrangles. Called North Fork Yuba River on Bidwell Bar (1897), Downieville (1897), and Smartsville (1895) 30' quadrangles, but United States Board on Geographic Names (1950, p. 6) rejected the names "North Fork," "North Fork of Yuba River," and "North Fork Yuba River" for the stream, and rejected the names "North Fork of North Yuba River" and "South Fork of North Fork Yuba River" for upper reaches of the stream. On Downieville (1897) 30' quadrangle, present Downie River [SIERRA] is called N. Fork of N. Fork Yuba River, and present Haypress Creek [SIERRA] is called South Fork of North Fork Yuba River; United States Board on Geographic Names (1950, p. 5) rejected both of these older names. On Downieville (1897) 30' quadrangle also, present Lavezzola Creek [SIERRA] is called Middle Fork of North Fork Yuba River, but United States Board on Geographic Names (1950, p. 5) rejected this name for the stream, and also rejected the name "North Fork of North Fork" for the upper part of the stream. On Downieville (1897) 30' quadrangle, present Pauley Creek [SIERRA] is called East Fork of North Fork Yuba River, but United States Board on Geographic Names (1950, p. 6) rejected this name. Gudde (1975, p. 73) listed a place called Churchman Bar that was situated on the east side of North Yuba River near the junction with Middle Yuba River.

Norton [YOLO]: *locality,* 4.25 miles north of Winters along Southern Pacific Railroad (lat. 38°35'10" N, long. 121°58'10" W; on W line sec. 34, T 9 N, R 1 W). Named on Winters (1953) 7.5' quadrangle. Called Ely on Winters (1916) 7.5' quadrangle.

Norton Ravine [EL DORADO]: *canyon,* drained by a stream that flows nearly 4 miles to South Fork American River 5 miles west of Coloma (lat. 38°47'35" N, long. 120°58'55" W; sec. 21, T 11 N, R 9 E). Named on Coloma (1949) and Pilot Hill (1954) 7.5' quadrangles.

Norway: see **Little Norway**, under **Meyers** [EL DORADO].

Noyes: see **Tarke** [SUTTER].

Nuestro [SUTTER]: *locality,* nearly 4 miles northwest of Yuba City along Sacramento Northern Railroad (lat. 39°11'05" N, long. 121° 39'40" W; sec. 5, T 15 N, R 3 E). Named on Sutter (1952) 7.5' quadrangle.

Nueva Helvecia: see **New Helvetia** [SACRAMENTO-SUTTER-YUBA].

Nueva Helvetia: see **Sacramento** [SACRAMENTO].

Nye's Crossing: see **Bridgeport** [NEVADA]

Nyes Crossing: see **Freemans Crossing** [NEVADA-YUBA].

Nyes Landing: see **Bridgeport** [NEVADA].

Nye's Ranch: see **Marysville** [YUBA].

—O—

Oahu: see **Craigs Flat** [SIERRA].
Oak Cove [COLUSA]: *relief feature*, 3.5 miles northwest of Wilbur Springs off of Freshwater Branch (lat. 39°04'15" N, long. 122°27'15" W). Named on Wilbur Springs (1961) 15' quadrangle.
Oak Flat [PLACER]: *area*, 11.5 miles west of Granite Chief (lat. 39°11'50" N, long. 120°29'55" W; near N line sec. 2, T 15 N, R 13 E). Named on Royal Gorge (1953) 7.5' quadrangle.
Oak Flat [SIERRA]: *area*, 1.5 miles south-southwest of Alleghany (lat. 39°27'10" N, long. 120°51'15" W; near S line sec. 4, T 18 N, R 10 E). Named on Alleghany (1949) 7.5' quadrangle.
Oak Flat [YUBA]: *area*, 3.25 miles east of Strawberry Valley (lat. 39°33'45" N, long. 121°02'40" W; sec. 26, T 20 N, R 8 E). Named on Strawberry Valley (1948) 7.5' quadrangle.
Oak Flat: see **Big Oak Flat** [PLACER]; **Grimes** [COLUSA]; **Little Oak Flat** [PLACER].
Oak Grove [EL DORADO]: *locality*, 2.5 miles east-northeast of Placerville (lat. 38°44'40" N, long. 120°45'40" W). Named on Placerville (1893) 30' quadrangle.
Oak Grove [YUBA]: *locality*, 2.5 miles west-southwest of Oregon House along Dry Creek (1) (lat. 39°20'50" N, long. 121°19'05" W). Named on Smartsville (1895) 30' quadrangle. Water of Virginia Ranch Reservoir now covers the site. Wescoatt's (1861) map shows a place called Abbott House located 2.5 miles west-southwest of Oregon House along Dry Creek (1). John M. Abbott built Abbott House in the early 1850's; it first was known as Oak Grove House (Hoover, Rensch, and Rensch, p. 592-593).
Oak Grove House: see **Oak Grove** [YUBA].
Oak Hall Bend [SACRAMENTO-YOLO]: *bend*, 3.5 miles south of West Sacramento along Sacramento River on Sacramento-Yolo County line (lat. 38°31'15" N, long. 121°31'25" W). Named on Sacramento West (1967) 7.5' quadrangle.
Oakland: see **Marysville** [YUBA].
Oakland Pond [SIERRA]: *lake*, 300 feet long, 8 miles north-northwest of Sierra City (lat. 39°40'40" N, long. 120°40'55" W; on W line sec. 18, T 21 N, R 12 E). Named on Gold Lake (1981) 7.5' quadrangle.
Oak Park [SACRAMENTO]: *district*, 2.25 miles southeast of downtown Sacramento (lat. 38°33' N, long. 121°28'15" W). Named on Sacramento East (1967) 7.5' quadrangle. Postal authorities established Oak Park post office in 1892 (Salley, p. 158).
Oaks: see **The Oaks** [NEVADA].
Oak Valley [YUBA]: *settlement*, 5.5 miles southeast of Strawberry Valley (lat. 39°30' N, long. 121°02'15" W; sec. 24, T 19 N, R 8 E). Named on Camptonville (1948) and Strawberry Valley (1948) 7.5' quadrangles.
Oak Valley Creek [SIERRA]: *stream*, flows 1.25 miles to Willow Creek 4 miles north-northwest of Pike (lat. 39°29'35" N, long. 121° 01'35" W; near N line sec. 25, T 19 N, R 8 E). Named on Camptonville (1948) 7.5' quadrangle.
Oat Creek [YOLO]: *stream*, formed by the confluence of North Fork and South Fork, flows 5.5 miles to lowlands nearly 4 miles northwest of Zamora (lat. 38°49'55" N, long. 121°56'05" W; sec. 2, T 11 N, R 1 W); the stream drains Oat Valley. Named on Bird Valley (1959) and Zamora (1953) 7.5' quadrangles. North Fork and South Fork both are 8 miles long and are named on Bird Valley (1959) 7.5' quadrangle.
Oat Hills [COLUSA]: *ridge*, north-trending, 3 miles long, 5 miles north-northeast of Wilbur Springs (lat. 39°06' N, long. 122°22'15" W). Named on Wilbur Springs (1961) 15' quadrangle.
Oat Hills [YUBA]: *ridge*, west-trending, 1.5 miles long, about 7 miles south-southwest of Oregon House (lat. 39°15'25" N, long. 121°18'45" W; sec. 8, 9, T 16 N, R 6 E). Named on Oregon House (1948) 7.5' quadrangle. On Smartsville (1895) 30' quadrangle, the name "Oat Hills" applies to a ridge that extends for 3 or 4 miles north-northwest from present Oat Hills across present High Prairie.
Oat Valley [COLUSA]: *valley*, 8 miles north of Wilbur Springs (lat. 39°09' N, long. 122°23'15" W; in and near sec. 14, T 15 N, R 5 W). Named on Wilbur Springs (1961) 15' quadrangle.
Oat Valley [YOLO]: *valley*, 6.5 miles west of Zamora in Dunnigan Hills (lat. 38°48'15" N, long. 122°00' W); the valley is along Oat Creek. Named on Bird Valley (1959) and Zamora (1953) 7.5' quadrangles.
Oat Valley: see **Capay** [YOLO].
Observatory Point: see **Dollar Point** [PLACER].
Occident: see **Maxwell** [COLUSA].
O'Connor Gulch [EL DORADO]: *canyon*, drained by a stream that flows 1 mile to Middle Fork Cosumnes River less than 1 mile north of Omo Ranch (lat. 38°35'30" N, long. 120°34'15" W; sec. 32, T 9 N, R 13 E). Named on Omo Ranch (1952) 7.5' quadrangle.
O'Connor Lakes [SUTTER]: *lakes*, 6.5 miles north of Nicolaus near Feather River (lat. 39°00' N, long. 121°35'20" W). Named on Nicolaus (1952) and Olivehurst (1952) 7.5' quadrangles.
O'Donnells Flat: see **Downieville** [SIERRA].
Ogden Bend [COLUSA-SUTTER]: *bend*, 1.5 miles south of Meridian along Sacramento River on Colusa-Sutter County line (lat. 39°07'20" N, long. 121°54'40" W; at W line sec. 30, T 15 N, R 1 E). Named on Grimes (1954) 7.5' quadrangle.
Ogilby Canyon [EL DORADO]: *canyon*, drained by a stream that flows 2.5 miles to South Fork American River, 1.5 miles west-southwest of Riverton (lat. 38°46' N, long. 120°28'45" W; sec. 25, T 11 N, R 11 E). Named on Riverton (1950) and Stump Spring (1951) 7.5' quadrangles.
Ohio Bar: see **South Yuba River** [NEVADA-PLACER].
Ohio Hill [AMADOR]: *peak*, 1.5 miles north of Jackson (lat. 38°22'15" N, long. 120°46'10" W; sec. 16, T 6 N, R 11 E). Named on Jackson (1962) 7.5' quadrangle.
Ohm: see **Camp Spaulding** [NEVADA].
Oil Spring: see **Wilbur Springs** [COLUSA].
Oilville: see **Colfax** [PLACER].
Oiyer Spring [EL DORADO]: *spring*, 6 miles northwest of Leek Spring Mill (lat. 38°41'45" N, long. 120°21' W; near N line sec. 30, T 10 N, R 15 E). Named on Leek Spring Hill (1951) 7.5' quadrangle.
Old Bar: see **Shirttail Canyon** [PLACER].
Old Condon Mill [NEVADA]: *locality*, 2.5 miles south of Graniteville (lat. 39°24'20" N, long. 120°44' W; near SW cor. sec. 22, T 18 N, R 11 E). Site named on Graniteville (1982) 7.5' quadrangle.
Old Cortina Creek: see **Cortina Creek** [COLUSA]
Old Craggy [SUTTER]: *peak*, 5 miles northwest of Sutter in Sutter Buttes (lat. 39°12'30" N, long. 121°48'45" W; sec. 25, T 16 N, R 1 E). Named on Sutter Buttes (1954) 7.5' quadrangle.
Old Dry Diggings: see **Placerville** [EL DORADO].
Old Fort Jim [EL DORADO]: *locality*, 3 miles southwest of Camino (lat. 38°42'40" N, long. 120°43' W; sec. 24, T 10 N, R 11 E). Named on Camino (1952) 7.5' quadrangle.
Old Galloway Ridge [SIERRA]: *ridge*, north-northwest-trending, 1.5 miles long, center 1.5 miles south of Downieville (lat. 39°32'30" N, long. 120°49'30" W). Named on Downieville (1951) 7.5' quadrangle.
Old Iron Mountain [EL DORADO]: *peak*, 8 miles northwest of Leek Spring Hill (lat. 38°42'20" N, long. 120°23'25" W; sec. 23, T 10 N, R 14 E); the peak is on Iron Mountain Ridge 2 miles west of Iron Mountain (2). Altitude 5903 feet. Named on Stump Spring (1951) 7.5' quadrangle.
Old Man Mountain [NEVADA]: *peak*, 6.25 miles northeast of Yuba Gap (lat. 39°22'15" N, long. 120°31'15" W; sec. 4, T 17 N, R 13 E). Altitude 7789 feet. Named on Cisco Grove (1955) 7.5' quadrangle. Logan's (1940) map shows a place called Carlysle located less than 1 mile south of Old Man Mountain (on S line sec. 4, T 17 N, R 13 E), where Cisco Grove (1955) 7.5' quadrangle shows Carlisle mine—the name is for Thomas Carlyle, one of the locators of U.S. Grant claim in 1866 (Gudde, 1975, p. 61).
Old Mill Campground [COLUSA]: *locality*, 3.25 miles south-southeast of Fouts Springs (lat. 39°18'35" N, long. 122°38'30" W; sec. 21, T 17 N, R 7 W). Named on Fouts Springs (1968) 7.5' quadrangle.
Old Mill Creek [SIERRA]: *stream*, flows 3.5 miles to Little Canyon Creek 8 miles south-southwest of Mount Fillmore (lat. 39°37'35" N, long. 120°54'20" W; at W line sec. 6, T 20 N, R 10 E). Named on La Porte (1951) and Mount Fillmore (1951) 7.5' quadrangles.
Old Mountain House [SIERRA]: *locality*, nearly 3 miles south of Goodyears Bar (lat. 39°30' N, long. 120°53'25" W; near E line sec. 19, T 19 N, R 10 E). Site named on Goodyears Bar (1951) and Pike (1949) 7.5' quadrangles. Called Mountain House on Colfax (1898) 30' quadrangle. Postal authorities established Mountain House post office in 1874 and discontinued it in 1911 (Frickstad, p. 184).
Old Pino [EL DORADO]: *locality*, 5 miles northwest of Pollock Pines in Water Canyon (lat. 38°49'05" N, long. 120°38'45" W; sec. 9, T 11 N, R 12 E). Named on Slate Mountain (1950) 7.5' quadrangle.
Old Rancheria: see **Drytown** [AMADOR]; **Rancheria** [AMADOR].
Old River [SUTTER-YOLO]: *water feature*, cutoff meander of Sacramento River 4 miles southeast of Knights Landing on Sutter-Yolo County line (lat. 38°45'30" N, long. 121°40'10" W). Named on Grays Bend (1953) and Knights Landing (1952) 7.5' quadrangles. Shown as part of Sacramento River on Knights Landing (1910) and Grays Bend (1916) 7.5' quadrangles.
Old Road: see **Squaw Creek** [PLACER].
Old Schaeffer Camp [PLACER]: *locality*, 7.25 miles west-southwest of Martis Peak (lat. 39°15'15" N, long. 120°09'35" W; on W line sec. 12, T 16 N, R 16 E). Site named on Truckee (1955) 7.5' quadrangle.
Old Schaeffer Mill [PLACER]: *locality*, 7 miles west of Martis Peak (lat. 39°16'50" N, long. 120°09'45" W; near E line sec. 35, T 17 N, R 16 E). Site named on Truckee (1955) 7.5' quadrangle.
Old Smith Mill [SIERRA]: *locality*, 15 miles south of Loyalton along Little Truckee River (lat. 39°27'55" N, long. 120°11'20" W; sec. 27, T 19 N, R 16 E). Site named on Hobart Mills (1981) 7.5' quadrangle.
Old Stanford Wood Camp [PLACER]: *locality*, 5 miles southeast of Donner Pass (lat. 39°16'15" N, long. 120°15'05" W; near NW cor. sec. 6, T 16 N,

R 16 E). Site named on Norden (1955) 7.5' quadrangle.

Oleta: see **Fiddletown** [AMADOR].

Olgert Canyon [COLUSA]: *canyon*, drained by a stream that flows 1.25 miles to Bear Creek 8 miles south-southeast of Wilbur Springs (lat. 38°56'35" N, long. 122°20'30" W; sec. 30, T 13 N, R 4 W). Named on Glascock Mountain (1958) 7.5' quadrangle.

Olive: see **Mount Olive** [NEVADA].

Olive Hill [YUBA]: *locality*, 3.25 miles west-southwest of Loma Rica (lat. 39°17'15" N, long. 121°28'10" W; sec. 36, T 17 N, R 4 E). Named on Loma Rica (1947) 7.5' quadrangle.

Olivehurst [YUBA]: *town*, 4 miles south-southeast of Marysville (lat. 39°05'45" N, long. 121°33' W; in and near sec. 5, T 14 N, R 4 E). Named on Olivehurst (1952) 7.5' quadrangle. Postal authorities established Olivehurst post office in 1941 (Frickstad, p. 223). California Mining Bureau's (1917c) map shows a place called Denniston located along Western Pacific Railroad at or near present Olivehurst.

Oliver [YUBA]: *locality*, less than 1 mile south of downtown Marysville along Western Pacific Railroad (lat. 39°08' N, long. 121°35'25" W). Named on Marysville (1952) 15' quadrangle.

Olympic Valley: see **Squaw Valley** [PLACER].

Omega [NEVADA]: *locality*, 3.25 miles east-southeast of Washington (lat. 39°20' N, long. 120°45' W; near S line sec. 16, T 17 N, R 11 E). Named on Blue Canyon (1955) and Washington (1950) 7.5' quadrangles. Postal authorities established Omega post office in 1857 and discontinued it in 1891 (Frickstad, p. 114). Reportedly, the place first was called Delirum Tremens (Gudde, 1975, p. 251). Whitney's (1873) map shows a community called Diamond Creek located 1.5 miles east of Omega, a community called Shellback located 1 mile south-southwest of Omega, and a community called Spiritsville located 1.5 miles south-southwest of Omega.

Omega Diggings [NEVADA]: *locality*, 2.5 miles east-southeast of Washington (lat. 39°20'15" N, long. 120°45'25" W; sec. 16, 17, T 17 N, R 11 E); the place is near Omega. Named on Washington (1950) 7.5' quadrangle.

Omits Flat: see **Secret Canyon** [SIERRA].

Omochumnes [SACRAMENTO]: *land grant*, 16 miles southeast of downtown Sacramento. Named on Buffalo Creek (1967), Elk Grove (1968), Galt (1968), and Sloughhouse (1968) 7.5' quadrangles. Joaquin Sheldon received 5 leagues in 1844; Catherine Sheldon claimed 18,662 acres patented in 1870 (Cowan, p. 55; Perez, p. 79). The name is from an Indian village that was situated at present Elk Grove (Kroeber, p. 52).

Omo Ranch [EL DORADO]: *village*, 12.5 miles south-southeast of Camino (lat. 38°34'50" N, long. 120°34'05" W; at N line sec. 5, T 8 N, R 13 E). Named on Omo Ranch (1952) 7.5' quadrangle. Postal authorities established Omo Ranch post office in 1888 and discontinued it in 1974 (Salley, p. 161). The name "Omo" is from an Indian village (Kroeber, p. 52).

One Eye Creek [EL DORADO]: *stream*, formed by the confluence of North Fork and South Fork, flows 3.25 miles to Rock Creek nearly 5 miles northeast of Chili Bar (lat. 38°49'10" N, long. 120°45'50" W; at W line sec. 9, T 11 N, R 11 E). Named on Garden Valley (1949) and Slate Mountain (1950) 7.5' quadrangles. North Fork is 2.5 miles long and South Fork is 1.5 miles long; both forks are named on Slate Mountain (1950) 7.5' quadrangle. The name "One Eye Creek" was given after one of the first prospectors along the stream lost an eye (Gudde, 1975, p. 251).

One Horse Bar: see **Green Valley** [PLACER].

Oneida: see **Loyalton** [SIERRA]; **Martell** [AMADOR].

Oneida Creek [AMADOR]: *stream*, flows 2 miles to North Fork Jackson Creek 1.25 miles north of Jackson (lat. 38°22'05" N, long. 120°46'30" W; sec. 16, T 6 N, R 11 E). Named on Amador City (1962) and Jackson (1962) 7.5' quadrangles.

Onemile Creek [COLUSA]: *water feature*, enters Colusa County from Glenn County 1.25 miles west-northwest of Princeton (lat. 39°24'40" N, long. 122°01'40" W). Named on Princeton (1918) 7.5' quadrangle.

1001 Ridge [SIERRA]: *ridge*, generally west-trending, 5 miles long, center 5 miles east-northeast of Sierra City (lat. 39°35'15" N, long. 120°33' W). Named on Haypress Valley (1981) 7.5' quadrangle, which shows 1001 mine near the west end of the ridge.

Onion Creek [EL DORADO]: *stream*, flows 5.25 miles to Silver Creek 7 miles north-northeast of Pollock Pines (lat. 38°51'20" N, long. 120°32'05" W; near E line sec. 29, T 12 N, R 13 E). Named on Devil Peak (1950), Pollock Pines (1950), and Robbs Peak (1950) 7.5' quadrangles.

Onion Creek [PLACER]: *stream*, flows 3.25 miles to North Fork American River 5 miles south-southwest of Donner Pass (lat. 39° 15'15" N, long. 120°22'15" W; sec. 14, T 16 N, R 14 E). Named on Norden (1955) 7.5' quadrangle.

Onion Creek [SIERRA]: *stream*, flows 2.5 miles to Cold Stream (1) 6.5 miles southeast of Sierraville in Onion Valley (lat. 39°31'05" N, long. 120°17'05" W; near N line sec. 11, T 19 N, R 15 E). Named on Sierraville (1981) 7.5' quadrangle.

Onion Creek Campground [PLACER]: *locality*, 3.5 miles south-southwest of Donner Pass (lat. 39°16'30" N, long. 120°21'45" W; near SE cor. sec. 2, T 16 N, R 14 E); the place is along Onion Creek. Named on Norden (1955) 7.5' quadrangle.

Onion Flat [EL DORADO]: *area*, 4.5 miles west-northwest of Phipps Peak (lat. 38°59'10" N, long. 120°13'10" W; near SW cor. sec. 9, T 13 N, R 16 E). Named on Rockbound Valley (1955) 7.5' quadrangle. Water of Rubicon Reservoir now covers much of the area.

Onion Valley [AMADOR]: *area*, 5.5 miles west-northwest of Mokelumne Peak (lat. 38°33'55" N, long. 120°06'15" W; near NW cor. sec. 11, T 8 N, R 16 E). Named on Bear River Reservoir (1979) 7.5' quadrangle.

Onion Valley [PLACER]: *valley*, 2.25 miles south-southeast of Emigrant Gap (1) (lat. 39°16'10" N, long. 120°39'05" W; mainly in sec. 8, T 16 N, R 12 E). Named on Blue Canyon (1955) 7.5' quadrangle. On Colfax (1898) 30' quadrangle, the stream in the valley is called Onion Valley Cr.

Onion Valley [SIERRA]: *valley*, 6.5 miles southeast of Sierraville (lat. 39°30'50" N, long. 120°17'05" W; sec. 11, T 19 N, R 15 E); the valley is along Cold Stream (1) at the mouth of Onion Creek. Named on Sierraville (1981) 7.5' quadrangle.

Onion Valley: see **Upper Onion Valley** [AMADOR].

Onion Valley Creek: see **Onion Valley** [PLACER].

Onion Valley Spring 2 [PLACER]: *spring*, 3 miles south-southeast of Emigrant Gap (1) (lat. 39°15'25" N, long. 120°39'05" W; sec. 17, T 16 N, R 12 E); the spring is less than 1 mile south of Onion Valley. Named on Blue Canyon (1955) 7.5' quadrangle.

Onisbo: see **Courtland** [SACRAMENTO].

On It Creek [EL DORADO]: *stream*, flows 3.25 miles to Scott Creek 5.5 miles east-southeast of Aukum (lat. 38°32'05" N, long. 120°37'40" W; sec. 23, T 8 N, R 12 E). Named on Aukum (1952) and Omo Ranch (1952) 7.5' quadrangles. Justice of the Peace Jinkerson gave the name to the stream after he ordered destruction of the buildings along the creek that gave Indian Diggins the nickname "Whore House Gulch" (Yohalem, p. 27).

O'Pera: see **Camp O'Pera**, under **Lancha Plana** [AMADOR].

Ophir [PLACER]: *village*, 2.5 miles west of Auburn in Auburn Ravine (lat. 38°53'30" N, long. 121°07'20" W; sec. 18, T 12 N, R 8 E). Named on Auburn (1953) 7.5' quadrangle. The place first was called Spanish Corral (Bancroft, 1888, p. 355). The name "Ophir" refers to the biblical source of King Solomon's treasure (Scamehorn, p. 191). Postal authorities established Ophirville post office before March 24, 1852, discontinued it in 1866, reestablished it with the name "Ophir" in 1872, and discontinued it in 1910 (Salley, p. 161). They established Coon Creek post office northwest of Ophir in 1856 and discontinued it in 1860 (Salley p. 50). A place called Frytown was located in Auburn Ravine 2 miles below Ophir—the name was from one of the owners of the merchandise firm of Fry and Bruce; a place called Crees Flat was situated on the road between Ophir and Auburn (Gudde, 1975, p. 88, 126).

Ophir Hill [NEVADA]: *peak*, 1.5 miles southeast of downtown Grass Valley (lat. 39°12'20" N, long. 121°02'30" W; sec. 35, T 16 N, R 8 E). Named on Grass Valley (1949) 7.5' quadrangle.

Ophirville: see **Ohir** [PLACER].

Orangevale [SACRAMENTO]: *town*, 2.5 miles west of Folsom (lat. 38°40'40" N, long. 121°13'30" W). Named on Folsom (1967) 7.5' quadrangle. Called Orange Vale on Sacramento (1892) 30' quadrangle. Postal authorities established Orangevale post office in 1891, discontinued it in 1901, and reestablished it in 1951 (Salley, p. 162).

Ora Spring [EL DORADO]: *spring*, 7.5 miles north-northwest of Leek Spring Hill (lat. 38°43'50" N, long. 120°19'50" W; sec. 8, T 10 N, R 15 E). Named on Leek Spring Hill (1951) 7.5' quadrangle.

Orchard Creek [PLACER]: *stream*, flows 9 miles to Auburn Ravine 9 miles north-northwest of Roseville (lat. 38°51'45" N, long. 121° 22'10" W; sec. 25, T 12 N, R 5 E). Named on Rocklin (1967) and Roseville (1967) 7.5' quadrangles. Called Rock Creek on Markham Ravine (1942) 15' quadrangle.

Orcum: see **Mount Orcum**, under **Mount Aukum** [EL DORADO].

Oregon Bar [EL DORADO]: *locality*, 3 miles northwest of the village of Pilot Hill along North Fork American River (lat. 38°51'50" N, long. 121°03'20" W; sec. 26, T 12 N, R 8 E). Named on Auburn (1954) 15' quadrangle.

Oregon Bar [PLACER]: *locality*, 9 miles east-northeast of Auburn along Middle Fork American River (lat. 38°57'45" N, long. 120° 55'45" W; sec. 24, T 13 N, R 9 E). Named on Greenwood (1949) 7.5' quadrangle.

Oregon Bar: see **Long Bar** [YUBA] (1).

Oregon Canyon [EL DORADO]: *canyon*, drained by a stream that flows 1.25 miles to Canyon Creek (1) 1.5 miles north-northwest of Georgetown (lat. 38°55'45" N, long. 120°51'05" W; sec. 34, T 13 N, R 10 E). Named on Georgetown (1949) 7.5' quadrangle. Three men from Oregon discovered gold in the canyon in 1848 or 1849 (Gudde, 1975, p. 254).

Oregon Creek [SIERRA-YUBA]: *stream*, formed in Sierra County by the confluence of North Fork and South Fork, flows 18 miles to to Middle Yuba River 4.25 miles south-southwest of Camptonville in Yuba County (lat. 39°23'40" N, long. 121°05' W; sec. 28, T 18 N, R 8 E). Named on Alleghany (1949), Camptonville (1948), and Pike (1949) 7.5' quadrangles. North Fork is 2 miles long and South Fork is 2.25 miles long; both forks are named on Alleghany (1949) and Downieville (1951) 7.5'

quadrangles.

Oregon Creek: see **Indian Creek** [EL DORADO] (5); **Little Oregon Creek** [YUBA].

Oregon Gulch [EL DORADO]: *canyon,* drained by a stream that flows 1.5 miles to Scott Creek 4.5 miles southeast of Omo Ranch (lat. 38°32' N, long. 120°30'40" W; sec. 23, T 8 N, R 13 E). Named on Caldor (1951), and Omo Ranch (1952) 7.5' quadrangles.

Oregon Hill: see **Greenville** [YUBA].

Oregon Hills [YUBA]: *ridge,* north-northwest-trending, 5.5 miles long, center 3 miles north-northeast of Dobbins (lat. 39°25' N, long. 121°11'25" W); Oregon Peak is at the south end of the ridge. Named on Challenge (1948) 7.5' quadrangle.

Oregon House [YUBA]: *village,* 22 miles northeast of Marysville (lat. 39°21'25" N, long. 121°16'40" W; at E line sec. 3, T 17 N, R 6 E). Named on Oregon House (1948) 7.5' quadrangle. Postal authorities established Oregon House post office in 1854, discontinued it in 1902, and reestablished it in 1903 (Salley, p. 162). The name is from a popular travelers stop built at the place in 1852 (Hoover, Rensch, and Rensch, p. 593). Wescoatt's (1861) map shows a place called Golden Ball located nearly 1 mile south-southeast of Oregon House, a place called Martins H. [House] located 2 miles west of Oregon House, and a place called Yuba County Ho. [House] located 5.5 miles southwest of Oregon House.

Oregon Peak [YUBA]: *peak,* 2 miles northeast of Dobbins (lat. 39° 23'20" N, long. 121°10'35" W; sec. 27, T 18 N, R 7 E). Altitude 3447 feet. Named on Challenge (1948) 7.5' quadrangle.

Orelli [EL DORADO]: *locality,* 1 mile east of Robbs Peak (lat. 38°55'15" N, long. 120°23' W). Named on Pyramid Peak (1896) 30' quadrangle.

Orleans: see **Orleans Flat** [NEVADA].

Orleans Flat [NEVADA]: *locality,* 5.25 miles northeast of North Bloomfield (lat. 39°25'45" N, long. 120°50' W; near NE cor. sec. 15, T 18 N, R 10 E). Site named on Alleghany (1949) 7.5' quadrangle. Called Orleans on Colfax (1898) 30' quadrangle. The place first was called Concord (Bancroft, 1888, p. 486).

Oro: see **Nicolaus** [SUTTER].

Oro City: see **Rio Oso** [SUTTER].

Orr City: see **Gold Hill** [PLACER].

Orr Creek [PLACER]: *stream,* flows 7.5 miles to join Dry Creek (1) and form Coon Creek 6.25 miles north-northwest of Auburn (lat. 38°58'30" N, long. 121°08'15" W; sec. 13, T 13 N, R 7 E). Named on Auburn (1953) and Gold Hill (1954) 7.5' quadrangles. Called North Fork Dry Creek on Sacramento (1892) 30' quadrangle.

Osborne Hill [NEVADA]: *peak,* 2.5 miles south-southeast of Nevada City (lat. 39°11'10" N, long. 121°02'10" W; sec. 1, T 15 N, R 8 E). Named on Grass Valley (1949) 7.5' quadrangle. On United States Geological Survey's (1901) map, the name "Osborne Hill" applies to the whole ridge on which present Osborne Hill is the high point.

Osceola Ravine [NEVADA]: *canyon,* drained by a stream that flows 1 mile to Squirrel Creek 4.5 miles north-northeast of Pilot Peak (lat. 39°13'30" N, long. 121°08'10" W; near N line sec. 25, T 16 N, R 7 E). Named on Rough and Ready (1949) 7.5' quadrangle.

Osceola Ridge: see **Deadmans Flat** [NEVADA] (1).

Osgood Swamp [EL DORADO]: *marsh,* 2.5 miles north-northwest of Echo Summit (lat. 38°50'50" N, long. 120°02'30" W; on E line sec. 36, T 12 N, R 17 E). Named on Echo Lake (1955) 7.5' quadrangle.

Osma Lake [EL DORADO]: *lake,* 425 feet long, 1.5 miles east-southeast of Pyramid Peak (lat. 38°50'20" N, long. 120°08'05" W). Named on Pyramid Peak (1955) 7.5' quadrangle.

Oso: see **East Arboga** [YUBA].

Oso Spring [EL DORADO]: *spring,* nearly 7 miles north of Leek Spring Hill (lat. 38°43'35" N, long. 120°17'10" W; near SW cor. sec. 11, T 10 N, R 15 E). Named on Leek Spring Hill (1951) 7.5' quadrangle.

Ostrom [YUBA]: *locality,* nearly 3 miles southeast of Olivehurst along Southern Pacific Railroad (lat. 39°04'10" N, long. 121°30'40" W; near N line sec. 15, T 14 N, R 4 E). Named on Olivehurst (1952) 7.5' quadrangle. Called Reed on Marysville (1895) 30' quadrangle. Postal authorities established Reeds Station post office 1871 and discontinued it the same year; the name was for Henry Reed, a settler of 1850 (Salley, p. 183).

Oswald [SUTTER]: *locality,* 5 miles south of Yuba City along Southern Pacific Railroad (lat. 39°04'10" N, long. 121°37'25" W). Named on Gilsizer Slough (1952) and Olivehurst (1952) 7.5' quadrangles. Postal authorities established Oswald post office in 1914 and discontinued it in 1918; the name commemorates August Oswald, a pioneer of 1850 (Salley, p. 163). California Division of Highways' (1934) map shows a place called Messick located 1.5 miles south of Oswald along Southern Pacific Railroad.

Otter Creek [EL DORADO]: *stream,* flows 10.5 miles to Middle Fork American River 3.5 miles north-northwest of Georgetown at Fords Bar (lat. 38°57'25" N, long. 120°51'20" W; near SW cor. sec. 22, T 13 N, R 10 E). Named on Georgetown (1949) and Tunnel Hill (1950) 7.5' quadrangles. Gudde (1975, p. 337) listed a place called Stony Bar that was situated at the confluence of Otter Creek and Middle Fork American River.

Oulton Landing: see **Oulton Point** [SACRAMENTO].

Oulton Point [SACRAMENTO]; *promontory,* 5.25 miles south-southwest of Isleton along San Joaquin River on Twitchell Island (lat. 38°05'25" N, long. 121°38'10" W). Named on Jersey Island (1978) 7.5' quadrangle. Jersey (1910) 7.5' quadrangle shows a place called Oulton Landing situated near the promontory.

Our House [SIERRA]: *locality,* nearly 2 miles southwest of Pike (lat. 39°25'05" N, long. 121°01'10" W; near NW cor. sec. 19, T 18 N, R 9 E). Named on Camptonville (1948, photorevised 1969) 7.5' quadrangle. Called Hour House on Nevada City (1948) 15' quadrangle. United States Board on Geographic Names (1970, p. 2) approved the name "Our House" for a meadow at the place, and gave the name "Hour House" as a variant. The Board also noted that the name is from the custom of the Abe Harris family, who lived at the place from the 1860's until 1903, of inviting people to "our house," a station on the old stage route.

Ousleys Bar: see **Dry Creek** [YUBA].

Outingdale [EL DORADO]: *settlement,* 4 miles north of Aukum along Middle Fork Cosumnes River (lat. 38°36'55" N, long. 120° 43'40" W; sec. 23, T 9 N, R 11 E). Named on Aukum (1952) 7.5' quadrangle. Called Mars on Placerville (1893) 30' quadrangle. Logan's (1938) map has the name "Outingdale Resort" at the place.

Owens Camp [EL DORADO]: *locality,* 9 miles west-northwest of Kirkwood (lat. 38°44'20" N, long. 120°14'10" W; near NE cor. sec. 7, T 10 N, R 16 E). Named on Silver Lake (1956) 15' quadrangle.

Owl Creek [NEVADA]: *stream,* flows 3 miles to South Yuba River nearly 2 miles south-southeast of French Corral (lat. 39°17'05" N, long. 121°08'40" W; near S line sec. 36, T 17 N, R 7 E). Named on French Corral (1948) and Nevada City (1948) 7.5' quadrangles.

Owl Creek [PLACER]: *stream,* formed by the confluence of North Branch, Middle Branch, and South Branch, flows 1.5 miles to North Fork American River 6.25 miles south-southeast of Colfax (lat. 39°00'45" N, long. 120°55' W; near N line sec. 1, T 13 N, R 9 E). Named on Colfax (1949) 7.5' quadrangle. Middle Branch is 2.5 miles long, North Branch is 2 miles long, and South Branch is 1 mile long; all three branches are named on Colfax (1949) and Foresthill (1949) 7.5' quadrangles.

Owl Gulch [YUBA]: *canyon,* drained by a stream that flows 2.25 miles to Deadwood Creek 1.5 miles south-southeast of Strawberry Valley (lat. 39°32'45" N, long. 121°05'35" W; at S line sec. 33, T 20 N, R 8 E). Named on Strawberry Valley (1948) 7.5' quadrangle.

Owsley's Bar: see **Dry Creek** [YUBA].

Oxbow: see **The Oxbow** [SACRAMENTO].

Oxbow Bar [EL DORADO]: *locality,* 3 miles northeast of Volcanoville along Middle Fork American River (lat. 38°00'15" N, long. 120°44'40" W; near W line sec. 3, T 13 N, R 11 E). Named on Duncan Peak (1952) 15' quadrangle.

Oyster Creek [AMADOR-EL DORADO]: *stream,* heads in Amador County and flows 2 miles to Silver Fork American River 3.5 miles west-southwest of Kirkwood in El Dorado County (lat. 38°40'45" N, long. 120°07'45" W; near NW cor. sec. 32, T 10 N, R 17 E). Named on Caples Lake (1979) 7.5' quadrangle.

Oyster Lake [AMADOR]: *intermittent lake,* 750 feet long, 9 miles north of Mokelumne Peak (lat. 38°40'15" N, long. 120°07' W; sec. 32, T 10 N, R 17 E). Named on Caples Lake (1979) 7.5' quadrangle.

—P—

Pace Flat [YOLO]: *area,* 3 miles north-northeast of Guinda (lat. 38° 52'10" N, long. 122°10'25" W; on S line sec. 22, T 12 N, R 3 W). Named on Guinda (1959) 7.5' quadrangle.

Pacific [EL DORADO]: *locality,* 4.25 miles east of Pollock Pines (lat. 38°45'35" N, long. 120°30'25" W; near E line sec. 34, T 11 N, R 13 E). Named on Pollock Pines (1950) 7.5' quadrangle. Postal authorities established Pacific post office in 1880, discontinued it in 1893, reestablished in it 1894, and changed the name to Pacific House in 1958 (Salley, p. 165). Pacific House was an early-day hostelry and Pony Express stop at the site (Hanna, p. 224).

Pacific House: see **Pacific** [EL DORADO].

Pacific Point [COLUSA]: *peak,* 8.5 miles southwest of Stonyford on Colusa-Lake County line (lat. 39°12'50" N, long. 122°35'45" W); the feature is on Pacific Ridge. Named on Clearlake Oaks (1960) 15' quadrangle.

Pacific Ridge [COLUSA]: *ridge,* generally east-trending, 11 miles long, 11 miles south of Stonyford on Colusa-Lake County line (center near lat. 39°13'15" N, long. 122°37' W). Named on Clearlake Oaks (1960) 15' quadrangle.

Packer Creek [SIERRA]: *stream,* flows 3.25 miles to Salmon Creek 4.25 miles north of Sierra City (lat. 39°37'40" N, long. 120°37'05" W; sec. 3, T 20 N, R 12 E); the stream goes through Packer Lake. Named on Gold Lake (1981) 7.5' quadrangles.

Packer Lake [SIERRA]: *lake,* 1150 feet long, 4 miles north-northwest of Sierra City (lat. 39°37'20" N, long. 120°39'20" W; near SW cor. sec. 5, T 20 N, R 12 E); the lake is along Packer Creek. Named on Sierra City (1981) 7.5' quadrangle.

Packer Lake Lodge [SIERRA]: *locality,* 4 miles north-northwest of Sierra City (lat. 39°37'20" N, long. 120°39'25" W; near SW cor. sec. 5, T 20 N, R 12 E); the place is along Packer Lake. Named on Sierra City (1981) 7.5' quadrangle.

Packer Lake Saddle [SIERRA]: *pass,* 4 miles north-northwest of Sierra City (lat. 39°37'10" N, long. 120°40' W; near N line sec. 7, T 20 N, R 12 E); the pass is 0.5 mile west-southwest of Packer Lake. Named on Sierra City (1981) 7.5' quadrangle.

Packsaddle Campground [SIERRA]: *locality,* about 4 miles north-northwest of Sierra City (lat. 39°37'25" N, long. 120°38'55" W; sec. 5, T 20 N, R 12 E). Named on Sierra City (1981) 7.5' quadrangle.

Page Meadows [PLACER]: *area,* 3 miles west-southwest of Tahoe City (lat. 39°09' N, long. 120°11'15" W; sec. 14, 15, T 15 N, R 16 E). Named on Tahoe City (1955, photorevised 1969) 7.5' quadrangle. Called Paige Meadow on Tahoe (1955) 15' quadrangle, but United States Board on Geographic Names (1969, p. 4) rejected this form of the name, which commemorates John Page and Frances Page, who grazed dairy cattle in the area from 1863 until 1880.

Pagge Creek [PLACER]: *stream,* flows 4.5 miles to North Shirttail Canyon 7 miles north of Foresthill (lat. 39°07'10" N, long. 120°47'45" W; sec. 25, T 15 N, R 10 E). Named on Foresthill (1949) and Michigan Bluff (1952) 7.5' quadrangles.

Pahatsi: see **Camp Pahatsi** [NEVADA].

Paige Meadow: see **Page Meadows** [PLACER].

Painsville: see **Indian Springs** [NEVADA].

Painted Rock [PLACER]:

(1) *peak,* 3.5 miles north-northwest of Granite Chief (lat. 39°14'30" N, long. 120°19'15" W; near N line sec. 16, T 16 N, R 15 E). Altitude 6682 feet. Named on Granite Chief (1953) 7.5' quadrangle.

(2) *ridge,* west-trending, 0.5 mile long, 3.5 miles north-northwest of Tahoe City (lat. 39°12'50" N, long. 120°10'35" W; at SW cor. sec. 23, T 16 N, R 16 E). Named on Tahoe City (1955) 7.5' quadrangle.

Painter's Station: see **Eight Mile House** [EL DORADO].

Paintersville [SACRAMENTO]: *locality,* less than 1 mile south-southwest of Courtland along Sacramento River (lat. 38°19'10" N, long. 121°34'30" W). Named on Courtland (1978) 7.5' quadrangle. The name commemorates Levi Painter, who came to California in 1853 and laid out lots at the place in 1879 (Dillon, p. 68).

Palen Reservoir [SIERRA]: *lake,* 1150 feet long, 5.5 miles north-northwest of Sierraville in Antelope Valley (lat. 39°39'10" N, long. 120°18'25" W; near S line sec. 21, T 21 N, R 15 E). Named on Antelope Valley (1981) 7.5' quadrangle.

Palisade Creek [PLACER]: *stream,* flows nearly 5 miles to North Fork American River 8 miles west-northwest of Granite Chief (lat. 39°14'45" N, long. 120°25'05" W; at E line sec. 17, T 16 N, R 14 E); the stream heads at Palisade Lake. Named on Royal Gorge (1953) and Soda Springs (1955) 7.5' quadrangles.

Palisade Lake [PLACER]: *lake,* 2900 feet long, 5 miles west-southwest of Donner Pass (lat. 39°17'55" N, long. 120°24'50" W; sec. 33, T 17 N, R 14 E). Named on Soda Springs (1955) 7.5' quadrangle.

Palmer [EL DORADO]: *locality,* 3.25 miles south-southwest of Robbs Peak (lat. 38°52'40" N, long. 120°25'15" W). Named on Pyramid Peak (1896) 30' quadrangle.

Palmer Canyon [COLUSA]: *canyon,* 1.25 miles long, 10.5 miles southeast of Wilbur Springs on upper reaches of Cortina Creek (lat. 38°56'10" N, long. 122°16'35" W; in and near sec. 35, T 13 N, R 4 W). Named on Glascock Mountain (1958) 7.5' quadrangle.

Palmer Canyon [YOLO]: *canyon,* drained by a stream that flows 2.5 miles to Capay Valley 5.25 miles south of Guinda (lat. 38°45'10" N, long. 122°10'45" W). Named on Brooks (1959) and Guinda (1959) 7.5' quadrangles. Rumsey (1945) 15' quadrangle has the name "Brooks Cr." for the stream that drains Palmer Canyon and joins Cache Creek less than 1 mile northeast of Brooks (lat. 38°45'10" N, long. 122°08'11" W). Durst's (1916) map has the possessive form "Brook's Creek" for the name.

Palmer Ridge [SIERRA]: *ridge,* southwest-trending, 5.25 miles long, center 4.5 miles east of Alleghany (lat. 39°28' N, long. 120°45'35" W). Named on Alleghany (1949) and Graniteville (1982) 7.5' quadrangles.

Pan Ravine [NEVADA]: *canyon,* drained by a stream that flows 1.5 miles to Humbug Creek 1.5 miles southwest of North Bloomfield (lat. 39°21'05" N, long. 120°55'20" W; near W line sec. 12, T 17 N, R 9 E). Named on North Bloomfield (1949) 7.5' quadrangle.

Panther Creek [AMADOR]: *stream,* formed by the confluence of East Panther Creek and West Panther Creek, flows 1.25 miles to North Fork Mokelumne River 5.25 miles south-southwest of Hams Station (lat. 38°28'25" N, long. 120°24'55" W; sec. 10, T 7 N, R 14 E). Named on Devils Nose (1979) 7.5' quadrangle.

Panther Creek: see **East Panther Creek** [AMADOR]; **West Panther Creek** [AMADOR].

Panther Ridge [AMADOR]: *ridge,* south-southeast of Hams Station (lat. 38°30'45" N, long. 120°21'10" W); the ridge is between East Panther Creek and West Panther Creek. Named on Devils Nose (1979) and Peddler Hill (1951) 7.5' quadrangles.

Papoose Creek [SIERRA]: *stream,* flows less than 0.5 mile to Jim Crow Creek 3 miles east-southeast of Downieville (lat. 39°32'30" N, long. 120°46'25" W; near E line sec. 6, T 19 N, R 11 E). Named on Downieville (1951) 7.5' quadrangle.

Paradise [PLACER]: *locality,* 10 miles east-northeast of Auburn (lat. 38°58'20" N, long. 120°54'10" W); the place is along Todd Creek above present Paradise Canyon. Named on Placerville (1893) 30' quadrangle.

Paradise Canyon [PLACER]: *canyon,* 0.5 mile long, opens into the canyon of Middle Fork American River 9.5 miles east-northeast of Auburn (lat. 38°57'40" N, long. 120°55'20" W; sec. 24, T 13 N, R 9 E). Named on Greenwood (1949) 7.5' quadrangle.

Paradise Creek [COLUSA]: *stream,* flows nearly 3 miles to Middle Fork Stony Creek 2 miles north of Fouts Springs (lat. 39°22'55" N, long. 122°39'55" W). Named on Saint John Mountain (1968) 7.5' quadrangle.

Paradise Flat [EL DORADO]: *area,* 6.5 miles north of Mount Tallac (lat. 39°00' N, long. 120°06'30" W; sec. 4, T 13 N, R 17 E). Named on Emerald Bay (1955) and Meeks Bay (1955) 7.5' quadrangles.

Paradise Lake [NEVADA]: *lake,* 1950 feet long, 6 miles north-northwest of Donner Pass (lat. 39°24' N, long. 120°21'40" W; on W line sec. 25, T 18 N, R 14 E); the lake is east of Paradise Valley. Named on Independence Lake (1981) 7.5' quadrangle.

Paradise Valley [NEVADA]: *valley,* 6.25 miles north-northwest of Donner Pass (lat. 39°24' N, long. 120°22'20" W; near N line sec. 26, T 18 N, R 14 E). Named on Independence Lake (1981) and Webber Peak (1981) 7.5' quadrangles.

Paradise Valley [YOLO]: *valley,* 2.5 miles east-northeast of Guinda (lat. 38°50'40" N, long. 122°09' W; at SW cor. sec. 36, T 12 N, R 3 W). Named on Guinda (1959) 7.5' quadrangle.

Paramount: see **Woodland** [YOLO].

Parazo Canyon: see **Perazzo Canyon** [NEVADA-SIERRA].

Pardee Reservoir [AMADOR]: *lake,* behind a dam on Mokelumne River 7.5 miles southwest of Jackson on Amador-Calaveras County line (lat. 38°15'25" N, long. 120°51' W; sec. 26, T 5 N, R 10 E). Named on Jackson (1962) and Mokelumne Hill (1948) 7.5' quadrangles. Channel Arm extends up Mokelumne River from the dam, and North Arm extends northwest from the river just behind the dam. Both arms are named on Jackson (1962) 7.5' quadrangle. The name "Pardee" honors George C. Pardee, mayor of Oakland from 1893 until 1895, governor of California from 1903 until 1907, and president of the board of directors of East Bay Municipal Utility District from 1924 until 1941 (Gudde, 1949, p. 253).

Pardoe Lake [AMADOR]: *lake,* 850 feet long, 3.5 miles north-northwest of Mokelumne Peak (lat. 38°35'30" N, long. 120°06'20" W; near N line sec. 33, T 9 N, R 17 E). Named on Mokelumne Peak (1979) 7.5' quadrangle.

Pardoes Camp: see **Upper Pardoes Camp** [AMADOR].

Park: see **Sly Park** [EL DORADO].

Park Creek: see **Sly Park Creek** [EL DORADO].

Parker Canyon [YOLO]: *canyon,* drained by a stream that flows 1.25 miles to Lamb Valley 3.5 miles west-southwest of Esparto (lat. 38°40'30" N, long. 122°04'45" W; near NW cor. sec. 34, T 10 N, R 2 W). Named on Esparto (1959) 7.5' quadrangle.

Park Reservoir: see **East Park Reservoir** [COLUSA].

Parks Bar [YUBA]: *locality,* 2 miles west-northwest of Smartville on the north side of Yuba River (lat. 39°13'15" N, long. 121°19'55" W; near NW cor. sec. 29, T 16 N, R 6 E). Site named on Smartville (1951) 7.5' quadrangle. Postal authorities established Parks Bar post office before October 7, 1851, and discontinued it in 1858 (Salley, p. 167). A party of prospectors that included Dr. John Marsh discovered gold at the site in 1848, and for a time the place was known as Marsh Diggings; later the same year David Parks opened a store there and the name became Parks Bar (Gudde, 1975, p. 259). Wescoatt's (1861) map shows a place called Bartons B. [Bar] situated 1.5 miles northeast of Parks Bar on the north side of Yuba River; the name was for Robert Barton and John Barton, who had a store at the site in the 1850's (Gudde, 1975, p. 28). Jackson's (1850) map shows a place called Foster's Lower Bar situated on the south side of Yuba River just below Barton's Bar. Gudde (1975, p. 309) listed a place called Saw Mill Bar that was located along Yuba River opposite Parks Bar—a sawmill was built there in 1849. Gudde (1975, p. 70) also listed a place called Chimney Hill that was situated along Yuba River between Parks Bar and Long Bar (2).

Parks Hill: see **Kings Hill** [PLACER].

Parkway [SACRAMENTO]: *city,* 6 miles south-southeast of downtown Sacramento (lat. 38°29'30" N, long. 121°26'45" W). Named on Florin (1968) 7.5' quadrangle.

Parry Spring [COLUSA]: *spring,* 5.5 miles east of Wilbur Springs (lat. 39°02'55" N, long. 122°19'15" W; sec. 20, T 14 N, R 4 W). Named on Wilbur Springs (1961) 15' quadrangle.

Parsley Bar [PLACER]: *locality,* 3 miles west-southwest of Bunker Hill along Rubicon River (lat. 39°02'10" N, long. 120°25'55" W; sec. 29, T 14 N, R 14 E). Named on Bunker Hill (1953) 7.5' quadrangle.

Parsley Bar Crossing [EL DORADO-PLACER]: *locality,* 3.25 miles west-southwest of Bunker Hill along Rubicon River on El Dorado-Placer County line (lat. 39°01'40" N, long. 120°26'05" W; at N line sec. 32, T 14 N, R 14 E); the place is below Parsley Bar. Named on Bunker Hill (1953) 7.5' quadrangle.

Parson Rock [EL DORADO]: *promontory,* 3.5 miles north of Mount Tallac on the northwest side of Emerald Bay (1) (lat. 38°57'20" N, long. 120°06'05" W; sec. 21, T 13 N, R 17 E). Named on Emerald Bay (1955) 7.5' quadrangle. The name is from the resemblance of the feature to a pulpit (Lekisch, p. 95).

Parsons Canyon [YOLO]: *canyon,* drained by a stream that flows 1.25 miles to Salt Arroyo 3 miles east of Berryessa Peak (lat. 38° 39'35" N, long. 122°08' W; sec. 6, T 9 N, R 2 W). Named on Brooks (1959) 7.5' quadrangle.

Pass Creek [SIERRA]: *stream,* flows 7.25 miles to Jackson Meadows Reservoir 7 miles southeast of Sierra City (lat. 39°30'10" N, long. 120°31'55" W; near NE cor. sec. 20, T 19 N, R 13 E). Named on Haypress Valley (1981), Sattley (1981), and Webber Peak (1981) 7.5' quadrangles.

Pass Creek Campground [SIERRA]: *locality,* 7 miles southeast of Sierra City along Jackson Meadows Reservoir (lat. 39°30'15" N, long. 120°32' W; near NE cor. sec. 20, T 19 N, R 13 E); the place is near the mouth of Pass Creek. Named on Haypress Valley (1981) 7.5' quadrangle.

Paterson: see **Cherokee** [NEVADA].

Pats Gulch [SIERRA]: *canyon,* drained by a stream that flows 2 miles to Slate Creek 8 miles southwest of Mount Fillmore (lat. 39° 39'35" N, long. 120°57'50" W; near SW cor. sec. 22, T 21 N, R 9 E). Named on La Porte (1951) 7.5' quadrangle.

Pats Meadow [SIERRA]: *area,* 9.5 miles southeast of Loyalton at the head of Smithneck Creek (lat. 39°33'35" N, long. 120°08'50" W; sec. 25, T 20 N, R 16 E). Named on Sardine Peak (1981) 7.5' quadrangle.

Patterson: see **Cherokee** [NEVADA].

Patterson Spring [YOLO]: *spring,* nearly 5 miles south of Guinda (lat. 38°45'35" N, long. 122°12'20" W; sec. 33, T 11 N, R 3 W). Named on Guinda (1959) 7.5' quadrangle.

Pattison: see **Poorman Creek** [NEVADA] (1).

Pat Yore Flat [NEVADA]: *area,* 2.5 miles southeast of Graniteville (lat. 39°24'45" N, long. 120°42'20" W; sec. 23, T 18 N, R 11 E). Named on Graniteville (1982) 7.5' quadrangle. Logan's (1940) map shows a place called Salina Flat located about 1 mile south of Pat Yore Flat (sec. 26, T 18 N, R 11 E).

Pauley Creek [SIERRA]: *stream,* flows 14 miles to Downie River 0.5 mile north-northeast of Downieville (lat. 39°34'10" N, long. 120°49'15" W; sec. 26, T 20 N, R 10 E). Named on Downieville (1951), Gold Lake (1981), and Sierra City (1981) 7.5' quadrangles. Called East Fork of North Fork Yuba River on Downieville (1897) 30' quadrangle, but United States Board on Geographic Names (1950, p. 6) rejected this name for the feature.

Paulinville: see **Hansonville** [YUBA].

Paynes Peak [YUBA]: *peak,* 2 miles east of Loma Rica (lat. 39°18'45" N, long. 121°22'45" W; sec. 23, T 17 N, R 5 E). Altitude 1156 feet. Named on Loma Rica (1947) 7.5' quadrangle.

Peace Valley [SUTTER]: *valley,* 7 miles north-northwest of Sutter in Sutter Buttes (lat. 39°15' N, long. 121°48'15" W). Named on Pennington (1954) and Sutter Buttes (1954) 7.5' quadrangles.

Peachstone Gulch [PLACER]: *canyon,* drained by a stream that flows nearly 2 miles to Middle Fork American River 13 miles east-northeast of Auburn (lat. 38°58' N, long. 120°51'15" W; at S line sec. 16, T 13 N, R 10 E). Named on Georgetown (1949) 7.5' quadrangle.

Peacock Ravine [EL DORADO]: *canyon,* drained by a stream that flows 2.25 miles to Skunk Canyon 3.5 miles south of the village of Pilot Hill (lat. 38°46'55" N, long. 121°01'20" W; sec. 30, T 11 N, R 9 E). Named on Pilot Hill (1954) 7.5' quadrangle.

Peardale [NEVADA]: *settlement,* 3.5 miles north-northwest of Chicago Park (lat. 39°11'30" N, long. 120°59'45" W; mainly in sec. 5, T 15 N, R 9 E). Named on Chicago Park (1949) and Grass Valley (1949) 7.5' quadrangles. Postal authorities established Peardale post office in 1916 and discontinued it in 1927 (Frickstad, p. 114). Colfax (1938) 30' quadrangle shows the place located along Nevada County Narrow Gauge Railroad.

Peardon Hill [NEVADA]: *peak,* 5.25 miles northwest of Pilot Peak (lat. 39°12'45" N, long. 121°15'45" W; sec. 26, T 16 N, R 6 E). Altitude 1264 feet. Named on Smartville (1951) 7.5' quadrangle.

Pearl Lake [EL DORADO]: *lake,* 700 feet long, 8 miles east-southeast of Robbs Peak (lat. 38°53'30" N, long. 120°15'20" W; sec. 18, T 12 N, R 16 E). Named on Loon Lake (1952, photorevised 1973) 7.5' quadrangle.

Pearls Hill: see **Anthony House** [NEVADA].

Pearson [YUBA]: *locality,* 2.5 miles south-southwest of Olivehurst along Sacramento Northern Railroad (lat. 39°03'45" N, long. 121° 34'30" W; near W line sec. 18, T 14 N, R 4 E). Named on Olivehurst (1952) 7.5' quadrangle.

Pearson Ravine [SIERRA]: *canyon,* drained by a stream that flows 2 miles to Potosi Creek 2.25 miles west of Mount Fillmore (lat. 39° 43'35" N, long. 120°53'35" W; near W line sec. 32, T 22 N, R 10 E). Named on La Porte (1951) and Mount Fillmore (1951) 7.5' quadrangles.

Pearson Tract: see **Vorden** [SACRAMENTO].

Peart [YOLO]: *locality,* nearly 3 miles north-northeast of Woodland along Southern Pacific Railroad (lat. 38°43' N, long. 121°45'30" W). Named on Yolo (1915) 7.5' quadrangle. Called Pearth on California Mining Bureau's (1917d) map, which shows a place called Howard located about 3 miles east-northeast of Pearth at the end of a railroad spur line. California Division of Highways' (1934) map shows a place called Garlic located along the railroad 0.5 mile south-southwest of Peart.

Pease [SUTTER]: *locality,* 3.25 miles northwest of Yuba City along Northern Electric Railroad (lat. 39°10'20" N, long. 121°39'40" W; near S line sec. 5, T 15 N, R 3 E). Named on Sutter (1911) 7.5' quadrangle. The name commemorates George Pease, who owned land at the place when the railroad was built in 1907 (Gudde, 1949, p. 256).

Peavine [SIERRA]: *locality,* 12.5 miles east of Loyalton along Western Pacific Railroad (lat. 39°40'40" N, long. 120°00'25" W; near N line sec. 19, T 21 N, R 18 E). Named on Evans Canyon (1978) 7.5' quadrangle.

Peavine Creek [EL DORADO]: *stream,* flows 3 miles to South Fork Silver Creek 4.5 miles northwest of Kyburz (lat. 38°49'05" N, long. 120°21'50" W; sec. 12, T 11 N, R 14 E); the stream heads on Peavine Ridge. Named on Kyburz (1952) 7.5' quadrangle.

Peavine Creek [PLACER]: *stream,* flows 7.5 miles to North Fork of Middle Fork American River 3 miles east-northeast of Michigan Bluff (lat. 39°03'10" N, long. 120°40'40" W; sec. 19, T 14 N, R 12 E); upper reaches of the stream are south of Peavine Ridge. Named on Greek Store (1952) and Michigan Bluff (1952) 7.5' quadrangles.

Peavine Flat: see **Chips Flat** [SIERRA].

Peavine Point [EL DORADO]: *ridge,* west- to north-trending, 4.5 miles long, 13 miles north-northwest of Pollock Pines (lat. 38°56'30" N, long. 120°19'45" W). Named on Tunnel Hill (1950) 7.5' quadrangle.

Peavine Ridge [EL DORADO]: *ridge,* west-trending, 17 miles long, center 2 miles east-northeast of Riverton (lat. 38°47'45" N, long. 120°25'45" W). Named on Kyburz (1952), Pollock Pines (1950), and Riverton (1950) 7.5' quadrangles.

Peavine Ridge [PLACER]: *ridge,* generally southwest-trending, 5 miles long, 7.5 miles southwest of Duncan Peak (lat. 39°04'30" N, long. 120°36'15" W); the ridge is north of Peavine Creek. Named on Greek Store (1952) and Michigan Bluff (1952) 7.5' quadrangles.

Pebble Canyon: see **Big Pebble Canyon** [EL DORADO]; **Little Pebble Canyon** [EL DORADO].

Peddler Creek [EL DORADO]: *stream,* flows 1.5 miles to Middle Fork Cosumnes River 8 miles east of Caldor (lat. 38°35'25" N, long. 120°17' W; sec. 35, T 9 N, R 15 E); the stream heads at Peddler Hill. Named on Peddler Hill (1951) 7.5' quadrangle.

Peddler Hill [AMADOR-EL DORADO]: *ridge,* south-southwest-trending, 1 mile long, 6.25 miles east-northeast of Hams Station on Amador-El Dorado County line (lat. 38°34'30" N, long. 120°15'50" W). Named on Peddler Hill (1951) 7.5' quadrangle.

Peethill [YOLO]: *locality,* 1 mile north-northeast of downtown West Sacramento along Sacramento Northern Railroad (lat. 38°35'05" N, long. 121°31'15" W). Named on Sacramento West (1967) 7.5' quadrangle.

Pegleg Creek [EL DORADO]: *stream,* flows about 1.5 miles to Bear Creek (2) 3.5 miles southeast of Georgetown (lat. 38°52'35" N, long. 120°47'10" W; sec. 19, T 12 N, R 11 E). Named on Georgetown (1949) 7.5' quadrangle.

Pelger: see **Everglade** [SUTTER].

Pelham Flat [PLACER]: *area,* 3 miles south of Cisco Grove (lat. 39° 16' N, long. 120°32'10" W; sec. 8, T 16 N, R 13 E). Named on Cisco Grove (1955) 7.5' quadrangle, which shows marsh and a lake at the place.

Pence Mountain [COLUSA]: *peak,* 4 miles southwest of Sites (lat. 39°16'05" N, long. 122°23'30" W; sec. 2, T 16 N, R 5 W). Altitude 1909 feet. Named on Lodoga (1960) 15' quadrangle.

Pendola: see **Camp Pendola**, under **Camptonville** [YUBA].

Pendola Ranch: see **Camp Pendola**, under **Camptonville** [YUBA].

Penner Lake [NEVADA]: *lake,* 1650 feet long, 4 miles west-southwest of English Mountain (lat. 39°25'10" N, long. 120°36'55" W; on S line sec. 15, T 18 N, R 12 E). Named on English Mountain (1983) 7.5' quadrangle.

Pennington [SUTTER]: *village,* 7.25 miles west of Live Oak at the north base of Sutter Buttes (lat. 39°17'30" N, long. 121°47'30" W; near SW cor. sec. 30, T 17 N, R 2 E). Named on Pennington (1954) 7.5' quadrangle, which shows North Butte cemetery situated less than 1 mile west of Pennington. Postal authorities established North Butte post office in 1874 and discontinued in in 1875; they reestablished it with the name "Pennington" at a new location in 1881 and discontinued it in 1917—the name is for John T. Pennington, who settled in Sutter County in 1862 and was county engineer from 1867 until 1871 (Salley, p. 155, 169).

Pennsylvania Point [PLACER]: *peak,* 9 miles west-northwest of Devil Peak (lat. 38°59'55" N, long. 120°42'05" W; on N line sec. 12, T 13 N, R 11 E). Altitude 3552 feet. Named on Tunnel Hill (1950) 7.5' quadrangle.

Penn Valley [NEVADA]: *valley,* 2.25 miles north of Pilot Peak along Squirrel Creek (lat. 39°12' N, long. 121°11' W). Named on Rough and Ready (1949) 7.5' quadrangle. Whitney's (1873) map shows Penn Valley Ho. [House] in or near present Penn Valley.

Penn Valley House: see **Penn Valley** [NEVADA].

Penobscot Creek [EL DORADO]: *stream,* flows 3.5 miles to Greenwood Creek 1.25 miles south-southwest of Greenwood (lat. 38°52'55" N, long. 120°55'25" W; sec. 24, T 12 N, R 9 E). Named on Greenwood (1949) 7.5' quadrangle.

Penryn [PLACER]: *town,* 5.5 miles northeast of Rocklin (lat. 38°51'10" N, long. 121°10'10" W; near NW cor. sec. 35, T 12 N, R 7 E). Named on Rocklin (1967) 7.5' quadrangle. Postal authorities established Penryn post office in 1873 (Frickstad, p. 121). Griffith Griffith, a Welshman who had granite quarries nearby, named the place for Penrhyn, Wales; a mining town called Stewarts Flat was located 1.5 miles east of Penryn in Secret Ravine (Hoover, Rensch, and Rensch, p. 271-272).

Peoria House: see **Prairie Creek** [YUBA].

Perazzo Canyon [NEVADA-SIERRA]: *canyon,* 9 miles south of Sierraville on Nevada-Sierra County line (lat. 39°26'45" N, long. 120°23'20" W). Named on Webber Peak (1981) 7.5' quadrangle. Called Parazo Canyon on Truckee (1940) 30' quadrangle, but United States Board on Geographic Names (1960a, p. 16) rejected the forms "Parazo" and "Perazza" for the name.

Perazzo Meadows [SIERRA]: *valley,* 7 miles south of Sierraville along Little Truckee River (lat. 39°29'15" N, long. 120°21'30" W). Named on Independence Lake (1981) and Webber Peak (1981) 7.5' quadrangles.

Perkins [SACRAMENTO]: *locality,* 5.5 miles east-southeast of downtown Sacramento along Southern Pacific Railroad (lat. 38°32'45" N, long. 121°23'45" W; sec. 14, T 8 N, R 5 E). Named on Sacramento East (1967) 7.5' quadrangle. Postal authorities established Perkins post office in 1886 (Frickstad, p. 134). The name commemorates Thomas C. Perkins, who settled at the place in 1861 (Gudde, 1949, p. 258).

Perkins Canyon [YOLO]: *canyon,* 3 miles long, opens into lowlands 4.5 miles south of Esparto (lat. 38°37'40" N, long. 122°00'50" W; sec. 18, T 9 N, R 1 W). Named on Esparto (1959) and Monticello Dam (1959) 7.5' quadrangles.

Perkins Spring [NEVADA]: *spring,* 2.25 miles east of Higgins Corner along Magonlia Creek (lat. 39°02'45" N, long. 121°03'15" W; near S line sec. 23, T 14 N, R 8 E). Named on Lake Combie (1949) 7.5' quadrangle.

Perks Corner [EL DORADO]: *locality,* 2.5 miles west-southwest of Placerville (lat. 38°42'40" N, long. 120°50'15" W; sec. 23, T 10 N, R 10 E). Named on Placerville (1949) 7.5' quadrangle.

Perley Landing [SACRAMENTO]: *locality,* 10.5 miles southwest of Isleton along Sacramento River on Sherman Island (lat. 38°04'20" N, long. 121°45'50" W). Named on Collinsville (1918) 7.5' quadrangle.

Perrington Creek [COLUSA]: *stream,* flows 2.5 miles to Trout Creek (3) 2.5 miles northwest of Pacific Point (lat. 39°14'30" N, long. 122°37'30" W; sec. 15, T 16 N, R 7 W). Named on Clearlake Oaks (1960) 15' quadrangle.

Perry Creek [EL DORADO]: *stream,* flows 7.5 miles to Middle Fork Cosumnes River 8 miles south of Camino (lat. 38°37'35" N, long. 120°42' W; at S line sec. 18, T 9 N, R 12 E). Named on Aukum (1952) and Omo Ranch (1952) 7.5' quadrangles.

Perry Creek [SIERRA]: *stream,* flows less than 0.25 mile to Sierra Valley 1.25 miles south of Sierraville (lat. 39°34'20" N, long. 120° 22' W; sec. 24, T 20 N, R 14 E). Named on Sattley (1981) and Sierraville (1981) 7.5' quadrangles.

Perry Mountain [EL DORADO]: *peak,* 1.5 miles north of Coloma (lat. 38°49'15" N, long. 120°53'20" W; sec. 8, T 11 N, R 10 E). Named on Coloma (1949) 7.5' quadrangle.

Perry Mountain Creek [EL DORADO]: *stream,* flows 1.5 miles to Indian Creek (1) 1.5 miles north-northwest of Coloma (lat. 38° 49'20" N, long. 120°54'15" W; sec. 7, T 11 N, R 10 E); the stream is west of Perry Mountain. Named on Coloma (1949) 7.5' quadrangle.

Peru: see **Garden Valley** [EL DORADO].

Peter Grubb Hut [NEVADA]: *locality,* 4 miles north-northwest of Donner Pass in Round Valley (2) (lat. 39°22'05" N, long. 120° 22' W; sec. 2, T 17 N, R 14 E). Named on Norden (1955) 7.5' quadrangle.

Peterson Ridge [YUBA]: *ridge,* south-trending, 4 miles long, 1.5 miles east-southeast of Strawberry Valley (lat. 39°33'15" N, long. 121°04'40" W). Named on Strawberry Valley (1948) 7.5' quadrangle.

Pet Hill: see **Mooney Flat** [NEVADA].

Petroleum Creek [COLUSA-YOLO]: *stream,* heads in Yolo County and flows 6 miles back and forth across Yolo-Colusa County line before ending in lowlands of Colusa County near Harrington (lat. 38°57'15" N, long. 122°00'45" W). Named on Rumsey (1959) and Wildwood School (1959) 7.5' quadrangles.

Petty Reservoir: see **Lake Tabeaud** [AMADOR].

Phelps Hill: see **Washington** [NEVADA].

Phelps Point: see **Washington** [NEVADA].

Philadelphia: see **New Philadelphia**, under **Bunker Hill** [AMADOR] (2).

Philadelphia Bar [EL DORADO]: *locality,* 3.5 miles northwest of Greenwood along Middle Fork American River (lat. 38°56'20" N, long. 120°57' W; on W line sec. 35, T 13 N, R 9 E). Named on Greenwood (1949) 7.5' quadrangle.

Phillips [EL DORADO]: *village,* 2.5 miles west of Echo Summit along South Fork American River (lat. 38°49' N, long. 120°04'40" W; near W line sec. 11, T 11 N, R 17 E). Named on Echo Lake (1955) 7.5' quadrangle. Fallen Leaf Lake (1955) 15' quadrangle shows Vade P.O. at the place. Joseph Wells Davis Phillips brought cattle to the site in 1859 and built a hotel there in 1863 (Yohalem, p. 162). Postal authorities established Vade post office at the place in 1912 and discontinued it in 1961 (Salley, p. 228); the post office name was for Phillips' daughter, Sierra Nevada Phillips, who had the nickname "Vade" (Yohalem, p. 164-165).

Phipps Creek [EL DORADO]: *stream,* flows 3.5 miles to Rubicon River 3 miles west-northwest of Phipps Peak in Rockbound Valley (lat. 38°57'55" N, long. 120°12'10" W; near W line sec. 22, T 13 N, R 16 E); the stream heads at Phipps Lake. Named on Rockbound Valley (1955) 7.5' quadrangle.

Phipps Lake [EL DORADO]: *lake,* 900 feet long, 0.5 mile north-northeast of Phipps Peak (lat. 38°57'40" N, long. 120°08'45" W; sec. 19, T 13 N, R 17 E). Named on Rockbound Valley (1955) 7.5' quadrangle.

Phipps Pass [EL DORADO]: *pass,* 0.5 mile east-northeast of Phipps Peak (lat. 38°57'30" N, long. 120°08'25" W; sec. 19, T 13 N, R 17 E). Named on Rockbound Valley (1955) 7.5' quadrangle.

Phipps Peak [EL DORADO]: *peak,* 7.5 miles north of Pyramid Peak (lat. 38°57'15" N, long. 120°08'55" W; at W line sec. 19, T 13 N, R 17 E). Named on Rockbound Valley (1955) 7.5' quadrangle. Altitude 9234 feet. The name commemorates General William Phipps, who came to Georgetown in 1854 (Gudde, 1949, p. 260).

Phoenix Lake [NEVADA]: *lake,* 1500 feet long, 5 miles south-southeast of English Mountain (lat. 39°22'35" N, long. 120°31'15" W; on S line sec. 33, T 18 N, R 13 E). Named on Cisco Grove (1955) and English Mountain (1983) 7.5' quadrangles.

Picachos: see **Sutter Buttes** [SUTTER].

Picayune Valley [PLACER]: *valley,* 2.5 miles south-southwest of Granite Chief (lat. 39°09'45" N, long. 120°18'40" W; at W line sec. 9, T 15 N, R 15 E). Named on Granite Chief (1953) 7.5' quadrangle.

Pickering Bar [PLACER]: *locality,* 4 miles south of Dutch Flat along North Fork American River (lat. 39°08'50" N, long. 120°50'30" W; sec. 15, T 15 N, R 10 E). Named on Dutch Flat (1950) 7.5' quadrangle.

Pierce Canyon [YOLO]: *canyon,* drained by a stream that flows 3.5 miles to Capay Valley 1.25 miles southwest of Guinda (lat. 38°48'55" N, long. 122°12'20" W; sec. 9, T 11 N, R 3 W). Named on Guinda (1959) 7.5' quadrangle.

Pierce Meadow [NEVADA]: *area,* 2.5 miles north-northeast of Yuba Gap (lat. 39°30'55" N, long. 120°35'35" W; at S line sec. 11, T 17 N, R 12 E). Named on Cisco Grove (1955) 7.5' quadrangle.

Pierces Bar: see **Ramshorn Creek** [SIERRA].

Pig Canyon [SIERRA]: *canyon,* drained by a stream that flows 2.25 miles to Hog Canyon 6 miles west-northwest of Sierra City (lat. 39°35'45" N, long. 120°44'20" W; sec. 16, T 20 N, R 11 E). Named on Sierra City (1981) 7.5' quadrangle.

Pigeon Creek [AMADOR]: *stream,* flows 6 miles to Big Indian Creek 5.5 miles west-northwest of Fiddletown near Enterprise (lat. 38°32'35" N, long. 120°50'50" W; sec. 14, T 8 N, R 10 E). Named on Fiddletown (1949) 7.5' quadrangle.

Pigeon Roost Canyon [PLACER]: *canyon,* drained by a stream that flows 1.5 miles to Rubicon River 3 miles southwest of Devil Peak (lat. 38°55'50" N, long. 120°35'10" W; sec. 36, T 13 N, R 12 E). Named on Devil Peak (1950) 7.5' quadrangle.

Pike [SIERRA]: *locality,* 8.5 miles west-southwest of Alleghany (lat. 39°26'20" N, long. 120°59'50" W; near W line sec. 8, T 18 N, R 9 E). Named on Pike (1949) 7.5' quadrangle. Postal authorities established Pike City post office in 1877, changed the name to Pike in 1895, discontinued it in 1901, reestablished it in 1902, and discontinued it in 1954; the named is for Pike County, Missouri (Salley, p. 171). Camptonville (1948) 7.5' quadrangle shows Pike P.O. located 0.5 mile northwest of Pike at Godfrey ranch.

Pike City: see **Pike** [SIERRA].

Pike County House [YUBA]: *locality,* less than 1 mile east-northeast of Challenge (lat. 39°29'10" N, long. 121°12'30" W); the place is 1 mile north-northwest of Pike County Peak. Named on Smartsville (1895) 30' quadrangle.

Pike County Peak [YUBA]: *peak,* 1.5 miles southeast of Challenge (lat. 39°28'30" N, long. 121°12'05" W; near W line sec. 28, T 19 N, R 7 E). Altitude 3695 feet. Named on Challenge (1948) 7.5' quadrangle.

Pike Mountain: see **Vandervere Mountain** [NEVADA].

Pilliken [EL DORADO]: *locality,* 5.5 miles northwest of Leek Spring Hill (lat. 38°41'10" N, long. 120°21'10" W; sec. 30, T 10 N, R 15 E). Named on Leek Spring Hill (1951) 15' quadrangle.

Pilot Creek [EL DORADO]:

(1) *stream,* flows 18 miles to Rubicon River 15 miles north-northwest of Pollock Pines (lat. 38°58'15" N, long. 120°40'55" W; near S line sec. 18, T 13 N, R 12 E). Named on Devil Peak (1950), Robbs Peak (1950), and Tunnel Hill (1950) 7.5' quadrangles.

(2) *stream,* flows 3.5 miles to North Fork American River 2.5 miles west-northwest of the village of Pilot Hill (lat. 38°50'40" N, long. 121°03'35" W; sec. 35, T 12 N, R 8 E); the stream heads near Pilot Hill (1). Named on Pilot Hill (1954) 7.5' quadrangle.

Pilot Hill [EL DORADO]:

(1) *peak,* 1.5 miles southwest of the village of Pilot Hill (lat. 38°49'05" N, long. 121°01'45" W; sec. 12, T 11 N, R 8 E). Altitude 1869 feet. Named on Pilot Hill (1954) 7.5' quadrangle.

(2) *village,* 13 miles west-northwest of Placerville (lat. 38°50'05" N, long. 121°00'50" W; sec. 6, T 11 N, R 9 E); the village is 1.5 miles northeast of Pilot Hill (1). Named on Pilot Hill (1954) 7.5' quadrangle. Mining began near the place in 1849 and mining camps called Pilot Hill, Centerville, and Pittsfield developed near one another there; the three camps soon consolidated under the name "Centerville," a designation that persisted even after the the post office at the place received the name "Pilot Hill" (Hoover, Rensch, and Rensch, p. 85). Postal authorities established Pilot Hill post office in 1854 (Frickstad, p. 28). Whitney (1880, p. 85) mentioned a place called Powningville that was located 3 or 4 miles east-northeast of Pilot Hill.

Pilot Hill: see **Pilot Peak** [NEVADA].

Pilot Peak [NEVADA]: *peak,* 7.25 miles west-southwest of Grass Valley (lat. 39°10'05" N, long. 121°10'55" W; sec. 10, T 15 N, R 7 E); the peak is 1 mile southeast of Indian Springs. Altitude 2239 feet. Named on Rough and Ready (1949) 7.5' quadrangle. Called Indian Springs Hill on Smartsville (1895) 30' quadrangle, and called Pilot Hill on Hobson's (1890a) map.

Pinchem Creek [EL DORADO]: *stream,* flows nearly 2 miles to Weber Creek 5.25 miles southwest of Coloma (lat. 38°45'25" N, long. 120°58'15" W; near SE cor. sec. 33, T 11 N, R 9 E). Named on Coloma (1949) and Shingle Springs (1949) 7.5' quadrangles. The name recalls an early mining camp called Pinchemtight; the name of the camp supposedly originated from the exclamation "Pinch 'em tight!" made by miners to a storekeeper who measured gold dust by gathering some between his fingers (Hoover, Rensch, and Rensch, p. 85).

Pinchemtight: see **Pinchem Creek** [EL DORADO].

Pine Creek [YOLO]: *stream,* flows 3.25 miles to Salt Creek 7 miles south-southwest of Esparto (lat. 38°35'50" N, long. 122°02'40" W; near E line sec. 26, T 9 N, R 2 W). Named on Monticello Dam (1959) 7.5' quadrangle.

Pinecrest [NEVADA]: *locality,* 1 mile north of Chicago Park along Nevada County Narrow Gauge Railroad (lat. 39°09'40" N, long. 120°58' W; near S line sec. 9, T 15 N, R 9 E). Named on Colfax (1938) 30' quadrangle.

Pinecrest Camp [EL DORADO]: *locality,* 4 miles west of Echo Summit along Tamarack Creek (lat. 38°48'35" N, long. 120°06'15" W; near S line sec. 9, T 11 N, R 17 E). Named on Echo Lake (1955) 7.5' quadrangle.

Pinecroft [PLACER]: *locality,* 2 miles southwest of Colfax (lat. 39° 04'55" N, long. 120°58'35" W; sec. 9, T 14 N, R 9 E). Named on Colfax (1949) 7.5' quadrangle.

Pine Grove [AMADOR]: *village,* 7.5 miles northeast of Jackson (lat. 38°24'50" N, long. 120°39'30" W; sec. 33, T 7 N, R 12 E). Named on Pine Grove (1948) 7.5' quadrangle. Postal authorities established Pine Grove post office in 1856 (Frickstad, p. 6). Camp's (1962) map shows a place called Irish Town located 1.5 miles south-southwest of Pine Grove, and a place called Armstrong's Mill situated 1 mile southwest of Pine Grove. Postal authorities established Wieland post office 1.5 miles southwest of Pine Grove in 1892 and discontinued it in 1893; they established Defender post office 5 miles northeast of Pine Grove at Defender mine in 1900 and discontinued it in 1915 (Salley, p. 56, 240).

Pine Grove: see **Kings Beach** [PLACER]; **Loomis** [PLACER].

Pine Grove Creek [SIERRA]: *stream,* flows 1 mile to East Branch Slate Creek 3.25 miles west of Mount Fillmore (lat. 39°43'10" N, long. 120°54'35" W; near SW cor. sec. 31, T 22 N, R 10 E). Named on La Porte (1951) 7.5' quadrangle.

Pine Grove Reservoir [NEVADA]: *lake,* behind a dam on Little Shady Creek 2 miles east-northeast of French Corral (lat. 39°19'05" N, long. 121°07'40" W; sec. 19, T 17 N, R 8 E). Named on French Corral (1948, photorevised 1969) and Nevada City (1948) 7.5' quadrangles.

Pine Hill [EL DORADO]: *peak,* 5 miles northwest of Shingle Springs (lat. 38°43'10" N, long. 120°59'20" W; sec. 16, T 10 N, R 9 E). Altitude 2059 feet. Named on Shingle Springs (1949) 7.5' quadrangle. Logan's (1938) map has the form "Pinehill" for the name.

Pine Hill [NEVADA]:

(1) *peak,* 7 miles south-southwest of Grass Valley (lat. 39°07'50" N, long. 121°07'15" W; at SW cor. sec. 20, T 15 N, R 8 E). Altitude 2134 feet. Named on Grass Valley (1949) 7.5' quadrangle.

(2) *peak,* less than 1 mile north of Wolf (lat. 39°04'20" N, long. 120°08'25" W; on N line sec. 13, T 14 N, R 7 E). Named on Wolf (1949) 7.5' quadrangle.

Pine Needle Point [COLUSA]: *ridge,* east-trending, less than 1 mile long, 3.25 miles northwest of Pacific Point (lat. 39°14'30" N, long. 122°38'35" W; near N line sec. 16, T 16 N, R 7 W). Named on Clearlake Oaks (1960) 15' quadrangle.

Pine Nut Canyon [PLACER]: *canyon,* drained by a stream that flows less than 1 mile to Duncan Canyon 6 miles south of Duncan Peak (lat. 39°04'10" N, long. 120°32' W; at N line sec. 16, T 14 N, R 13 E). Named on Greek Store (1952) 7.5' quadrangle.

Pine Ridge [COLUSA]: *ridge,* east-southeast-trending, 2 miles long, 3 miles northwest of Pacific Point (lat. 39°14'55" N, long. 122° 38' W). Named on Clearlake Oaks (1960) and Stonyford (1951) 15' quadrangles.

Pine Tree Reservoir: see **Grass Valley** [NEVADA].

Pine Tree Spring [PLACER]: *spring,* 3.5 miles northwest of Devil Peak (lat. 38°59'30" N, long. 120°36' W; sec. 11, T 13 N, R 12 E). Named on Devil Peak (1950) 7.5' quadrangle.

Ping Slough [SUTTER]: *stream,* flows 10 miles to Coon Creek 1.5 miles south-southeast of Nicolaus (lat. 38°53' N, long. 121°34'10" W; near S line sec. 18, T 12 N, R 4 E). Named on Nicolaus (1952, photorevised 1973) and Sheridan (1953, photorevised 1973) 7.5' quadrangles.

Pinnacles: see **The Pinnacles** [PLACER].

Pino: see **Loomis** [PLACER]; **Old Pino** [EL DORADO].

Pino Grande [EL DORADO]: *locality,* 8 miles north-northwest of Pollock Pines (lat. 38°52'10" N, long. 120°37'35" W; sec. 22, T 12 N, R 12 E). Named on Saddle Mountain (1950) 15' quadrangle. Called Pinogrande on California Mining Bureau's (1909a) map. Postal authorities established Pino Grande post office in 1892, moved it 5.5 miles south in 1893, discontinued it in 1899, reestablished it in 1902, and discontinued it in 1909 (Salley, p. 172).

Pinoli Peak [NEVADA]: *peak,* 6 miles northeast of Graniteville (lat. 39°29'25" N, long. 120°38'55" W; near N line sec. 29, T 19 N, R 12 E); the peak is at the west end of Pinoli Ridge. Altitude 7297 feet. Named on Graniteville (1982) 7.5' quadrangle.

Pinoli Ridge [NEVADA]: *ridge,* extends for 2.5 miles east-northeast and east from Pinole Peak; center 7 miles east-northeast of Graniteville (lat. 39°29'40" N, long. 120°37'35" W). Named on English Mountain (1983) and Graniteville (1982) 7.5' quadrangles.

Pioneer [AMADOR]: *village,* 5 miles east-northeast of Pine Grove (lat. 38°25'55" N, long. 120°34'20" W; sec. 29, T 7 N, R 13 E). Named on West Point (1948) 7.5' quadrangle. The place is called Pioneer Station on Mokelumne Hill (1948) 15' quadrangle. Postal authorities established Pioneer post office in 1947 (Frickstad, p. 6). Camp's (1962) map shows a place called Camp Contreras located less than 1 mile south of Pioneer; the name honored Pablo Contreras, the most influential citizen of the place (Sargent, p. 46).

Pioneer: see **Florin Road** [SACRAMENTO].

Pioneer Campground [SIERRA]: *locality,* 6 miles northeast of Sierra City along North Yuba River (lat. 39°37'50" N, long. 120° 33'40" W; near N line sec. 6, T 20 N, R 13 E). Named on Clio (1981) 7.5' quadrangle. Sierra City (1955) 15' quadrangle has the name "Pioneer Lodge" near the site of the campground.

Pioneer Creek [AMADOR]: *stream,* flows about 5.5 miles to Sutter Creek (1) 3 miles northeast of Pine Grove (lat. 38°26'35" N; long. 120°37'20" W; sec. 23, T 7 N, R 12 E). Named on West Point (1948) 7.5' quadrangle.

Pioneer Lodge: see **Pioneer Campground** [SIERRA].

Pioneer Station: see **Pioneer** [AMADOR].

Pipe Creek [SIERRA]: *stream,* flows 2 miles to Canyon Creek 6 miles northwest of Goodyears Bar (lat. 39°36'35" N, long. 120° 57' W; sec. 10, T 20 N, R 9 E). Named on Goodyears Bar (1951) 7.5' quadrangle.

Pipeline Canyon [YOLO]: *canyon,* drained by a stream that flows 1.5 miles to Lindermans Flat 5 miles west of Esparto (lat. 38°41'10" N, long. 122°06'20" W; sec. 29, T 10 N, R 2 W). Named on Esparto (1959) 7.5' quadrangle.

Piper Creek [NEVADA]: *stream,* flows 2 miles to Harry L. Englebright Lake (present Englebright Lake) 5 miles west-southwest of French Corral (lat. 39°16'45" N, long. 121°14'50" W; sec. 1, T 16 N, R 6 E); the stream heads at Piper Hill. Named on French Corral (1948) 7.5' quadrangle.

Piper Hill [NEVADA]: *peak,* 4.5 miles southwest of French Corral (lat. 39°15'40" N, long. 121°13'10" W; sec. 8, T 16 N, R 7 E). Named on French Corral (1948) 7.5' quadrangle.

Pi-Pi Creek [EL DORADO]: *stream,* flows 2.5 miles to Middle Fork Cosumnes River nearly 3 miles south of Caldor in Pi-Pi Valley (lat. 38°33'55" N, long. 120°25'50" W; near N line sec. 9, T 8 N, R 14 E). Named on Caldor (1951) 7.5' quadrangle.

Pi-Pi Valley [EL DORADO]: *valley,* 2.5 miles south of Caldor along Middle Fork Cosumnes River (lat. 38°34' N, long. 120°26' W; on S line sec. 4, T 8 N, R 14 E). Named on Caldor (1951) 7.5' quadrangle. Called Pi Pi Valley (without the hyphen) on Pyramid Peak (1896) 30' quadrangle.

Pirates Lair [SACRAMENTO]: *locality,* 5 miles south-southeast of Isleton along Mokelumne River on Andrus Island (lat. 38°05'55" N, long. 121°04' W). Named on Rio Vista (1952) 15' quadrangle.

Pitt Lake [EL DORADO]: *lake*, 400 feet long, 5.25 miles west-northwest of Echo Summit (lat. 38°50'10" N, long. 120°07'30" W). Named on Echo Lake (1955) and Pyramid Peak (1955) 7.5' quadrangles.

Pittsburg: see **Grass Valley** [NEVADA].

Pittsburgh Bar: see **Long Bar** [YUBA] (1).

Pittsburgh Hill [YUBA]: *peak*, 3.25 miles south of Strawberry Valley (lat. 39°30'55" N, long. 121°06' W; sec. 17, T 19 N, R 8 E). Named on Strawberry Valley (1948) 7.5' quadrangle.

Pittsfield: see **Pilot Hill** [EL DORADO] (2).

Placer: see **Loomis** [PLACER].

Placerville [EL DORADO]: *town*, near the center of the west half of El Dorado County (lat. 38°43'45" N, long. 120°47'55" W; around SE cor. sec. 7, T 10 N, R 11 E). Named on Placerville (1949) 7.5' quadrangle. Postal authorities established Placerville post office in 1850 (Frickstad, p. 28), and the town incorporated in 1854. In 1848 prospectors found gold at the place, which became known as Old Dry Diggings; after the hanging of three robbers there, the community bore the nickname "Hangtown," but officially it became Placerville in 1850 (Bancroft, 1888, p. 468). The place also was called simply Dry Diggings; the name "Placerville" recalls placer mining carried on in the streets of the town (Gudde, 1975, p. 270). Whitney's (1880) map shows a feature called Hangtown Hill situated just south of Placerville between the town and Coon Hollow. Bancroft's (1864) map shows a place called Sportsmans Hall located east of Placerville along the road to the State of Nevada. Postal authorities established Sportsmans Hall post office 11 miles east of Placerville in 1865 and discontinued it in 1867; the post office name was from a building used for the entertainment of stage and freight drivers who stopped there (Salley, p. 210). Postal authorities established Zodoc post office 5 miles south of Placerville in 1887 and discontinued it in 1888 (Salley, p. 246). Borthwick (p. 125, 166) in 1857 mentioned a mining camp called Middletown that was located 2 or 3 miles from Hangtown (present Placerville) on the road to Cold Springs. An early-day stopping place called Missouri House was situated 12 miles below Placerville (Paden, p. 456).

Plainfield [YOLO]: *locality*, 4.5 miles northwest of Davis (lat. 38°35'25" N, long. 121°48'10" W; near NW cor. sec. 31, T 9 N, R 2 E). Named on Merritt (1952) 7.5' quadrangle. Postal authorities established Plainfield post office in 1873 and discontinued it in 1908 (Frickstad, p. 221).

Planehaven [SACRAMENTO]: *locality*, 7.5 miles northeast of downtown Sacramento along Southern Pacific Railroad (lat. 38° 39' N, long. 121°23'30" W). Named on Fair Oaks (1954) 15' quadrangle.

Plasse [AMADOR]: *locality*, 7 miles north-northwest of Mokelumne Peak near Silver Lake (lat. 38°38'25" N, long. 120°07'40" W; sec. 8, T 9 N, R 17 E); Silver Lake post office is at the place. Both Silver Lake post office and Plasse are named on Tragedy Spring (1979) 7.5' quadrangle. Pyramid Peak (1896) 30' quadrangle has the form "Plassé" for the name. Postal authorities established Silver Lake post office in 1880, discontinued it in 1890, reestablished it in 1936, and discontinued it in 1973 (Salley, p. 205).

Plasse Trading Post [AMADOR]: *locality*, 5.25 miles north of Mokelumne Peak (lat. 38°36'50" N, long. 120°05'25" W; near W line sec. 22, T 9 N, R 17 E). Site named on Mokelumne Peak (1979) 7.5' quadrangle. Raymond Plasse started the place (Sargent, p. 13).

Pleasant: see **Mount Pleasant** [EL DORADO]; **Mount Pleasant** [SIERRA]; **Point Pleasant** [SACRAMENTO].

Pleasant Flat: see **Coloma** [EL DORADO]; **Newtown** [NEVADA].

Pleasant Grove [SUTTER]:

(1) *village*, 7.5 miles southeast of Nicolaus (lat. 38°49'25" N, long. 121°28'55" W; at N line sec. 12, T 11 N, R 4 E). Named on Pleasant Grove (1967) 7.5' quadrangle. Pleasant Grove (1910) 7.5' quadrangle shows both the village and an area with the label "Pleasant Grove" located just east of the village. California Mining Bureau's (1909a) map has the form "Pleasantgrove" for the name. Postal authorities established Pleasant Grove Creek post office in 1867, changed the name to Pleasant Grove in 1875, and moved it 1.5 miles east in 1940 (Salley, p. 174). Pleasant Grove was an early wagon and freight stop that had the nickname "Gouge-Eye" from a saloon fight there during which one man gouged out the eye of another (Hendrix, p. 107).

(2) *locality*, 6.5 miles east-northeast of Verona along Western Pacific Railroad (lat. 38°49'40" N, long. 121°30'25" W; at E line sec. 3, T 11 N, R 4 E); the place is 1.25 miles west of Pleasant Grove (1). Named on Verona (1967) 7.5' quadrangle. Called Pleasant Grove Station on Vernon (1910) 7.5' quadrangle, which shows another Pleasant Grove Station along Northern Electric Railroad 1 mile farther west (at SW cor. sec. 3, T 11 N, R 4 E). This second Pleasant Grove Station has the designation "Pleasant Grove (siding)" on Knights Landing (1952) 15' quadrangle, which shows it along Sacramento Northern Railroad.

Pleasant Grove Creek [PLACER-SUTTER]: *stream*, heads in Placer County and flows 10 miles to end in Sutter County nearly 6 miles east of Verona in American Basin (lat. 38°47'50" N, long. 121°30'30" W; sec. 15, T 11 N, R 4 E); the stream passes 1 mile south of Pleasant Grove [SUTTER] (1). Named on Pleasant Grove (1967), Rocklin (1967), Roseville (1967), and Verona (1967) 7.5' quadrangles. South Branch enters from the southeast 5 miles northwest of Roseville; it is 6.5 miles long and is named on Roseville (1967) 7.5' quadrangle.

Pleasant Grove Creek: see **Pleasant Grove** [SUTTER] (1).

Pleasant Grove Station: see **Pleasant Grove** [SUTTER] (2)

Pleasant Lake [EL DORADO]: *lake*, 2.5 miles east of Wentworth Springs (lat. 39°00'35" N, long. 120°17'40" W). Named on Granite Chief (1953) 15' quadrangle, where it is connected to Loon Lake. Wentworth Springs (1953, photorevised 1973) 7.5' quadrangle shows a larger lake with a wider connection to Loon Lake.

Pleasant Lake: see **Loon Lake** [EL DORADO].

Pleasant Point [NEVADA]: *peak*, 3.5 miles west of Washington (lat. 39°21'15" N, long. 120°52'10" W; at E line sec. 8, T 17 N, R 10 E). Named on Washington (1950) 7.5' quadrangle.

Pleasant Valley [EL DORADO]:

(1) *valley*, 8 miles east-southeast of Placerville (lat. 38°41' N, long. 120°40' W). Named on Placerville (1893) 30' quadrangle. Mormon men on their way across the Sierra Nevada to Salt Lake City in 1848 camped in the valley and named it (Hoover, Rensch, and Rensch, p. 83).

(2) *settlement*, 3.5 miles south of Camino (lat. 38°41' N, long. 120° 39'45" W; near SW cor. sec. 28, T 10 N, R 12 E); the place is near the south end of Pleasant Valley (1). Named on Camino (1952) 7.5' quadrangle. Postal authorities established Pleasant Valley post office in 1864 and discontinued it in 1917 (Frickstad, p. 28). They established Urban post office 5 miles southwest of Pleasant Valley post office in 1909 and discontinued it in 1912; the name was for Eva L. Urban, first postmaster (Salley, p. 228).

Pleasant Valley [NEVADA]: *valley*, 4 miles south-southwest of French Corral (lat. 39°15'30" N, long. 121°11'50" W; at and near sec. 9, T 16 N, R 7 E). Named on French Corral (1948) 7.5' quadrangle.

Pleasant View [SIERRA]: *locality*, 2 miles north-northeast of Pike (lat. 39°28' N, long. 120°58'50" W; near SW cor. sec. 33, T 19 N, R 9 E). Named on Pike (1949) 7.5' quadrangle.

Pliocene Ridge [SIERRA]: *ridge*, generally southwest-trending, 8 miles long, center 1 mile northwest of Alleghany (lat. 39°29' N, long. 120°51' W). Named on Alleghany (1949), Downieville (1951), and Pike (1949) 7.5' quadrangles.

Plug Point [SIERRA]: *peak*, 5.5 miles south-southwest of Mount Fillmore (lat. 39°39'10" N, long. 120°52'45" W; sec. 20, T 21 N, R 10 E). Altitude 5948 feet. Named on La Porte (1951) 7.5' quadrangle.

Plug Ugly Hill: see **Pug Ugly** [PLACER].

Plumas: see **Arboga** [YUBA]; **Plumas Landing** [YUBA].

Plumas City: see **Plumas Landing** [YUBA].

Plumas Lake [YUBA]: *lake*, 4 miles south of Olivehurst along Reeds Creek (lat. 39°02'30" N, long. 121°33' W). Named on Marysville (1952) 15' quadrangle. Ostrom (1911) 7.5' quadrangle shows a much larger lake, but now the lake is drained.

Plumas Landing [YUBA]: *locality*, 9 miles south of Marysville along Feather River (which also was called Rio de las Plumas) near the mouth of Reed Creek (lat. 39°00'30" N, long. 121°34'45" W). Named on Marysville (1895) 30' quadrangle. Eddy's (1851) map shows a place called Plumas City located on the east bank of Feather River near the site of Plumas Landing, and Eddy's (1854) map has the name "Plumas" at about the same place. Postal authorities established Plumas post office in 1860 and discontinued it in 1862 (Frickstad, p. 224). Messers. Sutter and Beach founded Plumas 15 miles below Marysville in 1850 as a trading center for miners (Bancroft, 1888, p. 487; Gudde, 1975, p. 271).

Plumbago [SIERRA]: *locality*, 2 miles southeast of Alleghany (lat. 39°27'10" N, long. 120°49' W; near SE cor. sec. 2, T 18 N, R 10 E). Named on Alleghany (1949) 7.5' quadrangle.

Plum Creek [EL DORADO]:

(1) *stream*, flows 2.25 miles to Pilot Creek (1) 5 miles west of Robbs Peak (lat. 38°54'50" N, long. 120°30' W; sec. 3, T 12 N, R 13 E). Named on Robbs Peak (1950) 7.5' quadrangle.

(2) *stream*, flows 6.5 miles to South Fork American River 0.5 mile east-southeast of Riverton (lat. 38°46'05" N, long. 120°26'25" W; sec. 29, T 11 N, R 14 E). Named on Leek Spring Hill (1951), Riverton (1950), and Stump Spring (1951) 7.5' quadrangles. West Fork enters 1.25 miles north of Old Iron Mountain; it is 1.5 miles long and is named on Stump Spring (1951) 7.5' quadrangle.

Plum Creek Mill [EL DORADO]: *locality*, 3 miles north-northwest of Old Iron Mountain (lat. 38°44'40" N, long. 120°24'55" W; near W line sec. 3, T 10 N, R 14 E); the place is along Plum Creek (2). Site named on Stump Spring (1951) 7.5' quadrangle. A sawmill was at the site (Beverly Cola, personal communication, 1985).

Plum Creek Ridge [EL DORADO]: *ridge*, north-northwest-trending, 5 miles long, center 2 miles north of Old Iron Mountain (lat. 38° 44' N, long. 120°23'10" W); the ridge is northeast of Plum Creek (2). Named on Leek Spring Hill (1951) and Stump Spring (1951) 7.5' quadrangles.

Plummer Ridge [EL DORADO]: *ridge*, generally west-trending, 16 miles long, center 3.5 miles northeast of Caldor (lat. 38°38' N, long. 120°22'45" W). Named on Caldor (1951), Leek Spring Hill (1951), Omo Ranch (1952), Peddler Hill (1951), Stump Spring (1951), and Tragedy Spring (1979)

7.5' quadrangles.

Plum Orchard [COLUSA]: *locality,* 7.25 miles east-southeast of Wilbur Springs (lat. 39°00'10" N, long. 122°17'40" W; sec. 3, T 13 N, R 4 W). Named on Wilbur Springs (1961) 15' quadrangle.

Plumtree [YOLO]: *locality,* 4.25 miles west of West Sacramento along Southern Pacific Railroad (lat. 38°34'20" N, long. 121°34'20" W). Named on Lovdal (1916) 7.5' quadrangle.

Plum Tree Crossing [NEVADA-PLACER]: *locality,* 2.5 miles southwest of Colfax along Bear River on Nevada-Placer County line (lat. 39°04'50" N, long. 120°59'40" W; sec. 8, T 14 N, R 9 E). Named on Colfax (1949) 7.5' quadrangle. On Colfax (1950) 15' quadrangle, the name has the form "Plumtree Crossing."

Plum Valley [SIERRA]:

(1) *area,* 2 miles east-northeast of Pike (lat. 39°26'50" N, long. 120° 57'35" W; at NW cor. sec. 10, T 18 N, R 9 E). Named on Pike (1949) 7.5' quadrangle.

(2) *locality,* 2.25 miles east-northeast of Pike (lat. 39°26'55" N, long. 120°57'10" W); the place is at Plum Valley (1). Named on Colfax (1898) 30' quadrangle. Postal authorities established Plum Valley post office in 1855 and discontinued it in 1877 (Frickstad, p. 184).

Plunkett Creek [EL DORADO]: *stream,* flows nearly 3 miles to Deer Creek (2) 3.5 miles south-southeast of Clarksville (lat. 38°36'25" N, long. 121°01'10" W; near W line sec. 29, T 9 N, R 9 E). Named on Clarksville (1953) and Folsom SE (1954) 7.5' quadrangles.

Pluto Peak: see **Mount Pluto** [PLACER].

Plymouth [AMADOR]: *town,* 10 miles north-northwest of Jackson (lat. 38°28'45" N, long. 120°50'45" W; mainly in sec. 11, T 7 N, R 10 E). Named on Amador City (1962) 7.5' quadrangle. Postal authorities established Plymouth post office in 1871 and named it for the hotel that housed it (Salley, p. 174). The town incorporated in 1917. Camp's (1962) map has the name "Puckerville" as an alternate designation for Plymouth. Gudde (1975, p. 271) mentioned the terms "Pokerville" or "Poker Camp" as other possible names for the community. According to Andrews (p. 109-110), the name "Pokerville" came when miners who were confined to the town in the winter of 1850 and 1851 played poker to relieve their boredom. Postal authorities established Figtree post office 4 miles northeast of Plymouth in 1917 and discontinued it in 1918; a fig tree was a landmark at the place (Salley, p. 74).

Pocket: see **Freeport** [SACRAMENTO] (1).

Pocket Canyon [COLUSA]: *canyon,* drained by a stream that flows 3.25 miles to the canyon of Cortina Creek 10 miles southeast of Wilbur Springs (lat. 38°57'30" N, long. 122°16'15" W; sec. 23, T 13 N, R 4 W). Named on Glascock Mountain (1958) 7.5' quadrangle.

Pocket Gulch [YOLO]: *canyon,* drained by a stream that flows 2 miles to Cache Creek 2.5 miles west-northwest of Rumsey (lat. 38° 54'35" N, long. 122°16'45" W; near SW cor. sec. 2, T 12 N, R 4 W). Named on Glascock Mountain (1958) 7.5' quadrangle.

Pocket Tract: see **Freeport** [SACRAMENTO] (1).

Podesta Camp [EL DORADO]: *locality,* 10.5 miles southwest of Kirkwood (lat. 38°37' N, long. 120°13'30" W; near E line sec. 20, T 9 N, R 16 E). Named on Bear River Reservoir (1979) 7.5' quadrangle.

Poffenbergers Landing [SUTTER]: *locality,* 3 miles northwest of Kirkville along Sacramento River (lat. 38°56'20" N, long. 121°49'40" W; at S line sec. 26, T 13 N, R 1 E). Named on Kirkville (1952) 7.5' quadrangle. Kirkville (1915) 7.5' quadrangle has the possessive form "Poffenberger's Landing" for the name.

Poho Ridge [EL DORADO]: *ridge,* generally west-trending, 3.25 miles long, center 3.5 miles northwest of Pollock Pines (lat. 38°48'10" N, long. 120°37'30" W). Named on Pollock Pines (1950) and Slate Mountain (1950) 7.5' quadrangles.

Point Burnett: see **Wood Island** [SACRAMENTO].

Point Defiance [NEVADA]: *relief feature,* 2.5 miles west-southwest of French Corral at the confluence of Yuba River and South Yuba River (lat. 39°17'45" N, long. 121°12'15" W; at SW cor. sec. 28, T 17 N, R 7 E). Named on French Corral (1948) 7.5' quadrangle.

Pointed Rocks [EL DORADO]: *peak,* 1.25 miles northwest of Cool (lat. 38°54' N, long. 121°02' W; near S line sec. 12, T 12 N, R 8 E). Altitude 1658 feet. Named on Auburn (1953) 7.5' quadrangle.

Point Ellis: see **Grand Island** [SACRAMENTO].

Point Hensley: see **Sevenmile Slough** [SACRAMENTO].

Point Larkin: see **Grand Island** [SACRAMENTO].

Point Pleasant [SACRAMENTO]: *settlement,* 7.5 miles southwest of Elk Grove (lat. 38°19'55" N, long. 121°27'45" W; on E line sec. 31, T 6 N, R 5 E). Named on Bruceville (1968) 7.5' quadrangle.

Point Rogers: see **Montezuma Island** [SACRAMENTO].

Point Sacramento [SACRAMENTO]: *promontory,* 14 miles west-southwest of Isleton at the west end of Sherman Island (lat. 38°33'45" N, long. 121°50'10" W); the feature is near the mouth of Sacramento River. Named on Antioch North (1978) 7.5' quadrangle.

Point Sutter: see **Sutter Island** [SACRAMENTO].

Poison Canyon [NEVADA]: *canyon,* 1 mile long, 4 miles west of English Mountain (lat. 39°26'40" N, long. 120°37'30" W). Named on English Mountain (1983) and Graniteville (1982) 7.5' quadrangles.

Poison Hole [EL DORADO]: *relief feature,* 5 miles east-northeast of Robbs Peak (lat. 38°56'55" N, long. 120°19'05" W; sec. 29, T 13 N, R 15 E). Named on Loon Lake (1952) 7.5' quadrangle.

Poker Bend [SUTTER-YOLO]: *bend,* 1.25 miles west of Kirkville along Sacramento River on Sutter-Yolo County line (lat. 38°54'40" N, long. 121°48'50" W; at S line sec. 1, T 12 N, R 1 E). Named on Kirkville (1952) 7.5' quadrangle.

Poker Bend: see **Little Poker Bend** [SUTTER-YOLO].

Poker Camp: see **Plymouth** [AMADOR].

Poker Flat [SIERRA]: *locality,* 2.5 miles south of Mount Fillmore along Canyon Creek (lat. 39°41'35" N, long. 120°50'40" W). Named on Mount Fillmore (1951) 7.5' quadrangle.

Pokerville: see **Plymouth** [AMADOR].

Polaris [NEVADA]: *locality,* 2.5 miles east-northeast of Truckee along Southern Pacific Railroad (lat. 39°20'20" N, long. 120°08'05" W; sec. 7, T 17 N, R 17 E). Named on Truckee (1955) 7.5' quadrangle. Postal authorities established Polaris post office in 1901 and discontinued it in 1923 (Frickstad, p. 114).

Pole Bridge Canyon [YOLO]: *canyon,* drained by a stream that flows 1 mile to Cache Creek 1.5 miles northwest of Rumsey (lat. 38°54'10" N, long. 122°15'45" W; at W line sec. 12, T 12 N, R 4 W). Named on Glascock Mountain (1958) 7.5' quadrangle.

Pole Creek [PLACER]: *stream,* flows 3.5 miles to Truckee River nearly 6 miles northwest of Tahoe City (lat. 39°14'10" N, long. 120°12'25" W; sec. 16, T 16 N, R 16 E). Named on Granite Chief (1953) and Tahoe City (1955) 7.5' quadrangles.

Polk [SACRAMENTO]: *locality,* 5.5 miles east-southeast of downtown Sacramento along Central California Traction Railroad (lat. 38°31'55" N, long. 121°24'25" W; near W line sec. 23, T 8 N, R 5 E). Named on Sacramento East (1967) 7.5' quadrangle. California Mining Bureau's (1917e) map shows a place called Gerber located along the railroad about halfway from Polk to Sheldon.

Pollock [SACRAMENTO]: *locality,* 6.5 miles south-southeast of downtown Sacramento along Western Pacific Railroad (lat. 38°29'20" N, long. 121°28'05" W; sec. 6, T 7 N, R 5 E). Named on Florin (1968) 7.5' quadrangle.

Pollock Pines [EL DORADO]: *town,* 12 miles east-northeast of Placerville (lat. 38°45'45" N, long. 120°35' W; mainly in sec. 36, T 11 N, R 12 E). Named on Pollock Pines (1950) 7.5' quadrangle. Postal authorities established Pollock Pines post office in 1936 (Frickstad, p. 28). The name is from a grove of pine trees that belonged to the Pollock family, first settlers at the site (Gudde, 1949, p. 269).

Pomegranate: see **Lancha Plana** [AMADOR].

Pomelo: see **Fair Oaks** [SACRAMENTO].

Pomins [EL DORADO]: *locality,* 2 miles north of the present town of Meeks Bay along Lake Tahoe (lat. 39°04' N, long. 120°07'20" W; near N line sec. 17, T 14 N, R 17 E). Named on Truckee (1940) 30' quadrangle. Postal authorities established Pomins post office in 1915 and discontinued it in 1942; the name was for Frank J. Pomin, first postmaster (Salley, p. 176).

Pond Creek [PLACER]: *stream,* flows 1.25 miles to Middle Fork American River 15 miles east-northeast of Auburn (lat. 38°59'25" N, long. 120°49'40" W; sec. 11, T 13 N, R 10 E). Named on Foresthill (1949) and Georgetown (1949) 7.5' quadrangles.

Poorman Creek [NEVADA]:

(1) *stream,* flows 13 miles to South Yuba River 0.5 mile southwest of Washington (lat. 39°21'10" N, long. 120°48'35" W; sec. 12, T 17 N, R 10 E). Named on Alleghany (1949), Graniteville (1982), and Washington (1950) 7.5' quadrangles. South Fork enters 2 miles north-northeast of Washington; it is 6 miles long and is named on Alleghany (1949) and Graniteville (1982) 7.5' quadrangles. A mining camp called South Fork was situated along South Fork Poorman Creek just above the mouth of the fork, and a mining place called Brandy Flat was located opposite the mouth of Poorman Creek (Slyter and Slyter, p. 7, 13). A place called Pattison was located along South Yuba River 0.5 mile above the mouth of Poorman Creek (Gudde, 1975, p. 261).

(2) *stream,* flows 2 miles to Rollins Reservoir 2 miles northeast of Chicago Park (lat. 39°09'55" N, long. 120°56'35" W; near W line sec. 11, T 15 N, R 9 E). Named on Chicago Park (1949, photorevised 1973) 7.5' quadrangle.

Poor Mans Canyon [PLACER]: *canyon,* drained by a stream that flows 1.5 miles to El Dorado Canyon 1.25 miles east-southeast of Michigan Bluff (lat. 39°02'15" N, long. 120°42'40" W; near N line sec. 26, T 14 N, R 11 E). Named on Michigan Bluff (1952) 7.5' quadrangle.

Poorman Valley [NEVADA]: *valley,* 4.5 miles northeast of Graniteville along East Fork Creek (lat. 39°29'05" N, long. 120°40'20" W; sec. 30, T 19 N, R 12 E). Named on Graniteville (1982) 7.5' quadrangle.

Pope Beach [EL DORADO]: *beach,* 4.25 miles east-northeast of Mount Tallac along Lake Tahoe (lat. 38°56'15" N, long. 120°01'40" W; sec. 6, T 12 N, R 18 E). Named on Emerald Bay (1955) 7.5' quadrangle. Lekisch (p. 97) associated the name with George A. Pope, who owned property at the place.

Poppy Campground [PLACER]: *locality,* 5.5 miles north-northwest of Bunker Hill along Middle Fork American River (lat. 39°07'10" N, long. 120°25'35" W; near E line sec. 29, T 15 N, R 14 E). Named on Granite Chief (1953) 15' quadrangle. Water of French Meadows Reservoir now covers the site.

Porthole Gap [AMADOR]: *pass,* 6.25 miles north-northwest of Mokelumne Peak (lat. 38°37'25" N, long. 120°07'55" W; near SE cor. sec. 18, T 9 N, R 17 E). Named on Bear River Reservoir (1979) 7.5' quadrangle.

Port of Sacramento [YOLO]: *locality,* less than 1 mile west-southwest of downtown West Sacramento at the upper end of Sacramento River Deep Water Ship Channel (lat. 38°34' N, long. 121° 32'45" W). Named on Sacramento West (1967) 7.5' quadrangle.

Portuguese Bar: see **American River** [EL DORADO-PLACER-SACRAMENTO].

Portuguese Bend [SUTTER-YOLO]: *bend,* 1.5 miles east of Knights Landing along Sacramento River on Sutter-Yolo County line (lat. 38°47'40" N, long. 121°41'25" W; at E line sec. 13, T 11 N, R 2 E). Named on Knights Landing (1952) 7.5' quadrangle.

Portuguese Point [PLACER]: *ridge,* generally west-trending, 1 mile long, 2.25 miles northwest of Foresthill (lat. 39°02'35" N, long. 120°50'50" W). Named on Foresthill (1949) 7.5' quadrangle.

Port Wine [SIERRA]: *locality,* 7 miles southwest of Mount Fillmore (lat. 39°39'40" N, long. 120°56'50" W; near SW cor. sec. 23, T 21 N, R 9 E). Named on La Porte (1951) 7.5' quadrangle. Called Portwine on California Mining Bureau's (1909a) map. Postal authorities established Port Wine post office in 1861, discontinued it in 1865, reestablished it in 1870, and discontinued it in 1918 (Frickstad, p. 184). Prospectors named the place after they found a cask of port wine hidden nearby (Hoover, Resnch, and Rensch, p. 497).

Port Wine Ravine [SIERRA]: *canyon,* drained by a stream that flows 1 mile to Pats Gulch 7.5 miles southwest of Mount Fillmore (lat. 39°39'35" N, long. 120°57'30" W; near S line sec. 22, T 21 N, R 9 E); the feature is south of Port Wine. Named on La Porte (1951) 7.5' quadrangle.

Port Wine Ridge [SIERRA]: *ridge,* southwest-trending, 6 miles long, between Slate Creek and Canyon Creek; center 6 miles southwest of Mount Fillmore (lat. 39°40' N, long. 120°55'40" W); the place called Port Wine is on the ridge. Named on La Porte (1951) 7.5' quadrangle. The feature first was called Sears Ridge (Gudde, 1975, p. 313)—Sears Ravine is on the side of the ridge.

Possum Bar: see **Grapevine Ravine** [AMADOR].

Post Flat [EL DORADO]: *area,* 4.5 miles east-southeast of Camino (lat. 38°42'35" N, long. 120°35'40" W; at NE cor. sec. 24, T 10 N, R 12 E). Named on Sly Park (1952) 7.5' quadrangle.

Potato Hill [COLUSA]: *ridge,* northeast-trending, nearly 1 mile long, 2 miles southwest of Fouts Springs (lat. 39°20'15" N, long. 122°41'30" W; sec. 7, T 17 N, R 7 W). Named on Fouts Springs (1968) 7.5' quadrangle.

Potosi [SIERRA]: *locality,* 1.5 miles southwest of Mount Fillmore (lat. 39°43' N, long. 120°52'30" W; at NW cor. sec. 4, T 21 N, R 10 E). Named on La Porte (1951) and Mount Fillmore (1951) 7.5' quadrangles.

Potosi Creek [SIERRA]: *stream,* flows 2.5 mile to East Branch Slate Creek 2.25 miles west of Mount Fillmore (lat. 39°43'35" N, long. 120°53'35" W; near W line sec. 32, T 22 N, R 10 E); the stream goes past Potosi. Named on La Porte (1951) and Mount Fillmore (1951) 7.5' quadrangles. Downieville (1897) 30' quadrangle has the name "Gold Canyon" along the stream.

Potts Cabin [EL DORADO]: *locality,* 5.5 miles north of Riverton (lat. 38°51' N, long. 120°26'40" W; near S line sec. 30, T 12 N, R 14 E). Named on Riverton (1950) 7.5' quadrangle.

Pourier Creek [SIERRA]: *stream,* flows 1.25 miles to Willow Creek 4 miles north-northwest of Pike (lat. 39°29'35" N, long. 121°01'45" W; near N line sec. 25, T 19 N, R 8 E). Named on Camptonville (1948) 7.5' quadrangle.

Poverty: see **Poverty Hill** [SIERRA] (2).

Poverty Bar [EL DORADO-PLACER]: *locality,* 3 miles north-northwest of Greenwood along Middle Fork American River on El Dorado-Placer County line (lat. 38°56'05" N, long. 120°56'25" W; sec. 35, T 13 N, R 9 E). Named on Greenwood (1949) 7.5' quadrangle.

Poverty Bar: see **Swiss Bar**, under **Long Bar** [YUBA] (2).

Poverty Hill [SIERRA]:

(1) *peak,* 9.5 miles southwest of Mount Fillmore (lat. 39°37'50" N, long. 120°58'25" W; near SE cor. sec. 33, T 21 N, R 9 E). Altitude 5518 feet. Named on La Porte (1951) 7.5' quadrangle.

(2) *locality,* 8 miles northwest of Goodyears Bar (lat. 39°37'20" N, long. 121°00'20" W; near SE cor. sec. 6, T 20 N, R 9 E). Named on Strawberry Valley (1948) 7.5' quadrangle. Called Poverty on Logan's (1929) map.

Poverty Point: see **Big Canyon** [EL DORADO] (1).

Powderhorn Creek [PLACER]: *stream,* flows 3.25 miles to Five Lakes Creek 6.25 miles northeast of Bunker Hill (lat. 39°06'30" N, long. 120°17'25" W; near W line sec. 34, T 15 N, R 15 E). Named on Wentworth Springs (1953) 7.5' quadrangle.

Powderhorn Creek: see **Little Powderhorn Creek** [PLACER].

Powell Slough [COLUSA]: *water feature,* 3 miles southwest of Colusa in Colusa Basin (lat. 39°10'45" N, long. 122°02'20" W). Named on Colusa (1952) 7.5' quadrangle.

Powningville: see **Pilot Hill** [EL DORADO] (2).

Prairie: see **Zamora** [YOLO].

Prairie Buttes: see **Sutter Buttes** [SUTTER].

Prairie City [SACRAMENTO]: *locality,* 2.5 miles south-southeast of Folsom (lat. 38°38'35" N, long. 121°09'10" W). Site named on Folsom (1967) 7.5' quadrangle. A mining place called Prairie Diggings was situated just north of Prairie City (Gudde, 1975, p. 276).

Prairie Creek [NEVADA]: *stream,* flows 2 miles to Jackson Creek 3 miles west-northwest of English Mountain (lat. 39°27'25" N, long. 120°36'05" W; near W line sec. 2, T 18 N, R 12 E). Named on English Mountain (1983) 7.5' quadrangle.

Prairie Creek [YUBA]: *stream,* flows nearly 7 miles to South Honcut Creek 4.25 miles west of Loma Rica (lat. 39°18'45" N, long. 121°29'50" W; sec. 23, T 17 N, R 4 E). Named on Loma Rica (1947) 7.5' quadrangle. Part of present South Honcut Creek is called Prairie Creek on Marysville (1895) 30' quadrangle. Loma Rica (1947) 7.5' quadrangle shows Peoria cemetery located 2.5 miles southeast of Loma Rica (near SE cor. sec. 34, T 17 N, R 5 E)—the name recalls Peoria House, a travelers stop that Captain Thomas Phillips operated in the early days near the site of the present cemetery (Hoover, Rensch, and Rensch, p. 592).

Prairie Diggings: see **Browns Valley** [YUBA]; **Prairie City** [SACRAMENTO].

Prairie House: see **Browns Valley** [YUBA]; **Marysville** [YUBA].

Prays [EL DORADO]: *locality,* 5 miles north of Omo Ranch (lat. 38° 39'15" N, long. 120°35' W). Named on Placerville (1893) 30' quadrangle.

Preston Reservoir [AMADOR]: *lake,* 1400 feet long, 1.25 miles north-northwest of Ione (lat. 38°22'10" N, long. 120°56'15" W). Named on Ione (1962) 7.5' quadrangle.

Preston Reservoir: see **Henderson Reservoir** [AMADOR].

Price: see **Mount Price** [EL DORADO].

Prince Albert Creek [YUBA]: *stream,* flows nearly 2 miles to Dry Creek (1) 4.5 miles east of Rackerby (lat. 39°25'40" N, long. 121° 15'15" W; sec. 12, T 18 N, R 6 E). Named on Challenge (1948) and Rackerby (1948) 7.5' quadrangles.

Princeton [COLUSA]: *town,* 13 miles north of Colusa on the west side of Sacramento River (lat. 39°24'10" N, long. 122°00'35" W). Named on Princeton (1952) 7.5' quadrangle. Postal authorities established Princeton post office in 1855 (Frickstad, p. 19). Dr. Almon Lull, a graduate of Princeton University, suggested the name (Gudde, 1949, p. 273). A place called Sixteen Mile House was at the site of present Princeton in the early 1850's (Hoover, Rensch, and Rensch, p. 49). Postal authorities established Moulton post office 5 miles south of Princeton in 1887 and discontinued it in 1888 (Salley, p. 147).

Princeton Siding [COLUSA]: *locality,* 0.5 mile west-southwest of Princeton along Southern Pacific Railroad (lat. 39°24' N, long. 122°01'15" W). Named on Princeton (1952) 7.5' quadrangle.

Prize[COLUSA]: *locality,* 3.5 miles northeast of Arbuckle (lat. 39°03'20" N, long. 122°00'50" W; near N line sec. 19, T 14 N, R 1 W). Named on Arbuckle (1918) 7.5' quadrangle. Postal authorities established Prize post office in 1900 and discontinued it in 1919 (Frickstad, p. 19).

Progress [SUTTER]: *locality,* 7.5 miles south-southwest of Sutter along Southern Pacific Railroad in Sutter Basin (lat. 39°03'50" N, long. 121°47'55" W). Named on Tisdale Weir (1952) 7.5' quadrangle.

Prospect Creek [EL DORADO]: *stream,* flows 2 miles to Middle Fork Cosumnes River 4 miles southeast of Caldor (lat. 38°33'55" N, long. 120°22'35" W; sec. 12, T 8 N, R 14 E); Prospect Rock is near the head of the stream. Named on Peddler Hill (1951) 7.5' quadrangle.

Prospect Hill [AMADOR]: *hill,* 2.5 miles northwest of Fiddletown (lat. 38°31'55" N, long. 120°47'15" W; sec. 20, T 8 N, R 11 E). Named on Fiddletown (1949) 7.5' quadrangle.

Prospect Hill [PLACER]: *ridge,* generally south-trending, 1.5 miles long, 5 miles north of Foresthill (lat. 39°05'20" N, long. 120° 50' W). Named on Foresthill (1949) 7.5' quadrangle.

Prospect Rock [EL DORADO]: *relief feature,* 6 miles southeast of Caldor (lat. 38°33'05" N, long. 120°20'55" W; near NW cor. sec. 17, T 8 N, R 15 E). Named on Peddler Hill (1951) 7.5' quadrangle.

Prosser [NEVADA]: *locality,* 4.25 miles northeast of Truckee (lat. 39°22'10" N, long. 120°07'30" W); the place is along Prosser Creek. Named on Truckee (1895) 30' quadrangle.

Prosser Campground [NEVADA]: *locality,* 2 miles southeast of Hobart Mills (lat. 39°22'40" N, long. 120°09'40" W; near E line sec. 26, T 18 N, R 16 E); the place is along Prosser Creek Reservoir. Named on Hobart Mills (1981) 7.5' quadrangle.

Prosser Creek [NEVADA]: *stream,* formed by the confluence of North Fork and South Fork, flows 8.5 miles to Truckee River 4.5 miles northeast of Truckee (lat. 39°22'15" N, long. 120°07' W; sec. 32, T 18 N, R 17 E). Named on Hobart Mills (1981), Martis Peak (1955), and Truckee (1955) 7.5' quadrangles. The stream also was called John Greenwood's Creek

(Morgan, p. 377) and Johns Creek (Clyman, p. 205). North Fork is 8 miles long and is named on Hobart Mills (1981) and Independence Lake (1981) 7.5' quadrangles. South Fork is 5.5 miles long and is named on Hobart Mills (1981), Independence Lake (1981), and Norden (1955) 7.5' quadrangles.

Prosser Creek: see **Boca** [NEVADA].

Prosser Creek Reservoir [NEVADA]: *lake,* behind a dam on Prosser Creek 3 miles east-southeast of Hobart Mills (lat. 39°22'45" N, long. 120°08'15" W; sec. 30, T 18 N, R 17 E). Named on Hobart Mills (1981) and Truckee (1955, photorevised 1969) 7.5' quadrangles. United States Board on Geographic Names (1977b, p. 5) gave the name "Prosser Reservoir" as a variant.

Prosser Hill [NEVADA]: *peak,* 2.5 miles southwest of Hobart Mills (lat. 39°22'30" N, long. 120°13' W; near SW cor. sec. 28, T 18 N, R 16 E). Altitude 7171 feet. Named on Hobart Mills (1981) and Truckee (1955) 7.5' quadrangles.

Prosser House [NEVADA]: *locality,* 4 miles north-northeast of Truckee (lat. 39°22'45" N, long. 120°09' W); the place is along Prosser Creek. Named on Truckee (1895) 30' quadrangle.

Prosser Reservoir: see **Prosser Creek Reservoir** [NEVADA].

Prothro Creek [EL DORADO]: *stream,* flows nearly 3 miles to Middle Fork Cosumnes River 5 miles east-southeast of Caldor (lat. 38°34'35" N, long. 120°20'45" W; sec. 5, T 8 N, R 15 E). Named on Peddler Hill (1951) 7.5' quadrangle.

Providence [NEVADA]: *locality,* 1.25 miles west-southwest of Nevada City on the south side of Deer Creek (lat. 39°15'25" N, long. 121°02'15" W). Named on Smartsville (1895) 30' quadrangle.

Puckerville: see **Plymouth** [AMADOR].

Pug Ugly [PLACER]: *relief feature,* less than 1 mile southwest of Dutch Flat (lat. 39°12' N, long. 120°51' W; near NE cor. sec. 4, T 15 N, R 10 E). Named on Dutch Flat (1950) 7.5' quadrangle. Whitney's (1870) map shows Plug Ugly Hill.

Punchbowl: see **The Punchbowl** [NEVADA].

Puny Dip Canyon [NEVADA]: *canyon,* drained by a stream that heads in the State of Nevada and flows less than 0.5 mile in Nevada County to Truckee River 12.5 miles northeast of Truckee (lat. 39°26'40" N, long. 120°00'30" W; sec. 7, T 18 N, R 18 E). Named on Boca (1955) 7.5' quadrangle.

Purdon Bridge: see **Purdon Crossing** [NEVADA].

Purdon Creek [NEVADA]: *stream,* flows 0.5 mile to South Yuba River 4.5 miles north-northwest of Nevada City (lat. 39°19'40" N, long. 121°02'50" W; sec. 23, T 17 N, R 8 E). Named on Nevada City (1948) 7.5' quadrangle.

Purdon Crossing [NEVADA]: *locality,* 4.5 miles north-northwest of Nevada City along South Yuba River (lat. 39°19'40" N, long. 121° 02'45" W; sec. 23, T 17 N, R 8 E); the place is near the mouth of Purdon Creek. Named on Nevada City (1948) 7.5' quadrangle. Called Purdon Bridge on Smartsville (1895) 30' quadrangle. The bridge at the place first was known as Wall's Bridge, then as Webber's Bridge, and finally as Purdon's Bridge (Hoover, Rensch, and Rensch, p. 249-250).

Purdue Lake [SUTTER]: *lake,* 0.5 mile long, 9 miles south-southwest of Sutter in Sutter Basin (lat. 39°02'15" N, long. 121°47'10" W; sec. 30, T 14 N, R 2 E). Named on Tisdale Weir (1952) 7.5' quadrangle. Called McIntyre Lake on Tisdale Weir (1912) 7.5' quadrangle.

Purdy [SIERRA]: *locality,* 13 miles east of Loyalton along Western Pacific Railroad (lat. 39°40'20" N, long. 120°00'10" W; sec. 19, T 21 N, R 18 E). Named on Loyalton (1955) 15' quadrangle. Called Purdys on California Mining Bureau's (1909a) map. Postal authorities established Purdys post office in 1889, moved it 2 miles west in 1891, and discontinued it in 1911; the name was for the Purdy family, who operated a store and travelers stop (Salley, p. 179).

Purdy Creek [SIERRA]: *stream,* flows 4 miles to Upper Long Valley 12 miles east of Loyalton (lat. 39°38'35" N, long. 120°01'35" W; sec. 25, T 21 N, R 17 E). Named on Dog Valley (1981) and Evans Canyon (1978) 7.5' quadrangles.

Purdys: see **Purdy** [SIERRA].

Puta Creek: see **Putah Creek** [YOLO].

Putah Creek [YOLO]: *stream,* heads in Lake County and Napa County, flows 26 miles along Yolo-Solano County line to finally enter Yolo County and end there 2.5 miles east of downtown Davis (lat. 38°32'35" N, long. 121°41'50" W; sec. 13, T 8 N, R 2 E). Named on Allendale (1953), Davis (1952), Merritt (1952), Monticello Dam (1959), Mount Vaca (1951), and Winters (1953) 7.5' quadrangles. Called Arroyo de los Putos on a diseño of 1844 (Becker), and called Puta Cr. on Eddy's (1854) map, but United States Board on Geographic Names (1933, p. 625) rejected the form "Puta" for the name. Williamson (p. 39) referred to Putos Creek in 1857. According to Gudde (1949, p. 276), the name is from the designation of Indians who lived along the stream, but Kroeber (p. 56) rejected an Indian origin for the name and attributed it to *puta,* which means "harlot" in Spanish. Malony (*in* Work, p. 93) identified Putah 'Creek as the stream that Duflet de Mofras called Young's River in 1844. South Fork diverges from Putah Creek into Solano County nearly 2 miles southwest of Davis, and then returns to Yolo County to flow 6 miles to Putah Creek Sinks 5.5 miles southwest of West Sacramento in Yolo Bypass (lat. 38°31'05" N, long. 121°36'15" W). South Fork is named on Davis (1952, photorevised 1968 and 1975) and Sacramento West (1967) 7.5' quadrangles.

Putah Creek Sinks [YOLO]: *area,* 5.5 miles southwest of West Sacramento in Yolo Bypass (lat. 38°31' N, long. 121°36'15" W); the place is at the lower end of South Fork Putah Creek. Named on Sacramento West (1967) 7.5' quadrangle.

Putnam Valley [PLACER]: *valley,* 1 mile south-southwest of Emigrant Gap (1) along present Fulda Creek (lat. 38°17'15" N, long. 120°40'15" W). Named on Colfax (1898) 30' quadrangle.

Putos Creek: see **Putah Creek** [YOLO].

Put's Bar: see **China Gulch** [AMADOR] (1).

Putt: see **Lake Putt** [PLACER].

Putts Bar: see **China Gulch** [AMADOR] (1).

Pyramid Campground [EL DORADO]: *locality,* 4 miles south-southwest of Pyramid Peak along South Fork American River (lat. 38°47'20" N, long. 120°11' W; sec. 23, T 11 N, R 16 E). Named on Pyramid Peak (1955) 7.5' quadrangle.

Pyramid Creek [EL DORADO]: *stream,* flows 5 miles to South Fork American River 3 miles south-southeast of Pyramid Peak (lat. 38° 48'25" N, long. 120°07'50" W; near N line sec. 17, T 11 N, R 17 E). Named on Echo Lake (1955) and Pyramid Peak (1955) 7.5' quadrangles.

Pyramid Lake [EL DORADO]: *lake,* 1500 feet long, 1 mile east-northeast of Pyramid Peak (lat. 38°50'55" N, long. 120°08'25" W). Named on Pyramid Peak (1955) 7.5' quadrangle.

Pyramid Peak [EL DORADO]: *peak,* 35 miles east of Placerville (lat. 38°50'45" N, long. 120°09'25" W). Altitude 9983 feet. Named on Pyramid Peak (1955) 7.5' quadrangle.

Pyramid Peak [NEVADA]: *peak,* 4.5 miles east-northeast of Graniteville (lat. 39°28'20" N, long. 120°39'50" W; sec. 31, T 19 N, R 12 E). Altitude 5925 feet. Named on Graniteville (1982) 7.5' quadrangle.

—Q—

Q Ranch: see **Ione** [AMADOR].

Quail Lake [PLACER]: *lake,* 1200 feet long, 1.25 miles south of Homewood (lat. 39°04'10" N, long. 120°09'55" W; on W line sec. 12, T 14 N, R 16 E). Named on Homewood (1955) 7.5' quadrangle.

Quail Trap Ravine [PLACER]: *canyon,* drained by a stream that flows less than 1 mile to Bunch Canyon 4.25 miles south-southeast of Colfax (lat. 39°02'35" N, long. 120°55'25" W; at N line sec. 25, T 14 N, R 9 E). Named on Colfax (1949) 7.5' quadrangle.

Quaker Hill [NEVADA]:

(1) *peak,* 7 miles south of North Bloomfield (lat. 39°16'05" N, long. 120°54'10" W; sec. 7, T 16 N, R 10 E). Named on North Bloomfield (1949) 7.5' quadrangle.

(2) *locality,* 7.25 miles south of North Bloomfield (lat. 39°15'45" N, long. 120°54'10" W; near W line sec. 7, T 16 N, R 10 E); the place is 0.25 mile south of present Quaker Hill (1). Named on Colfax (1938) 30' quadrangle. Gudde (1975, p. 25, 63, 286) listed a mining place called Red Diamond that was located about 3 miles northeast of Quaker Hill, a settlement called Balaklava that was located about 4 miles northeast of Quaker Hill, and a mining place called Cascade Diggings that was located about 3.5 miles northeast of Quaker Hill.

Quarry: see **Mills** [COLUSA].

Quartzburg: see **Nashville** [EL DORADO].

Quartz Canyon [EL DORADO]: *canyon,* drained by a stream that flows 1.25 miles to Otter Creek 4.25 miles north-northeast of Georgetown (lat. 38°57'40" N, long. 120°47'55" W; near W line sec. 19, T 13 N, R 11 E). Named on Georgetown (1949) 7.5' quadrangle.

Quartz Hill [NEVADA]: *ridge,* southwest- to west-trending, 1 mile long, 4.25 miles west-northwest of English Mountain (lat. 39°28'10" N, long. 120°37'30" W; on E line sec. 33, T 19 N, R 12 E). Named on English Mountain (1983) and Graniteville (1982) 7.5' quadrangles.

Quartz Mountain [AMADOR]: *peak,* 3 miles southeast of Plymouth (lat. 38°26'50" N, long. 120°48'35" W; sec. 19, T 7 N, R 11 E). Named on Amador City (1962) 7.5' quadrangle.

Quartz Point [SIERRA]: *peak,* 4 miles east-southeast of Downieville (lat. 39°32'30" N, long. 120°45'10" W; near W line sec. 4, T 19 N, R 11 E). Altitude 5403 feet. Named on Downieville (1951) 7.5' quadrangle.

Quartzville: see **Nashville** [EL DORADO].

Quayle Ravine [YUBA]: *canyon,* drained by a stream that flows 1 mile to North Yuba River 3.25 miles south-southeast of Strawberry Valley (lat. 39°31'10" N, long. 121°05'15" W; at N line sec. 16, T 19 N, R 8 E). Named on Strawberry Valley (1948) 7.5' quadrangle.

Queen City [SIERRA]: *locality,* 6.5 miles southwest of Mount Fillmore (lat. 39°39'50" N, long. 120°56'25" W; sec. 23, T 21 N, R 9 E). Named on La Porte (1951) 7.5' quadrangle.

Quesisosi: see **Guesisosi** [YOLO].
Quicksilver: see **Davis Creek** [YOLO].
Quinn: see **Jim Quinn Spring** [EL DORADO].
Quinn Canyon [NEVADA]: *canyon,* drained by a stream that flows 1.25 miles to Middle Yuba River 7.5 miles northeast of North Bloomfield (lat. 39°26'30" N, long. 120°47'35" W; sec. 7, T 18 N, R 11 E). Named on Alleghany (1949) 7.5' quadrangle, which shows Quinn ranch situated near the head of the canyon.
Quintette [EL DORADO]: *locality,* 12 miles north-northwest of Pollock Pines (lat. 38°54'55" N, long. 120°41'05" W; near SW cor. sec. 6, T 12 N, R 12 E). Named on Tunnel Hill (1950) 7.5' quadrangle. Postal authorities established Quintette post office in 1903, moved it 0.5 mile northwest in 1906, and discontinued it in 1912 (Salley, p. 180).

— R —

Rabbit Creek [AMADOR]: *stream,* flows 1.25 miles to Camanche Reservoir 6.5 miles south-southwest of Ione (lat. 38°15'50" N, long. 120°58'25" W). Named on Ione (1962) and Wallace (1962) 7.5' quadrangles.
Rabbit Flat [AMADOR]: *area,* 2.5 miles south-southwest of Jackson (lat. 38°18'40" N, long. 120°47'25" W; near S line sec. 5, T 5 N, R 11 E). Named on Jackson (1962) 7.5' quadrangle.
Rab Ravine [NEVADA]: *canyon,* 1.25 miles long, 3 miles west of Wolf (lat. 39°03'20" N, long. 121°11'55" W; on S line sec. 16, T 14 N, R 7 E). Named on Wolf (1949) 7.5' quadrangle.
Racetrack Bend: see **Bullock Bend** [SUTTER-YOLO].
Race Track Hill [PLACER]: *ridge,* west- to south-southwest-trending, 1 mile long, 3 miles east-southeast of Colfax (lat. 39°05'25" N, long. 120°54' W; sec. 6, T 14 N, R 10 E). Named on Colfax (1949) 7.5' quadrangle.
Race Track Point [YUBA]: *relief feature,* nearly 3 miles south-southeast of Strawberry Valley above North Yuba River near the mouth of Slate Creek (lat. 39°31'30" N, long. 121°05'25" W; sec. 9, T 19 N, R 8 E). Named on Strawberry Valley (1948) 7.5' quadrangle.
Rackerby [YUBA]: *village,* 24 miles north-northeast of Marysville (lat. 39°26'25" N, long. 121°20'25" W; at S line sec. 6, T 18 N, R 6 E). Named on Rackerby (1948) 7.5' quadrangle. Postal authorities established Rackerby post office in 1892, moved it to Butte County in 1930, and moved it back to Yuba County in 1934; the name is for William M. Rackerby, first postmaster (Salley, p. 180).
Raffetto [EL DORADO]: *locality,* 6.25 miles north of Riverton (lat. 38°51'50" N, long. 120°26'20" W; near NW cor. sec. 29, T 12 N, R 14 E). Named on Riverton (1950) 7.5' quadrangle.
Ragsdale Creek [NEVADA]: *stream,* flows 2 miles to Wolf Creek less than 1 mile west-northwest of Higgins Corner (lat. 39°02'45" N, long. 121°06'30" W; sec. 20, T 14 N, R 8 E). Named on Lake Combie (1949) 7.5' quadrangle.
Rail Canyon [COLUSA]: *canyon,* 3.5 miles long, 6 miles north of Lodoga on Colusa-Glenn County line (lat. 39°23' N, long. 122° 28' W). Named on Lodoga (1960) 15' quadrangle.
Rail Canyon: see **South Rail Canyon** [COLUSA].
Railroad Bend [SUTTER-YOLO]: *bend,* nearly 2 miles southwest of Robbins along Sacramento River on Sutter-Yolo County line (lat. 38°51'05" N, long. 121°43'25" W; at S line sec. 26, T 12 N, R 2 E). Named on Knights Landing (1952) 7.5' quadrangle.
Rail Road Gulch: see **Camptonville** [YUBA].
Rail Road Hill: see **Camptonville** [YUBA].
Rainbow [PLACER]: *settlement,* 1.5 miles east of Cisco Grove (lat. 38°18'35" N, long. 120°30'30" W; near W line sec. 27, T 17 N, R 13 E). Named on Cisco Grove (1955) 7.5' quadrangle.
Ralston [PLACER]: *locality,* 4 miles southeast of Michigan Bluff (lat. 39°00'20" N, long. 120°40'35" W; sec. 6, T 13 N, R 12 E). Named on Colfax (1938) 30' quadrangle. Michigan Bluff (1952) 7.5' quadrangle shows Ralston mine near the site—financier William C. Ralston owned a hydraulic-mining claim there (Salley, p. 180).
Ralston Divide: see **Ralston Ridge** [PLACER].
Ralston Lake [EL DORADO]: *lake,* 1150 feet long, 4.25 miles west-northwest of Echo Summit (lat. 38°50'30" N, long. 120°05'55" W; on W line sec. 34, T 12 N, R 17 E); the lake is 0.5 mile north of Ralston Peak. Named on Echo Lake (1955) 7.5' quadrangle.
Ralston Peak [EL DORADO]: *peak,* 4 miles west-northwest of Echo Summit (lat. 38°50' N, long. 120°06' W); the peak is 0.5 mile south of Ralston Lake. Altitude 9235 feet. Named on Echo Lake (1955) 7.5' quadrangle.
Ralston Ridge [PLACER]: *ridge,* extends southwest and west for 13 miles between Middle Fork American River and Long Canyon from near the site of French House to the junction of Middle Fork and Long Canyon. Named on Devil Peak (1950), Greek Store (1952), Michigan Bluff (1952), and Tunnel Hill (1950) 7.5' quadrangles. Gudde (1975, p. 282) called the feature Ralston Divide, and noted that it was named for William C. Ralston.
Ramirez [YUBA]: *locality,* 9 miles north-northeast of Marysville along Southern Pacific Railroad (lat. 39°16' N, long. 121°32'20" W; near SE cor. sec. 5, T 16 N, R 4 E). Named on Honcut (1952) 7.5' quadrangle. Postal authorities established Ramirez post office in 1889 and discontinued it in 1890 (Frickstad, p. 224). California Division of Highways' (1934) map shows a place called Mission located 1 mile north-northeast of Ramirez along the railroad (at S line sec. 33, T 17 N, R 4 E).
Ramms Ranch [YUBA]: *locality,* 2 miles west-northwest of Camptonville (lat. 39°28' N, long. 121°05' W). Named on Smartsville (1895) 30' quadrangle. Gudde (1975, p. 282) listed a mining community called Ramms Ranch that was named for John Ramm—it also was called Dutchmans Ranch.
Ramona [SACRAMENTO]: *locality,* 5 miles east-southeast of downtown Sacramento along Southern Pacific Railroad (lat. 38°32'50" N, long. 121°24'20" W; near W line sec. 14, T 8 N, R 5 E). Named on Sacramento East (1967) 7.5' quadrangle.
Rampart [PLACER]: *locality,* nearly 2 miles west-southwest of Tahoe City along Truckee River (lat. 39°09'55" N, long. 120°10'35" W; sec. 11, T 15 N, R 16 E). Named on Tahoe City (1955) 7.5' quadrangle. Truckee (1940) 30' quadrangle shows the place along Southern Pacific Railroad. California Division of Highways' (1934) map shows a place called Moss Hills situated along the railroad about halfway between Rampart and Tahoe (present Tahoe City) (sec. 12, T 15 N, R 16 E).
Ramsey Crossing [PLACER]: *locality,* 2.5 miles north of Devil Peak in Long Canyon (lat. 38°59'55" N, long. 120°13'10" W; near N line sec. 8, T 13 N, R 13 E). Named on Devil Peak (1950) 7.5' quadrangle.
Ramshorn Bar: see **Ramshorn Creek** [SIERRA].
Ramshorn Camp Ground [SIERRA]: *locality,* 1.5 miles west of Goodyears Bar (lat. 39°32'25" N, long. 120°54'45" W; sec. 1, T 19 N, R 9 E); the place is near the mouth of Ramshorn Creek. Named on Goodyears Bar (1951) 7.5' quadrangle. Called Ramshorn Camp on Downieville (1951) 15' quadrangle.
Ramshorn Creek [SIERRA]: *stream,* flows 2 miles to North Yuba River 1.5 miles west of Goodyears Bar (lat. 39°30'20" N, long. 120°54'40" W; sec. 1, T 19 N, R 9 E). Named on Goodyears Bar (1951) 7.5' quadrangle. A place called St. Joe Bar, or Ramshorn Bar, was located along Ramshorn Creek about 2 miles west of Goodyears Bar (Gudde, 1975, p. 301), and a place called Nigger Slide was situated on the steep slope above St. Joe's Bar (Hoover, Rensch, and Rensch, p. 491). A place called Pierces Bar was located near St. Joe Bar; later the name "Pierces Bar" was changed to Convicts Bar for the convicts who worked there on road crews between 1918 and 1920 (Gudde, 1975, p. 264).
Rancheria [AMADOR]: *locality,* 4 miles northwest of Pine Grove (lat. 38°27'35" N, long. 120°42'10" W; near W line sec. 18, T 7 N, R 12 E); the site is 1 mile north of Rancheria Creek. Named on Pine Grove (1948) 7.5' quadrangle. The place also was known as Upper Rancheria (Gudde, 1975, p. 283). A community also called Rancheria—or Old Rancheria, or Lower Rancheria to distinguish it from Upper Rancheria—was located along Dry Creek southwest of Drytown (Watson, p. 413).
Rancheria Creek [AMADOR]: *stream,* flows 14 miles to Amador Creek 4 miles south-southwest of Plymouth (lat. 38°25'30" N, long. 120°52'20" W; near NW cor. sec. 34, T 7 N, R 10 E). Named on Amador City (1962) and Pine Grove (1948) 7.5' quadrangles. North Fork enters from the east 4 miles east-southeast of Plymouth; it is 6 miles long and is named on Amador City (1962) 7.5' quadrangle.
Rancho Cordova [SACRAMENTO]: *city,* 2 miles southeast of downtown Carmichael (lat. 38°36' N, long. 121°17'45" W). Named on Carmichael (1967) 7.5' quadrangle. Postal authorities established Rancho Cordova post office in 1955; the name is from Cordova Vinyards (Salley, p. 181).
Randall [SACRAMENTO]: *locality,* 2 miles east-northeast of Courtland (lat. 38°20'45" N, long. 121°32'05" W; near W line sec. 27, T 6 N, R 4 E); the place is at the northeast end of Randall Island. Named on Courtland (1952) 7.5' quadrangle.
Randall: see **White Hall** [EL DORADO].
Randall Island [SACRAMENTO]: *ridge,* east-northeast-trending, 1.5 miles long, 1 mile northeast of Courtland near Sacramento River (lat. 38°20'25" N, long. 121°33' W). Named on Courtland (1978) 7.5' quadrangle. Shown as an island called Hensley I. on Ringgold's (1850b) map.
Randolph [SIERRA]: *locality,* less than 1 mile south of Sierraville (lat. 39°34'45" N, long. 120°22'10" W; near S line sec. 13, T 20 N, R 14 E). Named on Sierraville (1981) 7.5' quadrangle. Called Etta on Sierraville (1894) 30' quadrangle. Postal authorities established Etta post office in 1883 and discontinued it in 1895 (Frickstad, p. 184).
Randolph Canyon [EL DORADO]:
(1) *canyon,* drained by a stream that flows 1.25 miles to South Fork American River 1.5 miles northeast of Pollock Pines (lat. 38°46'35" N, long. 120°34' W; sec. 30, T 11 N, R 13 E). Named on Pollock Pines (1950) 7.5' quadrangle.
(2) *canyon,* drained by a stream that flows nearly 3 miles to Hangtown Creek 0.25 mile east-northeast of downtown Placerville (lat. 38°43'50" N, long. 120°47'25" W; sec. 8, T 10 N, R 11 E). Named on Placerville (1949) 7.5' quadrangle.
Randolph Flat [NEVADA]: *area,* nearly 3 miles west-northwest of Grass

Valley (lat. 39°14'05" N, long. 121°06'30" W; on W line sec. 20, T 16 N, R 8 E). Named on Grass Valley (1949) 7.5' quadrangle.

Randolph Hill [SIERRA]: *hill,* 1.25 miles south-southwest of Sierraville (lat. 39°34'25" N, long. 120°22'35" W; sec. 24, T 20 N, R 14 E); the hill is 0.5 mile southwest of Randolph. Altitude 5619 feet. Named on Sattley (1981) and Sierraville (1981) 7.5' quadrangles.

Randolph House: see **Rough and Ready** [NEVADA].

Ranlett: see **Sunnybrook** [AMADOR].

Ranse Doddler Bar: see **Rantedodler Bar**, under **Goodyears Bar** [SIERRA].

Rantedodler Bar: see **Goodyears Bar** [SIERRA].

Ranty Doddler Bar: see **Rantedodler Bar**, under **Goodyears Bar** [SIERRA].

Rapp Ravine [NEVADA]: *canyon,* drained by a stream that flows 1.5 miles to Kentucky Ravine 2.25 miles southwest of French Corral (lat. 39°16'50" N, long. 121°11'25" W; near NE cor. sec. 4, T 16 N, R 7 E). Named on French Corral (1948) 7.5' quadrangle. Smartsville (1895) 30' quadrangle shows Rapps ranch at the head of the canyon.

Rapps Ravine [SIERRA]: *canyon,* drained by a stream that flows 1 mile to Kanaka Creek 2 miles southwest of Alleghany (lat. 39°27'15" N, long. 120°52'05" W; near SE cor. sec. 5, T 18 N, R 10 E). Named on Alleghany (1949) 7.5' quadrangle.

Rattlesnake: see **Rattlesnake Bar** [PLACER].

Rattlesnake Bar [NEVADA-SIERRA]: *locality,* 3.5 miles east-southeast of Alleghany along Middle Yuba River on Nevada-Sierra County line (lat. 39°26'50" N, long. 120°47'50" W; at S line sec. 6, T 18 N, R 11 E). Named on Alleghany (1949) 7.5' quadrangle.

Rattlesnake Bar [PLACER]: *locality,* 6 miles south of Auburn along North Fork American River (lat. 38°49' N, long. 121°05'30" W; sec. 9, T 11 N, R 8 E). Site named on Auburn (1954) 15' quadrangle. Water of Folsom Lake now covers the site. Postal authorities established Rattlesnake Bar post office in 1854, discontinued it in 1869, reestablished it with the name "Rattlesnake" in 1882, and discontinued it in 1883 (Salley, p. 181). The community, which was named for a mining place along North Fork, was above the river on a level place known as Rattlesnake Flat (Hoover, Rensch, and Rensch, p. 268-269). Arrowsmith's (1860) map shows a place called Manhattan Bar located along North Fork about 1.5 miles north-northeast of Rattlesnake Bar. Gudde (1975, p. 199) listed a mining place called Lorenz Bar that was located on both sides of North Fork American River above Rattlesnake Bar, and (p. 30) a place called Beaver Bar, or Rich Bar, that was located on both sides of North Fork below Rattlesnake Bar.

Rattlesnake Bar: see **Little Rattlesnake Bar**, under **Auburn** [PLACER].

Rattlesnake Bridge [EL DORADO]: *locality,* 4.5 miles west-southwest of the village of Pilot Hill along North Fork American River (lat. 38°48'50" N, long. 121°05'20" W; near S line sec. 9, T 11 N, R 8 E). Named on Auburn (1944) 15' quadrangle, which shows the site of Rattlesnake Bar [PLACER] across North Fork from Rattlesnake Bridge. Water of Folsom Lake now covers the site.

Rattlesnake Creek [AMADOR]:

(1) *stream,* flows 3 miles to Bear River 6 miles east-southeast of Hams Station (lat. 38°31'10" N, long. 120°15'55" W; sec. 25, T 8 N, R 15 E). Named on Peddler Hill (1951) 7.5' quadrangle.

(2) *stream,* flows 1.5 miles to Butte Canyon 1.5 miles south of Jackson Butte (lat. 38°19' N, long. 120°43'15" W; sec. 1, T 5 N, R 11 E). Named on Mokelumne Hill (1948) 7.5' quadrangle.

Rattlesnake Creek [NEVADA]:

(1) *stream,* flows 1.5 miles to Middle Yuba River 1.5 miles north of Graniteville (lat. 39°27'40" N, long. 120°44'30" W; near N line sec. 4, T 18 N, R 11 E). Named on Graniteville (1982) 7.5' quadrangle.

(2) *stream,* flows 5.25 miles to Wolf Creek 6.5 miles south of Grass Valley (lat. 39°07'35" N, long. 121°05'05" W; near E line sec. 28, T 15 N, R 8 E). Named on Grass Valley (1949) 7.5' quadrangle.

Rattlesnake Creek [NEVADA-PLACER]: *stream,* heads in Nevada County and flows 7 miles to South Yuba River 3.5 miles east of Yuba Gap just inside Placer County (lat. 39°18'50" N, long. 120° 33' W; near NE cor. sec. 30, T 17 N, R 13 E). Named on Cisco Grove (1955) and Soda Springs (1955) 7.5' quadrangles.

Rattlesnake Creek [SIERRA]: *stream,* flows nearly 3 miles to Downie River 6 miles south of Mount Fillmore (lat. 39°38'30" N, long. 120°49'40" W). Named on Mount Fillmore (1951) 7.5' quadrangle.

Rattlesnake Flat: see **Rattlesnake Bar** [PLACER].

Rattlesnake Glade [COLUSA]: *area,* 2 miles west of Fouts Springs (lat. 39°21'30" N, long. 122°42' W; on E line sec. 1, T 17 N, R 8 W). Named on Fouts Springs (1968) 7.5' quadrangle.

Rattlesnake Mountain [NEVADA-PLACER]: *peak,* 0.5 mile northeast of Cisco Grove on Nevada-Placer County line (lat. 39°18'55" N, long. 120°31'45" W; at NE cor. sec. 29, T 17 N, R 13 E); the peak is 1 mile east of the mouth of Rattlesnake Creek [NEVADA-PLACER]. Altitude 6959 feet. Named on Cisco Grove (1955) 7.5' quadrangle.

Rattlesnake Peak [SIERRA]: *peak,* 4.5 miles southeast of Mount Fillmore (lat. 39°41' N, long. 120°47'15" W; sec. 18, T 21 N, R 11 E). Altitude 7219 feet. Named on Mount Fillmore (1951) 7.5' quadrangle.

Rawhide [PLACER]: *locality,* nearly 5 miles east of Dutch Flat (lat. 39°12'05" N, long. 120°44'45" W; at N line sec. 4, T 15 N, R 11 E). Named on Colfax (1938) 30' quadrangle. Westville (1952) 7.5' quadrangle shows Rawhide mine near the site.

Ray Hill [YUBA]: *peak,* 2.5 miles south of Smartville (lat. 39°10'10" N, long. 121°17'25" W; sec. 10, T 15 N, R 6 E). Altitude 1104 feet. Named on Smartville (1951) 7.5' quadrangle.

Rays Flat: see **Grass Valley** [NEVADA].

Red Ant [SIERRA]: *locality,* 2.5 miles northwest of Downieville (lat. 39°35'05" N, long. 120°51'30" W; sec. 21, T 20 N, R 10 E). Named on Downieville (1951) 7.5' quadrangle.

Red Bank: see **Mormon Island** [SACRAMENTO].

Redbird Canyon [EL DORADO]: *canyon,* 0.5 mile long, opens into the canyon of South Fork American River 7.25 miles west of Pollock Pines (lat. 38°46'40" N, long. 120°43' W; near N line sec. 26, T 11 N, R 11 E); the canyon is along lower reaches of Redbird Creek. Named on Slate Mountain (1950) 7.5' quadrangle.

Redbird Creek [EL DORADO]: *stream,* flows 2 miles to South Fork American River 7.25 miles west of Pollock Pines (lat. 38°46'40" N, long. 120°43' W; near N line sec. 26, T 11 N, R 11 E). Named on Slate Mountain (1950) 7.5' quadrangle. Placerville (1893) 30' quadrangle has the form "Red Bird Creek" for the name.

Red Bluff [YUBA]: *relief feature,* 2.5 miles southeast of Dobbins on the north side of Yuba River (lat. 39°20'40" N, long. 121°10'40" W; sec. 10, T 17 N, R 7 E). Named on French Corral (1948) 7.5' quadrangle.

Red Cliffs [PLACER]: *relief feature,* 2 miles east-northeast of Bunker Hill (lat. 39°03'20" N, long. 120°20'40" W; on W line sec. 18, T 14 N, R 15 E). Named on Wentworth Springs (1953) 7.5' quadrangle.

Red Diamond: see **Quaker Hill** [NEVADA] (2).

Red Diggins [EL DORADO]: *locality,* 5.5 miles northeast of Georgetown in Missouri Canyon (lat. 38°57'55" N, long. 120°46'15" W; sec. 20, T 13 N, R 11 E). Named on Georgetown (1949) 7.5' quadrangle.

Red Dog [NEVADA]: *locality,* 6 miles north-northeast of Chicago Park (lat. 39°13' N, long. 120°53'55" W; at S line sec. 30, T 16 N, R 10 E); the place is 1 mile west of Chalk Bluff. Named on Chicago Park (1949) 7.5' quadrangle. Postal authorities established Red Dog post office in 1855 and discontinued it in 1869 (Frickstad, p. 114). Goddard's (1857) map has the name "Brooklin" for a place located just south of Red Dog, and Whitney's (1873) map shows a community called Chalk Bluffs situated 1.5 miles east of Red Dog. Charlie Wilson of Illinois and his companions found gold in 1850 on an elevation that they named Red Dog Hill after a place in Illinois where Wilson had mined lead and zinc; two camps, called Red Dog and Chalk Bluffs, were started, but soon the residents of Chalk Bluffs moved to Red Dog, where the inhabitants voted to change the name of the place to Brooklyn, but postal authorities rejected the name "Brooklyn" and accepted the name "Red Dog" (Gudde, 1975, p. 286).

Red Dog Hill: see **Red Dog** [NEVADA].

Red Dog You Bet Diggings [NEVADA]: *locality,* 6.25 miles northeast of Chicago Park (lat. 39°12'45" N, long. 120°53'15" W); the place is east of Red Dog and You Bet. Named on Chicago Park (1949) 7.5' quadrangle.

Red Eye Spring [COLUSA]: *spring,* 0.25 mile west-southwest of Fouts Springs (lat. 39°21'05" N, long. 122°40'15" W; near SW cor. sec. 5, T 17 N, R 7 W). Named on Fouts Springs (1968) 7.5' quadrangle.

Red Hill [NEVADA]: *peak,* 3.5 miles west of English Mountain (lat. 39°26'40" N, long. 120°37' W; sec. 10, T 18 N, R 12 E). Altitude 7060 feet. Named on English Mountain (1983) 7.5' quadrangle.

Red Hill [PLACER]: *peak,* nearly 4 miles east of Colfax (lat. 39°05'50" N, long. 120°52'55" W; near NE cor. sec. 6, T 14 N, R 10 E). Named on Colfax (1949) 7.5' quadrangle.

Red Hill [YUBA]: *ridge,* northwest-trending, 1.5 miles long, 5.5 miles south-southwest of Oregon House (lat. 39°17'10" N, long. 121°19'55" W). Named on Oregon House (1948) 7.5' quadrangle.

Red Hill Spring [NEVADA]: *spring,* 10 miles northeast of Chicago Park (lat. 39°14'55" N, long. 120°50'50" W; sec. 15, T 16 N, R 10 E). Named on Dutch Flat (1950) 7.5' quadrangle.

Redlands: see **The Redlands** [COLUSA].

Red Mountain [EL DORADO]: *peak,* 1 mile west-southwest of Wentworth Springs (lat. 39°00'25" N, long. 120°21'20" W; near N line sec. 1, T 13 N, R 14 E). Altitude 6872 feet. Named on Wentworth Springs (1953) 7.5' quadrangle. Called Red Peak on Truckee (1895) 30' quadrangle.

Red Mountain [NEVADA]:

(1) *ridge,* east-northeast-trending, 1 mile long, 5 miles north-northeast of Donner Pass (lat. 39°23'05" N, long. 120°17'50" W; mainly in sec. 27, T 18 N, R 15 E). Named on Independence Lake (1981) 7.5' quadrangle. On Donner Pass (1955) 15' quadrangle, the name applies to a peak on the ridge.

(2) *ridge,* west-southwest-trending, 2.5 miles long, 4.5 miles east-northeast of Yuba Gap (lat. 39°20'15" N, long. 120°32'15" W). Named on Cisco Grove (1955) 7.5' quadrangle.

Red Oak Canyon [SIERRA]: *canyon,* drained by a stream that flows 3 miles to Empire Creek 7.25 miles southeast of Mount Fillmore (lat. 39°38'40" N, long. 120°46'30" W; near N line sec. 32, T 21 N, R 11 E). Named on Mount Fillmore (1951) 7.5' quadrangle.

Red Peak [EL DORADO]: *peak,* 4.25 miles west-southwest of Phipps Peak (lat. 38°55'30" N, long. 120°13'15" W; at N line sec. 4, T 12 N, R 16 E). Altitude 9307 feet. Named on Rockbound Valley (1955) 7.5' quadrangle.

Red Peak: see **Red Mountain** [EL DORADO].

Red Point [PLACER]: *relief feature,* 3.5 miles southwest of Westville (lat. 39°08'55" N, long. 120°42' W; sec. 14, T 15 N, R 11 E). Named on Westville (1952) 7.5' quadrangle. Colfax (1898) 30' quadrangle has the name "Red Point" for an inhabited place near the feature.

Red Ridge [COLUSA]: *ridge,* south-trending, 1.5 miles long, 4.5 miles east of Pacific Point on Colusa-Lake County line (lat. 39°12'05" N, long. 122°30'50" W). Named on Clearlake Oaks (1960) 15' quadrangle.

Red Star Point [PLACER]: *peak,* 7 miles south of Duncan Peak (lat. 39°03'10" N, long. 120°32' W; sec. 21, T 14 N, R 13 E); the peak is near the southwest end of Red Star Ridge. Altitude 4883 feet. Named on Greek Store (1952) 7.5' quadrangle.

Red Star Ravine [SIERRA]: *canyon,* drained by a stream that flows 0.5 mile to North Fork Kanaka Creek 0.25 mile east-northeast of Alleghany (lat. 39°28'25" N, long. 120°50'10" W; sec. 34, T 19 N, R 10 E). Named on Alleghany (1949) 7.5' quadrangle.

Red Star Ridge [PLACER]: *ridge,* south-southwest-trending, 13 miles long, between Duncan Canyon and Middle Fork American River; center 10 miles west-southwest of Granite Chief (lat. 39° 08' N, long. 120°27' W); Red Star Point is near the southwest end of the ridge. Named on Bunker Hill (1953), Greek Store (1952), and Royal Gorge (1953) 7.5' quadrangles.

Reed: see **Ostrom** [YUBA].

Reed Junction: see **Arboga** [YUBA].

Reeds: see **Reeds Creek** [YUBA].

Reeds Creek [YUBA]: *stream,* flows 6.5 miles to lowlands 6 miles south-southwest of Browns Valley (lat. 39°09'50" N, long. 121° 27' W; at W line sec. 8, T 15 N, R 5 E). Named on Browns Valley (1947) and Olivehurst (1952) 7.5' quadrangles. Ostrom (1911) 7.5' quadrangle shows the stream extending across lowlands to Plumas Lake. Wescoatt's (1861) map has the name "Reeds Dry Creek" for the stream, which it shows extending all the way to Feather River 9.5 miles south of Marysville. The same map has the name "Reeds" by a building near the stream (near S line sec. 16, T 14 N, R 4 E).

Reeds Dry Creek: see **Reeds Creek** [YUBA].

Reeds Station: see **Ostrom** [YUBA].

Reese Ravine [SIERRA]: *canyon,* drained by a stream that flows 1.5 miles to Little Canyon Creek nearly 5 miles south-southwest of Mount Fillmore (lat. 39°39'45" N, long. 120°52'30" W; at W line sec. 21, T 21 N, R 10 E). Named on Mount Fillmore (1951) 7.5' quadrangle, which shows Reese mine near the head of the canyon.

Refuge Canyon [PLACER]: *canyon,* drained by a stream that flows 1.5 miles to New York Canyon 4 miles north-northwest of Foresthill (lat. 39°04'20" N, long. 120°51'30" W; sec. 9, T 14 N, R 10 E). Named on Foresthill (1949) 7.5' quadrangle. Whitney's (1880) map shows an inhabited place called Wisconsin Hill located on the ridge between Refuge Canyon and New York Canyon, and shows an inhabited place called Elizabeth Hill situated between Refuge Canyon and Indian Canyon, which holds Indian Creek (2) of modern maps.

Reiff Canyon [YOLO]: *canyon,* drained by a stream that flows 1.5 miles to Capay Valley 4 miles northwest of Guinda (lat. 38°52'25" N, long. 122°14' W; sec. 19, T 12 N, R 3 W). Named on Knoxville (1958) and Guinda (1959) 7.5' quadrangles.

Relief [NEVADA]: *locality,* 3.25 miles west of Washington (lat. 39° 21'40" N, long. 120°51'35" W; sec. 4, T 17 N, R 10 E). Named on Washington (1950) 7.5' quadrangle. Called Relief Hill on Whitney's 1873) map, which shows a place called Louisa situated less than 1 mile south of Relief Hill along South Yuba River, and shows a feature called Cotton Hill located 1.5 miles southeast of Relief Hill. The name "Relief" is from a station established at the site by the first relief group sent to rescue Donner Party survivors in 1847 (Hanna, p. 253). The place also was called Grizzly Hill (Bancroft, 1888, p. 358). Gudde (1975, p. 96) listed a mining place called Diggers Bar that was located 1 mile below Relief on the south side of South Yuba River, and (p. 53) a mining place called Burks Bar that was situated 3 miles above Relief on the south side of the river.

Relief Hill [NEVADA]: *ridge,* west-southwest-trending, 2 miles long, 3 miles east-northeast of North Bloomfield (lat. 39°23' N, long. 120°51'30" W); the ridge is 2 miles north of Relief. Named on Colfax (1898) 30' quadrangle.

Relief Hill: see **Relief** [NEVADA].

Remington Hill [NEVADA]:

(1) *ridge,* southwest-trending, 1.5 miles long, 4.5 miles south of Washington (lat. 39°17'25" N, long. 120°47'05" W). Named on Washington (1950) 7.5' quadrangle.

(2) *locality,* 5.5 miles south of Washington (lat. 39°16'30" N, long. 120°47'40" W). Named on Colfax (1898) 30' quadrangle. Whitney's (1873) map shows a community called Melburn Hill located 1 mile southwest of Remington Hill (2), a community called Excelsior located 1.25 miles east-northeast of Remington Hill (2), a community called Bald Eagle located 1.25 miles northeast of Remington Hill (2), and a community called Negro Flat situated 0.25 mile southwest of Remington Hill (2).

Rena Canyon [COLUSA]: *canyon,* drained by a stream that flows 2.5 miles to Grapevine Creek 4 miles east-northeast of Lodoga (lat. 39°19'30" N, long. 122°25'15" W; sec. 16, T 17 N, R 5 W). Named on Lodoga (1960) 15' quadrangle.

Represa [SACRAMENTO]: *locality,* 1.5 miles north-northeast of Folsom (lat. 38°41'45" N, long, 121°09'40" W). Named on Folsom (1967) 7.5' quadrangle, which has the notation "Represa P.O." at Folsom state prison. Postal authorities established State Prison post office in 1886 and changed the name to Represa in 1892; the name "Repressa" refers to a dam nearby on American River—*represa* means "dam" in Spanish (Salley, p. 183, 212).

Republican Cañon: see **Jesse Canyon** [EL DORADO].

Rescue [EL DORADO]: *locality,* 3.5 miles north-northwest of Shingle Springs (lat. 38°42'40" N, long. 120°57'05" W; sec. 23, T 10 N, R 9 E). Named on Shingle Springs (1949) 7.5' quadrangle. Postal authorities established Rescue post office in 1895; the name is for a nearby mine (Salley, p. 184). California Mining Bureau's (1909a) map shows a place called Jurgens located 6 miles by stage line northwest of Rescue. Postal authorities established Jurgens post office in 1903 and discontinued it in 1914; the name was for Annie C. Jurgens, first postmaster (Salley, p. 109). They established Green Springs post office in 1851 and discontinued it in 1852; it was located along Weber Creek 8 miles southwest of Coloma in the neighborhood of present Rescue (Salley, p. 89).

Rex Reservoir [NEVADA]: *lake,* 700 feet long, 3.5 miles northeast of Pilot Peak (lat. 39°12'30" N, long. 121°08'10" W; sec. 36, T 16 N, R 7 E). Named on Rough and Ready (1949) 7.5' quadrangle.

Reynolds: see **Rose and Reynolds Bar**, under **Rose Bar** [YUBA].

Rhode Island Ravine [NEVADA]: *canyon,* drained by a stream that flows less than 1 mile to Wolf Creek 0.5 mile south-southwest of downtown Grass Valley (lat. 39°12'40" N, long. 121°04' W; near N line sec. 34, T 16 N, R 8 E). Named on Grass Valley (1949) 7.5' quadrangle. Rhode Island Company mined gold in the canyon (Morley and Foley, p. 22).

Rice Canyon [SIERRA]: *canyon,* drained by a stream that flows 4 miles to Cold Stream (1) 5 miles southeast of Sierraville (lat. 39° 31'55" N, long. 120°18'15" W; near N line sec. 3, T 19 N, R 15 E). Named on Sierraville (1981) 7.5' quadrangle.

Rice Creek [PLACER]: *stream,* flows 3.5 miles to Middle Fork American River nearly 7 miles west-southwest of Granite Chief (lat. 39°09'15" N, long. 120°23'45" W; sec. 15, T 15 N, R 14 E). Named on Granite Chief (1953) and Royal Gorge (1953) 7.5' quadrangles.

Rice Crossing [NEVADA-YUBA]: *locality,* 2.5 miles west of French Corral along Yuba River on Nevada-Yuba County line (lat. 39°18'45" N, long. 121°12'15" W; near SE cor. sec. 20, T 17 N, R 7 E). Site named on French Corral (1948) 7.5' quadrangle. Called Rices Ford on Smartsville (1895) 30' quadrangle, and called Rices Bridge on Wescoatt's (1861) map. It also was called Lousey Level (Bancroft, 1888, p. 360), Liars Flat, and Liases Flat (Gudde, 1975, p. 290). Wescoatt's (1861) map shows a place called Horse Bar located 1.25 miles south-southwest of Rices Bridge.

Rice Hill [SIERRA]: *peak,* 4 miles north of Sierraville (lat. 39°38'40" N, long. 120°21'35" W; sec. 25, T 21 N, R 14 E). Altitude 5406 feet. Named on Antelope Valley (1981) 7.5' quadrangle.

Rices [EL DORADO]: *locality,* 3.5 mile northwest of Omo Ranch (lat. 38°37'15" N, long. 120°37'20" W). Named on Placerville (1893) 30' quadrangle.

Rices Bridge: see **Rice Crossing** [NEVADA-YUBA].

Rices Ford: see **Rice Crossing** [NEVADA-YUBA].

Richardson: see **Camp Richardson** [EL DORADO].

Richardson Lake [EL DORADO]: *lake,* 1100 feet long, 5 miles west-southwest of the town of Meeks Bay (lat. 39°01'20" N, long. 120° 12'40" W; on N line sec. 33, T 14 N, R 16 E). Named on Homewood (1955) 7.5' quadrangle.

Rich Bar: see **Grapevine Ravine** [AMADOR]; **Rattlesnake Bar** [PLACER].

Rich Creek [COLUSA]: *stream,* flows 3 miles to the canyon of Sand Creek 6.25 miles west of Arbuckle (lat. 39°00'35" N, long. 122° 10'10" W; near NE cor. sec. 3, T 13 N, R 3 W). Named on Cortina Creek (1953) and Rumsey (1959) 7.5' quadrangles.

Rich Dry Diggins: see **Auburn** [PLACER].

Rich Gulch [YUBA]: *canyon,* drained by a stream that flows 1.25 miles to Deadwood Creek 1 mile east-northeast of Strawberry Valley (lat. 39°34'05" N, long. 121°05'25" W; near N line sec. 28, T 20 N, R 8 E). Named on Strawberry Valley (1948) 7.5' quadrangle.

Rich Gulch: see **Little Oregon Creek** [YUBA].

Richland: see **Hood** [SACRAMENTO].

Richmond Hill: see **Mormon Island** [SACRAMENTO].

Rickeyville: see **Ione** [AMADOR].

Riego [PLACER]: *locality,* 11 miles west of Roseville along the abandoned line of Sacramento Northern Railroad (lat. 38°45'05" N, long. 121°29' W; at NW cor. sec. 6, T 10 N, R 6 E). Named on Pleasant Grove (1967) and Rio Linda (1967) 7.5' quadrangles. Postal authorities established Riego post office in 1908 and discontinued it in 1919 (Frickstad, p. 121).

Riffle Box Ravine [NEVADA]: *canyon,* 2 miles long, opens into an unnamed canyon 5 miles west-northwest of Pilot Peak (lat. 39°11'45" N, long. 121°15'50" W; near S line sec. 35, T 16 N, R 6 E). Named on Rough and Ready (1949) and Smartville (1951) 7.5' quadrangles.

Ringgold: see **Weber Creek** [EL DORADO].

Ringgold Creek: see **Ringold Creek** [EL DORADO].

Ringold Creek [EL DORADO]: *stream,* flows 4.5 miles to Weber Creek 2 miles south of downtown Placerville (lat. 38°42'15" N, long. 120°47'30" W; sec. 20, T 10 N, R 11 E). Named on Camino (1952) and Placerville (1949) 7.5' quadrangles. United States Board on Geographic Names (1984a, p. 4) approved the name "Ringgold Creek" for the stream, and noted that the name is for Commander Cadwallader Ringgold, who was in charge of a party sent into the region in 1841 as part of Charles Wilkes' United States Exploring Expedition.

Rio de Jesus Maria: see **Cache Creek** [COLUSA-YOLO].

Rio de las Mukelemnes: see **Mokelumne River** [AMADOR-SACRAMENTO].

Rio de las Plumas: see **Feather River** [SUTTER-YUBA].

Rio de los Americanos [SACRAMENTO]: *land grant,* 16 miles east of downtown Sacramento between Rancho Cordova and Folsom; southeast of American River, which also was called Rio de los Americanos. Named on Buffalo Creek (1967), Carmichael (1967), Citrus Heights (1967), and Folsom (1967) 7.5' quadrangles. William A. Leidesdorff received 8 leagues in 1844; Joseph L. Folsom and Anna Maria Spark claimed 35,521 acres patented in 1864 (Cowan, p. 15).

Rio de los Americanos: see **American River** [EL DORADO-PLACER-SACRAMENTO].

Rio de los Cosumnes: see **Cosumnes River** [AMADOR-EL DORADO-SACRAMENTO].

Rio de los Putos: [YOLO]: *land grant,* along Putah Creek near Winters on Yolo-Solano County line. Named on Allendale (1953), Merritt (1952), Montecello Dam (1959), Mount Vaca (1951), and Winters (1953) 7.5' quadrangles. Francisco Guerrero y Palomares received 4 leagues in 1842; William Wolfskill claimed 17,755 acres patented in 1858 (Cowan, p. 66). According to Perez (p. 87), William Wolfskill was the grantee in 1842.

Rio de Yuba: see **Yuba River** [NEVADA-YUBA].

Rio Jesus Maria [YOLO]: *land grant,* west of Sacramento River between Knights Landing and Woodland. Named on Grays Bend (1953), Knights Landing (1952), Taylor Monument (1967), Venona (1967), and Woodland (1952) 7.5' quadrangles. Thomas M. Hardy received 6 leagues in 1843; J.M. Harbin and others claimed 26,637 acres patented in 1858 (Cowan, p. 42).

Rio Linda [SACRAMENTO]: *town,* 8.5 miles north-northeast of downtown Sacramento (lat. 38°41'30" N, long. 121°26'55" W); the town is near Dry Creek (1), which also was called Linda Creek. Named on Rio Linda (1967) 7.5' quadrangle. Postal authorities established Rio Linda post office in 1914 (Frickstad, p. 134).

Rio Linda Creek: see **Dry Creek** [PLACER-SACRAMENTO].

Rio Oso [SUTTER]: *locality,* 4.25 miles north-northeast of Nicolaus (lat. 38°57'40" N, long. 121°32'35" W; at E line sec. 20, T 13 N, R 4 E); the place is near Bear River. Named on Nicolaus (1952) 7.5' quadrangle. Nicolaus (1910) 7.5' quadrangle shows the place located along Northern Electric Railroad. Postal authorities established Rio Oso post office in 1920; the name is from nearby Bear River—*Rio Oso* means "Bear River" in Spanish (Salley, p. 186). Present Rio Oso is near the location given by Salley (p. 163) for Oro City post office, established in 1853 along Bear River 3 miles above the confluence of Bear River and Feather River, discontinued the same year, reestablished in 1855, and discontinued again in 1858—changes in Sutter-Placer County line moved the post office site in and out of Sutter County.

Rio Sacramento: see **Sacramento River** [COLUSA-SACRAMENTO-SUTTER-YOLO].

Rio San Joaquin: see **San Joaquin River** [SACRAMENTO].

Rio Tulare: see **San Joaquin River** [SACRAMENTO].

Ritchey: see **Ione** [AMADOR].

Riverbank: see **Bryte** [YOLO].

River Hill: see **Somerset** [EL DORADO].

Riverlands: see **Riverview** [YOLO].

River Pines [AMADOR]: *settlement,* 3 miles north-northeast of Fiddletown (lat. 38°32'45" N, long. 120°44'30" W; sec. 14, 15, T 8 N, R 11 E). Named on Aukum (1952) 7.5' quadrangle. Postal authorities established River Pines post office in 1948 (Frickstad, p. 6).

Riverside [SACRAMENTO]: *locality,* 4.5 miles south-southwest of downtown Sacramento along Sacramento River (lat. 38°31' N, long. 121°31'35" W). Named on Lovdal (1916) 7.5' quadrangle.

Riverton [EL DORADO]: *locality,* 8.5 miles west of Kyburz along South Fork American River (lat. 38°46'15" N, long. 120°26'50" W; sec. 30, T 11 N, R 14 E). Named on Riverton (1950) 7.5' quadrangle. Called Moores on Pyramid Peak (1896) 30' quadrangle. Postal authorities established Riverton post office in 1893 and discontinued it in 1898; the name was for the location of the site along a river (Salley, p. 186). The place first was known as Moore's Station—it was along a toll road built and operated by John M. Moore (Gudde, 1949, p. 287-288).

Riverview [YOLO]: *locality,* 5 miles south-southwest of West Sacramento along Sacramento Northern Railroad (lat. 38°30'15" N, long. 121°33'30" W); the place is on the west bank of Sacramento River. Named on Sacramento West (1967) 7.5' quadrangle. Called Glide Landing on Lovedal (1916) 7.5' quadrangle, which shows it along Oakland Antioch and Eastern Railroad. California Division of Highways' (1934) map has the name "Riverlands" at the place, and has the name "Glide Tract" for the area to the south.

Riviera [SUTTER]: *locality,* less than 2 miles north of Live Oak along Northern Electric Railroad (lat. 39°18'05" N, long. 121°39'45" W). Named on Gridley (1912) 7.5' quadrangle.

Riviere la Cache: see **Cache Creek** [COLUSA-YOLO].

Roach Hill [PLACER]: *ridge,* south-southwest- to west-trending, 2 miles long, 5.5 miles south of Dutch Flat (lat. 39°07'45" N, long. 120°49'45" W). Named on Dutch Flat (1950) and Foresthill (1949) 7.5' quadrangles.

Robbers Flat [COLUSA]: *area,* 8.5 miles north-northwest of Wilbur Springs (lat. 39°09'30" N, long. 122°27'50" W; near SE cor. sec. 12, T 15 N, R 6 W). Named on Wilbur Springs (1961) 15' quadrangle.

Robbers Ravine [PLACER]: *canyon,* 1.5 miles long, opens into an unnamed canyon 1.5 miles east-northeast of Colfax (lat. 39°06'50" N, long. 120°55'40" W; near NW cor. sec. 36, T 15 N, R 9 E). Named on Chicago Park (1949) and Colfax (1949) 7.5' quadrangles. Present Secret Ravine (1) is called Robbers Ravine on Colfax (1938) 30' quadrangle.

Robbins [SUTTER]: *village,* 19 miles south-southwest of Yuba City in Sutter Basin (lat. 38°52'15" N, long. 121°42'15" W; sec. 24, T 12 N, R 2 E). Named on Knights Landing (1952) 7.5' quadrangle. The place first was called Madox for a manager of Sutter Basin Company, but company officials changed the name in 1925 to honor the company president, George B. Robbins (Gudde, 1949, p. 288). Postal authorities established Robbins post office in 1926 (Frickstad, p. 202).

Robbs Peak [EL DORADO]: *peak,* 12 miles north-northwest of Kyburz (lat. 38°55'30" N, long. 120°24'10" W; near SW cor. sec. 34, T 13 N, R 14 E). Altitude 6686 feet. Named on Robbs Peak (1950) 7.5' quadrangle. The name commemorates either Hamilton D. Robb, a stockman in the early days, or Lieutenant Robb, who climbed the peak while he was exploring with a cavalry detachment (Gudde, 1969, p. 271).

Robbs Valley [EL DORADO]: *valley,* 1.5 miles east-northeast of Robbs Peak (lat. 38°55'40" N, long. 120°22'30" W). Named on Loon Lake (1952) and Robbs Peak (1950) 7.5' quadrangles.

Robert's Flat: see **Robinsons Flat** [PLACER].

Robertson Flat: see **Robinsons Flat** [PLACER].

Robertson Valley: see **Little Robertson Valley**, under **Little Robinsons Valley** [PLACER].

Robie Point [PLACER]: *peak,* 1.25 miles east-southeast of downtown Auburn (lat. 38°53'35" N, long. 121°03'05" W; sec. 14, T 12 N, R 8 E). Named on Auburn (1953) 7.5' quadrangle.

Robinson: see **Jack Robinson Ravine** [PLACER].

Robinson Cow Camp [SIERRA]: *locality,* 4.5 miles northwest of Sierra City (lat. 39°37'15" N, long. 120°40'50" W; near SE cor. sec. 1, T 20 N, R 11 E). Named on Sierra City (1981) 7.5' quadrangle.

Robinson Flat: see **Robinsons Flat** [PLACER].

Robinson Ravine: see **Montezuma Hill** [NEVADA] (1).

Robinson's Crossing: see **Edwards Crossing** [NEVADA].

Robinsons Crossing: see **Camp Far West** [YUBA].

Robinsons Flat [PLACER]: *area,* 0.5 mile east of Duncan Peak (lat. 39°09'20" N, long. 120°30'05" W; around SW cor. sec. 11, T 15 N, R 13 E). Named on Duncan Peak (1952) and Royal Gorge (1953) 7.5' quadrangles. Called Robert's Flat on Whitney's (1880) map. United States Board on Geographic Names (1961, p. 14) rejected the forms "Robertson Flat," "Robinson Flat," and "Robinson's Flat" for the name.

Robinsons Valley: see **Little Robinsons Valley** [PLACER].

Robla [SACRAMENTO]: *district,* 6.5 miles north-northeast of downtown Sacramento (lat. 38°39'40" N, long. 121°26'45" W). Named on Rio Linda (1967) 7.5' quadrangle.

Rob Roy Creek: see **Deadman Creek** [NEVADA].

Rock: see **Rumsey** [YOLO].

Rockbound Lake [EL DORADO]: *lake,* 4000 feet long, 5.5 miles west-northwest of Phipps Peak (lat. 38°59'50" N, long. 120°14'10" W). Named on Homewood (1955) and Rockbound Valley (1955) 7.5' quadrangles.

Rockbound Pass [EL DORADO]: *pass,* 4.5 miles southwest of Phipps Peak (lat. 38°54'10" N, long. 120°11'50" W); the pass is west of the upper end of Rockbound Valley. Named on Rockbound Valley (1955) 7.5' quadrangle.

Rockbound Valley [EL DORADO]: *valley,* on upper reaches of Rubicon River above a point 4.5 miles west-northwest of Phipps Peak (lat. 38°59'30" N, long. 120°13'15" W). Named on Rockbound Valley (1955) 7.5'

quadrangle.

Rock Canyon [EL DORADO]: *canyon,* drained by a stream that flows 4.5 miles to Traverse Creek 2.5 miles south-southeast of Georgetown (lat. 38°52'25" N, long. 120°49' W; sec. 24, T 12 N, R 10 E). Named on Georgetown (1949) 7.5' quadrangle.

Rock Creek [AMADOR]: *stream,* flows 6.5 miles to Jackson Creek 6 miles west-southwest of Jackson (lat. 38°18'25" N, long. 120°52'15" W; at E line sec. 9, T 5 N, R 10 E). Named on Jackson (1962) 7.5' quadrangle.

Rock Creek [EL DORADO]: *stream,* flows 14 miles to South Fork American River 2.5 miles east-northeast of Chili Bar (lat. 38°47' N, long. 120°46'40" W; sec. 20, T 11 N, R 11 E). Named on Garden Valley (1949), Slate Mountain (1950), and Tunnel Hill (1950) 7.5' quadrangles.

Rock Creek [NEVADA]: *stream,* flows 8.5 miles to South Yuba River 3.5 miles north-northwest of Nevada City (lat. 39°18'45" N, long. 121°02'55" W; sec. 26, T 17 N, R 8 E). Named on Nevada City (1948) and North Bloomfield (1949) 7.5' quadrangles.

Rock Creek [NEVADA-YUBA]: *stream,* heads in Nevada County and flows 8 miles to Camp Far West Reservoir 7.5 miles east-northeast of Wheatland in Yuba County (lat. 39°03'25" N, long. 121°17'50" W; near N line sec. 22, T 14 N, R 6 E). Named on Grass Valley (1949) and Wheatland (1949) 15' quadrangles. Camp Far West (1949, photorevised 1973) 7.5' quadrangle shows the stream entering an enlarged Camp Far West Reservoir in Nevada County (lat. 39°03'40" N, long. 121°16'40" W; sec. 14, T 14 N, R 6 E).

Rock Creek [PLACER]: *stream,* flows 4 miles to Dry Creek (1) 5 miles north-northwest of Auburn (lat. 38°58' N, long. 121°06'35" W; sec. 20, T 13 N, R 8 E). Named on Auburn (1953) 7.5' quadrangle.

Rock Creek [SIERRA]:

(1) *stream,* flows 3.5 miles to Smithneck Creek 8.5 miles southeast of Loyalton (lat. 39°34'20" N, long. 120°09'20" W; sec. 24, T 20 N, R 16 E). Named on Dog Valley (1981) and Sardine Peak (1981) 7.5' quadrangles.

(2) *stream,* flows 4.5 miles to North Yuba River at Goodyears Bar (lat. 39°32'20" N, long. 120°53'10" W; near SW cor. sec. 5, T 19 N, R 10 E). Named on Downieville (1951) and Goodyears Bar (1951) 7.5' quadrangles.

Rock Creek [SIERRA-YUBA]: *stream,* heads in Sierra County and flows 7.5 miles to Canyon Creek 4 miles east of Strawberry Valley in Yuba County (lat. 39°33'20" N, long. 121°01'55" W; near S line sec. 25, T 20 N, R 8 E). Named on Goodyears Bar (1951), La Porte (1951), and Strawberry Valley (1948) 7.5' quadrangles.

Rock Creek: see **Linda Creek** [PLACER-SACRAMENTO]; **Little Rock Creek** [SIERRA]; **Orchard Creek** [PLACER].

Rock Creek Lake [PLACER]: *lake,* behind a dam on Rock Creek 3.5 miles north-northwest of downtown Auburn (lat. 38°56'50" N, long. 121°05'20" W; sec. 28, T 13 N, R 8 E). Named on Auburn (1953) 7.5' quadrangle.

Rock Island Bar [YUBA]: *locality,* 4 miles east of Challenge (lat. 39°28'35" N, long. 121°08'45" W; near W line sec. 25, T 19 N, R 7 E). Named on Nevada City (1948) 15' quadrangle. Miners from Rock Island, Illinois, named the place in 1850 (Gudde, 1975, p. 294). Water of New Bullards Bar Reservoir now covers the site.

Rock Lake [NEVADA]: *lake,* 1650 feet long, 3.5 miles west-southwest of English Mountain at the head of Texas Creek (lat. 39°29'55" N, long. 120°36'55" W; near N line sec. 15, T 18 N, R 12 E). Named on English Mountain (1983) 7.5' quadrangle.

Rock Lake: see **Lower Rock Lake** [NEVADA].

Rocklin [PLACER]: *town,* 11 miles southwest of Auburn (lat. 38°47'25" N, long. 121°14'05" W). Named on Rocklin (1967) and Roseville (1967) 7.5' quadrangles. Postal authorities established Rocklin post office in 1868 (Frickstad, p. 121), and the town incorporated in 1893. The name is from rock quarries near the place (Hanna, p. 257).

Rock Mountain [NEVADA]: *peak,* 5 miles west of Wolf (lat. 39°03'35" N, long. 121°13'55" W; near SE cor. sec. 18, T 14 N, R 7 E); the peak is south of Rock Creek (2). Altitude 1409 feet. Named on Wolf (1949) 7.5' quadrangle.

Rockwell Gap [YOLO]: *pass,* 7.5 miles south-southeast of Berryessa Peak along Rocky Ridge on Yolo-Napa County line (lat. 38°34' N, long. 122°07'15" W; sec. 6, T 8 N, R 2 W). Named on Monticello Dam (1959) 7.5' quadrangle. Called Rosslyn Gap on Capay (1945) 15' quadrangle, but United States Board on Geographic Names (1962a, p. 15) rejected this name.

Rocky Bar: see **Ashland** [SACRAMENTO]; **Scotchman Creek** [NEVADA].

Rocky Basin Creek [EL DORADO]: *stream,* flows 2.5 miles to Gerle Creek nearly 5 miles north-northeast of Robbs Peak (lat. 38°59'25" N, long. 120°22'25" W; sec. 11, T 13 N, R 14 E). Named on Loon Lake (1952) 7.5' quadrangle.

Rocky Canyon [EL DORADO]: *canyon,* drained by a stream that flows 2 miles to South Fork American River 3 miles south-southeast of Pyramid Peak (lat. 38°48'25" N, long. 120°08'05" W; near NE cor. sec. 18, T 11 N, R 17 E). Named on Pyramid Peak (1955) 7.5' quadrangle.

Rocky Canyon [NEVADA]: *canyon,* drained by a stream that flows 2.25 miles to Boca Reservoir 7.5 miles northeast of Truckee (lat. 39°24'20" N, long. 120°05'05" W; near SW cor. sec. 15, T 18 N, R 17 E). Named on Boca (1955) 7.5' quadrangle.

Rocky Canyon Spring [NEVADA]: *spring,* 8 miles northeast of Truckee (lat. 39°24' N, long. 120°04'05" W; near NE cor. sec. 22, T 18 N, R 17 E); the spring is in Rocky Canyon. Named on Boca (1955) 7.5' quadrangle.

Rocky Glen [NEVADA]: *canyon,* drained by a stream that flows 1 mile to Poorman Creek (1) 9 miles east-northeast of North Bloomfield (lat. 39°25'40" N, long. 120°45'15" W; near W line sec. 16, T 18 N, R 11 E). Named on Alleghany (1949) and Graniteville (1982) 7.5' quadrangles.

Rocky Peak [SIERRA]: *peak,* 4.25 miles west-northwest of Goodyears Bar (lat. 39°34'25" N, long. 120°57'10" W; sec. 27, T 20 N, R 9 E). Altitude 5344 feet. Named on Goodyears Bar (1951) 7.5' quadrangle.

Rocky Point [AMADOR]: *peak,* 4.5 miles south-southwest of Plymouth (lat. 38°25'10" N, long. 120°53'20" W; near W line sec. 33, T 7 N, R 10 E). Altitude 760 feet. Named on Irish Hill (1962) 7.5' quadrangle.

Rocky Point [YUBA]: *relief feature,* 6 miles southwest of Camptonville on the north side of Middle Yuba River (lat. 39°22'55" N, long. 121°06'55" W; at E line sec. 31, T 18 N, R 8 E). Named on Camptonville (1948) 7.5' quadrangle.

Rocky Point: see **Sattley** [SIERRA].

Rocky Ridge [YOLO]: *ridge,* south-southeast-trending, 12.5 miles long, extends along Yolo-Napa County line from near Berryessa Peak to Putah Creek. Named on Brooks (1959), Lake Berryessa (1959), and Monticello Dam (1959) 7.5' quadrangles.

Rocky Wash [PLACER]: *stream,* flows less than 0.5 mile to Truckee River 10 miles west-southwest of Martis Peak (lat. 39°15'55" N, long. 120°12'30" W; sec. 4, T 16 N, R 16 E). Named on Truckee (1955) 7.5' quadrangle.

Rodwell: see **Somerset** [EL DORADO].

Rogers: see **Point Rogers**, under **Montezuma Island** [SACRAMENTO].

Rolleys Point [YUBA]: *relief feature,* 3.5 miles southeast of Dobbins on the north side of Yuba River (lat. 39°20'05" N, long. 121°09'35" W; sec. 14, T 17 N, R 7 E). Named on French Corral (1948) 7.5' quadrangle. Called Clincmans Point on Wescoatt's (1861) map.

Rolling Draw [SACRAMENTO]: *canyon,* drained by a stream that flows 2.25 miles to Laguna 5 miles northeast of Galt (lat. 38°18'30" N, long. 121°13'55" W; sec. 5, T 5 N, R 7 E). Named on Clay (1968) 7.5' quadrangle.

Rollins Reservoir [NEVADA-PLACER]: *lake,* behind a dam on Bear River 1 mile southeast of Chicago Park on Nevada-Placer County line (lat. 39°08'10" N, long. 120°57'05" W; sec. 22, T 15 N, R 9 E). Named on Chicago Park (1949, photorevised 1973) 7.5' quadrangle.

Ronda [YOLO]: *locality,* 9.5 miles southeast of Dunnigan along Southern Pacific Railroad (lat. 38°46'40" N, long. 121°51'30" W; near NE cor. sec. 28, T 11 N, R 1 E). Named on Ronda (1915) 7.5' quadrangle.

Ropi Lake [EL DORADO]: *lake,* 1900 feet long, 1.5 miles east-southeast of Pyramid Peak (lat. 38°50'20" N, long. 120°07'50" W). Named on Pyramid Peak (1955) 7.5' quadrangle. The word "Ropi" was coined from letters in the name "Ross Pierce" (Lekisch, p. 65).

Roscoe Creek [NEVADA]: *stream,* flows 2.25 miles to McKilligan Creek 1.5 miles west of Washington (lat. 39°21'50" N, long. 120° 49'50" W; at E line sec. 3, T 17 N, R 10 E). Named on Alleghany (1949) and Washington (1950) 7.5' quadrangles. The canyon of the stream is called Roscoe's Cañon on Whitney's (1873) map.

Roscoe's Cañon: see **Roscoe Creek** [NEVADA].

Rose and Reynolds Bar: see **Rose Bar** [YUBA].

Rose Bar [YUBA]: *locality,* less than 1 mile north of Smartville along Yuba River (lat. 39°13'05" N, long. 121°17'50" W; near E line sec. 28, T 16 N, R 6 E). Site named on Smartville (1951) 7.5' quadrangle. Called Rose's Bar on Derby's (1849b) map, and called Rose & Reynolds Bar on Jackson's (1850) map. John Rose and William J. Reynolds opened a store at the place in 1848 (Hoover, Rensch, and Rensch, p. 589). Trask's (1853) map shows a place called Syracuse B. [Bar] situated a short distance upstream from Rose Bar.

Roseberry Slough [YOLO]: *water feature,* 2.5 miles south-southeast of Knights Landing (lat. 38°46'15" N, long. 121°42'10" W); the feature is along the north part of present Knights Landing Ridge Cut. Named on Knights Landing (1910) 7.5' quadrangle.

Rose Briar Flat [YOLO]: *area,* 6.5 miles southwest of Esparto (lat. 38°38'35" N, long. 122°07'15" W; sec. 7, T 9 N, R 2 W). Named on Esparto (1959) 7.5' quadrangle.

Rose Canyon [YOLO]: *canyon,* drained by a stream that flows 1.5 miles to Capay Valley 1.25 miles west-northwest of Guinda (lat. 38°50' N, long. 122°12'50" W; sec. 5, T 11 N, R 3 W). Named on Guinda (1959) 7.5' quadrangle.

Rose Garden: see **Mikon** [YOLO].

Rose Hill [YUBA]: *ridge,* south-southeast-trending, 1 mile long, 1.5 miles south-southwest of Smartville (lat. 39°11'15" N, long. 121° 18'30" W; sec. 4, T 15 N, R 6 E). Named on Smartville (1951) 7.5' quadrangle.

Rosemont [SACRAMENTO]: *town,* 5 miles south-southwest of downtown Carmichael (lat. 38°33' N, long. 121°21'45" W; mainly in sec. 18, T 8 N, R 6 E). Named on Carmichael (1967) 7.5' quadrangle.

Rose Mountain Range: see **Carson Range** [EL DORADO].

Roseneath: see **Isleton** [SACRAMENTO].

Rose's Bar: see **Rose Bar** [YUBA].

Roseville [PLACER]: *city,* 15 miles southwest of Auburn (lat. 38° 45' N, long. 121°17' W; around NE cor. sec. 2, T 10 N, R 6 E). Named on Citrus Heights (1967), Folsom (1967), Rocklin (1967), and Roseville (1967) 7.5' quadrangles. Postal authorities established Roseville post office in 1864 (Frickstad, p. 121), and the city incorporated in 1909. A stage station called Griders was at the place before the railroad came; trainmen called the place Junction before the name "Roseville" was applied (Hanna, p. 260).

Roseville Reservoir [PLACER]: *lake,* 950 feet long, 1.5 miles south of Rocklin (lat. 38°46'05" N, long. 121°14'05" W; near S line sec. 30, T 11 N, R 7 E). Named on Rocklin (1967) 7.5' quadrangle.

Rossassco Ravine [SIERRA]: *canyon,* drained by a stream that flows 1 mile to North Yuba River 1.25 miles west of Downieville (lat. 39°33'30" N, long. 120°51'05" W; near E line sec. 33, T 20 N, R 10 E). Named on Downieville (1951) 7.5' quadrangle.

Rosslyn Gap: see **Rockwell Gap** [YOLO].

Rough and Ready [NEVADA]: *village,* 5 miles north-northeast of Pilot Peak (lat. 39°13'50" N, long. 121°08'10" W; sec. 24, T 16 N, R 7 E). Named on Rough and Ready (1949) 7.5' quadrangle. Postal authorities established Rough and Ready post office before July 28, 1851, discontinued it for a time in 1855, discontinued it again for a time in 1913, discontinued it in 1942, and reestablished it in 1948 (Salley, p. 189). Miners of Rough and Ready Company came to the place in 1849 and the community that developed there took the company's name; Captain A.A. Townsend, leader of the company, had served under General Zachary Taylor, who had the nickname "Old Rough and Ready" (Hoover, Rensch, and Rensch, p. 251). Whitney's (1873) map shows a place called Randolph Ho. [House] located 1.25 miles east of Rough and Ready. California Mining Bureau's (1909a) map shows a place called Fernley located 5 miles southwest of Rough and Ready. Postal authorities established Fernley post office in 1898 and discontinued it in 1913 (Frickstad, p. 113). They established Elida post office 5 miles southwest of Rough and Ready in 1882 and discontinued it in 1883; the name war for the postmaster's wife (Salley, p. 67).

Rough and Ready Landing [SUTTER]: *locality,* nearly 3 miles south of Kirkville along Sacramento River (lat. 38°52' N, long. 121°47'35" W; at S line sec. 19, T 12 N, R 2 E). Named on Ronda (1915) 7.5' quadrangle.

Rough and Ready Reservoir [NEVADA]: *intermittent lake,* 350 feet long, 5.25 miles north-northeast of Pilot Peak (lat. 39°14'10" N, long. 121°08' W; sec. 24, T 16 N, R 7 E); the feature is 0.5 mile north-northeast of Rough and Ready. Named on Rough and Ready (1949) 7.5' quadrangle.

Round Buttons: see **Maggies Peaks** [EL DORADO].

Round Hill [EL DORADO]: *peak,* 4.5 miles north-northeast of Chili Bar (lat. 38°49'40" N, long. 120°47'10" W; sec. 6, T 11 N, R 11 E). Altitude 2555 feet. Named on Garden Valley (1949) 7.5' quadrangle.

Round Lake [EL DORADO]: *lake,* 2100 feet long, 4.5 miles south-southeast of Echo Summit (lat. 38°45' N, long. 120°00'20" W; sec. 4, T 10 N, R 18 E). Named on Caples Lake (1979) and Echo Lake (1955) 7.5' quadrangles.

Round Lake [NEVADA]: *lake,* 850 feet long, 5 miles southwest of English Mountain (lat. 39°23'45" N, long. 120°36'45" W; sec. 27, T 18 N, R 12 E). Named on English Mountain (1983) 7.5' quadrangle.

Round Mountain [EL DORADO]: *peak,* 4 miles southwest of Omo Ranch (lat. 38°32'20" N, long. 120°36'55" W; near SE cor. sec. 14, T 8 N, R 12 E). Altitude 3501 feet. Named on Omo Ranch (1952) 7.5' quadrangle.

Round Mountain [NEVADA]: *peak,* 3.25 miles north-northeast of Nevada City (lat. 39°18'50" N, long. 121°00'05" W; near NE cor. sec. 30, T 17 N, R 9 E). Named on Nevada City (1948) and North Bloomfield (1949) 7.5' quadrangles.

Round Tent: see **Waldo Junction** [YUBA].

Round Tent Canyon [EL DORADO]: *canyon,* drained by a stream that flows 4.5 miles to Silver Creek 5 miles north-northeast of Pollock Pines (lat. 38°49'30" N, long. 120°32'15" W; near W line sec. 4, T 11 N, R 13 E). Named on Pollock Pines (1950) and Riverton (1950) 7.5' quadrangles.

Round Top: see **Little Round Top** [EL DORADO].

Roundtop: see **Kirkwood** [AMADOR].

Round Valley [NEVADA]:

(1) *valley,* 4 miles north-northwest of English Mountain (lat. 39°30'20" N, long. 120°33'50" W; near NW cor. sec. 19, T 19 N, R 13 E). Named on Haypress Valley (1981) 7.5' quadrangle.

(2) *valley,* 4.25 miles north-northwest of Donner Pass (lat. 39°22'10" N, long. 120°21'50" W; near E line sec. 2, T 17 N, R 14 E). Named on Norden (1955) 7.5' quadrangle.

Routier [SACRAMENTO]: *locality,* 2.5 miles south of present downtown Carmichael along Southern Pacific Railroad (lat. 38°34'45" N, long. 121°19'20" W). Named on Mills (1911) 7.5' quadrangle. The name commemorates Joseph Routier, who settled at the place in 1853 (Gudde, 1949, p. 291). Postal authorities established Routier Station post office in 1873 and discontinued it in 1899 (Frickstad, p. 134).

Routier Station: see **Routier** [SACRAMENTO].

Rowland: see **Al Tahoe** [EL DORADO].

Royal Gorge [PLACER]: *canyon,* 2.5 miles long, along North Fork American River above a point 9.5 miles west of Granite Chief (lat. 39°13'15" N, long. 120°27'30" W; at E line sec. 25, T 16 N, R 13 E). Named on Royal Gorge (1953) 7.5' quadrangle.

Rubicon: see **Emerald Bay** [EL DORADO] (2).

Rubicon Bay [EL DORADO]: *embayment,* 1.5 miles south-southeast of the town of Meeks Bay along Lake Tahoe (lat. 39°01'55" N, long. 120°06'30" W). Named on Meeks Bay (1955) 7.5' quadrangle.

Rubicon Creek [EL DORADO]: *stream,* flows nearly 2 miles to Lake Tahoe 2.5 miles south-southeast of the town of Meeks Bay (lat. 39° 00'05" N, long. 120°06'05" W; sec. 4, T 13 N, R 17 E). Named on Emerald Bay (1955) 7.5' quadrangle.

Rubicon Creek: see **Rubicon River** [EL DORADO-PLACER].

Rubicon Lake [EL DORADO]: *lake,* 1100 feet long, 1 mile northeast of Phipps Peak (lat. 38°58' N, long. 120°08' W; near SE cor. sec. 18, T 13 N, R 17 E). Named on Rockbound Valley (1955) 7.5' quadrangle.

Rubicon Lodge: see **Meeks Bay** [EL DORADO] (2).

Rubicon Peak [EL DORADO]: *peak,* 2.5 miles north-northeast of Phipps Peak (lat. 38°59'20" N, long. 120°07'55" W; on W line sec. 8, T 13 N, R 17 E). Altitude 9183 feet. Named on Rockbound Valley (1955) 7.5' quadrangle.

Rubicon Point [EL DORADO]: *promontory,* 6.5 miles north of Mount Tallac along Lake Tahoe (lat. 38°59'55" N, long. 120°05'40" W; sec. 3, T 13 N, R 17 E). Named on Emerald Bay (1955) 7.5' quadrangle.

Rubicon Reservoir [EL DORADO]: *lake,* 3500 feet long, behind a dam on Rubicon River 4.5 miles west-northwest of Phipps Peak (lat. 38°59'20" N, long. 120°13'20" W; at W line sec. 9, T 13 N, R 16 E); the lake covers most of Onion Flat. Named on Rockbound Valley (1955, photorevised 1969) 7.5' quadrangle.

Rubicon River [EL DORADO-PLACER]: *stream,* flows for 55 miles, first in El Dorado County, then in Placer County, and finally along El Dorado-Placer County line, to Middle Fork American River 3.25 miles east-northeast of Volcanoville (lat. 39°00'10" N, long. 120°43'50" W; sec. 3, T 13 N, R 11 E). Named on Bunker Hill (1953), Devil Peak (1950), Homewood (1955), Michigan Bluff (1952), Robbs Peak (1950), Rockbound Valley (1955), Tunnel Hill (1950), and Wentworth Springs (1953) 7.5' quadrangles. Wheeler's (1876-1877b) map has the name "Rubicon Creek" for the upper part of the stream, and has the name "Big Meadow Creek" for the lower part. South Fork enters from the east 4.5 miles northwest of Robbs Peak; it is 15 miles long and is named on Loon Lake (1952, photorevised 1973) and Robbs Peak (1950) 7.5' quadrangles. South Fork is called Little South Fork Rubicon River on Pyramid Peak (1896) 30' quadrangle.

Rubicon Springs [EL DORADO]: *springs,* nearly 7 miles west-southwest of the town of Meeks Bay (lat. 39°01'05" N, long. 120° 14'40" W; sec. 31, T 14 N, R 16 E). Named on Homewood (1955) 7.5' quadrangle. Truckee (1895) 30' quadrangle has the name for a locality at the site. The springs were the basis of a resort as early as the 1860's; in 1909 a small hotel and three log cabins were open to guests in the summer (Waring, G.A., p. 234).

Ruby Bluff [SIERRA]: *relief feature,* 3.5 miles south-southwest of Downieville (lat. 39°30'45" N, long. 120°50'50" W; sec. 15, T 19 N, R 10 E). Named on Downieville (1951) 7.5' quadrangle.

Ruby Canyon [EL DORADO]: *canyon,* drained by a stream that flows 1 mile to Pilot Creek (1) 9.5 miles north of Pollock Pines (lat. 38°53'50" N, long. 120°33'55" W; near S line sec. 7, T 12 N, R 13 E). Named on Devil Peak (1950) 7.5' quadrangle.

Ruck-A-Chuncky Rapids [EL DORADO-PLACER]: *water feature,* 4 miles north of Greenwood along Middle Fork American River on El Dorado-Placer County line (lat. 38°57'20" N, long. 120°54'45" W; on E line sec. 24, T 13 N, R 9 E). Named on Greenwood (1949) 7.5' quadrangle.

Rucker Creek [NEVADA]: *stream,* flows 3 miles to South Yuba River 4 miles west-northwest of Yuba Gap (lat. 39°20'40" N, long. 120°40'40" W; near NW cor. sec. 18, T 17 N, R 12 E); the stream goes through Rucker Lake. Named on Blue Canyon (1955) 7.5' quadrangle.

Rucker Lake [NEVADA]: *lake,* 3350 feet long, 3.25 miles northwest of Yuba Gap (lat. 39°21'20" N, long. 120°39'05" W; sec. 8, T 17 N, R 12 E); the lake is along Rucker Creek. Named on Blue Canyon (1955) 7.5' quadrangle.

Ruff Hill [YUBA]: *ridge,* west- to south-trending, 1 mile long, 4.5 miles east-northeast of Rackerby (lat. 39°27'45" N, long. 121°15'30" W). Named on Rackerby (1948) 7.5' quadrangle.

Rumsey [YOLO]: *village,* 18 miles northwest of Esparto in Capay Valley (lat. 38°53'20" N, long. 122°14'10" W). Named on Rumsey (1959) 7.5' quadrangle. Postal authorities established Rock post office in 1878, moved it 2 miles north to a railroad depot in 1888 and changed the name to Rumsey—the name "Rock" was from a rock landmark (Salley, p. 187). The name "Rumsey" is for Captain D.C. Rumsey, who owned land at the place (Gudde, 1949, p. 292).

Rumsey Canyon [YOLO]: *canyon,* drained by a stream that flows 3.25 miles to Capay Valley less than 1 mile west-northwest of Rumsey (lat. 38°53'35"

N, long. 122°15'05" W; near N line sec. 13, T 12 N, R 4 E). Named on Glascock Mountain (1958) and Knoxville (1958) 7.5' quadrangles.

Rumsey Hills: see **Capay Hills** [YOLO].

Rumsey Range: see **Blue Ridge** [YOLO].

Runyon: see **Franklin** [SACRAMENTO].

Rupert: see **Rupert Siding** [YUBA].

Rupert Siding [YUBA]: *locality,* 1.5 miles north-northwest of Olivehurst along Southern Pacific Railroad (lat. 39°09'10" N, long. 121°33'40" W). Named on Olivehurst (1952) 7.5' quadrangle. Called Rupert on Marysville (1952) 15' quadrangle, and called Yuba on Marysville (1895) 30' quadrangle.

Rupley Cabin [EL DORADO]: *locality,* 8 miles east-southeast of Robbs Peak (lat. 38°53'10" N, long. 120°15'35" W; sec. 18, T 12 N, R 16 E). Named on Loon Lake (1952) 7.5' quadrangle.

Rush Creek [NEVADA]: *stream,* flows nearly 4 miles to South Yuba River 5 miles west-northwest of Nevada City (lat. 39°17'35" N, long. 121°06'15" W; sec. 32, T 17 N, R 8 E). Named on Nevada City (1948) 7.5' quadrangle.

Russell: see **Mayhew** [SACRAMENTO].

Russell Hollow [EL DORADO]: *canyon,* 2 miles long, on upper reaches of Hancock Creek above a point 4.5 miles southwest of the village of Pilot Hill (lat. 38°47'20" N, long. 121°04'20" W; sec. 22, T 11 N, R 8 E). Named on Pilot Hill (1954) 7.5' quadrangle.

Russell Valley [NEVADA]: *valley,* 4 miles northeast of Hobart Mills along Dry Creek (1) (lat. 39°26'10" N, long. 120°07'30" W). Named on Boca (1955) and Hobart Mills (1981) 7.5' quadrangles.

Russian Embarcadero: see **Freeport Bend** [SACRAMENTO-YOLO].

Russville: see **Ashland** [SACRAMENTO].

Ryde [SACRAMENTO]: *village,* 6 miles north-northeast of Isleton along Sacramento River on Grand Island (lat. 38°14'20" N, long. 121°33'30" W). Named on Isleton (1978) 7.5' quadrangle. Postal authorities established Ryde post office in 1892 (Frickstad, p. 134). William A. Kesner laid out the community in 1892 on land that he bought from Judge Williams, who suggested the name "Ryde" from a town on the Isle of Wight (Gudde, 1949, p. 293).

— S —

Sabin Lake [COLUSA]: *intermittent lake,* 700 feet long, 1.5 miles north of Colusa (lat. 39°14'05" N, long. 122°00'35" W). Named on Colusa (1952) 7.5' quadrangle. Powell Slough (1918) 7.5' quadrangle shows a permanent lake.

Saccarus: see **Curtis** [YOLO].

Sacketts Gulch [SIERRA]: *canyon,* drained by a stream that flows 2 miles to Slate Creek 4.25 miles west-southwest of Mount Fillmore (lat. 39°42'35" N, long. 120°55'30" W; sec. 1, T 21 N, R 9 E). Named on La Porte (1951) 7.5' quadrangle.

Sacramento [SACRAMENTO]: *city,* east of Sacramento River at the mouth of American River (downtown and California State capitol building near lat. 38°34'35" N, long. 121°29'30" W). Named on Clarksburg (1967), Florin (1968), Rio Linda (1967), Sacramento East (1967), Sacramento West (1967), and Taylor Monument (1967) 7.5' quadrangles. Postal authorities established Sacramento City post office in 1849 and changed the name to Sacramento in 1883 (Frickstad, p. 134). The city incorporated in 1850. John A. Sutter settled at the site in 1839, and in 1841 he began building his well-known fort, generally referred to as Sutter's Fort, although he called the place Nueva Helvetia—*Helvetia* is the ancient name of Switzerland (Gudde, 1949, p. 348). The fort is called Fort Sutter on Jefferson's (1849) map, and Sutter himself used the name "Fort Sacramento" in 1846 (Whiting and Whiting, p. 81). Sutter's son, John A., Jr., and Sam Brannan had the city surveyed in the autumn of 1848 and named it for the river (Kanter *in* Grimshaw, p. 44). The city was laid out at what was known as Sutter's Embarcadero, the place along Sacramento River that goods and visitors for Sutter's Fort landed (Hussey *in* Swan, p. 48). Ringgold's (1850b) map shows a place called Boston situated along Sacramento River across American River from Sacramento City. J. Halls and Lieutenant Ringgold of the navy. surveyed the site of Boston (Buffum, p. 154) as a rival to Sacramento, but the enterprise failed. Postal authorities established Strauch post office 12 miles north of Sacramento in 1895 and discontinued it the same year; the name was for Victor F. Strauch, first postmaster (Salley, p. 214). California Division of Highways' (1934) map shows a place called Haggin located 1.5 miles northeast of downtown Sacramento along Western Pacific Railroad at the south end of the railroad crossing of American River, and shows a place called Globe situated about 1 mile north-northeast of Haggin across the river along the railroad. United States Board on Geographic Names (1992, p. 4) approved the name "Laguna West" for a populated place situated 8 miles south of the center of Sacramento (lat. 38°25'30" N, long, 121°28'20" W).

Sacramento: see **Camp Sacramento** [EL DORADO]; **North Sacramento** [SACRAMENTO]; **Point Sacramento** [SACRAMENTO]; **West Sacramento** [YOLO].

Sacramento Air Depot: see **McClellan Air Force Base** [SACRAMENTO].

Sacramento Bar: see **Fair Oaks** [SACRAMENTO].

Sacramento Bute: see **Sutter Buttes** [SUTTER].

Sacramento Bypass [YOLO]: *area,* low place that connects Sacramento River and Yolo Bypass 3 miles northwest of West Sacramento (lat. 38°36' N, long. 121°34'15" W). Named on Sacramento West (1967) 7.5' quadrangle.

Sacramento City: see **Sacramento** [SACRAMENTO].

Sacramento Deep Water Channel: see **Sacramento River Deep Water Ship Channel** [SACRAMENTO-YOLO].

Sacramento Hill [EL DORADO]: *ridge,* west-northwest- to west-trending, 1 mile long, less than 1 mile west-southwest of downtown Placerville (lat. 38°43'30" N, long. 120°48'35" W; near N line sec. 18, T 10 N, R 11 E). Named on Placerville (1949) 7.5' quadrangle.

Sacramento River [COLUSA-SACRAMENTO-SUTTER-YOLO]: *stream,* enters Colusa County from Glenn County; flows in Colusa County and along Colusa-Sutter, Sutter-Yolo, Sacramento-Yolo, and Sacramento-Solano County lines to the confluence of Sacramento River and San Joaquin River 15 miles west-southwest of Isleton (lat. 38°04' N, long. 121°51'45" W). Named on Chico (1958, limited revision 1966), Ukiah (1957), and Sacramento (1957) 1°x 2° quadrangles. Called Buenaventura River on Burr's (1839) map, and called Rio Sacramento on Fremont's (1845) map. Gabriel Moraga applied the name "Sacramento" to present Feather River, a tributary of Sacramento River, in 1808; present Sacramento River was called San Francisco and Buenaventura or Bonaventura before the name "Sacramento" was shifted to it (Hart, J.D., p. 364). Present Sutter Slough is called West Fork [of Sacramento River] on Ringgolds' (1850b) map.

Sacramento River Deep Water Ship Channel [SACRAMENTO-YOLO]: *channel,* artificially deepened and straightened waterway along the course of Sacramento River, generally on the Solano County side of Sacramento-Solano County line from the mouth of Sacramento River to the confluence of Steamboat Slough with the river, where the channel enters Solano County. Named on Antioch North (1978), Clarksburg (1967), Jersey Island (1978), Liberty Island (1978), Sacramento West (1967), and Saxon (1952, photorevised 1968) 7.5' quadrangles. Courtland (1952) 15' quadrangle shows a smaller water feature called West Cut along or near the line of present Sacramento River Deep Water Ship Channel. United States Board on Geographic Names (1978a, p. 7) rejected the names "Deep Water Ship Channel," "Sacramento Deep Water Channel," "Sacramento Ship Channel," and "Ship Channel" for present Sacramento River Deep Water Ship Channel.

Sacramento Ship Channel: see **Sacramento River Deep Water Ship Channel** [SACRAMENTO-YOLO].

Sacramento Slough [SUTTER]: *water feature,* joins Sacramento River 7.25 miles south-southeast of Robbins (lat. 38°47' N, long. 121°37'50" W). Named on Knights Landing (1952) 7.5' quadrangle.

Sacramento Valley: see "Regional setting."

Saddle Back: see **Saddleback Mountain** [SIERRA].

Saddleback Mountain [SIERRA]: *peak,* 6.5 miles south of Mount Fillmore (lat. 39°38'10" N, long. 120°51'45" W; sec. 33, T 21 N, R 10 E). Altitude 6690 feet. Named on Mount Fillmore (1951) 7.5' quadrangle Called Saddle Back on Logan's (1929) map.

Saddle Meadow [SIERRA]: *area,* 7.5 miles south-southeast of Sierraville (lat. 39°29'20" N, long. 120°18'30" W; at NE cor. sec. 21, T 19 N, R 15 E). Named on Independence Lake (1981) 7.5' quadrangle.

Saddle Mountain [EL DORADO]: *peak,* nearly 6 miles north of Pollock Pines (lat. 38°50'50" N, long. 120°34'55" W; sec. 36, T 12 N, R 12 E). Altitude 5165 feet. Named on Pollock Pines (1950) 7.5' quadrangle.

Saddle Spring Pass [YUBA]: *pass,* 2.25 miles southeast of Rackerby on Hedge Hill (lat. 39°24'25" N, long. 121°18'50" W; at W line sec. 16, T 18 N, R 6 E). Named on Rackerby (1948) 7.5' quadrangle.

Sagehen Campground [NEVADA]: *locality,* 9 miles north-northeast of Donner Pass (lat. 39°26'05" N, long. 120°15'25" W; near SE cor. sec. 1, T 18 N, R 15 E); the place is near Sagehen Creek. Named on Independence Lake (1981) 7.5' quadrangle.

Sagehen Creek [NEVADA-SIERRA]: *stream,* heads in Nevada County and flows 9.5 miles to Stampede Reservoir 15 miles south-southeast of Loyalton in Sierra County (lat. 39°27'15" N, long. 120°10'40" W; near W line sec. 35, T 19 N, R 16 E). Named on Hobart Mills (1981) and Independence Lake (1981) 7.5' quadrangles. The name has the form "Sage Hen Creek" on Truckee (1895) 30' quadrangle.

Sagehen Hills [NEVADA]: *ridge,* southwest- to west-northwest-trending, 4 miles long, center 3 miles west of Hobart Mills (lat. 39° 24'25" N, long. 120°14'40" W); the ridge is south of Sagehen Creek. Named on Hobart Mills (1981) and Independence Lake (1981) 7.5' quadrangles.

Sage Hill [PLACER]: *peak,* 3.5 miles east-northeast of Foresthill (lat. 39°02' N, long. 120°45'15" W; near W line sec. 28, T 14 N, R 11 E). Altitude 3655 feet. Named on Foresthill (1949) 7.5' quadrangle.

Sage Hill: see **Little Sage Hill** [PLACER].

Sailor Bar [SACRAMENTO]: *locality,* 4.5 miles southwest of Folsom on the north side of American River (lat. 38°38'15" N, long. 121° 14'35" W).

Named on Citrus Heights (1967) and Folsom (1967) 7.5' quadrangles. Called Sailor's Bar on Arrowsmith's (1860) map.

Sailor Canyon [PLACER]: *canyon,* drained by a stream that flows nearly 4 miles to North Fork American River 11.5 miles west of Granite Chief (lat. 39°13'05" N, long. 120°29'45" W; near SE cor. sec. 27, T 16 N, R 13 E). Named on Royal Gorge (1953) 7.5' quadrangle. Called Sailor Ravine on Truckee (1940) 30' quadrangle.

Sailor Creek: see **Big Sailor Creek** [EL DORADO]; **Little Sailor Creek** [EL DORADO].

Sailor Flat [NEVADA]:

(1) *area,* 5 miles southwest of North Bloomfield (lat. 39°18'50" N, long. 120°57'45" W; near NW cor. sec. 27, T 17 N, R 9 E). Named on North Bloomfield (1949) 7.5' quadrangle.

(2) *area,* 6 miles south of North Bloomfield (lat. 39°16'50" N, long. 120°53'05" W; sec. 5, T 16 N, R 10 E). Named on North Bloomfield (1949) 7.5' quadrangle.

Sailor Flat [PLACER]: *locality,* 1.25 miles north-northeast of Duncan Peak (lat. 39°10'25" N, long. 120°30'20" W; near SE cor. sec. 3, T 15 N, R 13 E). Named on Duncan Peak (1952) 7.5' quadrangle.

Sailor Flat Cañon: see **Blue Tent** [NEVADA].

Sailor Meadow [PLACER]: *area,* 10 miles west of Granite Chief (lat. 39°11'10" N, long. 120°28'30" W; sec. 1, T 15 N, R 13 E); the place is at the head of a branch of Sailor Canyon. Named on Royal Gorge (1953) 7.5' quadrangle.

Sailor Point [PLACER]: *ridge,* south-southwest-trending, 1 mile long, 3 miles south of Emigrant Gap (1) (lat. 39°15'30" N, long. 120°40'35" W); the ridge is east of Sailor Ravine. Named on Blue Canyon (1955) 7.5' quadrangle.

Sailor Ravine [EL DORADO]: *canyon,* drained by a stream that flows 2.5 miles to Whaler Creek 9 miles northwest of Pollock Pines (lat. 38°51'10" N, long. 120°42'10" W; at S line sec. 25, T 12 N, R 11 E). Named on Slate Mountain (1950) 7.5' quadrangle.

Sailor Ravine [PLACER]: *canyon,* drained by a stream that flows 2.5 miles to Fulda Creek 5 miles north-northwest of Westville (lat. 39°14'20" N, long. 120°41'20" W; sec. 24, T 16 N, R 11 E); the canyon is west of Sailor Point. Named on Blue Canyon (1955) and Westville (1952) 7.5' quadrangles.

Sailor Ravine [SIERRA]: *canyon,* drained by a stream that flows 1.25 miles to Downie River nearly 2 miles north of Downieville (lat. 39°35'05" N, long. 120°49'30" W; sec. 23, T 20 N, R 10 E). Named on Downieville (1951) 7.5' quadrangle.

Sailor Ravine: see **Sailor Canyon** [PLACER].

Sailor's Bar: see **Sailor Bar** [SACRAMENTO].

Sailors Flat: see **Garden Valley** [EL DORADO]; **Newtown** [NEVADA].

Sailors Gulch: see **Jackson Butte** [AMADOR].

Sailors Ravine [PLACER]: *canyon,* drained by a stream that flows nearly 4 miles to Doty Ravine 6.5 miles west of Auburn (lat. 38° 55'05" N, long. 121°11'20" W; near W line sec. 3, T 12 N, R 7 E). Named on Gold Hill (1954) 7.5' quadrangle.

Saint Catherine Creek [SIERRA]: *stream,* flows 2 miles to North Yuba River 3 miles west-southwest of Goodyears Bar (lat. 39°31'30" N, long. 120°56'10" W; sec. 11, T 19 N, R 9 E). Named on Goodyears Bar (1951) 7.5' quadrangle.

Saint Charles Hill [SIERRA]: *peak,* 2.5 miles northwest of Goodyears Bar (lat. 39°34'05" N, long. 120°54'40" W; sec. 25, T 20 N, R 9 E). Altitude 5411 feet. Named on Goodyears Bar (1951) 7.5' quadrangle.

Saint Joe Bar: see **Ramshorn Creek** [SIERRA].

Saint Lawrence: see **Kelsey** [EL DORADO].

Saint Lawrenceburgh: see **Kelsey** [EL DORADO].

Saint Louis [SIERRA]: *locality,* 4.5 miles west-southwest of Mount Fillmore (lat. 39°41'55" N, long. 120°55'25" W; sec. 12, T 21 N, R 9 E). Named on La Porte (1951) 7.5' quadrangle. Postal authorities established Saint Louis post office in 1855, discontinued it in 1895, reestablished it in 1898, and discontinued it in 1915 (Frickstad, p. 185). Miners from Missouri laid out a community in 1852 at a mining place called Sears' Diggings, and named it St. Louis for the city in their home state (Hoover, Rensch, and Rensch, p. 496). The name "Sears" was for Captain Sears, who discovered gold at the place in 1850 (Gudde, 1975, p. 313). A mining place called Challenge was located 2 miles south of St. Louis along a tributary to Slate Creek (Gudde, 1975, p. 66).

Salina Flat: see **Pat Yore Flat** [NEVADA].

Salmon Bend: see **Colusa** [COLUSA].

Salmon Creek [SIERRA]: *stream,* flows 4.25 miles to Sardine Creek 4.25 miles north of Sierra City (lat. 39°37'10" N, long. 120°36'35" W; near N line sec. 10, T 20 N, R 12 E); the stream goes through Upper Salmon Lake and Lower Salmon Lake. Named on Clio (1981), Gold Lake (1981), and Haypress Valley (1981) 7.5' quadrangles.

Salmon Creek Campground [SIERRA]: *locality,* 4 miles north-northeast of Sierra City (lat. 39°37'20" N, long. 120°36'35" W; at S line sec. sec. 3, T 20 N, R 12 E); the place is along Salmon Creek. Named on Sierra City (1955) 15' quadrangle.

Salmon Falls [EL DORADO]:

(1) *waterfall,* 6 miles south-southwest of the village of Pilot Hill along South Fork American River (lat. 38°45'30" N, long. 121°04'15" W; sec. 34, T 11 N, R 8 E). Named on Auburn (1954) 15' quadrangle. Water of Folsom Lake now covers the site. The place was a favorite fishing spot of aboriginal Indians (Hoover, Rensch, and Rensch, p. 85).

(2) *locality,* 5.5 miles south-southwest of the village of Pilot Hill along South Fork American River near Salmon Falls (1) (lat. 38° 45'40" N, long. 121°03'35" W; near E line sec. 34, T 11 N, R 8 E). Named on Auburn (1944) 15' quadrangle. Water of Folsom Lake now covers the site. Postal authorities established Salmon Falls post office in 1851, discontinued it for a time in 1875, discontinued it again for a time in 1893, and discontinued it finally in 1912 (Frickstad, p. 29). Mining began at the place in 1848, and a town was laid out in 1850 (Hoover, Rensch, and Rensch, p. 85). Arrowsmith's (1860) map shows a place called Higgins Point located along South Fork 0.5 mile west of Salmon Falls (2). The name was for an Australian who opened the first store at the place; gold was discovered there in 1849 (Gudde, 1975, p. 156).

Salmon Lake [PLACER]: *lake,* 650 feet long, 2.25 miles southeast of Cisco Grove (lat. 39°16'55" N, long. 120°30'55" W; sec. 4, T 16 N, R 13 E). Named on Cisco Grove (1955) 7.5' quadrangle.

Salmon Lake: see **Lower Salmon Lake** [SIERRA]; **Upper Salmon Lake** [SIERRA].

Salmon Lake Resort [SIERRA]: *locality,* 6.5 miles north of Sierra City (lat. 39°39'20" N, long. 120°39'15" W; sec. 29, T 21 N, R 12 E); the place is by Upper Salmon Lake. Named on Gold Lake (1981) 7.5' quadrangle.

Salmon Trout River: see **Truckee River** [NEVADA-PLACER-SIERRA].

Salsbury [SACRAMENTO]: *locality,* 4 miles east of present downtown Carmichael along Southern Pacific Railroad (lat. 38°36'50" N, long. 121°15'10" W). Named on Mills (1911) 7.5' quadrangle. Postal authorities established Salsbury post office in 1858 and discontinued it in 1869; the name was for Thompson G. Salsbury, first postmaster (Salley, p. 192).

Salt Arroyo [YOLO]: *canyon,* 5.25 miles long, opens into Capay Valley 5.5 miles west of Esparto (lat. 38°41'35" N, long. 122°07'10" W; at S line sec. 19, T 10 N, R 2 W). Named on Brooks (1959) and Esparto (1959) 7.5' quadrangles. Called Salt Canyon on Capay (1945) 15' quadrangle, but United States Board on Geographic Names (1962a, p. 15) rejected this name.

Salt Branch [COLUSA]: *stream,* flows 1.5 miles to West Fork Sulphur Creek nearly 3 miles west-northwest of Wilbur Springs (lat. 39°03'25" N, long. 122°28' W; near E line sec. 13, T 14 N, R 6 W). Named on Wilbur Springs (1961) 15' quadrangle.

Salt Canyon [COLUSA]: *canyon,* 2 miles long, along Salt Creek (2) above a point 8 miles northeast of Wilbur Springs (lat. 39°06'30" N, long. 122°18'15" W; sec. 33, T 15 N, R 4 W). Named on Wilbur Springs (1961) 15' quadrangle.

Salt Canyon [YOLO]: *canyon,* 2 miles long, along South Fork Buckeye Creek above a point 4.25 miles east of Guinda (lat. 38°50' N, long. 122°06'55" W; near W line sec. 5, T 11 N, R 2 W). Named on Bird Valley (1959) and Guinda (1959) 7.5' quadrangles.

Salt Canyon: see **Little Salt Canyon** [YOLO]; **Salt Arroyo** [YOLO].

Salt Creek [COLUSA]:

(1) *stream,* flows 7.5 miles to Stony Creek 0.5 mile northwest of Stonyford (lat. 39°22'55" N, long. 122°33'05" W; sec. 29, T 18 N, R 6 W). Named on Fouts Springs (1968), Gilmore Peak (1968), and Stonyford (1968) 7.5' quadrangles.

(2) *stream,* flows 22 miles to Freshwater Creek 3.25 miles north-northeast of Williams (lat. 39°11'35" N, long. 122°06'55" W; at W line sec. 32, T 16 N, R 2 W). Named on Colusa (1953) and Wilbur Springs (1961) 15' quadrangles.

(3) *stream,* flows to Sycamore Slough 4 miles northeast of Arbuckle (lat. 39°03'25" N, long. 121°59'50" W). Named on Arbuckle (1952), Rumsey (1959), and Wildwood School (1959) 7.5' quadrangles.

Salt Creek [EL DORADO]: *stream,* flows 2 miles to North Fork American River nearly 2 miles west of Cool (lat. 38°53'15" N, long. 121°02'55" W; sec. 14, T 12 N, R 8 E). Named on Auburn (1953) 7.5' quadrangle.

Salt Creek [NEVADA]: *stream,* flows 3.5 miles to South Wolf Creek 2.25 miles north-northeast of Higgins Corner (lat. 39°04'10" N, long. 121°04'05" W; near NE cor. sec. 15, T 14 N, R 8 E). Named on Lake Combie (1949) 7.5' quadrangle.

Salt Creek [YOLO]:

(1) *stream,* flows nearly 6 miles to Chickahominy Slough 6.5 miles south of Esparto (lat. 38°35'35" N, long. 122°02'10" W; sec. 25, T 9 N, R 2 W). Named on Monticello Dam (1959) 7.5' quadrangle.

(2) *stream,* flows 2.25 miles from the mouth of Salt Arroyo to Cache Creek 4.5 miles west-northwest of Esparto (lat. 38°42'35" N, long. 122°05'40" W). Named on Esparto (1959) 7.5' quadrangle

Salt Lake [COLUSA]: *intermittent lake,* 850 feet long, 4 miles north of Sites (lat. 39°22'05" N, long. 122°20'20" W; sec. 32, T 18 N, R 4 W). Named on Sites (1958) 7.5' quadrangle.

Salt Rock Creek [EL DORADO]: *stream,* flows 2 miles to Steely Fork

Cosumnes River 7.5 miles southwest of Old Iron Mountain (lat. 38°37'35" N, long. 120°29'05" W; near N line sec. 24, T 9 N, R 13 E). Named on Stump Spring (1951) 7.5' quadrangle.

Salt Springs Reservoir [AMADOR]: *lake,* behind a dam on North Fork Mokelumne River 7 miles west-southwest of Mokelumne Peak on Amador-Calaveras County line (lat. 38°29'55" N, long. 120°12'55" W; sec. 33, T 8 N, R 16 E). Named on Bear River Reservoir (1979) and Calaveras Dome (1979) 7.5' quadrangles.

Salvation Ravine [PLACER]: *canyon,* drained by a stream that flows 2 miles to North Fork American River 4 miles southeast of Colfax (lat. 39°03'15" N, long. 120°54'15" W; at N line sec. 19, T 14 N, R 10 E). Named on Colfax (1949) 7.5' quadrangle.

San Andreas Shoal [SACRAMENTO]: *shoal,* 4.5 miles south-southeast of Isleton in San Joaquin River (lat. 38°06'05" N, long. 121° 35'10" W). Named on Bouldin Island (1978) 7.5' quadrangle.

Sand Creek [COLUSA-YOLO]: *stream,* flows 20 miles to an artificial watercourse 4.25 miles north-northeast of Arbuckle (lat. 39°04'05" N, long. 122°00'35" W; sec. 18, T 14 N, R 1 W). Named on Arbuckle (1952), Cortina Creek (1953), and Rumsey (1959) 7.5' quadrangles. South Branch enters the main creek 2.25 miles west-northwest of Arbuckle; it is nearly 5 miles long and is named on Arbuckle (1952) and Cortina Creek (1953) 7.5' quadrangles. East Fork, which heads in Yolo County, enters the main creek 9.5 miles upstream from the mouth of South Fork; it is 5.25 miles long and is named on Rumsey (1959) 7.5' quadrangle. North Branch diverges northeast from Sand Creek 4.25 miles west-northwest of Arbuckle and flows 5.5 miles to an artificial watercourse in lowlands; it is named on Arbuckle (1952) and Cortina Creek (1953) 7.5' quadrangles.

Sanders [SUTTER]: *locality,* 5 miles north-northwest of Yuba City along Sacramento Northern Railroad (lat. 39°12'10" N, long. 121° 39'40" W; near N line sec. 32, T 16 N, R 3 E). Named on Sutter (1952) 7.5' quadrangle.

Sand Flat [NEVADA]: *area,* 3 miles northeast of Higgins Corner (lat. 39°04'15" N, long. 121°03'25" W; near N line sec. 14, T 14 N, R 8 E). Named on Lake Combie (1949) 7.5' quadrangle.

Sand Flat: see **Dry Creek** [YUBA].

Sand Hills [YUBA]: *ridge,* generally northwest-trending, 1.5 miles long, 1.25 miles northwest of Smartville at Timbuctoo Bend (lat. 39°13'20" N, long. 121°18'50" W). Named on Smartville (1951) 7.5' quadrangle.

Sand Mountain [EL DORADO]: *peak,* 8.5 miles north-northwest of Pollock Pines (lat. 38°52'20" N, long. 120°39'20" W; sec. 20, T 12 N, R 12 E). Altitude 4762 feet. Named on Slate Mountain (1950) 7.5' quadrangle.

Sand Mountain: see **Freel Peak** [EL DORADO].

Sand Pond [SIERRA]: *lake,* 350 feet long, 3.5 miles north of Sierra City (lat. 39°37' N, long. 120°37'15" W; near W line sec. 10, T 20 N, R 12 E). Named on Haypress Valley (1981) 7.5' quadrangle.

Sand Ridge [NEVADA]:

(1) *ridge,* east-trending, 1.25 miles long, 3 miles south-southwest of English Mountain (lat. 39°24'25" N, long. 120°34'45" W). Named on English Mountain (1983) 7.5' quadrangle.

(2) *ridge,* west-southwest-trending, 1 mile long, 5.5 miles northwest of Donner Pass (lat. 39°22'05" N, long. 120°23'55" W; on W line sec. 3, T 17 N, R 14 E). Named on Soda Springs (1955) 7.5' quadrangle.

Sand Ridge Lake [NEVADA]: *lake,* 600 feet long, 5.25 miles northwest of Donner Pass (lat. 39°22'35" N, long. 120°23'15" W; near S line sec. 34, T 18 N, R 14 E); the lake is northeast of Sand Ridge (2). Named on Webber Peak (1981) 7.5' quadrangle.

Sandusky Creek [SIERRA]: *stream,* flows 1.5 miles to Lucky Dog Creek 2 miles west-northwest of Alleghany (lat. 39°29'15" N, long. 120°52'20" W; near E line sec. 29, T 19 N, R 10 E). Named on Alleghany (1949) and Downieville (1951) 7.5' quadrangles.

Sanford Creek [YUBA]: *stream,* flows 2 miles to Big Ravine about 1 mile west-northwest of Smartville (lat. 39°12'40" N, long. 121° 18'50" W; at W line sec. 28, T 16 N, R 6 E). Named on Smartville (1951) 7.5' quadrangle.

Sanford Lake [NEVADA]: *lake,* 1150 feet long, 5 miles south-southwest of English Mountain (lat. 39°23'15" N, long. 120°36'10" W; near NW cor. sec. 35, T 18 N, R 12 E). Named on English Mountain (1983) 7.5' quadrangle.

San Joachin River: see **San Joaquin River** [SACRAMENTO].

San Joaquin River [SACRAMENTO]: *stream,* flows 20 miles along Sacramento-Contra Costa County line to join Sacramento River 15 miles west-southwest of Isleton at the west tip of Sacramento County (lat. 38°04' N, long. 121°51'45" W). Named on Antioch North (1978), Bouldin Island (1978), and Jersey Island (1978) 7.5' quadrangles. Called Rio San Joaquin on Fremont's (1845) map, called San Joachin R. on Wilkes' (1849) map, called Joaquin River on Jefferson's (1849) map, and called Rio Tulare or San Joaquin on Sage's (1846) map. Gabriel Moraga named the river about 1805 for Saint Joachim, father of the Virgin Mary (Hart, J.D., p. 379).

Sanjon de los Moquelumnes [SACRAMENTO]: *land grant,* 20 miles south-southeast of downtown Sacramento; extends south into San Joaquin County at and near Galt. Named on Bruceville (1968), Clay (1968), Elk Grove (1968), Galt (1968), Lodi North (1968), and Thornton (1978) 7.5' quadrangles. Anastacio Chabolla received 8 leagues in 1844; Angel Chabolla and Maria C. Chabolla claimed 35,508 acres patented in 1865 (Cowan, p. 49; Cowan listed the grant under the name "Zanjon de los Moquelumnes"). Perez (p. 96) used the surname "Chaboya" for the patentees.

San Juan [SACRAMENTO]: *land grant,* north of American River from Carmichael to Folsom. Named on Carmichael (1967), Citrus Heights (1967), and Folsom (1967) 7.5' quadrangles. Joel P. Dedmond received 4.5 leagues in 1844; Hiram Grimes claimed 19,983 acres patented in 1860 (Cowan, p. 81).

San Juan: see **North San Juan** [NEVADA].

San Juan Canyon [SIERRA]: *canyon,* drained by a stream that flows 2.5 miles to North Yuba River 2.5 miles east of Downieville (lat. 39°33'05" N, long. 120°46'45" W; near S line sec. 31, T 20 N, R 11 E). Named on Downieville (1951) 7.5' quadrangle.

San Juan Ridge [NEVADA]: *ridge,* extends for about 24 miles east-northeast between Middle Yuba River and South Yuba River. Named on Alleghany (1949), Camptonville (1948), French Corral (1948), Nevada City (1948), North Bloomfield (1949), and Pike (1949) 7.5' quadrangles.

Sankey [SUTTER]: *locality,* 3.25 miles south-southwest of Pleasant Grove (1) along an abandoned line of Sacramento Northern Railroad (lat. 38°46'40" N, long. 121°29'55" W; sec. 26, T 11 N, R 4 E). Named on Pleasant Grove (1967) 7.5' quadrangle.

Santa Clara Shoal [SACRAMENTO]: *shoal,* 5.25 miles south-southwest of Isleton in San Joaquin River on Sacramento-Contra Costa County line (lat. 38°05'25" N, long. 121°38'45" W). Named on Jersey Island (1978) 7.5' quadrangle.

Santa Maria Gulch [AMADOR]: *canyon,* drained by a stream that flows 1.5 miles to Grapevine Gulch (2) 3.5 miles south-southwest of Jackson (lat. 38°18'10" N, long. 120°48'30" W; sec. 7, T 5 N, R 11 E). Named on Jackson (1962) 7.5' quadrangle.

Sarahsville: see **Bath** [PLACER]; **Clinton** [AMADOR].

Sarahville: see **Clinton** [AMADOR].

Saratoga: see **Yeomet**, under **Entrprise** [AMADOR].

Sardine Bar [EL DORADO-PLACER]: *locality,* 3.5 miles northwest of Greenwood along Middle Fork American River on El Dorado-Placer County line (lat. 38°56'05" N, long. 121°56'05" W; sec. 34, T 13 N, R 9 E). Named on Greenwood (1949) 7.5' quadrangle.

Sardine Campground [SIERRA]: *locality,* 3.5 miles north-northeast of Sierra City (lat. 39°37'10" N, long. 120°37'05" W; sec. 10, T 20 N, R 12 E); the place is along Sardine Creek. Named on Sierra City (1955) 15' quadrangle.

Sardine Creek [SIERRA]: *stream,* flows 2 miles from Lower Sardine Lake to North Yuba River 3 miles north-northeast of Sierra City (lat. 39°36'15" N, long. 120°36'25" W; near NE cor. sec. 15, T 20 N, R 12 E). Named on Haypress Valley (1981) 7.5' quadrangle.

Sardine Lake: see **Lower Sardine Lake** [SIERRA]: **Upper Sardine Lake** [SIERRA].

Sardine Lake Resort [SIERRA]: *locality,* 3.5 miles north of Sierra City (lat. 39°37' N, long. 120°37'20" W; on W line sec. 10, T 20 N, R 12 E); the place is at the east end of Lower Sardine Lake. Named on Haypress Valley (1981) 7.5' quadrangle.

Sardine Peak [SIERRA]: *peak,* 10 miles south-southeast of Loyalton (lat. 39°32'25" N, long. 120°11'10" W; sec. 34, T 20 N, R 16 E). Altitude 8135 feet. Named on Sardine Peak (1981) 7.5' quadrangle.

Sardine Point [SIERRA]: *peak,* 9 miles south-southeast of Loyalton (lat. 39°33' N, long. 120°12'15" W; near S line sec. 28, T 20 N, R 16 E); the peak is 1 mile northwest of Sardine Peak. Altitude 7578 feet. Named on Sardine Peak (1981) 7.5' quadrangle.

Sardine Spring [NEVADA]: *spring,* nearly 4 miles south-southeast of Washington (lat. 39°18'35" N, long. 120°45'55" W; sec. 29, T 17 N, R 11 E). Named on Washington (1950) 7.5' quadrangle.

Sardine Spring [SIERRA]: *spring,* 9 miles south-southeast of Loyalton (lat. 39°32'20" N, long. 120°11'45" W; near NW cor. sec. 34, T 20 N, R 16 E); the spring is 3500 feet northwest of Sardine Peak. Named on Sardine Peak (1981) 7.5' quadrangle.

Sardine Valley [SIERRA]: *valley,* 12.5 miles south-southeast of Loyalton (lat. 39°31'10" N, long. 120°08' W). Named on Dog Valley (1981) and Sardine Peak (1981) 7.5' quadrangles, which show marsh in most of the valley.

Sattley [SIERRA]: *village,* 3.5 miles west-northwest of Sierraville (lat. 39°36'55" N, long. 120°25'30" W; sec. 4, T 20 N, R 14 E). Named on Sattley (1981) 7.5' quadrangle. Postal authorities established Sattley post office in 1884, discontinued it in 1918, and reestablished it in 1919 (Frickstad, p. 185). The name commemorates Harriet Sattley Church, wife of Ezra Bliss Church; the place first was called Churchs Corners (Hanna, p. 296). Postal authorities established Rocky Point post office 5 miles north of Sattley in 1876, changed the name to Rockypoint in 1895, and discontinued it in 1897 (Salley, p. 187).

Saucer Lake [EL DORADO]: *lake,* 350 feet long, 3 miles west-northwest of Echo Summit (lat. 38°50' N, long. 120°04'35" W; sec. 2, T 11 N, R 17 E);

the lake is 1 mile east-northeast of Cup Lake. Named on Echo Lake (1955) 7.5' quadrangle.

Sauterne [YOLO]: *locality,* 0.5 mile north-northwest of Guinda along Southern Pacific Railroad in Capay Valley (lat. 38°50'15" N, long. 122°11'55" W). Named on Rumsey (1921) 15' quadrangle.

Saw Mill Bar: see **Parks Bar** [YUBA].

Sawmill Creek [EL DORADO]: *stream,* flows 2.25 miles to French Creek 1.5 miles south-southeast of Shingle Springs (lat. 38°38'40" N, long. 120°54'30" W; near SW cor. sec. 8, T 9 N, R 10 E). Named on Shingle Springs (1949) 7.5' quadrangle.

Sawmill Creek [SIERRA]: *stream,* flows 2 miles to Salmon Creek 5 miles north of Sierra City (lat. 39°38'20" N, long. 120°37'30" W; near W line sec. 34, T 21 N, R 12 E). Named on Gold Lake (1981) 7.5' quadrangle.

Sawmill Flat [PLACER]: *area,* 5 miles southwest of Martis Peak (lat. 39°15'15" N, long. 120°06'30" W; sec. 8, T 16 N, R 17 E). Named on Martis Peak (1955) 7.5' quadrangle.

Sawmill Lake [NEVADA]: *lake,* behind a dam on Canyon Creek 2.5 miles west of English Mountain (lat. 39°26'45" N, long. 120°36'05" W; near NW cor. sec. 11, T 18 N, R 12 E). Named on English Mountain (1983) 7.5' quadrangle.

Sawmill Ravine [SIERRA]:

(1) *canyon,* drained by a stream that flows 1.5 miles to Slate Creek nearly 6 miles southwest of Mount Fillmore (lat. 39°41'05" N, long. 120°56'25" W; sec. 14, T 21 N, R 9 E). Named on La Porte (1951) 7.5' quadrangle.

(2) *canyon,* drained by a stream that flows 2 miles to Canyon Creek 6 miles northwest of Goodyears Bar (lat. 39°36'15" N, long. 120° 57'35" W; sec. 15, T 20 N, R 9 E). Named on Goodyears Bar (1951) 7.5' quadrangle.

Sawmill Ridge [SIERRA]: *ridge,* generally southwest-trending, 4 miles long, 2 miles west-northwest of Mount Fillmore (lat. 39° 44' N, long. 120°53'15" W). Named on Blue Nose Mountain (1951), La Porte (1951), and Mount Fillmore (1951) 7.5' quadrangles.

Sawpit Spring [PLACER]: *spring,* less than 1 mile west-northwest of Devil Peak (lat. 38°57'55" N, long. 120°33'30" W; near W line sec. 20, T 13 N, R 13 E). Named on Devil Peak (1950) 7.5' quadrangle.

Sawtooth Ridge [PLACER]:

(1) *ridge,* generally northwest-trending, 3 miles long, 5.5 miles north-northwest of Tahoe City (lat. 39°14'50" N, long. 120°10'15" W). Named on Tahoe City (1955) and Truckee (1955) 7.5' quadrangles.

(2) *ridge,* generally west-trending, 9 miles long, center 3.5 miles northwest of Westville (lat. 39°13' N, long. 120°41'15" W). Named on Duncan Peak (1952), Dutch Flat (1950), and Westville (1952) 7.5' quadrangles.

Saxon [YOLO]: *locality,* 7.5 miles west-northwest of Clarksburg along Sacramento Northern Railroad (lat. 38°28' N, long. 121°39'15" W; near W line sec. 9, T 7 N, R 3 E). Named on Saxon (1952) 7.5' quadrangle.

Saxon Creek [EL DORADO]: *stream,* flows 6 miles to Trout Creek 4.5 miles west-northwest of Freel Peak (lat. 38°53' N, long. 119° 58'45" W; sec. 15, T 12 N, R 18 E). Named on Freel Peak (1955) and South Lake Tahoe (1955) 7.5' quadrangles.

Saxonia Lake [SIERRA]: *lake,* 1050 feet long, 3.5 miles north of Sierra City (lat. 39°37'05" N, long. 120°38'15" W; near NW cor. sec. 9, T 20 N, R 12 E). Named on Sierra City (1981) 7.5' quadrangle.

Sayles Canyon [EL DORADO]: *canyon,* drained by a stream that flows nearly 5 miles to South Fork American River 4.5 miles west of Echo Summit (lat. 38°48'05" N, long. 120°06'40" W; sec. 16, T 11 N, R 17 E). Named on Echo Lake (1955) 7.5' quadrangle.

Sayles Flat [EL DORADO]: *locality,* nearly 5 miles west of Echo Summit along South Fork American River (lat. 38°48'10" N, long. 120°07' W; on W line sec. 16, T 11 N, R 17 E). Named on Echo Lake (1955) 7.5' quadrangle.

Scadden Flat [NEVADA]: *area,* 1 mile southwest of downtown Grass Valley (lat. 39°12'35" N, long. 121°04'40" W; near NE cor. sec. 33, T 16 N, R 8 E). Named on Grass Valley (1949) 7.5' quadrangle.

Scales [SIERRA]: *locality,* 7 miles northwest of Goodyears Bar (lat. 39°35'50" N, long. 120°59'30" W; sec. 17, T 20 N, R 9 E). Named on Goodyears Bar (1951) 7.5' quadrangle. Postal authorities established Scales Diggings post office in 1871, discontinued it in 1875, reestablished it with the name "Scales" in 1880, and discontinued it in 1923 (Salley, p. 199). A mining place called Council Hill was situated about 1.5 miles southwest of Scales Diggings on the same ridge (Marlette, p. 202).

Scales Diggings: see **Scales** [SIERRA].

Schad [SACRAMENTO]: *locality,* 8 miles south-southwest of Isleton on Sherman Island (lat. 38°03'50" N, long. 121°41' W). Named on Jersey (1910) 7.5' quadrangle. Postal authorities established Schad post office in 1910 and discontinued it in 1918 (Salley, p. 199).

Schaeffer Camp: see **Old Schaeffer Camp** [PLACER]

Schaeffer Mill: see **Old Schaeffer Mill** [PLACER].

Schallenberger Ridge [PLACER]: *ridge,* west-southwest- to southwest-trending, 2.5 miles long, 3 miles east-southeast of Donner Pass (lat. 39°18'20" N, long. 120°16'20" W). Named on Norden (1955) 7.5' quadrangle. The name is for Moses Schallenberger, a young emigrant who spent the winter of 1844 and 1845 in a log cabin below the ridge (Stewart, p. 11).

Schenck Camp [EL DORADO]: *locality,* 10 miles west-southwest of Kirkwood (lat. 38°39'20" N, long. 120°14'50" W; sec. 6, T 9 N, R 16 E). Named on Tragedy Spring (1979) 7.5' quadrangle.

Schleins Diggings: see **Tipton Hill** [EL DORADO].

Schmidell: see **Lake Schmidell** [EL DORADO].

Schneider: see **Jake Schneider Meadow** [EL DORADO].

Schneider Camp [EL DORADO]: *locality,* 2 miles northeast of Kirkwood (lat. 38°43'30" N, long. 120°03' W; sec. 7, T 10 N, R 18 E). Named on Caples Lake (1979) 7.5' quadrangle.

Schoolcraft Island: see **Sutter Island** [SACRAMENTO].

Schoolhouse Canyon [COLUSA]: *canyon,* drained by a stream that flows less than 1 mile to Sulphur Creek 1 mile west-southwest of Wilbur Springs (lat. 39°02'10" N, long. 122°26'15" W; sec. 29, T 14 N, R 5 W). Named on Wilbur Springs (1961) 15' quadrangle.

Schoolhouse Creek [YUBA]: *stream,* flows 0.5 mile to New Bullards Bar Reservoir 5 miles northeast of Dobbins (lat. 39°24'55" N, long. 121°07'55" W; near SE cor. sec. 13, T 18 N, R 7 E). Named on Camptonville (1948) and Challenge (1948, photorevised 1969) 7.5' quadrangles.

Schoolhouse Divide [COLUSA]: *ridge,* 8 miles east-southeast of Wilbur Springs (lat. 39°00'15" N, long. 122°16'45"). Named on Wilbur Springs (1961) 15' quadrangle.

School Land Gulch [AMADOR]: *canyon,* drained by a stream that flows 1 mile to Mokelumne River 4 miles south of Jackson (lat. 38°17'20" N, long. 120°46'25" W; sec. 16, T 5 N, R 11 E). Named on Jackson (1962) 7.5' quadrangle.

Sciata Creek: see **Curry Creek** [PLACER-SUTTER].

Sciots Camp [EL DORADO]: *locality,* 4 miles south of Pyramid Peak along South Fork American River (lat. 38°47'15" N, long. 120°09'10" W; near W line sec. 19, T 11 N, R 17 E). Named on Pyramid Peak (1955) 7.5' quadrangle.

Scotchman Creek [NEVADA]: *stream,* flows 3.5 miles to South Yuba River 1 mile east of Washington (lat. 39°21'25" N, long. 120°46'55" W; sec. 7, T 17 N, R 11 E). Named on Washington (1950) 7.5' quadrangle. Called Scotchman's Creek on Whitney's (1873) map, which has the name "Krumbacker's Rav." for a canyon that opens into the canyon of Scotchman's Creek from the southwest less than 0.5 mile above the mouth of Scotchman's Creek. Gudde (1975, p. 88) used the form "Crumbecker" for the name of the side canyon. Whitney's (1873) map also has the name "Baltimore Rav." for a canyon that enters the canyon of Scotchman's Creek from the southeast less than 1 mile above the mouth of Scotchman's Creek. Gudde (1975, p. 44, 295) listed two mining places, Boulder Bar and Rocky Bar, that were situated at the mouth of Scotchman Creek, but Bancroft (1888, p. 358) indicated that these two places were one and the same. Gudde (1975, p. 177, 197) also listed places called Long Bar and Jimmy Brown Bar that were situated along South Yuba River above the mouth of Scotchman Creek.

Scott Bar Creek: see **Empire Creek** [YUBA].

Scott Creek [EL DORADO]: *stream,* flows 16 miles to South Fork Cosumnes River 0.5 mile south-southeast of Aukum (lat. 38°32'50" N, long. 120°43'15" W; near W line sec. 13, T 8 N, R 11 E). Named on Aukum (1952), Caldor (1951), and Omo Ranch (1952) 7.5' quadrangles. Called South Fork Cosumnes River on Placerville (1893) 30' quadrangle, which has the name "South Fork of South Fork Cosumnes River" for present South Fork Cosumnes River.

Scott Hill [PLACER]: *ridge,* south-southwest-trending, 0.5 mile long, 3.25 miles south of Emigrant Gap (1) (lat. 39°15'15" N, long. 120° 39'50" W; sec. 18, T 16 N, R 12 E). Named on Blue Canyon (1955) 7.5' quadrangle.

Scott Hill [YUBA]: *peak,* 1.25 miles west of Dobbins (lat. 39°22'10" N, long. 121°13'40" W; near S line sec. 31, T 18 N, R 7 E). Named on French Corral (1948) 7.5' quadrangle.

Scotties Canyon [COLUSA]: *canyon,* drained by a stream that flows 1.5 miles to Grapevine Creek 3.5 miles east of Lodoga (lat. 39° 18'15" N, long. 122°25'10" W; near S line sec. 21, T 17 N, R 5 W). Named on Lodoga (1960) 15' quadrangle.

Scotties Canyon: see **East Scotties Canyon** [COLUSA].

Scotties Spring [COLUSA]: *spring,* 3.5 miles east of Lodoga along Grapevine Creek at the mouth of East Scotties Canyon (lat. 39°18'20" N, long. 122°25'15" W; sec. 21, T 17 N, R 5 W). Named on Lodoga (1960) 15' quadrangle.

Scott Peak [PLACER]: *peak,* 4.5 miles west-southwest of Tahoe City (lat. 39°09'30" N, long. 120°13'20" W; sec. 9, T 15 N, R 16 E). Altitude 8289 feet. Named on Tahoe City (1955) 7.5' quadrangle.

Scott Ravine [YUBA]: *canyon,* drained by a stream that flows less than 1 mile to Owl Creek 1 mile south-southwest of Strawberry Valley (lat. 39°32'55" N, long. 121°07' W; at E line sec. 31, T 20 N, R 8 E). Named on Clipper Mills (1948) and Strawberry Valley (1948) 7.5' quadrangles.

Scotts Flat [NEVADA]:

(1) *valley,* 6 miles south of North Bloomfield along Deer Creek (lat. 39°16'30" N, long. 120°55' W). Named on Colfax (1938) 30' quadrangle.

(2) *locality,* 6 miles south of North Bloomfield (lat. 39°16'45" N, long. 120°54'45" W); the place is at Scotts Flat (1). Named on Colfax (1898)

30' quadrangle. Whitney's (1873) map shows a place called Six Mile Ho. [House] located 1 mile west-northwest of Scotts Flat (2).

Scotts Flat Reservoir [NEVADA]: *lake,* behind a dam on Deer Creek 7 miles south-southwest of North Bloomfield (lat. 39°16'20" N, long. 120°55'50" W; on S line sec. 2, T 16 N, R 9 E); water of the reservoir covers Scotts Flat (1). Named on North Bloomfield (1949, photorevised 1973) 7.5' quadrangle.

Scotts Springs: see **Deer Park** [PLACER].

Scottsville [AMADOR]: *locality,* 1.5 miles southeast of Jackson (lat. 38°20'05" N, long. 120°45'20" W; sec. 34, T 6 N, R 11 E). Named on Jackson (1962) 7.5' quadrangle'

Screech Owl Canyon [EL DORADO]: *canyon,* drained by a stream that flows 1.5 miles to Alder Creek 4.5 miles west-southwest of Kyburz (lat. 38°45'20" N, long. 120°22'20" W; sec. 35, T 11 N, R 14 E). Named on Kyburz (1952), Leek Spring Hill (1951), Riverton (1950), and Stump Spring (1951) 7.5' quadrangles.

Screech Owl Creek [EL DORADO]: *stream,* flows 1.5 miles to Carson Creek near Clarksville (lat. 38°39'10" N, long. 121°03'20" W; sec. 12, T 9 N, R 8 E). Named on Clarksville (1953) 7.5' quadrangle.

Screwauger Canyon [PLACER]: *canyon,* drained by a stream that flows 6 miles to Middle Fork American River 5 miles west-southwest of Duncan Peak (lat. 39°07'20" N, long. 120°35'35" W; sec. 25, T 15 N, R 12 E). Named on Duncan Peak (1952) and Greek Store (1952) 7.5' quadrangles. Whitney's (1880) map has the form "Screw Auger Gulch" for the name.

Screw Auger Gulch: see **Screwauger Canyon** [PLACER].

Sears' Diggings: see **Saint Louis** [SIERRA].

Sears Ravine [SIERRA]: *canyon,* drained by a stream that flows 0.5 mile to Slate Creek 4.5 miles west-southwest of Mount Fillmore (lat. 39°42'15" N, long. 120°55'50" W; near SW cor. sec. 1, T 21 N, R 9 E). Named on La Porte (1951) 7.5' quadrangle.

Sears Ridge: see **Port Wine Ridge** [SIERRA].

Sebastopol [NEVADA]: *locality,* 1 mile west-southwest of North San Juan (lat. 39°21'45" N, long. 121°07'10" W; sec. 6, T 17 N, R 8 E). Named on Nevada City (1948) 7.5' quadrangle. The place was named at the time of the Crimean War, when the siege of Sebastopol was of world-wide interest (Gudde, 1975, p. 313).

Sebastopol [SACRAMENTO]: *locality,* 22 miles east-southeast of downtown Sacramento (lat. 38°27'30" N, long. 121°07' W). Named on Lodi (1894) 30' quadrangle. The place was a mining camp in the 1850's named during the Crimean War (Hoover, Rensch, and Rensch, p. 301).

Second Bannon Slough [SACRAMENTO]: *water feature,* joins Sacramento River 2.5 miles northwest of downtown Sacramento (lat. 38°36'20" N, long. 121°31'25" W); the feature is in American Basin 1 mile west of First Bannon Slough. Named on Lovedal (1916) 7.5' quadrangle.

Second Brushy Canyon [PLACER]: *canyon,* 2.25 miles long, opens into the head of Brushy Canyon (1) 2.25 miles west-northwest of Foresthill (lat. 39°02'15" N, long. 120°51'15" W; near N line sec. 28, T 14 N, R 10 E). Named on Foresthill (1949) 7.5' quadrangle.

Second Divide [SIERRA]: *pass,* nearly 3 miles north-northeast of Downieville on the ridge between Lavezzola Creek and Pauley Creek (lat. 39°35'40" N, long. 120°47'55" W; near SE cor. sec. 12, T 20 N, R 10 E); the pass is 1 mile northeast of First Divide. Named on Downieville (1951) 7.5' quadrangle.

Second Sugarloaf [PLACER]: *peak,* 6.25 miles north-northwest of Foresthill (lat. 38°06' N, long. 120°52'20" W; near S line sec. 32, T 15 N, R 10 E); the peak is less than 0.5 mile southwest of First Sugarloaf. Altitude 3066 feet. Named on Foresthill (1949) 7.5' quadrangle. This peak and First Sugarloaf together are called Sugar Loaves on Colfax (1898) 30' quadrangle.

Secreta: see **Clinton** [AMADOR].

Secret Canyon [PLACER]: *canyon,* drained by a stream that flows 9 miles to North Fork of Middle Fork American River 7.5 miles northeast of Michigan Bluff (lat. 39°07' N, long. 120°38' W; near E line sec. 28, T 15 N, R 12 E). Named on Duncan Peak (1952), Michigan Bluff (1952), and Westville (1952) 7.5' quadrangles.

Secret Canyon [SIERRA]: *canyon,* drained by a stream that flows 2.5 miles to North Yuba River 2.25 miles east-southeast of Downieville (lat. 39°33'10" N, long. 120°47'05" W; near S line sec. 31, T 20 N, R 11 E). Named on Downieville (1951) 7.5' quadrangle. Gudde (1975, p. 235) listed a mining place called Negro Bar that was located opposite Secret Canyon, and (p. 251) a mining place called Omits Flat that also was located opposite Secret Canyon.

Secret Canyon: see **Little Secret Canyon** [PLACER]; **Secret House** [PLACER].

Secret House [PLACER]: *locality,* 4.5 miles west-northwest of Duncan Peak (lat. 39°11'15" N, long. 120°35'05" W; sec. 1, T 15 N, R 12 E); the place is northwest of Little Secret Canyon. Named on Duncan Peak (1952) 7.5' quadrangle. Colfax (1898) 30' quadrangle has the name "Secret Canyon" for an inhabited place at or near present Secret House.

Secret Lake [EL DORADO]: *lake,* 400 feet long, 2.25 miles west-northwest of Pyramid Peak (lat. 38°51'10" N, long. 120°11'50" W). Named on Pyramid Peak (1955) 7.5' quadrangle.

Secret Lake [NEVADA]: *lake,* 550 feet long, 1 mile northeast of English Mountain (lat. 39°27'25" N, long. 120°32'15" W; sec. 5, T 18 N, R 13 E). Named on English Mountain (1983) 7.5' quadrangle.

Secret Meadow [SIERRA]: *area,* 10 miles south-southeast of Sierraville (lat. 39°27'40" N, long. 120°16'20" W; at SE cor. sec. 26, T 19 N, R 15 E). Named on Independence Lake (1981) 7.5' quadrangle.

Secret Ravine [PLACER]:

(1) *canyon,* drained by a stream that flows 3.5 miles to North Fork American River 3 miles east-northeast of Colfax (lat. 39°07' N, long. 120°53'55" W; near S line sec. 30, T 15 N, R 10 E); the canyon heads near the site of Secret Town. Named on Chicago Park (1949), Colfax (1949), and Dutch Flat (1950) 7.5' quadrangles. Called Robbers Ravine on Colfax (1938) 30' quadrangle.

(2) *canyon,* drained by a stream that flows 11 miles to Miners Ravine 1.5 miles east-northeast of downtown Roseville (lat. 38° 45'35" N, long. 121°15'20" W; sec. 36, T 11 N, R 6 E). Named on Rocklin (1967) and Roseville (1967) 7.5' quadrangles.

Secret Ravine: see **Newcastle** [PLACER].

Secret Ridge [SIERRA]: *ridge,* north-northeast-trending, 1.25 miles long, 1.5 miles southeast of Downieville (lat. 39°32'40" N, long. 120°48'15" W; sec. 1, T 19 N, R 10 E); the ridge is northwest of Secret Canyon. Named on Downieville (1951) 7.5' quadrangle.

Secret Town [PLACER]: *locality,* 5 miles northeast of Colfax (lat. 39°09'30" N, long. 120°52'45" W; near SW cor. sec. 8, T 15 N, R 10 E). Site named on Chicago Park (1949) 7.5' quadrangle.

Selby Flat [NEVADA]: *area,* 2 miles north-northwest of Nevada City (lat. 39°17'30" N, long. 121°01'45" W; sec. 36, T 17 N, R 8 E). Named on Nevada City (1948) 7.5' quadrangle. Smartsville (1895) 30' quadrangle shows a place called Shelby Flat situated 2 miles north-northwest of Nevada City.

Sellier Creek [PLACER]: *stream,* flows 2.25 miles to Brimstone Creek 5.5 miles north-northeast of Foresthill (lat. 39°05'10" N, long. 120°45'50" W; sec. 5, T 14 N, R 11 E). Named on Foresthill (1949) and Michigan Bluff (1952) 7.5' quadrangles.

Seminary Ridge [COLUSA]: *ridge,* south-southeast-trending, 1.5 miles long, 6.5 miles north-northwest of Sites on Colusa-Glenn County line, mainly in Glenn County (lat. 39°23'50" N, long. 122° 24' W). Named on Lodoga (1960) 15' quadrangle.

Seneca House: see **Eagleville** [YUBA].

Serena Creek [PLACER]: *stream,* flows 3 miles to North Fork American River 5.25 miles south-southwest of Donner Pass (lat. 39°15'20" N, long. 120°22'45" W; near W line sec. 14, T 16 N, R 14 E); the stream heads at Ice Lakes, one of which formerly was called Serena Lake. Named on Soda Springs (1955) 7.5' quadrangle. Called Sereno Creek on Truckee (1895) 30' quadrangle.

Serena Lake: see **Ice Lakes** [PLACER].

Sereno Creek: see **Serena Creek** [PLACER].

Sereno Lake: see **Ice Lakes** [PLACER].

Seven Mile House: see **Camino** [EL DORADO]; **Colusa** [COLUSA].

Sevenmile House [YUBA]: *locality,* 6.5 miles northeast of Marysville (lat. 39°12'50" N, long. 121°30'25" W). Named on Yuba City (1952) 7.5' quadrangle. Marysville (1895) 30' quadrangle has the form "7 Mile House" for the name.

Sevenmile Slough [SACRAMENTO]: *water feature,* joins Threemile Slough 5.25 miles southwest of Isleton (lat. 38°07' N, long. 121°40'55" W); the feature is between Brannan Island and Twichell Island. Named on Bouldin Island (1978) and Jersey Island (1978) 7.5' quadrangles. Called Hensley Slough on Ringgold's (1850a) map, which has the name "Pt. Hensley" at the southwest corner of present Twitchell Island, where present Threemile Slough joins San Joaquin River.

Seventeen Mile House: see **Colusa** [COLUSA].

Shadow Lake [EL DORADO]:

(1) *lake,* 850 feet long, 7.5 miles east-northeast of Robbs Peak (lat. 38°58'10" N, long. 120°16'20" W; on W line sec. 14, T 13 N, R 15 E). Named on Loon Lake (1952) 7.5' quadrangle.

(2) *lake,* 900 feet long, 2.25 miles north of Phipps Peak (lat. 38°59'20" N, long. 120°08'45" W; sec. 7, T 13 N, R 17 E). Named on Rockbound Valley (1955) 7.5' quadrangle.

Shady Creek [NEVADA]: *stream,* flows 10.5 miles to South Yuba River 6 miles west-northwest of Nevada City (lat. 39°17'40" N, long. 121°07'20" W; sec. 31, T 17 N, R 8 E). Named on Nevada City (1948) and North Bloomfield (1949) 7.5' quadrangles. A miner used the name "Big Shady Creek" for the stream in 1852 (Canfield, p. 230).

Shady Creek: see **Little Shady Creek** [NEVADA]; **Little Shady Creek**, under **Blind Shady Creek** [NEVADA].

Shady Flat: see **Mobile Ravine** [SIERRA].

Shady Glen [PLACER]: *settlement,* 1.25 miles north of Colfax (lat. 39°07'05" N, long. 120°56'55" W; near SE cor. sec. 27, T 15 N, R 9 E). Named on Colfax (1949) 7.5' quadrangle.

Shady Grove Run [PLACER]: *stream,* flows 1 mile to North Fork of Middle

Fork American River 6.5 miles west-southwest of Duncan Peak (lat. 39°07'10" N, long. 120°37'30" W; sec. 27, T 15 N, R 12 E). Named on Greek Store (1952) 7.5' quadrangle.

Shady Run [PLACER]: *stream,* flows 1.25 miles to Blue Canyon (1) 5 miles east of Dutch Flat (lat. 38°12' N, long. 120°44'50" W). Named on Colfax (1898) 30' quadrangle.

Shady Run: see **Midas** [PLACER].

Shag Slough [YOLO]: *water feature,* 11 miles southwest of Clarksburg on Yolo-Solano County line (lat. 38°19' N, long. 121°41'30" W). Named on Liberty Island (1978) 7.5' quadrangle.

Shake Hill: see **Washington** [NEVADA].

Shake Ridge: see **Lockwood** [AMADOR].

Shale Spring Canyon [COLUSA]: *canyon,* drained by a stream that flows 1 mile to Bear Creek 6.25 miles southeast of Wilbur Springs (lat. 38°58'25" N, long. 122°20'20" W; near E line sec. 18, T 13 N, R 4 W). Named on Glascock Mountain (1958) 7.5' quadrangle.

Shands [NEVADA]: *locality,* 2.5 miles west-southwest of Graniteville (lat. 39°24'55" N, long. 120°46'50" W). Named on Colfax (1898) 30' quadrangle.

Shanghai Bend [SUTTER-YUBA]: *bend,* 3 miles south-southeast of Yuba City along Feather River on Sutter-Yuba County line (lat. 39°06' N, long. 121°36'05" W). Named on Olivehurst (1952) 7.5' quadrangle. Ostrom (1911) 7.5' quadrangle has the name "Eliza Bend" for present Shanghai Bend, and has the name "Shanghai Bend" for present Eliza Bend.

Shanks Cove [PLACER]: *relief feature,* 4 miles south-southwest of Granite Creek (lat. 39°08'20" N, long. 120°18'05" W; near N line sec. 21, T 15 N, R 15 E). Named on Granite Chief (1953) 7.5' quadrangle.

Shannon Ravine [SIERRA]: *canyon,* drained by a stream that flows 1 mile to Jim Crow Creek nearly 4 miles east-southeast of Downieville (lat. 39°32' N, long. 120°45'55" W; near N line sec. 8, T 19 N, R 11 E). Named on Downieville (1951) 7.5' quadrangle.

Sharon Valley [YUBA]: *locality,* 1.25 miles west-southwest of Challenge (lat. 39°28'55" N, long. 121°14'45" W; at N line sec. 25, T 19 N, R 6 E). Named on Challenge (1948) 7.5' quadrangle.

Sharps Ravine [PLACER]: *canyon,* drained by a stream that flows less than 1 mile to Middle Fork American River 8 miles east-northeast of Auburn (lat. 38°56'35" N, long. 120°56'15" W; at S line sec. 26, T 13 N, R 9 E). Named on Greenwood (1949) 7.5' quadrangle.

Shaughnessy Place: see **Mobile Flat**, under **Mobile Ravine** [SIERRA].

Shaughnessy Ravine [SIERRA]: *canyon,* drained by a stream that flows nearly 2 miles to North Yuba River 4 miles east of Downieville (lat. 39°33'35" N, long. 120°45'10" W; at W line sec. 33, T 20 N, R 11 E). Named on Downieville (1951) 7.5' quadrangle.

Shaw Flat [EL DORADO]: *area,* 7 miles west-southwest of Kirkwood (lat. 38°39'15" N, long. 120°11'20" W; near SE cor. sec. 3, T 9 N, R 16 E). Named on Tragedy Spring (1979) 7.5' quadrangle.

Shealor Lakes [EL DORADO]: *lakes,* largest 700 feet long, 5.25 miles southwest of Kirkwood (lat. 38°39'30" N, long. 120°09' W; mainly in sec. 1, T 9 N, R 16 E). Named on Tragedy Spring (1979) 7.5' quadrangle.

Sheep Hollow: see **Steephollow Creek** [NEVADA].

Sheep Ranch Ravine [SIERRA]: *canyon,* drained by a stream that flows 0.5 mile to Cedar Grove Ravine 3.25 miles southwest of Mount Fillmore (lat. 39°41'55" N, long. 120°53'55" W; sec. 7, T 21 N, R 10 E). Named on La Porte (1951) 7.5' quadrangle.

Sheffield: see **Hinsdale** [SUTTER].

Shelby Flat: see **Selby Flat** [NEVADA].

Sheldon [SACRAMENTO]: *village,* 4 miles east-northeast of Elk Grove (lat. 38°25'50" N, long. 121°18' W). Named on Elk Grove (1968) 7.5' quadrangle. Postal authorities established Sheldon post office in 1860, discontinued it in 1874, reestablished it in 1887, discontinued it in 1888, reestablished it in 1896, and discontinued it in 1913; the name commemorates Jared Sheldon, who held Omochumnes grant (Salley, p. 203). California Division of Highways' (1934) map shows a place called Coffing located 2 miles northwest of Sheldon along Central California Traction Railroad, and a place called Kosova situated 3 miles northwest of Sheldon along the same rail line.

Sheldon Ravine [PLACER]: *canyon,* drained by a stream that flows less than 1 mile to North Fork American River 4.25 miles south of Dutch Flat (lat. 39°08'40" N, long. 120°50'35" W; near W line sec. 15, T 15 N, R 10 E). Named on Dutch Flat (1950) 7.5' quadrangle.

Shellback: see **Omega** [NEVADA].

Shenandoah Valley [AMADOR]: *valley,* 3.5 miles west-northwest of Fiddletown (lat. 38°31'15" N, long. 120°48'45" W). Named on Fiddletown (1949) 7.5' quadrangle. John Jameson settled in the valley in the early 1850's and named it for his birthplace in Virginia (Gudde, 1949, p. 328).

Shenanigan Flat [SIERRA]: *area,* 8 miles west-southwest of Goodyears Bar along North Yuba River (lat. 39°30'20" N, long. 121°01'25" W; near NE cor. sec. 24, T 19 N, R 8 E). Named on Strawberry Valley (1948) 7.5' quadrangle.

Sheridan [PLACER]: *village,* 7.5 miles northwest of Lincoln (lat. 38° 58'50" N, long. 121°22'20" W; sec. 13, T 13 N, R 5 E). Named on Lincoln (1953) and Sheridan (1953) 7.5' quadrangles. Postal authorities established Sheridan post office in 1868 and discontinued it for a brief time in 1870 (Frickstad, p. 121). A crossroads station called Union Shed was located 0.5 mile south of present Sheridan before the railroad came (Hoover, Rensch, and Rensch, p. 268).

Sheridans [PLACER]: *locality,* 7.5 miles east-northeast of Auburn (lat. 38°57'35" N, long. 120°57'15" W). Named on Placerville (1893) 30' quadrangle.

Sherman Canyon [EL DORADO]: *canyon,* drained by a stream that flows 5.5 miles to Silver Fork American River 7 miles west of Kirkwood (lat. 38°41'40" N, long. 120°12' W). Named on Tragedy Spring (1979) 7.5' quadrangle.

Sherman Island [SACRAMENTO]: *island* 7.5 miles long, 8.5 miles southwest of Isleton between Sacramento River, Threemile Slough, and San Joaquin River (lat. 38°04' N, long. 121°43' W). Named on Antioch North (1978) and Jersey Island (1978) 7.5' quadrangles. The name commemorates Sherman Day, United States surveyor general for California from 1868 until 1871, who had a ranch on the island (Gudde, 1949, p. 329).

Sherman Lake [SACRAMENTO]: *lake,* 13 miles southwest of Isleton at the west end of Sherman Island (lat. 38°02'30" N, long. 121° 48' W). Named on Antioch North (1978) 7.5' quadrangle.

Shields Camp [NEVADA]: *locality,* 3 miles west-northwest of North Bloomfield (lat. 39°22'40" N, long. 120°57'20" W; sec. 34, T 18 N, R 9 E). Named on Pike (1949) 7.5' quadrangle.

Shingle: see **Shingle Springs** [EL DORADO].

Shingle Creek [EL DORADO]:

(1) *stream,* flows nearly 3 miles to South Fork American River 1.25 miles west of Coloma (lat. 38°48' N, long. 120°54'45" W; near W line sec. 18, T 11 N, R 10 E). Named on Coloma (1949) 7.5' quadrangle.

(2) *stream,* flows 3 miles to French Creek 5 miles north-northeast of Latrobe (lat. 38°37'15" N, long. 120°55'45" W; near E line sec. 24, T 9 N, R 9 E); the stream heads near Shingle Springs. Named on Latrobe (1949) and Shingle Springs (1949) 7.5' quadrangles.

Shingle Mill Creek [EL DORADO]: *stream,* flows 3 miles to Middle Fork Cosumnes River 4.5 miles southeast of Caldor (lat. 38°34'05" N, long. 120°22'05" W; near SW cor. sec. 6, T 8 N, R 15 E). Named on Peddler Hill (1951) 7.5' quadrangle.

Shingle Mill Gulch [EL DORADO]: *canyon,* drained by a stream that flows 1.5 miles to Steely Fork Cosumnes River 11.5 miles southeast of Camino (lat. 38°37'50" N, long. 120°31'05" W; near SE cor. sec. 15, T 9 N, R 13 E). Named on Omo Ranch (1952) and Sly Park (1952) 7.5' quadrangles.

Shingle Spring: see **Shingle Springs** [EL DORADO].

Shingle Spring House: see **Shingle Springs** [EL DORADO].

Shingle Springs [EL DORADO]: *village,* 8 miles southwest of Placerville (lat. 38°39'55" N, long. 120°55'35" W; near W line sec. 6, T 9 N, R 10 E). Named on Shingle Springs (1949) 7.5' quadrangle. Called Shingle on California Mining Bureau's (1909a) map. Postal authorities established Shingle Spring post office in 1853 and discontinued it in 1855; they established Shingle Springs post office in 1865, changed the name to Shingle in 1895, and changed it back to Shingle Springs in 1955 (Salley, p. 203). The name is from springs at the place, and from a shingle mill built there in 1849; mining began at the site in 1850 and a hostelry called Shingle Spring House was erected the same year (Hoover, Rensch, and Rensch, p. 83). Postal authorities established Canyon post office 5 miles southeast of Shingle post office in 1897 and discontinued it in 1906; the name was from the location of the post office along Big Canyon Creek (Salley, p. 36). California Division of Highways' (1934) map shows a place called Bennett situated 2.25 miles southwest of Shingle Springs along Southern Pacific Railroad (near N line sec. 14, T 9 N, R 9 E). A mining camp of 1849 called Euchre Diggings was located near Shingle Springs; the name was for the game miners played in the winter (Gudde, 1975, p. 111).

Ship Channel: see **Sacramento River Deep Water Ship Channel** [SACRAMENTO-YOLO].

Shirley Lake [PLACER]: *lake,* 350 feet long, 1 mile east-northeast of Granite Chief (lat. 39°12'10" N, long. 120°16'10" W; near SW cor. sec. 25, T 16 N, R 15 E). Named on Granite Chief (1953) 7.5' quadrangle.

Shirttail Canyon [PLACER]: *canyon,* drained by a stream that flows 12 miles to North Fork American River 5 miles southeast of Colfax (lat. 39°02'30" N, long. 120°54'05" W; near S line sec. 19, T 14 N, R 10 E). Named on Colfax (1949) and Foresthill (1949) 7.5' quadrangles. The name was given in the summer of 1849 after two men chanced upon a miner who wore nothing but a shirt to cover his nakedness (Hoover, Rensch, and Rensch, p. 275). Whitney's (1873) map shows a place called Old Bar located along North Fork American River nearly 1 mile below the mouth of Shirttail Canyon.

Shirttail Canyon: see **North Shirttail Canyon** [PLACER].

Shirttail Peak [EL DORADO]: *peak,* 5 miles southwest of the village of Pilot Hill (lat. 38°47'35" N, long. 121°05'20" W; sec. 21, T 11 N, R 8 E). Altitude 1217 feet. Named on Pilot Hill (1954) 7.5' quadrangle.

Shoemaker Hill [EL DORADO]: *peak,* 2.25 miles southeast of Georgetown (lat. 38°53'05" N, long. 120°48'20" W; sec. 13, T 12 N, R 10 E). Named on Georgetown (1949) 7.5' quadrangle.

Shoemaker Valley [COLUSA]: *canyon,* 1 mile long, 12 miles north of Wilbur Springs (lat. 39°12'55" N, long. 122°26' W). Named on Wilbur Springs (1961) 15' quadrangle.

Shotgun Lake [NEVADA]: *lake,* 1000 feet long, 3.25 miles southwest of English Mountain along South Fork Canyon Creek (lat. 39° 25'20" N, long. 120°36'15" W; on W line sec. 14, T 18 N, R 12 E). Named on English Mountain (1983) 7.5' quadrangle.

Shower Branch [SIERRA]: *stream,* flows 2.25 miles to Canyon Creek 6 miles west-northwest of Goodyears Bar (lat. 39°34'55" N, long. 120°59' W; near E line sec. 20, T 20 N, R 9 E). Named on Goodyears Bar (1951) 7.5' quadrangle.

Showers Lake [EL DORADO]: *lake,* 750 feet long, 3.25 miles northeast of Kirkwood (lat. 38°44'30" N, long. 120°02'05" W; on E line sec. 6, T 10 N, R 18 E). Named on Caples Lake (1979) 7.5' quadrangle.

Shriner Lake [AMADOR]: *lake,* 750 feet long, 3.5 miles west of Mokelumne Peak (lat. 38°32'10" N, long. 120°09'30" W; on N line sec. 24, T 8 N, R 16 E). Named on Bear River Reservoir (1979) 7.5' quadrangle.

Shrub [EL DORADO]: *locality,* 2.5 miles north-northeast of Latrobe along Southern Pacific Railroad (lat. 38°35'30" N, long. 120°57'10" W; sec. 35, T 9 N, R 9 E). Named on Latrobe (1949) 7.5' quadrangle.

Shuckman Canyon [COLUSA]: *canyon,* 1 mile long, 7 miles north of Wilbur Springs (lat. 39°08'15" N, long. 122°23'40" W; near NE cor. sec. 22, T 15 N, R 5 W). Named on Wilbur Springs (1961) 15' quadrangle.

Sicard Flat [YUBA]: *locality,* 3 miles west-northwest of Smartville (lat. 39°13'55" N, long. 121°20'40" W; sec. 19, T 16 N, R 6 E); the place is nearly 1 mile north of Yuba River. Named on Smartville (1951) 7.5' quadrangle. The name commemorates Theodore Sicard, a French sailor who mined and traded at the place in 1848 (Gudde, 1949, p. 330). Sicard Flat was the name given to the community that developed about a mile back from Sicard's Bar on Yuba River (Hoover, Rensch, and Rensch, p. 589).

Sicard's Bar: see **Sicard Flat** [YUBA].

Sierra: see **Sierra City** [SIERRA].

Sierra Buttes [SIERRA]: *relief feature,* multiple peaks 2 miles north-northwest of Sierra City along a northwest-trending ridge (lat. 39°35'30" N, long. 120°38'20" W). Named on Sierra City (1981) 7.5' quadrangle. Called Yuba Butte on Goddard's (1857) map.

Sierra Campground [SIERRA]: *locality,* 6 miles northeast of Sierra City along North Yuba River (lat. 39°37'50" N, long. 120°33'30" W; at N line sec. 6, T 20 N, R 13 E). Named on Clio (1981) 7.5' quadrangle.

Sierra City [SIERRA]: *village,* 10.5 miles east of Downieville along North Yuba River (lat. 39°34' N, long. 120°38' W; at S line sec. 28, T 20 N, R 12 E). Named on Sierra City (1981) 7.5' quadrangle. Postal authorities established Sierra post office in 1855, discontinued in it 1856, reestablished it with the name "Sierra City" in 1864, discontinued it in 1865, and reestablished it in 1867 (Salley, p. 204). Kane Flat, also known as Buttes Flat, is at the west end of Sierra City; it was the site of a stamp mill for Sierra Buttes mine (Gudde, 1975, p. 182).

Sierra de San Marcos: see "Regional setting."

Sierra House [EL DORADO]: *locality,* 5 miles northwest of Freel Peak (lat. 38°54'25" N, long. 119°57'50" W; near NW cor. cor. sec. 11, T 12 N, R 18 E). Site named on South Lake Tahoe (1955) 7.5' quadrangle.

Sierra Nevada: see "Regional setting."

Sierra Valley [SIERRA]: *valley,* extends north and northeast from Sierraville into Plumas County. Named on Antelope Valley (1981), Calpine (1981), Loyalton (1981), Sattley (1981), and Sierraville (1981) 7.5' quadrangles.

Sierra Valley: see **Sierraville** [SIERRA].

Sierra Valley Channels [SIERRA]: *water feature,* braided streams that extend from the south part of Sierra Valley north into Plumas County, where they enter marsh. Named on Antelope Valley (1981) and Calpine (1981) 7.5' quadrangles. United States Board on Geographic Names (1974b, p. 3) noted that the feature is a network of ditches and drains that converge in Plumas County at the head of Middle Fork Feather River—the Board gave the variant name "Middle Fork Feather River" for Sierra Valley Channels.

Sierraville [SIERRA]: *village,* 25 miles east of Downieville (lat. 39° 35'20" N, long. 120°22' W; sec. 13, T 20 N, R 14 E); the place is at the south end of Sierra Valley. Named on Sierraville (1981) 7.5' quadrangle. Postal authorities established Sierra Valley post office in 1862 and changed the name to Sierraville in 1899 (Frickstad, p. 185).

Sierraville Creek [SIERRA]: *stream,* formed by the confluence of Bonita Creek and Cold Stream (1), flows less than 1 mile to Sierra Valley 1.25 miles south of Sierraville (lat. 39°34'20" N, long. 120° 21'55" W; sec. 24, T 20 N, R 14 E); the stream goes past Sierraville. Named on Sierraville (1981) 7.5' quadrangle.

Signal Peak [NEVADA]: *peak,* 4.5 miles east-northeast of Yuba Gap (lat. 39°20'20" N, long. 120°32'05" W; sec. 17, T 17 N, R 13 E). Altitude 7841 feet. Named on Cico Grove (1955) 7.5' quadrangle.

Signal Rock [COLUSA]: *relief feature,* 3.5 miles west-northwest of Wilbur Springs (lat. 39°03'50" N, long. 122°28'30" W; sec. 13, T 14 N, R 6 W). Named on Wilbur Springs (1961) 15' quadrangle.

Sills Lake [SUTTER]: *lake,* 1250 feet long, 5.25 miles south-southeast of Meridian (lat. 39°04'25" N, long. 121°52'25" W; on W line sec. 9, T 14 N, R 1 E). Named on Grimes (1954) and Tisdale Weir (1952) 7.5' quadrangles.

Silvas Grove [SACRAMENTO]: *locality,* 3.25 miles west-northwest of downtown Sacramento (lat. 38°36' N, long. 121°32'35" W). Named on Lovdal (1916) 7.5' quadrangle.

Silverado: see **Camp Silverado** [AMADOR].

Silver Creek [EL DORADO]: *stream,* heads at Union Valley Reservoir and flows 16 miles to South Fork American River 2 miles north of Pollock Pines (lat. 38°47'20" N, long. 120°35'20" W; sec. 24, T 11 N, R 12 E). Named on Pollock Pines (1950) and Riverton (1950) 7.5' quadrangles. Jones Fork flows 16 miles to Union Valley Reservoir 6.5 miles north-northwest of Riverton (near S line sec. 26, T 12 N, R 14 E); it is named on Kyburz (1952), Pyramid Peak (1955), and Rockbound Valley (1955) 7.5' quadrangles. Kyburz (1952) 7.5' quadrangle shows Jones place situated along Jones Fork (NE cor. sec. 35, T 12 N, R 14 E). Jones Fork has the name "Middle Fork Silver Creek" on Pyramid Peak (1896) 30' quadrangle. South Fork enters Silver Creek 5.5 miles north of Riverton (sec. 30, T 12 N, R 14 E); it is 25 miles long and is named on Kyburz (1952), Pyramid Peak (1955), and Riverton (1950) 7.5' quadrangles.

Silver Creek [PLACER]: *stream,* flows 2.5 miles to Truckee River 5 miles northwest of Tahoe City (lat. 39°13'30" N, long. 120°12' W; sec. 21, T 16 N, R 16 E); the stream heads near Silver Peak. Named on Tahoe City (1955) 7.5' quadrangle.

Silver Creek: see **Big Silver Creek** [EL DORADO]; **Deer Creek** [PLACER]; **Litttle Silver Creek** [EL DORADO].

Silver Creek Campground [EL DORADO]: *locality,* nearly 5 miles northeast of Riverton along South Fork Silver Creek (lat. 38°48'55" N, long. 120°22'45" W; sec. 11, T 11 N, R 14 E). Named on Riverton (1950) 7.5' quadrangle.

Silver Creek Campground [PLACER]: *locality,* 5 miles northwest of Tahoe City along Truckee River (lat. 39°13'25" N, long. 120°12'05" W; sec. 21, T 16 N, R 16 E); the place is near the mouth of Silver Creek. Named on Tahoe City (1955) 7.5' quadrangle.

Silverdale [YOLO]: *locality,* 6 miles southwest of Clarksburg along Sacramento Northern Railroad (lat. 38°21'20" N, long. 121°36'05" W). Named on Courtland (1952) 7.5' quadrangle.

Silver Fork: see **American River** [EL DORADO-PLACER-SACRAMENTO].

Silver Fork Meadow [EL DORADO]: *area,* 4.5 miles west-southwest of Kirkwood (lat. 38°41'30" N, long. 120°09' W); the place is north of Silver Fork American River. Named on Tragedy Spring (1979) 7.5' quadrangle.

Silver Hill [EL DORADO]: *peak,* 4 miles west-southwest of Robbs Peak (lat. 38°53'55" N, long. 120°28'05" W; sec. 12, T 12 N, R 13 E). Altitude 6081 feet. Named on Robbs Peak (1950) 7.5' quadrangle.

Silver Lake [AMADOR]: *lake,* 2 miles long, behind a dam 9 miles north of Mokelumne Peak (lat. 38°40'05" N, long. 120°07'15" W; sec. 32, T 10 N, R 17 E). Named on Caples Lake (1979) and Tragedy Spring (1979) 7.5' quadrangles. Postal authorities established Caminettis post office—probably at a resort near Silver Lake—in 1916 and discontinued it in 1920; the name was for for Elizabeth B. Caminetti, first postmaster (Salley, p. 33).

Silver Lake: see **Plasse** [AMADOR].

Silver Lake West Campground [AMADOR-EL DORADO]: *locality,* 3.5 miles southwest of Kirkwood (lat. 38°40'20" N, long. 120°07'15" W; sec. 32, T 10 N, R 17 E); the place is north of Silver Lake. Named on Caples Lake (1979) 7.5' quadrangle.

Silver Peak [EL DORADO]: *peak,* 4.5 miles west-southwest of Phipps Peak (lat. 38°56'05" N, long. 120°13'45" W; sec. 32, T 13 N, R 16 E). Altitude 8930 feet. Named on Rockbound Valley (1955) 7.5' quadrangle.

Silver Peak [PLACER]: *peak,* 6.5 miles west-northwest of Tahoe City (lat. 39°13'15" N, long. 120°14'45" W; sec. 19, T 16 N, R 16 E). Altitude 8424 feet. Named on Tahoe City (1955) 7.5' quadrangle.

Simmerly Slough [YUBA]: *stream,* joins Jack Slough 2.5 miles north-northeast of Marysville (lat. 39°10'45" N, long. 121°34'30" W). Named on Honcut (1952) and Yuba City (1952) 7.5' quadrangles.

Simmons Hot Springs: see **Wilbur Springs** [COLUSA].

Simon Ravine [YUBA]: *canyon,* drained by a stream that flows 1 mile to Slate Creek 5.25 miles northeast of Strawberry Valley (lat. 39°37' N, long. 121°02'10" W; near SW cor. sec. 1, T 20 N, R 8 E). Named on Strawberry Valley (1948) 7.5' quadrangle.

Simpson Gulch [EL DORADO]: *canyon,* drained by a stream that flows 2.5 miles to Middle Dry Creek 1.5 miles south-southwest of Caldor (lat. 38°35'05" N, long. 120°26'20" W; sec. 33, T 9 N, R 14 E). Named on Caldor (1951) 7.5' quadrangle.

Sims: see **Runyon**, under **Franklin** [SACRAMENTO].

Singleton Springs [EL DORADO]: *springs,* 10 miles west-southwest of Kirkwood at the head of North Fork Cosumnes River (lat. 38° 38'15" N, long. 120°14'20" W; near SW cor. sec. 8, T 9 N, R 16 E). Named on Tragedy Spring (1979) 7.5' quadrangle.

Sites [COLUSA]: *village,* 8 miles west-northwest of Maxwell along Stone Corral Creek (lat. 39°18'30" N, long. 122°20'10" W; sec. 20, T 17 N, R 4 W). Named on Sites (1958) 7.5' quadrangle. Postal authorities established

Sites post office in 1887 and discontinued it in 1968 (Salley, p. 205). C.E. Grunsky named the place in 1887 for John H. Sites, a landholder (Gudde, 1949, p. 334).

Sites Spring [COLUSA]: *spring,* 2 miles southeast of Lodoga (lat. 39°16'45" N, long. 122°28' W; sec. 31, T 17 N, R 5 W). Named on Lodoga (1960) 15' quadrangle.

Sixmile Bar [SACRAMENTO]: *shoal,* 5 miles northwest of downtown Sacramento in Sacramento River (lat. 38°37'30" N, long. 121°33'40" W). Named on Elkhorn Weir (1915) 7.5' quadrangle.

Six Mile House [EL DORADO]: *locality,* 5.5 miles east of Placerville (lat. 38°44'15" N, long. 120°41'55" W). Named on Placerville (1893) 30' quadrangle.

6 Mile House [SACRAMENTO]: *locality,* nearly 6 miles north of downtown Sacramento along Linda Creek (Dry Creek (1) of modern maps) (lat. 38°39'30" N, long. 121°29' W). Named on Sacramento (1892) 30' quadrangle.

Six Mile House: see **Scotts Flat** [NEVADA] (2).

Sixmile Station [YUBA]: *locality,* 5 miles north of Marysville (lat. 39°13'10" N, long. 121°36' W). Named on Yuba City (1952) 7.5' quadrangle.

Sixmile Valley [PLACER]: *valley,* 3.5 miles west of Cisco Grove (lat. 39°18'45" N, long. 120°36'15" W; on E line sec. 27, T 17 N, R 12 E). Named on Cisco Grove (1955) 7.5' quadrangle.

Sixteen Mile House: see **Princeton** [COLUSA].

Skillman Flat [NEVADA]: *area,* nearly 3 miles south of Washington (lat. 39°19'10" N, long. 120°47'25" W; near SW cor. sec. 19, T 17 N, R 11 E). Named on Washington (1950) 7.5' quadrangle.

Skinners [EL DORADO]: *locality,* 4.25 miles west-northwest of Shingle Springs (lat. 38°42' N, long. 120°59'40" W; near N line sec. 28, T 10 N, R 9 E). Named on Shingle Springs (1949) 7.5' quadrangle.

Skinnerville Spring [COLUSA]: *spring,* 10 miles north of Wilbur Springs (lat. 39°10'55" N, long. 122°24'50" W; sec. 4, T 15 N, T 5 W). Named on Wilbur Springs (1961) 15' quadrangle.

Skunk Canyon [EL DORADO]: *canyon,* 1.5 miles long, opens into the canyon of South Fork American River 4.25 miles south-southwest of the village of Pilot Hill (lat. 38°46'25" N, long. 121°02' W; sec. 25, T 11 N, R 8 E). Named on Pilot Hill (1954) 7.5' quadrangle.

Skunk Canyon [PLACER]: *canyon,* drained by a stream that flows 1.5 miles to North Fork of Middle Fork American River 1.5 miles south of Michigan Bluff (lat. 39°01'05" N, long. 120°44' W; sec. 34, T 14 N, R 11 E). Named on Michigan Bluff (1952) 7.5' quadrangle. Called Skunk Gulch on Whitney's (1873) map.

Skunk Creek [SACRAMENTO]: *stream,* flows 12 miles to marsh near Laguna Creek 3.5 miles north of Galt (lat. 38°18'10" N, long. 121°18'30" W). Named on Clay (1968) and Galt (1968) 7.5' quadrangles.

Skunk Gulch: see **Skunk Canyon** [PLACER].

Skunk Spring [PLACER]: *spring,* 3.5 miles northwest of Duncan Peak (lat. 39°11'15" N, long. 120°33'50" W; sec. 6, T 15 N, R 13 E). Named on Duncan Peak (1952) 7.5' quadrangle.

Skyhigh [SIERRA]: *peak,* 2.25 miles south-southwest of Mount Fillmore (lat. 39°42' N, long. 120°51'45" W; sec. 9, T 21 N, R 10 E). Altitude 6443 feet. Named on Mount Fillmore (1951) 7.5' quadrangle.

Skylake Camp [EL DORADO]: *locality,* 6 miles west-northwest of Freel Peak along Upper Truckee River (lat. 38°54'15" N, long. 119°59'35" W; sec. 9, T 12 N, R 18 E). Named on Freel Peak (1956) 15' quadrangle.

Slab Creek [EL DORADO]: *stream,* flows 12 miles to South Fork American River 5.5 miles west-northwest of Pollock Pines (lat. 38° 47'15" N, long. 120°41' W; sec. 19, T 11 N, R 12 E). Named on Pollock Pines (1950) and Slate Mountain (1950) 7.5' quadrangles.

Slab Creek Reservoir [EL DORADO]: *lake,* behind a dam on South Fork American River 6.25 miles west of Pollock Pines (lat. 38°46'40" N, long. 120°41'50" W; sec. 25, T 11 N, R 11 E); Slab Creek joins South Fork American River in the lake. Named on Slate Mountain (1950, photorevised 1973) 7.5' quadrangle.

Slabtown: see **Jackson Butte** [AMADOR].

Slacks Ravine [NEVADA]: *canyon,* drained by a stream that flows 4 miles to Deer Creek 6 miles northwest of Pilot Peak (lat. 39°13'25" N, long. 121°16'20" W; at S line sec. 23, T 16 N, R 6 E). Named on Rough and Ready (1949) and Smartville (1951) 7.5' quadrangles.

Slapjack Creek [YUBA]: *stream,* flows 3 miles to Indian Creek 3 miles east of Challenge (lat. 39°28'55" N, long. 121°10'05" W; sec. 27, T 19 N, R 7 E). Named on Challenge (1948) and Clipper Mills (1948) 7.5' quadrangles.

Slat Creek [EL DORADO]: *stream,* flows 2 miles to Traverse Creek 7.25 miles north of Chili Bar (lat. 38°52'20" N, long. 120°49' W; sec. 24, T 12 N, R 10 E). Named on Garden Valley (1949) and Georgetown (1949) 7.5' quadrangles.

Slate Bar: see **Folsom** [SACRAMENTO].

Slate Canyon [EL DORADO]: *canyon,* drained by a stream that flows 2.5 miles to Whaler Creek 9 miles northwest of Pollock Pines (lat. 38°50'40" N, long. 120°42'50" W; sec. 35, T 12 N, R 11 E); the canyon is on the northeast side of the ridge called Slate Mountains. Named on Slate Mountain (1950) 7.5' quadrangle. Logan's (1938) map has the name "Slate Mtn. Cr." for the stream in the canyon.

Slate Castle [SIERRA]: *relief feature,* 2 miles south-southeast of Downieville (lat. 39°32'10" N, long. 120°48'35" W; near N line sec. 12, R 19 N, R 10 E). Altitude 5236 feet. Named on Downieville (1951) 7.5' quadrangle.

Slate Castle Creek [SIERRA]: *stream,* flows 1.5 miles to North Yuba River less than 1 mile east-southeast of Downieville (lat. 39° 33'30" N, long. 120°48'50" W; near W line sec. 36, T 20 N, R 10 E); the stream heads near Slate Castle. Named on Downieville (1951) 7.5' quadrangle.

Slate Creek [AMADOR]: *stream,* flows 2.25 miles to South Fork Cosumnes River 3 miles north of Fiddletown (lat. 38°32'55" N, long. 120°44'45" W; sec. 15, T 8 N, R 11 E). Named on Aukum (1952) 7.5' quadrangle.

Slate Creek [EL DORADO]:

(1) *stream,* flows 2 miles to Dutch Creek 3.5 miles northwest of Chili Bar (lat. 38°48'30" N, long. 120°51'25" W; near NW cor. sec. 15, T 11 N, R 10 E). Named on Garden Valley (1949) 7.5' quadrangle.

(2) *stream,* flows 6.25 miles to Big Canyon Creek 4 miles east-northeast of Latrobe (lat. 38°34'40" N, long. 120°54'35" W; near E line sec. 6, T 8 N, R 10 E). Named on Fiddletown (1949), Latrobe (1949), and Placerville (1949) 7.5' quadrangles.

(3) *stream,* flows 6.5 miles to Dry Creek 3.5 miles north-northeast of Shingle Springs (lat. 38°42'40" N, long. 120°54'05" W; sec. 20, T 10 N, R 10 E). Named on Placerville (1949) and Shingle Springs (1949) 7.5' quadrangles. Called North Slate Cr. on Logan's (1938) map.

Slate Creek [NEVADA]: *stream,* flows 2.5 miles to Deer Creek 2.25 miles northwest of Grass Valley (lat. 39°14'35" N, long. 121°05'20" W; near SW cor. sec. 16, T 16 N, R 8 E). Named on Grass Valley (1949) 7.5' quadrangle.

Slate Creek [SACRAMENTO]: *stream,* flows 2.5 miles to Little Deer Creek 9 miles south-southeast of Folsom (lat. 38°33'45" N, long. 121°06' W; sec. 9, T 8 N, R 8 E). Named on Folsom SE (1954) 7.5' quadrangle.

Slate Creek [SIERRA-YUBA]: *stream,* heads in Sierra County and flows 26 miles, partly in Plumas County, to North Yuba River nearly 3 miles south-southeast of Strawberry Valley in Yuba County (lat. 39°31'35" N, long. 121°05'25" W; sec. 9, T 19 N, R 8 E). Named on American House (1948), Blue Nose Mountain (1951), La Porte (1951), Onion Valley (1950), and Strawberry Valley (1948) 7.5' quadrangles. The stream forms part of Sierra-Plumas County line. Downieville (1897) 30' quadrangle has the name "Little Slate Creek" for present Slate Creek above the mouth of East Branch, which enters the main stream 3.5 miles west of Mount Fillmore. East Branch is 5.5 miles long and is named on La Porte (1951) and Mount Fillmore (1951) 7.5' quadrangles.

Slate Creek: see **Dry Creek** [AMADOR-SACRAMENTO].

Slate Mountain [EL DORADO]: *peak,* 7 miles northwest of Pollock Pines (lat. 38°49'25" N, long. 120°41' W; at S line sec. 6, T 11 N, R 12 E). Altitude 3892 feet. Named on Slate Mountain (1950) 7.5' quadrangle.

Slate Mountain Creek: see **Slate Canyon** [EL DORADO].

Slate Mountains [EL DORADO]: *ridge,* generally southeast-trending, 5.5 miles long, 8.5 miles northwest of Pollock Pines (lat. 38°50' N, long. 120°42' W); Slate Mountain is near the southeast end of the ridge. Named on Slate Mountain (1950) 7.5' quadrangle.

Slate Range [YUBA]: *locality,* 4.5 miles south-southeast of Strawberry Valley (lat. 39°30'05" N, long. 121°04'25" W); the place is 1.5 miles south of Slate Range Bar. Named on Bidwell Bar (1897) 30' quadrangle. Borthwick (p. 214) reported stopping at Slate Range House, "so called from being situated at the spot where one begins to descend to Slate Range, a place where the banks of the river are composed of huge masses of slate."

Slate Range Bar [YUBA]: *locality,* 3.5 miles south-southeast of Strawberry Valley along North Yuba River (lat. 39°31'05" N, long. 121°04'30" W; sec. 15, T 19 N, R 8 E). Named on Strawberry Valley (1948) 7.5' quadrangle. Wescoatt's (1861) map shows Slate Range Bar on the north side of the river, and shows a place called Finleys directly across the river.

Slate Range House: see **Slate Range** [YUBA].

Slatington: see **Kelsey** [EL DORADO].

Slaughter Ravine [PLACER]: *canyon,* drained by a stream that flows 1.5 miles to North Fork American River 1.5 miles east of Colfax (lat. 39°05'55" N, long. 120°55'25" W; near N line sec. 1, T 14 N, R 9 E). Named on Colfax (1949) 7.5' quadrangle.

Slaughter's Bar: see **Goodyears Bar** [SIERRA].

Sleepy Hollow [PLACER]: *canyon,* drained by a stream that flows 0.5 mile to Live Oak Ravine 3.5 miles south of Colfax (lat. 39°03'05" N, long. 120°57'45" W; sec. 22, T 14 N, R 9 E). Named on Colfax (1949) 7.5' quadrangle.

Sleighville Creek [SIERRA-YUBA]: *stream,* heads in Sierra County and flows 1 mile to Williamson Creek nearly 2 miles north-northeast of Camptonville in Yuba County (lat. 39°28'35" N, long. 121° 02'20" W; near NW cor. sec. 36, T 19 N, R 8 E); the stream heads north of Sleighville House. Named on Camptonville (1948) 7.5' quadrangle.

Sleighville House [SIERRA]: *locality,* 2.25 miles north-northwest of Pike (lat. 39°28'15" N, long. 121°00'35" W; sec. 31, T 19 N, R 9 E). Named on Camptonville (1948) 7.5' quadrangle. Peter Yore built the original structure at the site in 1849; goods were transferred from wagons to sleighs at the place in winter months (Hoover, Rensch, and Rensch, p. 495).

Sleighville Ridge [SIERRA-YUBA]: *ridge,* generally west-trending, 2 miles long, 1.5 miles northeast of Camptonville on Sierra-Yuba County line (lat. 39°27'50" N, long. 121°01'20" W); Sleighville House is at the east end of the ridge. Named on Camptonville (1948) 7.5' quadrangle.

Slick Rock [EL DORADO]: *peak,* 7 miles east-southeast of Robs Peak (lat. 38°53' N, long. 120°17'15" W; near SW cor. sec. 15, T 12 N, R 15 E). Altitude 7242 feet. Named on Loon Lake (1952) 7.5' quadrangle.

Slide: see **The Slide** [YOLO].

Slide Ravine [NEVADA]: *canyon,* 0.5 mile long, in the north part of Grass Valley (lat. 39°13'35" N, long. 121°03'50" W; on S line sec. 22, T 16 N, R 8 E). Named on Grass Valley (1949) 7.5' quadrangle.

Slippery Ford: see **Kyburz** [EL DORADO].

Sloughhouse [SACRAMENTO]: *village,* 17 miles east-southeast of downtown Sacramento (lat. 38°29'20" N, long. 121°11'40" W). Named on Sloughhouse (1968) 7.5' quadrangle. Called Slough House on Cosumnes (1909) 7.5' quadrangle. Postal authorities established Sloughhouse post office in 1916 (Frickstad, p. 134). Jared Sheldon built a roadhouse at the site and called it Slough House after a wooden building known by that name that he had built nearby in 1845 (Ricketts, 1978, p. 4, 22).

Slug Canyon [SIERRA]: *canyon,* drained by a stream that flows 2 miles to North Yuba River 0.25 mile southwest of Downieville (lat. 39°33'25" N, long. 120°49'55" W; at E line sec. 34, T 20 N, R 10 E); the canyon is east of City of Six Ridge. Named on Downieville (1951) 7.5' quadrangle. Gudde (1975, p. 73) listed a mining place called City of Six Diggings that was located "on Slug Canyon," and noted (p. 172) that Jackassville was a popular name for City of Six—the popular name was an abbreviation of the name "Camp of Half a Dozen Jackasses." The name "Slug" is from the coarse lump gold, or slug gold, found at the place (Hoover, Rensch, and Rensch, p. 492).

Slug Gulch [EL DORADO]:

(1) *canyon,* 2 miles long, opens into the canyon of Middle Fork Cosumnes River 3.25 miles northwest of Omo Ranch (lat. 38°36'45" N, long. 120°37'15" W; near S line sec. 23, T 9 N, R 12 E). Named on Omo Ranch (1952) 7.5' quadrangle.

(2) *canyon,* 1.25 miles long, opens into an unnamed canyon 2.25 miles east of Latrobe (lat. 38°33'55" N, long. 120°56'25" W; sec. 12, T 8 N, R 9 E). Named on Latrobe (1949) 7.5' quadrangle.

(3) *locality,* 2 miles west-northwest of Omo Ranch (lat. 38°35'40" N, long. 120°37' W). Named on Placerville (1893) 30' quadrangle.

Slug Gulch [PLACER]: *canyon,* drained by a stream that flows 2 miles to Middle Fork American River 11 miles east-northeast of Auburn (lat. 38°57'35" N, long. 120°53'05" W; sec. 20, T 13 N, R 10 E). Named on Greenwood (1949) 7.5' quadrangle.

Sluice Box: see **Big Sluice Box** [EL DORADO]; **Little Sluice Box** [EL DORADO].

Sly Creek Reservoir [YUBA]: *lake,* mainly in Butte County, but extends into Yuba County 1.25 miles north of Strawberry Valley (lat. 39°34'55" N, long. 121°06'25" W). Named on Strawberry Valley (1948, photorevised 1975) 7.5' quadrangle.

Sly Park [EL DORADO]: *valley,* 13 miles east of Placerville (lat. 38° 43'15" N, long. 120°33'30" W). Named on Placerville (1893) 30' quadrangle. Water of Jenkinson Lake now covers the valley. The name is for James Sly, one of a group of Mormons who discovered the place in 1848 (Gudde, 1969, p. 313). Park post office was located at Sly Park (Beverly Cola, personal communication, 1985). Postal authorities established Park post office in 1891, moved it 1 mile east in 1900, moved it 2.5 miles northwest in 1907, and discontinued it in 1919 (Salley, p. 167).

Sly Park Creek [EL DORADO]: *stream,* flows 14 miles to Camp Creek 5.5 miles southeast of Camino (lat. 38°41'15" N, long. 120° 35'45" W; near E line sec. 25, T 10 N, R 12 E); the stream goes through Sly Park. Named on Sly Park (1952) 7.5' quadrangle. Called Park Creek on Stump Spring (1951) 7.5' quadrangle, but United States Board on Geographic Names (1978a, p. 8) rejected this name for the stream. On Placerville (1893) 30' quadrangle, the part of present Sly Park Creek above present Jenkinson Lake is called Empire Creek, and present Hazel Creek is shown as the upper part of Sly Park Creek.

Sly Park Creek: see **North Sly Park Creek** [EL DORADO].

Sly Park House [EL DORADO]: *locality,* 13 miles east of Placerville (lat. 38°43'30" N, long. 120°33'10" W); the place is located near the east end of Sly Park. Named on Placerville (1893) 30' quadrangle.

Sly Park Reservoir: see **Jenkinson Lake** [EL DORADO].

Smartsville: see **Smartville** [YUBA].

Smartville [YUBA]: *village,* 16 miles east-northeast of Marysville (lat. 39°12'25" N, long. 121°17'45" W; at NE cor. sec. 33, T 16 N, R 6 E). Named on Smartville (1951) 7.5' quadrangle. Called Smartsville on Smartsville (1895) 30' quadrangle, but United States Board on Geographic Names (1949a, p. 4) rejected this form of the name. Postal authorities established Smartville post office in 1865; the name is for James Smart, who settled at the site in 1856 (Salley, p. 206). Wescoatt's (1861) map shows a place called Landers Bar located 1.25 miles north-northeast of Smartsville along Yuba River. A mining place called Malay Camp, which was situated across the river from Landers Bar, was populated by miners from Malay Peninsula (Hoover, Rensch, and Rensch, p. 589).

Smelt Road Ridge [COLUSA]: *ridge,* generally east-northeast-trending, 1 mile long, 3 miles south-southwest of Stonyford (lat. 39°20'15" N, long. 122°34' W; sec. 7, 8, T 17 N, R 6 W). Named on Gilmore Peak (1968) 7.5' quadrangle.

Smith Canyon [YOLO]: *canyon,* drained by a stream that flows 3.5 miles to Capay Valley 4 miles south of Guinda (lat. 38°46'10" N, long. 122°11'20" W; sec. 27, T 11 N, R 3 W). Named on Brooks (1959) and Guinda (1959) 7.5' quadrangles.

Smith Creek [SIERRA]: *stream,* flows 1.25 miles to Levezzola Creek 8.5 miles northwest of Sierra City (lat. 39°39'20" N, long. 120°44'40" W; sec. 28, T 21 N, R 11 E); the stream heads at Smith Lake. Named on Gold Lake (1981) 7.5' quadrangle.

Smith Creek [YOLO]: *stream,* heads in Dunnigan Hills and flows 4 miles to lowlands 1.5 miles south of Zamora (lat. 38°46'25" N, long. 121°52'45" W; sec. 29, T 11 N, R 1 E). Named on Zamora (1953) 7.5' quadrangle.

Smith Flat [YOLO]:

(1) *area,* 5.25 miles south-southwest of Guinda (lat. 38°45'20" N, long. 122°13'30" W; near SW cor. sec. 32, T 11 N, R 3 W); the place is in Smith Canyon. Named on Guinda (1959) 7.5' quadrangle.

(2) *area,* 2.5 miles south-southwest of Rumsey in Johnson Canyon (lat. 38°51'30" N, long. 122°16' W). Named on Knoxville (1958) 7.5' quadrangle.

Smithflat [EL DORADO]: *village,* 2.5 miles east of downtown Placerville (lat. 38°44'10" N, long. 120°45'15" W; sec. 10, T 10 N, R 11 E). Named on Placerville (1949) 7.5' quadrangle. Called Smiths Flat on Placerville (1893) 30' quadrangle, but United States Board on Geographic Names (1965b, p. 11) rejected the forms "Smiths Flat" and "Smith Flat" for the name. Postal authorities established Smith's Flat post office in 1876 and changed the name to Smithflat in 1895 (Frickstad, p. 29). The name commemorates Jeb Smith, a pioneer rancher (Gudde, 1949, p. 335).

Smith Lake [EL DORADO]: *lake,* 850 feet long, 2 miles west-northwest of Pyramid Peak (lat. 38°51'30" N, long. 120°11'15" W). Named on Pyramid Peak (1955) 7.5' quadrangle.

Smith Lake [SIERRA]: *lake,* 450 feet long, 8 miles northwest of Sierra City (lat. 39°39'20" N, long. 120°43'15" W; at E line sec. 27, T 21 N, R 11 E); the lake is at the head of Smith Creek. Named on Gold Lake (1981) 7.5' quadrangle.

Smith Mill: see **Old Smith Mill** [SIERRA]; **Winnie Smith Mill** [SIERRA].

Smithneck Creek [SIERRA]: *stream,* flows 9.5 miles to Sierra Valley 1.25 miles south-southeast of Loyalton (lat. 39°39'40" N, long. 120°13'50" W; sec. 19, T 21 N, R 16 E). Named on Antelope Valley (1981), Loyalton (1981), and Sardine Peak (1981) 7.5' quadrangles.

Smiths: see **Colfax** [PLACER].

Smith's Flat: see **Smithflat** [EL DORADO].

Smith's Neck: see **Loyalton** [SIERRA].

Smiths Point [PLACER]: *ridge,* west-trending, less than 1 mile long, 1.5 miles northwest of Foresthill (lat. 39°02' N, long. 120°50'20" W; sec. 27, T 14 N, R 10 E). Named on Foresthill (1949) 7.5' quadrangle. Called Smith Point on Colfax (1950) 15' quadrangle.

Smithville: see **Loomis** [PLACER]; **Stonyford** [COLUSA].

Smoky Ravine [YUBA]: *canyon,* drained by a stream that flows 1.5 miles to Lake Mildred 5.5 miles southeast of Rackerby (lat. 39°22'35" N, long. 121°16'40" W; near E line sec. 34, T 18 N, R 6 E). Named on Rackerby (1948) 7.5' quadrangle.

Smuthers Ravine [PLACER]: *canyon,* drained by a stream that flows 2 miles to Bunch Canyon 3 miles south-southeast of Colfax (lat. 39°03'35" N, long. 120°56'20" W; sec. 14, T 14 N, R 9 E). Named on Colfax (1949) 7.5' quadrangle.

Snag Lake [SIERRA]: *lake,* 2050 feet long, 7.25 miles north of Sierra City (lat. 39°40'10" N, long. 120°37'40" W; near E line sec. 21, T 21 N, R 12 E). Named on Gold Lake (1981) 7.5' quadrangle.

Snag Lake Campground [SIERRA]: *locality,* 7.25 miles north of Sierra City (lat. 39°40'10" N, long. 120°37'30" W; at W line sec. 22, T 21 N, R 12 E); the place is at the northeast end of Snag Lake. Named on Sierra City (1955) 15' quadrangle.

Snail Canyon [PLACER]: *canyon,* drained by a stream that flows 1.5 miles to North Shirttail Canyon 6 miles north of Foresthill (lat. 39° 06'35" N, long. 120°48'15" W; at N line sec. 36, T 15 N, R 10 E). Named on Foresthill (1949) 7.5' quadrangle.

Snake Flat: see **Drytown** [AMADOR].

Snake Gulch [AMADOR]: *canyon,* drained by a stream that flows 1.25 miles to Dry Creek 2.5 miles south of Plymouth at Drytown (lat. 38°26'35" N, long. 120°51'05" W; sec. 23, T 7 N, R 10 E). Named on Amador City (1962) 7.5' quadrangle.

Snakehead Point [PLACER]: *peak,* 3.5 miles east-southeast of Dutch Flat (lat. 39°10'35" N, long. 120°46'50" W; sec. 6, T 15 N, R 11 E). Altitude 2437 feet. Named on Dutch Flat (1950) 7.5' quadrangle.

Snake Lake [SIERRA]: *lake,* 800 feet long, 8 miles north-northwest of Sierra City (lat. 39°40'40" N, long. 120°41'25" W; sec. 13, T 21 N, R 11 E). Named on Gold Lake (1981) 7.5' quadrangle.

Snake River [SUTTER]: *stream,* heads northeast of Sutter Buttes and flows 14 miles to a point 7.5 miles southwest of Yuba City (lat. 39° 05'30" N, long. 121°44'10" W; sec. 3, T 14 N, R 2 E). Named on Gilsizer Slough (1911) and Sutter (1911) 7.5' quadrangles. Called Snake Slough on Gridley (1912) 7.5' quadrangle.

Snake Slough [SUTTER]: *stream,* flows 2.5 miles to a canal 6.5 miles southwest of Yuba City (lat. 39°05' N, long. 121°43' W; at S line sec. 2, T 14 N, R 2 E). Named on Marysville (1952) 15' quadrangle.

Snake Slough: see **Snake River** [SUTTER].

Snodgrass Slough [SACRAMENTO]: *water feature,* joins North Mokelumne River 1.25 miles south-southeast of Walnut Grove (lat. 38°13'30" N, long. 121°30'20" W). Named on Bruceville (1968), Courtland (1978), Isleton (1978), and Thornton (1978) 7.5' quadrangles.

Snow Creek [EL DORADO]: *stream,* flows 4 miles to Camp Creek 4.5 miles west of Old Iron Mountain (lat. 38°42' N, long. 120°28'25" W; near SW cor. sec. 19, T 10 N, R 14 E). Named on Stump Spring (1951) 7.5' quadrangle.

Snow Creek [SIERRA]: *stream,* flows 1.5 miles to Eureka Creek 3 miles north of Goodyears Bar (lat. 39°35' N, long. 120°53'20" W; near E line sec. 19, T 20 N, R 10 E). Named on Goodyears Bar (1951) 7.5' quadrangle.

Snowden Hill [SIERRA]: *ridge,* west-southwest-trending, 1 mile long, 3.5 miles west-southwest of Goodyears Bar (lat. 39°30'55" N, long. 120°56'35" W; on W line sec. 14, T 19 N, R 9 E). Named on Goodyears Bar (1951) 7.5' quadrangle.

Snow Lake [EL DORADO]: *lake,* 1400 feet long, 1 mile northwest of Mount Tallac (lat. 38°55'05" N, long. 120°06'50" W; on E line sec. 5, T 12 N, R 17 E). Named on Emerald Bay (1955) 7.5' quadrangle. The feature first was called Katrine Lake for Katherine Brigham Ebright (Lekisch, p. 108).

Snowline Camp [EL DORADO]: *locality,* 3 miles east-northeast of Camino (lat. 38°44'45" N, long. 120°37'25" W; sec. 2, T 10 N, R 12 E). Named on Sly Park (1952) 7.5' quadrangle.

Snow Mountain [COLUSA]: *ridge,* generally west-northwest-trending, 1.5 miles long, 11.5 miles west of Stonyford on Colusa-Lake County line (lat. 39°22'30" N, long. 122°45'45" W; in and near sec. 28, T 18 N, R 8 W). Named on Crockett Peak (1967) 7.5' quadrangle.

Snow Mountain [PLACER]: *peak,* 10 miles west-northwest of Granite Chief (lat. 39°14'30" N, long. 120°27'40" W; sec. 24, T 16 N, R 13 E). Altitude 8014 feet. Named on Royal Gorge (1953) 7.5' quadrangle.

Snow Mountain East [COLUSA]: *peak,* 11 miles west of Stonyford on Colusa-Lake County line (lat. 39°23' N, long. 122°45'05" W; sec. 27, T 18 N, R 8 W); the feature is 0.5 mile northeast of Snow Mountain West on the ridge called Snow Mountain. Altitude 7056 feet. Named on Crockett Peak (1967) 7.5' quadrangle.

Snow Mountain West [COLUSA]: *peak,* 11 miles west of Stonyford (lat. 39°22'40" N, long. 122°45'30" W; near SE cor. sec. 28, T 18 N, R 8 W); the feature is 0.5 mile southwest of Snow Mountain East on the ridge called Snow Mountain. Altitude 7038 feet. Named on Crockett Peak (1967) 7.5' quadrangle.

Snow Point [NEVADA]: *locality,* 6.25 miles northeast of North Bloomfield (lat. 39°25'15" N, long. 120°48'45" W). Named on Colfax (1898) 30' quadrangle. Whitney's (1873) map shows a place called Eureka located 4 miles east of Snow Point.

Snow Ridge [EL DORADO]: *ridge,* generally west-trending, 3.25 miles long, 1.5 miles south of Camino (lat. 38°42'45" N, long. 120° 40'45" W). Named on Camino (1952) 7.5' quadrangle.

Snow Tent [NEVADA]: *locality,* 3 miles northeast of North Bloomfield (lat. 39°23'45" N, long. 120°51'55" W). Named on Colfax (1898) 30' quadrangle. Whitney's (1873) map shows a place called Mt. Zion located 1.5 miles east-southeast of Snow Tent.

Snowtent Spring [NEVADA]: *spring,* 3.25 miles north-northwest of Washington (lat. 39°24' N, long. 121°49'45" W; near W line sec. 26, T 18 N, R 10 E). Named on Alleghany (1949) 7.5' quadrangle. Colfax (1938) 30' quadrangle has the form "Snow Tent Spring" for the name.

Snowy Mountains: see "Regional setting."

Snyder Canyon [PLACER]: *canyon,* drained by a stream that flows 1.25 miles to Middle Fork American River 1.5 miles south-southeast of Foresthill (lat. 39°00'05" N, long. 120°48'30" W; sec. 1, T 13 N, R 10 E). Named on Foresthill (1949) 7.5' quadrangle. Called Yankee Jim Gulch on Whitney's (1880) map.

Snyder Gulch: see **Big Snyder Gulch** [PLACER[.

Snyders Bar: see **Coloma** [EL DORADO].

Soapstone Ridge [COLUSA]: *ridge,* generally northeast-trending, 1.5 miles long, 2.25 miles northwest of Pacific Point (lat. 39°14'10" N, long. 122°37'25" W). Named on Clearlake Oaks (1960) 15' quadrangle.

Soapweed [EL DORADO]: *locality,* 7.5 miles northwest of Pollock Pines (lat. 38°50'30" N, long. 120°40'30" W; sec. 31, T 12 N, R 12 E). Named on Slate Mountain (1950) 7.5' quadrangle. Placerville (1893) 30' quadrangle has the form "Soap Weed" for the name. Logan's (1938) map shows a place called Golden located at or near present Soapweed. Postal authorities established Golden post office in 1923 and discontinued it in 1926; the name was for Miss Callie L. Golden, first postmaster (Salley, p. 86).

Soapweed Creek [EL DORADO]: *stream,* flows 2.25 miles to Slab Creek 6 miles northwest of Pollock Pines (lat. 38°49'35" N, long. 120°39'30" W; sec. 5, T 11 N, R 12 E). Named on Slate Mountain (1950) 7.5' quadrangle.

Soda Springs [NEVADA]: *village,* nearly 3 miles west of Donner Pass (lat. 39°19'25" N, long. 120°22'45" W; on W line sec. 23, T 17 N, R 14 E). Named on Soda Springs (1955) 7.5' quadrangle. Truckee (1895) 30' quadrangle shows Soda Springs Station at the place. Postal authorities established Summit Valley post office in 1870, changed the name to Soda Springs in 1875, discontinued it in 1881, and reestablished it in 1929 (Frickstad, p. 115). They established Hopkins post office, named for Mark Hopkins, at the place in 1885 and discontinued it in 1886 (Salley, p. 100). The resort that Mark Hopkins and Leland Stanford developed at present Soda Springs in the 1870's was known as Hopkins Springs; from 1867 until 1873 the railroad station at the place was called Tinkers Station for J.A. Tinker, a teamster who hauled freight between Soda Springs and the mines (Gudde, 1969, p. 315, 339).

Soda Springs [PLACER]: *springs,* 4 miles north-northwest of Granite Chief along North Fork American River (lat. 39°14'50" N, long. 120°19'35" W; near W line sec. 9, T 16 N, R 15 E). Named on Granite Chief (1953) 7.5' quadrangle. Anderson (p. 95) used the name "Berkeley Soda Springs" for present Soda Springs. G.A. Waring (p. 231) used the name "Summit Soda Springs" for the resort that operated there before the hotel burned in 1898. G.A. Waring (p. 232) also listed Florence Spring, located 0.25 mile northeast of Summit Soda Springs.

Soda Springs Station: see **Soda Springs** [NEVADA].

Soldier Creek [EL DORADO]: *stream,* formed by the confluence of North Fork and South Fork, flows 3.5 miles to South Fork American River 1.5 miles northeast of Pollock Pines (lat. 38°46'40" N, long. 120°33'35" W; near E line sec. 19, T 11 N, R 13 E). Named on Pollock Pines (1950) 7.5' quadrangle. North Fork is 1.5 miles long and South Fork is 2.25 miles long; both forks are named on Pollock Pines (1950) and Riverton (1950) 7.5' quadrangles.

Soldier Creek: see **Little Soldier Creek** [EL DORADO].

Soldiers Gulch: see **Jackson Butte** [AMADOR]; **Volcano** [AMADOR].

Somerset [EL DORADO]: *village,* 6.25 miles south of Camino (lat. 38°38'50" N, long. 120°41'05" W; at W line sec. 8, T 9 N, R 12 E). Named on Camino (1952) 7.5' quadrangle. Placerville (1893) 30' quadrangle shows Sommerset House at the place. Called Youngs on California Division of Highways' (1934) map. Postal authorities established Youngs post office, named for Morgan W. Young, first postmaster, in 1924 and discontinued in 1950, when they moved it 1 mile south and changed the name to Somerset (Salley, p. 245). The first settlers, who came from Somerset, Ohio, named the village (Gudde, 1975, p. 327). California Division of Highway's (1934) map also shows a place called Rodwell located nearly 2 miles east of Youngs along Diamond Caldor Railroad (near E line sec. 9, T 9 N, R 12 E), and a place called River Hill located along the railroad nearly 2 miles northwest of Youngs (sec. 1, T 9 N, R 11 W).

Sommerset House: see **Somerset** [EL DORADO].

Sonntag Hill: see **Sontag Hill** [NEVADA].

Sonora Bar: see **Lancha Plana** [AMADOR].

Sontag Hill [NEVADA]: *peak,* nearly 3 miles north of Chicago Park (lat. 39°11'10" N, long. 120°57'45" W; near W line sec. 3, T 15 N, R 9 E). Named on Chicago Park (1949) 7.5' quadrangle. United States Board on Geographic Names (1984a, p. 5) approved the form "Sonntag Hill" for the name, and noted that it commemorates Herman E. Sonntag, who settled in the neighborhood in 1890 and owned part of the feature.

Sopiago Creek [EL DORADO]: *stream,* flows 11.5 miles to Middle Fork Cosumnes River 0.5 mile north-northeast of Omo Ranch (lat. 38°35'20" N, long. 120°33'45" W; sec. 32, T 9 N, R 13 E). Named on Caldor (1951) and Omo Ranch (1952) 7.5' quadrangles.

Sore Finger Point [PLACER]: *ridge,* southeast-trending, 0.5 mile long, 6 miles south-southeast of Colfax (lat. 39°01' N, long. 120° 55'20" W; sec. 36, T 14 N, R 9 E). Named on Colfax (1949) 7.5' quadrangle.

Sorroca [YOLO]: *locality,* 7 miles southwest of Clarksburg along Sacramento Northern Railroad (lat. 38°20'23" N, long. 121°36'35" W). Named on Courtland (1978) 7.5' quadrangle.

Soudan [SACRAMENTO]: *locality,* 3 miles east-southeast of present downtown Carmichael along Southern Pacific Railroad (lat. 38°36'10" N, long. 121°16'30" W). Named on Mills (1911) 7.5' quadrangle. Called Cornell on Sacramento (1892) 30' quadrangle. California Division of Highways' (1934) map shows a place called Mather located nearly 0.5 mile west-southwest of Soudan along Southern Pacific Railroad.

Sourdough Hill [EL DORADO]: *peak,* 5.25 miles west of the town of Meeks Bay (lat. 39°01'35" N, long. 120°13'05" W; near SW cor. sec. 28, T 14 N, R 16 E). Altitude 7976 feet. Named on Homewood (1955) 7.5' quadrangle.

South Butte [SUTTER]: *peak,* 5 miles northwest of Sutter in Sutter Buttes (lat. 39°12'20" N, long. 121°49'10" W; near E line sec. 26, T 16 N, R 1 E). Altitude 2117 feet. Named on Sutter Buttes (1954) 7.5' quadrangle.

South Butte: see **Sutter** [SUTTER].

South Canyon [EL DORADO]: *canyon,* drained by a stream that flows 3 miles to South Fork American River 8.5 miles west of Pollock Pines (lat. 38°46'20" N, long. 120°44'15" W); the canyon is west of North Canyon (2). Named on Camino (1952) and Slate Mountain (1950) 7.5' quadrangles.

South Canyon: see **Illinois Canyon** [EL DORADO].

South Creek [EL DORADO]: *stream,* flows 2 miles to South Fork Rubicon River 4 miles northwest of Robbs Peak (lat. 38°57'55" N, long. 120°27'30" W; near NW cor. sec. 19, T 13 N, R 14 E). Named on Robbs Peak (1950) 7.5' quadrangle.

South Fork: see **Poorman Creek** [NEVADA] (1).

South Fork Camp Ground [EL DORADO]: *locality,* 1.5 miles north of Robbs Peak (lat. 38°56'55" N, long. 120°24' W; sec. 27, T 13 N, R 14 E); the place is along South Fork Rubicon River. Named on Robbs Peak (1950) 7.5' quadrangle.

South Honcut Creek [YUBA]: *stream,* flows 27 miles to join North Honcut Creek, which is in Butte County, and form Honcut Creek 12 miles north of Marysville (lat. 39°18'50" N, long. 121°36'05" W). Named on Honcut (1952), Loma Rica (1947), Oregon House (1948), and Rackerby (1948) 7.5' quadrangles. Called Honcut Creek on Honcut (1912) 7.5' quadrangle. On Marysville (1895) 30' quadrangle, present Wilson Creek is called South Honcut Creek, and present South Honcut Creek is called Prairie Creek. On Wescoatt's (1861) map, the uppermost part of present South Honcut Creek is called Hansonville Branch—the map shows Hansonville near the creek. South Honcut Creek forms a large part of Yuba-Butte County line.

South Indian Creek: see **Little Indian Creek** [AMADOR].

South Jackson Canyon [COLUSA]: *canyon,* drained by a stream that flows 1.5 miles to Bear Creek 6 miles southeast of Wilbur Springs (lat. 38°58'40" N, long. 122°20'20" W; near NE cor. sec. 18, T 13 N, R 4 W); the canyon heads just south of the head of Jackson Canyon. Named on Glascock Mountain (1958) 7.5' quadrangle.

South Lake Tahoe [EL DORADO]: *town,* 7 miles northwest of Freel Peak at the south end of Lake Tahoe (lat. 38°56'30" N, long. 119° 59' W). Named on Emerald Bay (1955, photorevised 1969) and South Lake Tahoe (1955, photorevised 1969 and 1974) 7.5' quadrangles. Postal authorities established South Lake Tahoe post office in 1967 (Salley, p. 209). The communities of Al Tahoe, Bijou, Bijou Park, Stateline, Tahoe Valley, and Tallac Village combined to form the new town, which incorporated in 1965. United States Board on Geographic Names (1985, p. 2) approved the name "Jakes Peak" for a peak located 7 miles northwest of South Lake Tahoe (lat. 38°58'12" N, long. 120°07'18" W; sec. 17, T 13 N, R 17 E; altitude 9187 feet); the name commemorates Jeffery J. Smith, who died with others in an avalanche in 1982.

South Long Point [PLACER]: *ridge,* west-trending, 1.5 miles long, 3.25 miles north-northwest of Foresthill (lat. 39°03'40" N, long. 120°51' W); the ridge is situated south across Shirttail Canyon from Long Point (1). Named on Foresthill (1949) 7.5' quadrangle.

South Mokelumne River: see **Mokelumne River** [AMADOR-SACRAMENTO].

South Rail Canyon [COLUSA]: *canyon,* 2.5 miles long, opens into the canyon of Freshwater Creek 3.25 miles north-northeast of Wilbur Springs (lat. 39°04'45" N, long. 122°23'10" W; sec. 11, T 14 N, R 5 W). Named on Wilbur Springs (1961) 15' quadrangle.

South Shore Campground [AMADOR]: *locality,* 8 miles west of Mokelumne Peak (lat. 38°32' N, long. 120°14'30" W; on E line sec. 19, T 8 N, R 16 E); the place is on the south shore of Lower Bear River Reservoir. Named on Bear River Reservoir (1979) 7.5' quadrangle.

South Steely Creek [EL DORADO]: *stream,* flows 3.5 miles to join North Steely Creek and form Steely Fork Cosumnes River 2 miles west-northwest of Caldor (lat. 38°37' N, long. 120°28' W; sec. 19, T 9 N, R 14 E). Named on Caldor (1951) and Stump Spring (1951) 7.5' quadrangles.

South Wallace Canyon [PLACER]: *canyon,* drained by a stream that flows 4.5 miles to Wallace Canyon 2 miles north-northeast of Davis Peak (lat. 38°59' N, long. 120°31'35" W; near N line sec. 16, T 13 N, R 13 E). Named on Bunker Hill (1953), Devil Peak (1950), and Robbs Peak (1950) 7.5' quadrangles. Called Middle Wallace Canyon on Placerville (1893) 30' quadrangle.

South Wolf Creek [NEVADA]: *stream,* flows 10.5 miles to Wolf Creek 1.5 miles north of Higgins Corner (lat. 39°03'45" N, long. 121°05'20" W; sec. 16, T 14 N, R 8 E). Named on Chicago Park (1949), Grass Valley (1949), and Lake Combie (1949) 7.5' quadrangles.

South Yuba [YUBA]: *locality,* 1.5 miles south of downtown Marysville along Sacramento Northern Railroad (lat. 39°07'15" N, long. 121°35'10" W). Named on Marysville (1952) 15' quadrangle. The name appears on Yuba City (1952, photorevised 1973) 7.5' quadrangle, but there it applies to a district, and the railroad is not shown.

South Yuba River [NEVADA-PLACER]: *stream,* heads near Donner Pass in Placer County and flows 62 miles to Yuba River 2.5 miles west-southwest of French Corral in Nevada County (lat. 39°17'45" N, long. 121°12'25" W; near NE cor. sec. 32, T 17 N, R 7 E). Named on Blue Canyon (1955), Cisco Grove (1955), French Corral (1948), Nevada City (1948), Norden (1955), North Bloomfield (1949), Soda Springs (1955), and Washington (1950) 7.5' quadrangles. Called Yuba River on Truckee (1895) 30' quadrangle, and called South Fork Yuba River on Colfax (1898), Smartsville (1895), and Truckee (1940) 30' quadrangles. United States Board on Geographic Names (1950, p. 6) rejected the names "South Fork" and "South Fork Yuba River" for the feature. Giffen (*in* Decker, p. 291) noted that a mining place called Ohio Bar was located on the south side of Yuba River 1 mile below the mouth of South Fork (present South Yuba River).

Spanish Corral: see **Ophir** [PLACER].

Spanish Creek [EL DORADO]: *stream,* formed by the confluence of North Fork and South Fork, flows 4.5 miles to Middle Fork Cosumnes River 11 miles south of Placerville (lat. 38°34'30" N, long. 120°46'45" W; near E line sec. 5, T 8 N, R 11 E). Named on Aukum (1952) and Fiddletown (1949) 7.5' quadrangles. North Fork is 2 miles long and South Fork is 3 miles long; both forks are named on Aukum (1952) 7.5' quadrangle.

Spanish Diggings: see **Spanish Dry Diggings** [EL DORADO].

Spanish Dry Diggings [EL DORADO]: *locality,* 3.25 miles north of Greenwood (lat. 38°56'45" N, long. 120°54'45" W; near W line sec. 30, T 13 N, R 10 E). Named on Greenwood (1949) 7.5' quadrangle. Called Spanish Diggings on Placerville (1893) 30' quadrangle. Postal authorities established Spanish Dry Dggings post office in 1875 and discontinued it the same year (Frickstad, p. 29). Andreas Pico and a party of Spaniards were the first prospectors at the place in 1848; the next year a group of Germans set up a trading center nearby that was known as Dutchtown (Hoover, Rensch, and Rensch, p. 87).

Spanish Flat [EL DORADO]: *locality,* 4 miles north of Chili Bar (lat. 38°49'25" N, long. 120°48'25" W; on N line sec. 12, T 11 N, R 10 E). Named on Garden Valley (1949) 7.5' quadrangle. Postal authorities established Spanish Flat post office in 1853, discontinued it in 1872, reestablished it in 1888, and discontinued it that same year (Frickstad, p. 29). The name was for Spanish-speaking miners at the place (Gernes, p. 39). A mining camp called Union Flat started in 1852 about 0.5 mile north of Spanish Flat; many of the early miners there were from Union County, Ohio (Gernes, p. 41, 42). A mining camp called Stag Flat was located about 0.5 mile south of Spanish Flat (Gernes, p. 49), and a mining place called Chicken Flat was located north of South Fork American River 1 mile west of Spanish Flat (Gudde, 1975, p. 69).

Spanish Gulch [AMADOR]: *canyon,* drained by a stream that flows 1.25 miles to Dry Creek 6.5 miles southwest of Plymouth (lat. 38° 24'35" N, long. 120°55'40" W). Named on Irish Hill (1962) 7.5' quadrangle.

Spanish Hill [EL DORADO]: *ridge,* north-northwest-trending, less than 1 mile long, 4.5 miles north of Chili Bar (lat. 38°49'40" N, long. 120°48'45" W; sec. 1, T 11 N, R 10 E); the ridge is northwest of Spanish Flat. Named on Garden Valley (1949) 7.5' quadrangle.

Spanish Hill: see **Big Spanish Hill**, under **Spanish Ravine** [EL DORADO].

Spanish Ravine [EL DORADO]: *canyon,* drained by a stream that flows 0.5 mile to Hangtown Creek 0.5 mile east of downtown Placerville (lat. 38°43'50" N, long. 120°47'15" W; sec. 8, T 10 N, R 11 E). Named on Placerville (1949) 7.5' quadrangle. Whitney's (1880) map shows a feature called Big Spanish Hill located just east of Spanish Ravine, and has the name "Taylor's Rav." for the canyon east of Big Spanish Hill.

Spanish Ravine [PLACER]: *canyon,* drained by a stream that flows 0.5 mile to Duncan Canyon 5.5 miles south of Duncan Peak (lat. 39°04'30" N, long. 120°32' W; sec. 9, T 14 N, R 13 E). Named on Greek Store (1952) 7.5' quadrangle.

Spanish Spring [AMADOR]: *spring,* 6.5 miles southwest of Plymouth (lat. 38°24'50" N, long. 120°55'50" W; sec. 36, T 7 N, R 9 E); the spring is in Spanish Gulch. Named on Irish Hill (1962) 7.5' quadrangle.

Spaulding: see **Camp Spaulding** [NEVADA]; **Lake Spaulding** [NEVADA].

Spaulding Point [PLACER]: *peak,* 2.5 miles northeast of Dutch Flat (lat. 39°13'30" N, long. 120°48' W; sec. 25, T 16 N, R 10 E). Named on Dutch Flat (1950) 7.5' quadrangle.

Specimen Gulch [PLACER]: *canyon,* drained by a stream that flows 1.25 miles to Bunch Canyon 4.25 miles south-southeast of Colfax (lat. 39°02'35" N, long. 120°55'30" W; at S line sec. 24, T 14 N, R 9 E). Named on Colfax (1949) 7.5' quadrangle.

Specks's Bar: see **Cordua Bar**, under **Timbuctoo** [YUBA].

Spencer Canyon [YOLO]: *canyon,* drained by a stream that flows 1 mile to Salt Arroyo 3.25 miles east-southeast of Berryessa Peak (lat. 38°39'05" N, long. 122°07'45" W). Named on Brooks (1959) and Esparto (1959) 7.5' quadrangles.

Spencer Creek [SIERRA]: *stream,* flows 1.5 miles to Lavezzola Creek 11 miles north-northwest of Sierra City (lat. 39°41'55" N, long. 120°44'50" W; sec. 9, T 21 N, R 11 E); the stream heads at Spencer Lakes. Named on Gold Lake (1981) 7.5' quadrangle.

Spencer Lakes [SIERRA]: *lakes,* two, each 850 feet long, 10.5 miles north-northwest of Sierra City (lat. 39°41'55" N, long. 120°43'25" W; on and near E line sec. 10, T 21 N, R 11 E); the lakes are at the head of Spencer Creek. Named on Gold Lake (1981) 7.5' quadrangle.

Spenceville [NEVADA]: *locality,* 6 miles southwest of Pilot Peak along Dry Creek (2) at the mouth of Little Dry Creek (lat. 39°06'50" N, long. 121°16'

W; near NE cor. sec. 35, T 15 N, R 6 E). Site named on Camp Far West (1949) 7.5' quadrangle. Postal authorities established Spenceville post office in 1872, discontinued it in 1878, reestablished it in 1879, and discontinued it in 1932 (Frickstad, p. 115). The name commemorates Edward F. Spence of Nevada City, who donated lumber for the first school at the place in 1868 (Hanna, p. 313).

Spicer Canyon [EL DORADO]: *canyon,* drained by a stream that flows 1 mile to Sherman Canyon 9 miles west-southwest of Kirkwood (lat. 38°38'45" N, long. 120°13'15" W; at E line sec. 8, T 9 N, R 16 E). Named on Tragedy Spring (1979) 7.5' quadrangle.

Spicer Meadow [EL DORADO]: *area,* 9.5 miles west-southwest of Kirkwood (lat. 38°38'55" N, long. 120°13'55" W; near N line sec. 8, T 9 N, R 16 E); the place is in Spicer Canyon. Named on Tragedy Spring (1979) 7.5' quadrangle.

Spider Lake [EL DORADO]: *lake,* 3150 feet long, 3.5 miles east of Wentworth Springs (lat. 39°00'50" N, long. 120°16'20" W; on E line sec. 34, T 14 N, R 15 E). Named on Wentworth Springs (1953, photorevised 1973) 7.5' quadrangle.

Spirit Mountain: see **Sutter Buttes** [SUTTER].

Spiritsville: see **Omega** [NEVADA].

S.P. Lakes [PLACER]: *lakes,* largest 1000 feet long, about 1 mile west-southwest of Cisco Grove (lat. 39°18'15" N, long. 120°33'35" W; sec. 30, T 17 N, R 13 E). Named on Cisco Grove (1955) 7.5' quadrangle.

Sportsmans Hall: see **Placerville** [EL DORADO].

Spring Canyon [EL DORADO]: *canyon,* 1 mile long, opens into String Canyon 10 miles southeast of Camino (lat. 38°38'40" N, long. 120°32'20" W; near SE cor. sec. 9, T 9 N, R 13 E); the canyon heads at Spring Flat. Named on Sly Park (1952) 7.5' quadrangle.

Spring Canyon [PLACER]: *canyon,* drained by a stream that flows 1.5 miles to Grouse Creek 6.25 miles northeast of Michigan Bluff (lat. 39°05'30" N, long. 120°38'25" W; sec. 4, T 14 N, R 12 E). Named on Michigan Bluff (1952) 7.5' quadrangle.

Spring Creek [COLUSA]: *stream,* flows 13 miles to Salt Creek (2) 1.5 miles west of Williams (lat. 39°09'05" N, long. 122°10'45" W; sec. 15, T 15 N, R 3 W). Named on Colusa (1953) and Wilbur Springs (1961) 15' quadrangles. On Spring Valley (1918) 7.5' quadrangle, present Walters Creek is called South Fork [Spring Creek].

Spring Creek [NEVADA]: *stream,* flows 6 miles to South Yuba River 5.5 miles west-southwest of North Bloomfield (lat. 39°19'55" N, long. 120°59'15" W; sec. 17, T 17 N, R 9 E). Named on North Bloomfield (1949) and Pike (1949) 7.5' quadrangles. Called Knapp Cr. on Hobson's (1890a) map.

Springfield: see **Grays Bend** [SUTTER-YOLO].

Spring Flat [EL DORADO]: *area,* 11 miles southeast of Camino (lat. 38°38'55" N, long. 120°30'40" W; sec. 11, T 9 N, R 13 E). Named on Sly Park (1952) 7.5' quadrangle.

Spring Garden [PLACER]: *locality,* 11 miles northeast of Auburn (lat. 38°59'55" N, long. 120°54'45" W). Named on Placerville (1893) 30' quadrangle.

Spring Garden Ravine [PLACER]: *canyon,* drained by a stream that flows 2.5 miles to Gas Canyon 11 miles northeast of Auburn (lat. 38°59'50" N, long. 120°54'30" W; near SE cor. sec. 1, T 13 N, R 9 E); Spring Garden was in the canyon. Named on Foresthill (1949) and Greenwood (1949) 7.5' quadrangles.

Spring Hill [NEVADA]: *locality,* 1.25 miles northeast of Grass Valley (lat. 39°13'55" N, long. 121°02'35" W; sec. 23, T 16 N, R 8 E). Named on Grass Valley (1949) 7.5' quadrangle.

Spring Valley [COLUSA]: *valley,* along Spring Creek above a point 5.25 miles southwest of Williams (lat. 39°06' N, long. 122°13' W; at N line sec. 5, T 14 N, R 3 W). Named on Colusa (1953) and Wilbur Springs (1961) 15' quadrangles.

Spring Valley [EL DORADO]: *locality,* 3 miles east-northeast of Pollock Pines (lat. 38°46'45" N, long. 120°31'35" W; sec. 21, T 11 N, E 13 E). Named on Pollock Pines (1950) 7.5' quadrangle.

Spring Valley: see **Colusa** [COLUSA].

Spring Valley Branch [AMADOR]: *stream,* flows 1 mile to Little Indian Creek 2 miles west-northwest of Plymouth (lat. 38°29'05" N, long. 120°52'55" W; sec. 4, T 7 N, R 10 E). Named on Amador City (1962) and Irish Hill (1962) 7.5' quadrangles.

Spruce [PLACER]: *locality,* 5.5 miles west of Donner Pass along Southern Pacific Railroad (lat. 39°18'55" N, long. 120°25'40" W; near N line sec. 29, T 17 N, R 14 E). Named on Truckee (1940) 30' quadrangle.

Spruce Bar: see **Spruce Creek** [PLACER].

Spruce Cañon: see **Spruce Creek** [PLACER].

Spruce Creek [PLACER]: *stream,* flows 2.5 miles to Duncan Canyon 7.25 miles south-southwest of Duncan Peak (lat. 39°03'05" N, long. 120°32'35" W; sec. 20, T 14 N, R 13 E). Named on Greek Store (1952) 7.5' quadrangle. Logan's (1925) map shows a place called Spruce Bar located at the mouth of the stream, and has the name "Spruce Cañon" for the canyon of the stream. Logan's (1925) map also shows a place called Greek Store situated at the head of the canyon (near the center of W line sec. 8, T 14 N, R 13 E), where Greek Store (1952) 7.5' quadrangle shows Greek Store guard station.

Squaw Creek [COLUSA]: *stream,* flows 4.5 miles to East Park Reservoir 1 mile north of Lodoga (lat. 39°18'55" N, long. 122°29'20" W; at E line sec. 23, T 17 N, R 6 W). Named on Lodoga (1960) 15' quadrangle. Lodoga (1943) 15' quadrangle has the name "Squaw Creek" for a tributary of Wilson Creek that goes through present Deer Flat, and omits a name for present Squaw Creek.

Squaw Creek [PLACER]: *stream,* flows 5.5 miles to Truckee River 4.25 miles northwest of Tahoe City (lat. 39°12'40" N, long. 120° 11'55" W; near NE cor. sec. 28, T 16 N, R 16 E); the stream goes through Squaw Valley. Named on Granite Chief (1953) and Tahoe City (1955) 7.5' quadrangles. California Division of Highways' (1934) map has the name "Squaw Creek" for a locality along Southern Pacific Railroad near the mouth of Squaw Creek (near SE cor. sec. 21, T 15 N, R 16 E), and has the name "Old Road" for a place along the railroad about 1 mile farther south (near SE cor. sec. 28, T 16 N, R 16 E). Postal authorities established Squaw Creek post office at a vacation resort along Squaw Creek in 1917 and discontinued it in 1918 (Salley, p. 211). Hobson's (1890b) map shows a place called Claraville situated south of the mouth of Squaw Creek on the east side of Truckee River (near W line sec. 27, T 16 N, R 16 E); Wheeler (1877, p. 1237) described the place as a deserted mining camp. Hobson's (1890b) map also shows a place called Knoxville located north of the mouth of Squaw Creek on the east side of Truckee River (sec. 21, T 16 N, R 16 E); Wheeler (1877, p. 1237) identified this place as a tollhouse on Truckee and Tahoe turnpike road.

Squaw Flat [PLACER]:

(1) *area,* 5.5 miles east-northeast of Auburn (lat. 38°56'25" N, long. 120°59'10" W; near NW cor. sec. 33, T 13 N, R 9 E). Named on Greenwood (1949) 7.5' quadrangle.

(2) *area,* 8 miles west-northwest of Devil Peak (lat. 38°59'25" N, long. 120°41'30" W; sec. 12, T 13 N, R 11 E). Named on Tunnel Hill (1950) 7.5' quadrangle.

Squaw Gulch [PLACER]: *canyon,* flows 1.5 miles to Middle Fork American River 11 miles east-northeast of Auburn (lat. 38°57'35" N, long. 120°53' W; sec. 20, T 13 N, R 10 E). Named on Georgetown (1949) and Greenwood (1949) 7.5' quadrangles.

Squaw Hollow [EL DORADO]: *valley,* 5 miles south-southeast of Placerville (lat. 38°40'05" N, long. 120°44'55" W; at N line sec. 3, T 9 N, R 11 E). Named on Camino (1952) and Placerville (1949) 7.5' quadrangles.

Squaw Hollow Creek [EL DORADO]: *stream,* flows 9 miles to Martinez Creek 6.5 miles south of Placerville (lat. 38°38'05" N, long. 120°19' W; near E line sec. 13, T 9 N, R 10 E); the stream goes through Squaw Hollow. Named on Camino (1952) and Placerville (1949) 7.5' quadrangles.

Squaw Lake [SIERRA]: *lake,* 700 feet long, 7.25 miles north of Sierra City (lat. 39°40'10" N, long. 120°39'05" W; sec. 20, T 21 N, R 12 E). Named on Gold Lake (1981) 7.5' quadrangle.

Squaw Peak [PLACER]: *peak,* 1.5 miles southeast of Granite Chief (lat. 39°10'50" N, long. 120°16'05" W; sec. 2, T 15 N, R 15 E); the peak is west of Squaw Valley. Altitude 8885 feet. Named on Granite Chief (1953) 7.5' quadrangle.

Squaw Ridge [AMADOR]: *ridge,* southwest-trending, 8 miles long, 4.5 miles north of Mokelumne Peak on Amador-Alpine County line (lat. 38°36' N, long. 120°06'30" W). Named on Bear River Reservoir (1979), Caples Lake (1979), and Mokelumne Peak (1979) 7.5' quadrangles.

Squaw Valley [PLACER]: *valley,* 4.5 miles west-northwest of Tahoe City (lat. 39°12'15" N, long. 120°13' W); the feature is along Squaw Creek. Named on Tahoe City (1955) 7.5' quadrangle. The valley was called Ladies Paradise in the early days (Stewart, p. 85). Postal authorities established Squaw Village post office in the valley in 1959 and changed the name to Olympic Valley when Winter Olympic Games were held there in 1960 (Salley, p. 161, 211).

Squaw Village: see **Squaw Valley** [PLACER].

Squires Canyon [PLACER]: *canyon,* drained by a stream that flows nearly 2 miles to Bear River 2 miles southwest of Dutch Flat (lat. 39°11'20" N, long. 120°51'50" W" W; near E line sec. 5, T 15 N, R 10 E). Named on Dutch Flat (1950) 7.5' quadrangle.

Squirrel Creek [NEVADA]: *stream,* flows 11 miles to Deer Creek 5.25 miles northwest of Pilot Peak (lat. 39°13'45" N, long. 121°14'40" W; sec. 24, T 16 N, R 6 E). Named on Grass Valley (1949) and Rough and Ready (1949) 7.5' quadrangles.

Squirrel Creek [SIERRA]: *stream,* flows 2 miles to Grouse Creek 3 miles east of Pike (lat. 39°26'05" N, long. 120°56'30" W; near SW cor. sec. 11, T 18 N, R 9 E). Named on Pike (1949) 7.5' quadrangle.

Stafford [SUTTER]: *locality,* 6.25 miles north-northwest of Yuba City along Northern Electric Railroad (lat. 39°13'35" N, long. 121° 39'40" W; sec. 20, T 16 N, R 3 E). Named on Sutter (1911) 7.5' quadrangle.

Stafford Creek [EL DORADO]: *stream,* flows 1.5 miles to Big Canyon Creek nearly 3 miles southeast of Shingle Springs (lat. 38°37'50" N, long. 120°53'50" W; sec. 17, T 9 N, R 10 E). Named on Shingle Springs (1949) 7.5' quadrangle.

Stafford Mountain [SIERRA]: *peak,* 1.5 miles east-northeast of Mount Fillmore on Sierra-Plumas County line (lat. 39°44'30" N, long. 120°49'30" W; sec. 26, T 22 N, R 10 E). Altitude 7019 feet. Named on Mount Fillmore (1951) 7.5' quadrangle.

Stafford Ravine [SIERRA]: *canyon,* drained by a stream that flows 0.5 mile to West Branch Canyon Creek 1 mile east-northeast of Mount Fillmore (lat. 39°44'15" N, long. 120°49'55" W; sec. 26, T 22 N, R 10 E); the canyon is west of Stafford Mountain. Named on Mount Fillmore (1951) 7.5' quadrangle.

Stag Flat [COLUSA]: *area,* 4 miles north-northeast of Wilbur Springs (lat. 39°05'20" N, long. 122°22'55" W; sec. 2, T 14 N, R 5 W). Named on Wilbur Springs (1961) 15' quadrangle.

Stag Flat: see **Spanish Flat** [EL DORADO].

Stahls Ravine [SIERRA]: *canyon,* drained by a stream that flows 1 mile to Cedar Grove Ravine 4 miles southwest of Mount Fillmore (lat. 39°41'35" N, long. 120°54'35" W; sec. 7, T 21 N, R 10 E). Named on La Porte (1951) 7.5' quadrangle.

Stallman Corners [PLACER]: *locality,* 4.25 miles east-southeast of Rocklin (lat. 38°46' N, long. 121°09'45" W; on S line sec. 26, T 11 N, R 7 E). Named on Rocklin (1967) 7.5' quadrangle.

Stampede Canyon [PLACER]: *canyon,* drained by a stream that flows 1 mile to Bear River 5.25 miles north-northeast of Colfax (lat. 39°09'55" N, long. 120°54'20" W; near W line sec. 7, T 15 N, R 10 E). Named on Chicago Park (1949) 7.5' quadrangle.

Stampede Reservoir [SIERRA]: *lake,* behind a dam on Little Truckee River 5.5 miles south of Crystal Peak (lat. 39°28'30" N, long. 120°06'10" W; at NW cor. sec. 28, T 19 N, R 17 E). Named on Boca (1955, photorevised 1969), Dog Valley (1981), Hobart Mills (1981), and Sardine Peak (1981) 7.5' quadrangles.

Stampede Valley [SIERRA]: *valley,* 4.5 miles south-southwest of Crystal Peak (lat. 39°29'30" N, long. 120°07'30" W). Named on Loyalton (1955) and Truckee (1955) 15' quadrangles. Water of Stampede Reservoir now covers most of the valley.

Stanfield Hill [YUBA]:

(1) *ridge,* northwest-trending, 1 mile long, 3.25 miles southwest of Oregon House (lat. 39°19'45" N, long. 121°19'40" W; in and near sec. 17, T 17 N, R 6 E). Named on Oregon House (1948) 7.5' quadrangle.

(2) *locality,* 3 miles west-southwest of Oregon House (lat. 39°20'35" N, long. 121°20' W; near E line sec. 7, T 17 N, R 6 E); the place is at the northwest end of Stanfield Hill (1). Named on Oregon House (1948) 7.5' quadrangle. The name commemorates William Stanfield, who opened Stanfield House in 1856 (Gudde, 1949, p. 342).

Stanford [PLACER]: *locality,* 3.5 miles east-southeast of Donner Pass along Southern Pacific Railroad (lat. 39°17'45" N, long. 120° 15'45" W; sec. 25, T 17 N, R 15 E). Named on Truckee (1940) 30' quadrangle.

Stanford Rock [PLACER]: *peak,* 3.5 miles northwest of Homewood (lat. 39°07'25" N, long. 120°12'15" W; sec. 27, T 15 N, R 16 E). Altitude 8473 feet. Named on Homewood (1955) 7.5' quadrangle. The name commemorates Leland Stanford (Lekisch, p. 110).

Stanford Wood Camp: see **Old Stanford Wood Camp** [PLACER].

Star Bend [SUTTER-YUBA]: *bend,* 9 miles south of Yuba City along Feather River on Sutter-Yuba County line (lat. 39°00'45" N, long. 121°35'55" W). Named on Olivehurst (1952) 7.5' quadrangle.

Star Lake [EL DORADO]: *lake,* 1800 feet long, 1.25 miles north-northeast of Freel Peak (lat. 38°52'30" N, long. 119°53'15" W; sec. 30, T 12 N, R 19 E). Named on Freel Peak (1955) and South Lake Tahoe (1955) 7.5' quadrangles.

Starr Ravine [PLACER]: *canyon,* 1.25 miles long, opens into Deep Canyon 3.5 miles south-southwest of Duncan Peak (lat. 39°06'45" N, long. 120°32'45" W; at N line sec. 32, T 15 N, R 13 E). Named on Greek Store (1952) 7.5' quadrangle, which shows a mine called Millers Defeat at the head of the canyon. On Logan's (1925) map, present Starr Ravine is called Millers Defeat Cañon.

Starrs Landing [SUTTER]: *locality,* 8.5 miles south of Yuba City along Feather River (lat. 39°00'35" N, long. 121°36' W); the place is at present Star Bend. Named on Marysville (1895) 30' quadrangle.

Star Town [PLACER]: *locality,* 6 miles west-southwest of Duncan Peak (lat. 39°07'10" N, long. 120°36'20" W; sec. 26, T 15 N, R 12 E). Named on Greek Store (1952) 7.5' quadrangle.

Star Valley [COLUSA]: *area,* 9 miles south of Stonyford (lat. 39° 15' N, long. 122°31'10" W; sec. 10, T 16 N, R 6 W). Named on Clearlake Oaks (1960) and Stonyford (1951) 15' quadrangles.

Starvation Bar [NEVADA]: *locality,* nearly 2 miles south-southeast of French Corral along South Yuba River (lat. 39°17'05" N, long. 121°08'40" W; near S line sec. 36, T 17 N, R 7 E). Named on French Corral (1948) 7.5' quadrangle.

Stateline [EL DORADO]: *district,* 7.5 miles north-northwest of Freel Peak in the town of South Lake Tahoe (lat. 38°57'30" N, long. 119°56'45" W; sec. 27, T 13 N, R 18 E); the place is at California-Nevada State line. Named on South Lake Tahoe (1955, photorevised 1969 and 1974) 7.5' quadrangle. Postal authorities established Stateline post office in 1901 (Salley, p. 212). Markleeville (1889) 30' quadrangle shows a place called Lakeside situated in present Stateline near the intersection of the old Von Schmidt California-Nevada State line with Lake Tahoe. The name "Laphams" shown on an old map at present Stateline refers to the hotel and landing that William W. Lapham had there in the mid-1850's (Lekisch, p. 108).

Stateline Point [PLACER]: *promontory,* 1.5 miles southeast of Kings Beach along Lake Tahoe (lat. 39°13'20" N, long. 120°00'15" W; sec. 30, T 16 N, R 18 E); the feature is at California-Nevada State line. Named on Kings Beach (1955) 7.5' quadrangle. Truckee (1895) 30' quadrangle has the form "State Line Point" for the name.

State Prison: see **Represa** [SACRAMENTO].

State Ranch Bend [SUTTER-YOLO]: *bend,* 3.25 miles south-southeast of Kirkville along Sacramento River on Sutter-Yolo County line (lat. 38°52'05" N, long. 121°45'30" W; near S line sec. 21, T 12 N, R 2 E). Named on Eldorado Bend (1952) 7.5' quadrangle.

Station Creek [EL DORADO]: *stream,* flows 3.5 miles to South Fork American River 4.25 miles south-southwest of Pyramid Peak (lat. 38°47'15" N, long. 120°11' W; sec. 23, T 11 N, R 16 E). Named on Pyramid Peak (1955) 7.5' quadrangle.

Station Creek [NEVADA]: *stream,* flows 1 mile to Prosser Creek 4 miles northeast of Truckee (lat. 39°22'25" N, long. 120°07'55" W; near N line sec. 31, T 18 N, R 17 E). Named on Truckee (1955) 7.5' quadrangle.

Steamboat Canyon [PLACER]: *canyon,* drained by a stream that flows 2 miles to Five Lakes Creek 3.5 miles northeast of Bunker Hill (lat. 39°05'05" N, long. 120°19'50" W; near SE cor. sec. 6, T 14 N, R 15 E); the canyon heads near Steamboat Mountain. Named on Wentworth Springs (1953) 7.5' quadrangle.

Steamboat Mountain [PLACER]: *peak,* 4.5 miles north-northeast of Bunker Hill (lat. 39°06'40" N, long. 120°21'10" W; sec. 36, T 15 N, R 14 E). Altitude 7347 feet. Named on Wentworth Springs (1953) 7.5' quadrangle. Called Steamboat Rock on Truckee (1940) 30' quadrangle.

Steamboat Mountain: see **Little Steamboat Mountain** [PLACER].

Steamboat Rock: see **Steamboat Mountain** [PLACER].

Steamboat Slough [SACRAMENTO]: *water feature,* forms part of Sacramento-Solano County line, diverges southwest from Sacramento River nearly 2 miles south of Courtland, and rejoins the river 3.25 miles west-northwest of Isleton (lat. 38°10'45" N, long. 121°39'50" W). Named on Courtland (1978), Isleton (1978), and Rio Vista (1978) 7.5' quadrangles. Called Middle Fork [Sacramento River] on Ringgold's (1850a) map, and called Merritt's Slough in 1848 for Ezekiel Merritt, who came to California in 1841 (Grimshaw, p. 11, 39).

Steeley Fork: see **Steely Fork**, under **Cosumnes River** [AMADOR-EL DORADO-SACRAMENTO].

Steel Trap Rock [COLUSA]: *relief feature,* 5.5 miles south-southwest of Fouts Springs (lat. 39°17'05" N, long. 122°43'05" W; near W line sec. 36, T 17 N, R 8 W). Named on Fouts Springs (1968) 7.5' quadrangle. Called Steeltrap Rock on Stonyford (1951) 15' quadrangle.

Steely Creek: see **North Steely Creek** [EL DORADO]; **South Steely Creek** [EL DORADO].

Steely Fork: see **Cosumnes River** [AMADOR-EL DORADO-SACRAMENTO].

Steephollow Creek [NEVADA]: *stream,* flows 18 miles to Bear River 4.5 miles northeast of Chicago Park (lat. 39°10'35" N, long. 120°53'40" W; near S line sec. 6, T 15 N, R 10 E). Named on Blue Canyon (1955), Chicago Park (1949), Dutch Flat (1950), and Washington (1950) 7.5' quadrangles. Colfax (1898) 30' quadrangle has the name "Sheep Hollow" along the stream. North Fork enters from the northeast 6 miles south of Washington; it is 4.5 miles long and is named on Blue Canyon (1955) and Washington (1950) 7.5' quadrangles.

Steephollow Crossing [NEVADA]: *locality,* 5.5 miles northeast of Chicago Park along Steephollow Creek (lat. 39°11'45" N, long. 120°53'05" W; near NE cor. sec. 6, T 15 N, R 10 E). Named on Chicago Park (1949) 7.5' quadrangle.

Stegeman [COLUSA]: *locality,* 3.25 miles south-southwest of Princeton (lat. 39°21'25" N, long. 122°01'40" W). Named on Moulton Weir (1952) 7.5' quadrangle. Called Stegemann on California Division of Highways' (1934) map.

Steiner Bend [COLUSA-SUTTER]: *bend,* 4 miles north-northeast of Boyer Landing along Sacramento River on Colusa-Sutter County line (lat. 38°59'45" N, long. 121°47'45" W; at N line sec. 7, T 13 N, R 2 E). Named on Kirkville (1952) 7.5' quadrangle.

Stephens: see **Mount Stephens**, under **Donner Lake** [NEVADA].

Sterling: see **Lake Sterling** [NEVADA].

Sterling Ranch: see **Fourteen Mile House**, under **Colusa** [COLUSA].

Stevens Ravine [PLACER]: *canyon,* drained by a stream that flows 1 mile to the head of Third Brushy Canyon 2.5 miles north of Foresthill (lat. 39°03'20" N, long. 120°49'25" W; sec. 14, T 14 N, R 10 E). Named on Foresthill (1949) 7.5' quadrangle.

Stewart: see **George R. Stewart Peak**, under **Donner Pass** [NEVADA-PLACER].

Stewarts Flat: see **Penryn** [PLACER].

Still Gulch [YOLO]: *canyon,* drained by a stream that flows 1.25 miles to Cache Creek nearly 4 miles west-northwest of Rumsey (lat. 38°54'35" N, long. 122°18'15" W; near S line sec. 4, T 12 N, R 4 W). Named on Glascock Mountain (1958) 7.5' quadrangle.

Stinchfield Canyon [COLUSA]: *canyon,* 1 mile long, 8 miles north-northwest of Wilbur Springs (lat. 39°09'05" N, long. 122°27'45" W). Named on Wilbur Springs (1961) 15' quadrangle.

Stockings Flat: see **Newtown** [NEVADA].

Stockyards: see **Cicero** [SACRAMENTO].

Stohlmann: see **Tarke** [SUTTER].

Stolp: see **East Nicolaus** [SUTTER].

Stonebreaker Creek [EL DORADO]: *stream,* flows 4.5 miles to Camp Creek 8.5 miles east of Camino (lat. 38°43'30" N, long. 120° 31' W; near NE cor. sec. 15, T 10 N, R 13 E). Named on Sly Park (1952) and Stump Spring (1951) 7.5' quadrangles. Logan's (1938) map has the name "Bryant Cr." for the feature.

Stone Cellar [EL DORADO]: *locality,* 4 miles northeast of Robbs Peak (lat. 38°57'40" N, long. 120°20'45" W; at W line sec. 19, T 13 N, R 15 E). Named on Loon Lake (1952) 7.5' quadrangle.

Stone Corral Creek [COLUSA]: *stream,* flows 9 miles to lowlands 4 miles east-southeast of Sites (lat. 39°16'40" N, long. 122°16'30" W; sec. 35, T 17 N, R 4 W). Named on Lodoga (1960) and Maxwell (1952) 15' quadrangles, and on Moulton Weir (1952) 7.5' quadrangle. Lodoga (1960) 15' quadrangle shows Swifts Stone Corral along the stream (near NE cor. sec. 33, T 17 N, R 4 W). A stone fence built across a hollow that is hemmed in on the other three sides by high hills forms a corral; Granville P. Swift generally is credited with building the fence in the early 1850's (Hoover, Rensch, and Rensch, p. 49).

Stonehill: see **Westville** [PLACER].

Stone House [YUBA]: *locality,* 2 miles northeast of Loma Rica along Tennessee Creek (lat. 39°19'45" N, long. 121°23' W; sec. 14, T 17 N, R 5 E). Named on Loma Rica (1947) 7.5' quadrangle.

Stone Lake [SACRAMENTO]:

(1) *lake,* 3.5 miles east of Courtland (lat. 38°20' N, long. 121° 30' W). Named on Bruceville (1968) and Courtland (1978) 7.5' quadrangles. Vorden (1916) 7.5' quadrangle shows a much larger lake.

(2) *lake,* 7.25 miles west of Elk Grove (lat. 38°23'40" N, long. 121° 29'50" W). Named on Florin (1968) 7.5' quadrangle.

Stoney Creek [EL DORADO]: *stream,* flows 2 miles to Perry Creek 4.5 miles northeast of Aukum (lat. 38°36'05" N, long. 120°39'35" W; sec. 28, T 9 N, R 12 E). Named on Aukum (1952) 7.5' quadrangle.

Stony Bar [PLACER]: *locality,* 2 miles south of Michigan Bluff (lat. 39°00'45" N, long. 120°44'10" W; sec. 34, T 14 N, R 11 E). Named on Michigan Bluff (1952) 7.5' quadrangle.

Stony Bar: see **Coloma** [EL DORADO]; **Otter Creek** [EL DORADO].

Stony Creek [AMADOR]: *stream,* flows 2.5 miles to Sutter Creek (1) 7 miles south of Plymouth (lat. 38°22'35" N, long. 120°50'50" W; sec. 14, T 6 N, R 10 E). Named on Amador City (1962) and Jackson (1962) 7.5' quadrangles.

Stony Creek [COLUSA]: *stream,* formed by the confluence of Middle Fork and South Fork, flows 6 miles to Glenn County 0.5 mile north of Stonyford (lat. 39°23'05" N, long. 122°32'50" W; sec. 29, T 18 N, R 6 W). Named on Fouts Springs (1968), Gilmore Peak (1968), Saint John Mountain (1968), and Stonyford (1968) 7.5' quadrangles. Middle Fork heads in Glenn County and flows little more than 1 mile in Colusa County; it is named on Saint John Mountain (1968) 7.5' quadrangle. South Fork is 11 miles long and is named on Fouts Springs (1968), Potato Hill (1967), and Saint John Mountain (1968) 7.5' quadrangles. North Fork heads in Glenn County and flows 0.5 mile in Colusa County to join Stony Creek 0.25 mile below the confluence of South Fork and Middle Fork; it is named on Saint John Mountain (1968) 7.5' quadrangle.

Stony Creek [EL DORADO]: *stream,* flows nearly 2 miles to Rubicon River 5 miles north-northwest of Robbs Peak (lat. 38°59'15" N, long. 120°27' W). Named on Robbs Peak (1950) 7.5' quadrangle.

Stony Creek: see **Little Stony Creek** [COLUSA].

Stonyford [COLUSA]: *village,* 31 miles west-northwest of Colusa in Indian Valley (lat. 39°22'35" N, long. 122°32'45" W; sec. 29, 32, T 18 N, R 6 W); the village is near Stony Creek. Named on Gilmore Peak (1968) and Stonyford (1968) 7.5' quadrangles. Postal authorities established Little Stony post office along Little Stony Creek in 1879, moved it 4 miles northwest in 1880, moved it 0.25 mile northwest in 1886, changed the name to Stony Ford in 1891, and changed the name to Stonyford in 1894—water of East Park Reservoir now covers the original site of Little Stony post office (Salley, p. 123, 213). John L. Smith settled along Stony Creek near the junction with Little Stony Creek in 1863, and the place came to be known as Smithville; in 1890 Smith sold his holdings—including a mill and a three-story hotel—and the new owners moved the buildings from low ground to a new site about 0.5 mile to the southeast on a ridge; they gave the name "Stony Ford" to the community at the new spot (Cook, F.S., b, p. 27).

Stony Hill [PLACER]: *peak,* 6 miles northeast of Auburn (lat. 38°56'50" N, long. 120°59' W; sec. 28, T 13 N, R 9 E). Altitude 1898 feet. Named on Greenwood (1949) 7.5' quadrangle.

Stony Point [YUBA]: *relief feature,* nearly 4 miles east-southeast of Challenge on the east side of North Yuba River (lat. 39°27'50" N, long. 121°09'30" W; sec. 35, T 19 N, R 7 E). Named on Challenge (1948) 7.5' quadrangle.

Stony Ridge Lake [EL DORADO]: *lake,* 2900 feet long, nearly 2 miles north-northeast of Phipps Peak (lat. 38°58'45" N, long. 120° 08'15" W; on N line sec. 18, T 13 N, R 17 E). Named on Rockbound Valley (1955) 7.5' quadrangle. The feature also was known as Upper Tallant Lake (Lekisch, p. 114).

Storms' Station: see **Chicago Park** [NEVADA].

Stove Spring [YOLO]: *spring,* 11 miles south-southwest of Esparto (lat. 38°32'30" N, long. 122°04'40" W; near W line sec. 15, T 8 N, R 2 W). Named on Monticello Dam (1959) 7.5' quadrangle.

Stowman Ravine [YUBA]: *canyon,* drained by a stream that flows 1.25 miles to Slate Creek 3.5 miles northeast of Strawberry Valley (lat. 39°35'50" N, long. 121°03'20" W; near NW cor. sec. 14, T 20 N, R 8 E). Named on Strawberry Valley (1948) 7.5' quadrangle.

Strap Miner Creek [EL DORADO]: *stream,* flows 1.25 miles to Deer Creek (2) nearly 4 miles south-southeast of Clarksville (lat. 38°36'25" N, long. 121°01' W; sec. 29, T 9 N, R 9 E). Named on Folsom SE (1954) 7.5' quadrangle.

Strap Ravine [PLACER]: *canyon,* drained by a stream that flows 3.5 miles to Linda Creek 2.5 miles southeast of Roseville (lat. 38°43'50" N, long. 121°15' W; near S line sec. 7, T 10 N, R 7 E). Named on Folsom (1967) 7.5' quadrangle.

Strauch: see **Sacramento** [SACRAMENTO].

Strawberry [EL DORADO]: *locality,* 3.25 miles south-southeast of Pyramid Peak along South Fork American River (lat. 38°47'55" N, long. 120°08'35" W; sec. 18, T 11 N, R 17 E); the place is in Strawberry Valley. Named on Pyramid Peak (1955) 7.5' quadrangle.

Strawberry Bar [NEVADA-YUBA]: *locality,* nearly 3 miles northeast of North San Juan along Middle Yuba River on Nevada-Yuba County line (lat. 39°23'25" N, long. 121°03'40" W; near SE cor. sec. 27, T 18 N, R 8 E). Named on Camptonville (1948) 7.5' quadrangle.

Strawberry Creek [EL DORADO]: *stream,* flows 7.25 miles to South Fork American River 4 miles south of Pyramid Peak in Strawberry Valley (lat. 38°47'20" N, long. 120°09'10" W; near W line sec. 19, T 11 N, R 17 E). Named on Caples Lake (1979), Echo Lake (1955), and Pyramid Peak (1955) 7.5' quadrangles.

Strawberry Creek [SACRAMENTO]: *stream,* flows 3.25 miles to Beacon Creek 4.25 miles northwest of Elk Grove (lat. 38°27'30" N, long. 121°25' W; sec. 15, T 7 N, R 5 E). Named on Elk Grove (1968) and Florin (1968) 7.5' quadrangles.

Strawberry Flat [EL DORADO]: *locality,* 5 miles northwest of Kyburz (lat. 38°49'45" N, long. 120°21' W; at E line sec. 1, T 11 N, R 14 E). Named on Robbs Peak (1952) 15' quadrangle. Water of Ice House Reservoir now covers the place.

Strawberry Flat [PLACER]: *area,* 7 miles north of Foresthill (lat. 39°07'15" N, long. 120°49'30" W; at W line sec. 26, T 15 N, R 10 E). Named on Foresthill (1949) 7.5' quadrangle. Whitney's (1873) map has the name for an inhabited place at the site.

Strawberry Valley [EL DORADO]: *valley,* 3.5 miles south of Pyramid Peak along South Fork American River (lat. 38°47'30" N, long. 120°09' W). Named on Pyramid Peak (1896) 30' quadrangle. According to Gudde, 1949, p. 345), the name is from a Mr. Berry, who ran a travelers stop at the place, and from the straw that Berry used to stuff the mattresses that he provided for his customers.

Strawberry Valley [YUBA]: *village,* 8 miles northeast of Challenge (lat. 39°33'50" N, long. 121°06'25" W; sec. 29, T 20 N, R 8 E). Named on Strawberry Valley (1948) 7.5' quadrangle. Postal authorities established Strawberry Valley post office in 1855 (Frickstad, p. 224). The name may be either from wild strawberrys at the site, or from two early settlers, Mr. Straw and Mr. Berry (Hoover, Rensch, and Rensch, p. 594). Wescoatt's (1861) map shows a place called Bartons House located 1.5 miles southwest of Strawberry Valley.

String Canyon [EL DORADO]: *canyon,* drained by a stream that flows nearly 3 miles to Steely Fork Cosumnes River 9 miles southeast of Camino (lat. 38°37'45" N, long. 120°34'25" W; near SE cor. sec. 18, T 9 N, R 13 E). Named on Sly Park (1952) 7.5' quadrangle.

Striplin [SUTTER]: *locality,* 7 miles northeast of Verona along Sacramento Northern Railroad (lat. 38°52' N, long. 121°32'35" W; at SE cor. sec. 20, T 12 N, R 4 E). Named on Knights Landing (1952) 15' quadrangle.

Strode Canyon [COLUSA]: *canyon,* drained by a stream that flows 4.5 miles to the canyon of Cortina Creek 9 miles east of Wilbur Springs (lat. 39°01'20" N, long. 122°15'15" W; sec. 36, T 14 N, R 4 E). Named on Morgan Valley (1958) and Wilbur Springs (1961) 15' quadrangles

Strong Diggings: see **Damascus** [PLACER].

Strong Ranch Slough [SACRAMENTO]: *stream,* flows 5 miles to an artificial watercourse 4.5 miles east of downtown Sacramento (lat. 38°35'15" N, long. 121°24'10" W). Named on Carmichael (1967) and Sacramento East (1967) 7.5' quadrangles.

Stroud's: see **Milk Ranch** [YUBA].

Strychnine City: see **Brandy City** [SIERRA].

Studhorse Canyon [YUBA]: *canyon,* drained by a stream that flows 2.5 miles to Middle Yuba River nearly 4 miles south of Camptonville (lat. 39°23'45" N, long. 121°02'50" W; sec. 26, T 18 N, R 8 E). Named on Camptonville (1948) 7.5' quadrangle.

Studhorse Ravine [SIERRA]: *canyon,* drained by a stream that flows 1.25 miles to Canyon Creek 2.25 miles south-southeast of Mount Fillmore (lat. 39°41'50" N, long. 120°50'15" W). Named on Mount Fillmore (1951) 7.5' quadrangle.

Stump Canyon [NEVADA]: *canyon,* 0.5 mile long, opens into the canyon of Bear River 9.5 miles northeast of Chicago Park (lat. 39° 13'35" N, long. 120°49'15" W; sec. 26, T 16 N, R 10 E). Named on Dutch Flat (1950) 7.5' quadrangle.

Stumps Bar [PLACER]: *locality,* 2.25 miles south of Michigan Bluff along North Fork of Middle Fork American River (lat. 39°00'35" N, long. 120°44'30" W; near SW cor. sec. 34, T 14 N, R 11 E). Named on Michigan Bluff (1952) 7.5' quadrangle.

Stump Spring [EL DORADO]: *spring,* less than 1 mile west of Old Iron Mountain (lat. 38°42'20" N, long. 120°24'15" W; sec. 22, T 10 N, R 14 E). Named on Stump Spring (1951) 7.5' quadrangle. The name is from the location of the spring in the stump of a tree (Beverly Cola, personal communication, 1985).

Stumpy Meadows [EL DORADO]: *area,* 9.5 miles north of Pollock Pines along Pilot Creek (1) (lat. 38°54' N, long. 120°35'30" W). Named on Saddle Mountain (1950) 15' quadrangle. Water of Stumpy Meadows Lake now covers the place.

Stumpy Meadows Lake [EL DORADO]: *lake,* behind a dam on Pilot Creek (1) 10 miles north of Pollock Pines (lat. 38°54'15" N, long. 120°36'10" W; sec. 11, T 12 N, R 12 E). Named on Devil Peak (1950, photorevised 1973) 7.5' quadrangle. United States Board on Geographic Names (1973, p. 3) gave the names "Lake Edson" and "Mark Edson Reservoir" as variants.

Sturdevant Ridge [EL DORADO]: *ridge,* west-southwest-trending, 3 miles long, 6 miles southeast of Camino (lat. 38°40'30" N, long. 120°35'45" W). Named on Sly Park (1952) 7.5' quadrangle.

Subaco [SUTTER]: *locality,* 9 miles west of Nicolaus along Southern Pacific Railroad in Sutter Basin (lat. 38°55'40" N, long. 121°44'15" W; sec. 34, T 13 N, R 2 E). Named on Sutter Causeway (1952) 7.5' quadrangle.

Succor Flat [PLACER]: *area,* 7 miles north of Foresthill (lat. 39°07'15" N, long. 120°48'15" W; near W line sec. 25, T 15 N, R 10 E). Named on Foresthill (1949) 7.5' quadrangle. Colfax (1898) 30' quadrangle has the name for an inhabited place at the site—the inhabited place is called Sucker Flat on Whitney's (1873) map, but United States Board on Geographic Names (1933, p. 725) rejected this name.

Sucker Bar [YUBA]: *locality,* nearly 5 miles east-northeast of Challenge along North Yuba River (lat. 39°29'55" N, long. 121°08'10" W; at S line sec. 13, T 19 N, R 7 E). Named on Nevada City (1948) 15' quadrangle. Water of New Bullards Bar Reservoir now covers the site. Wescoatt's (1861) map shows Sucker Bar on the southeast side of North Yuba River, shows Willow Bar across the river opposite Sucker Bar, and shows N.Y. [New York] Bar situated 0.25 mile upstream from Willow Bar on the north side of the river.

Sucker Flat [YUBA]: *locality,* 0.25 mile north-northeast of Smartville (lat. 39°12'45" N, long. 121°17'45" W; at W line sec. 27, T 16 N, R 6 E). Named on Smartville (1951) 7.5' quadrangle. The place first was called Gatesville for Mr. Gates, an early settler from Illinois; the name "Sucker" is from the designation "Sucker State" for Illinois (Gudde, 1975, p. 339).

Sucker Flat: see **Succor Flat** [PLACER].

Suckertown: see **Dry Creek** [AMADOR-SACRAMENTO].

Sugar Bowl [PLACER]: *canyon,* drained by a stream that flows 1 mile to South Yuba River 1 mile southwest of Donner Pass (lat. 39°18'30" N, long. 120°20'25" W; sec. 20, T 17 N, R 15 E). Named on Norden (1955) 7.5' quadrangle.

Sugarfield [YOLO]: *locality,* 2.5 miles north-northeast of Woodland (lat. 38°42'50" N, long. 121°45'10" W). Named on Woodland (1952) 7.5' quadrangle.

Sugar Loaf [PLACER]: *peak,* less than 0.25 mile northeast of Michigan Bluff (lat. 39°02'40" N, long. 120°44' W; near W line sec. 22, T 14 N, R 11 E). Named on Michigan Bluff (1952) 7.5' quadrangle.

Sugar Loaf: see **Big Sugar Loaf**, under **China Mountain** [EL DORADO]; **Sugarloaf Mountain** [NEVADA] (1); **Sugarloaf Peak** [AMADOR]; **Sugarloaf Peak** [NEVADA].

Sugarloaf [COLUSA]:

(1) *peak,* 3.5 miles southwest of Sites (lat. 39°16'50" N, long. 122° 23'15" W; sec. 35, T 17 N, R 5 W). Altitude 1396 feet. Named on Lodoga (1960) 15' quadrangle.

(2) *peak,* 9.5 miles north-northwest of Wilbur Springs (lat. 39°10'20" N, long. 122°27'55" W; on W line sec. 6, T 15 N, R 5 W). Named on Wilbur Springs (1961) 15' quadrangle.

Sugarloaf [EL DORADO]:

(1) *peak,* 12 miles northwest of Pollock Pines (lat. 38°52'55" N, long. 120°44'05" W; near S line sec. 15, T 12 N, R 11 E). Altitude 3419 feet. Named on Tunnel Hill (1950) 7.5' quadrangle.

(2) *peak,* less than 1 mile west of Kyburz (lat. 38°46'35" N, long. 120°18'25" W; on N line sec. 28, T 11 N, R 15 E). Named on Kyburz (1952) 7.5' quadrangle. Pyramid Peak (1896) 30' quadrangle has the form "Sugar Loaf" for the name.

(3) *peak,* 2.25 miles northeast of Latrobe (lat. 38°34'50" N, long. 120°56'55" W; near E line sec. 2, T 8 N, R 9 E). Named on Latrobe (1949) 7.5' quadrangle. Logan's (1938) map has the form "Sugar Loaf" for the name.

Sugarloaf [PLACER]:

(1) *peak,* 5 miles east-northeast of Rocklin (lat. 38°49'40" N, long. 121°09'10" W; at W line sec. 1, T 11 N, R 7 E). Named on Rocklin (1967) 7.5' quadrangle.

(2) *peak,* 5 miles east-southeast of Dutch Flat (lat. 39°10'20" N, long. 120°45'20" W; sec. 5, T 15 N, R 11 E). Altitude 4184 feet. Named on Dutch Flat (1950) 7.5' quadrangle.

Sugarloaf [SIERRA]:

(1) *peak,* 2.5 miles west-southwest of Mount Fillmore (lat. 39°42'55" N, long. 120°53'50" W; near N line sec. 6, T 21 N, R 10 E). Altitude 5818 feet. Named on La Porte (1951) 7.5' quadrangle.

(2) *peak,* 4.5 miles north-northwest of Goodyears Bar (lat. 39°36'15" N, long. 120°55'05" W; sec. 13, T 20 N, R 9 E). Altitude 5663 feet. Named on Goodyears Bar (1951) 7.5' quadrangle.

Sugarloaf [YOLO]: *peak,* nearly 6 miles west-northwest of Esparto (lat. 38°43'50" N, long. 122°06'45" W). Named on Esparto (1959) 7.5' quadrangle.

Sugarloaf [YUBA]: *peak,* 4.5 miles south-southwest of Rackerby (lat. 39°22'30" N, long. 121°21'35" W; sec. 36, T 18 N, R 5 E). Named on Oregon House (1948) and Rackerby (1948) 7.5' quadrangles. Called Sugar Loaf Mount on Wescoatt's (1861) map.

Sugarloaf: see **First Sugarloaf** [PLACER]; **Second Sugarloaf** [PLACER].

Sugarloaf Hill [NEVADA]: *peak,* 6.5 miles northwest of Pilot Peak (lat. 39°14'40" N, long. 121°15'35" W; sec, 14, T 16 N, R 6 E). Named on Smartville (1951) 7.5' quadrangle.

Sugar Loaf Mount: see **Sugarloaf** [YUBA].

Sugarloaf Mountain [NEVADA]:

(1) *peak,* less than 1 mile north of downtown Nevada City (lat. 39°16'25" N, long. 121°01' W; near SW cor. sec. 6, T 16 N, R 9 E). Named on Nevada City (1948) 7.5' quadrangle. Called Sugar Loaf on Smartsville (1895) 30' quadrangle. California Division of Highways' (1934) map has the name "Sugar Loaf Res." for a lake about 1 mile north of downtown Nevada City.

(2) *peak,* 3.25 miles north-northwest of Wolf (lat. 39°06'15" N, long. 121°09'30" W; near SE cor. sec. 35, T 15 N, R 7 E). Altitude 1514 feet. Named on Wolf (1949) 7.5' quadrangle.

Sugarloaf Peak [AMADOR]: *peak,* 3 miles southwest of Plymouth (lat. 38°26'45" N, long. 120°52'55" W; sec. 21, T 7 N, R 10 E). Altitude 1070 feet. Named on Irish Hill (1962) 7.5' quadrangle. Called Sugar Loaf on Jackson (1902) 30' quadrangle.

Sugarloaf Peak [NEVADA]: *peak,* 7.25 miles north of Nevada City (lat. 39°22'15" N, long. 121°00'30" W; sec. 6, T 17 N, R 9 E). Named on Nevada City (1948) 7.5' quadrangle. Called Chimney Hill on Whitney's (1873) map, and called Sugar Loaf on Smartsville(1895) 30' quadrangle.

Sugar Loaf Reservoir: see **Sugarloaf Mountain** [NEVADA] (1).

Sugar Loaves: see **First Sugarloaf** [PLACER].

Sugar Pine Canyon [EL DORADO]: *canyon,* drained by a stream that flows 1.5 miles to Cat Creek 5.5 miles east of Caldor (lat. 38°35'35" N, long. 120°19'45" W; near NW cor. sec. 33, T 9 N, R 15 E). Named on Peddler Hill (1951) 7.5' quadrangle.

Sugar Pine Canyon [PLACER]: *canyon,* drained by a stream that flows 3 miles to Brimstone Creek 5.5 miles north-northeast of Foresthill (lat. 39°05'30" N, long. 120°45'50" W; near N line sec. 5, T 14 N, R 11 E). Named on Foresthill (1949) and Michigan Bluff (1952) 7.5' quadrangles.

Sugar Pine Creek [AMADOR]: *stream,* flows nearly 2 miles to Lower Bear River Reservoir 8 miles west of Mokelumne Peak (lat. 38°32'45" N, long. 120°14'20" W; sec. 17, T 8 N, R 16 E). Named on Bear River Reservoir (1979) 7.5' quadrangle.

Sugar Pine Creek [EL DORADO]: *stream,* flows 2.5 miles to Silver Creek 6 miles north-northeast of Pollock Pines (lat. 38°50'25" N, long. 120°32'10" W; at E line sec. 32, T 12 N, R 13 E). Named on Pollock Pines (1950) 7.5' quadrangle.

Sugarpine Flat: see **Sugar Pine Point** [PLACER] (2).

Sugar Pine Mill [PLACER]: *locality,* 7 miles north-northeast of Foresthill along Brimstone Creek (lat. 39°06'30" N, long. 120°45'40" W). Named on Colfax (1898) 30' quadrangle.

Sugar Pine Mountain [PLACER]: *ridge,* east-southeast-trending, 3 miles long, 6.5 miles north of Auburn (lat. 38°59'35" N, long. 121° 03'15" W). Named on Auburn (1953) and Lake Combie (1949) 7.5' quadrangles.

Sugar Pine Mountain: see **Little Sugar Pine Mountain** [EL DORADO].

Sugar Pine Point [EL DORADO]: *promontory*, 1.5 miles north-northeast of the town of Meeks Bay along Lake Tahoe (lat. 39°03'40" N, long. 120°06'45" W; sec. 16, T 14 N, R 17 E). Named on Meeks Bay (1955) 7.5' quadrangle. United States Board on Geographic Names (1963, p. 7) rejected the form "Sugarpine Point" for the name.

Sugar Pine Point [PLACER]:

(1) *relief feature*, 3.5 miles northeast of Dutch Flat (lat. 39°14'05" N, long. 120°46'50" W; sec. 19, T 16 N, R 11 E). Named on Dutch Flat (1950) 7.5' quadrangle.

(2) *peak*, 6.5 miles north-northwest of Duncan Peak (lat. 39°14'45" N, long. 120°32'40" W; near SW cor. sec. 17, T 16 N, R 13 E). Altitude 6322 feet. Named on Duncan Peak (1952) 7.5' quadrangle. Colfax (1898) 30' quadrangle shows Sugarpine Flat at or near present Sugar Pine Point (2).

Sullivan [SUTTER]: *locality*, 4.25 miles north-northwest of Yuba City along Southern Pacific Railroad (lat. 39°12'10" N, long. 121° 38'05" W; near NE cor. sec. 33, T 16 N, R 3 E). Named on Sutter (1952) 7.5' quadrangle.

Sullivan Creek [COLUSA]: *stream*, flows 5 miles to Little Stony Creek 7.25 miles south-southwest of Stonyford (lat. 39°16'35" N, long. 122°36'25" W; sec. 36, T 17 N, R 7 W); the stream is north of Sullivan Ridge. Named on Fouts Springs (1968) and Gilmore Peak (1968) 7.5' quadrangles.

Sullivan Creek: see **Little Sullivan Creek** [COLUSA].

Sullivan Ridge [COLUSA]: *ridge*, east-trending, 4.25 miles long, 5.5 miles south-southeast of Fouts Springs (lat. 39°16'25" N, long. 122°38'05" W); the ridge is south of Sullivan Creek. Named on Fouts Springs (1968) and Gilmore Peak (1968) 7.5' quadrangles.

Sullivan Ridge: see **Little Sullivan Ridge** [COLUSA].

Sullivan Valley [COLUSA]: *canyon*, 1.5 miles long, 5.25 miles south-southeast of Fouts Springs (lat. 39°16'25" N, long. 122° 38' W); the canyon is on the north side of Sullivan Ridge. Named on Stonyford (1951) 15' quadrangle.

Sulphur Canyon: see **Little Sulphur Canyon** [COLUSA].

Sulphur Creek [COLUSA]: *stream*, formed by the confluence of East Fork and West Fork, flows 4 miles to Bear Creek less than 1 mile east of Wilbur Springs (lat. 39°02'25" N, long. 122°24'25" W; near SW cor. sec. 22, T 14 N, R 5 W). Named on Wilbur Springs (1961) 15' quadrangle. East Fork in 3.5 miles long and West Fork is 2 miles long; both forks are named on Wilbur Springs (1961) 15' quadrangle. Many sulphur and mineral springs make the water in the stream brackish and salty, unfit even for irrigation (Chandler, p. 27).

Sulphur Creek [SIERRA]: *stream*, flows 5 miles to Plumas County 11 miles north-northeast of Sierra City (lat. 39°42'25" N, long. 120°31'50" W; at W line sec. 4, T 21 N, R 13 E). Named on Calpine (1981) and Clio (1981) 7.5' quadrangles. United States Board on Geographic Names (1960a, p. 17) rejected the name "Mohawk Creek" for the stream.

Sulphur Creek: see **Wilbur Springs** [COLUSA].

Sulphur Gap [COLUSA]: *pass*, 14 miles north-northeast of Wilbur Springs (lat. 39°13'40" N, long. 122°20'30" W; sec. 19, T 16 N, R 4 W). Named on Manor Slough (1958) 7.5' quadrangle.

Sulphur Spring [COLUSA]: *spring*, 11.5 miles north of Wilbur Springs (lat. 39°12'20" N, long. 122°24'45" W; near SW cor. sec. 27, T 16 N, R 5 W). Named on Wilbur Springs (1944) 15' quadrangle.

Sulphur Spring [YOLO]:

(1) *spring*, 4.25 miles west of Rumsey (lat. 38°53'35" N, long. 122° 19' W). Named on Glascock Mountain (1958) 7.5' quadrangle.

(2) *spring*, 4.25 miles east of Guinda in Burger Canyon (lat. 38° 49'15" N, long. 122°06'50" W; sec. 8, T 11 N, R 2 W). Named on Bird Valley (1959) 7.5' quadrangle.

Sulphur Spring: see **Campbell Hot Springs** [SIERRA]; **Little Sulphur Spring** [COLUSA].

Summit City [NEVADA]: *locality*, 3.5 miles southeast of English Mountain (lat. 39°24'35" N, long. 120°30'10" W; sec. 22, T 18 N, R 13 E). Site named on English Mountain (1983) 7.5' quadrangle. Postal authorities established Meadow Lake post office at the place in 1866 and discontinued it in 1869; the community also was called Excelsior (Salley, p. 137). A place called Hudsonville was situated across Meadow Lake from Summit City (Fatout, p. 48).

Summit Creek: see **Cold Creek** [NEVADA-PLACER].

Summit Hill [EL DORADO]: *peak*, 4 miles north of Greenwood (lat. 38°57'10" N, long. 120°55'25" W; sec. 25, T 13 N, R 9 E). Altitude 2168 feet. Named on Greenwood (1949) 7.5' quadrangle.

Summit Hill [YUBA]: *peak*, 3.25 miles northeast of Dobbins (lat. 39°24'25" N, long. 121°10' W; on W line sec. 23, T 18 N, R 7 E). Named on Challenge (1948) 7.5' quadrangle.

Summit House [SIERRA]: *locality*, 8 miles east-northeast of Sierra City along North Fork Yuba River (present North Yuba River) (lat. 39°37' N, long. 120°30'30" W). Named on Downieville (1897) 30' quadrangle.

Summit House [YUBA]: *locality*, 3.5 miles northeast of Dobbins (lat. 39°24' N, long. 121°09'25" W). Named on Smartsville (1895) 30' quadrangle. Wescoatt's (1861) map shows a place called Mountain Cottage at or near the site.

Summit Lake [NEVADA]: *lake*, 850 feet long, 2.25 miles north of Donner Pass (lat. 39°21' N, long. 120°19'25" W; sec. 4, T 17 N, R 15 E). Named on Norden (1955) 7.5' quadrangle.

Summit Lake [SIERRA]: *lake*, 350 feet long, 7 miles north-northwest of Sierra City (lat. 39°39'40" N, long. 120°40'30" W; at S line sec. 19, T 21 N, R 12 E). Named on Gold Lake (1981) 7.5' quadrangle.

Summit Soda Springs: see **Soda Springs** [PLACER].

Summit Spring [COLUSA]: *spring*, nearly 5 miles west of Fouts Springs (lat. 39°20'40" N, long. 122°45'10" W; sec. 10, T 17 N, R 8 W). Named on Potato Hill (1967) 7.5' quadrangle.

Summit Station: see **Donner Pass** [NEVADA-PLACER].

Summit Valley [COLUSA]: *area*, 5.25 miles southwest of Fouts Springs on Board Camp Ridge (lat. 39°17'35" N, long. 122°43'20" W; near SE cor. sec. 26, T 17 N, R 8 W). Named on Fouts Springs (1968) 7.5' quadrangle.

Summit Valley [NEVADA-PLACER]: *valley*, 2 miles west of Donner Pass along South Yuba River on Nevada-Placer County line (lat. 39°18'55" N, long. 120°21'45" W). Named on Norden (1955) 7.5' quadrangle. Water of Lake Van Norden now covers most of the valley. Morgan (p. 425) identified present Summit Valley as the place called Meadow-Vale on Jefferson's (1849) map, and noted that it was known as Yuba Valley in 1846.

Summit Valley: see **Lake Van Norden** [NEVADA-PLACER]; **Nigger Heaven** [YOLO]; **Soda Springs** [NEVADA].

Summy: see **Tarke** [SUTTER].

Sunbeam: see **Tallac** [EL DORADO].

Sunday Ridge [EL DORADO]: *ridge*, west-trending, 0.5 mile long, 9.5 miles southeast of Camino (lat. 38°39'10" N, long. 120°32'20" W). Named on Sly Park (1952) 7.5' quadrangle.

Sunflower Hill [PLACER]: *peak*, 9.5 miles west-southwest of Granite Chief (lat. 39°10'10" N, long. 120°27'15" W; sec. 7, T 15 N, R 14 E). Altitude 7045 feet. Named on Royal Gorge (1953) 7.5' quadrangle.

Sunnybrook [AMADOR]: *locality*, 3 miles east of Ione along Mountain Spring Creek (lat. 38°20'35" N, long. 120°52'30" W; sec. 28, T 6 N, R 10 E). Named on Ione (1962) and Jackson (1962) 7.5' quadrangles. Postal authorities established Vogans post office at the place in 1888 and discontinued it in 1889; the name was from the operator of Mountain Spring House, a travelers stop at present Sunnybrook (Salley, p. 233). They established Ranlett post office 0.5 mile west of present Sunnybrook at Newton mine in 1895 and discontinued it in 1905; the name was for Arthur G. Ranlett, first postmaster (Andrews, p. 47; Salley, p. 181).

Sunnyside [PLACER]: *settlement*, 2 miles south-southwest of Tahoe City along Lake Tahoe (lat. 39°08'30" N, long. 120°09'15" W). Named on Tahoe City (1955) 7.5' quadrangle. The name is from a resort that Mrs. Hayes developed in the early 1880's (Lekisch, p. 115).

Sunnyside Creek [SIERRA]: *stream*, flows 2.25 miles to Lavezzola Creek nearly 6 miles east-southeast of Mount Fillmore (lat. 39°41'45" N, long. 120°45'05" W; sec. 9, T 21 N, R 11 E); the stream heads near Sunnyside Meadow. Named on Mount Fillmore (1951) 7.5' quadrangle.

Sunnyside Meadow [SIERRA]: *area*, 4.5 miles east-southeast of Mount Fillmore (lat. 39°41'55" N, long. 120°46'45" W; on E line sec. 7, T 21 N, R 11 E); the stream is near the head of Sunnyside Creek. Named on Mount Fillmore (1951) 7.5' quadrangle.

Sunny South [PLACER]: *locality*, 4 miles north-northeast of Michigan Bluff (lat. 39°05'45" N, long. 120°42'40" W; near SW cor. sec. 35, T 15 N, R 11 E). Site named on Michigan Bluff (1952) 7.5' quadrangle. The place was in a sheltered nook that escaped the heavy winter snows of the surrounding neighborhood (Hoover, Rensch, and Rensch, p. 276).

Sunrise Creek [SIERRA]: *stream*, flows 2.5 miles to the State of Nevada 5 miles east-southeast of Crystal Peak (lat. 39°31'25" N, long. 120°00'05" W; at E line sec. 7, T 19 N, R 18 E). Named on Dog Valley (1981) 7.5' quadrangle.

Sun Rock [EL DORADO]: *peak*, nearly 4 miles east of Robbs Peak (lat. 38°55'35" N, long. 120°20' W; sec. 31, T 13 N, R 15 E). Named on Loon Lake (1952) 7.5' quadrangle.

Sunset [SUTTER]: *locality*, 2 miles south-southeast of Live Oak along Southern Pacific Railroad (lat. 39°15' N, long. 121°39'05" W). Named on Gridley (1952) and Sutter (1952) 7.5' quadrangles. Postal authorities established Sunset City post office 2.5 miles south of Live Oak in 1906 and discontinued it in 1913 (Salley, p. 216).

Sunset City: see **Sunset** [SUTTER].

Sunset View [NEVADA]: *settlement*, 2.25 miles west-northwest of Grass Valley (lat. 39°13'45" N, long. 121°05'50" W; near S line sec. 20, T 16 N, R 8 E). Named on Grass Valley (1949) 7.5' quadrangle.

Sunset View Reservoir [NEVADA]: *lake*, 150 feet long, 2 miles west-northwest of Grass Valley (lat. 39°13'50" N, long. 121°05'35" W; near E line sec. 20, T 16 N, R 8 E); the lake is near the northeast end of Sunset View. Named on Grass Valley (1949) 7.5' quadrangle.

Sunshine Valley [NEVADA]: *area*, nearly 2 miles west-northwest of Chicago Park (lat. 39°09'20" N, long. 120°59'40" W; sec. 17, T 15 N, R 9 E). Named on Chicago Park (1949) 7.5' quadrangle.

Surrey: see **Berwick** [YOLO].

Susie Lake [EL DORADO]: *lake*, 0.5 mile long, 5 miles south-southeast of

Phipps Peak (lat. 38°52'55" N, long. 120°07'35" W). Named on Emerald Bay (1955) and Rockbound Valley (1955) 7.5' quadrangles.

Sutter [SUTTER]: *town,* 7 miles west of Yuba City (lat. 39°09'40" N, long. 121°44'50" W; in and near sec. 9, T 15 N, R 2 E). Named on Sutter (1952) and Sutter Buttes (1954) 7.5' quadrangles. Postal authorities established South Butte post office in 1871, discontinued it in 1878, and reestablished it in 1879; they moved it 0.5 mile east in 1888, when they changed the name to Sutter City, and changed the name again to Sutter in 1895 (Salley, p. 208, 216). Camp Bethel, site of large religious camp meetings, operated 2 miles north of present Sutter from the early 1860's until the early 1880's (Hoover, Rensch, and Rensch, p. 546).

Sutter: see **Point Sutter**, under **Sutter Island** [SACRAMENTO]; **Sutter Creek** [AMADOR] (2); **Sutterville** [SACRAMENTO].

Sutter Basin [SUTTER]: *area,* lowlands east of Sacramento River between Meridian and the confluence of Sacramento River and Feather River. Named on Eldorado Bend (1952), Gilsizer Slough (1952), Kirkville (1952), Knights Landing (1952), Sutter Causeway (1952), and Tisdale Weir (1952) 7.5' quadrangles. Shown as marsh on Gilsizer Slough (1911), Kirkville (1915), Marcuse (1910), Marysville Buttes (1912), and Tisdale Weir (1912) 7.5' quadrangles.

Sutter Buttes [SUTTER]: *range,* 12 miles west-northwest of Yuba City (lat. 39°13' N, long. 121°48' W). Named on Gridley (1952), Meridian (1952), Pennington (1954), Sanborn Slough (1952), Sutter (1952), and Sutter Buttes (1954) 7.5' quadrangles. Called Marysville Buttes on Marysville (1895) 30' quadrangle. The feature has the name "Butes" on Wilkes' (1841) map, "Three Buttes" on Fremont's (1848) map—the range has three prominent peaks, "Los Picos de Sutter" on Larkin's (1848) map, "Sutter's Buttes" on Ord's (1848) map, "Bute Mountains" on Eddy's (1851) map, "Buttes" on Trask's (1853) map, and "Butte Mts" on Goddard's (1857) map. Luis Antonio Arguello saw the range in 1817 and called it *los Picachos,* which has the meaning "the peaks" in Spanish (Hendrix, p. 33-34). Dana (1849b, p. 259) called the feature both Sacramento Bute and Three Butes. United States Board on Geographic Names (1949c, p. 5) rejected the names "Bute Mountains," "Buttes," "Buttes Mountains," "Los Tres Picos," "Marysville Buttes," "Picachos," "Prairie Buttes," "Spirit Mountain," "Sutter County Buttes," "Sutter's Buttes," "The Buttes," "The Buttes of Sacramento," "The Three Buttes," and "The Mountain of the Breathing Spirit," for the range.

Sutter Bypass [SUTTER]: *area,* lowland that carries overflow from Sacramento River along the east side of Sutter Basin for 30 miles from Butte Slough 4.5 miles west of Sutter to Sacramento River 8 miles south-southeast of Robbins. Named on Gilsizer Slough (1952), Knights Landing (1952), Nicolaus (1952), Sutter Buttes (1954), Sutter Causeway (1952), Tisdale Weir (1952), and Verona (1967) 7.5' quadrangles.

Sutter City: see **Sutter** [SUTTER]; **Sutterville** [SACRAMENTO].

Sutter County Buttes: see **Sutter Buttes** [SUTTER].

Sutter Creek [AMADOR]:

(1) *stream,* flows 32 miles to Dry Creek 3.25 miles west of Ione (lat. 38°21'35" N, long. 120°59'30" W). Named on Amador City (1962), Ione (1962), Jackson (1962), Pine Grove (1948), and West Point (1948) 7.5' quadrangles. John A. Sutter came to mine at the stream in 1848 (Bancroft, 1888, p. 77). South Branch, which enters from the southeast near Volcano, is 7.25 miles long and is named on Pine Grove (1948) and West Point (1948) 7.5' quadrangles.

(2) *town,* 6.5 miles south-southeast of Plymouth (lat. 38°23'35" N, long. 120°48'05" W; around NE cor. sec. 7, T 6 N, R 11 E); the town is along Sutter Creek (1). Named on Amador City (1962) 7.5' quadrangle. Postal authorities established Sutter Creek post office in 1852 (Frickstad, p. 6), and the town incorporated in 1913. The town was named for the stream; it also was called Sutter and Suttersville in the early 1850's (Gudde, 1975, p. 342).

Sutter Hill [AMADOR]: *village,* 7.25 miles south-southeast of Plymouth (lat. 38°22'45" N, long. 120°48'05" W; near NE cor. sec. 18, T 6 N, R 11 E). Named on Amador City (1962) 7.5' quadrangle.

Sutter Island [SACRAMENTO]: *island,* 5.5 miles long, center 3 miles south-southwest of Courtland between Sacramento River, Steamboat Slough, and Sutter Slough (1) (lat. 38°17'45" N, long. 121°35'30" W). Named on Courtland (1978) 7.5' quadrangle. Called Schoolcraft I. on Ringgold's (1850b) map, which shows Pt. Sutter at the north tip of the island.

Sutter's Buttes: see **Sutter Buttes** [SUTTER].

Sutter's Embarcadero: see **Sacramento** [SACRAMENTO].

Sutter's Fort: see **Sacramento** [SACRAMENTO].

Sutter Slough [SACRAMENTO]: *water feature,* remnant of a watercourse 8 miles east of downtown Sacramento (lat. 38°33'30" N, long. 121°21' W). Named on Carmichael (1967) 7.5' quadrangle. Fair Oaks (1954) 15' quadrangle shows a longer watercourse.

Sutter Slough [SACRAMENTO-YOLO]: *water feature,* diverges northwest from Sacramento River 0.5 mile west-southwest of Courtland (lat. 38°19'40" N, long. 121°34'30" W) and extends west of Sutter Island to Steamboat Slough. Named on Courtland (1978) 7.5' quadrangle. Called West Fork [Sacramento River] on Ringgold's (1850b) map. The feature forms part of Sacramento-Yolo County line and Sacramento-Solano County line.

Sutters Mill [EL DORADO]: *locality,* along South Fork American River at Coloma (lat. 38°48'10" N, long. 120°53'30" W; sec. 17, T 11 N, R 10 E). Site named on Coloma (1949) 7.5' quadrangle. James Marshall's discovery of gold in the mill race set off the California gold rush.

Suttersville: see **Sutter Creek** [AMADOR] (2); **Sutterville** [SACRAMENTO].

Sutterville [SACRAMENTO]: *locality,* 2.25 miles south-southwest of downtown Sacramento along Southern Pacific Railroad (lat. 38° 32'45" N, long. 121°30'30" W). Named on Lovdal (1916) 7.5' quadrangle. The name recalls the town of Suttersville, later Sutterville, that John A. Sutter had laid out in 1844 on high ground about 2 miles south of his embarcadero; when the city of Sacramento developed at the embarcadero, Sutterville declined (Hoover, Rensch, and Rensch, p. 302). The original town is called Sutter on Derby's (1849b) map, called Suttersville on Ringgold's (1850b) map, and called Sutter City on Williamson's (1849) map. Postal authorities established Sutter post office in 1855 and discontinued it in 1860 (Frickstad, p. 135). Camp Union was at the site during the Civil War (Whiting and Whiting, p. 84).

Sutterville Lake: see **Mungers Lake** [SACRAMENTO].

Swan Lake Jr. [PLACER]: *lake,* 400 feet long, 3.5 miles south of Colfax (lat. 39°03' N, long. 120°57'45" W; sec. 22, T 14 N, R 9 E). Named on Colfax (1949) 7.5' quadrangle.

Swanson Range [COLUSA]: *range,* 6.5 miles south-southeast of Wilbur Springs (lat. 38°57'45" N, long. 122°21'30" W). Named on Glascock Mountain (1958) 7.5' quadrangle.

Swanston [SACRAMENTO]: *locality,* 3.5 miles northeast of downtown Sacramento along Southern Pacific Railroad (lat. 38°36'20" N, long. 121°26'20" W). Named on Sacramento East (1967) 7.5' quadrangle.

Sweeneys: see **Sweeneys Crossing** [EL DORADO].

Sweeneys Crossing [EL DORADO]: *locality,* 6.5 miles south-southeast of Camino along North Fork Cosumnes River (lat. 38°39'10" N, long. 120°37'25" W; near N line sec. 11, T 9 N, R 12 E). Named on Sly Park (1952) 7.5' quadrangle. Called Sweeneys on Placerville (1893) 30' quadrangle.

Sweetland [NEVADA]: *locality,* 2 miles south-southwest of North San Juan (lat. 39°20'35" N, long. 121°07'10" W; at S line sec. 7, T 17 N, R 8 E). Named on Nevada City (1948) 7.5' quadrangle. Postal authorities established Sweetland post office in 1857 and discontinued it in 1905 (Frickstad, p. 115). The name commemorates the Sweetland brothers, who started mining at the place in 1850 (Gudde, 1975, p. 343).

Sweetland Creek [NEVADA]: *stream,* flows 3.5 miles to Yuba River 3 miles north-northeast of French Corral (lat. 39°21' N, long. 121° 08'35" W; sec. 12, T 17 N, R 7 E); the stream goes past Sweetland. Named on French Corral (1948) and Nevada City (1948) 7.5' quadrangles.

Sweet Vengeance: see **Browns Valley** [YUBA].

Sweetwater Creek [AMADOR]: *stream,* flows 2.25 miles to Tiger Creek 5.5 miles southwest of Hams Station (lat. 38°29'15" N, long. 120°26'40" W; near W line sec. 4, T 7 N, R 14 E). Named on Caldor (1951) and Devils Nose (1979) 7.5' quadrangles.

Sweetwater Creek [EL DORADO]: *stream,* flows 7.5 miles to South Fork American River nearly 6 miles south-southwest of the village of Pilot Hill near the site of Salmon Falls (2) (lat. 38°45'25" N, long. 121°03'30" W; sec. 35, T 11 N, R 8 E). Named on Auburn (1954) 15' quadrangle, and on Clarksville (1953) and Shingle Springs (1949) 7.5' quadrangles. The creek now joins South Fork in Folsom Lake.

Sweitzer Hills [YOLO]: *ridge,* south-southeast-trending, 1 mile long, 2.25 miles south of Guinda in Capay Valley (lat. 38°47'45" N, long. 122°11'15" W). Named on Guinda (1959) 7.5' quadrangle.

Swift: see **Flonellis** [EL DORADO].

Swifts Stone Corral: see **Stone Corral Creek** [COLUSA].

Swingle [YOLO]: *locality,* 4 miles east of Davis along Southern Pacific Railroad (lat. 38°33'30" N, long. 121°40'15" W). Named on Davis (1952) 7.5' quadrangle.

Swiss Bar: see **Long Bar** [YUBA] (2).

Switch [PLACER]: *locality,* 0.5 mile east of Emigrant Gap (1) along Southern Pacific Railroad (lat. 39°18'10" N, long. 120°39'10" W). Named on Colfax (1898) 30' quadrangle.

Sycamore [COLUSA]: *village,* 6.25 miles south-southeast of Colusa near the mouth of Sycamore Slough (lat. 39°08' N, long. 121°56'25" W). Named on Meridian (1952) 7.5' quadrangle.

Sycamore Siding [COLUSA]: *locality,* 4 miles northwest of Grimes along Southern Pacific Railroad (lat. 39°06'55" N, long. 121°56'10" W); the place is 1.25 miles south of Sycamore. Named on Grimes (1954) 7.5' quadrangle.

Sycamore Slough [COLUSA]: *stream,* flows 8.5 miles to Sacramento River 6.25 miles south-southeast of Colusa (lat. 39°08'10" N, long. 121°56'20" W). Named on Colusa (1953) and Sutter Buttes (1954) 15' quadrangles.

Sycamore Slough [COLUSA-YOLO]: *water feature,* extends for 15 miles through Colusa Basin from Colusa County to Knights Landing in Yolo County (lat. 38°48'05" N, long. 121°43'30" W). Named on Dunnigan

(1953), Eldorado Bend (1952), Kirkville (1952), and Knights Landing (1952) 7.5' quadrangles.

Sylvan Corners [SACRAMENTO]: locality, nearly 6 miles north-northeast of downtown Carmichael (lat. 38°41'40" N, long. 121°17'20" W; sec. 26, T 10 N, R 6 E). Named on Citrus Heights (1967) 7.5' quadrangle.

Sylvia: see **Lake Sylvia** [EL DORADO].

Syracuse Bar: see **Rose Bar** [YUBA].

—T—

Tabeaud Reservoir: see **Lake Tabeaud** [AMADOR].

Table Mountain [SIERRA]: *ridge,* west-trending, 0.5 mile long, 3.5 miles south-southwest of Downieville (lat. 39°30'40" N, long. 120° 50'50" W; near SW cor. sec. 15, T 19 N, R 10 E). Named on Downieville (1951) 7.5' quadrangle.

Table Rock [EL DORADO]: *ridge,* southwest-trending, 0.5 mile long, 5 miles north of Kyburz (lat. 38°50'45" N, long. 120°17'15" W; sec. 34, T 12 N, R 15 E). Named on Kyburz (1952) 7.5' quadrangle.

Table Rock [SIERRA]: *peak,* 2.5 miles southwest of Mount Fillmore (lat. 39°42'15" N, long. 120°52'50" W; near S line sec. 5, T 21 N, R 10 E). Altitude 6908 feet. Named on La Porte (1951) 7.5' quadrangle.

Table Rock: see **Howland Flat** [SIERRA]; **Little Table Rock** [SIERRA].

Tadpole Campground [PLACER]: *locality,* 2.5 miles northwest of Duncan Peak (lat. 39°11'05" N, long. 120°32'10" W; sec. 4, T 15 N, R 13 E); the place is near the head of Tadpole Creek. Named on Duncan Peak (1952) 7.5' quadrangle. Colfax (1938) 30' quadrangle shows Tadpole Spring at present Tadpole Campground.

Tadpole Canyon: see **Tadpole Creek** [PLACER].

Tadpole Creek [PLACER]: *stream,* flows nearly 3 miles to North Fork American River 5 miles northwest of Duncan Peak (lat. 39° 12'50" N, long. 120°34'05" W; near NE cor. sec. 36, T 16 N, R 12 E). Named on Duncan Peak (1952) 7.5' quadrangle. Colfax (1898) 30' quadrangle has the name "Tadpole Canyon" for the canyon of the stream.

Tadpole Spring: see **Tadpole Campground** [PLACER].

Taho: see **Tallac** [EL DORADO].

Tahoe: see **Lake Tahoe** [EL DORADO-PLACER]; **Tahoe City** [PLACER].

Tahoe City [PLACER]: town, 14 miles southeast of Donner Pass along Lake Tahoe (lat. 39°10'15" N, long. 120°08'25" W; sec. 6, 7, T 15 N, R 17 E). Named on Tahoe City (1955) 7.5' quadrangle. Called Tahoe on Truckee (1940) 30' quadrangle, but United States Board on Geographic Names (1954, p. 4) rejected this name for the place. Postal authorities established Tahoe post office in 1871, discontinued it for a time in 1896, and changed the name to Tahoe City in 1949 (Frickstad, p. 122). The town site was surveyed in 1863, and William Pomin built Tahoe House there in 1864 (Hanna, p. 324).

Tahoe House: see **Tahoe City** [PLACER].

Tahoe Keyes: see **Tahoe Valley** [EL DORADO].

Tahoe Mountain [EL DORADO]: *ridge,* south- to east-trending, 2 miles long, 3.5 miles east of Mount Tallac (lat. 38°54'30" N, long. 120°01'55" W). Named on Emerald Bay (1955) 7.5' quadrangle.

Tahoe Paradise: see **Meyers** [EL DORADO].

Tahoe Pines [PLACER]: *settlement,* 1 mile north of Homewood along Lake Tahoe (lat. 39°06'15" N, long. 120°09'45" W; sec. 36, T 15 N, R 16 E). Named on Homewood (1955) 7.5' quadrangle. Postal authorities established Tahoe Pines post office in 1912 and discontinued it in 1959 (Salley, p. 218). Messers. Ferguson and Breuner started the settlement in 1909 and named it for the large number of ponderosa pine trees there (Hanna, p. 324).

Tahoe Tavern [PLACER]: *locality,* less than 1 mile south of Tahoe City along Lake Tahoe (lat. 39°09'40" N, long. 120°08'30" W; sec. 7, T 15 N, R 17 E). Named on Tahoe (1955) 15' quadrangle.

Tahoe Valley [EL DORADO]: *district,* 5 miles east of Mount Tallac in South Lake Tahoe (lat. 38°54'50" N, long. 120°00'10" W). Named on Emerald Bay (1955) and South Lake Tahoe (1955, photorevised 1969 and 1974) 7.5' quadrangles. Postal authorities established Tahoe Valley post office in 1940 (Salley, p. 218). They established Tahoe Keyes post office at a marina located 2 miles north of Tahoe Valley post office in 1959 and discontinued it in 1962 (Salley, p. 218). California Division of Highways' (1934) map shows a place called Mays located in present Tahoe Valley district (near SE cor. sec. 5, T 12 N, R 18 E).

Tahoe Vista [PLACER]: *settlement,* 1.5 miles west of Kings Beach along Lake Tahoe (lat. 39°14'25" N, long. 120°03' W; sec. 13, 14, T 16 N, R 17 E). Named on Kings Beach (1955) 7.5' quadrangle. Postal authorities established Tahoe Vista post office in 1911 (Frickstad, p. 122).

Tahoma [PLACER]: *town,* 2 miles southeast of Homewood along Lake Tahoe at El Dorado-Placer County line (lat. 39°04'10" N, long. 120°07'45" W; near SW cor. sec. 8, T 14 N, R 17 E). Named on Homewood (1955) and Meeks Bay (1955) 7.5' quadrangles. Truckee (1940) 30' quadrangle shows Chambers Lodge at the site. Postal authorities established Tahoma post office in 1946 (Frickstad, p. 122).

Talbot Campground [PLACER]: *locality,* 4.5 miles west of Granite Chief along Middle Fork American River (lat. 39°11'15" N, long. 120°22'20" W; near E line sec. 2, T 15 N, R 14 E); the place is at the mouth of Talbot Creek. Named on Granite Chief (1953) 7.5' quadrangle.

Talbot Creek [PLACER]: *stream,* flows 2.5 miles to Middle Fork American River 4.5 miles west of Granite Chief (lat. 39°11'15" N, long. 120°22'20" W; near E line sec. 2, T 15 N, R 14 E). Named on Granite Chief (1953) 7.5' quadrangle.

Talking Mountain [EL DORADO]: *peak,* 2.5 miles west-northwest of Echo Summit (lat. 38°50' N, long. 120°04'05" W; sec. 2, T 11 N, R 17 E). Altitude 8824 feet. Named on Echo Lake (1955) 7.5' quadrangle.

Tallac [EL DORADO]: *locality,* 3.25 miles northeast of Mount Tallac along Lake Tahoe (lat. 38°56'20" N, long. 120°03'30" W). Named on Pyramid Peak (1896) 30' quadrangle. Postal authorities established Lake Valley post office in 1861, changed the name to Taho in 1863, to Tallac in 1870, back to Lake Valley in 1871, and discontinued the post office in 1895; they established Tallac post office again in 1875, moved it 0.5 mile east in 1883, moved it 0.5 mile west in 1888, and discontinued it in 1927 (Salley, p. 116, 217, 218). Bancroft's (1864) map shows a locality called Lake Valley situated just south of Lake Tahoe about halfway between Yanks and California-Nevada State line. Postal authorities established Sunbeam post office 9 miles north of Tallac in 1888 and discontinued it in 1893 (Salley, p. 215).

Tallac: see **Mount Tallac** [EL DORADO].

Tallac Creek [EL DORADO]: *stream,* flows 3.5 miles to Lake Tahoe 3.25 miles northeast of Mount Tallac (lat. 38°56'25" N, long, 120° 03'30" W; near W line sec. 25, T 13 N, R 17 E); the stream heads near Mount Tallac. Named on Emerald Bay (1955) 7.5' quadrangle.

Tallac Lake [EL DORADO]: *lake,* 400 feet long, nearly 1 mile north-northwest of Mount Tallac (lat. 38°54'45" N, long. 120°06'40" W). Named on Emerald Bay (1955) 7.5' quadrangle.

Tallac Village [EL DORADO]: *district,* 4.25 miles east-northeast of Mount Tallac in South Lake Tahoe (lat. 38°55'15" N, long. 120°01'15" W; near W line sec. 5, T 12 N, R 18 E). Named on Emerald Bay (1955) 7.5' quadrangle.

Tallant Lake: see **Upper Tallant Lake**, under **Stony Ridge Lake** [EL DORADO].

Tamarack [PLACER]: *locality,* 9 miles west of Donner Pass along Southern Pacific Railroad (lat. 39°18'20" N, long. 120°29'20" W; near W line sec. 26, T 17 N, R 13 E). Named on Truckee (1940) 30' quadrangle.

Tamarack Canyon [YOLO]: *canyon,* drained by a stream that flows nearly 1 mile to Taylor Canyon 1 mile east-northeast of Berryessa Peak (lat. 38°40'05" N, long. 122°10'05" W). Named on Brooks (1959) 7.5' quadrangle.

Tamarack Creek [EL DORADO]: *stream,* flows 1.25 miles to South Fork American River 4 miles west of Echo Summit (lat. 38°48'15" N, long. 120°06'20" W; sec. 16, T 11 N, R 17 E). Named on Echo Lake (1955) 7.5' quadrangle.

Tamarack Flat [SIERRA]: *area,* 4 miles south of Mount Fillmore (lat. 39°40'25" N, long. 120°51'05" W). Named on Mount Fillmore (1951) 7.5' quadrangle.

Tamarack Lake [EL DORADO]: *lake,* 1750 feet long, 4.5 miles west-northwest of Echo Summit (lat. 38°50'50" N, long. 120°05'50" W; on W line sec. 34, T 12 N, R 17 E). Named on Echo Lake (1955) 7.5' quadrangle.

Tamarack Lakes [SIERRA]: *lakes,* largest 650 feet long, 3.25 miles north-northwest of Sierra City (lat. 39°36'35" N, long. 120°39'15" W; sec. 8, T 20 N, R 12 E). Named on Sierra City (1981) 7.5' quadrangle.

Tamaroo Bar [PLACER]: *locality,* 1.5 miles east-southeast of downtown Auburn along North Fork American River (lat. 38°53'15" N, long. 121°03' W; near S line sec. 14, T 12 N, R 8 E). Named on Auburn (1953) 7.5' quadrangle.

Tambo [YUBA]: *locality,* 6.5 miles north of Marysville along Western Pacific Railroad (lat. 39°14'20" N, long. 121°34'35" W). Named on Yuba City (1952) 7.5' quadrangle.

Tancred [YOLO]: *locality,* 4.5 miles south-southeast of Guinda in Capay Valley (lat. 38°45'55" N, long. 122°09'45" W). Named on Guinda (1959) 15' quadrangle. Rumsey (1921) 15' quadrangle shows the place along Southern Pacific Railroad. Postal authorities established Tancred post office in 1892 and discontinued it in 1932 (Frickstad, p. 221).

Tanglefoot Canyon [AMADOR]: *canyon,* drained by a stream that flows 4 miles to Salt Springs Reservoir 4 miles southwest of Mokelumne Peak (lat. 38°29'50" N, long. 120°09'05" W). Named on Bear River Reservoir (1979) and Calaveras Dome (1979) 7.5' quadrangles.

Tanner Reservoir [AMADOR]: *lake,* 600 feet long, 7.5 miles south-southeast of Plymouth (lat. 38°22'55" N, long. 120°47'15" W; sec. 8, T 6 N, R 11 E). Named on Amador City (1962) 7.5' quadrangle.

Tanners Point [PLACER]: *ridge,* northwest-trending, 0.5 mile long, 5.5 miles east of Michigan Bluff (lat. 39°01'55" N, long. 120°38'15" W; near E line sec. 28, T 14 N, R 12 E). Named on Michigan Bluff (1952) 7.5' quadrangle.

Tarke [SUTTER]: *locality,* 5.5 miles west-southwest of Sutter along Sacramento Northern Railroad (lat. 39°08'40" N, long. 121°50'50" W). Named on Sutter Buttes (1954) 7.5' quadrangle, which shows Stohlman Cem. [Cemetery] situated 1.25 miles east-northeast of Tarke. California Division of Highways' (1934) map shows a place called Stohlmann located nearly 2 miles east of Tarke along Sacramento Northern Railroad, a place called Summy located nearly 3 miles east of Tarke along the railroad, and a place called Noyes located 5 miles east of Tarke along the railroad.

Tars Mill [AMADOR]: *locality,* 13 miles east of present Fiddletown (lat. 38°30'15" N, long. 120°30'40" W). Named on Placerville (1893) 30' quadrangle.

Taylor Bluffs [YOLO]: *relief feature,* 2.5 miles south-southeast of Berryessa Peak on Yolo-Napa County line (lat. 38°37'50" N, long. 122°10' W). Named on Brooks (1959) and Lake Berryessa (1959) 7.5' quadrangles.

Taylor Canyon [YOLO]: *canyon,* drained by a stream that flows 4.5 miles to Capay Valley 4 miles north-northeast of Berryessa Peak (lat. 38°42'55" N, long. 122°09'25" W; sec. 14, T 10 N, R 3 W). Named on Brooks (1959) 7.5' quadrangle.

Taylor Creek [EL DORADO]: *stream,* heads at Fallen Leaf Lake and flows 2 miles to Lake Tahoe 3.25 miles northeast of Mount Tallac (lat. 38°56'25" N, long. 120°03'25" W; sec 25, T 13 N, R 17 E). Named on Emerald Bay (1955) 7.5' quadrangle.

Taylor Crossing [NEVADA-PLACER]: *locality,* 2 miles west-northwest of Colfax along Bear River on Nevada-Placer County line (lat. 39°06'40" N, long. 120°59' W; near W line sec. 33, T 15 N, R 9 E). Named on Colfax (1949) 7.5' quadrangle.

Taylor Island: see **Grand Island** [SACRAMENTO].

Taylor Reservoir [NEVADA]: *lake,* 350 feet long, 2.5 miles east-northeast of Grass Valley (lat. 39°14'15" N, long. 121°01'05" W; at W line sec. 19, T 16 N, R 9 E). Named on Grass Valley (1949) 7.5' quadrangle.

Taylor's Landing: see **Bijou** [EL DORADO].

Taylor's Ravine: see **Spanish Ravine** [EL DORADO].

Tehama Ravine [NEVADA]: *canyon,* drained by a stream that flows nearly 2 miles to Middle Yuba River 10 miles northeast of North Bloomfield (lat. 39°27'15" N, long. 120°45'15" W; at E line sec. 5, T 18 N, R 11 E). Named on Alleghany (1949) and Graniteville (1982) 7.5' quadrangles.

Tehuantepec Valley: see **Haypress Valley** [SIERRA].

Telegraph Hill [PLACER]: *peak,* 6 miles north of Roseville (lat. 38° 50'05" N, long. 121°15'50" W; at W line sec. 1, T 11 N, R 6 E). Named on Roseville (1967) 7.5' quadrangle.

Telegraph Ridge [COLUSA]: *ridge,* north-trending, 2 miles long, 5 miles east-southeast of Wilbur Springs (lat. 39°00' N, long. 122°20'35" W). Named on Wilbur Springs (1961) 15' quadrangle.

Telephone Ridge [EL DORADO]:

(1) *ridge,* generally west-trending, 4.5 miles long, center 4.5 miles east-northeast of Pollock Pines (lat. 38°47'20" N, long. 120°30'30" W). Named on Pollock Pines (1950) and Riverton (1950) 7.5' quadrangles.

(2) *ridge,* generally south-trending, 2.5 miles long, 3.5 miles east of Caldor (lat. 38°36'15" N, long. 120°21'45" W). Named on Peddler Hill (1951) 7.5' quadrangle.

Tells Creek [EL DORADO]: *stream,* flows 6.5 mile to Union Valley Reservoir nearly 2.5 miles southeast of Robbs Peak (lat. 38°53'55" N, long. 120°22'35" W; sec. 11, T 12 N, R 14 E). Named on Loon Lake (1952) 7.5' quadrangle.

Tells Peak [EL DORADO]: *peak,* 8.5 miles east-northeast of Robbs Peak (lat. 38°57'35" N, long. 120°15'15" W; sec. 19, T 13 N, R 16 E). Altitude 8872 feet. Named on Loon Lake (1952) 7.5' quadrangle. The name commemorates William Pedrini, a Swiss known as Bill Tell, who owned land in the neighborhood in the 1860's (Gernes, p. 58).

Temperance Creek [PLACER]: *stream,* flows about 1.5 miles to Shirttail Canyon 3.5 miles north-northeast of Foresthill (lat. 39°04'10" N, long. 120°47'20" W; at W line sec. 7, T 14 N, R 11 E). Named on Foresthill (1949) 7.5' quadrangle.

Ten Mile House: see **Colusa** [COLUSA].

Tenmile House [YUBA]: *locality,* 2.5 miles southwest of Browns Valley (lat. 39°13'15" N, long. 121°26'50" W; near NE cor. sec. 30, T 16 N, R 5 E). Named on Browns Valley (1911) 7.5' quadrangle. Whitney's (1873) map has the form "10 Mile Ho." for the name. The same map has the name "10 Mile Ho." for a second place, which is located 3.5 miles south of Brown Valley on the south side of Yuba River.

Tenmile Shoals [SACRAMENTO-YOLO]: *shoals,* 8 miles northwest of downtown Sacramento in Sacramento River on Sacramento-Yolo County line (lat. 38°39'25" N, long. 121°36'15" W). Named on Elkhorn Weir (1915) 7.5' quadrangle.

Tennessee Creek [EL DORADO]:

(1) *stream,* flows 4 miles to Dry Creek 4 miles north of Shingle Springs (lat. 38°43'20" N, long. 120°56' W; sec. 13, T 10 N, R 9 E). Named on Shingle Springs (1949) 7.5' quadrangle.

(2) *stream,* flows nearly 3 miles to North Fork Cosumnes River 7 miles south-southeast of Camino (lat. 38°39' N, long. 120°36'40" W; at W line sec. 12, T 9 N, R 12 E). Named on Sly Park (1952) 7.5' quadrangle.

Tennessee Creek [YUBA]: *stream,* flows 6.5 miles to South Honcut Creek 2 miles north-northeast of Loma Rica (lat. 39°20'25" N, long. 121°24'30" W; near SW cor. sec. 10, T 17 N, R 5 E). Named on Loma Rica (1947) and Oregon House (1948) 7.5' quadrangles.

Tennessee Mountain [SIERRA]: *peak,* 3 miles south-southeast of Mount Fillmore (lat. 39°41'20" N, long. 120°49'50" W); the peak is southwest of Tennessee Ravine. Altitude 6401 feet. Named on Mount Fillmore (1951) 7.5' quadrangle.

Tennessee Ravine [SIERRA]: *canyon,* drained by a stream that flows 1 mile to Canyon Creek 2.25 miles southeast of Mount Fillmore (lat. 39°42'15" N, long. 120°49'35" W); the canyon is northeast of Tennessee Mountain. Named on Mount Fillmore (1951) 7.5' quadrangle, which shows Tennessee mine in the canyon.

Terra Buena: see **Tierra Buena** [SUTTER].

Texas Bar [EL DORADO]: *locality,* nearly 5 miles west-northwest of Greenwood along Middle Fork American River (lat. 38°55'10" N, long. 120°59'45" W; sec. 5, T 12 N, R 9 E). Named on Greenwood (1949) 7.5' quadrangle.

Texas Bar: see **Beals Point** [PLACER]; **Chili Bar** [EL DORADO]; **Goodyears Bar** [SIERRA]; **Long Bar** [YUBA] (1).

Texas Canyon [EL DORADO]: *canyon,* drained by a stream that flows 1.5 miles to Kelsey Canyon nearly 1 mile north-northwest of Chili Bar (lat. 38°46'40" N, long. 120°49'40" W; sec. 26, T 11 N, R 10 E). Named on Garden Valley (1949) 7.5' quadrangle.

Texas Creek [EL DORADO]: *stream,* flows 1.25 miles to Slab Creek nearly 7 miles north-northwest of Pollock Pines (lat. 38°50'35" N, long. 120°39' W; at E line sec. 32, T 12 N, R 12 E). Named on Slate Mountain (1950) 7.5' quadrangle.

Texas Creek [NEVADA]: *stream,* flows 5 miles to Canyon Creek 4 miles southeast of Graniteville (lat. 39°24'15" N, long. 120°41'05" W; at S line sec. 24, T 18 N, R 11 E). Named on English Mountain (1983) and Graniteville (1982) 7.5' quadrangles.

Texas Diggins: see **Texas Hill** [PLACER].

Texas Flat: see **Anthony House** [NEVADA].

Texas Hill [EL DORADO]: *ridge,* generally west-trending, 2 miles long, 2 miles east-southeast of downtown Placerville (lat. 38°43'20" N, long. 120°45'45" W). Named on Placerville (1949) 7.5' quadrangle.

Texas Hill [PLACER]: *ridge,* generally northwest-trending, 1.5 miles long. 4.25 miles north of Westville (lat. 39°14'10" N, long. 120°38'30" W; on E line sec. 20, T 16 N, R 12 E). Named on Westville (1952) 7.5' quadrangle. Hobson's (1890b) map shows a place called Texas Diggins situated on the ridge.

Texas Hill [YUBA]: *ridge,* north-trending, 0.5 mile long, 2 miles west-southwest of Dobbins (lat. 39°21'25" N, long. 121°14'10" W; near SW cor. sec. 6, T 17 N, R 7 E). Named on French Corral (1948) 7.5' quadrangle.

Texas Hill: see **Folsom** [SACRAMENTO].

Texas Hill Diggings: see **Folsom** [SACRAMENTO].

Texas Hill Spring [PLACER]: *spring,* 4.5 miles north of Westville (lat. 39°14'15" N, long. 120°38'15" W; sec. 21, T 16 N, R 12 E); the feature is on the northeast side of Texas Hill. Named on Westville (1952) 7.5' quadrangle.

The Beartrap [NEVADA]: *relief feature,* 3.5 miles south-southeast of Graniteville (lat. 39°23'40" N, long. 120°42'25" W; sec. 26, T 18 N, R 11 E). Named on Graniteville (1982) 7.5' quadrangle.

The Berry Patch [SUTTER]: *locality,* 5 miles west of Pennington (lat. 39°18' N, long. 121°52'55" W; sec. 29, T 17 N, R 1 E). Named on Sanborn Slough (1952) 7.5' quadrangle.

The Buttes: see **Sutter Buttes** [SUTTER].

The Buttes of Sacramento: see **Sutter Buttes** [SUTTER].

The Cedars [PLACER]: *settlement,* 4.5 miles south-southwest of Donner Pass (lat. 39°15'15" N, long. 120°21' W; sec. 13, T 16 N, R 14 E); the place is along Cedar Creek. Named on Norden (1955) 7.5' quadrangle.

The Chemisal [AMADOR]: *peak,* 6.25 miles south-southeast of Ione (lat. 38°15'50" N, long. 120°54'20" W; sec. 29, T 5 N, R 10 E). Named on Ione (1962) 7.5' quadrangle.

The Cups [SIERRA]: *relief feature,* 1.25 miles west of Sierra City (lat. 39°34'10" N, long. 120°39'25" W; near SW cor. sec. 29, T 20 N, R 12 E). Named on Sierra City (1981) 7.5' quadrangle.

The Falls [SUTTER]: *waterfall,* 6.5 miles northwest of Sutter in Braggs Canyon (lat. 39°13'40" N, long. 121°50' W; near NW cor. sec. 23, T 16 N, R 1 E). Named on Sutter Buttes (1954) 7.5' quadrangle.

The Forks: see **Downieville** [SIERRA].

The Four Corners [COLUSA]: *locality,* 6 miles southwest of Colusa (lat. 39°08'40" N, long. 122°04'40" W; at SW cor. sec. 15, T 15 N, R 2 W). Named on Colusa (1952) 7.5' quadrangle.

The Gate: see **Jackson Gate** [AMADOR].

The Laguna: see **Laguna** [AMADOR-SACRAMENTO].

The Meadows Slough [SACRAMENTO]: *water feature,* 5.5 miles south-east of Courtland (lat. 38°15'55" N, long. 121°30'20" W). Named on Courtland (1978) 7.5' quadrangle.

The Mounds [SIERRA]: *hills,* 3 miles north-northwest of Sierraville in Sierra Valley (lat. 39°37'30" N, long. 120°23'50" W; sec. 34, T 21 N, R 14

E). Altitude of highest hill is 5027 feet. Named on Calpine (1981) and Sattley (1981) 7.5' quadrangles.

The Mountain of the Breathing Spirit: see **Sutter Buttes** [SUTTER].

The Narrows [YUBA]: *narrows*, 1.5 miles north-northeast of Smartville along Yuba River (lat. 39°13'45" N, long. 121°17'15" W; sec. 22, T 16 N, R 6 E). Named on Smartville (1951) 7.5' quadrangle.

The Oaks [NEVADA]: *settlement*, 1 mile west of downtown Grass Valley (lat. 39°13'15" N, long. 121°04'45" W; sec. 28, T 16 N, R 8 E). Named on Grass Valley (1949) 7.5' quadrangle.

Theodore: see **Lake Theodore** [PLACER].

The Oxbow [SACRAMENTO]: *bay*, 1.25 miles southeast of Isleton in a bend of Georgiana Slough (lat. 38°08'55" N, long. 121°35'20" W). Named on Isleton (1978) 7.5' quadrangle. United States Board on Geographic Names (1977a, p. 6) gave the name "Oxbow" as a variant.

The Pinnacles [PLACER]: *relief feature*, 1.25 miles northeast of Bunker Hill (lat. 39°03'30" N, long. 120°21'40" W; sec. 13, T 14 N, R 14 E). Named on Wentworth Springs (1953) 7.5' quadrangle.

The Punchbowl [NEVADA]: *relief feature*, 1.5 miles southwest of Grass Valley (lat. 39°11'55" N, long. 121°04'55" W; at S line sec. 33, T 16 N, R 8 E). Named on Grass Valley (1949) 7.5' quadrangle. Called Devils Punch Bowl on United States Geological Survey's (1901) map.

The Redlands [COLUSA]: *area*, 9.5 miles southeast of Wilbur Springs on the east side of the south part of Cortina Ridge (lat. 38° 56'15" N, long. 122°18'20" W). Named on Glascock Mountain (1958) 7.5' quadrangle.

The Slide [YOLO]: *relief feature*, 6 miles northwest of Esparto near Cache Creek (lat. 38°44'45" N, long. 122°06'20" W; sec. 5, T 10 N, R 2 W). Named on Esparto (1959) 7.5' quadrangle.

The Three Buttes [SUTTER]: see **Sutter Buttes** [SUTTER].

The Trees [YOLO]: *area*, 1.5 miles east-southeast of Berryessa Peak on Yolo-Napa County line (lat. 38°39'15" N, long. 120°09'50" W). Named on Brooks (1959) 7.5' quadrangle.

Thimbleberry Creek [NEVADA]: *stream*, flows less that 1 mile to Logan Canyon 2.5 miles west of Washington (lat. 39°21'40" N, long. 120°50'55" W; near SW cor. sec. 3, T 17 N, R 10 E). Named on Washington (1950) 7.5' quadrangle.

Third Brushy Canyon [PLACER]: *canyon*, formed by the junction of Blackhawk Canyon and Stevens Ravine, 1.5 miles long, opens into Brushy Canyon (1) 3 miles northwest of Foresthill (lat. 39°03'20" N, long. 120°51' W; sec. 16, T 14 N, R 10 E). Named on Foresthill (1949) 7.5' quadrangle.

Third Divide [SIERRA]: *pass*, 5.5 miles northeast of Downieville on the ridge between Lavezzola Creek and Pauley Creek (lat. 39°36'45" N, long. 120°45'05" W; near W line sec. 9, T 20 N, R 11 E); the pass is nearly 3 miles east-northeast of Second Divide. Named on Downieville (1951) 7.5' quadrangle.

Thompson Canyon [COLUSA]: *canyon*, 4.5 miles long, opens into the canyon of Bear Creek 6.5 miles southeast of Wilbur Springs (lat. 38°58'20" N, long. 122°20'25" W; sec. 18, T 13 N, R 4 W). Named on Glascock Mountain (1958) and Wilson Valley (1958) 7.5' quadrangles.

Thompson Canyon [YOLO]: *canyon*, drained by a stream that flows 2 miles to Putah Creek 13 miles south-southwest of Esparto (lat. 38°30'50" N, long. 122°05'50" W; near E line sec. 29, T 8 N, R 2 W). Named on Montecillo Dam (1959) 7.5' quadrangle.

Thompson Hill [EL DORADO]: *peak*, 2.5 miles south-southwest of Coloma (lat. 38°45'55" N, long. 120°54'15" W; sec. 31, T 11 N, R 10 E). Altitude 2035 feet. Named on Coloma (1949) 7.5' quadrangle.

Thompson Meadows [SIERRA]: *area*, 4 miles east-southeast of Sierra City (lat. 39°33'10" N, long. 120°33'40" W; near SW cor. sec. 31, T 20 N, R 13 E). Named on Haypress Valley (1981) 7.5' quadrangle. Sierra City (1955) 15' quadrangle shows marsh in the area.

Thompson Peak [EL DORADO]: *peak*, nearly 5 miles south-southwest of Freel Peak on El Dorado-Alpine County line (lat. 38°47'50" N, long. 119°56'35" W; near W line sec. 13, T 11 N, R 18 E). Altitude 9340 feet. Named on Freel Peak (1955) 7.5' quadrangle.

Thousand Dollar Canyon: see **Illinois Canyon** [EL DORADO].

Three Buttes: see **Sutter Buttes** [SUTTER].

Three Cornered Meadow [SIERRA]: *area*, 3 miles north-northwest of Calpine (lat. 39°42'20" N, long. 120°27'45" W; at NW cor. sec. 6, T 21 N, R 14 E). Named on Calpine (1981) 7.5' quadrangle.

Three Mile House [EL DORADO]: *locality*, 2 miles northeast of Georgetown (lat. 38°55'20" N, long. 120°48'10" W). Named on Placerville (1893) 30' quadrangle.

Threemile Slough [SACRAMENTO]: *water feature*, extends from Sacramento River to San Joaquin River 6.5 miles southwest of Isleton (lat. 38°05'15" N, long. 121°41'05" W). Named on Jersey Island (1978) 7.5' quadrangle.

Three Sisters [COLUSA]: *peaks*, 7.5 miles northeast of Wilbur Springs (lat. 39°07'20" N, long. 122°20' W; sec. 29, T 15 N, R 4 W). Altitude of the middle peak is 1932 feet. Named on Wilbur Springs (1961) 15' quadrangle.

Thunder Cliff [PLACER]: *relief feature*, 2.5 miles west of Tahoe City on the east side of Truckee River (lat. 39°10'30" N, long. 120° 11'05" W; sec. 2, T 15 N, R 16 E). Named on Tahoe City (1955) 7.5' quadrangle.

Thunder Mountain [AMADOR]: *peak*, 9.5 miles north of Mokelumne Peak (lat. 38°40'30" N, long. 120°05'25" W; sec. 33, T 10 N, R 17 E). Altitude 9408 feet. Named on Caples Lake (1979) 7.5' quadrangle. Forest Service personnel gave the name because "thunderheads appear to build up in that area" (United States Board on Geographic Names, 1980, p. 5).

Ticky Creek [EL DORADO]: *stream*, flows 1 mile to Slab Creek 7.5 miles north-northwest of Pollock Pines (lat. 38°52'05" N, long. 120°37'40" W; sec. 22, T 12 N, R 12 E). Named on Slate Mountain (1950) and Tunnel Hill (1950) 7.5' quadrangles.

Tierra Buena [SUTTER]: *locality*, 2.5 miles west-northwest of downtown Yuba City (lat. 39°09' N, long. 121°39'45" W; sec. 17, T 15 N, R 3 E). Named on Sutter (1952) 7.5' quadrangle. Postal authorities established Terra Buena post office in 1913 and discontinued it in 1918 (Frickstad, p. 202). United States Board on Geographic Names (1954, p. 4) rejected the form "Terra Buena" for the name.

Tiger Creek [AMADOR]: *stream*, flows 9 miles to Tiger Creek Reservoir 9 miles southwest of Hams Station (lat. 38°27' N, long. 120°29'30" W; sec. 24, T 7 N, R 13 E). Named on Caldor (1951) and Devils Nose (1979) 7.5' quadrangles.

Tiger Creek: see **Little Tiger Creek** [AMADOR].

Tiger Creek Reservoir [AMADOR]: *lake*, behind a dam on North Fork Mokelumne River 9 miles east-northeast of Pine Grove on Amador-Calaveras County line (lat. 38°26'30" N, long. 120°30'15" W; sec. 23, T 7 N, R 13 E); Tiger Creek joins North Fork Mokelumne River in the lake. Named on Devils Nose (1979) and West Point (1948) 7.5' quadrangles.

Tiger Lily [EL DORADO]: *locality*, 3.5 miles south-southeast of Placerville (lat. 38°40'55" N, long. 120°46'25" W; near NE cor. sec. 33, T 10 N, R 11 E). Named on Placerville (1949) 7.5' quadrangle.

Til Jones Spring [COLUSA]: *spring*, 4.25 miles northwest of Wilbur Springs (lat. 39°04' N, long. 122°29' W; near W line sec. 12, T 14 N, R 6 W). Named on Wilbur Springs (1961) 15' quadrangle.

Timbuctoo [YUBA]: *locality*, 1.25 miles west-northwest of Smartville (lat. 39°13' N, long. 121°19' W; near E line sec. 29, T 16 N, R 6 E). Named on Smartville (1951) 7.5' quadrangle. Postal authorities established Timbuctoo post office in 1858 and discontinued it in 1883 (Frickstad, p. 224). Mining began near the place in 1850, including in a ravine named for a Negro miner from Timbuctoo in Africa; the community began in 1855 (Hoover, Rensch, and Rensch, p. 591). Cordua Bar, named in 1848 for Theodore Cordua, who kept a trading post there, was on the north bank of Yuba River northwest of Timbuctoo (Gudde, 1975, p. 82). Derby (p. 6) referred to Cordua's or Specks's Bar. The name "Spect" was for Jonas Spect, who found the first gold along Yuba River (Bancroft, 1888, p. 360; Hoover, Rensch, and Rensch, p. 589). Cape Horn Bar, a mining camp started by a company that came from Connecticut in the summer of 1849 by way of Cape Horn, was situated along Yuba River just above Cordua Bar (Gudde, 1975, p. 60-61).

Timbuctoo Bend [YUBA]: *bend*, 2 miles north-northwest of Smartville along Yuba River (lat. 39°14' N, long. 121°19' W; sec. 20, 21, T 16 N, R 6 E); the feature is 1 mile north of Timbuctoo. Named on Smartville (1951) 7.5' quadrangle.

Timbucktoo Ravine: see **Big Ravine** [YUBA].

Tin Cup Diggings: see **Downieville** [SIERRA].

Tinker Knob [PLACER]: *peak*, 3.25 miles north of Granite Chief (lat. 39°14'40" N, long. 120°17'05" W; near SW cor. sec. 11, T 16 N, R 15 E). Altitude 8949 feet. Named on Granite Chief (1953) 7.5' quadrangle. Called Tinkerknob on Wheeler's (1876-1877b) map. The name is for J.A. Tinker, a teamster who hauled freight from Soda Springs to mines on Forest Hill Divide (Gudde, 1969, p. 339).

Tinkers Station: see **Soda Springs** [NEVADA].

Tippecanoe [SIERRA]: *locality*, 2.5 miles northeast of Pike (lat. 39° 27'50" N, long. 120°57'30" W). Named on Colfax (1898) 30' quadrangle.

Tipton Hill [EL DORADO]: *ridge*, south-trending, 1 mile long, 14 miles northwest of Pollock Pines (lat. 38°55'45" N, long. 120°44'25" W). Named on Tunnel Hill (1950) 7.5' quadrangle. Gudde (1975, p. 311) listed Schleins Diggings, a mining place located on Tipton Hill.

Tisdale [SUTTER]: *locality*, 8.5 miles south-southwest of Sutter along Southern Pacific Railroad in Sutter Basin (lat. 39°02'25" N, long. 121°47'05" W; on N line sec. 30, T 14 N, R 2 E). Named on Tisdale Weir (1952) 7.5' quadrangle.

Tisdale Bypass [SUTTER]: *area*, lowland that provides a route for overflow water of Sacramento River to travel 4.5 miles east to Sutter Bypass 10 miles southwest of Yuba City (lat. 39°01'35" N, long. 121°44'30" W; at S line sec. 27, T 14 N, R 2 E); the feature is south of Tisdale in Sutter Basin. Named on Gilsizer (1952) and Tisdale Weir (1952) 7.5' quadrangles.

Todd: see **Todd Valley** [PLACER].

Todd Creek [PLACER]: *stream*, flows 5.5 miles to Middle Fork American River 9.5 miles east-northeast of Auburn (lat. 38°57'40" N, long. 120°55'25" W; sec. 24, T 13 N, R 9 E). Named on Foresthill (1949), Georgetown (1949), and Greenwood (1949) 7.5' quadrangles. Called Todd's Valley Creek on Whitney's (1880) map.

Todd's Valley: see **Todd Valley** [PLACER].
Todd's Valley Creek: see **Todd Creek** [PLACER].
Todd Valley [PLACER]: *locality,* 13 miles east-northeast of Auburn (lat. 38°59'55" N, long. 120°51' W; at W line sec. 3, T 13 N, R 10 E); the place is along Todd Creek. Named on Georgetown (1949) 7.5' quadrangle. Postal authorities established Todd's Valley post office in 1856, discontinued it in 1884, reestablished it with the name "Todd" in 1885, and discontinued it in 1901 (Salley, p. 222). Dr. F. Walton Todd opened a store at the place in 1849 (Gudde, 1949, p. 363).
Todhunters Lake [YOLO]: *lake,* 6 miles northwest of West Sacramento (lat. 38°37'30" N, long. 121°36'55" W). Named on Elkhorn Weir (1915) and Lovdal (1916) 7.5' quadrangles.
Toe Drain [YOLO]: *water feature,* artificial watercourse that extends along the west side of Sacramento River Deep Water Ship Channel from near West Sacramento to Yolo-Solano County line 10 miles southwest of Clarksburg (lat. 38°18'50" N, long. 121°39'15" W). Named on Clarksburg (1967), Liberty Island (1978), Sacramento West (1967), and Saxon (1952) 7.5' quadrangles.
Toem Lake [EL DORADO]: *lake,* 1150 feet long, 1.25 miles east-southeast of Pyramid Peak (lat. 38°50'25" N, long. 120°08'10" W). Named on Pyramid Peak (1955) 7.5' quadrangle. The word "Toem" was coined from letters in the name "Tom Emery" (Lekisch, p. 65).
Tolles' New Diggings: see **Indiana Ranch** [YUBA].
Tollhouse Lake [NEVADA]: *lake,* 800 feet long, 2 miles east-southeast of English Mountain (lat. 39°26' N, long. 120°31' W; on N line sec. 16, T 18 N, R 13 E). Named on English Mountain (1983) 7.5' quadrangle. Called Little Catfish Lake on Colfax (1938) 30' quadrangle, but United States Board on Geographic Names (1965a, p. 16) rejected this name.
Tolpekocking Flat: see **Chips Flat** [SIERRA].
Tomato Slough [SACRAMENTO]: *water feature,* on Brannan Island, joins Sevenmile Slough 4 miles southwest of Isleton (lat. 38°07'25" N, long. 121°40'05" W). Named on Rio Vista (1978) 7.5' quadrangle.
Tombstone Mountain [EL DORADO]: *peak,* 5 miles south-southwest of Placerville (lat. 38°39'40" N, long. 120°49'35" W; sec. 1, T 9 N, R 10 E). Altitude 1785 feet. Named on Placerville (1949) 7.5' quadrangle.
Tommy Cain Ravine [PLACER]: *canyon,* drained by a stream that flows 1.5 miles to North Fork American River 4.5 miles south of Dutch Flat (lat. 39°08'25" N, long. 120°50'45" W; near NE cor. sec. 21, T 15 N, R 10 E). Named on Dutch Flat (1950) 7.5' quadrangle.
Toms Creek [NEVADA]: *stream,* flows 1.5 miles to East Fork Creek 5 miles northeast of Graniteville (lat. 39°28'40" N, long. 120°39'20" W; at N line sec. 32, T 19 N, R 12 E). Named on Graniteville (1982) 7.5' quadrangle.
Toms Valley [NEVADA]: *valley,* 9.5 miles north-northwest of Donner Pass (lat. 39°26'10" N, long. 120°24'35" W; near S line sec. 9, T 18 N, R 14 E). Named on Webber Peak (1981) 7.5' quadrangle.
Tongue Shoal: see **Chain Island** [SACRAMENTO].
Tonys Gulch [EL DORADO]: *canyon,* drained by a stream that flows 1.5 miles to Salt Rock Creek 7 miles southwest of Old Iron Mountain (lat. 38°37'40" N, long. 120°28'40" W; near SW cor. sec. 18, T 9 N, R 14 E). Named on Stump Spring (1951) 7.5' quadrangle.
Top Lake [EL DORADO]: *lake,* 850 feet long, 5 miles southwest of Phipps Peak (lat. 38°54'20" N, long. 120°12'55" W; sec. 9, T 12 N, R 16 E). Named on Rockbound Valley (1955) 7.5' quadrangle.
Towle [PLACER]: *locality,* 2 miles east of Dutch Flat along Southern Pacific Railroad (lat. 39°12'15" N, long. 120°48' W; sec. 36, T 16 N, R 10 E). Named on Dutch Flat (1950) 7.5' quadrangle. Called Towles on Hobson's (1890b) map. Postal authorities established Towle post office in 1891 and discontinued it in 1935 (Frickstad, p. 122). The name is for Allen Towle and George Towle, lumbermen in the region (Hanna, p. 332). California Mining Bureau's (1917c) map shows a place called Gorge located along the railroad about 1 mile east-southeast of Towle.
Towle Mill [NEVADA]: *locality,* 4 miles south of Washington (lat. 39°18'05" N, long. 120°48'40" W; near NW cor. sec. 36, T 17 N, R 10 E). Site named on Washington (1950) 7.5' quadrangle.
Townerville: see **Copper Mine Gulch** [AMADOR].
Town Talk [NEVADA]: *locality,* 2.5 miles northeast of Grass Valley (lat. 39°14'35" N, long. 121°01'50" W; near S line sec. 13, T 16 N, R 8 E). Named on Grass Valley (1949) 7.5' quadrangle.
Tragedy Creek [AMADOR]: *stream,* flows 6 miles to Bear River 7 miles west-northwest of Mokelumne Peak (lat. 38°35'15" N, long. 120°12'05" W; sec. 34, T 9 N, R 16 E); the stream heads at Tragedy Spring [EL DORADO]. Named on Bear River Reservoir (1979) and Tragedy Spring (1979) 7.5' quadrangles.
Tragedy Creek: see **Bear River** [AMADOR]; **North Tragedy Creek** [EL DORADO].
Tragedy Spring [AMADOR]: *locality,* 7.5 miles north-northwest of Mokelumne Peak (lat. 38°38'20" N, long. 120°08'40" W; sec. 7, T 9 N, R 17 E). Named on Silver Lake (1956) 15' quadrangle.
Tragedy Spring [EL DORADO]: *spring,* 6 miles southwest of Kirkwood (lat. 38°38'25" N, long. 120°08'45" W; sec. 7, T 9 N, R 17 E). Named on Tragedy Spring (1979) 7.5' quadrangle. The name was given after Indians killed three Mormons at the spring in 1848; the victims were in advance of a group traveling to Salt Lake City (Ricketts, 1983, p. 20).
Trailer Hill [NEVADA]: *ridge,* south-trending, 1.5 miles long, 3.25 miles north-northeast of Higgins Corner (lat. 39°05'15" N, long. 121°04'30" W; on N line sec. 10, T 14 N, R 8 E). Named on Lake Combie (1949) 7.5' quadrangle.
Trail Gulch [EL DORADO]: *canyon,* less than 1 mile long, opens into the canyon of Rock Creek 4 miles north-northeast of Chili Bar (lat. 38°49' N, long. 120°46'45" W; sec. 8, T 11 N, R 11 E). Named on Garden Valley (1949) 7.5' quadrangle.
Trainer Hills [YUBA]: *ridge,* south-southwest-trending, 1.5 miles long, 4.5 miles west of Brown Valley (lat. 39°14'30" N, long. 121° 29'40" W). Named on Browns Valley (1947) and Yuba City (1952) 7.5' quadrangles.
Trap Canyon [EL DORADO]: *canyon,* drained by a stream that flows 1.5 miles to Park Creek (present Sly Park Creek) 2.5 miles west-northwest of Old Iron Mountain (lat. 38°42'50" N, long. 120°26'10" W; near SW cor. sec. 16, T 10 N, R 14 E). Named on Stump Spring (1951) 7.5' quadrangle.
Trap Creek [NEVADA]: *stream,* flows 2.5 miles to Fall Creek 5 miles northwest of Yuba Gap (lat. 39°21'20" N, long. 120°41'40" W; sec. 12, T 17 N, R 11 E). Named on Blue Canyon (1955) 7.5' quadrangle.
Trask: see **Vorden** [SACRAMENTO].
Trasks Bar: see **Wambo Bar** [YUBA].
Trask's Landing: see **Vorden** [SACRAMENTO].
Travelers Home: see **Yolo** [YOLO].
Traverse Creek [EL DORADO]: *stream,* flows 7.25 miles to Bear Creek (2) nearly 5 miles north-northeast of Chili Bar (lat. 38°49'50" N, long. 120°46'55" W; near W line sec. 5, T 11 N, R 11 E). Named on Garden Valley (1949) and Georgetown (1949) 7.5' quadrangles.
Travis Saddle [YUBA]: *pass,* nearly 1 mile west-southwest of Strawberry Valley (lat. 39°33'35" N, long. 121°07'15" W; sec. 30, T 20 N, R 8 E). Named on Strawberry Valley (1948) 7.5' quadrangle.
Treasure Island [AMADOR]: *island,* 2000 feet long, 8 miles north of Mokelumne Peak in Silver Lake (lat. 39°39'10" N, long. 120°07'15" W; near S line sec. 5, T 9 N, R 17 E). Named on Caples Lake (1979) 7.5' quadrangle
Treasure Mountain [SIERRA]: *peak,* 3.5 miles south of Sierraville (lat. 39°32'25" N, long. 120°21'20" W; sec. 1, T 19 N, R 14 E). Altitude 7085 feet. Named on Sierraville (1981) 7.5' quadrangle.
Trees: see **The Trees** [YOLO].
Trestle Ravine [SIERRA]: *canyon,* drained by a stream that flows less than 0.5 mile to Middle Yuba River 4.5 miles southwest of Alleghany (lat. 39°25'30" N, long. 120°54'15" W; near W line sec. 18, T 18 N, R 10 E). Named on Pike (1949) 7.5' quadrangle.
Triangle Lake [EL DORADO]: *lake,* 450 feet long, 4.5 miles northwest of Echo Summit (lat. 38°51'35" N, long. 120°05'30" W). Named on Echo Lake (1955) 7.5' quadrangle. The name is from the shape of the lake (Lekisch, p. 141).
Trimmer Peak: see **Freel Peak** [EL DORADO].
Trojan: see **Fort Trojan**, under **Virginiatown** [PLACER].
Trosi Canyon [SIERRA]: *canyon,* drained by a stream that flows 3 miles to Smithneck Creek 9.5 miles southeast of Loyalton in Pats Meadow (lat. 39°33'35" N, long. 120°08'50" W; sec. 25, T 20 N, R 16 E). Named on Sardine Peak (1981) 7.5' quadrangle.
Trough Spring [COLUSA]: *spring,* 2.5 miles southeast of Fouts Springs (lat. 39°19'25" N, long. 122°37'50" W). Named on Fouts Springs (1968) 7.5' quadrangle.
Trough Spring Ridge [COLUSA]: *ridge,* generally south- to southwest-trending, 10 miles long, center about 3.5 miles south-southeast of Fouts Spring (lat. 39°18'30" N, long. 122°38'15" W); Trough Spring is on the ridge. Named on Fouts Springs (1968) 7.5 quadrangle.
Trout Creek [COLUSA]:
(1) *stream,* flows 4.25 miles to South Fork Stony Creek 0.5 mile west of Fouts Springs (lat. 39°21'05" N, long. 122°40'25" W; at W line sec. 5, T 17 N, R 7 W). Named on Fouts Springs (1968) 7.5' quadrangle.
(2) *stream,* flows 5.5 miles to Bear Creek 5 miles north of Wilbur Springs (lat. 39°06'35" N, long. 122°25'05" W; sec. 33, T 15 N, R 5 W). Named on Wilbur Springs (1961) 15' quadrangle.
(3) *stream,* flows 4.5 miles to Little Stony Creek 9 miles south-southwest of Stonyford (lat. 39°15'10" N, long. 122°36'30" W). Named on Clearlake Oaks (1960) and Stonyford (1951) 15' quadrangles.
Trout Creek [EL DORADO]: *stream,* flows 10 miles to Truckee Marsh 7 miles northwest of Freel Peak (lat. 38°56' N, long. 120°59'10" W; near E line sec. 4, T 12 N, R 18 E). Named on Freel Peak (1955) and South Lake Tahoe (1955) 7.5' quadrangles.
Trout Creek [NEVADA]: *stream,* flows 5.5 miles to Truckee River 1 mile east-northeast of downtown Truckee (lat. 39°19'55" N, long. 120°09'50" W; near SE cor. sec. 11, T 17 N, R 16 E). Named on Truckee (1955, photorevised 1969) 7.5' quadrangle.
Trowbridge [SUTTER]: *locality,* 3 miles east of Nicolaus along Western Pacific Railroad (lat. 38°54'35" N, long. 121°31'25" W; at NW cor. sec. 10, T 12 N, R 4 E). Named on Nicolaus (1952) 7.5' quadrangle. Postal

authorities established Trowbridge post office in 1915; the name is from the land-development firm of Trowbridge and Hill (Salley, p. 225).

Troy [PLACER]: *locality,* 7.5 miles west of Donner Pass along Southern Pacific Railroad (lat. 39°18'40" N, long. 120°27'40" W; sec. 25, T 17 N, R 13 E). Named on Soda Springs (1955) 7.5' quadrangle.

Truckee [NEVADA]: *town,* 47 miles east of Grass Valley (lat. 39° 19'45" N, long. 120°11' W; near NE cor. sec. 15, T 17 N, R 16 E). Named on Truckee (1955) 7.5' quadrangle. Postal authorities established Truckee post office in 1868 (Frickstad, p. 115). The place was called Coburn Station, for a saloon keeper, when the railroad reached the site in 1863-1864, but it was renamed for Truckee River in 1868 (Bancroft, 1888, p. 486). Postal authorities established Donner Lake post office 7 miles west of Truckee in 1866 and discontinued it in 1868 (Salley, p. 60).

Truckee Canyon [NEVADA-SIERRA]: *canyon,* along Truckee River in Nevada County and Sierra County below a point about 6.5 miles northeast of Truckee near Boca—the canyon extends into the State of Nevada. Named on Boca (1955) and Martis Peak (1955) 7.5' quadrangles.

Truckee Lake: see **Donner Lake** [NEVADA]; **Little Truckee Lake**, under **Webber Lake** [SIERRA].

Truckee Marsh [EL DORADO]: *marsh,* 5 miles east-northeast of Mount Tallac in Lake Valley near Lake Tahoe (lat. 38°56' N, long. 120°00'45" W). Named on Fallen Leaf Lake (1955) and Freel Peak (1956) 15' quadrangles. Called Upper Truckee Marsh on Taylor's (1902) map. Development of South Lake Tahoe now partly covers the marsh.

Truckee River [NEVADA-PLACER-SIERRA]: *stream,* heads at Lake Tahoe in Placer County and flows 35 miles through Nevada County and Sierra County to the State of Nevada 7.5 miles southeast of Crystal Peak (lat. 39°28' N, long. 120°00'05" W; at E line sec. 31, T 19 N, R 18 E). Named on Boca (1955), Martis Peak (1955), Tahoe City (1955), and Truckee (1955) 7.5' quadrangles. Called Salmon Trout R. on Fremont's (1848) map, and called Truckey R. on Jefferson's (1849) map. Elisha Stevens and his party of emigrants gave the name "Truckee" to the stream in 1844 to honor a helpful Indian whom they called Truckee (Stewart, p. 8).

Truckee River: see **Little Truckee River** [NEVADA-SIERRA]; **Upper Truckee River** [EL DORADO].

Truckee Summit: see **Little Truckee Summit** [SIERRA].

Truckey Pass: see **Donner Pass** [PLACER].

Truckey River: see **Truckee River** [NEVADA-PLACER-SIERRA].

Tucker Flat [EL DORADO]: *area,* 4.25 miles southwest of Freel Peak along Saxon Creek (lat. 38°49' N, long. 119°57'30" W; sec. 11, T 11 N, R 18 E). Named on Freel Peak (1955) 7.5' quadrangle. The name commemorates a stockman who took up land in the neighborhood of Upper Truckee River (Gudde, 1969, p. 346).

Tudor [SUTTER]: *settlement,* 9 miles south of Yuba City (lat. 39°00'20" N, long. 121°37'25" W; sec. 3, T 13 N, R 3 E). Named on Olivehurst (1952) 7.5' quadrangle. Postal authorities established Tudor post office in 1893 and discontinued it in 1942; the name commemorates a railroad official (Salley, p. 225).

Tule Basin: see **Cache Creek Settling Basin** [YOLO].

Tule Glade [COLUSA]: *area,* 2.25 miles north of Pacific Point (lat. 39°14'45" N, long. 122°35'45" W; on N line sec. 13, T 16 N, R 7 W). Named on Clearlake Oaks (1960) 15' quadrangle.

Tule Gulch [AMADOR]: *canyon,* less than 1 mile long, opens into the canyon of Mokelumne River 6.5 miles south-southwest of Jackson (lat. 38°16'05" N, long. 120°50'05" W; near SE cor. sec. 23, T 5 N, R 10 E). Named on Jackson (1962) 7.5' quadrangle. Water of Pardee Reservoir now covers the lower part of the canyon.

Tule Pond [COLUSA]: *lake,* about 300 feet long, 3 miles northwest of Pacific Point (lat. 39°14'25" N, long. 122°38'20" W; sec. 16, T 16 N, R 7 W). Named on Clearlake Oaks (1960) 15' quadrangle.

Tule Slough [COLUSA]: *water feature,* dry watercourse 4 miles south-southeast of Grimes (lat. 39°01'30" N, long. 121°51'40" W). Named on Hershey (1916) and Tisdale Weir (1912) 7.5' quadrangles.

Tuman Mill [EL DORADO]: *locality,* 2.5 miles west-northwest of Old Iron Mountain (lat. 38°42'50" N, long. 120°25'55" W; near SW cor. sec. 16, T 10 N, R 14 E). Site named on Stump Spring (1951) 7.5' quadrangle.

Tunnel Creek [EL DORADO]: *stream,* flows 1.25 miles to Whaler Creek 10 miles northwest of Pollock Pines (lat. 38°52'55" N, long. 120°41'05" W; near SW cor. sec. 18, T 12 N, R 12 E). Named on Tunnel Hill (1950) 7.5' quadrangle.

Tunnel Hill [AMADOR]: *hill,* 1 mile southeast of Jackson (lat. 38°20'20" N, long. 120°45'30" W; near SW cor. sec. 27, T 6 N, R 11 E). Altitude 1441 feet. Named on Jackson (1962) 7.5' quadrangle.

Tunnel Hill [EL DORADO]: *ridge,* north-trending, 2.5 miles long, 15 miles north-northwest of Pollock Pines (lat. 38°57' N, long. 120° 42'10" W); a tunnel along Georgetown Divide ditch is near the south end of the ridge. Named on Tunnel Hill (1950) 7.5' quadrangle. On Placerville (1893) 30' quadrangle, the name applies to a peak on the ridge.

Tunnel Mill Campground [PLACER]: *locality,* 3.5 miles south-southeast of Emigrant Gap (1) (lat. 39°15'05" N, long. 120°30'10" W; sec. 17, T 16 N, R 12 E). Named on Blue Canyon (1955) 7.5' quadrangle.

Tunnel Spring: see **Big Tunnel Spring** [NEVADA].

Turkey Camp [YOLO]: *locality,* 5 miles northwest of Esparto (lat. 38°44'45" N, long. 122°05' W; sec. 4, T 10 N, R 2 W). Named on Esparto (1959) 7.5' quadrangle.

Turner: see **Isleton** [SACRAMENTO].

Turner Canyon [SIERRA]:

(1) *canyon,* 2.5 miles long, along Turner Creek above a point 5 miles west-northwest of Sierraville (lat. 39°37'30" N, long. 120°26'40" W; near W line sec. 32, T 21 N, R 14 E). Named on Calpine (1981) and Sattley (1981) 7.5' quadrangles.

(2) *canyon,* drained by a stream that flows 2.25 miles to Bear Valley Creek 4.25 miles south-southeast of Loyalton (lat. 39°37' N, long. 120°13'10" W; sec. 5, T 20 N, R 16 E). Named on Sardine Peak (1981) and Sierraville (1981) 7.5' quadrangles.

Turner Creek [SIERRA]: *stream,* flows 4.25 miles to Sierra Valley 3.5 miles west-northwest of Sierraville (lat. 39°36'45" N, long. 120°25'30" W; sec. 4, T 20 N, R 14 E); the stream drains Turner Canyon (1). Named on Calpine (1981) and Sattley (1981) 7.5' quadrangles.

Tut Canyon [YOLO]: *canyon,* drained by a stream that flows 2 miles to South Fork Oat Creek 5 miles east-southeast of Guinda (lat. 38° 48'20" N, long. 122°06'15" W; sec. 17, T 11 N, R 2 W). Named on Bird Valley (1959) and Guinda (1959) 7.5' quadrangles.

Tuttle: see **Colusa** [COLUSA].

Tuttle Lake [NEVADA]: *lake,* 1100 feet long, 5 miles east of Yuba Gap (lat. 39°19'10" N, long. 120°31'35" W; near SW cor. sec. 21, T 17 N, R 13 E). Named on Cisco Grove (1955) 7.5' quadrangle.

TV Hill [SIERRA]: *peak,* 6.5 miles east-northeast of Sierraville (lat. 39°38'20" N, long. 120°15'50" W; near SE cor. sec. 26, T 21 N, R 15 E). Altitude 6706 feet. Named on Antelope Valley (1981) 7.5' quadrangle.

Twelvemile Bar [YOLO]: *relief feature,* 11 miles northeast of Davis in Sacramento River (lat. 38°39'40" N, long. 121°36'35" W). Named on Elkhorn Weir (1915) 7.5' quadrangle.

Twelve Mile House [EL DORADO]: *locality,* 8 miles east of Georgetown (lat. 38°54'40" N, long. 120°41' W). Named on Placerville (1893) 30' quadrangle.

Twelvemile House [SACRAMENTO]:

(1) *locality,* 4 miles north of present downtown Carmichael (lat. 38° 40'30" N, long. 121°19'30" W). Named on Antelope (1911) 7.5' quadrangle. Sacramento (1892) 30' quadrangle has the form "12 Mile House" for the name. Postal authorities established Twelve Mile House post office in 1875; they moved it to the railroad and changed the name to Antelope in 1877 (Salley, p. 226).

(2) *locality,* 7.5 miles south-southeast of present downtown Carmichael (lat. 38°30'50" N, long. 121°16'30" W; near SW cor. sec. 25, T 8 N, R 6 E). Named on Mills (1911) 7.5' quadrangle. Sacramento (1892) 30' quadrangle has the form "12 Mile House" for the name.

Twentyfive Mile Canyon [EL DORADO]: *canyon,* drained by a stream that flows 1.5 miles to South Fork American River less than 1 mile west-northwest of Riverton (lat. 38°46'40" N, long. 120°27'35" W; near NW cor. sec. 30, T 11 N, R 14 E). Named on Riverton (1950) 7.5' quadrangle.

Twentymile Bar [COLUSA]: *locality,* 2.25 miles north-northwest of Grimes along Sacramento River (lat. 39°06'25" N, long. 121°54'10" W; sec. 31, T 15 N, R 1 E). Named on Grimes (1954) 7.5' quadrangle.

Twin Bridges [EL DORADO]: *locality,* 5 miles west of Echo Summit along Pyramid Creek (lat. 38°48'40" N, long. 120°07'15" W; sec. 8, T 11 N, R 17 E). Named on Echo Lake (1955) 7.5' quadrangle. Postal authorities established Twin Bridges post office in 1947 (Frickstad, p. 30).

Twin Cities [SACRAMENTO]: *settlement,* 2.5 miles north of Galt (lat. 38°17'30" N, long. 121°18'30" W). Named on Galt (1968) 7.5' quadrangle.

Twin Crags [PLACER]: *relief feature,* 1.25 miles west-southwest of Tahoe City on the north side of Truckee River (lat. 39°09'55" N, long. 120°09'55" W; sec. 12, T 15 N, R 16 E). Named on Tahoe City (1955) 7.5' quadrangle.

Twin Gulch [EL DORADO]: *canyon,* drained by a stream that flows 2.5 miles to Middle Fork Cosumnes River nearly 4 miles southeast of Caldor (lat. 38°33'55" N, long. 120°23'05" W; near NW cor. sec. 12, T 8 N, R 14 E). Named on Caldor (1951) and Peddler Hill (1951) 7.5' quadrangles.

Twin Lakes [EL DORADO]: *lakes,* two, each about 1200 feet long, 2.5 miles northwest of Pyramid Peak (lat. 38°52'10" N, long. 120° 11'30" W). Named on Pyramid Peak (1955) 7.5' quadrangle.

Twin Lakes [PLACER]: *lakes,* two, largest 800 feet long, 4.5 miles west-southwest of Cisco Grove (lat. 39°17'20" N, long. 120°37' W; near N line sec. 3, T 16 N, R 12 E). Named on Cisco Grove (1955) 7.5' quadrangle.

Twin Peaks [EL DORADO]: *peaks,* 5 miles east-southeast of Mount Tallac (lat. 38°52'55" N, long. 120°00'35" W; at S line sec. 17, T 12 N, R 18 E). Altitude of highest is 6971 feet. Named on Emerald Bay (1955) 7.5' quadrangle.

Twin Peaks [PLACER]: *peaks,* 4.25 miles west-northwest of Homewood (lat. 39°06'45" N, long. 120°13'55" W; at SE cor. sec. 29, T 15 N, R 16 E). Altitude of the easternmost peak is 8878 feet. Named on Homewood (1955) 7.5' quadrangle. Called Twin Peak on Truckee (1895) 30' quadrangle.

Twin Peaks [SUTTER]: *peaks,* 5.25 miles northwest of Sutter in Sutter Buttes (lat. 39°12'50" N, long. 121°49' W; at NE cor. sec. 26, T 16 N, R 1 E). Named on Sutter Buttes (1954) 7.5' quadrangle.

Twin Sisters [YOLO]: *peaks,* 9 miles west of Rumsey on Yolo-Lake County line (lat. 38°53'05" N, long. 122°24'25" W). Named on Wilson Valley (1958) 7.5' quadrangle.

Twin Valley: see **Carpenter Valley** [NEVADA].

Twitchell Island [SACRAMENTO]: *island,* 4 miles long, 4.5 miles south-southwest of Isleton between San Joaquin River, Threemile Slough, and Sevenmile Slough (lat. 38°06'30" N, long. 121°39' W). Named on Bouldin Island (1978) and Jersey Island (1978) 7.5' quadrangles.

Two Peaks [EL DORADO]: *peaks,* 6.5 miles east-southeast of Robbs Peak (lat. 38°54'10" N, long. 120°17' W; sec. 10, T 12 N, R 15 E). Altitude of highest is 7594 feet. Named on Loon Lake (1952) 7.5' quadrangle.

Twin Pines [PLACER]: *settlement,* 5.5 miles south-southwest of Colfax (lat. 39°01'30" N, long. 120°58'40" W; sec. 33, T 14 N, R 9 E). Named on Colfax (1949) 7.5' quadrangle.

Two Sentinels [AMADOR]: *peaks,* 11 miles north of Mokelumne Peak (lat. 38°41'55" N, long. 120°05'15" W; sec. 21, T 10 N, R 17 E). Named on Caples Lake (1979) 7.5' quadrangle.

Two Sentinels: see **Camp Two Sentinels** [EL DORADO].

Tyler: see **Cherokee** [NEVADA].

Tyler Island [SACRAMENTO]: *island,* 9 miles long, 27 miles south of downtown Sacramento between Georgiana Slough and North Mokelumne River (lat. 38°11' N, long. 121°32'30" W). Named on Isleton (1978) 7.5' quadrangle.

Tyler Lake [EL DORADO]: *lake,* 500 feet long, 5.5 miles south-southwest of Phipps Peak (lat. 38°52'50" N, long. 120°11'50" W). Named on Rockbound Valley (1955) 7.5' quadrangle.

Tylers Corner [EL DORADO]: *locality,* 3 miles southeast of Aukum along South Fork Cosumnes River (lat. 38°31'40" N, long. 120°41'05" W; near W line sec. 20, T 8 N, R 12 E). Named on Aukum (1952) 7.5' quadrangle.

Tyndall: see **Tyndall Landing** [YOLO].

Tyndall Landing [YOLO]: *locality,* 8 miles east of Dunnigan along Sacramento River (lat. 38°53' N, long. 121°49' W; near SW cor. sec. 13, T 12 N, R 1 E); the place is near Tyndall Mound. Named on Kirkville (1952) 7.5' quadrangle. California Division of Highways' (1934) map shows a place called Tyndall located along Southern Pacific Railroad near present Tyndall Landing.

Tyndall Mound [YOLO]: *locality,* 8 miles east of Dunnigan near Sacramento River (lat. 38°53'05" N, long. 121°49'05" W; near W line sec. 13, T 12 N, R 1 E); the place is close to Tyndall Landing. Named on Kirkville (1952) 7.5' quadrangle. Called Indian Mound on Kirkville (1915) 7.5' quadrangle.

—U—

Uhlen Valley [NEVADA]: *valley,* 2 miles northwest of Donner Pass along Upper Castle Creek (lat. 39°20' N, long. 120°21'20" W). Named on Norden (1955) 7.5' quadrangle.

Umbrella Hill [EL DORADO]: *peak,* 1 mile north-northeast of the village of Pilot Hill (lat. 38°50'50" N, long. 121°00'15" W; at W line sec. 32, T 12 N, R 9 E). Named on Pilot Hill (1954) 7.5' quadrangle.

Umpa Lake [EL DORADO]: *lake,* 400 feet long, 3 miles northwest of Pyramid Peak (lat. 38°52'20" N, long. 120°12'05" W). Named on Pyramid Peak (1955) 7.5' quadrangle.

Uncles Canyon [COLUSA]: *canyon,* drained by a stream that flows nearly 2 miles to Howard Creek 5.5 miles northeast of Lodoga (lat. 39°21'15" N, long. 122°24'50" W; on E line sec. 4, T 17 N, R 5 W). Named on Lodoga (1960) 15' quadrangle.

Uncle Toms Cabin [EL DORADO]: *locality,* 4.5 miles west of Robbs Peak (lat. 38°55'45" N, long. 120°29'10" W; sec. 35, T 13 N, R 13 E). Named on Robbs Peak (1950) 7.5' quadrangle. The name "Uncle Tom" is said to be from a black man who lived at the place in the early days; later a roadhouse at the site was called Uncle Toms Cabin (Yohalem, p. 199).

Union: see **Camp Union**, under **Lancha Plana** [AMADOR]; **Camp Union**, under **Sutterville** [SACRAMENTO].

Union Bar: see **Woods Creek** [YUBA].

Union Canyon [NEVADA]: *canyon,* drained by a stream that flows 1.25 miles to South Yuba River nearly 4 miles west-southwest of Washington (lat. 39°20'40" N, long. 120°52'05" W; near NW cor. sec. 16, T 17 N, R 10 E). Named on Washington (1950) 7.5' quadrangle.

Union Creek: see **Woods Creek** [YUBA].

Union Flat: see **Spanish Flat** [EL DORADO]; **Volcano** [AMADOR].

Union Flat Campground [SIERRA]: *locality,* 6 miles west of Sierra City along North Yuba River (lat. 39°34' N, long. 120°44'40" W; near S line sec. 28, T 20 N, R 11 E). Named on Sierra City (1981) 7.5' quadrangle.

Union Hill [EL DORADO]: *peak,* 1.5 miles east of Pollock Pines (lat. 38°45'50" N, long. 120°33'10" W; near N line sec. 32, T 11 N, R 13 E). Named on Pollock Pines (1950) 7.5' quadrangle.

Union Hill [NEVADA]: *village,* 1.5 miles east-southeast of Grass Valley (lat. 39°12'25" N, long. 121°02'15" W; on E line sec. 35, T 16 N, R 8 E). Named on Grass Valley (1949) 7.5' quadrangle. California Division of Highways' (1934) map shows a place called Union Hill located about 1.5 miles farther east (sec. 31, T 16 N, R 9 E) along Nevada County Narrow Gauge Railroad, and a place called Cedar Kress located along the railroad 0.5 mile south of this second Union Hill (near S line sec. 31, T 16 N, R 9 E).

Union Hill [SIERRA]: *locality,* 7.25 miles west-northwest of Goodyears Bar (lat. 39°35'50" N, long. 121°00'10" W; near E line sec. 18, T 20 N, R 9 E). Named on Strawberry Valley (1948) 7.5' quadrangle.

Union Hotel: see **Brownsville** [YUBA]; **Eagleville** [YUBA].

Union House [SACRAMENTO]: *locality,* 6 miles northwest of Elk Grove (lat. 38°27'55" N, long. 121°26'45" W; near NE cor. sec. 17, T 7 N, R 5 E). Named on Florin (1909) 7.5' quadrangle. Postal authorities established Union House post office in 1871, changed the name to Unionhouse in 1895, and discontinued it in 1901 (Salley, p. 227).

Union House: see **Hidden Valley** [PLACER] (2).

Union Mills [NEVADA]: *locality,* 4.5 miles east-northeast of Truckee (lat. 39°21'15" N, long. 120°06'15" W; at E line sec. 5, T 17 N, R 17 E); the place is in Union Valley. Site named on Martis Peak (1955) 7.5' quadrangle.

Union Reservoir [YUBA]: *intermittent lake,* 800 feet long, 1 mile southeast of Smartville (lat. 39°11'50" N, long. 121°16'55" W; near SE cor. sec. 34, T 16 N, R 6 E). Named on Smartville (1951) 7.5' quadrangle.

Union School Slough [YOLO]: *stream,* flows 2.25 miles to lowlands 7 miles north-northwest of Winters (lat. 38°37'15" N, long. 122° 00' W; at S line sec. 17, T 9 N, R 1 W). Named on Monticello Dam (1959) and Winters (1953) 7.5' quadrangles.

Union Shed: see **Sheridan** [PLACER].

Uniontown: see **El Dorado** [EL DORADO]; **Lotus** [EL DORADO].

Union Valley [EL DORADO]: *valley,* 3.5 miles south of Robbs Peak (lat. 38°52'30" N, long. 120°24'30" W). Named on Robbs Peak (1952) 15' quadrangle. Water of Union Valley Reservoir now covers most of the valley.

Union Valley [NEVADA]: *valley,* 4.5 miles east-northeast of Truckee (lat. 39°21'05" N, long. 120°05'55" W; sec. 4, 5, T 17 N, R 17 E); the site of Union Mills is in the valley. Named on Martis Peak (1955) 7.5' quadrangle.

Union Valley Reservoir [EL DORADO]: *lake,* behind a dam on Silver Creek 6.5 miles north of Riverton (lat. 38°52' N, long. 120° 26'20" W; near SW cor. sec. 20, T 12 N, R 14 E); the lake is in Union Valley. Named on Loon Lake (1952, photorevised 1973), Riverton (1950, photorevised 1973), and Robbs Peak (1950, photorevised 1973) 7.5' quadrangles.

Uno: see **Aukum** [EL DORADO].

Upper Arkansas Bar: see **Green Valley** [PLACER].

Upper Castle Creek [NEVADA]: *stream,* flows 4 miles to Lake Van Norden 2.5 miles west of Donner Pass (lat. 39°19'20" N, long. 120°22'15" W; sec. 23, T 17 N, R 14 E); the stream heads at Castle Valley. Named on Norden (1955) 7.5' quadrangle.

Upper Corral: see **Illinoistown** [PLACER].

Upper Crossing: see **Amador Crossing**, under **Amador City** [AMADOR].

Upper Derbec Spring [NEVADA]: *spring,* 2.25 miles north-northeast of North Bloomfield (lat. 39°23'40" N, long. 120°52'35" W; sec. 29, T 18 N, R 10 E); the spring is 1000 feet north-northeast of Derbec Spring. Named on Pike (1949) 7.5' quadrangle.

Upper Echo Lake [EL DORADO]: *lake,* 3600 feet long, 3.25 miles northwest of Echo Summit (lat. 38°50'40" N, long. 120°04'30" W; sec. 35, T 12 N, R 17 E); the lake is west of Lower Echo Lake. Named on Echo Lake (1955) 7.5' quadrangle.

Upper Forni [EL DORADO]: *locality,* nearly 2 miles south-southwest of Pyramid Peak (lat. 38°49'20" N, long. 120°10'20" W; near NW cor. sec. 12, T 11 N, R 16 E); the place is 3.25 miles east-northeast of Lower Forni. Named on Pyramid Peak (1955) 7.5' quadrangle. Called Forni on Pyramid Peak (1896) 30' quadrangle.

Upper Hell Hole [PLACER]: *valley,* 2.5 miles north-northeast of Bunker Hill along Rubicon River (lat. 39°05' N, long. 120°21'30" W; on S line sec. 1, T 14 N, R 14 E). Named on Granite Chief (1953) 15' quadrangle. Called Hell Hole on Truckee (1895) 30' quadrangle. Truckee (1940) 30' quadrangle has the form "Upper Hellhole" for the name. Water of Hell Hole Reservoir now floods part of the valley.

Upper Independence Creek [NEVADA]: *stream,* flows nearly 3 miles to Independence Lake 8 miles north of Donner Pass (lat. 39° 25'55" N, long. 120°19'40" W; near SE cor. sec. 5, T 18 N, R 15 E). Named on Independence Lake (1981) 7.5' quadrangle.

Upper Jones Valley [NEVADA]: *valley,* 6.5 miles west-northwest of Donner Pass at the head of Rattlesnake Creek (2) (lat. 39°20'55" N, long. 120°26'30" W; near S line sec. 7, T 17 N, R 14 E); the feature is above Jones Valley. Named on Soda Springs (1955) 7.5' quadrangle.

Upper Letts Lake [COLUSA]: *lake,* 0.5 mile long, behind a dam 4.25 miles southwest of Fouts Springs (lat. 39°18'30" N, long. 122° 42'55" W; sec. 24, T 17 N, R 8 W); the lake is in Upper Letts Valley. Named on Fouts

Springs (1968) 7.5' quadrangle.

Upper Letts Valley [COLUSA]: *valley,* 4 miles southwest of Fouts Springs (lat. 39°18'20" N, long. 122°42'45" W; at S line sec. 24, T 17 N, R 8 W). Named on Stonyford (1951) 15' quadrangle. Water of Upper Letts Lake now covers most of the valley. Jack Lett and David Lett settled at Letts Valley in 1855; they died there in 1877 while defending their land from squatters (Hoover, Rensch, and Rensch, p. 49).

Upper Lola Montez Lake [NEVADA]: *lake,* 550 feet long, 6.25 miles west-northwest of Donner Pass (lat. 39°21'05" N, long. 120° 25'50" W; sec. 8, T 17 N, R 14 E); the lake is 0.25 mile west-northwest of Lower Lola Montez Lake. Named on Soda Springs (1955) 7.5' quadrangle.

Upper Long Valley [SIERRA]: *valley,* 11 miles east of Loyalton on Sierra-Lassen County line (lat. 39°42'30" N, long. 120°02'30" W). Named on Evans Canyon (1978) 7.5' quadrangle.

Upper Mud Spring [EL DORADO]: *spring,* 6.5 miles southeast of Caldor (lat. 38°32'50" N, long. 120°20' W; near E line sec. 17, T 8 N, R 15 E); the spring is less than 0.5 mile east-northeast of Mud Spring [AMADOR]. Named on Peddler Hill (1951) 7.5' quadrangle.

Upper Narrows Reservoir: see **Englebright Lake** [NEVADA-YUBA].

Upper Onion Valley [AMADOR]: *area,* 5.25 miles west-northwest of Mokelumne Peak (lat. 38°33'40" N, long. 120°11' W; sec. 11, T 8 N, R 16 E); the place is 0.5 mile south-southeast of Onion Valley. Named on Bear River Reservoir (1979) 7.5' quadrangle.

Upper Pardoes Camp [AMADOR]: *locality,* 4.25 miles west-northwest of Mokelumne Peak (lat. 38°33'45" N, long. 120°10' W; sec. 12, T 8 N, R 16 E). Site named on Bear River Reservoir (1979) 7.5' quadrangle.

Upper Rancheria: see **Rancheria** [AMADOR].

Upper Salmon Lake [SIERRA]: *lake,* 2100 feet long, 6.5 miles north of Sierra City (lat. 39°39'25" N, long. 120°39'05" W; sec. 29, T 21 N, R 12 E); the lake is along Salmon Creek 0.5 mile upstream from Lower Salmon Lake. Named on Gold Lake (1981) 7.5' quadrangle.

Upper Sardine Lake [SIERRA]: *lake,* 2950 feet long, 3 miles north of Sierra City (lat. 39°36'30" N, long. 120°38' W; sec. 9, 16, T 20 N, R 12 E); the lake is on upper reaches of Sardine Creek less than 0.25 mile upstream from Lower Sardine Lake. Named on Sierra City (1981) 7.5' quadrangle.

Upper Tallant Lake: see **Stony Ridge Lake** [EL DORADO].

Upper Truckee Marsh: see **Truckee Marsh** [EL DORADO].

Upper Truckee River [EL DORADO]: *stream,* heads in Alpine County and flows 18 miles to Lake Tahoe 8 miles northwest of Freel Peak in El Dorado County (lat. 38°56'30" N, long. 119° 59'45" W; sec. 31, T 13 N, R 18 E). Named on Caples Lake (1979), Echo Lake (1955), Emerald Bay (1955), and South Lake Tahoe (1955, photorevised 1969 and 1974) 7.5' quadrangles.

Upper Velma Lake [EL DORADO]: *lake,* 1300 feet long, 2 miles south of Phipps Peak (lat. 38°55'40" N, long. 120°08'50" W; on W line sec. 31, T 13 N, R 17 E); the lake is less than 1 mile south-southwest of Lower Velma Lake. Named on Rockbound Valley (1955) 7.5' quadrangle.

Upper Woolsey Spring [NEVADA]: *spring,* 3.25 miles north-northeast of North Bloomfield (lat. 39°24'40" N, long. 120°52' W; near W line sec. 21, T 18 N, R 10 E); the spring is 0.5 mile southwest of the site of Woolsey Flat (2). Named on Alleghany (1949) 7.5' quadrangle.

Urban: see **Pleasant Valley** [EL DORADO] (2).

Ure Mountain [YUBA]: *peak,* 3.25 miles south of Oregon House (lat. 39°18'35" N, long. 121°16'50" W; on S line sec. 22, T 17 N, R 6 E). Altitude 2212 feet. Named on Oregon House (1948) 7.5' quadrangle.

United States Canyon [PLACER]: *canyon,* drained by a stream that flows nearly 1 mile to Middle Fork American River 8.5 miles east-northeast of Auburn (lat. 38°57'45" N, long. 120°56'20" W; sec. 23, T 13 N, R 9 E). Named on Greenwood (1949) 7.5' quadrangle.

—V—

Vade: see **Phillips** [EL DORADO].

Valdez [YOLO]: *locality,* 8 miles south-southwest of Clarksburg along Sacramento Northern Railroad (lat. 38°19'35" N, long. 121° 36'45" W). Named on Courtland (1978) 7.5' quadrangle.

Valensin: see **Centralia** [SACRAMENTO].

Valley View [PLACER]: *locality,* 5.25 miles north of Lincoln (lat. 38°57'45" N, long. 121°16'30" W). Named on Sacramento (1892) 30' quadrangle. Gudde (1975, p. 369) noted that the place also was called Whiskey Diggings.

Valley View Reservoir [PLACER]: *lake,* 400 feet long, 10.5 miles west-northwest of Auburn (lat. 38°58' N, long. 121°14'45" W; on E line sec. 24, T 13 N, R 6 E). Named on Gold Hill (1954) 7.5' quadrangle.

Van Cliffe Canyon: see **Cliff Canyon** [PLACER].

Vandervere Mountain [NEVADA]: *peak,* 3 miles south of Pilot Peak (lat. 39°07'40" N, long. 121°10'35" W; near NE cor. sec. 27, T 15 N, R 7 E). Altitude 1846 feet. Named on Rough and Ready (1949) 7.5' quadrangle. Called Pike Mt. on Smartsville (1895) 30' quadrangle.

Vangeisen Combie Diversion Reservoir: see **Lake Combie** [NEVADA-PLACER].

Van Horn Creek [EL DORADO]: *stream,* flows 3.25 miles to North Fork Cosumnes River 4 miles southwest of Old Iron Mountain (lat. 38°39'45" N, long. 120°26'20" W; at W line sec. 4, T 9 N, R 14 E). Named on Stump Spring (1951) 7.5' quadrangle.

Van Norden: see **Lake Van Norden** [NEVADA-PLACER].

Vantrent: see **Lincoln** [PLACER].

Van Vleck [EL DORADO]: *locality,* 4 miles east-northeast of Pollock Pines (lat. 38°46'40" N, long. 120°30'50" W; sec. 22, T 11 N, R 13 E). Named on Pollock Pines (1950) 7.5' quadrangle.

Van Winkle [EL DORADO]: *locality,* 4.5 miles west-southwest of Kirkwood (lat. 38°41'15" N, long. 120°09'10" W). Named on Pyramid Peak (1896) 30' quadrangle.

Vaughn Cabin [EL DORADO]: *locality,* 11.5 miles north-northeast of Pollock Pines (lat. 38°55'05" N, long. 120°31'05" W; sec. 4, T 12 N, R 13 E). Named on Devil Peak (1950) 7.5' quadrangle.

Velma Lake: see **Lower Velma Lake** [EL DORADO]; **Middle Velma Lake** [EL DORADO]; **Upper Velma Lake** [EL DORADO].

Venado: see **Mountain House** [COLUSA].

Vera: see **Lake Vera** [NEVADA].

Verdi Peak [SIERRA]: *peak,* 6.25 miles south-southeast of Crystal Peak (lat. 39°28'20" N, long. 120°02'20" W; sec. 25, T 19 N, R 17 E); the peak is at the south end of Verdi Range. Altitude 8444 feet. Named on Boca (1955) 7.5' quadrangle. Called Crystal Peak on Truckee (1895) 30' quadrangle, but United States Board on Geographic Names (1939, p. 36) rejected this name and the name "Bald Mountain" for the feature. The name "Verdi" is from nearby Verdi, Nevada, which was named for the Italian composer, Giuseppe Verdi (Hanna, p. 344).

Verdi Range [SIERRA]: *ridge,* south-trending, 5 miles long, center 4.25 miles southeast of Crystal Peak (lat. 39°30' N, long. 120°02'45" W); Verdi Peak is near the south end of the ridge. Named on Boca (1955) and Dog Valley (1981) 7.5' quadrangles.

Vernon: see **Marchant** [SUTTER]; **Mount Vernon** [SUTTER]; **Verona** [SUTTER].

Verona [SUTTER]: *village,* 8 miles south-southwest of Nicolaus along Sacramento River at the mouth of Feather River (lat. 38°47'10" N, long. 121°37'05" W; on E line sec. 22, T 11 N, R 3 E). Named on Verona (1967) 7.5' quadrangle. Vernon (1910) 7.5' quadrangle has both the names "Vernon" and "Verona P.O." at the place. Postal authorities established Vernon post office in 1849, discontinued it in 1853, reestablished it at a new site in 1866, discontinued it in 1868, reestablished it in 1878, discontinued it the same year, reestablished it with the name "Verona" in 1897, and discontinued it in 1941 (Salley, p. 231). Vernon was laid out in the spring of 1849 at what was thought to be the head of navigation on Feather River, but high water the following winter allowed ships to pass on up the river beyond Vernon and the community failed to prosper (Bancroft, 1888, p. 463).

Victor Bend [SUTTER-YOLO]: *bend,* 2.25 miles west of Robbins along Sacramento River on Sutter-Yolo County line (lat. 38°52'20" N, long. 121°44'50" W; sec. 21, T 12 N, R 2 E). Named on Knights Landing (1952) 7.5' quadrangle.

Vin [YOLO]: *locality,* nearly 7 miles northwest of West Sacramento along Sacramento and Woodland Railroad (lat. 38°39' N, long. 121°36'05" W). Named on Elkhorn Weir (1915) 7.5' quadrangle.

Vineyard Creek [YUBA]: *stream,* flows 7 miles to Dry Creek (2) 9.5 miles northeast of Wheatland at Waldo Junction (lat. 39°06'40" N, long. 121°18'30" W; sec. 33, T 15 N, R 6 E). Named on Camp Far West (1949) and Smartville (1951) 7.5' quadrangles.

Viola: see **Folsom** [SACRAMENTO].

Virginia: see **Virginiatown** [PLACER].

Virginia House: see **Boca** [NEVADA].

Virginia Ranch Reservoir [YUBA]: *lake,* behind a dam on Dry Creek (1) 3 miles southwest of Oregon House (lat. 39°19'25" N, long. 121°18'45" W; near NW cor. sec. 21, T 17 N, R 6 E). Named on Oregon House (1948, photorevised 1969) 7.5' quadrangle. Smartsville (1895) 30' quadrangle shows Virginia ranch located nearly 3 miles southwest of Oregon House along Dry Creek (1) near the site of the dam that forms the present lake.

Virginiatown [PLACER]: *locality,* 7.5 miles west of Auburn along Auburn Ravine (lat. 38°54'05" N, long. 121°12'45" W; sec. 8, T 12 N, R 7 E). Named on Gold Hill (1954) 7.5' quadrangle. Called Virginia on Sacramento (1892) 30' quadrangle. A place called Fort Trojan, settled in 1858, was situated about 1 mile down Auburn Ravine from Virginiatown; when the town of Lincoln was founded, the inhabitants of Fort Trojan moved 3 miles on down Auburn Ravine to the new community (Hoover, Rensch, and Rensch, p. 271).

Virner: see **Balderson Station** [EL DORADO].

Vogans: see **Sunnybrook** [AMADOR].

Volcano [AMADOR]: *village,* 2.5 miles northeast of Pine Grove along Sutter Creek (lat. 38'26'35" N, long. 120°37'45" W; sec. 23, T 7 N, R 12 E). Named on Pine Grove (1948) 7.5' quadrangle. Postal authorities established Volcano post office in 1851 (Frickstad, p. 6). Doble (p. 101) noted in 1852 that the place was named "from the supposed Volcanic appearance that exist in & about it." Camp (map facing p. 99 *in* Doble) showed a canyon called Soldiers Gulch that opens into the canyon of Sutter Creek from the northwest at Volcano; Doble (p. 103) stated that soldiers made the first discovery of gold in Soldiers Gulch in 1848. Camp (*in* Doble, p. 301) noted that the name "Soldiers Gulch" was an early designation for Volcano. Camp (map facing p. 99 *in* Doble) also showed a canyon called Clapboard Gulch that opens into the canyon of Sutter Creek from the north at the edge of Volcano, a canyon called Jackass Gulch that opens into Clapboard Gulch from the northwest less than 0.5 mile north-northeast of Volcano, a canyon called Ballards Humbug that opens into the canyon of South Branch Sutter Creek from the south 0.5 mile south-southeast of Volcano, and a place called Mahala Flat located south-southeast of Volcano along South Branch Sutter Creek. Camp's (1962) map shows Fort Ann located 3.5 miles north of Volcano along Dry Creek (present South Fork Dry Creek), and Fort John located 4 miles northwest of Volcano along the same stream. According to local tradition, Fort Ann began as a military post (Andrews, p. 98), but Whiting and Whiting (p. 5) called the place an early mining camp and not a military post. Fort John was named for John Stuart (Gudde, 1975, p. 120). Gudde (1975, p. 356) mentioned a place called Union Flat that was situated about 1 mile north of Volcano.

Volcano: see **Bath** [PLACER].

Volcano Canyon [PLACER]: *canyon,* drained by a stream that flows 10 miles to Middle Fork American River 2 miles southeast of Foresthill (lat. 39°00' N, long. 120°47'15" W; sec. 6, T 13 N, R 11 E). Named on Foresthill (1949) and Michigan Bluff (1952) 7.5' quadrangles.

Volcano Hill [PLACER]: *peak,* 5 miles south-southeast of Rocklin (lat. 38°43'20" N, long. 121°11'50" W; sec. 15, T 10 N, R 7 E). Named on Folsom (1967) 7.5' quadrangle.

Volcano Lake [SIERRA]: *lake,* 750 feet long, 3 miles north of Sierra City (lat. 39°36'25" N, long. 120°37'25" W; at SE cor. sec. 9, T 20 N, R 12 E). Named on Haypress Valley (1981) 7.5' quadrangle.

Volcanoville [EL DORADO]: *village,* 6 miles north-northeast of Georgetown (lat. 38°58'55" N, long. 120°47'15" W; on N line sec. 18, T 13 N, R 11 E). Named on Georgetown (1949) 7.5' quadrangle. Postal authorities established Volcanoville post office in 1930 and discontinued it in 1953 (Frickstad, p. 30). The name is from the mistaken idea of early miners that a nearby peak was an extinct volcano (Gudde, 1969, p. 356). Postal authorities established Lava post office near present Volcanoville in 1880 and discontinued it in 1881 (Salley, p. 119). Whitney's (1880) map shows a place called Flora's located about 2 miles west of Volcanoville.

Vorden [SACRAMENTO]: *locality,* 4 miles south-southeast of Courtland along Sacramento River (lat. 38°16'40" N, long. 121°32'20" W). Named on Courtland (1978) 7.5' quadrangle. The place also was known as Trask's Landing (Dillon, p. 104). Postal authorities established Trask post office in 1894, changed the name to Vorden in 1902, and discontinued it in 1936; the name "Trask" was for Charles F. Trask, first postmaster (Salley, p. 224, 233). California Division of Highways' (1934) map has the name "Pearson Tract" for the area along Sacramento River north of Vorden.

Vormans Landing [SACRAMENTO]: *locality,* nearly 3 miles southeast of Isleton along Mokelumne River on Tyler Island (lat. 38°07'50" N, long. 121°34'35" W). Named on Isleton (1952) 7.5' quadrangle.

Voss [EL DORADO]: *locality,* 3.25 miles south of Old Iron Mountain (lat. 38°39'25" N, long. 120°23'10" W; sec. 2, T 9 N, R 14 E). Named on Stump Spring (1951) 7.5' quadrangle.

Votaw Camp [AMADOR]: *locality,* 5.5 miles west of Mokelumne Peak (lat. 38°31'45" N, long. 120°11'15" W; near E line sec. 22, T 8 N, R 16 E). Named on Bear River Reservoir (1979) 7.5' quadrangle.

– W –

Wabena Creek [PLACER]: *stream,* flows 4.25 miles to North Fork American River 8.5 miles west of Granite Chief (lat. 39°13'20" N, long. 120°26'35" W; sec. 30, T 16 N, R 14 E). Named on Royal Gorge (1953) 7.5' quadrangle.

Waca Lake [EL DORADO]: *lake,* 650 feet long, 1 mile northeast of Pyramid Peak (lat. 38°51'20" N, long. 120°08'25" W). Named on Pyramid Peak (1955) 7.5' quadrangle. The word "Waca" was coined from letters in the name "Walter Campbell" (Lekisch, p. 65).

Wagner [EL DORADO]: *locality,* 3.5 miles south-southwest of Robbs Peak (lat. 38°52'40" N, long. 120°26'10" W). Named on Pyramid Peak (1896) 30' quadrangle.

Wagner Creek [YUBA]: *stream,* flows 1 mile to Moonshine Creek 4.5 miles southwest of Camptonville (lat. 39°24'15" N, long. 121° 06'20" W; near S line sec. 20, T 18 N, R 8 E). Named on Camptonville (1948) 7.5' quadrangle.

Wagon Wheel Lake [NEVADA]: *lake,* 650 feet long, 4.25 miles south-southeast of English Mountain (lat. 39°23'05" N, long. 120° 31'45" W; on E line sec. 32, T 18 N, R 13 E). Named on English Mountain (1983) 7.5' quadrangle.

Wahoo [SIERRA]: *locality,* 5.5 miles southwest of Mount Fillmore (lat. 39°40'05" N, long. 120°54'55" W; near E line sec. 24, T 21 N, R 9 E). Named on La Porte (1951) 7.5' quadrangle.

Waits Station [AMADOR]: *locality,* 3.25 miles southwest of Plymouth (lat. 38°27' N, long. 120°53'50" W; sec. 20, T 7 N, R 10 E). Named on Irish Hill (1962) 7.5' quadrangle.

Waldo: see **Waldo Junction** [YUBA].

Waldo Junction [YUBA]: *locality,* 9.5 miles northeast of Wheatland along Dry Creek (2) (lat. 39°06'40" N, long. 121°17'55" W; sec. 33, T 15 N, R 6 E). Named on Camp Far West (1949) 7.5' quadrangle. Called Cabbage Patch on Smartsville (1895) 30' quadrangle. Postal authorities established Waldo post office in 1898 and discontinued it in 1915; the name was for William Waldo, a pioneer settler (Salley, p. 233-234). The name "Cabbage Patch" originated in 1852 when two negroes planted cabbage at the place; the name was changed to Waldo when the post office opened (Gudde, 1975, p. 55). Wescoatt's (1861) map shows a place called Round Tent located 1.25 miles east-southeast of Cabbage Patch. Postal authorities established Round Tent post office in 1853 and discontinued it in 1860; the name was from a large round tent used as a hotel at the place (Salley, p. 190).

Waldron Reservoir: see **Backbone House** [NEVADA].

Walerga [SACRAMENTO]: *locality,* 4.5 miles north-northwest of downtown Carmichael along Southern Pacific Railroad (lat. 38°40'30" N, long. 121°21'50" W). Named on Citrus Heights (1967) 7.5' quadrangle.

Walker: see **Bob Walker Canyon** [YOLO]; **Courtland** [SACRAMENTO].

Walker Landing [SACRAMENTO]: *locality,* 3.5 miles north of Isleton along Steamboat Slough on Grand Island (lat. 38°12'55" N, long. 121°36'10" W). Named on Isleton (1978) 7.5' quadrangle.

Walker Ridge [COLUSA]: *ridge,* south-trending, 4 miles long, 4.5 miles northwest of Wilbur Springs on Colusa-Lake County line (lat. 39°05' N, long. 122°29'10" W). Named on Wilbur Springs (1961) 15' quadrangle.

Walkers Ravine: see **Cirby Creek** [PLACER].

Wallace Canyon [PLACER]: *canyon,* formed by the junction of North Wallace Canyon and South Wallace Canyon, drained by a stream that flows 4.25 miles to Long Canyon 3.25 miles west-northwest of Devil Peak (lat. 38°58'50" N, long. 120°35'55" W; sec. 14, T 13 N, R 12 E). Named on Devil Peak (1950) 7.5' quadrangle. On Placerville (1893) 30' quadrangle, present North Wallace Canyon is shown as part of Wallace Canyon.

Wallace Canyon: see **Little Wallace Canyon** [PLACER]; **North Wallace Canyon** [PLACER]; **South Wallace Canyon** [PLACER].

Wallace Creek [SIERRA]: *stream,* flows 2.5 miles, partly in Plumas County, to Slate Creek 4.25 miles west-southwest of Mount Fillmore (lat. 39°42'35" N, long. 120°55'40" W; sec. 1, T 21 N, R 9 E). Named on La Porte (1951) 7.5' quadrangle.

Wallace Spring [PLACER]: *spring,* 3 miles west-northwest of Devil Peak (lat. 38°58'05" N, long. 120°35'55" W; near NE cor. sec. 23, T 13 N, R 12 E); the spring is 1 mile south of the mouth of Wallace Canyon. Named on Devil Peak (1950) 7.5' quadrangle.

Walloupa: see **You Bet** [NEVADA].

Wall's Bridge: see **Purdon Crossing** [NEVADA].

Walls Flat [NEVADA]: *area,* 2.5 miles north of North Bloomfield (lat. 39°24'15" N, long. 120°54' W; sec. 19, T 18 N, R 10 E). Named on Pike (1949) 7.5' quadrangle.

Walltown [SACRAMENTO]: *locality,* 8 miles south-southeast of Folsom (lat. 38°34'25" N, long. 121°06'10" W; sec. 4, T 8 N, R 8 E). Named on Folsom SE (1954) 7.5' quadrangle.

Walmort [SACRAMENTO]: *locality,* 7 miles east-southeast of Elk Grove along Central California Traction Railroad (lat. 38°22'50" N, long. 121°14'35" W). Named on Sloughhouse (1968) 7.5' quadrangle.

Walnut Grove [SACRAMENTO]: *town,* 7.5 miles northeast of Isleton along Sacramento River at the northeast end of Tyler Island (lat. 38°14'35" N, long. 121°30'40" W). Named on Isleton (1978) 7.5' quadrangle. Postal authorities established Walnut Grove post office in 1856 (Frickstad, p. 135). John Sharp, a ferryman, founded the community in 1851 (Dillon, p. 104).

Waloupa: see **You Bet** [NEVADA].

Walsh: see **Walsh Station** [SACRAMENTO].

Walsh Hill [YUBA]: *ridge,* north-trending, 1 mile long, 2.5 miles south of Smartville (lat. 39°10'10" N, long. 121°18'10" W; at E line sec. 9, T 15 N, R 6 E). Named on Smartville (1951) 7.5' quadrangle. Called Wash Hill on Wheatland (1949) 15' quadrangle.

Walsh Station [SACRAMENTO]: *locality,* 6 miles south of downtown Carmichael (lat. 38°31'45" N, long. 121°20' W). Named on Carmichael (1967) 7.5' quadrangle. Called Walsh on Sacramento (1892) 30' quadrangle. Postal authorities established Walsh Station post office in 1876 and discontinued in 1917; the name was for J.M. Walsh, first postmaster (Salley, p. 234).

Walters Creek [COLUSA]: *stream,* flows 8.5 miles to Spring Creek 5 miles southwest of Williams (lat. 39°06'05" N, long. 122°12'55" W; at N line sec. 5, T 14 N, R 3 W). Named on Colusa (1953) and Wilbur Springs (1961) 15' quadrangles. Called South Fork [Spring Creek] on Spring Valley (1918) 7.5' quadrangle.

Walton: see **Live Oak** [SUTTER].

Wambo Bar [YUBA]: *locality,* 2.5 miles south-southeast of Strawberry Valley along North Yuba River near the mouth of Deadwood Creek (lat. 39°31'50" N, long. 121°05'40" W; near W line sec. 9, T 19 N, R 8 E). Named on Strawberry Valley (1948) 7.5' quadrangle. The name commemorates Mahlon M. Wambough, an officer in Fremont's California Battalion, who founded the mining camp in 1849; the name also had the forms "Wombough," "Waubaugh," "Waurbaugh," "Wormbough," and "Wamba" (Dillon *in* Burrows and Hall, p. 64-65), as well as "Yamboo" (Osbun, p. 201). Wescoatt's (1861) map shows a place called Trasks Bar located along North Yuba River just below Wambo Bar. A place called Fraser's Bar was situated on the south bank of North Yuba River east of the mouth of Deadwood Creek (Hoover, Rensch, and Rensch, p. 595).

Ward Creek [PLACER]: *stream,* flows 5.5 miles to Lake Tahoe 3 miles south-southwest of Tahoe City (lat. 39°07'45" N, long. 120° 09'15" W; sec. 24, T 15 N, R 16 E). Named on Homewood (1955) and Tahoe City (1955) 7.5' quadrangles. Ward Rust and William Ferguson built a cabin at the mouth of Ward Creek in 1862 (Hoover, Rensch, and Rensch, p. 266).

Ward Peak [PLACER]: *peak,* nearly 6 miles west-southwest of Tahoe City (lat. 39°08'50" N, long. 120°14'40" W; at W line sec. 17, T 15 N, R 16 E). Altitude 8637 feet. Named on Tahoe City (1955) 7.5' quadrangle.

Warm Lake [PLACER]: *lake,* 650 feet long, 9.5 miles west-southwest of Donner Pass (lat. 39°15'55" N, long. 120°29'15" W; sec. 11, T 16 N, R 13 E). Named on Soda Springs (1955) 7.5' quadrangle.

Warner Ravine [EL DORADO]: *canyon,* drained by a stream that flows 1 mile to Middle Fork American River 2 miles north-northwest of Cool (lat. 38°54'50" N, long. 121°01'45" W; near N line sec. 12, T 12 N, R 8 E). Named on Auburn (1953) 7.5' quadrangle.

Warnick Canyon [COLUSA]: *canyon,* drained by a stream that flows 1.25 miles to Bear Creek nearly 3 miles southeast of Wilbur Springs (lat. 39°00'50" N, long. 122°22'45" W; sec. 35, T 14 N, R 5 W). Named on Wilbur Springs (1961) 15' quadrangle.

Warren Lake [NEVADA]: *lake,* 2450 feet long, 5.5 miles north-northwest of Donner Pass (lat. 39°23'45" N, long. 120°21' W; sec. 25, T 18 N, R 14 E). Named on Independence Lake (1981) 7.5' quadrangle.

Wash Clark Well [YOLO]: *well,* 6 miles west-southwest of Esparto (lat. 38°39'10" N, long. 122°07'05" W; near SE cor. sec. 6, T 9 N, R 2 W). Named on Esparto (1959) 7.5' quadrangle.

Wash Hill: see **Walsh Hill** [YUBA].

Washington [NEVADA]: *village,* 17 miles northeast of Grass Valley along South Yuba River (lat. 39°21'30" N, long. 120°28' W; at N line sec. 12, T 17 N, R 10 E). Named on Washington (1950) 7.5' quadrangle. Postal authorities established Washington South Yuba post office in 1852 and discontinued it in 1854; they reestablished it in 1862 with the name "Washington" (Salley, p. 235). Miners from Indiana settled at the site in 1849, and for a time the place was known as Indiana Camp; the name "Washington" was adopted in 1850 at a Fourth-of-July celebration—the village is at what is known as Washington Flat (Slyter and Slyter, p. 2). Logan's (1940) map shows a peak called Shake Hill located 3 miles south-southeast of Washington (sec. 23, T 17 N, R 10 E). Whitney's (1873) map shows a place called White Cloud located 3 miles south-southwest of Washington, a relief feature called Phelps Point situated 1 mile south-southwest of Washington, a relief feature called Phelps Hill located 2 miles south-southwest of Washington, and a relief feature called Gold Hill located 1 mile southwest of Washington—fire destroyed a mining town at Gold Hill in 1856 and the community never recovered (Slyter and Slyter, p. 10). Gudde (1975, p. 45) listed a place called Brass Wire Bar that was located along South Yuba River opposite Washington, and (p. 125) a place called Frenchmans Bar that was located along South Yuba River about 3 miles west of Washington.

Washington: see **Broderick** [YOLO]; **George Washington Hill** [NEVADA].

Washington Creek [NEVADA]: *stream,* flows nearly 3 miles to South Yuba River 0.25 mile southwest of Washington (lat. 39°21'20" N, long. 120°48'15" W; sec. 12, T 17 N, R 10 E). Named on Washington (1950) 7.5' quadrangle. The canyon of the stream is called Washington Rav. [Ravine] on Whitney's (1873) map.

Washington Flat: see **Washington** [NEVADA].

Washington Lake: see **Lake Washington** [YOLO].

Washington Mill [YUBA]: *locality,* 2 miles south of Brownsville along Dry Creek (1) (lat. 39°26'30" N, long. 121°16'20" W). Named on Smartsville (1895) 30' quadrangle. The place was a lumber camp with a sawmill from 1851 until 1863 (Hoover, Rensch, and Rensch, p. 593).

Washington Ravine: see **Washington Creek** [NEVADA].

Washington Ridge [NEVADA]: *ridge,* west- to west-southwest-trending, 5 miles long, center 4.5 miles southwest of Washington (lat. 39°19'20" N, long. 120°52'15" W). Named on North Bloomfield (1949) and Washington (1950) 7.5' quadrangles.

Washington South Yuba: see **Washington** [NEVADA].

Washingtonville: see **Durgans Flat**, under **Downieville** [SIERRA].

Wasiu: see **Camp Wasiu** [EL DORADO].

Water Canyon [EL DORADO]: *canyon,* drained by a stream that flows 2 miles to Slab Creek 5.5 miles northwest of Pollock Pines (lat. 38°48'50" N, long. 120°39'30" W; sec. 8, T 11 N, R 12 E). Named on Slate Mountain (1950) 7.5' quadrangle.

Waterhouse Peak [EL DORADO]: *peak,* 6.5 miles south-southwest of Freel Peak on El Dorado-Alpine County line (lat. 38°46'35" N, long. 119°57'50" W; sec. 26, T 11 N, R 18 E). Altitude 9497 feet. Named on Freel Peak (1955) 7.5' quadrangle. Forest Service officials named the peak to honor Clark Waterhouse, a Forest Service employee who died in World War I (Gudde, 1969, p. 359).

Waterman [AMADOR]: *settlement,* 0.5 mile north-northwest of Ione (lat. 38°21'40" N, long. 120°56'15" W). Named on Sutter Creek (1944) 15' quadrangle. Postal authorities established Waterman post office in 1895 and discontinued it in 1955; the name was for Robert W. Waterman, who promoted the place (Salley, p. 235).

Waters Campground: see **Middle Waters Campground** [SIERRA].

Waters Peak [AMADOR]: *peak,* 7.5 miles southwest of Jackson (lat. 38°16'10" N, long. 120°52'10" W; near W line sec. 22, T 5 N, R 10 E). Altitude 950 feet. Named on Jackson (1962) 7.5' quadrangle.

Watkins Bar: see **Electra** [AMADOR].

Watson: see **Mount Watson** [PLACER].

Watson Creek [PLACER]: *stream,* flows 3 miles to Lake Tahoe 3.5 miles west-southwest of Kings Beach (lat. 39°13'25" N, long. 120° 05'05" W; at E line sec. 21, T 16 N, R 17 E); the stream heads near Watson Lake. Named on Kings Beach (1955) and Tahoe City (1955) 7.5' quadrangles. The name commemorates Robert Montgomery Watson, who came to Lake Tahoe in 1875 and purchased Tahoe House in 1888 (Lekisch, p. 151).

Watson Lake [PLACER]: *lake,* 750 feet long, nearly 4 miles north of Tahoe City (lat. 39°13'30" N, long. 120°08'10" W; sec. 19, T 16 N, R 17 E); the lake is 0.5 mile northeast of Mount Watson. Named on Tahoe City (1955) 7.5' quadrangle. The name is for Robert Montgomery Waston of Watson Creek (Lekisch, p. 151).

Weaver Creek: see **Weber Creek** [EL DORADO].

Weaver Lake [NEVADA]: *lake,* 0.5 mile long, 4.5 miles east-northeast of Graniteville (lat. 39°27'55" N, long. 120°39'25" W; at SW cor. sec. 32, T 19 N, R 12 E). Named on Graniteville (1982) 7.5' quadrangle.

Weavertown: see **Weber Creek** [EL DORADO].

Weaverville: see **Weber Creek** [EL DORADO].

Webber [EL DORADO]: *locality,* 15 miles east of Georgetown (lat. 38°53'30" N, long. 120°33' W). Named on Placerville (1893) 30' quadrangle.

Webber Creek: see **Weber Creek** [EL DORADO].

Webber Creek Reservoir: see **Weber Reservoir** [EL DORADO].

Webber Lake [SIERRA]: *lake,* 4100 feet long, 7.5 miles south-southwest of Sierraville (lat. 39°29'10" N, long. 120°24'45" W; sec. 28, T 19 N, R 14 E); the lake is at the head of Little Truckee River. Named on Webber Peak (1981) 7.5' quadrangle. The name commemorates David Gould Webber, who bought land around the lake in 1852 for stock range—the feature previously was called Little Truckee Lake (Gudde, 1949, p. 385).

Webber Peak [SIERRA]: *peak,* 8.5 miles south-southwest of Sierraville (lat. 39°28'50" N, long. 120°26'40" W; sec. 30, T 19 N, R 14 E). Altitude 8093 feet. Named on Webber Peak (1981) 7.5' quadrangle.

Webber's Bridge: see **Purdon Crossing** [NEVADA].

Weber Creek [EL DORADO]: *stream,* formed by the confluence of North Fork and South Fork, flows 20 miles to South Fork American River 5 miles south of the village of Pilot Hill (lat. 38° 45'50" N, long. 121°00'25" W; near E line sec. 31, T 11 N, R 9 E). Named on Camino (1952), Coloma (1949), Pilot Hill (1954), Placerville (1949), and Shingle Springs (1949) 7.5' quadrangles. Called Webber Creek on Placerville (1893) 30' quadrangle. North Fork is 9 miles long and is named on Camino (1952) and Sly Park (1952) 7.5' quadrangles. South Fork is 7.5 miles long and is named on Camino (1952) and Sly Park (1952) 7.5' quadrangles. The name "Weber" is for Charles M. Weber, who mined in the neighborhood in 1848; it also had the forms "Webber" and "Weaver" (Gudde, 1975, p. 366). Weber started a store along Weber Creek about 2 miles from Placerville and it became the nucleus of a mining camp called Weberville (Hoover, Rensch, and Rensch, p. 82). The camp, which also was called Weaverville, was located at the confluence of Weber Creek and Ringgold Creek (Morgan *in* Pritchard, p. 170). The place also was called Weavertown; a mining camp called Ringgold was situated along Weber Creek between Weavertown and Diamond Springs (Becker *in* Christy, entry for August 7, 1850). Postal authorities established Ringgold post office in 1852 and discontinued it in 1853 (Frickstad, p. 29).

Weber Reservoir [EL DORADO]: *lake,* behind a dam on North Fork Weber Creek nearly 2 miles south-southwest of Camino (lat. 38° 42'55" N, long. 120°41'30" W; sec. 18, T 10 N, R 12 E). Named on Camino (1952) 7.5' quadrangle. Called Webber Creek Reservoir on California Division of Highways' (1934) map, which has the form "Webber Creek" for the name of present Weber Creek.

Weber's Island: see **West Island** [SACRAMENTO].

Weberville: see **Weber Creek** [EL DORADO].

Webster [YOLO]: *locality,* 5 miles east-northeast of Davis along Southern

Pacific Railroad (lat. 38°33'45" N, long. 121°39'15" W). Named on Davis (1952) 7.5' quadrangle.

Webster: see **Freeport Bend** [SACRAMENTO-YOLO]; **Michigan Bluff** [PLACER].

Webster Flat [NEVADA]: *area*, 9 miles west of Donner Pass (lat. 39°19'50" N, long. 120°29'25" W; near NW cor. sec. 23, T 17 N, R 13 E). Named on Soda Springs (1955) 7.5' quadrangle.

Weed Point [YUBA]: *relief feature*, 2 miles south-southeast of Strawberry Valley above North Yuba River (lat. 39°32'10" N, long. 121°05'35" W; near SW cor. sec. 4, T 19 N, R 8 E). Named on Strawberry Valley (1948) 7.5' quadrangle.

Weeds Point [YUBA]: *locality*, nearly 2 miles north of Camptonville (lat. 39°28'40" N, long. 121°02'55" W; near N line sec. 35, T 19 N, R 8 E). Named on Camptonville (1948) 7.5' quadrangle. The name commemorates a miner who abandoned his claim at the place in 1853, a dozen years before mining there proved profitable (Gudde, 1975, p. 367).

Weil Lake [NEVADA]: *lake*, 850 feet long, 1.5 miles south of English Mountain along Canyon Creek (lat. 39°25'30" N, long. 120°32'45" W; on W line sec. 17, T 18 N, R 13 E). Named on English Mountain (1983) 7.5' quadrangle.

Weimar [PLACER]: *settlement*, 4.5 miles south-southwest of Colfax (lat. 39°02'10" N, long. 120°58'25" W; near E line sec. 28, T 14 N, R 9 E). Named on Colfax (1949) 7.5' quadrangle. Postal authorities established Weimar post office in 1866 (Frickstad, p. 122). United States Board on Geographic Names (1933, p. 806) rejected the form "Weimer" for the name, which is from a local Indian chief (Stewart, p. 90).

Weiss Hill [YUBA]: *peak*, 4.5 miles north-northeast of Rackerby (lat. 39°29'45" N, long. 121°18'25" W; near N line sec. 21, T 19 N, R 6 E). Named on Rackerby (1948) 7.5' quadrangle.

Wellman Creek [YUBA]: *stream*, flows 4.25 miles to Hutchinson Creek 5 miles southwest of Smartville (lat. 39°09'45" N, long. 121° 22'10" W; sec. 12, T 15 N, R 5 E). Named on Smartville (1951) 7.5' quadrangle.

Welsh: see **Nick Welsh Spring** [PLACER].

Welton Glade [COLUSA]: *area*, 1.5 miles west of Fouts Springs (lat. 39°21'05" N, long. 122°41'40" W; near SW cor. sec. 6, T 17 N, R 7 W). Named on Fouts Springs (1968) 7.5' quadrangle.

Wench Flat [EL DORADO]: *area*, 3.5 miles east-southeast of Robbs Peak (lat. 38°54' N, long. 120°20'30" W; sec. 7, T 12 N, R 15 E). Named on Loon Lake (1952) 7.5' quadrangle.

Wentworth Springs [EL DORADO]: *locality*, 11.5 miles west of the town of Meeks Bay (lat. 39°00'45" N, long. 120°20'20" W; sec. 31, T 14 N, R 15 E). Named on Wentworth Springs (1953) 7.5' quadrangle.

Wentworth Springs Campground [EL DORADO]: *locality*, less than 1 mile east of Wentworth Springs (lat. 39°00'45" N, long. 120°19'25" W; sec. 32, T 14 N, R 15 E). Named on Wentworth Springs (1953) 7.5' quadrangle.

West: see **Camp Harvey West** [EL DORADO].

West Applegate: see **Applegate** [PLACER].

West Butte [SUTTER]:
(1) *peak*, 6.5 miles northwest of Sutter in Sutter Buttes (lat. 39°13'05" N, long. 121°50'45" W; near S line sec. 22, T 16 N, E 1 E). Altitude 1685 feet. Named on Sutter Buttes (1954) 7.5' quadrangle.
(2) *locality*, 3.25 miles north-northeast of Meridian (lat. 39°11'15" N, long. 121°53'10" W; on S line sec. 32, T 16 N, R 1 E); the place is 3 miles southwest of West Butte (1) at the west base of Sutter Buttes. Named on Meridian (1952) 7.5' quadrangle. Postal authorities established West Butte post office in 1863 and discontinued it in 1930; the post office name also had the form "Westbutte" (Salley, p. 237). They established Kent post office 3 miles west of West Butte post office in 1891 and discontinued it in 1911 (Salley, p. 110).

West Canyon [EL DORADO]: *canyon*, drained by a stream that flows 2 miles to Canyon Creek (1) 2 miles northwest of Georgetown (lat. 38°55'50" N, long. 120°51'40" W; sec. 33, T 13 N, R 10 E). Named on Georgetown (1949) 7.5' quadrangle.

West Cut: see **Sacramento River Deep Water Ship Channel** [SACRAMENTO-YOLO].

Westfalls [EL DORADO]: *locality*, 6 miles southwest of Leek Spring Hill (lat. 38°33'30" N, long. 120°30'50" W). Named on Pyramid Peak (1896) 30' quadrangle.

West Island [SACRAMENTO]: *island*, 1.5 miles long, 13 miles southwest of Isleton in San Joaquin River (lat. 38°01'25" N, long. 121°46'40" W). Named on Antioch North (1978) 7.5' quadrangle. Called Weber's I. on Ringgold's (1850a) map.

West Juniper Creek [NEVADA]: *stream*, flows nearly 2 miles to Juniper Creek 7.25 miles east of Truckee (lat. 39°20'15" N, long. 120°03'05" W; sec. 11, T 17 N, R 17 E). Named on Martis Peak (1955) 7.5' quadrangle.

West Lakes [NEVADA]: *lakes*, nearly 2 miles north-northwest of Donner Pass (lat. 39°20'25" N, long. 120°20'15" W; near NW cor. sec. 8, T 17 N, R 15 E). Named on Norden (1955) 7.5' quadrangle.

West Martis Creek [PLACER]: *stream*, flows 4.25 miles to Martis Creek nearly 5 miles west of Martis Peak (lat. 39°18'05" N, long. 120°07'15" W; near SW cor. sec. 20, T 17 N, R 17 E). Named on Martis Peak (1955) 7.5' quadrangle.

West Meadow Creek [PLACER]: *stream*, flows nearly 3 miles to Barker Creek 4.5 miles east of Bunker Hill (lat. 39°03'40" N, long. 120°17'50" W; sec. 16, T 14 N, R 15 E). Named on Wentworth Springs (1953) 7.5' quadrangle.

Westmoreland [AMADOR]: *locality*, 4.25 miles southeast of present Hams Station (lat. 38°30'05" N, long. 120°19'05" W). Named on Pyramid Peak (1896) 30' quadrangle.

Westmoreland Bridge: see **Chaparral Hill**, under **Lancha Plana** [AMADOR].

Westmoreland's Ferry: see **Chaparral Hill**, under **Lancha Plana** [AMADOR].

West Panther Creek [AMADOR]: *stream*, flows 6.5 miles to join East Panther Creek and form Panther Creek 4.25 miles south-southwest of Hams Station (lat. 38°29'10" N, long. 120°24'05" W; sec. 2, T 7 N, R 14 E); the stream is west of Panther Ridge. Named on Caldor (1951), Devils Nose (1979), and Peddler Hill (1951) 7.5' quadrangles. Called Panther Creek on Pyramid Peak (1896) 30' quadrangle, but United States Board on Geographic Names (1959, p. 7) rejected this name for the stream.

West Sacramento [YOLO]: *town*, 15 miles east-southeast of Woodland along Sacramento River (lat. 38°34'15" N, long. 121°31'45" W); the place is west of the city of Sacramento [SACRAMENTO]. Named on Sacramento West (1967) 7.5' quadrangle. Postal authorities established West Sacramento post office in 1915 (Frickstad, p. 221).

Westville [PLACER]: *locality*, 14 miles northeast of Foresthill on Forest Hill Divide (lat. 39°10'30" N, long. 120°38'50" W; at W line sec. 4, T 15 N, R 12 E). Named on Westville (1952) 7.5' quadrangle. Postal authorities established Westville post office in 1889 and discontinued it in 1919; the name was for George C. West, first postmaster (Salley, p. 238). They established Ackerman post office 4.5 miles east of Westville in 1896 and discontinued it in 1899; the name was for John Q. Ackerman, first postmaster (Salley, p. 1). They established Stonehill post office 5 miles south of Westville in 1900 and discontinued it in 1901; the name was for Frances H. Stone, first postmaster (Salley, p. 213).

Wet Ravine [SIERRA]:
(1) *canyon*, drained by a stream that flows 1 mile to Fiddle Creek 6.25 miles west-southwest of Goodyears Bar (lat. 39°31'10" N, long. 120°59'45" W; sec. 17, T 19 N, R 9 E). Named on Goodyears Bar (1951) 7.5' quadrangle.
(2) *canyon*, drained by a stream that flows 2 miles to Kanaka Creek 1.25 miles southwest of Alleghany (lat. 39°27'30" N, long. 120°51'25" W; sec. 4, T 18 N, R 10 E). Named on Alleghany (1949) 7.5' quadrangle.

Whaler Creek [EL DORADO]: *stream*, flows 8 miles to Rock Creek 10 miles west-northwest of Pollock Pines (lat. 38°49'45" N, long. 120°44'45" W; near W line sec. 3, T 11 N, R 11 E). Named on Slate Mountain (1950) and Tunnel Hill (1950) 7.5' quadrangles.

Wheatland [YUBA]: *town*, 12.5 miles southeast of Marysville (lat. 39°00'35" N, long. 121°25'20" W). Named on Wheatland (1947) 7.5' quadrangle. Postal authorities established Wheatland post office in 1866 (Frickstad, p. 224), and the town incorporated in 1874. A place called Greenhorn Bar was located on the north side of Bear River 6 miles east of Wheatland (Gudde, 1975, p. 143).

Wheelers Sheep Camp [SIERRA]: *locality*, 11 miles south of Loyalton (lat. 39°30'55" N, long. 120°14'40" W; sec. 7, T 19 N, R 16 E). Named on Sardine Peak (1981) 7.5' quadrangle.

Whiskey Bar [EL DORADO]: *locality*, 5.25 miles west-southwest of the village of Pilot Hill along North Fork American River (lat. 38° 48'55" N, long. 121°06'20" W; sec. 8, T 11 N, R 8 E). Site named on Auburn (1954) 15' quadrangle. Water of Folsom Lake now covers the spot.

Whiskey Creek [SIERRA]: *stream*, flows 1.5 miles to Slate Creek 2.25 miles northwest of Mount Fillmore (lat. 39°45'05" N, long. 120°52'55" W; sec. 20, T 22 N, R 10 E). Named on Blue Nose Mountain (1951) and Onion Valley (1950) 7.5' quadrangles.

Whiskey Creek [YUBA]: *stream*, flows 1.25 miles to Deadwood Creek 2 miles south-southeast of Strawberry Valley (lat. 39°32'15" N, long. 121°05'15" W; sec. 4, T 19 N, R 8 E). Named on Strawberry Valley (1948) 7.5' quadrangle.

Whiskey Diggings [SIERRA]: *locality*, 2.25 miles northwest of Mount Fillmore (lat. 39°45'10" N, long. 120°52'50" W; sec. 20, T 22 N, R 10 E); the place is near the mouth of Whiskey Creek. Named on Onion Valley (1950) 7.5' quadrangle. Downieville (1897) 30' quadrangle has the name for a community. The place also was called Newark (Bancroft, 1888, p. 362).

Whiskey Diggings: see **Valley View** [PLACER].

Whiskey Hill [COLUSA]: *relief feature*, 4.5 miles east-northeast of Wilbur Springs along Salt Creek (2) (lat. 39°03'30" N, long. 120° 20'30" W; sec. 18, T 14 N, R 4 W). Named on Wilbur Springs (1961) 15' quadrangle.

Whisky Creek [COLUSA]: *stream*, flows 8 miles to South Branch Sand Creek 3 miles west of Arbuckle (lat. 39°01'25" N, long. 122° 06'20" W; sec. 32, T 13 N, R 2 W). Named on Arbuckle (1952), Cortina Creek (1953), and Rumsey (1959) 7.5' quadrangles.

Whisky Creek [PLACER]: *stream,* flows 2 miles to Five Lakes Creek 2.5 miles south-southeast of Granite Chief (lat. 39°09'40" N, long. 120°16'10" W; sec. 11, T 15 N, R 15 E). Named on Granite Chief (1953) 7.5' quadrangle.

Whisky Creek Camp [PLACER]: *locality,* 2.25 mile south-southeast of Granite Chief (lat. 39°10' N, long. 120°16'15" W; sec. 11, T 15 N, R 15 E); the place is along Whisky Creek. Named on Granite Chief (1953) 7.5' quadrangle.

Whisky Gulch [AMADOR]: *canyon,* less than 1 mile long, 5.25 miles south-southeast of Plymouth (lat. 38°24'35" N, long. 120° 48' W). Named on Amador City (1962) 7.5' quadrangle.

Whisky Hill [PLACER]: *ridge,* west-southwest-trending, 1.5 miles long, 4.5 miles northwest of Duncan Peak (lat. 39°11'35" N, long. 120°34'35" W; on E line sec. 1, T 15 N, R 12 E). Named on Duncan Peak (1952) 7.5' quadrangle.

Whisky Hill [SACRAMENTO]: *hill,* 2.5 miles south-southeast of downtown Sacramento (lat. 38°32'30" N, long. 121°28'30" W; near S line sec. 18, T 8 N, R 5 E). Altitude 31 feet. Named on Sacramento East (1967) 7.5' quadrangle. On Brighton (1911) 7.5' quadrangle, the name applies to a hill located 1.5 miles farther east-southeast (lat. 38°32'10" N, long. 121°26'50" W).

Whisky Run [PLACER]: *stream,* flows 2 miles to Coon Creek 7 miles north-northeast of Lincoln (lat. 38°59'20" N, long. 121°15'15" W; sec. 12, T 13 N, R 6 E). Named on Gold Hill (1954) and Lincoln (1953) 7.5' quadrangles.

White [EL DORADO]: *locality,* 1.25 miles east of Leek Spring Hill in Leek Spring Valley (lat. 38°38' N, long. 120°15'20" W; sec. 18, T 9 N, R 16 E). Named on Leek Spring Hill (1951) 7.5' quadrangle.

White Azalea Campground [AMADOR]: *locality,* 7.5 miles southeast of Hams Station along North Fork Mokelumne River (lat. 38° 29'10" N, long. 120°15'40" W; near W line sec. 6, T 7 N, R 16 E). Named on Garnet Hill (1979) 7.5' quadrangle.

White Cloud: see **Washington** [NEVADA].

White Hall [EL DORADO]: *locality,* 2.5 miles east of Riverton along South Fork American River (lat. 38°46'30" N, long. 120°24'10" W; sec. 27, T 11 N, R 14 E). Named on Riverton (1950) 7.5' quadrangle. Logan's (1938) map has the form "Whitehall" for the name. Postal authorities established Randall post office at Whitehall in 1917 and discontinued it in 1937; the name was for Albert B. Randall, first postmaster (Salley, p. 181).

White Hall Canyon [EL DORADO]: *canyon,* drained by a stream that flows 1 mile to South Fork American River 2.25 miles east of Riverton at White Hall (lat. 38°46'35" N, long. 120°24'15" W; sec. 27, T 11 N, R 14 E). Named on Riverton (1950) 7.5' quadrangle.

Whitehouse Creek [SACRAMENTO]: *stream,* flows 2.5 miles to end 3 miles northwest of Elk Grove (lat. 38°26'10" N, long. 121°24'25" W; near NW cor. sec. 26, T 7 N, R 5 E). Named on Elk Grove (1968) and Florin (1968) 7.5' quadrangles.

White Man Ravine [EL DORADO]: *canyon,* drained by a stream that flows 1.5 miles to Little Indian Creek 2.5 miles east of Latrobe (lat. 38°33'15" N, long. 120°55'55" W; sec. 13, T 8 N, R 9 E). Named on Latrobe (1949) 7.5' quadrangle. Called White Mans Ravine on Placerville (1893) 30' quadrangle.

White Meadow [EL DORADO]: *area,* 2 miles west-northwest of Riverton (lat. 38°47' N, long. 120°29'05" W; near NE cor. sec. 23, T 11 N, R 13 E). Named on Riverton (1950) 7.5' quadrangle.

White Oak Creek [EL DORADO]: *stream,* flows 2.25 miles to Kelly Creek 3.5 miles north-northwest of Shingle Springs (lat. 38°42'45" N, long. 120°57' W; sec. 23, T 10 N, R 9 E); the stream goes through White Oak Flat. Named on Shingle Springs (1949) 7.5' quadrangle.

White Oak Flat [EL DORADO]: *area,* 3.25 miles northwest of Shingle Springs (lat. 38°42'20" N, long. 120°57'45" W). Named on Shingle Springs (1949) 7.5' quadrangle. The place first was called Cart Wheel Valley (Gudde, 1975, p. 370).

White Oak Point [EL DORADO]: *peak,* 6.5 miles west of Pollock Pines (lat. 38°46'45" N, long. 120°42'10" W; at N line sec. 25, T 11 N, R 12 E). Altitude 2888 feet. Named on Slate Mountain (1950) 7.5' quadrangle.

White Rock [SACRAMENTO]: *locality,* nearly 6 miles southeast of Folsom along Southern Pacific Railroad (lat. 38°37'35" N, long. 121°05'25" W; at N line sec. 22, T 9 N, R 8 E). Named on Clarksville (1953) 7.5' quadrangle. The name is from nearby White Rock Springs, which were named for white rocks above them (Ledyard *in* Loomis, p. 126).

White Rock Canyon: see **White Rock Creek** [EL DORADO].

White Rock Creek [EL DORADO]: *stream,* flows 3.5 miles to South Fork American River 2.25 miles east of Chili Bar (lat. 38°45'50" N, long. 120°46'50" W; near NW cor. sec. 32, T 11 N, R 11 E). Named on Camino (1952), Garden Valley (1949), and Slate Mountain (1950) 7.5' quadrangles. The canyon of the stream is called White Rock Canyon on Placerville (1893) 30' quadrangle.

White Rock Creek [NEVADA]: *stream,* flows 3.5 miles to North Creek 7.5 miles northwest of Donner Pass (lat. 39°23'50" N, long. 120°25'20" W; sec. 29, T 18 N, R 14 E). Named on Webber Peak (1981) 7.5' quadrangle.

White Rock Lake [NEVADA]: *lake,* 2900 feet long, 7.5 miles north-northwest of Donner Pass (lat. 39°25'10" N, long. 120°23' W; at SE cor. sec. 15, T 18 N, R 14 E); the lake is along White Rock Creek. Named on Webber Peak (1981) 7.5' quadrangle. Truckee (1940) 30' quadrangle has the form "Whiterock Lake" for the name.

White Rock Springs: see **White Rock** [SACRAMENTO].

Whites Bar: see **Electra** [AMADOR].

Whitmore [AMADOR]: *locality,* 8 miles east-northeast of Pine Grove (lat. 38°27'20" N, long. 120°31' W). Named on Jackson (1902) 30' quadrangle.

Whitmore Meadow [AMADOR]: *area,* 7.5 miles southwest of Hams Station (lat. 38°28'35" N, long. 120°28'40" W; sec. 7, T 7 N, R 14 E). Named on Devils Nose (1979) 7.5' quadrangle.

Whitney [PLACER]: *locality,* nearly 6 miles north-northwest of Roseville along Southern Pacific Railroad (lat. 38°49'55" N, long. 121°18'20" W; sec. 4, T 11 N, R 6 E). Named on Roseville (1967) 7.5' quadrangle. The name commemorates Joel Parker Whitney, who had a large ranch at the place (Hanna, p. 354).

Whore House Gulch: see **Indian Diggins** [EL DORADO].

Wickes: see **Floriston** [NEVADA].

Widow Creek: see **Burnt Shanty Creek** [EL DORADO].

Widow Flats [COLUSA]: *valley,* 3.25 miles northeast of Wilbur Springs (lat. 39°04' N, long. 122°22'15" W). Named on Wilbur Springs (1961) 15' quadrangle.

Wieland: see **Pine Grove** [AMADOR].

Wightman's Camp: see **Baltimore Town** [NEVADA].

Wilbur [SACRAMENTO]: *locality,* 26 miles east-southeast of downtown Sacramento (lat. 38°25'35" N, long. 121°03'10" W). Named on Lodi (1894) 30' quadrangle.

Wilbur Hot Springs: see **Wilbur Springs** [COLUSA].

Wilbur Springs [COLUSA]: *locality,* 17 miles west-southwest of Williams along Sulphur Creek (lat. 39°02'20" N, long. 122°25'10" W; at N line sec. 28, T 14 N, R 5 W). Named on Wilbur Springs (1961) 15' quadrangle. Postal authorities established Wilbur Springs post office in 1909 and discontinued it in 1945 (Frickstad, p. 20). The original resort known as Wilbur Hot Springs was situated 4 miles northwest of a resort called Simmons Hot Springs; when the hotel at the original site of Wilbur Hot Springs burned, the resort moved to the Simmons Hot Springs property, but kept the name "Wilbur Hot Springs" (Waring, G.A., p. 99). Clark's Springs were located along Sulphur Creek less than 1 mile above Simmons Hot Springs; Simmons Hot Springs, Wilbur Hot Springs, and Clark's Springs together were known as Colusa Sulphur Springs (Goodyear, p. 155). Logan (1929b, p. 291) used the name "Elgin Mine Hot Springs" for springs at the original site of Wilbur Hot Springs resort, and noted that they are at Elgin quicksilver mine—Wilbur Springs (1961) 15' quadrangle shows Elgin mine along Sulphur Creek (sec. 13, T 14 N, R 6 W). Postal authorities established Sulphur Creek post office 1.5 miles southwest of Wilbur Springs in 1874 and discontinued it in 1915 (Salley, p. 215). According to Logan (1929b, p. 288), the old village of Sulphur Creek was on the south side of the stream of the same name, and 1 mile west of present Wilbur Springs. Postal authorities established Gilmore post office 5 miles north of Sulphur Creek post office in 1881 and discontinued it in 1892; the name was for Giles U. Gilmore, first postmaster (Salley, p. 85). A spring situated on the west side of Bear Valley about 1.5 miles north of Wilbur Hot Springs is called Oil Spring because it produces water that tastes of petroleum (Waring, G.A., p. 194).

Wild Bill Canyon [SIERRA]: *canyon,* drained by a stream that flows 2 miles to Berry Creek 4.5 miles west of Sierraville (lat. 39°35'50" N, long. 120°27' W; sec. 8, T 20 N, R 14 E). Named on Sattley (1981) 7.5' quadrangle. On Sierraville (1955) 15' quadrangle, the stream in the canyon is called Berry Creek.

Wild Cat Bar: see **Hoosier Bar** [EL DORADO-PLACER].

Wildcat Canyon [EL DORADO]:

(1) *canyon,* drained by a stream that flows 1.5 miles to Middle Fork American River 4 miles west-northwest of Greenwood (lat. 38°55'45" N, long. 120°58'30" W; near SE cor. sec. 33, T 13 N, R 9 E). Named on Greenwood (1949) 7.5' quadrangle.

(2) *canyon,* drained by a stream that flows 1 mile to Weber Creek 6.5 miles west-southwest of Coloma (lat. 38°45'35" N, long. 121° 00' W). Named on Coloma (1949) and Pilot Hill (1954) 7.5' quadrangles.

Wildcat Canyon [PLACER]: *canyon,* drained by a stream that flows 3.5 miles to North Fork American River 10 miles west of Granite Chief (lat. 39°13'05" N, long. 120°28'25" W; near SE cor. sec. 26, T 16 N, R 13 E). Named on Royal Gorge (1953) 7.5' quadrangle.

Wildcat Creek [YOLO]: *stream,* flows nearly 7 miles to Mushoak Creek 9 miles east of Rumsey (lat. 38°53'05" N, long. 122°04'25" W; near S line sec. 15, T 12 N, R 2 W). Named on Bird Valley (1959), Guinda (1959), and Wildwood School (1959) 7.5' quadrangles.

Wildcat Ravine [YUBA]: *canyon,* drained by a stream that flows 0.5 mile to South Honcut Creek 2 miles east-northeast of Rackerby (lat. 39°27'05" N, long. 121°18'15" W; sec. 4, T 18 N, R 6 E). Named on Rackerby (1948) 7.5' quadrangle.

Wild Cow Mountain [YOLO]: *peak,* 9 miles south-southwest of Esparto (lat. 38°35'05" N, long. 122°06'40" W; sec. 32, T 9 N, R 2 W). Altitude 2266 feet. Named on Monticello Dam (1959) 7.5' quadrangle.

Wild Goose Flat: see **Goose Flat** [EL DORADO].

Wild Irishman Bend [SUTTER-YOLO]: *bend,* 3 miles southeast of Knights Landing along Sacramento River on Sutter-Yolo County line (lat. 38°46' N, long. 121°41'25" W; at W line sec. 30, T 11 N, R 3 E). Named on Knights Landing (1952) 7.5' quadrangle.

Wild Plum Campground [SIERRA]: *locality,* nearly 2 miles east of Sierra City along Haypress Creek (lat. 39°34' N, long. 120°36' W; near SW cor. sec. 26, T 20 N, R 12 E). Named on Sierra City (1955) 15' quadrangle.

Wildwood: see **Hidden Valley** [PLACER] (2).

Wiley: see **Cooks Station** [AMADOR].

Wilkins Slough [COLUSA]: *water feature,* joins Sacramento River 5.5 miles southeast of Grimes (lat. 39°00'45" N, long. 121°49'35" W; at N line sec. 2, T 13 N, R 1 E). Named on Tisdale Weir (1952) 7.5' quadrangle.

Williams [COLUSA]: *town,* 8 miles west-southwest of Colusa (lat. 39°09'15" N, long. 122°09' W; mainly in sec. 13, 14, T 15 N, R 3 W). Named on Williams (1952) 7.5' quadrangle. Postal authorities established Central post office in 1874 and changed the name to Williams in 1876; the name "Central" was for the central position of the place in Sacramento Valley (Salley, p. 41). The town incorporated in 1920. The name "Williams" commemorates W.H. Williams, who laid out the townsite (Hoover, Rensch, and Rensch, p. 48). Postal authorities established Freshwater post office 5 miles northwest of Williams in 1874 and discontinued it in 1877; the name was for the location of the place along Freshwater Creek (Salley, p. 81).

Williams Creek [SIERRA]: *stream,* flows 1 mile to Deer Creek 4 miles northeast of Sierra City (lat. 39°36'40" N, long. 120°35'15" W; near E line sec. 11, T 20 N, R 12 E). Named on Haypress Valley (1981) 7.5' quadrangle. On Sierra City (1955) 15' quadrangle, the name "Williams Creek" applies to present Deer Creek below its junction with Williams Creek.

Williamson Creek [SIERRA-YOLO]: *stream,* heads in Sierra County and flows 2.25 miles to Willow Creek nearly 2 miles north of Camptonville in Yuba County (lat. 39°28'40" N, long. 121°02'30" W; near NW cor. sec. 36, T 19 N, R 8 E). Named on Camptonville (1948) 7.5' quadrangle.

Williams Ravine: see **You Bet** [NEVADA].

Willmont Canyon [PLACER]: *canyon,* drained by a stream that flows 1 mile to Burnett Canyon 4 miles north-northwest of Westville (lat. 39°13'50" N, long. 120°40'35" W; at N line sec. 30, T 16 N, R 12 E). Named on Westville (1952) 7.5' quadrangle.

Willmont Saddle [PLACER]: *pass,* 3.25 miles north-northwest of Westville (lat. 39°13'10" N, long. 120°39'50" W; sec. 30, T 16 N, R 12 E); the pass is near the head of Willmot Canyon. Named on Westville (1952) 7.5' quadrangle.

Willow Bar [EL DORADO]: *locality,* 3 miles northeast of Volcanoville along Middle Fork American River (lat. 39°00'25" N, long. 120°44'45" W; near N line sec. 4, T 13 N, R 11 E). Named on Michigan Bluff (1952) 7.5' quadrangle.

Willow Bar: see **Hoosier Bar** [EL DORADO-PLACER]; **Sucker Bar** [YUBA].

Willow Creek [AMADOR-SACRAMENTO]: *stream,* heads in Amador County and flows 12.5 miles to Laguna in Sacramento County 27 miles east-southeast of downtown Sacramento (lat. 38°24'35" N, long. 121°02'50" W; at S line sec. 36, T 7 N, R 8 E). Named on Carbondale (1968) and Irish Hill (1962) 7.5' quadrangles. Called Laguna on Carbondale (1909) 7.5' quadrangle, but United States Board on Geographic Names (1964, p. 15) rejected this name.

Willow Creek [COLUSA]: *water feature,* enters Colusa County from Glenn County in an artificial watercourse 4 miles west of Princeton (lat. 39°24'50" N, long. 122°04'45" W). Named on Moulton Weir (1952) and Princeton (1952) 7.5' quadrangles.

Willow Creek [PLACER]: *stream,* flows 1 mile to Bear Pen Creek 7 miles northeast of Bunker Hill (lat. 39°06'50" N, long. 120°16'45" W; sec. 27, T 15 N, R 15 E). Named on Wentworth Springs (1953) 7.5' quadrangle.

Willow Creek [SACRAMENTO]:

(1) *stream,* flows 8 miles to Lake Natoma 2 miles south-southwest of Folsom (lat. 38°39' N, long. 121°11'05" W). Named on Clarksville (1953) and Folsom (1967) 7.5' quadrangles.

(2) *stream,* flows 4.25 miles to marsh near Badger Creek nearly 5 miles north-northwest of Galt (lat. 38°19'10" N, long. 121°19'15" W). Named on Galt (1968) 7.5' quadrangle. Clay (1953) 7.5' quadrangle shows the stream extending farther east.

Willow Creek [SIERRA-YUBA]: *stream,* heads in Sierra County and flows 5.25 miles to New Bullards Bar Reservoir 1.5 miles west of Camptonville in Yuba County (lat. 39°27'15" N, long. 121°04'35" W; near W line sec. 3, T 18 N, R 8 E). Named on Camptonville (1948, photorevised 1969) 7.5' quadrangle.

Willow Creek: see **Laguna** [AMADOR-SACRAMENTO]; **Little Willow Creek** [YUBA].

Willow Flat [AMADOR]: *area,* nearly 4 miles west-northwest of Mokelumne Peak (lat. 38°34'10" N, long. 120°09'20" W; near E line sec. 1, T 8 N, R 16 E). Named on Bear River Reservoir (1979) 7.5' quadrangle.

Willow Flat [EL DORADO]:

(1) *area,* 6 miles southwest of Phipps Peak (lat. 38°53'05" N, long. 120°13'05" W; sec. 16, T 12 N, R 16 E). Named on Rockbound Valley (1955) 7.5' quadrangle.

(2) *area,* 8 miles west-southwest of Kirkwood (lat. 38°38'55" N, long. 120°12'25" W; sec. 9, T 9 N, R 16 E). Named on Tragedy Spring (1979) 7.5' quadrangle.

Willow Flat Creek [EL DORADO]: *stream,* flows 3.25 miles to Sherman Canyon 7.5 miles west-southwest of Kirkwood (lat. 38° 40' N, long. 120°12'15" W; near S line sec. 33, T 10 N, R 16 E); the stream goes through Willow Flat (2). Named on Tragedy Spring (1979) 7.5' quadrangle.

Willow Glen Creek [YUBA]: *stream,* flows 5 miles to Virginia Ranch Reservoir 2.25 miles west-northwest of Oregon House (lat. 39°21'55" N, long. 121°19'10" W; near NE cor. sec. 5, T 17 N, R 6 E). Named on Oregon House (1948, photorevised 1969) and Rackerby (1948) 7.5' quadrangles. The canyon of the stream is called Doubtful Gulch on Wescoatt's (1861) map, which shows Willow Glen House situated in the canyon 3.5 miles west of Frenchtown.

Willow Glen House: see **Willow Glen Creek** [YUBA].

Willow Glen Ridge [YUBA]: *ridge,* generally south-trending, 2 miles long, 4.5 miles south-southeast of Rackerby (lat. 39°22'50" N, long. 121°18'35" W); the ridge is east of Willow Glen Creek. Named on Oregon House (1948) and Rackerby (1948) 7.5' quadrangles.

Willow Hill Reservoir [SACRAMENTO]: *lake,* 800 feet long, 2.25 miles south-southeast of Folsom (lat. 38°38'50" N, long. 121°09'15" W). Named on Folsom (1967) 7.5' quadrangle.

Willow Island [SUTTER]: *area,* less than 1 mile northeast of downtown Yuba City along Sacramento River (lat. 39°09' N, long. 121° 36'25" W). Named on Yuba City (1952, photorevised 1973) 7.5' quadrangle. Shown as an island on Yuba City (1911) 7.5' quadrangle.

Willow Point [YOLO]:

(1) *promontory,* 4 miles west-northwest of Clarksburg along the east edge of Yolo Basin (lat. 38°26'45" N, long. 121°35'30" W). Named on Babel Slough (1916) 7.5' quadrangle. The name appears on Clarksburg (1967) 7.5' quadrangle, but there the nature of the feature is uncertain

(2) *locality,* 1.5 miles west-northwest of Clarksburg along Sacramento Northern Railroad (lat. 38°25'30" N, long. 122°33'10" W); the place is 2.5 miles east-southeast of Willow Point (1). Named on Courtland (1952) 15' quadrangle..

Willow Slough [YOLO]: *stream,* formed by the confluence of North Fork and South Fork, flows 14 miles to an artificial watercourse 8 miles north-northeast of Davis in Yolo Bypass (lat. 38°38'50" N, long. 121°39'55" W; at N line sec. 8, T 9 N, R 3 E). Named on Davis (1954) and Woodland (1953) 15' quadrangles. North Fork is 3 miles long and is named on Woodland (1953) 15' quadrangle. South Fork is 15 miles long and is named on Lake Berryessa (1959) and Woodland (1953) 15' quadrangles.

Willow Slough Bypass [YOLO]: *water feature,* diverges from Willow Slough 4 miles north of Davis (lat. 38°36' N, long. 121°45'10" W; sec. 28, T 9 N, R 2 E) and extends for 7.5 miles to Yolo Bypass. Named on Davis (1952) and Merritt (1952) 7.5' quadrangles.

Willow Spring [NEVADA]:

(1) *spring,* nearly 2 miles north-northeast of North Bloomfield (lat. 39°23'35" N, long. 120°53'25" W; sec. 30, T 18 N, R 10 E). Named on Pike (1949) 7.5' quadrangle.

(2) *spring,* 2 miles east of Graniteville (lat. 39°26'05" N, long. 120° 41'55" W; near SE cor. sec. 11, T 18 N, R 11 E). Named on Graniteville (1982) 7.5' quadrangle.

Willow Spring Creek [YOLO]: *stream,* flows 3.25 miles to lowlands nearly 1 mile southwest of Zamora (lat. 38°47'20" N, long. 121°53'40" W; at W line sec. 20, T 11 N, R 1 E). Named on Zamora (1953) 7.5' quadrangle.

Willow Springs: see **Willow Springs Creek** [AMADOR].

Willow Springs Creek [AMADOR]: *stream,* flows 2.5 miles to Willow Creek 4.25 miles west-southwest of Plymouth (lat. 38°26'50" N, long. 120°54'45" W; sec. 19, T 7 N, R 10 E). Named on Irish Hill (1962) 7.5' quadrangle. Camp's (1962) map shows a place called Willow Springs situated near the confluence of present Willow Springs Creek and Willow Creek.

Willow Valley [NEVADA]:

(1) *valley,* 8 miles south-southwest of North Bloomfield along Deer Creek (lat. 39°16'05" N, long. 120°58'50" W; on E line sec. 8, T 16 N, R 9 E). Named on North Bloomfield (1949) 7.5' quadrangle.

(2) *locality,* 6.5 miles south-southwest of North Bloomfield in present Willow Valley (1) (lat. 39°16'40" N, long. 120°57'50" W). Named on Colfax (1898) 30' quadrangle.

Willow Valley: see **Castle Valley** [NEVADA].

Willow Valley Creek [NEVADA]: *stream,* flows 2 miles to Deer Creek 8 miles south-southwest of North Bloomfield in Willow Valley (1) (lat. 39°16'05" N, long. 120°58'40" W; sec. 9, T 16 N, R 9 E). Named on North Bloomfield (1949) 7.5' quadrangle.

Wilson [EL DORADO]: *locality,* 3.5 miles northeast of Slippery Ford (present Kyburz) (lat. 38°49' N, long. 120°15'30" W). Named on Pyramid Peak

(1896) 30' quadrangle.

Wilson [SUTTER]: *locality,* 5.5 miles north-northwest of Nicolaus along Southern Pacific Railroad (lat. 38°58'40" N, long. 121°37'25" W; sec. 15, T 13 N, R 3 E). Named on Nicolaus (1952) 7.5' quadrangle.

Wilson Camp [COLUSA]: *locality,* 4.25 miles west of Pacific Point (lat. 39°13'40" N, long. 122°40'20" W). Named on Clearlake Oaks (1960) 15' quadrangle.

Wilson Canyon [COLUSA]: *canyon,* 2.25 miles long, along Walters Creek above a point 7 miles east of Wilbur Springs (lat. 39°02'50" N, long. 122°17'30" W; sec. 22, T 14 N, R 4 W). Named on Wilbur Springs (1961) 15' quadrangle.

Wilson Creek [COLUSA]: *stream,* drained by a stream that flows 2.5 miles to Squaw Creek 1.5 miles north-northeast of Lodoga (lat. 39° 19'10" N, long. 122°28' W; near SW cor. sec. 18, T 17 N, R 5 W). Named on Lodoga (1960) 15' quadrangle.

Wilson Creek [YUBA]: *stream,* heads in Butte County and flows 3.5 miles along Yuba-Butte County line to South Honcut Creek 11.5 miles north of Marysville (lat. 39°18'40" N, long. 121°35' W). Named on Honcut (1952) 7.5' quadrangle. Called South Honcut Creek on Marysville (1895) 30' quadrangle.

Wilsons Ranch: see **Emigrant Gap** [PLACER] (2).

Wilson Valley: see **Carpenter Flat** [PLACER].

Wilton [SACRAMENTO]: *locality,* 5 miles east of Elk Grove along Central California Traction Railroad (lat. 38°24'40" N, long. 121° 16'15" W). Named on Elk Grove (1968) 7.5' quadrangle. Postal authorities established Wilton post office in 1914 (Frickstad, p. 135). The name commemorates Seth A. Wilton, who owned land at the place (Gudde, 1949, p. 391).

Winchester Lake [YOLO]: *lake,* extends for 2.5 miles from near Babel Slough almost to Sacramento River 1 mile north-northwest of Clarksburg (lat. 38°25'45" N, long. 121°32' W). Named on Clarksburg (1967) 7.5' quadrangle.

Windmill Draw [SACRAMENTO]: *canyon,* drained by a stream that flows 2.25 miles to Laguna 5.5 miles northeast of Galt (lat. 38°18'40" N, long. 121°13'25" W; near W line sec. 4, T 5 N, R 7 E). Named on Clay (1968) 7.5' quadrangle.

Windmiller Ravine [EL DORADO]: *canyon,* drained by a stream that flows 2 miles to South Fork Silver Creek 3 miles northeast of Riverton (lat. 38°48'10" N, long. 120°24'35" W; sec. 16, T 11 N, R 14 E). Named on Riverton (1950) 7.5' quadrangle.

Windmuller [EL DORADO]: *locality,* 9 miles southeast of Robbs Peak (lat. 38°49'55" N, long. 120°17'25" W). Named on Pyramid Peak (1896) 30' quadrangle. Kyburz (1952) 7.5' quadrangle shows Windmiller cabin at or near the place.

Wind River: see **Little Truckee River** [NEVADA-SIERRA].

Windy Point [COLUSA]: *relief feature,* at the end of a ridge 9 miles north of Wilbur Springs (lat. 39°10' N, long. 122°24' W). Named on Wilbur Springs (1961) 15' quadrangle.

Windy Point [PLACER]: *relief feature,* 2 miles east-southeast of Colfax (lat. 39°05'20" N, long. 120°54'55" W; sec. 1, T 14 N, R 9 E). Named on Colfax (1949) 7.5' quadrangle.

Windy Point [YOLO]: *peak,* 2 miles southeast of Berryessa Peak along Rocky Ridge on Yolo-Napa County line (lat. 38°38'40" N, long. 122°09'35" W). Named on Brooks (1959) 7.5' quadrangle.

Windy Point Cliffs [NEVADA]: *relief feature,* 4 miles east of Graniteville (lat. 39°25'45" N, long. 120°40' W; sec. 18, T 18 N, R 12 E). Named on Graniteville (1982) 7.5' quadrangle.

Winifred: see **Lake Winifred** [EL DORADO].

Winnie Smith Mill [SIERRA]:

(1) *locality,* 5 miles northeast of Sierraville in Antelope Valley (lat. 39°38' N, long. 120°17' W; near NW cor. sec. 34, T 21 N, R 15 E). Ruins named on Sierraville (1955) 15' quadrangle.

(2) *locality,* 16 miles south-southeast of Loyalton along Dry Creek (lat. 39°27' N, long. 120°08'25" W; near SW cor. sec. 31, T 31 N, R 17 E). Site named on Hobart Mills (1981) 7.5' quadrangle.

Winters [YOLO]: *town,* 15 miles southwest of Woodland (lat. 38°31'20" N, long. 121°58'15" W). Named on Winters (1953) 7.5' quadrangle. Postal authorities established Winters post office in 1875 (Frickstad, p. 222), and the town incorporated in 1898. The name is for Theodore W. Winters, who donated half of the land for the town (Gudde, 1949, p. 392). Postal authorities established Buckeye post office 6 miles northeast of Winters in 1855 and discontinued it in 1875; the name came from buckeye trees at the place (Salley, p. 28).

Winters Flat [YOLO]: *area,* 4.5 miles south-southwest of Guinda (lat. 38°46'05" N, long. 122°13'50" W; near SE cor. sec. 30, T 11 N, R 3 W). Named on Guinda (1959) 7.5' quadrangle.

Winton: see **Camp Winton** [AMADOR].

Wisconsin Bar: see **Bucks Bar** [EL DORADO]; **Grapevine Ravine** [AMADOR].

Wisconsin Gulch [EL DORADO]: *canyon,* drained by a stream that flows 1 mile to Steely Fork Cosumnes River 9 miles southeast of Camino (lat. 38°38'10" N, long. 120°34'45" W; sec. 18, T 9 N, R 13 E). Named on Sly Park (1952) 7.5' quadrangle.

Wisconsin Hill: see **Refuge Canyon** [PLACER].

Wisconsin House: see **Junction House** [YUBA].

Wolf [NEVADA]: *locality,* 11.5 miles south-southwest of Grass Valley (lat. 39°03'35" N, long. 121°08'20" W; near SE cor. sec. 13, T 14 N, R 7 E); the place is near the head of Little Wolf Creek (2). Named on Wolf (1949) 7.5' quadrangle. Postal authorities established Wolf post office in 1888, moved it 0.5 mile south in 1940, and discontinued it in 1956 (Salley, p. 242).

Wolf Creek [NEVADA]: *stream,* flows 22 miles to Bear River nearly 2 miles south-southeast of Wolf (lat. 39°02'05" N, long. 121°07'45" W; sec. 30, T 14 N, R 8 E). Named on Chicago Park (1949), Grass Valley (1949), Lake Combie (1949), and Wolf (1949) 7.5' quadrangles. South Fork enters the main stream in downtown Grass Valley; it is nearly 3 miles long and is named on Grass Valley (1949) 7.5' quadrangle.

Wolf Creek [SIERRA]: *stream,* flows 6.5 miles to Middle Yuba River 3 miles southeast of Alleghany (lat. 39°26'40" N, long. 120° 48'15" W; near N line sec. 12, T 18 N, R 10 E). Named on Alleghany (1949) and Graniteville (1982) 7.5' quadrangles.

Wolf Creek: see **Little Wolf Creek** [NEVADA]; **Little Wolf Creek** [SIERRA]; **Mill Creek** [EL DORADO] (2); **South Wolf Creek** [NEVADA].

Wolf Creek Mountain: see **Wolf Mountain** [NEVADA].

Wolf Glade [COLUSA]: *area,* 4.25 miles west-southwest of Stonyford (lat. 39°21'35" N, long. 122°37'20" W). Named on Gilmore Peak (1968) 7.5' quadrangle.

Wolf Mountain [NEVADA]: *peak,* 6 miles south-southwest of Grass Valley (lat. 39°08' N, long. 121°05'55" W; near SW cor. sec. 21, T 15 N, R 8 E). Altitude 2632 feet. Named on Grass Valley (1949) 7.5' quadrangle. Called Wolf Creek Mountain on Smartsville (1895) 30' quadrangle—the feature is west of Wolf Creek. Whitney's (1873) map has the name "Wolf Creek Mts." near present Wolf Mountain.

Wolverine: see **Monona Flat** [PLACER].

Woodcamp Campground [NEVADA]: *locality,* 2.5 miles north of English Mountain (lat. 39°29'10" N, long. 120°32'55" W; near E line sec. 30, T 19 N, R 13 E); the place is at the mouth of Woodcamp Creek. Named on English Mountain (1983) 7.5' quadrangle.

Woodcamp Creek [NEVADA]: *stream,* flows 1.25 miles to Jackson Meadows Reservoir 2.5 miles north of English Mountain (lat. 39° 29'10" N, long. 120°33' W; near E line sec. 30, T 19 N, R 13 E). Named on English Mountain (1983) 7.5' quadrangle.

Wood Canyon [YOLO]: *canyon,* 6 miles east-northeast of Guinda along South Fork Buckeye Creek (lat. 38°50'45" N, long. 122°05'30" W). Named on Bird Valley (1959) 7.5' quadrangle.

Woodchoppers Spring [NEVADA]: *spring,* 2.25 miles east of Hobart Mills (lat. 39°24'20" N, long. 120°08'30" W; near SW cor. sec. 18, T 18 N, R 17 E). Named on Hobart Mills (1981) 7.5' quadrangle.

Woodchuck Flat [NEVADA]: *area,* 5.5 miles east-northeast of Yuba Gap (lat. 39°20'05" N, long. 120°30'55" W; near SE cor. sec. 16, T 17 N, R 13 E). Named on Cisco Grove (1955) 7.5' quadrangle.

Wood-Curtis Landing [SACRAMENTO]:

(1) *locality,* 9.5 miles southwest of Isleton along Sacramento River on Sherman Island (lat. 38°04'50" N, long. 121°45'05" W). Named on Collinsville (1918) 7.5' quadrangle.

(2) *locality,* 12 miles southwest of Isleton along San Joaquin River on Sherman Island (lat. 38°01'50" N, long. 121°45'35" W). Named on Collinsville (1918) 7.5' quadrangle.

Wood Island [SACRAMENTO]: *island,* 7300 feet long, 4.25 miles west of Isleton in Sacramento River (lat. 38°09'10" N, long. 121° 41'05" W). Named on Rio Vista (1910) 7.5' quadrangle. Called Gillespie I. on Ringgold's (1850b) map, which shows Pt. Burnett at the south end of the feature. The island has disappeared.

Woodland [YOLO]: *city,* in the east-central part of Yolo County (lat. 38°40'40" N, long. 121°46'25" W; in and around sec. 29, 32, T 10 N, R 2 E). Named on Woodland (1952) 7.5' quadrangle. Postal authorities established Woodland post office in 1861 (Frickstad, p. 222), and the city incorporated in 1874. The place was settled in 1853 and had the name "Yolo City" before the post office opened (Hoover, Rensch, and Rensch, p. 585). Postal authorities established Paramount post office 8.5 miles east of Woodland (NE quarter sec. 34, T 10 N, R 3 E) in 1916 and discontinued it in 1919 (Salley, p. 167).

Woodleaf [YUBA]: *village,* 2.5 miles northeast of Challenge (lat. 39°31'05" N, long. 121°11'30" W; sec. 9, T 19 N, R 7 E). Named on Clipper Mills (1948) 7.5' quadrangle. Called Woodville on Bidwell Bar (1897) 30' quadrangle. Postal authorities established Woodleaf post office in 1898, discontinued it in 1945, reestablished it in 1947, and discontinued it in 1971 (Salley, p. 243). The place first was known as Barker's Ranch or Barker House; Charles Barker settled there in 1850 and James Wood bought the property in 1858 (Hoover, Rensch, and Rensch, p. 594).

Woodleaf Creek [YUBA]: *stream,* mainly in Butte County, but flows for 0.5 mile in Yuba County 3 miles north-northeast of Challenge (lat. 39°31'35" N, long. 121°11'25" W; sec. 9, T 19 N, R 7 E); the stream is 0.5 mile north-northeast of Woodleaf. Named on Clipper Mills (1948) 7.5'

quadrangle.

Woodpecker Gulch [EL DORADO]: *canyon,* drained by a stream that flows 0.5 mile to Cedar Canyon 9 miles southeast of Camino (lat. 38°39'05" N, long. 120°33'10" W; at W line sec. 9, T 9 N, R 13 E). Named on Sly Park (1952) 7.5' quadrangle.

Woodpecker Ravine [NEVADA]: *canyon,* drained by a stream that flows 4.5 miles to South Wolf Creek 6 miles south-southeast of Grass Valley (lat. 39°08'15" N, long. 121°00'55" W; sec. 19, T 15 N, R 9 E). Named on Grass Valley (1949) 7.5' quadrangle.

Woodpile Gulch [AMADOR]: *canyon,* 1 mile long, 7 miles southwest of Jackson (lat. 38°16'25" N, long. 120°51'35" W; sec. 22, T 5 N, R 10 E). Named on Jackson (1962) 7.5' quadrangle. Water of North Arm Pardee Reservoir now floods most of the canyon.

Woodruff Creek [SIERRA]: *stream,* flows about 2.5 miles to Rock Creek (3) 0.25 mile south-southwest of Goodyears Bar (lat. 39°32'10" N, long. 120°53'05" W; near S line sec. 5, T 19 N, R 10 E). Named on Goodyears Bar (1951) 7.5' quadrangle.

Woods Creek [YUBA]: *stream,* flows 4 miles to Englebright Reservoir (present Englebright Lake) 5.25 miles south of Oregon House (lat. 39°16'55" N, long. 121°15'50" W; near S line sec. 35, T 17 N, R 6 E). Named on French Corral (1948) and Oregon House (1948) 7.5' quadrangles. Called Union Creek on Wescoatt's (1861) map, which shows a place called Union Bar at the mouth of the stream.

Wood's Dry Diggings: see **Auburn** [PLACER].

Woods Lake [SUTTER]: *intermittent lake,* 1500 feet long, 2.5 miles north-northwest of Meridian near Sacramento River (lat. 39°10'35" N, long. 121°56' W; sec. 2, T 15 N, R 1 W). Named on Meridian (1952) 7.5' quadrangle.

Woodville: see **Woodleaf** [YUBA].

Woodville Creek: see **Indian Creek** [YUBA].

Wooley Creek [PLACER]: *stream,* flows 4 miles to Lake Combie 7.5 miles south-southwest of Colfax (lat. 39°00'20" N, long. 121° 02'30" W; at W line sec. 1, T 13 N, R 8 E). Named on Lake Combie (1949) 7.5' quadrangle. Called Coyote Creek on Smartsville (1895) 30' quadrangle.

Woolford: see **King Woolford Mill** [NEVADA].

Woolsey Flat [NEVADA]:

(1) *locality,* 8.5 miles northeast of North Bloomfield along Middle Yuba River (lat. 39°27' N, long. 120°46'35" W; near SE cor. sec. 6, T 18 N, R 11 E). Named on Alleghany (1949) 7.5' quadrangle. Colfax (1938) 30' quadrangle shows Woolsey cabin at or near the place.

(2) *locality,* 4 miles north-northeast of North Bloomfield (lat. 39° 25' N, long. 120°51'30" W; at N line sec. 21, T 18 N, R 10 E). Named on Alleghany (1949) 7.5' quadrangle.

Woolsey Spring: see **Upper Woolsey Spring** [NEVADA].

Woosterville: see **Ione** [AMADOR].

Worn Mill Canyon [SIERRA]: *canyon,* drained by a stream that flows 3.25 miles to Little Truckee River 6 miles south of Crystal Peak (lat. 39°28'05" N, long. 120°06'05" W; near W line sec. 28, T 19 N, R 17 E). Named on Boca (1955) 7.5' quadrangle.

Wrights Lake [EL DORADO]: *lake,* 3250 feet long, 4 miles west of Pyramid Peak (lat. 38°50'55" N, long. 120°13'55" W; near NE cor. sec. 32, T 12 N, R 16 E). Named on Pyramid Peak (1955) 7.5' quadrangle. Pyramid Peak (1896) 30' quadrangle has the name "Wrights Lakes" for present Wrights Lake, Dark Lake, and Beauty Lake together.

Wrights Lakes: see **Wrights Lake** [EL DORADO].

Wulffs [EL DORADO]: *locality,* 5 miles north-northeast of Clarksville (lat. 38°43'20" N, long. 121°01'05" W). Named on Sacramento (1892) 30' quadrangle.

Wycoff [YOLO]: *locality,* 5.5 miles northwest of Zamora along Southern Pacific Railroad (lat. 38°51'35" N, long. 121°56'45" W; sec. 26, T 12 N, R 1 E). Named on Zamora (1916) 7.5' quadrangle.

—X - Y—

Yagers Gulch [AMADOR]: *canyon,* drained by a stream that flows less than 0.5 mile to Pardee Reservoir 6.25 miles southwest of Jackson (lat. 38°17'05" N, long. 120°51'15" W; sec. 15, T 5 N, R 10 E). Named on Jackson (1962) 7.5' quadrangle.

Yankee Jim Gulch: see **Snyder Canyon** [PLACER].

Yankee Jims [PLACER]: *settlement,* 2.5 miles west-northwest of Foresthill (lat. 39°01'45" N, long. 120°51'40" W; sec. 28, T 14 N, R 10 E). Named on Foresthill (1949) 7.5' quadrangle. Called Yankee Jim on Colfax (1898) 30' quadrangle. Postal authorities established Yankee Jim's post office in 1852 and discontinued it in 1940 (Frickstad, p. 122). The name is for an Australian criminal who had the nickname "Yankee" and who held stolen horses at the site before the discovery of gold there (Jackson, J.H., p. 398-399). A mining camp called Yorkville was located 1.5 miles north of Yankee Jims, where gold was discovered in 1853 (Gudde, 1975, p. 379).

Yankee Jims Cañon: see **Mexican Gulch** [PLACER].

Yankee John Creek [EL DORADO]: *stream,* flows 2.25 miles to Slab Creek nearly 6 miles west-northwest of Pollock Pines (lat. 38° 47'40" N, long. 120°40'50" W; near S line sec. 18, T 11 N, R 12 E). Named on Slate Mountain (1950) 7.5' quadrangle. Placerville (1893) 30' quadrangle has the name "Yankee John Rav." for the canyon of the stream.

Yankee John Ravine: see **Yankee John Creek** [EL DORADO].

Yankee Slough [PLACER-SUTTER]: *water feature,* heads in Placer County and flows for 8 miles in Sutter County to Bear River nearly 5 miles north-northeast of Nicolaus (lat. 38°58'10" N, long. 121° 32'35" W; near SE cor. sec. 17, T 13 N, R 4 E). Named on Nicolaus (1952) and Sheridan (1953, photorevised 1973) 7.5' quadrangles.

Yanks [EL DORADO]: *locality,* 3.5 miles northeast of Mount Tallac along Lake Tahoe (lat. 38°56'10" N, long. 120°02'40" W). Named on Pyramid Peak (1896) 30' quadrangle.

Yanks: see **Meyers** [EL DORADO].

Yank's Station: see **Meyers** [EL DORADO].

Yellow Jacket Canyon [PLACER]: *canyon,* drained by a stream that flows 1 mile to Duncan Canyon 5.25 miles south-southwest of Duncan Peak (lat. 39°04'50" N, long. 120°32' W; sec. 9, T 14 N, R 13 E). Named on Greek Store (1952) 7.5' quadrangle.

Yellow Jacket Creek [PLACER]: *stream,* drained by a stream that flows less than 1 mile to Shirttail Canyon 3.5 miles north-northeast of Foresthill (lat. 39°04'10" N, long. 120°48'05" W; sec. 12, T 14 N, R 10 E). Named on Foresthill (1949) 7.5' quadrangle.

Yellowjacket Creek [YUBA]: *stream,* flows nearly 2 miles to Marys Ravine 4.25 miles east of Dobbins (lat. 39°22'55" N, long. 121°07'35" W). Named on Camptonville (1948) 7.5' quadrangle.

Yeomet: see **Enterprise** [AMADOR].

Yolo [YOLO]: *village,* 4.25 miles north-northwest of Woodland along Cache Creek (lat. 38°44' N, long. 121°48'25" W). Named on Woodland (1952) 7.5' quadrangle. Postal authorities established Yolo post office in 1853 (Frickstad, p. 222). In 1849 Thomas Cochran settled at the place, which became known as Cochrans Crossing; in 1853 James A. Hutton built a hostelry at the site, which then was called Huttons Ranch or Travelers Home until 1857, when the community was renamed Cacheville—a name that persisted until the post office opened (Hanna, p. 361). Hudson's Bay Company trappers occupied a site called French Camp that was situated on the north bank of Cache Creek about 1 mile east of present Yolo (Hoover, Rensch, and Rensch, p. 583).

Yolo Basin: see **Yolo Bypass** [YOLO].

Yolo Bypass [YOLO]: *area,* lowlands that extend south from Sacramento River 4.5 miles east-southeast of Knights Landing to Solano County 10 miles south-southwest of Clarksburg. Named on Clarksburg (1967), Davis (1952), Grays Bend (1953), Knights Landing (1952), Liberty Island (1978), Sacramento West (1967), Saxon (1952), and Taylor Monument (1967) 7.5' quadrangles. Courtland (1908) and Davisville (1907) 15' quadrangles have the name "Yolo Basin" in the vicinity of present Yolo Bypass.

Yolo City: see **Woodland** [YOLO].

Yolo House: see **Davis** [YOLO].

Yomana: see **Forest** [SIERRA].

Yore: see **Pat Yore Flat** [NEVADA].

York: see **Little York** [NEVADA].

York Diggings: see **Little York Diggings** [NEVADA].

Yorkville: see **Yankee Jims** [PLACER].

Yornet: see **Yeomet**, under **Enterprise** [AMADOR].

You Bet [NEVADA]: *locality,* 5.5 miles northeast of Chicago Park (lat. 39°12'35" N, long. 120°53'50" W; sec. 31, T 16 N, R 10 E). Named on Chicago Park (1949) 7.5' quadrangle. Postal authorities established You Bet post office in 1868 and discontinued it in 1903 (Frickstad, p. 115). The name is from the favorite expression of a saloonkeeper at the place (Browne, p. 21-22). Whitney's (1873) map shows a mining camp called Waloupa located less than 1 mile south of You Bet. The name "Waloupa" or "Walloupa" was for an Indian chief; the place started in 1852, but by 1860 the remains of the community had moved to You Bet (Browne, p. 21). Whitney's (1873) map also shows a canyon called Williams Ravine that heads near You Bet and extends west-northwest for 1.25 miles to Greenhorn Creek. Gudde (1975, p. 47) listed a feature called Browns Hill that was located about 0.25 mile east of You Bet and named for Giles S. Brown, one of the brothers who owned a mine there.

Young America Canyon [PLACER]: *canyon,* drained by a stream that flows less than 1 mile to Stevens Ravine 2 miles north of Foresthill (lat. 39°03' N, long. 120°49'10" W; sec. 23, T 14 N, R 10 E). Named on Foresthill (1949) 7.5' quadrangle.

Youngs: see **Dad Youngs Spring** [PLACER]; **Somerset** [EL DORADO].

Youngs Hill [YUBA]:

(1) *peak,* 2 miles north-northwest of Camptonville (lat. 39°28'45" N, long. 121°03'40" W; near SE cor. sec. 27, T 19 N, R 8 E). Named on Camptonville (1948) 7.5' quadrangle.

(2) *locality,* 2 miles north-northeast of Camptonville (lat. 39°28'55" N, long. 121°03'45" W); the place is near present Youngs Hill (1). Named on Smartsville (1895) 30' quadrangle. The name is for William Young and his brother, who discovered gold at the place in 1852 (Hanna, p. 362).

Young's River: see **Putah Creek** [YOLO].
Yuba: see **Camp Yuba** [SIERRA]; **Rupert Siding** [YUBA]; **South Yuba** [YUBA].
Yuba Butte: see **Sierra Buttes** [SIERRA].
Yuba City [SUTTER]: *town,* along Feather River at the east edge of the north part of Sutter County (lat. 39°08'25" N, long. 121°37' W); the town is opposite the mouth of Yuba River. Named on Olivehurst (1952), Sutter (1952), and Yuba City (1952) 7.5' quadrangles. Postal authorities established Yuba City post office in 1851 (Frickstad, p. 203), and the town incorporated in 1908. Samuel Brannan and others had the community laid out in 1849 (Hoover, Rensch, and Rensch, p. 546).
Yuba County House: see **Oregon House** [YUBA].
Yuba Gap [NEVADA]: *locality,* 2 miles west of Truckee near Nevada-Placer County line (lat. 39°19' N, long. 120°37' W; near N line sec. 27, T 17 N, R 12 E). Named on Emigrant Gap (1955) 15' quadrangle. Called Yuba Pass on Colfax (1938) 30' quadrangle.
Yuba Gold Field [YUBA]: *area,* along and south of Yuba River; center 4 miles south-southwest of Browns Valley (lat. 39°12'15" N, long. 121°26'15" W); tailings from gold dredging operations cover the area. Named on Browns Valley (1947, photorevised 1973) 7.5' quadrangle.
Yuba Pass [NEVADA]:
(1) *pass,* 1 mile northeast of Yuba Gap (lat. 39°19' N, long. 120°35'55" W; sec. 23, T 17 N, R 12 E). Named on Emigrant Gap (1955) 15' quadrangle.
(2) *locality,* 1 mile east-northeast of Yuba Gap along Southern Pacific Railroad (lat. 39°19'25" N, long. 120°35'55" W; sec. 23, T 17 N, R 12 E); the place is at Yuba Pass (1). Named on Cisco Grove (1955, photorevised 1973) 7.5' quadrangle.
Yuba Pass: see **Yuba Gap** [NEVADA].
Yuba Reservoir [NEVADA]: *lake,* 1100 feet long, 5.5 miles north-northwest of Chicago Park (lat. 39°13'25" N, long. 120°59'15" W; sec. 29, T 16 N, R 9 E). Named on Chicago Park (1949, photorevised 1973) 7.5' quadrangle.
Yuba River [NEVADA-YUBA]: *stream,* formed by the confluence of Middle Yuba River and North Yuba River, flows 37 miles, partly along Nevada-Yuba County line, to Feather River 1.25 miles south-southwest of downtown Marysville (lat. 39°07'40" N, long. 121°35'50" W). Named on Browns Valley (1947, photorevised 1973), French Corral (1948), Oregon House (1948), Smartville (1951, photorevised 1973), and Yuba City (1952, photorevised 1973) 7.5' quadrangles. Called Rio de Yuba on Larkin's (1848) map, and called Juba C. [Creek] on Ord's (1848) map. Work called the stream Middle Fork of Feather River in 1833 (Maloney *in* Work, p. 95). The name "Yuba" is derived from the designation of an Indian village that was near the mouth of the stream (Kroeber, p. 68). The name had a variety of forms in the early days, including "Yubah" (Dana, 1949a, p. 125), "Uba" (Lyman, p. 307), "Uber" and "Yu ba" (Cook, E.W., p. 36), and "Juber" (Ingersoll, p. 42). On Smartsville (1895) 30' quadrangle, the part of present Yuba River between the mouth of present Middle Yuba River and the mouth of present South Yuba River is called Middle Fork Yuba River, but United States Board on Geographic Names (1950, p. 7) rejected the names "Middle Fork" and "Middle Fork Yuba River" for this reach. Yuba City (1911) 7.5' quadrangle shows a distributary of Yuba River, also called Yuba River, located about 1 mile southeast of the lower part of present Yuba River, and nearly parallel to it; the dry course of the distributary has the label "Old River Channel" on Yuba City (1952) 7.5' quadrangle.
Yuba River: see **Middle Yuba River** [NEVADA-SIERRA-YUBA]; **North Yuba River** [SIERRA-YUBA]; **South Yuba River** [NEVADA-PLACER].
Yuba Valley: see **Summit Valley** [NEVADA-PLACER].

— Z —

Zachary: see **Lodoga** [COLUSA].
Zamora [YOLO]: *village,* 10 miles northwest of Woodland (lat. 38°47'45" N, long. 121°52'50" W; sec. 17, T 11 N, R 1 E). Named on Zamora (1953) 7.5' quadrangle. Dunnigan (1907) 15' quadrangle shows Blacks Station P.O. at the place, and California Mining Bureau's (1909c) map has the name "Blacks" there. Postal authorities established Prairie post office in 1857, changed the name to Black's Station in 1876, and to Zamora in 1915 (Frickstad, p. 221, 222).
Zamora Creek [YOLO]: *stream,* flows 2.5 miles to lowlands 1.25 miles west of Zamora (lat. 38°47'50" N, long. 121°54'25" W; sec. 18, T 11 N, R 1 E). Named on Zamora (1953) 7.5' quadrangle.
Zanjon de los Moquelumnes: see **Sanjon de los Moquelumnes** [SACRAMENTO].
Zero Spring [EL DORADO]: *spring,* 16 miles north-northwest of Pollock Pines (lat. 38°58'35" N, long. 120°41'40" W; sec. 13, T 13 N, R 11 E). Named on Tunnel Hill (1950) 7.5' quadrangle.
Zinc House: see **Mooney Flat** [NEVADA].
Zion: see **Mount Zion** [AMADOR]; **Mount Zion**, under **Snow Tent** [NEVADA].
Zion Hill [NEVADA]: *peak,* nearly 3 miles north-northwest of Yuba Gap (lat. 39°21'10" N, long. 120°38'05" W; sec. 9, T 17 N, R 12 E). Altitude 6204 feet. Named on Blue Canyon (1955) 7.5' quadrangle.
Zitella: see **Lake Zitella** [EL DORADO].
Zodoc: see **Placerville** [EL DORADO].
Zumwalt [EL DORADO]: *locality,* 9.5 miles northwest of Leek Spring Hill (lat. 38°43'10" N, long. 120°24'40" W). Named on Pyramid Peak (1896) 30' quadrangle.
Zumwalt Flat: see **Downieville** [SIERRA].
Zuver [PLACER]: *locality,* 3 miles west-northwest of Devil Peak (lat. 38°58'25" N, long. 120°35'55" W; sec. 14, T 13 N, R 12 E). Named on Devil Peak (1950) 7.5' quadrangle, which shows Zuver mine situated 0.5 mile east of the place

South Sacramento Valley Region
Amador, Colusa, El Dorado, Nevada, Placer, Sacramento, Sierra, Sutter, Yolo and Yuba Counties

References Cited

BOOKS AND ARTICLES

Anderson, Winslow. 1892. *Mineral springs and health resorts of California.* San Francisco: The Bancroft Company, 347 p.

Andrews, John R. 1978. *The ghost towns of Amador.* Fresno, California: Valley Publishers, 137 p.

Arreola, Daniel D. 1975. "The Chinese role in the making of the early cultural landscape of the Sacramento-San Joaquin Delta." *The California Geographer,* v. 15, p. 1-15.

Bancroft, Hubert Howe. 1888. *History of California, Volume VI, 1848-1859.* San Francisco: The History Company, Publishers, 787 p.

_____1890. *History of California, Volume VII, 1860-1890.* San Francisco: The History Company, Publishers, 826 p.

Becker, Robert H. 1969. *Designs on the land.* San Francisco: The Book Club of California, (no pagination).

Blenkle, Joe. 1976. *Gold, blood, water, Folsom-Auburn and the Mother Lode.* Sacramento, California: Western Wonder Publications, 44 p.

Borthwick, J.D. 1857. *Three years in California.* Edinburgh and London: William Blackwood and Sons, 384 p.

Boyd, William Harland. 1972. *A California middle boarder, The Kern River country, 1772-1880.* Richardson, Texas: The Havilah Press, 226 p.

Bradley, Walter W. 1915. "The counties of Colusa, Glenn, Lake, Marin, Napa, Solano, Sonoma, Yolo." *Report XIV of the State Mineralogist.* Sacramento: California State Mining Bureau, p. 173-370.

Brewer, William H.. 1949. *Up and down California in 1860-1864.* Berkeley and Los Angeles: University of California Press, 583 p.

Brotherton, I.N. 1982. *Annals of Stanislaus County, Volume I, River towns and ferries.* Santa Cruz: Western Tanager Press, 180 p.

Browne, J. Ross, and Taylor, James W. 1867. *Reports upon the mineral resources of the United States.* Washington: Government Printing Office, 360 p.

Browne, Juanita Kennedy. 1983. *Nuggets of Nevada County history.* Nevada City, California: Nevada County Historical Society, 143 p.

Buffum, E. Gould. 1850. *Six months in the gold mines; From a journal of three years' residence in Upper and Lower California, 1847-8-9.* Philadelphia: Lea and Blanchard, 172 p.

Burrows, Rufus, and Hall, Cyrus. 1971. *A long road to Stony Creek.* (Introduction and annotations by Richard Dillon.) Ashland: Lewis Osborne, 71 p.

California Division of Highways. 1934. *California highway transportation survey, 1934.* Sacramento: Department of Public Works, Division of Highways, 130 p. + appendices.

Canfield, Chauncey L. (editor). 1920. *The diary of a forty-niner.* Boston and New York: Houghton Mifflin Company, 253 p.

Chandler, Albert E. 1901. *Water storage, Cache Creek, California.* (United States Geological Survey Water-Supply and Irrigation Papers No. 45.) Washington: Government Printing Office, 48 p.

Christy, Thomas. 1969. *Thomas Christy's road across the Plains.* (Edited by Robert H. Becker.) Denver, Colorado: Old West Publishing Company, (no pagination).

Clark, William B. 1970. *Gold districts of California.* (California Division of Mines and Geology Bulletin 193.) San Francisco: California Division of Mines and Geology, 186 p.

Clyman, James. 1960. *James Clyman, frontiersman.* Portland, Oregon: Champoeg Press, 352 p.

Cook, Elliott Wilkinson. 1935. *Land Ho! The original diary of a forty-niner.* Baltimore: The Remington-Putnam Book Company, 43 p.

Cook, Fred S. (No date) a. *Legends of the Southern Mines.* (No place): California Traveler, 64 p.

_____(editor). (No date) b. *Historic legends of Colusa County.* Volcano, California: California Traveler, Inc., 32 p.

Cowan, Robert G. 1956. *Ranchos of California.* Fresno, California: Academy Library Guild, 151 p.

Coy, Owen C. 1923. *California county boundaries.* Berkeley: California Historical Survey Commission, 335 p.

Crawford, J.J. 1894. "Report of the State Mineralogist." *Twelfth report of the State Mineralogist, (Second Biennial,) two years ending September 15, 1894.* Sacramento: California State Mining Bureau, p. 8-412.

_____1896. "Report of the State Mineralogist." *Thirteenth report (Third Biennial) of the State Mineralogist for the two years ending September 15, 1896.* Sacramento: California State Mining Bureau, p. 10-646.

Dana, James D. 1849a. "Gold in California." *American Journal of Science and Arts* (series 2), v. 7, no. 19, p. 125-126.

_____1849b. "Notes on Upper California." *American Journal of Science and Arts* (series 2), v. 7, no. 20, p. 247-264.

Davis, Leonard M. 1975. *Dry diggings on the North Fork; Personal observations of Auburn, California, in the days of '49.* (No place): Placer County Museum Foundation, 47 p.

Day, Sherman. 1856. "Hon. Sherman Day's report on the immigrant wagon road explorations." *Annual Report of the Surveyor-General of the State of California.* (Sen. Doc.No. 5, Sess. of 1856.) Sacramento: State printer, p. 77-84.

Decker, Peter. 1966. *The diaries of Peter Decker, Overland to California in 1849 and life in the mines 1850-1851.* (Edited by Helen S. Giffen.) Georgetown, California: The Talisman Press, 338 p.

Derby, Geo. H., 1850. "Topographical memoir accompanying maps of the Sacramento valley, &c." *Report of the Secretary of War, Part II.* (31st Cong., 1st Sess., Sen. Ex. Doc. 47.) Washington: p. 3-16.

Dillon, Richard. 1982. *Delta country.* Novato, California: Presidio Press, 134 p.

Doble, John, 1962. *John Doble's journal and letters from the mines, Mokelumne Hill, Jackson, Volcano, and San Francisco, 1851-1865.* (Edited by Charles L. Camp.) Denver, Colorado: The Old West Publishing Company, 304 p.

Durst, David M. 1916. "Physiographic features of Cache Creek in Yolo County." *University of California Publications in Geography,* v. 1, no. 8, p. 331-372.

Farquhar, Francis P. 1930. "Fremont in the Sierra Nevada." *Sierra Club Bulletin,* v. 15, no. 1, p. 74-95.

_____1965. *History of the Sierra Nevada.* Berkeley, Los Angeles, London: University of California Press, 262 p.

Fatout, Paul. 1969. *Meadow Lake gold town.* Bloomington, London: Indiana University Press, 178 p.

Fremont, J.C. 1845. *Report of the exploring expedition to the Rocky Mountains in the year 1842, and to Oregon and North California in the years 1843-'44.* Washington: Blair and Rives, Printers, 583 p.

Frickstad, Walter N. 1955. *A century of California post offices, 1848 to 1954.* Oakland, California: Philatelic Research Society, 395 p.

Gernes, Phyllis. 1979. *Hidden in the chaparral.* Garden Valley, California: (Author), 209 p.

Goodyear, W.A. 1890. "Colusa County." *Tenth annual report of the State Mineralogist, for the year ending December 1, 1890.* Sacramento: California State Mining Bureau, p. 153-164.

Grimshaw, William Robinson. 1964. *Grimshaw's narrative.* (Edited by J.R.K. Kantor.) (No place): Sacramento Book Collectors Club, 59 p.

Gudde, Erwin G. 1949. *California place names.* Berkeley and Los Angeles: University of California Press, 431 p.

_____1969. *California place names.* Berkeley and Los Angeles: University of California Press, 416 p.

_____1975. *California gold camps.* Berkeley, Los Angeles, London: University of California Press, 467 p.

Gwinn, William H. 1971. "The Freeport Railroad 1863-1865." *Golden Notes* (Sacramento County Historical Society), v. 17, no. 1, p. 1-10.

Hanna, Phil Townsend. 1951. *The dictionary of California land names.* Los Angeles: The Automobile Club of Southern California, 392 p.

Hart, Herbert M. 1965. *Old forts of the Far West.* New York: Bonanza Books, 192 p.

Hart, James D. 1978. *A companion to California.* New York: Oxford University Press, 504 p.

Hendrix, Louise Butts. 1985. *Sutter Buttes, Land of Histum Yani.* (Third edition.) (Author), 152 p.

Hobson, J.B. 1890a. "Nevada County." *Tenth annual report of the State Mineralogist, for the year ending December 1, 1890.* Sacramento: California State Mining Bureau, p. 364-398.

_____1890b. "Placer County." *Tenth annual report of the State Mineralogist, for the year ending December 1, 1890.* Sacramento, California State Mining Bureau, p. 410-434.

Hoover, Mildred Brooke, Rensch, Hero Eugene, and Rensch, Ethel Grace. 1966. *Historic spots in California.* (Third edition, revised by William N. Abeloe.) Stanford, California: Stanford University Press, 642 p.

Ingersoll, Chester. 1937. *Overland to California in 1847.* Chicago: Black Cat Press., 50 p.

Jackson, Joseph Henry. 1941. *Anybody's gold, The story of California's mining towns.* New York, London: D. Appleton-Century Company, 468 p.

Jackson, Louise A. 1988. *Beulah, A biography of the Mineral King Valley of California.* Tucson, Arizona: Westernlore Press, 179 p.

Kelly, William. 1950. *A stroll through the diggings of California.* Oakland, California: Biobooks, 206 p.

Kip, Leonard. 1946. *California sketches, with recollections of the gold mines.* Los Angeles: N.A. Kovach, 58 p.

Kirby, J.M. 1943. "Rumsey Hills area." *Geologic formations and economic development of the oil and gas fields of California.* (California Division of Mines Bulletin 118.) San Francisco: Division of Mines, p. 601-605.

Kroeber, A.L. 1916. "California place names of Indian origin." *University of California Publications in American Archæology and Ethnology,* v. 12, no. 2, p. 31-69.

Lekisch, Barbara. 1988. *Tahoe place names.* Lafayette, California: Great West Books, 173 p.

Lindgren, Waldemar. 1897. "The gold-quartz veins of Nevada City and Grass Valley districts, California." *Seventeenth Annual Report of the United States Geological Survey, Part II,—Papers of an economic character, 1895.* Washington: Government Printing Office, p. 1-262.

_____1911. *The Tertiary gravels of the Sierra Nevada of California.* (United States Geological Survey Professional Paper 73.) Washington: Government Printing Office, 226 p.

Logan, C.A. 1925. "Sacramento field division (Ancient channels of the Duncan Canyon region, Placer County)." *Mining in California,* v. 21, no. 3, p. 275-280.

_____1929a. "Sacramento field division (Sierra County)." *Mining in California,* v. 25, no. 2, p. 151-212.

_____1929b. "Sacramento field division (Colusa County)." *Mining in California,* v. 25, no. 3, p. 284-300.

_____1938. "Mineral resources of El Dorado County." *California Journal of Mines and Geology,* v. 34, no. 3, p. 206-280.

_____1941. "Sacramento field district (Mineral resources of Nevada County)." *California Journal of Mines and Geology,* v. 37, no. 3, p. 374-468.

Long, Ileen Price (Chairman, The Centennial Book Committee). 1964. *Alpine heritage, One hundred years of history, recreation, lore, in Alpine County, California, 1864-1964.* Campbell, California: Craftsmen Typographers, Inc., 66 p.

Loomis, Leander V. 1928. *A journal of the Birmingham Emigrating Company.* (Edited by Edgar M. Ledyard.) Glendale, California: The Arthur H. Clark Company, 198 p.

Lyman, C.S. 1849. "Observations on California." *American Journal of Science and Arts* (series 2), v. 7, no. 20, p. 290-292, 305-309.

Marlette, S.H. 1856. *Annual report of the Surveyor-General, of the State of California.* (Sen. Doc. No. 5, Sess. of 1856.) Sacramento: State Printer, 334 p.

McKinstry, Bruce L. 1975. *The California gold rush overland diary of Byron N. McKinstry, 1850-1852.* Glendale, California: The Arthur H. Clark Company, 401 p.

Morgan, Dale (editor). 1963. *Overland in 1846, Diaries and letters of the California-Oregon trail.* Georgetown, California: The Talisman Press, 825 p.

Morley, Jim, and Foley, Doris. 1965. *Gold cities, Grass Valley and Nevada City.* Berkeley, California: Howell-North Books, 96 p.

Mosier, Dan L. 1979. *California coal towns, coaling stations, & landings.* San Leandro, California: Mines Road Books, 8 p.

Myrick, Thomas S. 1971. *The gold rush, Letters of Thomas S. Myrick from California to the Jackson, Michigan, American Citizen, 1849-1855.* Mount Pleasant, Michigan: The Cumming Press, 117 p.

O'Brien, J.C. 1950. "Mines and mineral resources of Yolo County." *California Journal of Mines and Geology,* v. 46, no. 3, p. 421-436.

Osbun, Albert G. 1966. *To California and the South Seas, The diary of Albert G. Osbun, 1849-1851.* San Marino, California: The Huntington Library. 233 p.

Paden, Irene D. 1943. *The wake of the prairie schooner.* New York: The Macmillan Company, 514 p.

Perez, Crisostomo N. 1996. *Land grants in Alta California.* Rancho Cordova, California: Landmark Enterprises, 264 p.

Preston, E.B. 1893. "Sierra County." *Eleventh report of the State Mineralogist, (First Biennial,) Two years ending September 15, 1892.* Sacramento: California State Mining Bureau, p. 400-412.

Pritchard, James A. 1959. *The overland diary of James A. Pritchard from Kentucky to California in 1849.* Denver, Colorado: The Old West Publishing Company, 221 p.

Ricketts, Norma Baldwin. 1978. *Historic Cosumnes and the Slough House Pioneer Cemetery.* Salt Lake City, Utah: Daughters of Utah Pioneers, 71 p.

_____1983. *Tragedy Spring and the pouch of gold.* Sacramento, California: Ricketts Publishing Company, 47 p.

Ringgold, Cadwalader 1852. *A series of charts, with sailing directions embracing surveys of the Farallones, entrance to the Bay of San Francisco, Bays of San Francisco and San Pablo, Straits of Carquines and Suisun Bay, confluence and deltaic branches of the Sacramento and San Joaquin Rivers, and the Sacramento River (with the Middle Fork) to the American River, including the cities of Sacramento and Boston, State of California.* (Fourth edition, with additions.) Washington: Jno. T. Towers, 48 p.

Salley, H.E. 1977. *History of California post offices, 1849-1976.* La Mesa, California: Postal History Associates, Inc., 300 p.

Sargent, Mrs. J.L. (editor). 1927. *Amador County history.* (No place): Amador County Federation of Women's Clubs, 127 p.

Scamehorn, Howard L. (editor). 1965. *The Buckeye Rovers in the gold rush.* Athens, Ohio: Ohio University Press, 195 p.

Sinclair, C.H. 1901. *Oblique boundary line between California and Nevada.* (United.States Coast and Geodetic Survey, Report for 1900, Appendix 3.) Washington: Government Printing Office, p. 255-484.

Slyter, Robert I., and Slyter, Grace I. (No date.) *Historical notes of the early Washington, Nevada, County, California, mining district.* (Authors), 160 p.

Stewart, George R. 1960. *Donner Pass and those who crossed it.* San Francisco, California: The California Historical Society, 96 p.

Swan, John A. 1960. *A trip to the gold mines of California in 1848.* (Edited by John A. Hussey.) San Francisco: The Book Club of California, 51 p.

Taylor, L.H. 1902. *Water storage in the Truckee basin, California-Nevada.* (United States Geological Survey Water-Supply and Irrigation Papers No. 68.) Washington: Government Printing Office, 90 p.

Tyson, Philip T. 1850. "Report of P.T. Tyson, esq., upon the geology of California." *Report of the Secretary of War, communicating information in relation to the geology and topography of California.* (31st Cong., 1st Sess., Sen. Ex. Doc. No. 47.) Washington: Government Printing Office, p. 3-74.

United States Board on Geographic Names (under name "United States Geographic Board"). 1933. *Sixth report of the United States Geographic Board, 1890 to 1932.* Washington: Government Printing Office, 834 p.

_____(under name "United States Board on Geographical Names"). 1936. *Decisions of the United States Board on Geographical Names, Decisions rendered between July 1, 1935, and June 30, 1936.* Washington: Government Printing Office, 44 p.

_____(under name "United States Board on Geographical Names"). 1939. *Decisions of the United States Board on Geographical Names, Decisions rendered between July 1, 1938, and June 30, 1939.* Washington: Government Printing Office, 41 p.

_____(under name "United States Board on Geographical Names"). 1942. *Decisions of the United States Board on Geographical Names, Decisions rendered between July 1, 1940, and June 30, 1941.* Washington: Government Printing Office, 89 p.

_____1949a. *Decision lists nos. 4810, 4811, 4812, October, November, December, 1948.* Washington: Department of the Interior, 25 p.

_____1949b. *Decision list no. 4903, March 1949.* Washington: Department of the Interior. 26 p.

_____1949c. *Decision lists nos. 4907, 4908, 4909, July, August, September, 1949.* Washington: Department of the Interior, 24 p.

_____1950. *Decisions on names in the United States and Alaska rendered during April, May, and June 1950.* (Decision list no. 5006.) Washington: Department of the Interior, 47 p.

_____1954. *Decisions on names in the United States, Alaska and Puerto Rico, Decisions rendered from July 1950 to May 1954.* (Decision list no. 5401.) Washington: Department of the Interior, 115 p.

_____1957. *Decisions on names in the United States, Alaska and Hawaii, Decisions rendered from May 1954 through March 1957.* (Decision list no. 5701.) Washington: Department of the Interior, 23 p.

_____1959. *Decisions on names in the United States, Decisions rendered from January, 1959 through April, 1959.* (Decision list no. 5902.) Washington: Department of the Interior, 49 p.

_____1960a. *Decisions on names in the United States and Puerto Rico, Decisions rendered in May, June, July, and August, 1959.* (Decision list no. 5903.) Washington: Department of the Interior, 79 p.

_____1960b. *Decisions on names in the United States, Decisions rendered from September 1959 through December 1959.* (Decision list no. 5904.) Washington: Department of the Interior, 68 p.

_____1961. *Decisions on names in the United States, Decisions rendered from May through August 1961.* (Decision list no. 6102.) Washington:

Department of the Interior, 81 p.
_____1962a. *Decisions on names in the United States, Decisions rendered from September through December 1961.* (Decision list no. 6103.) Washington: Department of the Interior, 75 p.
_____1962b. *Decisions on names in the United States, Decisions rendered from January through April 1962.* (Decision list no. 6201.) Washington: Department of the Interior, 72 p.
_____1962c. *Decisions on names in the United States, Decisions rendered from May through August 1962.* (Decision list no. 6202.) Washington: Department of the Interior, 81 p.
_____1963. *Decisions on names in the United States, Decisions rendered from September through December 1962.* (Decision list no. 6203.) Washington: Department of the Interior, 59 p.
_____1964. *Decisions on geographic names in the United States, September through December 1963.* (Decision list no. 6303.) Washington: Department of the Interior, 66 p.
_____1965a. *Decisions on geographic names in the United States, January through March 1965.* (Decision list no. 6501.) Washington: Department of the Interior, 85 p.
_____1965b. *Decisions on geographic names in the United States, July through September 1965.* (Decision list no. 6503.) Washington: Department of the Interior, 74 p.
_____1967. *Decisions on geographic names in the United States, January through March 1967.* (Decision list no. 6701.) Washington: Department of the Interior, 20 p.
_____1968a. *Decisions on geographic names in the United States, January through March 1968.* (Decision list no. 6801.) Washington: Department of the Interior, 51 p.
_____1968b. *Decisions on geographic names in the United States, April through June 1968.* (Decision list no. 6802.) Washington: Department of the Interior, 42 p.
_____1969. *Decisions on geographic names in the United States, April through June 1969.* (Decision list no. 6902.) Washington: Department of the Interior, 28 p.
_____1970. *Decisions on geographic names in the United States, January through March 1970.* (Decision list no. 7001.) Washington: Department of the Interior, 31 p.
_____1971. *Decisions on geographic names in the United States, January through March 1971.* (Decision list no. 7101.) Washington: Department of the Interior, 19 p.
_____1972. *Decisions on geographic names in the United States, January through March 1972.* (Decision list no. 7201.) Washington: Department of the Interior, 32 p.
_____1973. *Decisions on geographic names in the United States, January through March 1973.* (Decision list no. 7301.) Washington: Department of the Interior, 20 p.
_____1974a. *Decisions on geographic names in the United States, October through December 1973.* (Decision list no. 7304.) Washington: Department of the Interior, 15 p.
_____1974b. *Decisions on geographic names in the United States, January through March 1974.* (Decision list no. 7401.) Washington: Department of the Interior, 27 p.
_____1976. *Decisions on geographic names in the United States, October through December 1975.* (Decision list no. 7504.) Washington: Department of the Interior, 45 p.
_____1977a. *Decisions on geographic names in the United States, October through December 1976.* (Decision list no. 7604.) Washington: Department of the Interior, 34 p.
_____1977b. *Decisions on geographic names in the United States, April through June 1977.* (Decision list no. 7702.) Washington: Department of the Interior, 40 p.
_____1977c. *Decisions on geographic names in the United States, July through September 1977.* (Decision list no. 7703.) Washington: Department of the Interior, 25 p.
_____1978a. *Decisions on geographic names in the United States, October through December 1977.* (Decision list no. 7704.) Washington: Department of the Interior, 29 p.
_____1978b. *Decisions on geographic names in the United States, October through December 1978.* (Decision list no. 7804.) Washington: Department of the Interior, 48 p.
_____1980. *Decisions on geographic names in the United States, April through June 1980.* (Decision list no. 8002.) Washington: Department of the Interior, 33 p.
_____1981. *Decisions on geographic names in the United States, January through March 1981.* (Decision list no. 8101.) Washington: Department of the Interior, 23 p.
_____1982. *Decisions on geographic names in the United States, April through June 1982.* (Decision list no. 8202.) Washington: Department of the Interior, 21 p.
_____1984a. *Decisions on geographic names in the United States, April through June 1984.* (Decision list no. 8402.) Washington: Department of the Interior, 22 p.
_____1984b. *Decisions on geographic names in the United States, October through December 1984.* (Decision list no. 8404.) Washington: Department of the Interior, 18 p.
_____1985. *Decisions on geographic names in the United States, July through September 1985.* (Decision list no. 8503.) Washington: Department of the Interior, 19 p.
_____1986. *Decisions on geographic names in the United States, April through June 1986.* (Decision list no. 8602.) Washington: Department of the Interior, 10 p.
_____1991. *Decisions on geographic names in the United States.* (Decision list 1991.) Washington: Department of the Interior, 40 p.
_____1992. *Decisions on geographic names in the United States.* (Decision list 1992.) Washington: Department of the Interior, 21 p.
_____1994. *Decisions on geographic names in the United States.* (Decision list 1994.) Washington: Department of the Interior, 17 p.
_____1995. *Decisions on geographic names in the United States.* (Decision list 1995.) Washington: Department of the Interior, 19 p.
Waring, Clarence A. 1919. "Placer County." *Report XV of the State Mineralogist.* San Francisco: California State Mining Bureau, p. 309-399.
Waring, Gerald A. 1915. *Springs of California.* (United States Geological Survey Water-Supply Paper 338.) Washington: Government Printing Office, 410 p.
Watson, Jeanne Hamilton (editor). 1988. *To the land of gold and wickedness, The 1848-59 diary of Lorena L. Hayes.* St. Louis, Missouri: The Patrice Press, 486 p.
Wheat, Carl I. 1963. *Mapping the Transmississippi West.* Volume Five. San Francisco: The Institute of Historical Cartography, 487 p.
Wheeler, George M. 1877. *Annual report upon the geographical surveys west of the one-hundredth meridian in the states and territories of California, Oregon, Nevada, Texas, Arizona, Colorado, Idaho, Montana, New Mexico, Utah, and Wyoming.* (Appendix NN of *The Annual Report of the Chief of Engineers for 1877.*) Washington: Government Printing Office, p. 1211-1334.
_____1878. *Annual report upon the geographical surveys of the territory of the United States west of the 100th meridian, in the states and territories of California, Colorado, Kansas, Nebraska, Nevada, Oregon, Texas, Arizona, Idaho, Montana, New Mexico, Utah, Washington, and Wyoming.* (Appendix NN of *The Annual Report of the Chief of Engineers for 1878.*) Washington: Government Printing Office, 234 p.
_____1879. *Annual report upon the geographical surveys of the territory of the United States west of the 100th meridian, in the states and territories of California, Colorado, Kansas, Nebraska, Nevada, Oregon, Texas, Arizona, Idaho, Montana, New Mexico, Utah, Washington, and Wyoming.* (Appendix OO of *The Annual Report of the Chief of Engineers for 1879.*) Washington: Government Printing Office, 340 p.
Whiting, J.S., and Whiting, Richard J. 1960. *Forts of the State of California.* (Authors), 90 p.
Whitney, J.D. 1865. *Report of progress and synopsis of the field-work from 1860 to 1864.* (Geological Survey of California, Geology, Volume I.) Published by authority of the Legislature of California, 498 p.
_____1880. *The auriferous gravels of the Sierra Nevada of California.* Cambridge: University Press, John Wilson & Son, 569 p.
Wierzbicki, F.P. 1970. *California as it is & as it may be, or a guide to the gold region.* New York: Burt Franklin, 101 p.
Wilkes, Charles. 1958. *Columbia River to the Sacramento.* Oakland, California: Biobooks, 140 p.
Williamson, R.S. 1857. "General report." *Reports of explorations and surveys, to ascertain the most practicable and economical route for a railroad from the Mississippi River to the Pacific Ocean.* Volume VI, part I. (33d. Cong., 2d Sess., Sen. Ex. Doc. No. 78.) Washington: Beverly Tucker, Printer, 134 p.
Winterstein, Herb. 1981. *Tales of old Folsom.* Folsom, California: Folsom Historical Society, 35 p.
Work, John. 1945. *Fur brigade to the Bonaventura, John Work's California expedition, 1832-1833, for the Hudson's Bay Company.* (Edited by Alice Bay Malony.) San Francisco: California Historical Society, 112 p.
Yohalem, Betty. 1977. *"I remember . . .", Stories and pictures of El Dorado County pioneer families.* Placerville, California: El Dorado County Chamber of Commerce, 237 p.
Zauner, Phyllis. 1982. *Lake Tahoe.* Tahoe Paradise, California: Zanel Publications, 63 p.

QUADRANGLE MAPS

(All maps published by United States Geological Survey, except as noted. Dates identify the editions of the maps. If a reprinted or revised map was used, the year of reprinting or revision is given in parentheses, unless the reprinted or revised map is cited specifically in the text.)

Alleghany 15'—1950.
7.5'—1949.

Allendale 7.5' (same area as Wolfskill 7.5')—1953 (photorevised 1968 and 1973).
Amador City 7.5' (same area as Plytmouth 7.5')—1962.
American House 7.5'—1948.
Antelope 7.5' (same area as Citrus Heights 7.5')—1911.
Antelope Valley 7.5'—1981.
Antioch North 7.5' (same area as Collinsville 7.5')—1953 (photorevised 1965); 1978.
Arbuckle 7.5'—1918; 1952 (photorevised 1973).
Arcade 7.5' (same area as Rio Linda 7.5')—1911 (reprinted 1942).
Auburn 15'—1944 (reprinted 1948); 1954.
7.5'—1953 (photorevised 1973).
Aukum 7.5'—1952.
Babel Slough 7.5' (same area as Clarksburg 7.5')—1916.
Bangor 15'—1941.
Bartlett Springs 15' (same area as Clearlake Oaks 15')—1944.
Bear River Reservoir 7.5'—1979.
Bidwell Bar 30'—1897 (reprinted 1928).
Big Trees 30'—1891.
Bird Valley 7.5'—1959.
Blue Canyon 7.5'—1955; 1955, photorevised 1973.
Blue Nose Mountain 7.5'—1951.
Boca 7.5'—1955; 1955, photorevised 1969.
Bouldin Island 7.5' (same area as Bouldin 7.5')—1978.
Brighton 7.5' (same area as Sacramento East 7.5')—1911 (reprinted 1947).
Brooks 7.5'—1959.
Browns Valley 7.5'—1911; 1947; 1947, photorevised 1973.
Bruceville 7.5'—1910 (reprinted 1947); 1968.
Buffalo Creek 7.5'—1967.
Bunker Hill 7.5'—1953; 1953, photorevised 1973.
Butte City 7.5'—1952 (photorevised 1973).
Calaveras Dome 7.5'—1979).
Caldor 7.5'—1951 (photorevised 1973).
Calpine 7.5'—1981.
Camino 15'— 1952.
7.5'—1952 (photorevised 1973).
Camp Far West 7.5' (same area as Spenceville 7.5')—1949; 1949, photorevised 1973.
Camptonville 7.5'—1948; 1948, photorevised 1969.
Capay 15' (same area as Lake Berryessa 15')—1945.
Caples Lake 7.5'—1979.
Carbondale 7.5'—1909 (reprinted 1947); 1968.
Carmichael 7.5' (same area as Mills 7.5')—1967.
Challenge 7.5'—1948; 1948, photorevised 1969.
Chicago Park 7.5'—1949; 1949, photorevised 1973.
Chico 1°x 2°—1958, limited revision 1966.
Cisco Grove 7.5'—1955; 1955, photorevised 1973.
Citrus Heights 7.5' (same area as Antelope 7.5')—1967.
Clarksburg 7.5' (same area as Babel Slough 7.5')—1967.
Clarksville 7.5'—1953; 1953, photorevised 1980.
Clay 7.5'—1909 (reprinted 1943); 1953; 1968.
Clearlake Oaks 15' (same area as Bartlett Springs 15')—1960.
Clements 7.5'—1968.
Clio 7.5'—1981.
Clipper Mills 7.5'—1948; 1948, photorevised 1975).
Colfax 30'—1898; 1938 (reprinted 1941).
15'—1950.
7.5'—1949.
Collinsville 7.5' (same area as Antioch North 7.5')—1918 (reprinted 1947).
Coloma 7.5'—1949.
Colusa 15'—1942 (Army); 1953.
7.5' (same area as Powell Slough 7.5')—1952.
Compton Landing 7.5' (same area as Moulton Weir 7.5')—1917 (reprinted 1947).
Cortina Creek 7.5' (same area as Spring Valley 7.5')—1953 (photorevised 1973).
Cosumnes 7.5' (same area as Sloughhouse 7.5')—1909 (reprinted 1947).
Courtland 15'—1908 (reprinted 1914); 1952.
7.5' (same area as Vorden 7.5')—1952 (photorevised 1968); 1978.
Crockett Peak 7.5'—1967.
Davis 15' (same area as Davisville 15')—1954.
7.5' (same area as Swingle 7.5')—1952; 1952 photorevised 1968 and 1975.
Davisville 15' (same area as Davis 15')—1907.
Devil Peak 7.5'—1950; 1950, photorevised 1973.
Devils Nose 7.5'—1979.
Dog Valley 7.5'—1981.
Donner Pass 15'—1955.
Downieville 30'—1897 (reprinted 1946).
15'—1951.
7.5'—1951 (photorevised 1975).
Duncan Peak 15'—1952.
7.5'—1952 (photorevised 1973).
Dunnigan 15'—1907; 1953.
7.5' (same are as Hershey 7.5')—1953 (photorevised 1973).
Dutch Flat 7.5'—1950; 1950, photorevised 1973.
Echo Lake 7.5'—1955 (photorevised 1969).
Eldorado Bend 7.5' (same area as Ronda 7.5')—1952 (photorevised 1973).
Elk Grove 7.5'—1968.
Elkhorn Weir 7.5' (same area as Taylor Monument 7.5')—1915.
Emerald Bay 7.5'—1955; 1955, photorevised 1969.
Emigrant Gap 15'—1955.
English Mountain 7.5'—1983.
Esaparto 7.5'—1959.
Evans Canyon 7.5'—1978.
Fair Oaks 15'—1902 (with the form "Fairoaks" for the name; reprinted 1910); 1954.
Fairview 7.5' (same area as Manor Slough 7.5')—1918 (reprinted 1922).
Fallen Leaf Lake 15'—1955.
Fiddletown 7.5'—1949.
Florin 7.5'—1909 (reprinted 1947); 1968.
Folsom 15'—1941.
7.5'—1967.
Folsom SE 7.5'—1954.
Forbestown 7.5'—1970.
Foresthill 7.5'—1949 (photorevised 1973).
Fouts Springs 7.5'—1968.
Freel Peak 15'—1956.
7.5'—1955 (photorevised 1969).
French Corral 7.5'—1948; 1948, photorevised 1969.
Galt 7.5'—1910 (reprinted 1947); 1968.
Garden Valley 7.5'—1949 (photorevised 1973).
Garnet Hill 7.5'—1979.
Georgetown 15'—1949.
7.5'—1949 (photorevised 1973).
Gilmore Peak 7.5'—1968.
Gilsizer Slough 7.5'—1911; 1952 (photorevised 1973).
Glascock Mountain 7.5'—1958.
Gold Hill 7.5'—1954 (photorevised 1973).
Gold Lake 7.5'—1981.
Goodyears Bar 7.5'—1951.
Goose Creek 7.5'—1968.
Granite Chief 15'—1953.
7.5'—1953.
Graniteville 7.5'—1982.
Grass Valley 15'—1949.
7.5'—1949.
Grays Bend 7.5'—1916; 1953 (photorevised 1965).
Greek Store 7.5'—1952 (photorevised 1973).
Greenwood 7.5'—1949.
Gridley 7.5'—1912; 1952 (photorevised 1973).
Grimes 7.5'—1911; 1954 (photorevised 1973).
Guinda 15' (same area as Rumsey 15')—1959.
7.5'—1959.
Harrington 7.5' (same area as Wildwood School 7.5')—1916.
Haypress Valley 7.5'—1981.
Hershey 7.5' (same area as Dunnigan 7.5')—1916.
Hobart Mills 7.5'—1981.
Homewood 7.5'—1955; 1955, photorevised 1969.
Honcut 7.5'—1912; 1952 (photorevised 1973).
Independence Lake 7.5'—1981.
Ione 7.5'—1962.
Irish Hill 7.5'—1962.
Isleton 7.5'—1910 (reprinted 1947); 1952 (photorevised 1968); 1978.
Jackson 30'—1902 (reprinted 1948).
7.5'—1962.
Jacobs Corner 7.5' (same area as Madison 7.5')—1916.
Jericho Valley 7.5'—1958.
Jersey 7.5' (same area as Jersey Island 7.5')—1910 (reprinted 1932).
Jersey Island 7.5' (same area as Jersey 7.5')—1978.
Kings Beach 7.5'—1955 (photorevised 1969).
Kirkville 7.5'—1915; 1952 (photorevised 1973).
Knights Landing 15'—1952.
7.5'—1910; 1952 (photorevised 1973).
Knoxville 7.5'—1958.
Kyburz 7.5'—1952; 1952, photorevised 1973.
Lake Berryessa 15' (same area as Capay 15')—1959.
7.5'—1959.
Lake Combie 7.5'—1949 (photorevised 1973).
La Porte 7.5'—1951.
Latrobe 7.5'—1949 (photorevised 1973).
Leek Spring Hill 15'—1951.
7.5'—1951 (photorevised 1973).

Liberty Island 7.5' (same area as Cache Slough 7.5')—1978.
Lincoln 7.5'—1953 (photorevised 1973).
Lockeford 7.5'—1968.
Lodi 30'—1894 (reprinted 1906).
Lodi North 7.5' (same area as Woodbridge 7.5')—1968.
Lodoga 15'—1943; 1960.
Logandale 7.5'—1952 (photorevised 1973).
Logan Ridge 7.5' (same area as Logan Creek 7.5')—1958.
Loma Rica 7.5' (same area as Prairie Creek 7.5')—1947; 1947, photorevised 1969.
Loon Lake 7.5'—1952; 1952, photorevised 1973.
Lovdal 7.5' (same area as Sacramento West 7.5')—1916.
Loyalton 15'—1955.
7.5'—1981.
Madison 7.5' (same area as Jacobs Corner 7.5')—1953; 1953, photorevised 1968.
Manor Slough 7.5' (same area as Fairview 7.5')—1958.
Marcuse 7.5' (same area as Sutter Causeway 7.5')—1910 (marsh added 1911; reprinted 1947).
Markham Ravine 15' (same area as Lincoln 15')—1942 (Army).
Markleeville 30'—1889.
Martis Peak 7.5'—1955 (photorevised 1969).
Marysville 30'—1895 (reprinted 1911).
15'—1952.
Marysville Buttes 7.5' (same area as Sutter Buttes 7.5')—1912.
Maxwell 15'—1906 (reprinted 1936); 1952 (photorevised 1973).
7.5' (same area as Delevan 7.5')—1952 (photorevised 1973).
Meeks Bay 7.5'—1955 (photorevised 1969).
Meridian 7.5'—1912 (reprinted 1947); 1952 (photorevised 1973).
Merritt 7.5'—1952 (photorevised 1968 and 1975).
Michigan Bluff 7.5'—1952 (photorevised 1973).
Mills 7.5' (same area as Carmichael 7.5')—1911.
Mokelumne Hill 15'—1948.
7.5'—1948.
Mokelumne Peak 7.5'—1979.
Monticello Dam 7.5'—1959.
Morgan Valley 15' (same area as Reiff 15')—1958.
Moulton Weir 7.5' (same area as Compton Landing 7.5')—1952.
Mount Fillmore 7.5'—1951.
Mount Vaca 7.5'—1951 (photorevised 1968).
Nevada City 15'—1948.
7.5'—1948 (photorevised 1969).
New Hope 7.5' (same area as Thornton 7.5')—1910 (reprinted 1942).
Nicolaus 7.5'—1910 (reprinted 1947); 1952; 1952, photorevised 1973.
Norden 7.5'—1955.
North Bloomfield 7.5'—1949; 1949, photorevised 1973.
Olivehurst 7.5' (same area as Ostrom 7.5')—1952; 1952, photorevised 1973.
Omo Ranch 7.5'—1952 (photorevised 1973).
Onion Valley 7.5'—1950.
Oregon House 7.5'—1948; 1948, photorevised 1969.
Ostrom 7.5' (same area as Olivehurst 7.5')—1911.
Peddler Hill 7.5'—1951; 1951, photorevised 1973.
Pennington 7.5'—1954 (photorevised 1973).
Pike 7.5'—1949.
Pilot Hill 7.5'—1954; 1954, photorevised 1973.
Pine Grove 7.5'—1948.
Placerville 30'—1893 (reprinted 1947).
7.5'—1949 (photorevised 1973).
Pleasant Grove 7.5'—1910; 1967.
Pollock Pines 7.5'—1950; 1950, photorevised 1973.
Potato Hill 7.5'—1967.
Powell Slough 7.5' (same area as Colusa 7.5')—1918.
Princeton 7.5'—1918; 1952 (photorevised 1973).
Pyramid Peak 30'—1896 (corrected 1940; reprinted 1947).
7.5'—1955 (photorevised 1969).
Rackerby 7.5'—1948 (photorevised 1969).
Rail Road Flat 7.5' (the name also had the form "Railroad Flat")—1948.
Rio Linda 7.5' (same area as Arcade 7.5')—1967.
Rio Vista 15'—1952.
7.5'—1910 (reprinted 1936); 1978.
Riverton 7.5'—1950; 1950; photorevised 1973.
Robbs Peak 15'—1952.
7.5'—1950; 1950, photorevised 1973.
Rockbound Valley 7.5'—1955; 1955 (photorevised 1969)
Rocklin 7.5'—1967.
Ronda 7.5' (same area as Eldorado Bend 7.5')—1915.
Roseville 7.5'—1967.
Rough and Ready 7.5'—1949 (photorevised 1973).
Royal Gorge 7.5'—1953; 1953, photorevised 1973.
Rumsey 15' (same area as Guinda 15')—1921; 1945.
7.5'—1959.
Sacramento 1°x 2°—1957 (limited revision 1964).
30'—1892 (reprinted 1929).
Sacramento East 7.5' (same area as Brighton 7.5')—1967.
Sacramento West 7.5' (same area as Lovdal 7.5')—1967.
Saddle Mountain 15'—1950.
Saint John Mountain 7.5'—1968.
Sanborn Slough 7.5'—1952 (photorevised 1973).
Sardine Peak 7.5'—1981.
Sattley 7.5'—1981.
Saxon 7.5'—1952, photorevised 1968.
Sheridan 7.5'—1953; 1953, photorevised 1973.
Shingle Springs 7.5'—1949.
Sierra City 15'—1955.
7.5'—1981.
Sierraville 30'—1894 (reprinted (1951).
15'—1955.
7.5'—1981.
Silver Lake 15'—1956.
Sites 7.5'—1904; 1958.
Slate Mountain 7.5'—1950; 1950, photorevised 1973.
Sloughhouse 7.5' (same area as Cosumnes 7.5')—1968.
Sly Park 7.5'—1952; 1952, photorevised 1973.
Smartsville 30'—1895 (reprinted 1917); 1942 (Army).
Smartville 7.5'—1951; 1951, photorevised 1973.
Soda Springs 7.5'—1955; 1955, photorevised 1973.
South Lake Tahoe 7.5'—1955; 1955, photorevised 1969 and 1974.
Spring Valley 7.5' (same area as Cortina Creek 7.5')—1918 (reprinted 1942).
Stonyford 15'—1951.
7.5'—1968.
Strawberry Valley 7.5'—1948; 1948, photorevised 1975.
Stump Spring 7.5'—1951 (photorevised 1973).
Sutter 7.5'—1911; 1952; 1952, photorevised 1973.
Sutter Buttes 15'—1954.
7.5' (same area as Marysville Buttes 7.5')—1954 (photorevised, 1973).
Sutter Causeway 7.5' (same area as Marcuse 7.5')—1952 (photorevised 1973).
Sutter Creek 15'—1944.
Tahoe 15'—1955.
Tahoe City 7.5'—1955; 1955, photorevised 1969.
Tamarack 7.5'—1979.
Taylor Monument 7.5' (same area as Elkhorn Weir 7.5')—1967.
Thornton 7.5' (same area as New Hope 7.5')—1978.
Tisdale Weir 7.5'—1912; 1952 (photorevised 1973).
Tragedy Spring 7.5'—1979.
Truckee 30'—1895 (reprinted 1932); 1940 (reprinted 1951).
15'—1955.
7.5'—1955; 1955, photorevised 1969).
Tunnel Hill 7.5'—1950 (photorevised 1973).
Ukiah 1°x 2°—1957.
Valley Springs 7.5'—1962.
Venado 15' (same area as Wilbur Springs 15')—1920 (Army).
Vernon 7.5' (same area as Verona 7.5')—1910.
Verona 7.5' (same area as Vernon 7.5')—1967.
Vorden 7.5' (same area as Courtland 7.5')—1916.
Wallace 7.5'—1962.
Washington 7.5'—1950; 1950, photorevised 1979.
Webber Peak 7.5'—1981.
Wentworth Springs 7.5'—1953; 1953, photorevised 1973.
West Point 7.5'—1948.
Westville 7.5'—1952; 1952, photorevised 1973.
Wheatland 15'—1949.
7.5'—1910 (reprinted 1947); 1947; 1947, photorevised 1973.
Wilbur Springs 15' (same area as Venado 15')—1944 (reprinted 1948); 1961.
Wildwood School 7.5' (same area as Harrington 7.5')—1959 (photorevised 1973).
Williams 7.5'—1918; 1952 (photorevised 1973).
Wilson Valley 7.5'—1958.
Winters 7.5'—1916; 1953 (photorevised 1968).
Wolf 7.5'—1949 (photorevised 1973).
Woodland 15'—1953.
7.5' (same area as Yolo 7.5')—1952; 1952, photorevised 1968 and 1975.
Yolo 7.5' (same area as Woodland 7.5')—1915.
Yuba City 7.5'—1911 (reprinted 1934); 1952; 1952, photorevised 1973.
Zamora 7.5'—1916 (reprinted 1920); 1953 (photorevised 1973).

MISCELLANEOUS MAPS

Arrowsmith. 1860. "Map of the American River and Natoma Water and Mining Compys. Canals." A.T. Arrowsmith, C.E.

Bancroft. 1864. "Bancroft's map of the Pacific States." Compiled by Wm. H. Knight. Published by H.H. Bancroft & Co., Booksellers and Stationers, San Francisco, Cal.

Burr. 1839. "Map of the United States of North America with parts of the adjacent countries." By David N. Burr. (Late Topographer to the Post Office.) Geographer to the House of Representatives of the U.S.

California Division of Highways. 1934. (Appendix "A" *of* California Division of Highways.)

California Mining Bureau. 1909a. "Sutter, Yuba, Sierra, Nevada, Placer, and El Dorado Counties." (*In* California Mining Bureau Bulletin 56.)

_____1909b. "Sacramento, San Joaquin, Amador, and Calaveras Counties." (*In* California Mining Bureau Bulletin 56.)

_____1909c. "Sonoma, Marin, Napa, Yolo, and Solano Counties." (*In* California Mining Bureau Bulletin 56.)

_____1910. "Map of California showing the approximate location of the principal mineral deposits." Compiled by the State Mining Bureau.

_____1917a. (Untitled map *in* California Mining Bureau Bulletin 74, p. 161.)

_____1917b. (Untitled map *in* California Mining Bureau Bulletin 74, p. 162.)

_____1917c. (Untitled map *in* California Mining Bureau Bulletin 74, p. 163.)

_____1917d. (Untitled map *in* California Mining Bureau Bulletin 74, p. 164.)

_____1917e. (Untitled map *in* California Mining Bureau Bulletin 74, p. 165.)

Camp. 1962. (Untitled map *in* Doble.)

DeGroot. 1863. "Bancroft's map of Nevada Territory exhibiting a portion of southern Oregon & eastern California." Published by Warren Holt, San Francisco, Cal.

Derby. 1849a. "A Sketch of General Riley's route through the mining districts, July and Aug. 1849."

_____1849b. "The Sacramento Valley from the American River to Butte Creek." By Lieut. Derby, Topl. Engrs, September & October 1849.

Durst. 1916. "Sketch map of northwestern Yolo County." (Plate 37 *in* Durst.)

Eddy. 1851. "A complete map of the Feather & Yuba Rivers, with towns, ranches, diggings, roads, distances." Compiled from the recent surveys of M. Milleson & R. Adams, C. Engineers. Published by R.A. Eddy, Book & Stationer, Marysville Calia.

_____1854. "Approved and declared to be the official map of the State of California by an act of the Legislature passed March 25th 1853." Compiled by W.M. Eddy, State Surveyor General. Published for R.A. Eddy, Marysville, California, by J.H. Colton, New York.

Fremont. 1845. "Map of an exploring expedition to the Rocky Mountains in the year 1842 and to Oregon & North California in the years 1843-44." By Brevet Capt. J.C. Frémont.

_____1848. "Map of Oregon and Upper California from the surveys of John Charles Frémont, and other authorities." Drawn by Charles Preuss. Washington City.

Gibbes. 1852. "A new map of California." By Charles Drayton Gibbes, from his own and other recent surveys and explorations. Published by C.D. Gibbes, Stockton, Cal.

Goddard. 1857. "Britton & Rey's map of the State of California." By George H. Goddard.

Hobson. 1890a. "Geological map of Nevada County." By J.B. Hobson. (*In* Hobson, 1890a.)

_____1890b. "Geological map of Placer County." By J.B. Hobson. (*In* Hobson, 1890b.)

Jackson. 1850. "Map of the mining district of California." By Wm. A. Jackson.

Jefferson. 1849. "Map of the emigrant road from Independence, Mo. to St. Francisco, California." By T.H. Jefferson.

Larkin. 1848. "Map of the valley of the Sacramento, including the gold region." This map is a correct tracing of the map of Bidwell (land surveyor) by Thos. O. Larkin Esq. late Consul of the U.S. for California. Boston. Published by T. Wiley Jr.

Lindgren. 1911a. "Map of the northern part of the Sierra Nevada, California and Nevada." (Plate I *in* Lindgren, 1911.)

_____1911b. "Map of the deep placer mines near North Bloomfield and Relief, Nevada County, California." (Plate XX *in* Lindgren, 1911.)

Logan. 1925. "Region of Duncan Cañon, Placer County, Cal." (*In* Logan, 1925.)

_____1929. "Mineral map of western part of Sierra County, California." (*In* Logan, 1929a.)

_____1938. "Map of western portion of El Dorado County, showing mining claims." Prepared by C.A. Logan, District Mining Engineer, July 1938. (Plate 2 *in* Logan, 1938.)

_____1940. "Map of western portion Nevada County, California, showing mining claims." By C.A. Logan, District Mining Engineer, 1940. (*In* Logan, 1941.)

Ord. 1848. "Topographical sketch of the gold & quicksilver district of California, July 25th 1848." By E.O.C.O. [E.O.C. Ord] Lt. U.S.A.

Postal Route. 1884. (Map reproduced in *Early California, Northern Edition*. Corvallis, Oregon: Western Guide Publishers, p, 34-43.)

Ringgold. 1850a. "Chart of Suisun & Vallejo Bays, with the confluence of the Rivers Sacramento and San Joaquin, California." By Cadwalader Ringgold, Commander U.S. Navy, Assisted by Sam. R. Knox, Lieut. U.S.N., and Wm. P. Humphreys & J.H. Rowe Engineers. 1850.

_____1850b. "Chart of the Sacramento River from Suisun City to the American River, California." By Cadwalader Ringgold, Commander, U.S. Navy, Assisted by Edwin Cullbert, Lieut. of the Hydrotechnic Corps, Swedish Navy, and T.A. Emmet, Civil Engineer, 1850.

Sage. 1846. "Map of Oregon, California, New Mexico, N.W. Texas, & the proposed Territory of Ne-bras-ka." By Rufus B. Sage.

Scholfield. 1851. "Map of southern Oregon and northern California." Compiled from the best authorities, and from personal surveys and explorations, by N. Scholfield, Civil Engineer. Published by Marvin & Hitchcock, San Francisco.

Sinclair. 1901. "Oblique boundary between California and Nevada, Lake Tahoe to Colorado River." (In 7 sections.) By C.H. Sinclair, Assistant, Chief of Party. (*In* Sinclair.)

Taylor. 1902. "Map of Lake Tahoe." (Figure 5 *in* Taylor.)

Trask. 1853. "Topographical map of the mineral districts of California." Being the first map ever published from actual survey. By John B. Trask. Lithog. & Published by Britton & Rey. San Francisco.

United States Geological Survey. 1901. "Grass Valley quadrangle." (Scale 1:14,400.)

_____1922. "Parks Bar quadrangle". (Scale 1:31,680.)

Wescoatt. 1861. "Official surveys." By N. Wescoatt. [Nevada] County Surveyor.

Wheeler. 1876-1877a. "Parts of eastern California and western Nevada." (Atlas Sheet No. 56B.) Expeditions of 1876 & 1877 under the command of 1st Lieut. Geo. M. Wheeler.

_____1876-1877b. "Parts of eastern California and western Nevada." (Atlas Sheets 47(B) & 47 (D).) Expeditions of 1876 and 1877 under the command of 1st Lieut. Geo. M. Wheeler.

Whitney. 1870. "Map showing the extent of the hydraulic mining operations near Gold Run, Dutch Flat, Little York, You Bet, Chalk Bluffs, Red Dog, Hunt's Hill and Quaker Hill, on Bear River and Cañon, Steep Hollow and Greenhorn Creeks." From surveys made for the Geological Survey of California in 1870. By W.H. Pettee and A. Bowman. Revised and corrected in 1879 by W.H. Pettee. (*In* Whitney, 1880.)

_____1873. "Map of the Tertiary Auriferous Gravel deposits lying between the Middle Fork of the American and the Middle Yuba Rivers." (*In* Whitney, 1880.)

_____1880. "Sketch map showing the distribution of the volcanic and gravel formations over a portion of Placer and El Dorado Counties, California." (Plate B *in* Whitney, 1880.)

Wilkes. 1841. "Map of Upper California." By the U.S. Ex. Ex. and best authorities.

_____1849. "Map of Upper California." By the best authorities.

Williamson. 1849. "Sketch of the route of Capt. Warner's exploring party in the Sacramento Valley and Sierra Nevada. During the months of August, September, and October, 1849." By R.S. Williamson, Lieut. Top. Engrs.

Part Five
San Francisco Bay Region

Alameda, Contra Costa, Marin, Napa, San Francisco, San Mateo, Santa Clara, Solano and Sonoma Counties

Part Five—San Francisco Bay Region

San Francisco Bay Region
Alameda, Contra Costa, Marin, Napa, San Francisco, San Mateo, Santa Clara, Solano and Sonoma Counties

Regional Setting

General.—This section concerns geographic features in nine counties—Alameda, Contra Costa, Marin, Napa, San Francisco, San Mateo, Santa Clara, Solano, and Sonoma—that touch upon San Francisco Bay and adjacent water bodies. Townships (T) and Ranges (R) refer to Mount Diablo Base and Meridian. The region lies in the generally mountainous terrane between California's Central Valley and the sea. Cermeño first applied the name "San Francisco" in California in 1595 to present Drakes Bay (Treutlein, p. 12). Members of the Portola expedition in 1769 used the term "Puerto de San Francisco" for present Gulf of the Farallons before they discovered present San Francisco Bay (Davidson, p. 6); gradually the name "San Francisco" transferred to the bay (Treutlein, p. 14). The map on the facing page shows the location of the San Francisco Bay Region and the counties in it.

Alameda County.—Alameda County extends from San Francisco Bay eastward into and across Diablo Range. The county was organized in 1853 from territory of Contra Costa County and Santa Clara County; the county boundaries have had only minor changes (Coy, p. 61). The county seat first was at Alvarado, it moved in 1856 to San Leandro, and moved again in 1873 to Oakland, where it remains (Hoover, Rensch, and Rensch, p. 1). The county name, no doubt, is from Alameda Creek (Thompson and West, 1878. p. 15).

Contra Costa County.—Contra Costa County lies east of San Francisco Bay and San Pablo Bay, and south of Suisun Bay and Carquinez Strait. It includes the northernmost part of Diablo Range. The first state legislature created the county 1850; the southern third of the original territory of the county was lost in 1853 to newly created Alameda County (Coy, p. 91). Martinez is and always has been the county seat; the name "Contra Costa" is from the early designation of land east of San Francisco Bay—*contra costa* means "opposite coast" in Spanish (Hoover, Rensch, and Rensch, p. 50).

Marin County.—Marin County extends from the coast north of San Francisco eastward to San Francisco Bay and San Pablo Bay. The county is one of the original counties that the state legislature created in 1850; the only significant boundary change came in 1854 when the county line in San Francisco Bay was modified (Coy, p. 158-159). San Rafael was designated the seat of government when the county was organized, and has retained the honor (Hoover, Rensch, and Rensch, p. 174). The name "Marin" is thought to be from the word "Marinero," the name given by Spaniards to an Indian ferryman on San Francisco Bay—*marinero* means "mariner" in Spanish (Kroeber, p. 47).

Napa County.—Napa County lies north of San Francisco Bay along Napa River. The first state legislature created Napa County in 1850; the north part of the original county territory was lost in 1861 with the creation of Lake County; other boundary changes were made mainly to remedy deficiencies in the first county-boundary description (Coy, p. 187-193). The city of Napa has always been the county seat (Hoover, Rensch, and Rensch, p. 239).

San Francisco County.—San Francisco County is at the north end of the peninsula that separates San Francisco Bay from the sea; the county also includes some rocks and islands in the bay and in the sea. The county was created in 1850; much of the original area of the county was lost in 1856 to newly formed San Mateo County (Coy, p. 225-227). After this loss of territory, the governments of the county and of the city of San Francisco were consolidated; the name "San Francisco" is from San

Francisco de Asis mission, started within the limits of the present city in 1776 (Hoover, Rensch, and Rensch, p. 346).

San Mateo County.— San Mateo County is south of San Francisco between San Francisco Bay and the sea, and includes the north part of Santa Cruz Mountains. The county was created in 1856 from the south part of the original San Francisco County; San Mateo County annexed the north part of Santa Cruz County in 1868, but otherwise the boundaries of San Mateo County have changed only slightly (Coy, p. 238-239). Belmont was chosen the first county seat by a fraudulent election; within a year the seat of government moved to Redwood City, where it remains (Hoover, Rensch, and Rensch, p. 389).

Santa Clara County.—Santa Clara County covers most of Santa Clara Valley, which is the south part of the topographic depression occupied by San Francisco Bay. The county extends east to the crest of Diablo Range and west to the crest of Santa Cruz Mountains. It was created when California achieved statehood in 1850; the only significant change in county boundaries came in 1853, when territory was lost to newly organized Alameda County (Coy, p. 245). San Jose was the first, and remains the county seat; the name of the county is from Santa Clara de Asis mission, founded in 1777 (Hoover, Rensch, and Rensch, p. 425).

Solano County.—Solano County lies north of the mouth of Sacramento River and north of the connection of the river with San Pablo Bay through Suisun Bay and Carquinez Strait. The first state legislature created the county in 1850; except for the transfer of Mare Island from Sonoma County to Solano County in 1853, the original counties boundaries have changed only slightly (Coy, p. 259). The county seat first was at Benicia, but it moved in 1858 to Fairfield; the county name is from an Indian, a friend of the Mexicans, who was baptized Francisco Solano—the Indian's name was taken from San Francisco Solano mission at Sonoma in Sonoma County (Hoover, Rensch, and Rensch, p. 511).

Sonoma County.—Sonoma County extends from the sea to San Pablo Bay. The first state legislature created the county in 1850; some redefinition of county boundaries in the 1850's were made largely to rectify difficulties in the original boundary descriptions (Coy, p. 262-268). Sonoma was the county seat until 1854, when the county government moved to Santa Rosa (Hoover, Rensch, and Rensch, p. 525).

SAN FRANCISCO BAY REGION ALAMEDA, CONTRA COSTA, MARIN, NAPA, SAN FRANCISCO, SAN MATEO, SANTA CLARA, SOLANO AND SONOMA COUNTIES

— A —

Ababais Creek: see **Ebabias Creek** [SONOMA].

Abbey House: see **Daly City** [SAN MATEO].

Abbotts Lagoon [MARIN]: *lake,* 1.5 miles long, 9.5 miles north-northeast of the lighthouse at Point Reyes (lat. 38°07'15" N, long. 122°56'45" W). Named on Drakes Bay (1953) and Tomales (1954) 7.5' quadrangles. The name recalls John Abbott and his brother, Carlyle S. Abbott, who had a ranch in the neighborhood and took turns as justice of the peace at Point Reyes from 1859 until 1861 (Teather, p. 1).

Acalanes [CONTRA COSTA]: *land grant,* at and west of Lafayette. Named on Briones Valley (1959) and Walnut Creek (1959) 7.5' quadrangles. Candelario Valencia received 1 league in 1834 and Elam Brown claimed 3329 acres patented in 1858 (Cowan, p. 12). The name probably is from an Indian village located on or near the grant (Kroeber, p. 33).

Acelanus: see **Alamo** [CONTRA COSTA].

Adams: see **Corte Madera** [MARIN]; **Moon and Adams Landing**, under **Oakland** [ALAMEDA].

Adams Creek [NAPA]: *stream,* flows 6.5 miles to Eticuera Creek 5 miles northeast of Walter Springs (lat. 38°41'50" N, long. 122°17'15" W; sec. 22, T 10 N, R 4 W); the stream is south of Adams Ridge. Named on Walter Springs (1959) 7.5' quadrangle.

Adams Flat [NAPA]: *valley,* 9 miles northwest of Mount Vaca along Capell Creek (lat. 38°28'30" N, long. 122°14'05" W; on S line sec. 6, T 7 N, R 3 W). Named on Capell Valley (1951) 7.5' quadrangle.

Adams Ridge [NAPA]: *ridge,* generally northwest-trending, 2 miles long, 5 miles south of Knoxville (lat. 38°45' N, long. 122°20' W). Named on Knoxville (1958) and Walter Springs (1959) 7.5' quadrangles.

Adelante: see **Napa Junction** [NAPA].

Adeline [ALAMEDA]: *locality,* nearly 3 miles north of downtown Oakland along Southern Pacific Railroad (lat. 37°50'40" N, long. 122°16'25" W). Named on San Francisco (1899) 15' quadrangle.

Adeline [CONTRA COSTA]: *locality,* 6.5 miles north-northeast of the present Walnut Creek civic center along Oakland, Antioch and Eastern Railroad (lat. 37°59'45" N, long. 122°01'45" W). Named on Concord (1915) 15' quadrangle.

Adobe Canyon [SONOMA]: *canyon,* 4.5 miles long, along Sonoma Creek above a point 1.25 miles north-northwest of Kenwood (lat. 38°26' N, long. 122°33'10" W). Named on Kenwood (1954) and Rutherford (1951) 7.5' quadrangles. Called Sonoma Canyon on Santa Rosa (1916) 15' quadrangle.

Adobe Corner [SAN MATEO]: *locality,* 4.5 miles south-southwest of downtown Redwood City in Woodside (lat. 37°25'35" N, long. 122°15'55" W). Named on Woodside (1961) 7.5' quadrangle. John Coppinger built an adobe house at the site in 1841 (Brown, p. 1).

Adobe Creek [SANTA CLARA]: *stream,* flows 11 miles to flatlands 3 miles east-southeast of downtown Palo Alto near San Francisco Bay (lat. 37°25'50" N, long. 122°06'20" W). Named on Cupertino (1961), Mindego Hill (1961), and Mountain View (1961) 7.5' quadrangles. Called San Antonio Creek on Palo Alto (1899) 15' quadrangle, called Yeguas Cr. on Healy's (1866) map, and called San Antonio or Yeguas Creek on Thompson and West's (1876) map. Juan Prado Mesa gave the name "San Antonio" to the stream after he obtained nearby San Antonio grant in 1839 (Fava, p. 29). West Fork enters from the southwest 9 miles upstream from the flatlands; it is 2 miles long and is named on Mindego Hill (1961) 7.5' quadrangle.

Adobe Creek [SONOMA]: *stream,* flows 7.5 miles to Petaluma River 2 miles east-southeast of downtown Petaluma (lat. 38°13'25" N, long. 122°36'15" W); the stream goes past Petaluma Adobe state historical monument. Named on Glen Ellen (1954) and Petaluma River (1954) 7.5' quadrangles.

Adobe Gulch [SAN MATEO]: *canyon,* drained by a stream that flows 1 mile to marsh 6.5 miles north-northwest of Skeggs Point near Upper Crystal Springs Reservoir (lat. 37°29'50" N, long. 122°20'45" W; sec. 18, T 5 S, R 4 W). Named on Woodside (1961) 7.5' quadrangle. The name is from an adobe house built in the canyon in 1850 (Brown, p. 1).

Adobe Point [SAN MATEO]: *promontory,* 6 miles north-northwest of Skeggs Point on the west side of Upper Crystal Springs Reservoir (lat. 37°29'45" N, long. 122°20'15" W); the feature is near the mouth of Adobe Gulch. Named on Woodside (1961) 7.5' quadrangle.

Aetna Springs [NAPA]: *locality,* 10 miles north of Saint Helena (lat. 38°39'10" N, long. 122°29' W; near SW cor. sec. 1, T 9 N, R 6 W). Named on Aetna Springs (1958) 7.5' quadrangle. Crawford (1894, p. 341) used the form "Etna Springs" for the name. Postal authorities established Phoenix Mine post office, named for a quicksilver mine, in 1873 and discontinued it in 1880, when they moved the service 1 mile west to Lidell (Salley, p. 170). They established Lidell post office in 1880, moved it and changed the name to Aetna Springs in 1915, and discontinued it in 1945; the name "Lidell" was for William H. Lidell, first postmaster (Salley, p. 2, 122). The property at Aetna Springs post office belonged to Ætna Quicksilver Mining Company; after the company stopped mining in one of the tunnels, mineralized water from that tunnel was the basis of a resort as early as 1878 (Waring, p. 156-157). United States Board on Geographic Names (1991, p. 7) approved the name "Upper Bohn Lake" for a reservoir, 1 mile long, located 6 miles north-northeast of Aetna Springs on Napa-Lake County line (lat. 38°43'48" N, long. 122°26'28" W), and rejected the name "Eaton H. Magoon Lake" for the feature.

Agnes Island: see **Point San Quentin** [MARIN].

Agnew [SANTA CLARA]: *locality,* 2 miles south-southeast of Alviso along Southern Pacific Railroad (lat. 37°23'45" N, long. 121°57'30" W). Named on Milpitas (1961) 7.5' quadrangle. The name commemorates Abram Agnew, who settled in the neighborhood about 1873; the form "Agnews" also was used for the name (Rambo, 1964, p. 30). Postal authorities established Agnew post office in 1884 and discontinued it for a short time in 1890 (Frickstad, p. 172). In 1888 W.H. Peall, a real estate promoter, started a community called Bethlehem across the street from the community of Agnew; Bethlehem had a forty-room hotel, but the promotion failed (Joanne Grant in *San Jose Mercury News,* December 14, 1992). Postal authorities established Bethlehem post office less than 1 mile south of Agnew post office in 1890 and discontinued it the same year (Salley, p. 20).

Agnews: see **Agnew** [SANTA CLARA].

Agua Caliente [ALAMEDA-SANTA CLARA]: *land grant,* at and near Warm Springs district of Fremont on Alameda-Santa Clara County line, mainly in Alameda County. Named on Calaveras Reservoir (1961), Milpitas (1961), and Niles (1961) 7.5' quadrangles. Fulgencio Higuera received 2 leagues in 1834 and claimed 9564 acres patented in 1858 (Cowan, p. 12). Perez (p. 52) gave the year 1839 for the grant. The name is from hot springs—*agua caliente* means "hot water" in Spanish (Arbuckle, p. 13).

Agua Caliente [SONOMA]:

(1) *land grant,* at Agua Caliente (2) and Glen Ellen in Valley of the Moon. Named on Glen Ellen (1954), Kenwood (1954), and Sonoma (1951) 7.5' quadrangles. Lazaro Piña received 11 leagues in 1840; C.P. Stone claimed 212 acres patented in 1880; Mariano Guadalupe Vallejo claimed 1864 acres patented in 1880; T. M. Leavenworth claimed 592 acres patented in 1880; Joseph Hooker claimed 551 acres patented in 1866 (Cowan, p. 12).

(2) *locality,* nearly 3 miles northwest of Sonoma (lat. 38°19'25" N, long. 122°29'10" W); the place is on Agua Caliente grant. Named on Sonoma (1951) 7.5' quadrangle. Postal authorities established Agua Caliente post office in 1886 and discontinued it in 1951 (Frickstad, p. 193). Naturally occurring hot water at the place was the basis for a resort called Agua Caliente Springs (Bradley, p. 334). Postal authorities established Cave Dale post office 3 miles northeast of Agua Caliente (2) in 1913 and discontinued it in 1925 (Salley, p. 40).

Agua Caliente: see **Calistoga** [NAPA].

Agua Caliente Canyon [SONOMA]: *canyon,* 4 miles long, along Agua Caliente Creek above a point 1.5 miles northwest of Sonoma (lat. 38°18'35" N, long. 122°28'25" W). Named on Sonoma (1951) 7.5' quadrangle.

Agua Caliente Creek [ALAMEDA]: *stream,* flows 2.25 miles to lowlands 4.5 miles southeast of Fremont civic center (lat. 37°30'10" N, long. 121°54'40" W). Named on Milpitas (1961) and Niles (1961) 7.5' quadrangles. The stream also had the names "Arroyo del Agua Caliente" and

"Warm Springs Creek" (Mosier and Mosier, p. 4).

Agua Caliente Creek [SONOMA]: *stream,* flows nearly 5 miles to Sonoma Creek 1.5 miles west-northwest of Sonoma (lat. 38°18'10" N, long. 122°28'55" W); the stream goes through Agua Caliente Canyon. Named on Sonoma (1951) 7.5' quadrangle.

Agua Caliente Springs: see **Agua Caliente** [SONOMA] (2).

Agua de Vida Springs: see **Mendenhall Springs** [ALAMEDA].

Agua Fria Creek [ALAMEDA]: *stream,* flows 2.5 miles to lowlands 4.5 miles southeast of Fremont civic center (lat. 37°29'50" N, long. 121°55' W). Named on Milpitas (1961) 7.5' quadrangle. The stream first had the name "Arroyo de Agua Fria," and later the names "Agua Frio" and "Cold Springs Creek" (Mosier and Mosier, p. 4).

Agua Frio: see **Agua Fria Creek** [ALAMEDA].

Agua Rica Hot Sulphur Springs: see **Boyes Hot Springs** [SONOMA].

Air Base: see **Travis Air Force Base** [SOLANO].

Airport Channel [ALAMEDA]: *channel,* extends for 2.25 miles southeast from the Tidal Canal through San Leandro Bay to Metropolitan Oakland International Airport 3 miles west of downtown San Leandro (lat. 37°43'55" N, long. 122°12'35" W). Named on Oakland East (1959) and San Leandro (1959) 7.5' quadrangles.

Alambique Creek [SAN MATEO]: *stream,* flows 2.5 miles to marsh 5.5 miles south of downtown Redwood City near Searsville Lake (lat. 37°24'10" N, long. 122°14'15" W). Named on Woodside (1961) 7.5' quadrangle. The stream first was called Arroyo del Alambique for an illegal still built beside the creek in 1842—*alambique* means "stillhouse" in Spanish; the canyon along the upper part of the stream has been called Alambique Gulch, Mountain Home Gulch, and Jones Gulch (Brown, p. 1).

Alambique Gulch: see **Alambique Creek** [SAN MATEO].

Alameda [ALAMEDA]: *city,* 3 miles south-southeast of downtown Oakland on an island separated from the mainland by the Tidal Canal and Oakland Inner Harbor (lat. 37°45'45" N, long. 122°14'30" W). Named on Hunters Point (1956), Oakland East (1959), Oakland West (1959), and San Leandro (1959) 7.5' quadrangles. Postal authorities established Alameda post office in 1854 (Frickstad, p. 1), and the community incorporated the same year. The city was named for the county in the expectation that the name would influence settlers (Bancroft, 1888, p. 478). The site first was known as Bolsa de Encinal, or Encinal de San Antonio; soon after Alameda began on what then was a peninsula, a community called Encinal was laid out near the center of the peninsula and a community called Woodstock was laid out at the west end, but in 1872 the entire peninsula was united as Alameda under a town charter (Bancroft, 1888, p. 478). San Francisco and Alameda Railroad started Encinal Station in 1864 to serve the community of Encinal; the place also was known as Fasskings Station for Frederick Louis Fassking, a pioneer, and was called Grand Street Station (Mosier and Mosier, p. 35). Postal authorities established Encinal post office 4 miles south of Oakland post office in 1876, changed the name to West End in 1877, and discontinued it in 1891 (Salley, p. 69, 237). The settlement of West End first was called Bowman's Point for Charles C. Bowman, who settled at the place (Mosier and Mosier, p. 16).

Alameda Canyon: see **Niles Canyon** [ALAMEDA].

Alameda Creek [ALAMEDA-SANTA CLARA]: *stream,* heads in Santa Clara County and flow 46 miles to San Francisco Bay 7 miles south-southwest of downtown Hayward in Alameda County (lat. 37°34'55" N, long. 122°08'35" W). Named on Calaveras Reservoir (1961), Eylar Mountain (1955), La Costa Valley (1960), Mount Day (1955), Newark (1959), Niles (1961), and Redwood Point (1959) 7.5' quadrangles. The stream is called Rio de San Clemente and rio de la Alameda in Spanish documents of 1795 (Gudde, 1949, p. 6). The stream also had the local name "Arroyo de las Calaveras" (Mosier and Mosier, p. 11). Present Mount Eden Creek is called North Branch Alameda Creek on Thompson and West's (1878) map.

Alameda Naval Air Station [ALAMEDA]: *military installation,* 2.5 miles southwest of downtown Oakland along San Francisco Bay (lat. 37°47' N, long. 122°18'30" W); the installation is west of Alameda. Named on Oakland West (1959) 7.5' quadrangle.

Alameda Warm Springs: see **Warm Springs** [ALAMEDA].

Alamias Creek [SANTA CLARA]: *stream,* flows 2 miles to lowlands 3.5 miles northeast of Gilroy (lat. 37°02'30" N, long. 121°31' W). Named on Gilroy (1955) 7.5' quadrangle. On Chittenden (1955, photorevised 1968 and 1973) 7.5' quadrangle, the continuation of the stream in the lowlands is called Jones Creek.

Alamitos [SANTA CLARA]: *locality,* 6 miles south of downtown San Jose along Southern Pacific Railroad (lat. 37°15'05" N, long. 121° 52' W); the place is near the confluence of Alamitos Creek and Guadalupe River. Named on San Jose East (1961) and Santa Teresa Hills (1953) 7.5' quadrangles.

Alamitos Creek [SANTA CLARA]: *stream,* flows 12 miles to Guadalupe Creek 5.5 miles north-northwest of New Almaden (lat. 37° 14'50" N, long. 121°52'10" W). Named on Santa Teresa Hills (1953) 7.5' quadrangle; application of the name to upper reaches of the stream is unclear on the map. Called Arroyo de los Alamitos on Thompson and West's (1876) map.

Alamo [CONTRA COSTA]: *town,* 2.5 miles northwest of Danville (lat. 37°51' N, long. 122°01'50" W). Named on Las Trampas Ridge (1959) 7.5' quadrangle. Postal authorities established Alamo post office in 1852 (Frickstad, p. 20). The name is from poplar trees that were abundant near the place—*alamo* means "poplar" in Spanish (Hoover, Rensch, and Rensch, p. 56-57). Postal authorities established Acelanus post office 7 miles northwest of Alamo in 1854 and discontinued it in 1855; the name was from Acelanes grant (Salley, p. 1).

Alamo Creek [ALAMEDA-CONTRA COSTA]: *stream,* heads in Contra Costa County and flows 10 miles to Amador Valley 1.5 miles northeast of Dublin in Alameda County (lat. 37°42'50" N, long. 121°54'50" W). Named on Diablo (1953), Dublin (1961), and Tassajara (1953) 7.5' quadrangles. West Branch joins the main stream 6.5 miles southeast of Danville; it is 7.5 miles long and is named on Diablo (1953) 7.5' quadrangle.

Alamo Creek [SOLANO]: *stream,* flows 10 miles to lowlands 2 miles east-southeast of downtown Vacaville (lat. 38°20'35" N, long. 121°57'30" W). Named on Elmira (1953), Fairfield North (1951), and Mount Vaca (1951) 7.5' quadrangles.

Alamo Creek: see **Cottonwood Creek** [ALAMEDA-CONTRA COSTA].

Alamo Oaks [CONTRA COSTA]: *settlement,* 1.5 miles north-northeast of Danville (lat. 37°50'25" N, long. 121°59'30" W; sec. 17, T 1 S, R 1 W). Named on Diablo (1953) 7.5' quadrangle.

Alamo Ridge [CONTRA COSTA]: *ridge,* northwest- to west-northwest-trending, 2.25 miles long, center 1.5 miles north-northwest of Danville (lat. 37°50'40" N, long. 122°00'20" W); the ridge is east-southeast of Alamo. Named on Diablo (1953) and Las Trampas Ridge (1959) 7.5' quadrangles.

Alaska Packers Association Basin: see **Fortmann Basin** [ALAMEDA].

Albany [ALAMEDA]: *town,* 6.25 miles north-northwest of downtown Oakland (lat. 37°53'25" N, long. 122°17'55" W). Named on Richmond (1959) 7.5' quadrangle. Postal authorities established Albany post office in 1926 (Salley, p. 3). The town incorporated in 1908 under the name "Ocean View," but in 1909 the name was changed to Albany after the birthplace in New York of the town's first mayor, Frank J. Roberts (Gudde, 1949, p. 6).

Albany: see **Knights Valley** [SONOMA].

Albany Hill [ALAMEDA]: *hill,* 6.5 miles north-northwest of downtown Oakland (lat. 37°53'40" N, long. 122°18'20" W); the hill is in the town of Albany. Named on Richmond (1959) 7.5' quadrangle. Called Serrito de San Antonio on a diseño of San Pablo [CONTRA COSTA] grant made in 1830 (Becker, 1964). Called Cerritos San Antonio on Thompson and West's (1878) map. The hill also was called Signal Hill, Cerrito de San Antonio, Cerrito Hill, El Cerrito Hill, and Skunk Hill (Bowen, p. 339).

Albert Canyon [SAN MATEO]: *canyon,* drained by a stream that flows 1.5 miles to Pilarcitos Creek 3 miles northeast of downtown Half Moon Bay (lat. 37°29'30" N, long. 122°23' W; sec. 14, T 5 S, R 5 W). Named on Woodside (1961) 7.5' quadrangle. The William C. Albrecht (also called Albert) family ranch was in the canyon from the early 1870's until 1954 (Brown, p. 1; Brown called the feature Albert Gulch).

Albert Gulch: see **Albert Canyon** [SAN MATEO].

Albrae [ALAMEDA]: *locality,* 4 miles south-southwest of Fremont civic center along Southern Pacific Railroad (lat. 37°29'40" N, long. 121°59'15" W; sec. 17, T 5 S, R 1 W). Named on Milpitas (1961) 7.5' quadrangle. The name is from Albrae Gun Club, which incorporated in 1907; the club owned property at the place (Mosier and Mosier, p. 8).

Alcatraces Island: see **Alcatraz Island** [SAN FRANCISCO].

Alcatraz: see **Alcatraz Island** [SAN FRANCISCO]; **Lorin** [ALAMEDA].

Alcatraz Island [SAN FRANCISCO]: *island,* 1800 feet long, 1.25 miles north-northwest of North Point in San Francisco Bay (lat. 37°49'35" N, long. 122°25'20" W). Named on San Francisco North (1956) 7.5' quadrangle. Called Alcatraces on Ringgold's (1850a) map, and called Alcatraces Id. on Williamson's (1853) map. Ringgold (p. 25) referred to the feature as Isle of Alcatraces, and Fremont called it White Island or Bird Island in 1847 (Spence and Jackson, p. 317). The island was fortified in the 1850's, became a military prison in 1907, and a federal prison in 1934 (Frazer, p. 19). Postal authorities established Alcatraz post office in 1874 and discontinued it in 1963 (Salley, p. 4).

Alcatraz Shoal [SAN FRANCISCO]: *shoal,* 1.25 miles northwest of North Point in San Francisco Bay (lat. 37°49'30" N, long. 122° 26' W); the shoal is west of Alcatraz Island. Named on San Francisco North (1956, photorevised 1968 and 1973) 7.5' quadrangle.

Alden: see **Oakland** [ALAMEDA].

Alder Creek [CONTRA COSTA]: *stream,* flows 1.25 miles to Curry Canyon nearly 2 miles south-southeast of Mount Diablo (lat. 37° 51'30" N, long. 121°53'55" W; sec. 7, T 1 S, R 1 E). Named on Diablo (1953) 7.5' quadrangle.

Alder Creek [SONOMA]:

(1) *stream,* heads in Mendocino County and flows 3.5 miles to Squaw Creek 5 miles north-northwest of Geyser Peak (lat. 38°50'05" N, long. 122°52' W; sec. 4, T 11 N, R 9 W). Named on Asti (1959) and The Geysers (1959) 7.5' quadrangles.

(2) *stream,* flows less than 1 mile to Dutch Bill Creek nearly 2 miles north-

northwest of Occidental (lat. 38°25'50" N, long. 122° 57'40" W; near SW cor. sec. 22, T 7 N, R 10 W). Named on Camp Meeker (1954) 7.5' quadrangle.

Aldercroft Creek [SANTA CLARA]: *stream,* flows nearly 2 miles to Lexington Reservoir 3 miles south of downtown Los Gatos (lat. 37°10'40" N, long. 121°59'45" W; sec. 5, T 9 S, R 1 W). Named on Castle Rock Ridge (1955) and Los Gatos (1953) 7.5' quadrangles.

Aldercroft Heights [SANTA CLARA]: *settlement,* 4.25 miles south-southwest of Los Gatos (lat. 37°09'45" N, long. 121°58'15" W; sec. 9, 10, T 9 S, R 1 W); the place is 1.5 miles southeast of the mouth of Aldercroft Creek. Named on Los Gatos 1953) 7.5' quadrangle.

Alderglen Springs [SONOMA]: *locality,* 3 miles northwest of Cloverdale (lat. 38°50'05" N, long. 123°03'15" W; sec. 2, T 11 N, R 11 W). Named on Cloverdale (1960) 7.5' quadrangle. Called Alder Glen Sps. on Hopland (1944) 15' quadrangle. In 1909, a resort at the place had a hotel, cottages, and tents that provided accommodations for 75 guests (Waring, p. 166).

Alec Canyon [SANTA CLARA]: *canyon,* drained by a stream that flows 1.25 miles to Uvas Creek 3.5 miles east-southeast of Loma Prieta (lat. 37°05'05" N, long. 121°47' W; sec. 6, T 10 S, R 2 E). Named on Loma Prieta (1955) 7.5' quadrangle.

Alexander: see **Alexander Valley** [SONOMA].

Alexander Valley [SONOMA]: *valley,* along Russian River from Cloverdale southeast for 20 miles to the latitude of Healdsburg. Named on Asti (1959), Cloverdale (1960), Geyserville (1955), Healdsburg (1955), and Jimtown (1955) 7.5' quadrangles. The name commemorates Cyrus Alexander, a trapper and trader who came to California in 1833 and later owned land in the valley (Hoover, Rensch, and Rensch, p. 534). Postal authorities established Alexanderville post office 7 miles southeast of Geyserville in 1871 and discontinued it in 1872; They established Alexander post office at or near the site of Alexanderville post office in 1879 and discontinued it in 1880 (Salley, p. 4). They established Soda Rock post office 6 miles east of Healdsburg in 1889 and discontinued it in 1892, when they moved it 1 mile northwest and renamed it Alexander Valley; they discontinued Alexander Valley post office in 1903 (Salley, p. 4, 207).

Alexanderville: see **Alexander Valley** [SONOMA].

Alfalfa Patch Reservoir [NAPA]: *lake,* 150 feet long, nearly 3 miles south-southeast of Berryessa Peak (lat. 38°37'30" N, long. 122°10'30" W). Named on Brooks (1959) 7.5' quadrangle.

Alhambra: see **Lake Alhambra** [CONTRA COSTA].

Alhambra Creek [CONTRA COSTA]: *stream,* flows 2.5 miles to Arroyo del Hambre 6 miles northwest of Walnut Creek civic center (lat. 37°58'25" N, long. 122°07'30" W). Named on Briones Valley (1959) and Walnut Creek (1959) 7.5' quadrangles.

Alhambra Creek: see **Arroyo del Hambre** [CONTRA COSTA].

Alhambra Valley [CONTRA COSTA]: *valley,* along Arroyo del Hambre above a point 8.5 miles north-northeast of Orinda (lat. 37° 59'45" N, long. 122°07'50" W). Named on Briones Valley (1959) 7.5' quadrangle. According to Holmes (p. 248-249), Louisiana Strentzel gave the name "Alhambra" to the valley when she moved there in the 1850's. The feature first was called Cañada del Hambre—*Cañada del Hambre* means "Valley of Hunger" in Spanish—and later it was called Hungry Valley (Gudde, 1949, p. 7); this name came from the hunger that a company of Spanish soldiers suffered at the place (Davis, W.H., p. 16).

Alice Eastwood: see **Camp Alice Eastwood,** under **Camp Eastwood** [MARIN].

Alice Rock [SONOMA]: *relief feature,* 2.25 miles north-northwest of the village of Bodega Bay (lat. 38°21'55" N, long. 122°03'05" W). Named on Bodega Head (1942) 7.5' quadrangle.

Alisal: see **Pleasanton** [ALAMEDA].

Allen Creek [SONOMA]: *stream,* flows 2.5 miles to House Creek 7 miles southwest of Big Mountain (lat. 38°38'10" N, long. 123°13'40" W; sec. 7, T 9 N, R 12 W). Named on Tombs Creek (1978) 7.5' quadrangle.

Allendale [SOLANO]: *settlement,* 6.5 miles north-northeast of Vacaville (lat. 38°26'35" N, long. 121°56'30" W). Named on Allendale (1953) 7.5' quadrangle. Postal authorities established Allendale post office in 1876 and discontinued it in 1884; the name is for Morgan Allen, first postmaster (Salley, p. 4).

Allendale: see **Oakland** [ALAMEDA].

Allen's Landing: see **Mount Eden** [ALAMEDA].

Alliance Redwood [SONOMA]: *locality,* 2.25 miles northwest of Occidental (lat. 38°26' N, long. 122°58'20" W; sec. 21, T 7 N, R 10 W). Named on Camp Meeker (1954) 7.5' quadrangle.

Allison: see **Mount Allison** [ALAMEDA].

Allison Canyon [SANTA CLARA]: *canyon,* drained by a stream that flows 1 mile to Llagas Creek 3.5 miles south-southeast of New Almaden (lat. 37°08' N, long. 121°47'25" W). Named on Loma Prieta (1955) and Santa Teresa Hills (1953) 7.5' quadrangles.

Alma [SANTA CLARA]: *village,* 2.5 miles south of Los Gatos along Los Gatos Creek (lat. 37°11' N, long. 121°59'05" W; sec. 5, T 9 S, R 1 W); water of Lexington Reservoir now covers the site. Named on Los Gatos (1919) 15' quadrangle. The place began in 1862 with the opening there of a hotel called Forest House (Hoover, Rensch, and Rensch, p. 455). Postal authorities established Alma post office in 1873 and discontinued it in 1952 (Frickstad, p. 172). Gudde (1949, p. 8) related the name "Alma" to the first four letters of the name "*Alma*den."

Almaden: see **New Almaden** [SANTA CLARA].

Almaden Canyon [SANTA CLARA]: *canyon,* extends for at least 3 miles along Alamitos Creek at and above New Almaden (lat. 37° 10' N, long. 121°49'45" W). Named on Santa Teresa Hills (1953) 7.5' quadrangle.

Almaden Reservoir [SANTA CLARA]: *lake,* 1 mile long, behind a dam on Alamitos Creek less than 1 mile south-southwest of New Almaden (lat. 37°09'55" N, long. 121°49'40" W); the lake is in Almaden Canyon. Named on Santa Teresa Hills (1953) 7.5' quadrangle.

Alma Soda Spring: see **Soda Spring Canyon** [SANTA CLARA].

Almond Reservoir [ALAMEDA]: *intermittent lake,* 350 feet long, 3 miles north of downtown Hayward (lat. 37°42'50" N, long. 122°04'50" W). Named on Hayward (1959) 7.5' quadrangle. The name is from Almond Road, where the feature is located (Mosier and Mosier, p. 8).

Almonte [MARIN]: *locality,* nearly 6 miles south of downtown San Rafael along Northwestern Pacific Railroad (lat. 37°53'25" N, long. 122°31'25" W). Named on San Rafael (1954) 7.5' quadrangle. Called Mill Valley Junction on Tamalpais (1897) 15' quadrangle. The place first was called Bay Junction in 1890 (Teather, p. 1).

Alms House Canyon: see **Polhemus Creek** [SAN MATEO].

Alpine Creek [SAN MATEO]: *stream,* flows 4.5 miles to join La Honda Creek and form San Gorgonio Creek 0.5 mile south-southwest of La Honda (lat. 37°18'35" N, long. 122°16'35" W; near E line sec. 22, T 7 S, R 4 W). Named on La Honda (1961) and Mindego Hill (1961) 7.5' quadrangles. The name is from Alpine ranch, located at the head of the stream (Brown, p. 2).

Alpine Lake [MARIN]: *lake,* behind a dam on Lagunitas Creek 3.25 miles northwest of Bolinas (lat. 37°56'25" N, long. 122°38'15" W). Named on Bolinas (1954) and San Rafael (1954) 7.5' quadrangles.

Alston: see **Dresser** [ALAMEDA].

Alta Creek: see **Strawberry Creek** [ALAMEDA].

Alta Mesa [SANTA CLARA]: *locality,* 3.5 miles east-southeast of downtown Palo Alto along Southern Pacific Railroad (lat. 37°24'05" N, long. 122°08' W). Named on Palo Alto (1961) 7.5' quadrangle. The rail line no longer reaches the place.

Altamont [ALAMEDA]: *locality,* 7.5 miles northeast of Livermore (lat. 37°44'40" N, long. 121°39'45" W; sec. 20, T 2 S, R 3 E). Named on Altamont (1953) 7.5' quadrangle. Postal authorities established Altamont post office in 1872 and discontinued it in 1955 (Salley, p. 6). Irelan (p. 34) referred to the place as Alta Monte. The site was called The Summit before Central Pacific Railroad reached it in 1869 (Mosier and Mosier, p. 8).

Altamont Creek [ALAMEDA]: *stream,* flows 3.25 miles to Livermore Valley 2.5 miles southwest of Altamont (lat. 37°42'45" N, long. 121°41'45" W; near E line sec. 36, T 2 S, R 2 E); the stream heads near Altamont Pass. Named on Altamont (1953) 7.5' quadrangle.

Alta Monte: see **Altamont** [ALAMEDA].

Altamont Medical Springs: see **Occidental** [SONOMA].

Altamont Pass [ALAMEDA]: *pass,* 7.5 miles northeast of Livermore (lat. 37°44'50" N, long. 121°39'15" W; near W line sec. 21, T 2 S, R 3 E); the pass is near Altamont. Named on Altamont (1953) 7.5' quadrangle. Called Livermores Pass on Goddard's (1857) map. Williamson (1855, p. 11) called the feature Livermore's Pass, and Whitney (p. 33) called it Livermore Pass—Whitney (p. 32) noted that the name is for "Mr. Livermore, an old settler in the valley."

Alta Vista [SONOMA]: *locality,* 2 miles north-northeast of Sonoma (lat. 38°19'15" N, long. 122°26'30" W). Named on Sonoma (1942) 15' quadrangle.

Alten [SONOMA]: *locality,* 1.5 mile southeast of Sebastopol along Petaluma and Santa Rosa Railroad (lat. 38°23' N, long. 122°48'25" W; sec. 12, T 6 N, R 9 W). Named on Sebastopol (1942) 15' quadrangle.

Alto [MARIN]: *locality,* nearly 5 miles south of downtown San Rafael along Northwestern Pacific Railroad (lat. 37°54'15" N, long. 122°31'30" W). Named on San Rafael (1954) 7.5' quadrangle. The railroad station at the site was called Blithedale during the early 1880's, when carriages from Blithedale resort met trains there (Teather, p. 1).

Alton: see **Maine Prairie** [SOLANO].

Altruria: see **Fulton** [SONOMA].

Alum Rock [SANTA CLARA]:

(1) *relief feature,* a conspicuous outcrop of alum-bearing rock in Alum Rock Canyon 1 mile east of the mouth of the canyon (lat. 37°23'40" N, long. 121°48'35" W). Named on Calaveras Reservoir (1961) 7.5' quadrangle.

(2) *district,* on the east side of San Jose south of the mouth of Alum Rock Canyon. Named on Calaveras Reservoir (1961) and San Jose East (1961) 7.5' quadrangles. California Mining Bureau's (1917b) map shows a place called Alum Rock located beyond Berryessa at the end of a rail line.

Alum Rock Canyon [SANTA CLARA]: *canyon,* along Upper Penitencia Creek and the lower part of Arroyo Aguague; the name seems to apply to a canyon 3 miles long that opens into lowlands 5 miles northeast of downtown San Jose (lat. 37°23'40" N, long. 121°49'45" W); Alum Rock (1) is in the lower part of the canyon. Named on Calaveras Reservoir (1961) 7.5' quadrangle. Rancher John Martin Ogan named the canyon, and the state legislature used the name in the act that created a park there in 1872 (undated item from *San Jose Mercury*). Crawford (1894, p. 345) called the feature Penitentiary Cañon. Winslow Anderson (p. 78-80) described a resort called Alum Rock Springs that was situated in the canyon.

Alum Rock Springs: see **Alum Rock Canyon** [SANTA CLARA].

Alvarado [ALAMEDA]: *district,* 5 miles north-northwest of downtown Newark in Union City (lat. 37°35'45" N, long. 122°04'45" W). Named on Newark (1959) 7.5' quadrangle. Newark (1948) 7.5' quadrangle has the name for a community that in 1958 joined with the neighboring community of Decoto to form the new city of Union City (Hoover, Rensch, and Rensch, p. 17). Henry C. Smith founded a town at the site in 1851 and named it New Haven after the city in his home state of Connecticut; in 1853 the place became the seat of government of newly formed Alameda County, and took the name "Alvarado" from a nearby community that had been named for Juan B. Alvarado, Mexican governor of California from 1836 until 1842 (Gudde, 1949, p. 9). Postal authorities established Alvarado post office in 1853 (Frickstad, p. 1).

Alvirez Field [SANTA CLARA]: *land grant,* 1.5 miles northwest of Coyote. Named on Santa Teresa Hills (1953) 7.5' quadrangle. The land belonged to Juan Alvirez; title to 78.62 acres was confirmed in 1865 (Arbuckle, p. 37).

Alviso [SANTA CLARA]: *town,* 8 miles northwest of downtown San Jose near the head of navigation at the south end of San Francisco Bay (lat. 37°25'35" N, long. 121°58'30" W). Named on Milpitas (1961) and Mountain View (1961) 7.5' quadrangles. The place has been part of San Jose since 1968. The landing place for Santa Clara mission, called Embarcadero de Santa Clara de Asis, was at the head of present Alviso Slough; Ygnacio Alviso, owner of Ricon de los Esteros grant, settled at the site in 1840 (Hoover, Rensch, and Rensch, p. 428). The town, which was named for the owner of the grant, was laid out in 1849 and incorporated in 1852 (Bancroft, 1888, p. 525). Postal authorities established Alviso post office in 1854, discontinued it in 1855, and reestablished it in 1859 (Salley, p. 6). A city to be called New Chicago was proposed in the 1890's for lowlands north of Alviso, but it failed to develop (Butler, p. 57). San Jose Port Association was formed in 1928 to promote a deep-water port—to be called Port San Jose—at Alviso, but this project also failed (Curtis, p. 33).

Alviso Slough [SANTA CLARA]: *water feature,* extends for 4 miles from Alviso to Coyote Creek near the mouth of that stream (lat. 37°27'40" N, long. 122°01'20" W). Named on Milpitas (1961) and Mountain View (1961) 7.5' quadrangles. Called Steamboat Slough on Thompson and West's (1876) map.

Amador's: see **Dublin** [ALAMEDA].

Amador Valley [ALAMEDA]: *valley,* at and near Pleasanton; the feature is the western extension of Livermore Valley. Named on Dublin (1961) and Livermore (1961) 7.5' quadrangles. The name commemorates Jose Maria Amador, owner of San Ramon grant (Gudde, 1949, p. 9-10). Thompson and West's (1878) map shows Willow Marsh, which covers much of the west part of the valley.

Amador Valley: see **Dublin** [ALAMEDA]; **San Ramon Valley** [ALAMEDA-CONTRA COSTA].

Ambrose [CONTRA COSTA]: *locality,* 3.5 miles west of Pittsburg along Atchison, Topeka and Santa Fe Railroad (lat. 38°02'05" N, long. 121°56'55" W; near W line sec. 11, T 2 N, R 1 W). Named on Honker Bay (1918) 7.5' quadrangle.

America: see **Santa Rosa** [SONOMA].

American Canyon [NAPA]: *canyon,* 2.25 miles long, opens into lowlands 2 miles south-southeast of Napa Junction (lat. 38°09'50" N, long. 122°13'55" W); the canyon heads opposite the head of American Canyon [SOLANO]. Named on Cordelia (1951) 7.5' quadrangle, where the name "American Canyon" applies to American Canyon [NAPA] and to American Canyon [SOLANO] together. Postal authorities established American Canyon post office 5 miles north of Vallejo in the canyon in 1956 (Salley, p. 7).

American Canyon [SOLANO]: *canyon,* 3.5 miles long, opens into lowlands 1.25 miles southwest of Cordelia (lat. 38°11'45" N, long. 122°09' W; near W line sec. 13, T 4 N, R 3 W); the canyon heads opposite the head of American Canyon [NAPA]. Named on Cordelia (1951) 7.5' quadrangle, where the name "American Canyon" applies to American Canyon [SOLANO] and to American Canyon [NAPA] together.

American Canyon Creek [NAPA]: *stream,* flows 2.25 miles to lowlands nearly 2 miles south-southeast of Napa Junction (lat. 38°09'50" N, long. 122°13'55" W); the stream drains American Canyon. Named on Cordelia (1951) and Cuttings Wharf (1949) 7.5' quadrangles.

Americano Creek [MARIN-SONOMA]: *stream,* forms part of Marin-Sonoma County line, heads in Sonoma County and flows 11 miles to Estero Americano 4.5 miles north-northwest of Tomales in Marin County (lat. 38°18'45" N, long. 122°55'40" W). Named on Two Rock (1954) and Valley Ford (1954) 7.5' quadrangles. United States Board on Geographic Names (1943, p. 9) rejected the names "Ebabias Creek," "Estero Americano," and "Estero Americano Creek" for the stream, or for any part of it.

Ames Beach: see **Miramar Beach** [SAN MATEO].

Amesport: see **Miramar** [SAN MATEO].

Amesport Landing: see **Miramar** [SAN MATEO].

Analy: see **Freestone** [SONOMA].

Analy Valley: see **Freestone** [SONOMA].

Ancha Vista Spring: see **Red Hill** [MARIN] (2).

Anchor Creek [SONOMA]: *stream,* heads in Mendocino County and flows 1.5 miles to Cherry Creek 4.5 miles west-northwest of Cloverdale (lat. 38°49'30" N, long. 123°05'50" W; near SW cor. sec. 4, T 11 N, R 11 W). Named on Cloverdale (1960) 7.5' quadrangle.

Anderson Canyon [NAPA]: *canyon,* drained by a stream that flows 2.5 miles to lowlands along Lake Berryessa nearly 3 miles west-southwest of Berryessa Peak (lat. 38°39'20" N, long. 122°14'15" W); the canyon is south of Anderson Mountain. Named on Brooks (1959) 7.5' quadrangle.

Anderson Lake [SANTA CLARA]: *lake,* 5.25 miles long, behind a dam on Coyote Creek nearly 3 miles north-northeast of Morgan Hill (lat. 37°09'55" N, long. 121°37'40" W). Named on Morgan Hill (1955) and Mount Sizer (1955) 7.5' quadrangles.

Anderson Mountain [NAPA]: *peak,* 1.25 miles west-southwest of Berryessa Peak (lat. 38°39'35" N, long. 122°12'45" W); the peak is north of Anderson Canyon. Altitude 1807 feet. Named on Brooks (1959) 7.5' quadrangle.

Anderson's Landing: see **Patterson Landing** [ALAMEDA].

Andrews Landing: see **San Leandro Creek** [ALAMEDA-CONTRA COSTA].

Andy Mason Slough: see **Simmons Island** [SOLANO].

Angel Creek [SONOMA]: *stream,* flows 1.25 miles to Mill Creek (1) 7 miles north of Guerneville (lat. 38°36'20" N, long. 122°58'45" W; near NW cor. sec. 28, T 9 N, R 10 W). Named on Guerneville (1955) 7.5' quadrangle.

Angel Island [MARIN-SAN FRANCISCO]: *island,* mainly in Marin County, but two promontories on the east side extend into San Francisco County; 1.5 miles long, 3 miles east of downtown Sausalito in San Francisco Bay (lat. 37°51'45" N, long. 122°25'45" W). Named on San Francisco North (1956) 7.5' quadrangle. Called I. de los Angeles on Ringgold's (1850a) map, but in his text Ringgold (p. 11, 24) called the feature Angel Isle and Angel Island. Ayala in 1775 called it Isla de los Angeles, and his chaplain, Vicente Santa Maria, called it la Isla de Santa Maria de los Angeles (Galvin, p. 83). Postal authorities established Angel Island post office in 1875 and discontinued it in 1945 (Salley, p. 7).

Angelo Creek: see **Angelo Slough** [SAN MATEO]; **Belmont Slough** [SAN MATEO].

Angelo House: see **Belmont** [SAN MATEO].

Angelo's Creek: see **Belmont Slough** [SAN MATEO].

Angelo Slough [SAN MATEO]: *water feature,* extends from Seal Creek (present Seal Slough) to Belmont Slough 4 miles east-southeast of downtown San Mateo (lat. 37°32'45" N, long. 122°15'10" W). Named on San Mateo (1947) 7.5' quadrangle. Called Angelo Cr. on San Mateo (1915) 15' quadrangle. The name commemorates Charles Aubrey Angelo, who started Angelo House in 1850 at present Belmont (Brown, p. 2).

Angelo Slough: see **Seal Slough** [SAN MATEO].

Angwin [NAPA]: *town,* 5 miles north-northeast of Saint Helena (lat. 38°34'45" N, long. 122°26'45" W); the town is on La Jota grant. Named on Saint Helena (1960) 7.5' quadrangle. Postal authorities established Angwin post office in 1883 and discontinued it in 1910; they established La Jota post office 7 miles northeast of Saint Helena in 1923 and discontinued it in 1925, when they moved it and changed the name to Angwin (Salley, p. 8, 115). The name "Angwin" commemorates Edwin Angwin, who operated a summer resort at the site (Gudde, 1949, p. 11).

Anita Rock [SAN FRANCISCO]: *rock,* 1.25 miles east of Fort Point, and 900 feet offshore in San Francisco Bay (lat. 37°48'30" N, long. 122°27'10" W). Named on San Francisco North (1956) 7.5' quadrangle. Called Annita Rocks on Ringgold's (1850a) map.

Ann: see **Livermore** [ALAMEDA].

Anna Belcher Creek [SONOMA]: *stream,* flows 1.25 miles to Little Sulphur Creek 10 miles north-northeast of Healdsburg at Pine Flat (lat. 38°44'30" N, long. 122°46'15" W; sec. 5, T 10 N, R 8 W). Named on Jimtown (1955) 7.5' quadrangle. Called Florence Cr. on Healdsburg (1940) 15' quadrangle. Anne Belcher quicksilver mine was situated near the stream about 1.75 miles north of Pine Flat (Bailey, p. 228).

Annadel [SONOMA]: *locality,* 3.25 miles west-northwest of Kenwood along Southern Pacific Railroad (lat. 38°26'25" N, long. 122° 36' W). Named on Santa Rosa (1916) 15' quadrangle. Postal authorities established Annadel post office in 1892 and discontinued it in 1893 (Frickstad, p. 194). The name was derived from the first name of Annie Hutchinson, the daughter of a landowner at the place (Higgins, p. 235).

Annapolis [SONOMA]: *settlement,* 5 miles north-northeast of the village of Stewarts Point (lat. 38°43'15" N, long. 123°22'05" W). Named on Annapolis (1977) 7.5' quadrangle. Postal authorities established Annapolis post office in 1901 and moved it 0.5 mile east in 1940; the name is from Annapolis Orchards, started in the 1880's (Salley, p. 8).

Annita Rocks: see **Anita Rock** [SAN FRANCISCO].

Año Nuevo Bay [SAN MATEO]: *embayment,* east of Año Nuevo Point (present Point Año Nuevo) along the coast (lat. 37°06'45" N, long. 122°18'45" W). Named on Año Nuevo (1955) 7.5' quadrangle. Brown (p. 61) used the name "New Year's Bay." United States Board on Geographic Names (1962a, p. 4) rejected the name "New Year Bay" for the feature, and rejected the form "Ano Nuevo Bay" for the name. California Mining Bureau's (1917b) map has the name "Steele" for a place near the coast at the embayment.

Año Nuevo Creek [SAN MATEO]: *stream,* heads in Santa Cruz County and flows nearly 4 miles to the sea 1.25 miles east of Año Nuevo Point (present Point Año Nuevo) (lat. 37°07' N, long. 122° 18'20" W). Named on Año Nuevo (1955) and Franklin Point (1955) 7.5' quadrangles. United States Board on Geographic Names (1962a, p. 4) rejected the name "New Year Creek" for the feature, and rejected the form "Ano Nuevo Creek" for the name. Brown (p. 61) used the name "New Year's Creek" for the stream, and noted that in Spanish times the creek was called arroyo de Lucia for an incident involving Lucia Bolcof of Santa Cruz, and also was called arroyo de los Lobos—*lobos* is the Spanish term for "sea lion." Davidson (p. 37) stated that the name "Big Gulch" is a local designation for the canyon of the stream. Brown (p. 98) used the name "Waddell Beach" for the beach at and south of the mouth of the creek, and remarked that Waddell's Landing was situated at the north end of the beach from 1864 into the 1870's. Morrall (p. 51) mentioned that lumber was shipped from Waddell's Wharf at Point Año Nuevo.

Año Nuevo Island [SAN MATEO]: *island,* 0.25 mile long, 0.5 mile southwest of Año Nuevo Point (present Point Año Nuevo) (lat. 37° 06'30" N, long. 122°20'10" W). Named on Año Nuevo (1955) 7.5' quadrangle. Brown (p. 61) used the form "New Year's Island" for the name. United States Board on Geographic Names (1962a, p. 5) rejected the name "New Year Island" for the feature, and rejected the form "Ano Nuevo Island" for the name.

Año Nuevo Point [SAN MATEO]: *promontory,* 6 miles southeast of Pigeon Point along the coast (lat. 37°06'45" N, long. 122°19'40" W). Named on Año Nuevo (1955) 7.5' quadrangle. United States Board on Geographic Names (1962a, p. 4) approved the name "Point Año Nuevo" for the promontory, and rejected the names "New Years Point," "Año Nuevo Point," "Ano Nuevo Point," "Point Anno Nueva," "Point Anno Nuevo," "Point Ano Nuevo," and "Punta Año Nueva." The Board pointed out that Sebastian Vizcaino gave the name "Punta de Año Nuevo" to the feature on January 3, 1603, because it was the first promontory sighted in the new year—*Punta de Año Nuevo* means "New Year Point" in Spanish. Postal authorities established Point New Year post office 12 miles south of Pescadero in 1872 and discontinued it in 1874 (Salley, p. 175). Grant and Gale (p. 661) used the name "Purisima Rock" for a feature located seven-eighths of a mile east of Año Nuevo Point.

Antioch [CONTRA COSTA]: *city,* 10 miles north-northeast of Mount Diablo (lat. 38°00'40" N, long. 121°48'30" W). Named on Antioch North (1978) and Antioch South (1953) 7.5' quadrangles. Postal authorities established Antioch post office in 1851, discontinued it in 1852, reestablished it in 1855, discontinued it in 1862, and reestablished it in 1863 (Salley, p. 8). The city incorporated in 1872. Brothers W.W. Smith and Joseph Smith settled in 1849 at the site, which was known as Smith's Landing before it was named after the biblical city of Antioch (Gleason, p. 190). The place also was called Marshs Landing because John Marsh used it as a shipping point (Hanna, P.T., p. 14). Postal authorities established Junction post office in 1850 and discontinued it in 1853, when they moved it to Antioch (Salley, p. 108). A place called Horse Haven was situated 6 miles south of Antioch in the 1870's (Davis and Goldman, p. 516).

Antioch: see **East Antioch** [CONTRA COSTA].

Antioch Point [CONTRA COSTA]: *promontory,* 1.25 miles northwest of downtown Antioch along San Joaquin River (lat. 38°01'30" N, long. 121°49'30" W). Named on Antioch North (1978) 7.5' quadrangle.

Antioch Station [CONTRA COSTA]: *locality,* less than 1 mile south-southeast of present downtown Antioch along Southern Pacific Railroad (lat. 38°00'05" N, long. 121°48'20" W). Named on Collinsville (1918) 7.5' quadrangle.

Antonio Mountain [MARIN]: *peak,* 11 miles west-northwest of downtown Novato (lat. 38°11'35" N, long. 122°44' W); the peak is on Laguna de San Antonio grant. Altitude 1171 feet. Named on Petaluma (1953) 7.5' quadrangle.

Anza: see **Lake Anza** [CONTRA COSTA].

Apanolio Creek [SAN MATEO]: *stream,* flows 3.5 miles to Pilarcitos Creek 1.25 miles northeast of downtown Half Moon Bay (lat. 37°28'35" N, long. 122°24'40" W). Named on Half Moon Bay (1961) and Montara Mountain (1956) 7.5' quadrangles. The misspelled name is for Apolonio Rodriguez, who settled by the stream in 1858; the feature also was called Fillmore Creek for another rancher (Brown, p. 28). The stream drains Digges Canyon.

Apperson Creek [ALAMEDA]: *stream,* flows 3.25 miles to San Antonio Creek nearly 3 miles southeast of Sunol (lat. 37°34'20" N, long. 121°50'30" W). Named on La Costa Valley (1960) 7.5' quadrangle. The stream now enters San Antonio Reservoir. The name commemorates Elbert Apperson, who settled in the neighborhood in the 1890's (Mosier and Mosier, p. 10). South Fork enters from the south 1 mile upstream from the mouth of the main creek; it is 2.5 miles long and is named on La Costa Valley (1960) 7.5' quadrangle.

Apperson Ridge [ALAMEDA]: *ridge,* northwest-trending, 3.5 miles long, 5.5 miles southeast of Sunol (lat. 37°32'15" N, long. 121°47'30" W). Named on La Costa Valley (1960) 7.5' quadrangle. Pleasanton (1906) 15' quadrangle shows the feature as part of Valpe Ridge.

Appleby Bay [NAPA]: *marsh,* 5 miles west of Napa Junction along Napa Slough (lat. 38°11'30" N, long. 122°20'20" W; sec. 18, T 4 N, R 4 W). Named on Cuttings Wharf (1949) 7.5' quadrangle.

Apple Tree Canyon [NAPA]: *canyon,* drained by a stream that flows 1 mile to Gosling Canyon 7 miles south-southeast of Berryessa Peak (lat. 38°34'05" N, long. 122°09'10" W; sec. 2, T 8 N, R 3 W). Named on Lake Berryessa (1959) 7.5' quadrangle.

Appletree Gulch [SAN MATEO]: *canyon,* drained by a stream that flows 1.25 miles to West Union Creek 2.25 miles northeast of Skeggs Point (lat. 37°25'40" N, long. 122°16'10" W). Named on Woodside (1961) 7.5' quadrangle.

Arastradero Creek [SANTA CLARA]: *stream,* flows 2.25 miles to Matadero Creek 4.25 miles south of downtown Palo Alto (lat. 37° 23'05" N, long. 122°09'50" W). Named on Mindego Hill (1961) and Palo Alto (1961) 7.5' quadrangles.

Arched Rock [SONOMA]:

(1) *island,* 400 feet long, 1.25 miles south-southwest of Jenner, and 1250 feet offshore (lat. 38°26' N, long. 123°07'35" W). Named on Arched Rock (1977) 7.5' quadrangle.

(2) *rock,* 3 miles north-northwest of the village of Bodega Bay, and 150 feet offshore (lat. 38°22'10" N, long. 123°04'25" W). Named on Bodega Head (1972) 7.5' quadrangle.

Arched Rock Beach [SONOMA]: *beach,* nearly 3 miles north-northwest of the village of Bodega Bay along the coast (lat. 38°22'05" N, long. 123°04'20" W); the beach is southeast of Arched Rock (2). Named on Bodega Head (1972) 7.5' quadrangle.

Arch Rock [SAN FRANCISCO]: *rock,* 2 miles northwest of North Point in San Francisco Bay (lat. 37°49'45" N, long. 122°26'20" W). Named on San Francisco North (1956) 7.5' quadrangle. Called Bird Rock on Wackenreuder's (1861) map.

Arden: see **Dumbarton Point** [ALAMEDA].

Arff: see **Baumberg** [ALAMEDA].

Argus Island: see **Point San Pedro** [MARIN].

Armstrong's Creek: see **Kingston Creek** [SAN MATEO].

Army Point [SOLANO]: *promontory,* 1.5 miles east of downtown Benicia along Carquinez Strait (lat. 38°02'40" N, long. 122°17'45" W; sec. 6, T 2 N, R 2 W). Named on Benicia (1959) 7.5' quadrangle. Called Navy Pt. on Ringgold's (1850c) map.

Arrowhead Mountain [NAPA-SONOMA]: *ridge,* northwest-trending, 2 miles long, 3 miles east-southeast of Sonoma on Napa-Sonoma County line (lat. 38°16'35" N, long. 122°24'10" W). Named on Sonoma (1951) 7.5' quadrangle.

Arroya de la Alameda: see **Arroyo de la Alameda** [ALAMEDA].

Arroya Honda [MARIN]: *stream,* flows 3 miles to the sea 3 miles west-northwest of Bolinas (lat. 37°55'35" N, long. 122°44'10" W). Named on Bolinas (1954) 7.5' quadrangle.

Arroyo Aguague [SANTA CLARA]: *stream,* flows 8.5 miles to Upper Penitencia Creek 7.5 miles northeast of downtown San Jose (lat. 37°24'10" N, long. 121°47'25" W). Named on Calaveras Reservoir (1961), Lick Observatory (1955), and San Jose East (1961) 7.5' quadrangles. Whitney (p. 51) used the names "Arroyo de la Penitencia" and "Arroyo Aguage" for the stream.

Arroyo Arichi: see **Arroyo Avichi** [MARIN].

Arroyo Avichi [MARIN]: *stream,* flows 3 miles to Novato Creek 0.5 mile south-southeast of downtown Novato (lat. 38°05'55" N, long. 122°34' W). Named on Novato (1954) 7.5' quadrangle. Called Arroyo Arichi on Petaluma (1914) 15' quadrangle.

Arroyo Bayo [SANTA CLARA]: *stream,* flows 8 miles to San Antonio Creek 6.25 miles south of Eylar Mountain (lat. 37°23'05" N, long. 121°34'20" W; sec. 30, T 6 S, R 4 E). Named on Eylar Mountain (1955), Isabel Valley (1955), and Mount Stakes (1955) 7.5' quadrangles.

Arroyo Buenos Ayres: see **Corral Hollow** [ALAMEDA].

Arroyo Calero [SANTA CLARA]: *stream,* joins Alamitos Creek 2.5 miles north-northwest of New Almaden (lat. 37°12'50" N, long. 121°50' W). Named on Santa Teresa Hills (1953) 7.5' quadrangle. The stream extends for nearly 2 miles below Calero Reservoir, but application of the name above the reservoir is uncertain on the map. On Thompson and West's (1876) map, the lower part of the stream has the name "Arroyo Seco" and the upper part has the name "Calero Creek."

Arroyo Cañada Verde: see **Cañada Verde** [SAN MATEO].

Arroyo Cavelano: see **Cayetano Creek** [ALAMEDA-CONTRA COSTA].

Arroyo Cayetano: see **Cayetano Creek** [ALAMEDA-CONTRA COSTA].

Arroyo Corte Madera Del Presidio [MARIN]: *stream,* flows 4.5 miles to

Richardson Bay 5.5 miles south of downtown San Rafael (lat. 37°53'30" N, long. 122°31'15" W); the stream forms part of the boundary of Corte de Madera del Presidio grant. Named on San Rafael (1954) 7.5' quadrangle. Called Widow Reed Creek on Tamalpais (1897) 15' quadrangle—this name was for Mrs. John Reed, whose husband built the first sawmill in Marin County along the stream in 1834 (Gudde, 1949, p. 389).

Arroyo Covelano: see **Cayetano Creek** [ALAMEDA-CONTRA COSTA].

Arroyo Creek: see **Holmes Canyon** [SONOMA]; **Pulgas Creek** [SAN MATEO].

Arroyo de Agua Fria: see **Agua Fria Creek** [ALAMEDA].

Arroyo de Carnadero: see **Carnadero Creek** [SANTA CLARA].

Arroyo de en Medio [SAN MATEO]: *stream,* flows 2.5 miles to the sea 2.5 miles northwest of downtown Half Moon Bay (lat. 37°29'35" N, long. 122°27'35" W). Named on Half Moon Bay (1961) and Montara Mountain (1956) 7.5' quadrangles. The stream is the boundary between the two Corral de Tierra grants. The name is from an enclosure that was situated by the stream in the early nineteenth century and had the name "rodeo de en Medio" from its position between the two ranches—*rodeo de en medio* has the meaning "middle roundup corral" in Spanish; other names for the stream were Mullen's Creek and Bradley's Creek, both for ranchers (Brown, p. 59-60).

Arroyo de la Alameda [ALAMEDA]: *land grant,* at and near Union City. Named on Hayward (1959), Newark (1959), Niles (1961), and Redwood Point (1959) 7.5' quadrangles. Called Arroya de la Alameda on San Leandro (1959) 7.5' quadrangle. Jose de Jesus Vallejo received 4 leagues in 1842 and claimed 17,705 acres patented in 1858 (Cowan, p. 13-14).

Arroyo de la Bajada: see **Gazos Creek** [SAN MATEO].

Arroyo de la Ballena: see **Yankee Jim Gulch** [SAN MATEO].

Arroyo de la Bocana: see **Strawberry Creek** [ALAMEDA].

Arroyo de la Cienega: see **Cascade Creek** [SAN MATEO].

Arroyo de la Cuesta: see **Martini Creek** [SAN MATEO].

Arroyo de la Encarnation: see **Scott Creek** [ALAMEDA-SANTA CLARA].

Arroyo del Agua Caliente: see **Agua Caliente Creek** [ALAMEDA].

Arroyo de la Harina: see **San Lorenzo Creek** [ALAMEDA].

Arroyo de la Laguna [ALAMEDA]:

(1) *stream,* flows 7.25 miles to Alameda Creek 0.5 mile southwest of Sunol (lat. 37°35'20" N, long. 121°53'25" W; sec. 17, T 4 S, R 1 E). Named on Dublin (1961), La Costa Valley (1960), and Niles (1961) 7.5' quadrangles.

(2) *stream,* heads at The Lagoon (present Stivers Lagoon) near present Fremont civic center (lat. 37°32'30" N, long. 121°57'45" W), and flows south for 3.25 miles before ending. Named on Pleasanton (1906) 15' quadrangle.

Arroyo del Alambique: see **Alambique Creek** [SAN MATEO].

Arroyo de la Penitencia: see **Arroyo Aguague** [SANTA CLARA]; **Upper Penitencia Creek** [SANTA CLARA].

Arroyo de la Purisima: see **Cañada de Verde y Arroyo de la Purisima** [SAN MATEO].

Arroyo de la Purissima: see **Purisima Creek** [SAN MATEO].

Arroyo de las Calaveras: see **Alameda Creek** [ALAMEDA].

Arroyo de las Garzas: see **Gazos Creek** [SAN MATEO].

Arroyo de las Llagas: see **Llagas Creek** [SANTA CLARA].

Arroyo de las Nueces: see **Walnut Creek** [CONTRA COSTA] (1).

Arroyo de las Nueces y Bolbones [CONTRA COSTA]: *land grant,* extends from the city of Walnut Creek to Concord and eastward. Named on Clayton (1953), Diablo (1953), Las Trampas Ridge (1959), and Walnut Creek (1959) 7.5' quadrangles. Juan Sanchez Pacheco received 2 leagues in 1834; Pacheco's heirs claimed 17,782 acres patented in 1866 (Cowan, p. 53; Cowan listed the grant under the name "Arroyo de las Nueces y Sierra de Bolbones"). The term "Bolbones" probably is from the Spanish name for the inhabitants of an Indian village (Kroeber, p. 36).

Arroyo de las Nueces y Sierra de Bolbones: see **Arroyo de las Nueces y Bolbones** [CONTRA COSTA].

Arroyo de las Pulgas: see **Pulgas Creek** [SAN MATEO].

Arroyo de las Trampas: see **Bolinger Creek** [CONTRA COSTA].

Arroyo de las Trancas: see **Corinda Los Trancos Creek** [SAN MATEO].

Arroyo de las Tunitas: see **Tunitas Creek** [SAN MATEO].

Arroyo del Bosque: see **Sausal Creek** [ALAMEDA].

Arroyo del Cerro [CONTRA COSTA]: *stream,* flows nearly 3 miles to Ygnacio Valley 4.5 miles west-northwest of Mount Diablo (lat. 37°54'05" N, long. 121°59'35" W). Named on Clayton (1953) 7.5' quadrangle.

Arroyo del Coyote: see **Coyote Creek** [ALAMEDA-SANTA CLARA].

Arroyo del Hambre [CONTRA COSTA]: *stream,* flows 8 miles to Carquinez Strait at Martinez (lat. 38°01'25" N, long. 122°08'25" W). Named on Benicia (1959), Briones Valley (1959), and Walnut Creek (1959) 7.5' quadrangles. United States Board on Geographic Names (1943, p. 11) rejected the name "Alhambra Creek" for the stream. Whitney (p. 15) called the feature El Hambre Creek.

Arroyo del Ingreto: see **San Ramon Creek** [CONTRA COSTA].

Arroyo del Leona: see **Lion Creek** [ALAMEDA].

Arroyo del Matadero: see **Matadero Creek** [SANTA CLARA].

Arroyo del Monte: see **Frenchmans Creek** [SAN MATEO].

Arroyo del Monte Diablo: see **Mount Diablo Creek** [CONTRA COSTA].

Arroyo de los Alamitos: see **Alamitos Creek** [SANTA CLARA].

Arroyo de los Cadillos: see **Cordilleras Creek** [SAN MATEO].

Arroyo De Los Calabazas: see **Calabazas Creek** [SANTA CLARA].

Arroyo de los Capitancillos: see **Los Capitancillos Creek** [SANTA CLARA].

Arroyo de los Coches [SANTA CLARA]: *stream,* flows 2.25 miles to lowlands 2 miles east-northeast of Milpitas (lat. 37°26'20" N, long. 121°52'05" W), and continues in an artificial watercourse through lowlands to Lower Penitencia Creek. Named on Calaveras Reservoir (1961) and Milpitas (1961) 7.5' quadrangles.

Arroyo de los Frijoles [SAN MATEO]: *stream,* flows 5.5 miles to the sea 3 miles north-northwest of Pigeon Point at Bean Hollow Beach (lat. 37°13'30" N, long. 122°24'30" W). Named on Franklin Point (1955) and Pigeon Point (1955) 7.5' quadrangles. According to Brown (p. 6), the stream should be called Bean Hollow Creek, from the name "Bean Hollow" for the canyon of the stream; the early name for the canyon was Cañada del Frijol—*frijol* means "kidney bean" in Spanish.

Arroyo de Los Gatos: see **Los Gatos Creek** [SANTA CLARA].

Arroyo de los Guilicos: see **Calabazas Creek** [SONOMA].

Arroyo de los Laureles: see **Laurel Creek** [SAN MATEO].

Arroyo de los Lobitos: see **Lobitos Creek** [SAN MATEO].

Arroyo de los Lobos: see **Año Nuevo Creek** [SAN MATEO].

Arroyo de los Nogales: see **Walnut Creek** [CONTRA COSTA] (1).

Arroyo de los Pilarcitos: see **Miramontes** [SAN MATEO] (1); **Pilarcitos Creek** [SAN MATEO].

Arroyo de los Poblanos: see **Marsh Creek** [CONTRA COSTA].

Arroyo de los Taunamines: see **Arroyo Valle** [ALAMEDA-SANTA CLARA].

Arroyo del Pescadero: see **Pescadero Creek** [SAN MATEO].

Arroyo del Puetro: see **Lobos Creek** [SAN FRANCISCO].

Arroyo del Sanjon: see **Sausal Creek** [SAN MATEO].

Arroyo de Lucia: see **Año Nuevo Creek** [SAN MATEO].

Arroyo del Valle: see **Arroyo Valle** [ALAMEDA-SANTA CLARA].

Arroyo del Viaje: see **Arroyo Valle** [ALAMEDA-SANTA CLARA].

Arroyo de Matadera: see **Matadero Creek** [SANTA CLARA].

Arroyo de Monte Verde: see **Higgins Canyon** [SAN MATEO].

Arroyo de Nuestra Señora de los Dolores: see **Mission District** [SAN FRANCISCO].

Arroyo de Permanente: see **Santa Rosa Creek** [SONOMA].

Arroyo de Pescadero: see **Pescadero Creek** [SANTA CLARA].

Arroyo de San Antonio: see **San Antonio Creek** [MARIN-SONOMA].

Arroyo de San Bruno: see **Colma Creek** [SAN MATEO].

Arroyo de San Felipe: see **Pacheco Creek** [SANTA CLARA].

Arroyo de San Francisco: see **San Francisquito Creek** [SAN MATEO-SANTA CLARA].

Arroyo de San Francisquito: see **San Francisquito Creek** [SAN MATEO-SANTA CLARA].

Arroyo de San Geronimo: see **Lagunitas Creek** [MARIN].

Arroyo de San Gregorio: see **San Gregorio Creek** [SAN MATEO].

Arroyo de San Jose Cupertino: see **Stevens Creek** [SANTA CLARA].

Arroyo de San Leandro: see **San Leandro Creek** [ALAMEDA-CONTRA COSTA].

Arroyo de San Matheo: see **San Mateo Creek** [SAN MATEO].

Arroyo de San Pedro: see **San Pedro Creek** [SAN MATEO].

Arroyo de San Salvador de Horta: see **San Lorenzo Creek** [ALAMEDA].

Arroyo de San Simon y San Judas: see **Pilarcitos Creek** [SAN MATEO].

Arroyo de Santa Rosa: see **Santa Rosa Creek** [SONOMA].

Arroyo de Santa Toma Aquino: see **San Tomas Aquinas Creek** [SANTA CLARA].

Arroyo de San Vicente: see **San Vicente Creek** [SAN MATEO].

Arroyo de Soto: see **Whitehouse Creek** [SAN MATEO].

Arroyo Diablo: see **Belmont Creek** [SAN MATEO].

Arroyo Grande: see **Sonoma Creek** [SONOMA].

Arroyo Holon: see **Larkspur Creek** [MARIN].

Arroyo Hondo [SANTA CLARA]: *stream,* formed by the confluence of Isabel Creek and Smith Creek, flows 9 miles to Calaveras Reservoir 11 miles northeast of downtown San Jose (lat. 37°27'50" N, long. 121°46'30" W; sec. 29, T 5 S, R 2 E). Named on Calaveras Reservoir (1961) and Mount Day (1955) 7.5' quadrangles.

Arroyo Hondo: see **La Honda Creek** [SAN MATEO].

Arroyo las Positas [ALAMEDA]: *stream,* flows 14 miles to Arroyo Mocho 5 miles west of Livermore (lat. 37°41'40" N, long. 121°51'30" W). Named on Tesla (1907) 15' quadrangle, and on Livermore (1961) 7.5' quadrangle. The stream is called Posita Creek on Land Office maps of the 1850's, and it is called Las Posita Creek on a map of 1873 (Gudde, 1949, p. 270).

Arroyo Leon [SAN MATEO]: *stream,* flows 6.25 miles to Pilarcitos Creek near downtown Half Moon Bay (lat. 37°27'55" N, long. 122°25'30" W). Named on Half Moon Bay (1961) and Woodside (1961) 7.5' quadrangles. Called Leon Creek on Halfmoon Bay (1940) 15' quadrangle. The name commemorates Francisco de Leon, a Chilenian who settled by the stream in the 1850's (Brown, p. 47).

Arroyo Limpio: see **Clear Creek** [SAN MATEO].

Arroyo Mocho [ALAMEDA-SANTA CLARA]: *stream*, heads in Santa Clara County and flows 34 miles to Arroyo de la Laguna 2.25 miles southeast of Dublin in Alameda County (lat. 37°40'40" N, long. 121°54'40" W); the stream heads near Mount Mocho. Named on Altamont (1953), Cedar Mountain (1956), Dublin (1961), Eylar Mountain (1955), Livermore (1961), and Mendenhall Springs (1956) 7.5' quadrangles. Gudde (1949, p. 218) noted use of the name "Mocho Creek" as early as 1852, and attributed the name to disappearance of the water after the stream forms distributaries—*arroyo mocho* means "cut-off creek" in Spanish.

Arroyo Nicasio: see **Nicasio Creek** [MARIN].

Arroyo Ojo de Agua [SAN MATEO]: *stream*, flows 2 miles to lowlands 1.5 miles south-southwest of downtown Redwood City (lat. 37°27'45" N, long. 122°14'15" W). Named on Palo Alto (1961) and Woodside (1961) 7.5' quadrangles. The name is from a lake called el Ojo de Agua that was near the feature; the stream, or its canyon, also was called Deer Creek, Hawes Gulch—for Horace Hawes, who had a ranch along the stream in the late 1850's, and Schroeder Gulch—for J.B. Schroeder, who lived near the mouth of the canyon in the 1880's (Brown, p. 86).

Arroyo Olemus Loke: see **Olema Creek** [MARIN].

Arroyo Permanente: see **Permanente Creek** [SANTA CLARA].

Arroyo Quito: see **Saratoga Creek** [SANTA CLARA].

Arroyo Rodrigues: see **San Gregorio Creek** [SAN MATEO].

Arroyo Salinas: see **Redwood Creek** [SAN MATEO].

Arroyo San Antonio: see **Chileno Creek** [MARIN]; **Walker Creek** [MARIN].

Arroyo San Jose [MARIN]: *stream*, flows 4 miles to lowlands 3.25 miles south-southeast of downtown Novato at Ignacio (lat. 38°04'05" N, long. 122°32'15" W); the stream is on San Jose grant. Named on Novato (1954) 7.5' quadrangle.

Arroyo San Tomas Aquino: see **San Tomas Aquinas Creek** [SANTA CLARA].

Arroyo Sausal [MARIN]: *stream*, flows 11 miles to join Salmon Creek and form Walker Creek 9 miles southeast of Tomales (lat. 38°09'40" N, long. 122°46'50" W). Named on Petaluma (1953), Point Reyes NE (1954), and San Geronimo (1954) 7.5' quadrangles.

Arroyo Sausal: see **Sausal Creek** [SAN MATEO]; **Walker Creek** [MARIN].

Arroyo Seco [ALAMEDA]: *stream*, flows 7.25 miles to Livermore Valley 5.25 miles south-southwest of Altamont (lat. 37°40'30" N, long. 121°42'04" W; sec. 13, T 3 S, R 2 E). Named on Altamont (1953) and Midway (1953) 7.5' quadrangles. Called Muddy Creek on Thompson and West's (1878) map. The feature was known as Coal Mine Creek in the early 1870's, and also was called Bangs Creek, for Joseph L. Bangs, a local resident (Mosier and Mosier, p. 12). Thomas Harris and Jenkin Richards discovered coal in the canyon of Arroyo Seco 7 miles southeast of Livermore in 1862; a community called Harrisville, for Thomas Harris, flourished there in the 1870's (Mosier, p. 5).

Arroyo Seco [SONOMA]: *stream*, flows 6.5 miles to Schell Creek 5.25 miles south-southeast of Sonoma (lat. 38°14'55" N, long. 122° 26' W). Named on Sears Point (1951) and Sonoma (1951) 7.5' quadrangles.

Arroyo Seco: see **Arroyo Calero** [SANTA CLARA].

Arroyo Seco de los Capitancillos: see **Los Capitancillos Creek** [SANTA CLARA].

Arroyo Valle [ALAMEDA-SANTA CLARA]: *stream*, formed by the confluence of Arroyo Bayo and San Antonio Creek in Santa Clara County, flows 24 miles to Arroyo de la Laguna 3.25 miles south-southeast of Dublin in Alameda County (lat. 37°39'40" N, long. 121°54'20" W). Named on Cedar Mountain (1956), Dublin (1961), Eylar Mountain (1955), La Costa Valley (1960), Livermore (1961), and Mendenhall Springs (1956) 7.5' quadrangles. The name is from Valle de San Jose grant (Gudde, 1949, p. 376). Dall and Harris (p. 198) referred to "the Arroyo del Viaja, or Valle." United States Board on Geographic Names (1933, p. 104) rejected the name "Arroyo del Valle" for the feature. The stream first was called Arroyo de los Taunamines for an Indian tribe (Mosier and Mosier, p. 12).

Arroyo Verde [SONOMA]: see **Salmon Creek** [SONOMA] (1).

Arroyo Viejo [ALAMEDA]: *stream*, flows 5 miles to Lion Creek 5 miles southeast of downtown Oakland (lat. 37°45'15" N, long. 122° 12' W). Named on Oakland East (1959) 7.5' quadrangle.

Arthur Creek: see **Little Arthur Creek** [SANTA CLARA].

Artist Point [CONTRA COSTA]: *peak*, 2.5 miles south-southwest of Mount Diablo (lat. 37°50'55" N, long. 121°56' W; near E line sec. 14, T 1 S, R 1 W). Named on Diablo (1953) 7.5' quadrangle.

Asbury Creek [SONOMA]: *stream*, flows 2.5 miles to Sonoma Creek 0.5 mile south of Glen Ellen (lat. 38°21'20" N, long. 122° 31'25" W). Named on Glen Ellen (1954) 7.5' quadrangle.

Asco [ALAMEDA]: *locality*, nearly 6 miles west of Livermore along Southern Pacific Railroad (lat. 37°41' N, long. 121°52'20" W). Named on Livermore (1961) 7.5' quadrangle. The name is from Alameda Sugar Company, which raised sugar beets and other crops at the place from 1899 until 1917 (Mosier and Mosier, p. 12).

Ashland [ALAMEDA]: *town*, 2.5 miles northwest of downtown Hayward (lat. 37°41'40" N, long. 122°07' W). Named on Hayward (1959) 7.5' quadrangle. The place developed in the 1940's and was named for an Oregon ash tree growing there (Mosier and Mosier, p. 13).

Aspenwall Bay: see **Paradise Cay** [MARIN].

Associated: see **Avon** [CONTRA COSTA].

Asti [SONOMA]: *village*, 4 miles southeast of Cloverdale (lat. 38°45'45" N, long. 122°58'20" W). Named on Asti (1959) 7.5' quadrangle. Postal authorities established Asti post office in 1888 (Frickstad, p. 194). Andrea Sbarboro founded a cooperative enterprise in 1881 that he called Italian-Swiss Colony; Asti was part of the venture and was named for a city in northern Italy (Hansen and Miller, p. 56).

Asylum Slough: see **Tulucay Creek** [NAPA].

Atascadero Creek [SONOMA]: *stream*, flows 8.5 miles to Green Valley Creek 4.25 miles northeast of Occidental (lat. 38°26'55" N, long. 122°53'10" W). Named on Camp Meeker (1954) and Sebastopol (1954) 7.5' quadrangles.

Atchison: see **Richmond** [CONTRA COSTA].

Atherton [SAN MATEO]: *town*, center 2 miles southeast of downtown Redwood City (lat. 37°27'45" N, long. 122°12' W). Named on Palo Alto (1961) 7.5' quadrangle. The place, which began as a community of estates around Fair Oaks railroad station, was known as Fair Oaks; the town incorporated in 1923 and took the name "Atherton" for Faxon Dean Atherton, whose estate was there (Brown, p. 3). Postal authorities established Atherton post office in 1947 (Salley, p. 11).

Atherton Peak [SANTA CLARA]: *peak*, 2 miles northwest of Pajaro Gap on Santa Clara-Santa Cruz County line (lat. 36°56'15" N, long. 121°38'50" W). Altitude 1616 feet. Named on Watsonville East (1955) 7.5' quadrangle.

Atlas [NAPA]: *locality*, 8 miles west-northwest of Mount Vaca (lat. 38°25'45" N, long. 122°14'50" W; sec. 25, T 7 N, R 4 W); the place is 1.5 miles south-southeast of Atlas Peak. Named on Capell Valley (1951) 7.5' quadrangle. Postal authorities established Atlas post office in 1893, moved it 1 mile south in 1894, and discontinued it in 1934; the place was a resort community named for nearby Atlas Peak (Salley, p. 11).

Atlas Peak [NAPA]: *peak*, 6.25 miles east-northeast of Yountville (lat. 38°27'05" N, long. 122°15'45" W; near SW cor. sec. 14, T 7 N, R 4 W). Altitude 2663 feet. Named on Yountville (1951) 7.5' quadrangle.

Aurora Creek: see **Stemple Creek** [MARIN-SONOMA].

Ausaymas y San Felipe [SANTA CLARA]: *land grant*, 10 miles east of Gilroy; partly in San Benito County. Named on Gilroy Hot Springs (1955), Pacheco Peak (1955), San Felipe (1955), and Three Sisters (1954) 7.5' quadrangles. Francisco Perez Pacheco received 2 leagues in 1836 and claimed 35,504 acres patented in 1859 (Cowan, p. 17). According to Kroeber (p. 35), the term "Ausaymas" came from the name of Indians who lived near San Juan Bautista mission in San Benito County.

Austin [SANTA CLARA]: *locality*, 1.5 miles northwest of Los Gatos (lat. 37°14'30" N, long. 121°59'50" W). Named on Los Gatos (1919) 15' quadrangle.

Austin: see **Cazadero** [SONOMA]; **Melrose** [ALAMEDA].

Austin Creek [SOLANO]: *stream*, flows 1.25 miles to Napa River 2 miles north-northwest of downtown Vallejo (lat. 38°07'40" N, long. 122°16'20" W). Named on Mare Island (1959) 7.5' quadrangle.

Austin Creek [SONOMA]: *stream*, flows 15 miles to Russian River 3.5 miles southwest of Guerneville (lat. 38°27'55" N, long. 123°02'55" W). Named on Cazadero (1978), Duncans Mills (1979) and Fort Ross (1978) 7.5' quadrangles. Called Big Austin Creek on Cazadero (1943) and Fort Ross (1943) 7.5' quadrangles. On Healdsburg (1940) 15' quadrangle, present Gilliam Creek is called East Br. Austin Cr.

Austin Creek: see **East Austin Creek** [SONOMA]; **Little Austin Creek**, under **Gray Creek** [SONOMA].

Austin Gap [SONOMA]: *pass*, nearly 3 miles southwest of Guerneville (lat. 38°28'45" N, long. 123°02'20" W); the pass is east of Austin Creek. Named on Duncans Mills (1979) 7.5' quadrangle.

Austrian Gulch [SANTA CLARA]: *canyon*, drained by a stream that flows 2 miles to Lake Elsman 2.25 miles southwest of Mount Umunhum (lat. 37°08'05" N, long. 121°55'20" W; sec. 24, T 9 S, R 1 W). Named on Los Gatos (1953) 7.5' quadrangle. The name commemorates a group of Austro-Germans who settled in the canyon in the 1870's (Hoover, Rensch, and Rensch, p. 457). Water of Lake Elsman now covers the sites of communities called Austrian Gulch and Germantown, built by the settlers (Young, p. 63).

Avalis Beach [MARIN]: *beach*, 4.25 miles west-southwest of Tomales on Tomales Point at the mouth of Tomales Bay (lat. 38° 13'55" N, long. 122°58'50" W). Named on Tomales (1954) 7.5' quadrangle. The name commemorates an Indian (Mason, 1976a, p. 149).

Avisadero Point: see **Point Avisadero** [SAN FRANCISCO].

Avon [CONTRA COSTA]: *locality*, 3.5 miles east-northeast of Martinez along Southern Pacific Railroad (lat. 38°02' N, long. 122°04'30" W). Named on Vine Hill (1959) 7.5' quadrangle, which also has the name "Associated P.O." at the place. Postal authorities established Marsh post office in 1912, changed the name to Associated in 1913, and discontinued it in 1960; the name "Marsh" was for John Marsh, a pioneer in the region, and the name

"Associated" was for Tidewater Associated Oil Company, which owned the site (Salley, p. 11, 134).

Ayala Cove: see **Hospital Cove** [MARIN].

Azule Springs [SANTA CLARA]: *locality,* 1.5 miles west-northwest of Saratoga along Calabazas Creek (lat. 37°15'50" N, long. 122°03'25" W; sec. 2, T 8 S, R 2 W). Named on Palo Alto (1899) 15' quadrangle. Arthur S. Caldwell discovered a soda spring at the site in the early 1850's; the spring was called Caldwell Springs before L.R. Mills bought the property (Cunningham, p. 79). The place was called Mills Seltzer Spring until it received the name "Azule" from the blue appearance of the range to the southwest—*azule* means "blue" in Spanish; the owner sold bottled water and developed the property as a picnic resort (Waring, p. 212-213). Cunningham (p. 80-81) noted that a popular resort called Idlewild was started in the 1870's on the ridge above Azule Springs

— B —

Babb Creek [SANTA CLARA]: *stream,* flows 2.5 miles to lowlands 3 miles east-southeast of Berryessa (lat. 37°22'10" N, long. 121°48'45" W). Named on San Jose East (1961) 7.5' quadrangle.

Babb Creek: see **South Babb Creek** [SANTA CLARA].

Babbs Canyon [SANTA CLARA]: *canyon,* drained by a stream that flows 1 mile to lowlands nearly 2 miles southwest of Gilroy (lat. 36°59' N, long. 121°35'10" W). Named on Chittenden (1955) 7.5' quadrangle.

Baby Peak [SANTA CLARA]: *peak,* 3.5 miles north-northeast of Mount Day (lat. 37°27'45" N, long. 121°39'50" W; at SE cor. sec. 29, T 5 S, R 3 E). Altitude 2766 feet. Named on Mount Day (1955) 7.5' quadrangle.

Bache: see **Mount Bache**, under **Loma Prieta** [SANTA CLARA].

Back Creek [CONTRA COSTA]: *stream,* flows 2 miles to Donner Creek 3 miles north-northwest of Mount Diablo (lat. 37°55'20" N, long. 121°55'35" W; sec. 24, T 1 N, R 1 W). Named on Clayton (1953) 7.5' quadrangle.

Bacon Flat [SONOMA]: *area,* 5.5 miles northwest of Mount Saint Helena (lat. 38°43'35" N, long. 122°42'10" W; sec. 11, T 10 N, R 8 W). Named on Mount Saint Helena (1959) 7.5' quadrangle.

Baden: see **South San Francisco** [SAN MATEO].

Baden Creek: see **Twelvemile Creek** [SAN MATEO].

Baden Station [SAN MATEO]: *locality,* 1 mile west of present downtown South San Francisco along Southern Pacific Railroad (lat. 37°39'15" N, long. 122°26' W). Named on San Mateo (1915) 15' quadrangle. Postal authorities established Baden Station post office in 1895 and discontinued it in 1897 (Salley, p. 13).

Bahia [SOLANO]: *locality,* 4.25 miles northeast of Benicia along Southern Pacific Railroad (lat. 38°05'45" N, long. 122°06'10" W). Named on Vine Hill (1959) 7.5' quadrangle. Called Goodyear on Karquines (1898) 15' quadrangle, and called Benicia Junction on Carquinez (1938) 15' quadrangle. Postal authorities established Goodyear post office in 1907 and discontinued it in 1912; the name was for the operator of a boat landing near the place (Salley, p. 87).

Bahia de Nuestra Señora del Rosario la Marinera: see **San Rafael Bay** [MARIN].

Bahia de San Francisco: see **Drakes Bay** [MARIN].

Bahia de San Pablo: see **San Pablo Bay** [CONTRA COSTA-MARIN-SOLANO-SONOMA].

Bahia de Sonoma: see **San Pablo Bay** [CONTRA COSTA-MARIN-SOLANO-SONOMA].

Bahia Redondo: see **San Pablo Bay** [CONTRA COSTA-MARIN-SOLANO-SONOMA].

Bailhache [SONOMA]: *locality,* 1 mile southeast of Healdsburg along Northwestern Pacific Railroad (lat. 38°36'15" N, long. 122° 51'15" W). Named on Healdsburg (1955) 7.5' quadrangle.

Bair Island [SAN MATEO]: *island,* 2.5 miles long, 3.25 miles north of downtown Redwood City along San Francisco Bay (lat. 37°31'50" N, long. 122°13'15" W). Named on Redwood Point (1959) 7.5' quadrangle.

Bak [SONOMA]: *locality,* 2.5 miles east-northeast of downtown Santa Rosa along Southern Pacific Railroad (lat. 38°27'30" N, long. 122°40'15" W). Named on Santa Rosa (1916) 15' quadrangle. Bradley (p. 358) referred to Baku switch, located 2 miles east of Santa Rosa.

Baker: see **Fort Baker Military Reservation** [MARIN].

Baker Beach [SAN FRANCISCO]: *beach,* 1.25 miles south-southwest of Fort Point along the coast (lat. 37°47'40" N, long. 122°28'55" W). Named on San Francisco North (1956, photorevised 1968 and 1973) 7.5' quadrangle. Called Bakers Beach on San Francisco North (1956) 7.5' quadrangle, but United States Board on Geographic Names (1976b, p. 1) gave this name as a variant. The name commemorates the Baker family, who had a dairy ranch near the beach in the 1860's (Gudde, 1949, p. 20). United States Board on Geographic Names (1979b, p. 5) approved the name "China Beach" for the next beach along the coast southwest of Baker Beach.

Baker Creek: see **Langley Creek** [SAN MATEO].

Bakers Beach: see **Baker Beach** [SAN FRANCISCO].

Baker's Landing: see **Warm Springs Landing**, under **Mud Slough** [ALAMEDA].

Baku: see **Bak** [SONOMA].

Bald Hill [MARIN]: *ridge,* south-southwest-trending, 0.5 mile long, nearly 3 miles west-southwest of downtown San Rafael (lat. 37°57'55" N, long. 122°34'50" W). Named on San Rafael (1954) 7.5' quadrangle.

Bald Hill [NAPA]: *peak,* 2.5 miles north-northeast of Calistoga (lat. 38°36'35" N, long. 122°33'30" W; near SE cor. sec. 19, T 9 N, R 6 W). Named on Calistoga (1958) 7.5' quadrangle.

Bald Hill [SONOMA]: *peak,* 3.25 miles west-southwest of Big Mountain (lat. 38°41'45" N, long. 123°12' W; near SE cor. sec. 20, T 10 N, R 12 W). Named on Tombs Creek (1978) 7.5' quadrangle. Called Hayfield Hill on Tombs Creek (1943) 7.5' quadrangle.

Bald Hills [SONOMA]: *ridge,* southeast- to south-trending, 1 mile long, 3.5 miles north of Mark West Springs (lat. 38°36'05" N, long. 122°42'35" W). Named on Mark West Springs (1958) 7.5' quadrangle. California Division of Forestry's (1945) map shows Patty Clark Springs situated on the northeast side of the ridge.

Bald Knob [SAN MATEO]: *peak,* 3 miles west-northwest of Skeggs Point (lat. 37°25'25" N, long. 122°21'10" W). Altitude 2102 feet. Named on Woodside (1961) 7.5' quadrangle. Brown (p. 4) gave the name "Bald Mountain" as an alternate.

Bald Mountain [NAPA-SONOMA]:

(1) *peak,* 3.5 miles northeast of Kenwood on Napa-Sonoma County line (lat. 38°27'25" N, long. 122°30'30" W; sec. 15, T 7 N, R 6 W). Altitude 2729 feet. Named on Kenwood (1954) 7.5' quadrangle.

(2) *peak,* 4.25 miles west-southwest of Rutherford on Napa-Sonoma County line (lat. 38°25'45" N, long. 122°29'35" W; near N line sec. 26, T 7 N, R 6 W). Altitude 2275 feet. Named on Rutherford (1951) 7.5' quadrangle.

Bald Mountain [SANTA CLARA]: *peak,* 3 miles west-southwest of New Almaden (lat. 37°09'35" N, long. 121°52' W; sec. 9, T 9 S, R 1 E). Altitude 2387 feet. Named on Santa Teresa Hills (1953) 7.5' quadrangle.

Bald Mountain: see **Bald Knob** [SAN MATEO].

Bald Pate: see **Ox Hill** [SAN MATEO].

Bald Peak: see **Volimer Peak** [CONTRA COSTA].

Bald Peaks [SANTA CLARA]: *ridge,* east- to east-northeast-trending, 1 mile long, 2 miles southeast of New Almaden (lat. 37°09'30" N, long. 121°47'40" W). Named on Santa Teresa Hills (1953) 7.5' quadrangle.

Bald Ridge [CONTRA COSTA]: *ridge,* west-northwest-trending, 1 mile long, center 1 mile northwest of Mount Diablo (lat. 37°53'35" N, long 121°55'30" W). Named on Clayton (1953) 7.5' quadrangle.

Bald Ridge: see **Buri Buri Ridge** [SAN MATEO]; **Cahill Ridge** [SAN MATEO].

Baldy: see **Old Baldy** [NAPA].

Baldy Mountain [NAPA]: *peak,* 8.5 miles east-northeast of Saint Helena (lat. 38°33'05" N, long. 122°19'30" W). Altitude 2114 feet. Named on Chiles Valley (1958) 7.5' quadrangle.

Baldy Ryan [SANTA CLARA]: *canyon,* drained by a stream that flows 2.5 miles to Llagas Creek 3.5 miles southeast of New Almaden (lat. 37°08'55" N, long. 121°46'15" W). Named on Santa Teresa Hills (1953) 7.5' quadrangle. Called Longwall Canyon on Los Gatos (1919) 15' quadrangle.

Bale [NAPA]: *locality,* 4.25 miles east-southeast of Calistoga along Southern Pacific Railroad (lat. 38°33'15" N, long. 122°30'35" W); the place is on Carne Humana grant. Named on Calistoga (1945) 15' quadrangle. The name commemorates Edward F. Bale, who came to California in 1837 and received Carne Humana grant in 1841 (Gudde, 1949, p. 21).

Bale Slough [NAPA]: *water feature,* joins Napa River 0.5 mile northeast of Rutherford (lat. 38°27'50" N, long. 122°24'50" W). Named on Rutherford (1951) 7.5' quadrangle.

Ballenas: see **Bolinas** [MARIN].

Ballenas Bay: see **Bolinas Bay** [MARIN].

Baltimore Canyon [MARIN]: *canyon,* 2 miles long, along Larkspur Creek above a point 3 miles south of downtown San Rafael (lat. 37°55'50" N, long. 122°32'10" W). Named on San Rafael (1954) 7.5' quadrangle. Hoover, Rensch, and Rensch (p. 186) called the feature Baltimore Gulch, and noted that the name is from Baltimore and Frederick Trading Company, which sent a group of men to the region in 1849 to erect a sawmill on Corte de Madera grant.

Baltimore Gulch: see **Baltimore Canyon** [MARIN].

Baltimore Park [MARIN]: *locality,* 3 miles south of downtown San Rafael (lat. 37°55'50" N, long. 122°31'50" W); the place is near the mouth of Baltimore Canyon. Named on San Rafael (1954) 7.5' quadrangle.

Bancroft [CONTRA COSTA]: *locality,* 2.25 miles north-northeast of Walnut Creek civic center along Sacramento Northern Railroad (lat. 37°56'05" N, long. 122°02'45" W). Named on Walnut Creek (1959) 7.5' quadrangle. Concord (1915) 15' quadrangle has the name "Hookston" along Oakland Antioch and Eastern Railroad at present Bancroft, as well as at present Hookston.

Bangs Creek: see **Arroyo Seco** [ALAMEDA].

Bank Mills: see **Saratoga** [SANTA CLARA].

Banks of Braes: see **Los Altos** [SANTA CLARA].

Banta Spring [SANTA CLARA]: *spring,* 10.5 miles north-northeast of Mount Hamilton (lat. 37°28'30" N, long. 121°32'40" W; sec. 28, T 5 S, R 4 E). Named on Eylar Mountain (1955) 7.5' quadrangle.

Barcal Spring: see **Preston** [SONOMA].

Bar Channel [SAN FRANCISCO]: *channel,* southeast of Yerba Buena Island in San Francisco Bay (lat. 37°48'10" N, long. 122°21'15" W). Named on Oakland West (1959) 7.5' quadrangle. The feature leads to the entrance channels for harbors in Alameda County.

Barker Slough [SOLANO]: *water feature,* joins Lindsey Slough 10 miles southwest of Elmira (lat. 38°15'40" N, long. 121°46'15" W). Named on Dozier (1952) 7.5' quadrangle.

Barlow [SONOMA]: *locality,* 2.5 miles northwest of Sebastopol along Petaluma and Santa Rosa Railroad (lat. 38°25'25" N, long. 122°51'30" W). Named on Sebastopol (1954) 7.5' quadrangle.

Barnabe Creek [MARIN]: *stream,* flows 0.5 mile to Lagunita Creek 10.5 miles southwest of downtown Novato (lat. 38°01'10" N, long. 122°43'30" W); the stream heads at Bernabe Mountain. Named on San Geronimo (1954) 7.5' quadrangle.

Barnabe Mountain [MARIN]: *peak,* 10 miles southwest of downtown Novato (lat. 38°01'40" N, long. 122°42'55" W). Altitude 1466 feet. Named on San Geronimo (1954) 7.5' quadrangle. The peak was named for Barnabe, a white mule that grazed there (Teather, p. 6).

Barns Creek [SONOMA]: *stream,* flows 2.25 miles to Brooks Creek 6 miles east-southeast of Healdsburg (lat. 38°35'10" N, long. 122° 45'45" W; sec. 32, T 9 N, R 8 W). Named on Healdsburg (1955) and Mark West Springs (1958) 7.5' quadrangles.

Barrelli Creek [SONOMA]: *stream,* flows 3 miles to Russian River less than 1 mile northwest of Asti (lat. 38°46'05" N, long. 122°58'45" W). Named on Asti (1959) and Warm Springs Dam (1978) 7.5' quadrangles.

Barret Canyon [SANTA CLARA]: *canyon,* drained by a stream that flows nearly 3.5 miles to Alamitos Creek 2 miles southwest of New Almaden (lat. 37°09'20" N, long. 121°50'35" W). Named on Loma Prieta (1955) and Santa Teresa Hills (1953) 7.5' quadrangles. Called Berrocal Canyon on Los Gatos (1919) 15' quadrangle.

Barrett [CONTRA COSTA]: *locality,* 0.5 mile west of present Richmond civic center along Southern Pacific Railroad (lat. 37°56'15" N, long. 122°21'20" W). Named on San Francisco (1899) 15' quadrangle.

Barries Bay [MARIN]: *bay,* opens into Drakes Estero 5.25 miles northeast of the lighthouse at Point Reyes (lat. 38°02'50" N, long. 122°56'55" W). Named on Drakes Bay (1953) 7.5' quadrangle.

Barro [NAPA]: *locality,* 2 miles northwest of Saint Helena along Southern Pacific Railroad (lat. 38°31'35" N, long. 122°29'30" W). Named on Saint Helena (1960) 7.5' quadrangle.

Barron Creek [SANTA CLARA]: *stream,* flows 5.25 miles to flatlands near San Francisco Bay 3.5 miles north-northwest of downtown Mountain View (lat. 37°26' N, long. 122°06'30" W). Named on Mountain View (1961) and Palo Alto (1961) 7.5' quadrangles. Called Dry Creek on Mountain View (1953) 7.5' quadrangle. The stream passes through Barron Park, a residential and commercial development named for Edward Barron, a retired stock dealer and mine operator who came to the place in 1878 (Hoover, Rensch, and Rensch, p. 462).

Barron Park: see **Barron Creek** [SANTA CLARA].

Barron's Landing: see **Hayward Landing** [ALAMEDA]; **Mount Eden** [ALAMEDA].

Barry: see **Fort Barry Military Reservation** [MARIN].

Barths Creek [MARIN]: *stream,* flows 0.5 mile to Cataract Creek 6.25 miles southwest of downtown San Rafael (lat. 37°55'20" N, long. 122°37'55" W). Named on San Rafael (1954) 7.5' quadrangle. Teather (p. 7) associated the name with Emil Barth, who hiked and helped build trails in the neighborhood of Mount Tamalpais.

Barths Retreat [MARIN]: *locality,* nearly 6 miles southwest of downtown San Rafael (lat. 37°55'20" N, long. 122°36'55" W); the place is near the head of Barths Creek. Named on San Rafael (1954) 7.5' quadrangle.

Barton Hill [NAPA]: *peak,* 2.5 miles east-northeast of Walter Springs (lat. 38°40' N, long. 122°18'50" W; near E line sec. 32, T 10 N, R 4 W). Altitude 1041 feet. Named on Walter Springs (1959) 7.5' quadrangle.

Barton's Store: see **Suisun City** [SOLANO].

Barzilla: see **Pescadero** [SAN MATEO].

Basalt Creek [MARIN]: *stream,* 2 miles long, winds through lowlands 2 miles north-northeast of downtown Novato (lat. 38°08' N, long. 122°33'10" W). Named on Petaluma River (1954) 7.5' quadrangle.

Bascome: see **Meridian** [SANTA CLARA].

Bass Lake [MARIN]: *lake,* 1350 feet long, 1 mile east of Double Point (lat. 37°57'05" N, long. 122°45'50" W). Named on Double Point (1954) 7.5' quadrangle.

Batavia [SOLANO]: *locality,* 3.5 miles south-southwest of Dixon along Southern Pacific Railroad (lat. 38°24'25" N, long. 121°51'30" W; at W line sec. 34, T 7 N, R 1 E). Named on Dixon (1952) 7.5' quadrangle.

Batchelder Creek: see **Sinbad Creek** [ALAMEDA].

Bateman Creek [NAPA]: *stream,* flows 2 miles to James Creek 7 miles north-northeast of Calistoga (lat. 38°40'10" N, long. 122°31'40" W; sec. 33, T 10 N, R 6 W). Named on Detert Reservoir (1958) 7.5' quadrangle.

Bateria San Jose: see **Fort Mason Military Reservation** [SAN FRANCISCO].

Batto [SONOMA]: *locality,* 1.25 miles east-southeast of Sonoma along Northwestern Pacific Railroad (lat. 38°17' N, long. 122°26'05" W). Named on Sonoma (1951) 7.5' quadrangle.

Baulenas: see **Bolinas** [MARIN].

Baulenas Bay: see **Bolinas Bay** [MARIN].

Baumberg [ALAMEDA]: *locality,* 7 miles north-northwest of downtown Newark along Southern Pacific Railroad (lat. 37°37'10" N, long. 122°06' W). Named on Newark (1959) 7.5' quadrangle. South Pacific Coast Railroad established a station called Arff at the site in 1877—the name was for Frederic Danieh Arff, who settled at the place in 1856; officials of Southern Pacific Railroad changed the name to Baumberg after that company took over the line in 1887—the name Baumberg was from Baumberger's Salt Works, which was active in the 1880's and 1890's (Mosier and Mosier, p. 10, 14).

Baumert Springs [SONOMA]: *spring,* 1.25 miles northwest of Occidental (lat. 38°25'10" N, long. 122°57'50" W; sec. 28, T 7 N, R 10 W). Named on Camp Meeker (1954) 7.5' quadrangle.

Bay: see **Bodega Bay** [SONOMA].

Bay Farm Island [ALAMEDA]: *area,* 3.5 miles west of downtown San Leandro along San Francisco Bay (lat. 37°44' N, long. 122°13'15" W). Named on Hunters Point (1956) and San Leandro (1959) 7.5' quadrangles. Haywards (1899) 15' quadrangle has the name for an island, 1.25 miles long, that is separated from shore by mud flats. The area now is largely filled land between the original island and shore, and is the site of Metropolitan Oakland International Airport. The place was called Bay Island in the 1870's, but this name was changed to Bay Farm Island in the 1880's, when farming began there (Mosier and Mosier, p. 14).

Bay Island: see **Bay Farm Island** [ALAMEDA].

Bay Junction: see **Almonte** [MARIN].

Bay of Napa: see **Mare Island Strait** [SOLANO].

Bay of Sir Francis Drake: see **Drakes Bay** [MARIN].

Bay of Suisun: see **Suisin Bay** [CONTRA COSTA-SOLANO].

Bayo Vista [CONTRA COSTA]: *district,* 6 miles east-northeast of Pinole Point in Rodeo (lat. 38°02'15" N, long. 122°15'30" W). Named on Mare Island (1959) 7.5' quadrangle.

Bay Point: see **Port Chicago** [CONTRA COSTA].

Bay Point Yacht Harbor [CONTRA COSTA]: *water feature,* 7 miles east-northeast of Martinez (lat. 38°03'15" N, long. 122°01' W). Named on Carquinez (1938) 15' quadrangle.

Bayshore [SAN MATEO]: *district,* 3.5 miles north of downtown South San Francisco in Visitacion Valley (lat. 37°42'20" N, long. 122°24'50" W). Named on San Francisco South (1956) 7.5' quadrangle. Diller and others' (1915) map has the form "Bay Shore" for the name of the railroad station at the place.

Bay Slough [SAN MATEO]: *water feature,* extends for 1 mile from Belmont Slough to San Francisco Bay 4.5 miles north of downtown Redwood City (lat. 37°32'55" N, long. 122°13'30" W). Named on Redwood Point (1959) 7.5' quadrangle. United States Board on Geographic Names (1961b, p. 8) rejected the names "Seal Creek," "The Cut," and "The Cutoff" for the feature.

Bayview District [SAN FRANCISCO]: *district,* 3.5 miles east of Mount Davidson near San Francisco Bay (lat. 37°44'15" N, long. 122°23'15" W). Named on San Francisco South (1956) 7.5' quadrangle.

Baywood [SAN MATEO]: *district,* 1 mile south-southwest of downtown San Mateo (lat. 37°33'15" N, long. 122°20' W). Named on San Mateo (1947) 7.5' quadrangle.

Bean Hollow: see **Arroyo de los Frijoles** [SAN MATEO].

Bean Hollow Beach [SAN MATEO]: *beach,* 3 miles north-northwest of Pigeon Point along the coast at the mouth of Arroyo de los Frijoles (lat. 37°13'30" N, long. 122°24'30" W). Named on Pigeon Point (1955) 7.5' quadrangle.

Bean Hollow Creek: see **Arroyo de los Frijoles** [SAN MATEO].

Bean Hollow Lagoon: see **Lake Lucerne** [SAN MATEO].

Bean Hollow Lake [SAN MATEO]: *lake,* 1.25 miles long, behind a dam on Arroyo de los Frijoles 2.5 miles north-northeast of Pigeon Point (lat. 37°12'55" N, long. 122°22'20" W). Named on Año Nuevo (1948) 15' quadrangle. The lake is named from the stream—*frijoles* means "kidney beans" in Spanish. Franklin Point (1955) 7.5' quadrangle shows a dam dividing the lake into two nearly equal parts called Upper Bean Hollow Lake and Lower Bean Hollow Lake—together they sometimes are called Hidden Valley Lakes from the name of a hunting club started there after the lakes formed in the early 1930's (Brown, p. 96).

Bear Canyon [NAPA]: *canyon,* drained by a stream that flows 3 miles to Napa Valley 1 mile southwest of Rutherford (lat. 38°27'05" N, long. 122°26'15" W). Named on Rutherford (1951) 7.5' quadrangle.

Bear Canyon [SONOMA]:

(1) *canyon,* drained by a stream that flows 1.25 miles to Squaw Creek 4.5 miles north-northeast of Geyser Peak (lat. 38°49'40" N, long. 122°48'55"

W; sec. 1, T 11 N, R 9 W). Named on The Geysers (1959) 7.5' quadrangle.
(2) *canyon,* drained by a stream that flows nearly 1.5 miles to Sausal Creek 6.5 miles northeast of Healdsburg (lat. 38°41'15" N, long. 122°47'45" W; sec. 30, T 10 N, R 8 W). Named on Jimtown (1955) 7.5' quadrangle.

Bear Creek [CONTRA COSTA]: *stream,* flows 6.25 miles to San Pablo Reservoir 2.5 miles northwest of Orinda (lat. 37°54'25" N, long. 122°12'50" W). Named on Briones Valley (1959) 7.5' quadrangle.

Bear Creek [SAN MATEO]:
(1) *stream,* flows 1.25 miles to Peters Creek 3 miles southeast of Mindego Hill (lat. 37°16'35" N, long. 122°11'55" W; sec. 33, T 7 S, R 3 W). Named on Mindego Hill (1961) 7.5' quadrangle.
(2) *stream,* flows 6.5 miles to San Francisquito Creek 5 miles south of downtown Redwood City (lat. 37°24'35" N, long. 122°14'15" W); the stream drains Bear Gulch. Named on Palo Alto (1961) and Woodside (1961) 7.5' quadrangles. Brown (p. 6) used the name "Bear Gulch Creek" for at least part of the stream, and noted that it also was called Coppinger Creek, for John Coppinger, who dammed the creek about 1840.

Bear Creek [SONOMA]:
(1) *stream,* flows 3.25 miles to McDonnell Creek nearly 6 miles west-northwest of Mount Saint Helena (lat. 38°41'35" N, long. 122°44'10" W; near N line sec. 27, T 10 N, R 8 W). Named on Mount Saint Helena (1959) 7.5' quadrangle.
(2) *stream,* flows 1 mile to Warm Springs Creek 1 mile west of Skaggs Springs (lat. 38°41'50" N, long. 123°02'35" W; sec. 23, T 10 N, R 11 W). Named on Warm Springs Dam (1978) 7.5' quadrangle.
(3) *stream,* flows 2.5 miles to Sonoma Creek 2 miles north-northeast of Kenwood (lat. 38°26'35" N, long. 122°31'50" W; near N line sec. 21, T 7 N, R 6 W). Named on Kenwood (1954) 7.5' quadrangle.

Bear Creek: see **Tarwater Creek** [SAN MATEO].

Beard Creek [ALAMEDA]: *water feature,* enters San Francisco Bay 4.25 miles west-southwest of downtown Newark (lat. 37°3030" N, long. 122°06'45" W). Named on Haywards (1899) 15' quadrangle. The name commemorates E.L. Beard, who settled near Mission San Jose about 1846 (Gudde, 1949, p. 26).

Beard's Slough: see **Newark Slough** [ALAMEDA].

Bear Flat [NAPA]: *area,* 10 miles northwest of Mount Vaca along Capell Creek (lat. 38°29'15" N, long. 122°14'40" W; near E line sec. 1, T 7 N, R 4 W). Named on Capell Valley (1951) 7.5' quadrangle.

Bear Flat [SONOMA]: *area,* nearly 7 miles north-northeast of Guerneville along Mill Creek (1) (lat. 38°35'50" N, long. 122°57'50" W). Named on Guerneville (1955) 7.5' quadrangle.

Bear Gulch [ALAMEDA-SANTA CLARA]: *canyon,* drained by a stream that heads in Alameda County and flows 2.25 miles to Alameda Creek 4.5 miles north-northwest of Mount Day in Santa Clara County (lat. 37°28'50" N, long. 121°42'55" W; sec. 24, T 5 S, R 2 E). Named on Mount Day (1955) 7.5' quadrangle.

Bear Gulch [SAN MATEO]: *canyon,* 3.25 miles long, along Bear Creek (2) above a point 2 miles east-northeast of Skeggs Point (lat. 37°25' N, long. 122°16'05" W). Named on Woodside (1961) 7.5' quadrangle. The canyon first was called El Arroyo de la Presa for a dam that John Coppinger built there—*presa* means "dam" in Spanish; the feature received the name "Bear Gulch" after a bear mauled a man there (Stanger, 1967, p. 35).

Bear Gulch Creek: see **Bear Creek** [SAN MATEO] (2).

Bear Gulch Lake: see **Bear Gulch Reservoir** [SAN MATEO].

Bear Gulch Reservoir [SAN MATEO]: *lake,* 0.25 mile long, 3.5 miles south of downtown Redwood City (lat. 37°26' N, long. 122° 13'35" W). Named on Palo Alto (1961) 7.5' quadrangle. The name is from Bear Gulch Water Company, which piped water from Bear Gulch to the reservoir; the feature also was called Bear Gulch Lake, and before about 1900 it was called Corte Madera Lake (Brown, p. 6).

Bear House Creek: see **Bearpen Creek** [SONOMA] (1).

Bear Mountain [SANTA CLARA]: *peak,* 9 miles north-northeast of Gilroy Hot Springs on Santa Clara-Stanislaus County line (lat. 37° 13'55" N, long. 121°26'10" W; sec. 21, T 8 S, R 5 E). Altitude 2604 feet. Named on Mississippi Creek (1955) 7.5' quadrangle.

Bearpen Creek [SONOMA]:
(1) *stream,* flows 3 miles to Austin Creek 3.5 miles north-northwest of Cazadero (lat. 38°34'40" N, long. 123°06'55" W; sec. 31, T 9 N, R 11 W). Named on Cazadero (1978) and Fort Ross (1978) 7.5' quadrangles. Called Bear House Cr. on California Division of Forestry's (1945) map.
(2) *stream,* flows 1.25 miles to Warm Springs Creek 4 miles west-southwest of Skaggs Springs (lat. 38°39'55" N, long. 123°05'25" W; at SW cor. sec. 33, T 10 N, R 11 W). Named on Warm Springs Dam (1978) 7.5' quadrangle.

Bear Ridge [SONOMA]: *ridge,* west- to northwest-trending, 2.5 miles long, 10 miles northeast of the village of Stewarts Point (lat. 38°45'10" N, long. 123°16' W). Named on Ornbaun Valley (1960) 15' quadrangle, and on Annapolis (1977) and Tombs Creek (1978) 7.5' quadrangles.

Bear Springs [SANTA CLARA]: *spring,* 1 mile south-southeast of Bear Mountain (lat. 37°13'05" N, long. 121°25'50" W; at N line sec. 28, R 8 S, R 5 E). Named on Mississippi Creek (1955) 7.5' quadrangle.

Bear Trap Ridge: see **Mitchell Ravine** [ALAMEDA].

Beartrap Ridge [ALAMEDA-SANTA CLARA]: *ridge,* east-northeast-trending, 2 miles long, 15 miles east-southeast of Sunol on Alameda-Santa Clara County line (lat. 37°29' N, long. 121°38' W). Named on Eylar Mountain (1955) and Mount Day (1955) 7.5' quadrangles.

Bear Valley [MARIN]: *canyons,* two; one canyon extends for 1.25 miles from near Olema to the top of Inverness Ridge 3.5 miles south of Point Reyes Station (lat. 38°01'10" N, long. 122°48' W); the second canyon extends for 2.5 miles from the head of the first to the sea 3.25 miles north-northwest of Double Point (lat. 37°59'10" N, long. 122°48'45" W). Named on Double Point (1954) and Inverness (1954) 7.5' quadrangles. The name is from bears that preyed on cattle in the vicinity in the early days (Gilliam, p. 86).

Bear Valley [NAPA]: *valley,* 5 miles north-northeast of Calistoga along Van Ness Creek (lat. 38°38'50" N, long. 122°33'15" W; near NW cor. sec. 8, T 9 N, R 6 W). Named on Detert Reservoir (1958) 7.5' quadrangle.

Beatty Ridge [SONOMA]: *ridge,* west- to west-northwest-trending, 5 miles long, 5 miles north of the village of Stewarts Point (lat. 38° 43'20" N, long. 123°23'45" W). Named on Annapolis (1977) and Stewarts Point (1978) 7.5' quadrangles.

Beauregard Creek [SANTA CLARA]: *stream,* flows 6.5 miles to San Antonio Creek 5.5 miles northwest of Mount Stakes in San Antonio Valley (lat. 37°22'05" N, long. 121°29'15" W; sec. 36, T 6 S, R 4 E). Named on Mount Boardman (1955) and Mount Stakes (1955) 7.5' quadrangles. Thompson and West's (1876) map has the name "Beauregarde Cañon" along the stream.

Beauregarde Cañon: see **Beauregard Creek** [SANTA CLARA].

Bedrock Spring [SONOMA]: *spring,* 3 miles northeast of the village of Bodega Bay (lat. 38°22' N, long. 123°00'30" W). Named on Bodega Head (1942) 7.5' quadrangle.

Bee Flat [SONOMA]: *area,* 4.5 miles west-southwest of Big Mountain along Wheatfield Fork Gualala River (lat. 38°41'40" N, long. 123°13'40" W; sec. 19, T 10 N, R 12 W); the place is 0.5 mile southwest of Bee Knoll. Named on Tombs Creek (1978) 7.5' quadrangle.

Beehive: see **The Beehive** [NAPA].

Bee Knoll [SONOMA]: *peak,* 4.25 miles west of Big Mountain (lat. 38°42' N, long. 123°13'20" W; sec. 19, T 10 N, R 12 W). Altitude 861 feet. Named on Tombs Creek (1978) 7.5' quadrangle. On Tombs Creek (1943) 7.5' quadrangle, Bee Knoll is the high point on a ridge called Bee Tree Ridge.

Beenar: see **Point Beenar** [CONTRA COSTA].

Beeners Channel: see **Middle Slough** [CONTRA COSTA].

Bee Tree Ridge: see **Bee Knoll** [SONOMA].

Belcher: see **Anna Belcher Creek** [SONOMA].

Beldons Landing [SOLANO]: *locality,* 5 miles west-southwest of Denverton along Montezuma Slough (lat. 38°11'20" N, long. 121° 58'30" W; sec. 16, T 4 N, R 1 W). Named on Denverton (1953) 7.5' quadrangle. Pittsburg (1953) 15' quadrangle shows Grizzly Island Ferry at the site.

Bell Canyon [NAPA]: *canyon,* drained by a stream that flows 7.5 miles to Napa River 2.5 miles north-northwest of Saint Helena (lat. 38°32'05" N, long. 122°29'30" W). Named on Saint Helena (1960) 7.5' quadrangle.

Bell Canyon Reservoir [NAPA]: *lake,* behind a dam in Bell Canyon 3.5 miles north of Saint Helena (lat. 38°33'20" N, long. 122°28'55" W; sec. 12, T 8 N, R 6 W). Named on Saint Helena (1960) 7.5' quadrangle. Saint Helena (1942) 15' quadrangle shows Bell Valley at the site.

Belleair [SOLANO]: *locality,* 7 miles southeast of Dixon along Sacramento Northern Railroad (lat. 38°21'45" N, long. 121°44'50" W; near W line sec. 15, T 6 N, R 2 E). Named on Liberty Island (1952) 7.5' quadrangle.

Belle Monte [SAN MATEO]: *district,* 3.5 miles south-southeast of downtown San Mateo in Belmont (lat. 37°31'05" N, long. 122° 18' W). Named on San Mateo (1956) 7.5' quadrangle.

Bellevue [SONOMA]: *locality,* 2.5 miles south of downtown Santa Rosa (lat. 38°24'05" N, long. 122°43' W). Named on Santa Rosa (1954) 7.5' quadrangle.

Bell Mountain [SONOMA]: *peak,* 4.25 miles north-northwest of Mark West Springs (lat. 38°36'20" N, long. 122°45' W; near S line sec. 21, T 9 N, R 8 W). Named on Healdsburg (1955) and Mark West Springs (1958) 7.5' quadrangles.

Bello Beach: see **Muir Beach** [MARIN].

Belloma Slough [CONTRA COSTA]: *water feature,* joins Suisun Bay 7 miles east-northeast of Martinez (lat. 38°03'25" N, long. 122°01'05" W). Named on Vine Hill (1959) 7.5' quadrangle.

Bello's Bend: see **Muir Beach** [MARIN].

Bell Station [SANTA CLARA]: *locality,* 15 miles east of Gilroy (lat. 37°02'10" N, long. 121°18'35" W). Named on Pacheco Peak (1955) 7.5' quadrangle. Called Bells Station on Gilroy Hot Springs (1921) 15' quadrangle. The place first was called Hollenbeck's Station (Latta, 1976, p. 212), but after Lafayette F. Bell bought the toll road over Pacheco Pass in the 1860's, the tavern near the toll gate became known as Bell's Station (Shumate, p. 3). Postal authorities established Bell's Station post office in 1873 and discontinued it in 1914 (Frickstad, p. 173).

Bell Station: see **Zinfandel** [NAPA].

Bellvale [SAN MATEO]: *village,* 2.25 miles west of La Honda along San Gregorio Creek (lat. 37°18'45" N, long. 122°18'45" W). Named on Santa Cruz (1902) 30' quadrangle. Postal authorities established Bellvale post office in 1897 and discontinued it in 1922 (Frickstad, p. 167).

Bell Valley: see **Bell Canyon Reservoir** [NAPA].

Belmae Park: see **Lomita Park** [SAN MATEO].

Belmont [SAN MATEO]: *city,* 4.25 miles southeast of downtown San Mateo (lat. 37°31'05" N, long. 122°16'20" W). Named on San Mateo (1956) 7.5' quadrangle. Charles Aubrey Angelo opened a stage station called Angelo House in 1850 at the site of the present city (Hoover, Rensch, and Rensch, p. 406). The community that grew around Angelo House took the name "Belmont" from a beautiful hill nearby (Hynding, p. 123). Postal authorities established Belmont post office in 1854, discontinued it in 1856, and reestablished it in 1857 (Frickstad, p. 167). The city incorporated in 1926.

Belmont Channel [SAN MATEO]: *water feature,* joins Bay Slough 4.5 miles north-northwest of downtown Redwood City (lat. 37° 33' N, long. 122°14'30" W). Named on Redwood Point (1959) and San Mateo (1956) 7.5' quadrangles.

Belmont Creek [SAN MATEO]: *stream,* flows nearly 3 miles to lowlands along San Francisco Bay 4.5 miles southeast of downtown San Mateo in Belmont (lat. 37°31'05" N, long. 122°16'20" W). Named on San Mateo (1956) 7.5' quadrangle. The stream was called Arroyo Diablo in the 1850's, and the canyon of the stream was called Cañada del Diablo; Spanish missionaries gave the name "cañada de San Agustin" to the feature in the 1780's (Brown, p. 7, 27).

Belmont Creek: see **Belmont Slough** [SAN MATEO].

Belmont Embarcadero Creek: see **Belmont Slough** [SAN MATEO].

Belmont Hill [SAN MATEO]: *peak,* 4.5 miles southeast of downtown San Mateo (lat. 37°30'35" N, long. 122°16'30" W); the peak is in Belmont. Named on San Mateo (1956) 7.5' quadrangle. The feature has had several names: Hull Hill, for William Hull's brickyard, established in 1858; Van Court's Hill, for Jimmie Van Court, who lived there in the 1870's; and Picnic Hill, for a picnic ground at the base of the peak in the 1870's and 1880's (Brown, p. 7).

Belmont Landing: see **North Belmont Landing**, under **Belmont Slough** [SAN MATEO].

Belmont Slough [SAN MATEO]: *water feature,* enters San Francisco Bay 5 miles north of downtown Redwood City (lat. 37°33'15" N, long. 122°14'35" W). Named on Redwood Point (1959) and San Mateo (1956) 7.5' quadrangles. United States Board on Geographic Names (1961b, p. 8) rejected the names "Angelo Creek" and "Belmont Creek" for the feature. According to Brown (p. 7), it first was called Angelo's Creek, for Charles Aubrey Angelo of Angelo House, and later it was called Belmont Embarcadero Creek for a landing at its head. California Division of Highways (1934) map shows a place called North Belmont Landing located at the mouth of Belmont Slough.

Beltane [SONOMA]: *locality,* 2 miles southeast of Kenwood along Southern Pacific Railroad (lat. 38°23'20" N, long. 122°31'25" W). Named on Santa Rosa (1916) 15' quadrangle.

Belvedere [MARIN]: *town,* 1.5 miles northeast of downtown Sausalito across Richardson Bay (lat. 37°52'30" N, long. 122°28' W); the town is on Belvedere Island. Named on San Francisco North (1956) and San Quentin (1959) 7.5' quadrangles. Postal authorities established Belvedere post office in 1897 (Frickstad, p. 87), and the town incorporated in 1896.

Belvedere Cove [MARIN]: *embayment,* 1.5 miles east-northeast of downtown Sausalito off Raccoon Strait (lat. 38°52'15" N, long. 122°27'30" W); the feature is at Belvedere. Named on San Francisco North (1956) 7.5' quadrangle. Called Ensenada del Santo Evangelio on a map of 1775; about 1880 the place sometimes was called Stillwater Bay (Teather, p. 8).

Belvedere Island [MARIN]: *island,* 1.5 miles long, 1.25 miles northeast of downtown Sausalito across the mouth of Richardson Bay (lat. 37°52'15" N, long. 122°27'55" W). Named on San Francisco North (1956, photorevised 1968 and 1973) and San Quentin (1959) 7.5' quadrangles. The island was called El Potrero de la Punta del Tiburon in the early days, and later it was called Kashow's Island, for Israel Kashow and his family, who lived there; the feature also was known as Peninsula Island, Promontory Island, and Still Island (Teather, p. 7-8).

Belvedere Lagoon [MARIN]: *water feature,* 4.5 miles south of Point San Quentin (lat. 37°52'40" N, long. 122°28' W); the feature is at Belvedere. Named on San Quentin (1959) 7.5' quadrangle.

Benecia: see **Benicia** [SOLANO].

Benicia [SOLANO]: *town,* 15 miles south-southwest of Fairfield along Carquinez Strait (near lat. 38°03' N, long. 122°09'30" W). Named on Benicia (1959) 7.5' quadrangle. United States Board on Geographic Names (1933, p. 136) rejected the form "Benecia" for the name. Postal authorities established Benicia post office in 1849 (Frickstad, p. 191), and the town incorporated in 1850. Robert Semple laid out the community in 1847 on land that had belonged to Mariano Guadalupe Vallejo, and gave it the name "Francisca" for Vallejo's wife; when the name of the rival town of Yerba Buena was changed to San Francisco, the name "Francisca" was changed to Benicia, another of Mrs. Vallejo's names (Hoover, Rensch, and Rensch, p. 514) United States Board on Geographic Names (1984a, p. 3) approved the name "Port of Benicia" for the waterfront of Carquinez Strait between Benicia Point and Army Point (lat. 38°02'33" N, long. 122°08' W; sec. 1, T 2 N, R 3 W, and sec. 6, T 2 N, R 2 W). Postal authorities established Dalton Manor post office as a station of Benicia post office in 1944 and discontinued it in 1954; the name was from a real-estate development (Salley, p. 55).

Benicia Junction: see **Bahia** [SOLANO].

Benicia Point [SOLANO]: *promontory,* along Carquinez Strait at Benicia (lat. 38°02'40" N, long. 122°09'40" W). Named on Benicia (1959) 7.5' quadrangle. Ringgold's (1850c) map shows Seal I. off present Benicia Point, and Ringgold (p. 36) mentioned Seal isle.

Benicia Shoals [SOLANO]: *shoal,* 0.25 mile south-southeast of Benicia Point in Carquinez Strait (lat. 38°02'20" N, long. 122°09'35" W). Named on Benicia (1959) 7.5' quadrangle. Called Three fathom Shoal on Ringgold's (1850c) map. Officials of United States Bureau of Lighthouses applied the name "Benicia" to the shoal (Gudde, 1949, p. 28).

Bennett Mountain [SONOMA]: *peak,* 4 miles west of Kenwood (lat. 38°24'50" N, long. 122°37'25" W; sec. 34, T 7 N, R 7 W); the peak is northeast of Bennett Valley. Altitude 1887 feet. Named on Kenwood (1954) and Santa Rosa (1954) 7.5' quadrangles.

Bennett Tract [SANTA CLARA]: *land grant,* 1.5 miles west-southwest of downtown Santa Clara. Named on San Jose West (1961) 7.5' quadrangle. Narcisco Bennett received two tracts, one of 1000 varas and the other of 2000 varas, in 1845; Mary S. Bennett claimed 359 acres patented in 1871 (Cowan, p. 92; Cowan listed the grant under the name "Solar en Santa Clara").

Bennett Valley [SONOMA]: *valley,* along Matanzas Creek above a point 2 miles east of downtown Santa Rosa (lat. 38°26' N, long. 122°40'20" W). Named on Kenwood (1954) and Santa Rosa (1954) 7.5' quadrangles. The name commemorates James N. Bennett, who was a squatter in the valley (LeBaron and others, p. 21).

Beresford: see **Hillsdale** [SAN MATEO].

Berkeley [ALAMEDA]: *city,* 4.5 miles north of downtown Oakland (lat. 37°52'10" N, long. 122°16'20" W). Named on Briones Valley (1959), Oakland East (1959), Oakland West (1959), and Richmond (1959) 7.5' quadrangles. Postal authorities established Berkeley post office in 1872 (Salley, p. 19), and the city incorporated in 1878. The place was chosen as the site of the new state university and named in 1866 for George Berkeley, Bishop of Cloyne—Frederick Billings proposed the name (Gudde, 1949, p. 29).

Berkeley: see **North Berkeley** [ALAMEDA]; **South Berkeley**, under **Lorin** [ALAMEDA]; **West Berkeley** [ALAMEDA].

Berkeley Camp: see **Berkeley Music Camp** [SONOMA].

Berkeley Hills [ALAMEDA-CONTRA COSTA]: *range,* first range east of San Francisco Bay on Alameda-Contra Costa County line. Named on Briones Valley (1959), Oakland East (1959), and Richmond (1959) 7.5' quadrangles. The feature is part of what was known in the early days as Contra Costa Hills (Diller and others, p. 83).

Berkeley Music Camp [SONOMA]: *locality,* 0.5 mile south of Cazadero (lat. 38°31'20" N, long. 123°05'05" W; sec. 21, T 8 N, R 11 W). Named on Cazadero (1978) 7.5' quadrangle. Called Berkeley Camp on Cazadero (1943) 7.5' quadrangle.

Berkeley Yacht Harbor [ALAMEDA]: *water feature,* 5 miles northwest of downtown Oakland along the Berkeley water front (lat. 37° 52' N, long. 122°18'45" W). Named on Oakland West (1959) 7.5' quadrangle.

Bernal Heights [SAN FRANCISCO]: *ridge,* east-trending, 0.5 mile long, 2.25 miles east of Mount Davidson (lat. 37°44'35" N, long. 122°24'45" W); the ridge is on Rincon de las Salinas y Potrero Viejo grant, which belonged to the Bernal family. Named on San Francisco South (1956) 7.5' quadrangle.

Bernards Landing: see **Jagel Landing** [SANTA CLARA].

Berreyesa: see **Berryessa** [SANTA CLARA].

Berrocal Canyon: see **Barret Canyon** [SANTA CLARA].

Berry Creek [SAN MATEO]: *stream,* flows less than 0.5 mile to Santa Cruz County 6 miles east-northeast of Franklin Point (lat. 37°11'25" N, long. 122°15'35" W; at SE cor. sec. 35, T 8 S, R 4 W). Named on Franklin Point (1955) 7.5' quadrangle. T.G. Berry homesteaded along the stream in 1878 (Brown, p. 7).

Berryessa [SANTA CLARA]: *settlement,* 2 miles west-southwest of the mouth of Alum Rock Canyon (lat. 37°23'10" N, long. 121°51'35" W). Named on Calaveras Reservoir (1961) 7.5' quadrangle. Postal authorities established Berryessa post office in 1889, discontinued it in 1904, and reestablished it in 1976 (Salley, p. 20). The name commemorates Nicolas Berryessa, who claimed land at the place (Rambo, 1973, p. 39). United States Board on Geographic Names (1901, p. 33) rejected the forms "Berreyesa," "Berryesa," and "Bereyessa" for the name.

Berryessa: see **Lake Berryessa** [NAPA].

Berryessa Creek [SANTA CLARA]: *stream,* flows 5 miles to lowlands 2.25 miles north of Berryessa (lat. 37°25'10" N, long. 121° 51'15" W). Named on Calaveras Reservoir (1961) 7.5' quadrangle. Called Milpitas Creek on Hare's (1872) map.

Berryessa Marina [NAPA]: *locality,* 6.5 miles south-southwest of Berryessa Peak on the west side of Lake Berryessa (lat. 38°34'50" N, long. 122°14'55" W). Named on Lake Berryessa (1959) 7.5' quadrangle.

Berryessa Peak [NAPA]: *peak,* 18 miles northeast of Saint Helena on Napa-Yolo County line near the southeast end of Blue Ridge (lat. 38°39'50" N, long. 122°11'20" W). Altitude 3057 feet. Named on Brooks (1959) 7.5' quadrangle.

Berryessa Siding [SANTA CLARA]: *locality,* 1 mile west of Berryessa along Western Pacific Railroad (lat. 37°23'15" N, long. 121° 52'50" W). Named on Milpitas (1961) 7.5' quadrangle.

Berryessa Valley [NAPA]: *valley,* 15 miles northeast of Saint Helena along Putah Creek (lat. 38°37' N, long. 122°15' W); the valley is on Las Putas grant. Named on Capay (1945) and Saint Helena (1942) 15' quadrangles. The name is for Joe Jesus Berryessa and Sixto Berryessa, who received Las Putas grant in 1843 (Gudde, 1949, p. 30). Water of Lake Berryessa now covers a large part of the valley.

Berryman: see **North Berkeley** [ALAMEDA].

Berryman Reservoir [ALAMEDA]: *lake,* 600 feet long, 5.5 miles north of downtown Oakland (lat. 37°53'05" N, long. 122°15'40" W). Named on Richmond (1959) 7.5' quadrangle. The name is for Henry Burpee Berryman, who built the lake in 1884 (Mosier and Mosier, p. 15-16).

Beryessa: see **Berryessa** [SANTA CLARA].

Bessie: see **Camp Bessie** [SANTA CLARA].

Betabel [SANTA CLARA]: *locality,* 7.25 miles south of Gilroy along Southern Pacific Railroad (lat. 36°53'50" N, long. 121°33'45" W). Named on San Juan Bautista (1917) 15' quadrangle.

Bethany Reservoir [ALAMEDA]: *lake,* 1.5 miles long, 11 miles northeast of Livermore along California Aqueduct (lat. 37°46'45" N, long. 121°36'30" W). Named on Clifton Court Forebay (1978) 7.5' quadrangle. The reservoir was built in the 1960's and named for the town of Bethany, located in San Joaquin County (Mosier and Mosier, p. 16).

Bethel Island [CONTRA COSTA]:

(1) *island,* 4 miles long, 8 miles east of Antioch between Piper Slough, Sand Mound Slough, Dutch Slough, and Taylor Slough (lat. 38°01'45" N, long. 121°38'30" W). Named on Bouldin Island (1978) and Jersey Island (1978) 7.5' quadrangles. Called Bethel Tract on Bouldin Island (1952) and Jersey Island (1952) 7.5' quadrangles, but United States Board on Geographic Names (1977b, p. 3) approved the designation "Bethel Island" for the feature.

(2) *settlement,* about 9 miles east of Antioch (lat. 38°00'50" N, long. 121°38'20" W); the place is on Bethel Island (1). Named on Jersey Island (1978) 7.5' quadrangle. Bethell post office, named for Franklin C. Bethell, first postmaster, was established in 1897, discontinued in 1902, and reestablished with the name "Bethel Island" in 1947 (Salley, p. 20).

Bethell: see **Bethel Island** [CONTRA COSTA] (2).

Bethel Tract: see **Bethel Island** [CONTRA COSTA] (1).

Bethlehem: see **Agnew** [SANTA CLARA].

Beulah Heights: see **Oakland** [ALAMEDA].

Bidwell Creek [SONOMA]: *stream,* flows 4.5 miles to Franz Creek 4.25 miles north-northeast of Mark West Springs (lat. 38°36'30" N, long. 122°41'35" W). Named on Mark West Springs (1958) 7.5' quadrangle.

Bielawski Mountain [SANTA CLARA]: *peak,* 4.5 miles southwest of Saratoga on Santa Clara-Santa Cruz County line (lat. 37°13'25" N, long. 122°05'30" W; sec. 21, T 8 S, R 2 W). Altitude 3231 feet. Named on Castle Rock Ridge (1955) 7.5' quadrangle. Whitney (p. 70) gave the name "Mount Bielawski" to the peak to honor C. Bielawski, chief draughtsman of the Surveyor-General's Office. United States Board on Geographic Names (1960b, p. 16) approved this name for the feature, and rejected the names "Bielawski Mountain," "Bielwaski Mountain," and "Mount McPherson."

Big Austin Creek: see **Austin Creek** [SONOMA].

Big Basin [NAPA]: *valley,* 7.5 miles north-northeast of Aetna Springs along Putah Creek (lat. 38°45' N, long. 122°25' W). Named on Aetna Springs (1958) and Jericho Valley (1958) 7.5' quadrangles.

Big Basin [SONOMA]: *relief feature,* 5.25 miles west-northwest of Mount Saint Helena along Bear Creek (1) (lat. 38°42'45" N, long. 122°42'45" W; sec. 14, T 10 N, R 8 W). Named on Mount Saint Helena (1959) 7.5' quadrangle.

Big Bend [SONOMA]: *village,* 6 miles north of Sears Point (lat. 38°14'10" N, long. 122°27'35" W). Named on Sears Point (1951) 7.5' quadrangle.

Big Break [CONTRA COSTA]: *bay,* 4 miles west of the settlement of Bethel Island off San Joaquin River (lat. 38°01' N, long. 121°42'30" W). Named on Jersey Island (1978) 7.5' quadrangle.

Big Brush: see **The Big Brush** [SONOMA].

Big Bull Valley [CONTRA COSTA]: *canyon,* 1.5 miles long, 3.5 miles west-northwest of Martinez (lat. 38°02'25" N, long. 122°11'30" W); the canyon is 0.5 mile northwest of Little Bull Valley. Named on Benicia (1959) 7.5' quadrangle.

Big Canyon [CONTRA COSTA]: *canyon,* drained by a stream that flows 2.5 miles to lowlands 7.5 miles south-southeast of Danville (lat. 37°43'20" N, long. 121°56'40" W). Named on Dublin (1961) 7.5' quadrangle.

Big Canyon [SANTA CLARA]: *canyon,* formed by the junction of Rough Gulch and Little Rough Gulch, drained by a stream that flows nearly 1 mile to Coyote Creek 2.25 miles south-southeast of Manzanita Point (lat. 37°08'35" N, long. 121°29'10" W; near NW cor. sec. 24, T 9 S, R 4 E). Named on Mississippi Creek (1955) 7.5' quadrangle.

Big Carson Creek [MARIN]: *stream,* flows 1.5 miles to Kent Lake 5.5 miles north of Bolinas (lat. 37°59'30" N, long. 122°40'30" W). Named on Bolinas (1954) 7.5' quadrangle.

Big Chicken Hollow [SAN MATEO]: *canyon,* 1 mile long, 4.5 miles southwest of La Honda on the upper reaches of Honsinger Creek (lat. 37°16'50" N, long. 122°20'15" W); the canyon is south of Little Chicken Hollow. Named on La Honda (1961) 7.5' quadrangle.

Big Coyote: see **Tamalpais**, under **Mill Valley** [MARIN] (2); **The Big Coyote**, under **Coyote Point** [SAN MATEO].

Big Coyote Hill: see **Coyote Point** [SAN MATEO].

Big Coyote Point: see **Coyote Point** [SAN MATEO].

Big Creek Artesian Slough: see **Coyote Creek** [ALAMEDA-SANTA CLARA].

Big Ditch: see **The Big Ditch** [SOLANO].

Big Gulch: see **Año Nuevo Creek** [SAN MATEO].

Big Hill [SONOMA]: *peak,* 6 miles west-northwest of Mount Saint Helena (lat. 38°42' N, long. 122°44'05" W; sec. 22, T 10 N, R 8 W). Altitude 1075 feet. Named on Mount Saint Helena (1959) 7.5' quadrangle.

Big Lagoon [MARIN]: *intermittent lake,* 1100 feet long, 4 miles northwest of Point Bonita near the mouth of Redwood Creek (lat. 37°51'35" N, long. 122°34'30" W). Named on Point Bonita (1954) 7.5' quadrangle.

Big Lagoon [SAN MATEO]: *lake,* 650 feet long, nearly 3 miles southwest of La Honda (lat. 37°17'35" N, long. 122°18'35" W; sec. 28, T 7 S, R 4 W); the lake is 650 feet southwest of Little Lagoon. Named on La Honda (1961) 7.5' quadrangle.

Big Moody Creek: see **Saratoga Creek** [SANTA CLARA].

Big Mountain [SONOMA]: *peak,* 15 miles north-northeast of Fort Ross (lat. 38°42'35" N, long. 122°08'35" W; near SW cor. sec. 13, T 10 N, R 12 W). Altitude 2675 feet. Named on Tombs Creek (1978) 7.5' quadrangle.

Big Oat Creek [SONOMA]: *stream,* flows 1.5 miles to Ward Creek 6.5 miles east-northeast of Fort Ross (lat. 38°32'25" N, long. 123° 07'30" W; near E line sec. 13, T 8 N, R 12 W); the stream is east of Big Oat Mountain. Named on Fort Ross (1978) 7.5' quadrangle.

Big Oat Mountain [SONOMA]: *peak,* 6.5 miles east-northeast of Fort Ross (lat. 38°32'45" N, long. 123°07'55" W; near S line sec. 12, T 8 N, R 12 W); the peak is west of Big Oat Creek. Named on Fort Ross (1978) 7.5' quadrangle.

Big Pepperwood Creek [SONOMA]: *stream,* heads in Mendocino County and flows 3.5 miles to South Fork Gualala River 8.5 miles north-northwest of the village of Stewarts Point (lat. 38°45'45" N, long. 123°28'40" W; near NW cor. sec. 31, T 11 N, R 14 W). Named on Ornbaun Valley (1960) 15' quadrangle.

Big Ridge [SONOMA]: *ridge,* east-southeast- to southeast-trending, 3 miles long, 6 miles south-southwest of Geyserville (lat. 38°37'30" N, long. 122°56'15" W). Named on Geyserville (1955) and Guerneville (1955) 7.5' quadrangles.

Big Rock [MARIN]: *relief feature,* 5 miles southwest of downtown Novato (lat. 38°02'55" N, long. 122°37'15" W). Named on Novato (1954) 7.5' quadrangle.

Big Rock Ridge [MARIN]: *ridge,* west-northwest-trending, 5 miles long, 4 miles south-southwest of downtown Novato (lat. 38°03'05" N, long. 122°36'15" W); the ridge is northeast of Big Rock. Named on Novato (1954) and San Geronimo (1954) 7.5' quadrangles.

Big Spring [SONOMA]: *spring,* 5.5 miles east of Mark West Springs (lat. 38°32'25" N, long. 122°36'55" W; near SE cor. sec. 15, T 8 N, R 7 W). Named on Calistoga (1958) 7.5' quadrangle.

Big Sulphur Creek [SONOMA]: *stream,* flows 21 miles to Russian River 1 mile north-northeast of Cloverdale (lat. 38°49'05" N, long. 123°00'35" W). Named on Asti (1959), Cloverdale (1960), The Geysers (1959), and Whispering Pines (1958) 7.5' quadrangles. Called Sulphur Cr. on Calistoga (1945) and Lower Lake (1945) 15' quadrangles. Called Pluton R. on Goddard's (1857) map. Shepherd (p. 153) used the name "Pluton valley" for the canyon of the stream in the vicinity of The Geysers, and Goodyear (1890b, p. 674) used the name "Pluton Cañon" for the same feature.

Bihler Landing: see **Black Point Landing** [SONOMA].

Bihler Point: see **Black Point** [SONOMA].

Bills Hill [SANTA CLARA]: *peak,* nearly 5 miles south-southeast of Gilroy Hot Springs (lat. 37°02'45" N, long. 121°26'20" W; near SE cor. sec. 20, T 10 S, R 5 E). Altitude 1988 feet. Named on Gilroy Hot Springs (1955) 7.5' quadrangle.

Bill Williams Creek [MARIN]: *stream,* flows 1.25 miles to Phoenix Lake nearly 3 miles southwest of downtown San Rafael (lat. 37° 57' N, long. 122°34'20" W). Named on San Rafael (1954) 7.5' quadrangle.

Binghamton [SOLANO]: *locality,* 5 miles east of Elmira (lat. 38°21'05" N, long. 121°48'55" W; sec. 24, T 6 N, R 1 E). Named on Dozier (1952) 7.5' quadrangle. Postal authorities established Binghamton post office in 1864, discontinued it for a short time in 1874, and discontinued it finally in 1906; the place was named after Binghamton, New York (Salley, p. 22).

Bird Island [CONTRA COSTA]: *island,* 150 feet long, 3 miles south-southwest of Richmond civic center in San Francisco Bay (lat. 37° 53'45" N, long. 122°21'30" W). Named on Richmond (1959) 7.5' quadrangle.

Bird Island [MARIN]: *island,* 500 feet long, less than 1 mile northwest of Point Bonita, and 50 feet offshore (lat. 37°49'25" N, long. 122°32'10" W). Named on Point Bonita (1954) 7.5' quadrangle.

Bird Island: see **Alcatraz Island** [SAN FRANCISCO].

Bird Rock [MARIN]: *island,* 450 feet long, 5 miles west-southwest of Tomales, and 950 feet offshore west of Tomales Point (lat. 38° 13'50" N, long. 122°59'35" W). Named on Tomales (1954) 7.5' quadrangle.

Bird Rock: see **Arch Rock** [SAN FRANCISCO].

Birds Landing [SOLANO]:

(1) *locality,* 1 mile west-southwest of Birds Landing (2) along Montezuma Slough (lat. 38°07'20" N, long. 121°53'10" W). Named on Honker Bay (1918) 7.5' quadrangle. The name is for John Bird, who built a wharf at the place about 1869 and shipped hay and wheat from there (Hoover, Rensch, and Rensch, p. 524).

(2) *village,* 17 miles south-southeast of Vacaville (lat. 38°08' N, long. 121°52'10" W; sec. 4, T 3 N, R 1 E); 1 mile east-northeast of Birds Landing (1). Named on Birds Landing (1953) 7.5' quadrangle. Postal authorities established Birds Landing post office in 1876 (Frickstad, p. 192).

Bismark Knob [NAPA-SONOMA]: *peak,* 4.5 miles north of Sonoma on Napa-Sonoma County line (lat. 38°21'30" N, long. 122°26'20" W; on N line sec. 20, T 6 N, R 5 W). Named on Sonoma (1951) 7.5' quadrangle. The feature also was known as Mount Nebo (Gudde, 1949, p. 32). Eddy's (1854) map has the name "Carnero Mt." for the ridge where Bismark Knob lies.

Bitter Creek [NAPA]: *stream,* flows 2.25 miles to lowlands 3.25 miles east of Calistoga (lat. 38°34'40" N, long. 122°30'55" W). Named on Calistoga (1958) 7.5' quadrangle.

Bivalve [MARIN]: *locality,* 2 miles northwest of Point Reyes Station on the northeast side of Tomales Bay (lat. 38°05'30" N, long. 122° 49'30" W). Named on Inverness (1954) 7.5' quadrangle. Point Reyes (1918) 15' quadrangle shows the place along Northwestern Pacific Railroad. Pacific Oyster Company planted 450 acres of oyster beds in 1907 and shipped oysters (which are bivalves) to San Francisco from the railroad station at the place (Teather, p. 8).

Bixler [CONTRA COSTA]: *locality,* 4 miles east of Brentwood along Atchison, Topeka and Santa Fe Railroad (lat. 37°56'35" N, long. 121°37'30" W; near SE cor. sec. 10, T 1 N, R 3 E). Named on Brentwood (1978) and Woodward Island (1978) 7.5' quadrangles.

Blackberry Spring [SANTA CLARA]: *spring,* 2.5 miles west-southwest of Mount Sizer on Pine Ridge (lat. 37°11'50" N, long. 121°33'15" W). Named on Mount Sizer (1955) 7.5' quadrangle.

Blackbird Valley [SANTA CLARA]: *canyon,* 2.5 miles long, 1.5 miles south of Mount Mocho on upper reaches of Colorado Creek (lat. 37°26'10" N, long. 121°29' W). Named on Eylar Mountain (1955) and Mount Boardman (1955) 7.5' quadrangles. On Mount Hamilton (1897) 15' quadrangle, the name "Blackbird Valley" applies to present South Pocket.

Black Canyon [MARIN]: *canyon,* 1.25 miles long, 1.5 miles northeast of downtown San Rafael (lat. 37°59'30" N, long. 122°30'30" W). Named on San Rafael (1954) 7.5' quadrangle.

Black Creek [SANTA CLARA]: *stream,* flows nearly 0.5 mile to Lexington Reservoir 2.25 miles south of downtown Los Gatos (lat. 37°11'25" N, long. 121°59'40" W; sec. 32, T 8 S, R 1 W). Named on Los Gatos (1953) 7.5' quadrangle.

Black Creek Valley: see **Dry Creek** [ALAMEDA] (1).

Black Diamond: see **Pittsburg** [CONTRA COSTA].

Black Diamond Landing: see **Pittsburg** [CONTRA COSTA].

Blackhawk Canyon [SANTA CLARA]: *canyon,* drained by a stream that flows nearly 2 miles to Bodfish Creek 1.5 miles east-southeast of Mount Madonna (lat. 37°00'10" N, long. 121°40'50" W). Named on Mount Madonna (1955) 7.5' quadrangle.

Black Hawk Creek: see **Mills Creek** [SAN MATEO] (1).

Black Hawk Ridge [CONTRA COSTA]: *ridge,* west-northwest-trending, 1.25 miles long, 3 miles south of Mount Diablo (lat. 37°50'15" N, long. 121°54'15" W). Named on Diablo (1953) 7.5' quadrangle.

Black Head Rock [SAN FRANCISCO]: *rock,* less than 1 mile northeast of Point Lobos, and 500 feet offshore at Lands End (lat. 37°47'20" N, long. 122°30'25" W). Named on San Francisco North (1956) 7.5' quadrangle.

Black Hills [CONTRA COSTA]:

(1) *ridge,* west- to south-trending, 2.5 miles long, 3 miles north of Orinda (lat. 37°55'15" N, long. 122°11'30" W). Named on Briones Valley (1959) 7.5' quadrangle.

(2) *range,* center 5 miles southeast of Mount Diablo (lat. 37°49'45" N, long. 121°51'45" W). Named on Diablo (1953) and Tassajara (1953) 7.5' quadrangles.

Black Hills: see **Candlestick Point** [SAN FRANCISCO].

Black John Slough [MARIN]: *water feature,* enters Petaluma River 3.5 miles northeast of downtown Novato (lat. 38°08'10" N, long. 122°30'55" W). Named on Petaluma River (1954) 7.5' quadrangle. The name commemorates John Henry Pingston, known as Black John, who was an early settler in the neighborhood (Teather, p. 8).

Black Mountain [MARIN]: *peak,* 2.5 miles east-northeast of Point Reyes Station (lat. 38°04'50" N, long. 122°45'50" W). Altitude 1280 feet. Named on Inverness (1954) 7.5' quadrangle. The name commemorates James Black, who owned Nicasio (1) grant., where the peak is located. The feature also was called Black's Peak (Teather, p. 8), Seven Sisters, and Elephant Mountain (Mason, 1976a, p. 149).

Black Mountain [SAN MATEO]: *peak,* 2 miles southwest of downtown San Mateo (lat. 37°32'45" N, long. 122°21'05" W). Altitude 676 feet. Named on San Mateo (1956) 7.5' quadrangle.

Black Mountain [SANTA CLARA]:

(1) *peak,* 4.5 miles south-southwest of Los Altos on Monte Bello Ridge (lat. 37°19'05" N, long. 122°08'45" W; sec. 13, T 7 S, R 3 E). Named on Mindego Hill (1961) 7.5' quadrangle.

(2) *peak,* 1 mile north of Mount Day (lat. 37°26'15" N, long. 121° 42' W). Altitude 3951 feet. Named on Mount Day (1955) 7.5' quadrangle. Called Mt. Day on Mount Hamilton (1897) 15' quadrangle, where present Mount Day is called Black Mountain.

(3) *peak,* nearly 1 mile north of Mount Stakes on Santa Clara-Stanislaus County line (lat. 37°19'55" N, long. 121°24'30" W; at N line sec. 15, T 7 S, R 5 E). Named on Mount Stakes (1955) 7.5' quadrangle.

Black Mountain [SONOMA]:

(1) *peak,* 4.5 miles east of Fort Ross (lat. 38°30'05" N, long. 123° 09'35" W). Altitude 1632 feet. Named on Fort Ross (1978) 7.5' quadrangle.

(2) *peak,* 12 miles north-northeast of the village of Stewarts Point (lat. 38°47'40" N, long. 123°16'05" W; near S line sec. 14, T 11 N, R 13 W). Altitude 2646 feet. Named on Ornbaun Valley (1960) 15' quadrangle.

(3) *peak,* 4.25 miles east-northeast of Guerneville (lat. 38°31'30" N, long. 122°55'20" W; sec. 24, T 8 N, R 10 W). Named on Guerneville (1955) 7.5' quadrangle.

(4) *range,* 9.5 miles north-northeast of Healdsburg (lat. 38°44'40" N, long. 122°48'15" W). Named on Jimtown (1955) and The Geysers (1959) 7.5' quadrangles.

Black Mountain: see **Little Black Mountain** [SONOMA].

Black Mountain Conservation Camp: see **Murphy Mill** [SONOMA].

Black Mountain Ridge [SONOMA]: *ridge,* southeast- to south-southeast-trending, 1.25 miles long, 4.25 miles east of Fort Ross (lat. 38°30'30" N, long. 123°09'55" W); Black Mountain (1) is at the south end of the ridge. Named on Fort Ross (1978) 7.5' quadrangle.

Black Oak Ridge[SONOMA]: *ridge,* south-southwest- to west-trending, 1 mile long, 3 miles west-northwest of Big Mountain (lat. 38° 43'20" N, long. 123°11'50" W). Named on Tombs Creek (1978) 7.5' quadrangle.

Black Oaks [SONOMA]: *locality,* 4.5 miles north of Geyser Peak (lat. 38°49'50" N, long. 122°49'55" W; sec. 2, T 11 N, R 9 W). Named on The Geysers (1959) 7.5' quadrangle.

Black Peak [SONOMA]: *peak,* 3 miles east of Healdsburg (lat. 38°36'50" N, long. 122°48'35" W). Named on Healdsburg (1955) 7.5' quadrangle.

Black Point [CONTRA COSTA]: *peak,* 3.25 miles northwest of Mount Diablo (lat. 37°54'45" N, long. 121°07'30" W; near N line sec. 27, T 1 N, R 1 W). Altitude 1791 feet. Named on Clayton (1953) 7.5' quadrangle. Members of the Whitney survey named the peak in the 1860's (Whitney, p. 22).

Black Point [MARIN]: *town,* 3.5 miles east of downtown Novato on the west side of Petaluma River (lat. 38°06'40" N, long. 122°30'05" W). Named on Novato (1954) and Petaluma Point (1959) 7.5' quadrangles. Called Grandview on Petaluma (1914) 15' quadrangle, but United States Board on Geographic Names (1950, p. 4) rejected this name for the place. Postal authorities established Black Point post office in 1865 and discontinued it in 1891; they established Grandview post office in 1905, changed the name to Black Point in 1944, and discontinued it in 1952 (Salley, p. 22, 88). They established Fairford post office 4 miles southwest of Black Point in 1879 and discontinued it the same year; the post office was located at Pacheco station of Northwestern Pacific Railroad (Salley, p. 72).

Black Point [SAN FRANCISCO]: *promontory,* nearly 1 mile west of North Point along San Francisco Bay (lat. 37°48'30" N, long. 122° 25'35" W). Named on San Francisco North (1956) 7.5' quadrangle. Called Pta. de San Josef on Ringgold's (1850a) map, and called San Jose or Black Point on Wackenreuder's (1861) map. The feature also was called Punta Medanos in Spanish times (Whiting and Whiting, p. 44). Ringgold's (1850a) map shows a promontory called Tonquin Pt. located about 0.5 mile east of present Black Point.

Black Point [SONOMA]: *promontory,* 2.5 miles northwest of the village of Stewarts Point along the coast (lat. 38°40'45" N, long. 123°25'50" W). Named on Stewarts Point (1978) 7.5' quadrangle. Called Bihler Pt. on Plantation (1915) 15' quadrangle.

Black Point Landing [SONOMA]: *locality,* 2.5 miles northwest of the village of Stewarts Point along the coast (lat. 38°40'45" N, long. 123°25'45"

W); the place is just east of Black Point. Named on Stewarts Point (1978) 7.5' quadrangle. Called Bihler Landing on Plantation (1915) 15' quadrangle. The name "Bihler" was for William "Dutch Bill" Bihler, who came to California in 1848 and became a stock breeder in Sonoma County (Gudde, 1949, p. 31).

Black Rock [SONOMA]: *peak,* 3.5 miles north of Cazadero (lat. 38° 34'50" N, long. 123°04'45" W; sec. 33, T 9 N, R 11 W). Altitude 1332 feet. Named on Cazadero (1978) 7.5' quadrangle.

Black Rock Creek [SONOMA]: *stream,* flows 2.5 miles to East Austin Creek 1.5 miles northeast of Cazadero (lat. 38°33' N, long. 123°04' W; sec. 10, T 8 N, R 11 W); the stream heads west of Black Rock. Named on Cazadero (1978) 7.5' quadrangle.

Black's Peak: see **Black Mountain** [MARIN].

Black Sulphur Creek [SONOMA]: *stream,* flows less than 1 mile to Little Warm Springs Creek nearly 1 mile south-southwest of Skaggs Springs (lat. 38°40'50" N, long. 123°01'45" W; sec. 25, T 10 N, R 11 W). Named on Warm Springs Dam (1978) 7.5' quadrangle.

Blakes Landing [MARIN]: *locality,* 3.5 miles south of Tomales on the northeast side of Tomales Bay (lat. 38°11'40" N, long. 122°55'05" W). Named on Tomales (1954) 7.5' quadrangle. Jeremiah Blake owned the landing (Mason, 1976a, p. 33).

Blake's Ravine: see **Strawberry Creek** [ALAMEDA].

Blenheim: see **Moss Beach** [SAN MATEO].

Blind Beach [SONOMA]: *beach,* 1 mile south-southwest of Jenner along the coast (lat. 38°26'15" N, long. 123°07'15" W). Named on Duncans Mills (1979) 7.5' quadrangle.

Blind Point [CONTRA COSTA]: *promontory,* 4.5 miles west-northwest of the settlement of Bethel Island along San Joaquin River at the west end of Jersey Island (lat. 38°01'55" N, long. 121°43'10" W). Named on Jersey Island (1978) 7.5' quadrangle.

Blithedale: see **Alto** [MARIN].

Blithedale Ridge [MARIN]: *ridge,* southeast- to south-southeast-trending, 2 miles long, 3.5 miles south-southwest of downtown San Rafael (lat. 37°55'30" N, long. 122°32'55" W). Named on San Rafael (1954) 7.5' quadrangle. The name recalls a resort near the ridge that was called Blithedale from Hawthorne's novel, *The Blithedale Romance* (Teather, p. 9).

Blodgett Magic Spring: see **Bodfish Creek** [SANTA CLARA].

Blodgett Magnesia Spring: see **Bodfish Creek** [SANTA CLARA].

Blodgett Mineral Spring: see **Bodfish Creek** [SANTA CLARA].

Bloomfield [SONOMA]: *town,* 6 miles south-southwest of Sebastopol (lat. 38°18'50" N, long. 122°51'10" W). Named on Two Rock (1954) 7.5' quadrangle. Postal authorities established Bloomfield post office in 1856 and discontinued it in 1955 (Salley, p. 23). The name may commemorate F.G. Blume, who owned Cañada de Pogolimi grant where the town is situated, or the name may be from Bloomfield, Kentucky, hometown of Larkin Cockrill, one of the purchasers of the site (Hansen and Miller, p. 44, 46).

Bloomfield: see **Miller** [SANTA CLARA].

Bloomquist Creek [SAN MATEO]: *stream,* flows 1 mile to Pescadero Creek 3.5 miles south-southwest of La Honda (lat. 37°16'20" N, long. 122°17'50" W; near S line sec. 33, T 7 S, R 4 W). Named on La Honda (1961) 7.5' quadrangle. The Bloomquist family had a sawmill along the creek in the 1870's; the stream also is called Hoffman Creek (Brown, p. 9).

Blossom Creek [NAPA]: *stream,* flows nearly 3 miles to Napa River 1 mile west-northwest of Calistoga (lat. 38°35'15" N, long. 122°35'45" W). Named on Calistoga (1958) 7.5' quadrangle.

Blossom Hill [SANTA CLARA]: *ridge,* west-northwest-trending, 2.25 miles long, 3 miles east of downtown Los Gatos (lat. 37°13'40" N, long. 121°55'40" W). Named on Los Gatos (1953) 7.5' quadrangle. Postal authorities established a post office called Blossom Hill in 1968 (Salley, p. 23).

Blossom Rock [SAN FRANCISCO]: *rock,* nearly 1 mile northeast of North Point in San Francisco Bay (lat. 37°49'05" N, long. 122°24'05" W). Named on San Francisco North (1956) 7.5' quadrangle. Captain Beechey discovered the rock in 1826 while he was charting the bay, and named the feature for his ship *Blossom,* a British man-of-war (Davis, W.H., p. 138).

Blucher [MARIN-SONOMA]: *land grant,* inland from the coast along Estero San Antonio and Americano Creek on Marin-Sonoma County line. Named on Two Rock (1954) and Valley Ford (1954) 7.5' quadrangles. Jean Vioget received 6 leagues in 1844; heirs of Stephen Smith claimed 26,759 acres patented in 1858 (Cowan, p. 19). Vioget had the nickname "Blucher" because of his resemblance to Prussian Field Marshall Gebhard von Blucher, famous for his role at the Battle of Waterloo; from the nickname came the designation of the grant (Gudde, 1949, p. 34).

Blucher Creek [SONOMA]: *stream,* flows 5 miles to Laguna de Santa Rosa 3 miles southeast of Sebastopol (lat. 38°22'40" N, long. 122°46'55" W); the stream is mainly on Blucher grant. Named on Two Rock (1954) 7.5' quadrangle.

Blue Grouse Ridge [SONOMA]: *ridge,* south- to southeast-trending, 0.5 mile long, 2.5 miles north-northeast of Cazadero (lat. 38°33'45" N, long. 123°03'55" W). Named on Cazadero (1978) 7.5' quadrangle.

Bluegum Creek [SONOMA]: *stream,* flows 1.5 miles to McDonnell Creek 6 miles west of Mount Saint Helena (lat. 38°41'10" N, long. 122°44'30" W; near W line sec. 27, T 10 N, R 8 W). Named on Jimtown (1955) and Mount Saint Helena (1959) 7.5' quadrangles.

Blue Gums [MARIN]: *locality,* 4.25 miles west-southwest of Tomales on Tomals Point (lat. 38°13'35" N, long. 122°58'35" W). Named on Tomales (1954) 7.5' quadrangle.

Blue Hills [SANTA CLARA]: *locality,* 2 miles north of downtown Saratoga along Southern Pacific Railroad (lat. 37°17'15" N, long. 122°01'50" W; sec. 25, T 7 S, R 2 W). Named on Cupertino (1961) 7.5' quadrangle.

Blue Jay Creek [SONOMA]: *stream,* flows 2.5 miles to Ward Creek 6 miles east-northeast of Fort Ross (lat. 38°32'05" N, long. 123° 08'05" W; sec. 13, T 8 N, R 12 W); the stream is east of Blue Jay Ridge. Named on Fort Ross (1978) 7.5' quadrangle.

Blue Jay Ridge [SONOMA]: *ridge,* south-trending, 2 miles long, 6 miles east-northeast of Fort Ross (lat. 38°33'10" N, long. 123°08'35" W); the ridge is west of Blue Jay Creek. Named on Fort Ross (1978) 7.5' quadrangle.

Blue Mountain: see **Mount Davidson** [SAN FRANCISCO]; **Mount Sutro** [SAN FRANCISCO]; **Mount Vaca** [NAPA-SOLANO].

Blue Mountains: see **Vaca Mountains** [NAPA-SOLANO].

Blue Ridge [MARIN]: *ridge,* south-southeast-trending, 1 mile long, 4.5 miles west-northwest of San Rafael (lat. 37°59'15" N, long. 122°36'50" W). Named on San Rafael (1954) 7.5' quadrangle. United States Board on Geographic Names (1976a, p. 5) approved the name "Pams Blue Ridge" for the next ridge east of the south part of Blue Ridge; the name "Pam" commemorates Pamela Ettinger, who lived near the ridge and hiked there.

Blue Ridge [NAPA]: *ridge,* extends north-northwest for 20 miles from near Berryessa Peak to Cache Creek, mainly on Napa-Yolo County line. Named on Brooks (1959), Guinda (1959), and Knoxville (1958) 7.5' quadrangles. Called Rumsey Range on Durst's (1916) map.

Blue Ridge [NAPA-SOLANO]: *ridge,* generally south-trending, 15 miles long, extends from Putah Creek along Napa-Solano County line to the southeast corner of Napa County. Named on Capell Valley (1951), Fairfield North (1951), Monticello Dam (1959), and Mount Vaca (1951) 7.5' quadrangles.

Blue Ridge [SANTA CLARA]: *ridge,* northwest-trending, 7.5 miles long, 9.5 miles northeast of Morgan Hill (lat. 37°13'15" N, long. 121°31'15" W). Named on Isabel Valley (1955), Mississippi Creek (1955), and Mount Sizer (1955) 7.5' quadrangles.

Blue Rock [SONOMA]: *relief feature,* 5.25 miles north-northeast of Cazadero (lat. 38°36'05" N, long. 123°02'35" W). Named on Cazadero (1978) 7.5' quadrangle.

Blue Rocks [SANTA CLARA]: *peak,* 6 miles west-northwest of Mount Sizer (lat. 37°14'55" N, long. 121°36'35" W). Altitude 2441 feet. Named on Mount Sizer (1955) 7.5' quadrangle.

Blue Rock Springs: see **Sulphur Springs** [SOLANO].

Blue Rock Springs Creek [SOLANO[: *stream,* flows 3.5 miles to Lake Chabot 2.5 miles northeast of downtown Vallejo (lat. 38°08'05" N, long. 122°13'45" W; sec. 6, T 3 N, R 3 W). Named on Benicia (1959) 7.5' quadrangle. Called Sulphur Springs Creek on Karquines (1898) 15' quadrangle.

Bluff Point [MARIN]: *promontory,* nearly 5 miles south-southeast of Point San Quentin near the southeast end of Tiburon Peninsula (lat. 37°52'50" N, long. 122°26'15" W). Named on San Quentin (1959) 7.5' quadrangle. Called Pt. Reed on Ringgold's (1850a) map.

Blumbago Canyon [SANTA CLARA]: *canyon,* drained by a stream that flows nearly 2 miles to Arroyo Bayo 7 miles south-southwest of Eylar Mountain (lat. 37°22'50" N, long. 121°34'50" W; sec. 39, T 6 S, R 4 E). Named on Eylar Mountain (1955) 7.5' quadrangle. Thompson and West's (1876) map has the name "Plumbajo Flat" near the canyon.

Blunt Point [MARIN-SAN FRANCISCO]: *promontory,* at the southeast end of Angel Island on Marin-San Francisco County line (lat. 37°51'10" N, long. 122°25'05" W). Named on San Francisco North (1956) 7.5' quadrangle. Called Point Blunt on San Francisco (1942) 15' quadrangle, and United States Board on Geographic Names (1980, p. 3) approved this form of the name, which commemorates Lieutenant Simon F. Blunt, a member of Ringgold's expedition of 1849 (Teather, p. 2).

Blunt Point Rock [SAN FRANCISCO]: *rock,* 3 miles north of North Point in San Francisco Bay (lat. 37°51'10" N, long. 122°25' W); the rock is 100 feet off Blunt Point (present Point Blunt). Named on San Francisco North (1956) 7.5' quadrangle. United States Board on Geographic Names (1980, p. 4) approved the name "Point Blunt Rock" for the feature.

Boardman: see **Mount Boardman** [ALAMEDA-SANTA CLARA].

Boca del Puerto Dulce: see **Carquinez Strait** [CONTRA COSTA-SOLANO].

Bocus Creek: see **Bogess Creek** [SAN MATEO].

Bodega [SONOMA]:

(1) *land grant,* along the coast between Russian River and Estero Americano. Named on Arched Rock (1977), Bodega Head (1972), Camp Meeker (1954), Duncans Mills (1979), and Valley Ford (1954) 7.5' quadrangles. Stephen Smith received the land in 1844; M.T. Curtis and others claimed 35,488 acres patented in 1859 (Cowan, p. 19).

(2) *town,* 3.25 miles northwest of Valley Ford (lat. 38°20'45" N, long. 122°58'20" W); the town is on Bodega grant. Named on Valley Ford (1954) 7.5' quadrangle. Postal authorities established Bodega post office by 1852, discontinued it in 1867, reestablished it in 1882, and discontinued it in 1887; they established Smith's Ranch post office in 1854 and discontinued in 1901, when they moved it 5 miles west and changed the name to Bodega—the name "Smith's Ranch" was from Captain Stephen Smith, who received Bodega grant (Salley, p. 23, 200, 206). Present Bodega was called Bodega Corners in the early days (Hanna, P.T., p. 35). Russians had a settlement called Kuskov that was 1 mile north of present Bodega in the valley of Salmon Creek (1)—the name was for the Russian leader, Ivan Kuskov (Miller, J.T., p. 39).

Bodega: see **Point Bodega**, under **Tomales Bluff** [MARIN].

Bodega Bay [MARIN-SONOMA]: *embayment,* north-northwest of the mouth of Tomales Bay and southeast of Bodega Head along the coast on Marin-Somoma County line (lat. 38°16' N, long. 123° 00' W). Named on Bodega Head (1972), Tomales (1954) and Valley Ford (1954) 7.5' quadrangles. Called Puerto de la Bodega on Ringgold's (1850b) map. The name is for Juan Francisco Bodega y Quadra, who entered the embayment in 1775 (Wagner, H.R., p. 376-377). Ivan A. Ruskov built the first Russian structure in California at the place, which he called Port Rumyantsev (Schwartz, p. 37).

Bodega Bay [SONOMA]: *village,* 20 miles west-southwest of Santa Rosa on the east side of Bodega Harbor (lat. 38°20' N, long. 123° 02'45" W). Named on Bodega Head (1972) 7.5' quadrangle. Postal authorities established Bay post office in 1895 and changed the name to Bodega Bay in 1941 (Frickstad, p. 194). United States Board on Geographic Names (1950, p. 4) rejected the name "Bay" for the place.

Bodega Bay: see **Bodega Harbor** [SONOMA].

Bodega Corners: see **Bodega** [SONOMA] (2).

Bodega Harbor [SONOMA]: *bay,* opens into the northwest end of Bodega Bay [MARIN-SONOMA] 2 miles south of the village of Bodega Bay (lat. 38°18'20" N, long. 122°03'05" W). Named on Bodega Head (1972) 7.5' quadrangle. Called Bodega Bay on Duncans Mills (1921) 15' quadrangle, but United States Board on Geographic Names (1943, p. 10) rejected the names "Bodega Bay" and "Bodega Lagoon" for the feature.

Bodega Head [SONOMA]: *peninsula,* 2 miles south-southwest of the village of Bodega Bay (lat. 38°18'30" N, long. 123°03'40" W); the feature is west of the mouth of Bodega Harbor. Named on Bodega Head (1972) 7.5' quadrangle. Called C. Romanzoff on Ringgold's (1850c) map. The place is known locally as Campbells Point, for Captain John Campbell, a pioneer landowner in the neighborhood (Gudde, 1949, p. 53).

Bodaga Island [SONOMA]: *hill,* 1 mile southeast of the village of Bodega Bay in lowlands along Bodega Harbor (lat. 38°19'15" N, long. 123°02'05" W). Named on Bodega Head (1942) 7.5' quadrangle.

Bodega Lagoon [SONOMA]: see **Bodega Harbor** [SONOMA].

Bodega Point [SONOMA]: *locality,* 1.25 miles south-southeast of the present village of Bodega Bay in present Bodega Harbor (lat. 38° 19'10" N, long. 123°02' W). Named on Duncans Mills (1921) 15' quadrangle.

Bodega Rock [SONOMA]: *island,* 250 feet long, 2.5 miles south of the village of Bodega Bay and 1700 feet southeast of Bodega Head (lat. 38°17'45" N, long. 123°02'50" W). Named on Bodega Head (1972) 7.5' quadrangle. This probably is the feature that members of Vancouver's expedition called Gibson Island in 1793 (Hoover, Rensch, and Rensch, p. 525).

Bodfish Canon: see **Bodfish Creek** [SANTA CLARA].

Bodfish Creek [SANTA CLARA]: *stream,* flows 8 miles to Uvas Creek 3 miles west of Gilroy (lat. 37°00'50" N, long. 121°37'50" W). Named on Mount Madonna (1955) and Watsonville East (1955) 7.5' quadrangles. Thompson and West's (1876) map has the name "Bodfish Canon" on upper reaches of the stream. Waring (p. 273) described Blodgett Magic Spring, a summer camp and source of bottled mineral water located along Bodfish Creek nearly 7 miles west of Gilroy; Waring described another spring, called Blodgett Mineral Spring or Magnesia Spring, situated on a hillside above a branch of Bodfish Creek several miles north of Blodgett Magic Spring.

Bogess Creek [SAN MATEO]: *stream,* flows 5 miles to San Gregorio Creek 3.25 miles west of La Honda (lat. 37°18'55" N, long. 122° 19'40" W). Named on La Honda (1961) 7.5' quadrangle. The stream has been called Keiffer's Creek for a rancher of the 1860's; the name "Bogess" also had the forms "Bogus," "Bocus," and "Boggess" (Brown, p. 9).

Boggess Creek: see **Bogess Creek** [SAN MATEO].

Boggs Creek [SONOMA]: *stream,* heads in Mendocino County and flows 0.5 mile to Cascade Creek 6 miles north-northeast of Asti (lat. 38°50'35" N, long. 122°56'05" W; near E line sec. 35, T 12 N, R 10 W). Named on Asti (1959) 7.5' quadrangle.

Bogus Creek: see **Bogess Creek** [SAN MATEO].

Bohemian Grove [SONOMA]: *area,* 4.25 miles north-northwest of Occidental (lat. 38°28' N, long. 122°58'30" W). Named on Camp Meeker (1954) 7.5' quadrangle. The name was applied to the place in 1891 because the Bohemian Club of San Francisco held summer outings there (Gudde, 1949, p. 36).

Bohn Lake: see **Upper Bohn Lake**, under **Aetna Springs** [NAPA].

Bolinas [MARIN]: *town,* 10 miles west-southwest of downtown San Rafael along Bolinas Bay (lat. 37°54'35" N, long. 122°41'05" W). Named on Bolinas (1954) 7.5' quadrangle. Postal authorities established Bolinas post office in 1863 (Frickstad, p. 87). United States Board on Geographic Names (1933, p. 155) rejected the forms "Ballenas" and "Baulenas" for the name, which is from an Indian word (Gilliam, p. 86).

Bolinas Bay [MARIN]: *embayment,* between Duxbury Point and Rocky Point along the coast (lat. 37°53'30" N, long. 122°40' W); the feature is at Bolinas. Named on Bolinas (1954) 7.5' quadrangle. Called Rialto Cove on Ringgold's (1850b) map. United States Board on Geographic Names (1933, p. 155) rejected the forms "Ballenas" and "Baulenas" for the name.

Bolinas Creek [ALAMEDA]: *stream,* flows 3 miles to Crow Creek 14 miles east-southeast of downtown Oakland (lat. 37°45'35" N, long. 122°01'40" W; sec. 13, T 2 S, R 2 W). Named on Las Trampas Ridge (1959) 7.5' quadrangle. The name is from Antonio Bolena, who owned land along the stream in the 1870's; the canyon of the stream was called Davis Canyon in 1894 for J.H. Davis, a farmer who had land along the creek (Mosier and Mosier, p. 16, 28).

Bolinas Creek: see **Pine Gulch Creek** [MARIN].

Bolinas Lagoon [MARIN]: *bay,* opens into Bolinas Bay at Bolinas (lat. 37°54'30" N, long. 122°40'50" W). Named on Bolinas (1954) 7.5' quadrangle.

Bolinas Point [MARIN]: *promontory,* 2.25 miles west of Bolinas along the coast (lat. 37°54'15" N, long. 122°43'35" W). Named on Bolinas (1954) 7.5' quadrangle.

Bolinas Ridge [MARIN]: *ridge,* northwest-trending, 23 miles long, extends from Mount Tamalpais northwest to near Tomales. Named on Bolinas (1954), Inverness (1954), Point Reyes NE (1954), San Geronimo (1954), San Rafael (1954), and Tomales (1954) 7.5' quadrangles.

Bolinger Creek [CONTRA COSTA]: *stream,* flows 5.25 miles to San Ramon Creek 3.25 miles south of Danville (lat. 37°46'25" N, long. 121°59'45" W; sec. 8, T 2 S, R 1 W). Named on Diablo (1953) and Las Trampas Ridge (1959) 7.5' quadrangles. United States Board on Geographic Names (1981a, p. 2) approved the name "Bollinger Canyon Creek" for the feature, and rejected the names "Bolinger Creek" and "Bollinger Creek." At the same time the Board approved the name "Bollinger Canyon" for the canyon of the stream, and noted that the name commemorates Joshua Bollinger, who settled in the canyon in 1855. Becker (1969) identified a feature called Arroyo de las Trampas, shown on a diseño of Laguna de los Palos Colorados grant in 1835, as probably present Bollinger Canyon.

Bolitas Point: see **Bulls Head Point** [CONTRA COSTA].

Bollinger Canyon [SANTA CLARA]: *canyon,* drained by a stream that flows 2 miles to Arroyo Bayo 2.5 miles north-northeast of Isabel Valley (lat. 37°20'30" N, long. 121°31'10" W; sec. 10, T 7 S, R 4 E). Named on Isabel Valley (1955) and Mount Stakes (1955) 7.5' quadrangles.

Bollinger Canyon: see **Bolinger Creek** [CONTRA COSTA].

Bollinger Canyon Creek: see **Bolinger Creek** [CONTRA COSTA].

Bollinger Creek: see **Bolinger Creek** [CONTRA COSTA].

Bollinger Mountain [SANTA CLARA]: *peak,* 4 miles south of Isabel Valley (lat. 37°15'15" N, long. 121°32'40" W; sec. 9, T 8 S, R 4 E); the peak is near the southeast end of Bollinger Ridge. Named on Isabel Valley (1955) 7.5' quadrangle.

Bollinger Ridge [SANTA CLARA]: *ridge,* northwest- to west-trending, 5 miles long, 3.5 miles south of Isabel Valley. Named on Isabel Valley (1955) and Mount Sizer (1955) 7.5' quadrangles. On Morgan Hill (1917) and Mount Hamilton (1897) 15' quadrangles, the ridge is shown as part of a larger feature called Pine Ridge

Bolsa de Encinal: see **Alameda** [ALAMEDA].

Bolsa Point [SAN MATEO]: *promontory,* 1 mile north-northwest of Pigeon Point along the coast (lat. 37°11'45" N, long. 122°24'15" W). Named on Pigeon Point (1955) 7.5' quadrangle.

Bon Air Hill [MARIN]: *hill,* nearly 2 miles south of downtown San Rafael (lat. 37°56'50" N, long. 122°31'55" W). Named on San Rafael (1954) 7.5' quadrangle. The name recalls a resort hotel called Bon Air that was popular from the 1880's until the 1920's (Teather, p. 12).

Bone Creek [SONOMA]: *stream,* flows 0.5 mile to Austin Creek less than 1 mile north of Cazadero (lat. 38°32'35" N, long. 122°05'15" W; sec. 16, T 8 N, R 11 W). Named on Cazadero (1978) 7.5' quadrangle.

Bonilla [SONOMA]: *locality,* 1.5 miles southeast of Sonoma along Northwestern Pacific Railroad (lat. 38°16'40" N, long. 122°26'10" W). Named on Sonoma (1951) 7.5' quadrangle.

Bonita [CONTRA COSTA]: *locality,* 1.5 miles north of present Walnut Creek civic center along Oakland Antioch and Eastern Railroad (lat. 37°55'25" N, long. 122°03'30" W). Named on Concord (1915) 15' quadrangle.

Bonita: see **Point Bonita** [MARIN].

Bonita Channel [MARIN]: *water feature,* northwest of Point Bonita between Potatopatch Shoal and the coast (lat. 37°49'45" N, long. 122°33'25" W). Named on Point Bonita (1954) 7.5' quadrangle.

Bonita Cove [MARIN-SAN FRANCISCO]: *embayment,* east of Point Bonita along Marin County coast (lat. 37°49'20" N, long. 122° 31' W). Named on Point Bonita (1954) 7.5' quadrangle. Marin-San Francisco County line follows the low-water mark of Marin County coast from Point Bonita to Cavallo Point, which places the water area of the embayment in San Francisco County.

Bonita Creek [SANTA CLARA]: *stream,* flows 3.5 miles to Isabel Creek 2 miles north of Mount Hamilton (lat. 37°22'25" N, long. 121°38'25" W; sec. 34, T 6 S, R 3 E). Named on Lick Observatory (1955) and Mount Day (1955) 7.5' quadrangles. Called Bonito Creek on Mount Hamilton (1897) 15' quadrangle.

Bonito Creek: see **Bonita Creek** [SANTA CLARA].

Bonjetti Creek [SANTA CLARA]: *stream,* flows 2 miles to Saratoga Creek 2.25 miles west-southwest of Saratoga (lat. 37°14'55" N, long. 122°04'05" W; sec. 10, T 8 S, R 2 W). Named on Castle Rock Ridge (1955) 7.5' quadrangle. A resort called Long Bridge operated along Saratoga Creek near the mouth of Bonjetti Creek in the 1890's (Cunningham, p. 79).

Bon Tempe Creek [MARIN]: *stream,* flows 0.5 mile to Alpine Lake 4.5 miles west of downtown San Rafael (lat. 37°57'45" N, long. 122°36'40" W). Named on San Rafael (1954) 7.5' quadrangle.

Bon Tempe Lake [MARIN]: *lake,* behind a dam on Lagunitas Creek 4.5 miles west-southwest of downtown San Rafael (lat. 37°57'20" N, long. 122°36'40" W). Named on San Rafael (1954) 7.5' quadrangle. The Americanized name commemorates brothers Guiseppi Bautunpi and Pasquale Bautunpi, who started a dairy at the site of the present lake in 1868; Marin Municipal Water District built the lake in 1948 (Teather, p. 12).

Booker Creek [SANTA CLARA]: *stream,* flows 1.25 miles to Saratoga Creek 3 miles west of Saratoga (lat. 37°15'15" N, long. 122° 05'15" W; sec. 9, T 8 S, R 2 W). Named on Castle Rock Ridge (1955) and Cupertino (1961) 7.5' quadrangles.

Boon Hill [CONTRA COSTA]: *peak,* 1 mile east-northeast of Danville at the west end of Short Ridge (lat. 37°49'40" N, long. 121°58'40" W; sec. 21, T 1 S, R 1 W). Named on Diablo (1953) 7.5' quadrangle.

Bootjack Camp [MARIN]: *locality,* 6 miles southwest of downtown San Rafael (lat. 37°54'30" N, long. 122°36'05" W); the place is near Bootjack Creek. Named on San Rafael (1954) 7.5' quadrangle.

Bootjack Creek [MARIN]: *stream,* flows 1 mile to Rattlesnake Creek nearly 6 miles southwest of downtown San Rafael (lat. 37° 54'20" N, long. 122°35'35" W). Named on San Rafael (1954) 7.5' quadrangle.

Borel Hill [SAN MATEO]: *peak,* 2 miles east-northeast of Mindego Hill on Russian Ridge (lat. 37°19'10" N, long. 122°11'55" W; sec. 16, T 7 S, R 3 W). Altitude 2572 feet. Named on Mindego Hill (1961) 7.5' quadrangle.

Bothin [MARIN]: *locality,* 8 miles south-southwest of downtown Novato along Northwestern Pacific Railroad (lat. 38°00'15" N, long. 122°37'10" W). Named on Petaluma (1914) 15' quadrangle.

Bothin Creek [MARIN]: *stream,* flows less than 1 mile to Fairfax Creek 3.5 miles west-northwest of downtown San Rafael (lat. 37° 59'25" N, long. 122°35'35" W). Named on San Rafael (1954) 7.5' quadrangle.

Boulder Creek [SONOMA]: *stream,* flows 2.25 miles to Galloway Creek 11 miles west of Cloverdale (lat. 38°47'10" N, long. 123°12'55" W; sec. 20, T 11 N, R 12 W). Named on Hopland (1960) 15' quadrangle.

Boulder Creek: see **Little Boulder Creek** [SAN MATEO].

Bowman Canyon [MARIN]: *canyon,* 1 mile long, opens into the canyon of Novato Creek 3.25 miles west-northwest of downtown Novato (lat. 38°07'20" N, long. 122°37'30" W). Named on Petaluma (1954) 15' quadrangle.

Bowman's Point: see **West End**, under **Alameda** [ALAMEDA].

Boyd Creek [SONOMA]:
(1) *stream,* flows less than 1 mile to Mill Creek (1) 6.5 miles north of Guerneville (lat. 38°35'50" N, long. 122°59'15" W; sec. 29, T 9 N, R 10 W). Named on Guerneville (1955) 7.5' quadrangle.
(2) *stream,* flows 1.25 miles to Fuller Creek 2.5 miles southeast of Annapolis (lat. 38°41'50" N, long. 123°19'40" W; sec. 20, T 10 N, R 13 W). Named on Annapolis (1977) 7.5' quadrangle.

Boyer Creek [SONOMA]: *stream,* flows 1 mile to Pena Creek 3.25 miles south-southeast of Skaggs Springs (lat. 38°38'55" N, long. 123°00'20" W; near N line sec. 7, T 9 N, R 10 W). Named on Warm Springs Dam (1978) 7.5' quadrangle.

Boyes Hot Springs [SONOMA]: *town,* 2 miles northwest of Sonoma in Valley of the Moon (lat. 38°18'45" N, long. 122°28'40" W). Named on Sonoma (1951) 7.5' quadrangle. Called Boyes Springs on Sonoma (1942) 15' quadrangle. Postal authorities established Boyes Springs post office in 1911 and changed the name to Boyes Hot Springs in 1938 (Frickstad, p. 194). The name commemorates Captain Henry Boyes and his wife, who came to the place in 1888 and started a popular resort (Hansen and Miller, p. 133). Crawford (1896, p. 521) used the name "Agua Rica Hot Sulphur Springs" for 16 springs located 2 miles north of Sonoma along the railroad. A resort called Ohms Spring was situated about 0.5 mile southeast of Boyes Hot Springs, where in 1909 it had accommodations for 20 guests (Waring, p. 113).

Boyes Springs: see **Boyes Hot Springs** [SONOMA].

Boynton Slough [SOLANO]: *water feature,* joins Suisun Slough 2.5 miles south of Fairfield (lat. 38°12'40" N, long. 122°02'15" W). Named on Fairfield South (1949) 7.5' quadrangle.

Boysen: see **Cherry** [SONOMA].

Bozzo Gulch [SAN MATEO]: *canyon,* drained by a stream that flows 0.5 mile to Sausal Creek 4.25 miles north of Mindego Hill in Portola Valley (1) (lat. 37°22'25" N, long. 122°13'25" W). Named on Mindego Hill (1961) 7.5' quadrangle. Emmanuel Bozzo had a ranch at the head of the canyon in the late 1860's (Brown, p. 10).

Bradford Island [CONTRA COSTA]: *island,* 2.5 miles long, 4.25 miles north-northwest of the settlement of Bethel Island between San Joaquin River, Fishermans Cut, and False River (lat. 38°04'30" N, long. 121°39'45" W). Named on Jersey Island (1978) 7.5' quadrangle. Called Bradford Tract on Davis and Vernon's (1951) map.

Bradford Landing [CONTRA COSTA]: *locality,* 4.5 miles north-northwest of the present settlement of Bethel Island along San Joaquin River (lat. 38°04'35" N, long. 121°40'30" W); the place is on the west side of Bradford Island. Named on Jersey (1910) 7.5' quadrangle.

Bradford Mountain [SONOMA]: *peak,* 4 miles west-southwest of Geyserville (lat. 38°41'05" N, long. 122°58'20" W; sec. 28, T 10 N, R 10 W). Altitude 1229 feet. Named on Geyserville (1955) 7.5' quadrangle.

Bradford Tract: see **Bradford Island** [CONTRA COSTA].

Bradley Beach: see **Sand Beach** [SAN MATEO].

Bradley Creek [SAN MATEO]: *stream,* flows 3 miles to Pescadero Creek 5 miles south of the village of San Gregorio near Pescadero (lat. 37°15'10" N, long. 122°23'15" W). Named on San Gregorio (1961) 7.5' quadrangle. Charles Bradley had a dairy by the stream in the 1880's (Brown, p. 10).

Bradley's Creek: see **Arroyo de en Medio** [SAN MATEO].

Bradleys Store [SANTA CLARA]: *locality,* 4.5 miles west-southwest of Morgan Hill along Little Uvas Creek (lat. 37°06'30" N, long. 121°43'55" W). Named on Morgan Hill (1917) 15' quadrangle. This appears to be the place, or near the place, called Uvas on California Mining Bureau's (1917b) map. Postal authorities established Uvas post office in 1896, moved it 1.5 miles south in 1890, moved it 0.5 mile south in 1899, and discontinued it in 1908; the post office was located 9 miles southwest of Madrone (Salley, p. 228).

Bradmoor Island [SOLANO]: *island,* 2.5 miles south-southwest of Denverton along Nurse Slough (lat. 38°11'30" N, long. 121°55'15" W). Named on Denverton (1953) 7.5' quadrangle. Called Bradtmoor Island on Denverton (1918) 7.5' quadrangle.

Bradtmoor Island: see **Bradmoor Island** [SOLANO].

Brady Ridge [SONOMA]: *ridge,* south-trending, 1 mile long, 2.5 miles east-northeast of Guerneville (lat. 38°30'55" N, long. 122°57'05" W). Named on Guerneville (1955) 7.5' quadrangle.

Braen Canyon [SANTA CLARA]: *canyon,* drained by a stream that flows 2 miles to Hunting Hollow nearly 3 miles south-southeast of Gilroy Hot Springs (lat. 37°04'20" N, long. 121°27'20" W; near N line sec. 18, T 10 S, R 5 E). Named on Gilroy Hot Springs (1955) 7.5' quadrangle.

Brain Ridge [SONOMA]: *ridge,* northwest-trending, 1.25 miles long, 4.5 miles east-northeast of Fort Ross (lat. 38°32'15" N, long. 121° 10' W). Named on Fort Ross (1978) 7.5' quadrangle.

Brays: see **Fruitvale Station** [ALAMEDA].

Brazil Beach [MARIN]: *beach,* 3 miles west-southwest of Tomales along the northeast side of Tomales Bay (lat. 38°14' N, long. 122° 57'15" W). Named on Tomales (1954) 7.5' quadrangle. The name commemorates Antone Brazil, a farmer who shipped his produce by barge from the beach to San Francisco (United States Board on Geographic Names, 1967a, p. 2).

Brazoria: see **Rio Vista** [SOLANO].

Brazos [NAPA]: *locality,* 3.25 miles west-northwest of Napa Junction along Southern Pacific Railroad (lat. 38°12'30" N, long. 122° 18'10" W; sec. 9, T 4 N, R 4 W). Named on Cuttings Wharf (1949, photorevised 1968) 7.5' quadrangle.

Brazos del Rio: see **Rio Vista** [SOLANO].

Brentwood [CONTRA COSTA]: *town,* 12 miles east-northeast of Mount Diablo (lat. 37°55'55" N, long. 121°41'55" W). Named on Brentwood (1978) 7.5' quadrangle. Postal authorities established Brentwood post office in 1878 (Frickstad, p. 21), and the town incorporated in 1948. The name is from the town in England that was the ancestral home of John Marsh, owner of Los Meganos grant (Gudde, 1949, p. 40).

Brewer Island [SAN MATEO]: *island,* 2.5 miles long, 3 miles east of downtown San Mateo along San Francisco Bay (lat. 37°33'45" N, long. 122°16' W). Named on Redwood Point (1959) and San Mateo (1956) 7.5' quadrangles. Frank M. Brewer built levees and drained the island about 1905 to make a place for his dairy ranch (Brown, p. 11).

Bridgehaven [SONOMA]: *settlement,* 1.5 miles southeast of Jenner (lat. 38°26'05" N, long. 123°05'55" W); the place is at the south end of a highway bridge across Russian River. Named on Duncans Mills (1979) 7.5' quadrangle. Called Bridge Haven on Duncans Mills (1943) 7.5' quadrangle, but United States Board on Geographic Names (1979a, p. 2) rejected this form of the name.

Bridgehead [CONTRA COSTA]: *settlement,* 3.25 miles east of downtown Antioch (lat. 38°00'20" N, long. 121°45' W); the place is near the south end of a bridge across San Joaquin River. Named on Antioch North (1978) and Jersey Island (1978) 7.5' quadrangles.

Bridgeport: see **Cordelia** [SOLANO].

Briggs Creek [SANTA CLARA]: *stream,* flows 2.25 miles to Lexington Reservoir 3 miles south of downtown Los Gatos (lat. 37°10'55" N, long. 121°59'25" W; sec. 5, T 9 S, R 1 W). Named on Castle Rock Ridge (1955) and Los Gatos (1953) 7.5' quadrangles.

Briggs Creek [SONOMA]: *stream,* flows 5.5 miles to join McDonnell Creek and form Maacama Creek 6 miles west of Mount Saint Helena (lat. 38°40'25" N, long. 122°44'30" W; near W line sec. 34, T 10 N, R 8 W). Named on Mount Saint Helena (1959) 7.5' quadrangle.

Briggs Creek: see **Little Briggs Creek** [SONOMA].

Briggston [SOLANO]: *locality,* 7 miles north-northeast of Dixon along Southern Pacific Railroad (lat. 38°31'55" N, long. 121°44'50" W; near NW cor. sec. 22, T 8 S, R 2 E). Named on Swingle (1915) 7.5' quadrangle. The name commemorates Charles Briggs, a pioneer of Solano County (Hanna, P.T., p. 41).

Brighton Beach: see **Sharp Park** [SAN MATEO].

Brighton Lake: see **Laguna Salada** [SAN MATEO].

Brightside [ALAMEDA]: *locality,* 2.25 miles west of Sunol along Southern Pacific Railroad in Alameda (present Niles) Canyon (lat. 37°36' N, long. 121°55'25" W; sec. 12, T 4 S, R 1 W). Named on Pleasanton (1906) 15' quadrangle. The name is from the position of the place on the sunny, or bright, side of Alameda Creek (Mosier and Mosier, p. 17).

Brink Creek: see **Britain Creek** [SONOMA].

Briones Hills [CONTRA COSTA]: *ridge,* west-trending, 4.5 miles long, center 5 miles north-northeast of Orinda (lat. 37°56'35" N, long. 122°08'45" W). Named on Briones Valley (1959) and Walnut Creek (1959) 7.5' quadrangles. The name is from the Spanish Briones family (Gudde, 1949, p. 40).

Briones Reservoir [CONTRA COSTA]: *lake,* 3 miles long, behind a dam on Bear Creek 2.5 miles north-northwest of Orinda (lat. 37° 54'50" N, long. 122°12'30" W); water of the lake floods part of Briones Valley (1). Named on Briones Valley (1959, photorevised 1968) 7.5' quadrangle.

Briones Valley [CONTRA COSTA]:

(1) *canyon,* along Bear Creek above a point 3.5 miles north-northwest of Orinda (lat. 37°55'35" N, long. 122°12'05" W). Named on Briones Valley (1959) 7.5' quadrangle. Water of Briones Reservoir now covers part of the feature.

(2) *valley,* 8 miles east of Mount Diablo (lat. 37°53'50" N, long. 121°46'30" W). Named on Antioch South (1953) and Brentwood (1978) 7.5' quadrangles.

Brisbane [SAN MATEO]: *town,* 2 miles north-northeast of downtown South San Francisco (lat. 37°40'55" N, long. 122°24' W). Named on San Francisco South (1956) 7.5' quadrangle. Called Visitacion on San Mateo (1915) 15' quadrangle. A subdivision called Visitacion City was started at the place in 1908 to attract refugees from San Francisco after the earthquake of 1906, but the development failed to prosper; more than 20 years later Arthur Ennis, agent for the subdivision, renamed the place Brisbane for Arthur Brisbane, a popular newspaper columnist, and this time the community did prosper (Stanger, 1963, p. 163-164). Postal authorities established Visitacion post office in 1908 and discontinued it in 1914; they established Brisbane post office in 1931 (Frickstad, p. 167, 169), and Brisbane incorporated in 1961.

Brisbane Lagoon: see **Sierra Point** [SAN MATEO].

Britain Creek [SONOMA]: *stream,* flows 3.25 miles to House Creek 4.25 miles south-southwest of Big Mountain (lat. 38°39'20" N, long. 123°10'40" W; near W line sec. 3, T 9 N, R 12 W); the stream is north of Britain Ridge. Named on Tombs Creek (1978) 7.5' quadrangle. Called Brink Creek on Tombs Creek (1943) 7.5' quadrangle.

Britain Ridge [SONOMA]: *ridge,* west- to south-trending, about 1.25 miles long, 3.25 miles south-southwest of Big Mountain (lat. 38° 39'50" N, long. 123°09'40" W); the ridge is south of Britain Creek. Named on Tombs Creek (1978) 7.5' quadrangle. Called Shoeheart Ridge on Tombs Creek (1943) 7.5' quadrangle.

Brittan Knoll [SAN MATEO]: *peak,* 2.5 miles west-northwest of downtown Redwood City (lat. 37°30' N, long. 122°15'50" W). Named on Woodside (1961) 7.5' quadrangle. Brown (p. 11) called the feature Brittan's Knoll, and noted that Nat Brittan's ranch was there for nearly 70 years after 1856.

Brittan Park [SAN MATEO]: *district,* 5.5 miles south-southeast of downtown San Mateo in San Carlos (lat. 37°30'05" N, long. 122° 16'10" W). Named on San Mateo (1947) 7.5' quadrangle.

Broad Slough [CONTRA COSTA]: *water feature,* the lowermost reach of San Joaquin River 3 miles north-northwest of Antioch (lat. 38°02'50" N, long. 121°50'25" W). Named on Antioch North (1978) 7.5' quadrangle.

Broadway Wharf: see **Oakland** [ALAMEDA].

Brooklyn: see **Oakland** [ALAMEDA].

Brooklyn Basin [ALAMEDA]: *water feature,* 1 mile south-southeast of downtown Oakland in the east part of Oakland Inner Harbor (lat. 37°47'10" N, long. 122°15' W). Named on Oakland East (1959) and Oakland West (1959) 7.5' quadrangles. Concord (1897) and San Francisco (1899) 15' quadrangles have the name "Oakland Harbor" at the place. United States Board on Geographic Names (1949b, p. 3) rejected the name "North Channel" for the feature, and later the Board (1984c, p. 2) rejected the name "Embarcadero Cove" for it. The name "Brooklyn" is from the former town of Brooklyn, now part of Oakland (Gudde, 1969, p. 39).

Brooks Creek [SONOMA]: *stream,* flows 3.5 miles to Russian River 4.5 miles east of Healdsburg (lat. 38°36'20" N, long. 122°47'05" W). Named on Healdsburg (1955) and Mark West Springs (1958) 7.5' quadrangles.

Brooks Gulch [SONOMA]: *canyon,* drained by a stream that flows 1 mile to marsh along Bodega Harbor 1 mile southeast of the village of Bodega Bay (lat. 38°19'20" N, long. 123°02' W). Named on Bodega Head (1972) 7.5' quadrangle.

Brooks Island [CONTRA COSTA]: *island,* 3250 feet long, 3 miles south-southwest of Richmond civic center in San Francisco Bay (lat. 37°53'50" N, long. 122°21'15" W). Named on Richmond (1959) 7.5' quadrangle. United States Board on Geographic Names (1933, p. 166) rejected the names "Rocky Island" and "Sheep Island" for the feature. H.R. Wagner (p. 439) listed the early names "Isla del Carmen" or "Isla del Carmel" for it.

Brothers: see **The Brothers** [CONTRA COSTA].

Brown: see **Johnny Brown Springs** [SONOMA].

Brown Island: see **Turk Island** [ALAMEDA].

Browns Gulch [SONOMA]: *canyon,* drained by a stream that flows less than 1 mile to Russian River 3.5 miles east-northeast of Jenner (lat. 38°27'55" N, long. 123°03'05" W). Named on Duncans Mills (1979) 7.5' quadrangle.

Browns Hill [NAPA]: *peak,* 3.5 miles north-northeast of Calistoga (lat. 38°37'20" N, long. 122°32'15" W; near SW cor. sec. 16, T 9 N, R 6 W). Altitude 2768 feet. Named on Calistoga (1958) 7.5' quadrangle.

Browns Island [CONTRA COSTA]: *island,* 1.5 miles long, 3.5 miles west-northwest of Antioch (lat. 38°02'20" N, long. 121°51'50" W). Named on Antioch North (1978) and Honker Bay (1953) 7.5' quadrangles, which show the feature as marsh and water. Called Gwin I. on Ringgold's (1850b) map.

Browns Valley [NAPA]: *valley,* 3 miles west-northwest of downtown Napa (lat. 38°18'30" N, long. 122°20' W). Named on Napa (1951) 7.5' quadrangle.

Browns Valley Creek [NAPA]: *stream,* flows 4 miles to join Redwood Creek and form Napa Creek 1.5 miles west-northwest of downtown Napa (lat. 38°18'15" N, long. 122°18'45" W); the stream goes through Browns Valley. Named on Sonoma (1951) 7.5' quadrangle. On Napa (1902) 30' quadrangle, the stream is called South Branch [Napa Creek].

Brusha Peak: see **Brushy Peak** [ALAMEDA].

Brush Creek [SONOMA]: *stream,* flows 2.25 miles to Yorty Creek 5 miles southwest of Cloverdale (lat. 38°45'40" N, long. 123°05'10" W; sec. 33, T 11 N, R 11 W). Named on Cloverdale (1960) 7.5' quadrangle.

Brush Mountain [SANTA CLARA]: *peak,* 1 mile south of Isabel Valley (lat. 37°17'55" N, long. 121°31'55" W). Altitude 2920 feet. Named on Isabel Valley (1955) 7.5' quadrangle.

Brushy Canyon [NAPA]: *canyon,* drained by a stream that flows 2.5 miles to Gosling Canyon nearly 6 miles south-southeast of Berryessa Peak (lat. 38°35'05" N, long. 122°09'30" W). Named on Lake Berryessa (1959) 7.5' quadrangle.

Brushy Canyon [SANTA CLARA]: *canyon,* drained by a stream that flows 1.25 miles to Carlin Canyon 6 miles west-northwest of Mount Sizer (lat. 37°13'55" N, long. 121°37'20" W). Named on Mount Sizer (1955) 7.5' quadrangle.

Brushy Creek [ALAMEDA-CONTRA COSTA]: *stream,* heads just inside Alameda County and flows 8 miles to lowlands 7.5 miles south-southeast of Brentwood in Contra Costa County (lat. 37°50'20" N, long. 121°37'30" W; near S line sec. 15, T 1 S, R 3 E); the stream heads near Brushy Peak. Named on Byron Hot Springs (1953) and Clifton Court Forebay (1978) 7.5' quadrangles.

Brushy Peak [ALAMEDA]: *peak,* 7 miles north-northeast of Livermore (lat. 37°46'05" N, long. 121°42'05" W). Altitude 1702 feet. Named on Byron Hot Springs (1953) 7.5' quadrangle. Called Las Cuevas on California Mining Bureau's (1917b) map. Whitney (p. 33) referred to Bushy Knob or Las Cuevas. *Las Cuevas* means "the caves" in Spanish; outlaw Joaquin Murieta supposedly hid in caves at the base of the peak (Mosier and Mosier, p. 18). Hoover, Rensch, and Rensch (p. 1) described "Brushy (Brusha) Peak."

Brushy Ridge [SONOMA]: *ridge,* west-northwest-trending, 3 miles long, 6 miles north-northeast of the village of Stewarts Point (lat. 38°44'10" N, long. 123°22'30" W). Named on Annapolis (1977) and Stewarts Point (1978) 7.5' quadrangles.

Bryant: see **Orinda** [CONTRA COSTA].

Buchli [NAPA]: *locality,* 5 miles west-northwest of Napa Junction along Southern Pacific Railroad (lat. 38°12'55" N, long. 122°19'50" W). Named on Cuttings Wharf (1949) 7.5' quadrangle.

Buckeye Camp [CONTRA COSTA]: *locality,* 2 miles south-southwest of

Mount Diablo (lat. 37°51'20" N, long. 121°55'50" W; near SW cor. sec. 12, T 1 S, R 1 W). Named on Diablo (1953) 7.5' quadrangle.

Buckeye Creek [SONOMA]:

(1) *stream,* heads in Mendocino County and flows 2.5 miles to Galloway Creek 9.5 miles west of Cloverdale (lat. 38°47'30" N, long. 123°11'15" W; sec. 22, T 11 N, R 12 W). Named on Hopland (1960) 15' quadrangle.

(2) *stream,* flows 18 miles to South Fork Gualala River 7 miles north-northwest of the village of Stewarts Point (lat. 38°44'25" N, long. 123°27'25" W). Named on Ornbaun Valley (1960) 15' quadrangle, and on Annapolis (1977) and Stewarts Point (1978) 7.5' quadrangles. North Fork enters from the north 3 miles north-northeast of Annapolis; it is 5.5 miles long and is named on Ornbaun Valley (1960) 15' quadrangle.

Buckeye Creek: see **Wheatfield Fork**, under **Gualala River** [SONOMA].

Buckeye Spring [SONOMA]: *spring,* 9 miles north-northeast of Healdsburg (lat. 38°44'30" N, long. 122°49'40" W; sec. 2, T 10 N, R 9 W). Named on Jimtown (1955) 7.5' quadrangle.

Buckhorn Creek [ALAMEDA-CONTRA COSTA]: *stream,* heads in Contra Costa County and flows 3 miles to Kaiser Creek 10 miles east of downtown Oakland in Alameda County (lat. 37°47'20" N, long. 122°05'35" W; sec. 4, T 2 S, R 2 W). Named on Las Trampas Ridge (1959) 7.5' quadrangle. Called Kaiser Creek on Concord (1897) 15' quadrangle. The name "Buckhorn Creek" is from August Buchhorn and Frederick Buchhorn, who settled at the place in the 1890's (Mosier and Mosier, p. 18).

Buckhorn Ridge [SONOMA]: *ridge,* south-trending, 1 mile long, 3.5 miles south-southwest of Big Mountain (lat. 38°39'50" N, long. 123°10'35" W). Named on Tombs Creek (1978) 7.5' quadrangle.

Buck Knoll [SONOMA]: *peak,* 6 miles north-northeast of Cazadero (lat. 38°36'10" N, long. 123°01'50" W; sec. 25, T 9 N, R 11 W). Named on Cazadero (1978) 7.5' quadrangle.

Buck Knoll Ridge [SONOMA]: *ridge,* east- to southeast-trending, 1.5 miles long, 6 miles northeast of Cazadero (lat. 38°36'15" N, long. 123°01'10" W); Buck Knoll is at the west end of the ridge. Named on Cazadero (1978) 7.5' quadrangle.

Buckle Point [CONTRA COSTA]: *ridge,* west-southwest-trending, 0.5 mile long, 2.5 miles west of Mount Diablo (lat. 37°52'50" N, long. 121°57'50" W). Named on Clayton (1953) 7.5' quadrangle.

Buckler: see **Point Buckler** [SOLANO].

Buck Mountain [NAPA]: *peak,* 3.5 miles south of Knoxville (lat. 38°46'25" N, long. 122°19'45" W; sec. 29, T 11 N, R 4 W). Named on Knoxville (1958) 7.5' quadrangle.

Buck Mountain [SONOMA]:

(1) *peak,* 10 miles west of Cloverdale (lat. 38°48'20" N, long. 123° 11'40" W; sec. 16, T 11 N, R 12 W). Altitude 1575 feet. Named on Hopland (1960) 15' quadrangle.

(2) *peak,* 2.5 miles northwest of Big Mountain (lat. 38°44'20" N, long. 123°10'45" W; near SW cor. sec. 3, T 10 N, R 12 W). Named on Tombs Creek (1978) 7.5' quadrangle.

Bucks Canyon: see **Mix Canyon** [SOLANO].

Buck Spring [SONOMA]: *spring,* 7 miles southeast of Annapolis (lat. 38°38'50" N, long. 123°16'45" W; near NW cor. sec. 11, T 9 N, R 13 W). Named on Annapolis (1977) 7.5' quadrangle.

Bucktown [SOLANO]: *locality,* 4.5 miles east of Mount Vaca in Vaca Valley (lat. 38°23'25" N, long. 122°01'20" W). Named on Mount Vaca (1951) 7.5' quadrangle.

Buena Vista [SONOMA]: *settlement,* about 1.25 miles east of Sonoma (lat. 38°17'20" N, long. 122°26' W). Named on Sonoma (1951) 7.5' quadrangle. Called Buenavista on Sonoma (1942) 15' quadrangle.

Buenos Ayres Creek: see **Corral Hollow Creek** [ALAMEDA].

Bull Barn Gulch [SONOMA]: *canyon,* drained by a stream that flows less than 1 mile to Austin Creek 4 miles west of Guerneville (lat. 38°29'30" N, long. 123°03'55" W; sec. 34, T 8 N, R 11 W). Named on Duncans Mills (1979) 7.5' quadrangle.

Bull Canyon [NAPA]: *canyon,* drained by a stream that flows 2 miles to Lake Curry 2.5 miles south-southwest of Mount Vaca (lat. 38°21'55" N, long. 122°07' W). Named on Fairfield North (1951) 7.5' quadrangle.

Bull Canyon: see **East Bull Canyon** [NAPA]; **West Bull Canyon** [NAPA].

Bull Flat [SONOMA]: *area,* 4 miles south of Big Mountain (lat. 38° 39'10" N, long. 123°09'20" W; sec. 2, T 9 N, R 12 W). Named on Tombs Creek (1978) 7.5' quadrangle.

Bullhead Canyon [SANTA CLARA]: *canyon,* drained by a stream that flows 4 miles to North Fork Pacheco Creek 8 miles north-northwest of Pacheco Peak (lat. 37°07'05" N, long. 121°19'05" W; sec. 28, T 9 S, R 6 E). Named on Mustang Peak (1955) and Pacheco Peak (1955) 7.5' quadrangles.

Bull Head Point: see **Bulls Head Point** [CONTRA COSTA].

Bullhead Reservoir [SANTA CLARA]: *lake,* 175 feet long, nearly 3 miles east-southeast of Mustang Peak (lat. 37°09'50" N, long. 121° 19' W; sec. 9, T 9 S, R 6 E); the lake is at the head of a branch of Bullhead Canyon. Named on Mustang Peak (1955) 7.5' quadrangle.

Bull Hill [NAPA]: *peak,* nearly 3 miles south of Mount Vaca (lat. 38° 21'30" N, long. 122°07' W); the peak is south of the mouth of Bull Canyon. Altitude 702 feet. Named on Fairfield North (1951) 7.5' quadrangle.

Bull Island [NAPA]: *island,* 3300 feet long, 3.5 miles northwest of Napa Junction along Napa River (lat. 38°13'20" N, long. 122°18'15" W; on E line sec. 4, T 4 N, R 4 W). Named on Cuttings Wharf (1949) 7.5' quadrangle.

Bull Opening [SONOMA]: *area,* 3.5 miles west of Big Mountain (lat. 38°43' N, long. 123°12'25" W; sec. 17, T 10 N, R 12 W). Named on Tombs Creek (1978) 7.5' quadrangle.

Bull Point [MARIN]: *ridge,* south-southeast-trending, nearly 1 mile long, 6.5 miles northeast of the lighthouse at Point Reyes (lat. 38° 04' N, long. 122°56'45" W). Named on Drakes Bay (1953) 7.5' quadrangle.

Bull Run [SANTA CLARA]: *area,* nearly 2 miles west of New Almaden (lat. 37°10'50" N, long. 121°51' W). Named on Santa Teresa Hills (1953) 7.5' quadrangle. Workers at New Almaden mine held games and festivities at the place (Hoover, Rensch, and Rensch, p. 435).

Bull Run Creek [SAN MATEO]: *stream,* flows 1.25 miles to Sausal Creek nearly 7 miles south of downtown Redwood City in Portola Valley (1) (lat. 37°23'15" N, long. 122°14' W). Named on Palo Alto (1961) 7.5' quadrangle. A Southern sympathizer named the stream following the Union defeat at the Battle of Bull Run; the stream, or its canyon, has been called Sausal Creek, Willow Creek, and Kelley Gulch (Stanger, 1967, p. 27), as well as Uval Creek, Cañada de Sansevan—for William Nichols Sansevain, and Smith Gulch—for William R. Smith's steam-powered sawmill (Brown, p. 12).

Bulls Head Channel [CONTRA COSTA-SOLANO]: *channel,* 2.25 miles north-northeast of Martinez along Contra Costa-Solano County line near the junction of Suisun Bay and Carquinez Strait (lat. 38°02'30" N, long. 122°06'45" W); the feature is north of Bulls Head Point. Named on Vine Hill (1959) 7.5' quadrangle.

Bulls Head Channel: see **East Bulls Head Channel** [CONTRA COSTA-SOLANO].

Bulls Head Point [CONTRA COSTA]: *promontory,* nearly 2 miles north-northeast of Martinez on the south side of Carquinez Strait (lat. 38°02'10" N, long. 122°06'55" W). Named on Vine Hill (1959) 7.5' quadrangle. Called Pt. Bolitas on Ringgold's (1850b) map. United States Board on Geographic Names (1933, p. 173) rejected the names "Bolitas Point" and "Bull Head Point" for the feature.

Bull Tail Valley [MARIN]: *valley,* 5.5 miles southwest of downtown Novato (lat. 38°03'45" N, long. 122°39' W). Named on San Geronimo (1954) 7.5' quadrangle.

Bull Valley: see **Big Bull Valley** [CONTRA COSTA]; **Little Bull Valley** [CONTRA COSTA].

Bummer Peak [SONOMA]: *peak,* less than 1 mile north of Skaggs Springs (lat. 38°42'10" N, long. 123°01'30" W; sec. 24, R 10 N, R 11 W). Altitude 1150 feet. Named on Warm Springs Dam (1978) 7.5' quadrangle.

Bunker [SOLANO]: *locality,* 8 miles east of Elmira along Sacramento Northern Railroad (lat. 38°21'05" N, long. 121°45'25" W; sec. 21, T 6 N, R 2 E). Named on Dozier (1952) 7.5' quadrangle.

Burbank [SANTA CLARA]: *district,* 2 miles west-southwest of downtown San Jose. Named on San Jose West (1961) 7.5' quadrangle. The name honors Luther Burbank—the district originally was called Rose Lawn (Rambo, 1973, p. 39).

Burdell [MARIN]: *locality,* 3.5 miles north of downtown Novato along Northwestern Pacific Railroad (lat. 38°09'25" N, long. 122° 33'50" W); the place is 1.5 miles east-northeast of Burdell Mountain. Named on Petaluma River (1954) 7.5' quadrangle. The name recalls Dr. Burdell, owner of Olompali grant (Teather, p. 13).

Burdell Island [MARIN]: *island,* 3.5 miles north-northeast of downtown Novato in marsh lands (lat. 38°09'20" N, long. 122°33'10" W); the feature is 0.5 mile east of Burdell. Named on Petaluma River (1954) 7.5' quadrangle. James Burdell and his friends built Mira Monte Club on the island in 1895 (Mason, 1976b, p. 117-118).

Burdell Mountain [MARIN]: *ridge,* south-southeast-trending, 1.5 miles long, 3 miles north-northwest of downtown Novato (lat. 38° 08'45" N, long. 122°35'25" W). Named on Petaluma River (1954) 7.5' quadrangle. The peak is on Olompali grant, owned by Dr. Galen Burdell; the feature originally was called Mount Olompali (Teather, p. 13).

Buri Buri [SAN MATEO]: *land grant,* mainly between South San Francisco and Burlingame. Named on Montara Mountain (1956), San Francisco South (1956), and San Mateo (1956) 7.5' quadrangles. Jose Sanchez received the land in 1827 and 1835; Jose de la Cruz Sanchez and others claimed 14,639 acres patented in 1872 (Cowan, p. 21). The name is of Indian origin (Davis, W.H., p. 171).

Buri Buri Ridge [SAN MATEO]: *ridge,* southeast-trending, 5 miles long, center 3 miles south of downtown Millbrae (lat. 37°33'30" N, long. 122°22'20" W); the ridge is on Buri Buri grant. Named on Montara Mountain (1956) and San Mateo (1956) 7.5' quadrangles. On San Mateo (1915) 15' quadrangle, the name has the form "Buriburi Ridge." The feature was called Lomas Muertas in Spanish times because of the lack of vegetation there—*lomas muertas* means "bald hills" in Spanish; later it was called Bald Ridge before trees were planted there (Brown, p. 4).

Burke: see **Fulton** [SONOMA].

Burlingame [SAN MATEO]: *city,* 2.5 miles west-northwest of downtown San Mateo (lat. 37°35' N, long. 122°21'50" W). Named on Montara Mountain (1956) and San Mateo (1956) 7.5' quadrangles. William C. Ralston named the place in 1868 for his friend Anson Burlingame, United States minister to China in the 1860's (Gudde, 1949, p. 45). The first attempt to develop a town failed, but in the 1890's some wealthy San Francisco men organized Burlingame Country Club, and a railroad station called Burlingame was built; the town began to grow only after the earthquake of 1906, when refugees relocated there (Stanger, 1963, p. 151). Postal authorities established Burlingame post office in 1894 (Frickstad, p. 167), and the city incorporated in 1908. A railroad station called Oak Grove was at present Burlingame from the middle 1860's until Burlingame station was started in 1894 (Brown, p. 62).

Burned Mountain [SONOMA]: *ridge,* generally west-trending, 2 miles long, 4.5 miles east-northeast of Geyser Peak (lat. 38°47'50" N, long. 122°46'15" W). Named on The Geysers (1959) 7.5' quadrangle.

Burnett: see **Coyote** [SANTA CLARA].

Burns Chalks [SAN MATEO]: *relief feature,* 1.5 miles southwest of La Honda (lat. 37°18' N, long. 122°17'30" W; near NW cor. sec. 27, T 7 S, R 4 W). Named on La Honda (1961) 7.5' quadrangle, which shows Burns ranch 1 mile south of the feature.

Burns Creek [SONOMA]: *stream,* flows 1.5 miles to Sausal Creek 8 miles north-northeast of Healdsburg (lat. 38°43' N, long. 122°47'30" W; sec. 18, T 10 N, R 8 W). Named on Jimtown (1955) 7.5' quadrangle.

Burnt Hills [SANTA CLARA]: *range,* 5.5 miles south of Eyler Mountain (lat. 37°24' N, long. 121°32'30" W). Named on Eylar Mountain (1955) and Isabel Valley (1955) 7.5' quadrangles.

Burnt Knoll Ridge [SONOMA]: *ridge,* north-trending, 1 mile long, 3.25 miles southeast of Annapolis (lat. 38°41' N, long. 123°20' W). Named on Annapolis (1977) 7.5' quadrangle.

Burnt Ridge [SONOMA]:

(1) *ridge,* east-northeast-trending, 1 mile long, 10 miles north-northeast of Stewarts Point (2) (lat. 38°47'15" N, long. 123°20'15" W). Named on Ornbaun Valley (1960) 15' quadrangle.

(2) *ridge,* southeast- to south-trending, 3 miles long, 5 miles west-southwest of Big Mountain (lat. 38°41'20" N, long. 123°13'55" W). Named on Tombs Creek (1978) 7.5' quadrangle.

Burnt Ridge Creek [SONOMA]: *stream,* flows 1.25 miles to Rockpile Creek 11 miles north-northeast of the village of Stewarts Point at Sonoma-Mendocino County line (lat. 38°48'20" N, long. 123°20'45" W; at N line sec. 18, T 11 N, R 13 W); the stream is north of Burnt Ridge (1). Named on Ornbaun Valley (1960) 15' quadrangle.

Burra Burra Peak [SANTA CLARA]: *peak,* 8 miles north-northwest of Pacheco Peak (lat. 37°06'35" N, long. 121°21'50" W; sec. 31, T 9 S, R 6 E). Altitude 2281 feet. Named on Pacheco Peak (1955) 7.5' quadrangle.

Burrell: see **Wrights** [SANTA CLARA].

Burrell Canyon [NAPA]: *canyon,* drained by a stream that flows 1 mile to Steel Canyon 8 miles northwest of Mount Vaca (lat. 38°29'15" N, long. 122°11'30" W; near N line sec. 4, T 7 N, R 3 W). Named on Capell Valley (1951) 7.5' quadrangle.

Burton [CONTRA COSTA]: *locality,* 3.5 miles southwest of present Walnut Creek civic center along Oakland Antioch and Eastern Railroad (lat. 37°51'55" N, long. 122°06' W); the place is in present Burton Valley. Named on Concord (1915) 15' quadrangle.

Burton Creek [NAPA]: *stream,* flows 7.25 miles to Maxwell Creek 9 miles northeast of Saint Helena (lat. 38°36'15" N, long. 122°21'55" W). Named on Chiles Valley (1958) and Saint Helena (1960) 7.5' quadrangles.

Burton Valley [CONTRA COSTA]: *valley,* 6.25 miles west-northwest of Danville at the confluence of Grizzly Creek and Las Trampas Creek (lat. 37°52'15" N, long. 122°05'35" W). Named on Las Trampas Ridge (1959) 7.5' quadrangle.

Bush Hill [CONTRA COSTA]: *ridge,* north- to west-trending, 1 mile long, 4.5 miles west-northwest of Martinez (lat. 38°02'45" N, long. 122°12'20" W). Named on Benicia (1959) 7.5' quadrangle.

Bush Slough [SONOMA]: *water feature,* 2 miles north-northeast of Sears Point (lat. 38°10'45" N, long. 122°25'45" W). Named on Sears Point (1951) 7.5' quadrangle.

Bushy Knob: see **Brushy Peak** [ALAMEDA].

Butano [SAN MATEO]: *land grant,* along and near Butano Creek. Named on Franklin Point (1955), Pigeon Point (1955), and San Gregorio (1961) 7.5' quadrangles. Ramona Sanchez received 1 league in 1844; M. Rodriguez claimed 4439 acres patented in 1866 (Cowan, p. 21).

Butano Creek [SAN MATEO]: *stream,* flows 15 miles to Pescadero Creek 4.5 miles south-southwest of the village of San Gregorio (lat. 37°15'50" N, long. 122°24'20" W). Named on Big Basin (1955), Franklin Point (1955), Pigeon Point (1955), and San Gregorio (1961) 7.5' quadrangles. South Fork joins the main stream 7 miles north-northeast of Franklin Point. It is 4 miles long and is named on Big Basin (1955) and Franklin Point (1955) 7.5' quadrangles.

Butano Creek: see **Little Butano Creek** [SAN MATEO].

Butano Falls [SAN MATEO]: *waterfall,* nearly 7 miles north-northeast of Franklin Point (lat. 37°14'30" N, long. 122°18'55" W; sec. 17, T 8 S, R 4 W); the feature is along Butano Creek. Named on Franklin Point (1955) 7.5' quadrangle.

Butano Flat: see **Little Butano Flat**, under **Little Butano Creek** [SAN MATEO].

Butano Park [SAN MATEO]: *settlement,* 6 miles north-northeast of Franklin Point (lat. 37°14' N, long. 122°19'25" W; sec. 17, T 8 S, R 4 W); the place is along Butano Creek. Named on Franklin Point (1955) 7.5' quadrangle.

Butano Ridge [SAN MATEO]: *ridge,* east- to southeast-trending, 5 miles long, center 4.5 miles south of La Honda (lat. 37°15' N, long. 122°15'50" W). Named on Big Basin (1955), Franklin Point (1955), and La Honda (1961) 7.5' quadrangles.

Butcherknife: see **The Butcherknife** [SONOMA].

Butler Canyon [SONOMA]: *canyon,* drained by a stream that flows 1.5 miles to Valley of the Moon 5 miles north-northwest of Sonoma (lat. 38°21'25" N, long. 122°30' W). Named on Sonoma (1951) 7.5' quadrangle.

Butts Canyon [NAPA]: *canyon,* 4.5 miles long, on Napa-Lake County line along Butts Creek above a point 5 miles northeast of Aetna Springs (lat. 38°42'20" N, long. 122°25'25" W; near SW cor. sec. 16, T 10 N, R 5 W). Named on Aetna Springs (1958) 7.5' quadrangle.

Butts Creek [NAPA]: *stream,* heads in Lake County and flows 8 miles to Putah Creek 6.5 miles northeast of Aetna Springs (lat. 38°42'15" N, long. 122°22'50" W; near N line sec. 23, T 10 N, R 5 W). Named on Aetna Springs (1958) 7.5' quadrangle.

Buzzard Creek [SONOMA]: *stream,* flows 1.25 miles to Spanish Creek 3 miles southwest of Big Mountain (lat. 38°41'05" N, long. 123°11'25" W; sec. 28, T 10 N, R 12 W). Named on Tombs Creek (1978) 7.5' quadrangle.

Buzzard Peak [SONOMA]: *peak,* 4.5 miles northwest of Kenwood (lat. 38°28' N, long. 122°35'55" W; sec. 11, T 7 N, R 7 W). Altitude 1542 feet. Named on Kenwood (1954) 7.5' quadrangle.

Buzzard Rock [NAPA]: *peak,* 8 miles northwest of Mount Vaca (lat. 38°28'45" N, long. 122°12'30" W; sec. 5, T 7 N, R 3 W). Altitude 1701 feet. Named on Capell Valley (1951) 7.5' quadrangle.

Buzzard Rock [SONOMA]: *relief feature,* 1.5 miles west-northwest of Skaggs Springs (lat. 38°42' N, long. 123°03'15" W; at E line sec. 22, T 10 N, R 11 W). Named on Warm Springs Dam (1978) 7.5' quadrangle.

Buzzard Spring [SONOMA]: *spring,* 6 miles north-northeast of Guerneville (lat. 38°34'40" N, long. 122°56'15" W). Named on Guerneville (1955) 7.5' quadrangle.

Byrnes' Lake: see **Upper Crystal Springs Reservoir** [SAN MATEO].

Byron [CONTRA COSTA]: *town,* 5.5 miles southeast of Brentwood (lat. 37°52'05" N, long. 121°38'20" W; near SW cor. sec. 3, T 1 S, R 3 E). Named on Byron Hot Springs (1953) 7.5' quadrangle. Postal authorities established Byron post office in 1878; the name is for a railroad employee (Salley, p. 31). They established Point of Timber post office 2 miles north of Byron in 1869, discontinued it in 1871, reestablished it in 1872, and discontinued it in 1882 (Salley, p. 175). The names "Point of Timber" and "Eden Plain" were applied to part of the lowlands in the eastern section of Contra Costa County (Smith and Elliott, p. 28).

Byron Hot Springs [CONTRA COSTA]: *locality,* 7 miles south-southeast of Brentwood (lat. 37°50'50" N, long. 121°37'55" W; sec. 15, T 1 S, R 3 E); the place is 1.5 miles south-southeast of Bryon. Named on Byron Hot Springs (1953) 7.5' quadrangle. Postal authorities established Byron Hot Springs post office in 1889 and discontinued it in 1930 (Frickstad, p. 21). More that 50 springs were the basis of a resort at the site (Anderson, Winslow, p. 105). The place was an interrogation center for prisoners of war during World War II (Hillman and Covello, p. 70).

Byron Hot Springs Station [CONTRA COSTA]: *locality,* 7.5 miles southeast of Brentwood along Southern Pacific Railroad (lat. 37° 50'40" N, long. 121°37' W; sec. 14, T 1 S, R 3 E); the place is 1 mile east-southeast of Byron Hot Springs. Named on Byron (1916) 15' quadrangle.

Byron Tract [CONTRA COSTA]: *area,* 6 miles east-southeast of Brentwood (lat. 37°54' N, long. 121°35'45" W); the place is 3 miles northeast of Byron. Named on Clifton Court Forebay (1978) and Woodward Island (1978) 7.5' quadrangles.

— C —

Caballo Point: see **Cavallo Point** [MARIN].

Cabeza de Santa Rosa [SONOMA]: *land grant,* around Santa Rosa. Named on Santa Rosa (1954) 7.5' quadrangle. The name is from Santa Rosa Creek (Hanna, P.T., p. 292). Maria Ignacia Lopez received the land in 1841; Julio Carrillo claimed 4500 acres patented in 1866; F. Carrillo de Castro claimed 336 acres patented in 1881; James Eldridge claimed 1668 acres patented in 1880; John Hendley claimed 640 acres patented in 1879; Juana de J. Mallagh claimed 256 acres patented in 1879; J.R. Meyer and others claimed 1485 acres patented in 1879 (Cowan, p. 95).

Cabo de Fortunas: see **Pigeon Point** [SAN MATEO].

Cabo de Pinos: see **Point Reyes** [MARIN] (1).

Cache Slough [SOLANO]: *water feature,* joins Sacramento River 2 miles northeast of Rio Vista (lat. 38°10'45" N, long. 121°39'55" W). Named on Dozier (1952), Liberty Island (1978), and Rio Vista (1978) 7.5' quadrangles.

Cache Slough: see **Maine Prairie Slough** [SOLANO].

Cadwell [SONOMA]: *locality,* 5 miles northeast of Bloomfield along Petaluma and Santa Rosa Railroad (lat. 38°21'25" N, long. 122°46'35" W; near NW cor. sec. 20, T 6 N, R 8 W). Named on Two Rock (1954) 7.5' quadrangle.

Cahill Ridge [SAN MATEO]: *ridge,* northwest-trending, 5 miles long, 5.5 miles east-southeast of Montara Knob (lat. 37°31'45" N, long. 122°23'30" W). Named on Montara Mountain (1956), San Mateo (1956), and Woodside (1961) 7.5' quadrangles. Called Cahil Ridge on San Mateo (1915) 15' quadrangle. On Santa Cruz (1902) 30' quadrangle, the name applies along the ridge southeast as far as Kings Mountain. The feature was called Cuchilla de los Ajos by the 1840's—*ajos* means "garlic" in Spanish, and it was called Bald Ridge in the 1850's and 1860's; the name "Cahill" recalls Joseph Cahill, who started a ranch at the ridge in the late 1850's (Brown, p. 15).

Calabazas Creek [SANTA CLARA]: *stream,* flows 12.5 miles to Guadalupe Slough 1 mile southwest of Alviso (lat. 37°25' N, long. 121°59'10" W). Named on Cupertino (1961), Milpitas (1961), and San Jose West (1961) 7.5' quadrangles. San Jose (1899) 15' quadrangle, made before the lower course of the stream was altered, shows the creek continuing to Guadalupe Slough about 1 mile west-southwest of Alviso (lat. 37°25'10" N, long. 121°59'20" W), and it also shows that the watercourse is interrupted between the upper and lower parts. Called Arroyo De Los Calabazas on Thompson and West's (1876) map, which shows the stream entering Campbell Creek. The name "Calabazas" was given because Indians who lived along the creek raised and sold vegetables to early settlers—*calabazas* means "squash" or "pumpkin" in Spanish (Rambo, 1973, p. 39).

Calabazas Creek [SONOMA]: *stream,* flows 5.25 miles to Sonoma Creek in Glen Ellen (lat. 38°21'45" N, long. 122°31'25" W). Named on Glen Ellen (1954), Kenwood (1954), and Rutherford (1951) 7.5' quadrangles. Called Arroyo de los Guilicos on a diseño of Agua Caliente grant (Becker, 1964). United States Board on Geographic Names (1933, p. 183) rejected the forms "Calabezas" and "Calebezas" for the name.

Calaveras Creek [ALAMEDA-SANTA CLARA]: *stream,* flows 5.25 miles in Santa Clara County to Calaveras Reservoir, and from Calaveras Reservoir it flows 1 mile in Alameda County to Alameda Creek 7 miles south-southeast of Sunol (lat. 37°30'15" N, long. 121°49'15" W; sec. 13, T 5 S, R 1 E). Named on Calaveras Reservoir (1961), La Costa Valley (1960), and Mount Day (1955) 7.5' quadrangles. The name probably came after Spaniards discovered Indian skeletons near the stream—*calaveras* means "skulls" in Spanish (Rambo, 1973, p. 40).

Calaveras Point [ALAMEDA]: *promontory,* 5 miles south of downtown Newark on the north side of the mouth of Coyote Creek (lat. 37°28' N, long. 122°03' W). Named on Mountain View (1961) 7.5' quadrangle.

Calaveras Reservoir [ALAMEDA-SANTA CLARA]: *lake,* on Alameda-Santa Clara County line, mainly in Santa Clara County; 3.25 miles long, behind a dam on Calaveras Creek 8 miles south-southeast of Sunol (lat. 37°29'35" N, long. 121°49'10" W; sec. 13, T 5 S, R 1 E); water of the lake floods most of Calaveras Valley. Named on Calaveras Reservoir (1961) 7.5' quadrangle.

Calaveras Valley [ALAMEDA-SANTA CLARA]: *valley,* on Alameda-Santa Clara County line, mainly in Santa Clara County; along Calaveras Creek above a point 8 miles south-southeast of Sunol (lat. 37°29'35" N, long. 121°49'10" W). Named on Calaveras Reservoir (1961) 7.5' quadrangle. San Jose (1899) 15' quadrangle shows the valley before water of Calaveras Reservoir inundated it.

Caldwell Springs: see **Azule Springs** [SANTA CLARA].

Calebezas Creek: see **Calabazas Creek** [SONOMA].

Calera: see **Rockaway Beach** [SAN MATEO].

Calera Creek [SANTA CLARA]: *stream,* flows 2.25 miles to lowlands 2.25 miles north-northeast of Milpitas (lat. 37°27'45" N, long. 121°53'40" W), and continues in an artificial watercourse. Named on Calaveras Reservoir (1961) and Milpitas (1961) 7.5' quadrangles. The name records a limekiln built in the neighborhood as early as 1807—*calera* means "limekiln" in Spanish (Gudde, 1949, p. 50).

Calera Hill: see **Lime Hill**, under **Calera Valley** [SAN MATEO].

Calera Valley [SAN MATEO]: *valley,* 4 miles north of Montara Knob near the coast (lat. 37°36'50" N, long. 122°29'10" W). Named on Montara Mountain (1956) 7.5' quadrangle. The valley was called Cañada de la Calera in Spanish times because of a nearby limekiln—*calera* means "limekiln" in Spanish (Gudde, 1949, p. 50). Brown (p. 47) used the name "Lime Hill" for the ridge north of the mouth of the valley, and Eckel (p. 354) used the name "Calera Hill" for the same feature—limestone was mined at the place.

Calero Creek: see **Arroyo Calero** [SANTA CLARA].

Calero Reservoir [SANTA CLARA]: *lake,* 2.25 miles long, behind a dam on Arroyo Calero 1.5 miles east-northeast of New Almaden (lat. 37°11' N, long. 121°47'30" W). Named on Santa Teresa Hills (1953) 7.5' quadrangle.

Calhoun Cut [SOLANO]: *water feature,* joins Lindsey Slough 9.5 miles southeast of Elmira (lat. 38°15'40" N, long. 121°46'30" W). Named on Dozier (1952) 7.5' quadrangle.

California City: see **Paradise Cove** [MARIN].

California Point: see **Paradise Cay** [MARIN].

Calistoga [NAPA]: *town,* 8 miles northwest of Saint Helena (lat. 38° 34'45" N, long. 122°34'40" W). Named on Calistoga (1958) 7.5' quadrangle. Postal authorities established Calistoga post office in 1865 (Frickstad, p. 111), and the town incorporated in 1886. Samuel Brannan purchased land at the site in 1859 and built a resort based on hot springs there (Hoover, Rensch, and Rensch, p. 245). The place first was called Agua Caliente (Gudde, 1949, p. 51). It also was known as Little Geysers and as Hot Sulphur Springs before Brannan gave the name "Calistoga" to his resort to suggest a comparison with the famous spa at Saratoga, New York (Hanna, P.T., p. 51). The springs have been called Calistoga Hot Sulphur Springs (Goodyear, 1890a, p. 349), Calistoga Springs (Crawford, 1894, p. 341), and Calistoga Hot Springs (Waring, p. 108). A small bath establishment called Lathrop Hot Sulphur and Mud Spring was situated 1 mile south of Calistoga (Bradley, p. 278). Calistoga (1959) 15' quadrangle shows Silverado mine located 5.25 miles north-northwest of Calistoga (lat. 38°39'05" N, long. 122°36'15" W; sec. 2, T 9 N, R 7 W). Brannan's nephew, Alexander Badlam, built a stamp mill to process ore mined 7 miles north of Calistoga; the community that grew around the mill was called Silverado City, but the place was abandoned by 1877 (Archuleta, p. 61, 63).

Calistoga Hot Springs: see **Calistoga** [NAPA].

Calistoga Hot Sulphur Springs: see **Calistoga** [NAPA].

Calistoga Springs: see **Calistoga** [NAPA].

Callahan Gulch [ALAMEDA]: *canyon,* drained by a stream that flows 3.25 miles to Arroyo Mocho 4.25 miles southeast of Cedar Mountain (lat. 37°31'15" N, long. 121°32'45" W; near SW cor. sec. 4, T 5 S, R 4 E). Named on Cedar Mountain (1956) 7.5' quadrangle. The name commemorates Patrick Callaghan and John Callaghan, brothers who raised sheep in the neighborhood after 1868 (Mosier and Mosier, p. 19).

Calletano Creek: see **Cayetano Creek** [ALAMEDA-CONTRA COSTA].

Cambrian Park: see **Cambrian Village** [SANTA CLARA].

Cambrian Village [SANTA CLARA]: *district,* 3.5 miles north-northeast of downtown Los Gatos (lat. 37°15'25" N, long. 121°55'30" W). Named on San Jose West (1961) 7.5' quadrangle. Postal authorities established Cambrian Park post office in the district in 1954 (Salley, p. 33).

Camille: see **Lake Camille** [NAPA].

Campbell [SANTA CLARA]: *city,* 5 miles southwest of downtown San Jose (lat. 37°17'15" N, long. 121°57' W). Named on San Jose West (1961) 7.5' quadrangle. Benjamin Campbell subdivided his land and founded the community in 1885 (Butler, p. 124). Postal authorities established Campbell post office in 1885 (Frickstad, p. 173), and the city incorporated in 1952. Peninsular Railway Company's (1912) map shows a station called Hamilton located about one-quarter of the way from Campbell to San Jose, a station called Fairfield located along the railway about halfway, and a station called Lincoln located about three-quarters of the way. The same map shows a station called Union Ave. situated southeast of Campbell along a Southern Pacific Railroad branch line to New Almaden, and a station called LeFranc located farther southeast along the same branch line. MacGregor (p. 124) mentioned a place called Lovelady's that was located along the railroad near present Campbell in 1877, and noted (p. 135) that this station later was called Gravel Pit—a spur line ran from the spot to gravel deposits along Los Gatos Creek.

Campbell Canyon: see **Dry Creek** [NAPA].

Campbell Cove [SONOMA]: *embayment,* 2 miles south-southwest of the village of Bodega Bay (lat. 38°18'20" N, long. 123°03'20" W); the feature is on the east side of Bodega Head, which is known locally as Campbells Point (Gudde, 1949, p. 53). Named on Bodega Head (1972) 7.5' quadrangle.

Campbell Creek: see **Saratoga Creek** [SANTA CLARA].

Campbell Creek Cañon: see **Saratoga Creek** [SANTA CLARA].

Campbell Flat [NAPA]: *area,* 2.5 miles south-southwest of Rutherford (lat. 38°25'30" N, long. 122°26'05" W; sec. 29, T 7 N, R 5 W). Named on Rutherford (1951) 7.5' quadrangle.

Campbell Point [MARIN]: *promontory,* on the north shore of Angel Island (lat. 37°52'20" N, long. 122°25'45" W). Named on San Francisco North (1956) 7.5' quadrangle. United States Board on Geographic Names (1980, p. 3) approved the name "Point Campbell" for the feature. The name commemorates A.H. Campbell, a civil engineer with Ringgold's expedition of 1849 (Teather, p. 2).

Campbells Creek: see **Saratoga Creek** [SANTA CLARA].

Campbell's Gap: see **Saratoga** [SANTA CLARA].

Campbells Point: see **Bodega Head** [SONOMA].

Campbell's Redwoods: see **Saratoga Creek** [SANTA CLARA].

Camp Bessie [SANTA CLARA]: *locality,* 2.5 miles southeast of Eylar Mountain along Arroyo Mocho (lat. 37°27'20" N, long. 121°30'55" W; sec. 34, T 5 S, R 4 E). Named on Eylar Mountain (1955) 7.5' quadrangle.

Camp C.C. Moore: see **Camp Royaneh** [SONOMA].

Camp Cooley [SANTA CLARA]: *locality,* 4 miles southwest of Cupertino near Stevens Creek (lat. 37°16'50" N, long. 122°04'25" W; sec. 34, T 7 S, R 2 W). Named on Cupertino (1961) 7.5' quadrangle.

Camp Eastwood [MARIN]: *locality,* 5.5 miles south-southwest of downtown San Rafael (lat. 37°54'20" N, long. 122°34'50" W). Named on San Rafael (1954) 7.5' quadrangle. Called Eastwood Camp on Mount Tamalpais (1950) 15' quadrangle. Fairley (1987, p. 100) referred to Camp Alice Eastwood, located at the site of Mt. Tamalpais Camp, a former CCC facility.

Camp Five [SONOMA]: *locality,* 6.25 miles northeast of Sears Point (lat. 38°12'50" N, long. 122°22'10" W). Named on Cuttings Wharf (1949) 7.5' quadrangle.

Camp Four [SONOMA]: *locality,* 5 miles north-northeast of Sears Point (lat. 38°12'45" N, long. 122°24'10" W). Named on Sears Point (1951) 7.5' quadrangle.

Camp Fremont: see **Menlo Park** [SAN MATEO].

Camp Grizzly: see **Tanforan**, under **San Bruno** [SAN MATEO].

Camp Herms [CONTRA COSTA]: *locality,* 3 miles east-southeast of Richmond civic center (lat. 37°55'30" N, long. 122°17'20" W). Named on Richmond (1959) 7.5' quadrangle. United States Board on Geographic Names (1988a, p. 2) approved the name "William Rust Summit" for a peak located 0.25 mile northwest of Camp Herms (lat. 37°55'35" N, long. 122°17'23" W); the name is for a pioneer settler who was active in business and community affairs.

Camp Lilienthal [MARIN]: *locality,* 4.25 miles west of downtown San Rafael (lat. 37°58'20" N, long. 122°36'30" W). Named on San Rafael (1954) 7.5' quadrangle.

Camp Maacama [SONOMA]: *locality,* 6.5 miles east-northeast of Healdsburg (lat. 38°38'30" N, long. 122°45'05" W; sec. 9, T 9 N, R 8 W); the place is along Maacama Creek. Named on Jimtown (1955) 7.5' quadrangle.

Camp Meeker [SONOMA]: *settlement,* 1.5 miles north-northwest of Occidental (lat. 38°25'35" N, long. 122°57'30" W; in and near sec. 27, T 7 N, R 10 W). Named on Camp Meeker (1954) 7.5' quadrangle. Postal authorities established Camp Meeker post office in 1900; the name commemorates Melvin C. Meeker, an early lumberman (Salley, p. 35).

Campmeeting Ridge [SONOMA]: *ridge,* north-northwest-trending, 1.25 miles long, nearly 3 miles north of Fort Ross (lat. 38°33'15" N, long. 123°14'05" W). Named on Fort Ross (1978) 7.5' quadrangle.

Camp One [SONOMA]: *locality,* 3 miles north of Sears Point (lat. 38°11'40" N, long. 122°26' W). Named on Sears Point (1951) 7.5' quadrangle.

Camp Parks [ALAMEDA-CONTRA COSTA]: *military installation,* 2 miles east-northeast of Dublin on Alameda-Contra Costa County line, mainly in Alameda County (lat. 37°43' N, long. 121°54' W). Named on Dublin (1961) and Livermore (1961) 7.5' quadrangles. The camp operated from 1943 until 1945 as a naval training and distribution center, and again during the Korean War as an air force base; the name commemorates Rear Admiral Charles Wellman Parks (Mosier and Mosier, p. 19). A navy replacement center called Camp Shoemaker was situated east of Camp Parks in Livermore Valley (Mosier and Mosier, p. 19). Postal authorities established Shoemaker post office in Alameda County at the place in 1946 and discontinued it the same year (Salley, p. 203).

Camp Pistolesi: see **Camp Tomales** [MARIN].

Camp Pomponio [SAN MATEO]: *locality,* 3.5 miles south-southwest of Mindego Hill along Pescadero Creek (lat. 37°15'50" N, long. 122°14'50" W; sec. 1, T 8 S, R 4 W). Named on Mindego Hill (1961) 7.5' quadrangle.

Camp Reynolds: see **Fort McDowell** [MARIN-SAN FRANCISCO].

Camp Rose [SONOMA]: *settlement,* 2 miles east of Healdsburg along Russian River (lat. 38°36'55" N, long. 122°50' W). Named on Healdsburg (1955) 7.5' quadrangle.

Camp Rosenberg [SONOMA]: *locality,* 7 miles north of Guerneville along Mill Creek (1) (lat. 38°36'10" N, long. 122°58'15" W; sec. 28, T 9 N, R 10 W). Named on Guerneville (1955) 7.5' quadrangle.

Camp Royaneh [SONOMA]: *locality,* 1.25 miles east-southeast of Cazadero (lat. 38°31'10" N, long. 123°03'55" W; sec. 22, T 8 N, R 11 W). Named on Cazadero (1978) 7.5' quadrangle. Called Camp C.C. Moore on Cazadero (1943) 7.5' quadrangle.

Camp Saratoga [SANTA CLARA]: *locality,* 3.25 miles west of Saratoga (lat. 37°15'30" N, long. 122°05'30" W; near SW cor. sec. 4, T 8 S, R 2 W); the place is on upper reaches of Saratoga Creek. Named on Cupertino (1961) 7.5' quadrangle.

Camp Shoemaker: see **Camp Parks** [ALAMEDA-CONTRA COSTA].

Camp Six [SONOMA]: *locality,* 2.5 miles northeast of Sears Point (lat. 38°10'35" N, long. 122°24'50" W). Named on Sears Point (1951) 7.5' quadrangle.

Camp Stoneman [CONTRA COSTA]: *military installation,* 1.5 miles south-southeast of Pittsburg (lat. 38°00'30" N, long. 121°52'30" W). Named on Antioch North (1953), Clayton (1953), and Honker Bay (1953) 7.5' quadrangles. War Department officials named the place in 1942 to honor George Stoneman, governor of California from 1883 until 1887, who came to California in 1846 as a lieutenant in the Mormon Battalion (Hanna, P.T., p. 317).

Camp Sycamore [SANTA CLARA]: *locality,* nearly 3 miles west-northwest of Saratoga near Stevens Creek (lat. 37°16'55" N, long. 122°04'20" W; sec. 34, T 7 S, R 2 W). Named on Cupertino (1961) 7.5' quadrangle.

Camp Taylor [MARIN]: *locality,* 10.5 miles southwest of downtown Novato (lat. 38°01'10" N, long. 122°43'45" W). Named on San Geronimo (1954) 7.5' quadrangle. Petaluma (1914) 15' quadrangle shows the place along Northwestern Pacific Railroad. Postal authorities established Camp Taylor post office in 1894 and discontinued it in 1912 (Frickstad, p. 87).

Camp Thayer [SONOMA]: *locality,* 4 miles northeast of Jenner along Austin Creek (lat. 38°29'30" N, long. 122°03'45" W). Named on Duncans Mills (1943) 7.5' quadrangle. California Division of Highways' (1934) map shows a place called Fraser just southeast of Camp Thayer.

Camp Three [SONOMA]: *locality,* 3.5 miles north-northeast of Sears Point (lat. 38°12'05" N, long. 122°25'20" W). Named on Sears Point (1951) 7.5' quadrangle.

Camp Tomales [MARIN]: *locality,* 1.25 miles south-southwest of Tomales (lat. 38°13'50" N, long. 122°55' W). Named on Tomales (1954) 7.5' quadrangle. Called Camp Pistolesi on Point Reyes (1918) 15' quadrangle. The name "Pistolesi" is for Frank V. Pistolesi, who started a resort at the place in 1902 (Mason, 1976a, p. 149).

Camp Two [SONOMA]: *locality,* 5 miles north of Sears Point (lat. 38°13'20" N, long. 122°26'10" W). Named on Sears Point (1951) 7.5' quadrangle.

Cañada de Apolonio: see **Digges Canyon** [SAN MATEO].

Cañada de Guadalupe la Visitacion y Rodeo Viejo [SAN FRANCISCO-SAN MATEO]: *land grant,* at and near San Bruno Mountain, mainly in San Mateo County, but extends north into San Francisco west of Visitacion Valley. Named on San Francisco South (1956) 7.5' quadrangle. Jacob P. Leese received 2 leagues in 1841, and H.R. Payson claimed 5473 acres patented in 1865 (Cowan, p. 38).

Cañada de Guadalupe y Rodeo Viejo [SAN FRANCISCO-SAN MATEO]: *land grant,* at and near Visitacion Valley on San Francisco-San Mateo County line. Named on San Francisco South (1956) 7.5' quadrangle. Jacob P. Leese received the land in 1841, and William Pierce claimed 943 acres patented in 1865 (Cowan, p. 38).

Cañada de Herrera [MARIN]: *land grant,* around Fairfax. Named on Bolinas (1954), Novato (1954), and San Rafael (1954) 7.5' quadrangles. Domingo Sais received the land in 1839 and his heirs claimed 6648 acres patented in 1876 (Cowan, p. 39; Cowan gave the name "Providencia" as an alternate). According to Perez (p. 58), the grant has 6658.45 acres.

Cañada de Jonive [SONOMA]: *land grant,* mainly west of Sebastopol. Named on Camp Meeker (1954) and Sebastopol (1954) 7.5' quadrangles. James Black received 2 leagues in 1845, and Jasper O'Farrell claimed 10,787 acres patented in 1858 (Cowan, p. 42).

Cañada de la Brea: see **Las Animas** [SANTA CLARA].

Cañada de la Calera: see **Calera Valley** [SAN MATEO].

Cañada de la Dormida [SANTA CLARA]: *stream,* flows 5.5 miles to Cedar Creek 6 miles north-northwest of Pacheco Peak (lat. 37° 05' N, long. 121°20'40" W; near W line sec. 8, T 10 S, R 6 E). Named on Gilroy Hot Springs (1955) and Pacheco Peak (1955) 7.5' quadrangles.

Cañada del Aliso [ALAMEDA]: *stream,* flows 2 miles to lowlands 3 miles southeast of Fremont civic center (lat. 37°30'50" N, long. 121°56'10" W). Named on Niles (1961) 7.5' quadrangle. Pleasanton (1906) 15' quadrangle has the name "Canada del Aliso" for the canyon of the stream. Two large sycamore trees stood near the stream in the early days—*aliso* means "sycamore" in Spanish (Gudde, 1969, p. 7).

Cañada de la Puente: see **Digges Canyon** [SAN MATEO].

Cañada de las Auras: see **Feliz** [SAN MATEO].

Cañada del Cierbo [CONTRA COSTA]: *canyon,* 2.5 miles long, opens into lowlands along San Pablo Bay 7 miles west-northwest of Martinez near Tormey (lat. 38°03'05" N, long. 122°15' W). Named on Benicia (1959) 7.5' quadrangle.

Cañada del Corte de Madera [SAN MATEO-SANTA CLARA]: *land grant,* near Portola Valley (1) on San Mateo-Santa Clara County line, mainly in San Mateo County. Named on Mindego Hill (1961) and Palo Alto (1961) 7.5' quadrangles. Jose D. Peralta and Maximo Martinez received the land in 1833; Cipriano Thurn and H.W. Carpentier claimed 3566 acres patented in 1882 (Perez, p. 60).

Cañada del Diablo: see **Belmont Creek** [SAN MATEO].

Cañada de Leon: see **Nuff Creek** [SAN MATEO].

Cañada del Frijol: see **Arroyo de los Frijoles** [SAN MATEO].

Cañada del Hambre: see **Alhambra Valley** [CONTRA COSTA].

Cañada del Hambre y las Bolsas [CONTRA COSTA]: *land grant,* extends from near Crocket to the city of Walnut Creek. Named on Benicia (1959), Briones Valley (1959), and Walnut Creek (1959) 7.5' quadrangles. Teodora Soto received 2 leagues in 1842 and claimed 13,354 acres patented in 1866 (Cowan, p. 39; Cowan gave the grant the designation "Cañada del Hambre, (or) Las Bolsas del Hambre"). Perez (p. 60) used the name "Canada del Hambre y las Bolsas del Hambre" for the grant.

Cañada de los Capitancillos [SANTA CLARA]: *land grant,* 6 miles east of

Los Gatos. Named on Los Gatos (1953) 7.5' quadrangle. Justo Larios received the land in 1842; Guadalupe Mining Company claimed 1110 acres patented in 1871 (Cowan, p. 23-24; Cowan gave the grant the designation "Cañada de los Capitancillos, (or) New Almaden"). According to tradition, the name originated because Indians who lived at the place were small in stature, but brave—*cañada de los capitancillos* means "valley of the little captains" in Spanish (Johnson, p. 35).

Cañada de los Osos [SANTA CLARA]: *stream,* flows 8 miles to Coyote Creek 2.5 miles south of Gilroy Hot Springs (lat. 37°04'20" N, long. 121°28'35" W; near S line sec. 12, T 10 S, R 4 E). Named on Gilroy Hot Springs (1955) 7.5' quadrangle.

Cañada de los Poblanos [CONTRA COSTA]: *valley,* 7 miles east of Mount Diablo along Marsh Creek (lat. 37°53'15" N, long. 121°46'55" W). Named on Antioch South (1953) 7.5' quadrangle. Marsh Creek had the early name "Arroyo de los Poblanos" (Gudde, 1949, p. 206).

Cañada de los Vaqueros [ALAMEDA-CONTRA COSTA]: *land grant,* southwest of Byron on Alameda-Contra Costa County line, mainly in Contra Costa County. Named on Byron Hot Springs (1953) and Tassajara (1953) 7.5' quadrangles. Francisco Alviso received the land in 1844; Robert Livermore and Jose Noriega claimed 17,760 acres patented in 1889 (Cowan, p. 106).

Cañada de Novato: see **Novato Valley** [MARIN].

Cañada de Pala [SANTA CLARA]: *land grant,* in highlands east of San Jose. Named on Calaveras Reservoir (1961), Lick Observatory (1955), Mount Day (1955), and San Jose East (1961) 7.5' quadrangles. Jose Jesus Bernal received the land in 1839 and claimed 15,714 acres patented in 1863 (Cowan, p. 56). The name commemorates an Indian called Pala, who was mentioned in Spanish records as early as 1795 (Gudde, 1949, p. 249).

Cañada de Pogolimi [SONOMA]: *land grant,* at Bloomfield and Valley Ford. Named on Two Rock (1954) and Valley Ford (1954) 7.5' quadrangles. Antonio Caceres (or Cazares) received 2 leagues in 1844 and claimed 8781 acres patented in 1858 (Cowan, p. 62; Cowan listed the grant under the name "Cañada de Pogolomi," and gave the name "Cañada de Pogolimi" as an alternate).

Cañada de Polonio: see **Digges Canyon** [SAN MATEO].

Cañada de Raimundo: see **Cañada de Raymundo** [SAN MATEO]; **Upper Crystal Springs Reservoir** [SAN MATEO].

Cañada de Raymundo [SAN MATEO]: *land grant,* around Woodside. Named on Palo Alto (1961) and Woodside (1961) 7.5' quadrangles. John Coppinger received 2.5 leagues in 1840; Coppinger's widow and her new husband, Mr. Greer, claimed 12,545 acres patented in 1859 (Cowan, p. 67; Cowan gave the grant the designation "Cañada de Raimundo (or Raymundo)").

Cañada de San Agustin: see **Belmont Creek** [SAN MATEO].

Cañada de San Andres: see **San Andreas Lake** [SAN MATEO].

Cañada de San Felipe y las Animas [SANTA CLARA]: *land grant,* 5 miles north of Morgan Hill. Named on Morgan Hill (1955) and Mount Sizer (1955) 7.5' quadrangles. Thomas Bowen received 2 leagues in 1839; Charles M. Weber claimed 8788 acres patented in 1866 (Cowan, p. 75). Perez (p. 60) named Francisco Garcia as the grantee in 1844. Thompson and West's (1876) map has the name "Las Animas Hills" for the range located east of Coyote along the west edge of the grant.

Cañada de Sansevan: see **Bull Run Creek** [SAN MATEO]; **Neils Gulch** [SAN MATEO].

Cañada de Verde y Arroyo de la Purisima [SAN MATEO]: *land grant,* extends from the crest of Santa Cruz Mountains to the sea between Purisima Creek and Tunitas Creek. Named on Half Moon Bay (1961), San Gregorio (1961), and Woodside (1961) 7.5' quadrangles. Jose M. Alviso received 2 league in 1838; Jose Antonio Alviso claimed 8906 acres patented in 1865 (Cowan, p. 65). Perez (p. 60) listed Jose A. Alviso as the grantee in 1839.

Cañada Garcia [SANTA CLARA]: *canyon,* drained by a stream that flows 2.25 miles to Llagas Creek 4.25 miles west of Morgan Hill (lat. 37°07'35" N, long. 121°43'50" W). Named on Morgan Hill (1955), Mount Madonna (1955), and Santa Teresa Hills (1953) 7.5' quadrangles.

Canada Pomponio [MARIN]: *canyon,* 2.5 miles long, 7.5 miles west of downtown Novato along present Arroyo Sausal (lat. 38°07' N, long. 122°42' W). Named on Petaluma (1914) 15' quadrangle. The name commemorates an outlaw Indian (Mason, 1976b, p. 162).

Cañada Raimundo Creek: see **Upper Crystal Springs Reservoir** [SAN MATEO].

Cañada Verde [SAN MATEO]: *canyon,* drained by a stream that flows 1.5 miles to lowlands along the coast 2.5 miles south of downtown Half Moon Bay (lat. 37°25'35" N, long. 122°25'30" W; sec. 8, T 6 S, R 5 W). Named on Half Moon Bay (1961) 7.5' quadrangle. Brown (p. 16) noted the names "Cañada Verde Creek" and "Arroyo Cañada Verde" for the stream that drains the canyon.

Cañada Verde: see **Green Valley** [CONTRA COSTA].

Cañada Verde Creek: see **Cañada Verde** [SAN MATEO].

Candlestick Cove: see **Sierra Point** [SAN MATEO].

Candlestick Point [SAN FRANCISCO]: *promontory,* 4.25 miles east-southeast of Mount Davidson along San Francisco Bay (lat. 37°42'45" N, long. 122°23' W). Named on San Francisco South (1956) 7.5' quadrangle. San Francisco South (1956, photorevised 1980) 7.5' quadrangle shows the feature flanked by landfill. The name is from Candlestick Rock, a sharp pinnacle, 8 feet high, that was at the spot in the early days (Gudde, 1969, p. 52). Wackenreuder's (1861) map has the name "Black Hills" for the range that extends west from present Candlestick Point.

Candlestick Ridge [NAPA]: *ridge,* north-trending, nearly 1 mile long, 8 miles north of Saint Helena (lat. 38°37'05" N, long. 122°29'15" W). Named on Saint Helena (1960) 7.5' quadrangle.

Candlestick Rock: see **Candlestick Point** [SAN FRANCISCO].

Cannon [SOLANO]: *locality,* 4 miles southeast of Vacaville along Southern Pacific Railroad (lat. 38°18'15" N, long. 121°56'45" W; sec. 2, T 5 N, R 1 W). Named on Elmira (1953) 7.5' quadrangle.

Cannon Gulch [SONOMA]: *canyon,* drained by a stream that flows 1 mile to the sea 2.25 miles west-northwest of Plantation at Fisk Mill Cove (lat. 38°35'50" N, long. 123°21' W). Named on Plantation (1977) 7.5' quadrangle.

Cannons Resort [SANTA CLARA]: *locality,* 1 mile southwest of New Almaden (lat. 37°09'45" N, long. 121°50'05" W). Named on Los Gatos (1919) 15' quadrangle. Water of Almaden Reservoir now covers the site.

Canoas Creek [SANTA CLARA]: *stream,* flows 7.25 miles to Guadalupe River 3 miles south of downtown San Jose (lat. 37°17'20" N, long. 121°52'50" W). Named on San Jose East (1961), San Jose West (1961), and Santa Teresa Hills (1953) 7.5' quadrangles. The stream originally had the name "El Arroyo Tulares de los Canoas"—*el arroyo tulares de los canoas* means "the rivulet of the tules for canoes" in Spanish (Sawyer, p. 267). United States Board on Geographic Names (1943, p. 10) rejected the name "Cincas Creek" for the feature.

Canshea Creek: see **Conshea Creek** [SONOMA]; **Tiny Creek** [SONOMA].

Cape Horn Pass [SANTA CLARA]: *pass,* nearly 1 mile northwest of New Almaden (lat. 37°11' N, long. 121°49'55" W). Named on Santa Teresa Hills (1953) 7.5' quadrangle.

Capell [NAPA]: *locality,* nearly 6 miles west-northwest of Mount Vaca in Capell Valley (lat. 38°26'50" N, long. 122°11'45" W; near S line sec. 16, T 7 N, R 3 W). Named on Napa (1902) 30' quadrangle. Postal authorities established Capell post office in 1873, discontinued it for a time in 1901, and discontinued it finally in 1914 (Frickstad, p. 111).

Capell Creek [NAPA]: *stream,* flows 10.5 miles to Lake Berryessa 11 miles south of Berryessa Peak (lat. 38°30'25" N, long. 122°14'05" W; sec. 30, T 8 N, R 3 W). Named on Capell Valley (1951) and Lake Berryessa (1959) 7.5' quadrangles.

Capell Valley [NAPA]: *valley,* 6.5 miles northwest of Mount Vaca (lat. 38°27'15" N, long. 122°12'15" W); Capell Creek drains the valley. Named on Capell Valley (1951) 7.5' quadrangle.

Cape Romanzoff: see **Bodega Head** [SONOMA].

Carey Camp Creek [MARIN]: *stream,* flows 1 mile to San Anselmo Creek 4.5 miles west of downtown San Rafael (lat. 37°58'45" N, long. 122°36'50" W). Named on San Rafael (1954) 7.5' quadrangle.

Carillo: see **Sebastopol** [SONOMA].

Carlin Canyon [SANTA CLARA]: *canyon,* drained by a stream that flows nearly 4.5 miles to San Felipe Creek 5 miles east of Coyote (lat. 37°13'20" N, long. 121°38'50" W). Named on Morgan Hill (1955) and Mount Sizer (1955) 7.5' quadrangles.

Carlyle Hills [SANTA CLARA]: *range,* 3.5 miles south of Gilroy near the southeast end of Santa Cruz Mountains (lat. 36°57'10" N, long. 121°34'45" W). Named on Chittenden (1955) 7.5' quadrangle.

Carmet [SONOMA]: *village,* 3.25 miles north-northwest of the village of Bodega Bay (lat. 38°22'25" N, long. 123°04'30" W). Named on Bodega Head (1972) and Duncans Mills (1979) 7.5' quadrangles.

Carmet Beach [SONOMA]: *beach,* 3.25 miles north-northwest of the village of Bodega Bay along the coast (lat. 38°22'25" N, long. 123° 04'35" W); the beach is at Carmet. Named on Bodega Head (1972) 7.5' quadrangle. Bodega Head (1942) 7.5' quadrangle shows the place as part of Arched Rock Beach.

Carnadero [SANTA CLARA]: *locality,* 2.5 miles southeast of Gilroy along Southern Pacific Railroad, where the rail line branches to Hollister in San Benito County (lat. 36°58'35" N, long. 121°32'30" W). Named on Chittenden (1955) 7.5' quadrangle.

Carnadero: see **Las Animas** [SANTA CLARA].

Carnadero Creek [SANTA CLARA]: *stream,* joins Pajaro River 5.5 miles south-southeast of Gilroy (lat. 36°55'35" N, long. 121°32'25" W). Named on Chittenden (1955) 7.5' quadrangle, where the name applies to the southern extension for about 4 miles of the stream called Uvas Creek farther north. Morgan Hill (1917) 15' quadrangle has the name "Carnadero Creek" for present Uvas Creek below the confluence of present Uvas Creek and Bodfish Creek. On a diseño of Las Animas grant, present Carnadero Creek is called Arroyo de Carnadero (Becker, 1969). Bancroft's (1864) map has the name "Carniadero Cr." for the whole combined length of present Uvas Creek and present Carnadero Creek. Gudde (1949, p. 57) pointed out that *carnadero* probably refers to "butchering place" in Spanish, and was recorded in the neighborhood of Carnadero Creek as early as 1784. United States Board on Geographic Names (1973a, p. 2) approved the name "Gavilan Creek," from Gavilan College, for a stream that joins Carnadero Creek 4 miles south of Gilroy near the college (lat. 36°56'50" N, long. 121°31'55" W).

Carne Humana [NAPA]: *land grant,* near Calistoga and Saint Helena in Napa Valley. Named on Calistoga (1958), Mark West Springs (1958), Rutherford (1951), and Saint Helena (1960) 7.5' quadrangles. Edward T. Bale received 4 leagues in 1841, and his heirs claimed 17,962 acres patented in 1879 (Cowan, p. 24; Cowan gave the name "Colijolmanoc" as an alternate). Bale twisted the Indian name of the place into the designation for his grant—*carne humana* means "human flesh" in Spanish (Gudde, 1949, p. 21).

Carnero Mountain: see **Bismark Knob** [NAPA-SONOMA].

Carneros [NAPA]: *locality,* 4.5 miles northwest of Napa Junction along Southern Pacific Railroad (lat. 38°13'45" N, long. 122°18'30" W); the place is on Rincon de los Carneros grant. Named on Mare Island (1916) 15' quadrangle. Postal authorities established Carneros post office in 1867 and discontinued it in 1868 (Frickstad, p. 111).

Carneros Creek [NAPA]: *stream,* flows 10.5 miles to Napa River 4 miles northwest of Napa Junction (lat. 38°13'20" N, long. 122°18'35" W; sec. 4, T 4 N, R 4 W); the stream is on Rincon de los Carneros grant. Named on Cuttings Wharf (1949), Napa (1951), and Sonoma (1951) 7.5' quadrangles. Called Corneros Creek on Sonoma (1942) 15' quadrangle.

Carneros Valley [NAPA]: *valley,* 4.5 miles west-southwest of downtown Napa (lat. 38°16'50" N, long. 122°21'45" W); the valley is along Carneros Creek. Named on Napa (1951) and Sonoma (1951) 7.5' quadrangles.

Carniadero Creek: see **Carnadero Creek** [SANTA CLARA].

Caroline Livermore: see **Mount Caroline Livermore** [MARIN].

Carpenter [ALAMEDA]: *locality,* nearly 6 miles north of downtown Newark along Western Pacific Railroad (lat. 37°36'50" N, long. 122°02'35" W). Named on Newark (1959) 7.5' quadrangle.

Carpentier's Wharf: see **Oakland** [ALAMEDA].

Carquines Strait: see **Carquinez Strait** [CONTRA COSTA-SOLANO].

Carquinez Heights [SOLANO]: *district,* 2 miles south-southeast of downtown Vallejo along Carquinez Strait (lat. 38°04'35" N, long. 122°14'15" W). Named on Benicia (1959) 7.5' quadrangle. Postal authorities established Carquinez Heights post office in 1944 and discontinued it in 1954 (Salley, p. 38).

Carquinez Point: **Point Carquinez** [CONTRA COSTA].

Carquinez Strait [CONTRA COSTA-SOLANO]: *water feature,* extends for 9 miles from Suisun Bay to San Pablo Bay on Contra Costa-Solano County line; opens into San Pablo Bay 3 miles south of downtown Vallejo (lat. 38°03'35" N, long. 122°16' W). Named on Benicia (1959), Mare Island (1959), and Vine Hill (1959) 7.5' quadrangles. Called Karquines Strait on Karquines (1898) 15' quadrangle, but United States Board on Geographic Names (1933, p. 197) rejected the names "Karquines Strait," "Karquenas Strait," and "Carquines Strait" for the feature. The name "Carquinez" is derived from an Indian tribe or village called Carquin or Karkin (Kroeber, p. 37). Font gave the name "Boca del Puerto Dulce" to the strait in 1776—*boca del puerto dulce* means "mouth of the fresh-water port" in Spanish (Gudde, 1949, p. 58). Padre Ramon Abella gave the feature the name "Estrecho de las Karquines" in 1811 (Hanna, P.T., p. 56), and Crespi called it Rio de San Francisco in 1772 (Hoover, Rensch, and Rensch, p. 53). It is called Estrecho de Karquines on Beechey's (1827-1828) map. The name had a variety of forms in the early days: Wilkes (p. 47) called the feature Straits of Kaquines in 1841; Revere (p. 53) called it Straits of Karquin in 1846; Dana (p. 260) called it straits of Caquines in 1849; P.T. Tyson (p. 16) called it straits of Carquinos in 1850; and Ringgold (p. 27) called it Straits of Carquines in 1852. Ringgold's (1850b) map has the name "Vallejo Bay" for the east part of present Carquinez Strait opposite Martinez.

Carriger Creek [SAN MATEO]: *stream,* flows nearly 1 mile to Pescadero Creek 4 miles south-southeast of La Honda (lat. 37°15'50" N, long. 122°15'20" W; sec. 1, T 8 S, R 4 W). Named on La Honda (1961) 7.5' quadrangle. Officials of Santa Cruz Lumber Company named the stream about 1946 for Edward Carriger, secretary-treasurer of the company (Brown, p. 17).

Carriger Creek [SONOMA]: *stream,* flows 8 miles to join Felder Creek and form Fowler Creek 2 miles south-southwest of Sonoma (lat. 38°16'05" N, long. 122°28'30" W). Named on Glen Ellen (1954) and Sonoma (1951) 7.5' quadrangles. The name commemorates Nicholas Carriger, a farmer in the neighborhood after 1850 (Gudde, 1949, p. 58).

Carson Creek [SONOMA]: *stream,* flows 2.25 miles to join McKenzie Creek and form Marshall Creek 4 miles north-northeast of Fort Ross (lat. 38°33'50" N, long. 123°12'20" W; sec. 5, T 8 N, R 12 W). Named on Fort Ross (1978) 7.5' quadrangle.

Carson Creek: see **Big Carson Creek** [MARIN]; **Little Carson Creek** [MARIN].

Cascade [SONOMA]: *locality,* 2.5 miles south-southwest of Guerneville along Northwestern Pacific Railroad near Russian River (lat. 38°28' N, long. 123°01' W). Named on Duncans Mills (1921) 15' quadrangle.

Cascade: see **Lake Cascade** [CONTRA COSTA].

Cascade Creek [MARIN]:

(1) *stream,* flows 1 mile to San Anselmo Creek nearly 5 miles west of downtown San Rafael (lat. 37°58'50" N, long. 122°37'05" W). Named on Bolinas (1954) and San Rafael (1954) 7.5' quadrangles.

(2) *stream,* flows 1 mile to Old Mill Creek 4.5 miles south-southwest of downtown San Rafael (lat. 37°54'45" N, long. 122°33'50" W). Named on San Rafael (1954) 7.5' quadrangle.

Cascade Creek [SAN MATEO]: *stream,* heads in Santa Cruz County and flows 3.25 miles to the sea 1.5 miles southeast of Franklin Point (lat. 37°08'10" N, long. 122°20'15" W). Named on Franklin Point (1955) 7.5' quadrangle. The name is from Cascade dairy, started along the creek in 1863; the lower part of the stream was called Arroyo de la Cienega in Spanish times (Brown, p. 17).

Cascade Creek [SONOMA]: *stream,* flows 0.5 mile to Frasier Creek 6 miles north-northeast of Asti (lat. 38°50'35" N, long. 122°56' W; near E line sec. 35, T 12 N, R 10 W). Named on Asti (1959) 7.5' quadrangle.

Caslamayomi [SONOMA]: *land grant,* northeast of Asti and Geyserville. Named on Asti (1959), Geyserville (1955), Jimtown (1955), and The Geysers (1959) 7.5' quadrangles. Eugenio Montenegro received 8 leagues in 1844; William Forbes claimed 26,788 acres patented in 1874 (Cowan, p. 25; Cowan gave the name "Laguna de los Gentiles" as an alternate). Kroeber (p. 37) noted that the name "Caslamayomi" seems to be of Indian origin.

Castillo de San Joaquin: see **Fort Point** [SAN FRANCISCO].

Castle Canyon [SANTA CLARA]: *canyon,* drained by a stream that flows 3.5 miles to Smith Creek nearly 3 miles south of Mount Isabel (lat. 37°17'05" N, long. 121°36'55" W); the canyon heads on Castle Ridge. Named on Isabel Valley (1955) 7.5' quadrangle.

Castle Hill [CONTRA COSTA]: *peak,* 4 miles northwest of Danville (lat. 37°51'35" N, long. 122°03'05" W; sec. 11, T 1 S, R 2 W). Named on Las Trampas Ridge (1959) 7.5' quadrangle.

Castle Peak [NAPA]: *peak,* nearly 5 miles east of Yountville (lat. 38°23'50" N, long. 122°16'35" W; sec. 2, T 6 N, R 4 W). Altitude 1318 feet. Named on Yountville (1951) 7.5' quadrangle.

Castle Ridge [SANTA CLARA]: *ridge,* northwest-trending, 3 miles long, 2 miles southwest of Isabel Valley (lat. 37°17'45" N, long. 121°34' W). Named on Isabel Valley (1955) 7.5' quadrangle. The ridge is part of a larger feature called Pine Ridge on Morgan Hill (1917) and Mount Hamilton (1897) 15' quadrangles.

Castle Rock [CONTRA COSTA]: *peak,* 4 miles west of Mount Diablo (lat. 37°52'50" N, long. 121°59' W). Altitude 972 feet. Named on Clayton (1953) 7.5' quadrangle.

Castle Rock [NAPA]: *relief feature,* 8 miles west-northwest of downtown Napa (lat. 38°20'35" N, long. 122°24'45" W; near W line sec. 28, T 6 N, R 5 W). Named on Sonoma (1951) 7.5' quadrangle.

Castle Rock [SANTA CLARA]: *peak,* 0.5 mile north-northwest of Bielawski Mountain on Santa Clara-Santa Cruz County line (lat. 37°13'40" N, long. 122°05'40" W; at SW cor. sec. 16, T 8 S, R 2 W). Altitude 3214 feet. Named on Castle Rock Ridge (1955) 7.5' quadrangle.

Castle Rock [SONOMA]:

(1) *peak,* 10.5 miles northeast of Healdsburg (lat. 38°44'35" N, long. 122°45'10" W; sec. 4, T 10 N, R 8 W). Altitude 2662 feet. Named on Jimtown (1955) 7.5' quadrangle.

(2) *relief feature,* 6 miles north-northwest of Kenwood (lat. 38°29'45" N, long. 122°35'45" W; near E line sec. 35, T 8 N, R 7 W). Named on Kenwood (1954) 7.5' quadrangle.

Castle Rock Ridge [SANTA CLARA]: *ridge,* northwest-trending, 6 miles long, southeast of Saratoga Gap on Santa Clara-Santa Cruz County line (lat. 37°13'30" N, long. 122°05'30" W); Castle Rock is on the ridge. Named on Castle Rock Ridge (1955) and Cupertino (1961) 7.5' quadrangles.

Castro: see **Castro City** [SANTA CLARA].

Castro City [SANTA CLARA]: *locality,* 1.25 miles northwest of downtown Mountain View along Southern Pacific Railroad (lat. 37°24'10" N, long. 122°05'45" W). Named on Mountain View (1961) 7.5' quadrangle. Palo Alto (1899) 15' quadrangle has the name "Castro" at the place. Castro Station was named for Mariano Castro, owner of Pastoria de las Borregas grant, where the station is situated (Rambo, 1973, p. 40).

Castro Creek [CONTRA COSTA]: *stream,* enters San Pablo Bay 2 miles east-southeast of Point San Pablo (lat. 37°57'30" N, long. 122°23'35" W). Named on San Quentin (1959) 7.5' quadrangle.

Castro Flats: see **Castro Valley** [SANTA CLARA].

Castro Point [CONTRA COSTA]: *promontory,* 2.25 miles south-southeast of Point San Pablo along San Francisco Bay (lat. 37°56'10" N, long. 122°24'45" W). Named on San Quentin (1959) 7.5' quadrangle.

Castro Rocks [CONTRA COSTA]: *rocks,* 2.25 miles south-southeast of Point San Pablo in San Francisco Bay (lat. 37°55'55" N, long. 122°25' W); the rocks are 0.25 mile southwest of Castro Point. Named on San Quentin (1959) 7.5' quadrangle.

Castro Valley [ALAMEDA]:

(1) *valley,* 2 miles north-northeast of Haywards (present Hayward) (lat. 37°41'45" N, long. 122°04'15" W); the valley is on San Lorenzo (2) grant, which was owned by Guilleremo Castro. Named on Haywards (1899) 15' quadrangle.

(2) *city,* 2 miles north-northeast of downtown Hayward (lat. 37°41'45" N, long. 122°04'15" W); the city is in Castro Valley (1). Named on Hayward (1959) 7.5' quadrangle.

Castro Valley [SANTA CLARA]: *valley,* 3.5 miles south-southwest of Gilroy along upper reaches of Tar Creek (lat. 36°57'45" N, long. 121°36'45" W); the valley is partly on Las Animas grant, which belonged to the Castro family. Named on Chittenden (1955) 7.5' quadrangle. Called Castro Flats on San Juan Bautista (1917) 15' quadrangle.

Catacula [NAPA]: *land grant,* at and near Chiles Valley. Named on Chiles Valley (1958), Saint Helena (1960), and Yountville (1951) 7.5' quadrangles. Joseph B. Chiles received 2 leagues in 1844 and claimed 8546 acres patented in 1865 (Cowan, p. 25).

Cataract Canyon: see **Cataract Creek** [MARIN].

Cataract Creek [MARIN]: *stream,* flows 2.25 miles to Alpine Lake 3.25 miles northeast of Bolinas (lat. 37°56' N, long. 122°38'05" W). Named on Bolinas (1954) and San Rafael (1954) 7.5' quadrangles. The canyon of the stream is called Cataract Canyon on Mount Tamalpais (1950) 15' quadrangle. East Fork, which flows less than 1 mile to join the main stream in Alpine Lake, is named on Bolinas (1954) 7.5' quadrangle.

Cat Slough [SOLANO]: *water feature,* joins Volanti Slough nearly 5 miles south of Fairfield (lat. 38°10'50" N, long. 122°02' W). Named on Fairfield South (1949) 7.5' quadrangle.

Cattle Hill [SAN MATEO]: *peak,* 3.5 miles north of Montara Knob (lat. 37°36'25" N, long. 122°28'50" W). Named on Montara Mountain (1956) 7.5' quadrangle.

Cavallo Point [MARIN]: *promontory,* 2 miles south-southeast of downtown Sausalito along San Francisco Bay (lat. 37°49'55" N, long. 122°28'20" W). Named on San Francisco North (1956) 7.5' quadrangle. Called Pto. Cavallos on Ringgold's (1850a) map. United States Board on Geographic Names (1983a, p. 3) approved the name "Point Cavallo" for the promontory, and rejected the names "Cavallo Point," "Caballo Point," "Plaza de los Caballos," "Punta de los Caballos," and "Punto Cavallos." According to Gudde (1949, p. 61), the name "Cavallo" presumably is from horses that were kept at the place in Spanish times—*caballos* means "horses" in Spanish; the letters "b" and "v" commonly were interchanged.

Cavanaugh Gulch: see **Soda Spring Canyon** [SANTA CLARA].

Cave Dale: see **Agua Caliente** [SONOMA] (2).

Cavelano Creek: see **Cayetano Creek** [ALAMEDA].

Cave Point [CONTRA COSTA]: *peak,* 3.25 miles south-southeast of Mount Diablo (lat. 37°50'25" N, long. 121°52'55" W; sec. 17, T 1 S, R 1 E). Named on Diablo (1953) 7.5' quadrangle. Members of the Whitney survey named the feature for hollows in sandstone at the summit; they also gave the name "Tower Rocks" to outcrops of sandstone in the saddle just south of Cave Point (Whitney, p. 27).

Cayetano Creek [ALAMEDA-CONTRA COSTA]: *stream,* heads in Contra Costa County and flows 8 miles to Arroyo las Positas 1.5 miles northwest of Livermore in Alameda County (lat. 37°42'05" N, long. 121°47'05" W). Named on Livermore (1961) and Tassajara (1953) 7.5' quadrangles. Called Arroyo Cayetano on Mount Diablo (1898) 15' quadrangle. United States Board on Geographic Names (1933, p. 204) rejected the names "Arroyo Cavelano," "Arroyo Covelano," "Calletano Creek," and "Cavelano Creek" for the feature.

Cayetano Creek: see **Spencer Creek** [NAPA].

Cayle: see **Cayley** [ALAMEDA].

Cayley [ALAMEDA]: *locality,* 2.5 miles west-northwest of Midway along Southern Pacific Railroad (lat. 37°43'50" N, long. 121° 36' W; sec. 25, T 2 S, R 3 E). Named on Midway (1953) 7.5' quadrangle. Called Cayle on Tesla (1907) 15' quadrangle.

Caymus [NAPA]:

(1) *land grant,* near Rutherford and Yountville in Napa Valley. Named on Rutherford (1951) and Yountville (1951) 7.5' quadrangles. George C. Yount received 2 leagues in 1836 and claimed 11,887 acres patented in 1863 (Cowan, p. 25). Perez (p. 61) gave the size of the grant as 11,814.52 acres. The grant has the name of an Indian village that was at the site of present Yountville (Kroeber, p. 38).

(2) *locality,* 1.5 miles southeast of Rutherford along Southern Pacific Railroad (lat. 38°26'30" N, long. 122°24'20" W); the place is on Caymus grant. Named on Sonoma (1942) 15' quadrangle.

Cazadero [SONOMA]: *village,* 13 miles west-southwest of Healdsburg (lat. 38°31'50" N, long. 123°05'10" W; sec. 16, 21, T 8 N, R 11 W); the village is along Austin Creek. Named on Cazadero (1978) 7.5' quadrangle. Postal authorities established Austin post office in 1881, changed the name to Ingrams in 1886, and changed it to Cazadero in 1889; the name "Austin" was for Henry Austin, a pioneer settler, and the name "Ingrams" was for Silas D. Ingrams, first postmaster of Ingrams post office (Salley, p. 12, 40, 104). The place also was called Elim Grove in the early days (Mullen). California Mining Bureau's (1917a) map shows a place called Magnesite located north of Cazadero at the end of a rail line—this probably was at the property of Sonoma Magnesite Company described by Bradley (p. 328) as located along East Austin Creek at the end of a 24-inch gauge railroad (in and north of sec. 20, T 9 N, R 11 W).

C.C. Moore: see **Camp C.C. Moore**, under **Camp Royaneh** [SONOMA].

Cebada Flat [SANTA CLARA]: *area,* 6 miles northeast of Gilroy (lat. 37°03'40" N, long. 121°30'25" W). Named on Gilroy (1955) 7.5' quadrangle.

Cedar Canyon [NAPA]: *canyon,* drained by a stream that flows 2.25 miles to James Creek 7 miles north-northeast of Calistoga (lat. 38° 40'10" N, long. 122°31'20" W; near E line sec. 33, T 10 N, R 6 W). Named on Detert Reservoir (1958) 7.5' quadrangle.

Cedar Creek [NAPA]: *stream,* flows 4.25 miles to Hunting Creek 4.25 miles west-southwest of Knoxville (lat. 38°47'40" N, long. 122°24'20" W; sec. 22, T 11 N, R 5 W); the stream flows through Cedar Valley (1). Named on Jericho Valley (1958) and Knoxville (1958) 7.5' quadrangles.

Cedar Creek [SANTA CLARA]: *stream,* flows 6.25 miles to Pacheco Creek 2.5 miles east-northeast of Pacheco Peak (lat. 37°01'40" N, long. 121°19'30" W). Named on Pacheco Peak (1955) 7.5' quadrangle.

Cedar Creek [SONOMA]: *stream,* flows 3 miles to House Creek 4.25 miles south-southwest of Big Mountain (lat. 38°39'10" N, long. 123°10'05" W; sec. 3, T 9 N, R 12 W); the stream is south of Cedar Ridge. Named on Tombs Creek (1978) 7.5' quadrangle.

Cedar Hill: see **Cedar Mountain** [ALAMEDA].

Cedar Mountain [ALAMEDA]: *peak,* 3 miles southeast of Mendenhall Springs (lat. 37°33'35" N, long. 121°36'20" W; near W line sec. 25, T 4 S, R 3 E). Altitude 3675 feet. Named on Cedar Mountain (1956) 7.5' quadrangle. The peak also was known as Cedar Hill (Mosier and Mosier, p. 21).

Cedar Mountain Ridge [ALAMEDA]: *ridge,* northwest-trending, 8 miles long, center 2.25 miles southeast of Mendenhall Springs (lat. 37°33'10" N, long. 121°37'30" W); Cedar Mountain is near the ridge. Named on Cedar Mountain (1956) and Mendenhall Springs (1956) 7.5' quadrangles. The ridge was given the misspelled name "Chapparal Mountains" in 1874, and the name was changed to Cedar Mountain Ridge in 1878 (Mosier and Mosier, p. 22).

Cedar Opening [SONOMA]: *area,* 8 miles north of Guerneville (lat. 38°37'10" N, long. 122°59'25" W; near N line sec. 20, T 9 N, R 10 W). Named on Guerneville (1955) 7.5' quadrangle.

Cedar Ridge [SONOMA]: *ridge,* northwest- to west-trending, 1.5 miles long, nearly 4 miles south of Big Mountain (lat. 38°39'15" N, long. 123°09'05" W); the ridge is north of Cedar Creek. Named on Tombs Creek (1978) 7.5' quadrangle.

Cedar Roughs [NAPA]: *area,* 11 miles east-northeast of Saint Helena (lat. 38°34'30" N, long. 122°18' W). Named on Chiles Valley (1958) 7.5' quadrangle.

Cedars: see **The Cedars** [SONOMA].

Cedar Valley [NAPA]:

(1) *valley,* 4 miles south-southwest of Knoxville along Cedar Creek (lat. 38°46'15" N, long. 122°21'30" W; sec. 25, T 11 N, R 5 W). Named on Knoxville (1958) 7.5' quadrangle.

(2) *area,* 4.5 miles north-northeast of Walter Springs (lat. 38°43'10" N, long. 122°19'55" W). Named on Walter Springs (1959) 7.5' quadrangle.

Cement [SOLANO]: *locality,* 3.25 miles northeast of Fairfield (lat. 38°17'15" N, long. 122°00'10" W); the place is on the south side of present Cement Hill. Named on Suisun (1918) special quadrangle, which shows a cement mill near the place. Postal authorities established Cement post office in 1903 and discontinued it in 1928 (Frickstad, p. 192). Pacific Portland Cement Company completed a mill at the site in 1902 (Laizure, 1927b, p. 205).

Cement Creek [NAPA]: *stream,* flows 3 miles to Putah Creek 3.5 miles north-northwest of Walter Springs (lat. 38°42'15" N, long. 122°22'15" W; near NE cor. sec. 23, T 10 N, R 5 W). Named on Walter Springs (1959) 7.5' quadrangle.

Cement Hill [SOLANO]: *peak,* 4 miles north-northeast of Fairfield (lat. 38°18' N, long. 122°00'05" W; sec. 5, T 6 N, R 1 W). Named on Elmira (1953) and Fairfield North (1951) 7.5' quadrangles.

Cemetery [SANTA CLARA]: *locality,* 3 miles southeast of downtown San Jose along Southern Pacific Railroad (lat. 37°17'50" N, long. 121°51'30" W); the station for Oak Hill Memorial Park was at the site before the railroad was routed farther west. Named on San Jose (1899) 15' quadrangle.

Cemetery Creek: see **Glen Echo Creek** [ALAMEDA].

Centennial Mountain [SONOMA]: *peak,* 1 mile southeast of Big Mountain (lat. 38°42'05" N, long. 123°08' W; sec. 24, T 10 N, R 12 W). Altitude 2443 feet. Named on Tombs Creek (1978) 7.5' quadrangle.

Center Creek: see **Little Llagas Creek** [SANTA CLARA].

Center Flats [SANTA CLARA]: *area,* 4 miles east of Gilroy Hot Springs (lat. 37°06'40" N, long. 121°24'05" W; sec. 35, T 9 S, R 5 E). Named on Gilroy Hot Springs (1955) 7.5' quadrangle.

Centerville: see **Centerville District** [ALAMEDA].

Centerville District [ALAMEDA]: *district,* 2 miles west-northwest of Fremont civic center in Fremont (lat. 37°33'30" N, long. 122°00'20" W). Named on Newark (1959) and Niles (1961) 7.5' quadrangles. Newark (1948) 7.5' quadrangle has the name "Centerville" for the community that joined with other communities in 1956 to form the new city of Fremont. George Lloyd set up a tent at the site in 1850 and sold cold beer to horsemen and stage passengers; then Captain George Bond built a general store there, and the name "Centerville" was adopted for the place (MacGregor, p. 46). Postal authorities established Centreville post office in 1855, changed the name to Centerville in 1893, and discontinued it in 1956 (Salley, p. 41).

Centissima Reef [MARIN]: *shoal,* 1.5 miles northwest of Point Bonita, and 2200 feet offshore (lat. 37°49'40" N, long. 122°32'55" W). Named on Point Bonita (1954) 7.5' quadrangle.

Central Basin [SAN FRANCISCO]: *water feature,* 1.5 miles south of Rincon Point along San Francisco Bay (lat. 37°45'55" N, long. 122°23' W). Named on San Francisco North (1956) 7.5' quadrangle.

Central Reservoir [ALAMEDA]: *lake,* 1500 feet long, nearly 2.5 miles east-southeast of downtown Oakland (lat. 37°47'50" N, long. 122°13'20" W). Named on Oakland East (1959) 7.5' quadrangle. The lake also was called Highland Park Reservoir (Mosier and Mosier, p. 22).

Centreville: see **Centerville District** [ALAMEDA].

Cerrilo Creek: see **Cerrito Creek** [ALAMEDA-CONTRA COSTA].

Cerrito [CONTRA COSTA]: *hill,* 1 mile south of present Richmond civic center (lat. 37°55'20" N, long. 122°20'40" W). Named on San Francisco (1899) 15' quadrangle.

Cerrito Creek [ALAMEDA-CONTRA COSTA]: *stream,* forms part of Alameda-Contra Costa County line, flows 2 miles to San Francisco Bay 3.25 miles south-southeast of downtown Richmond (lat. 37° 53'50" N, long. 122°18'40" W). Named on Richmond (1959) 7.5' quadrangle. Called Cerritos Creek on Thompson and West's (1978) map. United States Board on Geographic Names (1933, p. 206) rejected the name "Cerrilo Creek" for the feature.

Cerrito de San Antonio: see **Albany Hill** [ALAMEDA].

Cerrito Hill: see **Albany Hill** [ALAMEDA].

Cerritos Creek: see **Cerrito Creek** [ALAMEDA].

Cerritos Hills: see **Coyote Hills** [ALAMEDA].

Cerritos San Antonio: see **Albany Hill** [ALAMEDA].

Cerro [MARIN]: *locality,* 1.25 miles north of downtown San Rafael along Northwestern Pacific Railroad (lat. 37°59'30" N, long. 122° 31'50" W). Named on San Rafael (1954) 7.5' quadrangle.

Cerro Alto de los Bolbones: see **Mount Diablo** [CONTRA COSTA].

Cerro Colorado: see **Red Mountain** [SANTA CLARA].

Cerro de las Calaveras: see **Monument Peak** [ALAMEDA-SANTA CLARA].

Cerro de San Bruno: see **San Bruno Mountain** [SAN MATEO].

Cerro de San Juan: see **Mount Diablo** [CONTRA COSTA].

Chabot: see **Lake Chabot** [ALAMEDA]; **Lake Chabot** [SOLANO]; **Lake Chabot**, under **Lake Temescal** [ALAMEDA].

Chabot Terrace [SOLANO]: *district,* 3 miles north-northeast of downtown Vallejo (lat. 38°08'50" N, long. 122°14'45" W); the district is northwest of Lake Chabot. Named on Cordelia (1951) and Cuttings Wharf (1949) 7.5' quadrangles. Postal authorities established Chabot Terrace post office in 1944 and discontinued it in 1956 (Salley, p. 41).

Chadbourne [SOLANO]: *locality,* 2.25 miles west of Fairfield along Sacramento Northern Railroad (lat. 38°14'40" N, long. 122°05' W). Named on Fairfield South (1949) 7.5' quadrangle.

Chadbourne Slough [SOLANO]: *water feature,* joins Wells Slough 5 miles south-southwest of Fairfield (lat. 38°10'50" N, long. 122° 04'15" W). Named on Fairfield South (1949) 7.5' quadrangle.

Chalk Hill [SONOMA]: *peak,* 5 miles east of Healdsburg (lat. 38°36'15" N, long. 122°46'35" W). Named on Healdsburg (1955) 7.5' quadrangle.

Chalk Mountain [SONOMA]: *ridge,* east-southeast-trending, less than 1 mile long, 2.5 miles east-northeast of Mark West Springs (lat. 38°33'35" N, long. 122°40'20" W). Named on Mark West Springs (1958) 7.5' quadrangle.

Chalk Point [SONOMA]: *peak,* 2 miles west of Mount Saint Helena (lat. 38°39'55" N, long. 122°40'15" W; near SE cor. sec. 31, T 10 N, R 7 W). Named on Mount Saint Helena (1959) 7.5' quadrangle.

Champagne Fountain [SANTA CLARA]: *locality,* nearly 2 miles northeast of downtown Saratoga along Southern Pacific Railroad (lat. 37°16'35" N, long. 122°00'25" W). Named on Cupertino (1961) 7.5' quadrangle. California Mining Bureau's (1909b) map has the name "Congress Jn." [Junction] at the place, which is the nearest railroad station to Congress Springs. The name "Congress Junction" was changed to "Champagne Fountain" in 1959 at the request of the management of a nearby winery (Willys Peck, *San Jose Mercury News,* July 22, 1981). Peninsular Railroad Company's (1912) map shows a railway station called Sorosis situated northeast of Congress Junction, about one-quarter of the way from Congress Junction to Meridian. The name "Sorosis" was from the large Sorosis fruit ranch (Willys Peck, *San Jose Mercury News,* July 22, 1981).

Champion Slough [SOLANO]: *water feature,* on Wheeler Island, joins Suisun Bay about 6 miles southwest of Birds Landing (2) (lat. 38°04'45" N, long. 121°57'30" W). Named on Honker Bay (1953) 7.5' quadrangle.

Champlin Creek [SONOMA]: *stream,* flows 3 miles to Rodgers Creek 3 miles south-southwest of Sonoma (lat. 38°15'20" N, long. 122°28'50" W). Named on Petaluma River (1954), Sears Point (1951), and Sonoma (1951) 7.5' quadrangles.

Chandler Gulch [SAN MATEO]: *canyon,* drained by a stream that flows 1.5 miles to Bradley Creek 3 miles south of the village of San Gregorio (lat. 37°16'55" N, long. 122°22'45" W). Named on La Honda (1961) 7.5' quadrangle. The name commemorates Lafayette Chandler, who had a ranch in the canyon in the late 1870's and 1880's (Brown, p. 18).

Chaparral Peak [ALAMEDA-CONTRA COSTA]: *peak,* 2.5 miles west of Orinda on Alameda-Contra Costa County line (lat. 37°52'40" N, long. 122°13'20" W; sec. 5, T 1 S, R 3 W). Named on Briones Valley (1959) 7.5' quadrangle.

Chaparral Spring [CONTRA COSTA]: *spring,* 3.25 miles north-northeast of Mount Diablo in Goethels Canyon (lat. 37°55'20" N, long. 121°52'55" W). Named on Clayton (1953) 7.5' quadrangle.

Chaplin: see **Dutton** [SOLANO].

Chapman: see **Point Chapman**, under **Steamboat Slough** [SOLANO].

Chapman Branch: see **Pena Creek** [SONOMA].

Chapman Canyon: see **East Chapman Canyon** [NAPA]; **West Chapman Canyon** [NAPA].

Chapparal Mountains: see **Cedar Mountain Ridge** [ALAMEDA].

Charleston Slough [SANTA CLARA]: *water feature,* meandering waterway that reaches mud flats near San Francisco Bay 4.25 miles north of downtown Mountain View (lat. 37°27'10" N, long. 122°05'25" W). Named on Mountain View (1961) 7.5' quadrangle.

Charley Haupt Creek: see **Haupt Creek** [SONOMA].

Chase Pond [CONTRA COSTA]: *lake,* 250 feet long, 1.5 miles south of Mount Diablo (lat. 37°51'40" N, long. 121°54'55" W; sec. 12, T 1 S, R 1 W). Named on Diablo (1953) 7.5' quadrangle.

Chauncey Point: see **Point Chauncey** [MARIN].

Chemeketa: see **Chemeketa Park** [SANTA CLARA].

Chemeketa Park [SANTA CLARA]: *settlement,* 4 miles south of Los Gatos (lat. 37°09'45" N, long. 121°58'45" W; sec. 9, T 9 S, R 1 W). Named on Los Gatos (1953) 7.5' quadrangle. The place also is called Chemeketa.

Cheney Gulch [SONOMA]: *canyon,* drained by a stream that flows nearly 4 miles to Bodega Harbor 1.25 miles south-southeast of the village of Bodega Bay (lat. 38°19' N, long. 123°02'10" W). Named on Bodega Head (1972) and Valley Ford (1954) 7.5' quadrangles.

Cherry [SONOMA]: *locality,* 3.5 miles southwest of Cotati along Petaluma and Santa Rosa Railroad (lat. 38°17'10" N, long. 122°44'50" W). Named on Santa Rosa (1944) 15' quadrangle. California Division of Highways' (1934) map shows a place called Garden and a place called Robinson located along the railroad between Cherry and Liberty, and a place called Houx and a place called Boysen located along the railroad between Cherry and Two Rock.

Cherry Canyon [SAN MATEO]: *canyon,* drained by a stream that flows 1.5 miles to lowlands along San Francisco Bay 1.5 miles west of downtown San Mateo (lat. 37°34'10" N, long. 122°21' W). Named on San Mateo (1956) 7.5' quadrangle.

Cherry Canyon [SANTA CLARA]: *canyon,* drained by a stream that flows 2 miles to Calero Reservoir nearly 2 miles east-southeast of New Almaden (lat. 37°10'20" N, long. 121°47'20" W). Named on Santa Teresa Hills (1953) 7.5' quadrangle.

Cherry Creek [SONOMA]: *stream,* heads in Mendocino County and flows 7.25 miles to Dry Creek 5 miles southwest of Cloverdale (lat. 38°45'55" N, long. 123°05'45" W; at S line sec. 28, T 11 N, R 11 W). Named on Cloverdale (1960) 7.5' quadrangle.

Cherry Flat Reservoir [SANTA CLARA]: *lake,* 0.5 mile long, behind a dam on Upper Penitencia Creek nearly 4 miles east of the mouth of Alum Rock Canyon (lat. 37°23'50" N, long. 121°45'25" W). Named on Calaveras Reservoir (1961) and Mount Day (1955) 7.5' quadrangles.

Cherry Glen [SOLANO]: *valley,* 5.5 miles north of Fairfield along Laguna Creek (lat. 38°20' N, long. 122°02'30" W; near SW cor. sec. 25, T 6 N, R 2 W). Named on Fairfield North (1951) 7.5' quadrangle.

Cherry Springs [SANTA CLARA]: *spring,* 2 miles north-northwest of Mount Umunhum (lat. 37°11'20" N, long. 121°54'45" W). Named on Los Gatos (1953) 7.5' quadrangle.

Cherry Valley [NAPA]: *area,* 5.5 miles north-northwest of Mount Vaca in Wragg Canyon (lat. 38°28'15" N, long. 122°09'20" W). Named on Capell Valley (1951) 7.5' quadrangle.

Chesbro Reservoir [SANTA CLARA]: *lake,* 2.25 miles long, behind a dam on Llagas Creek 2.5 miles west-southwest of Morgan Hill (lat. 37°07' N, long. 121°41'35" W). Named on Morgan Hill (1955) and Mount Madonna (1955) 7.5' quadrangles.

Chianti [SONOMA]: *locality,* 3 miles northwest of Geyserville along Northwestern Pacific Railroad (lat. 38°44'15" N, long. 123°56'30" W). Named on Geyserville (1955) 7.5' quadrangle.

Chicago: see **New Chicago** under **Alviso** [SANTA CLARA]; **Port Chicago** [CONTRA COSTA].

Chicken Hollow: see **Big Chicken Hollow** [SAN MATEO]; **Little Chicken Hollow** [SAN MATEO].

Chilanian Gulch [SANTA CLARA]: *canyon,* drained by a stream that flows 1 mile to Alamitos Creek 0.5 mile northeast of New Almaden (lat. 37°10'55" N, long. 121°48'55" W). Named on Santa Teresa Hills (1953) 7.5' quadrangle.

Childs: see **Chiles Valley** [NAPA].

Chileno: see **Chileno Valley** [MARIN].

Chileno Creek [MARIN]: *stream,* heads at Laguna Lake and flows 6.25 miles to Walker Creek 3.5 miles southeast of Tomales (lat. 38°12'45" N, long. 122°51'30" W); the stream drains Chileno Valley. Named on Point Reyes NE (1954) 7.5' quadrangle. United States Board on Geographic Names (1943, p. 10) rejected the name "Arroyo San Antonio" for the upper part of the stream, and rejected the name "North Fork, San Antonio Creek" for the entire stream.

Chileno Valley [MARIN-SONOMA]: *valley,* on Marin-Sonoma County line, mainly in Marin County, along Chileno Creek above a point 5 miles east-southeast of Tomales (lat. 38°12'50" N, long. 122°49'30" W). Named on Petaluma (1953) and Point Reyes NE (1954) 7.5' quadrangles. The name is from natives of Chili that Adrian Godoy, a Chilean immigrant himself, brought to the place after 1868 (Mason, 1976b, p. 163). Postal authorities established Offutt post office in Chileno Valley in Marin County in 1895, changed the name to Chileno in 1896, and discontinued it in 1900; the name was for Charles Alex Offutt (Salley, p. 43, 159).

Chiles: see **Chiles Valley** [NAPA].

Chiles Creek [NAPA]: *stream,* flows 4.5 miles to Lake Hennessey 6.25 miles east of Saint Helena (lat. 38°30'15" N, long. 122°21'15" W; sec. 31, T 8 N, R 4 W); the stream heads in Chiles Valley. Named on Chiles Valley (1958) and Yountville (1951) 7.5' quadrangles.

Chiles Valley [NAPA]: *valley,* 8 miles east-northeast of Saint Helena (lat. 38°32' N, long. 122°19'30" W); the valley is on upper reaches of Chiles Creek on Catacula grant. Named on Chiles Valley (1958) 7.5' quadrangle. The name commemorates Joseph B. Chiles, who came to California in 1841 and received Catacula grant in 1844 (Gudde, 1949, p. 65). California Division of Highways' (1934) map shows a place called Chiles located near the southeast end of present Chiles Valley, near where Saint Helena (1942) 15' quadrangle shows Chiles Valley Sch. Postal authorities established Childs post office in 1888, changed the name to Chiles the same year, moved it 0.75 mile east in 1894, moved it 1 mile northwest in 1908, and discontinued it in 1924 (Salley, p. 43).

Chimiles [NAPA]: *land grant,* southwest of Mount Vaca. Named on Capell Valley (1951), Fairfield North (1951), Mount George (1951), and Mount Vaca (1951) 7.5' quadrangles. Jose Ignacio Berryessa received 4 leagues in 1846; William Gordon and Nathan Coombs claimed 17,762 acres patented in 1860 (Cowan, p. 27).

Chimney Canyon [NAPA]: *canyon,* drained by a stream that flows 2 miles to Gordon Valley 3 miles south of Mount Vaca (lat. 38°21'20" N, long. 122°06'45" W). Named on Fairfield North (1951) 7.5' quadrangle.

Chimney Canyon [SANTA CLARA]: *canyon,* drained by a stream that flows 4.25 miles to East Fork Pacheco Creek nearly 7 miles north of Pacheco Peak (lat. 37°06'20" N, long. 121°15'50" W; sec. 36, T 9 S, R 6 E). Named on Mustang Peak (1955) and Pacheco Peak (1955) 7.5' quadrangles.

Chimney Gulch [SANTA CLARA]: *canyon,* drained by a stream that flows 2 miles to East Fork Pacheco Creek nearly 7 miles north-northeast of Pacheco Peak (lat. 37°06'30" N, long. 121°15'20" W). Named on Pacheco Pass (1955) and Pacheco Peak (1955) 7.5' quadrangles.

Chimney Ridge [SANTA CLARA]: *ridge,* northwest- to west-northwest-trending, 2.25 miles long, 13 miles east-southeast of Gilroy (lat. 36°58'30" N, long. 121°19' W). Named on Three Sisters (1954) 7.5' quadrangle.

Chimney Rock [MARIN]: *rock,* 3.25 miles east of the lighthouse at Point Reyes, and 100 feet off the east end of Point Reyes (lat. 37° 59'20" N, long. 122°57'45" W). Named on Drakes Bay (1953) 7.5' quadrangle.

Chimney Rock [SANTA CLARA]: *relief feature,* 5.5 miles north of Pacheco Peak (lat. 37°05'25" N, long. 121°17'05" W). Named on Pacheco Peak (1955) 7.5' quadrangle.

Chimney Rock [SONOMA]: *peak,* 2.5 miles southeast of Cazadero (lat. 38°30'10" N, long. 123°03' W; near NW cor. sec. 35, T 8 N, R 11 W). Altitude 1283 feet. Named on Cazadero (1978) 7.5' quadrangle. Water from Chimney Rock Spring, located near the peak, was bottled by hand for many years (Bradley, p. 336).

Chimney Rock Spring: see **Chimney Rock** [SONOMA].

China Basin [SAN FRANCISCO]: *water feature,* less than 1 mile south of Rincon Point along San Francisco Bay (lat. 37°46'40" N, long. 122°23'10" W). Named on San Francisco North (1956) 7.5' quadrangle.

China Beach: see **Baker Beach** [SAN FRANCISCO].

China Camp [MARIN]: *locality,* 9.5 miles southeast of downtown Novato along San Pabo Bay (lat. 38°00'05" N, long. 122°27'40" W). Named on Petaluma Point (1959) 7.5' quadrangle. A village of Chinese people who gathered shrimp was at the site (Teather, p. 16).

China Cove: see **Winslow Cove**, under **Simpton Point** [MARIN].

China Flat [SAN MATEO]: *area,* 5.5 miles southwest of La Honda (lat. 37°16'10" N, long. 122°21'10" W; sec. 1, T 8 S, R 5 W). Named on La Honda (1961) 7.5' quadrangle.

China Gulch: see **Old Womans Creek** [SAN MATEO].

Chinamans Cut: see **Chinese Cut** [SOLANO].

China Slough [NAPA-SONOMA]: *water feature,* on Napa-Sonoma County line, joins South Slough nearly 6 miles west-southwest of Napa Junction (lat. 38°09'50" N, long. 122°21'05" W; near W line sec. 30, T 4 N, R 4 W). Named on Cuttings Wharf (1949) 7.5' quadrangle.

Chinatown [SAN FRANCISCO]: *district,* 1.25 miles north-northeast of San Francisco civic center (lat. 37°47'45" N, long. 122°24'20" W). Named on San Francisco North (1956) 7.5' quadrangle. A small valley in the present district was the source of water for San Francisco in early American times; the feature was called Spring Valley and gave its name to Spring Valley Water Company, which later brought water to the city from outside the present city limits (Gudde, 1969, p. 318).

Chinese Cut [SOLANO]: *water feature,* 4 miles south-southwest of Rio Vista along Sacramento River (lat. 38°06'15" N, long. 121°43'30" W). Named on Jersey Island (1978) 7.5' quadrangle. Called Chinamans Cut on Jersey Island (1952) 7.5' quadrangle.

Chinese Gulch [SONOMA]: *canyon,* drained by a stream that flows 1 mile to the sea 2 miles west of Plantation (lat. 38°35'20" N, long. 123°20'35" W). Named on Plantation (1977) 7.5' quadrangle.

Chino Flat [NAPA]: *area,* 3.5 miles northwest of Calistoga (lat. 38° 37'15" N, long. 122°37'15" W). Named on Calistoga (1958) 7.5' quadrangle.

Chipps [SOLANO]: *locality,* 6.25 miles south-southwest of Birds Landing (2) along Sacramento Northern Railroad at the north end of a railroad ferry (lat. 38°03' N, long. 121°54'50" W); the place is on Chipps Island. Named on Honker Bay (1953) 7.5' quadrangle. Honker Bay (1953, photo-revised 1968 and 1973) quadrangle shows the place by an old railroad grade.

Chipps Island [SOLANO]: *island,* 5.5 miles south-southwest of Birds Landing (2) between Honker Bay, Spoonbill Creek, and Suisun Bay (lat. 38°03'30" N, long. 121°54'45" W). Named on Honker Bay (1953) 7.5' quadrangle. Called Knox I. on Ringgold's (1850c) map.

Chiquita [SONOMA]: *locality,* 1.25 miles north of Healdsburg along Northwestern Pacific Railroad (lat. 38°38'05" N, long. 122°52'25" W). Named on Jimtown (1955) 7.5' quadrangle.

Chisholm Landing: see **Sulphur Creek** [ALAMEDA].

Chisnantuck: see **Mount Chisnantuck**, under **New Almaden** [SANTA CLARA].

Choual: see **Mount Choual**, under **Mount Chual** [SANTA CLARA].

Christie [CONTRA COSTA]: *locality,* 4 miles west-southwest of Martinez along Atchison, Topeka and Santa Fe Railroad (lat. 38° 00' N, long. 122°12'15" W). Named on Benicia (1959) and Briones Valley (1959) 7.5' quadrangles.

Christmas Hill [SANTA CLARA]: *relief feature,* 1.5 miles southwest of Gilroy (lat. 36°59'20" N, long. 121°35'05" W). Named on Chittenden (1955) 7.5' quadrangle.

Chrysopylae: see **Golden Gate** [SAN FRANCISCO].

Chual: see **Mount Chual** [SANTA CLARA].

Church Creek: see **Little Llagas Creek** [SANTA CLARA].

Church Hill [SANTA CLARA]: *peak,* nearly 1 mile west of New Almaden (lat. 37°10'40" N, long. 121°50'10" W). Named on Santa Teresa Hills (1953) 7.5' quadrangle.

Cincas Creek: see **Canoas Creek** [SANTA CLARA].

Cinnabar: see **Petaluma** [SONOMA] (2).

Clairville: see **Geyserville** [SONOMA].

Clam Beach [SONOMA]: *beach,* 0.5 mile west of Fort Ross along the coast (lat. 38°30'55" N, long. 123°15'10" W). Named on Plantation (1977) 7.5' quadrangle.

Clamshell Cut [SOLANO]: *water feature,* joins Miner Slough 10 miles north-northeast of Rio Vista (lat. 38°17'30" N, long. 121°37'15" W). Named on Vorden (1916) 7.5' quadrangle.

Clank Hollow [SOLANO]: *canyon,* 2 miles long, opens into lowlands 1 mile south-southeast of Birds Landing (2) (lat. 38°07'05" N, long. 121°51'55" W; sec. 9, T 3 N, R 1 E). Named on Antioch North (1978) 7.5' quadrangle.

Claremont Creek [ALAMEDA]: *stream,* flows 1.5 miles to lowlands 4 miles north-northeast of downtown Oakland (lat. 37°51'35" N, long. 122°14'25" W). Named on Oakland East (1959) 7.5' quadrangle. The stream was called Harwood Creek as late as 1889, and the canyon of the stream was called Telegraph Canyon until 1886 or 1887 (Mosier and Mosier, p. 23, 87).

Clark: see **Patty Clark Springs**, under **Bald Hills** [SONOMA].

Clark Canyon [ALAMEDA]: *canyon,* drained by a stream that flows 1 mile to lowlands 0.5 mile north of Dublin (lat. 37°42'35" N, long. 121°56'20" W). Named on Dublin (1961) 7.5' quadrangle.

Clark Creek [SONOMA]: *stream,* flows 1 mile to Laguna de Santa Rosa less than 1 mile north-northwest of Cotati (lat. 38°20'10" N, long. 122°42'40" W). Named on Santa Rosa (1954) 15' quadrangle.

Clarks Canyon [SANTA CLARA]: *canyon,* 1 mile long, branches west-northwest from North Fork Otis Canyon 4.5 miles south-southwest of Mount Sizer (lat. 37°09'25" N, long. 121°33'10" W; sec. 17, T 9 S, R 4 E). Named on Mount Sizer (1955) 7.5' quadrangle.

Clarks Crossing [SONOMA]: *locality,* 5 miles southeast of Annapolis along Wheatfield Fork Gualala River (lat. 38°39'55" N, long. 123°18'45" W; sec. 33, T 10 N, R 13 W). Named on Annapolis (1977) 7.5' quadrangle.

Clark's Point: see **Telegraph Hill** [SAN FRANCISCO].

Clayburn [CONTRA COSTA]: *locality,* 1 mile southeast of Point San Pablo (lat. 37°57'15" N, long. 122°24'45" W). Named on San Francisco (1942) 15' quadrangle. Postal authorities established Ladrillo post office in 1906, changed the name to Clayburn in 1907, and discontinued it in 1910; the name "Ladrillo" is from bricks that were made at the place—*ladrillo* means "brick" in Spanish; the name "Clayburn" refers to the burning of clay to make bricks (Salley, p. 45, 114).

Clayton [CONTRA COSTA]: *town,* 4.25 miles north-northwest of Mount Diablo (lat. 37°56'25" N, long. 121°56'05" W; near NE cor. sec. 14, T 1 N, R 1 W). Named on Clayton (1953) 7.5' quadrangle. Postal authorities established Clayton post office in 1861 (Frickstad, p. 21), and the town incorporated in 1964. The name commemorates Joel Clayton, who laid out the townsite in 1856 during the early days of the coal boom in the vicinity (Mosier, p. 5). Brewer (p. 198) noted in 1861 that the place first was called Deadfall. The community also was called Clayton's and Claytonville (Gudde, 1949, p. 70).

Clayton's: see **Clayton** [CONTRA COSTA].

Clayton Valley [CONTRA COSTA]: *valley,* 7 miles northwest of Mount Diablo along Mount Diablo Creek (lat. 37°58' N, long. 121° 59' W); Clayton is near the southeast end of the valley. Named on Clayton (1953) and Walnut Creek (1959) 7.5' quadrangles.

Claytonville: see **Clayton** [CONTRA COSTA].

Clear Creek [NAPA]: *stream,* flows 3 miles to Sage Canyon 6.25 miles north-northeast of Yountville (lat. 38°29'15" N, long. 122°18'30" W; sec. 4, T 7 N, R 4 W). Named on Chiles Valley (1958) and Yountville (1951) 7.5' quadrangles.

Clear Creek [SAN MATEO]: *stream,* flows 3 miles to San Gregorio Creek 4.5 miles west of La Honda (lat. 37°19'30" N, long. 122°21'20" W). Named on La Honda (1961) 7.5' quadrangle. The stream was called Arroyo Limpio and Raynor Creek in the early days—*limpio* means "clear" in Spanish; the name "Raynor" was for a rancher who lived along the stream in the 1860's and 1870's (Brown, p. 19).

Clifton Court Ferry [CONTRA COSTA]: *locality,* 7.5 miles east-southeast of Byron along Old River on Contra Costa-San Joaquin County line (lat. 37°47'35" N, long. 121°33' W). Named on Bethany (1952) 7.5' quadrangle.

Clifton Court Forebay [CONTRA COSTA]: *lake,* 2.5 miles long, 9 miles southeast of Brentwood (lat. 37°50'20" N, long. 121°34'30" W). Named on Clifton Court Forebay (1978) 7.5' quadrangle. Bethany (1952) 7.5' quadrangle shows an area called Clifton Court Tract at the site of the lake.

Clifton Court Tract: see **Clifton Court Forebay** [CONTRA COSTA].

Clima [SOLANO]: *locality,* 1.5 miles west of downtown Fairfield along Sacramento Northern Railroad (lat. 38°14'55" N, long. 122° 04'15" W). Named on Fairfield South (1949) 7.5' quadrangle.

Clinton: see **Oakland** [ALAMEDA].

Clinton Basin [ALAMEDA]: *water feature,* 1.5 miles south-southeast of downtown Oakland on the north side of Oakland Inner Harbor (lat. 37°47'20" N, long. 122°15'30" W). Named on Oakland West (1959) 7.5' quadrangle. The feature is at the site of the old community of Clinton.

Cloudy Bend [SONOMA]: *bend,* 5 miles east-southeast of downtown Petaluma along Petaluma River (lat. 38°12' N, long. 122°33'45" W). Named on Petaluma River (1954) 7.5' quadrangle.

Cloverdale [SONOMA]: *town,* 15 miles north-northwest of Healdsburg near Russian River (lat. 38°48'20" N, long. 123°00'55" W). Named on Cloverdale (1960) 7.5' quadrangle. Postal authorities established Cloverdale post office in 1857 (Frickstad, p. 195), and the town incorporated in 1872. The site first was known as Markle's Place and Markleville, for R.B. Markle, who owned land there; the name "Cloverdale" was given for wild fodder growing in the vicinity (Gudde, 1949, p. 71; Salley, p. 46). California Mining Bureau's (1909a) map shows a place called Throop situated west of Cloverdale about halfway to the coast. Postal authorities established Throop post office 18 miles west of Cloverdale in 1906, discontinued it in 1911, reestablished it in 1916, and discontinued it in 1918; the name was for Charles W. Throop, first postmaster (Salley, p. 221). California Division of Highways' (1934) map shows a place called McCrays located just north of Cloverdale.

Cloverdale Creek [SONOMA]: *stream,* flows 3 miles to Russian River at Cloverdale (lat. 38°48'25" N, long. 123°00'25" W). Named on Cloverdale (1960) 7.5' quadrangle.

Clyde [CONTRA COSTA]: *town,* 6 miles east of Martinez (lat. 38°01'40" N, long. 122°01'40" W; on S line sec. 12, T 2 N, R 2 W). Named on Vine Hill (1959) 7.5' quadrangle. The name is from Clyde Shipyard, which was at the place during World War I (Gudde, 1949, p. 71).

Coal Creek [SAN MATEO]: *stream,* flows nearly 1 mile to Corte Madera Creek 2.5 miles north-northeast of Mindego Hill (lat. 37° 20'40" N, long. 122°12'20" W). Named on Mindego Hill (1961) 7.5' quadrangle.

Coal Mine Creek: see **Arroyo Seco** [ALAMEDA].

Coal Mine Ridge [SAN MATEO]: *ridge,* northwest-trending, 3 miles long, 3 miles north-northeast of Mindego Hill (lat. 37°20'45" N, long. 122°12'05" W). Named on Mindego Hill (1961) 7.5' quadrangle. A small low-grade coal mine was opened on the ridge in 1855 (Brown, p. 20).

Coast Campground [MARIN]: *locality,* 4.5 miles southwest of Point Reyes Station along the coast (lat. 38°01' N, long. 122°51'15" W). Named on Inverness (1954, photorevised 1971) 7.5' quadrangle.

Coast Guard Island: see **Government Island** [ALAMEDA].

Cobb Creek [SONOMA]: *stream,* flows 3 miles to Big Sulphur Creek 3.25 miles northeast of Geyser Peak (lat. 38°47'35" N, long. 122°47'40" W; sec. 19, T 11 N, R 8 W). Named on The Geysers (1959) 7.5' quadrangle.

Cobb Mountain Range: see **Mayacmas Mountains** [NAPA-SONOMA].

Cochiyunes: see **San Pablo** [CONTRA COSTA] (1).

Codornices Creek [ALAMEDA]: *stream,* flows 1.25 miles to land fill along San Francisco Bay 5.5 miles north-northwest of downtown Oakland (lat. 37°52'55" N, long. 122°18'25" W), and continues in an artificial watercourse around Golden Gate Fields racetrack. Named on Richmond (1959) 7.5' quadrangle. Jose Domingo Peralta named the stream in 1818 after he and his brother found a nest of quail eggs on its bank—*codorniz* means "quail" in Spanish (Gudde, 1949, p. 73). United States Board on Geographic Names (1933, p. 227) rejected the form "Cordonices Creek" for the name.

Coe's Spring: see **Madrone Soda Springs** [SANTA CLARA].

Coffey Mill Gulch [ALAMEDA-SANTA CLARA]: *canyon,* drained by a stream that heads in Santa Clara County and flows nearly 3 miles to Eylar Canyon 4.5 miles south of Cedar Mountain in Alameda County (lat. 37°29'30" N, long. 121°36'05" W; near S line sec. 13, T 5 S, R 3 E). Named on Eylar Mountain (1955) 7.5' quadrangle.

Cold Canyon [SOLANO]: *canyon,* drained by a stream that flows 2.5 miles to Putah Creek 7.5 miles north of Mount Vaca (lat. 38°30'45" N, long. 122°05'45" W; near W line sec. 28, T 8 N, R 2 W). Named on Monticello Dam (1959) and Mount Vaca (1951) 7.5' quadrangles.

Cold Flat [SANTA CLARA]: *area,* nearly 1 mile north of Mount Sizer along East Fork Coyote Creek (lat. 37°13'35" N, long. 121° 30'45" W). Named on Mount Sizer (1955) 7.5' quadrangle.

Cold Spring [NAPA]: *spring,* 5 miles northeast of Calistoga (lat. 38° 37'10" N, long. 122°30'05" W; near NW cor. sec. 23, T 9 N, R 6 W). Named on Calistoga (1958) 7.5' quadrangle.

Cold Springs [SONOMA]: *springs,* 1.25 miles southeast of Geyser Peak (lat. 38°45'10" N, long. 122°49'25" W; sec. 2, T 10 N, R 9 W). Named on The Geysers (1959) 7.5' quadrangle.

Cold Springs Creek: see **Agua Fria Creek** [ALAMEDA].

Cold Stream [MARIN]: *stream,* flows 1 mile to the sea 5 miles east-southeast of Bolinas (lat. 37°52'35" N, long. 122°36'15" W). Named on San Rafael (1954) 7.5' quadrangle.

Coldwater Canyon [SONOMA]: *canyon,* drained by a stream that flows 1 mile to Squaw Creek 4.5 miles north of Geyser Peak (lat. 38°49'50" N, long. 122°49'35" W; sec. 2, T 11 N, R 9 W). Named on The Geysers (1959) 7.5' quadrangle.

Coldwater Creek: see **Iverson Creek** [SAN MATEO].

Coldwater Gulch [SONOMA]: *canyon,* drained by a stream that flows 0.5 mile to Mill Creek (1) 6.5 miles north-northeast of Guerneville (lat. 38°35'35" N, long. 122°57'45" W). Named on Guerneville (1955) 7.5' quadrangle.

Cole Flat [NAPA]: *area,* 2.25 miles south-southwest of Rutherford (lat. 38°28'25" N, long. 122°29'20" W; near N line sec. 11, T 7 N, R 6 W). Named on Rutherford (1951) 7.5' quadrangle.

Coleman Beach [SONOMA]: *beach,* 2.5 miles north-northwest of the village of Bodega Bay along the coast (lat. 38°21'55" N, long. 123° 04'15" W). Named on Bodega Head (1972) 7.5' quadrangle.

Coleman Canyon [NAPA]: *canyon,* drained by a stream that flows 1 mile to Wragg Canyon 6.25 miles north-northwest of Mount Vaca (lat. 38°28'55" N, long. 122°09'30" W; sec. 2, T 7 N, R 3 W). Named on Capell Valley (1951) 7.5' quadrangle.

Coleman Field [SONOMA]: *area,* nearly 7 miles south-southwest of Big Mountain (lat. 38°37'35" N, long. 123°12'50" W; near NW cor. sec. 17, T 9 N, R 12 W). Named on Tombs Creek (1978) 7.5' quadrangle.

Coleman Hill [SONOMA]: *ridge,* west-northwest-trending, 1 mile long, 1.5 miles north of the village of Bodega Bay (lat. 38°21'15" N, long. 123°02'45" W). Named on Bodega Head (1972) 7.5' quadrangle.

Coleman Valley [SONOMA]: *valley,* 2.25 miles west of Occidental (lat. 38°24'25" N, long. 122°59'20" W). Named on Camp Meeker (1954) 7.5' quadrangle. The place first was called Kolmer Valley for Michael Kolmer, who settled there in 1848 (Gudde, 1949, p. 74).

Coleman Valley Creek [SONOMA]: *stream,* flows 5.5 miles to Salmon Creek (1) 2.5 miles northeast of the village of Bodega Bay (lat. 38°21'40" N, long. 123°00'55" W); the stream goes through Coleman Valley. Named on Bodega Head (1972), Camp Meeker (1954), and Duncans Mills (1979)

7.5' quadrangles.

Colijolmanoc: see **Carne Humana** [NAPA].

College Park [SANTA CLARA]: *district,* 1 mile northwest of downtown San Jose (lat. 37°20'30" N, long. 121°54'15" W). Named on San Jose West (1961) 7.5' quadrangle. The district was named for its proximity to College of the Pacific, which later moved to Stockton, California (Harry Farrell, *San Jose Mercury News,* January 6, 1980). Postal authorities established College Park post office in 1888 and changed the name to Substation No. 1 [of San Jose post office] in 1899 (Salley, p. 48).

College Terrace: see **Palo Alto** [SANTA CLARA].

Collier Canyon [ALAMEDA-CONTRA COSTA]: *canyon,* drained by a stream that heads in Contra Costa County and flows 4 miles to lowlands 3 miles northwest of Livermore in Alameda County (lat. 37°42'40" N, long. 121°48'15" W). Named on Livermore (1961) and Tassajara (1953) 7.5' quadrangles. The name commemorates Michael McCollier, who settled in the canyon in 1856 (Mosier and Mosier, p. 24).

Collier Spring [MARIN]: *spring,* 4.5 miles southwest of downtown San Rafael (lat. 37°55'50" N, long. 122°35'35" W). Named on San Rafael (1954) 7.5' quadrangle. Teather (p. 17) associated the name with John Munro Colier, who hiked and worked on trails in the neighborhood of Mount Tamalpais.

Collins [NAPA]: *locality,* 1.5 miles south of Napa Junction along Southern Pacific Railroad (lat. 38°09'55" N, long. 122°15'05" W; sec. 25, T 4 N, R 4 W). Named on Cuttings Wharf (1949) 7.5' quadrangle.

Collinsville [SOLANO]: *village,* 4 miles south-southeast of Birds Landing (2) near the mouth of Sacramento River (lat. 38°04'40" N, long. 121°51' W). Named on Antioch North (1978) 7.5' quadrangle. Postal authorities established Collinsville post office in 1862, discontinued it the same year, reestablished it in 1864, changed the name to Newport in 1867, and discontinued it in 1868; they reestablished Collinsville post office in 1871, discontinued it for a time in 1876, and discontinued it finally in 1960 (Salley, p. 48, 154). The name commemorates C.F. Collins, who settled in the neighborhood in 1856 and filed a map of the City of Collinsville in 1862 (Hoover, Rensch, and Rensch, p. 513-514). Ringgold's (1850c) map has the name "Montezuma House" east of the site of present Collinsville. In 1846 Lansford W. Hastings laid out a town and erected a building that he called Montezuma House about 1.25 miles east of present Collinsville, but this town failed to develop (Hoover, Rensch, and Rensch, p. 513).

Colma [SAN MATEO]: *village,* 3.5 miles west-northwest of downtown South San Francisco (lat. 37°40'30" N, long. 122°27'15" W). Named on San Francisco South (1956) 7.5' quadrangle. San Mateo (1942) 15' quadrangle has the name "Lawndale" at present Colma, and the name "Colma" at present Daly City. According to Stanger (1963, p. 157-158), a village called Colma began in present Daly City as an American farming center, but little by little it was annexed by Daly City until nothing was left but the name and post office; southeast of the village site some farmers and the proprietors of a group of cemeteries decided in 1924 to incorporate their property to avoid annexation by neighboring towns, and they chose the name "Lawndale" for their incorporated area, but because there already was a Lawndale post office in California, the newly incorporated area could not have a post office by that name; instead, the place took the name "Colma" from the already established post office in nearby Daly City. Postal authorities established Schoolhouse Station post office in 1869, changed the name to Colma Station in 1888, and changed it to Colma in 1943; the name "Colma" was coined from letters in the name of Thomas Coleman, a pioneer settler (Salley, p. 48, 199).

Colma Creek [SAN MATEO]: *stream,* flows nearly 6 miles to San Francisco Bay 1.25 miles east-southeast of downtown South San Francisco (lat. 37°38'55" N, long. 122°23'25" W); the creek goes through Colma. Named on San Francisco South (1956) 7.5' quadrangle. The stream was called Arroyo de San Bruno in Spanish times, and later it was called San Bruno Creek and Twelve Mile Creek (Brown, p. 21-22).

Colma Station: see **Colma** [SAN MATEO].

Colony: see **Moss Beach** [SAN MATEO].

Colorado Camp [SANTA CLARA]: *locality,* 2 miles south of Eylar Mountain (lat. 37°26'40" N, long. 121°32'25" W; near N line sec. 4, T 6 S, R 4 E); the place is along Colorado Creek. Named on Eylar Mountain (1955) 7.5' quadrangle.

Colorado Creek [SANTA CLARA]: *stream,* flows 11 miles to Arroyo Valle 2.5 miles east-southeast of Eylar Mountain (lat. 37°27'55" N, long. 121°35'35" W; sec. 25, T 5 S, R 3 E). Named on Eylar Mountain (1955) 7.5' quadrangle.

Colorado Ledge: see **Point Montara** [SAN MATEO].

Colorado Reef: see **Point Montara** [SAN MATEO].

Commission Rock: see **Mare Island Strait** [SOLANO].

Commodore Jones Point [SOLANO]: *promontory,* 1 mile northwest of downtown Benicia along Carquinez Strait (lat. 38°03'30" N, long. 122°10'25" W). Named on Benicia (1959, photorevised 1980) 7.5' quadrangle. The name commemorates Commodore Thomas ap Catesby Jones, United States Navy, who brought the storeship *Southampton* to Benicia in 1849 (United States Board on Geographic Names, 1975b, p. 4). Ringgold's (1850e) map has the name "Littles Pt." at or near present Commodore Jones Point, and has the name "Coopers Pt." for the next promontory to the southeast.

Comstock Canyon [SANTA CLARA]: *canyon,* drained by a stream that flows 1 mile to Wildcat Canyon (2) 18 miles east of Gilroy (lat. 36°57'35" N, long. 121°14'35" W). Named on Mariposa Peak (1969) 7.5' quadrangle.

Concord [CONTRA COSTA]: *city,* 5.25 miles north-northeast of Walnut Creek civic center (lat. 37°58'40" N, long. 122°01'50" W). Named on Walnut Creek (1959) 7.5' quadrangle. Postal authorities established Concord post office in 1872 (Frickstad, p. 21), and the city incorporated in 1905. Salvio Pacheco, owner of Monte del Diablo grant, founded the community and called it Todos Santos, but the strong New England influence of the population soon changed the name (Gudde, 1949, p. 76).

Cone Rock [MARIN]: *rock,* 1 mile east-northeast of downtown Sausalito near the mouth of Richardson Bay (lat. 37°51'50" N, long. 122°28'10" W). Named on San Francisco North (1956) 7.5' quadrangle.

Coney Island [CONTRA COSTA]: *island,* 2 miles long, 10 miles southeast of Brentwood along Old River (lat. 37°50'45" N, long. 121°32'50" W). Named on Clifton Court Forebay (1978) 7.5' quadrangle.

Congress Heights: see **Congress Springs** [SANTA CLARA].

Congress Junction: see **Champagne Fountain** [SANTA CLARA].

Congress Spring: see **Congress Valley** [NAPA].

Congress Springs [SANTA CLARA]: *locality,* 1 mile west of Saratoga along Campbell Creek (present Saratoga Creek) (lat. 37°15'05" N, long. 122°03'10" W; sec. 11, T 8 S, R 2 W). Named on Palo Alto (1899, reprinted 1930) 15' quadrangle. Palo Alto (1899) 15' quadrangle has the name "Congress Heights" at the site. A resort at the place opened to the public in 1866 and featured mineral springs discovered in the early 1850's; the resort closed in 1942 (Hoover, Rensch, and Rensch, p. 458). The place also was called Pacific Congress Springs, a name given because the water there was considered similar to water from the noted Congress Springs at Saratoga, New York (Anderson, Winslow, p. 213).

Congress Springs Canyon [SANTA CLARA]: *canyon,* drained by a stream that flows 1.5 miles to Saratoga Creek 1.25 miles west-southwest of Saratoga (lat. 37°15'05" N, long. 122°03'05" W; sec. 11, T 8 S, R 2 W); the mouth of the canyon is near the site of Congress Springs. Named on Castle Rock Ridge (1955) 7.5' quadrangle.

Congress Valley [NAPA]: *valley,* 2.5 miles west-southwest of downtown Napa (lat. 38°17'15" N, long. 122°19'45" W). Named on Napa (1951) 7.5' quadrangle. Waring (p. 156) listed Congress Spring, a spring of carbonated saline water located 3.5 miles southwest of Napa.

Conn Creek [NAPA]: *stream,* flows 20 miles to Napa River 1 mile northeast of Yountville (lat. 38°25'10" N, long. 122°21'10" W). Named on Rutherford (1951), Saint Helena (1960), and Yountville (1951) 7.5' quadrangles. Called Sage Creek on Pope Valley (1921) 15' quadrangle.

Conn Valley [NAPA]: *valley,* 4.5 miles east of Saint Helena (lat. 38° 30'30" N, long. 122°24'10" W); the valley is along Conn Creek. Named on Saint Helena (1960) 7.5' quadrangle. The name commemorates John Conn, who came to California in 1843 (Gudde, 1949, p. 77). Water of Lake Hennessey now covers part of the valley.

Conn Valley Reservoir: see **Lake Hennessey** [NAPA].

Conshea Creek [SONOMA]: *stream,* flows 1 mile to East Austin Creek 4.5 miles north of Cazadero (lat. 38°35'40" N, long. 123°05'05" W; near W line sec. 28, T 9 N, R 11 W). Named on Cazadero (1978) 7.5' quadrangle. Called Canshea Creek on Cazadero (1943) 7.5' quadrangle, which also has this name for present Tiny Creek, a tributary of present Conshea Creek.

Consolation Cove: see **Horesehoe Bay** [MARIN].

Consolli Gulch [SONOMA]: *canyon,* drained by a stream that flows 0.5 mile to Austin Creek 4 miles northeast of Jenner (lat. 38°29'05" N, long. 123°03'30" W). Named on Duncans Mills (1979) 7.5' quadrangle.

Contra Costa: see **Oakland** [ALAMEDA].

Contra Costa Hills: see **Berkeley Hills** [ALAMEDA-CONTRA COSTA].

Conyer Gulch: see **Soda Spring Canyon** [SANTA CLARA].

Cook: see **Dan Cook Canyon** [CONTRA COSTA].

Cook Canyon [ALAMEDA]: *canyon,* drained by a stream that flows 1.5 miles to Palomares Creek 4 miles southwest of Dublin (lat. 37° 39'50" N, long. 121°59'35" W; sec. 20, T 3 S, R 1 W). Named on Dublin (1961) 7.5' quadrangle. The name commemorates Charles Cook and Annie L. Cook, local ranchers (Mosier and Mosier, p. 25).

Cook Canyon [SOLANO]: *canyon,* drained by a stream that flows nearly 2 miles to Green Valley Creek 7 miles west-northwest of Fairfield (lat. 38°16'35" N, long. 122°09'45" W; sec. 14, T 5 N, R 3 W). Named on Mount George (1951) 7.5' quadrangle.

Cooksley Lake [NAPA]: *lake,* 750 feet long, 6.5 miles north of Saint Helena (lat. 38°36' N, long. 122°28'25" W; sec. 25, T 9 N, R 6 W). Named on Saint Helena (1960) 7.5' quadrangle.

Cooks Peak [SONOMA]: *peak,* 4 miles south-southeast of downtown Santa Rosa (lat. 38°23'30" N, long. 122°40'35" W). Named on Santa Rosa (1954) 7.5' quadrangle.

Cook's Pond: see **Santa Clara** [SANTA CLARA].

Cooley: see **Camp Cooley** [SANTA CLARA].

Cooley Landing [SAN MATEO]: *locality,* 5.5 miles east of downtown Redwood City along San Francisco Bay (lat. 37°28'35" N, long. 122°07'15" W). Named on Mountain View (1961) 7.5' quadrangle. Ravenswood Wharf was built at the site in the 1850's (Hoover, Rensch, and Rensch, p. 406).

Coon Creek [SANTA CLARA]: *stream,* flows 5.25 miles to North Fork Pacheco Creek 8.5 miles north-northwest of Pacheco Peak (lat. 37°07'25" N, long. 121°20'25" W; sec. 29, T 9 S, R 6 E). Named on Mustang Peak (1955) 7.5' quadrangle.

Coon Creek [SONOMA]: *stream,* flows nearly 3 miles to Briggs Creek 4.5 miles west of Mount Saint Helena (lat. 38°40'35" N, long. 122°42'45" W; near N line sec. 35, T 10 N, R 8 W). Named on Mount Saint Helena (1959) 7.5' quadrangle.

Coon Hunters Gulch [SANTA CLARA]: *canyon,* drained by a stream that flows nearly 5 miles to Hunting Hollow 3.5 miles south-southeast of Gilroy Hot Springs (lat. 37°03'50" N, long. 121°26'30" W; sec. 17, T 10 S, R 5 E). Named on Gilroy Hot Springs (1955) 7.5' quadrangle, where the name may apply only to the canyon along the lower 2.5 miles of the stream.

Coon Island [NAPA]: *marsh,* 4 miles west of Napa Junction between Napa Slough and Mud Slough (lat. 38°11'30" N, long. 122°19'15" W; sec. 17, T 4 N, R 4 W). Named on Cuttings Wharf (1949) 7.5' quadrangle.

Coopers Point: see **Commodore Jones Point** [SOLANO].

Copeland Creek [SONOMA]: *stream,* flows 6 miles to lowlands 2.5 miles east-northeast of Cotati (lat. 38°20'35" N, long. 122°40' W). Named on Cotati (1954) and Glen Ellen (1954) 7.5' quadrangles.

Copernicus Peak [SANTA CLARA]: *peak,* nearly 1 mile east-northeast of Mount Hamilton (lat. 37°20'50" N, long. 121°37'45" W; sec. 10, T 7 S, R 3 E). Named on Lick Observatory (1955) 7.5' quadrangle. The staff of Lick Observatory on nearby Mount Hamilton named the peak in 1895 for Nicolaus Copernicus (Gudde, 1949, p. 78).

Copper Mine Gulch [MARIN]: *canyon,* drained by a stream that heads on Bolinas Ridge and flows southwesterly for 2 miles to Pine Gulch Creek 3 miles north-northwest of Bolinas (lat. 37°56'50" N, long. 122°42'50" W). Named on Bolinas (1954) 7.5' quadrangle. Two or three companies worked on copper prospects in the neighborhood in 1863 (Laizure, 1926, p. 320). United States Board on Geographic Names (1980, p. 3-4) approved names for several canyons that lie parallel to Copper Mine Gulch: Lewis Gulch, located between Copper Mine Gulch and Wilkins Gulch, and named for the Lewis family who lived in the canyon in the late nineteenth century; Cronin Gulch, situated 0.25 mile northwest of Copper Mine Gulch; Cottinham Gulch, located 1.25 miles northwest of Copper Mine Gulch; and Mill Gulch, located 1.5 miles northwest of Copper Mine Gulch and named in 1979 for a sawmill that was at the mouth of the canyon. At the same time the Board approved the name "Pecks Ridge" for the ridge southeast of Cottinham Gulch.

Coppinger Creek: see **Bear Creek** [SAN MATEO] (2).

Corall Hollow: see **Corral Hollow** [ALAMEDA].

Cordelia [SOLANO]: *village,* 6 miles west-southwest of Fairfield (lat. 38°12'40" N, long. 122°08' W; on W line sec. 7, T 4 N, R 2 W). Named on Cordelia (1951) 7.5' quadrangle. Postal authorities established Cordelia post office in 1854, discontinued it in 1858, reestablished it in 1869, and discontinued it in 1943 (Salley, p. 50). The name was given to honor the wife of the founder of Fairfield, Captain Robert H. Waterman; in 1868 the original community of Cordelia moved a short distance south to a shipping point known as Bridgeport, which was along the railroad (Hoover, Rensch, and Rensch, p. 519). The name "Bridgeport" was for Bridgeport, Connecticut (Gudde, 1949, p. 78).

Cordelia Junction [SOLANO]: *locality,* 0.5 mile north-northwest of Cordelia (lat. 38°13' N, long. 122°08'15" W; near SE cor. sec. 1, T 4 N, R 3 W). Named on Cordelia (1951) 7.5' quadrangle.

Cordelia Slough [SOLANO]: *water feature,* joins Suisun Slough 8 miles south-southwest of Fairfield (lat. 38°08'10" N, long. 122°04'55" W). Named on Fairfield South (1949) 7.5' quadrangle.

Cordell Bank [MARIN]: *shoal,* 22 miles west of the lighthouse at Point Reyes (lat. 38°02' N, long. 123°26' W). Named on Santa Rosa (1958) 1°x 2° quadrangle. Captain Edward Cordell explored the feature in 1869 and named it Sutter Bank to honor John A. Sutter; members of United States Coast Survey renamed the shoal for Captain Cordell after Cordell's death in 1870 (Gudde, 1969, p. 74-75).

Cordero Junction [SOLANO]: *locality,* 5 miles south-southeast of Vacaville along Sacramento Northern Railroad (lat. 38°17'15" N, long. 121°57'15" W; near S line sec. 10, T 5 N, R 1 W). Named on Elmira (1953) 7.5' quadrangle.

Cordilleras Creek [SAN MATEO]: *stream,* flows 3.5 miles to lowlands along San Francisco Bay 1 mile west-northwest of downtown Redwood City (lat. 37°29'20" N, long. 122°14'45" W). Named on Palo Alto (1961) and Woodside (1961) 7.5' quadrangles. Brown (p. 33) called the stream Finger Creek, and noted that this name commemorates Theodore Finger, who settled near the creek in 1855; other names for the feature were Finger's Arroyo and Arroyo de los Cadillos—*Arroyo de los Cadillos* has the meaning "Cockleburr Creek" in Spanish.

Cordonices Creek: see **Codornices Creek** [ALAMEDA].

Cordoza Canyon [SANTA CLARA]: *canyon,* drained by a stream that flows nearly 2 miles to North Fork Otis Canyon 4.5 miles south-southeast of Mount Sizer (lat. 37°09'25" N, long. 121°33'10" W; sec. 17, T 9 S, R 4 E); the canyon heads on Cordoza Ridge. Named on Mount Sizer (1955) 7.5' quadrangle.

Cordoza Ridge [SANTA CLARA]: *ridge,* north- to northwest-trending, 1 mile long, 3.5 miles south of Mount Sizer (lat. 37°10' N, long. 121°31'30" W). Named on Mount Sizer (1955) 7.5' quadrangle.

Corinda Los Trancos [SAN MATEO]: *ridge,* southeast- to southwest-trending, 2 miles long, 5.5 miles southeast of Monara Knob (lat. 37°30'45" N, long. 122°24'20" W). Named on Montara Mountain (1956) 7.5' quadrangle.

Corinda Los Trancos Creek [SAN MATEO]: *stream,* flows 2.5 miles to Pilarcitos Creek 1.5 miles northeast of downtown Half Moon Bay (lat. 37°28'45" N, long. 122°24'15" W); the stream is east of the ridge called Corinda Los Trancos. Named on Half Moon Bay (1961) and Montara Mountain (1956) 7.5' quadrangles. According to Brown (p. 95), the stream should be called Trancas Creek—its original name was Arroyo de las Trancas.

Corkscrew Creek: see **Corkscrew Slough** [SAN MATEO].

Corkscrew Slough [SAN MATEO]: *water feature,* extends for nearly 4 miles along a circuitous course from Steinberger Slough to Redwood Creek 3 miles north-northeast of downtown Redwood City (lat. 37°31'25" N, long. 122°12'20" W). Named on Redwood Point (1959) 7.5' quadrangle. Called Corkscrew Cr. on Hayward (1915) 15' quadrangle.

Corneros Creek: see **Carneros Creek** [NAPA].

Cornwall: see **Pittsburg** [CONTRA COSTA].

Cornwall Station: see **Pittsburg** [CONTRA COSTA].

Corona [SONOMA]: *locality,* 5 miles south-southeast of Cotati along Petaluma and Santa Rosa Railroad (lat. 38°15'50" N, long. 122°39'30" W). Named on Santa Rosa (1944) 15' quadrangle.

Corporal [SANTA CLARA]: *locality,* about 5.5 miles south-southeast of Gilroy along Southern Pacific Railroad (lat. 36°55'45" N, long. 121°32'50" W). Named on Chittenden (1955) 7.5' quadrangle.

Corral de Tierra [SAN MATEO]:

(1) *land grant,* north of the north end of Half Moon Bay (1). Named on Half Moon Bay (1961) and Montara Mountain (1956) 7.5' quadrangles. Francisco Guerrero y Palomares received 1 league in 1839 and his heirs claimed 7766 acres patented in 1866 (Cowan, p. 103). According to Perez (p. 63), Francisco Palomeres was the grantee in 1844, and Josefa Guerrero was the patentee in 1866.

(2) *land grant,* north of the town of Half Moon Bay. Named on Half Moon Bay (1961) and Montara Mountain (1956) 7.5' quadrangles. Tiburcio Vasquez received 1 league in 1839 and claimed 4436 acres patented in 1873 (Cowan, p. 103).

Corral de Tierra: see **Pillar Point** [SAN MATEO].

Corral Hollow [ALAMEDA]: *canyon,* 10 miles long, 5.5 miles south of Midway on Alameda-San Joaquin County line (lat. 37°38'10" N, long. 121°33'20" W). Named on Midway (1953) 7.5' quadrangle. Called Corall Hollow on Goddard's (1857) map, and called Arroyo Buenos Ayres on Thompson and West's (1879) map. The feature is called Portezuela de Buenos Ayres on a Mexican map of 1834 (Gudde, 1949, p. 79). According to Mosier and Mosier (p. 25), the name "Corral" is from horse corrals built in the 1850's to hold captured wild horses, but Latta (1949, p. 234) cited a statement made by Mrs. Mamie Carroll Burns that the canyon was named for her stepfather, Edward Carroll.

Corral Hollow Creek [ALAMEDA]: *stream,* heads in San Joaquin County and flows 11 miles in Alameda County before reentering San Joaquin County 5.5 miles south of Midway (lat. 37°38'10" N, long. 121°33'20" W; at S line sec. 29, T 3 S, R 4 E); the stream goes through Corral Hollow. Named on Cedar Mountain (1956) and Midway (1953) 7.5' quadrangles. United States Board on Geographic Names (1933, p. 237) rejected the name "Buenos Ayres Creek" for the stream.

Corral Valley: see **Wooden Valley** [NAPA].

Corte de Madera Creek: see **Corte Madera Creek** [SAN MATEO]; **Sausal Creek** [SAN MATEO].

Corte de Madera del Presidio [MARIN]: *land grant,* at Corte Madera and Tiburon Peninsula. Named on San Quentin (1959) and San Rafael (1954) 7.5' quadrangles. John Reed received the land in 1834 and his heirs claimed 7845 acres patented in 1885 (Cowan, p. 30). The name is from lumber that was sent from the place to the presidio at San Francisco—*corte de madera* means "place where wood is cut" in Spanish (Gudde, 1949, p. 80).

Corte de Madera de Novato: see **Corte Madera de Novato** [MARIN].

Corte Madera [MARIN]: *town,* 3.25 miles south of downtown San Rafael (lat. 37°55'35" N, long. 122°31'40" W); the town is on Corte de Madera del Presidio grant. Named on San Quentin (1959) and San Rafael (1954) 7.5' quadrangles. Postal authorities established Corte Madera post office in 1878 and discontinued it in 1880; they established Adams post office, named for postmaster Jerry Adams, at the place in 1902 and changed the name to Corte Madera the same year (Salley, p. 1, 51). The town incorporated in 1916.

Corte Madera Channel: see **Corte Madera Creek** [MARIN].

Corte Madera Creek [MARIN]: *stream,* formed by the confluence of San Anselmo Creek and Rose Creek, flows 4.5 miles to San Francisco Bay 2.5 miles southeast of downtown San Rafael (lat. 37°56'35" N, long. 122°30'10" W). Named on San Rafael (1954) 7.5' quadrangle. United States Board on Geographic Names (1983c, p. 4) approved the name "Corte Madera Channel" for the waterway that extends for 2.25 miles from the mouth of Corte Madera Creek into San Francisco Bay.

Corte Madera Creek [SAN MATEO]: *stream,* flows 6.25 miles to marsh near Searsville Lake 6.25 miles south of downtown Redwood City (lat. 37°23'45" N, long. 122°14' W); the stream is on El Corte de Madera grant and on Cañada del Corte Madera grant. Named on Mindego Hill (1961) and Palo Alto (1961) 7.5' quadrangles. United States Board on Geographic Names (1939, p. 11) rejected the name "Corte de Madera Creek" for the feature. It was called Jones Creek in the 1850's and 1860's for Nathan Jones, a rancher (Brown, p. 23).

Corte Madera de Novato [MARIN]: *land grant,* 6 miles west-northwest of downtown Novato along Novato Creek. Named on Petaluma (1953) and San Geronimo (1954) 7.5' quadrangles. John Martin received 1 league in 1839 and claimed 8879 acres patented in 1863 (Cowan, p. 30; Cowan listed the grant under the name "Corte de Madera de Novato"). According to Perez (p. 63), the patent was issued in 1862.

Corte Madera Lake: see **Bear Gulch Reservoir** [SAN MATEO].

Corte Madera Ridge [MARIN]: *ridge,* southeast-trending, 1.25 mile long, 3.5 miles south of downtown San Rafael (lat. 37°55'20" N, long. 122°32'15" W); the ridge is southwest of Corte Madera. Named on San Rafael (1954) 7.5' quadrangle.

Costa: see **Port Costa** [CONTRA COSTA].

Cotate [SONOMA]: *land grant,* at and near Cotati. Named on Cotati (1954) and Santa Rosa (1954) 7.5' quadrangles. Juan Castañeda received 4 leagues in 1844; T.S. Page claimed 17,239 acres patented in 1858 (Cowan, p. 30). The name is from the chief of an Indian village on the grant (Mullen).

Cotati [SONOMA]: *town,* 7.5 miles south of Santa Rosa (lat. 38°19'35" N, long. 122°42'20" W); the town is on Cotate grant. Named on Cotati (1954) 7.5' quadrangle, which shows Cotati siding situated nearly 1 mile east-northeast of the center of the town along Northwestern Pacific Railroad. The railroad stop at Cotati originally was called Page's Station, for Dr. Thomas Stokes Page, owner of Cotate grant (Mullen). Postal authorities established Cotati post office in 1894 (Frickstad, p. 195), and the town incorporated in 1963.

Cotati Plain: see **Cotati Valley** [SONOMA].

Cotati Valley [SONOMA]: *valley,* between Cotati and Sonoma Mountains (lat. 38°19'30" N, long. 122°41'30" W). Named on Santa Rosa (1944) 15' quadrangle. Cardwell's (1958) map has the name "Cotati Plain" for the feature.

Cottinham Gulch [MARIN]: see **Copper Mine Gulch** [MARIN].

Cottonwood Canyon: see **Doolan Canyon** [ALAMEDA].

Cottonwood Creek [ALAMEDA-CONTRA COSTA]: *stream,* heads in Contra Costa County and flows 4.5 miles to lowlands 3.5 miles west-southwest of Livermore in Alameda County (lat. 37°42'10" N, long. 121°49'40" W); the creek drains Doolan Canyon, which originally was called Cottonwood Canyon. Named on Livermore (1961) 7.5' quadrangle. The stream first was called Los Alamos Creek, and then Alamo Creek (Mosier and Mosier, p. 25-26).

Cottrell [SAN MATEO]: *locality,* 3 miles southeast of downtown San Mateo along Southern Pacific Railroad (lat. 37°32' N, long. 122° 17'40" W). Named on San Mateo (1915) 15' quadrangle. The place was called Laurel Creek before about 1890 (Brown, p. 83).

Country Club Branch [ALAMEDA]: *stream,* flows 2 miles to Rifle Range Branch 7.5 miles east-southeast of downtown Oakland (lat. 37°45'25" N, long. 122°08'50" W). Named on Oakland East (1959) 7.5' quadrangle. The name is from Sequoyah Country Club, through which the stream flows (Mosier and Mosier, p. 26).

County Line: see **El Cerito** [CONTRA COSTA].

Cove: see **The Cove** [NAPA].

Cow Canyon [SANTA CLARA]: *canyon,* drained by a stream that flows 4.5 miles to Pine Spring Canyon 7 miles north of Pacheco Peak (lat. 37°06'30" N, long. 121°17'40" W; sec. 34, T 9 S, R 6 E). Named on Mustang Peak (1955) and Pacheco Peak (1955) 7.5' quadrangles.

Cow Creek [SANTA CLARA]: *stream,* flows nearly 4 miles to San Felipe Creek 6 miles south of Mount Hamilton (lat. 37°15'25" N, long. 121°39'20" W); the stream heads at Cow Hill. Named on Isabel Valley (1955) and Lick Observatory (1955) 7.5' quadrangles.

Cow Creek [SONOMA]: *stream,* flows nearly 1 mile to Danfield Creek 6 miles south-southwest of Big Mountain (lat. 38°38'05" N, long. 123°11'25" W; sec. 9, T 9 N, R 12 W). Named on Tombs Creek (1978) 7.5' quadrangle.

Cowell [CONTRA COSTA]: *locality,* 6.5 miles northwest of Mount Diablo (lat. 37°57'10" N, long. 121°59'20" W). Named on Clayton (1953) 7.5' quadrangle. Postal authorities established Cowell post office in 1922 and discontinued it in 1969; the name is for Joshua Cowell, who gave right of way at the place to Bay Point and Clayton Railroad (Salley, p. 52). Cowell was a company town for a cement operation (Hoover, Rensch, and Rensch, p. 67).

Cow Hill [SANTA CLARA]: *ridge,* north- to northwest-trending, 3 miles long, 4.5 miles south-southeast of Mount Isabel (lat. 37°15'25" N, long. 121°35'55" W). Named on Isabel Valley (1955) and Mount Sizer (1955) 7.5' quadrangles.

Cow Hollow: see **Marina District** [SAN FRANCISCO].

Coyote [SANTA CLARA]: *village,* 12 miles southeast of downtown San Jose along Coyote Creek (lat. 37°13' N, long. 121°44'15" W). Named on Morgan Hill (1955) 7.5' quadrangle. The community now is part of San Jose. Thompson and West's (1876) map has the names "Coyote Station" and "12 Mile House" at the place. Coyote was the site of a travelers stop called Laguna House, or Twelve Mile House, that operated as early as 1853 along the road south from San Jose (Hoover, Rensch, and Rensch, p. 431). Postal authorities established Burnett post office in 1862 and operated it until 1882, when they moved it and changed the name to Coyote; the name "Burnett" was for Peter H. Burnett, first governor of the state (Salley, p. 30).

Coyote: see **South Coyote** [SANTA CLARA]; **The Coyote**, under **Coyote Point** [SAN MATEO].

Coyote Creek [ALAMEDA-SANTA CLARA]: *stream,* formed by the confluence of East Fork and Middle Fork in Santa Clara County, flows 62 miles to the southeast end of San Francisco Bay 5 miles north-northeast of downtown Mountain View (lat. 37°27'30" N, long. 122°03' W). Near the bay, the stream marks part of Alameda-Santa Clara County line. Named on San Francisco (1956) and San Jose (1962) 1°x 2° quadrangles. Called Coyote River on New Almaden (1919) and San Jose (1899) 15' quadrangles, but United States Board on Geographic Names (1943, p. 10-11) decided against the names "Coyote River" and "Coyote Slough" for the feature. Font gave the name "Arroyo del Coyote" to the stream when the Anza expedition reached it in 1776 (Mosier and Mosier, p. 26). East Fork Coyote Creek is 13 miles long and is named on Mississippi Creek (1955) and Mount Stakes (1955) 7.5' quadrangles. United States Board on Geographic Names (1943, p. 11) rejected the names "Coyote Creek," "East Fork," and "East Fork Coyote River" for present East Fork Coyote Creek. Middle Fork Coyote Creek is 18 miles long and is named on Isabel Valley (1955), Mississippi Creek (1955), and Mount Sizer (1955) 7.5' quadrangles. On Thompson and West's (1876) map, Coyote River (present Coyote Creek) divides—about where modern maps show the creek reaching Alameda County—into two waterways, called North Coyote Slough and South Coyote Slough, which rejoin northeast of Alviso to form a single waterway, called Coyote Slough, that goes on to San Francisco Bay. On Milpitas (1961) 7.5' quadrangle, North Coyote Slough of the older map is called Coyote Creek, and South Coyote Slough of the older map is unnamed. Thompson and West's (1876) map also shows a waterway called Big Creek Artesian Slough that extends across mud flats north and east of Alviso to join Coyote Slough north of Alviso. Mathew William Dixon established Dixon's Landing along Coyote Creek in present Warm Springs district in 1868 (Mosier and Mosier, p. 30).

Coyote Creek [CONTRA COSTA]: *stream,* flows nearly 3 miles to South San Ramon Creek 5.5 miles south-southeast of Danville (lat. 37°45'10" N, long. 121°56'45" W). Named on Diablo (1953) 7.5' quadrangle.

Coyote Creek [MARIN]: *stream,* flows 2.5 miles to Richardson Bay 6.25 miles south of downtown San Rafael (lat. 37°52'55" N, long. 122°31'15" W); the stream heads on Coyote Ridge. Named on Point Bonita (1954) and San Rafael (1954) 7.5' quadrangles.

Coyote Creek [SAN MATEO]: *stream,* flows 2.25 miles to San Gregorio Creek 5.5 miles west of La Honda (lat. 37°19'40" N, long. 122°22'05" W). Named on La Honda (1961) 7.5' quadrangle.

Coyote Creek: see **Little Coyote Creek** [SANTA CLARA].

Coyote Hill [SANTA CLARA]: *hill,* 3 miles south-southeast of downtown Palo Alto (lat. 37°23'55" N, long. 122°08'50" W). Altitude 371 feet. Named on Palo Alto (1961) 7.5' quadrangle.

Coyote Hill: see **Big Coyote Hill**, under **Coyote Point** [SAN MATEO].

Coyote Hill Creek: see **Coyote Hills Slough** [ALAMEDA].

Coyote Hills [ALAMEDA]: *ridge,* northwest- to north-northwest-trending, nearly 3 miles long, 2.5 miles west-northwest of downtown Newark (lat. 37°32'45" N, long. 122°05'15" W). Named on Newark (1959) 7.5' quadrangle. The feature first was called Cerritos Hills, and later it was called Potrero Hills for Potrero de los Cerritos grant; the name "Coyote Hills" was given in the 1880's because coyotes at the place howled in response to the whistling of trains on the nearby tracks (Mosier and Mosier, p. 26). E.H. Dyer, a surveyor, gave the name "Hunter Island" in the 1850's to a hill situated north of Coyote Hills and surrounded by marsh; W.J. Lewis, another surveyor, renamed the feature Salmon Island in 1860 for Daniel E. Salmon, who owned it (Mosier and Mosier, p. 75).

Coyote Hills Slough [ALAMEDA]: *water feature,* enters San Francisco Bay 8 miles south-southwest of downtown Hayward (lat. 37° 33'45" N, long. 122°07'50" W); the feature is north of Coyote Hills. Named on Newark

(1948) and Redwood Point (1959) 7.5' quadrangles. Called Coyote Hill Creek on Haywards (1899) 15' quadrangle.

Coyote Knoll [SONOMA]: *peak,* 5.5 miles northeast of Guerneville (lat. 38°33' N, long. 122°55' W). Named on Guerneville (1955) 7.5' quadrangle.

Coyote Lake [SANTA CLARA]: *lake,* 3 miles long, behind a dam on Coyote Creek 4 miles northeast of San Martin (lat. 37°07'05" N, long. 121°32'55" W; sec. 29 T 9 S, R 4 E). Named on Gilroy (1955) 7.5' quadrangle.

Coyote Peak [SANTA CLARA]: *peak,* 3.5 miles northeast of New Almaden (lat. 37°12'30" N, long. 121°46'30" W). Altitude 1155 feet. Named on Santa Teresa Hills (1953) 7.5' quadrangle.

Coyote Point [SAN MATEO]: *promontory,* less than 2 miles north of downtown San Mateo along San Francisco Bay (lat. 37°35'30" N, long. 122°19'10" W). Named on San Mateo (1956) 7.5' quadrangle, which gives the name "Point San Mateo" as an alternate. Called San Mateo Pt. on San Mateo (1915) 15' quadrangle, and called Punta San Matheo on Beechey's (1827-1828) map. United States Board on Geographic Names (1961b, p. 10) rejected the names "San Mateo Point," "Point San Mateo," "Point San Matheo," and "Big Coyote Point" for the feature. The promontory had the names "The Coyote," "The Big Coyote," and "Big Coyote Hill" in the 1850's; the area along the shore for 1.5 miles west of present Coyote Point was called San Mateo Beach until the 1890's or later (Brown, p. 23, 84).

Coyote Point: see **Little Coyote Point** [SAN MATEO].

Coyote Point Yacht Harbor [SAN MATEO]: *water feature,* 1.5 miles north-northeast of downtown San Mateo along San Francisco Bay (lat. 37°35'20" N, long. 122°19' W); the feature is east of Coyote Point. Named on San Mateo (1956) 7.5' quadrangle.

Coyote Ridge [MARIN]: *ridge,* south-trending, 2 miles long, 3.5 miles north-northwest of Point Bonita (lat. 37°51'35" N, long. 122° 33'15" W). Named on Point Bonita (1954) 7.5' quadrangle.

Coyote River: see **Coyote Creek** [ALAMEDA-SANTA CLARA].

Coyote Slough: see **Coyote Creek** [ALAMEDA-SANTA CLARA]; **North Coyote Slough**, under **Coyote Creek** [ALAMEDA-SANTA CLARA]; **South Coyote Slough**, under **Coyote Creek** [ALAMEDA-SANTA CLARA].

Coyote Station: see **Coyote** [SANTA CLARA].

Coyote Valley: see **Tamalpais Valley** [MARIN].

Cozzens: see **Cozzens Corner** [SONOMA].

Cozzens Corner [SONOMA]: *locality,* 3 miles west of Geyserville (lat. 38°42'10" N, long. 122°57'20" W). Named on Healdsburg (1940) 15' quadrangle. Postal authorities established Cozzens post office 5 miles northwest of Clairville (present Geyserville) in 1881 and discontinued it in 1910; the name was for Davenport Cozzens, Jr., first postmaster (Salley, p. 52).

Crab Island [SONOMA]: *island,* 200 feet long, less than 0.5 mile west-southwest of Jenner in Russian River (lat. 38°26'50" N, long. 123°07'20" W). Named on Duncans Mills (1943) 7.5' quadrangle.

Crandall Creek [ALAMEDA]: *stream,* diverges southwest from Alameda Creek 3.25 miles north-northeast of Newark (lat. 37°34'30" N, long. 122°01'05" W), and continues for another 2.5 miles before ending. Named on Newark (1948) 7.5' quadrangle. The name "Crandall Creek" is for a family that lived along the stream (Mosier and Mosier, p. 26-27).

Crane [NAPA]: *locality,* nearly 3 miles northwest of Rutherford along Southern Pacific Railroad (lat. 38°29'30" N, long. 122°27'10" W). Named on Napa (1902) 30' quadrangle.

Crane Canyon [SONOMA]: *canyon,* 1 mile long, 4.25 miles northeast of Cotati (lat. 38°22'05" N, long. 122°38'45" W); the canyon is north of Crane Creek (2). Named on Cotati (1954) 7.5' quadrangle.

Crane Creek [SONOMA]:

(1) *stream,* flows 3 miles to Dry Creek 4 miles south-southwest of Geyserville (lat. 38°39' N, long. 122°55'25" W). Named on Geyserville (1955) 7.5' quadrangle.

(2) *stream,* flows 4 miles to lowlands 3 miles northeast of Cotati (lat. 38°21'20" N, long. 122°40' W). Named on Cotati (1954) and Glen Ellen (1954) 7.5' quadrangles.

Crane Peak [SONOMA]: *peak,* 2.25 miles northwest of Big Mountain (lat. 38°44'10" N, long. 123°10'15" W; on S line sec. 3, T 10 N, R 12 W). Named on Tombs Creek (1978) 7.5' quadrangle.

Crane Ridge [ALAMEDA]: *ridge,* northwest- to west-northwest-trending, 6 miles long, center 2 miles northeast of Mendenhall Springs (lat. 37°36'30" N, long. 121°37'30" W). Named on Altamont (1953), Cedar Mountain (1956), and Mendenhall Springs (1956) 7.5' quadrangles. The name is for Andrew Edward Crane, a settler of 1876 (Mosier and Mosier, p. 27).

Crawford Gulch [SONOMA]: *canyon,* less than 1 mile long, 4 miles south of Guerneville (lat. 38°26'45" N, long. 123°00'20" W). Named on Duncans Mills (1979) 7.5' quadrangle.

Creamery Bay [MARIN]: *bay,* opens into Drakes Estero 6 miles northeast of the lighthouse at Point Reyes (lat. 38°03'35" N, long. 122°57' W). Named on Drakes Bay (1953) 7.5' quadrangle.

Creed [SOLANO]: *locality,* 2.5 miles east-northeast of Denverton along Sacramento Northern Railroad (lat. 38°14'35" N, long. 121° 51'15" W; near S line sec. 27, T 5 N, R 1 E). Named on Birds Landing (1953) 7.5' quadrangle. Called Reservoir on Birds Landing (1918) 7.5' quadrangle.

Creighton Ridge [SONOMA]: *ridge,* generally west-trending, 1.5 miles long, nearly 4 miles northeast of Fort Ross (lat. 38°33'15" N, long. 123°11'35" W). Named on Fort Ross (1978) 7.5' quadrangle.

Creston [SOLANO]: *locality,* 3.5 miles west of Cordelia along Southern Pacific Railroad (lat. 38°12'30" N, long. 122°12' W; sec. 9, T 4 N, R 3 W). Named on Cordelia (1951) 7.5' quadrangle.

Crinkley Gulch: see **Kohute Gulch** [SONOMA].

Crocker Creek [SONOMA]: *stream,* flows nearly 3 miles to Russian River 0.5 mile north of Asti (lat. 38°46'10" N, long. 122°58'20" W). Named on Asti (1959) 7.5' quadrangle.

Crocker Mountain: see **San Bruno Mountain** [SAN MATEO].

Crockett [CONTRA COSTA]: *town,* 5 miles west-northwest of Martinez (lat. 38°03'15" N, long. 122°12'45" W). Named on Benicia (1959) 7.5' quadrangle. Postal authorities established Crockettville post office in 1883 and changed the name to Crockett the same year (Salley, p. 53). The name commemorates Joseph B. Crockett, who was a justice of California supreme court in 1867 (Hanna, P.T., p. 77). Thomas Edwards, Sr., purchased land from Judge Crockett and built a home in 1867 that became the nucleus of a company town of California and Hawaiian Sugar Refinery (Hoover, Rensch, and Rensch, p. 66-67).

Crockettville: see **Crockett** [CONTRA COSTA].

Cronin Gulch: see **Copper Mine Gulch** [MARIN].

Cronkhite: see **Fort Cronkhite Military Reservation** [MARIN].

Cropley Creek: see **Sweigert Creek** [SANTA CLARA].

Crosley Creek [SANTA CLARA]: *stream,* flows nearly 1 mile to lowlands 1.5 miles north-northeast of Berryessa (lat. 37°24'30" N, long. 121°50'35" W). Named on Calaveras Reservoir (1961) 7.5' quadrangle.

Cross Slough [SOLANO]: *water feature,* extends from Nurse Slough to Montezuma Slough 4.5 miles southwest of Denverton (lat. 38° 11' N, long. 121°57'45" W). Named on Denverton (1953) 7.5' quadrangle.

Crow Canyon: see **Crow Creek** [ALAMEDA].

Crow Creek [ALAMEDA]: *stream,* flows 8 miles to San Lorenzo Creek 2 miles northeast of downtown Hayward (lat. 37°41'35" N, long. 122°03'25" W). Named on Hayward (1959) and Las Trampas Ridge (1959) 7.5' quadrangles. Mosier and Mosier (p. 27) used the name "Crow Canyon" for the canyon of the creek, and noted that the name is for William Granville Crow, who settled at the place in the 1850's.

Crown [SONOMA]: *locality,* 5 miles southeast of Cotati along Northwestern Pacific Railroad (lat. 38°16'05" N, long. 122°39'20" W). Named on Cotati (1954) 7.5' quadrangle.

Croy Creek [SANTA CLARA]: *stream,* flows 2.5 miles to Uvas Creek 4.5 miles east-southeast of Loma Prieta (lat. 37°05'05" N, long. 121°46'05" W; sec. 5, T 10 S, R 2 E); the stream is west of Croy Ridge. Named on Loma Prieta (1955) 7.5' quadrangle.

Croy Ridge [SANTA CLARA]: *ridge,* north-trending, 2 miles long, 5.5 miles east-southeast of Loma Prieta (lat. 37°04' N, long. 121° 45'15" W). Named on Loma Prieta (1955) 7.5' quadrangle.

Crystal Lake [MARIN]: *lake,* 1750 feet long, nearly 1 mile northeast of Double Point (lat. 37°57'20" N, long. 122°46'10" W). Named on Double Point (1954) 7.5' quadrangle.

Crystal Lake [NAPA]: *intermittent lake,* 550 feet long, 9 miles northwest of Mount Vaca (lat. 38°28'35" N, long. 122°14'45" W; on S line sec. 1, T 7 N, R 4 W). Named on Capell Valley (1951) 7.5' quadrangle. Mount Vaca (1951) 15' quadrangle shows a perennial lake.

Crystal Peak: see **Sveadal** [SANTA CLARA].

Crystal Springs: see **Lower Crystal Springs Reservoir** [SAN MATEO]; **Sanitarium** [NAPA].

Crystal Springs Lake: see **Lower Crystal Springs Reservoir** [SAN MATEO].

Crystal Springs Reservoir: see **Lower Crystal Springs Reservoir** [SAN MATEO]; **Upper Crystal Springs Reservoir** [SAN MATEO].

Cuchilla de Almaden: see **New Almaden** [SANTA CLARA].

Cuchilla de la nema de la Luis Cheavoya: see **New Almaden** [SANTA CLARA].

Cuchilla de los Ajos: see **Cahill Ridge** [SAN MATEO].

Cuchillo de Pomponio: see **Pomponio Creek** [SAN MATEO].

Cuesta de los Gatos: see **Wrights** [SANTA CLARA].

Cull Canyon: see **Cull Creek** [ALAMEDA].

Cull Creek [ALAMEDA]: *stream,* flows 7.5 miles to Crow Creek 2.5 miles northeast of downtown Hayward (lat. 37°42'05" N, long. 122°03'10" W). Named on Hayward (1959) and Las Trampas Ridge (1959) 7.5' quadrangles. Mosier and Mosier (p. 27) used the name "Cull Canyon" for the canyon of the stream, and noted that it was named for William Slead Cull, who settled there in the 1850's.

Cunningham [SONOMA]: *locality,* 5.25 miles northeast of Bloomfield (lat. 38°21'50" N, long. 122°46'35" W; near E line sec. 18, T 6 N, R 8 W). Named on Two Rock (1954) 7.5' quadrangle. The name was given in 1904 for the Cunningham family, landholders in the neighborhood (Gudde, 1949, p. 86). California Division of Highways' (1934) map shows a place called

Stones located along Petaluma and Santa Rosa Railroad just northwest of Cunningham.

Cup and Saucer [NAPA]: *ridge,* south-southeast- to southeast-trending, less than 1 mile long, 1 mile northeast of downtown Napa (lat. 38°18'25" N, long. 122°15'55" W). Named on Napa (1951) 7.5' quadrangle.

Cupertino [SANTA CLARA]: *city,* 8 miles west of downtown San Jose (lat. 37°19'25" N, long. 122°01'55" W). Named on Cupertino (1961) 7.5' quadrangle. John T. Doyle purchased land along Stevens Creek in present Monte Vista, and in 1873 he built a house there that in 1882 became the site of Cupertino post office (Hoover, Rensch, and Rensch, p. 459). The name "Cupertino" came from Arroyo de San Jose Cupertino, the original name of Stevens Creek (Butler, p. 108). Postal authorities established this first Cupertino post office in 1882 and discontinued it in 1894 (Frickstad, p. 173). Meanwhile, a settlement called West Side developed in present Cupertino at the intersection of present Stevens Creek Boulevard and Saratoga-Sunnyvale Road—the place is named on Santa Cruz (1902) 30' quadrangle. Postal authorities established West Side post office in 1892 and changed the name to Cupertino in 1900 (Frickstad, p. 175). Cupertino incorporated in 1955.

Cupertino Creek: see **Stevens Creek** [SANTA CLARA].

Curry: see **Lake Curry** [NAPA].

Curry Canyon [CONTRA COSTA]: *canyon,* drained by a stream that flows 5 miles to Marsh Creek 2.5 miles east of Mount Diablo (lat. 37°52'50" N, long. 121°51'50" W; sec. 4, T 1 S, R 1 E). Named on Antioch South (1953), Diablo (1953), and Tassajara (1953) 7.5' quadrangles. Whitney (p. 26) mentioned Curry's Cañada, and Stanton (p. 1020) referred to Currys Creek, or Currys Cañada.

Curry's Cañada: see **Curry Canyon** [CONTRA COSTA].

Currys Creek: see **Curry Canyon** [CONTRA COSTA].

Curtis: see **Rio Vista Junction** [SOLANO].

Curtis Gulch: see **Liberty Gulch** [MARIN].

Curtner [ALAMEDA]: *locality,* 6 miles south-southeast of Fremont civic center along Western Pacific Railroad (lat. 37°28'10" N, long. 121°55'20" W). Named on Milpitas (1961) 7.5' quadrangle.

Cut: see **The Cut**, under **Bay Slough** [SAN MATEO].

Cut B [SONOMA]: *water feature,* artificial waterway 4 miles east-southeast of downtown Petaluma across the neck of a meander in Petaluma River (lat. 38°12'20" N, long. 122°34'25" W). Named on Petaluma River (1954) 7.5' quadrangle.

Cutoff: see **The Cutoff**, under **Bay Slough** [SAN MATEO].

Cutoff Slough [SOLANO]: *water feature,* extends from Montezuma Slough to Suisun Slough 4 miles south of Fairfield (lat. 38°11'35" N, long. 122°02'15" W). Named on Denverton (1953) and Fairfield South (1949) 7.5' quadrangles.

Cuttings Wharf [NAPA]: *locality,* 4 miles northwest of Napa Junction along Napa River (lat. 38°13'30" N, long. 122°18'30" W). Named on Cuttings Wharf (1949) 7.5' quadrangle.

Cygnus [SOLANO]: *locality,* 7 miles south-southwest of Fairfield along Southern Pacific Railroad (lat. 38°09'10" N, long. 122°05'20" W). Named on Fairfield South (1949) 7.5' quadrangle. Called Drawbridge on Karquines (1898) 15' quadrangle. Postal authorities established Cygnus post office in 1902 and discontinued it in 1907 (Frickstad, p. 192).

Cypress Dunes Campground [SONOMA]: *locality,* 0.5 mile north of the village of Bodega Bay (lat. 38°20'25" N, long. 123°02'50" W). Named on Bodega Head (1972) 7.5' quadrangle.

Cypress Grove [MARIN]: *locality,* 5.5 miles south of Tomales on the northeast side of Tomales Bay (lat. 38°09'55" N, long. 122°53'55" W). Named on Tomales (1954) 7.5' quadrangle. Point Reyes (1918) 15' quadrangle shows the place along Northwestern Pacific Railroad.

Cypress Point [CONTRA COSTA]: *promontory,* 3.5 miles southeast of Point San Pablo along San Francisco Bay (lat. 37°55'20" N, long. 122°23'25" W). Named on San Quentin (1959) 7.5' quadrangle.

Cyrus Creek [NAPA]: *stream,* flows 2.25 miles to Napa River 0.5 mile west-northwest of Calistoga (lat. 38°34'50" N, long. 122°35'10" W). Named on Calistoga (1958) 7.5' quadrangle.

—D—

Daglia Canyon [NAPA]: *canyon,* drained by a stream that flows 1.5 miles to Middle Creek 8 miles west-northwest of Mount Vaca (lat. 38°28' N, long. 122°14'40" W; sec. 12, T 7 N, R 4 W). Named on Capell Valley (1951) and Yountville (1951) 7.5' quadrangles.

Dago Valley [NAPA]: *valley,* 3.5 miles north-northwest of Saint Helena (lat. 38°33'10" N, long. 122°29'15" W). Named on Saint Helena (1960) 7.5' quadrangle.

Dairy Flat [SANTA CLARA]: *area,* 5.5 miles west-southwest of Mount Sizer (lat. 37°11'30" N, long. 121°36'30" W). Named on Mount Sizer (1955) 7.5' quadrangle.

Dairy Gulch [SAN MATEO]: *canyon,* drained by a stream that flows 1.25 miles to the sea 3 miles south-southwest of the village of San Gregorio (lat. 37°17'10" N, long. 122°24'25" W). Named on San Gregorio (1961, photorevised 1968) 7.5' quadrangle.

Dalton Manor: see **Benicia** [SOLANO].

Daly City [SAN MATEO]: *city,* 4.25 miles northwest of downtown South San Francisco (lat. 37°42'20" N, long. 122°27'40" W). Named on San Francisco South (1956) 7.5' quadrangle. A travelers stop called Abbey House was built at the site of present downtown Daly City in the 1850's, and it was still there when refugees from the 1906 earthquake began settling nearby on John D. Daly's dairy ranch; the citizens of the new community voted in 1911 to incorporate their town and named it for dairyman Daly (Stanger, 1963, p. 65, 157). Postal authorities established Vista Grande post office in 1908 and changed the name to Daly City in 1913 (Salley, p. 233).

Damiani Creek [SAN MATEO]: *stream,* flows less than 1 mile to Corte Madera Creek 3 miles north of Mindego Hill (lat. 37°21'20" N, long. 122°12'55" W). Named on Mindego Hill (1961) 7.5' quadrangle.

Damon Marsh: see **Fitchburg** [ALAMEDA].

Damon's Landing: see **Fitchburg** [ALAMEDA].

Damon Slough: see **Fitchburg** [ALAMEDA].

Dan Cook Canyon [CONTRA COSTA]: *canyon,* drained by a stream that flows 2 miles to Green Valley 3.5 miles south-southwest of Mount Diablo (lat. 37°50'15" N, long. 121°57' W; near NW cor. sec. 23, T 1 S, R 1 W). Named on Diablo (1953) 7.5' quadrangle.

Danfield Creek [SONOMA]: *stream,* flows 4.25 miles to Pepperwood Creek 6.25 miles south-southwest of Big Mountain (lat. 38° 37'45" N, long. 123°11'50" W; near SW cor. sec. 9, T 9 N, R 12 W); the stream is south of Danfield Ridge. Named on Tombs Creek (1978) 7.5' quadrangle.

Danfield Ridge [SONOMA]: *ridge,* east-northeast to east-southeast-trending, 1.5 miles long, 4.5 miles south-southwest of Big Mountain (lat. 38°39' N, long. 123°11' W); the ridge is north of Danfield Creek. Named on Tombs Creek (1978) 7.5' quadrangle.

Dangers: see **Liberty** [SONOMA].

Daniels Creek: see **Lagunitas Creek** [MARIN].

Danielson [SOLANO]: *locality,* 3.5 miles west-southwest of Fairfield along Sacramento Northern Railroad (lat. 38°14'15" N, long. 122° 06'15" W). Named on Fairfield South (1949) 7.5' quadrangle.

Danville [CONTRA COSTA]: *city,* 6.25 miles southwest of Mount Diablo (lat. 37°49'20" N, long. 121°59'55" W). Named on Diablo (1953) and Las Trampas Ridge (1959) 7.5' quadrangles. Postal authorities established Danville post office in 1860 (Frickstad, p. 21). The name is from Danville, Kentucky (Hoover, Rensch, and Rensch, p. 57).

Dardon Canyon [NAPA]: *canyon,* drained by a stream that flows nearly 1 mile to Gosling Canyon 7 miles south of Berryessa Peak (lat. 38°34' N, long. 122°10'25" W). Named on Lake Berryessa (1959) 7.5' quadrangle.

Dark Canyon [CONTRA COSTA]: *canyon,* 0.5 mile long, 4.25 miles east of Mount Diablo along Marsh Creek (lat. 37°53'05" N, long. 121°50'05" W; sec. 35, T 1 N, R 1 E). Named on Antioch South (1953) 7.5' quadrangle.

Dark Gulch [SAN MATEO]: *canyon,* drained by a stream that flows nearly 1 mile to Pescadero Creek 3.5 miles south-southeast of La Honda (lat. 37°15'55" N, long. 122°15'30" W; near W line sec. 1, T 8 S, R 4 W). Named on La Honda (1961) 7.5' quadrangle.

Davaney Canyon [ALAMEDA]: *canyon,* drained by a stream that flows 2.25 miles to Dublin Creek 0.5 mile southwest of Dublin (lat. 37°41'40" N, long. 121°56'50" W; near SW cor. sec. 2, T 3 S, R 1 W). Named on Dublin (1961) 7.5' quadrangle.

Davidson: see **Mount Davidson** [SAN FRANCISCO].

Davis Canyon: see **Bolinas Creek** [ALAMEDA].

Davis Point [CONTRA COSTA]: *promontory,* 6.25 miles east-northeast of Pinole Point on the south side of the mouth of Carquinez Strait (lat. 38°03'05" N, long. 122°15'35" W). Named on Mare Island (1959) 7.5' quadrangle. Called Pt. Davis on Ringgold's (1850a) map.

Day: see **Mount Day** [SANTA CLARA].

Day Creek: see **Lions Peak** [SANTA CLARA].

Day Island [MARIN]: *hill,* 4.5 miles east of downtown Novato near San Pablo Bay (lat. 38°06'10" N, long. 122°29'20" W). Named on Petaluma Point (1959) 7.5' quadrangle.

Deadfall: see **Clayton** [CONTRA COSTA].

Deadhorse Creek [SONOMA]: *stream,* flows 0.5 mile to Humbug Creek 4.5 miles east of Mark West Springs (lat. 38°32'25" N, long. 122°38'05" W; sec. 16, T 8 N, R 7 W). Named on Mark West Springs (1958) 7.5' quadrangle. Calistoga (1959) 15' quadrangle has the form "Dead Horse Creek" for the name.

Deadman Cliff [SONOMA]: *relief feature,* 2 miles north of Big Mountain on the north side of Rancheria Creek (lat. 38°44'25" N, long. 123°08'45" W; on E line sec. 2, T 10 N, R 12 W). Named on Tombs Creek (1978) 7.5' quadrangle.

Deadman Gulch [ALAMEDA]: *canyon,* flows 1 mile to Eylar Canyon 4 miles south of Cedar Mountain (lat. 37°29'40" N, long. 121°35'50" W; sec. 13, T 5 S, R 3 E). Named on Eylar Mountain (1955) 7.5' quadrangle.

Deadman Gulch [SONOMA]: *canyon,* drained by a stream that flows 1 mile to the sea 3 miles west-northwest of Plantation (lat. 38°36'05" N, long. 123°21'40" W). Named on Plantation (1977) 7.5' quadrangle.

Deadman Island [SOLANO]: *peninsula,* 2.25 miles south-southeast of Fairfield along Suisun Slough at the mouth of Hill Slough (lat. 38°13'15" N, long. 122°01'40" W). Named on Fairfield South (1949) 7.5' quadrangle.

Deadmans Gulch [MARIN]: *canyon,* drained by a stream that flows 0.5 mile to Lagunitas Creek 10.5 miles southwest of downtown Novato (lat. 38°01'40" N, long. 122°44'05" W). Named on San Geronimo (1954) 7.5' quadrangle.

Dean's Island: see **Wood Island** [MARIN].

Dearborn Gulch: see **Dearborn Park** [SAN MATEO].

Dearborn Park [SAN MATEO]: *settlement,* 5 miles south-southwest of La Honda (lat. 37°15'20" N, long. 122°18'55" W; near NE cor. sec. 8, T 8 S, R 4 W). Named on La Honda (1961) 7.5' quadrangle. Brown (p. 26) used the name "Dearborn Gulch" for the canyon in which the settlement lies, and noted that Henry Dearborn came to the place in the late 1880's.

Death Rock [SONOMA]: *promontory,* 4 miles south-southeast of Jenner along the coast (lat. 38°23'40" N, long. 123°05'45" W). Named on Duncans Mills (1979) 7.5' quadrangle.

Decker Canyon [NAPA]: *canyon,* drained by a stream that flows 1 mile to Lake Berryessa 7.25 miles north-northwest of Mount Vaca (lat. 38°29'45" N, long. 122°09'15" W). Named on Capell Valley (1951, photorevised 1968) 7.5' quadrangle.

Decker Island [SOLANO]: *island,* nearly 2 miles long, 4.5 miles south-southwest of Rio Vista in Sacramento River (lat. 38°05'30" N, long. 121°43' W). Named on Jersey Island (1978) 7.5' quadrangle. An artificial waterway across the neck of Horseshoe Bend forms the island.

Decoto [ALAMEDA]: *district,* 5 miles north of downtown Newark in Union City (lat. 37°36' N, long. 122°01'15" W). Named on Newark (1959) 7.5' quadrangle. Newark (1948) 7.5' quadrangle has the name on the community that joined with the neighboring community of Alvarado in 1958 to form the new city of Union City (Hoover, Rensch, and Rensch, p. 17). Postal authorities established Decoto post office in 1871, discontinued it in 1872, reestablished it in 1875, and discontinued it in 1959 (Salley, p. 56). The name commemorates Ezra Decoto, who sold right-of-way to the railroad in 1867 (Gudde, 1949, p. 90-91).

Deep Gulch [SANTA CLARA]: *canyon,* drained by a stream that flows almost 1 mile to Alamitos Creek near the south end of New Almaden (lat. 37°10'25" N, long. 121°49'25" W). Named on Santa Teresa Hills (1953) 7.5' quadrangle.

Deep Water Channel: see **Oakland Inner Harbor** [ALAMEDA].

Deep Water Ship Channel: see **Sacramento River Deep Water Ship Channel** [SOLANO].

Deepwater Slough [SAN MATEO]: *water feature,* 2.25 miles north of downtown Redwood City off Redwood Creek (lat. 37°31' N, long. 122°13' W). Named on Redwood Point (1959) 7.5' quadrangle.

Deer Creek [CONTRA COSTA]: *stream,* flows 8 miles to Marsh Creek less than 1 mile west-northwest of Brentwood (lat. 37°55'20" N, long. 121°42'40" W); the stream drains Deer Valley. Named on Antioch South (1953) and Brentwood (1954) 7.5' quadrangles. Called Dry Creek on Mount Diablo (1898) 15' quadrangle.

Deer Creek [SANTA CLARA]: *stream,* flows 3.25 miles to Matadero Creek 3 miles south of downtown Palo Alto (lat. 37°24'15" N, long. 122°09'05" W). Named on Palo Alto (1961, photorevised 1968 and 1973) 7.5' quadrangle. Called Purisima Creek on Mindego Hill (1961) and Palo Alto (1961) 7.5' quadrangles. United States Board on Geographic Names (1972, p. 2) listed the variant name "Purisima Creek" for the stream.

Deer Creek [SONOMA]: *stream,* flows 1 mile to Sausal Creek 6 miles northeast of Healdsburg (lat. 38°40'55" N, long. 122°48' W; sec. 25, T 10 N, R 9 W). Named on Jimtown (1955) 7.5' quadrangle.

Deer Creek: see **Arroyo Ojo de Agua** [SAN MATEO].

Deer Flat [CONTRA COSTA]: *area,* 1 mile west-northwest of Mount Diablo (lat. 37°53'20" N, long. 121°56' W; near E line sec. 35, T 1 N, R 1 W). Named on Clayton (1953) 7.5' quadrangle.

Deer Flat Creek [CONTRA COSTA]: *stream,* flows 1.5 miles to Mitchell Creek nearly 2 miles west-northwest of Mount Diablo (lat. 37°53'45" N, long. 121°56'25" W; sec. 35, T 1 N, R 1 W); the stream is north of Deer Flat. Named on Clayton (1953) 7.5' quadrangle.

Deer Horn Spring [SANTA CLARA]: *spring,* 1.5 miles west of Mount Sizer (lat. 37°12'45" N, long. 121°32'30" W; sec. 28, T 8 S, R 4 E). Named on Mount Sizer (1955) 7.5' quadrangle.

Deer Island [MARIN]: *hill,* 2 miles east-southeast of downtown Novato (lat. 38°05'50" N, long. 122°32'10" W). Named on Novato (1954) 7.5' quadrangle.

Deer Knoll [SONOMA]: *peak,* 8 miles north-northeast of Healdsburg (lat. 38°42'55" N, long. 122°47'25" W; sec. 18, T 10 N, R 8 W). Named on Jimtown (1955) 7.5' quadrangle.

Deer Lake [NAPA]: *lake,* 950 feet long, 6.25 miles north of Saint Helena (lat. 38°35'50" N, long. 122°28'20" W; sec. 25, T 9 N, R 6 W); the lake is north of Doe Lake. Named on Saint Helena (1960) 7.5' quadrangle.

Deer Park: see **Sanitarium** [NAPA].

Deer Park Creek [MARIN]: *stream,* flows 1.25 miles to San Anselmo Creek 3.25 miles west-northwest of downtown San Rafael (lat. 37°59' N, long. 122°35'20" W). Named on San Rafael (1954) 7.5' quadrangle.

Deer Park Ridge [SAN MATEO]: *ridge,* west-northwest-trending, 2.5 miles long, 3 miles west-southwest of La Honda (lat. 37°18' N, long. 122°19' W). Named on La Honda (1961) 7.5' quadrangle.

Deer Valley [CONTRA COSTA]: *valley,* 7 miles east-northeast of Mount Diablo (lat. 37°55'15" N, long. 121°47'30" W); the valley is along Deer Creek. Named on Antioch South (1953) 7.5' quadrangle.

De Forest: see **San Antonio Valley** [SANTA CLARA].

De Las Pulgas: see **Pulgas** [SAN MATEO].

De Laveaga [CONTRA COSTA]: *locality,* 1 mile northwest of present Orinda along California and Nevada Railroad (lat. 37°53'20" N, long. 122°11'35" W). Named on Concord (1897) 15' quadrangle.

Del Mar Landing [SONOMA]: *locality,* 8.5 miles northwest of the village of Stewarts Point along the coast (lat. 38°44'30" N, long. 123°30'25" W); the place is just east of Del Mar Point. Named on Stewarts Point (1978) 7.5' quadrangle.

Del Mar Point [SONOMA]: *promontory,* 8.5 miles northwest of the village of Stewarts Point along the coast (lat. 38°44'25" N, long. 123°30'30" W). Named on Stewarts Point (1978) 7.5' quadrangle.

Del Rio Woods [SONOMA]: *settlement,* 2 miles east-northeast of Healdsburg along Russian River (lat. 38°37'20" N, long. 122°50'15" W). Named on Healdsburg (1955) 7.5' quadrangle.

Del Valle: see **Lake Del Valle** [ALAMEDA].

Denman [SONOMA]: *locality,* 4 miles south-southeast of Cotati along Petaluma and Santa Rosa Railroad (lat. 38°16'25" N, long. 122°40'30" W); the place is at present Denman Flat. Named on Santa Rosa (1944) 15' quadrangle.

Denman Flat [SONOMA]: *area,* 4.25 miles south-southeast of Cotati (lat. 38°16'25" N, long. 122°40' W). Named on Cotati (1954) 7.5' quadrangle.

Denner Ridge [SONOMA]: *ridge,* east-southeast-trending, 1 mile long, 5.25 miles east-northeast of Guerneville (lat. 38°32'05" N, long. 122°54'30" W). Named on Guerneville (1955) 7.5' quadrangle.

Dennis Martin Creek: see **Martin Creek** [SAN MATEO].

Denniston Creek [SAN MATEO]: *stream,* flows 4.25 miles to the sea 3.5 miles south of Montara Knob at Princeton (lat. 37°30'10" N, long. 122°29'10" W). Named on Montara Mountain (1956) 7.5' quadrangle. The name commemorates James G. Denniston, who came to California with the New York Volunteers, and later settled by the stream (Hanna, P.T., p. 85).

Denverton [SOLANO]: *locality,* 10.5 miles south-southeast of Vacaville (lat. 38°13'30" N, long. 121°53'50" W; near E line sec. 6, T 4 N, R 1 E). Named on Denverton (1953) 7.5' quadrangle. The place first was called Nurse's Landing, for Dr. Stephen K. Nurse, who purchased land there in 1853 and built a house, store, and wharf; the name Denverton was given in 1858 to honor J.W. Denver, congressman from the district (Hoover, Rensch, and Rensch, p. 524). Postal authorities established Denverton post office in 1858 and discontinued it in 1911 (Frickstad, p. 192).

Denverton Creek [SOLANO]: *stream,* flows nearly 2 miles to Denverton Slough near Denverton (lat. 38°13'25" N, long. 121°53'50" W; near E line sec. 6, T 4 N, R 1 E). Named on Denverton (1953) 7.5' quadrangle.

Denverton Slough [SOLANO]: *water feature,* heads near Denverton and joins Nurse Slough 2 miles south-southwest of Denverton (lat. 38°12' N, long. 121°55'05" W). Named on Denverton (1953) 7.5' quadrangle.

Denverton Station [SOLANO]: *locality,* 1.25 miles east-southeast of Denverton along Sacramento Northern Railroad (lat. 38°13'15" N, long. 121°52'25" W; sec. 4, T 4 N, R 1 E). Named on Antioch (1908) 15' quadrangle.

Devil Creek [SONOMA]: *stream,* flows 4 miles to East Austin Creek 4.5 miles north of Cazadero (lat. 38°35'40" N, long. 123°04'40" W; sec. 28, T 9 N, R 11 W). Named on Cazadero (1978) 7.5' quadrangle. Called Devils Creek on California Division of Forestry's (1945) map, which names a North Fork of the stream.

Devils Backbone [SONOMA]: *ridge,* generally northeast-trending, 0.5 mile long, 2.25 miles northeast of Cazadero (lat. 38°32'50" N, long. 123°03' W). Named on Cazadero (1978) 7.5' quadrangle.

Devil's Cañon: see **Geyser Canyon** [SONOMA].

Devils Canyon [NAPA]: *canyon,* drained by a stream that flows 2.5 miles to Redwood Canyon 8.5 miles west-northwest of downtown Napa (lat. 38°21'15" N, long. 122°25'15" W; sec. 21, T 6 N, R 5 W). Named on Sonoma (1951) 7.5' quadrangle.

Devils Canyon [SAN MATEO]: *canyon,* on upper reaches of Peters Creek 3.25 miles east-southeast of Mindego Hill (lat. 37°17'20" N, long. 122°10'30" W). Named on Mindego Hill (1961) 7.5' quadrangle. According to Brown (p. 27), the stream in the canyon should be called Devil's Canyon Creek.

Devil's Canyon Creek: see **Devils Canyon** [SAN MATEO]; **Peters Creek** [SAN MATEO].

Devils Creek: see **Devil Creek** [SONOMA].

Devils Den Canyon [SONOMA]: *canyon,* 5.25 miles long, along North

Branch Little Sulphur Creek, which joins Little Sulphur Creek 4 miles east-northeast of Asti (lat. 38°47'25" N, long. 122° 54'40" W). Named on Asti (1959) and The Geysers (1959) 7.5' quadrangles.

Devils Elbow [NAPA]: *ridge,* east-southeast-trending, 0.5 mile long, 1 mile southeast of Berryessa Peak at the southeast end of Blue Ridge (1) (lat. 38°39'20" N, long. 122°10'30" W). Named on Brooks (1959) 7.5' quadrangle.

Devils Gate [SOLANO]: *narrows,* 7.5 miles north of Mount Vaca along Putah Creek on Solano-Yolo County line (lat. 38°30'45" N, long. 122°06' W; sec. 29, T 8 N, R 2 W). Named on Capay (1945) 15' quadrangle.

Devils Gulch [MARIN]: *canyon,* drained by a stream that flows 3 miles to Lagunitas Creek 10.5 miles west-southwest of downtown Novato (lat. 38°01'45" N, long. 122°44'05" W). Named on San Geronimo (1954) 7.5' quadrangle.

Devils Head: see **Devils Head Peak** [NAPA].

Devils Head Peak [NAPA]: *peak,* 8 miles northeast of Aetna Springs (lat. 38°44'55" N, long. 122°23'40" W). Altitude 1112 feet. Named on Aetna Springs (1958) 7.5' quadrangle. Called Devils Head on Pope Valley (1921) 15' quadrangle.

Devils Hole [ALAMEDA]: *relief feature,* 4.5 miles south of Mendenhall Springs (lat. 37°31'25" N, long. 121°37'55" W; sec. 3, T 5 S, R 3 E). Named on Mendenhall Springs (1956) 7.5' quadrangle.

Devils Kitchen [SONOMA]: *area,* 3 miles northeast of Mark West Springs (lat. 38°34'45" N, long. 122°40'45" W; near SW cor. sec. 31, T 9 N, R 7 W). Named on Mark West Springs (1958) 7.5' quadrangle.

Devil's Mount: see **Mount Saint Helena** [SONOMA].

Devils Pit [ALAMEDA]: *relief feature,* 2.25 miles south of Cedar Mountain (lat. 37°31'40" N, long. 121°36'10" W; sec. 1, T 5 S, R 3 E). Named on Cedar Mountain (1956) 7.5' quadrangle.

Devils Pulpit [CONTRA COSTA]: *relief feature,* 0.25 mile east-southeast of Mount Diablo (lat. 37°52'50" N, long. 121°54'30" W; near N line sec. 6, T 1 S, R 1 E). Named on Clayton (1953) 7.5' quadrangle.

Devils Ribs [SONOMA]: *ridge,* north-trending, 0.5 mile long, 6.5 miles northeast of Fort Ross (lat. 38°35'20" N, long. 123°09'50" W). Named on Fort Ross (1978) 7.5' quadrangle.

Devils Slide [CONTRA COSTA]: *relief feature,* 3 miles south of Mount Diablo on the north side of East Fork Sycamore Creek (1) (lat. 37°50'30" N, long. 121°54'20" W; sec. 18, T 1 S, R 1 E). Named on Diablo (1953) 7.5' quadrangle.

Devils Slide [SAN MATEO]: *promontory,* 2.25 miles west-northwest of Montara Knob along the coast (lat. 37°34'30" N, long. 122°31'10" W). Named on Montara Mountain (1956) 7.5' quadrangle. The feature had the early names "Saddle Rock" and "Striped Rock"; the name "Devils Slide" is used also for the steep slope on the coast just north of the promontory, where slides periodically destroy the highway (Brown, p. 27).

Devils Slough [NAPA]: *water feature,* extends from Napa Slough to China Slough 5 miles west-southwest of Napa Junction (lat. 38°10'10" N, long. 122°20'20" W; sec. 30, T 4 N, R 4 W). Named on Cuttings Wharf (1949) 7.5' quadrangle.

Devils Slough [SANTA CLARA]: *water feature,* opens into mud flats near San Francisco Bay 4.5 miles north-northeast of downtown Mountain View (lat. 37°26'55" N, long. 122°02'45" W). Named on Mountain View (1961, photorevised 1968 and 1973) 7.5' quadrangle, which shows Devils Slough and nearby Jagel Slough as artificial watercourses through salt ponds along opposite sides of a waterway that, together with adjacent marsh, is called Jagel Slough on Mountain View (1953) 7.5' quadrangle. Palo Alto (1899) 15' quadrangle has the name "Devils Slough" for a waterway that winds through tidal marshes to the bay south of the mouth of Coyote Creek (lat. 37°26'55" N, long. 122°02'55" W).

Dewing Park: see **Saranap** [CONTRA COSTA].

Dexter Canyon [SANTA CLARA]: *canyon,* drained by a stream that flows 3 miles to Coyote Creek 2.25 miles south-southwest of Gilroy Hot Springs (lat. 37°04'40" N, long. 121°29'35" W; sec. 11, T 10 S, R 4 E). Named on Gilroy (1955) and Gilroy Hot Springs (1955) 7.5' quadrangles. Called Leesley and Dexter Canyon on Morgan Hill (1917) 15' quadrangle.

Dexter Creek [SANTA CLARA]: *stream,* flows 1.25 miles to Jones Creek 1 mile east-southeast of Old Gilroy (lat. 36°59'30" N, long. 121°30'40" W). Named on Chittenden (1955, photorevised 1968 and 1973) 7.5' quadrangle. The name commemorates the Dexter family, ranchers who came to the neighborhood in the nineteenth century; the stream has the variant name "Furlong Creek" (United States Board on Geographic Names, 1973a, p. 2).

Diablo [CONTRA COSTA]: *settlement,* 2.5 miles east-northeast of Danville in Green Valley (lat. 37°50'05" N, long. 121°57'30" W; sec. 22, T 1 S, E 1 W). Named on Diablo (1953) 7.5' quadrangle. Postal authorities established Diablo post office in 1916 (Frickstad, p. 21).

Diablo: see **Mount Diablo** [CONTRA COSTA]; **Point Diablo** [MARIN].

Diablo Range [ALAMEDA-CONTRA COSTA-SANTA CLARA]: *range,* includes the east part of Alameda County and Santa Clara County, and most of the east part of Contra Costa County. Named on San Jose (1962) and Santa Cruz (1956) 1°x 2° quadrangles. The range extends from Carquinez Strait in Contra Costa County southeast to Antelope Valley in Kern County; Mount Diablo is near the northwest end. Called Sierra del Monte Diablo on Parke's (1854-1855) map. Whitney (p. 2) used the name "Monte Diablo Range," and stated that the range "is so called from the conspicuous point [Mount Diablo] of that name." United States Board on Geographic Names (1933, p. 264) rejected the names "Monte Diablo Range," "Mount Diablo Range," and "Sierra del Monte Diablo" for the feature. Carey and Miller (p. 153) referred to the part of the range east of San Jose in Santa Clara County as Mount Hamilton Range.

Diamond Canyon: see **Dimond Canyon** [ALAMEDA].

Diamond Creek: see **Dimond Canyon** [ALAMEDA].

Diamond Mountain [SONOMA]: *ridge,* extends west from Sonoma-Napa County line, 1.25 miles long, 7.25 miles east of Mark West Springs (lat. 38°32'20" N, long. 122°35'10" W). Named on Calistoga (1958) 7.5' quadrangle.

Dianna Rock [SONOMA]: *relief feature,* 4.25 miles east-northeast of Geyser Peak (lat. 38°47'05" N, long. 122°47'20" W; on S line sec. 19, T 11 N, R 8 W). Named on The Geysers (1959) 7.5' quadrangle.

Diavolo: see **Mount Diavolo**, under **Mount Diablo** [CONTRA COSTA].

Digger Bend [SONOMA]: *bend,* 2 miles east-northeast of Healdsburg along Russian River (lat. 38°37'45" N, long. 122°50'10" W). Named on Jimtown (1955) 7.5' quadrangle.

Digges Canyon [SAN MATEO]: *canyon,* drained by Apanolio Creek, which flows 3.5 miles to Pilarcitos Creek 1.25 miles northeast of downtown Half Moon Bay (lat. 37°28'35" N, long. 122°24'40" W). Named on Half Moon Bay (1961) and Montara Mountain (1956) 7.5' quadrangles. R. Montgomery Digges had a ranch in the canyon after 1866 (Brown, p. 27). Other names for the canyon, or for the stream in it, include Cañada de Polonio or Apolonio—Apolonio Rodriguez settled at the mouth of the canyon in 1858—and Cañada de la Puente (Brown, p. 28).

Dillon Beach [MARIN]: *village,* 3.25 miles west of Tomales near the coast (lat. 38°15' N, long. 122°57'50" W). Named on Tomales (1954) and Valley Ford (1954) 7.5' quadrangles. Postal authorities established Dillon Beach post office in 1922 (Frickstad, p. 87). The name commemorates George Dillon, who settled at the place in 1868 (Mason, 1976a, p. 126-127).

Dillon Point [SOLANO]: *promontory,* 2 miles west-northwest of Benicia along Carquinez Strait (lat. 38°03'35" N, long. 122°11'35" W; sec. 33, T 3 N, R 3 W). Named on Benicia (1959) 7.5' quadrangle. Called Ma lek ad el Pt. on Ringgold's (1850a) map; Ringgold (p. 36) also used the hyphenated form "Ma-lek-ad-el Point" for the name.

Dimond: see **Oakland** [ALAMEDA].

Dimond Canyon [ALAMEDA]: *canyon,* about 3 miles east of downtown Oakland along Sausal Creek (lat. 37°48'55" N, long. 122°12'40" W). Named on Oakland East (1959) 7.5' quadrangle. Called Diamond Canyon on Concord (1915) 15' quadrangle. Concord (1897) 15' quadrangle shows Diamond Creek in the canyon.

Dingee Reservoir [ALAMEDA]: *intermittent lake,* 300 feet long, 3 miles east-northeast of downtown Oakland (lat. 37°49'45" N, long. 122°13' W). Named on Oakland East (1959) 7.5' quadrangle. The name commemorates William Jackson Dingee, who founded Oakland Water Company in the late 1890's (Mosier and Mosier, p. 30).

Dini Gulch: see **Milagra Valley** [SAN MATEO].

Divide [SONOMA]: *locality,* 4.25 miles south of Cotati along Petaluma and Santa Rosa Railroad (lat. 38°17'35" N, long. 122°42'30" W). Named on Santa Rosa (1944) 15' quadrangle. California Division of Highways' (1934) map shows a place called Live Oaks located along the railroad north-northwest of Divide.

Divide Ridge [ALAMEDA-CONTRA COSTA]: *ridge,* north- to northwest-trending, 3.5 miles long, 2.5 miles northwest of Dublin, partly on Alameda-Contra Costa County line (lat. 37°43'45" N, long. 121°58'30" W). Named on Pleasanton (1906) 15' quadrangle. The ridge first was called Pita Navaga—*pita navaga* means "knife blade" in Spanish (Mosier and Mosier, p. 30).

Divide Ridge [SANTA CLARA]: *ridge,* west- to northwest-trending, 2.25 miles long, 1.5 miles north of Mount Sizer (lat. 37°14'25" N, long. 121°30'30" W). Named on Mississippi Creek (1955) and Mount Sizer (1955) 7.5' quadrangles.

Divide Springs [SANTA CLARA]: *spring,* 3.5 miles south-southeast of Mount Hamilton (lat. 37°17'25" N, long. 121°37'40" W). Named on Lick Observatory (1955) 7.5' quadrangle.

Dixon [SOLANO]: *town,* 11 miles northeast of Vacaville (lat. 38°26'50" N, long. 121°49'15" W; around SE cor. sec. 14, T 7 N, R 1 E). Named on Dixon (1952) 7.5' quadrangle. Postal authorities established Dixon post office in 1869 (Frickstad, p. 192), and the town incorporated in 1878. The misspelled name commemorates Thomas Dickson, who donated 10 acres at the place for a railroad station (Hoover, Rensch, and Rensch, p. 523). In 1852 Elijah S. Silvey built a house at a site that became a trading center called Silveyville; Silveyville was moved bodily 5 miles east in 1868 to the railroad, where Dixon developed (Hoover, Rensch, and Rensch, p. 523). Postal authorities established Putah post office along Putah Creek

13 miles north of Vacaville in 1854, discontinued it in 1856, reestablished it in 1858, changed the name to Silveyville in 1864, and discontinued it in 1871 (Salley, p. 179, 205).

Dixon Creek [SOLANO]: *stream,* flows 2 miles to end in Dixon (lat. 38°27'10" N, long. 121°49'55" W; sec. 14, T 7 N, R 1 E); the stream heads on Dixon Ridge. Named on Dixon (1952) 7.5' quadrangle.

Dixon Ridge [SOLANO]: *ridge,* north-trending, 5 miles long, center 1.25 miles west of Dixon (lat. 38°27' N, long. 121°50'50" W). Named on Dixon (1952) 7.5' quadrangle.

Dixon's Landing: see **Coyote Creek** [ALAMEDA-SANTA CLARA].

Dodgeville: see **Healdsburg** [SONOMA].

Dodonis Landing [SOLANO]: *locality,* 7 miles southwest of Denverton along Land Slough (present Tree Slough) (lat. 38°09'40" N, long. 121°59'50" W). Named on Denverton (1918) 7.5' quadrangle.

Doe Lake [NAPA]: *lake,* 500 feet long, 6 miles north of Saint Helena (lat. 38°35'40" N, long. 122°28'20" W; near S line sec. 25, T 9 N, R 6 W); the lake is between Deer Lake and Fawn Lake. Named on Saint Helena (1960) 7.5' quadrangle.

Doe Ridge [SONOMA]: *ridge,* west-northwest-trending, less than 1 mile long, 6 miles southwest of Big Mountain (lat. 38°39'30" N, long. 123°14'05" W). Named on Tombs Creek (1978) 7.5' quadrangle.

Dogtown: see **Woodville** [MARIN].

Doherty Ridge [SAN MATEO]: *ridge,* southwest-trending, 1 mile long, 4 miles southeast of Mindego Hill (lat. 37°16'25" N, long. 122°10'40" W). Named on Mindego Hill (1961) 7.5' quadrangle.

Donahue [SONOMA]: *locality,* 6.25 miles east-southeast of downtown Petaluma on the east side of Petaluma River at the end of a spur of Northwestern Pacific Railroad (lat. 38°11'20" N, long. 122° 32'30" W). Named on Petaluma (1914) 15' quadrangle. Postal authorities established Donahue post office in 1874 and discontinued it in 1875; the place also was known as Donahue Landing (Salley, p. 60). Peter Donahue built a landing at the place as the terminus of the railroad that he began constructing in 1870 (Miller, J.T., p. 19).

Donahue Landing: see **Donahue** [SONOMA].

Donahue Slough [SONOMA]: *water feature,* waterway that parallels Petaluma River in marsh west of the river—the midpoint of the feature is 7 miles southeast of downtown Petaluma (lat. 38°10'25" N, long. 122°32'10" W). Named on Petaluma River (1954) 7.5' quadrangle.

Donlan Canyon [ALAMEDA]: *canyon,* 1 mile long, on upper reaches of Dublin Creek above a point 1 mile west of Dublin (lat. 37°41'55" N, long. 121°57'20" W; sec. 3, T 3 S, R 1 W). Named on Dublin (1961) 7.5' quadrangle. The name commemorates John Donlan, who settled in the neighborhood in 1858 (Mosier and Mosier, p. 30).

Donland Point [ALAMEDA]: *peak,* 1.5 miles west of Dublin (lat. 37°42'05" N, long. 121°58' W; sec. 3, T 3 S, R 1 W); the peak is west of Donlan Canyon. Altitude 1138 feet. Named on Dublin (1961) 7.5' quadrangle.

Donner Canyon [CONTRA COSTA]: *canyon,* 3.25 miles long, along Donner Creek above a point 3 miles north-northwest of Mount Diablo (lat. 37°55'20" N, long. 121°55'35" W; sec. 24, T 1 N, R 1 W). Named on Clayton (1953) 7.5' quadrangle.

Donner Creek [CONTRA COSTA]: *stream,* flows nearly 4 miles to Mount Diablo Creek 4 miles north-northwest of Mount Diablo (lat. 37°56'10" N, long. 121°55'40" W; sec. 13, T 1 N, R 1 W); the stream drains Donner Canyon. Named on Clayton (1953) 7.5' quadrangle.

Doolan Canyon [ALAMEDA-CONTRA COSTA]: *canyon,* drained by Cottonwood Creek, which heads in Contra Costa County and flows 4.5 miles to lowlands 3.5 miles west-northwest of Livermore in Alameda County (lat. 37°42'10" N, long. 121°49'40" W). Named on Livermore (1961) and Tassajara (1953) 7.5' quadrangles. The name commemorates Michael Doolan, who settled in the canyon in 1871; the feature was known as Cottonwood Canyon in 1878 (Mosier and Mosier, p. 30).

Doran Beach [SONOMA]: *beach,* 2 miles long, center 1.5 miles south-southeast of the village of Bodega Bay (lat. 38°18'50" N, long. 123°02'20" W); the beach is at the northwest end of Bodega Bay (1). Named on Bodega Head (1972) 7.5' quadrangle.

Dorenda [CONTRA COSTA]: *locality,* 6 miles north-northeast of present Walnut Creek civic center along Oakland Antioch and Eastern Railroad (lat. 37°59'15" N, long. 122°01'55" W). Named on Concord (1915) 15' quadrangle.

Dorman Canyon [SONOMA]: *canyon,* drained by a stream that flows 1 mile to Crane Creek (1) 5 miles south-southwest of Geyserville (lat. 38°38'35" N, long. 122°56'55" W; sec. 10, T 9 N, R 10 W). Named on Geyserville (1955) 7.5' quadrangle.

Dos Piedras [SONOMA]: *relief feature,* 4.5 miles southeast of Bloomfield near the village of Two Rock (lat. 38°16'10" N, long. 122°47'30" W). Named on Two Rock (1954) 7.5' quadrangle.

Double Bowknot [MARIN]: *locality;* twisted road 4.25 miles south-southwest of downtown San Rafael (lat. 37°55'10" N, long. 122° 34'20"). Named on San Rafael (1954) 7.5' quadrangle.

Double Point [MARIN]: *promontory,* 6 miles west-northwest of Bolinas along the coast (lat. 37°56'50" N, long. 122°46'50" W); the feature has two high spurs less than 0.5 mile apart (United States Coast and Geodetic Survey, p. 124). Named on Double Point (1954) 7.5' quadrangle.

Double Rock [SAN FRANCISCO]: *rock,* 4.25 miles east-southeast of Mount Davidson in South Basin (lat. 37°43'15" N, long. 122°22'50" W). Named on San Francisco South (1956) 7.5' quadrangle.

Dougherty [ALAMEDA]: *locality,* 1.5 miles east-northeast of Dublin along Southern Pacific Railroad (lat. 37°42'35" N, long. 121°54'35" W). Named on Dublin (1961) 7.5' quadrangle.

Dougherty: see **Dublin** [ALAMEDA].

Dougherty Hills [ALAMEDA-CONTRA COSTA]: *ridge,* south-southeast-trending, 3.5 miles long, 7 miles southeast of Danville on Alameda-Contra Costa County line, mainly in Contra Costa County (lat. 37°44'45" N, long. 121°55'20" W). Named on Diablo (1953) and Dublin (1961) 7.5' quadrangles. The name commemorates James Witt Dougherty, who settled in the neighborhood in the 1850's (Mosier and Mosier, p. 31).

Dougherty's Station: see **Dublin** [ALAMEDA].

Dowdall Creek [SONOMA]: *stream,* flows 4 miles to Sonoma Creek 1.25 miles southwest of Sonoma (lat. 38°16'55" N, long. 122°28'30" W). Named on Glen Ellen (1954) and Sonoma (1951) 7.5' quadrangles.

Dowest Slough: see **New York Slough** [CONTRA COSTA].

Dozier [SOLANO]: *locality,* 7 miles southeast of Elmira along Sacramento Northern Railroad (lat. 38°17'10" N, long. 121°48'55" W; at S line sec. 12, T 5 S, R 1 E). Named on Dozier (1952) 7.5' quadrangle.

Drakes Bay [MARIN]: *embayment,* 7 miles southeast of Point Reyes Station along the coast east of Point Reyes (lat. 38°00'30" N, long. 122°55' W). Named on Drakes Bay (1953) and Inverness (1954) 7.5' quadrangles. Called Sir Francis Drake's Bay on Ringgold's (1850b) map, and called Bay of Sir F. Drake on Goddard's (1857) map. Sebastian Cermeño visited the embayment in 1595 and named it Puerto de San Francisco, or Bahia de San Francisco; Vizcaino came to the place in 1603—on January 6, the day of Los Reyes—and called it Puerto de los Reyes, or Puerto de Don Gaspar (Hanna, W.L., p. 39; Wagner, H.R., p. 405). Abraham Goos in 1624, and Henry Briggs in 1625, associated Sir Francis Drake's name with the place on maps, using the designation "P. Sr. Francisco Draco" (Wagner, H.R., p. 118, 304). The embayment was known as Jack's Harbor in the 1850's (Soule, Gihon, and Nisbet, p. 32). The present name is from the belief of some people that Francis Drake landed at the place in 1579.

Drakes Beach [MARIN]: *beach,* 4 miles northeast of the lighthouse at Point Reyes (lat. 38°01'40" N, long. 122°57'35" W); the beach is along Drakes Bay. Named on Drakes Bay (1953) 7.5' quadrangle.

Drakes Estero [MARIN]: *bay,* opens into Drakes Bay 5.5 miles east-northeast of the lighthouse at Point Reyes (lat. 38°01'55" N, long. 122°56' W). Named on Drakes Bay (1953) 7.5' quadrangle. Members of United States Coast Survey named the feature in 1860; before that time this bay and the adjoining bays together were called Estero de Limantour for the commander of a Mexican vessel lost at the entrance to the feature in 1841 (Hanna, W.L., p. 40-41).

Drakes Head [MARIN]: *ridge,* south-trending, less than 1 mile long, 6.5 miles east-northeast of the lighthouse at Point Reyes (lat. 38'02'20" N, long. 122°54'50" W). Named on Drakes Bay (1953) 7.5' quadrangle.

Drakes Peak: see **Drakes Point** [SOLANO].

Drakes Point [SOLANO]: *peak,* 5.25 miles south-southwest of Allendale (lat. 38°22'35" N, long. 121°59'15" W). Altitude 624 feet. Named on Allendale (1953) 7.5' quadrangle. United States Board on Geographic Names (1933, p. 272) rejected the name "Drakes Peak" for the feature.

Drawbridge [ALAMEDA]: *locality,* 6 miles south of Fremont civic center along Southern Pacific Railroad on an island between Coyote Creek and Mud Slough (lat. 37°28' N, long. 121°58'25" W). Named on Milpitas (1961) 7.5' quadrangle. The place was called Saline City about 1904, referring no doubt to the nearby salt ponds (Dick Barrett, *San Jose Mercury-News*, August 12, 1973).

Drawbridge: see **Cygnus** [SOLANO].

Dresser [ALAMEDA]: *locality,* 3 miles north-northeast of Fremont civic center along Southern Pacific Railroad in Niles Canyon (lat. 37°35'30" N, long. 121°57'15" W; near N line sec. 15, T 4 S, R 1 W). Named on Niles (1961) 7.5' quadrangle. According to Mosier and Mosier (p. 31), the place was called Merienda until 1915, and then was called Alston until 1957, when it received the present name.

Driftwood Beach [MARIN]: *beach,* 4.5 miles southwest of Tomales along the sea coast (lat. 38°11'45" N, long. 122°57'50" W). Named on Tomales (1954) 7.5' quadrangle.

Dry Arroyo [SOLANO]: *stream,* flows 5 miles to lowlands 2.5 miles north of Allendale (lat. 38°28'45" N, long. 121°56'45" W). Named on Allendale (1953) and Mount Vaca (1951) 7.5' quadrangles.

Dry Creek [ALAMEDA]:

(1) *stream,* flows 6.5 miles to Alameda Creek 4 miles north of downtown Newark (lat. 37°35'15" N, long. 122°02'15" W). Named on Newark (1959) 7.5' quadrangle. Thompson and West (1878, p. 17) used the designation "Segunda, or Dry Creek" for the feature. Spaniards applied the name "Segunda" to the stream because it was the second stream crossed by a traveler on the way north from San Jose mission—*segunda* means "sec-

ond" in Spanish; the canyon of the stream has the local name "Black Creek Valley" (Mosier and Mosier, p. 16, 79-80).

(2) *stream,* flows 4.5 miles to Arroyo Valle 3.25 miles south of Livermore (lat. 37°38'10" N, long. 121°45'50" W). Named on Altamont (1953), Livermore (1961), and Mendenhall Springs (1956) 7.5' quadrangles.

(3) *stream,* flows 4.5 miles to Arroyo Mocho 7 miles south-southwest of Altamont (lat. 37°39'35" N, long. 121°43'50" W; near W line sec. 23, T 3 S, R 2 E). Named on Tesla (1907) 15' quadrangle.

Dry Creek [CONTRA COSTA]: *stream,* flows 3.5 miles to Marsh Creek about 1 mile southwest of Brentwood (lat. 37°55'20" N, long. 121°42'40" W). Named on Antioch South (1953) and Brentwood (1978) 7.5' quadrangles.

Dry Creek [NAPA]: *stream,* flows 15 miles to Napa River 5.25 miles north-northwest of downtown Napa (lat. 38°22'20" N, long. 122° 18'20" W). Named on Napa (1951), Rutherford (1951), Sonoma (1951), and Yountville (1951) 7.5' quadrangles. The canyon of Dry Creek is called Wing Canyon on Sonoma (1942) 15' quadrangle. United States Board on Geographic Names (1986, p. 3) approved the name "Campbell Canyon" for a canyon, 1.5 miles long, that opens into the canyon of Dry Creek 3.5 miles south of Rutherford (lat. 34°24'27" N, long. 122°25'57" W; sec. 32, T 7 N, R 5 W); the name commemorates Duncan Campbell, who homesteaded at the place in 1875.

Dry Creek [SAN MATEO]: *stream,* flows 2.5 miles to Tunitas Creek 2.25 miles north of the village of San Gregorio (lat. 37°21'35" N, long. 122°23'25" W). Named on La Honda (1961) and San Gregorio (1961) 7.5' quadrangles.

Dry Creek [SANTA CLARA]:

(1) *stream,* flows nearly 3.5 miles to Los Gatos Creek 2 miles south-southwest of downtown San Jose (lat. 37°18'25" N, long. 121°54'35" W). Named on San Jose West (1961) 7.5' quadrangle. Called Old Channel Los Gatos [Creek] on Thompson and West's (1876) map.

(2) *stream,* flows nearly 3 miles to Sulphur Springs Creek 5.5 miles south-southeast of Eylar Mountain (lat. 37°23'55" N, long. 121°30'25" W; sec. 23, T 6 S, R 4 E). Named on Eylar Mountain (1955) 7.5' quadrangle. On Mount Hamilton (1897) 15' quadrangle, the stream is shown as part of Sulphur Spring Creek.

Dry Creek [SONOMA]: *stream,* heads in Mendocino County and flows 27 miles in Sonoma County to Russian River 2 miles south-southeast of Healdsburg (lat. 38°35'10" N, long. 122°51'25" W). Named on Hopland (1960) 15' quadrangle, and on Geyserville (1955), Guerneville (1955), Healdsburg (1955), and Warm Springs Dam (1978) 7.5' quadrangles. Hoods Hot Springs are in the canyon of Dry Creek near the north line of Sonoma County; they probably are the springs sometimes referred to as Fairmont Hot Springs (Waring, p. 82).

Dry Creek: see **Barron Creek** [SANTA CLARA]; **Deer Creek** [CONTRA COSTA]; **Martin Creek** [SAN MATEO]; **Thompson Creek** [SANTA CLARA].

Dublin [ALAMEDA]: *town,* 9.5 miles west of Livermore at the southwest end of San Ramon Valley (lat. 37°42'05" N, long. 121° 56'15" W). Named on Dublin (1961) 7.5' quadrangle. Pleasanton (1906) 15' quadrangle has both the names "Dublin" and "Dougherty P.O." at the place. James Witt Dougherty purchased a large part of Amador's San Ramon grant in 1852, including a two-story adobe building; the community that grew up around the building generally was known until 1860 as Amador's or Amador Valley, and the post office there was called Dougherty's Station—the south part of the community was called Dublin, supposedly because of the large number of Irish people there (Hoover, Rensch, and Rensch, p. 12-13). Postal authorities established Dougherty's Station post office in 1860, changed the name to Dougherty in 1896, and discontinued it in 1908; they established Dublin post office in 1963 (Salley, p. 61, 62).

Dublin Canyon [ALAMEDA]: *canyons,* two, each heads 2 miles west of Dublin (lat. 37°41'50" N, long. 121°58'30" W; sec. 4, T 3 S, R 1 W). Named on Dublin (1961) and Hayward (1959) 7.5' quadrangles. One canyon extends west for 2.5 miles to a point 4 miles east-northeast of downtown Hayward, and the other extends east for 2 miles to Dublin. The divide between the two canyons is called Haywards Pass on Pleasanton (1906) 15' quadrangle.

Dublin Creek [ALAMEDA]: *stream,* flows 2.25 miles to lowlands at Dublin (lat. 37°42' N, long. 121°56' W). Named on Dublin (1961) 7.5' quadrangle.

Duck Cove [MARIN]: *embayment,* 7 miles south of Tomales on the southwest side of Tomales Bay (lat. 38°08'35" N, long. 122° 54' W). Named on Tomales (1954) 7.5' quadrangle.

Ducker Creek [SONOMA]: *stream,* flows 3 miles to Rincon Creek 2.5 miles northeast of downtown Santa Rosa (lat. 38°27'50" N, long. 122°40'30" W). Named on Santa Rosa (1954) 7.5' quadrangle.

Duck Island: see **Hog Island** [MARIN].

Duck Slough [SOLANO]:

(1) *water feature,* joins Hass Slough 10.5 miles north of Rio Vista (lat. 38°18'25" N, long. 121°43'50" W). Named on Liberty Island (1978) 7.5' quadrangle.

(2) *water feature,* joins Hill Slough 2 miles south-southeast of downtown Fairfield (lat. 38°13'35" N, long. 122°01'20" W). Named on Fairfield South (1949) 7.5' quadrangle.

(3) *water feature,* in Yolo Basin (present Yolo Bypass), joins Miner Slough 10 miles north-northeast of Rio Vista (lat. 38°17'20" N, long. 121°36'45" W). Named on Vorden (1916) 7.5' quadrangle.

Duck Slough: see **Little Duck Slough** [SOLANO].

Dudley Creek [SOLANO]: *water feature,* dry watercourse that lies less than 1 mile northeast of Dixon (lat. 38°27'15" N, long. 121°48'45" W). Named on Dixon (1952) 7.5' quadrangle. Shown as an intermittent stream on Vacaville (1953) 15' quadrangle.

Dugans Pond [SONOMA]: *lake,* 300 feet long, 2.25 miles northwest of Cazadero (lat. 38°33'20" N, long. 123°06'45" W; sec. 7, T 8 N, R 11 W). Named on Cazadero (1978) 7.5' quadrangle.

Dug Road Creek [SOLANO]: *stream,* flows 2.5 miles to Wild Horse Creek 7.25 miles west of Fairfield (lat. 38°16'05" N, long. 122°10'10" W; near W line sec. 23, T 5 N, R 3 W). Named on Mount George (1951) 7.5' quadrangle.

Dumbarton [ALAMEDA]: *locality,* 3.25 miles west-southwest of downtown Newark along Southern Pacific Railroad (lat. 37°30'25" N, long. 122°05'35" W). Named on Hayward (1915) 15' quadrangle.

Dumbarton Point [ALAMEDA]: *promontory,* 4 miles west-southwest of downtown Newark at the edge of San Francisco Bay (lat. 37°29'55" N, long. 122°06'10" W). Named on Mountain View (1961) and Newark (1959) 7.5' quadrangles. Called Potrero Pt. on Palo Alto (1899) 15' quadrangle. A Scottish railroad surveyor named the feature for the city and county of Dumbarton in Scotland (Mosier and Mosier, p. 32). A place called Arden was situated along South Coast Railroad between Newark and Dumbarton Point; it was on land belonging to George Patterson, who called his estate Ardenwood (MacGregor, p. 90, 103).

Duncan Point: see **Duncans Point** [SONOMA].

Duncans Cove [SONOMA]: *embayment,* 4 miles south-southeast of Jenner along the coast (lat. 38°23'40" N, long. 123°05'30" W). Named on Duncans Mills (1979) 7.5' quadrangle. The cove is the site of Duncan's Landing, which was at the end of a horse-drawn railway that brought lumber from the mill of Alexander Duncan and Samuel Duncan for shipment in the 1860's and 1870's (Miller, J.T., p. 42).

Duncan's Landing: see **Duncans Cove** [SONOMA].

Duncans Mills [SONOMA]: *settlement,* 3.5 miles east of Jenner along Russian River (lat. 38°27'10" N, long. 123°03'10" W). Named on Duncans Mills (1979) 7.5' quadrangle. Postal authorities established Duncans Mills post office in 1862 (Frickstad, p. 195). Duncans Mills (1921) 15' quadrangle shows Duncans Mill situated south of Russian River near present Bridgehaven, where Alexander Duncan and Samuel Duncan operated a lumber mill, and where by 1860 a village called Duncansville had 300 inhabitants; Alexander Duncan moved the mill in 1876 to the site of present Duncans Mills (Hansen and Miller, p. 47-48).

Duncans Point [SONOMA]: *promontory,* 4.25 miles south-southeast of Jenner along the sea coast (lat. 38°23'35" N, long. 123°05'40" W). Named on Duncans Mills (1979) 7.5' quadrangle. Called Duncan Pt. on Duncans Mills (1943) 7.5' quadrangle.

Duncansville: see **Duncans Mills** [SONOMA].

Dunes Beach [SAN MATEO]: *beach,* 2 miles northwest of downtown Half Moon Bay along the coast (lat. 37°29' N, long. 122°27'05" W). Named on Half Moon Bay (1961) 7.5' quadrangle.

Dunn: see **Petaluma** [SONOMA] (2).

Dunn Canyon [SANTA CLARA]: *canyon,* drained by a stream that flows 1 mile to Hay Canyon 5 miles north of Mount Madonna (lat. 37°05'15" N, long. 121°42'15" W). Named on Mount Madonna (1955) 7.5' quadrangle.

Dunne Ridge [SANTA CLARA]: *ridge,* north-trending, 3 miles long, 12 miles east-southeast of Gilroy on Santa Clara-San Benito County line (lat. 36°58' N, long. 121°21'15" W). Named on Three Sisters (1954) 7.5' quadrangle.

Dunns Peak [SOLANO]: *peak,* 5 miles east of Mount Vaca (lat. 38° 23'45" N, long. 122°00'45" W). Altitude 804 feet. Named on Mount Vaca (1951) 7.5' quadrangle.

Du Pont [CONTRA COSTA]: *locality,* 5.5 miles west of the settlement of Bethel Island along Atchison, Topeka and Santa Fe Railroad (lat. 38°00'25" N, long. 121°44'15" W; sec. 22, T 2 N, R 2 E). Named on Jersey Island (1978) 7.5' quadrangle.

Durham Ridge [SAN MATEO]: *ridge,* southwest-trending, 1.5 miles long, 2.5 miles west-southwest of Skeggs Point (lat. 37°23'45" N, long. 122°20'50" W). Named on Woodside (1961) 7.5' quadrangle. Durham ranch was on the ridge in the middle and late 1850's (Brown, p. 30).

Dutard Creek [SANTA CLARA]: *stream,* flows 1.25 miles to Upper Penitencia Creek nearly 2 miles east-northeast of Berryessa (lat. 37°23'40" N, long. 121°49'40" W). Named on Calaveras Reservoir (1961) 7.5' quadrangle.

Dutch Bill Creek [SONOMA]: *stream,* flows 6.25 miles to Russian River 2.5 miles south-southwest of Guerneville at Monte Rio (lat. 38°27'55" N, long. 123°00'35" W; sec. 7, T 7 N, R 10 W). Named on Camp Meeker (1954) and Duncans Mills (1979) 7.5' quadrangles. The name is for William Howard, who came to the region in the 1840's (Hansen and Miller, p. 48).

Dutcher Creek [SONOMA]: *stream,* flows 3.5 miles to Dry Creek 4 miles west of Geyserville (lat. 38°42'25" N, long. 123°58'25" W). Named on Geyserville (1955) 7.5' quadrangle.

Dutch Henry Canyon [NAPA]: *canyon,* drained by a stream that flows 3 miles to Napa Valley 3.25 miles east of Calistoga (lat. 38° 34'40" N, long. 122°31'05" W). Named on Calistoga (1958) 7.5' quadrangle.

Dutchman Slough [SOLANO]: *water feature,* lies between Island Number 1 and Knight Island from South Slough to Napa River 2 miles northwest of downtown Vallejo (lat. 38°07'15" N, long. 122° 17' W). Named on Cuttings Wharf (1949) and Mare Island (1959) 7.5' quadrangles.

Dutch Slough [CONTRA COSTA]: *water feature,* extends for 6.25 miles from Sand Mound Slough to San Joaquin River 4.5 miles west of the settlement of Bethel Island (lat. 38°01'35" N, long. 121°43'25" W). Named on Brentwood (1954) and Jersey Island (1978) 7.5' quadrangles.

Dutton [SOLANO]: *locality,* 4 miles south of Birds Landing (2) along Sacramento Northern Railroad on Van Sickle Island (lat. 38°04'35" N, long. 121°53' W). Named on Honker Bay (1953) 7.5' quadrangle. Called Chaplin on Honker Bay (1918) 7.5' quadrangle, which shows the place along Oakland Antioch and Eastern Railroad. Honker Bay (1953, photorevised 1968 and 1973) 7.5' quadrangle shows it along an old railroad grade.

Dutton Island [SOLANO]: *island,* 6.5 miles west-southwest of Birds Landing (2) along Suisun Bay (lat. 38°04'50" N, long. 121°58'15" W). Named on Honker Bay (1953) 7.5' quadrangle.

Dutton Landing [NAPA]: *locality,* 3.5 miles west-northwest of Napa Junction along Napa River (lat. 38°12'40" N, long. 122°18'20" W; sec. 9, T 4 N, R 4 W). Named on Cuttings Wharf (1949, photorevised 1968) 7.5' quadrangle.

Dutton Ridge: see **Thompson Ridge** [SONOMA] (2).

Duttons Landing [SOLANO]: *locality,* 2.25 miles south-southwest of Birds Landing (2) along Montezuma Slough (lat. 38°06'35" N, long. 121°53'20" W). Named on Honker Bay (1918) 7.5' quadrangle. Postal authorities established Duttons Landing post office in 1887 and discontinued it in 1926; the name is from John W. Dutton, who operated the boat landing at the place (Salley, p. 63).

Duvall Lake [NAPA]: *lake,* 1100 feet long, 1 mile southeast of Aetna Springs (lat. 38°38'35" N, long. 122°28'20" W; sec. 12, T 9 N, R 6 W). Named on Aetna Springs (1958) 7.5' quadrangle.

Duvoul Creek [SONOMA]: *stream,* flows 2 miles to Dutch Bill Creek nearly 3 miles north-northwest of Occidental (lat. 38°26'35" N, long. 122°58'30" W; near N line sec. 21, T 7 N, R 10 W). Named on Camp Meeker (1954) 7.5' quadrangle.

Du Vrees Creek: see **Islais Creek Channel** [SAN FRANCISCO].

Duxbury Point [MARIN]: *promontory,* at Bolinas (lat. 37°53'40" N, long. 122°42' W); the feature is along the coast opposite Duxbury Reef. Named on Bolinas (1954) 7.5' quadrangle. Called Punta de Baulenes on a diseño of Las Baulenes grant made in 1846 (Becker, 1969).

Duxbury Reef [MARIN]: *shoal,* 1.5 miles south-southwest of Bolinas (lat. 37°53'30" N, long. 122°42' W). Named on Bolinas (1954) 7.5' quadrangle. The name is from the ship *Duxbury,* which ran aground at the place in 1849 (Mason, 1976b, p. 103).

Dyer Canyon [SANTA CLARA]: *canyon,* drained by a stream that flows 1 mile to Briggs Creek 3.25 miles south-southwest of Los Gatos (lat. 37°11'10" N, long. 122°00'25" W; near S line sec. 31, T 8 S, R 1 W). Named on Castle Rock Ridge (1955) 7.5' quadrangle.

Dyer Creek [NAPA]: *stream,* flows 3.5 miles to Lake Berryessa 3 miles east of Walter Springs (lat. 38°39'20" N, long. 122°18'20" W; sec. 4, T 9 N, R 4 W). Named on Walter Springs (1959) 7.5' quadrangle.

— E —

Ead's Island: see **Simmons Island** [SOLANO].

Eagle Hill [SAN MATEO]: *hill,* 1 mile southwest of downtown Redwood City (lat. 37°28'30" N, long. 122°14'35" W). Named on Palo Alto (1961) 7.5' quadrangle.

Eaglenest: see **Rio Nido** [SONOMA].

Eagle Peak [CONTRA COSTA]: *peak,* 2 miles northwest of Mount Diablo (lat. 37°54'05" N, long. 121°56'15" W; sec. 26, T 1 N, R 1 E). Altitude 2369 feet. Named on Clayton (1953) 7.5' quadrangle. Called Eagle Pt. on Mount Diablo (1898) 15' quadrangle—members of the Whitney survey gave this name to the feature (Whitney, p. 21).

Eagle Point: see **Eagle Peak** [CONTRA COSTA].

Eagle Rock [SANTA CLARA]: *relief feature,* 2.5 miles east-northeast of Berryessa near the mouth of Alum Rock Canyon (lat. 37°23'45" N, long. 121°48'50" W). Named on Calaveras Reservoir (1961) 7.5' quadrangle.

Eagle Rock [SONOMA]:

(1) *relief feature,* nearly 3 miles north of Geyser Peak (lat. 38°48'20" N, long. 122°50'20" W; near NW cor. sec. 14, T 11 N, R 9 W). Named on The Geysers (1959) 7.5' quadrangle.

(2) *relief feature,* 4 miles southeast of Jenner (lat. 38°24'15" N, long. 123°04'45" W). Named on Duncans Mills (1979) 7.5' quadrangle.

(3) *peak,* 5.5 miles west-northwest of Skaggs Springs (lat. 38°43' N, long. 123°07'15" W; sec. 18, T 10 N, R 11 W). Named on Warm Springs Dam (1978) 7.5' quadrangle.

East Antioch [CONTRA COSTA]: *settlement,* 2 miles east of downtown Antioch (lat. 38°00'30" N, long. 121°46'15" W). Named on Antioch North (1978) 7.5' quadrangle.

East Austin Creek [SONOMA]: *stream,* flows 13 miles to Austin Creek less than 2 miles southeast of Cazadero (lat. 38°30'35" N, long. 123°04' W). Named on Cazadero (1978) and Warm Springs Dam (1978) 7.5' quadrangles.

East Bull Canyon [NAPA]: *canyon,* nearly 2 miles long, opens into Wragg Canyon 4.5 miles northwest of Mount Vaca (lat. 38°27'15" N, long. 122°09'05" W; near W line sec. 13, T 7 N, R 3 W); the mouth of the canyon is opposite the mouth of West Bull Canyon. Named on Capell Valley (1951) 7.5' quadrangle.

East Bulls Head Channel [CONTRA COSTA-SOLANO]: *channel,* 3.5 miles northeast of Martinez in Suisun Bay along Contra Costa-Solano County line (lat. 38°03' N, long. 122°05'20" W); the feature is east-northeast of Bulls Head Channel. Named on Vine Hill (1959) 7.5' quadrangle.

East Chapman Canyon [NAPA]: *canyon,* 0.5 mile long, opens into Wragg Canyon nearly 5 miles north-northwest of Mount Vaca (lat. 38°27'35" N, long. 122°09'55" W; near NE cor. sec. 14, T 7 N, R 3 W); the mouth of the canyon is opposite the mouth of West Chapman Canyon. Named on Capell Valley (1951) 7.5' quadrangle.

East Creek: see **Lion Creek** [ALAMEDA].

East Guernewood [SONOMA]: *settlement,* less than 0.5 mile southwest of Guerneville along Russian River (lat. 38°29'50" N, long. 123°00'10" W; sec. 31, T 8 N, R 10 W). Named on Duncans Mills (1979) 7.5' quadrangle.

East Harbor [SAN FRANCISCO]: *water feature,* 1.25 miles west of North Point along San Francisco Bay (lat. 37°48'25" N, long. 122° 25'55" W). Named on San Francisco North (1956, photorevised 1968 and 1973) 7.5' quadrangle. United States Board on Geographic Names (1981b, p. 3) approved the name "Gashouse Cove" for the embayment that includes East Harbor, and noted that the name is from a gas works built near the embayment in the 1890's.

Eastland: see **Mill Valley** [MARIN] (2).

East Landing: see **Southeast Farallon** [SAN FRANCISCO].

Eastman Canyon [SANTA CLARA]: *canyon,* drained by a stream that flows 3.25 miles to Uvas Reservoir 4 miles north of Mount Madonna (lat. 37°04'20" N, long. 121°42'35" W; sec. 12, T 10 S, R 2 E). Named on Mount Madonna (1955, photorevised 1968 and 1973) 7.5' quadrangle.

East Marin Island [MARIN]: *island,* 1350 feet long, nearly 2 miles southwest of Point San Pedro in San Rafael Bay (lat. 37°57'50" N, long. 122°28' W); the feature is 400 feet east-southeast of West Marin Island. Named on San Quentin (1959) 7.5' quadrangle. East Marin Island and West Marin Island together are called Marin Is. on San Francisco (1915) 15' quadrangle.

East Mitchell Canyon [NAPA]: *canyon,* 1 mile long, opens into Wragg Canyon 5.5 miles north-northwest of Mount Vaca (lat. 38° 28'15" N, long. 122°09'15" W; sec. 11, T 7 N, R 3 W); the mouth of the canyon is opposite the mouth of West Mitchell Canyon. Named on Capell Valley (1951) 7.5' quadrangle.

East Napa Reservoir [NAPA]: *lake,* 600 feet long, 1 mile east-northeast of downtown Napa (lat. 38°18'10" N, long. 122°16' W). Named on Napa (1951) 7.5' quadrangle.

East Oakland: see **San Antonio**, under **Oakland** [ALAMEDA].

Easton: see **Easton Creek** [SAN MATEO].

Easton Creek [SAN MATEO]: *stream,* flows 1.5 miles to lowlands along San Francisco Bay 2.5 miles east-northeast of downtown San Mateo (lat. 37°35'05" N, long. 122°22'05" W). Named on Montara Mountain (1956) and San Mateo (1956) 7.5' quadrangles. A community called Easton developed near the mouth of present Easton Creek between 1900 and 1910; Burlingame annexed the place in 1910 (Brown, p. 11). Ansel Mills Easton subdivided land at Easton and built a depot that he named Easton Station (Hynding, p. 113). Postal authorities established Easton post office in 1909 and discontinued it in 1916 (Frickstad, p. 167).

East Palo Alto [SAN MATEO]: *town,* 5 miles east-southeast of downtown Redwood City (lat. 37°28'10" N, long. 122°08'10" W); the community is north of Palo Alto [SANTA CLARA]. Named on Palo Alto (1961) 7.5' quadrangle. Palo Alto (1953) 7.5' quadrangle gives the alternate name "Ravenswood" for East Palo Alto. Isaiah Woods laid out a townsite at the place in 1849 and called it Ravenswood; a cooperative colony called Runnymede was at the site from 1916 until the 1930's, but in 1925 residents chose the name "East Palo Alto" for the community (Hynding, p. 133, 135-136). The town incorporated in 1983. California Mining Bureau's (1917b) map shows a place called Sweeney along the railroad in present East Palo Alto at the edge of San Francisco Bay.

East Peak [MARIN]: *peak,* 4 miles southwest of downtown San Rafael on Mount Tamalpais (lat. 37°55'45" N, long. 122°34'35" W). Altitude 2571 feet. Named on San Rafael (1954) 7.5' quadrangle.

East Pleasanton [ALAMEDA]: *locality,* 3.5 miles west of Livermore (lat. 37°40'20" N, long. 121°49'45" W); the place is 2.5 miles east-northeast of Pleasanton. Named on Livermore (1961) 7.5' quadrangle.

Eastport [CONTRA COSTA]: *locality,* 2.5 miles south of Orinda (lat. 37°50'25" N, long. 122°10'50" W; sec. 15, T 1 S, R 3 W). Named on Oakland East (1959) 7.5' quadrangle. Concord (1915) 15' quadrangle shows the place at the east portal of a tunnel along Oakland Antioch and Eastern Railroad.

East San Jose [SANTA CLARA]: *district,* 1.5 miles east-northeast of present downtown San Jose, and east of Coyote Creek (lat. 37°20'30" N, long. 121°52' W). Named on San Jose (1899) 15' quadrangle.

East Side Reservoir [NAPA]: *lake,* 250 feet long, 1.5 miles north-northeast of downtown Napa (lat. 38°19'10" N, long. 122°16'05" W). Named on Napa (1951) 7.5' quadrangle.

East Slough [ALAMEDA]: *water feature,* enters San Leandro Bay 4.25 miles southeast of downtown Oakland (lat. 37°45'35" N, long. 122°13' W). Named on Oakland East (1959) 7.5' quadrangle.

East Vallejo: see **Vallejo** [SOLANO].

East Windsor [SONOMA]: *settlement,* 6 miles southeast of Healdsburg (lat. 38°32'45" N, long. 122°48'15" W; sec. 13, T 8 N, R 9 W); the place is 0.5 mile east of Windsor. Named on Healdsburg (1955) 7.5' quadrangle.

Eastwood Camp: see **Camp Eastwood** [MARIN].

Eastyard: see **Point Richmond** [CONTRA COSTA] (2).

Eaton H. Magoon Lake: see **Upper Bohn Lake**, under **Aetna Springs** [NAPA].

Ebabais Creek: see **Ebabias Creek** [SONOMA].

Ebabaza Creek: see **Ebabias Creek** [SONOMA].

Ebabias Creek [SONOMA]: *stream,* flows 5.25 miles to Estero Americano 0.5 mile west-southwest of Valley Ford (lat. 38°18'50" N, long. 122°56'05" W). Named on Valley Ford (1954) 7.5' quadrangle. United States Board on Geographic Names (1943, p. 11) rejected the forms "Ababais," "Ebabais," "Ebabaza," "Ebebais," and "Erabais" for the name.

Ebabias Creek: see **Americano Creek** [MARIN-SONOMA].

Ebebais Creek: see **Ebabias Creek** [SONOMA].

Eberly [ALAMEDA]: *locality,* 2 miles northwest of Fremont civic center along Western Pacific Railroad (lat. 37°34'20" N, long. 121° 59'30" W). Named on Niles (1961) 7.5' quadrangle. The name commemorates William V. Eberly, manager of California Nursery from 1904 until 1917 (Mosier and Mosier, p. 33).

Eckley [CONTRA COSTA]: *locality,* 4.5 miles northwest of Martinez along Southern Pacific Railroad (lat. 38°03'15" N, long. 122°12'05" W). Named on Benicia (1959) 7.5' quadrangle. The name commemorates Commodore John L. Eckley, who bought the cove at the place in the 1870's for a yacht harbor (Gudde, 1949, p. 103).

Eddicut Flat [SONOMA]: *area,* nearly 5 miles west of Big Mountain along Wheatfield Fork Gualala River (lat. 38°41'55" N, long. 123° 13'45" W; sec. 19, T 10 N, R 12 W). Named on Tombs Creek (1978) 7.5' quadrangle.

Eden: see **Mount Eden** [ALAMEDA].

Eden Canyon [ALAMEDA]: *canyon,* 2.5 miles long, on upper reaches of San Lorenzo Creek above a point 4.25 miles northeast of downtown Hayward (lat. 37°42'35" N, long. 122°01'05" W). Named on Dublin (1961) and Hayward (1959) 7.5' quadrangles. The stream in the canyon is called Eden Creek on Haywards (1899) and Pleasanton (1906) 15' quadrangles.

Eden Creek: see **Eden Canyon** [ALAMEDA].

Edendale [SONOMA]: *settlement,* 1 mile south-southwest of Guerneville along Russian River (lat. 38°29'10" N, long. 123°00'10" W; sec. 6, T 7 N, R 10 W). Named on Duncans Mills (1979) 7.5' quadrangle.

Edendale: see **Mount Eden** [ALAMEDA].

Eden Landing: see **Mount Eden** [ALAMEDA].

Eden Plain: see **Byron** [CONTRA COSTA].

Edenvale [SANTA CLARA]: *locality,* 6 miles southeast of downtown San Jose along Southern Pacific Railroad (lat. 37°15'55" N, long. 121°49' W). Named on San Jose East (1961) 7.5' quadrangle. An inn called Seven Mile House began operating at the place in the 1850's (Hoover, Rensch, and Rensch, p. 431). Another stopping place, called Eight Mile House, was situated about 1 mile farther southeast (*San Jose Mercury-News, California Today Magazine,* October 23, 1977). The names recorded the distance of the places from San Jose. Postal authorities established Eden Vale post office in 1893 and discontinued it in 1916 (Frickstad, p. 173). Rambo (1973, p. 41) attributed the name "Edenvale" to the Edenlike beauty of Hayes Estate, which was at the site. The low range 0.5 mile north of Edenvale is called Los Lagrimas Hills (Carey and Miller, p. 153) or Las Lagrimas (Hoover, Rensch, and Rensch, p. 431).

Edgemar [SAN MATEO]: *district,* 4 miles west of downtown South San Francisco near the coast (lat. 37°39'15" N, long. 122°29'15" W). Named on San Francisco South (1956) 7.5' quadrangle. The residents of the place voted in 1957 to join neighboring communities and form the new city of Pacifica (Gudde, 1969, p. 233).

Edgerley Island [NAPA]: *island,* nearly 4 miles west-northwest of Napa Junction along Napa River (lat. 38°12' N, long. 122°19' W). Named on Cuttings Wharf (1949) 7.5' quadrangle.

Edith Point: see **Point Edith** [CONTRA COSTA].

Edson Canyon [SANTA CLARA]: *canyon,* drained by a stream that flows nearly 1 mile to an unnamed stream 3 miles south-southeast of New Almaden (lat. 37°08'05" N, long. 121°48'40" W; near E line sec. 24, T 9 S, R 1 E). Named on Santa Teresa Hills (1953) 7.5' quadrangle.

Eel Rock [SAN MATEO]: *island,* 550 feet long, 4 miles south of downtown Half Moon Bay and 100 feet offshore (lat. 37°24'20" N, long. 122°25'40" W). Named on Half Moon Bay (1961) 7.5' quadrangle.

Egbert Cut [SOLANO]: *water feature,* joins Miner Slough 9.5 miles north-northeast of Rio Vista near Five Points (lat. 38°17'35" N, long. 121°38'40" W). Named on Courtland (1952) and Liberty Island (1952) 7.5' quadrangles.

Eighteen Mile House: see **Madrone** [SANTA CLARA].

Eight Mile House: see **Edenvale** [SANTA CLARA].

El Arroyo de Gallinas: see **Gallinas Creek** [MARIN].

El Arroyo de la Presa: see **Bear Gulch** [SAN MATEO].

El Arroyo Tulares de los Canoas: see **Canoas Creek** [SANTA CLARA].

El Bonita [SONOMA]: *settlement,* 1 mile northeast of Guerneville along Russian River (lat. 38°30'45" N, long. 122°59' W; sec. 29, T 8 N, R 10 W). Named on Guerneville (1955) 7.5' quadrangle.

El Campo]MARIN]: *locality,* 3 miles south-southeast of Point San Quentin on the northeast side of Tiburon Peninsula (lat. 37°53'50" N, long. 122°27'50" W). Named on San Quentin (1959) 7.5' quadrangle. Officials of San Francisco and North Pacific Railroad opened a resort called El Campo at the place in 1891; later the resort site was called Paradise Park (Teather, p. 23).

El Cañada de San Vicente: see **San Antonio Valley** [SANTA CLARA].

El Cerito [CONTRA COSTA]: *town,* 3 miles east-southeast of Richmond civic center (lat. 37°54'45" N, long. 122°17'45" W). Named on Richmond (1959) 7.5' quadrangle. The place first was called County Line (Gudde, 1949, p. 62). Postal authorities established Rust post office at the site in 1909 and changed the name to El Cerito in 1916; the name "Rust" was for William R. Rust, first postmaster (Salley, p 191). The town incorporated in 1917.

El Cerrito Hill: see **Albany Hill** [ALAMEDA].

El Cierbo: see **Tormey** [CONTRA COSTA].

El Corte de Madera [SAN MATEO-SANTA CLARA]: *land grant,* chiefly southwest of Portola Valley (1) on San Mateo-Santa Clara County line, mainly in San Mateo County. Named on La Honda (1961), Mindego Hill (1961), Palo Alto (1961), and Woodside (1961) 7.5' quadrangles. Maximo Martinez received 2 leagues in 1844 and claimed 13,316 acres patented in 1858 (Cowan, p. 30). *El corte de madera* has the meaning "the place where lumber is cut," "the lumber cutting," or "the timber clearing" in Spanish (Arbuckle, p. 15).

El Corte de Madera Creek [SAN MATEO]: *stream,* flows 8.5 miles to San Gregorio Creek nearly 4 miles west of La Honda (lat. 37°18'50" N, long. 122°20'20" W). Named on La Honda (1961) and Woodside (1961) 7.5' quadrangles.

Elder Valley [NAPA]: *valley,* 10 miles east of Saint Helena (lat. 38° 31'15" N, long. 122°17' W). Named on Chiles Valley (1958) 7.5' quadrangle.

Eldridge [SONOMA]: *locality,* 1.25 miles south-southeast of Glen Ellen (lat. 38°21' N, long. 122°30'40" W). Named on Santa Rosa (1944) 15' quadrangle. Santa Rosa (1916) 15' quadrangle shows the place along Southern Pacific Railroad. Glen Ellen (1954) 7.5' quadrangle has the designation "Sonoma State Home (Eldridge P.O.)" near the site. Postal authorities established Eldridge post office in 1894 and named it for a pioneer rancher (Salley, p. 67).

Eleda Hot Springs: see **Fetters Hot Springs** [SONOMA].

Elephant Head [SANTA CLARA]: *peak,* nearly 4 miles west-northwest of Pacheco Peak (lat. 37°01'30" N, long. 121°21' W; sec. 31, T 10 S, R 6 E). Altitude 1905 feet. Named on Pacheco Peak (1955) 7.5' quadrangle.

Elephant Head Creek [SANTA CLARA]: *stream,* flows 3.5 miles to Pacheco Creek 4 miles west of Pacheco Peak (lat. 37°00'20" N, long. 121°21'30" W); the stream is southwest of Elephant Head Ridge. Named on Pacheco Peak (1955) 7.5' quadrangle.

Elephant Head Ridge [SANTA CLARA]: *ridge,* north- to west-trending, 3.5 miles long, 5 miles west-northwest of Pacheco Peak (lat. 37°02'35" N, long. 121°21'45" W); Elephant Head is near the southeast end of the ridge. Named on Gilroy Hot Springs (1955) and Pacheco Peak (1955) 7.5' quadrangles.

Elephant Mountain [SANTA CLARA]: *peak,* 2 miles north of Black Mountain (1) (lat. 37°20'55" N, long. 122°09'10" W; sec. 2, T 7 S, R 3 W). Named on Mindego Hill (1961) 7.5' quadrangle.

Elephant Mountain: see **Black Mountain** [MARIN].

Elephant Rock [MARIN]: *island,* 300 feet long, 5.5 miles southwest of Tomales, and 350 feet offshore (lat. 38°10'50" N, long. 122°57'50" W). Named on Tomales (1954) 7.5' quadrangle.

El Granada [SAN MATEO]: *town,* 3.5 miles south-southeast of Montara Knob near the coast (lat. 37°30'15" N, long. 122°28'10" W). Named on Montara Mountain (1956) 7.5' quadrangle. San Mateo (1915) 15' quadrangle shows North Granada along Ocean Shore Railroad at the place. The town had railroad stations called North Granada, Granada, and South Granada; the main stop was North Granada (Wagner, J.R., p. 50). Postal authorities established El Granada post office in 1909, discontinued it in 1945, and reestablished it in 1948 (Frickstad, p. 167).

El Granada Beach [SAN MATEO]: *beach,* 4 miles south of Montara Knob along the coast (lat. 37°30'05" N, long. 122°28'15" W); the beach is at El Granada. Named on Half Moon Bay (1961) and Montara Mountain (1956) 7.5' quadrangles. Brown (p. 36) called the place Granada Beach.

El Hambre Creek: see **Arroyo del Hambre** [CONTRA COSTA].

Elim Grove: see **Cazadero** [SONOMA].

Elizabeth: see **Lake Elizabeth**, under **Stivers Lagoon** [ALAMEDA].

Elk Creek [SONOMA]: *stream,* flows 2 miles to Wheatfield Fork Gualala River 7 miles east-southeast of Annapolis (lat. 38°40'35" N, long. 123°15'15" W; sec. 25, T 10 N, R 13 W). Named on Annapolis (1977) and Tombs Creek (1978) 7.5' quadrangles.

Elkhead Creek [SONOMA]: *stream,* flows 1.5 miles to Tombs Creek 4 miles west of Big Mountain (lat. 38°43' N, long. 123°12'50" W; near W line sec. 17, T 10 N, R 12 W). Named on Tombs Creek (1978) 7.5' quadrangle.

Elk Horn: see **Mountain House** [ALAMEDA].

Elkhorn Peak [NAPA-SOLANO]: *peak,* 3.5 miles west-northwest of Cordelia on Napa-Solano County line (lat. 38°13'50" N, long. 122° 11'40" W; near S line sec. 33, T 5 N, R 3 W). Altitude 1330 feet. Named on Cordelia (1951) 7.5' quadrangle.

Elkhorn Slough [SOLANO]: *water feature,* on Ryer Island (1), joins Cache Slough 4 miles north-northeast of Rio Vista (lat. 38°12'35" N, long. 121°39'15" W). Named on Courtland (1978), Liberty Island (1978), and Rio Vista (1978) 7.5' quadrangles. Called West Fork [Sacramento River] on Ringgold's (1850c) map.

Elk Slough [CONTRA COSTA]: *water feature,* 5.5 miles north-northeast of the settlement of Bethel Island on Webb Track (lat. 38° 05' N, long. 121°35'20" W). Named on Bouldin Island (1952) 7.5' quadrangle.

Elk Valley: see **Tennessee Valley** [MARIN].

Ellen: see **Lake Ellen** [NAPA]; **Mount Ellen** [SAN MATEO].

Elliot [ALAMEDA]: *locality,* 4 miles west of Livermore along Southern Pacific Railroad (lat. 37°40'25" N, long. 121°50'15" W). Named on Pleasanton (1906) 15' quadrangle.

Elliot: see **Point Elliot**, under **Port Costa** [CONTRA COSTA]

Elliot Cove [SOLANO]: *embayment,* 3.25 miles west-northwest of Benicia along Carquinez Strait (lat. 38°04' N, long. 121°12'45" W). Named on Benicia (1959) 7.5' quadrangle.

Elliot Creek [SAN MATEO]: *stream,* heads in Santa Cruz County and flows 2 miles to the sea 2 miles east of Año Nuevo Point (present Point Año Nuevo) (lat. 37°06'40" N, long. 122°17'45" W). Named on Año Nuevo (1955) and Franklin Point (1955) 7.5' quadrangles.

Ellis Slough: see **Santa Fe Channel** [CONTRA COSTA].

Elmar Beach [SAN MATEO]: *beach,* 1.25 miles northwest of downtown Half Moon Bay along the coast (lat. 37°28'30" N, long. 122° 26'55" W). Named on Half Moon Bay (1961) 7.5' quadrangle.

Elmhurst [ALAMEDA]: *town,* nearly 2 miles north-northwest of downtown San Leandro in present Oakland (lat. 37°44'45" N, long. 122°10'05" W). Named on Haywards (1899) 15' quadrangle. Officials of San Francisco and Oakland Railroad established a station at the place in 1865 and called it Jones, for Edmond Jones; officials of Central Pacific Railroad changed the name of the station to Elmhurst in 1869 (Mosier and Mosier, p. 34). Postal authorities established Elmhurst post office in 1892 and discontinued it in 1911 (Frickstad, p. 1).

Elmira [SOLANO]: *village,* 4.5 miles east of Vacaville (lat. 38°21' N, long. 121°54'25" W; sec. 19, T 6 N, R 1 E). Named on Elmira (1953) 7.5' quadrangle. Postal authorities established Valta post office in 1868, changed the name to Vaca in 1870, and to Elmira in 1873 (Frickstad, p. 193). The name "Vaca" was given to the railroad station at the place because Vacaville was nearby; when the railroad came to Vacaville about 1875, the name of the station at Vaca was changed to Elmira, for the city in New York State (Gudde, 1949, p. 106).

El Pescadero [ALAMEDA-CONTRA COSTA]: *land grant,* mainly in Contra Costa and San Joaquin Counties, but extends into the extreme northeast part of Alameda County 15 miles northeast of Livermore. Named on Clifton Court Forebay (1978) 7.5' quadrangle. Antonio Maria Pico received 8 leagues in 1843; Pico and Henry M. Naglee claimed 35,546 acres patented in 1865 (Cowan, p. 59).

El Pinole: see **Pinole** [CONTRA COSTA] (1) and (2).

El Pinole Point: see **Pinole Point** [CONTRA COSTA] (1) and (2).

El Potrero de la Punta del Tiburon: see **Belvedere Island** [MARIN],

El Potrero de Santa Clara [SANTA CLARA]: *land grant,* 2 miles northwest of downtown San Jose near San Jose Municipal Airport. Named on San Jose West (1961) 7.5' quadrangle. Called Potrero de Santa Clara on San Jose (1899) 15' quadrangle. James Alexander Forbes received 1 league in 1844; Robert F. Stockton claimed 1939 acres patented in 1861 (Cowan, p. 91).

El Pueblo San Jose de Guadalupe: see **San Jose** [SANTA CLARA].

El Sereno [SANTA CLARA]: *peak,* 4 miles east of Castle Rock (lat. 37°13'10" N, long. 122°01'20" W). Named on Castle Rock Ridge (1955) 7.5' quadrangle.

Elsman: see **Lake Elsman** [SANTA CLARA].

El Sobrante [CONTRA COSTA]:

(1) *land grant,* extends from Orinda to the town of El Sobrante. Named on Briones Valley (1959) and Richmond (1959) 7.5' quadrangles. Juan Jose Castro received 11 leagues in 1841; V. Castro and Juan Jose Castro claimed 20,565 acres patented in 1883 (Cowan, p. 98-99). According to Perez (p. 100), the patentees received 19,982.49 acres.

(2) *town,* 4 miles northeast of Richmond civic center (lat. 37°58'40" N, long. 122°17'40" W); the town is on El Sobrante grant. Named on Richmond (1959) 7.5' quadrangle. Postal authorities established El Sobrante post office in 1941 (Salley, p. 68). When the railroad reached the place in 1878, the station there was called Sobrante, and only after the post office was established was the Spanish article "El" added to the name (Gudde, 1949, p. 337).

El Sombroso [SANTA CLARA]: *peak,* 1.5 miles north-northwest of Mount Umunhum (lat. 37°10'40" N, long. 121°54'35" W; sec. 6, T 9 S, R 1 E). Altitude 2999 feet. Named on Los Gatos (1953) 7.5' quadrangle.

El Toro [SANTA CLARA]: *peak,* 1 mile southwest of Morgan Hill (lat. 37°07'15" N, long. 121°40'20" W). Altitude 1420 feet. Named on Mount Madonna (1955) 7.5' quadrangle. Butler (p. 169) noted that the peak was known locally as Murphy's Peak, for Martin Murphy, Sr., whose ranch house was nearby. The peak also was called Oreja del Oso—*oreja del oso* means "bear's ear" in Spanish—and Twenty-one Mile Peak, presumably for Twenty-one Mile House, or for the distance from San Jose (Hoover, Rensch, and Rensch, p. 431).

El Valle de San Jose: see **Livermore Valley** [ALAMEDA].

El Verano [SONOMA]: *town,* 1.5 miles west-northwest of Sonoma (lat. 38°18' N, long. 122°29'15" W). Named on Sonoma (1951) 7.5' quadrangle. Napa (1902) 30' quadrangle has the form "Elverano" for the name. Postal authorities established El Verano post office in 1889 (Frickstad, p. 195). George H. Maxwell named the place for its climate—*el verano* means "the summer" in Spanish (Gudde, 1949, p. 107).

Ely [SONOMA]: *locality,* 4 miles southeast of Cotati along Northwestern Pacific Railroad (lat. 38°16'45" N, long. 122°39'50" W). Named on Santa Rosa (1944) 15' quadrangle.

Embarcadero [SONOMA]: *locality,* 6.25 miles north of Sears Point along Sonoma Creek (lat. 38°14'30" N, long. 122°26'55" W). Named on Mare Island (1916) 15' quadrangle.

Embarcadero: see **Redwood City** [SAN MATEO].

Embarcadero Cove: see **Brooklyn Basin** [ALAMEDA].

Embarcadero de San Francisquito: see **Mayfield Slough** [SANTA CLARA].

Embarcadero de Santa Clara [SANTA CLARA]: *land grant,* 1 mile south-southeast of Alviso. Named on Milpitas (1961) 7.5' quadrangle. Barcilla Bernal received the land in 1845, and was patentee for 196.25 acres in 1936—this is the last land grant in California to receive a United States patent (Arbuckle, p. 17; Perez, p. 65).

Embarcadero de Santa Clara de Asis: see **Alviso** [SANTA CLARA].

Emerald Lake: see **Lower Emerald Lake** [SAN MATEO]; **Upper Emerald Lake** [SAN MATEO].

Emerson Slough [CONTRA COSTA]: *water feature,* joins Dutch Slough 2 miles west of the settlement of Bethel Island (lat. 38° 00'40" N, long. 121°40'40" W). Named on Jersey Island (1978) 7.5' quadrangle.

Emery [ALAMEDA]: *locality,* 2 miles north-northwest of downtown Oakland along Southern Pacific Railroad (lat. 37°49'50" N, long. 122°17'30" W). Named on San Francisco (1899) 15' quadrangle.

Emeryville [ALAMEDA]: *town,* 2.5 miles north-northwest of downtown Oakland near San Francisco Bay (lat. 37°50'30" N, long. 122°17'15" W). Named on Oakland West (1959) 7.5' quadrangle. Postal authorities established Emeryville post office in 1884 (Frickstad, p. 1), and the town incorporated in 1896. The name, given in 1897, commemorates Joseph S. Emery, who in 1859 bought the land where the town is situated (Gudde, 1949, p. 107). Postal authorities established Stockyards post office 1.5 miles north of Emeryville in 1898 and discontinued it in 1909; the place was at a shipping point for cattle and sheep (Salley, p. 213).

Emmet: see **Point Emmet** [CONTRA COSTA].

Emmons Canyon [CONTRA COSTA]: *canyon,* drained by a stream that flows 1 mile to Green Valley Creek 4 miles west-southwest of Mount Diablo (lat. 37°51'20" N, long. 121°58'40" W; sec. 9, T 1 S, R 1 W). Named on Diablo (1953) 7.5' quadrangle.

Empire [CONTRA COSTA]: *locality,* less than 1 mile south of present downtown Antioch along Southern Pacific Railroad (lat. 38°00'15" N, long. 121°48'50" W). Named on Collinsville (1918) 7.5' quadrangle.

Enchanted Hills [NAPA]: *settlement,* 5.25 miles south of Rutherford (lat. 38°23' N, long. 122°25'30" W; sec. 8, 9, T 6 N, R 5 W). Named on Rutherford (1951) 7.5' quadrangle.

Encinal: see **Alameda** [ALAMEDA]; **Sunnyvale** [SANTA CLARA].

Encinal Basin [ALAMEDA]: *water feature,* 1.5 miles south-southeast of downtown Oakland on the south side of Oakland Inner Harbor (lat. 37°46'50" N, long. 122°15'35" W). Named on Oakland West (1959) 7.5' quadrangle.

Encinal de San Antonio: see **Alameda** [ALAMEDA].

Encinal Station: see **Alameda** [ALAMEDA].

Encinosa Creek [SOLANO]: *stream,* flows nearly 4 miles to Alamo Creek 8 miles north of Fairfield in Vacaville (lat. 38°21'35" N, long. 122°00'30" W). Named on Fairfield North (1951) 7.5' quadrangle.

Endor: see **Mountain View** [SANTA CLARA].

English Creek [SOLANO]: *stream,* flows 3.5 miles to Sweany Creek 2.5 miles west-southwest of Allendale (lat. 38°25'30" N, long. 121° 58'50" W; sec. 28, T 7 N, R 1 W); the stream is in English Hills. Named on Allendale (1953) and Mount Vaca (1951) 7.5' quadrangles. South Fork enters from the southwest 5.5 miles east of Mount Vaca; it is 1.5 miles long and is named on Mount Vaca (1951) 7.5' quadrangle.

English Hill [SONOMA]: *ridge,* south-southeast- to east-trending, 1.5 miles long, 2.5 miles north-northwest of Bloomfield (lat. 38°20'50" N, long. 122°51'55" W). Named on Two Rock (1954) 7.5' quadrangle.

English Hills [SOLANO]: *range,* north of Vacaville (lat. 38°26'15" N, long. 122°00'30" W). Named on Allendale (1953), Elmira (1953), and Mount Vaca (1951) 7.5' quadrangles.

English Town [SANTA CLARA]: *locality,* 1 mile west-northwest of New Almaden near New Almaden mine (lat. 37°10'45" N, long. 121°50'15" W). Site named on Santa Teresa Hills (1953) 7.5' quadrangle. The name is from English, particularly Cornish, miners who lived at the place (Lanyon and Bulmore, p. 63).

Enright Tract [SANTA CLARA]: *land grant,* southeast of Lawrence in Sunnyvale. Named on San Jose West (1961) 7.5' quadrangle. Francisco Garcia received the land in 1845; James Enright claimed 710.14 acres patented in 1866 (Arbuckle, p. 17-18).

Ensenada de Consolacion: see **Sausalito Point** [MARIN].

Ensenada de la Carmelita: see **Richardson Bay** [MARIN].

Ensenada de los Llorones: see **Mission Bay**, under **Mission District** [SAN FRANCISCO].

Ensenada del Santo Evangelio: see **Belvedere Cove** [MARIN].

Encinal de San Antonio: see **Alameda** [ALAMEDA].

Entre Napa [NAPA]: *land grant,* south of downtown Napa. Named on Napa (1951) 7.5' quadrangle. Nicolas Higuera received the land in 1836; between 1858 and 1897, eight people received patents for parcels ranging form 307 to 2558 acres (Perez, p. 65-66).

Ephlin Hill [NAPA]: *peak,* 3.25 miles south of Mount Vaca (lat. 38° 21'10" N, long. 122°06'05" W). Altitude 984 feet. Named on Fairfield North (1951) 7.5' quadrangle.

Erabais Creek: see **Ebabias Creek** [SONOMA].

Estero Americano [MARIN-SONOMA]: *water feature,* estuary that forms part of Marin-Sonoma County line; heads at the mouth of Americano Creek and extends to Bodega Bay [SONOMA] (1) 6.25 miles west-northwest of Tomales (lat. 38°17'45" N, long. 123°00'05" W). Named on Valley Ford (1954) 7.5' quadrangle. United States Board on Geographic Names (1943, p. 9) rejected the name "Estero de San Antonio" for the feature.

Estero Americano [SONOMA]: *land grant,* around Bodega and north of Estero Americano. Named on Camp Meeker (1954) and Valley Ford (1954) 7.5' quadrangles. Edward M. McIntosh received 2 leagues in 1839; Jasper O'Farrell claimed 8849 acres patented in 1858 (Cowan, p. 35).

Estero Americano: see **Americano Creek** [MARIN-SONOMA]; **Tomales Bay** [MARIN].

Estero Americano Creek: see **Americano Creek** [MARIN-SONOMA].

Estero de Americano: see **Estero de San Antonio** [MARIN].

Estero de las Mercedes: see **Petaluma River** [MARIN-SONOMA].

Estero de Limantour [MARIN]: *bay,* opens into Drakes Estero near the mouth of that feature 5.5 miles east-northeast of the lighthouse at Point Reyes (lat. 38°02'05" N, long. 122°55'50" W). Named on Drakes Bay (1953) 7.5' quadrangle. The name commemorates Jose Yves Limantour, who was shipwrecked at the mouth of present Drakes Estero in 1841 (Gilliam, p. 86). The name originally applied to present Drakes Estero and to nearby bays together, but after members of United States Coast Survey named Drakes Estero in 1860, the name "Estero de Limantour" was restricted to its present usage (Hanna, W.L., p. 40-41).

Estero de Nuestra Señora de la Merced: see **Petaluma River** [MARIN-SONOMA].

Estero de Petaluma: see **Petaluma River** [MARIN-SONOMA].

Estero de San Antonio [MARIN]: *water feature,* estuary that heads at the mouth of Stemple Creek and extends to Bodega Bay 4.25 miles west-northwest of Tomales (lat. 38°16'10" N, long. 122°58'40" W). Named on Valley Ford (1954) 7.5' quadrangle. United States Board on Geographic Names (1943, p. 12) rejected the names "Estero de Americano," "Stemple Creek," and "Tomales Creek" for all or part of the feature.

Estero de San Antonio: see **Estero Americano** [MARIN-SONOMA]; **Stemple Creek** [MARIN].

Estero de San Francisco: see **San Francisco Bay**.

Estero de San Rafael de Agnanni: see **San Rafael Creek** [MARIN].

Estero de Santa Clara: see **San Francisco Bay**.

Estrecho de Karquines: see **Carquinez Strait** [CONTRA COSTA-SOLANO].

Estrecho de las Karquines: see **Carquinez Strait** [CONTRA COSTA-SOLANO].

Estrecho de San Jose: see **San Francisco Bay**.

Eticuera Creek [NAPA]: *stream,* formed by the confluence of Knoxville Creek and Foley Creek, flows 12.5 miles to Lake Berryessa 4.5 miles northeast of Walter Springs (lat. 38°41'40" N, long. 122°17'15" W; sec. 22, T 10 N, R 4 W). Named on Knoxville (1958) and Walter Springs (1959) 7.5' quadrangles. United States Board on Geographic Names (1962a, p. 11) rejected the forms "Eticura Creek" and "Eticurea Creek" for the name.

Eticura Creek: see **Eticuera Creek** [NAPA].

Eticurea Creek: see **Eticuera Creek** [NAPA].

Etna Springs: see **Aetna Springs** [NAPA].

Eucalyptus Island [CONTRA COSTA]: *island,* 0.5 mile long, 8.5 miles southeast of Brentwood along Old River (lat. 37°51'35" N, long. 121°34'15" W). Named on Clifton Court Forebay (1978) 7.5' quadrangle, which shows the feature as marsh and water.

Eues Creek: see **Evans Creek** [SAN MATEO].

Eugene Spring [CONTRA COSTA]: *spring,* 7 miles south-southeast of Danville (lat. 37°43'35" N, long. 121°57'50" W; sec. 27, T 2 S, R 1 W). Named on Dublin (1961) 7.5' quadrangle.

Eureka Peak [CONTRA COSTA]: *peak,* 1.5 miles west of Orinda (lat. 37°52'45" N, long. 122°12'40" W; sec. 5, T 1 S, R 3 W). Named on Briones Valley (1959) 7.5' quadrangle.

Eu's Creek: see **Evans Creek** [SAN MATEO].

Eva [SANTA CLARA]: *locality,* 5.5 miles south-southeast of downtown Los Gatos along Southern Pacific Railroad (lat. 37°09' N, long. 121°57'30" W; sec. 15, T 9 S, R 1 W). Named on Los Gatos (1919) 15' quadrangle.

Evans Creek [SAN MATEO]: *stream,* flows nearly 2 miles to Peters Creek 3.5 miles south-southeast of Mindego Hill (lat. 37°15'35" N, long. 122°12'50" W; sec. 5, T 8 S, R 3 W). Named on Mindego Hill (1961) 7.5' quadrangle. Called Eues Creek on Palo Alto (1899) 15' quadrangle. The stream also was called Eu's Creek, for Eugenio Soto, whose ranch was near the head of the creek in the 1850's (Brown, p. 33).

Evans Ridge [SONOMA]: *ridge,* west-northwest-trending, 1.25 miles long, 2.5 miles east-northeast of Annapolis (lat. 38°44'05" N, long. 123°19'40" W). Named on Annapolis (1977) 7.5' quadrangle.

Evergreen [SANTA CLARA]: *settlement,* 6 miles east-southeast of downtown San Jose (lat. 37°18'35" N, long. 121°47' W). Named on San Jose East (1961) 7.5' quadrangle. Postal authorities established Evergreen post office in 1870, discontinued it in 1913, reestablished it in 1932, and discontinued it in 1935 (Frickstad, p. 173). Rambo (1973, p. 41) attributed the name to groves of live oaks at the place.

Ewing Hill [SANTA CLARA]: *peak,* 2 miles north of Black Mountain (1) (lat. 37°20'40" N, long. 122°08'50" W; on N line sec. 12, T 7 S, R 3 W). Named on Mindego Hill (1961) 7.5' quadrangle.

Excelsior: see **Healdsburg** [SONOMA].

Ex Mission San Jose [ALAMEDA]: *land grant,* at and near Fremont. Named on La Costa Valley (1960), Milpitas (1961), Newark (1959), and Niles (1961) 7.5' quadrangles. Andrés Pico and Juan Buatista Alvarado purchased the land in 1846, but their claim was rejected; the Catholic Church patented 28 acres in 1858 (Cowan, p. 80; Cowan listed the grant under the name "San José de Guadalupe Mision").

Eylar Canyon [ALAMEDA]: *canyon,* drained by a stream that flows 5.5 miles to Arroyo Valle 5 miles south of Cedar Mountain (lat. 37°29'25" N, long. 121°36'25" W; near NW cor. sec. 24, T 5 S, R 3 E); the canyon heads on the west side of Man Ridge near Eylar Mountain [SANTA CLARA]. Named on Cedar Mountain (1956) and Eylar Mountain (1955) 7.5' quadrangles. Called Man Gulch on Mount Hamilton (1897) and Tesla (1907) 15' quadrangles.

Eylar Mountain [SANTA CLARA]: *ridge,* west-northwest-trending, 1.5 miles long, 10.5 miles northeast of Mount Hamilton (lat. 37°28'30" N, long. 121°32'50" W). Named on Eylar Mountain (1955) 7.5' quadrangle.

—F—

Fagan Creek [NAPA]: *stream,* flows 4.5 miles to lowlands 2 miles north-northwest of Napa Junction (lat. 38°12'50" N, long. 122° 16' W; sec. 11, T 4 N, R 4 W). Named on Cordelia (1951) and Cuttings Wharf (1949) 7.5' quadrangles.

Fagan Slough [NAPA]: *water feature,* joins Napa River 3.5 miles west-northwest of Napa Junction (lat. 38°12'45" N, long. 122°18'20" W). Named on Cuttings Wharf (1949) 7.5' quadrangle.

Fairchild Gulch [ALAMEDA]: *canyon,* drained by a stream that flows 2 miles to Eylar Gulch 4 miles south-southeast of Cedar Mountain (lat. 37°30'15" N, long. 121°35'10" W; at S line sec. 7, T 5 S, R 4 E). Named on Cedar Mountain (1956) and Eylar Mountain (1955) 7.5' quadrangles.

The name commemorates P.R. Fairchild, who owned property in the canyon in 1900 (Mosier and Mosier, p. 36).

Fairfax [MARIN]: *town,* 3.25 miles west-northwest of downtown San Rafael (lat. 37°59'10" N, long. 122°35'30" W). Named on San Rafael (1954) 7.5' quadrangle. Postal authorities established Fairfax post office in 1910 (Frickstad, p. 87), and the town incorporated in 1931. The name commemorates Charles S. Fairfax, who purchased 40 acres in 1856 at the site of the present town (Hanna, P.T., p. 102).

Fairfax Creek [MARIN]: *stream,* flows 3.25 miles to San Anselmo Creek 3.25 miles west-northwest of downtown San Rafael (lat. 37° 59'10" N, long. 122°35'20" W). Named on Novato (1954) and San Rafael (1954) 7.5' quadrangles.

Fairfax Manor: see **Manor** [MARIN].

Fairfield [SOLANO]: *city,* in the west-central part of Solano County (lat. 38°15' N, long. 122°02'30" W). Named on Fairfield North (1951) and Fairfield South (1949) 7.5' quadrangles. Postal authorities established Fairfield post office in 1858, discontinued it in 1861, and reestablished it in 1879 (Frickstad, p. 192). The city incorporated in 1903. R.H. Waterman purchased part of Suisun grant in 1848 and made a gift of land for a new county seat in 1858; the new town was laid out in 1859 and named for Waterman's birthplace, Fairfield, Connecticut (Hoover, Rensch, and Rensch, p. 523). Postal authorities established Waterman Park post office as a station of Fairfield post office in 1944 and discontinued it in 1948; the name was for R.H. Waterman (Salley, p. 235).

Fairfield: see **Campbell** [SANTA CLARA].

Fairfield Unit Number 1: see **Travis Air Force Base** [SOLANO].

Fairford: see **Black Point** [MARIN].

Fairmont Hot Springs: see **Hoods Hot Springs**, under **Dry Creek** [SONOMA].

Fair Oaks: see **Atherton** [SAN MATEO].

Fairoaks [SAN MATEO]: *locality,* 2 miles southeast of downtown Redwood City along Southern Pacific Railroad (lat. 37°27'50" N, long. 122°11'55" W). Named on Palo Alto (1899) 7.5' quadrangle. Postal authorities established Fair Oaks post office in 1867 and discontinued it in 1871 (Frickstad, p. 167).

Fairville [SONOMA]: *locality,* 2 miles north of Sears Point along Northwestern Pacific Railroad (lat. 38°10'40" N, long. 122°26'40" W). Named on Sears Point (1951) 7.5' quadrangle.

Fall Creek [SAN MATEO]: *stream,* flows 1.25 miles to Pescadero Creek 4 miles south of Mindego Hill (lat. 37°14'55" N, long. 122° 13' W; sec. 8, T 8 S, R 3 W). Named on Big Basin (1955) 7.5' quadrangle.

Fall Creek [SONOMA]:

(1) *stream,* flows 2.5 miles to Dry Creek 4 miles west of Geyserville (lat. 38°42'25" N, long. 123°58'45" W). Named on Geyserville (1955) and Warm Springs Dam (1978) 7.5' quadrangles.

(2) *stream,* flows 1.5 miles to Warm Springs Creek nearly 4 miles southwest of Skaggs Springs (lat. 38°39'20" N, long. 123°04'35" W; at E line sec. 4, T 9 N, R 11 W). Named on Warm Springs Dam (1978) 7.5' quadrangle.

Fallon [MARIN]: *village,* 2 miles north of Tomales (lat. 38°16'30" N, long. 122°54'15" W). Named on Valley Ford (1954) 7.5' quadrangle. Postal authorities established Fallon post office in 1898 (Salley, p. 72). The name is from Luke Fallon and James Fallon, brothers who were early settlers in the region (Hanna, P.T., p. 103).

False Bay [SONOMA]: *water feature,* wide place in Petaluma River 8 miles southeast of downtown Petaluma (lat. 38°09'40" N, long. 122°31'35" W). Named on Petaluma (1914) 15' quadrangle. Water no longer covers the place.

False River [CONTRA COSTA]: *water feature,* extends for 6 miles from Old River to San Joaquin River 3.5 miles northwest of the settlement of Bethel Island (lat. 38°03'30" N, long. 121°40'40" W). Named on Bouldin Island (1978) and Jersey Island (1978) 7.5' quadrangles. Bouldin (1910) 7.5' quadrangle shows an artificial waterway called Washington Slough situated along the north side of False River at the south edge of Webb Tract; the former Washington Slough now is part of the west end of present False River.

Family Farm: see **The Family Farm** [SAN MATEO].

Farallon: see **Middle Farallon** [SAN FRANCISCO]; **North Farallon** [SAN FRANCISCO]; **Southeast Farallon** [SAN FRANCISCO]; **South Farallon**, under **Southeast Farallon** [SAN FRANCISCO].

Farallone [SAN MATEO]: *locality,* 2 miles west-southwest of present Montara Knob along Ocean Shore Railroad (lat. 37°32'25" N, long. 122°31' W). Named on San Mateo (1915) 15' quadrangle. Postal authorities established Farallone post office in 1909 and changed the name to Montara in 1918 (Salley, p. 73).

Farallones del Angel de la Guarda: see **Farallon Islands** [SAN FRANCISCO].

Farallones de los Frayles: see **Farallon Islands** [SAN FRANCISCO].

Farallones de San Francisco: see **Farallon Islands** [SAN FRANCISCO].

Farallones Islands: see **Farallon Islands** [SAN FRANCISCO].

Farallones Rocks: see **Farallon Islands** [SAN FRANCISCO].

Farallon Islands [SAN FRANCISCO]: *islands,* 30 miles west of the Golden Gate; the principal islands are—from northwest to southeast—North Farallon, Isle of St. James, Middle Farallon, and Southeast Farallon. Named on Farallon Islands (1988) 7.5' quadrangle. Called Los Farellones on Costanso's (1771) map, called Farellons of Sn. Francisco on Dalrymple's (1789) map, and called Farallones de los Freyles on Ringgold's (1850b) map. Smith (p. 103) mentioned Farallones Rocks in 1850, and Blake (1856, p. 397) used the name "Farallones Islands" in 1856. United States Board on Geographic Names (1933, p. 298) rejected the names "Farallones" and "Marallone" for the features. Francis Drake landed on the islands in 1579 and called them the Ilands of St. James (Hanna, W.L., p. 263). *Los Farallones* is a Spanish nautical term derived from the word meaning "cliff" or "small, pointed island in the sea" (Hoover, p. 1). In 1602, Vizcaino called the northwest group of the islands the Frayles, from the Spanish term with the meaning "friar" or "monk," but the name "Farallones de los Freyles" dates from Bodega's expedition of 1775; the islands sometimes were called Farallones de San Francisco and Farallones del Angel de la Guarda (Wagner, H.R., p. 387, 426).

Farman Canyon [SANTA CLARA]: *canyon,* drained by a stream that flows 1 mile to lowlands nearly 2 miles south-southwest of Gilroy (lat. 36°58'50" N, long. 121°34'40" W). Named on Chittenden (1955) 7.5' quadrangle.

Farwell [ALAMEDA]: *locality,* 3.5 miles north-northeast of Fremont civic center along Southern Pacific Railroad in Niles Canyon (lat. 37°35'35" N, long. 121°56'40" W; sec. 11, T 4 S, R 1 W). Named on Niles (1961) 7.5' quadrangle. The name commemorates James Dumaresy Farwell, who owned property north of the site; the place also was called Stonybrook after Stonybrook Creek (Mosier and Mosier, p. 36).

Fasskings Station: see **Alameda** [ALAMEDA].

Fawn Lake [NAPA]: *lake,* 500 feet long, 6 miles north of Saint Helena (lat. 38°35'35" N, long. 122°28'20" W; near N line sec. 36, T 9 N, R 6 W); the lake is south of Doe Lake. Named on Saint Helena (1960) 7.5' quadrangle.

Fay Creek [SONOMA]: *stream,* flows 4 miles to Salmon Creek (1) 3 miles northeast of the village of Bodega Bay (lat. 38°21'25" N, long. 123°00' W). Named on Bodega Head (1972), Camp Meeker (1954), and Valley Ford (1954) 7.5' quadrangles.

Federal Terrace: see **Vallejo** [SOLANO].

Felder Creek [SONOMA]: *stream,* flows nearly 4 miles to join Carriger Creek and form Fowler Creek 2 miles south-southwest of Sonoma (lat. 38°16'05" N, long. 122°28'30" W). Named on Glen Ellen (1954) and Sonoma (1951) 7.5' quadrangles.

Felice [SONOMA]: *locality,* 2 miles south-southeast of Kenwood along Southern Pacific Railroad (lat. 38°23'30" N, long. 122°31'55" W). Named on Santa Rosa (1916) 15' quadrangle.

Felix: see **Feliz** [SAN MATEO].

Feliz [SAN MATEO]: *land grant,* west of Upper Crystal Springs Reservoir and Lower Crystal Springs Reservoir. Named on Montara Mountain (1956), San Mateo (1956), and Woodside (1961) 7.5' quadrangles. Domingo Felix received 1 league in 1844 and claimed 4448 acres patented in 1873 (Cowan, p. 17; Cowan listed the grant under the designation "Cañada de las Auras, (or) Felix").

Felta Creek [SONOMA]: *stream,* flows 3.5 miles to Mill Creek (1) 2.5 miles south-southwest of Healdsburg (lat. 38°34'50" N, long. 122°52'55" W). Named on Guerneville (1955) 7.5' quadrangle.

Felt Lake [SANTA CLARA]: *lake,* 0.5 mile long, behind a dam on a tributary to Los Trancos Creek 4 miles south-southwest of downtown Palo Alto (lat. 37°23'40" N, long. 122°11'05" W). Named on Palo Alto (1961) 7.5' quadrangle. Palo Alto (1899) 15' quadrangle shows a natural lake. Thompson and West's (1876) map indicates that J.H. Felt owned land near the site

Fenton Canyon [SANTA CLARA]: *canyon,* drained by a stream that flows 3 miles to Black Bird Valley 3 miles south of Mount Boardman (lat. 37°26'10" N, long. 121°28'40" W; at W line sec. 6, T 6 S, R 5 E). Named on Mount Boardman (1955) 7.5' quadrangle.

Fern Creek [MARIN]: *stream,* formed by the confluence of East Fork and West Fork, flows 1.5 miles to Redwood Creek 5.5 miles south-southwest of downtown San Rafael (lat. 37°54'05" N, long. 122°34'40" W). Named on San Rafael (1954) 7.5' quadrangle. East Fork and West Fork each are 0.5 mile long; both forks are named on San Rafael (1954) 7.5' quadrangle.

Ferndale Springs: see **Vaca Canyon** [CONTRA COSTA].

Fern Hill: see **Fern Peak** [SANTA CLARA]; **Nob Hill** [SAN FRANCISCO].

Fern Lake [SONOMA]: *lake,* 1650 feet long, 1.25 miles south-southwest of Glen Ellen (lat. 38°20'40" N, long. 122°31'55" W). Named on Glen Ellen (1954) 7.5' quadrangle.

Fern Mountain [SOLANO]: *ridge,* northwest-trending, 0.5 mile long, 4.5 miles south of Big Mountain (lat. 38°38'40" N, long. 123°09'05" W). Named on Tombs Creek (1978) 7.5' quadrangle.

Fern Peak [SANTA CLARA]: *peak,* nearly 2 miles south-southeast of New Almaden (lat. 37°09'10" N, long. 121°48'40" W). Altitude 1710 feet. Named on Santa Teresa Hills (1953) 7.5' quadrangle. Called Fern Hill on Los Gatos (1919) 15' quadrangle.

Fern Spring [NAPA]: *spring,* 6 miles north-northwest of Berryessa Peak (lat. 38°44'15" N, long. 122°14'40" W; sec. 1, T 10 N, R 4 W). Named on Brooks (1959) 7.5' quadrangle.

Fern Spring [SONOMA]: *spring,* 5 miles south of Guerneville (lat. 38°25'50" N, long. 123°00'45" W). Named on Duncans Mills (1979) 7.5' quadrangle.

Fetters Hot Springs [SONOMA]: *town,* 2.25 miles northwest of Sonoma in Valley of the Moon (lat. 38°19'05" N, long. 122°29'05" W). Named on Sonoma (1951) 7.5' quadrangle. Postal authorities established Fetters Springs post office in 1913, changed the name to Fetters Hot Springs in 1939, and discontinued it in 1955; the name is for George Fetters, who discovered hot water at the site (Salley, p. 74). The first resort at the place was started in 1909 and was known as Eleda Hot Springs (Waring, p. 114).

Fetters Springs: see **Fetters Hot Springs** [SONOMA].

Fiege Reservoir [NAPA]: *intermittent lake,* 150 feet long, 1.25 miles west of Calistoga (lat. 38°34'30" N, long. 122°36'10" W; sec. 2, T 8 N, R 7 W). Named on Calistoga (1958) 7.5' quadrangle.

Fife Creek [SONOMA]: *stream,* flows 5 miles to Russian River at Guerneville (lat. 38°30' N, long. 123°00' W). Named on Cazadero (1978) and Guerneville (1955) 7.5' quadrangles.

Fifield Ridge [SAN MATEO]: *ridge,* southeast-trending, 1.5 miles long, 3 miles east-northeast of Montara Knob (lat. 37°34'10" N, long. 122°25'55" W). Named on Montara Mountain (1956) 7.5' quadrangle. The name commemorates Albert B. Fifield and Winfield J. Fifield, who in 1859 settled east of the ridge in Fifield Valley (Brown, p. 33)

Fifield Valley: see **Fifield Ridge** [SAN MATEO].

Fifteen Mile House: see **Perry** [SANTA CLARA].

Fillmore Creek: see **Apanolio Creek** [SAN MATEO].

Finger Creek: see **Cordilleras Creek** [SAN MATEO].

Finger's Arroyo: see **Cordilleras Creek** [SAN MATEO].

Finley Creek [SONOMA]: *stream,* flows 3.25 miles to Salmon Creek (1) 2.5 miles northeast of the village of Bodega Bay (lat. 38°21'35" N, long. 123°01'05" W). Named on Bodega Head (1972) and Duncans Mills (1979) 7.5' quadrangles.

Finley Ridge [SANTA CLARA]: *ridge,* northwest-trending, 2 miles long, 5 miles southwest of Mount Sizer (lat. 37°09'20" N, long. 121°34' W). Named on Mount Sizer (1955) 7.5' quadrangle.

Finney Creek [SAN MATEO]: *stream,* heads in Santa Cruz County and flows 1.5 miles to the sea 1.5 miles east of Año Nuevo Point (present Point Año Nuevo) (lat. 37°06'50" N, long. 122°18' W). Named on Año Nuevo (1955) and Franklin Point (1955) 7.5' quadrangles. Called Finny Creek on Año Nuevo (1948) 15' quadrangle. The name is for Seldon J. Finney, who lived along the creek; Finney was a state assemblyman from 1869 until 1870, and a state senator from 1871 until 1875 (Gudde, 1949, p. 116).

Finny Creek: see **Finney Creek** [SAN MATEO].

Fir Canyon [NAPA]: *canyon,* drained by a stream that flows 2.5 miles to Sage Canyon 6.5 miles north-northeast of Yountville (lat. 38°29'10" N, long. 122°17'45" W; sec. 3, T 7 N, R 4 W). Named on Yountville (1951) 7.5' quadrangle. Called Fur Canyon on Sonoma (1942) 15' quadrangle.

First Mallard Branch [SOLANO]: *water feature,* joins Cutoff Slough nearly 3 miles south of Fairfield (lat. 38°11'40" N, long. 122°01'55" W). Named on Fairfield South (1949) 7.5' quadrangle.

First Slough [SAN MATEO]: *water feature,* joins Westpoint Slough 2.5 miles northeast of downtown Redwood City (lat. 37°30'30" N, long. 122°11'35" W). Named on Redwood Point (1959) 7.5' quadrangle.

Fisherman Bay [SONOMA]: *embayment,* 0.25 mile south-southwest of the village of Stewarts Point along the coast (lat. 38°38'50" N, long. 123°24' W). Named on Stewarts Point (1978) 7.5' quadrangle. Postal authorities established Fisherman's Bay post office in 1863, moved it 3 miles north in 1888, and discontinued it in 1902 (Salley, p. 75). They established Monti post office 9 miles northeast of Fisherman's Bay post office in 1884 and discontinued it in 1888 (Salley, p. 145).

Fishermans Bay [SAN FRANCISCO]: *embayment,* on the north side of South Farallon (lat. 37°41'55" N, long. 123°00'35" W). Named on Farallon Islands (1988) 7.5' quadrangle. Hoover (frontispiece map) used the form "Fisherman's Bay" for the name.

Fisherman's Bay: see **Fisherman Bay** [SONOMA]; **Fishermans Bay** [SAN FRANCISCO].

Fishermans Channel: see **Fishermans Cut**, under **Roe Island** [SOLANO].

Fishermans Cut [CONTRA COSTA]: *water feature,* extends for 2 miles between Bradford Island and Webb Tract from San Joaquin River to False River 3 miles north of the community of Bethel Island (lat. 38°03'25" N, long. 121°38'50" W). Named on Jersey Island (1978) 7.5' quadrangle.

Fishermans Cut: see **Roe Island** [SOLANO].

Fishermans Slough [CONTRA COSTA]: *water feature,* 4.5 miles north of the settlement of Bethel Island on Webb Tract (lat. 38°04'55" N, long. 121°38' W). Named on Jersey Island (1952) 7.5' quadrangle.

Fishermans Wharf [SAN FRANCISCO]: *locality,* near North Point along San Francisco Bay (lat. 37°48'35" N, long. 122°24'55" W). Named on San Francisco North (1956) 7.5' quadrangle.

Fishermen's: see **Marconi** [MARIN].

Fisher Point [SONOMA]: *ridge,* northwest-trending, less than 0.5 mile long, 1.5 miles northwest of Mount Saint Helena (lat. 38°40'50" N, long. 122°39'05" W). Named on Mount Saint Helena (1959) 7.5' quadrangle.

Fisher's Ranche: see **La Laguna Seca** [SANTA CLARA].

Fish Gulch [MARIN]: *canyon,* drained by a stream that flows 0.5 mile to Phoenix Creek 3 miles west-southwest of downtown San Rafael (lat. 37°57'20" N, long. 122°35' W). Named on San Rafael (1954) 7.5' quadrangle.

Fisk: see **Plantation** [SONOMA].

Fisk Mill Cove [SONOMA]: *embayment,* 2.25 miles west of Plantation along the coast (lat. 38°35'50" N, long. 123°20'55" W). Named on Plantation (1977) 7.5' quadrangle.

Fisk's Mill: see **Plantation** [SONOMA].

Fitchburg [ALAMEDA]: *locality,* 5.5 miles southeast of downtown Oakland (lat. 37°45'25" N, long. 122°11'10" W). Named on Concord (1897) 15' quadrangle. The railroad stop at the place first was called Fitch's Station (Mosier and Mosier, p. 37). Postal authorities established Fitchburg post office in 1908, discontinued it in 1911, and reestablished it in 1954; the name is for Colonel Henry S. Fitch, a land developer (Salley, p. 75). Damon Slough is situated at the mouth of Lion Creek, Damon's Landing was located along the slough on the east side of San Leandro Bay, and Damon Marsh is north of the site of the landing; Nathaniel Damon came to the neighborhood in 1853 and established the landing, which served the community of Fitchburg—the place also was called Fitchburg Landing (Mosier and Mosier, p. 27-28, 36).

Fitchburg Landing: see **Damon's Landing**, under **Fitchburg** [ALAMEDA].

Fitch Mountain [SONOMA]: *peak,* 1.5 miles east of Healdsburg (lat. 38°37'05" N, long. 122°50'25" W). Altitude 991 feet. Named on Healdsburg (1955) 7.5' quadrangle. The name commemorates Captain Henry D. Fitch, owner of Sotoyome grant (Davis, W.H., p. 24).

Fitch's Station: see **Fitchburg** [ALAMEDA].

Fitzgerald Ridge [SANTA CLARA]: *ridge,* northwest- to west-trending, 1 mile long, 4.25 miles south-southwest of Mount Sizer (lat. 37°09'25" N, long. 121°32'30" W). Named on Mount Sizer (1955) 7.5' quadrangle.

Five Brooks [MARIN]: *locality,* 5.25 miles south-southeast of Point Reyes Station along Olema Creek (lat. 38°00'05" N, long. 122°45'25" W). Named on Inverness (1954) 7.5' quadrangle.

Five Creek [SONOMA]: *water feature,* artificial watercourse in lowlands 2.5 miles north of Cotati (lat. 38°21'50" N, long. 122°41'45" W). Named on Cotati (1954) 7.5' quadrangle.

Five Points [SOLANO]: *locality,* 9.5 miles north-northeast of Rio Vista in Yolo Bypass (lat. 38°17'25" N, long. 121°38'35" W). Named on Liberty Island (1978) 7.5' quadrangle.

Flat Ridge [SONOMA]: *ridge,* east-southeast-trending, 1.25 miles long, 10 miles north-northeast of the village of Stewarts Point (lat. 38°46'15" N, long. 123°18' W). Named on Ornbaun Valley (1960) 15' quadrangle.

Flat Ridge Creek [SONOMA]: *stream,* flows 4.5 miles to Buckeye Creek (2) 8.5 miles northeast of the village of Stewarts Point (lat. 38°15'15" N, long. 123°18'25" W; sec. 33, T 11 N, R 13 W); the stream is south of Flat Ridge. Named on Ornbaun Valley (1960) 15' quadrangle. On Ornbaun (1944) 15' quadrangle, the name has the form "Flatridge Creek."

Flat Top [NAPA]: *peak,* 4.5 miles east-northeast of Calistoga on Rattlesnake Ridge (lat. 38°36'20" N, long. 122°30'05" W; at NW cor. sec. 26, T 9 N, R 6 W). Named on Calistoga (1958) 7.5' quadrangle.

Fleming [ALAMEDA]: *locality,* 4.5 miles north-northwest of downtown Oakland along Southern Pacific Railroad (lat. 37°53'05" N, long. 122°18'30" W); the place is 0.5 mile east-northeast of Fleming Point. Named on San Francisco (1915) 15' quadrangle. The name commemorates John J. Fleming, a local meat-market proprietor (Mosier and Mosier, p. 37). The place is called Highland on San Francisco (1899) 15' quadrangle.

Fleming Point [ALAMEDA]: *promontory,* 6 miles north-northwest of downtown Oakland along San Francisco Bay (lat. 37°53'10" N, long. 122°18'55" W). Named on Richmond (1959) 7.5' quadrangle. Called Pt. Fleming on San Francisco (1942) 15' quadrangle, and called Flemings Pt. on San Francisco (1899) 15' quadrangle, which shows the feature as an island separated from the mainland by marsh. The name commemorates J.J. Fleming, who settled near the promontory in 1853 (Gudde, 1949, p. 116).

Flint Creek [SANTA CLARA]: *stream,* flows 3 miles to lowlands 3 miles north of Evergreen (lat. 37°21'10" N, long. 121°47'20" W). Named on San Jose East (1961) 7.5' quadrangle.

Flood Slough [SAN MATEO]: *water feature,* joins Westpoint Slough 3 miles east-northeast of downtown Redwood City (lat. 37°29'55" N, long. 122°10'35" W). Named on Palo Alto (1961) 7.5' quadrangle.

Florence Creek: see **Anna Belcher Creek** [SONOMA].

Flosden [SOLANO]: *locality,* 3 miles north of downtown Vallejo along Southern Pacific Railroad (lat. 38°08'45" N, long. 122°15'05" W). Named on Mare Island (1916) 15' quadrangle.

Flosden Acres [SOLANO]: *district,* 2.25 miles north of downtown Vallejo (lat. 38°08'10" N, long. 122°15' W; sec. 1, T 3 N, R 4 W). Named on Cordelia (1951) and Cuttings Wharf (1949) 7.5' quadrangles.

Floyd: see **Harry Floyd Terrace** [SOLANO].

Fly Bay [NAPA]: *marsh,* 4.25 miles west-northwest of Napa Junction (lat. 38°12'25" N, long. 122°19'20" W; sec. 8, T 4 N, R 4 W). Named on Cuttings Wharf (1949) 7.5' quadrangle.

Foam Gulch: see **Spring Bridge Gulch** [SAN MATEO].

Fog Whistle [SAN MATEO]: *locality,* 2.25 miles southwest of present Montara Knob along Ocean Shore Railroad near Montara Point (present Point Montara) (lat. 37°32'05" N, long. 122°31'05" W). Named on San Mateo (1915) 15' quadrangle.

Foley Creek [NAPA]: *stream,* flows 3.5 miles to join Knoxville Creek and form Eticuera Creek 2.25 miles southeast of Knoxville (lat. 38°47'55" N, long. 122°18'45" W; sec. 16, T 11 N, R 4 W). Named on Knoxville (1958) 7.5' quadrangle.

Foote Creek [SONOMA]: *stream,* flows 3 miles to Redwood Creek (1) 4.25 miles west-southwest of Mount Saint Helena in Knights Valley (lat. 38°38'20" N, long. 122°42' W). Named on Mount Saint Helena (1959) 7.5' quadrangle.

Forbes [MARIN]: *locality,* 7.5 miles south-southeast of downtown Novato along Northwestern Pacific Railroad (lat. 38°30' N, long. 122°32'20" W). Named on Petaluma (1914) and Tamalpais (1897) 15' quadrangles.

Forbes Mill: see **Los Gatos** [SANTA CLARA].

Forbestown: see **Los Gatos** [SANTA CLARA].

Forest Hills [SONOMA]: *settlement,* 4 miles east of Guerneville along Russian River (lat. 38°30'30" N, long. 122°55'30" W; sec. 25, T 8 N, R 10 W). Named on Guerneville (1955) 7.5' quadrangle.

Forest House: see **Alma** [SANTA CLARA].

Forest Knolls [MARIN]: *settlement,* 9 miles southwest of downtown Novato (lat. 38°00'55" N, long. 122°41'15" W). Named on San Geronimo (1954) 7.5' quadrangle. Postal authorities established Forest Knolls post office in 1916 (Frickstad, p. 87).

Forestville [SONOMA]: *town,* 5.5 miles north-northeast of Occidental (lat. 38°28'25" N, long. 122°53'20" W). Named on Camp Meeker (1954) 7.5' quadrangle. Postal authorities established Forestville post office in 1872 (Frickstad, p. 195). The name commemorates A.J. Forrest, an early settler (Hansen and Miller, p. 48).

Forgotten Valley [SONOMA]: *canyon,* 0.5 mile long, 1.5 miles northwest of Guerneville (lat. 38°31'10" N, long. 123°00'45" W). Named on Cazadero (1978) 7.5' quadrangle. The name was given about 1925 (Clar, p. 14-15).

Fort Baker Military Reservation [MARIN]: *military installation,* 2 miles south of downtown Sausalito at the southeast end of Marin Peninsula (lat. 37°50' N, long. 122°29'15" W). Named on San Francisco North (1956) 7.5' quadrangle. The federal government bought the property in 1866 and called it Lime Point Military Reservation (Teather, p. 5). A new installation built there in the 1890's was named Fort Baker in 1897 to honor Colonel Edward D. Baker, who was killed in 1861 at the Battle of Ball's Bluff in Virignia (Frazer, p. 20).

Fort Barry: see **Fort Barry Military Reservation** [MARIN].

Fort Barry Military Reservation [MARIN]: *military installation,* at and east of Point Bonita and Rodeo Cove (lat. 37°49'45" N, long. 122°31' W). Named on Point Bonita (1954) and San Francisco North (1956) 7.5' quadrangles. Postal authorities established Fort Barry post office in 1911 and discontinued it in 1918 (Frickstad, p. 87). The name, given in 1904, honors Brevet Major General William F. Barry (Whiting and Whiting, p. 10).

Fort Cronkhite Military Reservation [MARIN]: *military installation,* 1.5 miles north-northwest of Point Bonita (lat. 37°50'20" N, long. 122°32'30" W). Named on Point Bonita (1954) 7.5' quadrangle. The name, given in 1937, honors Major General Adelbert Cronkhite (Whiting and Whiting, p. 19).

Fort Funston Military Reservation [SAN FRANCISCO]: *military installation,* 3 miles west-southwest of Mount Davidson (lat. 37° 43' N, long. 122°30' W). Named on San Francisco South (1956) 7.5' quadrangle. San Mateo (1942) 15' quadrangle shows Fort Funston. The installation was acquired in 1901 and called Laguna Merced Military Reservation; the place was renamed in 1917 to honor Major General Frederick Funston (Whiting and Whiting, p. 28).

Fortmann Basin [ALAMEDA]: *water feature,* 2 miles south-southeast of downtown Oakland on the south side of Oakland Inner Harbor (lat. 37°46'45" N, long. 121°15'20" W). Named on Oakland West (1959) 7.5' quadrangle. The name commemorates Henry F. Fortmann, who was instrumental in formation of Alaska Packers Association, which purchased waterfront land in 1904 and had the basin dredged to accommodate a fishing fleet; the feature was called Alaska Packers Association Basin before 1926 (Mosier and Mosier, p. 37).

Fort Mason Military Reservation [SAN FRANCISCO]: *military installation,* 1 mile west of North Point at Black Point (lat. 37° 48'25" N, long. 122°25'40" W). Named on San Francisco North (1956) 7.5' quadrangle. The place was reserved for military use in 1850 and occupied by the army in 1863; it first was called Fort Point San Jose, from the designation "Bateria San Jose" for the old Spanish installation there, and then in 1882 the name was changed to Fort Mason to honor Brevet Brigadier General Richard B. Mason, military governor of California in early American times (Whiting and Whiting, p. 44-45).

Fort McDowell [MARIN-SAN FRANCISCO]: *military installation,* on the east shore of Angel Island on Marin-San Francisco County line (lat. 37°51'45" N, long. 122°25'10" W). Named on San Francisco North (1956) 7.5' quadrangle. Camp Reynolds, named for Major General John F. Reynolds, who was killed at the Battle of Gettysburg, was built at the site in 1864; the name of the installation was changed in 1900 to Fort McDowell, for Major General Irvin McDowell, (Frazer, p. 25-26).

Fort Miley Military Reservation [SAN FRANCISCO]: *military installation,* less than 0.5 mile east of Point Lobos (lat. 37°46'55" N, long. 122°30'25" W). Named on San Francisco North (1956) 7.5' quadrangle. The name, given in 1900, commemorates Lieutenant Colonel John D. Miley (Whiting and Whiting, p. 47).

Fort Montgomery: see **Telegraph Hill** [SAN FRANCISCO].

Fort Point [SAN FRANCISCO]: *promontory,* 4 miles northwest of San Francisco civic center on the south side of the Golden Gate (lat. 37°48'40" N, long. 122°28'35" W). Named on San Francisco North (1956) 7.5' quadrangle. Spaniards had a fortification with the name "Castillo de San Joaquin" at the place as early as 1794; Americans built a new fort at the site in the 1850's that first was called Fort Point and then given the name "Fort Winfield Scott" in 1882 (Hoover, Rensch, and Rensch, p. 351). The Spaniards called the promontory Punta del Cantil Blanco—*cantil blanco* means "white cliff" in Spanish—and Punta del Castillo (Davidson, p. 117; Davis, W.H., p. 4). Dalrymple's (1789) map has the designation "Punta del Cantil Blanco (White Cliff Pt.)" for the feature. The anchorage inside Fort Point was known as Presidio Anchorage, or Old Spanish Anchorage, in American times (Treutlein, p. 68).

Fort Point Rock [SAN FRANCISCO]: *rock,* 0.25 mile south-southwest of Fort Point, and 100 feet offshore (lat. 37°48'30" N, long. 122°28'40" W). Named on San Francisco North (1956) 7.5' quadrangle.

Fort Point San Jose: see **Fort Mason Military Reservation** [SAN FRANCISCO].

Fort Ross [SONOMA]: *locality,* 29 miles west of Santa Rosa near the coast (lat. 38°30'50" N, long. 123°14'35" W). Named on Fort Ross (1978) 7.5' quadrangle. Ivan A. Kuskov began construction of the principal Russian establishment in California at the site in 1812; he called the place Slavyansk or Ross—the name "Ross" is from an old form of the word *Rossiia,* which means "Russia" (Schwartz, p. 37).

Fort Ross Cove [SONOMA]: *embayment,* 0.25 mile southwest of Fort Ross along the coast (lat. 38°30'40" N, long. 123°14'45" W). Named on Fort Ross (1978) 7.5' quadrangle.

Fort Ross Creek [SONOMA]: *stream,* flows 2.25 miles to the sea 700 feet south of Fort Ross (lat. 38°30'40" N, long. 123°14'35" W). Named on Fort Ross (1978) 7.5' quadrangle.

Fort Ross Reef [SONOMA]: *shoal* and *rocks,* 1 mile south-southeast of Fort Ross (lat. 38°30'05" N, long. 123°14' W). Named on Fort Ross (1978) 7.5' quadrangle.

Fort Scott [SAN FRANCISCO]: *military installation,* 0.5 mile south-southeast of Fort Point on Presidio Military Reservation (lat. 37° 48'10" N, long. 122°28'20" W). Named on San Francisco North (1956) 7.5' quadrangle. This place and Fort Winfield Scott at Fort Point are separate installations.

Fort Winfield Scott: see **Fort Point** [SAN FRANCISCO].

Fossil Ridge [CONTRA COSTA]: *ridge,* west-northwest-trending, 1.5 miles long, 2.5 miles south-southwest of Mount Diablo (lat. 37°50'50" N, long. 121°55'55" W). Named on Diablo (1953) 7.5' quadrangle.

Foss Valley [NAPA]: *valley,* 6 miles east-northeast of Yountville (lat. 38°25'20" N, long. 122°15'30" W). Named on Capell Valley (1951) and Yountville (1951) 7.5' quadrangles.

Foster City [SAN MATEO]: *city,* 3 miles east of downtown San Mateo on Brewer Island (lat. 37°33'30" N, long. 122°16'15" W). Named on San Mateo (1956, photorevised 1980) 7.5' quadrangle. Postal authorities established Foster City post office in 1964 (Salley, p. 79), and the city incorporated in 1971. The name is for T. Jack Foster, who developed of the place (Hynding, p. 280).

Four Corners [CONTRA COSTA]: *locality,* nearly 4 miles north-northeast of Walnut Creek civic center (lat. 37°57'25" N, long. 122°02'15" W). Named on Walnut Creek (1959) 7.5' quadrangle.

Four Corners [NAPA]: *locality,* 3.5 miles north of Saint Helena (lat. 38°33'10" N, long. 122°27'20" W; near S line sec. 7, T 8 N, R 5 W). Named on Saint Helena (1960) 7.5' quadrangle.

Four Corners [SONOMA]: *locality,* 1 mile south of Sonoma (lat. 38° 16'35" N, long. 122°27'35" W). Named on Sonoma (1951) 7.5' quadrangle.

Four Fathom Bank: see **Potatopatch Shoal** [MARIN].

Four Mile House: see **Lick** [SANTA CLARA].

Fourteenmile House [ALAMEDA]: *locality,* 1.5 miles northeast of Cedar Mountain (lat. 37°34'40" N, long. 121°35'10" W; near NE cor. sec. 24, T 4 S, R 3 E). Named on Cedar Mountain (1956) 7.5' quadrangle.

Fowler Creek [SANTA CLARA]: *stream,* flows 2 miles to lowlands 1.5 miles east-northeast of Evergreen (lat. 37°19' N, long. 121°45'20" W). Named on San Jose East (1961) 7.5' quadrangle.

Fowler Creek [SONOMA]: *stream,* formed by the confluence of Carriger

Creek and Felder Creek, flows 2.5 miles to Sonoma Creek 6.25 miles north of Sears Point (lat. 38°14'30" N, long. 122° 27' W). Named on Sears Point (1951) and Sonoma (1951) 7.5' quadrangles.

Fox Canyon [SONOMA]: *canyon,* drained by a stream that flows 1 mile to Felta Creek 3.5 miles southwest of Healdsburg (lat. 38°34'30" N, long. 122°53'55" W). Named on Guerneville (1955) 7.5' quadrangle.

Fox Mountain [SONOMA]: *peak,* 3 miles north-northeast of Cazadero (lat. 38°34'15" N, long. 123°03'50" W; sec. 3, T 8 N, R 11 W). Named on Cazadero (1978) 7.5' quadrangle.

Franchini Creek [SONOMA]: *stream,* flows 2 miles to Buckeye Creek (2) 1.5 miles north of Annapolis (lat. 38°44'30" N, long. 123°22'05" W; sec. 1, T 10 N, R 14 W). Named on Ornbaun Valley (1960) 15' quadrangle, and on Annapolis (1977) 7.5' quadrangle.

Francis Beach [SAN MATEO]: *beach,* 1 mile west-northwest of downtown Half Moon Bay along the coast (lat. 37°28'10" N, long. 122°26'45" W). Named on Half Moon Bay (1961) 7.5' quadrangle. The Manuel Francis family settled in the 1870's at the place, which has the alternate name "Half Moon Bay Beach" (Brown, p. 34).

Francisca: see **Benicia** [SOLANO].

Franconia Bay: see **Maintop Bay** [SAN FRANCISCO].

Frank Canyon [MARIN]: *canyon,* drained by a stream that flows 2.5 miles to Walker Creek 6 miles southeast of Tomales (lat. 38°10'55" N, long. 122°50'10" W). Named on Point Reyes NE (1954) 7.5' quadrangle.

Frank Horan Slough [SOLANO]: *water feature,* 6.25 miles south-southwest of Fairfield in marsh lands (lat. 38°10'10" N, long. 122° 05'45" W). Named on Fairfield South (1949) 7.5' quadrangle.

Franklin Canyon [CONTRA COSTA]: *canyon,* nearly 3 miles long, along Franklin Creek above a point 8 miles north of Orinda (lat. 37°59'50" N, long. 122°09'10" W). Named on Benicia (1959) and Briones Valley (1959) 7.5' quadrangles. The name commemorates Edward Franklin, who lived in the canyon until 1875 (Gudde, 1969, p. 113).

Franklin Creek [CONTRA COSTA]: *stream,* flows 5 miles to Arroyo del Hambre 8.5 miles north-northeast of Orinda (lat. 37°59'45" N, long. 122°07'50" W); the stream drains Franklin Canyon. Named on Briones Valley (1959) 7.5' quadrangle.

Franklin Point [SAN MATEO]: *promontory,* nearly 3 miles southeast of Pigeon Point along the coast (lat. 37°09' N, long. 122°21'35" W). Named on Franklin Point (1955) 7.5' quadrangle. The name is for the ship *Sir John Franklin,* which was wrecked at the point in 1865; before the wreck, the promontory was called Middle Point (Gudde, 1949, p. 120).

Franklin Ridge [CONTRA COSTA]: *ridge,* northwest-trending, 6 miles long, center 8 miles north of Orinda (lat. 37°59'35" N, long. 122°10'15" W). Named on Benicia (1959) and Briones Valley (1959) 7.5' quadrangles.

Franklin Town: see **Santa Rosa** [SONOMA].

Frank's Lagoon: see **Muir Beach** [MARIN].

Franks Tract [CONTRA COSTA]: *area,* center 2.5 miles north-northeast of the settlement of Bethel Island (lat. 38°02'40" N, long. 121°36'45" W). Named on Bouldin Island (1978) and Jersey Island (1978) 7.5' quadrangles, which show the area mainly covered by water. The feature is shown as an island on Bouldin (1910) and Jersey (1910) 7.5' quadrangles.

Frank Valley [MARIN]: *canyon,* 2.5 miles long, along the lower reaches of Redwood Creek, which enters the sea 4 miles northwest of Point Bonita (lat. 37°51'35" N, long. 122°34'40" W). Named on Point Bonita (1954) and San Rafael (1954) 7.5' quadrangles.

Franz Creek [SONOMA]: *stream,* flows about 10 miles to Maacama Creek 5.25 miles east of Healdsburg (lat. 38°36'45" N, long. 122° 46'15" W); the stream goes through Franz Valley. Named on Healdsburg (1955) and Mark West Springs (1958) 7.5' quadrangles.

Franz Valley [SONOMA]: *valley,* 3.5 miles northeast of Mark West Springs (lat. 38°35' N, long. 122°40'15" W); the valley is along Franz Creek. Named on Mark West Springs (1958) 7.5' quadrangle. The name commemorates Captain Frederick W. Franz, who acquired land in the valley in 1875 (Archuleta, p. 33).

Fraser: see **Camp Thayer** [SONOMA].

Frasier Creek [SONOMA]: *stream,* heads just inside Mendocino County and flows nearly 3 miles to Big Sulphur Creek 5.5 miles northeast of Asti (lat. 38°49'40" N, long. 122°54'40" W; sec. 6, T 11 N, R 9 W). Named on Asti (1959) 7.5' quadrangle.

Frayles: see **Farallon Islands** [SAN FRANCISCO].

Frazer: see **Glen Frazer** [CONTRA COSTA].

Frazerville: see **Glen Frazer** [CONTRA COSTA].

Frazier Gulch [SONOMA]: *canyon,* drained by a stream that flows 0.5 mile to Austin Creek 4 miles east-northeast of Jenner (lat. 38° 28'55" N, long. 123°03'20" W). Named on Duncans Mills (1979) 7.5' quadrangle.

Fredericks [SONOMA]: *locality,* 2.5 miles southeast of Sebastopol along Petaluma and Santa Rosa Railroad (lat. 38°22'25" N, long. 122°47'45" W). Named on Sebastopol (1942) 15' quadrangle.

Freeman Island [SOLANO]: *island,* 3900 feet long, 7.25 miles west-southwest of Birds Landing (2) in Suisun Bay (lat. 38°04'50" N, long. 121°59'10" W). Named on Honker Bay (1953) 7.5' quadrangle. Called Holbrook Id. on Ringgold's (1850c) map.

Freestone [SONOMA]: *village,* nearly 4 miles north of Valley Ford (lat. 38°22'20" N, long. 122°54'55" W; near S line sec. 12, T 6 N, R 10 W). Named on Valley Ford (1954) 7.5' quadrangle. Postal authorities established Analy post office in 1860, discontinued it in 1861, reestablished it in 1866, changed the name to Freestone in 1870, and discontinued it in 1951 (Frickstad, p. 194, 195). Jasper O'Farrell, owner of Estero Americano grant, gave the name "Analy Valley" to the place that the village is situated—the misspelled name is from Annaly, Ireland, the O'Farrell family home (Gudde, 1949, p. 11). The name "Freestone" is from volcanic rock used to build fireplaces and chimneys (Goodyear, 1890b, p. 678).

Freezeout Creek [SONOMA]: *stream,* flows 2.5 miles to Russian River 3.5 miles east of Jenner (lat. 38°27' N, long. 123°03' W). Named on Duncans Mills (1979) 7.5' quadrangle.

Freezeout Flat [SONOMA]: *area,* nearly 4 miles east of Jenner (lat. 38°27' N, long. 123°02'50" W); place is near the mouth of Freezeout Creek. Named on Duncans Mills (1979) 7.5' quadrangle.

Fremont [ALAMEDA]: *city;* the civic center is 25 miles southeast of Oakland (lat. 37°33'05" N, long. 121°58'05" W; near SE cor. sec. 28, T 4 S, R 1 W). Named on Milpitas (1961), Mountain View (1961), Newark (1959), Niles (1961), and Redwood Point (1959) 7.5' quadrangles. The communities of Centerville, Irvington, Mission San Jose, Niles, and Warm Springs joined to form the new city of Fremont, incorporated in 1956; the incorporation committee chose the name "Fremont" for the place (Gudde, 1969, p. 114-115). Postal authorities established Fremont post office in 1956 (Salley, p. 80).

Fremont: see **Camp Fremont**, under **Menlo Park** [SAN MATEO].

Fremont House: see **Mountain View** [SANTA CLARA].

Fremont Well [ALAMEDA]: *well,* nearly 2 miles south-southeast of Fremont civic center (lat. 37°31'30" N, long. 121°57'25" W; sec. 3, T 5 S, R 1 W). Named on Niles (1961) 7.5' quadrangle.

French Island [SOLANO]: *island,* 2300 feet long, 7 miles north of Rio Vista at the junction of Cache Slough and Shag Slough (lat. 38°15'50" N, long. 121°41'35" W). Named on Liberty Island (1978) 7.5' quadrangle.

Frenchmans Creek [SAN MATEO]: *stream,* flows 4 miles to the sea 1.5 miles northwest of downtown Half Moon Bay (lat. 37°28'50" N, long. 122°27'05" W). Named on Half Moon Bay (1961) and Montara Mountain (1956) 7.5' quadrangles. Called Frenchman Cr. on Santa Cruz (1902) 30' quadrangle. The stream was called Arroyo del Monte in the early days; the canyon of the creek was called Jara Canyon for Sebastian Jara, a woodcutter who lived there in the 1860's and 1870's, and now it commonly is called Frenchman's Creek Canyon (Brown, p. 35, 43).

Frenchman's Creek Canyon: see **Frenchmans Creek** [SAN MATEO].

Frenchs Flat [SANTA CLARA]: *area,* nearly 4 miles south-southwest of Pacheco Pass on Santa Clara-Merced County line (lat. 37°00'45" N, long. 121°14'05" W; around NW cor. sec. 5, T 11 S, R 7 E). Named on Pacheco Pass (1955) 7.5' quadrangle.

Freshwater Bay: see **Suisun Bay** [CONTRA COSTA-SOLANO].

Frey: see **Lake Frey** [SOLANO].

Frick Lake [ALAMEDA]: *intermittent lake,* 2000 feet long, 3 miles west-southwest of Altamont (lat. 37°43'50" N, long. 121°42'35" W; sec. 25, T 2 S, R 2 E). Named on Altamont (1953) 7.5' quadrangle. The name is for John Frick, a farmer in the region (Mosier and Mosier, p. 38).

Frog Lake [SONOMA]: *lake,* 300 feet long, 5 miles east-northeast of Mark West Springs (lat. 38°34'20" N, long. 122°38' W; sec. 4, T 8 N, R 7 W). Named on Mark West Springs (1958) 7.5' quadrangle.

Frog Pond [ALAMEDA]: *lake,* 300 feet long, 9 miles southeast of Sunol along Alameda Creek (lat. 37°30'05" N, long. 121°46'20" W). Named on Pleasanton (1906) 15' quadrangle.

Frog Pond [CONTRA COSTA]: *lake,* 150 feet long, 1.5 miles southeast of Mount Diablo (lat. 37°51'55" N, long. 121°53'50" W; sec. 7, T 1 S, R 1 E). Named on Diablo (1953) 7.5' quadrangle.

Frohm: see **New Almaden** [SANTA CLARA].

Frost Slough [SOLANO]: *water feature,* on Grizzly Island, joins Montezuma Slough 5 miles southwest of Denverton (lat. 38°10'15" N, long. 121°57'15" W). Named on Denverton (1953) 7.5' quadrangle.

Frowning Ridge [ALAMEDA-CONTRA COSTA]: *ridge,* west-northwest-trending, 1 mile long, 2.5 miles west of Orinda on Alameda-Contra Costa County line (lat. 37°52'50" N, long. 122°13'30" W). Named on Briones Valley (1959) 7.5' quadrangle.

Fruitvale: see **Fruitvale Station** [ALAMEDA].

Fruitvale Creek: see **Sausal Creek** [ALAMEDA].

Fruitvale Station [ALAMEDA]: *locality,* 3.5 miles southeast of downtown Oakland along Southern Pacific Railroad (lat. 37°46'30" N, long. 122°13'35" W). Named on Oakland East (1959) 7.5' quadrangle. Concord (1897) 15' quadrangle shows a community called Fruitvale at the place. Postal authorities established Brays post office in 1891 and changed the name to Fruitvale in 1892; the name "Brays" was for Watson A. Bray, a pioneer rancher (Salley, p. 26).

Fuller Creek [SONOMA]: *stream,* formed by the confluence of North Fork and South Fork, flows 3.25 miles to Wheatfield Fork Gualala River 4 miles south-southeast of Annapolis (lat. 38°40'15" N, long. 123°20'05" W; sec.

32, T 10 N, R 13 W). Named on Annapolis (1977) 7.5' quadrangle. North Fork is 2.5 miles long and South Fork is 4.25 miles long; both forks are named on Annapolis (1977) 7.5' quadrangle.

Fuller Mountain [SONOMA]: *ridge,* west-northwest-trending, 1.25 miles long, 3.5 miles east-southeast of Annapolis (lat. 38°42' N, long. 123°18'15" W). Named on Annapolis (1977) 7.5' quadrangle.

Fulton [SONOMA]: *village,* 7 miles north-northeast of Sebastopol (lat. 38°29'45" N, long. 122°46'10" W). Named on Sebastopol (1954) 7.5' quadrangle. Postal authorities established Fulton post office in 1871, discontinued it in 1872, reestablished it in 1873, and discontinued it briefly in 1874; the name commemorates Thomas Fulton and James Fulton, who founded the community (Salley, p. 81-82). California Mining Bureau's (1909a) map shows a place called Mt. Olivet located 3 miles west of Fulton along the railroad. Postal authorities established Mount Olivet post office in 1890 and discontinued it in 1909 (Frickstad, p. 197). The same map shows a place called Burke located 3 miles east of Fulton along a stage line. Postal authorities established Altruria post office in 1895, changed the name to Burke in 1903; and discontinued it in 1925—founders of the place, who were altruists, coined the name "Altruria"; the name "Burke" was for William P. Burke, first postmaster (Salley, p. 6, 29).

Funston: see **Fort Funston Military Reservation** [SAN FRANCISCO].

Fur Canyon: see **Fir Canyon** [NAPA].

Furlong Creek: see **Dexter Creek** [SANTA CLARA].

Furlong Gulch [SONOMA]: *canyon,* drained by stream that flows 2 miles to the sea nearly 3 miles south-southeast of Jenner (lat. 38° 24'50" N, long. 123°06'05" W). Named on Duncans Mills (1979) 7.5' quadrangle.

—G—

Gabes Rock [SONOMA]: *peak,* 1 mile west of Guerneville (lat. 38° 30'20" N, long. 123°01' W; near SW cor. sec. 30, T 8 N, R 10 W). Altitude 942 feet. Named on Cazadero (1978) 7.5' quadrangle. The name of this isolated mass of rock commemorates George Gabriel (Clar, p. 48).

Gaffney Point [SONOMA]: *promontory,* 1.5 miles south-southwest of the village of Bodega Bay on the west side of Bodega Harbor (lat. 38°18'50" N, long. 123°03'20" W). Named on Bodega Head (1972) 7.5' quadrangle.

Galindo [CONTRA COSTA]: *locality,* 6.25 miles north of present Walnut Creek civic center along Southern Pacific Railroad (lat. 37° 59'40" N, long. 122°03'05" W). Named on Concord (1943) 15' quadrangle.

Galindo Creek [CONTRA COSTA]: *stream,* flows 8 miles to Pine Creek 4.5 miles north-northeast of Walnut Creek civic center (lat. 37°58' N, long. 122°02'30" W). Named on Clayton (1953) and Walnut Creek (1959) 7.5' quadrangles.

Gallinas [MARIN]: *locality,* 6.5 miles south-southeast of downtown Novato along Northwestern Pacific Railroad (lat. 38°01'10" N, long. 122°31'25" W); the place is on San Pedro Santa Margarita y las Gallinas grant. Named on Novato (1954) 7.5' quadrangle. Petaluma (1942) 15' quadrangle shows St. Vincent Station along the railroad about 1 mile north-northeast of Gallinas near St. Vincent School. Postal authorities established Saint Vincent post office in 1896 and discontinued it in 1922—the name was for St. Vincent School for Boys, founded in 1855 by Daughters of Charity of St. Vincent de Paul (Salley, p. 191).

Gallinas Beach [MARIN]: *beach,* 7.25 miles south-southeast of downtown Novato (lat. 38°00'55" N, long. 122°30'15" W); the beach is south of Gallinas Creek. Named on Novato (1954) 7.5' quadrangle.

Gallinas Creek [MARIN]: *water feature,* enters San Pablo Bay 7.5 miles south-southeast of downtown Novato (lat. 38°01' N, long. 122°29'45" W). Named on Novato (1954) and Petaluma Point (1959) 7.5' quadrangles. The diseño for Las Gallinas grant, made in 1844, shows El Arroyo de Gallinas (Becker, 1969). South Fork enters from the southwest about 1 mile above the mouth of the main stream; it is named on Novato (1954) 7.5' quadrangle.

Gallinas Valley [MARIN]: *valley,* 5.5 miles south of downtown Novato along Miller Creek (lat. 38°01'40" N, long. 122°34' W); the valley is on San Pedro Santa Margarita y las Gallinas grant. Named on Novato (1954) 7.5' quadrangle.

Galloway Creek [SONOMA]: *stream,* heads in Mendocino County and flows 8.5 miles to Dry Creek 8 miles west of Cloverdale (lat. 38°47'50" N, long. 123°09'50" W; sec. 14, T 11 N, R 12 W). Named on Hopland (1960) and Ornbaun Valley (1960) 15' quadrangles.

Gang Mill Gulch: see **Martin Creek** [SAN MATEO].

Garcia [MARIN]: *locality,* nearly 2 miles east of Point Reyes Station along Northwestern Pacific Railroad (lat. 38°04'05" N, long. 122° 46'25" W); the place is on Tomales y Bolinas (1) grant, patented to Rafael Garcia. Named on Point Reyes (1918) 15' quadrangle.

Garden: see **Cherry** [SONOMA].

Garfield [SOLANO]: *locality,* 3 miles south-southeast of Denverton along Sacramento Northern Railroad (lat. 38°11'05" N, long. 121° 53' W; at S line sec. 17, T 4 N, R 1 E). Named on Denverton (1953) 7.5' quadrangle. Denverton (1918) 7.5' quadrangle has the name for a place located nearly 0.5 mile farther east.

Garnet Point [SOLANO]: *promontory,* 7.25 miles east-northeast of Benicia in Suisun Bay at the northwest end of Ryer Island (2) (lat. 38°05'40" N, long. 122°02'20" W). Named on Vine Hill (1959) 7.5' quadrangle. United States Board on Geographic Names (1933, p. 318) rejected the name "Long Point" for the feature.

Garnett Creek [NAPA]: *stream,* flows 5 miles to Napa River less than 1 mile west-northwest of Calistoga (lat. 38°35'05" N, long. 122°35'30" W). Named on Calistoga (1958) and Detert Reservoir (1958) 7.5' quadrangles.

Garretson Point: see **Lion Creek** [ALAMEDA].

Garrity Creek [CONTRA COSTA]: *stream,* flows 3 miles to San Pablo Bay 2.25 miles east-southeast of Pinole Point (lat. 38°00'10" N, long. 122°19'40" W). Named on Mare Island (1959) and Richmond (1959) 7.5' quadrangles.

Garrity Ridge [SANTA CLARA]: *ridge,* south-southwest-trending, nearly 1 mile long, 2 miles west-northwest of Loma Prieta (lat. 37° 07'25" N, long. 121°52'45" W). Named on Laurel (1955) 7.5' quadrangle. The name commemorates an early settler who had a cabin at the head of Los Gatos Creek above present Williams Reservoir (Young, p. 66).

Gashouse Cove: see **East Harbor** [SAN FRANCISCO].

Gateley [CONTRA COSTA]: *locality,* 3 miles east of Pinole Point along Atchison, Topeka and Santa Fe Railroad (lat. 38°00'25" N, long. 122°18'35" W). Named on Mare Island (1959) 7.5' quadrangle.

Gates Canyon [SOLANO]: *canyon,* 3.5 miles long, on upper reaches of Alamo Creek, opens into Vaca Valley 4.5 miles east-southeast of Mount Vaca (lat. 38°22'30" N, long. 122°01'30" W). Named on Mount Vaca (1951) 7.5' quadrangle.

Gates Canyon [SONOMA]: *canyon,* 1 mile long, along Humbug Creek 4.5 miles east of Mark West Springs (lat. 38°32'30" N, long. 122°38' W). Named on Mark West Springs (1958) 7.5' quadrangle. California Division of Forestry's (1945) map shows a settlement called Sunbeam Acres situated along Humbug Creek near the mouth of Gates Canyon.

Gavilan Creek: see **Carnadero Creek** [SANTA CLARA].

Gavin [CONTRA COSTA]: *locality,* 3 miles east-northeast of present Walnut Creek civic center along a branch of Oakland Antioch and Eastern Railroad (lat. 37°55'15" N, long. 122°00'40" W). Named on Concord (1915) 15' quadrangle.

Gazos: see **Gazos Creek** [SAN MATEO].

Gazos Creek [SAN MATEO]: *stream,* heads just inside Santa Cruz County and flows 9 miles to the sea 1 mile north of Franklin Point (lat. 37°09'55" N, long. 122°21'40" W). Named on Big Basin (1955) and Franklin Point (1955) 7.5' quadrangles. The stream also had the names "Arroyo de las Garzas," "Arroyo de la Bajada," and "Rice's Creek" (Brown, p. 35-36). California Mining Bureau's (1917a) map shows a place called Gazos located along the coast at about the position of Gazos Creek. Postal authorities established Gazos post office 10 miles south of Pescadero along Gazos Creek in 1882 and discontinued it in 1883 (Salley, p. 83).

Gelston: see **Point Gelston**, under **Ryer Island** [SOLANO] (1).

George Mountain: see **Mount George** [NAPA].

George Young Creek [SONOMA]: *stream,* flows 2.5 miles to Sausal Creek 7.25 miles northeast of Healdsburg (lat. 38°41'55" N, long. 122°47'20" W; sec. 19, T 10 N, R 8 W). Named on Jimtown (1955) 7.5' quadrangle.

German [SONOMA]: *land grant,* along the coast between the mouth of Gualala River and Salt Point. Named on Ornbaun Valley (1960) 15' quadrangle, and on Annapolis (1977), Gualala (1960), Plantation (1977), and Stewarts Point (1978) 7.5' quadrangles. Ernest Rufus received 5 leagues in 1846; Charles Meyer and others claimed 17,580 acres patented in 1872 (Cowan, p. 37). Developers purchased the grant in 1962 and started the community called Sea Ranch (Miller, J.T., p. 50).

Germantown: see **Austrian Gulch** [SANTA CLARA].

Gerstle Cove [SONOMA]: *embayment,* 2 miles south-southwest of Plantation along the coast (lat. 38°33'50" N, long. 123°19'35" W). Named on Plantation (1977) 7.5' quadrangle.

Geyser Canyon [SONOMA]: *canyon,* drained by a stream that flows 1 mile to Big Sulphur Creek 3 miles northeast of Geyser Peak (lat. 38°48' N, long. 122°48'25" W; sec. 13, T 11 N, R 9 W); the canyon is near The Geysers. Named on The Geysers (1959) 7.5' quadrangle. Winslow Anderson (p. 152) called the feature Devil's Cañon.

Geyser Hotel: see **Geysers Resort** [SONOMA].

Geyser Peak [SONOMA]: *peak,* 7 miles east of Asti (lat. 38°45'50" N, long. 122°50'40" W). Altitude 3457 feet. Named on The Geysers (1959) 7.5' quadrangle. Called Sulphur Peak on Kelseyville (1944) 15' quadrangle, but United States Board on Geographic Names (1962b, p. 17) rejected this name for the feature.

Geyser Rock [SONOMA]: *relief feature,* 5.5 miles northeast of Geyser Peak on Sonoma-Lake County line (lat. 38°48'50" N, long. 122°45'55" W; at S line sec. 8, T 11 N, R 8 W). Named on The Geysers (1959) 7.5' quadrangle.

Geysers: see **The Geysers** [SONOMA]; **The Geysers**, under **Geysers Resort** [SONOMA].

Geyser Springs: see **Geyserville** [SONOMA].

Geysers Resort [SONOMA]: *locality,* 3 miles northeast of Geyser Peak (lat. 38°47'55" N, long. 122°48'25" W; sec. 13, T 11 N, R 9 W); the place is near The Geysers. Named on The Geysers (1959) 7.5' quadrangle. Called Geyser Hotel on Kelseyville (1921) 15' quadrangle. The resort began as early as 1852 (Allen and Day, p. 11). Postal authorities established The Geysers post office in 1893, discontinued it for a time in 1905, and discontinued it finally in 1935 (Frickstad, p. 198).

Geysers Spa: see **Lytton Springs**, under **Lytton** [SONOMA].

Geyserville [SONOMA]: *town,* nearly 7 miles north-northwest of Healdsburg near Russian River (lat. 38°42'25" N, long. 122°54'10" W). Named on Geyserville (1955) 7.5' quadrangle. Postal authorities established Clairville post office in 1858, changed the name to Guyserville in 1887, and to Geyserville in 1888 (Salley, p. 44, 84). Elisha Ely founded the community in 1851; the name "Clairville" was for John Clar, and the name "Geyserville" is from nearby thermal features (Gudde, 1949, p. 126). Postal authorities established Geyser Springs post office at a resort near present Geyserville in 1874 and discontinued it in 1887 (Salley, p. 84).

Giant [CONTRA COSTA]: *locality,* 3.5 miles north of Richmond civic center along Southern Pacific Railroad (lat. 37°59'25" N, long. 122°21'20" W). Named on Richmond (1959) 7.5' quadrangle. Postal authorities established Giant post office in 1895 and discontinued it in 1936 (Frickstad, p. 21). The name is from Giant Powder Company's plant located at the place (Gudde, 1949, p. 126).

Gibbon Point [ALAMEDA]: *promontory,* 2 miles west of downtown Oakland along San Francisco Bay (lat. 37°48'20" N, long. 122°18'35" W). Named on San Francisco (1899) 15' quadrangle. The name recalls Rodmond Gibbons, who in 1855 planned to build a ferry terminal at the place; the feature now is called Oakland Point (Mosier and Mosier, p. 39).

Gibson Canyon Creek [SOLANO]: *stream,* flows 3.5 miles to lowlands 2 miles south of Allendale (lat. 38°25' N, long. 121°57' W). Named on Allendale (1953) 7.5' quadrangle. On Vacaville (1953) 15' quadrangle, the stream extends through lowlands to Sweany Creek 4.5 miles south-southwest of Dixon.

Gibson Flat [NAPA]: area, 3.5 miles northeast of Walter Springs (lat. 38°41'10" N, long. 122°18'35" W; sec. 28, T 10 N, R 4 W). Named on Walter Springs (1959) 7.5' quadrangle.

Gibson Island: see **Bodega Rock** [SONOMA].

Gibson Ridge [SONOMA]: *ridge,* southwest- to west-trending, 1.5 miles long, 4.25 miles west-northwest of Big Mountain (lat. 38°43'45" N, long. 123°13'15" W). Named on Tombs Creek (1978) 7.5' quadrangle.

Gilbert: see **San Antonio Creek** [SANTA CLARA].

Gilbert's Camp: see **Grabtown** [SAN MATEO].

Gilder Ridge [SONOMA]: *ridge,* east- to southeast-trending, 2.25 miles long, 4.5 miles northeast of Guerneville (lat. 38°32'10" N, long. 122°55'30" W). Named on Guerneville (1955) 7.5' quadrangle.

Gill Creek [SONOMA]: *stream,* flows 3 miles to Russian River 1.5 miles north-northwest of Geyserville (lat. 38°43'35" N, long. 122° 55'05" W). Named on Asti (1959) and Geyserville (1955) 7.5' quadrangles.

Gillespie Point [SOLANO]: *promontory,* 8 miles east of Benicia along Suisun Bay at the east end of Roe Island (lat. 38°04'15" N, long. 122°01'15" W). Named on Vine Hill (1959) 7.5' quadrangle. Called Pt. Gillespie on Ringgold's (1850c) map.

Gilliam Creek [SONOMA]: *stream,* flows 4 miles to East Austin Creek 2.5 miles northeast of Cazadero (lat. 38°33'35" N, long. 123° 03'10" W; sec. 2, T 8 N, R 11 W); the stream is north of Gilliam Ridge. Named on Cazadero (1978) 7.5' quadrangle. Called East Br. Austin Cr. on Healdsburg (1940) 15' quadrangle, and called Gilman Creek on Cazadero (1943) 7.5' quadrangle.

Gilliam Ridge [SONOMA]: *ridge,* west-trending, 1 mile long, 4.5 miles east-northeast of Cazadero (lat. 38°33'45" N, long. 123°00'35" W); the ridge is south of Gilliam Creek. Named on Cazadero (1978) 7.5' quadrangle. Called Gilman Ridge on Cazadero (1943) 7.5' quadrangle.

Gilman Creek: see **Gilliam Creek** [SONOMA].

Gilman Ridge: see **Gilliam Ridge** [SONOMA].

Gilroy [SANTA CLARA]: *town,* 28 miles southeast of downtown San Jose (lat. 37°00'30" N, long. 121°34'15" W). Named on Chittenden (1955) and Gilroy (1955) 7.5' quadrangles. Scotsman John Gilroy arrived in California in 1814 and married Maria Clara Ortega, who inherited a third part of San Ysidro grant (Butler, p. 177-178). The first village in the neighborhood was called San Isidro (or San Ysidro), for the grant, but gradually it took Gilroy's name; eventually the name "Gilroy" shifted 2.5 miles west-northwest to a settlement around an inn established in 1850 on the main road down the valley—there the present town of Gilroy was laid out in 1868 and incorporated in 1870 (Bancroft, 1888, p. 525). Postal authorities established Gilroy post office in 1851 (Frickstad, p. 173). With the shift of the name to the new site, the old settlement at became known as Old Gilroy. The present site of Gilroy, when the place was only a stage stop, was called Pleasant Valley (Pierce, p. 161).

Gilroy Hot Springs [SANTA CLARA]: *locality,* 8.5 miles northeast of Gilroy along Coyote Creek (lat. 37°06'30" N, long. 121°28'40" W; sec. 36, T 9 S, R 4 E). Named on Gilroy Hot Springs (1955) 7.5' quadrangle. Anza may have camped at the place in 1776, but a Mexican sheepherder made the effective discovery of the springs at the site in 1865 (Rambo, 1973, p. 41). A resort developed at the springs as early as the 1870's, and by 1908 a hotel and other facilities provided rooms for about 125 guests (Waring, p. 80). Postal authorities established Gilroy Hot Springs post office in 1873 and discontinued it in 1934 (Frickstad, p. 173).

Gilroy Valley: see **Santa Clara Valley** [SANTA CLARA].

Gird Creek [SONOMA]: *stream,* flows 3.5 miles to Russian River 4.5 miles north-northeast of Healdsburg (lat. 38°40'35" N, long. 122°50'45" W). Named on Jimtown (1955) 7.5' quadrangle.

Girdle: see **The Girdle** [SONOMA].

Giubbini Point: see **Willow Point** [MARIN].

Glass Mountain [NAPA]: *ridge,* west-northwest-trending, less than 1 mile long, 2 miles north-northwest of Saint Helena (lat. 38°32' N, long. 122°29' W). Named on Saint Helena (1960) 7.5' quadrangle.

Gleason Beach [SONOMA]: *beach,* 4.5 miles south-southeast of Jenner along the coast (lat. 38°23'20" N, long. 123°05' W). Named on Duncans Mills (1979) 7.5' quadrangle.

Gleason Gulch: see **Scotty Creek** [SONOMA].

Glenbrook Creek [MARIN]: *stream,* flows 3.5 miles to an arm of Estero de Limantour 7.5 miles east-northeast of the lighthouse at Point Reyes (lat. 38°02'10" N, long. 122°53'30" W). Named on Drakes Bay (1953) 7.5' quadrangle. The name is from Glen Brook ranch (Teather, p. 27).

Glen Cove [SOLANO]: *embayment,* 3 miles west-northwest of Benicia along Carquinez Strait (lat. 38°04' N, long. 122°12'20" W; sec. 33, T 3 N, R 3 W). Named on Benicia (1959) 7.5' quadrangle.

Glencove [SOLANO]: *locality,* 3 miles west-northwest of Benicia (lat. 38°04'05" N, long. 122°12'20" W; near NW cor. sec. 33, T 3 N, R 3 W); the place is at at Glen Cove. Named on Benicia (1959) 7.5' quadrangle.

Glen Echo Creek [ALAMEDA]: *stream,* ends in downtown Oakland 0.25 mile north of Lake Merritt (lat. 37°48'55" N, long. 122°15'45" W). Named on Oakland West (1959) 7.5' quadrangle. Called Hayes Creek on Concord (1897) 15' quadrangle. The stream formerly was called Cemetery Creek and Hays' Creek—Wickham Havens, a developer, gave the present name to the stream in 1905; the canyon of the stream was called Hays Canyon, for John Coffee Hays, who had an estate at the head of the feature (Mosier and Mosier, p. 39, 42).

Glen Ellen [SONOMA]: *town,* 11.5 miles east-southeast of Santa Rosa in Valley of the Moon (lat. 38°21'50" N, long. 122°31'25" W). Named on Glen Ellen (1954) 7.5' quadrangle. Postal authorities established Glen Ellen post office in 1871; Colonel J.B. Armstrong named the place for his wife (Salley, p. 86). California Mining Bureau's (1917a) map shows a place called Triniti located about 5 miles east-northeast of Glen Ellen near Sonoma-Napa County line. Postal authorities established Triniti post office in 1907 and discontinued it in 1935 (Frickstad, p. 198).

Glen Frazer [CONTRA COSTA]: *locality,* 8 miles north of Orinda along Atchison, Topeka and Santa Fe Railroad in Franklin Canyon (lat. 37°59'50" N, long. 122°09'40" W; sec. 23, T 2 N, R 3 W). Named on Briones Valley (1959) 7.5' quadrangle. Postal authorities established Frazerville post office at the place in 1898 and discontinued it in 1899; they established Glen Frazer post office in 1906 and discontinued it in 1919—the name "Frazer" is from an early rancher in the neighborhood (Salley, p. 80, 86).

Glen Una: see **Saratoga** [SANTA CLARA].

Glorietta [CONTRA COSTA]: *settlement,* 1.25 miles southeast of Orinda (lat. 37°51'45" N, long. 122°10' W). Named on Oakland East (1959) 7.5' quadrangle.

Goat Hill [SAN MATEO]: *peak,* 4 miles southwest of La Honda (lat. 37°16'55" N, long. 122°19'35" W; sec. 32, T 7 S, R 4 W). Named on La Honda (1961) 7.5' quadrangle.

Goat Island [SOLANO]: *hill,* 2.5 miles south of Fairfield in marsh (lat. 38°12'50" N, long. 122°02' W). Named on Fairfield South (1949) 7.5' quadrangle. United States Board on Geographic Names (1983e, p. 2) approved the name "Japanese Point" for a promontory on Goat Island (lat. 38°12'52" N, long. 122°02' W; sec. 1, T 4 N, R 2 W), and rejected the name "Jap Rock" for the feature.

Goat Island: see **Yerba Buena Island** [SAN FRANCISCO].

Goat Rock [SONOMA]:

(1) *peak,* 4 miles north-northwest of Cazadero (lat. 38°34'55" N, long. 123°07'15" W; sec. 31, T 9 N, R 11 W). Altitude 874 feet. Named on Cazadero (1978) 7.5' quadrangle.

(2) *peak,* 8 miles north-northeast of Healdsburg (lat. 38°42'55" N, long. 123°47'35" W; sec. 18, T 10 N, R 8 W). Altitude 870 feet. Named on Jimtown (1955) 7.5' quadrangle.

(3) *promontory,* less than 1 mile southwest of Jenner along the coast (lat. 38°26'25" N, long. 123°07'35" W). Named on Arched Rock (1977) 7.5' quadrangle.

Goat Rock Beach [SONOMA]: *beach,* 0.5 mile west-southwest of Jenner along the coast south of the mouth of Russian River (lat. 38°26'50" N, long. 123°07'35" W); the beach is north of Goat Rock (3). Named on Arched Rock (1977) 7.5' quadrangle.

Goat Roost Rock [SONOMA]: *peak,* 1.25 miles north-northwest of Mount

Saint Helena (lat. 38°41' N, long. 122°38'35" W; sec. 28, T 10 N, R 7 W). Altitude 3263 feet. Named on Mount Saint Helena (1959) 7.5' quadrangle.

Goecken: see **Greenville** [ALAMEDA].

Goethels Canyon [CONTRA COSTA]: *canyon*, drained by a stream that flows 1.25 miles to Mount Diablo Creek nearly 3 miles north-northeast of Mount Diablo (lat. 37°55'10" N, long. 121°53'50" W; sec. 19, T 1 N, R 1 E). Named on Clayton (1953) 7.5' quadrangle.

Gold Creek [ALAMEDA]: *stream*, flows 1.5 miles to lowlands 1 mile south-southeast of Dublin (lat. 37°41'15" N, long. 121°55'45" W). Named on Dublin (1961) 7.5' quadrangle. Prospectors found placer gold in the creek in 1871 (Mosier and Finney, p. 8).

Golden Gate [ALAMEDA]: *locality*, 2.5 miles north-northwest of downtown Oakland along Southern Pacific Railroad (lat. 37°50'20" N, long. 122°17' W). Named on San Francisco (1899) 15' quadrangle. Postal authorities established Klinknerville post office in 1887, changed the name to Golden Gate in 1888, changed it to Goldengate in 1895, and discontinued the post office in 1905; the first name was for Charles A. Klinkner, who built 75 homes at the place (Salley, p. 87, 113).

Golden Gate [SAN FRANCISCO]: *narrows*, water connection between San Francisco Bay and the sea; 1 mile wide north of Fort Point (lat. 37°49'10" N, long. 122°28'40" W). Named on San Francisco North (1956) 7.5' quadrangle. Soldiers of Lieutenant Fages party first sighted the entrance to San Francisco Bay in 1770 from heights east of the bay; the first vessel to traverse Golden Gate was the Spanish ship *San Carlos*, under the command of Lieutenant Ayala, which entered San Francisco Bay in 1775 (Stanger and Brown, p. 19, 34). Fremont's (1848) map has the designation "Chrysopylae or Golden Gate" for the feature. Fremont (p. 29-30) bestowed the name by analogy with the harbor of Byzantium called Chrysoceras, or golden horn.

Golden Rock: see **Red Rock** [CONTRA COSTA-MARIN-SAN FRANCISCO].

Golden Spur: see **Monta Vista** [SANTA CLARA].

Golf [MARIN]: *locality*, 7.25 miles south-southeast of downtown Novato along Northwestern Pacific Railroad (lat. 38°00'20" N, long. 122°31'55" W). Named on Petaluma (1914) 15' quadrangle.

Good Luck Point [NAPA]: *promontory*, 3 miles west of Napa Junction along Napa River (lat. 38°11' N, long. 122°18'20" W; sec. 21, T 4 N, R 4 W). Named on Cuttings Wharf (1949) 7.5' quadrangle.

Goodyear: see **Bahia** [SOLANO].

Goodyear Landing: see **Goodyear Slough** [SOLANO].

Goodyear Slough [SOLANO]: *water feature*, joins Cordelia Slough 8 miles south-southwest of Fairfield (lat. 38°08'05" N, long. 122°05'05" W). Named on Fairfield South (1949) and Vine Hill (1959) 7.5' quadrangles. A place called Goodyear Landing was situated along Goodyear Slough in the early days (Hoover, Rensch, and Rensch, p. 525).

Goose Lake [SONOMA]: *intermittent lake*, 300 feet long, 4.25 miles north-northwest of Sears Point (lat. 38°12'20" N, long. 122°28'50" W). Named on Sears Point (1951) 7.5' quadrangle.

Gordon: see **John Gordon Creek** [SONOMA].

Gordon Ridge [SAN MATEO]: *ridge*, southwest- to west-trending, 3.5 miles long, 6 miles west-northwest of La Honda (lat. 37°21'05" N, long. 122°22' W). Named on La Honda (1961) and San Gregorio (1961, photorevised 1968) 7.5' quadrangles. Alexander Gordon settled on the ridge in the late 1860's (Brown, p. 36).

Gordon's Chute: see **Tunitas Creek** [SAN MATEO].

Gordon Valley [NAPA]: *valley*, along Suisun Creek above a point nearly 5 miles south-southwest of Mount Vaca (lat. 38°20'05" N, long. 122°07'35" W). Named on Capell Valley (1951), Fairfield North (1951), and Mount George (1951) 7.5' quadrangles.

Gordon Valley Creek [NAPA-SOLANO]: *stream*, heads in Napa County and flows 6.5 miles to Ledgewood Creek 4.5 miles west-northwest of Fairfield in Solano County (lat. 38°17'05" N, long. 122°06'50" W). Named on Fairfield North (1951) 7.5' quadrangle.

Gosling Canyon [NAPA]: *canyon*, drained by a stream that flows 6 miles to Lake Berryessa 7 miles south of Berryessa Peak (lat. 38° 33'50" N, long. 122°10'55" W). Named on Lake Berryessa (1959) 7.5' quadrangle.

Gossage Creek [SONOMA]: *stream*, flows 3.5 miles to lowlands 2 miles northwest of Cotati (lat. 38°20'30" N, long. 122°44' W). Named on Cotati (1954) and Two Rock (1954) 7.5' quadrangles.

Government Island [ALAMEDA]: *island*, 3000 feet long, nearly 2 miles southeast of downtown Oakland in Oakland Inner Harbor (lat. 37°47' N, long. 122°15' W). Named on Oakland East (1959) and Oakland West (1959) 7.5' quadrangles. United States Board on Geographic Names (1985a, p. 3) approved the name "Coast Guard Island" for the feature—the new name is for the continued presence of United States Coast Guard on the island since 1926.

Government Ranch [CONTRA COSTA]: *locality*, 6 miles east of Martinez along Oakland Antioch and Eastern Railroad (lat. 38°01'05" N, long. 122°01'35" W). Named on Carquinez Strait (1896) 15' quadrangle.

Government Spring [SONOMA]: *spring*, 2.25 miles northwest of Cazadero (lat. 38°33'05" N, long. 123°07' W; sec. 7, T 8 N, R 11 W). Named on Cazadero (1978) 7.5' quadrangle.

Government Trail Canyon [NAPA]: *canyon*, 1.25 miles long, 3 miles south-southeast of Mount Vaca (lat. 38°21'35" N, long. 122° 05'30" W). Named on Fairfield North (1951) 7.5' quadrangle.

Grabtown [SAN MATEO]: *locality*, 2.25 miles west-northwest of Skeggs Point (lat. 37°25'20" N, long. 122°20'35" W). Named on Woodside (1961) 7.5' quadrangle. A settlement called Gilbert's Camp developed at the site in the 1860's, but the place took the nickname "Grabtown," reportedly after one inhabitant "grabbed" the garden plot of another resident and built a barn on it (Morrall, p. 44).

Grabtown Gulch [SAN MATEO]: *canyon*, drained by a stream that flows 0.5 mile to Purisima Creek nearly 3 miles northwest of Skeggs Point (lat. 37°26'05" N, long. 122°20'50" W); the canyon heads near Grabtown. Named on Woodside (1961) 7.5' quadrangle.

Graham Creek [SONOMA]: *stream*, flows 2.5 miles to Sonoma Creek 1 mile northwest of Glen Ellen (lat. 38°22'10" N, long. 122° 32'20" W). Named on Glen Ellen (1954) 7.5' quadrangle.

Granada: see **El Granada** [SAN MATEO].

Granada Beach: see **El Granada Beach** [SAN MATEO].

Grand Canyon [MARIN]: *canyon*, drained by a stream that flows 3.25 miles to lowlands along Tomales Bay 1.5 miles north-northwest of Point Reyes Station (lat. 38°05'30" N, long. 122°49'10" W). Named on Inverness (1954) 7.5' quadrangle.

Grand Street Station: see **Alameda** [ALAMEDA].

Grandview: see **Black Point** [MARIN].

Grandville: see **Mesa Grande** [SONOMA].

Granite Lake [NAPA]: *lake*, 400 feet long, 6 miles north of Saint Helena (lat. 38°35'40" N, long. 122°28'10" W; near SE cor. sec. 25, T 9 N, R 6 W). Named on Saint Helena (1960) 7.5' quadrangle.

Grant [SONOMA]: *locality*, 2 miles southeast of Healdsburg along Northwestern Pacific Railroad (lat. 38°35'25" N, long. 122°50'50" W). Named on Healdsburg (1955) 7.5' quadrangle.

Grape Creek [SONOMA]: *stream*, flows nearly 3 miles to Dry Creek 3.5 miles south-southwest of Geyserville (lat. 38°39'35" N, long. 122°56'05" W). Named on Geyserville (1955) 7.5' quadrangle.

Grapevine Creek [SONOMA]: *stream*, flows 1.25 miles to Sausal Creek 8 miles north-northeast of Healdsburg (lat. 38°43'15" N, long. 122°47'45" W; at NW cor. sec. 18, T 10 N, R 8 W). Named on Jimtown (1955) 7.5' quadrangle.

Grass Creek: see **Grass Valley** [ALAMEDA].

Grasshopper Creek [SONOMA]:

(1) *stream*, flows 5 miles to Buckeye Creek (2) 1.5 miles north of Annapolis (lat. 38°44'30" N, long. 123°22'05" W; sec. 1, T 10 N, R 14 W). Named on Annapolis (1977) 7.5' quadrangle.

(2) *stream*, flows nearly 2 miles to Pepperwood Creek 8.5 miles north-northeast of Fort Ross (lat. 38°37'20" N, long. 123°09'45" W; near E line sec. 15, T 9 N, R 12 W). Named on Tombs Creek (1978) 7.5' quadrangle.

Grass Valley [ALAMEDA]: *canyon*, drained by a stream that flows 4 miles to Lake Chabot 5 miles north-northwest of downtown Hayward (lat. 37°44'25" N, long. 122°06'50" W). Named on Hayward (1959), Las Trampas Ridge (1959), and Oakland East (1959) 7.5' quadrangles. Haywards (1899) 15' quadrangle shows Grass Creek in the canyon.

Grass Valley [SONOMA]: *area*, 5 miles west of Geyserville (lat. 38° 41'35" N, long. 122°59'45" W; sec. 20, 29, T 10 N, R 10 W). Named on Geyserville (1955) 7.5' quadrangle.

Grassy Hill [NAPA]: *peak*, nearly 4 miles northeast of Calistoga (lat. 38°37' N, long. 122°31'40" W; sec. 21, T 9 N, R 6 W). Named on Calistoga (1958) 7.5' quadrangle.

Graton [SONOMA]: *town*, 3.25 miles northwest of Sebastopol (lat. 38°26'05" N, long. 122°52' W). Named on Sebastopol (1954) 7.5' quadrangle. Postal authorities established Graton post office in 1906 (Frickstad, p. 195). James H. Gray and J.H. Brush founded the town in 1904 and coined the name from letters in the word "Graytown" (Gudde, 1949, p. 134).

Gravelly Lake [SONOMA]: *lake*, 300 feet long, 5 miles north-northwest of Sears Point (lat. 38°12'50" N, long. 122°29'30" W). Named on Sears Point (1951) 7.5' quadrangle.

Gravelly Spring [SONOMA]: *spring*, 5.25 miles north-northwest of Cazadero (lat. 38°36'10" N, long. 123°07'30" W; near NW cor. sec. 30, T 9 N, R 11 W). Named on Cazadero (1978) 7.5' quadrangle.

Gravelly Springs Creek [SONOMA]: *stream*, flows less than 0.5 mile to Austin Creek 8.5 miles northeast of Fort Ross (lat. 38° 36' N, long. 123°07'45" W; near N line sec. 25, T 9 N, R 12 W); the stream heads at Gravelly Spring. Named on Fort Ross (1978) 7.5' quadrangle.

Gravel Pit: see **Lovelady's**, under **Campbell** [SANTA CLARA].

Gravenstein [SONOMA]: *locality*, 1 mile east of Sebastopol along Petaluma and Santa Rosa Railroad (lat. 38°24'20" N, long. 122°48'25" W). Named on Sebastopol (1954) 7.5' quadrangle.

Gray Creek [SONOMA]: *stream*, flows 5.5 miles to East Austin Creek 4.25 miles north-northeast of Cazadero (lat. 38°35'20" N, long. 123°03'40" W; at N line sec. 34, T 9 N, R 11 W). Named on Cazadero (1978) 7.5' quadrangle. Called Little Austin Creek on Guerneville (1955) 7.5' quadrangle, but United States Board on Geographic Names (1978b, p. 3) rejected this name, and noted that the name "Gray Creek" is for Isaac Gray, an early settler.

Grayson Creek [CONTRA COSTA]: *stream,* flows 8 miles to Walnut Creek (1) 4 miles east of Martinez (lat. 38°00'15" N, long. 122°03'35" W). Named on Vine Hill (1959) and Walnut Creek (1959) 7.5' quadrangles.

Graystone [SONOMA]: *locality,* 1.25 miles southwest of Guerneville along Northwestern Pacific Railroad near Russian River (lat. 38° 29'20" N, long. 123°01'05" W). Named on Duncans Mills (1921) 15' quadrangle.

Great Beach: see **The Great Beach**, under **Point Reyes Beach** [MARIN].

Great Farallon: see **Southeast Farallon** [SAN FRANCISCO].

Greco Island [SAN MATEO]: *marsh,* 3.25 miles northeast of downtown Redwood City along San Francisco Bay (lat. 37°31'05" N, long. 122°10'55" W). Named on Redwood Point (1959) 7.5' quadrangle. V.C. Greco had a salt works at the place from 1910 until 1923 (Brown, p. 37).

Greeg Mountain [NAPA]: *ridge,* northwest-trending, 2.5 miles long, 8 miles east of Saint Helena (lat. 38°31' N, long. 122°19'40" W). Named on Chiles Valley (1958) 7.5' quadrangle.

Green: see **Point Green**, under **Preston Point** [SOLANO].

Green Brae [MARIN]: *town,* 1.5 miles south-southeast of downtown San Rafael (lat. 37°56'55" N, long. 122°31'30" W). Named on San Rafael (1954) 7.5' quadrangle. The name is from a huge dairy ranch that James Ross, Jr., started in the 1860's (Teather, p. 27).

Green Canon [SAN MATEO]: *locality,* 1.5 miles west-northwest of present Montara Knob along Ocean Shore Railroad (lat. 37°33'50" N, long. 122°30'40" W); the place is near present Green Valley. Named on San Mateo (1915) 15' quadrangle.

Green Canyon [NAPA]: *canyon,* drained by a stream that flows 3.5 miles to Lake Berryessa 5.5 miles east-northeast of Walter Springs (lat. 38°40'20" N, long. 122°15'20" W). Named on Brooks (1959) and Walter Springs (1959) 7.5' quadrangles.

Green Creek [SONOMA]: *stream,* flows 0.5 mile to Coleman Valley Creek 3.25 miles north-northeast of the village of Bodega Bay (lat. 38°22'20" N, long. 123°00'50" W). Named on Duncans Mills (1979) 7.5' quadrangle.

Green Gulch [MARIN]: *canyon,* drained by a stream that flows 2 miles to Big Lagoon 4 miles northwest of Point Bonita (lat. 37°51'35" N, long. 122°34'25" W). Named on Point Bonita (1954) and San Rafael (1954) 7.5' quadrangles.

Green Hill [MARIN]: *peak,* 6 miles north of Bolinas (lat. 37°59'50" N, long. 122°40'15" W). Altitude 1418 feet. Named on Bolinas (1954) 7.5' quadrangle.

Green Island [NAPA]: *hill,* 3 miles west-northwest of Napa Junction (lat. 38°12'10" N, long. 122°18'10" W; on S line sec. 9, T 4 N, R 4 W). Named on Cuttings Wharf (1949, photorevised 1968) 7.5' quadrangle, which shows the hill surrounded by salt evaporators. Mare Island (1916) 15' quadrangle shows the hill surrounded by marsh.

Green Oaks Creek [SAN MATEO]: *stream,* heads in Santa Cruz County and flows nearly 4 miles to the sea 2 miles southeast of Franklin Point (lat. 37°07'50" N, long. 122°20'10" W). Named on Año Nuevo (1955) and Franklin Point (1955) 7.5' quadrangles. Called Greenoaks Creek on Año Nuevo (1948) 15' quadrangle. The name is from Green Oaks dairy ranch, started near the stream in 1863 (Brown, p. 37).

Green Point [MARIN]: *promontory,* 3.5 miles east of downtown Novato on the west side of Petaluma River (lat. 38°06'50" N, long. 122°30'25" W). Named on Novato (1954) 7.5' quadrangle.

Green Point Landing: see **Mowry Landing** [ALAMEDA].

Green Valley [CONTRA COSTA]: *valley,* 2.25 miles east-northeast of Danville (lat. 37°50'05" N, long. 121°57'30" W); the valley is along Green Valley Creek and East Branch Green Valley Creek. Named on Diablo (1953) 7.5' quadrangle. Called Cañada Verde on a diseño of San Ramon (2) grant made in 1834 (Becker, 1969).

Green Valley [SAN MATEO]: *canyon,* drained by a stream that flows less than 1 mile to the sea 1.5 miles west-northwest of Montara Knob (lat. 37°33'55" N, long. 122°30'45" W). Named on Montara Mountain (1956) 7.5' quadrangle.

Green Valley [SOLANO]: *valley,* 2.5 miles northwest of Cordelia (lat. 38°14'20" N, long. 122°09'30" W); the valley is along Green Valley Creek. Named on Cordelia (1951) and Mount George (1951) 7.5' quadrangles.

Green Valley Creek [CONTRA COSTA]: *stream,* flows nearly 4 miles to San Ramon Creek at Danville (lat. 37°49'25" N, long. 121°59'50" W); the stream drains Green Valley. Named on Diablo (1953) 7.5' quadrangle. East Branch enters from the east 1.5 miles northeast of Danville; it is 3.5 miles long and is named on Diablo (1953) 7.5' quadrangle.

Green Valley Creek [SOLANO]: *stream,* flows 8.5 miles to Cordelia Slough 0.25 mile east of Cordelia (lat. 38°12'45" N, long. 122°07'40" W); the stream goes through Green Valley. Named on Cordelia (1951) and Mount George (1951) 7.5' quadrangles.

Green Valley Creek [SONOMA]: *stream,* flows 10.5 miles to Russian River 4.5 miles east of Guerneville (lat. 38°30'15" N, long. 122°54'30" W; near SE cor. sec. 25, T 8 N, R 10 W). Named on Camp Meeker (1954) 7.5' quadrangle.

Green Valley Falls [SOLANO]: *waterfall,* 8 miles west-northwest of Fairfield along Wild Horse Creek (lat. 38°16'35" N, long. 122°10'50" W; sec. 15, T 5 N, R 3 W). Named on Mount George (1951) 7.5' quadrangle.

Greenville [ALAMEDA]: *locality,* 2.5 miles southwest of Altamont (lat. 37°43'15" N, long. 121°42' W; sec. 36, T 2 S, R 2 E). Named on Tesla (1907) 15' quadrangle. The name commemorates John Green, who started the first store at the place (Hoover, Rensch, and Rensch, p. 12). A Southern Pacific Railroad station called Goecken, situated north of Greenville, was named for Herman Bernard Goecken, a local rancher (Mosier and Mosier, p. 39).

Greenwood [SONOMA]: *locality,* 1.5 miles southwest of Sears Point along Northwestern Pacific Railroad (lat. 38°08' N, long. 122°27'40" W). Named on Mare Island (1916) 15' quadrangle.

Greenwood Creek: see **Honsinger Creek** [SAN MATEO].

Greersburg: see **Woodside** [SAN MATEO].

Greer's Creek: see **West Union Creek** [SAN MATEO].

Gregorio's Creek: see **Pine Gulch Creek** [MARIN].

Greystone [SANTA CLARA]: *locality,* 3.5 miles north-northwest of New Almaden along Southern Pacific Railroad (lat. 37°13'25" N, long. 121°50'45" W). Named on Los Gatos (1919) 15' quadrangle. Santa Teresa Hills (1953) 7.5' quadrangle shows Greystone quarry near the site.

Grizzly: see **Camp Grizzly**, under **San Bruno** [SAN MATEO].

Grizzly Bay [SOLANO]: *embayment,* 8 miles south of Fairfield off Suisun Bay (lat. 38°08' N, long. 122°01' W). Named on Denverton (1953), Fairfield South (1949), Honker Bay (1953), and Vine Hill (1959) 7.5' quadrangles. Karquines (1898) 15' quadrangle and Denverton (1918) 7.5' quadrangle show the embayment as part of Suisun Bay.

Grizzly Creek [CONTRA COSTA]: *stream,* flows 3 miles to Las Trampas Creek 6.25 miles west-northwest of Danville in Burton Valley (lat. 37°52' N, long. 122°05'50" W; near E line sec. 5, T 1 S, R 2 W). Named on Las Trampas Ridge (1959) 7.5' quadrangle.

Grizzly Creek [SANTA CLARA]: *stream,* flows nearly 5 miles to East Fork Coyote Creek 6 miles southwest of Mount Stakes (lat. 37°15'15" N, long. 121°28'35" W; sec. 7, T 8 S, R 5 E). Named on Isabel Valley (1955), Mississippi Creek (1955), Mount Sizer (1955), and Mount Stakes (1955) 7.5' quadrangles. North Fork enters from the northwest 1.5 miles upstream from the mouth of the main stream; it is 2.5 miles long and is named on Isabel Valley (1955) 7.5' quadrangle. The canyon of North Fork is called Skunk Hollow on Mount Hamilton (1897) 15' quadrangle.

Grizzly Flats [SANTA CLARA]: *area,* 4 miles south-southeast of Isabel Valley (lat. 37°15'40" N, long. 121°30' W); the place is at the confluence of Grizzly Creek and North Fork Grizzly Creek. Named on Isabel Valley (1955) and Mount Stakes (1955) 7.5' quadrangles.

Grizzly Island [SOLANO]: *island,* 14 miles south of Fairfield between Montezuma Slough, Grizzly Slough, and Grizzly Bay (lat. 38°09'15" N, long. 121°57'45" W). Named on Denverton (1953), Fairfield South (1949), and Honker Bay (1953) 7.5' quadrangles.

Grizzly Island Ferry: see **Beldons Landing** [SOLANO].

Grizzly Peak [ALAMEDA-CONTRA COSTA]: *peak,* 3 miles west of Orinda on Alameda-Contra Costa County line (lat. 37°52'55" N, long. 122°13'55" W). Named on Briones Valley (1959) 7.5' quadrangle. The name is from a grizzly bear killed at the place in the early days (Mosier and Mosier, p. 40).

Grizzly Slough [SOLANO]: *water feature,* joins Montezuma Slough nearly 3 miles south-southwest of Birds Landing (2) (lat. 38°05'45" N, long. 121°53'40" W); the feature is along the southwest side of Grizzly Island. Named on Honker Bay (1953) 7.5' quadrangle.

Grouse Spring [NAPA]: *spring,* 4.25 miles east-northeast of Calistoga (lat. 38°36'20" N, long. 122°30'20" W; near N line sec. 27, T 9 N, R 6 W). Named on Calistoga (1958) 7.5' quadrangle.

Groves: see **Skaggs Springs** [SONOMA].

Grub Creek [SONOMA]: *stream,* flows 1.25 miles to Dutch Bill Creek 2.5 miles northwest of Occidental (lat. 38°26'20" N, long. 122°58'25" W; sec. 21, T 7 N, R 10 W). Named on Camp Meeker (1954) 7.5' quadrangle.

Guadalcanal Village [SOLANO]: *locality,* 2.25 miles west-northwest of downtown Vallejo adjacent to the naval reservation (lat. 38°07'10" N, long. 122°17'25" W). Named on Mare Island (1959) 7.5' quadrangle.

Guadalupe [SANTA CLARA]: *settlement,* 3.5 miles north of Mount Umunhum (lat. 37°12'45" N, long. 121°54'20" W); the place is along Guadalupe Creek. Named on Los Gatos (1919) 15' quadrangle. Los Gatos (1953) 7.5' quadrangle shows Guadalupe mines near the site.

Guadalupe Creek [SANTA CLARA]: *stream,* flows 10 miles to join Alamitos Creek and form Guadalupe River 5.5 miles north-northwest of New Almaden (lat. 37°14'50" N, long. 121°52'10" W). Named on Los Gatos (1953) and Santa Teresa Hills (1953) 7.5' quadrangles. United States Board on Geographic Names (1960b, p. 17) rejected the name "Los Capitancillos Creek" for the stream.

Guadalupe Reservoir [SANTA CLARA]: *lake,* 1 mile long, behind a dam on Guadalupe Creek nearly 3 miles north-northeast of Mount Umunhum (lat. 37°11'55" N, long. 121°52'40" W). Named on Los Gatos (1953) and Santa Teresa Hills (1953) 7.5' quadrangles.

Guadalupe River [SANTA CLARA]: *stream,* formed by the confluence of Guadalupe Creek and Alamitos Creek, flows 17 miles through San Jose to Alviso Slough at Alviso (lat. 37°25'30" N, long. 121°58'35" W). Named on Mipitas (1961), San Jose East (1961), San Jose West (1961), and Santa Teressa Hills (1953) 7.5' quadrangles. On San Jose (1899) 15' quadrangle, the river joins Guadalupe Slough at Alviso. According to Gudde (1949, p. 137), Anza called the stream Rio de Nuestra Señora de Guadalupe in 1776 to honor the principal patron saint of the Anza expedition. Gudde (1949, p. 306) also noted that the stream is called Rio de San Jose on old maps. United States Board on Geographic Names (1933, p. 342) rejected the forms "Guadaloupe River" and "Guadelupe River" for the name, and later (1943, p. 11) rejected the name "Guadalupe Slough" for the stream.

Guadalupe River: see **Guadalupe Slough** [SANTA CLARA].

Guadalupe Slough [SANTA CLARA]: *water feature,* 4 miles long, enters mud flats near San Francisco Bay 4 miles west-northwest of Alviso near the mouth of Coyote Creek (lat. 37°27'10" N, long. 122°02'15" W). Named on Milpitas (1961) and Mountain View (1961) 7.5' quadrangles. Called Guadalupe River on Mountain View (1953) 7.5' quadrangle. Water of Guadalupe River once entered San Francisco Bay through Guadalupe Slough, but now reaches the bay about 1 mile farther north through Alviso Slough. United States Board on Geographic Names (1960b, p. 17) rejected the name "Guadalupe River" for present Guadalupe Slough.

Guadalupe Slough: see **Guadalupe River** [SANTA CLARA].

Guadalupe Valley [SAN MATEO]: *valley,* 2.25 miles north of downtown South San Francisco (lat. 37°41'20" N, long. 122°24'35" W); the valley is on Cañada de Guadalupe la Visitacion y Rodeo Viejo grant. Named on San Francisco South (1956) 7.5' quadrangle.

Gualala Point [SONOMA]: *promontory,* 1.25 miles south-southeast of the mouth of Gualala River along the coast (lat. 38°45'10" N, long. 123°31'35" W). Named on Gualala (1960) 7.5' quadrangle.

Gualala Point Island [SONOMA]: *island,* 500 feet long, 1.25 miles south-southeast of the mouth of Gualala River (lat. 38°45'05" N, long. 123°31'40" W); the island is 550 feet off Gualala Point. Named on Gualala (1960) 7.5' quadrangle.

Gualala River [SONOMA]: *stream,* formed by the confluence of North Fork (which is in Mendocino County) and South Fork at Sonoma-Mendocino County line, flows 3.5 miles along the county line to the sea 10.5 miles northwest of the village of Stewarts Point (lat. 38°46'10" N, long. 123°31'55" W). Named on Gualala (1960) 7.5' quadrangle. The stream also was called Walalla River (Gudde, 1949, p. 138). South Fork is 35 miles long and is named on Ornbaun Valley (1960) 15' quadrangle, and on Annapolis (1977), Fort Ross (1978), Plantation (1977), and Stewarts Point (1978) 7.5' quadrangles. South Fork is called Gualala River on Ornbaun (1944) 15' quadrangle. Wheatfield Fork joins South Fork 3.5 miles north-northwest of the village of Stewarts Point; it is 33 miles long and is named on Hopland (1960) 15' quadrangle, and on Annapolis (1977), Stewarts Point (1978), and Tombs Creek (1978) 7.5' quadrangles. Present Wheatfield Fork is called Buckeye Creek on Hopland (1944) 15' quadrangle.

Guano Island: see **Little Coyote Point** [SAN MATEO].

Gubserville [SANTA CLARA]: *village,* 2.5 miles west-northwest of Campbell (lat. 37°17'40" N, long. 121°59'15" W). Named on San Jose (1899) 15' quadrangle. Postal authorities established Gubserville post office in 1882 and discontinued it in 1899 (Frickstad, p. 173). The place had a stage station, post office, and a house or two; the name commemorates Frank Gubser, a Swiss immigrant (undated item from *San Jose Mercury*).

Gudde Ridge: see **Round Top** [CONTRA COSTA].

Guerne Park: see **Guernewood Park** [SONOMA].

Guerneville [SONOMA]: *town,* 10 miles southwest of Healdsburg along Russian River (lat. 38°30'05" N, long. 122°59'45" W). Named on Camp Meeker (1954), Cazadero (1978), and Guerneville (1955) 7.5' quadrangles. Postal authorities established Guerneville post office in 1870; the name commemorates George E. Guerne, who settled at the place in 1864 and built a sawmill there (Salley, p. 91). California Mining Bureau's (1909a) map shows a place called Mercury located 4 miles by stage line north of Guerneville. Postal authorities established Mercuryville post office in 1874, discontinued it in 1876, reestablished it in 1878, discontinued it in 1879, reestablished it with the name "Mercury" in 1899, and discontinued it in 1909 (Salley, p. 138).

Guernewood: see **East Guernewood** [SONOMA]; **Guernewood Park** [SONOMA]; **West Guernewood** [SONOMA].

Guernewood Park [SONOMA]: *settlement,* less than 1 mile southwest of Guerneville along Russian River (lat. 38°29'40" N, long. 122°00'35" W; sec. 31, T 8 N, R 10 W). Named on Duncans Mills (1979) 7.5' quadrangle. Called Guerne Park on Duncans Mills (1921) 15' quadrangle, and called Guernewood on California Division of Forestry's (1945) map. Postal authorities established Guernewood Park post office in 1925; the name is for Bert Guerne, who build a summer resort at the place (Salley, p. 91).

Gulf of the Farallones [MARIN-SAN FRANCISCO-SAN MATEO]: *embayment,* along the coast between Point Reyes [MARIN] and Point San Pedro [SAN MATEO] (United States Coast and Geodetic Survey, p. 123); Farallon Islands lie west of the embayment. Named on San Francisco (1956) 1°x 2° quadrangle. After Cermeño applied the name "San Francisco" to present Drakes Bay in 1595 (Treutlein, p. 12), members of the Portola expedition used the term "Puerto de San Francisco" for present Gulf of the Farallones in 1769, before they were aware of present San Francisco Bay (Davidson, p. 6).

Gull Rock [MARIN]: *rock,* 4.5 miles east-southeast of Bolinas, and 300 feet offshore (lat. 37°52'35" N, long. 122°36'55" W). Named on San Rafael (1954) 7.5' quadrangle.

Gull Rock [SONOMA]: *island,* 300 feet long, nearly 2 miles south of Jenner, and 1350 feet offshore (lat. 38°25'30" N, long. 123°07'15" W). Named on Duncans Mills (1979) 7.5' quadrangle.

Gulnac Peak [SANTA CLARA]: *peak,* 6.5 miles northeast of Pacheco Peak (lat. 37°04'25" N, long. 121°22' W; sec. 12, T 10 S, R 5 E). Altitude 2276 feet. Named on Pacheco Peak (1955) 7.5' quadrangle. The name commemorates the Gulnac family, whose first member in California arrived in 1833 (Hanna, P.T., p. 130).

Gushee Creek: see **Old Womans Creek** [SAN MATEO].

Guth Landing [SANTA CLARA]: *locality,* 3 miles north of downtown Mountain View along Stevens Creek in mud flats near San Francisco Bay (lat. 37°25'55" N, long. 122°04'30" W). Named on Palo Alto (1899) 15' quadrangle.

Guthrie: see **Napa Junction** [NAPA].

Guyserville: see **Geyserville** [SONOMA].

Gwin Island: see **Browns Island** [CONTRA COSTA].

— H —

Haakerville: see **Woodside** [SAN MATEO].

Haas Slough: see **Hass Slough** [SOLANO].

Hacienda [SONOMA]: *settlement,* 3.5 miles east of Guerneville (lat. 38°30'45" N, long. 122°55'40" W; near E line sec. 26, T 8 N, R 10 W). Named on Guerneville (1955) 7.5' quadrangle.

Hacienda: see **New Almaden** [SANTA CLARA]; **Pleasanton** [ALAMEDA].

Hagerman Canyon [SANTA CLARA]: *canyon,* drained by a stream that flows 5.25 miles to Cedar Creek 3.25 miles northwest of Pacheco Peak (lat. 37°02'35" N, long. 121°19'25" W). Named on Gilroy Hot Springs (1955) and Pacheco Peak (1955) 7.5' quadrangles. Called Harrigan Canyon on Gilroy Hot Springs (1921) 15' quadrangle.

Hagerman Peak [SANTA CLARA]: *peak,* 3.5 miles north-northwest of Pacheco Pass (lat. 37°06'45" N, long. 121°14'15" W; sec. 31, T 9 S, R 7 E). Altitude 1790 feet. Named on Pacheco Pass (1955) 7.5' quadrangle.

Haggerty Gulch [MARIN]: *canyon,* drained by a stream that flows 1.5 miles to Lagunitas Creek nearly 1 mile west-southwest of Point Reyes Station (lat. 38°03'50" N, long. 122°49'10" W). Named on Inverness (1954) 7.5' quadrangle. Teather (p. 28) associated the name with Martin Haggerty, a rancher in the neighborhood in the 1870's.

Haggin Creek: see **Willow Brook** [SONOMA].

Hale Creek [SANTA CLARA]: *stream,* flows 3.25 miles to Permanente Creek 1.5 miles east of downtown Los Altos (lat. 37°23' N, long. 122°05'15" W). Named on Cupertino (1961) and Mountain View (1961) 7.5' quadrangles. The name commemorates Joseph A. Hale, who owned most of San Antonio grant (Mary T. Fortney, *Times Tribune*, October 15, 1988).

Halfmile Rock [SONOMA]: *rock,* 1 mile west-southwest of Jenner, and nearly 0.5 mile off the coast (lat. 38°26'35" N, long. 123° 08' W). Named on Arched Rock (1977) 7.5' quadrangle.

Half Moon Bay [SAN MATEO]:

(1) *embayment,* east and southeast of Pillar Point along the coast (lat. 37°29' N, long. 122°28' W). Named on Half Moon Bay (1961) and Montara Mountain (1956) 7.5' quadrangles. Called Halfmoon Bay on Santa Cruz (1902) 30' quadrangle, but United States Board on Geographic Names (1960b, p. 17) rejected this form of the name, which. is from the shape of the feature (Gudde, 1949, p. 140).

(2) *town,* 11 miles west of Redwood City (lat. 37°27'50" N, long. 122°25'40" W); the town is near the coast at Half Moon Bay (1). Named on Half Moon Bay (1961) 7.5' quadrangle. Called Halfmoon Bay on Santa Cruz (1902) 30' quadrangle, but United States Board on Geographic Names (1960b, p. 17) rejected the names "Halfmoon Bay," "Half-Moon Bay," "Spanish Town," and "Spanish-Town" for the place. Postal authorities established Halfmoon Bay post office in 1861, discontinued it for a time in 1862, and changed the name to Half Moon Bay in 1905 (Salley, p. 92). A village at the site in the 1840's was called San Benito, but Americans began calling it Spanish Town or Spanishtown in the 1850's; this name lasted long after Halfmoon Bay post office opened (Brown, p. 39).

Half Moon Bay Beach: see **Francis Beach** [SAN MATEO].

Half Way House: see **San Mateo** [SAN MATEO] (2).

Halfway House [ALAMEDA]: *locality,* nearly 3 miles southeast of Cedar Mountain along Arroyo Mocho (lat. 37°32'20" N, long. 121° 33'55" W; near W line sec. 32, T 4 S, R 4 E). Named on Tesla (1907) 15' quadrangle.

Hall: see **Hall Station** [ALAMEDA].

Halleck Creek [MARIN]: *stream,* flows 7.5 miles to Nicasio Creek 8 miles west-southwest of downtown Novato (lat. 38°04'05" N, long. 122°42'10" W); the creek is on Nicasio (4) grant, which Henry W. Halleck owned. Named on San Geronimo (1954) 7.5' quadrangle.

Hallidie Gulch: see **Neils Gulch** [SAN MATEO].

Hall Station [ALAMEDA]: *locality,* 4 miles north-northwest of downtown Newark along Southern Pacific Railroad (lat. 37°35'10" N, long. 122°03'45" W). Named on Newark (1959) 7.5' quadrangle. Called Hall on Haywards (1899) 15' quadrangle. The name commemorates John Hall, a farmer who donated land for railroad construction (MacGregor, p. 90).

Halls Valley [SANTA CLARA]: *valley,* 4 miles west of Mount Hamilton on the upper reaches of San Felipe Creek (lat. 37°20'15" N, long. 121°42'50" W). Named on Lick Observatory (1955) 7.5' quadrangle. Called Hall's Valley on Thompson and West's (1876) map. The name commemorates Frederic Hall, San Jose lawyer and historian (Arbuckle, p. 14).

Halo-Chemuck: see **Rio Vista** [SOLANO].

Halvern [ALAMEDA]: *locality,* 3.5 miles south-southeast of Hayward along Southern Pacific Railroad (lat. 37°37'25" N, long. 122° 03'10" W). Named on Hayward (1915) 15' quadrangle.

Halverson's Landing: see **San Leandro Creek** [ALAMEDA-CONTRA COSTA].

Hamilton: see **Campbell** [SANTA CLARA]; **Hamilton Air Force Base** [MARIN]; **Mount Hamilton** [SANTA CLARA].

Hamilton Air Force Base [MARIN]: *military installation,* 4.5 miles southeast of downtown Novato (lat. 38°03'30" N, long. 122°30'50" W). Named on Novato (1954) and Petaluma Point (1959) 7.5' quadrangles. Postal authorities established Hamilton Field post office in 1936, changed the name to Hamilton in 1949, and changed it to Hamilton Air Force Base in 1956 (Salley, p. 92). The name commemorates Lieutenant Lloyd A Hamilton, an American aviator who was killed in action in World War I; the site was known as Marin Meadows before it became an air field (Gudde, 1949, p. 141).

Hamilton Field: see **Hamilton Air Force Base** [MARIN].

Hamilton Flat [ALAMEDA]: *area,* 12 miles east-southeast of Sunol (lat. 37°29'50" N, long. 121°41'15" W; sec. 18, T 5 S, R 3 E). Named on Mendenhall Springs (1956) and Mount Day (1955) 7.5' quadrangles.

Hamilton Gulch [ALAMEDA]: *canyon,* drained by a stream that flows 1 mile to Strawberry Creek nearly 5 miles north-northeast of downtown Oakland (lat. 37°52'50" N, long. 122°14'15" W). Named on Oakland East (1959) 7.5' quadrangle.

Hamlet [MARIN]: *locality,* 3 miles south-southwest of Tomales on the northeast side of Tomales Bay (lat. 38°12'25" N, long. 122°55'25" W). Named on Tomales (1954) 7.5' quadrangle. Shown along Northwestern Pacific Railroad on Point Reyes (1918) 15' quadrangle. John Hamlet bought land at the site in 1865 (Teather, p. 28). Postal authorities established Hamlet post office in 1876 and discontinued it in 1886 (Frickstad, p. 88). They established Telmat post office at the place in 1917 after they rejected the name "Hamlet," and discontinued it in 1931—the name "Telmat" was derived from the word "Hamlet" by reversing the order of letters and substituting "t" for "h" (Salley, p. 219).

Hammer Island [ALAMEDA-CONTRA COSTA]: *island,* 15 miles northeast of Livermore in a branch of Old River on Alameda-Contra Costa County line at the extreme northeast corner of Alameda County (lat. 37°49' N, long. 121°33'20" W). Named on Clifton Court Forebay (1978) 7.5' quadrangle.

Hammock Hill [MARIN]: *peak,* 9 miles west-northwest of downtown Novato (lat. 38°09'50" N, long. 122°43'20" W). Altitude 914 feet. Named on Petaluma (1953) 7.5' quadrangle.

Hammond Island [SOLANO]: *island,* between Grizzly Slough and Roaring River Slough 4 miles southwest of Birds Landing (2) (lat. 38°06'15" N, long. 121°56'30" W). Named on Denverton (1953) and Honker Bay (1953) 7.5' quadrangles.

Hamms Gulch [SAN MATEO]: *canyon,* drained by a stream that flows 1.25 miles to Corte Madera Creek 3.5 miles north of Mindego Hill (lat. 37°21'45" N, long. 122°13'15" W). Named on Mindego Hill (1961) 7.5' quadrangle. Alexander N. Hamm had a ranch at the head of the canyon after 1860 (Brown, p. 39).

Hansen: see **Point Hansen**, under **Van Sickle Island** [SOLANO].

Happersberger Point [MARIN]: *ridge,* east-trending, 1 mile long, nearly 6 miles north-northeast of Bolinas (lat. 37°58'40" N, long. 122°37'35" W). Named on Bolinas (1954) and San Rafael (1954) 7.5' quadrangles.

Happy Valley [CONTRA COSTA]: *valley,* 3 miles northeast of Orinda (lat. 37°54'15" N, long. 122°08'20" W). Named on Briones Valley (1959) 7.5' quadrangle. Called Pleasant Valley on Concord (1897) 15' quadrangle.

Happy Valley: see **Rincon Hill** [SAN FRANCISCO].

Haraszthy Creek [SONOMA]: *stream,* flows 2.25 miles to Arroyo Seco 2 miles east-southeast of Sonoma (lat. 38°16'35" N, long. 122°25'30" W). Named on Sonoma (1951) 7.5' quadrangle.

Haraszthy Falls [SONOMA]: *waterfall,* 2 miles east of Sonoma (lat. 38°17'35" N, long. 122°25'05" W); the feature is along Haraszthy Creek. Named on Sonoma (1951) 7.5' quadrangle.

Harbine [SONOMA]: *locality,* nearly 6 miles northwest of Sebastopol along Petaluma and Santa Rosa Railroad (lat. 38°27'50" N, long. 122°53'05" W). Named on Sebastopol (1942) 15' quadrangle.

Harbor View: see **Yacht Harbor** [SAN FRANCISCO].

Hardin Creek [NAPA]: *stream,* flows 6.5 miles to Maxwell Creek 9.5 miles northeast of Saint Helena (lat. 38°36'35" N, long. 122°21'20" W). Named on Chiles Valley (1958) 7.5' quadrangle.

Harding Rock [SAN FRANCISCO]: *rock,* 2.5 miles northwest of North Point in San Francisco Bay (lat. 37°50'10" N, long. 122°26'40" W). Named on San Francisco North (1956) 7.5' quadrangle.

Harlan Hill [CONTRA COSTA]: *peak,* 6 miles south-southeast of Danville (lat. 37°44'10" N, long. 121°58'50" W; near N line sec. 28, T 2 S, R 1 W). Altitude 1719 feet. Named on Dublin (1961) 7.5' quadrangle.

Harness Camp [SONOMA]: *locality,* 2.25 miles north of Geyser Peak (lat. 38°47'50" N, long. 122°50'30" W; sec. 15, T 11 N, R 9 W). Named on The Geysers (1959) 7.5' quadrangle.

Harper Canyon [SANTA CLARA]: *canyon,* drained by a stream that flows 3.5 miles to Pacheco Creek nearly 3 miles west-northwest of Pacheco Peak (lat. 37°01' N, long. 121°20'05" W). Named on Pacheco Peak (1955) and Three Sisters (1954) 7.5' quadrangles.

Harrigan Canyon: see **Hagerman Canyon** [SANTA CLARA].

Harrington Creek [SAN MATEO]: *stream,* flows 4.5 miles to San Gregorio Creek 1.5 miles west of La Honda (lat. 37°19'10" N, long. 122°18'05" W). Named on La Honda (1961) and Woodside (1961) 7.5' quadrangles. The name commemorates George Harrington, who built a cabin at the head of the creek in 1859 (Brown, p. 40).

Harrington's Pond: see **Upper Crystal Springs Reservoir** [SAN MATEO].

Harrisburg: see **Warm Springs District** [ALAMEDA].

Harris Canyon [NAPA]: *canyon,* drained by a stream that flows 2.5 miles to lowlands along Lake Berryessa 3 miles west of Berryessa Peak (lat. 38°39'45" N, long. 122°14'45" W). Named on Brooks (1959) 7.5' quadrangle. Capay (1945) 15' quadrangle shows Harris ranch located near the mouth of the canyon.

Harrison: see **Pescadero** [SAN MATEO].

Harrison Gulch [SONOMA]: *canyon,* drained by a stream that flows 0.5 mile to Russian River 2.5 miles south-southwest of Guerneville (lat. 38°28'05" N, long. 123°00'45" W; sec. 7, T 7 N, R 10 W). Named on Duncans Mills (1979) 7.5' quadrangle.

Harrisville: see **Arroyo Seco** [ALAMEDA].

Harry Floyd Terrace [SOLANO]: *district,* 2 miles north-northwest of downtown Vallejo (lat. 38°07'55" N, long. 122°14'45" W; sec. 6, T 3 N, R 3 W). Named on Cordelia (1951) 7.5' quadrangle.

Hartley [SOLANO]: *locality,* nearly 2 miles south of Allendale along Southern Pacific Railroad (lat. 38°25' N, long. 121°56'45" W). Named on Allendale (1953) 7.5' quadrangle.

Hartley: see **West Hartley** [CONTRA COSTA].

Harvey Slough [SOLANO]: *water feature,* joins Suisun Slough 8 miles south-southwest of Fairfield (lat. 38°08'20" N, long. 122°04'55" W). Named on Fairfield South (1949) 7.5' quadrangle.

Harwood Creek [SAN MATEO]: *stream,* flows 0.5 mile to Pescadero Creek 3.5 miles south of La Honda (lat. 37°16' N, long. 122° 15'45" W; sec. 2, T 8 S, R 4 W). Named on La Honda (1961) 7.5' quadrangle.

Harwood Creek: see **Claremont Creek** [ALAMEDA].

Haskins Hill [SAN MATEO]: *ridge,* east-southeast-trending, 0.5 mile long, 1 mile south-southwest of La Honda (lat. 37°18'10" N, long. 122°16'40" W). Named on La Honda (1961) 7.5' quadrangle. Aaron A. Haskins settled at the place in the early 1860's (Brown, p. 40).

Hass Slough [SOLANO]: *water feature,* joins Cache Slough 9 miles north of Rio Vista (lat. 38°17'30" N, long. 121°43'25" W). Named on Dozier (1952) and Liberty Island (1978) 7.5' quadrangles. Called Haas Slough on Liberty Island (1952) 7.5' quadrangle.

Hastings Creek: see **Hastings Slough** [CONTRA COSTA].

Hastings Cut [SOLANO]: *water feature,* artificial waterway that extends from Lindsey Slough to Cache Slough 9.5 miles north-northwest of Rio Vista (lat. 38°17'30" N, long. 121°44'25" W). Named on Dozier (1952) and Liberty Island (1978) 7.5' quadrangles. Liberty Island (1952) 7.5' quadrangle has the name "McCoy Slough" at the northeast end of present Hastings Cut, where Hastings Cut joins Cache Slough.

Hasting Slough [SOLANO]: *water feature,* joins Cross Slough 4 miles southwest of Denverton (lat. 38°10'50" N, long. 121°56'40" W). Named on Denverton (1953) 7.5' quadrangle.

Hastings Slough [CONTRA COSTA]: *water feature,* enters Suisun Bay 5 miles east-northeast of Martinez (lat. 38°03'05" N, long. 122°03'20" W). Named on Vine Hill (1959) 7.5' quadrangle. Called Hastings Creek on Karquinez (1898) 15' quadrangle.

Hastings Tract [SOLANO]: *area,* 8 miles north-northwest of Rio Vista (lat. 38°16'30" N, long. 121°44' W). Named on Dozier (1952), Liberty Island (1978), and Rio Vista (1978) 7.5' quadrangles.

Hastings Tract: see **Little Hastings Tract** [SOLANO].

Hatfield Canyon [SANTA CLARA]: *canyon,* drained by a stream that flows nearly 2 miles to Pescadero Creek 2.5 miles north of Pajaro Gap (lat.

36°56'55" N, long. 121°38' W). Named on Watsonville East (1955) 7.5' quadrangle.

Haupt Creek [SONOMA]: *stream,* flows 5.5 miles to Wheatfield Fork Gualala River 4.5 miles southeast of Annapolis (lat. 38°39'45" N, long. 123°19'15" W; near SW cor. sec. 33, T 10 N, R 13 W). Named on Annapolis (1977) and Plantation (1977) 7.5' quadrangles. United States Board on Geographic Names (1977b, p. 3) noted that the name commemorates Charles Haupt, who settled in the neighborhood in the 1860's. The stream is called Charley Haupt Creek on a map of 1879 (Gudde, 1949, p. 143).

Havens [ALAMEDA]: *locality,* 4.25 miles east-northeast of downtown Oakland along Oakland Antioch and Eastern Railroad (lat. 37°49'45" N, long. 122°11'45" W). Named on Concord (1915) 15' quadrangle. The name commemorates Frank Colton Havens, a developer (Mosier and Mosier, p. 41-42).

Hawes Gulch: see **Arroyo Ojo de Agua** [SAN MATEO].

Hay Canyon [SANTA CLARA]: *canyon,* drained by a stream that flows 1.5 miles to Uvas Reservoir 5 miles north of Mount Madonna (lat. 37°05' N, long. 121°42'30" W). Named on Mount Madonna (1955, photorevised 1968 and 1973) 7.5' quadrangle.

Hayes Creek [SANTA CLARA]: *stream,* flows 1.5 miles to Llagas Creek nearly 6 miles north-northeast of Mount Madonna (lat. 37°05'05" N, long. 121°39'05" W); the stream drains part of Hayes Valley. Named on Mount Madonna (1955, photorevised 1968 and 1973) 7.5' quadrangle. The name commemorates an early landowner in the neighborhood (United States Board on Geographic Names, 1973a, p. 2).

Hayes Creek: see **Glen Echo Creek** [ALAMEDA].

Hayes Reach [CONTRA COSTA]: *water feature,* part of San Joaquin River located 5.5 miles northeast of the settlement of Bethel Island on Contra Costa-San Joaquin County line at the mouth of Old River (lat. 38°04'35" N, long. 121°34'10" W). Named on Bouldin Island (1978) 7.5' quadrangle.

Hayes Valley [SANTA CLARA]: *valley,* about 5 miles northeast of Mount Madonna (lat. 37°04'15" N, long. 121°39' W); Hayes Creek drains part of the valley. Named on Mount Madonna (1955) 7.5' quadrangle.

Hayfield Hill: see **Bald Hill** [SONOMA].

Haynes Gulch [ALAMEDA]: *canyon,* drained by a stream that flows 1.25 miles to Alameda Creek 4.5 miles south-southeast of Sunol (lat. 37°32'05" N, long. 121°51'05" W; near N line sec. 3, T 5 S, R 1 E). Named on La Costa Valley (1960) 7.5' quadrangle.

Hays Camp [ALAMEDA]: *locality,* 4 miles south of Cedar Mountain (lat. 37°29'55" N, long. 121°36'50" W; near E line sec. 14, T 5 S, R 3 E). Named on Eylar Mountain (1955) 7.5' quadrangle.

Hays Canyon: see **Glen Echo Creek** [ALAMEDA].

Hays' Creek: see **Glen Echo Creek** [ALAMEDA].

Haystack [SONOMA]: *locality,* 2 miles east-southeast of downtown Petaluma along Northwestern Pacific Railroad (lat. 38°13'25" N, long. 122°36'30" W; near NE cor. sec. 3, T 4 N, R 7 W). Named on Petaluma River (1954) 7.5' quadrangle. Petaluma (1914) 15' quadrangle shows a place called Haystack Landing located along Petaluma River near the site. Steamers docked at Haystack Landing, which was named for some haystacks left there in the 1840's; the place also was known as Rudesill's Landing (Heig, p. 72).

Haystack [NAPA]: *peak,* 3.5 miles northeast of Yountville (lat. 38° 26'30" N, long. 122°18'55" W; near W line sec. 21, T 7 N, R 4 W). Altitude 1672 feet. Named on Yountville (1951) 7.5' quadrangle.

Haystack Landing: see **Haystack** [SONOMA].

Hayward [ALAMEDA]: *city,* 13 miles southeast of downtown Oakland (lat. 37°40'15" N, long. 122°04'50" W). Named on Hayward (1959), Redwood Point (1959), and San Leandro (1959) 7.5' quadrangles. Called Haywards on Haywards (1899) 15' quadrangle. United States Board on Geographic Names (1933, p. 358) rejected the names "Haywards," "Hayward's," "Haywards Station," and "Haywood" for the place. Postal authorities established Haywood post office in 1860, changed the name to Haywards in 1880, and changed it to Hayward in 1911 (Frickstad, p. 2). The city incorporated in 1876. The name commemorates William Hayward, an early settler at the site (Hoover, Rensch, and Rensch, p. 18). Postal authorities established Hayward Heath post office in 1916 and discontinued it in 1918, when they moved the service to Hayward; the name was from a real-estate promotion (Salley, p. 95).

Hayward Heath: see **Hayward** [ALAMEDA].

Hayward Landing [ALAMEDA]: *locality,* 4.5 miles west-southwest of downtown Hayward at the edge of San Francisco Bay (lat. 37° 38'40" N, long. 122°09'15" W). Named on San Leandro (1959) 7.5' quadrangle. Called Haywards Landing on Haywards (1899) 15' quadrangle. Richard Barron arrived in the neighborhood in 1855 and established Barron's Landing at the site; the name was changed in the 1860's to Simpson's Landing for John Simpson, who operated the place; Hans Peter Jensen bought the business from Barron in 1884, and for a time the place was known locally as Jensen's Landing (Mosier, and Mosier, p. 43).

Hayward Park [SAN MATEO]: *district,* 1 mile southeast of downtown San Mateo (lat. 37°33'20" N, long. 122°18'40" W). Named on San Mateo (1956) 7.5' quadrangle.

Haywards: see **Hayward** [ALAMEDA].

Haywards Pass: see **Dublin Canyon** [ALAMEDA].

Haywards Station: see **Hayward** [ALAMEDA]; **Hayward Station** [ALAMEDA].

Hayward Station [ALAMEDA]: *locality,* 1 mile southwest of Hayward along Southern Pacific Railroad (lat. 37°39'50" N, long. 122° 05'55" W). Named on Hayward (1915) 15' quadrangle. Called Haywards Station on Haywards (1899) 15' quadrangle.

Haywood: see **Hayward** [ALAMEDA].

Healdsburg [SONOMA]: *town,* 14 miles northwest of Santa Rosa near Russian River (lat. 38°36'40" N, long. 122°52'10" W). Named on Healdsburg (1955) 7.5' quadrangle. Postal authorities established Russian River post office in 1854 and changed the name to Healdsburgh (with the final "h") in 1857 (Frickstad, p. 198)—the name had the form "Healdsburg" by 1880 (Hansen and Miller, p. 47). The town incorporated in 1867. The name commemorates H.G. Heald, who opened a store at the site in 1852 (Bancroft, 1888, p. 508). Postal authorities established Dodgeville post office 13 miles northeast of Healdsburg in 1874, changed the name to Pine Flat the same year, discontinued it in 1876, reestablished it in 1878, discontinued it in 1880, reestablished it with the name "Pineflat" in 1900, moved it 4 miles northeast in 1906, and discontinued it in 1932 (Salley, p. 60, 172). They established Pacific Home post office 7 miles northeast of Healdsburg (sec. 36, T 10 N, R 9 W) in 1858 and discontinued it in 1860 (Salley, p. 164). They established Excelsior post office 8 miles northeast of Healdsburg at Excelsior mine (sec. 35, T 9 N, R 8 W) in 1875 and discontinued it in 1877 (Salley, p. 71) They established Lambert post office 4.5 miles north of Healdsburg in 1897 and discontinued it in 1903; the name was for Charles L. Lambert, a pioneer settler (Salley, p. 116).

Hearst: see **Pleasanton** [ALAMEDA].

Hearts Desire [MARIN]: *locality,* 8 miles south of Tomales on the southwest side of Tomales Bay (lat. 38°08' N, long. 122°53'35" W). Named on Tomales (1954) 7.5' quadrangle.

Heath Canyon [NAPA]: *canyon,* drained by a stream that flows 2.5 miles to Sulphur Creek 1.25 miles south-southwest of Saint Helena (lat. 38°29'15" N, long. 122°28'40" W). Named on Rutherford (1951) 7.5' quadrangle.

Hecker Pass [SANTA CLARA]: *pass,* 7.5 miles northwest of Pajaro Gap on Santa Clara-Santa Cruz County line (lat. 36°59'45" N, long. 121°43' W). Named on Watsonville East (1955) 7.5' quadrangle. The name honors Henry Hecker, a Santa Clara County supervisor when the road over the pass was completed in 1928 (Rambo, 1964, p. 36). Because of a change made in the county line in 1971, the pass now lies entirely in Santa Clara County (Clark, D.T., p. 149).

Hedd Canyon [ALAMEDA]: *canyon,* drained by a stream that flows 1 mile to Devaney Canyon 1.25 miles southwest of Dublin (lat. 37° 41'20" N, long. 121°57'30" W; sec. 10, T 3 S, R 1 W). Named on Dublin (1961) 7.5' quadrangle. The misspelled name commemorates William G. Head, who owned land in the canyon in 1879 (Mosier and Mosier, p. 43).

Hedgpeth Lake [SONOMA]: *lake,* 2800 feet long, 6 miles south-southwest of Big Mountain (lat. 38°37'45" N, long. 123°11' W). Named on Tombs Creek (1978) 7.5' quadrangle.

Helen: see **Mount Helen**, under **Martinez** [CONTRA COSTA]; **Mount Helen** [SANTA CLARA]; **Mount Helen**, under **Mount Saint Helena** [SONOMA].

Heller: see **Mount Heller** [SONOMA].

Hell Hole [SONOMA]: *canyon,* 5.5 miles east-northeast of Fort Ross along Ward Creek (lat. 38°33' N, long. 123°09'10" W). Named on Fort Ross (1978) 7.5' quadrangle.

Helmet Rock [SAN FRANCISCO]: *rock,* 0.5 mile south-southwest of Fort Point, and 600 feet offshore (lat. 37°48'05" N, long. 122°28'50" W). Named on San Francisco North (1956) 7.5' quadrangle.

Helm's Creek: see **Hulbert Creek** [SONOMA].

Hemme Hills [CONTRA COSTA]: *ridge,* south-trending, 1 mile long, 4.5 miles south of Mount Diablo (lat. 37°49'05" N, long. 121°55'35" W). Named on Diablo (1953) 7.5' quadrangle.

Henderson [SAN MATEO]: *locality,* 3.5 miles east of downtown Redwood City along Southern Pacific Railroad (lat. 37°28'45" N, long. 122°09'45" W). Named on Palo Alto (1961) 7.5' quadrangle.

Henderson Ridge [SANTA CLARA]: *ridge,* south-southwest- to west-trending, nearly 4 miles long, 5 miles south of Mount Hamilton (lat. 37°15' N, long. 121°37'30" W). Named on Isabel Valley (1955), Lick Observatory (1955), Morgan Hill (1955), and Mount Sizer (1955) 7.5' quadrangles.

Hendrys Creek [SANTA CLARA]: *stream,* flows 1.5 miles to Lexington Reservoir 4 miles south of downtown Los Gatos (lat. 37°10'10" N, long. 121°58'45" W; sec. 9, T 9 S, R 1 W). Named on Los Gatos (1953) 7.5' quadrangle.

Henne: see **Lake Henne** [NAPA].

Hennessey: see **Lake Hennessey** [NAPA].

Henry: see **Mount Henry**, under **Mount Saint John** [NAPA].

Herbert Creek [SANTA CLARA]: *stream,* flows 2 miles to Alamitos Creek nearly 3 miles southwest of New Almaden (lat. 37°09' N, long. 121°51'30" W; near W line sec. 15, T 9 S, R 1 E). Named on Los Gatos (1953) and

Santa Teresa Hills (1953) 7.5' quadrangles.

Hercules [CONTRA COSTA]: *town,* 4 miles east of Point Pinole (lat. 38°01' N, long. 122°17'20" W). Named on Benicia (1959), Briones Valley (1959), Mare Island (1959), and Richmond (1959) 7.5' quadrangles. The town incorporated in 1900. Postal authorities established Hercules post office in 1914 (Frickstad, p. 22). The name is from Hercules Powder Company's plant established at the place in the 1890's (Gudde, 1949, p. 147).

Hercules Wharf [CONTRA COSTA]: *locality,* 4 miles east of Point Pinole along San Pablo Bay (lat. 38°01'20" N, long. 122°17'20" W); the place is at Hercules. Named on Mare Island (1959) 7.5' quadrangle. Called Refugio Ldg. on Mare Island (1916) 15' quadrangle.

Herdlyn [CONTRA COSTA]: *locality,* 10 miles southeast of Brentwood along Southern Pacific Railroad (lat. 37°49'05" N, long. 121° 35'05" W; on E line sec. 25, T 1 S, R 3 E). Named on Bethany (1952) 7.5' quadrangle.

Herman: see **Lake Herman** [SOLANO].

Herms: see **Camp Herms** [CONTRA COSTA].

Herpoco [CONTRA COSTA]: *locality,* 5 miles east of Pinole Point along Atchison, Topeka and Santa Fe Railroad (lat. 38°00'40" N, long. 122°16'10" W). Named on Mare Island (1959) 7.5' quadrangle. Railroad officials coined the name in 1919 from letters of the term "Hercules Powder Company" (Gudde, 1949, p. 147).

Hessel [SONOMA]: *locality,* 4.5 miles east-northeast of Bloomfield along Petaluma and Santa Rosa Railroad (lat. 38°20'50" N, long. 122°46'35" W). Named on Two Rock (1954) 7.5' quadrangle.

Hicks Mountain [MARIN]: *peak,* 9 miles west of downtown Novato (lat. 38°07'45" N, long. 122°43'30" W); the peak is south-southwest of Hicks Valley. Altitude 1532 feet. Named on Petaluma (1953) 7.5' quadrangle.

Hicks Valley [MARIN]: *valley,* 8 miles west-northwest of downtown Novato on the upper reaches of Arroyo Sausal (lat. 38°08'45" N, long. 122°42'30" W); the valley is mainly on Corte Madera de Novato grant. Named on Petaluma (1953) 7.5' quadrangle. The name is for William Hicks, who bought Corte Madera de Novato grant in 1855 (Mason, 1976b, p. 147).

Hidden Lake [MARIN]: *marsh,* 5 miles west-southwest of downtown San Rafael (lat. 37°56'25" N, long. 122°36'50" W). Named on San Rafael (1954) 7.5' quadrangle.

Hidden Pond [CONTRA COSTA]: *lake,* 200 feet long, 1.5 miles south of Mount Diablo (lat. 37°51'45" N, long. 121°54'35" W; sec. 7, T 1 S, R 1 E). Named on Diablo (1953) 7.5' quadrangle.

Hidden Valley [ALAMEDA]: *canyon,* 1.5 miles long, 5 miles southeast of Fremont civic center along Agua Caliente Creek (lat. 37°30'20" N, long. 121°54' W). Named on Niles (1961) 7.5' quadrangle.

Hidden Valley [SONOMA]: *canyon,* drained by a stream that flows 1 mile to Hulbert Creek 1.25 miles west of Guerneville (lat. 38°29'55" N, long. 123°01'10" W; sec. 36, T 8 N, R 11 W). Named on Duncans Mills (1979) 7.5' quadrangle.

Hidden Valley Lakes: see **Bean Hollow Lake** [SAN MATEO].

Higgins Canyon [SAN MATEO]: *canyon,* along Arroyo Leon above a point 1 mile south-southeast of downtown Half Moon Bay (lat. 37°27'10" N, long. 122°25'15" W). Named on Half Moon Bay (1961) 7.5' quadrangle. John Higgins had a ranch at the place after about 1870; the stream in the canyon had the name "Arroyo de Monte Verde" in the early days (Brown, p. 41).

Highcroft [SONOMA]: *locality,* 3 miles east of Guerneville along Russian River (lat. 38°30'05" N, long. 122°56'35" W; near NW cor. sec. 35, T 8 N, R 10 W). Named on Sebastopol (1942) 15' quadrangle and Guerneville (1955) 7.5' quadrangle.

Highland: see **Fleming** [ALAMEDA].

Highland Park Reservoir: see **Central Reservoir** [ALAMEDA].

High Point [NAPA]: *peak,* 4 miles northeast of Calistoga (lat. 38°37'05" N, long. 122°31'20" W; near NE cor. sec. 21, T 9 N, R 6 W). Altitude 2758 feet. Named on Calistoga (1958) 7.5' quadrangle.

High Rock [SONOMA]: *peak,* 8 miles northeast of Fort Ross (lat. 38° 36'25" N, long. 123°09'30" W; sec. 23, T 9 N, R 12 W). Altitude 2003 feet. Named on Fort Ross (1978) 7.5' quadrangle.

Hilarita [MARIN]: *locality,* 4 miles south of Point San Quentin on Tiburon Peninsula (lat. 37°53' N, long. 122°27'55" W). Named on San Quentin (1959) 7.5' quadrangle.

Hillsborough [SAN MATEO]: *town,* 2 miles west of downtown San Mateo (lat. 37°33'45" N, long. 122°21'45" W). Named on Montara Mountain (1956) and San Mateo (1956) 7.5' quadrangles. Postal authorities established Hillsborough post office in 1956 (Salley, p. 97), and the town incorporated in 1910. The name is from a town in New Hampshire that was the ancestral home of W.D.M. Howard, former owner of land at the site (Gudde, 1969, p. 140).

Hillsborough Park [SAN MATEO]: *district,* 2 miles west-southwest of downtown San Mateo in Hillsborough (lat. 37°33'20" N, long. 122°21'45" W). Named on San Mateo (1956) 7.5' quadrangle.

Hillsdale [SAN MATEO]: *district,* 2.25 miles south-southeast of downtown San Mateo (lat. 37°32'15" N, long. 122°18'15" W). Named on San Mateo (1956) 7.5' quadrangle. Called Beresford on San Mateo (1947) 7.5' quadrangle. The name "Beresford" is from Beresford Park subdivision, begun in the 1890's; the name of the railroad station at the place was changed in 1940 to Hillsdale for another subdivision (Brown, p. 83).

Hillsdale: see **Lick** [SANTA CLARA].

Hillside: see **Vallejo** [SOLANO].

Hill Slough [SOLANO]: *water feature,* joins Suisun Slough 2.25 miles south-southeast of Fairfield (lat. 38°13'10" N, long. 122°01'40" W). Named on Denverton (1953) and Fairfield South (1949) 7.5' quadrangles.

Hilton [SONOMA]: *locality,* 3 miles east of Guerneville along Russian River (lat. 38°30'15" N, long. 122°58'20" W; sec. 26, T 8 N, R 10 W). Named on Guerneville (1955) 7.5' quadrangle. Postal authorities established Hilton post office in 1894 and discontinued it in 1953; the name is for Hilton Ridenhour, son of the founder of the community (Salley, p. 98).

Hinebaugh Creek [SONOMA]: *stream,* flows 1.5 miles to lowlands 2.5 miles northeast of Cotati (lat. 38°21'05" N, long. 122°40'10" W). Named on Cotati (1954) 7.5' quadrangle.

Hinman: see **Lake Hinman** [NAPA].

Hirsch Creek [NAPA]: *stream,* flows 0.5 mile to Napa Valley 5.25 miles southeast of Calistoga (lat. 38°31'50" N, long. 122°30'20" W; sec. 22, T 8 N, R 6 W). Named on Calistoga (1958) 7.5' quadrangle.

Hobson Creek [SONOMA]: *stream,* flows 2.5 miles to Russian River 4 miles east of Guerneville (lat. 38°30'25" N, long. 122°55'40" W; sec. 26, T 8 N, R 10 W). Named on Guerneville (1955) 7.5' quadrangle.

Hoffman Creek [SAN MATEO]: *stream,* flows 1 mile to Pescadero Creek 3 miles south of La Honda (lat. 37°16'30" N, long. 122° 17' W; sec. 34, T 7 S, R 4 W). Named on La Honda (1961) 7.5' quadrangle.

Hoffman Creek: see **Bloomquist Creek** [SAN MATEO].

Hogback [SONOMA]: *promontory,* 4 miles south-southeast of Jenner along the sea coast (lat. 38°23'45" N, long. 123°05'45" W). Named on Duncans Mills (1979) 7.5' quadrangle. Duncans Mills (1943) 7.5' quadrangle shows the feature as an island.

Hogback Mountain [SONOMA]: *peak,* 4 miles north-northeast of Sonoma (lat. 38°20'40" N, long. 122°25'35" W; at SW cor. sec. 21, T 6 N, R 5 W). Altitude 1753 feet. Named on Sonoma (1951) 7.5' quadrangle.

Hog Canyon [CONTRA COSTA]: *canyon,* drained by Sycamore Creek (2), which flows nearly 4 miles to Marsh Creek 5.5 miles east of Mount Diablo (lat. 37°53'10" N, long. 121°48'40" W). Named on Antioch South (1953) and Tassajara (1953) 7.5' quadrangles.

Hog Island [MARIN]: *island,* 650 feet long, nearly 4 miles south-southwest of Tomales in Tomales Bay (lat. 38°11'50" N, long. 122°56'05" W). Named on Tomales (1954) 7.5' quadrangle. The name reportedly came after a barge broke loose and left a number of hogs at the place; a small island of less than an acre located near Hog Island is called Duck Island (Mason, 1976a, p. 57, 59).

Hog Island [SONOMA]: *area,* 7.5 miles southeast of downtown Petaluma near Petaluma River (lat. 38°09'30" N, long. 122°32'10" W). Named on Petaluma River (1954) 7.5' quadrangle. Petaluma (1914) 15' quadrangle shows the area as marsh situated between Petaluma River and False Bay.

Hogsback [SANTA CLARA]: *ridge,* north-trending, 0.25 mile long, 3 miles southwest of Mount Sizer (lat. 37°11'15" N, long. 121°33'15" W; on N line sec. 5, T 9 S, R 4 E). Named on Mount Sizer (1955) 7.5' quadrangle.

Hog Slough [SANTA CLARA]: *stream,* flows nearly 2 miles to Isabel Creek 2.5 miles northwest of Mount Hamilton (lat. 37°22'10" N, long. 121°40'10" W; sec. 32, T 6 S, R 3 E). Named on Lick Observatory (1955) 7.5' quadrangle.

Holbrook Island: see **Freeman Island** [SOLANO].

Hole in Rock [SONOMA]: *relief feature,* 2 miles north of the village of Bodega Bay (lat. 38°21'50" N, long. 123°02'30" W). Named on Bodega Head (1942) 7.5' quadrangle.

Hole in the Head [SONOMA]: *locality;* water-filled excavation 2 miles south-southwest of the village of Bodega Bay (lat. 38°18'20" N, long. 123°03'30" W); the feature is on Bodega Head. Named on Bodega Head (1972) 7.5' quadrangle. The excavation was for a nuclear generating plant before construction stopped because the site is on the San Andreas fault.

Holland Cut [CONTRA COSTA]: *water feature,* 3.25 miles east of the settlement of Bethel Island on the east side of Holland Tract (lat. 38°01' N, long. 121°34'50" W). Named on Bouldin Island (1978) 7.5' quadrangle.

Holland Tract [CONTRA COSTA]: *island,* 3.5 miles long, 2.5 miles east-southeast of the settlement of Bethel Island between Sheep Slough, Old River, Rock Slough, and Sand Mound Slough (lat. 38° 00' N, long. 121°36' W). Named on Bouldin Island (1978) and Woodward Island (1978) 7.5' quadrangles.

Holland Tract: see **Little Holland Tract** [SOLANO].

Hollenbeck's Station: see **Bell Station** [SANTA CLARA].

Hollis Canyon [ALAMEDA]: *canyon,* 3.25 miles long, on upper reaches of San Lorenzo Creek above a point 4.25 miles northeast of downtown Hayward (lat. 37°42'25" N, long. 122°01'05" W). Named on Dublin (1961) and Hayward (1959) 7.5' quadrangles. The stream in the canyon is called Hollis Creek on Haywards (1899) and Pleasanton (1906) 15' quadrangles. The name commemorates James Lyman Hollis, who settled at the head of the canyon in 1853 (Mosier, and Mosier, p. 45).

Hollis Creek: see **Hollis Canyon** [ALAMEDA].

Hollydale [SONOMA]: *settlement*, 4 miles east of Guerneville along Russian River (lat. 38°30'20" N, long. 122°55'10" W; sec. 25, T 8 N, R 10 W). Named on Guerneville (1955) 7.5' quadrangle.

Holmes Canyon [SONOMA]: *canyon*, drained by a stream that flows 1.25 miles to Austin Creek 2.5 miles north-northwest of Cazadero (lat. 38°33'50" N, long. 123°06'15" W; sec. 5, T 8 N, R 11 W). Named on Cazadero (1978) 7.5' quadrangle. California Division of Forestry's (1945) map shows Arroyo Cr. in the canyon.

Holt Hill [SONOMA]: *ridge*, southeast-trending, less than 1 mile long, 6 miles southwest of Big Mountain (lat. 38°38'40" N, long. 123°13'20" W). Named on Tombs Creek (1978) 7.5' quadrangle.

Holy City [SANTA CLARA]: *village*, 4.5 miles south of downtown Los Gatos (lat. 37°09'25" N, long. 121°58'40" W; near S line sec. 9, T 9 S, R 1 W). Named on Los Gatos (1953) 7.5' quadrangle. Postal authorities established Holy City post office in 1927 (Frickstad, p. 173). William E. Riker, leader of a religious cult, founded the place in 1918 (Hoover, Rensch, and Rensch, p. 457).

Home Bay [MARIN]: *bay*, opens into Drakes Estero 6.5 miles northeast of the lighthouse at Point Reyes (lat. 38°03'35" N, long. 122° 55'45" W). Named on Drakes Bay (1953) 7.5' quadrangle, which shows Home ranch near the head of the bay.

Home Hill [NAPA]: *peak*, 4.5 miles northwest of Napa Junction (lat. 38°14'25" N, long. 122°17'45" W). Named on Cuttings Wharf (1949) 7.5' quadrangle.

Home Ranch Creek [MARIN]: *stream*, flows 2 miles to Home Bay 8 miles northeast of the lighthouse at Point Reyes (lat. 38°04'15" N, long. 122°54'40" W). Named on Drakes Bay (1953) 7.5' quadrangle, which shows Home ranch situated along the stream.

Homestead [SAN MATEO]: *settlement*, 1.25 miles south-southeast of downtown San Mateo (lat. 37°32'50" N, long. 122°19'10" W). Named on San Mateo (1915) 15' quadrangle. The name is from San Mateo City Homestead subdivision (Brown, p. 83). Diller and others' (1915) map shows a place called Leslie along the railroad at about the site of Homestead.

Homestead Valley [MARIN]: *canyon*, drained by a stream that flows 1.25 miles to Arroyo Corte Madera Del Presidio 5.25 miles south of downtown San Rafael (lat. 37°53'45" N, long. 122°32' W). Named on San Rafael (1954) 7.5' quadrangle. Teather (p. 29) associated the name with a hunting lodge called The Homestead that Samuel Throckmorton had built in 1866.

Honker Bay [SOLANO]: *embayment*, 5.5 miles southwest of Birds Landing (2) off Suisun Bay (lat. 38°04'15" N, long. 121°55'45" W). Named on Honker Bay (1953) 7.5' quadrangle.

Honker Bay: see **Little Honker Bay** [SOLANO].

Honsinger Creek [SAN MATEO]: *stream*, flows 3.5 miles to Pescadero Creek 7 miles southwest of La Honda (lat. 37°15'10" N, long. 122°22'10" W; sec. 11, T 8 S, R 5 W). Named on La Honda (1961) 7.5' quadrangle. The stream first had the name "Greenwood Creek" for the Green family ranch established about 1859; Mr. A. Honsinger had a dairy ranch along the stream after about 1870 (Brown, p. 41).

Hood: see **Mount Hood** [SONOMA].

Hoodoo Gulch [SANTA CLARA]: *canyon*, drained by a stream that flows 1.5 miles to Colorado Creek 1.5 miles south-southwest of Eylar Mountain (lat. 37°27'20" N, long. 121°33'50" W; sec. 32, T 5 S, R 4 E). Named on Eylar Mountain (1955) 7.5' quadrangle.

Hoods Hot Springs: see **Dry Creek** [SONOMA].

Hooker: see **Mount Hooker**, under **Mount Thayer** [SANTA CLARA].

Hooker Canyon [SONOMA]: *canyon*, 4 miles long, along Hooker Creek above a point 3.5 miles north-northwest of Sonoma (lat. 38° 20'20" N, long. 122°29'25" W). Named on Rutherford (1951) and Sonoma (1951) 7.5' quadrangles. The name commemorates Joseph Hooker, who purchased part of Agua Caliente grant in 1851, and lived there for several years (Gudde, 1949, p. 152-153).

Hooker Canyon: see **Stuart Canyon** [SONOMA].

Hooker Creek [SAN MATEO]: *stream*, flows 1.25 miles to Pescadero Creek 4 miles south of Mindego Hill (lat. 37°15'10" N, long. 122°13'35" W). Named on Big Basin (1955) 7.5' quadrangle. According to Brown (p. 78), the canyon of the stream had the name "Rooter Gulch" in the 1930's from a piece of construction machinery left there; the canyon also had the name "Oil Barrel Gulch" at about the same time because of oil stored there.

Hooker Creek [SONOMA]: *stream*, flows 5 miles to Wilson Creek 2.25 miles southeast of Glen Ellen (lat. 38°20'10" N, long. 122°30'05" W); the stream goes through Hooker Canyon. Named on Sonoma (1951) 7.5' quadrangle.

Hooker Gulch [SANTA CLARA]: *canyon*, drained by a stream that flows nearly 3 miles to Los Gatos Creek 5 miles south-southeast of Los Gatos (lat. 37°09'15" N, long. 121°57'45" W; sec. 15, T 9 S, R 1 W). Named on Los Gatos (1953) 7.5' quadrangle. The name commemorates Billy Hooker, a lumber-mill worker who had a cabin in the canyon (Young, p. 124).

Hookston [CONTRA COSTA]: *locality*, 2.5 miles north of Walnut Creek civic center along Southern Pacific Railroad (lat. 37°56'30" N, long. 122°03'05" W). Named on Walnut Creek (1959) 7.5' quadrangle. Concord (1915) 15' quadrangle also has the name "Hookston" at present Bancroft.

Hooper [CONTRA COSTA]: *locality*, 2.25 miles west of present downtown Antioch along Atchison, Topeka and Santa Fe Railroad (lat. 38°01'10" N, long. 121°51' W). Named on Collinsville (1918) 7.5' quadrangle.

Hoot Owl Creek [SONOMA]: *stream*, flows 2.25 miles to Russian River 4.5 miles east-northeast of Healdsburg (lat. 38°38'50" N, long. 122°47'45" W). Named on Jimtown (1955) 7.5' quadrangle.

Hoover Creek [SANTA CLARA]: *stream*, flows nearly 3 miles to Packwood Creek 5.25 miles west-southwest of Mount Sizer (lat. 37°11'30" N, long. 121°36'15" W); the stream drains Hoover Valley. Named on Mount Sizer (1955) 7.5' quadrangle.

Hoover Lake [SANTA CLARA]: *lake*, 750 feet long, 3.5 miles north-northeast of Gilroy Hot Springs (lat. 38°09'20" N, long. 120°26'50" W; sec. 17, T 9 S, R 5 E). Named on Mississippi Creek 1955) 7.5' quadrangle.

Hoover Ridge [SONOMA]: *ridge*, generally northwest-trending, 3.25 miles long, 3.25 miles east-northeast of Annapolis (lat. 38°44'30" N, long. 122°19' W). Named on Ornbaun Valley (1960) 15' quadrangle, and on Annapolis (1977) 7.5' quadrangle.

Hoover Valley [SANTA CLARA]: *valley*, 4.25 miles west-southwest of Mount Sizer (lat. 37°11'30" N, long. 121°35' W); the valley is along Hoover Creek. Named on Mount Sizer (1955) 7.5' quadrangle.

Hopkins Ravine [SOLANO]: *canyon*, drained by a stream that flows 2.5 miles to lowlands at Birds Landing (2) (lat. 38°07'55" N, long. 121°52'20" W; sec. 4, T 3 N, R 1 E). Named on Birds Landing (1953) 7.5' quadrangle.

Hopyard [SONOMA]: *locality*, 3 miles northwest of Sebastopol along Petaluma and Santa Rosa Railroad (lat. 38°25'50" N, long. 122°52' W). Named on Sebastopol (1942) 15' quadrangle.

Horan: see **Frank Horan Slough** [SOLANO].

Horn: see **The Horn** [SONOMA].

Horse Haven: see **Antioch** [CONTRA COSTA].

Horse Hill [SONOMA]: *ridge*, west- to south-southwest-trending, 1.5 miles long, 1.5 miles north of Mark West Springs (lat. 38°34'15" N, long. 122°43'05" W). Named on Mark West Springs (1958) 7.5' quadrangle.

Horse Opening [SONOMA]: *area*, 7 miles southwest of Big Mountain (lat. 38°38'25" N, long. 123°14' W; sec. 7, T 9 N, R 12 W). Named on Tombs Creek (1978) 7.5' quadrangle.

Horse Pasture Creek: see **Old Womans Creek** [SAN MATEO].

Horse Pond [NAPA]: *lake*, 400 feet long, 3 miles east-northeast of Calistoga (lat. 38°35'55" N, long. 122°31'35" W; sec. 28, T 9 N, R 6 W). Named on Calistoga (1958) 7.5' quadrangle.

Horseshoe Bay [MARIN-SAN FRANCISCO]: *embayment*, nearly 2 miles south-southeast of downtown Sausalito along San Francisco Bay (lat. 37°50' N, long. 122°28'30" W). Named on San Francisco North (1956) 7.5' quadrangle. Because Marin-San Francisco County line follows the low-water line of Marin County coast from Point Bonita to Cavallo Point, the water area of the embayment is in San Francisco County. The name is from the horseshoe shape of the feature (Gudde, 1949, p. 61). Galvin (p. 85) identified Horseshoe Bay as the place that Ayala called Consolation Cove in 1775.

Horseshoe Bend [NAPA]: *bend*, 3.25 miles south of downtown Napa along Napa River (lat. 38°15'05" N, long. 122°17'35" W). Named on Cuttings Wharf (1949) and Napa (1951) 7.5' quadrangles.

Horseshoe Bend [SOLANO]: *bend*, 5 miles south-southwest of Rio Vista along Sacramento River on Solano-Sacramento County line (lat. 38°05' N, long. 121°42'45" W). Named on Jersey Island (1978) 7.5' quadrangle. An artificial waterway now takes the main channel of the river across the neck of land at the bend. Ringgold's (1850c) map has the name "Sagadehock Reach" along this part of Sacramento River.

Horseshoe Cove [SONOMA]:

(1) *embayment*, 3.5 miles west-northwest of Plantation along the coast (lat. 38°36'45" N, long. 123°22' W). Named on Plantation (1977) 7.5' quadrangle.

(2) *embayment*, nearly 2 miles southwest of the village of Bodega Bay along the coast (lat. 38°18'55" N, long. 123°04'10" W). Named on Bodega Head (1972) 7.5' quadrangle.

Horseshoe Point [SONOMA]: *promontory*, 3.5 miles west-northwest of Plantation along the coast (lat. 38°36'25" N, long. 123°22'15" W); the feature is on the south side of Horseshoe Cove (1). Named on Plantation (1977) 7.5' quadrangle.

Horsethief Canyon [SANTA CLARA]: *canyon*, 0.5 mile long, opens into the canyon of Colorado Creek 3.5 miles southeast of Eylar Mountain (lat. 37°26'10" N, long. 121°30'40" W; near SW cor. sec. 2, T 6 S, R 4 E). Named on Eylar Mountain (1955) 7.5' quadrangle.

Horsethief Canyon [SONOMA]: *canyon*, 1.5 miles long, 9 miles north of the village of Stewarts Point on Sonoma-Mendocino County line (lat. 38°47'05" N, long. 123°22' W). Named on Ornbaun Valley (1960) 15' quadrangle.

Horse Valley [CONTRA COSTA]: *valley*, 7.5 miles east-northeast of Mount Diablo (lat. 37°56'10" N, long. 121°47'40" W). Named on Antioch South

(1953) 7.5' quadrangle.

Horse Valley [SANTA CLARA]: *valley,* 4 miles southwest of Isabel Valley on the upper reaches of Smith Creek (2) (lat. 37°16'35" N, long. 121°35'35" W). Named on Isabel Valley (1955) 7.5' quadrangle.

Hospital Cove [MARIN]: *embayment,* on the northwest shore of Angel Island (lat. 37°52'05" N, long. 122°26'05" W); the feature is off Raccoon Strait. Named on San Francisco North (1956) 7.5' quadrangle. Called Raccoon Cove on Ringgold's (1850a) map. United States Board on Geographic Names (1969, p. 8) approved the designation Ayala Cove for the feature, and noted that this name commemorates Don Juan Manuel de Ayala, who based his ship at the place while he explored San Francisco Bay in 1775. The embayment was known as Morgan's Cove before the army built two hospital buildings by it in 1870 (Gudde, 1969, p. 146).

Hot Springs: see **The Geysers** [SONOMA].

Hot Springs Creek [SONOMA]: *stream,* flows 1 mile to Big Sulphur Creek 3.5 miles east-northeast of Geyser Peak (lat. 38°47'15" N, long. 122°47' W; sec. 19, T 11 N, R 8 W). Named on Kelseyville (1959) 15' quadrangle.

Hot Sulphur Springs: see **Calistoga** [NAPA].

House Creek [SONOMA]: *stream,* flows 13 miles to Wheatfield Fork Gualala River 6 miles southwest of Big Mountain (lat. 38°39'45" N, long. 123°14' W; sec. 6, T 9 N, R 12 W). Named on Tombs Creek (1978) and Warm Springs Dam (1978) 7.5' quadrangles.

Houx: see **Cherry** [SONOMA].

Howard Slough [SOLANO]: *water feature,* on Hammond Island, joins Roaring River Slough 4 miles southwest of Birds Landing (2) (lat. 38°05'35" N, long. 121°55'45" W). Named on Honker Bay (1953) 7.5' quadrangle.

Howard's Station: see **Occidental** [SONOMA].

Howell Mountain [NAPA]:

(1) *ridge,* south-southeast-trending, 2 miles long, 5.5 miles north-northeast of Saint Helena (lat. 38°34'45" N, long. 122°26' W). Named on Saint Helena (1960) 7.5' quadrangle. Goodyear (1890a, p. 349) noted that the range northeast of the upper part of Napa Valley is known as Howell Mountains, and F.F. Davis (p. 161) stated that the northeast half of Napa County is separated from Napa Valley by Howell Range, which is the southeast extension of Mayacmas Mountains.

(2) *settlement,* 5.5 miles north-northeast of Saint Helena (lat. 38°34'50" N, long. 122°27' W); the place is west of present Howell Mountain (1). Named on Saint Helena (1942) 15' quadrangle. Pope Valley (1921) 15' quadrangle has the name "White Cottage" at the site. The place now is part of Angwin.

Howell Mountains: see **Howell Mountain** [NAPA] (1).

Howell Range: see **Howell Mountain** [NAPA] (1).

Howell Reservoirs [SANTA CLARA]: *lakes,,* largest 850 feet long, nearly 5 miles east-southeast of Bielawski Mountain (lat. 37°11'55" N, long. 122°00'55" W; sec. 31, T 8 S, R 1 W). Named on Castle Rock Ridge (1955) 7.5' quadrangle. The name commemorates Watkins F. Howell, who settled in the neighborhood in 1856 (Young, p. 21).

Huchones: see **Point Huchones**, under **Point San Pablo** [CONTRA COSTA].

Hudeman Slough [NAPA-SONOMA]: *water feature,* mainly in Sonoma County, but forms a small part of Napa-Sonoma County line; joins Napa Slough 5.5 miles west of Napa Junction (lat. 38° 11'35" N, long. 122°21' W; sec. 18, T 4 N, R 4 W). Named on Cuttings Wharf (1949) and Sears Point (1951) 7.5' quadrangles.

Huichica [NAPA-SONOMA]: *land grant,* southwest of the city of Napa on Napa-Sonoma County line. Named on Cuttings Wharf (1949), Napa (1951), Sears Point (1951), and Sonoma (1951) 7.5' quadrangles. Jacob P. Leese received 2 leagues in 1841 and claimed 18,704 acres patented in 1859 (Cowan, p. 41; Cowan used the form "Huichicha" for the name). The name of the grant is from an Indian village at the site of the present town of Sonoma (Kroeber, p. 43).

Huichica Creek [NAPA]: *stream,* flows 8 miles to marsh 6 miles west-northwest of Napa Junction (lat. 38°12'50" N, long. 122°21'20" W); the stream is on Huichica grant. Named on Cuttings Wharf (1949), Napa (1951), and Sonoma (1951) 7.5' quadrangles.

Hulbert Creek [SONOMA]: *stream,* flows 5.5 miles to Russian River less than 1 mile southwest of Guerneville (lat. 38°29'40" N, long. 123°00'20" W). Named on Cazadero (1978) and Duncans Mills (1979) 7.5' quadrangles. Called Hulburt Creek on Cazadero (1943) and Duncans Mills (1943) 7.5' quadrangles. The stream was called Helm's Creek in the 1860's (Clar, p. 15).

Hull Hill: see **Belmont Hill** [SAN MATEO].

Humbug Creek [SONOMA]: *stream,* flows 3 miles to Mark West Creek 4 miles east-southeast of Mark West Springs (lat. 38°31'10" N, long. 122°39'30" W; near S line sec. 20, T 8 N, R 7 W). Named on Mark West Springs (1958) 7.5' quadrangle.

Hummingbird Creek [SONOMA]: *stream,* heads in Mendocino County and flows 2 miles to Squaw Creek 5.25 miles north of Geyser Peak (lat. 38°50'20" N, long. 122°51'30" W; at E line sec. 33, T 12 N, R 9 W). Named on The Geysers (1959) 7.5' quadrangle.

Hungry Valley: see **Alhambra Valley** [CONTRA COSTA].

Hunter Island: see **Coyote Hills** [ALAMEDA].

Hunters Point [SAN FRANCISCO]: *peninsula,* modified by landfill, 4.5 miles east of Mount Davidson along San Francisco Bay (lat. 37°43'45" N, long. 122°22'30" W). Named on Hunters Point (1956, photorevised 1968) and San Francisco South (1956) 7.5' quadrangles. Called Hunter Point on San Mateo (1915) 15' quadrangle. H.R. Wagner (p. 443, 502) listed the obsolete names "Punta de Concha" and "San Juan Capistrano" for the feature.

Hunters Point: see **Point Avisadero** [SAN FRANCISCO].

Hunting Creek [NAPA]: *stream,* heads in Lake County and flows 9.5 miles along Napa-Lake County line to Putah Creek nearly 6 miles southwest of Knoxville (lat. 38°46'05" N, long. 122°24'55" W; near S line sec. 28, T 11 N, R 5 W). Named on Jericho Valley (1958) and Knoxville (1958) 7.5' quadrangles.

Hunting Hollow [SANTA CLARA]: *canyon,* drained by a stream that flows 4 miles to Coyote Creek 2.25 miles south-southeast of Gilroy Hot Springs (lat. 37°04'35" N, long. 121°28'05" W; sec. 7, T 10 S, R 5 E). Named on Gilroy Hot Springs (1955) 7.5' quadrangle.

Hurlbut [SONOMA]: *locality,* 1 mile northwest of Sebastopol along Petaluma and Santa Rosa Railroad (lat. 38°24'45" N, long. 122°50'10" W). Named on Sebastopol (1942) 15' quadrangle.

Hurley Creek [SONOMA]: *stream,* flows 1 mile to Little Sulphur Creek 10 miles northeast of Healdsburg at Pine Flat (lat. 38°44'20" N, long. 122°46' W; sec. 5, T 10 N, R 8 W). Named on Jimtown (1955) 7.5' quadrangle.

Hurricane Canyon [SANTA CLARA]: *canyon,* 3 miles long, 4 miles north-northwest of Pacheco Peak on lower reaches of Cedar Creek (lat. 37°03'30" N, long. 121°19'40" W). Named on Pacheco Peak (1955) 7.5' quadrangle.

Husman Canyon [NAPA]: *canyon,* drained by a stream that flows nearly 1 mile to Chiles Valley 7.5 miles east-northeast of Saint Helena (lat. 38°33'05" N, long. 122°20'40" W). Named on Chiles Valley (1958) 7.5' quadrangle.

—I—

Ibis Cut [SOLANO]: *water feature,* extends from Cordelia Slough to Frank Horan Slough 6.5 miles south-southwest of Fairfield (lat. 38°10'05" N, long. 122°06'10" W). Named on Fairfield South (1949) 7.5' quadrangle.

Icaria Creek [SONOMA]: *stream,* flows 4 miles to Russian River flood plain 1.5 miles northwest of Asti (lat. 38°46'35" N, long. 122°59'35" W). Named on Asti (1959) and Cloverdale (1960) 7.5' quadrangles. The name recalls the colony established in 1881 by Armand Dehay and Jules Leroux, two Frenchmen who bought land 3 miles south of Cloverdale for a community based upon the ideals of Icaria, the French utopia (Hine, p. 58-59).

Ida: see **Mount Ida**, under **Mount Caroline Livermore** [MARIN].

Idell: see **Lake Idell** [SONOMA].

Idlewild: see **Azule Springs** [SANTA CLARA].

Idlwood: see **Sunol** [ALAMEDA].

Ignacio [MARIN]: *town,* 3 miles southeast of downtown Novato (lat. 38°04'15" N, long. 122°32'15" W); the town is on San Jose grant, owned by Ignacio Pacheco. Named on Novato (1954) 7.5' quadrangle. Postal authorities established Ignacio post office in 1893, discontinued it in 1944, and reestablished it in 1961 (Salley, p. 103). They established Machin post office 4 miles north of Ignacio in 1896 and discontinued it in 1904; the name honored Timothy N. Machin, lieutenant governor of California in 1863, and later a real-estate man at Novato (Salley, p. 130).

Imola [NAPA]: *locality,* 1.25 miles south of downtown Napa along Southern Pacific Railroad (lat. 38°16'45" N, long. 122°16'45" W). Named on Napa (1951) 7.5' quadrangle, which has the designation "Napa State Hospital (Imola P.O.)" at a site less than 1 mile east-southeast of Imola. Postal authorities established Imola post office in 1920 and discontinued it in 1953 (Frickstad, p. 111). The railroad station and post office for the state hospital were named for Imola, Italy, apparently because the Italian city has a hospital for the insane (Gudde, 1949, p. 159).

India Basin [SAN FRANCISCO]: *embayment,* 4.5 miles east of Mount Davidson along San Francisco Bay on the north side of Hunters Point (lat. 37°44'05" N, long. 122°22' W). Named on Hunters Point (1956, photorevised 1980) 7.5' quadrangle. On San Francisco South (1956) 7.5' quadrangle, the name "India Basin" applies to an embayment located nearly 1 mile farther northwest—this earlier embayment now is filled.

Indian Beach [MARIN]: *beach,* 7.5 miles south of Tomales on the southwest side of Tomales Bay (lat. 38°08'15" N, long. 122°53'45" W). Named on Tomales (1954) 7.5' quadrangle.

Indian Cove: see **Tennessee Cove** [MARIN].

Indian Creek [ALAMEDA]: *stream,* flows 9.5 miles to San Antonio Creek 3.5 miles east of Sunol in La Costa Valley (lat. 37°35'20" N, long. 121°49'15" W). Named on La Costa Valley (1960) and Mendenhall Springs (1956) 7.5' quadrangles. Called South Fork San Antonio Cr. on Thompson and West's (1878) map. The stream now enters San Antonio Reservoir.

Indian Creek [CONTRA COSTA]: *stream,* flows nearly 2 miles to San Leandro Creek 4.5 miles south-southeast of Orinda (lat. 37°49'05" N, long. 122°08'45" W). Named on Oakland East (1959) 7.5' quadrangle.

Indian Creek [SANTA CLARA]: *stream,* flows nearly 1 mile to Stevens Creek 1 mile southwest of Black Mountain (1) (lat. 37°18'40" N, long. 122°09'35" W; sec. 23, T 7 S, R 3 W). Named on Mindego Hill (1961) 7.5' quadrangle.

Indian Gulch [ALAMEDA]: *canyon,* nearly 2 miles long, opens into lowlands 1.5 miles east of downtown Oakland (lat. 37°48'35" N, long. 122°14'45" W). Named on Oakland East (1959) 7.5' quadrangle. After trestles were built in 1893 to enable streetcars to travel to the head of Indian Gulch, the canyon was renamed Trestle Glen; the old name was restored after the trestles were removed (Mosier and Mosier, p. 45). Thompson and West's (1878) map shows a stream called Indian Gulch Creek that flows to Lake Merritt.

Indian Gulch Creek: see **Indian Gulch** [ALAMEDA].

Indian Joe Creek [ALAMEDA]: *stream,* flows 2.5 miles to Alameda Creek 6.25 miles south-southeast of Sunol (lat. 37°30'50" N, long. 121°49'35" W; sec. 11, T 5 S, R 1 E). Named on La Costa Valley (1960) 7.5' quadrangle. The name recalls Indian Joe, thought to be the last Ohlone Indian, who lived and worked in the neighborhood (Mosier and Mosier, p. 45).

Indian Mineral Spring [SONOMA]: *spring,* 3 miles northeast of Guerneville (lat. 38°31'50" N, long. 122°57'30" W; near N line sec. 22, T 8 N, R 10 W). Named on Healdsburg (1940) 15' quadrangle.

Indian Point [SAN MATEO]: *relief feature,* 3 miles south of La Honda on the south side of Pescadero Creek (lat. 37°16'25" N, long. 122°16'40" W; near SE cor. sec. 34, T 7 S, R 4 W). Named on La Honda (1961) 7.5' quadrangle.

Indian Slough [CONTRA COSTA]: *water feature,* joins Old River 7 miles east of Brentwood (lat. 37°54'55" N, long. 121°33'55" W). Named on Woodward Island (1978) 7.5' quadrangle.

Indian Spring: see **Pope Mineral Spring**, under **Samuel Springs** [NAPA].

Indian Springs [SANTA CLARA]: *springs,* near the southeast end of Isabel Valley (lat. 37°18'05" N, long. 121°30'40" W; sec. 26, T 7 S, R 4 E). Named on Isabel Valley (1955) 7.5' quadrangle.

Indian Valley [MARIN]: *valley,* nearly 2 miles southwest of downtown Novato (lat. 38°05'30" N, long. 122°35'40" W). Named on Novato (1954) 7.5' quadrangle.

Ingalls Bluff [SONOMA]: *relief feature,* 6.5 miles west-northwest of Mount Saint Helena (lat. 38°43'10" N, long. 122°44' W; near N line sec. 15, T 10 N, R 8 W); the feature is northwest of Ingalls Creek. Named on Mount Saint Helena (1959) 7.5' quadrangle. Called Ingalls Bluffs on Calistoga (1945) 15' quadrangle.

Ingalls Creek [SONOMA]: *stream,* flows 3 miles to McDonnell Creek 6.5 miles west-northwest of Mount Saint Helena (lat. 38°42'10" N, long. 122°44'35" W; at W line sec. 22, T 10 N, R 8 W). Named on Mount Saint Helena (1959) 7.5' quadrangle.

Ingleside [SAN FRANCISCO]: *district,* 1 mile south of Mount Davidson (lat. 37°43'20" N, long. 122°27'20" W). Named on San Francisco South (1956) 7.5' quadrangle.

Ingram Flat [SANTA CLARA]: *area,* 2 miles south-southeast of Eyler Mountain (lat. 37°27'10" N, long. 121°31'55" W; sec. 33, T 5 S, R 4 E). Named on Eyler Mountain (1955) 7.5' quadrangle.

Ingrams: see **Cazadero** [SONOMA].

Inner Harbor Basin [CONTRA COSTA]: *water feature,* 1.5 miles south-southwest of Richmond civic center off Richmond Inner Harbor (lat 37°54'40" N, long. 122°21' W). Named on Richmond (1959) 7.5' quadrangle. United States Board on Geographic Names (1981b, p. 4) approved the name "Richmond Marina Bay" for the feature.

Inner Signal Station: see **Telegraph Hill** [SAN FRANCISCO].

Inspiration Point [CONTRA COSTA]: *peak,* 4 miles west-northwest of Orinda on San Pablo Ridge (lat. 37°54'20" N, long. 122°14'35" W). Named on Briones Valley (1959) 7.5' quadrangle.

Inspiration Point [NAPA]: *peak,* 6.25 miles north of Saint Helena (lat. 38°35'45" N, long. 122°28' W; near SE cor. sec. 25, T 9 N, R 6 W). Named on Saint Helena (1960) 7.5' quadrangle.

Inverness [MARIN]: *town,* 3.5 miles northwest of Point Reyes Station on the southwest side of Tomales Bay (lat. 38°06' N, long. 122°51'15" W). Named on Inverness (1954) 7.5' quadrangle. Postal authorities established Inverness post office in 1897 (Frickstad, p. 88). The town was named for Inverness, Scotland (Mason, 1972, p. 75). Teather (p. 57) gave the name "Point Julia" for a promontory on the west side of Tomales Bay just north of Inverness—the name commemorates Julia Shaffer Hamilton, daughter of James M. Shaffer, a major landowner in the neighborhood.

Inverness Park [MARIN]: *settlement,* 1 mile west-southwest of Point Reyes Station (lat. 38°03'55" N, long. 122°49'20" W); the place is 3 miles south-east of Inverness. Named on Inverness (1954) 7.5' quadrangle. Development of the place began in 1909 (Mason, 1976a, p. 135).

Inverness Ridge [MARIN]: *ridge,* northwest-trending, 15 miles long, center 2.5 miles west of Point Reyes Station (lat. 38°04'30" N, long. 122°51'30" W); the ridge is west of Inverness. Named on Drakes Bay (1953), Inverness (1954), and Tomales (1954) 7.5' quadrangles.

Invincible Rock [CONTRA COSTA]: *rock,* nearly 1 mile southwest of Point San Pablo in San Francisco Bay (lat. 37°57'20" N, long. 122° 26'20" W). Named on San Quentin (1959) 7.5' quadrangle.

Ione: see **Point Ione** [MARIN].

Irish Canyon [CONTRA COSTA]: *canyon,* drained by a stream that flows nearly 3 miles to an unnamed canyon 4.25 miles north of Mount Diablo (lat. 37°56'35" N, long. 121°54'50" W; near W line sec. 7, T 1 N, R 1 E). Named on Antioch South (1953) and Clayton (1953) 7.5' quadrangles.

Irish Hill [SONOMA]:

(1) *ridge,* west-southwest-trending, 1 mile long, 2.5 miles north of the village of Bodega Bay (lat. 38°22'20" N, long. 123°02'50" W). Named on Bodega Head (1972) 7.5' quadrangle. On Bodega Head (1942) 7.5' quadrangle, the name applies to the peak at the west end of the ridge. Duncans Mills (1921) 15' quadrangle shows a place called Oceanview situated on present Irish Hill (1). Postal authorities established Ocean View post office 8 miles south of Duncans Mills (sec. 22, T 6 N, R 11 W) in 1870 and discontinued it in 1874 (Salley, p. 159).

(2) *peak,* 5.5 miles southeast of present Jenner (lat. 38°24'15" N, long. 123°02'30" W). Named on Duncans Mills (1921) 15' quadrangle.

Irish Ridge [SAN MATEO]: *ridge,* southwest-trending, 3 miles long, 3.5 miles west of Skeggs Point (lat. 37°24'10" N, long. 122°22'10" W). Named on Half Moon Bay (1961) and Woodside (1961) 7.5' quadrangles. Some Irish families grew potatoes on the ridge (Morrall, p. 28).

Irish Ridge: see **Sweeney Ridge** [SAN MATEO].

Iron Mountain [NAPA]: *peak,* 11.5 miles east-northeast of Saint Helena (lat. 38°33' N, long. 121°16'05" W). Altitude 2287 feet. Named on Chiles Valley (1958) 7.5' quadrangle.

Iron Spring [MARIN]: *spring,* 5 miles west-northwest of downtown San Rafael (lat. 37°59'55" N, long. 122°37'05" W). Named on San Rafael (1954) 7.5' quadrangle.

Irving [MARIN]: *locality,* 10.5 miles southwest of downtown Novato along Northwestern Pacific Railroad (lat. 38°01' N, long. 122°43'20" W). Named on Petaluma (1914) 15' quadrangle.

Irving: see **Irvington District** [ALAMEDA].

Irvington District [ALAMEDA]: *district,* 1.5 miles south-southeast of Fremont civic center in Fremont (lat. 37°31'45" N, long. 121°57'30" W). Named on Niles (1961) 7.5' quadrangle. On Pleasanton (1906) 15' quadrangle, the name "Irvington" applies to the community that joined with other communities in 1956 to form the new city of Fremont. Postal authorities established Washington Corners post office at Washington College—the first school for industrial education in California—in 1870, changed the name to Irving in 1884, and changed it to Irvington in 1887 (Salley, p. 105, 235).

Isabel: see **Mount Isabel** [SANTA CLARA].

Isabel Creek [SANTA CLARA]: *stream,* flows 18 miles to join Smith Creek and form Arroyo Hondo 2.5 miles south of Mount Day (lat. 37°23' N, long. 121°41'30" W; sec. 30, T 6 S, R 3 E). Named on Isabel Valley (1955), Lick Observatory (1955), and Mount Day (1955) 7.5' quadrangles. United States Board on Geographic Names (1933, p. 391) rejected the names "San Isabel Creek" and "Santa Ysabel Creek" for the stream.

Isabel Point: see **Point Isabel** [CONTRA COSTA].

Isabel Valley [SANTA CLARA]: *valley,* 6 miles east-southeast of Mount Hamilton (lat. 37°18'45" N, long. 121°32' W); the valley is along Isabel Creek. Named on Isabel Valley (1955) 7.5' quadrangle. United States Board on Geographic Names (1933, p. 391) rejected the names "San Isabel Valley" and "Santa Ysabel Valley" for the feature.

Isla de Alcatraces: see **Yerba Buena Island** [SAN FRANCISCO].

Isla de la Yegua: see **Mare Island** [SOLANO].

Isla del Carmel: see **Brooks Island** [CONTRA COSTA].

Isla del Carmen: see **Brooks Island** [CONTRA COSTA].

Isla de los Angeles: see **Angel Island** [MARIN-SAN FRANCISCO].

Isla de Santa Maria de los Angeles: see **Angel Island** [MARIN-SAN FRANCISCO].

Islais Creek: see **Islais Creek Channel** [SAN FRANCISCO].

Islais Creek Channel [SAN FRANCISCO]: *water feature,* 3.5 miles east of Mount Davidson off San Francisco Bay (lat. 37°44'50" N, long. 122°23'15" W). Named on San Francisco South (1956) 7.5' quadrangle. Called Islais Cr. on San Mateo (1915) 15' quadrangle, which shows the feature before it was modified. United States Board on Geographic Names (1983b, p. 5) rejected the names "Du Vrees Creek" and "Islais Creek" for present Islais Creek Channel.

Island: see **The Island** [SONOMA].

Island Number 1 [NAPA-SOLANO]: *island,* center 5 miles west-northwest of downtown Vallejo between by Napa Slough, South Slough, Dutchman Slough, and San Pablo Bay on Napa-Solano County line, mainly in Solano County (lat. 38°08'45" N, long. 122° 21' W). Named on Cuttings Wharf (1949), Mare Island (1959), and Sears Point (1951) 7.5' quadrangles.

Island Number 2 [NAPA-SOLANO]: *island,* 4.5 miles west-southwest of Napa Junction between China Slough and South Slough on Napa-Solano County line (lat. 38°09'20" N, long. 122°19'25" W). Named on Cuttings Wharf (1949) 7.5' quadrangle.

Island of Saint James see **Isle of Saint James** [SAN FRANCISCO].

Island Slough [SOLANO]: *water feature,* on Grizzly Island, joins Montezuma

Slough 5.5 miles west-southwest of Denverton (lat. 38°10'55" N, long. 121°59'15" W). Named on Denverton (1953) 7.5' quadrangle.

Isla Plana: see **Mare Island** [SOLANO].

Isle Hendida: see **Southeast Farallon** [SAN FRANCISCO].

Isle of Alcatraces: see **Alcatraz Island** [SAN FRANCISCO].

Isle of Saint James [SAN FRANCISCO]: *island,* one of Farallon Islands located 0.5 mile southeast of North Farallon (lat. 37°46' N, long. 123°06' W). Named on Farallon Islands (1988) 7.5' quadrangle. United States Board on Geographic Names (1985b, p. 2) noted that the feature is one of the North Farallon group, and used the form "Island of Saint James" for the name; the Board pointed out that Francis Drake gave the name "Iland of Saint James" to Farallon Islands in 1579. United States Coast and Geodetic Survey (p. 123) apparently included this island with nearby North Farallon under the name "North Farallon."

Italian Slough [CONTRA COSTA]: *water feature,* joins Old River 8 miles southeast of Brentwood (lat. 37°51'40" N, long. 121°34'45" W). Named on Clifton Court Forebay (1978) 7.5' quadrangle.

Iverson Creek [SAN MATEO]: *stream,* flows 0.5 mile to Pescadero Creek 4.25 miles south of Mindego Hill (lat. 37°14'45" N, long. 122°12'45" W; near S line sec. 8, T 8 S, R 3 W). Named on Big Basin (1955) 7.5' quadrangle. The stream first was called Coldwater Creek; Chris Iverson settled by the stream in the 1870's (Brown, p. 43).

Ivy Canyon [SANTA CLARA]: *canyon,* drained by a stream that flows 1.25 miles to Jumpoff Creek nearly 4 miles west-northwest of Mount Stakes (lat. 37°20'20" N, long. 121°28'25" W; sec. 7, T 7 S, R 5 E). Named on Mount Stakes (1955) 7.5' quadrangle.

Izabel: see **Point Izabel**, under **Point Isabel** [CONTRA COSTA].

Iverson Creek [SAN MATEO]: *stream,* flows 0.5 mile to Pescadero Creek 4.25 miles south of Mindego Hill (lat. 37°14'45" N, long. 122°12'45" W; near S line sec. 8, T 8 S, R 3 W). Named on Big Basin (1955) 7.5' quadrangle. The stream first was called Coldwater Creek; Chris Iverson settled by it in the 1870's (Brown, p. 43).

Ivy Canyon [SANTA CLARA]: *canyon,* drained by a stream that flows 1.25 miles to Jumpoff Creek nearly 4 miles west-northwest of Mount Stakes (lat. 37°20'20" N, long. 121°28'25" W; sec. 7, T 7 S, R 5 E). Named on Mount Stakes (1955) 7.5' quadrangle.

Izabel: see **Point Izabel**, under **Point Isabel** [CONTRA COSTA].

—J—

Jackass Point [CONTRA COSTA]: *promontory,* 2.25 miles north-northwest of the settlement of Bethel Island on Jersey Island at the confluence of Piper Slough and Taylor Slough (lat. 38°02'50" N, long. 121°39'10" W). Named on Jersey Island (1978) 7.5' quadrangle.

Jack Canyon [SANTA CLARA]: *canyon,* drained by a stream that flows 2 miles to Arroyo Bayo 3 miles north-northwest of Isabel Valley (lat. 37°21'20" N, long. 121°33'35" W; sec. 5, T 7 S, R 4 E). Named on Isabel Valley (1955) 7.5' quadrangle.

Jack Rabbit Flat [NAPA]: *area,* 8 miles northwest of Mount Vaca along Capell Creek (lat. 38°28'10" N, long. 122°13'40" W; sec. 7, T 7 N, R 3 W). Named on Capell Valley (1951) 7.5' quadrangle.

Jack's Harbor: see **Drakes Bay** [MARIN].

Jacksnipe [SOLANO]: *locality,* 4.25 miles south-southwest of Fairfield along Southern Pacific Railroad (lat. 38°11'30" N, long. 122° 04'05" W). Named on Fairfield South (1949) 7.5' quadrangle.

Jackson: see **Mount Jackson** [SONOMA].

Jackson Canyon [NAPA]: *canyon,* drained by a stream that flows less than 1 mile to Clear Creek 8.5 miles east of Saint Helena (lat. 38°30'10" N, long. 122°19' W; near W line sec. 33, T 8 N, R 4 W). Named on Chiles Valley (1958) 7.5' quadrangle.

Jackson Creek [NAPA]: *stream,* flows 2.5 miles to lowlands along Lake Berryessa 4 miles south-southwest of Berryessa Peak (lat. 38° 36'40" N, long. 122°12'50" W); the stream is south of Jackson Peak. Named on Lake Berryessa (1959) 7.5' quadrangle.

Jackson Peak [NAPA]: *peak,* 3 miles south of Berryessa Peak (lat. 38°37'15" N, long. 122°11'45" W); the peak is north of Jackson Creek. Altitude 1814 feet. Named on Lake Berryessa (1959) 7.5' quadrangle.

Jacksons Napa Soda Springs: see **Napa Soda Springs** [NAPA].

Jacques Gulch [SANTA CLARA]: *canyon,* drained by a stream that flows 2 miles to Almaden Reservoir 1.5 miles southwest of New Almaden (lat. 37°09'40" N, long. 121°50'30" W); the canyon is south of Jacques Ridge. Named on Santa Teresa Hills (1953) 7.5' quadrangle.

Jacques Ridge [SANTA CLARA]: *ridge,* northwest-trending, 1.5 miles long, 2 miles west of New Almaden (lat. 37°10'30" N, long. 121°51'35" W); the ridge is north of Jacques Gulch. Named on Santa Teresa Hills (1953) 7.5' quadrangle.

Jagel Landing [SANTA CLARA]: *locality,* 2.5 miles north-northeast of downtown Mountain View near the edge of mud flats along San Francisco Bay (lat. 37°25'30" N, long. 122°03'05" W); the landing is along Jagel Slough. Named on Palo Alto (1899) 15' quadrangle. The place appears to be at or near the site of Bernards Landing, which Thompson and West's (1876) map shows near the head of Whisman Slough (present Jagel Slough).

Jagel Slough [SANTA CLARA]: *water feature,* extends through marsh between salt evaporation ponds to enter San Francisco Bay 4.25 miles north-northeast of downtown Mountain View near the mouth of Coyote Creek (lat. 37°26'55" N, long. 122°02'50" W). Named on Mountain View (1953) 7.5' quadrangle. Called Whisman Slough on Thompson and West's (1876) map. On Mountain View (1961, photorevised 1968 and 1973) 7.5' quadrangle, a salt evaporation pond occupies the former position of the slough, and the name "Jagel Slough" applies to an artificial waterway located along the west side of the salt evaporation pond.

Jagels Slough: see **Moffett Channel** [SANTA CLARA].

James Creek [NAPA]: *stream,* flows nearly 5 miles to Pope Creek 1.5 miles north-northeast of Aetna Springs (lat. 38°40'20" N, long. 122°28'35" W; sec. 36, T 10 N, R 6 W). Named on Aetna Springs (1958) and Detert Reservoir (1958) 7.5' quadrangles.

Jameson Canyon [NAPA-SOLANO]: *canyons,* two canyons in Napa County and Solano County that head opposite one another, and that together are 4 miles long; one of the canyons opens into lowlands 1 mile west-southwest of Cordelia (lat. 38°12'25" N, long. 122° 09' W; near W line sec. 12, T 4 N, R 3 W). Named on Cordelia (1951) 7.5' quadrangle.

Japanese Point: see **Goat Island** [SOLANO].

Jap Rock: see **Japanese Point**, under **Goat Island** [SOLANO].

Jara Canyon: see **Frenchmans Creek** [SAN MATEO].

Jarvis Landing [ALAMEDA]: *locality,* 1.25 miles west of downtown Newark along Newark Slough (lat. 37°31'45" N, long. 122°03'45" W). Named on Newark (1959) 7.5' quadrangle. Called Mayhews Landing on Thompson and West's (1878) map. The embarcadero for San Jose mission was at the site—Captain Joseph A. Mayhews bought the landing in 1854 and turned it over to his uncle, Johnathan Mayhews; Francis Carr Jarvis bought the place in 1865 (Mosier and Mosier, p. 55).

Jasper Ridge [SAN MATEO]: *ridge,* east-trending, 1 mile long, 5.25 miles south of downtown Redwood City (lat. 37°24'30" N, long. 122°13'40" W). Named on Palo Alto (1961, photorevised 1968 and 1973) 7.5' quadrangle. Members of Stanford University geology department named the feature about 1901 (Brown, p. 43).

Jauiyomi: see **Russian River** [SONOMA].

Jays Ridge [SANTA CLARA]: *ridge,* north-trending, 2 miles long, 2 miles south of Isabel Valley (lat. 37°16'45" N, long. 121°31'40" W). Named on Isabel Valley (1955) 7.5' quadrangle.

Jenkins Rock [NAPA]: *relief feature,* 6.25 miles southwest of Mount Vaca (lat. 38°21'10" N, long. 122°12' W; sec. 21, T 6 N, R 3 W). Named on Mount George (1951) 7.5' quadrangle.

Jenner [SONOMA]: *village,* 7.5 miles west-southwest of Guerneville near the mouth of Russian River (lat. 38°27' N, long. 123°06'55" W). Named on Duncans Mills (1979) 7.5' quadrangle. Duncans Mills (1921) 15' quadrangle shows a place called Jenner-by-the-Sea situated nearly 1 mile southeast of present Jenner. Postal authorities established Jenner post office in 1904 (Frickstad, p. 196). The name is for Charles Jenner, a writer who built a cabin near the mouth of present Jenner Gulch in 1868; officials of A.B. Davis Lumber Company applied the name "Jenner" to the site in 1905, when they started a lumber mill there (Hanna, P.T., p. 154).

Jenner-by-the-Sea: see **Jenner** [SONOMA].

Jenner Gulch [SONOMA]: *canyon,* drained by a stream that flows 3.25 miles to Russian River at Jenner (lat. 38°26'55" N, long. 123° 06'50" W). Named on Duncans Mills (1979) 7.5' quadrangle.

Jensen's Landing: see **Hayward Landing** [ALAMEDA].

Jerd Creek [NAPA]: *stream,* flows 1.25 miles to Lake Berryessa 2 miles east of Walter Springs (lat. 38°39'05" N, long. 122°19'15" W; sec. 8, T 9 N, R 4 W). Named on Walter Springs (1959) 7.5' quadrangle.

Jericho Canyon [NAPA]: *canyon,* drained by a stream that flows 2.5 miles to Garnett Creek 2 miles north-northwest of Calistoga (lat. 38°36'20" N, long. 122°35'20" W). Named on Calistoga (1958) and Detert Reservoir (1958) 7.5' quadrangles.

Jersey [CONTRA COSTA]: *locality,* 3.5 miles northwest of the present settlement of Bethel Island along San Joaquin River (lat. 38°02'40" N, long. 121°41'30" W); the place is on Jersey Island. Named on Jersey (1910) 7.5' quadrangle. Postal authorities established Jersey Landing post office in 1878, discontinued it for a time in 1879, discontinued it in 1891, reestablished it with the name "Jersey" in 1898; and discontinued it in 1935 (Salley, p. 107). They established Sand Mound post office 3 miles west of Jersey Landing post office near Sand Mound Slough in 1888 and discontinued it in 1891 (Salley, p. 193).

Jersey Island [CONTRA COSTA]: *island,* 4 miles long, center 2.5 miles west-northwest of the settlement of Bethel Island between San Joaquin River, False River, Piper Slough, Taylor Slough, and Dutch Slough (lat. 38°02' N, long. 121°41' W). Named on Jersey Island (1978) 7.5' quadrangle. Davis and Vernon's (1951) map calls the feature Jersey Island Tract. Hagen and Davis, natives of Jersey Island off England, settled on the island in 1860 (Salley, p. 107).

Jersey Island Tract: see **Jersey Island** [CONTRA COSTA].

Jersey Landing: see **Jersey** [CONTRA COSTA].

Jersey Point [CONTRA COSTA]: *promontory,* 3.5 miles northwest of the settlement of Bethel Island along San Joaquin River (lat. 38°03'05" N, long. 121°41'20" W); the feature is on Jersey Island. Named on Jersey Island (1978) 7.5' quadrangle.

Jewell [MARIN]: *locality,* 11 miles west-southwest of downtown Novato (lat. 38°02'10" N, long. 122°44'40" W). Named on San Geronimo (1954) 7.5' quadrangle The place is near the ranch that Omar Jewell settled on in the 1860's (Teather, p. 32).

Jewel Lake [CONTRA COSTA]: *lake,* 550 feet long, behind a dam on Wildcat Creek 4.5 miles east-southeast of Richmond civic center (lat. 37°54'45" N, long. 122°16'05" W). Named on Richmond (1959) 7.5' quadrangle.

Jewell Gulch [SONOMA]: *canyon,* drained by a stream that flows 1 mile to the sea 5 miles northwest of Jenner (lat. 38°29'30" N, long. 123°11'40" W). Named on Arched Rock (1977) 7.5' quadrangle.

Jim Creek [SONOMA]: *stream,* flows 2.5 miles to Pepperwood Creek 8 miles north-northeast of Fort Ross (lat. 38°37'15" N, long. 123°11'20" W; sec. 16, T 9 N, R 12 W). Named on Fort Ross (1978) 7.5' quadrangle.

Jim McCall's Gulch: see **Jones Gulch** [SAN MATEO] (2).

Jimtown [SONOMA]: *village,* 4.5 miles northeast of Healdsburg (lat. 38°40' N, long. 122°49'05" W). Named on Jimtown (1955) 7.5' quadrangle.

Joaquin River: see **San Joaquin River** [CONTRA COSTA].

John Gordon Creek [SONOMA]: *stream,* flows 1.25 miles to Porter Creek (1) 4.5 miles northeast of Guerneville (lat. 38°32'35" N, long. 122°55'55" W; sec. 14, T 8 N, R 10 W). Named on Guerneville (1955) 7.5' quadrangle.

Johnny Brown Springs [SONOMA]: *springs,* 1.5 miles north-northwest of Big Mountain (lat. 38°43'55" N, long. 123°09'15" W; sec. 11, T 10 N, R 12 W). Named on Tombs Creek (1978) 7.5' quadrangle.

Johnson Camp [ALAMEDA]: *locality,* 4 miles south-southwest of Midway (lat. 37°39'45" N, long. 121°35'50" W; sec. 24, T 3 S, R 3 E). Named on Midway (1953) 7.5' quadrangle.

Johnson Canyon [NAPA]: *canyon,* drained by a stream that flows 1 mile to Lake Berryessa 7 miles north-northwest of Mount Vaca (lat. 38°29'25" N, long. 122°09'35" W; sec. 35, T 8 N, R 3 W). Named on Capell Valley (1951, photorevised 1968) 7.5' quadrangle.

Johnson Creek: see **Jones Creek** [SANTA CLARA].

Johnson Gulch [SONOMA]: *canyon,* drained by a stream that flows nearly 2 miles to Bodega Harbor at the village of Bodega Bay (lat. 38°20'05" N, long. 123°02'55" W). Named on Bodega Head (1972) 7.5' quadrangle.

Johnson Landing [ALAMEDA]: *locality,* 6.5 miles south of downtown San Leandro at the edge of San Francisco Bay (lat. 37°37'45" N, long. 122°09'05" W). Named on San Leandro (1959) 7.5' quadrangle. The name commemorates John Johnson, who came to the place in 1856 and built a wharf and warehouses (Mosier and Mosier, p., 47).

Johnson Spring [NAPA]: *spring,* 6.5 miles east-northeast of Saint Helena (lat. 38°32'10" N, long. 122°21'25" W; near NE cor. sec. 24, T 8 N, R 5 W). Named on Chiles Valley (1958) 7.5' quadrangle.

Johnston Creek: see **Mills Creek** [SAN MATEO] (2).

John West Ridge [SONOMA]: *ridge,* west-trending, 0.5 mile long, 2.5 miles northeast of Annapolis (lat. 38°44'45" N, long. 123°19'55" W). Named on Annapolis (1977) 7.5' quadrangle.

Joice Island [SOLANO]: *island,* 5.5 miles south of Fairfield between Cutoff Slough, Montezuma Slough, and Suisun Slough (lat. 38° 10" N, long. 121°03' W). Named on Denverton (1953), Fairfield South (1949), and Vine Hill (1959) 7.5' quadrangles. United States Board on Geographic Names (1933, p. 401) rejected the forms "Joice's Island" and "Joyce Island" for the name.

Joice's Island: see **Joice Island** [SOLANO].

Jones: see **Commodore Jones Point** [SOLANO]; **Elmhurst** [ALAMEDA].

Jones Creek [SANTA CLARA]: *stream,* joins Llagas Creek nearly 4 miles southeast of Gilroy (lat. 36°58'35" N, long. 121°30'40" W); the stream is the continuation in the lowlands of Alamias Creek. Named on Chittenden (1955, photorevised 1968 and 1973) 7.5' quadrangle. According to United States Board on Geographic Names (1973a, p. 2), the name commemorates an early landowner in the region; the Board gave the name "Johnson Creek" as a variant.

Jones Creek: see **Corte Madera Creek** [SAN MATEO]; **Los Gatos Creek** [SANTA CLARA].

Jones Gulch [SAN MATEO]:

(1) *canyon,* drained by a stream that flows 1.5 miles to Pescadero Creek 3 miles south of La Honda (lat. 37°16'30" N, long. 122° 16' W; sec. 35, T 7 S, R 4 W). Named on La Honda (1961) 7.5' quadrangle. J.C. Jones settled in the canyon in the early 1860's (Brown, p. 44).

(2) *canyon,* drained by a stream that flows 1 mile to Corte Madera Creek 3.5 miles north of Mindego Hill (lat. 37°21'45" N, long. 122°13'15" W). Named on Mindego Hill (1961) 7.5' quadrangle. William G. Jones settled near the head of the canyon about 1857; a common name for the feature in the twentieth century is Jim McCall's Gulch, for the owner of a cabin there (Brown, p. 44).

Jones Gulch: see **Alambique Creek** [SAN MATEO].

Jones Island: see **Van Sickle Island** [SOLANO].

Jones Mill: see **Lexington** [SANTA CLARA].

Josephine: see **Lake Josephine** [SONOMA].

Joyce Island: see **Joice Island** [SOLANO].

Judsonville: see **Stewartville** [CONTRA COSTA].

Julia: see **Point Julia**, under **Inverness** [MARIN].

Jumpoff Creek [SANTA CLARA]: *stream,* flows 9 miles to San Antonio Creek 4 miles north-northeast of Isabel Valley (lat. 37°22'05" N, long. 121°31'05" W; sec. 34, T 6 S, R 4 E). Named on Isabel Valley (1955) and Mount Stakes (1955) 7.5' quadrangles.

Junction: see **Antioch** [CONTRA COSTA]; **New Almaden Station** [SANTA CLARA].

Junction Camp [CONTRA COSTA]: *locality,* 1.5 miles southwest of Mount Diablo (lat. 37°51'55" N, long. 121°55'55" W; near NW cor. sec. 12, T 1 S, R 1 W). Named on Diablo (1953) 7.5' quadrangle.

Juniper Camp [CONTRA COSTA]: *locality,* 1 mile west-southwest of Mount Diablo (lat. 37°52'40" N, long. 121°55'50" W; at W line sec. 1, T 1 S, R 1 W). Named on Clayton (1953) 7.5' quadrangle.

Juristac [SANTA CLARA]: *land grant,* west of Pajaro River at the southernmost tip of Santa Clara County. Named on Chittenden (1955) 7.5' quadrangle. Antonio German and Faustino German received 1 league in 1835; J.L. Sargent claimed 4540 acres patented in 1871 (Cowan, p. 43). Kroeber (p. 44) gave an Indian origin for the name. The grant generally was known as Sargent Ranch for its American owner, James P. Sargent (Arbuckle, p. 18). The grant also was known as Los Germanos, for the original grantees, and as La Brea (Gudde, 1949, p. 169).

– K –

Kaiser Creek [ALAMEDA-CONTRA COSTA]: *stream,* heads in Contra Costa County and flows 3 miles to an arm of Upper San Leandro Reservoir 10 miles east of downtown Oakland in Alameda County (lat. 37°47'15" N, long. 122°05'35" W; sec. 4, T 2 S, R 2 W). Named on Las Trampas Ridge (1959) 7.5' quadrangle. Buckhorn Creek, a tributary of Kaiser Creek, is called Kaiser Creek on Concord (1897) 15' quadrangle.

Karquenas Strait: see **Carquinez Strait** [CONTRA COSTA].

Karquines Point: see **Point Carquinez** [CONTRA COSTA].

Karquines Strait: see **Carquinez Strait** [CONTRA COSTA-SOLANO].

Kashow's Island: see **Belvedere Island** [MARIN].

Kaufman Ridge [SANTA CLARA]: *ridge,* northwest- to west-trending, 2 miles long, 5 miles northwest of Pacheco Peak (lat. 37°03'45" N, long. 121°20'45" W). Named on Pacheco Peak (1955) 7.5' quadrangle.

Kawana Springs [SONOMA]: *spring,* 2.25 miles southeast of downtown Santa Rosa (lat. 38°24'55" N, long. 122°41'10" W; near NE cor. sec. 36, T 7 N, R 8 W). Named on Santa Rosa (1954) 7.5' quadrangle. The spring was the basis for a resort built in 1870 and known as Taylor's Springs, Taylor Sulphur Spring, and Taylor's White Sulphur Springs for J.S. Taylor, who owned the place (Bradley, p. 337; Goodyear, 1890b, p. 676; Waring, p. 256). Taylor asked Luther Burbank to rename the resort, and Burbank chose the name "Kawana Springs" (Hansen and Miller, p. 133).

Keiffer's Creek: see **Bogess Creek** [SAN MATEO].

Keil Cove [MARIN]: *embayment,* nearly 5 miles south-southeast of Point San Quentin near the southeast end of Tiburon Peninsula (lat. 37°52'45" N, long. 122°26'25" W). Named on San Quentin (1959) 7.5' quadrangle. The Keil family lived in the neighborhood (Teather, p. 32).

Keller Ridge [CONTRA COSTA]: *ridge,* generally west-trending, 1.5 miles long, 3.5 miles north-northeast of Mount Diablo (lat. 37° 55'40" N, long. 121°53'20" W). Named on Clayton (1953) 7.5' quadrangle.

Kelley Creek [SONOMA]: *stream,* flows nearly 3 miles to Dry Creek 5 miles south of Geyserville (lat. 38°37'55" N, long. 123°54' W). Named on Geyserville (1955) 7.5' quadrangle.

Kelley Gulch: see **Bull Run Creek** [SAN MATEO].

Kellogg [SONOMA]: *locality,* 3.25 miles southwest of Mount Saint Helena in Knights Valley (lat. 38°37'55" N, long. 122°40'25" W); the place is near Kellogg Creek. Named on Mount Saint Helena (1959) 7.5' quadrangle. Postal authorities established Kellogg post office in 1875, discontinued it in 1876, reestablished it in 1889, and discontinued it in 1935; the name is for a pioneer settler (Salley, p. 110).

Kellogg Creek [CONTRA COSTA]: *stream,* flows 14 miles to lowlands 2.5 miles south of Brentwood (lat. 37°53'35" N, long. 121° 41'35" W). Named on Brentwood (1978), Byron Hot Springs (1953), and Woodward Island (1978) 7.5' quadrangles.

Kellogg Creek [SONOMA]: *stream,* flows 4.5 miles to join Yellow Jacket Creek and form Redwood Creek (1) 3 miles southwest of Mount Saint Helena (lat. 38°38'05" N, long. 122°40'15" W). Named on Mount Saint Helena (1959) 7.5' quadrangle.

Kelly: see **Napa Junction** [NAPA].

Kelly Cabin Canyon [SANTA CLARA]: *canyon,* drained by a stream that flows 6.5 miles to East Fork Coyote Creek 4.5 miles north of Gilroy Hot

Springs (lat. 37°10'25" N, long. 121°28'50" W; at N line sec. 12, T 9 S, R 4 E). Named on Gilroy Hot Springs (1955) and Mississippi Creek (1955) 7.5' quadrangles.

Kelly Hill [SAN MATEO]: *peak,* 4 miles north-northwest of Mindego Hill (lat. 37°21'55" N, long. 122°14'50" W; sec. 36, T 6 S, R 4 W). Named on Mindego Hill (1961) 7.5' quadrangle.

Kenilworth: see **Sebastopol** [SONOMA].

Kensington [CONTRA COSTA]: *town,* 4 miles east-southeast of Richmond civic center (lat. 37°54'35" N, long. 122°16'45" W). Named on Richmond (1959) 7.5' quadrangle. Robert Bousefield named the place in 1911 for Kensington, England (Gudde, 1949, p. 172; Gudde listed it under the name "Kensington Park").

Kensington: see **Willow Glen** [SANTA CLARA].

Kensington Park: see **Kensington** [CONTRA COSTA].

Kent: see **Kentfield** [MARIN].

Kent Canyon [MARIN]: *canyon,* drained by a stream that flows 1.5 miles to Frank Valley nearly 7 miles south-southwest of downtown San Rafael (lat. 37°52'55" N, long. 122°34'35" W). Named on San Rafael (1954) 7.5' quadrangle. Congressman William Kent had a hunting cabin at the head of the canyon; the feature first was called Rocky Canyon (Teather, p. 32).

Kentfield [MARIN]: *town,* 2 miles southwest of downtown San Rafael (lat. 37°57' N, long. 122°33'15" W). Named on San Rafael (1954) 7.5' quadrangle. Tamalpais (1897) 15' quadrangle has the name "Tamalpais" along Northwestern Pacific Railroad at the place. Postal authorities established Kentfield post office in 1905 (Frickstad, p. 88). Albert Emmet Kent bought land at the place from the estate of James Ross in 1871; Ross Landing was at the site in the early days, when steamers came up Corte Madera Creek (Hoover, Rensch, and Rensch, p. 185). Kent called his home Tamalpais, and the nearby railroad station had that name before it was renamed Kent in the 1890's; the name "Kent" was changed to Kentfield when the post office came (Gudde, 1949, p. 172-173).

Kent Lake [MARIN]: *lake,* behind a dam on Lagunitas Creek 6 miles north of Bolinas (lat. 37°59'50" N, long. 122°42'10" W). Named on Bolinas (1954) 7.5' quadrangle. Teather (p. 33) associated the name with Thomas T. Kent, a director of Marin Municipal Water District from 1920 until 1959.

Kenwood [SONOMA]: *town,* 9 miles east of Santa Rosa on Los Guilicos grant (lat. 38°24'55" N, long. 122°32'50" W). Named on Kenwood (1954) 7.5' quadrangle. Postal authorities established Los Guilicos post office in 1888, changed the name to South Los Guilicos in 1889, and changed it to Kenwood in 1893 (Frickstad, p. 196, 198). The name "Kenwood" is from a town in Illinois (Gudde, 1949, p. 173). Cardwell's (1958) map has the name "Kenwood Valley" for the place where the town lies. Laizure (1926, p. 341) noted that Kenwood Springs, located 1.5 miles northwest of Kenwood along Sonoma Creek, were the basis of a resort with a hotel, cottages, and campground that accommodated about 100 people.

Kenwood Springs: see **Kenwood** [SONOMA].

Kenwood Valley: see **Kenwood** [SONOMA].

Keyes Creek [MARIN]: see **Keys Creek** [MARIN]; **Walker Creek** [MARIN].

Keys Creek [MARIN]: *stream,* flows 3.5 miles to Walker Creek 1 mile south-southwest of Tomales (lat. 38°14' N, long. 122°54'45" W). Named on Point Reyes NE (1954) and Tomales (1954) 7.5' quadrangles. United States Board on Geographic Names (1943, p. 11) rejected the name "Keyes Creek" for the stream, The name "Keys" commemorates John Keys, who took up land along the creek in the 1850's (Gudde, 1949, p. 174).

Keys Creek: see **Walker Creek** [MARIN].

Keys Embarcadero: see **Tomales** [MARIN].

Keyston Creek [SAN MATEO]: *stream,* flows less than 1 mile to Pescadero Creek 3.5 miles south-southwest of Mindego Hill (lat. 37°15'40" N, long. 122°14'55" W; sec. 1, T 8 S, R 4 W). Named on La Honda (1961) and Mindego Hill (1961) 7.5' quadrangles. Employees of Santa Cruz Lumber Company named the stream about 1946 for George N. Keyston, patron of a nearby Boy Scout camp (Brown, p. 44).

Kickham Peak [SANTA CLARA]: *peak,* 6.5 miles southeast of Gilroy Hot Springs on Elephant Head Ridge (lat. 37°02'50" N, long. 121°23'05" W; on W line sec. 24, T 10 S, R 5 E). Named on Gilroy Hot Springs (1955) 7.5' quadrangle.

Kid Creek: see **Kidd Creek** [SONOMA].

Kidd Canyon [NAPA]: *canyon,* 1.5 miles long, along James Creek above a point 7 miles north-northeast of Calistoga (lat. 38°40'10" N, long. 122°31'40" W; sec. 33, T 10 N, R 6 W). Named on Detert Reservoir (1958) 7.5' quadrangle.

Kidd Creek [SONOMA]: *stream,* flows 2.5 miles to Austin Creek 4 miles west of Guerneville (lat. 38°29'45" N, long. 123°04'05" W; sec. 34, T 8 N, R 11 W). Named on Cazadero (1978) and Duncans Mills (1979) 7.5' quadrangles. Called Kid Creek on Skaggs (1921) 15' quadrangle. California Mining Bureau's (1917a) map shows a place called Kid Creek located about halfway from Duncans Mills to Cazadero along a railroad near the mouth of present Kidd Creek—California Division of Highways' (1934) map has the name "Kidd Creek" at the place.

Kilcare Woods [ALAMEDA]: *settlement,* 5 miles south-southeast of Dublin along Sinbad Creek (lat. 37°37'45" N, long. 121°54'45" W). Named on Dublin (1961) 7.5' quadrangle.

Kilgore [CONTRA COSTA]: *locality,* 4 miles north-northeast of present Walnut Creek civic center along Oakland Antioch and Eastern Railroad (lat. 37°57'20" N, long. 122°01'40" W). Named on Concord (1915) 15' quadrangle.

Kimball Canyon [NAPA]: *canyon,* 1.5 miles long, along Napa River above a point 3.5 miles north-northwest of Calistoga (lat. 38°37'15" N, long. 122°36'40" W). Named on Detert Reservoir (1958) 7.5' quadrangle.

King: see **Mount King**, under **North Peak** [CONTRA COSTA].

King Canyon [ALAMEDA]: *canyon,* nearly 1 mile long, 8.5 miles east of downtown Oakland (lat. 37°48' N, long. 122°06'55" W; near E line sec. 31, T 1 S, R 2 W). Named on Las Trampas Ridge (1959) 7.5' quadrangle. Water of Upper San Leandro Reservoir nearly fills the canyon. The name commemorates Joaquin King, a stock rancher who settled at the place in the 1850's (Mosier and Mosier, p. 48).

King Mountain [MARIN]: *peak,* 2.5 miles south-southwest of downtown San Rafael (lat. 37°56'10" N, long. 122°32'50" W). Named on San Rafael (1954) 7.5' quadrangle.

King's Island: see **Ryer Island** [SOLANO] (2).

Kings Mountain [SAN MATEO]: *ridge,* northwest-trending, 2 miles long, 2 miles north-northwest of Skeggs Point (lat. 37°26'15" N, long. 122°19'15" W). Named on Woodside (1961) 7.5' quadrangle. The name is from a travellers stop called Kings Mountain House, operated by Mrs. Honora King (Gudde, 1949, p. 175).

Kings Ridge [SONOMA]: *ridge,* west-northwest-trending, 1.25 miles long, 8 miles northeast of Fort Ross (lat. 38°35'35" N, long. 123° 08'25" W). Named on Fort Ross (1978) 7.5' quadrangle.

Kings Rock [SAN MATEO]: *rock,* 3.5 miles west-northwest of downtown Half Moon Bay, and about 0.5 mile southeast of Pillar Point (lat. 37°29'15" N, long. 122°29'15" W). Named on Half Moon Bay (1961) 7.5' quadrangle.

Kingston Creek [SAN MATEO]: *stream,* flows nearly 2 miles to San Gregorio Creek 2.5 miles west-southwest of La Honda (lat. 37° 18'35" N, long. 122°19'10" W; sec. 20, T 7 S, R 4 W). Named on La Honda (1961) 7.5' quadrangle. J.R. Kingston had a ranch by the stream in the 1870's; the feature also was called Armstrong's Creek for the previous owner of the ranch (Brown, p. 45).

Kirby Beach: see **Point Diablo** [MARIN].

Kirby Hill [SOLANO]: *hill,* 4 miles south-southwest of Denverton (lat. 38°10'05" N, long. 121°55'10" W). Altitude 361 feet. Named on Denverton (1953) 7.5' quadrangle.

Kirker Creek [CONTRA COSTA]: *stream,* flows 4.25 miles to lowlands 8 miles north of Mount Diablo at Pittsburg (lat. 37°59'50" N, long. 121°53'35" W; near N line sec. 29, T 2 N, R 1 W). Named on Antioch North (1953), Clayton (1953), and Honker Bay (1953) 7.5' quadrangles.

Kirker Pass [CONTRA COSTA]:

(1) *pass,* 5.5 miles north of Mount Diablo (lat. 37°57'40" N, long. 121°55'15" W; sec. 1, T 1 N, R 1 W). Named on Mount Diablo (1898) 15' quadrangle. Whitney (p. 32) mentioned Kirker's Pass. United States Board on Geographic Names (1933, p. 430) rejected the names "Kirkers Pass," "Quercus Pass," and "Quereus Pass" for the feature. James Kirker lived near the place in the 1850's (Gudde, 1969, p. 166).

(2) *locality,* 5.5 miles north of Mount Diablo (lat. 37°57'40" N, long. 121°55'15" W; sec. 1, T 1 N, R 1 W); the place is at Kirker Pass (1). Named on Clayton (1953) 7.5' quadrangle.

Kitty Ridge [SONOMA]: *ridge,* east-trending, about 0.5 mile long, 3.5 miles west-southwest of Big Mountain (lat. 38°41'25" N, long. 123°12'25" W). Named on Tombs Creek (1978) 7.5' quadrangle.

Klinknerville: see **Golden Gate** [ALAMEDA].

Knife: see **The Knife** [ALAMEDA-CONTRA COSTA].

Knight Island [SOLANO]: *island,* 3 miles northwest of downtown Vallejo between Napa River, Dutchman Slough, and South Slough (lat. 38°08'15" N, long. 122°18'15" W). Named on Cuttings Wharf (1949) 7.5' quadrangle. On Mare Island (1916) 15' quadrangle, present Russ Island [NAPA] is has the name "Knight Island."

Knight's Creek: see **Redwood Creek** [SONOMA] (1).

Knightsen [CONTRA COSTA]: *town,* 3 miles north-northeast of Brentwood (lat. 37°58'10" N, long. 121°39'55" W; near S line sec. 32, T 2 N, R 3 E). Named on Brentwood (1978) 7.5' quadrangle. Postal authorities established Knightsen post office in 1900 (Frickstad, p. 22). G.M. Knight gave right of way at the place to the railroad, and suggested the name to combine his own name with the suffix of his wife's maiden name, Christensen (Gudde, 1949, p. 176).

Knights Valley [SONOMA]: *valley,* 4 miles southwest of Mount Saint Helena (lat. 38°38' N, long. 122°41'30" W). Named on Mark West Springs (1958) and Mount Saint Helena (1959) 7.5' quadrangles. Postal authorities established Knights Valley post office in Napa County 7 miles northwest of Calistoga in 1860 and discontinued it in 1862, when they moved the post office to Sonoma County and changed the name to Albany; they discontinued Albany post office in 1864—the name "Albany" was from Albany, New York (Salley, p. 3, 113). Thomas Knight, was the first permanent settler in the valley in the 1850's (Archuleta, p. 14). A hotel and houses in Knights Valley had the name "Knightsville" (Menefee, p. 264).

Knightsville: see **Knights Valley** [SONOMA].

Knob Hill [MARIN]: *peak,* 3.25 miles southwest of downtown San Rafael (lat. 37°56'05" N, long. 122°33'45" W). Altitude 1091 feet. Named on San Rafael (1954) 7.5' quadrangle.

Knob Point [CONTRA COSTA]: *peak,* 2.5 miles south-southeast of Mount Diablo (lat. 37°50'35" N, long. 121°53'55" W; sec. 18, T 1 S, R 1 E). Named on Diablo (1953) 7.5' quadrangle.

Knopf Canyon: see **Nuff Creek** [SAN MATEO].

Knowles Corner [SONOMA]: *locality,* 3.5 miles northeast of Bloomfield (lat. 38°21'10" N, long. 122°48'55" W). Named on Two Rock (1954) 7.5' quadrangle.

Knox Island: see **Chipps Island** [SOLANO].

Knox Point [MARIN]: *promontory,* at the southwest end of Angel Island (lat. 37°51'20" N, long. 122°26'30" W). Named on San Francisco North (1956) 7.5' quadrangle. United States Board on Geographic Names (1980, p. 4) approved the name "Point Knox" for the promontory. The name "Knox" commemorates Lieutenant Samuel R. Knox, who was an officer with Cadwallader Ringgold's expedition of 1849 (Teather, p. 2).

Knoxville [NAPA]: *village,* 23 miles north-northeast of Saint Helena (lat. 38°49'25" N, long. 122°20'10" W; near NE cor. sec. 7, T 11 N, R 4 W). Named on Knoxville (1958) 7.5' quadrangle. Postal authorities established Knoxville post office in 1863, moved it 2 miles northwest in 1904, moved it 1.5 miles southeast in 1907, and discontinued it in 1912; the name is for Ranar B. Knox, first postmaster and an owner of Reddington Quicksilver Mine Company (Salley, p. 113).

Knoxville Creek [NAPA]: *stream,* flows 4.25 miles to join Foley Creek and form Eticuera Creek 2.25 miles southeast of Knoxville (lat. 38°47'55" N, long. 122°18'45" W; sec. 16, T 11 N, R 4 W); the stream goes past Knoxville. Named on Knoxville (1958) 7.5' quadrangle.

Knuedler Lake [SAN MATEO]: *lake,* 350 feet long, less than 1 mile southwest of Mindego Hill (lat. 37°18'20" N, long. 122°14'25" W; near E line sec. 24, T 7 S, R 4 W). Named on Mindego Hill (1961) 7.5' quadrangle. John Knuedler had a ranch at the place (Brown, p. 45).

Kohler Creek: see **Temescal Creek** [ALAMEDA].

Kohute Gulch [SONOMA]: *canyon,* drained by a stream that flows nearly 2 miles to Austin Creek 3.5 miles west-southwest of Guerneville (lat. 38°28'55" N, long. 123°03'15" W). Named on Duncans Mills (1979) 7.5' quadrangle. Called Crinkley Gulch on Duncans Mills (1921) 15' quadrangle.

Kolmer Gulch [SONOMA]: *canyon,* drained by a stream that flows 3 miles to the sea 1.25 miles west-northwest of Fort Ross (lat. 38° 31'25" N, long. 123°15'50" W). Named on Fort Ross (1978) and Plantation (1977) 7.5' quadrangles. The name commemorates Michael Kolmer, who settled at the place in 1848 (Gudde, 1949, p. 177).

Kolmer Valley: see **Coleman Valley** [SONOMA].

Komandorski Village [ALAMEDA]: *locality,* nearly 2 miles northeast of Dublin (lat. 37°42'55" N, long. 121°54'35" W). Named on Dublin (1961) 7.5' quadrangle.

Koopman Canyon [ALAMEDA-CONTRA COSTA]: *canyon,* on Alameda-Contra Costa County line, mainly in Contra Costa County; drained by a stream that flows 1.5 miles to lowlands nearly 1 mile north of Dublin (lat. 37°42'50" N, long. 121°56'20" W). Named on Dublin (1961) 7.5' quadrangle. The name commemorates Martin Koopman and Mathew Koopman, who farmed in the neighborhood (Mosier and Mosier, p. 48).

Korbel [SONOMA]: *locality,* nearly 2 miles east of Guerneville along Russian River (lat. 38°30'25" N, long. 122°57'50" W; on E line sec. 28, T 8 N, R 10 W). Named on Guerneville (1955) 7.5' quadrangle. Postal authorities established Korbel's Mills post office 4 miles east of Guerneville (SE quarter sec. 28, T 8 N, R 10 W) in 1876 and discontinued in 1881; the name was from Korbel Lumber Company (Salley, p. 113).

Korbel's Mills: see **Korbel** [SONOMA].

Kortum Canyon [NAPA]: *canyon,* less than 1 mile long, opens into lowlands at Calistoga (lat. 38°34'25" N, long. 122°34'50" W). Named on Calistoga (1958) 7.5' quadrangle.

Krelling [CONTRA COSTA]: *locality,* 4.5 miles northwest of Danville along Oakland Antioch and Eastern Railroad (lat. 37°52'20" N, long. 122°02'45" W). Named on Concord (1915) 15' quadrangle.

Kreuse Canyon [NAPA]: *canyon,* nearly 2 miles long, along Kreuse Creek above a point 2.5 miles east-southeast of downtown Napa (lat. 38°16'50" N, long. 122°14'35" W; near W line sec. 18, T 5 N, R 3 W). Named on Mount George (1951) 7.5' quadrangle.

Kreuse Creek [NAPA]: *stream,* flows 3.25 miles to Tulacay Creek 1.25 miles east-southeast of downtown Napa (lat. 38°17'20" N, long. 122°15'35" W). Named on Mount George (1951) and Napa (1951) 7.5' quadrangles.

Krug [NAPA]: *locality,* 1 mile north-northwest of Saint Helena along Southern Pacific Railroad (lat. 38°31'05" N, long. 122°28'50" W). Named on Saint Helena (1960) 7.5' quadrangle.

Kuskov: see **Bodega** [SONOMA] (2).

— L —

La Boca de la Cañada del Pinole [CONTRA COSTA]: *land grant,* between Martinez and Lafayette. Named on Briones Valley (1959) and Walnut Creek (1959) 7.5' quadrangles. Manuel Valencia received the land in 1842 and claimed 13,316 acres patented in 1878 (Cowan, p. 61).

La Brea: see **Juristac** [SANTA CLARA]; **Las Animas** [SANTA CLARA]; **Sargent** [SANTA CLARA].

La Brea Creek: see **Tar Creek** [SANTA CLARA].

Lac [SONOMA]: *land grant,* 2 miles east-northeast of Sonoma. Named on Sonoma (1951) 7.5' quadrangle. Damasco Rodriguez received 100 varas in 1844; Jacob P. Leese claimed 177 acres patented in 1872 (Cowan, p. 43).

La Costa Creek [ALAMEDA]: *stream,* flows 7 miles to San Antonio Creek 6 miles east of Sunol (lat. 37°34'40" N, long. 121°46'25" W; sec. 20, T 4 S, R 2 E); the mouth of the stream is at the head of La Costa Valley. Named on La Costa Valley (1960) and Mendenhall Springs (1956) 7.5' quadrangles. The misspelled name is for Juan F. La Coste, who raised livestock in the region in the 1850's; the stream also was called San Antonio Creek (Mosier and Mosier, p. 48).

La Costa Valley [ALAMEDA]: *valley,* 4 miles east of Sunol along San Antonio Creek (lat. 37°35' N, long. 121°48'45" W). Named on La Costa Valley (1960) 7.5' quadrangle. Water of San Antonio Reservoir now covers part of the valley.

Lacresta [SONOMA]: *locality,* 5 miles northwest of Sebastopol along Petaluma and Santa Rosa Railroad (lat. 38°27'25" N, long. 122° 53' W). Named on Sebastopol (1942) 15' quadrangle.

La Cuchilla de la Mina de Louis Chabolla: see **New Almaden** [SANTA CLARA].

Laddville: see **Livermore** [ALAMEDA].

Ladrillo: see **Clayburn** [CONTRA COSTA].

Lafayette [CONTRA COSTA]: *town,* 3.25 miles west-southwest of Walnut Creek civic center (lat. 37°53'30" N, long. 122°07' W). Named on Briones Valley (1959), Las Trampas Ridge (1959), and Walnut Creek (1959) 7.5' quadrangles. Called La Fayette on California Mining Bureau's (1909b) map. Postal authorities established La Fayette post office in 1857 and changed the name to Lafayette in 1932 (Salley, p. 114). The town incorporated in 1968. Elam Brown, who settled at the place in 1846 and built a grist mill there in 1853, is considered the founder of the community (Smith and Elliott, p. 23).

Lafayette Branch: see **Lafayette Creek** [CONTRA COSTA].

Lafayette Creek [CONTRA COSTA]: *stream,* flows 3.25 miles to Las Trampas Creek 3 miles west-southwest of Walnut Creek civic center in Lafayette (lat. 37°53'35" N, long. 122°06'35" W). Named on Briones Valley (1959) and Walnut Creek (1959) 7.5' quadrangles. On Concord (1897) 15' quadrangle, present Lafayette Creek and Las Trampas Creek below their confluence have the name "Lafayette Branch."

Lafayette Reservoir [CONTRA COSTA]: *lake,* 4100 feet long, 2.25 miles east of Orinda (lat. 37°52'55" N, long. 122°08'25" W). Named on Briones Valley (1959) 7.5' quadrangle.

Lafayette Ridge [CONTRA COSTA]: *ridge,* east-southeast-trending, 2.5 miles long, center 3.25 miles west of Walnut Creek civic center (lat. 37°54'30" N, long. 122°07' W). Named on Briones Valley (1959) and Walnut Creek (1959) 7.5' quadrangles.

La Franchi: see **Santa Rosa** [SONOMA].

Lafranchi Creek [SONOMA]: *stream,* flows 2.5 miles to Redwood Creek (1) 5 miles west-southwest of Mount Saint Helena in Knights Valley (lat. 38°38'15 N, long. 122°42'50" W). Named on Mount Saint Helena (1959) 7.5' quadrangle.

Lagoon [SOLANO]: *intermittent lake,* 5.5 miles north-northeast of Fairfield in Lagoon Valley (lat. 38°19'45" N, long. 122°00'40" W). Named on Fairfield North (1951) 7.5' quadrangle, which shows two perennial lakes in the intermittent lake.

Lagoon: see **The Lagoon**, under **Stivers Lagoon** [ALAMEDA].

Lagoon Valley [SOLANO]: *valley,* 6.25 miles north of Fairfield (lat. 38°20'30" N, long. 122°01'15" W); Laguna Creek drains the valley. Named on Elmira (1953) and Fairfield North (1951) 7.5' quadrangles.

Laguna: see **The Laguna**, under **Upper Crystal Springs Reservoir** [SAN MATEO].

Laguna Alta [SAN MATEO]: *lake,* 1550 feet long, 3.5 miles west of downtown South San Francisco (lat. 37°39'35" N, long. 122°28'40" W). Named on San Francisco South (1956) 7.5' quadrangle. The lake now is filled, and the filled area is covered by buildings.

Laguna Creek [MARIN]: *stream,* flows 0.5 mile to Fern Creek 5 miles south-southwest of downtown San Rafael (lat. 37°54'40" N, long. 122°34'50" W). Named on San Rafael (1954) 7.5' quadrangle.

Laguna Creek [SOLANO]: *stream,* flows 4.5 miles to Alamo Creek less than 1 mile south-southwest of downtown Vacaville (lat. 38°20'35" N, long. 121°59'55" W); the stream goes through Lagoon Valley. Named on Fairfield North (1951) 7.5' quadrangle.

Laguna Creek: see **Lower Crystal Springs Reservoir** [SAN MATEO].

Laguna de la Merced [SAN FRANCISCO-SAN MATEO]: *land grant,* around Lake Merced on San Francisco-San Mateo County line, mainly in San Francisco. Named on San Francisco South (1956) 7.5' quadrangle. Jose Antonio Galindo received 1.5 leagues in 1835; Josefa de Haro and others claimed 2219 acres patented in 1872 (Cowan, p. 47-48).

Laguna de la Merced: see **Lake Merced** [SAN FRANCISCO].

Laguna del Corazon: see **Mindego Lake** [SAN MATEO].

Laguna de los Dolores: see **Mission District** [SAN FRANCISCO].

Laguna de los Gentiles: see **Caslamayomi** [SONOMA].

Laguna de los Palos Colorados [ALAMEDA-CONTRA COSTA]: *land grant,* mainly near and north of Moraga; almost entirely in Contra Costa County, but the southernmost tip of the grant extends into Alameda County. Named on Briones Valley (1959), Las Trampas Ridge (1959), Oakland East (1959), and Walnut Creek (1959) 7.5' quadrangles. Joaquin Moraga and Juan Bernal received 3 leagues in 1835 and 1841; Moraga and others claimed 13,316 acres patented in 1878 (Cowan, p. 57). The name is from a lake and some redwood trees on the grant (Gudde, 1949, p. 251).

Laguna del Presidio: see **Mountain Lake** [SAN FRANCISCO].

Laguna de Manantial: see **Mission District** [SAN FRANCISCO].

Laguna de Nuestra Señora de la Merced: see **Lake Merced** [SAN FRANCISCO].

Laguna de Nuestra Señora de los Dolores: see **Mission District** [SAN FRANCISCO].

Laguna de Raimundo: see **Upper Crystal Springs Reservoir** [SAN MATEO].

Laguna de San Antonio [MARIN-SONOMA]: *land grant,* around Laguna Lake on Marin-Sonoma County line. Named on Cotati (1954), Petaluma (1953), Point Reyes NE (1954), and Two Rock (1954) 7.5' quadrangles. Bartolo Bojorquez received 6 leagues in 1845 and claimed 24,903 acres patented in 1871 (Cowan, p. 72).

Laguna de San Antonio: see **Laguna Lake** [MARIN-SONOMA].

Laguna de San Benvenuto: see **Laguna Seca** [SANTA CLARA].

Laguna de Santa Rosa [SONOMA]: *water feature,* stream, with associated ponds and marsh, that joins Mark West Creek nearly 5 miles north of Sebastopol (lat. 38°28'15" N, long. 122°50'25" W). Named on Cotati (1954), Sebastopol (1954), and Two Rock (1954) 7.5' quadrangles. Called The Lagunas on Santa Rosa (1916) 15' quadrangle. A diseño of Llano de Santa Rosa grant has the Indian name "Livantuliyume" for the feature (Becker, 1969).

Laguna Grande: see **Upper Crystal Springs Reservoir** [SAN MATEO].

Laguna Honda [SAN FRANCISCO[: *lake,* 1200 feet long, 0.5 mile south-southwest of Mount Sutro (lat. 37°45'10" N, long. 122°27'40" W). Named on San Francisco North (1956) 7.5' quadrangle. Called Laguna Honda Reservoir on Wackenreuder's (1861) map.

Laguna Honda Reservoir: see **Laguna Honda** [SAN FRANCISCO].

Laguna House: see **Coyote** [SANTA CLARA].

Laguna Lake [MARIN-SONOMA]: *intermittent lake,* 2 miles long, 6 miles west-southwest of the city of Petaluma on Marin-Sonoma County line (lat. 38°12'45" N, long. 122°44'50" W). Named on Petaluma (1953) and Point Reyes NE (1954) 7.5' quadrangles. Mason (1976b, p. 163) called the feature Laguna de San Antonio.

Laguna Merced Military Reservation: see **Fort Funston Military Reservation** [SAN FRANCISCO].

Laguna Puerca [SAN FRANCISCO]: *lake,* 1250 feet long, nearly 2 miles east of Mount Davidson (lat. 37°44'05" N, long. 122°29'15" W). Named on San Mateo (1915) 15' quadrangle.

Laguna Ranch Canyon: see **Rough Gulch** [SANTA CLARA].

Lagunas: see **The Lagunas**, under **Laguna de Santa Rosa** [SONOMA].

Laguna Salada [SAN MATEO]: *lake,* 1850 feet long, nearly 5 miles west-southwest of downtown South San Francisco near the coast (lat. 37°37'35" N, long. 122°29'30" W). Named on Montara Mountain (1956) and San Francisco South (1956) 7.5' quadrangles. Brown (p. 78) used the name "Salt Lake" for the feature, and gave the name "Salt Lake Valley" to the valley that extends east from the lake; Brown also noted that the lake has the popular name "Brighton Lake" from Brighton Beach subdivision.

Laguna Seca [SANTA CLARA]: *marsh,* 1 mile south-southwest of Coyote (lat. 37°12'20" N, long. 121°44'40" W); the feature is on La Laguna grant. Named on Morgan Hill (1917) 15' quadrangle. Morgan Hill (1940) 15' quadrangle has the name, but shows no marsh. Morgan Hill (1955) 7.5' quadrangle omits the name and shows a drainage ditch through the place. Crespi called the feature Laguna de San Benvenuto in 1772 (Hoover, Rensch, and Rensch, p. 431).

Laguna Seca: see **La Laguna Seca** [SANTA CLARA].

Lagunita [SANTA CLARA]: *intermittent lake,* 1850 feet long, 4 miles south-southwest of downtown Palo Alto (lat. 37°25'20" N, long. 122°10'30" W). Named on Palo Alto (1961) 7.5' quadrangle. Called Lake Lagunita on Palo Alto (1940) 15' quadrangle.

Lagunitas [MARIN]: *settlement,* 10 miles southwest of downtown Novato (lat. 38°00'45" N, long. 122°42' W). Named on San Geronimo (1954) 7.5' quadrangle. Postal authorities established Lagunitas post office in 1906 (Frickstad, p. 88).

Lagunitas: see **Lake Lagunitas** [MARIN].

Lagunitas Creek [MARIN]: *stream,* heads at Lake Lagunitas, where East Fork, Middle Fork, and West Fork meet, flows 23 miles to marsh 1.5 miles northwest of Point Reyes Station at the southeast end of Tomales Bay (lat. 38°04'50" N, long. 122°49'35" W). Named on Bolinas (1954), Inverness (1954), and San Geronimo (1954) 7.5' quadrangles. Called Daniels C. on Goddard's (1857) map. United States Board on Geographic Names (1933, p. 444) rejected the name "Paper Mill Creek" for the stream. Samuel P. Taylor established the first paper mill on the Pacific Coast along the creek in 1856 (Gudde, 1949, p. 253). In Spanish times the stream was called Arroyo de San Geronimo, but the name "San Geronimo" now is restricted to San Geronimo Creek, a branch of Lagunitas Creek (Gudde, 1949, p. 180). East Fork is 1.5 miles long, Middle Fork is 1 mile long, and West Fork is nearly 1 mile long; all three forks are named on San Rafael (1954) 7.5' quadrangle. Postal authorities established Paper Mill post office 5.5 miles southeast of Olema at Taylor's paper mill in 1881, discontinued it in 1882, reestablished it with the name "Paperville" in 1884, and discontinued it in 1894 (Salley, p. 166).

La Honda [SAN MATEO]: *town,* 13 miles southeast of the town of Half Moon Bay (lat. 37°19'10" N, long. 122°16'15" W). Named on La Honda (1961) 7.5' quadrangle. John H. Sears built a store at the place about 1877 and named it for nearby Arroyo Hondo (present La Honda Creek) (Hoover, Rensch, and Rensch, p. 410). Postal authorities established La Honda post office in 1873, changed the name to Lahonda in 1894, and changed it back to La Honda in 1905 (Salley, p. 115). United States Board on Geographic Names (1974, p. 3) approved the name "Pearsons Pond" for a lake, 165 feet long, located 2.5 miles north of La Honda (lat. 37°21'08" N, long. 122°15'20" W); the name commemorates Charles A. Pearson and Edward J. Pearson, former owners of the feature.

La Honda Canyon: see **La Honda Creek** [SAN MATEO].

La Honda Creek [SAN MATEO]: *stream,* flows 7.5 miles to join Alpine Creek and form San Gregorio Creek 0.5 mile south-southwest of La Honda (lat. 37°18'35" N, long. 122°16'35" W; near E line sec. 22, T 7 S, R 4 W). Named on La Honda (1961) and Woodside (1961) 7.5' quadrangles. The stream first was called Arroyo Hondo; the canyon of the stream below Woodruff Creek is called La Honda Canyon (Brown , p. 46).

Lairds Landing [MARIN]: *locality,* 6 miles south of Tomales on the southwest side of Tomales Bay (lat. 38°09'35" N, long. 122°54'40" W). Named on Tomales (1954) 7.5' quadrangle. George Laird and Charles Laird leased the place in 1858 (Mason, 1976a, p. 33).

La Jota [NAPA]: *land grant,* 5 miles north-northeast of Saint Helena around Angwin. Named on Saint Helena (1960) 7.5' quadrangle. George C. Yount received 1 league in 1843 and claimed 4454 acres patented in 1857 (Cowan, p. 42-43).

La Jota: see **Angwin** [NAPA].

Lake Alhambra [CONTRA COSTA]: *lake,* 0.5 mile long, 1 mile east-southeast of downtown Antioch (lat. 38°00'30" N, long. 121°47'30" W). Named on Antioch North (1978) 7.5' quadrangle.

Lake Anza [CONTRA COSTA]: *lake,* 1000 feet long, behind a dam on Wildcat Creek 4 miles west-northwest of Orinda (lat. 37°53'50" N, long. 122°15' W). Named on Briones Valley (1959) and Richmond (1959) 7.5' quadrangles.

Lake Berryessa [NAPA]: *lake,* behind a dam on Putah Creek 11.5 miles south-southeast of Berryessa Peak (lat. 38°30'50" N, long. 122°06'10" W; sec. 29, T 8 N, R 2 W); the lake covers most of Berryessa Valley, including the site of the town of Monticello. Named on Aetna Springs (1958), Brooks (1959), Capell Valley (1951, photorevised 1968), Chiles Valley (1958), Lake Berryessa (1959), Monticello Dam (1959), Mount Vaca (1951), and Walter Springs (1959) 7.5' quadrangles. United States Board on Geographic Names (1957, p. 1) rejected the name "Monticello Reservoir" for the lake, and noted that the name "Lake Berryessa" was approved by congress on April 27, 1956.

Lake Camille [NAPA]: *lake,* 650 feet long, 2.25 miles southeast of downtown Napa (lat. 38°16'40" N, long. 122°15'10" W; sec. 13, T 5 N, R 4 W). Named on Napa (1951) 7.5' quadrangle.

Lake Cascade [CONTRA COSTA]: *lake,* 0.25 mile long, less than 1 mile north-northwest of Orinda (lat. 37°53'35" N, long. 122°11'05" W). Named on Briones Valley (1959) 7.5' quadrangle.

Lake Chabot [ALAMEDA]: *lake,* 2.25 miles long, behind a dam on San Leandro Creek 4.5 miles north-northwest of downtown Hayward (lat. 37°43'45" N, long. 122°07'15" W). Named on Hayward (1959) 7.5' quadrangle. The dam was built in 1868 and 1869; the name of the lake is for Anthony Chabot, a pioneer capitalist (Gudde, 1949, p. 63).

Lake Chabot [SOLANO]: *lake,* 3700 feet long, 2.5 miles north-northeast of downtown Vallejo (lat. 38°08'10" N, long. 122°14'10" W; sec. 6, T 3 N, R 3 W). Named on Cordelia (1951) 7.5' quadrangle.

Lake Chabot: see **Lake Temescal** [ALAMEDA].

Lake Creek: see **Lower Crystal Springs Reservoir** [SAN MATEO].

Lake Curry [NAPA]: *lake,* behind a dam on Suisun Creek 3.25 miles south-southwest of Mount Vaca (lat. 38°21'25" N, long. 122°07'25" W). Named on Fairfield North (1951) and Mount George (1951) 7.5' quadrangles. The name, given about 1925, honors Charles F. Curry; a congressman (Gudde, 1949, p. 86).

Lake Del Valle [ALAMEDA]: *lake,* 5.5 miles long, behind a dam on Arroyo Valle nearly 6 miles west-northwest of Mendenhall Springs (lat. 37°36'50" N, long. 121°44'40" W). Named on Mendenhall Springs (1956, photorevised 1971) 7.5' quadrangle.

Lake Elizabeth: see **Stivers Lagoon** [ALAMEDA].

Lake Ellen [NAPA]: *lake,* 1800 feet long, 4.25 miles northeast of Saint Helena (lat. 38°33'20" N, long. 122°25'20" W). Named on Saint Helena (1960) 7.5' quadrangle.

Lake Elsman [SANTA CLARA]: *lake,* nearly 1.5 miles long, behind a dam on Los Gatos Creek 7 miles south-southeast of downtown Los Gatos (lat. 37°07'50" N, long. 121°55'55" W; on W line sec. 24, T 9 S, R 1 W). Named on Laurel (1955) and Los Gatos (1953) 7.5' quadrangles.

Lake Frey [SOLANO]: *lake,* 3700 feet long, 8.5 miles west-northwest of Fairfield (lat. 38°17'35" N, long. 122°11'20" W; on W line sec. 10, T 5 N, R 3 W). Named on Mount George (1951) 7.5' quadrangle.

Lake Henne [NAPA]: *lake,* 1250 feet long, nearly 6 miles north of Saint Helena (lat. 38°35'15" N, long. 122°27'40" W; sec. 31, T 9 N, R 5 W). Named on Saint Helena (1960) 7.5' quadrangle.

Lake Hennessey [NAPA]: *lake,* behind a dam on Conn Creek 5 miles north of Yountville (lat. 38°28'50" N, long. 122°22'20" W; near SW cor. sec. 1, T 7 N, R 5 W); water of the lake covers most of Conn Valley. Named on Chiles Valley (1958), Rutherford (1951), Saint Helena (1960), and Yountville (1951) 7.5' quadrangles. Davis' (1948) map has the name "Conn Valley Res." for the feature.

Lake Herman [SOLANO]: *lake,* 4400 feet long, behind a dam on Sulphur Springs Creek 3 miles north of Benicia (lat. 38°05'35" N, long. 122°09' W; sec. 24, T 3 N, R 3 W). Named on Benicia (1959) 7.5' quadrangle. Herman Schussler had the dam built to form the lake by 1905 (Dillon, p. 217).

Lake Hinman [NAPA]: *lake,* 500 feet long, 5.25 miles south-southeast of Rutherford (lat. 38°23'30" N, long. 122°22'40" W; sec. 2, T 6 N, R 5 W). Named on Rutherford (1951) 7.5' quadrangle.

Lake Idell [SONOMA]: *lake,* 350 feet long, 0.5 mile west-northwest of Glen Ellen (lat. 38°22'05" N, long. 122°32'05" W). Named on Glen Ellen (1954) 7.5' quadrangle.

Lake Josephine [SONOMA]: *lake,* 700 feet long, 2.25 miles south of Glen Ellen (lat. 38°19'45" N, long. 122°31'20" W). Named on Glen Ellen (1954) 7.5' quadrangle.

Lake Lagunita: see **Lagunita** [SANTA CLARA].

Lake Lagunitas [MARIN]: *lake,* behind a dam on Lagunitas Creek 4 miles west-southwest of downtown San Rafael (lat. 37°56'50" N, long. 122°35'45" W). Named on San Rafael (1954) 7.5' quadrangle.

Lake Lucerne [SAN MATEO]: *lake,* nearly 1 mile long, 3 miles north of Pigeon Point along Arroyo de la Frijoles (lat. 37°13'25" N, long. 122°24'05" W). Named on Pigeon Point (1955) 7.5' quadrangle. Called Bean Hollow Lagoon on California Division of Highways' (1934) map. The lake called Bean Hollow Lagoon was made into a reservoir in 1923 and renamed Lucerne Lake by F.L. Lathrop, manager of the land company at the place (Brown, p. 50).

Lake Madigan [SOLANO]: *lake,* 1 mile long, 9 miles west-northwest of Fairfield (lat. 38°18'35" N, long. 122°11'35" W; sec. 4, T 5 N, R 3 W). Named on Mount George (1951) 7.5' quadrangle.

Lake Marie [NAPA]: *lake,* 1200 feet long, 12 miles south-southwest of Mount Vaca (lat. 38°15'30" N, long. 122°13'35" W; at SE cor. sec. 19, T 5 N, R 3 W). Named on Mount George (1951) 7.5' quadrangle.

Lake Mathilde [SAN MATEO]: *lake,* 650 feet long, 3 miles north-northwest of present Montara Knob (lat. 37°35'40" N, long. 122° 30'05" W). Named on San Mateo (1899) 15' quadrangle.

Lake McCoppin: see **Mission District** [SAN FRANCISCO].

Lake Merced [SAN FRANCISCO]: *lake,* 1.5 miles long, 2.5 miles west-southwest of Mount Davidson (lat. 37°43'10" N, long. 122° 29'35" W). Named on San Francisco South (1956) 7.5' quadrangle. A causeway divides the feature into two parts. Called Merced Lake on San Mateo (1915) 15' quadrangle, and called Laguna de la Merced on San Mateo (1942) 15' quadrangle, although United States Board on Geographic Names (1933, p. 513) rejected this name for the feature. Captain Heceta gave the name "Laguna de Nuestra Señora de la Merced" to the lake in 1775 (Davidson, p. 117). A United States Coast and Geodetic Survey map dated 1869 shows a tidal channel connecting the north end of the lake to the sea (Miller, R.C., p. 378).

Lake Merritt [ALAMEDA]: *lake,* nearly 1 mile long, in downtown Oakland (lat. 37°48'15" N, long. 122°15'15" W). Named on Oakland East (1959) and Oakland West (1959) 7.5' quadrangles. The feature originally was part of a tidal slough—called San Antonio Creek or San Antonio Slough—that forms present Oakland Inner Harbor; Dr. Samuel B. Merritt, mayor of Oakland in 1868, was instrumental in having a dam built to impound the tidal water and form present Lake Merritt, a salt-water lake with a broad causeway and a movable floodgate (Hoover, Rensch, and Rensch, p. 20). The lake first was called Lake Peralta, but was renamed Lake Merritt in 1891 (Gudde, 1969, p. 199).

Lake Mountain [SANTA CLARA]: *peak,* 6 miles north-northwest of Pacheco Peak (lat. 37°05'15" N, long. 121°19'15" W; near SW cor. sec. 4, T 10 S, R 6 E); the peak is 0.25 mile south-southwest of Shaeirn Lake. Named on Pacheco Peak (1955) 7.5' quadrangle.

Lake Newton [NAPA]: *lake,* 1000 feet long, 6 miles north of Saint Helena (lat. 38°35'35" N, long. 122°28'10" W; near NE cor. sec. 36, T 9 N, R 6 W). Named on Saint Helena (1960) 7.5' quadrangle.

Lake Oliver [SONOMA]: *lake,* 1600 feet long, 0.25 mile north-northwest of Plantation (lat. 38°35'40" N, long. 123°18'45" W). Named on Plantation (1977) 7.5' quadrangle. Plantation (1943) 7.5' quadrangle shows an intermittent lake.

Lake Orth [SONOMA]: *lake,* 800 feet long, 4 miles east-northeast of Mark West Springs (lat. 38°34'10" N, long. 122°39'10" W; sec. 5, T 8 N, R 7 W). Named on Mark West Springs (1958) 7.5' quadrangle.

Lake Orville [NAPA]: *lake,* 1050 feet long, 6 miles north of Saint Helena (lat. 38°35'25" N, long. 122°27'55" W; at W line sec. 31, T 9 N, R 5 W). Named on Saint Helena (1960) 7.5' quadrangle.

Lake Peralta: see **Lake Merritt** [ALAMEDA].

Lake Ralphine [SONOMA]: *lake,* 1750 feet long, 2.5 miles east-northeast of downtown Santa Rosa (lat. 38°27'20" N, long. 122° 40' W). Named on Santa Rosa (1954) 7.5' quadrangle.

Lake Ranch Reservoir [SANTA CLARA]: *lake,* 2000 feet long, 2.25 miles east of Bielawski Mountain (lat. 37°13'10" N, long. 122° 03' W; sec. 23, T 8 S, R 2 W). Named on Castle Rock Ridge (1955) 7.5' quadrangle.

Lake Sonoma [SONOMA]: *intermittent lake,* behind a dam on Dry Creek 2 miles north-northeast of Skaggs Springs (lat. 38°43'10" N, long. 123°00'30" W). Named on Warm Springs Dam (1978) 7.5' quadrangle.

Lake Suttonfield [SONOMA]: *lake,* 1700 feet long, 0.5 mile southeast of Glen Ellen (lat. 38°21'20" N, long. 122°30'55" W). Named on Glen Ellen (1954) 7.5' quadrangle.

Lake Temescal [ALAMEDA]: *lake,* 0.25 mile long, behind a dam on Temescal Creek 3.25 miles northeast of downtown Oakland (lat. 37°50'50" N, long. 122°13'50" W). Named on Oakland East (1959) 7.5' quadrangle. Called Temescal Lake on Concord (1897) 15' quadrangle. The feature first was called Lake Chabot, for Anthony Chabot (Mosier and Mosier, p. 49-50). The dam that forms the lake was built in 1866 (Hoover, Rensch, and Rensch, p. 4).

Lake Tolay: see **Lakeville** [SONOMA].

Lakeville [SONOMA]: *village,* 5.5 miles east-southeast of the city of Petaluma on the east bank of Petaluma River (lat. 38°11'55" N, long. 122°32'50" W). Named on Petaluma River (1954) 7.5' quadrangle. Postal authorities established Lakeville post office in 1859, discontinued it in 1874, reestablished it in 1875, and discontinued it in 1920 (Salley, p. 116). Lakeville was one of the earliest landing places along the river and was named for Lake Tolay, a large lake that lay in the hills east of the river (Miller, J.T., p. 19). William Bihler drained the lake after 1859 and planted potatoes and corn there—Lake Tolay was named for an Indian chief (Heig, p. 2).

Lake Whitehead [NAPA]: *lake,* 700 feet long, 6 miles north of Saint Helena (lat. 38°35'35" N, long. 122°27'55" W; near W line sec. 31, T 9 N, R 5 W). Named on Saint Helena (1960) 7.5' quadrangle.

La Laguna: see **Stivers Lagoon** [ALAMEDA].

La Laguna Seca [SANTA CLARA]: *land grant,* mainly between Coyote and Madrone. Named on Morgan Hill (1955), Mount Sizer (1955), and Santa Teresa Hills (1953) 7.5' quadrangles. Juan Alvirez received 4 leagues in 1834; L.C. Bull and others claimed 19,973 acres patented in 1865 (Cowan, p. 44). The lake called Laguna Seca is on the grant. The place also was known as Refugio de la Laguna Seca; after Alvirez sold the land to William Fisher in 1845, American travelers often referred to it as Fisher's Ranche (Arbuckle, p. 18). Postal authorities established Laguna Seca post office on the grant in 1853 and discontinued it in 1855 (Salley, p. 114).

Lambert: see **Healdsburg** [SONOMA].

Lambert Creek [SAN MATEO]: *stream,* flows 1.25 miles to Peters Creek 2.5 miles east-southeast of Mindego Hill (lat. 37°17'45" N, long. 122°11'05" W; sec. 27, T 7 S, R 3 W). Named on Mindego Hill (1961) 7.5' quadrangle. The name recalls Lambert Dornberger, who started a ranch at the head of the creek in the 1850's (Brown, p. 46).

Lamb Ridge [SANTA CLARA]: *ridge,* northwest-trending, 2.5 miles long, 5 miles northeast of Mount Day (lat. 37°28'15" N, long. 121° 37' W). Named on Eylar Mountain (1955) and Mount Day (1955) 7.5' quadrangles.

Lancel Creek [SONOMA]: *stream,* flows 1.25 miles to Dutch Bill Creek 1 mile north-northwest of Occidental (lat. 38°25'20" N, long. 122°57'05" W; sec. 27, T 7 N, R 10 W). Named on Camp Meeker (1954) 7.5' quadrangle. North Fork enters from the north less than 0.5 mile above the mouth of the main stream; it is 1.5 miles long and is named on Camp Meeker (1954) 7.5' quadrangle.

Lands End [SANTA CLARA]: *locality,* 4.5 miles southeast of Loma Prieta, where the land surface slopes abruptly into the canyon of Uvas Creek (lat. 37°03'55" N, long. 121°47'10" W; sec. 18, T 10 S, R 2 E). Named on Loma Prieta (1955) 7.5' quadrangle. Los Gatos (1919) 15' quadrangle shows a building situated at the end of the road leading to the place.

Lands End [SAN FRANCISCO]: *promontory,* 0.5 mile northeast of Point Lobos along the coast (lat. 37°47'20" N, long. 122°30'20" W). Named on San Francisco North (1956) 7.5' quadrangle.

Lands End: see **Point Bonita** [MARIN].

Land Slough: see **Tree Slough** [SOLANO].

Lane Hill [SAN MATEO]: *peak,* 5 miles southwest of La Honda (lat. 37°16'25" N, long. 122°20'25" W; near SE cor.sec. 36, T 7 S, R 5 W). Altitude 1240 feet. Named on La Honda (1961) 7.5' quadrangle.

Lang Canyon [ALAMEDA]: *canyon,* drained by a stream that flows 3 miles to Arroyo Valle 2.5 miles south-southwest of Mendenhall Springs (lat. 37°33'10" N, long. 121°39'55" W; sec. 29, T 4 S, R 3 E). Named on Cedar Mountain (1956) and Mendenhall Springs (1956) 7.5' quadrangles. The name commemorates Henry W. Lang, who worked in the neighborhood about 1900 (Mosier and Mosier, p. 50).

Langley Creek [SAN MATEO]: *stream,* flows 1.5 miles to La Honda Creek less than 1 mile north of La Honda (lat. 37°19'50" N, long. 122°16'10" W; near N line sec. 14, T 7 S, E 4 W); the stream heads near Langley Hill. Named on La Honda (1961) and Mindego Hill (1961) 7.5' quadrangles. The stream also was called Baker Creek for a rancher who had land along it during and after the 1860's (Brown, p. 46).

Langley Hill [SAN MATEO]: *peak,* 1.5 miles north-northwest of Mindego Hill (lat. 37°19'55" N, long. 122°14'25" W; near SW cor. sec. 7, T 7 S, R 3 W). Altitude 2256 feet. Named on Mindego Hill (1961) 7.5' quadrangle. Langley ranch was on the northeast side of the peak after 1857 (Brown, p. 46).

Lang's Landing: see **Patterson Landing** [ALAMEDA].

Lansdale: see **San Anselmo** [MARIN].

La Polka [SANTA CLARA]: *land grant,* 4.5 miles northeast of Gilroy. Named on Gilroy (1955) 7.5' quadrangle. Isabel Ortega received the land in 1833 as her share of San Ysidro grant; Bernard Murphy acquired the land in 1849 and reportedly gave it the name of the popular dance—the land was patented to Martin J.C. Murphy in 1860 (Arbuckle, p. 19).

La Punta de las Barrancas blancas: see **Point Reyes** [MARIN] (1).

La Purisima Concepcion [SANTA CLARA]: *land grant,* 5 miles south of downtown Palo Alto. Named on Cupertino (1961), Mindego Hill (1961), Mountain View (1961), and Palo Alto (1961) 7.5' quadrangles. Jose Gorgonio and others received 1 league in 1840; Juana Briones claimed 4439 acres patented in 1871 (Cowan, p. 65). United States Board on Geographic Names (1933, p. 449) rejected the form "La Purissima Concepcion" for the name.

Larios Canyon [SANTA CLARA]: *canyon,* drained by a stream that flows nearly 3.5 miles to Coyote Lake 4.25 miles east-northeast of San Martin (lat. 37°07'10" N, long. 121°32'40" W; near E line sec. 29, T 9 S, R 4 E). Named on Gilroy (1955) and Mount Sizer (1955) 7.5' quadrangle.

Larios Peak [SANTA CLARA]: *peak,* 5.5 miles east-northeast of San Martin (lat. 37°07'20" N, long. 121°31'10" W; sec. 27, T 9 S, R 4 E); the peak is south of Larios Canyon. Altitude 2766 feet. Named on Gilroy (1955) 7.5' quadrangle.

Larkin's Landing: see **Mowry Landing** [ALAMEDA].

Larkmead [NAPA]: *locality,* 3.25 miles east-southeast of Calistoga along Southern Pacific Railroad (lat. 38°33'30" N, long. 122°31'20" W). Named on Calistoga (1958) 7.5' quadrangle.

Larkspur [MARIN]: *city,* 3 miles south of downtown San Rafael (lat. 38°55'50" N, long. 122°32' W). Named on San Rafael (1954) 7.5' quadrangle. Postal authorities established Larkspur post office in 1891 (Frickstad, p. 88), and the city incorporated in 1908. Charles W. Wright bought the land in 1887 and laid out the town; Mrs. Wright is credited with naming the place for flowers in the neighborhood—she mistook native lupine for larkspur (Teather, p. 35).

Larkspur Creek [MARIN]: *stream,* flows 3.5 miles to Corte Madera Creek 2.5 miles south-southeast of downtown San Rafael (lat. 37° 56'25" N, long. 122°31'05" W). Named on San Rafael (1954) 7.5' quadrangle. Teather (p. 3) gave the alternate name "Arroyo Holon" for the stream, which drains Baltimore Canyon.

Larrabee Gulch [SANTA CLARA]: *canyon,* drained by a stream that flows 1.25 miles to Almaden Reservoir 1.25 miles south-southwest of New Almaden (lat. 37°09'30" N, long. 121°49'40" W). Named on Santa Teresa Hills (1953) 7.5' quadrangle.

Las Animas [SANTA CLARA]: *land grant,* mainly west and south of Gilroy. Named on Chittenden (1955), Gilroy (1955), Mount Madonna (1955), and Watsonville East (1955) 7.5' quadrangles. Mariano Castro received the land in 1802 and Josefa Romero de Castro received it in 1835; heirs of Jose Maria Sanchez claimed 26,519 acres patented in 1873 (Cowan, p. 15). *Las Animas* means "the souls" in Spanish and refers to All Souls' Day; the grant also was known by the names "Carnadero" and "La Brea" (Gudde, 1949, p. 12). American pioneers often referred to the grant by the name of its augmentation, Sitio de la Brea or Cañada de la Brea (Arbuckle, p. 19).

Las Animas: see **Cañada de San Felipe y las Animas** [SANTA CLARA].

Las Animas Creek [SANTA CLARA]: *stream,* flows 6.25 miles to Anderson Lake nearly 4.5 miles east-southeast of Coyote (lat. 37° 12'15" N, long. 121°39'40" W); the stream is partly on Cañada de San Felipe y las Animas grant. Named on Lick Observatory (1955) and Morgan Hill (1955) 7.5' quadrangles.

Las Animas Hills: see **Cañada de San Felipe y las Animas** [SANTA CLARA].

Las Baulines [MARIN]: *land grant,* around Bolinas Lagoon. Named on Bolinas (1954) and San Rafael (1954) 7.5' quadrangles. Gregorio Briones received the land in 1846 and claimed 8911 acres patented in 1866 (Cowan, p. 18).

Las Bolsas del Hambre: see **Cañada del Hambre y las Bolsas** [CONTRA COSTA].

Las Cuevas: see **Brushy Peak** [ALAMEDA].

Las Gallinas [MARIN]: *locality,* 6.25 miles south-southeast of downtown Novato (lat. 38°01'15" N, long. 122°32'15" W); the place is on San Pedro Santa Margarita y las Gallinas grant. Named on Novato (1954) 7.5' quadrangle.

Las Gallinas: see **San Pedro Santa Margarita y las Gallinas** [MARIN].

Lash Lighter Basin [SAN FRANCISCO]: *water feature,* 4.5 miles east of Mount Davidson along San Francisco Bay north of Hunters Point (lat. 37°44'20" N, long. 122°22' W). Named on Hunters Point (1956, photorevised 1980) 7.5' quadrangle. United States Board on Geographic Names (1976b, p. 2) gave the name "Lighter Basin" as a variant.

Las Juntas [CONTRA COSTA]:

(1) *land grant,* extends from the city of Walnut Creek to Martinez. Named on Benicia (1959), Briones Valley (1959), Vine Hill (1959), and Walnut Creek (1959) 7.5' quadrangles. William Welsh received 3 leagues in 1844; Welsh's estate claimed 13,293 acres patented in 1870 (Cowan, p. 43).

(2) *locality,* 2 miles north of Walnut Creek civic center along Southern Pacific Railroad (lat. 37°55'55" N, long. 122°03'10" W); the place is on Las Juntas grant. Named on Walnut Creek (1959) 7.5' quadrangle. Called Oakleigh on Concord (1915) 15' quadrangle.

Las Lagrimas: see **Edenvale** [SANTA CLARA].

Las Llagas de Nuestro Padre San Francisco: see **San Francisco de las Llagas** [SANTA CLARA].

Las Lomas [SONOMA]: *locality,* 2.25 miles south-southeast of Big Mountain (lat. 38°40'40" N, long. 123°08'05" W; near N line sec. 36, T 10 N, R 12 W). Named on Tombs Creek (1978) 7.5' quadrangle. Postal authorities established Las Lomas post office in 1915 and discontinued it in 1916 (Frickstad, p. 196).

Las Lomas Bajas: see **New Almaden** [SANTA CLARA].

Las Papas: see **Twin Peaks** [SAN FRANCISCO].

Las Papas Hill: see **Twin Peaks** [SAN FRANCISCO].

Las Posita Creek: see **Arroyo Las Positas** [ALAMEDA].

Las Positas [ALAMEDA]: *land grant,* at and near Livermore. Named on Altamont (1953), Livermore (1961), and Tassajara (1953) 7.5' quadrangles. Salvic Pacheco received 2 leagues in 1839; Jose Noriega and Robert Livermore claimed 8880 acres patented in 1872 (Cowan, p. 63; Cowan used the form "Pozitas" for the name).

Las Pulgas: see **Pulgas** [SAN MATEO].

Las Putas [NAPA]: *land grant,* at and near Lake Berryessa. Named on Brooks (1959), Chiles Valley (1958), Lake Berryessa (1959), and Walter Springs (1959) 7.5' quadrangles. Jose de Jesus Berryessa and Sixto Berryessa received 8 leagues in 1843; M. Anastasio Higuera de Berryessa and others claimed 35,516 acres patented in 1863 (Cowan, p. 65-66).

Las Tampas Peak: see **Las Trampas Peak** [CONTRA COSTA].

Las Trampas Creek [CONTRA COSTA]: *stream,* flows 11.5 miles to join San Ramon Creek and form Walnut Creek (1) near Walnut Creek civic center (lat. 37°53'50" N, long. 122°03'30" W). Named on Las Trampas Ridge (1959) and Walnut Creek (1959) 7.5' quadrangles.

Las Trampas Peak [CONTRA COSTA]: *peak,* 3.5 miles west-northwest of Danville (lat. 37°50' N, long. 122°03'50" W; sec. 22, T 1 S, R 2 W); the peak is near the northwest end of Las Trampas Ridge. Altitude 1827 feet. Named on Las Trampas Ridge (1959) 7.5' quadrangle. United States Board on Geographic Names (1933, p. 450) rejected the names "Las Tampas Peak" and "Sugarloaf Peak" for the feature.

Las Trampas Ridge [CONTRA COSTA]: *ridge,* northwest-trending, 6 miles long, center 2 miles west-southwest of Danville (lat. 37°48'45" N, long. 122°01'35" W). Named on Diablo (1953) and Las Trampas Ridge (1959) 7.5' quadrangles. Gudde (1969, p. 173) reported testimony that traps were set on or near the ridge to catch elk—*trampa* means "trap" or "snare" in Spanish.

Las Uvas [SANTA CLARA]: *land grant,* west of Morgan Hill and San Martin. Named on Loma Prieta (1955), Morgan Hill (1955), Mount Madona (1955), and Santa Teresa Hills (1953) 7.5' quadrangles. Lorenzo Pineda received the land in 1842; M.J.C. Murphy claimed 11,080 acres patented in 1860 (Cowan, p. 106). The name is from the abundance of wild grapes along watercourses in the neighborhood—*las uvas* means "the grapes" in Spanish (Arbuckle, p. 21).

Lathrop Hot Sulphur and Mud Spring: see **Calistoga** [NAPA].

Laton [SONOMA]: *locality,* 2 miles east-northeast of present Jenner at the end of a branch of Northwestern Pacific Railroad (lat. 38°27'55" N, long. 123°04'55" W). Named on Duncans Mills (1921) 15' quadrangle.

Laurel Creek [ALAMEDA]: *stream,* flows less than 1 mile to Amador Valley 0.5 mile south-southeast of Dublin (lat. 37°41'30" N, long. 121°55'50" W). Named on Dublin (1961) 7.5' quadrangle.

Laurel Creek [SAN MATEO]: *stream,* flows 2.5 miles to lowlands along San Francisco Bay 2.5 miles southeast of downtown San Mateo (lat. 37°32'10" N, long. 122°17'45" W). Named on San Mateo (1956) 7.5' quadrangle. The stream was called Arroyo de los Laureles in Spanish times, and Laureles Creek in early American times (Brown, p. 47).

Laurel Creek [SOLANO]: *stream,* flows 4 miles to lowlands 3 miles north-northeast of Fairfield (lat. 38°17'15" N, long. 122°01'10" W). Named on Fairfield North (1951) and Fairfield South (1949) 7.5' quadrangles.

Laurel Creek: see **Cottrell** [SAN MATEO].

Laurel Dell Camp [CONTRA COSTA]: *locality,* nearly 1 mile west-southwest of Mount Diablo (lat. 37°52'30" N, long. 121°55'35" W; sec. 1, T 1 S, R 1 W). Named on Clayton (1953) 7.5' quadrangle.

Laurel Dell Campground [MARIN]: *locality,* 3.5 miles east-northeast of Bolinas (lat. 37°55'25" N, long. 122°37'35" W). Named on Bolinas (1954) 7.5' quadrangle.

Laureles Creek: see **Laurel Creek** [SAN MATEO].

Laurel Hill [SANTA CLARA]: *peak,* 3.5 miles west of Madrone (lat. 37°09'15" N, long. 121°44' W). Altitude 1145 feet. Named on Morgan Hill (1955) 7.5' quadrangle.

Lauterwasser Creek [CONTRA COSTA]: *stream,* flows 2.5 miles to San Pablo Creek 1 mile northwest of Orinda (lat. 37°53'25" N, long. 122°11'40" W). Named on Briones Valley (1959) 7.5' quadrangle. The name commemorates F.P. Lauterwasser, an early settler in the neighborhood (Gudde, 1969, p. 174).

Laverne: see **Mill Valley** [MARIN] (2).

Lawhead Canyon: see **Lawhead Creek** [SONOMA].

Lawhead Creek [SONOMA]: *stream,* flows 1 mile to Gray Creek 6 miles northeast of Cazadero (lat. 38°35'30" N, long. 123°00'20" W). Named on Cazadero (1978) 7.5' quadrangle. On Guerneville (1955) 7.5' quadrangle, the canyon of the stream is called Lawhead Canyon.

Lawler Ravine [CONTRA COSTA]: *canyon,* drained by a stream that flows 2.25 miles to lowlands along Suisun Bay 3 miles west-southwest of Pittsburg (lat. 38°01'10" N, long. 121°56'05" W). Named on Clayton (1953) and Honker Bay (1953) 7.5' quadrangles.

Lawndale [SONOMA]: *locality,* 1.25 miles west-northwest of Kenwood (lat. 38°25'10" N, long. 122°39'15" W). Named on Kenwood (1954) 7.5' quadrangle.

Lawndale: see **Colma** [SAN MATEO].

Lawrence [SANTA CLARA]: *locality,* 6.5 miles west-northwest of downtown San Jose along Southern Pacific Railroad (lat. 37°22'15" N, long. 121°59'45" W; sec. 32, T 6 S, R 1 W). Named on San Jose West (1961) 7.5' quadrangle. Postal authorities established Lawrence post office in 1887 and discontinued it in 1935; the name is for Albert C. Lawrence, a settler in the 1850's (Salley, p. 120).

Lawson Hill [CONTRA COSTA]: *peak,* 4.5 miles north of Orinda (lat. 37°56'35" N, long. 122°11'30" W). Named on Briones Valley (1959) 7.5' quadrangle.

Leddy: see **Santa Rosa** [SONOMA].

Ledgewood Creek [NAPA-SOLANO]: *stream,* heads in Napa County and flows 12 miles to marsh 1.5 miles south-southwest of downtown Fairfield in Solano County (lat. 38°13'45" N, long. 122°03'15" W). Named on Fairfield North (1951) and Fairfield South (1949) 7.5' quadrangles.

Lee Lake [SONOMA]: *lake,* 300 feet long, 5.5 miles north-northwest of Sears Point (lat. 38°13'10" N, long. 122°29'45" W). Named on Sears Point (1951) 7.5' quadrangle.

Leesley and Dexter Canyon: see **Dexter Canyon** [SANTA CLARA].

Le Franc: see **Campbell** [SANTA CLARA].

Leisure Town [SOLANO]: *locality,* 3 miles east-northeast of downtown Vacaville (lat. 38°22'10" N, long. 121°56'45" W). Named on Allendale (1953, photorevised 1968 and 1973) and Elmira (1953, photorevised 1980) 7.5' quadrangles.

Lejuanjelua Bay: see **Point San Quentin** [MARIN].

Lemon Hill [NAPA]: *peak,* 3.5 miles south of Mount Vaca (lat. 38° 21' N, long. 122°07'10" W). Altitude 1060 feet. Named on Fairfield North (1951) 7.5' quadrangle.

Leoma Lakes [NAPA]: *lakes,* two connected, 1050 feet long, 7 miles southwest of Mount Vaca along White Creek (lat. 38°20'35" N, long. 122°12'25" W; near NE cor. sec. 29, T 6 N, R 3 W). Named on Mount George (1951) 7.5' quadrangle.

Leona [ALAMEDA]: *locality,* 5 miles east-southeast of downtown Oakland (lat. 37°46'55" N, long. 122°10'40" W). Named on Concord (1915) 15' quadrangle.

Leona Creek: see **Lion Creek** [ALAMEDA].

Leon Creek: see **Arroyo Leon** [SAN MATEO].

Leslie: see **Homestead** [SAN MATEO].

Letton Springs: see **Lytton** [SONOMA].

Levantahyume: see **Molinos** [SONOMA].

Lewis: see **Mococo** [CONTRA COSTA]; **Mount Lewis** [SANTA CLARA].

Lewis Creek [SONOMA]: *stream,* flows 1.25 miles to Felder Creek 6.25 miles south of Glen Ellen (lat. 38°16'20" N, long. 122°30'35" W). Named on Glen Ellen (1954) 7.5' quadrangle.

Lewis Gulch: see **Copper Mine Gulch** [MARIN].

Lexington [SANTA CLARA]: *locality,* 2 miles south of Los Gatos along Los Gatos Creek (lat. 37°11'50" N, long. 121°59'15" W; sec. 32, T 8 S, R 1 W). Named on Los Gatos (1919) 15' quadrangle. Water of Lexington Reservoir now covers the site. Postal authorities established Lexington post office in 1861 and discontinued it in 1873 (Frickstad, p. 174). Zachariah Jones bought a sawmill at the place and laid out a town that he called Jones Mill, but in 1860 he sold the mill and 480 acres; John P. Hennings bought some of the property and changed the name of the community to Lexington for his home town of Lexington, Kentucky (Bruntz, p. 7).

Lexington Reservoir [SANTA CLARA]: *lake,* 2.5 miles long, behind a dam on Los Gatos Creek 1.5 miles south-southwest of Los Gatos (lat. 37°12'05" N, long. 121°59'20" W; sec. 29, T 8 S, R 1 W); water of the lake covers the site of Lexington. Named on Castle Rock Ridge (1955) and Los Gatos (1953) 7.5' quadrangles.

Leyden Creek [ALAMEDA]: *stream,* flows 2.5 miles to Alameda Creek 6.5 miles south-southeast of Sunol (lat. 37°30'35" N, long. 121°49'40" W; sec. 11, T 5 S, R 1 E). Named on La Costa Valley (1960) 7.5' quadrangle. The name commemorates James Lydon, who settled near the mouth of the stream in the 1870's (Mosier and Mosier, p. 51).

Libantiliyami: see **Russian River** [SONOMA].

Liberty [MARIN]: *locality,* 4.5 miles northeast of Bolinas along Lagunitas Creek (lat. 37°57'15" N, long. 122°37'30" W). Named on Tamalpais (1897) 15' quadrangle. Water of Alpine Lake now covers the site. Vincent Liberty built a house for his family and accommodations for guests at the place in 1881 (Fairley, 1985, p. 38).

Liberty [SONOMA]: *locality,* 3 miles south of Cotati along Petaluma and Santa Rosa Railroad (lat. 38°17'05" N, long. 122°42'05" W). Named on Cotati (1954) 7.5' quadrangle. California Division of Highways' (1934) map shows a place called Merritt located along the railroad between Liberty and Denman, and a place called Dangers located along the railroad between Liberty and Divide.

Liberty Cut [SOLANO]: *water feature,* extends south from Yolo County into Solano County, where it joins Prospect Slough 9 miles north of Rio Vista (lat. 38°17'10" N, long. 121°39'50" W); the feature is east of Liberty Island. Named on Liberty Island (1978) 7.5' quadrangle.

Liberty Farms [SOLANO]: *locality,* 10.5 miles north of Rio Vista (lat. 38°18'45" N, long. 121°41'35" W). Named on Liberty Island (1978) 7.5' quadrangle. Postal authorities established Liberty Farms post office in 1952 (Frickstad, p. 192).

Liberty Gulch [MARIN]: *canyon,* drained by a stream that flows less than 1 mile to Alpine Lake 4.5 miles northeast of Bolinas (lat. 37° 57'35" N, long. 122°37'40" W); the place called Liberty was near the mouth of the canyon. Named on Bolinas (1954) 7.5' quadrangle. The feature first was called Curtis Gulch, for Loomis Curtis, who had a dairy ranch there in the 1850's before Vincent Liberty took over the property (Fairly, 1985, p. 38).

Liberty Island [SOLANO]: *area,* 9 miles north of Rio Vista in Yolo Bypass on Solano-Yolo County line, mainly in Solano County (lat. 38°17' N, long. 121°40'45" W). Named on Liberty Island (1978) and Rio Vista (1978) 7.5' quadrangles.

Liberty Island Ferry [SOLANO]: *locality,* 5.5 miles north of Rio Vista along Cache Slough (lat. 38°14'20" N, long. 121°41' W); the place is at the south end of Liberty Island. Named on Rio Vista (1978) 7.5' quadrangle.

Libfarm [SOLANO]: *locality,* 6.5 miles east-southeast of Dixon along Sacramento Northern Railroad (lat. 38°24'05" N, long. 121° 42'45" W; near NE cor. sec. 2, T 6 N, R 2 E). Named on Saxon (1952) 7.5' quadrangle.

Lichau Creek [SONOMA]: *stream,* flows 8.5 miles to Petaluma River 4 miles south-southeast of Cotati (lat. 38°16'25" N, long. 122°40'35" W). Named on Cotati (1954) and Glen Ellen (1954) 7.5' quadrangles.

Lick [SANTA CLARA]: *locality,* 4 miles southeast of downtown San Jose along Southern Pacific Railroad, where a rail line branches to Alamitos (lat. 37°17'10" N, long. 121°50'40" W). Named on San Jose East (1961) 7.5' quadrangle. Called Hillsdale on San Jose (1899) 15' quadrangle. Postal authorities established Hillsdale post office in 1887 and discontinued it in 1899 (Frickstad, p. 173). A stopping place called Four Mile House, named for its distance from San Jose, was near the site of Hillsdale before construction of the railroad (*San Jose Mercury-News, California Today Magazine,* October 23, 1977).

Lidell: see **Aetna Springs** [NAPA].

Lighter Basin: see **Lash Lighter Basin** [SAN FRANCISCO].

Lilienthal: see **Camp Lilienthal** [MARIN].

Lily Gulch [MARIN]: *canyon,* drained by a stream that flows less than 1 mile to Alpine Lake 4 miles northeast of Bolinas (lat. 37° 57'10" N, long. 122°37'55" W). Named on Bolinas (1954) 7.5' quadrangle.

Lily Lake [MARIN]: *lake,* 50 feet long, 4 miles northeast of Bolinas (lat. 37°57'15" N, long. 122°38'05" W); the feature is in Lily Gulch. Named on Bolinas (1954) 7.5' quadrangle.

Limantour Spit [MARIN]: *relief feature,* sand spit, 2.5 miles long, that separates Estero de Limantour from Drakes Bay 7 miles east-northeast of the lighthouse at Point Reyes (lat. 38°01'45" N, long. 122°54'15" W). Named on Drakes Bay (1953) 7.5' quadrangle. The name recalls Jose Yves Limantour, who wrecked the bark *Ayacucho* on the spit in 1841 (Teather, p. 36-37).

Lime Hill: see **Calera Valley** [SAN MATEO].

Limekiln Canyon [SANTA CLARA]:

(1) *canyon,* drained by a stream that flows 2.25 miles to Lexington Reservoir 1.5 miles south of Los Gatos (lat. 37°12'05" N, long. 121°58'35" W). Named on Los Gatos (1953) 7.5' quadrangle.

(2) *canyon,* drained by a stream that flows 1.25 miles to Llagas Creek 3.25 miles south-southeast of New Almaden (lat. 37°08'20" N, long. 121°47'05" W). Named on Santa Teresa Hills (1953) 7.5' quadrangle.

Lime Point [MARIN]: *promontory,* 2.25 miles south of downtown Sausalito along San Francisco Bay (lat. 37°49'30" N, long. 122°28'40" W). Named on San Francisco North (1956) 7.5' quadrangle. Called Lime Rks. on Ringgold's (1850a) map. Ayala named the feature Punta de San Carlos in 1775 for his ship (Galvin, p. 85; Wagner, H.R., p. 497).

Lime Point Military Reservation: see **Fort Baker Military Reservation** [MARIN].

Limerick: see **San Ramon** [CONTRA COSTA] (3).

Lime Ridge [CONTRA COSTA]: *ridge,* north- to northwest-trending, 4 miles long, 6 miles northwest of Mount Diablo (lat. 37°56'30" N, long. 121°59'30" W). Named on Clayton (1953) and Walnut Creek (1959) 7.5' quadrangles. Burned lime was produced from limestone that crops out on the ridge (Laizure, 1927a, p. 15).

Lime Rocks: see **Lime Point** [MARIN].

Lincoln: see **Campbell** [SANTA CLARA].

Linda Falls [NAPA]: *waterfall,* nearly 4 mile north-northeast of Saint Helena along Conn Creek (lat. 38°33'20" N, long. 122°26'30" W). Named on Saint Helena (1960) 7.5' quadrangle.

Linda Mar: see **Pedro Valley** [SAN MATEO].

Lindsey Slough [SOLANO]: *water feature,* joins Cache Slough 6 miles north of Rio Vista (lat. 38°14'40" N, long. 121°41'20" W). Named on Dozier (1952), Liberty Island (1978), and Rio Vista (1978) 7.5' quadrangles.

Lingos Landing [SOLANO]: *locality,* 4.5 miles south-southwest of Denverton along Montezuma Slough (lat. 38°09'35" N, long. 121° 55'30" W). Named on Denverton (1953) 7.5' quadrangle.

Lion Canyon [NAPA]: *canyon,* drained by a stream that flows 1.25 miles to Gosling Canyon 5.5 miles south-southeast of Berryessa Peak (lat. 38°35'25" N, long. 122°09'10" W). Named on Lake Berryessa (1959) 7.5' quadrangle.

Lion Canyon [SANTA CLARA]: *canyon,* drained by a stream that flows 1 mile to Grizzly Creek 4 miles south-southeast of Isabel Valley (lat. 37°15'30" N, long. 121°30'35" W; sec. 11, T 8 S, R 4 E). Named on Isabel Valley (1955) 7.5' quadrangle.

Lion Creek [ALAMEDA]: *stream,* enters San Leandro Bay 5 miles southeast of downtown Oakland (lat. 37°45'05" N, long. 122°12'40" W). Named on Oakland East (1959) 7.5' quadrangle, which does not show the stream through the urban area. Called East Creek on Concord (1897) 15' quadrangle. The stream first was called Arroyo del Leona, and then Leona Creek—*leona* means "lion" in Spanish (Mosier and Mosier, p. 51). A promontory at the mouth of Lion Creek was given the name "Garretson Point" in 1982 to honor Frederick Van Hon Garretson, a reporter for *Oakland Tribune,* who publicized the need for saving San Francisco Bay (Mosier and Mosier, p. 39).

Lions Head Rock [SONOMA]: *relief feature,* 3 miles north-northwest of Cazadero (lat. 38°34'15" N, long. 123°06'05" W; sec. 5, T 8 N, R 11 W). Named on Cazadero (1978) 7.5' quadrangle.

Lions Peak [SANTA CLARA]: *peak,* 5 miles south-southeast of Morgan Hill (lat. 37°03'25" N, long. 121°37'50" W). Named on Mount Madonna (1955) 7.5' quadrangle. United States Board on Geographic Names (1973a, p. 2) approved the name "Day Creek" for a stream that heads east of Lions Peak and flows 2 miles to an unnamed stream 2.2 miles northwest of Gilroy (lat. 37°02'09" N, long. 121°35'45" W); the name "Day" commemorates an early landowner in the neighborhood.

Little Arthur Creek [SANTA CLARA]: *stream,* flows 6.25 miles to Uvas Creek 3 miles east-northeast of Mount Madonna (lat. 37°01'40" N, long. 121°39'20" W). Named on Loma Prieta (1955) and Mount Madonna (1955) 7.5' quadrangles.

Little Austin Creek: see **Gray Creek** [SONOMA].

Little Black Mountain [SONOMA]:

(1) *peak,* 3 miles northwest of Jenner (lat. 38°29'05" N, long. 123° 09'20" W). Altitude 865 feet. Named on Arched Rock (1977) 7.5' quadrangle.

(2) *peak,* 2 miles southwest of Cazadero (lat. 38°30'50" N, long. 123°07'10" W; near NW cor. sec. 30, T 8 N, R 11 W). Named on Cazadero (1978) 7.5' quadrangle.

Little Boulder Creek [SAN MATEO]: *stream,* heads in Santa Cruz County and flows 1.5 miles to Pescadero Creek nearly 7 miles south-southeast of Mindego Hill (lat. 37°13'05" N, long. 122°11'05" W; sec. 22, T 8 S, R 3 W). Named on Big Basin (1955) 7.5' quadrangle.

Little Briggs Creek [SONOMA]: *stream,* flows 3 miles to Briggs Creek 5 miles west of Mount Saint Helena (lat. 38°40'40" N, long. 122°43'35" W; near NE cor. sec. 34, T 10 N, R 8 W). Named on Mount Saint Helena (1959) 7.5' quadrangle.

Little Bull Valley [CONTRA COSTA]: *canyon,* 1 mile long, 3 miles west-northwest of Martinez (lat. 38°02' N, long. 122°11'05" W); the feature is 0.5 mile southeast of Big Bull Valley. Named on Benicia (1959) 7.5' quadrangle.

Little Butano Creek [SAN MATEO]: *stream,* flows 4.5 miles to Butano Creek 4.5 miles north of Franklin Point (lat. 37°13' N, long. 122°21'05" W). Named on Franklin Point (1955) 7.5' quadrangle. Brown (p. 48) noted that an area located where Little Butano Creek leaves the highlands is called Little Butano Flat.

Little Butano Flat: see **Little Butano Creek** [SAN MATEO].

Little Carson Creek [MARIN]: *stream,* flows 2 miles to Lagunitas Creek 3.5 miles north-northeast of Bolinas (lat. 37°57'50" N, long. 122°39'50" W); the junction with Lagunitas Creek now is in Kent Lake. Named on Mount Tamalpais (1950) 15' quadrangle. On a map of 1873, the canyon of the stream is called Puerto Zuelo Lagunitas (Gudde, 1949, p. 180).

Little Chicken Hollow [SAN MATEO]: *canyon,* 1 mile long, 4.25 miles west-southwest of La Honda on the upper reaches of Honsinger Creek (lat. 37°17'15" N, long. 122°20'15" W); the canyon is north of Big Chicken Hollow. Named on La Honda (1961) 7.5' quadrangle.

Little Coyote Creek [SANTA CLARA]: *stream,* flows nearly 5 miles to Middle Fork Coyote Creek 2.25 miles south of Mount Sizer (lat. 37°10'55" N, long. 121°30'20" W; sec. 2, T 9 S, R 4 E). Named on Mount Sizer (1955) 7.5' quadrangle.

Little Coyote Point [SAN MATEO]: *promontory,* 3.5 miles east of downtown San Mateo along San Francisco Bay on Brewer Island (lat. 37°34'25" N, long. 122°15'50" W; sec. 23, T 4 S, R 4 W). Named on San Mateo (1956) 7.5' quadrangle. San Mateo (1915) 15' quadrangle shows Guano Island at the place.

Little Creek [SONOMA]: *stream,* flows about 2.5 miles to Buckeye Creek (2) 5.5 miles north of the village of Stewarts Point (lat. 38° 44'05" N, long. 123°24'25" W; near S line sec. 3, T 10 N, R 14 W). Named on Annapolis (1977) and Stewarts Point (1978) 7.5' quadrangles.

Little Duck Slough [SOLANO]: *water feature,* extends east from Suisun (present Suisun City) 1 mile south-southeast of downtown Fairfield (lat. 38°14'10" N, long. 122°02'10" W). Named on Suisun (1918) special quadrangle.

Little Geysers: see **Calistoga** [NAPA]; **The Geysers** [SONOMA].

Little Hastings Tract [SOLANO]: *area,* 6.5 miles north of Rio Vista (lat. 38°15' N, long. 121°41'30" W); Wright Cut separates the area from Hastings Tract. Named on Liberty Island (1978) and Rio Vista (1978) 7.5' quadrangles.

Little Holland Tract [SOLANO]: *area,* 11 miles north of Rio Vista in Yolo Bypass on Solano-Yolo County line (lat. 38°19' N, long. 121°39'15" W). Named on Liberty Island (1978) 7.5' quadrangle.

Little Honker Bay [SOLANO]: *bay,* 3 miles south-southwest of Denverton off of Nurse Slough (lat. 38°10'55" N, long. 121°54'45" W). Named on Denverton (1953) 7.5' quadrangle.

Little Island [NAPA]: *island,* 2 miles long, 5.5 miles west of Napa Junction between Napa Slough, Devils Slough, China Slough, and South Slough (lat. 38°10'45" N, long. 122°21' W). Named on Cuttings Wharf (1949) 7.5' quadrangle.

Little Lagoon [SAN MATEO]: *lake,* 150 feet long, 2.5 miles southwest of La Honda (lat. 37°17'40" N, long. 122°18'30" W; sec. 28, T 7 S, R 4 W); the lake is 650 feet northeast of Big Lagoon. Named on La Honda (1961) 7.5' quadrangle.

Little Llagas Creek [SANTA CLARA]: *stream,* flows 8.5 miles to Llagas Creek 2.5 miles southeast of San Martin (lat. 37°03'35" N, long. 121°34'25" W). Named on Gilroy (1955) and Mount Madonna (1955) 7.5' quadrangles. United States Board on Geographic Names (1973a, p. 2-3) approved names for several streams tributary to Little Llagas Creek: Church Creek, named for a pioneer landowner in the region, flows 3 miles to Little Llagas Creek 2 miles southeast of San Martin (lat. 37°04'05" N, long. 121°34'42" W); San Martin Creek flows 3.2 miles to Little Llagas Creek 1.2 miles west of San Martin (lat. 37°04'51" N, long. 121°35'15" W); Center Creek flows 2 miles to San Martin Creek 1.4 miles east-northeast of San Martin (lat. 37°15'25" N, long. 121° 35'01" W); and New Creek flows 2.5 miles to San Martin Creek 1.3 miles east of San Martin (lat. 37°05'04" N, long. 121°35'02" W).

Little Medora Lake [SOLANO]: *lake,* 1900 feet long, 11 miles north-northeast of Rio Vista in Yolo Basin (present Yolo Bypass) (lat. 38°18'25" N, long. 122°37'55" W); the lake is 0.5 mile east-southeast of Madora Lake. Named on Cache Slough (1916) 7.5' quadrangle.

Little Mile Rock [SAN FRANCISCO]: *rock,* less than 1 mile north-northeast of Point Lobos, and 1950 feet offshore at Lands End (lat. 37°47'35" N, long. 122°30'30" W); the feature is 100 feet southeast of Mile Rock. Named on San Francisco North (1956) 7.5' quadrangle. This rock and Mile Rock together are called Mile Rocks on San Francisco (1915) 15' quadrangle.

Little Mountain [MARIN]: *peak,* 3 miles west of downtown Novato (lat. 38°07' N, long. 122°37'45" W). Named on Novato (1954) and San Geronimo (1954) 7.5' quadrangles.

Little Oat Mountain [SONOMA]: *peak,* 2 miles west-northwest of Cazadero (lat. 38°32'45" N, long. 123°07'15" W; near SW cor. sec. 7, T 8 N, R 11 W). Named on Cazadero (1978) 7.5' quadrangle.

Little Peak Canyon [SANTA CLARA]: *canyon,* drained by a stream that flows nearly 2 miles to San Benito County 15 miles east-southeast of Gilroy (lat. 36°57'35" N, long. 121°18'05" W). Named on Three Sisters (1954) 7.5' quadrangle.

Little Pine Creek [CONTRA COSTA]: *stream,* flows 3.25 miles to Pine Creek 4.5 miles west of Mount Diablo (lat. 37°53'45" N, long. 121°59'30" W). Named on Clayton (1953) 7.5' quadrangle.

Little Portuguese Canyon [NAPA]: *canyon,* 2.25 miles long, opens into the canyon of Putah Creek 9.5 miles south-southeast of Berryessa Peak (lat. 38°32' N, long. 122°08'25" W; near S line sec. 13, T 8 N, R 3 W). Named on Lake Berryessa (1959) 7.5' quadrangle. Water of Lake Berryessa covers the lower part of the canyon.

Little Rancheria Creek [SONOMA]: *stream,* flows 2 miles to Rancheria Creek 5 miles west-northwest of Skaggs Springs (lat. 38°43'20" N, long. 123°06'20" W; near S line sec. 8, T 10 N, R 11 W). Named on Tombs Creek (1978) and Warm Springs Dam (1978) 7.5' quadrangles.

Little Rough Gulch [SANTA CLARA]: *canyon,* drained by a stream that flows nearly 2 miles to Rough Gulch 2.5 miles north-northwest of Gilroy Hot Springs (lat. 37°08'25" N, long. 121°29'50" W; sec. 23, T 9 S, R 4 E). Named on Mississippi Creek (1955) and Mount Sizer (1955) 7.5' quadrangles.

Littles Point: see **Commodore Jones Point** [SOLANO].

Little Strawberry Creek [SONOMA]: *stream,* flows 1.25 miles to Warm Springs Creek 4.5 miles west of Skaggs Springs (lat. 38°41'30" N, long. 123°06'30" W; near NW cor. sec. 29, T 10 N, R 11 W). Named on Warm Springs Dam (1978) 7.5' quadrangle.

Little Sugarloaf Peak [NAPA]: *peak,* 10 miles south-southwest of Berryessa Peak (lat. 38°31'25" N, long. 122°15' W); the peak is 0.5 mile south-southwest of Sugarloaf Peak. Altitude 1647 feet. Named on Chiles Valley (1958) and Lake Berryessa (1959) 7.5' quadrangles.

Little Sulphur Creek [SONOMA]: *stream,* flows 16 miles to Big Sulphur Creek 4 miles northeast of Asti (lat. 38°48'35" N, long. 122°55'30" W). Named on Asti (1959), Jimtown (1955), Mount Saint Helena (1959), and The Geysers (1959) 7.5' quadrangles. North Branch enters from the east 2.25 miles from the mouth of the main stream; it is 5.5 miles long and is named on Asti (1959) and The Geysers (1959) 7.5' quadrangles.

Little Uvas Creek [SANTA CLARA]: *stream,* flows 5 miles to Uvas Creek 6.25 miles north of Mount Madonna (lat. 37°06'05" N, long. 121°43'15" W). Named on Loma Prieta (1955) and Mount Madonna (1955) 7.5' quadrangles.

Little Valley [NAPA]: *canyon,* drained by a stream that flows 1.5 miles to Moskowite Reservoir 6 miles northwest of Mount Vaca (lat. 38°27'25" N, long. 122°11'15" W; near E line sec. 16, T 7 N, R 3 W). Named on Capell Valley (1951) 7.5' quadrangle.

Little Warm Springs Creek [SONOMA]: *stream,* flows 2.25 miles to Warm Springs Creek near Skaggs Springs (lat. 38°41'40" N, long. 123°01'35" W; sec. 24, T 10 N, R 11 W). Named on Warm Springs Dam (1978) 7.5' quadrangle.

Litton Springs: see **Lytton** [SONOMA].

Livantuliyume: see **Laguna de Santa Rosa** [SONOMA].

Live Oak Camp [CONTRA COSTA]: *locality,* 2.5 miles south-southwest of Mount Diablo (lat. 37°51'05" N, long. 121°56'10" W; sec. 14, T 1 S, R 1 W). Named on Diablo (1953) 7.5' quadrangle.

Live Oak Creek [SANTA CLARA]: *stream,* flows 3.25 miles to Llagas Creek nearly 2.5 miles northeast of Gilroy (lat. 37°02'10" N, long. 121°32'35" W). Named on Gilroy (1955) 7.5' quadrangle.

Live Oaks: see **Divide** [SONOMA].

Livereau Creek [SONOMA]: *stream,* flows 2 miles to Russian River at Guerneville (lat. 38°30' N, long. 123°15' W; sec. 31, T 8 N, R 10 W). Named on Cazadero (1978) 7.5' quadrangle.

Livermore [ALAMEDA]: *city,* 27 miles east-southeast of Oakland (lat. 37°40'55" N, long. 121°46' W); the city is in Livermore Valley. Named on Livermore (1961) 7.5' quadrangle. The name is for Robert Livermore, an English sailor who settled at the site in the 1830's; his home there was known as Livermore's after the American acquisition of California (Gudde, 1949, p. 189), and Goddard's (1857) map has the name "Livermores." Postal authorities established Livermore Ranch post office in 1851 and discontinued it in 1853 (Frickstad, p. 2). Alphonso Ladd built a hotel within the present city limits of Livermore in 1855 and the community that grew around the hotel was called Laddville, but when the railroad came through Livermore Valley, a station was built about 0.5 mile west of Laddville, and there in 1869 William M. Mendenhall had the present city of Livermore surveyed (Hoover, Rensch, and Rensch, p. 14-15). The first post office at present Livermore was called Nottingham, for Robert Livermore's home town in England (Gudde, 1949, p. 189); postal authorities established it in 1869 and changed the name to Livermore in 1870 (Frickstad, p. 3). The city incorporated in 1876. Postal authorities established Ann post office 11 miles southeast of Livermore in 1896 and discontinued it the same year (Salley, p. 8). A Military installation called Livermore Naval Air Station, and also called Wagoner Field, opened east of Livermore in 1942; the site now is occupied by Lawrence Livermore Laboratory (Mosier and Mosier, p. 51).

Livermore: see **Mount Caroline Livermore** [MARIN].

Livermore Naval Air Station: see **Livermore** [ALAMEDA].

Livermore Ranch: see **Livermore** [ALAMEDA].

Livermore's Pass: see **Altamont Pass** [ALAMEDA].

Livermore's Plain: see **Livermore Valley** [ALAMEDA].

Livermore Valley [ALAMEDA]: *valley,* at and near Livermore. Named on Altamont (1953) and Livermore (1961) 7.5' quadrangles. Williamson (1855, p. 10) called the feature Livermore's valley, and Parke (p. 7) called it Livermore's plain. Crespi called the place Santa Coleta in 1772, and it was known as El Valle de San Jose when Robert Livermore settled there in 1837 (Mosier and Mosier, p. 52). The range north of Livermore Valley was called Lomas de las Cuevas on a map of 1839 for the caves in weathered sandstone there—*lomas de las cuevas* means "small hills of the caves" in Spanish (Mosier and Mosier, p. 52).

Llagas: see **Llagas Creek** [SANTA CLARA].

Llagas Creek [SANTA CLARA]: *stream,* flows 30 miles to Pajaro River 4.5 miles southeast of Gilroy (lat. 36°57'50" N, long. 121°30'25" W). Named on Chittenden (1955), Gilroy (1955), Loma Prieta (1955), Morgan Hill (1955), Mount Madonna (1955), and Santa Teresa Hills (1953) 7.5' quadrangles. Called Arroyo de las Llagas on a diseño of Las Animas grant (Becker, 1969). West Branch flows 7 miles to Miller Slough at Gilroy and is named on Gilroy (1955) 7.5' quadrangle—Miller Slough joins Llagas Creek 2.25 miles east-southeast of Gilroy. California Mining Bureau's (1917b) map shows a place called Llagas located near Llagas Creek about where Morgan Hill (1917) 15' quadrangle shows Llagas school situated 4.25 west of Madrone (lat. 37°09'05" N, long. 121°44'40" W). Postal authorities established Llagas post office in 1892 and discontinued it in 1911 (Frickstad, p. 174). United States Board on Geographic Names (1973a, p. 3) approved names for several streams tributary to Llagas Creek: Panther Creek, which flows 2.3 miles to Llagas Creek 2.5 miles north-northeast of Gilroy (lat. 37°02'31" N, long. 121°32'57" W); South Panther Creek, which flows 1.5 miles nearly to Panther Creek 2.7 miles north-northeast of Gilroy (lat. 37°02'37" N, long. 121°32'50" W)—on Gilroy (1955) 7.5' quadrangle the stream stops short of Panther Creek, but on Morgan Hill (1917) 15' quadrangle it connects with Llagas Creek; Skillet Creek, which flows 3 miles to Llagas Creek 2.8 miles north of Gilroy (lat. 37°02'58" N, long. 121°33'35" W); and Rucker Creek, which flows 2.5 miles to Skillet Creek 3 miles north of Gilroy (lat. 37°03'03" N, long. 121°33'34" W).

Llagas Creek: see **Little Llagas Creek** [SANTA CLARA].

Llajome: see **Yajome** [NAPA].

Llano [SONOMA]: *locality,* 1.5 miles east-northeast of Sebastopol (lat. 38°24'45" N, long. 122°47'35" W); the place is on Llano de Santa Rosa grant. Named on Sebastopol (1954) 7.5' quadrangle.

Llano de las Llagas: see **Santa Clara Valley** [SANTA CLARA].

Llano del Tequisquita [SANTA CLARA]: *land grant,* mainly in San Benito County, but extends into Santa Clara County 7 miles east of Gilroy. Named on Gilroy Hot Springs (1955) and San Felipe (1955) 7.5' quadrangles. Jose Maria Sanchez received the land in 1835; Vicente Sanchez and others claimed 16,016 acres patented in 1871 (Cowan, p. 102; Cowan listed the grant under the name "Tequisquite"). Arbuckle (p. 23) used the form "Llano del Tequesquite" for the name.

Llano de Santa Rosa [SONOMA]: *land grant,* southwest of Santa Rosa. Named on Cotati (1954), Santa Rosa (1954), Sebastopol (1954), and Two Rock (1954) 7.5' quadrangles. Joaquin Carillo received 3 leagues in 1844 and claimed 13,316 acres patented in 1865 (Cowan, p. 95).

Lleguas Valley: see **Sheridan Creek** [ALAMEDA].

Lloyd Lake [SAN FRANCISCO]: *lake,* 500 feet long, nearly 2 miles east-southeast of Point Lobos (lat. 37°46'15" N, long. 122°28'50" W). Named on San Francisco North (1956) 7.5' quadrangle.

Lobatos Creek: see **Lobitos Creek** [SAN MATEO].

Lobitas Creek: see **Lobitos Creek** [SAN MATEO].

Lobitos [SAN MATEO]: *locality,* 5.5 miles south-southeast of downtown Half Moon Bay (lat. 37°23' N, long. 122°23'55" W); the place is along Lobitos Creek. Named on Half Moon Bay (1961) 7.5' quadrangle.

Lobitos Creek [SAN MATEO]: *stream,* flows 5 miles to the sea 6 miles south of downtown Half Moon Bay (lat. 37°22'35" N, long. 122°24'30"

W). Named on Half Moon Bay (1961) and Woodside (1961) 7.5' quadrangles. United States Board on Geographic Names (1933, p. 468) rejected the forms "Lobatos," "Lobitas," and "Lobitus" for the name. The stream was called Arroyo de los Lobitos in Spanish times (Gudde, 1949, p. 190).

Lobitus Creek: see **Lobitos Creek** [SAN MATEO].

Lobos: see **Point Lobos** [SAN FRANCISCO].

Lobos Creek [SAN FRANCISCO]: *stream,* flows nearly 1 mile to the sea 1.5 miles south-southwest of Fort Point (lat. 37°47'25" N, long. 122°29'05" W). Named on San Francisco North (1956) 7.5' quadrangle. Anza called the stream Arroyo del Puerto in 1776 (Davidson, p. 119).

Lobos Rock [SAN FRANCISCO]: *rock,* 0.5 mile north-northeast of Point Lobos, and 700 feet offshore (lat. 37°47'15" N, long. 122°30'35" W). Named on San Francisco North (1956) 7.5' quadrangle.

Locallome: see **Locoallomi** [NAPA].

Locks Creek [SAN MATEO]: *stream,* flows nearly 2 miles to Frenchmans Creek 4 miles southeast of Montara Knob (lat. 37° 31' N, long. 122°25'55" W; sec. 8, T 5 S, R 5 W). Named on Montara Mountain (1956) 7.5' quadrangle. Called Lock Creek on San Mateo (1915) 15' quadrangle. John B. Lock had a ranch near the stream in 1864 (Brown, p. 49).

Locoallomi [NAPA]: *land grant,* at and around Pope Valley (1). Named on Aetna Springs (1958), Chiles Valley (1958), and Saint Helena (1960) 7.5' quadrangles. Julian Pope received 2 leagues in 1841; Joseph Pope and others claimed 8873 acres patented in 1862 (Cowan, p. 45; Cowan used the form "Locallome" for the name). The grant name is from an Indian village (Kroeber, p. 46).

Locust [CONTRA COSTA]: *locality,* 1 mile north of present Walnut Creek civic center along Oakland Antioch and Eastern Railroad (lat. 37°55' N, long. 122°03'50" W). Named on Concord (1915) 15' quadrangle. Concord (1943) 15' quadrangle shows a place called Walden at or near the site.

Locust: see **Mill Valley** [MARIN] (2).

Lokoya [NAPA]: *settlement,* 9 miles northwest of downtown Napa (lat. 38°22'20" N, long. 122°25'25" W; around NW cor. sec. 16, T 6 N, R 5 W). Named on Sonoma (1951) 7.5' quadrangle, Postal authorities established Solid Comfort post office in 1918, changed the name to Lokoya in 1925, and discontinued it in 1951 (Frickstad, p. 111, 112). Sonoma (1951) 7.5' quadrangle shows Redwood cemetery situated southeast of Lokoya (near E line sec. 16, T 6 N, R 5 W). According to Salley (p. 211), postal authorities established Spruce Hill post office in 1874 and discontinued it in 1875; it was located 7 miles northeast of Sonoma [SONOMA] in Napa County at a site called Redwood (SE quarter sec. 16, T 6 N, R 5 W).

Loma Alta [MARIN]: *peak,* 6 miles south-southwest of downtown Novato (lat. 38°01'30" N, long. 122°36'40" W). Altitude 1592 feet. Named on Novato (1954) 7.5' quadrangle.

Loma Alta: see **Telegraph Hill** [SAN FRANCISCO].

Loma Alta Cove: see **Yerba Buena Cove**, under **Telegraph Hill** [SAN FRANCISCO].

Loma Chiquita [SANTA CLARA]: *peak,* 1.25 miles east-southeast of Loma Prieta (lat. 37°06'20" N, long. 121°49'20" W; sec. 35, T 9 S, R 1 E). Altitude 2607 feet. Named on Loma Prieta (1955) 7.5' quadrangle.

Loma Mar [SAN MATEO]: *village,* nearly 4 miles south-southwest of La Honda along Pescadero Creek (lat. 37°16'20" N, long. 122° 18'15" W). Named on La Honda (1961) 7.5' quadrangle. Postal authorities established Loma Mar post office in 1931 (Frickstad, p. 168).

Loma Prieta [SANTA CLARA]: *peak,* 15 miles south of downtown San Jose (lat. 37°06'40" N, long. 121°50'35" W). Altitude 3791 feet. Named on Loma Prieta (1955) 7.5' quadrangle. Called Loma Prieto on Goddard's (1857) map. United States Coast Survey used the peak as a primary triangulation station in 1854 and named it in honor of Alexander D. Bache, superintendent of the survey at the time (Gudde, 1949, p. 192). Whitney (p. 65) used the name "Mount Bache," but pointed out that *loma prieta,* which means "black mountain" in Spanish, was the name commonly given by the Spanish-speaking population to any high chaparral-covered point that appears black from a distance, including this one. On some maps, the name "Loma Prieta" applies mistakenly to present Mount Umunhum (Hoover, Rensch, and Rensch, p. 457).

Lomas de las Cuevas: see **Livermore Valley** [ALAMEDA].

Lomas Muertas: see **Buri Buri Ridge** [SAN MATEO].

Lombard [NAPA]: *locality,* 0.5 mile west-northwest of Napa Junction along Southern Pacific Railroad (lat. 38°11'30" N, long. 122°15'35" W; sec. 13, T 4 N, R 4 W). Named on Cuttings Wharf (1949) 7.5' quadrangle.

Lomita [SANTA CLARA]: *peak,* 3.5 miles south of Mount Umunhum on Santa Clara-Santa Cruz County line (lat. 37°06'40" N, long. 121°53'40" W). Named on Laurel (1955) 7.5' quadrangle.

Lomita de la Linares: see **Rucker** [SANTA CLARA].

Lomita Park [SAN MATEO]: *district,* 1 mile northwest of downtown Millbrae in San Bruno (lat. 37°37' N, long. 122°24'15" W). Named on Montara Mountain (1956) 7.5' quadrangle. Postal authorities established Belmae Park post office in 1927, changed the name to Lomita Park in 1933, and discontinued it in 1957—the name "Belmae" was coined from the names "Belmont" and "Millbrae" (Salley, p. 18, 125).

Lomitas: see **Rutherford** [NAPA].

Lone Hill [SANTA CLARA]: *hill,* 4 miles east-northeast of Los Gatos (lat. 37°14'40" N, long. 121°54'35" W; near NW cor. sec. 18, T 8 S, R 1 E). Named on Los Gatos (1953) 7.5' quadrangle. Housing development has destroyed the feature.

Lone Lake [SANTA CLARA]: *lake,* 250 feet long, 6.25 miles west-southwest of Mount Sizer (lat. 37°11'35" N, long. 121°37'20" W). Named on Mount Sizer (1955) 7.5' quadrangle. Called Lost Lake on Morgan Hill (1917) 15' quadrangle.

Lone Mountain [SAN FRANCISCO]: *peak,* 2.5 miles south-southeast of Fort Point (lat. 37°46'45" N, long. 122°27'05" W). Named on San Francisco North (1956) 7.5' quadrangle.

Lone Pine Thicket [NAPA]: *area,* 3.25 miles south of Knoxville (lat. 38°46'30" N, long. 122°20'30" W; sec. 30, T 11 N, R 4 W). Named on Knoxville (1958) 7.5' quadrangle.

Lone Point: see **Long Point** [SANTA CLARA].

Lone Tree Creek [MARIN]: *stream,* flows nearly 1.5 miles to the sea 4.5 miles east-southeast of Bolinas (lat. 37°52'40" N, long. 122°36'45" W). Named on San Rafael (1954) 7.5' quadrangle.

Lone Tree Creek: see **Scott Creek** [ALAMEDA-SANTA CLARA].

Lone Tree Island [SOLANO]: *island,* 1200 feet long, 6.25 miles southeast of Birds Landing (2) along Sacramento River (lat. 38°03'55" N, long. 121°47'15" W). Named on Collinsville (1918) 7.5' quadrangle.

Lone Tree Point [CONTRA COSTA]: *promontory,* 5.25 miles east-northeast of Pinole Point along San Pablo Bay at Rodeo (lat. 38°02'20" N, long. 122°16'20" W). Named on Mare Island (1959) 7.5' quadrangle.

Lone Tree Valley [CONTRA COSTA]: *valley,* 9 miles east-northeast of Mount Diablo along Sand Creek (lat. 37°57' N, long. 121°46'30" W). Named on Antioch South (1953) and Brentwood (1978) 7.5' quadrangles. Mendenhall's (1908) map has the form "Lonetree" for the name.

Long Branch [SANTA CLARA]: *stream,* flows 3.25 miles to Isabel Creek 2.5 miles northwest of Mount Hamilton (lat. 37°22'10" N, long. 121°40'10" W; sec. 32, T 6 S, R 3 E). Named on Lick Observatory (1955) and Mount Day (1955) 7.5' quadrangles.

Long Bridge: see **Bonjetti Creek** [SANTA CLARA]; **Princeton** [SAN MATEO]; **Tunitas Creek** [SAN MATEO].

Long Canyon [CONTRA COSTA]: *canyon,* drained by a stream that flows nearly 3 miles to Marsh Creek 5.5 miles east of Mount Diablo (lat. 37°53'15" N, long. 121°48'55" W; sec. 36, T 1 N, R 1 E). Named on Antioch South (1953) 7.5' quadrangle.

Long Canyon [NAPA]: *canyon,* drained by a stream that flows 3.5 miles to Eticuera Creek 2.5 miles southeast of Knoxville (lat. 38° 47'45" N, long. 122°18'05" W; near NE cor. sec. 21, T 11 N, R 4 W). Named on Knoxville (1958) 7.5' quadrangle.

Long Canyon [SANTA CLARA]: *canyon,* 5 miles long, along East Fork Coyote Creek above the mouth of Grizzly Creek, which is 6 miles southeast of Mount Stakes (lat. 37°15'15" N, long. 121°28'35" W). Named on Mount Stakes (1955) 7.5' quadrangle.

Long Gulch [SAN MATEO]: *canyon,* drained by a stream that flows 1 mile to the sea 2.5 miles south-southwest of the village of San Gregorio at Pomponio Beach (lat. 37°17'30" N, long. 122°24'20" W). Named on San Gregorio (1961, photorevised 1968) 7.5' quadrangle.

Long Gulch [SANTA CLARA]: *canyon,* drained by a stream that flows 2 miles to San Antonio Creek nearly 7 miles south of Eylar Mountain (lat. 37°22'40" N, long. 121°31'50" W; near SW cor. sec. 27, T 6 S, R 4 E). Named on Eylar Mountain (1955) 7.5' quadrangle.

Long Point [MARIN]: *promontory,* 5.5 miles southeast of downtown Novato along lowlands adjacent to San Pablo Bay (lat. 38°02'45" N, long. 122°30'20" W). Named on Novato (1954) 7.5' quadrangle.

Long Point [SANTA CLARA]: *promontory,* 4 miles north of downtown Mountain View at the edge of mud flats along San Francisco Bay (lat. 37°27' N, long. 122°04' W). Named on Mountain View (1961) 7.5' quadrangle. Called Lone Point on Thompson and West's (1876) map.

Long Point: see **Garnet Point** [SOLANO].

Long Point Island: see **Ryer Island** [SOLANO] (2).

Long Ridge [CONTRA COSTA]: *ridge,* west-trending, 1.5 miles long, 2.5 miles west of Mount Diablo (lat. 37°53'15" N, long. 121°57'45" W). Named on Clayton (1953) 7.5' quadrangle.

Long Ridge [SAN MATEO]: *ridge,* generally west-trending, 2.5 miles long, 3.5 miles east-southeast of Mindego Hill (lat. 37°17' N, long. 122°10'20" W). Named on Mindego Hill (1961) 7.5' quadrangle.

Long's Landing: see **Plummer Landing** [ALAMEDA].

Long Valley [CONTRA COSTA]: *canyon,* 1.25 miles long, 5.25 miles east-northeast of Mount Diablo (lat. 37°55' N, long. 121°49'45" W). Named on Mount Diablo (1898) 15' quadrangle.

Longwall Canyon: see **Baldy Ryan** [SANTA CLARA].

Lonoke [SANTA CLARA]: *locality,* 1.25 miles north-northwest of Gilroy along Southern Pacific Railroad (lat. 37°01'30" N, long. 121°34'35" W). Named on Gilroy (1955) 7.5' quadrangle.

Lookout Point [ALAMEDA]: *peak,* 5 miles south of Mendenhall Springs (lat. 37°30'50" N, long. 121°39'55" W; near E line sec. 8, T 5 S, R 3 E). Named on Mendenhall Springs (1956) 7.5' quadrangle.

Lookout Point [NAPA]: *peak,* 6 miles north of Saint Helena (lat. 38°35'40" N, long. 122°28'30" W; near S line sec. 25, T 9 N, R 6 W). Named on Saint Helena (1960) 7.5' quadrangle.

Lookout Point [SONOMA]: *peak,* 4 miles west of Big Mountain (lat. 38°42'30" N, long. 123°13'15" W; near SE cor. sec. 18, T 10 N, R 12 W). Named on Tombs Creek (1978) 7.5' quadrangle.

Lookout Rock [SONOMA]: *relief feature,* 0.5 mile northwest of Big Mountain (lat. 38°43' N, long. 123°09'10" W; sec. 14, T 10 N, R 12 W). Named on Tombs Creek (1978) 7.5' quadrangle.

Lookout Slough [SOLANO]: *water feature,* joins Shag Slough 10.5 miles north of Rio Vista (lat. 38°18'50" N, long. 121°41'35" W). Named on Liberty Island (1978) 7.5' quadrangle.

Lorenzo Station [ALAMEDA]: *locality,* 2.5 miles south-southeast of downtown San Leandro along Southern Pacific Railroad (lat. 37° 41'35" N, long. 122°07'45" W). Named on San Leandro (1959) 7.5' quadrangle.

Lorin [ALAMEDA]: *locality,* 3 miles north of downtown Oakland along Southern Pacific Railroad (lat. 37°50'50" N, long. 122°16'20" W). Named on San Francisco (1899) 15' quadrangle. Residents of the community applied for a post office under the name "Garfield," but the postal authorities assigned the name "Lorin" instead; Berkeley annexed Lorin in 1892 (Mosier and Mosier, p. 15, 82). Postal authorities established Lorin post office in 1882 and changed the name to South Berkeley in 1902 (Salley, p. 126). The railroad station at the place first was called Alcatraz, for Alcatraz Avenue (Mosier and Mosier, p. 53).

Los Alamos Creek: see **Cottonwood Creek** [ALAMEDA-CONTRA COSTA].

Los Altos [SANTA CLARA]: *city,* 13 miles west-northwest of downtown San Jose (lat. 37°22'55" N, long. 122°07' W). Named on Cupertino (1961) and Mountain View (1961) 7.5' quadrangles. When workmen for Southern Pacific Railroad began laying tracks to the place in 1906, Paul Shoup, a railroad executive, and some of his friends organized Los Altos Land Company, bought 100 acres, and laid out a town to be called Banks of Braes; after the railroad began operations in 1908, they changed the name of the place to Los Altos—*los altos* means "the heights" in Spanish (Butler, p. 43). Postal authorities established Los Altos post office in 1908 (Frickstad, p. 174), and the city incorporated in 1952. Healy's (1866) map has the name "Oak Grove" for a group of buildings situated in Los Altos at about the present intersection of El Camino Real and San Antonio Road.

Los Altos Hills [SANTA CLARA]: *locality,* the city hall is situated 14 miles west-northwest of downtown San Jose (lat. 37°23' N, long. 122°08'15" W). Named on Cupertino (1961), Mindego Hill (1961), Mountain View (1961), and Palo Alto (1961) 7.5' quadrangles. The community, which incorporated in 1956, has a rural setting.

Los Buellis Hills [SANTA CLARA]: *range,* 2.5 miles northeast of the mouth of Alum Rock Canyon (lat. 37°25'30" N, long. 121°48' W). Named on Calaveras Reservoir (1961) 7.5' quadrangle. According to Gudde (1949, p. 194), the name is from a misspelling of *bueyes,* which means "oxen" in Spanish.

Los Capitancillos [SANTA CLARA]: *land grant,* west-northwest of New Almaden. Named on Los Gatos (1953) and Santa Teresa Hills (1953) 7.5' quadrangles. Justo Larios received 4470.15 acres in 1842 (Arbuckle, p. 21).

Los Capitancillos Creek [SANTA CLARA]: *stream,* flows 1.25 miles to Guadalupe Creek nearly 3 miles west of New Almaden (lat. 37° 11'05" N, long. 121°52'15" W); the stream forms part of the border of Los Capitancillos grant. Named on Santa Teresa Hills (1953) 7.5' quadrangle. United States Board on Geographic Names (1943, p. 10) applied the name "Los Capitancillos Creek" to this stream and to Guadalupe Creek below their junction, while rejecting the names "Arroyo de los Capitancillos," "Arroyo Seco de los Capitancillos," and "Guadalupe Creek" for the combined streams. Later the Board (1960b, p. 17) decided against application of the name "Los Capitancillos Creek" to present Guadalupe Creek.

Los Capitancillos Ridge: see **New Almaden** [SANTA CLARA].

Los Coches [SANTA CLARA]: *land grant,* 2 miles west-southwest of downtown San Jose. Named on San Jose West (1961) 7.5' quadrangle. An Indian called Roberto received 0.5 league in 1844; Antonio Maria Suñol and others claimed 2219 acres patented in 1857 (Cowan, p. 28). The name is from use of the land as the swine range for Santa Clara mission—*los coches* means "the pigs" in colloquial Spanish (Hoover, Rensch, and Rensch, p. 440).

Los Farellones: see **Farallon Islands** [SAN FRANCISCO].

Los Gatos [SANTA CLARA]: *city,* 8.5 miles south-southwest of downtown San Jose (lat. 37°13'30" N, long. 121°58'55" W); the city is at the entrance of Los Gatos Creek to lowlands—partly on Rinconada de los Gatos grant. Named on Los Gatos (1953) and San Jose West (1961) 7.5' quadrangles. Postal authorities established Los Gatos post office in 1864 and discontinued it for a time in 1867 (Frickstad, p. 174). The city incorporated in 1887. After James Alexander Forbes built a flour mill there in the early 1850's, the place was known as Forbes Mill; the town that grew around the mill was called Forbestown first, and then Los Gatos (Hoover, Rensch, and Rensch, p. 454-455).

Los Gatos Creek [SANTA CLARA]: *stream,* flows 24 miles to Guadalupe River in downtown San Jose (lat. 37°20' N, long. 121°53'50" W). Named on Laurel (1955), Loma Prieta (1955), Los Gatos (1953), and San Jose West (1961) 7.5' quadrangles. Called Arroyo de Los Gatos on Hare's (1872) map. Zachariah Jones called the stream Jones Creek at the time that he laid out a town that he named Jones Mill, and that later was called Lexington (Bruntz, p. 7).

Los Gatos Creek, Old Channel: see **Dry Creek** [SANTA CLARA] (1).

Los Germanos: see **Juristac** [SANTA CLARA].

Los Guilicos [SONOMA]:

(1) *land grant,* at and near Kenwood. Named on Glen Ellen (1954), Kenwood (1954), Rutherford (1951), and Santa Rosa (1954) 7.5' quadrangles. John Wilson received 4 leagues in 1837 and claimed 18,834 acres patented in 1866 (Cowan, p. 39). The name is from an Indian village that was at the head of Sonoma Creek (Kroeber, p. 42).

(2) *locality,* 2 miles west-northwest of Kenwood along Southern Pacific Railroad (lat. 38°25'40" N, long. 122°34'50" W); the place is on Los Guilicos grant. Named on Santa Rosa (1916) 15' quadrangle.

Los Guilicos: see **Kenwood** [SONOMA].

Los Guilicos Warm Springs [SONOMA]: *spring,* 1.5 miles south of Kenwood along Sonoma Creek (lat. 38°23'40" N, long. 122° 33' W); the spring is on Los Guilicos grant. Named on Kenwood (1954) 7.5' quadrangle. Water from two springs was the basis of a resort at the place (Waring, p. 114).

Los Huecos [SANTA CLARA]: *land grant,* southeast of Mount Hamilton. Named on Isabel Valley (1955), Lick Observatory (1955), Morgan Hill (1955), and Mount Sizer (1955) 7.5' quadrangles. Luis Arenas and John Roland received 9 leagues in 1846; Roland and Hornsby claimed 39,951 acres patented in 1876 (Cowan, p. 40).

Los Lagrimas Hills: see **Edenvale** [SANTA CLARA].

Los Medanos [CONTRA COSTA]:

(1) *land grant,* at and near Pittsburg and Antioch. Named on Antioch North (1978), Antioch South (1953), Clayton (1953), and Honker Bay (1953) 7.5' quadrangles. Jose Antonio Mesa and others received 2 leagues in 1839; Johathan D. Stevenson claimed 8859 acres patented in 1872 (Cowan, p. 47). The name is from sand dunes located on the grant along San Joaquin River—*medanos* means "sand banks" in Spanish (Hoover, Rensch, and Rensch, p. 59).

(2) *locality,* 2.5 miles west of downtown Antioch along Southern Pacific Railroad (lat. 38°00'50" N, long. 121°51'10" W); the place is on Los Medanos grant. Named on Antioch North (1978) 7.5' quadrangle.

Los Meganos [CONTRA COSTA]: *land grant,* between Brentwood and Mount Diablo. Named on Brentwood (1978) and Byron Hot Springs (1953) 7.5' quadrangles. Jose Noriega received 4 leagues in 1835; John Marsh got the land in 1837 and claimed 13,316 acres patented in 1867 (Cowan, p. 47).

Los Putos [SOLANO]: *land grant,* at and north of Vacaville. Named on Allendale (1953), Davis (1952), Dixon (1952), Elmira (1953), Fairfield North (1951), Merritt (1952), Mount Vaca (1951), and Winters (1953) 7.5' quadrangles. Manuel Vaca and Juan Felipe Peña received 10 leagues in 1843 and claimed 44,384 acres patented in 1858 (Cowan, p. 65; Cowan listed the grant under the designation "Putas (or Putos, or Putah)").

Los Stancos Creek: see **Los Trancos Creek** [SAN MATEO-SANTA CLARA].

Lost Canyon [SANTA CLARA]: *canyon,* drained by a stream that flows 1.5 miles to San Antonio Creek 6.5 miles south-southeast of Eyler Mountain (lat. 37°22'55" N, long. 121°30'35" W; sec. 26, T 6 S, R 4 E). Named on Eylar Mountain (1955) 7.5' quadrangle.

Lost Lake: see **Lone Lake** [SANTA CLARA].

Los Trancos Creek [SAN MATEO-SANTA CLARA]: *stream,* flows 7 miles along part of San Mateo-Santa Clara County line to San Francisquito Creek nearly 3 miles southwest of downtown Palo Alto (lat. 37°24'50" N, long. 122°11'30" W). Named on Mindego Hill (1961) and Palo Alto (1961) 7.5' quadrangles. Called Stancos Creek on Thompson and West's (1876) map, but United States Board on Geographic Names (1933, p. 475) rejected the names "Los Stancos Creek" and "Stancos Creek" for the feature. The stream was called Maximo Creek in the 1850's for Maximo Martinez, a landholder near the feature, and was called Reynolds Creek for another early settler (Brown, p. 50).

Los Trancos Woods [SAN MATEO]: *settlement,* 3 miles north-northeast of Mindego Hill (lat. 37°20'55" N, long. 122°11'55" W); the place is near Los Trancos Creek. Named on Mindego Hill (1961) 7.5' quadrangle.

Los Ulpinos [SOLANO]: *land grant,* at and west of Rio Vista. Named on Antioch North (1978), Jersey Island (1978), and Rio Vista (1978) 7.5' quadrangles. John Bidwell received the land in 1845 and claimed 17,726 acres patented in 1866 (Cowan, p. 106). The name is from the designation of a group of Indians (Kroeber, p. 65).

Lovall Valley [NAPA]: *valley,* 6 miles west of downtown Napa on the headwaters of Huichica Creek (lat. 38°17'30" N, long. 122°23'45" W). Named on Sonoma (1951) 7.5' quadrangle. On Napa (1902) 30' quadrangle, the name has the form "Loveall Valley," and it extends west over a divide into Sonoma County. Sonoma (1942) 15' quadrangle has the name "Loveall Canyon" for the same extended feature.

Loveall Canyon: see **Lovall Valley** [NAPA].

Loveall Valley: see **Lovall Valley** [NAPA].

Lovelady's: see **Campbell** [SANTA CLARA].

Lovely Glen Resort: see **Twin Creeks** [SANTA CLARA].

Lovers Gulch Creek [SONOMA]: *stream,* flows 1.5 miles to Little Sulphur Creek 9 miles north of Healdsburg (lat. 38°44'50" N, long. 122°50'40" W). Named on Jimtown (1955) 7.5' quadrangle.

Lovers Leap [SANTA CLARA]: *peak,* 2 miles north-northwest of Pacheco Peak (lat. 37°02'05" N, long. 121°17'55" W). Altitude 1160 feet. Named on Pacheco Peak (1955) 7.5' quadrangle.

Lowell [NAPA]: *locality,* 1 mile south of Napa Junction (lat. 38°10'25" N, long. 122°15'10" W; sec. 24, T 4 N, R 4 W). Named on Cuttings Wharf (1949) 7.5' quadrangle.

Lower Bean Hollow Lake: see **Bean Hollow Lake** [SAN MATEO].

Lower Crystal Springs Reservoir [SAN MATEO]: *lake,* 3.5 miles long, behind a dam on San Mateo Creek 3.25 miles southwest of downtown San Mateo (lat. 37°31'45" N, long. 122°21'40" W); the feature is northeast of Upper Crystal Springs Reservoir, and separated from it by a low dam that forms a causeway. Named on Montara Mountain (1956) and San Mateo (1956) 7.5' quadrangles. Upper Crystal Springs Reservoir and Lower Crystal Springs Reservoir together are called Crystal Springs Lake on San Mateo (1915) 15' quadrangle. These two lakes and nearby San Andreas Lake commonly are called Spring Valley Lakes for Spring Valley Water Company, which owned them; the name "Crystal Springs" is from the settlement of Crystal Springs that grew at a resort hotel of the same name—water of Lower Crystal Springs Reservoir now covers the site of the settlement (Brown, p. 24). Water of the reservoir also covers the site of San Felix Station, a stage stop of the 1870's (Hoover, Rensch, and Rensch, p. 398). A stream called Lake Creek, or Laguna Creek, was located at the south end of present Lower Crystal Springs Reservoir; it received its name because it drained what was called The Laguna (Brown, p. 46).

Lower Emerald Lake [SAN MATEO]: *lake,* 550 feet long, 2.25 miles west-southwest of downtown Redwood City (lat. 37°28' N, long. 122°15'45" W); the lake is 0.5 mile north-northwest of Upper Emerald Lake. Named on Woodside (1961) 7.5' quadrangle.

Lower Lake [SONOMA]: *lake,* 1450 feet long, less than 1 mile northwest of Plantation (lat. 38°36' N, long. 123°19'05" W). Named on Plantation (1977) 7.5' quadrangle, which shows a marshy lake. Plantation (1943) 7.5' quadrangle has marsh at the place.

Lower Penitencia Creek [SANTA CLARA]: *stream,* flows 5.5 miles to Coyote Creek nearly 2 miles north-northwest of Milpitas (lat. 37°27'15" N, long. 121°55'25" W). Named on Milpitas (1961) 7.5' quadrangle. Both Upper Penitencia Creek and Lower Penitencia Creek have the name "Penitencia Creek" on San Jose (1899) 15' quadrangle, although they are shown as separate streams. United States Board on Geographic Names (1962a, p. 13, 18) rejected the name "Penitencia Creek" for both features. According to tradition, the creek was named for a house of penitence that priests used to hear confession (Hoover, Rensch, and Rensch, p. 444).

Loyola: see **Loyola Corners** [SANTA CLARA].

Loyola Corners [SANTA CLARA]: *locality,* 2.25 miles southeast of downtown Los Altos near Southern Pacific Railroad (now the route of Foothill Expressway) crossing of Permanente Creek (lat. 37°21'10" N, long. 122°05'10" W). Named on Cupertino (1961) 7.5' quadrangle. Palo Alto (1940) 15' quadrangle shows a place called Loyola in hills 1 mile west-southwest of Loyola Corners. Peninsular Railway Company's (1912) map has the name "Loyola" along the rail line at present Loyola Corners. University of Santa Clara acquired 650 acres near present Loyola Corners for a new campus, but the 1906 earthquake disrupted the project; the site of the proposed campus was given the name "Loyola" to honor one of the founders of the Society of Jesus, and Loyola Corners received its name from the campus site (Fava, p. 56-59).

Lucas Valley [MARIN]: *canyon,* 2.25 miles long, 6 miles southwest of downtown Novato along Nicasio Creek (lat. 38°03'25" N, long. 122°39'30" W); the canyon is on San Pedro Santa Margarita y las Gallinas grant. Named on San Geronimo (1954) 7.5' quadrangle. The name probably is from John Lucas, who inherited the grant (Gudde, 1949, p. 196).

Lucerne Lake: see **Lake Lucerne** [SAN MATEO].

Luco Hill [SOLANO]: *peak,* 2.5 miles west-southwest of Denverton near the east end of Potrero Hills (lat. 38°12'20" N, long. 121°56'15" W; sec. 11, T 4 N, R 1 W); the peak is west of Luco Slough. Altitude 303 feet. Named on Denverton (1953) 7.5' quadrangle.

Lucol Hollow [SOLANO]: *canyon,* drained by a stream that flows 3.5 miles to lowlands at Birds Landing (2) (lat. 38°07'55" N, long. 121°52'20" W; sec. 4, T 3 N, R 4 E). Named on Birds Landing (1953) 7.5' quadrangle.

Luco Slough [SOLANO]: *water feature,* joins Nurse Slough nearly 2 miles southwest of Denverton (lat. 38°12'20" N, long. 121°55'20" W); the feature is east of Luco Hill. Named on Denverton (1953) 7.5' quadrangle.

Luffley's: see **Barzilla**, under **Pescadero** [SAN MATEO].

Luzon [CONTRA COSTA]: *locality,* 6.25 miles west of Martinez along Atchison, Topeka and Santa Fe Railroad (lat. 38°00'55" N, long. 122°15' W). Named on Benicia (1959) and Mare Island (1959) 7.5' quadrangles. The place was named at the time of the Spanish-American War, when names from the Philippines were popular (Gudde, 1949, p. 197).

Lyle Ridge [SONOMA]: *ridge,* east-southeast-trending, 1 mile long, 9.5 miles west-southwest of Cloverdale (lat. 38°45'05" N, long. 123°11' W). Named on Hopland (1960) 15' quadrangle, and on Tombs Creek (1978) 7.5' quadrangle.

Lynch Creek [SONOMA]: *stream,* flows 6 miles to Petaluma River 1 mile north of downtown Petaluma (lat. 38°14'50" N, long. 122°38'10" W). Named on Cotati (1954), Glen Ellen (1954), and Petaluma (1953) 7.5' quadrangles.

Lynchville: see **San Ramon** [CONTRA COSTA] (3).

Lyndon Canyon [SANTA CLARA]: *canyon,* drained by a stream that flows 3 miles to Lexington Reservoir 2.25 miles south-southwest of downtown Los Gatos (lat. 37°11'45" N, long. 122°00'05" W; sec. 32, T 8 S, R 1 W). Named on Castle Rock Ridge (1955) 7.5' quadrangle.

Lynn: see **Oakland** [ALAMEDA].

Lytton [SONOMA]: *village,* 3 miles north of Healdsburg (lat. 38°39'35" N, long. 122°52'15" W). Named on Jimtown (1955) 7.5' quadrangle. Postal authorities established Letton Springs post office in 1887, discontinued it in 1888, reestablished it with the name "Litton Springs" in 1889, discontinued it in 1891, reestablished it with the name "Lytton" in 1895, moved it 0.5 mile east in 1897, and discontinued it in 1954 (Salley, p. 130). Lytton Springs are 0.5 mile west of Lytton; a resort at the springs was known as Geysers Spa (Waring, p. 165). The misspelled name "Lytton" is for Captain Litton, developer of the resort in 1875 (Gudde, 1949, p. 198).

– M –

Maacama: see **Camp Maacama** [SONOMA].

Maacama Creek [SONOMA]: *stream,* formed by the confluence of McDonnell Creek and Briggs Creek, flows 7 miles to Russian River 4.5 miles east of Healdsburg (lat. 38°36'50" N, long. 122°46'55" W). Named on Healdsburg (1955), Jimtown (1955), and Mount Saint Helena (1959) 7.5' quadrangles.

Macauley: see **Santa Rosa** [SONOMA].

Machado Creek [SANTA CLARA]: *stream,* flows 2 miles to Llagas Creek 2.5 miles south-southwest of Morgan Hill (lat. 37°05'30" N, long. 121°39'50" W). Named on Mount Madonna (1955, photorevised 1968 and 1973) 7.5' quadrangle. The name commemorates a pioneer family (United States Board on Geographic Names, 1973a, p. 2).

Machin: see **Ignacio** [MARIN].

Maclaytown: see **Saratoga** [SANTA CLARA].

Madera Creek: see **Matadero Creek** [SANTA CLARA].

Madigan: see **Lake Madigan** [SOLANO].

Madonna: see **Mount Madonna** [SANTA CLARA].

Madrone [SANTA CLARA]: *settlement,* 1.5 miles northwest of Morgan Hill (lat. 37°09' N, long. 121°40'10" W). Named on Morgan Hill (1955) 7.5' quadrangle. The community now is part of Morgan Hill. A stopping place called Madrone Station, or Eighteen Mile House, was on the stage route between Coyote and Morgan Hill (Hoover, Rensch, and Rensch, p. 431). Postal authorities established Sherman post office in 1867, discontinued it in 1870, reestablished it in 1871, changed the name to Madrone in 1882, and discontinued it in 1959 (Salley, p. 130, 203).

Madrone [SONOMA]: *locality,* nearly 2 miles south-southeast of Glen Ellen along Northwestern Pacific Railroad (lat. 38°20'25" N, long. 122°30'25" W). Named on Santa Rosa (1916) 15' quadrangle.

Madrone Mineral Springs: see **Madrone Soda Springs** [SANTA CLARA].

Madrone Soda Springs [SANTA CLARA]: *spring,* nearly 3.5 miles south of Mount Sizer (lat. 37°10' N, long. 121°30'45" W; sec. 10, T 9 S, R 4 E); the spring is in Soda Springs Canyon. Named on Mount Sizer (1955) 7.5' quadrangle. Morgan Hill (1917) 15' quadrangle shows a group of buildings at the site. Several cottages and a small hotel were built there as early as 1880; in 1892 and subsequent years, water from the spring was taken in barrels to San Jose and bottled (Waring, p. 214). Winslow Anderson (p. 191) referred to Madrone Mineral Springs. Postal authorities established Madrone Springs post office in 1883 and discontinued it in 1895 (Frickstad, p. 174). Crawford (1896, p. 518) noted that Coe's Spring was located 1 mile west of Madrone Soda Springs.

Madrone Springs: see **Madrone Soda Springs** [SANTA CLARA].

Madrone Station: see **Madrone** [SANTA CLARA].

Magnesite: see **Cazadero** [SONOMA].

Magoon: see **Eaton H. Magoon Lake**, under **Aetna Springs** [NAPA].

Maguire Peaks [ALAMEDA]: *peaks,*, 4.25 miles southeast of Sunol (lat. 38°32'45" N, long. 121°50' W; sec. 35, T 4 S, R 1 E). Altitude of highest, 1688 feet. Named on La Costa Valley (1960) 7.5' quadrangle. The name commemorates Peter Maguire, an Irish farmer who settled in the neighborhood in the 1870's (Mosier and Mosier, p. 54).

Mailliard [MARIN]: *locality,* 8 miles south-southwest of downtown Novato along Northwestern Pacific Railroad (lat. 38°00'25" N, long. 122°38'10" W). Named on Petaluma (1914) 15' quadrangle.

Maine Prairie [SOLANO]: *locality,* 9 miles east-southeast of Elmira (lat. 38°18'25" N, long. 121°45'20" W; sec. 4, T 5 N, R 2 E). Site named on Dozier (1952) 7.5' quadrangle. Postal authorities established Maine Prairie post office in 1861 and discontinued it in 1913 (Frickstad, p. 192). In the early days, the place was at the head of navigation on present Maine Prairie Slough, and was a shipping point for wild-oat hay and for wheat before 1859; after a flood destroyed the community in 1862, many residents moved to a new town called Alton that was built on higher ground about 0.25 mile from the flooded site, but some of the flooded-out residents rebuilt at the original place (Hoover, Rensch, and Rensch, p. 524).

Maine Prairie Slough [SOLANO]: *water feature,* joins Cache Slough 9 miles east-southeast of Elmira at the site of Maine Prairie (lat. 38°18'30" N, long. 121°45'30" W; sec. 4, T 5 N, R 2 E). Named on Dozier (1952) 7.5' quadrangle. The feature was called Cache Slough about 1877 (Hoover, Rensch, and Rensch, p. 524).

Maine Prairie Station: see **Vale** [SOLANO].

Main Ridge [ALAMEDA]: *ridge,* west- to north-trending, nearly 3 miles long, 2.5 miles south-southwest of Dublin (lat. 37°40' N, long. 121°57' W). Named on Dublin (1961) 7.5' quadrangle.

Maintop Bay [SAN FRANCISCO]: *embayment,* on the northwest side of Southeast Farallon (lat. 37°42'05" N, long. 123°00'30" W). Named on Farallon Islands (1988) 7.5' quadrangle. Hoover (p. 14-15) gave the name "Franconia Bay" as an alternate designation for the embayment, and noted that this name commemorates a ship that was wrecked at the place.

Maintop Island [SAN FRANCISCO]: *island,* 1800 feet long, west of Southeast Farallon and only slightly separated from it (lat. 37°41'55" N, long. 123°00'35" W). Named on Farallon Islands (1988) 7.5' quadrangle.

Malacomas Range: see **Mayacmas Mountains** [NAPA].

Maladero Creek: see **Matadero Creek** [SANTA CLARA].

Ma-lek-ad-el Point: see **Dillon Point** [SOLANO].

Mallacomes or Morristul [SONOMA]: *land grant,* around the northwest end of Knights Valley. Named on Mount Saint Helena (1959) 7.5' quadrangle. Jose de los Santos Berryessa received 2 leagues in 1843; Martin E. Cook and Rufus Ingalls claimed 2560 acres patented in 1859 (Cowan, p. 46—Cowan listed the grant under the designation "Malacomes, (or) Moristal"; Perez, p. 72). The name "Mallacomes" is from an Indian village that was situated 1 mile south of present Calistoga; another Indian village in the region had the name "Moristul" (Kroeber, p. 46, 49).

Mallacomes or Moristul y Plan de Agua Caliente [NAPA-SONOMA]: *land grant,* at and around the southeast end of Alexander Valley on Napa-Sonoma County line, mainly in Sonoma County. Named on Calistoga (1958), Detert Reservoir (1958), Mark West Springs (1958), and Mount Saint Helena (1959) 7.5' quadrangles. Jose de los Santos Berryessa received 4 leagues in 1843 and claimed 17,743 acres patented in 1873 (Cowan, p. 46; Cowan listed the grant under the designation "Seno de Malacomes, (or) Moristal y Plan de Agua Caliente").

Mallard [ALAMEDA]: *locality,* less than 1 mile east-southeast of present Fremont civic center along Southern Pacific Railroad (lat. 37°32'45" N, long. 121°57'20" W). Named on Pleasanton (1906) 15' quadrangle. Another station called Mallard was located along South Pacific Coast Railroad north of Drawbridge (Mosier and Mosier, p. 54).

Mallard [CONTRA COSTA]: *locality,* 2.25 miles west-northwest of Pittsburg along Suisun Bay at the end of a spur of Sacramento Northern Railroad (lat. 38°02'35" N, long. 121°55'10" W); the place is on Mallard Island. Named on Pittsburg (1953) 15' quadrangle.

Mallard Branch: see **First Mallard Branch** [SOLANO]; **Second Mallard Branch** [SOLANO].

Mallard Island [CONTRA COSTA]: *island,* nearly 1 mile long, 2 miles west-northwest of Pittsburg in Suisun Bay (lat. 38°02'30" N, long. 121°55'10" W). Named on Honker Bay (1953) 7.5' quadrangle.

Mallard Lake [SAN FRANCISCO]: *lake,* 600 feet long, nearly 2 miles east-southeast of Point Lobos (lat. 37°46' N, long. 122°29'05" W). Named on San Francisco North (1956) 7.5' quadrangle.

Mallard Reservoir [CONTRA COSTA]: *lake,* 4500 feet long, 5 miles east of Martinez (lat. 38°01' N, long. 122°02'20" W). Named on Vine Hill (1959) 7.5' quadrangle.

Mallard Slough [CONTRA COSTA]: *water feature,* 2 miles west-northwest of Pittsburg between Mallard Island and the mainland (lat. 38°02'30" N, long. 121°55'15" W). Named on Honker Bay (1953) 7.5' quadrangle.

Maloney Reservoir [CONTRA COSTA]: *lake,* 550 feet long, nearly 5 miles north-northeast of Richmond civic center (lat. 37°59'55" N, long. 122°17'50" W; sec. 21, T 2 N, R 4 W). Named on Richmond (1959) 7.5' quadrangle.

Maloney's Hill: see **Ox Hill** [SAN MATEO].

Maltby [CONTRA COSTA]: *locality,* 3.5 miles east of Martinez along Atchison, Topeka and Santa Fe Railroad (lat. 38°00'55" N, long. 122°04'10" W). Named on Vine Hill (1959) 7.5' quadrangle.

Man Gulch: see **Eylar Canyon** [ALAMEDA].

Manhattan Beach [SAN MATEO]: *beach,* 2.25 miles south-southwest of downtown Half Moon Bay along the coast (lat. 37°25'55" N, long. 122°26'20" W). Named on Halfmoon Bay (1940) 15' quadrangle.

Manka: see **Mankas Corner** [SOLANO].

Mankas Corner [SOLANO]: *locality,* 4.25 miles northwest of Fairfield (lat. 38°17'10" N, long. 122°06'20" W). Named on Fairfield North (1951) 7.5' quadrangle. California Mining Bureau's (1909a) map shows a place called Manka located at or near present Mankas Corner. Postal authorities established Manka post office in 1895 and discontinued it in 1902 (Frickstad, p. 192).

Mannings Flats [SONOMA]: *area,* 3.5 miles north-northeast of Cazadero along East Austin Creek (lat. 38°34'45" N, long. 123°03'50" W; sec. 34, T 9 N, R 11 W). Named on Cazadero (1978) 7.5' quadrangle

Manor [MARIN]: *locality,* 3.5 miles west-northwest of downtown San Rafael (lat. 37°59'30" N, long. 122°35'30" W). Named on San Rafael (1954) 7.5' quadrangle. Postal authorities established Manor post office in 1915 and discontinued it in 1953; the name was from a real-estate promotion called Fairfax Manor (Salley, p. 131).

Man Ridge [ALAMEDA]: *ridge,* north- to west-northwest-trending, 4 miles long, 4.5 miles southeast of Cedar Mountain (lat. 37°30'20" N, long. 121°33'20" W). Named on Cedar Mountain (1956) and Eylar Mountain (1955) 7.5' quadrangles. The misspelled name commemorates George Mann, who settled at the place in 1855 (Mosier and Mosier, p. 54).

Mantua Gulch [SONOMA]: *canyon,* drained by a stream that flows 1 mile to Cheney Gulch 1.5 miles southeast of the village on Bodega Bay (lat. 38°19'05" N, long. 123°01'35" W). Named on Bodega Head (1972) 7.5' quadrangle.

Manzana [SONOMA]: *locality,* 4 miles northwest of Sebastopol along Petaluma and Santa Rosa Railroad (lat. 38°26'40" N, long. 122°52'15" W). Named on Sebastopol (1954) 7.5' quadrangle.

Manzanita [MARIN]: *locality,* 6.25 miles south of downtown San Rafael along Northwestern Pacific Railroad (lat. 37°52'55" N, long. 122°31' W). Named on San Rafael (1954) 7.5' quadrangle.

Manzanita Point [SANTA CLARA]: *ridge,* east-trending, nearly 1 mile long, 9 miles east-northeast of Morgan Hill (lat. 37°10'30" N, long. 121°30' W). Named on Mississippi Creek (1955) and Mount Sizer (1955) 7.5' quadrangles.

Manzanita Ridge [SANTA CLARA]: *ridge,* north-northwest- to west-trending, 2.5 miles long, 5 miles west of Morgan Hill (lat. 37° 08'20" N, long. 121°45'10" W). Named on Morgan Hill (1955) and Santa Teresa Hills (1953) 7.5' quadrangles.

Maple Spring [NAPA]: *spring,* 4 miles north-northeast of Calistoga (lat. 38°37'45" N, long. 122°32'50" W; sec. 17, T 9 N, R 6 W). Named on Detert Reservoir (1958) 7.5' quadrangle.

Marallone Islands: see **Farallon Islands** [SAN FRANCISCO].

Marble Mine Ridge [SONOMA]: *ridge,* east-southeast to east-trending, 1 mile long, 5.5 miles northeast of Cazadero (lat. 38°34'55" N, long. 123°00'30" W). Named on Cazadero (1978) 7.5' quadrangle. Marble Mine Ridge and Thompson Ridge (2) together are called Dutton Ridge on California Division of Forestry's (1945) map.

Marconi [MARIN]: *locality,* 7 miles south-southeast of Tomales on the northeast side of Tomales Bay (lat. 38°08'40" N, long. 122° 52'35" W). Named on Tomales (1954) 7.5' quadrangle. An Indian village called Fishermen's was at the site in the early days when trains stopped there to take on clams and fish; in 1913 Marconi Wireless Company bought land at the place to build a trans-Pacific receiving station (Mason, 1976a, p. 120-121).

Mare Island [SOLANO]: *peninsula,* center 1 mile southwest of downtown Vallejo between Mare Island Strait and San Pablo Bay (lat. 38°05'45" N, long. 122°16'15" W). Named on Benicia (1959) and Mare Island (1959) 7.5' quadrangles. Mare Island (1916) 15' quadrangle shows marsh separating the feature from the mainland at the north end. Juan Manuel de Ayala called the place Isla Plana in 1775 (Hoover, Rensch, and Rensch, p. 522). It also was known in the early days as Isla de la Yegua—*isla de la yegua* means "mare island" in Spanish—either from a lone mare stranded there after a boat wreck, or from horses pastured there by Victor Castro, owner of the place (Bancroft, 1888, p. 475, 630). Ringgold (p. 26) referred to Napa or Mare Island. Ringgold's (1850a) map shows Spear Pt. at the southwest end of Mare Island, and shows Pt. Thompson at the southeast end. Postal authorities established Mare Island post office in 1854, changed the name to Mare Island Naval in 1917, and it changed back to Mare Island in 1924 (Salley, p. 132).

Mare Island Naval: see **Mare Island** [SOLANO].

Mare Island Strait [SOLANO]: *water feature,* estuary of Napa River that opens into Carquines Strait 2 miles south-southeast of downtown Vallejo (lat. 38°04'30" N, long. 122°14'30" W); the feature is between Mare Island and the mainland. Named on Benicia (1959) and Mare Island (1959) 7.5' quadrangles. Ringgold (p. 26) noted that Mare Island forms "the Strait and Bay of Napa, in connection with a stream of the same name." Ringgold's (1850a) map shows Commission Rk. [Rock] in present Mare Island Strait about opposite the site of present downtown Vallejo.

Mare Pasture Ridge [SANTA CLARA]: *ridge,* east-trending, 1.5 miles long, 4 miles west-southwest of Mount Sizer (lat. 37°12'05" N, long. 121°34'50" W). Named on Mount Sizer (1955) 7.5' quadrangle.

Marie: see **Lake Marie** [NAPA].

Marin: see **Point Reyes Station** [MARIN].

Marina District [SAN FRANCISCO]: *district,* 2 miles north-northwest of San Francisco civic center along San Francisco Bay (lat. 37°48'10" N, long. 122°26'15" W). Named on San Francisco North (1956) 7.5' quadrangle. A small fresh-water lake located in present Marina District in the 1850's was called Washerwoman's Lagoon because San Francisco housewives washed their clothes there (O'Brien, p. 191). Davidson (p. 130) identified Washerwoman's Lagoon as the lake that the Spaniards called Pequeña Laguna. At least 30 dairies that were in present Marina District in the 1870's gave it the name "Cow Hollow" (O'Brien, p. 192).

Marin City [MARIN]: *town,* 1.5 miles northwest of downtown Sausalito (lat. 37°52'20" N, long. 122°30'40" W). Named on Point Bonita (1954) and San Rafael (1954) 7.5' quadrangles. In 1851 Benjamin R. Buckelew laid out a town that he called Marin City at a site near Point San Quintin, but the place failed to develop; modern Marin City started during World War II as housing for workers in shipyards near Sausalito (Teather, p. 39).

Marine [SAN MATEO]: *locality,* 2.5 miles south-southwest of present Montara Knob along Ocean Shore Railroad at present Moss Beach (lat. 37°31'15" N, long. 122°12'35" W). Named on San Mateo (1915) 15' quadrangle. Morrall (p. 155) called the place Marine View.

Marine View: see **Marine** [SAN MATEO].

Marin Island: see **East Marin Island** [MARIN]; **West Marin Island** [MARIN].

Marin Islands: see **East Marin Island** [MARIN].

Marin Meadows: see **Hamilton Air Force Base** [MARIN].

Marin Peninsula [MARIN]: *peninsula,* at the extreme southeast end of Marin County between Richardson Bay and the sea. Named on Point Bonita (1954) and San Francisco North (1956) 7.5' quadrangles.

Markham [SONOMA]: *locality,* 1.25 miles east of present Jenner along Northwestern Pacific Railroad (lat. 38°27'10" N, long. 123° 05'45" W). Named on Duncans Mills (1921) 15' quadrangle. Postal authorities established Markham post office in 1883, discontinued it in 1900, reestablished it in 1903, and discontinued it in 1910; the name was for Andrew Markham, first postmaster (Salley, p. 133).

Markle's Place: see **Cloverdale** [SONOMA].

Markleville: see **Cloverdale** [SONOMA].

Markley Canyon [CONTRA COSTA]: *canyon,* 3 miles long, opens into lowlands 8 miles north-northeast of Mount Diablo (lat. 37°59'10" N, long. 121°51'10" W; sec. 27, T 2 N, R 1 E). Named on Antioch North (1953) and Antioch South (1953) 7.5' quadrangles.

Markley Canyon [NAPA]: *canyon,* 3 miles long, opens into the canyon of Putah Creek 11.5 miles south-southeast of Berryessa Peak (lat. 38°30'35" N, long. 122°07' W; near E line sec. 30, T 8 N, R 2 W). Named on Capell Valley (1951) and Monticello Dam (1959) 7.5' quadrangles. Called Martley Canyon on Capay (1945) 15' quadrangle. Water of Lake Berryessa now covers the lower part of the canyon.

Mark West [SONOMA]: *locality,* 8.5 miles southeast of Healdsburg along Northwestern Pacific Railroad (lat. 38°30'35" N, long. 122° 46'55" W; sec. 39, T 8 N, R 8 W); the place is near the railroad crossing of Mark West Creek. Named on Healdsburg (1955) 7.5' quadrangle. Postal authorities established Mark West post office in 1865, discontinued it in 1871, reestablished it in 1872, discontinued it in 1873, reestablished it in 1874, and discontinued it in 1917 (Salley, p. 134).

Mark West Creek [SONOMA]: *stream,* flows 28 miles to Russian River 5.5 miles east of Guerneville (lat. 38°29'35" N, long. 122°53'30" W; sec. 31, T 8 N, R 9 W). Named on Calistoga (1958), Camp Meeker (1954), Healdsburg (1955), Mark West Springs (1958), and Sebastopol (1954) 7.5' quadrangles. Called West C. [Creek] on Goddard's (1857) map. The name commemorates Mark West, owner of San Miguel grant (Gudde, 1949, p. 205).

Mark West Springs [SONOMA]: *locality,* 7.5 miles north of Santa Rosa (lat. 38°32'55" N, long. 122°48'10" W; near SW cor. sec. 11, T 8 N, R 8 W); the place is along Mark West Creek. Named on Mark West Springs (1958) 7.5' quadrangle. Mineralized water from springs at the site was the basis of a resort as early as 1880 (Waring, p. 115).

Marsh: see **Avon** [CONTRA COSTA].

Marshall [MARIN]: *village,* 6 miles south of Tomales on the northeast side of Tomales Bay (lat. 38°09'40" N, long. 122°53'35" W). Named on Tomales (1954) 7.5' quadrangle. Postal authorities established Marshall post office in 1872 (Frickstad, p. 88). The name commemorates the Marshall brothers, who had a wharf and warehouse at the place (Mason, 1976a, p. 33). United States Board on Geographic Names (1973b, p. 3) approved the name "Marshall Beach" for a beach located 1.2 miles west of Marshall on the west shore of Tomales Bay (lat. 38°09'45" N, long. 122°54'50" W).

Marshall Beach: see **Marshall** [MARIN].

Marshall Creek [SONOMA]: *stream,* formed by the confluence of McKenzie Creek and Carson Creek, flows 6.5 miles to South Fork Gualala River 1.25 miles east-northeast of Plantation (lat. 38° 36' N, long. 123°17'15" W; sec. 27, T 9 N, R 13 W). Named on Fort Ross (1978) and Plantation (1977) 7.5' quadrangles. Called Sproule Creek on Fort Ross (1943) and Plantation (1943) 7.5' quadrangles, and United States Board on Geographic Names (1977a, p. 4) gave this name as a variant.

Marshall Cut [SOLANO]: *water feature,* joins Sacramento River 4.5 miles south-southeast of Birds Landing (2) (lat. 38°04'20" N, long. 121°49'55" W). Named on Antioch North (1953) 7.5' quadrangle. Collinsville (1918) 7.5' quadrangle shows a place called Montezuma Landing located at the mouth of the feature.

Marshall Gulch [SONOMA]: *canyon,* drained by a stream that flows 1 mile to the sea 3 miles north-northwest of the village of Bodega Bay (lat. 38°22'10" N, long. 123°04'20" W). Named on Bodega Head (1972) 7.5' quadrangle.

Marsh Creek [CONTRA COSTA]: *stream,* flows 22 miles to lowlands 3 miles south-southwest of Brentwood (lat. 37°53'40" N, long. 121°43'05" W). Named on Antioch South (1953), Brentwood (1954), Byron Hot Springs (1953), Jersey Island (1978), and Tassajara (1953) 7.5' quadrangles. The name commemorates John Marsh, who lived by the stream; the Spaniards called the feature Arroyo de los Poblanos (Gudde, 1949, p. 206).

Marsh Creek Reservoir [CONTRA COSTA]: *lake,* behind a dam on Marsh Creek 3.25 miles south-southwest of Brentwood (lat. 37°53'25" N, long. 121°43'30" W). Named on Brentwood (1978) 7.5' quadrangle.

Marsh Creek Springs [CONTRA COSTA]: *locality,* 3.25 miles east of Mount Diablo (lat. 37°53'30" N, long. 121°51'20" W; sec. 34, T 1 N, R 1 E). Named on Antioch South (1953) 7.5' quadrangle.

Marsh Landing [CONTRA COSTA]: *locality,* 2.5 miles east of present downtown Antioch along San Joaquin River (lat. 38°01'10" N, long. 121°45'45" W). Named on Collinsville (1918) 7.5' quadrangle. Ringgold's (1850b) map shows Marsh's Landing situated about 3 miles farther west. According to Gudde (1949, p. 206), John Marsh's shipping point was 4 miles west of Antioch, and was known as Marsh's Landing. Postal authorities established Marsh's Landing post office in 1852 and discontinued it in 1854 (Salley, p. 134).

Marsh Point: see **Redwood Point** [SAN MATEO].

Marsh's Landing: see **Marsh Landing** [CONTRA COSTA].

Marshs Landing: see **Antioch** [CONTRA COSTA].

Martin Canyon [ALAMEDA]: *canyon,* drained by a stream that flows 2.5 miles to lowlands at Dublin (lat. 37°42'20" N, long. 121° 56'35" W). Named on Dublin (1961) 7.5' quadrangle. The name commemorates William Henry Martin, John Samuel Martin, and Denis David Martin, who settled at the head of the canyon in the late 1850's (Mosier and Mosier, p. 55).

Martin Creek [SAN MATEO]: *stream,* flows 1.25 miles to Portola Valley (1) 6 miles south of downtown Redwood City (lat. 37°23'45" N, long. 122°14'45" W). Named on Palo Alto (1961) and Woodside (1961) 7.5' quadrangles. Brown (p. 26) called the stream Dennis Martin Creek, and noted that the name is for a lumberman who settled by the creek in 1851; Dry Creek was another name for the feature, and the canyon of a north fork was called Gang Mill Gulch.

Martin Creek [SONOMA]: *stream,* flows 4 miles to Barnes Creek 6.5 miles east-southeast of Healdsburg (lat. 38°35'15" N, long. 122°45'20" W; sec. 33, T 9 N, R 8 W). Named on Healdsburg (1955) and Mark West Springs (1958) 7.5' quadrangles.

Martinez [CONTRA COSTA]: *town,* 14 miles west-northwest of Mount Diablo (lat. 38°00'50" N, long. 122°08' W). Named on Benicia (1959), Briones Valley (1959), Vine Hill (1959), and Walnut Creek (1959) 7.5' quadrangles. Postal authorities established Martinez post office in 1851 (Frickstad, p. 22), and the town incorporated in 1876. Colonel William M. Smith laid out the community in 1849 and named it for Ignacio Martinez, who owned the land there (Gudde, 1949, p. 206). United States Board on Geographic Names (1995, p. 5) approved the name "Mount Helen" for a peak located 1.2 miles south of Martinez in John Muir National Historic Site (lat. 37°58'54" N, long. 122°07'56" W); the name is for Helen Lillian Muir Funk, youngest daughter of John Muir. The Board at the same time approved the name "Mount Wanda" for another peak located 1.2 miles south of Martinez in John Muir National Historic Site (lat. 37°59'01" N, long. 122°08'09" W; the name is for Annie Wanda Muir Hanna, eldest daughter of John Muir.

Martinez Reservoir [CONTRA COSTA]: *lake,* 1200 feet long, 1.5 miles east of downtown Martinez (lat. 38°00'35" N, long. 122°06'25" W). Named on Vine Hill (1959) 7.5' quadrangle. United States Board on Geographic Names (1948, p. 5) rejected the name "Mountain View Reservoir" for the feature.

Martinez Ridge [CONTRA COSTA]: *ridge,* northwest-trending, 0.5 mile long, 6.5 miles north-northwest of Walnut Creek civic center (lat. 37°59'25" N, long. 122°07'05" W); the ridge is south of Martinez. Named on Walnut Creek (1959) 7.5' quadrangle.

Martini Creek [SAN MATEO]: *stream,* flows 1.5 miles to the sea 1.5 miles west-southwest of Montara Knob (lat. 37°33'10" N, long. 122°30'45" W; sec. 28, T 4 S, R 6 W). Named on Montara Mountain (1956) 7.5' quadrangle. Martini ranch was along the creek after the early 1890's; before then the stream was called Arroyo de la Cuesta (Brown, p. 51).

Martin Ridge [SAN MATEO]: *ridge,* south-trending, 1.25 miles long, 4.5 miles southwest of La Honda (lat. 37°16'20" N, long. 122°19'35" W). Named on La Honda (1961) 7.5' quadrangle. The name commemorates Andrew Martin, who had a ranch at the place in the 1860's and 1870's (Brown, p. 51).

Martins Beach [SAN MATEO]: *settlement,* 6.25 miles south of downtown Half Moon Bay (lat. 37°22'30" N, long. 122°24'25" W). Named on Half Moon Bay (1961) and San Gregorio (1961) 7.5' quadrangles. The name commemorates Nicholas Martin, who owned land at the site (Gudde, 1949, p. 206).

Martin Spring [NAPA]: *spring,* 6 miles north-northeast of Saint Helena (lat. 38°34'50" N, long. 122°25'10" W). Named on Saint Helena (1960) 7.5' quadrangle.

Martley Canyon: see **Markley Canyon** [NAPA].

Mason: see **Andy Mason Slough,** under **Simmons Island** [SOLANO]; **Fort Mason Military Reservation** [SAN FRANCISCO].

Mason Ridge: see **Mesa Ridge** [SANTA CLARA].

Massachusetts: see **Point Massachusetts**, under **Point Edith** [CONTRA COSTA].

Masters Hill [SANTA CLARA]: *peak,* 5.25 miles west of Mount Hamilton (lat. 37°20'15" N, long. 121°44'10" W). Named on Lick Observatory (1955) 7.5' quadrangle.

Matadera Creek: see **Matadero Creek** [SANTA CLARA].

Matadero Creek [SANTA CLARA]: *stream,* flows 4 miles to lowlands 1 mile north-northeast of Coyote Hill (lat. 37°24'45" N, long. 122°08'15" W), and continues to San Francisco Bay in an artificial watercourse. Named on Mindego Hill (1961) and Palo Alto (1961) 7.5' quadrangles. Called Madera Creek on Santa Cruz (1902) 30' quadrangle, and called Matadera Creek on Palo Alto (1899) 15' quadrangle, which shows the stream ending short of San Francisco Bay near Mayfield. Called Arroyo de Matadera on Healy's (1866) map, and called Maladero Creek on Thompson and West's (1876) map. Gudde (1949, p. 201) noted that the name "Arroyo del Matadero" appears on maps of the 1830's and 1840's—*matadero* means "slaughtering place" in Spanish.

Matanzas Creek [SONOMA]: *stream,* flows 10 miles to Santa Rosa Creek in downtown Santa Rosa (lat. 38°26'15" N, long. 122°42'40" W). Named on Glen Ellen (1954), Kenwood (1954), and Santa Rosa (1954) 7.5' quadrangles. South Fork enters from the south 5.5 miles east-southeast of downtown Santa Rosa; it is 4.5 miles long and is named on Glen Ellen (1954), Kenwood (1954), and Santa Rosa (1954) 7.5' quadrangles.

Mathilde: see **Lake Mathilde** [SAN MATEO].

Mattos [ALAMEDA]: *locality,* 1.5 miles northeast of downtown Newark (lat. 37°32'40" N, long. 122°01' W). Named on Hayward (1915) 15' quadrangle. The name commemorates John Garcia Mattos, Sr., who settled at the place in 1879 (Mosier and Mosier, p. 55).

Maxmo Creek: see **Los Trancos Creek** [SAN MATEO].

Maxwell Creek [NAPA]: *stream,* flows 9 miles to Pope Creek 1.5 miles southeast of Walter Springs (lat. 38°38'10" N, long. 122°20'35" W; sec. 18, T 9 N, R 4 W). Named on Chiles Valley (1958), Saint Helena (1960), and Walter Springs (1959) 7.5' quadrangles.

Mayacamas Mountains: see **Mayacmas Mountains** [NAPA-SONOMA].

Mayacmas Mountains [NAPA-SONOMA]: *range,* mainly in Sonoma and Lake Counties, but extends south along Napa-Sonoma County line. Named on Asti (1959), Detert Reservoir (1958), Mark West Springs (1958), Mount Saint Helena (1959), The Geysers (1959), and Whispering Pines (1958) 7.5' quadrangles. United States Board on Geographic Names (1933, p. 525) approved the name "Miyakma Range" for the feature, and rejected the names "Cobb Mountain Range," "Malacomas Range," "Mayacmis Range," and "St. Helena Range." Later the Board (1942, p. 35) approved the name "Mayacmas Mountains" for the same feature, and rejected the names "Miyakma Range," "Mayacamas Mountains," and "St. Helena Range."

Mayacmis Range: see **Mayacmas Mountains** [NAPA-SONOMA].

Mayfield [SANTA CLARA]: *town,* nearly 2 miles southeast of downtown Palo Alto, and now part of Palo Alto (lat. 37°25'30" N, long. 122°08'30" W). Named on Palo Alto (1899) 15' quadrangle. A village developed around a public house that James Otterson built at the site in 1853, and the town was laid out in 1867 (Hoover, Rensch, and Rensch, p. 462). The place took its name from nearby Mayfield farm (Butler, p. 11). Postal authorities established Mayfield post office in 1855 and changed the name to Palo Alto Station "A" in 1930 (Salley, p. 135). Palo Alto annexed Mayfield in 1925, and the name of the railroad station at Mayfield was changed to South Palo Alto (Brown, p. 52).

Mayfield Slough [SANTA CLARA]: *water feature,* consists of a series of elongate lakes and intermittent lakes that extend to flatlands near San Francisco Bay 5 miles north-northwest of downtown Mountain View (lat. 37°26'50" N, long. 122°06'15" W). Named on Mountain View (1961) 7.5' quadrangle. A landing called Embarcadero de San Francisquito was on a side channel of the slough in the 1850's; it was the shipping point for Mayfield (Brown, p. 52).

Mayhews Landing: see **Jarvis Landing** [ALAMEDA].

Mayhew Spring: see **Niles District** [ALAMEDA].

Mayhew's Sulphur Spring: see **Mayhew Spring**, under **Niles District** [ALAMEDA].

Mays Canyon [SONOMA]: *canyon,* drained by a stream that flows 2 miles to Pocket Canyon at the south edge of Guerneville (lat. 38° 29'50" N, long. 122°59'25" W; sec. 32, T 8 N, R 10 W). Named on Camp Meeker (1954) 7.5' quadrangle.

Mays Flat [NAPA]: *area,* 6.5 miles north-northwest of Berryessa Peak on Napa-Yolo County line (lat. 38°45' N, long. 122°14'30" W; near NE cor. sec. 1, T 10 N, R 4 W). Named on Brooks (1959) and Guinda (1959) 7.5' quadrangles.

McAvoy [CONTRA COSTA]: *locality,* 4.25 miles west of Pittsburg along Atchison, Topeka and Santa Fe Railroad (lat. 38°02'20" N, long. 121°57'30" W). Named on Honker Bay (1953) 7.5' quadrangle.

McAvoy Boat Harbor [CONTRA COSTA]: *water feature,* 4 miles west of Pittsburg along Suisun Bay (lat. 38°02'25" N, long. 121°57'25" W); the harbor is at McAvoy. Named on Honker Bay (1953) 7.5' quadrangle.

McCall: see **Jim McCall's Gulch**, under **Jones Gulch** [SAN MATEO] (2).

McCartysville: see **Saratoga** [SANTA CLARA].

McCauley [SONOMA]: *locality,* 4 miles east-northeast of Sebastopol along Petaluma and Santa Rosa Railroad (lat. 38°25'30" N, long. 122°45'30" W). Named on Sebastopol (1942) 15' quadrangle.

McChristian Creek [SONOMA]: *stream,* flows 1 mile to Mendocino County 6.5 miles west-northwest of Cloverdale (lat. 38°49'30" N, long. 123°08'05" W; near SW cor. sec. 6, T 11 N, R 11 W). Named on Hopland (1960) 15' quadrangle.

McClennon Gulch [SONOMA]: *canyon,* drained by a stream that flows 1 mile to Fisherman Bay 0.25 mile south-southeast of the village of Stewarts Point (lat. 38°38'50" N, long. 122°23'50" W). Named on Stewarts Point (1978) 7.5' quadrangle.

McClures Beach [MARIN]: *beach,* 5.25 miles southwest of Tomales along the coast (lat. 38°11'15" N, long. 122°57'50" W). Named on Tomales (1954) 7.5' quadrangle. James McClure and Margaret McClure bought the beach in 1929 (Teather, p. 45).

McCoppin: see **Lake McCoppin**, under **Mission District** [SAN FRANCISCO].

McCormick Creek [MARIN]: *stream,* flows 2 miles to Pine Gulch Creek 2.25 miles northwest of Bolinas (lat. 37°56'05" N, long. 122°42'50" W). Named on Bolinas (1954) 7.5' quadrangle.

McCormick Creek [SAN MATEO]: *stream,* flows nearly 2 miles to Pescadero Creek 3 miles south-southwest of La Honda (lat. 37° 16'35" N, long. 122°17'05" W; sec. 34, T 7 S, R 4 W). Named on La Honda (1961) 7.5' quadrangle.

McCoy Creek [SOLANO]: *stream,* flows 1.5 miles to Laurel Creek 3 miles north-northeast of Fairfield (lat. 38°17'20" N, long. 122°01'10" W). Named on Mount Vaca (1942) 15' quadrangle.

McCoy Slough: see **Hastings Cut** [SOLANO].

McCray Mountain [SONOMA]: *peak,* 4.25 miles north of Guerneville (lat. 38°33'50" N, long. 122°59'35" W; sec. 5, T 8 N, R 10 W). Altitude 1940 feet. Named on Guerneville (1955) 7.5' quadrangle.

McCrays: see **Cloverdale** [SONOMA].

McCune Creek [SOLANO]:

(1) *stream,* flows 3.5 miles to Putah Creek 4.5 miles northwest of Allendale (lat. 38°29'50" N, long. 121°59'50" W). Named on Allendale (1953) and Mount Vaca (1951) 7.5' quadrangles.

(2) *water feature,* artificial watercourse that joins Sweany Creek 3.5 miles southwest of Dixon (lat. 38°24'35" N, long. 121°52'50" W; sec. 33, T 7 N, R 1 E). Named on Dixon (1952, photorevised 1968 and 1975) 7.5' quadrangle. On Vacaville (1953) 15' quadrangle, the name applies to a stream that heads 9 miles west-northwest of Dixon and flows 11.5 miles to Sweany Creek 3.5 miles southwest of Dixon.

McCutchin Canyon [SANTA CLARA]: *canyon,* drained by a stream that flows 1 mile to lowlands 1.5 miles west-southwest of Gilroy (lat. 36°59'50" N, long. 121°35'45" W). Named on Chittenden (1955) 7.5' quadrangle.

McDonnell Creek [SONOMA]: *stream,* flows 4.25 miles to join Briggs Creek and form Maacama Creek 6 miles west of Mount Saint Helena (lat. 38°40'25" N, long. 122°44'30" W; near W line sec. 34, T 10 N, R 8 W). Named on Mount Saint Helena (1959) 7.5' quadrangle.

McDowell: see **Fort McDowell** [MARIN-SAN FRANCISCO].

McElroy Creek [SANTA CLARA]: *stream,* flows 1.25 miles to Bonjetti Creek 1.5 miles north-northeast of Bielawski Mountain (lat. 37°14'35" N, long. 122°05' W; near N line sec. 16, T 8 S, R 2 W). Named on Castle Rock Ridge (1955) 7.5' quadrangle.

McGarvey Gulch [SAN MATEO]: *canyon,* drained by a stream that flows nearly 2 miles to West Union Creek 2.5 miles north-northeast of Skeggs Point (lat. 37°26'40" N, long. 122°17'25" W). Named on Woodside (1961) 7.5' quadrangle. Owen McGarvey had a claim and cut wood in the canyon about 1860 (Brown, p. 53).

McGill [SONOMA]: *locality,* 3.25 miles north of Sears Point along Northwestern Pacific Railroad (lat. 38°11'55" N, long. 122°26'05" W). Named on Sears Point (1951) 7.5' quadrangle.

McGill's Wharf: see **Miramar** [SAN MATEO].

McGlinchey Spring [SANTA CLARA]: *spring,* 4 miles west of Eylar Mountain (lat. 37°28'55" N, long. 121°37'15" W; sec. 23, T 5 S, R 3 E). Named on Eylar Mountain (1955) 7.5' quadrangle.

McKenzie Creek [SONOMA]: *stream,* flows 4 miles to join Carson Creek and form Marshall Creek 4 miles north-northeast of Fort Ross (lat. 38°33'50" N, long. 123°12'20" W; sec. 5, T 8 N, R 12 W). Named on Fort Ross (1978) 7.5' quadrangle.

McKinnan Gulch [MARIN]: *canyon,* drained by a stream that flows 1.25 miles to Bolinas Lagoon 1.25 miles east of Bolinas (lat. 37° 54'45" N, long. 122°39'45" W). Named on Bolinas (1954) 7.5' quadrangle. The name commemorates Hugh McKennan, who bought land at Bolinas in 1867 and raised ducks there (Teather, p. 46).

McNear [SONOMA]: *locality,* 1.5 miles east-southeast of downtown Petaluma along Northwestern Pacific Railroad (lat. 38°13'45" N, long. 122°36'50" W). Named on Petaluma River (1954) 7.5' quadrangle.

McNear: see **McNears Beach** [MARIN].

McNear Landing: see **McNears Beach** [MARIN].

McNears Beach [MARIN]: *locality,* 0.5 mile north-northwest of Point San Pedro along San Pablo Bay (lat. 37°59'35" N, long. 122° 07'10" W). Named on San Quentin (1959) 7.5' quadrangle. United States Board on Geographic Names (1968a, p. 5) rejected the names "McNear" and "McNear Landing" for the place. California Mining Bureau's (1909a) map shows a place called McNear located at or near present Point San Pedro. Postal authorities established McNear post office 6 miles northeast of San Rafael in 1897 and discontinued it in 1910; the name was from McNears Point and McNears Landing (Salley, p. 136). The place developed as a fishing center in the 1870's; the name was taken from the firm of McNear and Brothers, owners of the land (Gudde, 1949, p. 200).

McNears Point: see **Point San Pedro** [MARIN].

McPherson: see **Mount McPherson**, under **Bielawski Mountain** [SANTA CLARA].

Meacham Hill [SONOMA]: *ridge,* southeast-trending, 1.5 miles long, 2.25 miles south-southeast of Cotati (lat. 38°17'35" N, long. 122°41'35" W). Named on Cotati (1954) 7.5' quadrangle. Called Meachim Hill on Santa Rosa (1944) 15' quadrangle.

Meachim Hill: see **Meacham Hill** [SONOMA].

Meadows: see **The Meadows** [SONOMA].

Meadowsweet [MARIN]: *locality,* 3.5 miles south-southeast of downtown San Rafael along Northwestern Pacific Railroad (lat. 37°55'25" N, long. 122°30'35" W). Named on San Rafael (1954) 7.5' quadrangle.

Medora Lake [SOLANO]: *lake,* 900 feet long, 11 miles north-northeast of Rio Vista in Yolo Bypass (lat. 38°18'35" N, long. 121°38'25" W). Named on Liberty Island (1978) 7.5' quadrangle.

Medora Lake: see **Little Medora Lake** [SOLANO].

Meeker: see **Camp Meeker** [SONOMA]; **Occidental** [SONOMA].

Meinert [CONTRA COSTA]: *locality,* 3.25 miles north-northeast of Walnut Creek civic center along Sacramento Northern Railroad (lat. 37°56'40" N, long. 122°01'35" W). Named on Walnut Creek (1959) 7.5' quadrangle.

Meins Landing [SOLANO]: *locality,* 6 miles south of Denverton along Montezuma Slough (lat. 38°08'25" N, long. 121°54'25" W; at N line sec. 6, T 3 N, R 1 E). Named on Denverton (1953) 7.5' quadrangle.

Melita [SONOMA]: *locality,* 4 miles east-northeast of downtown Santa Rosa (lat. 38°27'30" N, long. 122°38'20" W). Named on Santa Rosa (1954) 7.5' quadrangle. Called Melitta on Santa Rosa (1916) 15' quadrangle. Postal authorities established Melitta post office in 1891 and discontinued it in 1900 (Frickstad, p. 197).

Melita: see **Oakland** [ALAMEDA].

Melitta: see **Melita** [SONOMA].

Melrose [ALAMEDA]: *locality,* 4 miles southeast of downtown Oakland (lat. 37°46' N, long. 122°13' W). Named on Concord (1897) 15' quadrangle. Postal authorities established Melrose post office in 1881, discontinued it for a time in 1887, and discontinued it finally in 1908 (Frickstad, p. 2). Officials of San Francisco and Oakland Railroad had a station called Austin built at the place in 1862; the station was renamed for the community of Melrose in 1906—it also was called Simpson's for Robert Simson, who owned land at the place; Oakland annexed Melrose in 1909 (Mosier and Mosier, p. 56).

Melville: see **Mount Melville** [SAN MATEO].

Mendenhall Springs [ALAMEDA]: *spring,* 9 miles southeast of Livermore (lat. 37°35'15" N, long. 121°38'45" W; sec. 16, T 4 S, R 3 E). Named on Mendenhall Springs (1956) 7.5' quadrangle. Tesla (1907) 15' quadrangle has the name for a group of buildings at the spring. William M. Mendenhall opened a health resort at the place in the 1870's (Mosier and Mosier, p. 56). The resort had accommodations for 75 people in 1909; water that seeps from two short tunnels, dug to prospect for gold, is mineralized and was bottled under the name "Ague de Vida Springs Water" (Waring, p. 309-310).

Mendosoma: see **Tobacco Creek** [SONOMA].

Menlo Park [SAN MATEO]: *city,* 3.25 miles southeast of downtown Redwood City (lat. 37°27'15" N, long. 122°10'55" W). Named on Mountain View (1961) and Palo Alto (1961) 7.5' quadrangles. Dennis J. Oliver and his brother-in-law, D.C. McGlynn, built a wooden arch at the entrance to their property in present Menlo Park in the 1850's, and put the name "Menlo Park" on the arch in memory of their former home at Menlough, Ireland; when the railroad reached the place in 1863, the station there was called Menlo Park and the community around the station took that name—the city incorporated in 1874 and again in 1927 (Hoover, Rensch, and Rensch, p. 408-409). Postal authorities established Menlo Park post office in 1870 (Frickstad, p. 168). An army post called Camp Fremont occupied thousands of acres of leased land west of present downtown Menlo Park during World War I (Hynding, p. 199).

Menzesville: see **Redwood City** [SAN MATEO].

Merazo [SONOMA]: *locality,* 6.25 miles northeast of Sears Point along Southern Pacific Railroad (lat. 38°13' N, long. 122°22'10" W). Named on Cuttings Wharf (1949) 7.5' quadrangle.

Merced Lake: see **Lake Merced** [SAN FRANCISCO].

Mercury: see **Guerneville** [SONOMA].

Mercuryville [SONOMA]: *locality,* 1.5 miles east-northeast of Geyser Peak (lat. 38°46'35" N, long. 122°49'15" W; near NW cor. sec. 25, T 11 N, R 9 W). Named on The Geysers (1959) 7.5' quadrangle.

Mercuryville: see **Guerneville** [SONOMA].

Meridian [SANTA CLARA]: *locality,* 4.5 miles west of downtown San Jose (lat. 37°19'25" N, long. 121°58'10" W). Named on San Jose West (1961) 7.5' quadrangle. Peninsular Railway Company's (1912) map shows a station called Meridian located where a branch line to Saratoga leaves the main line between Cupertino and San Jose. The same map shows a place called Scotts Spur located just west of Meridian, a station called Bascome located about halfway from Meridian to downtown San Jose, a station called Moreland located about half way from Meridian to Congress Junction, and a place called Prospect Spur located a short distance beyond Moreland .

Meridian Ridge [CONTRA COSTA]: *ridge,* north-trending, 1.5 miles long, 2 miles north-northwest of Mount Diablo (lat. 37°54'30" N, long. 121°55'35" W); the ridge is 0.5 mile west of Mount Diablo Meridian. Named on Clayton (1953) 7.5' quadrangle.

Merienda: see **Dresser** [ALAMEDA].

Merritt: see **Lake Merritt** [ALAMEDA]; **Liberty** [SONOMA].

Mesa: see **The Mesa** [SAN MATEO].

Mesa Grande [SONOMA]: *settlement,* 2.5 miles southwest of Guerneville along Russian River (lat. 38°28'35" N, long. 123°01'05" W). Named on Duncans Mills (1979) 7.5' quadrangle. Duncans Mills (1921) 15' quadrangle shows both Mesa Grande and Grandville P.O. at the place. Postal authorities established Grandville post office in 1907 and discontinued it in 1921 (Frickstad, p. 195).

Mesa Grande Gulch [SONOMA]: *canyon,* drained by a stream that flows 0.5 mile to Russian River nearly 3 miles southwest of Guerneville (lat. 38°28'10" N, long. 123°01'50" W). Named on Duncans Mills (1979) 7.5' quadrangle.

Mesa Ridge [SANTA CLARA]: *ridge,* east-trending, 2.5 miles long, 2 miles southwest of Eylar Mountain (lat. 37°27' N, long. 121° 34' W). Named on Eylar Mountain (1955) 7.5' quadrangle. Called Mason Ridge on Mount Hamilton (1897) 15' quadrangle.

Metcalfe Canyon [SANTA CLARA]: *canyon,* drained by a stream that flows nearly 2 miles to lowlands 1 mile north-northwest of Coyote (lat. 37°13'50" N, long. 121°44'45" W). Named on Morgan Hill (1955) 7.5' quadrangle.

Mexican Camp [SANTA CLARA]: *locality,* 1.25 miles west of New Almaden near New Almaden mine (lat. 37°10'30" N, long. 121°50'35" W). Site named on Santa Teresa Hills (1953) 7.5' quadrangle. Lanyon and Bulmore (p. 45) called the place Spanishtown.

Meyer [SONOMA]: *locality,* 3 miles northwest of present Jenner (lat. 38°28'50" N, long. 123°09'50" W). Named on Duncans Mills (1921) 15' quadrangle.

Meyer Gulch [SONOMA]: *canyon,* drained by a stream that flows 0.5 mile to the sea 4.25 miles northwest of Jenner (lat. 38°29'05" N, long. 123°10'55" W). Named on Arched Rock (1977) 7.5' quadrangle.

Middle Creek [NAPA]: *stream,* flows nearly 2 miles to Capell Creek 9 miles northwest of Mount Vaca (lat. 38°28'30" N, long. 122°14'05' W; near N line sec. 7, T 7 N, R 3 W). Named on Capell Valley (1951) 7.5' quadrangle.

Middle Farallon [SAN FRANCISCO]: *island,* 2.5 miles northwest of Southeast Farallon (lat. 37°43'40" N, long. 123°01'50" W); the island is between Southeast Farallon and North Farallon. Named on Farallon Islands (1988) 7.5' quadrangle. According to United States Coast and Geodetic Survey (p. 123), the feature consists of a single 20-foot rock 150 feet in diameter.

Middlefield Reservoir [ALAMEDA]: *lake,* 450 feet long, 2 miles southeast of Fremont civic center (lat. 37°31'45" N, long. 121°56'45" W; sec. 2, T 5 S, R 1 W). Named on Niles (1961) 7.5' quadrangle. The reservoir, built in the 1950's, is named for Middlefield Avenue (Mosier and Mosier, p. 56).

Middle Ground Island [SOLANO]: *island,* 7.5 miles southwest of Birds

Landing (2) in Suisun Bay (lat. 38°03'45" N, long. 121°58'50" W). Named on Honker Bay (1953) 7.5' quadrangle.

Middle Lake [SAN FRANCISCO]: *lake,* 350 feet long, 1.25 miles southeast of Point Lobos (lat. 37°46'05" N, long. 122°29'55" W); the feature is between North Lake and South Lake. Named on San Francisco North (1956) 7.5' quadrangle.

Middle Pass: see **Patterson Pass** [ALAMEDA].

Middle Peak [MARIN]: *peak,* 4.5 miles southwest of downtown San Rafael on Mount Tamalpais (lat. 37°55'40" N, long. 122°35'15" W). Named on San Rafael (1954) 7.5' quadrangle.

Middle Point [CONTRA COSTA]: *promontory,* 6 miles west-northwest of Pittsburg along Suisun Bay (lat. 38°03'20" N, long. 121°59'30" W). Named on Honker Bay (1953) 7.5' quadrangle. Called Pt. Stephenson on Ringgold's (1850b) map.

Middle Point: see **Franklin Point** [SAN MATEO].

Middle Ridge [SANTA CLARA]: *ridge,* northwest-trending, 3.5 miles long, nearly 1.5 miles southwest of Mount Sizer (lat. 37°12' N, long. 121°31'45" W). Named on Mount Sizer (1955) 7.5' quadrangle.

Middle Slough [CONTRA COSTA]: *water feature,* extends for 1.25 miles, between Browns Island and Winter Island, from New York Slough to Suisun Bay 3.5 miles northwest of Antioch (lat. 38°02'50" N, long. 121°51'35" W). Named on Antioch North (1978) 7.5' quadrangle. Called Beeners Channel on Ringgold's (1850b) map.

Middleton [NAPA]: *locality,* 1.5 miles north-northwest of Napa Junction along Southern Pacific Railroad (lat. 38°12'20" N, long. 122°15'45" W; at W line sec. 12, T 4 N, R 4 W). Named on Cuttings Wharf (1949) 7.5' quadrangle.

Midshipman Point [SONOMA]: *promontory,* 2.5 miles south of Sears Point along San Pablo Bay (lat. 38°07' N, long. 122°27' W). Named on Petaluma Point (1959) 7.5' quadrangle. Postal Route (1884) map has the name "Sonoma Ldg." along San Pablo Bay near present Midshipman Point at the end of Sonoma Valley Railroad.

Midway [ALAMEDA]: *locality,* 6 miles east-southeast of Altamont along Southern Pacific Railroad (lat. 37°42'55" N, long. 121°33'30" W; sec. 32, T 2 S, R 4 E). Named on Midway (1953) 7.5' quadrangle. Postal authorities established Midway post office in 1870 and discontinued it in 1918 (Frickstad, p. 2).

Midway Siding [ALAMEDA]: *locality,* less than 1 mile south-southwest of Midway along Western Pacific Railroad (lat. 37°42'20" N, long. 121°34' W; at W line sec. 5, T 3 S, R 4 E). Named on Midway (1953) 7.5' quadrangle.

Miguelita Creek [SANTA CLARA]: *stream,* flows 0.5 mile to lowlands 2.5 miles east of Berryessa (lat. 37°23'05" N, long. 121°48'50" W); the same name applies to a stream that joins Coyote Creek in central San Jose (lat. 37°21'20" N, long. 121°52'20" W), but the two streams are unconnected through the intervening urban area. Named on Calaveras Reservoir (1961) and San Jose East (1961) 7.5' quadrangles.

Milagra Ridge [SAN MATEO]: *ridge,* northwest- to west-northwest-trending, 1.25 miles long, 4 miles west-southwest of downtown South San Francisco (lat. 37°38'25" N, long. 122°28'45" W); the ridge is south of Milagra Valley. Named on San Francisco South (1956) 7.5' quadrangle.

Milagra Valley [SAN MATEO]: *canyon,* drained by a stream that flows nearly 2 miles to the sea 4.5 miles west-southwest of downtown South San Francisco (lat. 37°38'40" N, long. 122°29'35" W). Named on San Francisco South (1956) 7.5' quadrangle. Brown (p. 58) gave the names "Morrissey's Gulch" and "Dini Gulch" as alternates, and noted that Lawrence Morrissey and Patrick Morrissey had a ranch at the place after 1900.

Mile Rock [SAN FRANCISCO]: *rock,* less than 1 mile north-northeast of Point Lobos, and 2100 feet offshore at Lands End (lat. 37°47'35" N, long. 122°30'35" W). Named on San Francisco North (1956) 7.5' quadrangle. This rock and nearby Little Mile Rock are called Mile Rocks on San Francisco (1915) 15' quadrangle. Beechey gave the two rocks the name "One-mile Rocks" in 1826 because they are 1 mile south of the channel leading to the Golden Gate (Gudde, 1949, p. 214). Ringgold (p. 24) used the form "One Mile Rocks" for the name.

Mile Rock: see **Little Mile Rock** [SAN FRANCISCO].

Mile Rocks [SONOMA]: *rocks,* 1.5 miles west-southwest of Jenner, and nearly 1 mile offshore (lat. 38°26'25" N, long. 123°08'30" W). Named on Arched Rock (1977) 7.5' quadrangle.

Mile Rocks: see **Mile Rock** [SAN FRANCISCO].

Miley: see **Fort Miley Military Reservation** [SAN FRANCISCO].

Millar [SOLANO]: *locality,* 6 miles east-southeast of Dixon along Oakland Antioch and Eastern Railroad (lat. 38°23'30" N, long. 121°43'15" W; sec. 2, T 6 N, R 2 E). Named on Saxon (1916) 7.5' quadrangle.

Millbrae [SAN MATEO]: *town,* 4 miles south-southeast of downtown South San Francisco (lat. 37°36'05" N, long. 122°23'25" W). Named on Montara Mountain (1956) and San Mateo (1956) 7.5' quadrangles. Darius Ogden Mills bought land at the place in 1860 and built an estate that he called Millbrae (Hoover, Rensch, and Rensch, p. 403). The name later was applied to the railroad station there (Gudde, 1949, p. 215). Postal authorities established Millbrae post office in 1866, discontinued it in 1874, and reestablished it in 1875 (Frickstad, p. 168). The town incorporated in 1948.

Millbrae Meadows [SAN MATEO]: *district,* 1.5 miles west of downtown Millbrae (lat. 37°36'15" N, long. 122°25' W). Named on Montara Mountain (1956) 7.5' quadrangle.

Mill Creek [NAPA]: *stream,* flows 3.5 miles to Napa River 3 miles north-northwest of Saint Helena (lat. 38°32'40" N, long. 122°29'45" W). Named on Calistoga (1958) and Saint Helena (1960) 7.5' quadrangles. Calistoga (1958) 7.5' quadrangle shows Bale Mill historical monument by the stream.

Mill Creek [SONOMA]:

(1) *stream,* flows 11 miles to Dry Creek less than 2 miles south of Healdsburg (lat. 38°35'20" N, long. 122°52'10" W). Named on Guerneville (1955) and Healdsburg (1955) 7.5' quadrangles. The name is from March's Mill, a lumber mill of 1850 (LeBaron and others, p. 13).

(2) *stream,* flows 2.5 miles to Sonoma Creek 1 mile south-southeast of Glen Ellen (lat. 38°21' N, long. 122°30'50" W). Named on Glen Ellen (1954) 7.5' quadrangle.

(3) *stream,* flows 2.25 miles to Mark West Creek 1.25 miles east of Mark West Springs (lat. 38°32'50" N, long. 122°41'50" W; at N line sec. 13, T 8 N, R 8 W). Named on Mark West Springs (1958) 7.5' quadrangle.

Mill Creek: see **Redwood Canyon** [NAPA].

Miller [MARIN]: *locality,* 6 miles south-southeast of downtown Novato along Northwestern Pacific Railroad (lat. 38°01'40" N, long. 122°31'20" W); the place is near the railroad crossing of present Miller Creek. Named on Petaluma (1914) 15' quadrangle. The name is for James Miller, who settled in present Marin County in 1845 (Gudde, 1949, p. 215).

Miller [SANTA CLARA]: *locality,* 3.5 miles south-southeast of Gilroy along Southern Pacific Railroad (lat. 36°57'25" N, long. 121°32'40" W). Named on Chittenden (1955) 7.5' quadrangle. Thompson and West's (1876) map shows a place called Miller's Station at the site, and shows Bloomfield farm nearby to the northwest. Miller-Lux ranch had its headquarters at Bloomfield, 3 miles south of Gilroy, where a self-contained community included a railroad station (Pierce, p. 177).

Miller Canyon [SOLANO]: *canyon,* 4.5 miles long, opens into Pleasants Valley 4 miles northeast of Mount Vaca (lat. 38°26'35" N, long. 122°03'30" W; near W line sec. 23, T 7 N, R 2 W); the feature is along upper reaches of Pleasants Creek. Named on Mount Vaca (1951) 7.5' quadrangle. United States Board on Geographic Names (1933, p. 520) rejected the name "Pleasants Canyon" for the feature. The stream in the canyon is called Miller Canyon Creek on Mount Vaca (1942) 15' quadrangle.

Miller Canyon: see **Miller Creek** [ALAMEDA].

Miller Canyon Creek: see **Miller Canyon** [SOLANO].

Miller Creek [ALAMEDA]: *stream,* flows 1.5 miles to San Leandro Creek 10.5 miles east-southeast of downtown Oakland (lat. 37°45'50" N, long. 122°05'30" W; sec. 16, T 2 S, R 2 W). Named on Las Trampas Ridge (1959) 7.5' quadrangle. The name commemorates William Hunt Miller, who settled at the head of the canyon of the stream—called Miller Canyon—in 1856 (Mosier and Mosier, p. 57).

Miller Creek [MARIN]: *stream,* flows 7 miles to lowlands 5.5 miles south-southeast of downtown Novato (lat. 38°01'55" N, long. 122° 31'30" W). Named on Novato (1954) 7.5' quadrangle.

Miller Creek [SONOMA]:

(1) *stream,* flows 4.5 miles to Russian River 1 mile east of Geyserville (lat. 38°42'20" N, long. 122°53'05" W). Named on Geyserville (1955) and Jimtown (1955) 7.5' quadrangles.

(2) *stream,* flows 3 miles to the sea 1.5 miles west-southwest of Plantation (lat. 38°34'50" N, long. 123°20'05" W). Named on Plantation (1977) 7.5' quadrangle.

Miller Flat [NAPA]: *area,* 3.5 miles east-northeast of Calistoga in Dutch Henry Canyon (lat. 38°36'05" N, long. 122°31'20" W; sec. 28, T 9 N, R 6 W). Named on Calistoga (1958) 7.5' quadrangle.

Miller Ridge [SONOMA]: *ridge,* northwest-trending, 4 mile long, center 2.25 miles north-northeast of the village of Stewarts Point (lat. 38°41' N, long. 123°23' W). Named on Annapolis (1977) and Stewarts Point (1978) 7.5' quadrangles.

Miller Slough [SANTA CLARA]: *stream,* the continuation of West Branch Llagas Creek has this name for 3.5 miles south from Gilroy to where it joins Llagas Creek (lat. 36°59'25" N, long. 121°31'50" W). Named on Chittenden (1955) and Gilroy (1955) 7.5' quadrangles.

Millers Peak: see **Putnam Peak** [SOLANO].

Miller's Station: see **Miller** [SANTA CLARA].

Millerton [MARIN]: *locality,* 3.5 miles northwest of Point Reyes Station (lat. 38°06'30" N, long. 122°50'40" W); the place is near the mouth of Millerton Gulch. Named on Inverness (1954) 7.5' quadrangle. James Miller had a large wharf at the place (Mason, 1976a, p. 33).

Millerton Gulch [MARIN]: *canyon,* drained by a stream that flows nearly 4 miles to Tomales Bay 3.5 miles northwest of Point Reyes Station (lat. 38°06'20" N, long. 122°50'25" W). Named on Inverness (1954) and Point Reyes NE (1954) 7.5' quadrangles.

Millerton Point [MARIN]: *promontory,* 3.5 miles northwest of Point Reyes Station on the northeast side of Tomales Bay (lat. 38°06'30" N, long. 122°51'05" W); the promontory is near Millerton. Named on Inverness

(1954) 7.5' quadrangle.

Mill Gulch [SONOMA]: *canyon,* drained by a stream that flows 1.5 miles to the sea 1.5 miles southeast of Fort Ross (lat. 38°30' N, long. 123°13'20" W). Named on Fort Ross (1978) 7.5' quadrangle.

Mill Gulch: see **Copper Mine Gulch** [MARIN].

Milliken Canyon [NAPA]: *canyon,* 6.25 miles long, along Milliken Creek above a point 4.25 miles north-northeast of downtown Napa (lat. 38°21'30" N, long. 122°15'30" W; sec. 24, T 6 N, R 4 W). Named on Capell Valley (1951), Mount George (1951), and Napa (1951) 7.5' quadrangles.

Milliken Creek [NAPA]: *stream,* flows 10.5 miles to Napa River 1.25 miles north-northeast of downtown Napa (lat. 38°19' N, long. 122°16'35" W); the stream drains Milliken Canyon. Named on Capell Valley (1951), Mount George (1951), Napa (1951), and Yountville (1951) 7.5' quadrangles.

Milliken Peak [NAPA]: *peak,* 4.5 miles west-southwest of downtown Napa (lat. 38°16'25" N, long. 122°21'35" W). Altitude 743 feet. Named on Napa (1951) 7.5' quadrangle.

Milliken Reservoir [NAPA]: *lake,* behind a dam on Milliken Creek 7 miles west-southwest of Mount Vaca (lat. 38°22'40" N, long. 122° 13'35" W; near E line sec. 7, T 6 N, R 3 W). Named on Capell Valley (1951) 7.5' quadrangle.

Mills [SONOMA]: *locality,* 1.25 miles northwest of Sebastopol along Petaluma and Santa Rosa Railroad (lat. 38°24'50" N, long. 122°50'30" W). Named on Sebastopol (1942) 15' quadrangle.

Mills College: see **Oakland** [ALAMEDA].

Mills Creek [SAN MATEO]:

(1) *stream,* flows 2.25 miles to San Francisco Bay 3 miles northwest of downtown San Mateo (lat. 37°35'50" N, long. 122°21'50" W). Named on Montara Mountain (1956) and San Mateo (1956) 7.5' quadrangles. The stream also has been called Black Hawk Creek for Black Hawk ranch, which was started in 1858 (Brown, p. 56).

(2) *stream,* flows 3.5 miles to Arroyo Leon nearly 2 miles southeast of downtown Half Moon Bay (lat. 37°26'45" N, long. 122°24'15" W). Named on Half Moon Bay (1961) and Woodside (1961) 7.5' quadrangles. Robert Mills had a ranch along the stream in the middle 1860's; the stream also had the names "Woods Creek," "Johnston Creek," and "Savage Creek," all for ranchers in the neighborhood (Brown, p. 56).

Mills Seltzer Spring: see **Azule Springs** [SANTA CLARA].

Mills Seminary: see **Oakland** [ALAMEDA].

Mills Switch Station: see **San Martin** [SANTA CLARA].

Mill Stream [SONOMA]: *stream,* flows 1.5 miles to Briggs Creek 2.5 miles west-northwest of Mount Saint Helena (lat. 38°41'25" N, long. 122°40'25" W; sec. 30, T 10 N, R 7 W). Named on Mount Saint Helena (1959) 7.5' quadrangle.

Mill Valley [MARIN]:

(1) *valley,* 5 miles south of downtown San Rafael along Arroyo Corte Madera Del Presidio (lat. 37°54'10" N, long. 122°32'15" W). Named on San Rafael (1954) 7.5' quadrangle. The name is from the sawmill that John Reed built in the valley in 1834 (Gudde, 1949, p. 214-215).

(2) *town,* 4.5 miles south of downtown San Rafael (lat. 37°54'25" N, long. 122°32'45" W); the town is in and around Mill Valley (1). Named on San Rafael (1954) 7.5' quadrangle. Postal authorities established Mill Valley post office in 1890, changed the name to Eastland in 1892, and changed it back to Mill Valley in 1904; the name "Eastland" was for Joseph G. Eastland, president of Tamalpais Land and Water Company, which developed the site (Salley, p. 64, 141). The town incorporated in 1900. Postal authorities established Tamalpais post office 8 miles west of Mill Valley post office in 1906 and discontinued it in 1929 (Salley, p. 218); according to Gudde (1969, p. 330), the place was known as Big Coyote before the post office came, and as Tamalpais Valley after 1908. Postal authorities established Laverne post office 1.5 miles west of Mill Valley post office in 1909 and discontinued it in 1914; they established Locust post office as a station of Mill Valley post office in 1938 and discontinued in 1948 (Salley, p. 119, 124).

Mill Valley [NAPA]: *valley,* 5.5 miles north-northeast of Saint Helena (lat. 38°34'45" N, long. 122°25'35" W). Named on Saint Helena (1960) 7.5' quadrangle.

Mill Valley Junction: see **Almonte** [MARIN].

Millwood [MARIN]: *locality,* 5 miles south of downtown San Rafael (lat. 37°53'50" N, long. 122°32'20" W). Named on Tamalpais (1897) 15' quadrangle.

Milpitas [SANTA CLARA]:

(1) *land grant,* at and east of the city of Milpitas. Named on Calaveras Reservoir (1961) and Milpitas (1961) 7.5' quadrangles. Jose Maria Alviso received the land in 1835 and his heirs claimed 4458 acres patented in 1871 (Cowan, p. 48). According to Arbuckle (p. 23), the name is from an Aztec word that means "corn patches" or "little corn fields."

(2) *city,* 7 miles north of downtown San Jose (lat. 37°25'45" N, long. 121°54'20" W); the city is partly on Milpitas grant. Named on Calaveras Reservoir (1961) and Milpitas (1961) 7.5' quadrangles. Postal authorities established Milpitas post office in 1856 (Frickstad, p. 174), and the city incorporated in 1954. The first structure at the place was built in 1855; the settlement that developed there was called Penitencia, presumably for nearby Penitencia Creek (present Lower Penitencia Creek), but the name "Penitencia" was changed to Milpitas, which already was in use for the post office (Hoover, Rensch, and Rensch, p. 453-454).

Milpitas Creek: see **Berryessa Creek** [SANTA CLARA].

Mimulus Spring [CONTRA COSTA]: *spring,* nearly 0.5 mile north-northeast of Mount Diablo (lat. 37°53'10" N, long. 121°54'35" W). Named on Clayton (1953) 7.5' quadrangle.

Mindego Creek [SAN MATEO]: *stream,* flows 4.25 miles to Alpine Creek 1.5 miles southeast of La Honda (lat. 37°17'50" N, long. 122°15'10" W; sec. 25, T 7 S, R 4 W); the stream goes past Mindego Hill. Named on La Honda (1961) and Mindego Hill (1961) 7.5' quadrangles. The stream also is called Wilbur's Creek (Brown, p. 53).

Mindego Hill [SAN MATEO]: *peak,* 12 miles south of Redwood City (lat. 37°18'40" N, long. 122°13'45" W; sec. 19, T 7 S, R 3 W). Altitude 2143 feet. Named on Mindego Hill (1961) 7.5' quadrangle. The misspelled name commemorates Juan Mendico, a Basque who settled at the place in 1859 (Brown, p. 53).

Mindego Lake [SAN MATEO]: *lake,* 650 feet long, 0.25 mile north-northwest of Mindego Hill (lat. 37°18'55" N, long. 122°13'50" W; near N line sec. 19, T 7 S, R 3 W). Named on Mindego Hill (1961) 7.5' quadrangle. The feature first had the name "Laguna del Corazon" for its shape—*corazon* means "heart" in Spanish (Brown, p. 53).

Mine Hill [SANTA CLARA]: *peak,* 1.5 miles west of New Almaden (lat. 37°10'35" N, long. 121°50'40" W); the feature is at New Almaden mine. Named on Santa Teresa Hills (1953) 7.5' quadrangle.

Mineral Spring [SONOMA]: *spring,* 4 miles north-northwest of Cazadero (lat. 38°35'05" N, long. 123°07'15" W). Named on Cazadero (1943) 7.5' quadrangle.

Mine Ridge: see **New Almaden** [SANTA CLARA].

Miner Slough [SOLANO]: *water feature,* extends from Sutter Slough to Cache Slough 5.25 miles north of Rio Vista (lat. 38°14' N, long. 121°40'25" W). Named on Courtland (1978), Liberty Island (1978), and Rio Vista (1978) 7.5' quadrangles.

Mining Hills: see **New Almaden** [SANTA CLARA].

Mirabel Heights [SONOMA]: *settlement,* nearly 6 miles east of Guerneville along Russian River (lat. 38°29'30" N, long. 122°53'30" W; sec. 31, T 8 N, R 9 W). Named on Camp Meeker (1954) 7.5' quadrangle. Called Mirabell Heights on Sebastopol (1954) 15' quadrangle.

Mirabel Park [SONOMA]: *settlement,* 5.5 miles east of Guerneville along Russian River (lat. 38°29'35" N, long. 122°53'50" W; sec. 31, T 8 N, R 9 W). Named on Camp Meeker (1954) 7.5' quadrangle. Called Mirabell Park on Sebastopol (1954) 15' quadrangle. The earliest resort along Russian River was opposite present Mirabel Park and was called Wall Springs—six mineral springs were the chief attraction there (Hansen and Miller, p. 133).

Miramar [SAN MATEO]: *district,* 2.5 miles northwest of downtown Half Moon Bay (lat. 37°29'35" N, long. 122°27'25" W). Named on Half Moon Bay (1961) 7.5' quadrangle. Josiah P. Ames and his partners constructed a wharf at the place in 1868, and the village that developed there was called Amesport (Morrall, p. 48-49). The wharf at the place was called Amesport Landing (Hoover, Rensch, and Rensch, p. 394), and later it was called McGill's Wharf (Wagner, J.R., p. 13).

Miramar Beach [SAN MATEO]: *beach,* 2.5 miles northwest of downtown Half Moon Bay along the coast (lat. 37°29'35" N, long. 122°27'35" W); the beach is at Miramar. Named on Half Moon Bay (1961) 7.5' quadrangle. The place sometimes is called Ames Beach, for J.P. Ames, for whom Amesport was named (Brown, p. 56).

Miramontes [SAN MATEO]:

(1) *land grant,* at and near the town of Half Moon Bay. Named on Half Moon Bay (1961) 7.5' quadrangle. Candelario Miramontes received 1 league in 1841; J.C. Miramontes claimed 4424 acres patented in 1882 (Cowan, p. 60; Cowan gave the names "Arroyo de los Pilarcitos" and "San Benito" as alternates). According to Perez (p. 73), Vincente Miramontes was the patentee in 1882.

(2) *ridge,* northwest-trending, 1.5 miles long, 3.5 miles south-southwest of present Montara Knob (lat. 37°30'20" N, long. 122° 30'15" W). Named on San Mateo (1915) 15' quadrangle.

Mira Monte Slough [SONOMA]: *water feature,* joins San Antonio Creek 7 miles southeast of downtown Petaluma (lat. 38°09'30" N, long. 122°33'05" W). Named on Petaluma River (1954) 7.5' quadrangle.

Miramontes Point [SAN MATEO]: *promontory,* 2.25 miles south-southwest of downtown Half Moon Bay along the coast (lat. 37° 26' N, long. 122°26'30" W); the feature is on Miramontes grant. Named on Half Moon Bay (1961) 7.5' quadrangle.

Misery: see **Mount Misery** [SANTA CLARA].

Mission Bay: see **Mission District** [SAN FRANCISCO].

Mission Canyon [SONOMA]: *canyon,* 2 miles long, along Hulbert Creek (present Hulbert Creek) above a point 2.25 miles northwest of Guerneville (lat. 38°31'25" N, long. 123°01'50" W; sec. 24, T 8 N, R 11 W). Named on Cazadero (1943) 7.5' quadrangle.

Mission Creek [ALAMEDA]: *stream,* flows 4.5 miles to lowlands 3 miles east-southeast of Fremont civic center (lat. 37°32'10" N, long. 121°55' W; sec. 36, T 4 S, R 1 W); the stream reaches lowlands at San Jose de Guadalupe mission. Named on Niles (1961) 7.5' quadrangle.

Mission Creek [SONOMA]: *stream,* flows 1.5 miles to Hulbert Creek less than 2 miles west of Guerneville at Monte Rosa (lat. 38° 30'15" N, long. 123°01'35" W). Named on Cazadero (1978) 7.5' quadrangle.

Mission Creek: see **Mission District** [SAN FRANCISCO]; **Santa Clara** [SANTA CLARA].

Mission District [SAN FRANCISCO]: *district,* 1.25 miles south of San Francisco civic center (lat. 37°45'40" N, long. 122°25' W); Mission Dolores is in the northwest part of the district. Named on San Francisco North (1956) 7.5' quadrangle. In 1776 Anza chose the site for San Francisco de Asis mission by a lake called Laguna de Manantial that covered much of present Mission District; the lake was fed by a stream that Anza called Arroyo de Nuestra Señora de los Dolores because he examined it on Friday of Our Lady of Sorrows—the mission became known popularly as Mission Dolores (Hoover, Rensch, and Rensch, p. 349). The lake also was called Laguna de Nuestra Señora de los Dolores; the word "Manantial" has to do with running water (Davidson, p. 121). The lake also had the names "Laguna de los Dolores"—as shown on Dalrymple's (1789) map—and "Lake McCoppin" (Hansen and Condon, p. 24). Mission Creek flowed from the lake, and a nearby embayment was called Mission Bay; earlier the embayment was called Ensenada de los Llorones (Davidson, p. 120). The earlier name dates from 1775, when Aguirre found three Indians weeping copiously at the place—*los llorones* means "the weepers" in Spanish (Bolton, p. 252). Wackenreuder's (1861) map shows Mission Bay between Rincon Point and Point San Quentin near present Mission Rock Terminal and China Basin. Soule, Gihon, and Nisbet's (1855) map shows the configuration of Mission Bay before the bay was filled.

Mission Highlands [SONOMA]: *settlement,* 2 miles north of Sonoma (lat. 38°19'15" N, long. 122°27'15" W; sec. 31, T 6 N, R 5 W). Named on Sonoma (1951) 7.5' quadrangle.

Mission Mountains: see **Twin Peaks** [SAN FRANCISCO].

Mission Pass [ALAMEDA]: *pass,* 3.25 miles east of Fremont civic center (lat. 37°33'35" N, long. 121°54'40" W; near W line sec. 30, T 4 S, R 1 E); the pass is nearly 2 miles north-northeast of San Jose de Guadalupe mission. Named on Niles (1961) 7.5' quadrangle. The feature also had the name "Stockton Pass" because it was on the road to Stockton in San Joaquin County (Mosier and Mosier, p. 57)

Mission Peak [ALAMEDA]: *peak,* 5.5 miles east-southeast of Fremont civic center (lat. 37°30'45" N, long. 121°52'50" W; sec. 8, T 5 S, R 1 E); the peak is 2.5 miles southeast of San Jose de Guadalupe mission. Altitude 2517 feet. Named on Niles (1961) 7.5' quadrangle.

Mission Peaks: see **Twin Peaks** [SAN FRANCISCO].

Mission Reservoir [ALAMEDA]: *lake,* 400 feet long, 3.5 miles east-southeast of Fremont civic center (lat. 37°31'50" N, long. 121°54'35" W; sec. 6, T 5 S, R 1 E); the lake is 0.5 mile east-southeast of San Jose de Guadalupe mission. Named on Niles (1961) 7.5' quadrangle.

Mission Rock [SAN FRANCISCO]: *island,* 850 feet long, 1 mile south-southeast of Rincon Point (lat. 37°46'25" N, long. 122°22'55" W). Named on San Francisco North (1947) 7.5' quadrangle. San Francisco North (1956) 7.5' quadrangle shows Mission Rock Terminal at the place, and indicates that the island is enlarged by landfill and is connected to shore by a causeway.

Mission Rock Terminal: see **Mission Rock** [SAN FRANCISCO].

Mission San Jose: see **Mission San Jose District** [ALAMEDA].

Mission San Jose District [ALAMEDA]: *district,* 3 miles east-southeast of Fremont civic center in Fremont (lat. 37°32' N, long. 121° 55'15" W); San Jose de Guadalupe mission is in the district. Named on Niles (1961) 7.5' quadrangle. Pleasanton (1906) 15' quadrangle has the name "Mission San Jose" for the community that in 1956 joined with neighboring communities to form the new city of Fremont. Postal authorities established Mission San Jose post office before April 9, 1850 (Salley, p. 143).

Mission San Jose Hot Springs: see **Warm Springs** [ALAMEDA].

Mississippi Creek [SANTA CLARA]: *stream,* flows 9 miles to North Fork Pacheco Creek nearly 6 miles east-northeast of Gilroy Hot Springs (lat. 37°08' N, long. 121°22'40" W; sec. 24, T 9 S, R 5 E). Named on Mississippi Creek (1955) 7.5' quadrangle.

Mitchell Canyon [CONTRA COSTA]: *canyon,* 4 miles long, opens into lowlands 4 miles north-northwest of Mount Diablo near Clayton (lat. 37°56'10" N, long. 121°56'15" W; sec. 14, T 1 N, R 1 W); Mitchell Creek drains the canyon. Named on Clayton (1953) 7.5' quadrangle. Captain Mitchell located a claim in the canyon in 1853 (Gudde, 1969, p. 205). Whitney (p. 24) mentioned Mitchell's Cañon.

Mitchell Canyon: see **East Mitchell Canyon** [NAPA]; **West Mitchell Canyon** [NAPA].

Mitchell Creek [CONTRA COSTA]: *stream,* flows 4.5 miles to Mount Diablo Creek nearly 4.5 miles north-northwest of Mount Diablo at Clayton (lat. 37°56'35" N, long. 121°56'05" W; near SE cor. sec. 11, T 1 N, R 1 W); the stream drains Mitchell Canyon. Named on Clayton (1953) 7.5' quadrangle.

Mitchell Creek [SAN MATEO]: *stream,* flows 1.25 miles to Tunitas Creek 2.5 miles west of Skeggs Point (lat. 37°24'30" N, long. 122° 21' W). Named on Woodside (1961) 7.5' quadrangle. The name is from the operator of a sawmill along the creek from 1910 until 1915 (Brown, p. 57).

Mitchell Ravine [ALAMEDA]: *canyon,* drained by a stream that heads in San Joaquin County and flows 6 miles to Corral Hollow Creek 5.5 miles south of Midway (lat. 37°38'10" N, long. 121°34'30" W; near S line sec. 30, T 3 S, R 4 E). Named on Cedar Mountain (1956) and Midway (1953) 7.5' quadrangles. A ridge known locally as Bear Trap Ridge is on the west side of Mitchell Ravine south of Corral Hollow; the name is from a bear trap that E.B. Carrell, Horatio P. Wright, and Grizzly Adams put on the ridge in 1856 (Mosier and Mosier, p. 14).

Mitchell Rock [CONTRA COSTA]: *peak,* 2.5 miles northwest of Mount Diablo (lat. 37°54'45" N, long. 121°56'25" W; near N line sec. 26, T 1 N, R 1 W). Altitude 1507 feet. Named on Clayton (1953) 7.5' quadrangle.

Mitchell's Cañon: see **Mitchell Canyon** [CONTRA COSTA].

Miwok Beach [SONOMA]: *beach,* 2.25 miles north-northwest of the village of Bodega Bay along the coast (lat. 38°21'35" N, long. 123° 04'05" W). Named on Bodega Head (1972) 7.5' quadrangle.

Mix Canyon [SOLANO]: *canyon,* 4 miles long, on upper reaches of Ulatis Creek, opens into lowlands 3.5 miles east of Mount Vaca (lat. 38°24'30" N, long. 122°02'30" W). Named on Mount Vaca (1951) 7.5' quadrangle. Called Weldon Canyon on Napa (1902) 30' quadrangle. United States Board on Geographic Names (1933, p. 807) once approved the name "Weldon Canyon" for the feature, and at the same time rejected the names "Bucks Canyon," "Mix Canyon," and "Mixs Canyon."

Mixs Canyon: see **Mix Canyon** [SOLANO].

Miyakma Range: see **Mayacmas Mountains** [NAPA-SONOMA].

Mocho: see **Mount Mocho** [SANTA CLARA].

Mocho Creek: see **Arroyo Mocho** [ALAMEDA-SANTA CLARA].

Mococo [CONTRA COSTA]: *locality,* 1.25 miles northeast of Martinez along Southern Pacific Railroad (lat. 38°01'35" N, long. 122°06'50" W). Named on Vine Hill (1959) 7.5' quadrangle. The name was coined in 1912 from letters in the term "Mountain Copper Company"—the company had a copper smelter at Bulls Head Point; the place first was called Lewis for the general manager of the company (Gudde, 1949, p. 218).

Moffett Channel [SANTA CLARA]: *water feature,* artificial waterway, nearly 1 mile long, that reaches Guadalupe Slough 3 miles southeast of the mouth of that slough (lat. 37°25'40" N, long. 122° 30' W). Named on Mountain View (1961, photorevised 1968 and 1973) 7.5' quadrangle. United States Board on Geographic Names (1968b, p. 8) rejected the names "Jagels Slough" and "Sunnyvale West Outfall Channel" for the feature.

Moffett Field [SANTA CLARA]: *military installation,* between downtown Sunnyvale and San Francisco Bay (lat. 37°25' N, long. 122°03' W). Named on Mountain View (1961) 7.5' quadrangle. According to an undated item from *San Jose Mercury*, the installation was commissioned in 1931 under the name "United States Naval Air Station, Sunnyvale, Mountain View, Calif.," and was a base for navy dirigibles; then in 1935 the army took charge of the place and used it as an air base until 1942, when the installation reverted to the navy as a base for lighter-than-air craft conducting anti-submarine activities off the West Coast—the name "Moffett" honors Admiral William A. Moffett, who was killed in the crash of the navy dirigible *Akron* in 1933. Postal authorities established Naval Air Station post office in 1933 and changed the name after a few months to Moffett Field (Frickstad, p. 174).

Mohrhardt Ridge [CONTRA COSTA]: *ridge,* generally east-trending, 3.5 miles long, 6.5 miles northeast of Fort Ross (lat. 38° 34'40" N, long. 123°09'15" W). Named on Fort Ross (1978) 7.5' quadrangle. On California Division of Forestry's (1945) map, a feature called Potatoe Patch Ridge extends south-southwest from Mohrhardt Ridge.

Molate Island: see **Red Rock** [CONTRA COSTA-MARIN-SAN FRANCISCO].

Molate Point: see **Point Molate** [CONTRA COSTA].

Molena [SOLANO]: *locality,* nearly 7 miles south of Denverton along Sacramento Northern Railroad (lat. 38°07'30" N, long. 121° 52'35" W; at S line sec. 4, T 3 N, R 1 E). Named on Denverton (1953) and Honker Bay (1953) 7.5' quadrangles.

Molino [SONOMA]: *locality,* 2 miles northwest of Sebastopol along Petaluma and Santa Rosa Railroad (lat. 38°25'25" N, long. 122°50'50" W; sec. 27, T 7 N, R 9 W). Named on Sebastopol (1954) 7.5' quadrangle. Postal authorities established Molino post office in 1899 and discontinued it in 1902; the name is from Molinos grant (Salley, p. 143).

Molino: see **Molinos** [SONOMA].

Molinos [SONOMA]: *land grant,* north-northwest of Sebastopol around Graton and Forestville. Named on Camp Meeker (1954), Guerneville (1955), Healdsburg (1955), and Sebastopol (1954) 7.5' quadrangles. John Bautista Roger Cooper received 10.5 leagues in 1836 and claimed 17,892 acres patented in 1858 (Cowan, p. 48-49; Cowan listed the grant under the designation "Molino, (or) Rio Ayoska, (or) Levantahyume").

Monclair: see **Thornhill** [ALAMEDA].

Monroe [SONOMA]: *locality,* 2 miles west-northwest of downtown Santa Rosa (lat. 38°27'10" N, long. 122°45' W). Named on Santa Rosa (1954) and Sebastopol (1954) 7.5' quadrangles.

Monsanto [CONTRA COSTA]: *locality,* 4.5 miles east of Martinez along Atchison, Topeka and Santa Fe Railroad (lat. 38°01'35" N, long. 122°03'20" W). Named on Vine Hill (1959) 7.5' quadrangle.

Montalvo [SANTA CLARA]: *locality,* 1 mile south of downtown Saratoga (lat. 37°14'35" N, long. 122°01'45" W; near S line sec. 12, T 8 S, R 2 W). Named on Castle Rock Ridge (1955) 7.5' quadrangle.

Montaña de San Juan Bautista: see **Mount Diablo** [CONTRA COSTA].

Montara [SAN MATEO]: *town,* 2 miles southwest of Montara Knob near the coast (lat. 37°32'30" N, long. 122°30'45" W). Named on Montara Mountain (1956) 7.5' quadrangle. Postal authorities established Montara post office in 1908 and discontinued it in 1918; later in 1918, they changed the name of Farallone post office to Montara (Salley, p. 144).

Montara Beach [SAN MATEO]: *beach,* nearly 2 miles west-southwest of Montara Knob along the coast (lat. 37°32'50" N, long. 122° 13'20" W); the beach is at Montara. Named on Montara Mountain (1956) 7.5' quadrangle.

Montara Creek: see **Point Montara** [SAN MATEO].

Montara Knob [SAN MATEO]: *peak,* 7.5 miles north-northwest of the town of Half Moon Bay (lat. 37°33'25" N, long. 122°29'05" W; sec. 26, T 4 S, R 6 W); the peak is on Montara Mountain. Named on Montara Mountain (1956) 7.5' quadrangle.

Montara Mountain [SAN MATEO]: *ridge,* northwest- to west-northwest-trending, 8 miles long, 13 miles west-northwest of Redwood City near the coast (lat. 37°33' N, long. 122°27' W). Named on Montara Mountain (1956) 7.5' quadrangle. United States Board on Geographic Names (1933, p. 528) rejected the form "Montora Mountain" for the name.

Montara Point: see **Point Montara** [SAN MATEO].

Monta Vista [SANTA CLARA]: *district,* 1.5 miles west of downtown Cupertino near Stevens Creek (lat. 37°19'20" N, long. 122°03'15" W). Named on Cupertino (1961) 7.5' quadrangle. Called Monte Vista on California Mining Bureau's (1909b) map. Rambo (1964, p. 38) described the place as "a turn of the century subdivision." Postal authorities established Monta Vista post office in 1946 (Salley, p. 144). Peninsular Railway Company's (1912) map shows a place called Simla located along the rail line about halfway from Monta Vista to Loyola, and a place called Golden Spur located about halfway from Monta Vista to Cupertino.

Monte Bello Ridge [SANTA CLARA]: *ridge,* northwest-trending, 6 miles long, 5 miles south of downtown Los Altos (lat. 37°18'30" N, long. 122°07'45" W). Named on Cupertino (1961) and Mindego Hill (1961) 7.5' quadrangles.

Monte Cristo [SONOMA]: *settlement,* 2 miles southwest of Guerneville along Russian River (lat. 38°28'35" N, long. 123°01'10" W). Named on Duncans Mills (1979) 7.5' quadrangle.

Monte Cristo Creek [SONOMA]: *stream,* flows less than 1 mile to Russian River 2.25 miles southwest of Guerneville (lat. 38°29'40" N, long. 123°01'25" W); the stream is west of Monte Cristo. Named on Duncans Mills (1979) 7.5' quadrangle.

Monte del Diablo [CONTRA COSTA]: *land grant,* extends from Clayton Valley to Pacheco and Suisun Bay Named on Clayton (1953), Honker Bay (1953), Vine Hill (1959), and Walnut Creek (1959) 7.5' quadrangles. Salvio Pacheco received the land in 1834 and 1844; he claimed 17,922 acres patented in 1859 (Cowan, p. 32).

Monte Diablo: see **Mount Diablo** [CONTRA COSTA].

Monte Diablo Creek: see **Mount Diablo Creek** [CONTRA COSTA].

Monte Diablo Range: see **Diablo Range** [ALAMEDA-CONTRA COSTA-SANTA CLARA].

Monte Rio [SONOMA]: *town,* 2.25 miles south-southwest of Guerneville along Russian River (lat. 38°27'50" N, long. 123°00'35" W; sec. 7, T 7 N, R 10 W). Named on Duncans Mills (1979) 7.5' quadrangle. Postal authorities established Montrio post office in 1902 and changed the name to Monte Rio in 1924 (Frickstad, p. 197).

Monte Rosa [SONOMA]: *settlement,* 1.5 miles west of Guerneville (lat. 38°30'15" N, long. 123°01'35" W; sec. 25, 36, T 8 N, R 11 W). Named on Cazadero (1978) 7.5' quadrangle.

Monte San Bruno: see **San Bruno Mountain** [SAN MATEO].

Montesano [SONOMA]: *settlement,* 1.5 miles southwest of Guerneville along Russian River (lat. 38°29'10" N, long. 123°00'50" W; near NW cor. sec. 6, T 7 N, R 10 W). Named on Duncans Mills (1979) 7.5' quadrangle.

Monte Sereno [SANTA CLARA]: *town,* between Los Gatos and Saratoga (lat. 37°14'15" N, long. 121°59'15" W). Named on Los Gatos (1953, photorevised 1968 and 1973) 7.5' quadrangle. Postal authorities established Monte Sereno post office in 1957 (Salley, p. 145), and the town incorporated in 1957.

Monte Vista: see **Monta Vista** [SANTA CLARA]; **Oakland** [ALAMEDA].

Montezuma [SOLANO]:

(1) *locality,* nearly 4 mile south of Denverton (lat. 38°10'10" N, long. 121°53'20" W; at N line sec. 29, T 4 N, R 1 E); the place is near the west end of Montezuma Hills. Named on Denverton (1953) 7.5' quadrangle.

(2) *locality,* nearly 3 miles south of Birds Landing (2) along Sacramento Northern Railroad (lat. 38°05'30" N, long. 121°52'30" W; sec. 21, T 3 N, R 1 E). Named on Antioch North (1978) and Honker Bay (1953) 7.5' quadrangles.

Montezuma Creek: see **Montezuma Slough** [SOLANO].

Montezuma Hills [SOLANO]: *range,* north of Sacramento River between Rio Vista and Birds Landing (2). Named on Antioch North (1978), Birds Landing (1953), Denverton (1953), Jersey Island (1978), and Rio Vista (1978) 7.5' quadrangles. Called Montezuma Range on Ringgold's (1850c) map.

Montezuma House: see **Collinsville** [SOLANO].

Montezuma Landing: see **Marshall Cut** [SOLANO].

Montezuma Range: see **Montezuma Hills** [SOLANO].

Montezuma Slough [SOLANO]: *water feature,* extends from Suisun Bay near the mouth of Sacramento River to Grizzly Bay 8 miles south of Fairfield (lat. 38°08' N, long. 122°03'30" W). Named on Antioch North (1978), Denverton (1953), Fairfield South (1949), and Honker Bay (1953) 7.5' quadrangles. Called Montezuma Creek on Karquines (1898) 15' quadrangle, but United States Board on Geographic Names (1943, p. 12) rejected this name.

Montgomery: see **Fort Montgomery** and **Point Montgomery**, under **Telegraph Hill** [SAN FRANCISCO].

Montgomery Creek [NAPA]: *stream,* flows 1.5 miles to Dry Creek nearly 4 miles south-southwest of Rutherford (lat. 38°24'20" N, long. 122°26'25" W). Named on Rutherford (1951) 7.5' quadrangle.

Montgomery Hill [SANTA CLARA]: *peak,* 2 miles east-southeast of Evergreen (lat. 37°17'55" N, long. 121°45' W). Named on San Jose East (1961, photorevised 1968 and 1973) 7.5' quadrangle. The name honors Professor John Joseph Montgomery, known for his research in aviation between 1879 and 1911 (United States Board on Geographic Names, 1964, p. 13).

Montgomery Village [SONOMA]: *district,* 1.5 miles east-northeast of downtown Santa Rosa (lat. 38°26'40" N, long. 122°41'15" W). Named on Santa Rosa (1954) 7.5' quadrangle.

Monti: see **Fisherman Bay** [SONOMA].

Monticello [NAPA]: *town,* 6 miles south of Berryessa Peak in Berryessa Valley (lat. 38°34'45" N, long. 122°12'20" W). Named on Capay (1945) 15' quadrangle. Postal authorities established Monticello post office in 1867 and discontinued it in 1956 (Salley, p. 145). Water of Lake Berryessa now covers the site.

Monticello Reservoir: see **Lake Berryessa** [NAPA].

Montora: see **Point Montora**, under **Point Montara** [SAN MATEO].

Montora Mountain: see **Montara Mountain** [SAN MATEO].

Montrio: see **Monte Rio** [SONOMA].

Monument Peak [ALAMEDA-SANTA CLARA]: *peak,* 7.5 miles south of Sunol on Alameda-Santa Clara County line (lat. 37°29'05" N, long. 121°51'50" W; sec. 21, T 5 S, R 1 E). Altitude 2594 feet. Named on Calaveras Reservoir (1961) 7.5' quadrangle. The name is from stone monuments that mark the county line (Mosier and Mosier, p. 58). The peak first was known as Cerro de las Calaveras (Gudde, 1949, p. 49).

Moody Creek: see **Big Moody Creek**, under **Saratoga Creek** [SANTA CLARA].

Moody Gulch [SANTA CLARA]: *canyon,* drained by a stream that flows 1.25 miles to Los Gatos Creek 4 miles south of downtown Los Gatos (lat. 37°10' N, long. 121°58'40" W; sec. 9, T 9 S, R 1 W). Named on Los Gatos (1953) 7.5' quadrangle. According to Rambo (1973, p. 24), David B. Moody owned part of an oil strike made in 1872 in what still is known as Moody's Gulch.

Moon and Adams Landing: see **Oakland** [ALAMEDA].

Moonshine Pond [SONOMA]: *lake,* 200 feet long, 1.5 miles northwest of Cazadero (lat. 38°32'55" N, long. 123°06'05" W; sec. 8, T 8 N, R 11 W). Named on Cazadero (1978) 7.5' quadrangle.

Moore: see **Camp C.C. Moore**, under **Camp Royaneh** [SONOMA].

Moore Creek [NAPA]: *stream,* flows 8 miles to Chiles Creek 6.25 miles east of Saint Helena (lat. 38°30'30" N, long. 122°21'15" W; near NE cor. sec. 31, T 8 N, R 4 W). Named on Chiles Valley (1958) and Saint Helena (1960) 7.5' quadrangles.

Moore Flat [NAPA]: *area,* 5.5 miles northeast of Walter Springs along lower reaches of Nevada Creek (lat. 38°42'45" N, long. 122° 17'30" W; near W line sec. 15, T 10 N, R 4 W). Named on Walter Springs (1959) 7.5' quadrangle.

Moore Hill [MARIN]: *ridge,* east-trending, 0.25 mile long, 0.5 mile west of downtown San Rafael (lat. 37°58'20" N, long. 122°32'25" W). Named on San Rafael (1954) 7.5' quadrangle.

Moore Tract [SOLANO]: *area,* 11 miles north of Rio Vista (lat. 38° 18'50" N, long. 121°43' W). Named on Liberty Island (1978) 7.5' quadrangle.

Moraga [CONTRA COSTA]: *town,* 4.25 miles southeast of Orinda (lat. 37°50'05" N, long. 122°07'45" W). Named on Las Trampas Ridge (1959) and Oakland East (1959) 7.5' quadrangles. Postal authorities established Moraga post office in 1886, discontinued it in 1887, and reestablished it in 1915 (Frickstad, p. 22). The town incorporated in 1974. The name is for Joaquin Moraga, a grantee of Laguna de los Palos Colorados grant

(Gudde, 1949, p. 224). Postal authorities established Saint Mary's College post office 1 mile northeast of Moraga post office in 1928 (Salley, p. 191).

Moraga Center: see **Moraga Valley** [CONTRA COSTA].

Moraga Valley [CONTRA COSTA]: *valley,* 4 miles southeast of Orinda at Moraga (lat. 37°50' N, long. 122°08' W). Named on Las Trampas Ridge (1959) and Oakland East (1959) 7.5' quadrangles. Postal authorities established Moraga Center post office in 1955 and discontinued it in 1956; the name was from the location of the post office in the center of Moraga Valley (Salley, p. 146).

Moreland: see **Meridian** [SANTA CLARA].

Morgan Hill [SANTA CLARA]: *town,* 19 miles southeast of downtown San Jose (lat. 37°07'45" N, long. 121°39'10" W). Named on Morgan Hill (1955) and Mount Madonna (1955) 7.5' quadrangles. Hiram Morgan Hill married Diana Murphy, who inherited 4900 acres of Ojo de Agua de la Coche grant; the couple built their home on the land, and when Hill subdivided the property in 1892, the community laid out there was named for him (Wyman, p. ix). Postal authorities established Morgan Hill post office in 1893 (Frickstad, p. 174), and the town incorporated in 1906.

Morgan's Cove: see **Hospital Cove** [MARIN].

Morgan Territory [CONTRA COSTA]: *area,* 3 miles east-southeast of Mount Diablo (lat. 37°52'15" N, long. 121°51'30" W). Named on Antioch South (1953) and Tassajara (1953) 7.5' quadrangles. The name commemorates Jeremiah Morgan, a Cherokee Indian who claimed 10,000 acres of unsurveyed land at the place in 1856 (Gudde, 1949, p. 225).

Mori Point [SAN MATEO]: *promontory,* 4.25 miles north of Montara Knob along the coast (lat. 37°37'10" N, long. 122°29'50" W). Named on Montara Mountain (1956) 7.5' quadrangle.

Moristul y Plan de Agua Caliente: see **Mallacomes or Moristul y Plan de Agua Caliente** [NAPA-SONOMA].

Morrison Canyon [ALAMEDA]: *canyon,* drained by a stream that flows 1.25 miles to lowlands 1.5 miles north-northeast of Fremont civic center (lat. 37°34'10" N, long. 121°57'15" W; sec. 22, T 4 S, R 1 W). Named on Niles (1961) 7.5' quadrangle. Perry Morrison and William Morrison settled in the canyon in 1849 (Mosier and Mosier, p. 58).

Morrison Ridge [SONOMA]: *ridge,* west-southwest-trending, 1.5 miles long, 4.5 miles northeast of Cazadero (lat. 38°34'25" N, long. 123°01'30" W). Named on Cazadero (1978) 7.5' quadrangle.

Morris Peak [SONOMA]: *peak,* 6 miles west-northwest of Cloverdale (lat. 38°49'40" N, long. 123°07'15" W; sec. 6, T 11 N, R 11 W). Altitude 1843 feet. Named on Cloverdale (1960) 7.5' quadrangle.

Morrissey's Gulch: see **Milagra Valley** [SAN MATEO].

Morristal: see **Mallacomes or Morristul** [SONOMA].

Morrow Cove [SOLANO]: *embayment,* nearly 3 miles south-southeast of downtown Vallejo along Carquinez Strait (lat. 38°04'05" N, long. 122°13'50" W). Named on Benicia (1959) 7.5' quadrangle.

Morrow Island [SOLANO]: *area,* 6 miles northeast of Benicia (lat. 38°07' N, long. 122°05'15" W). Named on Fairfield South (1949) and Vine Hill (1959) 7.5' quadrangles.

Morses Gulch [MARIN]: *canyon,* drained by a stream that flows 1.5 miles to Bolinas Lagoon 1 mile northeast of Bolinas (lat. 37°55'05" N, long. 122°40'10" W). Named on Bolinas (1954) 7.5' quadrangle. Teather (p. 47) associated the name with Benjamin G. Morse, a local carpenter and rancher.

Moscow [SONOMA]: *locality,* 4.25 miles southwest of Guerneville along Northwestern Pacific Railroad (lat. 38°27'20" N, long. 123° 02'55" W); the place is near Russian River. Named on Duncans Mills (1921) 15' quadrangle.

Moses Rock Ridge [CONTRA COSTA]: *ridge,* northwest- to west-trending, 1 mile long, 1.25 miles west of Mount Diablo (lat. 37°52'55" N, long. 121°56'05" W). Named on Clayton (1953) 7.5' quadrangle.

Moses Rock Spring [CONTRA COSTA]: *spring,* 2 miles west of Mount Diablo (lat. 37°53'05" N, long. 121°56'55" W); the spring is near the west end of Moses Rock Ridge. Named on Clayton (1953) 7.5' quadrangle.

Moskowite Reservoir [NAPA]: *lake,* 1650 feet long, 6 miles northwest of Mount Vaca (lat. 38°27'30" N, long. 122°11'30" W; sec. 16, T 7 N, R 3 W). Named on Capell Valley (1951) 7.5' quadrangle.

Moss Beach [SAN MATEO]: *town,* 2.5 miles southwest of Montara Knob near the coast (lat. 37°31'45" N, long. 122°30'45" W). Named on Montara Mountain (1956) 7.5' quadrangle. The name is from a marine plant found on rocks at the place, and goes back to the opening of Moss Beach hotel in 1880 (Brown, p. 59). Postal authorities established Colony post office at the place in 1894, changed the name to Blenheim in 1895, and discontinued it in 1901—the name "Colony" was from Half Moon Bay Colony Tract of 1881; they established Moss Beach post office in 1910 (Salley, p. 23, 48, 147).

Mountain Home [SANTA CLARA]: *locality,* nearly 3 miles east-northeast of Loma Prieta along Llagas Creek (lat. 37°07'15" N, long. 121°47'40" W; sec. 30, T 9 S, R 2 E). Named on Los Gatos (1919) 15' quadrangle.

Mountain Home Gulch: see **Alambique Creek** [SAN MATEO].

Mountain House [ALAMEDA]: *locality,* 12 miles east-northeast of Livermore (lat. 37°45'15" N, long. 121°34'30" W; sec. 18, T 2 S, R 4 E). Named on Clifton Court Forebay (1978) 7.5' quadrangle. Whitney (p. 33) referred to the place as Zimmerman's Mountain House. Postal authorities established Elk Horn post office at or near present Mountain House in 1852 and discontinued it in 1853; the post office was at a combined home, store, stage stop, and hotel that was decorated with the horns of tule elk (Salley, p. 67).

Mountain House: see **Pacheco Pass** [SANTA CLARA].

Mountain House Creek [ALAMEDA]: *stream,* flows 8 miles to San Joaquin County 13 miles east-northeast of Livermore (lat. 37° 46'20" N, long. 121°33'25" W; sec. 8, T 2 S, R 4 E). Named on Altamont (1953), Clifton Court Forebay (1978), and Midway (1953) 7.5' quadrangles. Called Mountainhouse Creek on Byron (1916) and Tesla (1907) 15' quadrangles.

Mountain Lake [SAN FRANCISCO]: *lake,* 650 feet long, 1.5 miles south-southeast of Fort Point (lat. 37°47'20" N, long. 122°28'10" W). Named on San Francisco North (1956) 7.5' quadrangle. The Spaniards called the feature Laguna del Presidio (Wagner, H.R., p. 486).

Mountain Rock [SONOMA]: *relief feature,* 2 miles east of the village of Bodega Bay (lat. 38°20' N, long. 123°00'45" W). Named on Bodega Head (1942) 7.5' quadrangle.

Mountain Springs Creek [CONTRA COSTA]: *stream,* flows nearly 2 miles to Curry Canyon 2 miles south-southeast of Mount Diablo (lat. 37°51'25" N, long. 121°54'05" W; sec. 7, T 1 S, R 1 E). Named on Diablo (1953) 7.5' quadrangle.

Mountain View [SANTA CLARA]: *city,* 11 miles west-northwest of downtown San Jose (lat. 37°23'30" N, long. 122°04'45" W). Named on Cupertino (1961) and Mountain View (1961) 7.5' quadrangles. James Campbell established a stage stop at the place in 1852, and nearby was an inn called Fremont House that was so well known that when the county organized in 1850, the area containing present Mountain View, Los Altos, and Palo Alto was named Fremont Township; Jacob Shumway, who had a store in the community, reportedly looked across the valley to the mountains and gave the name "Mountain View" to the place (Butler, p. 35). Postal authorities established Mountain View post office in 1854 (Frickstad, p. 174), and the city incorporated in 1902. With the coming of the railroad in 1865, a station called Mountain View was built about 1 mile north-northwest of the original community; the first site became known as Old Mountain View, and the village that developed around the railroad station became known as New Mountain View (Rambo, 1973, p. 43). Thompson and West's (1876) map shows both Old Mountain View and New Mountain View. Palo Alto (1899) 15' quadrangle has the name "Mountain View" near the railroad and the name "Old Mountain View" about 1 mile farther south-southeast—both places are in the present city. Peninsular Railroad Company's (1912) map shows a station called Endor along Southern Pacific Railroad less than halfway from Mountain View to Sunnyvale.

Mountain View Landing [SANTA CLARA]: *locality,* 2.5 miles north of downtown Mountain View near the edge of mud flats along San Francisco Bay (lat. 37°25'50" N, long. 122°04'50" W). Named on Palo Alto (1899) 15' quadrangle.

Mountain View Reservoir: see **Martinez Reservoir** [CONTRA COSTA].

Mountain View Slough [SANTA CLARA]: *water feature,* nearly 1.5 miles long, enters San Francisco Bay tidelands 2 miles southwest of the mouth of Coyote Creek (lat. 37°27' N, long. 122°04'35" W). Named on Mountain View (1961) 7.5' quadrangle. The feature is the outlet of Permanente Creek to San Francisco Bay.

Mount Allison [ALAMEDA]: *peak,* 6.5 miles south of Sunol (lat. 37° 29'55" N, long. 121°52'10" W; sec. 16, T 5 S, R 1 E). Altitude 2658 feet. Named on Calaveras Reservoir (1961) 7.5' quadrangle.

Mount Bache: see **Loma Prieta** [SANTA CLARA].

Mount Bielawski: see **Bielawski Mountain** [SANTA CLARA].

Mount Boardman [ALAMEDA-SANTA CLARA]: *peak,* 9 miles east-southeast of Cedar Mountain, where Alameda, San Joaquin, Santa Clara, and Stanislaus Counties meet (lat. 37°28'55" N, long. 121° 28'15" W; sec. 19, T 5 S, R 5 E). Altitude 3593 feet. Named on Mount Boardman (1955) 7.5' quadrangle. The name commemorates W.F. Boardman, county surveyor of Alameda County and city engineer of Oakland from 1864 until 1868 (Gudde, 1969, p. 33).

Mount Caroline Livermore [MARIN]: *peak,* 3 miles east of downtown Sausalito on Angel Island (lat. 37°51'40" N, long. 122°25'45" W). Altitude 781 feet. Named on San Francisco North (1956, photorevised 1968 and 1973) 7.5' quadrangle. Called Mount Ida on San Francisco North (1956) 7.5' quadrangle, but the peak—the highest point on the island—was renamed in 1959 for a Marin County conservation leader (Mason, 1976b, p. 214).

Mount Chisnantuck: see **New Almaden** [SANTA CLARA].

Mount Choual: see **Mount Chual** [SANTA CLARA].

Mount Chual [SANTA CLARA]: *peak,* nearly 1 mile northeast of Loma Prieta (lat. 37°07'10" N, long. 121°49'50" W; sec. 26, T 9 S, R 1 E). Altitude 3562 feet. Named on Loma Prieta (1955) 7.5' quadrangle. Gudde (1949, p. 67-68) traced the name back to a map of 1848, where it appeared as Picacho de Chual—*chual* is an Indian word for common pigweed. Whitney (p. 62) referred to Mount Choual.

Mount Davidson [SAN FRANCISCO]: *peak,* 5 miles south-southeast of Fort Point (lat. 37°44'20" N, long. 122°27'10" W). Named on San Francisco South (1956) 7.5' quadrangle. First called Blue Mountain, but San Francisco Board of Supervisors officially renamed the peak in 1911 to honor George Davidson, who had surveyed it in the 1860's (Lewis, p. 92-93).

Mount Day [SANTA CLARA]: *peak,* 6 miles north-northwest of Mount Hamilton (lat. 37°25'15" N, long. 122°41'55" W; near W line sec. 7, T 6 S, R 3 E). Altitude 3869 feet. Named on Mount Day (1955) 7.5' quadrangle. Called Black Mountain on Mount Hamilton (1897) 15' quadrangle, where Black Mountain (2) is called Mt. Day. The name probably is for Sherman Day, state senator representing Alameda and Santa Clara Counties from 1855 until 1856, and United States surveyor general for California from 1868 until 1871 (Gudde, 1949, p. 89).

Mount Diablo [CONTRA COSTA]: *peak,* near the center of Contra Costa County (lat. 37°52'55" N, long. 121°54'50" W; at NE cor. sec. 1, T 1 S, R 1 W). Altitude 3849 feet. Named on Clayton (1953) 7.5' quadrangle. Called Monte Diablo on Smith and Elliott's (1879) map. H.R. Wagner (p. 502) noted the early names "Cerro de San Juan" and "Montaña de San Juan Bautista" for the peak. According to Gudde (1949, p. 94), the feature also was known to the Spaniards by the names "Sierra de los Bolbones" and "Cerro Alto de los Bolbones" from Indians called Bolbones who lived near the base of the peak. Wilkes (p. 71) called the feature Mount Diavolo in 1841. According to one account, the name "Diablo" is from an incident following a battle between Spaniards and Indians in 1806, when an Indian appeared dressed in a devilish costume—*diablo* means "devil" in Spanish (Hanna, P.T., p. 86).

Mount Diablo Creek [CONTRA COSTA]: *stream,* flows 13 miles to marsh along Suisun Bay 5.25 miles east of Martinez (lat. 38°01'40" N, long. 122°02'20" W); the stream heads near Mount Diablo. Named on Clayton (1953) and Vine Hill (1959) 7.5' quadrangles. Ringgold (p. 27) called it Monte Diablo Creek, and Whitney (p. 23) called it Arroyo del Monte Diablo.

Mount Diablo Range: see **Diablo Range** [ALAMEDA-CONTRA COSTA-SANTA CLARA].

Mount Diavolo: see **Mount Diablo** [CONTRA COSTA].

Mount Eden [ALAMEDA]: *village,* 2.5 miles south-southwest of downtown Hayward (lat. 37°38'10" N, long. 122°05'55" W). Named on Hayward (1959) 7.5' quadrangle. The place was founded in 1850 by an association of farmers from Mount Eden, Kentucky; postal authorities established Mount Eden post office in 1862 and discontinued it for a short time in 1953 (Salley, p. 148). Thompson and West's (1878) map shows Eden Landing situated west-southwest of Mount Eden on Richard Barron's land along North Branch Alameda Creek (present Mount Eden Creek). Postal authorities established Edendale post office at Eden Landing in 1873 and discontinued it in 1875 (Salley, p. 65). Eden Landing was started in 1854 by farmers who were dissatisfied with freight charges at Allen's Landing, which was located 0.25 mile farther west; Richard Barron bought Eden Landing in 1855 (Mosier and Mosier, p. 33). Thompson and West's (1878) map shows Barrons Landing situated west of Mount Eden at the edge of San Francisco Bay; Thompson and West (1878, p. 25) noted that Barron's Landing also was called Mount Eden Landing. Eden Landing also was known locally as Peterman's Landing for Henry Louis Peterman and Mary F. Peterman, who operated Peterman's Salt Works (Mosier and Mosier, p. 33). James Johnstone Stokes established Stokes Landing east of Barron's Landing along Alameda Creek in 1858 (Mosier and Mosier, p. 84).

Mount Eden Creek [ALAMEDA]: *water feature,* enters San Francisco Bay 6 miles southwest of downtown Hayward (lat. 37°36'10" N, long. 122°08'40" W). Named on Newark (1959) and Redwood Point (1959) 7.5' quadrangles. Called North Branch Alameda Creek on Thompson and West's (1878) map.

Mount Eden Landing: see **Mount Eden** [ALAMEDA].

Mount Eden Station [ALAMEDA]: *locality,* 3 miles southwest of downtown Hayward along Southern Pacific Railroad (lat. 37°38'10" N, long. 122°07'05" W); the place is 1 mile west of Mount Eden. Named on Hayward (1959) 7.5' quadrangle.

Mount Ellen [SAN MATEO]: *peak,* 3 miles south-southwest of La Honda (lat. 37°16'45" N, long. 122°17'20" W; sec. 34, T 7 S, R 4 W). Named on La Honda (1961) 7.5' quadrangle. The name was given about 1890 to honor Miss Ellen Wurr by one of her admirers (Brown, p. 32).

Mount George [NAPA]: *peak,* 7.5 miles southwest of Mount Vaca (lat. 38°20'30" N, long. 122°13'10" W; sec. 29, T 6 N, R 3 W). Altitude 1877 feet. Named on Mount George (1951) 7.5' quadrangle. Called George Mt. on Napa (1902) 30' quadrangle.

Mount Hamilton [SANTA CLARA]: *peak,* 15 miles east of downtown San Jose (lat. 37°20'30" N, long. 121°38'30" W; sec. 9, T 7 S, R 3 E). Altitude 4213 feet. Named on Lick Observatory (1955) 7.5' quadrangle. William H. Brewer of the Whitney survey named the peak for Laurentine Hamilton, a San Jose clergyman who climbed the peak with Brewer in 1861 (Farquhar *in* Brewer, p. 167, 189). According to Irelan (p. 540), the feature first had the name "Mount Santa Isabel" and consists of a group of peaks, including one called Observatory Peak that has the principal building of Lick Observatory. Postal authorities established Mt. Hamilton post office in 1884 and discontinued it in 1886; they established Mount Hamilton post office in 1890 (Frickstad, p. 174).

Mount Hamilton Range: see **Diablo Range** [SANTA CLARA].

Mount Hamilton Springs [SANTA CLARA]: *spring,* 2.5 miles northwest of Mount Hamilton (lat. 37°22'15" N, long. 121°40' W; sec. 32, T 6 S, R 3 E). Named on Lick Observatory (1955) 7.5' quadrangle.

Mount Helen [SANTA CLARA]: *peak,* 2.5 miles south of Isabel Valley (lat. 37°16'35" N, long. 121°31'40" W; sec. 34, T 7 S, R 4 E). Altitude 3001 feet. Named on Isabel Valley (1955) 7.5' quadrangle.

Mount Helen: see **Martinez** [CONTRA COSTA]; **Mount Saint Helena** [SONOMA].

Mount Heller [SONOMA]: *peak,* nearly 3 miles south of Guerneville (lat. 38°27'40" N, long. 123°00'10" W; sec. 7, T 7 N, R 10 W). Altitude 865 feet. Named on Duncans Mills (1979) 7.5' quadrangle.

Mount Henry: see **Mount Saint John** [NAPA].

Mount Hood [SONOMA]: *peak,* 3 miles north of Kenwood (lat. 38° 27'35" N, long. 122°33'10" W; near S line sec. 8, T 7 N, R 6 W). Altitude 2730 feet. Named on Kenwood (1954) 7.5' quadrangle. The name commemorates William Hood, who arrived in California in 1846 and later bought part of Los Guilicos grant (Gudde, 1949, p. 152).

Mount Hooker: see **Mount Thayer** [SANTA CLARA].

Mount Ida: see **Mount Caroline Livermore** [MARIN].

Mount Isabel [SANTA CLARA]: *peak,* 4 miles west of Isabel Valley (lat. 38°19'35" N, long. 121°37'10" W; sec. 14, T 7 S, R 3 E). Altitude 4230 feet. Named on Isabel Valley (1955) 7.5' quadrangle. The name, originally given to Mount Hamilton, was applied to the peak after Mount Hamilton received its present name (Gudde, 1949, p. 141). United States Board on Geographic Names (1933, p. 391) rejected the names "Mount San Isabel" and "Mount Santa Ysabel" for the peak.

Mount Jackson [SONOMA]:

(1) *peak,* 3.25 miles northeast of Guerneville (lat. 38°32'20" N, long. 122°57'35" W; sec. 15, T 8 N, R 10 W). Altitude 1652 feet. Named on Guerneville (1955) 7.5' quadrangle.

(2) *settlement,* 5 miles east of Guerneville (lat. 38°30'50" N, long. 122°54'15" W; sec. 30, T 8 N, R 9 W). Named on Guerneville (1955) 7.5' quadrangle.

Mount King: see **North Peak** [CONTRA COSTA].

Mount Lewis [SANTA CLARA]: *peak,* 4.25 miles north-northeast of Mount Day near Santa Clara-Alameda County line (lat. 37°28'50" N, long. 121°40'45" W; sec. 20, T 5 S, R 3 E). Altitude 3768 feet. Named on Mount Day (1955) 7.5' quadrangle.

Mount Madonna [SANTA CLARA]: *peak,* 7.5 miles west of Gilroy (lat. 37°00'45" N, long. 121°42'15" W). Altitude 1897 feet. Named on Mount Madonna (1955) 7.5' quadrangle. Hiram Wentworth, a pioneer in the neighborhood, named the peak (Gudde, 1949, p. 201).

Mount McPherson: see **Bielawski Mountain** [SANTA CLARA].

Mount Melville [SAN MATEO]: *peak,* 2 miles north-northeast of Mindego Hill (lat. 37°20'15" N, long. 122°13'05" W; sec. 8, T 7 S, R 3 W). Named on Mindego Hill (1961) 7.5' quadrangle. The name honors Dr. Melville Best Anderson, who was professor of English literature at Stanford University (United States Board on Geographic Names, 1933, p. 512).

Mount Misery [SANTA CLARA]: *peak,* 5.5 miles southwest of Mount Hamilton (lat. 37°16'40" N, long. 121°42'20" W). Altitude 2502 feet. Named on Lick Observatory (1955) 7.5' quadrangle.

Mount Mocho [SANTA CLARA]: *peak,* 2.25 miles southwest of Mount Boardman (lat. 37°27'20" N, long. 121°29'35" W; near E line sec. 35, T 5 S, R 4 E). Altitude 3664 feet. Named on Mount Boardman (1955) 7.5' quadrangle. The name is from Arroyo Mocho (Gudde, 1949, p. 218).

Mount Nebo: see **Bismark Knob** [NAPA-SONOMA].

Mount Olivet: see **Fulton** [SONOMA].

Mount Olompali: see **Burdell Mountain** [MARIN].

Mount Olympus [SAN FRANCISCO]: *peak,* nearly 1 mile east-northeast of Mount Sutro (lat. 37°45'50" N, long. 122°26'40" W). Named on San Francisco North (1956) 7.5' quadrangle.

Mount Pajaro [SANTA CLARA]: *peak,* nearly 1 mile north of Pajaro Gap on Santa Clara-Santa Cruz County line (lat. 36°55'25" N, long. 121°37'40" W). Altitude 1573 feet. Named on Watsonville East (1955) 7.5' quadrangle.

Mount Palermo: see **Mount Tamalpais** [MARIN].

Mount Pisgah [SONOMA]:

(1) *ridge,* east-northeast-trending, 1 mile long, 3 miles northeast of Occidental (lat. 38°25'50" N, long. 122°53'55" W). Named on Camp Meeker (1954) 7.5' quadrangle.

(2) *peak,* 3.5 miles north of Sonoma (lat. 38°20'40" N, long. 122°27'35" W; near SW cor. sec. 19, T 6 N, R 5 W). Altitude 1349 feet. Named on Sonoma (1951) 7.5' quadrangle.

Mount Roscoe [SONOMA]: *peak,* 1 mile north-northeast of the village of Bodega Bay (lat. 38°20'45" N, long. 123°02'30" W). Altitude 621 feet. Named on Bodega Head (1972) 7.5' quadrangle.

Mount Saint Helena [SONOMA]: *peak,* 13 miles east-northeast of Healdsburg near the junction of Sonoma County, Lake County, and Napa

County (lat. 38°40'10" N, long. 122°37'55" W; near E line sec. 33, T 10 N, R 7 W). Altitude 4343 feet. Named on Mount Saint Helena (1959) 7.5' quadrangle. Called Mt. St. Hellens on Goddard's (1857) map. Trask (p. 10) called the feature Mount Helen. Whitney (p. 86-87) claimed that a Russian naturalist named Wosnessensky climbed the peak in 1841 and named it. It was called Devil's Mount in the early days of American settlement in California (Gudde, 1949, p. 295).

Mount Saint John [NAPA]: *peak,* 2.5 miles southwest of Rutherford (lat. 38°26'15" N, long. 122°27'35" W; sec. 19, T 7 N, R 5 W). Altitude 2375 feet. Named on Rutherford (1951) 7.5' quadrangle. Called St. John Mt. on Napa (1902) 30' quadrangle. Members of the Whitney survey named the peak Mount Henry for Joseph Henry of Princeton University and Smithsonian Institution, but the name was not adopted (Brewer, p. 224-225, 238).

Mount San Isabel: see **Mount Isabel** [SANTA CLARA].

Mount Santa Ysabel: see **Mount Isabel** [SANTA CLARA].

Mount Sizer [SANTA CLARA]: *peak,* 9.5 miles northeast of Morgan Hill (lat. 37°12'50" N, long. 121°30'45" W). Altitude 3216 feet. Named on Mount Sizer (1955) 7.5' quadrangle.

Mount Stakes [SANTA CLARA]: *peak,* 12 miles south-southeast of Mount Boardman on Santa Clara-Stanislaus County line (lat. 37° 19'20" N, long. 121°24'25" W; sec. 15, T 7 S, R 5 E). Altitude 3804 feet. Named on Mount Stakes (1955) 7.5' quadrangle.

Mount Sutro [SAN FRANCISCO]: *peak,* 2.5 miles southwest of San Francisco civic center (lat. 37°45'30" N, long. 122°27'20" W). Altitude 908 feet. Named on San Francisco North (1956) 7.5' quadrangle. Called Blue Mt. on San Francisco (1899, reprinted 1906) 15' quadrangle, but United States Board on Geographic Names (1933, p. 731) rejected the names "Blue Mountain" and "Sutro Crest" for the peak. The name "Sutro" commemorates Adolph Sutro, mayor of San Francisco from 1894 until 1898 (Gudde, 1949, p. 348).

Mount Tamalpais [MARIN]: *ridge,* west-southwest-trending, 2 miles long, center 4.5 miles southwest of downtown San Rafael (lat. 37°55'40" N, long. 122°35'30" W). Named on San Rafael (1954) 7.5' quadrangle. Called Table Hill on Beechey's (1827-1828) map. The feature was called Pico y Cerro de Reyes and Picacho Prieto in Spanish times; it was called Table Hill, Table Mountain, and Table Butte after Beechey's survey of San Francisco Bay in 1826, and it was called Mount Palermo by members of Wilkes' expedition in 1841 (Gudde, 1949, p. 353). The name "Tamalpais" is of Indian origin (Kroeber, p. 61).

Mount Tamalpais Camp: see **Camp Eastwood** [MARIN].

Mount Thayer [SANTA CLARA]: *peak,* 5.5 miles southeast of downtown Los Gatos (lat. 37°09'50" N, long. 121°55'05" W; sec. 12, T 9 S, R 1 W). Altitude 3483 feet. Named on Los Gatos (1953) 7.5' quadrangle. The peak first was called Mount Hooker (Young, p. 62).

Mount Tom [SONOMA]: *ridge,* east-southeast-trending, 1.25 miles long, 12.5 miles west-southwest of Cloverdale (lat. 38°46' N, long. 123°14'30" W). Named on Hopland (1960) 15' quadrangle.

Mount Umunhum [SANTA CLARA]: *peak,* 6.5 miles southeast of downtown Los Gatos (lat. 37°09'40" N, long. 121°53'50" W; sec. 7, T 9 S, R 1 E). Altitude 3486 feet. Named on Los Gatos (1953) 7.5' quadrangle. Gudde (1969, p. 350) related the name to an Indian word for hummingbird, and noted that the names "Picacho de Umunhum" and "Picacho de Umurhum" occur on maps of 1848. The peak mistakenly is called Loma Prieta on some maps (Hoover, Rensch, and Rensch, p. 457).

Mount Vaca [NAPA-SOLANO]: *peak,* 12 miles northeast of Napa on Blue Ridge (2) on Napa-Solano County line (lat. 38°24' N, long. 122°06'20" W; sec. 5, T 6 N, R 2 W); the peak is in Vaca Mountains. Altitude 2819 feet. Named on Mount Vaca (1951) 7.5' quadrangle. United States Board on Geographic Names (1970a, p. 3) gave the names "Blue Mountain" and "Vaca Peak" as variants, and pointed out that the feature is the highest point in Vaca Mountains.

Mount Veeder [NAPA-SONOMA]: *peak,* 5.5 miles south-southwest of Rutherford on Napa-Sonoma County line (lat. 38°22'45" N, long. 122°26'50" W; sec. 7, T 6 N, R 5 W). Named on Rutherford (1951) and Sonoma (1951) 7.5' quadrangles. Called Veeder Mt. on Napa (1902) 30' quadrangle. The name commemorates Peter V. Veeder, minister of the Presbyterian church in Napa from about 1858 until 1861 (Gudde, 1949, p. 377).

Mount Vision [MARIN]: *peak,* 4 miles west-northwest of Point Reyes Station on Inverness Ridge (lat. 38°05'20" N, long. 122°52'20" W). Altitude 1282 feet. Named on Inverness (1954) 7.5' quadrangle. F.M. Anderson (p. 123) referred to Vision Hill.

Mount Wallace [ALAMEDA]: *peak,* 3.5 miles east-southeast of Cedar Mountain on Alameda-San Joaquin County line (lat. 37°32'20" N, long. 121°33' W; sec. 32, T 4 S, R 4 E). Altitude 3112 feet. Named on Cedar Mountain (1956) 7.5' quadrangle. The name commemorates John Wallace, county surveyor of San Joaquin County, who helped establish Alameda-San Joaquin County line in 1868 (Mosier and Mosier, p. 59).

Mount Wanda: see **Martinez** [CONTRA COSTA].

Mount Wittenberg [MARIN]: *peak,* 2.25 miles south-southwest of Point Reyes Station on Inverness Ridge (lat. 38°02'20" N, long. 122°49'15" W). Altitude 1407 feet. Named on Inverness (1954) 7.5' quadrangle. United States Board on Geographic Names (1968b, p. 10) rejected the form "Mount Wittenburg" for the name, which commemorates Peter Wittenberg and Newton M. Wittenberg, who leased land in the neighborhood for a dairy ranch in the 1860's (Teather, p. 88). F.M. Anderson (p. 123) referred to Wittenberg Hill.

Mount Zion [CONTRA COSTA]: *peak,* 3.5 miles northwest of Mount Diablo (lat. 37°55'25" N, long. 121°57'10" W; near NE cor. sec. 22, T 1 N, R 1 W). Altitude 1635 feet. Named on Clayton (1953) 7.5' quadrangle. This apparently is the feature that members of the Whitney survey called Pyramid Hill (Whitney, p. 22).

Mowry Camp [SANTA CLARA]: *locality,* 1.25 miles west-southwest of Eylar Mountain (lat. 37°28'15" N, long. 121°34'05" W; sec. 30, T 5 S, R 4 E). Named on Eylar Mountain (1955) 7.5' quadrangle.

Mowry Landing [ALAMEDA]: *locality,* 2 miles southeast of downtown Newark (lat. 37°30'20" N, long. 122°00'45" W); the place is along Mowry Slough. Named on Newark (1959) 7.5' quadrangle. E.B. Perrin bought land on the north side of the mouth of Mowry Slough in 1870 and started Green Point Dairy Landing and Transportation Company; he built Green Point Landing there and named it for his company (Mosier and Mosier, p. 40). A place called Larkin's Landing was situated east of Mowry Landing along Mowry Slough; it was named for Stephen Larkin, who came to the neighborhood in 1851 (Mosier and Mosier, p. 50).

Mowry Slough [ALAMEDA]: *water feature,* joins San Francisco Bay 2.5 miles south-southwest of downtown Newark (lat. 37°29'30" N, long. 122°03'10" W). Named on Mountain View (1961) and Newark (1959) 7.5' quadrangles. The name commemorates Origin Mowry, who settled along the slough in 1850 (Mosier and Mosier, p. 59).

Mowry Station [ALAMEDA]: *locality,* 2.25 miles southeast of downtown Newark along Southern Pacific Railroad (lat. 37°30'35" N, long. 122°00'15" W). Named on Haywards (1899) 15' quadrangle.

Mowry Well [ALAMEDA]: *well,* 1 mile northwest of Fremont civic center (lat. 37°33'45" N, long. 121°58'45" W; sec. 28, T 4 S, R 1 W). Named on Niles (1961) 7.5' quadrangle.

Mud Creek: see **Mud Slough** [ALAMEDA].

Muddy Creek: see **Arroyo Seco** [ALAMEDA].

Muddy Hollow [MARIN]: *locality,* 3.5 miles west-southwest of Point Reyes Station (lat. 38°03' N, long. 122°52'05" W). Named on Inverness (1954) 7.5' quadrangle.

Mud Hen Slough [SONOMA]: *water feature,* joins San Antonio Creek 6.5 miles southeast of downtown Petaluma (lat. 38°10'10" N, long. 122°33'10" W). Named on Petaluma River (1954) 7.5' quadrangle.

Mudholes [SONOMA]: *water feature,* 7 miles north of Fort Ross (lat. 38°36'55" N, long. 123°13'30" W; at N line sec. 19, T 9 N, R 12 W). Named on Fort Ross (1978) 7.5' quadrangle.

Mud Lake [MARIN]: *lake,* 550 feet long, 2.25 miles northeast of Double Point (lat. 37°58'25" N, long. 122°45'20" W). Named on Double Point (1954) 7.5' quadrangle.

Mud Lake [NAPA]: *lake,* 550 feet long, 3 miles west of Mount Vaca (lat. 38°24' N, long. 122°09'30" W). Named on Capell Valley (1951, photorevised 1968) 7.5' quadrangle.

Mud Lake [SANTA CLARA]: *lake,* 200 feet long, 6 miles south-southwest of Mount Sizer (lat. 37°08'20" N, long. 121°34'30" W; sec. 19, T 9 S, R 4 E). Named on Mount Sizer (1955) 7.5' quadrangle.

Mud Slough [ALAMEDA]: *water feature,* joins Coyote Creek 6 miles south of Fremont civic center (lat. 37°27'55" N, long. 121° 59'15" W). Named on Milpitas (1961) 7.5' quadrangle. Thompson and West's (1878) map calls the slough Mud Creek, and shows a place called Warm Springs Landing situated near the head of the feature in present Warm Springs District—brothers Waitsell Baker and Joseph Baker started Baker's Landing at the place in 1857; the name was changed to Warm Springs Landing in 1860 (Mosier and Mosier, p. 13, 92).

Mud Slough [MARIN]: *water feature,* 0.5 mile long, connects two reaches of San Antonio Creek through marsh 5.25 miles north of downtown Novato (lat. 38°10'50" N, long. 122°34'05" W). Named on Petaluma River (1954) 7.5' quadrangle.

Mud Slough [NAPA]: *water feature,* joins Napa River 3.5 miles west of Napa Junction (lat. 38°11'25" N, long. 122°18'50" W). Named on Cuttings Wharf (1949) 7.5' quadrangle.

Mud Slough [SOLANO]: *water feature,* joins Roaring River Slough 5.5 miles west-southwest of Birds Landing (2) (lat. 38°05'50" N, long. 121°57'25" W). Named on Honker Bay (1953) 7.5' quadrangle.

Mud Spring [NAPA]: *spring,* 4.5 miles east-northeast of Calistoga on Rattlesnake Ridge (lat. 38°36'30" N, long. 122°30'20" W; sec. 22, T 9 N, R 6 W). Named on Calistoga (1958) 7.5' quadrangle.

Mud Springs [ALAMEDA]:

(1) *spring,* 1.5 miles northwest of Mendenhall Springs (lat. 37°36'20" N, long. 121°39'50" W; sec. 8, T 4 S, R 3 E). Named on Mendenhall Springs (1956) 7.5' quadrangle.

(2) *spring,* 5 miles south of Mendenhall Springs (lat. 37°30'45" N, long.

121°39'15" W; sec. 9, T 5 S, R 3 E). Named on Mendenhall Springs (1956) 7.5' quadrangle.

Mud Springs [SANTA CLARA]: *spring,* 3.5 miles east-southeast of New Almaden near the head of Pine Tree Canyon (lat. 37°09'30" N, long. 121°45'50" W). Named on Santa Teresa Hills (1953) 7.5' quadrangle.

Muir [CONTRA COSTA]: *locality,* 8 miles north-northeast of Orinda along Atchison, Topeka and Santa Fe Railroad in Alhambra Valley (lat. 37°59'25" N, long. 122°07'35" W). Named on Briones Valley (1959) 7.5' quadrangle.

Muir Beach [MARIN]: *beach,* 4 miles northwest of Point Bonita along the coast (lat. 37°51'35" N, long. 122°34'40" W); the beach is at the mouth of Redwood Creek. Named on Point Bonita (1954) 7.5' quadrangle. The name is from Muir Woods National Monument, located on the upper reaches of Redwood Creek (Gudde, 1949, p. 228). The place earlier was called Bello Beach, or Bello's Bend, for Anthony Nunes Bello, who filed a subdivision map in 1923 (Teather, p. 48). A lagoon, now filled, called Frank's Lagoon was at present Muir Beach in the 1850's (Teather, p. 26).

Muir Camp [CONTRA COSTA]: *locality,* 0.5 mile southwest of Mount Diablo (lat. 37°52'35" N, long. 121°55'15" W; sec. 1, T 1 S, R 1 W). Named on Clayton (1953) 7.5' quadrangle.

Mulford: see **West San Leandro** [ALAMEDA].

Mulford Gardens [ALAMEDA]: *district,* 2 miles southwest of downtown San Leandro (lat. 37°42'10" N, long. 122°10'45" W); the district is northeast of Mulford Landing. Named on San Leandro (1959) 7.5' quadrangle.

Mulford Landing [ALAMEDA]: *locality,* 2.5 miles southwest of downtown San Leandro at the edge of San Francisco Bay (lat. 37° 41'50" N, long. 122°11'10" W). Named on San Leandro (1959) 7.5' quadrangle. In 1853 Moses Wicks, Thomas W. Mulford, and others started business at the site, which was called Wicks Landing; Mulford bought the place in 1868 and renamed it—the landing is at what is known as Mulford Point (Mosier and Mosier, p. 60).

Mulford Point: see **Mulford Landing** [ALAMEDA].

Mulholland Hill [CONTRA COSTA]: *peak,* 2.5 miles southeast of Orinda (lat. 37°51'35" N, long. 122°08'40" W; sec. 12, T 1 S, R 3 W). Altitude 1157 feet. Named on Oakland East (1959) 7.5' quadrangle.

Mullen's Creek: see **Arroyo de en Medio** [SAN MATEO].

Mulligan Hill [CONTRA COSTA]: *ridge,* east-trending, nearly 1 mile long, 7 miles north of Mount Diablo (lat. 37°58'55" N, long. 121° 55'55" W). Altitude 1438 feet. Named on Clayton (1953) 7.5' quadrangle.

Muñis: see **Muniz** [SONOMA].

Muniz [SONOMA]: *land grant,* along the coast from Russian River to northwest of Fort Ross. Named on Arched Rock (1977), Duncans Mills (1979), Fort Ross (1978), and Plantation (1977) 7.5' quadrangles. Manuel Torres received 4 leagues in 1845 and claimed 17,761 acres patented in 1860 (Cowan, p. 50; Cowan used the form "Muñis" for the name).

Munroe: see **Point Munroe**, under **Paradise Cay** [MARIN].

Murphy: see **Sunnyvale** [SANTA CLARA].

Murphy Canyon [SANTA CLARA]: *canyon,* 2 miles long, 2.5 miles north-northwest of Mount Madonna on upper reaches of Little Arthur Creek (lat. 37°02'45" N, long. 121°43'45" W). Named on Mount Madonna (1955) 7.5' quadrangle.

Murphy Creek [NAPA]: *stream,* flows 3 miles to join Spencer Creek and form Tulucay Creek 10.5 miles southwest of Mount Vaca (lat. 38°17'35" N, long. 122°14'15" W). Named on Mount George (1951) 7.5' quadrangle.

Murphy Mill [SONOMA]: *locality,* 4.5 miles east of Fort Ross (lat. 38°30'55" N, long. 123°09'20" W; near N line sec. 26, T 8 N, R 12 W). Named on Fort Ross (1943) 7.5' quadrangle. Fort Ross (1978) 7.5' quadrangle has the name "Black Mountain Conservation Camp" at the site.

Murphy Rock [MARIN]: *rock,* 1.5 miles north-northwest of Point San Quentin in San Rafael Bay (lat. 37°57'40" N, long. 122°29'25" W). Named on San Quentin (1959) 7.5' quadrangle. Called Murphys Rock on Ringgold's (1850a) map, and called San Rafael Rock on San Francisco (1915) 15' quadrangle. The feature now is at the edge of filled land.

Murphy's Peak: see **El Toro** [SANTA CLARA].

Murray Park [MARIN]: *district,* 2.25 miles south-southwest of downtown San Rafael (lat. 37°56'50" N, long. 122°33'05" W). Named on San Rafael (1954) 7.5' quadrangle.

Mussel Point [SONOMA]: *promontory,* nearly 2 miles west-southwest of the village of Bodega Bay along the coast (lat. 38°19'20" N, long. 123°04'35" W). Named on Bodega Head (1972) 7.5' quadrangle.

Mussel Rock [SAN MATEO]:

(1) *rock,* 4.5 miles west of downtown South San Francisco, and 225 feet offshore (lat. 37°40' N, long. 122°29'45" W). Named on San Francisco South (1956) 7.5' quadrangle. The beach north from Mussel Rock to San Francisco-San Mateo-County line was called Seven Mile Beach (Brown, p. 88).

(2) *rock,* 1.5 miles north-northwest of the village of San Gregorio, and 250 feet offshore (lat. 37°20'50" N, long. 122°24'05" W). Named on San Gregorio (1961, photorevised 1968) 7.5' quadrangle.

Mustang Peak [SANTA CLARA]: *peak,* 8 miles northeast of Gilroy Hot Springs on Santa Clara-Stanislaus County line (lat. 37°11'10" N, long. 121°21'35" W; sec. 6, T 9 S, R 6 E). Altitude 2263 feet. Named on Mustang Peak (1955) 7.5' quadrangle.

Mustang Ridge [SANTA CLARA]: *ridge,* north-trending, nearly 4 miles long, 6 miles north of Pacheco Peak (lat. 37°07'10" N, long. 121°16'45" W). Named on Mustang Peak (1955) and Pacheco Peak (1955) 7.5' quadrangles.

Mysterious Creek [NAPA]: *stream,* flows nearly 2 miles to Putah Creek 6.25 miles south-southwest of Knoxville (lat. 38°45'05" N, long. 122°24'10" W; near N line sec. 3, T 10 N, R 5 W); the stream drains Mysterious Valley. Named on Jericho Valley (1958) and Knoxville (1958) 7.5' quadrangles.

Mysterious Valley [NAPA]: *valley,* 5.25 miles south-southwest of Knoxville (lat. 38°45'05" N, long. 122°22'05" W); Mysterious Creek drains the valley. Named on Knoxville (1958) and Walter Springs (1959) 7.5' quadrangles.

— N —

Nacio [CONTRA COSTA]: *locality,* 5 miles north of present Walnut Creek civic center along Southern Pacific Railroad (lat. 37°58'15" N, long. 122°02'50" W). Named on Concord (1943) 15' quadrangle.

Napa [NAPA]:

(1) *land grant,* mainly in Napa Valley at and northwest of the city of Napa. Named on Napa (1951), Rutherford (1951), Sonoma (1951), and Yountville (1951) 7.5' quadrangles. Salvador Vallejo received 4 leagues in 1838 and claimed 3178 acres patented in 1866; six other claimants received parcels ranging from 260 to 680 acres patented from 1866 to 1880 (Cowan, p. 51; Perez, p. 77-78). The name "Napa" may be from an Indian word for the detachable points of native fish harpoons (Kroeber, p. 50).

(2) *city,* near the south end of Napa Valley along Napa River (lat. 38°17'50" N, long. 122°17' W); the city is on Napa grant. Named on Napa (1951) 7.5' quadrangle. Called Nappa on Trask's (1853) map. Postal authorities established Napa City post office in 1850, and changed the name to Napa in 1890 (Frickstad, p. 111). Grigsby and Combs laid out the community in 1848 at what was known as the embarcadero at the head of navigation on Napa River (Bancroft, 1888, p. 510).

Napa City: see **Napa** [NAPA] (2).

Napa Creek [NAPA]: *stream,* formed by the confluence of Redwood Creek and Browns Valley Creek, flows 2 miles to Napa River in downtown Napa (lat. 38°17'55" N, long. 122°17' W). Named on Napa (1951) 7.5' quadrangle. On Napa (1902) 30' quadrangle, present Browns Valley Creek is called South Fork [Napa Creek], and the stream in present Pickel Canyon is called North Branch [Napa Creek].

Napa Creek: see **Napa River** [NAPA]; **Redwood Creek** [NAPA].

Napa Island: see **Mare Island** [SOLANO].

Napa Junction [NAPA]: *locality,* 7.5 miles south-southeast of Napa along Southern Pacific Railroad (lat. 38°11'15" N, long. 122° 15' W; near S line sec. 13, T 4 N, R 4 W). Named on Cordelia (1951) and Cuttings Wharf (1949) 7.5' quadrangles. Postal authorities established Adelante post office at the place in 1869 and discontinued it in 1871; they established Napa Junction post office in 1875, discontinued it for a time in 1880, and discontinued it finally in 1933 (Salley, p. 1, 150). California Division of Highways' (1934) map shows a place called Kelly located about 1.5 miles north of Napa Junction along San Francisco, Napa, and Calistoga Railway (sec. 12, T 4 N, R 4 W), and a place called Napa Wye nearly 1 mile farther north (sec. 1, T 4 N, R 4 W), apparently at a highway junction. California Mining Bureau's (1917a) map shows a place called Guthrie halfway from Napa Junction to Napa along a railroad.

Napa Reservoir: see **East Napa Reservoir** [NAPA]; **West Napa Reservoir** [NAPA].

Napa River [NAPA-SOLANO]: *stream,* heads in Napa County and flows 58 miles to Carquinez Strait (by way of Mare Island Strait) 2 miles south-southeast of downtown Vallejo in Solano County (lat. 38°04'30" N, long. 122°14'40" W). Named on Calistoga (1958), Cuttings Wharf (1949), Mare Island (1959), Napa (1951), Rutherford (1951), Saint Helena (1960), and Yountville (1951) 7.5' quadrangles. Called Nappa C.[Creek] on Trask's (1853) map, and called Napa Cr. on Eddy's (1854) map. United States Board on Geographic Names (1933, p. 544) rejected the name "Napa Creek" for the stream.

Napa Rock Soda Springs: see **Samuel Springs** [NAPA].

Napa Slough [NAPA-SONOMA]: *water feature,* forms part of Napa-Sonoma County line, joins Napa River 3.5 miles west of Napa Junction (lat. 38°11'05" N, long. 122°18'45" W). Named on Cuttings Wharf (1949) and Sears Point (1951) 7.5' quadrangles.

Napa Slough: see **Second Napa Slough** [SONOMA]; **Third Napa Slough** [SONOMA].

Napa Soda Springs [NAPA]: *locality,* 5 miles east-southeast of Yountville (lat. 38°23'30" N, long. 122°16'40" W; near SW cor. sec. 2, T 6 N, R 4 W). Named on Yountville (1951) 7.5' quadrangle. Postal authorities established Napa Soda Springs post office in 1882 and discontinued it in 1929 (Frickstad, p. 111). The place also was called Jacksons Napa Soda Springs

(Waring, p. 155).

Napa Valley [NAPA]: *valley,* along Napa River above the city of Napa. Named on Calistoga (1958), Napa (1951), Rutherford (1951), Saint Helena (1960), and Yountville (1951) 7.5' quadrangles. Called Nappa Valley on Jefferson's (1849) map, and called Valley of Nappa by Wilkes (p. 86) in 1841.

Napa Vichy Spring: see **Vichy Springs** [NAPA].

Napa Wye: see **Napa Junction** [NAPA].

Napland [CONTRA COSTA]: *locality,* 2 miles south-southwest of present Walnut Creek civic center along Oakland Antioch and Eastern Railroad (lat. 37°52'35" N, long. 122°04'20" W). Named on Concord (1915) 15' quadrangle.

Naples Beach [SAN MATEO]: *beach,* 2.25 miles northwest of downtown Half Moon Bay along the coast (lat. 37°29'20" N, long. 122° 27'20" W). Named on Half Moon Bay (1961) 7.5' quadrangle. The name is from an unsuccessful subdivision (Brown, p. 60).

Nappa: see **Napa** [NAPA] (2).

Nappa Creek: see **Napa River** [NAPA-SOLANO].

Nappa Valley: see **Napa Valley** [NAPA].

Narrows: see **The Narrows** [SANTA CLARA].

Nash Creek [NAPA]: *stream,* flows 2 miles to Napa River 2.5 miles east-southeast of Calistoga (lat. 38°33'50" N, long. 122°31'55" W). Named on Calistoga (1958) 7.5' quadrangle. William Nash built a house by the stream in or before 1848 (Archuleta, p. 16).

Nathanson Creek [SONOMA]: *stream,* flows 7.25 miles to Schell Creek 2.5 miles south of Sonoma (lat. 38°15'30" N, long. 122° 27' W). Named on Sonoma (1951) 7.5' quadrangle.

Naval Air Station: see **Moffett Field** [SANTA CLARA].

Navy Point: see **Army Point** [SOLANO]; **Voltani Slough** [SOLANO].

Neal [SANTA CLARA]: *locality,* 2.5 miles south-southeast of downtown Palo Alto along Southern Pacific Railroad (lat. 37°24'50" N, long. 122°08'25" W). Named on Palo Alto (1961) 7.5' quadrangle. Palo Alto (1961, photorevised 1968 and 1973) 7.5' quadrangle shows the rail line ending before it reaches Neal.

Neal Creek [SONOMA]: *stream,* flows 0.5 mile to Mark West Creek 7.5 miles east-southeast of Mark West Springs (lat. 38°31' N, long. 122°34'55" W; sec. 25, T 8 N, R 7 W). Named on Calistoga (1958) 7.5' quadrangle.

Nebo: see **Mount Nebo**, under **Bismark Knob** [NAPA-SOLANO].

Needles [SAN FRANCISCO]: *rocks,* 1.25 miles north of Fort Point, and 150 feet off of Marin County coast (lat. 37°49'45" N, long. 122°28'35" W). Named on San Francisco North (1956) 7.5' quadrangle.

Neeley Hill [SONOMA]: *peak,* less than 1 mile south-southwest of Guerneville (lat. 38°29'25" N, long. 123°00' W; at E line sec. 31, T 8 N, R 10 E). Named on Camp Meeker (1954) and Duncans Mills (1979) 7.5' quadrangles.

Neel Gulch: see **Neils Gulch** [SAN MATEO].

Neese Ridge [SONOMA]: *ridge,* south-southwest-trending, 1 mile long, 4 miles west-southwest of Big Mountain (lat. 38°40'45" N, long. 123°12'30" W). Named on Tombs Creek (1978) 7.5' quadrangle.

Negro Canyon [NAPA]: *canyon,* drained by a stream that flows 1 mile to Lake Berryessa 8 miles northwest of Mount Vaca (lat. 38° 29'35" N, long. 122°12'10" W; near W line sec. 33, T 8 N, R 3 W). Named on Capell Valley (1951, photorevised 1968) 7.5' quadrangle.

Neils Gulch [SAN MATEO]: *canyon,* drained by a stream that flows 1.25 miles to Sausal Creek 7 miles south of downtown Redwood City in Portola Valley (1) (lat. 37°22'50" N, long. 122°13'40" W). Named on Mindego Hill (1961) and Palo Alto (1961) 7.5' quadrangles. The stream in the canyon is called Sausal Cr. on Palo Alto (1899) 15' quadrangle. Brown (p. 60) called the feature Neel Gulch, and noted that it was named for David H. Neel, a settler in the neighborhood in the 1850's; the canyon also had the names "Cañada de Sansevan" and "Hallidie Gulch."

Neils Island [SONOMA]: *hill,* 4.5 miles southeast of downtown Petaluma in marsh southwest of Petaluma River (lat. 38°11'25" N, long. 122°34'40" W). Named on Petaluma River (1954) 7.5' quadrangle. Called Nell Island on Petaluma (1914) 15' quadrangle.

Nell Island: see **Neils Island** [SONOMA].

Nema [SANTA CLARA]: *locality,* at the end of a half-mile-long spur of Southern Pacific Railroad that branches southwest from the main line 3 miles south-southeast of Gilroy (lat. 36°57'30" N, long. 121°33' W). Named on San Juan Bautista (1917) 15' quadrangle.

Neroly [CONTRA COSTA]: *locality,* 4.25 miles northwest of Brentwood along Southern Pacific Railroad (lat. 37°58'55" N, long. 121° 44'25" W; near N line sec. 34, T 2 N, R 2 E). Named on Brentwood (1954) 7.5' quadrangle.

Nervo [SONOMA]: *locality,* 2 miles southeast of Geyserville along Northwestern Pacific Railroad (lat. 38°41'15" N, long. 122°52'45" W). Named on Geyserville (1955) 7.5' quadrangle.

Nesbit Ridge [SANTA CLARA]: *ridge,* U-shaped, 2.25 miles long, 6 miles south-southwest of Mount Sizer (lat. 37°07'55" N, long. 121° 32'15" W). Named on Mount Sizer (1955) 7.5' quadrangle.

Nevada Creek [NAPA]: *stream,* flows 7.5 miles to Adams Creek 5 miles northeast of Walter Springs (lat. 38°42'15" N, long. 122°17'30" W; near N line sec. 22, T 10 N, R 4 W). Named on Knoxville (1958) and Walter Springs (1959) 7.5' quadrangles.

Nevada Dock [CONTRA COSTA]: *locality,* 2.5 miles northwest of Martinez along Southern Pacific Railroad (lat. 38°02'10" N, long. 122°10'25" W). Named on Benicia (1959) 7.5' quadrangle.

New Almaden [SANTA CLARA]: *village,* 11 miles south-southeast of downtown San Jose (lat. 37°10'30" N, long. 121°49'15" W). Named on Santa Teresa Hills (1953) 7.5' quadrangle, which has both the names "New Almaden" and "Almaden P.O." at the place. Postal authorities established New Almaden post office in 1861, discontinued it the same year, reestablished it in 1873, and discontinued it in 1921; they established Almaden post office in 1934 and changed the name back to New Almaden in 1953 (Frickstad, p. 173, 174). The community name is for nearby New Almaden mine, which itself was named in 1848 after a famous quicksilver mine in Spain—*almaden* means "mine" or "mineral" in Spanish (Gudde, 1969, p. 7-8). The company that began producing quicksilver at New Almaden mine in 1847 selected a site along Alamitos Creek for its headquarters and furnaces; the place was referred to as Hacienda de Beneficio, or Reduction Works; the community that grew there was long called Hacienda, but eventually it became known as New Almaden (Lanyon and Bulmore, p. 91, 99). New Almaden mine is west of the village on a ridge that is unnamed on modern maps, but the name by which the ridge was known to Spanish-speaking residents in the vicinity was of considerable importance in legal proceedings that established ownership of the mine. Depositions of a number of witnesses in 1857 (United States Supreme Court, p. 30, 35, 46, 89) touched upon the question: Jose Fernandez stated that the ridge was called Cuchilla de Almaden, but previously had the name "Cuchilla de la nema [mina] de la Luis Cheavoya"; Jose Noriega testified that the ridge was called Las Lomas Bajas de las Minas, but before discovery of the mine it was called Las Lomas Bajas; James Alexander Forbes said that he first knew the ridge by the name "La Cuchilla de la Mina de Louis Chabolla," but later he knew it by the names "Mining Hills" or "Hills of the Mines"; and William J. Lewis referred to Sierra del Encino or Mine ridge. Davis and Jennings (p. 342) called the feature Los Capitancillos Ridge, and Whitney (p. 65-66) noted the name "Mount Chisnantuck" for the highest point on the ridge. A small mineral spring called Vichy Spring was on the south bank of the stream at New Almaden (Irelan, p. 549-550). Winslow Anderson (p. 208-209) used the name "New Almaden Vichy Springs" for the resort at the spring, but reported that the water had ceased to flow because of deep mine workings. Postal authorities established Frohm post office 4 miles north of New Almaden in 1887 and discontinued it in 1902; the name was for Chester C. Frohm, first postmaster (Salley, p. 81).

New Almaden: see **Cañada de los Capitanicillos** [SANTA CLARA].

New Almaden Station [SANTA CLARA]: *locality,* 2 miles north-northwest of New Almaden at the end of a branch line of Southern Pacific Railroad (lat. 37°12'05" N, long. 121°49'55" W). Named on Los Gatos (1919) 15' quadrangle. California Mining Bureau's (1909b) map shows a place called Junction located 1.5 miles northwest of New Almaden Station, where the rail line branches; Los Gatos (1919) 15' quadrangle shows the rail line branching only 0.5 mile north of New Almaden Station. California Mining Bureau's (1917b) map shows a place called Thona situated along the railroad about halfway between New Almaden Station and Campbell.

New Almaden Vichy Springs: see **New Almaden** [SANTA CLARA].

Newark [ALAMEDA]: *city,* 22 miles southeast of Oakland (lat. 37° 31'45" N, long. 122°02'20" W). Named on Newark (1959) and Niles (1961) 7.5' quadrangles. Postal authorities established Newark post office in 1878 (Frickstad, p. 3), and the city incorporated in 1955. The name is from the city in New Jersey, home state of the Davis brothers, who were involved in founding the California city (Thompson and West, 1878, p. 27).

Newark Creek: see **Newark Slough** [ALAMEDA].

Newark Slough [ALAMEDA]: *water feature,* enters San Francisco Bay 3 miles southwest of downtown Newark (lat. 37°30'10" N, long. 122°05'05" W). Named on Newark (1959) 7.5' quadrangle. Called Newark Creek on Haywards (1899) 15' quadrangle. The feature was called Beard's Slough in the 1870's (Mosier and Mosier, p. 61).

New Camp [SANTA CLARA]: *locality,* 4.25 miles east-northeast of Mount Day (lat. 37°26'45" N, long. 121°37'45" W; sec. 3, T 6 S, R 3 E); the place is 2.25 miles southeast of Old Camp. Named on Mount Day (1955) 7.5' quadrangle.

New Chicago: see **Alviso** [SANTA CLARA].

New Creek: see **Little Llagas Creek** [SANTA CLARA].

Newell Gulch [SAN MATEO]: *canyon,* drained by a stream that flows nearly 1 mile to Pescadero Creek 5.5 miles southwest of La Honda (lat. 37°15'25" N, long. 122°20'25" W; near N line sec. 12, T 8 S, R 5 W). Named on La Honda (1961) 7.5' quadrangle. Frank Newell lived in the canyon in the 1880's and 1890's (Brown, p. 60).

Newgate Ridge [SONOMA]: *ridge,* south-trending, 1 mile long, 5 miles northeast of Guerneville (lat. 38°33'25" N, long. 122°56'30" W). Named on Guerneville (1955) 7.5' quadrangle.

New Haven: see **Alvarado** [ALAMEDA]; **Union City** [ALAMEDA].

Newlove [CONTRA COSTA]: *locality,* 11.5 miles northeast of Mount Diablo along Southern Pacific Railroad (lat. 37°59'35" N, long. 121°45'45" W; sec. 28, T 2 N, R 2 E). Named on Antioch South (1953) 7.5' quadrangle.

New Mountain View: see **Mountain View** [SANTA CLARA].

New Philadelphia: see **Sonoma** [SONOMA].

Newport: see **Collinsville** [SOLANO].

Newton: see **Lake Newton** [NAPA].

Newtown [SOLANO]: *locality,* 1 mile north-northeast of Rio Vista along Sacramento River (lat. 38°10'10" N, long. 121°40'45" W). Named on Rio Vista (1910) 7.5' quadrangle.

Newtown [SONOMA]: *locality,* nearly 2 miles east of downtown Petaluma along Northwestern Pacific Railroad (lat. 38°13'55" N, long. 122°36'20" W). Named on Petaluma (1914) 15' quadrangle.

New Year Bay: see **Año Nuevo Bay** [SAN MATEO].

New Year Creek: see **Año Nuevo Creek** [SAN MATEO].

New Year Island: see **Año Nuevo Island** [SAN MATEO].

New Year's Bay: see **Año Nuevo Bay** [SAN MATEO].

New Year's Creek: see **Año Nuevo Creek** [SAN MATEO].

New Year's Island: see **Año Nuevo Island** [SAN MATEO].

New Years Point: see **Año Nuevo Point** [SAN MATEO].

New York Landing: see **Pittsburg** [CONTRA COSTA].

New York of the Pacific: see **Pittsburg** [CONTRA COSTA].

New York Point [CONTRA COSTA]: *promontory,* 0.5 mile north of downtown Pittsburg along Suisun Bay (lat. 38°02'30" N, long. 121°53'05" W); the feature is on the west side of the mouth of New York Slough. Named on Honker Bay (1953) 7.5' quadrangle.

New York Slough [CONTRA COSTA]: *water feature,* separates Browns Island and Winter Island from the mainland, extends for 3.5 miles from San Joaquin River to Suisun Bay 0.5 mile north of downtown Pittsburg (lat. 38°02'25" N, long. 121°52'55" W). Named on Antioch North (1978) and Honker Bay (1953) 7.5' quadrangles. United States Board on Geographic Names (1979b, p. 6) approved the name "Dowest Slough" for an inlet situated on the south shore of New York Slough 3 miles north-northwest of Antioch (lat. 38°01'30" N, long. 121°50'35" W).

Nibbs Knob [SANTA CLARA]: *peak,* 2.5 miles southeast of Loma Prieta (lat. 37°05'10" N, long. 121°48'40" W; sec. 1, T 10 S, R 1 E). Altitude 2694 feet. Named on Loma Prieta (1955) 7.5' quadrangle. The name also has the form "Nibs Knob" (Young, p. 64).

Nibs Knob: see **Nibbs Knob** [SANTA CLARA].

Nicasio [MARIN]:

(1) *land grant,* at and northeast of Point Reyes Station. Named on Inverness (1954), Point Reyes NE (1954), and San Geronimo (1954) 7.5' quadrangles. Pablo de la Guerra and John Bautista Roger Cooper received the land in 1844; James Black claimed 9479 acres patented in 1861 (Cowan, p. 52).

(2) *land grant,* 9 miles west-southwest of downtown Novato. Named on Inverness (1954) and San Geronimo (1954) 7.5' quadrangles. Pablo de la Guerra and John Bautista Roger Cooper received the land in 1844; B.R. Bucklew claimed 8695 acres patented in 1861 (Cowan, p. 52).

(3) *land grant,* 8 miles south-southeast of Tomales on the northeast side of Tomales Bay. Named on Inverness (1954), Point Reyes NE (1954), and Tomales (1954) 7.5' quadrangles. Pablo de la Guerra and John Bautista Roger Cooper received the land in 1844; Frink and Reynolds claimed 7598 acres patented in 1861 (Cowan, p. 52).

(4) *land grant,* in two parcels, one located 3 miles southeast of Tomales and the other located 6 miles west-southwest of downtown Novato. Named on Inverness (1954), Novato (1954), Petaluma (1953), Petaluma River (1954), Point Reyes NE (1954), San Geronimo (1954), and Tomales (1954) 7.5' quadrangles. Pablo de la Guerra and John Bautista Roger Cooper received the land in 1844; Henry W. Halleck claimed 30,843 acres patented in 1861 (Cowan, p. 52).

(5) *village,* 8 miles west-southwest of downtown Novato (lat. 38° 03'40" N, long. 122°41'50" W); the village is on Nicasio (2) grant. Named on San Geronimo (1954) 7.5' quadrangle. Postal authorities established Nicasio post office in 1871, discontinued it in 1899, and reestablished it in 1900 (Frickstad, p. 88).

Nicasio: see **San Geronimo** [MARIN] (2).

Nicasio Creek [MARIN]: *stream,* flows 11 miles to Lagunitas Creek 2 miles east of Point Reyes Station (lat. 38°04'10" N, long. 122°46'10" W). Named on Inverness (1954) and San Geronimo (1954) 7.5' quadrangles. Called Arroyo Nicasio on Petaluma (1914) 15' quadrangle.

Nicasio Reservoir [MARIN]: *lake,* behind a dam on Nicasio Creek 3 miles east-northeast of Point Reyes Station (lat. 38°04'35" N, long. 122°45'15" W). Named on Inverness (1954, photorevised 1971) and San Geronimo (1954, photorevised 1971) 7.5' quadrangles.

Nichols [CONTRA COSTA]: *locality,* 5.5 miles west of Pittsburg (lat. 38°02'30" N, long. 121°59'15" W; near SE cor. sec. 5, T 2 N, R 1 W). Named on Honker Bay (1953) 7.5' quadrangle. Officials of Atchison, Topeka and Santa Fe Railroad named the siding at the place in 1909 for William H. Nichols Syndicate, principal landholder there (Gudde, 1949, p. 236).

Nickols Knob [CONTRA COSTA]: *peak,* 4 miles southeast of Point San Pablo (lat. 37°55'15" N, long. 122°22'50" W). Altitude 371 feet. Named on San Quentin (1959) 7.5' quadrangle.

Nicks Cove [MARIN]: *locality,* 3.25 miles south-southwest of Tomales on the northeast side of Tomales Bay (lat. 38°11'55" N, long. 122°55'10" W). Named on Tomales (1954) 7.5' quadrangles. The name is from Nick Kojich, who opened a seafood restaurant by Tomales Bay in 1931 (Teather, p. 49).

Niles: see **Niles District** [ALAMEDA].

Niles Canyon [ALAMEDA]: *canyon,* 5 miles long, along Alameda Creek above a point 2 miles north of Fremont civic center (lat. 37° 34'45" N, long. 121°58' W). Named on Niles (1961) 7.5' quadrangle. Called Alameda Canyon on Pleasanton (1906) 15' quadrangle.

Niles District [ALAMEDA]: *district,* 2 miles north-northwest of Fremont civic center in Fremont (lat. 37°34'35" N, long. 121°59' W); the district is near the mouth of Niles Canyon. Named on Niles (1961) 7.5' quadrangle. Pleasanton (1906) 15' quadrangle has the name "Niles" for the community that joined in 1956 with neighboring communities to form the new city of Fremont. Postal authorities established Niles post office in 1873 (Salley, p. 154). Officials of Central Pacific Railroad named the place in 1869 for Judge Addison C. Niles, who was elected to the state supreme court in 1871 (Gudde, 1949, p. 236). The site first was known as Vallejo's Mills for the water-powered flouring mill that Jose Vallejo built there in 1853 (Thompson and West, 1878, p. 27). Mayhew Spring is about 600 feet north of the railroad depot at Niles (Waring, p. 270); it was owned by H.A. Meyhew, and also was called Meyhew's Sulphur Spring (Crawford, 1896, p. 508).

Niles Junction [ALAMEDA]: *locality,* nearly 2 miles north of Fremont civic center along Western Pacific Railroad (lat. 37°34'35" N, long. 121°57'50" W; sec. 22, T 4 S, R 1 W); the place is in Niles District. Named on Niles (1961) 7.5' quadrangle.

Nitro [CONTRA COSTA]: *locality,* at Pinole Point (lat. 38°00'35" N, long. 122°21'50" W). Named on Mare Island (1959) 7.5' quadrangle. The name is from a nitroglycerin works at the place (Gannett, p. 225).

Nob Hill [CONTRA COSTA]: *peak,* 3.5 miles east of Pinole Point (lat. 38°00'20" N, long. 122°18' W). Named on Mare Island (1959) 7.5' quadrangle.

Nob Hill [SAN FRANCISCO]: *peak,* 1 mile south of North Point (lat. 37°47'35" N, long. 122°24'50" W). Named on San Francisco North (1956) 7.5' quadrangle. The feature originally was called Fern Hill; the name "Nob" may be from the so-called nabob's who built pretentious mansions on the peak (Hoover, Rensch, and Rensch, p. 364).

Nob Hill [SANTA CLARA]: *ridge,* northeast-trending, 200 feet long, in Morgan Hill (lat. 37°07'30" N, long. 121°39'15" W). Named on Morgan Hill (1955) and Mount Madonna (1955) 7.5' quadrangles.

Nob Hill [SONOMA]: *peak,* 2.25 miles southeast of Annapolis (lat. 38°41'45" N, long. 123°20'20" W; sec. 20, T 10 N, R 13 W). Named on Annapolis (1977) 7.5' quadrangle.

Noble [ALAMEDA]: *locality,* 5 miles north-northwest of downtown Oakland along Southern Pacific Railroad (lat. 37°53'35" N, long. 122°18'35" W). Named on San Francisco (1899) 15' quadrangle.

Noel Heights [SONOMA]: *settlement,* 2 miles east-southeast of Guerneville in Picket Canyon (lat. 38°29'30" N, long. 122°57'30" W; sec. 34, T 8 N, R 10 W). Named on Camp Meeker (1954) 7.5' quadrangle.

Nolan Creek [SONOMA]: *stream,* flows about 3.5 miles to Salmon Creek (1) 2.5 miles northwest of Valley Ford (lat. 38°20'35" N, long. 122°57'45" W). Named on Camp Meeker (1954) and Valley Ford (1954) 7.5' quadrangles.

Nooday Rock [SAN FRANCISCO]: *rock,* 3.5 miles northwest of North Farallon (lat. 37°48'05" N, long. 123°08'30" W). Named on San Francisco (1947) 1°x 2° quadrangle. The name is from a clipper ship that struck the rock in 1862 (United States Coast and Geodetic Survey, p. 123).

Norris Canyon: see **Norris Creek** [ALAMEDA].

Norris Creek [ALAMEDA]: *stream,* flows 2 miles to Crow Creek 5 miles north-northeast of downtown Hayward (lat. 37°43'55" N, long. 122°01'55" W). Named on Hayward (1959) and Las Trampas Ridge (1959) 7.5' quadrangles. The stream first was called Wisener Creek for Joseph Hopson Wisenor, who settled along it in the 1850's; the canyon of the feature is called Norris Canyon for Leo Norris, who settled there in 1850 (Mosier and Mosier, p. 62, 95).

North Bay: see **North Point** [SAN FRANCISCO].

North Beach [SAN FRANCISCO]: *district,* 2 miles north of San Francisco civic center (lat. 37°48'20" N, long. 122°24'35" W). Named on San Francisco North (1956) 7.5' quadrangle.

North Belmont Landing: see **Belmont Slough** [SAN MATEO].

North Bend [MARIN]: *locality,* 1.5 miles northeast of Point Reyes Station along Northwestern Pacific Railroad (lat. 38°04'50" N, long. 122°46'50" W). Named on Point Reyes (1918) 15' quadrangle.

North Berkeley [ALAMEDA]: *district,* 5.5 miles north of downtown Oakland and north of University of California campus in Berkeley (lat. 37°52'50" N, long. 122°16'15" W). Named on San Francisco (1899) 15' quadrangle. Officials of Southern Pacific Railroad put a station at the place in 1878 and named it Berryman for Henry Burpee Berryman, of Berryman Reservoir; the station now is called North Berkeley (Mosier and Mosier, p. 16).

North Channel: see **Brooklyn Basin** [ALAMEDA]; **Oakland Inner Harbor** [ALAMEDA].

North Coyote Slough: see **Coyote Creek** [ALAMEDA-SANTA CLARA].

North Creek [ALAMEDA]: *water feature,* joins Alameda Creek 6.25 miles northwest of downtown Newark (lat. 37°35'35" N, long. 122° 09'20" W). Named on Newark (1948) 7.5' quadrangle.

Norther Slough [SOLANO]: *water feature,* 7 miles west-southwest of Birds Landing (2) on Simmons Island (lat. 38°05'40" N, long. 121°59' W). Named on Honker Bay (1953) 7.5' quadrangle.

North Farallon [SAN FRANCISCO]: *island,* 7 miles northwest of Southeast Farallon (lat. 37°46'20" N, long. 123°06'25" W); the feature is the northwesternmost of Farallon Islands. Named on Farallon Islands (1988) 7.5' quadrangle. Called N.W. Farallon on Ringgold's (1850b) map. United States Coast and Geodetic Survey (p. 123) described the feature as "two clusters of bare precipitous islets and rocks" 0.9 mile in extent—by this description, the Survey apparently includes present Isle of Saint James under the name "North Farallon."

North Gap [SONOMA]: *pass,* 8.5 miles northeast of Fort Ross (lat. 38°36'55" N, long. 123°08'50" W; near SE cor. sec. 14, T 9 N, R 12 W). Named on Fort Ross (1978) 7.5' quadrangle.

North Granada: see **El Granada** [SAN MATEO].

North Lake [SAN FRANCISCO]: *lake,* 1050 feet long, 1 mile southeast of Point Lobos (lat. 37°46'10" N, long. 122°30'05" W). Named on San Francisco North (1956) 7.5' quadrangle.

North Peak [CONTRA COSTA]: *peak,* 1 mile northeast of Mount Diablo (lat. 37°53'35" N, long. 121°53'55" W; sec. 31, T 1 N, R 1 E). Altitude 3557 feet. Named on Clayton (1953) 7.5' quadrangle. Brewer (p. 267) called the peak Mount King in 1862, but Whitney (p. 24) called it North Peak in 1865.

North Peak [SAN MATEO]: *peak,* 0.5 mile northeast of Montara Knob on Montara Mountain (lat. 37°33'40" N, long. 122°28'35" W; on W line sec. 25, T 4 S, R 6 W); the feature is nearly 0.5 mile north-northeast of South Peak. Altitude 1898 feet. Named on Montara Mountain (1956) 7.5' quadrangle.

North Point [SAN FRANCISCO]: *promontory,* 2 miles north of San Francisco civic center along San Francisco Bay (lat. 37°48'35" N, long. 122°24'40" W). Named on San Francisco North (1956) 7.5' quadrangle. Ringgold's (1850a) map has the name "North Bay" for the embayment west of present North Point.

North Reservoir [CONTRA COSTA]: *lake,* 850 feet long, 2.5 miles north-northeast of Richmond civic center (lat. 37°58'25" N, long. 122°19'35" W). Named on Richmond (1959) 7.5' quadrangle.

North Richmond [CONTRA COSTA]: *district,* nearly 2 miles northwest of Richmond civic center (lat. 37'57'25" N, long. 122°21'45" W). Named on Richmond (1959) 7.5' quadrangle.

North Salmon Creek Beach [SONOMA]: *beach,* 2 miles northwest of the village of Bodega Bay along the coast (lat. 38°21'25" N, long. 123°04' W); the beach is north of the mouth of Salmon Creek (1). Named on Bodega Head (1972) 7.5' quadrangle.

North Slough [NAPA]: *water feature,* enters lowlands along Napa River 1.5 miles west of Napa Junction (lat. 38°11'05" N, long. 122° 16'35" W; sec. 23, T 4 N, R 4 W). Named on Cuttings Wharf (1949) 7.5' quadrangle.

North Temescal: see **Oakland** [ALAMEDA].

Northwest Cape [SONOMA]: *promontory,* 0.5 mile west of Fort Ross along the coast (lat. 38°30'45" N, long. 123°15'15" W). Named on Fort Ross (1978) and Plantation (1977) 7.5' quadrangles.

Northwest Farallon: see **North Farallon** [SAN FRANCISCO].

Northwood [SONOMA]: *settlement,* 2 miles south of Healdsburg along Russian River (lat. 38°28'30" N, long. 123°00'05" W; sec. 6, T 7 N, R 10 W). Named on Duncans Mills (1979) 7.5' quadrangle. Postal authorities established Northwood post office in 1929 and discontinued it in 1938; the name is from nearby Northwood Heights (Salley, p. 157).

Northwood: see **Northwood Heights** [SONOMA].

Northwood Heights [SONOMA]: *settlement,* 1.5 miles south of Guerneville along Russian River (lat. 38°28'45" N, long. 122°59'50" W; sec. 5, 6, T 7 N, R 10 W). Named on Camp Meeker (1954) 7.5' quadrangle. Called Northwood on Sebastopol (1942) 15' quadrangle.

Northwood Lodge [SONOMA]: *locality,* nearly 2 miles south of Guerneville along Russian River (lat. 38°28'35" N, long. 122°59'45" W; sec. 5, T 7 N, R 10 W). Named on Camp Meeker (1954) 7.5' quadrangle.

Nortonville [CONTRA COSTA]: *locality,* 5.5 miles north-northeast of Mount Diablo along Kirker Creek (lat. 37°57'30" N, long. 121°52'45" W; near SE cor. sec. 5, T 1 N, R 1 E). Site named on Clayton (1953) 7.5' quadrangle. Postal authorities established Nortonville post office in 1874, discontinued it briefly in 1887, discontinued it in 1890, reestablished it in 1891, and discontinued it finally in 1910 (Frickstad, p. 22). The name was for Noah Norton, who started Black Diamond coal mine in 1861, and built the first house at the place (Hoover, Rensch, and Rensch, p. 65; Mosier, p. 6).

Nortonville Pass [CONTRA COSTA]: *pass,* 5.5 miles north-northeast of Mount Diablo (lat. 37°57'20" N, long. 121°52'25" W; sec. 4, T 1 N, R 1 E); the pass is 2000 feet east-southeast of Nortonville. Named on Antioch South (1953) 7.5' quadrangle.

Norwood Creek [SANTA CLARA]: *stream,* flows 1.5 miles to lowlands nearly 2 miles north-northeast of Evergreen (lat. 37°20' N, long. 121°46' W). Named on San Jose East (1961) 7.5' quadrangle.

Notley Junction [SAN MATEO]: *locality,* nearly 6 miles northeast of Franklin Point (lat. 37°11'40" N, long. 122°16'10" W). Named on Año Nuevo (1948) 15' quadrangle. Franklin Point (1955) 7.5' quadrangle shows Sandy Point guard station at the site. George Notley, Sr., settled at the place, which then was called Sandy Point, about 1910 (Brown, p. 62).

Nottingham: see **Livermore** [ALAMEDA].

Novato [MARIN]:

(1) *land grant,* at and near the city of Novato. Named on Petaluma (1953), Petaluma Point (1959), and Petaluma River (1954) 7.5' quadrangles. Fernando Felix received 2 leagues in 1839; assignees of B. Simmons claimed 8971 acres patented in 1866 (Cowan, p. 53). Perez (p. 79) gave the size of the grant as 8870.62 acres.

(2) *city,* 10 miles north-northwest of San Rafael along Novato Creek (lat. 38°06'30" N, long. 122°34'10" W). Named on Novato (1954) and Petaluma River (1954, photorevised 1968 and 1973) 7.5' quadrangles. Postal authorities established Novato post office in 1856, discontinued it in 1860, and reestablished it in 1891 (Salley, p. 157). The city incorporated in 1960.

Novato Creek [MARIN]: *stream,* flows 18 miles to San Pablo Bay 4.5 miles east of downtown Novato (lat. 38°05'40" N, long. 122° 29'15" W). Named on Novato (1954), Petaluma Point (1959), and San Geronimo (1954) 7.5' quadrangles.

Novato Heights [MARIN]: *ridge,* east-trending, 1 mile long, 1.25 miles southwest of downtown Novato (lat. 38°05'35" N, long. 122° 35'10" W). Named on Novato (1954) 7.5' quadrangle.

Novato Point: see **Petaluma Point** [MARIN].

Novato Valley [MARIN]: *valley,* at and west of the city of Novato along Novato Creek (lat. 38°06'30" N, long. 122°35'30" W). Named on Novato (1954) 7.5' quadrangle. Cañada de Novato of Spanish times was named for an Indian (Gudde, 1949, p. 239).

Noyce Slough [SOLANO]: *water feature,* joins Suisun Bay 7 miles west-southwest of Birds Landing (2) (lat. 38°04'45" N, long. 121° 58'35" W). Named on Honker Bay (1953) 7.5' quadrangle.

Nubble: see **The Nubble** [SONOMA].

Nuff Creek [SAN MATEO]: *stream,* flows 2 miles to Pilarcitos Creek 2.5 miles northeast of downtown Half Moon Bay (lat. 37°29'20" N, long. 122°23'30" W; sec. 22, T 5 S, R 5 W). Named on Half Moon Bay (1961) and Montara Mountain (1956) 7.5' quadrangles. Brown (p. 45) called the canyon of the stream Knopf Canyon—Knopf ranch was there in the middle 1870's. The stream was called Tollhouse Creek on a map made about 1868, and the canyon was called Cañada de Leon for Jose Maria Leon, who had a sheep ranch there about 1860 (Brown, p. 45).

Nunns Canyon [SONOMA]: *canyon,* 3 miles long, along Calabazas Creek above a point 2.25 miles southeast of Kenwood (lat. 38°23'30" N, long. 122°31' W). Named on Kenwood (1954) and Rutherford (1951) 7.5' quadrangles. Called Nuns Canyon on Santa Rosa (1944) and Sonoma (1951) 15' quadrangles.

Nunns Iron Spring [SONOMA]: *spring,* 4.25 miles east of Kenwood (lat. 38°24'30" N, long. 122°29'10" W; sec. 35, T 7 N, R 6 W); the spring is in Nunns Canyon. Named on Rutherford (1951) 7.5' quadrangle. Santa Rosa (1944) 15' quadrangle shows Nuns Iron Spring located 2.5 miles east-southeast of Kenwood in Nuns Canyon (present Nunns Canyon).

Nuns Canyon: see **Nunns Canyon** [SONOMA].

Nuns Iron Spring: see **Nunns Iron Spring** [SONOMA].

Nurse's Landing: see **Denverton** [SOLANO].

Nurse Slough [SOLANO]: *water feature,* joins Montezuma Slough 4.5 miles south-southwest of Denverton (lat. 38°10'05" N, long. 121°56' W). Named on Denverton (1953) 7.5' quadrangle. The name is from Nurse's Landing (present Denverton) (Gudde, 1949, p. 239).

Nut Tree: see **Vacaville** [SOLANO].

—O—

Oak Grove: see **Burlingame** [SAN MAETO]; **Los Altos** [SANTA CLARA].

Oak Knoll [NAPA]: *locality,* 5 miles north-northwest of downtown Napa along Southern Pacific Railroad (lat. 38°21'30" N, long. 122° 20' W). Named on Napa (1951) 7.5' quadrangle.

Oak Knolls [SONOMA]: *peak,* 2.25 miles north-northwest of Skaggs Springs (lat. 38°43'15" N, long. 123°02'45" W; at S line sec. 11, T 10 S, R 11 W). Named on Warm Springs Dam (1978) 7.5' quadrangle.

Oakland [ALAMEDA]: *city,* in the north part of Alameda County near San Francisco Bay (lat. 37°48'15" N, long. 122°16'15" W). Named on Hayward (1959), Hunters Point (1956), Las Trampas Ridge (1959), Oakland East

(1959), Oakland West (1959), and San Leandro (1959) 7.5' quadrangles. Andres Moon, Edson Adams, and Horace W. Carpentier built a cabin in 1850 on land belonging to Vincent Peralta; when Peralta threatened to eject these squatters, they each leased 160 acres from him and laid out a townsite that they called Oakland (Hoover, Rensch, and Rensch, p. 20). Oakland incorporated in 1852; the magnificent live-oak trees of the place suggested the name (Thompson and West, 1878, p. 17). In 1852, Moon and Adams built a wharf, called Moon and Adams Landing, at the foot of present Broadway; the same year, Carpentier built a wharf at the site that became known as Carpentier's Wharf, and that later was called Broadway Wharf (Mosier and Mosier, p. 17). In 1850, the Patten brothers leased land from Peralta, and in 1852 the brothers joined with other landholders to lay out a town that they called Clinton located on the east side of San Antonio Slough (Hoover, Rensch, and Rensch, p. 20). In 1851, J.B. Larue squatted on land west of Clinton across San Antonio Creek, where he started a store and built a wharf; the settlement that grew there was called San Antonio, after the creek and land grant (Bancroft, 1888, p. 478). San Francisco and Oakland Railroad built a station called San Antonio at the place; in 1870 Central Pacific Railroad took over the station and changed the name to Brooklyn, and in 1883 Southern Pacific Railroad changed the name to East Oakland (Mosier and Mosier, p. 17). Clinton and San Antonio joined in 1856 to form a new community called Brooklyn, named for the ship that brought Mormon pioneers to California in 1846; Brooklyn and a settlement located to the northeast known as Lynn incorporated under the name "Brooklyn" in 1870—residents of Brooklyn voted for annexation to Oakland in 1872 (Bancroft, 1888, p. 478). Lynn was named for Lynn, Massachusetts, because like the New England town, it had a large shoe and boot factory (Mosier and Mosier, p. 53). Postal authorities established Contra Costa post office at present Jack London Square section of Oakland in 1851, and changed the name to Oakland in 1855 (Salley, p. 49). They established Brooklyn post office in 1855 and it became a station of Oakland post office in 1878 (Frickstad, p. 1). They established Monte Vista post office 2.5 miles northeast of Oakland post office in 1865 and discontinued it in 1868 (Salley, p. 145). They established Melita post office 3.5 miles southwest of Brooklyn post office (SW quarter sec. 16, T 2 S, R 3 W) in 1869 and discontinued it in 1871 (Salley, p. 137). They established West Oakland post office in 1873 and discontinued it in 1966 (Salley, p. 238). They established North Temescal post office 2 miles north of the main Oakland post office in 1877, changed the name to Alden in 1899, and discontinued it in 1908—the name "Alden" was for S.E. Alden, a pioneer farmer who owned land at the site (Salley, p. 4, 156). They established Dimond post office 1.5 miles northeast of Alameda post office in 1891 and it became a station of Oakland post office in 1908—the name was for Hugh Dimond, a mine owner (Salley, p. 59). According to Mosier and Mosier (p. 29), the settlement of Dimond was in Dimond Canyon. Postal authorities established Allendale post office 1.5 miles northeast of Fruitvale in 1903 and it became a station of Oakland post office in 1908 (Salley, p. 4). Mosier and Mosier (p. 8) noted that Allendale probably was named for Charles E. Allen, a real-estate broker. Dr. Cyrus Mills and his wife moved their seminary for young ladies to the Oakland environs in 1871; in 1885 they changed the name of the school from Mills Seminary to Mills College (Hoover, Rensch, and Rensch, p. 22). Postal authorities established Mills Seminary post office in 1879 and changed the name to Mills College in 1888 (Frickstad, p. 2). They established Beulah Heights post office 2 miles northwest of Mills College post office in 1907 and discontinued it in 1911 (Salley, p. 20).

Oakland Estuary: see **Oakland Inner Harbor** [ALAMEDA].

Oakland Harbor: see **Brooklyn Basin** [ALAMEDA]; **Oakland Inner Harbor** [ALAMEDA].

Oakland Hills: see **San Leandro Hills** [ALAMEDA].

Oakland Inner Harbor [ALAMEDA]: *water feature,* between Oakland and Alameda, extends for 5 miles from San Francisco Bay to Tidal Canal (center near lat. 37°47'40" N, long. 122°17' W). Named on Oakland West (1959) 7.5' quadrangle. The feature includes what is called San Antonio Creek on San Francisco (1899) 15' quadrangle. United States Board on Geographic Names (1949b, p. 3) rejected the names "San Antonio Creek," "San Antonio Estuary," "Deep Water Channel," "North Channel," "Oakland Estuary," "Oakland Harbor," and "South Channel" for the place

Oakland Middle Harbor [ALAMEDA]: *water feature,* 3 miles west of downtown Oakland along the Oakland waterfront just north of the entrance to Oakland Inner Harbor (lat. 37°48'15" N, long. 122° 19'45" W). Named on Oakland West (1959) 7.5' quadrangle. United States Board on Geographic Names (1949b, p. 3) rejected the name "Southern Pacific Basin" for the feature.

Oakland Outer Harbor [ALAMEDA]: *water feature,* 3 miles west-northwest of downtown Oakland along Oakland water front 1 mile north of the entrance to Oakland Inner Harbor (lat. 37°49' N, long. 122°19' W). Named on Oakland West (1959) 7.5' quadrangle. Outer Harbor Entrance Channel leads to the place from San Francisco Bay.

Oakland Point: see **Gibbon Point** [ALAMEDA].

Oakleigh: see **Las Juntas** [CONTRA COSTA].

Oakley [CONTRA COSTA]: *town,* 4.5 miles north-northwest of Brentwood (lat. 37°59'45" N, long. 121°42'40" W; around NW cor. sec. 25, T 2 N, R 2 E). Named on Brentwood (1978) 7.5' quadrangle. Postal authorities established Oakley post office in 1898 (Frickstad, p. 22). R.C. Marsh, first postmaster, named the place for the native oak trees (Gudde, 1949, p. 240).

Oakmont [SONOMA]: *locality,* 3 miles west-northwest of Kenwood (lat. 38°26'20" N, long. 122°35'35" W). Named on Kenwood (1954, photorevised 1980) 7.5' quadrangle.

Oak Moss Creek [NAPA]: *stream,* flows 3.25 miles to Capell Creek 7 miles west-northwest of Mount Vaca (lat. 38°27'15" N, long. 122°12'50" W; sec. 17, T 7 N, R 3 W). Named on Capell Valley (1951) 7.5' quadrangle.

Oak Mountain [SONOMA]: *peak,* 5.25 miles south-southwest of Big Mountain (lat. 38°38'10" N, long. 123°10'05" W; sec. 10, T 9 N, R 12 W). Altitude 1693 feet. Named on Tombs Creek (1978) 7.5' quadrangle.

Oak Ridge [ALAMEDA-SANTA CLARA]: *ridge,* northwest- to west-trending, 6 miles long, 4 miles northwest of Mount Day on Alameda-Santa Clara County line, mainly in Santa Clara County (lat. 37°28' N, long. 121°44' W). Named on Calaveras Reservoir (1961) and Mount Day (1955) 7.5' quadrangles.

Oak Ridge [SANTA CLARA]: *ridge,* north-northwest-trending, 1 mile long, 3.5 miles southeast of Mount Day (lat. 37°22'55" N, long. 121°39'30" W). Named on Mount Day (1955) 7.5' quadrangle.

Oak Ridge [SONOMA]:

(1) *ridge,* northwest-trending, 2.25 miles long, 5.5 miles east of Annapolis (lat. 38°42'50" N, long. 123°15'50" W). Named on Annapolis (1977) 7.5' quadrangle.

(2) *ridge,* southwest-trending, 0.5 mile long, 7.5 miles southeast of Jenner (lat. 38°22'45" N, long. 123°00'40" W). Named on Duncans Mills (1979) 7.5' quadrangle.

Oak Springs: see **Orinda** [CONTRA COSTA].

Oak Springs Reservoir [SANTA CLARA]: *lake,* 1000 feet long, 6 miles east-southeast of Mustang Peak near Santa Clara-Stanislaus County line (lat. 37°08'55" N, long. 122°15'55" W; sec. 13, T 9 S, R 6 E). Named on Mustang Peak (1955) 7.5' quadrangle.

Oakville [NAPA]: *village,* 2 miles southeast of Rutherford (lat. 38° 26'10" N, long. 122°24'05" W). Named on Rutherford (1951) 7.5' quadrangle. Postal authorities established Oakville post office in 1857, discontinued it in 1859, and reestablished it in 1867 (Frickstad, p. 111).

Oakwood Valley [MARIN]: *canyon,* 1 mile long, 3.5 miles north of Point Bonita (lat. 37°52' N, long. 122°31'20" W). Named on Point Bonita (1954) 7.5' quadrangle.

Oat Creek: see **Big Oat Creek** [SONOMA].

Oat Hill [MARIN]: *peak,* 3.5 miles northeast of Bolinas (lat. 37°56'50" N, long. 122°38'20" W). Named on Bolinas (1954) 7.5' quadrangle.

Oat Hill [NAPA]:

(1) *peak,* 8 miles north-northeast of Calistoga (lat. 38°41'05" N, long. 122°30'50" W; sec. 27, T 10 N, R 6 W). Named on Detert Reservoir (1958) 7.5' quadrangle. California Mining Bureau's (1909a) map shows a locality called Oat Hill located 12 miles by stage line north-northeast of Calistoga near present Oat Hill (1). Postal authorities established Oat Hill post office in 1891 and discontinued it in 1910; the name also had the form "Oathill" (Salley, p. 159).

(2) *hill,* less than 1 mile west-southwest of Napa Junction (lat. 38° 11'05" N, long. 122°15'45" W; near NW cor. sec. 24, T 4 N, R 4 W). Named on Cuttings Wharf (1949) 7.5' quadrangle.

Oat Mountain: see **Big Oat Mountain** [SONOMA]; **Little Oat Mountain** [SONOMA].

Oat Valley [SONOMA]: *valley,* 1.5 miles north-northwest of Cloverdale (lat. 38°49'35" N, long. 123°01'45" W). Named on Cloverdale (1960) 7.5' quadrangle.

Oat Valley Creek [SONOMA]: *stream,* flows 4.5 miles to Russian River less than 1 mile north-northeast of Cloverdale (lat. 38°49' N, long. 123°00'40" W); the stream goes through Oat Valley. Named on Cloverdale (1960) 7.5' quadrangle.

Observatory Peak: see **Mount Hamilton** [SANTA CLARA].

Occidental [SONOMA]: *town,* 6.5 miles west of Sebastopol (lat. 38° 24'25" N, long. 122°56'45" W; sec. 34, T 7 N, R 10 W). Named on Camp Meeker (1954) 7.5' quadrangle. Postal authorities established Occidental post office in 1876; the name was from Occidental Methodist Church, the first building at the site (Salley, p. 159). In 1876 a narrow-gauge railroad reached the place, which then was called Howard's Station, Summit, and Meeker, as well as Occidental (Mullen). The name "Howard's" was for William Howard, an early settler; the name "Meeker" was for M.C. Meeker, who laid out the town (Gudde, 1949, p. 240). The name "Summit" reflects the position of the site at the highest point on the line of North Pacific Coast Railroad that ran up Dutch Bill Creek (Goodyear, 1890b, p. 678). A resort called Altamont Medical Springs was located at Occidental (Bradley, p. 335).

Ocean Beach [SAN FRANCISCO]: *beach,* south of Point Lobos along the coast (lat. 37°45'30" N, long. 122°30'35" W). Named on San Francisco

North (1956) 7.5' quadrangle.

Ocean Cove [SONOMA]: *embayment,* 2.5 miles south of Plantation along the coast (lat. 38°33'20" N, long. 123°18'15" W). Named on Plantation (1977) 7.5' quadrangle.

Ocean House [SAN FRANCISCO]: *locality,* 3 miles west of Mount Davidson near the coast (lat. 37°44'20" N, long. 122°30'25" W). Named on San Mateo (1915) 15' quadrangle.

Ocean Lake [MARIN]: *lake,* 725 feet long, 1 mile north-northwest of Double Point (lat. 37°57'40" N, long. 122°47'05" W). Named on Double Point (1954) 7.5' quadrangle.

Ocean Roar [MARIN]: *locality,* 2.25 miles south-southwest of Tomales (lat. 38°13' N, long. 122°55'20" W). Named on Tomales (1954) 7.5' quadrangle. Point Reyes (1918) 15' quadrangle shows the place along Northwestern Pacific Railroad.

Ocean View [SONOMA]: *settlement,* 4 miles south-southeast of Jenner (lat. 38°23'50" N, long. 123°05'35" W); the place is near the coast. Named on Duncans Mills (1979) 7.5' quadrangle.

Ocean View: see **Albany** [ALAMEDA]; **Irish Hill** [SONOMA] (1); **Thornton** [SAN MATEO].

Oceanview [SAN FRANCISCO]: *locality,* 2 miles south-southeast of Mount Davidson (lat. 37°42'45" N, long. 122°27'15" W); the place is on San Miguel grant. Named on San Mateo (1915) 15' quadrangle. Postal authorities established San Miguel post office in 1878, changed the name to Ocean View in 1881, and discontinued it in 1895 (Frickstad, p. 159).

Oceanview: see **Irish Hill** [SONOMA] (1).

Odd Fellows Park [SONOMA]: *settlement,* 2.5 miles east of Guerneville along Russian River (lat. 38°30'10" N, long. 122°56'45" W; on S line sec. 27, T 8 N, R 10 W). Named on Guerneville (1955) 7.5' quadrangle.

Offutt: see **Chileno Valley** [MARIN-SONOMA].

Ohmen Resort [SONOMA]: *locality,* 2.25 miles north-northwest of Cazadero (lat. 38°33'45" N, long. 123°06'05" W; sec. 5, T 8 N, R 11 W). Named on Cazadero (1943) 7.5' quadrangle.

Ohmer [CONTRA COSTA]: *locality,* 6 miles east of Martinez along Oakland Antioch and Eastern Railroad (lat. 38°00'10" N, long. 122°01'20" W). Named on Carquinez Strait (1896) 15' quadrangle.

Ohms Spring [SONOMA]: see **Boyes Hot Springs** [SONOMA].

Oil Barrel Gulch: see **Hooker Creek** [SAN MATEO].

Oil Canyon [CONTRA COSTA]: *canyon,* 2.5 miles long, opens into the canyon of Sand Creek 6 miles northeast of Mount Diablo (lat. 37°56'35" N, long. 121°50'10" W; sec. 11, T 1 N, R 1 E). Named on Antioch South (1953) 7.5' quadrangle. Mount Diablo (1898) 15' quadrangle shows Oil Creek in the canyon.

Oil Creek [SAN MATEO]: *stream,* heads in Santa Cruz County and flows 5 miles to Pescadero Creek 6 miles south-southeast of Mindego Hill (lat. 37°13'45" N, long. 122°11'25" W; at N line sec. 21, T 8 S, R 3 W). Named on Big Basin (1955) and Mindego Hill (1961) 7.5' quadrangles. Oil from natural seepages is noticeable in the water (Brown, p. 62).

Oil Creek: see **Oil Canyon** [CONTRA COSTA].

Oil Well Canyon [NAPA]:

(1) *canyon,* drained by a stream that flows 1.5 miles to Lake Berryessa 5.5 miles south of Berryessa Peak (lat. 38°35'10" N, long. 122°12' W). Named on Lake Berryessa (1959) 7.5' quadrangle.

(2) *canyon,* drained by a stream that flows 1.25 miles to Gosling Canyon 5.25 miles south-southeast of Berryessa Peak (lat. 38°35'40" N, long. 122°09'05" W). Named on Lake Berryessa (1959) 7.5' quadrangle, which shows an oil well in the canyon.

Ojo de Agua de la Coche: [SANTA CLARA]: *land grant,* near Morgan Hill. Named on Gilroy (1955), Morgan Hill (1955), Mount Madonna (1955), and Mount Sizer (1955) 7.5' quadrangles. Juan Maria Hernandez received 2 leagues in 1835; M.J.C. Murphy claimed 8927 acres patented in 1860 (Cowan, p. 54). Perez (p. 79) used the form "Ojo de Agua de la Coches" for the name.

Okell Hill [NAPA]: *peak,* 5.25 miles south of Mount Vaca (lat. 38° 19'35" N, long. 122°07'15" W). Altitude 1129 feet. Named on Fairfield North (1951) 7.5' quadrangle.

Olcott [SOLANO]: *locality,* 7 miles southeast of Elmira along Sacramento Northern Railroad (lat. 38°16'35" N, long. 121°49'25" W; near E line sec. 14, T 5 N, R 1 E). Named on Dozier (1952) 7.5' quadrangle.

Old Baldy [NAPA]: *peak,* 4.5 miles east-northeast of Calistoga on Rattlesnake Ridge (lat. 38°36'45" N, long. 122°30'15" W; near E line sec. 22, T 9 N, R 6 W). Named on Calistoga (1958) 7.5' quadrangle.

Old Camp [SANTA CLARA]: *locality,* 4.25 miles north-northeast of Mount Day (lat. 37°28'15" N, long. 121°39'20" W; sec. 28, T 5 S, R 3 E); the place is 2.25 miles northwest of New Camp. Named on Mount Day (1955) 7.5' quadrangle.

Old Gilroy [SANTA CLARA]: *settlement,* 2.25 miles east-southeast of Gilroy (lat. 37°00' N, long. 121°31'30" W). Named on Chittenden (1955) and Gilroy (1955) 7.5' quadrangles. The place first was called San Ysidro or San Isidro, then Gilroy or Gilroy's, and finally Old Gilroy (Bancroft, 1888, p. 525). Postal authorities established San Isidro post office in 1866 and discontinued it in 1877 (Frickstad, p. 175).

Old Landing: see **Princeton** [SAN MATEO].

Old Mill Creek [MARIN]: *stream,* flows 2.25 miles to Arroyo Corte Madera Del Presidio nearly 5 miles south of downtown San Rafael in the town of Mill Valley (lat. 37°54'20" N, long. 122°32'45" W). Named on San Rafael (1954) 7.5' quadrangle.

Old Mountain View: see **Mountain View** [SANTA CLARA].

Old River [CONTRA COSTA]: *stream,* heads in San Joaquin County and flows 33 miles along Contra Costa-San Joaquin County line to San Joaquin River 5.5 miles northeast of the settlement of Bethel Island (lat. 38°04'20" N, long. 121°34'15" W). Named on Bouldin Island (1978), Clifton Court Forebay (1978), and Woodward Island (1978) 7.5' quadrangles.

Old Spanish Anchorage: see **Fort Point** [SAN FRANCISCO].

Old Town [MARIN]: *settlement,* nearly 1 mile south of downtown Novato (lat. 38°05'45" N, long. 122°34'10" W). Named on Petaluma (1914) 15' quadrangle. The place is in the present city of Novato.

Old Womans Creek [SAN MATEO]: *stream,* heads in Santa Cruz County and flows 2.5 miles to Gazos Creek 2.5 miles north-northeast of Franklin Point (lat. 37°11'10" N, long. 122°20'20" W). Named on Franklin Point (1955) 7.5' quadrangle. Año Nuevo (1948) 15' quadrangle has the name on a tributary of Gazos Creek that is located 3.5 miles farther upstream. Brown (p. 18-19) noted that the name "Old Woman Creek" was an early designation of this second tributary of Gazos Creek, and mentioned that the canyon of that tributary was called China Gulch for Chinese laborers who built a sawmill there in 1882. Brown (p. 19) also noted that present Old Womans Creek was called Horse Pasture Creek or Gushee Creek before the name "Old Woman Creek" was applied to it by mistake on early maps.

Olema [MARIN]: *village,* 2.25 miles south-southeast of Point Reyes Station (lat. 38°02'25" N, long. 122°47'10" W); the place is along Olema Creek. Named on Inverness (1954) 7.5' quadrangle. Postal authorities established Olema post office in 1859, discontinued it in 1860, and reestablished it in 1864 (Frickstad, p. 88). Benjamin Winslow built a hotel called Olema House at the place, and is credited with naming the village (Mason, 1976a, p. 88). The name "Olema" probably is from an Indian village, and is derived from the Indian word for coyote (Kroeber, p. 51-52).

Olema Creek [MARIN]: *stream,* flows 10.5 miles to Lagunitas Creek nearly 0.5 mile south-southwest of Point Reyes Station (lat. 38°03'50" N, long. 122°48'35" W); the stream goes past Olema. Named on Bolinas (1954), Double Point (1954), and Inverness (1954) 7.5' quadrangles. Whitney (p. 84) called the stream Arroyo Olemus Loke.

Olema Station: see **Point Reyes Station** [MARIN].

Oleum [CONTRA COSTA]: *locality,* 6 miles east-northeast of Pinole Point along Southern Pacific Railroad (lat. 38°02'50" N, long. 122° 15'40" W). Named on Mare Island (1959) 7.5' quadrangle. On Benicia (1959) 7.5' quadrangle, the name applies to a group of oil tanks in the hills east of the place. Postal authorities established Oleum post office in 1910 and discontinued it in 1951 (Frickstad, p. 22). The name is from the word "petro<u>leum</u>"—an oil refinery is at the site (Gudde, 1949, p. 242).

Oliver: see **Lake Oliver** [SONOMA].

Olivet: see **Mount Olivet**, under **Fulton** [SONOMA].

Olofson Ridge [CONTRA COSTA]: *ridge,* north-northwest-trending, 1 mile long, 2.5 miles west-northwest of Mount Diablo (lat. 37°53'45" N, long. 121°57'15" W). Named on Clayton (1953) 7.5' quadrangle.

Olompali [MARIN]: *land grant,* 4 miles northwest of downtown Novato. Named on Petaluma (1953) and Petaluma River (1954) 7.5' quadrangles. Camilo Ynitia received 2 leagues in 1843 and claimed 8877 acres patented in 1862 (Cowan, p. 55). According to Perez (p. 79), Jose Ynitia was the grantee in 1843. The name is from the designation of an Indian village (Kroeber, p. 52).

Olompali: see **Mount Olompali**, under **Burdell Mountain** [MARIN].

Olympus: see **Mount Olympus** [SAN FRANCISCO].

Omus [SONOMA]: *locality,* 1.25 miles northwest of Geyserville along Northwestern Pacific Railroad (lat. 38°43'10" N, long. 122° 55'05" W). Named on Geyserville (1955) 7.5' quadrangle.

O'Neill Creek: see **O'Neill Slough** [SAN MATEO].

O'Neill Slough [SAN MATEO]: *water feature,* extends from Seal Slough to Belmont Slough 4 miles southeast of downtown San Mateo (lat. 37°31'45" N, long. 122°16'05" W). Named on San Mateo (1956) 7.5' quadrangle. San Mateo (1915) 15' quadrangle has the name "O'Neill Creek," but United States Board on Geographic Names (1961b, p. 13) rejected the names "O'Neill Creek," "O'Neil Slough," and "San Mateo Slough" for the feature. Captain Owen O'Neill started a landing place along the slough in the early 1860's (Brown, p. 63).

O'Neil Slough: see **O'Neill Slough** [SAN MATEO].

One Mile Rocks: see **Mile Rock** [SAN FRANCISCO].

Onion Pond [SONOMA]: *lake,* 50 feet long, 3 miles north-northwest of Cazadero (lat. 38°34'10" N, long. 123°06'25" W; sec. 6, T 8 N, R 11 W). Named on Cazadero (1943) 7.5' quadrangle.

Orchard [SONOMA]: *locality,* 4.5 miles east-northeast of Bloomfield along Petaluma and Santa Rosa Railroad (lat. 38°20'10" N, long. 122°46'20" W). Named on Sebastopol (1942) 15' quadrangle.

Oregon Canyon [SONOMA]: *canyon,* drained by a stream that flows 1.25 miles to Pocket Canyon nearly 5 miles north of Occidental (lat. 38°28'35" N, long. 122°57'05" W; sec. 3, T 7 N, R 10 W). Named on Camp Meeker (1954) 7.5' quadrangle.

Oreja del Oso: see **El Toro** [SANTA CLARA].

Orient: see **Point Orient** [CONTRA COSTA].

Original White Sulphur Springs: see **Sulphur Canyon** [NAPA].

Orinda [CONTRA COSTA]: *town,* 7 miles west-southwest of Walnut Creek civic center (lat. 37°52'45" N, long. 122°10'50" W). Named on Briones Valley (1959) and Oakland East (1959) 7.5' quadrangles. Concord (1897) 15' quadrangle shows a place called Bryant at the site of present Orinda, and has the name "Orinda" at present Orinda Village. Bryant was the eastern terminus of California and Nevada Railroad in 1893 (Hildebrand, p. 157). Theodore Wagner, United States surveyor general for California, had an estate in the 1880's that lay between Bear Creek and Lauterwasser Creek; he called the place Orinda Park (Gudde, 1969, p. 230). Postal authorities established Orinda Park post office in 1888, changed the name to Orinda in 1895, moved it 0.5 mile southeast to the site of Bryant in 1898, discontinued it in 1903, and reestablished it in 1927 (Salley, p. 162). United States Board on Geographic Names (1933, p. 575) rejected the name "Orinda Park" for the town. Bowen (p. 347) used the name "Orinda Crossroads" for the place formerly called Bryant. Oak Springs, located near Orinda (S half sec. 3, T 1 S, R 3 W), provided water for domestic use that was carried to Oakland by truck and bottled there (Davis and Vernon, p. 577).

Orinda Crossroads: see **Orinda** [CONTRA COSTA].

Orinda Park: see **Orinda** [CONTRA COSTA].

Orinda Village [CONTRA COSTA]: *town,* 1.5 miles northwest of Orinda (lat. 37°53'30" N, long. 122°12' W). Named on Briones Valley (1959) 7.5' quadrangle. Concord (1897) 15' quadrangle has the name "Orinda" at the place.

Orrs Creek [SONOMA]: *stream,* flows nearly 2 miles to Russian River 3.25 miles east of Jenner (lat. 38°26'55" N, long. 123°03'25" W). Named on Duncans Mills (1979) 7.5' quadrangle.

Ortega Creek [SANTA CLARA]: *stream,* flows 1.5 miles to lowlands near San Felipe (lat. 36°58'20" N, long. 121°24'55" W). Named on San Felipe (1955, photorevised 1971) 7.5' quadrangle. The name commemorates Ygnacio Ortega, original owner of San Ysidro grant (United States Board on Geographic Names, 1973a, p. 3).

Orth: see **Lake Orth** [SONOMA].

Orville: see **Lake Orville** [NAPA].

Orwood [CONTRA COSTA]: *locality,* 7 miles east of Brentwood along Atchison, Topeka and Santa Fe Railroad (lat. 37°56'25" N, long. 121°34' W). Named on Woodward Island (1978) 7.5' quadrangle. Postal authorities established Orwood post office in 1913 and discontinued it in 1921; the name is from Orville Y. Woodward, the promoter of Orwood Tract (Salley, p. 163).

Orwood Tract [CONTRA COSTA]: *area,* 6 miles east of Brentwood (lat. 37°55'40" N, long. 121°35' W). Named on Woodward Island (1978) 7.5' quadrangle.

Osage [CONTRA COSTA]: *locality,* 1.5 miles south-southeast of Danville along Southern Pacific Railroad (lat. 37°47'55" N, long. 121°58'55" W). Named on Mount Diablo (1898) 15' quadrangle.

Osborne Creek [SONOMA]: *stream,* flows 1 mile to Porter Creek (1) 4 miles northeast of Guerneville (lat. 38°33' N, long. 122°57'15" W; sec. 10, T 8 N, R 10 W). Named on Guerneville (1955) 7.5' quadrangle.

Osser Creek [SONOMA]: *stream,* flows nearly 4 miles to North Fork Buckeye Creek (2) 10 miles north-northeast of the village of Stewarts Point (lat. 38°46'55" N, long. 123°18'45" W; sec. 21, T 11 N, R 13 W). Named on Ornbaun Valley (1960) 15' quadrangle.

Otis Canyon [SANTA CLARA]: *canyon,* 1 mile long, drained by a stream that joins Coyote Creek 6 miles south-southwest of Mount Sizer (lat. 37°08'15" N, long. 121°33'50" W; near W line sec. 20, T 9 S, R 4 E). Named on Mount Sizer (1955) 7.5' quadrangle. The canyon splits at the head into North Fork and South Fork. North Fork is nearly 1 mile long and divides at its head into Clarks Canyon and Cordoza Canyon. South Fork is nearly 1.25 miles long. Both forks are named on Mount Sizer (1955) 7.5' quadrangle.

Oursan Ridge [CONTRA COSTA]: *ridge,* north- to northwest-trending, 2 miles long, 5.5 miles north-northwest of Orinda (lat. 37°57'15" N, long. 122°13' W). Named on Briones Valley (1959) 7.5' quadrangle.

Ousley Canyon [SANTA CLARA]: *canyon,* drained by a stream that flows nearly 2 miles to Uvas Creek 2.5 miles west of Gilroy (lat. 37°00'30" N, long. 121°36'45" W). Named on Chittenden (1955) and Gilroy (1955) 7.5' quadrangles.

Outer Harbor Entrance Channel: see **Oakland Outer Harbor** [ALAMEDA].

Outer Signal Station: see **Telegraph Hill** [SAN FRANCISCO].

Oxford [SOLANO]: *locality,* 11 miles north-northeast of Rio Vista along Sacramento Northern Railroad (lat. 38°18'25" N, long. 121° 37'10" W). Named on Courtland (1978) 7.5' quadrangle.

Ox Hill [SAN MATEO]: *peak,* 4 miles southeast of Montara Knob on Montara Mountain (lat. 37°31'25" N, long. 122°25'20" W; near E line sec. 5, T 5 S, R 5 W). Named on Montara Mountain (1956) 7.5' quadrangle. The peak was known locally as Bald Pate in the 1860's; the next peak north of Ox Hill is called Maloney's Hill—Michael Maloney had a ranch at the place in the 1860's (Brown, p. 51, 63).

Oxley [CONTRA COSTA]: *locality,* less than 1 mile north-northeast of present Walnut Creek civic center (lat. 37°54'50" N, long. 122° 03'15" W). Named on Concord (1943) 15' quadrangle.

Oyster Point [CONTRA COSTA]: *peak,* 4 miles south-southeast of Mount Diablo (lat. 37°49'50" N, long. 121°52'35" W; on E line sec. 20, T 1 S, R 1 E). Altitude 2106 feet. Named on Diablo (1953) and Tassajara (1953) 7.5' quadrangles.

Oyster Point [SAN MATEO]: *promontory,* 1.5 miles east-northeast of downtown South San Francisco along San Francisco Bay (lat. 37° 40' N, long. 122°23' W). Named on San Francisco South (1956) 7.5' quadrangle. Oyster beds were present near the point after the late 1860's (Brown, p. 63). The feature now is modified by filled land.

Oyster Point Channel [SAN MATEO]: *channel,* extends across San Francisco Bay north of Oyster Point to the shore 1.5 miles north-northeast of downtown South San Francisco (lat. 37°40' N, long. 122°23'15" W). Named on Hunters Point (1956) 7.5' quadrangle.

Ozol [CONTRA COSTA]: *locality,* about 1.5 miles west-northwest of Martinez along Southern Pacific Railroad (lat. 38°01'35" N, long. 122°09'45" W). Named on Benicia (1959) 7.5' quadrangle.

— P —

Pablo Bay: see **San Pablo Bay** [CONTRA COSTA-MARIN-SOLANO-SONOMA].

Pablo Point [MARIN]: *ridge,* south-southeast-trending, 1 mile long, 3 miles northwest of Bolinas (lat. 37°56'30" N, long. 122°43'20" W). Named on Bolinas (1954) 7.5' quadrangle.

Pabrico [ALAMEDA]: *locality,* 4 miles north-northeast of downtown Newark along Western Pacific Railroad (lat. 37°35' N, long. 122° 00'20" W). Named on Newark (1959) 7.5' quadrangle. The name is from Oakland Paving Brick Company, which operated at the site from 1910 until 1912 (Mosier and Mosier, p. 65).

Pacheco [CONTRA COSTA]: *town,* 5.5 miles north of Walnut Creek civic center (lat. 37°59'05" N, long. 122°04' W). Named on Walnut Creek (1959) 7.5' quadrangle. Postal authorities established Pacheco post office in 1859, discontinued it in 1913, and reestablished it in 1955 (Salley, p. 164). The name is for Salvio Pacheco; Dr. J.H. Carothers laid out the town (Smith and Elliott, p. 23-24).

Pacheco: see **Fairford**, under **Black Point** [MARIN].

Pacheco Canyon [SANTA CLARA]: *canyon,* drained by a stream that flows nearly 1 mile to Anderson Lake 4.5 miles north-northeast of Morgan Hill (lat. 37°11'30" N, long. 121°37'20" W). Named on Morgan Hill (1955) 7.5' quadrangle.

Pacheco Creek [CONTRA COSTA]: *stream,* flows 4 miles in an artificial watercourse to Suisun Bay 3 miles northeast of Martinez (lat. 38°02'35" N, long. 122°05'30" W). Named on Vine Hill (1959) 7.5' quadrangle. The stream is called San Ramon Creek on some early maps (Gudde, 1949, p. 313).

Pacheco Creek [SANTA CLARA]: *stream,* flows 15 miles to San Benito County 11 miles east-southeast of Gilroy (lat. 36°57'35" N, long. 121°22'15" W); the creek heads near Pacheco Pass. Named on Pacheco Peak (1955), San Felipe (1955), and Three Sisters (1954) 7.5' quadrangles. Called Arroyo de S. Felipe on a diseño of San Joaquin grant (which is in San Benito County) made in 1836 (Becker, 1964). Francisco Perez Pacheco had his ranch headquarters near the stream that bears his name (Shumate, p. 12). North Fork enters from the north 10 miles upstream from the entrance of Pacheco Creek into San Benito County; it is 18 miles long and is named on Mississippi Creek (1955), Mustang Peak (1955), and Pacheco Peak (1955) 7.5' quadrangles. North Fork is called Pacheco Creek on Gilroy Hot Springs (1921) 15' quadrangle. South Fork enters from the southeast 11 miles upstream from the entrance of Pacheco Creek into San Benito County; it heads in San Benito County, is 8 miles long, and is named on Pacheco Peak (1955) and Three Sisters (1954) 7.5' quadrangles. East Fork joins North Fork from the northeast nearly 4 miles upstream from the mouth of North Fork; it is 5 miles long and is named on Crevison Peak (1955) and Pacheco Peak (1955) 7.5' quadrangles.

Pacheco Hill [MARIN]: *peak,* 5 miles south-southeast of downtown Novato (lat. 38°02'35" N, long. 122°31'50" W); the peak is on San Jose grant, which Ignacio Pacheco owned. Altitude 454 feet. Named on Novato (1954) 7.5' quadrangle.

Pacheco Lake [SANTA CLARA]: *lake,* 2 miles long, behind a dam on North Fork Pacheco Creek 3 miles north of Pacheco Peak (lat. 37° 03' N, long. 121°17'25" W). Named on Pacheco Peak (1955) 7.5' quadrangle.

Pacheco Pass [SANTA CLARA]: *pass,* 20 miles east-northeast of Gilroy on

Santa Clara-Merced County line (lat. 37°03'50" N, long. 121°12'30" W). Named on Pacheco Pass (1955) 7.5' quadrangle. The name commemorates Francisco Perez Pacheco, who owned San Luis Gonzaga grant where the pass lies; the pass has the name "San Luis Gonzaga" in early records (Shumate, p. 1). Called Pacheco's Pass on Williamson's (1853) map. Mountain House station was at the summit of the pass (Latta, 1976, p. 246).

Pacheco Peak [SANTA CLARA]: *peak,* 16 miles east of Gilroy (lat. 37°00'30" N, long. 121°17'15" W). Altitude 2770 feet. Named on Pacheco Peak (1955) 7.5' quadrangle. Antisell (p. 17) used the form "Pacheco's Peak" for the name.

Pacifica [SAN MATEO]: *city,* center about 4.5 miles west-southwest of downtown South San Francisco (lat. 37°37'30" N, long. 122° 29' W). Named on Montara Mountain (1956, photorevised 1980) and San Francisco South (1956, photorevised 1980) 7.5' quadrangles. Residents of several communities in the vicinity voted in 1957 to form a new incorporated city called Pacifica (Gudde, 1969, p. 233). Postal authorities established Pacifica post office in 1959 (Salley, p. 164).

Pacific Congress Springs: see **Congress Springs** [SANTA CLARA].

Pacific Home: see **Healdsburg** [SONOMA].

Pacific Manor [SAN MATEO]: *district,* 4 miles west of downtown South San Francisco near the coast (lat. 37°39' N, long. 122°29'05" W). Named on San Francisco South (1956) 7.5' quadrangle. Residents of the place voted in 1957 to join neighboring communities and form the new city of Pacifica.

Packard Ridge [SANTA CLARA]: *ridge,* west- to north-northwest-trending, nearly 3 miles long, 4 miles east-southeast of Mount Day (lat. 37°23'45" N, long. 121°38' W). Named on Eylar Mountain (1955) and Mount Day (1955) 7.5' quadrangles.

Packwood Creek [SANTA CLARA]: *stream,* flows 7.5 miles to Anderson Lake 6.25 miles west-southwest of Mount Sizer (lat. 37° 10'30" N, long. 121°37' W). Named on Mount Sizer (1955) 7.5' quadrangle.

Packwood Valley [SANTA CLARA]: *valley,* 5 miles west of Mount Sizer (lat. 37°12'20" N, long. 121°36' W); the valley is along upper Packwood Creek. Named on Mount Sizer (1955) 7.5' quadrangle.

Paddy Lake [SOLANO]: *lake,* 1050 feet long, 4 miles north-northeast of Benicia (lat. 38°06'15" N, long. 122°08'10" W; sec. 13, T 3 N, R 3 W). Named on Benicia (1959) 7.5' quadrangle.

Page Flat [SOLANO]: *area,* 4.5 miles southwest of Cordelia (lat. 38° 09'25" N, long. 122°10'55" W; near S line sec. 27, T 4 N, R 3 W). Named on Cordelia (1951) 7.5' quadrangle.

Page Mill [SAN MATEO]: *locality,* 4.25 miles southeast of Mindego Hill along Slate Creek (lat. 37°15'40" N, long. 122°11'10" W; sec. 3, T 8 S, R 3 W). Site named on Mindego Hill (1961) 7.5' quadrangle.

Page's Station: see **Cotati** [SONOMA].

Pajaro: see **Mount Pajaro** [SANTA CLARA].

Pajaro River [SANTA CLARA]: *stream,* heads near the south end of Santa Clara Valley and flows 10 miles along Santa Clara-San Benito County line to the southeast end of Santa Cruz Mountains, where it leaves Santa Clara County and continues to the sea. Named on Chittenden (1955) and San Felipe (1955) 7.5' quadrangles. Called Sanjon de la Brea on a diseño of Llano de Tequesquet grant made in 1834 (Becker, 1969), called Payharo R. on Baker's (1855) map, and called R. Pajaros on Mitchell's (1856) map. Taylor (v. I, p. 175) called the stream Rio del Pajaro. Soldiers of the Portola expedition gave the name "Pajaro" to the stream in 1769 because of a huge stuffed bird displayed there by natives (Wagner, H.R., p. 401)—*pajaro* means "bird" in Spanish.

Pala [SANTA CLARA]: *land grant,* in Alum Rock district of San Jose. Named on Calaveras Reservoir (1961) 7.5' quadrangle. Jose Higuera received 1 league in 1835; Ellen E. White and others claimed 4454 acres patented in 1866 (Cowan, p. 56). According to Gudde (1949, p. 249), the name is from an Indian called Pala, who was mentioned in records as early as 1795.

Palassou Ridge [SANTA CLARA]: *ridge,* north-northwest-trending, 6 miles long, 9 miles east of Morgan Hill (lat. 37°07' N, long. 121° 29'45" W). Named on Gilroy (1955), Gilroy Hot Springs (1955), Mississippi Creek (1955), and Mount Sizer (1955) 7.5' quadrangles. Called Pellisier Ridge on Morgan Hill (1917) 15' quadrangle.

Palermo: see **Mount Palermo**, under **Mount Tamalpais** [MARIN].

Palisades: see **The Palisades** [NAPA].

Palmentto Landing [SOLANO]: *locality,* 2 miles west-southwest of Birds Landing (2) along Montezuma Slough (lat. 38°07'15" N, long. 121°54'10" W). Named on Honker Bay (1918) 7.5' quadrangle.

Palmer Canyon [SONOMA]: *canyon,* drained by a stream that flows 2 miles to Marshall Creek 4.5 miles north-northeast of Fort Ross (lat. 38°34'40" N, long. 123°13'20" W; sec. 31, T 9 N, R 12 W). Named on Fort Ross (1978) 7.5' quadrangle.

Palmer Creek [SONOMA]: *stream,* flows 3.5 miles to Mill Creek (1) 6.25 miles north-northeast of Guerneville (lat. 38°35'05" N, long. 122°56'50" W). Named on Guerneville (1955) 7.5' quadrangle.

Palmer Gulch [SAN MATEO]: *canyon,* drained by a stream that flows 0.5 mile to San Gregorio Creek at the village of San Gregorio (lat. 37°19'35" N, long. 122°23'05" W). Named on San Gregorio (1961, photorevised 1968) 7.5' quadrangle.

Palm Hill [MARIN]: *ridge,* east-southeast-trending, 0.5 mile long, 3 miles south of downtown San Rafael (lat. 37°55'55" N, long. 122° 31'35" W). Named on San Rafael (1954) 7.5' quadrangle.

Palm Tract [CONTRA COSTA]: *area,* 6 miles east-northeast of Brentwood (lat. 37°57'15" N, long. 121°35'15" W). Named on Woodward Island (1978) 7.5' quadrangle. Called Palms Tract on Davis and Vernon's (1951) map.

Palo Alto [SANTA CLARA]: *city,* 15 miles west-northwest of downtown San Jose (lat. 37°26'45" N, long. 122°09'30" W). Named on Mindego Hill (1961), Mountain View (1961), and Palo Alto (1961) 7.5' quadrangles. During construction of Stanford University campus in 1889 on Leland Stanford's Palo Alto farm, Mr. Stanford had a new town, to be called University Park, laid out next to the campus, but a developer bought 120 acres adjoining Stanford's land on the south and laid out another town, to be called Palo Alto; Stanford brought suit to prevent use of the name "Palo Alto" for the second town, and the matter was settled when the name of the second town was changed to College Terrace—Stanford's University Park was renamed Palo Alto (Butler, p. 11). The name "Palo Alto" is from a large redwood tree noted by early Spanish explorers near San Francisquito Creek—*palo alto* means "tall tree" in Spanish (Gudde, 1949, p. 250-251). Postal authorities established Palo Alto post office in 1892 (Frickstad, p. 174), and the town incorporated in 1894. According to Newhall (p. 21), present Palo Alto was the site of Twin Trees Station along the railroad in 1865.

Palo Alto: see **East Palo Alto** [SAN MATEO]; **South Palo Alto**, under **Mayfield** [SANTA CLARA].

Palo Alto Island: see **Snag Island** [SOLANO].

Palo Alto Point: see **Point Palo Alto** [SOLANO].

Palomares Canyon: see **Palomares Creek** [ALAMEDA].

Palomares Creek [ALAMEDA]: *stream,* flows 5.25 miles to San Lorenzo Creek 3.5 miles east-northeast of downtown Hayward (lat. 37°41'45" N, long. 122°01'30" W). Named on Dublin (1961) and Hayward (1959) 7.5' quadrangles. The name commemorates Francisco Palomares, who lived along the stream; the canyon of the creek is called Palomares Canyon (Mosier and Mosier, p. 66).

Palomar Park [SAN MATEO]: *district,* 2.25 miles west of downtown Redwood City (lat. 37°28'50" N, long. 122°15'50" W). Named on Woodside (1961) 7.5' quadrangle.

Palo Seco Creek [ALAMEDA]: *stream,* flows 2 miles to join Shephard Creek and form Sausal Creek 3.5 miles east-northeast of downtown Oakland (lat. 37°49'10" N, long. 122°12'25" W). Named on Oakland East (1959) 7.5' quadrangle.

Pams Blue Ridge: see **Blue Ridge** [MARIN].

Panochita Hill [SANTA CLARA]: *peak,* nearly 4 miles southwest of Mount Hamilton (lat. 37°18'15" N, long. 121°41'30" W). Altitude 1871 feet. Named on Lick Observatory (1955) 7.5' quadrangle.

Pansey Valley [SONOMA]: *valley,* 2 miles east of Sonoma (lat. 38° 17'10" N, long. 122°25'05" W). Named on Sonoma (1951) 7.5' quadrangle.

Panther Beds [SONOMA]: *area,* 4.25 miles northeast of Cazadero (lat. 38°34'50" N, long. 123°02'25" W; sec. 35, T 9 N, R 11 W). Named on Cazadero (1978) 7.5' quadrangle.

Panther Creek [SANTA CLARA]: see **Llagas Creek** [SANTA CLARA].

Panther Den [SONOMA]: *relief feature,* 0.5 mile north of Big Mountain (lat. 38°43'10" N, long. 123°08'40" W; near NE cor. sec. 14, T 10 N, R 12 E). Named on Tombs Creek (1978) 7.5' quadrangle.

Paper Mill: see **Lagunitas Creek** [MARIN].

Paper Mill Creek: see **Lagunitas Creek** [MARIN].

Paperville: see **Lagunitas Creek** [MARIN].

Paradise Cay [MARIN]: *locality,* 2 miles south of Point San Quentin along the northeast side of Tiburon Peninsula (lat. 37°54'45" N, long. 122°28'30" W). Named on San Quentin (1959) 7.5' quadrangle. Ringgold's (1850a) map shows Pt. Munroe at the place, and has the name "Aspinwall Bay" for the embayment between Point Munroe and Point Chauncey. San Francisco (1915) 15' quadrangle shows a promontory called California Point at the site, but United States Board on Geographic Names (1968a, p. 6) rejected this name.

Paradise Cove [MARIN]: *embayment,* 3.5 miles south-southeast of Point San Quentin on the northeast side of Tiburon Peninsula (lat. 37°53'40" N, long. 122°27'20" W). Named on San Quentin (1959) 7.5' quadrangle. San Francisco (1942) 15' quadrangle shows a place called California City located along San Francisco Bay 0.5 mile south-southeast of present Paradise Cove. Benjamin Buckelew laid out a townsite near Paradise Cove about 1850 and called it California City (Mason, 1976b, p. 62).

Paradise Creek [SANTA CLARA]: *stream,* flows 1 mile to Llagas Creek 2.25 miles west-southwest of Morgan Hill (lat. 37°06'50" N, long. 121°41'10" W). Named on Morgan Hill (1955, photorevised 1968 and 1973) and Mount Madonna (1955, photorevised 1968 and 1973) 7.5' quadrangles. The name is from Paradise Valley, which is at the mouth of the stream (United States Board on Geographic Names, 1973a, p. 3).

Paradise Park: see **El Campo** [MARIN].

Paradise Valley [MARIN]: *valley,* 1.25 miles northwest of Bolinas along Pine Gulch Creek (lat. 37°55'40" N, long. 122°42'10" W). Named on Bolinas (1954) 7.5' quadrangle.

Paradise Valley [NAPA]: *valley,* 4 miles west-southwest of Knoxville along Hunting Creek on Napa-Lake County line (lat. 38°48'15" N, long. 122°24' W; sec. 15, T 11 N, R 5 W). Named on Jericho Valley (1958) 7.5' quadrangle.

Paradise Valley [SANTA CLARA]: *valley,* 2.25 miles south-southwest of Morgan Hill along Llagas Creek (lat. 37°06' N, long. 121° 40'30" W). Named on Mount Madonna (1955) 7.5' quadrangle.

Parks: see **Camp Parks** [ALAMEDA-CONTRA COSTA].

Paso de las Trancas: see **Yajome** [NAPA].

Pasquini Canyon [SONOMA]: *canyon,* less than 1 mile long, 2 miles northeast of Guerneville (lat. 38°31'15" N, long. 122°57'45" W). Named on Guerneville (1955) 7.5' quadrangle.

Passionate Spring [SANTA CLARA]: *spring,* 2 miles south of Mount Boardman (lat. 37°27'05" N, long. 121°28'35" W; sec. 36, T 5 S, R 4 E). Named on Mount Boardman (1955) 7.5' quadrangle.

Passion River: see **Russian River** [SONOMA].

Pastoria de las Borregas [SANTA CLARA]: *land grant,* in Mountain View and Sunnyvale. Named on Cupertino (1961), Milpitas (1961), and Mountain View (1961) 7.5' quadrangles. Francisco Estrada received 2 leagues in 1842; Martin Murphy, Jr., claimed 4894 acres patented in 1865; Mariano Castro claimed 4172 acres, which he called Refugio, patented in 1881 (Cowan, p. 58).

Patapsco Point: see **Point Molate** [CONTRA COSTA].

Patchen Pass: see **Wrights** [SANTA CLARA].

Patchin: see **Wrights** [SANTA CLARA].

Patterson Creek [ALAMEDA]: *water feature,* joins Coyote Hills Slough 4.5 miles northwest of downtown Newark (lat. 37°34'05" N, long. 122°06'25" W). Named on Newark (1959) 7.5' quadrangle. The name commemorates George Washington Patterson, a local rancher; the feature first had the misspelled name "Sundburg Creek," for Edward Sundberg, who had a landing there in 1863 (Mosier and Mosier, p. 66).

Patterson Landing [ALAMEDA]: *locality,* 3.5 miles northwest of downtown Newark (lat. 37°34'05" N, long. 122°04'50" W); the place is near the head of Patterson Creek. Named on Haywards (1899) 15' quadrangle. Edward Lang built Lang's Landing at the site in the 1850's, and after Edward Sundberg bought the place, it had the misspelled name "Sundburg Landing" until Edward A. Anderson and Edward Anderson, Jr., bought it in 1870 and changed the name to Anderson's Landing; then George W. Patterson bought the landing before 1878 (Mosier and Mosier, p. 67).

Patterson Pass [ALAMEDA]: *pass,* 4.25 miles south-southeast of Altamont (lat. 37°41'15" N, long. 121°37'45" W; sec. 10, T 3 S, R 3 E). Named on Altamont (1953) 7.5' quadrangle. Thompson and West (1878, p. 17) referred to "Middle Pass, or Patterson Road" as a route east from Livermore Valley. The pass is said to have received its name after Mrs. Andrew Jackson Patterson broke her leg in an accident there in the 1850's (Gudde, 1949, p. 255).

Patterson Run [ALAMEDA]: *stream,* flows about 5.5 miles to San Joaquin County 0.5 mile north-northeast of Midway (lat. 37°43'20" N, long. 121°33'20" W; near S line sec. 29, T 2 S, R 4 E). Named on Midway (1953) 7.5' quadrangle.

Patty Clark Springs: see **Bald Hills** [SONOMA].

Peaches Creek: see **Pechaco Creek** [SONOMA].

Peachland: see **Sebastopol** [SONOMA].

Peach Tree Springs [CONTRA COSTA]: *springs,* 3 miles west-northwest of Mount Diablo (lat. 37°54' N, long. 121°57'50" W). Named on Clayton (1953) 7.5' quadrangle. Called Peachtree Springs on Mount Diablo (1898) 15' quadrangle. The name supposedly is from a tree that grew by the springs (Waring, p. 355).

Peacock Creek [CONTRA COSTA]: *stream,* flows 2.5 miles to Mount Diablo Creek at Clayton (lat. 37°56'30" N, long. 121°56'05" W; near SE cor. sec. 11, T 1 N, R 1 W). Named on Mount Diablo (1898) 15' quadrangle.

Peacock's: see **Harrisburg**, under **Warm Springs District** [ALAMEDA].

Peak: see **The Peak** [SANTA CLARA].

Peak Canyon: see **Little Peak Canyon** [SANTA CLARA].

Peaked Hill [SONOMA]: *peak,* 1.25 miles south of Jenner (lat. 38° 25'50" N, long. 123°07'05" W). Altitude 377 feet. Named on Duncans Mills (1979) 7.5' quadrangle.

Peak Mountain [SAN MATEO]: *peak,* about 0.25 mile north of Montara Knob on Montara Mountain (lat. 37°33'40" N, long. 122° 29' W; sec. 26, T 4 S, R 6 W). Named on Montara Mountain (1956) 7.5' quadrangle.

Pearl Gap [NAPA]: *pass,* 3.25 miles south of Mount Vaca (lat. 38° 21'10" N, long. 122°05'40" W). Named on Fairfield North (1951) 7.5' quadrangle.

Pearsons Pond: see **La Honda** [SAN MATEO].

Pebble Beach [MARIN]: *beach,* 8 miles south of Tomales on the southwest side of Tomales Bay (lat. 38°07'45" N, long. 122°53'10" W). Named on Tomales (1954) 7.5' quadrangle.

Pebble Beach [SAN MATEO]: *beach,* 4 miles north-northwest of Pigeon Point along the coast (lat. 37°14'10" N, long. 122°24'55" W). Named on Pigeon Point (1955) 7.5' quadrangle.

Pechaco Creek [SONOMA]: *stream,* flows nearly 3 miles to Pena Creek 3.5 miles south-southeast of Skaggs Springs (lat. 38°38'50" N, long. 123°00'25" W; sec. 7, T 9 N, R 10 W). Named on Geyserville (1955) and Warm Springs Dam (1978) 7.5' quadrangles. Called Peaches Creek on Healdsburg (1940) 15' quadrangle.

Pecks Ridge: see **Copper Mine Gulch** [MARIN].

Pedro Mountain: see **San Pedro Mountain** [SAN MATEO].

Pedro Point: see **Point San Pedro** [SAN MATEO].

Pedro Valley [SAN MATEO]: *district,* 2.5 miles north-northwest of Montara Knob in San Pedro Valley (lat. 37°35'30" N, long. 122°29'45" W); residents of the place voted in 1957 to join with neighboring communities to form the new city of Pacifica. Named on Montara Mountain (1956) 7.5' quadrangle. San Mateo (1915) 15' quadrangle shows a place called Tobin situated along Ocean Shore Railroad at the mouth of San Pedro Valley, and San Mateo (1942) 15' quadrangle shows a place called San Pedro Terrace at about the same site. Postal authorities established Tobin post office in 1894, moved it 1 mile east in 1897, discontinued it in 1901, reestablished it in 1908, changed the name to Pedro Valley in 1915, discontinued it in 1918, reestablished it in 1937, and discontinued it in 1960—the name "Tobin" was for a San Francisco financier who built a summer home at the site (Salley, p. 169, 222). Modern growth of the place began in 1953 with a large subdivision called Linda Mar (Hynding, p. 185).

Pelican Lake [MARIN]: *lake,* 1400 feet long, 750 feet from the coast at Double Point (lat. 37°57' N, long. 122°46'25" W). Named on Double Point (1954) 7.5' quadrangle.

Pelican Point [MARIN]: *promontory,* 4.25 miles south-southwest of Tomales on the southwest side of Tomales Bay (lat. 38°11'15" N, long. 122°55'50" W). Named on Tomales (1954) 7.5' quadrangle.

Pelican Point [SOLANO]: *promontory,* 7 miles west-southwest of Birds Landing (2) along Grizzly Bay (lat. 38°06'35" N, long. 121° 59'35" W). Named on Honker Bay (1953) 7.5' quadrangle.

Pellisier Ridge: see **Palassou Ridge** [SANTA CLARA].

Peltier Slough [SOLANO]: *water feature,* 5 miles southwest of Fairfield (lat. 38°11'25" N, long. 122°05'40" W). Named on Fairfield South (1949) 7.5' quadrangle.

Pena Creek [SONOMA]: *stream,* flows 10.5 miles to Dry Creek 3.25 miles west of Geyserville on Tzabaco grant, which belonged to Jose German Peña (lat. 38°42'05" N, long. 122°57'40" W). Named on Geyserville (1955) and Warm Springs Dam (1978) 7.5' quadrangles. Chapman Branch enters 4.5 miles above the mouth of the main stream; it is 1.5 miles long and is named on Geyserville (1955) 7.5' quadrangle.

Peninsula Island: see **Belvedere Island** [MARIN].

Peninsula Point [MARIN]: *promontory,* 1.5 miles east of downtown Sausalito at the southeast end of Belvedere Island (lat. 37°51'45" N, long. 122°27'30" W). Named on San Francisco North (1956) 7.5' quadrangle.

Penitencia: see **Milpitas** [SANTA CLARA] (2).

Penitencia Creek: see **Lower Penitencia Creek** [SANTA CLARA]; **Upper Penitencia Creek** [SANTA CLARA].

Penitentiary Cañon: see **Alum Rock Canyon** [SANTA CLARA].

Penn: see **Penngrove** [SONOMA].

Penngrove [SONOMA]: *village,* 3 miles southeast of Cotati (lat. 38° 18' N, long. 122°39'55" W). Named on Cotati (1954) 7.5' quadrangle. Postal authorities established Penn post office in 1882, changed the name to Penns Grove in 1883, and to Penngrove in 1894 (Frickstad, p. 197).

Penns Grove: see **Penngrove** [SONOMA].

Penny Island [SONOMA]: *island,* 0.5 mile long, in Russian River at Jenner (lat. 38°26'50" N, long. 123°07'05" W). Named on Duncans Mills (1979) 7.5' quadrangle.

Penole: see **Pinole** [CONTRA COSTA] (1) and (2); **Point Penole**, under **Pinole Point** [CONTRA COSTA].

Pepperwood Creek [SONOMA]: *stream,* flows 4.5 miles to House Creek 6.5 miles southwest of Big Mountain (lat. 38°38'05" N, long. 123°13' W; near E line sec. 7, T 9 N, R 12 W). Named on Fort Ross (1978) and Tombs Creek (1978) 7.5' quadrangles.

Pepperwood Creek: see **Big Pepperwood Creek** [SONOMA].

Pepperwood Gulch [SONOMA]: *canyon,* drained by a stream that flows 1 mile to Salmon Creek (1) 1.5 miles north of the village of Bodega Bay (lat. 38°21'25" N, long. 123°02'25" W). Named on Bodega Head (1972) 7.5' quadrangle.

Pequeña Laguna: see **Washerwoman's Lagoon**, under **Marina District** [SAN FRANCISCO].

Peralta [ALAMEDA]: *locality,* 5.5 miles north of downtown Oakland (lat. 37°52'55" N, long. 122°17' W). Named on San Francisco (1899) 15' quadrangle. Postal authorities established Peralta post office in 1890, discontinued it in 1901, reestablished it in 1949, and discontinued it in 1954 (Salley, p. 169).

Peralta: see **Lake Peralta**, under **Lake Merritt** [ALAMEDA].

Peralta Creek [ALAMEDA]: *stream,* flows nearly 2 miles to end in flatlands 3 miles east-southeast of downtown Oakland (lat. 37° 47' N, long. 122°13'05" W). Named on Oakland East (1959) 7.5' quadrangle. The name commemorates Don Luis Peralta, owner of San Antonio grant (Mosier and Mosier, p. 67).

Perkins Canyon [CONTRA COSTA]: *canyon,* drained by a stream that flows 2 miles to Marsh Creek 2.5 miles east-northeast of Mount Diablo (lat. 37°53'45" N, long. 121°52'10" W; near N line sec. 33, T 1 N, R 1 E). Named on Antioch South (1953) and Clayton (1953) 7.5' quadrangles.

Permanent Creek: see **Permanente Creek** [SANTA CLARA].

Permanente Creek [SANTA CLARA]: *stream,* flows 12 miles to Mountain View Slough 3 miles north of downtown Mountain View (lat. 37°26' N, long. 122°05'05" W). Named on Cupertino (1961), Mindego Hill (1961), and Mountain View (1961) 7.5' quadrangles. The stream is called Arroyo Permanente on a map of 1839 (Gudde, 1949, p. 258), and is called Permanent Creek on Thompson and West's (1876) map. The Spanish word *permanente* describes a stream that flows all year (Rambo, 1964, p. 40).

Perry [SANTA CLARA]: *locality,* 3 miles southeast of Coyote along Southern Pacific Railroad (lat. 37°10'55" N, long. 121°42'10" W). Named on Morgan Hill (1955) 7.5' quadrangle. Called Perrys on Morgan Hill (1917) 15' quadrangle. Perry Station was on the stage route between Coyote and Morgan Hill (Hoover, Rensch, and Rensch, p. 431). The hotel there was called Fifteen Mile House for its distance from San Jose (*San Jose Mercury-News, California Today Magazine*, October 23, 1977).

Perry Station: see **Perry** [SANTA CLARA].

Peruvian Island: see **Turk Island** [ALAMEDA].

Pescadero [SAN MATEO]: *town,* 5 miles south of the village of San Gregorio (lat. 37°15'20" N, long. 122°22'50" W); the town is along Pescadero Creek. Named on San Gregorio (1961) 7.5' quadrangle. Postal authorities established Pescadero post office in 1859 (Frickstad, p. 168). They established Harrison post office 7 miles northeast of Pescadero in 1889, moved it 1 mile west in 1896, discontinued it in 1899, reestablished it in 1909, discontinued it in 1916, reestablished it in 1917, and discontinued it in 1919; the name was for the operator of a logging camp at the place (Salley, p. 94). They established Barzilla post office 3 miles west of Harrison post office in 1891 and discontinued it in 1892; the name was for the operator of a combination lumber, shingle, and grist mill at the site—the place was known as Luffley's before 1874 (Salley, p. 15). They established Torquay post office 12 miles south of Pescadero in 1908 and discontinued it in 1911 (Salley, p. 223).

Pescadero: see **San Antonio or Pescadero** [SAN MATEO].

Pescadero Beach [SAN MATEO]: *beach* 4.5 miles south-southwest of the village of San Gregorio along the coast (lat. 37°15'45" N, long. 122°24'45" W); the beach is south of the mouth of Pescadero Creek. Named on San Gregorio (1961) 7.5' quadrangle.

Pescadero Creek [SAN MATEO]: *stream,* flows 25 miles to the sea 4.25 miles south-southwest of the village of San Gregorio, and 2 miles west-northwest of Pescadero (lat. 37°16' N, long. 122°24'40" W). Named on Big Basin (1955), Franklin Point (1955), La Honda (1961), Mindego Hill (1961), and San Gregorio (1961) 7.5' quadrangles. The stream was called Arroyo del Pescadero in Spanish times (Brown, p. 67).

Pescadero Creek [SANTA CLARA]: *stream,* flows nearly 6 miles to Pajaro River 7 miles south of Gilroy at the junction of Santa Clara County, Santa Cruz County, and San Benito County (lat. 36°54'05" N, long. 121°35'05" W). Named on Chittenden (1955) and Watsonville East (1955) 7.5' quadrangles. Called Arroyo de Pescadero on a diseño of Las Animas grant (Becker, 1969). According to Gudde (1949, p. 259), the name refers to the catching of fish in the stream—*pescadero* means "fishing place" in Spanish.

Pescadero Point [SAN MATEO]: *promontory,* 4.25 miles north-northwest of Pigeon Point along the coast (lat. 37°14'30" N, long. 122°25'05" W). Named on Pigeon Point (1955) 7.5' quadrangle.

Petaluma [SONOMA]:

(1) *land grant,* east of Petaluma River and north of San Pablo Bay. Named on Cotati (1954), Glen Ellen (1954), Petaluma (1953), Petaluma River (1954), Sears Point (1951), and Sonoma (1951) 7.5' quadrangles. Mariano Guadalupe Vallejo received 15 leagues in 1834, and in 1843 and 1844; he claimed 66,622 acres patented in 1874 (Cowan, p. 60). The name is from an Indian village that was located east of Petaluma River (Kroeber, p. 54).

(2) *city,* 15 miles south-southeast of Santa Rosa (lat. 38°14' N, long. 122°38'15" W); the city is along Petaluma River. Named on Cotati (1954, photorevised 1980), Glen Ellen (1954, photorevised 1968), Petaluma (1953), and Petaluma River (1954) 7.5' quadrangles. Postal authorities established Petaluma post office in 1852 (Frickstad, p. 197), and the city incorporated in 1858. Settlement of the place began in 1851 with construction of a trading post at the head of navigation on Petaluma River; Garrett W. Keller then laid out the community in 1852 (Heig, p. 28-29). In 1903 a group of Petaluma businessmen established Petaluma and Santa Rosa Electric Railway, which ran for 37 miles from Petaluma to Santa Rosa by way of Sebastopol; between Petaluma and Stony Point were eight station about 1 mile apart: Dunn, Cinnabar, Corona, Denman, Liberty, Dangers, Divide, and Live Oak (Heig, p. 91, 94). California Division of Forestry's (1945) map shows a place called Staubeville situated 2 miles west-northwest of downtown Petaluma.

Petaluma Creek: see **Petaluma River** [MARIN-SONOMA].

Petaluma Point [MARIN]: *promontory,* 4.5 miles east of downtown Novato on Day Island (lat. 38°06'20" N, long. 122°29'15" W); the feature is south of the mouth of Petaluma River. Named on Petaluma Point (1959) 7.5' quadrangle. Called Novato Pt. on Ringgold's (1850a) map.

Petaluma Reservoir [SONOMA]: *lake,* 1050 feet long, 5.25 miles south-southwest of Glen Ellen (lat. 38°17'50" N, long. 122°34'35" W). Named on Glen Ellen (1954) 7.5' quadrangle.

Petaluma River [MARIN-SONOMA]: *stream,* heads in Sonoma County and flows 21 miles to San Pablo Bay 3.5 miles southwest of Sears Point (lat. 38°06'40" N, long. 122°29'30" W). Named on Cotati (1954), Novato (1954), Petaluma (1953), Petaluma Point (1959), and Petaluma River (1954) 7.5' quadrangles. Called Petaluma Creek on Mare Island (1916) and Petaluma (1914) 15' quadrangles, but United States Board on Geographic Names (1959b, p. 7) rejected this form of the name. The feature is called Estero de Petaluma on the diseño of Olompali grant made in 1843 (Becker, 1964). The stream also had the Spanish names "Estero de las Mercedes" and "Estero de Nuestra Señora de la Merced" (Wagner, H.R., p. 472, 478). The river forms the Marin-Sonoma County line below the mouth of San Antonio Creek

Petaluma Valley [MARIN-SONOMA]: *valley,* along Petaluma River from north of the city of Petaluma to San Pablo Bay; on Marin-Sonoma County line. Named on Santa Rosa (1958) 1°x 2° quadrangle. P.T. Tyson (p. 19) referred to Petaloma valley in 1850.

Peter Hill [SONOMA]: *peak,* 5.5 miles west of Mount Saint Helena (lat. 38°40'25" N, long. 122°44' W; sec. 34, T 10 N, R 8 W). Altitude 841 feet. Named on Mount Saint Helena (1959) 7.5' quadrangle.

Peterman's Landing: see **Eden Landing**, under **Mount Eden** [ALAMEDA].

Peters Creek [SAN MATEO]: *stream,* heads just inside Santa Cruz County and flows 7 miles to Pescadero Creek 4 miles south of Mindego Hill (lat. 37°15'05" N, long. 122°13' W; sec. 8, T 8 S, R 3 W); the stream drains Devils Canyon. Named on Mindego Hill (1961) 7.5' quadrangle. Brown (p. 27) used the name "Devil's Canyon Creek" for the stream in Devils Canyon, and noted (p. 68) that the name "Peters" is for Jean Peter, who settled near the creek in 1860.

Peters Creek: see **Rail Creek** [SONOMA].

Petersen: see **Roblar** [SONOMA].

Peterson Creek [SAN MATEO]: *stream,* flows 1 mile to Pescadero Creek 3.25 miles south-southwest of La Honda (lat. 37°16'25" N, long. 122°17'30" W; sec. 34, T 7 S, R 4 W). Named on La Honda (1961) 7.5' quadrangle.

Peterson Creek [SONOMA]: *stream,* flows 3.5 miles to Russian River 2 miles east-southeast of Geyserville (lat. 38°41'40" N, long. 122°52'05" W). Named on Geyserville (1955) 7.5' quadrangle.

Peters Pocket [SOLANO]: *area,* 10 miles north-northwest of Rio Vista between Hass Slough and Cache Slough (lat. 38°18' N, long. 121°44'10" W). Named on Liberty Island (1978) 7.5' quadrangle.

Peters Springs [SONOMA]: *well,* 2.5 miles east of downtown Santa Rosa (lat. 38°26'45" N, long. 122°40'05" W). Named on Santa Rosa (1954) 7.5' quadrangle.

Petrified Forest [SONOMA]: *locality,* 4.5 miles east of Mark West Springs (lat. 38°33'20" N, long. 122°38'15" W; sec. 9, T 8 N, R 7 W). Named on Mark West Springs (1958) 7.5' quadrangle. William Travis discovered petrified trees at the site in 1857, and the place opened to the public in the 1870's (Miller, J.T., p. 32).

Peytonia Slough [SOLANO]: *water feature,* joins Suisun Slough 1.5 miles south-southeast of downtown Fairfield (lat. 38°13'35" N, long. 122°02' W). Named on Fairfield South (1949) 7.5' quadrangle.

Pheasant Creek [SANTA CLARA]: *stream,* flows 1.5 miles to Guadalupe Creek nearly 4.5 miles north-northwest of Mount Umunhum (lat. 37°12'50" N, long. 121°54'40" W). Named on Los Gatos (1953) 7.5' quadrangle.

Phegley Ridge [SANTA CLARA]: *ridge,* north-northwest-trending, nearly 2 miles long, 5 miles southeast of Gilroy Hot Springs (lat. 37°03'45" N, long. 121°24'40" W). Named on Gilroy Hot Springs (1955) 7.5' quadrangle.

Phelps: see **Point Phelps**, under **Point Carquinez** [CONTRA COSTA].

Phelps Slough [SAN MATEO]: *water feature,* enters Steinberger Slough nearly 3 miles north-northwest of downtown Redwood City (lat. 37°31'15" N, long. 122°14'50" W; sec. 1, T 5 S, R 4 W). Named on Redwood Point (1959) and San Mateo (1956) 7.5' quadrangles. Timothy Guy Phelps built a landing at the head of the slough in the late 1850's (Brown, p. 68).

Philadelphia: see **New Philadelphia**, under **Sonoma** [SONOMA].

Phillips Gulch [SONOMA]: *canyon,* drained by a stream that flows 1.25 miles to the sea 1.5 miles west-southwest of Plantation (lat. 38°35'05" N, long. 123°20'20" W). Named on Plantation (1977) 7.5' quadrangle.

Phillips Soda Springs: see **Samuel Springs** [NAPA].

Phoenix Creek [MARIN]: *stream,* flows 1 mile to Phoenix Lake 3 miles west-southwest of downtown San Rafael (lat. 37°57'20" N, long. 122°34'55" W). Named on San Rafael (1954) 7.5' quadrangle.

Phoenix Lake [MARIN]: *lake,* behind a dam on Ross Creek 2.5 miles west-southwest of downtown San Rafael (lat. 37°57'20" N, long. 122°34'30" W). Named on San Rafael (1954) 7.5' quadrangle.

Phoenix Mine: see **Aetna Springs** [NAPA].

Picacho de Chual: see **Mount Chual** [SANTA CLARA].

Picacho de Umunhum: see **Mount Umunhum** [SANTA CLARA].

Picacho de Umurhum: see **Mount Umunhum** [SANTA CLARA].

Picacho Prieto: see **Mount Tamalpais** [MARIN].

Picket: see **Point Picket**, under **Stake Point** [CONTRA COSTA].

Pickle Canyon [NAPA]: *canyon,* drained by a stream that flows 4 miles to Redwood Canyon 5.25 miles west-northwest of downtown Napa (lat. 38°20'05" N, long. 122°22'10" W). Named on Napa (1951) and Sonoma (1951) 7.5' quadrangles. The stream in Pickle Canyon is called North Branch [Napa Creek] on Napa (1902) 30' quadrangle.

Pickle Canyon [SONOMA]: *canyon,* 2 miles long, along Mill Creek (1) above a point 6.5 miles north of Guerneville (lat. 38°35'50" N, long. 122°59'30" W; sec. 29, T 9 N, R 10 W). Named on Cazadero (1978) and Guerneville (1955) 7.5' quadrangles.

Picnic Creek [SONOMA]: *stream,* flows 1.5 miles to Warm Springs Creek nearly 1 mile west-northwest of Skaggs Springs (lat. 38°41'45" N, long. 123°02'25" W; sec. 23, T 10 N, R 11 W). Named on Warm Springs Dam (1978) 7.5' quadrangle.

Picnic Hill: see **Belmont Hill** [SAN MATEO].

Pico y Cerro de Reyes: see **Mount Tamalpais** [MARIN].

Piedmont [ALAMEDA]: *town,* 2.5 miles east-northeast of downtown Oakland (lat. 37°49'30" N, long. 122°13'45" W). Named on Oakland East (1959) 7.5' quadrangle. Piedmont Springs Company bought land at the site about 1876 and built a hotel to exploit a sulphur spring located on the property; a community developed at the place about 1900 (Gudde, 1949, p. 261), and postal authorities established Piedmont post office in 1901 (Frickstad, p. 3). The town incorporated in 1907. Winslow Anderson (p. 222) referred to Piedmont White Sulphur Springs at the place.

Piedmont Creek [SANTA CLARA]: *stream,* formed by the confluence of North Branch and South Branch, flows 1 mile in an artificial watercourse to Berryessa Creek nearly 1 mile east of downtown Milpitas (lat. 37°25'35" N, long. 121°53'20" W). Named on Milpitas (1961) 7.5' quadrangle. North Branch is 1.25 miles long and South Branch is 1 mile long; both branches are named on Calaveras Reservoir (1961) 7.5' quadrangle.

Piedmont White Sulphur Springs: see **Piedmont** [ALAMEDA].

Pierce [SOLANO]: *locality,* 9 miles south-southwest of Fairfield along Southern Pacific Railroad (lat. 38°07'35" N, long. 122° 06' W). Named on Fairfield South (1949) 7.5' quadrangle.

Pierce Point: see **Tomales Point** [MARIN].

Pigeon Point [SAN MATEO]: *promontory,* 20 miles south of the town of Half Moon Bay along the coast (lat. 37°10'55" N, long. 122°23'35" W). Named on Pigeon Point (1955) 7.5' quadrangle. The name is for the clipper ship *Carrier Pigeon,* which was wrecked at the place in 1853; in Spanish times the promontory was called Punta de la Ballena, or Cabo de Fortunas (Reinstedt, p. 12). A small port community that developed at the place by the 1860's also was called Pigeon Point (Morrall, p. 60). Postal authorities established Pigeon Point post office in 1874 and discontinued it in 1875 (Frickstad, p. 168). The embayment on the coast under Pigeon Point is called Pigeon Point Cove; a rock in the cove was called Storehouse Rock in the 1850's, and was called Pirate's Rock during Prohibition times (Brown, p. 69, 70).

Pigeon Point [SANTA CLARA]:

(1) *ridge,* west-northwest-trending, 1 mile long, 3.25 miles north of Morgan Hill (lat. 37°10'40" N, long. 121°38'50" W). Named on Morgan Hill (1955) 7.5' quadrangle. On Morgan Hill (1917) 15' quadrangle, the name applies to a peak on the ridge.

(2) *peak,* 4 miles south of Gilroy Hot Springs (lat. 37°03'10" N, long. 121°29'35" W; sec. 23, T 10 S, R 4 E). Named on Gilroy Hot Springs (1955) 7.5' quadrangle.

Pigeon Point Cove: see **Pigeon Point** [SAN MATEO].

Pike County Gulch [MARIN]: *canyon,* drained by a stream that flows 1.5 miles to Bolinas Lagoon 1.5 miles north of Bolinas (lat. 37°55'55" N, long. 122°41'15" W). Named on Bolinas (1954) 7.5' quadrangle. Settlers reportedly named it for Pike County, Texas (Teather, p. 55).

Pilarcitos Canyon: see **Pilarcitos Creek** [SAN MATEO].

Pilarcitos Creek [SAN MATEO]: *stream,* flows 12.5 miles to the sea 1.25 miles northwest of downtown Half Moon Bay (lat. 37°28'30" N, long. 122°26'50" W). Named on Half Moon Bay (1961) and Montara Mountain (1956) 7.5' quadrangles. United States Board on Geographic Names (1933, p. 603) rejected the form "Pillarcitos" for the name. Crespi called the stream Arroyo de San Simon y San Judas in 1769, and later it was called Arroyo de los Pilarcitos (Gudde, 1949, p. 261). The canyon of the creek below Pilarcitos Lake is called Pilarcitos Canyon (Brown, p. 69).

Pilarcitos Lake [SAN MATEO]: *lake,* 1.25 miles long, behind a dam on Pilarcitos Creek 3.5 miles east of Montara Knob (lat. 37°32'55" N, long. 122°25'20" W; near NW cor. sec. 33, T 4 S, R 5 W). Named on Montara Mountain (1956) 7.5' quadrangle. United States Board on Geographic Names (1933, p. 603) rejected the form "Pillarcitos" for the name.

Pillar Point [SAN MATEO]: *promontory,* 4.25 miles west-northwest of downtown Half Moon Bay along the coast (lat. 37°29'45" N, long. 122°29'45" W). Named on Half Moon Bay (1961) 7.5' quadrangle. The feature is on a peninsula that was called Corral de Tierra in Spanish times, and was called Snake's Head in early American times (Brown, p. 69).

Pillar Point Harbor [SAN MATEO]: *water feature,* 3.5 miles south of Montara Knob at the north end of Half Moon Bay (1) (lat. 37° 30'10" N, long. 122°29' W); the feature is east of Pillar Point. Named on Montara Mountain (1956, photorevised 1980) 7.5' quadrangle.

Pillar Rock: see **Sail Rock** [SAN MATEO].

Pilot Knob [MARIN]: *peak,* 2.5 miles west of downtown San Rafael (lat. 37°56'55" N, long. 122°35'15" W). Altitude 1187 feet. Named on San Rafael (1954) 7.5' quadrangle.

Pilot Knob [SONOMA]: *peak,* 3 miles northwest of Mount Saint Helena (lat. 38°41'55" N, long. 122°40'25" W; sec. 19, T 10 N, R 7 W). Named on Mount Saint Helena (1959) 7.5' quadrangle.

Pine Canyon [CONTRA COSTA]: *canyon,* 4.25 miles long, along Pine Creek above a point 4.5 miles west of Mount Diablo (lat. 37° 53'35" N, long. 122°59'35" W). Named on Clayton (1953) and Diablo (1953) 7.5' quadrangles.

Pine Creek [CONTRA COSTA]: *stream,* flows 12.5 miles to Walnut Creek (1) 5 miles north of Walnut Creek civic center (lat. 37°58'35" N, long. 122°03'05" W); the stream drains Pine Canyon. Named on Clayton (1953) and Walnut Creek (1959) 7.5' quadrangles.

Pine Creek: see **Little Pine Creek** [CONTRA COSTA].

Pine Creek Reservoir [SONOMA]: *lake,* 400 feet long, less than 2 miles north-northeast of downtown Santa Rosa (lat. 38°28' N, long. 122°42'15" W; on E line sec. 11, T 7 N, R 8 W. Named on Santa Rosa (1954, photorevised 1968 and 1973) 7.5' quadrangle.

Pine Flat [SONOMA]: *area,* 10 miles northeast of Healdsburg along Little Sulphur Creek (lat. 38°44'20" N, long. 122°45'50" W; sec. 5, T 10 N, R 8 W). Named on Jimtown (1955) 7.5' quadrangle.

Pine Flat: see **Healdsburg** [SONOMA].

Pine Grove: see **Sebastopol** [SONOMA].

Pine Gulch Creek [MARIN]: *stream,* flows 7.5 miles to Bolinas Lagoon nearly 1 mile north of Bolinas (lat. 37°55'20" N, long. 122° 41'10" W). Named on Bolinas (1954) 7.5' quadrangle. Teather (p. 12) used the name "Bolinas Creek" for the stream, and noted that the feature also is called Gregorio's Creek, for Gregorio Briones, who received Las Baulines grant.

Pine Hill [SONOMA]: *peak,* 7.25 miles north-northeast of Fort Ross (lat. 38°36'50" N, long. 123°11'50" W; at SW cor. sec. 16, T 9 N, R 12 W). Altitude 1572 feet. Named on Fort Ross (1978) 7.5' quadrangle.

Pine Lake [SOLANO]: *lake,* 1400 feet long, 1 mile east of downtown Benicia (lat. 38°03'05" N, long. 122°08'10" W; sec. 1, T 2 N, R 3 W). Named on Benicia (1959) 7.5' quadrangle.

Pine Mountain [MARIN]: *peak,* 5 miles north-northeast of Bolinas (lat. 37°58'40" N, long. 122°39'05" W). Altitude 1762 feet. Named on Bolinas (1954) 7.5' quadrangle.

Pine Mountain [SONOMA]: *peak,* 6 miles northwest of Mount Saint Helena on Sonoma-Lake County line (lat. 38°43'55" N, long. 122° 42'20" W;

on E line sec. 11, T 10 N, R 8 W). Altitude 3614 feet. Named on Mount Saint Helena (1959) 7.5' quadrangle.

Pine Mountain Ridge [MARIN]: *ridge,* west- to northwest-trending, 2.25 miles long, 5 miles north of Bolinas (lat. 37°58'45" N, long. 122°40'10" W); Pine Mountain is at the east end of the ridge. Named on Bolinas (1954) 7.5' quadrangle.

Pine Ridge [CONTRA COSTA]: *ridge,* south-southeast-trending, 1 mile long, 3.25 miles west-southwest of Mount Diablo (lat. 37° 52' N, long. 121°58'20" W); the ridge is southwest of Pine Canyon. Named on Diablo (1953) 7.5' quadrangle.

Pine Ridge [SANTA CLARA]: *ridge,* northwest-trending, 4 miles long, 2.5 miles west-southwest of Mount Sizer (lat. 37°11'45" N, long. 121°33'15" W). Named on Mount Sizer (1955) 7.5' quadrangle.

Pine Ridge: see **Bollinger Ridge** [SANTA CLARA]; **Castle Ridge** [SANTA CLARA]; **Valpe Ridge** [ALAMEDA-SANTA CLARA].

Pine Ridge Canyon [SONOMA]: *canyon,* drained by a stream that flows 2 miles to Dry Creek 1 mile west-northwest of Healdsburg (lat. 38°37'10" N, long. 122°53'20" W). Named on Guerneville (1955) 7.5' quadrangle.

Pine Spring Canyon [SANTA CLARA]: *canyon,* drained by a stream that flows 6.25 miles to North Fork Pacheco Creek nearly 7 miles north of Pacheco Peak (lat. 37°06'20" N, long. 121°17'40" W; sec. 34, T 9 S, R 6 E). Named on Mustang Peak (1955) and Pacheco Peak (1955) 7.5' quadrangles.

Pine Springs Hill [SANTA CLARA]: *peak,* 4 miles east of Mustang Peak on Santa Clara-Stanislaus County line (lat. 37°10'50" N, long. 121°16'50" W; sec. 2, T 9 S, R 6 E); the peak is at the head of Pine Spring Canyon. Named on Mustang Peak (1955) 7.5' quadrangle.

Pine Station: see **Zinfandel** [NAPA].

Pine Tree Canyon [SANTA CLARA]: *canyon,* drained by a stream that flows 1 mile to an unnamed stream 3.5 miles east-southeast of New Almaden (lat. 37°09'50" N, long. 121°45'25" W). Named on Santa Teresa Hills (1953) 7.5' quadrangle.

Pine Tree Gulch [SAN MATEO]: *canyon,* drained by a stream that flows 0.5 mile to El Corte de Madera Creek 4 miles west-northwest of La Honda (lat. 37°21'05" N, long. 122°20' W). Named on La Honda (1961) 7.5' quadrangle.

Pinnacle Rock [SONOMA]: *rock,* 2.25 miles southeast of the village of Bodega Bay, and 300 feet offshore (lat. 38°18'25" N, long. 123° 01'10" W). Named on Bodega Head (1972) 7.5' quadrangle.

Pino Creek [SANTA CLARA]: *stream,* flows 2 miles to Arroyo Valle 5 miles south-southwest of Eylar Mountain (lat. 37°24'25" N, long. 121°35' W; sec. 18, T 6 S, R 4 E). Named on Eylar Mountain (1955) 7.5' quadrangle.

Pinole [CONTRA COSTA]:

(1) *land grant,* extends from the town of Pinole to Martinez. Named on Benicia (1959), Briones Valley (1959), Mare Island (1959), Richmond (1959), and Walnut Creek (1959) 7.5' quadrangles. United States Board on Geographic Names (1933, p. 606) rejected the names "El Pinole" and "Penole" for the grant. Ignacio Martinez held the land in 1829 and received 4 leagues in 1842; M.A. Martinez de Richardson claimed 17,761 acres patented in 1868 (Cowan, p. 61). The name "Pinole" is from the Spanish term for parched corn that the Mexicans ground up and used (Davis, W.H., p. 23).

(2) *town,* 4 miles east of Pinole Point (lat. 38°00'20" N, long. 122° 17'25" W). Named on Mare Island (1959), Petaluma Point (1959), and Richmond (1959) 7.5' quadrangles. United States Board on Geographic Names (1933, p. 606) rejected the names "El Pinole" and "Penole" for the town. Postal authorities established Pinole post office in 1878 (Frickstad, p. 23), and the town incorporated in 1903. Dr. Samuel J. Tennant founded the town, which is named for Pinole grant—Tennant was the son-in-law of the owner of the grant (Hanna, P.T., p. 236-237).

Pinole Creek [CONTRA COSTA]: *stream,* flows 10 miles to San Pablo Bay nearly 4 miles east of Pinole Point in the town of Pinole (lat. 38°00'50" N, long. 122°17'45" W). Named on Briones Valley (1959), Mare Island (1959), and Richmond (1959) 7.5' quadrangles.

Pinole Point [CONTRA COSTA]: *promontory,* 26 miles west-northwest of Mount Diablo along San Pablo Bay (lat. 38°00'45" N, long. 122°21'50" W). Named on Mare Island (1959) 7.5' quadrangle. Called Punta de Almejas on a diseño of San Pablo grant made in 1830 (Becker, 1969). Called Pt. Penole on Ringgold's (1850a) map, but United States Board on Geographic Names (1933, p. 606) rejected the forms "Penole" and "El Pinole" for the name.

Pinole Ridge [CONTRA COSTA]: *ridge,* northwest- to west-trending, 3.25 miles long, 6.25 miles northeast of Richmond civic center (lat. 37°59'30" N, long. 122°15' W). Named on Briones Valley (1959) and Richmond (1959) 7.5' quadrangles.

Pinole Shoal [CONTRA COSTA]: *shoal,* 3.5 miles northeast of Pinole Point in San Pablo Bay just west of Carquinez Strait (lat. 38°02'45" N, long. 122°18'45" W). Named on Mare Island (1959) 7.5' quadrangle.

Pioneer: see **Robertsville** [SANTA CLARA].

Pioneer Camp [CONTRA COSTA]: *locality,* less than 1 mile southwest of Mount Diablo (lat. 37°52'20" N, long. 121°55'20" W; sec. 1, T 1 S, R 1 W). Named on Diablo (1953) 7.5' quadrangle.

Piper Slough [CONTRA COSTA]: *water feature,* extends for 5 miles, mainly between Bethel Island (1) and Franks Tract, from Sand Mound Slough to False River 3 miles north-northwest of the settlement of Bethel island (lat. 38°03'20" N, long. 121°39'20" W). Named on Bouldin Island (1978) and Jersey Island (1978) 7.5' quadrangles.

Pirate Creek [ALAMEDA]: *stream,* flows 2.5 miles to Alameda Creek 3 miles south-southeast of Sunol (lat. 37°33'20" N, long. 121°51'50" W). Named on La Costa Valley (1960) and Niles (1961) 7.5' quadrangles. Mosier and Mosier (p. 68) suggested stream piracy as the probable source of the name; the stream flowed to Sheridan Creek before it was captured by a tributary of Alameda Creek.

Pirates Cove [MARIN]: *embayment,* 3 miles northwest of Point Bonita along the coast (lat. 37°51'05" N, long. 122°33'40" W). Named on Point Bonita (1954) 7.5' quadrangle.

Pirate's Cove: see **Shelter Cove** [SAN MATEO].

Pirate's Rock: see **Pigeon Point** [SAN MATEO].

Pisgah: see **Mount Pisgah** [SONOMA].

Pistolesi: see **Camp Pistolesi**, under **Camp Tomales** [MARIN].

Pita Navaga: see **Divide Ridge** [ALAMEDA-CONTRA COSTA].

Pitchers Range [SONOMA]: *locality,* 3 miles east-southeast of present Jenner along Willow Creek (lat. 38°25'50" N, long. 123°04'55" W). Named on Duncans Mills (1921) 15' quadrangle.

Pittsburg [CONTRA COSTA]: *city,* 10 miles north of Mount Diablo (lat. 38°01'55" N, long. 121°52'55" W). Named on Antioch North (1978), Clayton (1953), and Honker Bay (1953) 7.5' quadrangles. Ringgold's (1850b) map shows a town called New York of the Pacific at the site. Postal authorities established Black Diamond post office in 1868 and changed the name to Pittsburg in 1911 (Frickstad, p. 21). The city incorporated in 1903. Colonel Jonathan D. Stevenson of the New York Volunteers bought Los Medanos grant in 1849 and had a town laid out that he called New York of the Pacific (Hoover, Rensch, and Rensch, p. 64), but after 1850 the development was recognized as a failure (Bancroft, 1888, p. 528). With the discovery of coal in Diablo Range, the place became a shipping point for coal and was called Black Diamond until 1909, when the name was changed to Pittsburg in recognition of the industrial potential of the place (Hanna, P.T., p. 238). The site also was known as Black Diamond Landing (MacMullen, p. 78) and New York Landing (Mosier, p. 4). The name "Black Diamond" was from Black Diamond coal mine, located about 4 miles south of the center of Pittsburg (in and near SE quarter sec. 5, T 1 N, R 1 E) (Davis and Goldman, p. 520). California Mining Bureau's (1909b) map shows a place called Cornwall located near Black Diamond 7.25 miles east-southeast of Baypoint along a railroad. Postal authorities established Cornwall Station post office 1 mile south of Black Diamond in 1881, discontinued it in 1888, reestablished it with the name "Cornwall" in 1890, and discontinued it in 1911 (Salley, p. 50).

Pittsburg: see **West Pittsburg** [CONTRA COSTA].

Pittsburg Landing [CONTRA COSTA]: *locality,* 2.25 miles west-northwest of Antioch near the east end of New York Slough (lat. 38°01'40" N, long. 121°50'50" W). Named on Collinsville (1918) 7.5' quadrangle. Coal from mines in Diablo Range was shipped from the place, which was connected to the mines by Pittsburg Railroad (Mosier, p. 6).

Pittsburg Point [CONTRA COSTA]: *promontory,* 2.5 miles west-northwest of Antioch along New York Slough (lat. 38°01'50" N, long. 121°51'05" W). Named on Antioch North (1978) 7.5' quadrangle.

Pittsburg Station [CONTRA COSTA]: *locality,* less than 1 mile south-southwest of present downtown Pittsburg (lat. 38°01'25" N, long. 121°53'10" W). Named on Honker Bay (1918) 7.5' quadrangle.

Plan de Agua Caliente: see **Mallacomes or Muristul y Plan de Agua Caliente** [NAPA-SONOMA].

Planiel: see **Plantel** [SANTA CLARA].

Plantation [SONOMA]: *settlement,* 6.25 miles northwest of Fort Ross (lat. 38°35'25" N, long. 123°18'30" W). Named on Plantation (1977) 7.5' quadrangle. Postal authorities established Fisk's Mill post office in 1871, changed the name to Fisk in 1894, moved it 3 miles southeast in 1902 when they changed the name to Plantation, and discontinued it in 1933—the name "Fisk" was for Andrew J. Fisk, a lumber-mill operator, and the name "Plantation" was for Plantation House, a travelers stop (Salley, p. 75, 173).

Plantel [SANTA CLARA]: *locality,* 3 miles southeast of Gilroy along Southern Pacific Railroad (lat. 36°58' N, long. 121°31'50" W). Named on San Juan Bautista (1917) 15' quadrangle. Santa Cruz (1956) 1°x 2° quadrangle has the name "Planiel" at the place.

Plaza de los Caballos: see **Cavallo Point** [MARIN].

Pleasant Creek [SOLANO]: *stream,* flows 4.5 miles to McCune Creek (1) 3.5 miles northwest of Allendale (lat. 38°28'40" N, long. 121°59'20" W). Named on Allendale (1953) and Mount Vaca (1951) 7.5' quadrangles.

Pleasant Hill [CONTRA COSTA]: *city,* 2.5 miles north of Walnut Creek civic center (lat. 37°56'20" N, long. 122°04' W). Named on Walnut Creek (1959) 7.5' quadrangle. Postal authorities established Pleasant Hill post office in 1948 (Salley, p. 174), and the city incorporated in 1961.

Pleasanton [ALAMEDA]: *city,* 6 miles west-southwest of Livermore (lat. 37°39'45" N, long. 121°52'30" W). Named on Dublin (1961) and Livermore (1961) 7.5' quadrangles. The place first was called Alisal, but John Kottinger named the city in 1867 for General Alfred Pleasonton (Mosier and Mosier, p. 69). Postal authorities established the post office there with the misspelled name "Pleasanton" in 1867 (Frickstad, p. 3), and the city incorporated in 1894. A station along Western Pacific Railroad south of Pleasanton was called Hacienda because it served the Hearst estate called La Hacienda del Pozo de Verona; the station also was called Hearst (Mosier and Mosier, p. 40).

Pleasanton: see **East Pleasanton** [ALAMEDA].

Pleasanton Ridge [ALAMEDA]: *ridge,* northwest- to north-northwest-trending, 5.25 miles long, center 4.5 miles south-southeast of Dublin (lat. 37°38'15" N, long. 121°54'45" W); the ridge is 2.5 miles southwest of Pleasanton. Named on Dublin (1961) and Niles (1961) 7.5' quadrangles.

Pleasants Canyon: see **Miller Canyon** [SOLANO].

Pleasants Creek [SOLANO]: *stream,* flows 10 miles to Putah Creek 7.5 miles northeast of Mount Vaca (lat. 38°29'25" N, long. 122°01'10" W); the stream drains Pleasants Valley. Named on Mount Vaca (1951) 7.5' quadrangle. United States Board on Geographic Names (1933, p. 609) rejected the name "Pleasant Valley Creek" for the feature.

Pleasants Ridge [SOLANO]: *ridge,* north-trending, 4 miles long, 5.5 miles north-northeast of Mount Vaca (lat. 38°28'30" N, long. 122° 04'40" W); the ridge is northwest of Pleasants Valley. Named on Monticello Dam (1959) and Mount Vaca (1951) 7.5' quadrangles.

Pleasants Valley [SOLANO]: *valley,* 4.5 miles northeast of Mount Vaca along Pleasants Creek (lat. 38°27'15" N, long. 122°03'15" W). Named on Mount Vaca (1951) 7.5' quadrangle. The name commemorates James Marshall Pleasants and his son William James Pleasants, who arrived in the valley in 1850 and farmed there (Gudde, 1969, p. 251).

Pleasant Valley: see **Gilroy** [SANTA CLARA]; **Happy Valley** [CONTRA COSTA]; **Rincon Hill** [SAN FRANCISCO].

Pleasant Valley Creek: see **Pleasants Creek** [SOLANO].

Plumbajo Flat: see **Blumbago Canyon** [SANTA CLARA].

Plummer Creek [ALAMEDA]: *water feature,* joins Newark Slough 3 miles southwest of downtown Newark (lat. 37°30'20" N, long. 122°05' W). Named on Newark (1959) 7.5' quadrangle. The stream first was called Salt Work Slough for Crystal Salt Works, which John A. Plummer established in 1864 (Mosier and Mosier, p. 69).

Plummer Landing [ALAMEDA]: *locality,* 1.5 miles south-southwest of downtown Newark (lat. 37°30'35" N, long. 122°03'05" W); the place is along Plummer Creek. Named on Newark (1948) 7.5' quadrangle. Isaac Long established Long's Landing along present Plummer Creek in 1852; Long sold his landing to John Plummer in 1855 (Mosier and Mosier, p. 53).

Pluton Cañon: see **Big Sulphur Creek** [SONOMA].

Pluton River: see **Big Sulphur Creek** [SONOMA].

Pluton Valley: see **Big Sulphur Creek** [SONOMA].

Pocket Canyon [SONOMA]: *canyon,* drained by a stream that flows 5.5 miles to Russian River at Guerneville (lat. 38°30' N, long. 122° 59'45" W; sec. 32, T 8 N, R 10 W). Named on Camp Meeker (1954) and Guerneville (1955) 7.5' quadrangles.

Pocket Opening [SONOMA]: *area,* 4.5 miles north-northeast of Guerneville (lat. 38°33'45" N, long. 122°58' W). Named on Guerneville (1955) 7.5' quadrangle.

Pocket Peak [SONOMA]: *peak,* 4.5 miles east-northeast of Asti (lat. 38°47' N, long. 122°53'40" W). Altitude 2269 feet. Named on Asti (1959) 7.5' quadrangle.

Pocock Creek [NAPA]: *stream,* flows 2 miles to Hunting Creek 4.5 miles southwest of Knoxville (lat. 38°47'15" N, long. 122°24'30" W; near E line sec. 21, T 11 N, R 5 W). Named on Jericho Valley (1958) 7.5' quadrangle.

Point Anno Nuevo: see **Año Nuevo Point** [SAN MATEO].

Point Año Nuevo: see **Año Nuevo Point** [SAN MATEO].

Point Avisadero [SAN FRANCISCO]: *promontory,* 5.5 miles east of Mount Davidson along San Francisco Bay at the east end of Hunters Point (lat. 37°43'45" N, long. 122°21'20" W). Named on Hunters Point (1956) 7.5' quadrangle. Called Pta. Avisadera on Beechey's (1827-1828) map, and called Avisadero Pt. on San Mateo (1915) 15' quadrangle. United States Board on Geographic Names (1967b, p. 2) rejected the names "Avisadero Point," "Avisadera Point," and "Hunters Point" for the feature.

Point Beenar [CONTRA COSTA]: *promontory,* 2 miles northwest of Antioch along San Joaquin River at the southeast end of Winter Island (lat. 38°01'50" N, long. 121°50'10" W). Named on Antioch North (1978) 7.5' quadrangle.

Point Blunt: see **Blunt Point** [MARIN-SAN FRANCISCO].

Point Blunt Rock: see **Blunt Point Rock** [SAN FRANCISCO].

Point Bodega: see **Tomales Bluff** [MARIN].

Point Bolitas: see **Bulls Head Point** [CONTRA COSTA].

Point Boneta: see **Point Bonita** [MARIN].

Point Bonita [MARIN]: *promontory,* 11 miles south of downtown San Rafael along the coast (lat. 37°48'55" N, long. 122°31'40" W). Named on Point Bonita (1954) 7.5' quadrangle. Ayala called the promontory Punta de Santiago in 1775; the feature also was known as Punta Bonete and Punta de Bonetas in Spanish times (Gudde, 1949, p. 37). United States Board on Geographic Names (1933, p. 156) rejected the form "Point Boneta" for the name. The top of the promontory was called Lands End in the 1860's (Shanks and Shanks, p. 36).

Point Buckler [SOLANO]: *promontory,* 8 miles east-northeast of Benicia at the west end of Simmons Island (lat. 38°05'50" N, long. 122°01'10" W). Named on Vine Hill (1959) 7.5' quadrangle.

Point Campbell: see **Campbell Point** [MARIN].

Point Carquinez [CONTRA COSTA]: *promontory,* nearly 3 miles northwest of Martinez (lat. 38°02'20" N, long. 122°10'30" W); the promontory is along Carquinez Strait. Named on Benicia (1959) 7.5' quadrangle. Called Pt. Phelps on Ringgold's (1850a) map, Karquines Pt. on Karquines (1898) 15' quadrangle, and Carquinez Point on Carquinez Strait (1896) 15' quadrangle.

Point Cavallo: see **Cavallo Point** [MARIN].

Point Chapman: see **Steamboat Slough** [SOLANO].

Point Chauncey [MARIN]: *promontory,* 3.5 miles south-southeast of Point San Quentin on the northeast side of Tiburon Peninsula (lat. 37°53'40" N, long. 122°26'55" W). Named on San Quentin (1959) 7.5' quadrangle. Called Chauncey Pt. on San Francisco (1915) 15' quadrangle.

Point Davis: see **Davis Point** [CONTRA COSTA].

Point Diablo [MARIN]: *promontory,* nearly 3 miles south-southwest of downtown Sausalito along the coast (lat. 37°49'10" N, long. 122°29'50" W). Named on San Francisco North (1956) 7.5' quadrangle. Called Punta Diablo on Beechey's (1827-1828) map, and Kelley (p. 162) called it Punto Diavolo. United States Board on Geographic Names (1979b, p. 7) approved the name "Kirby Beach" for the beach, 1.7 miles long, that is situated about halfway between Point Diablo and Lime Point (west end at lat. 37°49'36" N, long. 122°29'25" W).

Point Edith [CONTRA COSTA]: *promontory,* 4.5 miles northeast of Martinez along Suisun Bay (lat. 38°03'10" N, long. 122°04'10" W). Named on Vine Hill (1959) 7.5' quadrangle. Called Edith Point on Karquines (1898) 15' quadrangle. Ringgold's (1850b) map shows Pt. Massachusetts situated about 0.5 mile east of Pt. Edith.

Point Edith Crossing Range [CONTRA COSTA-SOLANO]: *channel,* nearly 5 miles northeast of Martinez in Suisun Bay on Contra Costa-Solano County line (lat. 38°03'35" N, long. 122°04' W); the feature is north of Point Edith. Named on Vine Hill (1959) 7.5' quadrangle.

Point Elliot: see **Port Costa** [CONTRA COSTA].

Point Emmet [CONTRA COSTA]: *promontory,* 0.5 mile north of downtown Pittsburg at the west end of Browns Island on the west side of the mouth of New York Slough (lat. 38°02'25" N, long. 121°52'50" W). Named on Honker Bay (1953) 7.5' quadrangle.

Point Fleming: see **Fleming Point** [ALAMEDA].

Point Gelston: see **Ryer Island** [SOLANO] (1).

Point Gillespie: see **Gillespie Point** [SOLANO].

Point Green: see **Preston Point** [SOLANO].

Point Hansen: see **Van Sickle Island** [SOLANO].

Point Huchones: see **Point San Pablo** [CONTRA COSTA].

Point Ione [MARIN]: *promontory,* on the west side of Angel Island (lat. 37°52'05" N, long. 122°26'15" W). Named on San Francisco North (1956, photorevised 1968 and 1973) 7.5' quadrangle.

Point Isabel [CONTRA COSTA]: *promontory,* nearly 3 miles south-southeast of Richmond civic center along San Francisco Bay (lat. 37°53'55" N, long. 122°19'25" W). Named on Richmond (1959) 7.5' quadrangle. Called Isabel Pt. on San Francisco (1899) 15' quadrangle. United States Board on Geographic Names (1933, p. 392) rejected the names "Point Izabel" and "Point Potero" for the feature.

Point Izabel: see **Point Isabel** [CONTRA COSTA].

Point Julia: see **Inverness** [MARIN].

Point Knox: see **Knox Point** [MARIN].

Point Lobos [SAN FRANCISCO]: *promontory,* 3 miles southwest of Fort Point along the coast (lat. 37°46'50" N, long. 122°30'50" W). Named on San Francisco North (1956) 7.5' quadrangle. Called Pta. del Angel de la Guarda on Dalrymple's (1789) map, and called Punta de los Lobos on Ringgold's (1850a) map.

Point Massachusetts: see **Point Edith** [CONTRA COSTA].

Point Molate [CONTRA COSTA]: *promontory,* 1.25 miles south-southeast of Point San Pablo along San Francisco Bay (lat. 37°56'50" N, long. 122°25'15" W). Named on San Quentin (1959) 7.5' quadrangle. Called Patapsco Pt. on Ringgold's (1850a) map, and called Molate Pt. on San Francisco (1899) 15' quadrangle.

Point Montara [SAN MATEO]: *promontory,* 2.5 miles southwest of Montara Knob along the coast (lat. 37°32'15" N, long. 122°31'05" W). Named on Montara Mountain (1956) 7.5' quadrangle. Called Montara Pt. on San Mateo (1915) 15' quadrangle. United States Board on Geographic Names (1933, p. 528) rejected the form "Point Montora" for the name. Brown (p. 57) used the name "Montara Creek" for the stream that enters the sea on the north side of Point Montara. A rock situated offshore south of Point Montara is called Colorado Reef or Colorado Ledge for the steamship

Colorado, which was wrecked there in 1868; before this wreck, the feature was called Uncle Sam Rock for a ship wrecked there in 1855 (Brown, p. 22).

Point Montgomery: see **Telegraph Hill** [SAN FRANCISCO].

Point Montora: see **Point Montara** [SAN MATEO].

Point Munroe: see **Paradise Cay** [MARIN].

Point New Year: see **Año Nuevo Point** [SAN MATEO].

Point of Timber: see **Byron** [CONTRA COSTA].

Point Orient [CONTRA COSTA]: *promontory,* 0.5 mile south-southeast of Point San Pablo along San Francisco Bay (lat. 37°57'25" N, long. 122°25'25" W). Named on San Quentin (1959) 7.5' quadrangle.

Point Palo Alto [SOLANO]: *promontory,* 7 miles southwest of Birds Landing (2) at the east end of Snag Island (lat. 38°04'20" N long. 123°58'20" W). Named on Honker Bay (1953) 7.5' quadrangle. Called Palo Alto Pt. on Ringgold's (1850c) map, which has the name "Palo Alto Id." for present Snag Island.

Point Penole: see **Pinole Point** [CONTRA COSTA].

Point Picket: see **Stake Point** [CONTRA COSTA].

Point Phelps: see **Point Carquinez** [CONTRA COSTA].

Point Potrero [CONTRA COSTA]: *promontory,* 2.5 miles south-southwest of Richmond civic center (lat. 37°54'15" N, long. 122° 22' W). Named on Richmond (1959) 7.5' quadrangle. Called Shoal Pt. on San Francisco (1915) 15' quadrangle.

Point Potrero: see **Point Isabel** [CONTRA COSTA].

Point Reed: see **Bluff Point** [MARIN].

Point Reyes [MARIN]:

(1) *promontory,* 12 miles west-southwest of Point Reyes Station at the west end of Drakes Bay (the lighthouse at the end of the promontory is near lat. 37°59'45" N, long. 123°01'20" W). Named on Drakes Bay (1953) 7.5' quadrangle. Called Pta. de los Reyes on Costanso's (1771) map, called Punta de Reyes on Crespi's (1772) map, and called Punto de los Reyes on Ringgold's (1850b) map. Cabrillo discovered the promontory in 1542 and named it Cabo de Pinos; the present name comes from the Vizcaino expedition, which rounded the point and took shelter in present Drakes Bay on January 6, 1603, the day of Los Reyes (Wagner, H.R., p. 405). Vizcaino gave the name "La Punta de las Barrancas blancas" to the east end of present Point Reyes—*barrancas blancas* means "white cliffs" in Spanish (Davidson, p. 22-23), and no doubt refers to cliffs along present Drakes Bay.

(2) *locality,* 7.25 miles north-northeast of the lighthouse at Point Reyes (lat. 38°05'05" N, long. 122°57'15" W). Named on Point Reyes (1918) 15' quadrangle. Postal authorities established Point Reyes post office in 1891 at what was known as "F" Ranch, moved it 4 miles southeast in 1919 to "D" Ranch, moved it 4 miles southwest to the lighthouse at Point Reyes about 1942, and discontinued it in 1948 (Salley, p. 175).

Point Reyes: see **Point Reyes Station** [MARIN].

Point Reyes Beach [MARIN]: *beach,* extends for 10 miles along the coast north-northeast from Point Reyes (1) to a spot 6.5 miles south-southwest of Tomales (lat. 38°09'30" N, long. 122°56'55" W). Named on Drakes Bay (1953) and Tomales (1954) 7.5' quadrangles. The feature also is known as Ten Mile Beach and as The Great Beach (Mason, 1972, p. 62).

Point Reyes Hill [MARIN]: *peak,* 3.5 miles west-northwest of Point Reyes Station on Inverness Ridge (lat. 38°04'50" N, long. 122°52'05" W); the peak is 10 miles northeast of the lighthouse at Point Reyes. Altitude 1336 feet. Named on Inverness (1954) 7.5' quadrangle.

Point Reyes Station [MARIN]: *village,* 13 miles south-southeast of Tomales (lat. 38°04'10" N, long. 122°08'20" W); the village is 13 miles east-northeast of the lighthouse at Point Reyes. Named on Inverness (1954) 7.5' quadrangle. The place was called Olema Station when the railroad reached the site in 1875 (Mason, 1976b, p. 116). Postal authorities established Point Reyes post office at the place in 1882, changed the name to Marin by mistake in 1891, changed it back to Point Reyes the same year, and changed it to Point Reyes Station later in 1891 (Salley, p. 175).

Point Richmond [CONTRA COSTA]:

(1) *promontory,* 4.25 miles south-southeast of Point San Pablo along San Francisco Bay (lat. 37°54'35" N, long. 122°23'15" W). Named on San Quentin (1959) 7.5' quadrangle. Called Pt. Stephens on Ringgold's (1850a) map, and called Richmond Pt. on San Francisco (1899) 15' quadrangle.

(2) *district,* 3.5 miles southeast of Point San Pablo in Richmond (lat. 37°55'40" N, long. 122°23'10" W); the district is north of Point Richmond (1). Named on San Quentin (1959) 7.5' quadrangle. Atchison, Topeka and Santa Fe Railroad established a terminal at the place in 1897, and the community that developed there was called Santa Fe (Gudde, 1949, p. 286). Postal authorities established Eastyard post office in 1901 and changed the name to Point Richmond in 1902 (Salley, p. 65).

Point San Bruno [SAN MATEO]: *promontory,* 2 miles east of downtown South San Francisco along San Francisco Bay (lat. 37°39'10" N, long. 122°22'35" W). Named on San Francisco South (1956) 7.5' quadrangle, which shows that landfill modifies the feature. Called San Bruno Pt. on San Mateo (1915) 15' quadrangle, and called Punta San Bruno on Beechey's (1827-1828) map.

Point San Joaquin [CONTRA COSTA]: *promontory,* 4 miles northwest of Antioch at the north end of Winter Island (lat. 38°03'35" N, long. 121°51'20" W); the feature is west of the mouth of San Joaquin River. Named on Antioch North (1978) 7.5' quadrangle.

Point San Mateo: see **Coyote Point** [SAN MATEO].

Point San Matheo: see **Coyote Point** [SAN MATEO].

Point San Pablo [CONTRA COSTA]: *promontory,* 5 miles west-northwest of Richmond civic center along San Francisco Bay (lat. 37°57'55" N, long. 122°25'40" W). Named on San Quentin (1959) 7.5' quadrangle. Called San Pablo Pt. on San Francisco (1899) 15' quadrangle. Dalrymple's (1789) map has the name "Pta. de Sn. Antonio" for this or a nearby promontory, and Beechey's (1827-1828) map has the name "pta. San Pablo" for it. A diseño of San Pablo grant made in 1830 has the name "Punta de Sn. Pablo" (Becker, 1969). The feature was called Pt. Huchones before 1811—the Huchones Indians lived there (Bancroft, 1886, p. 321).

Point San Pablo Yacht Harbor [CONTRA COSTA]: *water feature,* 0.5 mile east-southeast of Point San Pablo along San Pablo Bay (lat. 37°57'45" N, long. 122°25'05" W). Named on San Quentin (1959) 7.5' quadrangle.

Point San Pedro [MARIN]: *promontory,* 4.5 miles east-northeast of downtown San Rafael on the northwest side of San Pablo Strait (lat. 37°59'05" N, long. 122°26'45" W). Named on San Quentin (1959) 7.5' quadrangle. Called Pta. San Pedro on Beechey's (1827-1828) map, and called San Pedro Pt. on San Francisco (1915) 15' quadrangle. The promontory was called Punta de San Pedro as early as 1811, and in the 1870's it was known as McNears Point from the firm of McNear and Brothers, which owned land there (Gudde, 1949, p. 200). Ringgold's (1850a) map shows a feature called Argus I. situated just off Pt. San Pedro.

Point San Pedro [SAN MATEO]: *promontory,* 3.25 miles northwest of Montara Knob along the coast (lat. 37°35'40" N, long. 122°31'10" W); the feature is on San Pedro grant. Named on Montara Mountain (1956) 7.5' quadrangle. Called San Pedro Pt. on San Mateo (1915) 15' quadrangle, and called Punta de Almejas on Font's (1777) map. Members of the Portola expedition in 1769 gave the name "Punta de Almejas" to the feature for mussels found nearby—*almejas* means "mussels" in Spanish; at the same time, Crespi gave it the name "Punta del Angel Custodio" (Wagner, H.R., p. 412). Brown (p. 65) called it Pedro Point.

Point San Quentin [MARIN]: *promontory,* 3.5 miles southeast of downtown San Rafael along San Francisco Bay (lat. 37°56'35" N, long. 122°28'35" W). Named on San Quentin (1959) 7.5' quadrangle. The promontory was called Punta de Quintin in Spanish times for an Indian named Quintin, who was captured there; members of United States Coast Survey Americanized the name and added the word "San" when they surveyed San Francisco Bay in 1850 (Gudde, 1949, p. 312). Ringgold's (1850a) map has the name "Lejuanjelua Bay" for the embayment south of Point San Quentin, and shows Agnes I. located just off of the point—landfill now connects the island to the promontory.

Point San Quentin: see **Potrero Point** [SAN FRANCISCO].

Point Semple: see **Semple Point** [SOLANO].

Point Sherman: see **Port Chicago** [CONTRA COSTA].

Point Simmons: see **Simmons Point** [SOLANO].

Point Simpton: see **Simpton Point** [MARIN].

Point Smith: see **Quarry Point** [MARIN-SAN FRANCISCO].

Point Stephens: see **Point Richmond** [CONTRA COSTA] (1).

Point Stephenson: see **Middle Point** [CONTRA COSTA].

Point Stuart: see **Stuart Point** [MARIN].

Point Thompson: see **Mare Island** [SOLANO].

Point Tiburon [MARIN]: *promontory,* 2 miles east-northeast of downtown Sausalito on the northwest side of Raccoon Strait (lat. 37°52'20" N, long. 122°26'55" W); the promontory is at Tiburon. Named on San Francisco North (1956) 7.5' quadrangle. Called Punta de Tiburon in Spanish times—*tiburon* means "shark" in Spanish (Gudde, 1949, p. 361).

Point Wall [SOLANO]: *promontory,* 5.5 miles south-southwest of Birds Landing (2) along Suisun Bay on Van Sickle Island (lat. 38° 03'10" N, long. 121°53'20" W). Named on Honker Bay (1953) 7.5' quadrangle. Called Wall Pt. on Ringgold's (1850c) map.

Point Wise [SOLANO]: *promontory,* 6 miles south-southwest of Birds Landing (2) along Suisun Bay on Chipps Island (lat. 38° 03' N, long. 121°53'50" W). Named on Honker Bay (1953) 7.5' quadrangle.

Pole Mountain [SONOMA]: *peak,* 2.5 miles southwest of Cazadero (lat. 38°30'20" N, long. 123°07'10" W; sec. 30, T 8 N, R 11 W). Altitude 2204 feet. Named on Cazadero (1978) 7.5' quadrangle.

Pole Mountain Creek [SONOMA]: *stream,* flows 2.25 miles to Ward Creek 6 miles east-northeast of Fort Ross (lat. 38°32'05" N, long. 123°08'05" W; sec. 13, T 8 N, R 12 W); the stream heads north of Pole Mountain. Named on Cazadero (1978) and Fort Ross (1978) 7.5' quadrangles.

Polhemus Creek [SAN MATEO]: *stream,* flows 1.5 miles to San Mateo Creek 2.5 miles south-southwest of downtown San Mateo (lat. 37°31'55" N, long. 122°21' W). Named on San Mateo (1956) 7.5' quadrangle. The canyon of the stream is called Alms House Canyon on San Mateo (1915) 15' quadrangle, which shows an alms house near the head of the canyon. C.B. Polhemus had a ranch along the stream in the 1860's and 1870's

(Brown, p. 70).

Pomar [SANTA CLARA]: *locality,* nearly 3 miles northwest of Coyote along Southern Pacific Railroad (lat. 37°14'30" N, long. 121°46'40" W). Named on Los Gatos (1919) 15' quadrangle.

Pomponio: see **Camp Pomponio** [SAN MATEO].

Pomponio Beach [SAN MATEO]: *beach,* 2.5 miles south-southwest of the village of San Gregorio along the coast (lat. 37°17'30" N, long. 122°24'20" W); the beach is south of the mouth of Pomponio Creek. Named on San Gregorio (1961) 7.5' quadrangle.

Pomponio Creek [SAN MATEO]: *stream,* flows 7 miles to the sea 2.25 miles south-southwest of the village of San Gregorio (lat. 37° 17'50" N, long. 122°24'20" W). Named on La Honda (1961) and San Gregorio (1961) 7.5' quadrangles. The name commemorates Jose Pomponio Lupugrim, a renegade neophyte Indian of Spanish times; the ridge at the head of the stream was called Cuchillo de Pomponio, or Pomponio Ridge (Stanger, 1963, p. 29).

Pomponio Reservoir [SAN MATEO]: *lake,* 1250 feet long, behind a dam on Pomponio Creek 3 miles southwest of La Honda (lat. 37° 17'25" N, long. 122°18'45" W; near W line sec. 28, T 7 S, R 4 W). Named on La Honda (1961) 7.5' quadrangle.

Pomponio Ridge: see **Pomponio Creek** [SAN MATEO].

Pool Creek [SONOMA]: *stream,* flows 8 miles to Windsor Creek 6.5 miles south-southeast of Healdsburg (lat. 38°31'20" N, long. 122° 49'50" W; sec. 23, T 8 N, R 9 W). Named on Healdsburg (1955) and Mark West Springs (1958) 7.5' quadrangles. United States Board on Geographic Names (1967c, p. 5) approved the name "Wright Creek" for a stream that flows 3 miles to Pool Creek 2.4 miles east of Windsor (lat. 38°32'48" N, long. 122°46'17" W); the name commemorates John Wright, a pioneer rancher of the neighborhood.

Pool Ridge [SONOMA]: *ridge,* south-southeast- to south-trending, 1 mile long, 1.25 miles west-northwest of Guerneville (lat. 38°30'45" N, long. 123°01' W). Named on Cazadero (1978) 7.5' quadrangle. Duncans Mills (1943) 7.5' quadrangle has the name on a ridge located 2.25 miles west-southwest of Guerneville. The name "Pool" is for a pioneer family (Clar, p. 87).

Poor Man's Flat: see **Windsor** [SONOMA].

Pope Creek [NAPA]: *stream,* flows 17 miles to Putah Creek 14 miles east-northeast of Saint Helena in Lake Berryessa (lat. 38°37'25" N, long. 122°15'55" W); the stream goes through Pope Valley. Named on Aetna Springs (1958), Chiles Valley (1958), and Walter Springs (1959) 7.5' quadrangles.

Pope Mineral Spring: see **Samuel Springs** [NAPA].

Pope Valley [NAPA]:

(1) *valley,* 9 miles north-northeast of Saint Helena (lat. 38°37' N, long. 122°24'30" W); the valley is on Locoallomi grant, and partly along Pope Creek. Named on Aetna Springs (1958), Chiles Valley (1958), and Saint Helena (1960) 7.5' quadrangles. The name commemorates William Pope, who received Locoallomi grant in 1841 (Menefee, p. 170).

(2) *settlement,* 8 miles north-northeast of Saint Helena along the south edge of Pope Valley (1) (lat. 38°36'55" N, long. 122°25'35" W). Named on Saint Helena (1960) 7.5' quadrangle. Postal authorities established Pope Valley post office in 1863 (Frickstad, p. 111).

Port Chicago [CONTRA COSTA]: *town,* 6.5 miles east-northeast of Martinez (lat. 38°02'45" N, long. 122°01'10" W). Named on Port Chicago (1959) 7.5' quadrangle. The site is abandoned and unnamed on Vine Hill (1959) 7.5' quadrangle. Karquines (1898) 15' quadrangle shows a place called Bay Point situated along Southern Pacific Railroad at the place, but United States Board on Geographic Names (1934, p. 3) rejected this name. Postal authorities established Baypoint post office in 1901, changed the name to Port Chicago in 1931, and discontinued it in 1969 (Salley, p. 16, 176). Ringgold's (1850b) map shows Pt. Sherman on the coast north of the later site of Port Chicago.

Port Chicago Reach [CONTRA COSTA-SOLANO]: *channel,* 7.5 miles east-northeast of Martinez in Suisun Bay on Contra Costa-Solano County line (lat. 38°03'30" N, long. 122°00'15" W); the feature is northeast of the site of Port Chicago. Named on Vine Hill (1959) 7.5' quadrangle.

Port Costa [CONTRA COSTA]: *village,* 3.5 miles northwest of Martinez (lat. 38°02'45" N, long. 122°11' W). Named on Benicia (1959) 7.5' quadrangle. Postal authorities established Port Costa post office in 1881 (Frickstad, p. 23). Ringgold's (1850a) map shows Pt. Elliot located along the shore at or near the site of present Port Costa.

Porter Creek [SONOMA]:

(1) *stream,* flows 6.5 miles to Russian River 6.25 miles east of Guerneville (lat. 38°30'55" N, long. 122°52'55" W; sec. 29, T 8 N, R 9 W). Named on Guerneville (1955) 7.5' quadrangle.

(2) *stream,* flows 1 mile to Buckeye Creek (2) 2 miles north-northeast of Annapolis (lat. 38°44'50" N, long. 123°21'15" W; sec. 6, T 10 N, R 13 W). Named on Ornbaun Valley (1960) 15' quadrangle, and on Annapolis (1977) 7.5' quadrangle.

(3) *stream,* flows 8 miles to Mark West Creek 1 mile east of Mark West Springs (lat. 38°32'50" N, long. 122°42'10" W; near SW cor. sec. 12, T 8 N, R 8 W). Named on Calistoga (1958) and Mark West Springs (1958) 7.5' quadrangles. Jerry Porter was the first known settler in the neighborhood (Archuleta, p. 29).

Porterfield Creek [SONOMA]: *stream,* formed by the confluence of North Branch and South Branch, flows 1.5 miles to the flood plain of Russian River 1.25 miles southeast of Cloverdale (lat. 38°47'20" N, long. 123°00'05" W). Named on Cloverdale (1960) 7.5' quadrangle. North Branch is 1.25 miles long and South Branch is 1.5 miles long; both branches are named on Cloverdale (1960) 7.5' quadrangle.

Portezuel [SANTA CLARA]: *pass,* 4 miles southeast of New Almaden at the head of Cañada Garcia (lat. 37°08'15" N, long. 121°45'50" W). Named on Santa Teresa Hills (1953) 7.5' quadrangle.

Portezuela de Buenos Ayres: see **Corral Hollow** [ALAMEDA].

Port of Benicia: see **Benicia** [SOLANO].

Port of Redwood City [SAN MATEO]: *locality,* 2 miles north-northeast of downtown Redwood City along Redwood Creek (lat. 37°30'45" N, long. 122°12'30" W). Named on Redwood Point (1959) 7.5' quadrangle.

Portola: see **Portola Valley** [SAN MATEO] (2).

Portola-Crespi Valley: see **Portola Valley** [SAN MATEO] (1).

Portola Valley [SAN MATEO]:

(1) *valley,* 7 miles south of downtown Redwood City along Sausal Creek (lat. 37°23' N, long. 122°13'45" W). Named on Mindego Hill (1961) and Palo Alto (1961) 7.5' quadrangles. The name stems from the designation "Portola-Crespi Valley" proposed in 1886 for the series of valleys between Crystal Springs and Searsville (Hoover, Rensch, and Rensch, p. 402).

(2) *town,* 7 miles south of downtown Redwood City in Portola Valley (1) (lat. 37°23' N, long. 122°13'45" W). Named on Mindego Hill (1961) and Palo Alto (1961) 7.5' quadrangles. Palo Alto (1953) 7.5' quadrangle has the name "Portola" at the place. Postal authorities established Portola post office in 1894 and discontinued it in 1901; they established Portola Valley post office in 1955 (Salley, p. 176). The town incorporated in 1964.

Port Rumyantsev: see **Bodega Bay** [MARIN-SONOMA].

Port San Jose: see **Alviso** [SANTA CLARA].

Portuguese Beach [SONOMA]: *beach,* 5.25 miles south-southeast of Jenner along the coast (lat. 38°22'50" N, long. 123°04'50" W). Named on Duncans Mills (1979) 7.5' quadrangle.

Portuguese Canyon [NAPA]: *canyon,* 3.5 miles long, opens into the canyon of Putah Creek 10 miles south-southeast of Berryessa Peak (lat. 38°31'05" N, long. 122°08'20" W; sec. 24, T 8 N, R 3 W). Named on Lake Berryessa (1959) 7.5' quadrangle. Water of Lake Berryessa covers the lower part of the canyon.

Portuguese Canyon: see **Little Portuguese Canyon** [NAPA].

Posita Creek: see **Arroyo las Positas** [ALAMEDA].

Posolmi [SANTA CLARA]: *land grant,* at Moffett Field. Named on Mountain View (1961) 7.5' quadrangle. An Indian called Lupe (or Lopez) Iñigo received the land in 1844; the Indian and Robert Walkinshaw claimed 1696 acres patented in 1881 (Cowan, p. 62; Cowan listed the grant under the designation "Posolmi, (or Posolomi, or) y Pozitas de las Animas").

Potatoe Cove: see **Tennessee Cove** [MARIN].

Potatoe Patch Ridge: see **Mohrhardt Ridge** [SONOMA].

Potato Hill [NAPA]: *peak,* 4.5 miles northeast of Calistoga (lat. 38° 37'10" N, long. 122°30'50" W; sec. 22, T 9 N, R 6 W). Named on Calistoga (1958) 7.5' quadrangle.

Potato Patch: see **The Potato Patch** [SAN MATEO].

Potatopatch Shoal [MARIN]: *shoal,* west of Point Bonita beyond Bonita Channel (lat. 37°49'20" N, long. 122°34'45" W). Named on Point Bonita (1954) 7.5' quadrangle. Mount Tamalpais (1950) 15' quadrangle has both the names "Potato Patch Shoal" and "Four Fathom Bank" for the feature. The name "Potatopatch Shoal" is said to have originated from the loss of potatoes from the decks of schooners from Bodega Bay as they crossed the feature (United States Coast and Geodetic Survey, p. 124).

Potrero: see **Point Potrero** [CONTRA COSTA]; **Point Potrero**, under **Point Isabel** [CONTRA COSTA].

Potrero de los Cerritos [ALAMEDA]: *land grant,* at and near Fremont. Named on Newark (1959) 7.5' quadrangle. Tomas Pacheco Alviso and Agustin Alviso received 3 leagues in 1844 and claimed 10,610 acres patented in 1866 (Cowan, p. 26).

Potrero de Santa Clara: see **El Potrero de Santa Clara** [SANTA CLARA].

Potrero District [SAN FRANCISCO]: *district,* 2 miles southeast of San Francisco civic center (lat. 37°45'30" N, long. 121°24' W); the district is around Potrero Hill. Named on San Francisco North (1956) 7.5' quadrangle.

Potrero Hill [SAN FRANCISCO]: *hill,* 2.25 miles south-southwest of Rincon Point (lat. 37°45'25" N, long. 122°23'55" W); the hill is west of Potrero Point. Named on San Francisco North (1956) 7.5' quadrangle. Called Potrero Nuevo on San Francisco (1899, reprinted 1913) 15' quadrangle.

Potrero Hills [SOLANO]: *range,* center 4.5 miles west-southwest of Denverton (lat. 38°12'30" N, long. 121°58'45" W). Named on Denverton (1953) and Fairfield South (1949) 7.5' quadrangles.

Potrero Hills: see **Coyote Hills** [ALAMEDA].

Potrero Meadows [MARIN]: *area,* 5.25 miles southwest of downtown San Rafael (lat. 37°55'30" N, long. 122°36'25" W). Named on San Rafael

(1954) 7.5' quadrangle.

Potrero Nuevo: see **Potrero Hill** [SAN FRANCISCO].

Potrero Point [SAN FRANCISCO]: *promontory,* 2 miles south of Rincon Point along San Francisco Bay (lat. 37°45'35" N, long. 122°22'50" W). Named on San Francisco North (1956) 7.5' quadrangle. Called Pt. San Quentin on Wackenreuder's (1861) map.

Potrero Point: see **Dumbarton Point** [ALAMEDA].

Potrero San Pablo [CONTRA COSTA]: *ridge,* extends 5.5 miles southeast from San Pablo Point to Potrero Point (present Point Potrero) (center near lat. 37°56' N, long. 122°23'45" W). Named on San Francisco (1899) 15' quadrangle. Before fences were common, the ridge was a convenient place to pasture horses because it was separated from the mainland by marshes (Dilller and others, p. 82)—*potrero* means "pasture-ground" in Spanish.

Potter's Beach: see **Tunitas Beach** [SAN MATEO].

Pottery [ALAMEDA]: *locality,* 5.25 miles south of Midway in Corral Hollow (lat. 37°38'20" N, long. 121°34'15" W; sec. 30, T 3 S, R 4 E). Site named on Midway (1953) 7.5' quadrangle. John Treadwell and James Treadwell built a brick and pottery plant at the site in the 1890's; they gave the name "Pottery" to the place, which was situated at Walden Spur on the rail line in Corral Hollow (Hoover, Rensch, and Rensch, p. 377).

Poverty Flat [SANTA CLARA]: *area,* 2.25 miles south-southeast of Mount Sizer along Little Coyote Creek (lat. 37°10'50" N, long. 121°30' W; sec. 2, T 9 S, R 4 E). Named on Mississippi Creek (1955) and Mount Sizer (1955) 7.5' quadrangles.

Poverty Ridge [SANTA CLARA]: *ridge,* northwest-trending, 5 miles long, 2.5 miles west-northwest of Mount Day (lat. 37°25'45" N, long. 121°44'15" W). Named on Calaveras Reservoir (1961) and Mount Day (1955) 7.5' quadrangles.

Pratt Valley [NAPA]: *valley,* 2.5 miles north-northwest of Saint Helena (lat. 38°32'25" N, long. 122°28'45" W). Named on Saint Helena (1960) 7.5' quadrangle.

Presidio: see **Presidio Military Reservation** [SAN FRANCISCO].

Presidio Anchorage: see **Fort Point** [SAN FRANCISCO].

Presidio Military Reservation [SAN FRANCISCO]: *military installation,* south of the Golden Gate at Fort Point (lat. 37°48' N, long. 122°28' W). Named on San Francisco North (1956) 7.5' quadrangle. Called Presidio of San Francisco on San Francisco (1942) 15' quadrangle. Spaniards established the presidio in 1776 and it became a permanent United States military installation in 1847 (Frazer, p. 30). Postal authorities established Presidio post office in 1888 (Frickstad, p. 159).

Presidio of San Francisco: see **Presidio Military Reservation** [SAN FRANCISCO].

Presidio Shoal [SAN FRANCISCO]: *shoal,* 1 mile east-northeast of Fort Point at the east end of the Golden Gate (lat. 37°48'55" N, long. 122°27'20" W). Named on San Francisco North (1956) 7.5' quadrangle.

Press Creek [SONOMA]: *stream,* flows about 2.25 miles to Porter Creek (1) 5.25 miles east-northeast of Guerneville (lat. 38°32'20" N, long. 122°54'45" W; sec. 13, T 8 N, R 10 W). Named on Guerneville (1955) 7.5' quadrangle.

Press Valley [SONOMA]: *area,* 5.5 miles northeast of Guerneville (lat. 38°32'50" N, long. 122°54'45" W); the place is along Press Creek. Named on Guerneville (1955) 7.5' quadrangle.

Preston [SONOMA]: *locality,* 2 miles north of Cloverdale along Northwestern Pacific Railroad (lat. 38°50'10" N, long. 123°00'55" W; near N line sec. 6, T 11 N, R 10 W). Named on Cloverdale (1960) 7.5' quadrangle. Postal authorities established Preston post office in 1890 and discontinued it in 1941; the name was for Madam Emily Preston, a cult leader (Salley, p. 178). Water from Barcal Spring, located 2 miles east of Preston (sec. 32, T 12 N, R 10 W), was bottled for sale (Bradley, p. 335).

Preston: see **Preston Point** [MARIN].

Preston Island: see **Roe Island** [SOLANO].

Preston Lake [SONOMA]: *lake,* 500 feet long, 3 miles north of Cloverdale (lat. 38°51' N, long. 123°00'50" W; sec. 31, T 12 N, R 10 W); the lake is 1 mile north of Preston. Named on Cloverdale (1960) 7.5' quadrangle.

Preston Point [MARIN]: *promontory,* 3 miles south-southwest of Tomales on the northeast side of Tomales Bay (lat. 38°12'40" N, long. 122°56' W). Named on Tomales (1954) 7.5' quadrangle. Postal authorities established Preston post office at the place in 1863 and discontinued it in 1866; the name was for Robert J. Preston, first postmaster, who operated a wharf and store (Salley, p. 178).

Preston Point [SOLANO]: *promontory,* 6.5 miles east-northeast of Benicia along Suisun Bay at the west end of Roe Island (lat. 38°04'15" N, long. 122°02'45" W). Named on Vine Hill (1959) 7.5' quadrangle. Called Pt. Green on Ringgold's (1850c) map, which has the name "Preston I." for present Roe Island.

Preston Point Reach [CONTRA COSTA-SOLANO]: *channel,* 5.5 miles northeast of Martinez in Suisun Bay on Contra Costa-Solano County line (lat. 38°03'50" N, long. 122°03'10" W); the feature is southeast of Preston Point. Named on Vine Hill (1959) 7.5' quadrangle.

Priest Rock [SANTA CLARA]: *peak,* 2 miles south-southeast of Los Gatos (lat. 37°11'45" N, long. 121°57'50" W). Altitude 1762 feet. Named on Los Gatos (1953) 7.5' quadrangle.

Priest Soda Springs: see **Samuel Springs** [NAPA].

Princeton [SAN MATEO]: *town,* 3.5 miles south of Montara Knob at the north end of Half Moon Bay (1) (lat. 37°30'15" N, long. 122° 29'10" W). Named on Montara Mountain (1956) 7.5' quadrangle. The place also was known as Old Landing—produce was shipped from there by schooner to San Francisco (Hoover, Rensch, and Rensch, p. 394). The name "Princeton" came from the Princeton-by-the-Sea subdivision of 1905 to 1906; the place sometimes was called Long Bridge in the early days (Brown, p. 73).

Pritchard Hill [NAPA]: *settlement,* 5.5 miles north of Yountville (lat. 38°29'10" N, long. 122°20'45" W; sec. 6, T 7 N, R 4 W). Named on Yountville (1951) 7.5' quadrangle.

Pritchett Peaks [SONOMA]: *peaks,* along a ridge 4 miles north-northwest of Skaggs Springs (lat. 38°44'45" N, long. 123°03'30" W). Named on Cloverdale (1960) and Warm Springs Dam (1978) 7.5' quadrangles.

Promontory Island: see **Belvedere Island** [MARIN].

Proschold Resort [SONOMA]; *locality,* 1.25 mile east of Cazadero (lat. 38°31'40" N, long. 123°03'45" W; sec. 22, T 8 N, R 11 W). Named on Cazadero (1943) 7.5' quadrangle.

Prospect Creek [SANTA CLARA]: *stream,* flows nearly 2 miles to Calabazas Creek 2 miles north of downtown Saratoga (lat. 37°17'20" N, long. 122°02'05" W). Named on Cupertino (1961, photorevised 1968 and 1973) 7.5' quadrangle.

Prospect Island [SOLANO]: *area,* 7 miles north-northeast of Rio Vista in Yolo Bypass (lat. 38°15'45" N, long. 121°39'25" W); the place is east of Prospect Slough. Named on Liberty Island (1978) and Rio Vista (1978) 7.5' quadrangles.

Prospectors Gap [CONTRA COSTA]: *pass,* less than 0.5 mile north-northeast of Mount Diablo (lat. 37°53'10" N, long. 121°54'35" W; sec. 31, T 1 N, R 1 E). Named on Clayton (1953) 7.5' quadrangle.

Prospect Slough [SOLANO]: *water feature,* joins Cache Slough 5.5 miles north of Rio Vista (lat. 38°14'15" N, long. 121°40'45" W); the feature is west of Prospect Island. Named on Liberty Island (1978) and Rio Vista (1978) 7.5' quadrangles.

Prospect Spur: see **Meridian** [SANTA CLARA].

Providencia: see **Cañada de Herrera** [MARIN].

Pueblo Saint Joseph: see **San Jose** [SANTA CLARA].

Puerto de Don Gaspar: see **Drakes Bay** [MARIN].

Puerto de la Asunta: see **Southampton Bay** [SOLANO].

Puerto de la Bodega: see **Bodega Bay** [MARIN-SONOMA].

Puerto de los Balleneros: see **Richardson Bay** [MARIN].

Puerto de los Reyes: see **Drakes Bay** [MARIN].

Puerto de San Francisco: see **Drakes Bay** [MARIN]; **Gulf of the Farallones** [MARIN-SAN FRANCISCO-SAN MATEO].

Puerto Dulce: see **Suisun Bay** [CONTRA COSTA-SOLANO].

Puerto Zuelo Lagunitas: see **Little Carson Creek** [MARIN].

Pulgas [SAN MATEO]: *land grant,* near Belmont, Redwood City, and Menlo Park. Named on Mountain View (1961), Palo Alto (1961), Redwood Point (1959), San Mateo (1956), and Woodside (1961) 7.5' quadrangles. United States Board on Geographic Names (1933, p. 623) rejected the names "De Las Pulgas," "Las Pulgas," and "Rancho de las Pulgas" for the grant. Luis Antonio Arguello received 4 leagues about 1824 and 1835; Maria Arguello claimed 35,240 acres patented in 1857 (Cowan, p. 64; Perez, p. 84).

Pulgas Creek [SAN MATEO]: *stream,* flows 2 miles to lowlands along San Francisco Bay 5.5 miles southeast of downtown San Mateo in San Carlos (lat. 37°30'10" N, long. 122°15'25" W). Named on Redwood Point (1959), San Mateo (1956), and Woodside (1961) 7.5' quadrangles. The stream was called Arroyo de las Pulgas in Spanish times, and more recently it was called San Carlos Creek and Arroyo Creek (Brown, p. 73).

Pulgas Ranch Embarcadero: see **Redwood City** [SAN MATEO].

Pulgas Ridge [SAN MATEO]: *ridge,* northwest-trending, 2 miles long, 3.5 miles south-southwest of downtown San Mateo (lat. 37° 31'05" N, long. 122°20'50" W). Named on San Mateo (1956) 7.5' quadrangle.

Pullman [CONTRA COSTA]: *locality,* less than 1 mile south-southeast of present Richmond civic center along Southern Pacific Railroad (lat. 37°55'30" N, long. 122°20'25" W). Named on San Francisco (1915) 15' quadrangle.

Pulse Canyon [SANTA CLARA]: *canyon,* drained by a stream that flows 1.5 miles to Arroyo Mocho 2 miles east-southeast of Eylar Mountain (lat. 37°27'40" N, long. 121°31' W; at N line sec. 34, T 5 S, R 4 E). Named on Eylar Mountain (1955) and Mount Boardman (1955) 7.5' quadrangles.

Pumpkin Flat [NAPA]: *area,* nearly 4 miles south-southeast of Mount Vaca (lat. 38°20'55" N, long. 122°04'50" W; sec. 21, T 6 N, R 2 W). Named on Fairfield North (1951) 7.5' quadrangle.

Punta Alvisadera: see **Point Avisadero** [SAN FRANCISCO].

Punta Año Nueva: see **Año Nuevo Point** [SAN MATEO].

Punta Bonete: see **Point Bonita** [MARIN].

Punta de Almejas: see **Pinole Point** [CONTRA COSTA]; **Point San Pedro** [SAN MATEO].

Punta de Año Nuevo: see **Año Nuevo Point** [SAN MATEO].

Punta de Baulenes: see **Duxbury Point** [MARIN].
Punta de Bonetas: see **Point Bonita** [MARIN].
Punta de Concha: see **Hunters Point** [SAN FRANCISCO].
Punta de la Ballena: see **Pigeon Point** [SAN MATEO].
Punta de la Loma Alta: see **Telegraph Hill** [SAN FRANCISCO].
Punta del Angel Custodio: see **Point San Pedro** [SAN MATEO].
Punta del Angel de la Guarda: see **Point Lobos** [SAN FRANCISCO].
Punta del Ano Nuevo [SAN MATEO]: *land grant,* at and north of Año Nuevo Point near the coast. Named on Año Nuevo (1955), Franklin Point (1955), and Pigeon Point (1955) 7.5' quadrangles. Simon Castro received 4 leagues in 1842; Maria A. Pico claimed 17,753 acres patented in 1857 (Cowan, p. 16; Perez, p. 84).
Punta del Cantil Blanco: see **Fort Point** [SAN FRANCISCO].
Punta del Castillo: see **Fort Point** [SAN FRANCISCO].
Punta del Embarcadero: see **Telegraph Hill** [SAN FRANCISCO].
Punta de los Caballos: see **Cavallo Point** [MARIN].
Punta de los Lobos: see **Point Lobos** [SAN FRANCISCO].
Punta de los Reyes: see **Point Reyes** [MARIN] (1).
Punta de Quintin: see **Point San Quentin** [MARIN].
Punta de Reyes: see **Point Reyes** [MARIN] (1).
Punta de San Antonio: see **Point San Pablo** [CONTRA COSTA].
Punta de San Carlos: see **Lime Point** [MARIN].
Punta de San Josef: see **Black Point** [SAN FRANCISCO].
Punta de San Pablo: see **Point San Pablo** [CONTRA COSTA].
Punta de San Pedro: see **Point San Pedro** [MARIN].
Punta de Santiago: see **Point Bonita** [MARIN].
Punta de Tiburon: see **Point Tiburon** [MARIN].
Punta Diablo: see **Point Diablo** [MARIN].
Punta Medanos: see **Black Point** [SAN FRANCISCO].
Punta Rena: see **Sand Point** [MARIN].
Punta San Bruno: see **Point San Bruno** [SAN MATEO].
Punta San Matheo: see **Coyote Point** [SAN MATEO].
Punta San Pablo: see **Point San Pablo** [CONTRA COSTA].
Punta San Pedro: see **Point San Pedro** [MARIN].
Punto Cavallos: see **Cavallo Point** [MARIN].
Punto de los Reyes: see **Point Reyes** [MARIN] (1).
Punto Diavolo: see **Point Diablo** [MARIN].
Purisima [SAN MATEO]: *settlement,* 4 miles south of the town of Half Moon Bay (lat. 37°24'20" N, long. 122°25'05" W); the place is near the mouth of Purisima Creek. Named on Santa Cruz (1902) 30' quadrangle. United States Board on Geographic Names (1960a, p. 18) rejected the form "Purissima" for the name. Postal authorities established Purissama (also called Purisima) post office in 1868, discontinued it in 1869, reestablished it in 1872, and discontinued it in 1901 (Salley, p. 179).
Purisima Creek [SAN MATEO]: *stream,* flows 7.5 miles to the sea 4 miles south of downtown Half Moon Bay (lat. 37°24'15" N, long. 122°25'30" W). Named on Half Moon Bay (1961) and Woodside (1961) 7.5' quadrangles. United States Board on Geographic Names (1933, p. 624) rejected the form "Purissima Creek" for the name. Spaniards called the stream Arroyo de la Purissima; the lower part of the canyon of the creek is called Purissima Valley (Brown, p. 74).
Purisima Creek: see **Deer Creek** [SANTA CLARA].
Purisima Rock: see **Año Nuevo Point** [SAN MATEO].
Purissima: see **Purisima** [SAN MATEO].
Purissima Valley: see **Purisima Creek** [SAN MATEO].
Purrington Creek [SONOMA]: *stream,* flows 3.5 miles to Green Valley Creek 3.5 miles east-northeast of Occidental (lat. 38°26'15" N, long. 122°53'20" W). Named on Camp Meeker (1954) 7.5' quadrangle.
Puta Creek: see **Putah Creek** [NAPA-SOLANO].
Putah: see **Dixon** [SOLANO].
Putah Creek [NAPA-SOLANO]: *stream,* heads in Lake County and flows 60 miles through Napa County and along Solano-Yolo County line to Yolo County 8.5 miles northeast of Dixon (lat. 38° 32'15" N, long. 121°42'35" W). Named on Aetna Springs (1958), Allendale (1953), Chiles Valley (1958), Davis (1952), Jericho Valley (1958), Lake Berryessa (1959), Merritt (1952), Monticello Dam (1959), Mount Vaca (1951), Walter Springs (1959) and Winters (1953) 7.5' quadrangles. Called Puta Cr. on Eddy's (1854) map, but United States Board on Geographic Names (1933, p. 625) rejected this form of the name. Williamson (1857, p. 39) referred to Putos creek. According to Gudde (1949, p. 276), the name "Putah" is from the designation of Indians who lived along the stream, but Kroeber (p. 56) rejected an Indian origin for the name, and attributed it to *puta,* which means "harlot" in Spanish. South Fork diverges southeast from the main stream 6 miles north-northeast of Dixon and flows 5 miles to Yolo County 8.5 miles northeast of Dixon; it is named on Davis (1952) and Merritt (1952) 7.5' quadrangles.
Putnam Peak [SOLANO]: *peak,* 4.5 miles northeast of Mount Vaca (lat. 38°26'45" N, long. 122°02'30" W); near NE cor. sec. 23, T 7 N, R 2 W). Altitude 1224 feet. Named on Mount Vaca (1951) 7.5' quadrangle. United States Board on Geographic Names (1933, p. 625) rejected the names "Millers Peak" and "Putnams Peak" for the feature. According to Gudde (1949, p. 276), the name "Putnam Peak" probably is for Ansel W. Putnam, who settled at Vacaville before 1867.
Putnams Peak: see **Putnam Peak** [SOLANO].
Putos Creek: see **Putah Creek** [NAPA-SOLANO].
Pyramid Hill: see **Mount Zion** [CONTRA COSTA].
Pyramid Point: see **Selby** [CONTRA COSTA].
Pyramid Rock [SAN FRANCISCO]: *rock,* less than 1 mile northeast of Point Lobos, and 500 feet offshore at Lands End (lat. 37°47'25" N, long. 122°30'20" W). Named on San Francisco North (1956) 7.5' quadrangle.
Pyramid Rock [SANTA CLARA]: *peak,* 3.25 miles west of Isabel Valley (lat. 37°18'20" N, long. 121°35'45" W). Altitude 4026 feet. Named on Isabel Valley (1955) 7.5' quadrangle.

– Q –

Quarries [SONOMA]: *locality,* 2.5 miles north of Sears Point along Northwestern Pacific Railroad (lat. 38°11'10" N, long. 122°26'20" W). Named on Mare Island (1916) 15' quadrangle. Postal authorities established Quarries post office in 1908 and discontinued it in 1926 (Frickstad, p. 197).
Quarry: see **Roblar** [SONOMA].
Quarry Beach: see **Quarry Point** [MARIN].
Quarry Canyon [NAPA]: *canyon,* drained by a stream that flows 2.5 miles to Lake Berryessa 8.5 miles south-southwest of Berryessa Peak (lat. 38°32'50" N, long. 122°14'05" W). Named on Chiles Valley (1958) and Lake Berryessa (1959) 7.5' quadrangles.
Quarry Point [MARIN-SAN FRANCISCO]: *promontory,* along the east shore of Angel Island on Marin-San Francisco County line (lat. 37°51'45" N, long. 122°25'05" W). Named on San Francisco North (1956) 7.5' quadrangle. Called Pt. Smith on Ringgold's (1850a) map. Army engineers opened a stone quarry at the point about 1890 (Bradley, p. 254). United States Board on Geographic Names (1980, p. 4) approved the name "Quarry Beach" for the beach that lies southeast of Quarry Point (lat. 37°51'33" N, long. 122°25'12" W).
Queens Peak [SONOMA]: *peak,* 5.5 miles north of Guerneville (lat. 38°34'50" N, long. 122°59'15" W; sec. 32, T 9 N, R 10 W). Altitude 1948 feet. Named on Guerneville (1955) 7.5' quadrangle.
Quercus Pass: see **Kirker Pass** [CONTRA COSTA] (1).
Quereus Pass: see **Kirker Pass** [CONTRA COSTA] (1).
Quicksilver Flat [SONOMA]: *area,* 3.5 miles west of Big Mountain (lat. 38°42'40" N, long. 123°12'45" W; sec. 17, T 10 N, R 12 W). Named on Tombs Creek (1978) 7.5' quadrangle.
Quimby Creek [SANTA CLARA]: *stream,* flows 1.25 miles to lowlands 1.5 miles northeast of Evergreen (lat. 37°19' N, long. 121°45'45" W). Named on San Jose East (1961) 7.5' quadrangle.
Quimby Island [CONTRA COSTA]: *island,* 2.25 miles long, 3.5 miles east-northeast of the settlement of Bethel Island between Old River and Sheep Slough (lat. 38°01'30" N, long. 121°34'15" W). Named on Bouldin Island (1978) 7.5' quadrangle.
Quinlan Gulch [SONOMA]: *canyon,* drained by a stream that flows 2 miles to Cheney Gulch 2 miles east-southeast of the village of Bodega Bay (lat. 38°19'05" N, long. 123°00'55" W). Named on Bodega Head (1972) 7.5' quadrangle.
Quito [SANTA CLARA]: *land grant,* northeast of Saratoga. Named on Cupertino (1961) and San Jose West (1961) 7.5' quadrangles. Jose Zenon Fernandez and Jose Noriega received 3 leagues in 1841; Jose M. Alviso and others claimed 13,310 acres patented in 1866 (Cowan, p. 66). According to Butler (p. 95), the grant originally was known by the name "Tito" for a neophyte Indian who ran a Santa Clara mission dairy ranch in the neighborhood in the 1830's.
Quito Creek: see **Saratoga Creek** [SANTA CLARA].

– R –

Rabbit Knoll [SONOMA]: *relief feature,* 6.25 miles northeast of Cazadero (lat. 38°35'55" N, long. 122°00'25" W; sec. 30, T 9 N, R 10 W). Named on Cazadero (1978) 7.5' quadrangle.
Raccoon Cove: see **Hospital Cove** [MARIN].
Raccoon Strait [MARIN]: *water feature,* 2.5 miles east-northeast of downtown Sausalito between Angel Island and Tiburon Peninsula (lat. 37°52'05" N, long. 122°26'35" W). Named on San Francisco North (1956) and San Quentin (1959) 7.5' quadrangles. The name commemorates the British ship *Racoon,* which visited San Francisco Bay in 1814 (Mason, 1976b, p. 214), but United States Board on Geographic Names (1933, p. 630) rejected the form "Racoon Strait" for the name.
Racetrack: see **The Racetrack** [SONOMA].
Rack Creek [SOLANO]: *water feature,* joins Honker Bay 4 miles south-southwest of Birds Landing (2) (lat. 38°05' N, long. 121°54'35" W). Named on Honker Bay (1953) 7.5' quadrangle.
Rafael Village [MARIN]: *district,* nearly 3 miles south-southeast of down-

town Novato (lat. 38°04'10" N, long. 122°33'15" W). Named on Novato (1954) 7.5' quadrangle.

Rag Cañon: see **Wragg Canyon** [NAPA].

Rail Creek [SONOMA]: *stream,* flows 3.5 miles, partly in Mendocino County, to Dry Creek 7.5 miles west of Cloverdale (lat. 38°47'30" N, long. 123°09'15" W; near E line sec. 23, T 11 N, R 12 W). Named on Hopland (1960) 15' quadrangle. Called Peters Creek on Hopland (1944) 15' quadrangle.

Railroad Slough [SONOMA]: *water feature,* joins Steamboat Slough 5.5 miles north-northeast of Sears Point (lat. 38°13'40" N, long. 122°25'25" W). Named on Sears Point (1951) 7.5' quadrangle.

Rainbow Slough [SONOMA]: *water feature,* 4.5 miles northeast of Sears Point (lat. 38°11'25" N, long. 122°22'30" W). Named on Cuttings Wharf (1949) and Sears Point (1951) 7.5' quadrangles.

Raleez Creek: see **Reliez Valley** [CONTRA COSTA].

Raliez [CONTRA COSTA]: *locality,* 2.25 miles west-southwest of present Walnut Creek civic center (lat. 37°53'15" N, long. 122°05'45" W); the place is near the mouth of present Reliez Valley. Named on Concord (1943) 15' quadrangle.

Ralphine: see **Lake Ralphine** [SONOMA].

Ramage Peak [ALAMEDA]: *peak,* 11 miles east of downtown Oakland (lat. 37°47'25" N, long. 122°04'05" W; sec. 3, T 2 S, R 2 W). Altitude 1401 feet. Named on Las Trampas Ridge (1959) 7.5' quadrangle. The name commemorates Charles Ramage, who owned the place (Mosier and Mosier, p. 70).

Ramal [SONOMA]: *locality,* 5.5 miles north-northeast of Sears Point along Southern Pacific Railroad (lat. 38°13'20" N, long. 122°23'40" W). Named on Sears Point (1951) 7.5' quadrangle.

Rancheria Creek [SONOMA]: *stream,* flows 6 miles to Warm Springs Creek 3 miles west-northwest of Skaggs Springs (lat. 38° 42'25" N, long. 123°04'40" W; near S line sec. 16, T 10 N, R 11 W). Named on Tombs Creek (1978) and Warm Springs Dam (1978) 7.5' quadrangles.

Rancheria Creek: see **Little Rancheria Creek** [SONOMA].

Ranchero Hill [SONOMA]: *peak,* 4 miles west-southwest of Big Mountain (lat. 38°41'40" N, long. 123°13' W; near SE cor. sec. 19, T 10 N, R 12 W). Altitude 1013 feet. Named on Tombs Creek (1978) 7.5' quadrangle.

Rancho de las Pulgas: see **Pulgas** [SAN MATEO].

Rancho Monticello [NAPA]: *locality,* 13 miles east-northeast of Saint Helena along Lake Berryessa (lat. 38°35'25" N, long. 122° 15'20" W). Named on Chiles Valley (1958) 7.5' quadrangle.

Raney Rock [NAPA]: *relief feature,* 6 miles west-northwest of Mount Vaca (lat. 38°26'45" N, long. 122°11'55" W; sec. 21, T 7 N, R 3 W). Named on Capell Valley (1951) 7.5' quadrangle.

Ransome [SAN MATEO]: *locality,* 3 miles northwest of present Montara Knob and 0.25 mile southeast of San Pedro Point (present Point San Pedro) along Ocean Shore Railroad (lat. 37°35'20" N, long. 122°31'05" W). Named on San Mateo (1915) 15' quadrangle.

Ransom Point [CONTRA COSTA]: *ridge,* extends 0.5 mile north-northwest from Mount Diablo (lat. 37°53'05" N, long. 121°54'50" W). Named on Clayton (1953) 7.5' quadrangle. The name commemorates Colonel Leander Ransom, who as deputy United States surveyor established Mount Diablo Base and Meridian lines in 1851 (United States Board on Geographic Names, 1933, p. 633).

Rat Rock [MARIN]: *rock,* 9.5 miles southeast of downtown Novato, and 300 feet offshore in San Pablo Bay (lat. 38°00'15" N, long. 122°27'40" W). Named on Petaluma Point (1959) 7.5' quadrangle.

Rattlesnake Butte [SANTA CLARA]: *peak,* 3.5 miles east-southeast of Mount Day (lat. 37°23'50" N, long. 121°38'40" W; on E line sec. 21, T 6 S, R 3 E). Named on Mount Day (1955) 7.5' quadrangle.

Rattlesnake Canyon [SONOMA]: *canyon,* 1.5 miles long, on upper reaches of Kellogg Creek above a point 1.25 miles west-southwest of Mount Saint Helena (lat. 38°39'40" N, long. 122°39'05" W; near NE cor. sec. 5, T 9 N, R 7 W). Named on Mount Saint Helena (1959) 7.5' quadrangle.

Rattlesnake Creek [MARIN]: *stream,* flows 1.25 miles to Redwood Creek 5.5 miles south-southwest of downtown San Rafael (lat. 37° 54'15" N, long. 122°35'20" W). Named on San Rafael (1954) 7.5' quadrangle.

Rattlesnake Ridge [NAPA]: *ridge,* generally north-northwest-trending, 3.25 miles long, 6.5 miles north of Saint Helena (lat. 38° 36' N, long. 122°29'45" W). Named on Calistoga (1958) and Saint Helena (1960) 7.5' quadrangles.

Rattlesnake Spring [NAPA]: *spring,* 6.5 miles north of Calistoga (lat. 38°40'20" N, long. 122°35'20" W; sec. 36, T 10 N, R 7 W). Named on Detert Reservoir (1958) 7.5' quadrangle.

Ratto Landing [NAPA]: *locality,* 3.5 miles northwest of Napa Junction along Napa River (lat. 38°13'55" N, long. 122°17'20" W). Named on Cuttings Wharf (1949, photorevised 1968) 7.5' quadrangle.

Ravenswood [SAN MATEO]: *locality,* 5 miles east of downtown Redwood City along Southern Pacific Railroad in East Palo Alto (lat. 37°28'35" N, long. 122°08'05" W). Named on Palo Alto (1961) 7.5' quadrangle. The name is from a town laid out in 1853 that failed to develop (Hoover, Rensch, and Rensch, p. 406). Palo Alto (1953) 7.5' quadrangle gives the alternate name "Ravenswood" for present East Palo Alto.

Ravenswood Point [SAN MATEO]: *promontory,* 5 miles east-northeast of downtown Redwood City along San Francisco Bay (lat. 37° 30'30" N, long. 122°08'15" W). Named on Redwood Point (1959) 7.5' quadrangle. The feature also was called West Point (Brown, p. 75, 99).

Ravenswood Slough [SAN MATEO]: *water feature,* enters San Francisco Bay 3.5 miles east-northeast of downtown Redwood City (lat. 37°30'10" N, long. 122°09'45" W). Named on Palo Alto (1961) and Redwood Point (1959) 7.5' quadrangles.

Ravenswood Wharf: see **Cooley Landing** [SAN MATEO].

Ray Hill: see **Rays Peak** [SAN MATEO].

Raynor Creek: see **Clear Creek** [SAN MATEO].

Rays Peak [SAN MATEO]: *peak,* 1.5 miles west-northwest of La Honda (lat. 37°19'45" N, long. 122°17'45" W). Altitude 1037 feet. Named on La Honda (1961) 7.5' quadrangle. Brown (p. 75) called the feature Ray Hill, and noted that Ray ranch was situated just east of the peak during and after the late 1860's.

Reclamation [SONOMA]: *locality,* 2 miles southwest of Sears Point along Northwestern Pacific Railroad (lat. 38°07'45" N, long. 122° 28'10" W). Named on Sears Point (1951) 7.5' quadrangle. Postal authorities established Reclamation post office in 1891 and discontinued it in 1903; the name was from a land-reclamation project (Salley, p. 182).

Recreation Flat [NAPA]: *area,* 5.5 miles northeast of Saint Helena (lat. 38°33'45" N, long. 122°24'10" W; sec. 10, T 8 N, R 5 W). Named on Saint Helena (1960) 7.5' quadrangle.

Rector [NAPA]: *locality,* 5.5 miles east of Yountville (lat. 38°25'05" N, long. 122°15'45" W). Named on Sonoma (1942) 15' quadrangle. Napa (1902) 30' quadrangle shows the place situated 1.5 miles farther west-northwest near the head of Rector Canyon (sec. 27, T 7 N, R 4 W). Postal authorities established Rector post office in 1896 and discontinued it in 1932; the name commemorates John P. Rector, an early settler in the neighborhood (Salley, p. 182).

Rector Canyon [NAPA]: *canyon,* nearly 4 miles long, opens into lowlands 2.5 miles north-northeast of Yountville (lat. 38°26'30" N, long. 122°20'55" W); Rector Creek drains the canyon. Named on Yountville (1951) 7.5' quadrangle.

Rector Creek [NAPA]: *stream,* flows 7 miles to Conn Creek 1.5 miles north of Yountville (lat. 38°25'45" N, long. 122°22'15" W). Named on Yountville (1951) 7.5' quadrangle.

Rector Reservoir [NAPA]: *lake,* behind a dam on Rector Creek 2.5 miles north-northeast of Yountville (lat. 38°26'30" N, long. 122°20'40" W; sec. 19, T 7 N, R 4 W). Named on Yountville (1951) 7.5' quadrangle.

Redbud Park [NAPA]: *locality,* 10.5 miles south-southeast of Berryessa Peak along Putah Creek (lat. 38°31'10" N, long. 122°08'10" W; near SE cor. sec. 24, T 8 N, R 3 W). Named on Capay (1945) 15' quadrangle. Water of Lake Berryessa now covers the site.

Red Hill [ALAMEDA]: *peak,* 3.5 miles west-northwest of downtown Newark (lat. 37°33'05" N, long. 122°05'35" W). Named on Newark (1948) 7.5' quadrangle.

Red Hill [MARIN]:

(1) *peak,* 7 miles west-northwest of downtown Novato (lat. 38° 09' N, long. 122°40'40" W). Altitude 1257 feet. Named on Petaluma (1953) 7.5' quadrangle.

(2) *peak,* 1.5 miles west-northwest of downtown San Rafael (lat. 37°58'45" N, long. 122°33'35" W). Altitude 464 feet. Named on San Rafael (1954) 7.5' quadrangle. Water from a mineral spring called Ancha Vista Spring, located on the slope of this peak, was used therapeutically at a resort (Bradley, p. 249).

Red Hill [NAPA]: *peak,* nearly 5 miles north-northwest of Calistoga (lat. 38°38'25" N, long. 122°36'50" W; near E line sec. 10, T 9 N, R 7 W). Altitude 2156 feet. Named on Detert Reservoir (1958) 7.5' quadrangle.

Red Hill [SONOMA]:

(1) *peak,* 10 miles northeast of Healdsburg (lat. 38°43'45" N, long. 122°45'25" W; on W line sec. 9, T 10 N, R 8 W). Altitude 2527 feet. Named on Jimtown (1955) 7.5' quadrangle.

(2) *peak,* 3 miles southeast of Jenner (lat. 38°25'15" N, long. 123° 04'50" W). Altitude 1062 feet. Named on Duncans Mills (1979) 7.5' quadrangle.

(3) *peak,* 3 miles south of Big Mountain (lat. 38°39'55" N, long. 123°08'15" W; near S line sec. 36, T 10 N, R 12 W). Named on Tombs Creek (1978) 7.5' quadrangle.

Red Lake [NAPA]: *lake,* 550 feet long, 6 miles north of Saint Helena (lat. 38°35'25" N, long. 122°27'40" W; sec. 31, T 9 N, R 5 W). Named on Saint Helena (1960) 7.5' quadrangle.

Redmond Cut [ALAMEDA]: *locality,* 2.25 miles east-southeast of Altamont along Western Pacific Railroad (lat. 37°43'45" N, long. 121°37'15" W; at E line sec. 27, T 2 S, R 3 E). Named on Altamont (1953) and Midway (1953) 7.5' quadrangles.

Red Mountain [NAPA]: *peak,* 9 miles northwest of Mount Vaca (lat. 38°28'20" N, long. 122°14'35" W; near E line sec. 12, T 7 N, R 4 W). Altitude 1360 feet. Named on Capell Valley (1951) 7.5' quadrangle.

Red Mountain [SANTA CLARA]: *ridge,* northwest-trending, nearly 2 miles long, 4.5 miles south of Mount Boardman on Santa Clara-Stanislaus

County line (lat. 37°24'55" N, long. 121°27'45" W). Named on Mount Boardman (1955) 7.5' quadrangle. Thompson and West's (1876) map has the label "Red Mountains or Cerro Colorado" along the crest of Diablo Range—including present Red Mountain—for a distance of about 11 miles south of Mount Boardman.

Red Mountain [SONOMA]:
(1) *peak,* 3.25 miles northeast of Kenwood (lat. 38°27'10" N, long. 122°30'30" W; sec. 15, T 7 N, R 6 W). Altitude 2548 feet. Named on Kenwood (1954) 7.5' quadrangle.
(2) *peak,* 2.5 miles west-southwest of Cloverdale (lat. 38°47'25" N, long. 123°03'25" W; sec. 23, T 11 N, R 11 W). Altitude 1494 feet. Named on Cloverdale (1960) 7.5' quadrangle.
(3) *peak,* 5.5 miles west of Cloverdale (lat. 38°47'50" N, long. 123° 06'55" W; at W line sec. 17, T 11 N, R 11 W). Named on Cloverdale (1960) 7.5' quadrangle.

Red Mountains: see **Red Mountain** [SANTA CLARA].

Red Oat Ridge [SONOMA]: *ridge,* south- to southeast-trending, 1.5 miles long, 2.5 miles north of Cazadero (lat. 38°34' N, long. 123° 05'25" W). Named on Cazadero (1978) 7.5' quadrangle.

Redondo Beach [SAN MATEO]: *beach,* 1.5 miles southwest of downtown Half Moon Bay along the coast (lat. 37°26'35" N, long. 122°26'35" W). Named on Halfmoon Bay (1940) 15' quadrangle.

Red Rock [CONTRA COSTA-MARIN-SAN FRANCISCO]: *island,* 850 feet long, 2.5 miles south of point San Pablo [CONTRA COSTA] in San Francisco Bay at the junction of Contra Costa, Marin, and San Francisco Counties (lat. 37°55'45" N, long. 122°25'50" W). Named on San Quentin (1959) 7.5' quadrangle. Called Molate I. on Ringgold's (1850a) map—the island is 1.25 miles south-southwest of Point Molate [CONTRA COSTA]. The feature also was called Treasure Rock and Golden Rock; these names were from a tradition that Spanish navigators buried a large treasure at the place (Smith and Elliott, p. 4). The name "Molate" is a misspelling by Beechey in 1826 of *moleta,* the Spanish word for the conical stone used by painters to grind colors (Gudde, 1949, p. 220).

Red Slide [SONOMA]:
(1) *relief feature,* 5.25 miles north of Cazadero (lat. 38°36'20" N, long. 123°06' W). Named on Cazadero (1978) 7.5' quadrangle.
(2) *relief feature,* 3.25 miles south of Big Mountain (lat. 38°39'50" N, long. 123°08'20" W; on S line sec. 36, T 10 N, R 12 W); the feature is on the southwest side of present Red Hill (3). Named on Tombs Creek (1943) 7.5' quadrangle.

Red Slide Creek [SONOMA]: *stream,* flows 2 miles to Austin Creek 4 miles north-northwest of Cazadero (lat. 38°35'05" N, long. 123° 06'55" W; sec. 31, T 9 N, R 11 W); the stream heads near Red Slide (1). Named on Cazadero (1978) 7.5' quadrangle.

Redwood: see **Lokoya** [NAPA]; **Redwood City** [SAN MATEO].

Redwood Canyon [ALAMEDA]: *canyon,* drained by a stream that flows 2.25 miles to Redwood Creek nearly 7 miles east of downtown Oakland (lat. 37°48'05" N, long. 122°08'35" W); the canyon heads near Redwood Peak [CONTRA COSTA]. Named on Oakland East (1959) 7.5' quadrangle.

Redwood Canyon [MARIN]:
(1) *canyon,* drained by a stream that flows 2.5 miles to Halleck Creek nearly 5 miles west-southwest of downtown Novato (lat. 38° 04'45" N, long. 122°38'55" W). Named on Novato (1954) and San Geronimo (1954) 7.5' quadrangles.
(2) *canyon,* 2 miles long, along Redwood Creek above a point 6 miles south-southwest of downtown San Rafael (lat. 37°53'20" N, long. 122°33'55" W). Named on San Rafael (1954) 7.5' quadrangle.

Redwood Canyon [NAPA]: *canyon,* 7 miles long, along Redwood Creek above a point 3.5 miles west-northwest of downtown Napa (lat. 38°19'15" N, long. 122°20'40" W). Named on Napa (1951) and Sonoma (1951) 7.5' quadrangles. On Napa (1902) 30' quadrangle, the stream in present Redwood Canyon above the mouth of present Pickle Canyon is called Mill Creek.

Redwood Canyon [SONOMA]: *canyon,* drained by a stream that flows nearly 1 mile to Pena Creek 3.5 miles south of Skaggs Springs (lat. 38°38'25" N, long. 123°01'35" W; sec. 12, T 9 N, R 11 W). Named on Warm Springs Dam (1978) 7.5' quadrangle.

Redwood City [SAN MATEO]: *city,* in the southeast part of San Mateo County near San Francisco Bay (lat. 37°29' N, long. 122°13'30" W). Named on Palo Alto (1961) and Woodside (1961) 7.5' quadrangles. Called Redwood on Palo Alto (1899) 15' quadrangle. Simon Menzes laid out the community along Redwood Creek in the 1850's and named it Menzesville, but this name failed to last; the place also was known in the early 1850's as Redwood Embarcadero, Red Woods City, Pulgas Ranch Embarcadero, Redwood Landing, and Embarcadero (Brown, p. 75-76; Hynding, p. 89-90). Postal authorities established Redwood post office in 1852, changed the name to Steinbergers in 1853, and changed it to Redwood City in 1856—the name "Steinbergers" was for the owner of the stage stop at the place (Salley, p. 183, 212). The city incorporated in 1868. Postal authorities established Redwood Park post office 11 miles southwest of Redwood City in 1940 and discontinued it in 1942 (Salley, p. 183).

Redwood Creek [ALAMEDA-CONTRA COSTA]: *stream,* heads in Contra Costa County and flows 4 miles to Upper San Leandaro Reservoir 7.5 miles east of downtown Oakland in Alameda County (lat. 37°47'30" N, long. 122°07'50" W; sec. 6, T 2 S, R 2 W). Named on Oakland East (1959) 7.5' quadrangle.

Redwood Creek [MARIN]: *stream,* flows 5.25 miles to the sea 4 miles north-west of Point Bonita at Muir Beach (lat. 37°51'35" N, long. 122°34'40" W). Named on Point Bonita (1954) and San Rafael (1954) 7.5' quadrangles.

Redwood Creek [NAPA]: *stream,* flows 9.5 miles to join Brown Valley Creek and form Napa Creek 1.5 miles west-northwest of downtown Napa (lat. 38°18'15" N, long. 122°18'45" W). Named on Napa (1951) 7.5' quadrangle. On Napa (1902) 30' quadrangle, the stream is called Napa Creek and North Branch [Napa Creek].

Redwood Creek [SAN MATEO]: *water feature,* enters San Francisco Bay 3.25 miles north-northeast of downtown Redwood City (lat. 37°31'35" N, long. 122°11'45" W). Named on Palo Alto (1961) and Redwood Point (1959) 7.5' quadrangles. Brown (p. 76) used the name "Redwood Slough" for lower reaches of the feature, and noted that in the 1850's the creek or slough was called Arroyo Salinas and Redwoods Embarcadero Creek—the name "Redwood Creek" is from redwood lumber stacked along the stream for shipment in the early days.

Redwood Creek [SONOMA]:
(1) *stream,* formed by the confluence of Kellogg Creek and Yellow Jacket Creek, flows 4.25 miles to Maacama Creek 6.5 miles west-southwest of Mount Saint Helena (lat. 38°38'30" N, long. 122°44'40" W; sec. 9, T 9 N, R 8 W); the stream originates in Knights Valley. Named on Mount Saint Helena (1959) 7.5' quadrangle. Bancroft's (1864) map has the name "Knights Cr.," apparently for present Redwood Creek (1) and for present Maacama Creek below its junction with Redwood Creek (1).
(2) *stream,* flows 2.5 miles to Fife Creek 1.5 miles north of Guerneville (lat. 38°31'35" N, long. 123°59'55" W; near E line sec. 19, T 8 N, R 10 W). Named on Guerneville (1955) 7.5' quadrangle.
(3) *stream,* flows 1.5 miles to Wheatfield Fork Gualala River 6.5 miles east of Annapolis (lat. 38°43'50" N, long. 123°14'55" W; at N line sec. 12, T 10 N, R 13 W). Named on Annapolis (1977) 7.5' quadrangle.

Redwood Embarcadero: see **Redwood City** [SAN MATEO].

Redwood Estates [SANTA CLARA]: *settlement,* 4.5 miles south of downtown Los Gatos (lat. 37°09'25" N, long. 121°59' W). Named on Los Gatos (1953) 7.5' quadrangle. Postal authorities established Redwood Estates post office in 1927 (Frickstad, p. 175).

Redwood Hill [SONOMA]: *peak,* 1 mile south of Mark West Springs (lat. 38°32'05" N, long. 122°43'10" W; near SW cor. sec. 14, T 8 N, R 8 W). Named on Mark West Springs (1958) 7.5' quadrangle.

Redwood Junction [SAN MATEO]: *locality,* 0.5 mile southeast of downtown Redwood City along Southern Pacific Railroad (lat. 37° 28'40" N, long. 122°13' W). Named on Palo Alto (1961) 7.5' quadrangle.

Redwood Lake [SONOMA]: *lake,* 450 feet long, 4.5 miles east-northeast of Cazadero (lat. 38°33'55" N, long. 123°00'35" W; sec. 6, T 8 N, R 10 W). Named on Cazadero (1978) 7.5' quadrangle.

Redwood Landing: see **Redwood City** [SAN MATEO].

Redwood Log Creek [SONOMA]: *stream,* flows 3.25 miles to Pena Creek 3.5 miles south of Skaggs Springs (lat. 38°38'40" N, long. 123°02' W; sec. 12, T 9 N, R 11 W). Named on Warm Springs Dam (1978) 7.5' quadrangle.

Redwood Mills: see **Saratoga** [SANTA CLARA].

Redwood Mountain [SONOMA]: *peak,* 3.25 miles north-northwest of Cloverdale (lat. 38°50'50" N, long. 123°02'35" W; on E line sec. 35, T 12 N, R 11 W). Altitude 1675 feet. Named on Cloverdale (1960) 7.5' quadrangle.

Redwood Park: see **Redwood City** [SAN MATEO].

Redwood Peak [CONTRA COSTA]: *peak,* 4.25 miles south of Orinda (lat. 37°49'05" N, long. 122°10'30" W). Altitude 1619 feet. Named on Oakland East (1959) 7.5' quadrangle.

Redwood Point [SAN MATEO]: *promontory,* 4 miles north-northeast of downtown Redwood City along San Francisco Bay (lat. 37°32'05" N, long. 122°11'35" W); the feature is near the mouth of Redwood Creek. Named on Redwood Point (1959) 7.5' quadrangle. United States Board on Geographic Names (1943, p. 12) rejected the name "Marsh Point" for the promontory.

Redwood Retreat [SANTA CLARA]: *settlement,* 2.5 miles north-northwest of Mount Madonna along Little Arthur Creek (lat. 37°02'30" N, long. 121°43' W; near SE cor.sec. 23, T 10 S, R 2 E). Named on Mount Madonna (1955) 7.5' quadrangle.

Red Woods City: see **Redwood City** [SAN MATEO].

Redwoods Embarcadero Creek: see **Redwood Creek** [SAN MATEO].

Redwood Slough: see **Redwood Creek** [SAN MATEO].

Redwood Terrace [SAN MATEO]: *settlement,* 1.25 miles west-southwest of La Honda (lat. 37°18'55" N, long. 122°17'35" W; near NW cor. sec. 22, T 7 S, R 4 W). Named on La Honda (1961) 7.5' quadrangle.

Reed [MARIN]: *locality,* 5 miles south-southeast of downtown San Rafael along Northwestern Pacific Railroad (lat. 37°54'20" N, long. 122°29'55"

W). Named on San Quentin (1959) 7.5' quadrangle. The name commemorates John Reed, who owned Corte de Madera del Presidio grant, where the place is situated (Gudde, 1949, p. 283).

Reed: see **Point Reed**, under **Bluff Point** [MARIN]; **Widow Reed Creek**, under **Arroyo Corte Madera Del Presidio** [MARIN].

Reese Gap [SONOMA]: *pass,* 4.5 miles south of Skaggs Springs (lat. 38°37'35" N, long. 123°02'05" W; near W line sec. 13, T 9 N, R 11 W). Named on Warm Springs Dam (1978) 7.5' quadrangle.

Reesley Valley: see **Reliez Valley** [CONTRA COSTA].

Reflection Lake [SAN MATEO]: *lake,* 650 feet long, at La Honda (lat. 37°19'05" N, long. 122°16'10" W; near S line sec. 14, T 7 S, R 4 W). Named on La Honda (1961) 7.5' quadrangle.

Refugio: see **Pastoria de las Borregas** [SANTA CLARA].

Refugio Creek [CONTRA COSTA]: *stream,* flows 4 miles to San Pablo Bay 4.5 miles east of Pinole Point (lat. 38°01'20" N, long. 122°17'05" W). Named on Briones Valley (1959) and Mare Island (1959) 7.5' quadrangles.

Refugio de la Laguna Seca: see **La Laguna Seca** [SANTA CLARA].

Refugio Landing: see **Hercules Wharf** [CONTRA COSTA].

Refugio Valley [CONTRA COSTA]: *valley,* 5 miles east of Pinole Point (lat. 38°00'50" N, long. 122°16'15" W); Refugio Creek and its tributaries drain the valley. Named on Mare Island (1959) 7.5' quadrangle.

Regnart Creek [SANTA CLARA]: *stream,* flows 1 mile to lowlands nearly 1.5 miles south of Monta Vista (lat. 37°18'10" N, long. 122° 03'10" W; sec. 23, T 7 S, R 2 W). Named on Cupertino (1961) 7.5' quadrangle.

Reliez Valley [CONTRA COSTA]: *valley,* 2.25 miles west-northwest of Walnut Creek civic center (lat. 37°55'05" N, long. 122°06'20" W). Named on Walnut Creek (1959) 7.5' quadrangle. Called Reesley Valley on Concord (1897) 15' quadrangle. Smith and Elliott (p. 23) referred to Raleez Creek.

Remillard [ALAMEDA]: *locality,* nearly 5 miles west of Livermore along Southern Pacific Railroad (lat. 37°40'15" N, long. 121°51'20" W). Named on Pleasanton (1906) 15' quadrangle. The name is from Remillard brick works, which was in business from 1889 until 1935 (Mosier and Mosier, p. 73).

Renevar Gulch [SONOMA]: *canyon,* drained by a stream that flows 0.5 mile to Palmer Creek 6 miles north-northeast of Guerneville (lat. 38°34'40" N, long. 122°56'30" W). Named on Guerneville (1955) 7.5' quadrangle.

Rengstorff Gulch [SAN MATEO]: *canyon,* drained by a stream that flows 0.5 mile to Corte Madera Creek 2.5 miles north-northeast of Mindego Hill (lat. 37°20'35" N, long. 122°12'20" W). Named on Mindego Hill (1961) 7.5' quadrangle. Rengstorff's ranch and silver mine were near the canyon in the 1870's and 1880's (Brown, p. 77).

Renz Gulch [SANTA CLARA]: *canyon,* drained by a stream that flows 1 mile to Bodfish Creek 2 miles east-southeast of Mount Madonna (lat. 37°00'10" N, long. 121°40'15" W). Named on Mount Madonna (1955) 7.5' quadrangle.

Reservoir: see **Creed** [SOLANO].

Reservoir Canyon [SANTA CLARA]: *canyon,* drained by a stream that flows nearly 1.5 miles to lowlands 1.5 miles southwest of Gilroy (lat. 36°59'35" N, long. 121°35'15" W). Named on Chittenden (1955) 7.5' quadrangle.

Reyes: see **Point Reyes** [MARIN].

Reynolds [MARIN]: *locality,* nearly 7 miles south of Tomales on the northeast side of Tomales Bay (lat. 38°08'55" N, long. 122°52'55" W); the place is on Nicasio (3) grant, which belonged to Messrs. Frank and Reynolds. Named on Tomales (1954) 7.5' quadrangle. On Point Reyes (1918) 15' quadrangle, the place is shown along Northwestern Pacific Railroad.

Reynolds: see **Camp Reynolds**, under **Fort McDowell** [MARIN].

Reynolds Creek: see **Los Trancos Creek** [SAN MATEO].

Rheem [CONTRA COSTA]:

(1) *locality,* 2.5 miles north-northwest of Richmond civic center along Southern Pacific Railroad (lat. 37°58'35" N, long. 122°21'25" W). Named on Richmond (1959) 7.5' quadrangle.

(2) *locality,* 7.5 miles west-northwest of Danville (lat. 37°51'35" N, long. 122°07'25" W; sec. 7, T 1 S, R 2 W). Named on Las Trampas Ridge (1959) and Oakland East (1959) 7.5' quadrangles. Donald I. Rheem started a development at the place in 1944 and called it Rheem Center (Gudde, 1969, p. 267).

Rheem Center: see **Rheem** [CONTRA COSTA] (2).

Rhine Canyon [CONTRA COSTA]: *canyon,* drained by a stream that flows nearly 2 miles to Curry Canyon 2 miles southeast of Mount Diablo (lat. 37°51'35" N, long. 121°53'35" W; sec. 8, T 1 S, R 1 E). Named on Clayton (1953) and Diablo (1953) 7.5' quadrangles.

Rhode Island [CONTRA COSTA]: *island,* 0.5 mile long, 3.5 miles east-southeast of the settlement of Bethel Island between Old River and Sheep Slough (lat. 38°00'05" N, long. 121°34'25" W). Named on Bouldin Island (1978) and Woodward Island (1978) 7.5' quadrangles.

Rhododendron Creek [SAN MATEO]: *stream,* flows 1 mile to Pescadero Creek 3.5 miles south of Mindego Hill (lat. 37°15'35" N, long. 122°14'20" W; near SW cor. sec. 6, T 8 S, R 3 W). Named on Mindego Hill (1961) 7.5' quadrangle.

Rialto Cove: see **Bolinas Bay** [MARIN].

Riccas Corner [SONOMA]: *locality,* 2.5 miles northeast of Sebastopol (lat. 38°25'25" N, long. 122°47'15" W). Named on Sebastopol (1954) 7.5' quadrangle. Called Smith Corner on Sebastopol (1942) 15' quadrangle.

Rice's Creek: see **Gazos Creek** [SAN MATEO].

Richardson Bay [MARIN]: *bay,* opens into San Francisco Bay at the town of Sausalito (lat. 37°51'30" N, long. 122°28' W). Named on Point Bonita (1954), San Francisco North (1956), San Quentin (1959), and San Rafael (1954) 7.5' quadrangles. Cañizares explored the bay in 1775 and called it Ensenada de la Carmelita because of a rock there that resembled a Carmelite nun (Bolton, p. 252). The bay also was known as Puerto de los Balleneros, a name later translated to Whaler's Harbor—the name "Richardson" commemorates William A. Richardson, who owned Sausalito grant (Gudde, 1969, p. 268).

Richardson Island [MARIN]: *hill,* 2.5 miles south-southeast of downtown San Rafael (lat. 37°56'10" N, long. 122°31' W). Named on San Rafael (1954) 7.5' quadrangle.

Richmond [CONTRA COSTA]: *city,* 23 miles west of Mount Diablo (civic center near lat. 37°56'15" N, long. 122°20'30" W). Named on Mare Island (1959), Petaluma Point (1959), Richmond (1959), and San Quentin (1959) 7.5' quadrangles. Postal authorities established Richmond post office in 1900 (Frickstad, p. 23), and the city incorporated in 1905. The community began when officials of Atchison, Topeka and Santa Fe Railroad made the place the western terminus of the rail line (Gleason, p. 189). Postal authorities established Atchison post office, named for the railroad, 1 mile southeast of Richmond post office in 1903 and discontinued it in 1912—it was at the local headquarters of the railroad (Salley, p. 11).

Richmond: see **North Richmond** [CONTRA COSTA].

Richmond District [SAN FRANCISCO]: *district,* 3 miles west of San Francisco civic center (lat. 37°46'45" N, long. 122°28'30" W). Named on San Francisco North (1956) 7.5' quadrangle.

Richmond Inner Harbor [CONTRA COSTA]: *water feature,* 2.5 miles south of Richmond civic center off of San Francisco Bay (lat. 37°54'10" N, long. 122°20'30" W). Named on Richmond (1959) 7.5' quadrangle.

Richmond Marina Bay: see **Inner Harbor Basin** [CONTRA COSTA].

Richmond Point: see **Point Richmond** [CONTRA COSTA] (1).

Richs Island: see **Simmons Island** [SOLANO].

Rien [SONOMA]: *locality,* 1.5 miles southeast of present Jenner along Russian River (lat. 38°26'15" N, long. 123°06'10" W). Named on Duncans Mills (1921) 15' quadrangle.

Rifle Camp [MARIN]: *locality,* 5.25 miles southwest of downtown San Rafael (lat. 37°55'35" N, long. 122°36'20" W). Named on San Rafael (1954) 7.5' quadrangle.

Rifle Range Branch [ALAMEDA]: *stream,* flows 3 miles to Arroyo Viejo 7.5 miles east-southeast of downtown Oakland (lat. 37°45'15" N, long. 122°09' W). Named on Oakland East (1959) 7.5' quadrangle. The name is from Oakland Pistol Club's range (Mosier and Mosier, p. 73).

Riggs Canyon [CONTRA COSTA]: *canyon,* drained by a stream that flows 2.25 miles to Tassajara Creek 5.25 miles southeast of Mount Diablo (lat. 37°49'20" N, long. 121°51'15" W; sec. 27, T 1 S, E 1 E). Named on Tassajara (1953) 7.5' quadrangle.

Right-Hand Canyon [NAPA]: *canyon,* drained by a stream that flows 1.5 miles to Gosling Canyon 6.25 miles south-southeast of Berryessa Peak (lat. 38°34'35" N, long. 122°09'15" W). Named on Lake Berryessa (1959) 7.5' quadrangle.

Riley Canyon [ALAMEDA]: *canyon,* 0.5 mile long, 10 miles east of downtown Oakland (lat. 37°46'40" N, long. 122°05'45" W). Named on Las Trampas Ridge (1959) 7.5' quadrangle. The name commemorates Eugene Riley, who settled at the place before 1889 (Mosier and Mosier, p. 73-74). Water of Upper San Leandro Reservoir floods the lower part of the canyon.

Riley Ridge [ALAMEDA]: *ridge,* west- to southwest-trending, 2 miles long, 10 miles east of downtown Oakland (lat. 37°46'45" N, long. 122°05'15" W). Named on Las Trampas Ridge (1959) 7.5' quadrangle.

Rinconada [SANTA CLARA]: *locality,* nearly 1 mile east of downtown Los Gatos (lat. 37°13'40" N, long. 121°58' W). Named on Los Gatos (1919) 15' quadrangle.

Rinconada del Arroyo de San Francisquito [SANTA CLARA]: *land grant,* extends from downtown Palo Alto to San Francisco Bay. Named on Mountain View (1961) and Palo Alto (1961) 7.5' quadrangles. Maria Antonio Mesa received 0.5 league in 1841 and claimed 2229 acres patented in 1872 (Cowan, p. 77—Cowan listed the grant under the name "Rinconada del San Francisquito"; Perez, p. 86).

Rinconada de los Gatos [SANTA CLARA]: *land grant,* at Los Gatos. Named on Castle Rock Ridge (1955), Los Gatos (1953), and San Jose West (1961) 7.5' quadrangles. Sebastian Peralta and Jose Hernandez received 1.5 leagues in 1840 and claimed 6631 acres patented in 1860 (Cowan, p. 37). *Rincon* means "corner" in Spanish; according to Arbuckle (p. 29), this word in the name of the grant comes from a sharp bend, or corner, made by Los Gatos Creek.

Rinconada del San Francisquito: see **Rinconada del Arroyo de San Francisquito** [SANTA CLARA].

Rincon Creek [SANTA CLARA]: *stream,* flows 2.5 miles to Guadalupe Creek nearly 3 miles west of New Almaden (lat. 37°10'55" N, long. 121°52'20" W). Named on Los Gatos (1953) and Santa Teresa Hills (1953) 7.5' quadrangles.

Rincon Creek [SONOMA]: *stream,* flows 4.25 miles to Santa Rosa Creek 2 miles east-northeast of downtown Santa Rosa (lat. 38°27'10" N, long. 122°40'35" W). Named on Mark West Springs (1958) and Santa Rosa (1954) 7.5' quadrangles.

Rincon de las Salinas y Potrero Viejo [SAN FRANCISCO-SAN MATEO]: *land grant,* at and near Hunters Point and Bernal Heights; a small part is in San Mateo County. Named on Hunters Point (1956, photorevised 1968) and San Francisco South (1956) 7.5' quadrangles. Jose Cornelio Bernal received 1 league in 1839 and 1840; his heirs claimed 4446 acres patented in 1857 (Cowan, p. 63). Perez (p. 85), gave the grant date as 1845.

Rincon de los Carneros [NAPA]: *land grant,* south of the city of Napa. Named on Cuttings Wharf (1949) and Napa (1951) 7.5' quadrangles. The place is part of Entre Napa grant that Nicolas Higuera received in 1836; Julius Martin claimed 2557 acres patented in 1858 (Cowan, p. 24).

Rincon de los Esteros [SANTA CLARA]: *land grant,* east of Alviso. Named on Milpitas (1961) 7.5' quadrangle. Ignacio Alviso received the land in 1838; Rafael Alviso and others claimed 2200 acres patented in 1872; Ellen E. White claimed 2308 acres patented in 1862; Francisco Berryessa and others claimed 1845 acres patented in 1873 (Cowan, p. 35).

Rincon de Musalacon [SONOMA]: *land grant,* along Russian River near Cloverdale. Named on Asti (1959), Cloverdale (1960), and Geyserville (1955) 7.5' quadrangles. Francisco Berreyessa received 2 leagues in 1846; Johnson Horrel and others claimed 8867 acres patented in 1866 (Cowan, p. 50; Cowan gave the name "Rincon de Musulacon" as an alternate). The name "Musalacon" probably is of Indian origin (Kroeber, p. 49).

Rincon de San Francisquito [SANTA CLARA]: *land grant,* in Palo Alto from the foothills to San Francisco Bay. Named on Mountain View (1961) and Palo Alto (1961) 7.5' quadrangles. Jose Peña received the land in 1841; Teodoro Robles and Secundino Robles claimed 8418 acres patented in 1868 (Cowan, p. 77).

Rincon Hill [SAN FRANCISCO]: *hill,* nearly 0.5 mile southwest of Rincon Point (lat. 37°47'10" N, long. 122°23'30" W). Named on San Francisco North (1956) 7.5' quadrangle. Soule, Gihon, and Nisbet's (1855) map shows two small valleys that were well known in the early days—Happy Valley, located northwest of present Rincon Hill, and Pleasant Valley, located southwest of the hill.

Rincon Point [SAN FRANCISCO]: *promontory*, nearly 2 miles east-northeast of San Francisco civic center along San Francisco Bay (lat. 37°47'25" N, long. 122°23'15" W). Named on San Francisco North (1956) 7.5' quadrangle.

Rincon Valley [SONOMA]: *valley,* 3.5 miles northeast of downtown Santa Rosa (lat. 38°28'30" N, long. 122°40' W); the valley is along Rincon Creek. Named on Santa Rosa (1954) 7.5' quadrangle.

Rindler Creek [SOLANO]: *stream,* flows 2.25 miles to an artificial watercourse 3 miles northeast of downtown Vallejo (lat. 38°08'15" N, long. 122°13'15" W; sec. 5, T 3 N, R 3 W). Named on Cordelia (1951) 7.5' quadrangle. Carquinez (1938) 15' quadrangle shows the stream extending to Lake Chabot.

Rings Gulch [SAN MATEO]: *canyon*, drained by a stream that flows 0.5 mile to Tunitas Creek 4 miles west-southwest of Skeggs Point (lat. 37°23'20" N, long. 122°22'10" W). Named on Woodside (1961) 7.5' quadrangle. Mr. E. Ring had a ranch in the canyon in the 1860's (Brown, p. 77).

Rio Ayoska: see **Molinos** [SONOMA].

Rio de la Alameda: see **Alameda Creek** [ALAMEDA].

Rio de la Harina: see **San Lorenzo Creek** [ALAMEDA].

Rio Dell [SONOMA]: *settlement,* 5 miles east of Guerneville along Russian River (lat. 38°29'55" N, long. 122°54'15" W; sec. 31, T 8 N, R 9 W). Named on Camp Meeker (1954) and Guerneville (1955) 7.5' quadrangles.

Rio de los Putos [SOLANO]: *land grant,* north of Allendale on Solano-Yolo County line. Named on Allendale (1953), Merritt (1952), Mount Vaca (1951), and Winters (1953) 7.5' quadrangles. Francisco Guerrero y Palomares received 4 leagues in 1842; William Wolfskill claimed 17,755 acres patented in 1858 (Cowan, p. 66). According to Perez (p. 87), Wolfskill was the grantee in 1842.

Rio del Pajaro: see **Pajaro River** [SANTA CLARA].

Rio de Nuestra Señora de Guadalupe: see **Guadalupe River** [SANTA CLARA].

Rio de San Clemente: see **Alameda Creek** [ALAMEDA].

Rio de San Francisco: see **Carquinez Strait** [CONTRA COSTA-SOLANO]; **San Francisquito Creek** [SAN MATEO-SANTA CLARA].

Rio de San Jose: see **Guadalupe River** [SANTA CLARA].

Rio de San Matheo: see **San Mateo Creek** [SAN MATEO].

Rio Farms [SOLANO]: *locality,* 7.5 miles north-northeast of Rio Vista on Ryer Island (1) (lat. 38°16' N, long. 121°38'20" W). Named on Liberty Island (1952) 7.5' quadrangle.

Rio Grande de San Sebastian: see **Tomales Bay** [MARIN].

Rio Nido [SONOMA]: *settlement,* 1.5 miles northeast of Guerneville on the north side of Russian River (lat. 38°31'15" N, long. 122°58'35" W; sec. 20, 21, T 8 N, R 10 W). Named on Guerneville (1955) 7.5' quadrangle. Called Rionido on Healdsburg (1940) 15' quadrangle, but United States Board on Geographic Names (1950, p. 6) rejected this form of the name. Postal authorities established Eaglenest post office in 1908, changed the name to Rionido in 1910, and changed it to Rio Nido in 1947; the name is from an eagle nest in a tree on the river bank—*rio nido* means "river nest" in Spanish (Salley, p. 63, 186).

Rio Pajaro: see **Pajaro River** [SANTA CLARA].

Rio Rusa: see **Russian River** [SONOMA].

Rio Sacramento: see **Sacramento River** [SOLANO].

Rio San Joaquin: see **San Joaquin River** [CONTRA COSTA].

Rio San Leandro: see **San Leandro Creek** [ALAMEDA-CONTRA COSTA].

Rio Tulare: see **San Joaquin River** [CONTRA COSTA].

Rio Vista [SOLANO]: *town,* 21 miles southeast of Vacaville along Sacramento River (lat. 38°09'20" N, long. 121°41'20" W). Named on Rio Vista (1978) 7.5' quadrangle. Postal authorities established Rio Vista post office in 1858 (Salley, p. 186), and the town incorporated in 1894. Colonel N.H. Davis first laid out the community near the entrance of Cache Slough into Sacramento River and called it Brazos del Rio—*brazos del rio* means "arms of the river" in Spanish; the name was changed to Rio Vista before a flood destroyed the town in 1862 and the inhabitants rebuilt on higher ground at the present site (Hoover, Rensch, and Rensch, p. 523-524). According to Bancroft (1888, p. 500), Bidwell and Hopps tried unsuccessfully to start a town in 1848 at or near the original site of Rio Vista; they called the place Brazoria, Sacramento Brazoria, or Halo-Chemuck. Ringgold's (1850c) map shows a place called Suisun City at the site of present Rio Vista.

Rio Vista Junction [SOLANO]: *locality,* 1.5 miles southeast of Denverton along Sacramento Northern Railroad (lat. 38°12'25" N, long. 121°52'30" W; sec. 9, T 4 N, R 1 E). Named on Birds Landing (1953) and Denverton (1953) 7.5' quadrangles. Called Curtis on Denverton (1918) 7.5' quadrangle, which shows the place along Oakland Antioch and Eastern Railroad.

Ritchey Creek: see **Ritchie Creek** [NAPA].

Ritchie Creek [NAPA]: *stream,* flows nearly 4 miles to Napa River 4 miles east-southeast of Calistoga (lat. 38°33'30" N, long. 122°30'30" W). Named on Calistoga (1958) 7.5' quadrangle. The name commemorates one of the purchasers of land from Edward T. Bale, owner of Carne Humana grant (Archuleta, p. 105). United States Board on Geographic Names (1991, p. 6) approved the name "Ritchey Creek" for the stream, and pointed out that the name is for Matthew Dill Ritchey, an early settler.

River Slavianka: see **Russian River** [SONOMA].

Roaring River Slough [SOLANO]: *water feature,* along the southwest side of Hammond Island, joins Montezuma Slough 3 miles south-southwest of Birds Landing (2) (lat. 38°05'25" N, long. 121°53'05" W). Named on Honker Bay (1953) 7.5' quadrangle.

Roberts Landing [ALAMEDA]: *locality,* nearly 4 miles south of downtown San Leandro at the edge of San Francisco Bay (lat. 37° 40'20" N, long. 122°09'50" W). Named on San Leandro (1959) 7.5' quadrangle. Robert Thompson, William Roberts, and Peter Anderson started the place in 1850, when it was known as Thompson's Landing; it was called Roberts Landing after Thompson sold out in 1856 (Mosier and Mosier, p. 74).

Robertsville [SANTA CLARA]: *locality,* 5 miles south of downtown San Jose near Guadalupe River (lat. 37°15'45" N, long. 121°52'35" W). Named on San Jose West (1961) 7.5' quadrangle. A village at the site was named for John Griffith Roberts, who farmed the surrounding land in the nineteenth century (Harry Farrell, *San Jose Mercury-News*, January 6, 1980). Thompson and West's (1876) map shows Pioneer P.O. near the site of Robertsville. Postal authorities established Pioneer post office in 1875 and discontinued it in 1886 (Frickstad, p. 175).

Robinson: see **Cherry** [SONOMA].

Robinson Ridge [SONOMA]: *ridge,* west-southwest-trending, 2 miles long, 8.5 miles north-northwest of the village of Stewarts Point (lat. 38°46' N, long. 122°27'10" W). Named on Ornbaun Valley (1960) 15' quadrangle.

Robinson Rock [SONOMA]: *relief feature,* 2 miles north of the village of Bodega Bay (lat. 38°21'55" N, long. 123°02'50" W). Named on Bodega Head (1942) 7.5' quadrangle.

Roblar [SONOMA]: *locality,* 5 miles east of Bloomfield along Petaluma and Santa Rosa Railroad (lat. 38°19'20" N, long. 122°45'30" W); the place is on Roblar de la Miseria grant. Named on Two Rock (1954) 7.5' quadrangle. California Division of Highways' (1934) map shows two places, Vestal and Petersen, located along the railroad between Roblar and Stony Point, and a place called Quarry located along the railroad just north of Roblar.

Roblar de la Miseria [SONOMA]: *land grant,* west and northwest of the city of Petaluma. Named on Cotati (1954), Petaluma (1953), and Two Rock (1954) 7.5' quadrangles. Juan Nepomuceno Padilla received 4 leagues in 1845; David Wright and others claimed 16,887 acres patented in 1858

(Cowan, p. 68).

Rockaway: see **Rockaway Beach** [SAN MATEO].

Rockaway Beach [SAN MATEO]: *district*, 3.5 miles north of Montara Knob near the coast at the mouth of Calera Valley (lat. 37°36'30" N, long. 122°29'40" W). Named on Montara Mountain (1956) 7.5' quadrangle. Called Rockaway on San Mateo (1915) 15' quadrangle. Postal authorities established Rockaway post office in 1908, changed the name to Rockaway Beach the same year, discontinued it in 1922, reestablished it in 1923, and discontinued it in 1959 (Salley, p. 187). Eckel (p. 354) used the designation "Calera or Rockaway Beach" for the community. Residents of the place voted in 1957 to join neighboring communities and form the new city of Pacifica.

Rock City [CONTRA COSTA]: *relief feature*, 2.5 miles south-southwest of Mount Diablo (lat. 37°51' N, long. 121°56'05" W; near E line sec. 14, T 1 S, R 1 W). Named on Diablo (1953) 7.5' quadrangle.

Rock Creek: see **Slate Creek** [SAN MATEO].

Rock Cut [ALAMEDA]: *locality*, 2 miles west-northwest of Midway along Southern Pacific Railroad (lat. 37°43'35" N, long. 121°35'45" W; sec. 25, T 2 S, R 3 E). Named on Tesla (1907) 15' quadrangle.

Rock House Ridge [SANTA CLARA]: *ridge*, west-northwest-trending, 2 miles long, just east of Mount Sizer (lat. 37°12'45" N, long. 121°29'30" W). Named on Mississippi Creek (1955) and Mount Sizer (1955) 7.5' quadrangles.

Rockpile Creek [SONOMA]: *stream*, heads in Mendocino County and flows 6 miles in Sonoma County to South Fork Gualala River 7.5 miles north-northwest of the village of Stewarts Point (lat. 38° 45'05' N, long. 123°28'10" W; sec. 31, T 11 N, R 14 W). Named on Ornbaun Valley (1960) 15' quadrangle.

Rock Point [SONOMA]: *promontory*, 4.25 miles south-southeast of Jenner along the coast (lat. 38°23'35" N, long. 123°05'20" W). Named on Duncans Mills (1979) 7.5' quadrangle. Called Rocky Point on Duncans Mills (1921) 15' quadrangle.

Rock Slough [CONTRA COSTA]: *water feature*, joins Old River 7 miles east-northeast of Brentwood (lat. 37°58'20" N, long. 121°34'35" W). Named on Brentwood (1978) and Woodward Island (1978) 7.5' quadrangles.

Rock Springs [MARIN]: *spring*, 6 miles southwest of downtown San Rafael (lat. 37°54'40" N, long. 122°36'40" W). Named on San Rafael (1954) 7.5' quadrangle.

Rock Springs Peak [SANTA CLARA]: *peak*, 5 miles east-southeast of Gilroy Hot Springs (lat. 37°05'05" N, long. 121°23'40" W; sec. 11, T 10 S, R 5 E). Named on Gilroy Hot Springs (1955) 7.5' quadrangle.

Rocktram [NAPA]: *locality*, nearly 3 miles south of downtown Napa along Southern Pacific Railroad (lat. 38°15'25" N, long. 122°16'45" W). Named on Napa (1951) 7.5' quadrangle. Called Rockfram on Sonoma (1942) 15' quadrangle.

Rockville [SOLANO]: *village*, 4.25 miles west of Fairfield (lat. 38° 14'40" N, long. 122°07'15" W). Named on Fairfield South (1949) 7.5' quadrangle. Postal authorities established Rockville post office in 1858, discontinued it in 1870, reestablished it in 1898, and discontinued it in 1902; the name is from a nearby rock quarry (Salley, p. 187).

Rockwell Gap [NAPA]: *pass*, 7.5 miles south-southeast of Berryessa Peak on Rocky Ridge on Napa-Yolo County line (lat. 38°34' N, long. 122°07'15" W; sec. 6, T 8 N, R 2 W). Named on Monticello Dam (1959) 7.5' quadrangle. Called Rosslyn Gap on Capay (1945) 15' quadrangle, but United States Board on Geographic Names (1962a), p. 15) rejected this name.

Rocky Canyon: see **Kent Canyon** [MARIN].

Rocky Island: see **Brooks Island** [CONTRA COSTA].

Rocky Mountain [SONOMA]:

(1) *peak*, 4.25 miles north-northeast of Guerneville (lat. 38°33'40" N, long. 122°58'45" W; near SW cor. sec. 4, T 8 N, R 10 W). Named on Guerneville (1955) 7.5' quadrangle.

(2) *peak*, nearly 5 miles north of Cazadero (lat. 38°36' N, long. 123° 04'20" W; sec. 28, T 9 N, R 11 W). Altitude 1482 feet. Named on Cazadero (1978) 7.5' quadrangle.

Rocky Point [MARIN]: *promontory*, 3.5 miles east-southeast of Bolinas along the coast (lat. 37°52'55" N, long. 122°37'40" W). Named on Bolinas (1954) 7.5' quadrangle. A spring of warm water known as Rocky Point Spring rises on the beach near the promontory (Waring, p. 80).

Rocky Point [SONOMA]: *promontory*, 1.5 miles south-southeast of the village of Stewarts Point along the coast (lat. 38°37'50" N, long. 123°23'20" W). Named on Stewarts Point (1978) 7.5' quadrangle.

Rocky Point: see **Rock Point** [SONOMA].

Rocky Point Spring: see **Rocky Point** [MARIN].

Rocky Ridge [ALAMEDA]: *ridge*, northwest-trending, 5.5 miles long, 4 miles west-southwest of Mendenhall Springs (lat. 37°33'45" N, long. 121°42'30" W). Named on Mendenhall Springs (1956) 7.5' quadrangle.

Rocky Ridge [ALAMEDA-CONTRA COSTA]: *ridge*, northwest-trending, 5 miles long, on Alameda-Contra Costa County line, mainly in Contra Costa County; center 3 miles southwest of Danville (lat. 37°48' N, long. 122°02'45" W). Named on Las Trampas Ridge (1959) 7.5' quadrangle.

Rocky Ridge [MARIN]: *ridge*, north-northwest- to northwest-trending, 2 miles long, 4.5 miles west-southwest of downtown San Rafael (lat. 37°56'35" N, long. 122°36'25" W). Named on San Rafael (1954) 7.5' quadrangle.

Rocky Ridge [NAPA]: *ridge*, extends south-southeast along Napa-Yolo County line for 12.5 miles from near Berryessa Peak to Putah Creek. Named on Brooks (1959), Lake Berryessa (1959), and Monticello Dam (1959) 7.5' quadrangles.

Rodeo [CONTRA COSTA]: *town*, 5.5 miles east-northeast of Pinole Point (lat. 38°02'05" N, long. 122°16' W); the town is along Rodeo Creek. Named on Mare Island (1959) 7.5' quadrangle. Postal authorities established Rodeo post office in 1892 (Frickstad, p. 23).

Rodeo Cove [MARIN]: *embayment*, 1 mile north-northwest of Point Bonita (lat. 37°49'45" N, long. 122°32'15" W). Named on Point Bonita (1954) 7.5' quadrangle.

Rodeo Creek [CONTRA COSTA]: *stream*, flows 8 miles to San Pablo Bay 5.5 miles east-northeast of Pinole Point (lat. 38°02'20" N, long. 122°16' W); the mouth of the stream is at Rodeo. Named on Benicia (1959), Briones Valley (1959), and Mare Island (1959) 7.5' quadrangles.

Rodeo Flat [SANTA CLARA]: *area*, 3.25 miles west of Mount Sizer (lat. 37°12'40" N, long. 121°34'15" W). Named on Mount Sizer (1955) 7.5' quadrangle.

Rodeo Lagoon [MARIN]: *lake*, 4400 feet long, 1 mile north of Point Bonita (lat. 37°49'50" N, long. 122°31'45" W); the lake is inland from Rodeo Cove. Named on Point Bonita (1954) 7.5' quadrangle. According to Teather (p. 62), the name appears to be derived from the word "Rodier"—the name "Rodier Lagoon" is on a Coast Survey chart of 1856.

Rodeo Viejo: see **Cañada de Guadalupe y Rodeo Viejo** [SAN FRANCISCO-SAN MATEO]; **Cañada de Guadalupe la Visitacion y Rodeo Viejo** [SAN FRANCISCO-SAN MATEO].

Rodgers Creek [SONOMA]: *stream*, flows 8 miles to Fowler Creek nearly 6.5 miles north of Sears Point (lat. 38°14'55" N, long. 122° 27'35" W). Named on Glen Ellen (1954), Sears Point (1951), and Sonoma (1951) 7.5' quadrangles.

Rodgers Gulch [SAN MATEO]: *canyon*, drained by a stream that flows 1.25 miles to Alpine Creek 1.5 miles southwest of Mindego Hill (lat. 37°17'50" N, long. 122°14'55" W; sec. 25, T 7 S, R 4 W). Named on Mindego Hill (1961) 7.5' quadrangle. Benjamin Rodgers had a ranch in the canyon in the 1860's (Brown, p. 78).

Rodier Lagoon: see **Rodeo Lagoon** [MARIN].

Roe Island [SOLANO]: *island*, nearly 1.5 miles long, 7 miles east-northeast of Benicia in Suisun Bay (lat. 38°04'20" N, long. 122° 02' W). Named on Vine Hill (1959) 7.5' quadrangle. Called Preston I. on Ringgold's (1850c) map. United States Board on Geographic Names (1989, p. 4) approved the name "Fishermans Cut" for a channel, 0.5 mile long, situated off of the east end of Roe Island in Suisun Bay (lat. 38°04'15" N, long. 121°01'02" W, at NE end) and rejected the name "Fishermans Channel" for the feature.

Roe Island Channel [CONTRA COSTA-SOLANO]: *channel*, 6.5 miles east-northeast of Martinez in Suisun Bay on Contra Costa-Solano County line (lat. 38°03'50" N, long. 122°01'45" W); the feature is south of Roe Island. Named on Vine Hill (1959) 7.5' quadrangle.

Rogers Canyon [SANTA CLARA]: *canyon*, drained by a stream that flows 3 miles to Sulphur Springs Creek 6.5 miles south-southwest of Mount Boardman (lat. 37°23'20" N, long. 121°29'45" W; sec. 26, T 6 S, R 4 E). Named on Eylar Mountain (1955) and Mount Boardman (1955) 7.5' quadrangles.

Rogers Gulch [SAN MATEO]: *canyon*, drained by a stream that flows 0.5 mile to Lobitos Creek 5.25 miles south-southeast of downtown Half Moon Bay (lat. 37°23'35" N, long. 122°23'35" W). Named on Half Moon Bay (1961) 7.5' quadrangle. Michael Rogers had a ranch in the canyon in the 1860's (Brown, p. 78).

Rohnert Park [SONOMA]: *town*, 1 mile north-northeast of Cotati (lat. 38°20'30" N, long. 122°41'45" W). Named on Cotati (1954, photorevised 1980) 7.5' quadrangle. Postal authorities established Rohnert Park post office in 1961 (Salley, p. 188), and the town incorporated in 1962. Development of the place began in 1957 on Waldo Rohnert seed farm (Mullen).

Rolands [SONOMA]: *settlement*, 1 mile northeast of Guerneville along Russian River (lat. 38°30'40" N, long. 122°58'50" W; on W line sec. 28, T 8 N, R 10 W). Named on Guerneville (1955) 7.5' quadrangle.

Romans Resort [SONOMA]: *locality*, 2.5 miles north-northwest of Cazadero (lat. 38°33'45" N, long. 123°06'25" W; near E line sec. 6, T 8 N, R 11 W). Named on Cazadero (1943) 7.5' quadrangle.

Romanzoff: see **Cape Romanzoff**, under **Bodega Head** [SONOMA].

Roos Cut [SOLANO]: *water feature*, joins Suisun Slough 6.5 miles south-southwest of Fairfield (lat. 38°09'25" N, long. 122°04'15" W). Named on Fairfield South (1949) 7.5' quadrangle.

Rooter Gulch: see **Hooker Creek** [SAN MATEO].

Roscoe: see **Mount Roscoe** [SONOMA].

Rose [SONOMA]: *locality*, 3.25 miles southwest of Sears Point along Northwestern Pacific Railroad (lat. 38°07'15" N, long. 122°29'25" W). Named

on Mare Island (1916) 15' quadrangle.
Rose: see **Camp Rose** [SONOMA].
Rose Flat [ALAMEDA]: *area,* 6 miles south-southwest of Mendenhall Springs (lat. 37°30'50" N, long. 121°42'05" W; near E line sec. 12, T 5 S, R 2 E). Named on Mendenhall Springs (1956) 7.5' quadrangle. The name commemorates Antonio Rose and Manuel Rose, landowners in the region (Mosier and Mosier, p. 74).
Rose Lawn: see **Burbank** [SANTA CLARA].
Rosenberg: see **Camp Rosenberg** [SONOMA].
Rosevelt Cut [CONTRA COSTA]: *water feature,* 1.5 miles east of the settlement of Bethel Island near Sand Mound Slough (lat. 38°01'10" N, long. 121°36' W). Named on Bouldin Island (1978) 7.5' quadrangle.
Ross [MARIN]: *town,* 1.5 miles west-southwest of downtown San Rafael (lat. 37°57'45" N, long. 122°33'30" W). Named on San Rafael (1954) 7.5' quadrangle. Postal authorities established Ross post office in 1887 (Frickstad, p. 89), and the town incorporated in 1908. The name commemorates James Ross, who settled at the place in 1859 (Hoover, Rensch, and Rensch, p. 185). The railroad station at the site first was called Sunnyside (Teather, p. 62).
Ross [SONOMA]: *locality,* nearly 5 miles northeast of Occidental along Petaluma and Santa Rosa Railroad (lat. 38°27'30" N, long. 122°53'05" W). Named on Camp Meeker (1954) 7.5' quadrangle.
Ross: see **Fort Ross** [SONOMA].
Ross Creek [MARIN]: *stream,* flows 1.25 miles from Phoenix Lake to join San Anselmo Creek and form Corte Madera Creek 1.5 miles west-southwest of downtown San Rafael in Ross (lat. 37°58' N, long. 122°33'30" W). Named on San Rafael (1954) 7.5' quadrangle.
Ross Creek [SANTA CLARA]: *stream,* flows 6.5 miles to Guadalupe River 5 miles south of downtown San Jose (lat. 37°15'55" N, long. 121°52'40" W). Named on Los Gatos (1953, photorevised 1968 and 1973) and San Jose West (1961) 7.5' quadrangles. The name is for John E. Ross, who settled in the vicinity in 1856 and farmed along the stream for nearly 40 years (Patricia Loomis, *San Jose Mercury,* January 21, 1980).
Ross Hill [MARIN]: *ridge,* northeast- to east-trending, 1 mile long, 2.25 miles southwest of downtown San Rafael (lat. 37°57'20" N, long. 122°33'55" W); the ridge is south of Ross. Named on San Rafael (1954) 7.5' quadrangle.
Ross Landing: see **Kentfield** [MARIN].
Rosslyn Gap: see **Rockwell Gap** [NAPA].
Ross Valley [MARIN]: *valley,* 1.5 miles west of downtown San Rafael along San Anselmo Creek and Corte Madera Creek (lat. 37° 58'30" N, long. 122°33'45" W). Named on San Rafael (1954) 7.5' quadrangle.
Rough Creek [SONOMA]: *stream,* flows 2.25 miles to Scotty Creek 5.5 miles southeast of Jenner (lat. 38°23'05" N, long. 123°03'20" W). Named on Duncans Mills (1979) 7.5' quadrangle.
Rough Gulch [SANTA CLARA]: *canyon,* drained by a stream that flows 2 miles to Big Canyon 2.5 miles north-northwest of Gilroy Hot Springs (lat. 37°08'25" N, long. 121°29'50" W; sec. 23, T 9 S, R 4 E). Named on Mississippi Creek (1955) and Mount Sizer (1955) 7.5' quadrangles. Called Laguna Ranch Canyon on Morgan Hill (1917) 15' quadrangle.
Rough Gulch: see **Little Rough Gulch** [SANTA CLARA].
Roughs: see **The Roughs** [SONOMA].
Round Corral [NAPA]: *locality,* 6.5 miles southwest of Knoxville along Putah Creek in Big Basin (lat. 38°45'10" N, long. 122°25'05" W; near S line sec. 33, T 11 N, R 5 W). Named on Jericho Valley (1958) 7.5' quadrangle.
Round Hill [SAN MATEO]: *hill,* 4.5 miles south of the village of San Gregorio near Pescadero Creek (lat. 37°15'40" N, long. 122°23'55" W). Named on San Gregorio (1961, photorevised 1968) 7.5' quadrangle.
Round Mountain [SANTA CLARA]: *peak,* 2 miles south-southwest of Isabel Valley (lat. 37°17'20" N, long. 121°32'55" W; near SW cor. sec. 28, T 7 S, R 4 E). Altitude 3085 feet. Named on Isabel Valley (1955) 7.5' quadrangle.
Round Top [CONTRA COSTA]: *peak,* 3 miles south-southwest of Orinda (lat. 37°51' N, long. 122°11'30" W; on S line sec. 9, T 1 S, R 3 W). Altitude 1763 feet. Named on Oakland East (1959) 7.5' quadrangle. United States Board on Geographic Names (1970b, p. 1) approved the name "Gudde Ridge" for the ridge on which Round Top is a high point; the name "Gudde" honors Erwin G. Gudde, professor at University of California, Berkeley, and author of California place-name books.
Round Valley [CONTRA COSTA]: *valley,* 8 miles east-southeast of Mount Diablo (lat. 37°51'10" N, long. 121°46'30" W). Named on Tassajara (1953) 7.5' quadrangle.
Routan Creek [NAPA]: *stream,* flows 4.25 miles to Butts Creek 6 miles northeast of Aetna Springs (lat. 38°41'55" N, long. 122°23'30" W; sec. 22, T 10 N, R 5 W). Named on Aetna Springs (1958) 7.5' quadrangle.
Royaneh: see **Camp Royaneh** [SONOMA].
Roy Creek [SONOMA]: *stream,* flows 2.5 miles to North Fork Buckeye Creek (2) 11 miles north-northeast of the village of Stewarts Point (lat. 38°48' N, long. 123°18'50" W; sec. 16, T 11 N, R 13 W). Named on Ornbaun Valley (1960) 15' quadrangle.
Roy Gulch [SAN MATEO]: *canyon,* drained by a stream that flows 1.25 miles to Pescadero Creek 5.25 miles southwest of La Honda (lat. 37°15'40" N, long. 122°20' W; sec. 6, T 8 S, R 4 W). Named on La Honda (1961) 7.5' quadrangle. Louis Roy had a ranch in the canyon in the late 1860's and 1870's (Brown, p. 78).
Ruby Canyon [SANTA CLARA]: *canyon,* 0.25 mile long, 4 miles northeast of Gilroy along Alamias Creek (lat. 37°02'40" N, long. 121°30'50" W). Named on Gilroy (1955) 7.5' quadrangle.
Ruckels Island: see **Winter Island** [CONTRA COSTA].
Rucker [SANTA CLARA]: *locality,* 3.25 miles north-northwest of Gilroy along Southern Pacific Railroad (lat. 37°03'15" N, long. 121°35'30" W). Named on Gilroy (1955) 7.5' quadrangle. Postal authorities established Rucker post office in 1894, moved it 0.5 mile west in 1896, and discontinued it in 1900; the name commemorates William B. Rucker, a pioneer settler (Salley, p. 190). According to tradition, a low hill on the west side of Santa Clara Valley between Rucker and Gilroy was called Lomita de la Linares for Señora Linares, who rested there when the first settlers bound for San Jose stopped to hunt elk (Hoover, Rensch, and Rensch, p. 431).
Rucker Creek: see **Llagas Creek** [SANTA CLARA].
Rudesill's Landing: see **Haystack Landing**, under **Haystack** [SONOMA].
Rule [SONOMA]: *locality,* less than 1 mile north-northwest of present Jenner (lat. 38°27'50" N, long. 123°07'15" W). Named on Duncans Mills (1921) 15' quadrangle.
Rumsey Range: see **Blue Ridge** [NAPA].
Rumyantsev: see **Port Rumyantsev**, under **Bodega Bay** [MARIN-SONOMA].
Runnymede: see **East Palo Alto** [SAN MATEO].
Rush Creek [MARIN]: *stream,* flows 1.5 miles to Black John Slough 2.5 miles north-northeast of downtown Novato (lat. 38°08' N, long. 122°33'05" W). Named on Novato (1954) and Petaluma River (1954) 7.5' quadrangles. Teather (p. 63) associated the name "Rush Creek" with Peter Rush, who bought land near present Novato in 1862.
Rush Landing [SOLANO]: *locality,* 2.25 miles south-southeast of Fairfield along Suisun Slough (lat. 38°13' N, long. 122°01'45" W; sec. 1, T 4 N, R 2 W). Named on Fairfield South (1949) 7.5' quadrangle.
Russell [SOLANO]: *locality,* 3 miles west-southwest of Fairfield along Sacramento Northern Railroad (lat. 38°14'20" N, long. 122° 05'40" W). Named on Fairfield South (1949) 7.5' quadrangle.
Russell: see **Russell City** [ALAMEDA].
Russel City [ALAMEDA]: *district,* 5.25 miles south-southeast of downtown San Leandro (lat. 37°39' N, long. 122°08' W). Named on San Leandro (1959) 7.5' quadrangle. United States Board on Geographic Names (1961a, p. 19) rejected the name "Russell" for the place. Frederick James Russell laid out the community in 1907 (Mosier and Mosier, p. 75).
Russellmann Creek [CONTRA COSTA]: *stream,* flows nearly 1 mile to Mount Diablo Creek 3 miles north of Mount Diablo (lat. 37°55'20" N, long. 121°54'20" W; sec. 19, T 1 N, R 1 E). Named on Clayton (1953) 7.5' quadrangle.
Russian Gulch [SONOMA]: *canyon,* 1 mile long, opens to the sea 2.25 miles west-northwest of Jenner (lat. 38°28' N, long. 123°09'15" W). Named on Arched Rock (1977) 7.5' quadrangle. The canyon divides at the head into three branches called East, Middle, and West. East Branch is 2.5 miles long and is named on Arched Rock (1977) and Duncans Mills (1979) 7.5' quadrangles. Middle Branch and West Branch each are 4 miles long and are named on Arched Rock (1977) and Fort Ross (1978) 7.5' quadrangles.
Russian Hill [SAN FRANCISCO]: *ridge,* northwest- to north-trending, 0.5 mile long, less than 1 mile south-southwest of North Point (lat. 37°47'55" N, long. 122°25' W). Named on San Francisco North (1956) 7.5' quadrangle. The name probably is from a graveyard for Russian sailors that was located on the hill in the early days (Hoover, Rensch, and Rensch, p. 363).
Russian Ridge [SAN MATEO]: *ridge,* west-northwest-trending, 2 miles long, 1.5 miles east-northeast of Mindego Hill (lat. 37°19'15" N, long. 122°12' W). Named on Mindego Hill (1961) 7.5' quadrangle.
Russian River [SONOMA]: *stream,* heads in Mendocino County and flows 68 miles in Sonoma County to the sea 0.5 mile west of Jenner (lat. 38°27'05" N, long. 123°07'40" W). Named on Santa Rosa (1958) 1°x 2° quadrangle. Called Rio Rusa on a diseño of San Miguel grant; the stream is designated by its Indian name "Jauiyomi" on a diseño of Llano de Santa Rosa grant—the name "Jauiyomi" often has the spelling "Satiyome" or "Saliyome" (Becker, 1964). A map of 1850 produced by the Topographical Engineers has the names "Passion River" and "River Slavianka" for present Russian River (Wheat, p. 113). Ivan Kuskov, who explored the river in 1811, gave it the name "Slavyanka" (Schwartz, p. 43). Arguello passed through the valley of Russian River in 1821 and called it Libantiliyami (Bancroft, 1886, p. 449).
Russian River: see **Healdsburg** [SONOMA].
Russian River Heights [SONOMA]: *locality,* 1.5 miles south-southwest of Guerneville along Northwestern Pacific Railroad near Russian River (lat. 38°28'50" N, long. 123°00'30" W). Named on Duncans Mills (1921) 15' quadrangle.
Russian River Terrace [SONOMA]: *settlement,* 3.5 miles east of Guerneville

along Russian River (lat. 38°30'15" N, long. 122°55'40" W; near SE cor. sec. 26, T 8 N, R 10 W). Named on Guerneville (1955) 7.5' quadrangle.

Russian Trough Spring [SONOMA]: *spring,* 2.25 miles northeast of Fort Ross (lat. 38°31'55" N, long. 123°12'25" W). Named on Fort Ross (1978) 7.5' quadrangle.

Russ Island [NAPA-SOLANO]: *island,* 3.25 miles west-southwest of Napa Junction between Napa River, South Slough, China Slough, and Devils Slough on Napa-Solano County line, mainly in Napa County (lat. 38°10'10" N, long. 122°18'30" W). Named on Cuttings Wharf (1949) 7.5' quadrangle. Called Knight Island on Mare Island (1916) 15' quadrangle.

Rust: see **El Cerito** [CONTRA COSTA]; **William Rust Summit**, under **Camp Herms** [CONTRA COSTA].

Rutherford [NAPA]: *village,* 4 miles southeast of Saint Helena (lat. 38°27'30" N, long. 122°25'20" W). Named on Rutherford (1951) 7.5' quadrangle. Postal authorities established Rutherford post office in 1871 (Frickstad, p. 112). The name commemorates Thomas L. Rutherford, who married a granddaughter of George C. Yount (Gudde, 1949, p. 293). Postal authorities established Lomitas post office 10 miles northeast of Rutherford in 1894 and discontinued it in 1906 (Salley, p. 125).

Ryer Island [SOLANO]:

(1) *island,* 6.5 miles north-northeast of Rio Vista between Miner Slough, Sutter Slough, Steamboat Slough, and Cache Slough (lat. 38°14' N, long. 121°38' W). Named on Courtland (1978), Isleton (1978), Liberty Island (1978), and Rio Vista (1978) 7.5' quadrangles. On Ringgold's (1850c) map, the part of the feature east of present Elkhorn Slough is called Sutter I., and the part west of the slough is called Taylor I. The same map has the name "Pt. Gelston" for the promontory at the south tip of present Ryer Island (1).

(2) *island,* 8 miles east-northeast of Benicia between Suisun Bay and Suisun Cutoff (lat. 38°05' N, long. 122°01' W). Named on Honker Bay (1953) and Vine Hill (1959) 7.5' quadrangles. Called Kings I. on Ringgold's (1850c) map, but United States Board on Geographic Names (1933, p. 654) rejected the names "King's Island," "Long Point Island," and "Ryer's Island" for the feature. The name commemorates Dr. W.M. Ryer, a pioneer physician who owned the island (Gudde, 1949, p. 293).

Ryer Island Ferry [SOLANO]: *locality,* 2.5 miles northeast of Rio Vista on Cache Slough near the south tip of Ryer Island (1) (lat. 38°11'10" N, long. 121°39'30" W). Named on Rio Vista (1978) 7.5' quadrangle.

Ryer's Island: see **Ryer Island** [SOLANO] (2).

— S —

Sacramento Brazoria: see **Rio Vista** [SOLANO].

Sacramento Deep Water Channel: see **Sacramento River Deep Water Ship Channel** [SOLANO].

Sacramento Landing [MARIN]: *locality,* 6.5 miles south of Tomales on the southwest side of Tomales Bay (lat. 38°09' N, long. 122°54'20" W). Named on Tomales (1954) 7.5' quadrangle. The place probably was named for an Indian (Mason, 1976a, p. 149).

Sacramento River [SOLANO]: *stream,* flows 15 miles along Solano-Sacramento County line to Suisun Bay 4.5 miles south of Birds Landing (2) (lat. 38°03'50" N, long. 121°51' W). Named on Antioch North (1978), Jersey Island (1978), and Rio Vista (1978) 7.5' quadrangles. Called Rio Sacramento on Fremont's (1845) map. In 1808 Gabriel Moraga applied the name "Sacramento" to present Feather River, a tributary of Sacramento River in Sutter County; present Sacramento River was called San Francisco and Buenaventura or Bonaventura before the name "Sacramento" shifted to it—*Sacramento* means "Holy Sacrament" in Spanish (Hart, p. 364). Present Elkhorn Slough is called West Fork [Sacramento River] on Ringgold's (1850c) map, present Steamboat Slough [SOLANO] is called Middle Fork [Sacramento River] on the same map, and present Sutter Slough [SOLANO] is called West Fork [Sacramento River] on Ringgold's (1850d) map.

Sacramento River: see **Suisun Bay** [CONTRA COSTA].

Sacramento River Deep Water Ship Channel [SOLANO]: *channel,* extends along Sacramento River from Suisun Bay past Rio Vista, and then along Cache Slough to Prospect Island, from which the channel follows an artificial waterway through Yolo Bypass to Yolo County. Named on Antioch North (1978), Jersey Island (1978), Liberty Island (1978), and Rio Vista (1978) 7.5' quadrangles. United States Board on Geographic names (1978a, p. 7) rejected the names "Deep Water Ship Channel," "Sacramento Deep Water Channel," "Sacramento Ship Channel," and "Ship Channel" for the feature.

Sacramento Ship Channel: see **Sacramento River Deep Water Ship Channel** [SOLANO].

Sacre Gap [SONOMA]: *pass,* 1 mile north of Mount Saint Helena on Sonoma-Lake County line (lat. 38°41'05" N, long. 122°38' W; sec. 28, T 10 N, R 7 W). Named on Mount Saint Helena (1959) 7.5' quadrangle.

Saddleback [NAPA]: *peak,* 2.5 miles east-northeast of Calistoga (lat. 38°35'40" N, long. 122°32'05" W; near SW cor. sec. 28, T 9 N, R 6 W). Named on Calistoga (1958) 7.5' quadrangle.

Saddle Rock: see **Devils Slide** [SAN MATEO]; **Seal Rock** [SAN FRANCISCO].

Sagadehock Reach: see **Horseshoe Bend** [SOLANO].

Sage Canyon [NAPA]: *canyon,* 4 miles long, opens into the canyon of Chiles Creek nearly 6 miles north of Yountville (lat. 38°29'25" N, long. 122°20'50" W; sec. 6, T 7 N, R 4 W). Named on Chiles Valley (1958) and Yountville (1951) 7.5' quadrangles. Water of Lake Hennessey floods the lowermost part of the canyon.

Sage Creek [NAPA]: *stream,* flows 5.5 miles to Lake Hennessey 6 miles north-northeast of Yountville (lat. 38°29'30" N, long. 122°20'25" W; sec. 6, T 7 N, R 4 W); the stream goes through Sage Canyon. Named on Chiles Valley (1958) 7.5' quadrangle.

Sage Creek: see **Conn Creek** [NAPA].

Sail Rock [SAN MATEO]: *rock,* 4.5 miles west-northwest of downtown Half Moon Bay off Pillar Point (lat. 37°29'35" N, long. 122° 29'55" W). Named on Half Moon Bay (1961) 7.5' quadrangle. United States Board on Geographic Names (1933, p. 656) rejected the names "Pillar Rock," "Seal Rock," and "Steeple Rock" for the feature. The name "Sail Rock" is from the shape of the rock (Brown, p. 78).

Saint Elmo Creek [SONOMA]: *stream,* flows 2 miles to Austin Creek 0.25 mile south of Cazadero (lat. 38°31'30" N, long. 123°05'15" W; sec. 21, T 8 N, R 11 W). Named on Cazadero (1978) 7.5' quadrangle.

Saint Helena [NAPA]: *town,* 17 miles northwest of the city of Napa (lat. 38°30'15" N, long. 122°28'10" W). Named on Rutherford (1951) and Saint Helena (1960) 7.5' quadrangles. Postal authorities established Saint Helena post office in 1856 (Frickstad, p. 112), and the town incorporated in 1876. The community began in 1853 when Henry Still built a store and house there; the name is from the designation of a division of Sons of Temperance established at the place (Menefee, p. 186).

Saint Helena: see **Mount Saint Helena** [SONOMA].

Saint Helena Creek [NAPA]: *stream,* flows 2 miles to Lake County nearly 7 miles north of Calistoga (lat. 38°40'35" N, long. 122°35'25" W; sec. 36, T 10 N, R 7 W). Named on Detert Reservoir (1958) 7.5' quadrangle.

Saint Helena Range: see **Mayacmas Mountains** [NAPA-SONOMA].

Saint Helena White Sulphur Springs: see **Sulphur Canyon** [NAPA].

Saint Hellens: see **Mount Saint Hellens**, under **Mount Saint Helena** [SONOMA].

Saint John Mountain: see **Mount Saint John** [NAPA].

Saint Joseph Camp [SONOMA]: *locality,* 3.5 miles southwest of Guerneville along Russian River (lat. 38°27'40" N, long. 123°02'35" W). Named on Duncans Mills (1979) 7.5' quadrangle.

Saint Josephs Hill [SANTA CLARA]: *peak,* 1.5 miles south of downtown Los Gatos (lat. 37°12'20" N, long. 121°58'35" W; sec. 28, T 8 S, R 1 W). Named on Los Gatos (1953) 7.5' quadrangle.

Saint Louis: see **Sonoma** [SONOMA].

Saint Marys Bay [CONTRA COSTA]: *water feature,* 6 miles east of Brentwood along Indian Slough (lat. 37°55'15" N, long. 121°35'15" W). Named on Woodward Island (1978) 7.5' quadrangle.

Saint Mary's College: see **Moraga** [CONTRA COSTA].

Saint Vincent: see **Gallinas** [MARIN].

Salada: see **Sharp Park** [SAN MATEO].

Salada Beach: see **Sharp Park** [SAN MATEO].

Saline City: see **Drawbridge** [ALAMEDA].

Saliyome: see **Russian River** [SONOMA].

Salmon Creek [MARIN]: *stream,* flows 5 miles to join Arroyo Sausal and form Walker Creek 9 miles southeast of Tomales (lat. 38°09'40" N, long. 122°46'50" W). Named on Petaluma (1953) and Point Reyes NE (1954) 7.5' quadrangles.

Salmon Creek [SONOMA]:

(1) *stream,* flows 17 miles to the sea 2 miles northwest of the village of Bodega Bay (lat. 38°21'20" N, long. 123°04' W). Named on Bodega Head (1972), Camp Meeker (1954), and Valley Ford (1954) 7.5' quadrangles. According to Bancroft (1886, p. 464), a party of Mexicans on the way to Fort Ross in 1822 called the stream Arroyo Verde for the color of the water after one of the party became ill and vomited into the stream—*verde* means "green" in Spanish.

(2) *village,* 1.5 miles northwest of the village of Bodega Bay (lat. 38°21'05" N, long. 123°03'40" W); the village is near the mouth of Salmon Creek (1). Named on Bodega Head (1972) 7.5' quadrangle.

Salmon Creek: see **Walker Creek** [MARIN].

Salmon Creek Beach: see **North Salmon Creek Beach** [SONOMA]; **South Salmon Creek Beach** [SONOMA].

Salmon Island: see **Coyote Hills** [ALAMEDA].

Salsipuedes [SANTA CLARA]: *land grant,* mainly in Santa Cruz County, but extends into Santa Clara County along the crest of Santa Cruz Mountains southwest of Gilroy. Named on Chittenden (1955), Mount Madonna (1955), and Watsonville East (1955) 7.5' quadrangles. Manuel Jimeno Casarin received 8 leagues in 1834 and 1840; James Blair and John P. Davidson claimed 31,201 acres patented in 1861 (Cowan, p. 71; Perez, p. 87). *Salsipuedes* means "get out if you can" in Spanish, and refers to rugged terrain on the grant (Arbuckle, p. 29-30).

Salt Creek [SONOMA]: *stream,* flows 1.5 miles to Santa Rosa Creek 5.25 miles north-northwest of Kenwood (lat. 38°29'25" N, long. 122°34' W; sec. 6, T 7 N, R 6 W). Named on Kenwood (1954) 7.5' quadrangle.

Salt Lake: see **Laguna Salada** [SAN MATEO].

Salt Lake Valley: see **Laguna Salada** [SAN MATEO].

Salt Marsh Creek [MARIN]: *stream,* flows 1.25 miles to San Francisco Bay 3.25 miles south-southeast of downtown San Rafael (lat. 37°55'55" N, long. 122°30'10" W). Named on San Rafael (1954) 7.5' quadrangle.

Salt Point [SONOMA]: *promontory,* 2 miles southwest of Plantation along the coast (lat. 38°33'55" N, long. 123°19'55" W). Named on Plantation (1977) 7.5' quadrangle.

Salt Tree Saddle [SONOMA]: *pass,* 3.25 miles north of Cazadero (lat. 38°34'40" N, long. 123°05'40" W; sec. 32, T 9 N, R 11 W). Named on Cazadero (1978) 7.5' quadrangle.

Salt Valley [SAN MATEO]: *valley,* 4.5 miles north of present Montara Knob at the south end of Laguna Salada (lat. 37°37'10" N, long. 122°29'15" W). Named on San Mateo (1915) 15' quadrangle.

Salt Work Slough: see **Plummer Creek** [ALAMEDA].

Salvador [NAPA]: *locality,* 3.5 miles north-northwest of downtown Napa (lat. 38°20'25" N, long. 122°19'10" W). Named on Napa (1951) 7.5' quadrangle.

Sams Canyon [SANTA CLARA]: *canyon,* drained by a stream that flows nearly 4 miles to Arroyo Valle 3.25 miles southwest of Eylar Mountain (lat. 37°26'15" N, long. 121°35' W; sec. 6, T 6 S, R 4 E). Named on Eylar Mountain (1955) 7.5' quadrangle.

Samson Canyon [SANTA CLARA]: *canyon,* drained by a stream that flows nearly 2 miles to Hoover Valley 4.25 miles west-southwest of Mount Sizer (lat. 37°11'35" N, long. 121°35' W); the canyon is south of Samson Ridge. Named on Mount Sizer (1955) 7.5' quadrangle.

Samson Ridge [SANTA CLARA]: *ridge,* west-northwest-trending, 1.5 miles long, 3.5 miles southwest of Mount Sizer (lat. 37°11'05" N, long. 121°34' W). Named on Mount Sizer (1955) 7.5' quadrangle.

Samuel Springs [NAPA]: *locality,* 11 miles northeast of Saint Helena (lat. 38°36'15" N, long. 122°18'40" W). Named on Chiles Valley (1958) 7.5' quadrangle. Springs at the place were the basis of a resort called Samuels' Soda Springs (Crawford, 1894, p. 341). Napa Rock Soda Springs, also known as Priest Soda Springs, were located about 6 miles south of Samuel Springs (Waring, p. 161)—water from these springs was bottled as early as 1898 (Bradley, p. 281). Phillips Soda Springs were situated about 350 yards north of Napa Rock Soda Springs; water there was used for bathing in the early days (Waring, p. 161). Pope Mineral Spring, also called Indian Spring, lies 1 mile west of Samuels Soda Springs; the proprietor began bottling the water in 1913 (Bradley, p. 281).

Samuels' Soda Springs: see **Samuel Springs** [NAPA].

San Andreas Lake [SAN MATEO]: *lake,* nearly 3 miles long, behind a dam 2 miles southwest of downtown Millbrae (lat. 37°34'50" N, long. 122°24'35" W). Named on Montara Mountain (1956) 7.5' quadrangle. United States Board on Geographic Names (1933, p. 664) rejected the form "San Andres Lake" for the name. The reservoir was created in 1875 in the valley that Palou called Cañada de San Andres in 1774 (Gudde, 1949, p. 297).

San Andres Lake: see **San Andreas Lake** [SAN MATEO].

San Anselmo [MARIN]: *town,* 1.5 miles west of downtown San Rafael (lat. 37°58'30" N, long. 122°33'45" W); the town is along San Anselmo Creek. Named on San Rafael (1954) 7.5' quadrangle. Postal authorities established San Anselmo post office in 1892 (Frickstad, p. 89), and the town incorporated in 1907. Postal authorities established Yolanda post office as a station of San Anselmo post office in 1924 and discontinued it in 1954; they established Lansdale post office as a station of San Anselmo post office in 1924 and discontinued it in 1962 (Salley, p. 117, 244).

San Anselmo Creek [MARIN]: *stream,* flows 6 miles to join Ross Creek and form Corte Madera Creek 1.5 miles west-southwest of downtown San Rafael (lat. 37°58' N, long. 122°33'30" W). Named on Bolinas (1954) and San Rafael (1954) 7.5' quadrangles.

San Antone Creek: see **San Antonio Creek** [SANTA CLARA].

San Antone Valley: see **San Antonio Valley** [SANTA CLARA].

San Antonio [ALAMEDA]:

(1) *land grant,* at and near Berkeley. Named on Briones Valley (1959), Oakland East (1959), Oakland West (1959), and Richmond (1959) 7.5' quadrangles. Luis Peralta received 11 leagues in 1820; his sons Domingo and Vicente claimed 18,849 acres patented in 1877 (Cowan, p. 71).

(2) *land grant,* at Oakland. Named on Oakland East (1959) 7.5' quadrangle. Luis Peralta received 11 leagues in 1820; his son Antonio Maria Peralta claimed 15,207 acres patented in 1874 (Cowan, p. 71).

(3) *land grant,* at and near San Leandro. Named on Hayward (1959), Las Trampas Ridge (1959), and San Leandro (1959) 7.5' quadrangles. Luis Peralta received 11 leagues in 1820; his son Ignacio Peralta claimed 9417 acres patented in 1858 (Cowan, p. 71). Perez (p. 88) gave the size of this grant as 9400.16 acres.

San Antonio [SANTA CLARA]: *land grant,* in Los Altos and Los Altos Hills. Named on Cupertino (1961) and Mindego Hill (1961) 7.5' quadrangles. Juan Prado Mesa received the land in 1839; Encarnacion Mesa and others claimed 4440 acres patented in 1866; William A. Dana and others claimed 3542 acres patented in 1857 (Cowan, p. 72).

San Antonio: see **Oakland** [ALAMEDA].

San Antonio Creek [ALAMEDA]: *stream,* flows 11.5 miles to Alameda Creek 1.5 miles south-southeast of Sunol (lat. 37°34'35" N, long. 121°52'10" W). Named on La Costa Valley (1960) and Mendenhall Springs (1956) 7.5' quadrangles. The stream, or part of it, also was called La Costa Creek (Mosier and Mosier, p. 76). Present Indian Creek, a tributary of San Antonio Creek, is called South Fork San Antonio Cr. on Thompson and West's (1878) map.

San Antonio Creek [MARIN-SONOMA]: *stream,* heads in Sonoma County and flows 17 miles, mainly along along Marin-Sonoma County line, to Petaluma River nearly 4 miles north-northeast of downtown Novato (lat. 38°09'30" N, long. 122°32'40" W). Named on Petaluma (1953) and Petaluma River (1954) 7.5' quadrangles. The stream was called Arroyo de San Antonio in Spanish days (Teather, p. 65).

San Antonio Creek [SANTA CLARA]: *stream,* flows 15 miles to Arroyo Bayo 6.25 miles south-southwest of Eylar Mountain (lat. 37°23'05" N, long. 121°34' W; sec. 30, T 6 S, R 4 E). Named on Eylar Mountain (1955), Isabel Valley (1955), Mount Boardman (1955), and Mount Stakes (1955) 7.5' quadrangles. Called San Antone Creek on Mount Boardman (1942) 15' quadrangle. Postal authorities established Gilbert post office along San Antonio Creek (T 7 S, R 4 E) in 1888 and discontinued it in 1889; the post office was on Charles Gilbert's ranch (Salley, p. 85).

San Antonio Creek: see **Adobe Creek** [SANTA CLARA]; **La Costa Creek** [ALAMEDA]; **Lake Merritt** [ALAMEDA]; **Oakland Inner Harbor** [ALAMEDA].

San Antonio Creek, North Fork: see **Chileno Creek** [MARIN].

San Antonio Estuary: see **Oakland Inner Harbor** [ALAMEDA].

San Antonio or Pescadero [SAN MATEO]: *land grant,* along the coast near Pescadero. Named on Pigeon Point (1955) and San Gregorio (1961) 7.5' quadrangles. Joaquin Solis and Jose Antonio Botiller received 4 leagues in 1829; Juan Jose Gonzales received three-quarters of a league in 1833 and claimed 3282 acres patented in 1866 (Cowan, p. 59).

San Antonio Reservoir [ALAMEDA]: *lake,* 3 miles long, behind a dam on San Antonio Creek 2.5 miles southeast of Sunol in La Costa Valley (lat. 37°34'20" N, long. 121°50'50" W). Named on La Costa Valley (1960, photorevised 1968) 7.5' quadrangle.

San Antonio Slough: see **Lake Merritt** [ALAMEDA].

San Antonio Valley [SANTA CLARA]: *valley,* 5 miles northwest of Mount Stakes (lat. 37°22' N, long. 121°28'45" W); the valley is on upper reaches of San Antonio Creek. Named on Mount Boardman (1955) and Mount Stakes (1955) 7.5' quadrangles. Called San Antone Valley on Mount Boardman (1942) 15' quadrangle. Anza traveled through the valley in 1776 and his soldiers called it El Cañada de San Vicente (Davidson, p. 123). Clark's (1924) map has the name "Deforest" for a group of buildings along San Antonio Creek, apparently in the northwest part of present San Antonio Valley. Postal authorities established DeForest post office in 1892, moved it 0.5 mile northwest in 1897, moved it 8 miles southeast in 1906, and discontinued it in 1909; the name was for Ransford S. DeForest, first postmaster (Salley, p. 56).

San Antonio Valley: see **Upper San Antonio Valley** [SANTA CLARA].

San Benito: see **Half Moon Bay** [SAN MATEO] (2); **Miramontes** [SAN MATEO] (1).

San Bernardino Valley: see **Santa Clara Valley** [SANTA CLARA].

San Bruno [SAN MATEO]: *city,* 2 miles south of downtown South San Francisco (lat. 37°37'40" N, long. 122°24'35" W). Named on Montara Mountain (1956) and San Francisco South (1956) 7.5' quadrangles. A travelers stop called San Bruno House opened at the place about 1852 and eventually it housed a railroad depot, post office, telegraph office, and freight station (Hynding, p. 53). Postal authorities established San Bruno post office in 1875, discontinued it for a time in 1890, discontinued it again for a time in 1891, discontinued it in 1893, and reestablished it in 1898 (Frickstad, p. 169). The city incorporated in 1914. A railroad station in present San Bruno was named Tanforan for nearby Tanforan Park race track—the track opened in the 1890's; the misspelled name is from Torribio Tanfaran, who inherited the land at the site; during World War I the race track was converted into a military installation called Camp Grizzly for an artillery regiment that had the name "California Grizzlies" (Brown, p. 93; Hynding, p. 120, 201).

San Bruno Canal [SAN MATEO]: *water feature,* opens into San Francisco Bay 1.25 miles east-southeast of downtown South San Francisco (lat. 37°39' N, long. 122°23'15" W). Named on San Francisco South (1956) 7.5' quadrangle. The feature now is filled.

San Bruno Canyon [SANTA CLARA]: *canyon,* drained by a stream that flows 1.25 miles to lowlands nearly 4 miles south-southeast of Coyote (lat. 37°09'55" N, long. 121°42'50" W). Named on Morgan Hill (1955) 7.5' quadrangle.

San Bruno Channel [SAN MATEO]: *channel,* extends through shallow water of San Francisco Bay south of Point San Bruno to the shore 1.5 miles southeast of downtown South San Francisco (lat. 37°38'30" N, long. 122°23'35" W). Named on Hunters Point (1956) 7.5' quadrangle.

San Bruno Creek [SAN MATEO]: *stream,* flows 2 miles to lowlands along San Francisco Bay less than 2 miles south of downtown South San Francisco in San Bruno (lat. 37°37'45" N, long. 122°25'05" W); the stream is on Buri Buri grant. Named on Montara Mountain (1956) and San Francisco South (1956) 7.5' quadrangles. The stream was called Sanjon de Buriburi in Spanish times (Brown, p. 80).

San Bruno Creek: see **Colma Creek** [SAN MATEO].

San Bruno House: see **San Bruno** [SAN MATEO].

San Bruno Mountain [SAN MATEO]: *ridge,* east-southeast-trending, 3.5 miles long, center 2 miles north-northwest of downtown South San Francisco (lat. 37°41' N, long. 122°25'45" W). Named on San Francisco South (1956) 7.5' quadrangle. The feature was called Sierra de San Bruno (Gudde, 1949, p. 299) and Cerro de San Bruno in Spanish times; later it also was called Crocker Mountain (Brown, p. 80). Blake (1856, p. 378) referred to San Bruno range, Antisell (p. 16) mentioned Monte San Bruno, and Whitney (p. 62) used the name "San Bruno Mountains."

San Bruno Point: see **Point San Bruno** [SAN MATEO].

San Bruno Range: see **San Bruno Mountain** [SAN MATEO].

San Bruno Shoal [SAN MATEO]: *shoal,* 7 miles east of downtown South San Francisco in San Francisco Bay (lat. 37°38'45" N, long. 122°17'20" W). Named on Hunters Point (1956) 7.5' quadrangle.

San Carlos [SAN MATEO]: *city,* 5.5 miles southeast of downtown San Mateo (lat. 37°30'15" N, long. 122°15'40" W). Named on Palo Alto (1961), Redwood Point (1959), San Mateo (1956), and Woodside (1961) 7.5' quadrangles. Postal authorities established San Carlos post office in 1895 (Frickstad, p. 169), and the city incorporated in 1925.

San Carlos Creek: see **Pulgas Creek** [SAN MATEO].

San Catanio Creek [CONTRA COSTA]: *stream,* flows 2.5 miles to San Ramon Creek 3.5 miles south-southeast of Danville (lat. 37° 46'25" N, long. 121°59' W). Named on Diablo (1953) 7.5' quadrangle.

Sanchez Creek [SAN MATEO]: *stream,* flows 2.5 miles to San Francisco Bay 2.5 miles northwest of downtown San Mateo (lat. 37°35'20" N, long. 122°21'25" W). Named on San Mateo (1956) 7.5' quadrangle.

San Clemente [MARIN]: *locality,* 4 miles south-southeast of downtown San Rafael along Northwestern Pacific Railroad (lat. 37°55'10" N, long. 122°30'35" W); the place is near present San Clemente Creek. Named on Mount Tamalpais (1950) 15' quadrangle.

San Clemente Creek [MARIN]: *stream,* flows 1.25 miles to San Francisco Bay 1.5 miles southwest of Point San Quentin (lat. 37° 55'35" N, long. 122°29'55" W). Named on San Quentin (1959) and San Rafael (1954) 7.5' quadrangles.

Sand Beach [SAN MATEO]: *beach,* 4 miles south-southwest of the village of San Gregorio along the coast north of the mouth of Pescadero Creek (lat. 37°16'15" N, long. 122°24'35" W). Named on San Gregorio (1961, photorevised 1968) 7.5' quadrangle. The place also was called Bradley Beach (Brown, p. 81).

Sand Creek [CONTRA COSTA]: *stream,* flows 10.5 miles to Marsh Creek 0.5 mile west-northwest of Brentwood (lat. 37°56'20" N, long. 121°42'20" W). Named on Antioch South (1953) and Brentwood (1978) 7.5' quadrangles.

Sand Hill [CONTRA COSTA]: *settlement,* 3 miles north of Brentwood (lat. 37°58'30" N, long. 121°41'35" W). Named on Brentwood (1978) 7.5' quadrangle.

Sand Mound: see **Jersey** [CONTRA COSTA].

Sand Mound Slough [CONTRA COSTA]: *water feature,* extends for 5.5 miles from Rock Slough to Old River 3.5 miles east-northeast of the settlement of Bethel Island (lat. 38°01'50" N, long. 121°34'50" W). Named on Bouldin Island (1978), Jersey Island (1978), and Woodward Island (1978) 7.5' quadrangles.

Sando [CONTRA COSTA]: *locality,* less than 1 mile east of downtown Antioch along Atchison, Topeka and Santa Fe Railroad (lat. 38°00'50" N, long. 121°47'40" W; sec. 18, T 2 N, R 2 E). Named on Antioch North (1953) 7.5' quadrangle.

Sand Point [MARIN]: *promontory,* nearly 4 miles west-southwest of Tomales on the east side of the entrance to Tomales Bay (lat. 38° 13'55" N, long. 122°58'15" W). Named on Tomales (1954) 7.5' quadrangle. The feature also was called Punta Rena (Teather, p. 65).

Sand Point [SANTA CLARA]: *promontory,* 5 miles north-northwest of downtown Mountain View at the edge of mud flats along San Francisco Bay (lat. 37°27'45" N, long. 122°06'05" W). Named on Mountain View (1961) 7.5' quadrangle.

Sandy Point [SONOMA]: *promontory,* 0.5 mile south of the village of Stewarts Point along the coast (lat. 38°38'40" N, long. 123°23'55" W). Named on Stewarts Point (1978) 7.5' quadrangle.

Sandy Point: see **Notley Junction** [SAN MATEO].

San Felipe [SANTA CLARA]: *locality,* 6 miles east-southeast of Gilroy (lat. 36°58'15" N, long. 121°25'05" W); the place is on Ausaymas y San Felipe grant. Named on San Felipe (1955) 7.5' quadrangle. Postal authorities established Felipe post office in 1868 and discontinued it in 1902 (Frickstad, p. 175).

San Felipe: see **Ausaymas y San Felipe** [SANTA CLARA].

San Felipe Creek [SANTA CLARA]: *stream,* flows 14 miles to Las Animas Creek nearly 6 miles north of Morgan Hill (lat. 37°12'50" N, long. 121°39'20" W). Named on Lick Observatory (1955) and Morgan Hill (1955) 7.5' quadrangles.

San Felipe Hills [SANTA CLARA]: *ridge,* northwest-trending, 2.25 miles long, 3 miles south-southeast of Mount Hamilton (lat. 37°17'50" N, long. 121°37'45" W). Named on Isabel Valley (1955) and Lick Observatory (1955) 7.5' quadrangles.

San Felipe Valley [SANTA CLARA]: *valley,* 5 miles south-southwest of Mount Hamilton (lat. 37°16'30" N, long. 121°40'35" W); the valley is along San Felipe Creek. Named on Lick Observatory (1955) 7.5' quadrangle.

San Felix Station: see **Lower Crystal Springs Reservoir** [SAN MATEO].

San Francisco [SAN FRANCISCO]: *city,* south of the Golden Gate between San Francisco Bay and the sea (civic center near lat. 37° 46'45" N, long. 122°25' W). Named on Hunters Point (1956, photorevised 1968), Oakland West (1959), Richmond (1959), San Francisco North (1956), San Francisco South (1956), and San Quentin (1959) 7.5' quadrangles. Postal authorities established San Francisco post office in 1848 (Frickstad, p. 159), and the city incorporated in 1850. Captain William A. Richardson built a house in 1835 near San Francisco Bay at Yerba Buena Cove, and the building became the nucleus of a village called Yerba Buena (Hoover, Rensch, and Rensch, p. 352). *Californian* newspaper for August 22, 1846, called the place Yerbabuano. *The California Star* newspaper for March 20, 1847, noted that the name "Yerba Buena" had been changed legally to San Francisco.

San Francisco: see **South San Francisco** [SAN MATEO].

San Francisco Bay: *bay,* lies between Contra Costa and Alameda Counties on the east side, and Marin, San Francisco, San Mateo and Santa Clara Counties on the west side. Named on San Francisco (1956) 1°x 2° quadrangle. Called Estero de S. Francisco on Costanso's (1771) map. Cermeño first applied the name "San Francisco" in the region to present Drakes Bay in 1595 (Treutlein, p. 12). Members of the Portola expedition used the term "Puerto de San Francisco" in 1769 for present Gulf of the Farallons before they discovered present San Francisco Bay (Davidson, p. 6), and gradually the name "San Francisco" transferred from the gulf to the bay (Treutlein, p. 14). On some old maps, the south arm of the bay is called Estrecho de San Jose and Estero de Santa Clara (Gudde, 1949, p. 306, 315).

San Francisco de las Llagas [SANTA CLARA]: *land grant,* near San Martin and Morgan Hill. Named on Gilroy (1955), Mount Madonna (1955), and Mount Sizer (1955) 7.5' quadrangles. Carlos Castro received 6 leagues in 1834; J. Murphy and M. Murphy claimed 22,283 acres patented in 1868 (Cowan, p. 76). Fages gave the name "Las Llagas de Nuestro Padre San Francisco" to his stopping place north of present San Martin in 1772; the name has the meaning "Stigmata of Our Father Saint Francis" in Spanish (Hoover, Rensch, and Rensch, p. 442).

San Francisquito [SANTA CLARA]: *land grant,* southwest of downtown Palo Alto at Stanford University. Named on Palo Alto (1961) 7.5' quadrangle. Antonio Buelna received 8 suertes in 1839; M. Concepcion V. de Rodrigues and others claimed 1471 acres patented in 1868 (Cowan, p. 77).

San Francisquito Creek [SAN MATEO-SANTA CLARA]: *stream,* heads in San Mateo County and flows 11.5 miles, mainly along San Mateo-Santa Clara County line, to mud flats along San Francisco Bay 2.25 miles east-northeast of downtown Palo Alto (lat. 37°27'55" N, long. 122°06'50" W). Named on Mountain View (1961) and Palo Alto (1961) 7.5' quadrangles. Called R. de Sn. Francisco on Font's (1777) map. Palou camped on the bank of the creek in 1774 and selected a spot there for a mission to be dedicated to St. Francis of Assisi; Anza mentioned the name "Arroyo de San Francisco" in 1776, and later the stream was called Arroyo de San Francisquito (Gudde, 1949, p. 304).

San Geronimo [MARIN]:

(1) *land grant,* 6 miles north of Bolinas. Named on Bolinas (1954), Novato (1954), and San Geronimo (1954) 7.5' quadrangles. Rafael Cacho received 2 leagues in 1844; Joseph Warren Revere claimed 8701 acres patented in 1860 (Cowan, p. 78).

(2) *village,* 8 miles southwest of downtown Novato (lat. 38°00'50" N, long. 122°39'50" W); the village is on San Geronimo grant. Named on San Geronimo (1954) 7.5' quadrangle. Postal authorities established San Geronimo post office in 1895, discontinued it in 1910, and reestablished it in 1911 (Frickstad, p. 89). The railroad station at the place first was called Nicasio, but the name was changed to San Geronimo in 1877 (Teather, p. 67).

San Geronimo Creek [MARIN]: *stream,* flows 5.25 miles to Lagunitas Creek 10.5 miles southwest of Novato (lat. 38°00'20" N, long. 122°42'25" W); the stream is on San Geronimo grant. Named on San Geronimo (1954) 7.5' quadrangle.

San Gregorio [SAN MATEO]:

(1) *land grant,* near La Honda. Named on La Honda (1961) 7.5' quadrangle. Antonio Buelna received 4 leagues in two parcels in 1839; Salvador Castro claimed one parcel of 4439 acres patented in 1861 (Cowan, p. 78).

(2) *land grant,* along the coast near San Gregorio Creek, and inland into nearby highlands. Named on La Honda(1961), San Gregorio (1961), and Woodside (1961) 7.5' quadrangles. Antonio Buelna received 4 leagues in two parcels in 1839; M. Concepcion V. de Rodriguez claimed one parcel of 13,344 acres patented in 1861 (Cowan, p. 78). According to Perez (p. 91), Encarnacion Buelna was the patentee in 1861.

(3) *village,* 10 miles south-southeast of the town of Half Moon Bay (lat. 37°19'35" N, long. 122°23'10" W); the village is along San Gregorio Creek on San Gregorio (2) grant. Named on San Gregorio (1961) 7.5' quadrangle. Postal authorities established San Gregorio post office in 1870 (Frickstad, p. 169).

San Gregorio Beach [SAN MATEO]: *beach,* 1 mile west-southwest of the village of San Gregorio (lat. 37°19'25" N, long. 122°24'10" W); the beach is at the mouth of San Gregorio Creek. Named on San Gregorio (1961) 7.5' quadrangle.

San Gregorio Creek [SAN MATEO]: *stream,* formed by the confluence of La Honda Creek and Alpine Creek, flows 10.5 miles to the sea 1 mile west-southwest of the village of San Gregorio (lat. 37° 19'20" N, long. 122°24'10" W). Named on La Honda (1961) and San Gregorio (1961) 7.5' quadrangles. The stream was called Arroyo de San Gregorio in Spanish times, and it was called Arroyo Rodrigues in the 1850's (Brown, p. 82-83).

San Isabel: see **Mount San Isabel**, under **Mount Isabel** [SANTA CLARA].

San Isabel Creek: see **Isabel Creek** [SANTA CLARA].

San Isabel Valley: see **Isabel Valley** [SANTA CLARA].

San Isidro: see **Gilroy** [SANTA CLARA]; **Old Gilroy** [SANTA CLARA]; **San Ysidro** [SANTA CLARA].

Sanitarium [NAPA]: *locality,* 2.5 miles north of Saint Helena (lat. 38°32'35" N, long. 122°28'25" W). Named on Saint Helena (1960) 7.5' quadrangle, which shows St. Helena Sanitarium at the place. Postal authorities established Sanitarium post office in 1901 and changed the name to Deer Park in 1970 (Salley, p. 195). Seventh-Day Adventists opened the sanitarium in 1878 and called the place Crystal Springs, but the community that developed there became known as Sanitarium (Gudde, 1949, p. 305).

San Joachin River: see **San Joaquin River** [CONTRA COSTA].

San Joaquin: see **Point San Joaquin** [CONTRA COSTA].

San Joaquin River [CONTRA COSTA]: *stream,* flows for 22 miles along Contra Costa-Sacramento County line to Suisun Bay 4 miles north-northwest of Antioch (lat. 38°03'45" N, long. 121°50'55" W). Named on Antioch North (1978), Bouldin Island (1978), and Jersey Island (1978) 7.5' quadrangles. Called R. San Joachim on Wilkes' (1841) map, Rio San Joaquin on Fremont's (1848) map, San Joachin R. on Wilkes' (1849) map, Joaquin River on Jefferson's (1849) map, River San Joarquin on Derby's (1850) map, and Rio Tulare or San Joaquin on Sage's (1846) map. Gabriel Moraga named the river about 1805 for St. Joaquim, father of the Virgin Mary (Hart, p. 379).

San Jon Creek: see **Saratoga Creek** [SANTA CLARA].

Sanjon Creek: see **Sausal Creek** [SAN MATEO].

Sanjon de Buriburi: see **San Bruno Creek** [SAN MATEO].

Sanjon de la Brea: see **Pajaro River** [SANTA CLARA].

Sanjon de los Alisos [ALAMEDA]: *stream,* flows 5.25 miles to Newark Slough 1.25 miles west of downtown Newark (lat. 37°31'40" N, long. 122°03'35" W). Named on Newark (1948) 7.5' quadrangle. Called Sanjen de los Alisos on Haywards (1899) 15' quadrangle.

San Jose [MARIN]: *land grant,* south of the city of Novato at and around Ignacio. Named on Novato (1954) 7.5' quadrangle. Ignacio Pacheco received 1.5 leagues in 1840 and claimed 6659 acres patented in 1861 (Cowan, p. 80).

San Jose [SANTA CLARA]: *city,* in the north part of Santa Clara Valley (downtown near lat. 37°20' N, long. 121°53' W). Named on Calaveras Reservoir (1961), Cupertino (1961), Milpitas (1961), San Jose East (1961), and San Jose West (1961) 7.5' quadrangles. Postal authorities established San Jose post office in 1849 (Frickstad, p. 175), and the city incorporated in 1850. The place was founded in 1777 on the bank of Guadalupe River and named El Pueblo San Jose de Guadalupe; floods caused removal of the community to higher ground within a couple of years (Hoover, Rensch, and Rensch, p. 427-428). Bidwell (p. 38) used the name "Pueblo of St. Joseph" in 1841, and Jefferson's (1849) map shows Pueblo St. Joseph.

San Jose: see **East San Jose** [SANTA CLARA]; **Port San Jose**, under **Alviso** [SANTA CLARA].

San Jose de Guadalupe Mision: see **Ex Mission San Jose** [ALAMEDA].

San Jose Point: see **Black Point** [SAN FRANCISCO].

San Jose Valley: see **Santa Clara Valley** [SANTA CLARA].

San Juan Bautista [SANTA CLARA]: *land grant,* south of downtown San Jose. Named on Los Gatos (1953), San Jose East (1961), San Jose West (1961) and Santa Teresa Hills (1953) 7.5' quadrangles. Jose Agustin Narvaez received 2 leagues in 1844 and claimed 8880 acres patented in 1865 (Cowan, p. 81). Thompson and West's (1876) map has the name "San Juan Bautista Hills" for highlands near the east edge of the grant and west of present Lick.

San Juan Bautista Hills: see **San Juan Bautista** [SANTA CLARA].

San Juan Capistrano: see **Hunters Point** [SAN FRANCISCO].

San Leandro [ALAMEDA]:

(1) *land grant,* at the city of San Leandro. Named on Hayward (1959) and San Leandro (1959) 7.5' quadrangles. Jose Joaquin Estudillo received 1 league in 1839 and 1842; he claimed 6830 acres patented in 1863 (Cowan, p. 83).

(2) *city,* 8 miles southeast of downtown Oakland (lat. 37°43'30" N, long. 122°09'20" W). Named on San Leandro (1959) 7.5' quadrangle. The Estudillo family, who owned the grant where the town lies, gave land for county buildings and reserved 200 acres for the community of San Leandro, which was surveyed in 1855; an election in 1854 brought the county seat to San Leandro from Alvarado (Hoover, Rensch, and Rensch, p. 15). Postal authorities established San Leandro post office in 1853 (Frickstad, p. 3), and the city incorporated in 1872.

San Leandro: see **West San Leandro** [ALAMEDA].

San Leandro Bay [ALAMEDA]: *embayment,* 4 miles west-northwest of downtown San Leandro off of San Francisco Bay (lat. 37°45' N, long. 122°13'30" W). Named on Oakland East (1959) and San Leandro (1959) 7.5' quadrangles.

San Leandro Creek [ALAMEDA-CONTRA COSTA]: *stream,* heads in Contra Costa County and flows 21 miles to San Leandro Bay 3 miles west-northwest of downtown San Leandro in Alameda County (lat. 37°44'35" N, long. 122°12'25" W). Named on Hayward (1959), Las Trampas Ridge (1959), Oakland East (1959), and San Leandro (1959) 7.5' quadrangles. The names "Arroyo de San Leandro" and "Rio San Leandro" were used in the 1820's and 1830's (Gudde, 1949, p. 308). Concord (1897) 15' quadrangle shows West Branch extending north from San Leandro Creek through Moraga Valley. Peter Andrews Halverson established Halverson's Landing at the mouth of San Leandro Creek in 1856—the place also was called Andrews Landing (Mosier and Mosier, p. 41).

San Leandro Hills [ALAMEDA]: *range,* 3.5 miles east-northeast of downtown San Leandro (lat. 37°45'30" N, long. 122°06'15" W). Named on Hayward (1959) and Las Trampas Ridge (1959) 7.5' quadrangles. The range also had the name "Oakland Hills" (Mosier and Mosier, p. 77).

San Leandro Reservoir: see **Upper San Leandro Reservoir** [ALAMEDA-CONTRA COSTA].

San Leandro Valley [ALAMEDA]: *area,* lowlands along San Francisco Bay at and near the city of San Leandro (lat. 37°41'45" N, long. 122°09'30" W). Named on San Leandro (1959) 7.5' quadrangle.

San Lorenzo [ALAMEDA]:

(1) *land grant,* at the town of San Lorenzo. Named on Hayward (1959) and San Leandro (1959) 7.5' quadrangles. Francisco Soto received 1.5 leagues in 1842 and 1844; Barbara Soto and others claimed 6686 acres patented in 1877 (Cowan, p. 83).

(2) *land grant,* at the city of Castro Valley. Named on Hayward (1959) and Las Trampas Ridge (1959) 7.5' quadrangles. Guillermo Castro received the land in 1841 and 1843; he claimed 26,724 acres patented in 1865 (Cowan, p. 83).

(3) *town,* center 2.25 miles west-northwest of downtown Hayward (lat. 37°40'45" N, long. 122°07'15" W). Named on Hayward (1959) and San Leandro (1959) 7.5' quadrangles. American squatters came to San Lorenzo (1) grant in 1851 and settled along San Lorenzo Creek at what they called Squattersville, now the town of San Lorenzo (Hanna, P.T., p. 279). Postal authorities established San Lorenzo post office in 1854 (Frickstad, p. 3).

San Lorenzo: see **West San Lorenzo** [ALAMEDA].

San Lorenzo Creek [ALAMEDA]: *stream,* flows 13 miles to San Francisco Bay 4 miles south of downtown San Leandro (lat. 37°40'15" N, long. 122°09'45" W). Named on Hayward (1959) and San Leandro (1959) 7.5' quadrangles. Called "R. de la Harina." on Font's (1777) map. Crespi called the stream Arroyo de San Salvador de Horta in 1772; the name "Arroyo de la Harina" for the feature was from a load of flour that got wet there—*harina* means "flour" in Spanish (Gudde, 1949, p. 308).

San Luis Gonzaga [SANTA CLARA]: *land grant,* mainly in Merced County, but extends over the crest of Diablo Range into Santa Clara County near Pacheco Pass. Named on Pacheco Pass (1955) and Pacheco Peak (1955) 7.5' quadrangles. Jose Ramon Estrada received the land in 1834 and Francisco Rivera received it in 1843; Francisco Perez Pacheco claimed 48, 821 acres patented in 1871 (Cowan, p. 83-84). According to Perez (p. 93), Juan Pacheco and Jose Mijira were the grantees in 1843.

San Martin [SANTA CLARA]: *town,* 5.5 miles north-northwest of Gilroy (lat. 37°05'05" N, long. 121°36'35" W). Named on Gilroy (1955) 7.5' quadrangle. According to Butler (p. 170), Martin Murphy built a chapel 2 miles east of the present town and named it San Martin for his patron saint; the name later was applied to the town that grew around a place called Mills Switch Station that was located along the railroad at present San Martin. Postal authorities established San Martin post office in 1894, discontinued it in 1900, and reestablished it in 1902 (Frickstad, p. 175).

San Martin Creek: see **Little Llagas Creek** [SANTA CLARA].

San Mateo [SAN MATEO]:

(1) *land grant,* at and west of the city of San Mateo. Named on Montara Mountain (1956) and San Mateo (1956) 7.5' quadrangles. Cayetano Arenas received 2 leagues in 1846; executors of W.D.M. Howard's estate claimed 6439 acres patented in 1857 (Cowan, p. 84-85).

(2) *city,* 7 miles northwest of downtown Redwood City (city hall near lat. 37°34' N, long. 122°19'25" W). Named on San Mateo (1956) 7.5' quadrangle. Nicholas de Peyster built a hostelry at the place in the early 1850's and called it San Mateo House, or Half Way House for its location halfway from San Francisco to San Jose (Stanger, 1963, p. 65). C.B. Polhemus laid out the modern city in 1863 (Gudde, 1949, p. 310). Postal authorities established San Mateo post office in 1857, discontinued it in 1858, and reestablished it in 1861 (Frickstad, p. 169). The city incorporated in 1894.

San Mateo Beach: see **Coyote Point** [SAN MATEO].

San Mateo Creek [SAN MATEO]: *stream,* flows 12 miles to San Francisco Bay 1.25 miles east-northeast of downtown San Mateo (lat. 37°34'05" N, long. 122°18'55" W). Named on Montara Mountain (1956) and San Mateo (1956) 7.5' quadrangles. Called R. de Sn. Matheo on Font's (1777) map. Anza and Font used the name "Arroyo de San Matheo" in 1776 (Gudde, 1949, p. 310), but United States Board on Geographic Names (1961b, p. 15) rejected the name "San Matheo Creek" for the stream.

San Mateo House: see **San Mateo** [SAN MATEO] (2).

San Mateo Park [SAN MATEO]: *district,* 1 mile west of downtown San Mateo (lat. 37°34'05" N, long. 122°20'30" W). Named on San Mateo (1956) 7.5' quadrangle.

San Mateo Point: see **Coyote Point** [SAN MATEO].

San Mateo Slough: see **O'Neill Slough** [SAN MATEO]; **Seal Slough** [SAN MATEO].

San Matheo Creek: see **San Mateo Creek** [SAN MATEO].

San Miguel [SAN FRANCISCO]: *land grant,* near Twin Peaks and Mount Davidson. Named on San Francisco North (1956) and San Francisco South (1956) 7.5' quadrangles. Jose de Jesus Noe received 1 league in 1845 and claimed 4443 acres patented in 1857 (Cowan, p. 85).

San Miguel [SONOMA]: *land grant,* northwest of Santa Rosa. Named on Healdsburg (1955), Mark West Springs (1958), Santa Rosa (1954), and Sebastopol (1954) 7.5' quadrangles. William Mark West received 1.5 leagues in 1840 and 1844; Guadalupe V. West claimed 6663 acres patented in 1865 (Cowan, p. 85; Perez, p. 94).

San Miguel: see **Oceanview** [SAN FRANCISCO].

San Miguel Hills [SAN FRANCISCO]: *range,* at and east of Mount Davidson (lat. 37°44'25" N, long. 122°26'30" W); the range is on San Miguel grant. Named on San Francisco South (1956) 7.5' quadrangle.

San Pablo [CONTRA COSTA]:

(1) *land grant,* extends from El Cerrito nearly to Pinole. Named on Mare Island (1959), Richmond (1959), and San Quentin (1959) 7.5' quadrangles. Francisco Maria Castro received the land in 1823 and 1834; Joaquin Isidro Castro claimed 17,939 acres patented in 1873 (Cowan, p. 86; Cowan listed the grant under the designation "San Pablo, (or) Cochiyunes"). Perez (p. 94) listed Joaquin Y. Castro as both the grantee in 1835, and as the patentee in 1873.

(2) *town,* 1.5 miles north-northwest of Richmond civic center (lat. 37°57'30" N, long. 122°20'55" W). Named on Richmond (1959) 7.5' quadrangle. Postal authorities established San Pablo post office in 1854 (Frickstad, p. 23), and the town incorporated in 1948.

San Pablo Bay [CONTRA COSTA-MARIN-SOLANO-SONOMA]: *bay,* between San Francisco Bay and Carquinez Strait in Contra Costa County, Marin County, Solano County, and Sonoma County. Named on Cuttings Wharf (1949), Mare Island (1959), Petaluma Point (1959), Richmond (1959), San Quentin (1959), and Sears Point (1951) 7.5' quadrangles. Called Bahia de San Pablo on Beechey's (1827-1828) map, and called Pablo Bay on Wilkes' (1849) map. Canizares named the feature Bahia Redondo in 1775—*bahia redondo* means "round bay" in Spanish (Hanna, W.L., p. 44). Gudde (1969, p. 291) gave the names "Bahia Redonda" and "Bahia de Sonoma" as early designations of the feature.

San Pablo Creek [CONTRA COSTA]: *stream,* flows 17 miles to San Pablo Bay 2.5 miles east-northeast of Point San Pablo (lat. 37°58'35" N, long. 122°22'55" W). Named on Brioncs Valley (1959), Oakland East (1959), Richmond (1959), and San Quentin (1959) 7.5' quadrangles. Concord (1915) 15' quadrangle shows West Branch, which is 3 miles long, joining the main stream from the southwest at Bryant (present Orinda).

San Pablo Point: see **Point San Pablo** [CONTRA COSTA].

San Pablo Reservoir [CONTRA COSTA]: *lake,* 4 miles long, behind a dam on San Pablo Creek 4.5 miles east of Richmond civic center (lat. 37°56'35" N, long. 122°15'40" W). Named on Briones Valley (1959) and Richmond (1959) 7.5' quadrangles.

San Pablo Ridge [CONTRA COSTA]: *ridge,* northwest-trending, 8 miles long, center 4 miles east of Richmond civic center (lat. 37° 56' N, long. 122°16' W). Named on Briones Valley (1959) and Richmond (1959) 7.5' quadrangles.

San Pablo Station [CONTRA COSTA]: *locality,* 1.25 miles north-northwest of present Richmond civic center along Southern Pacific Railroad (lat. 37°57'30" N, long. 122°21'35" W); the place is west of the town of San Pablo. Named on San Francisco (1899) 15' quadrangle.

San Pablo Strait [CONTRA COSTA-MARIN]: *water feature,* between San Francisco Bay and San Pablo Bay on Contra Costa-Marin County line (lat. 37°58'30" N, long. 122°26'15" W); the feature is northwest of Point San Pablo. Named on San Quentin (1959) 7.5' quadrangle. Called Straits of San Pablo on Ringgold's (1850a) map.

San Pedro [SAN MATEO]: *land grant,* near the coast at Pacifica. Named on Montara Mountain (1956) and San Francisco South (1956) 7.5' quadrangles. Francisco Sanchez received 2 leagues in 1839 and claimed 8926 acres patented in 1870 (Cowan, p. 87).

San Pedro Creek [SAN MATEO]: *stream,* formed by the confluence of Middle Fork and South Fork, flows 2.5 miles through San Pedro Valley to the sea 3 miles north-northwest of Montara Knob (lat. 37°35'45" N, long. 122°30'15" W). Named on Montara Mountain (1956) 7.5' quadrangle. Called Arroyo de San Pedro on maps of about 1860 (Brown, p. 65). Middle Fork is 1.5 miles long and South Fork is 1.25 miles long. North Fork, which enters from the northeast less than 0.5 mile downstream from the junction of South Fork and Middle Fork, is 1.5 miles long. All three forks are named on Montara Mountain (1956) 7.5' quadrangle.

San Pedro Hill [MARIN]: *peak,* 0.25 mile west-northwest of Point San Pedro (lat. 37°59'15" N, long. 122°27' W). Named on San Quentin (1959) 7.5' quadrangle.

San Pedro Mountain [SAN MATEO]: *ridge,* west- to northwest-trending, 1.25 miles long, 1.5 miles northwest of Montara Knob (lat. 37°34'30" N, long. 122°30'30" W). Named on Montara Mountain (1956) 7.5' quadrangle. Brown (p. 65) listed the names "Pedro Mountain," "Sierra de San Pedro," and "Sierra de Santa Clara" as former designations of the feature.

San Pedro Point: see **Point San Pedro** [MARIN]; **Point San Pedro** [SAN MATEO].

San Pedro Rock [SAN MATEO]: *island,* 1050 feet long, 3.25 miles northwest of Montara Knob and 300 feet offshore at Point San Pedro (lat. 37°35'40" N, long. 122°31'20" W). Named on Montara Mountain (1956) 7.5' quadrangle.

San Pedro Santa Margarita y las Gallinas [MARIN]: *land grant,* extends west-northwest from San Pablo Bay nearly to the village of Nicasio. Named on Novato (1954), Petaluma Point (1959), San Geronimo (1954), San Quentin (1959), and San Rafael (1954) 7.5' quadrangles. Timothy Murphy received 5 leagues in 1844 and claimed 21,679 acres patented in 1866 (Cowan, p. 87).

San Pedro Terrace: see **Pedro Valley** [SAN MATEO].

San Pedro Valley [SAN MATEO]: *valley,* 2 miles north-northwest of Montara Knob (lat. 37°35'15" N, long. 122°29'40" W); San Pedro Creek drains the valley. Named on Montara Mountain (1956) 7.5' quadrangle.

San Quentin [MARIN]: *town,* west of Point San Quentin (lat. 37°56'30" N, long. 122°29' W); the town is on Punta de Quentin grant. Named on San Quentin (1959) 7.5' quadrangle. Postal authorities established San Quentin post office in 1859, discontinued it the same year, and reestablished it in 1862 (Frickstad, p. 89). They established Tamal post office as a station of San Quentin post office in 1960 (Salley, p. 218).

San Quentin: see **Point San Quentin** [MARIN]; **Point San Quentin**, under **Potrero Point** [SAN FRANCISCO].

San Rafael [MARIN]: *city,* near the center of the east part of Marin County (lat. 37°58'25" N, long. 122°31'50" W). Named on Petaluma Point (1959), San Quentin (1959), and San Rafael (1954) 7.5' quadrangles. Postal authorities established San Rafael post office in 1851, discontinued it in 1853, and reestablished it in 1854 (Frickstad, p. 89). The city incorporated in 1874. Franciscan missionaries founded San Rafael Arcangel mission at the place in 1817; Timothy Murphy, who assumed charge of the mission estate and Indians there in 1837, built the first house at the site of the city in 1839 (Hoover, Rensch, and Rensch, p. 176-177). Postal authorities established Terra Linda post office 3 miles north of San Rafael post office in 1961; the name is from a residential development (Salley, p. 220)—Mrs. Joseph Rose, who as a child had lived on a ranch at the place, suggested the name "Terra Linda" (Teather, p. 81).

San Rafael Bay [MARIN]: *embayment,* off of San Francisco Bay between Point San Pedro and Point San Quentin (lat. 37°58' N, long. 122°28'30" W). Named on San Quentin (1959) 7.5' quadrangle. According to H.R. Wagner (p. 478), this probably is the feature that Ayala called Bahia de Nuestra Señora del Rosario la Marinera in 1775.

San Rafael Creek [MARIN]: *stream,* flows 3 miles through San Rafael to San Rafael Bay 2 miles east of downtown San Rafael (lat. 37°58'10" N, long. 122°29'35" W). Named on San Quentin (1959) and San Rafael (1954) 7.5' quadrangles. The stream was called Estero de San Rafael de Agnanni in Spanish days (Teather, p. 71).

San Rafael Hill [MARIN]: *ridge,* east-southeast-trending, 2.5 miles long, center 1 mile north-northwest of downtown San Rafael (lat. 37°59'15" N, long. 122°32'40" W). Named on San Rafael (1954) 7.5' quadrangle.

San Rafael Rock: see **Murphy Rock** [MARIN].

San Ramon [ALAMEDA-CONTRA COSTA]: *land grant,* southeast of the town of San Ramon on Alameda-Contra Costa County line. Named on Diablo (1953), Dublin (1961) Livermore (1961), and Tassajara (1953) 7.5' quadrangles. Jose Maria Amador received 4 leagues in 1835 and claimed 16,517 acres patented in 1865 (Cowan, p. 88).

San Ramon [CONTRA COSTA]:

(1) *land grant,* at and near Danville and Alamo. Named on Diablo (1953), Las Trampas Ridge (1959), and Walnut Creek (1959) 7.5' quadrangles. Rafael Soto de Pacheco received 2 leagues in 1833; H.W. Carpentier claimed 8917 acres patented in 1866 (Cowan, p. 88). According to Perez (p. 95), Bartolo Pacheco and Mariano Castro were the grantees in 1833, and Rafaela Pacheco and others were the patentees in 1866.

(2) *land grant,* in San Ramon Valley at and near the town of San Ramon. Named on Diablo (1953) and Dublin (1961) 7.5' quadrangles. Jose Maria Amador received 1 league in 1834; Leo Norris claimed 4451 acres patented in 1882 (Cowan, p. 88). According to Perez (p. 95), Jose M. Amador was the grantee in 1835.

(3) *town,* 3 miles south-southeast of Danville (lat. 37°46'45" N, long. 121°58'35" W); the town is in San Ramon Valley. Named on Diablo (1953) 7.5' quadrangle. Postal authorities established San Ramon post office in 1852 and discontinued it in 1859; they established San Ramoon post office in 1873 and changed the name to San Ramon in 1883 (Frickstad, p. 23). The place first was called Lynchville, and later Limerick—the last name for the preponderance of Irish settlers there (Hanna, P.T., p. 286).

San Ramon Creek [CONTRA COSTA]: *stream,* flows 12 miles to join Las Trampas Creek and form Walnut Creek (1) near Walnut Creek (2) civic center (lat. 37°53'50" N, long. 122°03'30" W); the stream goes through San Ramon Valley. Named on Diablo (1953), Las Trampas Ridge (1959), and Walnut Creek (1959) 7.5' quadrangles. Called Arroyo del Ingreto on a diseño of Arroyo de las Nueces y Bolbones grant made in 1834; the Spanish word *ingreto* refers to a grafted tree—here the reference is to an oak tree with a willow ingrafted on it (Becker, 1969). Gudde (1949, p. 313) cited testimony that San Ramon Creek was named not for a saint but for a Spaniard who ran sheep near the creek in the early days.

San Ramon Creek: see **Pacheco Creek** [CONTRA COSTA]; **South San Ramon Creek** [ALAMEDA-CONTRA COSTA].

San Ramon Siding [CONTRA COSTA]: *locality,* 3.5 miles southeast of Danville along Southern Pacific Railroad (lat. 37°46'45" N, long. 121°57'55" W). Named on Diablo (1953) 7.5' quadrangle.

San Ramon Valley [ALAMEDA-CONTRA COSTA]: *valley,* along San Ramon Creek southeast of Alamo on Alameda-Contra Costa County line, mainly in Contra Costa County. Named on Diablo (1953), Dublin (1961), and Las Trampas Ridge (1959) 7.5' quadrangles. The south part of the feature is called Amador Valley on Diablo (1953) 7.5' quadrangle. Pleasanton (1906) 15' quadrangle shows present San Ramon Valley as part of Amador Valley.

San Ramon Village [ALAMEDA]: *district,* north-northeast of Dublin in San Ramon Valley (lat. 37°43'15" N, long. 121°55'45" W). Named on Dublin (1961, photorevised 1980) 7.5' quadrangle.

San Ramoon: see **San Ramon** [CONTRA COSTA] (3).

Santa Clara [SANTA CLARA]: *city,* 3 miles west-northwest of downtown San Jose (lat. 37°21' N, long. 121°56'30" W). Named on Cupertino (1961), Milpitas (1961), and San Jose West (1961) 7.5' quadrangles. Postal authorities established Santa Clara post office in 1851 (Frickstad, p. 175), and the city incorporated in 1857. The name is from Santa Clara de Asis mission, founded in 1777 within the limits of the modern city about 2 miles from the present site of the mission; the original mission was by a stream called Mission Creek (Hoover, Rensch, and Rensch, p. 426-427). According to Rambo (1964, p. 38), Mission Creek headed at a large spring in the present Hanchett Park neighborhood, fed Cook's Pond, and joined Guadalupe River near the pear orchard of the original mission. Thompson and West's (1876) map shows Cooks Pond on the north side of The Alameda near present Hilmar Street on land belonging to Jane B. Cook. Rambo (1973, p. 40) noted that Cooks Pond was both a lake and a resort park.

Santa Clara Shoal [CONTRA COSTA]: *shoal,* 5.25 miles north of the settlement of Bethel Island in San Joaquin River on Contra Costa-Sacramento County line (lat. 38°05'25" N, long. 121°38'45" W). Named on Jersey Island (1978) 7.5' quadrangle.

Santa Clara Valley [SANTA CLARA]: *valley,* extends for 60 miles southeast from San Francisco Bay between Santa Cruz Mountains and Diablo Range. Drainage from the north part of the valley is to San Francisco Bay, mainly by way of Coyote Creek; drainage from the south part is to the sea by way of Pajaro River. Named on San Jose (1962) and Santa Cruz (1956) 1°x 2° quadrangles. Parke (p. 7) noted that the "entire valley is known by the general name Santa Clara, whilst that portion enveloping the head of the bay retains the name of the *pueblo* or town, San José." Antisell (p. 32) mentioned "The Santa Clara, or, as it is sometimes called, the San José valley." Blake (1854, p. 438) wrote that the Valley of San Jose is properly the south end of the great valley occupied by San Francisco Bay. Gudde (1949, p. 190) stated that Llano de las Llagas was the Spanish name for Gilroy Valley, meaning presumably the south part of present Santa Clara Valley near Gilroy. Bolton (p. 271) mentioned that Font referred to Gilroy Valley in 1766 by the name "San Bernardino Valley."

Santa Coleta: see **Livermore Valley** [ALAMEDA].

Santa Cruz Mountains [SAN MATEO-SANTA CLARA]: *range,* between the sea and the lowlands along San Francisco Bay in San Mateo, Santa Clara, and Santa Cruz Counties. Named on San Francisco (1956), San Jose (1962), and Santa Cruz (1956) 1°x 2° quadrangles. Called Sierra de la Santa Cruz on Parke's (1854-1855) map. Blake (1856, p. 378) used the name "Santa Cruz Range."

Santa Cruz Range: see **Santa Cruz Mountains** [SAN MATEO].

Santa Fe: see **Point Richmond** [CONTRA COSTA] (2).

Santa Fe Channel [CONTRA COSTA]: *channel,* 1.5 miles southwest of Richmond civic center (lat. 37°55'15" N, long. 122°22'05" W). Named on Richmond (1959) 7.5' quadrangle. United States Board on Geographic Names (1943, p. 13) rejected the name "Ellis Slough" for the feature.

Santa Isabel: see **Mount Santa Isabel**, under **Mount Hamilton** [SANTA CLARA].

Santa Margarita Valley [MARIN]: *valley,* 6.5 miles south of downtown Novato (lat. 38°00'50" N, long. 122°33'30" W); the valley is on San Pedro Santa Margarita y las Gallinas grant. Named on Novato (1954) 7.5' quadrangle.

Santa Nella [SONOMA]: *locality,* 1.5 miles east-southeast of Guerneville in Pocket Canyon (lat. 38°29'50" N, long. 122°57'55" W; near E line sec. 33, T 8 N, R 10 W). Named on Camp Meeker (1954) 7.5' quadrangle.

Santa Rita [ALAMEDA]: *land grant,* north of Pleasanton in Amador Valley. Named on Dublin (1961) and Livermore (1961) 7.5' quadrangles. Dolores Pacheco received the land in 1839; Yountz, administrator, claimed 8994 acres patented in 1865 (Cowan, p. 94).

Santa Rosa [SONOMA]: *city,* in the east-central part of Sonoma County (downtown near lat. 38°26'25" N, long. 122°42'45" W). Named on Santa Rosa (1954) and Sebastopol (1954, photorevised 1968) 7.5' quadrangles. Postal authorities established Santa Rosa post office in 1852 (Frickstad, p. 198), and the city incorporated in 1868. The name is from Cabeza de Santa Rosa grant, where the city lies; an earlier settlement located nearby was called Franklin Town (Hanna, P.T., p. 292). Franklin Town disappeared when its buildings were moved to the site of the new community of Santa Rosa, located farther down Santa Rosa Creek (Hansen and Miller, p. 44). Cardwell's (1958) map has the name "Santa Rosa Valley" for lowlands around Santa Rosa, and *Californian* newspaper for August 15, 1846, used the name "Santa Rosa Plains" for the same lowlands. A resort called Santa Rosa Springs operated 2 miles from Santa Rosa about 1890 (Anderson, Winslow, p. 231). Postal authorities established America post office 9 miles northeast of Santa Rosa in 1881, discontinued it for a time in 1887, and discontinued it finally in 1903; the name was from America S. Simpson, first postmaster (Salley, p. 6). California Division of Highways' (1934) map shows places called Wrights, Willow Grove, Macauley, Leddy, and La Franchi along Petaluma and Santa Rosa Railroad between Santa Rosa and Llano.

Santa Rosa Creek [SONOMA]: *stream,* flows 21 miles to Laguna de Santa Rosa 3.5 miles north of Sebastopol (lat. 38°27'05" N, long. 122°50' W). Named on Calistoga (1958), Kenwood (1954), Santa Rosa (1954), and Sebastopol (1954) 7.5' quadrangles. Sebastopol (1954, photorevised 1968) 7.5' quadrangle shows the stream modified to form Santa Rosa Flood Control Channel. According to one account, a Spanish priest named the creek in the late 1820's for St. Rose of Lima after the priest had baptized an Indian girl at the stream (Hoover, Rensch, and Rensch, p. 533). Called Arroyo de Permanente on a diseño of Cabeza de Santa Rosa grant in 1838, and called Arroyo de Sta. Rosa on a diseño of San Miguel grant (Becker, 1969).

Santa Rosa Creek Reservoir [SONOMA]: *lake,* 3700 feet long, 3.5 miles east-northeast of downtown Santa Rosa (lat. 38°27'15" N, long. 122°39'05" W). Named on Santa Rosa (1954) 7.5' quadrangle.

Santa Rosa Flood Control Channel: see **Santa Rosa Creek** [SONOMA].

Santa Rosa Plains: see **Santa Rosa** [SONOMA].

Santa Rosa Springs: see **Santa Rosa** [SONOMA].

Santa Rosa Valley: see **Santa Rosa** [SONOMA].

Santa Teresa [SANTA CLARA]: *land grant,* north of Santa Teresa Hills around Edenvale. Named on San Jose East (1961) and Santa Teresa Hills (1953) 7.5' quadrangles. Joaquin Bernal received 1 league in 1834; Agustin Bernal claimed 9647 acres patented in 1867 (Cowan, p. 96).

Santa Teresa Hills [SANTA CLARA]: *range,* west-northwest-trending, 7 miles long, 3 miles north of New Almaden (lat. 37°13' N, long. 121°49' W). Named on Santa Teresa Hills (1953) 7.5' quadrangle.

Santa Teresa Spring [SANTA CLARA]: *spring,* 3.5 miles north-northeast of New Almaden (lat. 37°13'35" N, long. 121°47'35" W); the spring is on Santa Teresa grant. Named on Santa Teresa Hills (1953) 7.5' quadrangle.

Santa Venetia [MARIN]: *town,* 1.5 miles north of downtown San Rafael (lat. 37°59'55" N, long. 122°31'30" W). Named on Novato (1954) and San Rafael (1954) 7.5' quadrangles. Mabry McMahon coined the name in 1914 for a development that he intended to have a resemblance to Venice, Italy; the project failed, but the name endured (Teather, p. 71).

Santa Ysabel: see **Mount Santa Ysabel**, under **Mount Isabel** [SANTA CLARA].

Santa Ysabel Creek: see **Isabel Creek** [SANTA CLARA].

Santa Ysabel Valley: see **Isabel Valley** [SANTA CLARA].

San Tomas [SANTA CLARA]: *district,* 2 miles southwest of downtown Campbell (lat. 37°16'10" N, long. 121°58'35" W); the place is near San Tomas Aquinas Creek. Named on San Jose West (1961) 7.5' quadrangle.

San Tomas Aquinas Creek [SANTA CLARA]: *stream,* flows 15 miles to Saratoga Creek nearly 3 miles south of Alviso (lat. 37°23'20" N, long. 121°58'05" W). Named on Castle Rock Ridge (1955), Los Gatos (1953), Milpitas (1961), and San Jose West (1961) 7.5' quadrangles. Called Arroyo San Tomas Aquino and Arroyo de Santa Toma Aquino on Tompson and West's (1876) map, and called Arroyo San Tomas Aquinas on Hare's (1872) map.

San Vicente [SANTA CLARA]: *land grant,* mainly between Santa Teresa Hills and New Almaden. Named on Santa Teresa Hills (1953) 7.5' quadrangle. Jose de los Reyes Berreyesa received 1 league in 1842 and Maria Berreyesa claimed 4438 acres patented in 1868 (Cowan, p. 89; Perez, p. 95).

San Vicente Creek [SAN MATEO]: *stream,* flows nearly 4 miles to the sea 3 miles southwest of Montara Knob at Moss Beach (lat. 37° 31'25" N, long. 122°31' W). Named on Montara Mountain (1956) 7.5' quadrangle. According to Brown (p. 85), the stream also is called Arroyo de San Vicente and Vicente Creek, and the canyon of the stream is called Torello Canyon, from Torello ranch.

San Ysidro [SANTA CLARA]: *land grant,* near Gilroy. Named on Chittenden (1955), Gilroy (1955), Gilroy Hot Springs (1955), and San Felipe (1955) 7.5' quadrangles. According to Arbuckle (p. 19, 34), Ygnacio Ortega received the land about 1809 or 1810 and divided it into thirds for this three children: Jose Quintin claimed 4439 acres patented in 1868; Clara, wife of John Gilroy, claimed 4461 acres patented in 1867; Ysabel got 4167 acres that Bernard Murphy bought in 1849 and gave the name "La Polka"—Martin J.C. Murphy claimed this part of the grant, patented in 1860. Cowan (p. 79) used the form "San Isidro" for the name of the grant.

San Ysidro: see **Gilroy** [SANTA CLARA]; **Old Gilroy** [SANTA CLARA].

San Ysidro Creek [SANTA CLARA]: *stream,* flows 5 miles to a point in lowlands 1.25 miles east-southeast of Old Gilroy (lat. 36° 59'40" N, long. 121°30'15" W). Named on Chittenden (1955, photorevised 1968 and 1973) 7.5' quadrangle. The stream flows through San Ysidro grant, and is named for the grant (United States Board on Geographic Names, 1973a, p. 3).

Saranap [CONTRA COSTA]: *locality,* 1.5 miles south-southwest of present Walnut Creek civic center along Oakland Antioch and Eastern Railroad (lat. 37°53'05" N, long. 122°04'35" W). Named on Concord (1915) 15' quadrangle. The place first was called Dewing Park, but in 1913 the new name was coined from the name of Sara Naphthaly, mother of Samuel Naphthaly, vice-president of the railroad (Gudde, 1949, p. 320).

Saratoga [SANTA CLARA]: *city,* 9 miles southwest of downtown San Jose (lat. 37°15'30" N, long. 122°01'55" W). Named on Cupertino (1961) and San Jose West (1961) 7.5' quadrangles. After William Campbell and his sons built a sawmill in the canyon of present Saratoga Creek in 1848, the little settlement that developed at the mouth of the canyon was identified on an early map by the name "Campbell's Gap" (Cunningham, p. 27). After lumberman Martin McCarty built a toll road up the canyon in 1850 and 1851, the settlement was called Toll Gate, and later the post office there was called McCartysville; in 1854 William Haun and John Whisman built a gristmill, called Redwood Mills, at the settlement (Hoover, Rensch, and Rensch, p. 457-458). Charles Maclay purchased the mill and renamed it Bank Mills in 1863; Maclay also planned a settlement, known as Maclaytown, around the mill (Cunningham, p. 51, 88). The place finally was named Saratoga because water at nearby Congress Springs was likened to water at Saratoga, New York (Butler, p. 95-96). Postal authorities established McCartysville post office in 1855, changed the name to Bank Mills in 1863, and changed it to Saratoga in 1865 (Frickstad, p. 173, 174). Saratoga incorporated in 1956. Peninsular Railway Company's (1912) map shows a station called Glen Una located nearly one-third of the way along the rail line from Saratoga to Los Gatos.

Saratoga: see **Camp Saratoga** [SANTA CLARA].

Saratoga Creek [SANTA CLARA]: *stream,* flows 18 miles to Alviso Slough at Alviso (lat. 37°25'20" N, long. 121°58'45" W); the stream leaves highlands at Saratoga. Named on Castle Rock Ridge (1955), Cupertino (1961), Milpitas (1961), and San Jose West (1961) 7.5' quadrangles. Thompson and West's (1876) map has the label "San Jon or Campbell Cr." on the lower part of present Saratoga Creek near Alviso, has the name "Campbells Creek" on the stream nearer the highlands, and has the name "Arroyo Quito" on the stream in the highlands. The feature is called Campbell Creek on Palo Alto (1899) 15' quadrangle. Until the early 1850's the stream was called Campbell Creek for William Campbell and his sons, who began construction of a sawmill along the creek in 1847 about 3 miles west of present Saratoga (Hoover, Rensch, and Rensch, p. 457). For many years the neighborhood around the sawmill was called Campbell's Redwoods (Cunningham, p. 27). Crawford (1896, p. 519) referred to Pacific Congress Springs as being in Campbell Creek Cañon. United States Board on Geographic Names (1933, p. 189) approved the name "Campbell Creek" for the stream, and rejected the names "Quito Creek" and "Arroyo Quito," but later the Board (1954, p. 3-4) approved the name "Saratoga Creek" for the stream, and rejected the names "Big Moody Creek" and "Campbell Creek" for it.

Saratoga Gap [SANTA CLARA]: *pass,* 5 miles west of Saratoga on Santa Clara-Santa Cruz County line (lat. 37°15'30" N, long. 122° 07'10" W; near S line sec. 6, T 8 S, R 2 W). Named on Cupertino (1961) 7.5' quadrangle.

Sarco Creek [NAPA]: *stream,* flows 4.5 miles to Milliken Creek nearly 2 miles north-northeast of downtown Napa (lat. 38°19'20" N, long. 122°16'25" W). Named on Mount George (1951) and Napa (1951) 7.5' quadrangles.

Sargent [SANTA CLARA]: *locality,* 6 miles south of Gilroy along Southern Pacific Railroad (lat. 36°55'10" N, long. 121°32'50" W). Named on Chittenden (1955) 7.5' quadrangle. J.P. Sargent owned a ranch at the place (Rambo, 1964, p. 42); a popular picnic resort called Sargent's was on the bank of Pajaro River there in 1895 (Pierce, p. 151-152). Postal authorities established La Brea post office along Tar Creek in 1874, changed the name to Sargent in 1876, discontinued it for a time in 1878, and discontinued it finally in 1933 (Salley, p. 114, 198).

Sargent Creek [SANTA CLARA]: *stream,* flows nearly 3 miles to Pajaro River 7.5 miles south of Gilroy (lat. 36°53'50" N, long. 121° 34'10" W); the stream is in Sargent Hills. Named on Chittenden (1955, photorevised 1968 and 1973) 7.5' quadrangle.

Sargent Hills [SANTA CLARA]: *range,* 6 miles south of Gilroy (lat. 36°55'15" N, long. 121°34'25" W); the range is west of Sargent. Named on Chittenden (1955) 7.5' quadrangle.

Sargent Ranch: see **Juristac** [SANTA CLARA].

Sarlandt Resort [SONOMA]: *locality,* 2 miles south of Cazadero (lat. 38°30'05" N, long. 123°05'10" W). Named on Cazadero (1943) 7.5' quadrangle.

Satiyome: see **Russian River** [SONOMA].

Saucelito: see **Sausalito** [MARIN] (1) and (2).

Sausal Creek [ALAMEDA]: *stream,* formed by the confluence of Shephard Creek and Palo Seco Creek, flows 3 miles to end in lowlands 3 miles east-southeast of downtown Oakland (lat. 37°47'15" N, long. 122°13'35" W). Named on Oakland East (1959) 7.5' quadrangle. Crespi called the stream Arroyo del Bosque in 1772—*bosque* means "woods" in Spanish; the stream also was known as Fruitvale Creek from the place called Fruitvale (Mosier and Mosier, p. 79).

Sausal Creek [SAN MATEO]: *stream,* flows 2.5 miles through Portola Valley (1) to marsh 6 miles south of downtown Redwood City near Searsville Lake (lat. 37°23'50" N, long. 122°14'30" W). Named on Mindego Hill (1961) and Palo Alto (1961) 7.5' quadrangles. Called Corte de Madera Creek on Palo Alto (1899) 15' quadrangle, but United States Board on Geographic Names (1968a, p. 7) rejected this designation for the feature. The stream also had the names "Arroyo Sausal," "Arroyo del Sanjon," and "Sanjon Creek" (Brown, p. 85).

Sausal Creek [SONOMA]: *stream,* flows 8 miles to Russian River 4 miles northeast of Healdsburg (lat. 38°39' N, long. 122°48'30" W). Named on Jimtown (1955) 7.5' quadrangle.

Sausal Creek: see **Bull Run Creek** [SAN MATEO]; **Neils Gulch** [SAN MATEO].

Sausalito [MARIN]:

(1) *land grant,* covers the south end of Marin Peninsula, including the town of Sausalito. Named on Point Bonita (1954) and San Francisco North (1950) 7.5' quadrangles. Called Saucelito on Bolinas (1954), San Francisco North (1956), and San Rafael (1954) 7.5' quadrangles. Jose Antonio Galindo received 3 leagues in 1835; William A. Richardson claimed 19,572 acres patented in 1879 (Cowan, p. 96-97; Cowan gave the forms "Sauzalito" and "Saucelito" as alternates). According to Perez (p. 98), Richardson was the grantee in 1838. The name is from *sausal,* the Spanish term for willows that grew around springs on the grant (Hoover, Rensch, and Rensch, p. 179).

(2) *town,* 8 miles south-southeast of downtown San Rafael (lat. 37° 51'30" N, long. 122°29' W); the town is on Sausalito grant. Named on Point Bonita (1954) and San Francisco North (1956) 7.5' quadrangles. United States Board on Geographic Names (1933, p. 674) rejected the form "Saucelito" for the name. Postal authorities established Saucelito post office in 1870 and changed the name to Sausalito in 1887 (Salley, p. 198). The town incorporated in 1893. The name took a number of forms in the 1840's and 1850's: San Saulito (Rogers and Johnston's (1857) map); San Salita (Agassiz, p. 380); San Solito (Kelly, p. 162); Sancolito (Tyson, J.L., p. 62); Sancilito (Delavan, p. 34); Sousolito (Taylor, volume I, p. 52); Sousalita (Bidwell, p. 39); Sousilito (*The California Star,* January 30, 1847); Sausilito (Dana, p. 261); Sauz Saulita (White, p. 61).

Sausalito Cove: see **Sausalito Point** [MARIN].

Sausalito Point [MARIN]: *promontory,* southwest of the mouth of Richardson Bay at the town of Sausalito (lat. 37°51'25" N, long. 122°28'40" W). Named on San Francisco North (1956) 7.5' quadrangle. Ringgold's (1850a) map has the name "Saucelito Bay" for the embayment south of present Sausalito Point—this embayment appears to be the Sausalito Cove that H.R. Wagner (p. 444) identified as the feature called Ensenada de Consolacion in Spanish times.

Sauselito Bay: see **Sausalito Point** [MARIN].

Sauzalito: see **Sausalito** [MARIN] (1).

Savage Creek: see **Mills Creek** [SAN MATEO] (2).

Sawmill Gulch [SONOMA]: *canyon,* 1 mile long, opens into the canyon of Russian River 1 mile east of Jenner (lat. 38°26'55" N, long. 123°05'45" W). Named on Duncans Mills (1979) 7.5' quadrangle.

Sawtooth Canyon [SANTA CLARA]: *canyon,* nearly 1 mile long, drained by a stream that joins San Antonio Creek 4 miles north-northeast of Isabel Valley (lat. 37°22'05" N, long. 121°31'05" W; sec. 34, T 6 S, R 4 E). Named on Isabel Valley (1955) 7.5' quadrangle.

Sawyer Ridge [SAN MATEO]: *ridge,* generally southeast-trending, 5.5 miles long, center 4 miles east of Montara Knob (lat. 37°33'30" N, long. 122°24'35" W). Named on Montara Mountain (1956) 7.5' quadrangle. Leander Sawyer trained performing horses in the 1860's and 1870's at a camp east of the ridge and near the north end of Lower Crystal Springs Lake; another name for the feature was Tunnel Ridge, for an aqueduct tunnel dug about 1860 (Brown, p. 85-86).

Sawyers Crossing [SANTA CLARA]: *locality,* 4 miles southeast of Gilroy along Southern Pacific Railroad (lat. 36°57'30" N, long. 121°31'15" W). Named on San Juan Bautista (1917) 15' quadrangle.

Scarpa Hill: see **Scarper Peak** [SAN MATEO].

Scarper Peak [SAN MATEO]: *peak,* 3.5 miles east-southeast of Montara Knob on Montara Mountain (lat. 37°31'45" N, long. 122° 25'35" W; sec. 5, T 5 S, R 5 W). Altitude 1944 feet. Named on Montara Mountain (1956) 7.5' quadrangle. Brown (p. 86) listed the peak under the name "Scarpa Hill," and noted that Giorgio Scarpa settled in the neighborhood in 1859; the feature also was called Spanish Peak in the early 1860's.

Schell Creek [SONOMA]: *stream,* flows 3.5 miles to Schell Slough 6 miles north of Sears Point (lat. 38°14'20" N, long. 122°25'50" W). Named on Sears Point (1951) and Sonoma (1951) 7.5' quadrangles.

Schell Slough [SONOMA]: *water feature,* extends from Schell Creek to Steamboat Slough 5.5 miles north-northeast of Sears Point (lat. 38°13'40" N, long. 121°25'25" W). Named on Sears Point (1951) 7.5' quadrangle.

Schellville [SONOMA]: *settlement,* 6.5 miles north of Sears Point along Northwestern Pacific Railroad (lat. 38°14'45" N, long. 122° 26'15" W); the place is near the mouth of Schell Creek. Named on Sears Point (1951) 7.5' quadrangle. Called Shellville on Mare Island (1916) 15' quadrangle. Postal authorities established Shellville post office in 1888 and discontinued it in 1931; the misspelled name was for Theodore L. Schell, pioneer rancher in the neighborhood (Salley, p. 203).

Schilling Lake [SAN MATEO]: *intermittent lake,* 375 feet long, 3 miles east-southeast of Skeggs Point (lat. 37°23'25" N, long. 122° 15'20" W). Named on Woodside (1961) 7.5' quadrangle. Brown (p. 86) called the feature Schilling's Lake, and noted that August Schilling had it built in the 1930's.

Schmidt [CONTRA COSTA]: *locality,* 2 miles east-southeast of present Richmond civic center along Atchison, Topeka and Santa Fe Railroad (lat. 37°55'10" N, long. 122°18'50" W). Named on San Francisco (1915) 15' quadrangle.

Schmidtville: see **Stege** [CONTRA COSTA].

Schocken Hill [SONOMA]: *peak,* 1 mile north-northeast of Sonoma (lat. 38°18'15" N, long. 122°27' W). Altitude 658 feet. Named on Sonoma (1951) 7.5' quadrangle.

Schoolhouse Beach [SONOMA]: *beach,* 5.5 miles south-southeast of Jenner (lat. 38°22'35" N, long. 123°04'40" W). Named on Duncans Mills (1979) 7.5' quadrangle.

Schoolhouse Creek [SAN MATEO]: *stream,* flows 0.5 mile to Lobitos Creek nearly 6 miles south-southeast of downtown Half Moon Bay at Lobitos (lat. 37°23' N, long. 122°24' W). Named on Half Moon Bay (1961) 7.5' quadrangle, which shows Tunitas Sch. near the head of the stream.

Schoolhouse Creek [SONOMA]:

(1) *stream,* flows 1.5 miles to Dry Creek 5 miles west of Geyserville (lat. 38°43'10" N, long. 123°59'30" W). Named on Geyserville (1955) and Warm Springs Dam (1978) 7.5' quadrangles.

(2) *stream,* flows 1 mile to Gilliam Creek 4 miles northeast of Cazadero (lat. 38°33'55" N, long. 123°01'55" W; sec. 1, T 8 N, R 11 W). Named on Cazadero (1978) 7.5' quadrangle.

Schoolhouse Gulch [SONOMA]: *canyon,* drained by a stream that flows 0.5 mile to Dutch Bill Creek 3 miles south-southwest of Guerneville (lat. 38°27'40" N, long. 123°00'35" W; sec. 7, T 7 N, R 10 W). Named on Duncans Mills (1979) 7.5' quadrangle.

Schoolhouse Point [SONOMA]: *ridge,* southwest-trending, 0.5 mile long, 1.5 miles northwest of Mount Saint Helena (lat. 38°41'25" N, long. 122°39'05" W). Named on Mount Saint Helena (1959) 7.5' quadrangle.

Schoolhouse Ridge [SANTA CLARA]: *ridge,* east-northeast-trending, 1 mile long, 3.5 miles southwest of Mount Sizer (lat. 37°10'30" N, long. 121°33'15" W). Named on Mount Sizer (1955) 7.5' quadrangle.

Schoolhouse Station: see **Colma** [SAN MATEO].

School Ridge [SONOMA]: *ridge,* south-trending, 1 mile long, 2 miles north of Annapolis (lat. 38°45' N, long. 123°22'20" W). Named on Annapolis (1977) 7.5' quadrangle.

Schooner Bay [MARIN]: *bay,* opens into Drakes Estero 6.5 miles northeast of the lighthouse at Point Reyes (lat. 38°03'45" N, long. 122°56'15" W). Named on Drakes Bay (1953) 7.5' quadrangle, which shows the site of a schooner landing on the west shore of the bay.

Schroeder Gulch: see **Arroyo Ojo de Agua** [SAN MATEO].

Schultz Slough [SONOMA]: *water feature,* 4 miles southeast of downtown Petaluma in marsh southwest of Petaluma River (lat. 38°12' N, long. 122°34'35" W). Named on Petaluma River (1954) 7.5' quadrangle.

Schwerin Valley: see **Visitacion Valley** [SAN FRANCISCO-SAN MATEO].

Scott: see **Fort Scott** [SAN FRANCISCO]; **Fort Winfield Scott**, under **Fort Point** [SAN FRANCISCO].

Scott Creek [ALAMEDA-SANTA CLARA]: *stream,* forms part of Alameda-Santa Clara County line, flows 2.5 miles to lowlands 7 miles southeast of the Fremont civic center (lat. 37°28' N, long. 121°53'50" W). Named on Calaveras Reservoir (1961) and Milpitas (1961) 7.5' quadrangles. Thompson and West's (1876) map has the label "Lone Tree Creek or Scotts Ravine" on the feature. The name "Scott" commemorates Joseph Scott, who settled by the creek in 1852; the name "Lone Tree Creek" was for a single sycamore tree that stood near the stream—Font called the feature Arroyo de la Encarnation in 1776 (Mosier and Mosier, p. 79).

Scotts Corner [ALAMEDA]: *locality,* 1 mile east-southeast of Sunol (lat. 37°35'20" N, long. 121°52'10" W). Named on La Costa Valley (1960) 7.5' quadrangle. Thomas Scott, Sr., opened a store at the place in the 1850's (Mosier and Mosier, p. 79). Thompson and West's (1878) map shows Scotts store situated east of Sunol beyond present Scotts Corner.

Scotts Creek [SONOMA]: *stream,* flows about 1.25 miles to Porter Creek (1) 4 miles northeast of Guerneville (lat. 38°32'50" N, long. 122°56'40" W; near SE cor. sec. 10, T 8 N, R 10 W); the stream is east of Scotts Ridge. Named on Guerneville (1955) 7.5' quadrangle.

Scotts Opening [SONOMA]: *area,* 4.5 miles northeast of Guerneville (lat. 38°33'25" N, long. 122°57' W); the place is on Scotts Ridge. Named on Guerneville (1955) 7.5' quadrangle.

Scotts Ravine: see **Scott Creek** [ALAMEDA-SANTA CLARA].

Scotts Ridge [SONOMA]: *ridge,* south-trending, 1 mile long, 4.5 miles northeast of Guerneville (lat. 38°33'25" N, long. 122°57' W). Named on Guerneville (1955) 7.5' quadrangle.

Scotts Spur: see **Meridian** [SANTA CLARA].

Scotty Creek [SONOMA]: *stream,* flows 2.5 miles to the sea 5 miles south-southeast of Jenner at Gleason Beach (lat. 38°23'05" N, long. 123°04'55" W). Named on Duncans Mills (1979) 7.5' quadrangle. On Duncans Mills (1921) 15' quadrangle, the canyon of the stream is called Gleason Gulch.

Scow Canyon [CONTRA COSTA]: *canyon,* 1 mile long, 5.5 miles northwest of Orinda (lat. 37°56'35" N, long. 122°14'30" W). Named on Briones Valley (1959) 7.5' quadrangle. Water of San Pablo Reservoir floods a large part of the canyon.

Scribner Mountain [NAPA]: *ridge,* west-northwest- to northwest-trending, 1 mile long, 2.25 miles south-southwest of Berryessa Peak (lat. 38°38'05" N, long. 122°12'35" W). Named on Brooks (1959) 7.5' quadrangle.

Seal Bluff Landing [CONTRA COSTA]: *locality,* 6 miles east-northeast of Martinez along Suisun Bay (lat. 38°03'15" N, long. 122°02'20" W); the place is east of Seal Islands. Named on Karquines (1898) 15' quadrangle.

Seal Cove [SAN MATEO]: *settlement,* 3 miles south-southwest of Montara Knob near the coast (lat. 37°31'10" N, long. 122°13'10" W). Named on Montara Mountain (1956) 7.5' quadrangle.

Seal Creek [CONTRA COSTA]: *water feature,* enters Hastings Slough 5 miles east-northeast of Martinez (lat. 38°02'10" N, long. 122°02'55" W); the feature is south of Seal Islands. Named on Vine Hill (1959) 7.5' quadrangle. On Karquines (1898) 15' quadrangle, the name extends up present Mount Diablo Creek.

Seal Creek: see **Bay Slough** [SAN MATEO]; **Seal Slough** [SAN MATEO].

Sea Lion Rock: see **Seal Rock** [SAN FRANCISCO]; **Seal Rock** [SAN MATEO].

Seal Islands [CONTRA COSTA]: *islands,* two, largest 2100 feet long, 5.5 miles east-northeast of Martinez in Suisun Bay (lat. 38°03'20" N, long. 122°02'45" W). Named on Vine Hill (1959) 7.5' quadrangle, which shows the islands as marsh.

Seal Isle: see **Benicia Point** [SOLANO].

Seal Rock [SAN FRANCISCO]: *island,* 600 feet long, 600 feet south of South Farallon (lat. 37°41'35" N, long. 123°00'10" W). Named on Farallon Islands (1988) 7.5' quadrangle. G.D. Hanna (p. 303) gave the designation "Sea Lion or Saddle Rock" for the feature.

Seal Rock [SAN MATEO]: *island,* 600 feet long, 5 miles south of downtown Half Moon Bay and 450 feet offshore (lat. 37°23'30" N, long. 122°25'25" W). Named on Half Moon Bay (1961) 7.5' quadrangle. The feature also has been called Sea Lion Rock (Brown, p. 87).

Seal Rock: see **Sail Rock** [SAN MATEO].

Seal Rocks [SAN FRANCISCO]: *rocks,* 0.25 mile south-southwest of Point

Lobos, and 500 feet offshore (lat. 37°46'40" N, long. 122°30'55" W). Named on San Francisco North (1956) 7.5' quadrangle.

Seal Slough [SAN MATEO]: *water feature,* between Brewer Island and the mainland, joins San Francisco Bay nearly 2 miles east of downtown San Mateo (lat. 37°34'15" N, long. 122°17'35" W). Named on San Mateo (1956) 7.5' quadrangle. Called Seal Creek on San Mateo (1947) 7.5' quadrangle, but United States Board on Geographic Names (1961b, p. 16) rejected the names "Seal Creek," "Angelo Slough," and "San Mateo Slough" for the feature.

Sea Ranch: see **German** [SONOMA].

Sears Point [SONOMA]: *locality,* 11 miles southeast of Petaluma along Northwestern Pacific Railroad (lat. 38°09' N, long. 122°26'45" W). Named on Sears Point (1951) 7.5' quadrangle. Postal authorities established Sears Point post office in 1903 and discontinued it in 1911; the name commemorates Franklin Sears, who settled near the place in 1851 (Salley, p. 200).

Searsville: see **Searsville Lake** [SAN MATEO].

Searsville Lake [SAN MATEO]: *lake,* 0.5 mile long, behind a dam on San Francisquito Creek 5.25 miles south of downtown Redwood City (lat. 37°24'25" N, long. 122°14'10" W). Named on Palo Alto (1961) 7.5' quadrangle. John H. Sears built a house at the site in 1854, and later the building was used as a hotel—the village of Searsville grew around the hotel (Hoover, Rensch, and Rensch, p. 400). Postal authorities established Searsville post office in 1858 and discontinued it in 1893 (Frickstad, p. 169). Water of the lake encroached on the site of the village of Searsville in 1890 (Brown, p. 87).

Seaview [SONOMA]: *locality,* 2.25 miles north-northeast of Fort Ross (lat. 38°32'45" N, long. 123°13'35" W; sec. 7, T 8 N, R 12 W). Named on Fort Ross (1943) 7.5' quadrangle. Skaggs (1921) 15' quadrangle has the form "Sea View" for the name. Postal authorities established Timber Cove post office in 1863, moved it 3 miles northeast and changed the name to Sea View in 1883, moved it 1 mile north in 1908, and discontinued it in 1914 (Salley, p. 200, 222).

Sebastopol [SONOMA]: *town,* 6.5 miles west-southwest of Santa Rosa (lat. 38°24'05" N, long. 122°49'25" W). Named on Sebastopol (1954) 7.5' quadrangle. Postal authorities established Sebastopol post office in 1867 (Salley, p. 200), and the town incorporated in 1902. The community began in 1852 with a store and settlement called Pine Grove; the name "Sebastopol" came in 1856 after a local quarrel was likened to the Crimean-War battle at Sebastopol (Miller, J.T., p. 32). California Mining Bureau's (1917a) map shows a place called Kenilworth located northeast of Sebastopol along the railroad about halfway from Sebastopol to Santa Rosa. Postal authorities established Peachland post office 5 miles northwest of Sebastopol in 1891 and discontinued it in 1901; the site was in peach orchards (Salley, p. 168). They established Carillo post office 3 miles east of Sebastopol in 1897 and discontinued it in 1899; the name was for an early settler (Salley, p. 37).

Sebastopol: see **Yountville** [NAPA].

Second Mallard Branch [SOLANO]: *water feature,* joins Cutoff Slough nearly 5 miles south-southeast of Fairfield (lat. 38°11' N, long. 122°00'45" W). Named on Fairfield South (1949) 7.5' quadrangle.

Second Napa Slough [SONOMA]: *water feature,* joins Sonoma Creek 3 miles north-northeast of Sears Point (lat. 38°11'15" N, long. 122°25'15" W). Named on Sears Point (1951) 7.5' quadrangle.

Secret Pasture [SONOMA]: *area,* 5.5 miles north-northwest of Sonoma (lat. 38°22'15" N, long. 122°29' W; near NE cor. sec. 14, T 6 N, R 6 W). Named on Sonoma (1951) 7.5' quadrangle.

Seeboy Ridge [SANTA CLARA]: *ridge,* north- to northwest-trending, 2.5 miles long, 5 miles northwest of Isabel Valley (lat. 37°22'30" N, long. 121°35'40" W). Named on Eylar Mountain (1955) and Isabel Valley (1955) 7.5' quadrangles.

Segassia Canyon [NAPA]: *canyon,* drained by a stream that flows 1.25 miles to Dry Creek 5 miles south of Rutherford (lat. 38°23'20" N, long. 122°24'30" W; near SE cor. sec. 4, T 6 N, R 5 W). Named on Rutherford (1951) and Sonoma (1951) 7.5' quadrangles.

Segunda Creek: see **Dry Creek** [ALAMEDA] (1).

Selby [CONTRA COSTA]: *locality,* 6.5 miles west-northwest of Martinez along Southern Pacific Railroad (lat. 38°03'25" N, long. 122° 14'35" W). Named on Benicia (1959) 7.5' quadrangle. Postal authorities established Selby post office in 1886 and discontinued it in 1967; the name is for Prentiss Selby, first postmaster (Salley, p. 201). Ringgold's (1850a) map has the name "Pyramid Pt." near present Selby.

Semple Point [SOLANO]: *promontory,* 3 miles south-southeast of downtown Vallejo along Carquinez Strait (lat. 38°03'55" N, long. 122°13'35" W). Named on Benicia (1959) 7.5' quadrangle. Called Pt. Semple on Ringgold's (1850a) map.

Seneca Reservoir [ALAMEDA]: *lake,* 550 feet long, 7 miles east-southeast of downtown Oakland (lat. 37°45'20" N, long. 122°09'20" W). Named on Oakland East (1959) 7.5' quadrangle. The reservoir was built in 1950 and named for Seneca Street, where it is located (Mosier and Mosier, p. 80).

Seno de Malacomes: see **Mallacomes or Moristul y Plan de Agua Caliente** [NAPA-SONOMA].

Sentinel Hill [NAPA]: *hill,* 4 miles north-northeast of Saint Helena (lat. 38°33'45" N, long. 122°26'50" W). Named on Saint Helena (1960) 7.5' quadrangle.

Serpentine Point [MARIN]: *peak,* 5 miles west-southwest of downtown San Rafael (lat. 37°56'15" N, long. 122°36'45" W). Named on San Rafael (1954) 7.5' quadrangle.

Serpents Slough [CONTRA COSTA]: *water feature,* 3.5 miles north of the settlement of Bethel Island on Webb Tract (lat. 38°03'50" N, long. 121°38'15" W). Named on Jersey Island (1952) 7.5' quadrangle. Called Serpent Slough on Jersey (1910) 7.5' quadrangle.

Serrito de San Antonio: see **Albany Hill** [ALAMEDA].

Seven Mile Beach: see **Mussel Rock** [SAN MATEO] (1).

Seven Mile House: see **Edenvale** [SANTA CLARA].

Seven Oaks Creek [SONOMA]: *stream,* flows 1.5 miles to Warm Springs Creek 1.5 miles west-northwest of Skaggs Springs (lat. 38° 42'05" N, long. 123°03'05" W; sec. 23, T 10 N, R 11 W). Named on Warm Springs Dam (1978) 7.5' quadrangle.

Seven Sisters: see **Black Mountain** [MARIN].

Seven Springs [NAPA]: *locality,* 4.25 miles north-northeast of Saint Helena (lat. 38°33'20" N, long. 122°25'45" W). Named on Pope Valley (1921) 15' quadrangle.

Seventy Acre Canyon [NAPA]: *canyon,* drained by a stream that flows 2.25 miles to Lake Curry 2.5 miles south-southwest of Mount Vaca (lat. 38°22' N, long. 122°07'15" W). Named on Fairfield North (1951) and Mount Vaca (1951) 7.5' quadrangles.

Shadow Spring [SANTA CLARA]: *spring,* 2 miles southwest of Pacheco Pass (lat. 37°02'25" N, long. 121°13'40" W). Named on Pacheco Pass (1955) 7.5' quadrangle.

Shaeirn Lake [SANTA CLARA]: *lake,* 600 feet long, 8.5 miles east of Gilroy Hot Springs (lat. 37°05'30" N, long. 121°19'10" W; sec. 4, T 10 S, R 6 E). Named on Pacheco Peak (1955) 7.5' quadrangle, which also shows Shaeirn ranch situated 1 mile west of the lake. Called Sharon Lake on Gilroy Hot Springs (1921) 15' quadrangle.

Shafer Creek [ALAMEDA]: *stream,* flows 1.25 miles to Trout Creek 5.5 miles south-southwest of Mendenhall Springs (lat. 37°30'45" N, long. 121°40'50" W; near W line sec. 8, T 5 S, R 3 E); the stream heads at Shafer Flat. Named on Mendenhall Springs (1956) 7.5' quadrangle.

Shafer Flat [ALAMEDA]: *area,* 5 miles south-southwest of Mendenhall Springs (lat. 37°31'40" N, long. 121°41'45" W; sec. 6, T 5 S, R 3 E). Named on Mendenhall Springs (1956) 7.5' quadrangle. The misspelled name commemorates Louis Schaffer, landowner at the site (Mosier and Mosier, p. 80-81).

Shafter [MARIN]: *locality,* 10.5 miles southwest of downtown Novato (lat. 38°00'20" N, long. 122°42'50" W). Named on San Geronimo (1954) 7.5' quadrangle. Petaluma (1914) 15' quadrangle shows the place along Northwestern Pacific Railroad.

Shag Rock [SAN FRANCISCO]: *rock,* in San Francisco Bay 5 miles east-southeast of Mount Davidson, and 2000 feet south of Hunters Point.(lat. 37°43' N, long. 122°22' W). Named on San Mateo (1915) 15' quadrangle.

Shag Rock: see **Shag Rocks** [SAN FRANCISCO].

Shag Rocks [SAN FRANCISCO]: *rocks,* 2.25 miles northwest of North Point in San Francisco Bay (lat. 37°50'05" N, long. 122°26'20" W). Named on San Francisco North (1956) 7.5' quadrangle. Called Shag Rock on San Francisco (1899, reprinted 1913) 15' quadrangle.

Shag Slough [SOLANO]: *water feature,* partly in Yolo County, joins Cache Slough 7 miles north of Rio Vista (lat. 38°15'35" N, long. 121°41'25" W). Named on Liberty Island (1978) 7.5' quadrangle. Cache Slough (1916) 7.5' quadrangle shows the feature before it was modified.

Shallow Beach [MARIN]: *beach,* 5.5 miles northwest of Point Reyes Station on the southwest side of Tomales Bay (lat. 38°07'25" N, long. 122°52'50" W). Named on Drakes Bay (1953) 7.5' quadrangle.

Shannon [SANTA CLARA]: *locality,* 1 mile west-northwest of downtown Los Gatos (lat. 37°13'50" N, long. 121°58' W). Named on Los Gatos (1919) 15' quadrangle.

Shanti Ashrama [SANTA CLARA]: *locality,* 3.5 miles west-southwest of Mount Stakes in Upper San Antonio Valley (lat. 37°18'30" N, long. 121°28'10" W; sec. 19, T 7 S, R 5 E). Named on Mount Stakes (1955) 7.5' quadrangle.

Sharon Lake: see **Shaeirn Lake** [SANTA CLARA].

Sharp Park [SAN MATEO]: *district,* 4.5 miles west-southwest of downtown South San Francisco near the coast (lat. 37°38'05" N, long. 122°29'20" W). Named on San Francisco South (1956) 7.5' quadrangle. Called Salada on San Mateo (1915) 15' quadrangle—the place is north of Laguna Salada. The community developed in 1905 with the name "Salada Beach" after nearby Laguna Salada (Gudde, 1949, p. 327). Salada Beach and Brighton Beach subdivision combined in 1935 to form the town of Sharp Park, named for land south of the place that the Sharp family donated to San Francisco for a park (Brown, p. 78-79). Residents of the town of Sharp Park voted in 1957 to join neighboring communities and form the new city of Pacifica. Postal authorities established Salada Beach post office in 1907, changed the name to Sharp Park in 1935, and discontinued it in

1959 (Salley, p. 191, 202).

Shaw Gulch [SAN MATEO]: *canyon,* 1 mile long, 6 miles west-southwest of La Honda (lat. 37°16'35" N, long. 122°21'55" W; sec. 35, T 7 S, R 5 W). Named on La Honda (1961) 7.5' quadrangle. The name commemorates the Shaw family, who had a ranch in the canyon after about 1870 (Brown, p. 88).

Sheehy Creek [NAPA]: *stream,* flows nearly 4 miles to salt evaporators 3.25 miles north-northwest of Napa Junction (lat. 38°13'45" N, long. 121°16'40" W; near N line sec. 2, T 4 N, R 4 W). Named on Cuttings Wharf (1949, photorevised 1968) 7.5' quadrangle.

Sheephouse Creek [SONOMA]: *stream,* flows nearly 3 miles to Russian River 1.25 miles east of Jenner (lat. 38°26'55" N, long. 123°05'40" W). Named on Duncans Mills (1979) 7.5' quadrangle.

Sheep Island: see **Brooks Island** [CONTRA COSTA].

Sheep Repose Ridge [SONOMA]: *ridge,* north- to northwest-trending, 1 mile long, 4.25 miles west-northwest of Big Mountain (lat. 38°44'35" N, long. 123°12'35" W). Named on Tombs Creek (1978) 7.5' quadrangle.

Sheep Ridge [SANTA CLARA]: *ridge,* northwest-trending, 2.5 miles long, 5.5 miles east of San Martin (lat. 37°06' N, long. 121°30'30" W). Named on Gilroy (1955) and Gilroy Hot Springs (1955) 7.5' quadrangles.

Sheep Ridge [SONOMA]: *ridge,* south-trending, 2.5 miles long, 7 miles southeast of Jenner (lat. 38°22'55" N, long. 122°01'20" W). Named on Bodega Head (1972) and Duncans Mills (1979) 7.5' quadrangles.

Sheepskin Rock [SONOMA]: *peak,* 7 miles northwest of Mount Saint Helena (lat. 38°44'35" N, long. 122°43' W; sec. 2, T 10 N, R 8 W). Named on Mount Saint Helena (1959) 7.5' quadrangle.

Sheep Slough [CONTRA COSTA]: *water feature,* 3.25 miles east of the settlement of Bouldin Island between Quimby Island and Holland Tract (lat. 38°01'15" N, long. 121°34'45" W). Named on Bouldin Island (1978) 7.5' quadrangle.

Sheldrake Slough [SOLANO]: *water feature,* joins Suisun Slough 3.5 miles south of Fairfield (lat. 38°11'50" N, long. 122°02'45" W). Named on Fairfield South (1949) 7.5' quadrangle.

Shell Beach [MARIN]: *beach,* 5 miles northwest of Point Reyes Station on the southwest side of Tomales Bay (lat. 38°07'05" N, long. 122°52'25" W). Named on Inverness (1954) 7.5' quadrangle.

Shell Beach [SONOMA]: *beach,* 2.5 miles south-southeast of Jenner along the coast (lat. 38°25' N, long. 123°06'15" W). Named on Duncans Mills (1979) 7.5' quadrangle.

Shell Mound [ALAMEDA]: *locality,* 2.5 miles north-northwest of downtown Oakland along Southern Pacific Railroad in Emoryville (lat. 37°50'05" N, long. 122°17'30" W). Named on San Francisco (1899) 15' quadrangle. Nelson's (1909) map shows the place situated near the site of a well-known Indian shell mound.

Shell Ridge [CONTRA COSTA]: *ridge,* west-northwest-trending, 3.5 miles long, center 3 miles east of Walnut Creek civic center (lat. 37°53'35" N, long. 122°00'30" W). Named on Clayton (1953) and Walnut Creek (1959) 7.5' quadrangles.

Shellville: see **Schellville** [SONOMA].

Shellville Colony [SONOMA]: *settlement,* 6.5 miles north-northeast of Sears Point (lat. 38°14'35" N, long. 122°25' W); the place is 1.25 miles east-southeast of Shellville (present Schellville). Named on Mare Island (1916) 15' quadrangle.

Shelter Cove [SAN MATEO]: *settlement,* 3 miles north-northwest of Montara Knob near the coast (lat. 37°35'50" N, long. 122°23'15" W). Named on Montara Mountain (1956) 7.5' quadrangle. The settlement began as a resort in the late 1930's; the embayment at the place was called Pirate's Cove for rum-running activity there during Prohibition times (Brown, p. 88). San Mateo (1942) 15' quadrangle has the name "Shelter Cove" for the embayment.

Shepard Creek: see **Shephard Creek** [ALAMEDA].

Shephard Creek [ALAMEDA]: *stream,* flows 1.5 miles to join Palo Seco Creek and form Sausal Creek 3.5 miles east-northeast of downtown Oakland (lat. 37°49'10" N, long. 122°12'25" W). Named on Oakland East (1959) 7.5' quadrangle. Called Shepard Creek on Concord (1897) 15' quadrangle. The misspelled name is for William Joseph Shepherd, who owned land along the stream; the canyon of the creek is called Shepherd Canyon (Mosier and Mosier, p. 81).

Shepherd Canyon: see **Shephard Creek** [ALAMEDA].

Sherburne Hills [CONTRA COSTA]: *ridge,* northwest-trending, 3 miles long, 3 miles east-southeast of Danville (lat. 37°47'55" N, long. 121°56'50" W). Named on Diablo (1953) 7.5' quadrangle.

Sheridan [SONOMA]: *locality,* 3.25 miles southwest of Guerneville along Russian River (lat. 38°27'55" N, long. 123°02'05" W). Named on Duncans Mills (1979) 7.5' quadrangle.

Sheridan Creek [ALAMEDA]: *stream,* flows 3 miles to Alameda Creek 1.25 miles south-southeast of Sunol (lat. 37°34'40" N, long. 121°52'35" W). Named on Niles (1961) 7.5' quadrangle. The stream was named in 1906 for Sheridan school, which was near the creek; the canyon of the stream was called Lleguas Valley (Mosier and Mosier, p. 81).

Sheridan Gulch [SONOMA]: *canyon,* drained by a stream that flows 0.5 mile to Russian River 3.25 miles southwest of Guerneville (lat. 38°27'50" N, long. 123°02'10" W). Named on Duncans Mills (1979) 7.5' quadrangle.

Sherman: see **Madrone** [SANTA CLARA]; **Point Sherman**, under **Port Chicago** [CONTRA COSTA].

Sherman Flats [SANTA CLARA]: *area,* 2 miles west-southwest of Eylar Mountain (lat. 37°27'40" N, long. 121°34'45" W). Named on Eylar Mountain (1955) 7.5' quadrangle.

Shiloh [SONOMA]: *locality,* 7.5 miles southeast of Healdsburg along Northwestern Pacific Railroad (lat. 38°31'25" N, long. 122°47'40" W; sec. 19, T 8 N, R 8 W). Named on Healdsburg (1955) 7.5' quadrangle.

Shingle Valley [SANTA CLARA]: *valley,* drained by a stream that joins Animas Creek 4.25 miles east of Coyote (lat. 37°12'35" N, long. 121°39'40" W). Named on Morgan Hill (1955) 7.5' quadrangle.

Shinn [ALAMEDA]: *locality,* 1.25 miles northwest of Fremont civic center along Southern Pacific Railroad (lat. 37°34' N, long. 121°58'55" W; sec. 21, T 4 S, R 1 W). Named on Niles (1961) 7.5' quadrangle. The name commemorates James Shinn, who settled at the place in 1856 (Mosier and Mosier, p. 81).

Ship Channel: see **Sacramento River Deep Water Ship Channel** [SOLANO].

Shipyard Acres [NAPA]: *locality,* 2.5 miles south-southeast of downtown Napa (lat. 38°15'35" N, long. 122°16'20" W). Named on Napa (1951) 7.5' quadrangle.

Shoal Point: see **Point Potrero** [CONTRA COSTA].

Shoeheart Ridge: see **Britain Ridge** [SONOMA].

Shoemaker: see **Camp Shoemaker**, under **Camp Parks** [ALAMEDA-CONTRA COSTA].

Shoquel Augmentation [SANTA CLARA]: *land grant,* mainly in Santa Cruz County, but extends over the crest of Santa Cruz Mountains into Santa Clara County 9 miles south-southeast of Los Gatos. Named on Laurel (1955) and Los Gatos (1953) 7.5' quadrangles. Martina Castro received the land in 1844 as an addition to her Soquel grant in present Santa Cruz County; she claimed 32,702 acres patented in 1860 (Arbuckle, p. 35; Arbuckle called the grant Soquel Augmentacion). The name "Soquel" is from an Indian village (Kroeber, p. 59).

Shore Acres [CONTRA COSTA]: *town,* 4.5 miles west of Pittsburg (lat. 38°02'10" N, long. 121°57'50" W). Named on Honker Bay (1953) 7.5' quadrangle.

Short Ridge [CONTRA COSTA]: *ridge,* west-northwest-trending, 2 miles long, 2 miles east of Danville (lat. 37°49'20" N, long. 121° 58' W). Named on Diablo (1953) 7.5' quadrangle.

Short Slough [CONTRA COSTA]: *water feature,* 3 miles north of the settlement of Bethel Island on Webb Tract (lat. 38°03'30" N, long. 121°37'45" W). Named on Bouldin Island (1978) and Jersey Island (1952) 7.5' quadrangles.

Shorttail Gulch [SONOMA]: *canyon,* drained by a stream that flows less than 1 mile to the sea nearly 3 miles southeast of the village of Bodega Bay (lat. 38°18'10" N, long. 123°00'45" W). Named on Bodega Head (1972) 7.5' quadrangle.

Shotgun Bend [SANTA CLARA]: *locality,* 2.5 miles northwest of Black Mountain (1), where Page Mill Road makes a sharp turn (lat. 37°20'45" N, long. 121°10'45" W). Named on Mindego Hill (1961) 7.5' quadrangle.

Shroyer Mountain [MARIN]: *peak,* 6.25 miles west-southwest of downtown Novato (lat. 38°03'55" N, long. 122°40'10" W). Altitude 1458 feet. Named on San Geronimo (1954) 7.5' quadrangle. Teather (p. 72) associated the name with Aaron Schroyer, who was justice of the peace for Nicasio from 1863 until 1873.

Shubrick Point: see **Southeast Farallon** [SAN FRANCISCO].

Sidney Flat [CONTRA COSTA]: *area,* 7 miles north-northeast of Mount Diablo in Markely Canyon (lat. 37°58'15" N, long. 121°51'45" W; near SE cor. sec. 33, T 2 N, R 1 E). Named on Antioch South (1953) 7.5' quadrangle.

Sierra Azul [SANTA CLARA]: *ridge,* northwest-trending, 8 miles long, in Santa Cruz Mountains northwest of Loma Prieta. Named on Loma Prieta (1955), Los Gatos (1953), and Santa Teresa Hills (1953) 7.5' quadrangles. *Sierra azul* means "blue mountain" in Spanish. According to testimony of James Alexander Forbes in 1857 (United States Supreme Court, p. 44), "The whole ridge from a considerable distance to the southeast, towards Monterey, up to the west of Santa Clara, is called the Sierra Azul, and sometimes the Santa Cruz mountains." Lyman (p. 270) noted that New Almaden mine is "in one of the ridges of Sierra Azul mountain."

Sierra Creek [SANTA CLARA]: *stream,* flows nearly 1 mile to lowlands 1.25 miles northeast of Berryessa (lat. 37°24' N, long. 121°50'30" W), and extends through lowlands in an artificial watercourse. Named on Calaveras Reservoir (1961) 7.5' quadrangle.

Sierra de Bolbones: see **Arroyo de las Nueces y Sierra de Bolbones**, under **Arroyo de las Nueces y Bolbones** [CONTRA COSTA].

Sierra de la Santa Cruz: see **Santa Cruz Mountains** [SAN MATEO-SANTA CLARA].

Sierra del Encino: see **New Almaden** [SANTA CLARA].

Sierra del Monte Diablo: see **Diablo Range** [ALAMEDA-CONTRA

COSTA-SANTA CLARA].

Sierra de los Bolbones: see **Mount Diablo** [CONTRA COSTA].

Sierra de San Bruno: see **San Bruno Mountain** [SAN MATEO].

Sierra de San Pedro: see **San Pedro Mountain** [SAN MATEO].

Sierra de Santa Clara: see **San Pedro Mountain** [SAN MATEO].

Sierra Morena [SAN MATEO]: *peak,* 850 feet west of Skeggs Point (lat. 37°24'35" N, long. 122°18'25" W; sec. 16, T 6 S, R 4 W). Altitude 2417 feet. Named on Woodside (1961) 7.5' quadrangle. In Spanish times, the name applied to the entire ridge on which this peak is a prominence—*sierra morena* means "dark mountain" in Spanish (Brown, p. 58). Irelan (p. 533) referred to the entire north part of Santa Cruz Mountains as Sierra Moreno.

Sierra Point [SAN MATEO]: *promontory,* 2 miles northeast of downtown South San Francisco along San Francisco Bay (lat. 37° 40'30" N, long. 122°23'15" W). Named on San Francisco South (1947) 7.5' quadrangle. The feature now protrudes into landfill. The embayment north of Sierra Point is called Candlestick Cove, from Candlestick Point [SAN FRANCISCO]; the causeway built to carry a highway across the cove forms a body of water called Brisbane Lagoon (Brown, p. 16).

Siesta Valley [CONTRA COSTA]: *canyon,* 1.5 miles west-southwest of Orinda (lat. 37°52'20" N, long. 122°12'20" W). Named on Briones Valley (1959) and Oakland East (1959) 7.5' quadrangles.

Signal Hill [NAPA-SOLANO]: *peak,* 2 miles south-southeast of Mount Vaca on Napa-Solano County line (lat. 38°22'35" N, long. 122°05' W; near S line sec. 9, T 6 N, R 2 W). Altitude 2394 feet. Named on Fairfield North (1951) and Mount Vaca (1951) 7.5' quadrangles.

Signal Hill: see **Albany Hill** [ALAMEDA]; **Telegraph Hill** [SAN FRANCISCO].

Silva Island [MARIN]: *island,* 0.25 mile long, 6 miles south of downtown San Rafael in Richardsons Bay (lat. 37°53'15" N, long. 122°30'55" W). Named on San Rafael (1954) 7.5' quadrangle. The feature now is connected to land.

Silverado City: see **Calistoga** [NAPA].

Silver Creek [SANTA CLARA]: *stream,* flows 14 miles to Miguelita Creek 2.5 miles northeast of downtown San Jose (lat. 37°21'35" N, long. 121°51'45" W). Named on Lick Observatory (1955), Morgan Hill (1955), and San Jose East (1961) 7.5' quadrangles. San Jose (1899) 15' quadrangle shows the stream ending in marsh less than 2 miles northwest of Evergreen.

Silveyville: see **Dixon** [SOLANO].

Simi [SONOMA]: *locality,* 1.5 miles north of Healdsburg along Northwestern Pacific Railroad (lat. 38°38'25" N, long. 122°52'25" W). Named on Jimtown (1955) 7.5' quadrangle.

Simla: see **Monta Vista** [SANTA CLARA].

Simmons Canyon [NAPA]: *canyon,* drained by a stream that flows 2 miles to lowlands nearly 2 miles east-northeast of Calistoga (lat. 38°35'30" N, long. 122°33' W). Named on Calistoga (1958) 7.5' quadrangle.

Simmons Island [SOLANO]: *island,* 7 miles west-southwest of Birds Landing (2) between Honker Bay and Suisun Bay (lat. 38°05'45" N, long. 121°59'15" W). Named on Honker Bay (1953) and Vine Hill (1959) 7.5' quadrangles. United States Board on Geographic Names (1933, p. 694) rejected the names "Ead's Island" and "Richs Island" for the feature. Later the Board (1988b, p. 4) approved the name "Andy Mason Slough" for a water passage, 0.4 mile long, that extends south from Grizzly Bay through Simmons Island to Suisun Cutoff (lat. 38°05'38" N, long. 122°00'45" W, at S end).

Simmons Point [SOLANO]: *promontory,* 6.25 miles south-southwest of Birds Landing (2) at the west end of Chipps Island (lat. 38°03'15" N, long. 121°56' W). Named on Honker Bay (1953) 7.5' quadrangle. Called Pt. Simmons on Ringgold's (1850c) map.

Simms Island [MARIN]: *hill,* 1.5 miles southeast of downtown San Rafael (lat. 37°57'30" N, long. 122°30'15" W). Named on San Rafael (1954) 7.5' quadrangle.

Simpson's: see **Melrose** [ALAMEDA].

Simpson's Landing: see **Hayward Landing** [ALAMEDA].

Simpton Point [MARIN]: *promontory,* on the north side of Angel Island (lat. 37°52'10" N, long. 122°25'25" W). Named on San Francisco North (1956) 7.5' quadrangle. United States Board on Geographic Names (1980, p. 4) approved the name "Point Simpton" for the feature. The Board at the same time approved the name "Winslow Cove" for the embayment just west of the promontory (lat. 37°52'15" N, long. 122°25'33" W). This feature was called China Cove after United States Immigration Service established a station there in 1910; the name "Winslow" is for Charles A. Winslow, a leader in making Angel Island a state park (Teather, p. 16).

Sinbad Creek [ALAMEDA]: *stream,* flows 7 miles to Sunol Valley at Sunol (lat. 37°35'40" N, long. 121°53'15" W; sec. 8, T 4 S, R 1 E). Named on Dublin (1961) and Niles (1961) 7.5' quadrangles. The stream first was called Batchelder Creek for Thomas Farwell Batchelder, who lived in the neighborhood in the 1870's (Mosier and Mosier, p. 82).

Sindicich Lagoons [CONTRA COSTA]: *lakes,* two, largest 325 feet long, 5 miles north-northeast of Orinda (lat. 37°56'40" N, long. 122°08'25" W). Named on Briones Valley (1959) 7.5' quadrangle.

Sir Francis Drake's Bay: see **Drakes Bay** [MARIN].

Sisters: see **The Sisters** [MARIN].

Sitio de la Brea: see **Las Animas** [SANTA CLARA].

Sizer: see **Mount Sizer** [SANTA CLARA].

Sizer Flat [SANTA CLARA]: *area,* 4 miles west-northwest of Mount Sizer (lat. 37°13'50" N, long. 121°34'45" W). Named on Mount Sizer (1955) 7.5' quadrangle.

Skaggs: see **Skaggs Springs** [SONOMA].

Skaggs Springs [SONOMA]: *springs,* 7.5 miles south of Cloverdale along Little Warm Springs Creek (lat. 38°41'35" N, long. 123°01'30" W; near S line sec. 24, T 10 N, R 11 W). Named on Warm Springs Dam (1978) 7.5' quadrangle. Skaggs Springs (1943) 7.5' quadrangle shows buildings at the place before water of Lake Sonoma inundated the site. Postal authorities established Skaggs Springs post office in 1878, discontinued it in 1884, reestablished it in 1889, changed the name to Skaggs in 1895, changed the name back to Skaggs Springs in 1927, and discontinued it in 1943—the name commemorates Alexander Skaggs, first postmaster and developer of a resort at the place (Salley, p. 205). The resort opened to the public in 1857, and by 1909 a hotel and cottages provided accommodations for 150 people to enjoy water from three hot springs (Waring, p. 81-82). Postal authorities established Groves post office 7 miles west of Skaggs post office in 1912 and discontinued it in 1914; the name was for James H. Groves, first postmaster (Salley, p. 90).

Skeggs Point [SAN MATEO]: *locality;* viewpoint 7.5 miles east-southeast of the town of Half Moon Bay (lat. 37°24'40" N, long. 122°18'20" W). Named on Woodside (1961) 7.5' quadrangle. California Division of Highways officials named the place in 1928 for John H. Skeggs, highway engineer, who was largely responsible for the road to the site (Brown, p. 89).

Skillet Creek: see **Llagas Creek** [SANTA CLARA].

Skunk Creek [SONOMA]: *stream,* flows 3 miles to Cherry Creek 3.5 miles west-southwest of Cloverdale (lat. 38°47'35" N, long. 123° 04'55" W; near NE cor. sec. 21, T 11 N, R 11 W). Named on Cloverdale (1960) 7.5' quadrangle.

Skunk Hill: see **Albany Hill** [ALAMEDA].

Skunk Hollow: see **Grizzly Creek** [SANTA CLARA]; **Skunk Hollow Gulch** [SANTA CLARA].

Skunk Hollow Gulch [SANTA CLARA]: *canyon,* 1 mile long, opens into an unnamed canyon 5 miles southeast of Mount Stakes (lat. 37°15'45" N, long. 121°27'50" W). Named on Mount Stakes (1955) 7.5' quadrangle. Called Skunk Hollow on Mount Boardman (1942) 15' quadrangle.

Sky Campground [MARIN]: *locality,* 2.25 miles south-southwest of Point Reyes Station on Inverness Ridge (lat. 38°02'25" N, long. 122°49'40" W). Named on Inverness (1954, photorevised 1971) 7.5' quadrangle.

Sky High [SONOMA]: *peak,* 5.5 miles west of Cloverdale (lat. 38°48'35" N, long. 123°07'15" W; near S line sec. 7, T 11 N, R 11 W). Altitude 2041 feet. Named on Cloverdale (1960) 7.5' quadrangle.

Skyland: see **Wrights** [SANTA CLARA].

Skyline Ridge [SONOMA]: *ridge,* southeast- to south-southeast-trending, 2.25 miles long, 8.5 miles southeast of Annapolis (lat. 38°38'10" N, long. 123°15' W). Named on Annapolis (1977), Fort Ross (1978), and Tombs Creek (1978) 7.5' quadrangles.

Sky Londa [SAN MATEO]: *settlement,* 3 miles southeast of Skeggs Point along La Honda Creek (lat. 37°23' N, long. 122°15'45" W). Named on Woodside (1961) 7.5' quadrangle.

Sky Valley [SOLANO]: *canyon,* 4.5 miles long, along Sulphur Springs Creek above a point 3.5 miles north of Benicia (lat. 38° 06' N, long. 122°09'40" W; near S line sec. 14, T 3 N, R 3 W). Named on Benicia (1959) and Cordelia (1951) 7.5' quadrangles.

Slate Creek [SAN MATEO]: *stream,* flows nearly 4 miles to Pescadero Creek 5 miles south-southeast of Mindego Hill (lat. 37°14'20" N, long. 122°12'10" W; sec. 16, T 8 S, R 3 W). Named on Big Basin (1955) and Mindego Hill (1961) 7.5' quadrangles. Stanger (1967, p. 93) gave the name "Rock Creek" as an alternate.

Slate Gap [SONOMA]: *pass,* 2.5 miles west-southwest of Guerneville (lat. 38°28'55" N, long. 123°02'10" W). Named on Duncans Mills (1979) 7.5' quadrangle.

Slaughterhouse Gulch [SONOMA]: *canyon,* drained by a stream that flows less than 1 mile to Russian River 3 miles east of Jenner (lat. 38°26'45" N, long. 123°03'45" W). Named on Duncans Mills (1979) 7.5' quadrangle.

Slaughterhouse Point [SOLANO]: *promontory,* 4 miles north-northwest of downtown Vallejo on the east side of Napa River (lat. 38° 09'15" N, long. 122°17'20" W; sec. 34, T 4 N, R 4 W). Named on Cuttings Wharf (1949) 7.5' quadrangle.

Slavianka: see **River Slavianda**, under **Russian River** [SONOMA].

Slavyansk: see **Fort Ross** [SONOMA].

Sleepy Hollow [CONTRA COSTA]: *valley,* 2 miles north of Orinda along Lauterwasser Creek (lat. 37°54'25" N, long. 122°11'10" W). Named on Briones Valley (1959) 7.5' quadrangle.

Sleepy Hollow [MARIN]: *valley,* 7 miles south of downtown Novato (lat. 38°00'30" N, long. 122°34'45" W). Named on Novato (1954) 7.5'

quadrangle.

Sleepy Hollow Creek [MARIN]: *stream,* flows 3.5 miles to San Anselmo Creek 2.25 miles west-northwest of downtown San Rafael (lat. 37°58'50" N, long. 122°34'10" W); the stream drains Sleepy Hollow. Named on San Rafael (1954) 7.5' quadrangle.

Smith: see **Point Smith**, under **Quarry Point** [MARIN].

Smith Corner: see **Riccas Corner** [SONOMA].

Smith Creek [SANTA CLARA]:
(1) *stream,* flows nearly 3 miles to San Tomas Aquinas Creek 1.25 miles west-southwest of downtown Campbell (lat. 37°16'35" N, long. 121°58'10" W). Named on San Jose West (1961) 7.5' quadrangle.
(2) *stream,* flows 14 miles to join Isabel Creek and form Arroyo Hondo 1.5 miles south of Mount Day (lat. 37°23' N, long. 121°41'30" W; sec. 30, T 6 S, R 3 E). Named on Isabel Valley (1955), Lick Observatory (1955), and Mount Day (1955) 7.5' quadrangles.

Smith Creek [SONOMA]:
(1) *stream,* flows 5.5 miles to Dry Creek 5.5 miles southwest of Cloverdale (lat. 38°45' N, long. 123°05'40" W; near NE cor. sec. 5, T 10 N, R 11 W). Named on Hopland (1960) 15' quadrangle, and on Warm Springs Dam (1978) 7.5' quadrangle.
(2) *stream,* flows 2.5 miles to Russian River 2 miles south of Guerneville (lat. 38°28'30" N, long. 122°59'25" W; near S line sec. 5, T 7 N, R 10 W). Named on Camp Meeker (1954) 7.5' quadrangle.

Smith Gulch [ALAMEDA]: *canyon,* drained by a stream that flows 1.25 miles to Arroyo Mocho 6.5 miles southeast of Cedar Mountain (lat. 37°29' N, long. 121°31'50" W; sec. 21, T 5 S, R 4 E). Named on Eylar Mountain (1955) 7.5' quadrangle. The name commemorates Elmer Smith, who owned the canyon before 1917 (Mosier and Mosier, p. 82).

Smith Gulch: see **Bull Run Creek** [SAN MATEO].

Smith Ridge [SONOMA]: *ridge,* generally east-trending, 1.5 miles long, 3.25 miles east of Fort Ross (lat. 38°30'55" N, long. 123°10'50" W). Named on Fort Ross (1978) 7.5' quadrangle.

Smiths Landing [MARIN]: *locality,* 3 miles west-southwest of Tomales on the northeast side of Tomales Bay (lat. 38°14'10" N, long. 122°57'30" W). Named on Point Reyes (1918) 15' quadrangle.

Smith's Landing: see **Antioch** [CONTRA COSTA].

Smith Slough [SAN MATEO]: *water feature,* extends 1.5 miles from Redwood Creek to Steinberger Slough nearly 2 miles north-northwest of downtown Redwood City (lat. 37°30'30" N, long. 122°14'35" W). Named on Redwood Point (1959) 7.5' quadrangle. The name commemorates William C.R. Smith, who built a landing along the slough in the 1850's (Brown, p. 90).

Smith Slough: see **Steinberger Slough** [SAN MATEO].

Smith's Ranch: see **Bodega** [SONOMA] (2).

Smittle Creek [NAPA]: *stream,* flows nearly 3 miles to Lake Berryessa 13 miles east-northeast of Saint Helena (lat. 38°34'40" N, long. 122°15'10" W). Named on Chiles Valley (1958) and Lake Berryessa (1959) 7.5' quadrangles.

Snag Island [SOLANO]: *island,* 7 miles southwest of Birds Landing (2) in Suisun Bay (lat. 38°04'20" N, long. 121°58'30" W). Named on Honker Bay (1953) 7.5' quadrangle. Called Palo Alto Id. on Ringgold's (1850c) map, which shows Palo Alto Pt. at the east end.

Snake's Head: see **Pillar Point** [SAN MATEO].

Snell Creek [NAPA]: *stream,* flows 2 miles to Butts Creek 5.25 miles northeast of Aetna Springs (lat. 38°42'15" N, long. 122°24'35" W; sec. 21, T 10 N, R 5 W); the stream heads near Snell Peak and joins Butts Creek in Snell Valley. Named on Aetna Springs (1958) 7.5' quadrangle.

Snell Peak [NAPA]: *peak,* 5 miles north-northeast of Aetna Springs (lat. 38°43'05" N, long. 122° 27' W; sec. 18, T 10 N, R 5 W). Altitude 1858 feet. Named on Aetna Springs (1958) 7.5' quadrangle.

Snell Valley [NAPA]: *valley,* 5 miles northeast of Aetna Springs along Snell Creek and Butts Creek (lat. 38°42'15" N, long. 122° 25' W). Named on Aetna Springs (1958) 7.5' quadrangle.

Snoboy [ALAMEDA]: *locality,* 3 miles south-southeast of Fremont civic center along Southern Pacific Railroad (lat. 37°30'40" N, long. 121°56'35" W). Named on Niles (1961) 7.5' quadrangle.

Snow Creek [SONOMA]: *stream,* flows 2 miles to Cherry Creek 4 miles west of Cloverdale (lat. 38°48'20" N, long. 123°05'15" W; sec. 16, T 11 N, R 11 W). Named on Cloverdale (1960) 7.5' quadrangle.

Snow Flat [NAPA]: *area,* 7.25 miles west-southwest of Mount Vaca (lat. 38°21'15" N, long. 122°13'15" W; sec. 20, T 6 N, R 3 W). Named on Mount George (1951) 7.5' quadrangle.

Sobey Creek [SANTA CLARA]: *stream,* flows 2 miles to Wildcat Creek nearly 3 miles west-southwest of downtown Campbell (lat. 37°16'05" N, long. 121°59'35" W). Named on Cupertino (1961, photorevised 1968 and 1973) and San Jose West (1961, photorevised 1968 and 1973) 7.5' quadrangles. Called Vasona Creek on Cupertino (1961) and San Jose West (1961) 7.5' quadrangles. United States Board on Geographic Names (1972, p. 3) gave the name "Vasona Creek" as a variant.

Sobrante [CONTRA COSTA]: *locality,* 1 mile southeast of Pinole Point along Southern Pacific Railroad (lat. 38°00'10" N, long. 122° 20'50" W). Named on Mare Island (1959) 7.5' quadrangle.

Sobrante: see **El Sobrante** [CONTRA COSTA] (2).

Sobrante Ridge [CONTRA COSTA]: *ridge,* northwest-trending, 7.5 miles long, center 6.25 miles northwest of Orinda (lat. 37°57'15" N, long. 122°14'45" W). Named on Briones Valley (1959) and Richmond (1959) 7.5' quadrangles.

Socayre: see **Yerba Buena** [SANTA CLARA].

Soda Canyon [NAPA]: *canyon,* 4 miles long, opens into lowlands 5 miles north of downtown Napa (lat. 38°22' N, long. 122°17'05" W); Soda Creek (1) drains the canyon. Named on Napa (1951) and Yountville (1951) 7.5' quadrangles.

Soda Creek [NAPA]:
(1) *stream,* flows 5 miles to Napa River nearly 4 miles north of downtown Napa (lat. 38°21'10" N, long. 122°17'25" W); the stream goes through Soda Canyon. Named on Napa (1951) and Yountville (1951) 7.5' quadrangles.
(2) *stream,* flows 4.5 miles to Capell Creek 10 miles northwest of Mount Vaca (lat. 38°29'45" N, long. 122°14'30" W; near SE cor. sec. 36, T 8 N, R 4 W); the stream drains Soda Valley. Named on Capell Valley (1951), Chiles Valley (1958), and Yountville (1951) 7.5' quadrangles.

Soda Gulch [SAN MATEO]: *canyon,* drained by a stream that flows less than 1 mile to Purisima Creek 2.5 miles northwest of Skeggs Point (lat. 37°26' N, long. 122°20'35" W; near S line sec. 6, T 6 S, R 4 W). Named on Woodside (1961) 7.5' quadrangle. The name is from the numerous springs of sulfurous water in the canyon; the feature was called Underwood Gulch in the 1860's—Joshua Underwood lived there in the late 1850's (Brown, p. 90).

Soda Rock [SONOMA]: *relief feature,* nearly 4 miles northeast of Healdsburg on the south bank of Russian River (lat. 38°39'05" N, long. 122°49' W). Named on Jimtown (1955) 7.5' quadrangle. Postal authorities established Soda Rock post office, named for the feature, 6 miles east of Healdsburg in 1889 and discontinued it in 1892, when they moved it 1 mile northwest and changed the name to Alexander Valley (Salley, p. 207).

Soda Spring [NAPA]: *spring,* 11.5 miles east of Saint Helena (lat. 38°31'05" N, long. 122°15'35" W); the spring is at the head of a branch of Soda Creek (2). Named on Chiles Valley (1958) 7.5' quadrangle.

Soda Spring Canyon [SANTA CLARA]: *canyon,* drained by a stream that flows 4.25 miles to Lexington Reservoir nearly 3 miles south of downtown Los Gatos (lat. 37°11'05" N, long. 121°58'40" W). Named on Los Gatos (1953) 7.5' quadrangle. Franke (p. 16) referred to this canyon when he noted a small carbonated spring called Alma Soda Spring "in Cavanaugh Gulch, about a mile from Alma Station." The canyon was known as Conyer Gulch in the 1860's, for a man who camped on the flat at its mouth; later John Cavance came to the canyon, and the name "Cavanaugh" is a misspelling of the word "Cavance" (Young, p. 125).

Soda Spring Creek [SONOMA]: *stream,* flows nearly 1 mile to House Creek 6.5 miles southwest of Big Mountain (lat. 38°38'55" N, long. 123°13'55" W; sec. 6, T 9 N, R 12 W). Named on Tombs Creek (1978) 7.5' quadrangle.

Soda Springs [SONOMA]: *locality,* 6.5 miles east-southeast of Annapolis along Wheatfield Fork Gualala River (lat. 38°40'20" N, long. 123°16' W; near NE cor. sec. 35, T 10 N, R 13 W). Site named on Annapolis (1977) 7.5' quadrangle.

Soda Springs Canyon [SANTA CLARA]: *canyon,* drained by a stream that flows 4 miles to Coyote Creek 3 miles south-southeast of Mount Sizer (lat. 37°10'15" N, long. 121°29'50" W); Madrone Soda Springs is in the canyon. Named on Mount Sizer (1955) 7.5' quadrangle.

Soda Springs Creek [SOLANO]: *stream,* flows 2.5 miles to Laurel Creek 3.25 miles north-northeast of Fairfield (lat. 38°17'40" N, long. 122°01'20" W; near W line sec. 7, T 5 N, R 1 W); the creek goes past Tolenas Springs. Named on Fairfield North (1951) 7.5' quadrangle.

Soda Springs Creek [SONOMA]: *stream,* flows 2 miles to Buckeye Creek (2) 2 miles north-northeast of Annapolis (lat. 38°44'50" N, long. 123°20'50" W; sec. 6, T 10 N, R 13 W). Named on Annapolis (1977) 7.5' quadrangle.

Soda Valley [NAPA]: *valley,* 11 miles east of Saint Helena on upper reaches of Soda Creek (2) (lat. 38°31'10" N, long. 122°16'10" W). Named on Chiles Valley (1958) 7.5' quadrangle.

Solano City [SOLANO]: *locality,* 1.5 miles east of Denverton along Oakland Antioch and Eastern Railroad (lat. 38°13'35" N, long. 121°52'15" W). Named on Birds Landing (1918) 7.5' quadrangle.

Solar en Santa Clara: see **Bennett Tract** [SANTA CLARA].

Solid Comfort: see **Lokoya** [NAPA].

Solis [SANTA CLARA]: *land grant,* west of Gilroy. Named on Gilroy (1955) and Mount Madonna (1955) 7.5' quadrangles. Mariano Castro received the land in 1835; Rufino Castro and others claimed 8875 acres patented in 1859 (Cowan, p. 99). According to Arbuckle (p. 34-35), Solis is a family name.

Somersville [CONTRA COSTA]: *locality,* 6 miles north-northeast of Mount Diablo in Markley Canyon (lat. 37°57'25" N, long. 121°51'45" W; sec. 4, T 1 N, R 1 E). Site named on Antioch South (1953) 7.5' quadrangle. Postal authorities established Somersville post office in 1863 and discontinued it in 1910 (Frickstad, p. 23); the name commemorates Francis Somers, who started coal mines near the place (Mosier, p. 7). United States Board on Geographic Names (1933, p. 706) rejected the forms "Sommerville" and "Summerville" for the name.

Sommerville: see **Somersville** [CONTRA COSTA].

Sonoma [SONOMA]: *town,* 17 miles southeast of Santa Rosa (lat. 38°17'35" N, long. 122°27'25" W). Named on Sonoma (1951) 7.5' quadrangle. Postal authorities established Sonoma post office in 1849 (Frickstad, p. 198), and the town incorporated in 1900. San Francisco Solano mission was founded at the place about 1823, and Mariano Guadalupe Vallejo started Pueblo de Sonoma there in 1835 (Hoover, Rensch, and Rensch, p. 527, 528). The name "Sonoma" most probably is of Indian origin (Kroeber, p. 59). Gibbes' (1852) map has the name "St. Louis" for a place situated south of Sonoma on the west side of Sonoma Creek. A description of a trip from San Francisco to Sonoma published in *The California Star* newspaper for December 25, 1847, described a new city of St. Louis located on the east side of Sonoma Creek near the embarcadero, and a rival new city of New Philadelphia laid out across the creek on the west side.

Sonoma: see **Lake Sonoma** [SONOMA].

Sonoma Canyon: see **Adobe Canyon** [SONOMA].

Sonoma Creek [SONOMA]: *stream,* flows 32 miles to San Pablo Bay 2.25 miles east of Sears Point (lat. 38°09'10" N, long. 122°24'15" W); the mouth of the stream is near the intersection of Sonoma-Napa County line with Sonoma-Solano County line. Named on Glen Ellen (1954), Kenwood (1954), Rutherford (1951), Sears Point (1951), and Sonoma (1951) 7.5' quadrangles. Called Arroyo Grande on a diseño of Agua Caliente grant (Becker, 1969).

Sonoma Landing: see **Midshipman Point** [SONOMA].

Sonoma Mountain [SONOMA]: *ridge,* southeast-trending, 1.25 miles long, 4 miles southwest of Glen Ellen (lat. 38°19'30" N, long. 122° 34'30" W); the feature is in Sonoma Mountains. Named on Glen Ellen (1954) 7.5' quadrangle.

Sonoma Mountains [SONOMA]: *range,* extends for 25 miles northwest from San Pablo Bay to the vicinity of Santa Rosa, and lies northeast of Petaluma Valley and Cotati Valley. Named on Cotati (1954), Glen Ellen (1954), Kenwood (1954), Petaluma River (1954), Santa Rosa (1954), and Sears Point (1951) quadrangles.

Sonoma Valley [SONOMA]: *valley,* along Sonoma Creek from near Sonoma southeast toward San Pablo Bay. Named on Sears Point (1951) and Sonoma (1951) 7.5' quadrangles. On Goddard's (1857) map, the name extends north-northwest through present Valley of the Moon.

Soquel Augmentacion: see **Shoquel Augmentation** [SANTA CLARA].

Sorenson [ALAMEDA]: *locality,* 2 miles south-southeast of Hayward along Western Pacific Railroad (lat. 37°38'35" N, long. 122° 04' W). Named on Hayward (1915) 15' quadrangle. The misspelled name commemorates Hansen Sorensen, a landowner who came to Hayward in 1881 (Mosier and Mosier, p. 82).

Sorosis: see **Champaign Fountain** [SANTA CLARA].

Soscol: see **Suscol** [NAPA].

Sotoyome [SONOMA]: *land grant,* near Healdsburg and the southeast end of Alexander Valley. Named on Geyserville (1955), Guerneville (1955), Healdsburg (1955), and Jimtown (1955) 7.5' quadrangles. Henry D. Fitch received 8 leagues in 1841; Fitch's heirs claimed 48,837 acres patented in 1858 (Cowan, p. 100; Cowan gave the name "Sotoyomi" as an alternate). According to Perez (p. 100), Fitch was the grantee in 1844. The name likely is an Indian place name derived in Spanish times from a personal name (Kroeber, p. 59-60).

Soulafate: see **Soulajule** [MARIN] (1).

Soulajule [MARIN]:

(1) *land grant,* 8 miles southeast of Tomales. Named on Point Reyes NE (1954) 7.5' quadrangle. Ramon Mesa received 20 leagues in 1844; J.S. Brackett claimed 2492 acres patented in 1879 (Cowan, p. 100; Cowan listed this and the other Soulajule grants under the designation "Soulajule, or Soulafate"). The name appears to be from an Indian word (Kroeber, p. 60).

(2) *land grant,* 9.5 miles west of downtown Novato. Named on Inverness (1954), Petaluma (1953), and Point Reyes NE (1954) 7.5' quadrangles. Ramon Mesa received 20 leagues in 1844; G.N. Cornwall claimed 919 acres patented in 1879 (Cowan, p. 100).

(3) *land grant,* 10 miles southeast of Tomales. Named on Inverness (1954) and Point Reyes NE (1954) 7.5' quadrangles. Ramon Mesa received 20 leagues in 1844; M.F. Gormley claimed 2266 acres patented in 1879 (Cowan, p. 100).

(4) *land grant,* 5.5 miles southeast of Tomales. Named on Point Reyes NE (1954) 7.5' quadrangle. Ramon Mesa received 20 leagues in 1844; P.J. Vasquez claimed 3774 acres patented in 1879 (Cowan, p. 100).

(5) *land grant,* 10 miles west-northwest of downtown Novato. Named on Petaluma (1953) and Point Reyes NE (1954) 7.5' quadrangles. Ramon Mesa received 20 leagues in 1844; L.D. Watkins claimed 1447 acres patented in 1879 (Cowan, p. 100).

Soup Bowl Creek [SANTA CLARA]: *stream,* flows 2.25 miles to Middle Fork Coyote Creek nearly 5 miles south-southwest of Isabel Valley (lat. 37°15'10" N, long. 121°34'45" W). Named on Isabel Valley (1955) 7.5' quadrangle.

Sousas Corner [SONOMA]: *locality,* 3.5 miles north-northwest of Sebastopol (lat. 38°26'45" N, long. 122°51'35" W). Named on Sebastopol (1954) 7.5' quadrangle. Called Sousa Corners on Sebastopol (1942) 15' quadrangle.

Southampton Bay [SOLANO]: *embayment,* 2 miles northwest of downtown Benicia along Carquinez Strait (lat. 38°04' N, long. 122°11'15" W). Named on Benicia (1959) 7.5' quadrangle. Cañizares called the feature Puerto de la Asunta in 1775 because he found it on the day of that feast—*Puerto de la Asunta* means "Asumption Harbor" in Spanish (Galvin, p. 96, 105). The present name is for the navy storeship *Southampton* that Commodore Thomas ap Catesby Jones brought to Benicia in 1849 (Bancroft, 1888, p. 473; Dillon, p. 31).

Southampton Shoal [SAN FRANCISCO]: *shoal,* 6 miles north of North Point in San Francisco Bay (lat. 37°53'30" N, long. 122°24'20" W). Named on San Quentin (1959) 7.5' quadrangle. The name is from the ship for which Southampton Bay was named (Dillon, p. 31).

Southampton Shoal Channel [SAN FRANCISCO]: *channel,* 7.5 miles north of North Point in San Francisco Bay (lat. 37°54'45" N, long. 122°25'20" W); the feature is north-northwest of Southampton Shoal. Named on San Quentin (1959) 7.5' quadrangle.

South Babb Creek [SANTA CLARA]: *stream,* flows 5 miles to Silver Creek 3.25 miles northwest of Evergreen (lat. 37°20'55" N, long. 121°49'05" W). Named on San Jose East (1961) 7.5' quadrangle.

South Basin [SAN FRANCISCO]: *embayment,* 4.25 miles east-southeast of Mount Davidson along San Francisco Bay (lat. 37°43'15" N, long. 122°22'45" W); the feature is on the south side of Hunters Point. Named on San Francisco South (1956) 7.5' quadrangle.

South Bay [SAN FRANCISCO]: *embayment,* along the coast 1.5 miles south-southwest of Fort Point (lat. 37°47'35" N, long. 122°29'30" W). Named on San Francisco North (1956) 7.5' quadrangle.

South Berkeley: see **Lorin** [ALAMEDA].

South Channel: see **Oakland Inner Harbor** [ALAMEDA].

South City: see **South San Francisco** [SAN MATEO].

South Coyote [SANTA CLARA]: *settlement,* 1.5 miles southeast of Coyote (lat. 37°12' N, long. 121°43'15" W). Named on Morgan Hill (1955) 7.5' quadrangle.

South Coyote Slough: see **Coyote Creek** [ALAMEDA-SANTA CLARA].

Southeast Farallon [SAN FRANCISCO]: *island,* about 4300 feet long, 30 miles west-southwest of the Golden Gate (lat. 37°41'55" N, long. 123°05' W); the feature is the largest of Farallon Islands. Named on Farallon Islands (1988) 7.5' quadrangle. Ringgold (p. 11) referred to South or Great Farallon. The island is believed to be the one that Vizcaino in 1603 called Isle Hendida (Hoover, p. 3). Hoover (frontispiece map) used the name "Shubrick Point" for a promontory at the east end of the island, and used the name "East Landing" at a narrow embayment at the southeast corner of the island.

Southeast Reef: see **Wash Rock** [SAN MATEO].

Southern Heights Ridge [MARIN]: *ridge,* southeast- to east-trending, 1.25 miles long, 1.5 miles south-southeast of downtown San Rafael (lat. 37°57'15" N, long. 122°31'10" W). Named on San Rafael (1954) 7.5' quadrangle.

Southern Pacific Basin: see **Oakland Middle Harbor** [ALAMEDA].

South Farallon: see **Southeast Farallon** [SAN FRANCISCO].

South Fork [SANTA CLARA]: *canyon,* drained by a stream that flows nearly 1 mile to lowlands 2 miles southwest of Gilroy (lat. 36°59' N, long. 121°35'10" W). Named on Chittenden (1955) 7.5' quadrangle.

South Granada: see **El Granada** [SAN MATEO].

South Lake [SAN FRANCISCO]: *lake,* 350 feet long, 1.25 miles southeast of Point Lobos (lat. 37°45'55" N, long. 122°29'55" W). Named on San Francisco North (1956) 7.5' quadrangle.

South Los Guilicos: see **Kenwood** [SONOMA].

South Palo Alto: see **Mayfield** [SANTA CLARA].

South Panther Creek: see **Llagas Creek** [SANTA CLARA].

South Peak [SAN MATEO]: *peak,* 0.25 mile east-southeast of Montara Knob on Montara Mountain (lat. 37°33'20" N, long. 122°28'45" W; sec. 26, T 4 S, R 6 W); the feature is nearly 0.5 mile south-southwest of North Peak. Altitude 1833 feet. Named on Montara Mountain (1956) 7.5' quadrangle.

South Pocket [SANTA CLARA]: *canyon,* drained by a stream that flows 1.5 miles to Arroyo Mocho 2.5 miles southeast of Eylar Mountain (lat. 37°27'05" N, long. 121°30'50" W; sec. 34, T 5 S, R 4 E). Named on Eylar Mountain (1955) and Mount Boardman (1955) 7.5' quadrangles. Called Blackbird Valley on Mount Hamilton (1897) 15' quadrangle.

South Salmon Creek Beach [SONOMA]: *beach,* 2.25 miles long, center 1.5 miles west-northwest of the village of Bodega Bay along the coast (lat. 38°20'15" N, long. 123°04'05" W); the beach is south of the mouth of Salmon Creek (1). Named on Bodega Head (1972) 7.5' quadrangle. Called Salmon Creek Beach on Bodega Head (1942) 7.5' quadrangle.

South San Francisco [SAN MATEO]: *city,* 15 miles northwest of downtown Redwood City (city hall near lat. 37°39'20" N, long. 122°24'45" W).

Named on San Francisco South (1956) and San Leandro (1959) 7.5' quadrangles. G.F. Swift gave the name "South San Francisco" to the industrial development that he started along San Francisco Bay east of the center of the present city; the residential and business district of the community originally was called Baden, from nearby Baden dairy farm (Brown, p. 90; Gudde, 1949, p. 20). Postal authorities established South San Francisco post office in 1892, discontinued it when they moved the post office to Baden Station in 1895, and reestablished it in 1897 (Salley, p. 209). The city incorporated in 1908. The place commonly is called South City (Brown, p. 91).

South San Ramon Creek [ALAMEDA-CONTRA COSTA]: *stream,* heads in Contra Costa County and flows 5 miles to a canal located 1 mile east of Dublin in Alameda County (lat. 37°42'05" N, long. 121°55'05" W); the stream drains the south part of San Ramon Valley. Named on Diablo (1953) and Dublin (1961) 7.5' quadrangles. Dublin (1961, photorevised 1980) 7.5' quadrangle shows the stream in an artificial watercourse in Alameda County.

South Slough [NAPA-SOLANO]: *water feature,* on Napa-Solano County line, joins Napa River 3.25 miles north-northwest of downtown Vallejo (lat. 38°09'40" N, long. 122°17'15" W; sec. 34, T 4 N, R 4 W). Named on Cuttings Wharf (1949) 7.5' quadrangle.

South Vallejo [SOLANO]: *district,* 1 mile southeast of downtown Vallejo (lat. 38°05'15" N, long. 122°14'35" W). Named on Karquines (1898) 15' quadrangle. Postal authorities established South Vallejo post office 2 miles south of Vallejo in 1870 and discontinued it in 1872 (Salley, p. 209).

Spanish Anchorage: see **Old Spanish Anchorage**, under **Fort Point** [SAN FRANCISCO].

Spanish Creek [SONOMA]: *stream,* flows 1.5 miles to Wolf Creek 3.5 miles southwest of Big Mountain (lat. 38°40'45" N, long. 123° 11'40" W; at S line sec. 28, T 10 N, R 12 W). Named on Tombs Creek (1978) 7.5' quadrangle.

Spanish Flat [NAPA]: *locality,* 9 miles south of Berryessa Peak (lat. 38°32'10" N, long. 122°13'20" W). Named on Lake Berryessa (1959) 7.5' quadrangle.

Spanish Flat Resort [NAPA]: *locality,* 10 miles south of Berryessa Peak on the west side of Lake Berryessa (lat. 38°31'10" N, long. 122°12'30" W; sec. 20, T 8 N, R 3 W); the place is 1 mile south-southeast of Spanish Flat. Named on Lake Berryessa (1959) 7.5' quadrangle.

Spanish Peak: see **Scarper Peak** [SAN MATEO].

Spanish Ranch Creek [SAN MATEO]: *stream,* flows 0.5 mile to Weeks Creek 2 miles north of La Honda (lat. 37°20'55" N, long. 122°16'05" W; sec. 2, T 7 S, R 4 W). Named on La Honda (1961) 7.5' quadrangle.

Spanish Town: see **Half Moon Bay** [SAN MATEO] (2).

Spanishtown: see **Mexican Camp** [SANTA CLARA].

Spanish Valley [NAPA]: *valley,* 5.5 miles east-northeast of Aetna Springs along Stone Corral Creek (lat. 38°40'45" N, long. 122° 23' W; in and near sec. 26, T 10 N, R 5 W). Named on Aetna Springs (1958) 7.5' quadrangle.

Spanish Valley Creek: see **Stone Corral Creek** [NAPA].

Sparkel [CONTRA COSTA]: *locality,* nearly 2 miles north of Walnut Creek civic center along Sacramento Northern Railroad (lat. 37°55'50" N, long. 122°03'15" W). Named on Walnut Creek (1959) 7.5' quadrangle.

Spear Point: see **Mare Island** [SOLANO].

Spencer Creek [NAPA]: *stream,* flows 3.25 miles to join Murphy Creek and form Tulucay Creek 10.5 miles southwest of Mount Vaca (lat. 38°17'35" N, long. 122°14'15" W). Named on Mount George (1951) 7.5' quadrangle. Called Cayetano Creek on Mount Vaca (1942) 15' quadrangle.

Spike Buck Creek [MARIN]: *stream,* flows 1.25 miles to Rattlesnake Creek 5.5 miles south-southwest of downtown San Rafael (lat. 37°54'15" N, long. 122°35'20" W). Named on San Rafael (1954) 7.5' quadrangle.

Spinner Island [SOLANO]: *island,* 3400 feet long, along Montezuma Slough 4.25 miles south of Birds Landing (2) (lat. 38°04'10" N, long. 121°52'05" W). Named on Antioch North (1978) 7.5' quadrangle.

Spoonbill [SOLANO]: *locality,* 5.25 miles south-southwest of Birds Landing (2) along Sacramento Northern Railroad on Van Sickle Island (lat. 38°03'05" N, long. 121°54'10" W); the place is along Spoonbill Creek. Named on Honker Bay (1953) 7.5' quadrangle.

Spoonbill Creek [SOLANO]: *water feature,* extends from Suisun Bay to Honker Bay between Chipps Island and Van Sickle Island; joins Honker Bay 5 miles south-southwest of Birds Landing (2) (lat. 38°04'20" N, long. 121°54'35" W). Named on Honker Bay (1953) 7.5' quadrangle.

Spreckels Lake [SAN FRANCISCO]: *lake,* 900 feet long, 1.25 miles east-southeast of Point Lobos (lat. 37°46'15" N, long. 122°29'35" W). Named on San Francisco North (1956) 7.5' quadrangle.

Sprig Lake [SANTA CLARA]: *lake,* 250 feet long, nearly 1.5 miles east-southeast of Mount Madonna (lat. 37°00'15" N, long. 121°40'50" W). Named on Mount Madonna (1955) 7.5' quadrangle.

Spring Branch [SOLANO]: *stream,* flows 4.5 miles to First Mallard Branch 3.25 miles south-southeast of Fairfield (lat. 38°12'20" N, long. 122°01'40" W). Named on Denverton (1953) and Fairfield South (1949) 7.5' quadrangles. Called Spring Brook on Carquinez (1938) 15' quadrangle, and called Spring Branch Cr. on Carquinez Strait (1940) 15' quadrangle.

Spring Branch Creek: see **Spring Branch** [SOLANO].

Spring Bridge Gulch [SAN MATEO]: *canyon,* drained by a stream that flows 1 mile to the sea nearly 2 miles north-northwest of Pigeon Point (lat. 37°12'20" N, long. 122°24'15" W). Named on Pigeon Point (1955) 7.5' quadrangle. Brown (p. 34) gave the name "Foam Gulch" as an early designation for the canyon—this name was from a bridge that was called Foam Bridge because sea foam blew over the road there.

Spring Brook: see **Spring Branch** [SOLANO].

Spring Canyon [SANTA CLARA]: *canyon,* drained by a stream that flows 2 miles to Arroyo Valle 5 miles south-southwest of Eylar Mountain (lat. 37°24'30" N, long. 121°34'45" W; sec. 18, T 6 S, R 4 E). Named on Eylar Mountain (1955) 7.5' quadrangle.

Spring Creek [SONOMA]:

(1) *stream,* flows about 0.5 mile to Ward Creek 5.5 miles east-northeast of Fort Ross (lat. 38°32'05" N, long. 123°08'40" W; sec. 14, T 8 N, R 12 W). Named on Fort Ross (1978) 7.5' quadrangle.

(2) *stream,* flows 5.5 miles to Matanzas Creek less than 1 mile east of downtown Santa Rosa (lat. 38°26'20" N, long. 122°41'55" W). Named on Kenwood (1954) and Santa Rosa (1954) 7.5' quadrangles.

Spring Ridge: see **Windy Hill** [SAN MATEO].

Springtowne: see **Vallejo** [SOLANO].

Spring Valley [NAPA]: *valley,* 3 miles east of Saint Helena (lat. 38°30'05" N, long. 122°24'50" W; sec. 33, T 8 N, R 5 W). Named on Rutherford (1951) and Saint Helena (1960) 7.5' quadrangles.

Spring Valley: see **Chinatown** [SAN FRANCISCO].

Spring Valley Creek: see **Spring Valley Ridge** [SAN MATEO].

Spring Valley Lakes: see **Lower Crystal Springs Reservoir** [SAN MATEO].

Spring Valley Ridge [SAN MATEO]: *ridge,* southeast-trending, 2 miles long, 2.5 miles east of Montara Knob (lat. 37°33'45" N, long. 122°26'05" W). Named on Montara Mountain (1956) 7.5' quadrangle. The name is from Spring Valley Water Company (Brown, p. 91). Brown, (p. 91) used the name "Spring Valley Creek" for the stream on the northeast side of the ridge.

Sproule Creek [SONOMA]: *stream,* flows 2.25 miles to Marshall Creek 5.5 miles north of Fort Ross (lat. 38°35'35" N, long. 123°14'55" W; sec. 25, T 9 N, R 11 W). Named on Plantation (1977) 7.5' quadrangle.

Sproule Creek: see **Marshall Creek** [SONOMA].

Spruce Hill: see **Lokoya** [NAPA].

Spud Point [SONOMA]: *promontory,* 0.5 mile southwest of the village of Bodega Bay on the west side of Bodega Harbor (lat. 38° 19'35" N, long. 123°03'15" W). Named on Bodega Head (1972) 7.5' quadrangle.

Squab [NAPA]: *locality,* 1.5 miles west-northwest of Napa Junction along Southern Pacific Railroad (lat. 38°11'55" N, long. 122°16'25" W; sec. 14, T 4 N, R 4 W). Named on Cuttings Wharf (1949) 7.5' quadrangle.

Squattersville: see **San Lorenzo** [ALAMEDA] (3).

Squaw Creek [SONOMA]: *stream,* flows 7 miles to Big Sulphur Creek 6.5 miles northeast of Asti (lat. 38°49'25" N, long. 122°52'35" W; at W line sec. 4, T 11 N, R 9 W). Named on The Geysers (1959) 7.5' quadrangle.

Squealer Gulch [SAN MATEO]: *canyon,* drained by a stream that flows 2.25 miles to West Union Creek 2 miles north-northeast of Skeggs Point (lat. 37°26'40" N, long. 122°17'25" W). Named on Woodside (1961) 7.5' quadrangle. According to Stanger (1967, p. 133), the name probably is for an early settler called Squealer Sam Alwell because of his high voice.

Squirrel Rock [SONOMA]: *relief feature,* 3 miles north of Cazadero (lat. 38°34'30" N, long. 123°05'10" W; at NW cor. sec. 4, T 8 N, R 11 W). Named on Cazadero (1978) 7.5' quadrangle.

Stafford Lake [MARIN]: *lake,* 3700 feet long, behind a dam on Novato Creek nearly 4 miles west of downtown Novato (lat. 38°07'05" N, long. 122°38'10" W). Named on San Geronimo (1954) 7.5' quadrangle. The name commemorates Dr. Charles Stafford, veterinarian and board member of North Marin County Water District (Teather, p. 73).

Stage Gulch [SONOMA]: *canyon,* 1 mile long, 5.25 miles east-southeast of downtown Petaluma (lat. 38°13'10" N, long. 122°32'35" W). Named on Petaluma River (1954) 7.5' quadrangle.

Stags Leap [NAPA]: *relief feature,* steep hillside 3 miles east-northeast of Yountville (lat. 38°25'10" N, long. 122°18'45" W; sec. 28, 33, T 7 N, R 4 W). Named on Yountville (1951) 7.5' quadrangle. Sonoma (1942) 15' quadrangle has the name for a feature situated about 1 mile farther southwest. California Division of Highways' (1934) map shows a place called Stags Leap located about 1.5 miles southwest of the relief feature shown on Yountville (1951) 7.5' quadrangle. Postal authorities established Stags Leap post office 11.5 miles north of Napa at a summer vacation resort in 1927 and discontinued it in 1944; the name "Stags Leap" is from a local legend (Salley, p. 211).

Stake Point [CONTRA COSTA]: *promontory,* 4 miles west-northwest of Pittsburg along Suisun Bay (lat. 38°03'05" N, long. 121°56'55" W). Named on Honker Bay (1953) 7.5' quadrangle. Called Pt. Picket on Ringgold's (1850b) map.

Stakes: see **Mount Stakes** [SANTA CLARA].

Staley Spring [SONOMA]: *spring,* 2 miles west-northwest of Big Mountain (lat. 38°43'25" N, long. 123°10'40" W; sec. 10, T 10 N, R 12 W). Named on Tombs Creek (1978) 7.5' quadrangle.

Stancos Creek: see **Los Trancos Creek** [SAN MATEO-SANTA CLARA].

Stanley [NAPA]: *locality*, 4.5 miles north-northwest of Napa Junction (lat. 38°14'40" N, long. 122°17'30" W). Named on Cuttings Wharf (1949) 7.5' quadrangle. Mare Island (1916) 15' quadrangle shows the place situated along Southern Pacific Railroad.

Stanley Ridge [SONOMA]: *ridge*, north- to west-trending, 3 miles long, 7 miles north of the village of Stewarts Point (lat. 38°45'15" N, long. 123°26' W). Named on Ornbaun Valley (1960) 15' quadrangle, and on Stewarts Point (1978) 7.5' quadrangle.

Star Canyon [SANTA CLARA]: *canyon*, drained by a stream that flows nearly 1 mile to Hoover Creek 3.5 miles west-southwest of Mount Sizer (lat. 37°11'25" N, long. 121°34'05" W). Named on Mount Sizer (1955) 7.5' quadrangle.

Star Creek [SANTA CLARA]: *stream*, flows nearly 1.5 miles to Pescadero Creek 5.5 miles southwest of Gilroy (lat. 36°56'20" N, long. 121°37'20" W). Named on Watsonville East (1955) 7.5' quadrangle.

Staubeville: see **Petaluma** [SONOMA] (2).

Steamboat Point [SAN FRANCISCO]: *promontory*, 0.5 mile south of Rincon Point along San Francisco Bay on the north side of present China Basin (lat. 37°46'40" N, long. 122°23'20" W). Named on San Francisco (1915) 15' quadrangle.

Steamboat Slough [NAPA]: *water feature*, passes around Bull Island and joins Napa River 4 miles northwest of Napa Junction (lat. 38° 13'10" N, long. 122°18'30" W; sec. 4, T 4 N, R 4 W). Named on Cuttings Wharf (1949) 7.5' quadrangle.

Steamboat Slough [SOLANO]: *water feature*, joins Cache Slough 2.5 miles northeast of Rio Vista (lat. 38°10'55" N, long. 121°39'30" W). Named on Courtland (1978), Isleton (1978), and Rio Vista (1978) 7.5' quadrangles. Called Middle Fork [Sacramento River] on Ringgold's (1850c) map, which shows Pt. Chapman along Sacramento River opposite the mouth of present Steamboat Slough.

Steamboat Slough [SONOMA]: *water feature*, 5 miles north-northeast of Sears Point (lat. 38°13'15" N, long. 122°25'25" W). Named on Sears Point (1951) 7.5' quadrangle.

Steamboat Slough: see **Alviso Slough** [SANTA CLARA].

Steel Canyon [NAPA]: *canyon*, 3.5 miles long, opens into the canyon of Capell Creek 11 miles south of Berryessa Peak (lat. 38° 30'20" N, long. 122°12'20" W; near SE cor. sec. 29, T 8 N, R 3 W); water of Lake Berryessa covers the lower part of the canyon. Named on Capell Valley (1951) and Lake Berryessa (1959) 7.5' quadrangles.

Steel Canyon Resort [NAPA]: *locality*, 11 miles south of Berryessa Peak (lat. 38°30'30" N, long. 122°12' W; sec. 28, T 8 N, R 3 W); the place is near the mouth of Steel Canyon. Named on Lake Berryessa (1959) 7.5' quadrangle.

Steele: see **Año Nuevo Bay** [SAN MATEO].

Steele Canyon [NAPA]: *canyon*, 1 mile long, 3 miles south-southeast of Mount Vaca (lat. 38°21'20" N, long. 122°05'20" W). Named on Fairfield North (1951) 7.5' quadrangle.

Steeple Rock: see **Sail Rock** [SAN MATEO].

Steep Ravine Canyon [MARIN]: *canyon*, along Webb Creek, which flows 2.25 miles to Bolinas Bay 3.5 miles east-southeast of Bolinas (lat. 37°53'05" N, long. 122°37'40" W). Named on San Rafael (1954) 7.5' quadrangle.

Stege [CONTRA COSTA]: *locality*, 1.5 miles south-southeast of Richmond civic center along Southern Pacific Railroad (lat. 37° 55' N, long. 122°19'35" W). Named on Richmond (1959) 7.5' quadrangle. Called Steige on Smith and Elliott's (1879) map. Postal authorities established Stege post office in 1889 and discontinued it in 1935 (Frickstad, p. 23). The name commemorates Richard Stege, who settled on a farm at the place about 1890 (Gudde, 1949, p. 343). Postal authorities established Schmidtville post office 2 miles northeast of Stege in 1900 and discontinued it in 1901 (Salley, p. 199).

Steige: see **Stege** [CONTRA COSTA].

Steiger Hill [SOLANO]: *peak*, 5.5 miles east of Mount Vaca (lat. 38° 23'55" N, long. 122°00'10" W). Named on Mount Vaca (1951) 7.5' quadrangle.

Steinbergen Creek: see **Steinberger Slough** [SAN MATEO].

Steinbergens Slough: see **Steinberger Slough** [SAN MATEO].

Steinberger Creek [SAN MATEO]: see **Steinberger Slough** [SAN MATEO].

Steinbergers: see **Redwood City** [SAN MATEO].

Steinberger Slough [SAN MATEO]: *water feature*, opens into San Francisco Bay 4 miles north of downtown Redwood City (lat. 37° 32'40" N, long. 122°13'20" W). Named on Redwood Point (1959) 7.5' quadrangle. Called Steinberger Creek on Hayward (1915) 15' quadrangle, but United States Board on Geographic Names (1961b, p. 16) rejected this name, and the names "Steinbergens Slough," "Steinbergen's Slough," "Steinbergen Slough," "Steinbergen Creek," and "Smith Slough" for the feature.

Stemple Creek [MARIN-SONOMA]: *stream*, heads in Sonoma County and flows 15 miles to Estero de San Antonio 1.5 miles north of Tomales in Marin County (lat. 38°16'15" N, long. 122°54'20" W). Named on Cotati (1954), Two Rock (1954) and Valley Ford (1954) 7.5' quadrangles. Teather (p. 75) associated the name with Henry M. Stemple, a rancher in the region. United States Board on Geographic Names (1943, p. 13) rejected the names "Aurora Creek," "Estero de San Antonio," and "Two Rock Creek" for the stream, or for any part of it.

Stemple Creek: see **Estero de San Antonio** [MARIN].

Stephens: see **Point Stephens**, under **Point Richmond** [CONTRA COSTA] (1).

Stephens Creek: see **Stevens Creek** [SANTA CLARA].

Stephenson: see **Point Stephenson**, under **Middle Point** [CONTRA COSTA].

Stevens Creek [SANTA CLARA]: *stream*, flows 21 miles to mud flats along San Francisco Bay 4 miles north-northeast of downtown Mountain View (lat. 37°26'45" N, long. 122°03'45" W). Named on Cupertino (1961), Mindego Hill (1961), and Mountain View (1961) 7.5' quadrangles. Members of the Anza expedition gave the name "Arroyo de San Jose Cupertino" to the stream in 1776 (Hoover, Rensch, and Rensch, p. 459). Called Cupertino Creek on Healy's (1866) map, and called Stephens Cr. on Hare's (1872) map. The modern name honors Elisha Stevens, who came overland to California in 1844 and settled by the stream in 1848 (Butler, p. 108). United States Board on Geographic Names (1933, p. 721) rejected the names "Cupertino Creek" and "Steven's Creek" for the stream, and later the Board (1968b, p. 9) rejected the names "Whishman Slough" and "Whisman Slough" for it.

Stevens Creek Reservoir [SANTA CLARA]: *lake*, 1.25 miles long, behind a dam on Stevens Creek 3 miles southwest of downtown Cupertino (lat. 37°17'55" N, long. 122°04'30" W; on W line sec. 27, T 7 S, R 2 W). Named on Cupertino (1961) 7.5' quadrangle.

Stewart Point [MARIN]: *ridge*, east-southeast- to southeast-trending, 1 mile long, 2.25 miles northwest of Bolinas (lat. 37°55'45" N, long. 122°42'55" W). Named on Bolinas (1954) 7.5' quadrangle.

Stewart Ridge [SONOMA]: *ridge*, south-trending, 1 mile long, 4.5 miles north-northeast of Fort Ross (lat. 38°34'20" N, long. 123°12'30" W). Named on Fort Ross (1978) 7.5' quadrangle.

Stewarts Creek [SONOMA]: *stream*, flows 1.25 miles to Fisherman Bay near the village of Stewarts Point (lat. 38°39' N, long. 123° 23'55" W). Named on Stewarts Point (1978) 7.5' quadrangle. Called Stewarts Point Creek on Annapolis (1943) and Stewarts Point (1943) 7.5' quadrangles.

Stewarts Point [SONOMA]:

(1) *promontory*, 0.5 mile north-northwest of the village of Stewarts Point along the coast (lat. 38°39'15" N, long. 123°24'25" W). Named on Stewarts Point (1978) 7.5' quadrangle. The name commemorates the Stewart family, who moved to the region in 1856 (Jackson, p. 8).

(2) *village*, 20 miles west of Healdsburg (lat. 38°39'05" N, long. 123°23'55" W); the village is near Stewarts Point (1). Named on Stewarts Point (1978) 7.5' quadrangle. Postal authorities established Stewarts Point post office in 1888, discontinued it in 1945, and reestablished it in 1946 (Frickstad, p. 198).

Stewarts Point Creek: see **Stewarts Creek** [SONOMA].

Stewarts Point Island [SONOMA]: *island*, 400 feet long, 0.5 mile west-northwest of the village of Stewarts Point (lat. 38°39'15" N, long. 123°24'30" W); the island is 50 feet offshore at Stewarts Point (1). Named on Stewarts Point (1978) 7.5' quadrangle.

Stewartville [CONTRA COSTA]: *locality*, 6 miles northeast of Mount Diablo (lat. 37°56'50" N, long. 121°50'55" W; sec. 10, T 1 N, R 1 E). Site named on Antioch South (1953) 7.5' quadrangle. Postal authorities established Stewartville post office in 1882 and discontinued it in 1902 (Frickstad, p. 24). The name was for William Stewart, owner of a coal mine at the place (Mosier, p. 7; Mosier called the place Stewartsville). Postal authorities established Judsonville post office 3 miles northeast of Stewartville in 1878, discontinued it for a time in 1879, and discontinued it finally in 1883 (Salley, p. 108). Judsonville was a coal-mine town named for Egbert Judson, a stockholder in the mine there (Mosier, p. 6).

Still Island: see **Belvedere Island** [MARIN].

Stillwater Bay: see **Belvedere Cove** [MARIN].

Stillwater Cove [SONOMA]: *embayment*, 3 miles south of Plantation along the sea coast (lat. 38°32'15" N, long. 123°17'55" W). Named on Plantation (1977) 7.5' quadrangle. Santa Rosa (1958) 1°x 2° quadrangle shows Stillwater Cove located about 1 mile farther southeast along the coast; United States Board on Geographic Names (1984b, p. 5) approved the name "Stillwater Cove" for this second place (lat. 38°32'20" N, long. 123°17'05" W), and at the same time rejected the name "Stillwater Harbor" for it.

Stillwater Harbor: see **Stillwater Cove** [SONOMA].

Stinson Beach [MARIN]: *town*, 2.5 miles east-southeast of Bolinas along Bolinas Bay (lat. 37°53'55" N, long. 122°38'20" W). Named on Bolinas (1954) 7.5' quadrangle. Postal authorities established Stinson Beach post office in 1916 (Frickstad, p. 89). The name "Stinson" commemorates Nathan H. Stinson, who bought land at the site in 1866 (Hanna, P.T., p. 316).

Stinson Gulch [MARIN]: *canyon,* drained by a stream that flows 1.25 miles to Bolinas Lagoon 2 miles east of Bolinas (lat. 37° 54'25" N, long. 122°39'05" W); the canyon is north of Stinson Beach. Named on Bolinas (1954) 7.5' quadrangle.

Stivers Lagoon [ALAMEDA]: *marsh,* center 0.5 mile southeast of present Fremont civic center (lat. 37°32'45" N, long. 121°57'35" W; in and near sec. 34, T 4 S, R 1 W). Named on Livermore (1961) 15' quadrangle. Called The Lagoon on Pleasanton (1906) 15' quadrangle, which shows a lake in the marsh. The name "Stivers" is for Simon Stivers, who settled at the place in 1850; the feature originally was called La Laguna, and it also was called Tule Pond for the vegetation there; a lake created from the marsh in 1968 is called Lake Elizabeth for Fremont's sister city, Elizabeth, Australia (Mosier and Mosier, p. 49).

Stockhoff Creek [SONOMA]: *stream,* flows 2 miles to the sea 3 miles south of Plantation (lat. 38°32'50" N, long. 123°17'50" W). Named on Plantation (1977) 7.5' quadrangle.

Stockton Pass: see **Mission Pass** [ALAMEDA].

Stockyards: see **Emeryville** [ALAMEDA].

Stokes Landing: see **Mount Eden** [ALAMEDA].

Stone Corral [NAPA]: *locality,* 2 miles north-northwest of Walter Springs (lat. 38°41' N, long. 122°22'10" W; near W line sec. 25, T 10 N, R 5 W). Named on Walter Springs (1959) 7.5' quadrangle.

Stone Corral Creek [NAPA]: *stream,* flows 3.5 miles to Putah Creek 2 miles north-northeast of Walter Springs (lat. 38°40'40" N, long. 122°20'55" W; sec. 30, T 10 N, R 4 W); the stream goes past Stone Corral. Named on Aetna Springs (1958) and Walter Springs (1959) 7.5' quadrangles. The stream passes through Spanish Valley, but United States Board on Geographic Names (1962a, p. 17) rejected the name "Spanish Valley Creek" for it.

Stone Dam Reservoir [SAN MATEO]: *lake,* 500 feet long, behind a dam on Pilarcitos Creek 5.25 miles east-southeast of Montara Knob (lat. 37°31'35" N, long. 122°23'50" W; sec. 3, T 5 S, R 5 W). Named on Montara Mountain (1956) 7.5' quadrangle.

Stoneman: see **Camp Stoneman** [CONTRA COSTA].

Stones: see **Cunningham** [SONOMA].

Stone Trough Canyon [NAPA]: *canyon,* 1 mile long, 3.5 miles south-southeast of Mount Vaca on upper reaches of Gordon Valley Creek (lat. 38°21' N, long. 122°05'10" W). Named on Fairfield North (1951) 7.5' quadrangle.

Stone Valley [CONTRA COSTA]: *valley,* 2.5 miles north-northwest of Danville (lat. 37°51'20" N, long. 122°01' W). Named on Las Trampas Ridge (1959) 7.5' quadrangle. The name commemorates Albert W. Stone, a settler in the valley (Hoover, Rensch, and Rensch, p. 58).

Stonybrook: see **Farwell** [ALAMEDA].

Stonybrook Canyon [ALAMEDA]: *canyon,* drained by a stream that flows 5 miles to Alameda Creek 3.5 miles north-northeast of Fremont civic center (lat. 37°35'55" N, long. 121°56'45" W; sec. 11, T 4 S, R 1 W). Named on Dublin (1961) and Niles (1961) 7.5' quadrangles. The name, which originally had the form "Stony Brook Canyon," is from large stones in the stream in the canyon—the stream is called Stonybrook Creek (Mosier and Mosier, p. 84).

Stonybrook Creek: see **Stonybrook Canyon** [ALAMEDA].

Stony Butte [SONOMA]: *peak,* 6 miles west-southwest of Glen Ellen (lat. 38°19'10" N, long. 122°37'05" W). Named on Glen Ellen (1954) 7.5' quadrangle.

Stony Creek [NAPA]: *stream,* flows 3 miles to Capell Creek nearly 7 miles west-northwest of Mount Vaca (lat. 38°26'55" N, long. 122° 12'45" W; sec. 17, T 7 N, R 3 W). Named on Capell Valley (1951) 7.5' quadrangle.

Stony Point [SONOMA]: *locality,* 2 miles southwest of Cotati along Petaluma and Santa Rosa Railroad (lat. 38°18'40" N, long. 122°44'05" W). Named on Cotati (1954) 7.5' quadrangle. Postal authorities established Stony Point post office in 1857 and discontinued it in 1911; the name was from Stony Point hotel, where the post office was located (Salley, p. 213).

Storehouse Rock: see **Pigeon Point** [SAN MATEO].

Stow Lake [SAN FRANCISCO]: *lake,* 1800 feet long, 2.25 miles east-southeast of Point Lobos (lat. 37°46'10" N, long. 122°28'25" W). Named on San Francisco North (1956) 7.5' quadrangle.

Strait of Napa: see **Mare Island Strait** [SOLANO].

Straits of Carquines: see **Carquinez Strait** [CONTRA COSTA].

Straits of San Pablo: see **San Pablo Strait** [MARIN].

Strawberry Canyon: see **Strawberry Creek** [ALAMEDA].

Strawberry Creek [ALAMEDA]: *stream,* flows 1.5 miles to lowlands 4.5 miles north of downtown Oakland (lat. 37°52'20" N, long. 122°15'10" W). Named on Briones Valley (1959), Oakland East (1959), and Oakland West (1959) 7.5' quadrangles. The stream also was called Alta Creek; Crespi called the canyon of the creek Arroyo de la Bocana in 1772—*bocana* means "mouth" in Spanish; the canyon also is called Strawberry Canyon, and in the 1860's it was known as Blake's Ravine for George Mansfield Blake, who owned land there (Mosier and Mosier, p. 84).

Strawberry Creek [SONOMA]: *stream,* flows 4 miles to Warm Springs Creek 3.5 miles west of Skaggs Springs (lat. 38°42'05" N, long. 123°05'35" W; near E line sec. 20, T 10 N, R 11 W). Named on Tombs Creek (1978) and Warm Springs Dam (1978) 7.5' quadrangles.

Strawberry Creek: see **Little Strawberry Creek** [SONOMA].

Strawberry Flat [SANTA CLARA]: *area,* 2.5 miles south-southeast of Eylar Mountain (lat. 37°26'35" N, long. 121°31'25" W; sec. 3, T 6 S, R 4 E). Named on Eylar Mountain (1955) 7.5' quadrangle.

Strawberry Hill [SAN FRANCISCO]: *island,* 1050 feet long, 2.25 miles east-southeast of Point Lobos in Stow Lake (lat. 37°46'10" N, long. 122°28'25" W). Named on San Francisco North (1956) 7.5' quadrangle.

Strawberry Point [MARIN]: *peninsula,* 6 miles south-southeast of downtown San Rafael along Richardson Bay (lat. 37°53'15" N, long. 122°30'20" W). Named on San Quentin (1959) and San Rafael (1954) 7.5' quadrangles. Postal authorities established Strawberry Point post office in 1960 and discontinued it in 1961 (Salley, p. 214).

Striped Rock: see **Devils Slide** [SAN MATEO].

Stuart Camp [SANTA CLARA]: *locality,* nearly 3 miles east-northeast of Bielawski Mountain (lat. 37°13'55" N, long. 122°02'30" W). Named on Castle Rock Ridge (1955) 7.5' quadrangle.

Stuart Canyon [SONOMA]: *canyon,* 3 miles long, along Stuart Creek above a point 1 mile east-northeast of Glen Ellen (lat. 38°22'10" N, long. 122°30'25" W). Named on Rutherford (1951) and Sonoma (1951) 7.5' quadrangles. Called Hooker Canyon on Napa (1902) 30' quadrangle.

Stuart Creek [SONOMA]: *stream,* flows 4.25 miles to Calabazas Creek in Glen Ellen (lat. 38°22'15" N, long. 122°31'25" W); the stream goes through Stuart Canyon. Named on Glen Ellen (1954) 7.5' quadrangle.

Stuart Point [MARIN]: *promontory,* on the west side of Angel Island (lat. 37°51'40" N, long. 122°26'45" W). Named on San Francisco North (1956) 7.5' quadrangle. United States Board on Geographic Names (1980, p. 4) approved the name "Point Stuart" for the feature. The name commemorates Frederick D.Stuart, hydrographer with Cadwalader Ringgold's expedition of 1849 (Teather, p. 2).

Stump Beach [SONOMA]: *beach,* 1.5 miles west-southwest of Plantation along the coast (lat. 38°34'55" N, long. 123°20'05" W). Named on Plantation (1977) 7.5' quadrangle.

Stump Gulch [SONOMA]: *canyon,* drained by a stream that flows 1.5 miles to the sea 4.5 miles south-southeast of present Jenner (lat. 35°23'40" N, long. 123°05'20" W). Named on Duncans Mills (1921) 15' quadrangle.

Subeet [SOLANO]: *locality,* 2.5 miles southwest of Fairfield along Southern Pacific Railroad (lat. 38°13'40" N, long. 122°04'55" W). Named on Fairfield South (1949) 7.5' quadrangle. The name is from words "sugar" and "beet," and is for the location of the place in a sugar-beet raising territory (Gannett, p. 292).

Sucro [SOLANO]: *locality,* nearly 2 miles north-northeast of Dixon along Southern Pacific Railroad (lat. 38°28'10" N, long. 121°48'10" W; at W line sec. 7, T 7 N, R 2 E). Named on Dixon (1952) 7.5' quadrangle.

Sugar Loaf: see **Sugarloaf Butte** [ALAMEDA].

Sugarloaf [MARIN]: *peak,* 3 miles west of Tomales near Dillon Beach (lat. 38°15'10" N, long. 122°57'30" W). Named on Valley Ford (1954) 7.5' quadrangle. Point Reyes (1918) 15' quadrangle has the name "Sugarloaf Hill" at or near this peak.

Sugarloaf [NAPA]: *peak,* 11.5 miles south-southwest of Mount Vaca (lat. 38°15'50" N, long. 122°13'15" W; sec. 20, T 5 N, R 3 W). Altitude 1630 feet. Named on Mount George (1951) 7.5' quadrangle.

Sugarloaf [SONOMA]:

(1) *peak,* 1 mile west of Big Mountain (lat. 38°42'45" N, long. 123° 09'45" W; on E line sec. 15, T 10 N, R 12 W). Altitude 1700 feet. Named on Tombs Creek (1978) 7.5' quadrangle.

(2) *peak,* 5 miles east of Mark West Springs (lat. 38°32'20" N, long. 122°37'50" W; at NW cor. sec. 22, T 8 N, R 7 W). Named on Mark West Springs (1958) 7.5' quadrangle.

(3) *peak,* 7 miles south of Guerneville (lat. 38°24'05" N, long. 123° 00'50" W). Altitude 1178 feet. Named on Duncans Mills (1979) 7.5' quadrangle.

Sugarloaf Butte [ALAMEDA]: *peak,* 1.5 miles south-southwest of Cedar Mountain (lat. 37°32'10" N, long. 121°37' W; sec. 35, T 4 S, R 3 E). Altitude 2726 feet. Named on Cedar Mountain (1956) 7.5' quadrangle. Called Sugar Loaf on California Mining Bureau's (1917b) map, and called Sugar Loaf Peak on Thompson and West's (1878) map

Sugarloaf Creek [SONOMA]: *stream,* flows 1.5 miles to Tombs Creek 1.5 miles west of Big Mountain (lat. 38°42'30" N, long. 123° 10'15" W; near S line sec. 15, T 10 N, R 12 W); the stream is south of Sugarloaf (1). Named on Tombs Creek (1978) 7.5' quadrangle.

Sugarloaf Hill [CONTRA COSTA]: *ridge,* northwest-trending, 2 miles long, 3 miles north-northwest of Danville (lat. 37°52'05" N, long. 122°02'05" W). Named on Las Trampas Ridge (1959) and Walnut Creek (1959) 7.5' quadrangles.

Sugarloaf Hill [SONOMA]: *peak,* 1.5 miles southwest of Mount Saint Helena (lat. 38°39'25" N, long. 122°39'20" W). Altitude 1717 feet. Named on Mount Saint Helena (1959) 7.5' quadrangle.

Sugarloaf Hill: see **Sugarloaf** [MARIN].

Sugarloaf Mountain [NAPA]: *peak,* 5 miles north-northeast of Calistoga (lat. 38°38'20" N, long. 122°31'45" W; sec. 9, T 9 N, R 6 W). Altitude 2988 feet. Named on Detert Reservoir (1958) 7.5' quadrangle.

Sugarloaf Mountain [SANTA CLARA]: *peak,* 2.5 miles north-northwest of Isabel Valley (lat. 37°20'50" N, long. 121°33'45" W; sec. 8, T 7 S, R 4 E). Altitude 2798 feet. Named on Isabel Valley (1955) 7.5' quadrangle.

Sugarloaf Park [NAPA]: *locality,* 9 miles south-southwest of Berryessa Peak (lat. 38°32'30" N, long. 122°14'15" W; sec. 18, T 8 N, R 3 W); the place is 1 mile north-northeast of Sugarloaf Peak. Named on Lake Berryessa (1959) 7.5' quadrangle.

Sugarloaf Peak [NAPA]: *peak,* 9.5 miles south-southwest of Berryessa Peak (lat. 38°31'50" N, long. 122°14'45" W). Altitude 1889 feet. Named on Lake Berryessa (1959) 7.5' quadrangle.

Sugar Loaf Peak: see **Las Trampas Peak** [CONTRA COSTA]; **Sugarloaf Butte** [ALAMEDA].

Sugarloaf Peak: see **Little Sugarloaf Peak** [NAPA].

Sugarloaf Ridge [SONOMA]: *ridge,* west-northwest- to west-trending, 2 miles long, 2 miles northeast of Kenwood (lat. 38°26'05" N, long. 122°31'15" W). Named on Kenwood (1954) 7.5' quadrangle.

Suisun [SOLANO]: *land grant,* at and west of Fairfield. Named on Cordelia (1951), Fairfield North (1951), Fairfield South (1949), and Mount George (1951) 7.5' quadrangles. Francisco Solano, an Indian, received 4 leagues in 1842; Archibald A. Ritchie claimed 17,755 acres patented in 1857, and J.H. Fine claimed 482 acres patented in 1882 (Cowan, p. 100).

Suisun: see **Suisun City** [SOLANO].

Suisun Bay [CONTRA COSTA-SOLANO]: *bay,* extends for 14 miles west along Contra Costa-Solano County line from the confluence of Sacramento River and San Joaquin River to Carquinez Strait. Named on Antioch North (1978), Honker Bay (1953), and Vine Hill (1959) 7.5' quadrangles. Called Middle Fork [Sacramento River] on Ringgold's (1850c) map, and the easternmost part of the bay is considered part of Sacramento River on Honker Bay (1918) 7.5' quadrangle. The feature had the early names "Puerto Dulce" and "Freshwater Bay" (Gudde, 1949, p. 346). Ringgold (p. 27) used the designation "Bay of Suisun." The name "Suisun" is from an Indian tribe or village (Kroeber, p. 60).

Suisun City [SOLANO]: *town,* less than 1 mile south of downtown Fairfield at the head of Suisun Slough (lat. 38°14'20" N, long. 122° 02'20" W). Named on Fairfield South (1949) 7.5' quadrangle. Called Suisun on Suisun (1918) special quadrangle. Postal authorities established Suisun post office in 1854 and changed the name to Suisun City in 1857 (Salley, p. 215). The town incorporated in 1868. Postal authorities established Barton's Store post office in 1857 when they split it off from Suisun City post office, and discontinued it in 1858; the name was for John W. Barton, store owner and first postmaster (Salley, p. 15). Captain Josiah Wing and John Owen laid out the town of Suisun near a shipping point already in use (Hoover, Rensch, and Rensch, p. 521).

Suisun City: see **Rio Vista** [SOLANO].

Suisun Creek [NAPA-SOLANO]: *stream,* heads in Napa County and flows 20 miles, including through Lake Curry, to marsh 5 miles southwest of Fairfield in Solano County (lat. 38°11'35" N, long. 122°06'10" W). Named on Capell Valley (1951), Fairfield North (1951), Fairfield South (1949), and Mount George (1951) 7.5' quadrangles.

Suisun Creek: see **Suisun Slough** [SOLANO].

Suisun Cutoff [SOLANO]: *water feature,* extends between Simmons Island and Ryer Island (2) from Suisun Bay to Grizzly Bay 8 miles east-northeast of Benicia (lat. 38°05'40" N, long. 122°01'15" W). Named on Honker Bay (1953) and Vine Hill (1959) 7.5' quadrangles.

Suisun Hill [SOLANO]: *peak,* 2.5 miles south-southeast of Fairfield (lat. 38°12'55" N, long. 122°01'05" W; near S line sec. 6, T 4 N, R 1 W). Altitude 212 feet. Named on Fairfield South (1949) 7.5' quadrangle.

Suisun Point [CONTRA COSTA]: *promontory,* 1.5 miles north-northeast of Martinez at the west end of Suisun Bay (lat. 38°02'05" N, long. 122°07'05" W). Named on Vine Hill (1959) 7.5' quadrangle.

Suisun Reservoir [SOLANO]: *lake,* 1000 feet long, 6.5 miles west-northwest of Fairfield (lat. 38°17'55" N, long. 122°08'40" W; sec. 12, T 5 N, R 3 W). Named on Mount George (1951) 7.5' quadrangle.

Suisun Slough [SOLANO]: *water feature,* extends from Suisun City to Grizzly Bay 9 miles south of Fairfield (lat. 38°07'15" N, long. 122°03'50" W). Named on Fairfield South (1949) and Vine Hill (1959) 7.5' quadrangles. Called Suisun Creek on Ringgold's (1850c) map, but United States Board on Geographic Names (1943, p. 13) rejected this name for the feature.

Suisun Valley [NAPA-SOLANO]: *valley,* 6 miles northwest of Fairfield along Suisun Creek, mainly in Solano County, but extends north into Napa County (lat. 38°18'45" N, long. 122°07'30" W). Named on Fairfield North (1951) and Mount George (1951) 7.5' quadrangles.

Sulfur Creek [SANTA CLARA]: *stream,* flows 2.5 miles to San Benito County 13 miles east-southeast of Gilroy (lat. 36°57'35" N, long. 121°20'40" W). Named on Three Sisters (1954) 7.5' quadrangle.

Sullivan Creek [SONOMA]: *stream,* flows 1.5 miles to Fuller Creek 3.25 miles southeast of Annapolis (lat. 38°41'05" N, long. 123°19'40" W; sec. 29, T 10 N, R 13 W). Named on Annapolis (1977) 7.5' quadrangle.

Sulphur Banks: see **The Geysers** [SONOMA].

Sulphur Canyon [NAPA]: *canyon,* 4 miles long, opens into lowlands 1.25 miles south-southwest of Saint Helena (lat. 38°29'15" N, long. 122°28'40" W); Sulphur Creek drains the canyon. Named on Kenwood (1954) and Rutherford (1951) 7.5' quadrangles. Called Sulphur Sprs. Canyon on Napa (1902) 30' quadrangle. California Division of Highways' (1934) map shows a place called White Sulphur Springs situated along Sulphur Creek about 2 miles west-southwest of Saint Helena (sec. 2, T 7 N, R 6 W); the springs at the place were discovered in 1845 and were the basis of a resort called White Sulphur Springs and Original White Sulphur Springs (Bradley, p. 280)—the resort also was called St. Helena White Sulphur Springs (Waring, p. 254).

Sulphur Creek [ALAMEDA]: *stream,* flows 3.5 miles to San Francisco Bay nearly 5 miles south of downtown San Leandro (lat. 37° 39'20" N, long. 122°09'25" W). Named on Hayward (1959) and San Leandro (1959) 7.5' quadrangles. Captain John Chisholm built Chisholm Landing at the mouth of Sulphur Creek after he landed there in 1851 (Mosier and Mosier, p. 22-23).

Sulphur Creek [NAPA]: *stream,* flows 6 miles to Napa River nearly 1 mile northeast of Saint Helena (lat. 38°30'40" N, long. 122°27'25" W). Named on Rutherford (1951) and Saint Helena (1960) 7.5' quadrangles.

Sulphur Creek [SANTA CLARA]:

(1) *stream,* flows nearly 5 miles to Smith Creek 1.5 miles south-southwest of Mount Hamilton (lat. 37°19'15" N, long. 121°39'20" W; sec. 16, T 7 S, R 3 E). Named on Isabel Valley (1955) and Lick Observatory (1955) 7.5' quadrangles.

(2) *stream,* flows 1.25 miles to Middle Fork Coyote Creek 4 miles northwest of Mount Sizer (lat. 37°14'45" N, long. 121°34'25" W; sec. 7, T 8 S, R 4 E). Named on Mount Sizer (1955) 7.5' quadrangle.

Sulphur Creek [SONOMA]: *stream,* flows 2.25 miles to East Austin Creek 6 miles north of Cazadero (lat. 38°37'05" N, long. 123°05'30" W). Named on Cazadero (1978) 7.5' quadrangle.

Sulphur Creek: see **Big Sulphur Creek** [SONOMA]; **Little Sulphur Creek** [SONOMA]; **Ward Creek** [ALAMEDA].

Sulphur Gulch [SANTA CLARA]: *canyon,* drained by a stream that flows 3.5 miles to Arroyo Valle 4.25 miles south-southwest of Eylar Mountain (lat. 37°25'05" N, long. 121°34'30" W; sec. 18, T 6 S, R 4 E). Named on Eylar Mountain (1955) 7.5' quadrangle.

Sulphur Peak: see **Geyser Peak** [SONOMA].

Sulphur Spring [CONTRA COSTA]: *spring,* 4.25 miles west of Mount Diablo in Pine Canyon (lat. 37°53'10" N, long. 121°59'25" W). Named on Clayton (1953) 7.5' quadrangle.

Sulphur Spring [NAPA]: *spring,* 2 miles southwest of Berryessa Peak (lat. 38°38'45" N, long. 122°13'15" W). Named on Brooks (1959) 7.5' quadrangle.

Sulphur Spring Canyon [ALAMEDA-CONTRA COSTA]: *canyon,* 1.5 miles long, 3 miles east-northeast of Cedar Mountain on Alameda-Contra Costa County line (lat. 37°34'35" N, long. 121°33'15" W). Named on Cedar Mountain (1956) 7.5' quadrangle.

Sulphur Spring Creek: see **Sulphur Springs Creek** [SANTA CLARA]; **Ward Creek** [ALAMEDA].

Sulphur Spring Gulch [SANTA CLARA]: *canyon,* drained by a stream that flows nearly 1 mile to San Antonio Creek 6.5 miles south-southeast of Eylar Mountain (lat. 37°23'05" N, long. 121°30'25" W; sec. 26, T 6 S, R 4 E). Named on Eylar Mountain (1955) 7.5' quadrangle.

Sulphur Springs [SOLANO]: *locality,* 4 miles east-northeast of downtown Vallejo (lat. 38°07'25" N, long. 122°11'25" W; near NW cor. sec. 10, T 3 N, R 3 W). Named on Karquines (1898) 15' quadrangle. Benicia (1959) 7.5' quadrangle shows the site in a place called Blue Rock Springs Park. A resort at the place was called Vallejo White Sulphur Springs, White Sulphur Springs, Vallejo Sulphur Springs (Bradley, p. 310), and Blue Rock Springs (Laizure, 1927b, p. 209).

Sulphur Springs Canyon: see **Sulphur Canyon** [NAPA].

Sulphur Springs Creek [SANTA CLARA]: *stream,* flows 3.5 miles to Beauregard Creek 7.25 miles south of Mount Boardman (lat. 37° 22'35" N, long. 121°29'10" W; near S line sec. 25, T 6 S, R 4 E). Named on Eylar Mountain (1955) and Mount Boardman (1955) 7.5' quadrangles. Called Sulphur Spring Creek on Mount Hamilton (1897) 15' quadrangle, where the name applies also to present Day Creek (2), a tributary of present Sulphur Springs Creek.

Sulphur Springs Creek [SOLANO]: *stream,* flows 9 miles to Carquinez Strait 2 miles east-northeast of Benicia (lat. 38°03'35" N, long. 122°07'15" W); the stream passes east of Sulphur Springs Mountain. Named on Benicia (1959) 7.5' quadrangle. Called Sulphur Springs Valley Creek on Karquines (1898) 15' quadrangle.

Sulphur Springs Creek: see **Blue Rock Springs Creek** [SOLANO].

Sulphur Springs Mountain [NAPA-SOLANO]: *ridge,* south-southeast to south-trending, 4.5 miles long, 6 miles south-southwest of Cordelia (lat. 38°08' N, long. 122°10'50" W); the north end of the ridge is in Napa County. Named on Benicia (1959) and Cordelia (1951) 7.5' quadrangles.

Sulphur Springs Valley Creek: see **Sulphur Springs Creek** [SOLANO].

Summerhome [SONOMA]: *settlement,* 3 miles east of Guerneville along Russian River (lat. 38°29'50" N, long. 122°56'20" W; sec. 35, T 8 N, R 10 W). Named on Camp Meeker (1954) and Guerneville (1955) 7.5' quadrangles. United States Board on Geographic Names (1992, p. 5) approved the name "Summerhome Park" for the place, and rejected the names "Summerhome" and "Summer Home Park."

Summerhome Park: see **Summerhome** [SONOMA].

Summerville: see **Somersville** [CONTRA COSTA].

Summit: see **Occidental** [SONOMA]; **The Summit**, under **Altamont** [ALAMEDA].

Summit Reservoir [ALAMEDA-CONTRA COSTA]: *lake,* 750 feet long, 4.5 miles east-southeast of Richmond civic center on Alameda-Contra Costa County line (lat. 37°54'20" N, long. 120°16'10" W). Named on Richmond (1959) 7.5' quadrangle.

Summit Rock [SANTA CLARA]: *peak,* 1.25 miles north-northwest of Bielawski Mountain (lat. 37°14'25" N, long. 122°05'50" W; sec. 17, T 8 S, R 2 W). Named on Castle Rock Ridge (1955) 7.5' quadrangle.

Summit Spring [NAPA]: *spring,* 4.5 miles east-northeast of Calistoga on Rattlesnake Ridge (lat. 38°36'45" N, long. 122°30'10" W; near E line sec. 22, T 9 N, R 6 W). Named on Calistoga (1958) 7.5' quadrangle.

Summit Spring [SAN MATEO]: *spring,* 1 mile north of Skeggs Point (lat. 37°25'35" N, long. 122°18'20" W). Named on Woodside (1961) 7.5' quadrangle. A travellers stop called Summit Springs House was built by the spring in the 1860's, and the village that grew around the hostelry was called Summit Springs—the village was gone by the 1880's (Brown, p. 93).

Summit Springs: see **Summit Spring** [SAN MATEO].

Summit Springs House: see **Summit Spring** [SAN MATEO].

Sunbeam Acres: see **Gates Canyon** [SONOMA].

Sundburg Creek: see **Patterson Creek** [ALAMEDA].

Sundburg Landing: see **Patterson Landing** [ALAMEDA].

Sunnyside: see **Ross** [MARIN].

Sunnyvale [SANTA CLARA]: *city,* 9 miles west-northwest of downtown San Jose (lat. 37°22'15" N, long. 122°02'15" W). Named on Cupertino (1961), Milpitas (1961), Mountain View (1961), and San Jose West (1961) 7.5' quadrangles. W.E. Crossman bought 200 acres from Patrick Murphy in 1898 and subdivided the land into lots for a town that first he called Encinal, and later called Sunnyvale (Butler, p. 36). Postal authorities established Encinal post office in 1897 and changed the name to Sunnyvale in 1901 (Frickstad, p. 173). The city incorporated in 1912. Palo Alto (1899) 15' quadrangle shows a place called Murphy located along Southern Pacific Railroad in present Sunnyvale (lat. 37°22'35" N, long. 122°01'45" W). The name was for Martin Murphy, Jr., who owned land at the site (Rambo, 1973, p. 44).

Sunnyvale West Outfall Channel: see **Moffett Channel** [SANTA CLARA].

Sunol [ALAMEDA]: *town,* 5.5 miles northeast of Fremont civic center (lat. 37°35'40" N, long. 121°53'05" W; near S line sec. 8, T 4 S, R 1 E); the town is in Sunol Valley. Named on Niles (1961) 7.5' quadrangle. Pleasanton (1906) 15' quadrangle has both the names "Sunol" and "Sunolglen P.O." at the place. The name "Sunol" commemorates Antonio Sunol, part owner of El Valle de San Jose grant (Gudde, 1949, p. 347). Postal authorities established Sunol post office in 1871, changed the name to Sunolglen the same year, and changed it back to Sunol in 1920 (Frickstad, p. 3). Idlwood, a station of Western Pacific Railroad, is situated west of Sunol (Mosier and Mosier, p. 45).

Sunolglen: see **Sunol** [ALAMEDA].

Sunol Ridge [ALAMEDA]: *ridge,* northwest-trending, nearly 7 miles long, center 4.5 miles south of Dublin (lat. 37°38'20" N, long. 121° 56'05" W); the ridge extends northwest from Sunol. Named on Dublin (1961) and Niles (1961) 7.5' quadrangles.

Sunol Valley [ALAMEDA]: *valley,* at and southeast of Sunol along Alameda Creek (lat. 37°35' N, long. 121°52'30" W). Named on La Costa Valley (1960) and Niles (1961) 7.5' quadrangles.

Sunrise Mountain [SONOMA]: *peak,* 2 miles south-southeast of Cazadero (lat. 38°30'15" N, long. 123°04'45" W; near S line sec. 28, T 8 N, R 11 W). Named on Cazadero (1978) 7.5' quadrangle.

Sunset District [SAN FRANCISCO]: *district,* 4 miles southwest of San Francisco civic center (lat. 37°45' N, long. 122°29' W). Named on San Francisco North (1956) and San Francisco South (1956) 7.5' quadrangles.

Sunset Point [NAPA]: *peak,* 3.5 miles north of Saint Helena (lat. 38° 33'25" N, long. 122°27'25" W; sec. 7, T 8 N, R 5 W). Named on Saint Helena (1960) 7.5' quadrangle.

Sunset Reservoir [SAN FRANCISCO]: *lake,* 1050 feet long, 1.5 miles west-southwest of Mount Sutro (lat. 37°45'05" N, long. 122°28'55" W); the feature is in Sunset District. Named on San Francisco North (1956) 7.5' quadrangle.

Sunshine Camp [CONTRA COSTA]: *locality,* 3 miles east-northeast of Mount Diablo (lat. 37°54' N, long. 121°51'50" W: sec. 28, T 1 N, R 1 E). Named on Antioch South (1953) 7.5' quadrangle.

Sun Valley [MARIN]: *valley,* less than 1 mile northwest of downtown San Rafael (lat. 37°58'50" N, long. 122°32'35" W). Named on San Rafael (1954) 7.5' quadrangle.

Surveyor's Gulch: see **Yankee Jim Gulch** [SAN MATEO].

Suscol [NAPA]: *locality,* 4.25 miles north-northwest of Napa Junction along Southern Pacific Railroad (lat. 38°14'40" N, long. 122° 17' W); the place is near the mouth of Suscol Creek. Named on Cuttings Wharf (1949) 7.5' quadrangle. Postal authorities established Suscol post office 4 miles south of Napa City post office in 1868, discontinued it in 1869, reestablished it with the name "Soscol" in 1872, and discontinued it finally in 1886 (Salley, p. 208).

Suscol Creek [NAPA]: *stream,* flows 4.5 miles to Napa River 4 miles north-northwest of Napa Junction (lat. 38°14'25" N, long. 122°17'05" W). Named on Cordelia (1951) and Cuttings Wharf (1949) 7.5' quadrangles. The name is from an Indian village (Kroeber, p. 60).

Sutro: see **Mount Sutro** [SAN FRANCISCO].

Sutro Crest: see **Mount Sutro** [SAN FRANCISCO].

Sutter Bank: see **Cordell Bank** [MARIN].

Sutter Island: see **Ryer Island** [SOLANO] (1).

Sutter Slough [SOLANO]: *water feature,* extends for 4.5 miles along Solano-Sacramento County line to Steamboat Slough 8 miles northeast of Rio Vista (lat. 38°15'15" N, long. 121°36' W). Named on Courtland (1978) 7.5' quadrangle. Called West Fork [Sacramento River] on Ringgold's (1850d) map.

Suttonfield: see **Lake Suttonfield** [SONOMA].

Suval [SOLANO]: *locality,* 2 miles west of downtown Fairfield along Sacramento Northern Railroad (lat. 38°14'50" N, long. 122°04'40" W). Named on Fairfield South (1949) 7.5' quadrangle.

Sveadal [SANTA CLARA]: *settlement,* 3.5 miles east-southeast of Loma Prieta along Uvas Creek (lat. 37°05'05" N, long. 121°47'15" W; near SE cor. sec. 6, T 10 S, R 2 E). Named on Loma Prieta (1955) 7.5' quadrangle. United States Board on Geographic Names (1983d, p. 4) approved the name "Crystal Peak" for a peak located 3.3 miles northwest of Sveadal (lat. 37°06'48" N, long. 121°50'05" W; sec. 35, T 9 S, R 1 E); the name is for a radio facility on the peak, and also for commemoration of early crystal-radio development.

Swallow City [SONOMA]: *relief feature,* 2 miles north-northeast of the village of Bodega Bay (lat. 38°21'45" N, long. 123°02'15" W). Named on Bodega Head (1942) 7.5' quadrangle.

Swanson Canyon [SANTA CLARA]: *canyon,* drained by a stream that flows nearly 1.5 miles to Uvas Creek 3.25 miles east-southeast of Loma Prieta (lat. 37°05'10" N, long. 121°47'30" W; sec. 6, T 10 S, R 2 E). Named on Loma Prieta (1955) 7.5' quadrangle.

Swanzy Lake: see **Swanzy Reservoir** [SOLANO].

Swanzy Reservoir [SOLANO]: *lake,* 950 feet long, 2.5 miles southeast of downtown Vallejo (lat. 38°04'35" N, long. 122°13'30" W). Named on Benicia (1959) 7.5' quadrangle. United States Board on Geographic Names (1962a, p. 17) rejected the names "Swanzy Lake" and "Vallejo Reservoir" for the feature.

Swartz Canyon [NAPA]: *canyon,* nearly 4 miles long, along Swartz Creek above a point 1 mile south-southwest of Aetna Springs (lat. 38°38'30" N, long. 122°29'15" W); sec. 11, T 9 N, R 6 W). Named on Detert Reservoir (1958) 7.5' quadrangle.

Swartz Creek [NAPA]: *stream,* flows 6 miles to Pope Creek 1.5 miles east-northeast of Aetna Springs in Popo Valley (lat. 38°39'35" N, long. 122°27'25" W; sec. 6, T 9 N, R 5 W). Named on Aetna Springs (1958) 7.5' quadrangle.

Sweany Creek [SOLANO]: *stream,* flows 6 miles to lowlands 1 mile west of Allendale (lat. 38°26'40" N, long. 121°57'30" W). Named on Allendale (1953), Dixon (1952), and Mount Vaca (1951) 7.5' quadrangles. Called Sweeny Creek on Napa (1902) 30' quadrangle, and called Sweeney Creek on Vacaville (1953) 15' quadrangle, which shows the stream extending through lowlands to Ulatis Creek 3.5 miles east of Elmira.

Swede George Canyon: see **Swede George Creek** [MARIN].

Swede George Creek [MARIN]: *stream,* flows 1.25 miles to Alpine Lake nearly 4 miles northeast of Bolinas (lat. 37°56'25" N, long. 122°37'35" W). Named on San Rafael (1954) 7.5' quadrangle. East Fork enters from the east near the mouth of the main stream and is 1.5 miles long. West Fork enters 0.25 mile from the mouth of the main stream and is nearly 1 mile long. Both forks are named on San Rafael (1954) 7.5' quadrangle. Mount Tamalpais (1950) 15' quadrangle has the name "Swede George Canyon" for the canyon of the stream.

Sweeney: see **East Palo Alto** [SAN MATEO].

Sweeney Creek: see **Sweany Creek** [SOLANO].

Sweeney Ridge [SAN MATEO]: *ridge,* northwest- to north-trending, 2 miles long, 3.5 miles north-northeast of Montara Knob (lat. 37° 36'10" N, long. 122°27'20" W). Named on Montara Mountain (1956) 7.5' quadrangle. The name is from Sweeney ranch, which was on the ridge in the 1880's; the feature also was called Irish Ridge (Brown, p. 93).

Sweeny Creek: see **Sweany Creek** [SOLANO].

Sweet Springs [ALAMEDA]: *springs,* 2.25 miles southeast of Cedar Mountain (lat. 37°32'20" N, long. 121°34'20" W; sec. 31, T 4 S, R 4 E). Named on Cedar Mountain (1956) 7.5' quadrangle. Water that comes from fourteen springs has a distinctly sweet taste (Waring, p. 310).

Sweetwater Creek [SANTA CLARA]: *stream,* flows 3.5 miles to Sulphur Springs Creek 7 miles south-southwest of Mount Boardman (lat. 37°23'

N, long. 121°29'45" W; sec. 26, T 6 S, R 4 E). Named on Eylar Mountain (1955) and Mount Boardman (1955) 7.5' quadrangles.

Sweetwater Creek [SONOMA]: *stream,* flows about 1 mile to Pena Creek 3.25 miles south of Skaggs Springs (lat. 38°38'45" N, long. 123°01'05" W; sec. 7, T 9 N, R 10 W). Named on Warm Springs Dam (1978) 7.5' quadrangle.

Sweigert Creek [SANTA CLARA]: *stream,* flows 0.5 mile to lowlands 2.25 miles north-northeast of Berryessa (lat. 37°24'55" N, long. 121°50'30" W). Named on Calaveras Reservoir (1961, photorevised 1968 and 1973) 7.5' quadrangle. Called Cropley Creek on Calaveras Reservoir (1961) 7.5' quadrangle. United States Board on Geographic Names (1972, p. 3) approved the name "Sweigert Creek" for the stream, and listed the name "Cropley Creek" as a variant.

Swiss Creek [SANTA CLARA]: *stream,* flows 2.5 miles to Stevens Creek 3.5 miles northwest of downtown Saratoga in Stevens Creek Reservoir (lat. 37°17'45" N, long. 122°04'45" W; sec. 28, T 7 S, R 2 W). Named on Cupertino (1961) 7.5' quadrangle.

Sycamore: see **Camp Sycamore** [SANTA CLARA].

Sycamore Canyon [SANTA CLARA]: *canyon,* drained by a stream that flows nearly 1 mile to Soda Springs Canyon 3.5 miles south of Mount Sizer (lat. 37°10' N, long. 121°30'45" W; sec. 10, T 9 S, R 4 E). Named on Mount Sizer (1955) 7.5' quadrangle.

Sycamore Creek [CONTRA COSTA]:

(1) *stream,* formed by the confluence of East Fork and West Fork, flows nearly 7 miles to San Ramon Creek 1 mile southeast of Danville (lat. 37°48'40" N, long. 121°59' W); the stream goes through Sycamore Valley. Named on Diablo (1953) 7.5' quadrangle. East Fork is 1 mile long and West Fork is 1.25 miles long; both forks are named on Diablo (1953) 7.5' quadrangle.

(2) *stream,* flows nearly 4 miles through Hog Canyon to Marsh Creek 5.5 miles east of Mount Diablo (lat. 37°53'10" N, long. 121° 48'40" W; sec. 36, T 1 N, R 1 E). Named on Antioch South (1953) and Tassajara (1953) 7.5' quadrangles.

Sycamore Creek [SANTA CLARA]:

(1) *stream,* flows 3.5 miles to Arroyo Valle 3.5 miles west-southwest of Eylar Mountain (lat. 37°27'05" N, long. 121°36'10" W; sec. 36, T 5 S, R 3 E). Named on Eylar Mountain (1955) and Mount Day (1955) 7.5' quadrangles.

(2) *stream,* flows 2 miles to Uvas Creek nearly 4 miles northeast of Mount Madonna (lat. 37°03'20" N, long. 121°39'50" W). Named on Mount Madonna (1955, photorevised 1968 and 1973) 7.5' quadrangle. The name is for the many sycamore trees on the banks of the stream (United States Board on Geographic Names, 1973a, p. 3).

Sycamore Slough [SOLANO]: *water feature,* 9.5 miles north of Rio Vista near Hass Slough (lat. 38°17'50" N, long. 121°43'25" W). Named on Liberty Island (1978) 7.5' quadrangle.

Sycamore Spring [ALAMEDA]: *spring,* 7 miles south of Sunol (lat. 37°29'45" N, long. 121°51'05" W; sec. 15, T 5 S, R 1 E). Named on Calaveras Reservoir (1961) 7.5' quadrangle.

Sycamore Spring [CONTRA COSTA]:

(1) *spring,* less than 1 mile northeast of Mount Diablo (lat. 37°53'15" N, long. 121°54'05" W; sec. 31, T 1 N, R 1 E). Named on Clayton (1953) 7.5' quadrangle.

(2) *spring,* 5.5 miles east-southeast of Mount Diablo (lat. 37°51'35" N, long. 121°48'50" W; sec. 12, T 1 S, R 1 E); the spring is near Sycamore Creek (2). Named on Tassajara (1953) 7.5' quadrangle.

Sycamore Valley [CONTRA COSTA]: *valley,* 3 miles east-southeast of Danville (lat. 37°48'30" N, long. 121°57' W); the valley is along Sycamore Creek (1). Named on Diablo (1953) 7.5' quadrangle.

Sykes Slough [SOLANO]: *water feature,* 8 miles northeast of Dixon between Putah Creek and South Fork Putah Creek (lat. 38°31'35" N, long. 121°43'50" W). Named on Swingle (1915) 7.5' quadrangle.

— T —

Table Butte: see **Mount Tamalpais** [MARIN].

Table Hill: see **Mount Tamalpais** [MARIN].

Table Mountain [NAPA]: *ridge,* northeast-trending, 1 mile long, 8 miles north-northeast of Calistoga (lat. 38°41'05" N, long. 122° 32' W). Named on Detert Reservoir (1958) 7.5' quadrangle.

Table Mountain [SANTA CLARA]:

(1) *peak,* 2 miles south-southeast of Black Mountain (1) (lat. 37°17'20" N, long. 122°08'20" W; sec. 25, T 7 S, R 3 W). Altitude 1852 feet. Named on Mindego Hill (1961) 7.5' quadrangle.

(2) *ridge,* east-trending, 1 mile long, 3 miles west of Saratoga (lat. 37°15'35" N, long. 122°04'40" W). Named on Cupertino (1961) 7.5' quadrangle.

Table Mountain [SONOMA]: *peak,* 5.5 miles north-northeast of Fort Ross (lat. 38°35'20" N, long. 123°12'35" W; sec. 29, T 9 N, R 12 W). Altitude 589 feet. Named on Fort Ross (1978) 7.5' quadrangle.

Table Mountain: see **Mount Tamalpais** [MARIN].

Table Rock [NAPA]: *peak,* 4.5 miles north of Calistoga (lat. 38°38'35" N, long. 122°34'45" W; sec. 12, T 9 N, R 7 W). Altitude 2462 feet. Named on Detert Reservoir (1958) 7.5' quadrangle.

Tahana Gulch [SAN MATEO]: *canyon,* drained by a stream that flows 1.5 miles to Bradley Creek 3 miles south of the village of San Gregorio (lat. 37°17'05" N, long. 122°22'45" W). Named on La Honda (1961) 7.5' quadrangle.

Tamal: see **San Quentin** [MARIN].

Tamalpais: see **Kentfield** [MARIN]; **Mill Valley** [MARIN] (2); **Mount Tamalpais** [MARIN].

Tamalpais Creek [MARIN]: *stream,* flows 1.25 miles to Corte Madera Creek 2 miles south-southwest of downtown San Rafael (lat. 37°56'55" N, long. 122°32'40" W). Named on San Rafael (1954) 7.5' quadrangle. The name was given to a previously unnamed stream during World War II so that a navy oiler ship constructed near Saucelito could have the name "Tamalpais"—the navy customarily named oilers for streams (Teather, p. 77).

Tamalpais Valley [MARIN]: *valley,* 6.5 miles south of downtown San Rafael along Coyote Creek (lat. 37°52'45" N, long. 122° 32' W). Named on San Rafael (1954) 7.5' quadrangle. Called Coyote Valley on a county map of 1873 (Teather, p. 79).

Tamalpais Valley: see **Tamalpais**, under **Mill Valley** [MARIN] (2).

Tamalpais Valley Junction [MARIN]: *locality,* 6.25 miles south of downtown San Rafael (lat. 37°52'55" N, long. 122°31'25" W); the place is near the mouth of Tamalpais Valley. Named on San Rafael (1954) 7.5' quadrangle.

Tanbark Canyon [SONOMA]: *canyon,* 1 mile long, 2.5 miles northwest of Mount Saint Helena along Mill Stream (lat. 38°41'45" N, long. 122°39'45" W). Named on Mount Saint Helena (1959) 7.5' quadrangle.

Tanforan: see **San Bruno** [SAN MATEO].

Tannery Creek [SONOMA]: *stream,* flows 2.5 miles to Salmon Creek (1) 4.25 miles northwest of Valley Ford (lat. 38°21'20" N, long. 122°59'20" W). Named on Camp Meeker (1954) and Valley Ford (1954) 7.5' quadrangles.

Tar Creek [SANTA CLARA]: *stream,* flows 8 miles to Carnadero Creek 5.5 miles south-southeast of Gilroy (lat. 36°55'50" N, long. 121°32'30" W). Named on Chittenden (1955) 7.5' quadrangle. Called La Brea Creek on San Juan Bautista (1917) 15' quadrangle. Goodyear (1888, p. 94) called the stream Tar Spring Creek, and described "copious seepages of black tar" along it.

Tar Creek: see **Tarwater Creek** [SAN MATEO].

Tarraville Canyon: see **Tarraville Creek** [ALAMEDA].

Tarraville Creek [ALAMEDA]: *stream,* flows 4 miles to Arroyo Mocho 6 miles southeast of Cedar Mountain (lat. 37°30' N, long. 121°32'10" W; sec. 16, T 5 S, R 4 E). Named on Eylar Mountain (1955) 7.5' quadrangle. On Mount Boardman (1955) 7.5' quadrangle, the canyon of the creek has the name "Tarraville Canyon."

Tar Spring Creek: see **Tar Creek** [SANTA CLARA].

Tarwater Creek [SAN MATEO]: *stream,* flows 2.25 miles to Pescadero Creek 3.5 miles south of Mindego Hill (lat. 37°15'40" N, long. 122°14'25" W; sec. 6, T 8 S, R 3 W). Named on Mindego Hill (1961) 7.5' quadrangle. Brown (p. 6, 93) used the name "Tar Creek" for the stream, and noted that asphalt and oil seep into the water; Brown also mentioned that the east branch of the stream was called Bear Creek

Tasajero: see **Tassajara** [CONTRA COSTA].

Tasajero Creek: see **Tassajara Creek** [CONTRA COSTA].

Tassajara [CONTRA COSTA]: *locality,* 6.5 miles south-southeast of Mount Diablo (lat. 37°47'45" N, long. 121°51'45" W; near S line sec. 33, T 1 S, R 1 E); the place is along Tassajara Creek. Named on Tassajara (1953) 7.5' quadrangle. Called Tassajero on Mount Diablo (1898) 15' quadrangle. United States Board on Geographic Names (1933, p. 745) first approved the name "Tassajero," and rejected the names "Tasajero" and "Tassajera" for the place; later the Board (1960a, p. 18) approved the name "Tassajara," and rejected the name "Tassajero." Postal authorities established Tassajara post office in 1896 and discontinued it in 1922 (Frickstad, p. 24). The name is from a Spanish-American term for a place where meat is cut in strips and dried in the sun (Gudde, 1949, p. 354).

Tassajara Creek [ALAMEDA-CONTRA COSTA]: *stream,* heads in Contra Costa County and flows 10.5 miles to lowlands 6.25 miles west-northwest of Livermore in Alameda County (lat. 37°42'50" N, long. 121°52'30" W). Named on Dublin (1961), Livermore (1961), and Tassajara (1953) 7.5' quadrangles. Called Tassajero Creek on Mount Diablo (1898) and Pleasanton (1906) 15' quadrangles. United States Board on Geographic Names (1933, p. 745) first approved the form "Tassajero," and rejected the forms "Tasajero" and "Tassajera" for the name; later the Board (1960a, p. 18) approved the form "Tassajara" and rejected the forms "Tassajero" and (1967c, p. 5) "Tassajera."

Tassajera: see **Tassajara** [CONTRA COSTA].

Tassajera Creek: see **Tassajara Creek** [ALAMEDA-CONTRA COSTA].

Tassajero: see **Tassajara** [CONTRA COSTA].

Tassajero Creek: see **Tassajara Creek** [ALAMEDA-CONTRA COSTA].

Tater Knoll [SONOMA]: *relief feature,* 5.5 miles north of Guerneville (lat. 38°35'05" N, long. 122°59'55" W; near W line sec. 32, T 9 N, R 10 W). Named on Guerneville (1955) 7.5' quadrangle.

Taylor: see **Camp Taylor** [MARIN].

Taylor Bluffs [NAPA]: *relief feature,* 2.5 miles south-southeast of Berryessa Peak on Napa-Yolo County line (lat. 38°37'50" N, long. 122°10' W). Named on Brooks (1959) and Lake Berryessa (1959) 7.5' quadrangles.

Taylor Island: see **Ryer Island** [SOLANO] (1).

Taylor Mountain [SONOMA]: *peak,* 3.5 miles southeast of downtown Santa Rosa (lat. 38°24'05" N, long. 122°40'25 W; near N line sec. 6, T 6 N, R 7 W); the peak is 1.25 miles southeast of Kawana Springs, which formerly were known as Taylor's Springs. Altitude 1401 feet. Named on Santa Rosa (1954) 7.5' quadrangle.

Taylor Slough [CONTRA COSTA]: *water feature,* extends for nearly 5 miles between Bethel Island (1) and Jersey Island from Piper Slough to Dutch Slough at the settlement of Bethel Island (lat. 38° 00'50" N, long. 121°38'45" W). Named on Jersey Island (1978) 7.5' quadrangle.

Taylor's Springs: see **Kawana Springs** [SONOMA].

Taylor Sulphur Spring: see **Kawana Springs** [SONOMA].

Taylor's White Sulphur Springs: see **Kawana Springs** [SONOMA].

Taylorville [MARIN]: *locality,* 11 miles west-southwest of downtown Novato along Northwestern Pacific Railroad (lat. 38°01'45" N, long. 122°44'20" W); the place is 1 mile northwest of Camp Taylor. Named on Petaluma (1914) 15' quadrangle. The name is for Samuel P. Taylor, who built the first paper mill on the Pacific Coast (Gudde, 1949, p. 354).

Teachers Beach [MARIN]: *beach,* 4.5 miles northwest of Point Reyes Station on the southwest side of Tomales Bay (lat. 38°06'50" N, long. 122°52'05" W). Named on Inverness (1954) 7.5' quadrangle.

Teague Hill [SAN MATEO]: *peak,* nearly 1 mile north-northeast of Skeggs Point (lat. 37°25'15" N, long. 122°17'50" W). Named on Woodside (1961) 7.5' quadrangle. Andrew Teague lived at the place from 1854 until 1860 (Brown, p. 94).

Teal [SOLANO]: *locality,* 5.5 miles south-southwest of Fairfield along Southern Pacific Railroad (lat. 38°10'25" N, long. 122°04'40" W). Named on Fairfield South (1949) 7.5' quadrangle.

Tehan Canyon [ALAMEDA]: *canyon,* drained by a stream that flows 1.5 miles to Amador Valley 1.5 miles south-southeast of Dublin (lat. 37°40'50" N, long. 121°55'25" W). Named on Dublin (1961) 7.5' quadrangle. The name is for William Tehan, who settled at the place in the 1860's—the stream in the canyon is called Tehan Creek (Mosier and Mosier, p. 86).

Tehan Creek: see **Tehan Canyon** [ALAMEDA].

Tehan Falls [ALAMEDA]: *waterfall,* 2 miles south of Dublin (lat. 37°40'25" N, long. 121°56'20" W; sec. 14, T 3 S, R 1 W); the feature is in Tehan Canyon. Named on Dublin (1961) 7.5' quadrangle.

Telegraph Canyon [ALAMEDA]: *canyon,* drained by a stream that flows 0.5 mile to Claremont Creek 5 miles north-northeast of downtown Oakland (lat. 37°52'10" N, long. 122°13'25" W). Named on Oakland East (1959) 7.5' quadrangle. A transcontinental telegraph line was built through the canyon in 1858; the canyon of present Claremont Creek was called Telegraph Canyon until 1886 or 1887 (Mosier and Mosier, p. 87).

Telegraph Hill [SAN FRANCISCO]: *hill,* 0.5 mile southeast of North Point (lat. 37°48'10" N, long. 122°24'20" W). Named on San Francisco North (1956) 7.5' quadrangle. Spaniards called the hill Loma Alta, but as early as 1849 it sometimes was called Signal Hill because it was used as a lookout for incoming ships; by 1853 it was called Inner Signal Station and was connected by telegraph to Outer Signal Station located near Point Lobos, where ships were sighted before they entered the Golden Gate (Hoover, Rensch, and Rensch, p. 362-363). The promontory formed by the southeast shoulder of the hill—which came to the edge of San Francisco Bay before landfill modified the shoreline—was called Punta de la Loma Alta and Punta del Embarcadero in Spanish days; later the promontory was known as Clark's Point for William S. Clark, who took land there as a squatter in 1848 (Hoover, Rensch, and Rensch, p. 357). The same promontory is called Pt. Montgomery on Ringgold's (1850a) map—Captain John Berrien Montgomery, commander of United States sloop *Portsmouth,* set up a gun battery called Fort Montgomery at the point in 1846 (Frazer, p. 27; Whiting and Whiting, p. 56). The embayment, now filled, that extended southeast from Clark's Point to Rincon Point was called Yerba Buena Cove (Soule, Gihon, and Nisbet, p. 157); the feature also was known as Loma Alta Cove (Davis, W.H., p. 2)—Soule, Gihon, and Nisbet's (1855) map shows the shoreline before the cove was filled. According to Bancroft (1886. p. 590), the name "Yerba Buena" applied before 1827 to an anchorage west of present North Point. The name no doubt is from mint that grew in abundance near the cove—*yerba buena* means "good herb" in Spanish (Soule, Gihon, and Nisbet, p. 157).

Telegraph Hill [SONOMA]: *peak,* 2 miles north-northeast of Mark West Springs (lat. 38°34'15" N, long. 122°42' W; sec. 1, T 8 N, R 8 W). Named on Mark West Springs (1958) 7.5' quadrangle.

Telmat: see **Hamlet** [MARIN].

Temescal [ALAMEDA]: *locality,* 2 miles north-northeast of downtown Oakland (lat. 37°49'50" N, long. 122°15'50" W); the place is near Temescal Creek. Named on San Francisco (1899) 15' quadrangle.

Temescal: see **North Temescal**, under **Oakland** [ALAMEDA].

Temescal Creek [ALAMEDA]: *stream,* flows 3 miles to lowlands 3 miles north-northeast of downtown Oakland (lat. 37°51' N, long. 122°14'15" W). Named on Oakland East (1959) and Oakland West (1959) 7.5' quadrangles. Called Kohler Creek on Concord (1897) 15' quadrangle. The name apparently is from an Indian sweat house near the stream—*temescal* means "sweat house" in Spanish (Hoover, Rensch, and Rensch, p. 3). The name "Kohler" recalls Andrew Kohler, who owned land in the neighborhood in the 1880's (Mosier and Mosier, p. 48).

Temescal Lake: see **Lake Temescal** [ALAMEDA].

Tenderfoot Flat [CONTRA COSTA]: *area,* 2.5 miles west-northwest of Mount Diablo (lat. 37°53'35" N, long. 121°57'25" W; sec. 34, T 1 N, R 1 W). Named on Clayton (1953) 7.5' quadrangle.

Ten Mile Beach: see **Point Reyes Beach** [MARIN].

Tennant [SANTA CLARA]: *locality,* 1.5 miles southeast of Morgan Hill along Southern Pacific Railroad (lat. 37°06'55" N, long. 121° 38' W). Named on Morgan Hill (1917) 15' quadrangle. The place was near the site of Twenty-one Mile House—named for the distance from San Jose—built in 1852, burned down in 1853, and soon rebuilt by William Tennant (*San Jose Mercury-News, California Today Magazine,* October 23, 1977). Postal authorities established Tennant post office in 1871, discontinued it for a time in 1879, and discontinued it finally in 1887 (Frickstad, p. 175).

Tennessee Cove [MARIN]: *embayment,* 2 miles northwest of Point Bonita along the coast (lat. 37°50'25" N, long. 122°33'05" W); the feature is at the mouth of Tennessee Valley. Named on Point Bonita (1954) 7.5' quadrangle. The name is from the steamer *Tennessee,* which went aground at the place in 1853 (Hoover, Rensch, and Rensch, p. 186). The feature also had the names "Indian Cove" and "Potatoe Cove" before application of the present name—the embayment is near Potato Patch Shoal (Teather, p. 79).

Tennessee Point [MARIN]: *promontory,* 1.5 miles northwest of Point Bonita along the coast (lat. 37°50'05" N, long. 122°32'55" W). Named on Point Bonita (1954) 7.5' quadrangle.

Tennessee Valley [MARIN]: *canyon,* drained by a stream that flows 2 miles to the sea 2.25 miles northwest of Point Bonita at Tennessee Cove (lat. 37°50'30" N, long. 122°33'05" W). Named on Point Bonita (1954) 7.5' quadrangle. Called Elk Valley on Tamalpais (1897) 15' quadrangle, but United States Board on Geographic Names (1962a, p. 17) rejected this name.

Tequisquite: see **Llano del Tequisquita** [SANTA CLARA].

Terra Linda: see **San Rafael** [MARIN].

Tesla [ALAMEDA]: *locality,* 5.5 miles south-southwest of Midway in Corral Hollow (lat. 37°38'25" N, long. 121°36' W; sec. 25, T 3 S, R 3 E). Site named on Midway (1953) 7.5' quadrangle. John Treadwell and James Treadwell founded a town at the place in 1890 for workers of nearby coal mines; they named the town for Nikola Tesla, a famous inventor of electrical devices (Mosier, p. 7). Postal authorities established Tesla post office in 1898 and discontinued it in 1915 (Frickstad, p. 3).

Thayer: see **Camp Thayer** [SONOMA]; **Mount Thayer** [SANTA CLARA].

The Beehive [NAPA]: *peak,* 7 miles north-northwest of Saint Helena on Rattlesnake Ridge (lat. 38°36'15" N, long. 122°29'50" W; sec. 26, T 9 N, R 6 W). Altitude 2750 feet. Named on Saint Helena (1960) 7.5' quadrangle.

The Big Brush [SONOMA]: *area,* 6 miles north-northeast of Cazadero (lat. 38°36'50" N, long. 123°02'45" W). Named on Cazadero (1978) 7.5' quadrangle.

The Big Coyote: see **Coyote Point** [SAN MATEO].

The Big Ditch [SOLANO]: *stream,* flows 9.5 miles to an intermittent lake 10 miles southeast of Elmira (lat. 38°15'10" N, long. 121°46'05" W). Named on Birds Landing (1953) and Dozier (1952) 7.5' quadrangles.

The Brothers [CONTRA COSTA]: *islands,* two, each 350 feet long, less than 0.5 mile west-southwest of Point San Pablo in San Francisco Bay (lat. 37°57'45" N, long. 122°26' W). Named on San Quentin (1959) 7.5' quadrangle. Buffum (p. 28) used the name "Two Brothers" for the islands.

The Butcherknife [SONOMA]: *ridge,* south-trending, 1 mile long, 4.5 miles north-northwest of Cazadero (lat. 38°35'35" N, long. 123°06'55" W). Named on Cazadero (1978) 7.5' quadrangle.

The Cedars [SONOMA]: *area,* 7 miles north-northwest of Cazadero (lat. 38°37'30" N, long. 123°07'30" W). Named on Cazadero (1978), Fort Ross (1978), Tombs Creek (1978), and Warm Springs Dam (1978) 7.5' quadrangles.

The Cove [NAPA]: *relief feature,* 5.5 miles south of Rutherford (lat. 38°22'40" N, long. 122°26'15" W; sec. 8, T 6 N, R 5 W). Named on Rutherford (1951) 7.5' quadrangle.

The Coyote: see **Coyote Point** [SAN MATEO].

The Cut: see **Bay Slough** [SAN MATEO].

The Cutoff: see **Bay Slough** [SAN MATEO].

The Family Farm [SAN MATEO]: *settlement,* 7 miles south of downtown Redwood City in present Portola Valley (1) (lat. 37°23'15" N, long. 122°14'

W). Named on Palo Alto (1953) 7.5' quadrangle.

The Geysers [SONOMA]: *water feature,* steam wells 3.25 miles northeast of Geyser Peak (lat. 38°48'05" N, long. 122°48'15" W; near E line sec. 13, T 11 N, R 9 W). Named on The Geysers (1959) 7.5' quadrangle. Called Hot Springs on Kelseyville (1921) 15' quadrangle. In 1847 William B. Elliott discovered the place where small hot springs and fumaroles occur on the north side of Big Sulphur Creek (Allen and Day, p. 11; Anderson, Winslow, p. 138). Steam from wells at the site now generates electricity. United States Board on Geographic Names (1981a, p. 2) approved the name "The Geysers" for an area of geothermal activity 10 miles long and 3 miles wide along the course of Big Sulphur Creek (NW end at lat. 38°49'40" N, long. 122°49'50" W; SE end at lat. 38°44'30" N, long. 122°41'45" W). An area of geothermal activity known as Little Geysers is in an amphitheater in a side canyon that opens into the canyon of Big Sulphur Creek from the northeast 5 miles above The Geysers (Allen and Day, p. 95). A mile downstream from The Geysers is a fumarole field known as Sulphur Banks (Allen and Day, p. 94), where extensive deposits of sulphur occur (Whitney, p. 94).

The Geysers: see **Geysers Resort** [SONOMA].

The Girdle [SONOMA]: *relief feature,* 0.5 mile west-northwest of Big Mountain (lat. 38°42'45" N, long. 122°09'15" W; sec. 14, T 10 N, R 12 W). Named on Tombs Creek (1978) 7.5' quadrangle.

The Great Beach: see **Point Reyes Beach** [MARIN].

The Horn [SONOMA]: *locality,* 9.5 miles northeast of Healdsburg along a road (lat. 38°43'30" N, long. 122°45'15" W; sec. 9, T 10 N, R 8 W). Named on Jimtown (1955) 7.5' quadrangle.

The Island [SONOMA]:

(1) *peak,* 7 miles north-northeast of Fort Ross (lat. 38°36'20" N, long. 123°10'50" W; sec. 21, T 9 N, R 12 W). Named on Fort Ross (1978) 7.5' quadrangle.

(2) *peak,* 5 miles north-northeast of Cazadero (lat. 38°36'05" N, long. 123°03'30" W). Altitude 1206 feet. Named on Cazadero (1978) 7.5' quadrangle.

The Knife [ALAMEDA-CONTRA COSTA]: *ridge,* northwest-trending, 1 mile long, 5.5 miles south of Danville on Alameda-Contra Costa County line (lat. 37°44'30" N, long. 122°00'15" W). Named on Hayward (1959) 7.5' quadrangle.

The Lagoon: see **Stivers Lagoon** [ALAMEDA].

The Laguna: see **Upper Crystal Springs Reservoir** [SAN MATEO].

The Lagunas: see **Laguna de Santa Rosa** [SONOMA].

The Meadows [SONOMA]: *area,* 3 miles south-southwest of Healdsburg (lat. 38°34'45" N, long. 122°54' W). Named on Guerneville (1955) 7.5' quadrangle.

The Mesa [SAN MATEO]: *relief feature,* 2 miles north-northeast of Pigeon Point (lat. 37°12'20" N, long. 122°22'30" W). Named on Franklin Point (1955) and Pigeon Point (1955) 7.5' quadrangles.

The Narrows [SANTA CLARA]: *narrows,* 4.5 miles south-southwest of Eylar Mountain along Arroyo Valle (lat. 37°24'45" N, long. 121°34'50" W). Named on Eylar Mountain (1955) 7.5' quadrangle.

The Nubble [SONOMA]: *relief feature,* nearly 4 miles west of Big Mountain (lat. 38°42'05" N, long. 123°12'45" W; sec. 20, T 10 N, R 12 W). Named on Tombs Creek (1978) 7.5' quadrangle.

The Palisades [NAPA]: *relief feature,* 4 miles north of Calistoga (lat. 38°38'10" N, long. 122°34' W; on N line sec. 18, T 9 N, R 6 W). Named on Detert Reservoir (1958) 7.5' quadrangle.

The Peak [SANTA CLARA]: *peak,* 1.25 miles east-southeast of Bielawski Mountain on Santa Clara-Santa Cruz County line (lat. 37°13'10" N, long. 122°04'15" W; sec. 22, T 8 S, R 2 W). Altitude 2886 feet. Named on Castle Rock Ridge (1955) 7.5' quadrangle.

The Potato Patch [SAN MATEO]: *area,* 3.5 miles southwest of La Honda along Pomponio Creek (lat. 37°17'25" N, long. 122°19'15" W; sec. 29, T 7 S, R 4 W). Named on La Honda (1961) 7.5' quadrangle.

The Racetrack [SONOMA]: *area,* 1.25 miles west of Cazadero (lat. 38°32' N, long. 123°06'20" W; at W line sec. 17, T 8 N, R 11 W). Named on Cazadero (1943) 7.5' quadrangle.

The Roughs [SONOMA]: *area,* 2 miles north of Cazadero (lat. 38°33'40" N, long. 123°05'35" W; at SE cor. sec. 5, T 8 N, R 11 W). Named on Cazadero (1978) 7.5' quadrangle.

The Sisters [MARIN]: *islands,* two, largest 200 feet long, 1800 feet northeast of Point San Pedro in San Pablo Bay (lat. 37°59'20" N, long. 120°26'30" W). Named on San Quentin (1959) 7.5' quadrangle.

The Summit: see **Altamont** [ALAMEDA].

The Trees [NAPA]: *area,* 1.5 miles east-southeast of Berryessa Peak on Napa-Yolo County line (lat. 38°39'15" N, long. 122°09'50" W). Named on Brooks (1959) 7.5' quadrangle.

The Tunnel: see **Wrights** [SANTA CLARA].

The Turnaround [SONOMA]: *locality,* 3.5 miles southwest of Skaggs Springs (lat. 38°39'15" N, long. 123°04'10" W). Named on Skaggs Springs (1943) 7.5' quadrangle.

The Willows: see **Willow Glen** [SANTA CLARA].

Third Napa Slough [SONOMA]: *water feature,* joins Second Napa Slough 4.5 miles northeast of Sears Point (lat. 38°11'50" N, long. 122°23'30" W). Named on Sears Point (1951) 7.5' quadrangle.

Thoman [NAPA]: *locality,* 1.5 miles southeast of Saint Helena along Southern Pacific Railroad (lat. 38°29'30" N, long. 122°27'05" W). Named on Rutherford (1951) 7.5' quadrangle.

Thomasson [SOLANO]: *locality,* 4.25 miles southwest of Fairfield along Southern Pacific Railroad (lat. 38°13' N, long. 122°06'25" W). Named on Fairfield South (1949) 7.5' quadrangle. Postal authorities established Thomasson post office in 1907 and discontinued it in 1913; the name is for a rancher who used the place as a shipping point (Salley, p. 221).

Thompson [NAPA]: *locality,* nearly 4 miles north-northwest of Napa Junction (lat. 38°14'15" N, long. 122°16'45" W; sec. 35, T 5 N, R 4 W). Named on Cuttings Wharf (1949) 7.5' quadrangle. Mare Island (1916) 15' quadrangle has the name nearby along Southern Pacific Railroad.

Thompson: see **Point Thompson**, under **Mare Island** [SOLANO].

Thompson Creek [SANTA CLARA]: *stream,* flows 9 miles to Silver Creek 4.25 miles east-southeast of downtown San Jose (lat. 37° 19'35" N, long. 121°48'35" W). Named on Lick Observatory (1955) and San Jose East (1961) 7.5' quadrangles. On San Jose East (1961, photorevised 1968 and 1973) 7.5' quadrangle, the stream ends before it reaches Silver Creek. Called Dry Creek on San Jose (1899) 15' quadrangle, which shows the stream ending in a marsh.

Thompson Creek [SONOMA]: *stream,* flows 2 miles to East Austin Creek 3.25 miles northeast of Cazadero (lat. 38°34'15" N, long. 123°02'55" W; sec. 2, T 8 N, R 11 W); the stream is south of Thompson Ridge (2). Named on Cazadero (1978) 7.5' quadrangle.

Thompson Ridge [SONOMA]:

(1) *ridge,* east- to east-southeast-trending, 4 miles long, 7 miles west-southwest of Cloverdale (lat. 38°46' N, long. 123°08' W). Named on Hopland (1960) 15' quadrangle.

(2) *ridge,* generally west-trending, 2 miles long, 4.25 miles northeast of Cazadero (lat. 38°34'45" N, long. 123°02'30" W). Named on Cazadero (1978) 7.5' quadrangle. This ridge and Marble Mine Ridge together are called Dutton Ridge on California Division of Forestry's (1945) map.

Thompson's Landing: see **Roberts Landing** [ALAMEDA].

Thona: see **New Almaden Station** [SANTA CLARA].

Thornhill [ALAMEDA]: *locality,* 3 miles east-northeast of downtown Oakland along Oakland Antioch and Eastern Railroad (lat. 37°49'50" N, long. 122°13' W). Named on Concord (1915) 15' quadrangle. Concord (1943) 15' quadrangle shows a place called Monclair situated at or near the site. Thornhill railroad station was established in 1913; the name commemorates Hiram Thorne, who was in the neighborhood in the 1850's (Mosier and Mosier, p. 88).

Thornton [SAN MATEO]: *locality,* 5.5 miles west-northwest of downtown South San Francisco along Ocean Shore Railroad (lat. 37°41'45" N, long. 122°29'50" W). Named on San Mateo (1915) 15' quadrangle. The name is for R.S. Thornton, an early settler in the neighborhood (Brown, p. 94). J.R. Wagner (p. 52) gave the name "Ocean View" as an alternate.

Three Fathom Shoal: see **Benicia Shoals** [SOLANO].

Three Peaks [MARIN]: *peak,* 9.5 miles southeast of Tomales (lat. 37°08'15" N, long. 122°48'05" W). Altitude 1161 feet. Named on Point Reyes NE (1954) 7.5' quadrangle.

Three Peaks [NAPA]: *peaks,* 7.5 miles north of Saint Helena (lat. 38°36'50" N, long. 122°29'45" W; sec. 23, T 9 N, R 6 W). Altitude of highest, 1889 feet. Named on Saint Helena (1960) 7.5' quadrangle.

Three Rocks [SAN MATEO]: *rocks,* 2.25 miles south-southwest of downtown Half Moon Bay off Miramontes Point (lat. 37°25'55" N, long. 122°26'35" W). Named on Half Moon Bay (1961) 7.5' quadrangle.

Throop: see **Cloverdale** [SONOMA].

Thurston Creek [SONOMA]: *stream,* flows 2.5 miles to Nolan Creek 3.25 miles northwest of Valley Ford (lat. 38°21'10" N, long. 122°57'45" N). Named on Camp Meeker (1954) and Valley Ford (1954) 7.5' quadrangles.

Tiburon [MARIN]: *town,* 2 miles east-northeast of downtown Sausalito (lat. 37°52'30" N, long. 122°27'15" W); the town is at the southeast end of Tiburon Peninsula. Named on San Francisco North (1956) and San Quentin (1959) 7.5' quadrangles. Postal authorities established Tiburon post office in 1884 (Frickstad, p. 89), and the town incorporated in 1964.

Tiburon: see **Point Tiburon** [MARIN].

Tiburon Peninsula [MARIN]: *peninsula,* extends 4.5 miles southeast between San Francisco Bay and Richardson Bay; center 5 miles south-southeast of downtown San Rafael (lat. 37°54' N, long. 122° 28'45" W). Named on San Quentin (1959) and San Rafael (1954) 7.5' quadrangles.

Tice Creek [CONTRA COSTA]: *stream,* flows 4 miles to Las Trampas Creek 0.5 mile south of Walnut Creek civic center (lat. 37°53'40" N, long. 122°03'30" W); the stream drains Tice Valley. Named on Las Trampas Ridge (1959) and Walnut Creek (1959) 7.5' quadrangles.

Tice Valley [CONTRA COSTA]: *valley,* 5 miles northwest of Danville (lat. 37°52' N, long. 122°04'10" W); the valley is along Tice Creek. Named on Las Trampas Ridge (1959) 7.5' quadrangle. The name commemorates James Tice, a landowner in the neighborhood (Hoover, Rensch, and Rensch, p. 58).

Tick Creek [SANTA CLARA]: *stream,* flows 3.25 miles to Carnadero Creek 5.25 miles south-southeast of Gilroy (lat. 36°55'55" N, long. 120°32'30" W). Named on Chittenden (1955) 7.5' quadrangle.

Tidal Canal [ALAMEDA]: *water feature,* extends for 1.5 miles between Oakland and Alameda from Oakland Inner Harbor to San Leandro Bay 4 miles southeast of downtown Oakland (lat. 37°45'30" N, long. 122°13'25" W). Named on Oakland East (1959) 7.5' quadrangle.

Timber Cove [SONOMA]: *embayment,* 4.5 miles south-southeast of Plantation along the coast (lat. 38°31'45" N, long. 123°16'15" W). Named on Plantation (1977) 7.5' quadrangle. W.R. Miller operated a sawmill at Timber Cove in 1856; schooners carried lumber, cordwood, and tanbark from the place to San Francisco (Miller, J.T., p. 50).

Timber Cove: see **Seaview** [SONOMA].

Timber Cove Creek [SONOMA]: *stream,* flows 2 miles to the sea 4.5 miles south-southeast of Plantation at Timber Cove (lat. 38° 32' N, long. 123°16'20" W). Named on Plantation (1977) 7.5' quadrangle.

Timber Gulch [SONOMA]: *canyon,* drained by a stream that flows less than 1 mile to the sea 6 miles northwest of Jenner (lat. 38°29'50" N, long. 123°12'40" W). Named on Arched Rock (1977) and Fort Ross (1978) 7.5' quadrangles.

Timber Ridge [SANTA CLARA]: *ridge,* north-northwest-trending, 2.5 miles long, 5.25 miles east of San Martin (lat. 37°05'30" N, long. 121°30'50" W). Named on Gilroy (1955) 7.5' quadrangle.

Tin Can Canyon [NAPA]: *canyon,* drained by a stream that flows 1.5 miles to lowlands along Lake Berryessa 4.5 miles south of Berryessa Peak (lat. 38°35'55" N, long. 122°12'30" W). Named on Lake Berryessa (1959) 7.5' quadrangle.

Tindle Spring [SOLANO]: *spring,* 7.5 miles northwest of Fairfield (lat. 38°18'30" N, long. 122°09'20" W; sec. 2, T 5 N, R 3 W). Named on Mount George (1951) 7.5' quadrangle.

Tiny Creek [SONOMA]: *stream,* flows less than 1 mile to Conchea Creek 4 miles north of Cazadero (lat. 38°35'25" N, long. 123°05'20" W). Named on Cazadero (1978) 7.5' quadrangle. Called Canshea Creek on Cazadero (1943) 7.5' quadrangle.

Tito: see **Quito** [SANTA CLARA].

Tobacco Creek [SONOMA]: *stream,* flows 1.5 miles to Wheatfield Fork Gualala River 5.5 miles southeast of Annapolis (lat. 38°40'15" N, long. 123°17'25" W; sec. 34, T 10 N, R 13 W). Named on Annapolis (1977) 7.5' quadrangle. California Division of Forestry's (1945) map shows a place called Mendosoma located along Wheatfield Fork Gualala River just downstream from the mouth of Tobacco Creek, where Annapolis (1977) 7.5' quadrangle shows Mendosoma Forest Fire Sta. (lat. 38°40'15" N, long. 123°17'40" W).

Tobin: see **Pedro Valley** [SAN MATEO].

Tocaloma [MARIN]: *locality,* 3 miles east-southeast of Point Reyes Station along Lagunitas Creek (lat. 38°03' N, long. 122°45'30" W). Named on Inverness (1954) 7.5' quadrangle. Point Reyes (1918) 15' quadrangle shows the place located along Northwestern Pacific Railroad. Postal authorities established Tocaloma post office in 1891 and discontinued it in 1919 (Frickstad, p. 89). The name probably is from an Indian word (Kroeber, p. 62-63).

Todd Creek [SANTA CLARA]: *stream,* flows 1.5 miles to Bonjetti Creek nearly 2 miles northeast of Bielawski Mountain (lat. 37°14'35" N, long. 122°04'10" W; sec. 10, T 8 S, R 2 W). Named on Castle Rock Ridge (1955) 7.5' quadrangle.

Todos Santos: see **Concord** [CONTRA COSTA].

Toe Drain [SOLANO]: *water feature,* artificial waterway in Yolo Bypass that parallels the west side of Sacramento River Deep Water Ship Channel; extends from Yolo County into Solano County as far as Prospect Slough 9 miles north of Rio Vista (lat. 38°17'15" N, long. 121°39'45" W). Named on Liberty Island (1978) 7.5' quadrangle.

Toland Landing [SOLANO]: *locality,* 6 miles south-southwest of Rio Vista along Sacramento River (lat. 38°05'15" N, long. 121°45'05" W); the place is on Los Ulpinos grant. Named on Antioch North (1978) 7.5' quadrangle. The name commemorates Dr. Hugh Hugar Toland, founder of University of California Medical School, and owner of 11,800 acres of Los Ulpinos grant (Hoover, Rensch, and Rensch, p. 524).

Tolay: see **Lake Tolay**, under **Lakeville** [SONOMA].

Tolay Creek [SONOMA]: *stream,* flows 11.5 miles to marsh along San Pablo Bay nearly 2 miles south-southwest of Sears Point (lat. 38°07'30" N, long. 122°27'10" W). Named on Petaluma River (1954) and Sears Point (1951) 7.5' quadrangles. The name is from former Lake Tolay (Gudde, 1949, p. 364). East Branch diverges from the main stream 1 mile north of Sears Point and extends nearly 2 miles to Sonoma Creek. North Branch enters East Branch from the north nearly 1.5 miles north-northeast of Sears Point. Both branches are named on Sears Point (1951) 7.5' quadrangle.

Tolenas [SOLANO]:

(1) *land grant,* northeast of Fairfield. Named on Denverton (1953), Elmira (1953), Fairfield North (1951), Fairfield South (1949), and Mount George (1951) 7.5' quadrangles. Jose F. Armijo received 3 leagues in 1840 and claimed 13,316 acres patented in 1868 (Cowan, p. 103-104). The name apparently is from an Indian village (Kroeber, p. 63).

(2) *locality,* 2.25 miles east-northeast of downtown Fairfield along Southern Pacific Railroad (lat. 38°16' N, long. 122°00'05" W; sec. 20, T 5 N, R 1 W); the place is on Tolenas grant. Named on Fairfield North (1951) 7.5' quadrangle. Postal authorities established Tolenas post office in 1872, discontinued it the same year, reestablished it in 1913, and discontinued it in 1914 (Frickstad, p. 193).

Tolenas Springs [SOLANO]: *springs,* 4 miles north of Fairfield (lat. 38°18'35" N, long. 122°03'10" W); the springs are on Tolenas grant. Named on Fairfield North (1951) 7.5' quadrangle. Nineteen springs at the site were the basis of a resort (Anderson, Winslow, p. 255-256).

Toll Canyon [NAPA]: *canyon,* drained by a stream that flows 2 miles to Eticuera Creek 6.5 miles northeast of Walter Springs (lat. 38°42'40" N, long. 122°15'40" W). Named on Brooks (1959) and Walter Springs (1959) 7.5' quadrangles. Capay (1945) 15' quadrangle shows Old Toll Road on the north side of the canyon.

Toll Gate: see **Saratoga** [SANTA CLARA].

Tollhouse Creek: see **Nuff Creek** [SAN MATEO].

Tolman Peak [ALAMEDA]: *peak,* 4.5 miles north-northwest of Fremont civic center (lat. 37°36'50" N, long. 121°59'25" W). Named on Niles (1961) 7.5' quadrangle. The name commemorates Professor Cyrus Fisher Tolman of Stanford University, who frequently brought geology students to the place (United States Board on Geographic Names, 1959a, p. 3).

Tom: see **Mount Tom** [SONOMA].

Tomales [MARIN]: *village,* 21 miles west-northwest of downtown Novato near Keyes Creek (lat. 38°14'45" N, long. 122°54'15" W). Named on Tomales (1954) and Valley Ford (1954) 7.5' quadrangles. Postal authorities established Tomalles post office in 1854 and changed the name to Tomales before 1879 (Salley, p. 223). John Keys arrived at the place in 1850, when present Keyes Creek was navigable, and built a home, stores, and a wharf called Keys Embarcadero (Donnelly, p. 48).

Tomales: see **Camp Tomales** [MARIN].

Tomales Bay [MARIN]: *bay,* extends southeast for 13 miles from Bodega Bay; the mouth of Tomales Bay is 4 miles west-southwest of Tomales (lat. 38°14' N, long. 122°58'30" W). Named on Drakes Bay (1953), Inverness (1954), Point Reyes NE (1954), and Tomales (1954) 7.5' quadrangles. Called Estero Americano on Ringgold's (1850b) map. Members of the Vizcaino expedition found the bay in 1603 and called it Rio Grande de San Sebasitan (Wagner, H.R., p. 419). The name "Tomales" comes from an Indian word that means "bay" (Kroeber, p. 63).

Tomales Bluff [MARIN]: *promontory,* 5 miles west of Tomales at the northwest end of Tomales Point (lat. 38°14'25" N, long. 122° 59'40" W). Named on Tomales (1954) 7.5' quadrangle. Called Pt. Bodega on Ringgold's (1850b) map.

Tomales Creek: see **Estero de San Antonio** [MARIN].

Tomales Point [MARIN]: *peninsula,* 4.25 miles west-southwest of Tomales (lat. 38°13'15" N, long. 122°58'30" W); the feature is southwest of the mouth of Tomales Bay. Named on Tomales (1954) 7.5' quadrangle. The place also is called Pierce Point for Solomon Pierce, who bought land there in 1858 (Mason, 1976a, p. 149).

Tomales y Baulines [MARIN]:

(1) *land grant,* 6 miles north-northwest of Bolinas. Named on Bolinas (1954), Double Point (1954), Inverness (1954), and San Geronimo (1954) 7.5' quadrangles. Called Tomales y Bolinas on Point Reyes (1918) 15' quadrangle. Rafael Garcia received 5 leagues in 1836 and claimed 9468 acres patented in 1883 (Cowan, p. 104).

(2) *land grant,* extends for 9 miles northwest from Mount Tamalpais. Named on Bolinas (1954), San Geronimo (1954), and San Rafael (1954) 7.5' quadrangles. Rafael Garcia received 5 leagues in 1836; Bethuel Phelps claimed 13,316 acres patented in 1866 (Cowan, p. 104).

Tomales y Bolinas: see **Tomales y Baulines** [MARIN] (1).

Tomalles: see **Tomales** [MARIN].

Tomasini Canyon [MARIN]: *canyon,* drained by a stream that flows 4 miles to lowlands along Tomales Bay near Point Reyes Station (lat. 38°04'15" N, long. 122°48'30" W). Named on Inverness (1954) 7.5' quadrangle. The name commemorates Battista Tomasini, who bought 830 acres in the neighborhood in 1880 (Mason, 1976a, p. 150).

Tombs Creek [SONOMA]: *stream,* flows 7.25 miles to Wheatfield Fork Gualala River 5.25 miles west of Big Mountain (lat. 38°43'05" N, long. 123°14'25" W; near W line sec. 18, T 10 N, R 12 W). Named on Tombs Creek (1978) 7.5' quadrangle.

Toms Point [MARIN]: *promontory,* 3.5 miles southwest of Tomales on the northeast side of Tomales Bay (lat. 38°12'50" N, long. 122° 57'05" W). Named on Tomales (1954) 7.5' quadrangle. The name commemorates Tom Wood, who deserted from the United States navy ship *Warren* in 1844 and lived among Indians of Tomales Bay (Mason, 1976b, p. 106).

Tonquin Point: see **Black Point** [SAN FRANCISCO].

Toole Pond [SONOMA]: *lake,* 350 feet long, 1.5 miles west-southwest of Cazadero (lat. 38°31'15" N, long. 123°06'30" W; near E line sec. 19, T 8 N, R 11 W). Named on Cazadero (1978) 7.5' quadrangle.

Torello Canyon: see **San Vicente Creek** [SAN MATEO].

Tormey [CONTRA COSTA]: *locality,* 6.5 miles west-northwest of Martinez near the mouth of Cañada del Cierbo (lat. 38°03' N, long. 122°14'55" W). Named on Benicia (1959) 7.5' quadrangle. Called El Cierbo on Karquines (1898) 15' quadrangle. Postal authorities established Tormey post office in 1891 and discontinued it in 1892 (Frickstad, p. 24). The name is for John and Patrick Tormey, who bought part of Pinole grant in 1867 (Gudde, 1949, p. 366).

Toroges Creek [ALAMEDA]: *stream,* flows 2 miles to lowlands 6 miles southeast of Fremont civic center (lat. 37°29' N, long. 121° 54'45" W). Named on Milpitas (1961) 7.5' quadrangle.

Torquay: see **Pescadero** [SAN MATEO].

Tosca [SONOMA]: *locality,* less than 1 mile northwest of Geyserville along Northwestern Pacific Railroad (lat. 38°42'50" N, long. 122° 54'45" W). Named on Healdsburg (1940) 15' quadrangle.

Tower Rocks: see **Cave Point** [CONTRA COSTA].

Toyon Camp [CONTRA COSTA]: *locality,* 1 mile south-southwest of Mount Diablo (lat. 37°52' N, long. 121°55'25" W; sec. 12, T 1 S, R 1 W). Named on Diablo (1953) 7.5' quadrangle.

Trail Canyon [SANTA CLARA]: *canyon,* drained by a stream that flows nearly 1 mile to San Antonio Creek 6.5 miles south-southeast of Eylar Mountain (lat. 37°23'10" N, long. 121°30'20" W). Named on Eylar Mountain (1955) 7.5' quadrangle.

Trancas Creek: see **Corinda Los Trancos Creek** [SAN MATEO].

Travis Air Force Base [SOLANO]: *military installation,* 7 miles south-southeast of Vacaville (lat. 38°15'45" N, long. 121°56'15" W). Named on Denverton (1953) and Elmira (1953) 7.5' quadrangles. Elmira (1953) 7.5' quadrangle also has the name "Travis Field" at the place. The name "Travis" honors Brigadier General Robert F. Travis, who was killed in an airplane accident at the site in 1950 (Hoover, Rensch, and Rensch, p. 523). Postal authorities established Fairfield Unit Number 1 post office in 1943, changed the name to Air Base in 1945, and changed it to Travis Air Force Base in 1950 (Salley, p. 2, 72).

Travis Field: see **Travis Air Force Base** [SOLANO].

Treasure Island [SAN FRANCISCO]: *island,* about 1 mile long, 2.25 miles east-northeast of North Point in San Francisco Bay (lat. 37° 49'30" N, long. 122°22'15" W); the feature is connected to Yerba Buena Island by a causeway. Named on Oakland West (1959) and San Francisco North (1956) 7.5' quadrangles. The island was built from 1936 to 1938 by pumping sand and mud dredged from the bay into an enclosure formed by a rock retaining wall; it was used for Golden Gate International Exposition in 1939 and 1940, and it became a navy installation during World War II (Bowen, p. 338-339).

Treasure Rock: see **Red Rock** [CONTRA COSTA-MARIN-SAN FRANCISCO].

Trees: see **The Trees** [NAPA].

Tree Slough [SOLANO]: *water feature,* on Grizzly Island, joins Montezuma Slough 6 miles west-southwest of Denverton (lat. 38° 10'45" N, long. 121°59'40" W). Named on Denverton (1953) and Fairfield South (1949) 7.5' quadrangles. Called Land Slough on Denverton (1918) 7.5' quadrangle.

Tremont [SOLANO]: *locality,* 4 miles northeast of Dixon along Southern Pacific Railroad (lat. 38°29'45" N, long. 121°46'45" W). Named on Dixon (1952) 7.5' quadrangle. Postal authorities established Tremont post office in 1876, discontinued it in 1878, reestablished it in 1889, discontinued it for a time in 1891, and discontinued it finally in 1896; the name is from a place in New York (Salley, p. 224).

Trenton [SONOMA]: *locality,* 6 miles north-northwest of Sebastopol (lat. 38°29'05" N, long. 122°51' W). Named on Sebastopol (1954) 7.5' quadrangle. Postal authorities established Trenton post office in 1887 and discontinued it in 1914 (Frickstad, p. 198).

Trestle Glen: see **Indian Gulch** [ALAMEDA].

Trevarno [ALAMEDA]: *locality,* 6 miles southwest of Altamont (lat. 37°41'25" N, long. 121°44'45" W). Named on Altamont (1953) 7.5' quadrangle. Officials of Coast Manufacturing and Supply Company named the place after George Bickford's home in England; the company made safety fuses invented by William Bickford, George's father (Gudde, 1949, p. 368).

Triniti: see **Glen Ellen** [SONOMA].

Tripp Creek: see **West Union Creek** [SAN MATEO].

Tripp Gulch [SAN MATEO]: *canyon,* drained by a stream that flows 1.25 miles to West Union Creek 2 miles northeast of Skeggs Point (lat. 37°25'50" N, long. 122°16'30" W). Named on Woodside (1961) 7.5' quadrangle. Dr. R.C. Tripp opened Woodside store near the mouth of the canyon in 1851 (Brown, p. 95).

Trospers Resort [SONOMA]: *locality,* less than 2 miles north of Cazadero (lat. 38°33'25" N, long. 123°05'30" W; sec. 8, T 8 N, R 11 W). Named on Cazadero (1943) 7.5' quadrangle.

Trout Creek [ALAMEDA]: *stream,* flows 4.25 miles to Arroyo Valle about 5.5 miles south of Mendenhall Springs (lat. 37°30'35" N, long. 121°38' W; sec. 10, T 5 S, R 3 E). Named on Mendenhall Springs (1956) 7.5' quadrangle. South Fork enters from the south 1.5 miles upstream from the mouth of the main creek; it is 1.5 miles long and is named on Mendenhall Springs (1956) and Mount Day (1955) 7.5' quadrangles.

Trout Creek [NAPA]: *stream,* flows 5.25 miles to Pope Creek 11 miles northeast of Saint Helena (lat. 38°36'40" N, long. 122°18'50" W). Named on Chiles Valley (1958) 7.5' quadrangle.

Trout Creek [SANTA CLARA]: *stream,* flows 2 miles to the canyon of Los Gatos Creek 1.5 miles south-southwest of downtown Los Gatos (lat. 37°12'10" N, long. 121°59'30" W; sec. 29, T 8 S, R 1 W). Named on Castle Rock Ridge (1955) and Los Gatos (1953) 7.5' quadrangles. According to Young (p. 122-123), the name recalls a Greek fish peddler of the 1850's who had the nickname "Trout."

Trout Creek Ridge [NAPA]: *ridge,* north-northwest-trending, 3 miles long, 12 miles east-northeast of Saint Helena (lat. 38°35'15" N, long. 122°16'55" W); the ridge is northeast of Trout Creek. Named on Chiles Valley (1958) 7.5' quadrangle.

Troutdale Creek [NAPA]: *stream,* flows 2.5 miles, partly in Lake County, to the canyon of Saint Helena Creek 6.25 miles north of Calistoga (lat. 38°40' N, long. 122°35'15" W; sec. 36, T 10 N, R 7 W). Named on Detert Reservoir (1958) 7.5' quadrangle.

Trubody [NAPA]: *locality,* nearly 6 miles north-northwest of downtown Napa along Southern Pacific Railroad (lat. 38°22'10" N, long. 122°20'20" W). Named on Napa (1902) 30' quadrangle. Postal authorities established Trubody post office in 1896 and discontinued it in 1906; the name was for members of the Trubody family, property owners at the place (Salley, p. 225).

Truitt Creek [SONOMA]: *stream,* flows 0.5 mile to Big Sulphur Creek 3.25 miles north of Geyser Peak (lat. 38°48'45" N, long. 122°51'20" W; sec. 10, T 11 N, R 9 W). Named on The Geysers (1959) 7.5' quadrangle.

Truth Home [SONOMA]: *locality,* 7.25 miles northeast of Fort Ross (lat. 38°34'50" N, long. 123°08'15" W; sec. 36, T 9 N, R 12 W). Named on Fort Ross (1943) 7.5' quadrangle.

Tubbs Island [SONOMA]: *island,* nearly 4 miles long, between Sears Point and the mouth of Sonoma Creek (lat. 38°09' N, long. 122°25'30" W). Named on Petaluma Point (1959) and Sears Point (1951) 7.5' quadrangles.

Tularcitos [SANTA CLARA]: *land grant,* northeast of the city of Milpitas. Named on Calaveras Reservoir (1961) and Milpitas (1961) 7.5' quadrangles. Jose Higuera received 2 leagues in 1821, and he or his son claimed 4394 acres patented in 1870 (Cowan, p. 105). According to Perez (p. 103), Jose Higuera was the grantee in 1839, and his heirs were the patentees in 1870.

Tularcitos Creek [SANTA CLARA]: *stream,* flows 1 mile to lowlands nearly 2 miles northeast of downtown Milpitas (lat. 37°26'50" N, long. 121°52'50" W); the stream is on Tularcitos grant. Named on Milpitas (1961) 7.5' quadrangle. South Branch Tularcitos Creek flows 1 mile to lowlands 10.5 mile east-southeast of the entrance of Tularcitos Creek to lowlands; it is named on Calaveras Reservoir (1961) 7.5' quadrangle. Tularcitos Creek and South Branch Tularcitos Creek are unconnected on the maps.

Tulare Hill [SANTA CLARA]: *hill,* 1 mile west-northwest of Coyote (lat. 37°13'15" N, long. 121°45'15" W). Altitude 565 feet. Named on Santa Teresa Hills (1953) 7.5' quadrangle.

Tule Lake [SANTA CLARA]: *lake,* 175 feet long, 6 miles west-southwest of Mount Sizer (lat. 37°10'45" N, long. 121°36'50" W). Named on Mount Sizer (1955) 7.5' quadrangle.

Tule Pond [ALAMEDA]: *intermittent lake,* 1800 feet long, 0.5 mile north-northwest of Fremont civic center (lat. 37°33'30" N, long. 121°58'25" W; sec. 28, T 4 S, R 1 W). Named on Niles (1961) 7.5' quadrangle. Cluff and Bolt (p. 61) gave the alternate name "Tysons Lagoon" for the feature.

Tule Pond: see **Stivers Lagoon** [ALAMEDA].

Tule Slough [SONOMA]: *water feature,* joins Petaluma River 6 miles east-southeast of downtown Petaluma (lat. 38°11'30" N, long. 122° 32'45" W). Named on Petaluma River (1954) 7.5' quadrangle.

Tulley Canyon: see **Tully Canyon** [NAPA].

Tully Canyon [NAPA]: *canyon,* drained by a stream that flows 4 miles to Lake Berryessa 4 miles south-southwest of Berryessa Peak (lat. 38°37' N, long. 122°13'25" W). Named on Brooks (1959) and Lake Berryessa (1959) 7.5' quadrangles. Called Tulley Canyon on Capay (1945) 15' quadrangle, but United States Board on Geographic Names (1962a, p. 18) rejected this form of the name. South Fork opens into the main canyon 2.5 miles south of Berryessa Peak; it is 1.5 miles long and is named on Brooks (1959) 7.5' quadrangle.

Tulucay [NAPA]: *land grant,* southeast of the city of Napa. Named on Cordellia (1951), Cuttings Wharf (1949), Mount George (1951), and Napa (1951) 7.5' quadrangles. Cayetano Juarez received 2 leagues in 1841 and claimed 8866 acres patented in 1861 (Cowan, p. 105-106). The name is from an Indian village that was located near present Napa (Kroeber, p. 63).

Tulucay Creek [NAPA]: *stream,* formed by the confluence of Murphy Creek and Spencer Creek, flows 3 miles to Napa River 1.25 miles south of downtown Napa (lat. 38°16'45" N, long. 122° 16'50" W); the stream is on Tulucay grant. Named on Mount George (1951) and Napa (1951) 7.5' quadrangles. United States Board on Geographic Names (1949a, p. 3) rejected the name

"Asylum Slough" for the stream, which is near Napa state hospital.

Tunitas [SAN MATEO]: *locality,* 6 miles south-southeast of the town of Half Moon Bay (lat. 37°22'50" N, long. 122°23'25" W); the place is on the divide between Tunitas Creek and Lobitos Creek. Named on Halfmoon Bay (1940) 15' quadrangle. Half Moon Bay (1961) 7.5' quadrangle shows Tunitas Sch. at the place.

Tunitas Beach [SAN MATEO]: *beach,* 2.25 miles north-northwest of the village of San Gregorio along the coast (lat. 37°21'25" N, long. 122°23'55" W); the beach is at the mouth of Tunitas Creek. Named on San Gregorio (1961) 7.5' quadrangle. The place first was called Potter's Beach for T.F. Potter ranch, which was near the beach in the 1860's and 1870's (Brown, p. 95).

Tunitas Creek [SAN MATEO]: *stream,* flows 6.5 miles to the sea 2.25 miles north-northwest of the village of San Gregorio (lat. 37° 21'25" N, long. 122°23'55" W). Named on Half Moon Bay (1961), San Gregorio (1961), and Woodside (1961) 7.5' quadrangles. The stream was called Arroyo de las Tunitas in Spanish times; *tunita* is the diminutive of *tuna,* the Spanish term for the fruit of a plant sometimes called the beach apple—the plant is abundant near the mouth of the stream (Gudde, 1949, p. 372; Brown, p. 95-96). East Fork enters from the east 2.25 miles upstream from the mouth of the main creek; it is 2.5 miles long and is named on Woodside (1961) 7.5' quadrangle. The railroad stop near the creek about 1910 was called Long Bridge for a structure built across the stream in 1869 (Brown, p. 49). Alexander Gordon built Gordon's Chute near the mouth of Tunitas Creek in the 1870's to load farm produce and lumber from a high bluff onto ships anchored just offshore (Stanger, 1963, p. 133).

Tunnel: see **The Tunnel**, under **Wrights** [SANTA CLARA]

Tunnel Creek [ALAMEDA]: *stream,* flows 2 miles to Arroyo Mocho 2 miles north-northwest of Cedar Mountain (lat. 37°35' N, long. 121°37'25" W; at W line sec. 14, T 4 S, R 3 E). Named on Cedar Mountain (1956) 7.5' quadrangle. A tunnel to carry water was dug near the mouth of the stream before 1921 (Mosier and Mosier, p. 89).

Tunnel Ridge: see **Sawyer Ridge** [SAN MATEO].

Turkey Flat [SANTA CLARA]: *area,* 5 miles north of Pacheco Peak along North Fork Pacheco Creek (lat. 37°04'50" N, long. 121°17'20" W). Named on Pacheco Peak (1955) 7.5' quadrangle.

Turk Island [ALAMEDA]: *hill,* 4.5 miles northwest of downtown Newark (lat. 37°34'20" N, long. 122°06'10" W). Altitude 116 feet. Named on Newark (1959) 7.5' quadrangle. The feature is unnamed on Haywards (1899) 15' quadrangle, which shows it as an island in marsh along San Francisco Bay. E.H. Dyer named the feature Peruvian Island in the 1850's, and W.J. Lewis named it Brown Island in 1860 for the owner, Charles Brown; John A. Plummer and sons established their Turk's Island Salt Works there in 1869 (Mosier and Mosier, p. 89).

Turnaround: see **The Turnaround** [SONOMA].

Turner [SONOMA]: *locality,* 4.5 miles east-northeast of Bloomfield along Petaluma and Santa Rosa Railroad (lat. 38°20'30" N, long. 122°46'35" W). Named on Two Rock (1954) 7.5' quadrangle.

Turner Canyon [SONOMA]: *canyon,* drained by a stream that flows 1.25 miles to South Fork Gualala River 3.5 miles east-northeast of Fort Ross (lat. 38°31'50" N, long. 123°10'50" W; near SE cor. sec. 16, T 8 N, R 12 W). Named on Fort Ross (1978) 7.5' quadrangle. Called Turner Gl. on California Division of Forestry's (1945) map.

Turner Gulch [SANTA CLARA]: *canyon,* drained by a stream that flows nearly 2 miles to Arroyo Mocho 1.5 miles east-southeast of Eylar Mountain (lat. 37°28'05" N, long. 121°31'10" W). Named on Eylar Mountain (1955) and Mount Boardman (1955) 7.5' quadrangles.

Turner Gulch: see **Turner Canyon** [SONOMA].

Turner Mountain [NAPA]: *peak,* 5.5 miles north of Walter Springs (lat. 38°44'10" N, long. 122°21'25" W; near SE cor. sec. 1, T 10 N, R 5 W). Altitude 1822 feet. Named on Walter Springs (1959) 7.5' quadrangle.

Turtle Rock [CONTRA COSTA]: *relief feature,* 2 miles west-southwest of Mount Diablo (lat. 37°52' N, long. 121°56'45" W). Named on Diablo (1953) 7.5' quadrangle.

Twelve Mile Creek: see **Colma Creek** [SAN MATEO].

Twelvemile Creek [SAN MATEO]: *stream,* flows 2.25 miles to Colma Creek nearly 1 mile west of downtown South San Francisco (lat. 37°39'25" N, long. 122°25'45" W). Named on San Francisco South (1956) 7.5' quadrangle. The name is for Twelve Mile House, established in 1851 near the creek; the stream also was called Baden Creek for the nearby community of Baden (Brown, p. 4), which now is part of South San Francisco.

Twelve Mile House: see **Coyote** [SANTA CLARA]; **Twelvemile Creek** [SAN MATEO].

Twenty-one Mile House: see **Tennant** [SANTA CLARA].

Twenty-one Mile Peak: see **El Toro** [SANTA CLARA].

Twin Creeks [SANTA CLARA]: *settlement,* nearly 2 miles southwest of New Almaden at the entrance of Alamitos Creek into Barret Canyon (lat. 37°09'20" N, long. 121°50'35" W; near NE cor. sec. 15, T 9 S, R 1 E). Named on Santa Teresa Hills (1953) 7.5' quadrangle. Los Gatos (1919) 15' quadrangle shows a place called Lovely Glen Resort at or near the site.

Twin Fall Creek [SANTA CLARA]: *stream,* flows 2 miles to Llagas Creek 3.5 miles south-southeast of New Almaden (lat. 37°07'50" N, long. 121°47'35" W). Named on Loma Prieta (1955) and Santa Teresa Hills (1953) 7.5' quadrangles.

Twin Lakes [SANTA CLARA]: *lakes,* two, largest 400 feet long, nearly 6 miles west-southwest of Mount Sizer (lat. 37°10'50" N, long. 121°36'40" W). Named on Mount Sizer (1955) 7.5' quadrangle.

Twin Peaks [CONTRA COSTA]: *peaks,* 2.25 miles north-northwest of Mount Diablo (lat. 37°54'40" N, long. 121°56'10" W; sec. 26, T 1 N, R 1 W). Named on Clayton (1953) 7.5' quadrangle.

Twin Peaks [NAPA]: *peaks,* two, 1 mile apart, 5.25 miles north-northeast of Calistoga (the westernmost peak is near lat. 37°39' N, long. 122°32'55" W; at N line sec. 8, T 9 N, R 6 W). Altitudes 2719 feet and 2837 feet. Named on Detert Reservoir (1958) 7.5' quadrangle.

Twin Peaks [SAN FRANCISCO]: *peaks,* two, 0.5 mile southeast of Mount Sutro (lat. 37°45'10" N, long. 122°26'45" W). Altitude of highest is 922 feet. Named on San Francisco North (1956) 7.5' quadrangle. The peaks were called Las Papas in Spanish times—*las papas* means "the potatoes" in Spanish; they were called Twin Sisters and Mission Peaks in later times (Gudde, 1949, p. 218, 373). The south end of the ridge on which the peaks lie is called Las Papas Hill on San Mateo (1899) 15' quadrangle. The range that includes present Twin Peaks has the name "Mission Mountains" on Wackenreuder's (1861) map.

Twin Peaks [SANTA CLARA]: *peaks,* two, nearly 5 miles north-northeast of Mount Madonna (lat. 37°04'45" N, long. 121°41'15" W). Named on Mount Madonna (1955) 7.5' quadrangle.

Twin Sisters [SOLANO]: *peaks,* two, 8 miles west-northwest of Fairfield (lat. 38°18'20" N, long. 122°10'10" W; sec. 2, 3, T 5 N, R 3 W). Altitudes 2177 and 2259 feet. Named on Mount George (1951) 7.5' quadrangle.

Twin Sisters: see **Twin Peaks** [SAN FRANCISCO].

Twin Sloughs [SOLANO]: *water features,* 4.5 miles south of Fairfield in marsh (lat. 38°11'05" N, long. 122°03'20" W). Named on Fairfield South (1949) 7.5' quadrangle.

Twin Trees Station: see **Palo Alto** [SANTA CLARA].

Two Brothers: see **The Brothers** [CONTRA COSTA].

Two Rock [SONOMA]:

(1) *relief feature,* nearly 2 miles west-southwest of Cazadero (lat. 38°31'10" N, long. 123°06'50" W; sec. 19, T 8 N, R 11 W). Named on Cazadero (1978) 7.5' quadrangle.

(2) *village,* 4.5 miles southeast of Bloomfield (lat. 38°16' N, long. 122°47'30" W). Named on Two Rock (1954) 7.5' quadrangle. Postal authorities established Two Rocks post office in 1857, discontinued it in 1858, reestablished it in 1863, discontinued it in 1877, reestablished it with the name "Two Rock" in 1914, and discontinued it in 1953—the name is a translation of the designation of a nearby relief feature called Dos Piedras (Salley, p. 226).

Two Rock Creek: see **Stemple Creek** [MARIN].

Two Rock Ranch Station Military Reservation [MARIN-SONOMA]: *military installation,* 5.5 miles southeast of Bloomfield near the village of Two Rock (lat. 38°15' N, long. 122°47'30" W). Named on Point Reyes NE (1954) and Two Rock (1954) 7.5' quadrangles. The installation is mainly in Sonoma County, but extends southwest into Marin County 6 miles east of Tomales

Two Rocks [SONOMA]: *relief feature,* 2 miles north of the village of Bodega Bay (lat. 38°21'45" N, long. 123°02'25" W). Named on Bodega Head (1942) 7.5' quadrangle.

Two Rocks: see **Two Rock** [SONOMA] (2).

Tyrone [SONOMA]: *locality,* 4 miles northwest of Occidental (lat. 38°26'55" N, long. 123°00' W; near SE cor. sec. 18, T 7 N, R 10 W). Named on Camp Meeker (1954) and Duncans Mills (1979) 7.5' quadrangles. Postal authorities established Tyrone post office in 1877, discontinued it in 1881, reestablished it in 1882, and discontinued it in 1883; the name is said to have been from a lumber mill (Salley, p. 227).

Tyrone Gulch [SONOMA]: *canyon,* 1 mile long, 4 miles south of Guerneville (lat. 38°26'30" N, long. 123°00'20" W); Tyrone is near the mouth of the canyon. Named on Duncans Mills (1979) 7.5' quadrangle

Tyson Lake [ALAMEDA]: *lake,* 425 feet long, 3 miles east-northeast of downtown Oakland (lat. 37°49'20" N, long. 122°13'05" W). Named on Oakland East (1959) 7.5' quadrangle. The name is for Dr. James Tyson, whose estate was near the lake (Mosier and Mosier, p. 89-90).

Tysons Lagoon: see **Tule Pond** [ALAMEDA].

Tzabaco [SONOMA]: *land grant,* at and near Geyserville. Named on Geyserville (1955), Jimtown (1955), and Warm Springs Dam (1978) 7.5' quadrangles. Jose German Peña received 4 leagues in 1843, and his heirs claimed 15,439 acres patented in 1859 (Cowan, p. 106).

—U—

Ualtis Creek: see **Ulatis Creek** [SOLANO].

Ulatis Creek [SOLANO]: *stream,* flows 11 miles to lowlands 1.5 miles east of downtown Vacaville (lat. 38°21'20" N, long. 121°57'55" W). Named on Allendale (1953), Elmira (1953), and Mount Vaca (1951) 7.5' quadrangles. United States Board on Geographic Names (1933, p. 780) rejected the name "Ualtis Creek" for the feature. The name "Ulatis" evidently is from the designation of Indians who lived in the neighborhood (Kroeber, p. 65).

Ulistac [SANTA CLARA]: *land grant,* 2 miles south-southeast of Alviso. Named on Milpitas (1961) 7.5' quadrangle. Marcelo Pico and an Indian called Cristobal received 0.5 league in 1845; J.D. Hoppe claimed 2217 acres patented in 1868 (Cowan, p. 106). Kroeber (p. 65) considered the name "Ulistac" to be of Indian origin.

Ulmar [ALAMEDA]: *locality,* 4 miles southwest of Altamont along Southern Pacific Railroad (lat. 37°42'10" N, long. 121°42'50" W). Named on Altamont (1953) 7.5' quadrangle.

Umunhum: see **Mount Umunhum** [SANTA CLARA].

Uncle John Creek [NAPA]: *stream,* flows nearly 1 mile to Moore Creek 5.5 miles northeast of Saint Helena (lat. 38°33'35" N, long. 122°23'55" W; sec. 10, T 8 N, R 5 W). Named on Saint Helena (1960) 7.5' quadrangle.

Uncle Sam Canyon [CONTRA COSTA]: *canyon,* drained by a stream that flows less than 1 mile to Mitchell Creek nearly 3 miles northwest of Mount Diablo (lat. 37°54'40" N, long. 121°56'50" W; near NW cor. sec. 26, T 1 N, R 1 W). Named on Clayton (1953) 7.5' quadrangle.

Uncle Sam Rock: see **Colorado Reef**, under **Point Montara** [SAN MATEO].

Underwood Gulch: see **Soda Gulch** [SAN MATEO].

Union [NAPA]: *locality,* 2.25 miles northwest of downtown Napa along Southern Pacific Railroad (lat. 38°19'20" N, long. 122°18'35" W). Named on Napa (1951) 7.5' quadrangle. California Mining Bureau's (1917a) map has the name "Upton" at or near present Union.

Union: see **Unon City** [ALAMEDA].

Union Avenue: see **Campbell** [SANTA CLARA].

Union City [ALAMEDA]: *city,* 5 miles north of downtown Newark (lat. 37°36' N, long. 122°03' W). Named on Newark (1959) 7.5' quadrangle. Newark (1948) 7.5' quadrangle has the name "Union City" on a small community near the west edge of present Union City (lat. 37°35'45" N, long. 122°05'20" W). According to Hoover, Rensch, and Rensch (p. 17), John M. Horner bought 110 acres in 1850 and laid out a town that he called Union City; then Henry C. Smith bought 465 acres next to Horner's Union City and began selling lots in 1851 in his own town of New Haven; finally Strode and Jones bought 750 acres south and west of the first two towns and laid out the town of Alvarado in 1852. Horner took the name "Union" from a river steamer, *The Union,* that he purchased and used to carry agricultural produce from Union City to San Francisco; the steamer was made in Union City, New Jersey (Mosier and Mosier, p. 90). In 1853 New Haven took the name of neighboring Alvarado, and in 1958 Alvarado and Decoto consolidated to form a new city that took the name "Union City" (Hoover, Rensch, and Rensch, p. 17). Postal authorities established Union post office 20 miles south of Oakland in 1851 and discontinued it in 1853; they established Union City post office in 1959 (Salley, p. 227), the year that Union City incorporated.

Union Creek [SOLANO]: *stream,* flows 4 miles to marsh 4.25 miles west of Denverton (lat. 38°13'45" N, long. 121°58'30" W). Named on Denverton (1953) and Elmira (1953) 7.5' quadrangles.

Union Creek: see **West Union Creek** [SAN MATEO].

University Avenue: see **West Berkeley** [ALAMEDA].

University Park: see **Palo Alto** [SANTA CLARA].

Upper Bean Hollow Lake: ee **Bean Hollow Lake** [SAN MATEO].

Upper Bohn Lake: see **Aetna Springs** [NAPA].

Upper Crystal Springs Reservoir [SAN MATEO]: *lake,* 2.5 miles long, center 5 miles south of downtown San Mateo (lat. 37°29'45" N, long. 122°20' W); the lake is southwest of Lower Crystal Springs Reservoir, and separated from it by a low dam that forms a causeway. Named on San Mateo (1956) and Woodside (1961) 7.5' quadrangles. Upper Crystal Springs Reservoir and Lower Crystal Springs Reservoir together are called Crystal Springs Lake on San Mateo (1915) 15' quadrangle. The lake that occupied the lower part of present Upper Crystal Springs Reservoir before 1877 was referred to in early times at Laguna de Raimundo, Laguna Grande, Harrington's Pond, Byrnes' Lake, and The Laguna (Brown, p. 74). The valley around and for about 2 miles southeast of this earlier lake was called Cañada de Raimundo in Spanish times; the stream in the valley is called Cañada Raimundo Creek (Brown, p. 16, 74).

Upper Emerald Lake [SAN MATEO]: *lake,* 550 feet long, 2.5 miles southwest of downtown Redwood City (lat. 37°27'35" N, long. 122°15'30" W); the lake is 0.5 mile south-southeast of Lower Emerald Lake. Named on Woodside (1961) 7.5' quadrangle.

Upper Penitencia Creek [SANTA CLARA]: *stream,* flows 11 miles to Coyote Creek 2.5 miles north-northeast of downtown San Jose (lat. 37°22'05" N, long. 121°52'45" W). Named on Calaveras Reservoir (1961), Mount Day (1955), San Jose East (1961), and San Jose West (1961) 7.5' quadrangles. Hare's (1872) map has the name "Penetencia Creek." Both Upper Penitencia Creek and Lower Penitencia Creek are called Penitencia Creek on San Jose (1899) 15' quadrangle, although they are shown as separate streams—United States Board on Geographic Names (1962a, p. 13, 18) rejected the name "Penitencia Creek" for both streams. Gudde (1949, p. 257) noted that the name "Arroyo de la Penitencia" appears on a map of 1840. Whitney (p. 51) mentioned that Arroyo de la Penitencia also is called Arroyo Aguage.

Upper San Antonio Valley [SANTA CLARA]: *valley,* 3.5 miles west of Mount Stakes on upper reaches of Jumpoff Creek (lat. 37°19' N, long. 121°28'15" W); the valley is south of San Antonio Valley. Named on Mount Stakes (1955) 7.5' quadrangle.

Upper San Leandro Reservoir [ALAMEDA-CONTRA COSTA]: *lake,* on Alameda-Contra Costa County line, behind a dam on San Leandro Creek 10 miles east-southeast of downtown Oakland (lat. 37°45'50" N, long. 122°05'45" W). Named on Las Trampas Ridge (1959) and Oakland East (1959) 7.5' quadrangles.

Upton: see **Union** [NAPA].

Uval Creek: see **Bull Run Creek** [SAN MATEO].

Uvas: see **Bradleys Store** [SANTA CLARA].

Uvas Creek [SANTA CLARA]: *stream,* flows 25 miles to a point 3 miles south-southeast of Gilroy, beyond which the stream is called Carnadero Creek. Named on Chittenden (1955), Gilroy (1955), Loma Prieta (1955), and Mount Madonna (1955) 7.5' quadrangles. On Morgan Hill (1917) 15' quadrangle, Uvas Creek appears to join Bodfish Creek to form Carnadero Creek 3 miles west of Gilroy, but the relation of the three streams is unclear on the map.

Uvas Creek: see **Little Uvas Creek** [SANTA CLARA].

Uvas Reservoir [SANTA CLARA]: *lake,* 2 miles long, behind a dam on Uvas Creek nearly 4 miles north-northeast of Mount Madonna (lat. 37°03'55" N, long. 121°41'25" W). Named on Mount Madonna (1955, photorevised 1968 and 1973) 7.5' quadrangle.

– V –

Vaca: see **Elmira** [SOLANO]; **Mount Vaca** [NAPA-SOLANO].

Vaca Canyon [CONTRA COSTA]: *canyon,* 2 miles long, opens into Alhambra Valley 6.25 miles north-northeast of Orinda (lat. 37°57'55" N, long. 122°08'50" W). Named on Briones Valley (1959) 7.5' quadrangle. Waring (p. 208) noted that two springs, called Ferndale Springs, were located in Vaca Canyon and provided water to a bottling works; the water was noticeably carbonated.

Vaca Mountains [NAPA-SOLANO]: *range,* south of Putah Creek on Napa-Solano County line; Blue Ridge (2) is at the crest of the range. Named on Capell Valley (1951), Fairfield North (1951), Monticello Dam (1959), and Mount Vaca (1951) 7.5' quadrangles. United States Board on Geographic Names (1970a, p. 3) gave the name "Blue Mountains" as a variant, and noted that the name "Vaca" commemorates the Vaca family, early residents of the region.

Vaca Peak: see **Mount Vaca** [NAPA-SOLANO].

Vacation: see **Vacation Beach** [SONOMA].

Vacation Beach [SONOMA]: *settlement,* 1.25 miles southwest of Guerneville along Russian River (lat. 38°29'20" N, long. 123°00'45" W; on S line sec. 31, T 8 N, R 10 W). Named on Duncans Mills (1979) 7.5' quadrangle. Postal authorities established Vacation post office, named for Vacation Beach, in 1904 and discontinued it in 1941 (Salley, p. 228).

Vaca Valley [SOLANO]: *valley,* at and northwest of Vacaville. Named on Allendale (1953), Elmira (1953), Fairfield North (1951), and Mount Vaca (1951) 7.5' quadrangles.

Vacaville [SOLANO]: *city,* 8 miles north-northeast of Fairfield (lat. 38°21'05" N, long. 121°59'35" W). Named on Elmira (1953) and Fairfield North (1951, photorevised 1968 and 1973) 7.5' quadrangles. Postal authorities established Vacaville post office in 1854 (Frickstad, p. 193), and the city incorporated in 1892. Manuel Vaca deeded 9 square miles of his Los Putos grant to William McDaniel in 1850 with the understanding that McDaniel would lay out a town on one of the square miles, give Vaca certain town lots, and name the place Vacaville; the town plat was filed in 1851 (Hoover, Rensch, and Rensch, p. 522-523). Postal authorities established Nut Tree post office 2.5 miles northeast of Vacaville post office in 1962 at a roadside attraction that Edwin Power started in 1921 when he set up a stand under a huge black-walnut tree (Salley, p. 157).

Vacaville Junction [SOLANO]: *locality,* 4 miles south-southeast of Vacaville along Sacramento Northern Railroad (lat. 38°17'50" N, long. 121°57'50" W; sec. 10, T 5 N, R 1 W). Named on Elmira (1953) 7.5' quadrangle.

Vale [SOLANO]: *locality,* 7 miles east-southeast of Elmira along Sacramento Northern Railroad (lat. 38°19'15" N, long. 121°47'05" W; near W line sec. 32, T 6 N, R 2 E); nearly 2 miles west-northwest of the site of Maine Prairie. Named on Dozier (1952) 7.5' quadrangle. Called Maine Prairie Sta. on Maine Prairie (1916) 7.5' quadrangle, which shows the place along Oakland Antioch and Eastern Railroad.

Vallecitos Creek [ALAMEDA]: *stream,* flows 5 miles to Arroyo de la Laguna at Sunol (lat. 37°35'40" N, long. 121°53' W); the stream drains Vallecitos Valley. Named on La Costa Valley (1960) 7.5' quadrangle.

Vallecitos Valley [ALAMEDA]: *valley,* 2 miles east of Sunol along Vallecitos Creek (lat. 37°36' N, long., 121°50'30" W). Named on La Costa Valley (1960) 7.5' quadrangle.

Valle de San Jose [ALAMEDA]: *land grant,* at and northeast of Sunol. Named on Altamont (1953), Dublin (1961), La Costa Valley (1960), Livermore (1961), Mendenhall Springs (1956), and Niles (1961) 7.5' quadrangles. Antonio Maria Pico and Antonio Maria Sunol received the land in 1839; Sunol and Bernal claimed 48,436 acres patented in 1865 (Cowan, p. 80).

Vallejo [SOLANO]: *city,* 15 miles southwest of Fairfield along Mare Island Strait (downtown near lat. 38°06'10" N, long. 122°15'20" W). Named on Benicia (1959), Cordelia (1951), Cuttings Wharf (1949), and Mare Island (1959) 7.5' quadrangles. Postal authorities established Vallejo post office in 1851, discontinued it in 1853, and reestablished it in 1855 (Frickstad, p. 193). The city incorporated in 1868. Mariano G. Vallejo founded the town in 1850 and offered land and money to the state legislature for public buildings if the state capital were moved to the place; the legislature moved to Vallejo early in 1852, but left almost immediately (Hoover, Rensch, and Rensch, p. 521-522). Postal authorities established East Vallejo post office in 1951 and changed the name to Springtowne in 1962 (Salley, p. 64). They established Federal Terrace post office as a branch of Vallejo post office in 1944 at a federal housing tract; they established Hillside post office as a branch of Vallejo post office at a wartime housing project in 1945, and discontinued it in 1946 (Salley, p. 73, 98).

Vallejo: see **East Valllejo**, under **Vallejo** [SOLANO]; **South Vallejo** [SOLANO].

Vallejo Bay: see **Carquinez Strait** [CONTRA COSTA-SOLANO].

Vallejo Beach [SAN MATEO]: *beach,* 3 miles northwest of downtown Half Moon Bay along the coast (lat. 37°29'45" N, long. 122° 27'45" W. Named on Half Moon Bay (1961) 7.5' quadrangle.

Vallejo Heights [SOLANO]: *ridge,* northwest-trending, less than 1 mile long, 1 mile north-northwest of downtown Vallejo (lat. 38° 07' N, long. 122°15'50" W). Named on Mare Island (1959) 7.5' quadrangle. Called Vallejo Hill on Mare Island (1916) 15' quadrangle.

Vallejo Hill: see **Vallejo Heights** [SOLANO].

Vallejo Junction [CONTRA COSTA]: *locality,* 6 miles west-northwest of Martinez at the south terminus of a railroad ferry across Carquinez Strait to Vallejo [SOLANO] (lat. 38°03'15" N, long. 122° 13'45" W). Named on Karquines (1898) 15' quadrangle.

Vallejo Reservoir: see **Swanzy Reservoir** [SOLANO].

Vallejo's Mills: see **Niles District** [ALAMEDA].

Vallejo Sulphur Springs: see **Sulphur Springs** [SOLANO].

Vallejo White Sulphur Springs: see **Sulphur Springs** [SOLANO].

Vallemar [SAN MATEO]: *district,* 4 miles north of Montara Knob in Calera Valley (lat. 37°36'45" N, long. 122°28'45" W). Named on Montara Mountain (1956) 7.5' quadrangle. Residents of the place voted in 1957 to join neighboring communities and form the new city of Pacifica.

Valle Vista [CONTRA COSTA]: *locality,* 4.5 miles south-southeast of Orinda (lat. 37°49'20" N, long. 122°08' W; near NE cor. sec. 25, T 1 S, R 3 W). Named on Oakland East (1959) 7.5' quadrangle. Concord (1915) 15' quadrangle shows the place located along Oakland Antioch and Eastern Railroad.

Valley Crossing [SONOMA]: *locality,* 3.25 miles north-northwest of the village of Stewarts Point along South Fork Gualala River (lat. 38°42' N, long. 123°24'45" W). Named on Stewarts Point (1978) 7.5' quadrangle.

Valley Ford [SONOMA]: *village,* 8 miles southwest of Sebastopol (lat. 38°19'05" N, long. 122°55'25" W). Named on Valley Ford (1954) 7.5' quadrangle. Postal authorities established Valley Ford post office in 1876; the name is from the crossing of Estero Americano at the place (Salley, p. 229).

Valley of Nappa: see **Napa Valley** [NAPA].

Valley of San Jose: see **Santa Clara Valley** [SANTA CLARA].

Valley of the Moon [SONOMA]: *valley,* along Sonoma Creek from northwest of Sonoma to near Glen Ellen. Named on Glen Ellen (1954), Kenwood (1954), and Sonoma (1951) 7.5' quadrangles. On Goddard's (1857) map, the name "Sonoma Vy." extends north-northwest through present Valley of the Moon.

Valona [CONTRA COSTA]: *town,* 5.5 miles west-northwest of Martinez (lat. 38°03'10" N, long. 122°13'20" W). Named on Benicia (1959) 7.5' quadrangle.

Valpe Creek [ALAMEDA-SANTA CLARA]: *stream,* heads in Alameda County and flows 5.5 miles to Alameda Creek 3.25 miles northeast of Mount Day in Santa Clara County (lat. 37°27'20" N, long. 121°39'30" W; sec. 33, T 5 S, R 3 E); the stream heads on Valpe Ridge. Named on Mendenhall Springs (1956) and Mount Day (1955) 7.5' quadrangles.

Valpe Ridge [ALAMEDA-SANTA CLARA]: *ridge,* north- to west-trending, 14 miles long, 5 miles north-northeast of Mount Day (lat. 37°29' N, long. 121°39'30" W); mainly in Santa Clara County, but extends northwest for 7.5 miles into Alameda County. Named on Eylar Mountain (1955), La Costa Valley (1960), Mendenhall Springs (1956), and Mount Day (1955) 7.5' quadrangles. Pleasanton (1906) 15' quadrangle shows Valpe Ridge extending northwest to include present Apperson Ridge. The misspelled name commemorates Calvin Valpey, who settled at the ridge in 1850; the feature first was called Pine Ridge (Mosier and Mosier, p. 91).

Valta: see **Elmira** [SOLANO].

Van Buren Creek [SONOMA]: *stream,* flows 3 miles to Mark West Creek 5 miles east-southeast of Mark West Springs (lat. 38°30'40" N, long. 122°38'15" W; sec. 28, T 8 N, R 7 W). Named on Calistoga (1958) and Mark West Springs (1958) 7.5' quadrangles.

Vance Canyon [SANTA CLARA]: *canyon,* drained by a stream that flows 1.5 miles to Packwood Valley 4.5 miles west of Mount Sizer (lat. 37°12'25" N, long. 121°35'45" W; sec. 25, T 8 S, R 3 E). Named on Mount Sizer (1955) 7.5' quadrangle.

Van Court's Hill: see **Belmont Hill** [SAN MATEO].

Vanden [SOLANO]: *locality,* 4.5 miles south-southeast of Vacaville along Southern Pacific Railroad (lat. 38°17'10" N, long. 121° 58' W). Named on Elmira (1917) 7.5' quadrangle. Postal authorities established Vanden post office in 1897 and discontinued it in 1899 (Frickstad, p. 193).

Van Horn Flats [SANTA CLARA]: *area,* 1.5 miles west of Mount Day (lat. 37°25'15" N, long. 121°43'30" W; sec. 11, T 6 S, R 2 E). Named on Mount Day (1955) 7.5' quadrangle.

Van Ness Creek [NAPA]: *stream,* flows 3.5 miles to Saint Helena Creek 6.25 miles north of Calistoga (lat. 38°40'05" N, long. 122° 35'10" W; sec. 36, T 10 N, R 7 W). Named on Detert Reservoir (1958) 7.5' quadrangle.

Van Sickle Island [SOLANO]: *island,* 4.5 miles south-southwest of Birds Landing (2) along Suisun Bay between Montezuma Slough and Spoonbill Creek (lat. 38°04'15" N, long. 121°53'30" W). Named on Antioch North (1978) and Honker Bay (1953) 7.5' quadrangles. Called Jones I. on Ringgold's (1850c) map, which shows Pt. Hansen at the east end of the island. United States Board on Geographic Names (1933, p. 787) rejected the form "Van Sickle's Island" for the name.

Van Wych Canyon: see **Van Wyck Creek** [MARIN].

Van Wyck Camp [MARIN]: *locality,* 5.5 miles southwest of downtown San Rafael (lat. 37°54'30" N, long. 122°35'45" W). Named on San Rafael (1954) 7.5' quadrangle.

Van Wyck Creek [MARIN]: *stream,* flows 1.25 miles to Alpine Lake 5.25 miles west-southwest of downtown San Rafael (lat. 37° 56'50" N, long. 122°37'20" W). Named on San Rafael (1954) 7.5' quadrangle. The canyon of the stream is called Van Wych Canyon on Mount Tamalpais (1950) 15' quadrangle. Teather (p. 85) associated the name with Sidney M. Van Wyck, Jr., who was a leader in the creation of Mount Tamalpais state park.

Vasona: see **Vasona Junction** [SANTA CLARA].

Vasona Creek [SANTA CLARA]: *stream,* flows nearly 1.5 miles to end in lowlands 1.25 miles east-northeast of Saratoga (lat. 37°15'55" N, long. 122°00'15" W). Named on Cupertino (1961, photorevised 1968 and 1973) 7.5' quadrangle. On Cupertino (1961) and San Jose West (1961) 7.5' quadrangles, present Sobey Creek is called Vasona Creek; United States Board on Geographic Names (1972, p. 3) listed the variant name "Vasona Creek" for Sobey Creek.

Vasona Junction [SANTA CLARA]: *locality,* 1.5 miles north-northeast of downtown Los Gatos along Southern Pacific Railroad, where two rail lines meet (lat. 37°15'25" N, long. 121°57'50" W). Named on San Jose West (1961) 7.5' quadrangle. Called Vasona on California Mining Bureau's (1917b) map. According to Patricia Loomis (*San Jose Mercury,* February 2, 1981), Albert August Vollmer asked officials of Southern Pacific Railroad about 1900 to put a flag stop near his home; when the officials agreed, they told Vollmer to name the stop, and he called it Vasona for a pony that he had owned.

Vasona Reservoir [SANTA CLARA]: *lake,* nearly 1 mile long, behind a dam on Los Gatos Creek 2 miles north-northeast of downtown Los Gatos (lat. 37°14'50" N, long. 121°57'50" W). Named on Los Gatos (1953) 7.5' quadrangle.

Vasquez Peak [SANTA CLARA]: *peak,* 4.5 miles east-southeast of Gilroy Hot Springs (lat. 37°04'50" N, long. 121°24' W; near W line sec. 11, T 10 S, R 5 E). Altitude 2210 feet. Named on Gilroy Hot Springs (1955) 7.5' quadrangle.

Veale Tract [CONTRA COSTA]: *area,* 4 miles east-northeast of Brentwood (lat. 37°58' N, long. 121°37' W). Named on Brentwood (1978) and Woodward Island (1978) 7.5' quadrangles.

Veeder Mountain: see **Mount Veeder** [NAPA-SONOMA].

Venado [SONOMA]: *locality,* 6.5 miles northeast of Cazadero (lat. 38°36'20" N, long. 123°00'25" W; near N line sec. 30, T 9 N, R 10 W). Named on Cazadero (1978) 7.5' quadrangle. Postal authorities established Venado post office in 1921 and discontinued it in 1941 (Frickstad, p. 199).

Venice Beach [SAN MATEO]: *beach,* 1.5 miles northwest of downtown Half Moon Bay along the coast (lat. 37°28'50" N, long. 122° 27'05" W). Named on Half Moon Bay (1961) 7.5' quadrangle.

Verano [SONOMA]: *locality,* 1 mile northwest of Sonoma (lat. 38° 18'05" N, long. 122°28'25" W). Named on Sonoma (1951) 7.5' quadrangle.

Verde Canyon [MARIN]: *canyon,* drained by a stream that flows 2.5 miles to Walker Creek 7.5 miles southeast of Tomales (lat. 38° 10' N, long. 122°48'40" W). Named on Point Reyes NE (1954) 7.5' quadrangle.

Verona [ALAMEDA]: *locality,* 2.25 miles north of Sunol along Western

Pacific Railroad and Southern Pacific Railroad (lat. 37°37'45" N, long. 121°52'50" W). Named on Pleasanton (1906) 15' quadrangle. The place was the station for Phoebe Hurst's estate, La Hacienda del Pozo de Verona, for which it was named (Mosier and Mosier, p. 91).

Vestal: see **Roblar** [SONOMA].

Veteran Heights [NAPA]: *locality,* 5 miles north-northeast of Saint Helena (lat. 38°34'25" N, long. 122°26'05" W). Named on Saint Helena (1960) 7.5' quadrangle.

Veterans Home: see **Yountville** [NAPA].

Veterans Peak [NAPA]: *peak,* nearly 2 miles south-southwest of Yountville (lat. 38°23' N, long. 122°22'35" W); the peak is less than 1 mile south-southwest of State Veterans Home. Altitude 1209 feet. Named on Rutherford (1951) 7.5' quadrangle.

Vicente Creek: see **San Vicente Creek** [SAN MATEO].

Vichy Spring: see **New Almaden** [SANTA CLARA].

Vichy Springs [NAPA]: *locality,* 3 miles north-northeast of downtown Napa (lat. 38°20'20" N, long. 122°15'40" W). Named on Napa (1951) 7.5' quadrangle. A spring called Napa Vichy Spring was the basis of a resort and a water-bottling enterprise at the place (Bradley, p. 280).

Villa Grande [SONOMA]: *settlement,* 2.5 miles southwest of Guerneville along Russian River (lat. 38°38'25" N, long. 123°01'25" W). Named on Duncans Mills (1979) 7.5' quadrangle. Postal authorities established Villa Grande post office in 1921 (Salley, p. 232).

Vincent Landing [MARIN]: *locality,* 2.5 miles southwest of Tomales along the northeast side of Tomales Bay (lat. 38°13'05" N, long. 122°56'20" W). Named on Tomales (1954) 7.5' quadrangle.

Vineburg [SONOMA]: *locality,* nearly 2 miles southeast of Sonoma (lat. 38°16'20" N, long. 122°26'15" W). Named on Sonoma (1951) 7.5' quadrangle. Called Vineyard on Napa (1902) 30' quadrangle. Postal authorities established Vineburg post office in 1897, discontinued it in 1900, and reestablished it in 1902 (Frickstad, p. 199).

Vine Hill [CONTRA COSTA]: *district,* 2.25 miles east of downtown Martinez (lat. 38°00'30" N, long. 122°05'40" W). Named on Vine Hill (1959) 7.5' quadrangle.

Vine Hill [SONOMA]: *ridge,* south-southeast-trending, 1.5 miles long, 5.25 miles north-northwest of Sebastopol (lat. 38°28'25" N, long. 122°51'45" W). Named on Sebastopol (1954) 7.5' quadrangle.

Vineyard: see **Vineburg** [SONOMA].

Violet [SOLANO]: *locality,* 4.5 miles south-southwest of Allendale along Southern Pacific Railroad (lat. 38°23' N, long. 121°58'15" W). Named on Wolfskill (1917) 7.5' quadrangle.

Vision: see **Mount Vision** [MARIN].

Vision Hill: see **Mount Vision** [MARIN].

Visitacion: see **Brisbane** [SAN MATEO].

Visitacion City: see **Brisbane** [SAN MATEO].

Visitacion Point [SAN MATEO]: *promontory,* 2.5 miles north-northeast of downtown South San Francisco along San Francisco Bay (lat. 37°41'35" N, long. 122°23'55" W). Named on San Francisco South (1947) 7.5' quadrangle. Called Visitation Pt. on San Mateo (1915) 15' quadrangle, but United States Board on Geographic Names (1949a, p. 4) rejected this form of the name; the Board pointed out that the name is from Cañada de Guadalupe y la Visitacion grant, where the promontory is located. The feature now protrudes into landfill. San Mateo (1899) 15' quadrangle has the name "Visitation Pt." at a place about 0.5 mile farther south-southeast on the south side of the mouth of Guadalupe Valley.

Visitacion Valley [SAN FRANCISCO-SAN MATEO]: *valley,* 3 miles southeast of Mount Davidson on San Francisco-San Mateo County line (lat. 37°42'30" N, long. 122°24'50" W). Named on San Francisco South (1956) 7.5' quadrangle. Called Visitation Valley on San Mateo (1915) 15' quadrangle, but United States Board on Geographic Names (1949a, p. 14) rejected this form of the name. The feature also was called Schwerin Valley for Henry Schwerin, a dairyman who lived there in the 1850's (Brown, p. 98).

Visitation Point: see **Visitacion Point** [SAN MATEO].

Visitation Valley: see **Visitacion Valley** [SAN FRANCISCO-SAN MATEO].

Vista Grande: see **Daly City** [SAN MATEO].

Volanti Slough [SOLANO]: *water feature,* joins Suisun Slough 4.5 miles south of Fairfield (lat. 38°10'50" N, long. 122°02'45" W). Named on Fairfield South (1949) 7.5' quadrangle. United States Board on Geographic Names (1983c, p. 6) approved the name "Navy Point" for a promontory on the west shore of Suisun Slough opposite the mouth of Volanti Slough (lat. 38°10'45" N, long. 122° 02'51" W).

Volimer Peak [CONTRA COSTA]: *peak,* 2.25 miles west of Orinda on San Pablo Ridge (lat. 37°53' N, long. 122°13'15" W). Altitude 1905 feet. Named on Briones Valley (1959) 7.5' quadrangle. Called Bald Peak on Concord (1897) 15' quadrangle, but United States Board on Geographic Names (1960b, p. 19) rejected this designation for the feature.

Vulture Ridge [SONOMA]: *ridge,* north- to northwest-trending, 0.5 mile long, 7 miles north-northeast of Cazadero (lat. 38°37'10" N, long. 123°00'50" W). Named on Cazadero (1978) 7.5' quadrangle.

– W –

Waddell Beach: see **Año Nuevo Creek** [SAN MATEO].

Waddell Creek: see **West Waddell Creek** [SAN MATEO].

Waddell's Landing: see **Waddell Beach**, under **Año Nuevo Creek** [SAN MATEO].

Waddell's Wharf: see **Waddell Beach**, under **Año Nuevo Creek** [SAN MATEO].

Wagoner Field: see **Livermore Naval Air Station**, under **Livermore** [ALAMEDA].

Walalla River: see **Gualala River** [SONOMA].

Walbridge Ridge [SONOMA]: *ridge,* generally northwest-trending, 2.5 miles long, 5.25 miles west-southwest of Skaggs Springs (lat. 38°39'30" N, long. 123°07' W). Named on Tombs Creek (1978) and Warm Springs Dam (1978) 7.5' quadrangles.

Walden: see **Locust** [CONTRA COSTA].

Walden Spur: see **Pottery** [ALAMEDA].

Waldo [MARIN]: *locality,* 1.25 miles northwest of downtown Sausalito along Western Pacific Railroad (lat. 37°52'20" N, long. 122° 30'10" W). Named on Point Bonita (1954) 7.5' quadrangle.

Waldo Point [MARIN]: *promontory,* 7 miles south-southeast of downtown San Rafael along Richardson Bay (lat. 37°52'15" N, long. 122°30'15" W). Named on Tamalpais (1897) 15' quadrangle.

Waldrue Heights [SONOMA]: *settlement,* 2.25 miles west of Glen Ellen (lat. 38°21'55" N, long. 122°33'55" W; sec. 18, T 6 N, R 6 W). Named on Glen Ellen (1954) 7.5' quadrangle.

Walker Canyon [CONTRA COSTA]: *canyon,* drained by a stream that flows 1.25 miles to Ygnacio Valley 4.5 miles west-northwest of Mount Diablo (lat. 37°54'15" N, long. 121°59'20" W). Named on Clayton (1953) 7.5' quadrangle.

Walker Canyon [SONOMA]: *canyon,* drained by a stream that flows 1.25 miles to Briggs Creek 4 miles west of Mount Saint Helena (lat. 38°40'35" N, long. 122°42'10" W; near N line sec. 36, T 10 N, R 8 W). Named on Mount Saint Helena (1959) 7.5' quadrangle.

Walker Creek [MARIN]: *stream,* formed by the confluence of Arroyo Sausal and Salmon Creek, flows 15 miles to Tomales Bay 2 miles south-southwest of Tomales (lat. 38°13'20" N, long. 122° 55'15" W). Named on Point Reyes NE (1954) and Tomales (1954) 7.5' quadrangles. United States Board on Geographic Names (1943, p. 14) rejected the names "Arroyo San Antonio," "Arroyo Sausal," "Keyes Creek," "Keys Creek," and "Salmon Creek" for the stream, or for any part of it. The name "Walker" commemorates the family of Lewis W. Walker, an early landowner in the neighborhood (Mason, 1976b, p. 153).

Walker Gulch [SAN MATEO]: *canyon,* drained by a stream that flows 1 mile to Purisima Creek 4 miles west-northwest of Skeggs Point (lat. 37°26'15" N, long. 122°22'05" W). Named on Woodside (1961) 7.5' quadrangle.

Wallace: see **Mount Wallace** [ALAMEDA].

Wallace Creek [SONOMA]: *stream,* flows 4 miles to Mill Creek (1) 2.5 miles west-southwest of Healdsburg (lat. 38°35'55" N, long. 122°54'40" W). Named on Geyserville (1955) and Guerneville (1955) 7.5' quadrangles.

Wallet Canyon [NAPA]: *canyon,* drained by a stream that flows less than 1 mile to Gosling Canyon 4.5 miles south-southeast of Berryessa Peak (lat. 38°36'20" N, long. 122°09'05" W). Named on Lake Berryessa (1959) 7.5' quadrangle.

Wall Point [CONTRA COSTA]: *peak,* 2.5 miles southwest of Mount Diablo (lat. 37°51'25" N, long. 121°57'10" W; sec. 10, T 1 S, R 1 W). Named on Diablo (1953) 7.5' quadrangle.

Wall Point: see **Point Wall** [SOLANO].

Wall Springs: see **Mirabel Park** [SONOMA].

Walnut Creek [CONTRA COSTA]:

(1) *stream,* formed by the confluence of San Ramon Creek and Las Trampas Creek, flows 10 miles to Pacheco Creek 3.5 miles east of Martinez (lat. 38°01'25" N, long. 122°04'10" W); the stream heads in the city of Walnut Creek. Named on Vine Hill (1959) and Walnut Creek (1959) 7.5' quadrangles. Called Arroyo de las Nueces on a diseño of Arroyo de las Nueces y Bolbones grant made in 1834 (Becker, 1969). The stream also was called Arroyo de los Nogales in the early days because of black-walnut trees that grew along it—*nogales* means "walnuts" in Spanish, and *nueces* means "nuts" (Gudde, 1949, p. 382).

(2) *city,* 8 miles west of Mount Diablo (civic center near lat. 37°54'10" N, long. 122°03'30" W); the city is along Walnut Creek (1). Named on Walnut Creek (1959) 7.5' quadrangle. Postal authorities established Walnut Creek post office in 1862 (Frickstad, p. 24), and the city incorporated in 1914.

Walnut Flat [NAPA]: *area,* 7 miles north of Saint Helena (lat. 38° 36'15" N, long. 122°29' W; on W line sec. 25, T 9 N, R 6 W). Named on Saint Helena (1960) 7.5' quadrangle.

Walpert Ridge [ALAMEDA]: *ridge,* southeast- to south-trending, 6.5 miles long, center 5 miles south-southwest of Dublin (lat. 37°38'20" N, long.

121°59'10" W). Named on Dublin (1961), Hayward (1959), and Niles (1961) 7.5' quadrangles. The name commemorates John Walpert, who owned land on the ridge (Mosier and Mosier, p. 91-92).

Walsh Landing [SONOMA]: *village,* 2.5 miles south-southeast of Plantation near the coast (lat. 38°33'20" N, long. 123°18' W). Named on Plantation (1977) 7.5' quadrangle.

Walshs Pocket [ALAMEDA]: *canyon,* drained by a stream that flows 0.5 mile to Martin Canyon 1.5 miles west-northwest of Dublin (lat. 37°42'50" N, long. 121°57'45" W; sec. 34, T 2 S, R 1 W). Named on Dublin (1961) 7.5' quadrangle. The name commemorates James Walsh, a local farmer (Mosier and Mosier, p. 92).

Walter Springs [NAPA]: *locality,* 12 miles north-northeast of Saint Helena (lat. 38°39'10" N, long. 122°21'25" W; near NE cor. sec. 12, T 9 N, R 5 W). Named on Walter Springs (1959) 7.5' quadrangle. Bradley (p. 282) used the name "Walters Springs," and noted that springs discovered at the place about 1869 were the basis of a resort.

Walters Ridge [SONOMA]: *ridge,* generally west-northwest-trending, 6 miles long, center 2.5 miles west-southwest of Big Mountain (lat. 38°42' N, long. 123°11'15" W). Named on Tombs Creek (1978) 7.5' quadrangle. Skaggs Springs (1943) and Tombs Creek (1943) 7.5' quadrangles have the name on a ridge located about 2 miles northeast of present Walters Ridge.

Walters Springs: see **Walter Springs** [NAPA].

Walwood [CONTRA COSTA]: *locality,* 3 miles east of the present Walnut Creek civic center at the end of a branch of Oakland Antioch and Eastern Railroad (lat. 37°54'15" N, long. 122°00'25" W). Named on Concord (1915) 15' quadrangle.

Wanda: see **Mount Wanda**, under **Martinez** [CONTRA COSTA].

Ward Creek [ALAMEDA]: *stream,* flows 3.5 miles to lowlands 0.5 mile southeast of downtown Hayward (lat. 37°39'55" N, long. 122° 04'35" W). Named on Hayward (1959) and Newark (1959) 7.5' quadrangles. The name commemorates Charles Trobridge Ward, who owned land along the upper part of the creek in the early 1870's; the stream originally was called Sulphur Spring Creek, but the upper part was renamed Ward Creek, and the lower part retains the name "Sulphur Creek" (Mosier and Mosier, p. 92).

Ward Creek [SONOMA]: *stream,* flows 6.5 miles to Austin Creek less than 1 mile north-northwest of Cazadero (lat. 38°32'30" N, long. 123°05'20" W; near W line sec. 16, T 8 N, R 11 W). Named on Cazadero (1978) and Fort Ross (1978) 7.5' quadrangles.

Warm Springs [ALAMEDA]: *springs,* 4.5 miles southeast of Fremont civic center (lat. 37°30'10" N, long. 121°54'25" W); the springs are near Agua Caliente Creek. Named on Niles (1961) 7.5' quadrangle. Berkstresser (p. A-3) gave the names "Alameda Warm Springs" and "Mission San Jose Hot Springs" as alternates.

Warm Springs: see **Warm Springs District** [ALAMEDA].

Warm Springs Creek [SONOMA]: *stream,* flows 13 miles to Dry Creek 2 miles north-northeast of Skaggs Springs (lat. 38°43'05" N, long. 123°00'25" W; sec. 18, T 10 N, R 10 W). Named on Warm Springs Dam (1978) 7.5' quadrangle.

Warm Springs Creek: see **Agua Caliente Creek** [ALAMEDA]; **Little Warm Springs Creek** [SONOMA].

Warm Springs District [ALAMEDA]: *district,* 5 miles south-southeast of Fremont civic center in Fremont (lat. 37°29'15" N, long. 121°55'35" W). Named on Milpitas (1961) 7.5' quadrangle. San Jose (1899) 15' quadrangle has the name "Warm Springs" for the community that joined in 1956 with neighboring communities to form the new city of Fremont. The springs called Warm Springs are in the district. Thompson and West (1878, p. 27) noted a hamlet called Harrisburg, or Peacock's, that was located a short distance east of Warm Springs railroad station. Postal authorities established Harrisburgh post office in 1865 and changed the post office name to Warm Springs in 1885; the name "Harrisburgh" was for Abram Harris, who settled at the site in 1858—George W. Peacock was the first postmaster (Salley, p. 94). Postal authorities changed the name of Warm Springs post office to Warmsprings in 1895 and back to Warm Springs in 1950 (Salley, p. 234).

Warm Springs Landing: see **Mud Slough** [ALAMEDA].

Warner Canyon [MARIN]: *canyon,* 1.5 miles long, 4 miles south of downtown San Rafael (lat. 37°54'50" N, long. 122°32'05" W). Named on San Rafael (1954) 7.5' quadrangle. Dr. Alexander Warner of San Francisco had a house and tent platforms in the canyon for use during his summer visits (Teather, p. 85).

Warren Creek [SONOMA]: *stream,* flows 1.5 miles to the sea 2 miles southwest of Plantation (lat. 38°34'15" N, long. 123°20'05" W). Named on Plantation (1977) 7.5' quadrangle.

Warrington Island: see **Wheeler Island** [SOLANO].

Washerwoman's Lagoon: see **Marina District** [SAN FRANCISCO].

Washington Corners: see **Irvington District** [ALAMEDA].

Washington Slough: see **False River** [CONTRA COSTA].

Washoe [SONOMA]: *locality,* nearly 2 miles west-southwest of Cotati along Washoe Creek (lat. 38°18'50" N, long. 122°44'05" W). Named on Santa Rosa (1944) 15' quadrangle.

Washoe Creek [SONOMA]: *stream,* flows 2.5 miles to lowlands 1.5 miles west-northwest of Cotati (lat. 38°20' N, long. 122°44' W). Named on Cotati (1954) 7.5' quadrangle.

Wash Rock [SAN MATEO]: *rock,* 2.5 miles west of downtown Half Moon Bay, and 2.25 miles south-southeast of Pillar Point (lat. 37° 28'05" N, long. 122°28'30" W). Named on Half Moon Bay (1961) 7.5' quadrangle. The rock is a high point on an underwater feature called Southeast Reef (United States Coast and Geodetic Survey, p. 122).

Watercress Gulch [SONOMA]: *canyon,* drained by a stream that flows less than 1 mile to Salmon Creek (1) nearly 2 miles north of the village of Bodega Bay (lat. 38°21'35" N, long. 123°03' W). Named on Bodega Head (1972) 7.5' quadrangle.

Water Gulch [SANTA CLARA]: *canyon,* drained by a stream that flows 3.5 miles to East Fork Coyote Creek 2.25 miles southwest of Bear Mountain (lat. 37°12'15" N, long. 121°27'35" W; sec. 29, T 8 S, R 5 E). Named on Mississippi Creek (1955) and Mount Sizer (1955) 7.5' quadrangles.

Waterman Creek [SAN MATEO]: *stream,* flows 3 miles to Pescadero Creek 7 miles south-southeast of Mindego Hill just inside of Santa Cruz County (lat. 37°12'50" N, long. 122°10'30" W; near N line sec. 27, T 8 S, R 3 W). Named on Big Basin (1955) 7.5' quadrangle.

Waterman Park: see **Fairfield** [SOLANO].

Watson Canyon [CONTRA COSTA]: *canyon,* drained by a stream that flows 1.5 miles to San Ramon Valley 4.25 miles southeast of Danville (lat. 37°46'20" N, long. 121°57'10" W). Named on Diablo (1953) 7.5' quadrangle.

Watson Hollow [SOLANO]: *valley,* 3 miles north-northwest of Rio Vista (lat. 38°11'40" N, long. 121°42'40" W). Named on Rio Vista (1978) 7.5' quadrangle.

Watsons [SONOMA]: *locality,* 2 miles south-southeast of Cazadero along Northwestern Pacific Railroad (lat. 38°30'25" N, long. 123° 04'10" W). Named on Skaggs (1921) 15' quadrangle.

Wauhab Ridge [ALAMEDA]: *ridge,* west- to northwest-trending, 6 miles long, 8 miles east-southeast of Sunol (lat. 38°32' N, long. 121°45'30" W). Named on La Costa Valley (1960) and Mendenhall Springs (1956) 7.5' quadrangles. The name commemorates Joshua W. Wauhab, who settled at the site in 1851 (Mosier and Mosier, p. 93).

Wayne [SANTA CLARA]: *locality,* 3 miles south of downtown Milpitas along Southern Pacific Railroad (lat. 37°23'10" N, long. 121° 53'50" W). Named on Milpitas (1961) 7.5' quadrangle.

Webb Creek [MARIN]: *stream,* flows 2.25 miles to Bolinas Bay 3.5 miles east-southeast of Bolinas (lat. 37°53'05" N, long. 122°37'40" W). Named on Bolinas (1954) and San Rafael (1954) 7.5' quadrangles. The name commemorates Johnathan E. Webb, a conservationist interested in preserving Mount Tamalpais and vicinity (Teather, p. 87).

Webb Point [CONTRA COSTA]: *promontory,* 6.25 miles north-northeast of the settlement of Bethel Island (lat. 38°05'30" N, long. 121°34'40" W); the feature is at the northeast corner of Webb Tract. Named on Bouldin Island (1978) 7.5' quadrangle.

Webb Reach [CONTRA COSTA]: *water feature,* part of San Joaquin River 6.5 miles north-northeast of the settlement of Bouldin Island (lat. 38°06' N, long. 121°35'45" W); the feature is north of Webb Tract. Named on Bouldin Island (1978) 7.5' quadrangle.

Webb's Landing: see **Webb Tract** [CONTRA COSTA].

Webb Tract [CONTRA COSTA]: *island,* 4.5 miles long, 4.5 miles north-northeast of the settlement of Bethel Island between San Joaquin River, Old River, False River, and Fishermans Cut (lat. 38°04'30" N, long. 121°36'45" W). Named on Bouldin Island (1978) and Jersey Island (1978) 7.5' quadrangles. Postal authorities established Webb's Landing post office on Webb Tract (NW quarter sec. 19, T 3 N, R 4 E) in 1873 and discontinued in 1879 (Salley, p. 236).

Weeks Creek [SAN MATEO]: *stream,* flows 1.5 miles to La Honda Creek 2 miles north of La Honda (lat. 37°20'45" N, long. 122°16'25" W; near S line sec. 2, T 7 S, R 4 W). Named on La Honda (1961) 7.5' quadrangle. The name is from Robinson J. Weeks ranch, the first American establishment in the neighborhood (Brown, p. 99).

Weeks Creek [SONOMA]: *stream,* flows 3.25 miles to Mark West Creek 4.5 miles southeast of Mark West Springs (lat. 38°30'30" N, long. 122°38'55" W; at E line sec. 29, T 8 N, R 7 W). Named on Kenwood (1954), Mark West Springs (1958), and Santa Rosa (1954) 7.5' quadrangles.

Welch Creek [ALAMEDA]: *stream,* flows 3 miles to Alameda Creek 4 miles south of Sunol (lat. 37°32'05" N, long. 121°51'05" W; at N line sec. 3, T 5 S, R 1 E). Named on La Costa Valley (1960) 7.5' quadrangle. The name is for a ranch owner (Mosier and Mosier, p. 93).

Weldon Canyon [SOLANO]: see **Mix Canyon** [SOLANO].

Wells Slough [SOLANO]: *water feature,* joins Suisun Slough 5.5 miles south-southwest of Fairfield (lat. 38°10'20" N, long. 122°03'45" W). Named on Fairfield South (1949) 7.5' quadrangle.

Werner [CONTRA COSTA]: *locality,* 5 miles east of Brentwood along Atchison, Topeka and Santa Fe Railroad (lat. 37°56'25" N, long. 121°36'25" W). Named on Woodward Island (1978) 7.5' quadrangle.

West: see **John West Ridge** [SONOMA]; **Mark West** [SONOMA].

West Berkeley [ALAMEDA]: *district,* 3 miles north-northwest of downtown Oakland near San Francisco Bay (lat. 37°52' N, long. 122°18' W). Named on San Francisco (1899) 15' quadrangle. The station along Southern Pacific Railroad in West Berkeley had the name "University Avenue" (Diller and others, p. 83).

West Bull Canyon [NAPA]: *canyon,* 1 mile long, opens into Wragg Canyon 4.5 miles northwest of Mount Vaca (lat. 38°27'10" N, long. 122°09'10" W; near E line sec. 14, T 7 N, R 3 W); the mouth of the canyon is opposite the mouth of East Bull Canyon. Named on Capell Valley (1951) 7.5' quadrangle.

West Chapman Canyon [NAPA]: *canyon,* 1 mile long, opens into Wragg Canyon 5 miles north-northwest of Mount Vaca (lat. 38°27'35" N, long. 122°09'15" W; near NE cor. sec. 14, T 7 N, R 3 W); the mouth of the canyon is opposite the mouth of East Chapman Canyon. Named on Capell Valley (1951) 7.5' quadrangle.

West Creek: see **Mark West Creek** [SONOMA].

West End: see **Alameda** [ALAMEDA].

Western Addition [SAN FRANCISCO]: *district,* 1.5 miles west-northwest of San Francisco civic center (lat. 37°47' N, long. 122° 26'45" W). Named on San Francisco North (1956) 7.5' quadrangle.

West Guernewood [SONOMA]: *settlement,* 1 mile west-southwest of Gueneville along Russian River (lat. 38°29'35" N, long. 123°00'45" W; sec. 31, T 8 N, R 10 W). Named on Duncans Mills (1979) 7.5' quadrangle.

West Hartley [CONTRA COSTA]: *locality,* 7 miles northeast of Mount Diablo (lat. 37°56'25" N, long. 121°48'45" W; near S line sec. 12, T 1 N, R 1 E). Site named on Antioch South (1953) 7.5' quadrangle. The place was a coal-mine town founded in the late 1880's; the name is from the famous West Hartley coal mine in England (Mosier, p. 7).

Westlake [SAN MATEO]: *district,* 5 miles northwest of downtown South San Francisco (lat. 37°41'55" N, long. 122°29'10" W). Named on San Francisco South (1956) 7.5' quadrangle.

West Marin Island [MARIN]: *island,* 700 feet long, 400 feet west-northwest of East Marin Island in San Rafael Bay (lat. 37°57'55" N, long. 122°28'20" W). Named on San Quentin (1959) 7.5' quadrangle. This island and East Marin Island together have the name "Marin Is." on San Francisco (1915) 15' quadrangle.

Westminister Woods [SONOMA]: *locality,* 2.5 miles northwest of Occidental (lat. 38°26'10" N, long. 122°58'20" W; sec. 21, T 7 N, R 10 W). Named on Camp Meeker (1954) 7.5' quadrangle.

West Mitchell Canyon [NAPA]: *canyon,* 1 mile long, opens into Wragg Canyon 5.5 miles north-northwest of Mount Vaca (lat. 38° 28'20" N, long. 122°09'25" W; sec. 11, T 7 N, R 3 W); the mouth of the canyon is opposite the mouth of East Mitchell Canyon. Named on Capell Valley (1951) 7.5' quadrangle.

West Napa Reservoir [NAPA]: *lake,* 225 feet long, 1.5 miles west-southwest of downtown Napa (lat. 38°17'35" N, long. 122°18'50" W). Named on Napa (1951) 7.5' quadrangle.

West Oakland: see **Oakland** [ALAMEDA].

West Peak [MARIN]: *peak,* 5 miles southwest of downtown San Rafael on Mount Tamalpais (lat. 37°55'25" N, long. 122°35'45" W). Named on San Rafael (1954) 7.5' quadrangle.

West Pittsburg [CONTRA COSTA]: *locality,* 3 miles west of Pittsburg (lat. 38°01'40" N, long. 121°56' W). Named on Honker Bay (1953) 7.5' quadrangle. Honker Bay (1918) 7.5' quadrangle has the name "West Pittsburg" at a place located 5 miles farther east along Oakland Antioch and Eastern Railroad.

West Point [MARIN]: *locality,* 5 miles southwest of downtown San Rafael on the southeast side of Mount Tamalpais (lat. 37°55' N, long. 122°35'35" W). Named on San Rafael (1954) 7.5' quadrangle.

West Point: see **Ravenswood Point** [SAN MATEO].

Westpoint Creek: see **Westpoint Slough** [SAN MATEO].

Westpoint Slough [SAN MATEO]: *water feature,* extends for 3.5 miles from Ravenswood Slough to Redwood Creek 2.5 miles north-northeast of downtown Redwood City (lat. 37°31'05" N, long. 122°12'10" W). Named on Palo Alto (1961) and Redwood Point (1959) 7.5' quadrangles. Called Westpoint Creek on Hayward (1915) 15' quadrangle.

West San Leandro [ALAMEDA]: *locality,* 1.5 miles southwest of downtown San Leandro along Southern Pacific Railroad (lat. 37° 42'15" N, long. 122°10'35" W). Named on Haywards (1899) 15' quadrangle. The railroad station at the place was called Mulford, for Mulford Landing, until 1887 (Mosier and Mosier, p. 94).

West San Lorenzo [ALAMEDA]: *locality,* 3.25 miles south of downtown San Leandro along Southern Pacific Railroad (lat. 37° 40'35" N, long. 122°09'20" W); the place is 1.5 miles west-southwest of San Lorenzo. Named on Haywards (1899) 15' quadrangle.

West Side: see **Cupertino** [SANTA CLARA].

West Union Creek [SAN MATEO]: *stream,* flows 4.25 miles to Bear Creek (2) 2.25 miles east-northeast of Skeggs Point (lat. 37°25'30" N, long. 122°15'55" W). Named on Woodside (1961) 7.5' quadrangle. West Union sawmill was built along the creek in the 1850's; other names for the stream were Tripp Creek, for Dr. R.O. Tripp, and Greer's Creek, for John Greer, who lived by the stream in the 1850's (Brown, p. 99-100).

West Waddell Creek [SAN MATEO]: *stream,* flows 1.25 miles to Santa Cruz County 8.5 miles south of Mindego Hill (lat. 37°11'25" N, long. 122°14'50" W; at S line sec. 36, T 8 S, R 4 W). Named on Big Basin (1955) 7.5' quadrangle. The name commemorates William W. Waddell, who had a sawmill in the neighborhood (Hoover, Rensch, and Rensch, p. 476).

Wether Ridge [SONOMA]: *ridge,* west-northwest-trending, less than 1 mile long, 3.25 miles northwest of Big Mountain (lat. 38°44'45" N, long. 123°11'05" W). Named on Tombs Creek (1978) 7.5' quadrangle.

Whale Point [SONOMA]: *promontory,* 0.5 mile southwest of Jenner along the coast south of the mouth of Russian River (lat. 38°26'40" N, long. 123°07'30" W). Named on Duncans Mills (1979) 7.5' quadrangle.

Whaler's Harbor: see **Richardson Bay** [MARIN].

Wheatfield Fork: see **Gualala River** [SONOMA].

Wheeler Island [SOLANO]: *island,* 5 miles southwest of Birds Landing (2) along Suisun Bay (lat. 38°05' N, long. 121°56'30" W). Named on Honker Bay (1953) 7.5' quadrangle. Shown as part of Warrington Island on Ringgold's (1850c) map.

Whishman Slough: see **Stevens Creek** [SANTA CLARA].

Whiskey Flat [SANTA CLARA]: *area,* 2.25 miles southwest of Pacheco Pass (lat. 37°02'25" N, long. 121°14'05" W). Named on Pacheco Pass (1955) 7.5' quadrangle.

Whiskey Hill: see **Woodside** [SAN MATEO].

Whisman Slough: see **Jagel Slough** [SANTA CLARA]; **Stevens Creek** [SANTA CLARA].

White Canyon [CONTRA COSTA]: *canyon,* drained by a stream that flows nearly 1 mile to Mitchell Creek 2.5 miles northwest of Mount Diablo (lat. 37°54'30" N, long. 121°56'55" W; near W line sec. 26, T 1 N, R 1 W). Named on Clayton (1953) 7.5' quadrangle.

White Cliff Point: see **Fort Point** [SAN FRANCISCO].

White Cottage: see **Howell Mountain** [NAPA] (2).

White Creek [NAPA]: *stream,* flows 4 miles to Wooden Valley Creek 4.5 miles southwest of Mount Vaca (lat. 38°21'25" N, long. 122°10'15" W). Named on Mount George (1951) 7.5' quadrangle.

White Creek [SONOMA]: *stream,* flows 1.25 miles to Galloway Creek 10 miles west of Cloverdale (lat. 38°47'10" N, long. 123°11'55" W; sec. 21, T 11 N, R 12 W); the stream heads southwest of White Mountain. Named on Hopland (1960) 15' quadrangle.

White Gulch [MARIN]: *canyon,* 0.5 mile long, 4.25 miles southwest of Tomales on the west side of Tomales Bay (lat. 38°11'50" N, long. 122°57'10" W). Named on Tomales (1954) 7.5' quadrangle. On Point Reyes (1918) 15' quadrangle, the name applies to the flooded lower part of the canyon.

Whitehead: see **Lake Whitehead** [NAPA].

White Hill [MARIN]: *peak,* 6.5 miles north-northwest of Bolinas (lat. 37°59'40" N, long. 122°37'35" W). Altitude 1430 feet. Named on Bolinas (1954) and San Rafael (1954) 7.5' quadrangles.

Whitehouse Creek [SAN MATEO]: *stream,* heads in Santa Cruz County and flows 5 miles to the sea less than 1 mile east-southeast of Franklin Point (lat. 37°08'45" N, long. 122°20'45" W). Named on Franklin Point (1955) 7.5' quadrangle. The name is for a white prefabricated building that was shipped around Cape Horn and erected near the stream in 1852; the creek was called Arroyo de Soto in the 1840's for Eugenio Soto, who lived near it (Brown, p. 100-101; Brown used the form "White House Creek" for the name).

White House Pool [MARIN]: *water feature,* less than 1 mile west-southwest of Point Reyes Station along Lagunitas Creek (lat. 38° 03'50" N, long. 122°49'10" W). Named on Inverness (1954) 7.5' quadrangle. A white house stood by the place until 1969 (Teather, p. 87).

White Island: see **Alcatraz Island** [SAN FRANCISCO].

White Mountain [SONOMA]: *peak,* 8.5 miles west of Cloverdale (lat. 38°47'10" N, long. 123°10'30" W; sec. 22, T 11 N, R 12 W). Altitude 1896 feet. Named on Hopland (1960) 7.5' quadrangle.

White Rock [SONOMA]: *relief feature,* 7 miles north-northeast of Jimtown (lat. 38°42'50" N, long. 123°49'50" W). Named on Jimtown (1955) 7.5' quadrangle.

White Slough [SOLANO]: *water feature,* joins Napa River 2.25 miles north-northwest of downtown Vallejo (lat. 38°08'05" N, long. 122°16'05" W; sec. 2, T 3 N, R 4 W). Named on Cuttings Wharf (1949) and Mare Island (1959) 7.5' quadrangles.

White Sulphur Springs: see **Sulphur Canyon** [NAPA]; **Sulphur Springs** [SOLANO].

Whiting Ridge [SAN MATEO]: *ridge,* west-southwest-trending, 1.5 miles long, 1.5 miles east-northeast of Montara Knob (lat. 37°34'05" N, long. 122°27'25" W). Named on Montara Mountain (1956) 7.5' quadrangle. Willard J. Whiting settled on the ridge about 1860 (Brown, p. 101).

Whiting Rock [CONTRA COSTA]: *rock,* 0.5 mile southwest of Point San Pablo in San Francisco Bay (lat. 37°57'35" N, long. 122°26'10" W). Named on San Quentin (1959) 7.5' quadrangle.

Whitlock Creek [ALAMEDA]: *stream,* flows 3 miles to Alameda Creek 10 miles southeast of Sunol (lat. 37°29'30" N, long. 121°44'55" W; near S line sec. 15, T 5 S, R 2 E). Named on Mendenhall Springs (1956) and Mount Day (1955) 7.5' quadrangles. Mount Hamilton (1897) 15' quadrangle has the name "Whitlock Gulch" for the canyon of the stream. The name commemorates Oscar Whitlock and Herman Whitlock, who settled along the stream in the 1870's (Mosier and Mosier, p. 94).

Whitlock Gulch: see **Whitlock Creek** [ALAMEDA].

Whitman [CONTRA COSTA]: *locality,* 3 miles northeast of present Walnut Creek civic center along a branch of Oakland Antioch and Eastern Railroad (lat. 37°56' N, long. 122°01'10" W). Named on Concord (1915) 15' quadrangle.

Whitman Canyon [SONOMA]: *canyon,* drained by a stream that flows 2 miles to Valley of the Moon 4 miles north-northwest of Sonoma (lat. 38°20'40" N, long. 122°29'30" W). Named on Sonoma (1951) 7.5' quadrangle.

Whittemore Gulch [SAN MATEO]: *canyon,* drained by a stream that flows nearly 2 miles to Purisima Creek 4 miles west-northwest of Skeggs Point (lat. 37°26'15" N, long. 122°22'05" W; sec. 2, T 6 S, R 5 W). Named on Woodside (1961) 7.5' quadrangle. Richard Whittemore settled at the place about 1860 (Brown, p. 101).

Wicks Landing: see **Mulford Landing** [ALAMEDA].

Widow Reed Creek: see **Arroyo Corte Madera Del Presidio** [MARIN].

Wiedman Hill [CONTRA COSTA]: *peak,* 6 miles south of Danville (lat. 37°44'15" N, long. 121°59'35" W; near S line sec. 20, T 2 S, R 1 W). Altitude 1854 feet. Named on Dublin (1961) 7.5' quadrangle.

Wiggins Hill [SONOMA]: *ridge,* northeast-trending, 1 mile long, 4 miles south-southwest of Cotati (lat. 38°16'15" N, long. 122°43'50" W). Named on Cotati (1954) 7.5' quadrangle.

Wilbur's Creek: see **Mindego Creek** [SAN MATEO].

Wildcat Canyon [NAPA]: *canyon,* drained by a stream that flows less than 1 mile to Moore Creek 5.25 miles northeast of Saint Helena (lat. 38°33'30" N, long. 122°24'05" W; sec. 10, T 8 N, R 5 W). Named on Saint Helena (1960) 7.5' quadrangle.

Wildcat Canyon [SANTA CLARA]:
(1) *canyon,* drained by a stream that flows nearly 1 mile to Castro Valley 3.25 miles southwest of Gilroy (lat. 36°58'10" N, long. 121° 36'05" W). Named on Chittenden (1955) 7.5' quadrangle.
(2) *canyon,* drained by a stream that heads in San Benito County and flows 3.5 miles to South Fork Pacheco Creek 7 miles south-southwest of Pacheco Pass (lat. 36°58'15" N, long. 121°15'30" W; near S line sec. 13, T 11 S, R 6 E). Named on Mariposa Peak (1969) 7.5' quadrangle.

Wildcat Canyon [SONOMA]: *canyon,* drained by a stream that flows 1.25 miles to Woods Creek 4.5 miles south of Skaggs Springs (lat. 38°37'40" N, long. 123°01'30" W; sec. 13, T 9 N, R 11 W). Named on Cazadero (1978) and Warm Springs Dam (1978) 7.5' quadrangles.

Wildcat Creek [CONTRA COSTA]: *stream,* flows 12 miles to Castro Creek 2.25 miles east-southeast of Point San Pablo (lat. 37°57'10" N, long. 121°23'15" W). Named on Briones Valley (1959), Richmond (1959), and San Quentin (1959) 7.5' quadrangles. Whitney (p. 15) used the form "Wild Cat Creek" for the name.

Wildcat Creek [SANTA CLARA]: *stream,* flows 4 miles to San Tomas Aquinas Creek 2.5 miles north-northwest of downtown Los Gatos (lat. 37°16'15" N, long. 121°59'25" W). Named on Castle Rock Ridge (1955), Cupertino (1961), and San Jose West (1961) 7.5' quadrangles.

Wildcat Creek [SONOMA]: *stream,* flows 1.25 miles to the sea 2.25 miles south of Plantation (lat. 38°33'30" N, long. 123°18'55" W). Named on Plantation (1977) 7.5' quadrangle.

Wildcat Lake [MARIN]: *lake,* 1050 feet long, 1.25 miles north of Double Point (lat. 37°58'05" N, long. 122°47'05" W). Named on Double Point (1954) 7.5' quadrangle.

Wildcat Mountain [SONOMA]: *peak,* 3.5 miles north-northwest of Sears Point (lat. 38°11'40" N, long. 122°28'20" W). Named on Sears Point (1951) 7.5' quadrangle.

Wild Cattle Canyon [SONOMA]: *canyon,* drained by a stream that flows 1.5 miles to Marshall Creek 5 miles north of Fort Ross (lat. 38°35'30" N, long. 123°14'20" W; near SW cor. sec. 30, T 9 N, R 12 W). Named on Fort Ross (1978) 7.5' quadrangle.

Wild Cattle Creek [SONOMA]: *stream,* flows nearly 3 miles to Warm Springs Creek 4.25 miles west of Skaggs Springs (lat. 38° 41' N, long. 123°06'20" W; sec. 29, T 10 N, R 11 W). Named on Tombs Creek (1978) and Warm Springs Dam (1978) 7.5' quadrangles.

Wild Hog Canyon [SONOMA]: *canyon,* drained by a stream that flows 1 mile to Carson Creek 4.5 miles north-northeast of Fort Ross (lat. 38°34'05" N, long. 123°11'55" W; sec. 5, T 8 N, R 12 W). Named on Fort Ross (1978) 7.5' quadrangle.

Wild Hog Hill [SONOMA]: *peak,* 5.5 miles northeast of Guerneville (lat. 38°33'35" N, long. 123°55'10" W). Altitude 1150 feet. Named on Guerneville (1955) 7.5' quadrangle.

Wild Horse Canyon [SOLANO]: *canyon,* drained by a stream that flows 6.25 miles to Cold Canyon 6.5 miles north of Mount Vaca (lat. 38°29'50" N, long. 122°05'55" W; sec. 32, T 8 N, R 2 W). Named on Mount Vaca (1951) 7.5' quadrangle.

Wild Horse Creek [SOLANO]: *stream,* flows 3.25 miles to Green Valley Creek 7 miles west of Fairfield in Green Valley (lat. 38°15'40" N, long. 122°09'55" W; sec. 23, T 5 N, R 3 W). Named on Mount George (1951) 7.5' quadrangle.

Wildhorse Creek [SONOMA]: *stream,* heads in Mendocino and Lake Counties, flows 2.25 miles to Squaw Creek 5 miles north of Geysers Peak (lat. 38°50'20" N, long. 122°50'30" W; sec. 34, T 12 N, R 9 W). Named on The Geysers (1959) 7.5' quadrangle.

Wild Horse Ridge [SONOMA]: *ridge,* west-southwest-trending, 0.25 mile long, 3.5 miles west of Big Mountain (lat. 38°42'25" N, long. 123°12'45" W). Named on Tombs Creek (1978) 7.5' quadrangle.

Wild Horse Valley [NAPA-SOLANO]: *valley,* 8 miles southwest of Mount Vaca on Napa-Solano County line (lat. 38°19' N, long. 122° 11'45" W; on S line sec. 33, T 6 N, R 3 W). Named on Mount George (1951) 7.5' quadrangle.

Wild Lake [NAPA]: *lake,* 650 feet long, 7 miles north of Saint Helena (lat. 38°36'25" N, long. 122°29'10" W; near NE cor. sec. 26, T 9 N, R 6 W). Named on Saint Helena (1960) 7.5' quadrangle

Wild Oat Canyon [CONTRA COSTA]: *canyon,* drained by a stream that flows 0.5 mile to Donner Canyon 1.25 miles north of Mount Diablo (lat. 37°54' N, long. 121°54'45" W; near SE cor. sec. 25, T 1 N, R 1 W). Named on Clayton (1953) 7.5;' quadrangle.

Wildwood [SONOMA]: *locality,* less than 1 mile south-southeast of Kenwood along Southern Pacific Railroad (lat. 38°24'25" N, long. 122°32'30" W). Named on Santa Rosa (1916) 15' quadrangle.

Wilfred [SONOMA]: *locality,* 3 miles north of Cotati along Northwestern Pacific Railroad (lat. 38°22'05" N, long. 122°42'54" W). Named on Cotati (1954) 7.5' quadrangle.

Wilkins Gulch [MARIN]: *canyon,* drained by a stream that flows 1.5 miles to Bolinas Lagoon nearly 2 miles north-northwest of Bolinas (lat. 37°56'05" N, long. 122°41'45" W). Named on Bolinas (1954) 7.5' quadrangle. Teather (p. 88) associated the name with William Wallace Wilkins, who bought a ranch in the neighborhood in 1869.

William Rust Summit: see **Camp Herms** [CONTRA COSTA].

Williams [SONOMA]: *locality,* 4.5 miles northwest of Sebastopol along Petaluma and Santa Rosa Railroad (lat. 38°27' N, long. 122° 52'40" W). Named on Sebastopol (1942) 15' quadrangle.

Williams: see **Bill Williams Creek** [MARIN].

Williams Cattle Station [SONOMA]: *locality,* 3.5 miles north-northeast of Cazadero (lat. 38°34'25" N, long. 123°03'05" W; sec. 2, T 8 N, R 11 W). Named on Cazadero (1943) 7.5' quadrangle.

Williams Gulch [ALAMEDA]: *canyon,* drained by a stream that flows 6.5 miles to San Antonio Creek 6.5 miles east of Sunol (lat. 37°34'30" N, long. 121°46'05" W; sec. 21, T 4 S, R 2 E). Named on La Costa Valley (1960) and Mendenhall Springs (1956) 7.5' quadrangles.

Williams Reservoir [SANTA CLARA]: *lake,* 2000 feet long, behind a dam on Los Gatos Creek nearly 3 miles south of Mount Umunhum (lat. 37°07'15" N, long. 121°54'20" W). Named on Laurel (1955) 7.5' quadrangle.

Willota [SOLANO]: *locality,* 3.5 miles west of Fairfield along Sacramento Northern Railroad (lat. 38°14'35" N, long. 122°06'20" W). Named on Fairfield South (1949) 7.5' quadrangle.

Willow Brook [SONOMA]: *stream,* flows 5 miles to Lichau Creek 3.5 miles southeast of Cotati (lat. 38°17'05" N, long. 122°39'50" W). Named on Cotati (1954) and Glen Ellen (1954) 7.5' quadrangles. Called Haggin Creek on Santa Rosa (1916) 15' quadrangle.

Willow Creek [CONTRA COSTA]: *water feature,* enters Sacramento River (present Suisun Bay) 1.5 miles west-northwest of Pittsburg (lat. 38°02'25" N, long. 121°54'25" W). Named on Honker Bay (1918) 7.5' quadrangle.

Willow Creek [SONOMA]: *stream,* flows 5.5 miles to Russian River 1.5 miles east-southeast of Jenner (lat. 38°26'20" N, long. 123°05'45" W). Named on Duncans Mills (1979) 7.5' quadrangle.

Willow Creek: see **Bull Run Creek** [SAN MATEO].

Willow Glen [SANTA CLARA]: *district,* 1.5 miles south of downtown San Jose (lat. 37°18'30" N, long. 121°53'45" W). Named on San Jose West (1961) 7.5' quadrangle. The place first was called The Willows because of a thick growth of willows there in the 1860's (Fox, p. 10). Postal authorities established Kensington post office in 1893, changed the name to Willowglen in 1895, and discontinued it in 1900, when they changed the name to San Jose Station No. 2 (Salley, p. 110, 241). United States Board on Geographic Names (1933, p. 820) rejected the form "Willowglen" for the name of the district.

Willow Grove: see **Santa Rosa** [SONOMA].

Willow Marsh: see **Amador Valley** [ALAMEDA].

Willow Point [MARIN]: *promontory,* 2.5 miles northwest of Point Reyes Station on the southwest side of Tomales Bay (lat. 38°05'25" N, long. 122°50'30" W). Named on Inverness (1954) 7.5' quadrangle. The feature also is called Giubbini Point for a Swiss dairyman who lived there (Mason, 1976a, p. 150).

Willow Ridge [SANTA CLARA]: *ridge,* north-trending, 1.5 miles long, 5 miles north-northeast of Gilroy Hot Springs (lat. 37°11'05" N, long. 121°27'40" W). Named on Mississippi Creek (1955) 7.5' quadrangle.

Willows: see **The Willows**, under **Willow Glen** [SANTA CLARA].

Willow Slough [CONTRA COSTA]: *water feature,* 3 miles east-northeast of the present settlement of Bethel Island (lat. 38°02' N, long. 121°35'45" W). Named on Bouldin (1910) 7.5' quadrangle.

Willow Spring [SANTA CLARA]: *spring,* 3.25 miles west-northwest of Mount Sizer (lat. 37°14' N, long. 121°34' W; near W line sec. 17, T 8 S, R 4 E). Named on Mount Sizer (1955) 7.5' quadrangle.

Willow Spring [SONOMA]: *spring,* 2.5 miles west of Skaggs Springs (lat. 38°41'20" N, long. 123°04'15" W; near W line sec. 27, T 10 N, R 11 W). Named on Warm Springs Dam (1978) 7.5' quadrangle.

Willow Springs Canyon [SANTA CLARA]: *canyon,* drained by a stream that flows 1.5 miles to lowlands 2.25 miles northwest of Morgan Hill (lat. 37°09' N, long, 121°41'15" W). Named on Morgan Hill (1955) 7.5' quadrangle.

Willow Springs Creek [SONOMA]: *stream,* flows 2.5 miles to Warm Springs Creek 4 miles west-southwest of Skaggs Springs (lat. 38°40'40" N, long. 123°05'55" W; at N line sec. 32, T 10 N, R 11 W); the stream heads at Willow Spring. Named on Warm Springs Dam (1978) 7.5' quadrangle.

Wilson Creek [SONOMA]: *stream,* flows 1.5 miles to Sonoma Creek 2.25 miles southeast of Glen Ellen (lat. 38°20'10" N, long. 122°30'05" W). Named on Glen Ellen (1954) and Sonoma (1951) 7.5' quadrangles.

Wilson Grove [SONOMA]: *locality,* 6.5 miles south of Healdsburg near Russian River (lat. 38°31' N, long. 122°51'15" W). Named on Healdsburg (1955) 7.5' quadrangle.

Wilson Gulch [SAN MATEO]: *canyon,* drained by a stream that heads in Santa Cruz County and flows less than 1 mile to the sea 2 miles east of Año Nuevo Point (present Point Año Nuevo) at San Mateo-Santa Cruz County line (lat. 37°06'25" N, long. 122°17'30" W). Named on Año Nuevo (1955) 7.5' quadrangle.

Wilson Peak [SANTA CLARA]: *peak,* 2.5 miles east-southeast of Gilroy Hot Springs (lat. 37°05'40" N, long. 121°26'05" W; sec. 4, T 10 S, R 5 E). Altitude 2651 feet. Named on Gilroy Hot Springs (1955) 7.5' quadrangle.

Wilson Point [CONTRA COSTA]: *promontory,* 2.5 miles east of Pinole Point along San Pablo Bay (lat. 38°00'40" N, long. 122°18'55" W). Named on Mare Island (1959) 7.5' quadrangle.

Windermere Point [SONOMA]: *promontory,* 5 miles south-southeast of Plantation along the coast (lat. 38°31'30" N, long. 123°16'05" W). Named on Plantation (1977) 7.5' quadrangle.

Windmill Gulch [SAN MATEO]: *canyon,* drained by a stream that flows 0.5 mile to Honsinger Creek 6.5 miles southwest of La Honda (lat. 37°15'35" N, long. 122°21'35" W; near S line sec. 2, T 8 S, R 5 W). Named on La Honda (1961) 7.5' quadrangle.

Windsor [SONOMA]: *town,* 5.5 miles southeast of Healdsburg (lat. 38°32'50" N, long. 122°48'55" W; around NE cor. sec. 14, T 8 N, R 9 W). Named on Healdsburg (1955) 7.5' quadrangle. Postal authorities established Windsor post office in 1855 (Frickstad, p. 199). The place also was known as Poor Man's Flat (Hansen and Miller, p. 48). The first postmaster chose the name "Windsor" for the fancied resemblance of the place to the oak-studded parks around Windsor Castle in England (Mullen).

Windsor: see **East Windsor** [SONOMA].

Windsor Creek [SONOMA]: *stream,* flows 8 miles to Mark West Creek 6.5 miles north of Sebastopol (lat. 38°29'45" N, long. 122° 50'55" W); the stream goes past Windsor. Named on Healdsburg (1955) and Sebastopol (1954) 7.5' quadrangles.

Windy Flat [NAPA]: *area,* nearly 6 miles west-southwest of Mount Vaca (lat. 38°22'25" N, long. 122°12'15" W; near NW cor. sec. 16, T 6 N, R 3 W). Named on Mount George (1951) 7.5' quadrangle.

Windy Gap [MARIN]: *pass,* 4.5 miles southwest of Tomales near the southeast end of Tomales Point (lat. 38°11'55" N, long. 122°57'40" W). Named on Tomales (1954) 7.5' quadrangle.

Windy Hill [SAN MATEO]: *peak,* 4 miles north-northwest of Mindego Hill (lat. 37°21'50" N, long. 122°14'45" W; sec. 36, T 6 S, R 4 W). Named on Mindego Hill (1961) 7.5' quadrangle. United States Board on Geographic Names (1975a, p. 11-12) approved the name "Spring Ridge" for the ridge on which Windy Hill is the high point.

Windy Point [CONTRA COSTA]: *peak,* 3 miles southeast of Mount Diablo (lat. 37°51'10" N, long. 121°52'30" W; on S line sec. 9, T 1 S, R 1 E). Altitude 2112 feet. Named on Diablo (1953) and Tassajara (1953) 7.5' quadrangles.

Windy Point [NAPA]: *peak,* 2 miles southeast of Berryessa Peak on Napa-Yolo County line (lat. 38°38'40" N, long. 122°09'35" W). Named on Brooks (1959) 7.5' quadrangle.

Windy Point [SONOMA]: *peak,* 3.5 miles southwest of Big Mountain (lat. 38°40'30" N, long. 123°11'50" W; near NW cor. sec. 33, T 10 N, R 12 W). Named on Tombs Creek (1978) 7.5' quadrangle.

Windy Ridge [MARIN]: *ridge,* north-northwest-trending, 1 mile long, 3 miles southwest of downtown San Rafael (lat. 37°56'35" N, long. 122°34'05" W). Named on San Rafael (1954) 7.5' quadrangle.

Wine Creek [SONOMA]: *stream,* flows 2.5 miles to Grape Creek 4.25 miles south-southwest of Geyserville (lat. 38°39'20" N, long. 123°56'45" W; near E line sec. 3, T 9 N, R 10 W). Named on Geyserville (1955) 7.5' quadrangle.

Winehaven [CONTRA COSTA]: *locality,* 1 mile south-southeast of Point San Pablo (lat. 37°57' N, long. 122°25' W). Named on San Francisco (1915) 15' quadrangle. Postal authorities established Winehaven post office in 1910 and discontinued it in 1925 (Salley, p. 241).

Winfield Scott: see **Fort Winfield Scott**, under **Fort Point** [SAN FRANCISCO].

Wing Canyon [NAPA]: *canyon,* drained by a stream that flows nearly 2 miles to Dry Creek 4.5 miles south of Rutherford (lat. 38° 23'40" N, long. 122°25' W; sec. 4, T 6 N, R 5 W). Named on Rutherford (1951) 7.5' quadrangle. On Sonoma (1942) 15' quadrangle, the name "Wing Canyon" applies to the canyon of Dry Creek.

Wingo [SONOMA]: *locality,* 4.25 miles north-northeast of Sears Point (lat. 38°12'35" N, long. 122°25'35" W). Named on Sears Point (1951) 7.5' quadrangle.

Winslow Cove: see **Simpton Point** [MARIN].

Winter Island [CONTRA COSTA]: *island,* 2.25 miles long, 3 miles northwest of Antioch (lat. 38°02'45" N, long. 121°51' W). Named on Antioch North (1978) 7.5' quadrangle, which shows the feature as mainly marsh and water. Called Ruckels I. on Ringgold's (1850b) map.

Wire Gate Saddle [SONOMA]: *pass,* 4.5 miles north of Cazadero (lat. 38°35'50" N, long. 123°06'05" W; sec. 29, T 9 N, R 11 W). Named on Cazadero (1978) 7.5' quadrangle.

Wise: see **Point Wise** [SOLANO].

Wisener Creek: see **Norris Creek** [ALAMEDA].

Wittenberg: see **Mount Wittenberg** [MARIN].

Wittenberg Hill: see **Mount Wittenberg** [MARIN].

Wolf Creek [SONOMA]: *stream,* flows 5 miles to Wheatfield Fork Gualala River nearly 5 miles southwest of Big Mountain (lat. 38° 40'10" N, long. 123°12'55" W; at W line sec. 32, T 10 N, R 12 W). Named on Tombs Creek (1978) 7.5' quadrangle.

Wolf Ridge [MARIN]: *ridge,* west-trending, 1.5 miles long, 2 miles north of Point Bonita (lat. 37°50'35" N, long. 122°32'05" W). Named on Point Bonita (1954) 7.5' quadrangle.

Wolfskill [SOLANO]: *locality,* 3.5 miles north of Allendale along Southern Pacific Railroad (lat. 38°29'50" N, long. 121°57'10" W); the place is on Rio de los Putos grant, which William Wolfskill owned. Named on Wolfskill (1917) 7.5' quadrangle.

Woloki Slough [SONOMA]: *water feature,* joins Donahue Slough 6 miles southeast of downtown Petaluma (lat. 38°11' N, long. 122° 32'45" W). Named on Petaluma River (1954) 7.5' quadrangle.

Woodacre [MARIN]: *settlement,* 8 miles south-southwest of downtown Novato (lat. 38°00'30" N, long. 122°38'15" W). Named on San Geronimo (1954) 7.5' quadrangle. Promoters began a subdivision at the place in 1912, and postal authorities established Woodacre post office there in 1925 (Salley, p. 242)

Wood Canyon [NAPA]: *canyon,* drained by a stream that flows nearly 1 mile to Chiles Valley 8 miles east-northeast of Saint Helena (lat. 38°32'40" N, long. 122°20'15" W). Named on Chiles Valley (1958) 7.5' quadrangle.

Wood Creek [SONOMA]: *stream,* flows nearly 3 miles to Russian River 0.5 mile east of Geyserville (lat. 38°42'30" N, long. 122°53'35" W). Named on Geyserville (1955) 7.5' quadrangle.

Wooden Valley [NAPA]: *valley,* 5 miles west-southwest of Mount Vaca (lat. 38°22'30" N, long. 122°11'30" W). Named on Capell Valley (1951) and Mount George (1951) 7.5' quadrangles. The place was called Corral Valley before John Wooden purchased land there in 1850 (Gudde, 1949, p. 393).

Wooden Valley Creek [NAPA]: *stream,* flows 6.5 miles to Suisun Creek 5.25 miles south-southwest of Mount Vaca (lat. 38°19'50" N, long. 122°08'10" W); the stream goes through Wooden Valley. Named on Capell Valley (1951) and Mount George (1951) 7.5' quadrangles.

Woodhams Creek [SAN MATEO]: *stream,* flows 2 miles to La Honda Creek near the north edge of La Honda (lat. 37°19'25" N, long. 122°16'15" W; sec. 14, T 7 S, R 4 W). Named on La Honda (1961) and Mindego Hill (1961) 7.5' quadrangles. Mr. A. Woodham had a dairy along the stream about 1860 (Brown, p. 102).

Woodhaven Camp [SAN MATEO]: *locality,* 3 miles north of La Honda (lat. 37°21'40" N, long. 122°15'40" W; near SE cor. sec. 35, T 6 S, R 4 W). Named on La Honda (1961) 7.5' quadrangle.

Wood Island [MARIN]: *hill,* 2.25 miles south-southeast of downtown San Rafael (lat. 37°56'40" N, long. 122°30'40" W). Named on San Rafael (1954) 7.5' quadrangle. The feature had the local name "Dean's Island" in the early 1920's (Teather, p. 89).

Wood Island: see **Yerba Buena Island** [SAN FRANCISCO].

Woodleaf [NAPA]: *locality,* 1.5 miles west-northwest of Calistoga (lat. 38°35'20" N, long. 122°36'20" W). Named on Calistoga (1945) 15' quadrangle.

Woodruff Creek [SAN MATEO]: *stream,* flows 3 miles to La Honda Creek

1.25 miles north of La Honda (lat. 37°20'15" N, long. 122° 16'05" W; sec. 11, T 7 S, R 4 W). Named on La Honda (1961) and Mindego Hill (1961) 7.5' quadrangles. Charles E. Woodruff had a ranch along the stream after about 1862 (Brown, p. 102).

Woods Creek [SONOMA]: *stream,* flows 3 miles to Pena Creek 3.5 miles south of Skaggs Springs (lat. 38°38'25" N, long. 123°02'05" W; sec. 12, T 9 N, R 11 W). Named on Cazadero (1978) and Warm Springs Dam (1978) 7.5' quadrangles.

Woods Creek: see **Mills Creek** [SAN MATEO] (2).

Woodside [SAN MATEO]: *town,* 4 miles south-southwest of downtown Redwood City (lat. 37°25'45" N, long. 122°15'30" W). Named on La Honda (1961), Palo Alto (1961), and Woodside (1961) 7.5' quadrangles. Parkhurst, Ellis, and Tripp had a lumber camp at the place as early as 1849, and in 1851 Tripp opened a store there that housed Woodside post office in 1854—the name "Woodside" then was used for the community near the store; in the early 1860's a new business center called Greersburg was started farther east at Adobe Corner, but by the 1870's the name "Woodside" applied to both places (Brown, p. 102). The name "Greersburg" was for the Greer family, owners of Cañada de Raymundo grant (Hoover, Rensch, and Rensch, p. 399). A group of saloons frequented by teamsters in the 1880's was located a little east of the first two settlements, and was called Whiskey Hill; the settlement that developed at Whiskey Hill took the name "Haakerville" for William Haaker, owner of a store there, but again use of the name "Woodside" was extended to apply to Haakerville (Brown, p. 100, 102). Postal authorities established Woodside post office in 1854, moved it 1.25 miles east in 1909, discontinued it in 1915, and reestablished it in 1949 (Salley, p. 243). The town incorporated in 1856.

Woodside Glens [SAN MATEO]: *district,* 3.25 miles south-southwest of downtown Redwood City (lat. 37°26'25" N, long. 122°15'20" W); the place is in Woodside. Named on Woodside (1961) 7.5' quadrangle.

Woodstock: see **Alameda** [ALAMEDA].

Woodville [MARIN]: *locality,* 2.5 miles north-northwest of Bolinas (lat. 37°56'40" N, long. 122°42'20" W). Named on Bolinas (1954) 7.5' quadrangle. The place first was called Dogtown (Laizure, 1926, p. 320).

Woodworth [SONOMA]: *locality,* 5.25 miles east-northeast of Bloomfield along Petaluma and Santa Rosa Railroad (lat. 38°19'55" N, long. 122°45'35" W). Named on Sebastopol (1942) 15' quadrangle.

Woolsey [SONOMA]: *locality,* 5.5 miles north of Sebastopol (lat. 38° 29' N, long. 122°49'05" W). Named on Sebastopol (1942) 15' quadrangle.

Worley Flat [SAN MATEO]: *area,* 3 miles south of La Honda along Pescadero Creek (lat. 37°16'30" N, long. 122°16'15" W; sec. 35, T 7 S, R 4 W). Named on La Honda (1961) 7.5' quadrangle.

Wragg Canyon [NAPA]: *canyon,* 8 miles long, opens into the canyon of Putah Creek 10 miles south of Berryessa Peak (lat. 38° 31'30" N, long. 122°09'30" W; sec. 23, T 8 N, R 3 W). Named on Capell Valley (1951, photorevised 1968) and Lake Berryessa (1959) 7.5' quadrangles. Water of Lake Berryessa covers the lower part of the canyon. The name commemorates the first settler in the neighborhood (Gudde, 1949, p. 393). Whitney (p. 105) called the feature Rag Cañon.

Wragg Creek [NAPA]: *stream,* flows nearly 6 miles to Lake Berryessa 6.25 miles north-northwest of Mount Vaca (lat. 38°28'55" N, long. 122°09'25" W; sec. 2, T 7 N, R 3 W); the stream is in Wragg Canyon. Named on Capell Valley (1951, photorevised 1968) 7.5' quadrangle.

Wragg Ridge [NAPA]: *ridge,* south-trending, 8 miles long, 7.5 miles northwest of Mount Vaca (lat. 38°29'15" N, long. 122°10'40" W); the ridge is west of Wragg Canyon. Named on Capell Valley (1951) and Lake Berryessa (1959) 7.5' quadrangles.

Wright [SONOMA]: *locality,* nearly 2 miles south-southeast of present Jenner (lat. 38°25'50" N, long. 123°06'30" W). Named on Duncans Mills (1921) 15' quadrangle.

Wright Beach: see **Wrights Beach** [SONOMA].

Wright Creek: see **Pool Creek** [SONOMA].

Wright Cut [SOLANO]: *water feature,* joins Lindsey Slough 6.25 miles north of Rio Vista (lat. 38°14'50" N, long. 121°41'40" W). Named on Liberty Island (1978) and Rio Vista (1978) 7.5' quadrangles.

Wright Gulch [SONOMA]: *canyon,* drained by a stream that flows 1.5 miles to the sea 3.5 miles south-southeast of present Jenner (lat. 38°24'20" N, long. 123°05'55" W); the mouth of the canyon is at present Wrights Beach. Named on Duncans Mills (1921) 15' quadrangle.

Wrights [SANTA CLARA]: *village,* 6.25 miles south-southeast of downtown Los Gatos along Los Gatos Creek (lat. 37°08'20" N, long. 121°56'45" W; sec. 23, T 9 S, R 1 W). Named on Los Gatos (1919) 15' quadrangle; the site is named on Los Gatos (1953) 7.5' quadrangle. The place began in 1877, when railroad construction reached the north portal of a tunnel there; it first was known as The Tunnel, and in 1880 as Wright's Station (Young, p. 42-43) for John Vincent Wright, son of James Richard Wright, the hotel operator at Burrell (Hoover, Rensch, and Rensch, p. 456). The settlement of Burrell was near the summit of Santa Cruz Mountains and was named for Lyman John Burrell, who lived there in the early 1850's (Hoover, Rensch, and Rensch, p. 455). Laurel (1955) 7.5' quadrangle has the label "Burrell Sch. (Abandoned)"—the principal evidence of Burrell on the map—at a point 1.5 miles south-southeast of the site of Wrights. Postal authorities established Wrights post office in 1879 and discontinued it in 1938 (Frickstad, p. 175). Postal Route (1884) map shows a place called Skyland situated 2 miles east of Wrights near Santa Clara-Santa Cruz County line; postal authorities established Skyland post office in 1884 and discontinued it in 1886 (Frickstad, p. 175). A place called Patchin was located 2 miles west-northwest of the site of Wrights at the junction of present Mountain Charley Road and the old Santa Cruz Highway; the place is said to have been named for a famous race horse, George M. Patchen (Hoover, Rensch, and Rensch, p. 456). Postal authorities established Patchin post office in 1872, discontinued it in 1895, reestablished it in 1897, and discontinued it in 1925 (Frickstad, p. 174). United States Board on Geographic Names (1979c, p. 5) approved the name "Patchen Pass" for the pass at the crest of Santa Cruz Mountains, near the site of Patchin, that is traversed by the main highway from Los Gatos to the coast. The Board at the same time approved the name "Cuesta de los Gatos" for the ridge, less than 2 miles long, where the pass is situated. The Board noted that city officials of Los Gatos proposed the name for the pass in 1976 to commemorate the community of Patchen (or Patchin); the name for the ridge was in use locally before 1831.

Wrights: see **Santa Rosa** [SONOMA].

Wrights Beach [SONOMA]: *beach,* 3.5 miles south-southeast of Jenner along the coast (lat. 38°24'15" N, long. 123°05'50" W). Named on Duncans Mills (1979) 7.5' quadrangle. Called Wright Beach on Duncans Mills (1943) 7.5' quadrangle.

Wright's Station: see **Wrights** [SANTA CLARA].

Wye [SONOMA]: *locality,* 1 mile west-northwest of downtown Santa Rosa along Northwestern Pacific Railroad (lat. 38°27' N, long. 122°43'45" W). Named on Santa Rosa (1954) 7.5' quadrangle.

—X-Y—

Yacht Harbor [SAN FRANCISCO]: *water feature,* 2 miles east of Fort Point along San Francisco Bay in Marina District (lat. 37°48'25" N, long. 122°26'35" W). Named on San Francisco North (1956) 7.5' quadrangle. The site was called Harbor View in the 1870's (O'Brien, p. 192).

Yajome [NAPA]: *land grant,* east of Napa River between Yountville and the city of Napa. Named on Napa (1951) and Yountville (1951) 7.5' quadrangles. Tomaso A. Rodriguez received 1.5 leagues in 1841; Salvador Vallejo and others claimed 6653 acres patented in 1864 (Cowan, p. 108; Cowan listed the grant under the designation "Yajome (or Llajome, or) Paso de las Trancas"). According to Perez (p. 104), Damaso Rodriguez was the grantee in 1841.

Yankee Jim Gulch [SAN MATEO]: *canyon,* drained by a stream that flows 1.5 miles to the sea less than 1 mile north-northwest of Pigeon Point (lat. 37°11'35" N, long. 122°23'50" W). Named on Franklin Point (1955) and Pigeon Point (1955) 7.5' quadrangles. The canyon was called Arroyo de la Ballena in Spanish times, and was called Surveyor's Gulch in the 1850's (Brown, p. 103).

Yeguas Creek: see **Adobe Creek** [SANTA CLARA].

Yellow Bluff [MARIN]: *promontory,* 1.5 miles south-southeast of downtown Sausalito along San Francisco Bay (lat. 37°50'10" N, long. 122°28'15" W). Named on San Francisco North (1956) 7.5' quadrangle.

Yellow Jacket Creek [SONOMA]: *stream,* flows 3.5 miles to join Kellogg Creek and form Redwood Creek (1) 3 miles southwest of Mount Saint Helena (lat. 38°38'05" N, long. 122°40'15" W). Named on Mount Saint Helena (1959) 7.5' quadrangle. Calistoga (1945) 15' quadrangle, which shows Yellowjacket mine near the stream, has the form "Yellowjacket Creek" for the name.

Yellowjacket Springs [SONOMA]: *springs,* 1 mile east-southeast of Big Mountain (lat. 38°42'15" N, long. 123°07'45" W; sec. 24, T 10 N, R 12 W). Named on Tombs Creek (1978) 7.5' quadrangle.

Yerba Buena [SANTA CLARA]: *land grant,* 5 miles southeast of downtown San Jose. Named on Lick Observatory (1955), Morgan Hill (1955), San Jose East (1961), and Santa Teresa Hills (1953) 7.5' quadrangles. Thompson and West's (1876) map has the name "Yerba Buena y Socayre" for the grant. Antonio Chabolla received the land in 1833 and claimed 24,332 acres patented in 1859; the grant also was called Socayre (Cowan, p. 108). According to Perez (p. 104), the grant was made in 1840.

Yerba Buena: see **San Francisco** [SAN FRANCISCO].

Yerba Buena Cove: see **Telegraph Hill** [SAN FRANCISCO].

Yerba Buena Creek [SANTA CLARA]: *stream,* flows nearly 3.5 miles to Thompson Creek 1 mile southeast of Evergreen (lat. 37° 17'55" N, long. 121°46'15" W); the stream is on Yerba Buena grant. Named on San Jose East (1961) 7.5' quadrangle.

Yerba Buena Island [SAN FRANCISCO]: *island,* 4300 feet long, 2.25 miles east-northeast of North Point in San Francisco Bay (lat. 37°48'40" N, long. 122°21'50" W). Named on Oakland West (1959) 7.5' quadrangle. Called Goat Id. on San Francisco (1899, reprinted 1913) 15' quadrangle, but United States Board on Geographic Names (1933, p. 829) rejected this name and noted that the California legislature restored the old Spanish name "Yerba Buena" to the island in 1931. The name "Goat Island" was from the goats turned loose to multiply on the island in the 1840's (Davis, W.H., p. 140). Ayala named the feature Isla de Alcatraces in 1775 for the abundance of pelicans there (Gudde, 1949, p. 6). It was known as Wood Island in the early nineteenth century (Wagner, H.R., p. 422).

Yerba Buena y Socayre: see **Yerba Buena** [SANTA CLARA].

Ygnacio Valley [CONTRA COSTA]: *valley*, 3 miles northeast of Walnut Creek civic center (lat. 37°55'30" N, long. 122°01' W). Named on Clayton (1953) and Walnut Creek (1959) 7.5' quadrangles.

Yolanda: see **San Anselmo** [MARIN].

Yolano [SOLANO]: *locality*, 7 miles east-southeast of Dixon along Sacramento Northern Railroad (lat. 38°24'35" N, long. 121°42'15' W; sec. 36, T 7 N, R 2 E). Named on Saxon (1952) 7.5' quadrangle. Railroad officials coined the name from the words "<u>Yo</u>lo" and "So<u>lano</u>"—the place is near Solano-Yolo County line (Hanna, P.T., p. 361).

Yolo Basin: see **Yolo Bypass** [SOLANO].

Yolo Bypass [SOLANO]: *area*, lowlands west of Sacramento River, mainly in Yolo County, but extends south nearly to Rio Vista in Solano County. Named on Liberty Island (1978) and Rio Vista (1978) 7.5' quadrangles. Called Yolo Basin on Cache Slough (1916) and Rio Vista (1910) 7.5' quadrangles, which show the feature as marsh and water.

Yolo Landing [SOLANO]: *locality*, 2.5 miles west-southwest of Birds Landing (2) along Montezuma Slough (lat. 38°07'25" N, long. 121°54'50" W). Named on Honker Bay (1918) 7.5' quadrangle.

York Creek [NAPA]: *stream*, flows 4.5 miles to Napa River 1.25 miles north-northwest of Saint Helena (lat. 38°31'20" N, long. 122° 28'30" W). Named on Calistoga (1958) and Saint Helena (1960) 7.5' quadrangles.

York Island [CONTRA COSTA]: *island*, 1 mile northwest of Pittsburg in present Suisun Bay (lat. 38°02'35" N, long. 121°53'50" W). Named on Honker Bay (1918) 7.5' quadrangle.

Yorty Creek [SONOMA]: *stream*, flows 3.25 miles to Dry Creek 5 miles southwest of Cloverdale (lat. 38°45'40" N, long. 123°05'25" W; sec. 33, T 11 N, R 11 W). Named on Cloverdale (1960) 7.5' quadrangle.

Young: see **George Young Creek** [SONOMA].

Yountville [NAPA]: *town*, 8.5 miles north-northwest of downtown Napa (lat. 38°24'25" N, long. 122°21'50" W). Named on Yountville (1951) 7.5' quadrangle, which shows the state veterans home located 1 mile south of Yountville. Postal authorities established Sebastopol post office in 1856, discontinued it in 1857, reestablished it in 1858, and changed the name to Yountville in 1867 (Frickstad, p. 112). The town incorporated in 1956. The name "Yountville" commemorates George C. Yount, first white settler in present Napa County, who arrived there in 1831 (Menefee, p. 19, 185). Postal authorities established Veterans Home post office at the state veterans home in 1892 (Frickstad, p. 112).

Yountville Hills [NAPA]: *range*, northwest of Yountville (lat. 38°25'10" N, long. 122°22'30" W). Named on Rutherford (1951) and Yountville (1951) 7.5' quadrangles.

Yulupa [SONOMA]: *locality*, nearly 2 miles southeast of Glen Ellen along Southern Pacific Railroad (lat. 38°20'30" N, long. 122°30'20" W). Named on Santa Rosa (1944) 15' quadrangle. Postal authorities established Yulupa post office 5.5 miles southeast of Santa Rosa—but not at this site along the railroad—in 1892 and discontinued it in 1897 (Salley, p. 245).

Yulupa Creek [SONOMA]: *stream*, flows 2.5 miles to Sonoma Creek 2.5 miles south of Kenwood (lat. 38°22'45" N, long. 122°33'05" W). Named on Kenwood (1954) 7.5' quadrangle.

– Z –

Zem Zem: see **Zim Zim Creek** [NAPA].

Zimmerman's Mountain House: see **Mountain House** [ALAMEDA].

Zim Zim Creek [NAPA]: *stream*, flows 6.25 miles to Eticuera Creek 5.5 miles south-southeast of Knoxville (lat. 38°45'15" N, long. 122°17' W; near SE cor. sec. 34, T 11 N, R 4 W). Named on Knoxville (1958) 7.5' quadrangle. Morgan Valley (1944) 15' quadrangle shows Zim Zim ranch at the mouth of the stream. According to Gudde (1949, p. 399), the creek is named for the ranch, and the ranch and creek names should have the form "Zem-Zem." Postal authorities established Zem Zem post office 14 miles north of Monticello in 1869 and discontinued it in 1890; the name is from a well in Mecca (Salley, p. 246).

Zinfandel [NAPA]: *locality*, 2 miles north-northwest of Rutherford along Southern Pacific Railroad (lat. 38°28'55" N, long. 122°26'30" W). Named on Rutherford (1951) 7.5' quadrangle. The place first was known as Pine Station, and later as Bell Station (Hoover, Rensch, and Rensch, p. 245).

Zion: see **Mount Zion** [CONTRA COSTA].

San Francisco Bay Region
Alameda, Contra Costa, Marin, Napa, San Francisco, San Mateo, Santa Clara, Solano and Sonoma Counties

References Cited

BOOKS AND ARTICLES

Agassiz, L. 1853. "Extraordinary fishes from California, constituting a new family." *American Journal of Science and Arts* (series 2), v. 16, no. 48, p. 380-390.

Allen, E.T., and Day, Arthur L. 1927. *Steam wells and other thermal activity at "The Geysers," California.* Washington: Carnegie Institution of Washington, 106 p.

Anderson, F.M. 1899. "The geology of Point Reyes Peninsula." *University of California, Bulletin of the Department of Geology,* v. 2, no. 5, p. 119-153.

Anderson, Winslow. 1892. *Mineral springs and health resorts of California.* San Francisco: The Bancroft Company, 347 p.

Antisell, Thomas. 1856. "Geological report." *Reports of explorations and surveys, to ascertain the most practicable and economical route for a railroad from the Mississippi River to the Pacific Ocean.* Volume VII, Part II. (33d Cong., 2d Sess., Sen. Ex. Doc. No. 78.) Washington: Beverley Tucker, Printer, 204 p.

Arbuckle, Clyde. 1968. *Santa Clara Co. Ranchos.* San Jose, California: The Rosicrucian Press, Ltd., 46 p.

Archuleta, Kay. 1977. *The Brannan saga.* (Author), 116 p.

Bailey, Edgar H. 1946. "Quicksilver deposits of the western Mayacmas district, Sonoma County, California." *California Journal of Mines and Geology,* v. 42, no. 3, p. 199-286.

Bancroft, Hubert Howe. 1886. *History of California, Volume II, 1801-1824.* San Francisco: The History Company, Publishers, 795 p.

_____1888. *History of California, Volume VI, 1848-1859.* San Francisco: The History Company, Publishers, 787 p.

Becker, Robert H. 1964. *Diseños of California ranchos.* San Francisco: The Book Club of California, (no pagination).

_____1969. *Designs on the land.* San Francisco: The Book Club of California, (no pagination).

Berkstresser, C.F., Jr. 1968. *Data for springs in the Southern Coast, Transverse, and Peninsular Ranges of California.* (United States Geological Survey, Water Resources Division, Open-file report.) Menlo Park, California, 21 p. + appendices.

Bidwell, John. 1964. *A journey to California, 1841, The first emigrant party to California by wagon train, The journal of John Bidwell.* Berkeley, California: The Friends of the Bancroft Library, 55 p. + 32 p.

Blake, W.P. 1854. "Quicksilver mine of Almaden, California." *American Journal of Science and Arts* (series 2), v. 17, no. 51, p. 438-440.

_____1856. "Observations on the physical geography and geology of the coast of California, from Bodega bay to San Diego." *United States Coast Survey, Report of the Superintendent 1855.* (34th Cong., 1st Sess., Sen. Ex. Doc. 22.) Appendix 65, p. 376-398.

Bolton, Herbert Eugene. 1931. *Outpost of empire.* New York: Alfred A. Knopf, 334 p.

Bowen, Oliver E., Jr. 1951. "Highways and byways of particular geologic interest." *Geologic guidebook of the San Francisco Bay Counties.* (California Division of Mines Bulletin 154.) San Francisco: Division of Mines, p. 315-379.

Bradley, Walter W. 1915. "The counties of Colusa, Glenn, Lake, Marin, Napa, Solano, Sonoma, Yolo." *Report XIV of the State Mineralogist.* Sacramento: California State Mining Bureau, p. 173-370.

Brewer, William H. 1949. *Up and down California in 1860-1864.* (Edited by Francis P. Farquhar.) Berkeley and Los Angeles: University of California Press, 583 p.

Brown, Alan K. 1975. *Place names of San Mateo County.* San Mateo, California: San Mateo County Historical Association, 118 p.

Bruntz, George G. 1971. *The history of Los Gatos, gem of the foothills.* Fresno, California: Valley Publishers, 173 p.

Buffum, E. Gould. 1850. *Six months in the gold mines; From a journal of three years' residence in Upper and Lower California, 1847-8-9.* Philadelphia: Lea and Blanchard, 172 p.

Butler, Phyllis Filiberti. 1975. *The valley of Santa Clara, Historic buildings, 1792-1920.* San Jose, California: Junior League of San Jose, Inc., 192 p.

California Division of Highways. 1934. *California highway transportation survey, 1934.* Sacramento: Department of Public Works, Division of Highways, 130 p. + appendices.

Cardwell, G.T. 1958. *Geology and ground water in the Santa Rosa and Petaluma Valley areas, Sonoma County, California.* (United States Geological Survey Water-Supply Paper 1427.) Washington: United States Government Printing Office, 273 p.

Carey, E.P, and Miller, W.J. 1907. "The crystalline rocks of the Oak Hill area near San Jose, California." *Journal of Geology,* v. 15, no. 2, p. 152-169.

Clar, C. Raymond. 1974. *Out of the river mist.* (Second edition.) Santa Cruz, California: Forest History Society, 135 p.

Clark, Donald Thomas. 1986. *Santa Cruz County place names.* Santa Cruz: Santa Cruz Historical Society, 552 p.

Clark, William O. 1924. *Ground water in Santa Clara Valley, California.* (United States Geological Survey Water-Supply Paper 519.) Washington: Government Printing Office, 209 p.

Cluff, Lloyd S., and Bolt, Bruce A. 1969. "Risk from earthquakes in the modern urban environment, with special emphasis on the San Francisco Bay area." *Urban environmental geology in the San Francisco Bay region.* San Francisco: Association of Engineering Geologists, San Francisco Section, p. 25-64.

Cowan, Robert G. 1956. *Ranchos of California.* Fresno, California: Academy Library Guild, 151 p.

Coy, Owen C. 1923. *California county boundaries.* Berkeley: California Historical Survey Commission, 335 p.

Crawford, J.J. 1894. "Report of the State Mineralogist." *Twelfth report of the State Mineralogist, (Second Biennial,) two years ending September 15, 1894.* Sacramento: California State Mining Bureau, p. 8-412.

_____1896. "Report of the State Mineralogist." *Thirteenth report (Third Biennial) of the State Mineralogist for the two years ending September 15, 1896.* Sacramento: California State Mining Bureau, p. 10-646.

Cunningham, Florence R. 1967. *Saratoga's first hundred years.* Fresno, California: Valley Publishers, 367 p.

Curtis, James R. 1978. "Whatever happened to Port San Jose?" *The California Geographer,* v. 18, p. 35-42.

Dall, William Healey, and Harris, Gilbert Dennison. 1892. *Correlation papers, Neocene.* (United States Geological Survey Bulletin 84.) Washington: Government Printing Office, 349 p.

Dana, James D. 1849. "Notes on Upper California." *American Journal of Science and Arts,* (series 2), v. 7, no. 20, p. 247-264.

Davidson, George. 1907. "The discovery of the Bay of San Francisco and the rediscovery of the Port of Monterey." *Transactions and Proceedings of the Geographical Society of the Pacific* (series. 2), v. 4, p. 1-153.

Davis, Fenelon F. 1948. "Mines and mineral resources of Napa County, California." *California Journal of Mines and Geology,* v. 44, no. 2, p. 159-188.

Davis, Fenelon F., and Goldman, Harold B. 1958. "Mines and mineral resources of Contra Costa County, California." *California Journal of Mines and Geology,* v. 54, no. 4, p. 501-581.

Davis, Fenelon F., and Jennings, Charles W. 1954. "Mines and mineral resources of Santa Clara County, California." *California Journal of Mines and Geology,* v. 50, no. 2, p. 321-430.

Davis, Fenelon F., and Vernon, James W. 1951. "Mines and mineral resources of Contra Costa County." *California Journal of Mines and Geology,* v. 47, no. 4, p. 561-617.

Davis, William Heath. 1962. *Seventy-five years in California.* San Francisco, California: John Howell—Books, 345 p.

Delavan, James. 1956. *Notes on California and the placers, How to get there, and what to do afterwards.* Oakland, California: Biobooks, 156 p.

Diller, J.S., and others. 1915. *Guidebook of the Western United States, Part D. The Shasta Route and Coast Line.* (United States. Geological Survey Bulletin 614.) Washington: Government Printing Office, 142 p.

Dillon, Richard. 1980. *Great expectations, The story of Benicia, California.* (No place): Benicia Heritage Book, Inc., 241 p.

Donnelly, Florence G. 1960. *Early days in Marin.* San Rafael, California: Marin County Savings and Loan Association, 63 p.
Durst, David M. 1916. "Physiographic features of Cache Creek in Yolo County." *University of California Publications in Geography,* v. 1, no. 8, p. 331-372.
Eckel, Edwin C. 1933. "Limestone deposits of the San Francisco region." *California Journal of Mines and Geology,* v. 29, no. 3-4, p. 348-361.
Fairley, Lincoln. 1985. "Mt. Tamalpais: Man and a mountain's resources." *The Californians,* v. 3, no. 1, p. 33-39.
_____1987. *Mount Tamalpais.* San Francisco, California: Scottwall Associates, 201 p.
Fava, Florence M. 1976. *Los Altos Hills.* Woodside, California: Gilbert Richards Publications, 135 p.
Fox, Frances L. 1978. *Land grant to landmark.*. San Jose, California: The Pied Piper Publishers, 131 p.
Franke, Herbert A. 1930. "Santa Clara County." *Mining in California,* v. 26, no. 1, p. 2-39.
Frazer, Robert W. 1965. *Forts of the West.* Norman: University of Oklahoma Press, 246 p.
Fremont, John Charles. 1964. *Geographical memoir upon Upper California in illustration of his map of Oregon and California, newly reprinted from the edition of 1848.* San Francisco: The Book Club of California, 65 p.
Frickstad, Walter N. 1955. *A century of California post offices, 1848 to 1954.* Oakland, California: Philatelic Research Society, 395 p.
Galvin, John (editor). 1971. *The first Spanish entry into San Francisco Bay, 1775.* San Francisco, California: John Howell—Books, 130 p.
Gannett, Henry. 1905. *The origin of certain place names in the United States.* (Second edition.) (United States Geological Survey Bulletin No. 258.) Washington: Government Printing Office, 334 p.
Gilliam, Harold. 1962. *Island in time, The Point Reyes Peninsula.* San Francisco: Sierra Club, 87 p.
Gleason, Duncan. 1958. *The islands and ports of California.* New York: The Devin-Adair Company, 201 p.
Goodyear, W.A. 1888. "Petroleum, asphaltum, and natural gas." *Seventh annual report of the State Mineralogist, for the year ending October 1, 1887.* Sacramento: California State Mining Bureau, p. 63-114.
_____1890a. "Napa County." *Tenth annual report of the State Mineralogist, for the year ending December 1, 1890.* Sacramento: California State Mining Bureau, p. 349-363.
_____1890b. "Sonoma County." *Tenth annual report of the State Mineralogist, for the year ending December 1, 1890.* Sacramento: California State Mining Bureau, p. 672-679.
Grant, U.S., IV, and Gale, Hoyt Rodney. 1931. *Catalogue of the marine Pliocene and Pleistocene Mollusca of California and adjacent regions.* (San Diego Society of Natural History Memoirs, Volume I.) San Diego, California: San Diego Society of Natural History, 1036 p.
Gudde, Erwin G. 1949. *California place names.* Berkeley and Los Angeles: University of California Press, 431 p.
_____1969. *California place names.* Berkeley and Los Angeles: University of California Press, 416 p.
Hanna, G. Dallas. 1951. "Geology of the Farallon Islands." *Geologic guidebook of the San Francisco Bay counties.* (California Division of Mines Bulletin 154.) San Francisco, California: Division of Mines, p. 301-310.
Hanna, Phil Townsend. 1951. *The dictionary of California land names.* Los Angeles: The Automobile Club of Southern California, 392 p.
Hanna, Warren L. 1979. *Lost harbor, The controversy over Drake's California anchorage.* Berkeley, Los Angeles, London: University of California Press, 459 p.
Hansen, Gladys, and Condon, Emmet. 1989. *Denial of disaster.* San Francisco: Cameron and Company, 160 p.
Hansen, Harvey J., and Miller, Jeanne Thurlow. 1962. *Wild oats in Eden, Sonoma County in the 19th century.* Santa Rosa, California: (Authors), 147 p.
Harlow, Neal. 1950. *The maps of San Francisco Bay, from the Spanish discovery in 1769 to the American occupation.* The Book Club of California, 140 p.
Hart, James D. 1978. *A companion to California.* New York: Oxford University Press, 504 p.
Heig, Adair. 1982. *History of Petaluma, A California river town.* Petaluma, California: Scottwall Associates, 166 p.
Higgins, Chris T. 1983. "Geology of Annadel State Park." *California Geology,* v. 36, no. 11, p. 235-241.
Hildebrand, George H. 1982. *Borax pioneer: Francis Marion Smith.* San Diego, California: Howell-North Books, 318 p.
Hillman, Raymond W., and Covello, Leonard A. 1985. *Cities and towns of San Joaquin County since 1847.* Fresno, California: Panorama West Books, 248 p.
Hine, Robert V. 1983. *California's utopian colonies.* Berkeley, Los Angeles, London: University of California Press, 209 p.
Holmes, Kenneth L. (editor). 1983. *Covered wagon women, Diaries & letters from the western trails, 1840-1890, Volume I, 1840-1848.* Glendale, California: The Arthur H. Clark Company, 272 p.
Honke, Martin T., Jr., and Ver Planck, William E., Jr. 1950. "Mines and mineral resources of Sonoma County, California." *California Journal of Mines and Geology,* v. 46, no. 1, p. 83-141.
Hoover, Mildred Brooke. 1932. *The Farallon Islands, California.* Stanford University, California: Stanford University Press, 18 p.
Hoover, Mildred Brooke, Rensch, Hero Eugene, and Rensch, Ethel Grace. 1966. *Historic spots in California.* (Third edition, revised by William N. Abeloe.) Stanford, California: Stanford University Press, 642 p.
Hynding, Alan. 1982. *From frontier to suburb, The story of the San Mateo peninsula.* Belmont, California: Star Publishing Company, 343 p.
Irelan, William, Jr. 1888. "Report of the State Mineralogist." *Eighth annual report of the State Mineralogist for the year ending October 1, 1888.* Sacramento: California State Mining Bureau, p. 12-695.
Jackson, Walter. 1976. *Bridgeport, Mendocino County, California.* Ukiah, California: Mendocino County Historical Society, *Inc.*, 16 p.
Johnson, Kenneth M. 1963. *The New Almaden quicksilver mine.* Georgetown, California: The Talisman Press, 115 p.
Kelly, William. 1950. *A stroll through the diggings of California.* Oakland, California: Biobooks, 206 p.
Kroeber, A.L. 1916. "California place names of Indian origin." *University of California Publications in American Archæology and Ethnology,* v. 12, no. 2, p. 31-69.
Laizure, C. McK. 1926. "San Francisco field division (Marin County)." *Mining in California,* v. 22, no. 3, p. 314-365.
_____1927a. "San Francisco field division (Contra Costa County)." *Mining in California,* v. 23, no. 1, p. 2-31.
_____1927b. "San Francisco field division (Solano County)." *Mining in California,* v. 23, no. 2, p. 203-213.
Lanyon, Milton, and Bulmore, Laurence. 1967. *Cinnabar Hills.* (Authors), 128 p.
Latta, Frank F. 1949. *Black gold in the Joaquin.* Caldwell, Idaho: The Caxton Printers, 344 p.
_____1976. *Saga of Rancho El Tejon.* Santa Cruz, California: Bear State Books, 293 p.
LeBaron, Gaye, and others. 1985. *Santa Rosa, a nineteenth century town.* (No place): Historia, Ltd. 224 p.
Lewis, Oscar. 1954. *George Davidson, Pioneer West Coast scientist.* Berkeley and Los Angeles: University of California Press, 146 p.
Lyman, C.S. 1848. "Mines of cinnabar in Upper California." *American Journal of Science and Arts* (series 2), v. 6, no. 17, p. 270-271.
MacGregor, Bruce A. 1968. *South Pacific Coast, An illustrated history of the narrow gauge South Pacific Coast Railroad.* Berkeley, California: Howell-North Books, 280 p.
MacMullen, Jerry. 1944. *Paddle-wheel days in California.* Stanford, California: Stanford University Press, 157 p.
Mason, Jack. 1972. *Point Reyes, The solemn land.* (Second edition.) Inverness, California: North Shore Books, 198 p.
_____1976a. *Earthquake Bay, A history of Tomales Bay, California.* Inverness, California: North Shore Books, 166 p.
_____1976b. *Early Marin.* (Second revised edition.) Inverness, California: North Shore Books, 228 p.
Mendenhall, Walter C. 1908. *Preliminary report on the ground waters of San Joaquin Valley, California.* (United States Geological Survey Water-Supply Paper 222.) Washington: Government Printing Office, 52 p.
Menefee, C.A. 1873. *Historical and descriptive sketch book of Napa, Sonoma, Lake and Mendocino.* Napa City: Reporter Publishing House, 356 p.
Miller, Jeanne Thurlow. 1967. *Seeing historic Sonoma today.* Santa Rosa, California: The Miller Associates, 50 p.
Miller, Robert C. 1958. "The relict fauna of Lake Merced, San Francisco." *Journal of Marine Research,* v. 17, p. 375-382.
Morrall, June. 1978. *Half Moon Bay memories.* El Granada, California: Moonbeam Press, 176 p.
Mosier, Dan L. 1979. *California coal towns, coaling stations, & landings.* San Leandro, California: Mines Road Books, 8 p.
Mosier, Dan, and Finney, Page. 1980. *Dublin gold, The story of Gold Creek.* San Leandro, California: Mines Road Books, 17 p.
Mosier, Page, and Mosier, Dan. 1986. *Alameda County place names.* Fremont, California: Mines Road Books, 105 p.
Mullen, Barbara Dorr. 1974. *Sonoma County crossroads.* San Rafael, California: C M Publications, (no pagination).
Nelson, N.C. 1909. "Shellmounds of the San Francisco Bay region." *University of California Publications in American Archæology and Ethnology,* v. 7, no. 4, p. 309-356.
Newhall, Ruth Waldo. 1958. *The Newhall ranch.* San Marino, California: The Huntington Library, 120 p.
O'Brien, Robert. 1948. *This is San Francisco.* San Carlos, California: Nourse Publishing Company, 351 p.
Parke, John G. 1857. "General report." *Reports of explorations and surveys, to ascertain the most practicable and economical route for a railroad from the Mississippi River to the Pacific Ocean.* Volume VII. (33d Cong.,

2d Sess., Sen. Ex. Doc. No. 78.) Washington: Beverley Tucker, Printer, 42 p.

Perez, Crisostomo N. 1996. *Land grants in Alta California.* Rancho Cordova, California: Landmark Enterprises, 264 p.

Pierce, Marjorie. 1977. *East of the Gabilans.* Fresno: Valley Publishers, 194 p.

Rambo, F. Ralph, 1964. *Almost forgotten.* (Author), 48 p.

____1973. *Pioneer blue book of the old Santa Clara Valley.* San Jose, California: The Rosicrucian Press, Ltd., 48 p.

Reinstedt, Randall A. 1975. *Shipwrecks & sea monsters of California's central coast.* Carmel, California: Ghost Town Publications, 168 p.

Revere, Joseph Warren. 1947. *Naval duty in California.* Oakland, California: Biobooks, 245 p.

Ringgold, Cadwalader. 1852. *A series of charts, with sailing directions, embracing surveys of the Farallones, entrance to the Bay of San Francisco, Bays of San Francisco and San Pablo, Straits of Carquines and Suisun Bay, confluence and deltaic branches of the Sacramento and San Joaquin Rivers, and the Sacramento River (with the Middle Fork) to the American River, including the cities of Sacramento and Boston, State of California.* (Fourth edition, with additions.) Washington: Jno. T. Towers, 48 p.

Salley, H.E. 1977. *History of California post offices, 1849-1976.* La Mesa, California: Postal History Associates, Inc., 300 p.

Sawyer, Eugene T. 1922. *History of Santa Clara County, California.* Los Angeles, California: Historic Record Company, 310 p.

Schwartz, Harvey. 1979. "Fort Ross, California, Imperial Russian outpost on America's western frontier, 1812-1841." *Journal of the West,* v. 18, no. 2, p. 35-48.

Shanks, Ralph C., Jr., and Shanks, Janetta Thompson. 1976. *Lighthouses of San Francisco Bay.* San Anselmo, California: Costaño Books, 125 p.

Shepherd, Forest. 1851. "Observations on the Pluton Geysers of California." *American Journal of Science and Arts* (series 2), v. 12, no. 35, p. 153-158.

Shumate, Albert. 1977. *Francisco Pacheco of Pacheco Pass.* Stockton, California: University of the Pacific, 47 p.

Smith and Elliott. 1979. *Facsimile reproduction of Illustrations of Contra Costa Co., California, with historical sketch, 1879, Smith & Elliott.* Fresno: Valley Publishers, 57 p.

Smith, Persifor F. 1850. "Report of General Persifor F. Smith." *Report of the Secretary of War, communicating information in relation to the geology and topography of California.* (31st Cong., 1st Sess., Sen. Ex. Doc. No. 47.) Washington: Government Printing Office, p. 75-108.

Soule, Frank, Gihon, John H., and Nisbet, James. 1855. *The annals of San Francisco.* New York: D. Appleton & Company, 852 p.

Spence, Mary Lee, and Jackson, Donald (editors). 1973. *The expeditions of John Charles Frémont, Volume 2, The Bear Flag revolt and the court-martial.* Urbana, Chicago, and London: University of Illinois Press, 519 p.

Stanger, Frank M. 1963. *South from San Francisco, San Mateo County, California, Its history and heritage.* San Mateo, California: San Mateo County Historical Association, 214 p.

____1967. *Sawmills in the redwoods, Logging on the San Francisco peninsula, 1849-1967.* San Mateo, California: San Mateo County Historical Association, 160 p.

Stanger, Frank M., and Brown, Alan K. 1969. *Who discovered the Golden Gate?* San Mateo, California: San Mateo County Historical Association, 173 p.

Stanton, Timothy W. 1896. "The faunal relations of the Eocene and Upper Cretaceous of the Pacific Coast." *Seventeenth Annual Report of the United States Geological Survey to the Secretary of the Interior, Part III, Mineral resources of the United States, 1895.* Washington: Government Printing Office, p. 1005-1060.

Taylor, Bayard. 1850. *Eldorado, or Adventures in the path of empire.* New York: George P. Putnam, (two volumes) 251 p + 247 p.

Teather, Louise. 1986. *Place names of Marin.* San Francisco, California: Scottwall Associates, 96 p.

Thompson & West. 1876. *Historical atlas map of Santa Clara County, California.* San Francisco, California: Thompson & West, 119 p.

____1878. *Official and historical atlas map of Alameda County, California.* Oakland, California: Thompson & West, 171 p.

____1879. *History of San Joaquin County, California.* Oakland, California: Thompson & West, 142 p.

Trask, John B., 1856. *Report on the geology of northern and southern California.* (Sen., Sess. of 1856, Doc. No. 14.) Sacramento: State Printer, 66 p.

Treutlein, Theodore E. 1968. *San Francisco Bay, Discovery and colonization, 1769-1776.* San Francisco: California Historical Society, 152 p.

Tyson, James L. 1955. *Diary of a physician in California.* Oakland, California: Biobooks, 124 p.

Tyson, Philip T. 1850. "Report of P.T. Tyson, esq., upon the geology of California." *Report of the Secretary of War, communicating information in relation to the geology and topography of California.* (31st Cong., 1st Sess., Sen. Ex. Doc. No. 47.) Washington: Government Printing Office, p. 3-74.

United States Board on Geographic Names. 1901. *Second report of the United States Board on Geographic Names, 1890-1899.* Washington: Government Printing Office, 150 p.

____(under name "United States Geographic Board"). 1933. *Sixth report of the United States Geographic Board, 1890 to 1932.* Washington: Government Printing Office, 834 p.

____(under name "United States Geographic Board"). 1934. *Decisions of the United States Geographic Board, No. 41—May 2, 1934.* Washington: Government Printing Office, 4 p.

____(under name "United States Board on Geographical Names"). 1939. *Decisions of the United States Board on Geographical Names, Decisions rendered between July 1, 1938, and June 30, 1939.* Washington: Government Printing Office, 41 p.

____(under name "United States Board on Geographical Names"). 1942. *Decisions of the United States Board on Geographical Names, Decisions rendered between July 1, 1940, and June 30, 1941.* Washington: Government Printing Office, 89 p.

____(under name "United States Board on Geographical Names"). 1943. *Decisions rendered between July 1, 1941, and June 30, 1943.* Washington: Department of the Interior, 104 p.

____1948. *Decision lists nos. 4801-4806, January-June, 1948.* Washington: Department of the Interior, 25 p.

____1949a. *Decision list no. 4903, March 1949.* Washington: Department of the Interior. 26 p.

____1949b. *Decision lists nos. 4905, 4906, May, June, 1949.* Washington: Department of the Interior, 10 p.

____1950. *Decisions on names in the United States and Alaska rendered during April, May, and June 1950.* (Decision list no. 5006.) Washington: Department of the Interior, 47 p.

____1954. *Decisions on names in the United States, Alaska and Puerto Rico, Decisions rendered from July 1950 to May 1954.* (Decision list no. 5401.) Washington: Department of the Interior, 115 p.

____1957. *Decisions on names in the United States, Alaska and Hawaii, Decisions rendered from May 1954 through March 1957.* (Decision list no. 5701.) Washington: Department of the Interior, 23 p.

____1959a. *Decisions on names in the United States, Puerto Rico and the Virgin Islands, Decisions rendered from April 1957 through December 1958.* (Decision list no. 5901.) Washington: Department of the Interior, 100 p.

____1959b. *Decisions on names in the United States, Decisions rendered from January, 1959 through April, 1959.* (Decision list no. 5902.) Washington: Department of the Interior, 49 p.

____1960a. *Decisions on names in the United States and Puerto Rico, Decisions rendered in May, June, July, and August, 1959.* (Decision list no. 5903.) Washington: Department of the Interior, 79 p.

____1960b. *Decisions on names in the United States, Puerto Rico and the Virgin Islands, Decisions rendered from January through April 1960.* (Decision list no. 6001.) Washington: Department of the Interior, 79 p.

____1961a. *Decisions on names in the United States, Decisions rendered from September through December 1960.* (Decision List No. 6003.) Washington: Department of the Interior, 73 p.

____1961b. *Decisions on names in the United States, Decisions rendered from May through August 1961.* (Decision list no. 6102.) Washington: Department of the Interior, 81 p.

____1962a. *Decisions on names in the United States, Decisions rendered from September through December 1961.* (Decision list no. 6103.) Washington: Department of the Interior, 75 p.

____1962b. *Decisions on names in the United States, Decisions rendered from January through April 1962.* (Decision list no. 6201.) Washington: Department of the Interior, 72 p.

____1964. *Decisions on geographic names in the United States, January through April 1964.* (Decision list no. 6401.) Washington: Department of the Interior, 74 p.

____1967a. *Decisions on geographic names in the United States, January through March 1967.* (Decision list no. 6701.) Washington: Department of the Interior, 20 p.

____1967b. *Decisions on geographic names in the United States, April through June 1967.* (Decision list no. 6702.) Washington: Department of the Interior, 26 p.

____1967c. *Decisions on geographic names in the United States, July through September 1967.* (Decision list no. 6703.) Washington: Department of the Interior, 29 p.

____1968a. *Decisions on geographic names in the United States, October through December 1967.* (Decision list no. 6704.) Washington: Department of the Interior, 46 p.

____1968b. *Decisions on geographic names in the United States, January through March 1968.* (Decision list no. 6801.) Washington: Department of the Interior, 51 p.

____1969. *Decisions on geographic names in the United States, July through September 1969.* (Decision list no. 6903.) Washington: Department of the

Interior, 36 p.
_____1970a. *Decisions on geographic names in the United States, April through June 1970.* (Decision list no. 7002.) Washington: Department of the Interior, 20 p.
_____1970b. *Decisions on geographic names in the United States, July through September 1970.* (Decision list no. 7003.) Washington: Department of the Interior, 15 p.
_____1972. *Decisions on geographic names in the United States, April through June 1972.* (Decision list no. 7202.) Washington: Department of the Interior, 30 p.
_____1973a. *Decisions on geographic names in the United States, October through December 1972.* (Decision list no. 7204.) Washington: Department of the Interior, 15 p.
_____1973b. *Decisions on geographic names in the United States, April through June 1973.* (Decision list no. 7302.) Washington: Department of the Interior, 16 p.
_____1974. *Decisions on geographic names in the United States, July through September 1974.* (Decision list no. 7403.) Washington: Department of the Interior, 34 p.
_____1975a. *Decisions on geographic names in the United States, January through March 1975.* (Decision list no. 7501.) Washington: Department of the Interior, 36 p.
_____1975b *Decisions on geographic names in the United States, July through September 1975.* (Decision list no. 7503.) Washington: Department of the Interior, 33 p.
_____1976a. *Decisions on geographic names in the United States, October through December 1975.* (Decision list no. 7504.) Washington: Department of the Interior, 45 p.
_____1976b. *Decisions on geographic names in the United States, April through June 1976.* (Decision list no. 7602.) Washington: Department of the Interior, 26 p.
_____1977a. *Decisions on geographic names in the United States, January through March 1977.* (Decision list no. 7701.) Washington: Department of the Interior, 32 p.
_____1977b. *Decisions on geographic names in the United States, July through September 1977.* (Decision List No. 7703.) Washington: Department of the Interior, 25 p.
_____1978a. *Decisions on geographic names in the United States, October through December 1977.* (Decision list no. 7704.) Washington: Department of the Interior, 29 p.
_____1978b. *Decisions on geographic names in the United States, January through March 1978.* (Decision list no. 7801.) Washington: Department of the Interior, 18 p.
_____1979a. *Decisions on geographic names in the United States, January through March 1979.* (Decision list no. 7901.) Washington: Department of the Interior, 27 p.
_____1979b. *Decisions on geographic names in the United States, April through June 1979.* (Decision list no. 7902.) Washington: Department of the Interior, 33 p.
_____1979c. *Decisions on geographic names in the United States, July through September 1979.* (Decision list no. 7903.) Washington: Department of the Interior, 38 p.
_____1980. *Decisions on geographic names in the United States, January through March 1980.* (Decision list no. 8001.) Washington: Department of the Interior, 23 p.
_____1981a. *Decisions on geographic names in the United States, October through December 1980.* (Decision list no. 8004.) Washington: Department of the Interior, 21 p.
_____1981b. *Decisions on geographic names in the United States, January through March 1981.* (Decision list no. 8101.) Washington: Department of the Interior, 23 p.
_____1983a. *Decisions on geographic names in the United States, July through September 1982.* (Decision list no. 8203.) Washington: Department of the Interior, 25 p.
_____1983b. *Decisions on geographic names in the United States, January through March 1983.* (Decision list no. 8301.) Washington: Department of the Interior, 33 p.
_____1983c. *Decisions on geographic names in the United States, April through June 1983.* (Decision list no. 8302.) Washington: Department of the Interior, 29 p.
_____1983d. *Decisions on geographic names in the United States, July through September 1983.* (Decision list no. 8303.) Washington: Department of the Interior, 26 p.
_____1983e. *Decisions on geographic names in the United States, October through December 1983.* (Decision list no. 8304.) Washington: Department of the Interior, 20 p.
_____1984a. *Decisions on geographic names in the United States, January through March 1984.* (Decision list no. 8401.) Washington: Department of the Interior, 29 p.
_____1984b. *Decisions on Geographic names in the United States, April through June 1984.* (Decision list no. 8402.) Washington: Department of the Interior, 22 p.
_____1984c. *Decisions on geographic names in the United States, October through December 1984.* (Decision list no. 8404.) Washington: Department of the Interior, 18 p.
_____1985a. *Decisions on geographic names in the United States, January through March 1985.* (Decision list no. 8501.) Washington: Department of the Interior, 18 p.
_____1985b. *Decisions on geographic names in the United States, October through December 1985.* (Decision list no. 8504.) Washington: Department of the Interior, 12 p.
_____1986. *Decisions on geographic names in the United States, October through December 1986.* (Decision list no. 8604.) Washington: Department of the Interior, 22 p.
_____1988a. *Decisions on geographic names in the United States, April through June 1988.* (Decision list no. 8802.) Washington: Department of the Interior, 19 p.
_____1988b. *Decisions on geographic names in the United States, October through December 1988.* (Decision list no. 8804.) Washington: Department of the Interior, 20 p.
_____1989. *Decisions on geographic names in the United States, January through March 1989.* (Decision list no. 8901.) Washington: Department of the Interior, 9 p.
_____1991. *Decisions on geographic names in the United States.* (Decision list 1991.) Washington: Department of the Interior, 40 p.
_____1992. *Decisions on geographic names in the United States.* (Decision list 1992.) Washington: Department of the Interior, 21 p.
_____1995. *Decisions on geographic names in the United States.* (Decision list 1995.) Washington: Department of the Interior, 19 p.
United States Coast and Geodetic Survey. 1963. *United States Coast Pilot 7, Pacific Coast, California, Oregon, Washington, and Hawaii.* (Ninth edition.) Washington: United States Government Printing Office, 336 p.
United States Supreme Court. 1857. *The United States, Appellants, vs. The Guadalupe Mining Company.* (Sen. Ex. Doc. 78.) 158 p.
Wagner, Henry R. 1968. *The cartography of the Northwest Coast of America to the year 1800.* (One-volume reprint of the 1937 edition.) Amsterdam: N. Israel, 543 p.
Wagner, Jack R. 1974. *The last whistle (Ocean Shore Railroad).* Berkeley, California: Howell-North Books, 135 p.
Waring, Gerald A. 1915. *Springs of California.* (United States Geological Survey Water-Supply Paper 338.) Washington: Government Printing Office, 410 p.
Wheat, Carl I. 1959. *Mapping the Transmississippi West.* Volume One. San Francisco: The Institute of Historical Cartography, 349 p.
White, Philo. 1965. *Philo White's narrative of a cruize in the Pacific to South America and California on the U.S. Sloop-of-War "Dale," 1841-1843.* Denver, Colorado: Old West Publishing Company, 84 p.
Whiting, J.S., and Whiting, Richard J. 1960. *Forts of the State of California.* (Authors), 90 p.
Whitney, J.D. 1865. *Report of progress and synopsis of the field-work from 1860 to 1864.* (Geological Survey of California, Geology, Volume I.) Published by authority of the Legislature of California, 498 p.
Wilkes, Charles. 1958. *Columbia River to the Sacramento.* Oakland, California: Biobooks, 140 p.
Williamson, R.S. 1855. "Report." *Reports of explorations and surveys, to ascertain the most practicable and economical route for a railroad from the Mississippi River to the Pacific Ocean.* Volume V, part I. (33d Cong., 2d Sess., Sen. Ex. Doc. No. 78) Washington: Beverley Tucker, Printer, 43 p.
_____1857. "General report." *Reports of explorations and surveys, to ascertain the most practicable and economical route for a railroad from the Mississippi River to the Pacific Ocean.* Volume VI, part I. (33d Cong., 2d Sess., Sen. Ex. Doc. No. 78.) Washington: Beverly Tucker, Printer, 134 p.
Wyman, Beth. 1983. *Hiram Morgan Hill.* (Author), 50 p.
Young, John V. 1979. *Ghost towns of the Santa Cruz Mountains.* Santa Cruz, California: Paper Vision Press, 156 p.

QUADRANGLE MAPS

(All maps published by United States Geological Survey, except as noted. Dates identify the editions of the maps. If a reprinted or revised map was used, the year of reprinting or revision is given in parentheses, unless the reprinted or revised map is cited specifically in the text.)

Aetna Springs 7.5'—1958.
Allendale 7.5' (same area as Wolfskill 7.5')—1953; 1953, photorevised 1968 and 1973.
Altamont 7.5'—1953.
Annapolis 7.5'—1943; 1977.
Año Nuevo 15'—1948 (Army).
7.5'—1955.
Antioch 15' (same area as Pittsburg 15')—1908.

Antioch North 7.5' (same area as Collinsville 7.5')—1953 (photorevised 1968); 1978.
Antioch South 7.5' (same area as Lone Tree Valley 7.5')—1953.
Arched Rock 7.5'—1977.
Asti 7.5'—1959.
Benicia 7.5'—1959; 1959, photorevised 1980.
Bethany 7.5' (same area as Clifton Court Forebay 7.5')—1952.
Big Basin 7.5'—1955.
Birds Landing 7.5'—1918; 1953 (photorevised 1968).
Bodega Head 7.5'—1942; 1972.
Bolinas 7.5'—1954.
Bouldin 7.5' (same area as Bouldin Island 7.5')—1910 (reprinted 1947).
Bouldin Island 7.5' (same area as Bouldin 7.5')—1952 (photorevised 1968); 1978.
Brentwood 7.5'—1954; 1978.
Briones Valley 7.5'—1959; 1959, photorevised 1968.
Brooks 7.5'—1959.
Byron 15'—1916 (reprinted 1941).
Bryon Hot Springs 7.5'—1953.
Cache Slough 7.5' (same area as Liberty Island 7.5')—1916.
Calaveras Reservoir 7.5'—1961; 1961, photorevised 1968 and 1973.
Calistoga 15'—1945; 1959.
7.5'—1958.
Camp Meeker 7.5'—1954 (photorevised 1971).
Capay 15' (same area as Lake Berryessa 15')—1945.
Capell Valley 7.5'—1951; 1951, photorevised 1968.
Carquinez 15' (same area as Karquines 15' and Carquinez Strait 15')—1938 (Army).
Carquinez Strait 15' (same area as Carquinez 15' and Karquines 15')—1896 (reprinted 1954); 1940 (Army).
Castle Rock Ridge 7.5'—1955.
Cazadero 7.5'—1943; 1978.
Cedar Mountain 7.5'—1956.
Chiles Valley 7.5'—1958.
Chittenden 7.5'—1955; 1955, photorevised 1968 and 1973.
Clayton 7.5'—1953.
Clifton Court Forebay 7.5' (same area as Bethany 7.5')—1978.
Cloverdale 7.5'—1960.
Collinsville 7.5' (same area as Antioch North 7.5')—1918 (reprinted 1947).
Concord 15'—1897 (reprinted 1913); 1915 (reprinted 1947); 1943 (Army).
Cordelia 7.5'—1951 (photorevised 1968).
Cotati 7.5'—1954; 1954, photorevised 1980.
Courtland 7.5' (same area as Vorden 7.5')—1952 (photorevised 1968); 1978.
Crevison Peak 7.5'—1955.
Cupertino 7.5'—1961; 1961, photorevised 1968 and 1973.
Cuttings Wharf 7.5'—1949; 1949, photorevised 1968.
Davis 7.5' (same area as Swingle 7.5')—1952 (photorevised 1968 and 1975).
Denverton 7.5'—1918; 1953 (photorevised 1968 and 1973).
Detert Reservoir 7.5'—1958.
Diablo 7.5'—1953.
Dixon 7.5'—1952; 1952, photorevised 1968 and 1975.
Double Point 7.5'—1954.
Dozier 7.5' (same area as Maine Prairie 7.5')—1952 (photorevised 1968).
Drakes Bay 7.5'—1953.
Dublin 7.5'—1961; 1961, photorevised 1980.
Duncans Mills 15'—1921 (Army).
7.5'—1943; 1979.
Elmira 7.5'—1917; 1953; 1953, photorevised 1980.
Eylar Mountain 7.5'—1955.
Fairfield North 7.5'—1951; 1951, photorevised 1968 and 1973.
Fairfield South 7.5'—1949 (photorevised 1968).
Farallon Islands 7.5'—1988.
Fort Ross 7.5'—1943; 1978.
Franklin Point 7.5'—1955.
Geyserville 7.5'—1955.
Gilroy 7.5'—1955.
Gilroy Hot Springs 15'—1921 (reprinted 1942).
7.5'—1955.
Glen Ellen 7.5'—1954; 1954, photorevised 1968.
Gualala 7.5'—1960.
Guerneville 7.5'—1955.
Guinda 7.5'—1959.
Half Moon Bay 7.5'—1961.
Halfmoon Bay 15'—1940 (Army).
Hayward 15' (same area as Haywards 15')—1915 (reprinted 1939).
7.5'—1959.
Haywards 15' (same area as Hayward 15')—1899 (reprinted 1913).
Healdsburg 15'—1940 (reprinted 1948).
7.5'—1955.
Honker Bay 7.5'—1918; 1953; 1953, photorevised 1968 and 1973.
Hopland 15'—1944 (Army); 1960.
Hunters Point 7.5'—1956; 1956, photorevised 1968; 1956, photorevised 1980.
Inverness 7.5'—1954; 1954, photorevised 1971.
Isabel Valley 7.5'—1955.
Isleton 7.5'—1978.
Jericho Valley 7.5'—1958.
Jersey 7.5' (same area as Jersey Island 7.5')—1910 (reprinted 1932).
Jersey Island 7.5' (same area as Jersey 7.5')—1952 (photorevised 1968); 1978.
Jimtown 7.5'—1955.
Karquines 15' (same area as Carquinez 15' and Carquinez Strait 15')—1898.
Kelseyville 15'—1921 (Army); 1944 (Army); 1959.
Kenwood 7.5'—1954; 1954, photorevised 1980.
Knoxville 7.5'—1958.
La Costa Valley 7.5'—1960; 1960, photorevised 1968.
La Honda 7.5'—1961.
Lake Berryessa 7.5'—1959.
Las Trampas Ridge 7.5'—1959.
Laurel 7.5'—1955.
Liberty Island 7.5' (same area as Cache Slough 7.5')—1952 (photorevised 1968); 1978.
Lick Observatory 7.5'—1955.
Livermore 15' (same area as Pleasanton 15')—1961.
7.5'—1961.
Loma Prieta 7.5'—1955.
Los Gatos 15' (same area as New Almaden 15')—1919 (reprinted 1942).
7.5'—1953; 1953, photorevised 1968 and 1973.
Lower Lake 15'—1945 (Army).
Maine Prairie 7.5' (same area as Dozier 7.5')—1916.
Mare Island 15'—1916.
7.5'—1959 (photorevised 1980).
Mariposa Peak 7.5'—1969.
Mark West Springs 7.5'—1958.
Mendenhall Springs 7.5'—1956; 1956, photorevised 1971.
Merritt 7.5'—1952 (photorevised 1968 and 1975).
Midway 7.5'—1953.
Milpitas 7.5'—1961 (photorevised 1968 and 1973).
Mindego Hill 7.5'—1961.
Mississippi Creek 7.5'—1955.
Montara Mountain 7.5'—1956; 1956, photorevised 1980.
Monticello Dam 7.5'—1959.
Morgan Hill 15' (same area as Reiff 15')—1917 (reprinted 1941); 1940 (Army).
7.5'—1955; 1955, photorevised 1968 and 1973.
Morgan Valley 15' (same area as Reiff 15')—1944.
Mountain View 7.5'—1953; 1961; 1961, photorevised 1968 and 1973.
Mount Boardman 15'—1942 (Army).
7.5'—1955.
Mount Day 7.5'—1955.
Mount Diablo 15'—1898 (reprinted 1941).
Mount George 7.5'—1951 (photorevised 1968).
Mount Hamilton 15'—1897 (reprinted 1932).
Mount Madonna 7.5'—1955; 1955, photorevised 1968 and 1973.
Mount Saint Helena 7.5'—1959.
Mount Sizer 7.5'—1955.
Mount Stakes 7.5'—1955.
Mount Tamalpais 15' (same area as Tamalpais 15')—1950.
Mount Vaca 15'—1942 (Army); 1951.
7.5'—1951 (photorevised 1968).
Mustang Peak 7.5'—1955.
Napa 30'—1902 (reprinted 1932).
7.5'—1951 (photorevised 1968 and 1973).
New Almaden 15' (same area as Los Gatos 15')—1919 (reprinted 1928).
Newark 7.5'—1948; 1959 (photorevised 1980).
Niles 7.5'—1961 (photorevised 1980).
Novato 7.5'—1954 (photorevised 1968).
Oakland East 7.5'—1959.
Oakland West 7.5'—1959.
Ornbaun 15' (same area as Ornbaun Valley 15')—1944 (Army).
Ornbaun Valley 15' (same area as Ornbaun 15')—1960.
Pacheco Pass 7.5'—1955.
Pacheco Peak 7.5'—1955.
Palo Alto 15'—1899; 1899, reprinted 1930; 1940 (Army).
7.5'—1953; 1961; 1961, photorevised 1968 and 1973.
Petaluma 15'—1914 (reprinted 1947); 1942 (Army); 1954.
7.5'—1953 (photorevised 1968).
Petaluma Point 7.5'—1959 (photorevised 1968).
Petaluma River 7.5'—1954; 1954, photorevised 1968 and 1973.
Pigeon Point 7.5'—1955.
Pittsburg 15' (same area as Antioch 15')—1953.
Plantation 15'—1915.
7.5'—1943; 1977.
Pleasanton 15' (same area as Livermore 15')—1906 (reprinted 1928).

Point Bonita 7.5'—1954.
Point Reyes 15'—1918 (reprinted 1951).
Point Reyes NE 7.5'—1954 (photorevised 1971).
Pope Valley 15' (same area as Saint Helena 15')—1921 (Army).
Port Chicago 7.5' (same area as Vine Hill 7.5')—1959 (photorevised 1968).
Redwood Point 7.5'—1959.
Richmond 7.5'—1959.
Rio Vista 7.5'—1910; 1978.
Rutherford 7.5'—1951 (photorevised 1968).
Saint Helena 15' (same area as Pope Valley 15')—1942.
7.5'—1960.
San Felipe 7.5'—1955; 1955; photorevised 1971.
San Francisco 1°x 2°—1947; 1956 (revised 1969).
15'—1899; 1899, reprinted 1906; 1899, reprinted 1913; 1915 (reprinted 1947); 1942 (Army).
San Francisco North 7.5'—1947; 1950; 1956; 1956, photorevised 1968 and 1973.
San Francisco South 7.5'—1947; 1956; 1956, photorevised 1980.
San Geronimo 7.5'—1954; 1954, photorevised 1971.
San Gregorio 7.5'—1961; 1961, photorevised 1968.
San Jose 1°x 2°—1962 (revised 1969).
15'—1899 (reprinted 1905).
San Jose East 7.5'—1961; 1961, photorevised 1968 and 1973.
San Jose West 7.5'—1961; 1961, photorevised 1968 and 1973.
San Juan Bautista 15'—1917 (reprinted 1931).
San Leandro 7.5'—1959.
San Mateo 15'—1899 (reprinted 1913); 1915 (reprinted 1947); 1942 (Army).
7.5'—1947; 1956; 1956, photorevised 1980.
San Quentin 7.5'—1959.
San Rafael 7.5'—1954.
Santa Cruz 1°x 2°—1956.
30'—1902 (reprinted 1939).
Santa Rosa 1°x 2°—1958 (limited revision 1967).
15'—1916; 1944 (reprinted 1951); 1954.
7.5'—1954; 1954, photorevised 1968 and 1973.
Santa Teresa Hills 7.5'—1953.
Saxon 7.5'—1916; 1952 (photorevised 1968).
Sears Point 7.5'—1951 (photorevised 1968).
Sebastopol 15'—1942 (reprinted 1948); 1954.
7.5'—1954; 1954, photorevised 1968.
Skaggs 15'—1921.
Skaggs Springs 7.5' (same area as Warm Springs Dam 7.5')—1943.
Sonoma 15'—1942 (Army); 1951.
7.5'—1951 (photorevised 1968).
Stewarts Point 7.5'—1943; 1978.
Suisun (special)—1918.
Swingle 7.5' (same area as Davis 7.5')—1915.
Tamalpais 15' (same area as Mount Tamalpais 15')—1897 (reprinted 1932).
Tassajara 7.5'—1953.
Telsa 15'—1907 (reprinted 1941).
The Geysers 7.5'—1959.
Three Sisters 7.5'—1954.
Tomales 7.5'—1954 (photorevised 1971).
Tombs Creek 7.5'—1943; 1978.
Two Rock 7.5'—1954 (photorevised 1971).
Vacaville 15'—1953.
Valley Ford 7.5'—1954 (photorevised 1971).
Vine Hill 7.5' (same area as Port Chicago 7.5')—1959 (photorevised 1980).
Vorden 7.5' (same area as Courtland 7.5')—1916.
Walnut Creek 7.5'—1959.
Walter Springs 7.5'—1959.
Warm Springs Dam 7.5' (same area as Skaggs Springs 7.5')—1978.
Watsonville East 7.5'—1955.
Whispering Pines 7.5'—1958.
Winters 7.5'—1953 (photorevised 1968).
Wolfskill 7.5' (same area as Allendale 7.5')—1917.
Woodside 7.5'—1961.
Woodward Island 7.5'—1978.
Yountville 7.5'—1951 (photorevised 1968).

MISCELLANEOUS MAPS

Baker. 1855. "Map of the mining region, of California." Drawn by Geo. H. Baker.

Bancroft. 1864. "Bancroft's map of the Pacific States." Compiled by Wm. H. Knight. Published by H.H. Bancroft & Co., Booksellers and Stationers, San Francisco, Cal.

Beechey. 1827-1828. "The harbor of San Francisco, Nueva California." By Captn. F.W. Beechey, R.N.F.R.S.

California Division of Forestry. 1945. "Sonoma County." (Used as base for plate 22 *in* Honke and Ver Planck.)

California Division of Highways. 1934. (Appendix "A" *of* California Division of Highways.)

California Mining Bureau. 1909a. "Sonoma, Marin, Napa, Yolo, and Solano Counties." (*In* California Mining Bureau Bulletin 56.)

_____1909b. "San Francisco, San Mateo, Contra Costa, Alameda, Santa Clara, and Santa Cruz Counties." (*In* California Mining Bureau Bulletin 56.)

_____1917a. (Untitled map *in* California Mining Bureau Bulletin 74, p. 164.)

_____1917b. (Untitled map in California Mining Bureau Bulletin 74, p. 166.)

Cardwell. 1958. "Geologic map of the Santa Rosa and Petaluma Valley areas, California, showing location of wells." (Plate 1 *in* Cardwell.)

Clark. 1924. "Map of the drainage basin of Alameda Creek and adjacent area." (Plate III *in* W.O. Clark.)

Costanso. 1771. "Carta reducida del Oceano Asiatico o mar del Sur." (Reproduced *in* Harlow.)

Crespi. 1772. "Mapa de lo substancial del famoso Puerto y Rio de San Francisco explorado por tierra en el mes de morzo del presente año de 1772." (Reproduced *in* Harlow.)

Dalrymple. 1789. "Plan of Port Sn francisco on the west coast of California." (Reproduced *in* Harlow.)

Davis. 1948. "Map of Napa County, California, showing locations of mines and mineral deposits." (Plate 22 *in* F.F. Davis.)

Davis and Vernon. 1951. "Mines and mineral deposits of Contra Costa County, California" (Plate 42 *in* Davis and Vernon.)

Derby. 1850. "Reconnaissance of the Tulares Valley." Lieut. G.H. Derby, Topl. Engrs., April and May, 1850.

Diller and others. 1915. "Geologic and topographic map of the Shasta route from Seattle, Washington, to San Francisco, California." (*In* Diller and others.)

Durst. 1916. "Sketch map of northwestern Yolo County." (Plate 37 *in* Durst.)

Eddy. 1854. "Approved and declared to be the official map of the State of California by an act of the Legislature passed March 25th 1853." Compiled by W.M. Eddy, State Surveyor General. Published for R.A. Eddy, Marysville, California, by J.H. Colton, New York.

Font. 1777. "Plan, o mapa del viage que bicimos desde Monterey al Puerto de Sn. francisco". (Reproduced *in* Harlow.)

Fremont. 1845. "Map of an exploring expedition to the Rocky Mountains in the year 1842 and to Oregon & North California in the years 1843-44." By Brevet Capt. J.C. Frémont.

_____1848. "Map of Oregon and Upper California from the surveys of John Charles Frémont, and other authorities." Drawn by Charles Preuss. Washington City.

Gibbes. 1852. "A new map of California." By Charles Drayton Gibbes, from his own and other recent surveys and explorations. Published by C.D. Gibbes, Stockton, Cal.

Goddard. 1857. "Britton & Rey's map of the State of California." By George H. Goddard.

Hare. 1872. "Map of vicinity of San Jose." Published by Geo. H. Hare, Book Dealer, San Jose.

Healy. 1866. (Untitled part of a map by Charles T. Healy, reproduced *in* Fava, p. 33.)

Jefferson. 1849. "Map of the emigrant road from Independence Mo. to St. Francisco, California." By T.H. Jefferson.

Mendenhall. 1908. "Artesian areas and groundwater levels in the San Joaquin Valley, California." (Plate I *in* Mendenhall.)

Mitchell. 1856. "Mitchell's new national map." Published by S. Augustus Mitchell.

Nelson. 1909. "Map of San Francisco Bay region showing distribution of shell heaps." (Map I *in* Nelson.)

Parke. 1854-1855. "Map No. 1, San Francisco Bay to the plains of Los Angeles." From explorations and surveys made by Lieut. John G. Parke. Constructed and drawn by H. Custer. (In *Reports of explorations and surveys, to ascertain the most practicable and economical route for a railroad from the Mississippi River to the Pacific Ocean.* Volume XI. 1861.)

Peninsular Railway Company. 1912. (Map showing interurban lines of Peninsular Railway Company, reproduced in *San Jose Mercury,* January 2, 1964.)

Postal Route. 1884. (Map reproduced in *Early California, Northern Edition.* Corvalis, Oregon: Western Guide Publishers, p. 34-43.)

Ringgold. 1850a. "Chart of the Bay of San Pablo, Straits of Carquines, and part of the Bay of San Francisco, California." By Cadwalader Ringgold, Commander, U.S. Navy, Assisted by Simon F. Blunt, Lieut. U.S.N. 1850.

_____1850b. "Chart of Suisun & Vallejo Bays, with the confluence of the Rivers Sacramento and San Joaquin, California." By Cadwalader Ringgold, Commander U.S. Navy, Assisted by Sam. R. Knox, Lieut. U.S.N., and Wm. P. Humphreys & J.H. Rowe Engineers. 1850.

_____1850c. "General chart embracing survey of the Farallones entrance to the Bay of San Francisco, Bays of San Francisco and San Pablo, Straits of Carquines and Suisun Bay, and the Sacramento and San Joaquin Rivers to the cities of Sacramento and San Joaquin, California." By Cadwalader Ringgold, Commander, U.S. Navy. 1850.

_____1850d. "Chart of the Sacramento River from Suisun City to the American River, California." By Cadwalader Ringgold, Commander, U.S. Navy, Assisted by Edwin Cullberg, Lieut. of the Hydrotechnic Corps, Swedish Navy, and T.A. Emmet, Civil Engineer. 1850.

_____1850e. "Straits of Carquines and Vallejo Bay." By Cadwalader Ringgold, U.S. N. 1850.

Rogers and Johnston (1857). "State of California." By Prof. H.D. Rogers & A. Keith Johnston.

Sage. 1846. "Map of Oregon, California, New Mexico, N.W. Texas, & the proposed Territory of Ne-Bras-ka." By Rufus B. Sage.

Smith and Elliott. 1879. "Map of Contra Costa and part of Alameda County." Published by Smith & Elliott, Engravers and lithographers, Oakland, Cal. (*In* Smith and Elliott.)

Soule, Gihon, and Nisbet. 1855. "Map of San Francisco." (*In* Soule, Gihon, and Nisbet, p. 20.)

Thompson and West. 1876. (Maps *in* Thompson and West, 1876.)

_____1878. (Maps *in* Thompson and West, 1878.)

_____1879. (Maps *in* Thompson and West, 1879.)

Trask. 1853. "Topographical map of the mineral districts of California." Being the first map ever published from actual survey. By John B. Trask. Lithog. and Published by Britton & Rey. San Francisco.

Wackenreuder. 1861. "City and County of San Francisco." Drawn by V. Wackenreuder, C.E. Published by Henry G. Langley for the San Francisco directory.

Wilkes. 1841. "Map of Upper California." By the U.S. Ex. Ex. and best authorities.

_____1849. "Map of Upper California." By the best authorities.

Williamson. 1853. "General map of explorations and surveys in California." By Lieut. R.S. Williamson, Topl. Engr., assisted by Lieut. J.G. Parke, Topl. Engr., and Mr. Isaac William Smith, Civ. Engr. (In *Reports of explorations and surveys, to ascertain the most practicable and economical route for a railroad from the Mississippi River to the Pacific Ocean.* Volume XI. 1861.)

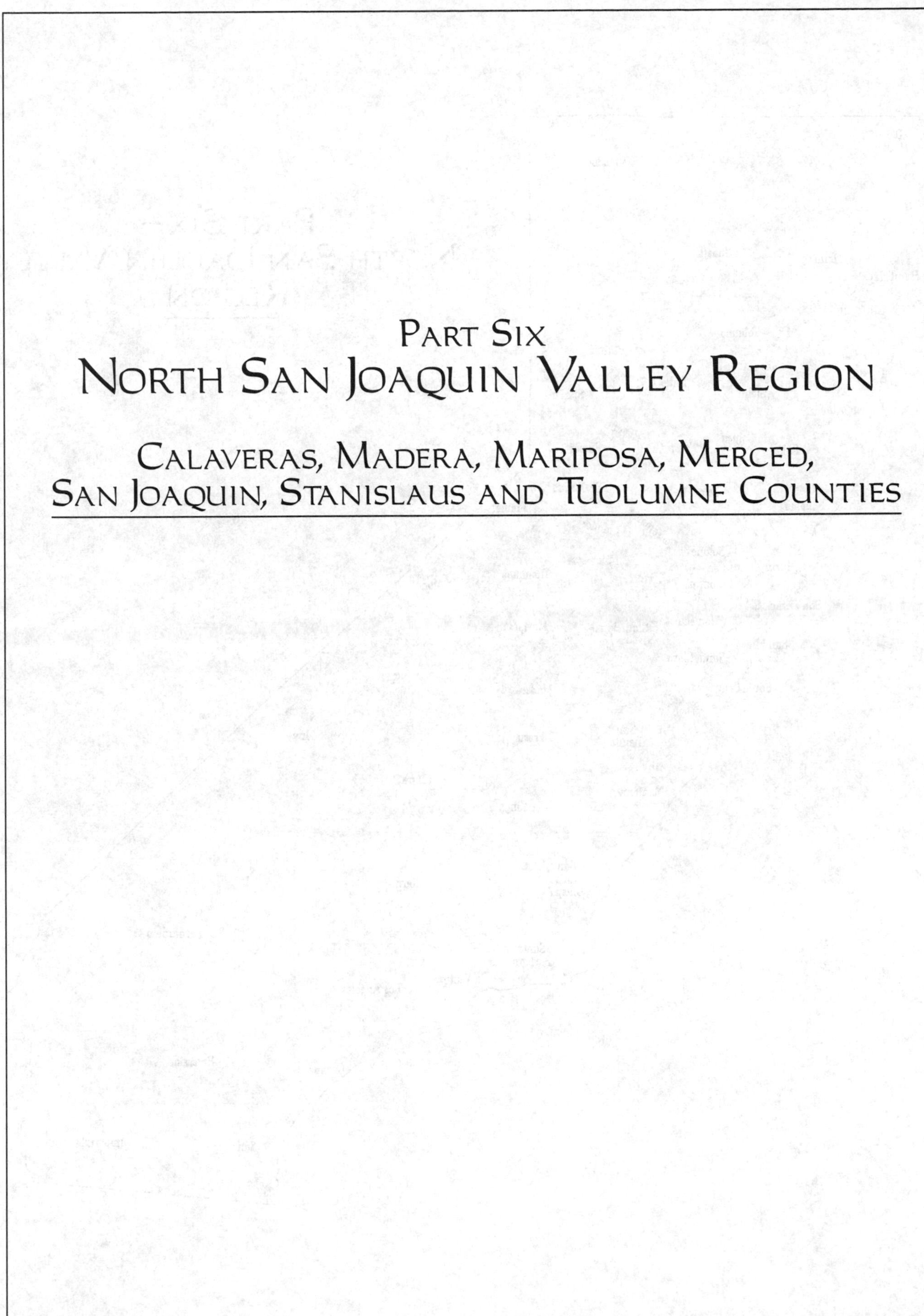

Part Six
North San Joaquin Valley Region

Calaveras, Madera, Mariposa, Merced, San Joaquin, Stanislaus and Tuolumne Counties

Part Six—North San Joaquin Valley Region

North San Joaquin Valley Region
Calaveras, Madera, Mariposa, Merced, San Joaquin, Stanislaus and Tuolumne Counties

Regional Setting

General.—This section concerns geographic features in seven counties—Calaveras, Madera, Mariposa, Merced, San Joaquin, Stanislaus, and Tuolumne—that lie in and around the north part of San Joaquin Valley. Townships (T) and Ranges (R) refer to Mount Diablo Base and Meridian. The map on the facing page shows the location of the North San Joaquin Valley Region and the counties in it. San Joaquin Valley is the south part of the Central Valley, or Great Valley, of California. It takes its name from San Joaquin River, which drains most of it. Early Spanish explorers in the valley found a lake that they called Laguna de los Tulares for the tules or cattails around it, and later the Spaniards began calling the valley itself Los Tulares (Mitchell, p. 5). The *Californian* newspaper for August 22, 1846, called it Toolary valley, Carson (p. 93, 95) called it Tulare Valley and Tulare Plains in 1852, and Derby's (1850) map shows Tulares Valley. The whole Central Valley is called Buena Ventura Valley on Wilkes' (1841) map. The highlands east of the Central Valley form the range called the Sierra Nevada. The United States Board on Geographic Names (1933a, p. 692) ruled against the form "Sierra Nevadas" for the name. The term "High Sierra" commonly is accepted for the part of the range that includes the high peaks (Gudde, 1949, p. 148). Garces called the range Sierra de San Marcos in 1776 (Boyd, p. 3), Wilkes (p. 44) called it California Range in 1841, Lyman (1849a, p. 307) called it "Sierra Nevada, or Snowy Mountains" in 1849, and Kip (p. 46) called it Snowy Range in 1850. Whitney (1865, p. 2) pointed out that the range was long known to the Spaniards as Sierra Nevada, or Snowy Range, because "the most distant and loftiest elevations are never entirely bare of snow, and for a large portion of the year are extensively covered with it." Diablo Range extends south along the west side of San Joaquin Valley from Contra Costa County to the northwest corner of Kern County. Parke's (1854-1855) map has the name "Sierra del Monte Diablo" for the feature, and Whitney (1865, p. 2), who called it Monte Diablo Range, stated that it "is so called from the conspicuous point of that name [Mount Diablo in Contra Costa County]." United States Board on Geographic Names (1933a, p. 264) rejected the names "Monte Diablo Range," "Mount Diablo Range," and "Sierra del Monte Diablo" for the feature.

Calaveras County.—Calaveras County extends from near the crest of the Sierra Nevada westward between Tuolumne River and Stanislaus River to the edge of San Joaquin Valley. It is one of 27 counties that the first state legislature created in 1850; part of its original territory was lost to Amador County in 1854, to Mono County in 1861, and to Alpine County in 1864 (Coy, p. 80-81). Pleasant Valley, later called Double Springs, was the first county seat; the county government moved to Jackson (now in Amador County) in 1851, to Mokelumne Hill in 1852, and to San Andreas in 1866, where it remains (Hoover, Rensch, and Rensch, p. 41-42).

Madera County.—Madera County extends from the crest of the Sierra Nevada southwestward into San Joaquin Valley. It was organized in 1893 from the part of Fresno County that lay north and west of San Joaquin River; the county boundaries have not changed (Coy, p. 157). The county name is from the principal town, Madera, which always has been the county seat (Hoover, Rensch, and Rensch, p. 170).

Mariposa County.—Mariposa County extends from the crest of the Sierra Nevada westward to near the east edge of San Joaquin Valley, and is largely in the drainage area of Merced River. It was one of 27 counties that the first state legislature formed in 1850; the county originally covered a huge area that included present Fresno, Kern, Kings, Madera, Mariposa, and Merced Counties, as well as parts of present Inyo, Los Angeles, Mono, San Benito, and San Bernardino Counties. By 1856 Mariposa County was reduced to the present size, and later changes in the county boundaries have been minor (Coy, p. 161-165). Agua Fria was the first seat of government, and Mariposa has been the county seat since 1851 (Hoover, Rensch, and Rensch, p. 189).

Merced County.—Merced County extends from the crest of Diablo Range northeastward across San Joaquin Valley to the foothills of the Sierra Nevada on the other side, where it includes lower reaches of Merced River. The state legislature created the county in 1855 from the west part of previously formed Mariposa County; much of the original territory of Merced County was lost in 1856 to newly organized Fresno County, and a smaller area was lost in 1887 to San Benito County (Coy, p. 178-180). The first county seat was at a ranch along Mariposa Creek about 7 miles southeast of present Merced; the county government moved in 1857 to Snelling's Ranch (at present Snelling), and moved again in 1872 to Merced (Hoover, Rensch, and Rensch, p. 205).

San Joaquin County.—San Joaquin County is at the north end of San Joaquin Valley, and extends southwest into Diablo Range. It is one of the counties that the first state legislature created in 1850; the only important change in the county boundaries came in 1860, when a triangular area north of Stanislaus River went to Stanislaus County (Coy, p. 230). Stockton is and always has been the county seat (Hoover, Rensch, and Rensch, p. 367).

Stanislaus County.—Stanislaus County extends eastward from the crest of Diablo Range across San Joaquin Valley into foothills on the other side. The county was organized in 1854 from territory of Tuolumne County; a triangular area north of the Stanislaus River was added to Stanislaus County in 1860 at the expense of San Joaquin County (Coy, p. 269-270). The first county seat was Adamsville; the county government moved after a few months to Empire City, then to La Grange in 1855, to Knight's Ferry in 1862, and finally to Modesto in 1872 (Hoover, Rensch, and Rensch, p. 539).

Tuolumne County.—Tuolumne County extends from the crest of the Sierra Nevada westward to near the east edge of San Joaquin Valley. It is one of the 27 counties that the first state legislature formed in 1850. Part of the original territory of Tuolumne County was lost to Stanislaus County when that county was organized in 1854, and part went to Alpine County when that county was formed in 1864 (Coy, p. 288-289). Sonora is the first and only seat of government for Tuolumne County (Hoover, Rensch, and Rensch, p. 565).

North San Joaquin Valley Region
Calaveras, Madera, Mariposa, Merced, San Joaquin, Stanislaus and Tuolumne Counties

— A —

Abbato [MERCED]: *locality,* 1.25 miles east-southeast of Los Banos along Southern Pacific Railroad (lat. 37°03'15" N, long. 120°49'35" W; sec. 24, T 10 S, R 10 E). Named on Los Banos (1921) 7.5' quadrangle.

Abbeys Ferry: see **Abbott Ferry** [CALAVERAS-TUOLUMNE].

Abbott Ferry [CALAVERAS-TUOLUMNE]: *locality,* nearly 3 miles southeast of Vallecito along Stanislaus River on Calaveras-Tuolumne County line (lat. 38°03'30" N, long. 120°26' W). Named on Big Trees (1891) 30' quadrangle. Whitney (1865, p. 242) referred to Abby's Ferry, and Gudde (1975, p. 13) listed Abbeys Ferry.

Abbotts Peak [CALAVERAS]: *peak,* 1 mile east-southeast of Copperopolis near the southeast end of Copperopolis Mountain (lat. 37°58'35" N, long. 120°37'15" W; sec. 35, T 2 N, R 12 E). Altitude 1545 feet. Named on Melones Dam (1962) 7.5' quadrangle.

Abby's Ferry: see **Abbott Ferry** [CALAVERAS-TUOLUMNE].

Acampo [SAN JOAQUIN]: *village,* 3 miles north of Lodi (lat. 38°10'25" N, long. 121°16'40" W; near NW cor. sec. 25, T 4 N, R 6 E). Named on Lodi North (1968) 7.5' quadrangle. Officials of Southern Pacific Railroad named the place in the 1870's (Gudde, 1949, p. 3). Postal authorities established Acampo post office in 1872 (Frickstad, p. 159). Acampo originally was at a place called New Liberty, located about 1.5 miles south of Liberty—*acampo* means "grazing land" in Spanish (Hillman and Covello, p. 109).

Ache: see **Billy Ache Canyon**, under **Bellyache Canyon** [MARIPOSA].

Aches: see **William Aches Canyon**, under **Bellyache Canyon** [MARIPOSA].

Acker Island [SAN JOAQUIN]: *island,* 1900 feet long, 9 miles west-northwest of downtown Stockton along San Joaquin River at the mouth of Turner Cut (lat. 37°59'50" N, long. 121°26'50" W). Named on Holt (1978) 7.5' quadrangle. United States Board on Geographic Names (1977c, p. 3) gave the variant name "Lost Isle" for the feature.

Acker Peak [TUOLUMNE]: *peak,* 3.25 miles southeast of Tower Peak (lat. 38°06'30" N, long. 119°30'30" W). Altitude 11,015 feet. Named on Tower Peak (1956) 15' quadrangle. Members of United States Geological Survey named the peak for William Bertrand Acker, head of National Park affairs for Department of the Interior (Browning, 1986, p. 1).

Ackerson Creek [TUOLUMNE]: *stream,* flows 6.25 miles to South Fork Tuolumne River 4.5 miles south-southwest of Mather (lat. 37°49'15" N, long. 119°52'30" W; sec. 27, T 1 S, R 19 E); the creek goes through Ackerson Meadow. Named on Lake Eleanor (1956) 15' quadrangle. The stream also was called Big Meadow Creek (Browning, 1986, p. 1).

Ackerson Meadow [TUOLUMNE]: *area,* 3 miles south-southeast of Mather (lat. 37°50'25" N, long. 119°50' W; mainly in sec. 24, T 1 S, R 19 E); the place is along Ackerson Creek. Named on Lake Eleanor (1956) 15' quadrangle. The area first was known as Buckley Meadows; the name "Ackerson" commemorates James T. Ackerson, who lived at the site (Paden and Schlichtmann, p. 207). Hoffmann and Gardner's (1863-1867) map has the notation "Wade's or big meadows" at the place. Hoffmann referred to the feature as Reservoir Meadows in 1867 (Browning, 1988, p. 1).

Ackerson Mountain [TUOLUMNE]: *peak,* 3 miles south-southwest of Mather (lat. 37°50'20" N, long. 119°52' W; sec. 22, T 1 S, R 19 E); the peak is 1.5 miles west of Ackerson Meadow. Altitude 5249 feet. Named on Lake Eleanor (1956) 15' quadrangle.

Acorn Lodge [MARIPOSA]: *locality,* 1.5 miles south of Midpines (lat. 37°31'25" N, long. 119°55'15" W; near W line sec. 5, T 5 S, R 19 E). Named on Feliciana Mountain (1947) 7.5' quadrangle. Laizure's (1935) map shows a place called Yosemite Oaks located a short distance west-northwest of Acorn Lodge (near E line sec. 6, T 5 S, R 19 E).

Acorn Peak: see **Ahwiyah Point** [MARIPOSA].

Adair Lake [MADERA]: *lake,* 850 feet long, 3.5 miles north-northwest of Merced Peak (lat. 37°41' N, long. 119°24'25" W). Named on Merced Peak (1953) 15' quadrangle. Browning (1988, p. 1) associated the name with Charles F. Adair, a ranger at Yosemite National Park from 1914 until 1935, who planted golden trout in the lake—Browning pointed out that the feature also was known as Obelisk Lake and as Cirque Lake.

Adair Lake: see **Obelisk Lake** [MARIPOSA].

Adams: see **Empire** [STANISLAUS]; **Mount Ansel Adams**, under **Foerster Peak** [MADERA].

Adamsville: see **Empire** [STANISLAUS].

Adela [STANISLAUS]: *locality,* 1.5 miles north-northwest of Oakdale along Southern Pacific Railroad (lat. 37°47'20" N, long. 120° 51'45" W). Named on Oakdale (1968) 7.5' quadrangle. Called Burnett on Oakdale (1915) 7.5' quadrangle.

Adeline: see **Mount Adeline**, under **Mount Savage** [MARIPOSA].

Adobe Canyon [STANISLAUS]: *canyon,* 2.5 miles long, opens into Del Puerto Canyon 6 miles southeast of Mount Boardman (lat. 37° 24'30" N, long. 121°24'30" W; sec. 15, T 6 S, R 5 E); Adobe Creek drains the canyon. Named on Copper Mountain (1956) and Mount Boardman (1955) 7.5' quadrangles.

Adobe Creek [STANISLAUS]: *stream,* flows 5.5 miles to Del Puerto Canyon 6 miles southeast of Mount Boardman (lat. 37°24'30" N, long. 121°24'30" W; sec. 15, T 6 S, R 5 E); the stream goes through Adobe Canyon. Named on Copper Mountain (1956) 7.5' quadrangle.

Adobe Gulch [CALAVERAS]: *canyon,* nearly 2 miles long, opens into the canyon of McKinney Creek 9.5 miles east of San Andreas (lat. 38°12'40" N, long. 120°30'30" W; sec. 11, T 4 N, R 13 E). Named on Calaveritas (1962) 7.5' quadrangle.

Adobe Hill [MADERA]: *hill,* 13 miles south of Raymond (lat. 37°02' N, long. 119°51'40" W; sec. 26, T 10 S, R 19 E). Altitude 669 feet. Named on Little Table Mountain (1962) 7.5' quadrangle.

A.E. Wood: see **Camp A.E. Wood**, under **Camp Hoyle** [MARIPOSA].

Agatha: see **Los Banos** [MERCED].

Agnew Meadows [MADERA]: *area,* 4.25 miles north-northwest of Devils Postpile (lat. 37°41'05" N, long. 119°05'45" W). Named on Devils Postpile (1953) 15' quadrangle. The name is for Theodore (Tom) Agnew, a miner who settled at the place in 1877 (Smith, p. 13).

Agnew Pass [MADERA]: *pass,* 8 miles north-northwest of Devils Postpile on Madera-Mono County line (lat. 37°44'05" N, long. 119°08'35" W; sec. 31, T 2 S, R 26 E). Named on Devils Postpile (1953) 15' quadrangle. The name commemorates Theodore Agnew of Agnew Meadows (Hanna, p. 2).

Agua Fria [MARIPOSA]: *locality,* 5.25 miles northeast of the settlement of Catheys Valley (lat. 37°29'10" N, long. 120°01'10" W); the place is along Agua Fria Creek. Site named on Catheys Valley (1962) 7.5' quadrangle. Called Lower Agua Fria on Hoffmann and Gardner's (1863-1867) map, which shows a place called Upper Agua Fria located about 1 mile upstream from Lower Agua Fria. Postal authorities established Agua Fria post office in 1851 and discontinued it in 1862 (Frickstad, p. 90). The name, which is from Agua Fria Creek, also had the forms "Agua Frio," "Agua Frie," and "Aqua Fria" (Wood, p. 11-12).

Agua Fria Creek [MARIPOSA]: *stream,* flows 9 miles to Mariposa Creek 5 miles south of Mariposa (lat. 37°24'45" N, long. 119°59' W; sec. 15, T 6 S, R 18 E). Named on Catheys Valley (1962) and Mariposa (1947) 7.5' quadrangles. The name is from two springs of cold water at a bend in the creek just below Agua Fria—*agua fria* means "cold water" in Spanish (Eccleston, p. 7).

Ahwahnee [MADERA]: *settlement,* 5.25 miles west of Yosemite Forks (lat. 37°22' N, long. 119°43'30" W; on W line sec. 31, T 6 S, R 21 E). Named on Bass Lake (1953) 15' quadrangle. The word "Ahwahnee" is from the Indian name for the largest Indian village in Yosemite Valley, and for the valley itself (Kroeber, p. 34). Postal authorities established Ahwahnee post office in 1893, discontinued it in 1896, reestablished it in 1900 when they moved Gertrude post office 2 miles north and changed the name to Ahwahnee, discontinued it in 1907, and reestablished it in 1917 (Salley, p. 2). They established Gertrude post office in 1881, discontinued it in 1893, reestablished it in 1896, moved it 2 miles south in 1899, and discontinued it in 1900; the name was for Gertrude Haley, first postmaster (Salley, p. 84). Gertrude post office was at a place called String Town before the post office was established (Clough, p. 79-80).

Ahwahnee: see **Wassamma** [MADERA].

Ahwiyah Point [MARIPOSA]: *relief feature*, 2.5 miles east of Yosemite Village (lat. 37°45' N, long. 119°32'10" W). Named on Hetch Hetchy Reservoir (1956) 15' quadrangle. The name is of Indian origin; the feature also had the names "Acorn Peak," "The Old Piute," and "Old Man of the Mountains" (Browning, 1988, p. 3).

Airola Camp [CALAVERAS]: *locality*, 6 miles east of Blue Mountain (lat. 38°21'55" N, long. 120°15'20" W; sec. 30, T 6 N, R 16 E); the place is along Airola Creek. Named on Dorrington (1979) 7.5' quadrangle.

Airola Creek [CALAVERAS]: *stream*, flows 3 miles to South Fork Mokelumne River 5.25 miles east-northeast of Blue Mountain (lat. 38°21'35" N, long. 120°16'05" W; sec. 24, T 6 N, R 15 E). Named on Boards Crossing (1979) and Dorrington (1979) 7.5' quadrangles.

Akers [SAN JOAQUIN]: *locality*, 3 miles north of downtown Stockton along Southern Pacific Railroad (lat. 37°59'55" N, long. 121° 16'50" W). Named on Stockton West (1952) 7.5' quadrangle.

Alabama Gulch: see **Alabama Hill** [CALAVERAS].

Alabama Hill [CALAVERAS]: *peak*, 4.25 miles west of Rail Road Flat near Glencoe (lat. 38°21'20" N, long. 120°35'25" W; sec. 19, T 6 N, R 13 E). Altitude 3012 feet. Named on Rail Road Flat (1948) 7.5' quadrangle. Miners from Alabama named the feature in 1849 (Camp *in* Doble, p. 297). Camp's (1962) map shows a canyon called Alabama Gulch that heads near Alabama Hill and opens into the canyon of Mokelumne River 2.5 miles south-southwest of the confluence of Middle Fork and North Fork Mokelumne River. Doble (p. 39) noted that Alabama Gulch sometimes was called Spring Gulch because of the numerous springs there.

Alabama House: see **Kentucky House** [CALAVERAS].

Alabama Settlement: see **Borden** [MADERA].

Aladdin: see **Cressey** [MERCED].

Alba [SAN JOAQUIN]: *locality*, 9.5 miles east of Manteca along Tidewater Southern Railroad (lat. 37°47'55" N, long. 121°02'20" W; near N line sec. 1, T 2 S, R 8 E). Named on Avena (1952) 7.5' quadrangle.

Albany: see **New Albany**, under **Stockton** [SAN JOAQUIN].

Albany Flat [CALAVERAS]: *area*, 2 miles south-southeast of Angels Camp (lat. 38°03' N, long. 120°31'40" W; near SE cor. sec. 3, T 2 N, R 13 E). Named on Angels Camp (1962) 7.5' quadrangle.

Alcant: see **Delhi** [MERCED].

Alder: see **Alder Creek** [MARIPOSA].

Alder Creek [MARIPOSA]: *stream*, flows 6.5 miles to South Fork Merced River 3.5 miles northwest of Wawona (lat. 37°34'40" N, long. 119°41'50" W; sec. 20, T 4 S, R 21 E). Named on Yosemite (1956) 15' quadrangle. Laizure's (1935) map shows a place called Alder located along Alder Creek about 1 mile east of the mouth of the stream (sec. 21, T 4 S, R 21 E).

Alder Creek [TUOLUMNE]: *stream*, flows 4 miles to Tuolumne River 9.5 miles south-southeast of Duckwall Mountain (lat. 37°50'55" N, long. 120°01'40" W; near SW cor. sec. 17, T 1 S, R 18 E). Named on Duckwall Mountain (1948) and Jawbone Ridge (1947) 7.5' quadrangles.

Alder Creek: see **Whiskey Creek** [MADERA] (2).

Alder Spring [TUOLUMNE]: *spring*, 2.25 miles east of Tuolumne (lat. 37°57'30" N, long. 120°11'35" W; near W line sec. 11, T 1 N, R 16 E). Named on Tuolumne (1948) 7.5' quadrangle.

Alexandria: see **Hopeton** [MERCED] (1).

Alfred Davis Reservoir: see **Turlock Lake** [STANISLAUS].

Algerine [TUOLUMNE]: *locality*, 5 miles south of Sonora (lat. 37°54'40" N, long. 120°22'55" W; sec. 25, T 1 N, R 14 E); the site is near Algerine Creek. Named on Sonora (1948) 7.5' quadrangle. The place first was called Providence Camp, then Algiers and Algerine Camp (Gudde, 1975, p. 15).

Algerine Camp: see **Algerine** [TUOLUMNE].

Algerine Creek [TUOLUMNE]: *stream*, flows nearly 3 miles to Curtis Creek 4.5 miles south of Sonora (lat. 37°55' N, long. 120° 22'40" W; near NE cor. sec. 25, T 1 N, R 14 E). Named on Sonora (1948) and Standard (1948) 7.5' quadrangles.

Algiers: see **Algerine** [TUOLUMNE].

Alkali Creek [TUOLUMNE]: *stream*, flows 5.5 miles to Conness Creek 8 miles west of Tioga Pass (lat. 37°55'05" N, long. 119°24'20" W). Named on Tuolumne Meadows (1956) 15' quadrangle. The stream is called Middle Fork on a Wheeler survey map of 1878-79 (Browning, 1988, p. 3).

Allen: see **John Allen Flat** [MARIPOSA].

Alpine Lake [MADERA]: *lake*, 450 feet long, 2.5 miles south-southeast of Merced Peak (lat. 37°36' N, long. 119°22'35" W). Named on Merced Peak (1953) 15' quadrangle. Ansel F. Hall and Al Solinski named the feature in 1922 (Browning, 1988, p. 3).

Altaville [CALAVERAS]: *town*, less than 1 mile northwest of Angels Camp (lat. 38°05' N, long. 120°33'30" W; sec. 28, 29, T 3 N, R 13 E). Named on Angels Camp (1962) 7.5' quadrangle. Postal authorities established Altaville post office in 1904, discontinued it in 1943, and reestablished it in 1944 (Salley, p. 6). The community first was known as Cherokee Flat, then as Forks of the Road, and as Winterton; residents of the town selected the name "Altaville" in 1857 (Hanna, p. 9). Angels Camp annexed the place in 1972 (Leonard, p. 3). Gudde (1949, p. 8) noted that the site also had the name "Low Divide."

Altha Lake [MADERA]: *lake*, 1100 feet long, 7 miles north-northwest of Devils Postpile (lat. 37°42'45" N, long. 119°08'40" W). Named on Devils Postpile (1953) 15' quadrangle.

Amelia Earhart Peak [TUOLUMNE]: *peak*, 8.5 miles south of Tioga Pass (lat. 37°47'15" N, long. 119°17'15" W). Altitude 11,982 feet. Named on Tuolumne Meadows (1956) 15' quadrangle. The name commemorates Amelia Earhart Putnam, who disappeared on a flight over the Pacific Ocean in 1937 (United States Board on Geographic Names, 1967b, p. 2). Rocketdyne Mountaineering Club proposed the name (Browning, 1988, p. 4).

American Camp: see **American Camp Station** [TUOLUMNE]; **Columbia** [TUOLUMNE]; **Jamestown** [TUOLUMNE].

American Camp Station [TUOLUMNE]: *locality*, 4.5 miles northeast of Columbia in Silver Gulch (lat. 38°05'15" N, long. 120°20'40" W; sec. 29, T 3 N, R 15 E). Named on Columbia SE (1948) 7.5' quadrangle. Big Trees (1891) 30' quadrangle shows a place called American Camp near the site.

Ampere [SAN JOAQUIN]: *locality*, 5.5 miles north-northwest of Waterloo along Central California Traction Railroad (lat. 38°06'10" N, long. 121°14'30" W; near SW cor. sec. 17, T 3 N, R 7 E). Named on Waterloo (1968) 7.5' quadrangle.

Amsterdam [MERCED]: *locality*, 6.5 miles north-northeast of Atwater (lat. 37°25'50" N, long. 120°32'20" W; near E line sec. 9, T 6 S, R 13 E). Named on Winton (1961) 7.5' quadrangle. Winton (1917) 7.5' quadrangle shows the place along Southern Pacific Railroad. Postal authorities established Amsterdam post office in 1893, discontinued it in 1895, reestablished it in 1900, discontinued it for a time in 1906, discontinued it in 1910, reestablished it in 1912, and discontinued it finally in 1925 (Frickstad, p. 99).

Anderson: see **Pick Anderson Slough**, under **Salt Slough** [MERCED].

Anderson Flat [MARIPOSA]: *area*, 8 miles west-northwest of El Portal (lat. 37°44'25" N, long. 119°54'25" W; near SE cor. sec. 19, T 2 S, R 19 E). Named on Kinsley (1947) 7.5' quadrangle.

Andrew Creek [TUOLUMNE]: *stream*, flows 3 miles to Mountain Pass Creek 2 miles north of Keystone (lat. 37°52'40" N, long. 120° 30'40" W; sec. 2, T 1 S, R 13 E). Named on Keystone (1962) and Melones Dam (1962) 7.5' quadrangles.

Andrews Lake [TUOLUMNE]: *lake*, 800 feet long, 10.5 miles southwest of Tower Peak (lat. 38°02'20" N, long. 119°41'20" W); the lake is 0.5 mile west of Andrews Peak. Named on Tower Peak (1956) 15' quadrangle.

Andrews Peak [TUOLUMNE]: *peak*, 10 miles southwest of Tower Peak (lat. 38°02'20" N, long. 119°40'45" W). Altitude 8570 feet. Named on Tower Peak (1956) 15' quadrangle.

Angels: see **Angels Camp** [CALAVERAS].

Angels Camp [CALAVERAS]: *town*, 11 miles southeast of San Andreas (lat. 38°04'30" N, long. 120°32'45" W); the place is along Angels Creek. Named on Angels Camp (1962) 7.5' quadrangle. Called Angel's on Derby's (1849) map, and called Angels and Angels Camp P.O. on San Andreas (1947) 15' quadrangle. Postal authorities established Carson's Creek post office at the place in 1851, and changed the name to Angels Camp in 1853 (Frickstad, p. 14). The town incorporated in 1912 under the name "Angels," but the post office kept the name "Angels Camp." The name "Angels" commemorates Henry P. Angel, who came to the neighborhood in July, 1848, and set up a trading post; the community first was called Angels Trading Post, and later was named Angels Camp (Leonard, p. 3).

Angels Creek [CALAVERAS]: *stream*, flows 17 miles to Melones Reservoir 4.5 miles south of Angels Camp (lat. 38°00'25" N, long. 120°33' W; sec. 21 T 2 N, R 13 E); the stream passes through Angels Camp. Named on Angels Camp (1962), Columbia (1948), Melones Dam (1962), and Murphys (1948) 7.5' quadrangles. The name commemorates Henry P. Angel of Angels Camp (Hanna, p. 13).

Angel's Trading Post: see **Angels Camp** [CALAVERAS].

Anne Lake [MADERA]: *lake*, 700 feet long, nearly 3 miles south-southeast of Merced Peak (lat. 37°36' N, long. 119°21'55" W). Named on Merced Peak (1953) 15' quadrangle.

Anona Lake [MADERA]: *lake*, 900 feet long, nearly 4 miles west-southwest of Devils Postpile (lat. 37°36'30" N, long. 119°08'55" W). Named on Devils Postpile (1953) 15' quadrangle.

Ansel Adams: see **Mount Ansel Adams**, under **Foerster Peak** [MADERA].

Antelope House: see **Jenny Lind** [CALAVERAS].

Antimony Mountain: see **Antimony Peak** [MERCED].

Antimony Peak [MERCED]: *peak*, 2.25 miles southwest of Mariposa Peak on Merced-San Benito County line (lat. 36°55'50" N, long. 121°13'55" W; sec. 32, T 11 S, R 7 E). Altitude 3297 feet. Named on Mariposa Peak (1969) 7.5' quadrangle. Angel (p. 516) called the feature Antimony Mountain, and noted that "As its name implies the mountain is characterized by its many veins of antimony." Irelan (p. 351) mentioned that Antimony Mountain (present Antimony Peak) was known locally as Gipsy Peak—Gipsy Mining Company had a mine there. Mariposa Peak (1969) 7.5' quadrangle shows Stayton mine located 1.25 miles southeast of Antimony Peak (near E line sec. 5, T 12 S, R 7 E). Postal authorities established Staytonville post office 10 miles southeast of Plainsburg in 1877 and discontinued it in

1878; the name was for the nearby Stayton copper mine (Salley, p. 212).

Apple Tree Spring [MARIPOSA]: *spring,* 3.5 miles east-northeast of the settlement of Catheys Valley (lat. 37°27'05" N, long. 120° 02' W). Named on Catheys Valley (1962) 7.5' quadrangle.

Aqua Fria: see **Agua Fria** [MARIPOSA].

Ararat: see **Mount Ararat** [CALAVERAS]: **Mount Ararat** [MERCED].

Arastraville [TUOLUMNE]: *locality,* 2.5 miles north-northeast of Tuolumne (lat. 37°59'50" N, long. 120°13'30" W; sec. 28, T 2 N, R 16 E). Named on Tuolumne (1948) 7.5' quadrangle. Reynolds' (1899) map has the form "Arrastraville" for the name.

Arburuas [MERCED]: *locality,* 19 miles west-southwest of Dos Palos along Piedra Azule Creek (lat. 36°52'55" N, long. 120°56'30" W). Named on Panoche (1913) 30' quadrangle. Ortigalita Peak NW (1956) 7.5' quadrangle shows Arburua ranch at the place.

Arcola: see **Borden** [MADERA].

Ardeth Lake [TUOLUMNE]: *lake,* 1650 feet long, 10 miles southwest of Tower Peak (lat. 38°03'05" N, long. 119°41'25" W). Named on Tower Peak (1956) 15' quadrangle. Otto M. Brown, a ranger at Yosemite National Park from 1927 until 1946, named the lake for his wife (Browning, 1986, p. 7).

Arena [MERCED]: *locality,* 4 miles west-northwest of Atwater along Southern Pacific Railroad (lat. 37°22'15" N, long. 120°40'35" W; sec. 32, T 6 S, R 12 E). Named on Arena (1960) 7.5' quadrangle.

Arkansas Canyon [STANISLAUS]: *canyon,* drained by a stream that flows 4.5 miles to Del Puerto Canyon about 2.5 miles west of Copper Mountain (lat. 37°25'20" N, long. 121°21'35" W; sec. 7, T 6 S, R 6 E). Named on Copper Mountain (1956) and Mount Boardman (1955) 7.5' quadrangles.

Arkansas Creek [STANISLAUS]: *stream,* flows 2.5 miles to lowlands 13 miles west-northwest of Patterson (lat. 37°34'30" N, long. 121°19'50" W; sec. 20, T 4 S, R 6 E). Named on Solyo (1953) 7.5' quadrangle.

Arkansas Flat: see **Carson** [MARIPOSA].

Armstrong [SAN JOAQUIN]: *locality,* 2.5 miles south of Lodi along Southern Pacific Railroad (lat. 38°05'20" N, long. 121°16'25" W; sec. 24, T 3 N, R 6 E). Named on Lodi South (1968) 7.5' quadrangle.

Arndt Lake [TUOLUMNE]: *lake,* 1300 feet long, 5.25 miles south-southeast of Tower Peak (lat. 38°04'30" N, long. 119°30'10" W). Named on Tower Peak (1956) 15' quadrangle. Lieutenant H.C. Benson named the feature in 1896 for Sergeant Alvin Arndt of Fourth Cavalry (Gudde, 1949, p. 15).

Arnold [CALAVERAS]: *settlement,* 6 miles south of Blue Mountain (lat. 38°15'15" N, long. 120°21'15" W; mainly in sec. 29, 30, T 5 N, R 15 E). Named on Dorrington (1979) 7.5' quadrangle. Postal authorities established Arnold post office in 1934; they named it for Robert Arnold and Bernice Arnold, who operated the local store (Salley, p. 10).

Arnold Creek [MADERA]: *stream,* flows 5.5 miles to Fine Gold Creek 5.5 miles west-southwest of the town of North Fork (lat. 37° 11'50" N, long. 119°36'10" W; near N line sec. 31, T 8 S, R 22 E). Named on North Fork (1965) 7.5' quadrangle.

Arnold Meadow [MADERA]: *area,* 5.5 miles northeast of Shuteye Peak (lat. 37°25' N, long. 119°22' W; sec. 8, T 6 S, R 24 E). Named on Shuteye Peak (1953) 15' quadrangle. James H. Arnold patented land in section 8 in 1892 (Browning, 1986, p. 7).

Arnold Spring [MADERA]: *spring,* nearly 4 miles west-southwest of the town of North Fork (lat. 37°12'25" N, long. 119°34'20" W; sec. 28, T 8 S, R 22 E); the spring is along Arnold Creek. Named on North Fork (1965) 7.5' quadrangle.

Arrastraville: see **Arastraville** [TUOLUMNE].

Arrojo del Osnita: see **Hospital Creek** [SAN JOAQUIN-STANISLAUS].

Arroyo Buenos Ayres: see **Corral Hollow** [SAN JOAQUIN].

Arroyo de las Garzas: see **Garzas Creek** [MERCED-STANISLAUS].

Arroyo de los Baños del Padre Arroyo: see **Los Banos Creek** [MERCED].

Arroyo de los Padres: see **Los Banos Creek** [MERCED].

Arroyo de los Piedras: see **Orestimba Creek** [STANISLAUS].

Arroyo Del Ospital: see **Hospital Creek** [SAN JOAQUIN-STANISLAUS].

Arroyo del Puerto: see **Del Puerto Creek** [STANISLAUS].

Arroyo de Orestimba: see **Orestimba Creek** [STANISLAUS].

Arroyo Padre Flat [MERCED]: *area,* 13 miles north of Ortigalita Peak along Los Banos Creek (lat. 36°59' N, long. 120°57'45" W; at NE cor. sec. 15, T 11 S, R 9 E). Named on Ortigalita Peak NW (1969) 7.5' quadrangle.

Artist Creek [MARIPOSA]: *stream,* flows 1.5 miles to Merced River 5.25 miles west-southwest of Yosemite Village (lat. 37°43'05" N, long. 119°40'20" W); the stream goes past Artist Point. Named on Yosemite (1956) 15' quadrangle.

Artist Point [MARIPOSA]: *relief feature,* 5.5 miles west-southwest of Yosemite Village on the south side of Yosemite Valley (lat. 37° 42'45" N, long. 119°40'30" W). Named on Yosemite (1956) 15' quadrangle. Artist Thomas Ayres drew the first picture of Yosemite Falls from the place; the feature is mislocated by 0.25 mile on early quadrangle maps (Browning, 1986, p. 8).

Arundel [MERCED]: *locality,* 7 miles north of Atwood along Southern Pacific Railroad (lat. 37°26'50" N, long. 120°35'50" W; near S line sec. 36, T 5 S, R 12 E). Named on Winton (1917) 7.5' quadrangle.

Ascension Mountain [TUOLUMNE]: *peak,* 4.25 miles southwest of Mather (lat. 37°50'05" N, long. 119°54'15" W; sec. 20, T 1 S, R 19 E). Named on Lake Eleanor (1956) 15' quadrangle.

Ash: see **Tillman** [MADERA].

Ashbrook Creek [MADERA]: *stream,* flows 2.5 miles to Coarse Gold Creek 4 miles south-southeast of Knowles (lat. 37°10'05" N, long. 119°50'15" W; sec. 7, T 9 S, R 20 E). Named on Knowles (1962) 7.5' quadrangle.

Ash Creek: see **Ash Slough** [MADERA]; **Little Ash Creek** [MADERA].

Ashley: see **Foppiano** [SAN JOAQUIN].

Ashley Lake [MADERA]: *lake,* 1200 feet long, 4 miles west of Devils Postpile (lat. 37°37' N, long. 119°09'20" W). Named on Devils Postpile (1953) 15' quadrangle.

Ash Slough [MADERA]: *stream,* diverges from Chowchilla River 8 miles northeast of Fairmead and flows 29 miles to Fresno River 16 miles west-southwest of Chowchilla (lat. 37°01'45" N, long. 120° 31'50" W; sec. 27, T 10 S, R 13 E). Named on Chowchilla (1960), Le Grand (1961), and Santa Rita Park (1962) 15' quadrangles. Called Ash Creek on Le Grand (1918) and Plainsburg (1919) 7.5' quadrangles.

Ashton Slough [MADERA]: *stream,* flows 2.25 miles to Merced County 15 miles west-southwest of Chowchilla (lat. 37°03'50" N, long. 120°31' W; sec. 14, T 10 S, R 13 E). Named on Santa Rita Bridge (1922) 7.5' quadrangle.

Aspen Meadow [TUOLUMNE]: *area,* 2.25 miles east-southeast of Pinecrest (lat. 38°10'40" N, long. 119°56'55" W; sec. 25, T 4 N, R 18 E). Named on Pinecrest (1979) 7.5' quadrangle.

Aspen Valley [TUOLUMNE]:

(1) *valley,* 6 miles southeast of Mather (lat. 37°50' N, long. 119°46'30" W). Named on Lake Eleanor (1956) 15' quadrangle.

(2) *settlement,* 6 miles southeast of Mather (lat. 37°49'40" N, long. 119°46'15" W; near E line sec. 28, T 1 S, R 20 E); the place is in Aspen Valley (1). Named on Lake Eleanor (1956) 15' quadrangle.

Aspinwall: see **Empire** [STANISLAUS].

Atherton: see **Davis and Atherton Ferry**, under **Bellota** [SAN JOAQUIN].

Athlone [MERCED]: *locality,* 6 miles west-southwest of Le Grand along Southern Pacific Railroad (lat. 37°12'35" N, long. 120°21'30" W; near W line sec. 29, T 8 S, R 15 E). Named on Chowchilla (1960) 15' quadrangle. When Central Pacific Railroad reached the place in 1872, the station there was called Plainsburg for a village located 2.5 miles to the northeast (Gudde, 1949, p. 17). Postal authorities established Athlone post office in 1881, discontinued it for a time in 1901, discontinued it in 1905, reestablished it in 1906, discontinued it in 1909, reestablished it in 1914, and discontinued it finally in 1937 (Frickstad, p. 99).

Atlanta [SAN JOAQUIN]: *locality,* 5.25 miles east-northeast of Manteca along Tidewater Southern Railroad (lat. 37°48'50" N, long. 121°07'15" W; near S line sec. 29, T 1 S, R 8 E). Named on Avena (1952) 7.5' quadrangle. Postal authorities established Atlanta post office in 1868, discontinued it for a time in 1876, discontinued it in 1887, reestablished it in 1888, discontinued it in 1911, reestablished it in 1914, and discontinued it finally in 1915; Lee Wilson built Atlanta store at the site in 1866 (Salley, p. 11).

Atlas Tract [SAN JOAQUIN]: *area,* 8 miles southeast of Terminous (lat. 38°02'25" N, long. 121°22'40" W). Named on Lodi South (1968) and Terminous (1978) 7.5' quadrangles.

Atwater [MERCED]: *town,* 8 miles west-northwest of Merced (lat. 37°21' N, long. 120°36'15" W; in and near sec. 1, T 7 S, R 12 E). Named on Atwater (1961) 15' quadrangle. The railroad station at the place was named in the 1870's for Marshall D. Atwater, a wheat rancher on whose property the station was situated; the town was founded and named for the station in 1888 (Gudde, 1949, p. 17). Postal authorities established Atwater post office in 1880 (Frickstad, p. 99), and the town incorporated in 1922.

Aurora [STANISLAUS]: *locality,* 1.5 miles north of downtown Modesto along Tidewater Southern Railroad (lat. 37°39'40" N, long. 121°00'10" W). Named on Salida (1969) 7.5' quadrangle.

Australia Gulch: see **Spring Creek** [MARIPOSA].

Aux-um-ne: see **Merced River** [MADERA-MARIPOSA-MERCED].

Ave Maria: see **Stockton Creek** [MARIPOSA].

Ave Maria River: see **Stockton Creek** [MARIPOSA].

Avena [SAN JOAQUIN]: *locality,* 9 miles east-northeast of Manteca along Atchison, Topeka and Santa Fe Railroad (lat. 37°50'35" N, long. 121°03'55" W; near S line sec. 14, T 1 S, R 8 E). Named on Avena (1952) 7.5' quadrangle. Avena (1914) 7.5' quadrangle has both the names "Avena" and "Ellisworth P.O." at the site. Railroad officials gave the place the name "Avena" in the early 1890's—*avena* means "oats" in Spanish (Gudde, 1949, p. 18). Postal authorities established Ellisworth post office in 1901 and discontinued it in 1927 (Frickstad, p. 160).

Avery [CALAVERAS]: *settlement,* 7 miles northeast of Murphys (lat. 38°12'20" N, long. 120°22'05" W; near N line sec. 18, T 4 N, R 15 E). Named on Stanislaus (1948) 7.5' quadrangle. Postal authorities established Avery post office in 1885, discontinued it in 1943, and reestablished it in 1949; the name is for George J. Avery, first postmaster (Salley, p. 12).

Avonelle Lake [TUOLUMNE]: *lake,* 2400 feet long, 8 miles southwest of Tower Peak (lat. 38°03'15" N, long. 119°38'30" W). Named on Tower Peak (1956) 15' quadrangle. Otto M. Brown, a ranger at Yosemite National Park from 1927 until 1946, named the lake for his daughter (Browning, 1986, p. 9).

—B—

Babcock Lake [MARIPOSA]: *lake,* 1500 feet long, 6.25 miles south of Cathedral Peak (lat. 37°45'25" N, long. 119°23'45" W). Named on Tuolumne Meadows (1956) 15' quadrangle. Lieutenant N.F. McClure named the lake in 1895 for J.P. Babcock, chief deputy of California State Board of Fish Commissioners (United States Board on Geographic Names, 1934, p. 2).

Bachelor Valley [STANISLAUS]: *valley,* 11 miles north of Oakdale along Hoods Creek (lat. 37°55'15" N, long. 120°49'30" W). Named on Bachelor Valley (1968) 7.5' quadrangle.

Bacon Island [SAN JOAQUIN]: *island,* 5 miles long, 14 miles west of downtown Stockton between Old River, Connection Slough, and Middle River (lat. 37°58'30" N, long. 121°33'15" W). Named on Bouldin Island (1978) and Woodward Island (1978) 7.5' quadrangles.

Badger Lake: see **Garnet Lake** [MADERA].

Badger Lakes [MADERA]: *lakes,* largest 700 feet long, 8 miles north-northwest of Devils Postpile (lat. 37°43'40" N, long. 119°08'55" W; sec. 31, T 2 S, R 26 E). Named on Devils Postpile (1953) 15' quadrangle.

Badger Pass [MARIPOSA]: *pass,* nearly 7 miles south-southwest of Yosemite Village (lat. 37°40' N, long. 119°39'15" W; near S line sec. 15, T 3 S, R 21 E). Named on Yosemite (1956) 15' quadrangle.

Bagby [MARIPOSA]: *locality,* 9.5 miles northeast of Hornitos along the north side of Merced River (lat. 37°36'45" N, long. 120°08' W). Named on Coulterville (1947) 15' quadrangle. Water of Lake McClure now covers the site. Postal authorities established Bagby post office in 1897 and discontinued it in 1951 (Frickstad, p. 90). The place opposite Bagby on the south side of the river was known from 1850 until 1860 as Ridleys Ferry for the ferry that Thomas E. Ridley operated there from 1850 until 1852 (Gudde, 1975, p. 32). John C. Fremont had a water-powered stamp mill built at the site of Ridleys Ferry and renamed the place Benton Mills for his father-in-law, Senator Thomas Hart Benton, but when postal authorities established the post office, they named it Bagby for Benjamin A. Bagby, who had a hotel, store, saloon, and boarding house across the river on the north side (Sargent, Shirley, 1976, p. 18). Stephen Bond had a store at a place called Bondville that was located 1 mile east of Benton Mills on the south side of the river (Gudde, 1975, p. 43). Postal authorities established Bondville post office in 1855 and discontinued it in 1860 (Frickstad, p. 90). A place called Kocher was situated 8 miles above Bagby along Yosemite Valley Railroad (Johnston, p. 51).

Bailey Flats [MADERA]: *area,* 10 miles north-northeast of Raymond (lat. 37°20'30" N, long. 119°49'20" W; in and near sec. 7, T 7 S, R 20 E). Named on Horsecamp Mountain (1947) 7.5' quadrangle. Mist post office was in a general store at Bailey Flats near Mariposa County line (Clough, p. 94). Postal authorities established Mist post office in 1913 and discontinued it in 1935; the name was from the mist of nearby waterfalls (Salley, p. 143).

Bailey Ridge [CALAVERAS]: *ridge,* generally west-trending, 18 miles long, between Middle Fork Mokelumne River and Forest Creek. Named on Calaveras Dome (1979), Devils Nose (1979), and Garnet Hill (1979) 7.5' quadrangles.

Bailey Ridge [TUOLUMNE]: *ridge,* southwest-trending, about 3 miles long, 7 miles southwest of Tower Peak (lat. 38°03'45" N, long. 119°38' W). Named on Tower Peak (1956) 15' quadrangle.

Baker: see **Baker Station** [TUOLUMNE].

Baker Campground [TUOLUMNE]: *locality,* 4.5 miles east-southeast of Dardanelle along Middle Fork Stanislaus River (lat. 38° 19'25" N, long. 119°45'10" W; sec. 35, T 6 N, R 20 E); the place is 0.5 mile south-southeast of Baker Station. Named on Dardanelle (1979) 7.5' quadrangle. Called Upper Baker Campground on Dardanelles Cone (1956) 15' quadrangle.

Baker Peak: see **Fletcher Peak** [MARIPOSA].

Bakers Crossing [TUOLUMNE]: *locality,* 5 miles west of Parsons (present Strawberry) along Middle Fork Stanislaus River (lat. 38° 11' N, long. 120°06'35" W). Named on Big Trees (1891) 30' quadrangle.

Baker's Ferry: see **Waterford** [STANISLAUS].

Baker Station [TUOLUMNE]: *locality,* 4.25 miles east of Dardanelle along Middle Fork Stanislaus River (lat. 38°19'50" N, long. 119° 45'20" W; near NW cor. sec. 35, T 6 N, R 20 E). Named on Dardanelle (1979) 7.5' quadrangle. Called Baker on California Mining Bureau's (1917a) map. Postal authorities established Baker post office in 1880 and discontinued it in 1881; the name was for Greenbury C. Baker, who built a stage station at the site (Salley, p. 13).

Bakersville: see **Waterford** [STANISLAUS].

Balaklava Hill: see **Vallecito** [CALAVERAS].

Bald Hill [CALAVERAS]: *hill,* 0.5 mile north of Angels Camp (lat. 38°05'05" N, long. 120°32'45" W; sec. 28, T 3 N, R 13 E). Altitude 1765 feet. Named on Angels Camp (1962) 7.5' quadrangle.

Bald Hill [MARIPOSA]: *peak,* 3.5 miles north of the settlement of Catheys Valley (lat. 37°29'15" N, long. 120°05'35" W; sec. 22, T 5 S, R 17 E). Named on Catheys Valley (1962) 7.5' quadrangle.

Bald Mountain [CALAVERAS]:

(1) *ridge,* northwest-trending, 1 mile long, 3 miles south-southwest of Devils Nose (lat. 38°25'25" N, long. 120°27' W). Named on Devils Nose (1979) 7.5' quadrangle.

(2) *hill,* 7.5 miles west-southwest of Valley Springs (lat. 38°08'20" N, long. 120°56'55" W; sec. 2, T 3 N, R 9 E). Altitude 506 feet. Named on Wallace (1962) 7.5' quadrangle.

(3) *peak,* 1 mile east-northeast of Vallecito (lat. 38°05'30" N, long. 120°27'20" W; on S line sec. 20, T 3 N, R 14 E). Named on Columbia (1948) 7.5' quadrangle.

Bald Mountain [MARIPOSA]: *peak,* 2 miles east-northeast of Coulterville (lat. 37°43'35" N, long. 120°09'45" W; near N line sec. 36, T 2 S, R 16 E). Named on Coulterville (1947) 7.5' quadrangle.

Bald Mountain [SAN JOAQUIN]: *peak,* 1.25 miles northeast of Eagle Mountain (lat. 37°34'50" N, long. 121°30'55" W; sec. 15, T 4 S, R 4 E). Altitude 2865 feet. Named on Cedar Mountain (1956) 7.5' quadrangle.

Bald Mountain [TUOLUMNE]:

(1) *peak,* nearly 3 miles southeast of Columbia (lat. 38°00'30" N, long. 120°21'45" W; sec. 19, T 2 N, R 15 E). Altitude 3342 feet. Named on Columbia SE (1948) 7.5' quadrangle. Perkins (p. 100) used the designation "Bear or Bare Mountain" for the feature.

(2) *peak,* 5.5 miles southwest of Strawberry (lat. 38°08'40" N, long. 120°05'10" W; sec. 3, T 3 N, R 17 E). Altitude 5802 feet. Named on Strawberry (1979) 7.5' quadrangle.

(3) *peak,* 4 miles east-southeast of Mather (lat. 37°51'20" N, long. 119°47'20" W; near E line sec. 17, T 1 S, R 20 E). Altitude 7261 feet. Named on Lake Eleanor (1956) 15' quadrangle. Called Wade's Mt. on Hoffmann and Gardner's (1863-1867) map.

Bald Peak [TUOLUMNE]: *peak,* nearly 4 miles northeast of Dardanelle (lat. 38°22'20" N, long. 119°46'35" W). Altitude 9715 feet. Named on Dardanelle (1979) 7.5' quadrangle.

Bald Rock [MARIPOSA]:

(1) *peak,* 8 miles south-southeast of Mariposa (lat. 37°22'25" N, long. 119°56'05" W; near N line sec. 31, T 6 S, R 19 E). Altitude 2067 feet. Named on Ben Hur (1947) 7.5' quadrangle.

(2) *relief feature,* 3.25 miles west of Fish Camp (lat. 37°29' N, long. 119°41'50" W; sec. 20, T 5 S, R 21 E). Named on Bass Lake (1953) 15' quadrangle.

Ballard Flat [STANISLAUS]: *area,* 4 miles north of Copper Mountain (lat. 37°28'25" N, long. 121°18' W; sec. 27, T 5 S, R 6 E). Named on Copper Mountain (1956) 7.5' quadrangle.

Ballico [MERCED]: *village,* 9 miles northwest of Atwater (lat. 37°27'15" N, long. 120°42'20" W; near E line sec. 36, T 5 S, R 11 E). Named on Atwater (1961) 15' quadrangle. Postal authorities established Ballico post office in 1924 and named it for <u>Ballin</u>tine <u>Co</u>mpany ranch, where it was located (Salley, p. 14).

Balloon Dome [MADERA]: *peak,* 13 miles northeast of Shuteye Peak (lat. 37°27'50" N, long. 119°13'30" W; sec. 27, T 5 S, R 25 E). Altitude 6881 feet. Named on Kaiser Peak (1953) 15' quadrangle. The feature reminded Brewer "of the top of a gigantic balloon struggling to get up through the rock" (Whitney, 1865, p. 401). The peak also was called Dome or Great Dome (Gudde, 1949, p. 22).

Balls [MADERA]: *relief feature,* 9 miles south-southeast of Merced Peak (lat. 37°30'25" N, long. 119°21'05" W). Named on Merced Peak (1953) 15' quadrangle.

Bandarita Ridge [MARIPOSA]: *ridge,* northwest-trending, 2 miles long, 5 miles northeast of Buckhorn Peak (lat. 37°42'20" N, long. 120°03'10" W). Named on Buckhorn Peak (1947) 7.5' quadrangle.

Bandereta: see **Coulterville** [MARIPOSA].

Banner Peak [MADERA]: *peak,* 8 miles northwest of Devils Postpile (lat. 37°41'50" N, long. 119°11'40" W). Altitude 12,945 feet. Named on Devils Postpile (1953) 15' quadrangle. Willard D. Johnson of United States Geological Survey gave the name in 1882 for banners of clouds that he saw streaming from the peak (Farquhar, 1923, p. 382). Members of the Whitney survey applied the name "Mammoth Mountain" to the feature (Browning, 1988, p. 8).

Banta [SAN JOAQUIN]: *town,* 15 miles south-southwest of downtown Stockton (lat. 37°45'10" N, long. 121°22'20" W; in and near sec. 24, T 2 S, R 5 E). Named on Lathrop (1952) 7.5' quadrangle. Called Bantas on Thompson and West's (1879) map. The community began with a stage stop called Elk Horn Inn, and a later stop called White House; the name "Banta" commemorates Henry C. Banta, who bought White House in 1863 (Hillman and Covello, p. 111). In the 1860's, officials of Western Pacific Railroad named their station at the site of the present town for Mr. Banta, whose Banta Inn was situated about 0.5 mile farther north (Gudde, 1949,

p. 23; Hanna, p. 25). Postal authorities established San Joaquin Valley post office in 1868 and changed the name to Banta in 1870; Henry C. Banta was the first postmaster (Salley, p. 195).

Banta Inn: see **Banta** [SAN JOAQUIN].

Bardi [SAN JOAQUIN]: *locality,* 3.5 miles southeast of Manteca along Southern Pacific Railroad (lat. 37°45'55" N, long. 121°09'50" W; sec. 14, T 2 S, R 7 E). Named on Manteca (1952) 7.5' quadrangle. Called Weston on Manteca (1914) 7.5' quadrangle.

Bare: see **McHenry** [STANISLAUS].

Bare Island Lake [MADERA]: *lake,* 1000 feet long, 10.5 miles north-northwest of Shuteye Peak (lat. 37°29'45" N, long. 119°29'25" W; sec. 18, T 5 S, R 23 E). Named on Shuteye Peak (1953) 15' quadrangle.

Bare Mountain: see **Bald Mountain** [TUOLUMNE] (1).

Bar Hill [MARIPOSA]: *peak,* 3 miles south-southeast of Mariposa (lat. 37°26'45" N, long. 119°56'30" W; near NW cor. sec. 6, T 6 S, R 19 E). Named on Mariposa (1912) 30' quadrangle.

Barnett [CALAVERAS]: *locality,* 7.5 miles north-northeast of Blue Mountain (lat. 38°26'15" N, long. 120°17'35" W; near S line sec. 23, T 7 N, R 15 E). Named on Blue Mountain (1956) 15' quadrangle.

Barnhart: see **Sargent-Barnhart Tract** [SAN JOAQUIN].

Barnhart Landing [SAN JOAQUIN]: *locality,* 4.5 miles west-northwest of downtown Stockton on the east side of San Joaquin River (lat. 37°58'35" N, long. 120°22'15" W); the place is on Sargent-Barnhart Tract. Named on Stockton (1913) 7.5' quadrangle.

Barn Meadow [TUOLUMNE]: *area,* 4 miles south-southwest of Dardanelle (lat. 38°17'20" N, long. 119°51'25" W; sec. 14, T 5 N, R 19 E). Named on Dardanelle (1979) 7.5' quadrangle.

Barrel Spring [MARIPOSA]:

(1) *spring,* 2.25 miles south-southeast of El Portal (lat. 37°38'50" N, long. 119°46'05" W; sec. 28, T 3 S, R 20 E). Named on El Portal (1947) 7.5' quadrangle.

(2) *spring,* 3 miles north-northeast of the settlement of Catheys Valley (lat. 37°28'35" N, long. 120°04'20" W). Named on Catheys Valley (1962) 7.5' quadrangle.

Barrett [MARIPOSA]: *locality,* 6.5 miles south-southwest of Penon Blanco Peak on the west side of Lake McClure (lat. 37°38'25" N, long. 120°17'05" W; sec. 26, T 3 S, R 15 E). Named on Penon Blanco Peak (1962) 7.5' quadrangle. Merced Falls (1944) 15' quadrangle shows the place situated along Yosemite Valley Railroad. In 1926 water of Lake McClure covered the site of a community called Barrett (Sargent, Shirley, 1976, p. 27).

Barth Mountain [CALAVERAS]: *peak,* 4.25 miles east of Copperopolis (lat. 37°59'10" N, long. 120°33'40" W; near E line sec. 32, T 2 N, R 13 E). Altitude 1916 feet. Named on Melones Dam (1962) 7.5' quadrangle.

Bartlett Creek [TUOLUMNE]: *stream,* flows 6.5 miles to join Kendrick Creek and form Eleanor Creek 16 miles southeast of Pinecrest (lat. 38°01'30" N, long. 119°48' W; near S line sec. 17, T 2 N, R 20 E); the stream heads near Bartlett Peak. Named on Pinecrest (1956) 15' quadrangle. The name is from Bartlett Peak (United States Board on Geographic Names, 1934, p. 2). The stream is called West Fork Eleanor Cr. on Dardanelles (1898) 30' quadrangle.

Bartlett Peak [TUOLUMNE]: *peak,* 14 miles east-southeast of Pinecrest (lat. 38°05'30" N, long. 119°46'35" W). Altitude 8238 feet. Named on Pinecrest (1956) 15' quadrangle.

Basalt Hill [MERCED]: *peak,* 7.5 miles east-southeast of Pacheco Pass (lat. 37°01'10" N, long. 121°05'10" W; near W line sec. 34, T 10 S, R 8 E). Altitude 1707 feet. Named on San Luis Dam (1969) 7.5' quadrangle. Anderson and Pack's (1909-1911) map shows basalt on the peak.

Basel: see **Ryer** [MERCED].

Base Line Camp [TUOLUMNE]: *locality,* 3 miles east-northeast of Mather (lat. 37°53'35" N, long. 119°48' W; near S line sec. 32, T 1 N, R 20 E); the place is near Mount Diablo Base line. Named on Lake Eleanor (1956) 15' quadrangle.

Basin: see **The Basin** [TUOLUMNE].

Basin Creek [TUOLUMNE]:

(1) *stream,* flows 2.5 miles to Shoofly Creek 5.5 miles southeast of Liberty Hill (lat. 38°18'40" N, long. 120°01'50" W; sec. 6, T 5 N, R 18 E). Named on Liberty Hill (1979) 7.5' quadrangle.

(2) *stream,* flows 4.5 miles to North Fork Tuolumne River 3.5 miles northeast of Tuolumne (lat. 37°59'35" N, long. 120°10'55" W; sec. 26, T 2 N, R 16 E); the stream goes through the feature called The Basin. Named on Duckwall Mountain (1948), Tuolumne (1948), and Twain Harte (1979) 7.5' quadrangles. Called Basin Slope Creek on Sonora (1897) 30' quadrangle.

Basin Slope Creek: see **Basin Creek** [TUOLUMNE] (2).

Basket Dome [MARIPOSA]: *peak,* 2 miles east-northeast of Yosemite Village (lat. 37°45'50" N, long. 119°33' W). Altitude 7612 feet. Named on Hetch Hetchy Reservoir (1956) 15' quadrangle. The name is from an Indian legend concerning a basket that turned to stone (Browning, 1986, p. 12).

Bassella Creek [CALAVERAS]: *stream,* flows 3 miles to O'Neil Creek 6 miles north of Murphys (lat. 38°13'35" N, long. 120° 28' W; sec. 6, T 4 N, R 14 E). Named on Fort Mountain (1979) and Murphys (1948) 7.5' quadrangles.

Bassett's Gulch: see **Sonora Creek** [TUOLUMNE].

Bass Lake [MADERA]:

(1) *lake,* about 4.5 miles long, behind a dam on North Fork Willow Creek (2) 7.5 miles southeast of Yosemite Forks (lat. 37°17'30" N, long. 119°31'45" W; sec. 26, T 7 S, R 22 E). Named on Bass Lake (1953) 15' quadrangle. Water of the lake covers most of Crane Valley, but United States Board on Geographic Names (1964b, p. 11) rejected the name "Crane Valley Lake" for the feature. A dam formed the lake in 1895, and a second dam enlarged the lake in 1910; the name "Bass Lake" was given after the lake was stocked with bass (Clough, p. 82-83).

(2) *settlement,* 4.5 miles southeast of Yosemite Forks (lat. 37°19'30" N, long. 119°34' W; sec. 15, 16, T 7 S, R 22 E); the place is on the northeast side of Bass Lake (1). Named on Bass Lake (1953) 15' quadrangle. Postal authorities established Bass Lake post office in 1912 (Frickstad, p. 84).

Bass Lake [MERCED]: *lake,* 700 feet long, 6.25 miles north-northeast of Pacheco Pass along Romero Creek (lat. 37°09' N, long. 121°10'35" W; near W line sec. 14, T 9 S, R 7 E). Named on Crevison Peak (1955) 7.5' quadrangle.

Bates: see **Bates Station** [MADERA].

Bates Station [MADERA]: *locality,* 10.5 miles south-southeast of Raymond (lat. 37°05'25" N, long. 119°48'05" W; near E line sec. 5, T 10 S, R 20 E). Named on Little Table Mountain (1962) 7.5' quadrangle. Called Bates on Mariposa (1912) 30' quadrangle. Postal authorities established Bates post office in 1883, moved it 5 miles south in 1891, and discontinued it in 1903 (Salley, p. 15). The post office name was for George Bates, who operated Bates Station and was the first postmaster; Henry J. Prewett became postmaster in 1889, and the place sometimes was called Prewett Station, but the post office retained the old name—the final site of Bates post office was about 3 miles down Cottonwood Creek from the original site (Clough, p. 83). Postal authorities established Media post office 5 miles southwest of Bates post office in 1894 and discontinued it in 1898; the name was from the belief that the place was at the geographical center of California (Salley, p. 137).

Bath Mountain [TUOLUMNE]: *peak,* 5.25 miles west-southwest of Matterhorn Peak (lat. 38°03'30" N, long. 119°27'50" W). Named on Matterhorn Peak (1956) 15' quadrangle.

Bathtub Spring [MARIPOSA]: *spring,* 3.5 miles east of Santa Cruz Mountain (lat. 37°28' N, long. 120°08'15" W; near W line sec. 29, T 5 S, R 17 E). Named on Indian Gulch (1962) 7.5' quadrangle.

Battalion Pass [MARIPOSA]: *pass,* 3.25 miles southwest of Wawona (lat. 37°30'20" N, long. 119°41'45" W; sec. 8, T 5 S, R 21 E). Named on Yosemite (1956) 15' quadrangle. Chester Versteeg suggested the name because the Mariposa Battalion is believed to have used the pass in 1851 (Browning, 1986, p. 12).

Baxter [MARIPOSA]: *locality,* 5 miles southwest of Coulterville (lat. 37°40' N, long. 120°16'15" W). Named on Sonora (1891) 30' quadrangle. Postal authorities established Baxter post office in 1890 and discontinued it in 1907 (Frickstad, p. 90).

Bean Creek [MARIPOSA]: *stream,* flows 11 miles to North Fork Merced River 7 miles northeast of Buckhorn Peak (lat. 37°44'30" N, long. 120°02'35" W; sec. 24, T 2 S, R 17 E). Named on Buckhorn Peak (1947) and Groveland (1947) 7.5' quadrangles. Called Bean's Creek on Hoffmann and Gardner's (1863-1867) map, which shows Bean's Mill situated on upper reaches of the stream.

Bean Gulch [CALAVERAS]: *canyon,* drained by a stream that flows 2.25 miles to Stanislaus River 6.25 miles east-southeast of Copperopolis (lat. 37°57'35" N, long. 120°32'10" W; sec. 15, T 1 N, R 13 E). Named on Melones Dam (1962) 7.5' quadrangle.

Bean Gulch [MADERA]: *canyon,* 1 mile long, 5.5 miles east-northeast of Knowles along Spangle Gold Creek (lat. 37°14'35" N, long. 119°46'45" W). Named on Knowles (1962) 7.5' quadrangle.

Bean's Mill: see **Bean Creek** [MARIPOSA].

Bear Creek [CALAVERAS]:

(1) *stream,* flows 9.5 miles to Middle Fork Mokelumne River nearly 7 miles southwest of Devils Nose (lat. 38°23'05" N, long. 120°29'45" W; sec. 12, T 6 N, R 13 E). Named on Devils Nose (1979) and West Point (1948) 7.5' quadrangles.

(2) *stream,* flows 5.5 miles to New Hogan Reservoir 5 miles east of Jenny Lind (lat. 38°06'35" N, long. 120°46'35" W; near W line sec. 16, T 3 N, R 11 E). Named on Jenny Lind (1962), Salt Spring Valley (1962), and Valley Springs (1962) 7.5' quadrangles.

(3) *stream,* flows 5 miles to Cherokee Creek 6.5 miles west-northwest of Angels Camp (lat. 38°06'50" N, long. 120°39'05" W; sec. 16, T 3 N, R 12 E). Named on Salt Spring Valley (1962) 7.5' quadrangle.

Bear Creek [CALAVERAS-SAN JOAQUIN]: *stream,* heads in Calaveras County and flows 39 miles to Disappointment Slough 7.5 miles southeast of Terminous in San Joaquin County (lat. 38°02'35" N, long. 121°23'10" W). Named on Clements (1968), Lockeford (1968), Lodi South (1968), Terminous (1978), Valley Springs (1962), Wallace (1962), and Waterloo

(1968) 7.5' quadrangles.

Bear Creek [MARIPOSA]: *stream,* flows 8.5 miles to Merced River 5 miles north-northwest of Midpines at Briceburg (lat. 37°36'15" N, long. 119°57'55" W; sec. 10, T 4 S, R 18 E). Named on Feliciana Mountain (1947) 7.5' quadrangle.

Bear Creek [MARIPOSA-MERCED]: *stream,* heads in Mariposa County and flows 69 miles to San Joaquin River 3.5 miles south-southeast of Stevinson in Merced County (lat. 37°16'45" N, long. 120°49'35" W; sec. 36, T 7 S, R 10 E). Named on Atwater (1961), Merced (1962), and Turlock (1962) 15' quadrangles, and on Bear Valley (1947), Catheys Valley (1962), Hornitos (1947), Indian Gulch (1962), and Owens Reservoir (1962), 7.5' quadrangles.

Bear Creek [MERCED]: *settlement,* 3.5 miles east of Merced (lat. 35°17'50" N, long. 120°24'55" W; near E line sec. 27, T 7 S, R 14 E); the settlement is 1 mile south of Bear Creek [MARIPOSA-MERCED]. Named on Merced (1961) 7.5' quadrangle.

Bear Creek [SAN JOAQUIN]: *locality,* 4.5 miles northwest of Waterloo along Central California Traction Railroad (lat. 38°05'05" N, long. 121°14'30" W; on W line sec. 29, T 3 N, R 7 E); the place is 1.25 miles north of the railroad crossing of Bear Creek [CALAVERAS-SAN JOAQUIN]. Named on Waterloo (1968) 7.5' quadrangle.

Bear Creek [TUOLUMNE]:

(1) *stream,* flows 3 miles to New Melones Lake 6.5 miles west-southwest of Sonora (lat. 37°56'35" N, long. 120°39'15" W; near E line sec. 13, T 1 N, R 13 E). Named on Sonora (1948, photorevised 1973) 7.5' quadrangle.

(2) *stream,* flows 3.5 miles to Reed Creek 5.5 miles east of Duckwall Mountain (lat. 37°58'40" N, long. 120°01'05" W; near N line sec. 5, T 1 N, R 18 E). Named on Lake Eleanor (1956), Pinecrest (1956), and Tuolumne (1948) 15' quadrangles.

Bear Creek: see **Briceburg** [MARIPOSA]; **Merced** [MERCED].

Beardsley Lake [TUOLUMNE]: *lake,* behind a dam on Middle Fork Stanislaus River 3.5 miles west of Strawberry (lat. 38°12'10" N, long. 120°04'30" W; sec. 14, T 4 N, R 17 E). Named on Strawberry (1979) 7.5' quadrangle.

Beardsley Point [TUOLUMNE]: *promontory,* 2.5 miles west-northwest of Strawberry on the south side of Beardsley Lake (lat. 38°12'40" N, long. 120°03'20" W; near S line sec. 12, T 4 N, R 17 E). Named on Strawberry (1979) 7.5' quadrangle.

Bear Gulch [STANISLAUS]: *canyon,* nearly 4 miles long, opens into the canyon of Garzas Creek 3.25 miles northeast of Crevison Peak (lat. 37°13'30" N, long. 121°08'50" W; sec. 24, T 8 S, R 7 E). Named on Crevison Peak (1955) 7.5' quadrangle.

Bear Hide Lake [MERCED]: *lake,* 400 feet long, 2.25 miles south of Pacheco Pass (lat. 37°01'45" N, long. 121°12'05" W). Named on Pacheco Pass (1955) 7.5' quadrangle.

Bear Lake [TUOLUMNE]:

(1) *lake,* 1750 feet long, 7.25 miles east of Pinecrest along Lily Creek (3) (lat. 38°10'30" N, long. 119°51'45" W; near W line sec. 26, T 4 N, R 19 E). Named on Pinecrest (1956) 15' quadrangle.

(2) *lake,* 1000 feet long, 9 miles west-southwest of Tower Peak (lat. 38°05'25" N, long. 119°41'55" W). Named on Tower Peak (1956) 15' quadrangle. Rangers Gallison and Wallis of Yosemite National Park named the lake in 1952 for a bear that they saw there (Browning, 1986, p. 13). United States Board on Geographic Names (1991, p. 3) approved the name "Big Island Lake" for the feature.

Bear Lake: see **Little Bear Lake** [TUOLUMNE].

Bear Lake Reservoir: see **Waterhouse Lake** [TUOLUMNE].

Bear Meadow [TUOLUMNE]: *area,* 8 miles southeast of Pinecrest (lat. 38°05'30" N, long. 119°54'25" W). Named on Cherry Lake North (1979) 7.5' quadrangle.

Bear Mountain [CALAVERAS]: *ridge,* northwest-trending, 2 miles long, 4.25 miles south-southwest of Angels Camp (lat. 38°01'20" N, long. 120°35'15" W). Named on Angels Camp (1962) 7.5' quadrangle.

Bear Mountain [STANISLAUS]: *peak,* 23 miles west-southwest of Newman on Stanislaus-Santa Clara County line (lat. 37°13'55" N, long. 121°26'10" W; sec. 21, T 8 S, R 5 E). Altitude 2604 feet. Named on Mississippi Creek (1955) 7.5' quadrangle.

Bear Mountain [TUOLUMNE]: *peak,* 2.5 miles southwest of Mather (lat. 37°51'20" N, long. 119°53'20" W; sec. 16, T 1 S, R 19 E). Altitude 5321 feet. Named on Lake Eleanor (1956) 15' quadrangle.

Bear Mountain: see **Bald Mountain** [TUOLUMNE] (1).

Bear Mountains [CALAVERAS]: *range,* extends southeast from Calaveras River to near Pools Station. Named on Jenny Lind (1962), Salt Spring Valley (1962), San Andreas (1962), and Valley Springs (1962) 7.5' quadrangles. On Jackson (1902) 30' quadrangle, application of the name extends farther southeast.

Bear Reservoir [MARIPOSA]: *lake,* behind a dam on Bear Creek (2) 9 miles west-southwest of the settlement of Catheys Valley (lat. 37°22'10" N, long. 120°13'40" W; sec. 33, T 6 S, R 16 E). Named on Indian Gulch (1962) and Owens Reservoir (1962) 7.5' quadrangles.

Bear Slough [MERCED]: *stream,* flows 2.25 miles to Bear Creek (1) 5 miles south-southeast of Stevinson (lat. 37°15'55" N, long. 120° 48'15" W; sec. 6, T 8 S, R 11 E). Named on Turlock (1962) 15' quadrangle.

Bear Springs Creek [TUOLUMNE]: *stream,* flows 3.5 miles to Clavey River 4.25 miles southeast of Duckwall Mountain (lat. 37° 55'20" N, long. 120°03'55" W; near W line sec. 24, T 1 N, R 17 E). Named on Duckwall Mountain (1948) 7.5' quadrangle.

Bear Trap Basin [CALAVERAS]: *canyon,* drained by a stream that flows 2.25 miles to Jelmini Creek 3.25 miles north-northwest of Tamarack (lat. 38°28'45" N, long. 120°06'20" W; near N line sec. 9, T 7 N, R 17 E). Named on Tamarack (1979) 7.5' quadrangle.

Beartrap Canyon [STANISLAUS]: *canyon,* drained by a stream that flows 2 miles to Orestimba Creek 6 miles south-southwest of Mikes Peak (lat. 37°16'50" N, long. 121°15'40" W; sec. 36, T 7 S, R 6 E). Named on Wilcox Ridge (1956) 7.5' quadrangle.

Bear Trap Gap [CALAVERAS]: *pass,* 7.5 miles west of Angels Camp (lat. 38°04'40" N, long. 120°41'15" W; near SE cor. sec. 30, T 3 N, R 12 E); the pass is in Bear Mountains. Named on Salt Spring Valley (1962) 7.5' quadrangle.

Beartrap Meadow [TUOLUMNE]: *area,* 3.25 miles east of Liberty Hill (lat. 38°22'10" N, long. 120°02'20" W; sec. 18, T 6 N, R 18 E). Named on Liberty Hill (1979) 7.5' quadrangle.

Bearup Lake [TUOLUMNE]: *lake,* 4400 feet long, 10 miles southwest of Tower Peak (lat. 38°03'45" N, long. 119°42' W). Named on Tower Peak (1956) 15' quadrangle. Lieutenant N.F. McClure named the lake in 1894 for a soldier in his detachment (United States Board on Geographic Names, 1934, p. 2).

Bear Valley [MARIPOSA]:

(1) *valley,* south-southeast of the village of Bear Valley along Bear Creek (2) (lat. 37°32' N, long. 120°06' W). Named on Sonora (1897) 30' quadrangle. John C. Fremont named the feature in 1848 (Richards *in* Davis, p. 115).

(2) *village,* 10.5 miles south-southeast of Coulterville (lat. 37°34'05" N, long. 120°07'05" W); the village is near the north end of Bear Valley (1). Named on Bear Valley (1947) 7.5' quadrangle. The place first was called Haydensville for David Hayden, Charles Hayden, and Willard Hayden, who mined gold nearby; later it had several names: Biddle's Camp and Biddleville for William C. Biddle; Simpsonville for Robert Simpson, who had a store there; Johnsonville for John F. "Quartz" Johnson; finally it was given the name "Bear Valley" in 1858 (Gudde, 1975, p. 29-30). Postal authorities established Haydensville post office before January 21, 1851, and discontinued it in 1852; they established Bear Valley post office in 1858, discontinued it in 1912, reestablished it in 1914, discontinued it in 1919, reestablished it in 1933, and discontinued it in 1955 (Salley, p. 17, 95).

Bear Valley [TUOLUMNE]: *area,* 8 miles south of Tower Peak (lat. 38°02' N, long. 119°34'30" W). Named on Tower Peak (1956) 15' quadrangle.

Bear Wallow Spur [MARIPOSA]: *ridge,* north-trending, 1.5 miles long, 6 miles west-northwest of Wawona (lat. 37°34'40" N, long. 119°45' W). Named on El Portal (1947) and Yosemite (1956) 15' quadrangles.

Beasore Creek [MADERA]: *stream,* flows 9 miles to Chiquito Creek 5.25 miles north-northeast of Shuteye Peak (lat. 37°25' N, long. 119°23'05" W; sec. 7, T 6 S, R 24 E). Named on Shuteye Peak (1953) 15' quadrangle.

Beasore Meadow Campground [MADERA]: *locality,* 7 miles north of Shuteye Peak (lat. 37°26'55" N, long. 119°27'10" W; near SE cor. sec. 33, T 5 S, R 23 E); the place is along Beasore Creek 1.5 miles downstream from Beasore Meadows. Named on Shuteye Peak (1953) 15' quadrangle.

Beasore Meadows [MADERA]: *area,* 7 miles north-northwest of Shuteye Peak (lat. 37°26'15" N, long. 119°28'45" W; mainly in sec. 5, T 6 S, R 23 E); the place is near the head of Beasore Creek. Named on Shuteye Peak (1953) 15' quadrangle. The name commemorates Tom Beasore, the first settler at the site (Crampton *in* Eccleston, p. 76). The place also was called Chiquito Meadows (Gudde, 1949, p. 66).

Beatitude: see **Mount Beatitude**, under **Old Inspiration Point** [MARIPOSA].

Beaver Canyon: see **Little Beaver Canyon** [TUOLUMNE].

Beaver Creek [TUOLUMNE]: *stream,* flows 19 miles to North Fork Stanislaus River 5.5 miles north-northeast of Stanislaus (lat. 38°12'25" N, long. 120°19' W; near SW cor. sec. 10, T 4 N, R 15 E). Named on Boards Crossing (1979), Dorrington (1979), Liberty Hill (1979), and Stanislaus (1948) 7.5' quadrangles.

Beaver Creek: see **Little Beaver Creek** [TUOLUMNE].

Beaver Creek Camp [TUOLUMNE]: *locality,* 8.5 miles southwest of Liberty Hill (lat. 38°17'10" N, long. 120°13'15" W; sec. 16, T 5 N, R 16 E); the place is along Beaver Creek. Named on Big Meadow (1956) 15' quadrangle.

Beaver Slough [SAN JOAQUIN]:

(1) *water feature,* joins South Mokelumne River nearly 4 miles southwest of Thornton (lat. 38°11'40" N, long. 121°28'40" W). Named on Thornton (1978) 7.5' quadrangle.

(2) *water feature,* on Mandeville Island, joins Connection Slough 15 miles west-southwest of Lodi (lat. 38°01'55" N, long. 121°32'15" W). Named on Bouldin (1910) 7.5' quadrangle.

Beck Lakes [MADERA]: *lakes*, two, largest 1900 feet long, 4.25 miles west-northwest of Devils Postpile (lat. 37°38'15" N, long. 119°09'30" W). Named on Devils Postpile (1953) 15' quadrangle. John Beck, a miner, named the lakes for himself about 1882 (Browning, 1986, p. 14).

Becknell Creek [MARIPOSA]: *stream*, flows 6 miles to Chapman Creek 13 miles south of Mariposa (lat. 37°17'55" N, long. 119°58'05" W; sec. 26, T 7 S, R 18 E). Named on Ben Hur (1947) 7.5' quadrangle. The name is for John Becknell, a pioneer rancher (Sargent, Shirley, 1976, p. 29).

Beehive [TUOLUMNE]: *locality*, 9 miles north-northeast of Mather Station (present Mather) (lat. 37°59'35" N, long. 119°46'45" W; sec. 28, T 2 N, R 20 E). Named on Yosemite (1909) 30' quadrangle. United States Board on Geographic Names (1991, p. 3) approved the name "Beehive" for a flat 4 miles east-northeast of Lake Eleanor (lat. 37°59'46" N, long. 119°46'36" W; sec. 28, T 2 N, R 20 E), and rejected the name "Beehive Meadow" for the feature.

Beehive Meadow: see **Beehive** [TUOLUMNE].

Bell Creek [TUOLUMNE]: *stream*, flows about 7.5 miles to join Lily Creek (3) and form Clavey River nearly 4 miles south-southeast of Pinecrest (lat. 38°08'30" N, long. 119°58' W; sec. 2, T 3 N, R 18 E). Named on Pinecrest (1956) 15' quadrangle. Bell Creek and Clavey River together are called Middle Fork Tuolumne River on Dardanelles (1898) 30' quadrangle. United States Board on Geographic Names (1963a, p. 5) rejected the names "Belle Creek," "Clavey Creek," and "Clavey River" for present Bell Creek.

Belle Creek: see **Bell Creek** [TUOLUMNE].

Belle Meadow: see **Bell Meadow** [TUOLUMNE].

Belleview [TUOLUMNE]: *locality*, 6.25 miles east-southeast of Columbia along Sullivan Creek (lat. 38°00'45" N, long. 120°17'25" W; sec. 23, T 2 N, R 15 E). Named on Columbia SE (1948) 7.5' quadrangle.

Bellevue [MERCED]: *locality*, 4 miles north of Merced along Yosemite Valley Railroad (lat. 37°21'40" N, long. 120°29'20" W; near S line sec. 36, T 6 S, R 13 E). Named on Merced (1917) 7.5' quadrangle.

Bellfour Canyon [CALAVERAS]: *canyon*, drained by a stream that flows 2.5 miles to Mattley Creek 5.25 miles northwest of Tamarack (lat. 38°29'45" N, long. 120°08'10" W). Named on Calaveras Dome (1979) 7.5' quadrangle.

Bell Hill [TUOLUMNE]: *peak*, 0.5 mile east-southeast of Columbia (lat. 38°02' N, long. 120°23'30" W; sec. 13, T 2 N, R 14 E). Named on Columbia (1948) 7.5' quadrangle. The feature was called Santiago Hill before about 1918 (Gudde, 1975, p. 305).

Bell Meadow [TUOLUMNE]: *area*, 4 miles east-southeast of Pinecrest (lat. 38°10' N, long. 119°55'45" W); the place is along Bell Creek. Named on Pinecrest (1979) 7.5' quadrangle. Called Belle Meadow on Dardanelles (1898) 30' quadrangle, but United States Board on Geographic Names (1963a, p. 5) rejected the names "Belle Meadow" and "Bell Meadows" for the area.

Bell Mountain [TUOLUMNE]: *peak*, 5 miles southeast of Pinecrest (lat. 38°08'55" N, long. 119°55'15" W). Altitude 7950 feet. Named on Pinecrest (1979) 7.5' quadrangle.

Bellota [SAN JOAQUIN]: *locality*, 4.5 miles east-northeast of Linden (lat. 38°03'10" N, long. 121°00'50" W; sec. 5, T 2 N, R 9 E). Named on Linden (1968) 7.5' quadrangle. Postal authorities established Bellota post office in 1860, discontinued it in 1863, reestablished it in 1870, discontinued it in 1871, reestablished it in 1874, and discontinued it in 1918 (Frickstad, p. 159). Indians considered the site a good place to gather acorns—*bellota* means "acorn" in Spanish (Hillman and Covello, p. 194). The locality first was known as Fisher's Bridge for William V. Fisher, who built a bridge and operated a stage station there (Hoover, Rensch, and Rensch, p. 376). Davis and Atherton Ferry was on the river a few miles east of the site of Bellota before Fisher built his bridge (Hoover, Rensch, and Rensch, p. 376).

Bellows' Butte: see **Liberty Cap** [MARIPOSA].

Bell's Gulch: see **Hoffs Gulch** [MARIPOSA].

Bellview [MADERA]: *locality*, 5.5 miles south-southwest of O'Neals (lat. 37°03'25" N, long. 119°42'50" W; sec. 18, T 10 S, R 21 E). Site named on Millerton Lake West (1965) 7.5' quadrangle. Called Sesame on Mariposa (1912) 30' quadrangle. Postal authorities established Bellview post office in 1894 and discontinued it in 1896; they established Sesame post office in 1902 and discontinued it in 1913 (Frickstad, p. 85, 86).

Bellyache Canyon [MARIPOSA]: *canyon*, drained by a stream that flows 1 mile to Cavallada Creek 4.25 miles north-northeast of the settlement of Catheys Valley (lat. 37°29'15" N, long. 120°03'10" W). Named on Catheys Valley (1962) 7.5' quadrangle. On Indian Gulch (1920) 15' quadrangle, the name applies to a canyon situated 1 to 2 miles farther southeast. United States Board on Geographic Names (1964a, p. 8) rejected the names "Billy Ache Canyon" and "William Aches Canyon" for the feature, but noted that the name "Bellyache" reportedly is derived from Billy Aike, or Ache, who was an early resident of the neighborhood.

Beltz Lake [STANISLAUS]: *intermittent lake*, 1000 feet long, 1.25 miles east-southeast of La Grange (lat. 37°39'20" N, long. 120°26'20" W; sec. 21, T 3 S, R 14 E). Named on La Grange (1962) 7.5' quadrangle.

Ben Brow Hill [TUOLUMNE]: *peak*, 2.5 miles south of Don Pedro Camp (lat. 37°40'45" N, long. 120°24'35" W; near NE cor. sec. 15, T 3 S, R 14 E). Altitude 1074 feet. Named on La Grange (1962) 7.5' quadrangle.

Bench Canyon [MADERA]: *canyon*, drained by a stream that flows 3 miles to North Fork San Joaquin River 9 miles west-northwest of Devils Postpile (lat. 37°40'05" N, long. 119°14'30" W). Named on Devils Postpile (1953) and Merced Peak (1953) 15' quadrangles.

Benedict Meadow [MADERA]: *area*, 7.25 miles south of Shuteye Peak (lat. 37°14'50" N, long. 119°25'50" W; sec. 11, T 8 S, R 23 E). Named on Shaver Lake (1953) 15' quadrangle. Called Ellis Meadow on Kaiser (1904) 30' quadrangle, but United States Board on Geographic Names (1960c, p. 15) rejected this name for the place, and approved the name "Benedict Meadow" to honor Maurice Abbott Benedict, supervisor of Sierra National Forest from 1909 until 1944.

Benedict's Ferry: see **Woodbridge** [SAN JOAQUIN].

Ben Hur [MARIPOSA]: *locality*, 9 miles south of Mariposa (lat. 37° 21'05" N, long. 119°57'25" W; sec. 1, T 7 S, R 18 E). Named on Ben Hur (1947) 7.5' quadrangle. Mariposa (1912) 30' quadrangle shows the place situated 1 mile farther north-northwest (near S line sec. 35, T 6 S, R 18 E). Postal authorities established Ben Hur post office in 1890, discontinued it in 1902, reestablished it 3 miles farther south in 1904, and discontinued it in 1951; the name is from the hero of Lew Wallace's romantic novel *Ben Hur* (Salley, p. 18).

Bennett Valley [STANISLAUS]: *valley*, 7 miles southwest of Newman (lat. 37°15' N, long. 121°07'30" W). Named on Crevison Peak (1955), Newman (1952), and Orestimba Peak (1955) 7.5' quadrangles.

Benson [SAN JOAQUIN]: *locality*, 12 miles northwest of Lodi near Mokelumne City (lat. 38°15'15" N, long. 121°26'15" W). Named on Franklin (1942) 15' quadrangle.

Benson Lake [TUOLUMNE]: *lake*, 9 miles south of Tower Peak along Piute Creek (2) (lat. 38°00'55" N, long. 119°01'40" W). Named on Tower Peak (1956) 15' quadrangle. The name, given in 1895, commemorates Harry C. Benson, an army officer in Yosemite National Park from 1895 until 1897, and acting superintendent of the park from 1905 until 1908 (Hanna, p. 30).

Benson Pass [TUOLUMNE]: *pass*, 7 miles southwest of Matterhorn Peak (lat. 38°00'50" N, long. 119°27'40" W). Named on Matterhorn Peak (1956) 15' quadrangle.

Benson's Ferry: see **Mokelumne City** [SAN JOAQUIN].

Benton Mills: see **Bagby** [MARIPOSA].

Berenda [MADERA]: *locality*, 3.5 miles southeast of Fairmead along Southern Pacific Railroad (lat. 37°02'25" N, long. 120°09'10" W; at W line sec. 30, T 10 S, R 17 E); the place is near Berenda Creek. Named on Berenda (1961) 7.5' quadrangle. Postal authorities established Berendo post office in 1873, discontinued it for a time in 1881, changed the name to Berenda in 1919, and discontinued it in 1935 (Frickstad, p. 85). The name is a corruption of *berrenda*, which means "antelope" in Spanish (Hanna, p. 30). United States Board on Geographic Names (1933a, p. 137) rejected the forms "Berendo" and "Berrendo" for the name.

Berenda Creek [MADERA]: *stream*, enters lowlands 11 miles east-northeast of Fairmead (lat. 37°08'30" N, long. 120°01' W) and flows 16 miles to a ditch 5.5 miles south-southwest of Fairmead. Named on Firebaugh (1962) and Le Grand (1961) 15' quadrangles.

Berenda Reservoir [MADERA]: *lake*, behind a dam on Berenda Slough 3.5 miles north of Fairmead (lat. 37°07'40" N, long. 120° 11'10" W; near S line sec. 23, T 9 S, R 16 E). Named on Le Grand (1961, photorevised 1981) 7.5' quadrangle.

Berenda Slough [MADERA]: *stream*, diverges from Ash Slough 7 miles north-northeast of Fairmead, and flows 25 miles to Fresno River 22 miles west of Madera (lat. 36°59'45" N, long. 120°28'15" W; sec. 8, T 11 S, R 14 E). Named on Chowchilla (1960) and Le Grand (1961) 15' quadrangles, and on Firebaugh NE (1961) and Poso Farm (1962) 7.5' quadrangles. United States Board on Geographic Names (1933a, p. 137) rejected the forms "Berendo Slough" and "Berrendo Slough" for the name.

Berendo: see **Berenda** [MADERA].

Berendo Slough: see **Berenda Slough** [MADERA].

Bernice Lake [MARIPOSA]: *lake*, 1600 feet long, nearly 7 miles southeast of Cathedral Peak (lat. 37°46' N, long. 119°19'55" W). Named on Tuolumne Meadows (1956) 15' quadrangle. The name commemorates the wife of Superintendent W.B. Lewis of Yosemite National Park (United States Board on Geographic Names, 1934, p. 2).

Berrendo: see **Berenda** [MADERA].

Berrendo Slough: see **Berenda Slough** [MADERA].

Berry Hill [MADERA]: *peak*, 5.5 miles south-southwest of O'Neals (lat. 37°03'05" N, long. 119°43'15" W; sec. 19, T 10 S, R 21 E). Named on Millerton Lake West (1965) 7.5' quadrangle.

Berry's Fish Camp: see **Fish Camp** [MARIPOSA].

Bethany [SAN JOAQUIN]: *locality*, 17 miles southwest of downtown Stockton along Southern Pacific Railroad (lat. 37°46'50" N, long. 121°31'35" W; near SW cor. sec. 3, T 2 S, R 4 E). Named on Bethany (1952) 7.5' quadrangle. Postal authorities established Bethany post office in 1879, discontinued it for a time in 1880, and discontinued finally it in 1940 (Frickstad, p. 159). The place first was called Burns' Landing for Maurice Burns (Hillman and Covello, p. 197). It also was called Mohr Station for John Mohr, who deeded the site to the railroad (Gudde, 1949, p. 30). Thompson and West's (1879) map shows a place called Mohr's Landing along Old River about 1 mile northeast of Bethany, and a community called Wickland nearby. Henry Mohr started the landing to ship coal from mines in Corral Hollow; a river town called Wicklund flourished near the landing until the mines failed (Mosier, 1979, p. 6).

Bethany Ferry [SAN JOAQUIN]: *locality,* 16 miles southwest of downtown Stockton on Old River (lat. 37°47'25" N, long. 121°30'50" W); the ferry is 1 mile northeast of Bethany. Named on Bethany (1914) 7.5' quadrangle

Bethel: see **North Fork** [MADERA].

Beulah Lake: see **Long Lake** [TUOLUMNE].

Biddle's Camp: see **Bear Valley** [MARIPOSA] (2)

Biddleville: see **Bear Valley** [MARIPOSA] (2).

Big Bar [CALAVERAS]: *locality,* 1 mile northwest of Mokelumne Hill along Mokelumne River (lat. 38°18'45" N, long. 120°43'05" W; sec. 1, T 5 N, R 11 E). Named on Mokelumne Hill (1948) 7.5' quadrangle. Gudde (1975, p. 34) noted that the place also had the names "Upper Bar" and "Upper Ferry." Whale Boat Ferry started at Big Bar in 1850 and operated until 1852 or 1853 (Hoover, Rensch, and Rensch, p. 29). Camp's (1962) map shows a place called Sandy Bar located less than 2 miles east-northeast of Big Bar, a place called Spanish Bar located nearly 3 miles east-northeast of Big Bar, and a place called Stony Bar located nearly 4 miles east-northeast of Big Bar—the map shows all three places on the south side of Moklumne River.

Big Bend [MADERA]: *bend,* 8 miles south-southeast of O'Neals along San Joaquin River on Madera-Fresno County line (lat. 37° 01'15" N, long. 119°38' W). The feature now is in Millerton Lake. Named on Millerton Lake West (1965) 7.5' quadrangle.

Big Brother Slough [SAN JOAQUIN]: *water feature,* on Mandeville Island, joins San Joaquin River 16 miles west-southwest of Lodi (lat. 38°03'20" N, long. 121°33' W); the feature is west of Little Brother Slough. Named on Bouldin Island (1952) 7.5' quadrangle.

Big Buttonwillow Lake [MERCED]: *lake,* 3400 feet long, 6.25 miles north-northeast of Los Banos (lat. 37°08'10" N, long. 120°47'35" W); the lake is south of Little Buttonwillow Lake. Named on San Luis Ranch (1961) 7.5' quadrangle.

Big Canon Creek: see **Clavey River** [TUOLUMNE].

Big Creek [MADERA-MARIPOSA]: *stream,* heads in Madera County and flows 15 miles to South Fork Merced River 0.5 mile west of Wawona in Mariposa County (lat. 37°32'20" N, long. 119°40' W; near E line sec. 33, T 4 S, R 21 E). Named on Bass Lake (1953) and Yosemite (1956) 15' quadrangles.

Big Creek [TUOLUMNE]:

(1) *stream,* flows 12.5 miles to Tuolumne River nearly 5 miles south of Tuolumne (lat. 37°53'35" N, long. 120°13'20" W; sec. 33, T 1 N, R 16 E). Named on Groveland (1947), Jawbone Ridge (1947), and Tuolumne (1948) 7.5' quadrangles. A large meadow at the head of the stream was called Savage Flat in the early days for James D. Savage, who probably grazed horses at the place (Gudde, 1975, p. 309).

(2) *stream,* flows nearly 7 miles to Don Pedro Reservoir 7.5 miles south of Chinese Camp (lat. 37°45'35" N, long. 120°25'05" W; sec. 15, T 2 S, R 14 E). Named on Chinese Camp (1947, photorevised 1973) and La Grange (1962) 7.5' quadrangles. Called Fortynine Creek on Merced Falls (1944) 15' quadrangle. West Fork enters from the northwest at the mouth of the main stream; it is nearly 5 miles long and is named on Chinese Camp (1947, photorevised 1973) 7.5' quadrangle.

(3) *stream,* flows 4.5 miles to South Fork Tuolumne River nearly 7 miles southwest of Mather (lat. 37°48'40" N, long. 119°56'20" W; near E line sec. 36, T 1 S, R 18 E). Named on Lake Eleanor (1956) 15' quadrangle. Called Hazel Green Creek on Yosemite (1909) 30' quadrangle, but United States Board on Geographic Names (1966, p. 7) rejected this name for the feature.

(4) *stream,* flows 3 miles to Tuolumne River 2 miles south-southwest of Don Pedro Camp (lat. 37°41'25" N, long. 120°25'20" W; sec. 10, T 3 S, R 14 E). Named on La Grange (1962) 7.5' quadrangle.

Big Creek: see **Hazel Green Creek** [TUOLUMNE].

Big Creek Basin [TUOLUMNE]: *valley,* 8 miles south-southwest of Mather (lat. 37°46'15" N, long. 119°54'15" W); the valley is at the head of Big Creek (3). Named on Lake Eleanor (1956) 15' quadrangle.

Big Dam Reservoir: see **Pinecrest Lake** [TUOLUMNE].

Big Deer Canyon [MERCED]: *canyon,* drained by a stream that flows less than 0.5 mile to Romero Creek 5.25 miles north of Pacheco Pass (lat. 37°08'45" N, long. 121°12'05" W; sec. 16, T 9 S, R 7 E); the feature is 1 mile west of Little Deer Canyon. Named on Crevison Peak (1955) 7.5' quadrangle.

Big Dome [CALAVERAS]: *peak,* nearly 2 miles north-northwest of Paloma (lat. 38°17' N, long. 120°46'30" W; sec. 16, T 5 N, R 11 E). Altitude 1436 feet. Named on Jackson (1962) 7.5' quadrangle.

Bigelow Lake [TUOLUMNE]: *lake,* 2300 feet long, 5 miles west of Tower Peak (lat. 38°09'20" N, long. 119°38'10" W); the lake is 0.5 mile north-west of Bigelow Peak. Named on Tower Peak (1956) 15' quadrangle.

Bigelow Peak [TUOLUMNE]: *peak,* 4.5 miles west of Tower Peak (lat. 38°09' N, long. 119°37'35" W). Altitude 10,539 feet. Named on Tower Peak (1956) 15' quadrangle. The name commemorates Major John Bigelow, Jr., acting superintendent of Yosemite National Park in 1904 (United States Board on Geographic Names, 1934, p. 2).

Big Falls: see **La Grange Reservoir** [STANISLAUS-TUOLUMNE].

Big Grizzly: see **Miller Gulch** [MARIPOSA].

Big Grizzly Creek [MARIPOSA]: *stream,* flows 1.5 miles to Ned Gulch (2) 5 miles west-northwest of El Portal (lat. 37°42'10" N, long. 119°51'50" W; sec. 4, T 3 S, R 19 E); the stream heads near Big Grizzly Mountain. Named on El Portal (1947) and Kinsley (1947) 7.5' quadrangles.

Big Grizzly Flat [MARIPOSA]: *area,* 6.25 miles west-northwest of El Portal (lat. 37°43'25" N, long. 119°52'40" W; at N line sec. 33, T 2 S, R 19 E); the place is 1 mile east-northeast of Big Grizzly Mountain. Named on El Portal (1947) and Kinsley (1947) 7.5' quadrangles.

Big Grizzly Mountain [MARIPOSA]: *peak,* 7 miles west-northwest of El Portal (lat. 37°43'05" N, long. 119°53'40" W; sec. 32, T 2 S, R 19 E); the peak is 1.25 miles east-northeast of Little Grizzly Mountain. Altitude 5192 feet. Named on Kinsley (1947) 7.5' quadrangle.

Big Hill: see **Rushing Mountain** [TUOLUMNE].

Big Humbug Creek [TUOLUMNE]: *stream,* flows 3.5 miles to Tuolumne River nearly 5 miles south-southeast of Tuolumne (lat. 37° 53'35" N, long. 120°13'05" W; sec. 33, T 1 N, R 16 E). Named on Groveland (1947) and Tuolumne (1948) 7.5' quadrangles.

Big Island [TUOLUMNE]: *island,* 325 feet long, 1 mile east-southeast of Don Pedro Camp in Don Pedro Reservoir (lat. 37°42'40" N, long. 120°23'10" W; near SW cor. sec. 36, T 2 N, R 14 E). Named on La Grange (1962) 7.5' quadrangle.

Big Island Lake: see **Bear Lake** [TUOLUMNE] (2).

Big Jackass Creek [TUOLUMNE]: *stream,* flows 7.5 miles to Moccasin Creek nearly 3 miles southeast of Moccasin (lat. 37°46'45" N, long. 120°16'15" W; sec. 12, T 2 S, R 15 E). Named on Groveland (1947) and Moccasin (1948) 7.5' quadrangles.

Big Lake [TUOLUMNE]: *lake,* 0.5 mile long, 12 miles east-southeast of Pinecrest (lat. 38°07'20" N, long. 119°47'50" W). Named on Pinecrest (1956) 15' quadrangle.

Big Meadow [CALAVERAS]:

(1) *area,* 2.25 miles southwest of Tamarack (lat. 38°25' N, long. 120°06'30" W; mainly in sec. 33, T 7 N, R 17 E). Named on Tamarack (1979) 7.5' quadrangle.

(2) *settlement,* 2.5 miles southwest of Tamarack (lat. 38°24'55" N, long. 120°06'50" W; sec. 33, T 7 N, R 17 E); the place is in Big Meadow (1). Named on Tamarack (1979) 7.5' quadrangle.

Big Meadow [MARIPOSA]: *area,* 2.5 miles northeast of El Portal (lat. 37°42'20" N, long. 119°45' W; near N line sec. 3, T 3 S, R 20 E). Named on El Portal (1947) and Yosemite (1956) 15' quadrangles.

Big Meadow Creek [CALAVERAS]: *stream,* flows 5 miles to North Fork Stanislaus River 3.5 miles southwest of Tamarack (lat. 38° 24' N, long. 120°07'15" W); the stream goes through Big Meadow (1). Named on Tamarack (1979) 7.5' quadrangle.

Big Meadow Creek [TUOLUMNE]: *stream,* flows 2.5 miles to Piute Creek (2) 5 miles southwest of Matterhorn Peak (lat. 38°03'10" N, long. 119°27'25" W). Named on Matterhorn Peak (1956) 15' quadrangle.

Big Meadow Creek: see **Ackerson Creek** [TUOLUMNE].

Big Oak Flat [TUOLUMNE]: *village,* 2.25 miles east-northeast of Moccasin near the head of Rattlesnake Creek (lat. 37°49'25" N, long. 120°15'25" W; sec. 30, T 1 S, R 16 E). Named on Moccasin (1948) 7.5' quadrangle. Postal authorities established Big Oak Flat post office in 1852 (Frickstad, p. 215). The name is from a huge oak tree at the place (Hanna, p. 33). James D. Savage began mining at the site in 1848, and it then became known as Savage Diggings; the place also was called Oak Flat and Oak Flats (Gudde, 1975, p. 37, 309).

Big Pine Canyon [MERCED-STANISLAUS]: *canyon,* drained by a stream that heads in Stanislaus County and flows 2.5 miles to Romero Creek 6.25 miles north-northeast of Pacheco Pass in Merced County (lat. 37°09'05" N, long. 121°10'50" W; near E line sec. 15, T 9 S, R 7 E); the feature is 1 mile west of Little Pine Canyon [MERCED]. Named on Crevison Peak (1955) 7.5' quadrangle. Called Pine Canyon on Pacheco Pass (1920) 15' quadrangle.

Big Prather Meadow [TUOLUMNE]: *valley,* less than 1 mile north of Liberty Hill (lat. 38°22'45" N, long. 120°06' W); the valley is 1 mile west of Little Prather Meadow. Named on Liberty Hill (1979) and Tamarack (1979) 7.5' quadrangles.

Big Rattlesnake Creek [TUOLUMNE]: *stream,* flows 5.25 miles to North Fork Stanislaus River 4.5 miles west of Liberty Hill (lat. 38° 21'30" N, long. 120°11'05" W; sec. 23, T 6 N, R 16 E); the stream generally is parallel to and about 1 mile north of Little Rattlesnake Creek. Named on

Boards Crossing (1979) and Liberty Hill (1979) 7.5' quadrangles.

Big Sandy Campground [MADERA]: *locality,* 7.25 miles north-northeast of Yosemite Forks (lat. 37°28' N, long. 119°34'55" W; sec. 29, T 5 S, R 22 E); the place is along Big Creek 1 mile downstream from Little Sandy Campground. Named on Bass Lake (1953) 15' quadrangle.

Big Seven Ridge [CALAVERAS]: *ridge,* northwest-trending, 2 miles long, 1.25 miles northeast of Copperopolis (lat. 37°59'45" N, long. 120°37'45" W); Big Seven mine is on the ridge. Named on Copperopolis (1962), Melones Dam (1962), and Salt Spring Valley (1962) 7.5' quadrangles.

Big Spring [MARIPOSA]: *spring,* 3 miles southeast of Mariposa (lat. 37°27'35" N, long. 119°55'10" W; near NW cor. sec. 32, T 5 S, R 19 E); the spring is along a branch of Spring Creek. Named on Mariposa (1947) 7.5' quadrangle.

Big Spring [STANISLAUS]: *spring,* 2.25 miles south-southwest of Crevison Peak (lat. 37°09'30" N, long. 121°12'05" W; near N line sec. 16, T 9 S, R 7 E). Named on Crevison Peak (1955) 7.5' quadrangle.

Big Springs Creek [CALAVERAS]: *stream,* flows 2.5 miles to Martells Creek 7.25 miles south-southwest of Copperopolis (lat. 37°53'10" N, long. 120°42'10" W). Named on Copperopolis (1962) 7.5' quadrangle. Called Big Spring Cr. on Copperopolis (1916) 15' quadrangle.

Big Tree [MARIPOSA]: *area,* 3.5 miles east-southeast of Wawona (lat. 37°30'30" N, long. 119°36' W). Named on Yosemite (1956) 15' quadrangle. The federal government gave the land to the State of California in 1864 as a park to preserve a grove of redwood trees (Whitney, 1870, p. 10). The place now is part of Yosemite National Park.

Big Trees [CALAVERAS]: *locality,* 5 miles south-southeast of Blue Mountain (lat. 38°16'45" N, long. 120°18'55" W; near NW cor. sec. 22, T 5 N, R 15 E); the place is in Calaveras Big Trees State Park. Named on Dorrington (1979) 7.5' quadrangle. Postal authorities established Big Trees post office in 1865, discontinued it for a time in 1903, and discontinued it finally in 1943 (Salley, p. 21).

Big Trees Creek [CALAVERAS]: *stream,* flows 3.5 miles to White Pine Lake 5.25 miles south-southeast of Blue Mountain (lat. 38° 16' N, long. 120°20'25" W; sec. 20, T 5 N, R 15 E). Named on Dorrington (1979) 7.5' quadrangle.

Big Trees Creek [TUOLUMNE]: *stream,* flows 3.5 miles to Beaver Creek 9 miles northeast of Stanislaus (lat. 38°14'30" N, long. 120° 16'15" W; sec. 36, T 5 N, R 15 E). Named on Boards Crossing (1979), Crandall Peak (1979), and Stanislaus (1948) 7.5' quadrangles.

Big Tree Station: see **Wawona** [MARIPOSA].

Big Water Lake [MERCED]: *lake,* 6 miles east-southeast of Los Banos (lat. 37°01'55" N, long. 120°45' W; sec. 27, T 10 S, R 11 E). Named on Los Banos (1961) and Santa Rita Park (1962) 15' quadrangles.

Biledo Meadow [MADERA]: *area,* 6.5 miles south-southwest of Buena Vista Peak (lat. 37°30'10" N, long. 119°34' W; on S line sec. 9, T 5 S, R 22 E). Named on Yosemite (1956) 15' quadrangle. United States Board on Geographic Names (1990, p. 5) rejected the form "Billiedo Meadow" for the feature. The name commemorates Thomas Biledo, or Biledeaux, a French-Canadian miner who built a log cabin at the place in 1890 (Uhte, p. 51).

Billiedo Meadow: see **Biledo Meadow** [MADERA].

Billy Ache Canyon: see **Bellyache Canyon** [MARIPOSA].

Bingaman Lake [TUOLUMNE]: *lake,* 1400 feet long, 4.5 miles south of Tioga Pass (lat. 37°50'45" N, long. 119°14'40" W). Named on Mono Craters (1953) 15' quadrangle. The name commemorates John W. Bingaman, a ranger at Yosemite National Park who planted trout in the lake in 1930, and who named the feature for himself (Browning, 1986, p. 19).

Bingham Lake: see **Calaveras Reservoir** [CALAVERAS].

Birch: see **Hildreth** [MADERA].

Birch Lake [TUOLUMNE]: *lake,* 850 feet long, at Mather (lat. 37°52'45" N, long. 119°51'15" W; sec. 2, T 1 S, R 19 E). Named on Lake Eleanor (1956) 15' quadrangle.

Birth Rock: see **Burst Rock** [TUOLUMNE].

Biscuit Point [STANISLAUS]: *promontory,* 5.25 miles north of Oakdale on the south side of Woodward Reservoir (lat. 37°50'40" N, long. 120°51'20" W). Named on Oakdale (1968) 7.5' quadrangle.

Bishop Creek [MARIPOSA]: *stream,* flows 4.5 miles to South Fork Merced River 6 miles northwest of Wawona (lat. 37°36'25" N, long. 119°43'10" W; near NW cor. sec. 12, T 4 S, R 20 E). Named on Yosemite (1956) 15' quadrangle. The name commemorates Samuel Addison Bishop, who served in the Mariposa Battalion during the Mariposa Indian War; the stream also is called Eleven Mile Creek (Mendershausen, p. 20).

Bishop Cut [SAN JOAQUIN]: *water feature,* watercourse that extends between Bishop Tract and King Island from White Slough to Disappointment Slough 6.5 miles southeast of Terminous (lat. 38° 02'40" N, long. 121°26'05" W). Named on Terminous (1978) 7.5' quadrangle.

Bishop Tract [SAN JOAQUIN]: *area,* 6.5 miles southeast of Terminous (lat. 38°03'30" N, long. 121°24' W); the area is east of Bishop Cut. Named on Terminous (1978) 7.5' quadrangle.

Black Bear Lake [TUOLUMNE]: *lake,* 1500 feet long, 5.5 miles west of Tower Peak (lat. 38°09'05" N, long. 119°38'55" W; sec. 34, T 4 N, R 21 E). Named on Tower Peak (1956) 15' quadrangle. Elden H. Vestal of California Department of Fish and Game named the lake in 1952 (Browning, 1986, p. 20).

Blackbird Lake [TUOLUMNE]: *lake,* 700 feet long, 7.25 miles west-northwest of Tower Peak (lat. 38°10'35" N, long. 119°40'20" W; sec. 21, T 4 N, R 21 E). Named on Tower Peak (1956) 15' quadrangle.

Black Butte [SAN JOAQUIN]: *peak,* 6.5 miles south-southwest of Tracy (lat. 37°39'10" N, long. 121°28'40" W; near E line sec. 24, T 3 S, R 4 E). Altitude 1083 feet. Named on Tracy (1954) 7.5' quadrangle.

Black Creek [CALAVERAS]:

(1) *stream,* flows 11 miles to Tulloch Lake 4 miles south-southeast of Copperopolis (lat. 37°55'30" N, long. 120°36'45" W; near W line sec. 24, T 1 N, R 12 E). Named on Copperopolis (1962), Melones Dam (1962), and Salt Spring Valley (1962) 7.5' quadrangles.

(2) *stream,* flows 1 mile to Texas Charley Gulch 4.5 miles east-northeast of Copperopolis (lat. 37°59'50" N, long. 120°33'35" W). Named on Melones Dam (1962) 7.5' quadrangle.

Black Gulch [STANISLAUS]: *canyon,* 2.5 miles long, opens into lowlands 2.5 miles west of Patterson (lat. 37°27'50" N, long. 121° 10'40" W; near NE cor. sec. 34, T 5 S, R 7 E). Named on Patterson (1953) 7.5' quadrangle.

Black Hawk Lake: see **Black Hawk Mountain** [TUOLUMNE].

Black Hawk Mountain [TUOLUMNE]: *peak,* 9.5 miles west-northwest of Tower Peak (lat. 38°12'25" N, long. 119°42'30" W). Altitude 10,348 feet. Named on Tower Peak (1956) 15' quadrangle. United States Board on Geographic Names (1965c, p. 7) approved the name "Black Hawk Lake" for a lake, 600 feet long, that lies 0.5 mile north-northwest of Black Hawk Mountain (lat. 38°12'45" N, long. 119°42'50" W).

Blackhawk Mountain [MADERA]: *ridge,* northeast-trending, 1.5 miles long, 2 miles north-northwest of O'Neals (lat. 37°09'15" N, long. 119°42'35" W). Named on O'Neals (1965) 7.5' quadrangle.

Black Hill [CALAVERAS-STANISLAUS]: *hill,* 9 miles west of Copperopolis on Calaveras-Stanislaus County line (lat. 37°58'30" N, long. 120°48'35" W; near S line sec. 31, T 2 N, R 11 E). Named on Bachelor Valley (1953) 7.5' quadrangle.

Black Hill [STANISLAUS]: *peak,* 5 miles east of Mustang Peak (lat. 37°11'30" N, long. 121°16'05" W; sec. 36, T 8 S, R 6 E). Altitude 1792 feet. Named on Mustang Peak (1955) 7.5' quadrangle.

Blackie Lake [MADERA]: *lake,* 400 feet long, 4 miles south-southeast of Merced Peak (lat. 37°34'45" N, long. 119°22'40" W). Named on Merced Peak (1953) 15' quadrangle. Warden Herb Black told employees of California Department of Fish and Game in 1946 that the lake sometimes was called Blackie Lake after himself (Browning, 1986, p. 21).

Blackland: see **Black Lands** [SAN JOAQUIN].

Black Lands [SAN JOAQUIN]: *locality,* 3.25 miles west-northwest of Waterloo along Central California Traction Railroad (lat. 38°03'25" N, long. 121°14'30" W; near NW cor. sec. 5, T 2 N, R 7 E). Named on Waterloo (1968) 7.5' quadrangle. California Division of Highways' (1934) map has the form "Blacklands" for the name, and also shows a place called Blackland situated 5 miles farther west.

Blackmans Bar [MADERA]: *locality,* 3 miles northeast of Shuteye Peak along West Fork Chiquito Creek (lat. 37°22'30" N, long. 119° 23' W; sec. 30, T 6 S, R 24 E). Named on Shuteye Peak (1953) 15' quadrangle.

Black Mountain [MARIPOSA]: *peak,* 6.5 miles east of Buckeye Peak (lat. 37°40' N, long. 120°00'20" W; near S line sec. 17, T 3 S, R 18 E). Altitude 3316 feet. Named on Buckhorn Peak (1947) 7.5' quadrangle. Called Texas Hill on Sonora (1897) 30' quadrangle.

Black Mountain [STANISLAUS]:

(1) *peak,* nearly 1 mile north of Mount Stakes on Stanislaus-Santa Clara County line (lat. 37°19'55" N, long. 121°24'30" W; at N line sec. 15, T 7 S, R 5 E). Named on Mount Stakes (1955) 7.5' quadrangle.

(2) *peak,* 12.5 miles west-southwest of Newman (lat. 37°16'05" N, long. 121°14'35" W; sec. 6, T 8 S, R 7 E). Altitude 2268 feet. Named on Orestimba Peak (1955) 7.5' quadrangle.

Black Mountain: see **Madera Peak** [MADERA].

Black Peak [TUOLUMNE]: *peak,* 2.5 miles southeast of Don Pedro Camp (lat. 37°41'40" N, long. 120°22'05" W; near NW cor. sec. 7, T 3 S, R 15 E). Altitude 1053 feet. Named on Penon Blanco Peak (1962) 7.5' quadrangle.

Black Peak: see **Madera Peak** [MADERA].

Black Peak Fork: see **Madera Creek** [MADERA].

Black Rascal Creek [MERCED]: *stream,* flows 29 miles to Bear Creek (1) 5.5 miles south of Atwater (lat. 37°16'05" N, long. 120° 37'25" W; sec. 2, T 8 S, R 12 W). Named on Atwater (1961) and Merced (1962) 15' quadrangles.

Blacks Creek [MARIPOSA]: *stream,* flows 5.25 miles to Maxwell Creek 1.5 miles west-southwest of Coulterville (lat. 37°42'15" N, long. 120°13'30" W; sec. 5, T 3 S, R 16 E). Named on Coulterville (1947) 7.5' quadrangle.

Black Slough [SAN JOAQUIN]: *water feature,* on Roberts Island, joins San Joaquin River 7.5 miles west-northwest of downtown Stockton (lat. 37°59'40" N, long. 121°25'10" W). Named on Holt (1978) 7.5' quadrangle.

Blackslough Landing [SAN JOAQUIN]: *locality,* 7.5 miles west-northwest of downtown Stockton at the north end of Roberts Island (lat. 37°59'40" N, long. 121°25'10" W); the place is on the south bank of San Joaquin River at the mouth of Black Slough. Named on Holt (1978) 7.5' quadrangle.

Black Spring [CALAVERAS]: *spring,* 7.5 miles southwest of Tamarack (lat. 38°22'35" N, long. 120°11'35" W; sec. 15, T 6 N, R 16 E). Named on Calaveras Dome (1979) 7.5' quadrangle, which indicates that the spring is dry.

Black Spring [MARIPOSA]: *spring,* 4.5 miles west-southwest of Yosemite Village in Yosemite Valley (lat. 37°43'10" N, long. 119° 39'35" W). Named on Yosemite (1956) 15' quadrangle. The name is from the color of the ground at the spring (Browning, 1986, p. 20).

Black Spring Creek [CALAVERAS]: *stream,* flows 1.5 miles to Murray Creek 5 miles east of San Andeas (lat. 38°12'40" N, long. 120°40'05" W; near E line sec. 12, T 4 N, R 12 E). Named on Calaveritas (1962) 7.5' quadrangle.

Blackstone Creek [MARIPOSA]: *stream,* flows 2.5 miles to Smith Creek 3.25 miles south of Smith Peak (lat. 37°45'15" N, long. 120° 05'30" W; near NW cor. sec. 22, T 2 S, R 17 E). Named on Jawbone Ridge (1947) 7.5' quadrangle.

Blade Creek [MARIPOSA]: *stream,* flows 6.25 miles to West Fork Chowchilla River 10 miles southeast of Mariposa (lat. 37°22'20" N, long. 119°51'30" W; sec. 35, T 6 S, R 19 E). Named on Horsecamp Mountain (1947), Mariposa (1947), and Stumpfield Mountain (1947) 7.5' quadrangles.

Blakes Landing [SAN JOAQUIN]: *locality,* 15 miles west-southwest of Lodi on the north side of San Joaquin River on Venice Island (lat. 38°03'45" N, long. 121°32'50" W). Named on Bouldin (1910) 7.5' quadrangle.

Blanchard [TUOLUMNE]: *locality,* 4.5 miles east-northeast of Don Pedro Camp (lat. 37°43'50" N, long. 120°19'25" W; sec. 28, T 2 S, R 15 E). Named on Penon Blanco Peak (1962) 7.5' quadrangle. Blanchard post office, named for Rosie M. Blanchard, first postmaster, was established in 1894, moved 0.5 mile southwest in 1938, and discontinued in 1953 (Salley p. 22).

Blanket Creek [TUOLUMNE]: *stream,* flows 5 miles to Rough and Ready Creek 7 miles south-southeast of Sonora (lat. 37°53'35" N, long. 120°19'50" W; sec. 33, T 1 N, R 15 E). Named on Standard (1948) 7.5' quadrangle. The stream received the name after some Indians stole blankets from a miner there (Gudde, 1975, p. 40).

Blewetts Point [TUOLUMNE]: *peak,* 2.5 miles northeast of Columbia (lat. 38°03'30" N, long. 120°21'55" W; sec. 6, T 2 N, R 15 E). Named on Columbia SE (1948) 7.5' quadrangle.

Blind Mans Gulch [STANISLAUS]: *canyon,* drained by a stream that flows 1.5 miles to Rocky Fork Canyon 5.25 miles north of Copper Mountain (lat. 37°29'35" N, long. 121°19'10" W; near NW cor. sec. 21, T 5 S, R 6 E). Named on Copper Mountain (1956) 7.5' quadrangle.

Bloods Creek [CALAVERAS]: *stream,* heads in Alpine County and flows 2.5 miles in Calaveras County to North Fork Stanislaus River 1.5 miles southeast of Tamarack (lat. 38°25" N, long. 120° 03'30" W). Named on Tamarack (1979) 7.5' quadrangle. Browning (1986, p. 21) associated the name with Harvey S. Blood, who owned and operated the main tollgate for Big Trees-Carson Valley turnpike.

Bloomer Lake [TUOLUMNE]: *lake,* 325 feet long, 5.25 miles south-southwest of Dardanelle (lat. 38°16' N, long. 119°51'40" W; on E line sec. 22, T 5 N, R 19 E). Named on Dardanelle (1979) 7.5' quadrangle.

Blue Canyon [TUOLUMNE]:

(1) *canyon,* drained by a stream that flows 2.25 miles to Beaver Creek 2.5 miles south of Liberty Hill (lat. 38°19'45" N, long. 120° 05'55" W; sec. 34, T 6 N, R 17 E). Named on Liberty Hill (1979) 7.5' quadrangle.

(2) *canyon,* drained by a stream that flows nearly 1.5 miles to Deadman Creek 1.5 miles west-southwest of Sonora Pass (lat. 38°19'05" N, long. 119°39'45" W). Named on Sonora Pass (1979) 7.5' quadrangle.

Blue Canyon Lake [TUOLUMNE]: *lake,* 1000 feet long, 2.5 miles southwest of Sonora Pass (lat. 38°17'50" N, long. 119°39'55" W); the lake is at the head of Blue Canyon (2). Named on Sonora Pass (1979) 7.5' quadrangle.

Blue Cottage: see **Eugene** [STANISLAUS].

Blue Creek [CALAVERAS]: *stream,* flows 15 miles to North Fork Mokelumne River 6.5 miles west of Garnet Hill (lat. 38°27'45" N, long. 120°22'25" W; sec. 13, T 7 N, R 14 E). Named on Calaveras Dome (1979) and Garnet Hill (1979) 7.5' quadrangles.

Blue Gulch [TUOLUMNE]: *canyon,* drained by a stream that flows 2 miles to Don Pedro Reservoir 2.25 miles east-southeast of Chinese Camp (lat. 37°51'45" N, long. 120°23'40" W; near E line sec. 11, T 1 S, R 14 E). Named on Chinese Camp (1947, photorevised 1973) and Sonora (1948) 7.5' quadrangles

Blue Hole [CALAVERAS]: *lake,* 200 feet long, 5.25 miles northwest of Tamarack at the mouth of Mattley Creek (lat. 38°29'50" N, long. 120°08'10" W). Named on Calaveras Dome (1979) 7.5' quadrangle.

Bluejay Creek [MARIPOSA]: *stream,* flows 2.5 miles to Yosemite Creek nearly 3 miles north-northwest of Yosemite Village (lat. 37° 46'55" N, long. 119°36'40" W). Named on Hetch Hetchy Reservoir (1956) 15' quadrangle.

Blue Jay Point [CALAVERAS]: *peak,* 3 miles east-southeast of Mokelumne Hill (lat. 38°16'40" N, long. 120°39'35" W; near N line sec. 21, T 5 N, R 12 E). Named on Mokelumne Hill (1948) 7.5' quadrangle.

Blue Lake [MADERA]: *lake,* 1200 feet long, 7 miles east-northeast of Merced Peak (lat. 37°40'50" N, long. 119°16'55" W). Named on Merced Peak (1953) 15' quadrangle.

Blue Mountain [CALAVERAS]: *peak,* 20 miles east-northeast of San Andreas (lat. 38°20'30" N, long. 120°21'50" W; sec. 30, T 6 N, R 15 E). Altitude 6071 feet. Named on Dorrington (1979) 7.5' quadrangle.

Blue Mountain: see **Mountain Ranch** [CALAVERAS].

Blue Mountain City: see **Mountain Ranch** [CALAVERAS].

Bluerock Spring [SAN JOAQUIN]: *spring,* 15 miles south-southwest of Tracy (lat. 37°32' N, long. 121°29'05" W; near S line sec. 36, T 4 S, R 4 E). Named on Lone Tree Creek (1955) 7.5' quadrangle.

Blue Tent Tavern: see **Escalon** [SAN JOAQUIN].

Bluff Meadow [TUOLUMNE]: *area,* 6.5 miles northeast of Pinecrest (lat. 38°14'45" N, long. 119°53'45" W; near W line sec. 33, T 5 N, R 19 E). Named on Pinecrest (1979) 7.5' quadrangle.

Boardman: see **Mount Boardman** [SAN JOAQUIN-STANISLAUS].

Boards Crossing [CALAVERAS-TUOLUMNE]: *locality,* 8.5 miles west-southwest of Liberty Hill [TUOLUMNE] along North Fork Stanislaus River on Calaveras-Tuolumne County line (lat. 38°18'15" N, long. 120°14' W; sec. 8, T 5 N, R 16 E). Named on Boards Crossing (1979) 7.5' quadrangle.

Board Springs [STANISLAUS]: *spring,* 3 miles west of Mustang Peak (lat. 37°11'20" N, long. 121°24'40" W; near SE cor. sec. 34, T 8 S, R 5 E). Named on Mississippi Creek (1955) 7.5' quadrangle.

Boggy Meadow [MADERA]:

(1) *area,* 7.5 miles north-northeast of Yosemite Forks along Big Creek (lat. 37°27'30" N, long. 119°33' W; sec. 34, T 5 S, R 22 E). Named on Bass Lake (1953) 15' quadrangle. Called Boggy Meadows on Mariposa (1912) 30' quadrangle.

(2) *area,* 5.25 miles northeast of Shuteye Peak (lat. 37°24'10" N, long. 119°21'30" W; on W line sec. 16, T 6 S, R 24 E). Named on Shuteye Peak (1953) 15' quadrangle.

Bonanza [MERCED]: *locality,* 8 miles south-southeast of Sweeney Hill (lat. 36°47'10" N, long. 121°00'05" W; sec. 21, T 13 S, R 9 E). Site named on Ruby Canyon (1968) 7.5' quadrangle. Postal authorities established Bonanza post office in 1906 and discontinued it in 1914 (Frickstad, p. 99). California Mining Bureau's (1917b) map shows a place called Cleveland located 8 miles northwest of Bonanza near Merced-San Benito County line. Postal authorities established Cleveland post office in 1893 in San Benito County, moved it 6.5 miles northwest into Merced County in 1905, and discontinued it in 1912; the name was for a mining company (Salley, p. 46).

Bond Pass [TUOLUMNE]: *pass,* 4 miles west-northwest of Tower Peak (lat. 38°10'20" N, long. 119°36'30" W). Named on Tower Peak (1956) 15' quadrangle. The name commemorates Frank Bond of General Land Office, a member of Yosemite Park Boundary Commission of 1904, and later chairman of United States Geographic Board (United States Board on Geographic Names, 1934, p. 3).

Bonds Flat [TUOLUMNE]: *area,* nearly 4 miles southeast of Don Pedro Camp (lat. 37°40'40" N, long. 120°21'40" W; sec. 18, T 3 S, R 15 E). Named on Penon Blanco Peak (1962) 7.5' quadrangle.

Bond's Flat: see **Rocky Gulch** [MARIPOSA].

Bond's Gulch: see **Rocky Gulch** [MARIPOSA].

Bondville: see **Bagby** [MARIPOSA].

Bonell Gulch [MARIPOSA]: *canyon,* 2 miles long, 10.5 miles west of El Portal (lat. 37°41'30" N, long. 119°58'15" W). Named on Kinsley (1947) 7.5' quadrangle. United States Board on Geographic Names (1933a, p. 156) rejected the form "Bonnel Gulch" for the name.

Bone Spring Hill [STANISLAUS]: *peak,* 3.25 miles southwest of Crevison Peak (lat. 37°09'45" N, long. 121°14'05" W; near E line sec. 7, T 9 S, R 7 E). Altitude 2509 feet. Named on Crevison Peak (1955) 7.5' quadrangle.

Boneyard Creek [MARIPOSA]: *stream,* flows 3.5 miles to Cuneo Creek 1 mile north-northeast of Coulterville (lat. 37°43'35" N, long. 120°11'10" W; near SE cor. sec. 27, T 2 S, R 16 E). Named on Coulterville (1947) and Groveland (1947) 7.5' quadrangles.

Boney Flat [TUOLUMNE]: *area,* 5.25 miles southeast of Long Barn (lat. 38°02'05" N, long. 120°04'05" W; near NE cor. sec. 14, T 2 N, R 17 E). Named on Hull Creek (1979) 7.5' quadrangle.

Bonita [MADERA]: *locality,* 8 miles west of Madera (lat. 36°57'10" N, long. 120°12'05" W; near NE cor. sec. 27, T 11 S, R 16 E). Named on Bonita Ranch (1963) 7.5' quadrangle.

Bonnel Gulch: see **Bonell Gulch** [MARIPOSA].

Bonsals: see **Mossdale** [SAN JOAQUIN].

Bonsell's Ferry: see **Mossdale** [SAN JOAQUIN].

Boothe Lake [MARIPOSA]: *lake,* 1300 feet long, 4.5 miles southeast of Cathedral Peak (lat. 37°48' N, long. 119°20'50" W). Named on Tuolumne

Meadows (1956) 15' quadrangle. The name commemorates Clyde Boothe, a ranger at Yosemite National Park from 1915 until 1927 (Browning, 1986, p 23).

Bootjack [MARIPOSA]: *locality,* 4.5 miles east-southeast of Mariposa (lat. 37°27'55" N, long. 119°53'05" W; on W line sec. 27, T 5 S, R 19 E). Named on Mariposa (1947) 7.5' quadrangle. Shirley Sargent (1976, p. 31) listed three possible explanations given for the name: first, a road fork at the place makes a "Y" or bootjack shape; second, a large tree at the site had a bootjack shape; and third, a bootjack had to be used to remove the boots from a horsethief after he was hung at the spot.

Borden [MADERA]: *locality,* 3 miles southeast of Madera along Southern Pacific Railroad (lat. 36°55'45" N, long. 120°01'30" W; sec. 32, T 11 S, R 18 E). Named on Madera (1963) 7.5' quadrangle. The place was populated in 1868 by families from Alabama and was called Alabama Settlement; an attempt was made to call it Arcola after a plantation in Alabama owned by one of the settlers, but when the railroad came in 1872 the name became Borden, for Dr. James Borden, a leader of the community (Clough, p. 77, 78). Postal authorities established Borden post office in 1873, discontinued it for a time in 1896, and discontinued it finally in 1906 (Frickstad, p. 85). They established Oak post office 13 miles southeast of Borden in 1894 and discontinued it the same year (Salley, p. 157).

Bostick Bar [CALAVERAS]: *locality,* 6 miles east of Copperopolis along Stanislaus River (lat. 37°58'30" N, long. 120°31'45" W; near N line sec. 3, T 1 N, R 13 E). Named on Copperopolis (1916) 15' quadrangle. Water of New Melones Lake now covers the site. Gudde (1975, p. 44) called the place Bostwick Bar.

Bostick Mountain [CALAVERAS]: *ridge,* northwest-trending, 2 miles long, 6 miles east-southeast of Copperopolis (lat. 37°57'45" N, long. 120°31'45" W); the ridge is south of the site of Bostick Bar. Named on Melones Dam (1962) 7.5' quadrangle.

Boston Flat [CALAVERAS]: *area,* 4.5 miles south-southwest of Devils Nose (lat. 38°23'55" N, long. 120°26'30" W; near SW cor. sec. 4, T 6 N, R 14 E). Named on Devils Nose (1979) 7.5' quadrangle.

Boston Flat Gulch [CALAVERAS]: *canyon,* drained by a stream that flows 2.5 miles to Forest Creek 5.25 miles south-southwest of Devils Nose (lat. 38°23'35" N, long. 120°27'30" W); the stream goes past Boston Flat. Named on Devils Nose (1979) 7.5' quadrangle.

Bostwick Bar: see **Bostick Bar** [CALAVERAS].

Boucher Mountain [CALAVERAS]: *peak,* 4.5 miles west-southwest of Copperopolis on Gopher Ridge (lat. 37°57'25" N, long. 120°42'55" W; near N line sec. 12, T 1 N, R 11 E). Altitude 1549 feet. Named on Copperopolis (1962) 7.5' quadrangle.

Boulder Flat [TUOLUMNE]: *area,* 2 miles northwest of Dardanelle along Middle Fork Stanislaus River (lat. 38°21'20" N, long. 119° 51'35" W). Named on Dardanelle (1979) 7.5' quadrangle.

Bouldin Island [SAN JOAQUIN]:

(1) *island,* 5 miles long, 14 miles west of Lodi between San Joaquin River, Mokelumne River, South Mokelumne River, Little Potato Slough, and Potato Slough (lat. 38°06' N, long. 121°32'15" W). Named on Bouldin Island (1978), Isleton (1978), and Terminous (1978) 7.5' quadrangles. Thompson and West's (1879) map shows a place called Bouldin Landing located along San Joaquin River near the southwest corner of Bouldin Island (near SW cor. sec. 20, T 3 N, R 4 E).

(2) *locality,* 17 miles west-southwest of Lodi (lat. 38°05'10" N, long. 121°34'05" W); the place is on Bouldin Island (1). Named on Bouldin (1910) 7.5' quadrangle. Postal authorities established Bouldin Island post office in 1878, moved it 1 mile south in 1906, and discontinued it in 1918; the name "Bouldin" was for an early settler (Salley, p. 25).

Bouldin Landing: see **Bouldin Island** [SAN JOAQUIN] (1)

Boundary Creek [MADERA]: *stream,* flows 2 miles to Middle Fork San Joaquin River 1.25 miles south of Devils Postpile (lat. 37°36'15" N, long. 119°04'35" W); the mouth of the stream is near the east boundary of Devils Postpile National Monument. Named on Devils Postpile (1953) 15' quadrangle.

Boundary Hill [MARIPOSA]: *peak,* 2.5 miles west-northwest of Yosemite Village (lat. 37°45'50" N, long. 119°37'40" W); the feature is at the boundary of the Yosemite grant. Named on Hetch Hetchy Reservoir (1956) 15' quadrangle. Lieutenant Macomb of the Wheeler survey named the feature (Browning, 1986, p. 24).

Boundary Lake [TUOLUMNE]: *lake,* 3500 feet long, 13 miles east-southeast of Pinecrest (lat. 38°05'15" N, long. 119°47'20" W); the lake is near the boundary of Yosemite National Park. Named on Pinecrest (1956) 15' quadrangle.

Bourland Creek [TUOLUMNE]: *stream,* flows 11 miles to join Reynolds Creek and form Reed Creek 8.5 miles southeast of Long Barn (lat. 38°01'10" N, long. 120°00'45" W; near W line sec. 21, T 2 N, R 18 E); the stream goes through Bourland Meadow. Named on Cherry Lake North (1979), Hull Creek (1979), and Pinecrest (1979) 7.5' quadrangles. The name commemorates John L. Bourland, sheriff of Tuolumne County from 1865 until 1868 (Browning, 1986, p. 24). Called Reed Creek on Big Trees (1891) and Dardanelles (1898) 30' quadrangles, but United States Board on Geographic Names (1963a, p. 5) rejected this name for the stream.

Bourland Meadow [TUOLUMNE]: *area,* 7.25 miles southeast of Pinecrest (lat. 38°06'55" N, long. 119°54'20" W; sec. 17, T 3 N, R 19 E); the place is along Bourland Creek. Named on Cherry Lake North (1979) 7.5' quadrangle.

Bourland Mountain [TUOLUMNE]: *peak,* 6.5 miles south-southeast of Pinecrest (lat. 38°06'30" N, long. 119°56'10" W; on N line sec. 19, T 3 N, R 19 E); the peak is north of Bourland Creek. Altitude 7691 feet. Named on Cherry Lake North (1979) 7.5' quadrangle.

Bowen: see **Moore and Bowen Camp**, under **Hodgdon Ranch** [TUOLUMNE].

Bower Cave [MARIPOSA]: *cave,* 7.5 miles northeast of Buckhorn Peak near North Fork Merced River (lat. 37°44'50" N, long. 120° 02'05" W; sec. 19, T 2 S, R 18 E). Named on Buckhorn Peak (1947) 7.5' quadrangle. The name is from the leafy boughs of maple trees that grow in the pitlike feature, which was discovered in the 1850's and developed into a tourist attraction (Sargent, Shirley, 1976, p. 22).

Bowie Flat [CALAVERAS]: *valley,* 4.5 miles southeast of Copperopolis on upper reaches of Loucks Creek (lat. 37°56'20" N, long. 120°34' W). Named on Melones Dam (1962) 7.5' quadrangle.

Bowman Gulch [CALAVERAS]: *canyon,* drained by a stream that flows 1 mile to Bean Gulch 5 miles east-southeast of Copperopolis (lat. 37°57'20" N, long. 120°33'05" W; sec. 9, T 1 N, R 13 E). Named on Melones Dam (1962) 7.5' quadrangle.

Box Canyon [CALAVERAS]: *narrows,* 3.5 miles west-northwest of Paloma along Mokelumne River on Calaveras-Amador County line (lat. 38°16'25" N, long. 120°49'35" W; sec. 24, T 5 N, R 10 E). Named on Jackson (1962) 7.5' quadrangle.

Box Spring [TUOLUMNE]:

(1) *spring,* nearly 6 miles southeast of Long Barn (lat. 38°01'35" N, long. 120°04'05" W; near E line sec. 14, T 2 N, R 17 E). Named on Hull Creek (1979) 7.5' quadrangle.

(2) *spring,* 6.5 miles southeast of Pinecrest (lat. 38°07'50" N, long. 119°54'15" W). Named on Pinecrest (1979) 7.5' quadrangle.

Brach's Landing: see **Brack Tract** [SAN JOAQUIN].

Brack: see **Thornton** [SAN JOAQUIN].

Brack Tract [SAN JOAQUIN]: *area,* 6 miles west-southwest of Thornton (lat. 38°09'15" N, long. 121°28' W). Named on Isleton (1978) and Thornton (1978) 7.5' quadrangles. The misspelled name recalls the now defunct Brach's Landing (Dillon, 1982, p. 104), which was the west terminus of the narrow gauge San Joaquin and Sierra Nevada Railroad; the railroad started service in 1882 (Hillman and Covello, p. 41).

Bradford [TUOLUMNE]: *locality,* 3 miles northeast of Long Barn along North Fork Tuolumne River (lat. 38°06'55" N, long. 120°05'30" W). Named on Big Trees (1891) 30' quadrangle.

Branch's Ferry: see **La Grange** [STANISLAUS].

Brandy Flat [CALAVERAS]: *area,* 3.5 miles southeast of San Andreas (lat. 38°10' N, long. 120°37'30" W; mainly in sec. 26, T 4 N, R 12 E). Named on Calaveritas (1962) and San Andreas (1962) 7.5' quadrangles.

Branigan Lake [TUOLUMNE]: *lake,* 2200 feet long, 11 miles southwest of Tower Peak (lat. 38°01'50" N, long. 119°41'10" W). Named on Tower Peak (1956) 15' quadrangle. Lieutenant N.F. McClure named the lake for a soldier under his command while the lieutenant was exploring Yosemite National Park in 1894 (United States Board on Geographic Names, 1934, p. 3).

Branigan Lake: see **Middle Branigan Lake** [TUOLUMNE]; **Upper Branigan Lake** [TUOLUMNE].

Bravel Slough [MERCED]: *water feature,* extends for about 2 miles from Deep Slough to Bear Creek (1) 5 miles south-southwest of Stevinson (lat. 37°16' N, long. 120°48'20" W; sec. 6, T 8 S, R 11 E). Named on Turlock (1962) 15' quadrangle.

Brazoria Bar: see **Moccasin Creek** [TUOLUMNE].

Breeze Creek [TUOLUMNE]: *stream,* flows 5.5 miles to Deep Canyon 7.5 miles north of White Wolf (lat. 37°58'50" N, long. 119°37'40" W). Named on Hetch Hetchy Reservoir (1956) and Tower Peak (1956) 15' quadrangles. The name commemorates William F. Breeze, brother-in-law of Lieutenant H.C. Benson; Breeze helped the lieutenant compile a map of Yosemite National Park (Browning, 1986, p. 25).

Breeze Lake [MADERA]: *lake,* 1600 feet long, 4 miles south of Merced Peak (lat. 37°34'35" N, long. 119°23'30" W). Named on Merced Peak (1953) 15' quadrangle. Lieutenant H.C. Benson named the lake for William H. Breeze of Breeze Creek (United States Board on Geographic Names, 1934, p. 3).

Brentwood Park [TUOLUMNE]: *settlement,* 1 mile west-northwest of Twain Harte (lat. 38°02'45" N, long. 120°14'45" W; on W line sec. 8, T 2 N, R 16 E). Named on Twain Harte (1979) 7.5' quadrangle.

Briceburg [MARIPOSA]: *locality,* 5 miles north-northwest of Midpines along Merced River (lat. 37°36'15" N, long. 119°57'55" W; sec. 10, T 4 S, R 18 E); the place is at the mouth of Bear Creek (1). Named on Feliciana Mountain (1947) 7.5' quadrangle. Called Bear Creek on Yosemite (1909) 30' quadrangle. The name "Briceburg" is for William M. Brice, who in 1909 started a general store across the river from the place, and who moved his business to the site of present Briceburg after a work camp there was abandoned in 1926 (Sargent, Shirley, 1976, p. 11). California Division of Highways' (1934) map shows a place called Drum located along the railroad 2.25 miles northeast of Briceburg (sec. 10, T 4 S, R 18 E).

Brickville: see **Merced** [MERCED].

Bridalveil Campground [MARIPOSA]: *locality,* 6.25 miles south-southwest of Yosemite Village (lat. 37°39'50" N, long. 119°37'15" W; sec. 24, T 3 S, R 21 E); the place is near Bridalveil Creek. Named on Yosemite (1956) 15' quadrangle.

Bridalveil Creek [MARIPOSA]: *stream,* flows 10.5 miles to Merced River 4.25 miles west-southwest of Yosemite Village (lat. 37°43'10" N, long. 119°39'10" W); Bridalveil Fall is along the stream. Named on Yosemite (1956) 15' quadrangle. King and Gardner's (1865) map has the form "Bridal Veil Creek" for the name.

Bridalveil Fall [MARIPOSA]: *waterfall,* 4 miles southwest of Yosemite Village (lat. 37°43' N, long. 119°38'45" W). Named on Yosemite (1956) 15' quadrangle. King and Gardner's (1865) map has the form "Bridal Veil Fall" for the name. Apparently Warren Baer, editor of the Mariposa *Democrat* newspaper, named the feature in 1856, although the Indian name "Pohono" still was in common use in the 1860's (Gudde, 1969, p. 38). United States Board on Geographic Names (1991, p. 3) approved the name "Bridalveil Moraine" for a ridge situated 0.6 mile west of Bridalveil Fall (lat. 37°43' N, long. 119°39'23" W).

Bridalveil Moraine: see **Bridalveil Fall** [MARIPOSA].

Bridgeport [MARIPOSA]: *locality,* 5 miles east of the settlement of Catheys Valley along Agua Fria Creek (lat. 37°26' N, long. 120°00'15" W). Named on Catheys Valley (1962) 7.5' quadrangle. The place was known as Suckertown (Hanna, p. 41) before Andrew Church opened a store there in 1852 and gave the present name (Gudde, 1975, p. 46).

Bright: see **Irwin Bright Lake** [TUOLUMNE]; **Irwin Bright Lake**, under **Saddle Horse Lake** [TUOLUMNE].

Brightman Flat [TUOLUMNE]: *area,* 1.25 miles northwest of Dardanelle along Middle Fork Stanislaus River (lat. 38°21'10" N, long. 119°51' W). Named on Dardanelle (1979) 7.5' quadrangle. Dardanelles Cone (1956) 15' quadrangle shows Brightman Flat Campground at the place. J.W. Brightman started a station at Brightman's Flat about 1860 (Wedertz, p. 61).

Brightman Flat Campground: see **Brightman Flat** [TUOLUMNE].

Brito [MERCED]: *locality,* 4.5 miles west of Dos Palos along Southern Pacific Railroad (lat. 36°59'30" N, long. 120°42'20" W; near W line sec. 7, T 11 S, R 12 E). Named on Dos Palos (1956) 7.5' quadrangle.

Broderick: see **Mount Broderick** [MARIPOSA]; **Mount Broderick**, under **Liberty Cap** [MARIPOSA].

Bronson Meadows: see **Hodgdon Ranch** [TUOLUMNE].

Bronson's Meadow: see **Crocker's Meadow**, under **Rush Creek** [TUOLUMNE] (3).

Brother Slough: see **Big Brother Slough** [SAN JOAQUIN]; **Little Brother Slough** [SAN JOAQUIN].

Brower Creek [CALAVERAS]: *stream,* flows nearly 3 miles to Angels Creek 2.5 miles south-southwest of Angels Camp (lat. 38° 02'20" N, long. 120°33'35" W; near W line sec. 9, T 2 N, R 13 E). Named on Angels Camp (1962) 7.5' quadrangle.

Brown Bear Pass [TUOLUMNE]: *pass,* 8 miles northwest of Tower Peak (lat. 38°12'45" N, long. 119°39'45" W). Named on Tower Peak (1956) 15' quadrangle.

Brownes Meadow [TUOLUMNE]: *area,* 3.5 miles northeast of Long Barn (lat. 38°07'15" N, long. 120°05' W; near NE cor. sec. 15, T 3 N, R 17 E). Named on Hull Creek (1979) 7.5' quadrangle. United States Board on Geographic Names (1965c, p. 8) rejected the names "Browns Meadow" and "Brownes Meadows" for the feature.

Brown Flat: see **Browns Flat** [TUOLUMNE].

Brown Gulch [MERCED-STANISLAUS]: *canyon,* drained by a stream that heads in Stanislaus County and flows 2.25 miles to Quinto Creek 8 miles north-northeast of Pacheco Pass in Merced County (lat. 37°10'15" N, long. 121°09'25" W; sec. 12, T 9 S, R 7 E). Named on Crevison Peak (1955) 7.5' quadrangle.

Brown Peak [MARIPOSA]: *peak,* 3 miles south-southwest of El Portal on Pinoche Ridge (lat. 37°38'10" N, long. 119°48'10" W; near N line sec. 31, T 3 S, R 20 E). Altitude 5648 feet. Named on El Portal (1947) 7.5' quadrangle.

Brown's: see **North Fork** [MADERA].

Browns Creek [MADERA]: *stream,* flows 5.5 miles to join Sand Creek and form Willow Creek (2) 5 miles southwest of Shuteye Peak (lat. 37°17'55" N, long. 119°29'40" W; near NE cor. sec. 30, T 7 S, R 23 E); the stream heads at Browns Meadow. Named on Shuteye Peak (1953) 15' quadrangle.

Browns Creek [MARIPOSA]: *stream,* flows 8 miles to Dry Creek just inside Merced County 9 miles northwest of Hornitos (lat. 37° 34'55" N, long. 120°21'30" W; sec. 18, T 4 S, R 15 E). Named on Merced Falls (1962) and Penon Blanco Peak (1962) 7.5' quadrangles.

Browns Flat [TUOLUMNE]: *village,* 2.5 miles south-southeast of Columbia along Woods Creek (lat. 38°00'15" N, long. 120°23' W; sec. 25, T 2 N, R 14 E). Named on Columbia (1948) 7.5' quadrangle. Wheeler (1879, p. 179) referred to Brown's Flat, and Bancroft (1888, p. 376) mentioned Brown Flat. The place was a mining camp started in 1851 (Hoover, Rensch, and Rensch, p. 573).

Brown's Hill: see **Mokelumne Hill** [CALAVERAS].

Browns Island [SAN JOAQUIN]: *island,* 950 feet long, 3.5 miles west of downtown Stockton along San Joaquin River (lat. 37°57'35" N, long. 121°21'20" W). Named on Stockton (1913) 7.5' quadrangle, which shows the island as marsh.

Browns Meadow [MADERA]: *area,* 1 mile southwest of Shuteye Peak (lat. 37°20'20" N, long. 119°26'25" W; sec. 10, T 7 S, R 23 E); the place is at the head of Browns Creek. Named on Shuteye Peak (1953) 15' quadrangle.

Browns Meadow: see **Brownes Meadow** [TUOLUMNE].

Browns Pass: see **Tioga Pass** [TUOLUMNE].

Brownsville: see **Murphys** [CALAVERAS].

Bruce: see **Mount Bruce**, under **Merced Peak** [MADERA].

Bruce Crossing [CALAVERAS]: *locality,* 2.25 miles east of Devils Nose along North Fork Mokelumne River on Calaveras-Amador County line (lat. 38°27'40" N, long. 120°22'35" W; sec. 13, T 7 N, R 14 E). Named on Devils Nose (1979) 7.5' quadrangle.

Bruener Meadow: see **Sonny Meadow** [MARIPOSA].

Brunner Hill [CALAVERAS]: *peak,* nearly 2.25 miles northwest of Angels Camp (lat. 38°05'55" N, long. 120°34'35" W; on W line sec. 20, T 3 N, R 13 E). Altitude 1851 feet. Named on Angels Camp (1962) 7.5' quadrangle.

Brush Gulch [TUOLUMNE]: *canyon,* drained by a stream that flows nearly 0.5 mile to Tuolumne River 1 mile southwest of Don Pedro Camp (lat. 37°42'25" N, long. 120°24'50" W; sec. 3, T 3 S, R 14 E). Named on La Grange (1962) 7.5' quadrangle.

Brush Lake [STANISLAUS]: *intermittent lake,* 4000 feet long, 8.5 miles southwest of Modesto (lat. 37°33'40" N, long. 121°07'15" W; on W line sec. 29, T 4 S, R 8 E). Named on Brush Lake (1969) and Westley (1969) 7.5' quadrangles. Brush Lake (1953) 7.5' quadrangle shows a permanent lake.

Brush Ridge [MARIPOSA]: *ridge,* south-southeast-trending, 2 miles long, 3 miles east-southeast of Smith Peak (lat. 37°46'55" N, long. 120°03' W). Named on Jawbone Ridge (1947) 7.5' quadrangle.

Brushy Canyon [MARIPOSA]: *canyon,* drained by a stream that flows 4 miles to Mariposa Creek 5.25 miles south-southeast of the settlement of Catheys Valley (lat. 37°21'40" N, long. 120°04'15" W; near SE cor. sec. 35, T 6 S, R 17 E). Named on Illinois Hill (1962) 7.5' quadrangle.

Brushy Creek [TUOLUMNE]: *stream,* flows 2 miles to Twomile Creek 5.25 miles southeast of Long Barn (lat. 38°02'25" N, long. 120°03'45" W; sec. 12, T 2 N, R 17 E). Named on Hull Creek (1979) 7.5' quadrangle.

Brushy Hollow Creek [TUOLUMNE]: *stream,* flows 3 miles to Beardsley Lake 3.25 miles north-northwest of Strawberry (lat. 38°14'15" N, long. 120°02'35" W; near SW cor. sec. 31, T 5 N, R 18 E). Named on Liberty Hill (1979) and Strawberry (1979) 7.5' quadrangles.

Buchanan [TUOLUMNE]: *locality,* 4 miles southeast of Tuolumne (lat. 37°54'55" N, long. 120°11'15" W; sec. 26, T 1 N, R 16 E). Named on Tuolumne (1948) 7.5' quadrangle.

Buchanan: see **Eastman Lake** [MADERA-MARIPOSA].

Buchanan Hollow: see **Eastman Lake** [MADERA-MARIPOSA].

Buchanan Reservoir: see **Eastman Lake** [MADERA-MARIPOSA].

Buck Camp [MADERA]: *locality,* 7.25 miles southwest of Merced Peak (lat. 37°33'50" N, long. 119°29'20" W; near N line sec. 30, T 4 S, R 23 E); the place is along Buck Creek. Named on Mount Lyell (1901) 30' quadrangle. The name supposedly is from the so-called buck privates who were on army duty at the place (Browning, 1988, p. 17).

Buck Creek [MADERA]: *stream,* flows 2.25 miles to South Fork Merced River 8 miles southwest of Merced Peak (lat. 37°32'30" N, long. 119°29'10" W); Buck Camp is along the stream.. Named on Merced Peak (1953) 15' quadrangle.

Buckeye Canyon [MERCED]: *canyon,* drained by a stream that flows 2 miles to Carrisalito Flat 7 miles northwest of Ortigalita Peak (lat. 36°52'35" N, long. 120°59'45" W). Named on Ortigalita Peak NW (1969) and Ruby Canyon (1968) 7.5' quadrangles.

Buckeye Canyon [STANISLAUS]: *canyon,* drained by a stream that flows nearly 2 miles to Garzas Creek 2.5 miles east of Mustang Peak (lat. 37°11'05" N, long. 121°19' W; sec. 4, T 9 S, R 6 E). Named on Mustang Peak (1955) 7.5' quadrangle.

Buckeye Creek [MARIPOSA]: *stream,* flows nearly 5 miles to Agua Fria Creek 4.25 miles south-southwest of Mariposa (lat. 37°25'25" N, long. 119°59'15" W; sec. 10, T 6 S, R 18 E). Named on Mariposa (1947) 7.5' quadrangle.

Buckeye Gulch [STANISLAUS]: *canyon,* 2 miles long, opens into Hospital Canyon 16 miles west-northwest of Patterson (lat. 37°31'25" N, long. 121°24'35" W). Named on Lone Tree Creek (1955) 7.5' quadrangle.

Buckeye Gulch: see **Happy Valley** [CALAVERAS].

Buckeye Hill [MARIPOSA]: *peak,* 10.5 miles south of Mariposa (lat.

37°19'50" N, long. 119°56'55" W; near N line sec. 13, T 7 S, R 18 E). Altitude 1904 feet. Named on Ben Hur (1947) 7.5' quadrangle.

Buckeye Hill: see **Mokelumne Hill** [CALAVERAS].

Buckeye Mountain [MADERA]: *ridge*, northwest- to west-trending, 3 miles long, 7 miles southwest of Yosemite Forks (lat. 37°18'10" N, long. 119°43'40" W). Named on Bass Lake (1953) and Mariposa (1947) 15' quadrangles.

Buckeye Pass [TUOLUMNE]: *pass*, 6 miles west-northwest of Matterhorn Peak on Tuolumne-Mono County line (lat. 38°07'50" N, long. 119°28'40" W). Named on Matterhorn Peak (1956) 15' quadrangle. The name is from Buckeye Mill Company, which was active during the 1860's (Browning, 1986, p. 27).

Buckeye Spring [MERCED]: *spring*, nearly 4 miles southeast of Pacheco Pass (lat. 37°01'10" N, long. 121°10'05" W; sec. 35, T 10 S, R 7 E). Named on Pacheco Pass (1955) 7.5' quadrangle.

Buck Field [CALAVERAS]: *area*, 4.5 miles northwest of Angels Camp (lat. 38°07'30" N, long. 120°36'20" W; sec. 12, T 3 N, R 12 E). Named on Angels Camp (1962) and Calaveritas (1962) 7.5' quadrangles.

Buckham Gulch [CALAVERAS]: *canyon*, drained by a stream that flows nearly 4 miles to Snow Creek 7.5 miles west-southwest of Copperopolis (lat. 37°56'55" N, long. 120°46'25" W; sec. 9, T 1 N, R 11 E). Named on Bachelor Valley (1968) and Copperopolis (1962) 7.5' quadrangles.

Buckhorn Creek [MARIPOSA]: *stream*, flows nearly 4 miles to Maxwell Creek 1.5 miles south of Coulterville (lat. 37°41'20" N, long. 120°11'50" W; sec. 10, T 3 S, R 16 E); the stream heads at Buckhorn Flat. Named on Coulterville (1947) 7.5' quadrangle.

Buckhorn Flat [MARIPOSA]: *area*, 4 miles southeast of Coulterville (lat. 37°40'40" N, long. 120°08'15" W; mainly in sec. 7, 18, T 3 S, R 17 E); the place is northwest of Buckhorn Peak. Named on Coulterville (1947) 7.5' quadrangle.

Buckhorn Mountain [TUOLUMNE]: *peak*, 6 miles east-southeast of Sonora (lat. 37°57'35" N, long. 120°16'30" W; sec. 12, T 1 N, R 15 E). Altitude 3311 feet. Named on Standard (1948) 7.5' quadrangle.

Buckhorn Mountain: see **Buckhorn Peak** [MARIPOSA].

Buckhorn Peak [MARIPOSA]: *peak*, 5 miles southeast of Coulterville (lat. 37°39'50" N, long. 120°07'20" W; on N line sec. 20, T 3 S, R 17 E). Altitude 3774 feet. Named on Buckhorn Peak (1947) 7.5' quadrangle. Called Buckhorn Mt. on Hoffmann and Gardner's (1863-1867) map.

Buckingham Mountain [MARIPOSA]: *ridge*, northwest-trending, 2 miles long, 11 miles south-southwest of El Portal (lat. 37°31'45" N, long. 119°51'55" W). Named on Buckingham Mountain (1947) 7.5' quadrangle. Gudde (1975, p. 228), who called the feature Mount Buckingham, noted that William Buckingham opened the first gold mine on the ridge in 1850.

Buck Lakes [TUOLUMNE]: *lakes*, largest 4250 feet long, 10.5 miles west of Tower Peak (lat. 38°09'40" N, long. 119°44'25" W); the lakes are along Buck Meadow Creek. Named on Tower Peak (1956) 15' quadrangle.

Buckley Cove [SAN JOAQUIN]: *bay*, opens into San Joaquin River 5 miles west-northwest of downtown Stockton (lat. 37°58'40" N, long. 121°22'45" W). Named on Holt (1978) and Stockton West (1952) 7.5' quadrangles.

Buckley Meadows: see **Ackerson Meadow** [TUOLUMNE].

Buck Meadow Creek [TUOLUMNE]: *stream*, flows 8.5 miles to West Fork Cherry Creek 10 miles east-southeast of Pinecrest (lat. 38°09'15" N, long. 119°48'45" W). Named on Pinecrest (1956) and Tower Peak (1956) 15' quadrangles.

Buck Meadows [MARIPOSA]: *locality*, 2 miles east-northeast of Smith Peak (lat. 37°48'50" N, long. 120°03'50" W; sec. 36, T 1 S, R 17 E). Named on Jawbone Ridge (1947) 7.5' quadrangle. Postal authorities established Buck Meadows post office in 1915 and discontinued it in 1925 (Frickstad, p. 90). Alva Hamilton started a stage stop called Hamilton's Station at the place in the early 1870's (Paden and Schlichtmann, p. 194).

Buck Mountain [CALAVERAS]: *ridge*, southwest-trending, 1 mile long, 7.5 miles northwest of Dorrington (lat. 38°22'20" N, long. 120°22'40" W). Named on Dorrington (1979), Fort Mountain (1979), and Garnet Hill (1979) 7.5' quadrangles.

Buck Pass [MERCED]: *pass*, 4 miles southeast of Mariposa Peak on Peckham Ridge (lat. 36°54'50" N, long. 121°09'45" W; near SW cor. sec. 1, T 12 S, R 7 E). Named on Mariposa Peak (1969) 7.5' quadrangle.

Buck Point [MARIPOSA]: *peak*, 3.5 miles north-northeast of the settlement of Catheys Valley (lat. 37°29'05" N, long. 120°04'35" W). Altitude 2513 feet. Named on Catheys Valley (1962) 7.5' quadrangle.

Budd Creek [TUOLUMNE]: *stream*, flows 2.5 miles to Tuolumne River 7.5 miles west-southwest of Tioga Pass in Tuolumne Meadows (lat. 37°52'35" N, long. 119°23' W; sec. 6, T 1 S, R 24 E); the creek heads at Budd Lake. Named on Tuolumne Meadows (1956) 15' quadrangle. The stream was called Cathedral Creek in 1883, no doubt because it heads just east of Cathedral Peak (Browning, 1988, p. 17).

Budd Lake [TUOLUMNE]: *lake*, 1400 feet long, 9 miles west-southwest of Tioga Pass (lat. 37°50'30" N, long. 119°23'40" W; sec. 13, T 1 S, R 23 E); the lake is at the head of Budd Creek. Named on Tuolumne Meadows (1956) 15' quadrangle. The name probably commemorates Governor Budd of California (United States Board on Geographic Names, 1934, p. 4).

Buena Ventura Valley: see "Regional setting."

Buena Vista [MARIPOSA]: *locality*, 2.5 miles north-northwest of El Portal (lat. 37°4240" N, long. 119°47'30" W; sec. 32, T 2 S, R 20 E). Named on El Portal (1947) 7.5' quadrangle.

Buena Vista: see **Knights Ferry** [STANISLAUS].

Buena Vista Creek [MADERA-MARIPOSA]: *stream*, heads in Madera County and flows 6 miles to Illilouette Creek 7.25 miles southeast of Yosemite Village in Mariposa County (lat. 37° 40' N, long. 119°30'05" W; near NE cor. sec. 24, T 3 S, R 22 E). Named on Merced Peak (1953) and Yosemite (1956) 15' quadrangles.

Buena Vista Crest [MADERA]: *ridge*, east- to northeast-trending, 4 miles long, 5 miles west-southwest of Merced Peak (lat. 37°36' N, long. 119°28'30" W); the ridge is east of Buena Vista Peak. Named on Merced Peak (1953) 15' quadrangle.

Buena Vista Lake [MADERA]: *lake*, 1500 feet long, less than 0.5 mile north of Buena Vista Peak (lat. 37°36' N, long. 119°31' W; sec. 12, T 4 S, R 22 E). Named on Yosemite (1956) 15' quadrangle.

Buena Vista Mountain [CALAVERAS]: *peak*, 4.5 miles west-southwest of San Andreas (lat. 38°09'55" N, long. 120°45' W; near S line sec. 27, T 4 N, R 11 E). Named on San Andreas (1962) and Valley Springs (1962) 7.5' quadrangles.

Buena Vista Peak [MADERA]: *peak*, 17 miles north-northeast of Yosemite Forks (lat. 37°35'40" N, long. 119°31' W; near SW cor. sec. 12, T 4 N, R 22 E). Altitude 9709 feet. Named on Yosemite (1956) 15' quadrangle.

Buenos Ayres Creek: see **Corral Hollow Creek** [SAN JOAQUIN].

Buffin Meadow [MADERA]: *area*, 8.5 miles north of Yosemite Forks (lat. 37°29'20" N, long. 119°35'50" W; near N line sec. 19, T 5 S, R 22 E). Named on Bass Lake (1953) 15' quadrangle. The misspelled name is for businessman Edward Wheaton Buffum (Browning, 1986, p. 28).

Buford Mountain [MADERA]: *peak*, 2.5 miles east of Knowles (lat. 37°13'15" N, long. 119°49'50" W; sec. 19, T 8 S, R 20 E). Altitude 2066 feet. Named on Knowles (1962, photorevised 1981) 7.5' quadrangle.

Bug Table [MADERA]: *ridge*, west-northwest-trending, 0.5 mile long, 8 miles south-southwest of the town of North Fork (lat. 37° 07'45" N, long. 119°34'45" W; sec. 21, T 9 S, R 22 E). Named on North Fork (1965) 7.5' quadrangle.

Buhach [MERCED]: *village*, 2 miles east-southeast of Atwater (lat. 37°20'10" N, long. 120°34'40" W; near E line sec. 7, T 7 S, R 13 E). Named on Atwater (1961) 15' quadrangle.

Bullard Mountain [MERCED]: *ridge*, east-trending, nearly 1 mile long, 3.5 miles west-southwest of Sweeney Hill (lat. 36°52'35" N, long. 121°06'25" W). Named on Los Banos Valley (1969) 7.5' quadrangle.

Bull Creek [MARIPOSA]: *stream*, flows 12 miles to North Fork Merced River 6 miles east-northeast of Buckhorn Peak (lat. 37°42'10" N, long. 120°01'40" W; sec. 6, T 3 S, R 18 E). Named on Coulterville (1947), El Portal (1947), and Lake Eleanor (1956) 15' quadrangles.

Bull Creek [TUOLUMNE]: *stream*, flows 1.25 miles to Middle Fork Stanislaus River 8.5 miles south-southeast of Liberty Hill (lat. 38° 15'30" N, long. 120°01'10" W; sec. 29, T 5 N, R 18 E). Named on Liberty Hill (1979) and Strawberry (1979) 7.5' quadrangles.

Bullion: see **Mount Bullion** [MARIPOSA].

Bullion Hill [MARIPOSA]: *ridge*, north- to north-northwest-trending, less than 1 mile long, 5 miles north-northwest of Hornitos (lat. 37° 34'15" N, long. 120°15'15" W). Named on Merced Falls (1962) 7.5' quadrangle.

Bullion Mountain [MARIPOSA]: *ridge*, northwest-trending, 5 miles long, center 2.25 miles east-southeast of the village of Bear Valley (lat. 37°33'30" N, long. 120°04'30" W). Named on Bear Valley (1947) 7.5' quadrangle. Called Mount Bullion Spur Ridge on Laizure's (1928) map, which has the name "Mount Bullion" for a peak on the ridge. Whitney (1865, p. 224) used the name "Mount Bullion Range" for the ridge. John C. Fremont named the feature for his father-in-law, Senator Thomas Hart Benton, who had the nickname "Old Bullion" from his monetary policy (Chamberlain, p. 4).

Bull Meadow [TUOLUMNE]: *area*, 6 miles southeast of Duckwall Mountain (lat. 37°53'45" N, long. 120°03'20" W; sec. 36, T 1 N, R 17 E). Named on Duckwall Mountain (1948) 7.5' quadrangle.

Bull Meadow Creek [TUOLUMNE]: *stream*, flows 3.5 miles to Clavey River 7.5 miles south-southeast of Duckwall Mountain (lat. 37°52'05" N, long. 120°03'40" W; sec. 12, T 1 S, R 17 E); the stream goes through Bull Meadow. Named on Duckwall Mountain (1948) and Jawbone Ridge (1947) 7.5' quadrangles.

Bull Run [MARIPOSA]: *stream*, flows 2.25 miles to Mariposa Creek 4.25 miles south-southeast of the settlement of Catheys Valley (lat. 37°22'50" N, long. 120°03'10" W; sec. 25, T 6 S, R 17 E). Named on Catheys Valley (1962) 7.5' quadrangle.

Bull Run [TUOLUMNE]: *area*, 9 miles southwest of Dardanelle along Cow Creek (1) (lat. 38°15' N, long. 119°57' W). Named on Donnell Lake (1979) and Pinecrest (1979) 7.5' quadrangles.

Bull Run Rock [TUOLUMNE]: *peak*, 8.5 miles southwest of Dardanelle (lat. 38°15'20" N, long. 119°56'30" W; sec. 25, T 5 N, R 18 E); the peak is 0.5 mile northeast of Bull Run. Named on Donnell Lake (1979) 7.5'

quadrangle.

Bull Run Valley [MARIPOSA]: *valley,* 3 miles southeast of the settlement of Catheys Valley (lat. 37°24' N, long. 120°03'15" W; sec. 24, T 6 S, R 17 E); Bull Run drains the valley. Named on Catheys Valley (1962) 7.5' quadrangle.

Bumblebee [TUOLUMNE]: *settlement,* 2.25 miles north of Pinecrest (lat. 38°13'35" N, long. 119°59'45" W; near SE cor. sec. 4, T 4 N, R 18 E); the place is by Bumblebee Creek. Named on Pinecrest (1979) 7.5' quadrangle.

Bumblebee Creek [TUOLUMNE]: *stream,* flows 2.25 miles to Cow Creek (1) 2.5 miles north of Strawberry (lat. 38°14'05" N, long. 120°01' W; near W line sec. 5, T 4 N, R 18 E). Named on Pinecrest (1979) and Strawberry (1979) 7.5' quadrangles.

Bummers Flat [TUOLUMNE]: *area,* 5.5 miles east-southeast of Liberty Hill (lat. 38°20'30" N, long. 120°00'15" W; sec. 28, T 6 N, R 18 E). Named on Liberty Hill (1979) 7.5' quadrangle.

Bummerville [CALAVERAS]: *village,* 1.25 miles east of West Point (lat. 38°24'05" N, long. 120°30'20" W; near E line sec. 2, T 6 N, R 13 E). Named on West Point (1948) 7.5' quadrangle. Camp's (1962) map shows a place called Camp Spirito situated 1.25 miles northwest of Bummerville, and a peak called Valentine Hill located less than 1 mile north-northwest of Bummerville. The name "Valentine" commemorates Valentine Granados, a Mexican prospector in Calaveras County (Camp *in* Doble, p. 300).

Bunnell Cascade [MARIPOSA]: *waterfall,* 8 miles south-southwest of Cathedral Peak along Merced River (lat. 37°44'45" N, long. 119°28'10" W); the feature is north-northwest of Bunnell Point. Named on Merced Peak (1953) 15' quadrangle, where the name has the misspelled form "Bunnel Cascade." The name commemorates Lafayette H. Bunnell (United States Board on Geographic Names, 1933a, p. 4). The feature also had the names "Washburn Cascade," "Diamond Shower Fall," and "Little Grizzly Falls" (Browning, 1986, p. 28).

Bunnell Point [MARIPOSA]: *peak,* 8.5 miles south-southwest of Cathedral Peak (lat. 37°44'20" N, long. 119°28' W). Altitude 8193 feet. Named on Merced Peak (1953) 15' quadrangle. The name commemorates Lafayette H. Bunnell, one of the group of men who discovered Yosemite Valley in 1851 (Hanna, p. 45). The peak was called Sugarbowl Dome before about 1920 (Browning, 1986, p. 28).

Burchell [MERCED]: *locality,* 2.5 miles southeast of Planada along Atchison, Topeka and Santa Fe Railroad (lat. 37°15'45" N, long. 120°17'15" W; near W line sec. 1, T 8 S, R 15 E). Named on Planada (1918) 7.5' quadrangle.

Burch Meadow [TUOLUMNE]: *area,* 6.5 miles east-southeast of Groveland (lat. 37°48'40" N, long. 120°07'05" W; near W line sec. 33, T 1 S, R 17 E). Named on Jawbone Ridge (1947) 7.5' quadrangle.

Burford [MADERA]: *locality,* 1.5 miles northwest of Yosemite Forks (lat. 37°22'55" N, long. 119°39'10" W; sec. 27, T 6 S, R 21 E). Site named on Bass Lake (1953) 15' quadrangle.

Burgeson Lake: see **Burgson Lake** [TUOLUMNE].

Burgson Lake [TUOLUMNE]: *lake,* 600 feet long, 6.5 miles west-northwest of Dardanelle (lat. 38°21'35" N, long. 119°56'50" W; sec. 24, T 6 N, R 18 E). Named on Donnell Lake (1979) 7.5' quadrangle. United States Board on Geographic Names (1981b, p. 3) rejected the form "Burgeson Lake" for the name.

Burnett: see **Adela** [STANISLAUS].

Burney's Ferry: see **Islip's Ferry**, under **Oakdale** [STANISLAUS].

Burneyville: see **Burneyville Ferry** [STANISLAUS].

Burneyville Ferry [STANISLAUS]: *locality,* 8 miles north-northeast of Modesto along Stanislaus River at Riverbank (lat. 37°44'30" N, long. 120°56'20" W; sec. 24, T 2 S, R 9 E). Named on Riverbank (1916) 7.5' quadrangle. The name "Burneyville" applied to a small community that grew at the site of a ferry constructed in 1867 by Major James Burney (Brotherton, p. 57, 59).

Burnham [SAN JOAQUIN]: *locality,* 8.5 miles east-southeast of downtown Stockton along Atchison, Topeka and Santa Fe Railroad (lat. 37°53'30" N, long. 121°08'50" W; sec. 36, T 1 N, R 7 E). Named on Stockton East (1952) 7.5' quadrangle.

Burnham: see **Hillyer and Burnham Ferry**, under **Stanislaus River** [SAN JOAQUIN].

Burns' Camp: see **Quartzburg**, under **Hornitos** [MARIPOSA].

Burns Creek [MARIPOSA-MERCED]: *stream,* heads in Mariposa County and flows 26 miles to Bear Creek (1) nearly 3 miles north of Planada in Merced County (lat. 37°20' N, long. 120°19'10" W; sec. 10, T 7 S, R 15 E). Named on Haystack Mountain (1962), Hornitos (1947), Indian Gulch (1962), and Planada (1961) 7.5' quadrangles. Blake (p. 15) referred to Burns' creek, and Wheeler (1879, p. 168) referred to Burns's Creek.

Burns' Creek: see **Quartzburg**, under **Hornitos** [MARIPOSA].

Burns Cutoff [SAN JOAQUIN]: *water feature,* diverges from San Joaquin River 3 miles west-southwest of downtown Stockton (lat. 37°56'30" N, long. 121°20'45" W). Named on Holt (1978) and Stockton West (1952) 7.5' quadrangles.

Burns' Diggings: see **Quartzburg**, under **Hornitos** [MARIPOSA].

Burns' Landing: see **Bethany** [SAN JOAQUIN].

Burns' Ranch: see **Quartzburg**, under **Hornitos** [MARIPOSA].

Burns Reach [SAN JOAQUIN]: *water feature,* part of San Joaquin River 14 miles west-southwest of Lodi between Venice and Medford Islands (lat. 38°03'10" N, long. 121°30'30" W). Named on Bouldin Island (1978) 7.5' quadrangle.

Burnt Corral [TUOLUMNE]: *locality,* 6 miles southwest of Liberty Hill (lat. 38°19'10" N, long. 120°11'25" W; sec. 3, T 5 N, R 16 E). Named on Big Meadow (1956) 15' quadrangle.

Burnt Corral Spring [TUOLUMNE]: *spring,* 5.5 miles southwest of Liberty Hill (lat. 38°19'05" N, long. 120°10'35" W; sec. 2, T 5 N, R 16 E); the spring is less than 1 mile east of the site of Burnt Corral. Named on Boards Crossing (1979) 7.5' quadrangle.

Burro Lake [MADERA]: *lake,* 400 feet long, 7 miles south-southeast of Merced Peak (lat. 37°31'55" N, long. 119°21'50" W; sec. 5, T 5 S, R 24 E); the lake is west-northwest of Jackass Lakes. Named on Merced Peak (1953) 15' quadrangle.

Burro Pass [TUOLUMNE]: *pass,* 0.5 mile west-southwest of Matterhorn Peak (lat. 38°05'20" N, long. 119°23'35" W). Named on Matterhorn Peak (1956) 15' quadrangle.

Burson [CALAVERAS]: *locality,* 3.25 miles west of Valley Springs (lat. 38°11' N, long. 120°53'20" W; on W line sec. 21, T 4 N, R 10 E). Named on Wallace (1962) 7.5' quadrangle. Jackson (1902) 30' quadrangle shows Burson along San Joaquin and Sierra Nevada Railroad. Postal authorities established Burson post office in 1884 (Frickstad, p. 14). The name commemorates David S. Burson, a railroad man (Gudde, 1969, p. 43).

Burst Rock [TUOLUMNE]: *relief feature,* 6.5 miles east of Pinecrest (lat. 38°12'05" N, long. 119°52'25" W; sec. 15, T 4 N, R 19 E). Named on Pinecrest (1956) 15' quadrangle. The feature also is known as Birth Rock because an emigrant mother gave birth there (Hoover, Rensch, and Rensch, p. 566).

Burwood: see **Escalon** [SAN JOAQUIN].

Butcher Knife Pocket [TUOLUMNE]: *canyon,* drained by a stream that flows less than 1 mile to Don Pedro Reservoir 1.25 miles north-northwest of Don Pedro Camp (lat. 37°44' N, long. 120°24'35" W; sec. 27, T 2 S, R 14 E). Named on La Grange (1962) 7.5' quadrangle.

Butcher Knife Ridge [TUOLUMNE]: *ridge,* south- to west-trending, 1.25 miles long, 6 miles south of Duckwall Mountain (lat. 37° 53' N, long. 120°06'35" W). Named on Duckwall Mountain (1948) 7.5' quadrangle.

Butler Mountain [MARIPOSA]: *ridge,* south-trending, 2.5 miles long, 9.5 miles southeast of Mariposa (lat. 37°23'15" N, long. 119° 50'45" W). Named on Horsecamp Mountain (1947) and Stumpfield Mountain (1947) 7.5' quadrangles.

Buttonwillow Lake: see **Big Buttonwillow Lake** [MERCED]; **Little Buttonwillow Lake** [MERCED].

Buttonwillow Slough [MADERA]: *water feature,* 21 miles west-southwest of Madera, and east of San Joaquin River. Named on Firebaugh (1956) and Poso Farm (1962) 7.5' quadrangles.

Buttresses: see **The Buttresses** [MADERA].

Buzzard Canyon [MADERA]: *canyon,* drained by a stream that flows 2 miles to Fresno River 5 miles south-southeast of Knowles (lat. 37°09' N, long. 119°51'20" W; sec. 13, T 9 S, R 19 E). Named on Knowles (1962) 7.5' quadrangle.

Buzzard Point [TUOLUMNE]: *peak,* 0.25 mile southwest of Don Pedro Camp (lat. 37°42'50" N, long. 120°24'35" W; near E line sec. 34, T 2 S, R 14 E). Named on La Grange (1962) 7.5' quadrangle.

Buzzard Roost [SAN JOAQUIN]: *relief feature,* part of South Ridge 12.5 miles south of Tracy (lat. 37°34' N, long. 121°28'30" W). Named on Lone Tree Creek (1955) 7.5' quadrangle.

Byersville: see **Crows Landing** [STANISLAUS].

Byrnes Ferry: see **O'Byrnes Ferry** [CALAVERAS].

— C —

Cabbage Patch [CALAVERAS]: *area,* 3.25 miles west-southwest of Tamarack (lat. 38°24'55" N, long. 120°07'55" W; sec. 32, T 7 N, R 17 E). Named on Calaveras Dome (1979) 7.5' quadrangle.

Cabin Lake [MADERA]: *lake,* 900 feet long, 5.5 miles northwest of Devils Postpile (lat. 37°41'05" N, long. 119°09'05" W). Named on Devils Postpile (1953) 15' quadrangle. David Nidever built a log cabin by the lake in the early 1900's (Smith, p. 61).

Calaveras: see **Waterloo** [SAN JOAQUIN].

Calaveras Dome [CALAVERAS]: *relief feature,* 8.5 miles west-northwest of Tamarack on the south side of North Fork Mokelumne River (lat. 38°29'10" N, long. 120°13'35" W; on E line sec. 5, T 7 N, R 16 E). Named on Calaveras Dome (1979) 7.5' quadrangle.

Calaveras Landing [SAN JOAQUIN]: *locality,* 3.5 miles west of downtown Stockton along San Joaquin River (lat. 37°58' N, long. 121°21'25" W); the place is at the mouth of Calaveras River. Named on Stockton (1913) 7.5' quadrangle.

Calaveras Reservoir [CALAVERAS]: *lake,* behind a dam on North Fork Calaveras River 7.5 miles west of Blue Mountain (lat. 38°19'30" N, long. 120°29'35" W; near S line sec. 36, T 6 N, R 13 E). Named on Fort Mountain (1979) 7.5' quadrangle. United States Board on Geographic Names (1990, p. 10) approved the name "Redhawk Lake" for the feature, and rejected the names "Calaveras Reservoir," "Bingham Lake," and "McCarty Reservoir."

Calaveras River [CALAVERAS-SAN JOAQUIN-STANISLAUS]: *stream,* formed by the confluence of North Fork and South Fork in New Hogan Reservoir, flows 50 miles to San Joaquin River 4.25 miles west of downtown Stockton (lat. 37°58' N, long. 121°22' W). Named on Jenny Lind (1962), Linden (1968), Lodi South (1968), San Andreas (1962), Stockton West (1952), Valley Springs (1962), Valley Springs SW (1962) and Waterloo (1968) 7.5' quadrangles. Alfrez Gabriel Moraga discovered the stream in 1806 and named it Rio de la Pasion; later Moraga renamed the river Rio de las Calaveras for the discovery near the stream of many skulls left from an Indian battle—*calaveras* means "skulls" in Spanish (Hanna, p. 49-50. North Fork is 25 miles long and is named on Fort Mountain (1979), Mokelumne Hill (1948), Rail Road Flat (1948), and San Andreas (1962) 7.5' quadrangles. United States Board on Geographic Names (1980a, p. 3) rejected the name "Calaveras River" for North Fork. South Fork, formed by the confluence of San Domingo Creek and Cherokee Creek, is 8 miles long; it is named on Salt Spring Valley (1962) and San Andreas (1962) 7.5' quadrangles.

Calaveras Valley [CALAVERAS]: *valley,* 1.25 miles south-southwest of Railroad Flat (present Rail Road Flat) (lat. 38°19'30" N, long. 120°31'15" W); the valley is along North Fork Calaveras River. Named on Jackson (1902) 30' quadrangle.

Calaveritas [CALAVERAS]: *village,* 4.5 miles southeast of San Andreas (lat. 38°09'25" N, long. 120°36'35" W; near W line sec. 36, T 4 N, R 12 E); the place is along Calaveritas Creek. Named on Calaveritas (1962) 7.5' quadrangle. The community was called Upper Calaveritas in the early days to distinguish it from Lower Calaveritas, which was located about 3.5 miles farther west and now has vanished (Gudde, 1975, p. 55-56).

Calaveritas Creek [CALAVERAS]: *stream,* formed by the confluence of McKinney Creek and O'Neil Creek, flows 10 miles to South Fork Calaveras River 2.5 miles south of San Andreas (lat. 38°09'35" N, long. 120°40'25" W; sec. 32, T 4 N, R 12 E); the stream goes past Calaveritas. Named on Calaveritas (1962) and San Andreas (1962) 7.5' quadrangles.

Califa [MADERA]: *locality,* 1 mile northwest of Fairmead along Southern Pacific Railroad (lat. 37°05'05" N, long. 120°12'25" W; near S line sec. 3, T 10 S, R 16 E). Named on Berenda (1918) 7.5' quadrangle. Postal authorities established Califa post office in 1912 and discontinued it in 1915 (Frickstad, p. 85).

California Creek [MADERA]: *stream,* flows 3 miles to Nelder Creek 3.5 miles north-northeast of Yosemite Forks (lat. 37°24'40" N, long. 119°35'45" W; at W line sec. 17, T 6 S, R 22 E). Named on Bass Lake (1953) 15' quadrangle.

California Falls [TUOLUMNE]: *waterfall,* 10 miles west of Tioga Pass on Tuolumne River (lat. 37°55' N, long. 119°26'20" W). Named on Tuolumne Meadows (1956) 15' quadrangle.

California Falls: see **LeConte Falls** [TUOLUMNE].

California Range: see "Regional setting."

Calla [SAN JOAQUIN]: *locality,* 2.25 miles southeast of Manteca along Southern Pacific Railroad (lat. 37°46'30" N, long. 121°10'55" W; sec. 10, T 2 S, R 7 E). Named on Manteca (1952) 7.5' quadrangle.

Calpack [MERCED]: *locality,* nearly 2 miles west of Planada (lat. 37°17'50" N, long. 120°21'05" W; sec. 29, T 7 S, R 15 E). Named on Planada (1961) 7.5' quadrangle.

Camanche [CALAVERAS]: *village,* 6 miles west-northwest of Valley Springs (lat. 38°12'45" N, long. 120°56' W; sec. 12, T 4 N, R 9 E); the place is along Camanche Creek. Named on Wallace (1962) 7.5' quadrangle. Water of Camanche Reservoir now covers the site. Postal authorities established Clay's Bar post office in 1861, changed the name to Camanche in 1864, discontinued it in 1886, reestablished it in 1887, and discontinued it in 1962; the name "Clay's Bar" was for the discoverer of gold at the place (Salley, p. 33, 45). Camanche first was called Limerick (Gudde, 1975, p. 56), but a miner renamed the place in 1849 for his hometown in Iowa (Cook, p. 3).

Camanche Creek [CALAVERAS]: *stream,* flows 1.5 miles to Camanche Reservoir 5 miles west of Valley Springs (lat. 38°12' N, long. 120°54'50" W; sec. 18, T 4 N, R 10 E); the stream once flowed past Camanche to Mokelumne River. Named on Wallace (1962) 7.5' quadrangle.

Camanche Reservoir [CALAVERAS-SAN JOAQUIN]: *lake,* extends up Mokelumne River along Calaveras-Amador County line from a dam located in San Joaquin County 4.25 miles northeast of Clements (lat. 38°13'30" N, long. 121°01'20" W; sec. 6, T 4 N, R 9 E). Named on Clements (1968), Jackson (1962), Valley Springs (1962), and Wallace (1962) 7.5' quadrangles. The name is from the village of Camanche; water of the reservoir now covers the site of the village.

Camiaca Peak [TUOLUMNE]: *peak,* 4 miles southeast of Matterhorn Peak on Tuolumne-Mono County line (lat. 38°03'35" N, long. 119° 19'25" W). Altitude 11,739 feet. Named on Matterhorn Peak (1956) 15' quadrangle.

Camino Campground [MADERA]: *locality,* 5.5 miles north of Shuteye Peak (lat. 37°25'55" N, long. 119°25'55" W; near SE cor. sec. 3, T 6 S, R 23 E); the place is along Camino Creek. Named on Shuteye Peak (1953) 15' quadrangle.

Camino Creek [MADERA]: *stream,* flows about 3 miles to Beasore Creek 5.25 miles north of Shuteye Peak (lat. 37°25'30" N, long. 119°24'25" W; sec. 12, T 6 S, R 23 E). Named on Shuteye Peak (1953) 15' quadrangle.

Camp A.E. Wood: see **Camp Hoyle** [MARIPOSA].

Campbell Creek [CALAVERAS]: *stream,* flows 1.5 miles to Black Creek (1) 2 miles east-southeast of Copperopolis (lat. 37°58'25" N, long. 120°36'20" W; near N line sec. 1, T 1 N, R 12 E). Named on Melones Dam (1962) 7.5' quadrangle.

Camp Clavey [TUOLUMNE]: *locality,* 6.25 miles east-southeast of Long Barn (lat. 38°04'15" N, long. 120°01'30" W; sec. 32, T 3 N, R 18 E); the place is along a tributary to Clavey River. Named on Hull Creek (1979) 7.5' quadrangle.

Camp Connell [CALAVERAS]: *settlement,* 5 miles east-southeast of Blue Mountain (lat. 38°18'45" N, long. 120°16'40" W; near W line sec. 1, T 5 N, R 15 E). Named on Dorrington (1979) 7.5' quadrangle. Postal authorities established Camp Connell post office in 1934; the name is for John F. Connell, first postmaster and owner of a vacation resort at the place (Salley, p. 34).

Camp Creek [TUOLUMNE]: *stream,* flows about 2 miles to Piute Creek (2) 5.5 miles southwest of Matterhorn Peak (lat. 38°02'50" N, long. 119°27'45" W). Named on Matterhorn Peak (1956) 15' quadrangle.

Camp Curry [MARIPOSA]: *locality,* 1 mile southeast of Yosemite Village in Yosemite Valley (lat. 37°44'15" N, long. 119°34'15" W). Named on Yosemite (1956) 15' quadrangle. Postal authorities established Camp Curry post office in 1909 and changed the name to Curry Village in 1970; David A. Curry and his wife founded the place in 1899 (Salley, p. 34).

Camp Curry [TUOLUMNE]: *locality,* 4 miles south-southwest of Liberty Hill near Beaver Creek (lat. 38°18'50" N, long. 120° 08' W). Named on Boards Crossing (1979) 7.5' quadrangle.

Camp Earnest [TUOLUMNE]: *settlement,* nearly 2 miles south of Twain Harte (lat. 38°00'50" N, long. 120°13'30" W; sec. 21, T 2 N, R 16 E). Named on Long Barn (1956) 15' quadrangle.

Camp 8 [TUOLUMNE]: *locality,* 5.5 miles east-southeast of Twain Harte (lat. 38°00'10" N, long. 120°08' W; sec. 29, T 2 N, R 17 E). Site named on Twain Harte (1979) 7.5' quadrangle.

Camp 45 [TUOLUMNE]: *locality,* 5.5 miles east of Duckwall Mountain (lat. 37°57'35" N, long. 120°01'15" W; sec. 8, T 1 N, R 18 E). Named on Duckwall Mountain (1948) 7.5' quadrangle.

Camp 44 [TUOLUMNE]: *locality,* 6.5 miles northwest of Mather (lat. 37°56'45" N, long. 119°56'45" W; sec. 13, T 1 N, R 18 E). Named on Lake Eleanor (1956) 15' quadrangle.

Camp 43 [TUOLUMNE]: *locality,* 8.5 miles northwest of Mather along Crane Creek (2) (lat. 37°58'30" N, long. 119°57'30" W; near E line sec. 2, T 1 N, R 18 E). Named on Lake Eleanor (1956) 15' quadrangle.

Camp High Sierra [TUOLUMNE]: *locality,* nearly 4 miles south-southwest of Strawberry along North Fork Tuolumne River (lat. 38°09'05" N, long. 120°02'45" W; near NW cor. sec. 6, T 3 N, R 18 E). Named on Strawberry (1979) 7.5' quadrangle.

Camp Hoyle [MARIPOSA]: *locality,* 1 mile west-northwest of Wawona (lat. 37°32'35" N, long. 119°40'20" W; sec. 32, T 4 S, R 21 E). Named on Yosemite (1909) 30' quadrangle. Camp A.E. Wood, an army encampment that was the hub of the army administration of Yosemite National Park, occupied the site from 1891 until 1905; the name "Wood" was for Captain Abram Epperson Wood, first acting superintendent of the park (Sargent, Shirley, 1961, p. 16). Bert Hoyle started Camp Hoyle at the site in 1922 to provide camping facilities for touring families; the place later became a public campground operated by the National Park Service (Sargent, Shirley, 1961, p. 36).

Camp Ida Spring [TUOLUMNE]: *spring,* 3.5 miles east of Long Barn on Dodge Ridge (lat. 38°06'15" N, long. 120°04' W; near E line sec. 23, T 3 N, R 17 E). Named on Hull Creek (1979) 7.5' quadrangle.

Camp Lake [TUOLUMNE]: *lake,* 1100 feet long, 6.5 miles east-southeast of Pinecrest (lat. 38°10' N, long. 119°52'45" W; on N line sec. 34, T 4 N, R 19 E). Named on Pinecrest (1979) 7.5' quadrangle.

Camp MacBride [TUOLUMNE]: *locality,* 1.5 miles east-northeast of Pinecrest on the east shore of Pinecrest Lake (lat. 38°12' N, long. 119°58'15" W; sec. 14, T 4 N, R 18 E). Named on Pinecrest (1956) 15' quadrangle.

Camp Meeting Creek [MARIPOSA]: *stream,* flows 4 miles to DeLong Creek 9 miles east of Mariposa (lat. 37°28'40" N, long. 119°48'15" W; sec. 20, T 5 S, R 20 E). Named on Buckingham Mountain (1947) and Stumpfield Mountain (1947) 7.5' quadrangles.

Camp Meeting Gulch [TUOLUMNE]: *canyon,* 1.5 miles long, 5.25 miles south of Sonora along Algerine Creek (lat. 37°54'30" N, long. 120°22' W; sec. 30, T 1 N, R 15 E). Named on Standard (1948) 7.5' quadrangle.

Camp Niagara [TUOLUMNE]: *locality,* 9 miles southeast of Long Barn (lat. 38°00'25" N, long. 120°00'15" W); the place is near Niagara Creek (1). Named on Hull Creek (1979) 7.5' quadrangle.

Campo de los Franceses [SAN JOAQUIN]: *land grant,* around Stockton. Named on Lathrop (1952), Lodi South (1968), Manteca (1952), Stockton East (1952), Stockton West (1952), and Waterloo (1968) 7.5' quadrangles. William Gulnac received 11 leagues in 1844, and Charles M. Weber claimed 48,747 acres patented in 1861 (Cowan, p. 22). The name is from the French-Canadian trappers who camped at the place in the 1830's (Gudde, 1949, p. 53).

Campoodle Creek [TUOLUMNE]: *stream,* flows 4.5 miles to Smoothwire Creek 8 miles south-southeast of Liberty Hill (lat. 38° 15'30" N, long. 120°02' W; sec. 30, T 5 N, R 18 E). Named on Liberty Hill (1979) 7.5' quadrangle. Called Compoodle Creek on Big Meadow (1956) 15' quadrangle, but United States Board on Geographic Names (1980a, p. 3) rejected this name for the stream.

Campo Salvador: see **Chinese Camp** [TUOLUMNE].

Campo Seco [CALAVERAS]: *village,* nearly 3 miles north-northwest of Valley Springs along a stream that reaches Mokelumne River at Oregon Bar (lat. 38°13'40" N, long. 120°51'10" W; on E line sec. 3, T 4 N, R 10 E). Named on Valley Springs (1962) 7.5' quadrangle. Postal authorities established Campo Seco post office in 1854 (Frickstad, p. 14). Mexican miners settled at the place in the summer of 1849 to work placer deposits in Oregon Gulch, which extended through the community; the village got its present name after high water prevented work on the bars in the gulch and mining activity had to move to higher ground—*campo seco* indicates "dry camp" in Spanish (Hanna, p. 53).

Campo Seco [TUOLUMNE]: *locality,* 3.5 miles south-southwest of Sonora (lat. 37°56'20" N, long. 120°24'55" W; sec. 15, T 1 N, R 14 E). Named on Sonora (1948) 7.5' quadrangle. Postal authorities established Camp Seco post office at the place in 1852 and discontinued it in 1853 (Salley, p. 35).

Camp Pardee [CALAVERAS]: *locality,* 4 miles north of Valley Springs (lat. 38°14'55" N, long. 120°50'40" W; sec. 35, T 5 N, R 10 E); the place is near Pardee Reservoir. Named on Valley Springs (1962) 7.5' quadrangle.

Camp Pendola [TUOLUMNE]: *locality,* nearly 4 miles north of Crandall Peak (lat. 38°12'55" N, long. 120°08'50" W; sec. 7, T 4 N, R 17 E); the place is near Soap Creek Pass. Named on Crandall Peak (1979) 7.5' quadrangle. Called Soap Cr. Pass Camp on Long Barn (1956) 15' quadrangle.

Camp Santa Teresita [MADERA]: *locality,* 3.5 miles southeast of Yosemite Forks at the northwest end of Bass Lake (1) (lat. 37°19'50" N, long 119°34'55" W; near SW cor. sec. 9, T 7 S, R 22 E). Named on Bass Lake (1953) 15' quadrangle.

Camp Seco: see **Campo Seco** [TUOLUMNE].

Camp Spirito: see **Bummerville** [CALAVERAS].

Camp Stanislaus: see **Oakdale** [STANISLAUS].

Camp Tamarack: see **Tamarack** [CALAVERAS].

Camp 13 [MERCED]: *locality,* 13 miles northeast of Ortigalita Peak (lat. 36°56'30" N, long. 120°45'25" W; near S line sec. 27, T 11 S, R 11 E). Named on Ortigalita Peak (1943) 15' quadrangle.

Camp 13 Slough [MERCED]: *water feature,* 7.5 miles west-southwest of Dos Palos (lat. 36°57'30" N, long. 120°45'15" W); the feature is near the site of Camp 13. Named on Charleston School (1956) 7.5' quadrangle.

Camp Twentyfive Creek [TUOLUMNE]: *stream,* flows nearly 3 miles to Twomile Creek 5.5 miles southeast of Long Barn (lat. 38° 02'10" N, long. 120°03'50" W; near S line sec. 12, T 2 N, R 17 E). Named on Hull Creek (1979) 7.5' quadrangle.

Camp Twentyfour [TUOLUMNE]: *locality,* 4.5 miles southeast of Long Barn (lat. 38°02'15" N, long. 120°05'20" W; near SE cor. sec. 10, T 2 N, R 17 E). Site named on Hull Creek (1979) 7.5' quadrangle.

Camp Twentyone Spring [TUOLUMNE]: *spring,* 6.5 miles south-southeast of Long Barn (lat. 38°00'25" N, long. 120°04'25" W; near N line sec. 26, T 2 N, R 17 E). Named on Hull Creek (1979) 7.5' quadrangle.

Camp Washington: see **Chinese Camp** [TUOLUMNE].

Camp Wolfeboro [CALAVERAS]: *locality,* nearly 2 miles south of Tamarack along North Fork Stanislaus River (lat. 38°24'45" N, long. 120°04'40" W). Named on Tamarack (1979) 7.5' quadrangle.

Cañada del Puerto: see **Del Puerto Canyon** [STANISLAUS].

Canady Gulch [TUOLUMNE]: *canyon,* drained by a stream that flows 0.5 mile to Sawmill Gulch 2 miles southeast of Columbia (lat. 38°01'05" N, long. 120°22'20" W; sec. 19, T 2 N, R 15 E). Named on Columbia SE (1948) 7.5' quadrangle.

Canal Creek [MERCED]: *stream,* flows 16 miles to Black Rascal Creek 3.5 miles southeast of Atwater (lat. 37°18'50" N, long. 120° 33'35" W; near E line sec. 20, T 7 S, R 13 E). Named on Atwater (1961) and Merced (1962) 15' quadrangles.

Canon Creek: see **Big Canon Creek**, under **Clavey River** [TUOLUMNE].

Canty Meadow [MARIPOSA]: *locality,* 3 miles south-southwest of El Portal (lat. 37°38'05" N, long. 119°47'55" W; near NE cor. sec. 31, T 3 S, R 20 E). Named on El Portal (1947) 7.5' quadrangle.

Capitol Dome: see **Wawona Dome** [MARIPOSA].

Cap of Liberty: see **Liberty Cap** [MARIPOSA].

Carbona [SAN JOAQUIN]: *locality,* 3 miles south-southeast of Tracy along Western Pacific Railroad (lat. 37°41'45" N, long. 121°24'40" W; near N line sec. 10, T 3 S, R 5 E). Named on Tracy (1954) 7.5' quadrangle. Postal authorities established Carbona post office in 1926 and discontinued it in 1927 (Frickstad, p. 160). The place began in 1895 as a coaling station on Alameda and San Joaquin Railroad (Mosier, 1979, p. 4). California Division of Highways' (1934) map shows a place called Kerlinger located 2 miles southwest of Carbona along Western Pacific Railroad (sec. 17, T 3 S, R 5 E), a place called River Rock located 3.5 miles southwest of Carbona along the railroad (sec. 19, T 3 S, R 5 E), and a place called Moy located 4.25 miles southwest of Carbona at the end of the rail line (near W line sec. 19, T 3 S, R 5 E).

Cardoza Lake [STANISLAUS]: *lake,* 350 feet long, 1.25 miles south-southeast of La Grange (lat. 37°38'45" N, long. 120°27'20" W; sec. 29, T 3 S, R 14 E). Named on La Grange (1962) 7.5' quadrangle.

Cardoza Ridge [STANISLAUS]: *ridge,* east-southeast-trending, 1.5 miles long, 3 miles southeast of La Grange (lat. 37°38'05" N, long. 120°25'35" W). Named on La Grange (1962) 7.5' quadrangle.

Cargyle Creek [MADERA]: *stream,* flows 4.5 miles to Middle Fork San Joaquin River 8 miles southwest of Devils Postpile (lat. 37° 31'55" N, long. 119°10'50" W; sec. 1, T 5 S, R 25 E). Named on Devils Postpile (1953) 15' quadrangle. East Fork enters from the northeast 2 miles upstream from the mouth of the main creek; it is 3.5 miles long and is named on Devils Postpile (1953) 15' quadrangle.

Cargyle Meadow [MADERA]: *area,* 5.5 miles southwest of Devils Postpile (lat. 37°34'25" N, long. 119°09'30" W); the place is east of East Fork Cargyle Creek. Named on Devils Postpile (1953) 15' quadrangle.

Carl Inn [TUOLUMNE]: *locality,* 4.5 miles south of Mather Station (present Mather) (lat. 37°48'50" N, long. 119°51'40" W; near NW cor. sec. 35, T 1 S, R 19 E). Named on Yosemite (1909) 30' quadrangle. Dan Carlon and Donna Carlon started a resort a the place in 1916 (Paden and Schlichtmann, p. 213).

Carlton: see **Clements** [SAN JOAQUIN].

Carmen City [CALAVERAS]: *locality,* 8 miles west-southwest of Angels Camp on the east side of Salt Spring Valley (lat. 38°02'50" N, long. 120°41'30" W; near S line sec. 6, T 2 N, R 12 E); the place is nearly 2 miles west-southwest of Carmen Peak. Named on Salt Spring Valley (1962) 7.5' quadrangle.

Carmen Peak [CALAVERAS]: *peak,* 6.5 miles west-southwest of Angels Camp (lat. 38°0315" N, long. 120°39'40" W; sec. 4, T 2 N, R 12 E). Altitude 2603 feet. Named on Salt Spring Valley (1962) 7.5' quadrangle. Called Harmon Peak on Jackson (1902) 30' quadrangle.

Carnazzani Island [SAN JOAQUIN]: *island,* 650 feet long, 2.5 miles west-southwest of downtown Stockton in San Joaquin River (lat. 37°57'05" N, long. 121°20'05" W). Named on Stockton (1913) 7.5' quadrangle, which shows marsh between the island and the river bank.

Carnegie [SAN JOAQUIN]: *locality,* 9.5 miles southwest of Tracy in Corral Hollow (lat. 37°37'45" N, long. 121°31'35" W; sec. 34, T 3 S, R 4 E). Site named on Midway (1953) 7.5' quadrangle. John Treadwell and James Treadwell founded a community at the site to serve employees of their Carnegie Brick and Pottery Company; the place was abandoned in 1906 after the company failed (Hanna, p. 56). California Mining Bureau's (1917a) map shows a place called Manganese located 2.5 miles northeast of Carnegie along a rail line.

Carnegie Ridge [SAN JOAQUIN]: *ridge,* northeast-trending, 1.5 miles long, 3.25 miles north of Eagle Mountain (lat. 37°37'05" N, long. 121°32'10" W); the ridge is south of the site of Carnegie. Named on Cedar Mountain (1956) 7.5' quadrangle.

Carranza Spring [MERCED]: *spring,* 3 miles west-northwest of Ortigalita Peak (lat. 36°49'05" N, long. 120°58' W; near W line sec. 11, T 13 S, R 9 E). Named on Ortigalita Peak (1969) 7.5' quadrangle.

Carrisalito Creek [MERCED]: *stream,* flows 4.5 miles to Los Banos Creek 4.5 miles north-northeast of Sweeney Hill (lat. 36°57'20" N, long. 121°00'30" W); the stream is on Panoche de San Juan y los Carrisalitos grant. Named on Los Banos Valley (1969) and Ortigalita Peak NW (1956) 7.5' quadrangles.

Carrisalito Flat [MERCED]: *valley,* 2.5 miles east of Sweeney Hill (lat. 36°54' N, long. 121°00'10" W); the feature is on Panoche de San Juan y los Carrisalitos grant. Named on Los Banos Valley (1969) and Ortigalita Peak NW (1969) 7.5' quadrangles.

Carrisalito Springs [MERCED]: *springs,* 2.5 miles east of Sweeney Hill (lat. 36°54'10" N, long. 121°00' W); the springs are at Carrisalito Flat. Named on Los Banos Valley (1969) and Ortigalita Peak NW (1956) 7.5' quadrangles.

Carrolton [SAN JOAQUIN]: *locality,* 8 miles east of Manteca along Tidewater Southern Railroad (lat. 37°47'55" N, long. 121°04'15" W; near SE cor. sec. 34, T 1 S, R 8 E). Named on Avena (1952) 7.5' quadrangle.

Carson [MARIPOSA]: *locality,* 5.5 miles northeast of the settlement of Catheys Valley (lat. 37°28'50" N, long. 120°00'35" W); the place is along Carson Creek at Carson Flat. Named on Catheys Valley (1962) 7.5' quadrangle. Laizure's (1928) map shows a place called Arkansas Flat located nearly 1 mile east-northeast of the site of Carson, and a canyon called Goday Gulch that opens into the canyon of Carson Creek at Arkansas Flat. The misspelled name "Goday" commemorates Alex Godey (Sargent, Shirley, 1976, p. 9), who discovered gold deposits on Fremont's Las Mariposas grant in 1849 (Gudde, 1975, p. 63).

Carson Creek [CALAVERAS]: *stream,* flows 4 miles to Melones Reservoir 5 miles south-southeast of Angels Camp (lat. 38°00'25" N, long. 120°31' W; sec. 23, T 2 N, R 13 E). Named on Angels Camp (1962) 7.5' quadrangle. The name commemorates Sergeant James H. Carson, who discovered gold in the stream in 1848 while he was on furlough (Gudde, 1975, p. 62).

Carson Creek [MARIPOSA]: *stream,* flows 2 miles to Agua Fria Creek 5 miles northeast of the settlement of Catheys Valley (lat. 37°28'55" N, long. 120°01'15" W); the stream goes past the site of Carson. Named on Catheys Valley (1962) and Mariposa (1947) 7.5' quadrangles. Alex Godey probably named the stream for Kit Carson (Gudde, 1975, p. 63).

Carson Creek: see **McBrides Gulch** [MARIPOSA].

Carson Flat [CALAVERAS]: *area,* 3 miles south-southeast of Angles Camp (lat. 38°02'25" N, long. 120°31' W; sec. 11, T 2 N, R 13 E); the place is near Carson Creek. Named on Angels Camp (1962) 7.5' quadrangle. Bancroft (1888, p. 513) referred to Carson's Flat, "the great camp of 1851."

Carson Flat [MARIPOSA]: *area,* 5.5 miles northeast of the settlement of Catheys Valley (lat. 37°28'50" N, long. 120°00'35" W); the place is along Carson Creek at the site of Carson. Named on Catheys Valley (1962) 7.5' quadrangle.

Carson Flat: see **Carson Hill** [CALAVERAS] (2).

Carson Gulch: see **McBrides Gulch** [MARIPOSA].

Carson Hill [CALAVERAS]:

(1) *peak,* 4.5 miles south-southeast of Angels Camp (lat. 38°01'20" N, long. 120°30'10" W; near SW cor. sec. 13, T 2 N, R 13 E); the peak is east of Carson Creek. Altitude 1983 feet. Named on Angels Camp (1962) and Columbia (1948) 7.5' quadrangles.

(2) *village,* nearly 4 miles south-southeast of Angels Camp (lat. 38°01'40" N, long. 120°30'20" W; near W line sec. 13, T 2 N, R 13 E); the village is north of Carson Hill (1) near Carson Creek. Named on Angels Camp (1962) 7.5' quadrangle. Called Carson Flat on Jackson (1902) 30' quadrangle, which shows the place along Sierra Railroad. The village originally was called Slumgullion, but later it was named for James H. Carson of Carson Creek (Gudde, 1949, p. 58). According to Hanna (p. 189), Slumgullion was the site of an 1849 gold camp called Melones, a name later applied to a place about 2 miles farther east. Postal authorities established Irvine post office in 1896, changed the name to Carson Hill in 1909, and discontinued it in 1935; the name "Irvine" was from a mining claim on Carson Hill (1) (Salley, p. 38, 105).

Carson's Creek: see **Angels Camp** [CALAVERAS].

Carson's Flat: see **Carson Flat** [CALAVERAS].

Carter Creek [MADERA]: *stream,* flows 3.25 miles to Fine Gold Creek 4.5 miles northeast of O'Neals (lat. 37°10'20" N, long. 119° 38' W; sec. 1, T 9 S, R 21 E). Named on North Fork (1965) and O'Neals (1965) 7.5' quadrangles.

Carter Creek [MADERA-MARIPOSA]: *stream,* heads in Mariposa County and flows 7.5 miles to Miami Creek 4.25 miles west of Yosemite Forks in Madera County (lat. 37°21'45" N, long. 119°42'20" W; near W line sec. 32, T 6 S, R 21 E). Named on Bass Lake (1953) 15' quadrangle.

Carters: see **Summersville**, under **Soulsbyville** [TUOLUMNE].

Casa Diablo [MARIPOSA]: *relief feature,* 4.5 miles southwest of El Portal (lat. 37°37'20" N, long. 119°49'55" W; near N line sec. 2, T 4 S, R 19 E). Named on Buckingham Mountain (1947) 7.5' quadrangle.

Cascade Creek [MARIPOSA]: *stream,* flows 8 miles to Merced River 7.25 miles west-southwest of Yosemite Village (lat. 37°43'20" N, long. 119°42'45" W; sec. 36, T 2 S, R 20 E). Named on Hetch Hetchy Reservoir (1956) and Yosemite (1956) 15' quadrangles.

Cascade Creek [TUOLUMNE]:

(1) *stream,* flows 5.5 miles to Middle Fork Stanislaus River 8 miles southeast of Liberty Hill (lat. 38°16'30" N, long. 120°00'40" W; sec. 20, T 5 N, R 18 E). Named on Donnell Lake (1979) and Liberty Hill (1979) 7.5' quadrangles.

(2) *locality,* 8.5 miles west-southwest of Dardanelle (lat. 38°16'45" N, long. 119°58'05" W; on N line sec. 23, T 5 N, R 18 E); the place is along Cascade Creek (1). Named on Donnell Lake (1979) 7.5" quadrangle.

Cascade Falls: see **The Cascades** [MARIPOSA].

Cascadel: see **North Fork** [MADERA].

Cascadel Point [MADERA]: *ridge,* east-trending, 1.5 miles long, 9.5 miles south of Shuteye Peak (lat. 37°13' N, long. 119°26'45" W). Named on Shaver Lake (1953) 15' quadrangle.

Cascades: see **The Cascades** [MARIPOSA].

Casey: see **Dan Casey Slough** [STANISLAUS].

Cashman Creek [STANISLAUS]: *stream,* flows 13 miles to Dry Creek 5 miles north-northeast of Waterford (lat. 37°42'05" N, long. 120°42'45" W; sec. 1, T 3 S, R 11 E). Named on Knights Ferry (1962) and Pausell (1968) 7.5' quadrangles.

Casnau Creek [TUOLUMNE]: *stream,* flows 1.5 miles to Mountain Pass Creek 32 miles north-northwest of Keystone (lat. 37°52'30" N, long. 120°31'10" W; near E line sec. 3, T 1 S, R 13 E). Named on Melones Dam (1962) 7.5' quadrangle.

Cassidy Meadows [MADERA]: *areas,* 16 miles northeast of Shuteye Peak (lat. 37°28'45" N, long. 119°11'15" W; sec. 24, T 5 S, R 25 E). Named on Kaiser Peak (1953) 15' quadrangle. Kaiser (1904) 30' quadrangle has the singular form "Cassidy Meadow" for the name, which commemorates James Cassidy, an early sheepman (Browning, 1986, p. 34).

Castle [SAN JOAQUIN]: *locality,* 6 miles south of Lodi along Southern Pacific Railroad (lat. 38°02'10" N, long. 121°16'40" W; sec. 11, T 2 N, R 6 E). Named on Lodi South (1968) 7.5' quadrangle.

Castle Air Force Base [MERCED]: *military installation,* 2.25 miles east-northeast of Atwater (lat. 37°21'50" N, long. 120°34'10" W). Named on Atwater (1961) 15' quadrangle.

Castle Cliffs [MARIPOSA]: *relief feature,* 0.5 mile north-northwest of Yosemite Village on the north side of Yosemite Valley (lat. 37° 45'20" N, long. 119°35'15" W). Named on Hetch Hetchy Reservoir (1956) 15' quadrangle.

Castle Gardens [MERCED]: *district,* 1.5 miles east-northeast of Atwater (lat. 37°21'25" N, long. 120°34'45" W; mainly in sec. 6, T 7 S, R 13 E); the place is near Castle Air Force Base. Named on Atwater (1961) 15' quadrangle. Grunsky's (1899) map has the name "Gracey" for a place at or near present Castle Gardens.

Castle Lake [MADERA]: *lake,* 600 feet long, nearly 4 miles northwest of Devils Postpile (lat. 37°40'10" N, long. 119°07'10" W). Named on Devils Postpile (1953) 15' quadrangle.

Castle Meadow [TUOLUMNE]: *area,* 6.25 miles south-southwest of Dardanelle along Willow Creek (1) (lat. 38°15'05" N, long. 119°51'30" W; near SW cor. sec. 26, T 5 N, R 19 E). Named on Dardanelle (1979) 7.5' quadrangle.

Castle Peak [MADERA]: *peak,* 11.5 miles south of Shuteye Peak (lat. 37°11'05" N, long. 119°26'30" W; near S line sec. 34, T 8 S, R 23 E). Altitude 4082 feet. Named on Shaver Lake (1953) 15' quadrangle. Called Oat Mt. on Kaiser (1904) 30' quadrangle.

Castle Peak: see **Tower Peak** [TUOLUMNE].

Castle Rock [CALAVERAS]: *relief feature,* 0.5 mile northeast of Valley Springs (lat. 38°11'50" N, long. 120°49'05" W; sec. 13, T 4 N, R 10 E). Named on Valley Springs (1962) 7.5' quadrangle.

Castle Rock [SAN JOAQUIN]: *peak,* 8 miles south-southwest of Tracy (lat. 37°38'10" N, long. 121°29'20" W; sec. 25, T 3 S, R 4 E). Named on Tracy (1954) 7.5' quadrangle.

Castle Rock [TUOLUMNE]: *peak,* 9.5 miles east-northeast of Pinecrest (lat. 38°14'55" N, long. 119°50'15" W; sec. 36, T 5 N, R 19 E). Named on Pinecrest (1956) 15' quadrangle. Members of the Wheeler survey named the feature before 1878 (Browning, 1986, p. 34).

Castoria: see **French Camp** [SAN JOAQUIN].

Cataract Gulch [CALAVERAS]: *canyon,* drained by a stream that flows 1 mile to Stanislaus River 4 miles east-northeast of Vallecitos (lat. 38°06'25" N, long. 120°24'10" W; near S line sec. 14, T 3 N, R 14 E). Named on Columbia (1948) 7.5' quadrangle.

Cat Camp [CALAVERAS]: *locality,* 6.5 miles west of Valley Springs (lat. 38°12'20" N, long. 120°56'40" W; near NW cor. sec. 13, T 4 N, R 9 E). Named on Wallace (1962) 7.5' quadrangle.

Catfish Camp [STANISLAUS]: *locality,* 7 miles east-southeast of Patterson on the west side of San Joaquin River (lat. 37°25'45" N, long. 121°00'50" W). Named on Crows Landing (1952) 7.5' quadrangle.

Catfish Lake [TUOLUMNE]: *lake,* 350 feet long, 1.5 miles northeast of Pinecrest (lat. 38°12'25" N, long. 119°58'40" W; near NE cor. sec. 15, T 4 N, R 18 E). Named on Pinecrest (1979) 7.5' quadrangle.

Cathay: see **Catheys Valley** [MARIPOSA] (2).

Cathay Mountain: see **Catheys Mountain** [MARIPOSA].

Cathay Valley: see **Catheys Valley** [MARIPOSA] (1).

Cathedral Creek [TUOLUMNE]: *stream,* flows 10 miles to Tuolumne River 13 miles west of Tioga Pass (lat. 37°55'55" N, long. 119°30' W); the creek heads near Cathedral Peak. Named on Hetch Hetchy Reservoir (1956) and Tuolumne Meadows (1956) 15' quadrangles. The stream was called Rocky Canyon Creek in the early 1880's (Browning, 1988, p. 22). South Fork enters from the south 2 miles upstream from the mouth of the main stream; it is 4.25 miles long and is named on Tuolumne Meadows (1956) 15' quadrangle.

Cathedral Creek: see **Budd Creek** [TUOLUMNE].

Cathedral Fork [MARIPOSA]: *stream,* flows 5 miles to Echo Creek 5.5 miles south of Cathedral Peak (lat. 37°46' N, long. 119°25' W); the stream heads south of Cathedral Peak. Named on Tuolumne Meadows (1956) 15' quadrangle. United States Board on Geographic Names (1970, p. 2) gave the names "Cathedral Fork Merced Creek," "Cathedral Fork Merced River," and "Cathedral Fork of Merced River" as variants.

Cathedral Fork: see **Echo Creek** [MARIPOSA].

Cathedral Lakes [MARIPOSA]: *lakes,* two, largest 1900 feet long, 1 mile southwest of Cathedral Peak (lat. 37°50'30" N, long. 119°25'10" W; mainly in sec. 14, T 1 S, R 23 E). Named on Tuolumne Meadows (1956) 15' quadrangle.

Cathedral Pass [MARIPOSA]: *pass,* 1.25 miles south-southwest of Cathedral Peak (lat. 37°50'10" N, long. 119°24'50" W; near N line sec. 23, T 1 S, R 23 E). Named on Tuolumne Meadows (1956) 15' quadrangle.

Cathedral Peak [MARIPOSA-TUOLUMNE]: *peak,* 9 miles west-southwest of Tioga Pass on Mariposa-Tuolumne County line (lat. 37°50'50" N, long. 119°24'20" W; near W line sec. 13, T 1 S, R 23 E). Altitude 10,940 feet. Named on Tuolumne Meadows (1956) 15' quadrangle. Brewer (p. 412) noted in 1863 that the peak is "something the shape of a huge cathedral."

Cathedral Peak [MERCED]: *peak,* 0.5 mile east-northeast of Mariposa Peak (lat. 36°57'40" N, long. 121°12'10" W; sec. 21, T 11 S, R 7 E). Named on Mariposa Peak (1969) 7.5' quadrangle.

Cathedral Point: see **Cathedral Rocks** [MARIPOSA].

Cathedral Range [MADERA-MARIPOSA-TUOLUMNE]: *ridge,* southeast-trending, 12 miles long, northwest of Mount Lyell; mainly on Mariposa-Tuolumne County line, but extends southeast for 4 miles along Madera-Tuolumne County line. Named on Merced Peak (1953) and Tuolumne Meadows (1956) 15' quadrangles.

Cathedral Rocks [MARIPOSA]: *relief feature,* 3.5 miles southwest of Yosemite Village on the south side of Yosemite Valley (lat. 37° 43' N, long. 119°38'15" W). Named on Yosemite (1956) 15' quadrangle. United States Board on Geographic Names (1933a, p. 202) rejected the name "Cathedral Point" for the feature, which had the early name "The Three Graces" (Browning, 1986, p. 35).

Cathedral Spires [MARIPOSA]: *relief features,* 3.5 miles southwest of Yosemite Village on the south side of Yosemite Valley (lat. 37° 42'50" N, long. 119°37'45" W). Named on Yosemite (1956) 15' quadrangle. Henry G. Hanks, James Hutchings, and Captain Corcoran named the features in 1862 (Chalfant, p. 170).

Catherine: see **Lake Catherine** [MADERA].

Cathewood Saddle [MARIPOSA]: *pass,* 2.25 miles south-southeast of El Portal (lat. 37°38'35" N, long. 119°46' W; sec. 28, T 3 S, R 20 E). Named on El Portal (1947) 7.5' quadrangle.

Cathey Pond [MARIPOSA]: *intermittent lake,* 125 feet long, nearly 2 miles northwest of Santa Cruz Mountain (lat. 37°28'25" N, long. 120°13'35" W; sec. 28, T 5 S, R 16 E). Named on Indian Gulch (1962) 7.5' quadrangle.

Catheys Mountain [MARIPOSA]: *peak,* nearly 3 miles north-northeast of the settlement of Catheys Valley (lat. 37°28'10" N, long. 120°03'50" W; sec. 25, T 5 S, R 17 E). Altitude 2867 feet. Named on Catheys Valley (1962) 7.5' quadrangle. Called Cathay Mtn. on Indian Gulch (1920) 15' quadrangle, but United States Board on Geographic Names (1964a, p. 8) rejected this form of the name.

Catheys Valley [MARIPOSA]:

(1) *valley,* 8 miles west-southwest of Mariposa (lat. 37°25'30" N, long. 120°05' W). Named on Catheys Valley (1962) 7.5' quadrangle. Called Cathay Valley on Indian Gulch (1920) 15' quadrangle, but United States Board on Geographic Names (1964a, p. 8) rejected this name, and noted that the name "Cathey" is for Andrew Cathey of North Carolina, who settled in the valley about 1850. The feature first was called Vallecita (Sargent, Shirley, 1976, p. 8).

(2) *settlement,* 8 miles southwest of Mariposa (lat. 37°26'05" N, long. 120°05'35" W; sec. 3, 10, T 6 S, R 17 E); the place is in Catheys Valley (1). Named on Catheys Valley (1962) 7.5' quadrangle. Postal authorities established Cathey's Valley post office in 1879, discontinued it in 1881, reestablished it with the name "Cathay" in 1882, discontinued it in 1918, reestablished it in 1919, and changed the name to Catheys Valley in 1964 (Salley, p. 40). United States Board on Geographic Names (1964a, p. 8) rejected the name "Cathay" for the settlement.

Cattle Mountain [MADERA]: *peak,* 11 miles southwest of Devils Postpile (lat. 37°31'05" N, long. 119°13'55" W; on W line sec. 3, T 5 S, R 25 E). Altitude 7946 feet. Named on Devils Postpile (1953) 15' quadrangle.

Cat Town [MARIPOSA]: *locality,* 2.25 miles southeast of Buckhorn Peak (lat. 37°38'40" N, long. 120°05'15" W; near W line sec. 27, T 3 S, R 17 E). Named on Buckhorn Peak (1947) 7.5' quadrangle.

Cavallada Creek [MARIPOSA]: *stream,* formed by the confluence of two unnamed streams and flows 1 mile to Sand Creek 4.25 miles northeast of the settlement of Catheys Valley (lat. 37°28'55" N, long. 120°02'15" W). Named on Catheys Valley (1962) 7.5' quadrangle. United States Board on Geographic Names (1964b, p. 12) rejected the name "Texas Creek" for the stream.

Cavallada Gulch: see **La Mineta Gulch** [MARIPOSA]; **Texas Gulch** [MARIPOSA].

Cavallado Creek: see **Sand Creek** [MARIPOSA].

Cave City [CALAVERAS]: *locality,* 9.5 miles east of San Andreas along McKinney Creek (lat. 38°12'10" N, long. 120°30'25" W; sec. 14, T 4 N, R 13 E). Named on Calaveritas (1962) 7.5' quadrangle. The place was a mining camp of the 1850's; Cave City cave was an early-day tourist attraction (Gudde, 1975, p. 64).

Cave Country [TUOLUMNE]: *area,* 3 miles north of Columbia (lat. 38°04'35" N, long. 120°23'50" W). Named on Columbia (1948) 7.5' quadrangle.

Cecile Lake [MADERA]: *lake,* 1900 feet long, 5.5 miles west-northwest of Devils Postpile at the head of Shadow Creek (lat. 37°39'50" N, long. 119°10' W). Named on Devils Postpile (1953) 15' quadrangle. The feature also is called Upper Iceberg Lake (Smith, p. 62).

Cedarbrook [MARIPOSA]: *locality,* 5 miles southwest of Fish Camp (lat. 37°25'10" N, long. 119°41'20" W; near SE cor. sec. 8, T 6 S, R 21 E). Named on Bass Lake (1953) 15' quadrangle.

Cedar Creek [CALAVERAS]: *stream,* flows 3.5 miles to North Fork Calaveras River 3 miles north of San Andreas (lat. 38°14'25" N, long. 120°41'25" W; sec. 31, T 5 N, R 12 E). Named on Mokelumne Hill (1948) and San Andreas (1962) 7.5' quadrangles.

Cedar Flat [TUOLUMNE]: *area,* 8.5 miles southwest of Liberty Hill (lat. 38°16'05" N, long. 120°11'25" W; sec. 22, T 5 N, R 16 E). Named on Boards Crossing (1979) 7.5' quadrangle.

Cedar Gulch [STANISLAUS]: *canyon,* drained by a stream that flows 1.5 miles to Quinto Creek 2.5 miles west of Crevison Peak (lat. 37°11'10" N, long. 121°14'10" W; sec. 6, T 9 S, R 7 E). Named on Crevison Peak (1955) 7.5' quadrangle.

Cedar Gulch [TUOLUMNE]: *canyon,* drained by a stream that flows nearly 2 miles to North Fork Tuolumne River 1.5 miles southeast of Tuolumne (lat. 37°56'30" N, long. 120°13'05" W; sec. 16, T 1 N, R 16 E). Named on Tuolumne (1948) 7.5' quadrangle.

Cedar Knob [STANISLAUS]: *peak,* 17 miles west of Patterson (lat. 37°30'45" N, long. 121°26'05" W; sec. 8, T 5 S, R 5 E). Altitude 2030 feet. Named on Lone Tree Creek (1955) 7.5' quadrangle.

Cedar Mountain: see **Streeter Mountain** [MARIPOSA].

Cedar Ridge [TUOLUMNE]: *settlement,* 7 miles east-northeast of Columbia (lat. 38°03'55" N, long. 120°16'40" W; sec. 36, T 3 N, R 15 E). Named on Columbia SE (1948) 7.5' quadrangle.

Cedar Rock Lodge [TUOLUMNE]: *locality,* 8 miles east of Columbia (lat. 38°01'15" N, long. 120°15' W; near N line sec. 19, T 2 N, R 16 E). Named on Columbia SE (1948) 7.5' quadrangle.

Cedar Spring Gulch [STANISLAUS]: *canyon,* 2.5 miles long, opens into Ingram Canyon 12 miles west-northwest of Patterson (lat. 37° 31'25" N, long. 121°20'25" W; near SE cor. sec. 6, T 5 S, R 6 E). Named on Solyo (1953) 7.5' quadrangle.

Cemetery Hill [MARIPOSA]: *hill,* 3.5 miles west-northwest of Hornitos on the south side of Merced River (lat. 37°30'55" N, long. 120° 18' W; near W line sec. 11, T 5 S, R 15 E). Named on Merced Falls (1962) 7.5' quadrangle.

Cemetery Ridge [MARIPOSA]: *ridge,* south-southeast-trending, 1 mile long, 8.5 miles north-northwest of Hornitos (lat. 37°37'10" N, long. 120°16'30" W). Named on Merced Falls (1962) 7.5' quadrangle.

Center Mountain [TUOLUMNE]: *peak,* 7 miles west-northwest of Matterhorn Peak on Tuolumne-Mono County line (lat. 38°08'40" N, long. 119°29'20" W). Altitude 11,273 feet. Named on Matterhorn Peak (1956) 15' quadrangle.

Central Camp [MADERA]: *locality,* 3 miles west of Shuteye Peak (lat. 37°21' N, long. 119°28'55" W; sec. 5, T 7 S, R 23 E). Named on Shuteye Peak (1953) 15' quadrangle. United States Board on Geographic Names (1994, p. 5) approved the name "Peckinpah Mountain" for a peak bounded by Peckinpah Creek 5.2 miles south-southeast of Central Camp (lat. 37°16'30" N, long. 119°28' W; sec. 33, T 17 S, R 23 E), and rejected the name "Mount Peckinpah" for it.

Central Ferry [CALAVERAS-TUOLUMNE]: *locality,* 6.25 miles east-southeast of Copperopolis along Stanislaus River on Calaveras-Tuolumne County line (lat. 37°56'20" N, long. 120°32'15" W; sec. 15, T 1 N, R 13 E). Site named on Melones Dam (1962) 7.5' quadrangle.

Central Hill [CALAVERAS]: *ridge,* south-southwest- to south-trending, 1.5 miles long, 3.5 miles west-northwest of San Andreas (lat. 38°13'30" N, long. 120°44'20" W). Named on San Andreas (1962) 7.5' quadrangle.

Central Landing [SAN JOAQUIN]: *locality,* 15 miles west of Lodi on the east side of Mokelumne River on Bouldin Island (lat. 38°06'05" N, long. 121°33'45" W). Named on Bouldin (1910) 7.5' quadrangle.

Central Point: see **Los Banos** [MERCED].

Central Valley: see "Regional setting."

Ceres [STANISLAUS]: *town,* 4 miles southeast of Modesto (lat. 37° 35'40" N, long. 120°57'10" W; around NW cor. sec. 14, T 4 S, R 9 E). Named on Ceres (1969) 7.5' quadrangle. Postal authorities established Ceres post office in 1870 (Frickstad, p. 199), and the town incorporated in 1918. Elma Carter, daughter of an early settler, named the place for the goddess of growing vegetation (Gudde, 1949, p. 62).

Cerro Colorado: see **Red Mountain** [STANISLAUS].

Chain Lakes [MADERA]: *lakes,* largest 1600 feet long, 4.5 miles south of Merced Peak (lat. 37°34'05" N, long. 119°24'15" W). Named on Merced Peak (1953) 15' quadrangle.

Chain Lakes [TUOLUMNE]: *lakes,* 7.5 miles east-southeast of Pinecrest (lat. 38°08'25" N, long. 119°52'30" W). Named on Pinecrest (1956) 15' quadrangle. United States Board on Geographic Names (1991, p. 3) re-

jected the form "Chain of Lakes" for the name.
Chain of Lakes: see **Chain Lakes** [TUOLUMNE].
Chalmers' Ranch: see **Collegeville** [SAN JOAQUIN].
Chalybeate Spring: see **Iron Spring** [MARIPOSA].
Chamberlain Slough [MERCED]: *stream,* flows 3 miles from Sand Slough to Mariposa Slough 7.5 miles north of Dos Palos Y (lat. 37°09'20" N, long. 120°36'50" W; near N line sec. 13, T 9 S, R 12 E). Named on Santa Rita Park (1962) 15' quadrangle.
Chambers Bar: see **Indian Bar** [TUOLUMNE].
Chamisal [MARIPOSA]: *locality,* 7 miles west-northwest of the village of Bear Valley (lat. 37°36'55" N, long. 120°14' W). Named on Sonora (1891) 30' quadrangle. The place was a gold-mining camp; the name also had the forms "Chemisal" and "Chimesal" (Gudde, 1975, p. 66).
Channel Arm: see **Pardee Reservoir** [CALAVERAS].
Chapman Creek [MADERA-MARIPOSA]: *stream,* heads in Mariposa County and flows 12.5 miles to Chowchilla River 3 miles northwest of Raymond in Madera County (lat. 37°15'15" N, long. 119°56'40" W; sec. 12, T 8 S, R 18 E). Named on Ben Hur (1947) 7.5' quadrangle. On Mariposa (1912) 30' quadrangle, the part of the stream above the mouth of Becknell Creek is called West Branch.
Charleston [SAN JOAQUIN]: *locality,* 7 miles east of downtown Stockton along Southern Pacific Railroad (lat. 37°58'45" N, long. 121°10'30" W). Named on Burnham (1914) 7.5' quadrangle.
Charleston: see **Los Banos** [MERCED].
Chase's Ferry: see **San Joaquin City** [SAN JOAQUIN].
Chemisal: see **Chamisal** [MARIPOSA].
Chemurgic [STANISLAUS]: *locality,* 4.5 miles west-southwest of Turlock along Tidewater Southern Railroad (lat. 37°27'50" N, long. 120°55'10" W; near SW cor. sec. 30, T 5 S, R 10 E). Named on Hatch (1962) 7.5' quadrangle.
Chepo Saddle [MADERA]: *pass,* 2.5 miles east-southeast of Yosemite Forks (lat. 37°20'55" N, long. 119°35'20" W; sec. 5, T 7 S, R 22 E). Named on Bass Lake (1953) 15' quadrangle.
Cherokee [SAN JOAQUIN]: *locality,* 5 miles west of Lockeford along Central California Traction Railroad (lat. 38°09'30" N, long. 121°14'30" W; near NW cor. sec. 32, T 4 N, R 7 E). Named on Lockeford (1968) 7.5' quadrangle.
Cherokee [TUOLUMNE]: *locality,* 1.5 miles north-northwest of Tuolumne (lat. 37°58'55" N, long. 120°14'30" W; sec. 32, T 2 N, R 16 E). Named on Tuolumne (1948) 7.5' quadrangle. Called Cherokee Camp on Sonora (1897) 30' quadrangle. The Scott brothers, who were of Cherokee Indian ancestry, discovered gold at the place in 1853 (Gudde, 1969, p. 61).
Cherokee Camp: see **Cherokee** [TUOLUMNE].
Cherokee Creek [CALAVERAS]: *stream,* flows 9.5 miles to join San Domingo Creek and form South Fork Calaveras River 6.5 miles west-northwest of Angels Camp (lat. 38°07'10" N, long. 120° 39' W; near S line sec. 9, T 3 N, R 12 E). Named on Angels Camp (1962) and Salt Spring Valley (1962) 7.5' quadrangles.
Cherokee Flat [CALAVERAS]: *area,* northwest of downtown Angels Camp at Altaville (lat. 38°05' N, long. 120°34' W; sec. 29, T 3 N, R 13 E); the place is along Cherokee Creek. Named on Angels Camp (1962) 7.5' quadrangle. Leonard (p. 14) noted that a stopping place called Cherokee House was located just north of Cherokee Creek along the trail leading to Angels Camp from the north—this location suggests that the place must have been at or near Cherokee Flat.
Cherokee Flat: see **Altaville** [CALAVERAS].
Cherokee House: see **Cherokee Flat** [CALAVERAS].
Cherry Creek [TUOLUMNE]: *stream,* formed by the confluence of East Fork and North Fork 13 miles east-southeast of Pinecrest, flows 26 miles to Tuolumne River 6.25 miles west of Mather (lat. 37°53'20" N, long. 119°58'15" W; sec. 2, T 1 S, R 18 E). Named on Lake Eleanor (1956) and Pinecrest (1956) 15' quadrangles. East Fork is 13 miles long and North Fork is 14 miles long; both forks are named on Pinecrest (1956) and Tower Peak (1956) 15' quadrangles. West Fork enters the main stream 11 miles south-southeast of Pinecrest; it is 16 miles long and is named on Pinecrest (1956) 15' quadrangle.
Cherry Creek Canyon [TUOLUMNE]: *canyon,* 7 miles long, along Cherry Creek above a point 11 miles south-southeast of Pinecrest (lat. 38°03'10" N, long. 119°54'05" W). Named on Pinecrest (1956) 15' quadrangle.
Cherry Creek Reservoir: see **Cherry Lake** [TUOLUMNE].
Cherry Lake [TUOLUMNE]: *lake,* behind a dam on Cherry Creek 7 miles north-northwest of Mather (lat. 37°58'30" N, long. 119°54'30" W; sec. 5, T 1 N, R 19 E). Named on Lake Eleanor (1956) and Pinecrest (1956) 15' quadrangles. Called Cherry Creek Res. on California Mining Bureau's (1917a) map. Yosemite (1909) 30' quadrangle shows Cherry Valley at the site before the lake formed.
Cherry Ridge [TUOLUMNE]: *ridge,* southwest-trending, 6 miles long, 9 miles southeast of Pinecrest (lat. 38°06' N, long. 119°52'30" W); the ridge is between Cherry Creek and West Fork Cherry Creek. Named on Pinecrest (1956) 15' quadrangle.
Cherry Valley: see **Cherry Lake** [TUOLUMNE].
Chester: see **Merced** [MERCED].
Chetwood Creek [MADERA]: *stream,* flows 2 miles to North Fork San Joaquin River 8.5 miles west-southwest of Devils Postpile (lat. 37°35'50" N, long. 119°14'10" W). Named on Devils Postpile (1953) and Merced Peak (1953) 15' quadrangles. Merced Peak (1953) 15' quadrangle shows Chetwood cabin near the stream.
Chewing Gum Lake [TUOLUMNE]: *lake,* 700 feet long, 8 miles east of Pinecrest (lat. 38°11'45" N, long. 119°51' W; near N line sec. 23, T 4 N, R 19 E). Named on Pinecrest (1956) 15' quadrangle.
Chichi: see **Mountain Ranch** [CALAVERAS].
Chicken Flat [STANISLAUS]: *area,* 14 miles west-northwest of Patterson (lat. 37°32'55" N, long. 121°21'50" W; sec. 36, T 4 S, R 5 E). Named on Solyo (1953) 7.5' quadrangle.
Chilanoialna Creek: see **Chilnualna Creek** [MARIPOSA].
Chilanoialna Fall: see **Chilnualna Fall** [MARIPOSA].
Chilean Gulch: see **Chili Gulch** [CALAVERAS].
Chile Gulch [TUOLUMNE]: *canyon,* drained by a stream that flows 0.5 mile to Deadman Gulch 2.5 miles west of Columbia (lat. 38°02'15" N, long. 120°26'55" W; sec. 9, T 2 N, R 14 E). Named on Columbia (1948) 7.5' quadrangle.
Chileno Creek [MERCED]: *stream,* flows 2.5 miles to Carrisalito Creek 3 miles east-northeast of Sweeney Hill (lat. 36°55'05" N, long. 121°00' W). Named on Los Banos Valley (1969) 7.5' quadrangle.
Chili: see **Chili Gulch** [CALAVERAS].
Chili Camp: see **Chili Camp Gulch** [CALAVERAS].
Chili Camp Gulch [CALAVERAS]: *canyon,* 1.25 miles long, 2 miles west-northwest of Valley Springs (lat. 38°11'55" N, long. 120°51'40" W; mainly in sec. 15, T 4 N, R 10 E). Named on Valley Springs (1962) 7.5' quadrangle. Camp's (1962) map shows a place called Chili Camp located in Chili Gulch (present Chili Camp Gulch).
Chili Gulch [CALAVERAS]: *canyon,* 7 miles long, opens into the canyon of North Fork Calaveras River 2 miles northwest of San Andreas (lat. 38°12'55" N, long. 120°42'25" W; sec. 12, T 4 N, R 11 E). Named on Mokelumne Hill (1948) and San Andreas (1962) 7.5' quadrangles. Apparently the original name was Chilean Gulch (Gudde, 1975, p. 70) for miners from Chili who worked in the canyon in 1848 and 1849 (Hanna, p. 62). Postal authorities established Chili post office 4 miles south of Mokelumne Hill in 1857, discontinued it in 1860, reestablished it in 1861, discontinued it in 1872, reestablished it in 1873, and discontinued it in 1877 (Salley, p. 43).
Chili Gulch: see **Chili Camp Gulch** [CALAVERAS].
Chili Hill [CALAVERAS]: *peak,* nearly 4 miles northwest of San Andreas (lat. 38°14'05" N, long. 120°43'50" W; sec. 2, T 4 N, R 11 E); the peak is west of Chili Gulch. Named on San Andreas (1962) 7.5' quadrangle.
Chilkoot Campground [MADERA]: *locality,* 5 miles east of Yosemite Forks (lat. 37°21'45" N, long. 119°32'20" W; sec. 35, T 6 S, R 22 E); the place is near the mouth of Chilkoot Creek. Named on Bass Lake (1953) 15' quadrangle.
Chilkoot Creek [MADERA]: *stream,* flows 5.5 miles to North Fork Willow Creek (2) 5 miles east of Yosemite Forks (lat. 37°21'55" N, long. 119°32'20" W; sec. 35, T 6 S, R 22 E); the stream heads at Chilkoot Lake. Named on Bass Lake (1953) and Shuteye Peak (1953) 15' quadrangles. United States Board on Geographic Names (1933a, p. 216) rejected the name "Willow Creek" for the feature.
Chilkoot Lake [MADERA]: *lake,* 1000 feet long, 5 miles northwest of Shuteye Peak (lat. 37°24'40" N, long. 119°28'50" W; sec. 17, T 6 S, R 23 E); the lake is at the head of Chilkoot Creek. Named on Shuteye Peak (1953) 15' quadrangle.
Chilnoalna Creek: see **Chilnualna Creek** [MARIPOSA].
Chilnoalna Fall: see **Chilnualna Fall** [MARIPOSA].
Chilnoialny Creek: see **Chilnualna Creek** [MARIPOSA].
Chilnoialny Fall: see **Chilnualna Fall** [MARIPOSA].
Chilnualna Creek [MADERA-MARIPOSA]: *stream,* heads along Madera-Mariposa County line and flows 7.5 miles to South Fork Merced River 1.25 miles east-northeast of Wawona (lat. 37°32'45" N, long. 119°38' W; sec. 35, T 4 S, R 21 E). Named on Yosemite (1956) 15' quadrangle. Called Chilnoialny Cr. on Hoffmann and Gardner's (1863-1867) map, but United States Board on Geographic Names (1933a, p. 216) rejected the forms "Chilnoialny Creek," "Chilanoialna Creek," and "Chilnoalna Creek" for the name.
Chilnualna Fall [MARIPOSA]: *waterfall,* 3 miles northeast of Wawona (lat. 37°33'50" N, long. 119°36'50" W; sec. 25, T 4 S, R 21 E); the feature is along Chilnualna Creek. Named on Yosemite (1956) 15' quadrangle. United States Board on Geographic Names (1933a, p. 216) rejected the forms "Chilnoialny Fall," "Chilanoialna Fall," and "Chilnoalna Fall" for the name.
Chilnualna Lakes [MADERA-MARIPOSA]: *lakes,* 1 mile west of Buena Vista Peak on Madera-Mariposa County line (lat. 37°35'45" N, long. 119°32'15" W); the lakes are on upper reaches of Chilnualna Creek. Named on Yosemite (1956) 15' quadrangle.
Chimesal: see **Chamisal** [MARIPOSA].
China Cabin Flat [STANISLAUS]: *area,* 2.5 miles northwest of Crevison

Peak along Garzas Creek (lat. 37°12'40" N, long. 121°13'30" W; sec. 29, T 8 S, R 7 E). Named on Crevison Peak (1955) 7.5' quadrangle.

China Creek [MADERA]: *stream,* flows 5.25 miles to Fresno River 3 miles south-southwest of Yosemite Forks at Oakhurst (lat. 37°19'45" N, long. 119°39'20" W; at N line sec. 15, T 7 S, R 21 E). Named on Bass Lake (1953) 15' quadrangle.

China Flat [MARIPOSA]: *area,* 1 mile east-southeast of Smith Peak (lat. 37°47'45" N, long. 120°04'55" W; near sec. 3, T 2 S, R 17 E). Named on Jawbone Ridge (1947) 7.5' quadrangle.

China Garden [MADERA]: *area,* 11 miles south of Raymond on the southeast side of Fresno River (lat. 37°03'30" N, long. 119°55' W; mainly in sec. 17, T 10 S, R 19 E). Named on Daulton (1962) 7.5' quadrangle.

China Gulch [MARIPOSA]: *canyon,* 3 miles long, opens into the canyon of Mariposa Creek 5.5 miles east-southeast of the settlement of Catheys Valley (lat. 37°24'10" N, long. 120°00'10"W). Named on Catheys Valley (1962) 7.5' quadrangle.

China Hat [MERCED]: *peak,* 13 miles northeast of Merced (lat. 37°27'25" N, long. 120°20'55" W; sec. 32, T 5 S, R 15 E). Altitude 700 feet. Named on Haystack Mountain (1962) 7.5' quadrangle.

Chinaman Creek [TUOLUMNE]: *stream,* flows 3.5 miles to Middle Fork Stanislaus River 8 miles north-northeast of Long Barn (lat. 38°12'05" N, long. 120°04'50" W; sec. 14, T 4 S, R 17 E). Named on Long Barn (1956) 15' quadrangle.

China Slough [MADERA]: *stream,* flows 3 miles to South Fork Fresno River 13 miles south-southwest of Raymond (lat. 37°01'25" N, long. 119°57'20" W; at N line sec. 36, T 10 S, R 18 E); the stream heads at China Garden. Named on Daulton (1962) 7.5' quadrangle.

China Wells [MADERA]: *locality,* 2 miles north-northwest of Yosemite Forks (lat. 37°23'25" N, long. 119°38'45" W; sec. 23, T 6 S, R 21 E). Site named on Bass Lake (1953) 15' quadrangle.

Chincapin: see **Chinquapin**, under **Wawona** [MARIPOSA].

Chinee: see **Chinese Camp** [TUOLUMNE].

Chinese: see **Chinese Station** [TUOLUMNE].

Chinese Camp [TUOLUMNE]: *village,* 8 miles south-southwest of Sonora (lat. 37°52'15" N, long. 120°25'55" W; near SE cor. sec. 4, T 1 S, R 14 E). Named on Chinese Camp (1947) 7.5' quadrangle. Postal authorities established Chinese Camp post office in 1854 (Frickstad, p. 215). The first settlement at the place was called Camp Washington, but after a large number of Orientals began mining at the site it became known as Chinese Camp, or Chinee (Paden and Schlichtmann, p. 68). Whitney (1865, p. 233) called the place Chinese Diggings. Whitney's (1880) map shows a place called Salvado located less than 1 mile east of present Chinese Camp. Paden and Schlichtmann (p. 68, 69) called the same place Campo Salvador, and noted that the name was from a group of miners from San Salvador in Central America who settled at the site; they mentioned also that the place sometimes was called East Chinee. California Mining Bureau's (1909b) map shows a place called Shawmut situated 2 miles by stage east of Chinese Camp. Postal authorities established Shawmut post office in 1907 and discontinued it in 1925; the name was from Eagle Shawmut mine (Salley, p. 202). California Mining Bureau's (1917a) map shows a place called McAlpine located 7 miles south-southeast of Chinese Camp on the west side of Tuolumne River. Postal authorities established McAlpine post office in 1902 and discontinued it in 1907 (Frickstad, p. 216).

Chinese Diggings: see **Chinese Camp** [TUOLUMNE].

Chinese Gulch [MARIPOSA]: *canyon,* drained by a stream that flows about 1.5 miles to Indian Gulch (1) 1.5 miles northeast of Buckhorn Peak (lat. 37°40'40" N, long. 120°06' W; sec. 16, T 3 S, R 17 E). Named on Buckhorn Peak (1947) 7.5' quadrangle.

Chinese Station [TUOLUMNE]: *locality,* 8 miles south-southwest of Sonora along Sierra Railway (lat. 37°52'45" N, long. 120°27'25" W; sec. 5, T 1 S, R 14 E); the place is 1.5 miles west-northwest of Chinese Camp. Named on Sonora (1948) 15' quadrangle. Called Chinese on Sonora (1897) 30' quadrangle. A place called Shoemake, both a ranch house and a roadhouse for travelers, was located about 2 miles northeast of Chinese Station (Gudde, 1975, p. 318).

Chinkapin: see **Chinquapin**, under **Wawona** [MARIPOSA].

Chinquapin: see **Wawona** [MARIPOSA].

Chinquapin Creek: see **Indian Creek** [MARIPOSA].

Chinquapin Falls [MARIPOSA]: *waterfall,* 1.5 miles east-southeast of El Portal along Indian Creek (lat. 37°40' N, long. 119°45'20" W; sec. 15, T 3 S, R 20 E). Named on El Portal (1947) 7.5' quadrangle.

Chipmunk Flat [TUOLUMNE]: *area,* 3 miles west of Sonora Pass (lat. 38°19'30" N, long. 119°41'30" W). Named on Sonora Pass (1979) 7.5' quadrangle.

Chipmunk Meadow [MADERA]: *area,* 7 miles east-northeast of Yosemite Forks along Chilkoot Creek (lat. 37°23'45" N, long. 119° 30'30" W; near E line sec. 24, T 6 S, R 22 E). Named on Bass Lake (1953) 15' quadrangle.

Chiquita Joaquin River: see **Chiquito Creek** [MADERA].

Chiquita Pass: see **Chiquito Pass** [MADERA].

Chiquito Campground: see **Lower Chiquito Campground** [MADERA]; **Upper Chiquito Campground** [MADERA].

Chiquito Creek [MADERA]: *stream,* flows 20 miles to Mammoth Pool Reservoir on San Joaquin River 5 miles east of Shuteye Peak (lat. 37°20'30" N, long. 119°20' W; sec. 3, T 7 S, R 24 E). Named on Merced Peak (1953) and Shuteye Peak (1953) 15' quadrangles. Called Chiquito Joaquin on Hoffmann and Gardner's (1863-1867) map, and called Chiquita Joaquin River on Lippincott's (1902) map. East Fork enters from the north-northeast 9 miles south of Merced Peak; it is 3.5 miles long and is named on Merced Peak (1953) 15' quadrangle. West Fork enters from the west 2 miles upstream from the mouth of the main creek; it is 11 miles long and is named on Shuteye Peak (1953) 15' quadrangle.

Chiquito Joaquin: see **Chiquito Creek** [MADERA].

Chiquito Lake [MADERA]: *lake,* 1400 feet long, 7 miles south-southwest of Merced Peak (lat. 37°32'10" N, long. 119°26'10" W; on N line sec. 3, T 5 S, R 23 E); the lake is along Chiquito Creek. Named on Merced Peak (1953) 15' quadrangle.

Chiquito Meadows: see **Beasore Meadows** [MADERA].

Chiquito Pass [MADERA]: *pass,* nearly 7 miles south-southwest of Merced Peak (lat. 37°32'30" N, long. 119°26'15" W); the pass is north of Chiquito Lake. Named on Merced Peak (1953) 15' quadrangle. United States Board on Geographic Names (1991, p. 3) rejected the form "Chiquita Pass" for the name.

Chiquito Ridge [MADERA]: *ridge,* generally south-southeast-trending, 6 miles long, Shuteye Peak is near the center of the feature (lat. 37°21' N, long. 119°25'40" W); the ridge is west of Chiquito Creek. Named on Shuteye Peak (1953) 15' quadrangle.

Chittenden Lake [MADERA]: *lake,* 1200 feet long, 5.5 miles south of Merced Peak (lat. 37°33'15" N, long. 119°22'30" W). Named on Merced Peak (1953) 15' quadrangle. Billy Brown, a packer, named the feature in the 1920's for members of the Chittenden family of Fresno (Browning, 1988, p. 24).

Chittenden Peak [TUOLUMNE]: *peak,* 5 miles southwest of Tower Peak (lat. 38°05'55" N, long. 119°37' W). Altitude 9685 feet. Named on Tower Peak (1956) 15' quadrangle. The name commemorates Hiram M. Chittenden of the army, who was one of a group that made a report in 1904 on revision of the boundaries of Yosemite National Park (United States Board on Geographic Names, 1934, p. 5). Lieutenant McClure gave the name "Jack Main Mountain" to the feature in the mid-1890's (Browning, 1986, p. 39).

Chowchilla [MADERA]: *town,* 15 miles northwest of Madera (lat. 37°07'10" N, long. 120°15'50" W; in and near sec. 30, T 9 S, R 16 E). Named on Chowchilla (1960) 15' quadrangle. Postal authorities established Chowchilla post office in 1912 (Frickstad, p. 85), and the town incorporated in 1923.

Chowchilla Creek: see **Old Chowchilla Creek** [MERCED].

Chowchilla Mountain: see **Chowchilla Mountains** [MARIPOSA].

Chowchilla Mountains [MARIPOSA]: *ridge,* northwest-trending, 6 miles long, 4 miles west of Wawona (lat. 37°31'30" N, long. 119° 44' W). Named on El Portal (1947) and Yosemite (1956) 15' quadrangles. Called Chowchilla Mtn. on Buckingham Mountain (1947) 7.5' quadrangle.

Chowchilla River [MADERA-MARIPOSA-MERCED]: *stream,* formed by the confluence of Middle Fork and West Fork in Madera County 9.5 miles northwest of Raymond, flows 80 miles near Madera-Mariposa County line, and then in Merced County, before ending 6 miles northeast of Dos Palos Y (lat. 37°06'30" N, long. 120°32'50" W; sec. 33, T 9 S, R 13 E). Named on Chowchilla (1960), Le Grand (1961), Mariposa (1947), Raymond (1962), and Santa Rita Park (1962) 15' quadrangles. The word "Chowchilla" is a corruption of the name of a warlike Indian tribe that lived along the river; the Indian name is said to have the meaning "murderers" (Hanna, p. 64). Eccleston (p. 31) in 1851 referred to the Indians as the Chou Chili. East Fork heads in Mariposa County and flows 16 miles to Chowchilla River 13 miles southeast of Mariposa in Madera County; it is named on Bass Lake (1953) and Mariposa (1947) 15' quadrangles. Middle Fork is formed in Mariposa County by the confluence of Magoon Creek and Fox Creek; it is 11.5 miles long and is named on Horsecamp Mountain (1947) and Stumpfield Mountain (1947) 7.5' quadrangles. West Fork is formed in Mariposa County by the confluence of Jones Creek and Snow Creek (2); it is 12.5 miles long and is named on Horsecamp Mountain (1947), Mariposa (1947), and Stumpfield Mountain (1947) 7.5' quadrangles. Mendenhall's (1908) map shows a place called Newton Crossing situated along Chowchilla River about 12 miles east-northeast of Chowchilla near the entrance of the river into lowlands (near SW cor. sec. 31, T 8 S, R 18 E). Goddard's (1857) map shows Newtons Crossing.

Christensen Landing [SAN JOAQUIN]: *locality,* 10 miles west of downtown Stockton along Whisky Slough (present Whiskey Slough) (lat. 37°58'20" N, long. 121°28'20" W). Named on Holt (1913) 7.5' quadrangle.

Christian Gulch [CALAVERAS]: *canyon,* drained by a stream that flows 2.25 miles to Black Creek 1.25 miles east-northeast of Copperopolis (lat. 37°59'05" N, long. 120°37' W; sec. 35, T 2 N, R 12 E). Named on Copperopolis (1962), Melones Dam (1962), and Salt Spring Valley (1962)

7.5' quadrangles.

Churchs Spring [CALAVERAS]: *spring,* 7 miles south-southwest of Copperopolis along Martells Creek (lat. 37°53'50" N, long. 120°42'40" W; sec. 36, T 1 N, R 11 E). Named on Copperopolis (1962) 7.5' quadrangle.

Church Tower [MARIPOSA]: *promontory,* 3.25 miles southwest of Yosemite Village on the south side of Yosemite Valley (lat. 37°42'55" N, long. 119°37'45" W). Named on Yosemite (1956) 15' quadrangle.

Ciatana Creek [MADERA]: *stream,* flows about 3.5 miles to Fish Creek (2) 4.25 miles south-southwest of the town of North Fork (lat. 37°10'05" N, long. 119°31'35" W; sec. 12, T 9 S, R 22 E). Named on North Fork (1965) 7.5' quadrangle.

Circle Island [MERCED]: *area,* 7.5 miles northeast of Los Banos (lat. 37°08'50" N, long. 120°45'45" W). Named on San Luis Ranch (1961) 7.5' quadrangle.

Circle Island Drain: see **Circle Island Slough** [MERCED].

Circle Island Slough [MERCED]: *water feature,* 8 miles north-northeast of Los Banos (lat. 37°09'15" N, long. 120°46' W); the feature is on the north side of Circle Island. Named on Los Banos (1961) 15' quadrangle. Called Circle Island Drain on San Luis Ranch (1961) 7.5' quadrangle.

Cirque Lake: see **Adair Lake** [MADERA].

Claribel [STANISLAUS]: *locality,* 6 miles northwest of Waterford along Southern Pacific Railroad (lat. 37°42'50" N, long. 120°49'25" W; sec. 36, T 2 S, R 10 E). Named on Waterford (1969) 7.5' quadrangle.

Clarice Lake [MADERA]: *lake,* 600 feet long, 6.5 miles north-northwest of Devils Postpile (lat. 37°42'20" N, long. 119°08'35" W). Named on Devils Postpile (1953) 15' quadrangle.

Clark: see **Mount Clark** [MARIPOSA].

Clark and Moore's: see **Wawona** [MARIPOSA].

Clark Canyon [MARIPOSA]: *canyon,* drained by a stream that flows 3.5 miles to Merced River 7.5 miles south of Cathedral Peak (lat. 37°44'35" N, long. 119°25'50" W); the canyon heads near Mount Clark. Named on Merced Peak (1953) 15' quadrangle.

Clarke: see **Sirey and Clarke's Ferry,** under **Stanislaus River** [CALAVERAS-SAN JOAQUIN-STANISLAUS-TUOLUMNE].

Clark Flat: see **Clarks Flat** [CALAVERAS].

Clark Fork [MARIPOSA]: *stream,* flows 5 miles to Illilouette Creek 6.5 miles southeast of Yosemite Village (lat. 37°40'35" N, long. 119°30'30" W); the stream heads near Mount Clark. Named on Merced Peak (1953) and Yosemite (1956) 15' quadrangles. United States Board on Geographic Names (1991, p. 4) rejected the name "Clark Fork Creek" for the feature.

Clark Fork [TUOLUMNE]: *stream,* heads in Alpine County and flows 18 miles, approximately along Tuolumne-Alpine County line, to Middle Fork Stanislaus River 3 miles west-northwest of Dardanelle (lat. 38°21'40" N, long. 119°52'30" W). Named on Dardanelle (1979), Dardanelles Cone (1979), Disaster Peak (1979), and Sonora Pass (1979) 7.5' quadrangles. Called Clark's Fork Stanislaus River on Wheeler's (1876-1877) map. The name "Clark" commemorates a member of the commission that the state legislature authorized in 1862 to locate a wagon road from Sonora eastward over the Sierra Nevada to Aurora in the present State of Nevada; the route decided upon follows the stream (Browning, 1986, p. 40).

Clark Fork Campground [TUOLUMNE]: *locality,* 4.5 miles north-northeast of Dardanelle on Tuolumne-Alpine County line (lat. 38° 23'45" N, long. 119°48' W); the place is along Clark Fork. Named on Dardanelles Cone (1979) 7.5' quadrangle.

Clark Fork Creek: see **Clark Fork** [MARIPOSA].

Clark Range [MADERA]: *ridge,* northwest- to north-trending, 5 miles long, northwest of Merced Peak (lat. 37°39' N, long. 119°24'30" W). Named on Merced Peak (1953) 15' quadrangle. The feature was known as Obelisk Group and Merced Group at the time of the Whitney survey (Browning, 1986, p. 144).

Clark Reservoir [CALAVERAS]: *lake,* 600 feet long, 0.5 mile south of Rail Road Flat (lat. 38°20'05" N, long. 120°30'50" W; sec. 35, T 6 N, R 13 E). Named on Rail Road Flat (1948) 7.5' quadrangle.

Clarks Flat [CALAVERAS]: *area,* 4.5 miles east of Murphys on the west side of Stanislaus River (lat. 38°08'35" N, long. 120°22'40" W; on E line sec. 1, T 3 N, R 14 E). Named on Stanislaus (1948) 7.5' quadrangle. Called Clark Flat on Murphys (1948) 7.5' quadrangle.

Clark's Fork Stanislaus River: see **Clark Fork** [TUOLUMNE].

Clarks Gulch [TUOLUMNE]: *canyon,* drained by a stream that flows 1 mile to South Fork Stanislaus River 3 miles northeast of Columbia (lat. 38°03'55" N, long. 120°21'25" W; near SE cor. sec. 31, T 3 N, R 15 E). Named on Columbia SE (1948) 7.5' quadrangle.

Clarks Mill [MARIPOSA]: *locality,* 9 miles east of Mariposa (lat. 37° 29'25" N, long. 119°48' W; near SE cor. sec. 17, T 5 S, R 20 E). Named on Mariposa (1912) 30' quadrangle.

Clark's Ranch: see **Wawona** [MARIPOSA].

Clark's Station: see **Wawona** [MARIPOSA].

Clarks Valley [MARIPOSA]: *valley,* 10 miles south-southwest of El Portal (lat. 37°32'45" N, long. 119°51'45" W). Named on Buckingham Mountain (1947) 7.5' quadrangle.

Claus [STANISLAUS]: *locality,* 5.5 miles northeast of Modesto along Atchison, Topeka and Santa Fe Railroad (lat. 37°41'10" N, long. 120°55'10" W; near W line sec. 7, T 3 S, R 10 E). Named on Riverbank (1969) 7.5' quadrangle. Postal authorities established Clauston post office in 1901, changed the name to Claus in 1902, and discontinued it in 1907; the name commemorates financier Claus Spreckels (Salley, p. 45).

Clauston: see **Claus** [STANISLAUS].

Clavey: see **Camp Clavey** [TUOLUMNE].

Clavey Creek: see **Bell Creek** [TUOLUMNE]; **Clavey River** [TUOLUMNE].

Clavey Meadow [TUOLUMNE]: *area,* 8.5 miles south of Pinecrest along Looney Creek (lat. 38°04'05" N, long. 120°00' W; sec. 33, T 3 N, R 18 E). Named on Cherry Lake North (1979) and Hull Creek (1979) 7.5' quadrangles. Browning (1986, p. 41) associated the name with Jane A. Clavey, who patented land in the neighborhood in 1897.

Clavey River [TUOLUMNE]: *stream,* formed by the confluence of Bell Creek and Lily Creek (3), flows 30 miles to Tuolumne River 7.25 miles south of Duckwall Mountain (lat. 37°51'50" N, long. 120°06'55" W; sec. 9, T 1 S, R 17 E). Named on Cherry Lake North (1979), Duckwall Mountain (1948), Hull Creek (1979), Jawbone Ridge (1947), and Pinecrest (1979) 7.5' quadrangles. Present Clavey River is called Clavey Creek on Sonora (1897) 30' quadrangle, and present Clavey River and present Bell Creek together are called Middle Fork Tuolumne River on Dardanelles (1898) 30' quadrangle, but United States Board on Geographic Names (1963a, p. 6) rejected the names "Clavey Creek," "Middle Fork Tuolumne River," and "Big Canon Creek" for Clavey River.

Clavey River: see **Bell Creek** [TUOLUMNE].

Clay's Bar: see **Camanche** [CALAVERAS].

Clearing House [MARIPOSA]: *locality,* nearly 5 miles west of El Portal on the north side of Merced River (lat. 37°39'55" N, long. 119°52' W; sec. 21, T 3 S, R 19 E). Named on El Portal (1947) 7.5' quadrangle. Postal authorities established Clearinghouse post office in 1913 and discontinued it in 1933; the name is from Clearinghouse mine, which received its name because it was the exchange place for clearinghouse certificates and gold bullion in the panic of 1907 (Salley, p. 45). Hoffmann and Gardner's (1863-1867) map shows a place called Yosemite Mill situated at or near present Clearing House. California Division of Highways' (1934) map shows a place called Sloss located along Yosemite Valley Railroad 1 mile southeast of Clearinghouse (present Clearing House), and a place called Emory located along the railroad 1 mile west of Clearinghouse. The name "Emory" is for A. Emory Wishon of Fresno, who headed a group that formed Yosemite Portland Cement Company in 1925 to use limestone at the site (Johnston, p. 51, 117, 119). The name "Emory" later was changed to "Richardsons" (Sargent, Shirley, 1976, p. 12).

Clear Lake [TUOLUMNE]: *lake,* 650 feet long, 5.5 miles southeast of Pinecrest (lat. 38°07'40" N, long. 119°56'15" W). Named on Pinecrest (1979) 7.5' quadrangle.

Clear View: see **Whiskey Slide** [CALAVERAS].

Clearwater Creek [MADERA]: *stream,* flows 2 miles to Ross Creek 9 miles south-southeast of Shuteye Peak (lat. 37°14'05" N, long. 119°21'10" W; sec. 16, T 8 S, R 24 E). Named on Shaver Lake (1953) 15' quadrangle.

Clements [SAN JOAQUIN]: *village,* 11 miles east-northeast of Lodi (lat. 38°11'25" N, long. 121°05'20" W; near N line sec. 22, T 4 N, R 8 E). Named on Clements (1968) 7.5' quadrangle. Postal authorities established Clements post office in 1882, changed the name to Carlton in 1887, and changed it back to Clements the same year (Frickstad, p. 160). The name "Clements" commemorates Thomas Clements, pioneer farmer and founder of the village (Elliott, p. 65). Postal authorities established Dexter post office in 1876 and discontinued it the same year; it probably was at or near present Clements (Salley, p. 59).

Cleveland: see **Bonanza** [MERCED].

Clifton Court Ferry [SAN JOAQUIN]: *locality,* 16 miles southwest of downtown Stockton along Old River on San Joaquin-Contra Costa County line (lat. 37°49'35" N, long. 121°33' W). Named on Bethany (1952) 7.5' quadrangle.

Cline Creek [TUOLUMNE]: *stream,* flows 2 miles to Big Jackass Creek 4.5 miles south-southeast of Groveland (lat. 37°46'50" N, long. 120°11'45" W; sec. 10, T 2 S, R 16 E). Named on Groveland (1947) 7.5' quadrangle.

Cloudman: see **Keystone** [TUOLUMNE].

Clouds Rest [MARIPOSA]: *peak,* 7 miles southwest of Cathedral Peak (lat. 37°46'05" N, long. 119°29'20" W). Altitude 9926 feet. Named on Tuolumne Meadows (1956) 15' quadrangle. Called Clouds' Rest on Hoffmann and Gardner's (1863-1867) map. Members of an exploring party gave the name in 1851 when they saw clouds settling on the peak before a snow storm (Gudde, 1969, p. 67).

Clover Creek [CALAVERAS]: *stream,* flows 4.5 miles to Littlejohns Creek 2.5 miles west-southwest of Copperopolis (lat. 37°58'10" N, long. 120°41' W; sec. 5, T 1 N, R 12 E). Named on Copperopolis (1962) and Salt Spring Valley (1962) 7.5' quadrangles.

Clover Meadow [TUOLUMNE]: *area,* 7.5 miles west-northwest of Dardanelle along Wheats Meadow Creek (lat. 38°22'10" N, long.

119°57'45" W; sec. 14, T 6 N, R 18 E). Named on Donnell Lake (1979) 7.5' quadrangle.

Coalpit Hill [MARIPOSA]: *peak,* 2.25 miles north of Buckhorn Peak (lat. 37°42' N, long. 120°07' W; sec. 5, T 3 S, R 17 E). Altitude 3375 feet. Named on Buckhorn Peak (1947) 7.5' quadrangle.

Coarsegold [MADERA]: *village,* 8 miles south-southwest of Yosemite Forks (lat. 37°15'45" N, long. 119°42' W; sec. 5, T 8 S, R 21 E); the village is along Coarse Gold Creek. Named on Bass Lake (1953) 15' quadrangle. Mariposa (1912) 30' quadrangle has the form "Coarse Gold" for the name. Postal authorities established Coarse Gold Gulch post office in 1878, changed the name to Goldgulch in 1895, and changed it to Coarsegold in 1899 (Frickstad, p. 85). Miners from Texas found gold at the place in 1849 and the community that developed there was known first as Texas Flat (Hoover, Rensch, and Rensch, p. 172). A map of 1874 has the name "Michaels" at the site—Charles Michael had a business there (Clough, p. 78). A Mexican mining camp called Oro Grosso probably was at the place (Gudde, 1975, p. 256). Postal authorities established Rallsville post office 20 miles northeast of Madera in 1881 and discontinued it in 1883, when they moved the service to Coarse Gold Gulch post office; the name "Rallsville" was for George W. Ralls, first postmaster (Salley, p. 180).

Coarse Gold Creek [MADERA]: *stream,* flows 23 miles to Fresno River 4 miles south-southeast of Knowles (lat. 37°10'05" N, long. 119°50'30" W; sec. 12, T 9 S, R 19 E). Named on Bass Lake (1953), Millerton Lake (1965), and Raymond (1962) 15' quadrangles. The name is from the coarseness of gold found in the stream (Hoover, Rensch, and Rensch, p. 172).

Coarse Gold Gulch: see **Coarsegold** [MADERA].

Cobbs Creek [TUOLUMNE]: *stream,* flows 2 miles to Big Jackass Creek 3.25 miles southeast of Moccasin (lat. 37°47' N, long. 120° 15'10" W; near N line sec. 7, T 2 S, R 16 E). Named on Groveland (1947) and Moccasin (1948) 7.5' quadrangles. Paden and Schlichtmann (p. 128) used the form "Cobb's Creek" for the name.

Cochrane [SAN JOAQUIN]: *locality,* 3.5 miles east of Tracy along Western Pacific Railroad (lat. 37°43'50" N, long. 121°21'30" W; near W line sec. 30, T 2 S, R 6 E). Named on Vernalis (1969) 7.5' quadrangle.

Cocklebur Beach [STANISLAUS]: *beach,* 7 miles north of Oakdale on the north shore of Woodward Reservoir (lat. 37°52' N, long. 120°52'10" W). Named on Oakdale (1968) 7.5' quadrangle.

Cockscomb [MARIPOSA-TUOLUMNE]: *peak,* 1 mile south-southeast of Cathedral Peak on Mariposa-Tuolumne County line (lat. 37°50'05" N, long. 119°23'40" W; sec. 24, T 1 S, R 23 E). Named on Tuolumne Meadows (1956) 15' quadrangle. François Matthes named the feature before 1923 (O'Neill, p. 96). United States Board on Geographic Named (1970, p. 2) gave the names "Cockscomb Crest" and "Cockscomb Peak" as variants.

Cockscomb Crest: see **Cockscomb** [MARIPOSA-TUOLUMNE].

Cockscomb Peak: see **Cockscomb** [MARIPOSA-TUOLUMNE].

Coe Gulch [MARIPOSA]: *canyon,* drained by a stream that flows nearly 1.5 miles to Whites Gulch 3 miles south-southeast of Coulterville (lat. 37°40'15" N, long. 120°10'40" W; sec. 14, T 3 S, R 16 E). Named on Coulterville (1947) 7.5' quadrangle.

Coffin Hollow [TUOLUMNE]: *canyon,* 2.25 miles long, 6 miles southeast of Pinecrest along Lily Creek (3) (lat. 38°08' N, long. 119°55'15" W). Named on Pinecrest (1979) 7.5' quadrangle.

Colby Mountain [TUOLUMNE]: *peak,* nearly 7 miles east-northeast of White Wolf (lat. 37°54'40" N, long. 119°32'20" W). Altitude 9631 feet. Named on Hetch Hetchy Reservoir (1956) 15' quadrangle. The name commemorates W.E. Colby of the Sierra Club (United States Board on Geographic Names, 1934, p. 5).

Cold Canyon [MARIPOSA]: *canyon,* drained by a stream that flows 3 miles to Merced River 1.5 miles west-southwest of El Portal (lat. 37°39'55" N, long. 119°48'30" W; near N line sec. 19, T 3 S, R 20 E). Named on El Portal (1947) 7.5' quadrangle.

Cold Canyon [TUOLUMNE]: *canyon,* drained by a stream that flows 5.25 miles to Tuolumne River 9 miles west of Tioga Pass (lat. 37° 54'35" N, long. 119°25'05" W). Named on Tuolumne Meadows (1956) 15' quadrangle.

Cold Creek [MADERA]: *stream,* flows 1 mile to Middle Fork San Joaquin River 4.5 miles south of Devils Postpile (lat. 37°33'20" N, long. 119°05'30" W). Named on Devils Postpile (1953) 15' quadrangle.

Cold Mountain [TUOLUMNE]: *peak,* 9.5 miles west-northwest of Tioga Pass (lat. 37°57' N, long. 119°25'35" W); the peak is west of Cold Canyon. Altitude 10,301 feet. Named on Tuolumne Meadows (1956) 15' quadrangle.

Cold Spring [CALAVERAS]: *spring,* 5.5 miles east-southeast of Blue Mountain in Dorrington (lat. 38°18'05" N, long. 120°16'40" W; near W line sec. 12, T 5 N, R 15 E). Named on Dorrington (1979) 7.5' quadrangle.

Cold Spring [MARIPOSA]: *spring,* 6 miles west of Fish Camp (lat. 37°28'15" N, long. 119°44'30" W; near W line sec. 25, T 5 S, R 20 E). Named on Bass Lake (1953) 15' quadrangle. Laizure's (1935) map shows a locality called Cold Springs at or near the spring. Postal authorities established Cold Springs post office in 1879 and discontinued it in 1883 (Frickstad, p. 90).

Cold Spring: see **Cold Springs** [TUOLUMNE].

Cold Spring Meadow [MADERA]: *area,* 5 miles south-southeast of Shuteye Peak (lat. 37°17' N, long. 119°23'50" W; near NW cor. sec. 31, T 7 S, R 24 E). Named on Shuteye Peak (1953) 15' quadrangle.

Cold Spring Meadow [MARIPOSA]: *area,* nearly 6 miles west of Fish Camp (lat. 37°28'30" N, long. 119°44'30" W); Cold Spring is in the meadow. Named on Bass Lake (1953) 15' quadrangle.

Cold Springs [TUOLUMNE]: *settlement,* 3.5 miles southwest of Strawberry (lat. 38°09'45" N, long. 120°03'15" W; sec. 36, T 4 N, R 17 E). Named on Strawberry (1979) 7.5' quadrangle. Big Trees (1891) 30' quadrangle shows a place called Cold Spring at the site.

Cold Springs: see **Cold Spring** [MARIPOSA].

Cold Springs Meadow [MADERA]:

(1) *area,* 9 miles south-southwest of Merced Peak (lat. 37°31'15" N, long. 119°28'45" W; near SW cor. sec. 5, T 5 S, R 23 E). Named on Merced Peak (1953) 15' quadrangle.

(2) *area,* nearly 6 miles northwest of Shuteye Peak (lat. 37°25' N, long. 119°29'30" W; near S line sec. 7, T 6 S, R 23 E). Named on Shuteye Peak (1953) 15' quadrangle.

Cold Springs Ranch: see **Dorrington** [CALAVERAS].

Coleman Flat [MARIPOSA]: *area,* 10.5 miles south-southeast of Mariposa (lat. 37°21'10" N, long. 119°52'50" W; sec. 3, T 7 S, R 19 E). Named on Ben Hur (1947) 7.5' quadrangle.

Colfax Gate: see **Colfax Spring** [TUOLUMNE].

Colfax Spring [TUOLUMNE]: *locality,* 11 miles east of Groveland (lat. 37°49'15" N, long. 120°01'30" W; sec. 29, T 1 S, R 18 E). Named on Jawbone Ridge (1947) 7.5' quadrangle. Sonora (1897) 30' quadrangle shows a place called Colfax Gate at the site. Charles Ewell built a modest stopping place at the locality for teamsters, who were attracted by an unfailing cold spring; about 1874 Ewell enlarged his establishment and called it Eagle Hotel for an eagle that his small son shot (Paden and Schlichtmann, p. 197-198).

Collegeville [SAN JOAQUIN]: *locality,* 8.5 miles east-southeast of downtown Stockton (lat. 37°54'20" N, long. 121°08'50" W; on E line sec. 25, T 1 N, R 7 E). Named on Stockton East (1952) 7.5' quadrangle. Dr. L.R. Chalmers settled at the site in 1850 and ran a travelers stop called Chalmers' Ranch, or Eight Mile House; the name "Collegeville" came when Cumberland Presbyterian Church started Morris College at the place in 1867— the school functioned for six years (Hillman and Covello, p. 207). Postal authorities established Collegeville post office in 1868 and discontinued it in 1903 (Frickstad, p. 160).

Collierville [CALAVERAS]: *locality,* 6 miles northeast of Vallecito (lat. 38°08' N, long. 120°23'10" W). Named on Big Trees (1891) 30' quadrangle. W. Collier owned nearby Homestake mine (Crawford, 1894, p. 93).

Collierville [SAN JOAQUIN]: *town,* 5.5 miles north of Lodi (lat. 38° 12'50" N, long. 121°16'05" W; mainly in sec. 12, T 4 N, R 6 E). Named on Lodi North (1968) 7.5' quadrangle.

Colony Center: see **Dos Palos** [MERCED].

Colorado [MARIPOSA]: *locality,* 13 miles southwest of El Portal (lat. 37°33'25" N, long. 119°58' W; sec. 27, T 4 S, R 18 E). Named on Yosemite (1909) 30' quadrangle. El Portal (1947) 15' quadrangle shows Colorado mine near the site. Postal authorities established Colorado post office in 1858 and discontinued it in 1860; the name was from the mine (Salley, p. 48).

Columbia [TUOLUMNE]: *village,* 3.5 miles north-northwest of Sonora (lat. 38°02'10" N, long. 120°24' W; sec. 11, 14, T 2 N, R 14 E). Named on Columbia (1948) 7.5' quadrangle. Postal authorities established Columbia post office in 1852 (Frickstad, p. 215), and the community incorporated in 1854. Dr. Thaddeus Hildreth and his brother George were with a group that found gold at the place in 1850, and for a time the mining camp there was called Hildreth's Diggings (Hoover, Rensch, and Rensch, p. 570). The camp also was called American Camp, Dry Diggings (Gudde, 1975, p. 78-79), and New Camp (Stoddart, p. 125) before Major Sullivan, the first alcalde, and others gave it the name "Columbia" in April of 1850 (Bancroft, 1888, p. 515). A feature called Main Gulch, first called Columbia Gulch, is in Columbia, and a feature called Lawnsdale Gulch is located about 1 mile west of the village (Gudde, 1975, p. 192, 203). A mining camp called Santiago, Santa Iago, or San Diego, was situated about 1 mile northeast of the site of Columbia; Mexicans mined there in 1849 before discovery of gold at Columbia (Morgan *in* Gardiner, p. 346).

Columbia Camp [TUOLUMNE]: *locality,* 5.5 miles west-southwest of Mather (lat. 37°51'15" N, long. 119°56'50" W; sec. 13, T 1 S, R 18 E). Named on Lake Eleanor (1956) 15' quadrangle.

Columbia Cut [SAN JOAQUIN]: *water feature,* artificial watercourse that extends from Middle River to San Joaquin River 5.5 miles south of Terminous (lat. 38°01'45" N, long. 121°29'30" W). Named on Bouldin Island (1978) and Terminous (1978) 7.5' quadrangles.

Columbia Finger [MARIPOSA]: *relief feature,* 2.25 miles south-southwest of Cathedral Peak (lat. 37°49'10" N, long. 119°25'20" W; sec. 26, T 1 S, R

23 E). Named on Tuolumne Meadows (1956) 15' quadrangle. United States Board on Geographic Names (1933a, p. 231) rejected the form "Columbia's Finger" for the name.

Columbia Gulch: see **Main Gulch**, under **Columbia** [TUOLUMNE].

Columbia Rock [MARIPOSA]: *relief feature,* 1 mile west-southwest of Yosemite Village on the north side of Yosemite Valley (lat. 37° 44'45" N, long. 119°36'05" W). Named on Yosemite (1956) 15' quadrangle.

Columbia's Finger: see **Columbia Finger** [MARIPOSA].

Columbia Well [MADERA]: *well,* 16 miles west of Madera (lat. 36° 56'25" N, long. 120°21'20" W; sec. 29, T 11 S, R 15 E). Named on Kentucky Well (1922) 7.5' quadrangle.

Columns of the Giants [TUOLUMNE]: *relief feature,* 1.5 miles east of Dardanelle (lat. 38°20'15" N, long. 119°48'10" W; sec. 29, T 6 N, R 20 E). Named on Dardanelle (1979) 7.5' quadrangle.

Cometa [SAN JOAQUIN]: *locality,* 5 miles north-northeast of Escalon along Southern Pacific Railroad (lat. 37°51'20" N, long. 120°56'40" W; near NE cor. sec. 14, T 1 S, R 9 E). Named on Escalon (1968) 7.5' quadrangle. Postal authorities established Cometa post office in 1892 and discontinued it the same year (Frickstad, p. 160).

Compoodle Creek: see **Campoodle Creek** [TUOLUMNE].

Cone Hill [TUOLUMNE]: *peak,* 4 miles northeast of Stanislaus (lat. 38°11'05" N, long. 120°19'45" W; sec. 21, T 4 N, R 15 E). Altitude 2649 feet. Named on Stanislaus (1948) 7.5' quadrangle.

Confidence [TUOLUMNE]: *settlement,* nearly 2 miles east-northeast of Twain Harte (lat. 38°02'50" N, long. 120°11'55" W; near N line sec. 10, T 2 N, R 16 E). Named on Twain Harte (1979) 7.5' quadrangle, which shows Confidence mine situated 0.5 mile west-southwest of the place. Postal authorities established Confidence post office in 1899, changed the name to Middle Camp in 1906, changed it back to Confidence the same year, and discontinued it in 1925 (Frickstad, p. 215). The name "Confidence" is from Confidence mine (Hanna, p. 71). California Mining Bureau's (1917a) map shows a place called Newell located along a rail line between Soulsbyville and Confidence, and a place called Lyons situated at the end of the rail line beyond Confidence. Postal authorities operated Godfrey post office for a few months in 1901—it was situated 8 miles north of Confidence and named for Godfrey Willer, first postmaster; they established Conlin post office in 1903 and discontinued it in 1904—it was located 18 miles northeast of Confidence and named for George F. Conlin, first postmaster (Salley, p. 49, 86).

Conlin: see **Confidence** [TUOLUMNE].

Connection Slough [SAN JOAQUIN]: *water feature,* joins Middle River 15 miles west-southwest of Lodi (lat. 38°01'55" N, long. 121°31'30" W); the feature connects Old River and Middle River. Named on Bouldin Island (1952) 7.5' quadrangle.

Connection Slough: see **Little Connection Slough** [SAN JOAQUIN].

Connell: see **Camp Connell** [CALAVERAS].

Conness: see **Mount Conness** [TUOLUMNE].

Conness Creek [TUOLUMNE]: *stream,* flows 7 miles to Tuolumne River 9 miles west of Tioga Pass (lat. 37°54'35" N, long. 119°25'05" W); the stream heads near Mount Conness. Named on Tuolumne Meadows (1956) 15' quadrangle.

Contention Ridge [TUOLUMNE]: *ridge,* west-southwest-trending, 3.5 miles long, 6.5 miles north-northeast of Columbia (lat. 38° 07' N, long. 120°20'15" W). Named on Columbia SE (1948) 7.5' quadrangle.

Cony Crags [MADERA]: *ridge,* southwest-trending, 0.5 mile long, 7 miles north-northeast of Merced Peak (lat. 37°44' N, long. 119° 21' W). Named on Merced Peak (1953) 15' quadrangle. The name is for the numerous "conies" that live in talus on the ridge (United States Board on Geographic Names, 1963b, p. 14).

Coon Creek [MADERA]: *stream,* flows nearly 3 miles to Fine Gold Creek 3.5 miles east-northeast of O'Neals (lat. 37°08'45" N, long. 119°38'15" W; sec. 13, T 9 S, R 21 E). Named on North Fork (1965) 7.5' quadrangle.

Cooper: see **Turlock** [STANISLAUS].

Cooper Meadow [TUOLUMNE]: *area,* 9.5 miles east-northeast of Pinecrest (lat. 38°14' N, long. 119°49'40" W; near NE cor. sec. 1, T 4 N, R 19 E). Named on Pinecrest (1956) 15' quadrangle. Browning (1986, p. 46) associated the name with W.F. Cooper, who ran cattle in the neighborhood from 1861 until 1900.

Cooper Peak [TUOLUMNE]: *peak,* 8 miles east-northeast of Pinecrest (lat. 38°14'30" N, long. 119°51'25" W; sec. 35, T 5 N, R 19 E); the peak is 1.5 miles west-northwest of Cooper Meadow. Altitude 9603 feet. Named on Pinecrest (1956) 15' quadrangle.

Cooper Pocket [TUOLUMNE]: *area,* 11 miles east-northeast of Pinecrest at the head of a tributary to South Fork Stanislaus River (lat. 38°14'30" N, long. 119°48'10" W; near W line sec. 32, T 5 N, R 20 E); the place is 1.5 miles east-northeast of Cooper Meadow. Named on Pinecrest (1956) 15' quadrangle.

Coopers Creek [CALAVERAS]: *stream,* flows 3.25 miles to San Domingo Creek 4.5 miles west-northwest of Angels Camp (lat. 38° 06'40" N, long. 120°37'15" W; sec. 14, T 3 N, R 12 E). Named on Angels Camp (1962) 7.5' quadrangle.

Cooperstown [STANISLAUS]: *locality,* 16 miles east of Oakdale along Sierra Railway (lat. 37°44'35" N, long. 120°32'35" W; sec. 21, T 2 S, R 13 E). Named on Cooperstown (1968) 7.5' quadrangle. Called Coopertown on Mendenhall's (1908) map. Postal authorities established Cooperstown post office in 1901 and discontinued it in 1932 (Frickstad, p. 199). The place was on the ranch of William F. Cooper (Paden and Schlichtmann, p. 50).

Copper Creek [CALAVERAS]: *stream,* flows about 3 miles to Black Creek (1) 2 miles southeast of Copperopolis (lat. 37°5730" N, long. 120°37' W; sec. 11, T 1 N, R 12 E). Named on Copperopolis (1962) and Melones Dam (1962) 7.5' quadrangles.

Copper Gulch [CALAVERAS]: *canyon,* drained by a stream that flows 2.5 miles to Stanislaus County 7.5 miles west-southwest of Copperopolis (lat. 37°56'25" N, long. 120°46'15" W; sec. 16, T 1 N, R 11 E). Named on Bachelor Valley (1968) and Copperopolis (1962) 7.5' quadrangles.

Copper Hill [MARIPOSA]: *peak,* 10 miles south-southeast of the settlement of Catheys Valley (lat. 37°17'25" N, long. 120°02'30" W; sec. 30, T 7 S, R 18 E). Named on Illinois Hill (1962) 7.5' quadrangle. Called Copper Mtn. on Indian Gulch (1920) 15' quadrangle.

Copper Mountain [STANISLAUS]: *peak,* 11 miles west-southwest of Patterson (lat. 37°25'05" N, long. 121°18'50" W; on W line sec. 15, T 6 S, R 6 E). Altitude 2678 feet. Named on Copper Mountain (1956) 7.5' quadrangle.

Copper Mountain: see **Copper Hill** [MARIPOSA].

Copperopolis [CALAVERAS]: *village,* 15 miles south of San Andreas (lat. 37°58'50" N, long. 120°38'25" W; sec. 34, T 2 N, R 12 E). Named on Copperopolis (1962) 7.5' quadrangle. Postal authorities established Copperopolis post office in 1861 (Frickstad, p. 14). Copper was discovered and the first house was built at the place in 1861 (Whitney, 1865, p. 255)

Copperopolis Mountain [CALAVERAS]: *ridge,* northwest-trending, nearly 3 miles long, northeast of Copperopolis (lat. 37°59'15" N, long. 120°37'55" W). Named on Copperopolis (1962), Melones Dam (1962), and Salt Spring Valley (1962) 7.5' quadrangles.

Copperopolis Reservoir [CALAVERAS]: *lake,* 2100 feet long, behind a dam on Penny Creek 0.5 mile west-northwest of Copperopolis (lat. 37°59' N, long. 120°38'55" W; sec. 34, T 2 N, R 12 E). Named on Copperopolis (1962) 7.5' quadrangle.

Cora Creek [MADERA]: *stream,* flows 3.5 miles to North Fork San Joaquin River 8.5 miles west-southwest of Devils Postpile (lat. 37° 35'25" N, long. 119°13'50" W); the stream heads at Cora Lakes. Named on Devils Postpile (1953) and Merced Peak (1953) 15' quadrangles.

Cora Lakes [MADERA]: *lakes,* largest 1300 feet long, 7.25 miles east-southeast of Merced Peak (lat. 37°35'45" N, long. 119°16'15" W); the lakes are at the head of Cora Creek. Named on Merced Peak (1953) 15' quadrangle. R.B. Marshall of United States Geological Survey named the lakes for Mrs. Cora Cressey Crow (Gudde, 1949, p. 78).

Corall Hollow: see **Corral Hollow** [SAN JOAQUIN].

Corbet Creek [MARIPOSA]: *stream,* flows 6.5 miles to Bear Creek (2) 3 miles east-northeast of Santa Cruz Mountain (lat. 37°28'15" N, long. 120°09'05" W; sec. 30, T 5 S, R 17 E). Named on Hornitos (1947) and Indian Gulch (1962) 7.5' quadrangles. Called Corbett's Creek on Laizure's (1935) map. The name is for Alexander Corbett, who had mining claims, a store, and a hotel near the stream in the early 1850's; the hotel was called Dog Pump Hotel because Corbett had a Newfoundland dog that worked a water pump (Sargent, Shirley, 1976, p. 24).

Corbett's Creek: see **Corbet Creek** [MARIPOSA].

Corcoran Flat [TUOLUMNE]: *area,* 6.5 miles south-southeast of Tuolumne (lat. 37°52'35" N, long. 120°10'25" W; near SW cor. sec. 1, T 1 S, R 16 E). Named on Tuolumne (1948) 7.5' quadrangle.

Corral: see **Ellis** [SAN JOAQUIN].

Corral Canyon [TUOLUMNE]: *canyon,* 1.5 miles long, 12.5 miles east of Pinecrest along Spring Creek (lat. 38°11'20" N, long. 119° 45'50" W). Named on Pinecrest (1956) 15' quadrangle.

Corral Creek [TUOLUMNE]: *stream,* flows nearly 6 miles to Tuolumne River 8.5 miles southeast of Duckwall Mountain (lat. 37°52'45" N, long. 120°00'45" W; sec. 5, T 1 S, R 18 E). Named on Duckwall Mountain (1948) 7.5' quadrangle.

Corral Flat: see **Mokelumne Hill** [CALAVERAS].

Corral Gulch [CALAVERAS]: *canyon,* drained by a stream that flows nearly 2 miles to Eldorado Creek 7.5 miles east-northeast of San Andreas (lat. 38°13'35" N, long. 120°32'40" W; sec. 4, T 4 N, R 13 E). Named on Calaveritas (1962) 7.5' quadrangle.

Corral Hollow [CALAVERAS]: *valley,* 3.5 miles north of Tamarack (lat. 38°29'15" N, long. 120°05' W; on W line sec. 2, T 7 N, R 17 E). Named on Tamarack (1979) 7'5' quadrangle.

Corral Hollow [SAN JOAQUIN]: *canyon,* 10 miles long, on San Joaquin-Alameda County line, opens into lowlands 5 miles south-southwest of Tracy (lat. 37°40'15" N, long. 121°27'05" W; near W line sec. 17, T 3 S, R 5 E). Named on Midway (1953) and Tracy (1954) 7.5' quadrangles. Called Corall Hollow on Goddard's (1857) map, and called Arroyo Buenos Ayres on Thompson and West's (1879) map. The feature is called Portezuela de

Buenos Ayres on a Mexican map of 1834 (Gudde, 1949, p. 79). According to Mosier and Mosier (p. 25), the name "Corral" is from horse corrals built in the 1850's to hold captured wild horses, but Latta (1949, p. 234) cited a statement made by Mrs. Mamie Carroll Burns that the feature was named for her stepfather, Edward Carroll.

Corral Hollow Creek [SAN JOAQUIN]: *stream,* flows 26 miles, partly in Alameda County, to lowlands 5 miles south-southwest of Tracy (lat. 37°49'15" N, long. 121°27'05" W; near W line sec. 17, T 3 S, R 5 E); the stream drains Corral Hollow. Named on Cedar Mountain (1956), Lone Tree Creek (1955), and Midway (1953) 7.5' quadrangles. United States Board on Geographic Names (1933a, p. 237) rejected the name "Buenos Ayres Creek" for the stream.

Corral Meadow [MADERA]: *area,* 6 miles southwest of Devils Postpile (lat. 37°34'25" N, long. 119°10'10" W). Named on Devils Postpile (1953) 15' quadrangle. Mount Lyell (1901) 30' quadrangle shows "77" Corral at about the site of present Corral Meadow—this corral was named for the dry summer of 1877 because it was at one of the few feeding places for stock available that year (Smith, p. 58).

Corral Meadow [TUOLUMNE]: *area,* 4 miles northeast of Liberty Hill (lat. 38°23'50" N, long. 120°02'25" W). Named on Tamarack (1979) 7.5' quadrangle.

Correia Ferry [SAN JOAQUIN]: *locality,* 2.5 miles south-southeast of Terminous along White Slough (lat. 38°05' N, long. 121°28'10" W). Named on Terminous (1952) 7.5' quadrangle.

Corrine Lake [MADERA]: *lake,* 1100 feet long, 13 miles south-southwest of Shuteye Peak (lat. 37°09'35" N, long. 119°29'45" W; on E line sec. 7, T 9 S, R 23 E). Named on Shaver Lake (1953) 15' quadrangle.

Cortez [MERCED]: *locality,* 11.5 miles northwest of Atwater along Atchison, Topeka and Santa Fe Railroad (lat. 37°28'30" N, long. 120°44'20" W; at E line sec. 27, T 5 S, R 11 E). Named on Atwater (1961) 15' quadrangle.

Cosgrove Creek [CALAVERAS]: *stream,* flows 10.5 miles to Calaveras River nearly 3 miles south of Valley Springs (lat. 38°09' N, long. 120°49'50" W; sec. 36, T 5 N, R 10 E). Named on Valley Springs (1962) 7.5' quadrangle.

Cottage Spring [CALAVERAS]:

(1) *spring,* 10 miles southwest of Tamarack (lat. 38°20'45" N, long. 120°12'45" W; sec. 28, T 6 N, R 16 E). Named on Boards Crossing (1979) 7.5' quadrangle.

(2) *locality,* 4 miles east-northeast of Valley Springs (lat. 38°12'45" N, long. 120°45'45" W). Named on Jackson (1902) 30' quadrangle.

Cottage Springs [CALAVERAS]: *locality,* 9 miles southwest of Tamarack (lat. 38°21'20" N, long. 120°12'40" W; sec. 21, T 6 N, R 16 E); the place is less than 1 mile north of Cottage Spring (1). Named on Boards Crossing (1979) 7.5' quadrangle.

Cotton Arm: see **Lake McClure** [MARIPOSA].

Cotton Creek [MARIPOSA]: *stream,* flows about 4 miles to Lake McClure 5.5 miles north of Hornitos (lat. 37°34'45" N, long. 120° 13'10" W; at S line sec. 16, T 4 S, R 16 E). Named on Hornitos (1947, photorevised 1973) 7.5' quadrangle.

Cotton's Ferry: see **Oakdale** [STANISLAUS].

Cottonwood Campground [TUOLUMNE]: *locality,* 3 miles north of present Dardanelle along Clark Fork (lat. 38°23' N, long. 119°49'30" W). Named on Dardanelles Cone (1956) 15' quadrangle.

Cottonwood Cow Camp [MADERA]: *locality,* 9.5 miles southwest of Madera along Cottonwood Creek (2) (lat. 36°52' N, long. 120° 11'10" W; near S line sec. 23, T 12 S, R 16 E). Named on Madera (1946) 15' quadrangle.

Cottonwood Creek [MADERA]:

(1) *stream,* flows 11.5 miles to San Joaquin River 9 miles south of O'Neals (lat. 36°59'50" N, long. 119°42'25" W; near W line sec. 5, T 11 S, R 21 E). Named on Little Table Mountain (1962) and Millerton Lake West (1965) 7.5' quadrangles.

(2) *stream,* diverges from Fresno River 10 miles south of Raymond (lat. 37°04'10" N, long. 119°54'35" W; near SW cor. sec. 9, T 10 S, R 19 E) and flows more than 30 miles before ending in lowlands southwest of Madera. Named on Firebaugh (1946), Herndon (1965), Madera (1946), and Raymond (1962) 15' quadrangles.

Cottonwood Creek [MERCED]:

(1) *stream,* flows 10 miles to San Luis Creek 7.5 miles east of Pacheco Pass (lat. 37°03'50" N, long. 121°04'15" W). Named on Pacheco Pass (1955) and San Luis Creek (1953) 7.5' quadrangles. The stream now enters San Luis Reservoir.

(2) *stream,* flows 2.5 miles to lowlands 3.25 miles northeast of Merced (lat. 37°20'05" N, long. 120°26'25" W; sec. 9, T 7 S, R 14 E). Named on Merced (1961) 7.5' quadrangle.

Cottonwood Creek [TUOLUMNE]:

(1) *stream,* flows 5 miles to Clavey River 3.5 miles east-northeast of Duckwall Mountain (lat. 37°58'50" N, long. 120°03'15" W; sec. 36, T 2 N, R 17 E). Named on Duckwall Mountain (1948) and Hull Creek (1979) 7.5' quadrangles.

(2) *stream,* flows 3 miles to Cherry Lake 7.5 miles north-northwest of Mather (lat. 37°58'40" N, long. 119°55' W; near N line sec. 5, T 1 N, R 19 E). Named on Lake Eleanor (1956) 15' quadrangle, and on Cherry Lake North (1979) 7.5' quadrangle.

(3) *stream,* flows 6 miles to Middle Tuolumne River 3.25 miles east of Mather (lat. 37°52'55" N, long. 119°47'45" W; sec. 5, T 1 S, R 20 E). Named on Hetch Hetchy Reservoir (1956) and Lake Eleanor (1956) 15' quadrangles.

Cottonwood Creek: see **Willow Creek** [MADERA] (3).

Cottonwood Gulch [CALAVERAS]: *canyon,* drained by a stream that flows nearly 2 miles to Blue Creek 5 miles west of Tamarack (lat. 38°26'20" N, long. 120°10'15" W; near SW cor. sec. 24, T 7 N, R 16 E). Named on Calaveras Dome (1979) 7.5' quadrangle.

Cottonwood Peak: see **Smith Peak** [TUOLUMNE].

Coulterville [MARIPOSA]: *village,* 20 miles northwest of Mariposa along Maxwell Creek (lat. 37°42'45" N, long. 120°11'40" W; on S line sec. 34, T 2 S, R 16 E). Named on Coulterville (1947) 7.5' quadrangle. Postal authorities established Maxwell's Creek post office at the place in 1852 and changed the name to Coulterville in 1872 (Frickstad, p. 92). The name "Coulterville" commemorates George W. Coulter, who came to the site in 1850 and lived in a tent beneath an American flag; the flag caused Mexican miners to call the place *bandereta,* which means "small flag" in Spanish (Hanna, p. 75). When Coulter and George Maxwell cast lots to determine whose name should be applied to the community, Coulter won and the place became Coulterville, while the stream and the post office there were called Maxwell's Creek (Hanna, p. 75). Postal authorities established Opie post office 6 miles northeast of Coulterville in 1896 and discontinued it in 1898; they established Wenger post office 15 miles east of Coulterville in 1882 and discontinued it in 1883—the name was for Frederick Wenger, first postmaster (Salley, p. 162, 236).

Court House Rock: see **Medlicott Dome** [MADERA].

Courthouse Rock [MARIPOSA]: *hill,* 9.5 miles west of the settlement of Catheys Valley (lat. 37°25'20" N, long. 120°16'50" W; sec. 12, T 6 S, R 15 E). Named on Haystack Mountain (1962) 7.5' quadrangle.

Covell [STANISLAUS]: *locality,* 5 miles northwest of downtown Modesto along Southern Pacific Railroad (lat. 37°41'20" N, long. 121°03'35" W; sec. 11, T 3 S, R 8 E). Named on Salida (1953) 7.5' quadrangle.

Cow and Calf Gulch [MARIPOSA]: *canyon,* drained by a stream that flows 2.5 miles to Bear Creek (2) 4.25 miles south-southeast of the village of Bear Valley (lat. 37°30'25" N, long. 120°05'50" W). Named on Bear Valley (1947) 7.5' quadrangle. Laizure's (1928) map has the designation "Humbug or Cow and Calf Gulch" for the feature.

Cow and Calf Mountain [MARIPOSA]: *peak,* 9.5 miles south of the settlement of Catheys Valley (lat. 37°17'40" N, long. 120°05'20" W; near E line sec. 27, T 7 S, R 17 E). Named on Illinois Hill (1962) 7.5' quadrangle.

Coward: see **Ham Coward Gulch** [MARIPOSA].

Cow Creek [MARIPOSA]: *stream,* flows nearly 3 miles to Chapman Creek 14 miles south of Mariposa (lat. 37°16'15" N, long. 119°57'30" W; near NW cor. sec. 1, T 8 S, R 18 E). Named on Ben Hur (1947) 7.5' quadrangle.

Cow Creek [TUOLUMNE]:

(1) *stream,* flows 6 miles to Beardsley Lake 3 miles northwest of Strawberry (lat. 38°13'55" N, long. 120°02'35" W; sec. 6, T 4 N, R 18 E). Named on Donnell Lake (1979), Pinecrest (1979), and Strawberry (1979) 7.5' quadrangles.

(2) *settlement,* 3.5 miles north of Pinecrest (lat. 38°14'30" N, long. 119°59'25" W; on E line sec. 33, T 5 N, R 18 E); the place is near Cow Creek (1). Named on Pinecrest (1979) 7.5' quadrangle.

Cowell: see **Manteca** [SAN JOAQUIN].

Cow Meadow Lake [TUOLUMNE]: *lake,* 2000 feet long, 10 miles west of Tower Peak along North Fork Cherry Creek (lat. 38°08'35" N, long. 119°44' W). Named on Tower Peak (1956) 15' quadrangle.

Coyote Creek [CALAVERAS]: *stream,* flows 12 miles to Stanislaus River 5.25 miles south of Vallecito (lat. 38°00'40" N, long. 120°29'30" W; sec. 24, T 2 N, R 13 E). Named on Columbia (1948) and Murphys (1948) 7.5' quadrangles. The name probably is from the so-called "coyote mining" done in the neighborhood (Goodman *in* Wood, p. 24).

Coyote Creek [SAN JOAQUIN]: *stream,* flows 12 miles to Dry Creek 6.5 miles north-northwest of Lockeford (lat. 38°14'55" N, long. 121°12'10" W; at N line sec. 34, T 5 N, R 7 E). Named on Clay (1968), Clements (1968), Goose Creek (1968), and Lockeford (1968) 7.5' quadrangles.

Coyote Meadow: see **Gully Meadow** [TUOLUMNE].

Coyote Meadows [TUOLUMNE]: *area,* 8 miles east-northeast of Pinecrest (lat. 38°14'30" N, long. 119°52'15" W; sec. 34, T 5 N, R 19 E). Named on Pinecrest (1979) 7.5' quadrangle.

Coyote Rocks [MARIPOSA]: *relief feature,* 5.25 miles north-northeast of Yosemite Village (lat. 37°48'50" N, long. 119°32'10" W; sec. 34, T 1 S, R 22 E). Named on Hetch Hetchy Reservoir (1956) 15' quadrangle.

Coyote Spring [MERCED]: *spring,* 4 miles southeast of Pacheco Pass (lat. 37°01'45" N, long. 121°09'05" W; near S line sec. 25, T 10 S, R 7 E). Named on Pacheco Pass (1955) 7.5' quadrangle.

Crabtree Campsite [TUOLUMNE]: *locality,* 5 miles east-southeast of Pinecrest (lat. 38°10'35" N, long. 119°54'20" W; sec. 29, T 4 N, R 19 E). Named on Pinecrest (1979) 7.5' quadrangle. Called Crabtree Camp on

Pinecrest (1956) 15' quadrangle. O.S. Crabtree tried to patent 160 acres at the site in 1898 (Browning, 1986, p. 48).

Craig Peak [TUOLUMNE]: *peak,* 1.25 miles south-southwest of Tower Peak (lat. 38°07'45" N, long. 119°33'30" W). Altitude 11,090 feet. Named on Tower Peak (1956) 15' quadrangle. R.B. Marshall of United States Geological Survey named the feature for Colonel John W. Craig (United States Board on Geographic Names, 1934, p. 6).

Cranberry Gulch [MARIPOSA]: *canyon,* drained by a stream that flows 1.25 miles to the canyon of Merced River 4 miles west-southwest of El Portal (lat. 37°39'45" N, long. 119°51' W; sec. 22, T 3 S, R 19 E). Named on El Portal (1947) 7.5' quadrangle.

Cranberry Peak: see **Trumbull Peak** [MARIPOSA].

Crandall Peak [TUOLUMNE]: *peak,* 4.5 miles north of Long Barn (lat. 38°09'30" N, long. 120°08'35" W; sec. 31, T 4 N, R 17 E). Altitude 5449 feet. Named on Crandall Peak (1979) 7.5' quadrangle.

Crane: see **Joe Crane Lake** [MADERA].

Crane Creek [MARIPOSA]: *stream,* flows 8.5 miles to Merced River at El Portal (lat. 37°40'35" N, long. 119°46'30" W). Named on El Portal (1947) and Lake Eleanor (1956) 15' quadrangles. Crane Flat ranger station is 6 miles north-northwest of El Portal near the head of Crane Creek; Hoffmann and Gardner's (1863-1867) map shows Crane Flat at the site of the ranger station. Members of a group that included George W. Coulter and Lafayette H. Bunnell named the flat in 1856 after they heard the cries of sandhill cranes there (Paden and Schlichtmann, p. 219).

Crane Creek [TUOLUMNE]:

(1) *stream,* flows 4 miles to Beaver Creek 6 miles southwest of Liberty Hill (lat. 38°18'05" N, long. 120°10'25" W; sec. 11, T 5 N, R 16 E). Named on Boards Crossing (1979) and Liberty Hill (1979) 7.5' quadrangles. Called Little Beaver Creek on Big Meadow (1956) 15' quadrangle.

(2) *stream,* flows 3.25 miles to Jawbone Creek 9 miles northwest of Mather (lat. 38°58'20" N, long. 119°58'50" W; sec. 3, T 1 N, T 18 E); the stream goes through Crane Meadow. Named on Lake Eleanor (1956) 15' quadrangle.

Crane Creek: see **Little Crane Creek** [MARIPOSA]; **North Crane Creek** [TUOLUMNE].

Crane Flat: see **Crane Creek** [MARIPOSA].

Crane Meadow [TUOLUMNE]: *area,* 9 miles northwest of Mather (lat. 37°59'15" N, long. 119°56'50" W; sec. 36, T 2 N, R 18 E); the place is near the head of Crane Creek (2). Named on Lake Eleanor (1956) 15' quadrangle.

Crane Mountain: see **El Capitan** [MARIPOSA].

Crane Valley [MADERA]: *valley,* 5 miles southeast of Yosemite Forks along North Fork Willow Creek (2) (lat. 37°19' N, long. 119°33'30" W). Named on Bass Lake (1953) 15' quadrangle. Water of Bass Lake (1) now covers most of the valley.

Crane Valley Creek: see **North Fork**, under **Willow Creek** [MADERA] (2).

Crane Valley Lake: see **Bass Lake** [MADERA] (1).

Crater Creek [MADERA]: *stream,* flows 6.5 miles to Middle Fork San Joaquin River 4.5 miles south of Devils Postpile (lat. 37°33'30" N, long. 119°05'30" W). Named on Devils Postpile (1953) 15' quadrangle.

Crazy Mule Gulch [TUOLUMNE]: *canyon,* drained by a stream that flows 2.5 miles to Piute Creek (2) 6.25 miles southwest of Matterhorn Peak (lat. 38°02'30" N, long. 119°28'35" W). Named on Matterhorn Peak (1956) 15' quadrangle.

Creegan [MERCED]: *locality,* 1.25 miles east-southeast of downtown Merced along Southern Pacific Railroad (lat. 37°17'35" N, long. 120°27'50" W; sec. 29, T 7 S, R 14 E). Named on Merced (1961) 7.5' quadrangle.

Creighton: see **Creightons Meadow** [CALAVERAS].

Creightons Meadow [CALAVERAS]: *locality,* 2.5 miles north-northwest of Blue Mountain (lat. 38°22'20" N, long. 120°23'10" W; sec. 13, T 6 N, R 14 E). Named on Fort Mountain (1979) 7.5' quadrangle. Big Trees (1891) 30' quadrangle has the name "Creighton" at the spot.

Crescent City: see **Empire** [STANISLAUS].

Crescent Creek [MADERA]: *stream,* flows 4.5 miles to South Fork Merced River 4.25 miles south-southwest of Buena Vista Peak (lat. 37°32'15" N, long. 119°33' W; at S line sec. 34, T 4 S, R 22 E). Named on Yosemite (1956) 15' quadrangle.

Crescent Lake [MADERA]: *lake,* 1700 feet long, 2.25 miles south-southwest of Buena Vista Peak (lat. 37°33'55" N, long. 119°32' W; on N line sec. 26, T 4 S, R 22 E); the lake is along Crescent Creek. Named on Yosemite (1956) 15' quadrangle.

Cressey [MERCED]: *town,* 6 miles north-northwest of Atwater (lat. 37°25'15" N, long. 120°39'55" W; near SW cor. sec. 9, T 6 S, R 12 E). Named on Atwater (1961) 15' quadrangle. Postal authorities established Cressy post office in 1882, discontinued it in 1883, reestablished it in 1909, and changed the name to Cressey in 1912 (Salley, p. 52). Officials of Atchison, Topeka and Santa Fe Railroad named the place for Calvin J. Cressey, owner of land there (Gudde, 1949, p. 84). Postal authorities established Aladdin post office 3.5 miles northwest of Cressey in 1914 and discontinued it in 1919 (Salley, p. 3).

Cressy: see **Cressey** [MERCED].

Crevison Peak [STANISLAUS]: *peak,* 12.5 miles southwest of Newman (lat. 37°11'25" N, long. 121°11'15" W; sec. 34, T 8 S, R 7 E). Altitude 2103 feet. Named on Crevison Peak (1955) 7.5' quadrangle.

Crimea House [TUOLUMNE]: *locality,* 3.5 miles southwest of Chinese Camp (lat. 37°49'55" N, long. 120°28'40" W; sec. 19, T 1 S, R 14 E). Named on Chinese Camp (1947) 7.5' quadrangle. Paden and Schlichtmann (p. 61-62) believed that the name came from interest in the Crimean War, and also from the Chinese Tong War of 1856, which inhabitants of the neighborhood called their local Crimean War.

Criminal Point: see **Prisoners Point** [SAN JOAQUIN].

Criminal Slough [SAN JOAQUIN]: *water feature,* extends from Potato Slough to San Joaquin River 15 miles west-southwest of Lodi (lat. 38°04' N, long. 121°32'30" W); the feature is northeast of Criminal Point (present Prisoners Point) on Venice Island. Named on Bouldin (1910) 7.5' quadrangle.

Crocker Meadow: see **Harden Flat** [TUOLUMNE].

Crocker Point [MARIPOSA]: *promontory,* 5 miles southwest of Yosemite Village on the south side of Yosemite Valley (lat. 37°42'25" N, long. 119°39'30" W). Named on Yosemite (1956) 15' quadrangle. The name commemorates Charles Crocker of Central Pacific Railroad (Browning, 1988, p. 30).

Crocker Ridge [TUOLUMNE]: *ridge,* west-northwest-trending, 2.5 miles long, 7 miles south-southwest of Mather (lat. 37°47' N, long. 119°53'15" W); the ridge is 2 miles south of Rush Creek (3), which had the early name "Crockers Creek." Named on Lake Eleanor (1956) 15' quadrangle. The name is for Henry Robinson Crocker of Crocker's Sierra Resort (Browning, 1988, p. 30).

Crockers: see **Rush Creek** [TUOLUMNE] (3).

Crocker's Meadow: see **Rush Creek** [TUOLUMNE] (3).

Crocker's Sierra Resort: see **Rush Creek** [TUOLUMNE] (3).

Crook Creek [MADERA]: *stream,* flows 4.5 miles to Fresno River 6.5 miles west of Yosemite Forks (lat. 37°21' N, long. 119°44'45" W); the stream is east of Crook Mountain (1). Named on Bass Lake (1953) 15' quadrangle. United States Board on Geographic Names (1984a, p. 3) approved the name "Crooks Creek" for the feature; the name commemorates William H. Crooks, a rancher along the stream from the 1850's until 1912.

Crooked Spring Gulch [CALAVERAS]: *canyon,* drained by a stream that flows nearly 1 mile to Straight Spring Gulch 3.5 miles east-northeast of San Andreas (lat. 38°12'50" N, long. 120°36'55" W; sec. 11, T 4 N, R 12 E). Named on Calaveritas (1962) 7.5' quadrangle.

Crook Mountain [MADERA]:

(1) *ridge,* north-trending, 3 miles long, 13 miles north-northeast of Raymond (lat. 37°22'30" N, long. 119°46'15" W). Named on Horsecamp Mountain (1947) and Stumpfield Mountain (1947) 7.5' quadrangles. United States Board on Geographic Names (1984a, p. 3) approved the name "Crooks Mountain" for the feature; the name commemorates William H. Crooks, of present Crooks Creek.

(2) *peak,* nearly 6 miles southeast of O'Neals (lat. 37°04'20" N, long. 119°37'05" W; sec. 7, T 10 S, R 22 E). Altitude 2006 feet. Named on Millerton Lake East (1965) 7.5' quadrangle.

Crooks Creek: see **Crook Creek** [MADERA].

Crooks Mountain: see **Crook Mountain** [MADERA] (1).

Crow Creek [STANISLAUS]: *stream,* flows 12.5 miles to lowlands 6.5 miles south of Patterson (lat. 37°22'25" N, long. 121°08' W; sec. 31, T 6 S, R 8 E). Named on Newman (1952), Orestimba Peak (1955), and Wilcox Ridge (1956) 7.5' quadrangles.

Crow Hill [STANISLAUS]: *peak,* 8 miles south of Patterson (lat. 37° 21'25" N, long. 121°08'50" W; sec. 1, T 7 S, R 7 E); the peak is south of Crow Creek. Named on Orestimba Peak (1955) 7.5' quadrangle.

Crown Point [TUOLUMNE]: *peak,* 4.25 miles west-northwest of Matterhorn Peak on Tuolumne-Mono County line (lat. 38°06'40" N, long. 119°27'25" W). Altitude 11,346 feet. Named on Matterhorn Peak (1956) 15' quadrangle. J.P. Walker named the peak in 1905 when he was surveying a new boundary for Yosemite National Park (Browning, 1988, p. 30).

Crowsfoot Campground [MARIPOSA]: *locality,* 4.25 miles west-southwest of Wawona (lat. 37°31'15" N, long. 119°43'45" W; near E cor. sec. 12, T 5 S, R 20 E). Named on Yosemite (1956) 15' quadrangle.

Crows Landing [STANISLAUS]: *village,* 6.25 miles south-southeast of Patterson (lat. 37°23'35" N, long. 121°04'15" W; mainly in sec. 22, T 6 S, R 8 E); the place is near Orestimba Creek and Orestimba grant. Named on Crows Landing (1952) 7.5' quadrangle. Watts (p. 682) referred to Crow's Landing. The name commemorates the Crow family, owners of a cattle ranch at the place in the early days (Hanna, p. 78). Postal authorities established Oristembra post office in 1870 at a little community called Newsom's Bridge, named for John M. Newsom, who took up land there in the early 1850's; they moved the post office 3 miles north and changed the name to Crow's Landing in 1870 (Brotherton, p. 32-33; Salley, p. 163). They established Byersville post office 4.5 miles northeast of Crows Landing in 1889 and discontinued it in 1894—the name was for William Byers, a stockman along San Joaquin River (Salley, p. 31).

Crow Spring Canyon [STANISLAUS]: *canyon,* drained by a stream that flows 2.5 miles to South Fork Orestimba Creek 4 miles south of Mikes Peak (lat. 37°17'55" N, long. 121°18'15" W; sec. 27, T 7 S, R 6 E). Named on Wilcox Ridge (1956) 7.5' quadrangle.

Croziers Landing [SAN JOAQUIN]: *locality,* nearly 3 miles west of downtown Stockton on the south side of San Joaquin River on Rough and Ready Island (lat. 37°57'05" N, long. 121°20'25" W). Named on Stockton (1913) 7.5' quadrangle.

Cuba [MERCED]: *locality,* 2.25 miles east-northeast of Atwater along Atchison, Topeka and Santa Fe Railroad (lat. 37°21'25" N, long. 120°34' W; sec. 5, T 7 S, R 13 E). Named on Atwater (1918) 7.5' quadrangle.

Culbertson's: see **Moccasin** [TUOLUMNE].

Cuneo Camp [CALAVERAS]: *locality,* 6 miles west of Tamarack (lat. 38°26'15" N, long. 120°11'25" W; near NW cor. sec. 26, T 7 N, R 16 E). Named on Calaveras Dome (1979) 7.5' quadrangle.

Cuneo Creek [MARIPOSA]: *stream,* flows 3 miles to Maxwell Creek nearly 1 mile northeast of Coulterville (lat. 37°43'15" N, long. 120° 11'05" W; near E line sec. 34, T 2 S, R 16 E). Named on Coulterville (1947) and Groveland (1947) 7.5' quadrangles.

Cunningham Flat: see **Rush Creek** [MARIPOSA].

Curran Creek: see **Kern Creek** [STANISLAUS].

Curry: see **Camp Curry** [MARIPOSA]; **Camp Curry** [TUOLUMNE].

Curry Village: see **Camp Curry** [MARIPOSA].

Curtis' Camp: see **Curtis Creek** [TUOLUMNE].

Curtis Creek [TUOLUMNE]: *stream,* flows 11 miles to Sullivan Creek 5 miles south-southwest of Sonora (lat. 37°54'40" N, long. 120°24'15" W; sec. 26, T 1 N, R 14 E). Named on Sonora (1948) and Standard (1948) 7.5' quadrangles. The name is for Kezia Darwin Curtis, a fortyniner (Dillon *in* Harris, p. 124). Curtis' Camp, or Curtisville, was located along Curtis Creek south of Sonora (Morgan and Scobie *in* Perkins, p. 198). Postal authorities established Curtisville post office in 1853 and discontinued it in 1856 (Frickstad, 215).

Curtisville: see **Curtis Creek** [TUOLUMNE].

Cypress Point [CALAVERAS]: *promontory,* 4 miles west of Paloma on the east side of Pardee Reservoir (lat. 38°15'55" N, long. 120° 50'05" W; near NE cor. sec. 26, T 5 N, R 10 E). Named on Jackson (1962) 7.5' quadrangle.

– D –

Dairyland [MADERA]: *locality,* 7.5 miles south-southwest of Chowchilla (lat. 37°01'05" N, long. 120°18'35" W; on W line sec. 35, T 10 S, R 15 E). Named on Chowchilla (1960) 7.5' quadrangle. Chowchilla (1918) 7.5' quadrangle shows the place 3 miles farther west at the end of Chowchilla Pacific Railroad, and California Division of Highways' (1934) map shows it at the end of a branch of Southern Pacific Railroad (SE quarter sec. 31, T 10 S, R 15 E).

Dallas' Ferry: see **Waterford** [STANISLAUS].

Dallas-Warner Reservoir: see **Modesto Reservoir** [STANISLAUS].

Dana Fork [TUOLUMNE]: *stream,* flows 8 miles to join Lyell Fork and form Tuolumne River nearly 6 miles west-southwest of Tioga Pass (lat. 37°52'30" N, long. 119°21' W; near SE cor. sec. 5, T 1 S, R 24 E); the stream heads 1 mile south of Mount Dana. Named on Mono Craters (1953) and Tuolumne Meadows (1956) 15' quadrangles. The name is from Mount Dana (United States Board on Geographic Names, 1934, p. 6).

Dana Meadows [TUOLUMNE]: *valley,* south of Tioga Pass (lat. 37° 53'30" N, long. 119°15'30" W). Named on Mono Craters (1953) and Tuolumne Meadows (1956) 15' quadrangles. The place first was known as Tioga Meadows (Browning, 1988, p. 31).

Dana Mountain: see **Mount Dana** [TUOLUMNE].

Dana Slough [MERCED]: *stream,* flows 4.25 miles to Hopeton Slough 9.5 miles north-northeast of Atwater (lat. 37°28'50" N, long. 120°33'35" W; sec. 20, T 5 S, R 13 E). Named on Atwater (1961) 15' quadrangle.

Dan Casey Slough [STANISLAUS]: *stream,* flows 0.5 mile to Tuolumne River 3.25 miles east of Waterford (lat. 37°38'40" N, long. 120°41'55" W; near W line sec. 30, T 3 S, R 12 E). Named on Paulsell (1968) 7.5' quadrangle.

Dan Sullivan Gulch [MARIPOSA]: *canyon,* 1.25 miles long, opens into lowlands 8.5 miles southwest of Penon Blanco Peak near Hayward (lat. 37°38'40" N, long. 120°22'10" W; near W line sec. 30, T 3 S, R 15 E). Named on Penon Blanco Peak (1962) 7.5' quadrangle.

Darby House: see **Knights Ferry** [STANISLAUS].

Darby Knob [CALAVERAS]: *peak,* 5 miles east-northeast of Murphys (lat. 38°10'15" N, long. 120°23'05" W; sec. 25, T 4 N, R 14 E). Altitude 3692 feet. Named on Murphys (1948) 7.5' quadrangle.

Dardanelle [TUOLUMNE]: *settlement,* 10.5 miles west of Sonora Pass (lat. 38°20'30" N, long. 119°50' W; sec. 25, T 6 N, R 19 E). Named on Dardanelle (1979) 7.5' quadrangle. Dardanelles Cone (1956) 15' quadrangle shows Dardanelle P.O. at the place. Postal authorities established Dardanelle post office in 1924 (Frickstad, p. 215).

Dardanelles Campground [TUOLUMNE]: *locality,* at present Dardanelle (lat. 38°20'30" N, long. 119°50' W; sec. 25, T 6 N, R 19 E). Named on Dardanelles Cone (1956) 15' quadrangle.

Dardanelles Creek [TUOLUMNE]: *stream,* heads in Alpine County and flows 4.25 miles to Donnell Lake 5.5 miles west of Dardanelle (lat. 38°21' N, long. 119°56'05" W); the stream heads west of The Dardanelles, which is in Alpine County. Named on Donnell Lake (1979) and Spicer Meadow Reservoir (1979) 7.5' quadrangles.

Dark Hole [MARIPOSA]: *locality,* 7 miles north of Yosemite Village (lat. 37°50'45" N, long. 119°36' W; near NW cor. sec. 19, T 1 S, R 22 E). Named on Hetch Hetchy Reservoir (1956) 15' quadrangle. It is believed that the place was a stage stop (Browning, 1988, p. 31).

Darrah [MARIPOSA]: *locality,* 11.5 miles south-southwest of El Portal (lat. 37°31' N, long. 119°50'05" W; near NE cor. sec. 12, T 5 S, R 19 E). Named on Buckingham Mountain (1947) 7.5' quadrangle. United States Board on Geographic Names (1933a, p. 255) rejected the names "Darrah's" and "Snow Creek" for the place. Postal authorities established Darrah post office in 1880, discontinued it in 1889, reestablished it in 1890, and discontinued it in 1907; the name was for Richard Darrah, first postmaster (Salley, p. 55).

Date Flat [MARIPOSA]: *area,* 3 miles north-northeast of Buckhorn Peak (lat. 37°42'05" N, long. 120°05'35" W; near E line sec. 4, T 3 S, T 17 E). Named on Buckhorn Peak (1947) 7.5' quadrangle.

Daulton [MADERA]: *locality,* 8 miles south-southwest of Raymond (lat. 37°07'10" N, long. 119°58'50" W; sec. 26, T 9 S, R 18 E); the place is along Daulton Creek. Named on Daulton (1962) 7.5' quadrangle. Postal authorities established Daulton post office in 1899 and discontinued it in 1908 (Frickstad, p. 85). Daulton (1921) 7.5' quadrangle shows the place along Southern Pacific Railroad. Officials of the railroad named the station there in the 1860's for Henry C. Daulton, who gave right of way through his property—Mr. Daulton was chairman of the commission that organized Madera County (Gudde, 1949, p. 89).

Daulton Creek [MADERA]: *stream,* flows 16 miles to Dry Creek 10.5 miles south-southwest of Raymond (lat. 37°04'30" N, long. 119°59'20" W; sec. 10, T 10 S, R 18 E). Named on Daulton (1962) and Raymond (1962) 7.5' quadrangles. The part of the stream above the mouth of Rawls Gulch is called Gnat Creek on Raymond (1944) 15' quadrangle, but United States Board on Geographic Names (1964a, p. 9) rejected this name for the stream.

Daulton Spring [MADERA]: *spring,* 5.5 miles southeast of Knowles (lat. 37°10'20" N, long. 119°47'30" W; sec. 4, T 9 S, R 20 E). Named on Knowles (1962) 7.5' quadrangle.

David Gulch [MARIPOSA]: *canyon,* drained by a stream that flows 4 miles to Lake McClure 2.5 miles north of the village of Bear Valley (lat. 37°36'20" N, long. 120°07'05" W). Named on Bear Valley (1947, photorevised 1973) and Buckhorn Peak (1947) 7.5' quadrangles.

Davis: see **Alfred Davis Reservoir**, under **Turlock Lake** [STANISLAUS].

Davis and Atherton Ferry: see **Bellota** [SAN JOAQUIN].

Davis' Crossing: see **Lockeford** [SAN JOAQUIN].

Davis Ferry: see **Empire** [STANISLAUS].

Davis Mountain: see **Mount Davis** [MADERA].

Dawson Lake [STANISLAUS]: *lake,* 1 mile long, 1.5 miles southwest of La Grange (lat. 37°38'50" N, long. 120°28'40" W). Named on La Grange (1962) 7.5' quadrangle.

Days Pass [STANISLAUS]: *pass,* 7.25 miles south-southeast of Mikes Peak (lat. 37°15'25" N, long. 121°16'40" W; sec. 11, T 8 S, R 6 E). Named on Wilcox Ridge (1956) 7.5' quadrangle.

Dead Horse Flat [CALAVERAS]: *area,* 1.5 miles north of Vallecito (lat. 38°06'30" N, long. 120°28'05" W; near SE cor. sec. 18, T 3 N, R 14 E). Named on Columbia (1948) 7.5' quadrangle.

Deadhorse Lake [MADERA]: *lake,* 1000 feet long, 4.5 miles west-northwest of Devils Postpile (lat. 37°39'05" N, long. 119°09'35" W). Named on Devils Postpile (1953) 15' quadrangle.

Deadman Bar [TUOLUMNE]: *locality,* 3 miles west of Columbia along Stanislaus River (lat. 38°02'20" N, long. 120°27'10" W; sec. 8, T 2 N, R 14 E); the place is at the mouth of Deadman Gulch. Named on Columbia (1948) 7.5' quadrangle.

Deadman Campground [TUOLUMNE]: *locality,* 6.25 miles west of Sonora Pass along Middle Fork Stanislaus River (lat. 38°19' N, long. 119°44'55" W; near N line sec. 2, T 5 N, R 20 E); the place is 0.25 mile north-northwest of the mouth of Deadman Creek. Named on Sonora Pass (1979) 7.5' quadrangle.

Deadman Creek [MARIPOSA]: *stream,* flows nearly 2 miles to Odom Creek 2.5 miles east-northeast of Santa Cruz Mountain (lat. 37°28'40" N, long. 120°09'45" W; sec. 24, T 5 S, R 16 E). Named on Indian Gulch (1962) 7.5' quadrangle.

Deadman Creek [MARIPOSA-MERCED]: *stream,* heads in Mariposa County and flows 52 miles, partly in an artificial watercourse, to Duck Slough 11 miles north-northwest of Dos Palos Y in Merced County (lat. 37°12'20" N, long. 120°40'40" W; sec. 29, T 8 S, R 12 E). Named on Chowchilla (1960) and Santa Rita Park (1962) 15' quadrangles, and on Illinois Hill (1962), Le Grand (1961), and Raynor Creek (1961) 7.5' quadrangles. Called Deadman's Creek on Laizure's (1935) map.

Deadman Creek [TUOLUMNE]: *stream,* heads in Alpine County and flows 8 miles to Middle Fork Stanislaus River 6 miles west of Sonora Pass (lat. 38°18'50" N, long. 119°44'50" W; sec. 2, T 5 N, R 20 E). Named on Sonora Pass (1979) 7.5' quadrangle.

Deadman Flat [CALAVERAS]: *area,* 8.5 miles west-northwest of Tamarack along North Fork Mokelumne River (lat. 38°29'45" N, long. 120°13' W; near S line sec. 33, T 8 N, R 16 E). Named on Calaveras Dome (1979) 7.5' quadrangle.

Deadman Gulch [TUOLUMNE]: *canyon,* drained by a stream that flows 1 mile to Stanislaus River 3 miles west of Columbia (lat. 38° 02'20" N, long. 120°27'10" W; sec. 8, T 2 N, R 14 E); the mouth of the canyon is at Deadman Bar. Named on Columbia (1948) 7.5' quadrangle.

Deadman Lake [TUOLUMNE]: *lake,* 950 feet long, nearly 3 miles south-southwest of Sonora Pass (lat. 38°17'35" N, long. 119°39'30" W). Named on Sonora Pass (1979) 7.5' quadrangle.

Deadman Pass [MADERA]: *pass,* 4.5 miles north of Devils Postpile on Madera-Mono County line (lat. 37°41'20" N, long. 119°04'10" W); the pass is near the head of Deadman Creek, which is in Mono County. Named on Devils Postpile (1953) 15' quadrangle. Deadman Creek was named for the headless body of a man found along it about 1868 (Browning, 1986, p. 53-54).

Deadman Reach [SAN JOAQUIN]: *water feature,* part of San Joaquin River 8 miles south-southeast of Terminous (lat. 38°00'15" N, long. 121°27'15" W). Named on Headreach (1910) 7.5' quadrangle. Terminous (1952) 7.5' quadrangle shows the feature as mainly marsh.

Deadmans Slough [MERCED]: *water feature,* 10 miles north-northeast of Los Banos on San Luis Island (lat. 37°12'15" N, long. 120° 48'30" W). Named on San Luis Ranch (1961) 7.5' quadrangle.

Deadwood [TUOLUMNE]: *locality,* 6 miles south-southeast of Long Barn along a logging railroad (lat. 38°00'20" N, long. 120°06'30" W; sec. 28, T 2 N, R 17 E). Named on Long Barn (1956) 15' quadrangle.

Deadwood Gulch [MADERA]: *canyon,* 1.5 miles long, 7.25 miles south-southwest of Yosemite Forks (lat. 37°16'45" N, long. 119° 42' W). Named on Bass Lake (1953) 15' quadrangle.

Deadwood Peak [MADERA]: *peak,* 4.5 miles southwest of Yosemite Forks on Potter Ridge (lat. 37°18'50" N, long. 119°41'05" W; sec. 21, T 7 S, R 21 E). Altitude 4540 feet. Named on Bass Lake (1953) 15' quadrangle.

Deadwood Spring [TUOLUMNE]: *spring,* 5 miles south-southeast of Long Barn (lat. 38°01'30" N, long. 120°06'40" W; sec. 16, T 2 N, R 17 E). Named on Hull Creek (1979) 7.5' quadrangle.

Deep Canyon [TUOLUMNE]: *canyon,* 1.5 miles long, 7.5 miles north of White Wolf along a tributary to Rancheria Creek (lat. 37°58'50" N, long. 119°38'10" W). Named on Hetch Hetchy Reservoir (1956) 15' quadrangle.

Deep Gulch [CALAVERAS]: *canyon,* drained by a stream that flows 0.5 mile to Stanislaus River 3 miles east of Vallecito (lat. 38°04'50" N, long. 120°25'05" W; sec. 27, T 3 N, R 14 E). Named on Columbia (1948) 7.5' quadrangle.

Deep Gulch [SAN JOAQUIN]: *canyon,* drained by a stream that flows 4.5 miles to lowlands 7.5 miles south of Tracy (lat. 37°37'55" N, long. 121°24' W; sec. 34, T 3 S, R 5 E). Named on Lone Tree Creek (1955) and Tracy (1954) 7.5' quadrangles.

Deep Hollow [MADERA]: *canyon,* drained by a stream that flows nearly 2 miles to Willow Creek (1) 3.5 miles north-northeast of Raymond (lat. 37°15'45" N, long. 119°53'30" W). Named on Ben Hur (1947) and Raymond (1962) 7.5' quadrangles.

Deep Slough [MERCED]: *stream,* formed by the confluence of Duck Slough and Owens Creek, flows 5.5 miles to Bear Creek (1) 6.25 miles southeast of Stevinson (lat. 37°15'20" N, long. 120°46'55" W). Named on Los Banos (1961), Santa Rita Park (1962), and Turlock (1962) 15' quadrangles.

Deer Camp [MARIPOSA]: *locality,* 5 miles north-northeast of Wawona (lat. 37°36'50" N, long. 119°37'45" W; at W line sec. 1, T 4 S, R 21 E). Named on Yosemite (1956) 15' quadrangle.

Deer Canyon: see **Big Deer Canyon** [MERCED]: **Little Deer Canyon** [MERCED].

Deer Creek [TUOLUMNE]:

(1) *stream,* flows 7.25 miles to South Fork Stanislaus River 8 miles east-northeast of Columbia (lat. 38°05'30" N, long. 120°16'10" W; near N line sec. 25, T 3 N, R 15 E). Named on Columbia SE (1948), Crandall Peak (1979), and Twain Harte (1979) 7.5' quadrangles.

(2) *stream,* flows 5 miles to Tuolumne River 4.25 miles north of Moccasin (lat. 37°52'25" N, long. 120°17'45" W; sec. 2, T 1 S, R 15 E). Named on Moccasin (1948) 7.5' quadrangle.

Deer Flat [MARIPOSA]: *area,* 9.5 miles west-northwest of El Portal (lat. 37°44'25" N, long. 119°56'15" W; near S line sec. 24, T 2 S, R 18 E). Named on Kinsley (1947) 7.5' quadrangle.

Deer Flat [TUOLUMNE]: *area,* 8 miles south of Tuolumne on upper reaches of Deer Creek (2) (lat. 37°50'30" N, long. 120°15'30" W). Named on Sonora (1897) 30' quadrangle.

Deer Lake [TUOLUMNE]: *lake,* 0.5 mile long, 12.5 miles east of Pinecrest (lat. 38°09'55" N, long. 119°45'50" W). Named on Pinecrest (1956) 15' quadrangle.

Deer Lick Creek [MARIPOSA]: *stream,* flows 3.5 miles to Moore Creek 4.25 miles southeast of Smith Peak (lat. 37°45'45" N, long. 120°02'15" W; near E line sec. 13, T 2 S, R 17 E). Named on Jawbone Ridge (1947) 7.5' quadrangle.

Deer Park Canyon [STANISLAUS]: *canyon,* drained by a stream that flows 7.5 miles to Del Puerto Canyon about 6.5 miles southeast of Mount Boardman (lat. 37°25'25" N, long. 121°22'45" W; sec. 12, T 6 S, R 5 E). Named on Mount Boardman (1955) 7.5' quadrangle.

Deer Peak [CALAVERAS]: *peak,* 3.25 miles west-southwest of San Andreas (lat. 38°10'15" N, long. 120°43'50" W; sec. 26, T 4 N, R 11 E). Altitude 1921 feet. Named on San Andreas (1962) 7.5' quadrangle.

Deer Ridge [CALAVERAS]: *ridge,* south-trending, 1.25 miles long, 4 miles north-northeast of San Andreas (lat. 38°14'55" N, long. 120° 39'15" W). Named on Mokelumne Hill (1948) and San Andreas (1962) 7.5' quadrangles.

Delaney Creek [TUOLUMNE]: *stream,* flows 5.5 miles to Tuolumne River 7 miles west-southwest of Tioga Pass (lat. 37°53' N, long. 119°23' W; sec. 6, T 1 S, R 24 E). Named on Tuolumne Meadows (1956) 15' quadrangle. John Muir named the stream for Pat Delaney, who accompanied Muir to the Sierra Nevada in 1869 (United States Board on Geographic Names, 1934, p. 6).

Delfino Landing [SAN JOAQUIN]: *locality,* 3 miles west of downtown Stockton on the southwest side of San Joaquin River on Rough and Ready Island (lat. 37°57'25" N, long. 121°20'45" W). Named on Stockton (1913) 7.5' quadrangle.

Delhi [MERCED]: *town,* 18 miles west-northwest of Merced (lat. 37° 25'45" N, long. 120°46'30" W; in and near sec. 8, 9, T 6 S, R 11 E). Named on Turlock (1962) 15' quadrangle. Postal authorities established Delhi post office in 1912, discontinued it in 1918, and reestablished it in 1920; the name is from letters in the name "Delta Highline Canal Company," an irrigation enterprise (Salley, p. 57). California Division of Highways' (1934) map shows a place called Alcant located 2.5 miles northwest of Delhi along Southern Pacific Railroad (sec. 31, T 5 S, R 11 E).

DeLong Creek [MARIPOSA]: *stream,* flows 4.5 miles to Oliver Creek 10 miles east-southeast of Mariposa (lat. 37°26'50" N, long. 119°47'15" W; near S line sec. 33, T 5 S, R 20 E). Named on Stumpfield Mountain (1947) 7.5' quadrangle. Mariposa (1947) 15' quadrangle has the name "DeLong Creek" for present Oliver Creek below the confluence of DeLong Creek and Oliver Creek. The name "DeLong" is for Charles DeLong, a rancher (Sargent, Shirley, 1976, p. 32).

Del Orto Camp [CALAVERAS]: *locality,* 2.25 miles west-southwest of Tamarack in Thompson Meadow (lat. 38°26' N, long. 120°06'55" W; sec. 28, T 7 N, R 17 E). Named on Tamarack (1979) 7.5' quadrangle.

Del Puerto Canyon [STANISLAUS]: *canyon,* 20 miles long, opens into lowlands 4.5 miles west-northwest of Patterson (lat. 37°29'20" N, long. 121°12'25" W; sec. 21, T 5 S, R 7 E); Del Puerto Creek drains the canyon. Named on Copper Mountain (1956), Mount Boardman (1955), and Patterson (1953) 7.5' quadrangles. Called Puerto Canyon on Patterson (1916) 7.5' quadrangle. Brewer (p. 279) used the name "Cañada del Puerto." Mount Boardman (1955) 7.5' quadrangle shows Phoenix mine near the head of Del Puerto Canyon (sec. 20, T 6 S, R 5 E). Postal authorities established Phoenix post office, named for the mine, near the upper end of the canyon in 1903 and discontinued it in 1904 (Salley, p. 170). Anderson and Pack's (1909-1911) map shows a prominent peak called Hammonds Hill located 1.25 miles north-northwest of the mouth of Del Puerto Canyon (sec. 17, T 5 S, R 7 E)—the name is from J.W. Hammonds, an early settler in the neighborhood (Anderson and Pack, p. 18).

Del Puerto Creek [STANISLAUS]: *stream,* flows 20 miles to lowlands 4.5 miles west-northwest of Patterson (lat. 37°29'20" N, long. 121°12'25" W; sec. 21, T 5 S, R 7 E); the stream goes through Del Puerto Canyon. Named on Brush Lake (1969), Patterson (1953), and Westley (1969) 7.5' quadrangles. Called Puerto Creek on Patterson (1916) and Westley (1915) 7.5' quadrangles. Whitney (1865, p. 41) mentioned Arroyo del Puerto and (p. 43) Puerto Creek. The name is from the natural cut in the hills through which the stream flows in the rainy season—*puerto* means "gate" in Spanish (Hoover, Rensch, and Rensch, p. 540). North Fork enters from the northwest 2 miles northwest of Copper Mountain; it is 4.5 miles long and is named on Copper Mountain (1956) and Mount Boardman (1955) 7.5' quadrangles.

Denair [STANISLAUS]: *town,* 13 miles east-northeast of Modesto (lat. 37°31'35" N, long. 120°47'40" W; sec. 5, 6, T 5 S, R 11 E). Named on Denair (1969) 7.5' quadrangle. The community first was called Elmdale, then Elmwood Colony before John Denair purchased the townsite in 1906 (Gudde, 1949, p. 93). Postal authorities established Elmdale post office in 1898; changed the name to Elmwood in 1904, and changed it to Denair in 1907 (Frickstad, p. 200).

Dentville: see **Knights Ferry** [STANISLAUS].

Denver Church Campground [MADERA]: *locality,* 4.25 miles southeast of Yosemite Forks on the west side of Bass Lake (1) (lat. 37°19'20" N, long. 119°34'40" W; sec. 16, T 7 S, R 22 E). Named on Bass Lake (1953)

15' quadrangle.

Detachment Meadow [MADERA]: *area,* 7.25 miles east-southeast of Merced Peak (lat. 37°36'10" N, long. 119°16'05" W). Named on Merced Peak (1953) 15' quadrangle.

Detwiler: see **Jasper** [MARIPOSA].

Devil Gulch [MARIPOSA]: *canyon,* drained by a stream that flows 8.5 miles to South Fork Merced River 5 miles south-southwest of El Portal (lat. 37°36'35" N, long. 119°49'15" W). Named on Buckingham Mountain (1947) 7.5' quadrangle.

Devil Peak [MARIPOSA]: *peak,* 4.5 miles west of Wawona in Chowchilla Mountains (lat. 37°31'45" N, long. 119°44'25" W; sec. 1, T 5 S, R 20 E). Altitude 6989 feet. Named on Yosemite (1956) 15' quadrangle. Called Devil's Mt. on Hoffmann and Gardner's (1863-1867) map. United States Board on Geographic Names (1933a, p. 263) rejected the names "Devil's Peak" and "Signal Peak" for the feature. According to Hanna (p. 306), the name "Signal Peak" was given because Indians used the place to send messages by smoke and fire.

Devils Canyon [TUOLUMNE]: *canyon,* drained by a stream that flows nearly 2 miles to Stanislaus River 3.5 miles west-southwest of Columbia (lat. 38°00'40" N, long. 120°27'40" W; sec. 20, T 2 N, R 14 E). Named on Columbia (1948) 7.5' quadrangle.

Devils Glen [MERCED]: *canyon,* 1 mile long, 3.5 miles south of Pacheco Pass along the lower part of Spicer Creek (lat. 37°00'50" N, long. 121°12'55" W). Named on Pacheco Pass (1955) 7.5' quadrangle.

Devils Isle: see **White Slough** [SAN JOAQUIN].

Devil's Mountain: see **Devil Peak** [MARIPOSA].

Devils Nose [CALAVERAS]: *peak,* 9 miles north-northwest of Blue Mountain (lat. 38°27'45" N, long. 120°25'10" W; sec. 15, T 7 N, R 14 E). Altitude 4802 feet. Named on Devils Nose (1979) 7.5' quadrangle.

Devil's Peak: see **Devil Peak** [MARIPOSA].

Devils Postpile [MADERA]: *relief feature,* 17 miles east of Merced Peak along Middle Fork San Joaquin River (lat. 37°37'30" N, long. 119°05' W). Named on Devils Postpile (1953) 15' quadrangle. The feature consists of columns of volcanic rock; it was known locally in 1894 as Devils Woodpile (Hanna, p. 86). McLaughlin and Bradley (p. 534) used the form "Devil's Post Pile" for the name. United States Board on Geographic Names (1954, p. 3) rejected the names "Devil Postpile" and "Devils Post Pile" for the feature.

Devils Woodpile: see **Devils Postpile** [MADERA].

Dewey Point [MARIPOSA]: *promontory,* 4.5 miles southwest of Yosemite Village on the south side of Yosemite Valley (lat. 37°42'15" N, long. 119°39'05" W). Named on Yosemite (1956) 15' quadrangle.

Dexter: see **Clements** [SAN JOAQUIN].

Diablo Range: see "Regional setting."

Diamond Lake [MERCED]: *lake,* 225 feet long, 2.5 miles south of Pacheco Pass (lat. 37°01'35" N, long. 121°12'45" W). Named on Pacheco Pass (1955) 7.5' quadrangle.

Diamond Shower Fall: see **Bunnell Cascade** [MARIPOSA].

Dickenson Ferry: see **Old Dickenson Ferry** [MERCED].

Dickenson's Ferry: see **Waterford** [STANISLAUS].

Dickinson [MERCED]: *locality,* 3.25 miles southeast of Le Grand along Atchison, Topeka and Santa Fe Railroad (lat. 37°11'55" N, long. 120°12'25" W; near N line sec. 34, T 8 S, R 16 E). Named on Le Grand (1918) 7.5' quadrangle. The name commemorates William Legrand Dickinson, for whom Le Grand was named (Gudde, 1949, p. 186).

Dickinson: see **Chester**, under **Merced** [MERCED].

Dike Creek [MADERA]: *stream,* flows 3.25 miles to North Fork San Joaquin River 7.5 miles west of Devils Postpile (lat. 37°38' N, long. 119°13'15" W). Named on Devils Postpile (1953) 15' quadrangle.

Dingley Creek [TUOLUMNE]: *stream,* flows nearly 4 miles to Tuolumne River 7.5 miles west of Tioga Pass (lat. 37°53'50" N, long. 119°23'40" W). Named on Tuolumne Meadows (1956) 15' quadrangle.

Dinosaur Lake [MERCED]: *lake,* 600 feet long, less than 1 mile south-southeast of Pacheco Pass (lat. 37°03'10" N, long. 121°12'10" W). Named on Pacheco Pass (1955) 7.5' quadrangle.

Dirty Gulch [CALAVERAS]: *canyon,* drained by a stream that flows 2.5 miles to McKinney Creek 9 miles east of San Andreas (lat. 38° 11'50" N, long. 120°30'50" W; sec. 14, T 4 N, R 13 E). Named on Calaveritas (1962) 7.5' quadrangle.

Disappointment Slough [SAN JOAQUIN]: *water feature,* joins San Joaquin River 5.25 miles south of Terminous (lat. 38°02'15" N, long. 121°29'10" W). Named on Terminous (1978) 7.5' quadrangle.

Diving Board [MARIPOSA]: *relief feature,* 2.5 miles east of Yosemite Village (lat. 37°44'30" N, long. 119°32'10" W). Named on Yosemite (1956) 15' quadrangle.

Dodge Meadow [TUOLUMNE]: *area,* nearly 4 miles south of Pinecrest along Trout Creek (lat. 38°08'15" N, long. 119°59'10" W; on S line sec. 3, T 3 N, R 18 E). Named on Pinecrest (1979) 7.5' quadrangle.

Dodge Ridge [TUOLUMNE]: *ridge,* southwest-trending, 12 miles long, 5 miles east-northeast of Long Barn (lat. 38°07' N, long. 120° 03'30" W). Named on Hull Creek (1979), Pinecrest (1979), and Strawberry (1979) 7.5' quadrangles.

Doe Lake [TUOLUMNE]: *lake,* 1500 feet long, 6 miles southwest of Matterhorn Peak (lat. 38°02'10" N, long. 119°28' W). Named on Matterhorn Peak (1956) 15' quadrangle.

Doghead Peak [TUOLUMNE]: *peak,* nearly 4 miles southwest of Matterhorn Peak (lat. 38°03'10" N, long. 119°25'45" W). Altitude 11,102 feet. Named on Matterhorn Peak (1956) 15' quadrangle.

Dog Lake [TUOLUMNE]: *lake,* 2300 feet long, 4.5 miles west-southwest of Tioga Pass (lat. 37°53'25" N, long. 119°20'20" W; sec. 4, T 1 S, R 24 E). Named on Tuolumne Meadows (1956) 15' quadrangle. R.B. Marshall of United States Geological Survey named the lake in 1898 after he found a sheep dog and a litter of puppies there (Gudde, 1969, p. 91).

Dog Pump Hotel: see **Corbet Creek** [MARIPOSA].

Dogtown [CALAVERAS]: *locality,* 7.5 miles southeast of San Andreas along San Domingo Creek (lat. 38°07'30" N, long. 120° 34'15" W; sec. 8, T 3 N, R 13 E). Named on Angels Camp (1962) and Calaveritas (1962) 7.5' quadrangles. The place was a mining camp of 1849 that was named for a stray dog (Gudde, 1975, p. 97).

Dogtown [MARIPOSA]: *locality,* nearly 4 miles east of Coulterville along Maxwell Creek (lat. 37°42'10" N, long. 120°07'40" W; near E line sec. 6, T 3 S, R 17 E). Named on Coulterville (1947) 7.5' quadrangle.

Dogtown [SAN JOAQUIN]: *locality,* 1.5 miles north of Clements (lat. 38°12'50" N, long. 121°05'15" W; sec. 10, T 4 N, R 8 E). Named on Clements (1968) 7.5' quadrangle.

Dome: see **Balloon Dome** [MADERA].

Domengine Spring [MERCED]: *spring,* 8 miles east-southeast of Pacheco Pass (lat. 37°01'45" N, long. 121°04' W; near S line sec. 26, T 10 S, R 8 E). Named on San Luis Dam (1969) 7.5' quadrangle.

Dome Rock [TUOLUMNE]: *peak,* 8 miles west of Dardanelle (lat. 38°20'20" N, long. 119°58'30" W). Named on Donnell Lake (1979) 7.5' quadrangle.

Domingo Flat [MARIPOSA]: *area,* 7 miles northwest of El Portal (lat. 37°43'55" N, long. 119°52'55" W; sec. 28, T 2 S, R 19 E). Named on Kinsley (1947) 7.5' quadrangle.

Domingo Peak [TUOLUMNE]: *peak,* 2.5 miles southwest of Moccasin (lat. 37°47'10" N, long. 120°19'50" W; sec. 4, T 2 S, R 15 E). Altitude 2486 feet. Named on Moccasin (1948) 7.5' quadrangle.

Dominici Creek: see **Lower Dominici Creek** [STANISLAUS]; **Upper Dominici Creek** [STANISLAUS].

Donnell Lake [TUOLUMNE]: *lake,* behind a dam on Middle Fork Stanislaus River 7 miles west of Dardanelle (lat. 38°19'50" N, long. 119°57'35" W). Named on Donnell Lake (1979) 7.5' quadrangle. Called Donnells Reservoir on Dardanelles Cone (1956) 15' quadrangle, but United States Board on Geographic Names (1960a, p. 14) approved the form "Donnell Lake" for the name, which commemorates one of the partners of Donnell and Parson, who in 1855 built a system to bring water to Columbia (Gudde, 1969, p. 92).

Donnells Reservoir: see **Donnell Lake** [TUOLUMNE].

Donohue Pass [TUOLUMNE]: *pass,* 10.5 miles south of Tioga Pass on Tuolumne-Mono County line (lat. 37°45'40" N, long. 119°14'50" W). Named on Mono Craters (1953) 15' quadrangle. Lieutenant N.F. McClure named the pass in 1895 for a sergeant in his command (United States Board on Geographic Names, 1934, p. 7).

Donohue Peak [TUOLUMNE]: *peak,* 9.5 miles south of Tioga Pass (lat. 37°46'30" N, long. 119°13'45" W); the peak is 1.5 miles northeast of Donohue Pass. Altitude 12,023 feet. Named on Mono Craters (1953) 15' quadrangle. Lieutenant N.F. McClure named the feature in 1895 for Sergeant Donohue of Troop K, Fourth Cavalry, after the sergeant made the first ascent of the peak (Browning, 1986, p. 58).

Donovan Ridge [CALAVERAS]: *ridge,* west-southwest-trending, less than 1 mile long, 6.5 miles southeast of San Andreas (lat. 38° 08' N, long. 120°35'30" W). Named on Calaveritas (1962) 7.5' quadrangle.

Don Pedro Bar [TUOLUMNE]: *locality,* 10 miles south-southeast of Chinese Camp along Tuolumne River (lat. 37°43'45" N, long. 120° 22'45" W). Named on Sonora (1897) 30' quadrangle. Water of Don Pedro Reservoir now covers the site. Postal authorities established Don Pedro's Bar post office in 1853 and discontinued it in 1866 (Salley, p. 60). The name commemorates Pierre "Don Pedro" Sainsevain, a carpenter who went to the mines in 1848 (Morgan *in* Gardiner, p. 325).

Don Pedro Camp [TUOLUMNE]: *locality,* 10.5 miles south of Chinese Camp (lat. 37°42'55" N, long. 120°24'15" W; sec. 35, T 2 S, R 14 E); the place is near Don Pedro Reservoir. Named on La Grange (1962) 7.5' quadrangle.

Don Pedro Reservoir [TUOLUMNE]: *lake,* behind a dam on Tuolumne River 10.5 miles south of Chinese Camp (lat. 37°42'45" N, long. 120°24'05" W; sec. 35, T 2 N, R 14 E); water of the lake covers the site of Don Pedro Bar. Named on Chinese Camp (1947, photorevised 1973), La Grange (1962), Moccasin (1948, photorevised 1973), and Penon Blanco Peak (1962, photorevised 1973) 7.5' quadrangles. United States Board on Geographic Names (1977a, p. 4) gave the names "Lake Don Pedro" and "New Don Pedro Reservoir" as variants. A dam completed in 1924 first formed the lake, and a dam completed in 1971 enlarged it (Gray, p. 38).

Dorothy Lake [TUOLUMNE]: *lake,* 3250 feet long, 3.25 miles northwest of Tower Peak (lat. 38°10'40" N, long. 119°35'15" W). Named on Tower Peak (1956) 15' quadrangle. R.B. Marshall of United States Geological Survey named the lake for the daughter of Major W.W. Forsyth; the major was acting superintendent of Yosemite National Park from 1909 until 1912 (United States Board on Geographic Names, 1934, p. 7).

Dorothy Lake Pass [TUOLUMNE]: *pass,* 3.25 miles northwest of Tower Peak on Tuolumne-Mono County line (lat. 38°10'50" N, long. 119°34'50" W); the pass is northeast of Dorothy Lake. Named on Tower Peak (1956) 15' quadrangle.

Dorrington [CALAVERAS]: *settlement,* 5.5 miles east-southeast of Blue Mountain (lat. 38°18' N, long. 120°16'30" W). Named on Dorrington (1979) 7.5' quadrangle. Postal authorities established Dorrington post office in 1902, discontinued it in 1919, reestablished it in 1921, and discontinued it in 1934; the post office name was from the maiden name of the postmaster's wife—the place also was known as Cold Springs Ranch (Salley, p. 60).

Dos Palos [MERCED]: *town,* 23 miles south-southwest of Merced (lat. 36°59'10" N, long. 120°37'30" W; in and near sec. 11, T 11 S, R 12 E). Named on Dos Palos (1956) and Oxalis (1956) 7.5' quadrangles. Postal authorities established Dospalos post office in 1891, discontinued it in 1906, and reestablished it with the name "Dos Palos" the same year (Salley, p. 61). The town incorporated in 1935. According to local tradition, the name is from two sticks used by surveyors to mark the boundary of Sanjon de Santa Rita grant—*dos palos* means "two trees" or "two sticks" in Spanish (Hanna, p. 228). Postal authorities established Colony Center post office 3 miles northeast of Dos Palos in 1905 and discontinued it in 1906; the name was from a farming enterprise called Dos Palos Colony (Salley, p. 48). They established Elgin post office 3.5 miles southwest of Dos Palos in 1896 and discontinued it in 1900 (Salley, p. 67).

Dos Palos: see **South Dos Palos** [MERCED].

Dos Palos Slough [MERCED]: *stream,* between Dos Palos and South Dos Palos on Merced-Fresno County line (lat. 36°58' N, long. 120° 38' W). Named on Panoche (1913) 30' quadrangle.

Dos Palos Station: see **South Dos Palos** [MERCED].

Dos Palos Wye: see **Dos Palos Y** [MERCED].

Dos Palos Y [MERCED]: *village,* 11.5 miles east of Dos Palos (lat. 37°02'55" N, long. 120°38'05" W; on W line sec. 23, T 10 S, R 12 E). Named on Santa Rita Park (1962) 15' quadrangle. The name also had the form "Dos Palos Wye."

Double Dome Rock [TUOLUMNE]: *peaks,* two, 2.25 miles west of Dardanelle (lat. 38°20'30" N, long. 119°52'30" W). Named on Dardanelle (1979) and Donnell Lake (1979) 7.5' quadrangles.

Double Rock [MARIPOSA]: *peak,* 10.5 miles north of Yosemite Village on Mariposa-Tuolumne County line (lat. 37°54' N, long. 119°34'20" W). Altitude 9782 feet. Named on Hetch Hetchy Reservoir (1956) 15' quadrangle.

Double Rock [TUOLUMNE]: *peak,* 5 miles east-northeast of White Wolf on Tuolumne-Mariposa County line (lat. 37°54' N, long. 119° 34'20" W). Altitude 9782 feet. Named on Hetch Hetchy Reservoir (1956) 15' quadrangle.

Double Springs: see **Wheats** [CALAVERAS].

Doud Hill [CALAVERAS]: *peak,* 8.5 miles northeast of Murphys (lat. 38°12'45" N, long. 120°20'10" W; near E line sec. 8, T 4 N, R 15 E). Altitude 4155 feet. Named on Stanislaus (1948) 7.5' quadrangle.

Douds Landing [CALAVERAS]: *locality,* 9 miles northeast of Murphys and high above North Fork Stanislaus River (lat. 38°12'45" N, long. 120°19'25" W; sec. 9, T 4 N, R 15 E); the place is less than 1 mile east of Doud Hill. Named on Stanislaus (1948) 7.5' quadrangle.

Dougherty [SAN JOAQUIN]: *locality,* 5 miles west of Lockeford along Central California Traction Railroad (lat. 38°09'45" N, long. 121°14'30" W; near SW cor. sec. 29, T 4 N, R 7 E). Named on Lockeford (1968) 7.5' quadrangle.

Douglas Creek [TUOLUMNE]: *stream,* flows 4.25 miles to Middle Fork Stanislaus River 3 miles east of Dardanelle (lat. 38°20'15" N, long. 119°46'45" W; sec. 28, T 6 N, R 20 E). Named on Dardanelle (1979) and Sonora Pass (1979) 7.5' quadrangles. Browning (1986, p. 59) associated the name with Francis Douglass, who patented land in section 28 in 1891.

Douglas Flat [CALAVERAS]: *settlement,* 2.25 miles north-northeast of Vallecito (lat. 38°06'55" N, long. 120°27'10" W; sec. 17, T 3 N, R 14 E). Named on Columbia (1948) 7.5' quadrangle. Postal authorities established Douglas Flat post office in 1879, discontinued it in 1891, and reestablished it with the name "Douglasflat" the same year—the name "Douglas" commemorates Tom Douglas, who built a store at the place in the 1850's (Salley, p. 61). Whitney (1865, p. 259) called the settlement Douglass Flat, and mentioned a feature called Silver Knoll located less than 1 mile northwest of the place.

Douglas Resort [TUOLUMNE]: *locality,* 3 miles east of present Dardanelle (lat. 38°20'25" N, long. 119°46'30" W); the place is near the mouth of Douglas Creek. Named on Dardanelles Cone (1956) 15' quadrangle.

Douglasville: see **Union Hill** [TUOLUMNE].

Dover: see **San Joaquin River** [MADERA-MERCED-SAN JOAQUIN-STANISLAUS].

Dragoon Flat: see **Shaws Flat** [TUOLUMNE].

Dragoon Gulch [TUOLUMNE]: *canyon,* drained by a stream that flows 1.25 miles to Woods Creek in Sonora (lat. 37°58'55" N, long. 120°23'25" W; sec. 36, T 2 N, R 14 E). Named on Sonora (1948) 7.5' quadrangle. The name is for a discharged dragoon who discovered gold in the canyon (Stoddart, p. 64).

Draper: see **Ralph** [TUOLUMNE].

Drew Creek [TUOLUMNE]:

(1) *stream,* flows 3 miles to Tuolumne River 10 miles south-southeast of Duckwall Mountain (lat. 37°50'35" N, long. 120°02'20" W; sec. 19, T 1 S, R 18 E); the stream heads at Drew Meadow. Named on Jawbone Ridge (1947) 7.5' quadrangle

(2) *stream,* heads in Alpine County and flows 3.5 miles, mainly in Alpine County, to Middle Fork Stanislaus River 3.25 miles west-northwest of Dardanelle (lat. 38°21'30" N, long. 119°53'15" W). Named on Donnell Lake (1979) 7.5' quadrangle.

Drew Meadow [TUOLUMNE]: *area,* 8 miles west-southwest of Mather (lat. 37°51'10" N, long. 120°00' W; sec. 16, T 1 S, R 18 E); the place is at the head of Drew Creek (1). Named on Lake Eleanor (1956) and Tuolumne (1948) 15' quadrangles.

Drexler Tract [SAN JOAQUIN]: *area,* 9.5 miles west-southwest of downtown Stockton on Roberts Island (lat. 37°54' N, long. 121°26'30" W). Named on Holt (1978) 7.5' quadrangle.

Drum: see **Briceburg** [MARIPOSA].

Drunken Gulch [MARIPOSA]: *canyon,* drained by a stream that flows 2.25 miles to Sherlock Creek 3.25 miles east-northeast of the village of Bear Valley (lat. 37°35'15" N, long. 120°03'40" W; sec. 14, T 4 S, R 17 E). Named on Bear Valley (1947) 7.5' quadrangle.

Dry Creek [CALAVERAS]:

(1) *stream,* flows 10 miles to Whisky Creek nearly 5 miles east of Jenny Lind (lat. 38°05'55" N, long. 120°46'55" W; sec. 20, T 3 N, R 11 E); the stream goes through Heiser Canyon. Named on Jenny Lind (1962) and Salt Spring Valley (1962) 7.5' quadrangles. On San Andreas (1947) 15' quadrangle, the part of the stream north of Salt Spring Valley is called Heiser Creek.

(2) *stream,* flows 2.25 miles to Coyote Creek 0.25 mile north-northeast of Vallecito (lat. 38°05'30" N, long. 120°28'15" W; near N line sec. 30, T 3 N, R 14 E). Named on Columbia (1948) 7.5' quadrangle.

Dry Creek [MADERA]: *stream,* flows 20 miles to an artificial watercourse 8.5 miles west of Madera (lat. 36°59' N, long. 120°12'30" W; sec. 10, T 11 S, R 16 E). Named on Le Grand (1961), Madera (1946), and Raymond (1962) 15' quadrangles.

Dry Creek [MARIPOSA-MERCED]: *stream,* heads in Mariposa County and flows 32 miles to Merced River 7 miles north of Atwood in Merced County (lat. 37°27'10" N, long. 120°37'10" W; sec. 35, T 5 S, R 12 E). Named on Merced Falls (1962), Snelling (1962), Turlock Lake (1968), and Winton (1961) 7.5' quadrangles. South Fork heads in Mariposa County and flows 10.5 miles to join the main stream 3.5 miles north of Snelling in Merced County; South Fork is named on Merced Falls (1962) and Snelling (1962) 7.5' quadrangles.

Dry Creek [SAN JOAQUIN]: *stream,* enters lowlands from Amador County and flows 25 miles on and near San Joaquin-Sacramento County line to Mokelumne River less than 1 mile northeast of Thornton (lat. 38°13'55" N, long. 121°24'35" W). Named on Clay (1968), Galt (1968), Goose Creek (1968), Lockeford (1968), Lodi North (1968), and Thornton (1978) 7.5' quadrangles.

Dry Creek [STANISLAUS]: *stream,* heads just inside Tuolumne County and flows 50 miles to Tuolumne River in Modesto (lat. 37° 37'40" N, long. 120°59' W; sec. 33, T 3 S, R 9 E). Named on Cooperstown (1968), La Grange (1962), Paulsell (1968), Riverbank (1969) and Waterford (1969) 7.5' quadrangles. On La Grange (1919) 7.5' quadrangle, the name "Dry Creek" applies to present Gallup Creek (a tributary of present Dry Creek). North Fork heads in Tuolumne County and flows 8.5 miles to Dry Creek 1.5 miles west-southwest of Cooperstown in Stanislaus County. North Fork is named on Cooperstown (1968) and Keystone (1962) 7.5' quadrangles—it is called Dry Creek on Copperopolis (1916) 15' quadrangle.

Dry Creek [TUOLUMNE]: *stream,* flows 2.5 miles to Deer Creek (1) 9 miles east-northeast of Columbia (lat. 38°05'30" N, long. 120°15'20" W; near N line sec. 30, T 3 N, R 16 E). Named on Columbia SE (1948) and Twain Harte (1979) 7.5' quadrangles.

Dry Creek: see **Gallup Creek** [STANISLAUS-TUOLUMNE]; **Little Dry Creek** [CALAVERAS]; **Little Dry Creek** [MADERA]; **Rydberg Creek** [STANISLAUS-TUOLUMNE].

Dry Diggings: see **Columbia** [TUOLUMNE].

Dry Gulch [MARIPOSA]: *canyon,* drained by a stream that flows 2.5 miles to Merced River 3 miles west of El Portal (lat. 37°40'25" N, long. 119°50' W; sec. 14, T 3 S, R 19 E). Named on El Portal (1947) 7.5' quadrangle.

Dry Hollow [CALAVERAS]: *area,* 4 miles northeast of San Andreas (lat. 38°14'10" N, long. 120°37'40" W; near SW cor. sec. 35, T 5 N, R 12 E). Named on San Andreas (1962) 7.5' quadrangle.

Dry Lake [MERCED]: *intermittent lake,* 425 feet long, 6.25 miles north-northeast of Pacheco Pass along Romero Creek (lat. 37°09'05" N, long. 121°10'50" W; at E line sec. 15, T 9 S, R 7 E). Named on Crevison Peak (1955) 7.5' quadrangle.

Dry Meadow [TUOLUMNE]: *area,* 6.25 miles west-northwest of Strawberry (lat. 38°13'25" N, long. 120°07'25" W; on N line sec. 8, T 4 N, R 17 E). Named on Strawberry (1979) 7.5' quadrangle.

Dry Meadow Creek [TUOLUMNE]: *stream,* flows 5.25 miles to Middle Fork Stanislaus River 2 miles north of Crandall Peak (lat. 38°11'10" N, long. 120°08'35" W; sec. 19, T 4 N, R 17 E); the stream goes through Dry Meadow. Named on Crandall Peak (1979) and Strawberry (1979) 7.5' quadrangles.

Dry Meadow Station [TUOLUMNE]: *locality,* nearly 5 miles north of Crandall Peak (lat. 38°13'35" N, long. 120°07'30" W; sec. 5, T 4 N, R 17 E); the place is at Dry Meadow. Named on Crandall Peak (1979) 7.5' quadrangle.

Duck Bar [CALAVERAS]: *locality,* 3.25 miles east of Vallecito along Stanislaus River (lat. 38°05' N, long. 120°24'50" W; near E line sec. 27, T 3 N, R 14 E). Named on Columbia (1948) 7.5' quadrangle.

Duck Cove [STANISLAUS]: *embayment,* 5 miles north of Oakdale along Woodward Reservoir (lat. 37°50'20" N, long. 120°51' W). Named on Oakdale (1968) 7.5' quadrangle.

Duck Creek [SAN JOAQUIN]: *stream,* flows 9.5 miles to Calaveras River 4.5 miles east-northeast of Linden (lat. 38°03'10" N, long. 121°00'35" W; sec. 5, T 2 N, R 9 E). Named on Clements (1968), Linden (1968), and Valley Springs SW (1962) 7.5' quadrangles.

Duck Creek [SAN JOAQUIN-STANISLAUS]: *stream,* heads in Stanislaus County and flows 33 miles before ending nearly 3 miles south-southeast of downtown Stockton in San Joaquin County (lat. 37°55'15" N, long. 121°16'15" W). Named on Farmington (1953), Jenny Lind (1962), Peters (1952), Stockton East (1952), Stockton West (1952), and Valley Springs SW (1962) 7.5' quadrangles. North Fork heads in Stanislaus County and flows 10 miles to join the main stream 1 mile east-northeast of Farmington in San Joaquin County; it is named on Farmington (1968) and Valley Springs SW (1962) 7.5' quadrangles.

Duck Slough [MERCED]: *stream,* flows 30 miles to join Owens Creek and form Deep Slough 12.5 miles north-northwest of Dos Palos Y (lat. 37°13'15" N, long. 120°42'45" W; sec. 24, T 8 S, R 11 E). Named on El Nido (1960), Merced (1961), Planada (1961), Sandy Mush (1962), and Turner Ranch (1961) 7.5' quadrangles.

Duckwall Creek [TUOLUMNE]: *stream,* flows 4 miles to North Fork Tuolumne River 1 mile east-southeast of Tuolumne (lat. 37°57'20" N, long. 120°13'05" W; sec. 9, T 1 N, R 16 E). Named on Tuolumne (1948) 7.5' quadrangle.

Duckwall Mountain [TUOLUMNE]: *peak,* 6.5 miles east of Tuolumne (lat. 37°58'05" N, long. 120°07'10" W; sec. 4, T 1 N, R 17 E). Altitude 5835 feet. Named on Duckwall Mountain (1948) 7.5' quadrangle. The name recalls the Duckwall family, emigrants who crossed Sonora Pass by wagon in 1853 (Hoover, Rensch, and Rensch, p. 566).

Duckwall Ridge [TUOLUMNE]: *ridge,* extends 3.5 miles east from Duckwall Mountain (lat. 37°57'20" N, long. 120°05'30" W). Named on Duckwall Mountain (1948) 7.5' quadrangle.

Dudley [MARIPOSA]: *locality,* 5.5 miles east-northeast of Coulterville along Smith Creek (lat. 37°45'15" N, long. 120°06'30" W). Named on Sonora (1891) 30' quadrangle. Dudley's Station was a stage stop that Hosea E. Dudley and Fanny Chase Dudley operated on the road to Yosemite Valley (Sargent, Shirley, 1976, p. 21).

Dudley Hill [MARIPOSA]: *peak,* 6 miles north of Buckhorn Peak (lat. 37°44'50" N, long. 120°07'10" W; sec. 20, T 2 S, R 17 E). Named on Buckhorn Peak (1947) 7.5' quadrangle.

Dudley's Station: see **Dudley** [MARIPOSA].

Dunbar [CALAVERAS]: *locality,* nearly 7 miles south of Blue Mountain (lat. 38°14'30" N, long. 120°21'45" W). Named on Big Trees (1891) 30' quadrangle.

Dunlap Gulch [CALAVERAS]: *canyon,* drained by a stream that flows 2 miles to San Antonio Creek 5.5 miles north-northeast of Murphys (lat. 38°12'50" N, long. 120°25'30" W; sec. 10, T 4 N, R 14 E). Named on Murphys (1948) 7.5' quadrangle.

Dunn Creek [TUOLUMNE]: *stream,* flows 2.5 miles to Stanislaus County 4.5 miles south of Don Pedro Camp (lat. 37°38'55" N, long. 120°24'25" W; near W line sec. 26, T 3 S, R 14 E); the stream is west of Dunn Ridge. Named on La Grange (1962) 7.5' quadrangle.

Dunn Ridge [MARIPOSA-TUOLUMNE]: *ridge,* north- to northwest-trending, 2 miles long, 3.5 miles south-southeast of Don Pedro Camp on Tuolumne-Mariposa County line (lat. 37°40' N, long. 120°23'25" W). Named on La Grange (1962) 7.5' quadrangle.

Dunow's Camp: see **Keystone** [TUOLUMNE].

Durham's Ferry: see **San Joaquin City** [SAN JOAQUIN].

Dutch Creek [CALAVERAS]: *stream,* flows 2.5 miles to Licking Fork 3 miles west-northwest of Blue Mountain (lat. 38°21'10" N, long. 120°25'05" W; near S line sec. 22, T 6 N, R 14 E). Named on Fort Mountain (1979) 7.5' quadrangle.

Dutch Creek [MARIPOSA]: *stream,* flows 4.5 miles to Bean Creek 6 miles north-northeast of Buckhorn Peak (lat. 37°44'25" N, long. 120°04'30" W; near NE cor. sec. 27, T 2 S, R 17 E). Named on Buckhorn Peak (1947) and Coulterville (1947) 7.5' quadrangles. The name is for "Dutch Frank" Laumeister, quartermaster of the Mariposa Battalion (Gudde, 1975, p. 104).

Dutch Ed Gulch [CALAVERAS]: *canyon,* drained by a stream that flows less than 1 mile to San Antonio Creek 5 miles south-southeast of San Andreas (lat. 38°08' N, long. 120°37'50" W; near SE cor. sec. 3, T 3 N, R 12 E). Named on Calaveritas (1962) and San Andreas (1962) 7.5' quadrangles.

Dutchman Creek [MARIPOSA-MERCED]: *stream,* heads in Mariposa County and flows 35 miles to Deadman Creek 12 miles west-southwest of Le Grand in Merced County (lat. 37°11'35" N, long. 120°27'50" W; sec. 32, T 8 S, R 14 E). Named on Chowchilla (1960) and Le Grand (1961) 15' quadrangles, and on Illinois Hill (1962) and Raynor Creek (1961) 7.5' quadrangles. Laizure's (1935) map has the form "Dutchman's Cr." for the name.

Dyer Creek [TUOLUMNE]: *stream,* flows nearly 1 mile to North Fork Tuolumne River 2 miles northeast of Tuolumne (lat. 37°58'45" N, long. 120°12'15" W; sec. 34, T 2 N, R 16 E). Named on Tuolumne (1948) 7.5' quadrangle.

— E —

Eagle Creek [MARIPOSA]: *stream,* flows 2 miles to Merced River nearly 2 miles southwest of Yosemite Village (lat. 37°43'55" N, long. 119°36'35" W); the stream heads west of Eagle Peak (1). Named on Yosemite (1956) 15' quadrangle.

Eagle Creek [TUOLUMNE]:

(1) *stream,* flows 8 miles to Rose Creek 6.25 miles northeast of Columbia (lat. 38°06'20" N, long. 120°19'50" W; near N line sec. 21, T 3 N, R 15 E). Named on Columbia SE (1948), Crandall Peak (1979), and Twain Hart (1979) 7.5' quadrangles.

(2) *stream,* flows 7.5 miles to Middle Fork Stanislaus River at Dardanelle (lat. 38°20'35" N, long. 119°49'55" W; sec. 25, T 6 N, R 19 E); the stream goes through Eagle Meadow. Named on Dardanelle (1979) 7.5' quadrangle. On Dardanelles (1898) 30' quadrangle, the name applies to present Long Valley Creek

Eagle Creek Camp [TUOLUMNE]: *locality,* 3.5 miles west of Crandall Peak (lat. 38°09'15" N, long. 120°12'30" W; sec. 34, T 4 N, R 16 E); the place is along Eagle Creek (1). Named on Crandall Peak (1979) 7.5' quadrangle.

Eagle Island [TUOLUMNE]: *island,* 150 feet long, less than 1 mile north-northeast of Don Pedro Camp in Don Pedro Reservoir (lat. 37°43'35" N, long. 120°24' W; near S line sec. 26, T 2 S, R 14 E). Named on La Grange (1962) 7.5' quadrangle.

Eagle Meadow [TUOLUMNE]: *area,* 4 miles south of Dardanelle (lat. 38°16'50" N, long. 119°50'05" W; near S line sec. 13, T 5 N, R 19 E); the place is less than 1 mile east-northeast of Eagle Peak along Eagle Creek (2). Named on Dardanelle (1979) 7.5' quadrangle.

Eagle Mountain [SAN JOAQUIN]: *peak,* 13 miles south-southwest of Tracy (lat. 37°34'10" N, long. 121°32'10" W; sec. 21, T 4 S, R 4 E). Altitude 3033 feet. Named on Cedar Mountain (1956) 7.5' quadrangle.

Eagle Pass [TUOLUMNE]: *pass,* 10 miles east-northeast of Pinecrest (lat. 38°14'55" N, long. 119°49'35" W; near NE cor. sec. 36, T 5 N, R 19 E); the pass is near the head of Eagle Creek (2). Named on Pinecrest (1956) 15' quadrangle.

Eagle Peak [MARIPOSA]:

(1) *peak,* 1.5 miles west of Yosemite Village (lat. 37°44'45" N, long. 119°36'55" W). Altitude 7779 feet. Named on Yosemite (1956) 15' quadrangle. The feature also was called Eagle Point (Browning, 1986, p. 61). The peak is one of the group called Three Brothers.

(2) *peak,* 1 mile north-northwest of El Portal (lat. 37°41'20" N, long. 119°47'20" W; sec. 8, T 3 S, R 20 E). Altitude 4578 feet. Named on El Portal (1947) 7.5' quadrangle.

Eagle Peak [TUOLUMNE]: *peak,* 4.5 miles south of Dardanelle (lat. 38°16'30" N, long. 119°50'50" W; sec. 23, T 5 N, R 19 E); the peak is less than 1 mile west-southwest of Eagle Meadow. Altitude 9370 feet. Named on Dardanelle (1979) 7.5' quadrangle.

Eagle Peak Creek [MARIPOSA]: *stream,* flows 1.5 miles to Yosemite Creek 2 miles northwest of Yosemite Village (lat. 37° 46' N, long. 119°36'10" W); the stream heads near Eagle Peak (1). Named on Hetch Hetchy Reservoir (1956) 15' quadrangle.

Eagle Peak Meadows [MARIPOSA]: *area,* 2 miles west-northwest of Yosemite Village along Eagle Peak Creek (lat. 37°45'30" N, long. 119°36'45" W); the place is 1 mile north of Eagle Peak (1). Named on Hetch Hetchy Reservoir (1956) 15' quadrangle.

Eagle Point: see **Eagle Peak** [MARIPOSA] (1).

Eagle Spring [STANISLAUS]: *spring,* 3 miles southwest of Crevison Peak (lat. 37°09'30" N, long. 121°13'15" W; near N line sec. 17, T 9 S, R 7 E). Named on Crevison Peak (1955) 7.5' quadrangle.

Eagle Tent: see **Eugene** [STANISLAUS].

Eagle Tree [SAN JOAQUIN]: *locality,* 13 miles west-northwest of Lodi along North Mokelumne River on Staten Island (lat. 38°12'10" N, long. 121°30'35" W). Named on Isleton (1952) 7.5' quadrangle. Postal authorities established Staten post office in 1894, moved it 2 miles south in 1903 when they changed the name to Eagle Tree, and discontinued it in 1904—the name "Staten" was from Staten Island, and the name "Eagle Tree" was from a landmark tree that had the nest of an eagle in it (Salley, p. 63, 212).

Eagle Well [MERCED]: *well,* 4.5 miles east of Ingomar (lat. 37° 11'05" N, long. 120°53'05" W; on E line sec. 5, T 9 S, R 10 E). Named on Ingomar (1960) 7.5' quadrangle. Ingomar (1919) 7.5' quadrangle shows Eagle ranch at the place.

Earhart: see **Amelia Earhart Peak** [TUOLUMNE].

Earnest: see **Camp Earnest** [TUOLUMNE].

East Chinee: see **Campo Salvador**, under **Chinese Camp** [TUOLUMNE].

East Flange Rock [TUOLUMNE]: *relief feature,* 13 miles east-northeast of Pinecrest (lat. 38°14'50" N, long. 119°46'10" W; near SW cor. sec. 27, T 5 N, R 20 E). Named on Pinecrest (1956) 15' quadrangle.

Eastman Lake [MADERA-MARIPOSA]: *lake,* on Madera-Mariposa County line behind a dam on Chowchilla River 4.25 miles west of Raymond (lat. 37°13' N, long. 119°59' W; sec. 22, T 8 S, R 18 E). Named on Raymond (1962, photorevised 1981) 7.5' quadrangle, which has the name "Buchanan Dam" for the dam that forms the lake. United States Board on Geographic Names (1975, p. 5) noted that the name "H.V. Eastman Lake" was mandated by Congressional action and gave the name "Buchanan Reservoir" as a variant. Logan's (1950) map shows a place called Buchanan located about 5 miles west of Raymond near the site of the dam that forms the present lake. Buchanan took its name from Buchanan Hollow, which extends along Chowchilla River for about 2 miles just northeast of the place that Madera County, Mariposa County, and Merced County meet (Clough, p. 78). Postal authorities established Buchanan post office in 1873 and discontinued it in 1904—Buchanan Hollow was named for an early settler (Salley, p. 28).

East Side [SAN JOAQUIN]: *locality,* 5.5 miles west-southwest of Lockeford along Central California Traction Railroad (lat. 38°08'05" N, long. 121°14'30" W; at W line sec. 5, T 3 N, R 7 E). Named on Lockeford (1968) 7.5' quadrangle.

Eaton: see **Mount Eaton** [TUOLUMNE].

Echo Creek [MARIPOSA]: *stream,* flows 8 miles to Merced River 7.5 miles south-southwest of Cathedral Peak (lat. 37°44'30" N, long. 119°26'35" W). Named on Merced Peak (1953) and Tuolumne Meadows (1956) 15' quadrangles. United States Board on Geographic Names (1970, p. 2-3) gave the name "Cathedral Fork" as a variant

Echo Lake [MARIPOSA]: *lake,* 750 feet long, 2 miles south of Cathedral Peak (lat. 37°49' N, long. 119°24'30" W; near E line sec. 26, T 1 S, R 23 E); the lake is 1 mile south-southwest of Echo Peaks. Named on Tuolumne Meadows (1956) 15' quadrangle.

Echo Peaks [MARIPOSA]: *relief features,* about 1 mile south of Cathedral Peak on Mariposa-Tuolumne County line (lat. 37°50' N, long. 119°24' W; sec. 24, T 1 S, R 23 E). Named on Tuolumne Meadows (1956) 15' quadrangle.

Echo Valley [MARIPOSA]: *valley,* 7.25 miles south-southwest of Cathedral Peak (lat. 37°44'45" N, long. 119°26' W); the feature is at the mouth of Echo Creek. Named on Merced Peak (1953) 15' quadrangle.

Edendale [MERCED]: *locality,* 9 miles northeast of Atwood along Yosemite Valley Railroad (lat. 37°26'55" N, long. 120°30'10" W; near SE cor. sec. 35, T 5 S, R 13 E). Named on Winton (1917) 7.5' quadrangle.

Edendale Creek [MERCED]: *stream,* flows 4.25 miles to Canal Creek 6.5 miles northeast of Atwater (lat. 37°25'20" N, long. 120° 31'40" W; sec. 10, T 6 S, R 13 E). Named on Winton (1961) and Yosemite Lake (1962) 7.5' quadrangles.

Edith Lake: see **Edyth Lake** [TUOLUMNE].

Ediza Lake [MADERA]: *lake,* 1700 feet long, 6.25 miles northwest of Devils Postpile along Shadow Creek (lat. 37°41'05" N, long. 119°09'55" W); the lake is 1.5 miles west-southwest of Shadow Lake. Named on Devils Postpile (1953) 15' quadrangle. The feature also was called Little Shadow Lake (Browning, 1988, p. 37).

Edna Lake [MADERA]: *lake,* 0.5 mile long, nearly 1 mile northeast of Merced Peak (lat. 37°38'35" N, long. 119°22'50" W). Named on Merced Peak (1953) 15' quadrangle. R.B. Marshall of United States Geological Survey named the lake for Edna Bowman of San Jose, who later became Mrs. Charles J. Kuhn (United States Board on Geographic Names, 1934, p. 7).

Edna Lake: see **Pinecrest Lake** [TUOLUMNE].

Edna Lake Reservoir: see **Pinecrest Lake** [TUOLUMNE].

Edson Lake [MARIPOSA]: *lake,* 800 feet long, 9 miles south-southeast of Yosemite Village (lat. 37°37'55" N, long. 119°31'25" W; sec. 35, T 3 S, R 22 E). Named on Yosemite (1956) 15' quadrangle. This name is a perversion of the name "Edison Lake" suggested by park rangers Bingaman and Ernst (Browning, 1988, p, 38).

Edwards' Creek: see **Wildcat Creek** [STANISLAUS-TUOLUMNE].

Edyth Lake [TUOLUMNE]: *lake,* 3500 feet long, 16 miles southeast of Pinecrest along Kendrick Creek (lat. 38°03'35" N, long. 119° 45' W; sec. 2, T 2 N, R 20 E). Named on Pinecrest (1956) and Tower Peak (1956) 15' quadrangles. Called Edith Lake on Dardanelles (1898, reprinted 1947) 30' quadrangle. Major W.W. Forsyth named the lake for Edyth Nance, daughter of Colonel Nance (United States Board on Geographic Names, 1934, p. 7). United States Board on Geographic Names (1990, p. 7) approved the form "Edith Lake" for the name—the daughter's name has the form "Edith."

Ehrnbeck Peak [TUOLUMNE]: *peak,* less than 2 miles east-southeast of Tower Peak on Tuolumne-Mono County line (lat. 38°08'15" N, long. 119°30'50" W). Altitude 11,240 feet. Named on Tower Peak (1956) 15' quadrangle. Browning (1986, p. 62-63) associated the name with Lieutenant Arthur R. Ehrnbeck, who reported in 1909 on a road and trail project for Yosemite National Park.

Eighteen Mile House [MADERA]: *locality,* 6.25 miles south-southeast of Raymond (lat. 37°07'40" N, long. 119°52'10" W; sec. 23, T 9 S, R 19 E). Named on Daulton (1921) 7.5' quadrangle.

Eightmile: see **Wawona** [MARIPOSA].

Eight Mile Corners: see **Stockton** [SAN JOAQUIN].

Eight Mile House: see **Collegeville** [SAN JOAQUIN].

Eightmile House [SAN JOAQUIN]: *locality,* 5 miles south-southeast of Lodi (lat. 38°03'25" N, long. 121°15'30" W; near SE cor. sec. 36, T 3 N, R 6 E). Named on Castle (1910) 7.5' quadrangle.

Eight Square Leagues on Stanislaus River [SAN JOAQUIN-STANISLAUS]: *land grant,* at and near Oakdale on San Joaquin-Stanislaus County line. Named on Bachelor Valley (1968), Escalon (1968), Farmington (1968), Oakdale (1968), Riverbank (1969), and Waterford (1969) 7.5' quadrangles. Called Thompson Rancho on Bachelor Valley (1916), Oakdale (1915), Riverbank (1916), Thalheim (1915), Trigo (1915), and Waterford (1916) 7.5' quadrangles. Alpheus B. Thompson received 8 leagues in 1846 and claimed 35,533 acres patented in 1858 (Cowan, p. 35; Cowan listed the grant under the designation "Estanislao, (or) Thompson's").

El Arroyo del Ortigalito: see **Ortigalita Creek** [MERCED].

El Arroyo de Quinto: see **Quinto Creek** [MERCED-SAN JOAQUIN].

El Arroyo de Romero: see **Romero Creek** [MERCED-SAN JOAQUIN].

Elbow Hill [TUOLUMNE]: *peak,* 9 miles west-northwest of Tioga Pass (lat. 37°58'20" N, long. 119°24'10" W). Named on Tuolumne Meadows (1956) 15' quadrangle.

El Capitan [MARIPOSA]: *relief feature,* 3 miles west-southwest of Yosemite Village on the north side of Yosemite Valley (lat. 37° 44' N, long. 119°38'10" W). Named on Yosemite (1956) 15' quadrangle. Lafayette H. Bunnell named the feature in 1880 (United States Board on Geographic Names, 1934, p 8). According to Browning (1986, p. 63), the feature also had the names "Crane Mountain," from sandhill cranes that flew over it, and "Giant's Tower."

El Capitan Gully [MARIPOSA]: *canyon,* drained by a stream that flows 1 mile to Ribbon Creek 3.5 miles west-southwest of Yosemite Village (lat. 37°44' N, long. 119°38'40" W); the feature is 0.5 mile west of El Capitan. Named on Yosemite (1956) 15' quadrangle.

El Capitan Meadow [MARIPOSA]: *area,* 3.25 miles southwest of Yosemite Village (lat. 37°43'20" N, long. 119°38' W); the place is at the base of El Capitan. Named on Yosemite (1956) 15' quadrangle.

Elder Spring [SAN JOAQUIN]: *spring,* 9 miles south of Tracy (lat. 37°36'50" N, long. 121°27'25" W; sec. 6, T 4 S, R 5 E). Named on Lone Tree Creek (1955) 7.5' quadrangle.

El Dorado: see **Mountain Ranch** [CALAVERAS].

El Dorado Bar: see **Melones** [CALAVERAS].

El Dorado Creek [CALAVERAS]: *stream,* flows 4.25 miles to Murry Creek 6.25 miles east-northeast of San Andreas (lat. 38°13'20" N, long. 120°34'15" W; sec. 5, T 4 N, R 13 E). Named on Calaveritas (1962) 7.5' quadrangle.

Eldorado Creek [MARIPOSA]: *stream,* flows 8 miles to Burns Creek 3.5 miles northwest of Santa Cruz Mountain (lat. 37°29'50" N, long. 120°14'15" W; sec. 17, T 5 S, R 16 E). Named on Indian Gulch (1962) 7.5' quadrangle. On Hornitos (1947) 7.5' quadrangle, the name has the form "El Dorado Creek."

Eldorado Landing [SAN JOAQUIN]: *locality,* 6 miles west-northwest of downtown Stockton along San Joaquin River on Roberts Island (lat. 37°59'10" N, long. 121°23'35" W). Named on Holt (1913) 7.5' quadrangle.

Eleanor: see **Lake Eleanor**, under **Lake Eleanor Reservoir** [TUOLUMNE].

Eleanor Creek [TUOLUMNE]: *stream,* formed by the confluence of Bartlett Creek and Kendrick Creek, flows 9.5 miles to Cherry Creek 4.25 miles north-northwest of Mather (lat. 37°56'10" N, long. 119°53'45" W; near S line sec. 16, T 1 N, R 19 E). Named on Lake Eleanor (1956) and Pinecrest (1956) 15' quadrangles. United States Board on Geographic Names (1933a, p. 285) rejected the name "Lake River" for present Eleanor Creek. On

Dardanelles (1898) 30' quadrangle, present Kendrick Creek is called East Fork Eleanor Cr.

Eleanor Lake [TUOLUMNE]: *lake,* 2200 feet long, 1.5 miles east-northeast of present Pinecrest along South Fork Stanislaus River (lat. 38°12'05" N, long. 119°58'10" W). Named on Dardanelles (1898, reprinted 1947) 30' quadrangle. Pinecrest (1979) 7.5' quadrangle does not show Eleanor Lake, which apparently is encompassed by present Pinecrest Lake.

Eleanor Lake Reservoir: see **Lake Eleanor Reservoir** [TUOLUMNE].

Electra Peak [MADERA]: *peak,* 8.5 miles northeast of Merced Peak (lat. 37°42'20" N, long. 119°15'35" W). Altitude 12,442 feet. Named on Merced Peak (1953) 15' quadrangle.

Elephant Rock [MARIPOSA]: *relief feature,* 7.5 miles west-southwest of Yosemite Village (lat. 37°42'50" N, long. 119°42'45" W; sec. 36, T 2 S, R 20 E). Named on Yosemite (1956) 15' quadrangle.

Elevenmile: see **Wawona** [MARIPOSA].

Eleven Mile Creek: see **Bishop Creek** [MARIPOSA].

Elevenmile Creek [MARIPOSA]: *stream,* flows 4 miles to Bishop Creek 11 miles south-southwest of Yosemite Village (lat. 37°36'45" N, long. 119°41'40" W; sec. 5, T 4 S, R 21 E). Named on Yosemite (1956) 15' quadrangle. The name is from Eleven Mile Station, a stage stop located 11 miles from Wawona (Browning, 1986, p. 64). United States Board on Geographic Names (1991, p. 6) approved the name "Rail Creek" for a stream, 2 miles long, that joins Elevenmile Creek 6.4 miles north-northwest of Wawona (lat. 37°37'44" N, long. 119°41'40" W; sec. 32, T 3 S, R 21 E), and rejected the name "Elevenmile Creek" for this stream.

11-Mile House: see **Wawona** [MARIPOSA].

Eleven Mile Station: see **Wawona** [MARIPOSA].

Elgin: see **Dos Palos** [MERCED].

Eli Hill [STANISLAUS]: *peak,* 3 miles west of Crevison Peak (lat. 37°11'50" N, long. 121°14'30" W; sec. 31, T 8 S, R 7 E). Altitude 2042 feet. Named on Crevison Peak (1955) 7.5' quadrangle.

Elizabeth Lake [TUOLUMNE]: *lake,* 1500 feet long, 7.5 miles southwest of Tioga Pass (lat. 37°50'45" N, long. 119°22'05" W). Named on Tuolumne Meadows (1956) 15' quadrangle. R.B. Marshall of United States Geological Survey named the lake in 1909 for a daughter of Dr. and Mrs. Samuel E. Simmons (United States Board on Geographic Names, 1934, p. 8).

Elizabeth Peak [TUOLUMNE]: *peak,* 2 miles north-northwest of Twain Harte (lat. 38°03'45" N, long. 120°14'50" W; near NW cor. sec. 5, T 2 N, R 16 E). Altitude 4939 feet. Named on Twain Harte (1979) 7.5' quadrangle. Called Mount Elizabeth on Big Trees (1891) 30' quadrangle.

Elkhorn: see **Indian Gulch** [MARIPOSA] (3).

Elk Horn Inn: see **Banta** [SAN JOAQUIN].

Elkhorn Station [CALAVERAS]: *locality,* 4.5 miles west-southwest of Angels Camp (lat. 38°03'05" N, long. 120°37'25" W; sec. 2, T 2 N, R 12 E). Named on Angels Camp (1962) 7.5' quadrangle.

Elk Ravine [SAN JOAQUIN]: *canyon,* drained by a stream that flows 4.25 miles to Corral Hollow 6.5 miles south-southwest of Tracy (lat. 37°39'20" N, long. 121°29'15" W; sec. 24, T 3 S, R 4 E). Named on Midway (1953) and Tracy (1954) 7.5' quadrangles.

Elliott [SAN JOAQUIN]: *locality,* 5.25 miles north-northwest of Lockeford (lat. 38°14'05" N, long. 121°10'50" W). Named on Lockeford (1908) 7.5' quadrangle. The place first was called Hawk's Corners (Hillman and Covello, p. 208). Postal authorities established Orr's Ranch post office in 1858, changed the name to Elliott in 1863, discontinued it in 1871, reestablished it in 1872, and discontinued it in 1901—the name "Orr" was for Fountain J. Orr, pioneer rancher and first postmaster at Orr's Ranch post office; the name "Elliott" was for J. Elliott, a pioneer rancher (Salley, p. 67, 163).

Elliott Corner [MARIPOSA]: *locality,* 10.5 miles east of Mariposa (lat. 37°27'45" N, long. 119°46'25" W; near SW cor. sec. 27, T 5 S, R 20 E). Named on Stumpfield Mountain (1947) 7.5' quadrangle.

Ellis [MARIPOSA]: *locality,* 8 miles north-northwest of Hornitos along Yosemite Valley Railroad (lat. 37°37' N, long. 120°16'20" W; sec. 1, T 4 S, R 15 E). Named on Merced Falls (1944) 15' quadrangle.

Ellis [SAN JOAQUIN]: *locality,* 2.5 miles southwest of Tracy along Southern Pacific Railroad (lat. 37°43'15" N, long. 121°27'35" W; sec. 31, T 2 S, R 5 E). Named on Tracy (1916) 7.5' quadrangle. Postal authorities established Ellis post office in 1870 and discontinued it in 1878 (Frickstad, p. 160). The place first was called Corral because a branch line to Corral Hollow left the main rail line there (Mosier, 1983, p. 47).

Ellis Meadow: see **Benedict Meadow** [MADERA].

Ellisworth: see **Avena** [SAN JOAQUIN].

Elmdale: see **Denair** [STANISLAUS].

Elmwood: see **Denair** [STANISLAUS].

Elmwood Colony: see **Denair** [STANISLAUS].

Elmwood Tract [SAN JOAQUIN]: *area,* 5 miles west-northwest of downtown Stockton (lat. 37°59'15" N, long. 121°22'45" W). Named on Holt (1978) and Stockton West (1952) 7.5' quadrangles. Holt (1913) 7.5' quadrangle shows the place as part of Wright Tract.

El Nido [MERCED]: *village,* 15 miles west-southwest of Le Grand (lat. 37°08' N, long. 120°29'30" W; on W line sec. 19, T 9 S, R 14 E). Named on El Nido (1960) 7.5' quadrangle. Postal authorities established El Nido post office in 1920 (Frickstad, p. 100).

El Nido Reservoir [MERCED]: *lake,* 1650 feet long, 11.5 miles west-southwest of Le Grand (lat. 37°08'40" N, long. 120°25'35" W; sec. 15, T 9 S, R 14 E); the lake is 3.5 miles east-northeast of El Nido. Named on El Nido (1960) 7.5' quadrangle.

El Pescadero [SAN JOAQUIN]: *land grant,* 13 miles south-southwest of downtown Stockton. Named on Clifton Court Forebay (1978), Lathrop (1952), Union Island (1978), and Vernalis (1969) 7.5' quadrangles. Antonio Maria Pico received 8 leagues in 1843; Pico and Henry M. Naglee claimed 35,546 acres patented in 1865 (Cowan, p. 59).

El Pescadero [SAN JOAQUIN-STANISLAUS]: *land grant,* west of Modesto and west of San Joaquin River on San Joaquin-Stanislaus County line. Named on Brush Lake (1969), Lathrop (1952), Ripon (1969), Solyo (1953), Vernalis (1969), and Westley (1969) 7.5' quadrangles. Valentin Higuera and Rafael Felix received 8 leagues in 1843; Hiram Grimes and others claimed 34,446 acres patented in 1858 (Cowan, p. 59).

El Pinal [SAN JOAQUIN]: *locality,* 1.5 miles north-northeast of downtown Stockton along Southern Pacific Railroad (lat. 37°58'55" N, long. 121°16'55" W). Named on Stockton West (1952) 7.5' quadrangle.

El Portal [MARIPOSA]: *village,* 11.5 miles west-southwest of Yosemite Village along Merced River (lat. 37°40'35" N, long. 119° 46'45" W; on E line sec. 17, T 3 S, R 20 E). Named on El Portal (1947) 7.5' quadrangle. Postal authorities established El Portal post office in 1907 (Frickstad, p. 91). The place was Yosemite Valley Railroad's railhead near the entrance to Yosemite National Park—*el portal* means "the gateway" in Spanish (Johnston, p. 15).

El Rio de Nuestra Senora de la Merced: see **Merced River** [MADERA-MARIPOSA-MERCED].

Emerald Lake [MADERA]: *lake,* 900 feet long, 8 miles north-northwest of Devils Postpile (lat. 37°43'35" N, long. 119°09'50" W); the lake is north of Garnet Lake and Ruby Lake. Named on Devils Postpile (1953) 15' quadrangle.

Emerald Pool [MARIPOSA]: *lake,* 400 feet long, 3 miles east-southeast of Yosemite Village (lat. 37°43'40" N, long. 119°32'30" W). Named on Yosemite (1956) 15' quadrangle. The name dates from 1856; that same year the lake also was given the name "Frances" for Mrs. Jane Frances Neal, the first white woman to visit the place (Browning, 1988, p. 40-41).

Emeric Creek [MARIPOSA]: *stream,* flows 3.25 miles to Fletcher Creek 5.25 miles south of Cathedral Peak (lat. 37°46'20" N, long. 119°23'15" W); the stream goes through Emeric Lake. Named on Tuolumne Meadows (1956) 15' quadrangle. Lieutenant N.F. McClure named the creek for Henry F. Emeric, for whom he named Emeric Lake (Browning, 1986, p. 65).

Emeric Lake [MARIPOSA]: *lake,* 2400 feet long, 5 miles south-southeast of Cathedral Peak (lat. 37°46'35" N, long. 119°23'05" W). Named on Tuolumne Meadows (1956) 15' quadrangle. Lieutenant N.F. McClure named the lake in 1895 for Henry F. Emeric, president of California Board of Fish Commissioners (United States Board on Geographic Names, 1934, p. 8).

Emery Reservoir [CALAVERAS]: *lake,* behind a dam on McKinney Creek 10 miles east-northeast of San Andreas (lat. 38°14'50" N, long. 120°30'10" W; sec. 35, T 5 N, R 13 E). Named on Calaveritas (1962), Murphys (1948), and Rail Road Flat (1948) 7.5' quadrangles.

Emigrant Lake [TUOLUMNE]: *lake,* 1.5 miles long, 8.5 miles west-northwest of Tower Peak along North Fork Cherry Creek (lat. 38° 10'25" N, long. 119°41'50" W). Named on Tower Peak (1956) 15' quadrangle. United States Board on Geographic Names (1965c, p. 9, 11, 12) approved the name "Fraser Lakes" for a group of four small lakes located about 0.3 mile south of Emigrant Lake (lat. 38°10'10" N, long. 119°41'55" W), approved the name "Ridge Lake" for a small lake situated about 4 miles northwest of Emigrant Lake (lat. 38°13'15" N, long. 119°44'40" W), and approved the name "W Lake" for a small lake found about 0.6 mile southeast of the northeast end of Emigrant Lake (lat. 38°10'18" N, long. 119° 40'45" W).

Emigrant Lake: see **High Emigrant Lake** [TUOLUMNE]; **Middle Emigrant Lake** [TUOLUMNE].

Emigrant Meadow [TUOLUMNE]: *valley,* 7 miles northwest of Tower Peak at the head of North Fork Cherry Creek (lat. 38°12'15" N, long. 119°39' W); the valley is west of Emigrant Pass. Named on Tower Peak (1956) 15' quadrangle.

Emigrant Meadow Lake [TUOLUMNE]: *lake,* 0.5 mile long, nearly 7 miles northwest of Tower Peak (lat. 38°12'05" N, long. 119°38'50" W); the lake is in Emigrant Meadow. Named on Tower Peak (1956) 15' quadrangle.

Emigrant Pass [TUOLUMNE]: *pass,* 6 miles northwest of Tower Peak on Tuolumne-Mono County line (lat. 38°12' N, long. 119°37'50" W); the pass is east of Emigrant Meadow. Named on Tower Peak (1956) 7.5' quadrangle.

Emily Lake [MADERA]: *lake,* 800 feet long, 4 miles northwest of Devils Postpile (lat. 37°40'20" N, long. 119°07'15" W). Named on Devils Postpile

(1953) 15' quadrangle.

Emory: see **Clearing House** [MARIPOSA].

Emory's Ferry: see **Oakdale** [STANISLAUS].

Empire [STANISLAUS]: *town,* 5 miles east of Modesto (lat. 37°38'25" N, long. 120°54'10" W; around SE cor. sec. 30, T 3 S, R 10 E). Named on Riverbank (1969) 7.5' quadrangle. John Gage Marvin founded Empire City in April of 1850 (DeFerrari *in* Stoddart, p. 111) on the south side of Tuolumne River at the head of navigation about 1 mile south of present Empire—the town of Empire was laid out later as a trade center for farmers (Hoover, Rensch, and Rensch, p. 541-542). Postal authorities established Empire post office in 1851 and discontinued it the same year; they established modern Empire post office in 1910 (Frickstad, p. 200, 215). Gibbes' (1850) map shows Empire City on the south bank of Tuolumne River, and shows a place called Crescent City located on the north bank of the river 2 miles below Empire City. Goddard's (1857) map shows a place called Adams located on the south side of the river between Empire City and Tuolumne City. Bancroft (1888, p. 514) noted that in 1849 Dr. Adams founded Adamsville—this apparently is at the place called Adams on Goddard's (1857) map. Goddard's (1857) map also shows a place called Davis Ferry located on Tuolumne River 8 miles east of Empire City. Hoover, Rensch, and Rensch (p. 542) noted that a place called Aspinwall was on the south side of the river several miles above Empire City.

Empire Camp: see **Empire Meadow** [MARIPOSA].

Empire City: see **Empire** [STANISLAUS].

Empire Creek [CALAVERAS]: *stream,* flows 3.5 miles to Black Creek (1) nearly 2 miles east of Copperopolis (lat. 37°58'30" N, long. 120°36'20" W; at S line sec. 36, T 2 N, R 12 E). Named on Angels Camp (1962) and Melones Dam (1962) 7.5' quadrangles.

Empire Cut [SAN JOAQUIN]: *water feature,* joins Middle River 13 miles west of downtown Stockton (lat. 37°58'10" N, long. 121°31'50" W). Named on Holt (1978) and Woodward Island (1978) 7.5' quadrangles. Called Empire Slough on Woodward Island (1913) 7.5' quadrangle.

Empire Meadow [MARIPOSA]: *area,* 5.5 miles north of Wawona (lat. 37°37' N, long. 119°38'30" W; sec. 2, T 4 S, R 21 E). Named on Yosemite (1956) 15' quadrangle. Hoffmann and Gardner's (1863-1867) map shows a place called Empire Camp located along Alder Creek, probably at or near present Empire Meadow.

Empire Slough: see **Empire Cut** [SAN JOAQUIN].

Empire Tract [SAN JOAQUIN]: *island,* 3.5 miles long, 3 miles south of Terminous between Little Potato Slough, White Slough, Honker Cut, Disappointment Slough, Little Connection Slough, and San Joaquin River (lat. 38°04' N, long. 121°29' W). Named on Terminous (1978) 7.5' quadrangle.

Ensalada Creek: see **Salado Creek** [STANISLAUS].

Erickson Slough [STANISLAUS]: *water feature,* 6.5 miles north of Oakdale in Woodward Reservoir between Whale Island and the north shore of the reservoir (lat. 37°51'35" N, long. 120°50'50" W). Named on Oakdale (1968) 7.5' quadrangle.

Escalon [SAN JOAQUIN]: *town,* 12 miles east of Manteca (lat. 37° 47'45" N, long. 120°59'30" W; in and near sec. 4, T 2 S, R 9 E). Named on Avena (1952) and Escalon (1968) 7.5' quadrangles. Postal authorities established Escalon post office in 1898 (Frickstad, p. 160), and the town incorporated in 1957. James W. Jones laid out the community on his land in 1895 and 1896; supposedly he chose the name "Escalon" simply because he liked the sound of the word—*escalon* means "step of a stair" in Spanish (Gudde, 1949, p. 109). Thompson and West's (1879) map shows Burwood post office situated about 3 miles southeast of the site of present Escalon (SE quarter sec. 14, T 2 S, R 9 E); postal authorities established it in 1859 and discontinued it in 1898 (Salley, p. 30). Thompson and West's (1879) map shows a place called Lone Tree House (near NE cor. sec. 28, T 1 S, R 9 E) that was started in the early 1850's 3 miles north of present Escalon (Hoover, Rensch, and Rensch, p. 370). A travelers stop called Blue Tent Tavern was 1 mile east of present Escalon (Hoover, Rensch, and Rensch, p. 373).

Esmar [STANISLAUS]: *locality,* 6 miles southeast of Modesto along Southern Pacific Railroad (lat. 37°34' N, long. 120°55'40" W; near S line sec. 24, T 4 S, R 9 E). Named on Ceres (1918) 7.5' quadrangle.

Esmeralda [CALAVERAS]: *locality,* 8 miles east-southeast of San Andreas (lat. 38°09'15" N, long. 120°32'10" W). Named on Jackson (1902) 30' quadrangle. Postal authorities established Esmeralda post office in 1887, changed the name to Esmerelda in 1902, and discontinued it in 1943—the name is from Esmeralda mine (Salley, p. 70).

Esperanza: see **Esperanza Creek** [CALAVERAS].

Esperanza Creek [CALAVERAS]: *stream,* flows 11.5 miles to North Fork Calaveras River 5 miles west-southwest of Rail Road Flat (lat. 38°19'05" N, long. 120°35'50" W; near E line sec. 1, T 5 N, R 12 E). Named on Fort Mountain (1979) and Rail Road Flat (1948) 7.5' quadrangles. Doble (p. 86) recorded a visit in 1852 to a mining camp called Esperanza that was along what he called "North fork of the Caliveras [River]." Camp (*in* Doble, p. 299) noted that Esperanza may have been a short distance up Esperanza Creek from the mouth.

Esperanza Valley [CALAVERAS]: *valley,* 6.5 miles west-southwest of Blue Mountain (lat. 38°17'55" N, long. 120°28'15" W; near S line sec. 7, T 5 N, R 14 E); the valley is along Esperanza Creek. Named on Fort Mountain (1979) 7.5' quadrangle.

Estanislao: see **Eight Square Leagues on Stanislaus River** [SAN JOAQUIN-STANISLAUS].

Eugene [STANISLAUS]: *locality,* 9 miles north of Oakdale (lat. 37° 53'35" N, long. 120°50'45" W; sec. 35, T 1 N, R 10 E). Named on Bachelor Valley (1968) 7.5' quadrangle. Eugene is the site of an early hostelry called Eagle Tent, and later known as Twenty-eight Mile House (Brotherton, p. 86). Postal authorities established Twenty Six Mile House post office in 1870, moved it 2 miles east and changed the name to Eugene in 1894, and discontinued it in 1930; the place was a stage stop located 26 miles from Stockton on the Sonora Road (Salley, p. 71, 226). The name "Eugene" was for Eugene Kelliher, whose parents operated a store, post office, and bar at the site (Paden and Schlichtmann, p. 21). A stopping place called Blue Cottage was about 6 miles beyond Eugene on the road to Knights Ferry (Brotherton, p. 87).

Eureka Valley [TUOLUMNE]: *area,* 2.5 miles east of Dardanelle along Middle Fork Stanislaus River (lat. 38°20'25" N, long. 119° 47'10" W; sec. 28, T 6 N, R 20 E). Named on Dardanelle (1979) 7.5' quadrangle.

Evans Creek [STANISLAUS]: *stream,* flows about 2.5 miles to a watercourse 0.5 mile south-southwest of La Grange (lat. 37°39'10" N, long. 120°27'30" W; sec. 20, T 3 S, R 14 E). Named on La Grange (1962) 7.5' quadrangle.

Evans Gulch: see **Rocky Gulch** [MARIPOSA].

Evelyn Lake [TUOLUMNE]: *lake,* 2100 feet long, 8 miles south-southwest of Tioga Pass (lat. 37°48'20" N, long. 119°19'30" W). Named on Tuolumne Meadows (1956) 15' quadrangle. The name commemorates Evelyn Clough (United States Board on Geographic Names, 1934, p. 8).

Evergreen Lodge [TUOLUMNE]: *locality,* 0.5 mile south-southwest of Mather (lat. 37°52'30" N, long. 119°51'25" W; near N line sec. 11, T 1 S, R 19 E). Named on Lake Eleanor (1956) 15' quadrangle.

Excelsior Mountain [TUOLUMNE]: *peak,* 6.25 miles southeast of Matterhorn Peak on Tuolumne-Mono County line (lat. 38°01'25" N, long. 119°18'15" W; near W line sec. 14, T 2 N, R 24 E). Altitude 12,446 feet. Named on Matterhorn Peak (1956) 15' quadrangle.

Exchequer [MARIPOSA]:

(1) *locality,* 6.25 miles north-northwest of Hornitos along Yosemite Valley Railroad (lat. 37°35'15" N, long. 120°16' W). Named on Sonora (1897) 30' quadrangle. Postal authorities established Exchequer post office in 1907, discontinued it in 1919, reestablished it in 1922, and discontinued it in 1926 (Frickstad, p. 91). Water of Lake McClure now covers the site. California Mining Bureau's (1909b) map shows a place called Varain located along the railroad 5 miles north of Exchequer. Postal authorities established Varain post office in 1907 and discontinued it in 1919; the name was for John B. Varain, first postmaster (Salley, p. 230).

(2) *locality,* 6.25 miles north-northwest of Hornitos along Yosemite Valley Railroad (lat. 37°35' N, long. 120°17'15" W; sec. 14, T 4 S, R 15 E). Named on Merced Falls (1944) 15' quadrangle.

Exchequer Reservoir: see **Lake McClure** [MARIPOSA].

Experimental Gulch [TUOLUMNE]: *canyon,* drained by a stream that flows 1.25 miles to South Fork Stanislaus River 2.5 miles north-northeast of Columbia (lat. 38°04'05" N, long. 120°23'05" W; sec. 36, T 3 N, R 14 E). Named on Columbia (1948) 7.5' quadrangle, which shows Experimental mine in the canyon.

— F —

Fahey Meadow [TUOLUMNE]: *area,* 4 miles south-southeast of Long Barn (lat. 38°02'10" N, long. 120°06'45" W; near S line sec. 9, T 2 N, R 17 E). Named on Hull Creek (1979) 7.5' quadrangle.

Fahrens Creek [MERCED]: *stream,* flows 13 miles to a ditch 1.5 miles north-northwest of Merced (lat. 37°19'30" N, long. 120°29'45" W; sec. 13, T 7 S, R 13 E). Named on Merced (1961) and Yosemite Lake (1962) 7.5' quadrangles. Called Farahns Creek on Hopeton (1916) 7.5' quadrangle.

Fairchild: see **French Camp** [SAN JOAQUIN].

Fairmead [MADERA]: *village,* 11 miles northwest of Madera (lat. 37°04'35" N, long. 120°11'35" W; sec. 11, T 10 S, R 16 E). Named on Berenda (1961) 7.5' quadrangle. Postal authorities established Fairmead post office in 1913 and discontinued it in 1940 (Frickstad, p. 85).

Fair Oaks [SAN JOAQUIN]: *district,* 2 miles east of downtown Stockton (lat. 37°57'30" N, long. 121°15' W). Named on Stockton East (1952) and Stockton West (1952) 7.5' quadrangles. On Stockton (1913) 7.5' quadrangle, the name has the form "Fairoaks."

Fairview Dome [TUOLUMNE]: *peak,* 8.5 miles west-southwest of Tioga Pass (lat. 37°52'15" N, long. 119°24'10" W; near NW cor. sec. 12, T 1 S, R 23 E). Altitude 9731 feet. Named on Tuolumne Meadows (1956) 15' quadrangle. United States Board on Geographic Names (1933a, p. 296) rejected the names "Soda Spring Dome" and "Soda Springs Butte" for the feature. John Muir used the names "Glacier Monument" and "Tuolumne Glacier Monument" for the peak (Browning, 1986, p. 67).

Fall Canyon [STANISLAUS]: *canyon,* drained by a stream that flows 2.25 miles to Del Puerto Canyon 1.5 miles northwest of Copper Mountain (lat. 37°25'45" N, long. 121°20'10" W; sec. 8, T 6 S, R 6 E). Named on Copper Mountain (1956) 7.5' quadrangle.

Fall River: see **Falls Creek** [TUOLUMNE].

Falls: see **The Falls** [MADERA].

Falls Creek [TUOLUMNE]: *stream,* flows 21 miles to Hetch Hetchy Reservoir 7.5 miles northeast of Mather (lat. 37°57'50" N, long. 119°45'50" W; sec. 10, T 1 N, R 20 E). Named on Hetch Hetchy Reservoir (1956), Lake Eleanor (1956), and Tower Peak (1956) 15' quadrangles. United States Board on Geographic Names (1933a, p. 297) rejected the name "Fall River" for the stream.

Falls Ridge [TUOLUMNE]: *ridge,* west-northwest-trending, 3.5 miles long, 11 miles west of Tioga Pass (lat. 37°55' N, long. 119°28' W); the ridge is southwest of Waterwheel Falls, LeConte Falls, and California Falls. Named on Tuolumne Meadows (1956) 15' quadrangle.

Farahns Creek: see **Fahrens Creek** [MERCED].

Farmington [SAN JOAQUIN]: *village,* 16 miles east of downtown Stockton (lat. 37°55'50" N, long. 120°59'55" W; around NW cor. sec. 21, T 1 N, R 9 E). Named on Farmington (1968) and Peters (1952) 7.5' quadrangles. George Theyer and David Wells settled at the site in 1848 on what they called Oregon ranch, and later they opened a travelers stop there that they called Oregon Tent; Dr. W.B. Stamper laid out a town at the place in 1858 and named it Farmington for its location in rich farming country (Hoover, Rensch, and Rensch, p. 373). A travelers stop located 3 miles east of present Farmington was called Murietta House, a hostelry located 4 miles east of present Farmington was called Texas Tent, and a hostelry built in 1850 less than 1 mile west of present Farmington was called Wisconsin House (Brotherton, p. 85). Postal authorities established Fourteen Mile House post office 14 miles east of Stockton on the route to the mines in 1857, discontinued it the same year, and reestablished it in 1858; they changed the post office name to Marietta in 1858 and to Farmington in 1862—a group of farmers from Marietta, Georgia, gave the name "Marietta" to the place (Salley, p. 79, 133).

Farmington Flood Control Basin [SAN JOAQUIN-STANISLAUS]: *intermittent lake,* on San Joaquin-Stanislaus County line behind a dam on Littlejohns Creek and Rock Creek 4 miles east-southeast of Farmington (lat. 37°54'30" N, long. 120°56' W; sec. 25, T 1 N, R 9 E). Named on Bachelor Valley (1968), Escalon (1968), and Farmington (1968) 7.5' quadrangles.

Fawn Canyon: see **Little Fawn Canyon** [STANISLAUS].

Fawn Lake [TUOLUMNE]: *lake,* 1000 feet long, 9 miles west-southwest of Tower Peak (lat. 38°06'50" N, long. 119°42'20" W). Named on Tower Peak (1956) 15' quadrangle.

Fay Island [SAN JOAQUIN]: *island,* 3300 feet long, 15 miles west of Stockton along Old River (lat. 37°56'55" N, long. 121°33'45" W). Named on Woodward Island (1978) 7.5' quadrangle.

Feldspar Valley: see **Long Meadow** [MARIPOSA].

Feliciana Creek [MARIPOSA]: *stream,* flows 4.5 miles to Merced River 9 miles west-southwest of El Portal (lat. 37°38'05" N, long. 119°56' W; sec. 36, T 3 S, R 18 E). Named on Feliciana Mountain (1947) and Kinsley (1947) 7.5' quadrangles. According to Gudde (1975, p. 114), this stream should be called Slate Gulch, and the name "Feliciana Creek" should be applied to a stream that heads near Feliciana mine and flows westerly into Bear Creek (1) about 1 mile south of the confluence of Bear Creek (1) and Merced River.

Feliciana Mountain [MARIPOSA]: *peak,* 3.5 miles north of Midpines (lat. 37°35'40" N, long. 119°55'05" W; near S line sec. 7, T 4 S, R 19 E). Altitude 4174 feet. Named on Feliciana Mountain (1947) 7.5' quadrangle.

Felix [CALAVERAS]: *locality,* 9.5 miles west-southwest of Angels Camp in Salt Spring Valley (lat. 38°01'45" N, long. 120°42'50" W; sec. 13, T 2 N, R 11 E). Named on Salt Spring Valley (1962) 7.5' quadrangle. Postal authorities established Felix post office in 1896 and discontinued it in 1923; the name is for Madame Felix of Salt Spring Valley (Salley, p. 73).

Fellows Spring [STANISLAUS]: *spring,* 2 miles south-southwest of Copper Mountain along Adobe Creek (lat. 37°23'35" N, long. 121° 20'05" W; sec. 20, T 6 S, R 6 E). Named on Copper Mountain (1956) 7.5' quadrangle.

Femmon: see **Nipinnawasee** [MADERA].

Femmons [TUOLUMNE]: *locality,* nearly 6 miles east-southeast of Duckwall Mountain (lat. 37°56'20" N, long. 120°01'15" W; sec. 17, T 1 N, R 18 E). Named on Duckwall Mountain (1948) 7.5' quadrangle.

Fennessy [TUOLUMNE]: *locality,* 9.5 miles northwest of Parsons (present Strawberry) along Griswold Creek (present North Fork Griswold Creek) (lat. 38°16'40" N, long. 120°09'25" W). Named on Big Trees (1891) 30' quadrangle.

Fergus [MERCED]: *locality,* 4.5 miles east-southeast of Atwater along Southern Pacific Railroad (lat 37°19'10" N, long. 120°32'05" W; sec. 15, T 7 S, R 13 E). Named on Atwater (1961) 15' quadrangle. Atwater (1918) 7.5' quadrangle has the name at a place along the railroad 1 mile closer to Atwood (near center sec. 16, T 7 S, R 13 E).

Ferguson Ridge [MARIPOSA]: *ridge,* north-northwest-trending, 4 miles long, 7 miles west-southwest of El Portal (lat. 37°38'30" N, long. 119°54' W). Named on El Portal (1947) 15' quadrangle.

Fernandez Creek [MADERA]: *stream,* flows 1.25 miles to West Fork Granite Creek nearly 4 miles southeast of Merced Peak (lat. 37°35'25" N, long. 119°21'10" W); the stream heads near Fernandez Pass. Named on Merced Peak (1953) 15' quadrangle.

Fernandez Lakes [MADERA]: *lakes,* largest 800 feet long, nearly 4 miles south-southeast of Merced Peak (lat. 37°35' N, long. 119°22'20" W); the lakes are east of Fernandez Pass. Named on Merced Peak (1953) 15' quadrangle.

Fernandez Pass [MADERA]: *pass,* 3.25 miles south of Merced Peak (lat. 37°35'15" N, long. 119°23' W); the pass is near the head of Fernandez Creek. Named on Merced Peak (1953) 15' quadrangle. Captain H.C. Benson, acting superintendent of Yosemite National Park, named the pass for First Sergeant Joseph Fernandez, who was commended for his assistance in planting fish (United States Board on Geographic Names, 1934, p. 9).

Fern Island [SAN JOAQUIN]: *island,* 0.5 mile long, 5.5 miles south of Terminous in San Joaquin River (lat. 38°02' N, long. 121°29'15" W). Named on Terminous (1978) 7.5' quadrangle, which shows the feature made up largely of marsh and water.

Fern Lake [MADERA]: *lake,* 750 feet long, 3 miles west-southwest of Devils Postpile (lat. 37°36'25" N, long. 119°08' W). Named on Devils Postpile (1953) 15' quadrangle.

Fern Spring [MARIPOSA]: *spring,* 5 miles west-southwest of Yosemite Village in Yosemite Valley (lat. 37°42'55" N, long. 119° 39'50" W). Named on Yosemite (1956) 15' quadrangle.

Ferrin: see **Nairn** [MERCED].

Fiddlers Green [TUOLUMNE]: *area,* 2.5 miles north-northeast of Pinecrest (lat. 38°13'20" N, long. 119°58'20" W; sec. 11, T 4 N, R 18 E). Named on Pinecrest (1979) 7.5' quadrangle.

Fifteen Mile House: see **Linden** [SAN JOAQUIN].

Fine Gold [MADERA]: *locality,* 6.5 miles west-southwest of North Fork (lat. 37°11'30" N, long. 119°37' W; near E line sec. 36, T 8 S, R 21 E); the place is along Fine Gold Creek. Named on Millerton Lake (1945) 15' quadrangle. Postal authorities established Fine Gold post office in 1881 and discontinued it in 1882 (Frickstad, p. 85). When they established a new post office called Gold a little way to the east in 1894, the inhabitants of the community called Fine Gold moved there; postal authorities discontinued Gold post office in 1907 (Clough, p. 79; Frickstad, p. 85). The name "Fine Gold" is the Anglicized form of the Spanish term *Oro Fino* (Gudde, 1975, p. 115).

Fine Gold Creek [MADERA]: *stream,* flows 18 miles to Millerton Lake 5.25 miles south-southeast of O'Neals (lat. 37°03'30" N, long. 119°38'55" W; sec. 14, T 10 S, R 21 E). Named on Bass Lake (1953) and Millerton Lake (1965) 15' quadrangles. North Fork enters from the northwest 6.5 miles northeast of O'Neals; it is 6.5 miles long and is named on Bass Lake (1953) and Millerton Lake (1965) 15' quadrangles. Clough (p. 79) used the name "Finegold Gulch" for the canyon of Fine Gold Creek.

Fine Gold Creek: see **Little Fine Gold Creek** [MADERA].

Finegold Gulch: see **Fine Gold Creek** [MADERA].

Finger Peaks [TUOLUMNE]: *relief features,* 1.5 miles west-southwest of Matterhorn Peak (lat. 38°05'15" N, long. 119°24'20" W). Named on Matterhorn Peak (1956) 15' quadrangle.

Finnegan Cut [STANISLAUS]: *water feature,* 3 miles long, diverges from San Joaquin River and carries water past a series of meanders of that river before returning to the main stream 11 miles west of Modesto (lat. 37°38'10" N, long. 121°12'15" W). Named on Ripon (1969) and Westley (1969) 7.5' quadrangles. Ripon (1915) 7.5' quadrangle has the name "Finnegan Cutoff" for present Riley Slough as well as for the connection of present Riley Slough to present Finnegan Cut. Dillon (1982, p. 31) noted that a series of sloughs called Lagunas de Guadalupe in early Spanish days formerly occupied the site of present Finnegan's Cut-off.

Finnegan Cutoff: see **Finnegan Cut** [STANISLAUS].

Finnegan Falls [STANISLAUS]: *waterfall,* 12.5 miles east of Modesto along Finnegan Cutoff (present Riley Slough) (lat. 37°39'30" N, long. 121°13'40" W; sec. 20, T 3 S, R 7 E). Named on Ripon (1915) 7.5' quadrangle.

Fireplace Bluffs [MARIPOSA]: *relief feature,* 5.5 miles west-southwest of Yosemite Village on the north side of Yosemite Valley (lat. 37°43'55" N, long. 119°41' W). Named on Yosemite (1956) 15' quadrangle.

Fireplace Creek [MARIPOSA]: *stream,* flows 2 miles to Merced River 5.5 miles west-southwest of Yosemite Village (lat. 37°43'10" N, long. 119°40'55" W); the stream goes past Fireplace Bluffs. Named on Yosemite (1956) 15' quadrangle.

First Creek [TUOLUMNE]: *stream,* flows nearly 3 miles to Hatch Creek 4.5 miles south-southwest of Moccasin (lat. 37°45'05" N, long. 120°19'45" W; sec. 21, T 2 S, R 15 E); the stream is south of Second Creek. Named on Moccasin (1948) 7.5' quadrangle.

First Garrote: see **Groveland** [TUOLUMNE].

Fish Camp [MARIPOSA]: *settlement,* 18 miles east of Mariposa along Big Creek (lat. 37°28'40" N, long. 119°38'15" W; sec. 23, T 5 S, R 21 E). Named on Bass Lake (1953) 15' quadrangle. Called Happy Camp on Mariposa (1912) 30' quadrangle. Postal authorities established Fish Camp post office in 1924, discontinued it in 1933, and reestablished it in 1939; the name is from a fish hatchery at the site—the official name of the place is Berry's Fish Camp (Salley, p. 75).

Fish Camp Landing [SAN JOAQUIN]: *locality,* 10.5 miles west-southwest of downtown Stockton on the south side of Middle River on Union Island (lat. 37°52'55" N, long. 121°27'15" W). Named on Holt (1913) 7.5' quadrangle.

Fish Creek [MADERA]:

(1) *stream,* flows 5 miles to San Joaquin River 8 miles southeast of Shuteye Peak (lat. 37°15'45" N, long. 119°19'30" W; sec. 2, T 8 S, R 24 E). Named on Shuteye Peak (1953) 15' quadrangle.

(2) *stream,* flows 4.5 miles to Kerckhoff Lake 5.25 miles south of the town of North Fork (lat. 37°09'05" N, long. 119°31'10" W; sec. 13, T 9 S, R 22 E). Named on North Fork (1965) 7.5' quadrangle.

(3) *stream,* heads in Fresno County and flows 2.5 miles in Madera County to Middle Fork San Joaquin River 6 miles south-southwest of Devils Postpile (lat. 37°32'40" N, long. 119°07'55" W). Named on Devils Postpile (1953) 15' quadrangle.

Fish Creek Campground [MADERA]: *locality,* 7.5 miles southeast of Shuteye Peak (lat. 37°15'35" N, long. 119°21'10" W; sec. 4, T 8 S, R 24 E); the place is along Fish Creek (1). Named on Shuteye Peak (1953) 15' quadrangle.

Fish Creek Mountain [MADERA]: *ridge,* east-trending, 1.5 miles long, 5.5 miles southwest of the town of North Fork (lat. 37°09'50" N, long. 119°34'25" W); the ridge is south of the headwaters of Fish Creek (2). Named on North Fork (1965) 7.5' quadrangle.

Fisher Creek [TUOLUMNE]: *stream,* flows 6.25 miles to Skull Creek 6 miles north-northwest of Crandall Peak (lat. 38°14'15" N, long. 120°11'35" W; sec. 34, T 5 N, R 16 E). Named on Crandall Peak (1979), Liberty Hill (1979), and Strawberry (1979) 7.5' quadrangles.

Fisher Lakes: see **Lertora Lake** [TUOLUMNE].

Fisher's Bridge: see **Bellota** [SAN JOAQUIN].

Fisher's Landing: see **French Camp** [SAN JOAQUIN].

Fissures: see **The Fissures** [MARIPOSA].

Fitz [SAN JOAQUIN]: *locality,* 8 miles north-northeast of Vernalis along Western Pacific Railroad (lat. 37°44'20" N, long. 121°20'45" W). Named on Vernalis (1952) 7.5' quadrangle.

Five Corners [SAN JOAQUIN]: *locality,* 4.5 miles east-northeast of Manteca (lat. 37°49'35" N, long. 121°08'35" W; near NE cor. sec. 25, T 1 S, R 7 E). Named on Manteca (1952) 7.5' quadrangle.

Fivemile Creek [SAN JOAQUIN]: *stream,* flows 2 miles to Fivemile Slough 8.5 miles south-southwest of Lodi in the north part of Stockton (lat. 38°00'50" N, long. 121°20'15" W; near N line sec. 20, T 2 N, R 6 E). Named on Lodi South (1968) 7.5' quadrangle.

Fivemile Creek [TUOLUMNE]: *stream,* flows 6 miles to South Fork Stanislaus River 3.25 miles northeast of Columbia (lat. 38°04' N, long. 120°21'10" W; sec. 32, T 3 N, R 15 E). Named on Columbia SE (1948) 7.5' quadrangle.

Fivemile House [SAN JOAQUIN]: *locality,* 8 miles south-southwest of Lodi in present Stockton (lat. 38°01'10" N, long. 121°19'25" W; sec. 16, T 2 N, R 6 E); the place is along present Fivemile Creek. Named on Castle (1910) 7.5' quadrangle.

Fivemile Slough [SAN JOAQUIN]: *water feature,* artificial watercourse that joins Fourteenmile Slough 9.5 miles south-southwest of Lodi (lat. 38°00'50" N, long. 121°22'05" W). Named on Lodi South (1968) 7.5' quadrangle.

Flagpole Point [CALAVERAS]: *peak,* 2.25 miles northwest of Tamarack (lat. 38°27'35" N, long. 120°06'35" W; sec. 16, T 7 N, R 17 E). Altitude 7933 feet. Named on Tamarack (1979) 7.5' quadrangle.

Flange Rock: see **East Flange Rock** [TUOLUMNE].

Flat Lake [MADERA]: *lake,* 650 feet long, 4.5 miles south-southeast of Merced Peak (lat. 37°34'30" N, long. 119°21'40" W). Named on Merced Peak (1953) 15' quadrangle.

Flat Pond [MERCED]: *lake,* 5.25 miles east of Los Banos (lat. 37°02'40" N, long. 120°45'25" W; in and near sec. 22, T 10 S, R 11 E). Named on Los Banos (1960) 7.5' quadrangle.

Flat Top Mountain [MARIPOSA]: *peak,* 11.5 miles south of the settlement of Catheys Valley (lat. 37°16'15" N, long. 120°06'35" W; near NE cor. sec. 4, T 8 S, R 17 E). Altitude 838 feet. Named on Illinois Hill (1962) 7.5' quadrangle.

Fleming Creek [TUOLUMNE]: *stream,* flows nearly 2 miles to Don Pedro Reservoir 3 miles east of Don Pedro Camp (lat. 37°42'45" N, long. 120°21'20" W; sec. 31, T 2 S, R 15 E). Named on Penon Blanco Peak (1962, photorevised 1973) 7.5' quadrangle.

Fletcher Creek [MARIPOSA]: *stream,* flows 7 miles to Lewis Creek 7.25 miles south of Cathedral Peak (lat. 37°44'40" N, long. 119° 23'30" W). Named on Merced Peak (1953) and Tuolumne Meadows (1956) 15' quadrangles. Lieutenant N.F. McClure named the stream in 1895 for A.G. Fletcher, a state fish commissioner instrumental in having streams in Yosemite National Park stocked with fish (Gudde, 1949, p. 116).

Fletcher Gulch [CALAVERAS]: *canyon,* drained by a stream that flows 1.25 miles to Mokelumne River 2.25 miles north-northwest of Paloma (lat. 38°17'15" N, long. 120°46'50" W; sec. 17, T 5 N, R 11 E). Named on Jackson (1962) 7.5' quadrangle.

Fletcher Lake: see **Upper Fletcher Lake** [MARIPOSA]; **Upper Fletcher Lake**, under **Townsley Lake** [MARIPOSA].

Fletcher Peak [MARIPOSA]: *peak,* 5.5 miles southeast of Cathedral Peak (lat. 37°47'30" N, long. 119°20'10" W). Named on Tuolumne Meadows (1956) 15' quadrangle. The peak first was named for a Mr. Baker, who was a camp cook at Boothe Lake (United States Board on Geographic Names, 1934, p. 9).

Flora Lake [TUOLUMNE]: *lake,* 1400 feet long, 14 miles southeast of Pinecrest (lat. 38°03' N, long. 119°48'25" W; near N line sec. 8, T 2 N, R 20 E). Named on Pinecrest (1956) 15' quadrangle. The name is for Flora Coleman of Mannsboro, Virginia, a cousin of R.B. Marshall of United States Geological Survey (Browning, 1986, p. 71).

Florence: see **Mount Florence** [MADERA].

Florence Creek [MADERA-MARIPOSA]: *stream,* heads in Madera County and flows 6 miles to Lewis Creek 7 miles south-southeast of Cathedral Peak in Mariposa County (lat. 37°45'20" N, long. 119°21'15" W). Named on Merced Peak (1953) and Tuolumne Meadows (1956) 15' quadrangles. Browning (1986, p. 72) associated the name with Florence Hutchings, for whom Mount Florence was named.

Florence Lake [MADERA]: *lake,* 850 feet long, 8 miles north-northeast of Merced Peak (lat. 37°45' N, long. 119°20'35" W); the lake is along Florence Creek. Named on Merced Peak (1953) and Tuolumne Meadows (1956) 15' quadrangles. Browning (1986, p. 72) associated the name with Florence Hutchings, for whom Mount Florence was named.

Floto Lake [STANISLAUS]: *lake,* 1000 feet long, 2.25 miles southwest of La Grange (lat. 37°38'10" N, long. 120°29'10" W; near N line sec. 36, T 3 S, R 13 E). Named on La Grange (1962) 7.5' quadrangle.

Flowers Mountain [CALAVERAS]: *ridge,* northwest-trending, 1 mile long, nearly 5 miles south-southwest of Copperopolis (lat. 37° 55' N, long. 120°40'30" W). Named on Copperopolis (1962) 7.5' quadrangle.

Fluhr [MERCED]: *locality,* 2 miles east-northeast of Atwater along Atchison, Topeka and Santa Fe Railroad (lat. 37°21'45" N, long. 120°34'35" W; near SE cor. sec. 31, T 6 S, R 13 E). Named on Atwater (1961) 15' quadrangle.

Flyaway Creek: see **Flyaway Gulch** [MARIPOSA].

Flyaway Gulch [MARIPOSA]: *canyon,* drained by a stream that flows 3.5 miles to Lake McClure 9.5 miles northeast of Hornitos near Bagby (lat. 37°36'45" N, long. 120°08'10" W). Named on Coulterville (1947) and Hornitos (1947, photorevised 1973) 7.5' quadrangles. Hoffmann and Gardner's (1863-1867) map has the form "Fly away Gulch" for the name. Laizure's (1928) map shows Flyaway Cr. in the canyon.

Foerster Creek [MADERA]: *stream,* flows 2.5 miles to Triple Peak Fork 4.5 miles northeast of Merced Peak (lat. 37°41' N, long. 119° 20'10" W); the stream heads near Foerster Peak. Named on Merced Peak (1953) 15' quadrangle.

Foerster Peak [MADERA]: *peak,* 7 miles northeast of Merced Peak (lat. 37°41'25" N, long. 119°17'20" W). Altitude 12,058 feet. Named on Merced Peak (1953) 15' quadrangle. Lieutenant N.F. McClure named the peak in 1895 for Sergeant Lewis Foerster (United States Board on Geographic Names, 1934, p. 9). United States Board on Geographic Names (1985, p. 1) approved the name "Mount Ansel Adams" for a peak, altitude 11,760 feet, located 0.8 mile northeast of Foerster Peak (lat. 37°41'52" N, long. 119°16'49" W); the name honors Ansel Easton Adams, photographer and conservationist.

Folsom [CALAVERAS]: *locality,* nearly 7 miles north of Blue Mountain (lat. 38°26'25" N, long. 120°22'10" W). Named on Big Trees (1891) 30' quadrangle.

Folsom Campground [CALAVERAS]: *locality,* 5.5 miles north-northeast of Blue Mountain (lat. 38°25'10" N, long. 120°14'40" W; sec. 33, T 7 N, R 15 E). Named on Blue Mountain (1956) 15' quadrangle.

Footman Mountain: see **Footman Ridge** [MADERA].

Footman Ridge [MARIPOSA]: *ridge,* north-northwest-trending, 2.25 miles long, 9 miles south-southwest of El Portal (lat. 37°32'45" N, long. 119°49'20" W). Named on Buckingham Mountain (1947) 7.5' quadrangle. Called Footman Mtn. on Yosemite (1909) 30' quadrangle.

Foppiano [SAN JOAQUIN]: *locality,* 3 miles west-southwest of Waterloo along Central California Traction Railroad (lat. 38°01'20" N, long. 121°14'25" W). Named on Waterloo (1968) 7.5' quadrangle. California Division of Highways' (1934) map shows a place called Ashley located 1.25 miles north of Foppiano along the railroad (near SW cor. sec. 5, T 2 N, R 9 E).

Foremans: see **Fourth Crossing** [CALAVERAS].

Foreman's Ranch: see **Linden** [SAN JOAQUIN].

Foresta [MARIPOSA]: *settlement,* 2.25 miles northeast of El Portal (lat.

37°41'50" N, long. 119°45' W; sec. 3, T 3 S, R 20 E). Named on El Portal (1947) and Yosemite (1956) 15' quadrangles. Yosemite (1909) 30' quadrangle has the name "McCauley" at the place. The name "Foresta" recalls Foresta Land Company that A.B. Davis started in 1913; Davis built a resort at the site, but abandoned it in 1915 (Browning, 1986, p. 72-73). Postal authorities established Opim post office at the place in 1882 and discontinued it in 1884 (Salley, p. 162).

Foresta Falls [MARIPOSA]: *waterfall,* 1.5 miles northeast of El Portal along Crane Creek (lat. 37°41'35" N, long. 119°45'30" W; near W line sec. 10, T 3 S, R 20 E); the feature is 0.5 mile southwest of Foresta. Named on El Portal (1947) 7.5' quadrangle.

Forest Creek [CALAVERAS]: *stream,* flows 17 miles to Middle Fork Mokelumne River 6 miles south-southwest of Devils Nose (lat. 38°23'05" N, long. 120°28'05" W; sec. 7, T 6 N, R 14 E). Named on Calaveras Dome (1979), Devils Nose (1979), and Garnet Hill (1979) 7.5' quadrangles. Called North Fork of Middle Fork Mokelumne River on Big Trees (1891) 30' quadrangle, but United States Board on Geographic Names (1960a, p. 14) rejected this name for the stream.

Forest Lake [SAN JOAQUIN]: *locality,* 6.5 miles north of Lodi along Southern Pacific Railroad (lat. 38°13'35" N, long. 121°17'45" W; sec. 2, T 4 N, R 6 E). Named on Lodi North (1968) 7.5' quadrangle. Postal authorities established Forest Lake post office in 1890, changed the name to Forestlake in 1895, and discontinued it in 1903 (Salley, p. 77). They established Jakesville post office at the place in 1917 and discontinued it in 1918; the name was for Jacob Small, first postmaster (Salley, p. 106).

Forked Meadow [MADERA]: *area,* 5.25 miles northeast of Shuteye Peak (lat. 37°23'35" N, long. 119°20'45" W; sec. 21, T 6 S, R 24 E). Named on Shuteye Peak (1953) 15' quadrangle.

Forks: see **The Forks** [MADERA].

Forks Campground [MADERA]: *locality,* 5 miles southeast of Yosemite Forks on the west side of Bass Lake (1) (lat. 37°18'45" N, long. 119°34'10" W; near N line sec. 21, T 7 S, R 22 E); the place is near The Forks. Named on Bass Lake (1953) 15' quadrangle.

Forks of the Road: see **Altaville** [CALAVERAS].

Forlorn Hope: see **Hopeton** [MERCED] (1).

Forsyth Peak [TUOLUMNE]: *peak,* 2 miles west-northwest of Tower Peak (lat. 38°09'30" N, long. 119°34'50" W). Altitude 11,180 feet. Named on Tower Peak (1956) 15' quadrangle. The name commemorates Colonel William W. Forsyth, acting superintendent of Yosemite National Park from 1909 until 1912 (United States Board on Geographic Names, 1934, p. 9).

Fort Hill: see **Fort Mountain** [CALAVERAS].

Fort Monroe [MARIPOSA]: *locality,* 6.5 miles west-southwest of Yosemite (present Yosemite Village) (lat. 37°42'30" N, long. 119° 41'30" W). Named on Yosemite (1909) 30' quadrangle. The place was a stage station of the 1880's named for driver George F. Monroe (Whiting and Whiting, p. 49).

Fort Mountain [CALAVERAS]: *peak,* 6 miles west of Blue Mountain (lat. 38°20'35" N, long. 120°28'20" W; sec. 30, T 6 N, R 14 E). Altitude 3322 feet. Named on Fort Mountain (1979) 7.5' quadrangle. Blue Mountain (1956) 15' quadrangle shows the peak situated 0.5 mile farther south-southeast. Whitney (1865, p. 267), who illustrated the feature, called it Fort Hill.

Fortynine Creek [TUOLUMNE]: *stream,* flows 3 miles to Don Pedro Reservoir 1.5 miles north of Don Pedro Camp (lat. 37°44'25" N, long. 120°24'35" W; sec. 22, T 2 S, R 14 E). Named on La Grange (1962) 7.5' quadrangle.

Fortynine Creek: see **Big Creek** [TUOLUMNE] (2).

Fortynine Gap [MARIPOSA]: *pass,* 7.5 miles south-southwest of Penon Blanco Peak (lat. 37°37'35" N, long. 120°18'25" W; sec. 34, T 3 S, R 15 E). Named on Penon Blanco Peak (1962) 7.5' quadrangle.

Fort Yosemite: see **Yosemite Village** [MARIPOSA].

Fosteria: see **Paloma** [CALAVERAS].

Four Corners [MADERA]: *locality,* 15 miles south-southeast of Raymond (lat. 37°00'35" N, long. 119°47'35" W; at S line sec. 33, T 10 S, R 20 E). Named on Little Table Mountain (1962) 7.5' quadrangle.

Four Corners [MERCED]: *locality,* 11.5 miles north-northeast of Atwood (lat. 37°29'35" N, long. 120°30'05" W; near SE cor. sec. 14, T 5 S, R 13 E). Named on Winton (1961) 7.5' quadrangle.

Four Corners [SAN JOAQUIN]: *locality,* 1.25 miles west of Thornton (lat. 38°13'30" N, long. 121°26'45" W). Named on Thornton (1978) 7.5' quadrangle.

Fourmile [MARIPOSA]: *locality,* 2.5 miles south-southeast of Wawona (lat. 37°30'20" N, long. 119°38' W; near W line sec. 12, T 5 S, R 21 E). Named on Yosemite (1909) 30' quadrangle.

Fourteen Mile House: see **Farmington** [SAN JOAQUIN].

Fourteenmile Slough [SAN JOAQUIN]: *water feature,* extends from Disappointment Slough to San Joaquin River 7.5 miles west-northwest of downtown Stockton (lat. 37°59'50" N, long. 121°25'10" W). Named on Holt (1978), Lodi South (1968), Stockton West (1952), and Terminous (1978) 7.5' quadrangles.

Fourth Crossing [CALAVERAS]: *locality,* 5 miles south-southeast of San Andreas along San Antonio Creek (lat. 38°07'20" N, long. 120°38' W; sec. 10, T 3 N, R 12 E). Named on San Andreas (1962) 7.5' quadrangle. Postal authorities established Fourth Crossing post office in 1855, discontinued it in 1888, reestablished it in 1892, and discontinued it in 1925 (Frickstad, p. 15). Alexander Beritzhoff and David Foreman operated a hotel and ferry at the place; the site was called Foremans—it also was called Fourth Crossing because it was at the fourth river crossing along the road from Stockton to the mines (Gudde, 1975, p. 118, 121).

Fowler Mountain [MADERA]: *ridge,* south-southeast-trending, 1 mile long, 6 miles south of the town of North Fork (lat. 37°08'30" N, long. 119°31'40" W; on S line sec. 13, T 9 S, R 22 E). Named on North Fork (1965) 7.5' quadrangle.

Fox Creek [MARIPOSA]: *stream,* flows 2.25 miles to join Magoon Creek and form Middle Fork Chowchilla River 8 miles east of Mariposa (lat. 37°29'10" N, long. 119°49'10" W; sec. 19, T 5 S, R 20 E). Named on Buckingham Mountain (1947) and Stumpfield Mountain (1947) 7.5' quadrangles.

Fox Gulch [TUOLUMNE]: *canyon,* drained by a stream that flows less than 1 mile to South Fork Stanislaus River 2.5 miles north of Columbia (lat. 38°04'15" N, long. 120°23'50" W; near E line sec. 35, T 3 N, R 14 E). Named on Columbia (1948) 7.5' quadrangle.

Frances: see **Mount Frances**, under **Liberty Cap** [MARIPOSA].

Franceses: see **The Homestead** [SAN JOAQUIN].

Frank Harris Point [MARIPOSA]: *peak,* 4.5 miles east-southeast of Smith Peak (lat. 37°47'05" N, long. 120°01'20" W; near S line sec. 6, T 2 S, R 18 E). Named on Jawbone Ridge (1947) 7.5' quadrangle.

Franklyn: see **Lodi** [SAN JOAQUIN].

Frank Young Gulch [TUOLUMNE]: *canyon,* drained by a stream that flows less than 1 mile to Tuolumne River 0.5 mile south-southwest of Don Pedro Camp (lat. 37°42'35" N, long. 120°24'30" W; at NW cor. sec. 2, T 3 S, R 14 E). Named on La Grange (1962) 7.5' quadrangle.

Fraser Flat [TUOLUMNE]: *area,* nearly 4 miles west-southwest of Strawberry along South Fork Stanislaus River (lat. 38°10'10" N, long. 120°04'15" W; sec. 26, T 4 N, R 17 E). Named on Strawberry (1979) 7.5' quadrangle.

Fraser Lakes: see **Emigrant Lake** [TUOLUMNE].

Frazier Spring [MERCED]: *spring,* 3.5 miles south-southeast of Pacheco Pass (lat. 37°01' N, long. 121°11' W; sec. 34, T 10 S, R 7 E). Named on Pacheco Pass (1955) 7.5' quadrangle.

Freeze-out Spring [TUOLUMNE]: *spring,* 2.25 miles north-northwest of Don Pedro Camp (lat. 37°44'45" N, long. 120°25'30" W; near W line sec. 22, T 2 S, R 14 E). Named on La Grange (1962) 7.5' quadrangle.

Fremont Ford [MERCED]: *locality,* 5.25 miles northeast of Gustine along San Joaquin River (lat. 37°18'35" N, long. 120°55'45" W; sec. 24, T 7 S, R 9 E). Named on Turlock (1962) 15' quadrangle.

Fremont Peak [MARIPOSA]: *peak,* 2.25 miles east-southeast of the village of Bear Valley on Bullion Mountain (lat. 37°33'35" N, long. 120°04'30" W; sec. 27, T 4 S, R 17 E). Altitude 4199 feet. Named on Bear Valley (1947) 7.5' quadrangle.

Fremont's Channel: see **McLeod Lake** [SAN JOAQUIN].

Fremont's Crossing: see **Oakdale** [STANISLAUS].

Fremont Spring [MARIPOSA]: *spring,* 2.5 miles east of the village of Bear Valley (lat. 37°33'40" N, long. 120°04'20" W; sec. 27, T 4 S, R 17 E); the spring is 1000 feet northeast of Fremont Peak. Named on Bear Valley (1947) 7.5' quadrangle. Sonora (1891) 30' quadrangle has the plural form "Fremont Springs" for the name.

Fremont Valley: see **Jenny Lind** [CALAVERAS].

French Bar: see **La Grange** [STANISLAUS]:

French Camp [SAN JOAQUIN]: *town,* 5.25 miles south-southeast of downtown Stockton (lat. 37°53' N, long. 121°16'15" W). Named on Stockton West (1952) 7.5' quadrangle. The name is from use of the site by French-Canadian fur trappers in the 1830's and 1840's; Charles Weber had a town that he called Castoria laid out at the place in 1850, but the name "French Camp" was retained by popular usage—the name "Castoria" signified "place of beavers" (Hoover, Rensch, and Rensch, p. 368, 371). Postal authorities established French Camp post office in 1854, discontinued it in 1862, reestablished it in 1865, discontinued it in 1870, and reestablished it in 1874 (Frickstad, p. 160). Thompson and West's (1879) map shows a place called Fisher's Landing located along San Joaquin River about 3.5 miles southwest of French Camp on Roberts Island (near S line sec. 9, T 1 S, R 6 E), and a place called Frewert's Ferry located less than 1 mile farther upstream (sec. 16, T 1 S, R 6 E). Postal authorities established Merry Oaks post office perhaps 10 miles southwest of French Camp in 1853, discontinued it in 1855, reestablished it in 1859, and discontinued it in 1860; the post office name was transferred from North Carolina (Salley, p. 138). They established Montevideo post office 8 miles east of French Camp (sec. 5, T 1 S, R 8 E) in 1857 and discontinued it the same year; they established Fairchild post office 7 miles northwest of French Camp in 1900 and discontinued it in 1902 (Salley, p. 72, 145).

French Camp [TUOLUMNE]: *locality,* 3.5 miles north-northeast of Columbia (lat. 38°04'40" N, long. 120°22' W; near N line sec. 31, T 3 N, R 15 E). Site named on Columbia SE (1948) 7.5' quadrangle.

French Camp: see **Mariposa** [MARIPOSA].

French Camp Slough [SAN JOAQUIN]: *stream,* formed by the confluence of Littlejohns Creek and Lone Tree Creek (2), flows 6.25 miles to San Joaquin River 3 miles south-southwest of downtown Stockton (lat. 37°55'15" N, long. 121°19'05" W); the feature is northeast of French Camp. Named on Stockton East (1952) and Stockton West (1952) 7.5' quadrangles. Jarves' (1849) map shows French Creek joining present San Joaquin River south of Stockton. French Camp Slough was called San Juan River in the early days (Dillon, 1975, p. 343).

French Creek [CALAVERAS]: *stream,* flows 2.5 miles to Bean Gulch 6 miles east-southeast of Copperopolis (lat. 37°56'45" N, long. 120°32'20" W; near N line sec. 15, T 1 N, R 13 E). Named on Melones Dam (1962) 7.5' quadrangle.

French Creek [TUOLUMNE]: *stream,* flows 1 mile to Silver Gulch 4.5 miles northeast of Columbia (lat. 38°04'45" N, long. 120°20'25" W; near SE cor. sec. 29, T 3 N, R 15 E). Named on Columbia SE (1948) 7.5' quadrangle.

French Creek: see **French Camp Slough** [SAN JOAQUIN].

French Flat [TUOLUMNE]: *area,* 5 miles west of Sonora (lat. 37°58'25" N, long. 120°28'15" W; near NE cor. sec. 6, T 1 N, R 14 E). Named on Sonora (1948) 7.5' quadrangle.

French Gulch [CALAVERAS]:

(1) *canyon,* drained by a stream that flows 6.25 miles to San Domingo Creek 4 miles north-northwest of Angels Camp at Dogtown (lat. 38°07'35" N, long. 120°34'20" W; sec. 8, T 3 N, R 13 E). Named on Angels Camp (1962) 7.5' quadrangle.

(2) *canyon,* drained by a stream that flows 2 miles to Coyote Creek nearly 5 miles south of Vallecito (lat. 38°01'05" N, long. 120°29'20" W; near NE cor. sec. 24, T 2 N, R 13 E). Named on Columbia (1948) 7.5' quadrangle.

French Gulch [MADERA]: *canyon,* drained by a stream that flows 1.5 miles to Fresno River 7.25 miles west-southwest of Yosemite Forks (lat. 37°19' N, long. 119°44'45" W; near S line sec. 14, T 7 S, R 20 E). Named on Bass Lake (1953) 15' quadrangle.

French Hill [CALAVERAS]: *peak,* less than 1 mile northeast of Mokelumne Hill (lat. 38°18'25" N, long. 120°41'35" W; sec. 7, T 5 N, R 12 E). Named on Mokelumne Hill (1948) 7.5' quadrangle.

Frenchman's Ranch: see **Paloma** [CALAVERAS].

French Meadow [CALAVERAS]: *area,* 6 miles east-southeast of Blue Mountain at Dorrington (lat. 38°17'45" N, long. 120°16'25" W; near S line sec. 12, T 5 N, R 15 E). Named on Dorrington (1979) 7.5' quadrangle.

French Pit [STANISLAUS]: *locality,* an excavation, partly filled with water, 0.25 mile south-southwest of La Grange (lat. 37°39'35" N, long. 120°27'30" W; sec. 20, T 3 S, R 14 E). Named on La Grange (1962) 7.5' quadrangle.

Frenchs Flat [MERCED]: *area,* nearly 4 miles south-southwest of Pacheco Pass on Merced-Santa Clara County line (lat. 37°00'45" N, long. 121°14'05" W; around NW cor. sec. 5, T 11 S, R 7 E). Named on Pacheco Pass (1955) 7.5' quadrangle.

Frenchs Pass [MERCED]: *pass,* 1.5 miles southwest of Mariposa Peak on Merced-San Benito County line (lat. 36°56'25" N, long. 121°13'40" W; sec. 32, T 11 S, R 7 E). Named on Mariposa Peak (1969) 7.5' quadrangle, which shows French ranch northwest of the pass.

Fresno Crossing [MADERA]: *locality,* 5.5 miles east-northeast of Knowles along Fresno River near the mouth of Spangle Gold Creek (lat. 37°14'15" N, long. 119°46'25" W; sec. 15, T 8 S, R 20 E). Named on Knowles (1962) 7.5' quadrangle. The place was the main crossing of Fresno River in the mining region (Crampton *in* Eccleston, p. 74).

Fresno Dome [MADERA]: *peak,* 8 miles northeast of Yosemite Forks (lat. 37°27'15" N, long. 119°32'10" W; sec. 35, T 5 S, R 22 E). Altitude 7540 feet. Named on Bass Lake (1953) 15' quadrangle. United States Board on Geographic Names (1991, p. 4) rejected the names "Hogans Dome," "Walemo Rock," "Wameloo Rock," and "Wamelo Rock" for the feature.

Fresno Dome Campground [MADERA]: *locality,* 7.5 miles northeast of Yosemite Forks along Big Creek (lat. 37°27'20" N, long. 119°32'50" W; sec. 34, T 5 S, R 22 E); the place is less than 1 mile west of Fresno Dome. Named on Bass Lake (1953) 15' quadrangle.

Fresno Flats [MADERA]: *valley,* 4.5 miles west-southwest of Yosemite Forks along Fresno River (lat. 37°20'15" N, long. 119° 42' W). Named on Bass Lake (1953) 15' quadrangle.

Fresno Flats: see **Oakhurst** [MADERA].

Fresno River [MADERA-MERCED]: *stream,* formed by the confluence of Lewis Fork and Nelder Creek in Madera County, flows 80 miles to San Joaquin River 4.25 miles east-northeast of Dos Palos Y in Merced County (lat. 37°04'35" N, long. 120°33'30" W). Named on Bass Lake (1953), Chowchilla (1960), Firebaugh (1946), Le Grand (1961), Madera (1946), Mariposa (1947), Raymond (1962), and Santa Rita Park (1962) 15' quadrangles. South Fork branches southwest from Fresno River 13 miles south of Raymond and flows 5.5 miles before rejoining the main stream 2.5 miles northeast of Madera; it is named on Herndon (1965) and Raymond (1962) 15' quadrangles. United States Board on Geographic Names (1964c, p. 15) rejected the name "North Fork of Fresno River" for present Lewis Fork [MADERA-MARIPOSA].

Frewert's Ferry: see **French Camp** [SAN JOAQUIN].

Frog Creek [TUOLUMNE]: *stream,* flows 16 miles to Lake Eleanor 7 miles north of Mather (lat. 37°59' N, long. 119°50'30" W; sec. 36, T 2 N, R 19 E). Named on Lake Eleanor (1956), Pinecrest (1956), and Tower Peak (1956) 15' quadrangles.

Frog Lake: see **Lertora Lake** [TUOLUMNE].

Frogtown [CALAVERAS]: *locality,* 2.25 miles south-southeast of Angles Camp (lat. 38°02'50" N, long. 120°31'35" W; near NE cor. sec. 10, T 2 N, R 13 E). Named on San Andreas (1947) 15' quadrangle.

Frying Pan Lake [MADERA]: *lake,* 300 feet long, 2 miles east-southeast of Merced Peak (lat. 37°37'15" N, long. 119°21'50" W). Named on Merced Peak (1953) 15' quadrangle. John Handley of California Department of Fish and Game named the lake in 1940 (Browning, 1986, p. 75).

Fuchs [CALAVERAS]: *locality,* 5 miles west of Blue Mountain (lat. 38°21' N, long. 120°27'25" W; sec. 29, T 6 N, R 14 E). Named on Blue Mountain (1956) 15' quadrangle.

Fugitt: see **Lockeford** [SAN JOAQUIN].

Fuller Buttes [MADERA]: *peaks,* two, 9 miles east-northeast of Shuteye Peak (lat. 37°24'55" N, long. 119°17'05" W; near SW cor. sec. 7, T 6 S, R 25 E). Named on Shuteye Peak (1953) 15' quadrangle.

Fuller Meadow [MADERA]: *area,* 6.25 miles east of Shuteye Peak (lat. 37°21'20" N, long. 119°18'55" W; sec. 35, T 6 S, R 24 E). Named on Shuteye Peak (1953) 15' quadrangle. Called Fullers Meadow on Kaiser (1904) 30' quadrangle. Frank F. Fuller homesteaded in section 35 in 1900 (Browning, 1986, p. 75).

Funk Hill [CALAVERAS]: *peak,* 4 miles east of Copperopolis (lat. 37°58'45" N, long. 120°33'55" W; sec. 32, T 2 N, R 13 E). Named on Melones Dam (1962) 7.5' quadrangle.

Funks Meadow [TUOLUMNE]: *area,* 3.5 miles southeast of Long Barn along Hull Creek (lat. 38°02'50" N, long. 120°05'45" W; sec. 10, T 2 N, R 17 E). Named on Hull Creek (1979) 7.5' quadrangle.

Fuqua Ridge [MARIPOSA]: *ridge,* south-trending, 1.5 miles long, 2.25 miles west-northwest of Coulterville (lat. 37°43'20" N, long. 120°14' W). Named on Coulterville (1947) 7.5' quadrangle..

– G –

Gadwall [MERCED]: *locality,* 5.5 miles east-southeast of Los Banos along Southern Pacific Railroad (lat. 37°01'20" N, long. 120°45'50" W; near E line sec. 33, T 10 S, R 11 E). Named on Los Banos (1921) 7.5' quadrangle.

Gaggs Camp [MADERA]: *locality,* 2.5 miles west-northwest of Shuteye Peak (lat. 37°21'40" N, long. 119°28' W; sec. 33, T 6 S, R 23 E). Named on Shuteye Peak (1953) 15' quadrangle.

Gale Lake [MADERA]: *lake,* 300 feet long, 5.25 miles south of Merced Peak (lat. 37°33'40" N, long. 119°22'50" W); the lake is 0.5 mile south-southeast of Gale Peak. Named on Merced Peak (1953) 15' quadrangle. William A. Dill and a group from California Department of Fish and Game named the lake in 1946 for nearby Gale Peak (Browning, 1986, p. 77).

Gale Peak [MADERA]: *peak,* 4.5 miles south of Merced Peak (lat. 37°34'05" N, long. 119°23'10" W). Altitude 10,693 feet. Named on Merced Peak (1953) 15' quadrangle. Lieutenant N.F. McClure named the peak for Captain G.H.G. Gale, acting superintendent of Yosemite National Park in 1894 (United States Board on Geographic Names, 1934, p. 10).

Gales Ridge [CALAVERAS]: *ridge,* north-northwest-trending, 1.5 miles long, 1.5 miles northwest of Paloma (lat. 38°16'30" N, long. 120°46'50" W). Named on Jackson (1962) 7.5' quadrangle.

Gallison Lake [MARIPOSA]: *lake,* 1100 feet long, 6.5 miles southeast of Cathedral Peak (lat. 37°46'30" N, long. 119°19'40" W). Named on Tuolumne Meadows (1956) 15' quadrangle. Rangers Bingaman and Eastman of Yosemite National Park proposed the name to honor Arthur L. Gallison, a fellow ranger who planted fish in the lake in 1916 (Browning, 1986, p. 77).

Gallup Creek [STANISLAUS-TUOLUMNE]: *stream,* heads in Tuolumne County and flows 10 miles to Dry Creek nearly 3 miles south-southeast of Cooperstown in Stanislaus County (lat. 37°42'35" N, long. 120°31'05" W; near NE cor. sec. 3, T 3 S, R 13 E). Named on Cooperstown (1968) and La Grange (1962) 7.5' quadrangles. Called Salt Spring Creek on Merced Falls (1944) 15' quadrangle, and on Chinese Camp (1947) 7.5' quadrangle; called Dry Creek on La Grange (1919) 7.5' quadrangle.

Galt Basin [MADERA]: area, 7.5 miles southwest of the town of North Fork (lat. 37°08'50" N, long. 119°36'05" W; near W line sec. 17, T 9 S, R 22 E). Named on North Fork (1965) 7.5' quadrangle.

Ganns [CALAVERAS]: *locality,* 5 miles west-southwest of Tamarack (lat. 38°24'15" N, long. 120°09'30" W; sec. 1, T 6 N, R 16 E). Named on Calaveras Dome (1979) 7.5' quadrangle.

Ganns Creek [MARIPOSA]: *stream,* flows 5.5 miles to Mariposa Reservoir 9.5 miles south-southwest of the settlement of Catheys Valley (lat. 37°18'05" N, long. 120°07'35" W; near N line sec. 29, T 7 S, R 17 E). Named on Illinois Hill (1962) 7.5' quadrangle.

Garden Canyon [STANISLAUS]: *canyon,* 2 miles long, opens into Del

Puerto Canyon 3 miles northeast of Copper Mountain (lat. 37° 27'10" N, long. 121°16'40" W; sec. 35, T 5 S, R 6 E). Named on Copper Mountain (1956) 7.5' quadrangle.

Gardener's Station: see **Gardner** [CALAVERAS].

Gardner [CALAVERAS]: *locality,* 5.5 miles east-southeast of Blue Mountain at present Dorrington (lat. 38°18' N, long. 120°16'30" W). Named on Big Trees (1891) 30' quadrangle. Wheeler (1879, p. 178) listed Gardener's Station.

Gardner Meadow [TUOLUMNE]: *area,* 4.25 miles northeast of Liberty Hill (lat. 38°24'40" N, long. 120°02'50" W). Named on Tamarack (1979) 7.5' quadrangle.

Garnet Hill [CALAVERAS]: *peak,* 11 miles north-northeast of Blue Mountain (lat. 38°28'50" N, long. 120°15'10" W; near N line sec. 7, T 7 N, R 16 E). Altitude 4512 feet. Named on Garnet Hill (1979) 7.5' quadrangle.

Garnet Lake [MADERA]: *lake,* 1.5 miles long, 7.25 miles northwest of Devils Postpile (lat. 37°42'35" N, long. 119°09'30" W); the feature is south of Emerald Lake and Ruby Lake. Named on Devils Postpile (1953) 15' quadrangle. Called Badger Lake on maps of the 1890's, where the name "Garnet Lake" applies to present Shadow Lake (Browning, 1988, p. 48). United States Board on Geographic Names (1976c, p. 4) approved the name "Red Top Mountain" for a peak, altitude 10,532 feet, situated 5 miles southeast of Garnet Lake (lat. 37°38'12" N, long. 119°08'04" W).

Garnet Point [MARIPOSA]: *peak,* 3.5 miles north of the settlement of Catheys Valley (lat. 37°29'15" N, long. 120°06'05" W; on W line sec. 22, T 5 S, R 17 E). Altitude 2013 feet. Named on Catheys Valley (1962) 7.5' quadrangle.

Garrison: see **Lathrop** [SAN JOAQUIN].

Garrotte: see **Groveland** [TUOLUMNE]; **Second Garrotte** [TUOLUMNE].

Garrotte Creek [TUOLUMNE]: *stream,* flows nearly 3 miles to Pine Mountain Lake 1.5 miles east-northeast of Groveland (lat. 37°50'55" N, long. 120°12' W; near S line sec. 15, T 1 S, R 16 E); the stream goes through Second Garrotte. Named on Groveland (1947, photorevised 1973) 7.5' quadrangle.

Garzas Creek [MERCED-STANISLAUS]: *stream,* heads in Stanislaus County and flows 29 miles to Los Banos Creek 12 miles north-northwest of Los Banos in Merced County (lat. 37°12'55" N, long. 120°56'25" W). Named on Crevison Peak (1955), Howard Ranch (1953), Ingomar (1960), and Mustang Peak (1955) 7.5' quadrangles. The stream was called Arroyo de las Garzas in the early days—*las garzas* means "the herons" in Spanish (Hoover, Rensch, and Rensch, p. 539); however, United States Board on Geographic Names (1962a, p. 16) rejected this name for the feature.

Garzas Creek: see **Los Banos Creek** [MERCED].

Gasburg Creek [STANISLAUS-TUOLUMNE]: *stream,* heads in Tuolumne County and flows 6 miles to Tuolumne River opposite La Grange in Stanislaus County (lat. 37°40' N, long. 120°27'50" W; near S line sec. 18, T 3 S, R 14 E). Named on La Grange (1962) 7.5' quadrangle.

Gaylor Lakes [TUOLUMNE]: *lakes,* largest 2000 feet long, just west of Tioga Pass (lat. 37°54'45" N, long. 119°16'10" W). Named on Tuolumne Meadows (1956) 15' quadrangle. The name is for Jack Gaylor, a ranger in Yosemite National Park who died in service in 1921 (United States Board on Geographic Names, 1934, p. 10).

Gaylor Peak [TUOLUMNE]: *peak,* less than 1 mile north-northwest of Tioga Pass on Tuolumne-Mono County line (lat. 37°55'10" N, long. 119°15'50" W; sec. 30, T 1 N, R 25 E); the peak is east of Gaylor Lakes. Altitude 11,004 feet. Named on Tuolumne Meadows (1956) 15' quadrangle. Hubbard used the name "Tioga Hill" either for the peak, or for the ridge where it lies.

Geers Gulch [CALAVERAS]: *canyon,* drained by a stream that flows 0.5 mile to Chili Gulch 4.25 miles northwest of San Andreas (lat. 38°14'35" N, long. 120°43'45" W; sec. 35, T 5 N, R 11 E). Named on San Andreas (1962) 7.5' quadrangle.

Gem Lake [TUOLUMNE]: *lake,* 750 feet long, 11 miles east of Pinecrest (lat. 38°09'45" N, long. 119°47'35" W). Named on Pinecrest (1956) 15' quadrangle. Theodore C. Agnew, an early miner, gave the name "Gem-o'-the-Mountains" to the lake (Browning, 1986, p. 78).

Geneva: see **Planada** [MERCED].

Genness [TUOLUMNE]: *locality,* 2 miles north-northeast of Long Barn along Sugarpine Creek (lat. 38°06'50" N, long. 120°07'20" W). Named on Big Trees (1891) 30' quadrangle.

Gentry Gulch [MARIPOSA]: *canyon,* drained by a stream that flows 5 miles to North Fork Merced River 5 miles east-northeast of Buckhorn Peak (lat. 37°41'20" N, long. 120°02'15" W; near W line sec. 7, T 3 S, R 18 E). Named on Buckhorn Peak (1947) 7.5' quadrangle. Called Gentry's Gulch on Hoffmann and Gardner's (1863-1867) map.

German Ridge [CALAVERAS]: *ridge,* south-trending, 0.5 mile long, 2.5 miles north of Angels Camp (lat. 38°06'45" N, long. 120°32'20" W; near W line sec. 15, T 3 N, R 13 E). Named on Angels Camp (1962) 7.5' quadrangle.

Gertrude: see **Ahwahnee** [MADERA].

Gertrude Creek [MADERA]: *stream,* flows 3 miles to Whiskey Creek (2) 8 miles south of Shuteye Peak (lat. 37°14'10" N, long. 119°27'15" W; at W line sec. 15, T 8 S, R 23 E). Named on Shaver Lake (1953) and Shuteye Peak (1953) 15' quadrangles.

Gertrude Lake [MADERA]: *lake,* 800 feet long, 3.5 miles west of Devils Postpile (lat. 37°37'10" N, long. 119°08'45" W). Named on Devils Postpile (1953) 15' quadrangle.

Gertrude Lake [TUOLUMNE]: *lake,* 3200 feet long, 6 miles east-northeast of present Pinecrest along South Fork Stanislaus River (lat. 38°12'55" N, long. 119°54'30" W). Named on Dardanelles (1898, reprinted 1947) 30' quadrangle. Pinecrest (1979) 7.5' quadrangle does not show a lake at the place.

Giant's Tower: see **El Capitan** [MARIPOSA].

Gibbs: see **Mount Gibbs** [TUOLUMNE].

Gibson: see **Mount Gibson** [TUOLUMNE].

Giles Pond [MARIPOSA]: *lake,* 500 feet long, 2.25 miles west-northwest of Santa Cruz Mountain (lat. 37°28'20" N, long. 120°14'20" W; sec. 29, T 5 S. R 16 E). Named on Indian Gulch (1962) 7.5' quadrangle.

Gillett Mountain [TUOLUMNE]: *peak,* 12.5 miles east-southeast of Pinecrest (lat. 38°06'50" N, long. 119°47'35" W). Altitude 8361 feet. Named on Pinecrest (1956) 15' quadrangle. R.B. Marshall of United States Geological Survey named the peak in 1909 for James Norris Gillett, governor of California from 1907 until 1911 (Hanna, p. 120).

Gillis [SAN JOAQUIN]: *locality,* 5 miles west-southwest of downtown Stockton along Atchison, Topeka and Santa Fe Railroad on Roberts Island (lat. 37°56'05" N, long. 121°22'55" W). Named on Holt (1978) 7.5' quadrangle.

Gillman Gulch [TUOLUMNE]: *canyon,* drained by a stream that flows 1.25 miles to Tuolumne River 0.25 mile south of Don Pedro Camp (lat. 37°42'40" N, long. 120°24'20" W; near S line sec. 35, T 2 S, R 14 E). Named on La Grange (1962) 7.5' quadrangle. Called Gilman Gulch on Merced Falls (1962) 15' quadrangle.

Gilman [STANISLAUS]: *locality,* 6 miles south of Modesto along Tidewater Southern Railroad (lat. 37°33'05" N, long. 120°59' W; near S line sec. 28, T 4 S, R 9 E). Named on Ceres (1953) 7.5' quadrangle.

Gilman Gulch: see **Gillman Gulch** [TUOLUMNE].

Gimasol Ridge [MARIPOSA]: *ridge,* east-trending, 2 miles long, 6 miles southwest of El Portal (lat. 37°37'35" N, long. 119°52' W). Named on El Portal (1947) 15' quadrangle.

Gin Flat [MARIPOSA]: *area,* 6.25 miles north of El Portal (lat. 37° 45'55" N, long. 119°46'25" W; near N line sec. 16, T 2 S, R 20 E). Named on Lake Eleanor (1956) 15' quadrangle. Paden and Schlichtmann (p. 229) connected the name to a story about a barrel of gin that fell off of a wagon at the place.

Gipsy Peak: see **Antimony Peak** [MERCED].

Gitana [CALAVERAS]: *locality,* 2.5 miles northwest of present Tamarack in or near present Jelmini Basin (lat. 38°28'05" N, long. 120°06'30" W). Named on Big Trees (1891) 30' quadrangle.

Givens Creek [MADERA]: *stream,* flows 4.5 miles to South Fork Merced River 7.5 miles south-southwest of Merced Peak (lat. 37° 32'40" N, long. 119°28'20" W). Named on Merced Peak (1953) 15' quadrangle.

Givens Gulch [MARIPOSA]: *canyon,* drained by a stream that flows 1.5 miles to Eldorado Creek 2.5 miles north-northwest of Santa Cruz Mountain (lat. 37°29'25" N, long. 120°13' W; at S line sec. 16, T 5 S, R 16 E). Named on Indian Gulch (1962) 7.5' quadrangle.

Givens Lake [MADERA]: *lake,* 900 feet long, 5.25 miles southwest of Merced Peak (lat. 37°35' N, long. 119°27'55" W); the lake is at the head of a branch of Givens Creek. Named on Merced Peak (1953) 15' quadrangle.

Givens Meadow [MADERA]: *area,* 6 miles southwest of Merced Peak (lat. 37°34'45" N, long. 119°28'20" W); the place is 0.5 mile southwest of Givens Lake along Givens Creek. Named on Merced Peak (1953) 15' quadrangle.

Glacier Brook: see **Snow Creek** [MARIPOSA] (1).

Glacier Lake: see **Johnson Lake** [MADERA].

Glacier Monument: see **Fairview Dome** [TUOLUMNE].

Glacier Point [MARIPOSA]: *relief feature,* 1.5 miles south-southeast of Yosemite Village on the south side of Yosemite Valley (lat. 37°43'50" N, long. 119°34'20" W). Named on Yosemite (1956) 15' quadrangle.

Gladys Lake [MADERA]: *lake,* 600 feet long, 4.5 miles north-northwest of Devils Postpile (lat. 37°40'55" N, long. 119°07'05" W). Named on Devils Postpile (1953) 15' quadrangle.

Glasier Lake: see **Johnson Lake** [MADERA].

Glen Aulin [TUOLUMNE]: *valley,* 9 miles west of Tioga Pass along Tuolumne River (lat. 37°54'45" N, long. 119°25'35" W). Named on Tuolumne Meadows (1956) 15' quadrangle. R.B. Marshall of United States Geological Survey named the place in 1913 or 1914 at the suggestion of James McCormick, who later was secretary of United States Geographic Board; the name is from *gleann alainn,* which means "beautiful valley" or "beautiful glen" in Gaelic (United States Board on Geographic Names, 1934, p. 10).

Glen Aulin High Sierra Camp [TUOLUMNE]: *locality,* 9 miles west of Tioga Pass (lat. 37°54'35" N, long. 119°25'05" W); the camp is at Glen Aulin. Named on Tuolumne Meadows (1956) 15' quadrangle.

Glencoe [CALAVERAS]: *village,* 4 miles west of Rail Road Flat near the head of Mosquito Gulch (lat. 38°21'15" N, long. 120°35' W; near S line sec. 19, T 6 N, R 13 E). Named on Rail Road Flat (1948) 7.5 quadrangle. The place formerly was called Mosquito Gulch (California Department of Parks and Recreation, p. 15). Postal authorities established Musquito post office in 1858, discontinued it in 1869, and reestablished it in 1873 with the name "Musquito Gulch"; they changed the name to Glencoe in 1878, discontinued it in 1916, and reestablished it in 1947 (Salley, p. 85, 149). L.P. Terwilliger, a pioneer of Calaveras County, applied the name "Glencoe" to the place (Hanna, p. 121).

Glenwood [SAN JOAQUIN]: *locality,* 5.5 miles east-northeast of downtown Stockton (lat. 37°59'20" N, long. 121°11'40" W). Named on San Jose (1962) 1°x 2° quadrangle. Stockton East (1952) 7.5' quadrangle shows the Glenwood school at the place.

Globe Rock [MADERA]: *peak,* 9.5 miles north of Shuteye Peak (lat. 37°29'10" N, long. 119°24'45" W; sec. 23, T 5 S, R 23 E). Altitude 7152 feet. Named on Shuteye Peak (1953) 15' quadrangle.

Gnat Creek: see **Daulton Creek** [MADERA].

Goat Mountain [MADERA]: *ridge,* south- to southeast-trending, 3 miles long, 7 miles southeast of Yosemite Forks (lat. 37°17' N, long. 119°33'35" W). Named on Bass Lake (1953) 15' quadrangle.

Goday Gulch: see **Carson** [MARIPOSA].

Godfrey: see **Confidence** [TUOLUMNE].

Goff [MARIPOSA]: *locality,* 10.5 miles south-southwest of Coulterville along Yosemite Valley Railroad (lat. 37°34'40" N, long. 120° 17'30" W). Named on Sonora (1897) 30' quadrangle.

Gold: see **Fine Gold** [MADERA].

Golden Gate Butte: see **Golden Gate Hill** [CALAVERAS].

Golden Gate Hill [CALAVERAS]: *peak,* 5 miles northwest of San Andreas (lat. 38°14'55" N, long. 120°44'35" W; near E line sec. 34, T 5 N, T 11 E). Altitude 2064 feet. Named on San Andreas (1962) 7.5' quadrangle. The feature also was known as Golden Gate Butte (Gudde, 1975, p. 133).

Goldgulch: see **Coarsegold** [MADERA].

Gold Spring [TUOLUMNE]: *spring,* 1 mile north-northwest of Columbia (lat. 38°02'50" N, long. 120°24'35" W; sec. 11, T 2 N, R 14 E). Named on Columbia (1948) 7.5' quadrangle. Big Trees (1891) 30' quadrangle shows a locality called Gold Spring at the site. Charles M. Radcliff, justice of the peace for the mining camp at the spring, gave the name "Gold Spring" to the camp after watching an old man and his two sons mining there (Stoddart, p. 129). A place called Texas Flat was situated just south of Gold Spring (Gudde, 1975, p. 347).

Good Gulch [MARIPOSA]: *canyon,* drained by a stream that flows 3 miles to Merced River 7 miles east-northeast of the village of Bear Valley (lat. 37°36'30" N, long. 120°00'10" W; near S line sec. 5, T 4 S, R 18 E). Named on Bear Valley (1947) and Feliciana Mountain (1947) 7.5' quadrangles. Called Goods Gulch on Kinsley (1947) 7.5' quadrangle.

Goodmans Corner [CALAVERAS-SAN JOAQUIN]: *locality,* 5.5 miles east of Clements on San Joaquin-Calaveras County line (lat. 38°12'15" N, long. 120°59'10" W; sec. 16, T 4 N, R 9 E). Named on Wallace (1962) 7.5' quadrangle.

Goods Gulch: see **Good Gulch** [MARIPOSA].

Goodwin Creek [STANISLAUS]: *stream,* flows 2.5 miles to Evans Creek 1 mile south-southeast of La Grange (lat. 37°39'05" N, long. 120°27'20" W; sec. 29, T 3 S, R 14 E). Named on La Grange (1962) 7.5' quadrangle.

Goodwin's: see **Yosemite Junction** [TUOLUMNE].

Gooseberry Canyon [STANISLAUS]: *canyon,* drained by a stream that flows 2.5 miles to North Fork Orestimba Creek nearly 2 miles west-southwest of Mikes Peak (lat. 37°20'50" N, long. 121°20'45" W; near NW cor. sec. 8, T 7 S, R 6 E). Named on Mount Stakes (1955) and Wilcox Ridge (1956) 7.5' quadrangles.

Gooseberry Creek [TUOLUMNE]: *stream,* flows less than 1 mile to North Fork Tuolumne River 1.5 miles east of Pinecrest (lat. 38°11'20" N, long. 119°58'05" W; sec. 23, T 4 N, R 18 E). Named on Pinecrest (1979) 7.5' quadrangle.

Gooseberry Flat [MADERA]: *area,* 3.25 miles northeast of Yosemite Forks along Nelder Creek (lat. 37°24'20" N, long. 119°35'35" W; near SW cor. sec. 17, T 6 S, R 22 E). Named on Bass Lake (1953) 15' quadrangle.

Gooseberry Spring [CALAVERAS]: *spring,* 7 miles west-southwest of Angels Camp (lat. 38°01'35" N, long. 120°39'15" W; sec. 16, T 2 N, R 12 E). Named on Salt Spring Valley (1962) 7.5' quadrangle.

Goose Creek [SAN JOAQUIN]: *stream,* heads just inside Amador County and flows 11 miles to Dry Creek 10 miles northeast of Lodi (lat. 38°15'35" N, long. 121°09'55" W; sec. 25, T 5 N, R 7 E). Named on Clay (1953) and Goose Creek (1968) 7.5' quadrangles.

Gopher Hills: see **Gopher Ridge** [CALAVERAS].

Gopher Ridge [CALAVERAS]: *range,* extends south-southeast from Calaveras River to Littlejohns Creek. Named on Copperopolis (1962), Jenny Lind (1962), Salt Spring Valley (1962), and Valley Springs (1962) 7.5' quadrangles. Whitney (1865, p. 255) used the name "Gopher Hills" for the feature.

Gordon Creek [MADERA]: *stream,* flows 1.5 miles to Rock Creek 2.5 miles south-southeast of Shuteye Peak (lat. 37°19'05" N, long. 119°24'20" W; sec. 13, T 7 S, R 23 E); the stream heads at Gordon Meadow. Named on Shuteye Peak (1953) 15' quadrangle.

Gordon Meadow [MADERA]: *area,* 2.5 miles south of Shuteye Peak (lat. 37°18'45" N, long. 119°25'45" W; on S line sec. 14, T 7 S, R 23 E); the place is at the head of Gordon Creek. Named on Shuteye Peak (1953) 15' quadrangle.

Gothic Peak: see **Mount Clark** [MARIPOSA].

Gotri [SAN JOAQUIN]: *locality,* 3.25 miles south-southeast of Farmington along Southern Pacific Railroad (lat. 37°53'10" N, long. 120°58'20" W; near N line sec. 3, T 1 S, R 9 E). Named on Farmington (1953) 7.5' quadrangle. Called Trigo on Trigo (1915) 7.5' quadrangle. The name "Gotri" obviously is the name "Trigo" with the syllables reversed.

Gourley Reservoir [CALAVERAS]: *lake,* 650 feet long, 4 miles northwest of San Andreas (lat. 38°14'15" N, long. 120°44'10" W; on S line sec. 35, T 5 N, R 11 E). Named on San Andreas (1962) 7.5' quadrangle.

Grace Meadow [TUOLUMNE]: *area,* 3.5 miles west of Tower Peak along Falls Creek (lat. 38°08'20" N, long. 119°36'50" W). Named on Tower Peak (1956) 15' quadrangle. The name commemorates Grace Sovulewski, whose father Gabriel Sovulewski was in government service at Yosemite National Park (United States Board on Geographic Names, 1934, p. 10).

Gracey: see **Castle Gardens** [MERCED].

Graham Meadow [MADERA]: *area,* 7.5 miles east-southeast of Yosemite Forks (lat. 37°18'45" N, long. 119°30'45" W; on N line sec. 24, T 7 S, R 22 E). Named on Bass Lake (1953) 15' quadrangle.

Graham Mountain [MADERA]: *ridge,* northwest-trending, 1 mile long, 6.25 miles east of Yosemite Forks (lat. 37°21'30" N, long. 119°30'55" W; on S line sec. 36, T 6 S, R 22 E). Named on Bass Lake (1953) 15' quadrangle.

Grand Canyon of the Tuolumne River [TUOLUMNE]: *canyon,* 18 miles long, along Tuolumne River above a point 6 miles northeast of Mather (lat. 37°56'50" N, long. 119°47'15" W). Named on Hetch Hetchy Reservoir (1956) 15' quadrangle. Called Grand Canyon of the Tuolumne on Yosemite (1909) 30' quadrangle.

Grand Mountain [TUOLUMNE]: *peak,* nearly 8 miles east-northeast of White Wolf (lat. 37°54'45" N, long. 119°31'05" W). Altitude 9491 feet. Named on Hetch Hetchy Reservoir (1956) 15' quadrangle. John Muir reportedly gave the name "Grand Mountain" to the peak, which Theodore S. Solomons called Tuolumne Castle (Browning, 1986, p. 85).

Grange: see **Harp** [STANISLAUS].

Granite Creek [MADERA]: *stream,* formed by the confluence of East Fork and West Fork, flows 6.5 miles to San Joaquin River 13 miles northeast of Shuteye Peak (lat. 37°28'35" N, long. 119° 14' W; near E line sec. 21, T 5 S, R 25 E). Named on Devils Postpile (1953), Kaiser Peak (1953), and Merced Peak (1953) 15' quadrangles. East Fork is 10 miles long and West Fork is 9.5 miles long; both forks are named on Merced Peak (1953) 15' quadrangle.

Granite Creek [MARIPOSA]: *stream,* flows 3 miles to South Fork Merced River 5 miles south-southeast of El Portal (lat. 37°36'10" N, long. 119°45'25" W). Named on Buckingham Mountain (1947) 7.5' quadrangle.

Granite Creek [TUOLUMNE]: *stream,* flows 3.5 miles to Cherry Creek 6.25 miles west of Mather (lat. 37°53'45" N, long. 119°58' W; sec. 35, T 1 N, R 18 E). Named on Lake Eleanor (1956) 15' quadrangle.

Granite Creek Campground [MADERA]: *locality,* 9.5 miles southeast of Merced Peak near the confluence of East Fork Granite Creek and West Fork Granite Creek (lat. 37°32'30" N, long. 119° 16' W). Named on Merced Peak (1953) 15' quadrangle.

Granite Creek Saddle [MARIPOSA]: *pass,* 8 miles south of El Portal (lat. 37°33'25" N, long. 119°45'45" W); the pass is at the head of Granite Creek. Named on Buckingham Mountain (1947) 7.5' quadrangle.

Granite Dome [TUOLUMNE]: *peak,* 12 miles west-northwest of Tower Peak (lat. 38°12'55" N, long. 119°44'45" W). Altitude 10,322 feet. Named on Tower Peak (1956) 15' quadrangle. United States Board on Geographic Names (1965c, p. 11) approved the name "Sardella Lake" for a lake, 0.1 mile across, located 0.7 mile northeast of Granite Dome (lat. 38°13'20" N, long. 119°44'05" W); the name is for Giovanni Domenico Sardella, who lived by the lake.

Granite Dome: see **Wawona Dome** [MARIPOSA].

Granite Lake [TUOLUMNE]: *lake,* 800 feet long, 9 miles east of Pinecrest (lat. 38°11' N, long. 119°50' W; sec. 24, T 4 N, R 19 E). Named on Pinecrest (1956) 15' quadrangle.

Granite Lakes [TUOLUMNE]: *lakes,* two, largest 0.5 mile long, 1.25 miles northwest of Tioga Pass (lat. 37°55'20" N, long. 119°16'35" W). Named on Tuolumne Meadows (1956) 15' quadrangle. United States Board on Geographic Names (1962a, p. 17) decided that Granite Lakes are not part of the group called Gaylor Lakes.

Granite Ridge [TUOLUMNE]: *ridge,* southwest-trending, 5 miles long, 5 miles north-northeast of Twain Harte (lat. 38°06'45" N, long. 120°12'15" W). Named on Crandall Peak (1979) and Twain Harte (1979) 7.5' quadrangles.

Granite Springs [MARIPOSA]: *settlement,* nearly 3 miles southwest of Penon Blanco Peak (lat. 37°42' N, long. 120°17'30" W; near W line sec. 2,

T 3 S, R 15 E). Named on Penon Blanco Peak (1962, photorevised 1973) 7.5' quadrangle.

Granite Stairway [MADERA]: *relief feature,* 3 miles southwest of Devils Postpile (lat. 37°35'40" N, long. 119°07'30" W). Named on Devils Postpile (1953) 15' quadrangle.

Grant Lakes [MARIPOSA]: *lakes,* two, largest 1000 feet long, 10 miles north-northeast of Yosemite Village (lat. 37°53'15" N, long. 119°32' W; mainly in sec. 3, T 1 S, R 22 E). Named on Hetch Hetchy Reservoir (1956) 15' quadrangle.

Grapevine Canyon [MADERA]: *canyon,* drained by a stream that flows 1.5 miles to San Joaquin River 6.5 miles south-southwest of the town of North Fork (lat. 37°08'30" N, long. 119°33'40" W; at S line sec. 15, T 9 S, R 22 E). Named on North Fork (1965) 7.5' quadrangle.

Grapevine Creek [TUOLUMNE]: *stream,* flows 3.5 miles to Tuolumne River 7 miles southeast of Tuolumne (lat. 37°53'10" N, long. 120°08'45" W; sec. 6, T 1 S, R 17 E). Named on Duckwall Mountain (1948) and Tuolumne (1948) 7.5' quadrangles.

Grapevine Gulch [CALAVERAS]: *canyon,* drained by a stream that flows 2.5 miles to Stanislaus River 3.5 miles east of Vallecito (lat. 38°05'35" N, long. 120°24'35" W; near SW cor. sec. 23, T 3 N, R 14 E). Named on Columbia (1948) 7.5' quadrangle.

Grapevine Point [TUOLUMNE]: *peak,* 5.25 miles south of Duckwall Mountain (lat. 37°53'30" N, long. 120°07'25" W; near SE cor. sec. 32, T 1 N, R 17 E). Altitude 3650 feet. Named on Duckwall Mountain (1948) 7.5' quadrangle.

Gravelly Fork [MADERA]: *locality,* nearly 7 miles south-southwest of Merced Peak along South Fork Merced River (lat. 37°32'50" N, long. 119°27'10" W). Named on Merced Peak (1953) 15' quadrangle.

Gravel Pit Lake [TUOLUMNE]: *lake,* 1050 feet long, 6 miles north-northeast of Mather along Miguel Creek (lat. 37°57'55" N, long. 119°49'40" W; near NW cor. sec. 7, T 1 N, R 20 E). Named on Lake Eleanor (1956) 15' quadrangle.

Gravel Range [TUOLUMNE]: *ridge,* south-southwest-trending, 3 miles long, 10 miles southeast of Duckwall Mountain (lat. 37°51'30" N, long. 120°00'15" W). Named on Lake Eleanor (1956) and Tuolumne (1948) 15' quadrangles.

Graveyard Creek [TUOLUMNE]: *stream,* flows less than 1 mile to Don Pedro Reservoir 2 miles east-northeast of Don Pedro Camp (lat. 37°43'20" N, long. 120°22'30" W; near NE cor. sec. 36, T 2 S, R 14 E). Named on Penon Blanco Peak (1962, photorevised 1973) 7.5' quadrangle.

Graveyard Meadow [MADERA]: *area,* 11 miles northeast of Shuteye Peak (lat. 37°27'50" N, long. 119°17'40" W; sec. 25, T 5 S, R 24 E). Named on Shuteye Peak (1953) 15' quadrangle.

Gray Butte: see **Grey Butte** [TUOLUMNE].

Gray Creek [MARIPOSA]: *stream,* flows 2 miles to Clark Fork 12 miles south-southwest of Cathedral Peak (lat. 37°40'55" N, long. 119°27'50" W); the stream heads near Gray Peak [MADERA]. Named on Merced Peak (1953) 15' quadrangle.

Grayling Lake [MADERA]: *lake,* 750 feet long, 3.5 miles west-northwest of Merced Peak (lat. 37°39'40" N, long. 119°26'50" W). Named on Merced Peak (1953) 15' quadrangle. The name was given in 1930 when grayling first were planted in the lake (Browning, 1986, p. 87).

Gray Peak [MADERA]: *peak,* 3 miles north-northwest of Merced Peak (lat. 37°40'25" N, long. 119°25'05" W). Altitude 11,574 feet. Named on Merced Peak (1953) 15' quadrangle. Members of the Whitney survey named the peak for the color of its upper part (Browning, 1988, p. 53). United States Board on Geographic Names (1933a, p. 336) rejected the name "Hayes Peak" for the feature.

Gray Peak Fork [MADERA-MARIPOSA]: *stream,* heads in Madera County and flows 7.5 miles to Merced River 8.5 miles south of Cathedral Peak in Mariposa County (lat. 37°43'45" N, long. 119° 23'25" W); the stream heads near Gray Peak [MADERA]. Named on Mount Lyell (1901) 30' quadrangle.

Grayson [STANISLAUS]: *village,* 1.5 miles northeast of Westley (lat. 37°33'50" N, long. 121°10'40" W). Named on Westley (1969) 7.5' quadrangle. Called Grayson City on Gibbes' (1850) map. A.J. Grayson started a ferry in 1850 on San Joaquin River 8 miles above the mouth of Tuolumne River, and a community known as Grayson developed there; although the ferry continued to operate, the place was nearly deserted from 1852 until 1868, when the site was surveyed and a town laid out (Hoover, Rensch, and Rensch, p. 542). Postal authorities established Graysonville post office in 1870, changed the name to Grayson in 1874, and discontinued it in 1906 (Frickstad, p. 200). Blake (p. 11) crossed San Joaquin River at Grayson's Ferry in 1853. Gibbes' (1850) map shows Lippincott's Ferry above Grayson City on Rio San Joaquin.

Grayson City: see **Grayson** [STANISLAUS].

Grayson's Ferry: see **Grayson** [STANISLAUS].

Graysonville: see **Grayson** [STANISLAUS].

Greaser Gulch [MARIPOSA]: *canyon,* drained by a stream that flows 4.5 miles to Burns Creek 1.25 miles east of Courthouse Rock (lat. 37°25'15" N, long. 120°15'25" W; sec. 7, T 6 S, R 16 E). Named on Haystack Mountain (1962) and Indian Gulch (1962) 7.5' quadrangles.

Greasertown: see **San Andreas** [CALAVERAS].

Great Dome: see **Balloon Dome** [MADERA].

Great Valley: see "Regional setting."

Greeley Hill [MARIPOSA]:

(1) *peak,* 3 miles northeast of Coulterville (lat. 37°44'35" N, long. 120°09'15" W; near S line sec. 24, T 2 S, R 16 E). Altitude 3629 feet. Named on Coulterville (1947) 7.5' quadrangle.

(2) *settlement,* 4.25 miles northeast of Coulterville (lat. 37°44'45" N, long. 120°07'50" W; on E line sec. 19, T 2 S, R 17 E); the place is 1.25 miles east of Greeley Hill (1). Named on Coulterville (1947) 7.5' quadrangle. The name commemorates Josiah F. Greely (who spelled his name without the third "e"), owner of a sawmill at the place (Sargent, Shirley, 1976, p. 21).

Green Gulch [MARIPOSA]: *canyon,* drained by a stream that flows 3 miles to Bear Creek (2) 4.25 miles south-southeast of Bear Valley (2) (lat. 37°30'30" N, long. 120°05'35" W). Named on Bear Valley (1947) 7.5' quadrangle. Called Green's Gulch on Laizure's (1928) map.

Greenhorn Creek [CALAVERAS]: *stream,* flows 3 miles to Angels Creek 2.5 miles south-southwest of Angels Camp (lat. 38°02'30" N, long. 120°33'30" W; sec. 9, T 2 N, R 13 E); the stream goes through Greenhorn Gulch. Named on Angels Camp (1962) 7.5' quadrangle.

Greenhorn Gulch [CALAVERAS]: *canyon,* 1 mile long, 2 miles south-southwest of Angels Camp (lat. 38°02'50" N, long. 120°33'50" W); the canyon is along lower reaches of Greenhorn Creek. Named on Angels Camp (1962) 7.5' quadrangle.

Greenleaf: see **Gregg** [MADERA].

Green Mountain [MADERA]: *ridge,* east- to southeast-trending, 1.5 miles long, 10 miles west-southwest of Devils Postpile (lat. 37°34'20" N, long. 119°15' W). Named on Devils Postpile (1953) and Merced Peak (1953) 15' quadrangles.

Green Mountain [MARIPOSA]: *peak,* 15 miles south of Mariposa (lat. 37°15'50" N, long. 119°59'25" W; sec. 3, T 8 S, R 18 E). Altitude 1374 feet. Named on Ben Hur (1947) 7.5' quadrangle.

Green's Gulch: see **Green Gulch** [MARIPOSA].

Green Spring Run [TUOLUMNE]: *stream,* flows nearly 7 miles to Tulloch Lake 3.5 miles northwest of Keystone (lat. 37°52'30" N, long. 120°32'55" W; sec. 4, T 1 S, R 13 E). Named on Keystone (1962) and Melones Dam (1962) 7.5' quadrangles.

Green Springs: see **Keystone** [TUOLUMNE].

Gregg [MADERA]: *locality,* 2.5 miles south-southeast of Trigo along Atchison, Topeka and Santa Fe Railroad (lat. 36°52'55" N, long. 119°56'10" W; near S line sec. 18, T 12 S, R 19 E). Named on Gregg (1965) 7.5' quadrangle. Called Greenleaf on Mendenhall's (1908) map. Postal authorities established Greenleaf post office in 1904 and discontinued it in 1905; they established Gregg post office in 1917, discontinued it for a time in 1928, and discontinued it finally in 1931 (Frickstad, p. 85).

Greve [CALAVERAS]: *locality,* 3 miles west-northwest of Blue Mountain near present Hamilton Camp (lat. 38°21' N, long. 120° 25' W). Named on Big Trees (1891) 30' quadrangle.

Grey Butte [TUOLUMNE]: *peak,* 3.5 miles south-southeast of Matterhorn Peak (lat. 38°03'05" N, long. 119°20'50" W). Altitude 11,365 feet. Named on Matterhorn Peak (1956) 15' quadrangle. United States Board on Geographic Names (1970, p. 3) gave the name "Gray Butte" as a variant.

Grider Island [STANISLAUS]: *area,* 3.5 miles east of Westley on the south side of San Joaquin River (lat. 37°33'30" N, long. 121° 07'55" W). Named on Westley (1952) 7.5' quadrangle.

Griswold Creek [TUOLUMNE]: *stream,* formed by the confluence of North Fork and South Fork, flows 12.5 miles to North Fork Stanislaus River 3.25 miles north-northeast of Stanislaus (lat. 38°10'40" N, long. 120°20'10" W; at SW cor. sec. 21, T 4 N, R 15 E). Named on Boards Crossing (1979), Crandall Peak (1979), and Stanislaus (1948) 7.5' quadrangles. North Fork is 6 miles long and South Fork is 4 miles long; both forks are named on Boards Crossing (1979) and Liberty Hill (1979) 7.5' quadrangles.

Grizzly: see **Big Grizzly**, under **Miller Gulch** [MARIPOSA].

Grizzly Creek [MADERA]: *stream,* flows 5 miles to South Fork Merced River 8 miles southwest of Merced Peak (lat. 37°32'30" N, long. 119°29' W); the stream heads at Grizzly Lake. Named on Merced Peak (1953) and Shuteye Peak (1953) 15' quadrangles. Called Quartz Cr. on Mount Lyell (1901) 30' quadrangle, but United States Board on Geographic Names (1969, p. 3) rejected this name for the stream, which is west of Quartz Mountain (1).

Grizzly Creek [TUOLUMNE]: *stream,* flows 3.5 miles to Beaver Creek 10 miles southwest of Liberty Hill (lat. 38°16'10" N, long. 120°14'05" W; sec. 20, T 5 N, R 16 E). Named on Boards Crossing (1979) 7.5' quadrangle.

Grizzly Creek: see **Big Grizzly Creek** [MARIPOSA]; **Little Grizzly Creek** [MARIPOSA].

Grizzly Falls: see **Little Grizzly Falls**, under **Bunnel Cascade** [MARIPOSA].

Grizzly Flat: see **Big Grizzly Flat** [MARIPOSA]; **Little Grizzly Flat**

[MARIPOSA].

Grizzly Gulch [TUOLUMNE]:

(1) *canyon,* drained by a stream that flows 0.5 mile to Devils Canyon 3.5 miles west-southwest of Columbia (lat. 38°00'35" N, long. 120°27'30" W; sec. 20, T 2 N, R 14 E). Named on Columbia (1948) 7.5' quadrangle.

(2) *canyon,* drained by a stream that flows nearly 3 miles to Moccasin Lake at Moccasin (lat. 37°48'40" N, long. 120°18'10" W; near N line sec. 34, T 1 S, R 15 E). Named on Moccasin (1948) 7.5' quadrangle.

Grizzly Lake [MADERA]: *lake,* 600 feet long, 10 miles north-northwest of Shuteye Peak (lat. 37°29'10" N, long. 119°29' W; near W line sec. 20, T 5 S, R 23 E); the lake is at the head of Grizzly Creek. Named on Shuteye Peak (1953) 15' quadrangle.

Grizzly Meadow [MADERA]: *area,* 4 miles north of Shuteye Peak (lat. 37°24'15" N, long. 119°24'45" W; sec. 13, T 6 S, R 23 E). Named on Shuteye Peak (1953) 15' quadrangle.

Grizzly Meadow [TUOLUMNE]:

(1) *area,* 7 miles south-southwest of Liberty Hill (lat. 38°16'40" N, long. 120°09'10" W; sec. 24, T 5 N, R 16 E). Named on Boards Crossing (1979) 7.5' quadrangle.

(2) *area,* 5.5 miles northwest of Tower Peak (lat. 38°11'30" N, long. 119°37'45" W); the place is 0.5 mile west of Grizzly Peak. Named on Tower Peak (1956) 15' quadrangle.

Grizzly Mountain: see **Big Grizzly Mountain** [MARIPOSA]; **Little Grizzly Mountain** [MARIPOSA].

Grizzly Peak [MARIPOSA]: *peak,* 2.5 miles east-southeast of Yosemite Village (lat. 37°43'50" N, long. 119°33' W). Named on Yosemite (1956) 15' quadrangle. The feature was called Grizzly Point in the early days (Browning, 1986, p. 88).

Grizzly Peak [TUOLUMNE]: *peak,* 5.25 miles northwest of Tower Peak on Tuolumne-Mono County line (lat. 38°11'35" N, long. 119° 37'15" W). Named on Tower Peak (1956) 15' quadrangle.

Grizzly Point: see **Grizzly Peak** [MARIPOSA].

Grohl: see **Grohl Meadow** [TUOLUMNE].

Grohl Meadow [TUOLUMNE]: *area,* 4.5 miles northwest of Crandall Peak (lat. 38°12'15" N, long. 120°12'10" W; sec. 15, T 4 N, R 16 E). Named on Crandall Peak (1979) 7.5' quadrangle. Big Trees (1891) 30' quadrangle has the name "Grohl" at the place.

Grohls Upper Camp [TUOLUMNE]: *locality,* 4 miles east-southeast of Liberty Hill (lat. 38°20'25" N, long. 120°02'10" W; sec. 30, T 6 N, R 18 E). Named on Big Meadow (1956) 15' quadrangle.

Groundhog Meadow [TUOLUMNE]:

(1) *area,* 6 miles south-southwest of Dardanelle (lat. 38°15'35" N, long. 119°52' W; sec. 27, T 5 N, R 19 E). Named on Dardanelle (1979) 7.5' quadrangle.

(2) *area,* 9 miles east-southeast of Pinecrest along Piute Creek (1) (lat. 38°09'20" N, long. 119°50' W; sec. 36, T 4 N, R 19 E). Named on Pinecrest (1956) 15' quadrangle.

Grouse Creek [MARIPOSA]: *stream,* flows 4.5 miles to Merced River 9 miles west-southwest of Yosemite Village (lat. 37°41'20" N, long. 119°43'40" W; sec. 11, T 3 S, R 20 E). Named on Yosemite (1956) 15' quadrangle.

Grouse Creek [TUOLUMNE]: *stream,* flows 2.25 miles to Relief Reservoir 6.5 miles southwest of Sonora Pass (lat. 38°16'10" N, long. 119°44' W; at W line sec. 24, T 5 N, R 20 E). Named on Sonora Pass (1979) 7.5' quadrangle.

Grouse Lake [MADERA]: *lake,* 500 feet long, 2.25 miles southwest of Buena Vista Peak (lat. 37°34'20" N, long. 119°32'45" W; sec. 22, T 4 S, R 22 E). Named on Yosemite (1956) 15' quadrangle.

Grouse Lake [TUOLUMNE]: *lake,* 650 feet long, 7.5 miles east-southeast of Pinecrest (lat. 38°09'05" N, long. 119°52'10" W; near S line sec. 34, T 4 N, R 19 E). Named on Pinecrest (1956) 15' quadrangle.

Grouse Meadow [MADERA]: *area,* 6.25 miles north-northeast of Yosemite Forks (lat. 37°26'55" N, long. 119°34'40" W; at SW cor. sec. 33, T 5 S, R 22 E). Named on Bass Lake (1953) 15' quadrangle.

Grove: see **The Grove** [MERCED].

Groveland [TUOLUMNE]: *village,* 13 miles southeast of Sonora (lat. 37°50'20" N, long. 120°13'45" W; sec. 20, 21, T 1 S, R 16 E). Named on Groveland (1947) 7.5' quadrangle. Postal authorities established Garrotte post office in 1851 and changed the name to Groveland in 1875 (Frickstad, p. 215). Following the hanging of two Mexican thieves there in 1849, the place became known as Garrote from the Spanish term for death by choking or hanging; later the community was called First Garrote—to distinguish it from Second Garrote—until the middle 1870's, when Benjamin Savory suggested the more genteel name "Groveland," taken from his hometown in Massachusetts (Paden and Schlichtmann, p. 167-168).

Groves Meadow: see **Sonny Meadow** [MARIPOSA].

Grubb Gulch [TUOLUMNE]: *canyon,* drained by a stream that flows 1.5 miles to Rose Creek 5.5 miles north of Twain Harte (lat. 38° 07'10" N, long. 120°14'15" W; sec. 17, T 3 N, R 16 E). Named on Twain Harte (1979) 7.5' quadrangle.

Grub Gulch [MADERA]:

(1) *canyon,* 10.5 miles northeast of Raymond (lat. 37°19'25" N, long. 119°46'10" W; sec. 15, T 7 S, R 20 E). Named on Horsecamp Mountain (1947) 7.5' quadrangle. The name is from the local tradition that miners, unsuccessful elsewhere, could always "grub out" enough gold in the canyon to make a living (Hanna, p. 128).

(2) *locality,* 10.5 miles northeast of Raymond (lat. 37°19'30" N, long. 119°46'15" W; sec. 15, T 7 S, R 20 E); the place is in Grub Gulch (1). Named on Mariposa (1912) 30' quadrangle. Postal authorities established Grubgulch post office in 1883 and discontinued it in 1918 (Salley, p 90). They established Miami post office 8 miles southwest of Grub Gulch (2) in 1884 and discontinued it in 1887; the name was from the Miami River region of Ohio (Salley, p. 139).

Grummett Creek [STANISLAUS]: *stream,* flows 2 miles to Ingram Canyon 12 miles west-northwest of Patterson (lat. 37°31'25" N, long. 121°20'25" W; near SE cor. sec. 6, T 5 S, R 6 E). Named on Solyo (1953) 7.5' quadrangle.

Guadalupe: see **Guadalupe Mountains** [MARIPOSA].

Guadalupe Creek [MARIPOSA]: *stream,* flows 2.5 miles to Agua Fria Creek 4 miles east-northeast of the settlement Catheys Valley (lat. 37°27'15" N, long. 120°01'10" W). Named on Catheys Valley (1962) 7.5' quadrangle. United States Board on Geographic Names (1964a, p. 10) rejected the names "La Minita Creek" and "Minita Creek" for the stream. The canyon of the creek is called Minita Gulch on Indian Gulch (1920) 15' quadrangle, and is called Guadalupe Gulch on Laizure's (1928) map.

Guadalupe Gulch: see **Guadalupe Creek** [MARIPOSA].

Guadalupe Mountains [MARIPOSA]: *ridge,* northwest-trending, 6 miles long, center 3 miles east of the settlement of Catheys Valley (lat. 37°25'45" N, long. 120°02'30" W). Named on Catheys Valley (1962) 7.5' quadrangle. The name is from the old mining town of Guadalupe (Gudde, 1949, p. 137), which Hoffmann and Gardner's (1863-1867) map shows situated nearly 2 miles north-northwest of Bridgeport along Agua Fria Creek.

Guadalupe Valley [MARIPOSA]: *valley,* 4.5 miles east of the settlement of Catheys Valley along Agua Fria Creek (lat. 37°26'50" N, long. 120°00'35" W); the valley is northeast of Guadalupe Mountains. Named on Catheys Valley (1962) 7.5' quadrangle.

Guild [SAN JOAQUIN]: *locality,* 5.25 miles west-southwest of Lockeford along Central California Traction Railroad (lat. 38°08'40" N, long. 121°14'30" W; near NW cor. sec. 5, T 3 N, R 7 E). Named on Lockeford (1968) 7.5' quadrangle.

Guishetti [CALAVERAS]: *locality,* 3.25 miles west-southwest of present Tamarack (lat. 38°25' N, long. 120°08' W). Named on Big Trees (1891) 30' quadrangle.

Gully Meadow [TUOLUMNE]: *area,* 7 miles east-northeast of Pinecrest (lat. 38°14'45" N, long. 119°53'05" W; sec. 33, T 5 N, R 19 E). Named on Pinecrest (1979) 7.5' quadrangle. Called Coyote Meadows on Pinecrest (1956) 15' quadrangle. United States Board on Geographic Names (1980a, p. 3) described Gully Meadow as the northernmost of the group called Three Meadows, and rejected the names "Coyote Meadow" and "Coyote Meadows" for the feature.

Gunsite [MARIPOSA]: *relief feature,* nearly 4 miles west-southwest of Yosemite Village on the south side of Yosemite Valley (lat. 37° 43'10" N, long. 119°38'45" W). Named on Yosemite (1956) 15' quadrangle. Rangers of Yosemite National Park named the feature because the view along it has Leaning Tower centered as in a gunsite (Browning, 1986, p. 89).

Gustine [MERCED]: *town,* 29 miles west of Merced (lat. 37°15'15" N, long. 120°59'45" W; in and near sec. 8, T 8 S, R 9 E). Named on Los Banos (1961) and Turlock (1962) 15' quadrangles, and on Howard Ranch (1953) and Newman (1952) 7.5' quadrangles. Postal authorities established Gustine post office in 1907 (Frickstad, p. 100), and the town incorporated under the name "Gustine City" in 1915. According to local tradition, cattle baron Henry Miller named the place using his intimate name for his daughter Augusta (Hanna, p. 130).

Gustine City: see **Gustine** [MERCED].

Gwin: see **Le Grand** [MERCED]; **Rich Gulch** [CALAVERAS] (1).

Gwin Mine: see **Rich Gulch** [CALAVERAS] (1).

Gwin Mine Canyon: see **Rich Gulch** [CALAVERAS] (1).

Gwin's Peak: see **Liberty Cap** [MARIPOSA].

— H —

Haight [SAN JOAQUIN]: *locality,* 5 miles northwest of Waterloo along Central California Traction Railroad (lat. 38°05'35" N, long. 121°14'30" W; on W line sec. 20, T 3 N, R 7 E). Named on Waterloo (1968) 7.5' quadrangle. Called Hawes on Bellota (1939) 15' quadrangle.

Hale [TUOLUMNE]: *locality,* 3 miles north of Long Barn along South Fork Stanislaus River (lat. 38°07'50" N, long. 120°08'30" W). Named on Big Trees (1891) 30' quadrangle.

Half Dome [MARIPOSA]: *relief feature,* 3 miles east of Yosemite Village (lat. 37°44'40" N, long. 119°32' W). Named on Yosemite (1956) 15' quadrangle. The men who discovered Yosemite Valley named the domelike feature in 1851 (Hanna, p. 131). United States Board on Geographic Names (1934, p. 11) rejected the names "Tesaiyak," "Tisayac," and "Tis-sa-ack" for it.

Half Moon Meadow [MARIPOSA]: *area,* 10.5 miles north of Yosemite Village (lat. 37°53'40" N, long. 119°32'45" W). Named on Hetch Hetchy Reservoir (1956) 15' quadrangle.

Half Way Gulch [MARIPOSA]: *canyon,* drained by a stream that flows nearly 2 miles to Bear Creek (2) 2.5 miles south-southeast of the village of Bear Valley (lat. 37°32'15" N, long. 120°05'50" W). Named on Bear Valley (1947) 7.5' quadrangle. Coulterville (1947) 15' quadrangle has the form "Halfway Gulch" for the name. Laizure's (1928) map shows a place called Half Way House located along Half Way Gulch.

Half Way House: see **Half Way Gulch** [MARIPOSA]; **Mokelumne River** [CALAVERAS-SAN JOAQUIN].

Halfway House: see **Woods Creek** [TUOLUMNE].

Halleck Hill [CALAVERAS]: *peak,* 1.5 miles south-southwest of Vallecito (lat. 38°03'55" N, long. 120°29'20" W; sec. 36, T 3 N, R 13 E). Altitude 2235 feet. Named on Columbia (1948) 7.5' quadrangle.

Halley: see **Hally** [STANISLAUS].

Halls Gulch [MARIPOSA]: *canyon,* drained by a stream that flows 8.5 miles to Merced River 6.5 miles northeast of the village of Bear Valley (lat. 37°37'15" N, long. 120°01'15" W; sec. 6, T 4 S, R 18 E). Named on Buckhorn Peak (1947) and Kinsley (1947) 7.5' quadrangles. Called Hall Gulch on Bear Valley (1947) 7.5' quadrangle, but United States Board on Geographic Names (1978a, p. 4) rejected this form of the name. North Fork opens into the main canyon from the north 5 miles above the mouth of the main canyon; it is nearly 4 miles long and is named on Kinsley (1947) 7.5' quadrangle.

Hally [STANISLAUS]: *locality,* 4 miles northwest of Westley along Southern Pacific Railroad (lat. 37°35'40" N, long. 121°14'50" W; near N line sec. 18, T 4 S, R 7 E). Named on Westley (1952) 7.5' quadrangle. On California Mining Bureau's (1917b) map, the name has the form "Halley."

Ham Coward Gulch [MARIPOSA]: *canyon,* drained by a stream that flows nearly 2 miles to Gentry Gulch 4 miles northeast of Buckhorn Peak (lat. 37°41'40" N, long. 120°03'55" W; near S line sec. 2, T 3 S, R 17 E). Named on Buckhorn Peak (1947) 7.5' quadrangle.

Hamilton Camp [CALAVERAS]: *locality,* 3 miles east of Fort Mountain along Licking Fork (lat. 38°21'05" N, long. 120°25' W; sec. 27, T 6 N, R 14 E). Named on Fort Mountain (1979) 7.5' quadrangle.

Hamilton's Station: see **Buck Meadows** [MARIPOSA].

Hammer Hill [STANISLAUS]: *peak,* 4.25 miles east-northeast of Mustang Peak (lat. 37°12'50" N, long. 121°17'25" W; near W line sec. 26, T 8 S, R 6 E). Altitude 2429 feet. Named on Mustang Peak (1955) 7.5' quadrangle.

Hammill Canyon [TUOLUMNE]: *canyon,* 2.5 miles long, along Herring Creek above a point 7.5 miles southwest of Dardanelle (lat. 38°15'20" N, long. 119°55'15" W; sec. 30, T 5 N, R 19 E). Named on Donnell Lake (1979) 7.5' quadrangle.

Hammils Mountain [TUOLUMNE]: *peak,* 4 miles northwest of Keystone (lat. 37°52'35" N, long. 120°33'25" W; near E line sec. 5, T 1 S, R 13 E). Altitude 1044 feet. Named on Melones Dam (1962) 7.5' quadrangle.

Hammonds Hill: see **Del Puerto Canyon** [STANISLAUS].

Hams [CALAVERAS]: *locality,* 5.5 miles west-northwest of Blue Mountain (lat. 38°22'25" N, long. 120°27'40" W; sec. 17, T 6 N, R 14 E). Named on Blue Mountain (1956) 15' quadrangle.

Hanging Basket Lake [MARIPOSA]: *lake,* 750 feet long, 5.5 miles southeast of Cathedral Peak (lat. 37°47'20" N, long. 119°19'50" W). Named on Tuolumne Meadows (1956) 15' quadrangle.

Happy Camp [MARIPOSA]: *locality,* less than 1 mile south-southwest of Fish Camp (lat. 37°28'10" N, long. 119°38'40" W; sec. 26, T 5 S, R 21 E). Named on Bass Lake (1953) 15' quadrangle.

Happy Camp: see **Fish Camp** [MARIPOSA].

Happy Hollow [MADERA]: *canyon,* drained by a stream that flows 3.5 miles to Coarse Gold Creek 6 miles southeast of Knowles (lat. 37°09'35" N, long. 119°47'45" W; sec. 9, T 9 S, R 20 E). Named on Knowles (1962) and Little Table Mountain (1962) 7.5' quadrangles.

Happy Isles [MARIPOSA]: *islands,* 2 miles southeast of Yosemite Village in Merced River (lat. 37°43'50" N, long. 119°33'30" W). Named on Yosemite (1956) 15' quadrangle. W.E. Dennison named the islands for their effect on the emotions of visitors; James M Hutchings earlier called the place Island Rapids (Browning, 1986, p. 92).

Happy Valley [CALAVERAS]: *valley,* 1 mile east of Mokelumne Hill (lat. 38°18' N, long. 120°41'05" W; sec. 7, 8, T 5 N, R 12 E). Named on Mokelumne Hill (1948) 7.5' quadrangle. According to McKinstry (p. 358, 369), two canyons, Indian Gulch and Buckeye Gulch, join near the valley.

Harden Flat [TUOLUMNE]: *settlement,* 7 miles southwest of Mather along South Fork Tuolumne River (lat. 37°48'40" N, long. 119°56'45" W; sec. 36, T 1 S, R 18 E). Named on Lake Eleanor (1956) 15' quadrangle. According to Paden and Schlichtmann (p. 202), the name recalls James Hardin, an Englishman who owned land at the place. Yosemite (1909) 30' quadrangle shows Harden ranch at the site. United States Board on Geographic Names (1991, p. 4) approved the name "Crocker Meadow" for a flat located 3 miles east of Harden Flat (lat. 37°48'40" N, long. 119°53'30" W; sec. 33, T 1 S, R 19 E).

Harden Lake [TUOLUMNE]: *lake,* 1050 feet long, 2.25 miles northwest of White Wolf (lat. 37°53'45" N, long. 119°40'30" W). Named on Hetch Hetchy Reservoir (1956) 15' quadrangle. United States Board on Geographic Names (1933a, p. 352) rejected the names "Hardin Lake," "Hardins Lake," "Hardin's Lake," and "Rardin Lake" for the feature.

Hardin Lake: see **Harden Lake** [TUOLUMNE].

Hardscrabble Gulch [TUOLUMNE]: *canyon,* drained by a stream that flows 1 mile to Rattlesnake Gulch 1.5 miles east of Columbia (lat. 38°02' N, long. 120°22'15" W; near N line sec. 18, T 2 N, R 15 E). Named on Columbia SE (1948) 7.5' quadrangle.

Hardscratch Point: see **Potato Point** [SAN JOAQUIN].

Harmon Peak: see **Carmen Peak** [CALAVERAS].

Harp [STANISLAUS]: *locality,* 4 miles south of Modesto along Tidewater Southern Railroad (lat. 37°34'50" N, long. 120°59' W; on S line sec. 16, T 4 S, R 9 E). Named on Ceres (1969) 7.5' quadrangle. California Division of Highways' (1934) map shows a place called Grange located nearly 1 mile south of Harp along the railroad.

Harriet Lake [MADERA]: *lake,* 2000 feet long, 5.5 miles east-northeast of Merced Peak (lat. 37°40'25" N, long. 119°18'25" W). Named on Merced Peak (1953) 15' quadrangle.

Harris: see **Frank Harris Point** [MARIPOSA].

Hart: see **Kingdon** [SAN JOAQUIN].

Hart Lakes [MARIPOSA]: *lakes,* three, largest 800 feet long, 9 miles northeast of Wawona (lat. 37°37'15" N, long. 119°36'40" W; sec. 2, T 4 S, R 22 E). Named on Yosemite (1956) 15' quadrangle.

Hartley Slough [MERCED]: *stream,* heads near Merced and flows 4 miles to Owens Creek 14 miles north-northeast of Dos Palos Y (lat. 37°14'20" N, long. 120°32'45" W; sec. 16, T 8 S, R 13 E). Named on Atwater (1961) and Santa Rita Park (1962) 15' quadrangles.

Hartman Creek [STANISLAUS]: *stream,* flows 3.25 miles to South Fork Orestimba Creek 1.5 miles northwest of Mustang Peak (lat. 37°12'05" N, long. 121°22'40" W; sec. 36, T 8 S, R 5 E). Named on Mississippi Creek (1955) 7.5' quadrangle.

Harveys Bar: see **Horseshoe Bend** [MARIPOSA].

Haskell Meadow [MADERA]: *area,* nearly 2 miles south of Shuteye Peak (lat. 37°19'25" N, long. 119°25'55" W; on W line sec. 14, T 7 S, R 23 E). Named on Shuteye Peak (1953) 15' quadrangle. The name is for Bill Haskell and John Haskell, early sheepmen in the neighborhood (Browning, 1986, p. 93).

Hatch [STANISLAUS]: *locality,* 6 miles west of Turlock along Tidewater Southern Railroad (lat. 37°29'25" N, long. 120°57'15" W; sec. 23, T 5 S, R 9 E). Named on Hatch (1962) 7.5' quadrangle.

Hatch Creek [TUOLUMNE]: *stream,* flows 5.5 miles to Don Pedro Reservoir 4.5 miles south-southwest of Moccasin (lat. 37°45'05" N, long. 120°20'35" W; sec. 20, T 2 S, R 15 E). Named on Moccasin (1948) and Penon Blanco Peak (1962) 7.5' quadrangles.

Hathaway Pines [CALAVERAS]: *settlement,* 6.5 miles northeast of Murphys (lat. 38°11'30" N, long. 120°21'50" W; sec. 18, 19, T 4 N, R 15 E). Named on Stanislaus (1948) 7.5' quadrangle. Postal authorities established Hathaway Pines post office in 1943; the name is for Robert B. Hathaway, first postmaster and promoter of a vacation resort at the place (Salley, p. 94).

Haupt Creek [CALAVERAS]: *stream,* flows 4 miles to New Hogan Reservoir 4 miles east of Valley Springs (lat. 38°12' N, long. 120° 45'20" W; sec. 15, T 4 N, R 11 E). Named on San Andreas (1962) and Valley Springs (1962) 7.5' quadrangles.

Hawes: see **Haight** [SAN JOAQUIN].

Hawkeye [CALAVERAS]: *locality,* 4.25 miles northwest of Angels Camp along present Coopers Creek (lat. 38°06'30" N, long. 120° 36' W). Named on Jackson (1902) 30' quadrangle. Gudde (1975, p. 153) used the form "Hawk Eye" for the name.

Hawkins Bar: see **Red Mountain Bar** [TUOLUMNE].

Hawk Rock [STANISLAUS]: *peak,* 1.25 miles west of Crevison Peak (lat. 37°11'20" N, long. 121°12'35" W; at S line sec. 33, T 8 S, R 7 E). Altitude 1930 feet. Named on Crevison Peak (1955) 7.5' quadrangle.

Hawksbeak Peak [TUOLUMNE]: *peak,* 2.5 miles east-northeast of Tower Peak on Tuolumne-Mono County line (lat. 38°09'30" N, long. 119°30'10" W). Named on Tower Peak (1956) 15' quadrangle.

Hawk's Corners: see **Elliott** [SAN JOAQUIN].

Haydensville: see **Bear Valley** [MARIPOSA] (2).

Hayes Peak: see **Gray Peak** [MADERA].

Hayes Point [SAN JOAQUIN]: *promontory,* 17 miles west-southwest of Lodi along San Joaquin River near the north end of Mandeville Island (lat. 38°04'05" N, long. 121°33'35" W). Named on Bouldin Island (1978) 7.5' quadrangle.

Hayes Reach [SAN JOAQUIN]: *water feature,* part of San Joaquin River 17 miles west-southwest of Lodi on San Joaquin-Contra Costa County line (lat. 38°04'35" N, long. 121°34'10" W); the feature is northwest of Hayes Point. Named on Bouldin Island (1978) 7.5' quadrangle.

Hayes Slough [SAN JOAQUIN]: *water feature,* on Lower Jones Tract, joins

Middle River 12 miles west of downtown Stockton (lat. 37°57'10" N, long. 121°31'25" W). Named on Woodward Island (1978) 7.5' quadrangle.

Hay Gulch [CALAVERAS]: *canyon,* drained by a stream that flows 2 miles to Blue Creek nearly 5 miles west of Tamarack (lat. 38°26'15" N, long. 120°09'50" W; at S line sec. 24, T 7 N, R 16 E). Named on Calaveras Dome (1979) 7.5' quadrangle.

Haypress Lake [TUOLUMNE]: *lake,* 1300 feet long, 4.5 miles east-southeast of Dardanelle (lat. 38°18'25" N, long. 119°45'50" W; sec. 3, T 5 N, R 20 E); the lake is in Haypress Meadow. Named on Dardanelle (1979) 7.5' quadrangle.

Haypress Meadow [TUOLUMNE]: *area,* 4.5 miles southeast of Dardanelle (lat. 38°18'15" N, long. 119°45'50" W; on S line sec. 3, T 5 N, R 20 E). Named on Dardanelle (1979) 7.5' quadrangle.

Haypress Reach [SAN JOAQUIN]: *water feature,* part of San Joaquin River 7.5 miles south-southeast of Terminous between Spud Island and McDonald Island (lat. 38°00'30" N, long. 121°27'35" W). Named on Terminous (1978) 7.5' quadrangle.

Hays Meadow [TUOLUMNE]: *area,* 10 miles east-northeast of Pinecrest (lat. 30°13'30" N, long. 119°49'15" W). Named on Pinecrest (1956) 15' quadrangle.

Haystack Mountain [MERCED]: *peak,* 10 miles northeast of Merced (lat. 37°23'05" N, long. 120°19'40" W; sec. 28, T 6 S, R 15 E). Altitude 472 feet. Named on Haystack Mountain (1962) 7.5' quadrangle.

Haystack Peak [TUOLUMNE]: *peak,* 8 miles west-southwest of Tower Peak (lat. 38°06'20" N, long. 119°40' W). Altitude 10,015 feet. Named on Tower Peak (1956) 15' quadrangle.

Hayward [MARIPOSA]: *locality,* 8.5 miles southwest of Penon Blanco Peak (lat. 37°38'30" N, long. 120°22'15" W; near E line sec. 25, T 3 S, R 14 E); the place is near Hayward Creek. Named on Penon Blanco Peak (1962) 7.5' quadrangle.

Hayward Creek [CALAVERAS]: *stream,* flows 3.5 miles to South Fork Mokelumne River 3 miles east of Blue Mountain (lat. 38°20'40" N, long. 120°18'20" W; sec. 27, T 6 N, R 15 E). Named on Dorrington (1979) 7.5' quadrangle.

Hayward Creek [MARIPOSA-MERCED]: *stream,* heads in Mariposa County and flows 9 miles to Dry Creek 4.5 miles north-northeast of Snelling in Merced County (lat. 37°34'50" N, long. 120°24'35" W; near SE cor. sec. 15, T 4 S, R 14 E). Named on La Grange (1962), Penon Blanco Peak (1962), and Snelling (1962) 7.5' quadrangles.

Hazel Dell Gulch [CALAVERAS]: *canyon,* 1 mile long, opens into the canyon of Jack Nelson Creek 4 miles southwest of Rail Road Flat (lat. 38°17'50" N, long. 120°33'20" W; near SE cor. sec. 8, T 5 N, R 13 E). Named on Rail Road Flat (1948) 7.5' quadrangle.

Hazel Green [MARIPOSA]: *locality,* 8 miles northwest of El Portal (lat. 37°46' N, long. 119°52' W; at S line sec. 10, T 2 S, R 19 E). Named on Yosemite (1909) 30' quadrangle. Lake Eleanor (1956) 15' quadrangle shows Hazel Green ranch at the place.

Hazel Green Creek [TUOLUMNE]: *stream,* flows 2.5 miles to North Crane Creek 6 miles south of Mather (lat. 37°48' N, long. 119°50'45" W; near SE cor. sec. 35, T 1 S, R 19 E). Named on Lake Eleanor (1956) 15' quadrangle. United States Board on Geographic Names (1933a, p. 358) rejected the name "Big Creek" for the stream. Lafayette H. Bunnell gave the name "Hazel Green" in 1856 to a campsite on the trail to Yosemite Valley because of the hazel bushes growing near the site (Hanna, p. 135).

Hazel Green Creek: see **Big Creek** [TUOLUMNE] (3).

Hazelton: see **Stockton** [SAN JOAQUIN].

Head Reach [SAN JOAQUIN]: *water feature,* part of San Joaquin River 5.5 miles south of Terminous (lat. 38°02' N, long. 121°28'50" W). Named on Headreach (1910) 7.5' quadrangle.

Headreach Cutoff [SAN JOAQUIN]: *water feature,* part of San Joaquin River 6 miles south of Terminous (lat. 38°01'35" N, long. 121°29' W); the feature is south of Headreach Island. Named on Terminous (1978) 7.5' quadrangle. Headreach (1910) 7.5' quadrangle shows the feature crossing a neck of land to cut off Head Reach, a meander of San Joaquin River.

Headreach Island [SAN JOAQUIN]: *island,* 0.5 mile long, nearly 6 miles south of Terminous in San Joaquin River (lat. 38°01'50" N, long. 121°29' W). Named on Terminous (1978) 7.5' quadrangle, which shows that the island consists largely of marsh and water.

Headreach Landing [SAN JOAQUIN]: *locality,* 6 miles south of Terminous along San Joaquin River (lat. 38°01'35" N, long. 121° 28'55" W); the place is at the upstream end of Headreach Cutoff. Named on Headreach (1910) 7.5' quadrangle.

Heath and Emory's Ferry: see **Oakdale** [STANISLAUS].

Hebron Mill [TUOLUMNE]: *locality,* 6.5 miles east-southeast of Groveland (lat. 37°47'30" N, long. 120°07'30" W); the place is 0.5 mile west of present Hobron Hill. Named on Sonora (1897) 30' quadrangle.

Heiser Canyon [CALAVERAS]: *canyon,* 3.5 miles long, on upper reaches of Dry Creek (1) above a point 9 miles west of Angels Camp (lat. 38°04'15" N, long. 120°42'50" W; sec. 36, T 3 N, R 11 E). Named on Salt Spring Valley (1962) 7.5' quadrangle. San Andreas (1947) 15' quadrangle has the name "Heiser Creek" for the stream in the canyon.

Heiser Creek: see **Dry Creek** [CALAVERAS] (1); **Heiser Canyon** [CALAVERAS].

Helen Lake [TUOLUMNE]: *lake,* 2100 feet long, 6 miles south-southeast of Tioga Pass (lat. 37°49'50" N, long. 119°13'40" W). Named on Mono Craters (1953) 15' quadrangle. R.B. Marshall of United States Geological Survey named the lake in 1900 for Helen Coburn Smith, daughter of George Otis Smith (United States Board on Geographic Names, 1934, p. 11).

Helen Lake: see **Maxwell Lake** [TUOLUMNE]; **Starr King Lake** [MARIPOSA].

Helisma Station [CALAVERAS]: *locality,* 3.25 miles west of Valley Springs along Southern Pacific Railroad at Burson (lat. 38°11' N, long. 120°53'20" W; on W line sec. 21, T 4 N, R 10 E). Named on Wallace (1962) 7.5' quadrangle.

Hell Hollow [MARIPOSA]: *canyon,* 1.5 miles long, opens into the canyon of Merced River 9 miles northeast of Hornitos opposite Bagby (lat. 37°36'35" N, long. 120°08'10" W). Named on Hornitos (1947) 7.5' quadrangle. Called Hell's Hollow Gulch on Laizure's (1928) map. Shirley Sargent (1976, p. 17) called the feature Hell's Hollow, and attributed the name to the danger, difficulty of access, and summer heat of the place.

Hells Half Acre [MADERA]: *area,* 9 miles east-northeast of Shuteye Peak near San Joaquin River (lat. 37°24'15" N, long. 119°16'25" W). Named on Shuteye Peak (1953) 15' quadrangle.

Hells Half Acre [TUOLUMNE]: *area,* 3.5 miles north-northwest of Strawberry along Middle Fork Stanislaus River (lat. 38°14'50" N, long. 120°02' W; sec. 31, T 5 N, R 18 E). Named on Strawberry (1979) 7.5' quadrangle.

Hells Hollow [TUOLUMNE]: *area,* 5 miles east-southeast of Groveland (lat. 37°47'55" N, long. 120°09' W; near NE cor. sec. 1, T 2 S, R 16 E). Named on Groveland (1947) 7.5' quadrangle. Paden and Schlichtmann (p. 186) used the form "Hell's Hollow" for the name.

Hell's Hollow: see **Hell Hollow** [MARIPOSA].

Hells Hollow Creek [TUOLUMNE]: *stream,* flows 2.5 miles to Big Creek 5.5 miles east-southeast of Groveland (lat. 37°48'40" N, long. 120°08'05" W; sec. 32, T 1 S, R 17 E); the stream goes through Hells Hollow. Named on Groveland (1947) 7.5' quadrangle.

Hell's Hollow Gulch: see **Hell Hollow** [MARIPOSA].

Hells Hollow Ridge [TUOLUMNE]: *ridge,* northeast-trending, nearly 1 mile long, 4 miles southeast of Groveland (lat. 37°48'25" N, long. 120°10'10" W); the ridge is northwest of Hells Hollow. Named on Groveland (1947) 7.5' quadrangle.

Hellsinger Canyon [SAN JOAQUIN]: *canyon,* drained by a stream that flows 2.5 miles to Corral Hollow Creek 15 miles south-southwest of Tracy (lat. 37°32'05" N, long. 121°29'55" W; near S line sec. 35, T 4 S, R 4 E). Named on Lone Tree Creek (1955) 7.5' quadrangle.

Hells Kitchen [CALAVERAS-TUOLUMNE]: *area,* 2 miles south of Tamarack along North Fork Stanislaus River on Calaveras-Tuolumne County line (lat. 38°24'35" N, long. 120°04'45" W). Named on Tamarack (1979) 7.5' quadrangle.

Hells Mountain [TUOLUMNE]: *peak,* 9 miles south-southeast of Pinecrest (lat. 38°04'25" N, long. 119°54'55" W). Altitude 6996 feet. Named on Cherry Lake North (1979) 7.5' quadrangle.

Helms Creek [MADERA]: *stream,* flows 2.25 miles to Fine Gold Creek 5 miles west-southwest of the town of North Fork (lat. 37° 12'15" N, long. 119°35'45" W; sec. 29, T 8 S, R 22 E). Named on North Fork (1965) 7.5' quadrangle.

Hemlock Crossing [MADERA]: *locality,* 8 miles west of Devils Postpile along North Fork San Joaquin River (lat. 37°38'20" N, long. 119°13'25" W). Named on Devils Postpile (1953) 15' quadrangle.

Henderson Village [SAN JOAQUIN]: *settlement,* 2.5 miles southwest of Lodi (lat. 38°06' N, long. 121°18'30" W; near N line sec. 22, T 3 N, R 6 E). Named on Lodi South (1968) 7.5' quadrangle.

Henness [MARIPOSA]: *locality,* 1.25 miles west of El Portal along Yosemite Valley Railroad (lat. 37°40'15" N, long. 119°48' W). Named on Yosemite (1909) 30' quadrangle. The name recalls James A. Hennessy, who had an extensive truck garden at present El Portal in the 1870's (Mendershausen, p. 21).

Henness Branch [MARIPOSA]: *stream,* flows 2 miles to Merced River 0.5 mile west-southwest of El Portal (lat. 37°40'15" N, long. 119°47'20" W). Named on El Portal (1947) 15' quadrangle. United States Board on Geographic Names (1933a, p. 361) rejected the names "Hennessy Branch," "Ward's Branch," and "Wilsons Branch" for the stream.

Henness Ridge [MARIPOSA]: *ridge,* generally west-trending, 2.5 miles long, 11 miles southwest of Yosemite Village (lat. 37°38'30" N, long. 119°43'45" W). Named on Yosemite (1956) 15' quadrangle.

Hennessy Branch: see **Henness Branch** [MARIPOSA].

Henning Island: see **McDonald Island** [SAN JOAQUIN].

Hensley Lake [MADERA]: *lake,* behind a dam on Fresno River 7.5 miles south of Raymond (lat. 37°06'40" N, long. 119°53' W; near N line sec. 34, T 9 S, R 19 E). Named on Daulton (1962, photorevised 1981), Knowles (1962, photorevised 1981), Little Table Mountain (1962, photorevised 1981), and Raymond (1962, photorevised 1981) 7.5' quadrangles.

Herbeck Flat [MARIPOSA]: *area,* 1 mile west-southwest of Penon Blanco

Peak (lat. 37°43'45" N, long. 120°16'30" W; on W line sec. 25, T 2 S, R 15 E). Named on Penon Blanco Peak (1962) 7.5' quadrangle.

Herbert: see **Raymond** [MADERA].

Hermit Spring [CALAVERAS]: *spring,* 9 miles west of Tamarack (lat. 38°25'25" N, long. 120°14'15" W; sec. 29, T 7 N, R 16 E). Named on Calaveras Dome (1979) 7.5' quadrangle.

Herrero Canyon [MERCED]: *canyon,* drained by a stream that flows 2 miles to Carrisalito Flat 2.25 miles east of Sweeney Hill (lat. 36° 54'10" N, long. 121°00'25" W). Named on Los Banos Valley (1969) 7.5' quadrangle.

Herring Creek [TUOLUMNE]: *stream,* flows 11 miles to South Fork Stanislaus River 0.5 mile north of Pinecrest (lat. 38°12'05" N, long. 119°59'55" W; sec. 16, T 4 N, R 18 E). Named on Dardanelle (1979), Donnell Lake (1979), and Pinecrest (1979) 7.5' quadrangles.

Herring Creek Reservoir [TUOLUMNE]: *lake,* behind a dam on Herring Creek 8 miles southwest of Dardanelle (lat. 38°15'05" N, long. 119°55'35" W; sec. 30, T 5 N, R 19 E). Named on Donnell Lake (1979) 7.5' quadrangle. Called Herring Reservoir on California Division of Highways' (1934) map.

Herring Reservoir: see **Herring Creek Reservoir** [TUOLUMNE].

Hess Mill [TUOLUMNE]: *locality,* 4.5 miles north of Twain Harte along Dry Creek (lat. 38°06'10" N, long. 120°14'15" W; sec. 20, T 3 N, R 16 E). Site named on Twain Harte (1979) 7.5' quadrangle.

Hetch Hetchy: see **Mather** [TUOLUMNE].

Hetch Hetchy Dome [TUOLUMNE]: *peak,* 8 miles northeast of Mather (lat. 37°57'55" N, long. 119°45'10" W; near NW cor. sec. 11, T 1 N, R 20 E); the peak is on the north side of Hetch Hetchy Reservoir. Named on Lake Eleanor (1956) 15' quadrangle. Called Hetch Hetchy Mtn. on Yosemite (1909) 30' quadrangle. United States Board on Geographic Names (1934, p. 11) rejected the name "North Dome" for the feature.

Hetch Hetchy Fall: see **Wapama Falls** [TUOLUMNE].

Hetch Hetchy Junction [TUOLUMNE]: *locality,* 5.5 miles south-southwest of Chinese Camp along Sierra Railway (lat. 37°48'05" N, long. 120°29'15" W; sec. 36, T 1 S, R 13 E); the place is near the railroad crossing of Hetch Hetchy aqueduct. Named on Chinese Camp (1947) 7.5' quadrangle. Postal authorities established Hetch Hetchy Junction post office in 1926 and discontinued it in 1930 (Frickstad, p. 215).

Hetch Hetchy Mountain: see **Hetch Hetchy Dome** [TUOLUMNE].

Hetch Hetchy Reservoir [TUOLUMNE]: *lake,* behind a dam on Tuolumne River 6 miles northeast of Mather (lat. 37°56'50" N, long. 119°47'15" W; sec. 16, T 1 N, R 20 E). Named on Hetch Hetchy Reservoir (1956) and Lake Eleanor (1956) 15' quadrangles.

Hetch Hetchy Valley [TUOLUMNE]: *valley,* 4 miles long, along Tuolumne River above a point 6 miles northeast of Mather Station (present Mather) (lat. 37°56'50" N, long. 119°47'15" W). Named on Yosemite (1909) 30' quadrangle. Water of Hetch Hetchy Reservoir now floods most of the Yosemitelike valley. The term "Hetch Hetchy" is from the Indian name for a kind of grass with edible seeds that was abundant in the valley (Kroeber, p. 42). Hoffmann (p. 266) referred to "Tuolumne Valley, or Hetch-Hetchy, as it is called by the Indians."

Hetch Hetchy Valley: see **Little Hetch Hetchy Valley** [TUOLUMNE].

Hewitt Valley [MADERA]: *valley,* 7 miles east-southeast of O'Neals (lat. 37°05'05" N, long. 119°34'55" W). Named on Millerton Lake East (1965) 7.5' quadrangle.

Hickman [STANISLAUS]: *village,* 1.5 miles south-southeast of Waterford (lat. 37°37'15" N, long. 120°45' W; sec. 3, T 4 S, R 11 E). Named on Denair (1969) and Montpelier (1968) 7.5' quadrangles. Postal authorities established Hickman post office in 1891 (Frickstad, p. 200). The name commemorates Louis M. Hickman, landowner in the neighborhood in the 1860's (Hanna, p. 138).

Hicks Spring [CALAVERAS]: *spring,* 1.25 miles west-northwest of Copperopolis (lat. 37°59'15" N, long. 120°39'45" W; near N line sec. 33, T 2 N, R 12 E). Named on Copperopolis (1962) 7.5' quadrangle.

Hidden Creek [MERCED]: *stream,* flows 1.5 miles to Salt Creek (1) 2.5 miles south-southeast of Pacheco Pass (lat. 37°01'40" N, long. 121°11'30" W; near N line sec. 34, T 10 S, R 7 E). Named on Pacheco Pass (1955) 7.5' quadrangle.

Hidden Lake [MARIPOSA]: *lake,* 800 feet long, nearly 6 miles west-southwest of Cathedral Peak (lat. 37°48'20" N, long. 119°29'40" W; near E line sec. 36, T 1 S, R 22 E). Named on Tuolumne Meadows (1956) 15' quadrangle.

Hidden Lake: see **Ruth Lake** [MADERA].

Hideaway Lake: see **Ruth Lake** [MADERA].

Hideout Canyon [STANISLAUS]: *canyon,* drained by a stream that flows nearly 3 miles to Del Puerto Canyon 5.5 miles south-southeast of Mount Boardman (lat. 37°24'40" N, long. 121°25'40" W; sec. 16, T 5 S, R 5 E). Named on Mount Boardman (1955) 7.5' quadrangle. On Mount Boardman (1942) 15' quadrangle, the name has the form "Hide Out Canyon."

High Emigrant Lake [TUOLUMNE]: *lake,* 700 feet long, 6.5 miles northwest of Tower Peak (lat. 38°12'30" N, long. 119°37'50" W); the lake is 0.5 mile north of Emigrant Pass. Named on Tower Peak (1956) 15' quadrangle.

Highland Creek [TUOLUMNE]: *stream,* heads in Alpine County and flows 8 miles in Tuolumne County to North Fork Stanislaus River 2.5 miles north-northeast of Liberty Hill (lat. 38°24'15" N, long. 120°05'20" W). Named on Spicer Meadow Reservoir (1979) and Tamarack (1979) 7.5' quadrangles. The name recalls Highland City, an early mining camp in Alpine County (Gudde, 1949, p. 148).

High Mountain [CALAVERAS]: *peak,* 9.5 miles east-southeast of San Andreas (lat. 38°10'10" N, long. 120°30'35" W; sec. 26, T 4 N, R 13 E). Altitude 2450 feet. Named on Calaveritas (1962) 7.5' quadrangle.

High Sierra: see **Camp High Sierra** [TUOLUMNE]; "Regional setting."

High Sierra Campground [MARIPOSA]: *locality,* 7.5 miles south of Cathedral Peak along Merced River (lat. 37°44'20" N, long. 119° 24'15" W); the place is in the Sierra Nevada. Named on Merced Peak (1953) 15' quadrangle.

High Sierra Park [TUOLUMNE]: *settlement,* 5.25 miles northeast of Twain Harte (lat. 38°04'45" N, long. 120°08'55" W; sec. 30, 31, T 3 N, R 17 E). Named on Twain Harte (1979) 7.5' quadrangle.

Hildreth [MADERA]: *locality,* 3.5 miles east-southeast of O'Neals (lat. 37°06'35" N, long. 119°37'55" W; sec. 36, T 9 N, R 21 E). Named on Millerton Lake West (1965) 7.5' quadrangle. Postal authorities established Hildreth post office in 1886 and discontinued it in 1896 (Frickstad, p. 86). The place began in the late 1870's when Tom Hildreth opened a store there (Clough, p. 85). Logan's (1950) map shows a place called Birch located about 3 miles west-northwest of Hildreth.

Hildreth Creek [MADERA]: *stream,* flows 14 miles to Cottonwood Creek (2) 5.5 miles north-northeast of Trigo (lat. 36°59'20" N, long. 119°56' W; sec. 7, T 11 S, R 19 E). Named on Herndon (1965) and Raymond (1962) 15' quadrangles.

Hildreth Mountain [MADERA]: *peak,* 3 miles east of O'Neals (lat. 37°07'15" N, long. 119°38'15" W; near W line sec. 25, T 9 S, R 21 E); the peak is less than 1 mile north-northwest of Hildreth. Altitude 2058 feet. Named on Millerton Lake West (1965) 7.5' quadrangle.

Hildreth's Diggings: see **Columbia** [TUOLUMNE].

Hills [CALAVERAS]: *locality,* 7.5 miles west-northwest of Valley Springs (lat. 38°12'50" N, long. 120°57'50" W). Named on Jackson (1902) 30' quadrangle. Water of Camanche Reservoir now covers the site.

Hills Ferry [STANISLAUS]: *settlement,* 12 miles southwest of Turlock on the west side of San Joaquin River (lat. 37°21' N, long. 120°58'45" W; sec. 4, T 7 S, R 9 E). Named on Turlock (1962) 15' quadrangle. Postal authorities established Hill's Ferry post office in 1855 and discontinued it in 1856; they established Hills Ferry post office (without the apostrophe) in 1870 and discontinued it in 1888, when they moved it 3.5 miles west to Newman (Salley, p. 98). The site had a ferry as early as the autumn of 1849, and Jesse Hill ran the enterprise until 1865; when the town of Newman was laid out nearby in 1887, most of the residents of Hills Ferry moved there (Hoover, Rensch, and Rensch, p. 540).

Hillside: see **Knowles** [MADERA].

Hillyer and Burnham Ferry: see **Stanislaus River** [CALAVERAS-SAN JOAQUIN-STANISLAUS-TUOLUMNE].

Hilmar [MERCED]: *town,* 4.25 miles west-southwest of Delhi (lat. 37°24'35" N, long. 120°51' W; near E line sec. 15, T 6 S, R 10 E). Named on Turlock (1962) 15' quadrangle. The town was started in 1917 and named for Hilmar Colony, a community of Swedes (Gudde, 1949, p. 149). Postal authorities established Hilmar post office in 1920 (Frickstad, p. 100). California Division of Highways' (1934) map shows a place called Tegner located 3 miles northwest of Hilmar along Tidewater Southern Railroad (near NW cor. sec. 9, T 6 S, R 10 E).

Hite: see **Hite Cove** [MARIPOSA].

Hite Cove [MARIPOSA]: *locality,* 4.5 miles west-southwest of El Portal along South Fork Merced River (lat. 37°38'25" N, long. 119°50'50" W; sec. 27, T 3 S, R 19 E). Named on El Portal (1947) 7.5' quadrangle. Hoffmann and Gardner's (1863-1867) map shows a place called Hite's Cove located near the confluence of South Fork with Merced River. The name commemorates John Hite, who discovered gold at the place (Chamberlain, p. 4). Postal authorities established Hites Cove post office in 1868, discontinued it in 1869, reestablished it in 1878, and discontinued it in 1889; they established Hite post office at a new site in 1901 and discontinued it in 1902 (Salley, p. 98).

Hites Cove: see **Hite Cove** [MARIPOSA].

Hobart Creek [TUOLUMNE]: *stream,* heads in Alpine County and flows 3 miles to Spicer Meadow Reservoir 9.5 miles west-northwest of Dardanelle (lat. 38°23'40" N, long. 119°59'45" W). Named on Spicer Meadow Reservoir (1979) 7.5' quadrangle.

Hobron Hill [MARIPOSA-TUOLUMNE]: *peak,* less than 1 mile southwest of Smith Peak on Mariposa-Tuolumne County line (lat. 37°47'40" N, long. 120°06'40" W; near E line sec. 5, T 2 S, R 17 E). Altitude 3805 feet. Named on Jawbone Ridge (1947) 7.5' quadrangle.

Hocks Corners [SAN JOAQUIN]: *locality,* 5 miles north-northwest of Lockeford at or near present Elliott (lat. 38°14'05" N, long. 121°10'45" W). Named on Lodi (1894) 30' quadrangle.

Hodgdon Meadows: see **Hodgdon Ranch** [TUOLUMNE].

Hodgdon Ranch [TUOLUMNE]: *locality,* 6 miles south of Mather (lat. 37°47'50" N, long. 119°51'25" W; near N line sec. 3, T 2 S, R 19 E). Named on Lake Eleanor (1956) 15' quadrangle. The site first was called Moore and Bowen Camp, then Bronson Meadows, and finally Hodgdon Meadows after T.J. Hodgdon settled there in 1865 (Uhte, p. 63-64). Hodgdon eventually built an inn for travelers going to Yosemite Valley (Paden and Schlichtmann, p. 216).

Hodson [CALAVERAS]: *village,* 2.5 miles west-northwest of Copperopolis (lat. 37°59'50" N, long. 120°41' W; sec. 29, T 2 N, R 12 E). Named on Copperopolis (1916) 15' quadrangle. Postal authorities established Hodson post office in 1898, discontinued it in 1906, reestablished it in 1915, and discontinued it in 1917; the name is for J.J. Hodson, a financier who backed copper mining (Salley, p. 99).

Hoff [MERCED]: *locality,* 3.5 miles east of Atwater along Atchison, Topeka and Santa Fe Railroad (lat. 37°20'25" N, long. 120°32'20" W; near W line sec. 10, T 7 S, R 13 E). Named on Atwater (1918) 7.5' quadrangle.

Hoffman Canyon [MERCED]: *canyon,* drained by a stream that flows 2.5 miles to Carrisalito Flat 2.5 miles east-southeast of Sweeney Hill (lat. 36°53'15" N, long. 121°00'20" W). Named on Los Banos Valley (1969) 7.5' quadrangle.

Hoffman Creek: see **Snow Creek** [MARIPOSA] (1).

Hoffmann: see **Mount Hoffmann** [MARIPOSA].

Hoffmann Creek [MARIPOSA]: *stream,* flows 2.25 miles to Snow Creek (1) 5.5 miles northeast of Yosemite Village (lat. 37°48'30" N, long. 119°31' W; sec. 35, T 1 S, R 22 E); the stream heads southwest of Mount Hoffmann. Named on Hetch Hetchy Reservoir (1956) 15' quadrangle.

Hoffmann Creek: see **Snow Creek** [MARIPOSA] (1).

Hoffs Gulch [MARIPOSA]: *canyon,* drained by a stream that flows 1 mile to Agua Fria Creek 5.5 miles northeast of the settlement of Catheys Valley (lat. 37°29'25" N, long. 120°01'05" W). Named on Catheys Valley (1962) 7.5' quadrangle. Laizure's (1928) map has the designation "Bell's Gulch (Hof's G.)" for the canyon.

Hogan Meadow: see **Sonny Meadow** [MARIPOSA].

Hogan Mountain [MARIPOSA]: *ridge,* west-southwest-trending, 2.5 miles long, 2.25 miles west-northwest of Fish Camp (lat. 37°29' N, long. 119°40'45" W). Named on Bass Lake (1953) 15' quadrangle.

Hogan Reservoir: see **New Hogan Reservoir** [CALAVERAS].

Hogans Dome: see **Fresno Dome** [MADERA].

Hogan's Meadow: see **Sonny Meadow** [MARIPOSA].

Hogback Mountain [CALAVERAS]: *ridge,* north-northwest-trending, 5.5 miles long, 2.5 miles south-southwest of San Andreas (lat. 38°09'45" N, long. 120°42'15" W). Named on San Andreas (1962) 7.5' quadrangle.

Hog Canyon [STANISLAUS]: *canyon,* drained by a stream that flows 1.5 miles to Garzas Creek 2.5 miles east of Mustang Peak (lat. 37° 10'55" N, long. 121°19' W; sec. 4, T 9 S, R 6 E). Named on Mustang Peak (1955) 7.5' quadrangle.

Hoggem Lake [MADERA]: *lake,* 600 feet long, 10 miles north-northeast of Yosemite Forks (lat. 37°29'35" N, long. 119°31'45" W; sec. 14, T 5 S, R 22 E). Named on Bass Lake (1953) 15' quadrangle.

Hog Hill [CALAVERAS]: *peak,* 6.25 miles southwest of Copperopolis (lat. 37°55'15" N, long. 120°43'45" W; sec. 23, T 1 N, R 11 E). Altitude 1300 feet. Named on Copperopolis (1962) 7.5' quadrangle.

Hog Island [SAN JOAQUIN]: *island,* 1 mile long, 8 miles south-southeast of Terminous along San Joaquin River (lat. 38°00'20" N, long. 121°26'50" W). Named on Terminous (1978) 7.5' quadrangle.

Hog Island Cut [SAN JOAQUIN]: *water feature,* artificial watercourse 8 miles south-southeast of Terminous along Stockton Deep Water Channel between Hog Island and Spud Island (lat. 38° 00'20" N, long. 121°27'05" W). Named on Terminous (1952) 7.5' quadrangle.

Hog Mountain [TUOLUMNE]: *peak,* 7 miles south-southeast of Sonora (lat. 37°53' N, long. 120°21'10" W; sec. 5, T 1 S, R 15 E). Altitude 2481 feet. Named on Standard (1948) 7.5' quadrangle.

Hog Ranch: see **Mather** [TUOLUMNE].

Hog Slough [SAN JOAQUIN]: *water feature,* joins South Mokelumne River 5.5 miles southwest of Thornton (lat. 38°10' N, long. 121°29'30" W). Named on New Hope (1952) 7.5' quadrangle.

Holcomb Lake [MADERA]: *lake,* 1400 feet long, 4 miles west of Devils Postpile (lat. 37°37'45" N, long. 119°09'15" W). Named on Devils Postpile (1953) 15' quadrangle.

Holden [SAN JOAQUIN]: *locality,* 10 miles east of downtown Stockton along Southern Pacific Railroad (lat. 37°58'45" N, long. 121° 06'20" W; sec. 33, T 2 N, R 8 E). Named on Peters (1915) 7.5' quadrangle. Postal authorities established Holden post office in 1871 and discontinued it the same year (Frickstad, p. 161).

Holden's Ferry: see **Oakdale** [STANISLAUS].

Holman Slough [SAN JOAQUIN]: *water feature,* joins Old River 15 miles west of downtown Stockton on Bacon Island (lat. 37°59'35" N, long. 121°34'25" W). Named on Woodward Island (1913) 7.5' quadrangle.

Holt [SAN JOAQUIN]: *locality,* 7.5 miles west of downtown Stockton along Atchison, Topeka and Santa Fe Railroad on Roberts Island (lat. 37°56'05" N, long. 121°25'30" W). Named on Holt (1952) 7.5' quadrangle. Postal authorities established Holt post office in 1902 (Frickstad, p. 161). The name is from the Holt brothers, who founded Stockton Wheel Company in 1883; the enterprise eventually became Holt Catepillar Tractor Company (Hanna, p. 140).

Homestead: see **The Homestead** [SAN JOAQUIN].

Homestead Ridge [CALAVERAS]: *ridge,* north-northwest-trending, 2 miles long, 1.25 miles northwest of Copperopolis (lat. 37°59'30" N, long. 120°39'35" W). Named on Copperopolis (1962) and Salt Spring Valley (1962) 7.5' quadrangles.

Honda: see **Lake Honda** [MERCED].

Honker Cut [SAN JOAQUIN]: *water feature,* artificial watercourse that extends between Empire Tract and King Island from White Slough to Disappointment Slough 4.5 miles south-southeast of Terminous (lat. 38°03'15" N, long. 121°27'30" W). Named on Terminous (1978) 7.5' quadrangle.

Honker Lake Tract [SAN JOAQUIN]: *area,* 7 miles west-southwest of downtown Stockton on Roberts Island (lat. 37°55'15" N, long. 121°25' W). Named on Holt (1978) 7.5' quadrangle.

Hoods Creek [CALAVERAS-STANISLAUS]: *stream,* heads in Calaveras County and flows 16 miles to Rock Creek 11 miles north-northwest of Oakdale in Stanislaus County (lat. 37°55'20" N, long. 120°54'20" W; sec. 20, T 1 N, R 10 E). Named on Bachelor Valley (1953), Copperopolis (1962), and Farmington (1968) 7.5' quadrangles.

Hookers Cove [MADERA]: *valley,* 11 miles south-southeast of Shuteye Peak (lat. 37°11'50" N, long. 119°22' W; sec. 29, 32, T 8 S, R 24 E); the valley is along Hookers Creek. Named on Shaver Lake (1953) 15' quadrangle.

Hookers Creek [MADERA]: *stream,* flows 3 miles to San Joaquin River 12 miles south-southeast of Shuteye Peak (lat. 37°11'10" N, long. 119°21'05" W; sec. 33, T 8 S, R 24 E); the stream goes through Hookers Cove. Named on Shaver Lake (1953) 15' quadrangle.

Hooper Creek: see **South Fork,** under **San Joaquin River** [MADERA-MERCED-SAN JOAQUIN-STANISLAUS].

Hooper Peak [TUOLUMNE]: *peak,* 12 miles west-northwest of Tioga Pass (lat. 37°57'15" N, long. 119°28'10" W). Named on Tuolumne Meadows (1956) 15' quadrangle.

Hoover Creek [MADERA-MARIPOSA]: *stream,* heads in Madera County and flows 3.5 miles to Buena Vista Creek 8.5 miles southeast of Yosemite Village in Mariposa County (lat. 37°38'55" N, long. 119°30'05" W); the stream heads at Hoover Lakes. Named on Merced Peak (1953) 15' quadrangle. Forest S. Townsley, chief ranger of Yosemite National Park, named Hoover Creek and Hoover Lakes for his friend Herbert C. Hoover (Browning, 1986, p. 99).

Hoover Lakes [MADERA]: *lakes,* three, largest 950 feet long, 4.5 miles west-southwest of Merced Peak (lat. 37°36'35" N, long. 119° 28'20" W); the lakes are at the head of Hoover Creek. Named on Merced Peak (1953) 15' quadrangle.

Hopeton [MERCED]:

(1) *locality,* 10.5 miles north-northeast of Atwater (lat. 37°29'30" N, long. 120°31'45" W; on N line sec. 22, T 5 S, R 13 E). Named on Winton (1961) 7.5' quadrangle. The place first was called Forlorn Hope (Hoover, Rensch, and Rensch, p. 206). Postal authorities established Forlorn Hope post office in 1854, discontinued it in 1859, reestablished it in 1860, and discontinued it in 1861—the name was from a mine at the site; they established Hopeton post office in 1866, discontinued it in 1894, reestablished it in 1911, and discontinued it in 1914 (Salley, p. 100). They established Alexandria post office 8 miles southwest of Hopeton (SW quarter sec. 9, T 6 S, R 12 E) in 1869 and discontinued it in 1871; the name was from the given name of postmaster Alexander C. McSwain (Salley, p. 4).

(2) *locality,* 2.5 miles southwest of Snelling along Yosemite Valley Railroad (lat. 37°30' N, long. 120°28'40" W; sec. 18, T 5 S, R 14 E). Named on Hopeton (1916) and Snelling (1918) 7.5' quadrangles.

Hopeton Slough [MERCED]: *stream,* flows 6 miles to Ingalsbe Slough 9 miles north of Atwater (lat. 37°28'45" N, long. 120°34'15" W); the stream goes past Hopeton (1). Named on Winton (1961) 7.5' quadrangle.

Horizon Ridge [MARIPOSA]: *ridge,* northwest-trending, 2 miles long, 7.25 miles south of Yosemite Village (lat. 37°38'45" N, long. 119°34' W). Named on Yosemite (1956) 15' quadrangle.

Hornitas: see **Hornitos** [MARIPOSA].

Hornitos [MARIPOSA]: *village,* 14 miles south of Coulterville along Burns Creek (lat. 37°30'10" N, long. 120°14'15" W; sec. 17, T 5 S, R 16 E). Named on Hornitos (1947) 7.5' quadrangle. Postal authorities established Hornitas post office in 1856 and changed the name to Hornitos in 1877 (Frickstad, p. 91). The name is from the resemblance of above-ground graves at the place to little outdoor ovens—*hornitos* means "little ovens" in Spanish (Salazar, p. 2). A mining camp located about 2 miles upstream from Hornitos was called Burns' Creek, Burns' Camp, Burns' Ranch, or Burns' Diggings before it became known as Quartzburg in 1851 (Crampton *in* Eccleston, p. 11). The name "Burns" was for John Burns and Robert Burns, who settled at the place in 1847 (Gudde, 1975, p. 53). Postal authorities established Quartzburg post office in 1851 and discontinued it in 1861 (Frickstad, p. 92). Thomas Thorn gave the name "Quartzburg" to the community because of numerous quartz ledges nearby (Sargent, Shirley, 1976, p. 26). Postal authorities established Phillip's Flat post office on the bank of Merced River 7 miles north of Hornitos in 1857 and discontinued it in 1858 (Salley, p. 170).

Hornitos Creek [MARIPOSA]: *stream,* flow 4.5 miles to Burns Creek 1.25 miles north-northwest of Hornitos (lat. 37°31'05" N, long. 120°14'40" W; sec. 8, T 5 S, R 16 E). Named on Hornitos (1947) 7.5' quadrangle.

Horr: see **Waterford** [STANISLAUS].

Horr's Ranch: see **Waterford** [STANISLAUS].

Horrsville: see **Waterford** [STANISLAUS].

Horse and Cow Meadow [TUOLUMNE]: *area,* 8 miles east-northeast of Pinecrest (lat. 38°14'05" N, long. 119°51' W; on S line sec. 35, T 5 N, R 19 E). Named on Pinecrest (1956) 15' quadrangle.

Horsecamp Mountain [MADERA]: *ridge,* north-northwest- to northwest-trending, 1.25 miles long, 8 miles north-northeast of Raymond (lat. 37°19'50" N, long. 119°50'45" W). Named on Horsecamp Mountain (1947) 7.5' quadrangle.

Horse Creek [MARIPOSA]: *stream,* flows 4.25 miles to Striped Rock Creek 10.5 miles south-southeast of Mariposa (lat. 37°20'45" N, long. 119°53'30" W; on S line sec. 4, T 7 S, R 19 E). Named on Ben Hur (1947) and Mariposa (1947) 7.5' quadrangles.

Horse Gulch [CALAVERAS]: *canyon,* drained by a stream that flows 1.25 miles to Hay Gulch 4.25 miles west of Tamarack (lat. 38° 26'30" N, long. 120°09'20" W; near E line sec. 24, T 7 N, R 16 E). Named on Calaveras Dome (1979) 7.5' quadrangle.

Horse Gulch [MARIPOSA]: *canyon,* drained by a stream that flows 1 mile to Agua Fria Creek 5.5 miles northeast of the settlement of Catheys Valley (lat. 37°29'25" N, long. 120°01'05" W). Named on Catheys Valley (1962) 7.5' quadrangle.

Horse Meadow [TUOLUMNE]:
(1) *area,* 8 miles west of Dardanelle (lat. 38°20'40" N, long. 119° 58' W). Named on Donnell Lake (1979) 7.5' quadrangle.
(2) *area,* 6.25 miles west-northwest of Tower Peak along East Fork Cherry Creek (lat. 38°09'45" N, long. 119°39'35" W; sec. 27, T 4 N, R 21 E). Named on Tower Peak (1956) 15' quadrangle.

Horse Ridge [MARIPOSA]: *ridge,* west-northwest-trending, 2 miles long, 9.5 miles south-southeast of Yosemite Village (lat. 37°37' N, long. 119°32'25" W). Named on Yosemite (1956) 15' quadrangle.

Horseshoe Bend [CALAVERAS]: *bend,* 5.25 miles south of Vallecito along Stanislaus River (lat. 38°00'40" N, long. 120°27'45" W; near W line sec. 20, T 2 N, R 14 E). Named on Columbia (1948) 7.5' quadrangle.

Horseshoe Bend [MADERA]: *bend,* 16 miles south of Shuteye Peak along San Joaquin River on Madera-Fresno County line (lat. 37°06'40" N, long. 119°28'15" W). Named on Shaver Lake (1953) 15' quadrangle.

Horseshoe Bend [MARIPOSA]: *bend,* 3.25 miles southwest of Coulterville along Merced River (lat. 37°40'30" N, long. 120°13'45" W; sec. 17, T 3 S, R 16 E); the feature now is in Lake McClure. Named on Coulterville (1947) 15' quadrangle. A mining place called Harveys Bar was at Horseshoe Bend in the 1850's (Gudde, 1975, p. 152-153).

Horseshoe Bend Mountain [MARIPOSA]: *ridge,* southeast-trending, 3 miles long, 2.25 miles south-southwest of Coulterville (lat. 37° 40'50" N, long. 120°12'30" W); the ridge is northeast of Horseshoe Bend. Named on Coulterville (1947) 7.5' quadrangle.

Horseshoe Lake [SAN JOAQUIN]: *lake,* 1250 feet long, 15 miles southwest of Lodi on Roberts Island (present McDonald Tract) (lat. 38°01'10" N, long. 121°30'50" W); the lake is at the head of Horseshoe Slough. Named on Bouldin (1910) 7.5' quadrangle.

Horseshoe Slough [SAN JOAQUIN]: *water feature,* on Roberts Island (present McDonald Tract), joins Whiskey Slough 15 miles southwest of Lodi (lat. 38°01' N, long. 121°30'25" W); the slough heads at Horseshoe Lake. Named on Bouldin (1910) 7.5' quadrangle.

Horseshoe Slough [STANISLAUS]: *water feature,* 9 miles south-southwest of Modesto on the east side of San Joaquin River (lat. 37°31'50" N, long. 121°05'10" W). Named on Brush Lake (1953) 7.5' quadrangle.

Hospital Canyon [SAN JOAQUIN-STANISLAUS]: *canyon,* 24 miles west-southwest of Modesto on San Joaquin-Stanislaus County line (lat. 37°32' N, long. 121°24'45" W); Hospital Creek drains the canyon. Named on Copper Mountain (1956), Lone Tree Creek (1955), and Mount Boardman (1955) 7.5' quadrangles. West Fork opens into the main canyon from the west 8.5 miles upstream from the mouth of the main canyon; it is 4.25 miles long and is named on Lone Tree Creek (1955) 7.5' quadrangle.

Hospital Creek [SAN JOAQUIN-STANISLAUS]: *stream,* heads in Stanislaus County and flows 14 miles to lowlands 10.5 miles south-southeast of Tracy in San Joaquin County (lat. 37°36'10" N, long. 121°21' W; sec. 7, T 4 S, R 6 E); the stream drains Hospital Canyon. Named on Lone Tree Creek (1955), Solyo (1953), and Westley (1952) 7.5' quadrangles. Called Arrojo del Osnita on Goddard's (1857) map, and called Arroyo Del Ospital on Thompson and West's (1876) map. Carbona (1922) 15' quadrangle shows West Fork of the creek in present West Fork Hospital Canyon. The name "Hospital Creek" recalls a band of Spaniards who were ill and rested by the stream until they recovered their health (Hoover, Rensch, and Rensch, p. 540). Mendenhall's (1908) map shows a place called Seegar located along Hospital Creek (sec. 24, T 4 S, R 5 E).

Hoyle: see **Camp Hoyle** [MARIPOSA].

Huckleberry Lake [TUOLUMNE]: *lake,* 2 miles long, 9 miles west of Tower Peak along East Fork Cherry Creek (lat. 38°07'45" N, long. 119°42'45" W). Named on Tower Peak (1956) 15' quadrangle. United States Board on Geographic Names (1965c, p. 10) approved the name "Olive Lake" for a feature, 0.2 mile long, located 0.6 mile north-northwest of the southwest end of Huckleberry Lake (lat. 38°07'30" N, long. 119°43'52" W); the name commemorates Olive Hall, a local resident and conservationist.

Hughes and Keyes Ferry: see **Islip's Ferry**, under **Oakdale** [STANISLAUS].

Hughson [STANISLAUS]: *town,* 8 miles east-southeast of Modesto (lat. 37°35'50" N, long. 120°51'50" W). Named on Denair (1969) 7.5' quadrangle. Postal authorities established Hughson post office in 1908 (Frickstad, p. 200), and the town incorporated in 1972. The name is for Hiram Hughson, owner of the land where the town was laid out in 1907 (Gudde, 1949, p. 156).

Hulbert Mountain [MADERA]: *peak,* 5 miles south-southeast of O'Neals (lat. 37°03'20" N, long. 119°40'15" W; near S line sec. 15, T 10 S, R 21 E). Altitude 1847 feet. Named on Millerton Lake West (1965) 7.5' quadrangle.

Hull Creek [TUOLUMNE]: *stream,* flows 14 miles to Clavey River 7.5 miles southeast of Long Barn (lat. 38°00'05" N, long. 120°03'35" W; sec. 25, T 2 N, R 17 E). Named on Hull Creek (1979) and Strawberry (1979) 7.5' quadrangles.

Hull Creek Spring [TUOLUMNE]: *spring,* 5.25 miles east of Long Barn (lat. 38°05'35" N, long. 120°02'35" W); the spring is along Hull Creek. Named on Hull Creek (1979) 7.5' quadrangle.

Hulls Meadows [TUOLUMNE]: *area,* 4 miles east-southeast of Long Barn (lat. 38°04' N, long. 120°04'15" W; on S line sec. 35, T 3 N, R 17 E); the place is along Hull Creek. Named on Hull Creek (1979) 7.5' quadrangle.

Humbug Creek [MARIPOSA]: *stream,* flows nearly 3 miles to West Fork Chowchilla River 6.25 miles southeast of Mariposa (lat. 37° 25'35" N, long. 119°52'35" W; sec. 10, T 6 S, R 19 E). Named on Mariposa (1947) 7.5' quadrangle.

Humbug Creek: see **Big Humbug Creek** [TUOLUMNE].

Humbug Gulch [CALAVERAS]: *canyon,* drained by a stream that flows 1 mile to South Fork Mokelumne River 3.25 miles northwest of Rail Road Flat (lat. 38°22'15" N, long. 120°33'45" W; sec. 17, T 6 N, R 13 E). Named on Rail Road Flat (1948) 7.5' quadrangle. Camp's (1962) map shows Kohlberg's Humbug at the place.

Humbug Gulch: see **Cow and Calf Gulch** [MARIPOSA].

Hungry Flat [TUOLUMNE]: *locality,* 4.5 miles northeast of Stanislaus (lat. 38°10'55" N, long. 120°18'10" W; sec. 22, T 4 N, R 15 E). Named on Stanislaus (1948) 7.5' quadrangle.

Hungry Hill [TUOLUMNE]: *peak,* 2.25 miles south-southeast of Chinese Camp (lat. 37°50'25" N, long. 120°24'50" W; near NE cor. sec. 22, T 1 S, R 14 E). Named on Chinese Camp (1947) 7.5' quadrangle.

Hunter Bend [TUOLUMNE]: *bend,* 8.5 miles south-southeast of Duckwall Mountain along Clavey River (lat. 37°51'25" N, long. 120°03'20" W; sec. 13, T 1 S, R 17 E); the feature is 1.25 miles southeast of Hunter Point. Named on Jawbone Ridge (1947) 7.5' quadrangle.

Hunter Creek [CALAVERAS]: *stream,* flows 4.5 miles to Forest Creek 3.5 miles south of Devils Nose (lat. 38°24'50" N, long. 120° 25'35" W; sec. 34, T 7 N, R 14 E); the stream goes through Hunter Flat. Named on Devils Nose (1979) 7.5' quadrangle.

Hunter Creek [TUOLUMNE]: *stream,* flows 9 miles to North Fork Tuolumne River 2.5 miles south-southeast of Tuolumne (lat. 37° 55'35" N, long. 120°13'30" W; sec. 21, T 1 N, R 16 E). Named on Duckwall Mountain (1948) and Tuolumne (1948) 7.5' quadrangles.

Hunter Creek Camp Ground [TUOLUMNE]: *locality,* 5.5 miles east-southeast of Tuolumne (lat. 37°55'45" N, long. 120°08'40" W; sec. 19, T 1 N, R 17 E); the place is along Hunter Creek. Named on Tuolumne (1948) 7.5' quadrangle.

Hunter Flat [CALAVERAS]: *area,* 2.5 miles southeast of Devils Nose (lat. 38°26'15" N, long. 120°23'15" W; near NW cor. sec. 25, T 7 N, R 14 E); the place is along Hunter Creek. Named on Devils Nose (1979) 7.5' quadrangle.

Hunter Point [TUOLUMNE]: *peak,* 7 miles south-southeast of Duckwall Mountain (lat. 37°52' N, long. 120°04'25" W; sec. 11, T 1 S, R 17 E). Named on Jawbone Ridge (1947) 7.5' quadrangle.

Hunter Reservoir [CALAVERAS]: *lake,* behind a dam on Mill Creek (2) 7 miles northeast of Murphys (lat. 38°11'55" N, long. 120°21'30" W; sec. 18, T 4 N, R 15 E). Named on Stanislaus (1948) 7.5' quadrangle.

Hunters Valley: see **Hunter Valley** [MARIPOSA].

Hunter Valley [MARIPOSA]: *area,* 7 miles north-northeast of Hornitos (lat. 37°36' N, long. 120°11'45" W). Named on Coulterville (1947) and Hornitos (1947) 7.5' quadrangles. Postal authorities established Hunters Valley post office 10 miles northeast of Hornitos in 1907 and discontinued it in 1923 (Salley, p. 102). The name commemorates William W. Hunter, a well-known engineer (Gudde, 1975, p. 164).

Hunter Valley Mountain [MARIPOSA]: *ridge,* east-southeast to southeast-trending, 2 miles long, 5 miles south of Coulterville (lat. 37°38'25" N, long. 120°12'50" W); the ridge is northeast of the northwest end of Hunter Valley. Named on Coulterville (1947) 7.5' quadrangle.

Huntley [SAN JOAQUIN]: *locality,* 3.5 miles southeast of Escalon along the Atchison, Topeka and Santa Fe Railroad (lat. 37°45'35" N, long. 120°56'50" W; sec. 14, T 2 S, R 9 E). Named on Escalon (1968) 7.5' quadrangle.

Hutching Creek [MADERA]: *stream,* flows 3.5 miles to Lyell Fork nearly 7 miles northeast of Merced Peak (lat. 37°42'35" N, long. 119°18'40" W). Named on Merced Peak (1953) 15' quadrangle. United States Board on Geographic Names (1978b, p. 2-3) approved the form "Hutchings Creek" for the name, and rejected the names "Hutching Creek" and "North Fork Merced River" for it; the name is for James M. Hutchings, who wrote of Yosemite Valley.

Hutchings Creek: see **Hutching Creek** [MADERA].

H.V. Eastman Lake: see **Eastman Lake** [MADERA-MARIPOSA].

Hyatt Lake [TUOLUMNE]: *lake,* 3000 feet long, 10 miles east-southeast of Pinecrest (lat. 38°07'20" N, long. 119°50' W). Named on Pinecrest (1956) 15' quadrangle. R.B. Marshall of United States Geological Survey named the lake in 1909 for Edward Hyatt, Jr., who was with a Survey field party that year, and who later was California state engineer (Browning, 1986, p. 104).

— I —

Iceberg Lake [MADERA]: *lake,* about 2000 feet long, 5.5 miles west-northwest of Devils Postpile along Shadow Creek (lat. 37°40'15" N, long. 119°10'05" W). Named on Devils Postpile (1953) 15' quadrangle. The name is for the ice that sometimes floats in the lake until the late summer months (Smith, p. 62).

Iceberg Lake: see **Upper Iceberg Lake**, under **Cecile Lake** [MADERA].

Iceberg Meadow [TUOLUMNE]: *area,* 8.5 miles northwest of Sonora Pass on Tuolumne-Alpine County line (lat. 38°25'05" N, long. 119°44'50" W); the place is 0.5 mile south-southwest of a feature called The Iceberg, which is in Alpine County. Named on Disaster Peak (1979) 7.5' quadrangle.

Iceland Lake [TUOLUMNE]: *lake,* 1300 feet long, 12 miles west-northwest of Tower Peak (lat. 38°13'45" N, long. 119°44'40" W). Named on Tower Peak (1956) 15' quadrangle. United States Board on Geographic Names (1965a, p. 14) decided that Iceland Lake is not one of the group called Lewis Lakes.

Ida: see **Camp Ida Spring** [TUOLUMNE].

Illilouette Creek [MADERA-MARIPOSA]: *stream,* heads in Madera County and flows 14 miles to Merced River 2.25 miles southeast of Yosemite Village in Mariposa County (lat. 37°43'30" N, long. 119°33'25" W). Named on Merced Peak (1953) and Yosemite (1956) 15' quadrangles. Called Illilouette Fork on Hoffmann and Gardner's (1863-1867) map. King and Gardner's (1865) map has the designation "Illilouette or South Fork" for the stream. Whitney (1870, p. 65) called it "the South Fork, or the Illilouette." He added: "This is the South Fork of the Middle Fork [Merced River] and not the main South Fork," and, "To avoid confusion, it will be well to call it by the Indian name, Illilouette, one not yet much in use in the Valley." United States Board on Geographic Names (1933a, p. 385) rejected the names "South Canyon Creek" and "Tu-lu-la-wi-ak" for the stream.

Illilouette Fall [MARIPOSA]: *waterfall,* 3 miles south-southeast of Yosemite Village along Illilouette Creek (lat. 37°42'50" N, long. 119°33'40" W). Named on Yosemite (1956) 15' quadrangle.

Illilouette Fork: see **Illilouette Creek** [MADERA-MARIPOSA].

Illilouette Gorge [MARIPOSA]: *canyon,* less than 1 mile long, 2.25 miles southeast of Yosemite Village (lat. 37°43'10" N, long. 119° 33'30" W); the canyon is along Illilouette Creek below Illilouette Fall. Named on Yosemite (1956) 15' quadrangle.

Illilouette Ridge [MARIPOSA]: *ridge,* north-trending, 2 miles long, 3 miles south of Yosemite Village (lat. 37°42'10" N, long. 119°34'30" W); the ridge is west of Illilouette Creek. Named on Yosemite (1956) 15' quadrangle.

Illinois Hill [MARIPOSA]: *peak,* 8.5 miles south-southeast of the settlement of Catheys Valley (lat. 37°19'55" N, long. 120°00'45" W; near SW cor. sec. 9, T 7 S, R 18 E). Altitude 1670 feet. Named on Illinois Hill (1962) 7.5' quadrangle.

Incline [MARIPOSA]: *locality,* 4 miles west-southwest of El Portal on the south side of Merced River (lat. 37°39'40" N, long. 119° 51' W; sec. 22, T 3 S, R 19 E). Named on El Portal (1947) 7.5' quadrangle. Postal authorities established Incline post office in 1924 and discontinued it in 1953 (Frickstad, p. 91). Officials of Yosemite Valley Railroad named the place in 1923 for a precipitous incline railway that carried logs to the railroad from the timber belt about 12 miles away (Gudde, 1949, p. 159; Johnston, p. 51).

Independence [CALAVERAS]: *settlement,* 0.5 mile north of Rail Road Flat (lat. 38°21' N, long. 120°30'40" W; near N line sec. 26, T 6 N, R 13 E). Named on Railroad Flat (1948) 7.5' quadrangle.

Independence Flat: see **Mokelumne Hill** [CALAVERAS]; **Rail Road Flat** [CALAVERAS].

Independence Gulch [CALAVERAS]: *canyon,* drained by a stream that flows nearly 2 miles to South Fork Mokelumne River 2 miles northwest of Rail Road Flat (lat. 38°21'55" N, long. 120°31'50" W; near N line sec. 22, T 6 N, R 13 E); the canyon heads at Independence. Named on Rail Road Flat (1948) 7.5' quadrangle.

Indian Bar [TUOLUMNE]: *locality,* 7.5 miles south-southeast of Chinese Camp along Tuolumne River (lat. 37°46'30" N, long. 120° 22' W). Named on Sonora (1897) 30' quadrangle. Water of Don Pedro Reservoir now covers the site. A mining camp called Swetts Bar was located along the river 2 miles above Indian Bar (Gardiner, p. 229), and a mining camp called Chambers Bar was situated along the river 0.5 mile above Swetts Bar (Gudde, 1975, p. 66).

Indian Burying Gulch [CALAVERAS]: *canyon,* drained by a stream that flows 1.5 miles to San Antonio Creek 5.5 miles north-northeast of Murphys (lat. 38°12'55" N, long. 120°25'20" W; sec. 10, T 4 N, R 14 E). Named on Murphys (1948) 7.5' quadrangle.

Indian Canyon Creek [MARIPOSA]: *stream,* flows 3.5 miles to Merced River at Yosemite Village (lat. 37°44'45" N, long. 119°34'50" W). Named on Hetch Hetchy Reservoir (1956) 15' quadrangle. Indian prisoners of the Mariposa Battalion escaped up the stream course in 1851, and Mono Indians came down the stream to attack Indians in Yosemite Valley in 1853 (Browning, 1986, p. 105). United States Board on Geographic Names (1934, p. 12) rejected the name "Indian Creek" for the stream to avoid confusion with another tributary of Merced River that is called Indian Creek.

Indian Creek [CALAVERAS]:

(1) *stream,* flows 10 miles to San Antonio Creek 6.5 miles east-southeast of San Andreas (lat. 38°08'55" N, long. 120°34'25" W; near N line sec. 5, T 3 N, R 13 E). Named on Calaveritas (1962) and Murphys (1948) 7.5' quadrangles.

(2) *stream,* flows nearly 4 miles to Sixmile Creek 1.25 miles south-southeast of Angels Camp (lat. 38°03'25" N, long. 120°32'10" W; sec. 3, T 2 N, R 13 E). Named on Angels Camp (1962) 7.5' quadrangle.

Indian Creek [CALAVERAS-SAN JOAQUIN]: *stream,* heads in Calaveras County and flows 14 miles to Calaveras River 8 miles east-northeast of Linden in San Joaquin County (lat. 38°04'10" N, long. 120°57' W; sec. 35, T 3 N, R 9 E). Named on Valley Springs (1962) and Valley Springs SW (1962) 7.5' quadrangles.

Indian Creek [MARIPOSA]: *stream,* flows 6 miles to Merced River 0.5 mile east of El Portal (lat. 37°40'35" N, long. 119°46'10" W; sec. 16, T 3 S, R 20 E). Named on El Portal (1947) and Yosemite (1956) 15' quadrangles. Chinquapin Falls is along the creek, but United States Board on Geographic Names (1933a, p. 387) rejected the name "Chinquapin Creek" for the stream. Present Lehamite Creek once was called East Fork of Indian Creek (Browning, 1986, p. 125).

Indian Creek [TUOLUMNE]: *stream,* flows 4 miles to Tuolumne River 7 miles southeast of Tuolumne (lat. 37°53' N, long. 120°09'10" W; sec. 6, T 1 S, R 17 E). Named on Groveland (1947) and Tuolumne (1948) 7.5' quadrangles.

Indian Creek: see **Indian Canyon Creek** [MARIPOSA].

Indian Gulch [CALAVERAS]: *canyon,* drained by a stream that flows 1 mile to New Melones Lake 5.25 miles south-southeast of Angels Camp (lat. 38°00'30" N, long. 120°30' W; sec. 24, T 2 N, R 13 E). Named on Angels Camp (1962) 7.5' quadrangle.

Indian Gulch [MARIPOSA]:

(1) *canyon,* drained by a stream that flows 4.5 miles to North Fork Merced River 4 miles east of Buckhorn Peak (lat. 37°39'30" N, long. 120°03'05" W; near W line sec. 24, T 3 S, R 17 E). Named on Buckhorn Peak (1947) 7.5' quadrangle.

(2) *canyon,* drained by a stream that flows 3.5 miles to Slate Gulch 1.5 miles east-southeast of Santa Cruz Mountain (lat. 37°26'25" N, long. 120°10'25" W; sec. 1, T 6 S, R 16 E). Named on Indian Gulch (1962) 7.5' quadrangle.

(3) *locality,* 1.25 miles south-southeast of Santa Cruz Mountain (lat. 37°26'25" N, long. 120°11'45" W; near E line sec. 3, T 6 S, R 16 E); the place is in Indian Gulch (2). Named on Indian Gulch (1962) 7.5' quadrangle. California Mining Bureau's (1909b) map has the form "Indiangulch" for the name. Postal authorities established Indian Gulch post office in 1855, discontinued it for a time in 1901, and discontinued it finally in 1912 (Frickstad, p. 91). The place originally was called Santa Cruz (Chamberlain, p. 153). Laizure's (1935) map shows a place called Elkhorn located 3 miles north of Indiangulch.

Indian Gulch: see **Happy Valley** [CALAVERAS]; **Mokelumne River** [CALAVERAS-SAN JOAQUIN]; **West Point** [CALAVERAS].

Indian Hill [MADERA]: *peak,* 11 miles northeast of Raymond (lat. 37°19'40" N, long. 119°45'45" W; sec. 15, T 7 S, R 20 E). Named on Horsecamp Mountain (1947) 7.5' quadrangle.

Indian Hill [STANISLAUS]: *peak,* 0.5 mile east-northeast of La Grange (lat. 37°40'05" N, long. 120°27'10" W; sec. 17, T 3 S, R 14 E). Named on La Grange (1962) 7.5' quadrangle.

Indian Meadow [MADERA]: *area,* 10 miles southwest of Devils Postpile (lat. 37°32'35" N, long. 119°14'05" W). Named on Devils Postpile (1953) 15' quadrangle.

Indian Mountain [MARIPOSA]: *peak,* 2 miles east of Mariposa (lat. 37°29'25" N, long. 119°55'50" W; on N line sec. 19, T 5 S, R 19 E). Named on Mariposa (1947) 7.5' quadrangle.

Indian Peak [MARIPOSA]:

(1) *peak,* 1.5 miles south-southeast of Santa Cruz Mountain (lat. 37° 26'05" N, long. 120°11'15" W; sec. 2, T 6 S, R 16 E); the peak is 0.5 mile east-southeast of Indian Gulch (3). Named on Indian Gulch (1962) 7.5' quadrangle.

(2) *peak,* 10.5 miles southeast of Mariposa (lat. 37°23'35" N, long. 119°48'40" W; sec. 20, T 6 S, R 20 E). Altitude 3083 feet. Named on Stumpfield Mountain (1947) 7.5' quadrangle.

Indian Ridge [MARIPOSA]: *ridge,* south-southwest-trending, 2 miles long, 2 miles northeast of Yosemite Village (lat. 37°46'15" N, long. 119°33'25" W); Indian Rock is at the north-northeast end of the ridge. Named on Hetch Hetchy Reservoir (1956) 15' quadrangle.

Indian Rock [MARIPOSA]: *peak,* 3 miles northeast of Yosemite Village (lat. 37°47' N, long. 119°33' W); the peak is at the north-northeast end of Indian Ridge. Altitude 8522 feet. Named on Hetch Hetchy Reservoir (1956) 15' quadrangle.

Indian Spring [TUOLUMNE]:

(1) *spring,* 1.5 miles west-northwest of Crandall Peak (lat. 38°09'50" N, long. 120°10'20" W; at SE cor. sec. 26, T 4 N, R 16 E). Named on Crandall Peak (1979) 7.5' quadrangle.

(2) *spring,* 4.25 miles south-southeast of Duckwall Mountain (lat. 37°54'50" N, long. 120°05' W; near W line sec. 26, T 1 N, R 17 E). Named on Duckwall Mountain (1948) 7.5' quadrangle.

Indian Springs [MADERA]: *locality,* 5.5 miles south-southwest of O'Neals along Cottonwood Creek (1) (lat. 37°03'05" N, long. 119° 43'55" W; sec. 24, T 10 S, R 20 E). Named on Millerton Lake West (1965) 7.5' quadrangle.

Indian Wells Canyon [STANISLAUS]: *canyon,* drained by a stream that flows 1 mile to Garzas Creek 2.25 miles northwest of Crevison Peak (lat. 37°12'45" N, long. 121°13'10" W; sec. 29, T 8 S, R 7 E). Named on Crevison Peak (1955) 7.5' quadrangle.

Inferno Lakes [TUOLUMNE]: *lakes,* two, each about 1100 feet long, 15 miles east-southeast of Pinecrest (lat. 38°05'20" N, long. 119° 45'25" W). Named on Pinecrest (1956) 15' quadrangle.

Ingalsbe Slough [MERCED]: *stream,* heads near Snelling and flows 11 miles to Merced River 8.5 miles north of Atwater (lat. 37°28'15" N, long. 120°35'05" W; sec. 30, T 5 S, R 13 E). Named on Snelling (1962), Turlock Lake (1968), and Winton (1961) 7.5' quadrangles. Surface flow of the stream is discontinuous through an area of dredge tailings west of Snelling

Ingomar [MERCED]: *locality,* 10.5 miles northwest of Los Banos along Southern Pacific Railroad (lat. 37°10'45" N, long. 120° 58' W; sec. 3, T 9 S, R 9 E). Named on Ingomar (1960) 7.5' quadrangle. Postal authorities established Ingomar post office in 1890 and discontinued it in 1921 (Frickstad, p. 100). Gudde (1969, p. 151) believed that the name "Ingomar" may have been suggested by Friedrich Halm's play *Ingomar, the Barbarian,* which was revived on the American stage in 1885. Postal authorities established Sturgeon post office 11 miles southwest of Hills Ferry [STANISLAUS] in 1884 and discontinued it in 1890, when they moved the service to Ingomar; the name was for Inis Sturgeon, first postmaster (Salley, p. 214).

Ingram Canyon [STANISLAUS]: *canyon,* 5.5 miles long, opens into lowlands 9 miles west-northwest of Patterson (lat. 37°32'25" N, long. 121°16'05" W; at E line sec. 35, T 4 S, R 6 E); Ingram Creek drains the canyon. Named on Solyo (1953) 7.5' quadrangle.

Ingram Creek [STANISLAUS]: *stream,* flows 8 miles to lowlands 9 miles west-northwest of Patterson (lat. 37°32'25" N, long. 121°16'05" W; at E line sec. 35, T 4 S, R 6 E); the stream drains Ingram Canyon. Named on Solyo (1953) and Westley (1969) 7.5' quadrangles.

Inspiration Point [MARIPOSA]: *relief feature,* 6 miles west-southwest of Yosemite Village on the south side of Yosemite Valley (lat. 37°42'50" N, long. 119°41'15" W). Named on Yosemite (1956) 15' quadrangle.

Inspiration Point: see **Old Inspiration Point** [MARIPOSA].

Iowa Cabin: see **North Branch** [CALAVERAS].

Ireland Creek [TUOLUMNE]: *stream,* flows 3 miles to Lyell Fork 6 miles south of Tioga Pass (lat. 37°49'30" N, long. 119°16'40" W); the stream heads at Ireland Lake. Named on Tuolumne Meadows (1956) 15' quadrangle. Lieutenant H.C. Benson named the stream for Merritte Weber Ireland of the medical corps, who was on duty with the army in Yosemite National Park in 1897 (United States Board on Geographic Names, 1934, p. 12).

Ireland Lake [TUOLUMNE]: *lake,* 2900 feet long, 8.5 miles south-southwest of Tioga Pass (lat. 37°47'20" N, long. 119°18'15" W); the lake is at the head of Ireland Creek. Named on Tuolumne Meadows (1956) 15' quadrangle. Lieutenant H.C. Benson named the lake for Merritte Weber Ireland, for whom he named Ireland Creek (United States Board on Geographic Names, 1934, p. 12).

Iron Canyon [CALAVERAS-TUOLUMNE]: *narrows,* 7 miles east-southeast of Copperopolis along Stanislaus River on Calaveras-Tuolomne County line (lat. 37°57' N, long. 120°31'15" W; sec. 10, 11, T 1 N, R 13 E). Named on Melones Dam (1962) 7.5' quadrangle.

Iron Creek [MADERA]:

(1) *stream,* flows 3.5 miles to South Fork Merced River 4 miles south of Buena Vista Peak (lat. 37°32' N, long. 119°31'30" W; sec. 2, T 5 S, R 22 E); the stream heads at Iron Lakes. Named on Bass Lake (1953) and Yosemite (1956) 15' quadrangles.

(2) *stream,* flows 3 miles to Middle Fork San Joaquin River 7.5 miles west of Devils Postpile (lat. 37°37'10" N, long. 119°13'15" W); the stream heads at Iron Lake on the west side of Iron Mountain (2). Named on Devils Postpile (1953) 15' quadrangle.

Iron Creek [MARIPOSA]: *stream,* flows 3.5 miles to South Fork Merced River 3.25 miles northwest of Wawona (lat. 37°34'10" N, long. 119°41'55" W; sec. 20, T 4 S, R 21 E); the stream heads south of Iron Mountain. Named on Yosemite (1956) 15' quadrangle.

Iron Lake [MADERA]: *lake,* 950 feet long, nearly 5 miles west of Devils Postpile (lat. 37°36'45" N, long. 119°10'05" W); the lake is 0.25 mile west of Iron Mountain (2). Named on Devils Postpile (1953) 15' quadrangle.

Iron Lakes [MADERA]: *lakes,* largest 1400 feet long, 10.5 miles north-northwest of Shuteye Peak (lat. 37°29'30" N, long. 119°29'45" W; sec. 18, T 5 S, R 23 E). Named on Shuteye Peak (1953) 15' quadrangle.

Iron Mountain [CALAVERAS]: *peak,* 7.25 miles south-southwest of Copperopolis (lat. 37°52'50" N, long. 120°40'50" W). Altitude 990 feet. Named on Copperopolis (1962) 7.5' quadrangle.

Iron Mountain [MADERA]:

(1) *peak,* 10 miles north-northwest of Shuteye Peak (lat. 37°28'55" N, long. 119°29'15" W; sec. 19, T 5 S, R 23 E). Altitude 9165 feet. Named on Shuteye Peak (1953) 15' quadrangle.

(2) *peak,* 4.5 miles west-southwest of Devils Postpile (lat. 37°36'45" N, long. 119°09'50" W). Altitude 11,149 feet. Named on Devils Postpile (1953) 15' quadrangle.

(3) *peak,* 3.5 miles southwest of Raymond (lat. 37°11'10" N, long. 119°57'35" W; at SW cor. sec. 36, T 8 S, R 18 E). Altitude 984 feet. Named on Raymond (1962) 7.5' quadrangle.

Iron Mountain [MARIPOSA]: *ridge,* north-trending, 2 miles long, 5.25 miles northwest of Wawona (lat. 37°35' N, long. 119°43'55" W). Named on Yosemite (1956) 15' quadrangle.

Iron Spring [MARIPOSA]: *spring,* nearly 2 miles east-southeast of Yosemite Village along Tenaya Creek (lat. 37°44'35" N, long. 119° 33'10" W). Named on Yosemite (1956) 15' quadrangle. The feature also had the name "Chalybeate Spring" (Browning, 1986, p. 107).

Ironton Flats [MADERA]: *area,* 6.5 miles southwest of the town of North Fork (lat. 37°09'35" N, long. 119°35'45" W; sec. 8, T 9 S, R 22 E). Named on North Fork (1965) 7.5' quadrangle.

Irrigosa [MADERA]: *locality,* 2 miles southwest of Trigo along Southern Pacific Railroad (lat. 36°53'30" N, long. 119°59'10" W; sec. 15, T 12 S, R 18 E). Named on Gregg (1965) 7.5' quadrangle. California Division of Highways' (1934) map shows a place called Tharsa located along the railroad 3.25 miles southeast of Irrigosa (near SW cor. sec. 30, T 12 S, R 19 E).

Irvine: see **Carson Hill** [CALAVERAS] (2).

Irving Bright Lake: see **Irwin Bright Lake** [TUOLUMNE]; **Saddle Horse Lake** [TUOLUMNE].

Irwin [MERCED]: *settlement,* 4.5 miles west-southwest of Delhi, and less than 1 mile south of Hilmar (lat. 37°23'50" N, long. 120° 51' W). Named on Turlock (1962) 15' quadrangle. Postal authorities established Irwin post office in 1911 and discontinued it in 1958; the name commemorates W.A. Irwin, who laid out the settlement (Salley, p. 105).

Irwin Bright Lake [TUOLUMNE]: *lake,* 1750 feet long, 9.5 miles north-northeast of White Wolf (lat. 37°59'25" N, long. 119°33'30" W). Named on Hetch Hetchy Reservoir (1956) 15' quadrangle. The name commemorates the man who planted rainbow trout in the lake (Browning, 1986, p. 107). United States Board on Geographic Names (1960b, p. 17) rejected the names "Lily Lake," "Irving Bright Lake," and "Saddle Horse Lake" for the feature.

Isberg Lakes [MADERA]: *lakes,* two, each about 700 feet long, 4.5 miles east of Merced Peak (lat. 37°38'50" N, long. 119°18'50" W); the lakes are less than 1 mile east of Isberg Pass. Named on Merced Peak (1953) 15' quadrangle.

Isberg Pass [MADERA]: *pass,* nearly 4 miles east of Merced Peak (lat. 37°38'40" N, long. 119°19'30" W). Named on Merced Peak (1953) 15' quadrangle. Lieutenant N.F. McClure named the pass for the soldier who found it in 1895 (United States Board on Geographic Names, 1934, p. 12).

Isberg Peak [MADERA]: *peak,* 4.25 miles east-northeast of Merced Peak (lat. 37°39'15" N, long. 119°19'15" W); the peak is less than 1 mile north-northeast of Isberg Pass. Altitude 10,996 feet. Named on Merced Peak (1953) 15' quadrangle.

Island Pass [MADERA]: *pass,* 10 miles northwest of Devils Postpile on Madera-Mono County line (lat. 37°44'10" N, long. 119°11'35" W); the pass is north of Thousand Island Lake. Named on Devils Postpile (1953) 15' quadrangle

Island Rapids: see **Happy Isles** [MARIPOSA].

Island Slough: see **Islemouth Slough** [SAN JOAQUIN].

Islemouth Slough [SAN JOAQUIN]: *water feature,* joins South Mokelumne River 0.5 mile north-northeast of Terminus (lat. 38° 07'20" N, long. 121°29'30" W). Named on Terminous (1952) 7.5' quadrangle. Called Island Slough on Headreach (1910) and New Hope (1910) 7.5' quadrangles.

Islip's Ferry: see **Oakdale** [STANISLAUS].

Italian Bar [MADERA]: *locality,* 13 miles south of Shuteye Peak along San Joaquin River on Madera-Fresno County line (lat. 37°09'25" N, long. 119°24'15" W; near SW cor. sec. 7, T 9 S, R 24 E). Named on Shaver Lake (1953) 15' quadrangle.

Italian Bar [TUOLUMNE]: *locality,* 4.5 miles northeast of Columbia along South Fork Stanislaus River (lat. 38°04'30" N, long. 120°20'05" W; sec. 33, T 3 N, R 15 E). Named on Columbia SE (1948) 7.5' quadrangle.

Italian Creek [MARIPOSA]: *stream,* flows 5.5 miles to West Fork Chowchilla River 7.5 miles southeast of Mariposa (lat. 37°24'55" N, long. 119°51'45" W; sec. 14, T 6 S, R 19 E). Named on Stumpfield Mountain (1947) 7.5' quadrangle.

Italian Point [CALAVERAS]: *peak,* 5.5 miles southeast of San Andreas (lat. 38°08'25" N, long. 120°36'20" W; sec. 1, T 3 N, R 12 E). Named on Calaveritas (1962) 7.5' quadrangle.

Italian Ranch [TUOLUMNE]: *locality,* 4.25 miles east-southeast of Columbia (lat. 38°01'10" N, long. 120°19'35" W; near NE cor. sec. 21, T 2 N, R 15 E). Named on Columbia SE (1948) 7.5' quadrangle.

Isberg Peak [MADERA]: *peak,* 4.25 miles east-northeast of Merced Peak (lat. 37°39'15" N, long. 119°19'15" W); the peak is less than 1 mile north-northeast of Isberg Pass. Altitude 10,996 feet. Named on Merced Peak (1953) 15' quadrangle.

Island Pass [MADERA]: *pass,* 10 miles northwest of Devils Postpile on Madera-Mono County line (lat. 37°44'10" N, long. 119°11'35" W); the pass is north of Thousand Island Lake. Named on Devils Postpile (1953) 15' quadrangle

Island Rapids: see Happy Isles [MARIPOSA].

Island Slough: see **Islemouth Slough** [SAN JOAQUIN].

Islemouth Slough [SAN JOAQUIN]: *water feature,* joins South Mokelumne River 0.5 mile north-northeast of Terminus (lat. 38°07'20" N, long. 121°29'30" W). Named on Terminous (1952) 7.5' quadrangle. Called Island Slough on Headreach (1910) and New Hope (1910) 7.5' quadrangles.

Islip's Ferry: see **Oakdale** [STANISLAUS].

Italian Bar [MADERA]: *locality,* 13 miles south of Shuteye Peak along San Joaquin River on Madera-Fresno County line (lat. 37°09'25" N, long. 119°24'15" W; near SW cor. sec. 7, T 9 S, R 24 E). Named on Shaver Lake (1953) 15' quadrangle.

Italian Bar [TUOLUMNE]: *locality,* 4.5 miles northeast of Columbia along South Fork Stanislaus River (lat. 38°04'30" N, long. 120°20'05" W; sec. 33, T 3 N, R 15 E). Named on Columbia SE (1948) 7.5' quadrangle.

Italian Creek [MARIPOSA]: *stream,* flows 5.5 miles to West Fork Chowchilla River 7.5 miles southeast of Mariposa (lat. 37°24'55" N, long. 119°51'45" W; sec. 14, T 6 S, R 19 E). Named on Stumpfield Mountain (1947) 7.5' quadrangle.

Italian Point [CALAVERAS]: *peak,* 5.5 miles southeast of San Andreas (lat. 38°08'25" N, long. 120°36'20" W; sec. 1, T 3 N, R 12 E). Named on Calaveritas (1962) 7.5' quadrangle.

Italian Ranch [TUOLUMNE]: *locality,* 4.25 miles east-southeast of Columbia (lat. 38°01'10" N, long. 120°19'35" W; near NE cor. sec. 21, T 2 N, R 15 E). Named on Columbia SE (1948) 7.5' quadrangle.

— J —

Jackass Butte [MADERA]: *peak,* 11 miles north-northeast of Shuteye Peak (lat. 37°29' N, long. 119°18'30" W; sec. 23, T 5 S, R 24 E); the peak is near Jackass Creek. Altitude 7238 feet. Named on Shuteye Peak (1953) 15' quadrangle.

Jackass Campground: see **Little Jackass Campground** [MADERA].

Jackass Creek [MADERA]: *stream,* flows 15 miles to Mammoth Pool Reservoir 7 miles east-northeast of Shuteye Peak (lat. 37°22'20" N, long. 119°18'15" W; sec. 25, T 6 S, R 24 E); the stream heads at Jackass Lakes and goes past Jackass Butte and Jackass Rock. Named on Merced Peak (1953) and Shuteye Peak (1953) 15' quadrangles. West Fork enters from the northwest 0.5 mile upstream from the mouth of the main stream; it is 6.5 miles long and is named on Shuteye Peak (1953) 15' quadrangle.

Jackass Creek: see **Big Jackass Creek** [TUOLUMNE]; **Little Jackass Creek** [TUOLUMNE].

Jackass Flat [STANISLAUS]: *area,* 6 miles south-southeast of Mikes Peak along Orestimba Creek (lat. 37°16'55" N, long. 121°16' W; sec. 36, T 7 S, R 6 E). Named on Wilcox Ridge (1956) 7.5' quadrangle.

Jackass Gulch: see **Middle Bar** [CALAVERAS]; **Norwegian Gulch** [TUOLUMNE].

Jackass Hill [TUOLUMNE]: *locality,* 5.25 miles west-northwest of Sonora (lat. 37°59'50" N, long. 120°28'30" W; sec. 30, T 2 N, R 14 E). Named on Columbia (1948) and Sonora (1948) 7.5' quadrangles. The name is from noisy pack-train animals that paused overnight at the place on the way to and from the mines (Hoover, Rensch, and Rensch, p. 573).

Jackass Lakes [MADERA]: *lakes,* largest 1500 feet long, 7.5 miles south-southeast of Merced Peak (lat. 37°31'40" N, long. 119°21'10" W; sec. 4, 5, T 5 S, R 24 E); the lakes are at the head of Jackass Creek. Named on Merced Peak (1953) 15' quadrangle.

Jackass Meadow [MADERA]: *area,* 11.5 miles north-northeast of Shuteye Peak (lat. 37°30' N, long. 119°20' W); the place is along Jackass Creek. Named on Merced Peak (1953) and Shuteye Peak (1953) 15' quadrangles.

Jackass Meadow: see **Little Jackass Meadow**, under **Soldier Meadow** [MADERA].

Jackass Mountain [MARIPOSA]: *ridge,* west-trending, 1 mile long, 7.25 miles northeast of Buckhorn Peak (lat. 37°43'50" N, long. 120°01' W). Named on Buckhorn Peak (1947) 7.5' quadrangle.

Jackass Ridge [TUOLUMNE]: *ridge,* north-northwest-trending, 2 miles long, 4 miles south-southeast of Groveland (lat. 37°46'50" N, long. 120°12'15" W). Named on Groveland (1947) 7.5' quadrangle.

Jackass Rock [MADERA]: *peak,* 9 miles northeast of Shuteye Peak (lat. 37°26' N, long. 119°18' W; sec. 1, T 6 S, R 24 E). Altitude 7112 feet. Named on Shuteye Peak (1953) 15' quadrangle.

Jack Main Canyon [TUOLUMNE]: *canyon,* 12 miles long, along upper reaches of Falls Creek above a point 11 miles southwest of Tower Peak (lat. 38°02'15" N, long. 119°42'15" W). Named on Tower Peak (1956) 15' quadrangle. The corrupted name commemorates Jack Means, an early-day sheepherder (United States Board on Geographic Names, 1934, p. 13).

Jack Main Mountain: see **Chittenden Peak** [TUOLUMNE].

Jack Nelson Creek [CALAVERAS]: *stream,* flows 3.25 miles to Esperanza Creek 4 miles southwest of Rail Road Flat (lat. 38°17'40" N, long. 120°33'20" W; near NE cor. sec. 17, T 5 N, R 13 E). Named on Rail Road Flat (1948) 7.5' quadrangle.

Jackson Gulch [TUOLUMNE]: *canyon,* drained by a stream that flows nearly 2 miles to Big Jackass Creek 3.25 miles south-southeast of Groveland (lat. 37°47'40" N, long. 120°12'55" W; sec. 4, T 2 S, R 16 E). Named on Groveland (1947) 7.5' quadrangle.

Jacksonville [TUOLUMNE]: *village,* 9.5 miles south of Sonora near the confluence of Woods Creek and Tuolumne River (lat. 37°50'45" N, long. 120°22'35" W; on E line sec. 13, T 1 S, R 14 E). Named on Sonora (1948) 15' quadrangle. Water of Don Pedro Reservoir now covers the site. Colonel Alden M. Jackson founded the place in June of 1849 (Paden and Schlichtmann, p. 97). Postal authorities established Jacksonville post office in 1851, discontinued it in 1868, reestablished it in 1895, discontinued it in 1896, reestablished it in 1900, and discontinued it in 1918 (Frickstad, p. 216).

Jahant Slough [SAN JOAQUIN]: *stream,* flows 7 miles to Tracy Lake 5.5 miles north-northwest of Lodi (lat. 38°12'30" N, long. 121°18'45" W; sec. 10, T 4 N, R 6 E). Named on Lockeford (1968) and Lodi North (1968) 7.5' quadrangles.

Jakesville: see **Forest Lake** [SAN JOAQUIN].

James Bar: see **Rich Gulch** [CALAVERAS] (1).

James Canyon [SAN JOAQUIN]: *canyon,* drained by a stream that flows 1 mile to a branch of Corral Hollow Creek 1 mile south-southeast of Eagle Mountain (lat. 37°33'20" N, long. 121°31'45" W). Named on Cedar Mountain (1956) 7.5' quadrangle.

Jamestown [TUOLUMNE]: *town,* 3 miles southwest of Sonora (lat. 37°57'10" N, long. 120°25'20" W; sec. 10, T 1 N, R 14 E). Named on Sonora (1948) 7.5' quadrangle. The name commemorates Colonel James, a San Francisco lawyer and a mining speculator at the place in 1848; the town was called American Camp for a time after the colonel's departure (Stoddart, p. 61). Postal authorities established Jamestown post office in 1853 (Frickstad, p. 216). Gudde (1975, p. 186, 214, 369) listed a place called Whiskey Hill that was located 1 mile southwest of Jamestown, a place called Mexican Flat that was situated on the east side of Whiskey Hill, and a place called Kincades Flat that was located about 3 miles east of Jamestown. Rossland post office, located 5 miles northwest of Jamestown, operated for a a few months in 1898 (Salley, p. 189).

Janes Gulch [CALAVERAS]: *canyon,* drained by a stream that flows 1 mile to Walla Gulch 4 miles east of San Andreas (lat. 38°12'25" N, long. 120°36'35" W; near SW cor. sec. 12, T 4 N, R 12 E). Named on Calaveritas (1962) 7.5' quadrangle.

Janney: see **Tracy** [SAN JOAQUIN].

Jarbau Creek: see **Jawbone Creek** [TUOLUMNE].

Jarn: see **Stockton** [SAN JOAQUIN].

Jasper [MARIPOSA]: *locality,* 5 miles southwest of Coulterville along Yosemite Valley Railroad (lat. 37°39'25" N, long. 120°15'20" W); the place is near present Jasper Point. Named on Sonora (1897) 30' quadrangle. Jasper Point post office, named for Jasper, was established 9 miles northwest of Bagby in 1909 and discontinued in 1916 (Salley, p. 106-107). California Division of Highways' (1934) map shows a place called Detwiler situated 1.5 miles east-northeast of Jasper along the railroad.

Jasper Point [MARIPOSA]: *promontory,* 5 miles south of Penon Blanco Peak on the south side of Lake McClure (lat. 37°39'35" N, long. 120°15'10" W; sec. 19, T 3 S, R 16 E). Named on Penon Blanco Peak (1962) 7.5' quadrangle.

Jasper Point: see **Jasper** [MARIPOSA].

Jawbone Creek [TUOLUMNE]: *stream,* flows 13 miles to Tuolumne River 7.5 miles west of Mather (lat. 37°53' N, long. 119°59'25" W; sec. 3, T 1 S, R 18 E). Named on Lake Eleanor (1956) and Pinecrest (1956) 15' quadrangles. A Frenchman named Jarbau had a cabin in the 1860's at the confluence of present Jawbone Creek and Skunk Creek; present Jawbone Creek was called Jarbau Creek before the name was corrupted to the form "Jawbone" (Browning, 1986, p. 109). United States Board on Geographic Names (1933a, p. 397) rejected the name "Pile Creek" for present Jawbone Creek.

Jawbone Falls [TUOLUMNE]: *waterfall,* nearly 13 miles south of Pinecrest along Jawbone Creek (lat. 38°00'30" N, long. 119°58'15" W). Named on Cherry Lake North (1979) 7.5' quadrangle.

Jawbone Pass [TUOLUMNE]: *pass,* 11 miles south-southeast of Pinecrest (lat. 38°02'10" N, long. 119°56'25" W; near SE cor. sec. 12, T 2 N, R 18 E); the pass is near the head of Jawbone Creek. Named on Cherry Lake North (1979) 7.5' quadrangle.

Jawbone Pass Pond [TUOLUMNE]: *lake,* 150 feet long, 11 miles south of Pinecrest (lat. 38°02' N, long. 119°57'40" W; sec. 14, T 2 N, R 18 E); the lake is 1.25 miles west-southwest of Jawbone Pass. Named on Cherry Lake North (1979) 7.5' quadrangle.

Jawbone Ridge [TUOLUMNE]: *ridge,* south- to west-trending, 4.5 miles long, 8 miles south-southeast of Duckwall Mountain (lat. 37° 51' N, long. 120°03'30" W). Named on Jawbone Ridge (1947) 7.5' quadrangle.

Jeffers Canyon [MERCED]: *canyon,* drained by a stream that flows 1 mile to Romero Creek 6 miles north of Pacheco Pass (lat. 37°08'50" N, long. 121°11'20" W; sec. 15, T 9 S, R 7 E). Named on Crevison Peak (1955) 7.5' quadrangle.

Jeffersonville: see **Tuttletown** [TUOLUMNE].

Jelmini Basin [CALAVERAS]: *area,* nearly 3 miles northwest of Tamarack (lat. 38°28'15" N, long. 120°06'15" W; sec. 9, T 7 N, R 17 E); the place is near Jelmini Creek. Named on Tamarack (1979) 7.5' quadrangle.

Jelmini Creek [CALAVERAS]: *stream,* flows 3.25 miles to North Fork Mokelumne River 4.5 miles north-northwest of Tamarack (lat. 38°29'45" N, long 120°07'15" W); the stream goes past Jelmini Basin. Named on Tamarack (1979) 7.5' quadrangle.

Jenkins Hill [MARIPOSA]: *ridge,* south-southeast-trending, less than 1 mile long, 8.5 miles west of El Portal (lat. 37°39'50" N, long. 119°56'35" W). Named on Kinsley (1947) 7.5' quadrangle.

Jenkins Hill [TUOLUMNE]: *peak,* 1.5 miles east of Don Pedro Camp (lat. 37°43' N, long. 120°22'30" W; sec. 36, T 2 S, R 14 E). Named on La Grange (1962) and Penon Blanco Peak (1962) 7.5' quadrangles.

Jenny Lind [CALAVERAS]: *village,* 7 miles south-southwest of Valley Springs near Calaveras River (lat. 38°05'45" N, long. 120° 52'10" W; near W line sec. 22, T 3 N, R 10 E). Named on Jenny Lind (1962) 7.5' quadrangle. Postal authorities established Jenny Lind post office in 1857, discontinued it in 1944, reestablished it in 1947, and discontinued it in 1951 (Frickstad, p. 15). The village, which began in the early 1850's as a mining camp, was named for the famous Swedish songstress who toured the eastern United States from 1850 until 1852 (Gudde, 1949, p. 166). Postal authorities operated Fremont Valley post office 6 miles northeast of Jenny Lind for a time in 1879; they established Pattees Ranch post office 8 miles northeast of Jenny Lind in 1865 and discontinued it in 1871 (Salley, p. 80, 168). A stopping place called Antelope House was situated across Calaveras River from Jenny Lind (Leonard, p. 14).

Jerseydale [MARIPOSA]: *locality,* nearly 9 miles south-southwest of El Portal (lat. 37°33'50" N, long. 119°51'20" W; near NW cor. sec. 27, T 4 S, R 19 E). Named on Buckingham Mountain (1947) 7.5' quadrangle. Postal authorities established Jerseydale post office in 1889 and discontinued it in 1930 (Frickstad, p. 91). They established Minear post office 6 miles north of Jerseydale in 1895 and discontinued it in 1896; the name was for John J. Minear, first postmaster (Salley, p. 141).

Jesbel [MADERA]: *locality,* 5.25 miles south-southwest of Raymond along Southern Pacific Railroad (lat. 37°09' N, long. 119°57'15" W; sec. 13, T 9 S, R 18 E). Named on Raymond (1944) 15' quadrangle.

Jesus Maria [CALAVERAS]: *locality,* 3.25 miles east-southeast of Mokelumne Hill (lat. 38°17'10" N, long. 120°38'45" W; near W line sec. 15, T 5 N, R 12 E). Named on Mokelumne Hill (1948) 7.5' quadrangle. The site was settled in the early 1850's and named for a Mexican who grew vegetables and melons there (California Department of Parks and Recreation, p. 16).

Jesus Maria Creek [CALAVERAS]: *stream,* flows 17 miles to North Fork Calaveras River 2.5 miles east-southeast of Mokelumne Hill (lat. 38°17'15" N, long. 120°39'35" W; sec. 16, T 5 N, R 12 E); the stream goes past Jesus Maria. Named on Fort Mountain (1979), Mokelumne Hill (1948), and Rail Road Flat (1948) 7.5' quadrangles.

Jet [STANISLAUS]: *locality,* 3 miles south-southeast of Patterson along Southern Pacific Railroad (lat. 37°25'55" N, long. 121°05'55" W; sec. 9, T 6 S, R 8 E). Named on Crows Landing (1952) 7.5' quadrangle.

Jewelry Lake [TUOLUMNE]: *lake,* 1200 feet long, 12 miles east of Pinecrest (lat. 38°09'45" N, long. 119°46'55" W). Named on Pinecrest (1956) 15' quadrangle. The name is from some jeweled spinners used by a fishermen at the lake about 1915 (Browning. 1986, p. 110).

Joaquin Gulch [CALAVERAS]: *canyon,* drained by a stream that flows 1.5 miles to Calaveritas Creek 8.5 miles east of San Andreas (lat. 38°10'55" N, long. 120°31'25" W; sec. 22, T 4 N, R 13 E). Named on Calaveritas (1962) 7.5' quadrangle.

Joaquin Peak [CALAVERAS]: *peak,* nearly 4 miles south of San Andreas near the south end of Hogback Mountain (lat. 38°08'30" N, long. 120°41'25" W; sec. 6, T 3 N, R 12 E). Altitude 2812 feet. Named on San Andreas (1962) 7.5' quadrangle. Called Mt. Joaquin on Jackson (1902) 30' quadrangle. The name "Joaquin" is for the Mexican outlaw Joaquin Murieta, who is said to have been involved in a skirmish near the peak in 1853 (Gudde, 1969, p. 215).

Joe Crane Lake [MADERA]: *lake,* 1000 feet long, 4.5 miles east of Merced Peak (lat. 37°37'30" N, long. 119°18'50" W). Named on Merced Peak (1953) 15' quadrangle.

Joes Point [TUOLUMNE]: *peak,* 5.5 miles west of Mather (lat. 37°53'10" N, long. 119°57'15" W; near W line sec. 1, T 1 S, R 18 E). Altitude 4219 feet. Named on Lake Eleanor (1956) 15' quadrangle.

John Allen Flat [MARIPOSA]: *area,* 6.5 miles southeast of Mariposa along Blade Creek (lat. 37°24'40" N, long. 119°53'35" W; sec. 16, T 6 S, R 19 E). Named on Mariposa (1947) 7.5' quadrangle.

John Bull Peak [CALAVERAS]: *peak,* 3.25 miles west of Paloma (lat. 38°15'25" N, long. 120°49'25" W; sec. 25, T 5 N, R 10 E). Altitude 1053 feet. Named on Jackson (1962) 7.5' quadrangle.

Johnnie Gulch [TUOLUMNE]: *canyon,* drained by a stream that flows 1 mile to North Fork Tuolumne River 2.5 miles east of Twain Harte (lat. 38°02' N, long. 120°11' W; near N line sec. 14, T 2 N, R 16 E). Named on Twain Harte (1979) 7.5' quadrangle.

Johnson Creek [MADERA]:

(1) *stream,* flows 3.5 miles to South Fork Merced River 4 miles south of Buena Vista Peak (lat. 37°32'15" N, long. 119°31'20" W; near SE cor. sec. 35, T 4 S, R 22 E). Named on Yosemite (1956) 15' quadrangle.

(2) *stream,* flows 4.5 miles to Chiquito Creek 5.5 miles north-northeast of Shuteye Peak (lat. 37°25' N, long. 119°23'05" W; sec. 7, T 6 S, R 24 E). Named on Shuteye Peak (1953) 15' quadrangle.

Johnson Creek [STANISLAUS-TUOLUMNE]: *stream,* heads in Tuolumne County and flows 4 miles to Dry Creek 3.25 miles northwest of La Grange in Stanislaus County (lat. 37°42' N, long. 120°30' W; near W line sec. 1, T 3 S, R 13 E). Named on La Grange (1962) 7.5' quadrangle.

Johnson Lake [MADERA]: *lake,* 900 feet long, 1.5 miles south of Buena Vista Peak (lat. 37°34'05" N, long. 119°31' W; near SW cor. sec. 24, T 4 S, R 22 E); the lake is along Johnson Creek (1). Named on Yosemite (1956) 15' quadrangle. United States Board on Geographic Names (1933a, p. 400) rejected the names "Glacier Lake" and "Glasier Lake" for the feature.

Johnson Lake: see **Johnston Lake** [MADERA].

Johnson Meadow: see **Johnston Meadow** [MADERA].

Johnson Meadows [MADERA]: *area,* 6 miles north-northeast of Shuteye Peak (lat. 37°25'50" N, long. 119°23'30" W; sec. 6, T 6 S, R 24 E). Named on Shuteye Peak (1953) 15' quadrangle.

Johnson Peak [TUOLUMNE]: *peak,* 7 miles southwest of Tioga Pass (lat. 37°50'10" N, long. 119°20'50" W). Altitude 11,070 feet. Named on Tuolumne Meadows (1956) 15' quadrangle. R.B. Marshall of United States Geological Survey named the peak in the 1890's for a teamster who worked for the Survey and was especially useful as a guide (United States Board on Geographic Names, 1934, p. 13).

Johnson's Ferry: see **Lathrop** [SAN JOAQUIN].

Johnsonville: see **Bear Valley** [MARIPOSA] (2).

Johnston Lake [MADERA]: *lake,* 600 feet long, nearly 2 miles northwest of Devils Postpile (lat. 37°38'45" N, long. 119°06' W); the lake is in Johnston Meadow. Named on Devils Postpile (1953) 15' quadrangle. It first was called Minaret Lake, but Stephen T. Mather suggested the name "Johnston Lake" to honor Taylor Johnston, as well as Mr. Johnston's father and brother—the three men began mining in the neighborhood in 1919 (Browning, 1988, p. 69). United States Board on Geographic Names (1962b, p. 20) rejected the names "Minaret Lake" and "Johnson Lake" for the feature.

Johnston Meadow [MADERA]: *area,* 2 miles northwest of Devils Postpile along Minaret Creek (lat. 37°38'45" N, long. 119°06' W). Named on Devils Postpile (1953) 15' quadrangle. Stephen T. Mather suggested the name "Johnston Meadow" for what had been called Minaret Meadow; the new name honors the Johnstons for whom Johnston Lake was named (Browning, 1988, p. 69). United States Board on Geographic Names (1962b, p. 20) rejected the names "Johnson Meadow" and "Minaret Meadow" for the place.

Jones Creek [MARIPOSA}: *stream,* flows 4.25 miles to join Snow Creek (2) and form West Fork Chowchilla River 5 miles east of Mariposa (lat. 37°28'55" N, long. 119°52'25" W; sec. 22, T 5 S, R 19 E). Named on Feliciana Mountain (1947) and Mariposa (1947) 7.5' quadrangles.

Jones Flat [MARIPOSA]: *area,* 5 miles north-northwest of Hornitos (lat. 37°34'20" N, long. 120°16'15" W; sec. 24, T 4 S, R 15 E). Named on Merced Falls (1962) 7.5' quadrangle.

Jones Hill [TUOLUMNE]: *ridge,* north-northeast-trending, 1 mile long, 1 mile north of Groveland (lat. 37°51'05" N, long. 120°13'50" W). Named on Groveland (1947) 7.5' quadrangle.

Jones Tract: see **Lower Jones Tract** [SAN JOAQUIN]; **Upper Jones Tract** [SAN JOAQUIN].

Jordan Creek [MARIPOSA]: *stream,* flows 5.5 miles to North Fork Merced River 5 miles southeast of Smith Peak (lat. 37°45'05" N, long. 120°02'05" W; sec. 19, T 2 S, R 18 E). Named on Jawbone Ridge (1947) 7.5' quadrangle. West Fork enters from the northwest 3 miles upstream from the mouth of the main stream; it is 2.5 miles long and is named on Jawbone Ridge (1947) 7.5' quadrangle.

Jordan Flat [MARIPOSA]: *area,* 1 mile south of Smith Peak (lat. 37° 47'05" N, long. 120°06'10" W; near S line sec. 4, T 2 S, R 17 E); the place is along West Fork Jordan Creek. Named on Jawbone Ridge (1947) 7.5' quadrangle.

Joyce: see **Turlock** [STANISLAUS].

Jumping Off Place: see **The Jumping Off Place**, under **Lovers Leap** [STANISLAUS].

Junction Bluffs [MADERA]: *relief feature,* 7 miles south-southwest of Devils Postpile (lat. 37°31'30" N, long. 119°08' W); the feature is on the south side of Middle Fork San Joaquin River east of the junction with North Fork. Named on Devils Postpile (1953) 15' quadrangle.

Junction Butte [MADERA]: *ridge,* north-trending, 2 miles long, 9 miles southwest of Devils Postpile (lat. 37°31'40" N, long. 119°11'45" W; near E line sec. 2, T 5 S, R 25 E); the ridge is southwest of the junction of West Fork San Joaquin River and Middle Fork San Joaquin River. Named on Devils Postpile (1953) 15' quadrangle.

Junction Lake [MADERA]: *lake,* about 600 feet long, 10.5 miles north-northwest of Shuteye Peak (lat. 37°29'45" N, long. 119°29'45" W; sec. 18, T 5 S, R 23 E). Named on Shuteye Peak (1953) 15' quadrangle.

Jupiter [TUOLUMNE]: *locality,* 9 miles northeast of Columbia (lat. 38°07'20" N, long. 120°16'55" W; sec. 12, T 3 N, R 15 E). Named on Columbia SE (1948) 7.5' quadrangle. Postal authorities established Jupiter post office, named for Jupiter mine, in 1901 and discontinued it in 1922 (Salley, p. 109). The post office was at a place called Philadelphia Diggings (Gudde, 1975, p. 264).

—K—

Kadota [MERCED]: *locality,* 4 miles east of Merced along Atchison, Topeka and Santa Fe Railroad (lat. 37°17'40" N, long. 120°24'40" W; sec. 26, T 7 S, R 14 E). Named on Merced (1961) 7.5' quadrangle.

Kaiser Creek Ford [MADERA]: *locality,* 7 miles east of Shuteye Peak along San Joaquin River (lat. 37°22' N, long. 119°18' W; sec. 36, T 6 S, R 24 E); the place is above the mouth of Kaiser Creek, which is in Fresno County. Named on Kaiser (1904) 30' quadrangle.

Kaiser's Landing: see **Roberts Island** [SAN JOAQUIN].

Kanaka Bar: see **Kanaka Creek** [TUOLUMNE].

Kanaka Creek [TUOLUMNE]: *stream,* flows 3 miles to Don Pedro Reservoir 4 miles northwest of Moccasin (lat. 37°50'40" N, long. 120°21'25" W; sec. 18, T 1 S, R 15 E). Named on Moccasin (1948, photorevised 1973) 7.5' quadrangle. Kanaka Bar was located along Tuolumne River at the mouth of Kanaka Creek—water of Don Pedro Reservoir now covers the site of the bar (Gudde, 1975, p. 181).

Karls Lake [TUOLUMNE]: *lake,* 0.5 miles, long, 13 miles east-southeast of Pinecrest (lat. 38°08'50" N, long. 119°45'45" W). Named on Pinecrest (1956) 15' quadrangle. The name commemorates Karl Defiebre, a hotelman at Pinecrest before World War II (Browning, 1986, p. 114).

Kassabaum Flats [MARIPOSA]: *area,* 6.5 miles south-southwest of Penon Blanco Peak along Browns Creek (lat. 37°38'45" N, long. 120°19' W). Named on Penon Blanco Peak (1962) 7.5' quadrangle.

Kassabaum Meadow [TUOLUMNE]: *area,* 5.5 miles east of Groveland (lat. 37°49'25" N, long. 120°07'40" W; mainly in sec. 29, T 1 S, R 17 E). Named on Groveland (1947) 7.5' quadrangle.

Kates Cow Camp [MADERA]: *locality,* 8 miles north of Shuteye Peak (lat. 37°27'55" N, long. 119°24'15" W; sec. 25, T 5 S, R 23 E). Named on Shuteye Peak (1953) 15' quadrangle.

Keeler's Ferry: see **Lovers Leap** [STANISLAUS].

Keeler's Flat: see **Lovers Leap** [STANISLAUS].

Kelly Flat [TUOLUMNE]: *locality,* 6.25 miles west of Mather along Cherry Creek (lat. 37°53'30" N, long. 119°58'10" W; on S line sec. 35, T 1 N, R 18 E). Named on Lake Eleanor (1956) 15' quadrangle.

Kelsey [MERCED]: *locality,* 5 miles east of Snelling along Yosemite Valley Railroad (lat. 37°31'20" N, long. 120°21' W; sec. 5, T 5 S, R 15 E). Named on Merced Falls (1944) 15' quadrangle.

Kelsey Reservoir [MERCED]: *lake,* 3150 feet long, nearly 5 miles east-northeast of Snelling (lat. 37°32'30" N, long. 120°21'15" W; on E line sec. 31, T 4 S, R 15 E); the lake is 1.25 miles north of the site of Kelsey. Named on Merced Falls (1962) 7.5' quadrangle.

Kelshaw Corners [MADERA]: *locality,* 2.5 miles northwest of O'Neals (lat. 37°09'05" N, long. 119°44' W; sec. 13, T 9 S, R 20 E). Named on O'Neals (1965) 7.5' quadrangle.

Kelty Meadow [MADERA]: *area,* 7 miles northeast of Yosemite Forks (lat. 37°26'30" N, long. 119°32'35" W; near E line sec. 3, T 6 S, R 22 E). Named on Bass Lake (1953) 15' quadrangle. The misspelled name is for Frank Keltie, who homesteaded in sections 2 and 3 in 1886 (Browning, 1986, p. 116).

Kelty Meadow Campground [MADERA]: *locality,* 7 miles northeast of Yosemite Forks (lat. 37°26'25" N, long. 119°32'35" W; sec. 3, T 6 S, R 22 E); the place is at Kelty Meadow. Named on Bass Lake (1953) 15' quadrangle.

Kendrick Creek [TUOLUMNE]: *stream,* flows 13 miles to join Bartlett Creek and form Eleanor Creek 16 miles southeast of Pinecrest (lat. 38°01'30" N, long. 119°48' W; near S line sec. 17, T 2 N, R 20 E); the stream heads near Kendrick Peak. Named on Pinecrest (1956) and Tower Peak (1956) 15' quadrangles. The name is from Kendrick Peak (United States Board on Geographic Names, 1934, p. 13). Called East Fork Eleanor Cr. on Dardanelles (1898) 30' quadrangle.

Kendrick Peak [TUOLUMNE]: *peak,* 5 miles west-southwest of Tower Peak (lat. 38°07'30" N, long. 119°38'15" W). Altitude 10,390 feet. Named on Tower Peak (1956) 15' quadrangle. Colonel W.W. Forsyth named the peak in 1912 for Henry L. Kendrick, professor of chemistry at West Point (United States Board on Geographic Names, 1934, p. 13).

Kenefick: see **Peltier** [SAN JOAQUIN].

Kennebec Hill [TUOLUMNE]: *hill,* 0.5 mile south-southeast of Columbia (lat. 38°01'40" N, long. 120°23'45" W; sec. 13, 14, T 2 N, R 14 E). Named on Columbia (1948) 7.5' quadrangle.

Kennedy Creek [TUOLUMNE]: *stream,* flows 8 miles to join Summit Creek and form Middle Fork Stanislaus River 5.5 miles west-southwest of Sonora Pass (lat. 38°17'40" N, long. 119°43'45" W; sec. 12, T 5 N, R 20 E). Named on Sonora Pass (1956) and Tower Peak (1956) 15' quadrangles. Called East Fork [Relief Creek] on Dardanelles (1898) 30' quadrangle, where present Summit Creek is called Relief Creek. United States Board on Geographic Names (1980a, p. 3) rejected the names "East Fork Summit Creek" and "Middle Fork Stanislaus River" for Kennedy Creek.

Kennedy Lake [TUOLUMNE]: *lake,* 0.5 mile long, 4.5 miles south-southwest of Sonora Pass along Kennedy Creek (lat. 38°15'35" N, long. 119°39'05" W; on S line sec. 22, T 5 N, R 21 E). Named on Sonora Pass (1979) 7.5' quadrangle. The name is for Andrew L. Kennedy, who patented land at the lake in 1886 (Gudde, 1949, p. 172).

Kennedy Meadow [TUOLUMNE]:

(1) *area,* 6 miles west-southwest of Sonora Pass along Middle Fork Stanislaus River (lat. 38°18'05" N, long. 119°44'20" W; near N line sec. 11, T 5 N, R 20 E). Named on Sonora Pass (1979) 7.5' quadrangle.

(2) *locality,* 6 miles west of Sonora Pass along Middle Fork Stanislaus River (lat. 38°18'40" N, long. 119°44'40" W; sec. 2, T 5 N, R 20 E). Named on Sonora Pass (1979) 7.5' quadrangle.

Kennedy Peak [TUOLUMNE]: *peak,* 9 miles northwest of Tower Peak (lat. 38°14'45" N, long. 119°39'15" W; near S line sec. 27, T 5 N, R 21 E); the peak is 1 mile south of Kennedy Lake. Altitude 10,718 feet. Named on Tower Peak (1956) 15' quadrangle. United States Board on Geographic Names (1976a, p. 5) approved the name "Molo Mountain" for a peak, altitude 10,885 feet, located less than 1 mile south of Kennedy Peak (lat. 38°14'04" N, long. 119°39'20" W; sec. 34, T 5 N, R 21 E).

Kennedy Table [MADERA]: *ridge,* south southeast-trending, 4.5 miles long, 6 miles east-southeast of O'Neals (lat. 37°06'30" N, long. 119°35'45" W). Named on Millerton Lake East (1965) and North Fork (1965) 7.5' quadrangles.

Kentucky House [CALAVERAS]: *locality,* 2.25 miles south of San Andreas near the confluence of Calaveritas Creek and South Fork Calaveras River (lat. 38°09'45" N, long. 120°40'20" W; near N line sec. 32, T 4 N, R 12 E). Named on San Andreas (1962) 7.5' quadrangle. Camp's (1962) map gives the name "Third Crossing" as an alternate, and shows a place called Alabama House situated 1 mile north-northwest of Kentucky House along South Fork Calaveras River. Postal authorities established Third Crossing post office in 1852 and discontinued it in 1854 (Salley, p. 221).

Kentucky Well [MADERA]: *well,* 15 miles west of Madera (lat. 36°59'50" N, long. 120°20'20" W; near S line sec. 4, T 11 S, R 15 E). Named on

Kentucky Well (1922) 7.5' quadrangle.

Kerckhoff Lake [MADERA]: *lake,* 2.25 miles long, behind a dam on San Joaquin River 7 miles south of the town of North Fork on Madera-Fresno County line (lat. 37°07'40" N, long. 119°31'30" W; near S line sec. 24, T 9 S, R 22 E). Named on North Fork (1965) 7.5' quadrangle. The name is from Kerckhoff power plant, which San Joaquin Power Company put into operation in 1920; the name of the plant commemorates William G. Kerckhoff, one of the organizers of the power company (Gudde, 1949, p. 173).

Kerlinger: see **Carbona** [SAN JOAQUIN].

Kern Canyon [STANISLAUS]: *canyon,* 3.5 miles long, opens into lowlands 3.25 miles southwest of Westley (lat. 37°30'55" N, long. 121°14'25" W; sec. 7, T 5 S, R 7 E). Named on Copper Mountain (1956), Solyo (1953), and Westley (1969) 7.5' quadrangles.

Kern Creek [STANISLAUS]: *stream,* flows 3.5 miles to lowlands 3.25 miles southwest of Westley (lat. 37°30'55" N, long. 121°14'25" W; sec. 7, T 5 S, R 7 E); the stream drains Kern Canyon. Named on Westley (1952) 7.5' quadrangle. Called Curran Cr. on Mendenhall's (1908) map.

Kerrick Canon [TUOLUMNE]: *canyon,* 7 miles long, along Rancheria Creek above a point 8.5 miles south-southwest of Tower Peak (lat. 38°02' N, long. 119°36'45" W). Named on Tower Peak (1956) 15' quadrangle. Members of the Wheeler survey named the canyon for James D. Kerrick, who took sheep into the region about 1880 (Browning, 1986, p. 118).

Kerrick Meadow [TUOLUMNE]: *valley,* 5.5 miles west-northwest of Matterhorn Peak at the head of Rancheria Creek (lat. 38°06'30" N, long. 119°28'45" W). Named on Matterhorn Peak (1956) 15' quadrangle.

Kerrick's Ranch: see **Stockton** [SAN JOAQUIN].

Ketcham Slough [STANISLAUS]: *stream,* flows nearly 1 mile to Tuolumne River 6.5 miles east of Waterford (lat. 37°38'25" N, long. 120°38'35" W; near SW cor. sec. 27, T 3 S, R 12 E). Named on Paulsell (1968) 7.5' quadrangle.

Kettleman [SAN JOAQUIN]: *locality,* 6.5 miles north-northwest of Waterloo along Central California Traction Railroad (lat. 38°07' N, long. 121°14'30" W; at SW cor. sec. 8, T 3 N, R 7 E). Named on Waterloo (1968) 7.5' quadrangle.

Keyes [STANISLAUS]: *town,* 8 miles southeast of Modesto (lat. 37° 33'30" N, long. 120°54'45" W; sec. 30, T 4 S, R 10 E). Named on Ceres (1969) 7.5' quadrangle. Postal authorities established Keyes post office in 1868, discontinued it in 1888, and reestablished it in 1913; the name commemorates Thomas J. Keyes, a state senator from 1871 until 1874 (Salley, p. 111).

Keyes: see **Hughes and Keyes Ferry**, under **Oakdale** [STANISLAUS].

Keyes Peak [TUOLUMNE]: *peak,* 2.25 miles west of Tower Peak (lat. 38°08'25" N, long. 119°35'20" W). Altitude 10,670 feet. Named on Tower Peak (1956) 15' quadrangle. Colonel W.W. Forsyth named the peak in 1912 for his son-in-law, Edward Appleton Keyes (United States Board on Geographic Names, 1934, p. 13).

Keystone [TUOLUMNE]: *locality,* 12.5 miles south-southwest of Sonora along Sierra Railway (lat. 37°50'05" N, long. 120°30'25" W; sec. 23, T 1 S, R 13 E). Named on Keystone (1962) 7.5' quadrangle. Postal authorities established Cloudman post office in 1882, changed the name to Keystone in 1905, and discontinued it in 1913; the name "Cloudman" was for Daniel C. Cloudman, first postmaster (Salley, p. 46, 111). Paden and Schlichtmann (p. 60) noted both a place called Dunow's Camp, which was located less than 0.5 mile beyond Keystone at the site of Green Springs school, and (p. 55) "the forgotten community of Green Springs," a stopping place of the early 1850's situated 0.6 mile along the road to Sonora beyond the turnoff into present Keystone. Postal authorities established Green Springs post office in 1852 and discontinued it in 1869 (Frickstad, p. 215)—the name was from a double spring (Morgan *in* Gardiner, p. 315).

Kibbie Creek [TUOLUMNE]: *stream,* flows 8.5 miles to Lake Eleanor Reservoir 7.5 miles north of Mather (lat. 37°59'25" N, long. 119°51'55" W; near W line sec. 35, T 2 N, R 19 E). Named on Lake Eleanor (1956) and Pinecrest (1956) 15' quadrangles. Browning (1986, p. 119) associated the misspelled name with Horace G. Kibbe, who planted trout in Lake Eleanor and Lake Vernon in 1877.

Kibbie Lake [TUOLUMNE]: *lake,* 1 mile long, 12.5 miles southeast of Pinecrest (lat. 38°03'15" N, long. 119°50'45" W; sec. 1, 12, T 2 N, R 19 E); the lake is along Kibbie Creek. Named on Pinecrest (1956) 15' quadrangle.

Kibbie Ridge [TUOLUMNE]: *ridge,* generally south-southwest-trending, 12 miles long, 12 miles south-southeast of Pinecrest between Kibbie Creek and Cherry Creek. Named on Lake Eleanor (1956) and Pinecrest (1956) 15' quadrangles.

Kiefer Reservoir [CALAVERAS]: *lake,* 950 feet long, 2.5 miles north-northeast of Angels Camp in French Gulch (1) (lat. 38°06'35" N, long. 120°32'10" W; sec. 15, T 3 N, R 13 E). Named on Angels Camp (1962) 7.5' quadrangle.

Kincades Flat: see **Jamestown** [TUOLUMNE].

King: see **Mount Starr King** [MARIPOSA]; **Starr King Lake** [MARIPOSA]; **Starr King Meadow** [MARIPOSA].

King Creek [MADERA]: *stream,* flows 6 miles to Middle Fork San Joaquin River 2 miles south-southwest of Devils Postpile (lat. 37° 35'50" N, long. 119°05'30" W). Named on Devils Postpile (1953) 15' quadrangle.

Kingdon [SAN JOAQUIN]: *locality,* 4.25 miles west-southwest of Lodi along Western Pacific Railroad (lat. 38°06'15" N, long. 121° 21' W; near W line sec. 17, T 3 N, R 6 E). Named on Lodi South (1968) 7.5' quadrangle. The place was called West Lodi when the railroad first reached it in 1909, but in 1915 railroad officials named their station for Kingdon Gould, a grandson of Jay Gould (Gudde, 1949, p. 174). California Mining Bureau's (1917a) map shows a place called Hart located 5 miles south-southeast of Kingdon along the railroad.

King Island [SAN JOAQUIN]: *island,* 3 miles long, 4.5 miles southeast of Terminous between White Slough, Bishop Cut, Disappointment Slough, and Honker Cut (lat. 38°03'45" N, long. 121°26'15" W). Named on Terminous (1978) 7.5' quadrangle.

Kings Island [SAN JOAQUIN]: *island,* 1000 feet long, 16 miles west-southwest of downtown Stockton along Old River (lat. 37°51'30" N, long. 121°34'05" W). Named on Clifton Court Forebay (1978) 7.5' quadrangle.

Kinsley [MARIPOSA]: *locality,* 11.5 miles west of El Portal (lat. 37° 42'05" N, long. 119°59' W; near W line sec. 3, T 3 S, R 18 E). Named on Yosemite (1909) 30' quadrangle. Postal authorities established Kinsley post office in 1896, moved it 2 miles northwest in 1910, and discontinued it in 1928; the name was for James B. Kinsley, first postmaster (Salley, p. 112).

Kinsman Flat [MADERA]: *area,* 11 miles south-southeast of Shuteye Peak (lat. 37°12'15" N, long. 119°21'15" W; sec. 28, T 8 S, R 24 E). Named on Shaver Lake (1953) 15' quadrangle.

Kirby Peak [MARIPOSA]: *peak,* 10.5 miles south of El Portal (lat. 37°31'20" N, long. 119°47'45" W; near NW cor. sec. 9, T 5 S, R 20 E). Altitude 5448 feet. Named on Buckingham Mountain (1947) 7.5' quadrangle.

Kismet [MADERA]: *locality,* 6 miles east-southeast of Fairmead along Atchison, Topeka and Santa Fe Railroad (lat. 37°02'50" N, long. 120°05'35" W; near E line sec. 22, T 10 S, R 17 E). Named on Kismet (1961) 7.5' quadrangle. Called Miller on California Mining Bureau's (1917b) map.

Kittridge [MARIPOSA]: *locality,* 5 miles south-southeast of Coulterville along Yosemite Valley Railroad (lat. 37°38'25" N, long. 120° 10'30" W). Named on Sonora (1897) 30' quadrangle.

Knickerbocker Flat: see **Yankee Hill** [TUOLUMNE] (2).

Knight: see **Mount Knight** [TUOLUMNE].

Knight Creek [TUOLUMNE]: *stream,* flows 11 miles to Rose Creek nearly 5 miles north of Columbia (lat. 38°06'20" N, long. 120°23'40" W; near W line sec. 24, T 3 N, R 14 E). Named on Columbia (1948), Columbia SE (1948), Crandall Peak (1979), and Stanislaus (1948) 7.5' quadrangles.

Knight's Crossing: see **Knights Ferry** [STANISLAUS].

Knights Ferry [STANISLAUS]: *town,* 9 miles east-northeast of Oakdale on the north side of Stanislaus River (lat. 37°49'10" N, long. 120°40'15" W). Named on Knights Ferry (1962) 7.5' quadrangle. The name "Knight's Ferry" or "Knight's Crossing" commemorates William Knight, who came to Stanislaus River in 1849 with his partner, Captain Vantine; the two men operated a crude hotel, trading post, and row-boat ferry until Knight was killed in a gun battle in the autumn of 1849 (Criswell, p. 10-11). The place also was called Vantine's Crossing (Salley, p. 113). After Knight's death, John Dent and Lewis Dent took over the ferry, and in 1856 a town was laid out that some people called Dentville, but that officially was named Knight's Ferry (Hoover, Rensch, and Rensch, p. 540). Postal authorities established Knights Ferry post office in 1851 (Frickstad, p. 200). A settlement called Buena Vista sprang up on the south side of Stanislaus River opposite Knight's Ferry (Criswell, p. 24), and a stopping place, first called Mountain Inn and later called Darby House, was started in 1850 at a fork in the road about 3.5 miles northwest of Knights Ferry (Brotherton, p. 87).

Knob Hill [MARIPOSA]: *peak,* 9 miles south of Mariposa (lat. 37°21'15" N, long. 119°58'10" W; sec. 2, T 7 S, R 18 E). Altitude 2159 feet. Named on Ben Hur (1947) 7.5' quadrangle.

Knowles [MADERA]: *settlement,* less than 2 miles east of Raymond (lat. 37°13'10" N, long. 119°52'20" W; sec. 22, T 8 S, R 19 E). Named on Knowles (1962) and Raymond (1962) 7.5' quadrangles. Postal authorities established Knowles post office in 1902 and discontinued it in 1955; the name is for F.E. Knowles, who operated a granite quarry at the place (Salley, p. 113). California Division of Highways' (1934) map shows a place called Hillside located just southwest of Knowles along Southern Pacific Railroad (near N line sec. 27, T 8 S, R 19 E).

Knowles Junction [MADERA]: *locality,* 1 mile south of Raymond (lat. 37°12'10" N, long. 119°54'30" W; sec. 29, T 8 S, R 19 E); the place is 2.25 miles west-southwest of Knowles. Named on Raymond (1962) 7.5' quadrangle.

Kocher: see **Bagby** [MARIPOSA].

Kohlberg's Humbug: see **Humbug Gulch** [CALAVERAS].

Koip Crest [TUOLUMNE]: *ridge,* trends south along Tuolumne-Mono County line, then southeast into Mono County, 3.5 miles long, 9 miles south-southeast of Tioga Pass (lat. 37°47'30" N, long. 119°12'15" W). Named on Mono Craters (1953) 15' quadrangle. Kroeber (p. 45) considered the word "Koip" of Indian origin. United States Board on Geographic Names (1988, p. 4) rejected the names "Ko-it Ridge" and "Koip Ridge" for the feature

Koip Ridge: see **Koip Crest** [TUOLUMNE].

Ko-it Ridge: see **Koip Crest** [TUOLUMNE].

Kolana Rock [TUOLUMNE]: *peak,* 7 miles northeast of Mather (lat. 37°57'10" N, long. 119°45'30" W; near S line sec. 10, T 1 N, R 20 E). Named on Lake Eleanor (1956) 15' quadrangle. The feature had the early name "Sugar Loaf" (Browning, 1988, p. 71).

Kramer Meadow [MADERA]: *area,* 7 miles north-northeast of Yosemite Forks (lat. 37°27'10" N, long. 119°33'35" W; at E line sec. 33, T 5 S, R 22 E). Named on Bass Lake (1953) 15' quadrangle.

Krappeau Gulch [CALAVERAS]: *canyon,* drained by a stream that flows 1.5 miles to Coyote Creek nearly 3 miles south-southwest of Vallecito (lat. 38°02'45" N, long. 120°29'05" W; sec. 7, T 2 N, R 14 E). Named on Columbia (1948) 7.5' quadrangle.

Kuna Creek [TUOLUMNE]: *stream,* flows 3 miles to Lyell Fork 8 miles south of Tioga Pass (lat. 37°47'30" N, long. 119°15'35" W); the stream heads near Kuna Peak. Named on Mono Craters (1953) and Tuolumne Meadows (1956) 15' quadrangles.

Kuna Crest [TUOLUMNE]: *ridge,* generally northwest-trending, 4.5 miles long, 6 miles south of Tioga Pass (lat. 37°49'45" N, long. 119°14'45" W); Kuna Peak is at the southeast end of the ridge. Named on Mono Craters (1953) and Tuolumne Meadows (1956) 15' quadrangles. W.D. Johnson of United States Geological Survey named the feature about 1883—the word "kuna" is of Indian origin (United States Board on Geographic Names, 1934, p. 13).

Kuna Lake [TUOLUMNE]: *lake,* 1800 feet long, 4 miles south of Tioga Pass (lat. 37°51'05" N, long. 119°15'05" W); the lake is northeast of Kuna Crest. Named on Mono Craters (1953) and Tuolumne Meadows (1956) 15' quadrangles.

Kuna Peak [TUOLUMNE]: *peak,* 7 miles south-southeast of Tioga Pass on Tuolumne-Mono County line (lat. 37°48'55" N, long. 119° 12'40" W); the peak is at the southeast end of Kuna Crest. Named on Mono Craters (1953) 15' quadrangle. W.D. Johnson of United States Geological Survey named the peak about 1883 (United States Board on Geographic Names, 1934, p. 13).

— L —

La Baig Spring [MERCED]: *spring,* 5 miles southeast of Pacheco Pass (lat. 37°01'20" N, long. 121°08'05" W; sec. 31, T 10 S, R 8 E). Named on Pacheco Pass (1955) 7.5' quadrangle.

La Branza [MERCED]: *locality,* 5.5 miles southwest of Le Grand along Southern Pacific Railroad (lat. 37°10'30" N, long. 120° 19' W; sec. 3, T 9 S, R 15 E). Named on Plainsberg (1919) 7.5' quadrangle.

La Commodedad: see **Pine Log** [TUOLUMNE].

Lacto [SAN JOAQUIN]: *locality,* 10 miles west of downtown Stockton along Atchison, Topeka and Santa Fe Railroad (lat. 37°56'15" N, long. 121°28'45" W). Named on Holt (1952) 7.5' quadrangle. Called Quito on Holt (1913) 7.5' quadrangle.

Lacy Hill [MARIPOSA]: *peak,* 9.5 miles south of Mariposa (lat. 37° 20'50" N, long. 119°56'45" W; sec. 1, T 7 S, R 18 E). Altitude 2203 feet. Named on Ben Hur (1947) 7.5' quadrangle.

Ladd Creek [MADERA]: *stream,* flows 4.25 miles to Fine Gold Creek 4 miles northeast of O'Neals (lat. 37°09'50" N, long. 119°38'20" W; sec. 12, T 9 S, R 21 E). Named on O'Neals (1965) 7.5' quadrangle. Millerton Lake (1945) 15' quadrangle shows Ladd ranch near the mouth of the stream.

Lady Lake [MADERA]: *lake,* 1100 feet long, 6.5 miles south-southeast of Merced Peak (lat. 37°32'35" N, long. 119°21'40" W); the lake is one of the group called Madera Lakes. Named on Merced Peak (1953) 15' quadrangle.

Lafayette: see **Lodi** [SAN JOAQUIN].

La Garzas Creek: see **Los Banos Creek** [MERCED].

La Grange [STANISLAUS]: *village,* 16 miles east of Waterford on the south side of Tuolumne River (lat. 37°39'50" N, long. 120°27'40" W; on W line sec. 20, T 3 S, R 14 E). Named on La Grange (1962) 7.5' quadrangle. A group of French miners settled on the south side of Tuolumne River in 1850 at what was called French Bar, located between 0.5 mile and 1.25 miles west of present La Grange; after floods in the winter of 1851 and 1852, the community moved to higher ground at the site of present La Grange, and eventually the name "French Bar" was changed to La Grange (Brotherton, p. 161, 162). Gudde (1949, p. 179) noted that Owen's Ferry was at French Bar. Postal authorities established La Grange post office in 1854 (Frickstad, p. 200). The name "La Grange" reportedly is from the first location of the post office in a barn—*la grange* means "the barn" in French (Gray, p. 5). A mining place called Spanish Bar was situated just upstream from the upper end of French Bar, and Spark's Ferry was on the river at Spanish Bar (Brotherton, p. 162-163). George C. Branch started Branch's Ferry in 1851 on Tuolumne River 2 miles below present La Grange, and Calvin Salter and I.D. Morley started Salter and Morley's Ferry 4 miles below Branch's Ferry (Hoover, Rensch, and Rensch, p. 541, 542). A mining settlement of the late 1850's or early 1860's called Patricksville was located about 1.5 miles south of La Grange (Brotherton, p. 167).

La Grange Reservoir [STANISLAUS-TUOLUMNE]: *lake,* on Stanislaus-Tuolumne County line behind a dam on Tuolumne River 3.5 miles south-west of Don Pedro Camp in Stanislaus County (lat. 37° 40'20" N, long. 120°26'35" W; on W line sec. 16, T 3 S, R 14 E). Named on La Grange (1962) 7.5' quadrangle. The dam that forms the lake was built at a place called Big Falls (Gray, p. 1).

Lagunas de Guadalupe: see **Finnegan Cutoff** [STANISLAUS].

Laguna Seca Creek [MERCED]: *stream,* flows 6 miles to lowlands 9.5 miles northeast of Ortigalita Peak (lat. 36°53'30" N, long. 120° 48'05" W; sec. 18, T 12 S, R 11 E). Named on Charleston School (1956) 7.5' quadrangle. United States Board on Geographic Names (1933a, p. 444) rejected the names "Salt Creek" and "Wildcat Creek" for the stream.

La Honda Park [CALAVERAS]: *settlement,* 2.5 miles north-northwest of Vallecito (lat. 38°07'15" N, long. 120°29'40" W; near S line sec. 12, T 3 N, R 13 E). Named on Columbia (1948) 7.5' quadrangle.

Laird's Ferry: see **Lockeford** [SAN JOAQUIN].

Laird Slough [STANISLAUS]: *water feature,* 2 miles long, diverges from San Joaquin River and carries water past a series of meanders in the river before rejoining the main stream 3.25 miles northeast of Westley (lat. 37°34'50" N, long. 121°09'50" W). Named on Westley (1969) 7.5' quadrangle. John Willison Laird settled on the bank of the slough about 1852 or 1853 (Brotherton, p. 24).

Lake Catherine [MADERA]: *lake,* 1800 feet long, 8 miles northwest of Devils Postpile (lat. 37°41'55" N, long. 119°11'25" W). Named on Devils Postpile (1953) 15' quadrangle.

Lake Don Pedro: see **Don Pedro Reservoir** [TUOLUMNE].

Lake Eleanor: see **Lake Eleanor Reservoir** [TUOLUMNE].

Lake Eleanor Reservoir [TUOLUMNE]: *lake,* behind a dam on Eleanor Creek 6.5 miles north of Mather (lat. 37°58'30" N, long. 119°52'45" W; sec. 3, T 1 N, R 19 E). Named on Lake Eleanor (1956) 15' quadrangle. The dam, constructed in 1917 and 1918, enlarged a natural lake (Hanna, p. 96) that is called Lake Eleanor on Yosemite (1909) 30' quadrangle. United States Board on Geographic Names (1965b, p. 11) approved the name "Lake Eleanor" for the present reservoir, and rejected the names "Lake Eleanor Reservoir" and "Eleanor Lake Reservoir." Members of the Whitney survey named the natural lake in the 1860's for Eleanor Goddard Whitney, daughter of Josiah Dwight Whitney (United States Board on Geographic Names, 1934, p. 8).

Lake Helen: see **Maxwell Lake** [TUOLUMNE].

Lake Honda [MERCED]: *intermittent lake,* 800 feet long, 2 miles east-southeast of Stevinson (lat. 37°19'10" N, long. 120°49' W; sec. 13, T 7 S, R 10 E). Named on Stevinson (1961) 7.5' quadrangle.

Lake McClure [MARIPOSA]: *lake,* behind a dam 6 miles north-northwest of Hornitos on Merced River (lat. 37°35'05" N, long. 120°16'10" W; sec. 13, T 4 S, R 15 E). Named on Bear Valley (1947, photorevised 1973), Coulterville (1947, photorevised 1973), Hornitos (1947, photorevised 1973), and Penon Blanco Peak (1962, photorevised 1973) 7.5' quadrangles. Called Lake McClure Reservoir on Sonora (1897) 30' quadrangle. Merced Falls (1962) 7.5' quadrangle has the designation "Lake McClure (Exchequer Reservoir)" for the lake, but United States Board on Geographic Names (1964c, p. 15) rejected the name "Exchequer Reservoir" for the feature. Exchequer dam formed the lake in 1926, and the lake was enlarged when the dam was raised; the name "Exchequer" is from the first bank in Mariposa County—water of the lake now covers the site of the bank (Sargent, Shirley, 1976, p. 26-27). The name "McClure" commemorates Wilbur Fiske McClure, who was state engineer of California from 1912 until 1926 (Hanna, p. 181). Cotton Arm of the lake occupies the lower part of the canyon of Cotton Creek, and Temperance Arm occupies the lower part of the canyon of Temperance Creek; both arms are named on Merced Falls (1962) 7.5' quadrangle.

Lake McClure Reservoir: see **Lake McClure** [MARIPOSA].

Lake Moic [MADERA]: *lake,* 600 feet long, 7.5 miles south-southeast of Yosemite Forks along Little Fine Gold Creek (lat. 37°16' N, long. 119°34'20" W; sec. 4, T 8 S, R 22 E). Named on Bass Lake (1953) 15' quadrangle.

Lake Moran [TUOLUMNE]: *lake,* 1400 feet long, nearly 2 miles northwest of Liberty Hill (lat. 38°23' N, long. 120°07'45" W). Named on Calaveras Dome (1979) 7.5' quadrangle.

Lake Nina: see **Tilden Lake** [TUOLUMNE].

Lake Ramona [STANISLAUS]: *lake,* 3.25 miles east of Patterson near San Joaquin River (lat. 37°28'50" N, long. 121°04'10" W). Named on Crows Landing (1952) 7.5' quadrangle.

Lake River: see **Eleanor Creek** [TUOLUMNE].

Lakeside Campground [MADERA]: *locality,* nearly 6 miles southeast of Yosemite Forks on the southwest side of Bass Lake (1) (lat. 37°18'35" N, long. 119°32'45" W; near E line sec. 22, T 7 S, R 22 E). Named on Bass

Lake (1953) 15' quadrangle.

Lake Tent House: see **Turlock Lake** [STANISLAUS].

Lake Valley [TUOLUMNE]: *valley,* 8 miles east of Pinecrest (lat. 38° 12' N, long. 119°50'40" W; in and near sec. 13, T 4 N, R 19 E). Named on Pinecrest (1956) 15' quadrangle.

Lake Vernon [TUOLUMNE]: *lake,* 0.5 mile long, 13 miles southwest of Tower Peak along Falls Creek (lat. 38°00'50" N, long. 119°43'25" W; sec. 24, T 2 N, R 20 E). Named on Tower Peak (1956) 15' quadrangle. Called Vernon Lake on Dardanelles (1898) 30' quadrangle.

Lake Yosemite: see **Yosemite Lake** [MERCED].

Lambert: see **San Luis Gonzaga** [MERCED].

Lambert Dome: see **Lembert Dome** [TUOLUMNE].

Lambert Soda Springs: see **Soda Springs** [TUOLUMNE].

La Mineta: see **Mount Bullion** [MARIPOSA].

La Mineta Gulch [MARIPOSA]: *canyon,* drained by a stream that flows 2.5 miles to Agua Fria Creek 4.5 miles east-northeast of the settlement of Catheys Valley (lat. 37°28'05" N, long. 120°01'20" W). Named on Catheys Valley (1962) 7.5' quadrangle. Called Cavallada Gulch on Indian Gulch (1920) 15' quadrangle, but United States Board on Geographic Names (1964a, p. 11) rejected the names "Cavallada Gulch" and "Minita Gulch" for the feature.

La Minita Creek: see **Guadalupe Creek** [MARIPOSA].

Lane [SAN JOAQUIN]: *locality,* about 4 miles west-southwest of Waterloo along Central California Traction Railroad (lat. 38°00'10" N, long. 121°14'55" W). Named on Waterloo (1968) 7.5' quadrangle.

Langston Spring [MERCED]: *spring,* 2.5 miles south-southeast of Pacheco Pass (lat. 37°01'45" N, long. 121°11'30" W). Named on Pacheco Pass (1955) 7.5' quadrangle.

Langworth: see **Oakdale** [STANISLAUS].

Lankershim: see **Trigo** [MADERA].

Larson [SAN JOAQUIN]: *locality,* 5 miles east-southeast of downtown Stockton along Atchison, Topeka and Santa Fe Railroad (lat. 37°55'45" N, long. 121°12'35" W). Named on Burnham (1914) 7.5' quadrangle.

Las Mariposas [MARIPOSA]: *land grant,* around Bear Valley (1). Named on Bear Valley (1947), Catheys Valley (1962), Feliciana Mountain (1947), Hornitos (1947), Indian Gulch (1962), and Mariposa (1947) 7.5' quadrangles. Called Mariposa Estate on Hoffmann and Gardner's (1863-1867) map. Juan Bautista Alvarado received 10 leagues in 1844; John C. Fremont purchased the grant in 1847 and claimed 44,387 acres patented in 1856 (Cowan, p. 46-47).

Last Chance Meadow [MADERA]: *area,* 6.5 miles south-southwest of Buena Vista Peak (lat. 37°30'10" N, long. 119°33' W; near N line sec. 15, T 5 S, R 22 E). Named on Yosemite (1956) 15' quadrangle.

Las Vinas [SAN JOAQUIN]: *locality,* 5 miles south-southeast of Thornton along Western Pacific Railroad (lat. 38°09'45" N, long. 121°23' W; sec. 25, T 4 N, R 5 E). Named on New Hope (1952) 7.5' quadrangle.

Latham Slough [SAN JOAQUIN]: *water feature,* joins Empire Cut 12 miles west of downtown Stockton (lat. 37°58'20" N, long. 121° 30'30" W). Named on Woodward Island (1978) 7.5' quadrangle. Woodward Island (1913) 7.5' quadrangle shows East Fork joining Latham Slough from the southeast near the north end of the slough.

Lathrop [SAN JOAQUIN]: *town,* 9 miles south of downtown Stockton (lat. 37°49'20" N, long. 121°16'35" W; sec. 26, T 1 S, R 6 E). Named on Lathrop (1952) 7.5' quadrangle. The name commemorates Charles Lathrop, Leland Stanford's brother-in-law (Hillman and Covello, p. 139). Postal authorities established Lathrop post office in 1871, discontinued it in 1875, and reestablished it the same year (Frickstad, p. 161). The place first was known as Wilson's Station, for Thomas A. Wilson, a principal landowner there (Hillman and Covello, p. 139). Postal authorities established Morano post office 8 miles southeast of Lathrop in 1872 and discontinued in 1875; they established Morrissey post office 7 miles west of Lathrop in 1881 and discontinued it the same year; they established Undine post office 7 miles west of Lathrop on Union Island in 1881 and it discontinued in 1906—the name was from Undine ranch (Salley, p. 146, 227). California Mining Bureau's (1917a) map shows a place called Garrison located about 2 miles southeast of Lathrop along the railroad. Thompson and West's (1879) map shows Johnson's Ferry on San Joaquin River about 2.5 miles southwest of Lathrop.

Latimer Gulch [CALAVERAS]: *canyon,* drained by a stream that flows 1.5 miles to New Hogan Reservoir 2 miles west of San Andreas (lat. 38°12'05" N, long. 120°43'20" W; near W line sec. 13, T 4 N, R 11 E). Named on San Andreas (1962) 7.5' quadrangle. David Latimer had a store in the canyon at the community of North Branch, where he was postmaster (Camp *in* Doble, p. 296-297).

Laughlin Ridge [TUOLUMNE]: *ridge,* west-northwest-trending, 0.5 mile long, 1.5 miles southeast of Don Pedro Camp (lat. 37°42'15" N, long. 120°23'05" W; sec. 1, T 3 S, R 14 E). Named on La Grange (1962) 7.5' quadrangle.

Laura Lake [MADERA]: *lake,* 700 feet long, 6.25 miles north-northwest of Devils Postpile (lat. 37°42'20" N, long. 119°08'15" W). Named on Devils Postpile (1953) 15' quadrangle.

Laurel Creek [MARIPOSA]: *stream,* flows 3 miles to Big Creek 1.5 miles south-southwest of Wawona (lat. 37°30'55" N, long. 119°39'55" W; sec. 10, T 5 S, R 21 E). Named on Bass Lake (1953) and Yosemite (1956) 15' quadrangles.

Laurel Lake [TUOLUMNE]: *lake,* 2600 feet long, 8.5 miles north-northeast of Mather (lat. 37°59'55" N, long. 119°47'40" W; on E line sec. 29, T 2 N, R 20 E). Named on Lake Eleanor (1956) and Pinecrest (1956) 15' quadrangles.

Laurel Spring [STANISLAUS]: *spring,* 1.25 miles south-southwest of Crevison Peak (lat. 37°10'20" N, long. 121°11'45" W; near NW cor. sec. 10, T 9 S, R 7 E). Named on Crevison Peak (1955) 7.5' quadrangle.

Laveaga Peak [MERCED]: *peak,* 5 miles south-southeast of Mariposa Peak on Merced-San Benito County line (lat. 36°53'25" N, long. 121°10'35" W; sec. 14, T 12 S, R 7 E). Altitude 3801 feet. Named on Mariposa Peak (1969) 7.5' quadrangle.

La Vina [MADERA]: *village,* 6.5 miles south-southwest of Madera (lat. 36°52'50" N long. 120°06'45" W; on S line sec. 16, T 12 S, R 17 E). Named on Madera (1963) 7.5' quadrangle. Postal authorities established La Vina post office in 1891 and discontinued it in 1895 (Frickstad, p. 86). The place began as part of an unsuccessful land-development scheme (Clough, p. 86).

Lawnsdale Gulch: see **Columbia** [TUOLUMNE].

Leaning Tower [MARIPOSA]: *relief feature,* 4 miles southwest of Yosemite Village on the south side of Yosemite Valley (lat. 37°42'45" N, long. 119°38'50" W). Named on Yosemite (1956) 15' quadrangle.

Leavitt Peak [TUOLUMNE]: *peak,* 3 miles south-southeast of Sonora Pass on Tuolumne-Mono County line (lat. 38°17'10" N, long. 119° 39' W). Altitude 11,569 feet. Named on Sonora Pass (1979) 7.5' quadrangle. Called Leavitts Pk. on Wheeler's (1876-1877) map. The name recalls Hiram L. Leavitt, who lived in Sonora about 1865 and later had a stage station in Mono County on the road that extended from Sonora into Mono County (Wedertz, p. 89).

LeConte Cascade: see **LeConte Falls** [TUOLUMNE].

LeConte Falls [TUOLUMNE]: *waterfall,* 10.5 miles west of Tioga Pass along Tuolumne River (lat. 37°55'25" N, long. 119°27'05" W). Named on Tuolumne Meadows (1956) 15' quadrangle. R.M. Price gave the name "LeConte Cascade" to present Waterwheel Falls in 1894 to honor Professor Joseph N. LeConte of University of California, but the name "LeConte" somehow was transferred to present LeConte Falls, which had been known as California Falls (Browning, 1988, p. 72-73).

LeConte Point [TUOLUMNE]: *peak,* 6 miles north-northwest of White Wolf (lat. 37°56'45" N, long. 119°42'20" W). Named on Hetch Hetchy Reservoir (1956) 15' quadrangle. R.B. Marshall of United States Geological Survey named the peak for Professor Joseph N. LeConte of University of California (United States Board on Geographic Names, 1934, p. 14).

Ledger Island [MADERA]: *area,* 18 miles east of Madera on the west side of San Joaquin River (lat. 36°56'55" N, long. 119°44'20" W; sec. 25, T 11 S, R 20 E). Named on Friant (1964) 7.5' quadrangle.

Lee Price Camp [TUOLUMNE]: *locality,* 4 miles east-southeast of Long Barn in Hulls Meadows (lat. 38°03'50" N, long. 120°04'30" W; near N line sec. 2, T 2 N, R 17 E). Named on Hull Creek (1979) 7.5' quadrangle.

Le Grand [MERCED]: *town,* 14 miles east-southeast of Merced (lat. 37°13'45" N, long. 120°15' W; sec. 17, 20, T 8 S, R 16 E). Named on Chowchilla (1960) and Le Grand (1961) 15' quadrangles. Athlone (1942) 15' quadrangle has the form "Legrand" for the name. Postal authorities established Le Grand post office in 1896; the name commemorates William Le Grand Dickinson, who sold land at the place to the railroad (Salley, p. 120). They established Gwin post office 4 or 5 miles northeast of present Le Grand (sec. 2, T 8 S, R 16 E) in 1855 and discontinued it in 1864; the name was for Senator William M. Gwin of California (Salley, p. 91). They established Union post office 5 miles northeast of present Le Grand in 1864, discontinued it in 1876, reestablished it in 1878, and discontinued it in 1896; Fremont had given the name "Union" to his base camp in the neighborhood (Salley, p. 227). Smith and Weber (*in* Churchill, p. 104) noted that Gwin post office and Union post office were at the same place—both were in a building called McDermott's Tavern.

Lehamite Creek [MARIPOSA]: *stream,* flows 2.25 miles to Indian Canyon Creek 0.5 mile north-northwest of Yosemite Village (lat. 37°45'30" N, long. 119°34'50" W). Named on Hetch Hetchy Reservoir (1956) 15' quadrangle. The word "Lehamite" is of Indian origin (United States Board on Geographic Names, 1934, p. 14). Called Little Winkle Branch on a map of the Wheeler survey in 1883, and later called East Fork of Indian Creek (Browning, 1986, p. 125).

Leidig Meadow [MARIPOSA]: *area,* 1.25 miles southwest of Yosemite Village in Yosemite Valley (lat. 37°44'15" N, long. 119° 36'10" W). Named on Yosemite (1956) 15' quadrangle. The name commemorates Charlie Leidig, a ranger in Yosemite National Park (United States Board on Geographic Names, 1934, p. 14).

Leighton Lake [TUOLUMNE]: *lake,* 3300 feet long, 13 miles east-southeast of Pinegrove (lat. 38°08'30" N, long. 119°46'10" W). Named on Pinecrest (1956) 15' quadrangle. Browning (1986, p. 125) associated the name with Fred Leighton, a sportsman and conservationist.

Leitch's Ferry: see **Oakdale** [STANISLAUS].

Leland Creek [TUOLUMNE]: *stream,* flows 2.5 miles to Cow Creek (1) 3.25 miles north of Pinecrest (lat. 38°14'20" N, long. 119°59'55" W; sec. 33, T 5 N, R 18 E). Named on Pinecrest (1979) 7.5' quadrangle.

Leland Gulch [MADERA]: *canyon,* drained by a stream that flows 1.5 miles to Chowchilla River 8 miles northeast of Raymond (lat. 37°18'30" N, long. 119°49'05" W; sec. 19, T 7 S, R 20 E). Named on Horsecamp Mountain (1947) 7.5' quadrangle.

Leland Meadow: see **Leland Reservoir** [TUOLUMNE].

Leland Reservoir [TUOLUMNE]: *lake,* 1000 feet long, 3 miles north-northeast of Pinecrest (lat. 38°14' N, long. 119°58'45" W; sec. 3, T 4 N, R 18 E); the lake is at the head of Leland Creek. Named on Pinecrest (1979) 7.5' quadrangle. Pinecrest (1956) 15' quadrangle shows Leland Mdw. at the site. G.A. Leland patented land there in 1898 (Browning, 1986, p. 125).

Lembert Dome [TUOLUMNE]: *peak,* 5.25 miles west-southwest of Tioga Pass on the north side of Tuolumne Meadows (lat. 37°52'55" N, long. 119°20'45" W; near W line sec. 4, T 1 S, R 24 E). Altitude 9450 feet. Named on Tuolumne Meadows (1956) 15' quadrangle. The name commemorates John Baptist Lembert, who homesteaded in Tuolumne Meadows in 1885 (Hanna, p. 170). United States Board on Geographic Names (1933a, p. 454) rejected the form "Lambert Dome" for the name.

Leopold Lake [TUOLUMNE]: *lake,* 1350 feet long, 10.5 miles east of Pinecrest (lat. 38°10'40" N, long. 119°48'15" W). Named on Pinecrest (1956) 15' quadrangle.

Lertora Lake [TUOLUMNE]: *lake,* 2900 feet long, 9.5 miles west of Tower Peak (lat. 38°08'20" N, long. 119°43'10" W). Named on Tower Peak (1956) 15' quadrangle. United States Board on Geographic Names (1965c, p. 8) approved the name "Fisher Lakes" for a group of five small lakes situated just north of Lertora Lake (lat. 38°08'40" N, long. 119°43'10" W), and (p. 9) approved the name "Frog Lake" for a small lake located about 0.3 mile east-northeast of Lertora Lake (lat. 38°08'30" N, long. 119°42'40" W).

Lesnini Creek [STANISLAUS]: *stream,* flows 5.5 miles to Stanislaus River 3.25 miles east-northeast of Oakdale (lat. 37°47'20" N, long. 120°47'35" W). Named on Oakdale (1968) 7.5' quadrangle.

Lewis [MARIPOSA]: *locality,* 8.5 miles south of the present settlement of Catheys Valley along Ganns Creek (lat. 37°18'15" N, long. 120°06'35" W; sec. 21, T 7 S, R 17 E). Named on Indian Gulch (1920) 15' quadrangle. Postal authorities established Lewis post office in 1879 and discontinued it in 1927 (Frickstad, p. 91).

Lewis [TUOLUMNE]: *locality,* 5 miles south-southwest of Long Barn (lat. 38°01'15" N, long. 120°10'15" W); the place is 1 mile southwest of Mount Lewis. Named on Big Trees (1891) 30' quadrangle.

Lewis: see **Mount Lewis** [TUOLUMNE].

Lewis Creek [MADERA-MARIPOSA]: *stream,* heads just inside Madera County and flows 7.5 miles to Merced River 7.5 miles south of Cathedral Peak (lat. 37°44'15" N, long. 119°24' W). Named on Merced Peak (1953) and Tuolumne Meadows (1956) 15' quadrangles. United States Board on Geographic Names (1934, p. 14) rejected the name "Maclure Fork" for the stream, and pointed out that the name "Lewis" is for W.B. Lewis, a superintendent of Yosemite National Park.

Lewis Creek: see **Lewis Fork** [MADERA-MARIPOSA].

Lewis Fork [MADERA-MARIPOSA]: *stream,* heads just inside Mariposa County and flows 8.5 miles to join Nelder Creek and form Fresno River less than 0.5 mile south-southwest of Yosemite Forks in Madera County (lat. 37°21'40" N, long. 119°37'55" W; near SW cor. sec. 36, T 6 S, R 21 E). Named on Bass Lake (1953) 15' quadrangle. Browning (1986, p. 127) associated the name with Jonathan Lewis, who homesteaded in the neighborhood in 1886. United States Board on Geographic Names (1964c, p. 15) rejected the names "Lewis Creek" and "North Fork of Fresno River" for the stream.

Lewis Gulch [MARIPOSA]: *canyon,* drained by a stream that flows 3 miles to Bull Creek 7.25 miles east-northeast of Buckhorn Peak (lat. 37°42'45" N, long. 120°00'20" W; sec. 32, T 2 S, R 18 E). Named on Buckhorn Peak (1947) and Kinsley (1947) 7.5' quadrangles.

Lewis Lakes [TUOLUMNE]: *lakes,* three, largest 2200 feet long, 11 miles west-northwest of Tower Peak (lat. 38°13'15" N, long. 119° 43'40" W). Named on Tower Peak (1956) 15' quadrangle. The name honors Bert Lewis, a Forest Service employee who died in France during World War I (United States Board on Geographic Names, 1933a, p. 456).

Liberty: see **Lockeford** [SAN JOAQUIN]; **New Liberty**, under **Acampo** [SAN JOAQUIN].

Liberty Cap [MARIPOSA]: *peak,* 3 miles east-southeast of Yosemite Village (lat. 37°43'45" N, long. 119°31'55" W). Altitude 7076 feet. Named on Yosemite (1956) 15' quadrangle. King and Gardner's (1865) map has the designation "Cap of Liberty or Mt. Broderick" for the peak. The feature also was called Mount Frances, Gwin's Peak, and Bellows' Butte in the early days, but when Governor Leland Stanford viewed the peak he asked that a more appropriate name be found; he then approved the name "Liberty Cap" suggested by the resemblance of the feature to the Cap of Liberty depicted on the half-dollar coin of the time (Browning, 1986, p. 127).

Liberty Hill [TUOLUMNE]: *peak,* 28 miles northeast of Columbia (lat. 38°22'05" N, long. 120°06' W; near NE cor. sec. 21, T 6 N, R 17 E). Altitude 7537 feet. Named on Liberty Hill (1979) 7.5' quadrangle.

Licking Fork [CALAVERAS]: *stream,* flows 14 miles to South Fork Mokelumne River 1.5 miles north of Rail Road Flat (lat. 38°21'45" N, long. 120°30'25" W; sec. 23, T 6 N, R 13 E). Named on Dorrington (1979), Fort Mountain (1979), Garnet Hill (1979), and Railroad Flat (1948) 7.5' quadrangles.

Lightner Peak [CALAVERAS]: *peak,* nearly 4 miles southeast of Copperopolis (lat. 37°56'40" N, long. 120°35'15" W; near N line sec. 18, T 1 N, R 13 E). Altitude 1543 feet. Named on Melones Dam (1962) 7.5' quadrangle.

Lightning Creek [CALAVERAS]: *stream,* flows 2 miles to South Fork Mokelumne River 2.5 miles east of Blue Mountain (lat. 38° 20'20" N, long. 120°19'05" W; near SW cor. sec. 27, T 6 N, R 15 E). Named on Dorrington (1979) 7.5' quadrangle.

Lillian Lake [MADERA]: *lake,* 1550 feet long, 5.25 miles south-southeast of Merced Peak (lat. 37°33'45" N, long. 119°21'50" W). Named on Merced Peak (1953) 15' quadrangle.

Lilly Mountain [MADERA]: *peak,* 5 miles east-southeast of Knowles (lat. 37°10'55" N, long. 119°47'40" W; sec. 4, T 9 S, R 20 E). Named on Knowles (1962) 7.5' quadrangle.

Lily Creek [TUOLUMNE]:

(1) *stream,* flows 2.25 miles to Middle Fork Stanislaus River 8.5 miles south-southeast of Liberty Hill (lat. 38°15'45" N, long. 120° 00'55" W; sec. 29, T 5 N, R 18 E). Named on Donnell Lake (1979) and Liberty Hill (1979) 7.5' quadrangles.

(2) *stream,* flows 4 miles to Hull Creek 3.5 miles southeast of Long Barn (lat. 38°03'25" N, long. 120°05' W; sec. 2, T 2 N, R 17 E). Named on Hull Creek (1979) 7.5' quadrangle.

(3) *stream,* flows 10 miles to join Bell Creek and form Clavey River nearly 4 miles south-southeast of Pinecrest (lat. 38°08'30" N, long. 119°58' W; sec. 2, T 3 N, R 18 E). Named on Pinecrest (1956) 15' quadrangle.

Lily Gap [CALAVERAS]: *locality,* nearly 3 miles southwest of Devils Nose along Bear Creek (1) (lat. 38°25'45" N, long. 120° 27' W; sec. 29, T 7 N, R 14 E). Named on Devils Nose (1979) 7.5' quadrangle.

Lily Lake [MADERA]: *lake,* 500 feet long, 8.5 miles west of Devils Postpile (lat. 37°36'15" N, long. 119°13'50" W). Named on Devils Postpile (1953) 15' quadrangle.

Lily Lake [TUOLUMNE]: *intermittent lake,* 1000 feet long, 2.5 miles southeast of Pinecrest (lat. 38°09'35" N, long. 119°57'55" W; sec. 35, T 4 N, R 18 E). Named on Pinecrest (1979) 7.5' quadrangle.

Lily Lake: see **Irwin Bright Lake** [TUOLUMNE]; **Mud Lake** [TUOLUMNE].

Lily Valley [CALAVERAS]: *valley,* 1.5 miles south-southwest of Devils Nose (lat. 38°26'30" N, long. 120°25'45" W). Named on Devils Nose (1979) 7.5' quadrangle.

Limerick: see **Camanche** [CALAVERAS].

Lincoln [MADERA]: *locality,* 8 miles south-southwest of Chowchilla along Chowchilla Pacific Railroad (lat. 37°01'10" N, long. 120°20'40" W; near W line sec. 33, T 10 S, R 15 E). Named on Chowchilla (1918) 7.5' quadrangle.

Lincoln Village [SAN JOAQUIN]: *district,* in the north part of Stockton (lat. 38°00'15" N, long. 121°19'30" W). Named on Lodi South (1968) 7.5' quadrangle.

Lind: see **Jenny Lind** [CALAVERAS].

Linden [SAN JOAQUIN]: *town,* 13 miles southeast of Lodi (lat. 38° 01'20" N, long. 121°05'05" W; sec. 15, T 2 N, R 8 E). Named on Linden (1968) 7.5' quadrangle. Dr. W.D. Treblecock started a tavern called Fifteen Mile House at the site in 1849, and the town of Linden was laid out there in 1862; John Wasley named the place, presumably for his former home of Linden, Ohio (Hoover, Rensch, and Rensch, p. 376). Postal authorities established Foreman's Ranch post office in 1855 and discontinued it in 1863, when they moved it 2 miles southwest and changed the name to Linden; the name "Foreman" was for Samuel Foreman, pioneer rancher and first postmaster (Salley, p. 76-77).

Lindsay's Lake: see **Mormon Slough** [SAN JOAQUIN].

Lingard [MERCED]: *locality,* 8 miles west of Le Grand along Southern Pacific Railroad (lat. 37°14'25" N, long. 120°23'50" W; near E line sec. 14, T 8 S, R 14 E). Named on El Nido (1960) 7.5' quadrangle.

Linora [MERCED]: *locality,* 2.5 miles north-northwest of Los Banos along Southern Pacific Railroad (lat. 37°12'40" N, long. 120°58'45" W; sec. 28, T 8 S, R 9 E). Named on Ingomar (1919) 7.5' quadrangle.

Lion Canyon [STANISLAUS]: *canyon,* drained by a stream that flows 2.5 miles to South Fork Orestimba Creek 7.5 miles south-southwest of Mikes Peak (lat. 37°15' N, long. 121°20'55" W; sec. 7, T 8 S, R 6 E). Named on Mustang Peak (1955) and Wilcox Ridge (1956) 7.5' quadrangles.

Lion Creek [CALAVERAS]: *stream,* flows 3.5 miles to Forest Creek 3.5 miles south of Devils Nose (lat. 38°24'35" N, long. 120°25'50" W; near

SE cor. sec. 33, T 7 N, R 14 E). Named on Devils Nose (1979) 7.5' quadrangle.

Lion Creek [TUOLUMNE]: *stream,* flows 4.5 miles to Middle Fork Stanislaus River nearly 7 miles southeast of Liberty Hill (lat. 38° 18'25" N, long. 120°00'10" W; sec. 9, T 5 N, R 18 E). Named on Liberty Hill (1979) 7.5' quadrangle.

Lion Lake [CALAVERAS]: *lake,* 300 feet long, located 2 miles east of Tamarack (lat. 38°26'10" N, long. 120°02'25" W). Named on Tamarack (1979) 7.5' quadrangle.

Lion Point [MADERA]:

(1) *peak,* 11 miles south of Shuteye Peak (lat. 37°11'40" N, long. 119°23'35" W; sec. 31, T 8 S, R 24 E). Altitude 4970 feet. Named on Shaver Lake (1953) 15' quadrangle.

(2) *peak,* nearly 5 miles south-southwest of Devils Postpile (lat. 37° 33'50" N, long. 119°07'30" W). Altitude 8866 feet. Named on Devils Postpile (1953) 15' quadrangle.

Lions Canyon [STANISLAUS]: *canyon,* drained by a stream that flows 3.5 miles to North Fork Orestimba Creek 3.25 miles west-northwest of Mikes Peak (lat. 37°22'10" N, long. 121°22'25" W; sec. 36, T 6 S, R 5 E). Named on Mount Stakes (1955) and Wilcox Ridge (1956) 7.5' quadrangles.

Lippincott's Ferry: see **Grayson** [STANISLAUS].

Little Ash Creek [MADERA]: *stream,* diverges west from Ash Creek (present Ash Slough) 8.5 miles west-southwest of Chowchilla (lat. 37°04'05" N, long. 120°23'50" W; near NW cor. sec. 13, T 10 S, R 14 E), and flows for 5 miles in a westerly direction. Named on Bliss Ranch (1918) 7.5' quadrangle.

Little Bear Lake [TUOLUMNE]: *lake,* 2000 feet long, 14 miles southeast of Pinecrest (lat. 38°04'50" N, long. 119°47' W). Named on Pinecrest (1956) 15' quadrangle. Elden H. Vestal of California Department of Fish and Game named the lake in 1952 (Browning, 1986, p. 128).

Little Beaver Canyon [TUOLUMNE]: *canyon,* 1.25 miles long, on upper reaches of Beaver Creek above a point 2 miles south-southeast of Liberty Hill (lat. 38°20'30" N, long. 120°05'10" W). Named on Liberty Hill (1979) 7.5' quadrangle.

Little Beaver Creek [TUOLUMNE]: *stream,* flows 3 miles to Beaver Creek 8 miles southwest of Liberty Hill (lat. 38°17'15" N, long. 120°12'50" W; sec. 16, T 5 N, R 16 E). Named on Boards Crossing (1979) 7.5' quadrangle. On Big Meadow (1956) 15' quadrangle, the name applies to present Crane Creek (1).

Little Brother Slough [SAN JOAQUIN]: *water feature,* on Mandeville Island, joins San Joaquin River 16 miles west-southwest of Lodi (lat. 38°03'30" N, long. 121°32'45" W); the feature is east of Big Brother Slough. Named on Bouldin (1910) 7.5' quadrangle.

Little Buttonwillow Lake [MERCED]: *lake,* 1 mile long, 6.5 miles north-northeast of Los Banos (lat. 37°08'25" N, long. 120°47'30" W); the lake is north of Big Buttonwillow Lake. Named on San Luis Ranch (1961) 7.5' quadrangle.

Little Connection Slough [SAN JOAQUIN]: *water feature,* joins San Joaquin River 5 miles south of Terminous (lat. 38°02'40" N, long. 121°29'55" W). Named on Bouldin Island (1978) and Terminous (1978) 7.5' quadrangles.

Little Crane Creek [MARIPOSA]: *stream,* flows 4.5 miles to Crane Creek 1.25 miles north-northeast of El Portal (lat. 37°41'30" N, long. 119°46'15" W; sec. 9, T 3 S, R 20 E). Named on El Portal (1947) 7.5' quadrangle.

Little Deer Canyon [MERCED]: *canyon,* drained by a stream that flows 1.25 miles to Romero Creek 6 miles north of Pacheco Pass (lat. 37°09' N, long. 121°11'10" W; sec. 15, T 9 S, R 7 E); the feature is 1 mile east of Big Deer Canyon. Named on Crevison Peak (1955) 7.5' quadrangle.

Little Dry Creek [CALAVERAS]: *stream,* flows 1 mile to Dry Creek (2) 1 mile northeast of Vallecitos (lat. 38°05'50" N, long. 120°27'35" W; sec. 20, T 3 N, R 14 E). Named on Columbia (1948) 7.5' quadrangle.

Little Dry Creek [MADERA]: *stream,* flows 16 miles to Cottonwood Creek (2) 3 miles northwest of Trigo (lat. 36°57' N, long. 119°59'15" W; sec. 27, T 11 S, R 18 E). Named on Herndon (1965) and Raymond (1962) 15' quadrangles.

Little Fawn Canyon [STANISLAUS]: *canyon,* drained by a stream that flows 1 mile to Adobe Canyon about 7 miles southeast of Mount Boardman (lat. 37°24'10" N, long. 121°23'20" W; sec. 23, T 6 S, R 5 E). Named on Mount Boardman (1955) 7.5' quadrangle.

Little Fine Gold Creek [MADERA]: *stream,* flows 12 miles to Fine Gold Creek 6.25 miles west-southwest of North Fork (lat. 37°11'45" N, long. 119°37' W; near W line sec. 31, T 8 S, R 22 E). Named on Bass Lake (1953) and Millerton Lake (1965) 15' quadrangles.

Little Grizzly Creek [MARIPOSA]: *stream,* flows 2.5 miles to Ned Gulch (2) 5.5 miles west-northwest of El Portal (lat. 37°41'25" N, long. 119°52'50" W); the stream heads at Big Grizzly Mountain. Named on Kinsley (1947) 7.5' quadrangle. Called Little Grizzly on Yosemite (1909) 30' quadrangle.

Little Grizzly Falls: see **Bunnell Cascade** [MARIPOSA].

Little Grizzly Flat [MARIPOSA]: *area,* 7.5 miles west-northwest of El Portal (lat. 37°42'45" N, long. 119°54'35" W; near SE cor. sec. 31, T 2 S, R 19 E); the place is 0.25 mile east of Little Grizzly Mountain. Named on Kinsley (1947) 7.5' quadrangle.

Little Grizzly Mountain [MARIPOSA]: *peak,* 8 miles west-northwest of El Portal (lat. 37°42'40" N, long. 119°55' W; sec. 31, T 2 S, R 19 E); the peak is 1.25 miles west-southwest of Big Grizzly Mountain. Altitude 4341 feet. Named on Kinsley (1947) 7.5' quadrangle.

Littlehales [CALAVERAS]: *locality,* 3.25 miles north-northeast of Valley Springs (lat. 38°14' N, long. 120°48'30" W). Named on Jackson (1902) 7.5' quadrangle.

Little Hetch Hetchy Valley [TUOLUMNE]: *canyon,* 2 miles long, along Tuolumne River 5 miles north-northwest of White Wolf (lat. 37°56' N, long. 119°42' W); the valley is upstream from Hetch Hetchy Valley, and now holds part of the water of Hetch Hetchy Reservoir. Named on Yosemite (1909) 30' quadrangle.

Little Jackass Campground [MADERA]: *locality,* 6 miles northeast of Shuteye Peak (lat. 37°24' N, long. 119°20'10" W; near S line sec. 15, T 6 S, R 24 E); the place is along West Fork Jackass Creek. Named on Shuteye Peak (1953) 15' quadrangle.

Little Jackass Creek [TUOLUMNE]: *stream,* flows 2.25 miles to Big Jackass Creek 3.25 miles south of Groveland (lat. 37°47'35" N, long. 120°13'20" W; near E line sec. 5, T 2 S, R 16 E). Named on Groveland (1947) 7.5' quadrangle.

Little Jackass Meadow: see **Soldier Meadow** [MADERA].

Littlejohns Creek [CALAVERAS-SAN JOAQUIN-STANISLAUS]: *stream,* heads in Calaveras County and flows 65 miles to join Lone Tree Creek (2) and form French Camp Slough 6 miles south-southeast of downtown Stockton in San Joaquin County (lat. 37°52'35" N, long. 121°14'05" W). Named on Bachelor Valley (1968), Copperopolis (1962), Farmington (1968), Knights Ferry (1962), Melones Dam (1962), Oakdale (1968), Peters (1952), Salt Spring Valley (1962), and Stockton East (1952) 7.5' quadrangles. Burnham (1914) and Peters (1915) 7.5' quadrangles have the form "Little Johns Creek" for the name. Watts (p. 685) called the feature Little John Creek. United States Board on Geographic Names (1954, p. 3) rejected the forms "Littlejohn Creek" and "Little Johns Creek" for the name.

Little Mandeville Island [SAN JOAQUIN]: *island,* 1.25 miles long, 18 miles west-southwest of Lodi between Old River and Connection Slough (lat. 38°00'35" N, long. 121°33'50" W); the feature is southwest of Mandeville Island. Named on Bouldin Island (1978) 7.5' quadrangle.

Little Mokelumne River [CALAVERAS]: *stream,* flows 4 miles to South Fork Mokelumne River nearly 2 miles south of Blue Mountain (lat. 38°18'55" N, long. 120°22' W; sec. 6, T 5 N, R 15 E). Named on Dorrington (1979) 7.5' quadrangle.

Little Nellie Falls [MARIPOSA]: *waterfall,* 3 miles north of El Portal along Little Crane Creek (lat. 37°43'15" N, long. 119°46'55" W; sec. 32, T 2 S, R 20 E). Named on El Portal (1947) 7.5' quadrangle.

Little Otter Lake [TUOLUMNE]: *lake,* 1000 feet long, 7.25 miles south-west of Tower Peak (lat. 38°04'50" N, long. 119°39'20" W); the lake is 0.25 mile south of Otter Lake. Named on Tower Peak (1956) 15' quadrangle.

Little Panoche Valley [MERCED]: *valley,* mainly in Fresno County, but extends north into Merced County 3 miles southeast of Ortigalita Peak (lat. 36°46' N, long. 120°53'10" W). Named on Ortigalita Peak (1969) 7.5' quadrangle. United States Board on Geographic Names (1933a, p. 466) rejected the name "Panochita Valley" for the feature.

Little Pine Canyon [MERCED]: *canyon,* drained by a stream that flows 0.5 mile to Romero Creek 6.25 miles north-northeast of Pacheco Pass (lat. 37°08'50" N, long. 121°09'50" W; sec. 14, T 9 S, R 7 E); the canyon is 1 mile east of Big Pine Canyon [MERCED-STANISLAUS]. Named on Crevison Peak (1955) 7.5' quadrangle.

Little Potato Slough [SAN JOAQUIN]: *water feature,* diverges from South Mokelumne River at Terminous and extends to Potato Slough 13 miles west-southwest of Lodi (lat. 38°04'20" N, long. 121°30'10" W). Named on Bouldin Island (1978) and Terminous (1978) 7.5' quadrangles. Called Potato Slough on Bouldin (1910) and Headreach (1910) 7.5' quadrangles.

Little Prather Meadow [TUOLUMNE]: *valley,* 1.5 miles east-northeast of Liberty Hill (lat. 38°22'20" N, long. 120°04'30" W; sec. 14, T 6 N, T 17 E); the valley is 1 mile east of Big Prather Meadow. Named on Liberty Hill (1979) and Tamarack (1979) 7.5' quadrangles.

Little Rattlesnake Creek [TUOLUMNE]: *stream,* flows 5.25 miles to North Fork Stanislaus River 6 miles west-southwest of Liberty Hill (lat. 38°19'55" N, long. 120°12'10" W; sec. 34, T 6 N, R 16 E); the stream is generally parallel to and about 1 mile south of Big Rattlesnake Creek. Named on Boards Crossing (1979) and Liberty Hill (1979) 7.5' quadrangles.

Little Reynolds Creek [TUOLUMNE]: *stream,* flows 4 miles to Reynolds Creek 11 miles south of Pinecrest (lat. 38°01'45" N, long. 119°59'10" W; sec. 15, T 2 N, R 18 E). Named on Cherry Lake North (1979) 7.5' quadrangle.

Little Salado Creek [STANISLAUS]: *stream,* flows 7 miles to lowlands 5 miles south of Patterson (lat. 37°23'50" N, long. 121°07'45" W; sec. 19, T 6 S, R 8 E); the stream is south of Salado Creek. Named on Patterson (1953) 7.5' quadrangle.

Little Sandy Campground [MADERA]: *locality,* 7 miles north-northeast of Yosemite Forks (lat. 37°27'30" N, long. 119°34' W; sec. 33, T 5 S, R 22 E); the place is along Big Creek 1 mile upstream from Big Sandy Campground. Named on Bass Lake (1953) 15' quadrangle.

Little Shadow Lake: see **Ediza Lake** [MADERA].

Little Shuteye Pass [MADERA]: *pass,* 2 miles north-northwest of Shuteye Peak (lat. 37°22'45" N, long. 119°26'10" W; sec. 27, T 6 S, R 23 E); the pass is 2 miles east-southeast of Little Shuteye Peak. Named on Shuteye Peak (1953) 15' quadrangle.

Little Shuteye Peak [MADERA]: *peak,* 4 miles northwest of Shuteye Peak (lat. 37°23'40" N, long. 119°28'10" W; near E line sec. 20, T 6 S, R 23 E). Altitude 8362 feet. Named on Shuteye Peak (1953) 15' quadrangle.

Little Table Mountain [MADERA]: *ridge,* south- to south-southeast-trending, 3 miles long, 12 miles east-northeast of Trigo (lat. 36°59' N, long. 119°46' W). Named on Herndon (1965) and Raymond (1962) 15' quadrangles.

Little Twin Gulch [TUOLUMNE]: *canyon,* drained by a stream that flows 0.25 mile to Twin Gulch (2) 3 miles south-southwest of Don Pedro Camp (lat. 37°40'45" N, long. 120°25'40" W; sec. 16, T 3 S, R 14 E). Named on La Grange (1962) 7.5' quadrangle.

Little Venice Island [SAN JOAQUIN]: *island,* 0.5 mile long, 4.5 miles south of Terminous along San Joaquin River (lat. 38°03' N, long. 121°30' W); the feature is southeast of Venice Island. Named on Bouldin Island (1978) and Terminous (1978) 7.5' quadrangles, which show the feature made up largely of marsh. Called Venice Island on Lodi (1939) 7.5' quadrangle.

Little Winkle Branch: see **Lehamite Creek** [MARIPOSA].

Little Yosemite Valley [MARIPOSA]: *valley,* 4.5 miles east-southeast of Yosemite Village along Merced River above Nevada Fall (lat. 37°44' N, long. 119°30'30" W). Named on Merced Peak (1953) and Yosemite (1956) 15' quadrangles. Members of the Mariposa Battalion named the valley in 1851 (Browning, 1986, p. 129).

Live Oak: see **Lodi** [SAN JOAQUIN].

Livingston [MERCED]: *town,* 7 miles west-northwest of Atwater (lat. 37°23' N, long. 120°43'15" W; in and near sec. 25, 26, T 6 S, R 11 E). Named on Atwater (1961) 15' quadrangle. Postal authorities established Livingston post office in 1873, discontinued it in 1882, and reestablished it in 1883; the name was for Charles C. Livingston, a station operator for Southern Pacific Railroad (Salley, p. 124).

Lockeford [SAN JOAQUIN]: *town,* 7 miles east-northeast of Lodi (lat. 38°09'50" N, long. 121°08'55" W; near SE cor. sec. 25, T 4 N, R 7 E). Named on Lockeford (1968) 7.5' quadrangle. Dr. Dean J. Locke and his two brothers purchased land along Mokelumne River in 1850, and in 1859 the town of Lockeford was laid out there (Hoover, Rensch, and Rensch, p. 374). Postal authorities established Lockeford post office in 1861 (Frickstad, p. 161). Laird's Ferry operated on Mokelumne River about 2 miles west of present Lockeford in 1849; David J. Staples, J.F. Staples, and W.H. Nichols took over the ferry in 1850, after which time it was called Staples' Ferry (Hoover, Rensch, and Rensch, p. 374). Postal authorities established Staples Ranch post office at the place in 1851 and discontinued it in 1863, when they moved it south and changed the name to Locust Shade (Salley, p. 212). They discontinued Locust Shade post office in 1868; it was located 4 miles southwest of Lockeford (NW quarter sec. 14, T 3 N, R 7 E), and was named for locust trees at the place (Salley, p. 124). In 1852 Chism Cooper Fugitt founded a community first called Davis' Crossing, then Fugitt's, and finally in 1859 it became Liberty, a name derived from Fugitt's former home in Missouri (Hillman and Covello, p. 215). The community of Liberty was situated about 6 miles north of present Lockeford; the residents moved 1 mile south in 1868 in hope of obtaining a station there on the new Central Pacific Railroad, but the hope was unrealized (Hoover, Rensch, and Rensch, p. 374). The new site along the railroad was called New Liberty and was located at present Acampo (Hillman and Covello, p. 109). Postal authorities established Fugitt post office in 1857, changed the name to Liberty in 1860, and discontinued it in 1874; C.C. Fugitt was the first postmaster of Fugitt post office (Salley, p. 81, 122).

Locust Shale: see **Lockeford** [SAN JOAQUIN].

Lodi [SAN JOAQUIN]: *city,* 12 miles north of Stockton (lat. 38°07'50" N, long. 121°16'40" W). Named on Lockeford (1968), Lodi North (1968), and Lodi South (1968) 7.5' quadrangles. Officials of Central Pacific Railroad gave their station at the place the name "Mokelumne" when the railroad reached the site in 1869, but later changed the name to Lodi (Gudde, 1949, p. 191). Postal authorities established Mokelumne post office in 1869 and changed the name to Lodi in 1873 (Frickstad, p. 162). The city incorporated in 1906. California Division of Highways' (1934) map shows a place called Lafayette located 4.5 miles west-southwest of Lodi. Lodi South (1968) 7.5' quadrangle shows Lafayette school in the neighborhood. The same map also shows a place called Franklyn located nearly 2 miles east of Lodi along Southern Pacific Railroad. Postal authorities established Snugville post office 8 miles northwest of Lodi in 1864 and discontinued it in 1869 (Hillman and Covello, p. 225; Salley, p. 207). They established Live Oak post office 5 miles south of present Lodi (SE quarter sec. 25, T 3 N, R 6 E) in 1869 and discontinued it in 1871 (Salley, p. 123). They established Tuleville post office 12 miles northwest of Lodi (NW quarter sec. 14, T 4 N, R 5 E) in 1875 and discontinued it in 1876 (Salley, p. 225).

Lodi: see **West Lodi**, under **Kingdon** [SAN JOAQUIN].

Lodi Junction [SAN JOAQUIN]: *locality,* 5.5 miles west-southwest of Lockeford along Central California Traction Railroad (lat. 38° 07'45" N, long. 121°14'30" W; near NW cor. sec. 8, T 3 N, R 7 E). Named on Lockeford (1968) 7.5' quadrangle.

Lodi Municipal Lake: see **Smith Lake** [SAN JOAQUIN].

Logan Meadow [MADERA]: *area,* 5 miles east of Shuteye Peak (lat. 37°21' N, long. 118°20'10" W; in and near sec. 3, T 7 S, R 24 E). Named on Kaiser (1904) 30' quadrangle.

Logan Meadow Campground [MADERA]: *locality,* 5 miles east of Shuteye Peak along Chiquito Creek (lat. 37°21'05" N, long. 119° 20'10" W; near N line sec. 3, T 7 S, R 24 E); the place is at Logan Meadow. Named on Shuteye Peak (1953) 15' quadrangle.

Logtown: see **Mariposa** [MARIPOSA].

Log Trough Spring [MERCED]: *spring,* 4.5 miles south-southeast of Mariposa Peak (lat. 36°53'45" N, long. 121°10'20" W; sec. 14, T 12 S, R 7 E). Named on Mariposa Peak (1969) 7.5' quadrangle.

Lois Lake [MADERA]: *lake,* 650 feet long, 4.25 miles northwest of Devils Postpile (lat. 37°40'30" N, long. 119°07'40" W). Named on Devils Postpile (1953) 15' quadrangle.

Lombardi: see **Sherman Acres** [CALAVERAS].

Lombardi Gulch [CALAVERAS]: *canyon,* drained by a stream that flows less than 1 mile to North Fork Calaveras River 2 miles southeast of Mokelumne Hill (lat. 38°16'55" N, long. 120° 40'45" W; sec. 17, T 5 N, R 12 E). Named on Mokelumne Hill (1948) 7.5' quadrangle, which shows Lombardi ranch near the mouth of the canyon.

Lone Gulch [CALAVERAS]: *canyon,* drained by a stream that flows 2.5 miles to Coopers Creek 4 miles northwest of Angels Camp (lat. 36°06'30" N, long. 120°36'40" W; near W line sec. 13, T 3 N, R 12 E). Named on Angels Camp (1962) 7.5' quadrangle.

Lone Gulch [TUOLUMNE]: *canyon,* drained by a stream that flows 0.25 mile to Don Pedro Reservoir 1 mile southeast of Don Pedro Camp (lat. 37°42'20" N, long. 120°23'25" W; sec. 2, T 3 S, R 14 E). Named on La Grange (1962) 7.5' quadrangle.

Lone Sequoia Campground [MARIPOSA]: *locality,* nearly 4 miles south-southwest of Fish Camp (lat. 37°25'40" N, long. 119°40' W; sec. 10, T 6 S, R 21 E). Named on Bass Lake (1953) 15' quadrangle.

Lone Tree Camp [MERCED]: *locality,* 20 miles southwest of Merced (lat. 37°03'50" N, long. 120°42'25" W; near W line sec. 18, T 10 S, R 12 E). Named on Delta Ranch (1922) 7.5' quadrangle.

Lone Tree Canyon: see **Lone Tree Creek** [SAN JOAQUIN].

Lone Tree Creek [SAN JOAQUIN]: *stream,* formed by the confluence of Middle Fork and North Fork, flows nearly 6 miles to lowlands 9 miles south-southeast of Tracy (lat. 37°37' N, long. 121°21'40" W; sec. 1, T 4 S, R 5 E). Named on Lone Tree Creek (1955), Solyo (1953), and Vernalis (1969) 7.5' quadrangles. Carbona (1922) 15' quadrangle has the form "Lonetree Creek" for the name. Brewer (p. 277) mentioned Lone Tree Canyon in 1862, and noted that "a lone tree stands near its mouth and gives the canyon a name." Middle Fork is 5 miles long and North Fork is nearly 4 miles long; both forks are named on Lone Tree Creek (1955) 7.5' quadrangle.

Lone Tree Creek [SAN JOAQUIN-STANISLAUS]: *stream,* heads in Stanislaus County and flows 24 miles to join Littlejohns Creek and form French Camp Slough 6 miles south-southeast of downtown Stockton in San Joaquin County (lat. 37°52'35" N, long. 121°14'05" W). Named on Avena (1952), Escalon (1968), Manteca (1952), and Stockton East (1952) 7.5' quadrangles.

Lone Tree House: see **Escalon** [SAN JOAQUIN].

Lone Tree Mineral Spring [SAN JOAQUIN]: *spring,* 11.5 miles south of Tracy (lat. 37°34'25" N, long. 121°26'40" W; sec. 20, T 4 S, R 5 E); the spring is along North Fork Lone Tree Creek (1). Named on Lone Tree Creek (1955) 7.5' quadrangle. Carbona (1922) 15' quadrangle has the form "Lonetree Mineral Springs" for the name.

Lone Willow: see **Los Banos** [MERCED].

Lone Willow Slough [MADERA]: *stream,* diverges northwest from San Joaquin River 18 miles southwest of Madera (lat. 36°46'25" N, long. 120°17'10" W; sec. 25, T 13 S, R 15 E) and flows 23 miles to an artificial watercourse. Named on Firebaugh (1956), Mendota Dam (1956), and Poso Farm (1962) 7.5' quadrangles.

Long Barn [TUOLUMNE]: *settlement,* 15 miles east-northeast of Sonora (lat. 38°05'30" N, long. 120°08' W; near N line sec. 29, T 3 N, R 17 E). Named on Twain Harte (1979) 7.5' quadrangle. Postal authorities established Long Barn post office in 1930 (Frickstad, p. 216). The name is from a large barn used in the early days to house logging and freighter teams (Quimby, p. 195).

Long Canyon [CALAVERAS]: *canyon,* drained by a stream that flows less than 1 mile to Stanislaus River 6.5 miles southeast of Copperopolis (lat. 37°55'20" N, long. 120°32'45" W; sec. 21, T 1 N, R 13 E). Named on

Melones Dam (1962) 7.5' quadrangle.

Long Canyon [MARIPOSA]: *canyon,* drained by a stream that flows 1.25 miles to Saxon Creek 3.25 miles west-northwest of Midpines (lat. 37°33'45" N, long. 119°58'25" W; sec. 27, T 4 S, R 18 E). Named on Feliciana Mountain (1947) 7.5' quadrangle.

Long Canyon [STANISLAUS]:

(1) *canyon,* drained by a stream that flows 3.5 miles to North Fork Orestimba Creek 2 miles west-southwest of Mikes Peak (lat. 37° 20'55" N, long. 121°21' W; sec. 6, T 7 S, R 6 E). Named on Copper Mountain (1956) and Wilcox Ridge (1956) 7.5' quadrangles.

(2) *canyon,* drained by a stream that flows 2.5 miles to Garzas Creek 3.25 miles west-northwest of Mustang Peak (lat. 37°12'55" N, long. 121°14'10" W; sec. 30, T 8 S, R 7 E). Named on Crevison Peak (1955) 7.5' quadrangle.

Long Canyon [TUOLUMNE]: *canyon,* drained by a stream that flows 3 miles to Griswold Creek 7 miles northeast of Stanislaus (lat. 38° 12'20" N, long. 120°16'30" W; near N line sec. 13, T 4 N, R 15 E). Named on Crandall Peak (1979) and Stanislaus (1948) 7.5' quadrangles.

Long Creek [MADERA]: *stream,* flows 5 miles to North Fork San Joaquin River 8 miles west of Devils Postpile (lat. 37°38'35" N, long. 119°13'40" W); the stream heads near Long Mountain. Named on Devils Postpile (1953) and Merced Peak (1953) 15' quadrangles.

Long Gulch [CALAVERAS]:

(1) *canyon,* 2 miles long, opens into the canyon of Blue Creek 5.5 miles west of Tamarack (lat. 38°26'15" N, long. 120°10'45" W; near S line sec. 23, T 7 N, R 16 E). Named on Calaveras Dome (1979) 7.5' quadrangle.

(2) *canyon,* drained by a stream that flows 1.5 miles to Shad Gulch 2.5 miles west-northwest of Paloma (lat. 38°16'25" N, long. 120° 48'30" W; sec. 19, T 5 N, R 11 E). Named on Jackson (1962) 7.5' quadrangle.

(3) *canyon,* drained by a stream that flows nearly 2 miles to North Fork Calaveras River 2.5 miles south-southeast of Mokelumne Hill (lat. 38°15'55" N, long. 120°41'20" W; near S line sec. 19, T 5 N, R 12 E). Named on Mokelumne Hill (1948) 7.5' quadrangle.

(4) *canyon,* drained by a stream that flows 2.25 miles to Rock Creek nearly 7 miles southeast of Jenny Lind (lat. 38°01'15" N, long. 120°47'20" W; sec. 17, T 2 N, R 11 E). Named on Jenny Lind (1962) 7.5' quadrangle.

(5) *canyon,* drained by a stream that flows 1 mile to Coyote Creek 2.5 miles south of Vallecito (lat. 38°03' N, long. 120°28'50" W; near S line sec. 6, T 2 N, R 14 E). Named on Columbia (1948) 7.5' quadrangle.

(6) *canyon,* drained by a stream that flows 1.5 miles to Calaveritas Creek 7 miles east-southeast of San Andreas (lat. 38°10'15" N, long. 120°33'15" W; near W line sec. 28, T 4 N, R 13 E). Named on San Andreas (1947) 15' quadrangle.

Long Gulch [MERCED-STANISLAUS]: *canyon,* drained by a stream that heads in Stanislaus County and flows nearly 2 miles to Quinto Creek 7.5 miles north-northeast of Pacheco Pass in Merced County (lat. 37°10'15" N, long. 121°09'55" W; sec. 11, T 9 S, R 7 E). Named on Crevison Peak (1955) 7.5' quadrangle.

Long Gulch [TUOLUMNE]:

(1) *canyon,* drained by a stream that flows 1.5 miles to South Fork Stanislaus River nearly 3 miles north-northeast of Columbia (lat. 38°04'10" N, long. 120°22'25" W; sec. 31, T 3 N, R 15 E). Named on Columbia (1948) 7.5' quadrangle.

(2) *canyon,* drained by a stream that flows 1.5 miles to New Melones Lake 6.5 miles west-southwest of Sonora (lat. 37°56'25" N, long. 120°29'15" W; sec. 13, T 1 N, R 13 E). Named on Sonora (1948, photorevised 1973) 7.5' quadrangle.

(3) *canyon,* drained by a stream that flows 2.5 miles to Big Creek (1) 3 miles east of Groveland (lat. 37°50'25" N, long. 120° 10'35" W; near W line sec. 24, T 1 S, R 16 E). Named on Groveland (1947) 7.5' quadrangle.

(4) *canyon,* drained by a stream that flows 4.5 miles to South Fork Tuolumne River 7.25 miles southeast of Mather (lat. 37°48'30" N, long. 119°45'40" W; sec. 34, T 1 S, R 20 E). Named on Hetch Hetchy Reservoir (1956) and Lake Eleanor (1956) 15' quadrangles.

Long Hollow [MADERA]: *canyon,* nearly 3 miles long, opens into the canyon of Coarse Gold Creek 7 miles east-southeast of Knowles (lat. 37°09'40" N, long. 119°46'25" W; sec. 10, T 9 S, R 20 E). Named on Knowles (1962) 7.5' quadrangle.

Long Lake [TUOLUMNE]: *lake,* 3500 feet long, 13 miles east of Pinecrest (lat. 38°10'30" N, long. 119°45'10" W). Named on Pinecrest (1956) and Tower Peak (1956) 15' quadrangles. Called Beulah Lake on Dardanelles (1898, reprinted 1947) 30' quadrangle, but United States Board on Geographic Names (1960b, p. 17) rejected this name for the feature.

Long Meadow [MADERA]:

(1) *area,* 8.5 miles north-northeast of Yosemite Forks (lat. 37°29'10" N, long. 119°34'45" W; near E line sec. 20, T 5 S, R 22 E). Named on Bass Lake (1953) 15' quadrangle.

(2) *area,* 9 miles north of Shuteye Peak (lat. 37°29' N, long. 119° 25' W; sec. 23, T 5 S, R 23 E). Named on Shuteye Peak (1953) 15' quadrangle.

(3) *area,* 4.5 miles north-northeast of Shuteye Peak (lat. 37°24'30" N, long. 119°23'45" W; near W line sec. 18, T 6 S, R 24 E). Named on Shuteye Peak (1953) 15' quadrangle.

Long Meadow [MARIPOSA]: *area,* 3 miles south-southeast of Cathedral Peak (lat. 37°48'45" N, long. 119°25'45" W). Named on Tuolumne Meadows (1956) 15' quadrangle. Joseph LeConte gave the name "Feldspar Valley" to the feature in 1872 (Browning, 1988, p. 79).

Long Meadow Creek [MADERA]: *stream,* flows 2.5 miles to Rainier Creek 8 miles north-northeast of Yosemite Forks (lat. 37° 28'55" N, long. 119°35'55" W; sec. 19, T 5 S, R 22 E); the stream goes through Long Meadow (1). Named on Bass Lake (1953) 15' quadrangle.

Long Mountain [MADERA]: *peak,* 6 miles east-northeast of Merced Peak (lat. 37°40'05" N, long. 119°17'40" W). Altitude 11,502 feet. Named on Merced Peak (1953) 15' quadrangle.

Long Ridge [MADERA]: *ridge,* south-trending, 2.5 miles long, 15 miles south of Shuteye Peak (lat. 37°08'15" N, long. 119°28'30" W). Named on Shaver Lake (1953) 15' quadrangle.

Long Valley [TUOLUMNE]: *valley,* 5 miles south-southeast of Dardanelle (lat. 38°16'30" N, long. 119°48' W). Named on Dardanelle (1979) 7.5' quadrangle.

Long Valley Creek [TUOLUMNE]: *stream,* flows 5 miles to Eagle Creek (2) nearly 3 miles south of Dardanelle (lat. 38°17'55" N, long. 119°49'55" W; sec. 12, T 5 N, R 19 E); the stream goes through Long Valley. Named on Dardanelles Cone (1956) 15' quadrangle. Called Eagle Creek on Dardanelles (1898) 30' quadrangle.

Lookout Mountain [MARIPOSA]: *peak,* 5.5 miles south-southeast of Mariposa (lat. 37°24'25" N, long. 119°56'25" W; on E line sec. 13, T 6 S, R 18 E). Altitude 2633 feet. Named on Mariposa (1947) 7.5' quadrangle.

Lookout Mountain [MERCED]: *peak,* nearly 3 miles west-southwest of Sweeney Hill (lat. 36°52'55" N, long. 121°05'40" W). Named on Los Banos Valley (1969) 7.5' quadrangle.

Lookout Point [TUOLUMNE]: *locality,* 11.5 miles southeast of Pinecrest (lat. 38°03'25" N, long. 119°52'40" W; sec. 3, T 2 N, R 19 E). Named on Cherry Lake North (1979) 7.5' quadrangle.

Looney Creek [TUOLUMNE]: *stream,* flows 5.25 miles to Bourland Creek 8 miles east-southeast of Long Barn (lat. 38°01'50" N, long. 120°00'15" W; sec. 16, T 2 N, R 18 E). Named on Long Barn (1956) and Pinecrest (1956) 15' quadrangles. The misspelled name recalls Jerome Loney, Joseph Loney, and James Loney, all of whom patented land in the neighborhood about 1890 (Browning, 1986, p. 131).

Lord [TUOLUMNE]: *locality,* 3.5 miles southeast of Long Barn along Rush Creek (2) (lat. 38°03'30" N, long. 120°04'50" W). Named on Big Trees (1891) 30' quadrangle.

Lord Meadow [TUOLUMNE]: *area,* 13 miles east-southeast of Pinecrest along Cherry Creek (lat. 38°05'50" N, long. 119°47'30" W). Named on Pinecrest (1956) 15' quadrangle.

Lord Spring [TUOLUMNE]: *spring,* 2 miles north-northwest of Columbia (lat. 38°03'50" N, long. 120°24'50" W; near NE cor. sec. 3, T 2 N, R 14 E). Named on Columbia (1948) 7.5' quadrangle.

Los Banos [MERCED]: *town,* 26 miles southwest of Merced (lat. 37° 03'30" N, long. 120°51' W; sec. 14, 15, 22, 23, T 10 S, R 10 E). Named on Los Banos (1960) 7.5' quadrangle. Postal authorities established Los Banos post office in 1873 (Frickstad, p. 101), and the town incorporated in 1907. Gustave Kreyenhagen opened a store in 1865 at what had been Lone Willow stage station, built in 1858 on the west bank of present Mud Slough; Kreyenhagen soon moved the building and business 3 miles east to a road junction about 8 miles northeast of present Los Banos, and relocated again in 1870 to a site 12 miles farther west on the Gilroy-Visalia road and about 2 miles south of present Volta, where postal authorities established Los Banos post office before the post office and businesses moved 5 miles farther east in 1889 to the railroad (Hoover, Rensch, and Rensch, p. 204-205). Postal authorities established Central Point post office 4 miles southeast of Los Banos in 1876 and discontinued it in 1890 (Salley, p. 41). They established Ortigalito post office 20 miles southwest of Central Point post office in 1876, discontinued it in 1877, reestablished it in 1879, and discontinued it in 1881 (Salley, p. 163). They established Wyruck post office 6 miles south of Los Banos in 1876, changed the name to Charleston in 1878, and discontinued it in 1884—the name "Charleston" was from the given name of Charles Bambauer, first postmaster (Salley, p. 42, 244). California Mining Bureau's (1917b) map shows a place called Agatha located about 7 miles east-southeast of Los Banos between Los Banos and South Dos Palos.

Los Banos Creek [MERCED]: *stream,* formed by the confluence of North Fork and South Fork 5.25 miles northwest of Sweeney Hill, flows 14 miles to lowlands 16 miles west of Dos Palos (lat. 37° 00' N, long. 120°54'45" W; near N line sec. 7, T 11 S, R 10 E). Named on Los Banos (1961) and Turlock (1962) 15' quadrangles, and on Los Banos Valley (1969) and Ortigalita Peak NW (1956) 7.5' quadrangles. Padre Felipe Arroyo of San Juan Bautista mission in present San Benito County occasionally visited the stream at pools that became known as Los Baños del Padre Arroyo (Shumate, p. 11)—*los baños* means "the baths" in Spanish. The creek itself became known as Arroyo de los Baños del Padre Arroyo (Hanna, p. 24-25); United States Board on Geographic Names (1962a, p. 18) rejected the names "Arroyo de los Padres," "Garzas Creek," and "La Garzas Creek" for the stream. The canyon of Los Banos Creek near the entrance of the stream into lowlands is called Menjoulet Canyon, for John Menjoulet, a French sheepman (Hoover, Rensch, and Rensch, p. 201). North Fork is 7 miles long and is named on Los Banos Valley (1969) and Mariposa Peak (1969) 7.5' quadrangles. South Fork heads in San Benito County, is 17 miles long, and is named on Los Banos Valley (1969) and Ruby Canyon (1968) 7.5' quadrangles.

Los Baños del Padre Arroyo: see **Los Banos Creek** [MERCED].

Los Banos Reservoir [MERCED]: *lake,* behind a dam on Los Banos Creek 13 miles north of Ortigalita Peak (lat. 36°59'30" N, long. 120°55'50" W; sec. 12, T 11 S, R 9 E). Named on Ortigalita Peak NW (1969) 7.5' quadrangle.

Los Banos Valley [MERCED]: *valley,* 5 miles north of Sweeney Hill (lat. 36°58' N, long. 121°03'15" W); the valley is along Los Banos Creek. Named on Los Banos Valley (1969) 7.5' quadrangle.

Lost Bear Meadow [MARIPOSA]: *area,* 7 miles south of Yosemite Village (lat. 37°38'45" N, long. 119°35'45" W; sec. 30, T 3 S, R 22 E). Named on Yosemite (1956) 15' quadrangle. Browning (1986, p. 132) attributed the name to an incident concerning a small girl who was lost in 1957, and after she was found unharmed she claimed that she was not lost, but that a bear that she saw went away and was lost.

Lost City [CALAVERAS]: *locality,* 11 miles west of Angels Camp along Bear Creek (3) (lat. 38°05'10" N, long. 120°44'55" W; sec. 27, T 3 N, R 11 E). Named on Salt Spring Valley (1962) 7.5' quadrangle. The place also was called Stone City and Stone Creek Settlement (Gudde, 1975, p. 199).

Lost Claim Camp Ground [TUOLUMNE]: *locality,* 10 miles east of Groveland (lat. 37°49'15" N, long. 120°02'50" W; at E line sec. 25, T 1 S, R 17 E). Named on Jawbone Ridge (1947) 7.5' quadrangle.

Lost Creek [TUOLUMNE]: *stream,* flows 2.5 miles to Reynolds Creek 11 miles south of Pinecrest (lat. 38°01'50" N, long. 119°59'45" W; sec. 16, T 2 N, R 18 E). Named on Cherry Lake North (1979) 7.5' quadrangle.

Lost Dog Lake [MADERA]: *lake,* 300 feet long, 2.25 miles west-northwest of Devils Postpile (lat. 37°38'20" N, long. 119°07' W). Named on Devils Postpile (1953) 15' quadrangle.

Lost Isle: see **Acker Island** [SAN JOAQUIN].

Lost Lake [MADERA]:

(1) *lake,* 750 feet long, 10 miles north of Shuteye Peak (lat. 37°29'45" N, long. 119°27'40" W; sec. 16, T 5 S, R 23 E). Named on Shuteye Peak (1953) 15' quadrangle.

(2) *lake,* 500 feet long, nearly 9 miles west of Devils Postpile (lat. 37°38'10" N, long. 119°14'30" W). Named on Devils Postpile (1953) 15' quadrangle.

Lost Lake [TUOLUMNE]: *lake,* 1000 feet long, 8 miles northwest of Tower Peak (lat. 38°13'50" N, long. 119°38'50" W; on S line sec. 34, T 5 N, R 21 E). Named on Tower Peak (1956) 15' quadrangle.

Lost Lake Creek [MADERA]: *stream,* flows 1 mile to Mugler Creek nearly 10 miles north of Shuteye Peak (lat. 37°29'25" N, long. 119° 26'40" W; near SW cor. sec. 15, T 5 S, R 23 E); the stream heads at Lost Lake (1). Named on Shuteye Peak (1953) 15' quadrangle.

Lost Valley [MARIPOSA]: *area,* 8.5 miles south-southwest of Cathedral Peak along Merced River (lat. 37°44'35" N, long. 119° 28'25" W). Named on Merced Peak (1953) 15' quadrangle.

Lotta Creek [STANISLAUS]: *stream,* flows 3.25 miles to Salado Creek 3.25 miles south-southeast of Copper Mountain (lat. 37°22'45" N, long. 121°16'55" W; sec. 26, T 6 S, R 6 E). Named on Copper Mountain (1956) 7.5' quadrangle.

Loucks Creek [CALAVERAS]: *stream,* flows 4 miles to Tulloch Lake 4.5 miles south-southeast of Copperopolis (lat. 37°55'30" N, long. 120°35'55" W; sec. 24, T 1 N, R 12 E). Named on Melones Dam (1962) 7.5' quadrangle.

Louise Point [MARIPOSA]: *peak,* 0.5 mile south of Coulterville (lat. 37°42'20" N, long. 120°11'35" W; sec. 3, T 3 S, R 16 E). Named on Coulterville (1947) 7.5' quadrangle.

Louse Canyon [TUOLUMNE]: *canyon,* 2 miles long, 10 miles east-southeast of Pinecrest along West Fork Cherry Creek (lat. 38°08'40" N, long. 119°49'15" W). Named on Pinecrest (1956) 15' quadrangle.

Love Creek [CALAVERAS]: *stream,* flows 6 miles to join Moran Creek and form Mill Creek (2) 8 miles northeast of Murphys (lat. 38°13' N, long. 120°21'25" W; sec. 7, T 4 N, R 15 E). Named on Dorrington (1979) and Stanislaus (1948) 7.5' quadrangles.

Lovers Leap [STANISLAUS]: *relief feature,* 1.5 miles southwest of Knights Ferry on the south side of Stanislaus River (lat. 37°48'25" N, long. 120°41'25" W; sec. 31, T 1 S, R 12 E). Named on Knights Ferry (1962) 7.5' quadrangle. The feature also was called The Jumping Off Place (Paden and Schlichtmann, p. 28). G.W. Keeler started Keeler's Ferry in 1850 on the river just below Lovers Leap (Paden and Schlichtmann,p. 28, 305). The ferry was at what was known as Keeler's Flat (Hoover, Rensch, and Rensch, p. 540).

Loving's Ferry: see **Oakdale** [STANISLAUS].

Low Divide: see **Altaville** [CALAVERAS].

Lower Agua Fria: see **Agua Fria** [MARIPOSA].

Lower Brother [MARIPOSA]: *relief feature,* nearly 2 miles west-southwest of Yosemite Village on the north side of Yosemite Valley (lat. 37°44'15" N, long. 119°36'50" W); the feature is one of the group called Three Brothers. Named on Yosemite (1956) 15' quadrangle.

Lower Calaveritas: see **Caliveritas** [CALAVERAS].

Lower Chiquito Campground [MADERA]: *locality,* 5 miles north-northeast of Shuteye Peak (lat. 37°24'50" N, long. 119°23' W; near N line sec. 18, T 6 S, R 24 E); the place is along Chiquito Creek 7 miles downstream from Upper Chiquito Campground. Named on Shuteye Peak (1953) 15' quadrangle.

Lower Dominici Creek [STANISLAUS]: *stream,* flows 3.25 miles to Tuolumne River 2 miles west-southwest of La Grange (lat. 37°39'05" N, long. 129°29'35" W; near W line sec. 25, T 3 S, R 13 E); the mouth of the stream is 1 mile south-southwest of the mouth of Upper Dominici Creek. Named on Cooperstown (1968) and La Grange (1962) 7.5' quadrangles.

Lower Falls [MADERA]: *waterfall,* 2 miles south of Devils Postpile on Middle Fork San Joaquin River (lat. 37°35'40" N, long. 119°05'15" W). Named on Devils Postpile (1953) 15' quadrangle.

Lower Ferry: see **Bonsells Ferry**, under **Mossdale** [SAN JOAQUIN].

Lower Jones Tract [SAN JOAQUIN]: *area,* 11 miles west of downtown Stockton (lat. 37°57'15" N, long. 121°29'30" W); the place is north of Upper Jones Tract. Named on Holt (1978) and Woodward Island (1978) 7.5' quadrangles.

Lower Merced Pass Lake [MADERA]: *lake,* 1000 feet long, 3 miles west of Merced Peak (lat. 37°37'35" N, long. 119°26'50" W); the lake is less than 0.5 mile west-northwest of Upper Merced Pass Lake. Named on Merced Peak (1953) 15' quadrangle.

Lower Ottoway Lake [MADERA]: *lake,* 1900 feet long, 1.5 miles west-northwest of Merced Peak (lat. 37°38'35" N, long. 119°25'05" W); the lake is along Ottoway Creek 1.5 miles west of Ottoway Peak. Named on Merced Peak (1953) 15' quadrangle.

Lower Relief Valley [TUOLUMNE]: *valley,* 13 miles east-northeast of Pinecrest (lat. 38°15' N, long. 119°45'30" W); the valley is along Relief Creek 1.5 miles north-northeast of Upper Relief Valley. Named on Dardanelles Cone (1956) and Pinecrest (1956) 15' quadrangles. Called Relief Valley on Dardanelles (1898) 30' quadrangle. Relief Valley took its name from an incident in the early 1850's, when a party of emigrants waited at the place until assistance arrived (Hoover, Rensch, and Rensch, p. 566).

Lower Ruth Lake [MERCED]: *lake,* 1950 feet long, 4.5 miles north-northeast of Los Banos (lat. 37°07'15" N, long. 120°48'50" W; sec. 30, T 9 S, R 11 E); the lake is north of Upper Ruth Lake. Named on Los Banos (1960) 7.5' quadrangle.

Lower Virginia Falls: see **White Cascade** [TUOLUMNE].

Lower White Lake [STANISLAUS]: *intermittent lake,* 450 feet long, 4.25 miles north of Westley (lat. 37°36'40" N, long. 121°12'20" W); the feature is 2.5 miles northwest of Upper White Lake. Named on Westley (1952) 7.5' quadrangle. Westley (1915) 7.5' quadrangle has the name on a dry depression.

Lower Yosemite Fall [MARIPOSA]: *waterfall,* 0.5 mile west-northwest of Yosemite Village along Yosemite Creek (lat. 37°45'05" N, long. 119°35'45" W); the feature is nearly 0.5 mile south of Upper Yosemite Fall. Named on Hetch Hetchy Reservoir (1956) 15' quadrangle. Upper Yosemite Fall and Lower Yosemite Fall together are called Yosemite Falls on Yosemite (1909) 30' quadrangle. Hoffmann and Gardner's (1863-1867) map has the name "Yosemite Fall" for the pair of waterfalls.

Lucas Gulch [TUOLUMNE]: *canyon,* drained by a stream that flows 1.5 miles to Don Pedro Reservoir 2 miles southeast of Don Pedro Camp (lat. 37°42'05" N, long. 120°22'35" W; sec. 1, T 3 S, R 14 E). Named on La Grange (1962) and Penon Blanco Peak (1962) 7.5' quadrangles.

Lucky Point [TUOLUMNE]: *peak,* 2 miles south-southeast of Don Pedro Camp (lat. 37°41'15" N, long. 120°23'45" W; sec. 11, T 3 S, R 14 E). Named on La Grange (1962) 7.5' quadrangle.

Lucky Spring [MERCED]: *spring,* nearly 3 miles south-southwest of Pacheco Pass (lat. 37°01'45" N, long. 121°14'10" W). Named on Pacheco Pass (1955) 7.5' quadrangle.

Luke Camp [TUOLUMNE]: *locality,* 3 miles south-southeast of Duckwall Mountain (lat. 37°55'30" N, long. 120°05'55" W). Named on Sonora (1897) 30' quadrangle.

Lukens Lake [TUOLUMNE]: *lake,* 1200 feet long, 2 miles east-southeast of White Wolf (lat. 37°51'35" N, long. 119°36'55" W; sec. 13, T 1 S, R 21 E). Named on Hetch Hetchy Reservoir (1956) 15' quadrangle. R.B. Marshall of United States Geological Survey named the lake in 1894 to honor Theodore Parker Lukens, mayor of Pasadena and a conservationist (Hanna, p. 178).

Lunch Meadow [TUOLUMNE]: *area,* 9 miles northwest of Tower Peak along Summit Creek (lat. 38°13'05" N, long. 119°41'20" W; near S line sec. 5, T 4 N, R 21 E). Named on Tower Peak (1956) 15' quadrangle.

Lupine Campground [MADERA]: *locality,* 6.25 miles southeast of Yosemite Forks on the southwest side of Bass Lake (1) (lat. 37°18'30" N, long.

119°32'35" W; near W line sec. 23, T 7 S, R 22 E). Named on Bass Lake (1953) 15' quadrangle.

Lyell: see **Mount Lyell** [MADERA-TUOLUMNE].

Lyell Canyon [TUOLUMNE]: *canyon,* 9 miles long, opens into Tuolumne Meadows 4.5 miles southwest of Tioga Pass (lat. 37°52'10" N, long. 119°20'15" W); the canyon is along Lyell Fork. Named on Tuolumne Meadows (1956) 15' quadrangle.

Lyell Fork [MADERA]: *stream,* flows 6 miles to join Merced Peak Fork and form Merced River 5.25 miles north-northeast of Merced Peak (lat. 37°42'05" N, long. 119°20'50" W). Named on Merced Peak (1953) 15' quadrangle. United States Board on Geographic Names (1978b, p. 3) rejected the names "Merced River" and "North Fork" for the stream.

Lyell Fork [TUOLUMNE]: *stream,* flows 12 miles to join Dana Fork and form Tuolumne River 5.5 miles west-southwest of Tioga Pass (lat. 37°52'30" N, long. 119°21' W; near SE cor. sec. 5, T 1 S, R 24 E); the stream heads near Mount Lyell and goes through Lyell Canyon. Named on Tuolumne Meadows (1956) 15' quadrangle.

Lyell Glacier [TUOLUMNE]: *glacier,* 11.5 miles south of Tioga Pass (lat. 37°44'35" N, long. 119°16'10" W); the glacier is north of Mount Lyell. Named on Merced Peak (1953) 15' quadrangle.

Lyons: see **Confidence** [TUOLUMNE].

Lyons Creek [TUOLUMNE]: *stream,* flows 4 miles to Lyons Reservoir 5.5 miles northeast of Twain Harte (lat. 38°05'50" N, long. 120°09'35" W; sec. 24, T 3 N, R 16 E). Named on Hull Creek (1979), Strawberry (1979), and Twain Harte (1979) 7.5' quadrangles.

Lyons Gulch [MARIPOSA]: *canyon,* drained by a stream that flows 4 miles to Sherlock Creek nearly 4 miles east-northeast of Bear Valley (2) (lat. 37°35' N, long. 120°03'05" W; sec. 13, T 4 S, R 17 E). Named on Bear Valley (1947) 7.5' quadrangle.

Lyons Reservoir [TUOLUMNE]: *lake,* behind a dam on South Fork Stanislaus River 5 miles northeast of Twain Harte (lat. 38°05'40" N, long. 120°10' W); Lyons Creek joins South Fork Stanislaus River in the lake. Named on Twain Harte (1979) 7.5' quadrangle.

Lyoth [SAN JOAQUIN]: *locality,* 3 miles southeast of Tracy along Western Pacific Railroad (lat. 37°42'55" N, long. 121°22'55" W; near E line sec. 35, T 2 S, R 5 E). Named on Tracy (1954) 7.5' quadrangle. Postal authorities established Lyoth post office in 1912 and discontinued it in 1938; Standard Oil Company had a pumping station at the place, which officials of the company named (Salley, p. 130).

– M –

MacBride: see **Camp MacBride** [TUOLUMNE].

Macks Gulch [CALAVERAS]: *canyon,* drained by a stream that flows 3.5 miles to O'Neil Creek 5.5 miles north of Murphys (lat. 38°13'15" N, long. 120°28'10" W; sec. 7, T 4 N, R 14 E). Named on Murphys (1948) 7.5' quadrangle.

Maclure: see **Mount Maclure** [MADERA-TUOLUMNE].

Maclure Creek [TUOLUMNE]: *stream,* flows 2 miles to Lyell Fork 9.5 miles south of Tioga Pass (lat. 37°46'30" N, long. 119°15'40" W); the stream heads north of Mount Maclure. Named on Tuolumne Meadows (1956) 15' quadrangle. The name is for William Maclure, a pioneer American geologist (United States Board on Geographic Names, 1934, p. 15).

Maclure Fork: see **Lewis Creek** [MADERA-MARIPOSA].

Macnider Switch [CALAVERAS]: *locality,* 1.5 miles west-southwest of San Andreas along Southern Pacific Railroad (lat. 38°11'25" N, long. 120°42'35" W; sec. 24, T 4 N, R 11 E). Named on San Andreas (1947) 15' quadrangle.

Macomb Falls: see **Wapama Falls** [TUOLUMNE].

Macomb Ridge [TUOLUMNE]: *ridge,* southwest-trending, 3.5 miles long, 6 miles south-southwest of Tower Peak (lat. 38°04'10" N, long. 119°36'30" W). Named on Tower Peak (1956) 15' quadrangle. The name commemorates Lieutenant M.M. Macomb, who was in charge of a party of the Wheeler survey in California in 1878 and 1879 (United States Board on Geographic Names, 1934, p. 15).

Madera [MADERA]: *town,* in the southwest-central part of Madera County along Fresno River (lat. 36°57'45" N, long. 120°03'30" W). Named on Madera (1963) 7.5' quadrangle. Postal authorities established Madera post office in 1877 (Frickstad, p. 86), and the town incorporated in 1907. Officials of California Lumber Company had the town laid out in 1876 at the end of a flume that brought lumber 63 miles from the mountains to the railroad—madera means "wood" or "timber" in Spanish (Hoover, Rensch, and Rensch, p. 173).

Madera Creek [MADERA]: *stream,* flows 4 miles to West Fork Granite Creek 6.5 miles southeast of Merced Peak (lat. 37°33'45" N, long. 119°18'50" W); the stream heads near Madera Peak. Named on Merced Peak (1953) 15' quadrangle. United States Board on Geographic Names (1933b, p. 19) rejected the name "Black Peak Fork" for the stream.

Madera Equalization Reservoir [MADERA]: *lake,* 1 mile long, 10 miles south of Raymond (lat. 37°04' N, long. 119°56'15" W; on N line sec. 18, T 10 S, R 19 E). Named on Daulton (1962) 7.5' quadrangle.

Madera Lake [MADERA]: *lake,* 1.5 miles long, 14 miles south-southwest of Raymond near Fresno River (lat. 37°01'20" N, long. 119°59'15" W). Named on Daulton (1962) 7.5' quadrangle.

Madera Lakes [MADERA]: *lakes,* three, largest 1100 feet long, 6.5 miles south-southeast of Merced Peak along Madera Creek (lat. 37°32'40" N, long. 119°21'25" W); the group includes Lady Lake and Vandeburg Lake. Named on Merced Peak (1953) 15' quadrangle.

Madera Peak [MADERA]: *peak,* 6.5 miles south of Merced Peak (lat. 37°32'15" N, long. 119°22'30" W). Altitude 10,509 feet. Named on Merced Peak (1953) 15' quadrangle. Called Black Mt. on Hoffmann and Gardner's (1863-1867) map. Members of the Wheeler survey called the feature Black Peak (Browning, 1986, p. 134), but United States Board on Geographic Names (1933a, p. 487) rejected this name.

Madera Station: see **Storey** [MADERA].

Magnet: see **O'Neals** [MADERA].

Magoon Creek [MARIPOSA]: *stream,* flows 3.5 miles to join Fox Creek and form Middle Fork Chowchilla River 8 miles east of Mariposa (lat. 37°29'10" N, long. 119°49'10" W; sec. 19, T 5 S, R 20 E); the stream is east of Magoon Hill. Named on Buckingham Mountain (1947) and Stumpfield Mountain (1947) 7.5' quadrangles.

Magoon Hill [MARIPOSA]: *peak,* 7 miles east of Mariposa (lat. 37° 29'35" N, long. 119°50'10" W; sec. 13, T 5 S, R 19 E). Named on Stumpfield Mountain (1947) 7.5' quadrangle.

Mahan Lake [TUOLUMNE]: *lake,* 2400 feet long, 9 miles southwest of Tower Peak (lat. 38°03'15" N, long. 119°40' W); the lake is less than 1 mile east-northeast of Mahan Peak. Named on Tower Peak (1956) 15' quadrangle.

Mahan Peak [TUOLUMNE]: *peak,* 10 miles southwest of Tower Peak (lat. 38°03'10" N, long. 119°41'05" W). Altitude 9146 feet. Named on Tower Peak (1956) 15' quadrangle. Browning (1986, p. 135) associated the name with Dennis H. Mahan, professor of military engineering at West Point before the Civil War.

Mahoney Gulch [MARIPOSA]: *canyon,* drained by a stream that flows 1 mile to Blacks Creek 1 mile west of Coulterville (lat. 37° 42'40" N, long. 120°13' W; sec. 4, T 3 S, R 16 E). Named on Coulterville (1947) 7.5' quadrangle.

Main: see **Jack Main Canyon** [TUOLUMNE]; **Jack Main Mountain**, under **Chittenden Peak** [TUOLUMNE].

Main Gulch: see **Columbia** [TUOLUMNE].

Malum Ridge [MADERA]: *ridge,* south-southeast-trending, 5 miles long, 10.5 miles southeast of Yosemite Forks (lat. 37°15' N, long. 119°30'30" W). Named on Bass Lake (1953), Millerton Lake (1965), and Shaver Lake (1953) 15' quadrangles.

Mammoth Cave: see **Mountain Ranch** [CALAVERAS].

Mammoth Crest [MADERA]: *ridge,* extends for 7 miles south-southeast and east from Mammoth Pass on Madera-Mono County line and on Fresno-Mono County line (center near lat. 37°34'15" N, long. 119°00' W). Named on Devils Postpile (1953) 15' quadrangle.

Mammoth Lake [MERCED]: *lake,* 600 feet long, 1.5 miles south-southeast of Pacheco Pass (lat. 37°02'35" N, long. 121°11'30" W). Named on Pacheco Pass (1955) 7.5' quadrangle.

Mammoth Mountain [MADERA]: *peak,* nearly 3 miles east of Devils Postpile on Madera-Mono County line (lat. 37°37'50" N, long. 119°01'55" W); the peak is northwest of Mammoth Lakes, which are in Mono County. Altitude 11,053 feet. Named on Devils Postpile (1953) 15' quadrangle. Called Mammoth Pk. on California Mining Bureau's (1917b) map.

Mammoth Mountain: see **Banner Peak** [MADERA].

Mammoth Pass [MADERA]: *pass,* 3 miles east-southeast of Devils Postpile on Madera-Mono County line (lat. 37°36'35" N, long. 119°01'45" W); the pass is west of Mammoth Lakes, which are in Mono County. Named on Devils Postpile (1953) 15' quadrangle. The pass also is called Pumice Gap (Smith *in* Wright, p. 92).

Mammoth Peak [TUOLUMNE]: *peak,* nearly 4 miles south of Tioga Pass (lat. 37°51'20" N, long. 119°15'45" W). Altitude 12,117 feet. Named on Tuolumne Meadows (1956) 15' quadrangle.

Mammoth Peak: see **Mammoth Mountain** [MADERA].

Mammoth Pool Reservoir [MADERA]: *lake,* 7.5 miles long, behind a dam on San Joaquin River 6.5 miles east-southeast of Shuteye Peak on Madera-Fresno County line (lat. 37°19'25" N, long. 119° 18'55" W; near N line sec. 14, T 7 S, R 24 E. Named on Shuteye Peak (1953) 15' quadrangle.

Mandeville: see **Stockton** [SAN JOAQUIN].

Mandeville Cut [SAN JOAQUIN]: *water feature,* artificial watercourse that cuts off a meander of San Joaquin River 15 miles west-southwest of Lodi (lat. 38°03'25" N, long. 121°32'20" W); the feature is part of Stockton Deep Water Channel on Mandeville Island. Named on Bouldin Island (1978) 7.5' quadrangle. United States Board on Geographic Names (1979, p. 8) approved the name "Singapore Cut" for an artificial watercourse located 0.5 mile north-northeast of Mandeville Cut (lat. 38°03'50" N, long. 121°32'10" W) that connects Mandeville Reach and Venice Reach.

Mandeville Island [SAN JOAQUIN]: *island,* 6 miles long, 16 miles west-southwest of Lodi between San Joaquin River, Middle River, Connection Slough, and Old River (lat. 38°02'15" N, long. 121° 33' W). Named on Bouldin Island (1978) 7.5' quadrangle.

Mandeville Island: see **Little Mandeville Island** [SAN JOAQUIN].

Mandeville Point [SAN JOAQUIN]: *promontory,* 15 miles west-southwest of Lodi along San Joaquin River (lat. 38°04' N, long. 121°32' W); the feature is on the northeast side of Mandeville Island. Named on Bouldin Island (1978) 7.5' quadrangle.

Mandeville Reach [SAN JOAQUIN]: *water feature,* part of San Joaquin River situated 15 miles west-southwest of Lodi (lat. 38°03'20" N, long. 121°32' W); the feature is south of Mandeville Point. Named on Bouldin Island (1978) 7.5' quadrangle.

Manganese: see **Carnegie** [SAN JOAQUIN].

Manley: see **Titus and Manley Ferry**, under **San Joaquin City** [SAN JOAQUIN].

Mann Creek [TUOLUMNE]: *stream,* flows 1.25 miles to South Fork Wildcat Creek 5.25 miles west of Keystone (lat. 37°49'20" N, long. 120°36'05" W; sec. 25, T 1 S, R 12 E). Named on Keystone (1962) 7.5' quadrangle.

Mansion House [SAN JOAQUIN]: *locality,* 15 miles west-southwest of downtown Stockton at the northwest corner of Victoria Island (lat. 37°54'40" N, long. 121°33'35" W). Named on Woodward Island (1952) 7.5' quadrangle.

Manteca [SAN JOAQUIN]: *city,* 11.5 miles south-southeast of downtown Stockton (lat. 37°47'50" N, long. 121°12'55" W; around SE cor. sec. 32, T 1 S, R 7 E). Named on Manteca (1952) 7.5' quadrangle. Postal authorities established Manteca post office in 1908 (Frickstad, p. 161), and the city incorporated in 1918. The railroad station at the place first was called Cowell, for Joshua Cowell, who gave the right of way there to the railroad in 1870; railroad officials gave the name "Manteca" to the place about 1904 or 1905—according to one account, the new name was from a local creamery that had taken its name from *manteca,* which means "butter" or "lard" in Spanish (Gudde, 1949, p. 203). Postal authorities established Mingesdale post office 5 miles northwest of Manteca (SE quarter sec. 15, T 1 S, R 7 E) in 1914 and discontinued it in 1915 (Salley, p. 141).

Manteca: see **West Manteca** [SAN JOAQUIN].

Manteca Junction [SAN JOAQUIN]: *locality,* 4.5 miles north of Manteca along Tidewater Southern Railroad (lat. 37°51'50" N, long. 121°13'40" W, sec. 8, T 1 S, R 7 E). Named on Manteca (1952) 7.5' quadrangle.

Manuel Mill [CALAVERAS]: *locality,* 5.5 miles south of Blue Mountain along San Antonio Creek (lat. 38°15'40" N, long. 120° 21'30" W; sec. 30, T 5 N, R 15 E). Site named on Blue Mountain (1956) 15' quadrangle.

Many Island Lake [TUOLUMNE]: *lake,* 1850 feet long, 12.5 miles southeast of Pinecrest (lat. 38°05' N, long. 119°48'40" W). Named on Pinecrest (1956) 15' quadrangle.

Manzanita Lake [MADERA]: *lake,* behind a dam on North Fork Willow Creek (2) 1.25 miles north-northwest of North Fork (lat. 37°14'40" N, long. 119°30'55" W; sec. 12, T 8 S, R 22 E). Named on Bass Lake (1953) and Millerton Lake (1965) 15' quadrangles.

Marble Gulch [MARIPOSA]: *canyon,* 1.5 miles long, 8 miles northeast of Buckhorn Peak (lat. 37°44'15" N, long. 120°00'40" W). Named on Buckhorn Peak (1947) 7.5' quadrangle.

Marble Mountain [TUOLUMNE]: *peak,* 5.5 miles east of Twain Harte (lat. 38°01'30" N, long. 120°07'40" W; sec. 17, T 2 N, R 17 E). Altitude 5477 feet. Named on Twain Harte (1979) 7.5' quadrangle.

Marble Point [MARIPOSA]: *promontory,* 5 miles southwest of El Portal on the west side of South Fork Merced River (lat. 37°37'15" N, long. 119°50'25" W; on W line sec. 2, T 4 S, R 19 E). Named on Buckingham Mountain (1947) 7.5' quadrangle.

Marguerite [MERCED]: *locality,* 5.5 miles southeast of Le Grand along Atchison, Topeka and Santa Fe Railroad (lat. 37°10'10" N, long. 120°10'10" W; on N line sec. 12, T 9 S, R 16 E). Named on Le Grand (1918) 7.5' quadrangle.

Mariana Gulch [CALAVERAS]: *canyon,* drained by a stream that flows less than 1 mile to Stanislaus River 3.25 miles east of Vallecito (lat. 38°05'05" N, long. 120°24'50" W; near E line sec. 27, T 3 N, R 14 E). Named on Columbia (1948) 7.5' quadrangle.

Marietta: see **Farmington** [SAN JOAQUIN].

Mariposa [MARIPOSA]: *town,* in the west-central part of Mariposa County along Mariposa Creek (lat. 37°29'05" N, long. 119°57'50" W); the town is on Las Mariposas grant. Named on Mariposa (1947) 7.5' quadrangle. Postal authorities established Mariposa post office in 1851 (Frickstad, p. 91). In 1849 the town was situated about 0.5 mile downstream from the present site (Chamberlain, p. 15). Miners who were flooded out of the town in the winter of 1849 and 1850 moved to slightly higher ground and formed a camp called Logtown (Sargent, Shirley, 1976, p. 15). Laizure's (1928) map shows a place called French Camp located 3.5 miles north-northwest of Mariposa (sec. 4, T 5 S, R 18 E).

Mariposa Creek [MARIPOSA-MERCED]: *stream,* heads in Mariposa County and flows 35 miles to Merced County 12.5 miles south-southwest of the settlement of Catheys Valley (lat. 37°16'20" N, long. 120°11' W; near N line sec. 2, T 8 S, R 16 E). Named on Chowchilla (1960) and Le Grand (1961) 15' quadrangles, and on Bear Valley (1947), Catheys Valley (1962), Feliciana Mountain (1947), Illinois Hill (1962), Mariposa (1947), and Owens Reservoir (1962) 7.5' quadrangles. According to Bancroft (1886, p. 52), members of a Spanish expedition applied the name "Mariposas" in the region in 1806 because of the abundance of butterflies there—*mariposas* means "butterflies" in Spanish. Fremont in his memoirs attributed the name to the resemblance of wind-blown poppies to fluttering butterflies (Spence and Jackson, p. 37).

Mariposa Estate: see **Las Mariposas** [MARIPOSA].

Mariposa Peak [MERCED]: *peak,* 21 miles west-southwest of Los Banos on Merced-San Benito County line (lat. 36°57'25" N, long. 121°12'40" W; near S line sec. 21, T 11 S, R 7 E). Altitude 3448 feet. Named on Mariposa Peak (1969) 7.5' quadrangle.

Mariposa Reservoir [MARIPOSA]: *lake,* behind a dam on Mariposa Creek 10.5 miles south-southwest of the settlement of Catheys Valley (lat. 37°17'30" N, long. 120°08'50" W; sec. 30, T 7 S, R 17 E). Named on Illinois Hill (1962) and Owens Reservoir (1962) 7.5' quadrangles.

Mariposa Slough [MERCED]: *stream,* flows 14 miles to San Joaquin River 11 miles north-northeast of Los Banos (lat. 37°12'15" N, long. 120°45'45" W). Named on Sandy Mush (1962), San Luis Ranch (1961), Santa Rita Bridge (1962), and Turner Ranch (1961) 7.5' quadrangles.

Marshs Flat [TUOLUMNE]: *valley,* 1.5 miles south-southwest of Moccasin (lat. 37°47'20" N, long. 120°18'20" W; sec. 3, T 2 S, R 15 E). Named on Moccasin (1948) 7.5' quadrangle. Sonora (1897) 30' quadrangle has the form "Marsh's Flat" for the name.

Martel Creek [CALAVERAS]: *stream,* flows 2 miles to South Fork Mokelumne River nearly 2 miles east-southeast of Blue Mountain (lat. 38°19'40" N, long. 120°20'05" W; sec. 33, T 6 N, R 15 E). Named on Dorrington (1979) 7.5' quadrangle.

Martells Creek [CALAVERAS-STANISLAUS]: *stream,* heads in Calaveras County and flows 12 miles to Littlejohns Creek 8 miles north-northeast of Oakdale in Stanislaus County (lat. 37°52'25" N, long. 120°47'45" W). Named on Copperopolis (1962), Knights Ferry (1962), and Oakdale (1968) 7.5' quadrangles.

Martin Creek [STANISLAUS]: *stream,* flows 2.5 miles to lowlands 11.5 miles northwest of Patterson (lat. 37°33'55" N, long. 121°18'20" W; at N line sec. 28, T 4 S, R 6 E). Named on Solyo (1953) 7.5' quadrangle.

Martinez [TUOLUMNE]: *locality,* 1.5 miles southeast of Columbia (lat. 38°01'25" N, long. 120°22'45" W; near SE cor. sec. 13, T 2 N, R 14 E). Named on Columbia (1948) 7.5' quadrangle. The place was known as Spanish Camp in 1850, but later it was called Martinez to honor the first female resident there (Stoddart, p. 144).

Martin Gulch [CALAVERAS]: *canyon,* drained by a stream that flows 2 miles to McKinney Creek 9.5 miles east of San Andreas (lat. 38°12'15" N, long. 120°30'25" W; sec. 14, T 4 N, R 13 E). Named on Calaveritas (1962) and Murphys (1948) 7.5' quadrangles.

Martins Cow Camp [TUOLUMNE]: *locality,* 3.5 miles south of Dardanelle (lat. 38°17'20" N, long. 119°50' W; sec. 13, T 5 N, R 19 E). Named on Dardanelle (1979) 7.5' quadrangle. Browning (1986, p. 138) related the name to Joe Martin, who had the cattle permit in Eagle Meadow in the 1850's.

Mary Lake [TUOLUMNE]: *lake,* 2900 feet long, 0.5 mile west of Tower Peak (lat. 38°08'40" N, long. 119°33'40" W). Named on Tower Peak (1956) 15' quadrangle. The name commemorates Mary Forsyth, daughter of Colonel W.W. Forsyth, acting superintendent of Yosemite National Park from 1909 until 1912 (Browning, 1988, p. 86).

Mast [MARIPOSA]: *locality,* 3.5 miles south-southwest of Coulterville along Yosemite Valley Railroad (lat. 37°40' N, long. 120°13'25" W). Named on Sonora (1897) 30' quadrangle. Water of Lake McClure now covers the site.

Matelot Gulch [TUOLUMNE]: *canyon,* 1 mile long, opens into lowlands at Columbia (lat. 38°02'20" N, long. 120°24' W; sec. 11, T 2 N, R 14 E). Named on Columbia (1948) 7.5' quadrangle. Stoddart (p. 127) referred to Matelot or Sailor's gulch.

Matelot Reservoir [TUOLUMNE]: *lake,* 350 feet long, 1.25 miles north-northeast of Columbia (lat. 38°03'05" N, long. 120°23'35" W; sec. 1, T 2 N, R 14 E); the lake is at the head of Matelot Gulch. Named on Columbia (1948) 7.5' quadrangle.

Mather [TUOLUMNE]: *village,* 33 miles west of Tioga Pass (lat. 37° 53' N, long. 119°51'20" W; sec. 2, T 1 S, R 19 E). Named on Lake Eleanor (1956) 15' quadrangle. Called Mather Sta. on Yosemite (1909) 30' quadrangle, where it is shown at the end of Hetch Hetchy Railroad. Postal authorities established Mather post office in 1921 (Frickstad, p. 216). The name is for Stephen Tyng Mather, director of the National Park Service from 1917 until 1929 (Hanna, p. 187). Hoffmann and Gardner's (1863-1867) map shows a place called Hog Ranch located at or near present Mather—an early sheepman drew a picture of a sheep on a rock there, but because the drawing looked more like a hog than a sheep, the place became known as Hog Ranch (Browning, 1986, p. 138-139). Hetch Hetchy post office, located 9 miles northeast of Mather at the construction camp for the dam that forms Hetch Hetchy Reservoir, was established in 1921, discontinued in 1923, reestablished in 1935, and discontinued in 1937 (Salley, p. 96).

Mather Station: see **Mather** [TUOLUMNE].

Matterhorn Canyon [TUOLUMNE]: *canyon,* drained by a stream that flows 9 miles to Regulation Creek 11 miles west-northwest of Tioga Pass (lat. 37°58'15" N, long. 119°26'50" W); the canyon heads near Matterhorn Peak. Named on Matterhorn Peak (1956) and Tuolumne Meadows (1956) 15' quadrangles.

Matterhorn Peak [TUOLUMNE]: *peak,* 21 miles southeast of Sonora Pass on Tuolumne-Mono County line (lat. 38°05'30" N, long. 119° 22'50" W). Altitude 12,264 feet. Named on Matterhorn Peak (1956) 15' quadrangle. Members of the Wheeler survey named the feature in 1878 (Browning, 1986, p. 139).

Matthes Crest [MARIPOSA]: *ridge,* south-southwest-trending, 2 miles long, 1.5 miles south-southeast of Cathedral Peak (lat. 37°49'20" N, long. 119°23'50" W). Named on Tuolumne Meadows (1956) 15' quadrangle. The name commemorates François Matthes of United States Geological Survey (O'Neill, p. 96).

Matthes Dome: see **Pywiak Dome** [MARIPOSA].

Matthes Lake [MARIPOSA]: *lake,* 900 feet long, 2.5 miles south of Cathedral Peak (lat. 37°48'35" N, long. 119°23'50" W; near S line sec. 25, T 1 S, R 23 E). Named on Tuolumne Meadows (1956) 15' quadrangle.

Mattie Lake [TUOLUMNE]: *lake,* 1250 feet long, 10 miles west of Tioga Pass (lat. 37°56' N, long. 119°26'20" W). Named on Tuolumne Meadows (1956) 15' quadrangle.

Mattley [CALAVERAS]: *locality,* 4.5 miles west-northwest of present Tamarack along Moore Creek (lat. 38°27'45" N, long. 120° 09'20" W). Named on Big Trees (1891) 30' quadrangle.

Mattley Creek [CALAVERAS]: *stream,* flows 3.25 miles to North Fork Mokelumne River 5.25 miles northwest of Tamarack (lat. 38° 29'50" N, long. 120°08'10" W); the stream is near Mattley Meadow. Named on Calaveras Dome (1979) and Tamarack (1979) 7.5' quadrangles.

Mattley Meadow [CALAVERAS]: *area,* 3 miles northwest of Tamarack (lat. 38°27'45" N, long. 120°07'30" W; sec. 17, T 7 N, R 17 E); the place is along a branch of Mattley Creek. Named on Calaveras Dome (1979) and Tamarack (1979) 7.5' quadrangles. Big Meadow (1956) 15' quadrangle shows Mattley cabin located 1.25 miles west of Mattley Meadow.

Maxwell Creek [CALAVERAS]: *stream,* flows 3.5 miles to Bear Creek (4) 7 miles west of Angels Camp (lat. 38°05'30" N, long. 120°40'05" W; near NE cor. sec. 29, T 3 N, R 12 E). Named on Salt Spring Valley (1962) 7.5' quadrangle.

Maxwell Creek [MARIPOSA]: *stream,* flows 11.5 miles to Lake McClure 2 miles west-southwest of Coulterville (lat. 37°41'55" N, long. 120°13'40" W; near S line sec. 5, T 3 S, R 16 E). Named on Buckhorn Peak (1947) and Coulterville (1947, photorevised 1973) 7.5' quadrangles. The name commemorates George Maxwell, an early settler at Coulterville (Hanna, p. 75).

Maxwell Lake [TUOLUMNE]: *lake,* 2100 feet long, 7 miles west of Tower Peak (lat. 38°09'30" N, long. 119°40'20" W; on S line sec. 28, T 4 N, R 21 E). Named on Tower Peak (1956) 15' quadrangle. Called Helen Lake on Dardanelles (1898, reprinted 1947) 30' quadrangle, but United States Board on Geographic Names (1960b, p. 18) rejected the names "Helen Lake" and "Lake Helen" for the feature.

Maxwell's Creek: see **Coulterville** [MARIPOSA].

May Lake [MARIPOSA]: *lake,* 2100 feet long, nearly 5 miles west of Cathedral Peak (lat. 37°50'50" N, long. 119°29'30" W; on W line sec. 18, T 1 S, R 23 E). Named on Tuolumne Meadows (1956) 15' quadrangle. Charles F. Hoffmann of the Whitney survey named the peak for Lucy Mayotta Browne, daughter of J. Ross Browne (United States Board on Geographic Names, 1934, p. 16).

May Lake High Sierra Camp [MARIPOSA]: *locality,* 4.5 miles west of Cathedral Peak (lat. 37°50'40" N, long. 119°29'20" W; sec. 18, T 1 S, R 23 E); the place is on the east shore of May Lake. Named on Tuolumne Meadows (1956) 15' quadrangle.

May Rock [MARIPOSA]: *relief feature,* 2 miles southeast of the village of Bear Valley (lat. 37°32'40" N, long. 120°05'50" W). Named on Bear Valley (1947) 7.5' quadrangle. Jessie Fremont named the feature in remembrance of a picnic held there in the month of May (Sargent, Shirley, 1976, p. 16).

McAfee Gulch [CALAVERAS]: *canyon,* drained by a stream that flows less than 1 mile to Pardee Reservoir 3 miles west-northwest of Paloma (lat. 38°16'10" N, long. 120°49' W; near E line sec. 24, T 5 N, R 10 E). Named on Jackson (1962) 7.5' quadrangle.

McAlpine: see **Chinese Camp** [TUOLUMNE].

McBrides Gulch [MARIPOSA]: *canyon,* drained by a stream that flows 1 mile to Carson Creek 5.5 miles northeast of the settlement of Catheys Valley (lat. 37°28'50" N, long. 120°00'40" W). Named on Catheys Valley (1962) 7.5' quadrangle. Laizure's (1928) map has the form "McBride's Gulch" for the name. The stream in the canyon is called Carson Creek on Indian Gulch (1920) 15' quadrangle. United States Board on Geographic Names (1964a, p. 11) rejected the name "Carson Gulch" for the canyon.

McCabe Creek [TUOLUMNE]: *stream,* flows 3.5 miles to Return Creek 6 miles south of Matterhorn Peak (lat. 38°00'20" N, long. 119°22'35" W). Named on Matterhorn Peak (1956) 15' quadrangle. The stream also was called East Fork [Return Creek] (Browning, 1988, p. 89).

McCabe Flat [MARIPOSA]: *area,* 6.5 miles east-northeast of the village of Bear Valley along Merced River (lat. 37°35'50" N, long. 120°00'10" W; sec. 8, T 4 S, R 18 E). Named on Bear Valley (1947) 7.5' quadrangle. On Sonora (1891) 30' quadrangle, the name "McCabe Flat" applies to a place situated about 2 miles farther northwest along Merced River.

McCabe Lake: see **Upper McCabe Lake** [TUOLUMNE].

McCabe Lakes [TUOLUMNE]: *lakes,* largest 1900 feet long, 7 miles northwest of Tioga Pass (lat. 37°59'30" N, long. 119°20'30" W). Named on Tuolumne Meadows (1956) 15' quadrangle. The name is for Edward R.W. McCabe, son-in-law of Colonel W.W. Forsyth, acting superintendent of Yosemite National Park from 1909 until 1912 (Browning, 1986, p. 141).

McCarthy Creek: see **McCarty Creek** [CALAVERAS].

McCarty Creek [CALAVERAS]: *stream,* flows 7 miles to Littlejohns Creek 2.5 miles south-southwest of Copperopolis (lat. 37°56'50" N, long. 120°39'45" W; sec. 9, T 1 N, R 12 E). Named on Copperopolis (1962) and Salt Spring Valley (1962) 7.5' quadrangles. Called McCarthy Creek on Copperopolis (1916) 15' quadrangle, but United States Board on Geographic Names (1963b, p. 14) rejected this designation for the stream.

McCarty Reservoir: see **Calaveras Reservoir** [CALAVERAS].

McCauley: see **Foresta** [MARIPOSA].

McCauley Hill [MARIPOSA]: *peak,* 12.5 miles west-northwest of El Portal (lat. 37°44'15" N, long. 119°59'30" W; sec. 28, T 2 S, R 18 E). Named on Kinsley (1947) 7.5' quadrangle, which has the designation "McCauley Ranch (Old Stage Station)" for a place located 0.5 mile north of the peak.

McCauley Ranch: see **McCauley Hill** [MARIPOSA].

McCleod Flat [MADERA]: *area,* 4 miles east of Yosemite Forks along North Fork Willow Creek (2) (lat. 37°21'20" N, long. 119° 33'25" W; near NW cor. sec. 3, T 7 S, R 22 E). Named on Bass Lake (1953) 15' quadrangle. United States Board on Geographic Names (1990, p. 9) approved the name "McLeod Flat" for the feature, and noted that the name is for Malcolm McLeod, district ranger for Fresno Flats in 1911.

Mc. Cloud's Lake: see **McLeod Lake** [SAN JOAQUIN].

McClure: see **Lake McClure** [MARIPOSA]; **Mount McClure**, under **Mount Maclure** [MADERA-TUOLUMNE].

McClure Lake [MADERA]: *lake,* 1100 feet long, 4.5 miles east of Merced Peak (lat. 37°38'30" N, long. 119°18'50" W). Named on Merced Peak (1953) 15' quadrangle. The name commemorates Lieutenant N.F. McClure, who was stationed in Yosemite National Park in 1894 and 1895 (Farquhar, 1924, p. 57).

Mc. Cormick: see **McCormick Meadows** [TUOLUMNE].

McCormick Creek [TUOLUMNE]:

(1) *stream,* flows 2.5 miles to Griswold Creek 4 miles northeast of Stanislaus (lat. 38°10'55" N, long. 120°19'30" W; sec. 21, T 4 N, R 15 E); the stream heads near McCormick Meadows. Named on Stanislaus (1948) 7.5' quadrangle.

(2) *stream,* heads in Alpine County and flows 5 miles to Middle Fork Stanislaus River 3.5 miles west-northwest of Dardanelle (lat. 38°21'30" N, long. 119°53'45" W). Named on Donnell Lake (1979) and Spicer Meadow Reservoir (1979) 7.5' quadrangles. The name commemorates an early settler (Browning, 1986, p. 141).

McCormick Meadows [TUOLUMNE]: *locality,* 5.5 miles northeast of Stanislaus (lat. 38°11'30" N, long. 120°17'20" W). Named on Stanislaus (1948) 7.5' quadrangle. Big Trees (1891) 30' quadrangle has the name "Mc. Cormick" at the place.

McCormick Pocket [TUOLUMNE]: *relief feature,* 5.5 miles south of Dardanelle (lat. 38°15'35" N, long. 119°50'45" W; near E line sec. 26, T 5 N, R 19 E). Named on Dardanelle (1979) 7.5' quadrangle.

McCormick Reservoir: see **Old McCormick Reservoir** [CALAVERAS].

McCreary Meadow [MADERA]: *area,* 13 miles northeast of Shuteye Peak (lat. 37°29'25" N, long. 119°16'20" W; sec. 18, T 5 S, R 25 E). Named on Shuteye Peak (1953) 15' quadrangle.

McDermott's Bridge: see **Mokelumne River** [CALAVERAS-SAN JOAQUIN].

McDermott's Tavern: see **Le Grand** [MERCED].

McDonald Creek [STANISLAUS]: *stream,* flows 1 mile from Beltz Lake to Evans Creek nearly 1 mile south of La Grange (lat. 37° 39'10" N, long. 120°27'25" W; near S line sec. 20, T 3 S, R 14 E). Named on La Grange (1962) 7.5' quadrangle.

McDonald Island [SAN JOAQUIN]: *island,* 4 miles long, 10 miles west-northwest of downtown Stockton between San Joaquin River, Empire Cut, Middle River, Columbia Cut, Latham Slough, and Turner Cut (lat. 38°00' N, long. 121°28'30" W). Named on Bouldin Island (1978), Holt (1978), Terminous (1978), and Woodward Island (1978) 7.5' quadrangles. The island is called McDonald Tract on Bouldin Island (1952) and Terminous (1952) 7.5' quadrangles. Headreach (1910) and Woodward Island (1913) 7.5' quadrangles show it as marsh that is part of Roberts Island. United

States Board on Geographic Names (1977c, p. 3) gave the names "Henning Island" and "Roberts Island" as variants.

McDonald Island Ferry [SAN JOAQUIN]: *locality,* 10 miles west of downtown Stockton on Turner Cut between McDonald Island and Roberts Island (lat. 37°58'45" N, long. 121°28'25" W). Named on Holt (1978) 7.5' quadrangle.

McDonald Tract: see **McDonald Island** [SAN JOAQUIN].

McDowell Spring [STANISLAUS]: *spring,* 1.25 miles south-southeast of Crevison Peak along Quinto Creek (lat. 37°10'25" N, long. 121°10'55" W; near NE cor. sec. 10, T 9 S, R 7 E). Named on Crevison Peak (1955) 7.5' quadrangle.

McGee Lake [MADERA]: *lake,* 550 feet long, 5.5 miles east-northeast of Merced Peak (lat. 37°39'15" N, long. 119°18' W). Named on Merced Peak (1953) 15' quadrangle.

McGee Lake [TUOLUMNE]: *lake,* 1400 feet long, 9.5 miles west of Tioga Pass (lat. 37°54'10" N, long. 119°25'45" W). Named on Tuolumne Meadows (1956) 15' quadrangle.

McGill: see **Turlock** [STANISLAUS].

McGill Creek: see **Miguel Creek** [TUOLUMNE].

McGill Meadow: see **Miguel Meadow** [TUOLUMNE].

McGurk Meadow [MARIPOSA]: *area,* 5.25 miles south-southwest of Yosemite Village (lat. 37°40'50" N, long. 119°37'45" W; at SW cor. sec. 12, T 3 S, R 21 E). Named on Yosemite (1956) 15' quadrangle. The name commemorates John J. McGurk, who lived at the place in the 1890's (Uhte, p. 55).

McHenry [STANISLAUS]: *locality,* 4.5 miles north of downtown Modesto along Tidewater Southern Railroad (lat. 37°42'25" N, long. 121°00'10" W; sec. 5, T 3 S, R 9 E). Named on Salida (1969) 7.5' quadrangle. California Division of Highways' (1934) map shows a place called Bare located 1 mile south of McHenry along the railroad (near N line sec. 8, T 3 S, R 9 E).

McKay [CALAVERAS]: *locality,* 11.5 miles northeast of Murphys (lat. 38°14'50" N, long. 120°18'20" W; sec. 34, T 5 N, R 15 E). Named on Stanislaus (1948) 7.5' quadrangle.

McKays Point [CALAVERAS]: *relief feature,* 11.5 miles northeast of Murphys (lat. 38°14'40" N, long. 120°17'35" W; sec. 35, T 5 N, R 15 E); the feature is 0.5 mile east-southeast of McKay above North Fork Stanislaus River. Named on Stanislaus (1948) 7.5' quadrangle.

McKee Hill [TUOLUMNE]: *peak,* 6.5 miles south of Liberty Hill (lat. 38°16'25" N, long. 120°07' W; sec. 20, T 5 N, R 17 E). Altitude 6363 feet. Named on Liberty Hill (1979) 7.5' quadrangle.

McKinney Creek [CALAVERAS]: *stream,* flows 6.25 miles to join O'Neil Creek and form Calaveritas Creek 8.5 miles east of San Andreas (lat. 38°11' N, long. 120°31'15" W; near E line sec. 22, T 4 N, R 13 E). Named on Calaveritas (1962) and Murphys (1948) 7.5' quadrangles. Called McKinneys Creek on Jackson (1902) 30' quadrangle. Gudde (1975, p. 202) noted that a mining camp of the early 1850's located along McKinney Creek 9 miles east of San Andreas was called McKinneys Secret Diggings, McKinneys Humbug, or McKinneys.

McKinneys: see **McKinney Creek** [CALAVERAS].

McKinneys Humbug: see **McKinney Creek** [CALAVERAS].

McKinneys Secret Diggings: see **McKinney Creek** [CALAVERAS].

McLeans Bar: see **Melones** [CALAVERAS].

McLeans Ferry: see **Melones** [CALAVERAS].

McLean's Pass: see **Tioga Pass** [TUOLUMNE].

McLeod Flat: see **McCleod Flat** [MADERA].

McLeod Lake [SAN JOAQUIN]: *water feature,* connected to the head of Stockton Deep Water Channel in downtown Stockton (lat. 38°57'25" N, long. 121°17'35" W). Named on Stockton West (1952) 7.5' quadrangle. Called Mc. Cloud's Lake on Hammond's (1849) map, which has the name "Fremont's Channel" for a water feature extending inland northeast from the lake.

McNeal: see **Modesto** [STANISLAUS].

McNulty Ridge [MARIPOSA-TUOLUMNE]: *ridge,* west-northwest-trending, 1 mile long, 2.5 miles south-southeast of Don Pedro Camp on Mariposa-Tuolumne County line (lat. 37°41'05" N, long. 120°23'05" W). Named on La Grange (1962) 7.5' quadrangle.

McNulty Spring [TUOLUMNE]: *spring,* 2 miles south of Don Pedro Camp (lat. 37°41'05" N, long. 120°24'20" W; near W line sec. 11, T 3 N, R 14 E). Named on La Grange (1962) 7.5' quadrangle.

McSwain Meadows [TUOLUMNE]: *area,* 1.25 miles southeast of White Wolf (lat. 37°51'20" N, long. 119°38' W; sec. 14, T 1 S, R 21 E). Named on Hetch Hetchy Reservoir (1956) 15' quadrangle.

Meadow Brook [MARIPOSA]: *stream,* flows 2 miles to Yosemite Valley 5 miles west-southwest of Yosemite Village (lat. 37°42'50" N, long. 119°40' W). Named on Yosemite (1956) 15' quadrangle.

Meadowview Campground [TUOLUMNE]: *locality,* less than 1 mile south-southeast of Strawberry (lat. 38°11'10" N, long. 120°00'15" W; sec. 21, T 4 N, R 18 E). Named on Strawberry (1979) 7.5' quadrangle.

Medal: see **Tracy** [SAN JOAQUIN].

Medano [MADERA]: *locality,* 4.5 miles north-northeast of Fairmead (lat. 37°07'50" N, long. 120°09'10" W; sec. 19, T 9 S, R 17 E). Named on Le Grand (1918) 7.5' quadrangle.

Medford Island [SAN JOAQUIN]: *island,* 2 miles long, 15 miles west-southwest of Lodi between San Joaquin River, Whiskey Slough, Columbia Cut, and Middle River (lat. 38°02'15" N, long. 121°30'45" W). Named on Bouldin Island (1978) and Terminous (1978) 7.5' quadrangles. Bouldin (1910) 7.5' quadrangle shows the feature as part of Roberts Island.

Media: see **Bates Station** [MADERA].

Medlicott Dome [MARIPOSA]: *peak,* 1.25 miles west-northwest of Cathedral Peak (lat. 37°51'20" N, long. 119°25'30" W; near NE cor. sec. 15, T 1 S, R 23 E). Named on Tuolumne Meadows (1956) 15' quadrangle. The name commemorates Harry P. Medlicott, who helped survey the Tioga Road in 1882; the feature also had the names "Court House Rock" and "Mount Medlicott" (Browning, 1988, p. 91).

Meentzen Gulch [TUOLUMNE]: *canyon,* drained by a stream that flows 0.5 mile to Sawmill Gulch 2.25 miles southeast of Columbia (lat. 38°01' N, long. 120°22'15" W; sec. 19, T 2 N, R 15 E). Named on Columbia SE (1948) 7.5' quadrangle.

Meinecke: see **Stanislaus River** [CALAVERAS-SAN JOAQUIN-STANISLAUS-TUOLUMNE].

Melones [CALAVERAS]: *settlement,* 5.25 miles south-southwest of Vallecito on the north side of Stanislaus River (lat. 38°00'40" N, long. 120°29'45" W; sec. 24, T 2 N, R 13 E). Named on Columbia (1948) 7.5' quadrangle. Called Robinson on Big Trees (1891) 30' quadrangle. The first community to have the name "Melones" was the present village of Carson Hill, which was situated about 2 miles west of present Melones on the west slope of Carson Hill (1); present Melones is at the site of Robinsons Ferry, where John W. Robinson and Stephen Mead settled in 1848, and later operated a ferry (Hanna, p. 189). Postal authorities established Robinson's Ferry post office in 1879, changed the name to Robinson's in 1895, changed it to Melones in 1902, discontinued it in 1932, reestablished it in 1933, and discontinued it in 1942 (Salley, p. 137, 187). Gudde (1975, p. 202) listed McLeans Bar and McLeans Ferry, both located about 1 mile upstream from Robinsons Ferry near the confluence of Coyote Creek and Stanislaus River. Wood (p. 24) noted a place called El Dorado Bar that was situated between McLeans Ferry and Coyote Creek.

Melones Lake: see **New Melones Lake** [CALAVERAS-TUOLUMNE].

Melones Reservoir: see **New Melones Lake** [CALAVERAS-TUOLUMNE].

Mendota Pool [MADERA]: *water feature,* behind a dam on San Joaquin River 21 miles south west of Madera on Madera-Fresno County line (lat. 36°47'15" N, long. 120°22'15" W; sec. 19, T 13 S, R 15 E). Named on Mendota Dam (1956) 7.5' quadrangle.

Menjoulet Canyon: see **Los Banos Creek** [MERCED].

Merced [MERCED]: *city,* in northeast-central part of Merced County (lat. 37°18'10" N, long. 120°29' W). Named on Atwater (1961) and Merced (1962) 15' quadrangles. Postal authorities established Merced post office in 1870 (Salley, p. 138), and the city incorporated in 1889. Grunsky's (1899) map shows a place called Chester located on the east side of San Joaquin River 17 miles southwest of Merced. Postal authorities established Chester post office in 1880 and discontinued it in 1886; the place also was known as Dickinson (Salley, p. 42). They established Bear Creek post office in 1871 and discontinued it in 1872, when they moved it 1 mile southwest and consolidated it with Merced post office (Salley, p. 17). They established Brickville post office 2 miles west of Merced in 1870 and discontinued it in 1871; the name was from brick manufacturing plants at the site (Salley, p. 26).

Merced Colonies Number 1 and **Number 2**: see **Winton** [MERCED].

Mercedes River: see **Merced River** [MADERA-MARIPOSA-MERCED].

Merced Falls [MERCED]: *locality,* 6 miles east of Snelling on the north side of Merced River (lat. 37°31'25" N, long. 120°19'45" W; sec. 4, T 5 S, R 15 E). Named on Merced Falls (1962) 7.5' quadrangle. Postal authorities established Merced Falls post office in 1856 and discontinued it in 1957 (Salley, p. 138). The principal crossings of Merced River on the old Stockton to Fort Miller road in the early days were called Murray's Ferry, Young's Ferry, and Phillips' Ferry; all three river crossings were situated within 2 miles downstream from Merced Falls (Hoover, Rensch, and Rensch, p. 206).

Merced Gorge [MARIPOSA]: *canyon,* 4 miles long, along Merced River above a point about 10 miles west-southwest of Yosemite Village (lat. 37°40'30" N, long. 119°44'30" W). Named on Yosemite (1956) 15' quadrangle.

Merced Group: see **Clark Range** [MADERA].

Merced Lake [MARIPOSA]: *lake,* 2500 feet long, 7.5 miles south of Cathedral Peak (lat. 37°44'20" N, long. 119°24'45" W); the lake is along Merced River. Named on Merced Peak (1953) 15' quadrangle. John Muir called the feature Shadow Lake (Browning, 1986, p. 144).

Merced Pass [MADERA]: *pass,* 3 miles west-southwest of Merced Peak (lat. 37°37' N, long. 119°26'30" W). Named on Merced Peak (1953) 15' quadrangle.

Merced Pass Lake: see **Lower Merced Pass Lake** [MADERA]; **Upper Merced Pass Lake** [MADERA].

Merced Peak [MADERA]: *peak,* 22 miles north-northeast of Yosemite Forks (lat. 37°38'05" N, long. 119°23'35" W); the peak is near the headwaters of Merced River. Altitude 11,726 feet. Named on Merced Peak (1953) 15' quadrangle. United States Board on Geographic Names (1976b, p. 1-2) approved the name "Mount Bruce" for a peak (altitude 9728 feet) located 6 miles southwest of Merced Peak (lat. 37°35'48" N, long. 119°29'32" W); the name commemorates the Bruce family, pioneers in the region in the 1850's.

Merced Peak Fork [MADERA]: *stream,* flows 6 miles to join Lyell Fork and form Merced River 5.25 miles north-northeast of Merced Peak (lat. 37°42'05" N, long. 119°20'50" W); the stream heads north of Merced Peak. Named on Merced Peak (1953) 15' quadrangle.

Merced Reservoir: see **Yosemite Lake** [MERCED].

Merced River [MADERA-MARIPOSA-MERCED]: *stream,* formed in Madera County by the confluence of Lyell Fork and Merced Peak Fork, flows 140 miles, partly in Mariposa County, to San Joaquin River 27 miles west of Merced in Merced County (lat. 37°20'55" N, long. 120°58'30" W; near W line sec. 3, T 7 S, R 9 E). Named on Atwater (1961), Coulterville (1947), El Portal (1947), Merced (1962), Merced Falls (1962), Merced Peak (1953), Turlock (1962), and Yosemite (1956) 15' quadrangles. Called Rio de los Merced on Ord's (1848) map, R. de la Merced on Wyld's (1849) map, and Mercedes River on Ellis' (1850) map. United States, Board on Geographic Names (1978b, p. 3) rejected the names "Aux-um-ne," "Aux-um-nes," "Rio de la Merced," "Wa-kal-la," and "El Rio de Nuestra Senora de la Merced" for the stream, and pointed out that Spanish explorers under Sergeant Gabriel Moraga named the river on September 29, 1806, five days after the feast day of Our Lady of Mercy—*merced* means "mercy" in Spanish. North Fork enters the main stream from the north 4.5 miles northeast of the village of Bear Valley in Mariposa County; it is 18 miles long and is named on Coulterville (1947), Lake Eleanor (1956), and Tuolumne (1948) 15' quadrangles. South Fork heads in Madera County and enters the main stream from the southeast 6 miles west-southwest of El Portal in Mariposa County; it is 43 miles long and is named on El Portal (1947), Merced Peak (1953), and Yosemite (1956) 15' quadrangles. United States Board on Geographic Names (1978b, p. 3) rejected the name "North Fork Merced River" for Lyell Fork. Gardiner (p. 139) noted a place called New York Camp that was started in Mariposa County near the mouth of Merced River in 1850.

Merced River: see **Lyell Fork** [MADERA].

Mercer Cave [CALAVERAS]: *cave,* 1 mile northwest of Murphys (lat. 38°09'05" N, long. 120°28'35" W; sec. 31, T 4 N, R 14 E). Named on Murphys (1948) 7.5' quadrangle.

Mercer Mountain [MADERA]: *peak,* 1 mile east of O'Neals (lat. 37° 07'40" N, long. 119°40'40" W; near SE cor. sec. 21, T 9 S, R 21 E). Altitude 1921 feet. Named on O'Neals (1965) 7.5' quadrangle.

Mercur Peak [TUOLUMNE]: *peak,* 12 miles southeast of Pinecrest (lat. 38°05'45" N, long. 119°48'50" W). Named on Pinecrest (1956) 15' quadrangle. Colonel W.W. Forsyth named the peak in 1912 for James Mercur, professor of engineering at West Point (United States Board on Geographic Names, 1934, p. 16).

Merrill Spring [TUOLUMNE]: *spring,* 1.25 miles east-northeast of Long Barn (lat. 38°05'45" N, long. 120°06'55" W; sec. 21, T 3 N, R 17 E). Named on Hull Creek (1979) 7.5' quadrangle.

Merry Oaks: see **French Camp** [SAN JOAQUIN].

Metcalf Gap [MADERA]: *pass,* 15 miles north-northeast of Raymond (lat. 37°24'15" N, long. 119°45'55" W; sec, 15, T 6 S, R 20 E). Named on Stumpfield Mountain (1947) 7.5' quadrangle.

Mexican Flat: see **Jamestown** [TUOLUMNE].

Mexican Gulch [CALAVERAS]: *canyon,* drained by a stream that flows 2.5 miles to Jesus Maria Creek nearly 7 miles south-southwest of Rail Road Flat (lat. 38°15'30" N, long. 120°34'20" W; near W line sec. 29, T 5 N, R 13 E). Named on Calaveritas (1962) and Rail Road Flat (1948) 7.5' quadrangles.

Mexican Gulch [TUOLUMNE]: *canyon,* drained by a stream that flows 1 mile to Tuolumne River 1.25 miles southwest of Don Pedro Camp (lat. 37°42'10" N, long. 120°25'15" W; sec. 3, T 3 S, R 14 E). Named on La Grange (1962) 7.5' quadrangle. On Merced Falls (1944) 15' quadrangle, the name applies to a nearby canyon (sec. 34, T 2 S, R 14 E).

Meyers [SAN JOAQUIN]: *locality,* 12 miles east-southeast of Manteca along Tidewater Southern Railroad (lat. 37°45'35" N, long. 121°00'05" W; sec. 17, T 2 S, R 9 E). Named on Avena (1952) 7.5' quadrangle.

Miami [MARIPOSA]: *locality,* 5 miles west of Happy Camp (present Fish Camp) (lat. 37°28'35" N, long. 119°43'30" W; near SE cor. sec. 24, T 5 S, R 20 E). Named on Mariposa (1912) 30' quadrangle. Postal authorities established Miami post office in 1894, moved it 3 miles north in 1898, and discontinued it in 1926; the name is from Miami Mountain (Salley, p. 139). California Division of Highways' (1934) map shows a place called Oakvale Retreat located 3 miles south-southeast of Miami.

Miami: see **Grub Gulch** [MADERA] (2).

Miami Creek [MADERA-MARIPOSA]: *stream,* heads in Mariposa County and flows 17 miles to Fresno River 5.5 miles west-southwest of Yosemite Forks in Mariposa County (lat. 37°20'30" N, long. 119°43'40" W; near NE cor. sec. 12, T 7 S, R 20 E). Named on Bass Lake (1953) 15' quadrangle. Called North Fork on Mariposa (1912) 30' quadrangle, but United States Board on Geographic Names (1964b, p. 13) rejected the name "North Fork Fresno River" for the stream.

Miami Mill: see **Old Miami Mill**, under **Timberloft Camp** [MARIPOSA].

Miami Mountain [MARIPOSA]: *peak,* 7 miles southwest of Fish Camp (lat. 37°25'10" N, long. 120°44'40" W; near SE cor. sec. 11, T 6 S, R 20 E). Altitude 4327 feet. Named on Bass Lake (1953) and Mariposa (1947) 15' quadrangles.

Michaels: see **Coarsegold** [MADERA].

Michie Peak [TUOLUMNE]: *peak,* 6 miles west-southwest of Tower Peak (lat. 38°07'25" N, long. 119°39'15" W). Altitude 10,365 feet. Named on Tower Peak (1956) 15' quadrangle. Colonel W.W. Forsyth named the peak for Peter Smith Michie, professor of engineering at West Point (Hanna, p. 191).

Middle Bar [CALAVERAS]: *locality,* 2.25 miles west of Mokelumne Hill along Mokelumne River (lat. 38°17'55" N, long. 120°44'50" W; sec. 10, T 5 N, R 11 E). Site named on Mokelumne Hill (1948) 7.5' quadrangle. Camp's (1962) map has the name "Jackass Gulch" for a canyon that opens into the canyon of Mokelumne River near Middle Bar.

Middle Branigan Lake [TUOLUMNE]: *lake,* 3000 feet long, 10.5 miles southwest of Tower Peak (lat. 38°01'55" N, long. 119°40'40" W); the feature is between Branigan Lake and Upper Branigan Lake. Named on Tower Peak (1956) 15' quadrangle.

Middle Brother [MARIPOSA]: *relief feature,* 1.5 miles west-southwest of Yosemite Village on the north side of Yosemite Valley (lat. 37°44'35" N, long. 119°36'45" W); the feature is one of the group called Three Brothers. Named on Yosemite (1956) 15' quadrangle.

Middle Camp: see **Confidence** [TUOLUMNE].

Middle Emigrant Lake [TUOLUMNE]: *lake,* 1400 feet long, 6.5 miles west-northwest of Tower Peak along North Fork Cherry Creek (lat. 38°11'25" N, long. 119°39'15" W); the feature is about halfway between Emigrant Lake and High Emigrant Lake. Named on Tower Peak (1956) 15' quadrangle.

Middle Ferry: see **Islip's Ferry**, under **Oakdale** [STANISLAUS].

Middle Fork Campground [TUOLUMNE]: *locality,* 2 miles south-southwest of Mather (lat. 37°51'20" N, long. 119°51'50" W; near E line sec. 15, T 1 S, R 19 E); the place is along Middle Tuolumne River; which formerly was called Middle Fork Tuolumne River. Named on Lake Eleanor (1956) 15' quadrangle.

Middle Gulch [CALAVERAS]: *canyon,* drained by a stream that flows 1.5 miles to Blue Creek 4.25 miles west of Tamarack (lat. 38°25'50" N, long 120°09'20" W; near E line sec. 25, T 7 N, R 16 E). Named on Calaveras Dome (1979) 7.5' quadrangle.

Middle Paddy Creek [SAN JOAQUIN]: *stream,* flows 6.5 miles to Paddy Creek 5.25 miles north-northeast of Waterloo (lat. 38°06'35" N, long. 121°09'35" W; sec. 13, T 3 N, R 7 E). Named on Linden (1968) and Waterloo (1968) 7.5' quadrangles.

Middle River [SAN JOAQUIN]:

(1) *stream,* diverges from San Joaquin River and flows 25 miles before rejoining the river 15 miles west-southwest of Lodi (lat. 38° 02'30" N, long. 121°31'35" W). Named on Bouldin Island (1978), Holt (1978), Lathrop (1952), Union Island (1978), and Woodward Island (1978) 7.5' quadrangles. Gabriel Moraga visited the stream in 1776 and called it San Francisco Xavier (Dillon, 1982, p. 30).

(2) *locality,* 12.5 miles west of downtown Stockton on Lower Jones Tract (lat. 37°56'30" N, long. 121°31'50" W); the place is on the west side of Middle River (1). Named on Woodward Island (1978) 7.5' quadrangle. Woodward Island (1913) 7.5' quadrangle has both the names "Middle River" and "Moorland P.O." at the place. Postal authorities established Moorland post office in 1902, changed the name to Middle River in 1915, and discontinued it in 1944 (Frickstad, p. 162).

Middle Slough Mariposa Creek: see **North Slough Mariposa Creek** [MERCED].

Middle Three Meadow [TUOLUMNE]: *area,* 7.25 miles east-northeast of Pinecrest (lat. 38°14'40" N, long. 119°52'45" W; on E line sec. 33, T 5 N, R 19 E); the place is one of the group called Three Meadows. Named on Pinecrest (1979) 7.5' quadrangle.

Middle Tuolumne River [TUOLUMNE]: *stream,* flows 30 miles to South Fork Tuolumne River 11 miles south-southeast of Duckwall Mountain (lat. 37°49'40" N, long. 120°01'10" W; sec. 29, T 1 S, R 18 E). Named on Hetch Hetchy Reservoir (1956) and Lake Eleanor (1956) 15' quadrangles. Called Middle Fork Tuolumne River on Tuolumne (1948) 15' quadrangle, but United States Board on Geographic Names (1934, p. 17) rejected this name for the stream.

Midpines [MARIPOSA]: *locality,* 12 miles southwest of El Portal (lat. 37°32'35" N, long. 119°55'10" W; sec. 31, T 4 S, R 19 E). Named on Feliciana Mountain (1947) 7.5' quadrangle. Postal authorities established Midpines post office in 1929 (Frickstad, p. 92). Newell D. Chamberlain began a resort at the place in 1926, and named the resort for its position in the pine forest midway between Merced and Yosemite Valley (Sargent, Shirley, 1976, p. 11).

Midway Slough [SAN JOAQUIN]: *water feature,* joins Empire Slough (present Empire Cut) 11 miles west of downtown Stockton (lat. 37°58'15" N, long. 121°29'30" W). Named on Holt (1913) 7.3' quadrangle.

Miguel Creek [TUOLUMNE]: *stream,* flows 4.5 miles to Eleanor Creek 5 miles north-northwest of Mather (lat. 37°57'15" N, long. 119°52'45" W; sec. 10, T 1 N, R 19 E); the stream goes through Miguel Meadow. Named on Lake Eleanor (1956) 15' quadrangle. United States Board on Geographic Names (1933a, p. 519) rejected the name "McGill Creek" for the stream.

Miguel Meadow [TUOLUMNE]: *area,* 5.5 miles north of Mather (lat. 37°57'35" N, long. 119°50'15" W; sec. 12, T 1 N, R 19 E); the place is along Miguel Creek. Named on Lake Eleanor (1956) 15' quadrangle. Miguel Herrara and his partner owned the area and grazed cattle and horses there (Uhte, p. 66). The name "Miguel" was corrupted to "McGill" in the early days (Browning, 1986, p. 146), but United States Board on Geographic Names (1933a, p. 519) rejected the name "McGill Meadow" for the place.

Mikes Peak [STANISLAUS]: *peak,* 12 miles southeast of Mount Boardman (lat. 37°21'25" N, long. 121°19' W; sec. 4, T 7 S, R 6 E). Altitude 2620 feet. Named on Wilcox Ridge (1956) 7.5' quadrangle.

Mike Walker Canyon [MADERA]: *canyon,* drained by a stream that flows 1.5 miles to San Joaquin River 6.25 miles south-southwest of the town of North Fork (lat. 37°08'40" N, long. 119°33'15" W; sec. 15, T 9 S, R 22 E). Named on North Fork (1965) 7.5' quadrangle.

Mildred Island [SAN JOAQUIN]: *island,* 2 miles long, 12 miles west of downtown Stockton between Middle River, Latham Slough, and Empire Cut (lat. 37°59' N, long. 121°31'15" W). Named on Woodward Island (1978) 7.5' quadrangle.

Mildred Island Ferry [SAN JOAQUIN]: *locality,* 13 miles west of downtown Stockton along Empire Cut (lat. 37°58'20" N, long. 121°01'15" W); the place is on the south side of Mildred Island. Named on Woodward Island (1978) 7.5' quadrangle.

Mildred Lake [MARIPOSA]: *lake,* 1400 feet long, nearly 3 miles southwest of Cathedral Peak (lat. 37°49'15" N, long. 119°26'25" W; sec. 27, T 1 S, R 23 E). Named on Tuolumne Meadows (1956) 15' quadrangle. The name commemorates Mildred Sovulewski, who was the daughter of Gabriel Sovulewski, a ranger and supervisor in Yosemite National Park from 1906 until 1936 (Browning, 1986, p. 146).

Mile High Curve [MADERA]: *locality,* 5.25 miles east-southeast of Shuteye Peak (lat. 37°18'40" N, long. 119°20'50" W); the feature is along a road 2500 feet above San Joaquin River. Named on Shuteye Peak (1953) 15' quadrangle.

Miles Creek [MARIPOSA-MERCED]: *stream,* heads in Mariposa County and flows 31 miles to Hartley Slough 14 miles north-northeast of Dos Palos Y in Merced County (lat. 37°14'40" N, long. 120°32'30" W; at SW cor. sec. 10, T 8 S, R 13 E). Named on El Nido (1960), Indian Gulch (1962), Merced (1961), Owens Reservoir (1962), Planada (1961), and Sandy Mush (1962) 7.5' quadrangles.

Milk Ranch Spring [TUOLUMNE]: *spring,* 4.5 miles southeast of Long Barn (lat. 38°02'40" N, long. 120°04'20" W; sec. 11, T 2 N, R 17 E). Named on Hull Creek (1979) 7.5' quadrangle.

Mill Creek [CALAVERAS]:

(1) *stream,* flows 2.5 miles to North Fork Stanislaus River 12.5 miles southwest of Tamarack near Boards Crossing (lat. 38°18'25" N, long. 120°14' W; sec. 8, T 5 N, R 16 E). Named on Boards Crossing (1979) 7.5' quadrangle.

(2) *stream,* formed by the confluence of Love Creek and Moran Creek, flows 3.5 miles to North Fork Stanislaus River 7.5 miles east-northeast of Murphys (lat. 38°10'55" N, long. 120°20'15" W; near E line sec. 20, T 4 N, R 15 E). Named on Stanislaus (1948) 7.5' quadrangle.

Mill Creek [TUOLUMNE]: *stream,* flows 8 miles to Middle Fork Stanislaus River 7.5 miles southeast of Liberty Hill (lat. 38°17'20" N, long. 120°00'30" W; near E line sec. 17, T 5 N, R 18 E). Named on Donnell Lake (1979) and Liberty Hill (1979) 7.5' quadrangles.

Mill Creek Campground [TUOLUMNE]: *locality,* 6.25 miles west-southwest of Dardanelle (lat. 38°18'05" N, long. 118°56'10" W; near E line sec. 12, T 5 N, R 18 E); the place is along Mill Creek. Named on Dardanelles Cone (1956) 15' quadrangle.

Miller: see **Kismet** [MADERA].

Miller Creek [MADERA]: *stream,* flows 4.5 miles to Granite Creek 14 miles northeast of Shuteye Peak (lat. 37°29'35" N, long. 119°14'40" W; sec. 16, T 5 S, R 25 E). Named on Kaiser Peak (1953), Merced Peak (1953), and Shuteye Peak (1953) 15' quadrangles.

Miller Crossing [MADERA]: *locality,* 10 miles southwest of Devils Postpile along San Joaquin River (lat. 37°30'35" N, long. 119° 12' W; sec. 11, T 5 S, R 25 E). Named on Devils Postpile (1953) 15' quadrangle. The name is for William C. Miller, an early-day sheepman (Browning, 1986, p. 147).

Miller Gulch [MARIPOSA]: *canyon,* drained by a stream that flows 3.25 miles to Merced River 8 miles west of El Portal (lat. 37°40'05" N, long. 119°55'15" W). Named on Kinsley (1947) 7.5' quadrangle. Yosemite (1909) 30' quadrangle has the name "Big Grizzly" for the stream in this canyon.

Miller Lake [STANISLAUS]: *lake,* 1 mile long, 11 miles west of Modesto (lat. 37°40'10" N, long. 121°12'15" W; mainly in sec. 16, T 3 S, R 7 E). Named on Ripon (1969) 7.5' quadrangle.

Miller Lake [TUOLUMNE]: *lake,* 1600 feet long, 10.5 miles west-northwest of Tioga Pass (lat. 37°59'30" N, long. 119°25'05" W). Named on Tuolumne Meadows (1956) 15' quadrangle. Lieutenant N.F. McClure named the lake in 1894 for a soldier in his command (United States Board on Geographic Names, 1934, p. 17).

Miller Meadow [MADERA]: *area,* 12.5 miles northeast of Shuteye Peak (lat. 37°29'50" N, long. 119°17'30" W; sec. 13, T 5 S, R 24 E). Named on Shuteye Peak (1953) 15' quadrangle.

Miller Meadow Campground [MADERA]: *locality,* 10.5 miles south-southeast of Merced Peak (lat. 37°30'15" N, long. 119°17'20" W; near S line sec. 12, T 5 S, R 24 E). Named on Merced Peak (1953) 15' quadrangle.

Millers Corner: see **Twentytwo Mile House** [MADERA].

Millerton Lake [MADERA]: *lake,* behind a dam on San Joaquin River 9 miles south of O'Neals on Madera-Fresno County line (lat. 37°00' N, long. 119°42'15" W; sec. 5, T 11 S, R 21 E). Named on Friant (1964), Millerton Lake East (1965), and Millerton Lake West (1965) 7.5' quadrangles. Water of the lake covers the site of Old Millerton in Fresno County.

Millerton Ridge [MADERA]: *ridge,* southwest-trending, 1.5 miles long, 5.5 miles south of O'Neals (lat. 37°02'45" N, long. 119° 41' W); the ridge is north of Millerton Lake. Named on Millerton Lake West (1965) 7.5' quadrangle.

Mill Gulch [STANISLAUS]: *canyon,* drained by a stream that flows 1.25 miles to Tuolumne River 0.5 mile east of La Grange (lat. 37° 39'50" N, long. 120°26'50" W; sec. 20, T 3 S, R 14 E). Named on La Grange (1962) 7.5' quadrangle.

Million Dollar Spring [TUOLUMNE]: *spring,* 10 miles northeast of Stanislaus (lat. 38°15'25" N, long. 120°15'15" W; sec. 30, T 5 N, R 16 E). Named on Dorrington (1979) 7.5' quadrangle.

Mill Valley: see **Mokelumne Hill** [CALAVERAS].

Milton [CALAVERAS]: *settlement,* 4.5 miles south-southeast of Jenny Lind (lat. 38°01'55" N, long. 120°51'05" W; near NW cor. sec. 14, T 2 N, R 10 E). Named on Jenny Lind (1962) 7.5' quadrangle. Jackson (1902) 30' quadrangle shows the place at the end of Stockton and Copperopolis Railroad. Postal authorities established Milton post office in 1871 and discontinued it in 1942 (Frickstad, p. 15). The name is for Milton Latham, a construction engineer for Southern Pacific Railroad when the rail line was built to the place in 1871 (Hanna, p. 193).

Minaret Creek [MADERA]: *stream,* flows 5 miles to Middle Fork San Joaquin River less than 1 mile north-northwest of Devils Postpile (lat. 37°38'05" N, long. 119°05'05" W); the stream heads at Minaret Lake. Named on Devils Postpile (1953) 15' quadrangle.

Minaret Falls [MADERA]: *waterfall,* 1.25 miles north-northwest of Devils Postpile (lat. 37°38'25" N, long. 119°05'30" W); the feature is along Minaret Creek. Named on Devils Postpile (1953) 15' quadrangle.

Minaret Falls Campground [MADERA]: *locality,* 1 mile north of Devils Postpile along Middle Fork San Joaquin River (lat. 37°38'20" N, long. 119°05' W); the place is 0.5 mile east-southeast of Minaret Falls. Named on Devils Postpile (1953) 15' quadrangle.

Minaret Lake [MADERA]: *lake,* 2000 feet long, nearly 5 miles west-northwest of Devils Postpile (lat. 37°39'35" N, long. 119°09'25" W); the lake is 1 mile east of Minarets. Named on Devils Postpile (1953) 15' quadrangle.

Minaret Lake: see **Johnston Lake** [MADERA].

Minaret Meadow: see **Johnston Meadow** [MADERA].

Minarets [MADERA]: *relief features,* 6 miles west-northwest of Devils Postpile (lat. 37°39'50" N, long. 119°10'45" W). Named on Devils Postpile (1953) 15' quadrangle. Members of the Whitney survey named the features for their resemblance to mosque spires (Smith, p. 26).

Minarets: see **North Fork** [MADERA].

Minaret Summit [MADERA]: *pass,* 2.5 miles north-northeast of Devils Postpile on Madera-Mono County line (lat. 37°39'15" N, long. 119°03'25" W). Named on Devils Postpile (1953) 15' quadrangle.

Minear: see **Jerseydale** [MARIPOSA].

Mine Creek [MERCED]: *stream,* flows 5.5 miles to Fresno County 3 miles south-southeast of Ortigalita Peak (lat. 36°45'15" N, long. 120°54'05" W; sec. 32, T 13 S, R 10 E). Named on Ortigalita Peak (1969) 7.5' quadrangle.

Miner Creek [MERCED]: *stream,* flows 5.5 miles to Piedra Azul Creek 19 miles west-southwest of Dos Palos (lat. 36°52'45" N, long. 120°56'35" W). Named on Ortigalita Peak (1969) and Ortigalita Peak NW (1956) 7.5' quadrangles.

Mingesdale: see **Manteca** [SAN JOAQUIN].

Minita Creek: see **Guadalupe Creek** [MARIPOSA].

Minita Gulch: see **Guadalupe Creek** [MARIPOSA]; **La Mineta Gulch** [MARIPOSA].

Minnow Gulch [TUOLUMNE]: *canyon,* drained by a stream that flows 1.5 miles to Six-bit Gulch 2.5 miles south of Chinese Camp (lat. 37°50'05" N, long. 120°25'55" W; sec. 21, T 1 S, R 14 E). Named on Chinese Camp

(1947) 7.5' quadrangle.

Minnow Lake [MADERA]: *lake,* 600 feet long, 1 mile south of Buena Vista Peak (lat. 37°34'45" N, long. 119°30'50" W; sec. 24, T 4 S, R 22 E). Named on Yosemite (1956) 7.5' quadrangle.

Minturn [MADERA]: *locality,* 1.5 miles north-northwest of Chowchilla along Southern Pacific Railroad (lat. 37°08'25" N, long. 120° 16'25" W; on W line sec. 19, T 9 S, R 16 E). Named on Chowchilla (1960) 15' quadrangle. Postal authorities established Minturn post office in 1884 and discontinued it in 1922 (Frickstad, p. 86). The name commemorates Jonas Minturn and Thomas Minturn, who raised wheat and arranged for a freight siding when the railroad reached the place in 1872 (Clough, p. 80).

Mirror Lake [MARIPOSA]: *lake,* 900 feet long, 2 miles east of Yosemite Village along Tenaya Creek (lat. 37°44'55" N, long. 119°32'55" W). Named on Yosemite (1956) 15' quadrangle. C.H. Spencer of Utica, New York., a member of the Mariposa Battalion, named the lake (United States Board on Geographic Names, 1934, p. 17; Browning, 1988, p. 95).

Missouri Bar: see **Moccasin Creek** [TUOLUMNE].

Mist: see **Bailey Flats** [MADERA].

Mitchell Ravine [SAN JOAQUIN]: *canyon,* drained by a stream that flows 3.5 miles to Alameda County 3.25 miles north-northwest of Eagle Mountain (lat. 37°36'50" N, long. 121°33'20" W; sec. 5, T 4 S, R 4 E). Named on Cedar Mountain (1956) 7.5' quadrangle. Local settlers named the feature in the 1860's (Mosier and Mosier, p. 57).

Mitchells Mill [CALAVERAS]: *locality,* 2.5 miles northeast of Fort Mountain (lat. 38°21'55" N, long. 120°25'55" W; near N line sec. 21, T 6 N, R 14 E). Named on Fort Mountain (1979) 7.5' quadrangle. Called Mitchell Mill on California Division of Highways' (1934) map. Postal authorities established Mitchells Mill post office in 1912 and discontinued it in 1955 (Salley, p. 143).

Miwok Lake [TUOLUMNE]: *lake,* 1700 feet long, 10 miles southwest of Tower Peak (lat. 38°03'20" N, long. 119°42' W). Named on Tower Peak (1956) 15' quadrangle.

Mi-Wuk Village [TUOLUMNE]: *town,* about 3 miles northeast of Twain Harte (lat. 38°03'45" N, long. 120°11' W; on S line sec. 35, T 3 N, R 16 E). Named on Twain Harte (1979) 7.5' quadrangle.

Moaning Caves [CALAVERAS]: *relief feature,* 1.25 miles south-southeast of Vallecito (lat. 38°04'10" N, long. 120°27'55" W; near W line sec. 32, T 3 N, R 14 E). Named on Columbia (1948) 7.5' quadrangle. The feature first was called Solomons Hole, and then renamed for the curious sound heard at the entrance to the place (Gudde, 1969, p. 205).

Moccasin [TUOLUMNE]: *village,* 13 miles south-southeast of Sonora (lat. 37°48'40" N, long. 120°18' W; near NE cor. sec. 34, T 1 S, R 15 E); the village is near Moccasin Creek. Named on Moccasin (1948) 7.5' quadrangle. Postal authorities established Moccasin post office in 1923 (Frickstad, p. 216). George F. Culbertson settled at the place in 1856; the traveler's stop there was called Culbertson's in 1878 (Paden and Schlichtmann, p. 114, 116).

Moccasin Creek [TUOLUMNE]: *stream,* flows 8.5 miles to Don Pedro Reservoir 2 miles northwest of Moccasin (lat. 37°49'50" N, long. 120°19'50" W; sec. 21, T 1 S, R 15 E). Named on Moccasin (1948, photorevised 1973) 7.5' quadrangle. Paden and Schlichtmann (p. 114) reported two theories concerning the name: one, it came from the abundance in the stream of water snakes that may have been mistaken for water moccasins; and the other, early prospectors found an Indian moccasin by the stream. A place called Brazoria Bar, and later called Missouri Bar, was on the south side of Tuolumne River a short distance above the mouth of Moccasin Creek (Gudde, 1975, p. 45)—water of Don Pedro Reservoir now covers the site.

Moccasin Peak [TUOLUMNE]: *peak,* 1.5 miles west-southwest of Moccasin (lat. 37°48'20" N, long. 120°19'40" W; sec. 33, T 1 S, R 15 E). Altitude 2948 feet. Named on Moccasin (1948) 7.5' quadrangle.

Moccasin Reservoir [TUOLUMNE]: *lake,* behind a dam on Moccasin Creek 0.25 mile west of Moccasin (lat. 37°48'40" N, long. 120°18'20" W; near N line sec. 34, T 1 S, R 15 E). Named on Moccasin (1948, photorevised 1973) 7.5' quadrangle.

Mockingbird Ridge [MARIPOSA]: *ridge,* east-southeast-trending, 1.5 miles long, 3.5 miles northeast of the settlement of Catheys Valley (lat. 37°27'45" N, long. 120°02'25" W). Named on Catheys Valley (1962) 7.5' quadrangle. On Indian Gulch (1920) 15' quadrangle, the name "Mocking Bird Ridge" applies to a feature located about 2 miles farther south. United States Board on Geographic Names (1964a, p. 11) rejected the form "Mocking Bird Ridge" for the name.

Modesto [STANISLAUS]: *city,* in the north-central part of Stanislaus County, mainly on the north side of Tuolumne River (lat. 37°38'15" N, long. 120°59'45" W). Named on Brush Lake (1969), Ceres (1969), Riverbank (1969), and Salida (1969) 7.5' quadrangles. The town was laid out in 1870 and called Ralston for railroad magnate W.C. Ralston, but. Mr. Ralston declined the honor; citizens of the place then named their community Modesto because of Ralston's modesty—*modesto* means "modesty" in Spanish (Hanna, p. 196). Postal authorities established Modesto post office in 1870 (Frickstad, p. 200), and the city incorporated in 1884. Mendenhall's (1908) map shows a place called McNeal located about 10 miles west-northwest of Modesto (sec. 14, T 3 S, R 7 E). Postal authorities established McNeal post office in 1902 and discontinued it in 1904 (Frickstad, p. 200). California Division of Highways' (1934) map shows an area called Palm Tract situated 12 miles west of Modesto on the east side of San Joaquin River.

Modesto Reservoir [STANISLAUS]: *lake,* 5.5 miles east-northeast of Waterford (lat. 37°40' N, long. 120°39'45" W). Named on Paulsell (1968) 7.5' quadrangle. Called Dallas-Warner Reservoir on Paulsell (1953) 7.5' quadrangle.

Mohr's Landing: see **Bethany** [SAN JOAQUIN].

Mohr Station: see **Bethany** [SAN JOAQUIN].

Moic: see **Lake Moic** [MADERA].

Mokelumne: see **Lodi** [SAN JOAQUIN].

Mokelumne Beach [SAN JOAQUIN]: *area,* 1.25 miles north-northeast of Clements on the south side of Mokelumne River (lat. 38°12'25" N, long. 121°04'45" W). Named on Bellota (1939) 15' quadrangle.

Mokelumne City [SAN JOAQUIN]: *locality,* 12 miles northwest of Lodi (lat. 38°15'10" N, long. 121°26'10" W); the place is on the south side of Mokelumne River. Named on Bruceville (1968) 7.5' quadrangle. A town laid out at the place in 1854 prospered before a flood destroyed it in 1862 (Hoover, Rensch, and Rensch, p. 374). Postal authorities established Mokelumne City post office in 1861 and discontinued it in 1864 (Frickstad, p. 162). Thompson and West's (1879) map shows Benson's Ferry located along Mokelumne River (near W line sec. 28, T 5 N, R 4 E). The ferry was less than 0.5 mile west of Mokelumne City (Gudde, 1975, p. 220). Edward Stokes and A.M. Woods started the ferry in 1849, and John A. Benson bought it in 1850 (Hoover, Rensch, and Rensch, p. 374).

Mokelumne Hill [CALAVERAS]: *town,* 7.5 miles north-northwest of San Andreas on the ridge between Mokelumne River and North Fork Calaveras River (lat. 38°18' N, long. 120°42'15" W; on E line sec. 12, T 5 N, R 11 E). Named on Mokelumne Hill (1948) 7.5' quadrangle. Postal authorities established Mokelumne Hill post office in 1851 (Frickstad, p. 16). They established Mill Valley post office 9.5 miles northeast of Mokelumne Hill in 1856 and discontinued it in 1861 (Salley, p. 141). Camp's (1962) map shows a place called Independence Flat located less than 2 miles west of Mokelumne Hill. McKinstry (p. 355, 356, 358) noted a feature called Brown's Hill located at the north edge of the town, a shoulder of French Hill called Nigger Hill situated just east of Brown's Hill, a high meadow called Corral Flat found just south of the town, and a feature called Sport Hill located at the southeast edge of the town next to Corral Flat. Gudde (1975, p. 49-50) listed a place called Buckeye Hill that was 2 miles east of Mokelumne Hill; people from Ohio who had a store there named the place in 1849.

Mokelumne River [CALAVERAS-SAN JOAQUIN]: *stream,* formed by the confluence of Middle Fork and North Fork 7.25 miles northeast of Mokelumne Hill, flows 75 miles to San Joaquin River 16 miles west of Lodi (lat. 38°05'50" N, long. 121°34'10" W). Named on Bouldin Island (1978), Bruceville (1968), Clements (1968), Isleton (1978), Jackson (1962), Lockeford (1968), Lodi North (1968), Mokelumne Hill (1948), Rail Road Flat (1948), Thornton (1978), Valley Springs (1962), and Wallace (1962) 7.5' quadrangles. Part of San Joaquin-Sacramento County line follows the river, and Calaveras-Amador County line follows the river and its North Fork. Ord's (1848) map has the names "Rio de las McGuelentes" and "Mokelamy" for the stream. The name "Mokelumne" is from an Indian expression meaning "people of Mokel"—Mokel was an Indian village near the stream (Kroeber, p. 48). Middle Fork is 28 miles long and is named on Calaveras Dome (1979), Devils Nose (1979), Garnet Hill (1979), Rail Road Flat (1948), and West Point (1948) 7.5' quadrangles. On Big Trees (1891) 30' quadrangle, present Forest Creek is called North Fork Middle Fork Mokelumne River. North Fork heads in Alpine County, is 32 miles long, and is named on Calaveras Dome (1979), Devils Nose (1979), Garnet Hill (1979), Mokelumne Peak (1979), Rail Road Flat (1948), Tamarack (1979), and West Point (1948) 7.5' quadrangles. South Fork joins Middle Fork 1.5 miles upstream from the confluence of Middle Fork and North Fork; it is 27 miles long and is named on Boards Crossing (1979), Calaveras Dome (1979), Dorrington (1979), Fort Mountain (1979), and Rail Road Flat (1948) 7.5' quadrangles. Camp's (1962) map shows a canyon called Indian Gulch that opens into the canyon of Mokelumne River 1 mile south-southwest of the confluence of Middle Fork and North Fork Mokelumne River, and shows a canyon called Nigger Gulch that opens into the canyon of Mokelumne River nearly 2 miles southwest of the confluence of North Fork and Middle Fork. Mokelumne River divides 13 miles west-northwest of Lodi to form two streams, North Mokelumne River and South Mokelumne River, which join again 16 miles west of Lodi to reform Mokelumne River. North Mokelumne River, which forms part of San Joaquin-Sacramento County line, is 10 miles long and is named on Isleton (1978) and Thornton (1978) 7.5' quadrangles; it is called North Fork Mokelumne River on Isleton (1910) and New Hope (1910) 7.5' quadrangles. South Mokelumne River is 15 miles long and is named on Bouldin Island (1978), Isleton (1978), Terminous (1978), and

Thornton (1978) 7.5' quadrangles; it is called South Fork Mokelumne River on Isleton (1910) and New Hope (1910) 7.5' quadrangles. Postal authorities established McDermott's Bridge post office in 1854, changed the name to Half Way House in 1856, and discontinued it in 1860; the name "McDermott" was for W.F. McDermott, first postmaster, who built a bridge across Mokelumne River halfway between Stockton and Sacramento (Salley, p. 92, 136).

Mokelumne River: see **Little Mokelumne River** [CALAVERAS].

Molina Canyon [MERCED]: *canyon,* drained by a stream that flows 3.25 miles to Piedra Azul Creek 5 miles northwest of Ortigalita Peak (lat. 36°51'15" N, long. 120°58'15" W). Named on Ortigalita Peak (1969) and Ruby Canyon (1968) 7.5' quadrangles. Called Molino Canyon on Quien Sabe (1922) 15' quadrangle.

Molino Canyon: see **Molina Canyon** [MERCED].

Molo Mountain: see **Kennedy Peak** [TUOLUMNE].

Mono Camp [MARIPOSA]: *locality,* nearly 2 miles west-southwest of Midpines (lat. 37°32'10" N, long. 119°57'05" W; at S line sec. 35, T 4 S, R 18 E); the place is in Mono Gulch. Named on Feliciana Mountain (1947) 7.5' quadrangle.

Mono Gulch [MARIPOSA]: *canyon,* drained by a stream that flows nearly 2 miles to Stockton Creek 2.5 miles southwest of Midpines (lat. 37°31'10" N, long. 119°56'55" W). Named on Feliciana Mountain (1947) 7.5' quadrangle.

Mono Meadow [MARIPOSA]: *area,* 5 miles south of Yosemite Village (lat. 37°40'30" N, long. 119°34'55" W; sec. 17, T 3 S, R 22 E). Named on Yosemite (1956) 15' quadrangle.

Mono Pass [TUOLUMNE]: *pass,* 4.5 miles south-southeast of Tioga Pass on Tuolumne-Mono County line (lat. 37°51'20" N, long. 119° 12'45" W). Named on Mono Craters (1953) 15' quadrangle. The name "Mono" is from Mono Indians who lived in the region (Kroeber, p. 48).

Monotti Hill [MARIPOSA]: *peak,* nearly 5 miles north-northeast of Buckhorn Peak (lat. 37°43'55" N, long. 120°06' W; sec. 28, T 2 S, R 17 E). Named on Buckhorn Peak (1947) 7.5' quadrangle.

Mono Vista [TUOLUMNE]: *settlement,* 6.25 miles east of Sonora (lat. 37°59'50" N, long. 120°16'05" W; near E line sec. 25, T 2 N, R 15 E). Named on Standard (1948) 7.5' quadrangle.

Monroe: see **Fort Monroe** [MARIPOSA].

Monroe Meadows [MARIPOSA]: *area,* 7.5 miles southwest of Yosemite Village (lat. 37°39'45" N, long. 119°39'45" W; sec. 22, T 3 S, R 21 E). Named on Yosemite (1956) 15' quadrangle. The name commemorates George Monroe, a black man who came to California from Georgia as a child, and who became a Pony Express rider on the route between Merced and Mariposa, and a stage driver in Yosemite Valley (Hart, p. 280).

Monte Diablo Range: see "Regional setting."

Montevideo: see **French Camp** [SAN JOAQUIN].

Montezuma [TUOLUMNE]: *locality,* 6.5 miles southwest of Sonora (lat. 37°54'15" N, long. 120°27'10" W; near SE cor. sec. 29, T 1 N, R 14 E). Named on Sonora (1948) 7.5' quadrangle. Postal authorities established Oak Spring post office 2 miles northwest of Chinese Camp in 1851 and moved it 1 mile northeast in 1854, when it took the name "Montezuma" from a trading post called Montezuma House; they discontinued Montezuma post office for a time in 1884 and discontinued it finally in 1887 (Salley, p. 145, 158).

Montgomery Gulch [MARIPOSA]: *canyon,* drained by a stream that flows 5.25 miles to Bull Creek 10 miles west-northwest of El Portal (lat. 37°42'15" N, long. 119°57'10" W; sec. 2, T 3 S, R 18 E). Named on El Portal (1947) and Lake Eleanor (1956) 15' quadrangles.

Montgomery Meadow [TUOLUMNE]: *area,* 4.5 miles west-northwest of Dardanelle (lat. 38°21'45" N, long. 119°55'20" W). Named on Donnell Lake (1979) 7.5' quadrangle.

Montgomery Ridge [MARIPOSA]: *ridge,* southwest- to south-trending, 5.5 miles long, 11.5 miles west-northwest of El Portal (lat. 37° 44'30" N, long. 119°58'15" W). Named on El Portal (1947) and Lake Eleanor (1956) 15' quadrangles.

Montpelier [STANISLAUS]: *locality,* 7 miles south-southeast of Waterford along Southern Pacific Railroad (lat. 37°32'40" N, long. 120°42'20" W; sec. 36, T 4 S, R 11 E). Named on Montpelier (1968) 7.5' quadrangle. Postal authorities established Montpelier post office in 1891 and discontinued it in 1937 (Frickstad, p. 200).

Monument Lake [MADERA]: *lake,* 450 feet long, 4.25 miles south-southeast of Merced Peak (lat. 37°34'45" N, long. 119°21'40" W). Named on Merced Peak (1953) 15' quadrangle.

Moody Gap [TUOLUMNE]: *pass,* 7.5 miles northwest of Crandall Peak (lat. 38°14'40" N, long. 120°13'55" W; sec. 32, T 5 N, R 16 E). Named on Crandall Peak (1979) 7.5' quadrangle.

Moore: see **Clark and Moore's**, under **Wawona** [MARIPOSA].

Moore and Bowen Camp: see **Hodgdon Ranch** [TUOLUMNE].

Moore Creek [CALAVERAS]: *stream,* flows nearly 7 miles to North Fork Mokelumne River less than 1 mile west of Garnet Hill (lat. 38°28'50" N, long. 120°15'55" W; near N line sec. 12, T 7 N, R 15 E); Moore mine is along the stream. Named on Calaveras Dome (1979) and Garnet Hill (1979) 7.5' quadrangles.

Moore Creek [MARIPOSA]: *stream,* flows 7 miles to Jordan Creek 4.5 miles southeast of Smith Peak (lat. 37°45'05" N, long. 120°02'25" W; sec. 24, T 2 S, R 17 E). Named on Jawbone Ridge (1947) 7.5' quadrangle.

Moore Hill [MARIPOSA]: *peak,* 6.5 miles south of Mariposa (lat. 37° 23'25" N, long. 119°59'10" W; near S line sec. 22, T 6 S, R 18 E). Named on Mariposa (1947) 7.5' quadrangle.

Moorland: see **Middle River** [SAN JOAQUIN] (2).

Moraine Dome [MARIPOSA]: *peak,* 8.5 miles southwest of Cathedral Peak (lat. 37°44'35" N, long. 119°29'20" W). Altitude 8055 feet. Named on Merced Peak (1953) 15' quadrangle.

Moraine Flat [TUOLUMNE]: *area,* 3 miles west-southwest of Tioga Pass (lat. 37°54' N, long. 119°18'35" W). Named on Tuolumne Meadows (1956) 15' quadrangle.

Moraine Meadow [MADERA]: *area,* 3 miles south-southwest of Merced Peak along South Fork Merced River (lat. 37°35'45" N, long. 119°25'30" W); the place is 1.5 miles east-northeast of Moraine Mountain. Named on Merced Peak (1953) 15' quadrangle. Mount Lyell (1901) 30' quadrangle has the form "Moraine Meadows" for the name.

Moraine Mountain [MADERA]: *peak,* 4.5 miles southwest of Merced Peak (lat. 37°35'30" N, long. 119°27'10" W). Altitude 9754 feet. Named on Merced Peak (1953) 15' quadrangle.

Moraine Ridge [TUOLUMNE]: *ridge,* southwest-trending, 4 miles long, 13 miles southwest of Tower Peak (lat. 38°01' N, long. 119° 44'15" W). Named on Pinecrest (1956) and Tower Peak (1956) 15' quadrangles.

Moran [CALAVERAS]: *locality,* 6.25 miles south-southeast of Blue Mountain along Moran Creek (lat. 38°15' N, long. 120°20'10" W). Named on Big Trees (1891) 30' quadrangle.

Moran: see **Lake Moran** [TUOLUMNE].

Moran Creek [CALAVERAS]: *stream,* flows 5 miles to join Love Creek and form Mill Creek (2) 8 miles northeast of Murphys (lat. 38°13' N, long. 120°21'25" W; sec. 7, T 4 N, R 15 E). Named on Dorrington (1979) and Stanislaus (1948) 7.5' quadrangles.

Moran Gulch [STANISLAUS]: *canyon,* about 1 mile long, 1.5 miles east of La Grange (lat. 37°39'45" N, long. 120°26'10" W; sec. 21, T 3 S, R 14 E). Named on La Grange (1962) 7.5' quadrangle.

Morano: see **Lathrop** [SAN JOAQUIN].

Moran Point [MARIPOSA]: *promontory,* 1 mile south-southeast of Yosemite Village on the south side of Yosemite Valley (lat. 37° 44'05" N, long. 119°34'45" W). Named on Yosemite (1956) 15' quadrangle.

Morgan Meadow [MADERA]: *area,* 1.5 miles northwest of Shuteye Peak (lat. 37°21'40" N, long. 119°26'15" W; sec. 34, T 6 S, R 23 E). Named on Shuteye Peak (1953) 15' quadrangle.

Morgan's Bar: see **Red Mountain Bar** [TUOLUMNE].

Morley: see **Salter and Morley's Ferry**, under **La Grange** [STANISLAUS].

Mormon [SAN JOAQUIN]: *locality,* less than 2 miles east-southeast of downtown Stockton along Atchison, Topeka and Santa Fe Railroad (lat. 37°57' N, long. 121°15'40" W); the place is near Mormon Slough. Named on Stockton West (1952) 7.5' quadrangle.

Mormon Bar [MARIPOSA]: *locality,* 2 miles south-southeast of Mariposa near Mariposa Creek (lat. 37°27'45" N, long. 119°56'45" W). Named on Mariposa (1947) 7.5' quadrangle. Some Mormons camped at the place in the winter of 1849 and 1850 (Sargent, Shirley, 1976, p. 28).

Mormon Channel: see **Mormon Slough** [SAN JOAQUIN].

Mormon Creek [TUOLUMNE]: *stream,* flows 8 miles to Melones Reservoir 9 miles north of Keystone (lat. 37°58' N, long. 120°30'20" W; at W line sec. 1, T 1 N, R 13 E). Named on Columbia (1948), Melones Dam (1962), and Sonora (1948) 7.5' quadrangles. The name is from Mormons who made the first discovery of gold along the creek—before the gold discovery, the stream was called Tuttle's Creek (Stoddart, p. 62).

Mormon Gulch: see **Tuttletown** [TUOLUMNE].

Mormon Hill [MADERA]: *peak,* 8 miles south of Shuteye Peak (lat. 37°14' N, long. 119°25'35" W; sec. 14, T 8 S, R 23 E). Named on Shaver Lake (1953) 15' quadrangle.

Mormon Slough [SAN JOAQUIN]: *stream,* diverges from Calaveras River near Bellota and flows for 20 miles to join Stockton Deep Water Channel 1.25 miles west-southwest of downtown Stockton (lat. 37°57'05" N, long. 121°18'45" W). Named on Linden (1968), Peters (1952), Stockton East (1952), and Stockton West (1952) 7.5' quadrangles. Called Mormon Channel on Hammond's (1849) map. Bancroft (1888, p. 466) noted that the city of Stockton was along what was called "Stockton or Mormon Slough" at the head of summer navigation on San Joaquin River. Hammond and Morgan (p. 17) mentioned that Stockton Slough was known as Lindsay's Lake in 1847.

Morning Star Spring [MARIPOSA]: *spring,* 8 miles north-northeast of Hornitos (lat. 37°36'20" N, long. 120°09'55" W; sec. 12, T 4 S, R 16 E); the spring is 0.5 mile north-northwest of Morning Star mine. Named on Hornitos (1947) 7.5' quadrangle.

Morrison Creek [TUOLUMNE]: *stream,* flows 5.25 miles to Tuolumne River 3.5 miles north-northeast of White Wolf (lat. 37°55'05" N, long. 119°37'30" W). Named on Hetch Hetchy Reservoir (1956) 15' quadrangle.

Morrison Island [SAN JOAQUIN]: *island,* 2350 feet long, 7.25 miles west-northwest of downtown Stockton along San Joaquin River (lat. 37°59'50" N, long. 121°24'50" W). Named on Holt (1978) 7.5' quadrangle.

Morrissey: see **Lathrop** [SAN JOAQUIN].

Morse [MARIPOSA]: *locality,* 3.25 miles west-northwest of Hornitos along Yosemite Valley Railroad (lat. 37°31'40" N, long. 120°17'10" W; sec. 2, T 5 S, R 15 E). Named on Merced Falls (1944) 15' quadrangle.

Mortar Gulch: see **Morton Gulch** [STANISLAUS].

Morton Gulch [STANISLAUS]: *canyon,* drained by a stream that flows nearly 1 mile to the canyon of Tuolumne River less than 1 mile west-northwest of La Grange (lat. 37°40'10" N, long. 120°28'20" W; sec. 18, T 3 S, R 14 E). Named on La Grange (1962) 7.5' quadrangle. Called Mortar Gulch on La Grange (1919) 7.5' quadrangle.

Mosher Creek [SAN JOAQUIN]: *stream,* flows 17 miles, partly in an artificial watercourse, to Mosher Slough 7 miles south-southwest of Lodi near the north edge of Stockton (lat. 38°01'40" N, long. 121°18'30" W; at N line sec. 15, T 2 N, R 6 E). Named on Linden (1968), Lodi South (1968), and Waterloo (1968) 7.5' quadrangles.

Mosher Slough [SAN JOAQUIN]: *water feature,* artificial watercourse that joins Disappointment Slough 7.5 miles southeast of Terminous (lat. 38°02'35" N, long. 121°23'10" W). Named on Lodi South (1968) and Terminous (1978) 7.5' quadrangles.

Mosquito Gulch [CALAVERAS]: *canyon,* drained by a stream that flows 2 miles to South Fork Mokelumne River 4 miles northwest of Rail Road Flat (lat. 38°22'30" N, long. 120°34'20" W; sec. 17, T 6 N, R 13 E). Named on Rail Road Flat (1948) 7.5' quadrangle.

Mosquito Gulch: see **Glenco** [CALAVERAS].

Mosquito Lake [TUOLUMNE]: *lake,* 1400 feet long, 8 miles west-northwest of Tower Peak (lat. 38°12'10" N, long. 119°40'20" W; at S line sec. 9, T 4 N, R 21 E). Named on Tower Peak (1956) 15' quadrangle.

Mosquito Slough [SAN JOAQUIN]: *water feature,* on Roberts Island (present Medford Island), joins San Joaquin River 15 miles west-southwest of Lodi (lat. 38°02'35" N, long. 121°31'25" W). Named on Bouldin (1910) 7.5' quadrangle.

Moss Canon: see **Moss Creek** [MARIPOSA].

Moss Canyon [MARIPOSA]:

(1) *canyon,* 3 miles long, 1.5 miles west-northwest of El Portal (lat. 37°41' N, long. 119°48'30" W); the canyon is along lower reaches of Moss Creek. Named on El Portal (1947) 7.5' quadrangle.

(2) *locality,* 2.25 miles west of El Portal along Yosemite Valley Railroad (lat. 37°40'15" N, long. 119°49'10" W); the place is near the mouth of present Moss Canyon (1). Named on Yosemite (1909) 30' quadrangle.

Moss Creek [MARIPOSA]: *stream,* flows 7.25 miles to Merced River 2 miles west of El Portal (lat. 37°40'10" N, long. 119°49'05" W). Named on El Portal (1947) and Lake Eleanor (1956) 15' quadrangles. United States Board on Geographic Names (1933a, p. 533) rejected the name "Moss Canon" for the feature.

Mossdale [SAN JOAQUIN]: *settlement,* 12 miles south of downtown Stockton on the west side of San Joaquin River (lat. 37°47'05" N, long. 121°18'30" W). Named on Lathrop (1952) 7.5' quadrangle. Postal authorities established Mossdale post office in 1911 and discontinued it the same year (Frickstad, p. 162). Trask's (1853) map has the name "Bonsals" at the place. John Doak and Jacob Bonsell started a ferry at the site in 1848; Doak left, and after Bonsell's widow married James Shepherd, the ferry was known as Shepherd's Ferry until 1856, when it was sold to William T. Moss, for whom Mossdale was named (Hoover, Rensch, and Rensch, p. 376-377). Thompson and West's (1879) map shows Moss's Ferry along San Joaquin River about 3 miles south-southwest of Lathrop. Martin (p. 29) recorded crossing San Joaquin River in 1849 at Bonsells Ferry, "or as it was sometimes called Lower Ferry." Slocum's Ferry was started 3 miles south of Bonsell's Ferry in 1849 (Hoover, Rensch, and Rensch, p. 377).

Moss's Ferry: see **Mossdale** [SAN JOAQUIN].

Moss Spring [MARIPOSA]: *spring,* 5 miles west-southwest of Yosemite Village in Yosemite Valley (lat. 37°42'50" N, long. 119° 39'50" W). Named on Yosemite (1956) 15' quadrangle.

Moss Tract [SAN JOAQUIN]: *area,* 2 miles south-southwest of downtown Stockton (lat. 37°55'50" N, long. 121°18'40" W). Named on Stockton West (1952) 7.5' quadrangle.

Mother Lode Acres [CALAVERAS]: *area,* 7.5 miles south-southwest of Valley Springs (lat. 38°05'45" N, long. 120°53'45" W; sec. 20, T 3 N, R 10 E). Named on Valley Springs SW (1962) 7.5' quadrangle.

Mount Adeline: see **Mount Savage** [MARIPOSA].

Mountain House: see **Pacheco Pass** [MERCED].

Mountain House Creek [SAN JOAQUIN]: *stream,* heads in Alameda County and flows 2.5 miles in San Joaquin County to Old River 16 miles southwest of downtown Stockton (lat. 37°47'50" N, long. 121°31'25" W). Named on Clifton Court Forebay (1978) 7.5' quadrangle. Bethany (1914) 7.5' quadrangle has the form "Mountainhouse Creek" for the name, which is from a place in Alameda County (Mosier and Mosier, p. 59).

Mountain Inn: see **Knights Ferry** [STANISLAUS].

Mountain King [MARIPOSA]: *locality,* 6 miles northeast of the village of Bear Valley along Yosemite Valley Railroad (lat. 37°37'15" N, long. 120°02' W). Named on Sonora (1897) 30' quadrangle. Postal authorities established Mountain King post office in 1907 and discontinued it in 1922; the name is from Mountain King mine (Salley, p. 147).

Mountain Pass [TUOLUMNE]: *pass,* 7.5 miles southwest of Sonora (lat. 37°54' N, long. 120°28'30" W). Named on Sonora (1897) 30' quadrangle.

Mountain Pass Creek [TUOLUMNE]: *stream,* flows 5 miles to Green Spring Run 3 miles north-northwest of Keystone (lat. 37°52'15" N, long. 120°32'20" W; near NE cor. sec. 9, T 1 S, R 13 E); the stream heads near Mountain Pass. Named on Keystone (1962), Melones Dam (1962), and Sonora (1948) 7.5' quadrangles.

Mountain Ranch [CALAVERAS]: *village,* 8 miles east-northeast of San Andreas along Eldorado Creek (lat. 38°13'45" N, long. 120°32'25" W; sec. 4, T 4 N, R 13 E). Named on Calaveritas (1962) 7.5' quadrangle. Postal authorities established Mountain Ranch post office in 1858 at a stopping place called Mountain Ranch House; they moved the post office 2 miles west in 1868 to the community of El Dorado, which then had its name changed to Mountain Ranch to match the post office designation (Hoover, Rensch, and Rensch, p. 46; Salley, p. 147). They established Blue Mountain post office 20 miles northeast of Mountain Ranch post office in 1863 and discontinued it in 1864 (Salley, p. 23); Blue Mountain City was along Licking Fork (Gudde, 1975, p. 41). They established Mammoth Cave post office 3 miles southeast of Mountain Ranch post office in 1883 and discontinued it in 1887; the name was from a nearby cave (Salley, p. 131). Gudde (1975, p. 69) noted a place called Chichi that was located 2 miles northwest of Mountain Ranch.

Mountain Ranch House: see **Mountain Ranch** [CALAVERAS].

Mountain Top [CALAVERAS]: *peak,* 4 miles east-southeast of Copperopolis (lat. 37°57'45" N, long. 120°34'25" W; near S line sec. 5, T 1 N, R 13 E). Altitude 1716 feet. Named on Melones Dam (1962) 7.5' quadrangle.

Mountain Valley [STANISLAUS]: *area,* 1.5 miles west-southwest of Crevison Peak (lat. 37°10'50" N, long. 121°12'35" W; sec. 4, T 9 S, R 7 E). Named on Crevison Peak (1955) 7.5' quadrangle.

Mountain View House: see **Westfall Meadows** [MARIPOSA].

Mountain View Peak [MADERA]: *ridge,* east-trending, 1 mile long, 6.5 miles southwest of North Fork (lat. 37°10'35" N, long. 119°36'30" W). Named on North Fork (1965) 7.5' quadrangle.

Mount Ansel Adams: see **Foerster Peak** [MADERA].

Mount Ararat [CALAVERAS]: *peak,* 9 miles west-northwest of Angels Camp (lat. 38°06'55" N, long. 120°42'15" W; near E line sec. 13, T 3 N, R 11 E). Altitude 2279 feet. Named on Salt Spring Valley (1962) 7.5' quadrangle.

Mount Ararat [MERCED]: *peak,* 2 miles east-northeast of Mariposa Peak (lat. 36°58'05" N, long. 121°10'40" W; sec. 23, T 11 S, R 7 E). Altitude 3274 feet. Named on Mariposa Peak (1969) 7.5' quadrangle.

Mount Beatitude: see **Old Inspiration Point** [MARIPOSA].

Mount Boardman [SAN JOAQUIN-STANISLAUS]: *peak,* 17 miles south of Tracy where San Joaquin County, Stanislaus County, Alameda County, and Santa Clara County meet at a point (lat. 37° 28'55" N, long. 121°28'15" W; sec. 19, T 5 S, R 5 E). Altitude 3593 feet. Named on Mount Boardman (1955) 7.5' quadrangle. The name commemorates William Fayette Boardman, county surveyor of Alameda County from 1864 until 1868 (Mosier and Mosier, p. 58).

Mount Broderick [MARIPOSA]: *peak,* 3 miles east-southeast of Yosemite Village (lat. 37°44' N, long. 119°32'05" W). Altitude 6706 feet. Named on Yosemite (1956) 15' quadrangle. The name commemorates David C. Broderick, senator from California from 1857 until 1859 (United States Board on Geographic Names, 1934, p. 3).

Mount Broderick: see **Liberty Cap** [MARIPOSA].

Mount Bruce: see **Merced Peak** [MADERA].

Mount Buckingham: see **Buckingham Mountain** [MARIPOSA].

Mount Bullion [MARIPOSA]: *village,* 6 miles southeast of the village of Bear Valley (lat. 37°30'30" N, long. 120°02'40" W). Named on Bear Valley (1947) 7.5' quadrangle. Called Princeton on Hoffmann and Gardner's (1863-1867) map. Postal authorities established Mount Bullion post office in 1862, discontinued it for a time in 1887, and discontinued it finally in 1955 (Salley, p. 147). The place first was called La Mineta—*la mineta* means "the little mine" in Spanish; it then was called Princeton for Princeton mine, which in turn was named for one of its discoverers, Prince Steptoe; finally the place was renamed Mount Bullion in 1862 to honor Fremont's father-in-law, Senator Thomas Hart Benton, whose monetary policy earned him the nickname "Old Bullion" (Sargent, Shirley, 1976, p. 15).

Mount Bullion: see **Bullion Mountain** [MARIPOSA].

Mount Bullion Range: see **Bullion Mountain** [MARIPOSA].

Mount Bullion Spur Ridge: see **Bullion Mountain** [MARIPOSA].

Mount Clark [MARIPOSA]: *peak,* 10.5 miles south of Cathedral Peak (lat. 37°41'50" N, long. 119°25'40" W). Altitude 11,522 feet. Named on Merced Peak (1953) 15' quadrangle. Members of the Whitney survey called the peak the Obelisk for its peculiar shape (Whitney, 1870, p. 108). Browning (1986, p. 41) associated the name "Clark" with Galen Clark of Clark's

Station (present Wawona), and pointed out that the feature also was called Gothic Peak.

Mount Conness [TUOLUMNE]: *peak*, 5.25 miles northwest of Tioga Pass on Tuolumne-Mono County line (lat. 37°58' N, long. 119°19'15" W). Altitude 12,590 feet. Named on Tuolumne Meadows (1956) 15' quadrangle. Members of the Whitney survey named the peak in 1864 for John Conness, senator from California (United States Board on Geographic Names, 1934, p. 6). Conness had promoted the Whitney survey while he was a member of the state legislature (Brewster, p. 184).

Mount Dana [TUOLUMNE]: *peak*, 2.25 miles east-southeast of Tioga Pass on Tuolumne-Mono County line (lat. 37°54' N, long. 119°13'15" W); the feature is 1 mile north of the head of Dana Fork. Altitude 13,053 feet. Named on Mono Craters (1953) 15' quadrangle. Members of the Whitney survey named the peak in 1863 to honor geologist James Dwight Dana (United States Board on Geographic Names, 1934, p. 6). The feature also was called Dana Mountain (Browning, 1988, p. 31).

Mount Davis [MADERA]: *peak*, 9.5 miles northwest of Devils Postpile on Madera-Mono County line (lat. 37°42'55" N, long. 119°13'05" W). Altitude 12,311 feet. Named on Devils Postpile (1953) 15' quadrangle. The name commemorates Milton F. Davis, who climbed the peak in 1891 when he was a Lieutenant under Captain A.E. Wood, first acting superintendent of Yosemite National Park (Farquhar, 1926, p. 305). The feature also was called Davis Mountain (Browning, 1988, p. 31).

Mount Diablo Range: see "Regional setting."

Mount Eaton [TUOLUMNE]: *peak*, 1.5 miles south-southeast of Tuolumne (lat. 37°56'25" N, long. 120°13'40" W; near W line sec. 16, T 1 N, T 16 E). Altitude 3134 feet. Named on Tuolumne (1948) 7.5' quadrangle. United States Board on Geographic Names (1978a, p. 4) rejected the name "Point Eaton" for the feature.

Mount Elizabeth: see **Elizabeth Peak** [TUOLUMNE].

Mount Florence [MADERA]: *peak*, 8 miles north-northeast of Merced Peak (lat. 37°44'25" N, long. 119°19' W); the peak is south of Florence Creek. Altitude 12,561 feet. Named on Merced Peak (1953) 15' quadrangle. The name commemorates Florence Hutchings, daughter of James M. Hutchings and the first white child born in Yosemite Valley (United States Board on Geographic Names, 1934, p. 9).

Mount Frances: see **Liberty Cap** [MARIPOSA].

Mount Gibbs [TUOLUMNE]: *peak*, 3.5 miles southeast of Tioga Pass on Tuolumne-Mono County line (lat. 37°52'35" N, long. 119° 12'40" W). Altitude 12,764 feet. Named on Mono Craters (1953) 15' quadrangle. Frederick Law Olmsted named the peak in 1864 for Oliver Wolcott Gibbs, professor of science at Harvard (Farquhar *in* Brewer, p. 549).

Mount Gibson [TUOLUMNE]: *peak*, 9 miles north-northwest of White Wolf (lat. 37°59'55" N, long. 119°42'15" W). Named on Hetch Hetchy Reservoir (1956) 15' quadrangle.

Mount Hoffmann [MARIPOSA]: *peak*, 8 miles north-northeast of Yosemite Village (lat. 37°50'50" N, long. 119°30'35" W; sec. 13, T 1 S, R 22 E). Altitude 10,850 feet. Named on Hetch Hetchy Reservoir (1956) 15' quadrangle. Members of the Whitney survey named the peak for Charles Frederick Hoffmann, topographer for the survey (Brewer, p. 407). United States Board on Geographic Names (1933a, p. 368) rejected the form "Hoffman" for the name.

Mount Joaquin: see **Joaquin Peak** [CALAVERAS].

Mount Knight [TUOLUMNE]: *peak*, 5.25 miles west of Crandall Peak (lat. 38°10' N, long. 120°14'20" W; sec. 29, T 4 N, R 16 E). Altitude 4783 feet. Named on Crandall Peak (1979) 7.5' quadrangle.

Mount Lewis [TUOLUMNE]: *peak*, 3.5 miles east of Twain Harte (lat. 38°02'10" N, long. 120°09'40" W; on S line sec. 12, T 2 N, R 16 E). Named on Twain Harte (1979) 7.5' quadrangle.

Mount Lyell [MADERA-TUOLUMNE]: *peak*, 12 miles south of Tioga Pass on Madera-Tuolumne County line (lat. 37°44'25" N, long. 119°16'15" W); the peak is near the head of Lyell Fork [TUOLUMNE]. Altitude 13,114 feet. Named on Merced Peak (1953) 15' quadrangle. Members of the Whitney survey named the peak for Sir Charles Lyell, distinguished English geologist (United States Board on Geographic Names, 1934, p. 15).

Mount Maclure [MADERA-TUOLUMNE]: *peak*, 11.5 miles south of Tioga Pass on Madera-Tuolumne County line (lat. 37°44'40" N, long. 119°16'45" W). Named on Merced Peak (1953) 15' quadrangle. Members of the Whitney survey named the peak for William Maclure, pioneer American geologist (Whitney, 1870, p. 101). United States Board on Geographic Names (1933a, p. 486) rejected the form "Mount McClure" for the name.

Mount McClure: see **Mount Maclure** [MADERA-TUOLUMNE].

Mount Medlicott: see **Medlicott Dome** [MARIPOSA].

Mount Ophir [CALAVERAS]: *ridge*, south-southwest-trending, 0.5 mile long, 4.25 miles northwest of San Andreas (lat. 38°14'50" N, long. 120°43'35" W; near E line sec. 35, T 5 N, R 11 E). Named on San Andreas (1962) 7.5' quadrangle.

Mount Ophir [MARIPOSA]: *locality*, 4.5 miles southeast of the village of Bear Valley (lat. 37°30'55" N, long. 120°04' W); the place is in Norwegian Gulch. Named on Bear Valley (1947) 7.5' quadrangle. Postal authorities established Ophir post office before February 20, 1852, they changed the name to Mount Ophir in 1856, and discontinued it in 1868 (Salley, p. 148, 161). The place also was called Norwegian Gulch Center (Burchfield, p. 43).

Mount Oso [STANISLAUS]: *peak*, 13 miles west of Patterson (lat. 37°30'30" N, long. 121°22'55" W; on S line sec. 12, T 5 S, R 5 E). Altitude 3347 feet. Named on Solyo (1953) 7.5' quadrangle. Brewer (p. 279) noted in 1862 that the peak was rightly named, "for the whole summit had been dug over by bears for roots"—*oso* means "bear" in Spanish.

Mount Peckinpah: see **Peckinpah Mountain**, under **Central Camp** [MADERA].

Mount Pleasant: see **Taylor Hill** [TUOLUMNE].

Mount Provo [TUOLUMNE]: *peak*, 2.25 miles southeast of Twain Harte (lat. 38°00'45" N, long. 120°12'20" W; sec. 22, T 2 N, R 16 E). Altitude 4845 feet. Named on Twain Harte (1979) 7.5' quadrangle.

Mount Raymond Camp [MADERA]: *locality*, 7 miles south-southwest of Buena Vista Peak (lat. 37°30' N, long. 119°29'20" W; sec. 16, T 5 S, R 22 E); the place is 1.5 miles west-southwest of Raymond Mountain. Named on Yosemite (1956) 15' quadrangle.

Mount Ritter [MADERA]: *peak*, 8 miles northwest of Devils Postpile (lat. 37°41'20" N, long. 119°11'55" W); the peak is on Ritter Ridge. Altitude 13,157 feet. Named on Devils Postpile (1953) 15' quadrangle. Members of the Whitney survey named the peak for German geographer Karl Ritter (Whitney, 1870, p. 101).

Mount Savage [MARIPOSA]: *peak*, 2 miles south of Wawona (lat. 37°30'35" N, long. 119°39' W; sec. 11, T 5 S, R 21 E). Altitude 5745 feet. Named on Yosemite (1956) 15' quadrangle. Chester Versteeg suggested the name in the early 1950's to commemorate Major James D. Savage of the Mariposa Battalion; the feature earlier was known locally as Twin Peaks and as Mount Adeline (Browning, 1986, p. 192).

Mount Stakes [STANISLAUS]: *peak*, 12 miles south-southeast of Mount Boardman on Stanislaus-Santa Clara County line (lat. 37° 19'20" N, long. 121°24'25" W; sec. 15, T 7 S, R 5 E). Altitude 3804 feet. Named on Mount Stakes (1955) 7.5' quadrangle.

Mount Starr King [MARIPOSA]: *peak*, 5 miles southeast of Yosemite Village (lat. 37°42'10" N, long. 119°31' W). Altitude 9092 feet. Named on Yosemite (1956) 15' quadrangle. The name honors Thomas Starr King, well-known Unitarian preacher and orator for the Union cause in California during the Civil War (United States Board on Geographic Names, 1934, p. 24).

Mount Trumbull: see **Trumbull Peak** [MARIPOSA].

Mount Wallace [SAN JOAQUIN]: *peak*, 2.25 miles south-southwest of Eagle Mountain on San Joaquin-Alameda County line (lat. 37° 32'20" N, long. 121°33' W; sec. 32, T 4 S, R 4 E). Altitude 3112 feet. Named on Cedar Mountain (1956) 7.5' quadrangle. The name is for John Wallace, who was county surveyor of San Joaquin County in 1868 (Mosier and Mosier, p. 59).

Mount Watkins [MARIPOSA]: *peak*, 4.5 miles east-northeast of Yosemite Village (lat. 37°47' N, long. 119°31' W). Altitude 8500 feet. Named on Hetch Hetchy Reservoir (1956) 15' quadrangle. The name commemorates photographer Carleton E. Watkins, whose early photographs of Yosemite Valley did much to publicize the place (Whitney, 1870, p. 69).

Moy: see **Carbona** [SAN JOAQUIN].

Mud Lake [CALAVERAS]: *lake*, 800 feet long, 3 miles east of Tamarack on Calaveras-Alpine County line (lat. 38°26'10" N, long. 120°01'10" W). Named on Tamarack (1979) 7.5' quadrangle.

Mud Lake [TUOLUMNE]: *lake*, 625 feet long, nearly 6 miles east-southeast of Pinecrest (lat. 38°09'05" N, long. 119°54'10" W). Named on Pinecrest (1979) 7.5' quadrangle, which shows the lake in a marsh. On Dardanelles (1898) 30' quadrangle, a feature called Lily Lake covers present Mud Lake and its adjacent marsh. United States Board on Geographic Names (1963a, p. 7) rejected the name "Lily Lake" for present Mud Lake.

Mud Slough [MERCED]:

(1) *water feature*, east of Gustine between Los Banos Creek and Salt Slough. Named on Los Banos (1961) and Turlock (1962) 15' quadrangles.

(2) *water feature*, joins Salt Slough 7 miles north-northeast of Los Banos (lat. 37°09'15" N, long. 120°48'25" W; sec. 18, T 9 S, R 11 E). Named on Los Banos (1960) and San Luis Ranch (1961) 7.5' quadrangles.

Mud Spring [CALAVERAS]: *spring*, 7 miles west-southwest of Tamarack (lat. 38°22'55" N, long. 120°11'15" W; near SE cor. sec. 10, T 6 N, R 16 E). Named on Calaveras Dome (1979) 7.5' quadrangle, which indicates that the spring is dry.

Mud Spring Creek [MADERA]: *stream*, flows 8 miles to Fresno River 9.5 miles south of Raymond (lat. 37°04'40" N, long. 119°53'55" W; sec. 9, T 10 S, R 19 E). Named on Daulton (1962), Knowles (1962), and Little Table Mountain (1962) 7.5' quadrangles.

Mugler Creek [MADERA]: *stream*, flows 6 miles to Chiquito Creek 6.5 miles north-northeast of Shuteye Peak (lat. 37°26'15" N, long. 119°23' W; sec. 6, T 6 S, R 24 E); the stream goes through Muglers Meadow. Named on Shuteye Peak (1953) 15' quadrangle.

Muglers Meadow [MADERA]: *area*, 9 miles north of Shuteye Peak (lat. 37°28'45" N, long. 119°26' W; sec. 22, T 5 S, R 23 E); the place is along

Mugler Creek. Named on Shuteye Peak (1953) 15' quadrangle. Christopher Mugler, a sheepman who was in the neighborhood as early as 1852, had his base camp at the place (Browning, 1986, p. 155).

Muir Gorge [TUOLUMNE]: *narrows,* 8 miles northeast of White Wolf along Tuolumne River (lat. 37°56'15" N, long. 119°31'45" W). Named on Hetch Hetchy Reservoir (1956) 15' quadrangle. R.M. Price named the feature in 1895 for naturalist John Muir (United States Board on Geographic Names, 1934, p. 17).

Mule Gulch [STANISLAUS]: *canyon,* 3.5 miles long, opens into the canyon of Garzas Creek 3.25 miles northeast of Crevison Peak (lat. 37°13'40" N, long. 121°08'40" W; sec. 24, T 8 S, R 7 E). Named on Crevison Peak (1955) 7.5' quadrangle.

Mullen Ridge [MADERA-MARIPOSA]: *ridge,* south-trending, 2 miles long, 6.5 miles north of Raymond on Madera-Mariposa County line (lat. 37°18'40" N, long. 119°53'35" W). Named on Ben Hur (1947) 7.5' quadrangle.

Murderers Gulch [CALAVERAS]: *canyon,* drained by a stream that flows 1 mile to Coyote Creek 1 mile south of Vallecito (lat. 38°04'10" N, long. 120°28'20" W; sec. 31, T 3 N, R 14 E). Named on Columbia (1948) 7.5' quadrangle.

Murderers Gulch [STANISLAUS]: *canyon,* drained by a stream that flows 1 mile to Del Puerto Canyon 2.25 miles northeast of Copper Mountain (lat. 37°26'30" N, long. 121°17'05" W; sec. 2, T 6 S, R 6 E). Named on Copper Mountain (1956) 7.5' quadrangle.

Murderers' Gulch: see **Wards Ferry** [TUOLUMNE].

Murdock Lake [TUOLUMNE]: *lake,* 700 feet long, 10 miles south-southeast of Tower Peak (lat. 38°00'10" N, long. 119°30'15" W). Named on Tower Peak (1956) 15' quadrangle. Lieutenant N.F. McClure named the lake in 1895 for William C. Murdock of California State Board of Fish Commissioners (Gudde, 1949, p. 229).

Murietta House: see **Farmington** [SAN JOAQUIN].

Murphy: see **Murphys** [CALAVERAS].

Murphy Creek [MARIPOSA]: *stream,* flows 3 miles to Tenaya Lake 3.25 miles west-southwest of Cathedral Peak (lat. 37°50' N, long. 119°27'45" W; near W line sec. 21, T 1 S, R 23 E). Named on Tuolumne Meadows (1956) 15' quadrangle. The name is for John L. Murphy, an early settler by Tenaya Lake (United States Board on Geographic Names, 1934, p. 17).

Murphy Creek [SAN JOAQUIN]: *stream,* heads in Amador County and flows 3.25 miles in San Joaquin County to Mokelumne River 4 miles northeast of Clements (lat. 38°13'40" N, long. 121°01'40" W; sec. 6, T 4 N, R 9 E). Named on Clements (1968) and Goose Creek (1968) 7.5' quadrangles.

Murphy Peak [TUOLUMNE]: *peak,* 4 miles east-northeast of Tuolumne (lat. 37°58'55" N, long. 120°09'50" W; sec. 36, T 2 N, R 16 E). Named on Tuolumne (1948) 7.5' quadrangle.

Murphys [CALAVERAS]: *town,* 12 miles east-southeast of San Andreas (lat. 38°08'15" N, long. 120°27'45" W; in and near sec. 5, T 3 N, R 14 E). Named on Murphys (1948) 7.5' quadrangle. The place is called Murphy's on Ellis' (1850) map, and called Murphy on Big Trees (1891) 30' quadrangle. Postal authorities established Murphy's post office in 1851, changed the name to Murphy in 1894, and changed it to Murphys in 1935 (Frickstad, p. 16). The name is for Daniel Murphy and John Murphy, brothers who set up a mining camp in 1848 that became known as Murphy's Diggings, Murphy's Camp, and Murphy's (Hoover, Rensch, and Rensch, p. 46). Gudde (1975, p. 258) noted that places called Owlsburg and Owlburrow Flat were rich diggings on a north-trending ridge located in present Murphys, and (p. 337) that a place called Stoutenburg, named for a German miner, was situated along Coyote Creek near Murphys. A mining camp of the 1850's and 1860's called Brownsville was located 1 mile east of Murphys; the name was for Alfred Brown (California Department of Parks and Recreation, p. 17).

Murphy's Camp: see **Murphys** [CALAVERAS].

Murphy's Diggings: see **Murphys** [CALAVERAS].

Murphy's Dome: see **Pywiack Dome** [MARIPOSA].

Murphy's Ferry: see **Ripon** [SAN JOAQUIN]; **Salida** [STANISLAUS].

Murray Creek [CALAVERAS]: *stream,* flows 14 miles to North Fork Calaveras River 1.5 miles northwest of San Andreas (lat. 38° 12'40" N, long. 120°42'15" W; near E line sec. 12, T 4 N, R 11 E). Named on Calaveritas (1962), Rail Road Flat (1948), and San Andreas (1962) 7.5' quadrangles. North Fork enters from the north 2.5 miles upstream from the mouth of Murray Creek; it is 5 miles long and is named on Mokelumne Hill (1948) and San Andreas (1962) 7.5' quadrangles.

Murray's Ferry: see **Merced Falls** [MERCED].

Musquito: see **Glencoe** [CALAVERAS].

Musquito Gulch: see **Glencoe** [CALAVERAS].

Mustang Canyon [STANISLAUS]: *canyon,* drained by a stream that flows 2.5 miles to Garzas Creek 2.5 miles northeast of Mustang Peak (lat. 37°12'20" N, long. 121°19'05" W; sec. 28, T 8 S, R 6 E); the canyon heads near Mustang Peak. Named on Mustang Peak (1955) 7.5' quadrangle.

Mustang Creek [MERCED]: *stream,* flows 3.25 miles to lowlands 12 miles northeast of Pacheco Pass (lat. 37°12'30" N, long. 121° 05' W; near W line sec. 27, T 8 S, R 8 E). Named on Crevison Peak (1955) and Howard Ranch (1953) 7.5' quadrangles.

Mustang Flat [STANISLAUS]: *area,* 1 mile north-northwest of Mustang Peak (lat. 37°11'55" N, long. 121°21'50" W; sec. 31, T 8 S, R 6 E). Named on Mustang Peak (1955) 7.5' quadrangle.

Mustang Peak [STANISLAUS]: *peak,* 20 miles west-southwest of Newman on Stanislaus-Santa Clara County line (lat. 37°11'10" N, long. 121°21'35" W; sec. 6, T 9 S, R 6 E). Altitude 2263 feet. Named on Mustang Peak (1955) 7.5' quadrangle.

Mustang Ridge [MERCED]: *ridge,* east-trending, 1.25 miles long, 3.5 miles west-northwest of Sweeney Hill (lat. 36°55'05" N, long. 121°06'20" W). Named on Los Banos Valley (1969) 7.5' quadrangle.

Myers Creek [MARIPOSA]: *stream,* flows 2.5 miles to South Fork Dry Creek 6.5 miles northwest of Hornitos (lat. 37°34'10" N, long. 120°19'35" W; sec. 21, T 4 S, R 15 E). Named on Merced Falls (1962) 7.5' quadrangle.

— N —

Nairn [MERCED]: *locality,* 6 miles east-northeast of Atwater along Southern Pacific Railroad (lat. 37°22'30" N, long. 120°30'05" W; near NW cor. sec. 36 ,T 6 S, R 13 E). Named on Atwater (1918) 7.5' quadrangle. California Division of Highways' (1934) map shows a place called Ferrin located 1 mile south of Nairn along Southern Pacific Railroad (near NE cor. sec. 35, T 6 S, R 13 E).

Nance Peak [TUOLUMNE]: *peak,* 15 miles east-southeast of Pinecrest (lat. 38°04'05" N, long. 119°45'10" W). Named on Pinecrest (1956) 15' quadrangle. The name commemorates John Torrence Nance, professor of military science at University of California (United States Board on Geographic Names, 1934, p. 17).

Narbo: see **Quartz Mountain** [MADERA] (2).

Narrows: see **The Narrows** [MERCED]; **The Narrows** [STANISLAUS].

Nashton: see **Soulsbyville** [TUOLUMNE].

Nassau: see **Nassau Valley** [CALAVERAS].

Nassau Creek [CALAVERAS]: *stream,* flows 7.5 miles to Cherokee Creek 5 miles west-northwest of Angels Camp (lat. 38°05'30" N, long. 120°37'55" W; near SE cor. sec. 22, T 3 N, R 12 E); the stream goes through Nassau Valley. Named on Angels Camp (1962) and Salt Spring Valley (1962) 7.5' quadrangles.

Nassau Valley [CALAVERAS]: *valley,* 5 miles southwest of Angels Camp (lat. 38°02' N, long. 120°37'10" W); the valley is on upper reaches of Nassau Creek. Named on Angels Camp (1962) 7.5' quadrangle. California Mining Bureau's (1909a) map shows a place called Nassau located 6.5 miles by stage line west-southwest of Altaville. Postal authorities established Nassau post office 6 miles west of Angels Camp in 1892, moved it 1.5 miles west in 1905, and discontinued it in 1910 (Salley, p. 150).

Neall Lake [TUOLUMNE]: *lake,* 950 feet long, 11.5 miles northwest of White Wolf (lat. 37°59'15" N, long. 119°30'15" W). Named on Hetch Hetchy Reservoir (1956) 15' quadrangle. The name is for John Mitchell Neall, who was stationed in Yosemite National Park with the Fourth Cavalry from 1892 until 1897 (United States Board on Geographic Names, 1934, p. 17). Lieutenant H.C. Benson named the feature, which first was called Rodgers Lake for Captain Alexander Rodgers—this name was dropped because it duplicated another name in the park (Browning, 1988, p. 102).

Ned Gulch [MARIPOSA]:

(1) *canyon,* drained by a stream that flows 1.25 miles to Willow Creek 2.25 miles south of Penon Blanco Peak (lat. 37°42' N, long. 120°15'35" W; sec. 1, T 3 S, R 15 E). Named on Penon Blanco Peak (1962) 7.5' quadrangle.

(2) *canyon,* drained by a stream that flows 7.5 miles to Merced River 6.5 miles west of El Portal (lat. 37°40'10" N, long. 119° 54' W). Named on El Portal (1947) and Lake Eleanor (1956) 15' quadrangles. Called Ned's Gulch on Hoffmann and Gardner's (1863-1867) map.

Neds Gulch [CALAVERAS]: *canyon,* drained by a stream that flows nearly 3 miles to San Antonio Creek 5.5 miles north-northeast of Murphys (lat. 38°12'50" N, long. 120°25'50" W; sec. 9, T 4 N, R 14 E). Named on Murphys (1948) 7.5' quadrangle.

Ned's Gulch: see **Ned Gulch** [MARIPOSA] (2).

Negro Hill [CALAVERAS]: *peak,* 2 miles west of Angels Camp (lat. 38°04'25" N, long. 120°34'55" W; sec. 31, T 3 N, R 13 E). Named on Angels Camp (1962) 7.5' quadrangle. Called Nigger Hill on San Andreas (1947) 15' quadrangle.

Negro Hill [MARIPOSA]: *ridge,* west-northwest-trending, 1.5 miles long, 5 miles northeast of the settlement of Catheys Valley (lat. 37° 28'30" N, long. 120°00'45" W). Named on Catheys Valley (1962) 7.5' quadrangle. Called Nigger Hill on Indian Gulch (1920) 15' quadrangle, but United States Board on Geographic Names (1964a, p. 12) rejected this name for the feature.

Negro Hill [MERCED]: *peak,* less than 1 mile northwest of Snelling (lat. 37°31'45" N, long. 120°26'40" W; near W line sec. 4, T 5 S, R 14 E). Altitude 331 feet. Named on Snelling (1962) 7.5' quadrangle.

Negro Jack Gulch [TUOLUMNE]: *canyon,* drained by a stream that flows nearly 1 mile to Tulloch Lake 5 miles northwest of Keystone (lat. 37°53'15" N, long. 120°34' W; at N line sec. 5, T 1 S, R 13 E); the canyon is east of Negro Jack Point. Named on Melones Dam (1962) 7.5' quadrangle. Called Nigger Jack Gulch on Copperopolis (1916) 15' quadrangle.

Negro Jack Point [TUOLUMNE]: *promontory,* 5.5 miles northwest of Keystone on the south side of Tulloch Lake (lat. 37°53'20" N, long. 120°34'40" W; near SW cor. sec. 32, T 1 N, R 13 E). Named on Melones Dam (1962) 7.5' quadrangle. Called Nigger Jack Pt. on Copperopolis (1916) 15' quadrangle. The name is for Jack Wade, a slave who came to California, bought his freedom, and settled near the feature (Paden and Schlichtmann, p. 52-53).

Nehouse Creek [MADERA]: *stream,* flows 3 miles to West Fork Jackass Creek 6.5 miles east-northeast of Shuteye Peak (lat. 37°23'30" N, long. 119°19'20" W; sec. 23, T 6 S, R 24 E). Named on Shuteye Peak (1953) 15' quadrangle.

Nelder Creek [MADERA]: *stream,* flows 7.5 miles to join Lewis Fork and form Fresno River less than 0.5 mile south-southwest of Yosemite Forks (lat. 37°21'40" N, long. 119°37'55" W; near SW cor. sec. 36, T 6 S, R 21 E). Named on Bass Lake (1953) 15' quadrangle.

Nelder Grove Campground [MADERA]: *locality,* 5 miles north-northeast of Yosemite Forks (lat. 37°15'20" N, long. 119°35' W; sec. 8, T 6 S, R 22 E). Named on Bass Lake (1953) 15' quadrangle. Nelder Grove is a group of redwood trees—John Muir found John A. Nelder living in a cabin at the place in 1875 (Browning, 1986, p. 157).

Nellie Falls: see **Little Nellie Falls** [MARIPOSA].

Nelson: see **Jack Nelson Creek** [CALAVERAS].

Nelson Cove [MARIPOSA]: *valley,* 11 miles east-southeast of Mariposa along East Fork Chowchilla Creek (lat. 37°24'35" N, long. 119°47' W; sec. 16, T 6 S, R 20 E). Named on Stumpfield Mountain (1947) 7.5' quadrangle.

Nelson Lake [MARIPOSA]: *lake,* 1400 feet long, 3 miles south-southeast of Cathedral Peak (lat. 37°48'35" N, long. 119°22'35" W). Named on Tuolumne Meadows (1956) 15' quadrangle. The name commemorates William Henry Nelson, a ranger in Yosemite National Park from 1917 until 1936, and from 1943 until 1945 (Browning, 1988, p. 103).

Nevada Fall [MARIPOSA]: *waterfall,* 3.5 miles east-southeast of Yosemite Village on Merced River (lat. 37°43'30" N, long. 119° 32' W). Named on Yosemite (1956) 15' quadrangle. Lafayette H. Bunnell, who was with the group that discovered the waterfall in 1851, suggested the name because the white foaming water resembled an avalanche of snow (United States Board on Geographic Names, 1934, p. 18)—*nevada* means "snowy" in Spanish.

New Albany: see **Stockton** [SAN JOAQUIN].

New Camp: see **Columbia** [TUOLUMNE].

New Don Pedro Reservoir: see **Don Pedro Reservoir** [TUOLUMNE].

Newell: see **Confidence** [TUOLUMNE].

New Hogan Lake: see **New Hogan Reservoir** [CALAVERAS].

New Hogan Reservoir [CALAVERAS]: *lake,* behind a dam on Calaveras River 3 miles south-southeast of Valley Springs (lat. 38° 09' N, long. 120°48'45" W; near SW cor. sec. 31, T 4 N, R 11 E). Named on Jenny Lind (1962), San Andreas (1962), and Valley Springs (1962) 7.5' quadrangles. United States Board on Geographic Names (1972, p. 4) approved the name "New Hogan Lake" for the feature, and gave the names "Hogan Reservoir" and "Valley Springs Reservoir" as variants. Valley Springs (1944) 15' quadrangle shows a smaller, unnamed lake behind a dam just upstream from the dam that forms present New Hogan Lake.

New Hope: see **Stanislaus River** [CALAVERAS-SAN JOAQUIN-STANISLAUS-TUOLUMNE]; **Thornton** [SAN JOAQUIN].

New Hope Landing [SAN JOAQUIN]: *locality,* 4 miles west of Thornton on the east side of Mokelumne River (lat. 38°13'40" N, long. 121°29'25" W); the place is on New Hope Tract. Named on Thornton (1978) 7.5' quadrangle.

New Hope Tract [SAN JOAQUIN]: *area,* 11 miles west-northwest of Lodi at and near Thornton (lat. 38°14' N, long. 121°27' W). Named on Bruceville (1968) and Thornton (1978) 7.5' quadrangles. Arthur Thornton started his New Hope ranch about 1855 at the site of present Thornton (Gudde, 1949, p. 235).

New Liberty: see **Acampo** [SAN JOAQUIN]; **Lockeford** [SAN JOAQUIN].

Newman [STANISLAUS]: *town,* 12 miles south-southeast of Patterson (lat. 37°18'55" N, long. 121°01'20" W; mainly in sec. 19, T 7 S, R 9 E). Named on Newman (1952) 7.5' quadrangle. The town was laid out when the railroad reached the place in 1887; it was named for Simon Newman, a founder of the community (Gudde, 1949, p. 235). Postal authorities established Newman post office in 1888 (Salley, p. 154). They established Vernon post office 3.5 miles northeast of Newman in 1889 and discontinued it in 1892 (Salley, p. 231).

New Melones Lake [CALAVERAS-TUOLUMNE]: *lake,* behind a dam on Stanislaus River 7 miles east-southeast of Copperopolis on Calaveras-Tuolumne County line (lat. 37°57'10" N, long. 120°30'50" W; sec. 11, T 1 N, R 13 E). Named on Columbia (1948, photorevised 1973) and Sonora (1948, photorevised 1973) 7.5' quadrangles. Called Melones Reservoir on Columbia (1948) and Sonora (1948) 15' quadrangles, and on Angels Camp (1962) and Melones Dam (1962) 7.5' quadrangles. United States Board on Geographic Names (1972, p. 4) gave the names "Melones Reservoir" and "New Melones Reservoir" as variants.

New Melones Reservoir: see **New Melones Lake** [CALAVERAS-TUOLUMNE].

Newsom's Bridge: see **Oristembra**, under **Crows Landing** [STANISLAUS].

Newton Crossing: see **Chowchilla River** [MADERA-MARIPOSA-MERCED].

New York Camp: see **Merced River** [MADERA-MARIPOSA-MERCED].

New York Tent: see **Yosemite Junction** [TUOLUMNE].

Niagara: see **Camp Niagara** [TUOLUMNE].

Niagara Creek [TUOLUMNE]:

(1) *stream,* flows 4.5 miles to Reed Creek 5.5 miles east-northeast of Duckwall Mountain (lat. 37°59'40" N, long. 120°01'15" W; near S line sec. 29, T 2 N, R 18 E). Named on Cherry Lake North (1979), Duckwall Mountain (1948), and Hull Creek (1979) 7.5' quadrangles.

(2) *stream,* flows 6.5 miles to Donnell Reservoir 6 miles west of Dardanelle (lat. 38°19'55" N, long. 119°56'25" W). Named on Dardanelle (1979) and Donnell Lake (1979) 7.5' quadrangles.

Niagara Creek Campground [TUOLUMNE]: *locality,* 4.5 miles west-southwest of present Dardanelle (lat. 38°19'35" N, long. 119° 54'45" W; sec. 32, T 6 N, R 19 E); the place is along Niagara Creek (2). Named on Dardanelles Cone (1956) 15' quadrangle.

Nibs Lake [SAN JOAQUIN]: *lake,* 1500 feet long, 15 miles west-southwest of Lodi on Roberts (present Medford) Island (lat. 38°01'35" N, long. 121°31' W). Named on Rio Vista (1952) 15' quadrangle.

Nibs Slough [SAN JOAQUIN]: *water feature,* on Mandeville Island, joins San Joaquin River 15 miles west-southwest of Lodi (lat. 38° 02'35" N, long. 121°31'50" W). Named on Bouldin Island (1952) 7.5' quadrangle.

Nichols: see **Robert Nichols Spring** [TUOLUMNE].

Nigger Creek: see **White Fir Creek** [TUOLUMNE].

Nigger Gulch: see **Mokelumne River** [CALAVERAS-SAN JOAQUIN].

Nigger Hill: see **Mokelumne Hill** [CALAVERAS]; **Negro Hill** [CALAVERAS]; **Negro Hill** [MARIPOSA].

Nigger Jack Gulch: see **Negro Jack Gulch** [TUOLUMNE].

Nigger Jack Point: see **Negro Jack Point** [TUOLUMNE].

Night Cap: see **Night Cap Peak** [TUOLUMNE].

Night Cap Peak [TUOLUMNE]: *peak,* 3.25 miles west-southwest of Sonora Pass (lat. 38°18'25" N, long. 119°41'25" W). Named on Sonora Pass (1979) 7.5' quadrangle. Called simply Night Cap on Dardanelles (1898) 30' quadrangle.

Nina: see **Lake Nina**, under **Tilden Lake** [TUOLUMNE].

Nipinnawasee [MADERA]: *settlement,* 6.25 miles west-northwest of Yosemite Forks (lat. 37°24'15" N, long. 119°43'55" W; on S line sec. 13, T 6 S, R 20 E). Called Nipinnawassee on Bass Lake (1953) 15' quadrangle, but United States Board on Geographic Names (1981a, p. 2) rejected the forms "Nipinnawassee" and "Nippinnawasee" for the name. Postal authorities established Femmon post office 3 miles north of Ahwahnee in 1912, and then moved it and changed the name to Nipinnawasee the same year; the name "Femmon" honored Frank Femmon, who developed a prize-winning apple (Salley, p. 73-74). They discontinued Nipinnawasee post office in 1961; the name is of Indian origin and was transferred from Michigan (Salley, p. 154).

Noname Lake [MADERA]: *lake,* 500 feet long, 3.5 miles west of Devils Postpile (lat. 37°37'40" N, long. 119°08'50" W). Named on Devils Postpile (1953) 15' quadrangle.

Norris Creek [MADERA]: *stream,* flows 4.5 miles to Jackass Creek 11.5 miles north-northeast of Shuteye Peak (lat. 37°29'45" N, long. 119°19'15" W); the stream heads near Norris Lake. Named on Merced Peak (1953) 15' quadrangle.

Norris Lake [MADERA]: *lake,* 400 feet long, 8 miles south-southeast of Merced Peak (lat. 37°31'35" N, long. 119°20'15" W; near W line sec. 3, T 5 S, R 24 E). Named on Merced Peak (1953) 15' quadrangle.

North American House: see **Valley Springs** [CALAVERAS].

North Branch [CALAVERAS]: *locality,* 2.5 miles west-northwest of San Andreas (lat. 38°12'25" N, long. 120°43'30" W). Named on Jackson (1902) 30' quadrangle. Camp's (1962) map has the designation "North Branch (old site)" for a place located about 1 mile east-northeast of present North Branch at the confluence of North Fork Calaveras River and Murray Creek. The same map shows a place called Iowa Cabin, or Second Crossing, situated about 0.5 mile down North Fork Calaveras River from the confluence. Postal authorities established North Branch post office before March 19, 1852, discontinued it in 1870, and reestablished it in 1876; they changed the name to Northbranch in 1895, discontinued it in 1911, reestablished it in 1912, and discontinued it in 1925 (Salley, p. 155).

North Crane Creek [TUOLUMNE]: *stream,* flows 4 miles to South Fork Tuolumne River 5.5 miles south of Mather (lat. 37°48'10" N, long.

19°50'50" W; sec. 35, T 1 S, R 19 E); the stream heads just north of the head of Crane Creek [MARIPOSA]. Named on Lake Eleanor (1956) 15' quadrangle

North Dome [MARIPOSA]: *peak,* 1.5 miles east-northeast of Yosemite Village (lat. 37°45'25" N, long. 119°33'35" W); the peak is on the north side of Yosemite Valley. Altitude 7542 feet. Named on Hetch Hetchy Reservoir (1956) 15' quadrangle. Members of the Mariposa Battalion named the peak in 1851 (Gudde, 1949, p. 238).

North Dome: see **Hetch Hetchy Dome** [TUOLUMNE].

North Fork [MADERA]: *town,* 22 miles east of Raymond (lat. 37°13'40" N, long. 119°30'30" W; around SE cor. sec. 13, T 8 S, R 22 E); the town is along North Fork Willow Creek (2). Named on North Fork (1965) 7.5' quadrangle. Called Northfork on California Mining Bureau's (1909c) map. Postal authorities established North Fork post office in 1888 (Frickstad, p. 86). Milton Brown was the first settler at the site, and the community that grew there was called Brown's; the place took the name "North Fork" after postal authorities started North Fork post office in the store building of North Fork Lumber Company (Clough, p. 80-81). Postal authorities established Cascadel post office 4 miles east of North Fork in 1892 and discontinued it in 1896; the name was from Cascadel ranch, which in turn was named for Cascadel Point (Salley, p. 39). Shaver Lake (1953) 15' quadrangle shows Cascadel ranch situated along Whiskey Creek (2) (sec. 16, T 8 S, R 23 E). Postal authorities established a post office called Minarets about 5 miles southeast of North Fork in 1925 and discontinued it in 1933; the place was the terminus of Minarets and Western Railroad (Salley, p. 141). The name "Minarets" was used much earlier, however, when Madera County separated from Fresno County and residents of the mountainous part of Madera County planned to build a town called Minarets 15 miles east of Madera and have the county seat there (Clough, p. 15-16). Postal authorities established Bethel post office 4 miles west of North Fork in 1881 and discontinued it in 1885; James W. Bethel owned the store that housed the post office (Salley, p. 20).

North Fork [MARIPOSA]: *locality,* 4.5 miles northeast of the village of Bear Valley along Yosemite Valley Railroad (lat. 37°36'35" N, long. 120°23'40" W). Named on Sonora (1897) 30' quadrangle.

North Grove Campground [CALAVERAS]: *locality,* 5.5 miles southeast of Blue Mountain along Big Trees Creek (lat. 38°16'30" N, long. 120°18'20" W; sec. 22, T 5 N, R 15 E). Named on Dorrington (1979) 7.5' quadrangle.

North Gulch [CALAVERAS]: *canyon,* drained by a stream that flows 2.5 miles to Calaveras River 1 mile east-northeast of Jenny Lind (lat. 38°06'15" N, long. 120°50'55" W; sec. 23, T 3 N, R 10 E). Named on Jenny Lind (1962) 7.2' quadrangle.

North Mokelumne River: see **Mokelumne River** [SAN JOAQUIN].

North Mountain [TUOLUMNE]: *peak,* 2.5 miles northwest of Mather Station (present Mather) (lat. 37°54'05" N, long. 119°53'55" W; near N line sec. 33, T 1 N, R 19 E). Named on Yosemite (1909) 30' quadrangle.

North Peak [TUOLUMNE]: *peak,* 6 miles north-northwest of Tioga Pass on Tuolumne-Mono County line (lat. 37°59' N, long. 119°18'50" W; sec. 34, T 2 N, R 24 E). Altitude 12,242 feet. Named on Tuolumne Meadows (1956) 15' quadrangle.

North Ridge [SAN JOAQUIN]: *ridge,* generally east-trending, 3 miles long, 11 miles south-southwest of Tracy (lat. 37°35'15" N, long. 121°28'30" W); the ridge is north of North Fork Lone Tree Creek (1). Named on Lone Tree Creek (1955) 7.5' quadrangle.

North Slough Mariposa Creek [MERCED]: *stream,* flows 10 miles before ending 14 miles north-northeast of Dos Palos Y (lat. 37°13'30" N, long. 120°30'20" W; at W line sec. 24, T 8 S, R 13 E). Named on Chowchilla (1960) 15' quadrangle. Called Middle Slough Mariposa Creek on Lingard (1918) 7.5' quadrangle.

North Wawona [MARIPOSA]: *settlement,* 1.25 miles northeast of Wawona (lat 37°32'50" N, long. 119°38'20" W; sec. 35, T 4 S, R 21 E); the place is 0.5 mile north of South Wawona. Named on Yosemite (1956) 15' quadrangle.

Norton [SAN JOAQUIN]: *locality,* 4.5 miles northwest of Waterloo along Central California Traction Railroad (lat. 38°04'50" N, long. 121°14'30" W; on W line sec. 29, T 3 N, R 7 E). Named on Waterloo (1968) 7.5' quadrangle.

Norval [CALAVERAS]: *locality,* less than 1 mile southwest of Valley Springs along Southern Pacific Railroad (lat. 38°11'05" N, long. 120°50'20" W; sec. 23, T 4 N, R 10 E). Named on Valley Springs (1944) 15' quadrangle.

Norwegian Gulch [MARIPOSA]: *canyon,* 2.25 miles long, opens into the canyon of Bear Creek (2) 4 miles south-southeast of the village of Bear Valley (lat. 37°31'05" N, long. 120°05'15" W). Named on Bear Valley (1947) 7.5' quadrangle.

Norwegian Gulch [TUOLUMNE]: *canyon,* drained by a stream that flows nearly 1 mile to Stanislaus River 5 miles west-southwest of Columbia (lat. 38°00'30" N, long. 120°29'15" W; near E line sec. 24, T 2 N, R 13 E). Named on Columbia (1948) 7.5' quadrangle. The canyon also was called Jackass Gulch (Gudde, 1975, p. 247)—the owner of a strayed jackass discovered gold in the canyon while he was hunting for the animal (Stoddart, p. 62).

Norwegian Gulch Center: see **Mount Ophir** [MARIPOSA].

Notarb [MADERA]: *locality,* 6 miles southeast of Fairmead along Southern Pacific Railroad (lat. 37°00'40" N, long. 120°07'05" W; near N line sec. 4, T 11 S, R 17 E). Named on Kismet (1961) 7.5' quadrangle.

Number Nine [MARIPOSA]: *locality,* 6 miles southwest of Bear Valley (2) (lat. 37°30'45" N, long. 120°11'55" W). Named on Sonora (1891) 30' quadrangle. Coulterville (1947) 15' quadrangle shows Number Nine mine at the place.

Nun Lake [MERCED]: *lake,* 150 feet long, 3 miles south-southwest of Pacheco Pass (lat. 37°01'35" N, long. 121°13'55" W). Named on Pacheco Pass (1955) 7.5' quadrangle.

Nutcracker Lake: see **Ruth Lake** [MADERA].

Nutmeg Gulch [MARIPOSA]: *canyon,* drained by a stream that flows 3.25 miles to South Fork Merced River 5 miles southwest of El Portal (lat. 37°37'35" N, long. 119°50'40" W; sec. 34, T 3 S, R 19 E). Named on Buckingham Mountain (1947) 7.5' quadrangle.

Nydiver Lakes [MADERA]: *lakes,* largest 1000 feet long, 7 miles northwest of Devils Postpile (lat. 37°41'35" N, long. 119°10'15" W). Named on Devils Postpile (1953) 15' quadrangle. Browning (1986, p. 160) associated the name with David Nidever, a prospector of the early 1900's.

– O –

Oak: see **Borden** [MADERA].

Oakdale [STANISLAUS]: *town,* 12 miles northeast of Modesto on the south side of Stanislaus River (lat. 37°46' N, long. 120°50'45" W). Named on Oakdale (1968) 7.5' quadrangle. A.J. Patterson founded the community in 1871, and a committee of citizens chose the name "Oakdale" because of oak trees at the place (Hanna, p. 216). Postal authorities established Oakdale post office in 1871 (Frickstad, p. 200), and the town incorporated in 1906. The present town is near a site long known as Fremont's Crossing because Fremont used the spot to cross Stanislaus River in 1844 (Paden and Schlichtmann, p. 18). In 1860 Henry Langworthy laid out a town called Langworth near present Oakdale on a hill above a ferry owned by Major James Burney (Hoover, Rensch, and Rensch, p. 542). Eslcalon (1968) 7.5' quadrangle shows Langworth cemetery situated 1.5 miles west-southwest of Oakdale, and Thalheim (1915) 7.5' quadrangle shows Langworth school in the vicinity of the cemetery. Postal authorities established Langworth post office in 1864 and moved it 2 miles east in 1871 when they changed the name to Oakdale (Salley, p. 117). Nelson Taylor operated Taylor's Ferry in 1849 at present Oakdale; later the ferry was called Emory's Ferry and was called Heath and Emory's Ferry (Morgan and Scobie *in* Perkins, p. 315; Brotherton, p. 73). A cantonment of United States troops at Taylor's Ferry in 1849 was called Camp Stanislaus (M'Collum, p. 130; Morgan *in* M'Collum, p. 202-203). Islip's Ferry operated in 1850 on Stanislaus River 6 miles below Taylor's Ferry (Morgan and Scobie *in* Perkins, p. 315; Brotherton, p. 63). Islip's Ferry also was known as Middle Ferry (Gudde, 1975, p. 171), Burney's Ferry, Warren's Ferry, Hughes and Keyes Ferry, and Walker's Ferry (Brotherton, p. 66). Cotton's Ferry began operations on Stanislaus River near present Oakdale in 1850; the site of the ferry now is more than 0.5 mile north of the present river because the river changed its course in the winter of 1861 and 1862 (Brotherton, p. 69). Postal authorities established Leitch's Ferry post office 1.5 miles east of present Oakdale along Stanislaus River in 1864 and discontinued it in 1866; the post office name was for Archibald Leitch, a partner in Leitch and Cottle Ferry Company (Salley, p. 120). They established Loving's Ferry post office 1.5 miles east of present Oakdale on the north side of Stanislaus River in 1855 and moved it to the south bank of the river in 1858, when they changed the name to Holden's Ferry; they moved the post office again in 1858 to the north side of the river and changed the name back to Loving's Ferry; they discontinued this Loving's Ferry post office in 1862—the name "Loving" was for John Loving, owner of the ferry, and the name "Holden" was for William Holden, ferry operator and later lieutenant governor of California (Salley, p. 99, 128). Postal authorities established Wanda post office 6 miles northeast of Oakdale in 1896 and discontinued it in 1901; the name was for Mrs. Wanda Muir Hanna, daughter of John Muir (Salley, p. 234). A ford on Stanislaus River near Wanda was called Rutherford's Crossing for W.W. Rutherford, who had land there on the south side of the river (Brotherton, p. 79).

Oak Flat: see **Big Oak Flat** [TUOLUMNE].

Oak Grove [CALAVERAS]: *locality,* 6 miles south-southwest of Valley Springs (lat. 38°07' N, long. 120°53'10" W; sec. 16, T 3 N, R 10 E). Named on Valley Springs SW (1962) 7.5' quadrangle.

Oakhurst [MADERA]: *settlement,* 3 miles south-southwest of Yosemite Forks along Fresno River (lat. 37°19'45" N, long. 119° 39' W; near NW cor. sec. 14, T 7 S, R 21 E); the place is at the east end of Fresno Flats. Named on Bass Lake (1953) 15' quadrangle. The settlement is called Fresno Flats on Mariposa (1912) 30' quadrangle. Postal authorities established Fresno Flats post office in 1873, and moved it and changed the name to

Oakhurst in 1912 (Salley, p. 81, 158). They established Starville post office 23 miles northeast of Fresno Flats post office in 1889 and discontinued it in 1891; the name was from Star mine (Salley, p. 212).

Oak Island [SAN JOAQUIN]: *island,* 1050 feet long, 13 miles southwest of downtown Stockton in Old River (lat. 37°48'15" N, long. 121°27'20" W). Named on Union Island (1978) 7.5' quadrangle

Oak Leaf Spring [TUOLUMNE]: *spring,* 10 miles north-northeast of Stanislaus (lat. 38°15'45" N, long. 120°15'55" W; sec. 25, T 5 N, R 15 E). Named on Dorrington (1979) 7.5' quadrangle.

Oak Point: see **Stockton** [SAN JOAQUIN].

Oak Spring: see **Montezuma** [TUOLUMNE].

Oakvale Retreat: see **Miami** [MARIPOSA].

Oat Gulch [STANISLAUS]: *canyon,* drained by a stream that flows 6.25 miles to Garzas Creek 3.5 miles northeast of Crevison Peak (lat. 37°13'50" N, long. 121°08'40" W; sec. 24, T 8 S, R 7 E). Named on Crevison Peak (1955) and Orestimba Peak (1955) 7.5' quadrangles.

Oat Hills [TUOLUMNE]: *range,* 3.5 miles east-northeast of Don Pedro Camp (lat. 37°44'25" N, long. 120°21' W). Named on Penon Blanco Peak (1962) 7.5' quadrangle.

Oat Mountain: see **Castle Peak** [MADERA].

Obelisk: see **Mount Clark** [MARIPOSA].

Obelisk Group: see **Clark Range** [MADERA].

Obelisk Lake [MARIPOSA]: *lake,* 1100 feet long, 10 miles south of Cathedral Peak (lat. 37°42'15" N, long. 119°24'55" W); the lake is less than 1 mile northeast of Mount Clark, which members of the Whitney survey called the Obelisk. Named on Merced Peak (1953) 15' quadrangle. United States Board on Geographic Names (1934, p. 18) rejected the name "Adair Lake" for the feature.

Obelisk Lake: see **Adair Lake** [MADERA].

O'Byrnes Ferry [CALAVERAS-TUOLUMNE]: *locality,* 7 miles south-southeast of Copperopolis along Stanislaus River on Calaveras-Tuolumne County line (lat. 37°53'40" N, long. 120°34'10" W; sec. 32, T 1 N, R 13 E). Named on Copperopolis (1916) 15' quadrangle. Water of Tulloch Lake now covers the site. Postal authorities established O'Byrnes Ferry post office in Calaveras County in 1855 and discontinued it in 1860 (Frickstad, p. 16). Patrick O. Byrne, or O'Byrne, operated a ferry there before the flood of 1852 (Paden and Schlichtmann, p. 58). A mining camp at the place in 1849 and 1850 was called Byrnes Ferry (Gudde, 1975, p. 55).

O'Connells Spring [MERCED]: *spring,* nearly 2 miles north of Pacheco Pass (lat. 37°05'20" N, long. 121°12'50" W). Named on Pacheco Pass (1955) 7.5' quadrangle.

Odom Creek [MARIPOSA]: *stream,* flows nearly 4 miles to Bear Creek (2) 2.5 miles east-northeast of Santa Cruz Mountain (lat. 37° 28'05" N, long. 120°09'40" W; sec. 25, T 5 S, R 16 E). Named on Hornitos (1947) and Indian Gulch (1962) 7.5' quadrangles.

Ohio Diggings: see **Soulsbyville** [TUOLUMNE].

Ohm [STANISLAUS]: *locality,* 15 miles west of Modesto along Southern Pacific Railroad (lat. 37°37'35" N, long. 121°16'55" W; sec. 35, T 3 S, R 6 E). Named on Vernalis (1969) 7.5' quadrangle. Railroad officials named the place for Ohm ranch, started in 1868 by Thomas Ohm (Gudde, 1949, p. 241).

Olaine Lake [MADERA]: *lake,* 1000 feet long, 5 miles north-northwest of Devils Postpile (lat. 37°41'40" N, long. 119°06'45" W). Named on Devils Postpile (1953) 15' quadrangle. Charles Olaine prospected at the lake about 1910 (Browning, 1986, p. 161).

Old Chowchilla Creek [MERCED]: *water feature,* stream and an interrupted watercourse that nearly parallels Chowchilla River 10 miles southwest of Le Grand. Named on Chowchilla (1960) 15' quadrangle.

Old Dickenson Ferry [MERCED]: *locality,* 12 miles north-northwest of Los Banos along San Joaquin River (lat. 37°13'25" N, long. 120°47' W; sec. 20, T 8 S, R 11 E). Named on San Luis Ranch (1919) 7.5' quadrangle.

Old Gulch [CALAVERAS]:

(1) *canyon,* drained by a stream that flows 4.5 miles to Calaveritas Creek 5.5 miles east-southeast of San Andreas (lat. 38°09'25" N, long. 120°35'30" W; near W line sec. 31, T 4 N, R 13 E). Named on Calaveritas (1962) 7.5' quadrangle.

(2) *village,* 5 miles east-southeast of San Andreas (lat. 38°10'20" N, long. 120°35'40" W); the village was in present Old Gulch (1). Named on Jackson (1902) 30' quadrangle. The place also was known as Washington Flat (Gudde, 1975, p. 250).

Old Inspiration Point [MARIPOSA]: *relief feature,* 5.5 miles west-southwest of Yosemite Village on the south side of Yosemite Valley (lat. 37°42'20" N, long. 119°49'25" W); the feature is 1 mile southeast of Inspiration Point. Named on Yosemite (1956) 15' quadrangle. The place first was called Mount Beatitude (Browning, 1986, p. 14).

Old Man of the Mountains: see **Ahwiyah Point** [MARIPOSA].

Old McCormick Reservoir [CALAVERAS]: *intermittent lake,* 1000 feet long, 3.5 miles east-southeast of Jenny Lind (lat. 38°04'55" N, long. 120°48'20" W; sec. 30, T 3 N, R 11 E). Named on Jenny Lind (1962) 7.5' quadrangle.

Old Miami Mill: see **Timberloft Camp** [MARIPOSA].

Old Piute: see **The Old Piute**, under **Ahwiyah Point** [MARIPOSA].

Old River [SAN JOAQUIN]: *stream,* diverges west from San Joaquin River and flows 50 miles, partly on San Joaquin-Contra Costa County line, to rejoin the river 17 miles west-southwest of Lodi (lat. 38°04'20" N, long. 121°34'15" W). Named on Bouldin Island (1978), Clifton Court Forebay (1978), Lathrop (1952), Union Island (1978), and Woodward Island (1952) 7.5' quadrangles. Present Old River was called Rio del Pescadero in early Spanish times (Dillon, 1982, p. 30). Union Island (1914) 7.5' quadrangle has the name "Salmon Slough" for present Old River between Middle River and present Salmon Slough.

Old Woman Gulch [CALAVERAS]: *canyon,* drained by a stream that flows 3 miles to Chili Gulch nearly 4 miles northwest of San Andreas (lat. 38°14'30" N, long. 120°43'15" W; near W line sec. 36, T 5 N, R 11 E). Named on Mokelumne Hill (1948) and San Andreas (1962) 7.5' quadrangles. On San Andreas (1947) 15' quadrangle, present Spring Gulch (3) is called Old Woman Gulch.

Olive Lake: see **Huckleberry Lake** [TUOLUMNE].

Oliver Creek [MARIPOSA]: *stream,* flows 7.25 miles to East Fork Chowchilla River 11.5 miles east-southeast of Mariposa (lat. 37° 25'20" N, long. 119°46'35" W; sec. 10, T 6 S, R 20 E). Named on Buckingham Mountain (1947) and Stumpfield Mountain (1947) 7.5' quadrangles. Mariposa (1947) 15' quadrangle has the name "DeLong Creek" for present Oliver Creek below the confluence of DeLong and Oliver Creeks.

Oliver Lake [SAN JOAQUIN]: *lake,* 2100 feet long, 3.25 miles northwest of Lodi (lat. 38°10'20" N, long. 121°18'40" W; sec. 27, T 4 N, R 6 E). Named on Woodbridge (1910) 7.5' quadrangle.

Olson Pond [MERCED]: *lake,* 0.5 mile long, nearly 6 miles northeast of Los Banos (lat. 37°07'25" N, long. 120°47'05" W; sec. 29, T 9 S, R 11 E). Named on Los Banos (1960) and San Luis Ranch (1961) 7.5' quadrangles.

O'Neals [MADERA]: *locality,* 13 miles east-southeast of Raymond along Willow Creek (4) (lat. 37°07'40" N, long. 119°41'40" W; near SW cor. sec. 21, T 9 S, R 21 E). Named on O'Neals (1965) 7.5' quadrangle. Postal authorities established O'Neals post office in 1887 (Frickstad, p. 86). Charles O'Neal bought the store at the place in 1887, operated a small hotel, and was named postmaster of the new post office that took his name (Clough, p. 82). Postal authorities established Magnet post office 4 miles northeast of O'Neals in 1900 and discontinued in 1907; the name was for Magnet mine (Salley, p. 131).

O'Neals Meadow [MARIPOSA]: *area,* 4.25 miles southwest of Fish Camp (lat. 37°26'05" N, long. 119°41'40" W; sec. 5, T 6 S, R 21 E). Named on Bass Lake (1953) 15' quadrangle. John Ruffin O'Neal patented land in section 5 in 1884, and homesteaded in sections 5 and 8 in 1892 (Browning, 1986, p. 162).

O'Neil Creek [CALAVERAS]: *stream,* flows 13 miles to join McKinney Creek and form Calaveritas Creek 8.5 miles east of San Andreas (lat. 38°11' N, long. 120°31'15" W; near E line sec. 22, T 4 N, R 13 E). Named on Calaveritas (1962), Dorrington (1979), Fort Mountain (1979), and Murphys (1948) 7.5' quadrangles. Jackson (1902) 30' quadrangle has the form "O'Neils Creek" for the name.

O'Neill Forebay [MERCED]: *lake,* 9 miles east of Pacheco Pass along San Luis Creek below San Luis Reservoir (lat. 37°05' N, long. 121°03' W). Named on San Luis Dam (1969) 7.5' quadrangle. United States Board on Geographic Names (1967a, p. 7) rejected the names "O'Neill Reservoir" and "San Luis Forebay" for the feature, and noted that the name "O'Neill Forebay" commemorates J.E. O'Neill, a San Joaquin Valley rancher and business leader whose efforts helped to create the lake.

O'Neill Reservoir: see **O'Neill Forebay** [MERCED].

O'Neil Reservoir [TUOLUMNE]: *lake,* 500 feet long, 3.25 miles west-southwest of Sonora (lat. 37°58'10" N, long. 120°26'10" W; sec. 4, T 1 N, R 14 E). Named on Sonora (1948, photorevised 1973) 7.5' quadrangle.

O'Neils Creek: see O'Neil Creek [CALAVERAS].

Onion Lake [TUOLUMNE]: *lake,* 600 feet long, nearly 5 miles southeast of Matterhorn Peak (lat. 38°02'30" N, long. 119°19'10" W; on N line sec. 10, T 2 N, R 24 E). Named on Matterhorn Peak (1956) 15' quadrangle.

Onion Valley [CALAVERAS]: *valley,* at Tamarack (lat. 38°26'25" N, long. 120°04'30" W; near S line sec. 23, T 7 N, R 17 E). Named on Big Meadow (1956) 15' quadrangle. The name is from the abundance of wild onions at the place (Browning, 1986, p. 212).

Opal Hill [CALAVERAS]: *hill,* 7.5 miles south-southwest of Valley Springs (lat. 38°05'35" N, long. 120°53'25" W; near SE cor. sec. 20, T 3 N, R 10 E). Altitude 385 feet. Named on Valley Springs SW (1962) 7.5' quadrangle.

Ophir: see **Mount Ophir** [CALAVERAS]; **Mount Ophir** [MARIPOSA].

Opie: see **Coulterville** [MARIPOSA].

Opim: see **Forestsa** [MARIPOSA].

Oregon Bar [CALAVERAS]: *locality,* 4 miles northwest of Valley Springs along Mokelumne River (lat. 38°13'45" N, long. 120° 53' W; sec. 4, T 4 N, R 10 E). Named on Wallace (1962) 7.5' quadrangle. Water of Camanche Reservoir now covers the site.

Oregon Gulch: see **Campo Seco** [CALAVERAS].

Oregon Tent: see **Farmington** [SAN JOAQUIN].

Orestimba [MERCED-STANISLAUS]: *land grant,* 28 miles west of Merced on the west side of San Joaquin River in Merced and Stanislaus Counties. Named on Turlock (1962) 15' quadrangle. Sebastian Nuñez received 6 leagues in 1844 and claimed 26,666 acres patented in 1863 (Cowan, p. 55).

Orestimba Cañon: see **Orestimba Creek** [STANISLAUS].

Orestimba Creek [STANISLAUS]: *stream,* formed by the confluence of North Fork and South Fork 4 miles south-southeast of Mikes Peak, flows 25 miles to San Joaquin River 8 miles east-southeast of Patterson (lat. 37°25'20" N, long. 121°00'10" W). Named on Crows Landing (1952), Newman (1952), Orestimba Peak (1955), and Wilcox Ridge (1956) 7.5' quadrangles. Called Arroyo de los Piedras on Bancroft's (1864) map. Early Spaniards called the stream Arroyo de Orestimba because the padres, after gathering the first Indians in the region, made an agreement with the remaining natives to meet at the stream the next year—*orestimba* means "meeting place" in Spanish (Hoover, Rensch, and Rensch, p. 539-540). Whitney (1865, p. 44) mentioned Orestimba Cañon. North Fork is 12 miles long and is named on Mount Stakes (1955) and Wilcox Ridge (1956) 7.5' quadrangles. South Fork is 15 miles long and is named on Wilcox Ridge (1956) 7.5' quadrangle—it is called Orestimba Creek on Mississippi Creek (1955) and Mustang Peak (1955) 7.5' quadrangles.

Orestimba Narrows [STANISLAUS]: *narrows,* 12.5 miles west of Newman (lat. 37°17'05" N, long. 121°14'30" W; sec. 31, T 7 S, R 7 E); the place is along Orestimba Creek. Named on Orestimba Peak (1955) and Wilcox Ridge (1956) 7.5' quadrangles.

Orestimba Peak [STANISLAUS]: *peak,* 11 miles west of Newman (lat. 37°19'25" N, long. 121°13'30" W; sec. 17, T 7 S, R 7 E); the peak is north of Orestimba Creek. Altitude 2074 feet. Named on Orestimba Peak (1955) 7.5' quadrangle.

Orford [SAN JOAQUIN]: *locality,* 5.5 miles east-northeast of downtown Stockton along Southern Pacific Railroad (lat. 37°58'40" N, long. 121°11'20" W). Named on Stockton East (1952) 7.5' quadrangle. Called Windsor on Burnham (1914) 7.5' quadrangle.

Oristembra: see **Crows Landing** [STANISLAUS].

Orogenen Canyon [MERCED]: *canyon,* drained by a stream that flows 3 miles to South Fork Los Banos Creek 4.5 miles south-southwest of Sweeney Hill (lat. 36°50'15" N, long. 121°04'20" W). Named on Ruby Canyon (1968) 7.5' quadrangle.

Oro Grosso: see **Coarsegold** [MADERA].

Orr's Ranch: see **Elliott** [SAN JOAQUIN].

Ortega [SAN JOAQUIN]: *locality,* 4 miles south-southeast of downtown Stockton along Southern Pacific Railroad (lat. 37°54'25" N, long. 121°16'20" W). Named on Stockton West (1952) 7.5' quadrangle.

Ortigalita Creek [MERCED]: *stream,* flows 16 miles to lowlands 14 miles west of Dos Palos (lat. 36°57'25" N, long. 120°52'35" W; sec. 21, T 11 S, R 10 E). Named on Ortigalita Peak (1969) and Ortigalita Peak NW (1956) 7.5' quadrangles. It also was called El Arroyo del Ortigalito—*ortigalito* means "little nettle" in Spanish (Hoover, Rensch, and Rensch, p. 202).

Ortigalita Peak [MERCED]: *peak,* 21 miles southwest of Dos Palos (lat. 36°47'40" N, long. 120°55'20" W; near S line sec. 18, T 13 S, R 10 E). Altitude 3304 feet. Named on Ortigalita Peak (1969) 7.5' quadrangle.

Ortigalita Ridge [MERCED]: *ridge,* generally northwest-trending, 14 miles long, 24 miles west-southwest of Dos Palos (lat. 36°48'30" N, long. 121°00' W). Named on Los Banos Valley (1969), Ortigalita Peak (1969), and Ruby Canyon (1968) 7.5' quadrangles.

Ortigalito: see **Los Banos** [MERCED].

Oso: see **Mount Oso** [STANISLAUS].

Oso Creek [STANISLAUS]: *stream,* flows 5 miles to Orestimba Creek 8 miles west of Newman (lat. 37°17'50" N, long. 121°10'05" W; sec. 26, T 7 S, R 7 E). Named on Orestimba Peak (1955) 7.5' quadrangle.

Ostrander Lake [MARIPOSA]: *lake,* 1750 feet long, 9 miles south-southeast of Yosemite Village (lat. 37°37'30" N, long. 119°33' W; sec. 34, T 3 S, R 22 E). Named on Yosemite (1956) 15' quadrangle. Members of the Whitney survey named the lake for Harvey J. Ostrander, who homesteaded near it (Hanna, p. 222). The feature first was called Pohono Lake (Browning, 1986, p. 162).

Ostrander Rocks [MARIPOSA]: *relief feature,* 4 miles south of Yosemite Village (lat. 37°41'30" N, long. 119°35'30" W; near W line sec. 8, T 3 S, R 22 E). Named on Yosemite (1956) 15' quadrangle. Called Ostrander's Rocks on Hoffmann and Gardner's (1863-1867) map. Members of the Whitney survey named the feature for Harvey J. Ostrander of Ostrander Lake (Browning, 1986, p. 162).

Otter Lake [TUOLUMNE]: *lake,* 2200 feet long, 7 miles southwest of Tower Peak (lat. 38°05'20" N, long. 119°39'15" W). Named on Tower Peak (1956) 15' quadrangle.

Otter Lake: see **Little Otter Lake** [TUOLUMNE].

Ottoway Creek [MADERA]: *stream,* flows 3 miles to Illilouette Creek 3.25 miles west of Merced Peak (lat. 37°38' N, long. 119°27'10" W); the stream heads near Ottoway Peak. Named on Merced Peak (1953) 15' quadrangle.

Ottoway Lake: see **Lower Ottoway Lake** [MADERA]; **Upper Ottoway Lake** [MADERA].

Ottoway Peak [MADERA]: *peak,* 0.5 mile north of Merced Peak (lat. 37°38'30" N, long. 119°23'30" W). Named on Merced Peak (1953) 15' quadrangle. Lieutenant N.F. McClure named the peak in 1895 for a corporal in his detachment (United States Board on Geographic Names, 1934, p. 18).

Ovejo: see **Tillman** [MADERA].

Owens Creek [MARIPOSA-MERCED]: *stream,* heads in Mariposa County and flows 53 miles to join Duck Slough and form Deep Slough 12.5 miles north-northwest of Dos Palos Y in Merced County (lat. 37°13'15" N, long. 120°42'45" W; sec. 24, T 8 S, R 11 E). Named on Catheys Valley (1962), Indian Gulch (1962), Merced (1961), Owens Reservoir (1962), Planada (1961), Sandy Mush (1962), and Turner Ranch (1961) 7'5' quadrangles.

Owen's Ferry: see **La Grange** [STANISLAUS].

Owens Reservoir [MARIPOSA]: *lake,* behind a dam on Owens Creek 9.5 miles south-southwest of the settlement of Catheys Valley (lat. 37°18'55" N, long. 120°11'05" W; near N line sec. 23, T 7 S, R 16 E). Named on Owens Reservoir (1962) 7.5' quadrangle.

Owlburrow Flat: see **Murphys** [CALAVERAS].

Owl Creek [MADERA]: *stream,* flows 2 miles to Whiskey Creek (2) 5.5 miles south of Shuteye Peak (lat. 37°16' N, long. 119°26'15" W; sec. 3, T 8 S, R 23 E). Named on Shuteye Peak (1953) 15' quadrangle.

Owl Creek [MARIPOSA]:

(1) *stream,* flows 2.5 miles to Devil Gulch 9 miles south of El Portal (lat. 37°33'45" N, long. 119°48'20" W; near E line sec. 25, T 4 S, R 19 E). Named on Buckingham Mountain (1947) 7.5' quadrangle.

(2) *stream,* flows 3 miles to West Fork Chowchilla River 5.25 miles east-southeast of Mariposa (lat. 37°27'55" N, long. 119°52'25" W; sec. 27, T 5 S, R 19 E). Named on Stumpfield Mountain (1947) 7.5' quadrangle.

Owl Creek [TUOLUMNE]: *stream,* flows 5.5 miles to Stanislaus River 7.25 miles west of Keystone (lat. 37°51'05" N, long. 120°38'10" W; sec. 15, T 1 S, R 12 E). Named on Keystone (1962) and Knights Ferry (1962) 7.5' quadrangles.

Owlsburg: see **Murphys** [CALAVERAS].

Oxendine [TUOLUMNE]: *locality,* 15 miles north-northeast of Columbia (lat. 38°12'55" N, long. 120°15'30" W). Named on Big Trees (1891) 30' quadrangle.

— P —

Pacheco Pass [MERCED]: *pass,* 43 miles west-southwest of Merced on Merced-Santa Clara County line (lat. 37°03'05" N, long. 121° 12'30" W). Named on Pacheco Pass (1955) 7.5' quadrangle. Called Pacheco's Pass on Wiliamson's (1853) map. The pass is on San Luis Gonzaga grant, which was owned by Francisco Perez Pacheco; it has the name "San Luis Gonzaga" in early records (Shumate, p. 1). A place called Mountain House station was at the summit of the pass (Latta, 1976, p. 246).

Pacific Placer Reservoir [CALAVERAS]: *lake,* 450 feet long, nearly 2 miles east of Valley Springs (lat. 38°11'20" N, long. 120°47'45" W; on E line sec. 19, T 4 N, R 11 E). Named on Valley Springs (1962) 7.5' quadrangle.

Paddle Creek [TUOLUMNE]: *stream,* flows 1.25 miles to Bourland Creek 9 miles south of Pinecrest (lat. 38°03'50" N, long. 119°59'25" W; near N line sec. 3, T 2 N, R 18 E). Named on Cherry Lake North (1979) 7.5' quadrangle.

Paddy Creek [SAN JOAQUIN]: *stream,* flows 10 miles to Bear Creek (1) 4 miles north of Waterloo (lat. 38°05'35" N, long. 121° 10'35" W; sec. 23, T 3 N, R 7 E). Named on Clements (1968), Linden (1968), Lockeford (1968), and Waterloo (1968) 7.5' quadrangles. Called Pattie Slough on Lodi (1894) 30' quadrangle.

Paddy Creek: see **Middle Paddy Creek** [SAN JOAQUIN]; **South Paddy Creek** [SAN JOAQUIN].

Page Mountain [TUOLUMNE]: *peak,* 6.5 miles south of Sonora (lat. 37°53'25" N, long. 120°22'45" W; on S line sec. 36, T 1 N, R 14 E). Altitude 2136 feet. Named on Sonora (1948) 7.5' quadrangle.

Paine: see **Tom Paine Slough** [SAN JOAQUIN].

Pain Flat: see **Payne Flat** [MARIPOSA].

Palm Tract: see **Modesto** [STANISLAUS].

Paloma [CALAVERAS]: *village,* 6.5 miles northwest of San Andreas (lat. 38°15'35" N, long. 120°45'40" W; near E line sec. 28, T 5 N, R 11 E). Named on Jackson (1962) 7.5' quadrangle. Camp's (1962) map shows a place called Frenchman's Ranch at Paloma. California Mining Bureau's (1909a) map shows a place called Fosteria situated 7.5 miles northeast of Valley Springs by stage line, and Hanna (p. 110) noted that Fosteria had the early name "Paloma." Postal authorities established Fosteria post office in 1903 and discontinued it in 1918; the name was for the Foster family, pioneers of the neighborhood (Salley, p. 79).

Paloni Mountain [MARIPOSA]: *ridge,* north-northeast-trending, 1.25 miles long, 11 miles east-southeast of Mariposa (lat. 37°26'50" N, long. 119°46'25" W). Named on Stumpfield Mountain (1947) 7.5' quadrangle.

Pandola Ferry: see **Parrott Ferry** [CALAVERAS-TUOLUMNE].

Panoche de San Juan y los Carrisalitos [MERCED]: *land grant,* southwest of Los Banos. Named on Los Banos Valley (1969), Ortigalita Peak (1969), and Ortigalita Peak NW (1956) 7.5' quadrangles. Julian Ursua received 5 leagues in 1844; Ursua and Pedro Romo claimed 22,175 acres patented in 1867 (Cowan, p. 57; Perez, p. 80). According to Hanna (p. 229), the name "Panoche" is a corruption of *panocha,* which is a Mexican-Spanish word for a confection of brown sugar. According to Gudde (1949, p. 252), the word "panoche," or "panocha," describes a sweet substance that Indians extracted from reeds and wild fruit.

Panoche Valley: see **Little Panoche Valley** [MERCED].

Panochita Valley: see **Little Panoche Valley** [MERCED].

Panorama Cliff [MARIPOSA]: *relief feature,* 2.5 miles southeast of Yosemite Village (lat. 37°43'10" N, long. 119°33' W); the feature is below Panorama Point. Named on Yosemite (1956) 15' quadrangle.

Panorama Point [MARIPOSA]: *peak,* 3 miles southeast of Yosemite Village (lat. 37°43' N, long. 119°33'05" W). Altitude 7007 feet. Named on Yosemite (1956) 15' quadrangle.

Paper Cabin Ridge [TUOLUMNE]: *ridge,* west- to south-trending, 3.5 miles long, 3 miles south-southeast of Tuolumne (lat. 37°55' N, long. 120°12'15" W). Named on Tuolumne (1948) 7.5' quadrangle.

Paps Gulch [MARIPOSA]: *canyon,* drained by a stream that flows 1.25 miles to Bull Creek 8.5 miles west-northwest of El Portal (lat. 37°43'30" N, long. 119°55'05" W; near S line sec. 30, T 2 S, R 19 E). Named on Kinsley (1947) 7.5' quadrangle.

Paradise: see **Tuolumne City** [STANISLAUS].

Paradise Cut [SAN JOAQUIN]: *water feature,* diverges northwest from San Joaquin River and joins Old River 12.5 miles south-southwest of downtown Stockton (lat. 37°48'10" N, long. 121°24'50" W). Named on Lathrop (1952) and Union Island (1978) 7.5' quadrangles.

Paradise Flat [STANISLAUS]: *area,* 3 miles north-northwest of Mustang Peak (lat. 37°13'45" N, long. 121°22'30" W). Named on Mississippi Creek (1955) and Mustang Peak (1955) 7.5' quadrangles.

Paradise Point [SAN JOAQUIN]: *promontory,* 6.25 miles southeast of Terminous at the southwest corner of Bishop Tract (lat. 38°02'35" N, long. 121°25' W). Named on Terminous (1978) 7.5' quadrangle.

Paradise Valley: see **Tuolumne City** [STANISLAUS].

Paramae Gulch [CALAVERAS]: *canyon,* 1 mile long, opens into the canyon of Jack Nelson Creek 4 miles southwest of Rail Road Flat (lat. 38°17'50" N, long. 120°33'20" W; near SE cor. sec. 8, T 5 N, R 13 E). Named on Rail Road Flat (1948) 7.5' quadrangle.

Pardee: see **Camp Pardee** [CALAVERAS].

Pardee Reservoir [CALAVERAS]: *lake,* behind a dam on Mokelumne River nearly 5 miles west of Paloma on Calaveras-Amador County line (lat. 38°15'25" N, long. 120°51' W; sec. 26, T 5 N, R 10 E). Named on Jackson (1962), Mokelumne Hill (1948), and Valley Springs (1962) 7.5' quadrangles. Channel Arm extends up the river from the dam and is named on Jackson (1962) 7.5' quadrangle. South Arm extends south-southeast along a canyon that lies perpendicular to the river and is named on Jackson (1962) and Valley Springs (1962) 7.5' quadrangles. Officials of East Bay Utility District named the lake in 1929 for George C. Pardee, governor of California from 1903 to 1907, and president of the board of directors of the district from 1924 until 1941 (Gudde, 1949, p. 253).

Parker Pass [TUOLUMNE]: *pass,* 6 miles south-southeast of Tioga Pass on Tuolumne-Mono County line (lat. 37°50'20" N, long. 119° 12'25" W); the pass is at the head of Parker Creek, which is in Mono County. Named on Mono Craters (1953) 15' quadrangle.

Parker Pass Creek [TUOLUMNE]: *stream,* flows 5.5 miles to Dana Fork 2 miles south-southwest of Tioga Pass (lat. 37°52'50" N, long. 119°16' W); the stream heads at Parker Pass. Named on Mono Craters (1953) and Tuolumne Meadows (1956) 15' quadrangles.

Parker Pass Lake [TUOLUMNE]: *lake,* 1000 feet long, 6 miles south-southeast of Tioga Pass (lat. 37°50'05" N, long. 119°12'35" W); the lake is 0.25 mile southwest of Parker Pass. Named on Mono Craters (1953) 15' quadrangle.

Parkinson Creek [MERCED]: *stream,* flows 9.5 miles to Fahrens Creek 4.5 miles north of Merced (lat. 37°21'45" N, long. 120°28'50" W; sec. 31, T 6 S, R 14 E). Named on Yosemite Lake (1962) 7.5' quadrangle.

Parnel Canyon [STANISLAUS]: *canyon,* drained by a stream that flows 1.25 miles to Garzas Creek 1.5 miles north-northwest of Crevison Peak (lat. 37°12'50" N, long. 121°11'50" W; at W line sec. 27, T 8 S, R 7 E). Named on Crevison Peak (1955) 7.5' quadrangle.

Parrott Ferry [CALAVERAS-TUOLUMNE]: *locality,* 2.5 miles west-northwest of Columbia along Stanislaus River on Calaveras-Tuolumne County line (lat. 38°02'35" N, long. 120°27' W). Named on Big Trees (1891) 30' quadrangle. Columbia (1948) 7.5' quadrangle shows Parrotts Ferry bridge at about the site of Parrott Ferry. Thomas H. Parrott started Parrott's Ferry in 1860 (Hoover, Rensch, and Rensch, p. 572). According to Wheeler (1879, p. 179), the place had the early name "Pandola Ferry."

Parsons: see **Strawberry** [TUOLUMNE].

Parsons Peak [MADERA-TUOLUMNE]: *peak,* 9.5 miles south-southwest of Tioga Pass on Madera-Tuolumne County line (lat. 37°46'30" N, long. 119°18'25" W). Named on Tuolumne Meadows (1956) 15' quadrangle. R.B. Marshall of United States Geological Survey named the peak for Edward Taylor Parsons, who for many years was a director of the Sierra Club (United States Board on Geographic Names, 1934, p. 19).

Paso Del Pino: see **Pine Log** [TUOLUMNE].

Pate Valley [TUOLUMNE]: *area,* 5.5 miles northeast of White Wolf along Tuolumne River (lat. 37°56' N, long 119°35'50" W). Named on Hetch Hetchy Reservoir (1956) 15' quadrangle.

Patricksville: see **La Grange** [STANISLAUS].

Pattees Ranch: see **Jenny Lind** [CALAVERAS].

Patterson [STANISLAUS]: *town,* 14 miles south-southwest of Modesto (lat. 37°28'20" N, long. 121°07'45" W; sec. 30, T 5 S, R 8 E). Named on Crows Landing (1952) and Patterson (1953) 7.5' quadrangles. Thomas W. Patterson laid out the town about 1910 and named it for his uncle, John D. Patterson, who had purchased the land there in 1864 (Gudde, 1949, p. 255). Postal authorities established Patterson post office in 1909 (Frickstad, p. 201).

Patterson: see **Trigo** [MADERA].

Patterson Bend [MADERA]: *bend,* 6 miles south-southwest of the town of North Fork along San Joaquin River on Madera-Fresno County line (lat. 37°08'40" N, long. 119°33'15" W). Named on North Fork (1965) 7.5' quadrangle.

Patterson Run [SAN JOAQUIN]: *stream,* heads in Alameda County and flows 6.25 miles to lowlands 6 miles west of Tracy (lat. 37°44'30" N, long. 121°32'30" W; sec. 21, T 2 S, R 4 E). Named on Bethany (1952) and Midway (1953) 7.5' quadrangles.

Pattie Slough: see **Paddy Creek** [SAN JOAQUIN].

Paulsell [STANISLAUS]: *locality,* 6.5 miles north-northeast of Waterford along Sierra Railway (lat. 37°43'05" N, long. 120°41'20" W; sec. 31, T 2 S, R 12 E). Named on Paulsell (1968) 7.5' quadrangle. Officials of the railway named the place in 1897 for A.C. Paulsell, landowner there (Gudde, 1949, p. 255).

Payne Flat [MARIPOSA]: *area,* 3.5 miles north-northeast of the settlement of Catheys Valley (lat. 37°28'50" N, long. 120°04' W). Named on Catheys Valley (1962) 7.5' quadrangle. Called Pain Flat on Indian Gulch (1920) 15' quadrangle, but United States Board on Geographic Names (1964a, p. 13) rejected this name for the feature. The place is called Payne's Flat on Laizure's (1928) map.

Payton Saddle [TUOLUMNE]: *pass,* nearly 3 miles southeast of Liberty Hill (lat. 38°20'40" N, long. 120°03'25" W; sec. 25, T 6 N, R 17 E). Named on Liberty Hill (1979) 7.5' quadrangle.

Peachtree Bar [MARIPOSA]: *locality,* 4.5 miles south of El Portal along South Fork Merced River (lat. 37°36'40" N, long. 119°47'20" W). Named on Buckingham Mountain (1947) 7.5' quadrangle. A man named Blair, who mined at the place until 1919, planted peach trees there (Mendershausen, p. 18, 20).

Peach Tree Creek [STANISLAUS]: *stream,* flows 2.25 miles to Del Puerto Canyon nearly 6 miles south-southeast of Mount Boardman (lat. 37°24'20" N, long. 121°25'50" W; near N line sec. 21, T 6 S, R 5 W). Named on Mount Boardman (1955) 7.5' quadrangle. Mount Boardman (1942) 15' quadrangle has the form "Peachtree Creek" for the name.

Peachys Creek [CALAVERAS-STANISLAUS]: *stream,* heads in Calaveras County and flows 10 miles to Littlejohns Creek 2 miles north-northwest of Knights Ferry in Stanislaus County (lat. 37°50'45" N, long. 120°41'20" W). Named on Copperopolis (1962) and Knights Ferry (1962) 7.5' quadrangles.

Pear Slough [STANISLAUS]: *water feature,* 4 miles east of Patterson (lat. 37°28'20" N, long. 121°03'10" W). Named on Crows Landing (1952) 7.5' quadrangle. The feature is a cutoff meander of San Joaquin River that lies west of the river.

Pearson [SAN JOAQUIN]: *locality,* 6 miles west-southwest of Lockeford along Central California Traction Railroad (lat. 38°07'50" N, long. 121°14'50" W; near S line sec. 6, T 3 N, R 7 E). Named on Lockeford (1968) 7.5' quadrangle.

Peaslee Creek [STANISLAUS]: *stream,* flows 6 miles to Tuolumne River 12.5 miles east of Waterford (lat. 37°37'35" N, long. 120°31'30" W; sec. 34, T 3 S, R 13 E). Named on Snelling (1962) and Turlock Lake (1968) 7.5' quadrangles.

Pecan Spring [MADERA]: *spring,* 5 miles southeast of Knowles (lat. 37°09'35" N, long. 119°49'05" W; sec. 8, T 9 S, R 20 E). Named on Knowles (1962) 7.5' quadrangle.

Peckham Ridge [MERCED]: *ridge,* east-trending, 3 miles long, 4 miles southeast of Mariposa Peak (lat. 36°54'50" N, long. 121°09'45" W). Named on Mariposa Peak (1969) 7.5' quadrangle.

Peckinpah Creek [MADERA]: *stream,* flows 4 miles to South Fork Willow Creek (2) 9 miles south-southwest of Shuteye Peak (lat. 37°14'10" N, long. 119°29'45" W; sec. 18, T 8 S, R 23 E); the stream goes through Peckinpah Meadow. Named on Shaver Lake (1953) and Shuteye Peak (1953) 15' quadrangles.

Peckinpah Meadow [MADERA]: *area,* 6 miles south-southwest of Shuteye Peak (lat. 37°15'55" N, long. 119°27'45" W; sec. 4, T 8 S, R 23 E); the place is along Peckinpah Creek. Named on Shuteye Peak (1953) 15'

quadrangle.

Peckinpah Mill [MADERA]: *locality,* 6.25 miles south-southwest of Shuteye Peak (lat. 37°15'50" N, long. 119°27'45" W; sec. 4, T 8 S, R 23 E); the place is along Peckinpah Creek. Named on Kaiser (1904) 30' quadrangle. Charlie Peckinpah and his brothers started a sawmill at the spot in 1884 (Browning, 1986, p. 167).

Peckinpah Mountain: see **Central Camp** [MADERA].

Pegleg Creek [MARIPOSA]: *stream,* flows 5 miles to West Fork Chowchilla River nearly 5 miles east-southeast of Mariposa (lat. 37°27'05" N, long. 119°53'20" W; sec. 33, T 5 S, R 19 E). Named on Mariposa (1947) 7.5' quadrangle.

Pegleg Creek [SAN JOAQUIN]: *stream,* flows 4 miles to Middle Fork Lone Tree Creek (1) 12.5 miles south of Tracy (lat. 37°33'45" N, long. 121°30'10" W; sec. 29, T 4 S, R 5 E); the stream is south of Pegleg Ridge. Named on Lone Tree Creek (1955) 7.5' quadrangle.

Pegleg Ridge [SAN JOAQUIN]: *ridge,* east-trending, 3.25 miles long, 13 miles south of Tracy (lat. 37°33'05" N, long. 121°27'45" W); the ridge is north of Pegleg Creek. Named on Lone Tree Creek (1955) 7.5' quadrangle.

Peltier [SAN JOAQUIN]: *locality,* 5.25 miles west-northwest of Lockeford along Central California Traction Railroad (lat. 38°11'20" N, long. 121°14'35" W). Named on Lockeford (1968) 7.5' quadrangle. California Division of Highways' (1934) map shows a place called Kenefick located 3 miles north of Peltier along the railroad (near NW cor. sec. 5, T 4 N, R 7 E).

Pena Blanca Point: see **Penon Blanco Point** [MARIPOSA].

Pena Blanca Ridge: see **Penon Blanco Ridge** [MARIPOSA-TUOLUMNE].

Pendola: see **Camp Pendola** [TUOLUMNE].

Pendola Gardens [MARIPOSA]: *locality,* 3.5 miles south-southeast of the village of Bear Valley in Cow and Calf Gulch (lat. 37°31'05" N, long. 120°06'20" W). Named on Bear Valley (1947) 7.5' quadrangle.

Peninsula Lake [TUOLUMNE]: *lake,* 3300 feet long, 8 miles west-southwest of Tower Peak (lat. 38°06' N, long. 119°40'20" W); a peninsula divides the lake into two parts. Named on Tower Peak (1956) 15' quadrangle.

Peninsula Lake: see **Upper Peninsula Lake** [TUOLUMNE].

Pennsylvania Gulch [CALAVERAS]: *canyon,* 1 mile long, 1.5 miles east of Murphys (lat. 38°08'15" N, long. 120°26'05" W; sec. 4, 9, T 3 N, R 14 E). Named on Murphys (1948) 7.5' quadrangle. A group of men from Pennsylvania began mining in the canyon in December of 1849 (Gudde, 1975, p. 262).

Penny Creek [CALAVERAS]: *stream,* flows 2.5 miles to Sawmill Creek 1 mile south-southwest of Copperopolis (lat. 37°58'05" N, long. 120°38'55" W; sec. 3, T 1 N, R 12 E). Named on Copperopolis (1962) 7.5' quadrangle.

Penole Peak [TUOLUMNE]: *peak,* nearly 3 miles southeast of Don Pedro Camp (lat. 37°41'35" N, long. 120°21'50" W; sec. 7, T 3 S, R 15 E). Named on Penon Blanco Peak (1962) 7.5' quadrangle.

Penon Blanco [MARIPOSA]: *locality,* 2.5 miles northwest of Coulterville along Blacks Creek (lat. 37°44'15" N, long. 120°13'30" W); the site is 1 mile southeast of present Penon Blanco Point. Named on Sonora (1891) 30' quadrangle.

Penon Blanco Peak [MARIPOSA]: *peak,* 4 miles west-northwest of Coulterville (lat. 37°43'55" N, long. 120°15'35" W; sec. 25, T 2 S, R 15 E); the peak is near the southeast end of Penon Blanco Ridge. Altitude 2878 feet. Named on Penon Blanco Peak (1962) 7.5' quadrangle.

Penon Blanco Point [MARIPOSA]: *peak,* 3.25 miles northwest of Coulterville (lat. 37°44'45" N, long. 120°14'15" W; on E line sec. 19, T 2 S, R 16 E); the peak is near the southeast end of Penon Blanco Ridge. Altitude 2470 feet. Named on Coulterville (1947) 7.5' quadrangle. United States Board on Geographic Names (1933a, p. 597) rejected the forms "Pena Blanca Point," "Peña Blanca Point," and "Peñon Blanco Point" for the name.

Penon Blanco Ridge [MARIPOSA-TUOLUMNE]: *ridge,* northwest-trending, 5 miles long, on Mariposa-Tuolumne County line, mainly in Tuolumne County; center 5 miles west-northwest of Coulterville (lat. 37°45' N, long. 120°16' W); the ridge extends northwest from Penon Blanco Peak. Named on Moccasin (1948) and Penon Blanco Peak (1962) 7.5' quadrangles. Whitney (1865, p. 231) noted that the feature is "a prominent elevation, of which the crest is a great white mass of quartz, visible from a great distance"—*peñon blanco* means "white rock" in Spanish. United States Board on Geographic Names (1933a, p. 597) rejected the forms "Pena Blanca Ridge," "Peña Blanca Ridge," and "Peñon Blanco Ridge" for the name.

Peon Gulch [CALAVERAS]: *canyon,* drained by a stream that flows 1.5 miles to Shad Gulch 2.5 miles west-northwest of Paloma (lat. 38°16'25" N, long. 120°48'30" W; sec. 19, T 5 N, R 11 E). Named on Jackson (1962) 7.5' quadrangle.

Peoria Basin [TUOLUMNE]: *valley,* 6.25 miles north of Keystone (lat. 37°55'20" N, long. 120°31'15" W; sec. 22, 23, T 1 N, R 13 E); Peoria Creek drains the place. Named on Melones Dam (1962) 7.5' quadrangle.

Peoria Creek [TUOLUMNE]: *stream,* flows 3.5 miles to Stanislaus River 6.5 miles north-northwest of Keystone (lat. 37°55'30" N, long. 120°32'10" W; sec. 22, T 1 N, R 13 E); the stream goes through Peoria Basin and Peoria Flat. Named on Melones Dam (1962) and Sonora (1948) 7.5' quadrangles.

Peoria Flat [TUOLUMNE]: *area,* 4.5 miles north of Keystone (lat. 37°54'15" N, long. 120°30' W; sec. 25, 36, T 1 N, R 13 E); the place is along Peoria Creek. Named on Melones Dam (1962) and Sonora (1948) 7.5' quadrangles.

Peoria Mountain [TUOLUMNE]: *ridge,* northwest-trending, 3 miles long, 7.25 miles west-southwest of Sonora (lat. 37°55'45" N, long. 120°29'45" W). Named on Melones Dam (1962) and Sonora (1948) 7.5' quadrangles.

Peoria Pass [TUOLUMNE]: *pass,* 4.25 miles north of Keystone (lat. 37°53'45" N, long. 120°30'10" W; sec. 36, T 1 N, R 13 E). Named on Melones Dam (1962) 7.5' quadrangle.

Peppermint Creek [CALAVERAS]: *stream,* flows 2.25 miles to Coyote Creek 2 miles east-southeast of Murphys (lat. 38°07'45" N, long. 120°25'50" W; at W line sec. 10, T 3 N, R 14 E). Named on Murphys (1948) 7.5' quadrangle.

Peppermint Creek [TUOLUMNE]: *stream,* flows 3.5 miles to Woods Creek 3 miles southwest of Sonora at Jamestown (lat. 37°57'20" N, long. 120°25'25" W; sec. 10, T 11 N, R 14 E). Named on Sonora (1948) 7.5' quadrangle.

Peregoy Meadow [MARIPOSA]: *area,* 6 miles south-southwest of Yosemite Village (lat. 37°40'10" N, long. 119°37'20" W; sec. 13, T 3 S, R 21 E). Named on Yosemite (1956) 15' quadrangle. The name commemorates Charles E. Peregoy, a native of Maryland who built Mountain View House in 1869 (Hanna, p. 233).

Peruvian Gulch [CALAVERAS]: *canyon,* drained by a stream that flows less than 1 mile to Coyote Creek nearly 3 miles south of Vallecito (lat. 38°02'50" N, long. 120°29' W; sec. 7, T 2 N, R 14 E). Named on Columbia (1948) 7.5' quadrangle.

Peters [SAN JOAQUIN]: *locality,* 13 miles east of downtown Stockton along Southern Pacific Railroad (lat. 37°58'50" N, long. 121°02'55" W; sec. 36, T 2 N, R 8 E). Named on Peters (1952) 7.5' quadrangle. Postal authorities established Peters post office in 1871, discontinued it in 1873, reestablished it in 1881, discontinued it in 1904, reestablished it in 1908, and discontinued it in 1951 (Frickstad, p. 162). The name commemorates J.D. Peters, landowner at the site (Gudde, 1949, p. 259). Mendenhall's (1908) map shows a place called Waverly located 5 miles east-northeast of Peters along the railroad.

Petersburg: see **San Andreas** [CALAVERAS].

Petersen [TUOLUMNE]: *locality,* 3.25 miles east of Columbia (lat. 38°02'30" N, long. 120°20'30" W). Named on Big Trees (1891) 30' quadrangle.

Peterson Creek [MADERA-MARIPOSA]: *stream,* heads in Mariposa County and flows 4.5 miles to Carter Creek 4.5 miles west of Yosemite Forks in Madera County (lat. 37°22'10" N, long. 119°42'40" W; sec. 31, T 6 S, R 21 E). Named on Bass Lake (1953) 15' quadrangle.

Petes Pond [MARIPOSA]: *lake,* 800 feet long, 3 miles south of Santa Cruz Mountain (lat. 37°24'45" N, long. 120°12'20" W; sec. 15, T 6 S, R 16 E). Named on Indian Gulch (1962) 7.5' quadrangle.

Pettit Peak [TUOLUMNE]: *peak,* 13 miles west-northwest of Tioga Pass (lat. 37°59'10" N, long. 119°28'45" W). Altitude 10,788 feet. Named on Tuolumne Meadows (1956) 15' quadrangle. United States Board on Geographic Names (1934, p. 19) rejected the form "Petit Peak" for the name; Colonel W.W. Forsyth named the feature for James Seymour Pettit.

Petty Reservoir: see **Stanislaus** [TUOLUMNE].

Philadelphia Diggings: see **Jupiter** [TUOLUMNE].

Phillips' Ferry: see **Merced Falls** [MERCED].

Phillip's Flat: see **Hornitos** [MARIPOSA].

Phoenix: see **Del Puerto Canyon** [MARIPOSA].

Phoenix Reservoir [TUOLUMNE]: *lake,* behind a dam on Sullivan Creek 3.25 miles east-northeast of Sonora (lat. 37°59'55" N, long. 120°19'35" W; sec. 28, T 2 N, R 15 E). Named on Columbia SE (1948) and Standard (1948) 7.5' quadrangles.

Picayune Creek [MADERA]: *stream,* flows 4.5 miles to Coarse Gold Creek 6.5 miles north of O'Neals (lat. 37°13'10" N, long. 119°42'35" W; sec. 19, T 8 S, R 21 E). Named on O'Neals (1965) 7.5' quadrangle.

Pick Anderson Slough: see **Salt Slough** [MERCED].

Picture Gallery Gulch [MARIPOSA]: *canyon,* drained by a stream that flows 1.5 miles to Lake McClure 3.25 miles southwest of Coulterville (lat. 37°40'50" N, long. 120°14'20" W; near E line sec. 18, T 3 S, R 16 E). Named on Coulterville (1947, photorevised 1973) and Penon Blanco Peak (1962) 7.5' quadrangles.

Piedra Azul Canyon [MERCED]: *canyon,* 3.5 miles long, along Piedra Azul Creek above a point 5 miles northwest of Ortigalita Peak (lat. 36°51'05" N, long. 120°58'30" W; sec. 34, T 12 S, R 9 E). Named on Ortigalita Peak (1969) and Ruby Canyon (1968) 7.5' quadrangles.

Piedra Azul Creek [MERCED]: *stream,* flows 5 miles to Ortigalita Creek 17 miles west-southwest of Dos Palos (lat. 36°52'55" N, long. 120°54'45" W); the stream drains Piedra Azul Canyon. Named on Ortigalita Peak (1969) and Ortigalita Peak NW (1956) 7.5' quadrangles.

Piedra Azul Spring [MERCED]: *spring,* 4.5 miles northwest of Ortigalita Peak (lat. 36°51' N, long. 120°58'10" W). Named on Ortigalita Peak (1969) 7.5' quadrangle.

Pietra Blanca: see **Springfield** [TUOLUMNE].

Pigeon Creek Fall: see **Ribbon Fall** [MARIPOSA].

Pigeon Flat [MARIPOSA]: *area,* 4 miles east of Jawbone Ridge (lat. 37°48'10" N, long. 120°01'25" W; near SW cor. sec. 32, T 1 S, R 18 E). Named on Jawbone Ridge (1947) 7.5' quadrangle.

Pigeon Flat [TUOLUMNE]: *area,* 1.5 miles east of Dardanelle along Middle Fork Stanislaus River (lat. 38°20'20" N, long. 119°48'20" W). Named on Dardanelle (1979) 7.5' quadrangle. Dardanelles Cone (1956) 15' quadrangle shows Pigeon Flat Campground at the place.

Pigeon Flat Campground: see **Pigeon Flat** [TUOLUMNE].

Pigeon Gulch [MARIPOSA]: *canyon,* drained by a stream that flows nearly 1 mile to the canyon of Merced River 1.5 miles west-southwest of El Portal (lat. 37°39'55" N, long. 119°48'20" W; sec. 19, T 3 S, R 20 E). Named on El Portal (1947) 7.5' quadrangle.

Pigeon Gulch [TUOLUMNE]: *canyon,* drained by a stream that flows nearly 1 mile to Woods Creek 1.25 miles east-southeast of Columbia (lat. 38°01'30" N, long. 120°22'50" W; sec. 13, T 2 N, R 14 E). Named on Columbia SE (1948) 7.5' quadrangle.

Pigs Bath Tub [MERCED]: *spring,* 3 miles southwest of Pacheco Pass (lat. 37°01'50" N, long. 121°14'20" W). Named on Pacheco Pass (1955) 7.5' quadrangle.

Pikes Peak [TUOLUMNE]: *peak,* 9 miles southwest of Dardanelle (lat. 38°15'40" N, long. 119°58'05" W; sec. 26, T 5 N, R 18 E). Altitude 7235 feet. Named on Donnell Lake (1979) 7.5' quadrangle.

Pile Creek: see **Jawbone Creek** [TUOLUMNE].

Pilot Peak [MARIPOSA]: *peak,* 4.5 miles southwest of Fish Camp (lat. 37°26'15" N, long. 119°42' W; sec. 5, T 6 S, R 21 E). Altitude 5246 feet. Named on Bass Lake (1953) 15' quadrangle.

Pilot Peak [MARIPOSA-TUOLUMNE]: *peak,* 10.5 miles northwest of El Portal on Mariposa-Tuolumne County line (lat. 37°45'45" N, long. 119°56'05" W; sec. 13, T 2 S, R 18 E); the peak is on Pilot Ridge. Altitude 6004 feet. Named on Lake Eleanor (1956) 15' quadrangle.

Pilot Ridge [MARIPOSA-TUOLUMNE]: *ridge,* northwest-trending, 9 miles long, 13 miles northwest of El Portal on Mariposa-Tuolumne County line (lat. 37°47' N, long. 119°58' W); Pilot Peak is on the ridge. Named on Lake Eleanor (1956) and Tuolumne (1948) 15' quadrangles.

Pine Canyon: see **Big Pine Canyon** [MERCED-STANISLAUS]; **Little Pine Canyon** [MERCED].

Pine Creek, North Fork: see **Sulphur Spring Gulch** [SAN JOAQUIN].

Pinecrest [TUOLUMNE]: *settlement,* 21 miles west-southwest of Sonora Pass (lat. 38°11'30" N, long. 119°59'45" W). Named on Pinecrest (1979) and Strawberry (1979) 7.5' quadrangles. Postal authorities established Pinecrest post office in 1917, discontinued it in 1921, and reestablished it in 1923 (Frickstad, p. 216).

Pinecrest Lake [TUOLUMNE]: *lake,* behind a dam on South Fork Stanislaus River 0.5 mile northeast of Pinecrest (lat. 38°12' N, long. 119°59'15" W). Named on Pinecrest (1979) 7.5' quadrangle. Called Edna Lake on Dardanelles (1898, reprinted 1947) 30' quadrangle, and called Strawberry Lake on California Division of Highways' (1934) map, but United States Board on Geographic Names (1959b, p. 7) rejected the names "Edna Lake," "Edna Lake Reservoir," and "Strawberry Lake" for the feature. R.B. Marshall of United States Geological Survey gave the name "Edna Lake" to honor Edna Bowman, later Mrs. Charles J. Kuhn (Hanna, p. 95). California Division of Highways' (1934) map shows a lake called Big Dam Reservoir located 5.25 miles east-northeast of Strawberry Lake (present Pinecrest Lake) along South Fork Stanislaus River, where current maps show no lake.

Pinecrest Peak [TUOLUMNE]: *ridge,* southwest-trending, 1.5 miles long, 4.5 miles east-northeast of Pinecrest (lat. 38°13'45" N, long. 119°55'20" W). Named on Pinecrest (1979) 7.5' quadrangle.

Pine Crossing: see **Pine Log** [TUOLUMNE].

Pine Flat [MADERA]: *area,* 9.5 miles southwest of Devils Postpile along San Joaquin River (lat. 37°30'50" N, long. 119°11'25" W; near NW cor. sec. 12, T 5 S, R 25 E). Named on Devils Postpile (1953) 15' quadrangle.

Pine Log [TUOLUMNE]: *locality,* 2.5 miles north-northeast of Columbia along South Fork Stanislaus River (lat. 38°04'10" N, long. 120°23'15" W; sec. 36, T 3 N, R 14 E). Named on Columbia (1948) 7.5' quadrangle. The place also was called Paso Del Pino, Pine Crossing, and Pine Log Crossing (Todd *in* Wayman, p. 93). Gudde (1975, p. 189) listed a mining camp of the 1850's called La Commodedad that was located 5 miles northeast of Pine Log Crossing.

Pine Log Crossing: see **Pine Log** [TUOLUMNE].

Pine Mountain Lake [TUOLUMNE]: *lake,* 1.25 miles long, behind a dam on Big Creek 2 miles northeast of Groveland (lat. 37°51'25" N, long. 120°12' W; sec. 15, T 1 S, R 16 E). Named on Groveland (1947, photorevised 1973) 7.5' quadrangle.

Pine Peak [CALAVERAS]: *peak,* 4 miles north-northwest of San Andreas (lat. 38°14'55" N, long. 120°42'40" W; sec. 36, T 5 N, R 11 E). Altitude 1402 feet. Named on San Andreas (1962) 7.5' quadrangle.

Pine Point Campground [MADERA]: *locality,* 6.5 miles southeast of Yosemite Forks on the southwest side of Bass Lake (1) (lat. 37° 18'20" N, long. 119°32'25" W; sec. 23, T 7 S, R 22 E). Named on Bass Lake (1953) 15' quadrangle.

Pine Ridge [CALAVERAS]: *ridge,* west-trending, 2 miles long, 5.5 miles west-southwest of Blue Mountain (lat. 38°18'35" N, long. 120°27'45" W). Named on Fort Mountain (1979) 7.5' quadrangle.

Pines: see **The Pines** [MADERA].

Pines Creek [MADERA]: *stream,* flows nearly 2 miles to Bass Lake (1) 5.5 miles southeast of Yosemite Forks (lat. 37°19'20" N, long. 119°32'45" W; near E line sec. 15, T 7 S, R 22 E). Named on Bass Lake (1953) 15' quadrangle.

Pine Slope Campground [MADERA]: *locality,* nearly 5 miles southeast of Yosemite Forks on the west side of Bass Lake (1) (lat. 37°18'55" N, long. 119°34'20" W; near S line sec. 16, T 7 S, R 22 E). Named on Bass Lake (1953) 15' quadrangle.

Pine Springs Hill [STANISLAUS]: *peak,* 4 miles east of Mustang Peak on Stanislaus-Santa Clara County line (lat. 37°10'50" N, long. 121°16'50" W; sec. 2, T 9 S, R 6 E). Named on Mustang Peak (1955) 7.5' quadrangle.

Pine Valley [TUOLUMNE]: *canyon,* nearly 1 mile long, 6.5 miles east-southeast of Pinecrest along Lily Creek (3) (lat. 38°09'25" N, long. 119°53'15" W; sec. 33, 34, T 4 N, R 19 E). Named on Pinecrest (1979) 7.5' quadrangle.

Piney Creek [MARIPOSA]: *stream,* flows 5 miles to Lake McClure 4.25 miles southwest of Penon Blanco Peak (lat. 37°41'25" N, long. 120°19' W; sec. 9, T 3 S, R 15 E); the stream is east of Piney Ridge. Named on Penon Blanco Peak (1962, photorevised 1973) 7.5' quadrangle. East Fork enters near the mouth of the main stream; it is 5.5 miles long and is named on Penon Blanco Peak (1962, photorevised 1973) 7.5' quadrangle.

Piney Ridge [MARIPOSA-TUOLUMNE]: *ridge,* south-southeast-trending, 4 miles long, 4.5 miles southwest of Penon Blanco Peak on Mariposa-Tuolumne County line (lat. 37°40'45" N, long. 120° 18'50" W); the ridge is west of Piney Creek. Named on Penon Blanco Peak (1962) 7.5' quadrangle.

Pingree Lake [TUOLUMNE]: *lake,* 1800 feet long, 11.5 miles east-southeast of Pinecrest (lat. 38°08'05" N, long. 119°47'55" W). Named on Pinecrest (1956) 15' quadrangle.

Pinoche Peak [MARIPOSA]: *peak,* 3 miles south of El Portal (lat. 37° 38'05" N, long. 119°46'30" W; near NW cor. sec. 33, T 3 S, R 20 E); the peak is on Pinoche Ridge. Altitude 5765 feet. Named on El Portal (1947) 7.5' quadrangle.

Pinoche Ridge [MARIPOSA]: *ridge,* mainly west-northwest-trending, 5 miles long, 3 miles south-southwest of El Portal (lat. 37°38'10" N, long. 119°48' W); Pinoche Peak is on the ridge. Named on El Portal (1947) 7.5' quadrangle.

Pinto Creek [STANISLAUS]: *stream,* flows 3 miles to Robinson Creek 3.25 miles south-southeast of Mount Stakes (lat. 37°16'45" N, long. 121°22'50" W; sec. 36, T 7 S, R 5 E). Named on Mount Stakes (1955) 7.5' quadrangle.

Pinto Lakes [TUOLUMNE]: *lakes,* two, largest 700 feet long, 13 miles east of Pinecrest (lat. 38°12'25" N, long. 119°45'10" W). Named on Pinecrest (1956) 15' quadrangle.

Piute Creek [TUOLUMNE]:

(1) *stream,* flows 5 miles to West Fork Cherry Creek 9 miles east-southeast of Pinecrest (lat. 38°07'55" N, long. 119°51' W); the stream goes through Piute Meadow. Named on Pinecrest (1956) 15' quadrangle. Bill Woods, who named Piute Meadow, named the stream for Piute Indians who fished there (Browning, 1986, p. 171).

(2) *stream,* flows 20 miles to Tuolumne River 5 miles northeast of White Wolf in Pate Valley (lat. 37°55'50" N, long. 119°36' W). Named on Hetch Hetchy Reservoir (1956), Matterhorn Peak (1956), and Tower Peak (1956) 15' quadrangles.

Piute Lake [TUOLUMNE]: *lake,* 550 feet long, 10 miles east of Pinecrest (lat. 38°09'45" N, long. 119°48'35" W); the lake is 1.25 miles east of Piute Meadow. Named on Pinecrest (1956) 15' quadrangle. The name is from a Piute Indian that Bill Woods killed during a fight and then sank in the lake (Browning, 1986, p. 171-172).

Piute Meadow [TUOLUMNE]: *area,* 9 miles east-southeast of Pinecrest (lat. 38°09'45" N, long. 119°50' W; sec. 36, T 4 N, R 19 E); the area is along Piute Creek (1). Named on Pinecrest (1956) 15' quadrangle. Bill Woods named the place for Piute Indians that came there from Nevada to hunt and fish (Browning, 1986, p. 171).

Piute Mountain [TUOLUMNE]: *peak,* 7.5 miles south of Tower Peak (lat. 38°02' N, long. 119°32'50" W); the peak is northwest of Piute Creek (2). Altitude 10,541 feet. Named on Tower Peak (1956) 15' quadrangle.

Pixley Slough [SAN JOAQUIN]: *stream,* flows 13 miles to Disappointment Slough 7.5 miles southeast of Terminous (lat. 38°02'40" N, long. 121°23'10" W). Named on Lodi South (1968), Terminous (1978), and Waterloo (1968) 7.5' quadrangles.

Plains: see **Tillman** [MADERA].

Plainsberg: see **Plainsburg** [MERCED].
Plainsburg [MERCED]: *village,* 4 miles west of Le Grand (lat. 37°14'05" N, long. 120°19'30" W; on W line sec. 15, T 8 S, R 15 E). Named on Chowchilla (1960) 15' quadrangle. Plainsberg (1919) 7.5' quadrangle has the form "Plainsberg" for the name. Postal authorities established Plainsberg post office in 1869 and discontinued it in 1907 (Salley, p. 173).
Plainsburg: see **Athlone** [MERCED].
Planada [MERCED]: *town,* 9 miles east of Merced (lat. 37°17'30" N, long. 120°19' W; sec. 27, T 7 S, R 15 E). Named on Planada (1961) 7.5' quadrangle. Called Geneva on Grunsky's (1899) map. Postal authorities established Geneva post office in 1896, discontinued it in 1897, reestablished it in 1898, and changed the name to Planada in 1911; a group of Swiss dairymen named the place "Geneva" for the city in their homeland (Salley, p. 83-84). The name "Planada" was the winner of a contest held in 1911 to select a new name for the town—*planada* means "plain" in Spanish; the railroad station at the place was called Whitton (Gudde, 1949, p. 266-267).
Pleasant: see **Mount Pleasant**, under **Taylor Hill** [TUOLUMNE].
Pleasant Springs: see **Rich Gulch** [CALAVERAS] (5).
Pleasant Valley [MARIPOSA]:
(1) *canyon,* 5 miles long, along Merced River above a point 9.5 miles south-southwest of Coulterville (lat. 37°35'15" N, long. 120°16' W). Named on Sonora (1891) 30' quadrangle. Water of Lake McClure now floods the canyon. Postal authorities established Pleasant Valley post office on the bank of Merced River 12 miles northeast of La Grange in 1855 and discontinued it in 1856 (Salley, p. 174).
(2) *village,* 6.5 miles southwest of Coulterville along Yosemite Valley Railroad (lat. 37°39' N, long. 120°17'25" W); the village is near the north end of Pleasant Valley (1). Named on Sonora (1897) 30' quadrangle.
Pleasant Valley [TUOLUMNE]: *area,* about 9 miles north-northeast of White Wolf along Piute Creek (2) (lat. 37°59'10" N, long. 119° 34'15" W). Named on Hetch Hetchy Reservoir (1956) 15' quadrangle. Members of the Bright family named the place and ran stock there before creation of Yosemite National Park (Browning, 1988, p. 109).
Pleasant Valley: see **Wheats** [CALAVERAS].
Plumbar Creek [MARIPOSA]: *stream,* flows 4.25 miles to Bear Creek (1) less than 0.5 mile southeast of Midpines (lat. 37°32'20" N, long. 119°54'55" W; sec. 31, T 4 S, R 19 E). Named on Feliciana Mountain (1947) 7.5' quadrangle.
Plum Flat [TUOLUMNE]: *area,* 4.5 miles west-northwest of Mather (lat. 37°54'20" N, long. 119°56'15" W; near SW cor. sec. 30, T 1 N, R 19 E). Named on Lake Eleanor (1956) 15' quadrangle.
Pocket: see **The Pocket** [SAN JOAQUIN].
Pohono: see **Bridalveil Fall** [MARIPOSA].
Pohono Lake: see **Ostrander Lake** [MARIPOSA].
Point Eaton: see **Mount Eaton** [TUOLUMNE].
Poison Meadow [MADERA]: *area,* 6.25 miles east-northeast of Yosemite Forks (lat. 37°23'50" N, long. 119°31'15" W; sec. 24, T 6 S, R 22 E). Named on Bass Lake (1953) 15' quadrangle.
Poison Spring [CALAVERAS]: *spring,* 6.5 miles west-southwest of Tamarack (lat. 38°23'40" N, long. 120°10'55" W; near N line sec. 11, T 6 N, R 16 E). Named on Calaveras Dome (1979) 7.5' quadrangle.
Poison Switch: see **Wassamma** [MADERA].
Poland: see **Poland House** [SAN JOAQUIN].
Poland House [SAN JOAQUIN]: *locality,* 1 mile east-northeast of Clements (lat. 38°11'50" N, long. 121°04'05" W). Named on Lodi (1894) 30' quadrangle. Postal authorities established Poland post office on the south side of Mokelumne River (sec. 14, T 4 N, R 8 E) in 1858 and discontinued it in 1867 (Salley, p. 175).
Polly Dome [MARIPOSA]: *peak,* 2.5 miles west of Cathedral Peak (lat. 37°51'15" N, long. 119°26'55" W; near N line sec. 16, T 1 S, R 23 E). Altitude 8910 feet. Named on Tuolumne Meadows (1956) 15' quadrangle. R.B. Marshall of United States Geological Survey named the peak for Polly McCabe, daughter of Colonel W.W. Forsyth (United States Board on Geographic Names, 1934, p. 19).
Polly Dome Lakes [MARIPOSA]: *lakes,* largest 1300 feet long, 3 miles west-northwest of Cathedral Peak (lat. 37°51'45" N, long. 119°27'10" W; sec. 9, T 1 S, R 23 E); the lakes are 0.5 mile north-northwest of Polly Dome. Named on Tuolumne Meadows (1956) 15' quadrangle.
Pond Lily Lake [MADERA]: *lake,* nearly 6 miles south of Devils Postpile (lat. 37°32'30" N, long. 119°06'05" W). Named on Devils Postpile (1953) 15' quadrangle.
Pond Lily Lake: see **Sotcher Lake** [MADERA].
Pooley's Ranch: see **Soulsbyville** [TUOLUMNE].
Pools Station [CALAVERAS]: *locality,* 6 miles west-southwest of Angels Camp (lat. 38°02'40" N, long. 120°38'50" W; sec. 10, T 2 N, R 12 E). Named on Salt Spring Valley (1962) 7.5' quadrangle.
Poopenaut Valley [TUOLUMNE]: *valley,* 4 miles northeast of Mather along Tuolumne River (lat. 37°55'30" N, long. 119°48'45" W). Named on Lake Eleanor (1956) 15' quadrangle. United States Board on Geographic Names (1933a, p. 614) rejected the forms "Poo Poo Valley" and "Poopenant Valley" for the name.
Poo Poo Valley: see **Poopenaut Valley** [TUOLUMNE].
Poorman Gulch [CALAVERAS]: *canyon,* drained by a stream that flows 2.5 miles to Mokelumne River 2.5 miles west-southwest of Mokelumne Hill (lat. 38°17'25" N, long. 120°45'05" W; sec. 15, T 5 N, R 11 E). Named on Mokelumne Hill (1948) 7.5' quadrangle.
Poor Mans Gulch [TUOLUMNE]: *canyon,* drained by a stream that flows 3.5 miles to Don Pedro Reservoir 4.25 miles south-southeast of Chinese Camp (lat. 37°48'50" N, long. 120°24'25" W; near S line sec. 26, T 1 S, R 14 E). Named on Chinese Camp (1947) 7.5' quadrangle.
Pope [SAN JOAQUIN]: *locality,* 5.25 miles west-southwest of Lockeford along Central California Traction Railroad (lat. 38°08'30" N, long. 121°14'30" W; on W line sec. 5, T 3 N, R 7 E). Named on Lockeford (1968) 7.5' quadrangle.
Porath Gulch [MARIPOSA]: *canyon,* drained by a stream that flows 2.5 miles to Bull Creek 11 miles west-northwest of El Portal (lat. 37°42'25" N, long. 119°58'50" W; sec. 3, T 3 S, R 18 E). Named on Kinsley (1947) 7.5' quadrangle.
Porcupine Creek [MARIPOSA]: *stream,* flows 4.5 miles to Snow Creek (1) 4 miles northeast of Yosemite Village (lat. 37°47'30" N, long. 119°32'10" W). Named on Hetch Hetchy Reservoir (1956) 15' quadrangle.
Porcupine Flat [MARIPOSA]: *area,* 4.25 miles north-northeast of Yosemite Village (lat. 37°48'20" N, long. 119°33'50" W; near W line sec. 33, T 1 S, R 22 E); the place is along Porcupine Creek. Named on Hetch Hetchy Reservoir (1956) 15' quadrangle.
Porphyry Lake [MADERA]: *lake,* 500 feet long, 3.25 miles east of Merced Peak (lat. 37°37'45" N, long. 119°20' W). Named on Merced Peak (1953) 15' quadrangle.
Porter [CALAVERAS]: *locality,* nearly 5 miles northwest of Blue Mountain (lat. 38°23'40" N, long. 120°25'30" W; near N line sec. 10, T 6 N, R 14 E). Named on Blue Mountain (1956) 15' quadrangle.
Portezuela de Buenos Ayres: see **Corral Hollow** [SAN JOAQUIN].
Port of Stockton [SAN JOAQUIN]: *locality,* in the city of Stockton near the end of Stockton Deep Water Channel (lat. 37°57'05" N, long. 121°19'30" W). Named on Stockton West (1952) 7.5' quadrangle.
Portuguese Creek [MADERA]: *stream,* flows 3.5 miles to Chiquito Creek 8.5 miles north-northeast of Shuteye Peak (lat. 37°28'10" N, long. 119°22'45" W; sec. 30, T 5 S, R 24 E). Named on Merced Peak (1953) and Shuteye Peak (1953) 15' quadrangles.
Portuguese Creek [MERCED]: *stream,* flows 2.25 miles to San Luis Creek 4.5 miles east-northeast of Mariposa Peak (lat. 36°59'15" N, long. 121°08' W). Named on Mariposa Peak (1969) 7.5' quadrangle.
Portuguese Gulch [TUOLUMNE]: *canyon,* drained by a stream that flows nearly 1 mile to Woods Creek 2.5 miles south-southeast of Columbia (lat. 38°00'05" N, long. 120°22'55" W; sec. 25, T 2 N, R 14 E). Named on Columbia (1948) and Columbia SE (1948) 7.5' quadrangles.
Portuguese Ridge [MARIPOSA]: *ridge,* north-northwest-trending, 2.5 miles long, 9.5 miles south-southwest of El Portal (lat. 37°32'35" N, long. 119°51' W). Named on Buckingham Mountain (1947) 7.5' quadrangle.
Post Corral [TUOLUMNE]: *locality,* 3 miles east of Liberty Hill (lat. 38°22'05" N, long. 120°02'45" W; near SW cor. sec. 18, T 6 N, R 18 E). Named on Liberty Hill (1979) 7.5' quadrangle.
Post Corral Canyon [TUOLUMNE]: *canyon,* 2 miles long, along Spring Creek above a point 11.5 miles east of Pinecrest (lat. 38°10'55" N, long. 119°47' W). Named on Pinecrest (1956) 15' quadrangle.
Post Corral Meadow [TUOLUMNE]: *area,* 2.5 miles east of Liberty Hill (lat. 38°21'45" N, long. 120°03'05" W; sec. 24, T 6 N, R 17 E); the place is 0.5 mile south-southwest of Post Corral. Named on Liberty Hill (1979) 7.5' quadrangle.
Post Creek [MADERA]: *stream,* flows 3.25 miles to West Fork Granite Creek 5.25 miles southeast of Merced Peak (lat. 37°34'50" N, long. 119°19'40" W); the stream heads near Post Peak. Named on Merced Peak (1953) 15' quadrangle.
Post Lakes [MADERA]: *lakes,* two, each about 700 feet long, nearly 3 miles east-southeast of Merced Peak (lat. 37°37'35" N, long. 119°20'40" W); the lakes are 1 mile west of Post Peak. Named on Merced Peak (1953) 15' quadrangle.
Post Peak [MADERA]: *peak,* 3.5 miles east of Merced Peak (lat. 37° 37'45" N, long. 119°19'40" W). Altitude 11,009 feet. Named on Merced Peak (1953) 15' quadrangle. R.B. Marshall of United States Geological Survey named the peak for William S. Post, an employee of the Survey (United States Board on Geographic Names, 1934, p. 19).
Post Peak Pass [MADERA]: *pass,* 3.5 miles east of Merced Peak (lat. 37°37'50" N, long. 119°19'40" W); the pass is north of Post Peak. Named on Merced Peak (1953) 15' quadrangle.
Potato Point [SAN JOAQUIN]: *promontory,* 16 miles west-southwest of Lodi at the west end of Venice Island (lat. 38°04'50" N, long. 121°34'05" W); the feature is at the confluence of Potato Slough and San Joaquin River. Named on Bouldin Island (1978) 7.5' quadrangle. Called Hardscratch Pt. on Bouldin (1910) 7.5' quadrangle.
Potato Slough [SAN JOAQUIN]: *water feature,* joins San Joaquin River 17

miles west-southwest of Lodi (lat. 38°05'05" N, long. 121°34' W). Named on Bouldin Island (1978) 7.5' quadrangle.

Potato Slough: see **Little Potato Slough** [SAN JOAQUIN].

Pothole Meadows [MARIPOSA]: *area,* 3.25 miles south of Yosemite Village (lat. 37°42'10" N, long. 119°35'10" W). Named on Yosemite (1956) 15' quadrangle. The name is from some bowl-shaped depressions about 5 feet in diameter (Browning, 1986, p. 173).

Potrero Peak [MERCED]: *peak,* 7.5 miles south-southeast of Mariposa Peak on Merced-San Benito County line (lat. 36°51'25" N, long. 121°08'55" W; sec. 25, T 12 S, R 7 E). Altitude 3742 feet. Named on Quien Sabe Valley (1968) 7.5' quadrangle.

Potter Point [TUOLUMNE]: *peak,* 7 miles south of Tioga Pass (lat. 37°48'40" N, long. 119°16'45" W). Altitude 10,728 feet. Named on Tuolumne Meadows (1956) 15' quadrangle. R.B. Marshall of United States Geological Survey named the feature in 1909 for Dr. Charles Potter, an army doctor (Browning, 1988, p. 112).

Potter Ridge [MARIPOSA]: *ridge,* west- to northwest-trending, 6.5 miles long, 5.5 miles southwest of Yosemite Forks (lat. 37°18'30" N, long. 119°42' W). Named on Bass Lake (1953) 15' quadrangle.

Poverty Bar [CALAVERAS]: *locality,* 5 miles west-northwest of Valley Springs along Mokelumne River (lat. 38°13'30" N, long. 120°54'30" W; on E line sec. 6, T 4 N, R 10 E). Named on Wallace (1962) 7.5' quadrangle. Postal authorities established Poverty Bar post office in 1858 and discontinued it in 1864 (Frickstad, p. 16). Water of Camanche Reservoir now covers the place.

Poverty Flat [STANISLAUS]: *canyon,* 4.5 miles west-southwest of Newman (lat. 37°17' N, long. 121°05'45" W; mainly in sec. 33, T 7 S, R 8 E). Named on Newman (1952) 7.5' quadrangle.

Poverty Hill: see **Stent** [TUOLUMNE].

Powell Lake [TUOLUMNE]: *lake,* 600 feet long, 7.5 miles east of Pinecrest (lat. 38°12'15" N, long. 119°50'30" W; sec. 14, T 4 N, R 19 E). Named on Pinecrest (1956) 15' quadrangle.

Prather Meadow: see **Big Prather Meadow** [TUOLUMNE]; **Little Prather Meadow** [TUOLUMNE].

Prewett Station: see **Bates Station** [MADERA].

Price: see **Lee Price Camp** [TUOLUMNE].

Price Peak [TUOLUMNE]: *peak,* 5.5 miles south of Tower Peak (lat. 38°03'50" N, long. 119°31'50" W). Altitude 10,716 feet. Named on Tower Peak (1956) 15' quadrangle. The name commemorates George Ehler Price of the Seventh Cavalry (United States Board on Geographic Names, 1934, p. 19).

Priest [TUOLUMNE]: *locality,* 1.5 miles east of Moccasin along Rattlesnake Creek (lat. 37°48'50" N, long. 120°16'20" W; near S line sec. 25, T 1 S, R 15 E). Named on Moccasin (1948) 7.5' quadrangle. The name is for William Priest and his wife, who ran a hotel at the place; Alexander Kirkwood and his wife founded the hotel in 1855, and after Mr. Kirkwood's death Mrs. Kirkwood married William Priest (Paden and Schlichtmann, p. 118). The hotel was called Rattlesnake House before 1872, and later it usually was called Priest's Station (Gudde, 1975, p. 276).

Priest Reservoir [TUOLUMNE]: *lake,* behind a dam on Rattlesnake Creek 2 miles east-southeast of Moccasin (lat. 37°48'05" N, long. 120°15'55" W; near W line sec. 31, T 1 S, R 16 E); the lake is 1 mile south-southeast of Priest. Named on Moccasin (1948) 7.5' quadrangle.

Priest's Station: see **Priest** [TUOLUMNE].

Princeton: see **Mount Bullion** [MARIPOSA].

Prisoners Point [SAN JOAQUIN]: *promontory,* 16 miles west-southwest of Lodi along San Joaquin River on the south side of Venice Island (lat. 38°03'40" N, long. 121°33'15" W). Named on Bouldin Island (1978) 7.5' quadrangle. Called Criminal Pt. on Bouldin (1910) 7.5' quadrangle.

Profile Cliff [MARIPOSA]: *relief feature,* 2.5 miles south-southwest of Yosemite Village on the south side of Yosemite Valley (lat. 37° 42'55" N, long. 119°36' W). Named on Yosemite (1956) 15' quadrangle.

Providence Camp: see **Algerine** [TUOLUMNE].

Provo: see **Mount Provo** [TUOLUMNE].

Pruitt Lake [TUOLUMNE]: *lake,* 1150 feet long, 14 miles east-southeast of Pinecrest (lat. 38°06'45" N, long. 119°45'40" W). Named on Pinecrest (1956) 15' quadrangle.

Puerto [STANISLAUS]: *locality,* 2.25 miles southeast of Westley along Southern Pacific Railroad (lat. 37°31'25" N, long. 121°10'10" W; near S line sec. 2, T 5 S, R 7 E); the place is less than 1 mile northwest of the railroad crossing of Del Puerto Creek. Named on Westley (1952) 7.5' quadrangle.

Puerto: see **Rancho del Puerto** [STANISLAUS].

Puerto Canyon: see **Del Puerto Canyon** [STANISLAUS]..

Puerto Creek: see **Del Puerto Creek** [STANISLAUS].

Pulpit Rock [MARIPOSA]: *relief feature,* 5.5 miles west-southwest of Yosemite Village in Yosemite Valley (lat. 37°43' N, long. 119° 41' W). Named on Yosemite (1956) 15' quadrangle.

Pulpit Rock [TUOLUMNE]: *relief feature,* 3.25 miles west-southwest of Sonora (lat. 37°57'35" N, long. 120°26'05" W; sec. 9, T 1 N, R 14 E). Named on Sonora (1948) 7.5' quadrangle.

Pumice Flat [MADERA]: *area,* 1.5 miles north of Devils Postpile along Middle Fork San Joaquin River (lat. 37°39' N, long. 119°04'30" W). Named on Devils Postpile (1953) 15' quadrangle. Waring (p. 239) noted that a meadow located 2 miles south of Pumice Flat is known as Soda Spring Flat for a small spring of carbonated water there that is well known to campers.

Pumice Gap: see **Mammoth Pass** [MADERA].

Pumpkin Hollow [CALAVERAS]: *area,* 5 miles west-southwest of Tamarack (lat. 38°25'20" N, long. 120°10'10" W; at N line sec. 36, T 7 N, R 16 E). Named on Calaveras Dome (1979) 7.5' quadrangle.

Punch Bowl [TUOLUMNE]: *valley,* 4 miles north-northeast of Pinecrest (lat. 38°14'20" N, long. 119°57'30" W; sec. 35, T 5 N, R 18 E). Named on Pinecrest (1979) 7.5' quadrangle.

Pywiack Cascade [MARIPOSA]: *waterfall,* 6.25 miles southwest of Cathedral Peak along Tenaya Creek (lat. 37°47'15" N, long. 119° 29'20" W). Named on Tuolumne Meadows (1956) 15' quadrangle. United States Board on Geographic Names (1934, p. 20) rejected the name "Slide Fall" for the feature, and noted that the name "Pywiack" is of Indian origin.

Pywiack Dome [MARIPOSA]: *peak,* 2 miles west of Cathedral Peak (lat.. 37°50'45" N, long. 119°26'30" W; near W line sec. 15, T 1 S, R 23 E). Named on Tuolumne Meadows (1956) 15' quadrangle. David Brower recommended the name in the early 1950's; before that time the feature had the names "Murphy's Dome," "Teapot Dome," "Matthes Dome," "Tenieya Dome," and "Turtle Rock" (Browning, 1986, p. 176).

—Q—

Quail Gulch [TUOLUMNE]: *canyon,* drained by a stream that flows 1.25 miles to Stanislaus River 3.5 miles west-southwest of Columbia (lat. 38°00'50" N, long. 120°27'45" W; sec. 20, T 2 N, R 14 E). Named on Columbia (1948) 7.5' quadrangle.

Quail Hill [CALAVERAS]: *peak,* 6 miles southwest of Copperopolis (lat. 37°55'25" N, long. 120°43'15" W; sec. 24, T 1 N, R 11 E). Named on Copperopolis (1962) 7.5' quadrangle.

Quarry Peak [TUOLUMNE]: *peak,* 4 miles south-southwest of Matterhorn Peak (lat. 38°02'45" N, long. 119°25'05" W). Altitude 11,161 feet. Named on Matterhorn Peak (1956) 15' quadrangle.

Quarter Domes [MARIPOSA]: *relief feature,* 4.25 miles east-northeast of Yosemite Village (lat. 37°45'30" N, long. 119°30'30" W). Named on Hetch Hetchy Reservoir (1956) 15' quadrangle. François Matthes named the feature (Browning, 1986, p. 176).

Quartz [TUOLUMNE]: *settlement,* 4.25 miles south-southwest of Sonora (lat. 37°55'40" N, long. 120°25'15" W; sec. 22, T 1 N, R 14 E); the place is north of Quartz Mountain. Named on Sonora (1948) 7.5' quadrangle. Postal authorities established Quartz post office in 1897 and discontinued it in 1924 (Frickstad, p. 216). The settlement also was called Quartz Hill and Quartz Mountain (Gudde, 1975, p. 278).

Quartzburg: see **Hornitos** [MARIPOSA].

Quartz Creek [CALAVERAS]: *stream,* flows less than 1 mile to San Domingo Creek 1.5 miles northwest of Murphys (lat. 38°09'10" N, long. 120°29'05" W; sec. 36, T 4 N, R 13 E). Named on Murphys (1948) 7.5' quadrangle.

Quartz Creek: see **Grizzly Creek** [MADERA].

Quartz Hill: see **Quartz** [TUOLUMNE].

Quartzite Peak [MARIPOSA]: *peak,* 9 miles south of Cathedral Peak (lat. 37°43' N, long. 119°25'30" W). Altitude 10,440 feet. Named on Merced Peak (1953) 15' quadrangle. Called Quartz Peak on Mount Lyell (1901) 30' quadrangle.

Quartz Mountain [MADERA]:

(1) *ridge,* northwest-trending, 1 mile long, 8.5 miles south-southwest of Merced Peak (lat. 37°31'10" N, long. 119°26'45" W). Named on Merced Peak (1953) 15' quadrangle.

(2) *peak,* 4.25 miles north of O'Neals (lat. 37°11'30" N, long. 119° 41'05" W; sec. 33, T 8 S, R 21 E). Altitude 2752 feet. Named on O'Neals (1965) 7.5' quadrangle. Quartz Mountain Mill Company, financed in France, started a mining community called Narbo on land that the company had near the peak (Clough, p. 89-90). Postal authorities established Narbo post office in 1884 (SW quarter sec. 33, T 8 S, R 21 E), moved it in 1887 (SW quarter sec. 20, T 8 S, R 21 E), and discontinued it the same year. The name "Narbo" was from the word "Narbonne," which was the name of one of the promoters of the French company (Salley, p. 150).

Quartz Mountain [MARIPOSA]:

(1) *peak,* 5 miles east-southeast of Buckhorn Peak (lat. 37°37'35" N, long. 120°02'35" W; sec. 36, T 3 S, R 17 E). Altitude 2475 feet. Named on Buckhorn Peak (1947) 7.5' quadrangle.

(2) *ridge,* west-trending, 1 mile long, nearly 2 miles northwest of Santa Cruz Mountain (lat. 37°28'35" N, long. 120°13'30" W). Named on Indian Gulch (1962) 7.5' quadrangle.

Quartz Mountain [TUOLUMNE]: *hill,* 4.5 miles south-southwest of Sonora (lat. 37°55'25" N, long. 120°25'10" W; sec. 22, T 1 N, R 14 E).

Altitude 1673 feet. Named on Sonora (1948) 7.5' quadrangle.

Quartz Mountain: see **Quartz** [TUOLUMNE].

Quartz Peak: see **Quartzite Peak** [MARIPOSA].

Quartz Rock [MARIPOSA]: *relief feature,* 12 miles south of the settlement of Catheys Valley along Dutchman Creek (lat. 37°15'50" N, long. 120°03'15" W; sec. 1, T 8 S, R 17 E). Named on Illinois Hill (1962) 7.5' quadrangle.

Quien Sabe Point [MERCED]: *promontory,* 6 miles east-southeast of Pacheco Pass on the east side of San Luis Reservoir (lat. 37°02'05" N, long. 121°06'40" W; sec. 29, T 10 S, R 8 E). Named on San Luis Dam (1969) 7.5' quadrangle.

Quiggs Mountain [CALAVERAS]: *peak,* 4.25 miles east-northeast of San Andreas (lat. 38°13'50" N, long. 120°36'50" W; near E line sec. 2, T 4 N, R 12 E). Altitude 2785 feet. Named on Calaveritas (1962) 7.5' quadrangle. Called Sierra Vista Mountain on San Andreas (1947) 15' quadrangle.

Quigley Creek [TUOLUMNE]: *stream,* flows 4 miles to Rydberg Creek 8 miles south-southwest of Chinese Camp (lat. 37°46'05" N, long. 120°29'40" W; near N line sec. 13, T 2 S, R 13 E). Named on Chinese Camp (1947) 7.5' quadrangle.

Quilty Creek [TUOLUMNE]: *stream,* flows 2 miles to Clavey River 4.5 miles southeast of Duckwall Mountain (lat. 37°55'05" N, long. 120°04'10" W; sec. 26, T 1 N, R 17 E). Named on Duckwall Mountain (1948) 7.5' quadrangle.

Quinto Creek [MERCED-STANISLAUS]: *stream,* heads in Stanislaus County and flows 15 miles to lowlands 11.5 miles northeast of Pacheco Pass in Merced County (lat. 37°09'55" N, long. 121°02'35" W; sec. 12, T 9 S, R 8 E). Named on Crevison Peak (1955), Howard Ranch (1953), and Mustang Peak (1955) 7.5' quadrangles. The stream first was called El Arroyo de Quinto, which means "The Fifth Creek" in Spanish (Hoover, Rensch, and Rensch, p. 202).

Quito: see **Lacto** [SAN JOAQUIN].

—R—

Rabbit Hill [MADERA]: *peak,* 5.5 miles south-southwest of Raymond (lat. 37°08'10" N, long. 119°55'50" W; near E line sec. 19, T 9 S, R 10 E). Altitude 886 feet. Named on Raymond (1962) 7.5' quadrangle.

Rackerby Jack Spring [TUOLUMNE]: *spring,* 5.25 miles east-southeast of Duckwall Mountain (lat. 37°56' N, long. 120°02' W; near N line sec. 19, T 1 N, R 18 E). Named on Duckwall Mountain (1948) 7.5' quadrangle.

Rafferty Creek [TUOLUMNE]: *stream,* flows 4.5 miles to Lyell Fork 4.5 miles southwest of Tioga Pass (lat. 37°52'10" N, long. 119°19'25" W); the stream heads near Rafferty Peak. Named on Tuolumne Meadows (1956) 15' quadrangle.

Rafferty Peak [MARIPOSA]: *peak,* 3.5 miles southeast of Cathedral Peak on Mariposa-Tuolumne County line (lat. 37°48'55" N, long. 119°21'15" W). Named on Tuolumne Meadows (1956) 15' quadrangle. Lieutenant N.F. McClure named the peak in 1895 for Captain Ogden Rafferty of the Medical Corps; the captain accompanied the lieutenant on a patrol of Yosemite National Park (United States Board on Geographic Names, 1934, p. 20).

Ragged Peak [TUOLUMNE]: *peak,* 5.5 miles west-northwest of Tioga Pass (lat. 37°56' N, long. 119°21'10" W). Altitude 10,912 feet. Named on Tuolumne Meadows (1956) 15' quadrangle.

Ragtown: see **Salt Gulch** [CALAVERAS].

Rail Creek: see **Elevenmile Creek** [MARIPOSA].

Rail Road Flat [CALAVERAS]: *village,* 11 miles east-northeast of Mokelumne Hill (lat. 38°20'35" N, long. 120°30'40" W; sec. 26, T 6 N, R 13 E). Named on Rail Road Flat (1948) 7.5' quadrangle. Jackson (1902) 30' quadrangle has the form "Railroad Flat" for the name, and United States Board on Geographic Names (1972, p. 4) gave this form as a variant. Postal authorities established Rail Road Flat post office in 1857, discontinued it in 1858, and reestablished it in 1869 (Frickstad, p. 16). The name came into use because miners at the place moved ore cars on rails; the place first was called Independence Flat (Cook, p. 17).

Rainbow Falls [MADERA]: *waterfall,* 1.5 miles south of Devils Postpile on Middle Fork San Joaquin River (lat. 37°36'05" N, long. 119°05' W). Named on Devils Postpile (1953) 15' quadrangle.

Rainbow Lake [MADERA]: *lake,* 950 feet long, 4 miles south-southeast of Merced Peak (lat. 37°34'40" N, long. 119°22' W). Named on Merced Peak (1953) 15' quadrangle.

Rainbow View [MARIPOSA]: *locality,* 5.25 miles west-southwest of Yosemite Village on the north side of Yosemite Valley (lat. 37°43'25" N, long. 119°40'25" W). Named on Yosemite (1956) 15' quadrangle. A rainbow at Bridalveil Fall sometimes can be seen from the place (Browning, 1986, p. 178).

Rainier Creek [MADERA]: *stream,* flows 5 miles to Big Creek 7.5 miles north of Yosemite Forks (lat. 37°28'40" N, long. 119°36'50" W; near SW cor. sec. 19, T 5 S, R 22 E). Named on Bass Lake (1953) and Yosemite (1956) 15' quadrangles.

Rairden Gulch [STANISLAUS]: *canyon,* drained by a stream that flows 4 miles to Tuolumne River 12.5 miles east of Waterford (lat. 37°37'50" N, long. 120°31'55" W; sec. 34, T 3 S, R 13 E). Named on Cooperstown (1968) 7.5' quadrangle.

Rallsville: see **Coarsegold** [MADERA].

Ralph [TUOLUMNE]: *locality,* 6.25 miles east-southeast of Sonora along Sierra Railway (lat. 37°57'55" N, long. 120°16'10" W; sec. 1, T 1 N, R 15 E). Named on Standard (1948) 7.5' quadrangle. California Division of Highways' (1934) map shows a place called Draper located 1.25 miles northwest of Ralph along Sierra Railway.

Ramona: see **Lake Ramona** [STANISLAUS].

Ramos Creek [TUOLUMNE]: *stream,* flows 1.25 miles to Don Pedro Reservoir 2.25 miles east of Don Pedro Camp (lat. 37°42'45" N, long. 120°21'50" W; sec. 31, T 2 S, R 15 E). Named on Merced Falls (1962) 15' quadrangle.

Ramsey [CALAVERAS]: *locality,* 7.25 miles southwest of Tamarack (lat. 38°22'20" N, long. 120°10'30" W; sec. 14, T 6 N, R 16 E). Site named on Boards Crossing (1979) 7.5' quadrangle.

Ramsey Gulch [CALAVERAS]: *canyon,* less than 1 mile long, 4 miles south of Copperopolis (lat. 37°55'15" N, long. 120°38'05" W; in and near sec. 22, T 1 N, R 12 E). Named on Copperopolis (1962) 7.5' quadrangle.

Rancheria Creek [MADERA]: *stream,* flows 1.5 miles to China Creek 4.25 miles south of Yosemite Forks (lat. 37°18'15" N, long. 119°37'20" W; sec. 24, T 7 S, R 21 E). Named on Bass Lake (1953) 15' quadrangle.

Rancheria Creek [MARIPOSA]: *stream,* flows about 1 mile to Bear Creek (1) nearly 4 miles northwest of Midpines (lat. 37°35'15" N, long. 119°57'35" W; near W line sec. 14, T 4 S, R 18 E). Named on Feliciana Mountain (1947) 7.5' quadrangle.

Rancheria Creek [TUOLUMNE]: *stream,* flows 23 miles to Hetch Hetchy Reservoir 7.25 miles northwest of White Wolf (lat. 37°57'10" N, long. 119°43'35" W; sec. 12, T 1 N, R 20 E). Named on Hetch Hetchy Reservoir (1956), Matterhorn Peak (1956), and Tower Peak (1956) 15' quadrangles.

Rancheria del Rio Estanislao [CALAVERAS-STANISLAUS]: *land grant,* near Stanislaus River on Calaveras-Stanislaus County line. Named on Bachelor Valley (1968), Copperopolis (1962), Keystone (1962), Knights Ferry (1962), Melones Dam (1962), and Oakdale (1968) 7.5' quadrangles. Francisco Rico and Jose Antonio Castro received the land in 1843 and claimed 48,887 acres patented in 1863 (Cowan, p. 35).

Rancheria Falls [TUOLUMNE]: *waterfall,* nearly 7 miles north-northwest of White Wolf on Rancheria Creek (lat. 37°57'20" N, long. 119°42'15" W). Named on Hetch Hetchy Reservoir (1956) 15' quadrangle.

Rancheria Flat [MARIPOSA]: *area,* 1.5 miles west of El Portal (lat. 37°40'20" N, long. 119°48'20" W; sec. 18, T 3 S, R 20 E). Named on El Portal (1947) 7.5' quadrangle.

Rancheria Mountain [TUOLUMNE]: *ridge,* west-southwest-trending, 3 miles long, 6.5 miles north-northeast of White Wolf (lat. 37°57'30" N, long. 119°36'30" W); the ridge is southeast of Rancheria Creek. Named on Hetch Hetchy Reservoir (1956) 15' quadrangle.

Ranchero Creek [TUOLUMNE]: *stream,* flows about 2 miles to Big Creek (2) 2.25 miles north-northwest of Don Pedro Camp (lat. 37° 44'50" N, long. 120°25'05" W; sec. 22, T 2 S, R 14 E). Named on La Grange (1962) 7.5' quadrangle.

Rancho del Oro Gulch [MARIPOSA]: *canyon,* drained by a stream that flows 1.25 miles to Lake McClure 4 miles southwest of Coulterville (lat. 37°40'20" N, long. 120°14'50" W). Named on Penon Blanco Peak (1962) 7.5' quadrangle.

Rancho del Puerto [STANISLAUS]: *land grant,* west of San Joaquin River and northeast of Patterson. Named on Brush Lake (1969), Crows Landing (1952), and Westley (1969) 7.5' quadrangles. Mariano Hernandez and Pedro Hernandez received 3 leagues in 1844; Samuel G. Reed and Rueben Wade claimed 13,340 acres patented in 1864 (Cowan, p. 64; Perez, p. 84—Perez listed the grant under the name "Puerto").

Randall Canon: see **Spiller Creek** [TUOLUMNE].

Randalls Meadow [TUOLUMNE]: *valley,* 2 miles east of Liberty Hill (lat. 38°22' N, long. 120°03'45" W). Named on Liberty Hill (1979) 7.5' quadrangle.

Rardin Lake: see **Harden Lake** [TUOLUMNE].

Raspberry: see **Sugarpine** [TUOLUMNE].

Raster Gulch [MARIPOSA]: *canyon,* drained by a stream that flows 2.5 miles to Bear Creek (2) 2.5 miles north-northwest of the settlement of Catheys Valley (lat. 37°28' N, long. 120°06'45" W; sec. 28, T 5 S, R 17 E). Named on Catheys Valley (1962) 7.5' quadrangle.

Rattlesnake Creek [TUOLUMNE]: *stream,* flows 4 miles to Big Jackass Creek 3 miles southeast of Moccasin (lat. 37°46'55" N, long. 120°15'30" W; near NE cor. sec. 12, T 2 S, R 15 E). Named on Moccasin (1948) 7.5' quadrangle.

Rattlesnake Creek: see **Big Rattlesnake Creek** [TUOLUMNE]; **Little Rattlesnake Creek** [TUOLUMNE].

Rattlesnake Gulch [MARIPOSA]: *canyon,* 1.5 miles long, 2.5 miles south-

southwest of Santa Cruz Mountain (lat. 37°25'20" N, long. 120°13'15" W). Named on Indian Gulch (1962) 7.5' quadrangle.

Rattlesnake Gulch [TUOLUMNE]: *canyon,* drained by a stream that flows nearly 2 miles to Woods Creek 1.25 miles east-southeast of Columbia (lat. 38°01'50" N, long. 120°22'40" W; near E line sec. 13, T 2 N, R 14 E). Named on Columbia SE (1948) 7.5' quadrangle.

Rattlesnake Hill [CALAVERAS]: *peak,* 6.5 miles east-northeast of Murphys (lat. 38°10'40" N, long. 120°21'30" W; at S line sec. 19, T 4 N, R 15 E). Altitude 3414 feet. Named on Stanislaus (1948) 7.5' quadrangle.

Rattlesnake House: see **Priest** [TUOLUMNE].

Rattlesnake Lake [MADERA]: *lake,* 850 feet long, 15 miles northeast of Shuteye Peak (lat. 37°28'40" N, long. 119°11'20" W; sec. 24, T 5 S, R 25 E). Named on Kaiser Peak (1953) 15' quadrangle.

Rattlesnake Well [MADERA]: *well,* 12.5 miles west of Madera (lat. 36°57'10" N, long. 120°16'45" W; near N line sec. 25, T 11 S, R 15 E). Named on Kentucky Well (1922) 7.5' quadrangle.

Rawhide [TUOLUMNE]: *locality,* 4 miles west-southwest of Sonora (lat. 37°57'30" N, long. 120°27'05" W); the place is at present Rawhide Flat. Named on Sonora (1897) 30' quadrangle. Postal authorities established Rawhide post office in 1904 and discontinued it in 1906 (Frickstad, p. 216).

Rawhide Flat [TUOLUMNE]: *area,* 3.5 miles west-southwest of Sonora (lat. 37°57'45" N, long. 120°26'35" W; on S line sec. 4, T 1 N, R 14 E). Named on Sonora (1948) 7.5' quadrangle.

Rawls Gulch [MADERA]: *canyon,* drained by a stream that flows 2.5 miles to Daulton Creek 4 miles south-southwest of Raymond (lat. 37°09'50" N, long. 119°56' W; sec. 7, T 9 S, R 19 E). Named on Raymond (1962) 7.5' quadrangle.

Raymond [MADERA]: *village,* 20 miles north-northeast of Madera (lat. 37°13'10" N, long. 119°54'20" W; mainly in sec. 20, 21, T 8 S, R 19 E). Named on Raymond (1962) 7.5' quadrangle. Postal authorities established Raymond post office in 1886 (Frickstad, p. 86). The place first was called Wildcat Station, but when Southern Pacific Railroad reached the site in 1886, the rail stop there was called Raymond for Mr. T. Raymond of Raymond-Whitcomb Travel Association (Clough, p. 90). California Division of Highways' (1934) map shows a place called Herbert located along the railroad 2.25 miles south of Raymond.

Raymond: see **Mount Raymond Camp** [MADERA].

Raymond Mountain [MADERA]: *peak,* 6 miles south-southwest of Buena Vista Peak (lat. 37°30'30" N, long. 119°32'50" W; sec. 10, T 5 S, R 22 E). Altitude 8712 feet. Named on Yosemite (1956) 15' quadrangle. Members of the Whitney survey named the peak for Israel Ward Raymond, who played an active part in persuading the federal government to give Yosemite Valley to the State of California for a park, and who served on the supervisory commission for the park from 1864 until 1866 (Hanna, p. 251).

Raynor Creek [MADERA-MARIPOSA]: *stream,* heads in Mariposa County and flows 10 miles to Chowchilla River 13 miles northeast of Fairmead in Madera County (lat. 37°12'05" N, long. 120°00'25" W; sec. 28, T 8 S, R 18 E). Named on Ben Hur (1947), Illinois Hill (1962), and Raynor Creek (1961) 7.5' quadrangles.

Real Pass: see **Vogelsang Pass**, under **Vogelsang Lake** [MARIPOSA].

Red Apple [CALAVERAS]: *locality,* 5.25 miles east-northeast of Murphys (lat. 38°10'45" N, long. 120°22'50" W; near S line sec. 24, T 4 N, R 14 E). Named on Murphys (1948) 7.5' quadrangle.

Red Bridge Slough [SAN JOAQUIN]: *water feature,* east of San Joaquin River 5 miles north-northeast of Vernalis (lat. 37°42' N, long. 121°15'10" W). Named on Ripon (1952) and Vernalis (1969) 7.5' quadrangles.

Red Can Lake [TUOLUMNE]: *lake,* 1000 feet long, 13 miles east-southeast of Pinecrest (lat. 38°08'40" N, long. 119°45'10" W). Named on Pinecrest (1956) 15' quadrangle.

Red Cones [MADERA]: *peaks,* two, 2.5 miles south-southeast of Devils Postpile (lat. 37°35'30" N, long. 119°03'25" W). Altitudes 8985 and 9015 feet. Named on Devils Postpile (1953) 15' quadrangle.

Red Creek [MADERA-MARIPOSA]: *stream,* heads near Red Peak in Madera County and flows 4.5 miles to Clark Fork 12.5 miles south-southwest of Cathedral Peak in Mariposa County (lat. 37° 40'55" N, long. 119°29'15" W). Named on Merced Peak (1953) 15' quadrangle.

Red Creek [STANISLAUS]: *stream,* flows 8 miles to South Fork Orestimba Creek 2 miles north of Mustang Peak (lat. 37°12'50" N, long. 121°21'50" W; sec. 30, T 8 S, R 6 E). Named on Mississippi Creek (1955), Mount Stakes (1955), and Mustang Peak (1955) 7.5' quadrangles.

Red Devil Lake [MADERA]: *lake,* 1500 feet long, 2 miles north of Merced Peak (lat. 37°39'55" N, long. 119°23'10" W). Named on Merced Peak (1953) 15' quadrangle.

Red Gulch [TUOLUMNE]: *canyon,* less than 0.5 mile long, opens into the canyon of Woods Creek 1.25 miles southeast of Columbia (lat. 38°01'25" N, long. 120°22'55" W; sec. 13, T 2 N, R 14 E). Named on Columbia (1948) 7.5' quadrangle.

Redhawk Lake: see **Calaveras Reservoir** [CALAVERAS].

Red Hill [CALAVERAS]: *peak,* less than 1 mile west-southwest of Vallecito (lat. 38°04'55" N, long. 120°29'10" W; near E line sec. 25, T 3 N, R 13 E). Named on Columbia (1948) 7.5' quadrangle.

Red Hill [MERCED]: *ridge,* southeast-trending, 2 miles long, 4 miles north-northeast of Pacheco Pass (lat. 37°07'30" N, long. 121°11'35" W). Named on Crevison Peak (1955) and Pacheco Pass (1955) 7.5' quadrangles.

Red Hills [TUOLUMNE]: *range,* south and west of Chinese Camp. Named on Chinese Camp (1947) and Keystone (1962) 7.5' quadrangles.

Red Mountain [MARIPOSA]: *peak,* 10 miles south-southeast of Mariposa (lat. 37°21'35" N, long. 119°53'05" W; on S line sec. 34, T 6 S, R 19 E). Altitude 1821 feet. Named on Ben Hur (1947) 7.5' quadrangle. Postal authorities established Red Mountain post office in 1918 and discontinued in 1919; it was located 2 miles north-northeast of the peak (near NE cor. sec. 27, T 6 S, R 19 E) and was named for the peak (Salley, p. 182).

Red Mountain [STANISLAUS]: *ridge,* northwest-trending, nearly 2 miles long, 4.5 miles south of Mount Boardman on Stanislaus-Santa Clara County line (lat. 37°24'55" N, long. 121°27'45" W). Named on Mount Boardman (1955) 7.5' quadrangle. Thompson and West's (1876) map has the label "Red Mountains or Cerro Colorado" along the crest of Diablo Range, including Red Mountain, for a distance of about 11 miles south from Mount Boardman.

Red Mountain: see **Red Peak** [MADERA]; **Taylor Hill** [TUOLUMNE].

Red Mountain Bar [TUOLUMNE]: *locality,* 5 miles south-southeast of Chinese Camp along Tuolumne River (lat. 37°48' N, long. 120° 24'35" W). Named on Sonora (1897) 30' quadrangle. Water of Don Pedro Reservoir now covers the site. Several mining camps were located along Tuolumne River near Red Mountain Bar: Hawkins Bar, named for "Old Hawkins," who kept a store at the place (Gudde, 1975, p. 153), was about 1 mile by path down the river from Red Mountain Bar (Gardiner, p. 80); Morgan's Bar was about 7 miles below Hawkins Bar along the river (Gardiner, p. 104); and Texas Bar was 9 miles below Hawkins Bar (Gudde, 1975, p. 347).

Red Mountains: see **Red Mountain** [STANISLAUS].

Red Peak [MADERA]: *peak,* 1.5 miles north-northwest of Merced Peak (lat. 37°39'15" N, long. 119°24'30" W). Altitude 11,699 feet. Named on Merced Peak (1953) 15' quadrangle. Members of the Whitney survey gave the name "Red Mountain" to the feature for the dominant color of its upper part (Browning, 1988, p. 116).

Red Peak [TUOLUMNE]: *peak,* 7 miles west-northwest of Sonora Pass (lat. 38°22'55" N, long. 119°44'30" W). Altitude 10,009 feet. Named on Disaster Peak (1979) 7.5' quadrangle.

Red Peak: see **Virginia Peak** [TUOLUMNE].

Red Peak Fork [MADERA]: *stream,* flows 4 miles to Merced River 5.25 miles north-northeast of Merced Peak (lat. 37°42'20" N, long. 119°21'40" W); the stream heads near Red Peak. Named on Merced Peak (1953) 15' quadrangle.

Red Rock Meadow [TUOLUMNE]: *area,* 4 miles southeast of Dardanelle (lat. 38°18'05" N, long. 119°46'40" W; near N line sec. 9, T 5 N, R 20 E). Named on Dardanelle (1979) 7.5' quadrangle.

Reds Creek [MADERA]: *stream,* flows 1.5 miles to Middle Fork San Joaquin River 1.25 miles north of Devils Postpile (lat. 37°38'35" N, long. 119°04'40" W); the stream heads near Reds Lake. Named on Devils Postpile (1953) 15' quadrangle.

Reds Creek: see **Reds Meadow Hot Springs** [MADERA].

Reds Lake [MADERA]: *lake,* 500 feet long, 1.5 miles northeast of Devils Postpile (lat. 37°38'20" N, long. 119°03'20" W); the lake is near the head of Reds Creek. Named on Devils Postpile (1953) 15' quadrangle.

Reds Meadow Hot Springs [MADERA]: *springs,* 0.5 mile southeast of Devils Postpile (lat. 37°37'05" N, long. 119°04'25" W); the springs are at Reds Meadows. Named on Devils Postpile (1953) 15' quadrangle. Waring (p. 55) reported that water in a bathing pool at the largest of several small thermal springs at the east side of Reds Meadows has a temperature of 120° Fahrenheit. United States Board on Geographic Names (1984b, p. 2) approved the name "Reds Creek" for a stream that flows 3.5 miles to San Joaquin River 0.5 mile west-southwest of Reds Meadow Hot Springs (lat. 37°36'58" N, long. 119°04'57" W)—the hot springs are along this stream.

Reds Meadows [MADERA]: *area,* 0.5 mile southeast of Devils Postpile (lat. 37°37' N, long. 119°04'30" W). Named on Mount Lyell (1901) 30' quadrangle. The name commemorates Red Sotcher, or Satcher, who came to the place in 1879 to herd sheep (Smith, p. 14).

Red Top [MADERA]:

(1) *locality,* 12 miles west-southwest of Chowchilla (lat. 37°05' N, long. 120°29'30" W; near SW cor. sec. 6, T 10 S, R 14 E). Named on Bliss Ranch (1960) 7.5' quadrangle. Postal authorities established Red Top post office in 1952 (Salley, p. 183).

(2) *peak,* 6 miles south of Merced Peak (lat. 37°32'45" N, long. 119°24'10" W). Altitude 9977 feet. Named on Merced Peak (1953) 15' quadrangle. The name also had the form "Redtop" (Browning, 1986, p. 180).

Red Top Mountain: see **Garnet Lake** [MADERA].

Redwood Creek [MADERA]: *stream,* flows 1.5 miles to Nelder Creek 1 mile east of Yosemite Forks (lat. 37°22' N, long. 119°36'35" W; sec. 13, T 6 S, R 22 E). Named on Bass Lake (1953) 15' quadrangle.

Reed Creek [TUOLUMNE]: *stream,* formed by the confluence of Bourland Creek and Reynolds Creek, flows 6 miles to Clavey River nearly 4 miles east of Duckwall Mountain (lat. 37°57'40" N, long. 120°02'55" W; near E line sec. 12, T 1 N, R 17 E). Named on Duckwall Mountain (1948) and Hull Creek (1979) 7.5' quadrangles.

Reed Creek: see **Bourland Creek** [TUOLUMNE].

Reeves Spring [MERCED]: *spring,* 6.25 miles north-northeast of Pacheco Pass (lat. 37°09'10" N, long. 121°10'35" W; sec. 14, T 9 S, R 7 E). Named on Crevison Peak (1955) 7.5' quadrangle.

Register Creek [TUOLUMNE]: *stream,* flows 6.5 miles to Tuolumne River 8 miles northeast of White Wolf (lat. 37°56'25" N, long. 119°32' W). Named on Hetch Hetchy Reservoir (1956) and Tuolumne Meadows (1956) 15' quadrangles.

Regulation Creek [TUOLUMNE]: *stream,* flows 2.5 miles to Return Creek 11 miles west-northwest of Tioga Pass (lat. 38°57'55" N, long. 119°26'45" W); the creek is east of Regulation Peak. Named on Tuolumne Meadows (1956) 15' quadrangle. The stream first was called West Fork Return Creek (Browning, 1986, p. 181).

Regulation Peak [TUOLUMNE]: *peak,* 13 miles west-northwest of Tioga Pass (lat. 38°55'10" N, long. 119°28'15" W). Named on Tuolumne Meadows (1956) 15' quadrangle. A trumpeter named McBride suggested the name to Lieutenant H.C. Benson after he and the lieutenant had posted regulations for Yosemite National Park throughout the park—the name originally was meant for present Volunteer Peak (Browning, 1986, p. 181).

Regulation Peak: see **West Peak** [TUOLUMNE].

Relief Creek [TUOLUMNE]: *stream,* flows 3.5 miles to Summit Creek 13 miles northwest of Tower Peak (lat. 38°14'55" N, long. 119°44'30" W; sec. 26, T 5 N, R 20 E); the stream heads in Upper Relief Valley and goes through Lower Relief Valley. Named on Pinecrest (1956) and Tower Peak (1956) 15' quadrangles.

Relief Creek: see **Summit Creek** [TUOLUMNE].

Relief Peak [TUOLUMNE]: *peak,* 10.5 miles northwest of Tower Peak (lat. 38°14'15" N, long. 119°41'45" W); the peak is 3 miles east of Lower Relief Valley. Altitude 10,808 feet. Named on Tower Peak (1956) 15' quadrangle.

Relief Reservoir [TUOLUMNE]: *lake,* 1.5 miles long, behind a dam on Summit Creek 6 miles west-southwest of Sonora Pass (lat. 38° 16'50" N, long. 119°43'55" W; near W line sec. 13, T 5 N, R 20 E). Named on Sonora Pass (1979) 7.5' quadrangle.

Relief Valley: see **Lower Relief Valley** [TUOLUMNE]; **Upper Relief Valley** [TUOLUMNE].

Repeater Hill [TUOLUMNE]: *peak,* 10 miles southwest of Liberty Hill (lat. 38°15'10" N, long. 120°13'10" W; near S line sec. 28, T 5 N, R 16 E). Altitude 5510 feet. Named on Boards Crossing (1979) 7.5' quadrangle.

Reservoir Meadows: see **Ackerson Meadow** [TUOLUMNE].

Return Creek [TUOLUMNE]: *stream,* flows 14 miles to Tuolumne River 11.5 miles west of Tioga Pass (lat. 37°55'55" N, long. 119° 27'55" W). Named on Matterhorn Peak (1956) 15' quadrangle. United States Board on Geographic Names (1934, p. 21) rejected the name "North Fork of Tuolumne River" for the stream. Present Regulation Creek first was called West Fork Return Creek (Browning, 1986, p. 181).

Return Creek: see **North Fork**, under **Tuolumne River** [STANISLAUS-TUOLUMNE].

Revis Mountain [MADERA]: *peak,* 5.5 miles north-northwest of O'Neals (lat. 37°11'40" N, long. 119°44'45" W; near E line sec. 35, T 8 S, R 20 E). Named on Knowles (1962) and O'Neals (1965) 7.5' quadrangles.

Reymann Lake [MARIPOSA]: *lake,* 900 feet long, 3 miles southeast of Cathedral Peak (lat. 37°49'15" N, long. 119°21'30" W). Named on Tuolumne Meadows (1956) 15' quadrangle. The name commemorates William M. Reymann, who was a ranger in Yosemite National Park (Browning, 1986, p. 182).

Reynolds Creek [TUOLUMNE]: *stream,* flows 8.5 miles to join Bourland Creek and form Reed Creek 8.5 miles southeast of Long Barn (lat. 38°01'10" N, long. 120°00'45" W; near W line sec. 21, T 2 N, R 18 E). Named on Cherry Lake North (1979) and Hull Creek (1979) 7.5' quadrangles.

Reynolds Creek: see **Little Reynolds Creek** [TUOLUMNE].

Reynolds Ferry [CALAVERAS-TUOLUMNE]: *locality,* 5.5 miles east of Copperopolis along Stanislaus River on Calaveras-Tuolumne County line (lat. 37°58'50" N, long. 120°32'20" W; sec. 34, T 2 N, R 13 E). Named on Copperopolis (1916) 15' quadrangle. Water of New Melones Lake now covers the site. Postal authorities established Reynolds Ferry post office in Calaveras County in 1856, discontinued it for a time in 1860, and discontinued it finally in 1868 (Frickstad, p. 16).

Rhodes [SAN JOAQUIN]: *locality,* 8 miles north-northeast of Vernalis along Western Pacific Railroad (lat. 37°43'55" N, long. 121°21'35" W; near W line sec. 30, T 2 S, R 6 E). Named on Vernalis (1952) 7.5' quadrangle.

Rhodes Lake [TUOLUMNE]: *lake,* 600 feet long, 4.25 miles east of Liberty Hill (lat. 38°22'15" N, long. 120°01'15" W; sec. 17, T 6 N, R 18 E). Named on Liberty Hill (1979) 7.5' quadrangle.

Ribbon Creek [MARIPOSA]: *stream,* flows 3.5 miles to Merced River 3.5 miles west-southwest of Yosemite Village (lat. 37°43'25" N, long. 119°38'20" W); Ribbon Fall is along the stream. Named on Hetch Hetchy Reservoir (1956) and Yosemite (1956) 15' quadrangles. Called Virgin Tears Creek on King and Gardner's (1865) map. Whitney (1870, p. 60) used the the form "Virgin's Tears Creek" for the name.

Ribbon Fall [MARIPOSA]: *waterfall,* 3.5 miles west-southwest of Yosemite Village on the north side of Yosemite Valley (lat. 37°44'10" N, long. 119°38'50" W). Named on Yosemite (1956) 15' quadrangle. Called Virgin Tear's Fall on King and Gardner's (1865) map. The Mariposa Battalion knew the feature as Pigeon Creek Fall (Browning, 1988, p. 118). James M. Hutchings gave it the name "Ribbon Fall" (Gudde, 1969, p. 268).

Ribbon Meadow [MARIPOSA]: *area,* 4 miles west of Yosemite Village (lat. 37°44'50" N, long. 119°39'30" W); the place is along a tributary to Ribbon Creek. Named on Yosemite (1956) 15' quadrangle.

Richard Creek [STANISLAUS]: *stream,* flows 3 miles to Garzas Creek 4 miles northwest of Crevison Peak (lat. 37°13'20" N, long. 121°14'40" W; sec. 19, T 8 S, R 7 E). Named on Crevison Peak (1955) and Mustang Peak (1955) 7.5' quadrangles.

Richards Creek [TUOLUMNE]: *stream,* flows nearly 2 miles to Cherry Lake 14 miles south-southeast of Pinecrest (lat. 38°00'05" N, long. 119°54'55" W; sec. 29, T 2 N, R 19 E). Named on Cherry Lake North (1979) 7.5' quadrangle.

Richardson Peak [TUOLUMNE]: *peak,* 9 miles west-southwest of Tower Peak (lat. 38°05' N, long. 119°41'30" W). Altitude 9884 feet. Named on Tower Peak (1956) 15' quadrangle. Lieutenant M.M. Macomb named the peak in 1897 for Thomas Richardson, who ran sheep in the neighborhood (United States Board on Geographic Names, 1934, p. 21).

Richardsons: see **Emory**, under **Clearing House** [MARIPOSA].

Richey Camp [STANISLAUS]: *locality,* 4 miles northwest of Crevison Peak along Garzas Creek (lat. 37°13'20" N, long. 121°14'35" W; sec. 19, T 8 S, R 7 E); the place is near the mouth of Richard Creek. Named on Crevison Peak (1955) 7.5' quadrangle.

Rich Gulch [CALAVERAS]:

(1) *canyon,* drained by a stream that flows 2.25 miles to Mokelumne River 2 miles north of Paloma (lat. 38°17'15" N, long. 120° 45'25" W; sec. 15, T 5 N, R 11 E). Named on Jackson (1962) 7.5' quadrangle. Camp's (1962) map shows a place called James Bar located on the south side of Mokelumne River just downstream from the mouth of Rich Gulch (1). The name "James" was for Colonel George F. James, who mined at the place in 1849, and for whom Jamestown [TUOLUMNE] was named (Gudde, 1975, p. 174). Gwin mine is in Rich Gulch (1), which also had the name "Gwin Mine Canyon" (Sargent, Mrs. J.L., p. 65). Postal authorities established Gwin Mine post office at the mine in 1870, discontinued it in 1882, reestablished it with the name "Gwin" in 1895, changed the name to Gwinmine in 1895; and discontinued it in 1910—the name "Gwin" was for W.M. Gwin, who had the mine in the 1850's (Salley, p. 91).

(2) *canyon,* drained by a stream that flows 3 miles to North Fork Calaveras River 2.5 miles east of Mokelumne Hill (lat. 38°18'25" N, long. 120°39'20" W; near N line sec. 9, T 5 N, R 12 E). Named on Mokelumne Hill (1948) 7.5' quadrangle. Camp's (1962) map has the designation "Rich Gulch (upper)" for the canyon.

(3) *canyon,* drained by a stream that flows 1.5 miles to Calaveras River nearly 1 mile east-southeast of Jenny Lind (lat. 38°05'20" N, long. 120°51'20" W; near NE cor. sec. 27, T 3 N, R 10 E). Named on Jenny Lind (1962) 7.5' quadrangle.

(4) *canyon,* drained by a stream that flows 0.5 mile to Snake Gulch 3.5 miles south-southeast of Vallecito (lat. 38°02'20" N, long. 120° 27'20" W; sec. 8, T 2 N, R 14 E). Named on Columbia (1948) 7.5' quadrangle.

(5) *locality,* 5 miles east-northeast of Mokelumne Hill (lat. 38°19'50" N, long. 120°37'30" W; sec. 35, T 6 N, R 12 E); the place is near the head of Rich Gulch (2). Named on Mokelumne Hill (1948) and Rail Road Flat (1948) 7.5' quadrangles. Postal authorities established Pleasant Springs post office in 1855, changed the name to Rich Gulch in 1857, discontinued it in 1867, reestablished it in 1887, and discontinued it in 1903 (Salley, p. 174, 185).

Richie Slough [STANISLAUS]: *water feature,* 4 miles east of Westley (lat. 37°33' N, long. 121°07'40" W). Named on Brush Lake (1969) and Westley (1969) 7.5' quadrangles.

Ridge Lake: see **Emigrant Lake** [TUOLUMNE].

Ridleys Ferry: see **Bagby** [MARIPOSA].

Riley Ridge [TUOLUMNE]: *ridge,* north-northwest-trending, 0.5 mile long, 1.25 miles south-southwest of Don Pedro Camp (lat. 37° 41'55" N, long. 120°24'55" W; sec. 3, T 3 N, R 14 E). Named on La Grange (1962) 7.5' quadrangle.

Riley Slough [STANISLAUS]: *water feature,* 12 miles west of Modesto near the confluence of Stanislaus River and San Joaquin River (lat. 37°39'25" N, long. 121°12'45" W). Named on Ripon (1969) 7.5' quadrangle.

Rincon Creek [MERCED]: *stream,* flows 6.25 miles to South Fork Los Banos Creek 2.5 miles west of Sweeney Hill (lat. 36°54'20" N, long. 121°05'30" W). Named on Los Banos Valley (1969) and Mariposa Peak (1969) 7.5' quadrangles.

Rindge Tract [SAN JOAQUIN]: *island,* 7.5 miles south-southeast of Terminous between San Joaquin River, Fourteen Mile Slough, and Disappointment Slough (lat. 38°01'15" N, long. 121°25'30" W). Named on Holt (1978) and Terminous (1978) 7.5' quadrangles.

Rio Blanco Tract [SAN JOAQUIN]: *area,* 5.5 miles east-southeast of Terminous (lat. 38°04'45" N, long. 121°24'15" W). Named on Terminous (1978) 7.5' quadrangle.

Rio de la Merced: see **Merced River** [MADERA-MARIPOSA-MERCED].

Rio de la Pasion: see **Calaveras River** [CALAVERAS-SAN JOAQUIN-STANISLAUS].

Rio de las Calaveras: see **Calaveras River** [CALAVERAS-SAN JOAQUIN-STANISLAUS].

Rio de la Towalumnes: see **Tuolumne River** [STANISLAUS-TUOLUMNE].

Rio del Laquisimes: see **Stanislaus River** [CALAVERAS-SAN JOAQUIN-STANISLAUS-TUOLUMNE].

Rio de los Merced: see **Merced River** [MADERA-MARIPOSA-MERCED].

Rio del Pescadero: see **Old River** [SAN JOAQUIN].

Rio de Nuestra Señora de Guadalupe: see **Stanislaus River** [CALAVERAS-SAN JOAQUIN-STANISLAUS-TUOLUMNE].

Rio Estanislao: see **Stanislaus River** [CALAVERAS-SAN JOAQUIN-STANISLAUS-TUOLUMNE].

Rio San Joaquin: see **San Joaquin River** [MADERA-MERCED-SAN JOAQUIN-STANISLAUS].

Rio Tulare: see **San Joaquin River** [MADERA-MERCED-SAN JOAQUIN-STANISLAUS].

Ripon [SAN JOAQUIN]: *town,* 6 miles southeast of Manteca (lat. 37° 44'20" N, long. 121°07'40" W; around NE cor. sec. 30, T 2 S, R 8 E). Named on Ripon (1969) and Salida (1969) 7.5' quadrangles. Postal authorities established Ripon post office in 1874 (Frickstad, p. 162), and the town incorporated in 1945. The place first was called Stanislaus City, but Applias Crooks, first postmaster, named the post office "Ripon" after his former home in Wisconsin (Gudde, 1949, p. 287). Thompson and West's (1879) map shows Murphy's Ferry on Stanislaus River 1 mile east of Ripon; the ferry operated from 1850 until 1870 (Hillman and Covello, p. 85).

Ripperdan [MADERA]: *village,* 7.5 miles south of Madera (lat. 36° 51'05" N, long. 120°03'20" W; at NE cor. sec. 36, T 12 S, R 17 E). Named on Biola (1963) 7.5' quadrangle.

Ritter: see **Mount Ritter** [MADERA].

Ritter Range [MADERA]: *ridge,* north-northwest-trending, 8 miles long, 8 miles northwest of Devils Postpile (lat. 37°41'30" N, long. 119°12' W); Mount Ritter is near the middle of the ridge. Named on Devils Postpile (1953) 15' quadrangle.

Riverbank [STANISLAUS]: *town,* 7.5 miles north-northeast of Modesto on the south side of Stanislaus River (lat. 37°44'10" N, long. 120°56'15" W; sec. 25, 26, T 2 S, R 9 E). Named on Riverbank (1969) 7.5' quadrangle. Postal authorities established Riverbank post office in 1898 (Frickstad, p. 201). Major James Burney gave the name "Riverbank" to an earlier community located at a site at the edge of the present town (Gudde, 1949, p. 288).

River Rock: see **Carbona** [SAN JOAQUIN].

Riverside [STANISLAUS]: *locality,* 2.5 miles east of downtown Modesto along an electric railroad (lat. 37°38'15" N, long. 120°56'50" W; on N line sec. 35, T 3 S, R 9 E). Named on Riverbank (1916) 7.5' quadrangle.

Riverside Station [TUOLUMNE]: *locality,* 2.25 miles northeast of Tuolumne along North Fork Tuolumne River (lat. 37°58'55" N, long. 120°12'20" W; sec. 34, T 2 N, R 16 E). Named on Tuolumne (1948) 7.5' quadrangle.

River View: see **Valley View** [MARIPOSA].

Robert Nichols Spring [TUOLUMNE]: *spring,* 5 miles east-northeast of Twain Harte (lat. 38°04'30" N, long. 120°08'55" W; sec. 31, T 3 N, R 17 E). Named on Twain Harte (1979) 7.5' quadrangle.

Roberts' Ferry: see **Waterford** [STANISLAUS].

Roberts Island [SAN JOAQUIN]: *island,* 14 miles long, between San Joaquin River, Turner Cut, Whiskey Slough, Trapper Slough, and Middle River; center 5 miles southwest of downtown Stockton (lat. 37°54' N, long. 121°22' W). Named on Holt (1978), Lathrop (1952), Stockton West (1952), and Union Island (1978) 7.5' quadrangles. On Bouldin (1910) 7.5' quadrangle, present Medford Island and present McDonald Island are shown as part of Roberts Island. Thompson and West's (1879) map shows a place called Robert's Landing located along San Joaquin River at the north edge of Roberts Island. Postal authorities established Roberts Landing post office 10 miles south of Bouldin Island [SAN JOAQUIN] (2) (NW quarter sec. 13, T 2 N, R 4 E) in 1877 and discontinued it in 1881; Martin Roberts was the first postmaster—the landing was named for Captain William Roberts, who owned hay and grain warehouses there (Salley, p. 187). Thompson and West's (1879) map also shows a place called Kaiser's Landing situated less than 1 mile east of Roberts Landing along San Joaquin River (near S line sec. 12, T 2 N, R 4 E).

Roberts Landing: see **Roberts Island** [SAN JOAQUIN].

Robinson: see **Melones** [CALAVERAS].

Robinson Creek [STANISLAUS]: *stream,* flows 5 miles to south Fork Orestimba Creek 5.5 miles south-southwest of Mikes Peak (lat. 37°16'55" N, long. 121°21'10" W; sec. 31, T 7 S, R 6 E). Named on Mount Stakes (1955) and Wilcox Ridge (1956) 7.5' quadrangles.

Robinson's: see **Melones** [CALAVERAS].

Robinson's Ferry: see **Melones** [CALAVERAS].

Rockbound Lake [MADERA]: *lake,* 6.5 miles east-northeast of Merced Peak (lat. 37°40'10" N, long. 119°16'50" W). Named on Merced Peak (1953) 15' quadrangle.

Rock Canyon [TUOLUMNE]: *canyon,* 1 mile long, 5.5 miles west-southwest of Matterhorn Peak (lat. 38°03'35" N, long. 119°28'35" W); the canyon is along lower reaches of Rock Creek (2). Named on Matterhorn Peak (1956) 15' quadrangle.

Rock Creek [CALAVERAS-SAN JOAQUIN-STANISLAUS]: *stream,* heads in Calaveras County and flows 19 miles, partly in Stanislaus County, to Littlejohns Creek 2.5 miles east-southeast of Farmington in San Joaquin County (lat. 37°54'50" N, long. 121°57'35" W; sec. 26, T 1 N, R 9 E). Named on Bachelor Valley (1968), Farmington (1968), and Jenny Lind (1962) 7.5' quadrangles.

Rock Creek [MADERA]: *stream,* flows 7 miles to San Joaquin River 7.5 miles southeast of Shuteye Peak (lat. 37°16'30" N, long. 119° 19'55" W; sec. 34, T 7 S, R 24 E). Named on Shuteye Peak (1953) 15' quadrangle.

Rock Creek [TUOLUMNE]:

(1) *stream,* flows 5.5 miles to Clavey River 7 miles east of Long Barn (lat. 38°05'45" N, long. 120°00'20" W; sec. 21, T 3 N, R 18 E). Named on Cherry Lake North (1979) and Hull Creek (1979) 7.5' quadrangles.

(2) *stream,* flows 3.5 miles to Crazy Mule Gulch 6 miles west-southwest of Matterhorn Peak (lat. 38°03'05" N, long. 119°28'30" W); the stream goes through Rock Canyon. Named on Matterhorn Peak (1956) 15' quadrangle.

Rock Island Lake [TUOLUMNE]: *lake,* 3800 feet long, 5.25 miles west-southwest of Matterhorn Peak (lat. 38°04'20" N, long. 119° 28'25" W); the lake is along Rock Creek (2). Named on Matterhorn Peak (1956) 15' quadrangle. Lieutenant N.F. McClure named the lake for a large island of granite near the north end (United States Board on Geographic Names, 1934, p. 21).

Rock Island Pass [TUOLUMNE]: *pass,* 4.5 miles west of Tower Peak on Tuolumne-Mono County line (lat. 38°05'55" N, long. 119°27'50" W); the pass is 1.5 miles north-northeast of Rock Island Lake. Named on Matterhorn Peak (1956) 15' quadrangle.

Rockslides [MARIPOSA]: *relief feature,* 4 miles west-southwest of Yosemite Village on the north side of Yosemite Valley (lat. 37°43'40" N, long. 119°39'10" W). Named on Yosemite (1956) 15' quadrangle.

Rock Spring [MARIPOSA]: *locality,* 3.5 miles south-southwest of Coulterville along Yosemite Valley Railroad (lat. 37°39'30" N, long. 120°12'30" W). Named on Sonora (1897) 30' quadrangle.

Rocky Canyon Creek: see **Cathedral Creek** [TUOLUMNE].

Rocky Creek [CALAVERAS]: *stream,* flows 1.25 miles to Littlejohns Creek 3.5 miles south-southwest of Copperopolis (lat. 37° 56' N, long. 120°39'45" W; sec. 16, T 1 N, R 12 E). Named on Copperopolis (1962) 7.5' quadrangle.

Rocky Ford Canyon [STANISLAUS]: *canyon,* drained by a stream that flows about 4 miles to Ingram Canyon 6.5 miles north of Copper Mountain (lat. 37°30'35" N, long. 121°19'05" W; sec. 9, T 5 S, R 6 E). Named on Copper Mountain (1956) 7.5' quadrangle.

Rocky Gulch [MARIPOSA]: *canyon,* drained by a stream that flows 1.5 miles to Lake McClure 2.5 miles north-northeast of the village of Bear Valley (lat. 37°36'20" N, long. 120°06'30" W). Named on Bear Valley (1947, photorevised 1973) 7.5' quadrangle. Called Bond's Gulch on Laizure's (1928) map, which shows Bond's Flat at the mouth of the canyon. The same map shows a canyon called Evans Gulch located about 0.5 mile east of Bond's Gulch (present Rocky Gulch).

Rocky Gulch [TUOLUMNE]: *canyon,* drained by a stream that flows nearly 0.5 mile to Tulloch Lake 5 miles northwest of Keystone (lat. 37°53'25" N, long. 120°34'10" W; sec. 32, T 1 N, R 13 E). Named on Melones Dam (1962) 7.5' quadrangle.

Rocky Hill [CALAVERAS]: *peak,* 4 miles east-southeast of San Andreas (lat. 38°10'25" N, long. 120°36'40" W; on E line sec. 26, T 4 N, R 12 E). Altitude 1803 feet. Named on Calaveritas (1962) 7.5' quadrangle.

Rocky Point [MARIPOSA]: *relief feature,* 2 miles southwest of Yosemite Village on the north side of Yosemite Valley (lat. 37° 44' N, long. 119°36'50" W). Named on Yosemite (1956) 15' quadrangle. United States Board on Geographic Names (1991, p. 6) rejected the name "We-ack" for the feature.

Rocky Point Campground [MADERA]: *locality,* 6.5 miles southeast of Yosemite Forks on the southwest side of Bass Lake (1) (lat. 37° 18'10" N, long. 119°32'20" W; sec. 23, T 7 S, R 22 E). Named on Bass Lake (1953) 15' quadrangle.

Rodden Creek [STANISLAUS]: *stream,* flows 2.5 miles to Stanislaus River 2.5 miles northeast of Oakdale (lat. 37°47'25" N, long. 120°48'30" W). Named on Oakdale (1968) 7.5' quadrangle.

Rodden Lake [STANISLAUS]: *lake,* 0.5 mile long, behind a dam on Lesnini Creek 5.5 miles northeast of Oakdale (lat. 37°49'05" N, long. 120°45'50" W). Named on Oakdale (1968) 7.5' quadrangle.

Rodger Peak [MADERA]: *peak*, 9.5 miles northeast of Merced Peak on Madera-Mono County line (lat. 37°43'30" N, long. 119°15'25" W). Altitude 12,978 feet. Named on Merced Peak (1953) 15' quadrangle. Called Rodgers Peak on Mount Lyell (1901) 30' quadrangle. United States Board on Geographic Names (1934, p. 21) approved the form "Rodgers Peak" for the name, which Lieutenant N.F. McClure gave in 1895 to honor Captain Alexander Rodgers.

Rodgers Canyon [TUOLUMNE]: *canyon*, drained by a stream that flows 4.5 miles to Tuolumne River 8 miles northeast of White Wolf (lat. 37°56'25" N, long. 119°32' W). Named on Hetch Hetchy Reservoir (1956) 15' quadrangle.

Rodgers Lake [TUOLUMNE]: *lake*, 3400 feet long, 14 miles west-northwest of Tioga Pass (lat. 37°59'45" N, long. 119°29'30" W). Named on Tuolumne Meadows (1956) 15' quadrangle. The name commemorates Captain Alexander Rodgers of the Fourth Cavalry, who was acting superintendent of Yosemite National Park from 1895 until 1897 (United States Board on Geographic Names, 1934, p. 21).

Rodgers Lake: see **Neall Lake** [TUOLUMNE].

Rodgers Peak: see **Rodger Peak** [MADERA].

Roger Creek [TUOLUMNE]: *stream*, flows 3.5 miles to Don Pedro Reservoir 4 miles southeast of Don Pedro Camp (lat. 37°41' N, long. 120°20'40" W; near S line sec. 8, T 3 S, R 15 E). Named on Penon Blanco Peak (1962, photorevised 1973) 7.5' quadrangle.

Rogers Creek [CALAVERAS]: *stream*, flows less than 1 mile to French Creek 6 miles east-southeast of Copperopolis (lat. 37°56'35" N, long. 120°32'35" W; near E line sec. 16, T 1 N, R 13 E). Named on Melones Dam (1962) 7.5' quadrangle.

Rogers Meadow [TUOLUMNE]: *area*, 11.5 miles northeast of White Wolf (lat. 37°59'35" N, long. 119°30'15" W). Named on Hetch Hetchy Reservoir (1956) 15' quadrangle.

Rogers Spring [MADERA]: *spring*, 2.5 miles east of Knowles (lat. 37°13'30" N, long. 119°49'40" W; sec. 19, T 8 S, R 20 E). Named on Knowles (1962) 7.5' quadrangle. Called Rogers Sprs. on Raymond (1944) 15' quadrangle, but United States Board on Geographic Names (1965c, p. 11) rejected this form of the name.

Roma [SAN JOAQUIN]: *locality*, 5.25 miles west-southwest of Lockeford along Southern Pacific Railroad (lat. 38°08'15" N, long. 121°14'20" W). Named on Bellota (1939) 15' quadrangle.

Romain: see **Solyo** [STANISLAUS].

Romero Creek [MERCED-STANISLAUS]: *stream*, heads in Stanislaus County and flows 14 miles to lowlands 9 miles east-northeast of Pacheco Pass in Merced County (lat. 37°07'15" N, long. 121°03'15" W; sec. 26, T 9 S, R 8 E). Named on Crevison Peak (1955), Howard Ranch (1953), and San Luis Creek (1953) 7.5' quadrangles. The stream was called El Arroyo de Romero in Spanish days; the name "Romero" is for a Spaniard whom Indians killed near the creek (Hoover, Rensch, and Rensch, p. 202).

Roosevelt Lake [TUOLUMNE]: *lake*, 4600 feet long, 6 miles northwest of Tioga Pass (lat. 37°58'15" N, long. 119°20' W; on S line sec. 33, T 2 N, R 24 E). Named on Tuolumne Meadows (1956) 15' quadrangle. The name commemorates Eleanor Roosevelt, who visited Tuolumne Meadows in 1934 (O'Neill, p 116).

Rooster Comb [STANISLAUS]: *ridge*, east-trending, less than 1 mile long, 4 miles north of Mustang Peak (lat. 37°14'40" N, long. 121° 21'25" W; sec. 18, T 8 S, R 6 E). Named on Mustang Peak (1955) 7.5' quadrangle.

Root Creek [MADERA]: *stream*, flows 11.5 miles before ending in lowlands 2 miles east-southeast of Trigo (lat. 36°53'50" N, long. 119°55'45" W; sec. 8, T 12 S, R 19 E). Named on Herndon (1965) 15' quadrangle.

Rosalie Lake [MADERA]: *lake*, 1100 feet long, nearly 5 miles north-northwest of Devils Postpile (lat. 37°41'15" N, long. 119°07'20" W). Named on Devils Postpile (1953) 15' quadrangle.

Rosasco: see **Rosasco Meadow** [TUOLUMNE].

Rosasco Lake [TUOLUMNE]: *lake*, 700 feet long, 10 miles east-southeast of Pinecrest (lat. 38°08'30" N, long. 119°49' W). Named on Pinecrest (1956) 15' quadrangle. The name commemorates Dave Rosasco, an early cattleman (Browning, 1986, p. 187).

Rosasco Meadow [TUOLUMNE]: *area*, 9 miles southeast of Long Barn (lat. 38°00'25" N, long. 120°00'45" W; at NW cor. sec. 28, T 2 N, R 18 E). Named on Hull Creek (1979) 7.5' quadrangle. Big Trees (1891) 30' quadrangle has the name "Rosasco" at or near the place.

Rose Creek [TUOLUMNE]: *stream*, flows 16 miles to Stanislaus River 5 miles north of Columbia (lat. 38°06'35" N, long. 120°23'50" W; near SE cor. sec. 14, T 3 N, R 14 E). Named on Columbia (1948), Columbia SE (1948), Crandall Peak (1979), and Twain Harte (1979) 7.5' quadrangles.

Rosedale [MADERA]: *locality*, 4.5 miles north-northwest of O'Neals (lat. 37°11'25" N, long. 119°43'40" W; near W line sec. 31, T 8 S, R 21 E). Named on Mariposa (1912) 30' quadrangle.

Ross Creek [MADERA]: *stream*, flows 5 miles to San Joaquin River 10 miles southeast of Shuteye Peak (lat. 37°13'35" N, long. 119° 20' W; near N line sec. 22, T 8 S, R 24 E). Named on Shaver Lake (1953) and Shuteye Peak (1953) 15' quadrangles.

Rossland: see **Jamestown** [TUOLUMNE].

Ross Reservoir [CALAVERAS]: *lake*, 1300 feet long, 3.25 miles northeast of Angels Camp (lat. 38°07' N, long. 120°30'45" W; sec. 14, T 3 N, R 13 E). Named on Angels Camp (1962) 7.5' quadrangle. Called Utica Reservoir on San Andreas (1947) 15' quadrangle.

Rough and Ready Creek [TUOLUMNE]: *stream*, flows 6.25 miles to Tuolumne River 8 miles south-southeast of Sonora (lat. 37°52'30" N, long. 120°20' W; sec. 4, T 1 S, R 15 E). Named on Standard (1948) 7.5' quadrangle.

Rough and Ready Island [SAN JOAQUIN]: *island*, 2.5 miles long, 4 miles west of downtown Stockton between San Joaquin River and Burns Cutoff (lat. 37°57' N, long. 121°21'30" W). Named on Holt (1978) and Stockton West (1952) 7.5' quadrangles.

Rough Gulch [STANISLAUS]: *canyon*, drained by a stream that flows 1.5 miles to Garzas Creek 1.5 miles northwest of Crevison Peak (lat. 37°12'25" N, long. 121°12'40" W; sec. 28, T 7 S, R 7 E). Named on Crevison Peak (1955) 7.5' quadrangle.

Round Hills [MARIPOSA]: *peaks*, two, nearly 4 miles south of the settlement of Catheys Valley (lat. 37°22'50" N, long. 120°05'30" W; sec. 27, T 6 S, R 17 E). Altitudes 1455 feet and 1588 feet. Named on Catheys Valley (1962) 7.5' quadrangle.

Round Meadow [TUOLUMNE]: *area*, 3 miles south of Duckwall Mountain (lat. 37°55'20" N, long. 120°07'25" W; near SE cor. sec. 20, T 1 N, R 17 E). Named on Duckwall Mountain (1948) 7.5' quadrangle.

Roundtree Saddle [MARIPOSA]: *pass*, 11.5 miles south of El Portal (lat. 37°30'35" N, long. 119°45'45" W; near SE cor. sec. 10, T 5 S, R 20 E). Named on Buckingham Mountain (1947) 7.5' quadrangle.

Roush Creek [MADERA]: *stream*, flows nearly 2 miles to Whiskey Creek (2) 5.5 miles south of Shuteye Peak (lat. 37°15'50" N, long. 119°26'15" W; sec. 3, T 8 S, R 23 E). Named on Shuteye Peak (1953) 15' quadrangle. Charley Roush had a sawmill in section 3 in the 1920's (Browning, 1986, p. 188).

Royal Arch Cascade [MARIPOSA]: *waterfall*, less than 1 mile east of Yosemite Village on the north side of Yosemite Valley (lat. 37° 44'55" N, long. 119°34'15" W); the waterfall is along Royal Arch Creek. Named on Yosemite (1956) 15' quadrangle.

Royal Arch Creek [MARIPOSA]: *stream*, flows 2.25 miles to Merced River less than 1 mile east-southeast of Yosemite Village (lat. 37°44'45" N, long. 119°34'15" W); the stream is west of Royal Arches. Named on Hetch Hetchy Reservoir (1956) 15' quadrangle.

Royal Arches [MARIPOSA]: *relief feature*, 1 mile east of Yosemite Village on the north side of Yosemite Valley (lat. 37°44'55" N, long. 119°33'50" W). Named on Yosemite (1956) 15' quadrangle. The name was used as early as 1851 (Browning, 1986, p. 188).

Royal Arch Lake [MADERA]: *lake*, 900 feet long, 1.25 miles southeast of Buena Vista Peak (lat. 37°34'40" N, long. 119°30'10" W; near E line sec. 24, T 4 S, R 22 E). Named on Yosemite (1956) 15' quadrangle.

Ruby Canyon [MERCED]: *canyon*, drained by a stream that flows 3 miles to South Fork Los Banos Creek 3.25 miles southwest of Sweeney Hill (lat. 36°51'40" N, long. 121°04'50" W). Named on Ruby Canyon (1968) 7.5' quadrangle.

Ruby Hill Spring [TUOLUMNE]: *spring*, 5 miles north of Twain Harte (lat. 38°06'50" N, long. 120°14'10" W; sec. 17, T 3 N, R 16 E). Named on Twain Harte (1979) 7.5' quadrangle.

Ruby Lake [MADERA]: *lake*, 1000 feet long, 8 miles north-northwest of Devils Postpile (lat. 37°43'20" N, long. 119°09'35" W); the feature is between Emerald Lake and Garnet Lake. Named on Devils Postpile (1953) 15' quadrangle.

Rudberg Creek: see **Rydberg Creek** [STANISLAUS-TUOLUMNE].

Rush Creek [MARIPOSA]: *stream*, flows 4.5 miles to South Fork Merced River 1.5 miles west-northwest of Wawona (lat. 37°32'50" N, long. 119°40'45" W; sec. 33, T 4 S, R 21 E). Named on Yosemite (1956) 15' quadrangle. Shirley Sargent (1961, p. 28) referred to a place called Cunningham Flat that was located at the mouth of Rush Creek and named for Stephen Mandeville Cunningham, who homesteaded there.

Rush Creek [TUOLUMNE]:

(1) *stream*, flows 2.25 miles to South Fork Tuolumne River 4.5 miles south-southwest of Mather (lat. 37°49'20" N, long. 119°53'35" W; in sec. 28, T 1 S, R 19 E). Named on Lake Eleanor (1956) 15' quadrangle.

(2) *stream*, flows 2.25 miles to Hull Creek 5.25 miles east of Long Barn (lat. 38°05'25" N, long. 120°02'30" W; sec. 30, T 3 N, R 18 E). Named on Hull Creek (1979) 7.5' quadrangle.

(3) *locality*, 5.25 miles south-southwest of Mather (lat. 37°48'40" N, long. 119°53'25" W; sec. 33, T 1 S, R 19 E); the place is near Rush Creek (1). Named on Lake Eleanor (1956) 15' quadrangle. Called Crockers on Yosemite (1909) 30' quadrangle. Henry Robinson Crocker arrived in California in 1853 and eventually built a cabin in what then was called Bronson's Meadow, and later became known as Crocker's Meadow; the cabin was the nucleus of a stage stop (Paden and Schlichtmann, p. 207, 211). Crocker built an inn at the place in 1880 that he called Crocker's Sierra Resort (Gudde, 1949, p. 84). California Mining Bureau's (1910) map shows a place called Sequoia located at or near present Rush Creek

(3). Postal authorities established Sequoia post office in 1886 and discontinued it in 1915 (Salley, p. 201). Sequoia first was called Santa Maria because the group of Mexicans who started the community worked at Santa Maria mine (Paden and Schlichtmann, p. 205). United States Board on Geographic Names (1933a, p. 682) rejected the names "Crocker" and "Crocker's" for Sequoia.

Rushing Hill: see **Rushing Mountain** [TUOLUMNE].

Rushing Lake [STANISLAUS]: *lake,* 900 feet long, 4.5 miles south of Cooperstown (lat. 37°40'30" N, long. 120°32'10" W; on W line sec. 15, T 3 S, R 13 E). Named on Cooperstown (1968) 7.5' quadrangle.

Rushing Meadow [TUOLUMNE]: *area,* nearly 7 miles northeast of Twain Harte along South Fork Stanislaus River (lat. 38°06'50" N, long. 120°09' W; sec. 18, T 3 N, R 17 E). Named on Twain Harte (1979) 7.5' quadrangle.

Rushing Mountain [TUOLUMNE]: *peak,* 3.25 miles west of Keystone (lat. 37°49'40" N, long. 120°34'05" W; near S line sec. 20, T 1 S, R 13 E). Altitude 1519 feet. Named on Keystone (1962) 7.5' quadrangle. Called Big Hill on Copperopolis (1916) 15' quadrangle, which shows Rushing ranch located 1 mile south-southeast of the peak. United States Board on Geographic Names (1965c, p. 11) rejected the names "Big Hill," "Rushing Hill," "Rushings Hill," and "Rushings Mountain" for the feature.

Russell Creek [TUOLUMNE]: *stream,* flows 1.5 miles to Clavey River 3.5 miles east of Duckwall Mountain (lat. 37°58'15" N, long. 120°03'10" W; sec. 1, T 1 N, R 17 E). Named on Duckwall Mountain (1948) 7.5' quadrangle.

Rutherford Lake [MADERA]: *lake,* 1900 feet long, nearly 3 miles south-southeast of Merced Peak (lat. 37°35'55" N, long. 119°22'15" W). Named on Merced Peak (1953) 15' quadrangle. The name commemorates Lieutenant Samuel M. Rutherford, who was stationed in Yosemite National Park in 1896 (Farquhar, 1925, p. 130).

Rutherford's Crossing: see **Oakdale** [STANISLAUS].

Ruth Lake [MADERA]: *lake,* 700 feet long, 4.25 miles south-southeast of Merced Peak (lat. 37°34'35" N, long. 119°22'15" W). Named on Merced Peak (1953) 15' quadrangle. A group from California Department of Fish and Game and from the Forest Service named the lake in 1934 to honor Ruth Burghduff, wife of A.E. Burghduff of the Department of Fish and Game; the feature had been called Hidden Lake, Nutcracker Lake, and Hideaway Lake (Browning, 1986. p. 189).

Ruth Lake: see **Lower Ruth Lake** [MERCED]; **Upper Ruth Lake** [MERCED].

Ryans Lower Cow Camp [MADERA]. *locality,* 4 miles north of Shuteye Peak (lat. 37°24'15" N, long. 119°25' W; near E line sec. 14, T 6 S, R 23 E); the place is 2 miles south-southeast of Ryans Upper Cow Camp. Named on Shuteye Peak (1953) 15' quadrangle.

Ryans Upper Cow Camp [MADERA]: *locality,* 5.5 miles north of Shuteye Peak (lat. 37°26' N, long. 119°25'55" W; near SW cor. sec. 2, T 6 S, R 23 E); the place is 2 miles north-northwest of Ryans Lower Cow Camp. Named on Shuteye Peak (1953) 15' quadrangle.

Rydberg Creek [STANISLAUS-TUOLUMNE]: *stream,* heads in Tuolumne County and flows 10.5 miles to Dry Creek 1.25 miles south-southwest of Cooperstown in Stanislaus County (lat. 37°43'30" N, long. 120°33'10" W; near SW cor. sec. 28, T 2 S, R 13 E). Named on Chinese Camp (1947), Cooperstown (1968), Keystone (1962), and La Grange (1962) 7.5' quadrangles. Called Dry Creek on Copperopolis (1916) 15' quadrangle. United States Board on Geographic Names (1978a, p. 5) rejected the name "Rudberg Creek" for the stream.

Ryer [MERCED]: *locality,* 9 miles north of Atwater along Southern Pacific Railroad (lat. 37°28'30" N, long. 120°38'25" W; sec. 27, T 5 S, R 12 E). Named on Cressey (1916) 7.5' quadrangle. California Division of Highways' (1934) map shows a place called Basel located 1.5 miles southeast of Ryer (near N line sec. 35, T 5 S, R 12 E).

Ryer's Ferry: see **Tuolumne City** [STANISLAUS].

— S —

Sachse Monument [TUOLUMNE]: *peak,* nearly 7 miles west of Tower Peak (lat. 38°09'10" N, long. 119°40'15" W; sec. 33, T 4 N, R 21 E). Altitude 9405 feet. Named on Tower Peak (1956) 15' quadrangle. The name commemorates a cowboy who was credited with discovering routes that later became trails (Browning, 1986, p. 190).

Saddle Horse Lake [TUOLUMNE]: *lake,* 2400 feet long, 9.5 miles north-northeast of White Wolf (lat. 37°59'50" N, long. 119°34'10" W). Named on Hetch Hetchy Reservoir (1956) 15' quadrangle. Members of the Bright family pastured saddle horses at the lake and named it (Browning, 1988, p. 124). The United States Board on Geographic Names (1960b, p. 18) rejected the names "Irving Bright Lake" and "Irwin Bright Lake" for the feature.

Sadler Lake [MADERA]: *lake,* 1100 feet long, 5 miles east of Merced Peak (lat. 37°38'35" N, long. 119°18'10" W); the lake is 1.5 miles west of Sadler Peak. Named on Merced Peak (1953) 15' quadrangle.

Sadler Peak [MADERA]: *peak,* 6.5 miles east of Merced Peak (lat. 37°38'20" N, long. 119°16'20" W). Altitude 10,567 feet. Named on Merced Peak (1953) 15' quadrangle. Lieutenant N.F. McClure named the peak in 1895 for a corporal in his detachment (Farquhar, 1925, p. 130).

Sage Mill [MADERA]: *locality,* 5.5 miles south of Shuteye Peak (lat. 37°16'15" N, long. 119°25'30" W; near S line sec. 35, T 7 S, R 23 E). Named on Kaiser (1904) 30' quadrangle.

Saginaw Creek [MADERA]: *stream,* flows 4.5 miles to San Joaquin River 13 miles south of Shuteye Peak (lat. 37°09'50" N, long. 119° 25' W; sec. 12, T 9 S, R 23 E). Named on Shaver Lake (1953) 15' quadrangle.

Sailor Gulch [CALAVERAS]: *canyon,* drained by a stream that flows 0.5 mile to Shirley Gulch 5 miles southwest of Copperopolis (lat. 37°56'15" N, long. 120°42'45" W; sec. 13, T 1 N, R 11 E). Named on Copperopolis (1962) 7.5' quadrangle.

Sailor's Gulch: see **Matelot Gulch** [TUOLUMNE].

Saint Catherines: see **Stockton** [SAN JOAQUIN].

Saint Louis: see **San Luis Gonzaga** [MERCED].

Saint Marys Peak [MERCED]: *peak,* 6 miles southeast of Mariposa Peak (lat. 36°53'15" N, long. 121°08'50" W; sec. 13, T 12 S, R 7 E). Altitude 2455 feet. Named on Mariposa Peak (1969) 7.5' quadrangle.

Saint Michele Meadow [CALAVERAS]: *area,* 3.25 miles west-southwest of Tamarack (lat. 38°25'15" N, long. 120°08' W; near NW cor. sec. 32, T 7 N, R 17 E). Named on Calaveras Dome (1979) 7.5' quadrangle.

Salada Creek: see **Salado Creek** [STANISLAUS].

Salado Creek [STANISLAUS]: *stream,* flows 14 miles to lowlands 3.25 miles south-southwest of Patterson (lat. 37°25'35" N, long. 121°09'05" W; sec. 12, T 6 S, R 7 E). Named on Copper Mountain (1956), Crows Landing (1952), Patterson (1953), and Wilcox Ridge (1956) 7.5' quadrangles. Called Salida Creek on Mendenhall's (1908) map, and Watts (p. 681) called the stream both Ensalada Creek and (p. 683) Salada Creek.

Salado Creek: see **Little Salado Creek** [STANISLAUS].

Salamander Creek [CALAVERAS]: *stream,* flows 3 miles to Jesus Maria Creek 8 miles southwest of Rail Road Flat (lat. 38°15'50" N, long. 120°36'45" W; near NE cor. sec. 26, T 5 N, R 12 E). Named on Calaveritas (1962) and Rail Road Flat (1948) 7.5' quadrangles.

Salida [STANISLAUS]: *town,* 6.5 miles northwest of Modesto (lat. 37°42'20" N, long. 121°05' W; sec. 3, 4, T 3 S, R 8 E). Named on Salida (1969) 7.5' quadrangle. Postal authorities established Salida post office in 1875 (Frickstad, p. 201). Officials of Southern Pacific Railroad named the town in 1870—*salida* means "departure" in Spanish (Gudde, 1949, p. 295). The place first was known as Murphys Ferry for John Murphy, who operated a ferry at the site (Hanna, p. 264).

Salida Creek: see **Salado Creek** [STANISLAUS].

Salmon Slough [SAN JOAQUIN]: *water feature,* joins Old River 12.5 miles south-southwest of downtown Stockton (lat. 37°48'20" N, long. 121°24'25" W). Named on Union Island (1978) 7.5' quadrangle. On Union Island (1914) 7.5' quadrangle, the name "Salmon Slough" applies to present Old River between Middle River and present Salmon Slough.

Salt Canyon [MERCED]: *canyon,* 6 miles long, 4.5 miles east of Ortigalita Peak on Merced-Fresno County line (lat. 36°48'15" N, long. 120°50'20" W). Named on Laguna Seca Ranch (1956) 7.5' quadrangle.

Salt Creek [CALAVERAS]: *stream,* flows 4.5 miles to Salt Spring Valley Reservoir 10 miles west-southwest of Angels Camp (lat. 38°02' N, long. 120°43'20" W; at E line sec. 11, T 2 N, R 11 E). Named on Salt Spring Valley (1962) 7.5' quadrangle.

Salt Creek [MERCED]:

(1) *stream,* flows 3.5 miles to San Luis Creek 3.25 miles south-southeast of Pacheco Pass (lat. 37°01'05" N, long. 121°11'20" W; sec. 34, T 10 S, R 7 E). Named on Pacheco Pass (1955) 7.5' quadrangle.

(2) *stream,* flows nearly 6 miles to lowlands 15 miles west of Dos Palos (lat. 36°58'45" N, long. 120°53'30" W; near E line sec. 17, T 11 S, R 10 E). Named on Ortigalita Peak NW (1956) 7.5' quadrangle.

Salt Creek: see **Laguna Seca Creek** [MERCED].

Salter and Morely's Ferry: see **La Grange** [STANISLAUS].

Salter Gulch [STANISLAUS]: *canyon,* 1 mile long, opens into the canyon of Tuolumne River 9 miles east of Waterford (lat. 37°38'30" N, long. 120°35'20" W; near SE cor. sec. 25, T 3 S, R 12 E). Named on Cooperstown (1968) 7.5' quadrangle.

Salter's Ferry: see **Waterford** [STANISLAUS].

Salt Grass Canyon [STANISLAUS]: *canyon,* drained by a stream that flows 1.5 miles to Del Puerto Canyon 1.5 miles north of Copper Mountain (lat. 37°26'15" N, long. 121°18'55" W; sec. 4, T 6 S, R 6 E). Named on Copper Mountain (1956) 7.5' quadrangle.

Salt Grass Springs [STANISLAUS]: *springs,* 1 mile north-northeast of Copper Mountain (lat. 37°25'55" N, long. 121°18'30" W; sec. 10, T 6 S, R 6 E); the springs are in Salt Grass Canyon. Named on Copper Mountain (1956) 7.5' quadrangle.

Salt Gulch [CALAVERAS]: *canyon,* drained by a stream that flows 0.5 mile to Pardee Reservoir 3 miles north of Valley Springs (lat. 38°14'05" N, long. 120°49'20" W; near N line sec. 1, T 4 N, R 10 E). Named on Valley Springs (1962) 7.5' quadrangle. Water of South Arm Pardee Reservoir now floods most of the canyon of the stream. Camp's (1962) map shows a place called Ragtown situated 2 miles north-northeast of Campo Seco in the part of Salt Gulch now under water.

Salt Lick Meadow [TUOLUMNE]: *area,* 11.5 miles east of Pinecrest (lat. 38°11'55" N, long. 119°47'15" W). Named on Pinecrest (1956) 15' quadrangle.

Salt Slough [MERCED]: *stream,* formed by the confluence of Wood Slough and Santa Rita Slough, flows 30 miles, partly in a ditch, to San Joaquin River 6.25 miles east-northeast of Gustine (lat. 37° 17'40" N, long. 120°53'50" W). Named on Los Banos (1961), Santa Rita Park (1962), and Turlock (1962) 15' quadrangles. United States Board on Geographic Names (1964a, p. 13) rejected the names "Pick Anderson Slough," "Salt Slough Ditch," and "Santa Rita Slough" for the feature. East Branch diverges from Salt Slough and extends for 2.5 miles before rejoining Salt Slough 2.5 miles upstream from the mouth of the slough. Middle Branch is between Salt Slough and East Branch. Both branches are named on Turlock (1962) 15' quadrangle.

Salt Slough Ditch: see **Salt Slough** [MERCED].

Salt Spring [MARIPOSA]: *spring,* 11.5 miles east-southeast of Mariposa (lat. 37°25'15" N, long. 119°46'15" W; sec. 10, T 6 S, R 20 E). Named on Mariposa (1947) 15' quadrangle. Mariposa (1912) 30' quadrangle has the plural form "Salt Springs" for the name.

Salt Spring [MERCED]: *spring,* 14 miles north of Ortigalita Peak (lat. 36°59'40" N, long. 120°57'55" W; sec. 10, T 11 S, R 9 E). Named on Ortigalita Peak NW (1969) 7.5' quadrangle.

Salt Spring [TUOLUMNE]:

(1) *spring,* 3.5 miles west of Don Pedro Camp (lat. 37°43'30" N, long. 120°28'05" W; near S line sec. 30, T 2 S, R 14 E). Named on La Grange (1962) 7.5' quadrangle.

(2) *spring,* 3 miles south of Dardanelle (lat. 38°17'50" N, long. 119° 49'15" W; sec. 7, T 5 N, R 20 E). Named on Dardanelle (1979) 7.5' quadrangle.

Salt Spring Creek: see **Gallup Creek** [STANISLAUS-TUOLUMNE].

Salt Springs [CALAVERAS]: *lake,* 300 feet long, 5.25 miles northwest of Tamarack (lat. 38°29'45" N, long. 120°08'10" W). Named on Calaveras Dome (1979) 7.5' quadrangle.

Salt Springs [MADERA]: *locality,* 2 miles south-southwest of present Yosemite Forks along Fresno River (lat. 37°20'30" N, long. 119°38'30" W; sec. 11, T 7 S, R 21 E). Named on Mariposa (1912) 30' quadrangle.

Salt Springs: see **Salt Spring** [MARIPOSA].

Salt Springs Reservoir [CALAVERAS]: *lake,* 4 miles long, behind a dam on North Fork Mokelumne River 8.5 miles west-northwest of Tamarack on Calaveras-Amador County line (lat. 38°29'55" N, long. 120°12'50" W; sec. 33, T 8 N, R 16 E). Named on Calaveras Dome (1979) 7.5' quadrangle.

Salt Spring Valley [CALAVERAS]: *valley,* 10 miles west-southwest of Angels Camp (lat. 38°02'30" N, long. 120°43'30" W). Named on Jenny Lind (1962) and Salt Spring Valley (1962) 7.5' quadrangles. Postal authorities established Salt Spring Valley post office about 8 miles east of Milton in 1878 and discontinued it in 1880 (Salley, p. 192).

Salt Spring Valley Reservoir [CALAVERAS]: *lake,* behind a dam on Rock Creek 7.5 miles southeast of Jenny Lind (lat. 38°01'40" N, long. 120°45'40" W; near E line sec. 16, T 2 N, R 11 E); the lake is in Salt Spring Valley. Named on Jenny Lind (1962) and Salt Spring Valley (1962) 7.5' quadrangles.

Salvada Gulch [TUOLUMNE]: *canyon,* drained by a stream that flows 1 mile to Woods Creek 1.25 miles east of Chinese Camp (lat. 37°52'25" N, long. 120°24'40" W; sec. 2, T 1 S, R 14 E). Named on Sonora (1948) 15' quadrangle.

Salvado: see **Chinese Camp** [TUOLUMNE].

Sam Williams Spring [TUOLUMNE]: *spring,* 1.5 miles east-southeast of Long Barn (lat. 38°05'15" N, long. 120°06'10" W; near E line sec. 28, T 3 N, R 17 E). Named on Hull Creek (1979) 7.5' quadrangle.

San Andreas [CALAVERAS]: *town,* 2 miles east of the confluence of North Fork Calaveras River and South Fork Calaveras River (lat. 38°11'45" N, long. 120°40'45" W; in and near sec. 17, T 4 N, R 12 E). Named on San Andreas (1962) 7.5' quadrangle. Postal authorities established San Andreas post office in 1854 (Salley, p. 192). Camp's (1962) map shows a place called Greasertown, or Petersburg, located 4 miles west of San Andreas on the west side of Calaveras River, a place called Taylors Bar situated 6 miles west-southwest of San Andreas on the south side of the river, and a place called Yaqui Camp located 2 miles southeast of San Andreas along Willow Creek.

San Andreas Creek [CALAVERAS]: *stream,* flows 3 miles to Murray Creek less than 1 mile northwest of San Andreas (lat. 38° 12'25" N, long. 120°41'20" W; near N line sec. 18, T 4 N, R 12 E). Named on San Andreas (1962) 7.5' quadrangle.

San Antone: see **San Antonio Camp** [CALAVERAS].

San Antonio Camp [CALAVERAS]: *locality,* 8 miles east-southeast of San Andreas (lat. 38°09'45" N, long. 120°32'15" W; near NW cor. sec. 34, T 4 N, R 13 E); the place is along San Antonio Creek. Named on Calaveritas (1962) 7.5' quadrangle. A Mexican mining camp probably was at the site by 1849 or 1850; the place also was called San Antone (Gudde, 1975, p. 304).

San Antonio Creek [CALAVERAS]: *stream,* flows 31 miles to South Fork Calaveras River nearly 4 miles south-southeast of San Andreas (lat. 38°08'35" N, long. 120°39'45" W; sec. 4, T 3 N, R 12 E). Named on Calaveritas (1962), Dorrington (1979), Fort Mountain (1979), Murphys (1948), and San Andreas (1962) 7.5' quadrangles.

San Antonio Spring [CALAVERAS]: *spring,* 4.5 miles south-southeast of Blue Mountain (lat. 38°17' N, long. 120°19'10" W; sec. 16, T 5 N, R 15 E); the spring is above San Antonio Creek. Named on Dorrington (1979) 7.5' quadrangle.

Sand Bar [TUOLUMNE]: *locality,* 4 miles southeast of Duckwall Mountain along Clavey River (lat. 37°56' N, long. 120°03'30" W; near N line sec. 24, T 1 N, R 17 E). Named on Duckwall Mountain (1948) 7.5' quadrangle.

Sand Creek [MADERA]: *stream,* flows 7 miles to join Browns Creek and form South Fork Willow Creek (2) 5 miles southwest of Shuteye Peak (lat. 37°17'55" N, long. 119°29'40" W; near NE cor. sec. 30, T 7 S, R 23 E). Named on Shuteye Peak (1953) 15' quadrangle. North Fork enters from the north-northwest 2.25 miles upstream from the mouth of the main creek; it is 4.5 miles long and is named on Shuteye Peak (1953) 15' quadrangle. Kaiser (1904) 30' quadrangle shows present North Fork as the main stream.

Sand Creek [MARIPOSA]: *stream,* flows 2 miles to Agua Fria Creek 4.5 miles northeast of the settlement of Catheys Valley (lat. 37°28'45" N, long. 120°01'45" W). Named on Catheys Valley (1962) 7.5' quadrangle. United States Board on Geographic Names (1964a, p. 14) rejected the name "Cavallado Creek" for the stream.

Sand Flat [CALAVERAS-TUOLUMNE]: *area,* 3.25 miles north-northeast of Liberty Hill along North Fork Stanislaus River on Calaveras-Tuolumne County line (lat. 38°24'35" N, long. 120° 04'35" W). Named on Tamarack (1979) 7.5' quadrangle.

Sand Flat Campground [CALAVERAS]: *locality,* 2 miles south of Tamarack along North Fork Stanislaus River (lat. 38°24'35" N, long. 120°04'50" W); the place is at Sand Flat. Named on Tamarack (1979) 7.5' quadrangle.

Sand Hill [CALAVERAS]: *hill,* 6.5 miles west-northwest of Valley Springs (lat. 38°13'10" N, long. 120°56'50" W). Altitude 205 feet. Named on Wallace (1962) 7.5' quadrangle. The feature now is in Camanche Reservoir.

San Diego: see **Columbia** [TUOLUMNE].

San Diego Reservoir [TUOLUMNE]: *lake,* 600 feet long, 0.5 mile east-southeast of Columbia (lat. 38°01'50" N, long. 120°23'20" W; sec. 13, T 2 N, R 14 E). Named on Columbia (1948) 7.5' quadrangle.

San Domingo Creek [CALAVERAS]: *stream,* flows 19 miles to join Cherokee Creek and form South Fork Calaveras River 6.5 miles west-northwest of Angels Camp (lat. 38°07'10" N, long. 120° 39' W; near S line sec. 9, T 3 N, R 12 E). Named on Angels Camp (1962), Calaveritas (1962), Murphys (1948), and Salt Spring Valley (1962) 7.5' quadrangles.

Sand Slough [MERCED]: *stream,* flows 7.5 miles to Mariposa Slough 9.5 miles north-northwest of Dos Palos Y (lat. 37°10'50" N, long. 120°41' W). Named on Sandy Mush (1962) and Turner Ranch (1961) 7.5' quadrangles.

Sands Meadow [TUOLUMNE]: *area,* nearly 2 miles southeast of Liberty Hill (lat. 38°20'55" N, long. 120°04'35" W; sec. 26, T 6 N, R 17 E). Named on Liberty Hill (1979) 7.5' quadrangle.

Sandy Bar: see **Big Bar** [CALAVERAS].

Sandy Campground: see **Big Sandy Campground** [MADERA]; **Little Sandy Campground** [MADERA].

Sandy Gulch [CALAVERAS]: *locality,* 1.25 miles south of West Point (lat. 38°22'50" N, long. 120°31'55" W; near N line sec. 15, T 6 N, R 13 E). Named on West Point (1948) 7.5' quadrangle. The place was named for a nearby canyon and was a trading center in 1849 (California Department of Parks and Recreation, p. 12).

Sandy Mush Country [MERCED]: *area,* 9 miles north-northeast of Dos Palos Y (lat. 37°10' N, long. 120°33' W). Named on Sandy Mush (1962) 7.5' quadrangle.

Sandy Wash [TUOLUMNE]: *stream,* flows nearly 2 miles to Wolf Gulch 2.25 miles northwest of Columbia (lat. 38°03'30" N, long. 120°25'45" W; sec. 3, T 2 N, R 14 E). Named on Columbia (1948) 7.5' quadrangle.

San Francisco Xavier: see **Middle River** [SAN JOAQUIN] (1).

San Joaquin: see **Vernalis** [SAN JOAQUIN].

San Joaquin City [SAN JOAQUIN]: *locality,* 3 miles north-northeast of Vernalis on the west side of San Joaquin River (lat. 37°40'15" N, long. 121°15'55" W). Site named on Vernalis (1969) 7.5' quadrangle. Captain Charles Imus founded a town at the spot in 1849 (Brotherton, p. 7). Thompson and West's (1879) map shows Durham's Ferry situated along the river less than 1 mile north-northeast of San Joaquin City. Titus and Manley Ferry operated on the river north of San Joaquin City in the early 1850's, and later it was called Durham's Ferry; Chase's Ferry operated 0.5 mile upstream from Titus and Manley Ferry in the 1850's (Brotherton, p. 7).

San Joaquin Mountain [MADERA]: *peak,* 6.5 miles north of Devils Postpile on Madera-Mono County line (lat. 37°43'10" N, long. 119°06'20" W).

Altitude 11,600 feet. Named on Devils Postpile (1953) 15' quadrangle. A pair of peaks, this one and the nearby peak now called Two Teats, together formerly had the name "Two Teats" (Gudde, 1949, p. 373-374).

San Joaquin River [MADERA-MERCED-SAN JOAQUIN-STANISLAUS]: *stream,* formed by the confluence of North Fork and Middle Fork in Madera County 8.5 miles southwest of Devils Postpile, flows 320 miles to Contra Costa and Sacramento Counties 17 miles west of Lodi (lat. 38°05'55" N, long. 121°34'40" W). Named on Fresno (1962, revised 1967), Mariposa (1957, revised 1970), Sacramento (1957, limited revision 1964), San Jose (1962), and Santa Cruz (1958) 1°x 2° quadrangles. Present San Joaquin River is called R. San Joachim on Wilkes' (1841) map, Rio San Joaquin on Fremont's (1848) map, River San Joarquin on Derby's (1850) map, and Rio Tulare or San Joaquin on Sage's (1846) map. Gabriel Moraga named the river about 1805 for Saint Joaquin, father of the Virgin Mary (Hart, p. 379). North Fork is 16 miles long and Middle Fork is 21 miles long; both forks are named on Devils Postpile (1953) 15' quadrangle. South Fork heads in Fresno County and flows 4 miles in Madera County to join San Joaquin River 12 miles east-northeast of Shuteye Peak; it is named on Kaiser Peak (1953) 15' quadrangle. United States Board on Geographic Names (1965b, p. 12) rejected the name "Hooper Creek" for South Fork. A landing place called Dover was situated along San Joaquin River 5 miles above the mouth of Merced River in present Merced County (Hoover, Rensch, and Rensch, p. 206). Postal authorities established Dover post office in 1870 and discontinued it in 1874; wheat was shipped from the place to Dover, England, which suggested the name (Salley, p. 61). The artificially deepened and straightened channel that extends along San Joaquin River, and off the river along Stockton Channel into the Port of Stockton, is called Stockton Deep Water Channel on Bouldin Island (1978), Holt (1978), Stockton West (1952), and Terminous (1978) 7.5' quadrangles.

San Joaquin Valley: see **Banta** [SAN JOAQUIN]; "Regional setting."

Sanjon de los Moquelumnes [SAN JOAQUIN]: *land grant,* mainly in Sacramento County, but extends south into San Joaquin County 8 miles north-northwest of Lodi. Named on Lodi North (1968) and Thornton (1978) 7.5' quadrangles. Anastacio Chabolla received 8 leagues in 1844; Angel Chabolla and Maria C. Chabolla claimed 35,508 acres patented in 1865 (Cowan, p. 49; Cowan listed the grant under the name "Zanjon de los Moquelumnes").

Sanjon de Santa Rita [MERCED]: *land grant,* southwest of Merced on the west side of San Joaquin River. Named on Los Banos (1961) and Santa Rita Park (1962) 15' quadrangles. Francisco Soberanes received 11 leagues in 1841 and claimed 48,824 acres patented in 1865 (Cowan, p. 94; Cowan listed the grant under the name "Zanjon de Santa Rita"). Perez (p. 96) gave 1862 as the date of the patent.

San Juan River: see **French Camp Slough** [SAN JOAQUIN].

San Luis Creek [MERCED]: *stream,* flows 20 miles to lowlands 8.5 miles east of Pacheco Pass (lat. 37°04'30" N, long. 121°03'20" W). Named on Los Banos (1961) 15' quadrangle, and on Mariposa Peak (1969), Pacheco Pass (1955), and San Luis Creek (1953) 7.5' quadrangles. The stream now enters San Luis Reservoir. Gabriel Moraga named the stream in 1805 when he discovered Pacheco Pass on the feast day of San Luis Gonzaga (Shumate, p. 1).

San Luis Flat [MERCED]: *valley,* 5 miles east of Pacheco Pass (lat. 37°03'45" N, long. 121°07' W). Named on Pacheco Pass (1955) 7.5' quadrangle. Water of San Luis Reservoir now covers the valley.

San Luis Forebay: see **O'Neill Forebay** [MERCED].

San Luis Gonzaga [MERCED]: *land grant,* at and near Pacheco Pass on Merced-Santa Clara County line. Named on Pacheco Pass (1955) and San Luis Creek (1953) 7.5' quadrangles. Jose Ramon Estrada received the land in 1834, and Francisco Rivera received it in 1843; Francisco Perez Pacheco claimed 48,821 acres patented in 1871 (Cowan, p. 83-84). According to Perez (p. 93), Juan Pacheco and Jose Mejira were the grantees in 1843, and Juan P. Pacheco was the patentee in 1871. The headquarters of the ranch on the grant was at San Luis Flat, and was a stop on Butterfield Overland stage line; it was called St. Louis on maps of that period (Shumate, p. 3-4). Postal authorities established San Luis Ranch post office 9 miles west of Los Banos in 1871, discontinued it in 1876, reestablished it in 1889, and discontinued it in 1890 (Salley, p. 195). They established Lambert post office about 10 miles northeast of San Luis Ranch post office (SW quarter sec. 31, T 8 S, R 9 E) in 1872 and discontinued it in 1874 (Salley, p. 116).

San Luis Holding Reservoir [MERCED]: *intermittent lake,* 6 miles northwest of Los Banos (lat. 37°07'30" N, long. 120°55' W). Named on Los Banos (1961) 15' quadrangle.

San Luis Island [MERCED]: *area,* 11 miles north of Los Banos between San Joaquin River and Salt Slough (lat. 37°12'30" N, long. 120°48'30" W). Named on Los Banos (1961) and Turlock (1962) 15' quadrangles.

San Luis Ranch: see **San Luis Gonzaga** [MERCED].

San Luis Reservoir [MERCED]: *lake,* behind a dam on San Luis Creek 7.5 miles east of Pacheco Pass (lat. 37°03'30" N, long. 121° 04'30" W). Named on Los Banos Valley (1969), Mariposa Peak (1969), Pacheco Pass (1955, photorevised 1971), and San Luis Dam (1969) 7.5' quadrangles.

Santa Cruz: see **Indian Gulch** [MARIPOSA] (3).

Santa Cruz Mountain [MARIPOSA]: *peak,* 6.25 miles west-northwest of the settlement of Catheys Valley (lat. 37°27'25" N, long. 120°12'05" W; sec. 34, T 5 S, T 16 E). Altitude 1525 feet. Named on Indian Gulch (1962) 7.5' quadrangle.

Santa Iago: see **Columbia** [TUOLUMNE].

Santa Maria: see **Sequoia**, under **Rush Creek** [TUOLUMNE] (3).

Santa Nella Village [MERCED]: *locality,* 11 miles east-northeast of Pacheco Pass (lat. 37°05'50" N, long. 121°01' W; sec. 6, T 10 S, R 9 E). Named on San Luis Dam (1969) 7.5' quadrangle.

Santa Rita Park [MERCED]: *settlement,* 2.25 miles east of Dos Palos Y (lat. 37°02'50" N, long. 120°35'40" W; sec. 19, T 10 S, R 13 E). Named on Santa Rita Bridge (1962) 7.5' quadrangle. Postal authorities established Santa Rita Park post office in 1940 and moved it 3 miles west in 1966 (Salley, p. 198).

Santa Rita Slough [MERCED]: *stream,* flows 7.5 miles to join Wood Slough and form Salt Slough 3.5 miles north-northeast of Dos Palos Y (lat. 37°06' N, long. 120°37' W; near SE cor. sec. 35, T 9 S, R 12 E); the stream heads near Santa Rita Park. Named on Santa Rita Park (1962) 15' quadrangle.

Santa Rita Slough: see **Salt Slough** [MERCED].

Santa Teresita: see **Camp Santa Teresita** [MADERA].

Santiago: see **Columbia** [TUOLUMNE].

Santiago Hill: see **Bell Hill** [TUOLUMNE].

Sapps Camp: see **Sapps Meadow** [TUOLUMNE].

Sapps Hill [TUOLUMNE]: *peak,* 5 miles northeast of Liberty Hill (lat. 38°24'50" N, long. 120°01'35" W); the peak is 1.25 miles west-northwest of Sapps Meadow. Altitude 7307 feet. Named on Tamarack (1979) 7.5' quadrangle.

Sapps Meadow [TUOLUMNE]: *area,* 6 miles east-northeast of Liberty Hill (lat. 38°24'35" N, long. 120°00'20" W); the place is 1.25 miles east-southeast of Sapps Hill. Named on Tamarack (1979) 7.5' quadrangle. Big Meadow (1956) 15' quadrangle shows a place called Sapps Camp at the site.

Sardella Lake: see **Granite Dome** [TUOLUMNE].

Sardine Meadow [TUOLUMNE]: *area,* 3.25 miles southeast of Dardanelle (lat. 38°18'25" N, long. 119°47'15" W; on W line sec. 4, T 5 N, R 20 E). Named on Dardanelle (1979) 7.5' quadrangle.

Sargent-Barnhart Tract [SAN JOAQUIN]: *area,* 4 miles west-northwest of downtown Stockton (lat. 37°59' N, long. 121°21'40" W). Named on Stockton West (1952) 7.5' quadrangle. Called Sargent Barnhart Tract (without the hyphen) on Stockton (1913) 7.5' quadrangle.

Sargent Slough [SAN JOAQUIN]: *water feature,* joins Little Potato Slough 1 mile south-southeast of Terminous (lat. 38°06'05" N, long. 121°29'10" W). Named on Terminous (1952) 7.5' quadrangle.

Satcher Lake: see **Sotcher Lake** [MADERA].

Saucer Meadow [TUOLUMNE]: *area,* 12 miles northwest of Tower Peak along Summit Creek (lat. 38°14'35" N, long. 119°43'40" W; near N line sec. 36, T 5 N, R 20 E). Named on Tower Peak (1956) 15' quadrangle.

Saurian Crest [TUOLUMNE]: *ridge,* southwest-trending, 1.5 miles long, 1 mile west-northwest of Tower Peak (lat. 38°08'45" N, long. 119°34'15" W). Named on Tower Peak (1956) 15' quadrangle. William E. Colby named the ridge in 1911 for its supposed resemblance to the serrated back of some ancient saurian creature (Gudde, 1949, p. 321).

Savage: see **Mount Savage** [MARIPOSA].

Savage Diggings: see **Big Oak Flat** [TUOLUMNE].

Savage Flat: see **Big Creek** [TUOLUMNE] (1).

Savages Trading Post [MARIPOSA]: *locality,* 4.5 miles southeast of the settlement of Catheys Valley along Mariposa Creek (lat. 37° 23' N, long. 120°02'35" W; sec. 30, T 6 S, R 18 E). Named on Catheys Valley (1962) 7.5' quadrangle.

Sawmill Creek [CALAVERAS]: *stream,* flows 4.5 miles to Black Creek (1) 3.25 miles south-southeast of Copperopolis (lat. 37°56'05" N, long. 120°37'20" W; sec. 14, T 1 N, R 12 E). Named on Copperopolis (1962) and Melones Dam (1962) 7.5' quadrangles.

Sawmill Flat [TUOLUMNE]: *locality,* 1.5 miles southeast of Columbia along Woods Creek (lat. 38°01'10" N, long. 120°22'50" W; near S line sec. 13, T 2 N, R 14 E). Named on Columbia (1948) 7.5' quadrangle. The name is from two sawmills built at the place to supply timbers for mines in the early 1850's; it also has the form "Saw Mill Flat" (Hoover, Rensch, and Rensch, p. 572).

Sawmill Gulch [TUOLUMNE]: *canyon,* drained by a stream that flows 1 mile to Woods Creek 1.5 miles southeast of Columbia at Sawmill Flat (lat. 38°01'15" N, long. 120°22'50" W; near S line sec. 13, T 2 N, R 14 E). Named on Columbia (1948) and Columbia SE (1948) 7.5' quadrangles.

Sawmill Mountain [TUOLUMNE]: *peak,* 6 miles southwest of Mather (lat. 37°49'35" N, long. 119°56'05" W; near W line sec. 30, T 1 S, R 19 E). Altitude 5300 feet. Named on Lake Eleanor (1956) 15' quadrangle.

Sawtooth Ridge [TUOLUMNE]: *ridge,* extends for 2.5 miles west-northwest from Matterhorn Peak along Tuolumne-Mono County line (lat. 38°06'15" N, long. 119°23'45" W). Named on Matterhorn Peak (1956) 15' quadrangle.

Saxon Creek [MARIPOSA]: *stream,* flows 5 miles to Merced River 5 miles northwest of Midpines (lat. 37°35'35" N, long. 119°59'15" W; near S line sec. 9, T 4 S, R 18 E). Named on Feliciana Mountain (1947) 7.5' quadrangle. Yosemite (1909) 30' quadrangle has the name "Saxon Gulch" for the canyon of the stream.

Saxon Gulch: see **Saxon Creek** [MARIPOSA].

Schaads Reservoir [CALAVERAS]: *lake,* behind a dam on Middle Fork Mokelumne River 5.5 miles south of Devils Nose (lat. 38° 23'05" N, long. 120°26'30" W; sec. 9, T 6 N, R 14 E). Named on Devils Nose (1979) 7.5' quadrangle.

Schmidt Creek [MADERA]: *stream,* flows 7.5 miles to end 6.5 miles southeast of Fairmead near Notarb (lat. 37°00'15" N, long. 120°07'05" W; sec. 4, T 11 S, R 17 E). Named on Kismet (1961) 7.5' quadrangle.

Schoettgen Pass [TUOLUMNE]: *pass,* 1.5 miles west-northwest of Crandall Peak (lat. 38°10'10" N, long. 120°10'10" W; near W line sec. 25, T 4 N, R 16 E). Named on Crandall Peak (1979) 7.5' quadrangle. Big Trees (1891) 30' quadrangle has the name "Shotgun" near the site.

Schofield Peak [TUOLUMNE]: *peak,* 8 miles west-southwest of Tower Peak (lat. 38°05'35" N, long. 119°40'40" W). Altitude 9935 feet. Named on Tower Peak (1956) 15' quadrangle. Major W.W. Forsyth, acting superintendent of Yosemite National Park, named the peak for Lieutenant General John McAllister Schofield (United States Board on Geographic Names, 1934, p. 22).

Schoolhouse Gulch [CALAVERAS]: *canyon,* drained by a stream that flows less than 1 mile to Chili Gulch 4 miles northwest of San Andreas (lat. 38°14'30" N, long. 120°43'30" W; sec. 35, T 5 N, R 11 E). Named on San Andreas (1962) 7.5' quadrangle.

Scorpion Gulch [CALAVERAS]: *canyon,* 1 mile long, opens into the canyon of Stanislaus River 6.5 miles south-southeast of Copperopolis (lat. 37°53'25" N, long. 120°35'45" W). Named on Melones Dam (1962) 7.5' quadrangle. Water of Tulloch Lake floods much of the canyon.

Scotch Gulch [MARIPOSA]: *canyon,* drained by a stream that flows nearly 3 miles to Lake McClure 5.5 miles south-southeast of Coulterville (lat. 37°28'10" N, long. 120°09'50" W; sec. 36, T 3 S, R 16 E). Named on Coulterville (1947, photorevised 1973) 7.5' quadrangle.

Scott Creek [MARIPOSA]: *stream,* flows 2.25 miles to North Fork Merced River 6 miles east-southeast of Smith Peak (lat. 37°45'20" N, long. 120°00'20" W; sec. 17, T 2 S, R 18 E); the stream is east of Scott Ridge. Named on Jawbone Ridge (1947) 7.5' quadrangle.

Scott Ridge [MARIPOSA]: *ridge,* south- to southwest-trending, 2.25 miles long, 5.25 miles east-southeast of Smith Peak (lat. 37°46'30" N, long. 120°00'35" W); the ridge is west of Scott Creek. Named on Jawbone Ridge (1947) 7.5' quadrangle.

Scraperville: see **Sonora** [TUOLUMNE].

Seavey Pass [TUOLUMNE]: *pass,* 7 miles south-southeast of Tower Peak (lat. 38°02'45" N, long. 119°31'15" W). Named on Tower Peak (1956) 15' quadrangle. R.B. Marshall of United States Geological Survey named the pass for Clyde L. Seavey, a member of California State Board of Control from 1911 until 1915 and from 1917 until 1921, state civil service commissioner from 1921 until 1923, and president of the California State Railroad Commission after 1923 (Hanna, p. 298).

Second Creek [TUOLUMNE]: *stream,* flows nearly 2 miles to Hatch Creek 4 miles south-southwest of Moccasin (lat. 37°45'25" N, long. 120°19'30" W; sec. 16, T 2 S, R 15 E); the stream is north of First Creek. Named on Moccasin (1948) and Penon Blanco Peak (1962) 7.5' quadrangles.

Second Crossing: see **North Branch** [CALAVERAS].

Second Garrotte [TUOLUMNE]: *locality,* 2 miles east-southeast of Groveland (lat. 37°49'30" N, long. 120°11'40" W; near W line sec. 26, T 1 S, R 16 E); the place is along Garrotte Creek. Named on Groveland (1947) 7.5' quadrangle. After present Groveland became known as Garrotte from the hanging there of Mexican thieves, Second Garrotte received its name from a similar incident—*garrote* is the Spanish term for capital punishment by strangulation (Gudde, 1949, p. 324). Wheeler (1879, p. 161) referred to "2[d] Garrotta, a mining village."

Second Garrotte Basin [TUOLUMNE]: *valley,* 2 miles southeast of Groveland (lat. 37°49'20" N, long. 120°12' W; mainly in sec. 27, T 1 S, R 16 E); the valley is west-southwest of Second Garrotte. Named on Groveland (1947) 7.5' quadrangle.

Second Garrotte Ridge [TUOLUMNE]: *ridge,* south- to west-trending, 2 miles long, center 3 miles southeast of Groveland (lat. 37°48'40" N, long. 120°11'20" W); the ridge is 1 mile south-southeast of Second Garrotte. Named on Groveland (1947) 7.5' quadrangle.

Seegar: see **Hospital Creek** [SAN JOAQUIN-STANISLAUS].

Sentinel Creek [MARIPOSA]: *stream,* flows 3 miles to Merced River 1.5 miles southwest of Yosemite Village (lat. 37°44'10" N, long. 119°36'15" W); the stream goes past Sentinel Dome and Sentinel Rock. Named on Yosemite (1956) 15' quadrangle.

Sentinel Dome [MARIPOSA]: *peak,* nearly 2 miles south of Yosemite Village (lat. 37°43'25" N, long. 119°35' W). Altitude 8122 feet. Named on Yosemite (1956) 15' quadrangle. The men who discovered Yosemite Valley in 1851 called the peak South Dome (Hanna, p. 131).

Sentinel Fall [MARIPOSA]: *waterfall,* 1.5 miles south-southwest of Yosemite Village (lat. 37°43'30" N, long. 119°35'40" W); the feature is along Sentinel Creek.. Named on Yosemite (1956) 15' quadrangle.

Sentinel Rock [MARIPOSA]: *promontory,* 1.5 miles south-southwest of Yosemite Village on the south side of Yosemite Valley (lat. 37° 43'45" N, long. 119°35'35" W). Named on Yosemite (1956) 15' quadrangle. The name is from the resemblance of the feature to a gigantic watch tower (Whitney, 1870, p. 62).

Sequoia: see **Rush Creek** [TUOLUMNE] (3).

Sesame: see **Bellview** [MADERA].

"77" Corral: see **Corral Meadow** [MADERA].

Sexton: see **Volstead** [SAN JOAQUIN].

Shad Gulch [CALAVERAS]: *canyon,* 0.5 mile long, 3 miles west-northwest of Paloma (lat. 38°16'30" N, long. 120°48'45" W; on W line sec. 19, T 5 N, R 11 E). Named on Jackson (1962) 7.5' quadrangle. Water of Pardee Reservoir floods the lower part of the canyon.

Shadow Creek [MADERA]: *stream,* flows 4.5 miles to Middle Fork San Joaquin River 5.25 miles north-northwest of Devils Postpile (lat. 37°41'45" N, long. 119°07'05" W); the stream goes through Shadow Lake. Named on Devils Postpile (1953) 15' quadrangle.

Shadow Lake [MADERA]: *lake,* 2400 feet long, 5.5 miles north-northwest of Devils Postpile (lat. 37°41'40" N, long. 119°07'50" W). Named on Devils Postpile (1953) 15' quadrangle. Called Garnet Lake on some early maps (Browning, 1988, p. 128).

Shadow Lake: see **Little Shadow Lake**, under **Ediza Lake** [MADERA]; **Merced Lake** [MARIPOSA].

Shag Slough [MERCED]: *water feature,* 4.5 miles west of Stevinson on the east side of San Joaquin River (lat. 37°19'40" N, long. 120° 56' W). Named on Turlock (1962) 15' quadrangle.

Shakeflat Creek [MADERA]: *stream,* flows 3.25 miles to San Joaquin River 5.5 miles east-southeast of Shuteye Peak (lat. 37°18'50" N, long. 119°20' W). Named on Shuteye Peak (1953) 15' quadrangle.

Shallow Lake [TUOLUMNE]: *lake,* 2000 feet long, 8 miles west of Tower Peak (lat. 38°09'40" N, long. 119°41'55" W). Named on Tower Peak (1956) 15' quadrangle.

Shamrock Lake [TUOLUMNE]: *lake,* 700 feet long, 6.25 miles southwest of Matterhorn Peak (lat. 38°01'25" N, long. 119°27'15" W). Named on Matterhorn Peak (1956) 15' quadrangle.

Shanahan Flat [TUOLUMNE]: *area,* 5 miles east-southeast of Groveland (lat. 37°43'30" N, long. 120°08'50" W; sec. 31, T 1 S, R 17 E). Named on Groveland (1947) 7.5' quadrangle.

Shanghai Ridge [MARIPOSA]: *ridge,* southeast-trending, 1 mile long, 4.25 miles north-northwest of the settlement of Catheys Valley (lat. 37°29'30" N, long. 120°07'30" W). Named on Catheys Valley (1962) and Indian Gulch (1962) 7.5' quadrangles.

Sharon [MADERA]: *locality,* 4 miles east-northeast of Fairmead along Atchison, Topeka and Santa Fe Railroad (lat. 37°06' N, long. 120°07'50" W; near SE cor. sec. 32, T 9 S, R 17 E). Named on Berenda (1961) 7.5' quadrangle. Postal authorities established Sharon post office in 1898 and discontinued it in 1927 (Frickstad, p. 86). The place began as part of a real estate promotion on land that had been owned by San Francisco financier William Sharon (Clough, p. 91). California Mining Bureau's (1917b) map shows a place called Watt located 2.5 miles north-northwest of Sharon along the railroad.

Sharon Lake [TUOLUMNE]: *lake,* 725 feet long, 5 miles southwest of Sonora Pass (lat. 38°16'35" N, long. 119°42' W; near SE cor. sec. 18, T 5 N, R 21 E). Named on Sonora Pass (1979) 7.5' quadrangle.

Shawmut: see **Chinese Camp** [TUOLUMNE].

Shaws Flat [TUOLUMNE]: *locality,* 2 miles south-southwest of Columbia (lat. 38°00'25" N, long. 120°24'30" W; near S line sec. 23, T 2 N, R 14 E). Named on Columbia (1948) 7.5' quadrangle. Mandeville Shaw planted an orchard at the place in 1849 (Hoover, Rensch, and Rensch, p. 572). Perkins (p. 199) referred to Shaw's Flats in 1851. Stoddart (p. 64) mentioned a place called Dragoon Flat that was located "at the lower end of Shaws Flat"—a group of discharged dragoons settled there to mine gold in 1848.

Sheepcamp Spring [MARIPOSA]: *spring,* less than 0.5 mile northeast of Santa Cruz Mountain (lat. 37°27'40" N, long. 120°11'50" W; at N line sec. 34, T 5 S, R 16 E). Named on Indian Gulch (1962) 7.5' quadrangle.

Sheep Crossing [MADERA]: *locality,* 8 miles west-southwest of Devils Postpile along North Fork San Joaquin River (lat. 37°33'40" N, long. 119°12'30" W). Named on Devils Postpile (1953) 15' quadrangle. A trail used by cattlemen crossed the river at the place on a bridge known as Sheep Crossing (McLaughlin and Bradley, p. 556).

Sheep Gap [MARIPOSA]: *pass,* 4 miles east-southeast of the settlement of Catheys Valley (lat. 37°24'10" N, long. 120°01'40" W; near NW cor. sec. 20, T 6 S, R 18 E). Named on Catheys Valley (1962) 7.5' quadrangle.

Sheep Peak [TUOLUMNE]: *peak,* 6.5 miles northwest of Tioga Pass (lat. 37°59' N, long. 119°20'25" W; sec. 33, T 2 N, R 24 E). Named on Tuolumne Meadows (1956) 15' quadrangle.

Sheep Ranch [CALAVERAS]: *village,* 5 miles north of Murphys (lat. 38°12'35" N, long. 120°27'50" W; near SW cor. sec. 7, T 4 N, R 14 E).

Named on Murphys (1948) 7.5' quadrangle. Postal authorities established Sheep Ranch post office in 1877 and changed the name to Sheepranch in 1895; the name was from Sheep Ranch mine (Salley, p. 202).

Sheep Thief Creek [STANISLAUS]: *stream,* flows 5.25 miles to South Fork Orestimba Creek 4.5 miles south of Mikes Peak (lat. 37°17'35" N, long. 121°20' W; sec. 29, T 7 S, R 6 E). Named on Mount Stakes (1955) and Wilcox Ridge (1956) 7.5' quadrangles.

Sheering Creek [TUOLUMNE]: *stream,* flows nearly 2 miles to North Fork Tuolumne River 0.5 mile south-southeast of Pinecrest (lat. 38°11' N, long. 119°59'35" W; at W line sec. 22, T 4 N, R 18 E). Named on Pinecrest (1979) 7.5' quadrangle.

Shellenbarger Lake [MADERA]: *lake,* 450 feet long, 6.25 miles west of Devils Postpile (lat. 37°38'35" N, long. 119°11'40" W). Named on Devils Postpile (1953) 15' quadrangle.

Shennel Island [SAN JOAQUIN]: *island,* 900 feet long, 4 miles west of downtown Stockton in Calaveras River (lat. 37°58' N, long. 121°21'35" W). Named on Stockton West (1952) 7.5' quadrangle.

Shepherd Crest [TUOLUMNE]: *ridge,* northwest-trending, 2 miles long, 6.5 miles south-southeast of Matterhorn Peak (lat. 38°00'35" N, long. 119°19'30" W). Named on Matterhorn Peak (1956) 15' quadrangle.

Shepherd Lake [TUOLUMNE]: *lake,* 700 feet long, 6 miles southeast of Matterhorn Peak (lat. 38°01'10" N, long. 119°19'05" W; sec. 15, T 2 N, R 24 E); the lake is northeast of Shepherd Crest. Named on Matterhorn Peak (1956) 15' quadrangle.

Shepherd's Ferry: see **Mossdale** [SAN JOAQUIN].

Sherlock: see **Sherlock Creek** [MARIPOSA].

Sherlock Creek [MARIPOSA]: *stream,* flows 7 miles to Merced River 3.25 miles northeast of the village of Bear Valley (lat. 37°35'50" N, long. 120°04'10" W; sec. 11, T 4 S, R 17 E). Named on Bear Valley (1947) and Feliciana Mountain (1947) 7.5' quadrangles. The name commemorates Jimmy Sherlock, who discovered gold in the stream in 1849; a mining camp by the creek was called Sherlock, Sherlock Town (Sargent, Shirley, 1976, p. 34-35), and Sherlock's Diggings (Morgan *in* Gardiner, p. 351).

Sherlock's Diggings: see **Sherlock Creek** [MARIPOSA].

Sherlock Town: see **Sherlock Creek** [MARIPOSA].

Sherman Acres [CALAVERAS]: *settlement,* 0.5 mile north-northeast of Tamarack (lat. 38°26'45" N, long. 120°04'20" W; sec. 23, T 7 N, R 17 E). Named on Tamarack (1979) 7.5' quadrangle. Called Lombardi on Big Meadow (1956) 15' quadrangle.

Sherwood Forest [TUOLUMNE]: *settlement,* less than 1 mile southeast of Twain Harte (lat. 38°01'45" N, long. 120°13'20" W; sec. 16, T 2 N, R 16 E). Named on Twain Harte (1979) 7.5' quadrangle.

Shima Bend [SAN JOAQUIN]: *bend,* 7 miles south-southeast of Terminous along San Joaquin River (lat. 38°00'55" N, long. 121° 27'20" W). Named on Terminous (1978) 7.5' quadrangle.

Shima Tract [SAN JOAQUIN]: *area,* 8.5 miles southeast of Terminous (lat. 38°01'45" N, long. 121°23' W). Named on Lodi South (1968) and Terminous (1978) 7.5' quadrangles. The name commemorates George Shima, a Japanese immigrant who farmed the area in the early 1900's (Dillon, 1982, p. 98).

Shingle Hill [MARIPOSA]: *ridge,* southeast- to east-trending, 2.5 miles long, 4 miles south-southeast of Smith Peak (lat. 37°45' N, long. 120°04' W). Named on Buckhorn Peak (1947) and Jawbone Ridge (1947) 7.5' quadrangles.

Shingle Spring [TUOLUMNE]: *spring,* 14 miles south-southeast of Pinecrest on Kibbie Ridge (lat. 38°00'45" N, long. 119°53' W; near W line sec. 22, T 2 N, R 19 E). Named on Cherry Lake North (1979) 7.5' quadrangle.

Shin Kee Tract [SAN JOAQUIN]: *area,* 4 miles east-southeast of Terminous (lat. 38°05'45" N, long. 121°25' W). Named on Terminous (1978) 7.5' quadrangle.

Shipyard Island: see **Vulcan Island** [SAN JOAQUIN].

Shirley Creek [CALAVERAS-STANISLAUS]: *stream,* heads in Calaveras County and flows 10 miles to Hoods Creek 10.5 miles north of Oakdale in Stanislaus County (lat. 37°55'20" N, long. 120°49'30" W; sec. 24, T 1 N, R 10 E); the stream goes through Shirley Gulch. Named on Bachelor Valley (1968) 7.5' quadrangle.

Shirley Creek [MADERA]: *stream,* flows 1 mile to Madera Creek nearly 6 miles south-southeast of Merced Peak (lat. 37°33'30" N, long. 119°20'50" W). Named on Merced Peak (1953) 15' quadrangle.

Shirley Gulch [CALAVERAS-STANISLAUS]: *canyon,* on Calaveras-Stanislaus County line, along Shirley Creek above a point 10.5 miles north-northeast of Oakdale (lat. 37°54' N, long. 120°45'50" W; near N line sec. 33, T 1 N, R 11 E). Named on Bachelor Valley (1968) and Copperopolis (1962) 7.5' quadrangles.

Shirley Lake [MADERA]: *lake,* 600 feet long, 5.25 miles south of Merced Peak (lat. 37°33'35" N, long. 119°22'30" W). Named on Merced Peak (1953) 15' quadrangle.

Shirley Mountain [CALAVERAS]: *ridge,* west-trending, 1 mile long, about 5 miles southwest of Copperopolis (lat. 37°55'45" N, long. 120°42'35" W); the ridge is south of Shirley Gulch. Named on Copperopolis (1962) 7.5' quadrangle.

Shoemake: see **Chinese Station** [TUOLUMNE].

Shoemake Siding [STANISLAUS]: *locality,* 6.5 miles south of Modesto along Tidewater Southern Railroad (lat. 37°32'15" N, long. 120°59' W). Named on Modesto East (1939) 15' quadrangle.

Shoofly Creek [TUOLUMNE]: *stream,* flows 6 miles to Middle Fork Stanislaus River nearly 7 miles southeast of Liberty Hill (lat. 38° 18'05" N, long. 120°00'30" W; at E line sec. 8, T 5 N, R 18 E). Named on Liberty Hill (1979) 7.5' quadrangle.

Shoofly Meadow [TUOLUMNE]: *area,* 4 miles east of Liberty Hill (lat. 38°21'30" N, long. 120°01'40" W; near E line sec. 19, T 6 N, R 18 E); the place is by the head of Shoofly Creek. Named on Liberty Hill (1979) 7.5' quadrangle.

Shotgun: see **Schoettgen Pass** [TUOLUMNE].

Shotgun Creek [TUOLUMNE]: *stream,* flows 1.5 miles to Stanislaus River nearly 6 miles north-northwest of Keystone (lat. 37°54'15" N, long. 120°33'45" W; sec. 29, T 1 N, R 13 E). Named on Melones Dam (1962) 7.5' quadrangle.

Shultz Mountain [MARIPOSA]: *ridge,* south- to southeast-trending, 2.5 miles long, 3.25 miles east-southeast of Santa Cruz Mountain (lat. 37°26'45" N, long. 120°08'35" W). Named on Indian Gulch (1962) 7.5' quadrangle.

Shumake Knoll [TUOLUMNE]: *ridge,* east- to east-northeast-trending, nearly 1 mile long, 8 miles south-southwest of Liberty Hill (lat. 38°15'30" N, long. 120°09'50" W). Named on Boards Crossing (1979) 7.5' quadrangle.

Shuteye Creek [MADERA]: *stream,* flows 2.5 miles to West Fork Chiquito Creek 3 miles northeast of Shuteye Peak (lat. 37°22'50" N, long. 119°23'20" W; sec. 30, T 6 S, R 24 E); the stream heads at Shuteye Peak. Named on Shuteye Peak (1953) 15' quadrangle.

Shuteye Pass [MADERA]: *pass,* 1 mile southeast of Shuteye Peak (lat. 37°20'20" N, long. 119°24'45" W; near NW cor. sec. 12, T 7 S, R 23 E). Named on Shuteye Peak (1953) 15' quadrangle.

Shuteye Pass: see **Little Shuteye Pass** [MADERA].

Shuteye Peak [MADERA]: *peak,* 11 miles east of Yosemite Forks (lat. 37°21' N, long. 119°25'40" W; sec. 2, T 7 S, R 23 E). Altitude 8351 feet. Named on Shuteye Peak (1953) 15' quadrangle. The name commemorates a mountaineer who was called Old Shuteye because he was blind in one eye (Hanna, p. 304).

Shuteye Peak: see **Little Shuteye Peak** [MADERA].

Siberia [CALAVERAS]: *area,* 7 miles south-southeast of Valley Springs between Whiskey Creek and Slate Creek (lat. 38°06' N, long. 120°47'30" W). Named on Jenny Lind (1962) and Valley Springs (1962) 7.5' quadrangles.

Sibley [SAN JOAQUIN]: *locality,* 7.5 miles east-northeast of downtown Stockton along Southern Pacific Railroad (lat. 37°58'45" N, long. 121°09'25" W). Named on Burnham (1914) 7.5' quadrangle.

Sierra Campground [TUOLUMNE]: *locality,* 3.5 miles south-southwest of Strawberry along North Fork Tuolumne River (lat. 38°09'15" N, long. 120°02'35" W). Named on Strawberry (1979) 7.5' quadrangle.

Sierra del Monte Diablo: see "Regional setting."

Sierra de San Marcos: see "Regional setting."

Sierra Nevada: see "Regional setting."

Sierra Point [MARIPOSA]: *promontory,* 2.25 miles southeast of Yosemite Village on the north side of Merced River (lat. 37°43'40" N, long. 119°33'15" W). Named on Yosemite (1956) 15' quadrangle. Charles A. Bailey named the place in 1897 to honor the Sierra Club after he found that Illilouette Fall, Vernal Fall, Nevada Fall , Upper Yosemite Fall, and Lower Yosemite Fall all can be seen from the spot (Browning, 1986, p. 198).

Sierra Village [TUOLUMNE]: *settlement,* 4 miles northeast of Twain Harte (lat. 38°04'20" N, long. 120°10'20" W; near W line sec. 36, T 3 N, R 16 E). Named on Twain Harte (1979) 7.5' quadrangle.

Sierra Vista [MADERA]: *locality,* 2.5 miles north-northwest of Chowchilla along Southern Pacific Railroad (lat. 37°09' N, long. 120°17'10" W; sec. 13, T 9 S, R 15 E). Named on Plainsburg (1919) 7.5' quadrangle.

Sierra Vista Mountain: see **Quiggs Mountain** [CALAVERAS].

Siesta Lake [TUOLUMNE]: *lake,* 500 feet long, 1.5 miles south-southwest of White Wolf (lat. 37°51' N, long. 119°39'35" W; near SE cor. sec. 16, T 1 S, R 21 E). Named on Hetch Hetchy Reservoir (1956) 15' quadrangle.

Signal Peak: see **Devil Peak** [MARIPOSA].

Silver Gulch [TUOLUMNE]: *canyon,* 1.25 miles long, opens into the canyon of South Fork Stanislaus River 4.5 miles northeast of Columbia (lat. 38°04'30" N, long. 120°20'10" W; sec. 33, T 3 N, R 15 E). Named on Columbia SE (1948) 7.5' quadrangle.

Silver Knob [MARIPOSA]: *peak,* 4 miles southwest of Fish Camp (lat. 37°26' N, long. 119°41' W; near S line sec. 4, T 6 S, R 21 E). Named on Bass Lake (1953) 15' quadrangle.

Silver Knoll: see **Douglas Flat** [CALAVERAS].

Silver Mine Creek [TUOLUMNE]: *stream,* flows 2.5 miles to Relief Reservoir 6.5 miles west-southwest of Sonora Pass (lat. 38°16'35" N, long. 119°44'10" W; sec. 14, T 5 N, R 20 E). Named on Dardanelle (1979) and

Sonora Pass (1979) 7.5' quadrangles.

Silver Strand Falls [MARIPOSA]: *waterfall,* 5.5 miles southwest of Yosemite Village along Meadow Brook (lat. 37°42'15" N, long. 119°40'05" W). Named on Yosemite (1956) 15' quadrangle. United States Board on Geographic Names (1933a, p. 694) rejected the name "Widows Tears Falls" for the feature. Early stage drivers told tourists that the name "Widows Tears Falls" was given to the feature because the waterfall lasted only two weeks; François E. Matthes suggested the present name (Browning, 1986, p. 201).

Simmons Creek [STANISLAUS]: *stream,* flows 11 miles to Littlejohns Creek 9 miles north-northwest of Oakdale (lat. 37°53'15" N, long. 120°54'40" W; near S line sec. 31, T 1 N, R 10 E). Named on Escalon (1968), Farmington (1968), and Oakdale (1915) 7.5' quadrangles. Oakdale (1968) 7.5' quadrangle shows the upper part of the stream in canals.

Simmons Peak [MADERA-TUOLUMNE]: *peak,* 10.5 miles south of Tioga Pass on Madera-Tuolumne County line (lat. 37°45'40" N, long. 119°17'35" W). Altitude 12,503 feet. Named on Tuolumne Meadows (1956) 15' quadrangle. R.B. Marshall of United States Geological Survey named the peak in 1909 for Dr. Samuel E. Simmons of Sacramento (United States Board on Geographic Names, 1934, p. 22).

Simmons Point [CALAVERAS]: *peak,* 5.5 miles southeast of San Andreas (lat. 38°08'05" N, long. 120°36'50" W; near SE cor. sec. 2, T 3 N, R 12 E). Named on Calaveritas (1962) 7.5' quadrangle.

Simms [SAN JOAQUIN]: *locality,* 6.5 miles east of Manteca along Tidewater Southern Railroad (lat. 37°47'55" N, long. 121°05'45" W; near S line sec. 33, T 1 S, R 8 E). Named on Avena (1952) 7.5' quadrangle.

Simpsonville: see **Bear Valley** [MARIPOSA] (2).

Sims Cove [MARIPOSA]: *locality,* nearly 5 miles south-southwest of El Portal along South Fork Merced River (lat. 37°37'10" N, long. 119°49'40" W; sec. 2, T 4 S, R 19 E). Named on Buckingham Mountain (1947) 7.5' quadrangle. The name should have the form "Simm's Cove" (Mendershausen, p. 18).

Singapore Cut: see **Mandeville Cut** [SAN JOAQUIN].

Sing Peak [MADERA]: *peak,* 5.5 miles south of Merced Peak (lat. 37°33'15" N, long. 119°23'15" W). Altitude 10,552 feet. Named on Merced Peak (1953) 15' quadrangle. R.B. Marshall of United States Geological Survey named the peak in 1899 for Tie Sing, cook for the Survey from 1888 until he died in an accident in 1918 (United States Board on Geographic Names, 1934, p. 22).

Sirey and Clarke's Ferry: see **Stanislaus River** [SAN JOAQUIN-STANISLAUS].

Sister Lake [TUOLUMNE]: *lake,* 1500 feet long, 7.25 miles southwest of Matterhorn Peak (lat. 38°01'05" N, long. 119°28'30" W). Named on Matterhorn Peak (1956) 15' quadrangle.

Sivels Mountain [MARIPOSA]: *peak,* 3.5 miles northeast of Yosemite Forks (lat. 37°23'50" N, long. 119°34'45" W; at W line sec. 21, T 6 S, R 22 E). Altitude 5813 feet. Named on Bass Lake (1953) 15' quadrangle, which shows Sivels ranch situated 0.5 mile southwest of the peak. The misspelled name recalls Thomas Sivils, who patented land in section 20 in 1891 (Browning, 1986, p. 201).

Six-Bit Gulch [TUOLUMNE]: *canyon,* drained by a stream that flows 5.5 miles to Don Pedro Reservoir 4 miles south-southeast of Chinese Camp (lat. 37°49'05" N, long. 120°24'45" W; sec. 27, T 1 S, R 14 E). Named on Chinese Camp (1947, photorevised 1973) 7.5' quadrangle. Sonora (1897) 30' quadrangle has the form "Sixbit Gulch" for the name, which was given in derision because of the scarcity of gold at the place (Paden and Schlichtmann, p. 63).

Sixmile Creek [CALAVERAS]: *stream,* flows nearly 7 miles to Angels Creek less than 1 mile south of Angels Camp (lat. 38°03'25" N, long. 120°32'30" W; near W line sec. 3, T 2 N, R 13 E). Named on Angels Camp (1962) and Columbia (1948) 7.5' quadrangles. Jackson (1902) 30' quadrangle has the form "Six Mile Creek" for the name.

Sixmile House [MADERA]: *locality,* 14 miles south-southwest of Raymond (lat. 37°00'45" N, long. 119°57'50" W; near SW cor. sec. 36, T 10 S, R 18 E). Named on Daulton (1921) 7.5' quadrangle.

Skelton Creek [MARIPOSA]: *stream,* flows 4.5 miles to Devil Gulch 7 miles south-southwest of El Portal (lat. 37°34'45" N, long. 119° 48'45" W; near N line sec. 24, T 4 S, R 19 E). Named on Buckingham Mountain (1947) 7.5' quadrangle.

Skelton Lakes [TUOLUMNE]: *lakes,* two, largest 1000 feet long, 3 miles northwest of Tioga Pass (lat. 37°56'05" N, long. 119°18' W). Named on Tuolumne Meadows (1956) 15' quadrangle. Browning (1986, p. 202) associated the name with Henry A. Skelton, who was a ranger at Yosemite National Park from 1916 until 1932.

Skull Creek [TUOLUMNE]: *stream,* formed by the confluence of North Fork and South Fork, flows nearly 6 miles to Griswold Creek 6.5 miles northwest of Crandall Peak (lat. 38°14'20" N, long. 120°12'35" W; sec. 33, T 5 N, R 15 E). Named on Boards Crossing (1979), Crandall Peak (1979), and Liberty Hill (1979) 7.5' quadrangles. North Fork is 3 miles long and South Fork is 2.5 miles long. Both forks are named on Liberty Hill (1979) 7.5' quadrangle.

Skull Flat [CALAVERAS]: *area,* 1.5 miles north-northeast of West Point (lat. 38°25'15" N, long. 120°30'50" W; mainly in sec. 35, T 7 N, R 13 E). Named on West Point (1948) 7.5' quadrangle.

Skunk Creek [TUOLUMNE]: *stream,* flows 5 miles to Jawbone Creek 8 miles west-northwest of Mather (lat. 37°55'40" N, long. 119°59'30" W; sec. 22, T 1 N, R 18 E). Named on Lake Eleanor (1956) and Tuolumne (1948) 15' quadrangles.

Skunk Gulch [CALAVERAS]: *canyon,* drained by a stream that flows nearly 2 miles to Stanislaus River 2.5 miles southeast of Vallecito (lat. 38°03'40" N, long. 120°26'35" W; sec. 4, T 2 N, R 14 E). Named on Columbia (1948) 7.5' quadrangle.

Skunk Gulch [MARIPOSA]: *canyon,* drained by a stream that flows 2.25 miles to Bull Creek 11.5 miles west of El Portal (lat. 37°42'25" N, long. 119°58'55" W; near E line sec. 4, T 3 S, R 18 E). Named on Buckhorn Peak (1947) and Kinsley (1947) 7.5' quadrangles.

Skyhigh [CALAVERAS]: *settlement,* 1.5 miles southwest of Tamarack (lat. 38°25'30" N, long. 120°05'45" W; sec. 27, T 7 N, R 17 E). Named on Tamarack (1979) 7.5' quadrangle.

Slab Lakes [MADERA]: *lakes,* largest 800 feet long, 2.5 miles east-southeast of Merced Peak (lat. 37°37'05" N, long. 119°21'25" W). Named on Merced Peak (1953) 15' quadrangle.

Slate Creek [CALAVERAS]: *stream,* flows 5.5 miles to New Hogan Reservoir nearly 6 miles south-southeast of Valley Springs (lat. 38°07'35" N, long. 120°48'35" W; sec. 7, T 3 N, R 11 E). Named on Jenny Lind (1962) and Valley Springs (1962) 7.5' quadrangles.

Slate Creek [TUOLUMNE]: *stream,* flows 1.5 miles to Woods Creek 6.5 miles south-southwest of Sonora (lat. 37°53'50" N, long. 120° 26' W; sec. 33, T 1 N, R 14 E). Named on Sonora (1948) 7.5' quadrangle.

Slate Gulch [MARIPOSA]: *canyon,* drained by a stream that flows 5 miles to Bear Creek (2) 2 miles east-southeast of Santa Cruz Mountain (lat. 37°26'35" N, long. 120°10'20" W; sec. 1, T 6 S, R 16 E). Named on Indian Gulch (1962) 7.5' quadrangle.

Slate Gulch [TUOLUMNE]: *canyon,* drained by a stream that flows 1 mile to Algerine Creek 6 miles south of Sonora (lat. 37°53'55" N, long. 120°21'40" W; near E line sec. 31, T 1 N, R 15 E). Named on Standard (1948) 7.5' quadrangle.

Slate Gulch: see **Feliciana Creek** [MARIPOSA].

Slaughter Pass [STANISLAUS]: *canyon,* less than 0.5 mile long, 3.25 miles west of Crevison Peak (lat. 37°11'10" N, long. 121°14'45" W; sec. 6, T 9 S, R 7 E). Named on Crevison Peak (1955) 7.5' quadrangle.

Slick Rock Canyon [STANISLAUS]: *canyon,* drained by a stream that flows 1.5 miles to Del Puerto Canyon 1.5 miles north-northwest of Copper Mountain (lat. 37°26'20" N, long. 121°19'45" W; at E line sec. 5, T 6 S, R 6 E). Named on Copper Mountain (1956) 7.5' quadrangle.

Slide: see **The Slide** [TUOLUMNE].

Slide Canyon [TUOLUMNE]: *canyon,* 5 miles long, on upper reaches of Piute Creek (2) above a point 5 miles southwest of Matterhorn Peak (lat. 38°03'10" N, long. 119°27'25" W); the canyon is east of the feature called The Slide. Named on Matterhorn Peak (1956) 15' quadrangle.

Slide Creek [MADERA]:

(1) *stream,* flows 3.5 miles to Bass Lake (1) nearly 4 miles southeast of Yosemite Forks (lat. 37°19'50" N, long. 119°34'40" W; sec. 9, T 7 S, R 22 E). Named on Bass Lake (1953) 15' quadrangle.

(2) *stream,* flows 2.5 miles to Rock Creek 5.5 miles southeast of Shuteye Peak (lat. 37°17'15" N, long. 119°21'25" W; sec. 28, T 7 S, R 24 E). Named on Shuteye Peak (1953) 15' quadrangle.

(3) *stream,* flows 2.5 miles to North Fork San Joaquin River 8 miles west of Devils Postpile (lat. 37°38'20" N, long. 119°13'25" W). Named on Devils Postpile (1953) 15' quadrangle.

Slide Fall: see **Pywiack Cascade** [MARIPOSA].

Slide Mountain [TUOLUMNE]:

(1) *peak,* 3.5 miles west of Tower Peak on Tuolumne-Mono County line (lat. 38°05'35" N, long. 119°26'45" W); the peak is at the head of the feature called The Slide. Named on Matterhorn Peak (1956) 15' quadrangle.

(2) *ridge,* west-southwest-trending, 1.25 miles long, 5.5 miles southwest of Matterhorn Peak (lat. 38°02'05" N, long. 119°27'15" W). Named on Matterhorn Peak (1956) 15' quadrangle.

Slocum Gulch [CALAVERAS]: *canyon,* drained by a stream that flows 0.5 mile to Mokelumne River 1 mile northwest of Mokelumne Hill at Big Bar (lat. 38°18'50" N, long. 120°43' W; sec. 1, T 5 N, R 11 E). Named on Mokelumne Hill (1948) 7.5' quadrangle.

Slocum's Ferry: see **Mossdale** [SAN JOAQUIN].

Sloss: see **Clearing House** [MARIPOSA].

Slumgullion: see **Carson Hill** [CALAVERAS] (2).

Smarts Gulch [TUOLUMNE]: *canyon,* drained by a stream that flows nearly 2 miles to Don Pedro Reservoir 3.25 miles east-southeast of Chinese Camp (lat. 37°51'05" N, long. 120°22'35" W; near E line sec. 13, T 1 S, R 14 E). Named on Chinese Camp (1947) 7.5' quadrangle.

Smedberg Lake [TUOLUMNE]: *lake,* 0.5 mile long, 8 miles southwest of Matterhorn Peak (lat. 38°00'50" N, long. 119°29' W). Named on Matterhorn

Peak (1956) 15' quadrangle. Lieutenant H.C. Benson named the lake in 1895 for Lieutenant William Renwick Smedberg, Jr. (United States Board on Geographic Names, 1934, p. 23).

Smiley Mountain [MADERA]: *peak,* 3.25 miles west-northwest of the town of North Fork (lat. 37°14'35" N, long. 119°33'55" W; near SE cor. sec. 9, T 8 S, R 22 E). Altitude 3648 feet. Named on North Fork (1965) 7.5' quadrangle.

Smith Creek [CALAVERAS]: *stream,* flows 2 miles to Peachy Creek 7.5 miles south-southwest of Copperopolis (lat. 37°52'25" N, long. 120°40'20" W); the stream goes through Smith Flat. Named on Copperopolis (1962) and Knights Ferry (1962) 7.5' quadrangles.

Smith Creek [MARIPOSA]: *stream,* flows 6.5 miles to Bean Creek 6.5 miles north-northeast of Buckhorn Peak (lat. 37°44'45" N, long. 120°04'10" W; sec. 23, T 2 S, R 17 E). Named on Buckhorn Peak (1947), Groveland (1947), and Jawbone Ridge (1947) 7.5' quadrangles.

Smith Creek [STANISLAUS]: *stream,* flows 6.25 miles to Hoods Creek 10.5 miles north of Oakdale (lat. 37°55'10" N, long. 120°52'10" W; near W line sec. 22, T 1 N, R 10 E). Named on Bachelor Valley (1968) 7.5' quadrangle.

Smith Flat [CALAVERAS]: *area,* nearly 7 miles south of Copperopolis (lat. 37°53' N, long. 120°39'30" W); the place is along Smith Creek. Named on Copperopolis (1962) 7.5' quadrangle.

Smith Lake [SAN JOAQUIN]: *lake,* 1900 feet long, 1.5 miles northwest of downtown Lodi (lat. 38°08'50" N, long. 121°17'40" W; near SW cor. sec. 35, T 4 N, R 6 E). Named on Woodbridge (1910) 7.5' quadrangle. The feature now is called Lodi Municipal Lake (Hillman and Covello, p. 50).

Smith Meadow [TUOLUMNE]: *area,* 6.25 miles east-northeast of Mather along Cottonwood Creek (3) (lat. 37°55'15" N, long. 119° 45'05" W; near NE cor. sec. 27, T 1 N, R 20 E); the place is southwest of Smith Peak (2). Named on Hetch Hetchy Reservoir (1956) and Lake Eleanor (1956) 15' quadrangles. Cyril C. Smith built a cabin in the area in 1885 (Uhte, p. 64).

Smith Peak [MARIPOSA-TUOLUMNE]: *peak,* 7.5 miles east-southeast of Groveland on Mariposa-Tuolumne County line (lat. 37°48'05" N, long. 120°06' W; sec. 34, T 1 S, R 17 E); the peak is 1.5 miles southeast of Smith Station. Altitude 3877 feet. Named on Jawbone Ridge (1947) 7.5' quadrangle.

Smith Peak [TUOLUMNE]: *peak,* 6 miles northwest of White Wolf (lat. 37°55'35" N, long. 119°44' W; on W line sec. 24, T 1 N, R 20 E); the peak is 1 mile east-northeast of Smith Meadow at the head of Cottonwood Creek (3). Altitude 7751 feet. Named on Hetch Hetchy Reservoir (1956) 15' quadrangle. United States Board on Geographic Names (1933a, p. 701) rejected the names "Smith's Peak" and "Cottonwood Peak" for the feature.

Smith Ridge [MARIPOSA]: *ridge,* south- to southeast-trending, 2.5 miles long, 2 miles southeast of Smith Peak (lat. 37°46'45" N, long. 120°04'35" W). Named on Jawbone Ridge (1947) 7.5' quadrangle.

Smith's Flat: see **Smith Station** [TUOLUMNE].

Smith's Peak: see **Smith Peak** [TUOLUMNE].

Smiths Ridge [SAN JOAQUIN]: *ridge,* generally northeast-trending, 5 miles long, 13 miles south of Tracy (lat. 37°33'15" N, long. 121° 25'30" W). Named on Lone Tree Creek (1955) 7.5' quadrangle.

Smith Station [TUOLUMNE]: *locality,* 6.25 miles east-southeast of Groveland in Burch Meadow (lat. 37°48'45" N, long. 120°07'15" W; near W line sec. 33, T 1 S, R 17 E). Named on Jawbone Ridge (1947) 7.5' quadrangle. The name commemorates John B. Smith, who homesteaded at the place and ran a stage station there at what became known as Smith's Flat (Paden and Schlichtmann, p. 186, 188).

Smith Tract [SAN JOAQUIN]: *area,* 2.5 miles west-northwest of downtown Stockton (lat. 37°58'15" N, long. 121°20' W). Named on Stockton (1913) 7.5' quadrangle.

Smoky Jack Campground [TUOLUMNE]: *locality,* 5 miles southwest of White Wolf (lat. 37°49'05" N, long. 119°42'45" W; near NW cor. sec. 31, T 1 S, R 21 E). Named on Hetch Hetchy Reservoir (1956) 15' quadrangle. Browning (1986, p. 203) associated the name with John Connell, a sheepman who had the nickname "Smoky Jack."

Smoky Mountain [MARIPOSA]: *peak,* 3 miles east of the settlement of Catheys Valley in the Guadalupe Mountains (lat. 37°26'25" N, long. 120°02'05" W; sec. 6, T 6 S, R 18 E). Named on Catheys Valley (1962) 7.5' quadrangle.

Smoothwire Camp [TUOLUMNE]: *locality,* 8 miles south-southeast of Liberty Hill (lat. 38°15'45" N, long. 120°02'40" W; near NE cor. sec. 25, T 5 N, R 17 E); the place is along Smoothwire Creek. Named on Big Meadow (1956) 15' quadrangle.

Smoothwire Creek [TUOLUMNE]: *stream,* flows 2.5 miles to Middle Fork Stanislaus River 9 miles south-southeast of Liberty Hill (lat. 38°15'15" N, long. 120°01'40" W; near E line sec. 30, T 5 N, R 18 E). Named on Liberty Hill (1979) 7.5' quadrangle.

Snake Gulch [CALAVERAS]: *canyon,* drained by a stream that flows 2 miles to Stanislaus River 3.5 miles south-southeast of Vallecito (lat. 38°02'15" N, long. 120°27'15" W; sec. 8, T 2 N, R 14 E). Named on Columbia (1948) 7.5' quadrangle.

Snake Meadow [MADERA]: *area,* 7.5 miles southwest of Devils Postpile (lat. 37°33'35" N, long. 119°11'20" W). Named on Devils Postpile (1953) 15' quadrangle.

Snake Ravine [STANISLAUS]: *canyon,* less than 0.5 mile long, 0.5 mile east-southeast of La Grange (lat. 37°39'40" N, long. 120° 27' W; sec. 20, T 3 S, R 14 E). Named on La Grange (1962) 7.5' quadrangle.

Snake Slough [MERCED]: *stream,* flows 3 miles to marsh 11.5 miles west of Le Grand (lat. 37°14'30" N, long. 120°27'35" W; sec. 17, T 8 S, R 14 E). Named on El Nido (1960) and Merced (1961) 7.5' quadrangles.

Snelling [MERCED]: *village,* 15 miles north of Merced on the north side of Merced River (lat. 37°31'10" N, long. 120°26'15" W; on N line sec. 9, T 5 S, R 14 E). Named on Snelling (1962) 7.5' quadrangle. The name is for the Snelling family, who purchased the way station at the place in 1851 and operated it under the name "Snelling's Hotel" (Hoover, Rensch, and Rensch, p. 205). Postal authorities established Snelling's Ranch post office in 1853, discontinued it for a time in 1861, and changed the name to Snelling in 1870 (Salley, p. 207).

Snelling's Ranch: see **Snelling** [MERCED].

Snow Canyon [MADERA]: *canyon,* 2.5 miles long, 1.5 miles southwest of Devils Postpile along King Creek (lat. 37°36'35" N, long. 119°06'45" W). Named on Devils Postpile (1953) 15' quadrangle.

Snow Creek [CALAVERAS-STANISLAUS]: *stream,* heads in Calaveras County and flows 5 miles to Hoods Creek 12 miles north-northeast of Oakdale in Stanislaus County (lat. 37°56'50" N, long. 120°47'30" W; sec. 8, T 1 N, R 11 E). Named on Bachelor Valley (1968) 7.5' quadrangle.

Snow Creek [MARIPOSA]:

(1) *stream,* flows 7.25 miles to Tenaya Creek 3 miles east-northeast of Yosemite Village (lat. 37°45'35" N, long. 119°32' W). Named on Hetch Hetchy Reservoir (1956) and Tuolumne Meadows (1956) 15' quadrangles. United States Board on Geographic Names (1933a, p. 703) rejected the names "Glacier Brook," "Hoffman Creek," and "Hoffmann Creek" for the stream.

(2) *stream,* flows 8 miles to join Jones Creek and form West Fork Chowchilla River 5 miles east of Mariposa (lat. 37°28'55" N, long. 119°52'25" W; sec. 22, T 5 S, R 19 E). Named on Buckingham Mountain (1947) and Stumpfield Mountain (1947) 7.5' quadrangles.

Snow Creek: see **Darrah** [MARIPOSA].

Snow Creek Falls [MARIPOSA]: *waterfall,* 3 miles east-northeast of Yosemite Village on Snow Creek (1) (lat. 37°46' N, long. 119° 32' W). Named on Hetch Hetchy Reservoir (1956) 15' quadrangle.

Snow Flat [MARIPOSA]: *area,* 5 miles west-southwest of Cathedral Peak (lat. 37°50' N, long. 119°29'30" W; near W line sec. 19, T 1 S, R 23 E); the area is along Snow Creek (1). Named on Tuolumne Meadows (1956) 15' quadrangle. The place was called Snow's Flat in 1893 (Browning, 1988, p. 133).

Snow Lake [TUOLUMNE]: *lake,* 2300 feet long, 4.5 miles west-northwest of Tower Peak (lat. 38°10'20" N, long. 119°37'30" W). Named on Tower Peak (1956) 15' quadrangle.

Snow Peak [TUOLUMNE]: *peak,* 2.25 miles south-southwest of Tower Peak (lat. 38°06'55" N, long. 119°34'15" W). Altitude 10,950 feet. Named on Tower Peak (1956) 15' quadrangle.

Snowshoe Lake [CALAVERAS]: *lake,* 600 feet long, 6 miles east-southeast of Blue Mountain (lat. 38°17'35" N, long. 120°16'25" W; near W line sec. 13, T 5 N, R 15 E). Named on Dorrington (1979) 7.5' quadrangle.

Snowy Mountains: see "Regional setting."

Snowy Range: see "Regional setting."

Snugville: see **Lodi** [SAN JOAQUIN].

Snyder Camp [TUOLUMNE]: *locality,* 2 miles east of Liberty Hill in Randalls Meadow (lat. 38°22'20" N, long. 120°03'40" W; sec. 13, T 6 N, R 17 E). Named on Liberty Hill (1979) 7.5' quadrangle.

Snyder Gulch [MARIPOSA]: *canyon,* drained by a stream that flows nearly 3 miles to Devil Gulch 5.5 miles south-southwest of El Portal (lat. 37°36'20" N, long. 119°49'20" W); the canyon is north of Snyder Ridge. Named on Buckingham Mountain (1947) 7.5' quadrangle. Browning (1988, p. 134) associated the name with John W. Snyder, a homesteader in the neighborhood in 1885.

Snyder Ridge [MARIPOSA]: *ridge,* south-trending, 2 miles long, 7 miles south-southwest of El Portal (lat. 37°34'50" N, long. 119°50'15" W); the ridge is south of Snyder Gulch. Named on Buckingham Mountain (1947) 7.5' quadrangle.

Soap Creek [TUOLUMNE]: *stream,* flows 7.25 miles to Griswold Creek 7.5 miles northeast of Stanislaus (lat. 38°12'25" N, long. 120°15'50" W; near NE cor. sec. 13, T 4 N, R 15 E). Named on Crandall Peak (1979) and Stanislaus (1948) 7.5' quadrangles.

Soap Creek Pass [TUOLUMNE]: *pass,* 4 miles north of Crandall Peak (lat. 38°13' N, long. 120°08'45" W; sec. 7, T 4 N, R 17 E); the pass is near the head of Soap Creek. Named on Crandall Peak (1979) 7.5' quadrangle.

Soap Creek Pass Camp: see **Camp Pendola** [TUOLUMNE].

Soapstone Hill [CALAVERAS]: *peak,* 10.5 miles east-southeast of San Andreas (lat. 38°08'15" N, long. 120°30'05" W; near W line sec. 1, T 3 N, R 13 E). Altitude 1625 feet. Named on Calaveritas (1962) 7.5' quadrangle.

Soapstone Ridge [MARIPOSA]: *ridge,* south-trending, 2 miles long, 8.5

miles west-northwest of El Portal (lat. 37°42' N, long. 119°56'15" W). Named on Kinsley (1947) 7.5' quadrangle.

Soda Canyon [TUOLUMNE]: *canyon,* drained by a stream that flows 2.5 miles to Kennedy Creek 4.5 miles south-southwest of Sonora Pass (lat. 38°16'15" N, long. 119°40'45" W; near E line sec. 20, T 5 N, R 21 E); Soda Spring is in the canyon. Named on Sonora Pass (1956) and Tower Peak (1956) 15' quadrangles.

Soda Gulch [MERCED]: *canyon,* drained by a stream that flows nearly 3 miles to San Luis Creek 5.25 miles southeast of Pacheco Pass (lat. 37°00'05" N, long. 121°09'05" W; sec. 1, T 11 S, R 7 E). Named on Mariposa Peak (1969) and Pacheco Pass (1955) 7.5' quadrangles.

Soda Spring [MADERA]: *spring,* 8 miles southwest of Devils Postpile near Sheep Crossing (lat. 37°33'15" N, long. 119°12'30" W). Named on Mount Lyell (1901) 30' quadrangle.

Soda Spring [TUOLUMNE]: *spring,* 5.5 miles south-southwest of Sonora Pass (lat. 38°15'15" N, long. 119°40'25" W; sec. 28, T 5 N, R 21 E); the spring is in Soda Canyon. Named on Sonora Pass (1979) 7.5' quadrangle.

Soda Spring Dome: see **Fairview Dome** [TUOLUMNE].

Soda Spring Flat: see **Pumice Flat** [MADERA].

Soda Springs [TUOLUMNE]: *spring,* 6.25 miles west-southwest of Tioga Pass in Tuolumne Meadows (lat. 37°52'45" N, long. 119°21'55" W; sec. 5, T 1 S, R 24 E). Named on Tuolumne Meadows (1956) 15' quadrangle. Waring (p. 237-238) called the feature Lambert Soda Springs, and noted that the water could be used to make biscuits without baking soda, the carbon dioxide in the water serving to lighten the dough.

Soda Springs Butte: see **Fairview Dome** [TUOLUMNE].

Soda Springs Campground [MADERA]: *locality,* 3 miles northeast of Shuteye Peak (lat. 37°22'50" N, long. 119°23'20" W; sec. 30, T 6 S, R 24 E). Named on Shuteye Peak (1953) 15' quadrangle.

Soldier Creek [TUOLUMNE]: *stream,* flows 1.5 miles to South Fork Tuolumne River 6.25 miles southwest of Mather (lat. 37°48'40" N, long. 119°55'40" W; sec. 31, T 1 S, R 19 E). Named on Lake Eleanor (1956) 15' quadrangle.

Soldier Gulch [TUOLUMNE]: *canyon,* drained by a stream that flows 1 mile to New Melones Lake 6.5 miles west-northwest of Sonora (lat. 38°00' N, long. 120°29'50" W; sec. 25, T 2 N, R 13 E). Named on Sonora (1948) 7.5' quadrangle. A group of soldiers discovered gold in the canyon in 1848 (Stoddart, p. 64).

Soldier Lake [TUOLUMNE]: *lake,* 1300 feet long, 3.5 miles south-southeast of Matterhorn Peak (lat. 38°02'50" N, long. 119°21'20" W). Named on Matterhorn Peak (1956) 15' quadrangle.

Soldier Meadow [MADERA]: *area,* 10 miles southeast of Merced Peak (lat. 37°32'35" N, long. 119°15' W). Named on Devils Postpile (1953) and Merced Peak (1953) 15' quadrangles. The place first was called Little Jackass Meadow; the present name is from use of the area as a patrol camp when the army administered Yosemite National Park (Browning, 1986, p. 204).

Solinsky Camp [CALAVERAS]: *locality,* 4 miles northeast of Blue Mountain (lat. 38°23' N, long. 120°18'50" W; sec. 10, T 6 N, R 15 E); the place is 0.5 mile west-southwest of Solinsky Crossing. Named on Blue Mountain (1956) 15' quadrangle.

Solinsky Crossing [CALAVERAS]: *locality,* 7 miles south-southwest of Garnet Hill along Middle Fork Mokelumne River (lat. 38°23'20" N, long. 120°18'35" W; sec. 10, T 6 N, R 15 E). Named on Garnet Hill (1979) 7.5' quadrangle.

Solomon Gulch [MARIPOSA]: *canyon,* drained by a stream that flows 6 miles to Lake McClure 2.5 miles north-northeast of the village of Bear Valley (lat. 37°36'20" N, long. 120°06'20" W; sec. 9, T 4 S, R 17 E). Named on Bear Valley (1947, photorevised 1973) and Buckhorn Peak (1947) 7.5' quadrangles.

Solomons Hole: see **Moaning Caves** [CALAVERAS].

Solsbury: see **Soulsbyville** [TUOLUMNE].

Solsby: see **Soulsbyville** [TUOLUMNE].

Solyo [STANISLAUS]: *locality,* 12 miles northwest of Patterson along Southern Pacific Railroad (lat. 37°36'35" N, long. 121°15'50" W; on W line sec. 12, T 4 S, R 6 E). Named on Solyo (1953) 7.5' quadrangle. Called Romain on Romain (1916) 7.5' quadrangle. The name "Solyo" is from El Solyo ranch, started in 1918 by Roy Melville Pike—it is a corruption of *sollo,* which means "pike" (the fish) in Spanish (Hanna, p. 311).

Somerville: see **Summersville**, under **Soulsbyville** [TUOLUMNE].

Sonny Meadow [MARIPOSA]: *area,* 4 miles west-southwest of Fish Camp (lat. 37°27' N, long. 119°42' W). Named on Bass Lake (1953) 15' quadrangle. Called Sonny Meadows on Mariposa (1912) 30' quadrangle; United States Board on Geographic Names (1947, p. 2) once approved this plural form of the name, while rejecting the names "Bruener Meadow," "Groves Meadow," "Hogan Meadow," and "Hogan's Meadow" for the feature.

Sonora [TUOLUMNE]: *town,* at the confluence of Woods Creek and Sonora Creek (lat. 37°59' N, long. 120°22'50" W; in and near sec. 36, T 2 N, R 14 E). Named on Sonora (1948) 7.5' quadrangle. Called Sonoran Camp on Derby's (1849) map. Postal authorities established Sonora post office in 1851 (Frickstad, p. 217), and the town incorporated the same year. The place started with a preponderance of miners from Sonora in Mexico, and was called Sonora Camp in the middle of 1848 (Bancroft, 1888, p. 469). When the town was made the seat of government of newly formed Tuolumne County, the state legislature gave the name "Stewart" to the community, probably to honor Malcolm M. Stewart, assemblyman from San Joaquin district, but soon restored the name "Sonora" to the place (DeFerrari *in* Stoddart, p. 86). Gudde (1975, p. 312) listed a place called Scraperville that was located about 2 miles west of Sonora on the east side of Table Mountain.

Sonora Camp: see **Sonora** [TUOLUMNE].

Sonora Creek [TUOLUMNE]: *stream,* flows 4 miles to Woods Creek in Sonora (lat. 37°58'45" N, long. 120°23'15" W; sec. 36, T 2 N, R 14 E). Named on Columbia SE (1948), Sonora (1948), and Standard (1948) 7.5' quadrangles. The canyon of the stream was called Bassett's Gulch for Charles Bassett, who prospected there early in 1849 (Stoddart, p. 82- 83).

Sonoran Camp: see **Sonora** [TUOLUMNE].

Sonora Pass [TUOLUMNE]: *pass,* 47 miles east-northeast of Sonora, where Tuolumne County, Mono County, and Alpine County meet (lat. 38°19'40" N, long. 119°38'10" W). Named on Sonora Pass (1979) 7.5' quadrangle. The name is from the town of Sonora—the wagon road from Sonora to mining camps east of the crest of the Sierra Nevada went through the pass (Hanna, p. 311).

Soquel Campground [MADERA]: *locality,* 4.5 miles northeast of Yosemite Forks along North Fork Willow Creek (2) (lat. 37°24'15" N, long. 119°33'40" W; near SE cor. sec. 16, T 6 S, R 22 E). Named on Bass Lake (1953) 15' quadrangle.

Soquel Meadow [MADERA]: *area,* 6 miles northeast of Yosemite Forks (lat. 37°25'40" N, long. 119°33'15" W; in and near sec. 10, T 6 S, R 22 E). Named on Bass Lake (1953) 15' quadrangle. Smith Comstock moved his sawmill to the place from Soquel in Santa Cruz County in 1881, and applied the name of the old site to the new one (Browning, 1986, p. 205).

Sotcher Lake [MADERA]: *lake,* 1600 feet long, 0.5 mile east of Devils Postpile (lat. 37°37'35" N, long. 119°04'25" W). Named on Devils Postpile (1953) 15' quadrangle. Called Satcher Lake on Mount Lyell (1901) 30' quadrangle. The name commemorates "Red" Sotcher (or Satcher), for whom Reds Meadows was named; the feature also is known as Pond Lily Lake for the mass of yellow lilies that cover its surface near the outlet (Smith, p. 14).

Soulsbys Flat: see **Soulsbyville** [TUOLUMNE].

Soulsbyville [TUOLUMNE]: *village,* 6.5 miles east of Sonora (lat. 37°59'05" N, long. 120°15'45" W; near W line sec. 31, T 2 N, R 16 E). Named on Standard (1948) 7.5' quadrangle. Postal authorities established Soulsbyville post office in 1877 (Frickstad, p. 217). The name commemorates Benjamin Soulsby and his sons, who found a rich gold mine at the place in 1858 (Gudde, 1969, p. 317). The village also was known as Solsby, Solsbury, and Soulsbys Flat (Gudde, 1975, p. 328). A place called Summersville was situated about 2.5 miles southeast of Soulsbyville; the name, which also had the form "Somerville," was from Franklin Summers and Elizabeth Summers, who settled near the site in 1854 (Gudde, 1975, p. 341). Postal authorities established Carters post office at Summersville in 1888 and discontinued it in 1908; the name was for Charles H. Carter, first postmaster (Salley, p. 39). California Mining Bureau's (1917a) map shows a place called Nashton located about 7 miles east of Soulsbyville between North Fork and Middle Fork Tuolumne River. Postal authorities established Nashton post office in 1900 and discontinued it in 1904; the name was for John F. Nash, first postmaster (Salley, p. 150). Gudde (1975, p. 249) listed a place called Ohio Diggings that was located 3 miles north of Soulsbyville. California Division of Highways' (1934) map shows Pooley's Ranch located 1.5 miles north-northwest of Soulsbyville (at E line sec. 25, T 2 N, R 15 E).

Source Point [MADERA]: *peak,* 9 miles south-southeast of Shuteye Peak (lat. 37°13'30" N, long. 119°23'20" W; near N line sec. 19, T 8 S, R 24 E). Altitude 6182 feet. Named on Shaver Lake (1953) 15' quadrangle.

Sourgrass Lake [TUOLUMNE]: *intermittent lake,* 250 feet long, 5 miles west of Strawberry (lat. 38°12'30" N, long. 120°06'10" W); the feature is 0.5 mile east-northeast of Sourgrass Meadow. Named on Strawberry (1979) 7.5' quadrangle.

Sourgrass Meadow [TUOLUMNE]: *area,* 5.5 miles west of Strawberry (lat. 38°12'15" N, long. 120°06'45" W; sec. 16, T 4 N, R 17 E); the place is 0.5 mile west-southwest of Sourgrass Lake. Named on Strawberry (1979) 7.5' quadrangle.

South Canyon Creek: see **Illilouette Creek** [MADERA-MARIPOSA].

South Dome: see **Sentinel Dome** [MARIPOSA].

South Dos Palos [MERCED]: *town,* 2 miles southwest of Dos Palos (lat. 36°57'50" N, long. 120°39'05" W; on W line sec. 22, T 11 S, R 12 E). Named on Dos Palos (1956) 7.5' quadrangle, which has the notation "Dos Palos Station" after the name. Postal authorities established South Dos Palos post office in 1906, when they moved Dos Palos post office there (Salley, p. 208).

South Fork [MADERA]: *village,* 9 miles south-southeast of Shuteye Peak along South Fork Willow Creek (2) (lat. 37°14' N, long. 119° 29'30" W;

sec. 18, T 8 S, R 23 E). Named on Shaver Lake (1953) 15' quadrangle.

South Fork [MARIPOSA]: *locality,* 6 miles west-southwest of El Portal (lat. 37°39'15" N, long. 119°53'10" W); the place is at the mouth of South Fork Merced River. Named on Kinsley (1947) 7.5' quadrangle.

South Fork Bluffs [MADERA]: *relief feature,* 6 miles south-southwest of Shuteye Peak on the east side of South Fork Willow Creek (2) (lat. 37°16'30" N, long. 119°29' W). Named on Shuteye Peak (1953) 15' quadrangle.

South Gulch [CALAVERAS-STANISLAUS]: *canyon,* mainly in Calaveras County, but a small part is in Stanislaus County; drained by a stream that flows 9 miles to Calaveras River 9.5 miles south-southwest of Valley Springs (lat. 38°04'10" N, long. 120°54'15" W; sec. 32, T 3 N, R 10 E). Named on Jenny Lind (1962) and Valley Springs SW (1962) 7.5' quadrangles.

South Hill [CALAVERAS]: *peak,* 1.25 miles southeast of Jenny Lind (lat. 38°04'55" N, long. 120°51'05" W; near W line sec. 26, T 3 N, R 10 E); the peak is between South Gulch and Calaveras River. Named on Jenny Lind (1962) 7.5' quadrangle.

South Mokelumne River: see **Mokelumne River** [CALAVERAS-SAN JOAQUIN].

South Paddy Creek [SAN JOAQUIN]: *stream,* flows 2.5 miles to Paddy Creek; 4.25 miles north-northeast of Waterloo (lat. 38°05'40" N, long. 121°10'05" W). Named on Waterloo (1968) 7.5' quadrangle.

South Ridge [SAN JOAQUIN]: *ridge,* east-trending, 3.25 miles long, 12.5 miles south of Tracy (lat. 37°33'55" N, long. 121°28'15" W); the ridge is parallel to and south of North Ridge. Named on Lone Tree Creek (1955) 7.5' quadrangle.

South San Joaquin Irrigation Reservoir: see **Woodward Reservoir** [STANISLAUS].

South Slough [MERCED]:

(1) *stream,* heads near Merced and flows 13 miles to end 14 miles north-northwest of Dos Palos Y (lat. 37°14'35" N, long. 120°42'20" W; near W line sec. 18, T 8 S, R 12 E). Named on Atwater (1961) and Santa Rita Park (1962) 15' quadrangles.

(2) *stream,* 7 miles west of Le Grand (lat. 37°13'35" N, long. 120° 23'30" W). Named on Chowchilla (1960) 15' quadrangle.

South Wawona [MARIPOSA]: *settlement,* 1 mile east-northeast of Wawona (lat. 37°32'25" N, long. 119°38'20" W; sec. 35, T 4 S, R 21 E); the place is 0.5 mile south of North Wawona. Named on Yosemite (1956) 15' quadrangle.

Spangle Gold Creek [MADERA]: *stream,* flows 3.5 miles to Fresno River 5.5 miles east-northeast of Knowles (lat. 37°14'15" N, long. 119°46'25" W; sec. 15, T 8 S, R 20 E). Named on Horsecamp Mountain (1947) and Knowles (1962) 7.5' quadrangles. Crawford (1896, p. 207) referred to Spangle Gold Gulch.

Spangle Gold Gulch: see **Spangle Gold Creek** [MADERA].

Spanish Bar: see **Big Bar** [CALAVERAS]; **La Grange** [STANISLAUS].

Spanish Camp: see **Martinez** [TUOLUMNE].

Spanish Gulch [CALAVERAS]: *canyon,* drained by a stream that flows 1.25 miles to Mokelumne River 2 miles north of Paloma (lat. 38°17'25" N, long. 120°46' W; sec. 16, T 5 N, R 11 E). Named on Jackson (1962) 7.5' quadrangle.

Spark's Ferry: see **La Grange** [STANISLAUS].

Specimen Gulch [MARIPOSA]: *canyon,* drained by a stream that flows 0.5 mile to Agua Fria Creek 5.5 miles northeast of Catheys Valley (2) (lat. 37°29'15" N, long. 120°21'05" W). Named on Catheys Valley (1962) 7.5' quadrangle.

Specimen Springs [MADERA]: *spring,* 6.25 miles north-northeast of Raymond (lat. 37°18'25" N, long. 119°52'05" W; sec. 23, T 7 S, R 19 E). Named on Horsecamp Mountain (1947) 7.5' quadrangle.

Speckerman Mountain [MADERA]: *peak,* 6.5 miles north-northeast of Yosemite Forks (lat. 37°27'15" N, long. 119°34'45" W; near E line sec. 32, T 5 S, R 22 E). Altitude 7137 feet. Named on Bass Lake (1953) 15' quadrangle. The name, given in the 1850's, commemorates a settler who lived near the feature (Gudde, 1949, p. 340).

Sperry Springs [STANISLAUS]: *spring,* 16 miles west of Patterson in Hospital Canyon (lat. 37°31'05" N, long. 121°24'40" W; near W line sec. 10, T 5 S, R 5 E). Named on Lone Tree Creek (1955) 7.5' quadrangle.

Spicer Creek [MERCED]: *stream,* flows 4.5 miles to San Luis Creek 3.25 miles south of Pacheco Pass (lat. 37°01'05" N, long. 121°13'10" W; sec. 32, T 10 S, R 7 E). Named on Mariposa Peak (1969) and Pacheco Pass (1955) 7.5' quadrangles.

Spicer Meadow Reservoir [TUOLUMNE]: *lake,* behind a dam on Highland Creek 10 miles west-northwest of Dardanelle (lat. 38°23'35" N, long. 119°59'45" W). Named on Spicer Meadow Reservoir (1979) 7.5' quadrangle.

Spikes Peak [MERCED]: *peak,* 2 miles south-southwest of Pacheco Pass (lat. 37°02'05" N, long. 121°13'10" W). Altitude 1927 feet. Named on Pacheco Pass (1955) 7.5' quadrangle.

Spiller Creek [TUOLUMNE]: *stream,* flows 6.5 miles to Return Creek 6.5 miles south of Matterhorn Peak (lat. 38°00' N, long. 119° 23'05" W). Named on Matterhorn Peak (1956) 15' quadrangle. Members of the Wheeler survey named the stream for J. Calvert Spiller, a topographer (United States Board on Geographic Names, 1934, p. 23). A Wheeler survey map has the name "Spiller's Cañon," and a map of the 1890's has the designation "Spiller or Randall Canon" (Browning, 1988, p. 135).

Spiller Lake [TUOLUMNE]: *lake,* 1700 feet long, 3 miles south of Matterhorn Peak (lat. 38°02'50" N, long. 119°22'10" W); the lake is at the head of a tributary to Spiller Creek. Named on Matterhorn Peak (1956) 15' quadrangle.

Spiller's Cañon: see **Spiller Creek** [TUOLUMNE].

Spillway Lake [TUOLUMNE]: *lake,* 1700 feet long, 5 miles south-southeast of Tioga Pass along Parker Pass Creek (lat. 37°50'30" N, long. 119°13'55" W). Named on Mono Craters (1953) 15' quadrangle.

Spinecup Ridge [MADERA]: *ridge,* southwest-trending, 1.5 miles long, 1.5 miles east-northeast of Raymond (lat. 37°13'30" N, long. 119°53' W). Named on Raymond (1962) 7.5' quadrangle.

Spirito: see **Camp Spirito**, under **Bummerville** [CALAVERAS].

Split Pinnacle [MARIPOSA]: *relief feature,* 2.25 miles west-southwest of Yosemite Village on the north side of Yosemite Valley (lat. 37°44'10" N, long. 119°37'15" W). Named on Yosemite (1956) 15' quadrangle. Members of the Sierra Club began using the name in the 1930's (Browning, 1986, p. 206).

Split Rock [MARIPOSA]: *peak,* 9.5 miles south of Mariposa (lat. 37° 21' N, long. 119°55'55" W; sec. 6, T 7 S, R 19 E). Named on Ben Hur (1947) 7.5' quadrangle.

Split Rock: see **Split Rock Ferry** [MARIPOSA].

Split Rock Creek [MARIPOSA]: *stream,* flows 5.5 miles to Chowchilla River 14 miles south of Mariposa at Mariposa-Madera County line (lat. 37°17' N, long. 119°55'35" W; near E line sec. 31, T 7 S, R 19 E). Named on Ben Hur (1947) 7.5' quadrangle.

Split Rock Ferry [MARIPOSA]: *locality,* 4.5 miles south-southeast of Coulterville along Merced River (lat. 37°38'40" N, long. 120°10'30" W). The site of the abandoned ferry is named on Coulterville (1947) 15' quadrangle. Split Rock post office, named for the ferry, was established in 1855 and discontinued in 1858 (Salley, p. 210).

Sport Hill: see **Mokelumne Hill** [CALAVERAS].

Spotted Fawn Lake [TUOLUMNE]: *lake,* 3000 feet long, 14 miles southeast of Pinecrest (lat. 38°04'20" N, long. 119°46'35" W). Named on Pinecrest (1956) 15' quadrangle.

Spotted Lakes [MADERA]: *lakes,* largest 1400 feet long, nearly 6 miles south of Merced Peak (lat. 37°33'05" N, long. 119°24' W). Named on Merced Peak (1953) 15' quadrangle.

Sprague [CALAVERAS]: *locality,* nearly 3 miles east-northeast of Blue Mountain (lat. 38°21'35" N, long. 120°19'20" W). Named on Big Trees (1891) 30' quadrangle.

Spring Cove Campground [MADERA]: *locality,* 6.5 miles southeast of Yosemite Forks on the southwest side of Bass Lake (1) (lat. 37° 18' N, long. 119°32'30" W; near S line sec. 23, T 7 S, R 22 E). Named on Bass Lake (1953) 15' quadrangle.

Spring Creek [MARIPOSA]: *stream,* flows 2 miles to Mariposa Creek 2.5 miles south-southeast of Mariposa (lat. 37°27'05" N, long. 119°56'45" W). Named on Mariposa (1947) 7.5' quadrangle. The canyon of the stream is called Spring Gulch on Mariposa (1912) 30' quadrangle, and it is called Australia Gulch on Laizure's (1928) map.

Spring Creek [TUOLUMNE]: *stream,* flows 4 miles to West Fork Cherry Creek 11 miles east of Pinecrest (lat. 38°11' N, long. 119° 47'25" W). Named on Pinecrest (1956) and Tower Peak (1956) 15' quadrangles.

Springfield [TUOLUMNE]: *locality,* 1 mile south-southwest of Columbia (lat. 38°01'20" N, long. 120°24'45" W; near SW cor. sec. 14, T 2 N, R 14 E). Named on Columbia (1948) 7.5' quadrangle. Postal authorities established Springfield post office in 1857 and discontinued it in 1868 (Frickstad, p. 217). The name is from large springs at the place (Hanna, p. 314). Stoddart (p. 127) noted the early names "Pietra Blanca" and "Tim's Springs" for the locality; Timothy Eastman filed a preemption claim on the site in 1850 (DeFerrari *in* Stoddart, p. 130).

Spring Gap [TUOLUMNE]: *locality,* 5.5 miles west-southwest of Strawberry (lat. 38°10'05" N, long. 120°06'05" W; near SW cor. sec. 27, T 4 N, R 17 E). Named on Strawberry (1979) 7.5' quadrangle.

Spring Gulch [CALAVERAS]:

(1) *canyon,* 1.25 miles long, 1 mile south-southeast of Mokelumne Hill (lat. 38°17'20" N, long. 120°41'45" W; in and near sec. 18, T 5 N, R 12 E). Named on Mokelumne Hill (1948) 7.5' quadrangle.

(2) *canyon,* drained by a stream that flows 2.25 miles to Jesus Maria Creek 7 miles southwest of Rail Road Flat (lat. 38°15'35" N, long. 120°35'10" W; sec. 30, T 5 N, R 13 E). Named on Rail Road Flat (1948) 7.5' quadrangle.

(3) *canyon,* drained by a stream that flows nearly 2 miles to Chili Gulch 2.5 miles northwest of San Andreas (lat. 38°13'35" N, long. 120°42'30" W). Named on San Andreas (1962) 7.5' quadrangle. Called Old Woman Gulch on San Andreas (1947) 15' quadrangle.

Spring Gulch [MARIPOSA]: *canyon,* drained by a stream that flows 1 mile to Willow Creek 2.5 miles south of Penon Blanco Peak (lat. 37°42' N, long. 120°15'45" W; sec. 1, T 3 S, R 15 E). Named on Penon Blanco Peak (1962) 7.5' quadrangle.

Spring Gulch [STANISLAUS]: *canyon,* drained by a stream that flows 2.5 miles to Rocky Fork Canyon 6 miles north of Copper Mountain (lat. 37°30'15" N, long. 121°19'15" W; near W line sec. 16, T 5 S, R 6 E). Named on Copper Mountain (1956) 7.5' quadrangle.

Spring Gulch: see **Alabama Gulch**, under **Alabama Hill** [CALAVERAS]; **Spring Creek** [MARIPOSA].

Spring Meadow [TUOLUMNE]: *area,* 12 miles east of Pinecrest (lat. 38°11'15" N, long. 119°46'35" W); the place is along Spring Creek. Named on Pinecrest (1956) 15' quadrangle.

Spring Valley [CALAVERAS]: *valley,* 2.25 miles east-northeast of Valley Springs (lat. 38°12'25" N, long. 120°47'25" W; on S line sec. 8, T 4 N, R 11 E). Named on Valley Springs (1962) 7.5' quadrangle.

Spring Valley: see **Valley Springs** [CALAVERAS].

Spring Valley Creek [CALAVERAS]: *stream,* flows 4.5 miles to Cosgrove Creek less than 1 mile south-southeast of Valley Springs (lat. 38°11' N, long. 120°49'25" W; sec. 24, T 4 N, R 10 E); the stream goes through Spring Valley. Named on Valley Springs (1962) 7.5' quadrangle.

Spring Valley House: see **Wheats** [CALAVERAS].

Spruce Gulch [CALAVERAS]: *canyon,* drained by a stream that flows nearly 4 miles to South Fork Mokelumne River 1.25 miles north-northeast of Rail Road Flat (lat. 38°21'35" N, long. 120°30'10" W; near W line sec. 24, T 6 N, R 13 E). Named on Fort Mountain (1979) and Rail Road Flat (1948) 7.5' quadrangles.

Spud Island [SAN JOAQUIN]: *island,* 4400 feet long, 7.5 miles south-southeast of Terminous between Haypress Reach, Hog Island Cut, and Twentyone Mile Cut (lat. 38°00'25" N, long. 121° 27'25" W). Named on Terminous (1978) 7.5' quadrangle.

Squabbletown [TUOLUMNE]: *locality,* 1.5 miles south-southeast of Columbia along Woods Creek (lat. 38°00'55" N, long. 120°23'05" W; sec. 24, T 2 N, R 14 E). Named on Columbia (1948) 7.5' quadrangle. According to Jackson (p. 326), the place was noted for fights.

Squaw Dome [MADERA]: *peak,* about 13 miles northeast of Shuteye Peak (lat. 37°28'55" N, long. 119°15'50" W; sec. 20, T 5 S, R 25 E). Altitude 7818 feet. Named on Shuteye Peak (1953) 15' quadrangle. Called Squaw Nipple Peak on California Mining Bureau's (1917b) map.

Squaw Hill [MARIPOSA]: *peak,* 11.5 miles east of Mariposa (lat. 37° 27'45" N, long. 119°45'25" W; near SW cor. sec. 26, T 5 S, R 20 E). Named on Stumpfield Mountain (1947) 7.5' quadrangle.

Squaw Hollow [CALAVERAS]: *area,* 6.25 miles southeast of Blue Mountain (lat. 38°16'10" N, long. 120°17'15" W; sec. 23, T 5 N, R 15 E). Named on Blue Mountain (1956) 15' quadrangle. Big Trees (1891) 30' quadrangle has the name "Squaw Hollow" for a cluster of buildings at or near the place.

Squaw Hollow Campground [CALAVERAS]: *locality,* 6.25 miles southeast of Blue Mountain (lat. 38°16'25" N, long. 120°17'20" W; sec. 23, T 5 N, R 15 E); the place is at or near Squaw Hollow. Named on Dorrington (1979) 7.5' quadrangle.

Squaw Nipple Peak: see **Squaw Dome** [MADERA].

Squirrel Creek [MARIPOSA]: *stream,* flows 1.5 miles to South Fork Merced River 2 miles west-northwest of Wawona (lat. 37°33' N, long. 119°41'05" W; near NE cor. sec. 32, T 4 S, R 21 E). Named on Yosemite (1956) 15' quadrangle.

Squirrel Gulch [CALAVERAS]: *canyon,* drained by a stream that flows less than 0.5 mile to Coyote Creek 5 miles south-southwest of Vallecito (lat. 38°00'55" N, long. 120°29'35" W; sec. 24, T 2 N, R 13 E). Named on Columbia (1948) 7.5' quadrangle.

Stack Spring [MERCED]: *spring,* 3.25 miles south-southeast of Pacheco Pass (lat. 37°01'10" N, long. 121°10'55" W; sec. 34, T 10 S, R 7 E). Named on Pacheco Pass (1955) 7.5' quadrangle.

Stage [TUOLUMNE]: *locality,* 10 miles northeast of Columbia near Knight Creek (lat. 38°08' N, long. 120°16'20" W). Named on Big Trees (1891) 30' quadrangle.

Staircase Falls [MARIPOSA]: *waterfall,* 1.25 miles southeast of Yosemite Village on the south side of Yosemite Valley (lat. 37°44'10" N, long. 119°34'30" W). Named on Yosemite (1956) 15' quadrangle.

Stairway Creek [MADERA]: *stream,* flows 4.5 miles to Middle Fork San Joaquin River 6.5 miles south-southwest of Devils Postpile (lat. 37°32'25" N, long. 119°08'15" W); the stream heads near Granite Stairway. Named on Devils Postpile (1953) 15' quadrangle.

Stairway Meadow [MADERA]: *area,* 3.25 miles southwest of Devils Postpile (lat. 37°35'50" N, long. 119°07'45" W); the place is northwest of Granite Stairway. Named on Devils Postpile (1953) 15' quadrangle.

Stakes: see **Mount Stakes** [STANISLAUS].

Standard [TUOLUMNE]: *village,* 4 miles east-southeast of Sonora (lat. 38°58' N, long. 120°18'40" W; sec. 3, T 1 N, R 15 E). Named on Standard (1948) 7.5' quadrangle. Postal authorities established Standard post office in 1910; Standard Lumber Company had a lumber mill, box factory, and homes for employees at the place (Salley, p. 211).

Standard Mill [MADERA]: *locality,* 4 miles northeast of O'Neals (lat. 37°09'55" N, long. 119°38'20" W; near W line sec. 12, T 9 S, R 21 E). Named on Mariposa (1912) 30' quadrangle.

Standiford [STANISLAUS]: *locality,* 3.5 miles north of downtown Modesto along Tidewater Southern Railroad (lat. 37°41'20" N, long. 121°00'10" W; sec. 8, T 3 S, R 9 E). Named on Salida (1953) 7.5' quadrangle.

Stanford Lakes [MADERA]: *lakes,* largest 1100 feet long, nearly 6 miles south-southeast of Merced Peak (lat. 37°33'15" N, long. 119° 21'40" W). Named on Merced Peak (1953) 15' quadrangle. Billy Brown, a local packer, applied the misspelled name about 1920; he intended to honor the Kenneth J. Staniford family of Fresno (Browning, 1986, p. 207).

Stanford Point [MARIPOSA]: *promontory,* 5.25 miles southwest of Yosemite Village on the south side of Yosemite Valley (lat. 37°42'25" N, long. 119°40' W). Named on Yosemite (1956) 15' quadrangle. The name commemorates Leland Stanford (Browning, 1988, p. 137).

Stanislaus [TUOLUMNE]: *locality,* 7.25 miles north-northeast of Columbia (lat. 38°08'15" N, long. 120°22'10" W; sec. 6, T 3 N, R 15 E); the place is along Stanislaus River. Named on Stanislaus (1948) 7.5' quadrangle. Postal authorities established Stanislaus post office in 1911 and discontinued it in 1962 (Salley, p. 211). California Division of Highways' (1934) map shows Petty Reservoir 1 mile northeast of Stanislaus (near NW cor. sec. 5, T 3 N, R 15 E).

Stanislaus: see **Camp Stanislaus**, under **Oakdale** [STANISLAUS]; **Stanislaus River** [CALAVERAS-SAN JOAQUIN-STANISLAUS-TUOLUMNE].

Stanislaus City: see **Ripon** [SAN JOAQUIN]; **Stanislaus River** [CALAVERAS-SAN JOAQUIN-STANISLAUS-TUOLUMNE].

Stanislaus Mesa: see **Table Mountain** [CALAVERAS-TUOLUMNE].

Stanislaus Pit: see **Stewart** [STANISLAUS].

Stanislaus River [CALAVERAS-SAN JOAQUIN-STANISLAUS-TUOLUMNE]: *stream,* formed by the confluence of North Fork and Middle Fork in Tuolumne County, flows 93 miles to San Joaquin River 13 miles west of Modesto in Stanislaus County (lat. 37°39'50" N, long. 121°14'25" W). Named on Sacramento (1957, limited revision 1964) and San Jose (1962) 1°x 2° quadrangles. Ensign Gabriel Moraga and Padre Pedro Muñoz gave the name "Rio de Nuestra Señora de Guadalupe" to the stream in 1806, but in mission records it usually has the designation "Rio del Laquisimes," a name derived from an Indian tribe that lived along its lower reaches (Brotherton, p. 47). In 1829 some Mexicans had a bloody battle near the river with a band of Indians led by a mission-trained Indian called Estanislao, who probably was named for a Polish saint; by 1839 the stream was known as Rio Estanislao, and later it was called Stanislaus River (Gudde, 1949, p. 342). Middle Fork, formed by the confluence of Summit Creek and Kennedy Creek, is 45 miles long; it is named on Crandall Peak (1979), Dardanelle (1979), Donnell Lake (1979), Liberty Hill (1979), Sonora Pass (1979), Stanislaus (1948), and Strawberry (1979) 7.5' quadrangles. United States Board on Geographic Names (1980a, p. 3) rejected the name "Middle Fork Stanislaus River" for Kennedy Creek. North Fork heads in Alpine County and flows for 31 miles along Calaveras-Tuloumne County line; it is named on Boards Crossing (1979), Calaveras Dome (1979), Dorrington (1979), Stanislaus (1948), and Tamarack (1979) 7.5' quadrangles. South Fork is 45 miles long and joins Stanislaus River 3 miles north-northeast of Columbia; it is named on Pinecrest (1956) 15' quadrangle, and on Columbia (1948), Columbia SE (1948), Crandall Peak (1979), Strawberry (1979), and Twain Harte (1979) 7.5' quadrangles. In 1846 a party of Mormons under Samuel Brannan started a community called New Hope on the north side of Stanislaus River about 1.5 miles above the mouth of the stream, but the place was abandoned by the autumn of 1847; another attempt at settlement, called Stanislaus City, was made at the same place during the gold rush (Hoover, Rensch, and Rensch, p. 376). Bancroft's (1864) map shows Stanislaus City situated on the south side of Stanislaus River near the mouth of the stream. Postal authorities established Stanislaus post office at the junction of Stanislaus River and San Joaquin River in 1874 and discontinued it in 1875 (Salley, p. 211). Sirey and Clarke's Ferry operated in 1850 on Stanislaus River about 5 miles above the mouth of the stream (Morgan and Scobie *in* Perkins, p. 315). Hillyer and Burnham Ferry was started on Stanislaus River in 1864 about 4.5 miles in a strait line from the mouth of the stream; C. and Frederick Meineckes took over the ferry in 1866, and a small settlement grew nearby, chiefly on the north side of the river (Brotherton, p. 51-52). Postal authorities established Meinecke post office at the place (NW quarter sec. 2, T 3 S, R 7 E) in 1866 and discontinued it in 1872 (Salley, p. 137). The ferry was called Taylor's Ferry after C.E. Taylor acquired it in 1869 (Brotherton, p. 52). Thompson and West's (1879) map shows Taylor's Ferry along Stanislaus River nearly 4 miles southwest of Ripon.

Stanislaus River Campground [CALAVERAS]: *locality,* 2 miles southeast of Tamarack (lat. 38°25'20" N, long. 120°02'45" W); the place is along North Fork Stanislaus River. Named on Tamarack (1979) 7.5' quadrangle.

Stanton Peak [TUOLUMNE]: *peak,* 2.5 miles south-southeast of Matterhorn Peak (lat. 38°03'30" N, long. 119°21'45" W). Altitude 11,695 feet. Named on Matterhorn Peak (1956) 15' quadrangle.

Staples' Ferry: see **Lockeford** [SAN JOAQUIN].

Staples Ranch: see **Lockeford** [SAN JOAQUIN].

Star [TUOLUMNE]: *locality,* 7.5 miles northeast of Columbia along Rose Creek (lat. 38°06' N, long. 120°17'30" W). Named on Big Trees (1891) 30' quadrangle. Columbia SE (1948) 7.5' quadrangle shows Star mine near the place. Postal authorities established Star post office in 1896 and discontinued it in 1901; the name was from Star mine (Salley, p. 212).

Starkweather Lake [MADERA]: *lake,* 600 feet long, 2.5 miles north of Devils Postpile (lat. 37°39'50" N, long. 119°04'25" W). Named on Devils Postpile (1953) 15' quadrangle. The name commemorates a prospector who had claims above the lake in the 1920's (Smith, p. 13).

Star Lakes [MADERA]: *lakes,* largest 900 feet long, 5.5 miles south-southwest of Buena Vista Peak (lat. 37°30'55" N, long. 119°32'45" W; sec. 10, T 5 S, R 22 E). Named on Yosemite (1956) 15' quadrangle, which shows Star mine southwest of the lakes.

Starr [MARIPOSA]: *locality,* 5.25 miles north-northwest of Hornitos along Yosemite Valley Railroad (lat. 37°34'05" N, long. 120°16'55" W; sec. 23, T 4 S, R 15 E). Named on Merced Falls (1944) 15' quadrangle.

Star Ridge [TUOLUMNE]: *ridge,* southwest- to west-trending, 9 miles long, 6 miles west-northwest of Long Barn between Rose Creek and Eagle Creek (1). Named on Columbia SE (1948), Crandall Peak (1979), and Twain Harte (1979) 7.5' quadrangles. Columbia SE (1948) 7.5' quadrangle shows Star mine near the west end of the ridge.

Starr King: see **Mount Starr King** [MARIPOSA].

Starr King Lake [MARIPOSA]: *lake,* 600 feet long, 4.5 miles east-southeast of Yosemite Village (lat. 37°43'05" N, long. 119°30'30" W); the lake is 1 mile north-northeast of Mount Starr King. Named on Yosemite (1956) 15' quadrangle. United States Board on Geographic Names (1934, p. 24) rejected the name "Helen Lake" for the feature.

Starr King Meadow [MARIPOSA]: *area,* 5.5 miles southeast of Yosemite Village (lat. 37°42' N, long. 119°30'10" W); the place is east of Mount Starr King. Named on Merced Peak (1953) and Yosemite (1956) 15' quadrangles. The name is from Mount Starr King (United States Board on Geographic Names, 1934, p. 24).

Starvation Lake [TUOLUMNE]: *lake,* 350 feet long, 12.5 miles east of Pinecrest (lat. 38°11'10" N, long. 119°45'40" W). Named on Pinecrest (1956) 15' quadrangle.

Starville: see **Oakhurst** [MADERA].

Staten: see **Eagle Tree** [SAN JOAQUIN].

Staten Island [SAN JOAQUIN]: *island,* 8 miles long, 13 miles west of Lodi between North Mokelumne River and South Mokelumne River (lat. 38°10' N, long. 121°31' W). Named on Bouldin Island (1978), Isleton (1978), Terminous (1978), and Thornton (1978) 7.5' quadrangles.

Staytonvile: see **Antimony Peak** [MERCED].

Steele Creek [CALAVERAS]: *stream,* flows nearly 4 miles to South Fork Calaveras River 7 miles west-northwest of Angels Camp (lat. 38°07'25" N, long. 120°39'25" W; sec. 9, T 3 N, R 12 E). Named on Salt Spring Valley (1962) and San Andreas (1962) 7.5' quadrangles.

Steep Gulch: see **Volunteer Gulch** [CALAVERAS].

Stent [TUOLUMNE]: *village,* 5 miles south-southwest of Sonora (lat. 37°55' N, long. 120°24'45" W; near NW cor. sec. 26, T 1 N, R 14 E). Named on Sonora (1948) 7.5' quadrangle. Stent post office, which originally was 2 miles south of present Stent, was established in 1895 and discontinued in 1925; the place also was known as Utterville (Salley, p. 213). William Utter settled at the site in 1850, which then was called Utters Bar (Gudde, 1975, p. 275). The village is on a prominence known as Poverty Hill, and was itself sometimes called by that name (Gudde, 1975, p. 335). DeFerrari (*in* Stoddart, p. 93) noted that a place called Yorktown was situated about 0.5 mile from Poverty Hill.

Stevenson Meadow [MADERA]: *area,* 8.5 miles west-northwest of Devils Postpile (lat. 37°39'35" N, long. 119°13'50" W). Named on Devils Postpile (1953) 15' quadrangle.

Stevinson [MERCED]: *village,* 20 miles west of Merced (lat. 37°19'40" N, long. 120°51' W; on E line sec. 15, T 7 S, R 10 E). Named on Turlock (1962) 15' quadrangle. Postal authorities established Stevinson post office in 1907 (Frickstad, p. 101). The name is for James J. Stevinson, who acquired land along lower reaches of Merced River in 1852 (Gudde, 1949, p. 343).

Stewart [STANISLAUS]: *locality,* 6.5 miles north of downtown Modesto along Tidewater Southern Railroad (lat. 37°44' N, long. 121°00'10" W; sec. 29, T 2 S, R 9 E). Named on Salida (1953) 7.5' quadrangle. California Division of Highways' (1934) map shows a place called Stanislaus Pit located 1 mile north of Stewart along the railroad (sec. 20, T 2 S, R 9 E).

Stewart: see **Sonora** [TUOLUMNE].

Stewarton: see **Stockton** [SAN JOAQUIN].

Stewart Tract [SAN JOAQUIN]: *island,* 6 miles long, 11 miles south-southwest of downtown Stockton between San Joaquin River, Paradise Cut, and Old River (lat. 37°48' N, long. 121°20'30" W). Named on Lathrop (1952) and Union Island (1978) 7.5' quadrangles.

Stockton [SAN JOAQUIN]: *city,* mainly between San Joaquin River and Calaveras River (near lat. 37°57'30" N, long. 121°17'30" W). Named on Lodi South (1968), Stockton East (1952), and Stockton West (1952) 7.5' quadrangles. Charles M. Weber had the town laid out in 1847 on his Campo de los Franceses grant on the south side of Laguna, later known as Stockton Channel; the town was resurveyed in 1849 and named Stockton in honor of Commodore Robert F. Stockton (Hoover, Rensch, and Rensch, p. 369). The place reportedly had the names "Weber's Embarcadero" (Kanton *in* Grimshaw, p. 37), "Tuleburg" for the dense tule swamps around the site (Hoover, Rensch, and Rensch, p. 369), "Weberville" (Gudde, 1949, p. 344), and "New Albany" for the birthplace in New York of Weber's partner, William Gulnac (Bancroft, 1888, p. 465), but Hammond and Morgan (p. 17) concluded that Weber chose the name "Stockton" for his townsite at the beginning. Thompson and West's (1879) map shows a place called Wakefield located on the west side of San Joaquin River 5 miles west of Stockton (sec. 1, T 1 N, R 5 E). Postal authorities established Wakefield post office in 1880, discontinued it in 1881, reestablished it in 1889, and discontinued it in 1891 (Salley, p. 233). Thompson and West's (1879) map also shows a place called Stewarton situated on the south side of San Joaquin River about 3 miles northwest of Wakefield (near E line sec. 28, T 2 N, R 5 E), and a place called St. Catherines located on the south side of the river about 3.5 miles west-southwest of Stockton (sec. 17, T 1 N, R 6 E). California Division of Highways' (1934) map shows a place called Jarn located about 1 mile north of the center of Stockton along Southern Pacific Railroad. Postal authorities established Kerrick's Ranch post office 14 miles southeast of Stockton (sec. 26, T 1 S, R 7 E) in 1858, moved it 1.5 miles north the same year when they changed the name to to Oak Point, and discontinued it in 1859 (Salley, p. 111, 158). They established Eight Mile Corners post office in 1861 and discontinued it in 1863—the name was for the distance north of Stockton to the place (Salley, p. 66). They established Mandeville post office 21 miles west of Stockton in 1876 and discontinued the same year—the name was for James W. Mandeville, assemblyman, state senator, and United States surveyor general (Salley, p. 131). They established Hazelton post office 1.5 miles east of Stockton in 1899 and discontinued in 1900 (Salley, p. 95).

Stockton Channel [SAN JOAQUIN]: *water feature,* extends for 2.5 miles east from a point along San Joaquin River (lat. 37°57'05" N, long. 121°20'05" W) to downtown Stockton. Named on Stockton (1913) 7.5' quadrangle. The feature is called Stockton Slough on Beaumont's (1858) map.

Stockton Creek [MARIPOSA]: *stream,* flows 5.5 miles to Mariposa Creek 1.5 miles southeast of Mariposa (lat. 37°28'10" N, long. 119°56'55" W). Named on Feliciana Mountain (1947) and Mariposa (1947) 7.5' quadrangles. The stream first was called Ave Maria River, and a mining camp at the mouth of the stream was called Ave Maria (Gudde, 1975, p. 23-24). Laizure's (1928) map has the name "Stockton Ridge" for the ridge located between Stockton Creek and Mariposa Creek.

Stockton Deep Water Channel: see **San Joaquin River** [MADERA-MERCED-SAN JOAQUIN-STANISLAUS].

Stockton Hill [CALAVERAS]: *peak,* at the southwest edge of the town of Mokelumne Hill (lat. 38°17'50" N, long. 120°42'30" W; sec. 12, T 5 N, R 11 E). Named on Mokelumne Hill (1948) 7.5' quadrangle.

Stockton Ridge: see **Stockton Creek** [MARIPOSA].

Stockton Slough: see **Mormon Slough** [SAN JOAQUIN]; **Stockton Channel** [SAN JOAQUIN].

Stoddard Spring [TUOLUMNE]: *spring,* nearly 7 miles southwest of Strawberry (lat. 38°07'50" N, long. 120°06' W; sec. 10, T 3 N, R 17 E). Named on Strawberry (1979) 7.5' quadrangle.

Stomar [STANISLAUS]: *locality,* 3.5 miles north-northwest of Newman along Southern Pacific Railroad (lat. 37°21'40" N, long. 121° 02'40" W; near N line sec. 1, T 7 S, R 8 E). Named on Newman (1952) 7.5' quadrangle.

Stone City: see **Lost City** [CALAVERAS].

Stone Corral [CALAVERAS]: *locality,* 3 miles west of Jenny Lind (lat. 38°06' N, long. 120°55'40" W). Named on Jackson (1902) 30' quadrangle. The place consisted of a hotel, barns, and the corral for which it was named (California Department of Parks and Recreation, p. 13).

Stone Creek Settlement: see **Lost City** [CALAVERAS].

Stonehouse [MARIPOSA]: *locality,* nearly 2 miles south of the settlement of Catheys Valley (lat. 37°24'35" N, long. 120°05'05" W; near E line sec. 15, T 6 S, R 17 E). Named on Catheys Valley (1962) 7.5' quadrangle.

Stony Bar: see **Big Bar** [CALAVERAS].

Stony Creek [MERCED]: *stream,* flows 3.5 miles to Merced River 4.5 miles east of Snelling (lat. 37°30'25" N, long. 120°21'25" W; near SE cor. sec. 7, T 5 S, R 15 E). Named on Haystack Mountain (1962) and Merced Falls (1962) 7.5' quadrangles.

Stony Gulch [TUOLUMNE]:

(1) *canyon,* drained by a stream that flows 4.25 miles to Stanislaus River 5.5 miles north of Columbia (lat. 38°06'50" N, long. 120°23'20" W; sec. 13, T 3 N, R 14 E). Named on Columbia (1948), Columbia SE (1948), and Stanislaus (1948) 7.5' quadrangles.

(2) *canyon,* drained by a stream that flows 1.5 miles to South Fork Stanislaus River 2.5 miles north of Columbia (lat. 38°04'25" N, long. 120°24'20"

W; sec. 35, T 3 N, R 14 E). Named on Columbia (1948) 7.5' quadrangle.

Storey [MADERA]: *locality,* 2.5 miles east-northeast of Madera along Atchison, Topeka and Santa Fe Railroad (lat. 37°58'30" N, long. 120°01'05" W; near W line sec. 16, T 11 S, R 18 E). Named on Madera (1963) 7.5' quadrangle. Madera (1946) 15' quadrangle has the designation "Storey (Madera Sta.)" at the place.

Stoutenburg: see **Murphys** [CALAVERAS].

Stovepipe Campground [MARIPOSA]: *locality,* 4.5 miles west of Wawona (lat. 37°32'30" N, long. 119°44' W; sec. 35, T 4 S, R 20 E). Named on Yosemite (1956) 15' quadrangle.

Straight Spring Gulch [CALAVERAS]: *canyon,* drained by a stream that flows less than 1 mile to Walla Gulch 3.5 miles east-northeast of San Andreas (lat. 38°12'45" N, long. 120°37' W; sec. 11, T 4 N, R 12 E). Named on Calaveritas (1962) 7.5' quadrangle.

Strand Falls [MARIPOSA]: *waterfall,* 5.5 miles southwest of Yosemite Village along Meadow Brook (lat. 37°42'15" N, long. 119°40'05" W). Named on Yosemite (1956) 15' quadrangle.

Strawberry [TUOLUMNE]: *settlement,* 10 miles northeast of Long Barn (lat. 38°11'50" N, long. 120°00'35" W). Named on Pinecrest (1979) and Strawberry (1979) 7.5' quadrangles. Postal authorities established Strawberry post office in 1949 (Frickstad, p. 217). Big Trees (1891) 30' quadrangle has the name "Parsons" at the place. Postal authorities established Parsons post office in 1891 and discontinued it in 1895; the name was for Edmond Parsons, who settled in Tuolumne County in 1856 and was a county supervisor (Salley, p. 167).

Strawberry Creek [MARIPOSA]: *stream,* flows 1.5 miles to Elevenmile Creek 9.5 miles southwest of Yosemite Village (lat. 37°38'10" N, long. 119°41'10" W; near NE cor. sec. 32, T 3 S, R 21 E). Named on Yosemite (1956) 15' quadrangle.

Strawberry Lake: see **Pinecrest Lake** [TUOLUMNE].

Strawberry Peak [TUOLUMNE]: *peak,* 1.25 miles west of Strawberry (lat. 38°11'45" N, long. 120°01'55" W; near SE cor. sec. 18, T 4 N, R 18 E). Named on Strawberry (1979) 7.5' quadrangle.

Streeter Mountain [MARIPOSA]: *peak,* 5.5 miles east-southeast of Mariposa (lat. 37°26'50" N, long. 119°52'45" W; near S line sec. 34, T 5 S, R 19 E). Altitude 2553 feet. Named on Mariposa (1947) and Stumpfield Mountain (1947) 7.5' quadrangles. Called Cedar Mtn. on Mariposa (1912) 30' quadrangle.

String Town: see **Gertrude**, under **Ahwanee** [MADERA].

Striped Rock [MARIPOSA]: *peak,* 6.5 miles south-southeast of Mariposa (lat. 37°23'50" N, long. 119°55'05" W; sec. 20, T 6 S, R 19 E). Altitude 2152 feet. Named on Mariposa (1947) 7.5' quadrangle.

Striped Rock Creek [MADERA-MARIPOSA]: *stream,* heads in Mariposa County and flows 11 miles to Chowchilla River 6.25 miles north-northeast of Raymond in Madera County (lat. 37°18'05" N, long. 119°51'45" W); the stream goes past Striped Rock. Named on Ben Hur (1947), Horsecamp Mountain (1947), and Mariposa (1947) 7.5' quadrangles.

Stubblefield Canyon [TUOLUMNE]: *canyon,* drained by a stream that flows 9.5 miles to Rancheria Creek 8 miles south-southwest of Tower Peak (lat. 38°02'20" N, long. 119°37'10" W). Named on Tower Peak (1956) 15' quadrangle.

Studhorse Meadow [TUOLUMNE]: *locality,* 9 miles east-southeast of Pinecrest along Piute Creek (1) (lat. 38°08'45" N, long. 119° 50'40" W). Named on Pinecrest (1956) 15' quadrangle.

Stumpfield Mountain [MARIPOSA]: *ridge,* north-trending, 2 miles long, 9.5 miles east-southeast of Mariposa (lat. 37°26'30" N, long. 119°48'10" W). Named on Stumpfield Mountain (1947) 7.5' quadrangle.

Sturgeon: see **Ingomar** [MERCED].

Sturgeon Bend [SAN JOAQUIN]: *bend,* 9 miles south of Manteca along San Joaquin River (lat. 37°40'15" N, long. 121°14'35" W). Named on Ripon (1969) 7.5' quadrangle.

Suckertown: see **Bridgeport** [MARIPOSA].

Sugarbowl Dome: see **Bunnell Point** [MARIPOSA].

Sugar Cut [SAN JOAQUIN]: *water feature,* joins Tom Paine Slough 13 miles south-southwest of downtown Stockton (lat. 37°47'25" N, long. 121°25'10" W). Named on Union Island (1978) 7.5' quadrangle.

Sugar Loaf: see **Kolana Rock** [TUOLUMNE].

Sugarloaf [CALAVERAS]: *peak,* nearly 6 miles west-northwest of Valley Springs (lat. 38°13'20" N, long. 120°55'40" W; near NE cor. sec. 12, T 4 N, R 9 E). Altitude 390 feet. Named on Wallace (1962) 7.5' quadrangle.

Sugarloaf [MERCED]: *peak,* 4 miles northwest of Ortigalita Peak (lat. 36°49'50" N, long. 120°58'30" W; sec. 3, T 13 S, R 9 E). Altitude 2830 feet. Named on Ortigalita Peak (1969) 7.5' quadrangle.

Sugarloaf [TUOLUMNE]: *peak,* 6.5 miles southeast of Tuolumne (lat. 37°53'50" N, long. 120°08'40" W; sec. 31, T 1 N, R 17 E). Altitude 3880 feet. Named on Tuolumne (1948) 15' quadrangle.

Sugarloaf Hill [CALAVERAS]: *peak,* 2.25 miles south-southeast of Vallecito (lat. 38°03'20" N, long. 120°27'50" W; sec. 5, T 2 N, R 14 E). Altitude 2179 feet. Named on Columbia (1948) 7.5' quadrangle.

Sugarloaf Mountain [CALAVERAS]: *peak,* 6 miles southeast of Copperopolis (lat. 37°55'10" N, long. 120°33'45" W; near SE cor. sec. 20, T 1 N, R 13 E). Altitude 1072 feet. Named on Melones Dam (1962) 7.5' quadrangle.

Sugar Pine [MADERA]: *village,* 5 miles north of Yosemite Forks (lat. 37°26'30" N, long. 119°37'45" W; near W line sec. 1, T 6 S, R 21 E). Named on Bass Lake (1953) 15' quadrangle. Postal authorities established Sugar Pine post office in 1907 and discontinued it in 1934 (Frickstad, p. 86). Madera Sugar Pine Company built a town at the site in 1899 and 1900 (Clough, p. 47).

Sugarpine [TUOLUMNE]: *settlement,* 2.25 miles northeast of Twain Harte (lat. 38°03'35" N, long. 120°11'50" W; sec. 3, T 2 N, R 16 E). Named on Twain Harte (1979) 7.5' quadrangle. Postal authorities established Sugar Pine post office in 1866 and discontinued it in 1900; the place was the site of Sugar Pine Lumber Company's sawmill (Salley, p. 215). They established Raspberry post office 15 miles east of Sugar Pine in 1880 and discontinued it in 1881 (Salley, p. 181).

Sugarpine Creek [TUOLUMNE]: *stream,* flows 6.5 miles to North Fork Tuolumne River 4.5 miles east-northeast of Twain Harte (lat. 38°03'40" N, long. 120°09'05" W; sec. 6, T 2 N, R 17 E). Named on Hull Creek (1979), Strawberry (1979), and Twain Harte (1979) 7.5' quadrangles.

Sugar Pine Gap [TUOLUMNE]: *pass,* 8 miles northwest of Crandall Peak (lat. 38°14'50" N, long. 120°14'55" W; sec. 31, T 5 N, R 16 E). Named on Crandall Peak (1979) 7.5' quadrangle.

Sugar Spring [CALAVERAS]: *spring,* less than 1 mile east-southeast of Devils Nose (lat. 38°27'25" N, long. 120°24'25" W; sec. 14, T 7 N, R 14 E). Named on Devils Nose (1979) 7.5' quadrangle.

Suicide Ridge [TUOLUMNE]: *ridge,* south-southwest-trending, 3 miles long, 4.5 miles west-southwest of Matterhorn Peak (lat. 38° 04'35" N, long. 119°27'45" W). Named on Matterhorn Peak (1956) 15' quadrangle.

Sullivan: see **Dan Sullivan Gulch** [MARIPOSA].

Sullivan Creek [TUOLUMNE]: *stream,* flows 20 miles to Woods Creek nearly 7 miles south-southwest of Sonora (lat. 37°53'25" N, long. 120°25'15" W; at S line sec. 34, T 1 N, R 14 E). Named on Columbia SE (1948), Sonora (1948), Standard (1948), and Twain Harte (1979) 7.5' quadrangles. The name commemorates John Sullivan, an Irishman who discovered gold in the canyon in 1848; the mining camp there was called Sullivan's Diggings (Buffum, p. 126).

Sullivan's Diggings: see **Sullivan Creek** [TUOLUMNE].

Sulphur Gulch [SAN JOAQUIN-STANISLAUS]: *canyon,* drained by a stream that heads in Stanislaus County and flows 1.5 miles to Hospital Canyon 14 miles south of Tracy in San Joaquin County (lat. 37°32'25" N, long. 121°24'35" W; sec. 34, T 4 S, R 5 E); a spring called Sulphur Springs is in the canyon. Named on Lone Tree Creek (1955) 7.5' quadrangle.

Sulphur Spring [MERCED]: *spring,* 5.5 miles southeast of Pacheco Pass (lat. 37°01'10" N, long. 121°07'30" W; sec. 31, T 10 S, R 8 E). Named on Pacheco Pass (1955) 7.5' quadrangle. Water of San Luis Reservoir now covers the feature

Sulphur Spring Canyon [SAN JOAQUIN]: *canyon,* 1.5 miles long, 1 mile west-northwest of Eagle Mountain on San Joaquin-Alameda County line (lat. 37°34'35" N, long. 121°33'15" W). Named on Cedar Mountain (1956) 7.5' quadrangle.

Sulphur Spring Gulch [MERCED]: *canyon,* drained by a stream that flows 1.5 miles to Quinto Creek 8 miles north-northeast of Pacheco Pass (lat. 37°10'15" N, long. 121°08'10" W; sec. 7, T 9 S, R 8 E). Named on Crevison Peak (1955) 7.5' quadrangle.

Sulphur Spring Gulch [SAN JOAQUIN]: *canyon,* drained by a stream that flows 5 miles to North Fork Lone Tree Creek (1) 12 miles south of Tracy (lat. 37°34'15" N, long. 121°26'25" W; sec. 20, T 4 S, R 5 E). Named on Cedar Mountain (1956) and Lone Tree Creek (1955) 7.5' quadrangles. Tesla (1907) 15' quadrangle shows North Fork Pine Cr. in the canyon.

Sulphur Springs [STANISLAUS]: *spring,* 15 miles west-northwest of Patterson (lat. 37°32'25" N, long. 121°23'55" W; sec. 34, T 4 S, R 5 E); the feature is in Sulphur Gulch. Named on Lone Tree Creek (1955) 7.5' quadrangle.

Summerdale [MARIPOSA]: *locality,* 0.25 mile north of Happy Camp (present Fish Camp) (lat. 37°28'50" N, long. 119°38'15" W; sec. 23, T 5 S, R 21 E). Named on Mariposa (1912) 30' quadrangle. Postal authorities established Summerdale post office in 1893 and discontinued it in 1908; the place was a summer-vacation camp (Salley, p. 215).

Summerdale Campground [MARIPOSA]: *locality,* less than 1 mile north of Fish Camp (lat. 37°29'20" N, long. 119°38'10" W; sec. 23, T 5 S, R 21 E). Named on Bass Lake (1953) 15' quadrangle.

Summer Home [SAN JOAQUIN]: *locality,* 4 miles north-northeast of Manteca along Tidewater Southern Railroad (lat. 37°50'50" N, long. 121°11' W; sec. 15, T 1 S, R 7 E). Named on Manteca (1952) 7.5' quadrangle.

Summersville: see **Soulsbyville** [TUOLUMNE].

Summit Campground [MARIPOSA]: *locality,* 3.25 miles southwest of Wawona (lat. 37°30'20" N, long. 119°42' W; sec. 8, T 5 S, R 21 E). Named on Yosemite (1956) 15' quadrangle.

Summit Creek [TUOLUMNE]: *stream,* flows 10 miles to join Kennedy Creek and form Middle Fork Stanislaus River 5.5 miles west-southwest of Sonora Pass (lat. 38°17'40" N, long. 119°43'45" W; sec. 12, T 5 N, R

20 E). Named on Sonora Pass (1956) and Tower Peak (1956) 15' quadrangles. Called Relief Creek on Dardanelles (1898) 30' quadrangle, which also applies the name "Relief Creek" to present Middle Fork Stanislaus River on its course through present Kennedy Meadow (1), and has the name "East Fork" for present Kennedy Creek.

Summit House [MADERA]: *locality,* 6 miles northeast of Raymond (lat. 37°16'50" N, long. 119°49'30" W; sec. 31, T 7 S, R 20 E). Named on Horsecamp Mountain (1947) 7.5' quadrangle.

Summit Inn [MARIPOSA]: *locality,* nearly 2 miles south-southwest of Midpines (lat. 37°31'15" N, long. 119°56'10" W; near SW cor. sec. 6, T 5 S, R 19 E). Named on Feliciana Mountain (1947) 7.5' quadrangle.

Summit Lake [MADERA]: *lake,* 600 feet long, 8 miles north-northwest of Devils Postpile (lat. 37°44' N, long. 119°08'35" W; sec. 31, T 2 S, R 26 E). Named on Devils Postpile (1953) 15' quadrangle.

Summit Lake [TUOLUMNE]: *lake,* 600 feet long, 4.5 miles south-southeast of Tioga Pass (lat. 37°51'15" N, long. 119°12'50" W). Named on Mono Craters (1953) 15' quadrangle.

Summit Level Ridge [CALAVERAS]: *ridge,* generally southwest- to west-trending, 11 miles long, extends from Cottage Springs to a point 3.5 miles south-southwest of Blue Mountain. Named on Boards Crossing (1979), Dorrington (1979), and Fort Mountain (1979) 7.5' quadrangles.

Summit Meadow [MADERA]:

(1) *area,* 5.5 miles east-northeast of Shuteye Peak (lat. 37°22'30" N, long. 119°19'45" W; sec. 27, T 6 S, R 24 E). Named on Shuteye Peak (1953) 15' quadrangle.

(2) *area,* nearly 3 miles southwest of Devils Postpile (lat. 37°36' N, long. 119°07'15" W). Named on Devils Postpile (1953) 15' quadrangle.

Summit Meadow [TUOLUMNE]: *area,* 4.5 miles west-northwest of Tower Peak (lat. 38°10'35" N, long. 119°37' W). Named on Tower Peak (1956) 15' quadrangle.

Summit Ridge [TUOLUMNE]: *ridge,* south-southwest-trending, 0.5 mile long, 4.25 miles east-northeast of Twain Harte (lat. 38°01'30" N, long. 120°09'15" W). Named on Twain Harte (1979) 7.5' quadrangle.

Sunburnt Spring [MERCED]: *spring,* 2.25 miles south of Pacheco Pass (lat. 37°01'50" N, long. 121°12'25" W). Named on Pacheco Pass (1955) 7.5' quadrangle.

Sunrise Creek [MARIPOSA]: *stream,* flows 5.5 miles to Merced River 4 miles east-southeast of Yosemite Village in Little Yosemite Valley (lat. 37°44' N, long. 119°30'45" W); the stream heads at the south end of Sunrise Mountain. Named on Merced Peak (1953), Tuolumne Meadows (1956), and Yosemite (1956) 15' quadrangles.

Sunrise Lakes [MARIPOSA]: *lakes,* largest 1100 feet long, 4 miles southwest of Cathedral Peak (lat. 37°48'20" N, long. 119°26'45" W; sec. 33, 34, T 1 S, R 23 E); the lakes are north of Sunrise Mountain. Named on Tuolumne Meadows (1956) 15' quadrangle.

Sunrise Mountain [MARIPOSA]: *ridge,* south-trending, 2.5 miles long, 4.5 miles south-southwest of Cathedral Peak (lat. 37°47'15" N, long. 119°26'30" W). Named on Tuolumne Meadows (1956) 15' quadrangle.

Sunset Camp [TUOLUMNE]: *locality,* 5.5 miles south-southwest of Mather (lat. 37°48'25" N, long. 119°53'45" W; sec. 33, T 1 S, R 19 E). Named on Lake Eleanor (1956) 15' quadrangle.

Sunshine Camp [TUOLUMNE]: *settlement,* 5.5 miles east of Sonora (lat. 37°59'15" N, long. 120°16'55" W; sec. 36, T 2 N, R 15 E). Named on Sonora (1948) 15' quadrangle.

Superior Lake [MADERA]: *lake,* 850 feet long, 3.25 miles west of Devils Postpile (lat. 37°38'05" N, long. 119°08'25" W). Named on Devils Postpile (1953) 15' quadrangle.

Surprise Lake [TUOLUMNE]: *lake,* 800 feet long, 7.5 miles southwest of Matterhorn Peak (lat. 38°01'20" N, long. 119°29'15" W). Named on Matterhorn Peak (1956) 15' quadrangle.

Swamp Creek [CALAVERAS]: *stream,* flows 5 miles to South Fork Mokelumne River 2 miles southeast of Blue Mountain (lat. 38°19'20" N, long. 120°20'20" W; near N line sec. 5, T 5 N, R 15 E). Named on Dorrington (1979) 7.5' quadrangle.

Swamp Lake [MADERA]: *lake,* 500 feet long, 7 miles south-southwest of Merced Peak (lat. 37°32'50" N, long. 119°27'15" W). Named on Merced Peak (1953) 15' quadrangle.

Swamp Lake [TUOLUMNE]:

(1) *lake,* 650 feet long, 2.5 miles west-northwest of Liberty Hill (lat. 38°22'35" N, long. 120°08'35" W). Named on Calaveras Dome (1979) 7.5' quadrangle.

(2) *lake,* 1200 feet long, 5 miles north-northeast of Mather (lat. 37° 57' N, long. 119°49'40" W; at NW cor. sec. 18, T 1 N, R 20 E). Named on Lake Eleanor (1956) 15' quadrangle.

Sweeney Hill [MERCED]: *peak,* 10 miles east-northeast of Mariposa Peak (lat. 36°53'55" N, long. 121°02'55" W). Altitude 2165 feet. Named on Los Banos Valley (1969) 7.5' quadrangle.

Sweetwater [MARIPOSA]: *locality,* 9 miles southwest of El Portal (lat. 37°34'20" N, long. 119°52'40" W; sec. 21, T 4 S, R 19 E); the place is near the head of Sweetwater Creek. Named on Yosemite (1909) 30' quadrangle.

Sweet Water Campground [MADERA]: *locality,* 4.5 miles east of Shuteye Peak along Chiquito Creek (lat. 37°21'30" N, long. 119° 20'40" W; near E line sec. 33, T 6 S, R 24 E). Named on Shuteye Peak (1953) 15' quadrangle.

Sweetwater Creek [MARIPOSA]: *stream,* flows 6.25 miles to Merced River 8 miles west-southwest of El Portal (lat. 37°38'15" N, long. 119°55'30" W); the stream heads near Sweetwater Point. Named on Feliciana Mountain (1947) and Kinsley (1947) 7.5' quadrangles.

Sweetwater Point [MARIPOSA]: *peak,* 2.5 miles northeast of Midpines (lat. 37°34'10" N, long. 119°53'05" W; sec. 20, T 4 S, R 10 E); the peak is near the head of Sweetwater Creek. Altitude 4615 feet. Named on Feliciana Mountain (1947) 7.6' quadrangle.

Sweetwater Ridge [MARIPOSA]: *ridge,* northwest-trending, 3.5 miles long, 8 miles west-southwest of El Portal (lat. 37°37'15" N, long. 119°54'45" W); the ridge is west of Sweetwater Creek. Named on El Portal (1947) 15' quadrangle.

Swetts Bar: see **Indian Bar** [TUOLUMNE].

Swiss Ranch [CALAVERAS]: *locality,* 6.5 miles southwest of Blue Mountain along Jesus Maria Creek (lat. 38°16'30" N, long. 120°27'30" W). Named on Big Trees (1891) 30' quadrangle.

Swortzels Camp [MADERA]: *locality,* 5.5 miles north of Shuteye Peak (lat. 37°26' N, long. 119°24'45" W; near E line sec. 2, T 6 S, R 23 E). Named on Shuteye Peak (1953) 15' quadrangle.

Sycamore Canyon [STANISLAUS]: *canyon,* drained by a stream that flows nearly 2 miles to Garzas Creek 2.5 miles west-northwest of Crevison Peak (lat. 37°12'45" N, long. 121°13'40" W; sec. 29, T 8 S, R 7 E). Named on Crevison Peak (1955) 7.5' quadrangle.

Sycamore Slough [SAN JOAQUIN]: *water feature,* joins South Mokelumne River 13 miles west of Lodi (lat. 38°08'30" N, long. 121°30'10" W). Named on Thornton (1978) 7.5' quadrangle.

Sylvan Lodge [TUOLUMNE]: *locality,* 1.5 miles west-southwest of Long Barn (lat. 38°05' N, long. 120°09'20" W; near E line sec. 25, T 3 N, R 16 E). Named on Long Barn (1956) 15' quadrangle.

— T —

Table Lake [TUOLUMNE]: *lake,* 1700 feet long, 9 miles north-northeast of White Wolf (lat. 37°59' N, long. 119°33'45" W). Named on Hetch Hetchy Reservoir (1956) 15' quadrangle.

Table Mountain [CALAVERAS-TUOLUMNE]: *ridge,* on Calaveras-Tuolumne County line, mainly in Tuolumne County; extends along Stanislaus River for 28 miles from a point northeast of Murphys to the entrance of the river into Stanislaus County 10 miles south of Copperopolis. Named on Columbia (1948), Keystone (1962), Knights Ferry (1962), Melones Dam (1962), Murphys (1948), and Sonora (1948) 7.5' quadrangles. The feature also is called Stanislaus Mesa (Gudde, 1975, p. 344).

Table Mountain [MARIPOSA]: *peak,* 16 miles south of the settlement of Catheys Valley (lat. 37°11'35" N, long. 120°03'10" W; near E line sec. 36, T 8 S, R 17 E). Named on Raynor Creek (1961) 7.5' quadrangle.

Table Mountain: see **Little Table Mountain** [MADERA].

Table Top Mountain [MERCED]: *hill,* 6.5 miles east of Snelling on the south side of Merced River opposite Merced Falls (lat. 37°30'40" N, long. 120°19'15" W; on E line sec. 9, T 5 S, R 15 E). Altitude 669 feet. Named on Merced Falls (1962) 7.5' quadrangle.

Taft Point [MARIPOSA]: *promontory,* 2.5 miles south-southwest of Yosemite Village on the south side of Yosemite Valley (lat. 37° 42'45" N, long. 119°36'15" W). Named on Yosemite (1956) 15' quadrangle. R.B. Marshall of United States Geological Survey named the feature for President William Howard Taft (United States Board on Geographic Names, 1934, p. 24).

Tailings Gulch [MARIPOSA]: *canyon,* less than 1 mile long, 5 miles north-northeast of the settlement of Catheys Valley on upper reaches of Sand Creek (lat. 37°29'40" N, long. 120°02'25" W). Named on Catheys Valley (1962) 7.5' quadrangle.

Taison [SAN JOAQUIN]: *locality,* 1.5 miles south-southeast of Thornton (lat. 38°12'20" N, long. 121°24'35" W). Named on New Hope (1910) 7.5' quadrangle. Postal authorities established Taison post office in 1883 and discontinued it in 1889 (Frickstad, p. 162). The name commemorates Captain G.P. Taison, who operated a vessel on Mokelumne River in the 1860's (Hillman and Covello, p. 225).

Talbot [MADERA]: *locality,* 9 miles east of Fairmead along Southern Pacific Railroad (lat. 37°04'30" N, long. 120°11'45" W; sec. 8, T 10 S, R 18 E). Named on Kismet (1920) 7.5' quadrangle.

Tallulah Lake [TUOLUMNE]: *lake,* 1000 feet long, nearly 6 miles southwest of Matterhorn Peak (lat. 38°01'50" N, long. 119°27' W). Named on Matterhorn Peak (1956) 15' quadrangle.

Tamarack [CALAVERAS]: *settlement,* 36 miles east-northeast of San Andreas (lat. 38°26'20" N, long. 120°04'35" W; near S line sec. 23, T 7 N, R 17 E). Named on Tamarack (1979) 7.5' quadrangle. W.H. Hutchins built the first store at the site in the early 1920's and called the place Camp Tamarack—the word "Camp" in the name was from a cow camp located at the place (Browning, 1986, p. 212).

Tamarack Creek [MARIPOSA]: *stream,* flows 5 miles to Cascade Creek 7 miles west-southwest of Yosemite Village (lat. 37°43'40" N, long. 119°42'45" W; sec . 25, T 2 S, R 20 E); the stream goes past Tamarack Flat. Named on Hetch Hetchy Reservoir (1956) and Yosemite (1956) 15' quadrangles.

Tamarack Flat [MARIPOSA]: *area,* 8.5 miles west of Yosemite Village (lat. 37°45'05" N, long. 119°44'20" W; near NW cor. sec. 23, T 2 S, R 20 E); the place is near Tamarack Creek. Named on Hetch Hetchy Reservoir (1956) 15' quadrangle. George W. Coulter and Lafayette H. Bunnell named the area in 1856; Alva Hamilton operated a small stopping place there that he called Tamarack House (Paden and Schlichtmann, p. 235).

Tamarack House: see **Tamarack Flat** [MARIPOSA].

Taylor Canyon [SAN JOAQUIN]: *canyon,* drained by a stream that flows 3 miles to Corral Hollow Creek 1.5 miles south-southwest of Eagle Mountain (lat. 37°32'50" N, long. 121°32'35" W; near N line sec. 33, T 4 S, R 4 E); the canyon is north of Taylor Ridge. Named on Cedar Mountain (1956) 7.5' quadrangle.

Taylor Hill [TUOLUMNE]: *peak,* 1.25 miles south-southwest of Chinese Camp (lat. 37°51'20" N, long. 120°26'35" W; on S line sec. 9, T 1 S, R 14 E). Altitude 1680 feet. Named on Chinese Camp (1947) 7.5' quadrangle. The feature also was called Red Mountain, Mount Pleasant, and Taylor Mountain (Paden and Schlichtmann, p. 62).

Taylor Mountain [MADERA]: *ridge,* west-northwest-trending, 1.5 miles long, 2 miles southeast of Yosemite Forks (lat. 37°20'50" N, long. 119°36' W; on E line sec. 6, T 7 S, R 22 E). Named on Bass Lake (1953) 15' quadrangle.

Taylor Mountain: see **Taylor Hill** [TUOLUMNE].

Taylor Ridge [SAN JOAQUIN]: *ridge,* west- to southwest-trending, 2 miles long, 2 miles southeast of Eagle Mountain (lat. 37°32'40" N, long. 121°31' W); the ridge is south of Taylor Canyon. Named on Cedar Mountain (1956) 7.5' quadrangle.

Taylors Bar: see **San Andreas** [CALAVERAS].

Taylor's Ferry: see **Oakdale** [STANISLAUS]; **Stanislaus River** [CALAVERAS-SAN JOAQUIN-STANISLAUS-TUOLUMNE].

Teaford Saddle [MADERA]: *pass,* 6 miles south-southeast of Yosemite Forks (lat. 37°17'15" N, long. 119°34'55" W; near SW cor. sec. 28, T 7 S, R 22 E). Named on Bass Lake (1953) 15' quadrangle, which shows Teaford ranch located 1 mile south of the pass.

Teapot Dome: see **Pywiack Dome** [MARIPOSA].

Tegner: see **Hilmar** [MERCED].

Telegraph City [CALAVERAS]: *locality,* 6.25 miles west-southwest of Copperopolis (lat. 37°56'10" N, long. 120°44'25" W; near W line sec. 14, T 1 N, R 11 E); the place is along Telegraph Creek. Named on Copperopolis (1962) 7.5' quadrangle. Postal authorities established Telegraph City post office in 1862 and discontinued it in 1894; the post office name was from a telegraph station on the Stockton to Sonora line (Salley, p. 219).

Telegraph Creek [CALAVERAS-STANISLAUS]: *stream,* heads in Calaveras County and flows 8 miles to Shirley Creek 10.5 miles north of Oakdale in Stanislaus County (lat. 37°54'55" N, long. 120° 48'50" W; near SW cor. sec. 19, T 1 N, R 11 E); the stream goes past Telegraph City. Named on Bachelor Valley (1968) and Copperopolis (1962) 7.5' quadrangles.

Telegraph Hill [MARIPOSA]: *peak,* 5 miles east-northeast of the village of Bear Valley (lat. 37°35'55" N, long. 120°02'05" W; near E line sec. 12, T 4 S, R 17 E). Altitude 3402 feet. Named on Bear Valley (1947) 7.5' quadrangle.

Telegraph Hill [TUOLUMNE]: *peak,* nearly 3 miles east of Columbia (lat. 38°01'55" N, long. 120°21' W; sec. 17, T 2 N, R 15 E). Altitude 3738 feet. Named on Columbia SE (1948) 7.5' quadrangle.

Telephone Cut [SAN JOAQUIN]: *water feature,* artificial watercourse that joins Bishop Cut 5 miles east-southeast of Terminous (lat. 38°04'20" N, long. 121°25' W). Named on Terminous (1978) 7.5' quadrangle.

Temperance Arm: see **Lake McClure** [MARIPOSA].

Temperance Creek [MARIPOSA]: *stream,* flows 3.5 miles to Lake McClure 7.25 miles north of Hornitos (lat. 37°36'25" N, long. 120° 14'25" W; near NW cor. sec. 8, T 4 S, R 16 E). Named on Hornitos (1947, photorevised 1973) 7.5' quadrangle.

Tenaya Canyon: see **Tenaya Creek** [MARIPOSA].

Tenaya Creek [MARIPOSA]: *stream,* flows 12.5 miles to Merced River 1 mile east-southeast of Yosemite Village (lat. 37°44'40" N, long. 119°34'10" W). Named on Hetch Hetchy Reservoir (1956), Tuolumne Meadows (1956), and Yosemite (1956) 15' quadrangles. Called Tenaya Fork on King and Gardner's (1865) map. Whitney (1870, p. 65) used the name "Tenaya Fork of the Merced" for the stream. On Yosemite (1909) 30' quadrangle, the name "Tenaya Canyon" applies to the canyon of Tenaya Creek above Yosemite Valley.

Tenaya Fork: see **Tenaya Creek** [MARIPOSA].

Tenaya Lake [MARIPOSA]: *lake,* 1 mile long, 3 miles west-southwest of Cathedral Peak (lat. 37°49'50" N, long. 119°27'30" W; sec. 20, 21, T 1 S, R 23 E). Named on Tuolumne Meadows (1956) 15' quadrangle. Lafayette H. Bunnell named the lake for the chief of the Indians who occupied Yosemite Valley when the valley was discovered by white men (Bunnell, p. 163).

Tenaya Peak [MARIPOSA]: *peak,* 2.5 miles southwest of Cathedral Peak (lat. 37°49'45" N, long. 119°26'30" W; near W line sec. 22, T 1 S, R 23 E). Altitude 10,301 feet. Named on Tuolumne Meadows (1956) 15' quadrangle.

Tenaya Peak: see **Tresidder Peak** [MARIPOSA].

Ten-ieya Dome: see **Pywiack Dome** [MARIPOSA].

Ten Lakes [TUOLUMNE]: *lakes,* largest 1400 feet long, 7.5 miles east-northeast of White Wolf (lat. 37°54' N, long. 119°31'15" W). Named on Hetch Hetchy Reservoir (1956) 15' quadrangle.

Tenmile Slough [SAN JOAQUIN]: *water feature,* between Elmwood Tract and Sargent-Barnhart Tract, joins Fourteenmile Slough 5 miles west-northwest of downtown Stockton (lat. 37°59'40" N, long. 121°22'05" W). Named on Stockton West (1952) 7.5' quadrangle.

Tennessee Gulch [TUOLUMNE]: *canyon,* drained by a stream that flows 1 mile to Woods Creek 2.5 miles south-southeast of Columbia at Browns Flat (lat. 38°00'10" N, long. 120°23' W; sec. 25, T 2 N, R 14 E). Named on Columbia (1948) and Columbia SE (1948) 7.5' quadrangles.

Terminous [SAN JOAQUIN]: *village,* 12 miles west of Lodi (lat. 38° 06'50" N, long. 121°29'40" W); the place is on Terminous Tract. Named on Terminous (1978) 7.5' quadrangle. John Dougherty founded the village and called it Terminus because it was at the end of a road; postal authorities, who misspelled the name given by Dougherty, established Terminous post office in 1895 and discontinued it in 1918 (Frickstad, p. 163; Gudde, 1949, p. 359).

Terminous Tract [SAN JOAQUIN]: *area,* 10 miles west-southwest of Lodi (lat. 38°06'30" N, long. 121°27'30" W). Named on Isleton (1978), Terminous (1978), and Thornton (1978) 7.5' quadrangles.

Tesaiyak: see **Half Dome** [MARIPOSA].

Texas Bar: see **Red Mountain Bar** [TUOLUMNE].

Texas Charlie Gulch [CALAVERAS]: *canyon,* drained by a stream that flows 3.5 miles to Melones Reservoir 5 miles east of Copperopolis (lat. 37°59'35" N, long. 120°33'05" W; sec. 28, T 2 N, R 13 E). Named on Angels Camp (1962) and Melones Dam (1962) 7.5' quadrangles.

Texas Creek: see **Cavallada Creek** [MARIPOSA].

Texas Flat [MADERA]: *area,* 7.25 miles north-northwest of Shuteye Peak (lat. 27°26'25" N, long. 119°29'45" W; sec. 6, T 6 S, R 23 E). Named on Shuteye Peak (1953) 15' quadrangle.

Texas Flat: see **Coarsegold** [MADERA]; **Gold Spring** [TUOLUMNE].

Texas Gulch [CALAVERAS]: *canyon,* drained by a stream that flows less than 1 mile to Buckham Gulch 5 miles west-southwest of Copperopolis (lat. 37°57'20" N, long. 120°43'35" W; sec. 11, T 1 N, R 11 E). Named on Copperopolis (1962) 7.5' quadrangle.

Texas Gulch [MARIPOSA]: *canyon,* drained by a stream that flows 1 mile to Agua Fria Creek 4.5 miles northeast of the settlement of Catheys Valley (lat. 37°28'45" N, long. 120°01'45" W). Named on Catheys Valley (1962) 7.5' quadrangle. United States Board on Geographic Names (1964a, p. 15) rejected the name "Cavallada Gulch" for the feature.

Texas Gulch [TUOLUMNE]: *canyon,* drained by a stream that flows less than 1 mile to Big Creek (1) 3 miles east of Groveland (lat. 37°50'05" N, long. 120°10'20" W; sec. 24, T 1 S, R 16 E). Named on Groveland (1947) 7.5' quadrangle.

Texas Hill [MARIPOSA]: *peak,* 6.25 miles east-northeast of Buckhorn Peak (lat. 37°41'35" N, long. 120°00'55" W; near NW cor. sec. 8, T 3 S, R 18 E). Altitude 3251 feet. Named on Buckhorn Peak (1947) 7.5' quadrangle.

Texas Hill: see **Black Mountain** [MARIPOSA].

Texas Tent: see **Farmington** [SAN JOAQUIN].

Tex Flat [MADERA]: *area,* 6.5 miles north-northeast of Shuteye Peak (lat. 37°26'15" N, long. 119°22'45" W; near E line sec. 6, T 6 S, R 24 E). Named on Shuteye Peak (1953) 15' quadrangle.

Thalheim: see **Valley Home** [STANISLAUS].

Tharsa: see **Irrigosa** [MADERA].

Thatchers Gulch [CALAVERAS]: *canyon,* drained by a stream that flows less than 1 mile to Pardee Reservoir 4 miles west of Paloma (lat. 38°15'40" N, long. 120°50' W; near W line sec. 25, T 5 N, R 10 E). Named on Jackson (1962) 7.5' quadrangle.

The Basin [TUOLUMNE]: *area,* 5 miles east-southeast of Twain Harte (lat. 38°00' N, long. 120°08'45" W); Basin Creek goes through the place. Named on Tuolumne (1948) and Twain Harte (1979) 7.5' quadrangles.

The Buttresses [MADERA]: *escarpment,* 1 mile south-southwest of Devils Postpile on the west side of Middle Fork San Joaquin River (lat. 37°36'45" N, long. 119°05'15" W). Named on Devils Postpile (1953) 15' quadrangle.

The Cascades [MARIPOSA]: *waterfall,* 7 miles west-southwest of Yosemite Village (lat. 37°43'40" N, long. 119°42'45" W; sec. 25, T 2 S, R 20 E); the feature is along Cascade Creek. Named on Yosemite (1956) 15' quadrangle. Lafayette H. Bunnell named the waterfall in 1851; the feature also was called Cascade Falls (Browning, 1988, p. 21).

The Falls [MADERA]: *locality,* 4 miles southeast of Yosemite Forks near the northwest end of Bass Lake (1) (lat. 37°19'55" N, long. 119°34'15" W;

sec. 9, T 7 S, R 22 E). Named on Bass Lake (1953) 15' quadrangle.

The Fissures [MARIPOSA]: *relief feature,* 2.5 miles south-southwest of Yosemite Village on the south side of Yosemite Valley (lat. 37° 42'45" N, long. 119°36' W). Named on Yosemite (1956) 15' quadrangle.

The Forks [MADERA]: *locality,* 5 miles southeast of Yosemite Forks on the west side of Bass Lake (1) (lat. 37°18'50" N, long. 119°34'20" W; on N line sec. 21, T 7 S, R 22 E). Named on Bass Lake (1953) 15' quadrangle.

The Grove [MERCED]: *locality,* 3.5 miles north of Atwater (lat. 37° 24'10" N, long. 120°35'30" W; near NW cor. sec. 19, T 6 S, R 13 E). Named on Winton (1961) 7.5' quadrangle.

The Homestead [SAN JOAQUIN]: *district,* 1.5 miles south-southeast of downtown Stockton (lat. 37°56'10" N, long. 121°16'45" W). Named on Stockton West (1952) 7.5' quadrangle. Postal authorities established Homestead post office 1.5 miles south of Stockton post office in 1898 and discontinued it in 1900 (Salley, p. 99). Mendenhall's (1908) map shows a place called Franceses located near Stockton on the road to French Camp, apparently in what is now The Homestead district.

The Jumping Off Place: see **Lovers Leap** [STANISLAUS].

The Narrows [MERCED]: *narrows,* 6.25 miles north-northeast of Pacheco Pass along Romero Creek (lat. 37°09'05" N, long. 121°10'30" W; sec. 14, T 9 S, R 7 E). Named on Crevison Peak (1955) 7.5' quadrangle.

The Narrows [STANISLAUS]: *narrows,* 6.5 miles northeast of Mustang Peak along Garzas Creek (lat. 37°14'10" N, long. 121°15'35" W; sec. 13, T 8 S, R 6 E). Named on Mustang Peak (1955) 7.5' quadrangle.

The Old Piute: see **Ahwiyah Point** [MARIPOSA].

The Pines [MADERA]: *settlement,* 5.25 miles southeast of Yosemite Forks on the northeast side of Bass Lake (1) (lat. 37°19'10" N, long. 119°33'15" W; sec. 15, T 7 S, R 22 E). Named on Bass Lake (1953) 15' quadrangle.

The Pocket [SAN JOAQUIN]: *area,* 8 miles southwest of downtown Stockton on Roberts Island (lat. 37°53'45" N, long. 121°25'05" W). Named on Holt (1978) 7.5' quadrangle.

The Slide [TUOLUMNE]: *relief feature,* 3.25 miles west of Matterhorn Peak (lat. 38°05'20" N, long. 119°26'20" W); the feature is on the southeast side of Slide Mountain (1). Named on Matterhorn Peak (1956) 15' quadrangle.

The Three Chimneys [TUOLUMNE]: *relief features,* 6.25 miles south-southeast of Dardanelle (lat. 38°15'10" N, long. 119°48'05" W; sec. 29, T 5 N, R 20 E). Named on Dardanelle (1979) 7.5' quadrangle.

The Three Graces: see **Cathedral Rocks** [MARIPOSA].

Third Crossing: see **Kentucky House** [CALAVERAS].

Thirteenmile Creek [TUOLUMNE]: *stream,* flows 2.5 miles to Cottonwood Creek (1) nearly 3 miles east-northeast of Duckwall Mountain (lat. 37°59'10" N, long. 120°04'20" W; sec. 35, T 2 N, R 17 E). Named on Duckwall Mountain (1948) 7.5' quadrangle.

Thirtyfive Spring [MERCED]: *spring,* 3.5 miles south-southeast of Pacheco Pass (lat. 37°01'10" N, long. 121°10'30" W; sec. 35, T 10 S, R 7 E). Named on Pacheco Pass (1955) 7.5' quadrangle.

Thompson Canyon [TUOLUMNE]: *canyon,* drained by a stream that flows 9.5 miles to Stubblefield Canyon 6.25 miles south-southwest of Tower Peak (lat. 38°03'30" N, long. 119°35'20" W). Named on Matterhorn Peak (1956) and Tower Peak (1956) 15' quadrangles.

Thompson Creek [CALAVERAS]: *stream,* flows nearly 3 miles to Greenhorn Gulch 2.25 miles south-southwest of Angels Camp (lat. 38°02'40" N, long. 120°33'35" W; sec. 9, T 2 N, R 13 E). Named on Angels Camp (1962) 7.5' quadrangle.

Thompson Flat [CALAVERAS]: *valley,* 4.5 miles southwest of Copperopolis near the head of Martells Creek (lat. 37°55'45" N, long. 120°41'45" W; on N line sec. 19, T 1 N, R 12 E). Named on Copperopolis (1962) 7.5' quadrangle.

Thompson Meadow [CALAVERAS]: *area,* 2.25 miles west of Tamarack along Big Meadow Creek (lat. 38°26' N, long. 120°07' W; near W line sec. 28, T 7 N, R 17 E). Named on Tamarack (1979) 7.5' quadrangle.

Thompson Meadow [TUOLUMNE]: *area,* 2.25 miles northeast of Duckwall Mountain (lat. 37°59'40" N, long. 120°05'35" W; on S line sec. 27, T 2 N, R 17 E); the place is 1.5 miles west-southwest of Thompson Peak. Named on Duckwall Mountain (1948) 7.5' quadrangle.

Thompson Peak [TUOLUMNE]: *peak,* 3.5 miles northeast of Duckwall Mountain (lat. 37°59'55" N, long. 120°04'05" W; near E line sec. 26, T 2 N, R 17 E). Altitude 5294 feet. Named on Duckwall Mountain (1948) 7.5' quadrangle.

Thompson Rancho: see **Eight Square Leagues on Stanislaus River** [SAN JOAQUIN-STANISLAUS].

Thompson's: see **Eight Square Leagues on Stanislaus River** [SAN JOAQUIN-STANISLAUS].

Thornberry Mountain [MADERA]: *ridge,* east- to east-northeast-trending, 4.5 miles long, 6.5 miles south of Yosemite Forks (lat. 37°16'15" N, long. 119°37' W). Named on Bass Lake (1953) 15' quadrangle.

Thornton [SAN JOAQUIN]: *town,* 10 miles northwest of Lodi (lat. 38°13'30" N, long. 121°25'15" W). Named on Thornton (1978) 7.5' quadrangle. Called New Hope on Lodi (1939) 7.5' quadrangle. Arthur Thornton started his New Hope ranch at the place about 1855, and the community that grew on the ranch was called New Hope before officials of Western Pacific Railroad gave the name "Thornton" to their station there (Gudde, 1949, p. 360). Postal authorities established New Hope post office in 1878 and changed the name to Thornton in 1909 (Frickstad, p. 162). California Mining Bureau's (1917a) map shows a place called Brack located about 5 miles south-southeast of Thornton along the railroad.

Thorps Creek [TUOLUMNE]: *stream,* flows 1.25 miles to North Fork Dry Creek 2.5 miles west of Keystone (lat. 37°50'25" N, long. 120°33' W; sec. 21, T 1 S, R 13 E). Named on Keystone (1962) 7.5' quadrangle.

Thousand Island Lake [MADERA]: *lake,* 1.5 miles long, 8.5 miles northwest of Devils Postpile (lat. 37°43'15" N, long. 119°11' W). Named on Devils Postpile (1953) 15' quadrangle.

Three Brothers [MARIPOSA]: *relief feature,* 1.5 miles west-southwest of Yosemite Village on the north side of Yosemite Valley (lat. 37°44'30" N, long. 119°36'45" W); the feature comprises Lower Brother, Middle Brother, and Eagle Peak (1). Named on Yosemite (1956) 15' quadrangle. The name is from three Indian brothers who were captured near the feature in 1851 by members of the Mariposa Battalion (Bunnell, p. 107-108).

Three Buttes [MARIPOSA]: *peaks,* 3 miles south-southwest of Santa Cruz Mountain (lat. 37°25'10" N, long. 120°13'35" W; near S line sec. 8, 9, T 6 S, R 16 E). Named on Indian Gulch (1962) 7.5' quadrangle.

Three Chimneys: see **The Three Chimneys** [TUOLUMNE].

Three Graces: see **The Three Graces**, under **Cathedral Rocks** [MARIPOSA].

Three Meadows [TUOLUMNE]: *areas,* 7 miles east-northeast of Pinecrest (lat. 38°14'35" N, long. 119°53' W). Named on Pinecrest (1979) 7.5' quadrangle. The group comprises Gully Meadow, Middle Three Meadow, and Upper Three Meadow (United States Board on Geographic Names, 1980b, p. 5).

Three Pine Gulch: see **Yankee Hill** [TUOLUMNE] (2).

Three River Reach [SAN JOAQUIN]: *water feature,* part of San Joaquin River 15 miles west-southwest of Lodi and northeast of the mouth of Middle River (lat. 38°02'50" N, long. 121°31'20" W). Named on Bouldin Island (1978) 7.5' quadrangle.

Three Tree Flat [STANISLAUS]: *valley,* 17 miles east-northeast of Turlock (lat. 37°36'20" N, long. 120°32'55" W). Named on Three Tree Flat (1916) 7.5' quadrangle. Water of Turlock Lake now covers the valley.

Thunder Hill [TUOLUMNE]: *ridge,* north-northeast-trending, less than 1 mile long, 7 miles southwest of Liberty Hill (lat. 38°17'10" N, long. 120°10'20" W; near E line sec. 14, T 5 N, R 16 E). Named on Boards Crossing (1979) 7.5' quadrangle.

Tice [CALAVERAS]: *locality,* 6 miles west of present Tamarack along Blue Creek (lat. 38°26'10" N, long. 120°11'35" W). Named on Big Trees (1891) 30' quadrangle.

Tick-Tack-Toe Hill [MADERA]: *ridge,* west-southwest-trending, 1 mile long, nearly 7 miles south of O'Neals (lat. 37°01'45" N, long. 119°42'15" W). Named on Millerton Lake West (1965) 7.5' quadrangle. Millerton Lake (1945) 15' quadrangle has the form "Tick-tack-toe Hill" for the name.

Tiger Creek Reservoir [CALAVERAS]: *lake,* behind a dam on North Fork Mokelumne River 3 miles north-northeast of West Point on Calaveras-Amador County line (lat. 38°26'30" N, long. 120°30'15" W; sec. 23, T 7 N, R 13 E); Tiger Creek enters the lake in Amador County. Named on Devils Nose (1979) and West Point (1948) 7.5' quadrangles.

Tilden Canyon [TUOLUMNE]: *canyon,* 0.5 mile long, 8.5 miles southwest of Tower Peak (lat. 38°02'25" N, long. 119°38'15" W). Named on Tower Peak (1956) 15' quadrangle.

Tilden Canyon Creek [TUOLUMNE]: *stream,* flows 5.5 miles to Rancheria Creek 9 miles south-southwest of Tower Peak (lat. 38° 01'35" N, long. 119°37'40" W); the stream goes through Tilden Canyon. Named on Tower Peak (1956) 15' quadrangle.

Tilden Creek [TUOLUMNE]: *stream,* flows 6 miles to Falls Creek 5.5 miles southwest of Tower Peak (lat. 38°05'35" N, long. 119° 37'45" W). Named on Tower Peak (1956) 15' quadrangle.

Tilden Lake [TUOLUMNE]: *lake,* 2 miles long, 4 miles southwest of Tower Peak (lat. 38°06'15" N, long. 119°36'10" W); the lake is along Tilden Creek. Named on Tower Peak (1956) 15' quadrangle. United States Board on Geographic Names (1986, p. 1) rejected the name "Lake Nina" for the feature.

Tile Canyon [MERCED]: *canyon,* drained by a stream that flows less than 1 mile to Romero Creek 6 miles north-northeast of Pacheco Pass (lat. 37°08'35" N, long. 121°09'30" W; sec. 24, T 9 S, R 7 E). Named on Crevison Peak (1955) 7.5' quadrangle.

Tillman [MADERA]: *locality,* 6.25 miles south-southwest of Chowchilla along Chowchilla Pacific Railroad (lat. 37°02'30" N, long. 120°19'35" W; near SW cor. sec. 22, T 10 S, R 15 E). Named on Chowchilla (1918) 7.5' quadrangle. California Division of Highways' (1934) map shows a place called Plains located along Southern Pacific Railroad nearly 2 miles southwest of Tillman (near E line sec. 32, T 10 S, R 15 E), a place called Ovejo located along the railroad 1.25 miles northeast of Tillman (near N line sec. 22, T 10 S, R 15 E), and a place called Ash located along the railroad 1.5 miles northeast of Ovejo (near S line sec. 11, T 10 S, R 15 E).

Tiltill Creek [TUOLUMNE]: *stream,* flows 6.25 miles to Hetch Hetchy Reservoir 7.5 miles northwest of White Wolf (lat. 37° 57'25" N, long. 119°43'40" W; sec. 12, T 1 N, R 20 E); the stream heads near Tiltill Mountain and goes through Tiltill Valley. Named on Hetch Hetchy Reservoir (1956) and Tower Peak (1956) 15' quadrangles.

Tiltill Mountain [TUOLUMNE]: *peak,* 10 miles southwest of Tower Peak (lat. 38°01'40" N, long. 119°39'55" W). Altitude 9005 feet. Named on Tower Peak (1956) 15' quadrangle.

Tiltill Valley [TUOLUMNE]: *valley,* 7.5 miles north-northwest of White Wolf (lat. 37°58'25" N, long. 119°41'35" W); the valley is along Tiltill Creek and a tributary to Tiltill Creek. Named on Hetch Hetchy Reservoir (1956) 15' quadrangle. Eugene Y. Ellwell homesteaded in the valley and named it in 1887 (Browning, 1986, p. 217). United States Board on Geographic Names (1933a, p. 756) rejected the forms "Til Till," "Tiltil," and "Tilltill" for the name.

Timba [STANISLAUS]: *locality,* 2 miles north of Newman along Southern Pacific Railroad (lat. 37°20'35" N, long. 121°01'50" W); the place is 2 miles southeast of Orestimba Creek. Named on Newman (1952) 7.5' quadrangle.

Timber Creek [MADERA]:

(1) *stream,* flows 2 miles to West Fork Granite Creek 6 miles southeast of Merced Peak (lat. 37°34'20" N, long. 119°19' W); the stream heads near Timber Knob. Named on Merced Peak (1953) 15' quadrangle.

(2) *stream,* flows 2.5 miles to Sand Creek 3.5 miles west-southwest of Shuteye Peak (lat. 37°19'45" N, long. 119°29'25" W; near SE cor. sec. 7, T 7 S, R 23 E). Named on Shuteye Peak (1953) 15' quadrangle.

Timber Knob [MADERA]: *peak,* 6 miles east-southeast of Merced Peak (lat. 37°35'20" N, long. 119°18' W); the peak is east of Timber Creek (1). Altitude 9945 feet. Named on Merced Peak (1953) 15' quadrangle.

Timber Lodge [MARIPOSA]: *locality,* 0.5 mile north-northwest of Midpines (lat. 37°33'05" N, long. 119°55'25" W; near SW cor. sec. 30, T 4 S, R 19 E). Named on Feliciana Mountain (1947) 7.5' quadrangle.

Timberloft Camp [MARIPOSA]: *locality,* 3 miles southwest of Fish Camp (lat. 37°26'30" N, long. 119°40'20" W; sec. 4, T 6 S, R 21 E). Named on Bass Lake (1953) 15' quadrangle. Mariposa (1912) 30' quadrangle shows Old Miami Mill at the place.

Tim's Springs: see **Springfield** [TUOLUMNE].

Tinsley Island [SAN JOAQUIN]: *island,* 0.5 mile long, 5.25 miles south of Terminous in San Joaquin River (lat. 38°02'15" N, long. 121°29'40" W). Named on Terminous (1978) 7.5' quadrangle.

Tioga Hill: see **Gaylor Peak** [TUOLUMNE].

Tioga Meadows: see **Dana Meadows** [TUOLUMNE].

Tioga Pass [TUOLUMNE]: *pass,* 60 miles east of Sonora on Tuolumne-Mono County line (lat. 37°54'40" N, long. 119°15'25" W; near N line sec. 31, T 1 N, R 25 E). Named on Tuolumne Meadows (1956) 15' quadrangle. The name is from Tioga County, New York (United States Board on Geographic Names, 1934, p. 25), and was applied to a mine near the pass and then to the pass itself (Smith, p. 29). The feature also was known as McLean's Pass (Hubbard). Bancroft's (1864) map had the name "Browns Pass" at or near present Tioga Pass.

Tip Top Peak [TUOLUMNE]: *peak,* 2.5 miles east-northeast of Moccasin (lat. 37°49'45" N, long. 120°15'40" W; sec. 30, T 1 S, R 16 E). Altitude 3361 feet. Named on Moccasin (1948) 7.5' quadrangle.

Tisaiyak: see **Half Dome** [MARIPOSA].

Tisayac: see **Half Dome** [MARIPOSA].

T Island [STANISLAUS]: *island,* 800 feet long, 5.5 miles north-northwest of Oakdale in Woodward Reservoir (lat. 37°50'50" N, long. 120°52'20" W). Named on Oakdale (1968) 7.5' quadrangle.

Tis-sa-ack: see **Half Dome** [MARIPOSA].

Titcomb Flat [MADERA]: *area,* 5.25 miles southwest of North Fork (lat. 37°10'35" N, long. 119°34'40" W; sec. 4, T 9 S, R 22 E). Named on North Fork (1965) 7.5' quadrangle.

Titus and Manly Ferry: see **San Joaquin City** [MADERA].

Tojam Lake [TUOLUMNE]: *lake,* 950 feet long, 10.5 miles east of Pinecrest (lat. 38°11'25" N, long. 119°48' W). Named on Pinecrest (1956) 15' quadrangle.

Toledo [MARIPOSA]: *locality,* nearly 2 miles west of Santa Cruz Mountain (lat. 37°27'30" N, long. 120°14'10" W; sec. 32, T 5 S, R 16 E). Site named on Indian Gulch (1962) 7.5' quadrangle.

Toledo Gulch [MARIPOSA]: *canyon,* drained by a stream that flows 3.25 miles to Burns Creek 1.5 miles north-northeast of Courthouse Rock (lat. 37°26'35" N, long. 120°16'15" W; sec. 1, T 6 S, R 15 E); the site of Toledo is in the canyon. Named on Haystack Mountain (1962) and Indian Gulch (1962) 7.5' quadrangles.

Toledo Pond [MARIPOSA]: *lake,* 550 feet long, 1.5 miles west-northwest of Santa Cruz Mountain (lat. 37°27'45" N, long. 120°13'50" W; near SE cor. sec. 29, T 5 S, R 16 E); the lake is 0.5 mile northeast of the site of Toledo. Named on Indian Gulch (1962) 7.5' quadrangle.

Tom Paine Slough [SAN JOAQUIN]: *water feature,* joins Old River 13 miles south-southwest of downtown Stockton (lat. 37°48' N, long. 121°06' W). Named on Lathrop (1952) and Union Island (1978) 7.5' quadrangles. Called Tom Paine's Slough on Thompson and West's (1879) map.

Toms Canyon [TUOLUMNE]: *canyon,* 1 mile long, 9.5 miles east of Pinecrest along upper reaches of Piute Creek (1) (lat. 38°10'40" N, long. 119°49'15" W). Named on Pinecrest (1956) 15' quadrangle.

Tomspur [SAN JOAQUIN]: *locality,* 5 miles south of Lodi along Southern Pacific Railroad (lat. 38°03'25" N, long. 121°16'35" W; near NW cor. sec. 1, T 2 N, R 6 E). Named on Lodi South (1968) 7.5' quadrangle.

Toutch Mill [CALAVERAS]: *locality,* 3.5 miles southwest of Blue Mountain (lat. 38°18'20" N, long. 120°24'20" W; near W line sec. 11, T 5 N, R 14 E). Site named on Blue Mountain (1956) 15' quadrangle.

Tower Peak [TUOLUMNE]: *peak,* 13 miles south-southeast of Sonora Pass (lat. 38°08'35" N, long. 119°32'50" W). Altitude 11,755 feet. Named on Tower Peak (1956) 15' quadrangle. First called Castle Peak, but members of the Whitney survey renamed the feature Tower Peak after the name "Castle Peak" was transferred by mistake to another feature (United States Board on Geographic Names, 1934, p. 25).

Towers [CALAVERAS]: *locality,* 10 miles west-southwest of Angels Camp in Salt Spring Valley (lat. 38°01'35" N, long. 120°43' W). Named on Jackson (1902) 30' quadrangle.

Townsley Lake [MARIPOSA]: *lake,* 1900 feet long, 5.5 miles southeast of Cathedral Peak along Fletcher Creek (lat. 37°47'40" N, long. 119°19'55" W). Named on Tuolumne Meadows (1956) 15' quadrangle. The name commemorates Forest Sanford Townsley, chief ranger of Yosemite National Park from 1916 until 1943, who planted golden trout in the lake; the feature first was called Upper Fletcher Lake (Browning, 1986, p. 219), but United States Board on Geographic Names (1991, p. 7) rejected this name.

Toyon [CALAVERAS]: *locality,* 3.5 miles east-northeast of Valley Springs along Southern Pacific Railroad (lat. 38°12'15" N, long. 120°46' W; sec. 16, T 4 N, R 11 E). Named on Valley Springs (1962) 7.5' quadrangle.

Trabucco Creek [MARIPOSA]: *stream,* flows about 1 mile to Bear Creek (1) 2.5 miles north-northwest of Midpines (lat. 37°34'30" N, long. 119°56'40" W; near E line sec. 23, T 4 S, R 18 E). Named on Feliciana Mountain (1947) 7.5' quadrangle.

Trabucco Flat [MARIPOSA]: *area,* 3 miles east-southeast of the settlement of Catheys Valley (lat. 37°25'40" N, long. 120°02'25" W; sec. 7, T 6 S, R 18 E). Named on Catheys Valley (1962) 7.5' quadrangle.

Trabucco Gardens [MARIPOSA]: *locality,* less than 1 mile south-southeast of the village of Bear Valley (lat. 37°33'35" N, long. 120°06'40" W). Named on Bear Valley (1947) 7.5' quadrangle. Louis Trabucco had his home and a store at the place in 1851 (Sargent, Shirley, 1976, p. 16-17).

Trabuco Mountain [MADERA]: *peak,* 8.5 miles north-northwest of O'Neals (lat. 37°14'50" N, long. 119°44'10" W; sec. 12, T 8 S, R 20 E). Altitude 2647 feet. Named on Bass Lake (1953) and Millerton Lake (1965) 15' quadrangles.

Tracy [SAN JOAQUIN]: *city,* 16 miles south-southwest of downtown Stockton (lat. 37°44'25" N, long. 121°25'03" W; in and near sec. 21, 28, T 2 S, R 5 E). Named on Tracy (1954) and Union Island (1978) 7.5' quadrangles. According to Gudde (1949, p. 367), the name commemorates Lathrop J. Tracy, an official of Central Pacific Railroad. According to Hanna (p. 332), the name is for Judge F.P. Tracy, a political colleague of Leland Stanford. Postal authorities established Tracy post office in 1878 (Frickstad, p. 163), and the city incorporated in 1910. California Division of Highways' (1934) map shows a place called Janney located 3 miles west-northwest of Tracy along Southern Pacific Railroad (near NE cor. sec. 24, T 2 S, R 4 E). The same map shows a place called Medal located 2 miles west-southwest of Tracy along the same railroad (sec. 31, T 2 S, R 5 E).

Tracy Lake [SAN JOAQUIN]: *intermittent lake,* 6 miles north-northwest of Lodi (lat. 38°12'45" N, long. 121°19'40" W; in and near sec. 8, T 4 N, R 6 E). Named on Lodi North (1968) 7.5' quadrangle.

Traner Slough [SAN JOAQUIN]: *water feature,* on Mandeville Island, joins Old River 15 miles west-southwest of Lodi (lat. 38° 03'25" N, long. 121°34'50" W). Named on Bouldin (1910) 7.5' quadrangle.

Trapper Slough [SAN JOAQUIN]: *water feature,* joins Middle River 11 miles west-southwest of downtown Stockton (lat. 37°53'35" N, long. 121°29'15" W). Named on Holt (1978) 7.5' quadrangle.

Tremont House: see **Valley Springs** [CALAVERAS].

Trent [MERCED]: *locality,* 2 miles northwest of Los Banos along Southern Pacific Railroad (lat. 37°04'40" N, long. 120°52'50" W; sec. 9, T 10 S, R 10 E). Named on Los Banos (1961) 15' quadrangle.

Tresidder Peak [MARIPOSA]: *peak,* 1.5 miles southwest of Cathedral Peak (lat. 37°49'50" N, long. 119°25'15" W; sec. 23, T 1 S, R 23 E). Named on Tuolumne Meadows (1956) 15' quadrangle. United States Board on Geographic Names (1959a, p. 3) rejected the name "Tenaya Peak" for the feature, and noted that the name "Tresidder" commemorates Donald E. Tresidder, president of Stanford University from 1943 until 1948. Tresidder also was president of Yosemite Park & Curry Company from 1925 until 1948 (Browning, 1986, p. 220).

Trigo [MADERA]: *village,* 7 miles east-southeast of Madera (lat. 36° 54'35" N, long. 119°57'30" W; sec. 1, T 12 S, R 18 E). Named on Gregg (1965) 7.5' quadrangle. Called Patterson on Mendenhall's (1908) map. Postal authorities established Trigo post office in 1912 and discontinued it in 1942 (Frickstad, p. 86). Logan's (1950) map shows a place called Lankershim located about 3.5 miles northwest of Trigo along Atchison, Topeka and Santa Fe Railroad.

Trigo: see **Gotri** [SAN JOAQUIN].

Trinity Lakes [MADERA]: *lakes,* 3.25 miles north-northwest of Devils Postpile (lat. 37°40' N, long. 119°06' W). Named on Devils Postpile (1953) 15' quadrangle.

Triple Divide Peak [MADERA]: *peak,* 1.5 miles east of Merced Peak (lat. 37°37'55" N, long. 119°22'10" W). Altitude 11,607 feet. Named on Merced Peak (1953) 15' quadrangle. Lieutenant N.F. McClure named the peak in 1895 (Browning, 1988, p. 147).

Triple Peak Fork [MADERA]: *stream,* flows 5.5 miles to Merced Peak Fork 5 miles north-northeast of Merced Peak (lat. 37°41'45" N, long. 119°20'50" W); the stream heads near Triple Divide Peak. Named on Merced Peak (1953) 15' quadrangle. United States Board on Geographic Names (1978b, p. 4) rejected the form "Tripple Peak Fork" for the name.

Trout Creek [TUOLUMNE]: *stream,* flows 6 miles to Clavey River nearly 7 miles east of Long Barn (lat. 38°04'55" N, long. 120°00'35" W; sec. 28, T 3 N, R 18 E). Named on Hull Creek (1979) and Pinecrest (1979) 7.5' quadrangles.

Trull [SAN JOAQUIN]: *locality,* 11.5 miles west of downtown Stockton along Atchison, Topeka and Santa Fe Railroad (lat. 37°56'20" N, long. 121°30'15" W). Named on Woodward Island (1978) 7.5' quadrangle.

Trumbull Peak [MARIPOSA]: *peak,* 4.5 miles west-northwest of El Portal (lat. 37°41'15" N, long. 119°51'35" W). Altitude 5004 feet. Named on El Portal (1947) 7.5' quadrangle. United States Board on Geographic Names (1901, p. 125) rejected the names "Cranberry Peak" and "Mount Trumbull" for the feature. The name "Trumbull" is for a Senator Trumbull, who visited Yosemite National Park (Browning, 1988, p. 147).

Tueculala Falls: see **Tueeulala Falls** [TUOLUMNE].

Tueeulala Falls [TUOLUMNE]: *waterfall,* 7 miles northeast of Mather on the north side of Hetch Hetchy Reservoir (lat. 37°57'45" N, long. 119°46'35" W; sec. 9, T 1 N, R 20 E). Named on Lake Eleanor (1956) 15' quadrangle. The name is of Indian origin (Browning, 1986, p. 221). United States Board on Geographic Names (1991, p. 7) rejected the name "Tueculala Falls" for the feature.

Tulare Plains: see "Regional setting."

Tulare Valley: see "Regional setting."

Tuleburg: see **Stockton** [SAN JOAQUIN].

Tule Island [SAN JOAQUIN]: *island,* 2200 feet long, 6 miles south of Terminous in San Joaquin River (lat. 38°01'40" N, long. 121°28'35" W). Named on Terminous (1978) 7.5' quadrangle.

Tule Lake [MERCED]: *lake,* 1350 feet long, 6.5 miles northeast of Pacheco Pass along Romero Creek (lat. 37°07'45" N, long. 121°07'40" W; sec. 30, T 9 S, R 8 E). Named on Crevison Peak (1955) 7.5' quadrangle.

Tuleville: see **Lodi** [SAN JOAQUIN].

Tulloch Gulch [TUOLUMNE]: *canyon,* drained by a stream that flows 1.25 miles to Tulloch Lake nearly 5 miles northwest of Keystone (lat. 37°53'10" N, long. 120°33'50" W; sec. 5, T 1 S, R 18 E). Named on Keystone (1962) and Melones Dam (1962) 7.5' quadrangles. Copperopolis (1916) 15' quadrangle has the form "Tullock Gulch" for the name.

Tulloch Lake [CALAVERAS-TUOLUMNE]: *lake,* behind a dam on Stanislaus River 7 miles south of Copperopolis on Calaveras-Tuolumne County line (lat. 37°52'35" N, long. 120°36'15" W). Named on Melones Dam (1962) 7.5' quadrangle. United States Board on Geographic Names (1977b, p. 6) approved the name "Tulloch Reservoir" for the feature, and gave the name "Tulloch Lake" as a variant.

Tulloch Mountain [TUOLUMNE]: *peak,* 4.5 miles northwest of Keystone (lat. 37°53' N, long. 120°33'40" W; sec. 5, T 1 S, R 13 E). Altitude 943 feet. Named on Melones Dam (1962) 7.5' quadrangle. Called Tullock Mtn. on Copperopolis (1916) 15' quadrangle, but United States Board on Geographic Names (1965c, p. 12) rejected this form of the name.

Tulloch Reservoir: see **Tulloch Lake** [CALAVERAS-TUOLUMNE].

Tullock Gulch: see **Tulloch Gulch** [TUOLUMNE].

Tullock Mountain: see **Tulloch Mountain** [TUOLUMNE].

Tu-lu-la-wi-ak: see **Illilouette Creek** [MADERA-MARIPOSA].

Tunnel Creek [TUOLUMNE]: *stream,* flows 1.5 miles to Middle Fork Stanislaus River 6.25 miles west of Strawberry (lat. 38°11'10" N, long. 120°07'25" W). Named on Strawberry (1979) 7.5' quadrangle.

Tuolumne [TUOLUMNE]: *town,* 8 miles east-southeast of Sonora (lat. 37°57'45" N, long. 120°14'15" W; on N line sec. 8, T 1 N, R 16 E). Named on Tuolumne (1948) 7.5' quadrangle. Postal authorities established Tuolumne post office in 1891, discontinued it in 1893, and reestablished it in 1901 (Frickstad, p. 217).

Tuolumne Camp [TUOLUMNE]: *locality,* 6.5 miles southwest of Mather (lat. 37°48'40" N, long. 119°55'50" W; sec. 31, T 1 S, R 19 E); the place is along South Fork Tuolumne River. Named on Lake Eleanor (1956) 15' quadrangle.

Tuolumne Castle: see **Grand Mountain** [TUOLUMNE].

Tuolumne City [STANISLAUS]: *locality,* 5.25 miles northeast of Westley (lat. 37°36'10" N, long. 121°07'50" W; sec. 7, T 4 S, R 8 E); the place is on the north side of Tuolumne River. Named on Westley (1952) 7.5' quadrangle. Postal authorities established Tuolumne City post office in 1867, discontinued it for a time in 1871, and discontinued it finally in 1872 (Frickstad, p. 201). Paxson McDowell started the place in the spring of 1850, but when in the summer the river was too low for navigation, the site was deserted; Tuolumne City was revived as a small farming community in the middle 1860's (Hoover, Rensch, and Rensch, p. 542). Ryer's Ferry, named for Dr. William M. Ryer, began operating at Tuolumne City in 1850 (Brotherton, p. 111). In 1867 John Mitchell laid out a community called Paradise located 5 miles east of Tuolumne City in Paradise Valley (Hoover, Rensch, and Rensch, p. 542). Postal authorities established Paradise post office in 1867 about 3.5 miles southwest of Modesto and discontinued it in 1870 (Salley, p. 167). A stopping place called Westport Landing began operating across Tuolumne River from Paradise in 1868 (Hoover, Rensch, and Rensch, p. 542).

Tuolumne Falls [TUOLUMNE]: *waterfall,* 8.5 miles west of Tioga Pass (lat. 37°54'10" N, long. 119°24'45" W); the feature is along Tuolumne River. Named on Tuolumne Meadows (1956) 15' quadrangle. United States Board on Geographic Names (1992, p. 5) rejected the name "White Cascade" for the feature.

Tuolumne Glacier Monument: see **Fairview Dome** [TUOLUMNE].

Tuolumne Meadows [TUOLUMNE]: *valley,* 5.5 miles west-southwest of Tioga Pass (lat. 37°52'30" N, long. 119°21' W); the valley is along upper reaches of Tuolumne River and lower reaches of Lyell Fork. Named on Tuolumne Meadows (1956) 15' quadrangle. Members of the Whitney survey named the feature in 1863 (O'Neill, p. 17).

Tuolumne Meadows High Sierra Camp [TUOLUMNE]: *locality,* 4.5 miles west-southwest of Tioga Pass (lat. 37°52'40" N, long. 119°19'55" W; near E line sec. 4, T 1 S, R 24 E); the place is in Tuolumne Meadows. Named on Tuolumne Meadows (1956) 15' quadrangle.

Tuolumne Pass [MARIPOSA-TUOLUMNE]: *pass,* 8.5 miles south-southwest of Tioga Pass on Mariposa-Tuolumne County line (lat. 37°48'15" N, long. 119°20'20" W). Named on Tuolumne Meadows (1956) 15' quadrangle.

Tuolumne Peak [TUOLUMNE]: *peak,* 12.5 miles west of Tioga Pass (lat. 37°52'30" N, long. 119°29' W; sec. 6, T 1 S, R 23 E). Altitude 10,845 feet. Named on Tuolumne Meadows (1956) 15' quadrangle.

Tuolumne River [STANISLAUS-TUOLUMNE]: *stream,* formed in Tuolumne County by the confluence of Lyell Fork and Dana Fork, flows 135 miles to San Joaquin River 4 miles north-northeast of Westley in Stanislaus County (lat. 37°36'20" N, long. 121°10'20" W; sec. 11, T 4 S, R 7 E). Named on Mariposa (1957, revised 1970) and San Jose (1962) 1°x 2° quadrangles. Called Touleme River on Ellis' (1850) map, Rio d. l. Towalumnes on Fremont's (1848) map, and Tualumne River on Gibbes' (1850) map. The name also had a variety of other forms in the early days, including: Tuwalumnes (Lyman, 1849b, p. 418), Tawallamie (Turner, p. 127), Towallamie (Evans, p. 215), Tuwaleme (Keller, p. 38), Towallome, and Towallernes (M'Collum, p. 129, 150). In the journal of the first session of California state senate the name "Tualumne" is described as a corruption of an Indian word that signifies a "cluster of stone wigwams" (DeFerrari *in* Stoddart, p. 173). North Fork enters from the north 9 miles south of Sonora; it is 33 miles long and is named on Long Barn (1956), Pinecrest (1956), Sonora (1948), and Tuolumne (1948) 15' quadrangles. United States Board on Geographic Names (1933a, p. 560) rejected the name "Return Creek" for North Fork, and also rejected the name "North Fork" without the further designation "Tuolumne River." South Fork enters from the southeast 10 miles east of Groveland; it is 27 miles long and is named on Hetch Hetchy Reservoir (1956), Lake Eleanor (1956), and Tuolumne (1948) 15' quadrangles. United States Board on Geographic Names (1934, p. 17) rejected the name "Middle Fork Tuolumne River" for present Middle Tuolumne River.

Tuolumne River: see **Middle Tuolumne River** [TUOLUMNE].

Tuolumne Valley: see **Hetch Hetchy Valley** [TUOLUMNE].

Turlock [STANISLAUS]: *city,* 13 miles southeast of Modesto (lat. 37°29'35" N, long. 120°50'55" W; in and near sec. 14, 15, 22, 23, T 5 S, R 10 E). Named on Turlock (1962) 15' quadrangle, and on Denair (1969) 7.5' quadrangle. Postal authorities established Turlock post office in 1871 (Frickstad, p. 201), and the city incorporated in 1908. Clark P. Lander and his brother Henry Lander suggested that the place be named for a lake in Scotland that they had read about in *Harpers Magazine* (Hanna, p. 337). California Division of Highways' (1934) map shows a place called Cooper located 1.25 miles west of Turlock along Tidewater Southern Railroad (near NW cor. sec. 22, T 5 S, R 10 E), a place called McGill located 1.25 miles west of Cooper along the railroad (near NE cor. sec. 20, T 5 S, R 10 E), and a place called Joyce located nearly 1 mile west of McGill along the railroad (near NW cor. sec. 20, T 5 S, R 10 E).

Turlock Lake [STANISLAUS]: *lake,* 17 miles east-northeast of Turlock (lat. 37°36'30" N, long. 120°34' W). Named on Cooperstown (1968) and Turlock Lake (1968) 7.5' quadrangles. Called Alfred Davis Reservoir on San Jose (1947) 1°x 2° quadrangle, and called Turlock Reservoir on

Cooperstown (1916) 7.5' quadrangle. Water of the lake covers the site of Lake Tent House, a stopping place of the 1860's (Brotherton, p. 149).

Turlock Reservoir: see **Turlock Lake** [STANISLAUS].

Turnback Creek [TUOLUMNE]: *stream*, flows 13 miles to Tuolumne River 9 miles southeast of Sonora (lat. 37°53'20" N, long. 120°16'20" W; sec. 1, T 1 S, R 15 E). Named on Standard (1948), Tuolumne (1948), and Twain Harte (1979) 7.5' quadrangles. The name supposedly records an incident involving a group of miners who turned back after an indecisive fight with Indians at the stream (Gudde, 1969, p. 348).

Turner [SAN JOAQUIN]: *locality*, 4.25 miles north of Manteca along Tidewater Southern Railroad (lat. 37°51'30" N, long. 121°12'50" W; sec. 9, T 1 S, R 7 E). Named on Manteca (1952) 7.5' quadrangle.

Turner: see **Tuttle** [MERCED].

Turner Cut [SAN JOAQUIN]: *water feature*, between McDonald Island and Roberts Island, joins San Joaquin River 9 miles west-northwest of downtown Stockton (lat. 37°59'45" N, long. 121° 26'40" W). Named on Holt (1978) 7.5' quadrangle.

Turner Island [MERCED]: *area*, 8 miles north-northwest of Dos Palos Y between San Joaquin River and Mariposa Slough. Named on Sandy Mush (1962), San Luis Ranch (1961), and Turner Ranch (1961) 7.5' quadrangles.

Turner Lake [MADERA]: *lake*, 1200 feet long, 2.5 miles east of Merced Peak (lat. 37°38'30" N, long. 119°20'50" W). Named on Merced Peak (1953) 15' quadrangle. The name is for Henry Ward Turner of United States Geological Survey, who pioneered geologic mapping in and near Yosemite National Park (United States Board on Geographic Names, 1963b, p. 15).

Turner Lake [SAN JOAQUIN]: *lake*, 1000 feet long, 17 miles west-southwest of Lodi (lat. 38°01'45" N, long. 121°33'25" W); the lake is at the head of Turner Slough. Named on Bouldin (1910) 7.5' quadrangle.

Turner Meadows [MARIPOSA]: *area*, 5 miles northeast of Wawona (lat. 37°35'45" N, long. 119°35'50" W; sec. 7, T 4 S, R 22 E). Named on Yosemite (1956) 15' quadrangle. United States Board on Geographic Names (1991, p. 7) approved the singular form "Turner Meadow" for the name. Browning (1986, p. 224) associated the name with Will Turner, who ran cattle in the vicinity in the 1880's, and was a ranger at Yosemite National Park for 37 years.

Turner Ridge [MARIPOSA]: *ridge*, southwest-trending, 2 miles long, 2.5 miles north of Wawona (lat. 37°34'15" N, long. 119°39'30" W). Named on Yosemite (1956) 15' quadrangle.

Turner Slough [SAN JOAQUIN]: *water feature*, on Mandeville Island, joins Old River 17 miles west-southwest of Lodi (lat. 38° 01'50" N, long. 121°33'50" W); the slough heads at Turner Lake. Named on Bouldin (1910) 7.5' quadrangle.

Turners Spring [CALAVERAS]: *spring*, 0.25 mile east-southeast of Copperopolis (lat. 37°58'45" N, long. 120°38'10" W; sec. 34, T 2 N, R 12 E). Named on Copperopolis (1962) 7.5' quadrangle.

Turtleback Dome [MARIPOSA]: *promontory*, 7 miles west-southwest of Yosemite Village on the south side of Merced River (lat. 37°42'45" N, long. 119°42'15" W). Named on Yosemite (1956) 15' quadrangle. United States Board on Geographic Names (1962a, p. 21) rejected the names "Turtle Dome" and "Turtle Back Dome" for the name.

Turtle Dome: see **Turtleback Dome** [MARIPOSA].

Turtle Rock: see **Pywiack Dome** [MARIPOSA].

Tuttle [MERCED]: *settlement*, 5.5 miles east of Merced (lat. 37°17'50" N, long. 120°22'40" W; on E line sec. 25, T 7 S, R 14 E). Named on Merced (1961) 7.5' quadrangle. Called Turner on Grunsky's (1899) map. Officials of Atchison, Topeka and Santa Fe Railroad named their station there about 1900 for R.H. Tuttle, a railroad official at Fresno (Gudde, 1949, p. 373).

Tuttle's Creek: see **Mormon Creek** [TUOLUMNE].

Tuttletown [TUOLUMNE]: *settlement*, 4.25 miles west of Sonora near Mormon Creek (lat. 37°59'30" N, long. 120°27'30" W; on S line sec. 29, T 2 N, R 14 E). Named on Sonora (1948) 7.5' quadrangle. The name is for Judge A.A.H. Tuttle, the earliest settler at the place (Stoddart, p. 61). Postal authorities established Tuttletown post office in 1857, discontinued it in 1858, reestablished it in 1890, and discontinued it in 1922 (Frickstad, p. 217). Wheeler (1878, p. 64) used the form "Tuttle Town" for the name. The community was known as Mormon Gulch in 1850 because some Mormons mined there (Jackson, p. 331). A place called Jeffersonville was situated about 1 mile southeast of Tuttletown (Gudde, 1975, p. 176); it thrived in the 1850's (Hoover, Rensch, and Rensch, p. 570).

Twain Harte [TUOLUMNE]: *town*, 9.5 miles east of Columbia (lat. 38°02'15" N, long. 120°13'45" W). Named on Twain Harte (1979) 7.5' quadrangle. Postal authorities established Twain Harte post office in 1931 (Frickstad, p. 217). Katurah F. Wood named the place in 1924 for writers Mark Twain and Bret Harte (Gudde, 1949, p. 373).

Twain Harte Lake [TUOLUMNE]: *lake*, 1150 feet long, less than 1 mile southwest of Twain Harte (lat. 38°01'45" N, long. 120°14'30" W; sec. 17, T 2 N, R 16 E). Named on Twain Harte (1979) 7.5' quadrangle.

Twain Harte Valley [TUOLUMNE]: *valley*, 1 mile north of Twain Harte (lat. 38°03'15" N, long. 120°13'55" W; near E line sec. 5, T 2 N, R 16 E). Named on Twain Harte (1979) 7.5' quadrangle.

Twelvemile House [MADERA]: *locality*, 10 miles south of Raymond (lat. 37°04'20" N, long. 119°54'10" W; sec. 9, T 10 S, R 19 E). Named on Daulton (1921) 7.5' quadrangle.

Twenty-eight Mile House: see **Eugene** [STANISLAUS].

Twentyone Mile Cut [SAN JOAQUIN]: *water feature*, about 8 miles south-southeast of Terminous along San Joaquin River (lat. 38°00'05" N, long. 121°27'15" W). Named on Terminous (1978) 7.5' quadrangle.

Twentyonemile Slough [SAN JOAQUIN]: *water feature*, joins San Joaquin River 8 miles south-southeast of Terminous (lat. 38°00'25" N, long. 121°26'40" W). Named on Headreach (1910) 7.5' quadrangle.

Twenty six Mile House: see **Eugene** [STANISLAUS].

Twentytwo Mile House [MADERA]: *locality*, 14 miles south-southeast of Raymond (lat. 37°02'20" N, long. 119°46'50" W; near S line sec. 22, T 10 S, R 20 E). Named on Little Table Mountain (1962) 7.5' quadrangle. Called Millers Corner on Raymond (1944) 15' quadrangle.

Twin Gulch [TUOLUMNE]:

(1) *canyon*, drained by a stream that flows nearly 1 mile to La Grange Reservoir 2.5 miles south-southwest of Don Pedro Camp opposite the mouth of Twin Gulch (2) (lat. 37°40'55" N, long. 120° 25'45" W; near S line sec. 9, T 3 S, R 14 E). Named on La Grange (1962) 7.5' quadrangle.

(2) *canyon*, drained by a stream that flows 1 mile to La Grange Reservoir 2.5 miles south-southwest of Don Pedro Camp opposite the mouth of Twin Gulch (1) (lat. 37°40'50" N, long. 120°25'40" W; near N line sec. 16, T 3 S, R 14 E). Named on La Grange (1962) 7.5' quadrangle.

Twin Gulch: see **Little Twin Gulch** [TUOLUMNE].

Twin Island Lakes [MADERA]: *lakes*, two, largest 1800 feet long, 9.5 miles west-northwest of Devils Postpile (lat. 37°41'30" N, long. 119°13'55" W); each lake contains a small island. Named on Devils Postpile (1953) 15' quadrangle.

Twin Lakes [MADERA]: *lakes*, two, largest 400 feet long, 5 miles southeast of Merced Peak (lat. 37°34'30" N, long. 119°20'25" W). Named on Merced Peak (1953) 15' quadrangle.

Twin Lakes [TUOLUMNE]: *lakes*, two, largest 1.25 miles long, 6.5 miles west of Tower Peak along Kendrick Creek (lat. 38°08' N, long. 119°40' W). Named on Tower Peak (1956) 15' quadrangle.

Twin Meadows [TUOLUMNE]: *areas*, two, 8 miles west-northwest of Dardanelle (lat. 38°23' N, long. 119°58' W). Named on Spicer Meadow Reservoir (1979) 7.5' quadrangle, which shows marsh in the areas.

Twin Meadows Lake [TUOLUMNE]: *lake*, 400 feet long, 8 miles west-northwest of Dardanelle (lat. 38°23'25" N, long. 119°57'45" W); the lake is 0.5 mile north-northeast of Twin Meadows. Named on Spicer Meadow Reservoir (1979) 7.5' quadrangle.

Twin Peaks [MERCED]: *peaks*, two, 3.5 miles east-southeast of Mariposa Peak (lat. 37°56' N, long. 121°09'15" W; sec. 36, T 11 S, R 7 E). Altitudes 2525 and 2682 feet. Named on Mariposa Peak (1969) 7.5' quadrangle.

Twin Peaks [TUOLUMNE]: *peaks*, two, 1.5 miles east-southeast of Matterhorn Peak on Tuolumne-Mono County line (lat. 38°04'55" N, long. 119°21'15" W). Named on Matterhorn Peak (1956) 15' quadrangle.

Twin Peaks: see **Mount Savage** [MARIPOSA].

Twin Sisters [MADERA]: *peaks*, two, 11 miles northeast of Raymond (lat. 37°20'25" N, long. 119°46'15" W; sec. 10, T 7 S, R 20 E). Altitudes 2697 and 2789 feet. Named on Horsecamp Mountain (1947) 7.5' quadrangle.

Twin Slough [SAN JOAQUIN]: *water feature*, joins Middle River 15 miles west-southwest of Lodi (lat. 38°02'20" N, long. 121°31'20" W). Named on Bouldin (1910) 7.5' quadrangle.

Two Dog Pass [TUOLUMNE]: *pass*, 4.5 miles east-northeast of Tuolumne (lat. 37°58'55" N, long. 120°09'25" W; near W line sec. 31, T 2 N, R 17 E). Named on Tuolumne (1948) 7.5' quadrangle.

Two Dollar Gulch [CALAVERAS]: *canyon*, drained by a stream that flows less than 1 mile to Spruce Gulch 0.25 mile east of Rail Road Flat (lat. 38°20'35" N, long. 120°30'15" W; near E line sec. 26, T 6 N, R 13 E). Named on Rail Road Flat (1948) 7.5' quadrangle.

Twomile Creek [TUOLUMNE]: *stream*, flows 5.25 miles to Clavey River 7 miles southeast of Long Barn (lat. 38°00'50" N, long. 120° 03' W; near E line sec. 24, T 2 N, R 17 E). Named on Hull Creek (1979) 7.5' quadrangle.

Two Springs: see **Wheats** [CALAVERAS].

Two Springs Campground [MADERA]: *locality*, 5 miles southeast of Yosemite Forks on the south side of Bass Lake (1) (lat. 37°18'50" N, long. 119°33'50" W; near SW cor. sec. 15, T 7 S, R 22 E). Named on Bass Lake (1953) 15' quadrangle.

Two Teats [MADERA]: *peak*, 6 miles north of Devils Postpile on Madera-Mono County line (lat. 37°42'45" N, long. 119°05'55" W). Altitude 11,387 feet. Named on Devils Postpile (1953) 15' quadrangle. This peak and nearby San Joaquin Mountain together also were called Two Teats (Gudde, 1949, p. 373-374).

Tyler [MADERA]: *locality*, 5 miles south-southwest of Chowchilla along Chowchilla Pacific Railroad (lat. 37°03'20" N, long. 120°18'50" W; sec. 15, T 10 S, R 15 E). Named on Chowchilla (1918) 7.5' quadrangle.

– U –

Underwood Creek [CALAVERAS]: *stream,* flows 2.5 miles to Littlejohns Creek 2.5 miles west-northwest of Copperopolis (lat. 37°59'45" N, long. 120°41' W; sec. 29, T 2 N, R 12 E). Named on Copperopolis (1962) and Salt Spring Valley (1962) 7.5' quadrangles.

Undine: see **Lathrop** [SAN JOAQUIN].

Unicorn Creek [TUOLUMNE]: *stream,* flows 2.5 miles to Tuolumne River 6.5 miles west-southwest of Tioga Pass in Tuolumne Meadows (lat. 37°52'30" N, long. 119°22'05" W; near W line sec. 5, T 1 S, R 24 E); the stream heads near Unicorn Peak. Named on Tuolumne Meadows (1956) 15' quadrangle.

Unicorn Peak [TUOLUMNE]: *peak,* 8 miles southwest of Tioga Pass (lat. 37°50'45" N, long. 119°22'50" W). Named on Tuolumne Meadows (1956) 15' quadrangle. Members of the Whitney survey named the peak (United States Board on Geographic Names, 1934, p. 26). Brewer (p. 412) described the feature in 1863 as a "sharp needle."

Union: see **Le Grand** [MERCED].

Union Hill [TUOLUMNE]: *hill,* 1 mile south of Columbia (lat. 38°01'10" N, long. 120°24'05" W; sec. 23, T 2 N, R 14 E). Named on Columbia (1948) 7.5' quadrangle. Gudde (1975, p. 99) listed a place called Douglasville that was situated opposite Union Hill.

Union Island [SAN JOAQUIN]: *island,* 10 miles southwest of downtown Stockton, mainly between Middle River and Old River (lat. 37°51' N, long. 121°27' W). Named on Clifton Court Forebay (1978), Holt (1978), Union Island (1978), and Woodward Island (1978) 7.5' quadrangles.

Union Point [MARIPOSA]: *promontory,* 1 mile south of Yosemite Village on the south side of Yosemite Valley (lat. 37°44'10" N, long. 119°35'10" W). Named on Yosemite (1956) 15' quadrangle.

Union Point [SAN JOAQUIN]: *locality,* 11.5 miles west-southwest of downtown Stockton at the southwest extremity of Roberts Island (lat. 37°53'30" N, long. 121°29'10" W). Named on Holt (1978) 7.5' quadrangle.

Upper Agua Fria: see **Agua Fria** [MARIPOSA].

Upper Baker Campground: see **Baker Campground** [TUOLUMNE].

Upper Bar: see **Big Bar** [CALAVERAS].

Upper Branigan Lake [TUOLUMNE]: *lake,* 900 feet long, 10 miles southwest of Tower Peak (lat. 38°02'20" N, long. 119°40'15" W); the lake is 0.25 mile upstream from Middle Branigan Lake. Named on Tower Peak (1956) 15' quadrangle.

Upper Calaveritas: see **Calaveritas** [CALAVERAS].

Upper Chiquito Campground [MADERA]: *locality,* 10 miles north of Shuteye Peak (lat. 37°29'55" N, long. 119°24'30" W; sec. 13, T 5 S, R 23 E); the place is along Chiquito Creek 7 miles upstream from Lower Chiquito Campground. Named on Shuteye Peak (1953) 15' quadrangle.

Upper Dominici Creek [STANISLAUS]: *stream,* flows 1.5 miles to the canyon of Tuolumne River 1.5 miles west of La Grange (lat. 37°39'55" N, long. 120°29'10" W; sec. 24, T 3 S, R 13 E); the mouth of the stream is 1 mile north-northeast of the mouth of Lower Dominici Creek. Named on La Grange (1962) 7.5' quadrangle.

Upper Ferry: see **Big Bar** [CALAVERAS].

Upper Fletcher Lake [MARIPOSA]: *lake,* 1100 feet long, 5 miles southeast of Cathedral Peak (lat. 37°47'50" N, long. 119°20'25" W); the lake is along Fletcher Creek. Named on Tuolumne Meadows (1956) 15' quadrangle. Called Fletcher Lake on Mount Lyell (1901) 30' quadrangle, and United States Board on Geographic Names (1991, p. 4) approved this name for it. Lieutenant N.F. McClure gave the name "Fletcher Lake" to the feature in 1895 to honor Arthur C. Fletcher of California State Board of Fish Commissioners (United States Board on Geographic Names, 1934, p. 9).

Upper Fletcher Lake: see **Townsley Lake** [MARIPOSA].

Upper Iceberg Lake: see **Cecile Lake** [MADERA].

Upper Jones Tract [SAN JOAQUIN]: *area,* 11 miles west-southwest of downtown Stockton (lat. 37°55' N, long. 121°29' W); the place is south of Lower Jones Tract. Named on Holt (1978) and Woodward Island (1978) 7.5' quadrangles. Holt (1913) 7.5' quadrangle shows the area as part of Roberts Island.

Upper McCabe Lake [TUOLUMNE]: *lake,* 0.5 mile long, 7 miles north-northwest of Tioga Pass (lat. 37°59'45" N, long. 119°19'20" W; on W line sec. 27, T 2 N, R 24 E); the lake is about 1 mile east of McCabe Lakes. Named on Tuolumne Meadows (1956) 15' quadrangle. On Mount Lyell (1901) 30' quadrangle, the lake apparently is included with the group called McCabe Lakes. United States Board on Geographic Names (1962a, p. 21) rejected the name "McCabe Lake" for present Upper McCabe Lake.

Upper Merced Pass Lake [MADERA]: *lake,* 450 feet long, 2.5 miles west-southwest of Merced Peak (lat. 37°37'25" N, long. 119°26'30" W); the lake is 0.5 mile north of Merced Pass. Named on Merced Peak (1953) 15' quadrangle.

Upper Ottoway Lake [MADERA]: *lake,* 1650 feet long, 0.5 mile west-northwest of Merced Peak (lat. 37°38'25" N, long. 119°24'15" W); the lake is less than 1 mile east of Lower Ottoway Lake. Named on Merced Peak (1953) 15' quadrangle.

Upper Peninsula Lake [TUOLUMNE]: *lake,* 1100 feet long, 8 miles west-southwest of Tower Peak (lat. 38°06' N, long. 119°40'45" W); the lake is 0.5 mile east of Peninsula Lake. Named on Tower Peak (1956) 15' quadrangle.

Upper Relief Valley [TUOLUMNE]: *valley,* 12 miles east-northeast of Pinecrest at the head of Relief Creek (lat. 38°13'30" N, long. 119°46'30" W); the valley is about 1.5 miles south-southwest of Lower Relief Valley. Named on Pinecrest (1956) 15' quadrangle.

Upper Ruth Lake [MERCED]: *lake,* 2200 feet long, 4.5 miles north-northeast of Los Banos (lat. 37°06'50" N, long. 120°48'50" W; at NE cor. sec. 31, T 9 S, R 11 E); the lake is south of Lower Ruth Lake. Named on Los Banos (1960) 7.5' quadrangle.

Upper Three Meadow [TUOLUMNE]: *area,* 7.25 miles east-northeast of Pinecrest (lat. 38°14'25" N, long. 119°52'40" W; sec. 34, T 5 N, R 19 E); the feature is one of the group called Three Meadows. Named on Pinecrest (1979) 7.5' quadrangle.

Upper White Lake [STANISLAUS]: *intermittent lake,* 350 feet long, 2.5 miles north-northeast of Westley (lat. 37°34'55" N, long. 121° 10'55" W); the feature is 2.5 miles southeast of Lower White Lake. Named on Westley (1952) 7.5' quadrangle. On Westley (1915) 7.5' quadrangle, the name applies to a larger permanent lake.

Upper Yosemite Fall [MARIPOSA]: *waterfall,* less than 1 mile northwest of Yosemite Village (lat. 37°45'20" N, long. 119°35'45" W); the feature is along Yosemite Creek above Lower Yosemite Fall. Named on Hetch Hetchy Reservoir (1956) 15' quadrangle. Yosemite (1909) 30' quadrangle has the name "Yosemite Falls" for Upper Yosemite Fall and Lower Yosemite Fall together. Hoffmann and Gardner's (1863-1867) map has the name "Yosemite Fall" for the two waterfalls together.

Urgon [SAN JOAQUIN]: *locality,* 2 miles north of downtown Lodi along Southern Pacific Railroad (lat. 38°09'30" N, long. 121°16'15" W; sec. 36, T 4 N, R 6 E). Named on Lodi North (1968) 7.5' quadrangle.

Usona [MARIPOSA]: *locality,* 8 miles east-southeast of Mariposa (lat. 37°27'15" N, long. 119°49'35" W; sec. 31, T 5 S, R 20 E). Named on Mariposa (1947) 15' quadrangle. Postal authorities established Usona post office in 1913, moved it 5.5 miles north in 1940, and discontinued it in 1942; the name is from the initial letters of the term "United States of North America" (Salley, p. 228).

Utica Reservoir [TUOLUMNE]: *lake,* nearly 2 miles long, 7 miles northeast of Liberty Hill on Tuolumne-Alpine County line, mainly in Alpine County (lat. 38°26' N, long. 120°00' W). Named on Tamarack (1979) 7.5' quadrangle.

Utica Reservoir: see **Ross Reservoir** [CALAVERAS].

Utters Bar: see **Stent** [TUOLUMNE].

Utterville: see **Stent** [TUOLUMNE].

– V –

Valentine Gulch [CALAVERAS]: *canyon,* drained by a stream that flows 1 mile to Middle Fork Mokelumne River nearly 5 miles west-northwest of Rail Road Flat (lat. 38°22'25" N, long. 120°35'25" W; sec. 18, T 6 N, R 13 E). Named on Rail Road Flat (1948) 7.5' quadrangle. The name commemorates Valentine Granados, a well-known Mexican prospector of Calaveras County (Camp *in* Doble, p. 300).

Valentine Hill: see **Bummerville** [CALAVERAS].

Vallecita: see **Catheys Valley** [MARIPOSA] (1).

Vallecito [CALAVERAS]: *village,* 4 miles east-northeast of Angels Camp (lat. 38°05'15" N, long. 120°28'20" W; sec. 30, T 3 N, R 14 E). Named on Columbia (1948) 7.5' quadrangle. Postal authorities established Vallicita post office in 1854 and changed the name to Vallecito in 1940 (Salley, p. 229). United States Board on Geographic Names (1950, p. 7) ruled against the name "Vallicita" for the place. Balaklava Hill, named for a battle site of the Crimean War, was located 2.5 miles south of Vallecito (Gudde, 1975, p. 25).

Valley Home [STANISLAUS]: *village,* 5 miles northwest of Oakdale (lat. 37°49'45" N, long. 120°54'45" W). Named on Escalon (1968) 7.5' quadrangle. Called Thalheim on Thalheim (1915) 7.5' quadrangle. Thalheim began as a community of Germans; during World War I the name of the place was changed to Valley Home, a translation of the German name "Thalheim" (Gudde, 1949, p. 376). Postal authorities established Thalheim post office in 1903 and changed the name to Valley Home in 1918 (Frickstad, p. 201).

Valley Springs [CALAVERAS]: *town,* 8 miles west of San Andreas (lat. 38°11'35" N, long. 120°49'45" W; sec. 13, 24, T 4 N, R 10 E). Named on Valley Springs (1962) 7.5' quadrangle. Postal authorities established Valley Springs post office in 1872, discontinued it in 1879, and reestablished it in 1882 (Frickstad, p. 17). The place first was called Spring Valley for mineral springs there, but the words of this name were reversed when the site became the terminous of San Joaquin and Sierra Nevada Railroad

(Gudde, 1949, p. 376). Camp's (1962) map has the name "Tremont House" for a stopping place located 3 miles south of Valley Springs, and the name "N. American House" for a stopping place situated 2 miles south of Valley Springs.

Valley Springs Peak [CALAVERAS]: *peak,* 1 mile north-northwest of Valley Springs (lat. 38°12'25" N, long. 120°50'15" W; near N line sec. 14, T 4 N, R 10 E). Altitude 1211 feet. Named on Valley Springs (1962) 7.5' quadrangle.

Valley Springs Reservoir: see **New Hogan Reservoir** [CALAVERAS].

Valley View [MARIPOSA]: *locality,* 5 miles west-southwest of Yosemite Village in Yosemite Valley (lat. 37°43'05" N, long. 119° 40' W). Named on Yosemite (1956) 15' quadrangle. This is the first spot from which most of Yosemite Valley can be viewed on the approach from the west; the place is called River View on a map of 1883 (Browning, 1988, p. 150).

Vallicita: see **Vallecito** [CALAVERAS].

Van Allen [SAN JOAQUIN]: *locality,* 9 miles east of Manteca along Tidewater Southern Railroad (lat. 37°47'55" N, long. 121°03'05" W; near SE cor. sec. 35, T 1 S, R 8 E). Named on Avena (1952) 7.5' quadrangle.

Vandeburg Lake [MADERA]: *lake,* 900 feet long, 6 miles south-southeast of Merced Peak (lat. 37°32'55" N, long. 119°21'05" W); the lake is one of the group called Madera Lakes. Named on Merced Peak (1953) 15' quadrangle. United States Board on Geographic Names (1991, p. 7) approved the form "Vanderburgh Lake" for the name.

Vanderburgh Lake: see **Vandeburg Lake** [MADERA].

Vanormer [STANISLAUS]: *locality,* 2 miles north-northwest of Patterson along Southern Pacific Railroad (lat. 37°29'55" N, long. 121°08'50" W; sec. 13, T 5 S, R 7 E). Named on Patterson (1916) 7.5' quadrangle.

Vantine's Crossing: see **Knights Ferry** [STANISLAUS].

Varain: see **Exchequer** [MARIPOSA] (1).

Venice: see **Venice Island** [SAN JOAQUIN].

Venice Cut [SAN JOAQUIN]: *water feature,* part of Stockton Deep Water Channel that cuts off a meander in San Joaquin River 15 miles west-southwest of Lodi (lat. 38°03'20" N, long. 121°31'25" W); the feature is on Venice Island. Named on Bouldin Island (1978) 7.5' quadrangle.

Venice Ferry [SAN JOAQUIN]: *locality,* 13 miles west-southwest of Lodi along Little Connection Slough (lat. 38°03'40" N, long. 121° 30'05" W); the place at the east end of Venice Island. Named on Bouldin Island (1978) 7.5' quadrangle.

Venice Island [SAN JOAQUIN]: *island,* 4 miles long, 15 miles west-southwest of Lodi between San Joaquin River, Potato Slough, and Little Connection Slough. (lat. 38°04'30" N, long. 121°31'30" W). Named on Bouldin Island (1978) 7.5' quadrangle. Thompson and West's (1879) map shows a place called Venice located along San Joaquin River on the south edge of Venice Island (near S line sec. 2, T 2 N, R 4 E).

Venice Island: see **Little Venice Island** [SAN JOAQUIN].

Venice Reach [SAN JOAQUIN]: *water feature,* part of San Joaquin River between Venice Island and Mandeville Island 15 miles west-southwest of Lodi (lat. 38°03'45" N, long. 121°32'30" W). Named on Bouldin Island (1978) 7.5' quadrangle.

Vermont Bar [TUOLUMNE]: *locality,* 9 miles north of Keystone along Stanislaus River (lat. 37°58'05" N, long. 120°31'30" W; on E line sec. 3, T 1 N, R 13 E). Named on Copperopolis (1916) 15' quadrangle. Water of New Melones Lake now covers the site.

Vernal Fall [MARIPOSA]: *waterfall,* 3 miles east-southeast of Yosemite Village along Merced River (lat. 37°43'40" N, long. 119° 32'35" W). Named on Yosemite (1956) 15' quadrangle. Lafayette H. Bunnell named the waterfall in 1851 (United States Board on Geographic Names, 1934, p. 26).

Vernalis [SAN JOAQUIN]: *village,* 10.5 miles southeast of Tracy (lat. 37°37'50" N, long. 121°17'10" W; near W line sec. 35, T 3 S, R 6 E). Named on Vernalis (1969) 7.5' quadrangle. Postal authorities established San Joaquin post office 25 miles south of Stockton in 1851, discontinued it in 1852, reestablished it in 1874, and moved it 3 miles southwest to the railroad in 1888, when they changed the name to Vernalis (Salley, p. 195).

Vernon: see **Newman** [STANISLAUS].

Vernon Lake: see **Lake Vernon** [TUOLUMNE].

Vichy Spring [MADERA]: *spring,* 7.25 miles east-southeast of Raymond (lat. 37°09'35" N, long. 119°47'35" W; sec. 9, T 9 S, R 20 E). Named on Raymond (1944) 15' quadrangle.

Victor [SAN JOAQUIN]: *village,* 3.5 miles west-southwest of Lockeford (lat. 38°08'20" N, long. 121°12'15" W; on W line sec. 3, T 3 N, R 7 E). Named on Lockeford (1968) 7.5' quadrangle. Postal authorities established Victor post office in 1922 (Frickstad, p. 163). Officials of Southern Pacific Railroad named the place in 1908 for Victor Morden, whose father, A.E. Morden, was instrumental in securing a railroad station there (Gudde, 1949, p. 379).

Victoria Gulch [MARIPOSA]: *canyon,* drained by a stream that flows 3 miles to Bear Creek (2) 4.25 miles north of the settlement of Catheys Valley (lat. 37°29'45" N, long. 120°06'05" W). Named on Catheys Valley (1962) 7.5' quadrangle.

Victoria Island [SAN JOAQUIN]: *island,* 14 miles west-southwest of downtown Stockton between Old River and Middle River (lat. 37° 53'15" N, long. 121°32' W). Named on Clifton Court Forebay (1978), Holt (1978), and Woodward Island (1978) 7.5' quadrangles.

Villinger [SAN JOAQUIN]: *locality,* 5 miles west of Lodi along Western Pacific Railroad (lat. 38°08'40" N, long. 121°22'20" W; near NE cor. sec. 1, T 3 N, R 5 E). Named on Lodi North (1968) 7.5' quadrangle.

Vine Spring [TUOLUMNE]: *spring,* nearly 2 miles north-northwest of Columbia (lat. 38°03'30" N, long. 120°25'10" W; sec. 3, T 2 N, R 14 E). Named on Columbia (1948) 7.5' quadrangle.

Virginia Canyon [TUOLUMNE]: *canyon,* 10 miles long, along Return Creek above a point 11 miles west-northwest of Tioga Pass (lat. 37°58' N, long. 119°26'25" W). Named on Matterhorn Peak (1956) and Tuolumne Meadows (1956) 15' quadrangles.

Virginia Creek [MARIPOSA]: *stream,* flows 1 mile to Devil Gulch 9 miles south of El Portal (lat. 37°32'25" N, long. 119°47'25" W). Named on Buckingham Mountain (1947) 7.5' quadrangle.

Virginia Falls: see **Lower Virginia Falls**, under **White Cascade** [TUOLUMNE].

Virginia Lake [TUOLUMNE]: *lake,* 1700 feet long, 10 miles west-northwest of Tioga Pass (lat. 37°57'45" N, long. 119°25'35" W); the lake is less than 1 mile east-southeast of the mouth of Virginia Canyon. Named on Tuolumne Meadows (1956) 15' quadrangle.

Virginia Pass [TUOLUMNE]: *pass,* 3 miles southeast of Matterhorn Peak on Tuolumne-Mono County line (lat. 38°04' N, long. 119°20'05" W); the pass is near the head of Virginia Canyon. Named on Matterhorn Peak (1956) 15' quadrangle.

Virginia Peak [TUOLUMNE]: *peak,* 2.25 miles southeast of Matterhorn Peak (lat. 38°03'55" N, long. 119°21'25" W). Altitude 12,001 feet. Named on Matterhorn Peak (1956) 15' quadrangle. Officials of the National Park Service recommended the name "Virginia Peak" to replace the earlier name "Red Peak" (United States Board on Geographic Names, 1934, p. 27).

Virginia Point [MARIPOSA]: *relief feature,* nearly 4 miles southeast of Coulterville (lat. 37°40'15" N, long. 120°09'05" W; near SE cor. sec. 13, T 3 S, R 16 E). Named on Coulterville (1947) 7.5' quadrangle.

Virgin Tears Creek: see **Ribbon Creek** [MARIPOSA].

Virgin Tear's Fall: see **Ribbon Fall** [MARIPOSA].

Vizard Creek [STANISLAUS-TUOLUMNE]: *stream,* heads in Tuolumne County and flows 7 miles to Beltz Lake 1.5 miles east-southeast of La Grange in Stanislaus County (lat. 37°39'20" N, long. 120°26'15" W). Named on La Grange (1962) 7.5' quadrangle.

Vogelsang High Sierra Camp [MARIPOSA]: *locality,* 5 miles southeast of Cathedral Peak (lat. 37°47'45" N, long. 119°20'40" W); the place is 1.25 miles north of Vogelsang Peak. Named on Tuolumne Meadows (1956) 15' quadrangle.

Vogelsang Lake [MARIPOSA]: *lake,* 1700 feet long, 5.25 miles southeast of Cathedral Peak (lat. 37°47'10" N, long. 119°20'35" W); the lake is 0.5 mile north-northeast of Vogelsang Peak. Named on Tuolumne Meadows (1956) 15' quadrangle. A pass located 0.5 mile south of the lake is called Vogelsang Pass; the same feature is called Real Pass on a map of 1896 made by Lieutenant McClure (Browning, 1988, p. 153).

Vogelsang Pass: see **Vogelsang Lake** [MARIPOSA].

Vogelsang Peak [MARIPOSA]: *peak,* nearly 6 miles south-southeast of Cathedral Peak (lat. 37°46'40" N, long. 119°20'55" W). Altitude 11,516 feet. Named on Tuolumne Meadows (1956) 15' quadrangle. Lieutenant H.C. Benson named the peak for Alexander T. Vogelsang, who was president of California State Board of Fish Commissioners from 1896 until 1901 (United States Board on Geographic Names, 1934, p. 27).

Volcanic Ridge [MADERA]: *ridge,* west- to southwest-trending, 2.25 miles long, 5.5 miles northwest of Devils Postpile (lat. 37°40'40" N, long. 119°09'15" W). Named on Devils Postpile (1953) 15' quadrangle.

Volstead [SAN JOAQUIN]: *locality,* 10.5 miles east of Manteca along Tidewater Southern Railroad (lat. 37°47'55" N, long. 121°01'30" W; near N line sec. 6, T 2 S, R 9 E). Named on Avena (1952) 7.5' quadrangle. California Division of Highways' (1934) map shows a place called Sexton located nearly 0.5 mile west of Volstead (near NW cor. sec. 6, T 2 S, R 8 E).

Volta [MERCED]: *village,* 5 miles west-northwest of Los Banos (lat. 37°05'45" N, long. 120°55'35" W; near NE cor. sec. 1, T 10 S, R 9 E). Named on Los Banos (1961) 15' quadrangle. Postal authorities established Volta post office in 1890 and discontinued it in 1972; the name recalls Volta Improvement Company (Salley, p. 233).

Volunteer Gulch [CALAVERAS]: *canyon,* drained by a stream that flows 1 mile to Mokelumne River 1 mile north-northwest of Mokelumne Hill (lat. 38°18'50" N, long. 120°42'45" W; sec. 1, T 5 N, R 11 E). Named on Mokelumne Hill (1948) 7.5' quadrangle. McKinstry (p. 362) mentioned a canyon called Steep Gulch that, from his description, probably is a branch of Volunteer Gulch.

Volunteer Peak [TUOLUMNE]: *peak,* 8.5 miles southwest of Matterhorn Peak (lat. 38°00'20" N, long. 119°29'15" W). Altitude 10,479 feet. Named on Matterhorn Peak (1956) 15' quadrangle. The feature originally had the name "Regulation Peak" (Browning, 1986, p. 181).

Vonich Gulch [CALAVERAS]: *canyon,* nearly 2 miles long, opens into the canyon of Angels Creek 5 miles south of Angels Camp (lat. 38°00'15" N, long. 120°33'10" W; near S line sec. 21, T 2 N, R 13 E). Named on Angels Camp (1962) 7.5' quadrangle.

Vulcan Island [SAN JOAQUIN]: *island,* 2350 feet long, 6.5 miles west-northwest of downtown Stockton along San Joaquin River (lat. 37°59'20" N, long. 121°24'15" W). Named on Holt (1952) 7.5' quadrangle. Called Shipyard I. on Holt (1913) 7.5' quadrangle, and shown connected to Roberts Island on Holt (1978) 7.5' quadrangle. United States Board on Geographic Names (1978b, p. 4) approved the name "Windmill Cove" for an embayment on the west side of Vulcan Island 6 miles northwest of Stockton along San Joaquin River (lat. 37°59'23" N, long. 121°24'27" W).

– W –

Wades Flat Gulch [CALAVERAS]: *canyon,* drained by a stream that flows 1.5 miles to Coyote Creek 1.5 miles south of Vallecito (lat. 38°03'45" N, long. 120°28'05" W; near NW cor. sec. 5, T 2 N, R 14 E). Named on Columbia (1948) 7.5' quadrangle.

Wade's Meadows: see **Ackerson Meadow** [TUOLUMNE].

Wade's Mountain: see **Bald Mountain** [TUOLUMNE] (3).

Wagner [SAN JOAQUIN]: *locality,* 7.25 miles east of Manteca along Tidewater Southern Railroad (lat. 37°47'50" N, long. 121°04'50" W; near N line sec. 3, T 2 S, R 8 E). Named on Avena (1952) 7.5' quadrangle.

Wagner [TUOLUMNE]: *settlement,* 2.5 miles west-northwest of Dardanelle (lat. 38°21'35" N, long. 119°52'40" W). Named on Donnell Lake (1979) 7.5' quadrangle.

Wagner Ridge [MARIPOSA-TUOLUMNE]: *ridge,* east-southeast-trending, 4.5 miles long, 2.5 miles west-southwest of Smith Peak on Mariposa-Tuolumne County line (lat. 37°47' N, long. 120°08'15" W). Named on Groveland (1947) and Jawbone Ridge (1947) 7.5' quadrangles.

Wagner Valley [MARIPOSA]: *valley,* 2.5 miles southwest of Smith Peak along Smith Creek (lat. 37°46'10" N, long. 120°07'45" W); the valley is south of Wagner Ridge. Named on Groveland (1947) and Jawbone Ridge (1947) 7.5' quadrangles.

Wa-kal-la: see **Merced River** [MADERA-MARIPOSA-MERCED].

Wakefield: see **Stockton** [SAN JOAQUIN].

Walden Slough [STANISLAUS]: *stream,* diverges from San Joaquin River nearly 5 miles north-northeast of Westley (lat. 37°36'50" N, long. 121°09'55" W; sec. 2, T 4 S, R 7 E), and flows 2 miles to Finnegan Cutoff (present Finnegan Cut). Named on Westley (1915) 7.5' quadrangle. The stream course is shown dry on Westley (1952) 7.5' quadrangle, and is omitted from Westley (1969) 7.5' quadrangle.

Walemo Rock: see **Fresno Dome** [MADERA].

Walker [CALAVERAS]: *locality,* 2.25 miles southwest of Garnet Hill (lat. 38°27'10" N, long. 120°16'35" W; near S line sec. 13, T 7 N, R 15 E). Named on Garnet Hill (1979) 7.5' quadrangle.

Walker: see **Mike Walker Canyon** [MADERA].

Walker's Ferry: see **Islip's Ferry**, under **Oakdale** [STANISLAUS].

Walker Slough [SAN JOAQUIN]: *water feature,* joins French Camp Slough 3 miles south of downtown Stockton (lat. 37°54'55" N, long. 121°18' W). Named on Stockton West (1952) 7.5' quadrangle.

Wallace [CALAVERAS]: *village,* 8 miles west of Valley Springs (lat. 38°11'40" N, long. 120°58'35" W; sec. 15, T 4 N, R 9 E). Named on Wallace (1962) 7.5' quadrangle. Postal authorities established Wallace post office in 1883, discontinued it in 1945, and reestablished it in 1951; the name is for J.H. Wallace, chief engineer for San Joaquin and Sierra Nevada Railroad (Salley, p. 234).

Wallace: see **Mount Wallace** [CALAVERAS].

Walla Gulch [CALAVERAS]: *canyon,* drained by a stream that flows 2.25 miles to Murray Creek 3.5 miles east of San Andreas (lat. 38° 12'05" N, long. 120°36'55" W; sec. 14, T 4 N, R 12 E). Named on Calaveritas (1962) 7.5' quadrangle.

Wally Hill [CALAVERAS]: *ridge,* west-northwest-trending, 1 mile long, 7.5 miles east-southeast of San Andreas (lat. 38°09'50" N, long. 120°33' W; on S line sec. 28, T 4 N, R 13 E). Named on Calaveritas (1962) 7.5' quadrangle.

Walters Island [SAN JOAQUIN]: *island,* 1050 feet long, 8 miles west-northwest of downtown Stockton in San Joaquin River (lat. 37°49'50" N, long. 121°25'30" W). Named on Holt (1978) 7.5' quadrangle.

Walthall [SAN JOAQUIN]: *locality,* 8 miles east of downtown Stockton along Southern Pacific Railroad (lat. 37°58'45" N, long. 121° 08'40" W; near W line sec. 31, T 2 N, R 8 E). Named on Stockton East (1952) 7.5' quadrangle.

Walthall Slough [SAN JOAQUIN]: *water feature,* enters Weatherbee Lake 13 miles south of downtown Stockton (lat. 37°46'15" N, long. 121°17'25" W). Named on Lathrop (1952) and Vernalis (1969) 7.5' quadrangles.

Walton Cabin Spring [TUOLUMNE]: *spring,* 6.25 miles south-southeast of Duckwall Mountain (lat. 37°52'40" N, long. 120°05'45" W; sec. 3, T 1 S, R 17 E). Named on Duckwall Mountain (1948) 7.5' quadrangle.

Walton Lake [MADERA]: *lake,* 500 feet long, 2 miles east-southeast of Merced Peak (lat. 37°37'20" N, long. 119°21'50" W). Named on Merced Peak (1953) 15' quadrangle. John Handley of California Department of Fish and Game named the lake in 1940 (Browning, 1986, p. 231).

Wamelo Rock: see **Fresno Dome** [MADERA].

Wanda: see **Oakdale** [STANISLAUS].

Wapama Falls [TUOLUMNE]: *waterfall,* 7.5 miles northeast of Mather on Falls Creek (lat. 37°58' N, long. 119°45'50" W; at S line sec. 3, T 1 N, R 20 E). Named on Lake Eleanor (1956) 15' quadrangle. Called Hetch Hetchy Fall on Hoffmann and Gardner's (1863-1867) map, and the feature has the name "Macomb Falls" on a map of 1896 (Browning, 1986, p. 231).

Ward Cut [SAN JOAQUIN]: *water feature,* artificial watercourse 5 miles south of Terminous along Stockton Deep Water Channel (lat. 38°02'25" N, long. 121°29'35" W); the feature cuts off a meander of San Joaquin River east of Ward Island. Named on Terminous (1978) 7.5' quadrangle. United States Board on Geographic Names (1977c, p. 4) listed the form "Wards Cut" as a variant..

Ward Island [SAN JOAQUIN]: *island,* 1600 feet long, 5 miles south of Terminous in San Joaquin River (lat. 38°02'30" N, long. 121° 30' W). Named on Bouldin Island (1978) and Terminous (1978) 7.5' quadrangles. United States Board on Geographic Names (1977c, p. 4) listed the form "Wards Island" as a variant.

Ward Lakes [MADERA]: *lakes,* two, largest 1200 feet long, 4 miles east of Merced Peak (lat. 37°38'15" N, long. 119°19'10" W). Named on Merced Peak (1953) 15' quadrangle.

Ward Mountain [MADERA]: *peak,* nearly 5 miles north-northeast of O'Neals (lat. 37°11'10" N, long. 119°38'50" W; near S line sec. 35, T 8 S, R 21 E). Altitude 2788 feet. Named on O'Neals (1965) 7.5' quadrangle.

Ward Mountain [MARIPOSA]: *ridge,* northwest- to west-trending, 1.25 miles long, 6 miles southeast of the settlement of Catheys Valley (lat. 37°22'40" N, long. 120°00'30" W). Named on Catheys Valley (1962) and Illinois Hill (1962) 7'5' quadrangles.

Ward's Branch: see **Henness Branch** [MARIPOSA].

Wards Cut: see **Ward Cut** [SAN JOAQUIN].

Wards Ferry [TUOLUMNE]: *locality,* 9 miles southeast of Sonora along Tuolumne River (lat. 37°52'40" N, long. 120°17'35" W). Named on Sonora (1897) 30' quadrangle. Standard (1948) 7.5' quadrangle shows Wards Ferry bridge at the place. Joseph Ward ran a ferry at the site in 1850; a canyon on the south side of Tuolumne River at Ward's Ferry was called Murderers' Gulch for the danger of bandits there (Paden and Schlichtmann, p. 148-149).

Wards Island: see **Ward Island** [SAN JOAQUIN].

Warm Gulch [STANISLAUS]: *canyon,* drained by a stream that flows 1.25 miles to Quinto Creek 1 mile south of Crevison Peak (lat. 37°10'35" N, long. 121°11'25" W; sec. 3, T 9 S, R 7 E). Named on Crevison Peak (1955) 7.5' quadrangle.

Warner: see **Dallas-Warner Reservoir**, under **Modesto Reservoir** [STANISLAUS].

Warner Gulch [STANISLAUS]: *canyon,* 0.5 mile long, opens into the canyon of Tuolumne River 8 miles east of Waterford (lat. 37° 38'20" N, long. 120°36'30" W). Named on Cooperstown (1968) 7.5' quadrangle.

Warnerville [STANISLAUS]: *locality,* 14 miles east of Oakdale along Sierra Railway (lat. 37°43'55" N, long. 120°35'45" W; sec. 25, T 2 S, R 12 E). Named on Cooperstown (1968) 7.5' quadrangle. Called Warnersville on Cooperstown (1953) 7.5' quadrangle. Postal authorities established Warnerville post office in 1898 and discontinued it in 1909; the name commemorates James Warner, a rancher and county supervisor in the 1880's (Salley, p. 234).

Warren's Ferry: see **Islip's Ferry**, under **Oakdale** [STANISLAUS].

Washburn Cascade: see **Bunnell Cascade** [MARIPOSA].

Washburn Lake [MADERA]: *lake,* 0.5 mile long, 5.5 miles north-northeast of Merced Peak along Merced River (lat. 37°42'55" N, long. 119°22'15" W). Named on Merced Peak (1953) 15' quadrangle. Lieutenant N.F. McClure named the lake in 1895 for Albert Henry Washburn of Wawona (United States Board on Geographic Names, 1934, p. 27).

Washburn Point [MARIPOSA]: *relief feature,* 2 miles south-southeast of Yosemite Village on the south side of Yosemite Valley (lat. 37°43'15" N, long. 119°34'20" W). Named on Yosemite (1956) 15' quadrangle. Browning (1986, p. 232) associated the name with Albert Henry Washburn, for whom Washburn Lake was named.

Washburn Slide [MARIPOSA]: *relief feature,* 5.25 miles west-southwest of Yosemite Village on the south side of Yosemite Valley (lat. 37°42'40" N, long. 119°40'05" W). Named on Yosemite (1956) 15' quadrangle.

Washington: see **Camp Washington**, under **Chinese Camp** [TUOLUMNE].

Washington Canyon [STANISLAUS]: *canyon,* drained by a stream that flows 4.5 miles to Del Puerto Canyon 2.25 miles north-northeast of Copper Mountain (lat. 37°26'40" N, long. 121°17'30" W; sec. 3, T 6 S, R 6 E). Named on Copper Mountain (1956) 7.5' quadrangle.

Washington Column [MARIPOSA]: *relief feature,* 1.5 miles east of Yosemite Village on the north side of Yosemite Valley (lat. 37° 44'55" N, long. 119°33'35" W). Named on Yosemite (1956) 15' quadrangle. The feature also was called Washington Tower (Browning, 1986, p. 232).

Washington Flat [MARIPOSA]: *area,* 2.5 miles north of the village of Bear Valley on the north side of Merced River (lat. 37°36'30" N, long. 120°07'15" W; on S line sec. 5, T 4 S, R 17 E). Named on Bear Valley (1947) 7.5' quadrangle.

Washington Flat: see **Old Gulch** [CALAVERAS] (2).

Washington Tower: see **Washington Column** [MARIPOSA].

Wassamma [MADERA]: *locality,* 6 miles west-southwest of present Yosemite Forks (lat. 37°21' N, long. 119°44' W; sec. 1, T 7 S, R 20 E); the place is 1.25 miles west-southwest of present Ahwahnee. Named on Mariposa (1912) 30' quadrangle. The name is from an Indian village located nearby (Kroeber, p. 66). United States Board on Geographic Names (1933a, p. 803) rejected the name "Ahwahnee" for the place, which was a stage station. McLaughlin and Bradley (p. 532) gave the name "Poison Switch" as an alternate. Clough (p. 80) described Poison Switch as a crossroads just outside of Gertrude, where teamsters after unloading their cargo of lumber at the head of the flume to Madera would "switch off" to a saloon.

Waterford [STANISLAUS]: *town,* 13 miles east of Modesto on the north side of Tuolumne River (lat. 37°38'30" N, long. 120°45'40" W; in and near sec. 28, T 3 S, R 11 E). Named on Paulsell (1968) and Waterford (1969) 7.5' quadrangles. The community also was known as Bakersville for William Baker, who started the first business at the place in 1862 (Brotherton, p. 146). Postal authorities established Waterford post office in 1872 (Frickstad, p. 201). Gallant Duncan Dickenson started Dickenson's Ferry on Tuolumne River about 8 miles east of Waterford in the early 1850's, and after John W. Roberts bought the ferry in 1862, it was known as Roberts' Ferry (Hoover, Rensch, and Rensch, p. 542). Charles Dallas started Dallas' Ferry in 1861 about 4 miles above Waterford, and Calvin W. Salter started Salter's Ferry in 1862 about 1.75 miles upstream from Robert's Ferry (Brotherton, p. 148, 158). Baker's Ferry began operations on Tuolumne River near Waterford in 1878 (Hoover, Rensch, and Rensch, p. 542). Dr. B.D. Horr attempted in the 1860's to found a town called Horrsville on his ranch near Dickenson's Ferry (Hoover, Rensch, and Rensch, p. 542). Postal authorities established Horr's Ranch post office in 1851, changed the name to Horr in 1895, and discontinued it in 1896 (Frickstad, p. 200).

Water Gulch [CALAVERAS]: *canyon,* drained by a stream that flows 1.25 miles to Blue Creek nearly 4 miles west-southwest of Tamarack (lat. 38°25'20" N, long. 120°08'35" W; near N line sec. 31, T 7 N, R 17 E). Named on Calaveras Dome (1979) 7.5' quadrangle.

Water Gulch [MADERA]: *canyon,* drained by a stream that flows 3.5 miles to Fresno River 5.5 miles east of Knowles (lat. 37°13'20" N, long. 119°46'25" W). Named on Knowles (1962) and O'Neals (1965) 7.5' quadrangles.

Waterhouse Lake [TUOLUMNE]: *lake,* 1150 feet long, 5.5 miles east-northeast of Pinecrest (lat. 38°13'20" N, long. 119°54'05" W; on W line sec. 9, T 4 N, R 19 E). Named on Pinecrest (1979) 7.5' quadrangle. Called Bear Lake Reservoir on California Division on Highways' (1934) map.

Waterloo [SAN JOAQUIN]: *settlement,* 8 miles south-southeast of Lodi (lat. 38°02'05" N, long. 121°11'10" W; on W line sec. 11, T 2 N, R 7 E). Named on Waterloo (1968) 7.5' quadrangle. The name is from a dispute, likened to the battle of Waterloo, over a land title at the place in the early 1860's (Gudde, 1949, p. 384). Postal authorities established Waterloo post office in 1865 and discontinued it in 1875 (Frickstad, p. 163). The place first was known as Calaveras Post Office or Waterloo House (Hillman and Covello, p. 231). Postal authorities established Calaveras post office in 1861 and discontinued it in 1862 (Salley, p. 32).

Waterloo House: see **Waterloo** [SAN JOAQUIN].

Waterman Creek [CALAVERAS]: *stream,* flows nearly 4 miles to Cherokee Creek 4 miles west of Angels Camp (lat. 38°05'05" N, long. 120°37'15" W; sec. 26, T 3 N, R 12 E). Named on Angels Camp (1962) 7.5' quadrangle.

Watershed Falls: see **Waterwheel Falls** [TUOLUMNE].

Waterwheel Falls [TUOLUMNE]: *waterfall,* 11 miles west of Tioga Pass on Tuolumne River (lat. 37°55'35" N, long. 119°27'30" W). Named on Tuolumne Meadows (1956) 15' quadrangle. R.M. Price gave the name "Le Conte Cascade" to the feature in 1894 to honor Professor J.N. Le Conte of University of California (Browning, 1988, p. 72-73). United States Board on Geographic Names (1991, p. 7) rejected the name "Watershed Falls" for the feature.

Watkins: see **Mount Watkins** [MARIPOSA].

Watt: see **Sharon** [MADERA].

Waverley: see **Peters** [SAN JOAQUIN].

Wawona [MARIPOSA]: *settlement,* 18 miles east of Mariposa (lat. 37°32'10" N, long. 119°39'15" W; near NW cor. sec. 2, T 5 S, R 21 E). Named on Yosemite (1956) 15' quadrangle. Called Clark's Ranch on Hoffmann and Gardner's (1863-1867) map. Galen Clark camped at the site in 1855 and returned in 1856 to build a rough overnight lodging place for tourists that was known at different times as Clark's Station, Clark and Moore's, and Big Tree Station; Clark sold out to Edward Washburn, John Washburn, and Henry Washburn in 1874—Henry Washburn's wife renamed the place Wawona (Sargent, Shirley, 1961, p. 6-9). Postal authorities established Clark's Station post office in 1878, changed the name to Wawona in 1883, and discontinued it in 1935 (Frickstad, p. 90, 92). The name "Wawona" supposedly is from an Indian term meaning "a Big Tree" (Bunnell, p. 37), but Kroeber (p. 66) stated that the word "wawona" does not appear to be Indian. Laizure's (1935) map shows a place called Chinquapin located 8.5 miles north-northwest of Wawona, where Yosemite (1956) 15' quadrangle shows Chinquapin Ranger Sta. (near SW cor. sec. 20, T 3 S, R 21 E). The name "Chinquapin" is from a kind of shrub common at the place (Hanna, p. 63). United States Board on Geographic Names (1933a, p. 217) approved the name "Chinquapin" for a settlement, and rejected the forms "Chincapin" and "Chinkapin." Laizure's (1935) map also shows a place called Elevenmile located about 1 mile south-southeast of Chinquapin and west of present Elevenmile Creek (near S line sec. 29, T 3 S, R 21 E). A stage stop called Eleven Mile Station and 11-Mile House was at the place, which was 11 miles from Wawona (Browning, 1988, p. 40). In addition, Laizure's (1935) map shows a place called Eightmile situated about 3 miles south-southeast of Chinquapin (near SW cor. sec. 4, T 4 S, R 21 E).

Wawona: see **North Wawona** [MARIPOSA]; **South Wawona** [MARIPOSA].

Wawona Campground [MARIPOSA]: *locality,* nearly 2 miles west-northwest of Wawona (lat. 37°33' N, long. 119°41' W; near NW cor. sec. 33, T 4 S, R 21 E). Named on Yosemite (1956) 15' quadrangle.

Wawona Dome [MARIPOSA]: *peak,* 2.5 miles east-northeast of Wawona (lat. 37°33'20" N, long. 119°36'45" W; near E line sec. 25, T 4 S, R 21 E). Altitude 6903 feet. Named on Yosemite (1956) 15' quadrangle. The feature also had the names "Granite Dome" and "Capitol Dome" (Browning, 1986, p. 233).

Wawona Point [MARIPOSA]: *peak,* 3.25 miles east-southeast of Wawona (lat. 37°31'05" N, long. 119°36' W). Altitude 6810 feet. Named on Yosemite (1956) 15' quadrangle.

We-ack: see **Rocky Point** [MARIPOSA].

Weatherbee Lake [SAN JOAQUIN]: *water feature,* inlet off San Joaquin River 12.5 miles south of downtown Stockton (lat. 37°46'25" N, long. 121°17'30" W). Named on Lathrop (1952) 7.5' quadrangle.

Webb: see **Webb Station** [MARIPOSA].

Webb Station [MARIPOSA]: *locality,* 8 miles north-northwest of Hornitos along Dry Creek (lat. 37°36'20" N, long. 120°18'25" W; sec. 10, T 4 S, R 15 E). Named on Merced Falls (1962) 7.5' quadrangle. Called Webb on Sonora (1891) 30' quadrangle.

Weber's Embarcadero: see **Stockton** [SAN JOAQUIN].

Weber Tract [SAN JOAQUIN]: *area,* 2 miles west of downtown Stockton (lat. 37°57'30" N, long. 121°19'40" W). Named on Stockton (1913) 7.5' quadrangle.

Weberville: see **Stockton** [SAN JOAQUIN].

Weed Meadow [TUOLUMNE]: *area,* 6.5 miles southeast of Pinecrest (lat. 38°07'15" N, long. 119°55' W; sec. 17, T 3 N, R 19 E). Named on Cherry Lake North (1979) 7.5' quadrangle.

Wegner Lake [MARIPOSA]: *lake,* 1000 feet long, 7 miles north-northeast of Yosemite Village (lat. 37°50'30" N, long. 119°32'10" W; sec. 22, T 1 S, R 22 E). Named on Hetch Hetchy Reservoir (1956) 15' quadrangle. The name commemorates John H. Wegner, a ranger in Yosemite National Park from 1916 until 1949 (Browning, 1986, p. 234).

Well Pond [MERCED]: *lake,* 2000 feet long, 5.25 miles east-southeast of Los Banos (lat. 37°02'15" N, long. 120°45'40" W; on W line sec. 27, T 10 S, R 11 E). Named on Los Banos (1960) 7.5' quadrangle.

Wells Peak [TUOLUMNE]: *peak,* 2 miles southeast of Tower Peak (lat. 38°07'20" N, long. 119°31'40" W). Altitude 11,118 feet. Named on Tower Peak (1956) 15' quadrangle. R.B. Marshall of United States Geological Survey named the peak for Rush Spencer Wells, an army officer (Browning, 1986, p. 234).

Wenger: see **Coulterville** [MARIPOSA].

Westfall Campground [MARIPOSA]: *locality,* 2.5 miles south-southwest of Fish Camp (lat. 37°26'40" N, long. 119°39'05" W; near NE cor. sec. 3, T 6 S, R 21 E). Named on Bass Lake (1953) 15' quadrangle.

Westfall Meadows [MARIPOSA]: *area,* 7 miles south-southwest of Yosemite Village (lat. 37°39'10" N, long. 119°38' W; near SE cor. sec. 23, T 3 S, R 21 E). Named on Yosemite (1956) 15' quadrangle. Hoffmann and Gardner's (1863-1867) map has the name "Westfall's" at or near present Westfall Meadows. Westfall's was a sheep camp; Charles Peregoy built Mountain View House at the site in 1869 (Russell, p. 51).

Westfall's: see **Westfall Meadows** [MARIPOSA].

Westley [STANISLAUS]: *village,* 13 miles west-southwest of Modesto (lat. 37°32'55" N, long. 121°11'55" W). Named on Westley (1969) 7.5' quadrangle. The name is for John Westley Van Benschoten, who came to California in 1846 with Fremont and settled by San Joaquin River in 1850 (Gudde, 1949, p. 387). Postal authorities established Westley post office in 1889 (Frickstad, p. 201).

West Lodi: see **Kingdon** [SAN JOAQUIN].

West Manteca [SAN JOAQUIN]: *settlement,* 2 miles west of Manteca (lat. 37°47'50" N, long. 121°15'50" W; near SE cor. sec. 36, T 1 S, R 6 E).

Named on Lathrop (1952) 7.5' quadrangle.

Weston: see **Bardi** [SAN JOAQUIN].

West Peak [TUOLUMNE]: *peak,* 14 miles west-northwest of Tioga Pass (lat. 37°58'50" N, long. 119°29'50" W). Named on Tuolumne Meadows (1956) 15' quadrangle. The feature also was called Regulation Peak (Browning, 1986, p. 234).

West Point [CALAVERAS]: *town,* 16 miles north-northeast of San Andreas on the ridge between North Fork and Middle Fork Mokelumne River (lat. 38°24' N, long. 120°31'35" W; sec. 3, T 6 N, R 13 E). Named on West Point (1948) 7.5' quadrangle. The place was called Indian Gulch in 1852, and it was called West Point in 1854 (Gudde, 1949, p. 387). Postal authorities established West Point post office in 1856, changed the name to Westpoint in 1895, and changed it back to West Point in 1947 (Salley, p. 238). United States Board on Geographic Names (1950, p. 7) rejected the form "Westpoint" for the name. According to Hanna (p. 352), Kit Carson gave the name "West Point" to his camp at the site in 1844 because it was as far west as he could go on his route before he had to retreat in order to cross North Fork Mokelumne River.

Westport Landing: see **Tuolumne City** [STANISLAUS].

Wet Gulch [CALAVERAS]:

(1) *canyon,* drained by a stream that flows 5.25 miles to Jesus Maria Creek 4 miles east-southeast of Mokelumne Hill (lat. 38°16'45" N, long. 120°38' W; sec. 15, T 5 N, R 12 E). Named on Rail Road Flat (1948) 7.5' quadrangle.

(2) *canyon,* drained by a stream that flows nearly 3 miles to South Fork Mokelumne River 2.5 miles northwest of Rail Road Flat (lat. 38°22'05" N, long. 120°32'40" W; near S line sec. 16, T 6 N, R 13 E). Named on Rail Road Flat (1948) 7.5' quadrangle.

Wet Gulch [TUOLUMNE]: *canyon,* drained by a stream that flows 1 mile to South Fork Stanislaus River 2.5 miles north-northeast of Columbia (lat. 38°04'05" N, long. 120°22'50" W; sec. 36, T 3 N, R 14 E). Named on Columbia (1948) and Columbia SE (1948) 7.5' quadrangles.

Wet Meadow [TUOLUMNE]: *area,* 5 miles east-southeast of Tuolumne (lat. 37°55'20" N, long. 120°09'40" W; near SE cor. sec. 24, T 1 N, R 16 E). Named on Tuolumne (1948) 7.5" quadrangle.

Wet Meadow Hill [TUOLUMNE]: *peak,* 5 miles southeast of Tuolumne (lat. 37°55' N, long. 120°09'45" W; sec. 25, T 1 N, R 16 E); the peak is less than 0.5 mile south-southwest of Wet Meadow. Named on Tuolumne (1948) 7.5' quadrangle.

Wet Meadows Springs [TUOLUMNE]: *springs,* two, 4.5 miles southeast of Long Barn (lat. 38°02'30" N, long. 120°04'50" W; sec. 11, T 2 N, R 17 E). Named on Hull Creek (1979) 7.5' quadrangle.

Wet Prong [CALAVERAS]: *stream,* flows 1.25 miles to Salamander Creek 5.5 miles east-northeast of San Andreas (lat. 38°14'20" N, long. 120°35'25" W; sec. 31, T 5 N, R 13 E). Named on Calaveritas (1962) 7.5' quadrangle.

Whale Boat Ferry: see **Big Bar** [CALAVERAS].

Whale Island [STANISLAUS]: *island,* 0.5 mile long, 6.25 miles north of Oakdale in Woodward Reservoir (lat. 37°51'25" N, long. 120°50'50" W). Named on Oakdale (1968) 7.5' quadrangle.

Wheats [CALAVERAS]: *locality,* 3.25 miles east-northeast of Valley Springs (lat. 38°12'45" N, long. 120°46'30" W). Named on Jackson (1902) 30' quadrangle. Called Double Springs on Camp's (1962) map. The place also was called Pleasant Valley (Hoover, Rensch, and Rensch, p. 41) and Two Springs (Gudde, 1975, p. 99). Postal authorities established Double Springs post office in 1851 and discontinued it in 1860 (Frickstad, p. 14). Valley Springs (1944) 15' quadrangle shows Double Springs ranch located 3 miles east-northeast of Valley Springs, and Camp's (1962) map shows Spring Valley House situated 1 mile west-southwest of Double Springs.

Wheats Cow Camp [TUOLUMNE]: *locality,* 7.25 miles west-northwest of Dardanelle (lat. 38°21'55" N, long. 119°57'40" W; near N line sec. 23, T 6 N, R 18 E); the place is in Wheats Meadow. Named on Donnell Lake (1979) 7.5' quadrangle.

Wheats Meadow [TUOLUMNE]: *area,* 7.25 miles west-northwest of Dardanelle (lat. 38°21'50" N, long. 119°57'40" W; near N line sec. 23, T 6 N, R 18 E). Named on Donnell Lake (1979) 7.5' quadrangle. The name commemorates an early settler (Browning, 1986, p. 235).

Wheats Meadow Creek [TUOLUMNE]: *stream,* flows 5 miles to Donnell Lake 5.5 miles west of Dardanelle (lat. 38°21' N, long. 119°56'05" W); the stream goes through Wheats Meadow. Named on Donnell Lake (1979) and Spicer Meadow Reservoir (1979) 7.5' quadrangles.

Wheeler Canyon [SAN JOAQUIN]: *canyon,* drained by a stream that flows 1 mile to Corral Hollow Creek 1.5 miles south-southwest of Eagle Mountain (lat. 37°32'50" N, long. 121°32'35" W; near N line sec. 33, T 4 S, R 4 E). Named on Cedar Mountain (1956) 7.5' quadrangle.

Wheeler Gulch [MARIPOSA]: *canyon,* drained by a stream that flows 3 miles to Lake McClure 3 miles west-southwest of Coulterville (lat. 37°41'50" N, long. 120°14'45" W; near N line sec. 7, T 3 S, R 16 E). Named on Coulterville (1947, photorevised 1973) 7.5' quadrangle.

Wheeler Peak [TUOLUMNE]: *peak,* 10.5 miles west-southwest of Tower Peak (lat. 38°06' N, long. 119°43'45" W). Altitude 9001 feet. Named on Tower Peak (1956) 15' quadrangle.

Whiskers Campground [MADERA]: *locality,* nearly 4 miles west-southwest of Shuteye Peak along North Fork Sand Creek (lat. 37° 20'05" N, long. 119°29'35" W; sec. 7, T 7 S, R 23 E). Named on Shuteye Peak (1953) 15' quadrangle.

Whiskey Creek [MADERA]:

(1) *stream,* flows nearly 3 miles to Willow Creek (3) at Knowles (lat. 37°12'55" N, long. 119°52'35" W; sec. 2, T 8 S, R 19 E). Named on Knowles (1962) 7.5' quadrangle.

(2) *stream,* flows 11.5 miles to Willow Creek (2) 13 miles south of Shuteye Peak (lat. 37°09'50" N, long. 119°28'20" W; sec. 9, T 9 S, R 23 E). Named on Shaver Lake (1953) and Shuteye Peak (1953) 15' quadrangles. The stream first was called Alder Creek, but after a store that sold a lot of whiskey opened near the feature at present Cascadel, Indians gave the stream the name "Whiskey Creek" (Clough, p. 80).

Whiskey Falls [MADERA]: *locality,* 4.5 miles south of Shuteye Peak along Whiskey Creek (2) (lat. 37°17'10" N, long. 119°26'25" W; sec. 27, T 7 S, R 23 E). Named on Shuteye Peak (1953) 15' quadrangle.

Whiskey Flat [MARIPOSA]: *area,* 6 miles east of the village of Bear Valley along Sherlock Creek (lat. 37°34'10" N, long. 120°00'35" W; sec. 20, T 4 S, R 18 E). Named on Bear Valley (1947) 7.5' quadrangle.

Whiskey Hill: see **Jamestown** [TUOLUMNE].

Whiskey Ridge [MADERA]: *ridge,* south-trending, 6 miles long, 5.5 miles south of Shuteye Peak (lat. 37°16' N, long. 119°24'45" W); the ridge is east of Whiskey Creek (2). Named on Shaver Lake (1953) and Shuteye Peak (1953) 15' quadrangles.

Whiskey Slide [CALAVERAS]: *locality,* 5.25 miles east of Mokelumne Hill (lat. 38°17'30" N, long. 120°36'30" W). Named on Jackson (1902) 30' quadrangle, which has the name along a road grade. The mining camp called Whiskey Slide later was called Clear View (Hoover, Rensch, and Rensch, p. 44). Clear View post office was established 8 miles east of Mokelumne Hill in 1902 and discontinued in 1903 (Salley, p. 45).

Whiskey Slough [SAN JOAQUIN]: *water feature,* on McDonald Island, enters San Joaquin River 5.5 miles south of Terminous (lat. 38°02'05" N, long. 121°29'50" W). Named on Holt (1978) and Terminous (1978) 7.5' quadrangles. Bouldin Island (1978) 7.5' quadrangle has the form "Whiskey Slu" for the name. Called Whisky Slough on Bouldin Island (1952), Holt (1952), and Terminous (1952) 7.5' quadrangles. United States Board on Geographic Names (1977a, p. 6) gave the form "Whisky Slough" as a variant, and noted that the name is from the beverage that Chinese railroad-construction workers made on a barge outside of Holt about 1900.

Whisky Creek [CALAVERAS]: *stream,* flows nearly 4 miles to New Hogan Reservoir 4.25 miles east-northeast of Jenny Lind (lat. 38° 06'35" N, long. 120°47'30" W; sec. 17, T 3 N, R 11 E). Named on Jenny Lind (1962) and Valley Springs (1962) 7.5' quadrangles.

Whisky Flat [MARIPOSA]: *area,* 3 miles west-southwest of Penon Blanco Peak (lat. 37°43' N, long. 120°18'55" W; on W line sec. 34, T 2 S, R 15 E). Named on Penon Blanco Peak (1962) 7.5' quadrangle.

Whisky Slough: see **Whiskey Slough** [SAN JOAQUIN].

White Cascade [TUOLUMNE]: *waterfall,* 9 miles west of Tioga Pass on Tuolumne River (lat. 37°54'45" N, long. 119°25' W). Named on Tuolumne Meadows (1956) 15' quadrangle. Members of the Whitney survey named the feature in 1866 (Browning, 1986, p. 235). United States Board on Geographic Names (1992, p. 5) rejected the name "Lower Virginia Falls" for the feature.

White Cascade: see **Tuolumne Falls** [TUOLUMNE].

White Chief Branch [MADERA]: *stream,* flows 2.5 miles to Big Creek 7.5 miles north-northeast of Yosemite Forks (lat. 37°28'20" N, long. 119°35'05" W; sec. 29, T 5 S, R 22 E); the stream heads near White Chief Mountain. Named on Bass Lake (1953) 15' quadrangle.

White Chief Mountain [MADERA]: *peak,* 10 miles north-northeast of Yosemite Forks (lat. 37°29'20" N, long. 119°32' W; near N line sec. 23, T 5 S, R 22 E). Altitude 8676 feet. Named on Bass Lake (1953) 15' quadrangle.

White Fir Creek [TUOLUMNE]: *stream,* flows 2.5 miles to Cherry Lake 7.5 miles north-northwest of Mather (lat. 37°59' N, long. 119°55' W; sec. 32, T 2 N, R 19 E). Named on Cherry Lake North (1979) 7.5' quadrangle. United States Board on Geographic Names (1969, p. 5) rejected the name "Nigger Creek" for the stream.

White Gulch: see **Whites Gulch** [MARIPOSA].

White House: see **Banta** [SAN JOAQUIN].

White House Landing [SAN JOAQUIN]: *locality,* 16 miles southwest of downtown Stockton along Old River on Union Island (lat. 37° 47'50" N, long. 121°31'15" W). Named on Bethany (1914) 7.5' quadrangle.

White Lake: see **Lower White Lake** [STANISLAUS]; **Upper White Lake** [STANISLAUS].

White Mountain [TUOLUMNE]: *peak,* 3.5 miles northwest of Tioga Pass on Tuolumne-Mono County line (lat. 37°56'45" N, long. 119° 18'30" W). Named on Tuolumne Meadows (1956) 15' quadrangle.

White Oak Creek [MARIPOSA]: *stream,* flows 1.5 miles to Moore Creek 2 miles east of Smith Peak (lat. 37°47'50" N, long. 120°03'45" W; near N line sec. 2, T 2 S, R 17 E). Named on Jawbone Ridge (1947) 7.5' quadrangle.

White Pines [CALAVERAS]: *village,* 5.5 miles south-southeast of Blue Mountain (lat. 38°15'50" N, long. 120°20'25" W; on N line sec. 29, T 5 N, R 15 E). Named on Dorrington (1979) 7.5' quadrangle. Postal authorities established White Pines post office at a lumber camp in 1940 and discontinued it in 1975 (Salley, p. 239).

White Pines Lake [CALAVERAS]: *lake,* behind a dam on San Antonio Creek 5.25 miles south-southeast of Blue Mountain (lat. 38°16'05" N, long. 120°20'35" W; sec. 20, T 5 N, R 15 E). Named on Dorrington (1979) 7.5' quadrangle.

White Rock [MARIPOSA]: *peak,* 7.25 miles south of the present settlement of Catheys Valley (lat. 37°19'50" N, long. 120°05' W; near NW cor. sec. 14, T 7 S, R 17 E). Altitude 1117 feet. Named on Indian Gulch (1920) 15' quadrangle.

Whites Gulch [MARIPOSA]: *canyon,* drained by a stream that flows 2.5 miles to Lake McClure 4.5 miles south-southeast of Coulterville (lat. 37°38'55" N, long. 120°10'25" W; sec. 26, T 3 S, R 16 E). Named on Coulterville (1947, photorevised 1973) 7.5' quadrangle. Called White Gulch on Hoffmann and Gardner's (1863-1867) map.

Whites Gulch [TUOLUMNE]: *canyon,* drained by a stream that flows less than 1 mile to Big Creek (1) 2.5 miles east of Groveland (lat. 37°50'30" N, long. 120°11'05" W; sec. 23, T 1 S, R 16 E). Named on Groveland (1947) 7.5' quadrangle.

Whitesides Meadow [TUOLUMNE]: *area,* 10 miles east of Pinecrest (lat. 38°12'35" N, long. 119°48'40" W). Named on Pinecrest (1956) 15' quadrangle.

White Slough [SAN JOAQUIN]: *water feature,* joins Little Potato Slough 1.5 miles south of Terminous (lat. 38°05'30" N, long. 121° 29'30" W). Named on Terminous (1978) 7.5' quadrangle. United States Board on Geographic Names (1983, p. 1) approved the name "Devils Isle" for an island, about 0.1 mile long, located 1.5 miles south of Terminous at the junction of White Slough and Little Potato Slough (lat. 38°05'32" N, long. 121°29'30" W).

White Spring [TUOLUMNE]: *spring,* 7.5 miles south-southeast of Liberty Hill (lat. 38°15'50" N, long. 120°03'15" W; sec. 24, T 5 N, R 17 E). Named on Liberty Hill (1979) 7.5' quadrangle.

White Wolf [TUOLUMNE]: *locality,* 22 miles west of Tioga Pass (lat. 37°52'10" N, long. 119°38'55" W; sec. 10, T 1 S, R 21 E). Named on Hetch Hetchy Reservoir (1956) 15' quadrangle. Brothers Diedrich Meyer and Heinrich Meyer named the place for the chief of a group of Indians that lived there; later the brothers owned the land (Paden and Schlichtmann, p. 153).

Whitlock: see **Whitlock Creek** [MARIPOSA].

Whitlock Creek [MARIPOSA]: *stream,* flows nearly 2 miles to Sherlock Creek 6 miles east of the village of Bear Valley (lat. 37°33'35" N, long. 120°00'45" W; sec. 29, T 4 S, R 18 E). Named on Bear Valley (1947) 7.5' quadrangle. Postal authorities established Whitlock post office 3.5 miles northwest of Mariposa in 1899, moved it 1 mile north in 1904, and discontinued it in 1910 (Salley, p. 239-240).

Whitney Canyon [MERCED-STANISLAUS]: *canyon,* drained by a stream that heads in Merced County and flows 2.5 miles to the canyon of Garzas Creek 5 miles northeast of Crevison Peak in Stanislaus County (lat. 37°14' N, long. 121°07'05" W; near S line sec. 17, T 8 S, R 8 E). Named on Crevison Peak (1955) 7.5' quadrangle.

Whittakers Dardanelles [TUOLUMNE]: *ridge,* northeast-trending, 3 miles long, 9 miles west-northwest of Dardanelle (lat. 38°22' N, long. 120°00' W). Named on Donnell Lake (1979), Liberty Hill (1979), and Spicer Meadow Reservoir (1979) 7.5' quadrangles.

Whittles Upper Camp [TUOLUMNE]: *locality,* 3.25 miles southwest of Liberty Hill (lat. 38°20'25" N, long. 120°09'05" W; sec. 30, T 6 N, R 17 E). Named on Boards Crossing (1979) 7.5' quadrangle.

Whitton: see **Planada** [MERCED].

Whorl Mountain [TUOLUMNE]: *peak,* 1.25 miles south of Matterhorn Peak (lat. 38°04'25" N, long. 119°22'55" W). Altitude 12,029 feet. Named on Matterhorn Peak (1956) 15' quadrangle.

Wickland: see **Bethany** [SAN JOAQUIN].

Widdows Island [SAN JOAQUIN]: *island,* 0.5 mile long, 16 miles west-southwest of downtown Stockton along Old River (lat. 37°51'40" N, long. 121°34'25" W). Named on Clifton Court Forebay (1978) 7.5' quadrangle.

Widows Tears Falls: see **Silver Strand Falls** [MARIPOSA].

Wilcox Ridge [STANISLAUS]: *ridge,* northwest-trending, 3 miles long, 4.25 miles southeast of Mikes Peak (lat. 37°18'30" N, long. 121°16'10" W). Named on Wilcox Ridge (1956) 7.5' quadrangle.

Wildcat Canyon [MERCED]: *canyon,* 6 miles east-northeast of Ortigalita Peak on Merced-Fresno County line, mainly in Fresno County (lat. 36°49'10" N, long. 120°49'15" W). Named on Laguna Seca Ranch (1956) 7.5' quadrangle.

Wildcat Creek [MADERA]: *stream,* flows 7 miles to Chowchilla River 5 miles west of Raymond (lat. 37°12'15" N, long. 119°59'55" W; sec. 28, T 8 S, R 18 E). Named on Raymond (1962) 15' quadrangle.

Wildcat Creek [MARIPOSA]: *stream,* flows 2 miles to Merced River 7.25 miles west-southwest of Yosemite Village (lat. 37°43'20" N, long. 119°42'45" W; sec. 36, T 2 S, R 20 E). Named on Yosemite (1956) 15' quadrangle.

Wildcat Creek [MERCED]: *stream,* flows 4.25 miles to Los Banos Creek 4 miles north-northeast of Sweeney Hill (lat. 36°57'10" N, long. 121°01'05" W). Named on Los Banos Valley (1969) 7.5' quadrangle.

Wildcat Creek [STANISLAUS-TUOLUMNE]: *stream,* formed by the confluence of North Fork and South Fork, flows nearly 5 miles to Stanislaus River 1.25 miles southwest of Knights Ferry in Stanislaus County (lat. 37°48'30" N, long. 120°41'05" W; sec. 31, T 1 S, R 12 E). Named on Knights Ferry (1962) 7.5' quadrangle. The stream first was called Edwards' Creek (Criswell, p. 16). North Fork is 4.5 miles long and South Fork is 5 miles long; both forks head in Tuolumne County and are named on Keystone (1962) and Knights Ferry (1962) 7.5' quadrangles.

Wildcat Creek: see **Laguna Seca Creek** [MERCED].

Wildcat Falls [MARIPOSA]: *waterfall,* 7.25 miles west-southwest of Yosemite Village on Wildcat Creek (lat. 37°43'25" N, long. 119° 42'55" W; near N line sec. 36, T 2 S, R 20 E). Named on Yosemite (1956) 15' quadrangle.

Wildcat Mountain [MARIPOSA]:

(1) *ridge,* north-northwest-trending, 1 mile long, 1 mile west-northwest of the settlement of Catheys Valley (lat. 37°26'30" N, long. 120°06'30" W; sec. 4, T 6 S, R 17 E). Named on Catheys Valley (1962) 7.5' quadrangle.

(2) *peak,* 8 miles east-southeast of Mariposa (lat. 37°26'25" N, long. 119°50'05" W; sec. 1, T 6 S, R 19 E). Altitude 2920 feet. Named on Stumpfield Mountain (1947) 7.5' quadrangle.

Wildcat Point [TUOLUMNE]: *peak,* 10 miles west of Tioga Pass (lat. 37°5540" N, long. 119°26'30" W). Altitude 9455 feet. Named on Tuolumne Meadows (1956) 15' quadrangle.

Wildcat Station: see **Raymond** [MADERA].

Wilderness Creek [TUOLUMNE]: *stream,* heads in Alpine County and flows less than 0.25 mile in Tuolumne County to Spicer Meadow Reservoir 8.5 miles west-northwest of Dardanelle (lat. 38°24'25" N, long. 119°58'05" W). Named on Spicer Meadow Reservoir (1979) 7.5' quadrangle.

Wild Goose Gulch [CALAVERAS]: *canyon,* drained by a stream that flows less than 1 mile to Coyote Creek 2 miles northeast of Vallecito (lat. 38°06'50" N, long. 120°27'05" W; sec. 17, T 3 N, R 14 E). Named on Columbia (1948) 7.5' quadrangle.

Wild Hog Canyon [MADERA]: *canyon,* drained by a stream that flows 2.5 miles to Fresno River 4.25 miles east of Knowles (lat. 37°12'35" N, long. 119°47'50" W; near W line sec. 28, T 8 S, R 20 E). Named on Knowles (1962) 7.5' quadrangle.

William Aches Canyon: see **Bellyache Canyon** [MARIPOSA].

Williams: see **Sam Williams Spring** [TUOLUMNE].

Williams Canyon [MERCED]: *canyon,* drained by a stream that flows 1.5 miles to Romero Creek 5.5 miles north of Pacheco Pass (lat. 37°08'35" N, long. 121°12'30" W; sec. 21, T 9 S, R 7 E). Named on Crevison Peak (1955) 7.5' quadrangle.

Williams Peak [MARIPOSA]: *peak,* 7.5 miles north-northeast of Hornitos (lat. 37°36' N, long. 120°10'10" W; near E line sec. 11, T 4 S, R 16 E). Altitude 3205 feet. Named on Hornitos (1947) 7.5' quadrangle. The name commemorates William H. Williams, a Cornishman who settled in Hunter Valley (Sargent, Shirley, 1976, p. 27).

Willow Creek [CALAVERAS]: *stream,* formed by the confluence of North Fork and South Fork, flows 5.5 miles to Calaveritas Creek 3 miles southeast of San Andreas (lat. 38°09'45" N, long. 120°38'50" W; near NE cor. sec. 33, T 4 N, R 12 E). Named on Calaveritas (1962) and San Andreas (1962) 7.5' quadrangles. North Fork is 2 miles long and South Fork is nearly 3 miles long; both forks are named on Calaveritas (1962) 7.5' quadrangle.

Willow Creek [MADERA]:

(1) *stream,* flows 6 miles to Chowchilla River nearly 4 miles north-northeast of Raymond (lat. 37°16'20" N, long. 119°53'40" W; near N line sec. 4, T 8 S, R 19 E). Named on Ben Hur (1947), Horsecamp Mountain (1947), and Knowles (1962) 7.5' quadrangles. North Branch enters from the northeast 3 miles northeast of Raymond; it is 4.5 miles long and is named on Horsecamp Mountain (1947) 7.5' quadrangle.

(2) *stream,* formed by the confluence of North Fork and South Fork, flows 6.25 miles to San Joaquin River 14 miles south of Shuteye Peak (lat. 37°08'45" N, long. 119°27'40" W; sec. 16, T 9 S, R 23 E). Named on Shaver Lake (1953) 15' quadrangle. United States Board on Geographic Names (1937, p. 32) rejected the name "North Fork, San Joaquin River" for the stream and (p. 21) for its North Fork. North Fork Willow Creek is 24 miles long and is named on Bass Lake (1953), Millerton Lake (1965), Shaver Lake (1953), and Shuteye Peak (1953) 15' quadrangles. North Fork is called Willow Creek on Mariposa (1912) 30' quadrangle. United States Board on Geographic Names (1933a, p. 216), under the entry "Chilkoot," called present North Fork Willow Creek by the name "Crane Valley Creek." South Fork is formed by the confluence of Browns Creek and Sand Creek; it is 6.5 miles long and is named on Bass Lake (1953), Shaver Lake (1953),

and Shuteye Peak (1953) 15' quadrangles.
(3) *stream,* flows 12 miles to Fresno River 7.5 miles south of Raymond (lat. 37°06'15" N, long. 119°53'15" W; sec. 34, T 9 S, R 19 E). Named on Daulton (1962), Knowles (1962), and Raymond (1962) 7.5' quadrangles. Called Cottonwood Cr. on Mariposa (1912) 30' quadrangle.
(4) *stream,* flows 8 miles to Fine Gold Creek 4.5 miles south-southeast of O'Neals (lat. 37°04'15" N, long. 119°38'55" W; sec. 11, T 10 S, R 21 E). Named on Millerton Lake West (1965) and O'Neals (1965) 7.5' quadrangles.

Willow Creek [MARIPOSA]: *stream,* flows 2.5 miles to Lake McClure 3 miles west-southwest of Coulterville (lat. 37°41'50" N, long. 120°14'45" W; near N line sec. 7, T 3 S, R 16 E). Named on Penon Blanco Peak (1962) 7.5' quadrangle.

Willow Creek [TUOLUMNE]:
(1) *stream,* flows 4.5 miles to Herring Creek 8 miles southwest of Dardanelle (lat. 38°15'10" N, long. 119°55'20" W; sec. 30, T 5 N, R 19 E). Named on Dardanelles Cone (1956) and Pinecrest (1956) 15' quadrangles.
(2) *stream,* flows 1.25 miles to Don Pedro Reservoir 3.5 miles northeast of Don Pedro Camp (lat. 37°44'35" N, long. 120°21'10" W; sec. 19, T 2 S, R 15 E). Named on Penon Blanco Peak (1962, photorevised 1973) 7.5' quadrangle.

Willow Creek: see **Chilkoot Creek** [MADERA].

Willow Glen [MADERA]: *locality,* 6 miles north of O'Neals (lat. 37° 12'45" N, long. 119°42'30" W; near NW cor. sec. 29, T 8 S, R 21 E). Named on Mariposa (1912) 30' quadrangle.

Willow Gulch [TUOLUMNE]: *canyon,* drained by a stream that flows 1.5 miles to Rose Creek nearly 5 miles north-northeast of Columbia (lat. 38°06'10" N, long. 120°22'45" W; sec. 24, T 3 N, R 14 E). Named on Columbia (1948) 7.5' quadrangle.

Willow Meadow [TUOLUMNE]:
(1) *area,* 6.5 miles south-southwest of Dardanelle (lat. 38°15'20" N, long. 119°53'35" W; sec. 28, T 5 N, R 19 E); the place is along Willow Creek (1). Named on Donnell Lake (1979) 7.5' quadrangle.
(2) *area,* 1.5 miles north-northeast of Duckwall Mountain (lat. 37° 59'25" N, long. 120°06'20" W; near NE cor. sec. 33, T 2 N, R 17 E). Named on Duckwall Mountain (1948) 7.5' quadrangle.

Willow Spring [MERCED]: *spring,* 6.5 miles east-southeast of Pacheco Pass (lat. 37°01'40" N, long. 121°06' W; near N line sec. 33, T 10 S, R 8 E). Named on San Luis Dam (1969) 7.5' quadrangle.

Willow Springs [STANISLAUS]: *spring,* 16 miles west of Patterson in Hospital Canyon (lat. 37°30'20" N, long. 121°24'25" W; sec. 15, T 5 S, R 5 E). Named on Lone Tree Creek (1955) 7.5' quadrangle.

Wilma Lake [TUOLUMNE]: *lake,* 1700 feet long, 7 miles southwest of Tower Peak (lat. 38°04'15" N, long. 119°38'25" W). Named on Tower Peak (1956) 15' quadrangle. Called Wilmer Lake on Dardanelles (1898, reprinted 1947) 30' quadrangle, but United States Board on Geographic Names (1964c, p. 16) rejected this designation. R.B. Marshall of United States Geological Survey named the lake for the daughter of Clyde L. Seavey (United States Board on Geographic Names, 1934, p. 28).

Wilmer Lake: see **Wilma Lake** [TUOLUMNE].

Wilseyville [CALAVERAS]: *village,* 1.5 miles south-southeast of West Point (lat. 38°22'45" N, long. 120°30'50" W; near N line sec. 14, T 6 N, R 13 E). Named on West Point (1948) 7.5' quadrangle. Postal authorities established Wilseyville post office in 1947 and named it for Lawrence A. Wilsey, an official of Forest Products Company (Salley, p. 241).

Wilson Creek [TUOLUMNE]: *stream,* flows 4.5 miles to Matterhorn Canyon (lat. 38°00'15" N, long. 119°25'30" W). Named on Matterhorn Peak (1956) 15' quadrangle. Lieutenant H.C. Benson named the stream for his friend Mountford Wilson (Browning 1986, p. 239).

Wilson Lake [CALAVERAS]: *lake,* 800 feet long, 3.25 miles southwest of Devils Nose along Bear Creek (1) (lat. 38°25'55" N, long. 120°27'45" W; near W line sec. 29, T 7 N, R 14 E). Named on Devils Nose (1979) 7.5' quadrangle.

Wilson Meadow [TUOLUMNE]: *area,* 6 miles north-northwest of Mather (lat. 37°57'40" N, long. 119°53'50" W; sec. 9, T 1 N, R 19 E). Named on Lake Eleanor (1956) 15' quadrangle. Browning (1986, p. 239) associated the name with William B. Wilson, who patented land in the neighborhood in 1892.

Wilsons Branch: see **Henness Branch** [MARIPOSA].

Wilson's Station: see **Lathrop** [SAN JOAQUIN].

Windfield: see **Winton** [MERCED].

Windlass Ridge [MARIPOSA]: *ridge,* north-northwest-trending, 2.5 miles long, 9 miles south of El Portal (lat. 37°32'30" N, long. 119° 48'10" W). Named on Buckingham Mountain (1947) 7.5' quadrangle.

Windmill Canyon [MARIPOSA]: *canyon,* drained by a stream that flows 2.25 miles to Del Puerto Canyon 3.5 miles northeast of Copper Mountain (lat. 37°27'15" N, long. 121°16'10" W; sec. 35, T 5 S, R 6 E). Named on Copper Mountain (1956) 7.5' quadrangle.

Windmill Cove: see **Vulcan Island** [SAN JOAQUIN].

Windmill Spring [MERCED]: *spring,* 2.5 miles southeast of Pacheco Pass (lat. 37°02'35" N, long. 121°10'25" W). Named on Pacheco Pass (1955) 7.5' quadrangle.

Windsor: see **Orford** [SAN JOAQUIN].

Windy Gap [MADERA]: *pass,* 11.5 miles northeast of Raymond (lat. 37°20'55" N, long. 119°46'10" W; sec. 3, T 7 S, R 20 E). Named on Horsecamp Mountain (1947) 7.5' quadrangle.

Windy Gap [TUOLUMNE]: *pass,* 10 miles southwest of Liberty Hill (lat. 38°15' N, long. 120°13'20" W; near N line sec. 33, T 5 N, R 16 E). Named on Boards Crossing (1979) 7.5' quadrangle.

Windy Lake [MADERA]: *lake,* 700 feet long, 1.25 miles north-northeast of Buena Vista Peak (lat. 37°36'45" N, long. 119°30'40" W; sec. 1, T 4 S, R 22 E). Named on Yosemite (1956) 15' quadrangle.

Winkle Branch: see **Little Winkle Branch**, under **Lehamite Creek** [MARIPOSA].

Winter Bar [CALAVERAS]: *locality,* 4 miles northwest of Valley Springs along Mokelumne River (lat. 38°13'25" N, long. 120°53'20" W; near SW cor. sec. 4, T 4 N, R 10 E). Named on Wallace (1962) 7.5' quadrangle. Water of Camanche Reservoir now covers the site. Andrews (p. 118) referred to Winter's Bar, and Cook (p. 4) mentioned Winters Bar.

Winterton: see **Altaville** [CALAVERAS].

Winton [MERCED]: *town,* 2.5 miles north of Atwood (lat. 37°23'20" N, long. 120°36'45" W; around NE cor. sec. 26, T 6 S, R 12 E). Named on Winton (1961) 7.5' quadrangle. Postal authorities established Yam post office in 1911 and discontinued it in 1912, when they moved it 1.5 miles northwest and changed the name to Winton; the name "Yam" was for the yams grown near the place, and name "Winton" commemorates J.E. Winton, who was county surveyor—the town also was known as Windfield and as Merced Colonies No. 1 and No. 2 (Salley, p. 242, 244).

Wire Lakes [TUOLUMNE]: *lakes,* largest 2200 feet long, 12 miles east of Pinecrest (lat. 38°10'30" N, long. 119°46'45" W). Named on Pinecrest (1956) 15' quadrangle.

Wisconsin House: see **Farmington** [SAN JOAQUIN].

Wiseman Flat: see **Wisenor Flat** [MERCED].

Wisenor Flat [MERCED]: *valley,* 2 miles north-northwest of Oretigalita Peak along Ortigalita Creek (lat. 36°49'15" N, long. 120°56'15" W). Named on Ortigalita Peak (1969) 7.5' quadrangle. Called Wiseman Flat on Ortigalita Peak (1956) 15' quadrangle.

Wishon: see **Wishon Cove** [MADERA].

Wishon Campground [MADERA]: *locality,* 7 miles southeast of Yosemite Forks on the west side of Bass Lake (1) (lat. 37°17'15" N, long. 119°32' W; sec. 26, T 7 S, R 22 E); the place is near Wishon Cove. Named on Bass Lake (1953) 15' quadrangle.

Wishon Cove [MADERA]: *embayment,* nearly 7 miles southeast of Yosemite Forks on the west side of Bass Lake (1) (lat. 37°18' N, long. 119°32'15" W; on N line sec. 26, T 7 S, R 22 E). Named on Bass Lake (1953) 15' quadrangle. The name "Wishon" commemorates A. Emory Wishon of San Joaquin Light and Power Corporation, later vice-president and general manager of Pacific Gas and Electric Company (Gudde, 1969, p. 366). A place called Wishon is situated along Minaret and Western Railroad on the south shore of Bass Lake (1) near the dam that forms the lake (Clough, p. 95). Postal authorities established Wishon post office in 1923 to serve a vacation community (Salley, p. 242).

W Lake: see **Emigrant Lake** [TUOLUMNE].

Wolfeboro: see **Camp Wolfeboro** [CALAVERAS].

Wolf Gulch [TUOLUMNE]: *canyon,* drained by a stream that flows 1.25 miles to Stanislaus River 2.25 miles northwest of Columbia (lat. 38°03'35" N, long. 120°25'50" W; sec. 3, T 2 N, R 14 E). Named on Columbia (1948) 7.5' quadrangle.

Wolfin Meadow [TUOLUMNE]: *area,* 8 miles southeast of Long Barn (lat. 38°00'50" N, long. 120°01'35" W; sec. 20, T 2 N, R 18 E). Named on Hull Creek (1979) 7.5' quadrangle.

Wolf Lake [MERCED]: *lake,* 350 feet long, 1.5 miles east-southeast of Pacheco Pass (lat. 37°03'05" N, long. 121°10'55" W). Named on Pacheco Pass (1955) 7.5' quadrangle.

Wood [CALAVERAS]: *locality,* 7 miles east of Blue Mountain (lat. 38°19'50" N, long. 120°14'15" W). Named on Big Trees (1891) 30' quadrangle.

Wood: see **Camp A.E. Wood**, under **Camp Hoyle** [MARIPOSA].

Woodbridge [SAN JOAQUIN]: *town,* 2 miles northwest of downtown Lodi on the southwest side of Mokelumne River (lat. 38°09'15" N, long. 121°18'15" W; sec. 34, T 4 N, R 6 E). Named on Lodi North (1968) 7.5' quadrangle. In 1852 Jeremiah H. Woods and Alexander McQueen put rock in the river to create what they called Wood's Ford (Hillman and Covello, p. 185). Later the same year they started Wood's Ferry at the place; Woods built a bridge—known as Wood's Bridge—there in 1858, and the town laid out at the site in 1859 took its name from the bridge (Hoover, Rensch, and Rensch, p. 375). Postal authorities established Wood's Ferry post office in 1857 and changed the name to Woodbridge in 1862 (Frickstad, p. 163). C.L. Benedict started Benedict's Ferry in 1850 on Mokelumne River about halfway between Wood's Ferry and Staples' Ferry (Hoover, Rensch, and Rensch, p. 374).

Woodchopper Canyon [MERCED]: *canyon,* drained by a stream that flows 1 mile to Romero Creek 6.25 miles north-northeast of Pacheco Pass (lat.

37°08'45" N, long. 121°09'45" W; near SE cor. sec. 14, T 9 S, R 7 E). Named on Crevison Peak (1955) 7.5' quadrangle.

Woodchopper Gulch [STANISLAUS]: *canyon,* drained by a stream that flows less than 1 mile to Quinto Creek 1.25 miles west-southwest of Crevison Peak (lat. 37°10'55" N, long. 121°12'25" W; sec. 4, T 9 S, R 7 E). Named on Crevison Peak (1955) 7.5' quadrangle.

Woodcock [CALAVERAS]: *locality,* 7.5 miles west-northwest of Blue Mountain (lat. 38°22'40" N, long. 120°29'50" W). Named on Big Trees (1891) 30' quadrangle.

Wood Lake [TUOLUMNE]: *lake,* nearly 1 mile long, 13 miles east of Pinecrest along Buck Meadow Creek (lat. 38°09'05" N, long. 119° 45'20" W). Named on Pinecrest (1956) 15' quadrangle.

Woodlake [SAN JOAQUIN]: *locality,* 5 miles west of Lockeford along Central California Traction Railroad (lat. 38°09'05" N, long. 121°14'30" W; on W line sec. 32, T 4 N, R 7 E). Named on Lockeford (1968) 7.5' quadrangle.

Wood Meadow [TUOLUMNE]: *area,* 7.5 miles northwest of Mather (lat. 37°57'20" N, long. 119°57'25" W; on W line sec. 12, T 1 N, R 18 E). Named on Lake Eleanor (1956) 15' quadrangle.

Woods Creek [TUOLUMNE]: *stream,* flows 17 miles to Don Pedro Reservoir 1.25 miles east-northeast of Chinese Camp (lat. 37°52'30" N, long. 120°24'40" W). Named on Columbia (1948), Columbia SE (1948), and Sonora (1948) 7.5' quadrangles. According to Morgan (*in* Gardiner, p. 317), the name possibly is for Benjamin Wood, who was killed by Indians in 1849. The first discovery of gold in Tuolumne County was made in August of 1848 along Woods Creek 1 mile southwest of Jamestown at Woods' Crossing (Hoover, Rensch, and Rensch, p. 568). Derby's (1849) map has the name "Woods" southeast of Sonoran Camp (present Sonora) on upper reaches of Tuolumne River drainage. Postal authorities established Wood's Diggings post office in 1851 and discontinued it in 1853 (Frickstad, p. 217). A travelers stop called Halfway House was situated along Woods Creek halfway from Sonora to Jamestown (Gudde, 1975, p. 149).

Woods' Crossing: see **Woods Creek** [TUOLUMNE].

Wood's Diggings: see **Woods Creek** [TUOLUMNE].

Wood's Ferry: see **Woodbridge** [SAN JOAQUIN].

Wood's Ford: see **Woodbridge** [SAN JOAQUIN].

Wood Slough [MERCED]: *stream,* flows 2.5 miles to join Santa Rita Slough and form Salt Slough 3.5 miles north-northeast of Dos Palos Y (lat. 37°06' N, long. 120°37' W; near SE cor. sec. 35, T 9 S, R 12 E). Named on Santa Rita Bridge (1962) 7.5' quadrangle.

Woodward [SAN JOAQUIN]: *locality,* 14 miles west of downtown Stockton (lat. 37°56'20" N, long. 121°33'35" W); the place is at the northwest corner of Woodward Island. Named on Woodward Island (1913) 7.5' quadrangle. Postal authorities established Woodward post office in 1901 and discontinued it in 1913; the name was for Orville Y. Woodward, first postmaster (Salley, p. 243).

Woodward Island [SAN JOAQUIN]: *island,* 3 miles long, 14 miles west of downtown Stockton between Old River and Middle River (lat. 37°55'45" N, long. 121°32'45" W). Named on Woodward Island (1978) 7.5' quadrangle.

Woodward Island Ferry [SAN JOAQUIN]: *locality,* 12.5 miles west-southwest of downtown Stockton along Middle River (lat. 37°55'10" N, long. 121°31' W); the place is near the southeast end of Woodward Island. Named on Woodward Island (1978) 7.5' quadrangle.

Woodward Reservoir [STANISLAUS]: *lake,* behind a dam on Simmons Creek 6.5 miles north-northwest of Oakdale (lat. 37°51'50" N, long. 120°52'35" W). Named on Escalon (1968) and Oakdale (1968) 7.5' quadrangles. Called South San Joaquin Irrigation Reservoir on California Division of Highways' (1934) map. The name "Woodward" commemorates W.J. Woodward, who was a member of the first board of directors of South San Joaquin Irrigation District; the dam that created the lake was completed in 1918 (Hanna, p. 358).

Wool Hollow [CALAVERAS]: *canyon,* drained by a stream that flows 1 mile to Stanislaus River 3.5 miles east-northeast of Vallecito (lat. 38°06'05" N, long. 120°24'35" W; sec. 23, T 3 N, R 14 E). Named on Columbia (1948) 7.5' quadrangle.

Wrights Creek [TUOLUMNE]: *stream,* flows 8 miles to North Fork Tuolumne River 5.25 miles east-northeast of Twain Harte (lat. 38°03'55" N, long. 120°08'15" W; at W line sec. 32, T 3 N, R 17 E). Named on Hull Creek (1979) and Twain Harte (1979) 7.5' quadrangles. Called Wright Creek on Big Trees (1891) 30' quadrangle.

Wright Tract [SAN JOAQUIN]: *area,* 6 miles west-northwest of downtown Stockton (lat. 38°00' N, long. 121°23'15" W). Named on Holt (1978), Lodi South (1968), Stockton West (1952), and Terminous (1978) 7.5' quadrangles.

Wyruck: see **Los Banos** [MERCED].

—X - Y—

Yam: see **Winton** [MERCED].

Yankee Hill [TUOLUMNE]:

(1) *ridge,* west-southwest-trending, 1.25 miles long, 2 miles east of Columbia (lat. 38°02'30" N, long. 120°21'30" W; sec. 7, 8, T 2 N, R 15 E). Named on Columbia (1948) 15' quadrangle.

(2) *locality,* 1 mile east of Columbia (lat. 38°02'20" N, long. 120° 22'40" W; near E line sec. 12, T 2 N, R 14 E); the place is 1 mile west of Yankee Hill (1). Named on Columbia (1948) 7.5' quadrangle. According to Stoddart (p. 89), Thomas Hill of New York City, a veteran of Stevenson's New York Volunteers, won the right to name the camp and he called it Yankee Hill. Other accounts attribute the name to other men named Hill; a camp called Knickerbocker Flat was at or south of Yankee Hill (Gudde, 1975, p. 188, 377; Jackson, p. 326). Gudde (1975, p. 349) listed a feature called Three Pine Gulch that was situated between Yankee Hill and Columbia.

Yaqui Camp: see **San Andreas** [CALAVERAS].

Yaqui Gulch [MARIPOSA]: *canyon,* 1.5 miles long, opens into the canyon of Carson Creek 5.5 miles northeast of the settlement of Catheys Valley at the site of Carson (lat. 37°28'45" N, long. 120°00'35" W). Named on Catheys Valley (1962) 7.5' quadrangle.

Yarmouth [SAN JOAQUIN]: *locality,* 5 miles northwest of Vernalis along Southern Pacific Railroad (lat. 37°41'10" N, long. 121°20'55" W; sec. 7, T 3 S, R 6 E). Named on Vernalis (1952) 7.5' quadrangle.

Yea Hoo Gulch [CALAVERAS]: *canyon,* drained by a stream that flows less than 1 mile to Stanislaus River 4.5 miles east-southeast of Murphys (lat. 38°07'25" N, long. 120°23' W; sec. 12, T 3 N, R 14 E). Named on Murphys (1948) 7.5' quadrangle.

Yellowhammer Lake [TUOLUMNE]: *lake,* 2300 feet long, 12.5 miles east-southeast of Pinecrest (lat. 38°07'10" N, long. 119° 47' W). Named on Pinecrest (1956) 15' quadrangle.

York Creek [CALAVERAS]: *stream,* flows 2.5 miles to Empire Creek 2.25 miles east-northeast of Copperopolis (lat. 37°59' N, long. 120°35'50" W; sec. 36, T 2 N, R 12 E). Named on Angels Camp (1962) and Melones Dam (1962) 7.5' quadrangles.

Yorktown: see **Stent** [TUOLUMNE].

Yosemite [MARIPOSA]: *area,* in and around Yosemite Valley; this is the original grant of land made by the United States Government to the State of California for the purpose of preserving Yosemite Valley as a park (Whitney, 1870, p. 9-10). Named on Hetch Hetchy Reservoir (1956), Tuolumne Meadows (1956), and Yosemite (1956) 15' quadrangles.

Yosemite: see **Fort Yosemite**, under **Yosemite Village** [MARIPOSA]; **Yosemite Village** [MARIPOSA].

Yosemite Creek [MARIPOSA]: *stream,* flows 12.5 miles to Merced River at Yosemite Village (lat. 37°44'30" N, long. 119°35'40" W). Named on Hetch Hetchy Reservoir (1956) 15' quadrangle.

Yosemite Creek Campgrounds [MARIPOSA]: *locality,* 5.5 miles north of Yosemite Village along Yosemite Creek (lat. 37°49'50" N, long. 119°35'15" W; sec. 30, T 1 S, R 22 E). Named on Hetch Hetchy Reservoir (1956) 15' quadrangle.

Yosemite Fall: see **Lower Yosemite Fall** [MARIPOSA]; **Upper Yosemite Fall** [MARIPOSA].

Yosemite Falls: see **Upper Yosemite Fall** [MARIPOSA]

Yosemite Forks [MADERA]: *locality,* 18 miles northeast of Raymond, where the road to Yosemite Valley branches from the road to Bass Lake (1) (lat. 37°22' N, long. 119°37'45" W; sec. 36, T 6 S, R 21 E). Named on Bass Lake (1953) 15' quadrangle.

Yosemite Junction [TUOLUMNE]: *locality,* 8.5 miles southwest of Sonora, where the road to Yosemite National Park branches from the road to Sonora (lat. 37°53'30" N, long. 120°29'15" W; near E line sec. 36, T 1 N, R 13 E). Named on Sonora (1948) 7.5' quadrangle. J.W. Goodwin founded a travelers stop known as Goodwin's at the site in 1854 and ran it for 27 years (Paden and Schlichtmann, p. 56, 57). A stopping place called New York Tent was located about 0.5 mile southwest of present Yosemite Junction (Gudde, 1975, p. 243).

Yosemite Lake [MERCED]: *lake,* 1.5 miles long, 6 miles north-northeast of Merced (lat. 37°22'35" N, long. 120°25'45" W; sec. 27, 28, 33, 34, T 6 S, R 14 E). Named on Merced (1961) and Yosemite Lake (1962) 7.5' quadrangles. Called Merced Reservoir on Grunsky's (1899) map, and called Lake Yosemite on California Mining Bureau's (1917b) map.

Yosemite Lake [SAN JOAQUIN]: *lake,* 900 feet long, 1 mile northwest of downtown Stockton (lat. 37°58'05" N, long. 121°18'25" W). Named on Stockton West (1952) 7.5' quadrangle.

Yosemite Mill: see **Clearing House** [MARIPOSA].

Yosemite National Park [post office]: see **Yosemite Village** [MARIPOSA].

Yosemite Oaks: see **Acorn Lodge** [MARIPOSA].

Yosemite Point [MARIPOSA]: *promontory,* less than 1 mile north-northwest of Yosemite Village on the north side of Yosemite Valley (lat. 37°45'30" N, long. 119°35'30" W). Named on Hetch Hetchy Reservoir (1956) 15' quadrangle.

Yosemite Valley [MARIPOSA]: *valley,* along Merced River above a point about 7 miles west-southwest of Yosemite Village (lat. 37° 43'30" N, long. 119°42'30" W). Named on Yosemite (1956) 15' quadrangle. Bunnell (p. 58-59) claimed that he proposed the name "Yosemite" in 1851 in the belief that the Indians in the valley had that designation. The name is from an Indian word that has the meaning "bear," or "grizzly bear" (Kroeber, p. 68).

Yosemite Valley: see **Little Yosemite Valley** [MARIPOSA].

Yosemite Village [MARIPOSA]: *settlement,* 27 miles northeast of Mariposa in Yosemite Valley (lat. 37°44'45" N, long. 119°35' W). Named on Hetch Hetchy Reservoir (1956) and Yosemite (1956) 15' quadrangles. Called Yosemite on Yosemite (1909) 30' quadrangle. Postal authorities established Yo Semite post office in 1869, changed the name to Yosemite in 1908, and changed it to Yosemite National Park in 1922 (Salley, p. 245). Major H.C. Benson started Fort Yosemite in 1906 at the later site of Yosemite Lodge, and troops were stationed there until creation of the National Park Service in 1916 (Whiting and Whiting, p. 88).

Young: see **Frank Young Gulch** [TUOLUMNE].

Young Lakes [TUOLUMNE]: *lakes,* three, largest 1900 feet long, 5 miles west-northwest of Tioga Pass (lat. 37°56'10" N, long. 119° 20'10" W). Named on Tuolumne Meadows (1956) 15' quadrangle. The name commemorates General S.M.B. Young, acting superintendent of Yosemite National Park in 1896 (United States Board on Geographic Names, 1962a, p. 21).

Youngs Creek [CALAVERAS]: *stream,* flows 4 miles to Spring Valley Creek 2.5 miles east-northeast of Valley Springs in Spring Valley (lat. 38°12'30" N, long. 120°47'20" W; near S line sec. 8, T 4 N, R 11 E). Named on Jackson (1962) and Valley Springs (1962) 7.5' quadrangles.

Young's Ferry: see **Merced Falls** [MERCED].

Youngs Slough [SAN JOAQUIN]: *water feature,* on Bacon Island, joins Connection Slough 17 miles west-southwest of Lodi (lat. 38° 00'20" N, long. 121°32'50" W). Named on Bouldin Island (1978) 7.5' quadrangle. Woodward Island (1978) 7.5' quadrangle has the form "Youngs Slu" for the name.

Youngston: see **Youngstown** [SAN JOAQUIN].

Youngstown [SAN JOAQUIN]: *locality,* 5 miles west of Lockeford along Central California Traction Railroad (lat. 38°10'20" N, long. 121°14'30" W; near NW cor. sec. 29, T 4 N, R 7 E). Named on Lockeford (1968) 7.5' quadrangle. Called Youngston on Bellota (1939) 15' quadrangle. Settlers from Youngstown, Pennsylvania, named the place in 1903 for their former home (Gudde, 1949, p. 397).

— Z —

Zanjon de los Moquelumnes: see **Sanjon de los Moquelumnes** [SAN JOAQUIN].

Zanjon de Santa Rita: see **Sanjon de Santa Rita** [MERCED].

Zebra: see **Zebra Station** [MADERA].

Zebra Station [MADERA]: *locality,* 10 miles southeast of Raymond (lat. 37°06'45" N, long. 119°46'40" W; sec. 27, T 9 S, R 20 E). Named on Little Table Mountain (1962) 7.5' quadrangle. Postal authorities established Zebra post office 6 miles northeast of Bates in 1886, discontinued it in 1888, reestablished it in 1890, discontinued it for a time in 1894, moved it 4.5 miles southwest in 1901, and discontinued it in 1904; the name was from Zebra mine, which had light and dark ore veins that suggested the stripes of a zebra (Salley, p. 246).

Zip Creek [MARIPOSA]: *stream,* flows 2.5 miles to South Fork Merced River nearly 5 miles south-southeast of El Portal (lat. 37° 36'35" N, long. 119°45'05" W). Named on Buckingham Mountain (1947) and El Portal (1947) 7.5' quadrangles.

North San Joaquin Valley Region Calaveras, Madera, Mariposa, Merced, San Joaquin, Stanislaus and Tuolumne Counties

References Cited

BOOKS AND ARTICLES

Anderson, Robert, and Pack, Robert W. 1915. *Geology and oil resources of the west border of the San Joaquin Valley north of Coalinga, California.* (United States. Geological Survey Bulletin 603.) Washington: Government Printing Office, 220 p.

Andrews, John R. 1978. *The ghost towns of Amador*. Fresno, California: Valley Publishers, 137 p.

Angel, Myron. 1890. "San Benito County." *Tenth annual report of the State Mineralogist, for the year ending December 1, 1890.* Sacramento: California State Mining Bureau, p. 515-517.

Bancroft, Hubert Howe, 1886. *History of California, Volume II, 1801-1824.* San Francisco: The History Company, Publishers, 795 p.

_____1888. *History of California, Volume VI, 1848-1859.* San Francisco: The History Company, Publishers, 787 p.

Blake, William P. 1857. "Geological report." *Reports of explorations and surveys, to ascertain the most practicable and economical route for a railroad from the Mississippi River to the Pacific Ocean.* Volume V, Part II. (33d Cong., 2d Sess., Sen. Ex. Doc. No. 78.) Washington: Beverley Tucker, Printer, 370 p.

Boyd, William Harland. 1972. *A California middle border, The Kern River country, 1772-1880.* Richardson, Texas: The Havilah Press, 226 p.

Brewer, William H. 1949. *Up and down California in 1860-1864.* (Edited by Francis P. Farquhar.) Berkeley and Los Angeles: University of California Press, 583 p.

Brewster, Edwin Tenney. 1909. *Life and letters of Josiah Dwight Whitney.* Boston and New York: Houghton Mifflin Company, 411 p.

Brotherton, I.N. 1982. *Annals of Stanislaus County, Volume I, River towns and ferries.* Santa Cruz: Western Tanager Press, 180 p.

Browning, Peter. 1986. *Place names of the Sierra Nevada.* Berkeley: Wilderness Press, 253 p.

_____1988. *Yosemite place names.* Lafayette, California: Great West Books, 241 p.

Buffum, E. Gould. 1850. *Six months in the gold mines; From a journal of three years' residence in Upper and Lower California, 1847-8-9.* Philadelphia: Lea and Blanchard, 172 p.

Bunnell, Lafayette Houghton. 1977. *Discovery of the Yosemite.* (Reprinted from *Discovery of the Yosemite and the Indian War of 1851 which led to that event,* first published in 1880.) Olympic Valley, California: Outbooks, 184 p.

Burchfield, Chris. 1986. "Demolishing two Mariposa legends." *The Californians*, v. 4, no. 6, p. 42-43.

California Department of Parks and Recreation. 1979. *California historical landmarks.* Sacramento: Department of Parks & Recreation. 174 p.

California Division of Highways. 1934. *California highway transportation survey, 1934.* Sacramento: Department of Public Works, Division of Highways, 130 p. + appendices.

Carson, James H. 1950. *Recollections of the California mines.* Oakland, California: Biobooks, 113 p.

Chalfant, W.A. 1933. *The story of Inyo.* (Revised edition.) (Author), 430 p.

Chamberlain, Newell D. 1936. *The call of gold, True tales on the gold road to Yosemite.* Mariposa, California: Gazette Press, 183 p.

Churchill, Charles William. 1977. *Fortunes are for the few, Letters of a forty-niner.* (Edited by Duane A. Smith and David J. Weber.) (No place): San Diego Historical Society, 136 p.

Clough, Charles W. 1968. *Madera*. Madera, California: Madera County History, 96 p.

Cook, Fred S. (No date.) *Legends of the Southern Mines.* (No place): California Traveler, 64 p.

Cowan, Robert G. 1956. *Ranchos of California.* Fresno, California: Academy Library Guild, 151 p.

Coy, Owen C. 1923. *California county boundaries*. Berkeley: California Historical Survey Commission, 335 p.

Crawford, J.J. 1894. "Report of the State Mineralogist." *Twelfth report of the State Mineralogist, (Second Biennial,) two years ending September 15, 1894.* Sacramento: California State Mining Bureau, p. 8-412.

_____1896. "Report of the State Mineralogist." *Thirteenth report (Third Biennial) of the State Mineralogist for the two years ending September 15, 1896.* Sacramento: California State Mining Bureau, p. 10-646.

Criswell, John F. 1972. *Knight's Ferry's golden past.* (Author), 64 p.

Davis, Stephen Chapin. 1956. *California gold rush merchant, The journal of Stephen Chapin Davis.* (Edited by Benjamin B. Richards.) San Marino, California: The Huntington Library, 124 p.

Dillon, Richard. 1975. *Siskiyou trail.* New York: McGraw-Hill Book Company, 381 p.

_____1982. *Delta country*. Novato, California: Presidio Press, 134 p.

Doble, John. 1962. *John Doble's journal and letters from the mines, Mokelumne Hill, Jackson, Volcano, and San Francisco, 1851-1865.* (Edited by Charles L. Camp.) Denver, Colorado: The Old West Publishing Company, 304 p.

Eccleston, Robert. 1957. *The Mariposa Indian War, 1850-1851.* (Edited by C. Gregory Crampton.) Salt Lake City: University of Utah Press, 168 p.

Elliott, W.W. 1885. *Calaveras County illustrated and described, showing its advantages for homes.* Oakland, California: W.W. Elliott & Co., 104 p.

Evans, George W.B. 1945. *Mexican gold trail, The journal of a forty-niner.* San Marino, California: The Huntington Library, 340 p.

Farquhar, Francis P. 1923. "Place names of the High Sierra [Part I]." *Sierra Cub Bulletin*, v. 11, no. 4, p. 380-407.

_____1924. "Place names of the High Sierra, Part II." *Sierra Club Bulletin*, v. 12, no. 1, p. 47-64.

_____1925. "Place names of the High Sierra, Part III." *Sierra Cub Bulletin*, v. 12, no. 2, p. 126-157.

_____1926. "Mountaineering notes." *Sierra Club Bulletin*, v. 12, no. 3, p. 304-307.

Frickstad, Walter N. 1955. *A century of California post offices, 1848 to 1954*: Oakland, California: Philatelic Research Society, 395 p.

Gardiner, Howard C. 1970. *In pursuit of the golden dream, Reminiscences of San Francisco and the Northern and Southern Mines, 1849-1857.* (Edited by Dale L. Morgan.) Stoughton, Massachusetts: Western Hemisphere, Inc., 390 p.

Gray, Thorne B. 1973. *Quest for deep gold, The story of La Grange, California.* La Grange, California: Southern Mines Press, 44 p.

Grimshaw, William Robinson. 1964. *Grimshaw's narrative*. (Edited by J.R.R. Kantor.) (No place): Sacramento Book Collectors Club, 59 p.

Grunsky, Carl Ewald. 1899. *Irrigation near Merced, California.* (United States Geological Survey Water-Supply and Irrigation Papers No. 19.) Washington: Government Printing Office, 59 p.

Gudde, Erwin G. 1949. *California place names.* Berkeley and Los Angeles: University of California Press, 431 p.

_____1969. *California place names*. Berkeley and Los Angeles: University of California Press, 416 p.

_____1975. *California gold camps*. Berkeley, Los Angeles, London: University of California Press, 467 p.

Hammond, George P. 1982. *The Weber era in Stockton history.* Berkeley, California: The Friends of the Bancroft Library, 170 p.

Hammond, George P., and Morgan, Dale L. 1966. *Captain Charles M. Weber, Pioneer of the San Joaquin and founder of Stockton, California.* Berkeley, California: The Friends of the Bancroft Library, 118 p.

Hanna, Phil Townsend. 1951. *The dictionary of California land names*. Los Angeles: The Automobile Club of Southern California, 392 p.

Harris, Benjamin Butler. 1960. *The Gila Trail, The Texas argonauts and the California gold rush.* (Edited by Richard H. Dillon.) Norman: University of Oklahoma Press, 175 p.

Hart, James D. 1978. *A companion to California*. New York: Oxford University Press, 504 p.

Hillman, Raymond W., and Covello, Leonard A. 1985. *Cities and towns of San Joaquin County since 1847.* Fresno, California: Panorama West Books, 248 p.

Hoffmann, C.F. 1868. "Notes on Hetch-Hetchy Valley." *American Journal of Science and Arts* (series 2), v. 46, no. 137, p. 266-267.

Hoover, Mildred Brooke, Rensch, Hero Eugene, and Rensch, Ethel Grace. 1966. *Historic spots in California*. (Third edition, revised by William N. Abeloe.) Stanford, California: Stanford University Press, 642 p.

Hubbard, Douglass. 1958. *Ghost mines of Yosemite*. Fredericksburg, Texas: The Awani Press, (no pagination).

Irelan, William, Jr. 1888. "Report of the State Mineralogist." *Eighth annual report of the State Mineralogist for the year ending October 1, 1888*. Sacramento: California State Mining Bureau, p. 12-695.

Jackson, Joseph Henry. 1941. *Anybody's gold, The story of California's mining towns*. New York, London: D. Appleton-Century Company, 468 p.

Johnston, Hank. 1963. *Railroads of the Yosemite Valley*. Corona del Mar, California: Trans-Anglo Books, 206 p.

Keller, George. 1955. *A trip across the plains and life in California*. Oakland, California: Biobooks, 44 p.

Kip, Leonard. 1946. *California sketches, with recollections of the gold mines*. Los Angeles: N.A. Kovach, 58 p.

Kroeber, A.L. 1916. "California place names of Indian origin." *University of California Publications in American Archæology and Ethnology*, v. 12, no. 2, p. 31-69.

Laizure, C. McK. 1928. "San Francisco field division (Mariposa County)." *Mining in California*, v. 24, no. 2, p. 72-153.

_____1935. "Current mining activities in the San Francisco district with special reference to gold." *California Journal of Mines and Geology*, v. 31, no. 1, p. 24-48.

Latta, Frank F. 1949. *Black gold in the Joaquin*. Caldwell, Idaho: The Caxton Printers, 344 p.

_____1976. *Saga of Rancho El Tejon*. Santa Cruz, California: Bear State Books, 293 p.

Leonard, Edward C. 1973. *A brief history of Angels Camp*. Murphys, California: Old Timer's Museum, 40 p.

Lippincott, Joseph Barlow. 1902. *Storage of water on Kings River, California*. (United States Geological Survey Water-Supply and Irrigation Paper 58.) Washington: Government Printing Office, 101 p.

Logan, C.A. 1950. "Mines and mineral resources of Madera County, California." *California Journal of Mines and Geology*, v. 46, no. 4, p. 445-482.

Lyman, C.S. 1849a. "Observations on California." *American Journal of Science and Arts* (series 2), v. 7, no. 20, p. 290-292, 305-309.

_____1849b. "Notes on the California gold regions." *American Journal of Science and Arts* (series 2), v. 8, no. 24, p. 415-419.

Martin, Thomas S. 1975. *With Fremont to California and the Southwest, 1845-1849*. Ashland: Lewis Osborne, 48 p.

McKinstry, Bruce L. 1975. *The California gold rush overland diary of Byron N. McKinstry, 1850-1852*. Glendale, California: The Arthur H. Clark Company, 401 p.

McLaughlin, R.P., and Bradley, Walter W. 1916. "Madera County." *Report XIV of the State Mineralogist*. Sacramento: California State Mining Bureau, p. 531-568.

M'Collum, William. 1960. *California as I saw it*. (Edited by Dale L. Morgan.) Los Gatos, California: The Talisman Press, 219 p.

Mendenhall, Walter C. 1908. *Preliminary report on the ground waters of San Joaquin Valley, California*. (United States Geological Survey Water-Supply Paper 222.) Washington: Government Printing Office, 52 p.

Mendershausen, Ralph Rene. 1984. *Treasures of the South Fork*. (Revised.) (Author), 96 p.

Mitchell, Annie R. 1972. *Land of the tules*. Fresno, California: Valley Publishers, 80 p.

Mosier, Dan L. 1979. *California coal towns, coaling stations, & landings*. San Leandro, California: Mines Road Books, 8 p.

_____1983. *Corral Hollow coal mining district*. Fremont, California: Mines Road Books, 86 p.

Mosier, Page, and Mosier, Dan, 1986. *Alameda County place names*. Fremont, California: Mines Road Books, 105 p.

O'Neill, Elizabeth Stone. 1983. *Meadow in the sky, A history of Yosemite's Tuolumne Meadows region*. Fresno, California: Panorama West Books, 162 p.

Paden, Irene D., and Schlichtmann, Margaret E. 1959. *The Big Oak Flat road, An account of freighting from Stockton to Yosemite Valley*. Yosemite National Park: Yosemite Natural History Association, 356 p.

Perez, Crisostomo N. 1996. *Land grants in Alta California*. Rancho Cordova, California: Landmark Enterprises, 264 p.

Perkins, William. 1964. *Three years in California, Williams Perkins' journal of life at Sonora, 1849-1852*. (Introduction and annotations by Dale L. Morgan and James R. Scobie.) Berkeley and Los Angeles: University of California Press, 424 p.

Quimby, Myron J. 1969. *Scratch Ankle, U.S.A., American place names and their derivation*. New York: A.S. Barnes and Company, 390 p.

Russell, Carl Parcher. 1968. *One hundred years in Yosemite*. Yosemite National Park: Yosemite Natural History Association, 206 p.

Salazar, Francisco. 1964. *The gold of old Hornitos*. Fresno, California: Saga-West Publishing Co., 32 p.

Salley, H.E. 1977. *History of California post offices, 1849-1976*. La Mesa, California: Postal History Associates, Inc., 300 p.

Sargent, Mrs. J.L. (editor). 1927. *Amador County history*. Amador County Federation of Women's Clubs, 127 p.

Sargent, Shirley. 1961. *Wawona's yesterdays*. Yosemite National Park: Yosemite Natural History Association, 44 p.

_____1976. *Mariposa County guidebook*. Yosemite, California: Flying Spur Press, 37 p.

Shumate, Albert. 1977. *Francisco Pacheco of Pacheco Pass*. Stockton, California: University of the Pacific, 47 p.

Smith, Genny (editor). 1976. *Mammoth Lakes Sierra*. (Fourth edition.) Palo Alto, California: Genny Smith Books, 147 p.

Spence, Mary Lee, and Jackson, Donald (editors). 1973. *The expeditions of John Charles Frémont, Volume 2, The Bear Flag revolt and the court-martial*. Urbana, Chicago, and London: University of Illinois Press, 519 p.

Stoddart, Thomas Robertson. 1963. *Annals of Tuolumne County*. (With introduction, critical notes, and index by Carlo M. DeFerrari.) Sonora, California: The Mother Lode Press. 188 p.

Thompson and West. 1876. *Historical atlas map of Santa Clara County, California*. San Francisco, California: Thompson & West. 119 p.

_____1879. *History of San Joaquin County, California*. Oakland, California: Thompson & West, 142 p.

Turner, Henry Smith. 1966. *The original journals of Henry Smith Turner, with Stephen Watts Kearney to New Mexico and California, 1846-1847*. Norman: University of Oklahoma Press, 173 p.

Uhte, Robert F. 1951. "Yosemite's pioneer cabins." *Sierra Club Bulletin*, v. 36, no. 5, p. 49-71.

United States Board on Geographic Names. 1901. *Second report of the United States Board on Geographic Names, 1890-1899*. Washington: Government Printing Office, 150 p.

_____(under name "United States Geographic Board"). 1933a. *Sixth report of the United States Geographic Board, 1890 to 1932*. Washington: Government Printing Office, 834 p.

_____(under name "United States Geographic Board"). 1933b. *Decisions of the United States Geographic Board—No. 20, Decisions October 5, 1932*. Washington: Government Printing Office, 29 p.

_____(under name "United States Geographic Board"). 1934. *Decisions of the United States Geographic Board, No. 30—June 30, 1932*. (Yosemite National Park, California.) Washington: Government Printing Office, 29 p.

_____(under name "United States Board on Geographical Names"). 1937. *Decisions of the United States Board on Geographical Names, Decisions rendered between July 1, 1936, and June 30, 1937*. Washington: Government Printing Office, 33 p.

_____(under name "United States Board on Geographical Names"). 1947. *Decision lists nos. 4701, 4702, 4703*. Washington: Department of the Interior, 14 p.

_____1950. *Decisions on names in the United States and Alaska rendered during April, May, and June 1950*. (Decision list no. 5006.) Washington: Department of the Interior, 47 p.

_____1954. *Decisions on names in the United States, Alaska and Puerto Rico, Decisions rendered from July 1950 to May 1954*. (Decision list no. 5401.) Washington: Department of the Interior, 115 p.

_____1959a. *Decisions on names in the United States, Puerto Rico and the Virgin Islands, Decisions rendered from April 1957 through December 1958*. (Decision list no. 5901.) Washington: Department of the Interior, 100 p.

_____1959b. *Decisions on names in the United States, Decisions rendered from January, 1959 through April, 1959*. (Decision list no. 5902.) Washington: Department of the Interior, 49 p.

_____1960a. *Decisions on names in the United States and Puerto Rico, Decisions rendered in May, June, July, and August, 1959*. (Decision list no. 5903.) Washington: Department of the Interior, 79 p.

_____1960b. *Decisions on names in the United States, Puerto Rico and the Virgin Islands, Decisions rendered from January through April 1960*. (Decision list no. 6001.) Washington: Department of the Interior, 79 p.

_____1960c. *Decisions on names in the United States and the Virgin Islands, Decisions rendered from May 1960 through August 1960*. (Decision list no. 6002.) Washington: Department of the Interior, 77 p.

_____1962a. *Decisions on names in the United States, Decisions rendered from January through April 1962*. (Decision list no. 6201.) Washington: Department of the Interior. 72 p.

_____1962b. *Decisions on names in the United States, Decisions rendered from May through August 1962*. (Decision list no. 6202.) Washington: Department of the Interior, 81 p.

_____1963a. *Decisions on names in the United States, Decisions rendered from September through December 1962*. (Decision list no. 6203.) Washington: Department of the Interior, 59 p.

_____1963b. *Decisions on geographic names in the United States, May through August 1963*. (Decision list no. 6302.) Washington: Department of the Interior. 81 p.

_____1964a. *Decisions on geographic names in the United States, September through December 1963.* (Decision list no. 6303.) Washington: Department of the Interior, 66 p.

_____1964b. *Decisions on geographic names in the United States, January through April 1964.* (Decision list no. 6401.) Washington: Department of the Interior, 74 p.

_____1964c. *Decisions on geographic names in the United States, May through August 1964.* (Decision list no. 6402.) Washington: Department of the Interior, 85 p.

_____1965a. *Decisions on geographic names in the United States, January through March 1965.* (Decision list no. 6501.) Washington: Department of the Interior, 85 p.

_____1965b. *Decisions on geographic names in the United States, April through June 1965.* (Decision list no. 6502.) Washington: Department of the Interior, 39 p.

_____1965c. *Decisions on geographic names in the United States, July through September 1965.* (Decision list no. 6503.) Washington: Department of the Interior, 74 p.

_____1966. *Decisions on geographic names in the United States, October through December 1965.* (Decision list no. 6504.) Washington: Department of the Interior, 38 p.

_____1967a. *Decisions on geographic names in the United States, October through December 1966.* (Decision list no. 6604.) Washington: Department of the Interior, 36 p.

_____1967b. *Decisions on geographic names in the United States, April through June 1967.* (Decision list no. 6702.) Washington: Department of the Interior, 26 p.

_____1969. *Decisions on geographic names in the United States, October through December 1968.* (Decision list no. 6804.) Washington: Department of the Interior, 33 p.

_____1970. *Decisions on geographic names in the United States, April through June 1970.* (Decision list no. 7002.) Washington: Department of the Interior, 20 p.

_____1972. *Decisions on geographic names in the United States, January through March 1972.* (Decision list no. 7201.) Washington: Department of the Interior, 32 p.

_____1975. *Decisions on geographic names in the United States, April through June 1975.* (Decision list no. 7502.) Washington: Department of the Interior, 32 p.

_____1976a. *Decisions on geographic names in the United States, October through December 1975.* (Decision list no. 7504.) Washington: Department of the Interior, 45 p.

_____1976b. *Decisions on geographic names in the United States, April through June 1976.* (Decision list no. 7602.) Washington: Department of the Interior, 26 p.

_____1976c. *Decisions on geographic names in the United States, July through September 1976.* (Decision list no. 7603.) Washington: Department of the Interior, 25 p.

_____1977a. *Decisions on geographic names in the United States, January through March 1977.* (Decision list no. 7701.) Washington: Department of the Interior, 32 p.

_____1977b. *Decisions on geographic names in the United States, April through June 1977.* (Decision list no. 7702.) Washington: Department of the Interior, 40 p.

_____1977c. *Decisions on geographic names in the United States, July through September 1977.* (Decision list no. 7703.) Washington: Department of the Interior, 25 p.

_____1978a. *Decisions on geographic names in the United States, April through June 1978.* (Decision list no. 7802.) Washington: Department of the Interior, 30 p.

_____1978b. *Decisions on geographic names in the United States, October through December 1978.* (Decision list no. 7804.) Washington: Department of the Interior, 48 p.

_____1979. *Decisions on geographic names in the United States, April through June 1979.* (Decision list no. 7902.) Washington: Department of the Interior, 33 p.

_____1980a. *Decisions on geographic names in the United States, October through December 1979.* (Decision list no. 7904.) Washington: Department of the Interior, 26 p.

_____1980b. *Decisions on geographic names in the United States, April through June 1980.* (Decision list no. 8002.) Washington: Department of the Interior, 33 p.

_____1981a. *Decisions on geographic names in the United States, October through December 1980.* (Decision list no. 8004.) Washington: Department of the Interior, 21 p.

_____1981b. *Decisions on geographic names in the United States, April through June 1981.* (Decision list no. 8102.) Washington: Department of the Interior, 28 p.

_____1983. *Decisions on geographic names in the United States, October through December 1982.* (Decision list no. 8204.) Washington: Department of the Interior, 26 p.

_____1984a. *Decisions on geographic names in the United States, April through June 1984.* (Decision list no. 8402.) Washington: Department of the Interior, 22 p.

_____1984b. *Decisions on geographic names in the United States, July through September 1984.* (Decision list no. 8403.) Washington: Department of the Interior, 10 p.

_____1985. *Decisions on geographic names in the United States, April through June 1985.* (Decision list no. 8502.) Washington: Department of the Interior, 12 p.

_____1986. *Decisions on geographic names in the United States, April through June 1986.* (Decision list no. 8602.) Washington: Department of the Interior, 10 p.

_____1988. *Decisions on geographic names in the United States, October through December 1988.* (Decision list no. 8804.) Washington: Department of the Interior, 20 p.

_____1990. *Decisions on geographic names in the United States.* (Decision list 1990.) Washington: Department of the Interior, 35 p.

_____1991. *Decisions on geographic names in the United States.* (Decision list 1991.) Washington: Department of the Interior, 40 p.

_____1992. *Decisions on geographic names in the United States.* (Decision list 1992.) Washington: Department of the Interior, 21 p.

_____1994. Decisions on geographic names in the United States. (Decision list 1994.) Washington: Department of the Interior, 17 p.

Waring, Gerald A. 1915. *Springs of California.* (United States Geological Survey Water-Supply Paper 338.) Washington: Government Printing Office, 410 p.

Watts, W.L. 1890. "Stanislaus County." *Tenth Annual report of the State Mineralogist, for the year ending December 1, 1890.* Sacramento: California State Mining Bureau, p. 680-690.

Wayman, John Hudson. 1971. *A doctor on the California Trail, The diary of Dr. John Hudson Wayman from Cambridge City, Indiana, to the gold fields in 1852.* (Edited by Edgeley Woodman Todd.) Denver, Colorado: Old West Publishing Company, 136 p.

Wedertz, Frank S. 1978. *Mono Diggings.* Bishop, California: Chalfant Press, Inc., 245 p.

Wheeler, George M. 1878. *Annual report upon the geographical surveys of the territory of the United States west of the 100th meridian, in the states and territories of California, Colorado, Kansas, Nebraska, Nevada, Oregon, Texas, Arizona, Idaho, Montana, New Mexico, Utah, Washington, and Wyoming.* (Appendix NN of *The Annual Report of the Chief of Engineers for 1878.*) Washington: Government Printing Office, 234 p.

_____1879. *Annual report upon the geographical surveys of the territory of the United States west of the 100th meridian, in the states and territories of California, Colorado, Kansas, Nebraska, Nevada, Oregon, Texas, Arizona, Idaho, Montana, New Mexico, Utah, Washington, and Wyoming.* (Appendix OO of *The Annual Report of the Chief of Engineers for 1879.*) Washington: Government Printing Office, 340 p.

Whiting, J.S., and Whiting, Richard J. 1960. *Forts of the State of California.* (Authors), 90 p.

Whitney, J.D. 1865. *Report of progress and synopsis of the field-work from 1860 to 1864.* (Geological Survey of California, Geology, Volume I.) Published by authority of the Legislature of California, 498 p.

_____1870. *The Yosemite guide-book.* Published by authority of the Legislature [of California], 155 p.

_____1880. *The auriferous gravels of the Sierra Nevada of California.* Cambridge: University Press, John Wilson & Son, 569 p.

Wilkes, Charles. 1958. *Columbia River to the Sacramento.* Oakland, California: Biobooks, 140 p.

Wood, Harvey. 1954. *Personal recollections of Harvey Wood.* (Introduction and notes by John B. Goodman, III.) Pasadena, California: (Privately published), 27 p.

Wright, James W.A. 1984. *The Lost Cement mine.* (Edited by Jenny Smith.) Mammoth Lakes, California: Genny Smith Books, 95 p.

QUADRANGLE MAPS

(All maps published by United States Geological Survey, except as noted. Dates identify the editions of the maps. If a reprinted or revised map was used, the year of reprinting or revision is given in parentheses, unless the reprinted or revised map is cited specifically in the text.)

Angels Camp 7.5'—1962.
Arena 7.5'—1960.
Athlone 15' (same area as Chowchilla 15')—1942 (Army).
Atwater 15'—1961.
7.5'—1918.
Avena 7.5'—1914; 1952.
Bachelor Valley 7.5'—1916; 1953; 1968.
Bass Lake 15'—1953.
Bear Valley 7.5'—1947; 1947, photorevised 1973.

Bellota 15'—1939 (Army).
Ben Hur 7.5'—1947.
Berenda 7.5'—1918; 1961.
Bethany 7.5' (same area as Clifton Court Forebay 7.5')—1914; 1952.
Big Meadow 15'—1956.
Big Trees 30'—1891.
Biola 7.5'—1963.
Bliss Ranch 7.5'—1918; 1960.
Blue Mountain 15'—1956.
Boards Crossing 7.5'—1979.
Bonita Ranch 7.5'—1963.
Bouldin 7.5' (same area as Bouldin Island 7.5')—1910 (reprinted 1947).
Bouldin Island 7.5' (same area as Bouldin 7.5')—1952; 1978.
Bruceville 7.5'—1968.
Brush Lake 7.5' (same area as Westport 7.5')—1953; 1969.
Buckhorn Peak 7.5'—1947.
Buckingham Mountain 7.5'—1947.
Burnham 7.5' (same area as Stockton East 7.5')—1914.
Calaveras Dome 7.5'—1979.
Calaveritas 7.5'—1962.
Carbona 15'—1922 (reprinted 1942).
Castle 7.5' (same area as Lodi South 7.5')—1910 (reprinted 1942).
Catheys Valley 7.5'—1962.
Cedar Mountain 7.5'—1956.
Ceres 7.5'—1918; 1953; 1969.
Charleston School 7.5'—1956.
Cherry Lake North 7.5'—1979.
Chinese Camp 7.5'—1947; 1947 photorevised 1973.
Chowchilla 15' (same area as Athlone 15')—1960.
7.5'—1918; 1960.
Clay 7.5'—1953; 1968.
Clements 7.5'—1968.
Clifton Court Forebay 7.5' (same areas as Bethany 7.5')—1978.
Columbia 15'—1948.
7.5'—1948; 1948, photorevised 1973.
Columbia SE 7.5'—1948.
Cooperstown 7.5'—1916; 1953; 1968.
Copper Mountain 7.5'—1956.
Copperopolis 15'—1916 (reprinted 1947).
7.5'—1962.
Coulterville 15'—1947.
7.5'—1947; 1947, photorevised 1973.
Crandall Peak 7.5'—1979.
Cressey 7.5'—1916.
Crevison Peak 7.5'—1955.
Crows Landing 7.5'—1952.
Dardanelle 7.5'—1979.
Dardanelles 30'—1898; 1898, reprinted 1947.
Dardanelles Cone 15'—1956.
7.5'—1979.
Daulton 7.5'—1921; 1962; 1962, photorevised 1981.
Delta Ranch 7.5'—1922.
Denair 7.5'—1969.
Devils Nose 7.5'—1979.
Devils Postpile 15'—1953.
Disaster Peak 7.5'—1979.
Donnell Lake 7.5'—1979.
Dorrington 7.5'—1979.
Dos Palos 7.5'—1956.
Duckwall Mountain 7.5'—1948.
El Nido 7.5' (same area as Lingard 7.5')—1960.
El Portal 15'—1947.
7.5'—1947.
Escalon 7.5' (same area as Thalheim 7.5')—1968.
Farmington 7.5' (same area as Trigo 7.5')—1953; 1968.
Feliciana Mountain 7.5'—1947.
Firebaugh 15'—1946; 1962.
7.5'—1956.
Firebaugh NE 7.5' (same area as Kentucky Well 7.5')—1961.
Fort Mountain 7.5'—1979.
Franklin 15'—1942 (Army).
Fresno 1°x 2°—1962, revised 1967.
Friant 7.5'—1964.
Galt 7.5'—1968.
Garnet Hill 7.5'—1979.
Goose Creek 7.5'—1968.
Gregg 7.5'—1965.
Groveland 7.5'—1947; 1947, photorevised 1973.
Hatch 7.5' (same area as Mitchell School 7.5')—1962.
Haystack Mountain 7.5'—1962.
Headreach 7.5' (same area as Terminous 7.5')—1910 (reprinted 1942).
Herndon 15'—1965.
Hetch Hetchy Reservoir 15'—1956.
Holt 7.5'—1913 (reprinted 1947); 1952; 1978.
Hopeton 7.5' (same area as Yosemite Lake 7.5')—1916.
Hornitos 7.5'—1947; 1947, photorevised 1973.
Horsecamp Mountain 7.5'—1947.
Howard Ranch 7.5'— 1953.
Hull Creek 7.5'—1979.
Illinois Hill 7.5'—1962.
Indian Gulch 15'—1920.
7.5'—1962.
Ingomar 7.5'—1919; 1960 (photorevised 1971).
Isleton 7.5'—1910 (reprinted 1947); 1952 (photorevised 1968); 1978.
Jackson 30'—1902 (reprinted 1948).
7.5'—1962.
Jawbone Ridge 7.5'—1947.
Jenny Lind 7.5'—1962.
Kaiser 30'—1904 (reprinted 1946).
Kaiser Peak 15'—1953.
Kentucky Well 7.5' (same area as Firebaugh NE 7.5')—1922.
Keystone 7.5'—1962.
Kinsley 7.5'—1947.
Kismet 7.5'—1920; 1961.
Knights Ferry 7.5'—1962.
Knowles 7.5'—1962; 1962, photorevised 1981.
La Grange 7.5'—1919 (reprinted 1922); 1962.
Laguna Seca Ranch 7.5'—1956.
Lake Eleanor 15'—1956.
Lathrop 7.5'—1952 (photorevised 1968).
Le Grand 15'—1961.
7.5'—1918; 1961; 1961, photorevised 1981.
Liberty Hill 7.5'—1979.
Linden 7.5'—1968.
Lingard 7.5' (same area as El Nido 7.5')—1918.
Little Table Mountain 7.5'—1962; 1962, photorevised 1981.
Lockeford 7.5'—1908 (reprinted 1942); 1968.
Lodi 30'—1894 (reprinted 1906).
7.5'—1939 (Army).
Lodi North 7.5' (same area as Woodbridge 7.5')—1968.
Lodi South 7.5' (same area as Castle 7.5')—1968.
Lone Tree Creek 7.5'—1955.
Long Barn 15'—1956.
Los Banos 15'—1961.
7.5'—1921; 1960.
Los Banos Valley 7.5'—1969.
Madera 15'—1946.
7.5'—1963.
Manteca 7.5'—1914; 1952.
Mariposa 1°x 2°—1957, revised 1970.
30'—1912 (reprinted 1951).
15'—1947.
7.5'—1947.
Mariposa Peak 7.5'—1969.
Matterhorn Peak 15'—1956.
Melones Dam 7.5'—1962.
Mendota Dam 7.5' (same area as Mendota 7.5')—1956.
Merced 15'—1962.
7.5'—1917; 1961.
Merced Falls 15'—1944; 1962.
7.5'—1962.
Merced Peak 15'—1953.
Midway 7.5'—1953.
Millerton Lake 15'—1945 (Army); 1965.
Millerton Lake East 7.5'—1965.
Millerton Lake West 7.5'—1965.
Mississippi Creek 7.5'—1955.
Moccasin 7.5'—1948; 1948, photorevised 1973.
Modesto East 15'—1939 (Army).
Mokelumne Hill 7.5'—1948.
Mokelumne Peak 7.5'—1979.
Mono Craters 15'—1953.
Montpelier 7.5'—1968.
Mount Boardman 15'—1942 (Army).
7.5'—1955.
Mount Lyell 30'—1901 (reprinted 1948).
Mount Stakes 7.5'—1955.
Murphys 7.5'—1948.
Mustang Peak 7.5'—1955.
New Hope 7.5' (same area as Thornton 7.5')—1910; 1952 (photorevised 1968).
Newman 7.5'—1952.

North Fork 7.5'—1965.
Oakdale 7.5'—1915; 1968.
O'Neals 7.5'—1965.
Orestimba Peak 7.5' (same area as Orestimba Creek 7.5')—1955.
Ortigalita Peak 15'—1943; 1956.
7.5'—1969.
Ortigalita Peak NW 7.5' (same area as Ortigalita 7.5')—1956; 1969.
Owens Reservoir 7.5' (same area as Owens Creek 7.5')—1962.
Oxalis 7.5'—1956.
Pacheco Pass 15'—1920 (reprinted 1947).
7.5'—1955; 1955, photorevised 1971.
Panoche 30'—1913 (reprinted 1948).
Patterson 7.5'—1916 (reprinted 1947); 1953.
Paulsell 7.5'—1953; 1968.
Penon Blanco Peak 7.5'—1962; 1962, photorevised 1973.
Peters 7.5'—1915; 1952.
Pinecrest 15'—1956.
7.5'—1979.
Plainsberg 7.5'—1919.
Planada 7.5'—1918; 1961.
Poso Farm 7.5'—1962.
Quien Sabe 15'—1922.
Quien Sabe Valley 7.5'—1968.
Rail Road Flat 7.5'—1948.
Raymond 15'—1944; 1962.
7.5'—1962; 1962, photorevised 1981.
Raynor Creek 7.5'—1961.
Rio Vista 15'—1952.
Ripon 7.5'—1915; 1952; 1969.
Riverbank 7.5'—1916; 1969.
Romain 7.5' (same area as Solyo 7.5')—1916 (reprinted 1922).
Ruby Canyon 7.5'—1968.
Sacramento 1°x 2°—1957, limited revision 1964.
Salida 7.5'—1953; 1969.
Salt Spring Valley 7.5'—1962.
San Andreas 15'—1947.
7.5'—1962.
Sandy Mush 7.5'—1962.
San Jose 1°x 2°—1947 (Army); 1962 (revised 1969).
San Luis Creek 7.5' (same area as San Luis Dam 7.5')—1953.
San Luis Dam 7.5' (same area as San Luis Creek 7.5')—1969.
San Luis Ranch 7.5'—1919; 1961.
Santa Cruz 1°x 2°—1958.
Santa Rita Bridge 7.5'—1922; 1962 (photorevised 1977).
Santa Rita Park 15'—1962.
Shaver Lake 15'—1953.
Shuteye Peak 15'—1953 (limited revision 1965).
Snelling 7.5'—1918 (reprinted 1943); 1962.
Solyo 7.5' (same area as Romain 7.5')—1953.
Sonora 30'—1891; 1897 (reprinted 1939).
15'—1948.
7.5'—1948; 1948, photorevised 1973.
Sonora Pass 15'—1956.
7.5'—1979.
Spicer Meadow Reservoir 7.5'—1979.
Standard 7.5'—1948.
Stanislaus 7.5'—1948.
Stevinson 7.5'—1961.
Stockton 7.5' (same area as Stockton West 7.5')—1913 (reprinted 1943).
Stockton East 7.5' (same area as Burnham 7.5')—1952.
Stockton West 7.5' (same area as Stockton 7.5')—1952.
Strawberry 7.5'—1979.
Stumpfield Mountain 7.5'—1947.
Tamarack 7.5'—1979.
Terminous 7.5' (same area as Headreach 7.5')—1952 (photorevised 1968); 1978.
Tesla 15'—1907 (reprinted 1941).
Thalheim 7.5' (same area as Escalon 7.5')—1915.
Thornton 7.5' (same area as New Hope 7.5')—1978.
Three Tree Flat 7.5' (same area as Turlock Lake 7.5')—1916.
Tower Peak 15'—1956.
Tracy 7.5'—1916 (reprinted 1928); 1954.
Trigo 7.5' (same area as Farmington 7.5')—1915.
Tuolumne 15'—1948.
7.5'—1948.
Tuolumne Meadows 15'—1956.
Turlock 15' (same area as Irwin 15')—1962.
Turlock Lake 7.5' (same area as Three Tree Flat 7.5')—1968.
Turner Ranch 7.5'—1961.
Twain Harte 7.5'—1979.
Union Island 7.5'—1914; 1978.
Valley Springs 15'—1944.
7.5'—1962.
Valley Springs SW 7.5'—1962.
Vernalis 7.5'—1952; 1969.
Wallace 7.5'—1962.
Waterford 7.5'—1916; 1969.
Waterloo 7.5'—1968.
Westley 7.5'—1915 (reprinted 1936); 1952; 1969.
West Point 7.5'—1948.
Wilcox Ridge 7.5'—1956.
Winton 7.5'—1917; 1961.
Woodbridge 7.5' (same area as Lodi North 7.5')—1910.
Woodward Island 7.5'—1913; 1952; 1978.
Yosemite 30'—1909 (reprinted 1938).
15'—1956.
Yosemite Lake 7.5' (same area as Hopeton 7.5')—1962.

MISCELLANEOUS MAPS

Anderson and Pack. 1909-1911. "Geologic map of the western border of San Joaquin Valley, California, between the Coalinga oil field and Livermore Pass." (Plate I *in* Anderson and Pack.)
Bancroft. 1864. "Bancroft's map of the Pacific States." Compiled by Wm. H. Knight. Published by H.H. Bancroft & Co., Booksellers and Stationers, San Francisco, Cal.
Beaumont. 1858. "Plan of El Rancho del Campo de los Franceces." Using the final survey made by the instructions of J.W. Mandeville, U.S. Surveyor General, Issued Feb. 12, 1858. Prepared by Duncan Beaumont, U.S. Deputy Surveyor. (Reproduced *in* Hammond.)
California Division of Highways. 1934. (Appendix "A" *of* California Division of Highways.)
California Mining Bureau. (1909a). "Sacramento, San Joaquin, Amador, and Calaveras Counties." (*In* California Mining Bureau Bulletin 56.)
_____1909b. "Stanislaus, Merced, Tuolumne, and Mariposa Counties." (*In* California Mining Bureau Bulletin 56.)
_____1909c. "Madera and Fresno Counties." (*In* California Mining Bureau Bulletin 56.)
_____1910. "Map of California showing the approximate location of the principal mineral deposits." Compiled by the State Mining Bureau.
_____1917a. (Untitled map *in* California Mining Bureau Bulletin 74, p. 165.)
_____1917b. (Untitled map *in* California Mining Bureau Bulletin 74, p. 167.)
Camp. 1962. (Untitled map *in* Doble.)
Derby. 1849. "A Sketch of General Riley's route through the mining districts, July and Aug. 1849."
_____1850. "Reconnaissance of the Tulares Valley." Lieut. G.H. Derby, Topl. Engrs., April and May, 1850.
Ellis. 1850. "Map of the gold region of California." Taken from a recent survey by Robert H. Ellis.
Fremont. 1848. "Map of Oregon and Upper California from the surveys of John Charles Frémont and other authorities." Drawn by Charles Preuss. Washington City.
Gibbes. 1850. "Map of San Joaquin River." By Charles D. Gibbes.
Goddard. 1857. "Britton & Rey's map of the State of California." By George H. Goddard.
Grunsky. 1899. "East side of San Joaquin Valley, from Chowchilla River to Merced River." (Plate IV *in* Grunsky.)
Hammond. 1849. "City of Stockton." Surveyed for the proprietor. Richd. P. Hammond, Bvt. Major 3d Artillery, June 1849. (Reproduced *in* Hammond.)
Hoffmann and Gardner. 1863-1867. "Map of a portion of the Sierra Nevada adjacent to Yosemite Valley." From surveys made by Chs. F. Hoffmann and J.T. Gardner, 1863-1867. Geological Survey of California.
Jarves. 1849. "A correct map of the Bay of San Francisco and the gold region." From actual survey June 20th 1849, for J.J. Jarves. Published by James Munroe & Co. 134 Washington St. Boston.
King and Gardner. 1865. "Map of the Yosemite Valley." From surveys made by order of the Commissioners to Manage the Yosemite Valley and Mariposa Big Tree Grove, by C. King and J.T. Gardner.
Laizure. 1928. "'Las Mariposa' of the Mariposa Commercial & Mining Company, Mariposa County, California." (*In* Laizure, 1928.)
_____1935. "Map of Mariposa County showing principal gold mines." (*In* Laizure, 1935.)
Lippincott. 1902. "Map of drainage basin of Kings River, California, showing route traversed by exploring parties." (Plate I *in* Lippincott.)
Logan. 1950. "Map of Madera County showing location of mines and mineral deposits." (Plate 73 *in* Logan.)
Mendenhall. 1908. "Artesian areas and groundwater levels in the San Joaquin Valley, California." (Plate I *in* Mendenhall.)
Ord. 1848. "Topographical sketch of the gold and quicksilver district of California, July 25th 1848." By E.O.C.O. [E.O.C. Ord]. Lt. U.S.A.
Parke. 1854-1855. "Map No. 1, San Francisco Bay to the plains of Los Angeles." From explorations and surveys made by Lieut. John G. Parke.

Constructed and drawn by H. Custer. (In *Reports of explorations and surveys, to ascertain the most practicable and economical route for a railroad from the Mississippi River to the Pacific Ocean.* Volume XI. 1861.)

Reynolds. 1899. "Mining map of Tuolumne County, California." By A.M. Reynolds, mining engineer. (Follows p. 358 in *California mines and minerals,* published by California Miners' Association in 1899 at San Francisco.)

Sage. 1846. "Map of Oregon, California, New Mexico, N.W. Texas, & the proposed Territory of Ne-Bras-ka." By Rufus B. Sage.

Thompson and West. 1876. (Maps *in* Thompson and West, 1876.)

____1879. (Maps *in* Thompson and West, 1879.)

Trask. 1853. "Topographical map of the mineral districts of California." Being the first map ever published from actual survey. By John B. Trask. Lithog. and Published by Britton & Rey. San Francisco.

Wheeler. 1876-1877. "Parts of eastern California and western Nevada." (Atlas Sheet No. 56B.) Expeditions of 1876 & 1877 under the command of 1st Lieut. Geo. M. Wheeler.

Whitney. 1880. "Diagram showing the position of the Table Mountain lava flow of Tuolumne County." (Plate D *in* Whitney, 1880.)

Wilkes. 1841. "Map of Upper California." By the U.S. Ex. Ex. and best authorities.

Williamson. 1853. "General map of explorations and surveys in California." By Lieut. R.S. Williamson, Topl. Engr., assisted by Lieut. J.G. Parke, Topl. Engr., and Mr. Isaac William Smith, Civ. Engr. (In *Reports of explorations and surveys, to ascertain the most practicable and economical route for a railroad from the Mississippi River to the Pacific Ocean.* Volume XI. 1861.)

Wyld. 1849. "Map of the gold regions of California." Compiled from original surveys by James Wyld, Geographer to the Queen & Prince Albert, Charing Cross East & 2 Royal Exchange, London.

Part Seven
Central Coast Region

Monterey, San Benito, San Luis Obispo, Santa Barbara and Santa Cruz Counties

Part Seven–Central Coast Region

Central Coast Region
Monterey, San Benito, San Luis Obispo, Santa Barbara and Santa Cruz Counties

Regional Setting

General.—This section concerns geographic features in five counties—Monterey, San Benito, San Luis Obispo, Santa Barbara, and Santa Cruz—that lie near the coast of California from Monterey Bay south to Santa Barbara Channel; all but San Benito County front on the sea. Townships (T) South refer to Mount Diablo Base and Meridian; Townships North refer to San Bernardino Base and Meridian. The region generally is mountainous and includes islands on the south side of Santa Barbara Channel. The map on the facing page shows the location of the Central Coast Region and the counties in it.

Monterey County.—Monterey County covers the north part of the valley of Salinas River and highlands east and west of the valley. The first state legislature created the county in 1850. Officials changed the boundary between Monterey and San Luis Obispo Counties several times before they fixed it at its present position in 1863; Monterey County lost part of its original territory when San Benito County was organized in 1874 (Coy, p. 184-186). The city of Monterey was the county seat until the county government moved to Salinas in 1873 (Hoover, Rensch, and Rensch, p. 216). The name "Monterey" in the region dates from 1602, when Vizcaino gave his anchorage near present Monterey the designation "Puerto de Monterey" to honor the Conde de Monterey, Viceroy of New Spain (Wagner, H.R., p. 398).

San Benito.—San Benito County is mostly mountainous; extensive lowlands occur only in the north part. The state legislature created the county in 1874 from part of Monterey County, and added territory in 1887 at the expense of Fresno County (Coy, p. 213-214). Hollister is and always has been the county seat; the county name is from San Benito River, which flows nearly the entire length of the county (Hoover, Rensch, and Rensch, p. 309, 315).

San Luis Obispo.—San Luis Obispo County includes part or all of several mountain ranges as well as lowlands along the coast, near Santa Maria River, and along part of Salinas River. The state legislature created the county in 1850; the original boundaries of the county have been modified only slightly (Coy, p. 233-237). The city of San Luis Obispo has been the county seat from the beginning; the name "San Luis Obispo" for city and county is from San Luis Obispo de Tolusa mission, founded in 1772 (Hoover, Rensch, and Rensch, p. 378-380).

Santa Barbara.—Santa Barbara County lies along the coast where the general south-southeast trend of the coastline turns eastward at Point Conception, and includes offshore islands. It is one of the original counties that the first state legislature created in 1850. Officials modified Santa Barbara-San Luis Obispo County line several times before 1872, when they fixed the present boundary; the east part of the original territory of Santa Barbara County was lost in 1872 with the formation of Ventura County (Coy, p. 242-244). The county name is from Santa Barbara Channel, which Vizcaino named; the city of Santa Barbara has always been the county seat (Hoover, Rensch, and Rensch, p. 413).

Santa Cruz.—Santa Cruz County extends inland from the coast to the crest of Santa Cruz Mountains. It is one of the counties that the state legislature created in 1850 when California achieved statehood; the north part of the original territory of the county was lost to San Mateo County in 1868, but otherwise the county boundaries differ little from those of 1850—the county was called Branciforte for a brief time before the name was changed to Santa Cruz (Coy, p. 248). The city of Santa Cruz is the first and only county seat; the county name is from Santa Cruz mission, founded in 1891 (Hoover, Rensch, and Rensch, p. 464).

CENTRAL COAST REGION
MONTEREY, SAN BENITO, SAN LUIS OBISPO, SANTA BARBARA AND SANTA CRUZ COUNTIES

- A -

Abalone Point: see **Carmel Beach** [MONTEREY]; **Point Alones** [MONTEREY].

Abbott Canyon [SAN LUIS OBISPO]: *canyon*, drained by a stream that flows 3.5 miles to Carrizo Plain 25 miles southeast of Simmler (lat. 35°03'50" N, long. 119°42'50" W; sec. 1, T 11 N, R 27 W). Named on Caliente Mountain (1959) and Wells Ranch (1954) 7.5' quadrangles.

Abel Canyon [SANTA BARBARA]: *canyon*, drained by a stream that flows 6.5 miles to Sisquoc River 6.25 miles west of Montgomery Potrero (lat. 34°49'25" N, long. 119°51'45" W). Named on Hurricane Deck (1964) and Peak Mountain (1964) 7.5' quadrangles.

Abel Canyon Campground [SANTA BARBARA]: *locality*, 6.25 miles west of Montgomery Potrero along Sisquoc River (lat. 34°49'20" N, long. 119°51'40" W); the place is near the mouth of Abel Canyon. Named on Hurricane Deck (1964) 7.5' quadrangle.

Abel Canyon Spring [SANTA BARBARA]: *spring*, 4.25 miles northwest of Montgomery Potrero (lat. 34°52'15" N, long. 119°48'50" W); the spring is in a branch of Abel Canyon. Named on Hurricane Deck (1964) 7.5' quadrangle.

Adams Cove [SANTA BARBARA]: *embayment*, 0.5 mile east of Point Bennett on the south side of San Miguel Island (lat. 34°01'50" N, long. 120°26'25" W). Named on San Miguel Island West (1950) 7.5' quadrangle.

Adelaida [SAN LUIS OBISPO]: *locality*, 10 miles west of Paso Robes (lat. 35°38'45" N, long. 120°52'20" W; near NE cor. sec. 27, T 26 S, R 10 E). Named on Adelaida (1948) 7.5' quadrangle. The place was the site of a Mennonite settlement (Lee and others, p. 8). Called Adelaide on California Mining Bureau's (1909b) map, and Crawford (1894, p. 394) referred to Adelaide P.O. Postal authorities established Adelaida post office in 1877 when they moved Josephine post office to the place; they moved Adelaida post office 1 mile northeast in 1880 and discontinued it in 1936—the name "Adelaida" was for the daughter of the postmaster (Salley, p. 1). They established Josephine post office in 1873, discontinued it for a time in 1877, and discontinued it finally in 1883; the name "Josephine" was for the first white child born at the site, which was 14 miles west of Paso Robles (Salley, p. 108). Josephine post office may have been at Josephine mine, a quicksilver mine discovered in 1862 about 5 miles southwest of present Adelaida (Logan, p. 711). California Mining Bureau's (1909b) map shows a place called Gibbons located 7.5 miles by stage line northwest of Adelaide (present Adelaida); postal authorities established Gibbons post office in 1894 and discontinued it in 1909 (Frickstad, p. 164).

Adelaide: see **Adelaida** [SAN LUIS OBISPO].

Adobe Canyon [SAN LUIS OBISPO]:

(1) *canyon*, drained by a stream that flows 1.5 miles to Rocky Canyon 6 miles north of Santa Margarita (lat. 35°28'35" N, long. 120°36'30" W; sec. 19, T 28 S, R 13 E). Named on Santa Margarita (1965) 7.5' quadrangle.

(2) *canyon*, drained by a stream that flows 2 miles to Los Berros Canyon 5 miles east-southeast of the town of Arroyo Grande (lat. 35°05'40" N, long. 120°30'05" W; sec. 32, T 32 S, R 14 E). Named on Oceano (1965) 7.5' quadrangle.

Adobe Canyon [SANTA BARBARA]: *canyon*, drained by a stream that flows 4 miles to Santa Ynez River 2.5 miles southeast of Buellton (lat. 34°35'30" N, long. 120°01'50" W). Named on Solvang (1959) and Zaca Creek (1959) 7.5' quadrangles.

Adobe Creek [SAN LUIS OBISPO]: *stream*, flows 2 miles to the sea nearly 2 miles west-northwest of the village of San Simeon (lat. 35°39'05" N, long. 121°13'20" W). Named on San Simeon (1958) 7.5' quadrangle.

Adobe Springs [SAN LUIS OBISPO]: *spring*, 4 miles west of Cholame (2) in McMillan Canyon (lat. 35°44' N, long. 120°21'55" W; sec. 21, T 25 S, R 15 E). Named on Cholame (1961) 7.5' quadrangle.

Agenda: see **Buena Vista** [MONTEREY] (2).

Agua Caliente Canyon [SANTA BARBARA]: *canyon*, drained by a stream that flows 14 miles to Santa Ynez River 6.5 miles south-southwest of Hildreth Peak (lat. 34°30'30" N, long. 119°34'45" W). Named on Hildreth Peak (1964) and Old Man Mountain (1943) 7.5' quadrangles.

Agua Caliente Spring [SANTA BARBARA]: *spring*, 4.5 miles south of Hildreth Peak (lat. 34°32'25" N, long. 119°33'45" W); the spring is in Agua Caliente Canyon. Named on Hildreth Peak (1964) 7.5' quadrangle.

Agua del Gavilan: see **Gabilan Creek** [MONTEREY] (2).

Aguadulce Spring [SANTA BARBARA]: *spring*, 2 miles east of Salisbury Potrero (lat. 34°49'10" N, long. 119°39'50" W). Named on Salisbury Potrero (1964) 7.5' quadrangle.

Agua Escondida Spring [SAN LUIS OBISPO]: *spring*, 7.5 miles west of Branch Mountain near the head of Arroyo Seco (lat. 35°10'55" N, long. 120°13'40" W; sec. 35, T 31 S, R 16 E). Named on Branch Mountain (1952) 15' quadrangle. Called Aqua Escondida Spr. on Branch Mountain (1942) 15' quadrangle.

Agua Escondido Campground [SAN LUIS OBISPO]: *locality*, 7.5 miles west of Branch Mountain (lat. 35°10'45" N, long. 120°13'40" W; on N line sec. 2, T 32 S, R 16 E). Named on Los Machos Hills (1967) 7.5' quadrangle. Branch Mountain (1952) 15' quadrangle shows Agua Escondida Spring near the site.

Agua Fria Creek [MONTEREY]: *stream*, flows nearly 3 miles to Gabilan Creek (2) 6 miles south-southwest of Jolon (lat. 35°53'40" N, long. 121°13'35" W). Named on Jolon (1949) 7.5' quadrangle.

Agua Grande Canyon [MONTEREY]: *canyon*, flows 6.25 miles to lowlands 5 miles east-southeast of Greenfield (lat. 36°18'10" N, long. 121°09'15" W). Named on Greenfield (1956) and Pinalito Canyon (1969) 7.5' quadrangles.

Aguajita [SANTA CRUZ]: *land grant*, 2.25 miles north-northwest of Soquel Point at the east edge of Santa Cruz. Named on Soquel (1954) 7.5' quadrangle. Miguel Villagrana received the land in 1837; 40 acres were patented to Villagrana or his son (Rowland, p. 41; Rowland used the form "Aguajito" for the name).

Aguajito [MONTEREY]: *land grant*, south and southeast of Monterey. Named on Monterey (1947) and Seaside (1947) 7.5' quadrangles. Gregorio Tapia received 0.5 league in 1835 and claimed 3323 acres patented in 1868 (Cowan, p. 13). Gudde (1949, p. 5) noted that *aguajito* is the diminutive of *aguaje*, which means "reservoir," "spring," or "watering place" in Spanish.

Aguajito: see **Aguajita** [SANTA CRUZ].

Aguajito Canyon [SANTA BARBARA]: *canyon*, drained by a stream that flows 2.5 miles to Cañada del Refugio 8.5 miles east of Gaviota (lat. 34°28'35" N, long. 120°04'05" W). Named on Santa Ynez (1959) and Tajiguas (1953) 7.5' quadrangles.

Agua Mala Creek [MONTEREY]: *stream*, flows 6.25 miles to Rana Creek 6.5 miles east-southeast of the town of Carmel Valley (lat. 36°26'20" N, long. 121°37'35" W). Named on Rana Creek (1956) 7.5' quadrangle.

Agua Puerca y las Trancas [SANTA CRUZ]: *land grant*, 4 miles north-northwest of Davenport along the coast at El Jarro Point. Named on Año Nuevo (1955) and Davenport (1955) 7.5' quadrangles. Ramon Rodriguez and Francisco Alviso received 1 league in 1843; their heirs claimed 4421 acres patented in 1867—the grant also was called El Jarro (Cowan, p. 13).

Airbase [SANTA BARBARA]: *locality*, 3 miles south of Santa Maria along Santa Maria Valley Railroad (lat. 34°54'25" N, long. 120°26'40" W; near N line sec. 34, T 10 N, R 34 W). Named on Santa Maria (1959) 7.5' quadrangle.

Airstrip Pond [SAN BENITO]: *intermittent lake*, 450 feet long, 12.5 miles east-southeast of Bitterwater (lat. 36°18'35" N, long. 120°47'50" W; sec. 5, T 19 S, R 11 E); the feature is near a landing strip situated along upper reaches of Laguna Creek. Named on Hepsedam Peak (1969) 7.5' quadrangle.

Ajax: see **Surf** [SANTA BARBARA].

Ajax Mountain: see **Alder Peak** [MONTEREY].

Alamar Campground: see **Lower Alamar Campground** [SANTA BARBARA].

Alamar Canyon [SANTA BARBARA]: *canyon*, drained by a stream that flows 9 miles to Mono Creek 2 miles northwest of Hildreth Peak (lat.

34°37'05" N, long. 119°34'20" W). Named on Hildreth Peak (1964) and Madulce Peak (1964) 7.5' quadrangles. Called Roble Canyon on Santa Ynez (1905) 30' quadrangle. Strawberry Peak (1944) 7.5' quadrangle shows Alamar Canyon as a branch of Roble Canyon.

Alamar Hill [SANTA BARBARA]: *ridge*, southeast-trending, less than 1 mile long, about 4 miles south of Madulce Peak (lat. 34°37'50" N, long. 119°35'25" W); the ridge is west of Alamar Canyon. Named on Madulce Peak (1964) 7.5' quadrangle.

Alamo Canyon [SANTA BARBARA]: *canyon*, drained by a stream that flows 4.5 miles to Santa Barbara Canyon 3 miles south-southeast of Fox Mountain (lat. 34°46'30" N, long. 119°34'20" W). Named on Fox Mountain (1964) and Strawberry Peak (1944) 7.5' quadrangles.

Alamo Creek [SAN LUIS OBISPO]:

(1) *stream*, flows 5.5 miles to Santa Margarita Lake 4 miles west-northwest of Pozo (lat. 35°19'40" N, long. 120°26'20" W; sec. 11, T 30 S, R 14 E). Named on Santa Margarita Lake (1967) 7.5' quadrangle.

(2) *stream*, flows 23 miles to Cuyama River 2.5 miles southeast of Huasna Peak (lat. 35°00'30" N, long. 120°18'50" W). Named on Chimney Canyon (1967), Huasna Peak (1967), and Los Machos Hills (1967) 7.5' quadrangles. Called Alamos Creek on Nipomo (1922) 15' quadrangle. The stream now joins Cuyama River in Twitchell Reservoir. California Mining Bureau's (1909b) map shows a place called Avenal located 14.5 miles by stage line southeast of Pozo, probably along Alamo Creek (2) at or near the place that Los Machos Hills (1967) 7.5' quadrangle shows Avenales ranch (lat. 35°12'20" N, long. 120°11'25" W). Postal authorities established Avenal post office in 1887 and discontinued it in 1905 (Frickstad, p. 163).

Alamo Creek [SANTA BARBARA]: *stream*, flows 2.5 miles to El Jaro Creek 12 miles southeast of the city of Lompoc (lat. 34°31'05" N, long. 120°18'20" W). Named on Santa Rosa Hills (1959) 7.5' quadrangle.

Alamo Pintado: see **Ballard** [SANTA BARBARA].

Alamo Pintado Creek [SANTA BARBARA]: *stream*, flows 18 miles to Santa Ynez River 3.5 miles southeast of Buellton near Solvang (lat. 34°35' N, long. 120°08'15" W). Named on Los Olivos (1959), Santa Ynez (1959), and Solvang (1959) 7.5' quadrangles.

Alamos Anchorage [SANTA BARBARA]: *anchorage*, 2.5 miles east of Punta Arena on the south side of Santa Cruz Island (lat. 33°57'40" N, long. 119°46'10" W). Named on Santa Cruz Island B (1943) 7.5' quadrangle. Bremner's (1932) map has the name "Cñ. del Alamo" for a canyon that opens to the sea 0.5 mile west of present Alamos Anchorage.

Alamos Creek: see **Alamo Creek** [SAN LUIS OBISPO] (2).

Alba Creek [SANTA CRUZ]: *stream*, flows 1.25 miles to San Lorenzo River 2 miles south-southeast of the town of Boulder Creek (lat. 37°06'10" N, long. 122°06'10" W; sec. 32, T 9 S, R 2 W). Named on Felton (1955) 7.5' quadrangle.

Albañez Spring [SAN BENITO]: *spring*, 7.5 miles west of Panoche (lat. 36°35'40" N, long. 120°58'05" W; sec. 27, T 15 S, R 9 E). Named on Llanada (1969) 7.5' quadrangle.

Albert Anchorage [SANTA BARBARA]: *embayment*, 3.5 miles south of Prisoners Harbor on the south side of Santa Cruz Island (lat. 33° 58'10" N, long. 119°41'50" W). Named on Santa Cruz Island C (1943) 7.5' quadrangle.

Alcatraz [SANTA BARBARA]: *locality*, less than 1 mile east of Gaviota (lat. 34°28'15" N, long. 120°12'15" W); the place is near the mouth of present Cañada Alcatraz. Named on Lompoc (1905) 30' quadrangle. Postal authorities established Alcatraz Landing post office at the site in 1898 and discontinued it in 1901—the landing was a shipping point for oil (Salley, p. 4).

Alcatraz Landing: see **Alcatraz** [SANTA BARBARA].

Alder Creek [MONTEREY]: *stream*, flows 4.5 miles to the sea 3.5 miles southeast of Cape San Martin (lat. 35°51'30" N, long. 121° 25' W; sec. 10, T 14 S, R 5 E); the stream heads near Alder Peak. Named on Villa Creek (1949) 7.5' quadrangle. Irelan (p. 406) mentioned a mining town called Alder Creek—Cape San Martin (1921) 15' quadrangle shows mines situated 1 to 1.5 miles west and southwest of Alder Peak on the upper reaches of Alder Creek. Reinstedt (1973, p. 13-14) noted that the community of Alder Creek later was called Manchester for a blacksmith who lived there in the early days; when a post office opened, the name of the place was changed to Mansfield for the Mansfield family of Gorda, the earliest residents in the neighborhood. Postal authorities established Mansfield post office in 1889 and discontinued it in 1897 (Frickstad, p. 107). Davis (p. 696) noted that an old townsite called Los Burros was situated "upon a fairly level piece of ground sloping into a gulch opening into Alder creek . . . just below the old Last Chance mine (now the Buclimo)." This site is about 2.5 miles from the mouth of Alder Creek (sec. 2, T 24 S, R 5 E).

Alder Creek [SANTA BARBARA]: *stream*, flows 3 miles to Santa Ynez River 6.25 miles north of Carpinteria (lat. 34°29'15" N, long. 119°31'10" W; sec. 29, T 5 N, R 25 W). Named on Carpinteria (1952) and White Ledge Peak (1952) 7.5' quadrangles.

Alder Creek Mountain: see **Alder Peak** [MONTEREY].

Alder Peak [MONTEREY]: *peak*, 5.5 miles east of Cape San Martin (lat. 35°53'05" N, long. 121°22'05" W; at E line sec. 36, T 23 S, R 5 E); the peak is near the head of Alder Creek. Altitude 3744 feet. Named on Alder Peak (1949) 7.5' quadrangle. The feature also was known as Alder Creek Mountain, and perhaps as Ajax Mountain (Clark, 1991, p. 5).

Alegria Canyon: see **Cañada de Alegria** [SANTA BARBARA].

Alejandro Campground [SANTA BARBARA]: *locality*, 1.25 miles east-southeast of Tepusquet Peak (lat. 34°54'20" N, long. 120°09'45" W); the place is in Alejandro Canyon. Named on Tepusquet Canyon (1964) 7.5' quadrangle. The name commemorates Alejandro Ontiveras, head of the Spanish family that held land in the vicinity (Gagnon, p. 65).

Alejandro Canyon [SANTA BARBARA]: *canyon*, drained by a stream that flows 5.5 miles to La Brea Creek 3.5 miles south-southeast of Tepusquet Peak (lat. 34°51'35" N, long. 120°09'55" W). Named on Foxen Canyon (1964) and Tepusquet Canyon (1964) 7.5' quadrangles. Called Alejandra Canyon on Tepusquet Peak (1943) 15' quadrangle, but United States Board on Geographic Names (1965c, p. 10) rejected this form for the name.

Alexander Canyon: see **Powell Canyon** [MONTEREY].

Alexander Peak [SANTA BARBARA]: *peak*, 7 miles north-northeast of San Marcos Pass (lat. 34°35'55" N, long. 119°45'45" W). Altitude 4107 feet. Named on San Marcos Pass (1959) 7.5' quadrangle.

Alisal [MONTEREY]: *district*, east of downtown Salinas (lat. 36°40'45" N, long. 121°36'45" W); the district is on and near El Alisal (1) grant. Named on Natividad (1947) and Salinas (1947) 7.5' quadrangles. Unnamed and shown as part of Salinas on Natividad (1947, photorevised 1968) and Salinas (1947, photorevised 1968 and 1975) 7.5' quadrangles. Alisal became part of Salinas in 1963 (Clark, 1991, p. 6). Postal authorities established Alisal post office in 1866 and discontinued it in 1869, when they moved it and changed the name to Gabilan; they discontinued Gabilan post office in 1883, reestablished it in 1898, discontinued it in 1900, and reestablished it in 1950; they established East Salinas post office in 1940 and discontinued it in 1947, when they changed the name to Alisal—they changed the name back to East Salinas in 1949, and changed it to Alisal again in 1950 (Salley, p. 4, 64, 82).

Alisal Creek [MONTEREY]: *stream*, flows 5.5 miles to lowlands 5 miles east of Salinas (lat. 36°41'30" N, long. 121°34'05" W). Named on Mount Harlan (1968) and Natividad (1947) 7.5' quadrangles.

Alisal Creek [SANTA BARBARA]: *stream*, flows 8 miles to Santa Ynez River 3.5 miles southeast of Buellton (lat. 34°35'05" N, long. 120°08'35" W). Named on Santa Ynez (1959) and Solvang (1959) 7.5' quadrangles.

Alisal Slough [MONTEREY]: *stream* and *dry wash*, branches north from Salinas River 5 miles southeast of Salinas (lat. 36°37'15" N, long. 121°36'20" W) and meanders for 20 miles toward the coast. Named on Chualar (1947), Natividad (1947), and Salinas (1947) 7.5' quadrangles.

Aliso Campground [SANTA BARBARA]: *locality*, 3 miles east-northeast of McPherson Peak (lat. 34°54'30" N, long. 119°46'05" W); the place is in Aliso Canyon (1). Named on Peak Mountain (1964) 7.5' quadrangle.

Aliso Canyon [SAN LUIS OBISPO]: *canyon*, drained by a stream that flows 2.5 miles to Alamo Creek (2) 8 miles west-northwest of Branch Mountain (lat. 35°13'25" N, long. 120°12'25" W). Named on La Panza (1967) and Los Machos Hills (1967) 7.5' quadrangles.

Aliso Canyon [SANTA BARBARA]:

(1) *canyon*, drained by a stream that flows 9.5 miles to Cuyama River 7 miles north-northeast of McPherson Peak (lat. 34°59'15" N, long. 119°46'40" W). Named on Peak Mountain (1964) 7.5' quadrangle.

(2) *canyon*, drained by a stream that flows nearly 2 miles to Santa Ynez River 3 miles northeast of San Marcos Pass (lat. 34°32'40" N, long. 119°47'20" W). Named on San Marcos Pass (1959) 7.5' quadrangle.

Aliso Creek [SANTA BARBARA]: *stream*, flows 7.25 miles to Cuyama River 9 miles west of Miranda Pine Mountain (lat. 35°01'55" N, long. 120°11'15" W). Named on Chimney Canyon (1967) and Miranda Pine Mountain (1967) 7.5' quadrangles.

Aliso Creek: see **Carrie Creek** [SAN LUIS OBISPO].

Alkali Canyon [SANTA BARBARA]: *canyon*, drained by a stream that flows 4 miles to Sisquoc River 5.25 miles north-northwest of Zaca Lake (lat. 34°51'05" N, long. 120°04'05" W). Named on Manzanita Mountain (1964) and Zaca Lake (1964) 7.5' quadrangles.

Alley Camp [SAN LUIS OBISPO]: *locality*, 9.5 miles south-southwest of Shandon on the east side of present Camatta Canyon (lat. 35°31'25" N, long. 120°19'15" W). Named on Commatti Canyon (1943) 7.5' quadrangle.

Allison Creek [MONTEREY]: *stream*, flows 1 mile to an unnamed stream 4 miles west-northwest of Fremont Peak (lat. 36°47'20" N, long. 121°34' W). Named on San Juan Bautista (1917) 15' quadrangle.

Almaden Flats [SAN LUIS OBISPO]: *area*, 7 miles east-northeast of the village of San Simeon (lat. 35°41'05" N, long. 121°04'50" W; sec. 11, T 26 S, R 8 E). Named on Pebblestone Shut-in (1959) 7.5' quadrangle, which shows Alamden mine at the place.

Almeja: see **Point Almeja**, under **Mussel Point** [MONTEREY].

Alones: see **Point Alones** [MONTEREY].

Alta Peak [SAN BENITO]: *peak*, 4 miles south of Idria (lat. 36°21'30" N, long. 120°39'40" W; sec. 16, T 18 S, R 12 E). Altitude 4709 feet. Named on San Benito Mountain (1969) 7.5' quadrangle.

Alva Paul Creek: see **Morro Bay** [SAN LUIS OBISPO] (2).

Alvarez Creek: see **Tully Creek** [SAN BENITO].

Alvisa Canyon [SAN BENITO]: *canyon,* drained by a stream that flows 1.25 miles to Three Troughs Canyon 6 miles south of Paicines (lat. 36°38'25" N, long. 121°17'15" W; sec. 11, T 15 S, R 6 E). Named on Paicines (1968) 7.5' quadrangle.

Amaya Creek [SANTA CRUZ]: *stream,* flows 2.5 miles to Soquel Creek 6.5 miles north-northeast of Soquel (lat. 37°04'30" N, long. 121°55'30" W). Named on Laurel (1955) 7.5' quadrangle. The name commemorates Casimero Amaya and Dario Amaya, brothers who owned land along the stream as early as 1860 (Clark, 1986, p. 4).

Amaya Lagoon: see **Brush Lagoon** [SANTA CRUZ].

American Canyon [SAN LUIS OBISPO]: *canyon,* drained by a stream that flows nearly 7 miles to Salinas River 6 miles east-southeast of Pozo (lat. 35°15'45" N, long. 120°17' W). Named on La Panza (1967) and Pozo Summit (1967) 7.5' quadrangles.

American Canyon Campground [SAN LUIS OBISPO]: *locality,* 6.25 miles east-southeast of Pozo (lat. 35°17' N, long. 120°15'55" W); the place is in American Canyon. Named on Pozo Summit (1967) 7.5' quadrangle.

American Canyon Spring [SAN LUIS OBISPO]: *spring,* 7 miles east of Pozo (lat. 35°17'30" N, long. 120°15'05" W); the spring is in a branch of American Canyon. Named on Pozo Summit (1967) 7.5' quadrangle.

Anacapa: see **Gato** [SANTA BARBARA].

Anacapa Passage [SANTA BARBARA]: *water feature,* strait between Santa Cruz Island and Anacapa Island (Anacapa Island is in Ventura County); the islands are only 4.5 miles apart where they are closest. Named on Santa Cruz Island D (1943) 7.5' quadrangle.

Anastasia Canyon [MONTEREY]: *canyon,* drained by a stream that flows 3.25 miles to Finch Creek nearly 3 miles east-southeast of Jamesburg (lat. 36°21'05" N, long. 121°32'35" W; sec. 21, T 18 S, R 4 E). Named on Chews Ridge (1956) 7.5' quadrangle.

Andersen Canyon [MONTEREY]: *canyon,* drained by a stream that flows nearly 3 miles to the sea less than 2.5 miles southeast of Partington Point (lat. 36°09'10" N, long. 121°39'55" W; sec. 32, T 20 N, R 13 E). Named on Partington Ridge (1956) 7.5' quadrangle. Called Anderson Canyon on Lucia (1921) 15' quadrangle, and United States Board on Geographic Names (1960c, p. 16) approved this form of the name. According to Fink (p. 209), Jim Anderson homesteaded near the canyon; according to Lussier (p. 33), the name is for Peter Andersen, a homesteader of 1883.

Andersen Landing [MONTEREY]: *locality,* nearly 1 mile southeast of the mouth of Andersen Canyon (present Anderson Canyon) along the coast (lat. 36°08'40" N, long. 121°39'25" W; sec. 32, T 20 S, R 3 E). The abandoned site is named on Partington Ridge (1956) 7.5' quadrangle. Called Anderson Landing on Lucia (1921) 15' quadrangle. The place also was known as Hot Springs Landing (Clark, 1991, p. 12-13).

Andersen Peak [MONTEREY]: *peak,* 3.25 miles east of Partington Point (lat. 36°10'50" N, long. 121°38'30" W; sec. 21, T 20 S, R 3 E). Altitude 4099 feet. Named on Partington Ridge (1956) 7.5' quadrangle. Called Anderson Peak on Lucia (1921) 15' quadrangle, and United States Board on Geographic Names (1960c, p. 16) approved this form of the name.

Anderson Canyon [SAN LUIS OBISPO]: *canyon,* drained by a stream that flows 3.25 miles to San Juan Creek 3 miles west-northwest of Freeborn Mountain (lat. 35°17'55" N, long. 120°06'05" W; sec. 24, T 30 S, R 17 E). Named on California Valley (1966) 7.5' quadrangle.

Anderson Canyon: see **Andersen Canyon** [MONTEREY].

Anderson Landing: see **Andersen Landing** [MONTEREY].

Anderson Peak: see **Andersen Peak** [MONTEREY].

Andrews Peak [MONTEREY]: *peak,* 3.5 miles southeast of Smith Mountain (lat. 36°02'20" N, long. 120°33'10" W; sec. 3, T 22 S, R 13 E). Altitude 3502 feet. Named on Smith Mountain (1969) 7.5' quadrangle. The name commemorates the family of George Leslie Andrews; the family moved to Stone Canyon below the peak in 1878 (Clark, 1991, p. 14).

Angle Canyon [SANTA BARBARA]: *canyon,* drained by a stream that flows 1 mile to Windmill Canyon 4 miles southwest of New Cuyama (lat. 34°54'35" N, long. 119°44'35" W; near W line sec. 35, T 10 N, R 27 W). Named on New Cuyama (1964) and Peak Mountain (1964) 7.5' quadrangles.

Angostura Pass [SANTA BARBARA]: *pass,* 5 miles north of downtown Santa Barbara (lat. 34°29'45" N, long. 119°41'55" W; sec. 22, T 5 N, R 27 W). Named on Santa Barbara (1952) 7.5' quadrangle.

Año Nuevo Creek [SANTA CRUZ]: *stream,* flows 3.25 miles to San Mateo County 2.5 miles north-northwest of the mouth of Waddell Creek (lat. 37°07'40" N, long. 122°17'50" W; sec. 28, T 9 S, R 4 W); the stream reaches the sea 1.5 miles east of Año Nuevo Point, which is in San Mateo County. Named on Franklin Point (1955) 7.5' quadrangle. United States Board on Geographic Names (1933, p. 97) rejected the name "New Year Creek" for the stream, and (1962a, p. 4) the form "Ano Nuevo Creek" for the name. According to Brown (p. 61), the name "New Year's Creek" is proper, and the name "Año Nuevo Creek" has never been used; the stream was called arroyo de Lucía in the 1840's and 1850's from an incident involving Lucia Bolcof of Santa Cruz—earlier the stream had the name "arroyo de los Lobos."

Antelope Creek [SAN BENITO]: *stream,* flows 3.5 miles to Tres Pinos Creek 1.5 miles north-northwest of Panoche Pass (lat. 36° 38'45" N, long. 121°01'55" W; at N line sec. 7, T 15 S, R 9 E); the stream joins Tres Pinos Creek near the northwest end of Antelope Valley. Named on Panoche Pass (1968) 7.5' quadrangle.

Antelope Valley [SAN BENITO]: *valley,* nearly 1 mile northwest of Panoche Pass along Payne Creek (lat. 36°38'15" N, long. 121°01'15" W). Named on Panoche Pass (1968) 7.5' quadrangle.

Anthony Creek [MONTEREY]: *stream,* flows nearly 3.5 miles to San Miguel Creek 8.5 miles east-northeast of Cape San Martin (lat. 35°56'40" N, long. 121°20' W; near E line sec. 8, T 23 S, R 6 E). Named on Alder Peak (1949) 7.5' quadrangle. The stream had the early name "Potrancas Creek"—*potrancas* means "little mares" in Spanish (Clark, 1991, p. 16).

Antimony Mountain: see **Antimony Peak** [SAN BENITO].

Antimony Peak [SAN BENITO]: *peak,* 2.25 miles southwest of Mariposa Peak on San Benito-Merced County line (lat. 36°55'50" N, long. 121°13'55" W; sec. 32, T 11 S, R 7 E). Altitude 3297 feet. Named on Mariposa Peak (1969) 7.5' quadrangle. Angel (1890b, p. 516) called the feature Antimony Mountain, and noted that "As its name implies the mountain is characterized by its many veins of antimony." Irelan (p. 351) mentioned that Antimony Mountain was known locally as Gipsy Peak—Gipsy Mining Company had a mine there.

Antone Canyon [MONTEREY]: *canyon,* drained by a stream that flows 4 miles to Lynch Canyon 3.5 miles east-southeast of San Ardo (lat. 36°00'30" N, long. 120°50'20" W; at S line sec. 13, T 22 S, R 10 E). Named on Pancho Rico Valley (1967) 7.5' quadrangle.

Antonio [SANTA BARBARA]: *locality,* 2.25 miles west of the village of Casmalia along Southern Pacific Railroad (lat. 34°50'05" N, long. 120°34'05" W). Named on Casmalia (1959) 7.5' quadrangle.

Anzar Lake [SAN BENITO]: *lake,* 1100 feet long, 4.5 miles northwest of San Juan Bautista (lat. 36°53'20" N, long. 121°36' W); the lake is on Las Aromitas y Agua Caliente grant, received by Juan M. Ansar, or Anzar. Named on Chittenden (1955) 7.5' quadrangle.

Apple Camp: see **Chalk Peak Camp** [MONTEREY].

Apple Tree Camp: see **Chalk Peak Camp** [MONTEREY]; **Turner Creek Camp** [MONTEREY].

Apricot: see **Vineyard Canyon** [MONTEREY-SAN LUIS OBISPO].

Aptos [SANTA CRUZ]:

(1) *land grant,* at and inland from the town of Aptos. Named on Laurel (1955), Soquel (1954), and Watsonville West (1954) 7.5' quadrangles. Rafael Castro received 1 league in 1833 and claimed 6686 acres patented in 1860 (Cowan, p. 16). The word "Aptos" is from the name of an Indian community (Rowland, p. 61).

(2) *town,* 4.5 miles east-northeast of Soquel Point (lat. 36°58'35" N, long. 121°53'55" W); the place is along Aptos Creek on Aptos grant. Named on Soquel (1954) 7.5' quadrangle. Postal authorities established Aptos post office in 1870 (Frickstad, p. 176). They established Glenecho post office 3.5 miles east of Aptos in 1894 and discontinued it in 1897; they established Rancho del Mar post office, named for a real estate development, 1 mile south of Aptos in 1962 and discontinued it in 1963 (Salley, p. 86, 181).

Aptos Creek [SANTA CRUZ]: *stream,* flows 9.5 miles to the sea 4 miles east-northeast of Soquel Point (lat. 36°58'10" N, long. 121° 54'20" W). Named on Laurel (1955), Loma Prieta (1955), and Soquel (1954) 7.5' quadrangles. Hamman's (1980a) map shows a tributary called Spring Creek that joins Aptos Creek 0.5 mile east-northeast of the confluence of Aptos Creek and Bridge Creek. The same map shows several named branches of the canyon of Aptos Creek: Long Gulch, which enters 1.5 miles north of Aptos; Love Gulch, which enters 3450 feet south-southwest of the confluence of Aptos Creek and Bridge Creek; Porter Gulch, which enters just west of the confluence of Aptos Creek and Bridge Creek; and Bassett Gulch, which enters near the head of Aptos Creek about 1 mile south of Santa Rosalita Mountain. Hamman's (1980a) map also has the name "Hell's Gate" for narrows in the canyon of Aptos Creek 1.25 miles east-northeast of the confluence of Aptos Creek and Bridge Creek, and shows several localities situated along Aptos Creek: a railroad siding called Hihn Spur or Ready, located 1 mile north of Aptos on land purchased from Mrs. Ruth Ready (Hamman, p. 78); Molino, located along the railroad nearly 1 mile south-southwest of the confluence of Aptos Creek and Bridge Creek, where a spur line ran to a lumber mill (Hamman, p. 43)—*molino* means "mill" in Spanish; Loma Prieta, located along the railroad 0.25 mile south-southwest of the confluence of Aptos Creek and Bridge Creek, where Loma Prieta Lumber Company had a mill (Hamman, p. 50); Camp Number 1, located 0.5 mile north-northeast of the confluence of Aptos Creek and Bridge Creek; and two places called Monte Vista, the first located 1 mile east of the confluence of Aptos Creek and Bridge Creek, and the second located nearly 2 miles northeast of the first—both along the railroad. Postal authorities established Loma Prieta post office in 1884, discontinued it in 1885, reestablished it in 1887, and discontinued it in 1901 (Frickstad, p. 177). The lumber mill at Loma Prieta was torn down in 1899 (Hamman,

p. 56). The settlement of Schillings Camp, situated about 1 mile below Loma Prieta along Aptos Creek, was run by the Schilling family, who hauled out shingle bolts, pickets, posts, ties, and cordwood by pack train (Hamman, p. 78). A place called The Island was located just below the confluence of Aptos Creek and Valencia Creek; it now is called Treasure Island, although it no longer is surrounded by water (Hoover, Rensch, and Rensch, p. 469).

Aqua Buena Spring [SAN BENITO]: *spring*, 6.5 miles southeast of Idria (lat. 36°20'45" N, long. 120°35'50" W; near E line sec. 24, T 18 S, R 12 E). Named on Santa Rita Peak (1969) 7.5' quadrangle.

Aqua Escondida Spring: see **Agua Escondida Spring** [SAN LUIS OBISPO].

Arana Gulch [SANTA CRUZ]: *canyon*, drained by a stream that flows nearly 4 miles to Woods Lagoon 2 miles northwest of Soquel Point (lat. 36°58'30" N, long. 121°59'50" W). Named on Laurel (1955) and Soquel (1954) 7.5' quadrangles. The name commemorates Jose Arana (Gudde, 1949, p. 13), who received Potreros y Rincon de San Pedro de Reglado grant

Arbolado: see **Big Sur** [MONTEREY].

Archibald Creek [SANTA CRUZ]: *stream*, flows nearly 1 mile to Scott Creek 3.5 miles north-northwest of Davenport (lat. 37°03'25" N, long. 122°13'35" W). Named on Davenport (1955) 7.5' quadrangle. The name recalls James Archibald, who purchased Agua Puerca y las Trancas grant, which includes the mouth of the stream (Hoover, Rensch, and Rensch, p. 473). On Hamman's (1980c) map, this stream has the name "Winter Creek" and the name "Archibald Creek" applies to the next tributary of Scott Creek to the south.

Arch Point [SANTA BARBARA]: *promontory*, at the north end of Santa Barbara Island (lat. 33°29'15" N, long. 119°01'40" W). Named on United States Geological Survey's (1973) map.

Arch Rock [SANTA BARBARA]: *rock*, 2.5 miles west of Diablo Point on the north side of Santa Cruz Island, and 700 feet offshore (lat. 34°03'25" N, long. 119°48' W). Named on Santa Cruz Island B (1943) 7.5' quadrangle. United States Board on Geographic Names (1978a, p. 3) rejected the form "Arch Rocks" for the name.

Arguelia: see **Point Arguelia**, under **Point Arguello** [SANTA BARBARA].

Arguello [SANTA BARBARA]:
(1) *locality*, less than 0.5 mile east of Point Arguello (lat. 34°34'40" N, long. 120°38'35" W). Named on Point Arguello (1959) 7.5' quadrangle.
(2) *locality*, 2.5 miles east-southeast of Point Arguello along Southern Pacific Railroad (lat. 34°33'30" N, long. 120°36'45" W). Named on Guadalupe (1905) 30' quadrangle.

Arguello: see **Point Arguello** [SANTA BARBARA]; **Tranquillon Mountain** [SANTA BARBARA].

Arguello Mountain: see **Tranquillon Mountain** [SANTA BARBARA].

Argyle Creek: see **Murry Creek** [MONTEREY].

Argyle District: see **Jolon Valley** [MONTEREY].

Arlight [SANTA BARBARA]: *locality*, 0.5 mile east of Point Arguello along Southern Pacific Railroad (lat. 34°34'40" N, long. 120°38'20" W). Named on Point Arguello (1959) 7.5' quadrangle. Postal authorities established Arlight post office in 1917 and discontinued it in 1951; the coined name was from the words "Arguello Lighthouse" (Salley, p. 9).

Arlington Canyon [SANTA BARBARA]: *canyon*, drained by a stream that flows 6 miles to the sea 4.25 miles east of Sandy Point on Santa Rosa Island (lat. 34°00'20" N, long. 120°10'35" W). Named on Santa Rosa Island North (1943) and Santa Rosa Island West (1943) 7.5' quadrangles. Called Cañada Corral on Kew's (1927) map.

Aromas [MONTEREY-SAN BENITO]: *village*, 6.5 miles west-northwest of San Juan Bautista on Monterey-San Benito County line (lat. 36°53'20" N, long. 121°38'30" W); the village is at the edge of Las Aromitas y Agua Caliente grant. Named on Watsonville East (1955) 7.5' quadrangle. The place first was known as Sand Cut because of a tunnel built there in the 1870's by workmen for Southern Pacific Railroad (Gudde, 1949, p. 15). Postal authorities established Aromas post office in Monterey County in 1894, moved it 100 rods into San Benito County in 1897, and returned it to Monterey County in 1924 (Salley, p. 10).

Arrowhead Island [SANTA BARBARA]: *island*, 100 feet long, 4.5 miles northeast of Santa Ynez Peak in Lake Cachuma (lat. 34°33'50" N, long. 119°54'40" W). Named on Lake Cachuma (1959) 7.5' quadrangle.

Arrowhead Point [MONTEREY]: *promontory*, 3500 feet east of Pescadero Point on the north side of Carmel Bay (lat. 36°33'40" N, long. 121°56'20" W). Named on Monterey (1947) 7.5' quadrangle. Called Sunium Pt. on Lawson's (1893) map. The name "Arrowhead" is from the shape of the promontory (Clark, 1991, p. 20).

Arroyo Burro [SANTA BARBARA]:
(1) *canyon*, drained by a stream that flows 2.5 miles to Santa Ynez River 4 miles east-northeast of San Marcos Pass (lat. 34°32'20" N, long. 119°45'50" W). Named on San Marcos Pass (1959) 7.5' quadrangle.
(2) *stream*, flows 1.5 miles to San Antonio Creek 4.25 miles northeast of present downtown Goleta (lat. 34°28'15" N, long. 119° 46' W). Named on Goleta (1903) 30' quadrangle.
(3) *stream*, flows nearly 6 miles to the sea 3 miles west-southwest of downtown Santa Barbara (lat. 34°24'10" N, long. 119°44'30" W); the stream drains Barger Canyon.. Named on Santa Barbara (1952) 7.5' quadrangle. Called San Roque Cr. on Santa Barbara (1903) 15' quadrangle, but United States Board on Geographic Names (1961b, p. 9) rejected the names "San Roque Creek," "Arroyo Burro Creek," and "Barger Canyon" for the feature.

Arroyo Burro: see **Barger Canyon** [SANTA BARBARA].

Arroyo Burro Creek: see **Arroyo Burro** [SANTA BARBARA] (3).

Arroyo Center [MONTEREY]: *settlement*, 14 miles west-southwest of Greenfield (lat. 36°14' N, long. 121°28'05" W; in and near sec. 31, T 19 S, R 5 E); the place is along Arroyo Seco (1). Named on Junipero Serra (1961) 15' quadrangle.

Arroyo de Agalia: see **Eagle Canyon** [SANTA BARBARA].

Arroyo de la Casa Blanca: see **Whitehouse Creek** [SANTA CRUZ].

Arroyo de la Cruz [SAN LUIS OBISPO]: *stream*, formed by the confluence of Burnett Creek and Marmolejo Creek, flows 10 miles to the sea 3.5 miles north-northwest of Piedras Blancas Point (lat. 35°42'35" N, long. 121°18'35" W). Named on Piedras Blancas (1959) and San Simeon (1958) 7.5' quadrangles. On San Simeon (1919) 15' quadrangle, Marmolejo Creek is shown as a tributary of Arroyo de la Cruz.

Arroyo de la Laguna [SANTA CRUZ]: *land grant*, 8 miles west-northwest of Point Santa Cruz along the coast and inland. Named on Davenport (1955) and Santa Cruz (1954) 7.5' quadrangles. Gil Sanchez received the land in 1840; James Williams and Squire Williams claimed 4418 acres patented in 1882 (Cowan, p. 16; Rowland, p. 42). Perez (p. 53) gave the date of the grant as 1839, and gave the date of the patent as 1881.

Arroyo de la Laguna: see **Laguna Creek** [SANTA CRUZ].

Arroyo de las Garrapatas: see **Garrapata Creek** [MONTEREY].

Arroyo de las Ortegas: see **Romero Creek** [SANTA BARBARA].

Arroyo de las Piedras: see **Stony Creek** [MONTEREY].

Arroyo de las Viboras [SAN BENITO]: *stream*, flows 14 miles to join Arroyo Dos Picachos and form Tequisquita Slough 4.5 miles north of Hollister (lat. 36°55' N, long. 121°23'20" W). Named on Mariposa Peak (1969), San Felipe (1955), and Three Sisters (1954) 7.5' quadrangles. According to Gudde (1949, p. 379), the stream is called Viboras Creek—*las viboras* means "the rattlesnakes" in Spanish.

Arroyo del Corral [SAN LUIS OBISPO]: *stream*, flows 2.5 miles to the sea 1.5 miles north of Piedras Blancas Point (lat. 35°41'05" N, long. 121°17'10" W). Named on Piedras Blancas (1959) 7.5' quadrangle.

Arroyo del Huasna: see **Huasna River** [SAN LUIS OBISPO].

Arroyo del Molino: see **Molino Creek** [SANTA CRUZ].

Arroyo del Montecito: see **Montecito Creek** [SANTA BARBARA].

Arroyo de los Alamos: see **San Antonio Creek** [SANTA BARBARA] (1).

Arroyo de los Chinos [SAN LUIS OBISPO]: *stream*, flows 3.5 miles to the sea 4.5 miles north-northwest of Piedras Point (lat. 35°43'30" N, long. 121°18'55" W). Named on Piedras Blancas (1959) 7.5' quadrangle.

Arroyo de los Lobos: see **Año Nuevo Creek** [SANTA CRUZ].

Arroyo del Oso [SAN LUIS OBISPO]: *stream*, flows 1.5 miles to the sea nearly 2 miles north-northwest of Piedras Blancas Point (lat. 35°41'30" N, long. 121°17'20" W). Named on Piedras Blancas (1959) 7.5' quadrangle.

Arroyo del Padre Juan [SAN LUIS OBISPO]: *stream*, flows 2.5 miles to the sea 3.25 miles southeast of the village of San Simeon (lat. 35°36'40" N, long. 121°08'45" W). Named on Cambria (1959), Pebblestone Shut-in (1959), and Pico Creek (1959) 7.5' quadrangles.

Arroyo del Palo Colorado: see **Palo Colorado Canyon** [MONTEREY].

Arroyo del Pecho: see **Pecho Creek** [SAN LUIS OBISPO].

Arroyo del Pedregoso: see **Mission Creek** [SANTA BARBARA].

Arroyo del Pino: see **Pine Canyon** [MONTEREY] (2).

Arroyo del Puerto [SAN LUIS OBISPO]: *stream*, flows 4 miles to San Simeon Bay at the village of San Simeon (lat. 35°38'35" N, long. 121°11'15" W). Named on San Simeon (1958) 7.5' quadrangle.

Arroyo del Puerto del Rosario: see **Tres Pinos Creek** [SAN BENITO].

Arroyo del Rodeo [SANTA CRUZ]: *land grant*, at and inland from Soquel Point east of Rodeo Creek Gulch. Named on Soquel (1954) 7.5' quadrangle. Francisco Rodriguez received 1.25 leagues in 1834; John Hames and John Daubenbis claimed 1473 acres patented in 1882 (Cowan, p. 69). The name alludes to cattle roundups, or rodeos, held at the place in the early days (Hoover, Rensch, and Rensch, p. 471).

Arroyo del Rosario: see **Tres Pinos Creek** [SAN BENITO].

Arroyo del Tulare: see **Oak Creek** [SANTA BARBARA].

Arroyo de Lucía: see **Año Nuevo Creek** [SANTA CRUZ].

Arroyo de Salispuedes: see **Corralitos Creek** [SANTA CRUZ].

Arroyo de San Augustin: see **Arroyo San Augustin** [SANTA BARBARA].

Arroyo de San Felipe: see **Pacheco Creek** [SAN BENITO].

Arroyo de San Joaquin y Santana: see **Arroyo Dos Picachos** [SAN BENITO].

Arroyo de San Nicolas: see **San Simeon Creek** [SAN LUIS OBISPO].

Arroyo de San Vicente: see **Arroyo Laguna** [SAN LUIS OBISPO]; **San Vicente Creek** [SANTA CRUZ].

Arroyo de Soto: see **Whitehouse Creek** [SANTA CRUZ].

Arroyo de Tepusque: see **Tepusquet Canyon** [SANTA BARBARA].

Arroyo de Villa: see **Branciforte Creek** [SANTA CRUZ].

Arroyo Dos Picachos [SAN BENITO]: *stream*, flows 12 miles to join Arroyo de las Viboras and form Tequisquita Slough 4.5 miles north of Hollister (lat. 36°55' N, long. 121°23'20" W). Named on Mariposa Peak (1969), San Felipe (1955), and Three Sisters (1954) 7.5' quadrangles. Called Arroyo de San Joaquin y Santana on a diseño of San Joaquin grant made in 1836 (Becker, 1964).

Arroyo El Bulito [SANTA BARBARA]: *canyon*, drained by a stream that flows 3.5 miles to the sea 8 miles east of Point Conception (lat. 34°27'45" N, long. 120°19'25" W). Named on Sacate (1953) 7.5' quadrangle. According to Bolton (p. 240), the name should have the form "Bullillo."

Arroyo Grande [SAN LUIS OBISPO]:

(1) *land grant*, 10 miles east-northeast of the town of Arroyo Grande along Arroyo Grande Creek. Named on Tar Spring Ridge (1967) 7.5' quadrangle. Seferino Carlon received the land in 1841; Francis Branch claimed 4437 acres patented in 1867 (Cowan, p. 16; Cowan gave the name "San Ramon" as an alternate). According to Perez (p. 54), Carlon received the grant in 1842. Angel (1883, p. 215) noted that the grant commonly was known as the Ranchita.

(2) *town*, 12 miles south-southeast of San Luis Obispo near the coast (lat. 35°07'15" N, long. 120°35' W); the town is along Arroyo Grande Creek. Named on Arroyo Grande NE (1965) and Oceano (1965) 7.5' quadrangles. The community began about 1867 with a schoolhouse and a blacksmith shop (Angel, 1883, p. 351). Postal authorities established Arroyo Grande post office in 1869 (Frickstad, p. 163), and the town incorporated in 1911.

Arroyo Grande Creek [SAN LUIS OBISPO]: *stream*, flows 22 miles to the sea 3 miles west-southwest of downtown Arroyo Grande (lat. 35°06'05" N, long. 120°37'50" W). Named on Arroyo Grande NE (1965), Oceano (1965), and Tar Spring Ridge (1967) 7.5' quadrangles. Called Rio Grande on Goddard's (1857) map.

Arroyo Grande Station [SAN LUIS OBISPO]: *locality*, 11 miles north-northeast of the town of Nipomo (lat. 35°11'35" N, long. 120°25'55" W); the place is along Arroyo Grande Creek. Named on Tar Spring Ridge (1967) 7.5' quadrangle.

Arroyo Grande Valley [SAN LUIS OBISPO]: *valley*, opens into lowlands near the sea 2 miles south-southeast of downtown Arroyo Grande (lat. 35°05'45" N, long. 120°36' W); Arroyo Grande Creek drains the valley. Named on Arroyo Grande NE (1965) and Oceano (1965) 7.5' quadrangles.

Arroyo Hondo [SAN BENITO]:

(1) *canyon*, drained by a stream that flows 3 miles to Tres Pinos Creek 1 mile south-southeast of Tres Pinos (lat. 36°46'35" N, long. 121°18'35" W). Named on Tres Pinos (1955) 7.5' quadrangle.

(2) *stream*, flows 1.5 miles to Fresno County 4.5 miles east-northeast of Idria (lat. 36°26' N, long. 120°35'45" W; at E line sec. 24, T 17 S, R 12 E). Named on Ciervo Mountain (1969) 7.5' quadrangle.

Arroyo Hondo [SAN LUIS OBISPO]: *stream*, flows nearly 2.5 miles to the sea 6 miles north-northwest of Piedras Blancas Point (lat. 35°45' N, long. 121°18'50" W). Named on Piedras Blancas (1959) 7.5' quadrangle.

Arroyo Hondo [SANTA BARBARA]: *stream*, flows 3.5 miles to the sea 4.5 miles east of Gaviota (lat. 34°28'25" N, long. 120°08'25" W). Named on Gaviota (1953) 7.5' quadrangle. On Solvang (1959) 7.5' quadrangle, the name applies to the canyon of the stream.

Arroyo Hondo: see **Arroyo Laguna** [SAN LUIS OBISPO].

Arroyo Joaquin Soto: see **Tres Pinos Creek** [SAN BENITO].

Arroyo Laguna [SAN LUIS OBISPO]: *stream*, flows nearly 3 miles to Oak Knoll Creek 1.5 miles northwest of the village of San Simeon (lat. 35°39'50" N, long. 121°12'40" W). Named on San Simeon (1958) 7.5' quadrangle. According to H.R. Wagner (p. 462, 508), Crespi gave the name "Arroyo de San Vicente" to the stream in 1769, but other members of the Portola expedition called it Arroyo Hondo.

Arroyo la Mission: see **Mission Creek** [MONTEREY].

Arroyo las Trancas [SANTA CRUZ]: *stream*, flows nearly 1 mile to the sea 0.5 mile south-southeast of the mouth of Waddell Creek (lat. 37°05'10" N, long. 122°16'15" W; sec. 2, T 10 S, R 4 W); the stream is near the northwest boundary of Agua Puerca y las Trancas grant. Named on Año Nuevo (1955) 7.5' quadrangle. United States Board on Geographic Names (1978c, p. 5) approved the name "Laguna de las Trancas" for a lake, 0.1 mile long, that is located less than 1 mile east of the mouth of Arroyo las Trancas on Agua Puerca y las Trancas grant. A stage station called Seaside was situated on the bluff at the mouth of Las Trancas Creek in 1872 (Hoover, Rensch, and Rensch, p. 478). Postal authorities established Sea Side post office in 1873 and discontinued it in 1881 (Frickstad, p. 177). Rowland (p. 131) reported that a village and post office known as Seaside were at a saw mill that William W. Waddell built along Waddell Creek. A place called China Ladder, located at the sea cliff about 1.5 miles southeast of the mouth of Arroyo las Trancas, received its name because Chinese abalone gatherers used a ladder there to reach the rocks at the base of the cliff (Hoover, Rensch, and Rensch, p. 474).

Arroyo Paredon [SANTA BARBARA]: *stream*, flows 5.25 miles to the sea 2.5 miles west-southwest of Carpinteria (lat. 34°24'45" N, long. 119°33'25" W). Named on Carpinteria (1952) 7.5' quadrangle. Called Arroyo Parida on Santa Barbara (1903) 15' quadrangle, but United States Board on Geographic Names (1961b, p. 13) rejected the names "Arroyo Parida," "Arroyo Parida Creek," and "Parida Creek" for the stream.

Arroyo Parida: see **Arroyo Paredon** [SANTA BARBARA].

Arroyo Parida Creek: see **Arroyo Paredon** [SANTA BARBARA].

Arroyo Quemado [SANTA BARBARA]: *stream*, flows 3 miles to the sea 5.25 miles east of Gaviota (lat. 34°28'10" N, long. 120°07'05" W). Named on Tajiguas (1953) 7.5' quadrangle. On Santa Ynez (1959) 7.5' quadrangle, the name applies to the canyon of the stream.

Arroyo San Agustin: see **Arroyo San Augustin** [SANTA BARBARA].

Arroyo San Augustin [SANTA BARBARA]: *stream*, flows 2.5 miles to the sea nearly 7 miles east of Point Conception (lat. 34°27'30" N, long. 120°21'10" W). Named on Sacate (1953) 7.5' quadrangle. Called Arroyo de San Augustin on Lompoc (1905) 30' quadrangle. United States Board on Geographic Names (1978b, p. 5) approved the form "Arroyo San Agustin" for the name, and rejected the names "Arroyo de San Augustin," "Arroyo San Augustin," and "Arroyo San Augustine" for the stream.

Arroyo San Carpoforo: see **San Carpoforo Creek** [MONTEREY-SAN LUIS OBISPO].

Arroyo San Carpojo: see **San Carpoforo Creek** [MONTEREY-SAN LUIS OBISPO].

Arroyo San Miguel: see **Mission Creek** [MONTEREY].

Arroyo San Ysidro: see **San Ysidro Creek** [SANTA BARBARA].

Arroyo Seco [MONTEREY]:

(1) *stream*, flows 44 miles to Salinas River 1 mile south-southwest of Soledad (lat. 36°24'45" N, long. 121°20'15" W). Named on Cone Peak (1949), Junipero Serra Peak (1949), Paraiso Springs (1956), Soledad (1955), Sycamore Flat (1956), and Tassajara Hot Springs (1956) 7.5' quadrangles.

(2) *land grant*, near Greenfield; includes the lowermost course of Arroyo Seco (1). Named on Greenfield (1956), Paraiso Springs (1956), and Soledad (1955) 7.5' quadrangles. Joaquin de la Torre received 4 leagues in 1840 and claimed 16,523 acres patented in 1859 (Cowan, p. 17). Soon after 1900 some promoters began a real-estate development that they called Clark Colony after one of the promoters; the development was on the grant near the mouth of the canyon of Arroyo Seco (1) at a place called Three Mile Flat (Fink, p. 164).

Arroyo Seco [SAN LUIS OBISPO]: *stream*, flows 10.5 miles to Huasna River 9.5 miles northeast of Nipomo (lat. 35°08'30" N, long. 120°21'30" W). Named on Caldwell Mesa (1967) and Los Machos Hills (1967) 7.5' quadrangles.

Arsenic Springs: see **Hot Springs** [SANTA BARBARA] (2).

Artillery Hill [MONTEREY]: *hill*, 3.5 miles south of Marina (lat. 36° 38'10" N, long. 121°47'20" W); the hill is on Fort Ord Military Reservation. Named on Marina (1947) 7.5' quadrangle.

Asbury Creek [SAN LUIS OBISPO]: *stream*, flows 3 miles to Nacimiento Reservoir 12 miles northeast of the village of San Simeon (lat. 35°45'40" N, long. 121°02'10" W; near N line sec. 18, T 25 S, R 9 E). Named on Bryson (1949, photorevised 1979) 7.5' quadrangle.

Ascension: see **Asuncion** [SAN LUIS OBISPO] (1) and (2).

Ashbury Gulch [SANTA CRUZ]: *canyon*, drained by a stream that flows 1.25 miles to Soquel Creek 8 miles north-northeast of Soquel (lat. 37°05'35" N, long. 121°53'30" W). Named on Laurel (1955) 7.5' quadrangle. According to Clark (1986, p. 13), the word "Ashbury" is a misspelling of the name "Asbury."

Ashurst Spring [SAN BENITO]: *spring*, 12 miles east-northeast of Bitterwater (lat. 36°27'05" N, long. 120°48'35" W; sec. 18, T 17 S, R 11 E). Named on Hernandez Reservoir (1969) 7.5' quadrangle. Called Henry Ashurst Spr. on Hernandez Valley (1943) 15' quadrangle.

Asilomar [MONTEREY]: *locality*, 1.25 miles south of Point Pinos (lat. 36°37'15" N, long. 121°56'10" W). Named on Monterey (1947) 7.5' quadrangle. The place began in 1913 as a campground for Young Women's Christian Association; the name is a contraction of *asilo del mar*, which means "refuge by the sea" in Spanish (Fink, p. 176). Postal authorities established Asilomar post office in 1914 and discontinued it in 1935 (Frickstad, p. 106).

Asilomar Beach: see **Moss Beach** [MONTEREY].

Asphaltea: see **Sisquoc** [SANTA BARBARA] (3).

Asphaltum Creek [SANTA BARBARA]: *stream*, flows 5.25 miles to join the stream in Foxen Canyon 7.5 miles south of Tepusquet Peak (lat. 34°48' N, long. 120°11'40" W). Named on Foxen Canyon (1964) and Zaca Lake (1964) 7.5' quadrangles. Zaca Lake (1964) 7.5' quadrangle shows an asphaltum mine near the head of the creek.

Asuncion [SAN LUIS OBISPO]:

(1) *land grant*, mainly west of Atascadero. Named on Atascadero (1965), Creston (1948), Morro Bay North (1965), Santa Margarita (1965), Templeton (1948), and York Mountain (1948) 7.5' quadrangles. Pedro Estrada received the land in 1845 and claimed 39,225 acres patented in 1866 (Cowan, p. 17). The name refers to the Ascension of the Virgin Mary; the form "Ascension" also has been used for the name (Gudde, 1949, p. 17).

(2) *locality*, nearly 2 miles north of Atascadero along Southern Pacific Railroad (lat. 35°30'50" N, long. 120°40'35" W); the place is on Asuncion

grant. Named on Templeton (1948) 7.5' quadrangle. Postal authorities established Ascension post office in 1879 and discontinued it in 1881 (Frickstad, p. 163).

Atascadero [SAN LUIS OBISPO]:

(1) *land grant,* along Salinas River at the town of Atascadero. Named on Atascadero (1965), Santa Margarita (1965), and Templeton (1948) 7.5' quadrangles. Trifon Garcia received 1 league in 1842; Henry Haight claimed 4348 acres patented in 1860 (Cowan, p. 17). According to Hanna (p. 19), *atascadero* means "boggy ground" in Spanish.

(2) *town,* 10 miles south of Paso Robles (lat. 35°29'20" N, long. 120°40'05" W); the town is on and near Atascadero grant. Named on Atascadero (1965) and Templeton (1948) 7.5' quadrangles. San Luis Obispo (1897) 15' quadrangle shows a place called Atascadero located along Southern Pacific Railroad where later maps have the name "Henry." Postal authorities established Atascadero post office in 1914 (Frickstad, p. 163), and the town incorporated in 1979. Edward Gardner Lewis bought 23,000 acres in 1913 and began promoting a model community called Atascadero Colony, but financial problems and a jail term for Lewis ended the development as he proposed it (Lee and others, p. 17).

Atascadero Creek [SAN LUIS OBISPO]: *stream,* flows 10 miles to Salinas River 1.25 miles north-northeast of downtown Atascadero (lat. 35°30'20" N, long. 120°39'35" W). Named on Atascadero (1965) 7.5' quadrangle.

Atascadero Creek [SANTA BARBARA]: *stream,* flows 6.25 miles to San Pedro Creek 1 mile south of downtown Goleta (lat. 34°25'10" N, long. 119°49'45" W). Named on Goleta (1950) 7.5' quadrangle.

Atascadero Lake [SAN LUIS OBISPO]: *lake,* 0.5 mile long, 1.5 miles south of downtown Atascadero (lat. 35°27'50" N, long. 120°39'55" W). Named on Atascadero (1965) 7.5' quadrangle.

Atascoso Creek [SANTA BARBARA]: *stream,* flows 1.25 miles to El Jaro Creek 12 miles southeast of the city of Lompoc (lat. 34°31'05" N, long. 120°18'45" W). Named on Santa Rosa Hills (1959) 7.5' quadrangle.

Atherton Peak [SANTA CRUZ]: *peak,* 6 miles east-northeast of Watsonville on Santa Cruz-Santa Clara County line (lat. 36°56'15" N, long. 121°38'50" W). Altitude 1616 feet. Named on Watsonville East (1955) 7.5' quadrangle. The name commemorates Faxon Dean Atherton; the feature was called Vanoni Peak on a map of 1913 (Clark, 1986, p. 13-14).

Augustine Creek [SAN BENITO]: *stream,* flows 3 miles to San Benito River 14 miles east of Bitterwater (lat. 36°20'45" N, long. 120°45'20" W; sec. 22, T 18 S, R 11 E). Named on Hepsedam Peak (1969) 7.5' quadrangle.

Aulon: see **Point Aulon**, under **Lovers Point** [MONTEREY].

Aumentos Rock [MONTEREY]: *rock,* less than 1 mile east-southeast of Point Pinos, and 700 feet offshore (lat. 36°38'05" N, long. 121° 55'10" W). Named on Monterey (1913) 15' quadrangle. United States Coast Survey officials applied the name in 1856 and 1857; the feature probably first had the name "Armenta's," for Jose Maria Armenta, who received Punta de Pinos grant where the rock is situated (Gudde, 1949, p. 18).

Ausaymas y San Felipe [SAN BENITO]: *land grant,* 8 miles north-northeast of Hollister on San Benito-Santa Clara County line. Named on San Felipe (1955) and Three Sisters (1954) 7.5' quadrangles. Francisco Perez Pacheco received 2 leagues in 1836 and claimed 35,504 acres patented in 1859 (Cowan, p. 17). According to Kroeber (1916, p. 35), the name "Ausaymas" came from the designation of Indians who lived near San Juan Bautista mission.

Austin Peak [MONTEREY]: *peak,* 16 miles north-northeast of San Ardo on Mustang Ridge (lat. 36°14'50" N, long. 120°50'25" W; sec. 25, T 19 S, R 10 E). Altitude 2594 feet. Named on Monarch Peak (1967) 7.5' quadrangle.

Avenal: see **Alamo Creek** [SAN LUIS OBISPO] (2).

Avenal's Station [SAN LUIS OBISPO]: *locality,* 19 miles northeast of the town of Nipomo along Salinas River (lat. 35°14'50" N, long. 120°15'55" W). Named on Caldwell Mesa (1967) 7.5' quadrangle.

Avila: see **Avila Beach** [SAN LUIS OBISPO].

Avila Beach [SAN LUIS OBISPO]: *village,* 8 miles south-southwest of downtown San Luis Obispo along the coast (lat. 35°10'45" N, long. 120°43'50" W). Named on Pismo Beach (1965) 7.5' quadrangle. Called Avila on Arroyo Grande (1942) 15' quadrangle, but United States Board on Geographic Names (1967a, p. 8) rejected this designation for the place. Postal authorities established Avila post office in 1907 and changed the name to Avila Beach in 1955 (Salley, p. 12). The name commemorates Miguel Avila, who received San Miguelito grant (Hoover, Rensch, and Rensch, p. 385). The community developed around a place called People's Wharf that John Harford built in 1869; when Harford built another wharf in 1872 at Port Harford, shipping activity transferred to that place (Angel, 1883, p. 322, 350). Postal authorities established Laplaya post office in 1876 at or near present Avila Beach; they changed the name to La Playa the same year, and discontinued it in 1878 (Salley, p. 117-118).

Avila Rock [SAN LUIS OBISPO]: *rock,* 100 feet long, nearly 1 mile southeast of Avila Beach, and 0.25 mile offshore (lat. 35°10'25" N, long. 120°43'25" W). Named on Pismo Beach (1965) 7.5' quadrangle.

Azalea Canyon [SAN BENITO]: *canyon,* drained by a stream that flows 2 miles to Bird Creek nearly 6.5 miles south-southwest of Hollister (lat. 36°46' N, long. 121°26'35" W). Named on Hollister (1955) 7.5' quadrangle.

- B -

Babies Gulch [SAN BENITO]: *canyon,* drained by a stream that flows 2 miles to Pimental Creek nearly 6 miles south of Panoche (lat. 36°30'45" N, long. 120°50'40" W; sec. 26, T 16 S, R 10 E). Named on Hernandez Reservoir (1969) and Panoche (1969) 7.5' quadrangles.

Bachelder Gulch: see **Granite Creek** [SANTA CRUZ].

Badger Spring [SANTA CRUZ]: *spring,* 6.5 miles north-northeast of Soquel (lat. 37°04'35" N, long. 121°55'05" W). Named on Laurel (1955) 7.5' quadrangle.

Bad Gulch [MONTEREY]: *canyon,* drained by a stream that flows nearly 1 mile to Big Sur River 9 miles east-southeast of Point Sur (lat. 36°15'05" N, long. 121°45'05" W; sec. 28, T 19 S, R 2 E). Named on Partington Ridge (1956) 15' quadrangle. The name reportedly is from conditions at the place during construction of a trail there in 1916 (Clark, 1991, p. 26).

Badlands [SAN BENITO]: *area,* 14 miles east-southeast of Bitterwater (lat. 36°17'10" N, long. 120°46'35" W; sec. 9, T 19 S, R 11 E). Named on Hepsedam Peak (1969) 7.5' quadrangle.

Bahia de los Pinos: see **Monterey Bay** [MONTEREY].

Bahia de San Pedro: see **Monterey Bay** [MONTEREY].

Baker Canyon [SAN BENITO]: *canyon,* drained by a stream that flows nearly 4 miles to Hernandez Reservoir 11 miles east of Bitterwater (lat. 36°22'50" N, long. 120°48'40" W; sec. 7, T 18 S, R 11 E). Named on Hernandez Reservoir (1969) 7.5' quadrangle. Called Cane Canyon on Hernandez Valley (1943) 15' quadrangle.

Balconies [SAN BENITO]: *relief feature,* 7 miles west of San Benito (lat. 36°30'15" N, long. 121°12'15" W; near SE cor. sec. 28, T 16 S, R 7 E). Named on Bickmore Canyon (1968) 7.5' quadrangle.

Bald Hill [SAN LUIS OBISPO]: *peak,* 2 miles south of Lopez Mountain (lat. 35°16'35" N, long. 120°34'35" W; near E line sec. 33, T 30 S, R 13 E). Named on Lopez Mountain (1965) 7.5' quadrangle.

Bald Knob [SAN LUIS OBISPO]: *peak,* 2.5 miles north-northwest of Point San Luis (lat. 35°11'50" N, long. 120°46'10" W). Altitude 1186 feet. Named on Port San Luis (1965) 7.5' quadrangle.

Bald Mountain [MONTEREY]:

(1) *ridge,* north-northwest-trending, nearly 1 mile long, 5 miles north-northeast of Charley Mountain on Monterey-Fresno County line (lat. 36°12'25" N, long. 120°37'40" W; sec. 12, T 20 S, R 12 E). Named on Priest Valley (1969) 7.5' quadrangle.

(2) *peak,* 8 miles south-southeast of Jolon (lat. 35°51'50" N, long. 121°07'25" W; sec. 8, T 24 S, R 8 E). Altitude 2132 feet. Named on Bryson (1949) and Burnett Peak (1949) 7.5' quadrangles.

Bald Mountain [SAN BENITO]: *peak,* 4.25 miles north of San Benito (lat. 36°34'15" N, long. 121°05'20" W). Altitude 2923 feet. Named on San Benito (1968) 7.5' quadrangle.

Bald Mountain [SAN LUIS OBISPO]:

(1) *peak,* 6.5 miles east-northeast of Edna (lat. 35°14'25" N, long. 120°30'10" W; near W line sec. 8, T 31 S, R 14 E). Altitude 2834 feet. Named on Arroyo Grande NE (1965) 7.5' quadrangle.

(2) *ridge,* northeast-trending, 1.25 miles long, 12 miles northeast of the town of Nipomo (lat. 35°09' N, long. 120°18'30" W). Named on Caldwell Mesa (1967) 7.5' quadrangle.

Bald Mountain [SANTA BARBARA]:

(1) *peak,* 8.5 miles southwest of McPherson Peak (lat. 34°48'45" N, long. 119°56'05" W). Altitude 4087 feet. Named on Bald Mountain (1964) 7.5' quadrangle.

(2) *peak,* 5.5 miles south of Santa Ynez (lat. 34°31'50" N, long. 120°05'25" W; sec. 11, T 5 N, R 31 W). Altitude 2614 feet. Named on Santa Ynez (1959) 7.5' quadrangle.

Bald Mountain [SANTA CRUZ]: *peak,* 3 miles east-northeast of Davenport (lat. 37°01'30" N, long. 122°08'20" W; near N line sec. 36, T 10 S, R 3 W). Altitude 1296 feet. Named on Davenport (1955) 7.5' quadrangle.

Bald Mountain Canyon [SANTA BARBARA]: *canyon,* drained by a stream that flows nearly 3 miles to Sisquoc River 2.25 miles west-northwest of Bald Mountain (1) (lat. 34°49'40" N, long. 119°58'15" W); the canyon heads near Bald Mountain (1). Named on Bald Mountain (1964) 7.5' quadrangle.

Bald Peak [MONTEREY-SAN BENITO]: *peak,* 9.5 miles north-northwest of Charley Mountain on Monterey-San Benito County line (lat. 36°16'40" N, long. 120°41'40" W; sec. 17, T 19 S, R 12 E). Altitude 3676 feet. Named on San Benito Mountain (1969) 7.5' quadrangle.

Bald Ridge [SANTA CRUZ]: *ridge,* west-southwest-trending, 1.5 miles long, 5 miles northeast of Watsonville (lat. 36°57'30" N, long. 121°40'45" W). Named on Watsonville East (1955) 7.5' quadrangle.

Bald Top [SAN LUIS OBISPO]: *peak,* nearly 2 miles east-northeast of the mouth of San Carpoforo Creek (lat. 35°46'35" N, long. 121°17'45" W; sec. 11, T 25 S, R 6 E). Named on Burro Mountain (1949) 7.5' quadrangle.

Baldwin Creek [SANTA CRUZ]: *stream*, flows 4 miles to the sea 5.5 miles west-northwest of Point Santa Cruz (lat. 36°58' N, long. 122° 07'20" W). Named on Felton (1955) and Santa Cruz (1954) 7.5' quadrangles.

Ballard [SANTA BARBARA]: *village*, 2 miles south of Los Olivos (lat. 34°38'10" N, long. 120°06'50" W; on S line sec. 35, T 7 N, R 31 W); the place is along Alamo Pintado Creek. Named on Los Olivos (1959) 7.5' quadrangle. The name commemorates W.N. Ballard, who from 1862 until 1870 had a stage station at the site, which then was called Alamo Pintado; George W. Lewis, who married Ballard's widow, gave the name "Ballard" to the place (Gudde, 1949, p. 21). Postal authorities established Ballards post office in 1870, discontinued it in 1872, reestablished it with the name "Ballard" in 1881, and discontinued it in 1918 (Salley, p. 14).

Ballard Campground [SANTA BARBARA]: *locality*, 2.5 miles southeast of Zaca Lake (lat. 34°45'05" N, long. 120°00'40" W). Named on Zaca Lake (1964) 7.5' quadrangle.

Ballard Canyon [SANTA BARBARA]: *canyon*, drained by a stream that flows 6 miles to lowlands 2 miles east-southeast of Buellton (lat. 34°36'15" N, long. 120°09'30" W). Named on Los Olivos (1959), Solvang (1959), and Zaca Creek (1959) 7.5' quadrangles.

Ballard Canyon: see **Birabent Canyon** [SANTA BARBARA].

Ballard Creek [SANTA BARBARA]: *stream*, flows 0.5 mile to Birbent Canyon (present Birabent Canyon) 8 miles northeast of Los Olivos (lat. 34°45' N, long. 120°01'05" W; at NW cor. sec. 25, T 8 N, R 30 W). Named on Los Olivos (1959) 7.5' quadrangle.

Ballard Creek: see **Quiota Creek** [SANTA BARBARA].

Ballards: see **Ballard** [SANTA BARBARA].

Ballinger Canyon [SANTA BARBARA]: *canyon*, drained by a stream that heads in Ventura and Kern Counties, and flows 3 miles in Santa Barbara County to Cuyama Valley 8.5 miles east-southeast of the village of Cuyama (lat. 34°53' N, long. 119°29'15" W). Named on Ballinger Canyon (1943) 7.5' quadrangle.

Ballinger Canyon Wash [SANTA BARBARA]: *stream*, flows 1.25 miles from the mouth of Ballinger Canyon to Cuyama River 7 miles east-southeast of the village of Cuyama (lat. 34°52'45" N, long. 119°30'25" W). Named on Cuyama (1964) 7.5' quadrangle.

Balloon Spring [SAN LUIS OBISPO]: *spring*, 6.25 miles north of Pozo (lat. 35°23'30" N, long. 120°21'35" W; near SW cor. sec. 15, T 29 S, R 15 E). Named on Camatta Ranch (1966) 7.5' quadrangle.

Balm of Gilead Campground [SAN LUIS OBISPO]: *locality*, 4.5 miles southeast of Pozo (lat. 35°15'25" N, long. 120°18'55" W; near NE cor. sec. 1, T 31 S, R 15 E). Named on Pozo Summit (1967) 7.5' quadrangle.

Banchero Rock [MONTEREY]: *peak*, 0.5 mile east-northeast of Monarch Peak on Mustang Ridge (lat. 36°13'10" N, long. 120°47'35" W; sec. 4, T 20 S, R 11 E). Named on Monarch Peak (1967) 7.5' quadrangle. The name is for the Banchero family; the feature has been mistakenly called Ranchero Rock (Clark, 1991, p. 27).

Banks Canyon [SANTA CRUZ]: *canyon*, nearly 2 miles long, drained by Casserly Creek above a point 5.25 miles north-northeast of Watsonville (lat. 36°59'25" N, long. 121°44'05" W). Named on Mount Madonna (1955) and Watsonville East (1955) 7.5' quadrangles.

Bardin [MONTEREY]: *locality*, 3 miles south-southeast of the mouth of Salinas River along Southern Pacific Railroad (lat. 36°42'25" N, long. 121°47'20" W). Named on Monterey (1913) 15' quadrangle.

Barger Canyon [SANTA BARBARA]: *canyon*, nearly 2 miles long, along Arroyo Burro (3) above a point 3.5 miles northwest of downtown Santa Barbara (lat. 34°27'15" N, long. 119°44'40" W). Named on Santa Barbara (1952) 7.5' quadrangle. United States Board on Geographic Names (1961b, p. 7) rejected the name "Arroyo Burro" for the feature.

Barger Canyon: see **Arroyo Burro** [SANTA BARBARA] (3).

Barka Slough [SANTA BARBARA]: *marsh*, 6.5 miles south of Orcutt in San Antonio Valley (lat. 34°46'15" N, long. 120a28' W). Named on Orcutt (1959) 7.5' quadrangle.

Barlow Flat Camp [MONTEREY]: *locality*, 5 miles north of Partington Point along the upper reaches of Big Sur River (lat. 36°14'50" N, long. 121°42'40" W; sec. 26, T 19 S, R 2 E). Named on Partington Ridge (1956) 7.5' quadrangle.

Barloy Canyon [MONTEREY]: *canyon*, drained by a stream that flows 2.25 miles to an unnamed stream 5 miles west of Spreckels (lat. 36°37'30" N, long. 121°44'20" W). Named on Spreckels (1947) 7.5' quadrangle.

Barn Springs: see **Lower Barn Springs**, under **Hot Springs** [SANTA BARBARA] (2); **Upper Barn Springs**, under **Hot Springs** [SANTA BARBARA] (2).

Baroda [SANTA BARBARA]: *locality*, less than 1 mile east-northeast of Surf along Southern Pacific Railroad (lat. 34°41'10" N, long. 120°35'25" W). Named on Surf (1959) 7.5' quadrangle.

Barranca Honda [SANTA BARBARA]: *canyon*, drained by a stream that flows 2.25 miles to the sea 5 miles east of Point Conception (lat. 34°27'25" N, long. 120°22'55" W). Named on Point Conception (1953) 7.5' quadrangle. Called Canada del Gato on Lompoc (1905) 30' quadrangle, but United States Board on Geographic Names (1962a, p. 5) rejected the names "Canada del Gato" and "Cañada del Gato" for the feature.

Barr Canyon [MONTEREY]: *canyon*, nearly 3 miles long, opens into lowlands 3.5 miles northeast of Jolon (lat. 36°00'30" N, long. 121° 08' W; near NW cor. sec. 20, T 22 S, R 8 E). Named on Cosio Knob (1949) and Espinosa Canyon (1949) 7.5' quadrangles. The name commemorates Harry Barr, who homesteaded about 2 miles east of the mouth of the canyon (NE quarter sec. 23, T 22 S, R 8 E) (Clark, 1991, p. 29).

Barrell Canyon [MONTEREY]: *canyon*, drained by a stream that flows nearly 5 miles to lowlands 5 miles west-northwest of San Ardo (lat. 36°03' N, long. 120°59'20" W). Named on Espinosa Canyon (1949) and San Ardo (1967) 7.5' quadrangles.

Barrel Springs [SANTA BARBARA]: *spring*, 2.5 miles east-southeast of Tepusquet Peak (lat. 34°54'05" N, long. 120°08'40" W). Named on Tepusquet Canyon (1964) 7.5' quadrangle.

Barrett Creek [SAN LUIS OBISPO]: *stream*, flows 11.5 miles to San Juan Creek 3.5 miles northeast of Branch Mountain (lat. 35°13'40" N, long. 120°02'40" W; sec. 16, T 31 S, R 18 E). Named on Branch Mountain (1967) and Chimineas Ranch (1959) 7.5' quadrangles.

Barsug [SANTA BARBARA]: *locality*, at the south edge of the town of Guadalupe, where Southern Pacific Railroad and Santa Maria Valley Railroad cross (lat. 34°57'25" N, long. 120°34'20" W). Named on Guadalupe (1959) 7.5' quadrangle.

Bartlett Canyon [SANTA BARBARA]: *canyon*, 4 miles long, along Carneros Creek above a point 2 miles west-northwest of downtown Goleta (lat. 34°26'45" N, long. 119°51'20" W). Named on Goleta (1950) 7.5' quadrangle.

Basin: see **The Basin** [MONTEREY].

Basin Creek [MONTEREY]: *stream*, flows nearly 5 miles to Sand Creek 11.5 miles south-southwest of Soledad (lat. 36°17' N, long. 121°25'45" W; sec. 16, T 19 S, R 5 E); the stream goes through The Basin. Named on Sycamore Flat (1956) 7.5' quadrangle.

Basket Spring [MONTEREY]: *spring*, 6 miles east-northeast of Cape San Martin (lat. 35°54'35" N, long. 121°21'40" W; sec. 30, T 23 S, R 6 E). Named on Alder Peak (1949) 7.5' quadrangle.

Basquez Creek: see **Vasquez Creek** [SAN LUIS OBISPO].

Bassett Gulch: see **Aptos Creek** [SANTA CRUZ].

Bates Canyon [SANTA BARBARA]: *canyon*, drained by a stream that flows nearly 4.5 miles to Cottonwood Canyon 7.25 miles northwest of McPherson Peak (lat. 34°58'15" N, long. 119°53'05" W; near NW cor. sec. 9, T 10 N, R 28 W). Named on Bates Canyon (1964) 7.5' quadrangle.

Bates Canyon Campground [SANTA BARBARA]: *locality*, 7.25 miles northwest of McPherson Peak (lat. 34°57'15" N, long. 119° 54'25" W); the place is in Bates Canyon. Named on Bates Canyon (1964) 7.5' quadrangle.

Bates Creek [SANTA CRUZ]: *stream*, flows 3 miles to Soquel Creek 3 miles north-northeast of Soquel Point (lat. 36°59'45" N, long. 121°57'15" W). Named on Laurel (1955) and Soquel (1954) 7.5' quadrangles. The name commemorates Joel Bates, who settled in the neighborhood as early as 1853; the feature also was called Picnic Gulch Creek (Clark, 1986, p. 18).

Bat Rock [SANTA BARBARA]: *rock*, 4.25 miles northwest of Cardwell Point, and 50 feet offshore on the north side of San Miguel Island (lat. 34°03'35" N, long. 120°21'15" W). Named on San Miguel Island East (1950) 7.5' quadrangle.

Battles [SANTA BARBARA]: *locality*, 2.25 miles southeast of Santa Maria along Santa Maria Valley Railroad (lat. 34°55'50" N, long. 120°24'20" W). Named on Santa Maria (1959) 7.5' quadrangle.

Bay de los Esteros: see **Estero Bay** [SAN LUIS OBISPO].

Bay of San Luis: see **San Luis Obispo Bay** [SAN LUIS OBISPO].

Bay-Osos: see **Los Osos** [SAN LUIS OBISPO].

Bay Point [SANTA BARBARA]: *promontory*, 2 miles northwest of Cardwell Point on the north side of San Miguel Island (lat. 34°02'30" N, long. 120°19'05" W). Named on San Miguel Island East (1950) 7.5' quadrangle. Bremner's (1933) map shows a feature called Eagle Cliff located along the coast less than 0.5 mile west-northwest of present Bay Point.

Baywood Park [SAN LUIS OBISPO]: *town*, 3.5 miles south-southeast of Morro Rock on the southeast side of Morro Bay (1) (lat. 35°19'35" N, long. 120°50'10" W). Named on Morro Bay South (1965) 7.5' quadrangle. Lots in a subdivision called El Moro were sold at the place in 1894 (Nicholson, p. 168). Walter Redfield resumed development of the subdivision in 1919, and changed the name from El Moro to Baywood Park; the community later was combined with Los Osos for census and postal purposes (Lee and others, p. 21). Postal authorities established Baywood Park post office in 1948 and discontinued it in 1967 (Salley, p. 16).

Beacon Reef: see **Carrington Point** [SANTA BARBARA].

Beam Flat [SAN LUIS OBISPO]: *area*, 36 miles southeast of Simmler near the southeast end of Elkhorn Plain (lat. 35°01'15" N, long. 119°29'25" W; near SE cor. sec. 24, T 11 N, R 25 W). Named on Maricopa (1951) 7.5' quadrangle.

Bean Canyon [SAN LUIS OBISPO]: *canyon*, drained by a stream that flows 3 miles to Pozo Creek 2.25 miles east-northeast of Pozo (lat. 35°18'45" N, long. 120°20'15" W; sec. 14, T 30 S, R 15 E). Named on Pozo Summit (1967) 7.5' quadrangle. Called Fraser Canyon on Pozo (1922) 15' quadrangle, but United States Board on Geographic Names (1968b, p. 5) rejected this name.

Bean Creek [SANTA CRUZ]: *stream,* flows 9 miles to Zayante Creek 6 miles southeast of the town of Boulder Creek (lat. 37°03'05" N, long. 122°03'35" W). Named on Felton (1955), Laurel (1955), and Los Gatos (1953) 7.5' quadrangles. John Bean settled along the stream in 1853 (Young, p. 10).

Bean Hill [SANTA CRUZ]: *peak,* 3.25 miles northwest of Corralitos (lat. 37°01'25" N, long. 121°50'50" W). Named on Loma Prieta (1955) 7.5' quadrangle.

Bean Hollow: see **Glenwood** [SANTA CRUZ].

Bear Basin [MONTEREY]: *area,* 2 miles east of Ventana Cone (lat. 36°17'10" N, long. 121°38'25" W; on N line sec. 16, T 19 S, R 3 E). Named on Ventana Cones (1956) 7.5' quadrangle.

Bear Basin Camp [MONTEREY]: *locality,* 2 miles east of Ventana Cone (lat. 36°17' N, long. 121°38'35" W; sec. 16, T 19 S, R 3 E); the place is on the south side of Bear Basin. Named on Ventana Cones (1956) 7.5' quadrangle.

Bear Basin Creek [MONTEREY]: *stream,* flows nearly 1 mile to Carmel River 2 miles east-northeast of Ventana Cone (lat. 36°17'50" N, long. 121°38'55" W; sec. 9, T 19 S, R 3 E); the stream heads in Bear Basin. Named on Ventana Cones (1956) 7.5' quadrangle.

Bear Campground [SANTA BARBARA]: *locality,* 1.25 miles east-northeast of Big Pine Mountain along Sisquoc River (lat. 34°42'15" N, long. 119°38' W). Named on Big Pine Mountain (1964) 7.5' quadrangle.

Bear Campground: see **Lower Bear Campground** [SANTA BARBARA].

Bear Canyon [MONTEREY]:
(1) *canyon,* drained by a stream that flows nearly 4 miles to Robertson Creek 4 miles east of Jamesburg (lat. 36°22'05" N, long. 121°31'20" W; near E line sec. 15, T 18 S, R 4 E). Named on Chews Ridge (1956) and Rana Creek (1956) 7.5' quadrangles.
(2) *canyon,* drained by a stream that flows 7.5 miles to San Antonio River 10 miles northwest of Jolon (lat. 36°04' N, long. 121°19'15" W); the canyon heads near Bear Mountain. Named on Bear Canyon (1949) and Reliz Canyon (1949) 7.5' quadrangles.

Bear Canyon [SAN BENITO]:
(1) *canyon,* drained by a stream that flows 3.25 miles to Stone Canyon 6 miles south of Paicines (lat. 36°38'25" N, long. 121°15'30" W; sec. 12, T 15 S, R 6 E). Named on Mount Johnson (1968) and Paicines (1968) 7.5' quadrangles.
(2) *canyon,* drained by a stream that flows 1 mile to Payne Creek 4 miles northeast of San Benito (lat. 36°33'25" N, long. 121°02'15" W). Named on San Benito (1968) 7.5' quadrangle.

Bear Canyon [SANTA BARBARA]: *canyon,* drained by a stream that flows 5.5 miles to North Fork La Brea Creek 2.5 miles east-northeast of Tepusquet Peak (lat. 34°55'10" N, long. 120°08'20" W). Named on Tepusquet Canyon (1964) 7.5' quadrangle.

Bear Canyon: see **Deer Canyon** [SAN LUIS OBISPO] (3); **De Vaul Canyon** [SANTA BARBARA].

Bear Creek [SAN BENITO]: *stream,* flows 3.25 miles to Chalone Creek 3 miles north-northeast of North Chalone Peak (lat. 36°29'05" N, long. 121°09'50" W; sec. 1, T 17 S, R 7 E); the stream drains Bear Gulch (1). Named on North Chalone Peak (1969) 7.5' quadrangle.

Bear Creek [SANTA BARBARA]:
(1) *stream,* flows 3.25 miles to lowlands along the coast 2.5 miles south of Surf (lat. 34°38'50" N, long. 120°36' W). Named on Surf (1959) and Tranquillon Mountain (1959) 7.5' quadrangles.
(2) *stream,* flows 2.5 miles to Kelly Creek 2.5 miles northwest of San Marcos Pass (lat. 34°32'30" N, long. 119°51'15" W). Named on San Marcos Pass (1959) 7.5' quadrangle.

Bear Creek [SANTA CRUZ]: *stream,* flows 8 miles to San Lorenzo River at the town of Boulder Creek (lat. 37°07'40" N, long. 122°07'15" W; near N line sec. 30, T 9 S, R 2 W). Named on Castle Rock Ridge (1955) 7.5' quadrangle.

Bear Creek: see **Rancho Nuevo Creek** [SANTA BARBARA].

Bear Gulch [SAN BENITO]:
(1) *canyon,* drained by Bear Creek, which flows 3.25 miles to Chalone Creek 3 miles north-northeast of North Chalone Peak (lat. 36°29'05" N, long. 121°09'50" W; sec. 1, T 17 S, R 7 E). Named on North Chalone Peak (1969) 7.5' quadrangle.
(2) *canyon,* drained by a stream that flows 1.5 miles to Rock Springs Creek 7.5 miles north-northeast of Bitterwater (lat. 36°28'20" N, long. 120°55'45" W; near N line sec. 7, T 17 S, R 10 E). Named on Rock Spring Peak (1969) 7.5' quadrangle.

Bear Gulch Reservoir [SAN BENITO]: *lake,* 1200 feet long, behind a dam in Bear Gulch (1) nearly 2 miles north-northeast of North Chalone Peak (lat. 36°28'20" N, long. 121°11'10" W; near NW cor. sec. 11, T 17 S, R 7 E). Named on North Chalone Peak (1969) 7.5' quadrangle.

Bear Mountain [MONTEREY]: *peak,* 14 miles west-southwest of King City (lat. 36°09'30" N, long. 121°22'30" W; sec. 25, T 20 S, R 5 E). Altitude 4771 feet. Named on Junipero Serra Peak (1949) and Reliz Canyon (1949) 7.5' quadrangles.

Bear Spring [MONTEREY]: *spring,* 7.5 miles north of Charley Mountain (lat. 36°14'50" N, long. 120°41'05" W; sec. 28, T 19 S, R 12 E). Named on Priest Valley (1969) 7.5' quadrangle.

Bear Trap: see **Little Bear Trap** [MONTEREY]; **The Bear Trap** [MONTEREY].

Bear Trap Canyon [MONTEREY]: *canyon,* drained by a stream that flows nearly 1 mile to Anastasia Canyon 3 miles south-southeast of Jamesburg (lat. 36°20' N, long. 121°33'55" W; sec. 29, T 18 S, R 4 E); the canyon is southwest of The Bear Trap. Named on Chews Ridge (1956) 7.5' quadrangle.

Beartrap Canyon [MONTEREY]: *canyon,* drained by a stream that flows 1 mile to Bixby Creek 5 miles north-northeast of Point Sur (lat. 36°22'10" N, long. 121°51'40" W; sec. 16, T 18 S, R 1 E). Named on Big Sur (1956) 7.5' quadrangle.

Beartrap Creek [SAN LUIS OBISPO]: *stream,* flows 5.5 miles to San Juan Creek 4 miles east-northeast of Castle Crags (lat. 35°20'05" N, long. 120°08'25" W; sec. 10, T 30 S, R 17 E). Named on La Panza (1967) 7.5' quadrangle.

Beartrap Flat [MONTEREY]: *area,* 7.5 miles south-southeast of Jolon (lat. 35°51'50" N, long. 121°08'30" W; sec. 6, 7, T 24 S, R 8 E). Named on Burnett Peak (1949) 7.5' quadrangle.

Bear Trap Gulch: see **San Vicente Creek** [SANTA CRUZ].

Bear Trap Spring [MONTEREY]: *spring,* 1 mile west-northwest of Charley Mountain (lat. 36°08'50" N, long. 120°40'50" W; sec. 33, T 20 S, R 12 E). Named on Priest Valley (1969) 7.5' quadrangle.

Beartrap Spring [SAN LUIS OBISPO]: *spring,* 2 miles east-northeast of Castle Crags (lat. 35°19'10" N, long. 120°10'10" W); the spring is along Beartrap Creek. Named on La Panza (1967) 7.5' quadrangle.

Beartree Canyon [MONTEREY]: *canyon,* drained by a stream that flows nearly 1.5 miles to Gabilan Creek 10 miles east-northeast of Salinas (lat. 36°44' N, long. 121°28'50" W). Named on Mount Harlan (1968) 7.5' quadrangle.

Bear Valley [SAN BENITO]: *valley,* opens into the canyon of Chalone Creek 3 miles northeast of North Chalone Peak (lat. 36° 28'50" N, long. 121°09'20" W; sec. 1, T 17 S, R 7 E). Named on Bickmore Canyon (1968) and North Chalone Peak (1969) 7.5' quadrangles.

Bear Valley [SANTA CRUZ]: *canyon,* nearly 1 mile long, opens into lowlands 3.25 miles west-northwest of Corralitos (lat. 37°00'30" N, long. 121°51'35" W). Named on Loma Prieta (1955) 7.5' quadrangle.

Beasley Flat [SAN LUIS OBISPO]: *area,* 11 miles northeast of the village of San Simeon (lat. 35°46'10" N, long. 121°04'20" W; near E line sec. 11, T 25 S, R 8 E). Named on Bryson (1949) 7.5' quadrangle.

Beatty Ridge [SANTA CRUZ]: *ridge,* south- to south-southeast-trending, 1.5 miles long, 6 miles north-northeast of the town of Boulder Creek (lat. 37°12' N, long. 122°03'55" W). Named on Castle Rock Ridge (1955) 7.5' quadrangle. The name is for G.W. Beatty and W.J. Beatty, brothers who settled in the neighborhood about 1905 and had a ranch on the ridge (Clark, 1986, p. 23).

Beatty Slide [SANTA CRUZ]: *relief feature,* nearly 6 miles north-northeast of the town of Boulder Creek (lat. 37°11'55" N, long. 122°04'10" W; near N line sec. 34, T 8 S, R 2 W); the slide is on the west side of Beatty Ridge. Named on Castle Rock Ridge (1955) 7.5' quadrangle. The feature is a landslide caused by the 1906 earthquake (Clark, 1986, p. 23).

Beauty Spring [SAN LUIS OBISPO]: *spring,* 9 miles northeast of the mouth of Morro Creek (lat. 35°28'55" N, long. 120°46'10" W). Named on Morro Bay North (1965) 7.5' quadrangle.

Bechers Bay: see **Beechers Bay** [SANTA BARBARA].

Becker Valley [SAN BENITO]: *canyon,* drained by a stream that flows nearly 5 miles to an unnamed canyon at Monterey-San Benito County line 5.25 miles south-southwest of Bitterwater (lat. 36°18'35" N, long. 121°02'20" W; sec. 6, T 19 S, R 9 E). Named on Lonoak (1969) and Pinalito Canyon (1969) 7.5' quadrangles.

Beckett: see **Emmett Station** [SAN BENITO].

Beck Lake [SAN LUIS OBISPO]: *intermittent lake,* 350 feet long, 8 miles north-northeast of Santa Margarita (lat. 35°29'30" N, long. 120°32' W). Named on Santa Margarita (1965) 7.5' quadrangle.

Bee Camp [MONTEREY]: *locality,* 3 miles east-northeast of Slates Hot Springs (lat. 36°08'10" N, long. 121°35'05" W; sec. 1, T 21 S, R 3 E). Named on Tassajara Hot Springs (1956) 7.5' quadrangle. The place also was called Upper Bee Camp to distinguish it from Lower Bee Camp (Clark, 1991, p. 32).

Bee Camp: see **Lower Bee Camp** [MONTEREY].

Bee Canyon [SAN LUIS OBISPO]: *canyon,* drained by a stream that flows nearly 0.5 mile to Corbit Canyon 4.5 miles southeast of Edna (lat. 35°09'25" N, long. 120°33'25" W). Named on Arroyo Grande NE (1965) 7.5' quadrangle. Called Deer Canyon on Arroyo Grande (1897) 15' quadrangle, where present Deer Canyon (2) is called Bee Canyon.

Bee Cave Canyon [MONTEREY]: *canyon,* drained by a stream that flows nearly 1 mile to Loeber Canyon 8.5 miles east of Jolon (lat. 35°57'35" N, long. 121°01'45" W; sec. 5, T 32 S, R 9 E). Named on Williams Hill (1949)

7.5' quadrangle.

Beechers Bay [SANTA BARBARA]: *embayment*, 5.5 miles northwest of East Point on the north side of Santa Rosa Island (lat. 34°00' N, long. 120°02'15" W). Named on Santa Rosa Island East (1943) and Santa Rosa Island North (1943) 7.5' quadrangles. United States Board on Geographic Names (1995, p. 5) approved the name "Bechers Bay" for the feature.

Beehive [SANTA CRUZ]: *peak*, 2.25 miles northwest of Laurel (lat. 37°08'30" N, long. 121°59'30" W; on N line sec. 20, T 9 S, R 1 W). Named on Los Gatos (1919) 15' quadrangle. The name is from the resemblance of the feature to a beehive (Gudde, 1949, p. 27).

Beeman Canyon [MONTEREY]: *canyon*, drained by a stream that flows 3.5 miles to Peachtree Valley (lat. 36°13'45" N, long. 120° 53' W). Named on Hepsedam Peak (1969), Monarch Peak (1967), and Nattrass Valley (1967) 7.5' quadrangles.

Bee Rock [SAN LUIS OBISPO]: *locality*, nearly 3 miles east-northeast of Tierra Redonda Mountain (lat. 35°47'15" N, long. 120°56'20" W; sec. 6, T 25 S, R 10 E); the place is in the upper part of Bee Rock Canyon (1). Named on Tierra Redonda Mountain (1949) 7.5' quadrangle.

Bee Rock [SANTA BARBARA]:

(1) *relief feature*, 5.5 miles northwest of Zaca Lake along Sisquoc River (lat. 34°50' N, long. 120°06'15" W). Named on Zaca Lake (1964) 7.5' quadrangle.

(2) *peak*, 2 miles north of Santa Ynez Peak (lat. 34°33'20" N, long. 119°58'40" W). Altitude 2091 feet. Named on Lake Cachuma (1959) 7.5' quadrangle.

(3) *rock*, 4 miles south-southeast of Sandy Point on the west side of Santa Rosa Island, and 4400 feet offshore (lat. 33°57' N, long. 120°12'45" W). Named on Santa Rosa Island West (1943) 7.5' quadrangle.

Bee Rock Canyon [MONTEREY-SAN LUIS OBISPO]: *canyon*, drained by a stream that heads in San Luis Obispo County and flows 4.5 miles to San Antonio River 6.5 miles southwest of Bradley in Monterey County (lat. 35°48'05" N, long. 120°53'25" W; sec. 33, T 24 S, R 10 E). Named on Tierra Redonda Mountain (1949) 7.5' quadrangle. The stream in the canyon is called Lynch's Creek on an unpublished map used about 1915. Water of San Antonio Reservoir (present Lake San Antonio) now floods the lower part of the canyon.

Bee Rock Canyon [SAN LUIS OBISPO]: *canyon*, drained by a stream that flows 3 miles to Cuyama Valley 2.5 miles northwest of New Cuyama [SANTA BARBARA] (lat. 34°58'30" N, long. 119°42'35" W). Named on New Cuyama (1964) 7.5' quadrangle.

Bee Rock Canyon [SANTA BARBARA]: *canyon*, drained by a stream that flows 2.25 miles to Sisquoc River 0.5 mile east of Bee Rock (1) (lat. 34°50'05" N, long. 120°05'45" W). Named on Zaca Lake (1964) 7.5' quadrangle.

Beeswax Canyon [MONTEREY]: *canyon*, drained by a stream that flows 1 mile to lowlands 5 miles west-southwest of Greenfield (lat. 36°18'05" N, long. 121°19'30" W). Named on Paraiso Springs (1956) 7.5' quadrangle.

Bee Tree Spring [SAN LUIS OBISPO]: *spring*, 2 miles west of Cholame (lat. 35°43'05" N, long. 120°19'50" W; sec. 26, T 25 S, R 15 E). Named on Cholame (1961) 7.5' quadrangle.

Bell Canyon [SANTA BARBARA]:

(1) *canyon*, drained by a stream that flows 2.25 miles to Zaca Creek 3 miles west of Zaca Lake (lat. 34°46'45" N, long. 120°05'25" W). Named on Zaca Lake (1964) 7.5' quadrangle.

(2) *canyon*, 1.25 miles long, opens to the sea 2.5 miles northwest of Coal Oil Point (lat. 34°25'45" N, long. 119°54'45" W). Named on Dos Pueblos Canyon (1951) 7.5' quadrangle.

Bello Spring [SAN LUIS OBISPO]: *spring*, 8.5 miles north-northwest of San Luis Obispo (lat. 35°23'25" N, long. 120°43'45" W; sec. 19, T 29 S, R 12 E). Named on Atascadero (1965) 7.5' quadrangle.

Bellyache Spring [SAN LUIS OBISPO]: *spring*, 14 miles southeast of Shandon (lat. 35°30'30" N, long. 120°11'40" W; sec. 12, T 28 S, R 16 E). Named on Holland Canyon (1961) 7.5' quadrangle.

Ben Graves Canyon [MONTEREY]: *canyon*, drained by a stream that flows 2.25 miles to McCoy Canyon 6 miles east-northeast of Gonzales (lat. 36°33' N, long. 121°21'05" W; sec. 7, T 16 S, R 6 E). Named on Mount Johnson (1968) 7.5' quadrangle. The name commemorates Benjamin Graves, who owned land in and near the canyon (Clark, 1991, p. 33).

Benham: see **Carpinteria** [SANTA BARBARA].

Ben Lomond [SANTA CRUZ]: *town*, 3.25 miles southeast of the town of Boulder Creek along San Lorenzo River (lat. 37°05'20" N, long. 122°05'15" W; in and near sec. 4, T 10 S, R 2 W). Named on Felton (1955) 7.5' quadrangle. Postal authorities established Ben Lomond post office in 1887 (Frickstad, p. 176). James J. Pierce, owner of timber operations in the neighborhood, laid out the town in the 1880's (Hoover, Rensch, and Rensch, p. 479-480). The community first was called Pacific Mills, but when postal authorities objected to this name, the place was renamed Ben Lomond for nearby Ben Lomond Mountain (Rowland, p. 173). Hamman's (1980b) map shows a place called Shingle Springs located along the railroad just south of Ben Lomond, and north of the confluence of Newell Creek and San Lorenzo River. Rowland (p. 172) mentioned two places situated along San Lorenzo River near Ben Lomond: Hicks' ford near the south edge of the present town, named for Napoleon Bonaparte Hicks, who settled there in 1868; and Priest's ford near the north end of the present town, named for James Priest, who had a sawmill nearby.

Ben Lomond: see **Camp Ben Lomond** [SANTA CRUZ].

Ben Lomond Mountain [SANTA CRUZ]: *ridge*, north-northwest-trending, 9 miles long, 11 miles northwest of Santa Cruz (lat. 37°06' N, long. 122°08'30" W). Named on Big Basin (1955), Davenport (1955), and Felton (1955) 7.5' quadrangles. John Burns, a native of Scotland, took up land on the ridge in 1850, planted a vineyard, and named the ridge after the Scotch wine-grape district of Ben Lomond (Rowland, p. 173).

Bennett: see **Point Bennett** [SANTA BARBARA].

Bennett Creek [SANTA CRUZ]: *stream*, flows nearly 2 miles to Fall Creek 5.5 miles south-southeast of the town of Boulder Creek (lat. 37°03'05" N, long. 122°05' W; sec. 21, T 10 S, R 2 W). Named on Felton (1955) 7.5' quadrangle. The name commemorates Eben Bennett, who came to Santa Cruz in 1866 and operated lime kilns near the stream (Clark, 1986, p. 26).

Bennett Slough [MONTEREY]: *water feature*, nearly 2 miles long, joins Elkhorn Slough at Moss Landing (lat. 36°48'35" N, long. 121°47'10" W). Named on Moss Landing (1954) 7.5' quadrangle.

Ben Willow Spring [SAN LUIS OBISPO]: *spring*, 4.25 miles southwest of Wilson Corner (lat. 35°25'15" N, long. 120°25'40" W; sec. 12, T 29 S, R 14 E). Named on Wilson Corner (1966) 7.5' quadrangle.

Bern [SAN LUIS OBISPO]: *locality*, 9.5 miles east-northeast of Paso Robles near Estrella Creek (lat. 35°41'20" N, long. 120°32'15" W; near S line sec. 2, T 26 S, R 13 E). Named on Paso Robles (1919) 15' quadrangle. Postal authorities established Bern post office in 1904 and discontinued it in 1932 (Frickstad, p. 164).

Bernard's Bay: see **Morro Bay** [SAN LUIS OBISPO] (1).

Berros [SAN LUIS OBISPO]: *settlement*, 4 miles southeast of downtown Arroyo Grande (lat. 35°04'40" N, long. 120°32'20" W); the place is along Los Berros Creek. Named on Oceano (1965) 7.5' quadrangle. Called Los Berros on Arroyo Grande (1897) 15' quadrangle, which shows the place located along Pacific Coast Railroad, and United States Board on Geographic Names (1991, p. 5) approved this name for the settlement. Postal authorities established Berros Creek post office in 1870 and discontinued it in 1872; they established Los Berros post office in 1888, changed the name to Berros in 1901, discontinued it in 1920, reestablished it in 1921, and discontinued it in 1940 (Salley, p. 19). *Berros* means "watercress" in Spanish (Gudde, 1949, p. 29).

Berros Creek: see **Berros** [SAN LUIS OBISPO].

Berry Creek [SANTA CRUZ]:

(1) *stream*, heads just inside San Mateo County and flows nearly 2 miles to West Waddell Creek 5 miles north of the mouth of Waddell Creek (lat. 37°10'05" N, long. 122°15'50" W; sec. 11, T 9 S, R 4 W). Named on Franklin Point (1955) 7.5' quadrangle. T.G. Berry homesteaded along the stream in 1878 (Brown, p. 7).

(2) *stream*, flows 1.25 miles to Big Creek nearly 5 miles north-northwest of Davenport (lat. 37°04'40" N, long. 122°13'05" W; sec. 8, T 10 S, R 3 W). Named on Davenport (1955) 7.5' quadrangle. The name is for Andrew Warren Berry, who homesteaded and had a cabin along the stream in the 1850's (Clark, 1986, p. 27).

Berry Creek Falls [SANTA CRUZ]: *waterfall*, 5 miles north of the mouth of Waddell Creek (lat. 37°10'10" N, long. 122°15'50" W; sec. 11, T 9 S, R 4 W); the waterfall is along Berry Creek (1). Named on Franklin Point (1955) 7.5' quadrangle. The feature also is called Lower Berry Creek Falls to distinguish it from other waterfalls on Berry Creek (Clark, 1986, p. 27).

Berry Falls: see **Davenport Landing** [SANTA CRUZ].

Berta Canyon [MONTEREY]: *canyon*, drained by a stream that flows 1 mile to an unnamed canyon nearly 1 mile north-northeast of Prunedale (lat. 36°47'15" N, long. 121°39'50" W). Named on Prunedale (1954) 7.5' quadrangle.

Berwick Canyon [MONTEREY]: *canyon*, drained by a stream that flows 2 miles to Carmel Valley (1) 6.5 miles east of the mouth of Carmel River (lat. 36°31'25" N, long. 121°48'35" W). Named on Seaside (1947) 7.5' quadrangle. The name commemorates Edward Berwick, who bought land in Carmel Valley (1) in 1867 (Clark, 1991, p. 34).

Bethany Park [SANTA CRUZ]: *settlement*, 6.5 miles north-northwest of Soquel (lat. 37°04'35" N, long. 121°59'35" W). Named on Laurel (1955) 7.5' quadrangle. The name is from Bethany Bible College (Clark, 1986, p. 28).

Bethel District: see **Templeton** [SAN LUIS OBISPO].

Betteravia [SANTA BARBARA]: *village*, 5 miles southeast of Guadalupe (lat. 34°55' N, long. 120°31' W). Named on Guadalupe (1959) 7.5' quadrangle. Postal authorities established Betteravia post office in 1900 and discontinued it in 1970 (Salley, p. 20). *Betterave* means "beet" in French; a sugar-beet processing plant opened at the site in 1897 (Gudde, 1949, p. 30).

Betteravia Junction [SANTA BARBARA]: *locality*, 4 miles southeast of the town of Guadalupe along Santa Maria Valley Railroad (lat. 34°55'40"

N, long. 120°31'55" W); the place is 1 mile northwest of Betteravia. Named on Guadalupe (1959) 7.5' quadrangle.

Betteravia Stockyards [SANTA BARBARA]: *locality,* 4.25 miles southeast of the town of Guadalupe along Santa Maria Valley Railroad (lat. 34°55'45" N, long. 120°31' W); the place is nearly 1 mile north of Betteravia. Named on Guadalupe (1959) 7.5' quadrangle. California Division of Highways' (1934) map has the name "Springer" for a place situated along the railroad at or near present Betteravia Stockyards.

Betteravia Storage [SANTA BARBARA]: *locality,* 4 miles southeast of the town of Guadalupe along Santa Maria Valley Railroad (lat. 34°55'40" N, long. 120°31'35" W); the place is 1 mile northwest of Betteravia. Named on Guadalupe (1959) 7.5' quadrangle.

Beulah Park [SANTA CRUZ]: *settlement,* 9.5 miles southeast of the town of Boulder Creek (lat. 37°00'40" N, long. 122°01'15" W). Named on Felton (1955) 7.5' quadrangle. The place grew around Beulah Park Conference Grounds, a church summer camp (Clark, 1986, p. 28).

Bickmore Canyon [SAN BENITO]: *canyon,* 5 miles long, opens into Bear Valley nearly 6 miles west-northwest of San Benito (lat. 36° 03'05" N, long. 121°10' W; near E line sec. 11, T 16 S, R 7 E). Named on Bickmore Canyon (1968) 7.5' quadrangle.

Bicknell [SANTA BARBARA]:

(1) *locality,* 4.25 miles southeast of Orcutt (lat. 34°49' N, long. 120° 23'30" W). Named on Orcutt (1959) 7.5' quadrangle. Postal authorities established Bicknell post office in 1909 and discontinued it in 1940 (Frickstad, p. 170). The name commemorates John Dustin Bicknell, a pioneer in the development of oil in Santa Maria Valley (Hanna, p. 31).

(2) *locality,* 10.5 miles south of Santa Maria along Pacific Coast Railroad in Harris Canyon (lat. 34°47'45" N, long. 120°26'25" W). Named on Lompoc (1905) 30' quadrangle.

Bielawski Mountain [SANTA CRUZ]: *peak,* 7 miles north-northeast of the town of Boulder Creek on Santa Cruz-Santa Clara County line (lat. 37°13'25" N, long. 122°05'30" W; sec. 21, T 8 S, R 2 W). Altitude 3231 feet. Named on Castle Rock Ridge (1955) 7.5' quadrangle. Whitney (p. 70) called the feature Mount Bielawski to honor C. Bielawski, chief draughtsman of the Surveyor-General's Office. United States Board on Geographic Names (1960c, p. 16) approved the name "Mount Bielawski" for the peak, and rejected the names "Bielawski Mountain," "Bielwaski Mountain," and "Mount McPherson."

Big Baldy [SAN LUIS OBISPO]: *peak,* 14 miles north-northeast of the town of Nipomo (lat. 35°13'40" N, long. 120°23'50" W; sec. 17, T 31 S, R 15 E). Altitude 2686 feet. Named on Tar Spring Ridge (1967) 7.5' quadrangle. Angel (1883, p. 354-355) called the feature Mount Hasbrouck for a landowner in the vicinity.

Big Basin [SANTA CRUZ]: *valley,* 6.5 miles west-northwest of the town of Boulder Creek (lat. 37°10'05" N, long. 122°13'15" W; sec. 7, 8, T 9 S, R 3 W). Named on Big Basin (1955) 7.5' quadrangle. On Ben Lomond (1946) 15' quadrangle, the name "Big Basin" applies to a group of buildings that represent the headquarters of Big Basin Redwoods State Park. Big Basin (1955) 7.5' quadrangle shows Big Basin P.O. at park headquarters in Big Basin. Postal authorities established Redwood Park post office in 1907 and changed the name to Big Basin in 1928 (Frickstad, p. 177).

Big Bend Canyon [SANTA BARBARA]: *canyon,* drained by a stream that flows 3.5 miles to Sisquoc River 5 miles west-southwest of Montgomery Potrero (lat. 34°48'40" N, long. 19°50'05" W). Named on Bald Mountain (1964) and Hurricane Deck (1964) 7.5' quadrangles.

Big Cone Spruce Camp [SANTA BARBARA]: *locality,* 2 miles west-northwest of San Rafael Mountain along Manzana Creek (lat. 34°43'35" N, long. 119°50'45" W; near E line sec. 5, T 7 N, R 28 W). Named on San Rafael Mountain (1959) 7.5' quadrangle.

Big Creek [MONTEREY]:

(1) *stream,* flows 5 miles to Finch Creek 1.5 miles east of Jamesburg (lat. 36°22'45" N, long. 121°33'50" W; sec. 8, T 18 S, R 4 E). Named on Rana Creek (1956) 7.5' quadrangle.

(2) *stream,* flows 6.25 miles to the sea 1.5 miles north-northwest of Gamboa Point (lat. 36°04'10" N, long. 121°36' W; sec. 26, T 21 S, R 3 E). Named on Lopez Point (1956) 7.5' quadrangle. North Fork enters from the north nearly 3 miles upstream from the mouth of the creek; it is 4 miles long and is named on Lopez Point (1956) and Tassajara Hot Springs (1956) 7.5' quadrangles. G.A. Waring (p. 57) described a spring called Dolans Hot Spring located along North Fork Big Creek—actually along Big Creek—about 1.5 miles from the coast. Crawford (1894, p. 340) mentioned Dolan's Hot Sulphur Spring, and Berkstresser (p. A-9) listed Dolans Hot Springs (sec. 24, T 21 S, R 3 E). The feature was called Hollins Hot Springs in the early 1930's, for Marion Hollins, who owned the land at the site; it also had the local name "Big Creek Hot Springs" (Clark, 1991, p. 142).

Big Creek [SANTA CRUZ]: *stream,* flows 7 miles to Scott Creek 4.5 miles north-northwest of Davenport (lat. 37°04' N, long. 122°13'45" W). Named on Big Basin (1955) and Davenport (1955) 7.5' quadrangles.

Big Creek Hot Springs: see **Dolans Hot Spring**, under **Big Creek** [MONTEREY] (2).

Big Dome: see **Big Dome Cove** [MONTEREY].

Big Dome Cove [MONTEREY]: *embayment,* 1000 feet east of Point Lobos on the south shore of Carmel Bay (lat. 36°31'20" N, long. 121°56'50" W). Named on Monterey (1947) 7.5' quadrangle. California Department of Parks and Recreation's map has the name "Big Dome" for the promontory just east of the cove, and has the name "Terminal Rock" for a small island northeast of Big Dome.

Big Falls Canyon [SAN LUIS OBISPO]: *canyon,* drained by a stream that flows 3 miles to Lopez Canyon 4.5 miles southeast of Lopez Mountain (lat. 35°15'35" N, long. 120°30'45" W; near N line sec. 6, T 31 S, R 14 E). Named on Lopez Mountain (1965) 7.5' quadrangle. Called Little Falls Canyon on San Luis Obispo (1897) 15' quadrangle.

Big Gulch: see **Waddell Creek** [SANTA CRUZ].

Big Meadow [MONTEREY]: *area,* 0.5 mile east-southeast of Point Lobos (lat. 36°31'05" N, long. 121°56'35" W). Named on Monterey (1947) 7.5' quadrangle.

Big Mountain [SAN BENITO]: *peak,* 6.5 miles north-northeast of San Benito (lat. 36°35'30" N, long. 121°01'30" W; sec. 30, T 15 S, R 9 E). Altitude 3992 feet. Named on San Benito (1968) 7.5' quadrangle.

Big Oak Flat [SAN BENITO]: *area,* 4 miles northeast of San Benito (lat. 36°32'45" N, long. 121°01'45" W; near SE cor. sec. 7, T 16 S, R 9 E). Named on San Benito (1968) 7.5' quadrangle.

Big Panoche Creek: see **Panoche Creek** [SAN BENITO].

Big Pine Campground [SANTA BARBARA]: *locality,* 0.25 mile west of Big Pine Mountain (lat. 34°41'50" N, long. 119°39'35" W). Named on Big Pine Mountain (1964) 7.5' quadrangle.

Big Pine Canyon [SANTA BARBARA]: *canyon,* drained by a stream that flows 2.5 miles to Sisquoc River 2.5 miles north-northwest of Big Pine Mountain (lat. 34°43'50" N, long. 119°40'25" W); the canyon heads at Big Pine Mountain. Named on Big Pine Mountain (1964) 7.5' quadrangle.

Big Pine Mountain [SANTA BARBARA]: *ridge,* west-trending, 1 mile long, 8 miles northeast of Little Pine Mountain (lat. 34°41'50" N, long. 119°39'10" W). Named on Big Pine Mountain (1964) 7.5' quadrangle.

Big Pines [MONTEREY]: *locality,* 3 miles northwest of Uncle Sam Mountain (lat. 36°22'15" N, long. 121°45' W). Named on Big Sur (1956) and Ventana Cones (1956) 7.5' quadrangles.

Big Pocket Lake [SAN LUIS OBISPO]: *intermittent lake,* 1750 feet long, 3.25 miles south-southwest of downtown Arroyo Grande near the coast (lat. 35°04'55" N, long. 120°36'50" W). Named on Oceano (1965) 7.5' quadrangle

Big Rocks [SAN LUIS OBISPO]: *peak,* 4 miles south-southwest of Branch Mountain (lat. 35°07'50" N, long. 120°07' W). Named on Branch Mountain (1967) 7.5' quadrangle.

Big Sand Creek [MONTEREY]: *stream,* flows 4 miles to Paloma Creek 14 miles west of Greenfield (lat. 36°19'30" N, long. 121°29'20" W; sec. 36, T 18 S, R 4 E). Named on Sycamore Flat (1956) 7.5' quadrangle. Called Little Sand Creek on Soledad (1915) 15' quadrangle.

Big Sandy Creek [MONTEREY]: *stream,* flows 28 miles to Salinas River 6.5 miles southeast of Bradley (lat. 35°47'30" N, long. 120° 43'30" W; near SW cor. sec. 31, T 24 S, R 12 E). Named on San Miguel (1948), Smith Mountain (1969), Stockdale Mountain (1948), and Valleton (1948) 7.5' quadrangles. The lower part of the stream flows through Indian Valley (3) for 15 miles. A map of Monterey County used about 1900 has the name "Nelson's Cr." for present Big Sandy Creek above Indian Valley (3). The stream in Indian Valley (3) is called Indian Valley Cr. on California Mining Bureau's (1917b) map, which fails to name the valley itself; the same map shows a locality called Oak Flat situated along Stone Canyon Railroad by present Big Sandy Creek between places called Pope and Hill that also are along the railroad.

Big Spring [SAN LUIS OBISPO]:

(1) *spring,* 2 miles southeast of Pozo (lat. 35°16'50" N, long. 120° 21'10" W; sec. 27, T 30 S, R 15 E). Named on Pozo Summit (1967) 7.5' quadrangle.

(2) *spring,* 8.5 miles south of Simmler (lat. 35°14' N, long. 119°59'50" W; near N line sec. 13, T 31 S, R 18 E). Named on Chimineas Ranch (1959) 7.5' quadrangle.

Big Spring [SANTA BARBARA]:

(1) *spring,* 5 miles northwest of McPherson Peak (lat. 34°55'40" N, long. 119°52'45" W); the feature is in Big Spring Canyon 850 feet south of Little Spring. Named on Bates Canyon (1964) 7.5' quadrangle.

(2) *spring,* 8.5 miles south of the city of Lompoc along Escondido Creek (lat. 34°31'30" N, long. 120°27'20" W). Named on Lompoc Hills (1959) 7.5' quadrangle.

Big Spring Canyon [SANTA BARBARA]: *canyon,* drained by a stream that flows 1 mile to Schoolhouse Canyon (1) 5 miles northwest of McPherson Peak (lat. 34°55'50" N, long. 119°52'30" W); Big Spring (1) is in the canyon. Named on Bates Canyon (1964) 7.5' quadrangle.

Big Sur [MONTEREY]: *settlement,* 5.5 miles east-southeast of Point Sur (lat. 36°16'10" N, long. 121°48'25" W; sec. 24, T 19 S, R 1 E); the place is by Big Sur River. Named on Big Sur (1956) 7.5' quadrangle. Postal authorities established Arbolado post office in 1910 and changed the name to Big Sur in 1915; they established Rainbow Lodge post office at a vacation resort along Bixby Creek 11 miles northwest of Big Sur in 1922 and discontinued it in 1925 (Salley, p. 9, 180).

Big Sur Hot Springs: see **Slates Hot Springs** [MONTEREY].

Big Sur River [MONTEREY]: *stream,* formed by the confluence of North Fork and South Fork, flows 15 miles to the sea 3 miles southeast of Point Sur (lat. 36°16'50" N, long. 121°51'30" W); the mouth of the stream is on El Sur grant. Named on Big Sur (1956), Partington Ridge (1956), Pfeiffer Point (1956), and Ventana Cones (1956) 7.5' quadrangles. Called Sur River on Point Sur (1925) 15' quadrangle. United States Board on Geographic Names (1943, p. 14) decided in favor of the name "Sur River," and later (1960b, p. 6) reversed the decision in favor of the name "Big Sur River." According to Lussier (p. 4), the early Spaniards at Carmel mission called the wilderness south of the mission *El Pais Grande del Sur*, which means "The Big Country to the South" in Spanish, and called the largest river there *El Rio Grande del Sur*, which means "The Big River to the South"—eventually the name of the stream became the partial translation "Big Sur River." North Fork is nearly 6.5 miles long and South Fork is 6.25 miles long; both forks are named on Partington Ridge (1956) and Tassajara Hot Springs (1956) 7.5' quadrangles.

Big Tree Gulch: see **Bridge Creek** [SANTA CRUZ].

Big Trees [SANTA CRUZ]: *locality,* 1.5 miles southeast of Felton along Southern Pacific Railroad (lat. 37°02'10" N, long. 122°03'30" W). Named on Santa Cruz (1902) 30' quadrangle.

Big Twin Lake [SAN LUIS OBISPO]: *lake,* 2100 feet long, nearly 4 miles south-southwest of downtown Arroyo Grande near the coast (lat. 35°04'10" N, long. 120°36'30" W); the lake is west of Small Twin Lake. Named on Oceano (1965) 7.5' quadrangle.

Bill Faris Campground [SANTA BARBARA]: *locality,* less than 1 mile south-southwest of Madulce Peak in Alamar Canyon (lat. 34° 40'50" N, long. 119°35'50" W). Named on Madulce Peak (1964) 7.5' quadrangle. The name commemorates a Boy Scout leader of Santa Barbara (Gagnon, p. 69).

Billiard Flats [SANTA BARBARA]: *area,* 8 miles north of Rincon Point along Santa Ynez River (lat. 34°29'20" N, long. 119°29' W; sec. 27, T 5 N, R 25 W). Named on White Ledge Peak (1952) 7.5' quadrangle. On Ventura (1904) 15' quadrangle, the name applies to a place located 1 mile farther west at a site that water of Jamesan Lake now covers.

Birabent Canyon [SANTA BARBARA]: *canyon,* 5 miles long, along Alamo Pinto Creek above a point 6 miles north-northeast of Los Olivos (lat. 34°44'30" N, long. 120°03'40" W). Named on Zaca Lake (1964) 7.5' quadrangle. Called Birbent Canyon on Tepusquet Peak (1943) 15' quadrangle, and on Figueroa Mountain (1959) and Los Olivos (1959) 7.5' quadrangles, but United States Board on Geographic Names (1965d, p. 7) rejected the names "Birbent Canyon" and "Ballard Canyon" for the feature.

Birbent Canyon: see **Birabent Canyon** [SANTA BARBARA].

Bird Creek [SAN BENITO]: *stream,* flows 7.5 miles to San Benito River 5 miles south-southeast of Hollister (lat. 36°47' N, long. 121° 22'15" W). Named on Hollister (1955), Mount Harlan (1968), and Tres Pinos (1955) 7.5' quadrangles. Left Fork enters nearly 5 miles upstream from the mouth of the main stream; it is 2.5 miles long and is named on Hollister (1955) and Mount Harlan (1968) 7.5' quadrangles. Jesse Whitton, who was in the neighborhood with Fremont in 1846, named the stream (Pierce, p. 69).

Bird Island [MONTEREY]: *island,* 500 feet long, 1 mile south-southeast of Point Lobos and 300 feet offshore (lat. 36°30'25" N, long. 121°56'35" W). Named on Monterey (1947) 7.5' quadrangle. The feature has a colony of sea birds in the spring and summer (Clark, 1991, p. 41).

Bird Rock [MONTEREY]:

(1) *rock,* 300 feet long, 1 mile northeast of Cypress Point and 400 feet offshore (lat. 36°35'30" N, long. 121°58' W). Named on Monterey (1947) 7.5' quadrangle.

(2) *rock,* 100 feet long, 1.25 miles southeast of Cape San Martin, and 1050 feet offshore (lat. 35°52'35" N, long. 121°27'10" W). Named on Cape San Martin (1949) 7.5' quadrangle. United States Coast and Geodetic Survey (p. 117) described Whaleboat Rock, which is near Bird Rock (2).

Bird Rock [SAN LUIS OBISPO]: *rock,* 75 feet long, 0.5 mile offshore at Shell Beach (lat. 35°08'55" N, long. 120°41' W). Named on Pismo Beach (1965) 7.5' quadrangle.

Bird Spring [MONTEREY]: *spring,* 12 miles east of San Ardo (lat. 36°02'05" N, long. 120°41'15" W; sec. 9, T 22 S, R 12 E). Named on Slack Canyon (1969) 7.5' quadrangle.

Bishop Peak [SAN LUIS OBISPO]: *peak,* nearly 2.5 miles northwest of downtown San Luis Obispo (lat. 35°18'10" N, long. 120°41'50" W; sec. 21, T 30 S, R 12 E). Altitude 1546 feet. Named on San Luis Obispo (1965) 7.5' quadrangle. Goodyear (1888, p. 99) called the feature Obispo Peak—*obispo* means "bishop" in Spanish.

Bitter Creek [SANTA BARBARA]: *stream,* formed by the confluence of the streams in Central Canyon and East Canyon, flows 4 miles to Cuyama River 2.25 miles northwest of New Cuyama (lat. 34°58'15" N, long. 119°43' W). Named on New Cuyama (1964) 7.5' quadrangle.

Bitter Creek Spring [SANTA BARBARA]: *spring,* 3.5 miles east of McPherson Peak (lat. 34°53'20" N, long. 119°45'05" W). Named on Peak Mountain (1964) 7.5' quadrangle.

Bitterwater [SAN BENITO]: *settlement,* 10 miles south-southeast of San Benito (lat. 36°22'50" N, long. 121°00' W; sec. 9, T 18 S, R 9 E); the place is in Bitterwater Valley. Named on Topo Valley (1969) 7.5' quadrangle. Postal authorities established Bitterwater post office in 1878, discontinued it in 1888, reestablished it in the same year with the name "Bitter Water," changed the name back to Bitterwater in 1894, changed it again to Bitter Water in 1905, and discontinued the post office in 1907 (Salley, p. 22).

Bitterwater Canyon [SAN BENITO]: *canyon,* drained by a stream that flows 8 miles to Panoche Valley nearly 5 miles west of Panoche at Llanada (lat. 36°36'35" N, long. 120°54'55" W; sec. 19, T 15 S, R 10 E). Named on Llanada (1969) and San Benito (1968) 7.5' quadrangles.

Bitterwater Canyon [SAN LUIS OBISPO]: *canyon,* 5 miles long, 20 miles east-southeast of Shandon on San Luis Obispo-Kern County line (lat. 35°30'30" N, long. 120°03'30" W); the canyon is along upper reaches of Bitterwater Creek. Named on La Panza NE (1966) and Packwood Creek (1961) 7.5' quadrangles.

Bitterwater Canyon: see **Little Bitterwater Canyon** [MONTEREY].

Bitterwater Creek [SAN BENITO]: *stream,* flows 6.5 miles to Lewis Creek 6.5 miles southeast of Bitterwater (lat. 36°18'35" N, long. 120°55'20" W; sec. 6, T 19 S, R 10 E); the stream drains the southeast part of Bitterwater Valley. Named on Lonoak (1969) 7.5' quadrangle.

Bitterwater Creek [SAN LUIS OBISPO]: *stream,* formed by the confluence of Walnut Creek and Yeguas Creek, flows 6.25 miles in and out of Kern County to enter Kern County finally 19 miles east-southeast of Shandon (lat. 35°31'35" N, long. 120°04'20" W; at S line sec. 31, T 27 S, R 18 E). Named on La Panza NE (1966) and Packwood Creek (1961) 7.5' quadrangles.

Bitterwater Lake [SAN BENITO]: *intermittent lake,* 3300 feet long, 1 mile southeast of Bitterwater (lat. 36°22'20" N, long. 120°59'10" W; sec. 10, 15, T 18 S, R 9 E); the feature is in the northwest part of Bitterwater Valley. Named on Lonoak (1969) and Rock Spring Peak (1969) 7.5' quadrangles.

Bitterwater Spring: see **Little Bitterwater Spring** [MONTEREY].

Bitterwater Valley [SAN BENITO]: *valley,* around Bitterwater (lat. 36°21'45" N, long. 120°58'15" W); the southeast part of the valley is drained by Bitterwater Creek. Named on Lonoak (1969), Rock Spring Peak (1969), and Topo Valley (1969) 7.5' quadrangles.

Bixby Creek [MONTEREY]: *stream,* formed by the confluence of Turner Creek and Mill Creek (1), flows 4.5 miles to the sea 4.5 miles north of Point Sur (lat. 36°22'20" N, long. 121°54'10" W; sec. 18, T 18 S, R 1 E). Named on Big Sur (1956) and Point Sur (1956) 7.5' quadrangles. Present Mill Creek (1) is called Bixby Creek on Point Sur (1925) 15' quadrangle. The name "Bixby" commemorates Charles Bixby, who filed for a homestead along the creek; the stream originally was called Mill Creek (Fink, p. 208).

Bixby Landing [MONTEREY]: *locality,* 0.25 mile west of the mouth of Bixby Creek along the coast (lat. 36°22'20" N, long. 121°54'20" W; sec. 18, T 18 S, R 1 E). Site named on Point Sur (1956) 7.5' quadrangle.

Bixby Mountain [MONTEREY]: *peak,* 4.5 miles northeast of Point Sur (lat. 36°21'15" N, long. 121°50'20" W; sec. 23, T 18 S, R 1 E). Altitude 2920 feet. Named on Big Sur (1956) 7.5' quadrangle.

Bixby's Mill: see **Point Sur** [MONTEREY].

Blackburn Gulch [SANTA CRUZ]: *canyon,* 2.25 miles long, on upper reaches of Branciforte Creek above a point 5 miles north-northwest of Soquel (lat. 37°03'25" N, long. 121°58'45" W; sec. 16, T 10 S, R 1 W). Named on Laurel (1955) 7.5' quadrangle. The name commemorates William F. Blackburn, who arrived in the neighborhood in the 1840's (Clark, 1986, p. 32).

Black Butte [MONTEREY]: *peak,* 7.5 miles south-southeast of Jamesburg (lat. 36°16' N, long. 121°32'25" W; sec. 21, T 19 S, R 4 E). Altitude 4941 feet. Named on Chews Ridge (1956) 7.5' quadrangle.

Black Butte [SAN LUIS OBISPO]: *peak,* 1 mile northwest of Lopez Mountain (lat. 35°18'45" N, long. 120°35'30" W; sec. 16, T 30 S, R 13 E). Altitude 2749 feet. Named on Lopez Mountain (1965) 7.5' quadrangle.

Black Canyon [SAN BENITO]: *canyon,* drained by a stream that flows 6 miles to San Lorenzo Creek 7.5 miles south-southwest of Bitterwater (lat. 36°16'30" N, long. 121°02'05" W; sec. 18, T 19 S, R 9 E). Named on Lonoak (1969) and Pinalito Canyon (1969) 7.5' quadrangles.

Black Canyon [SANTA BARBARA]:

(1) *canyon,* drained by a stream that flows 3.5 miles to Santa Cruz Creek 6 miles south-southeast of San Rafael Mountain (lat. 34° 37'55" N, long. 119°45'55" W; at N line sec. 6, T 6 N, R 27 W). Named on San Rafael Mountain (1959) 7.5' quadrangle.

(2) *canyon,* drained by a stream that flows 2.5 miles to the sea 1.5 miles north of Point Conception (lat. 34°28'25" N, long. 120°28'30" W). Named on Point Conception (1953) 7.5' quadrangle. On Point Conception (1942) 15' quadrangle, the stream in the canyon has the name "Las Animas Creek."

Black Cone [MONTEREY]: *peak,* 6.5 miles east-northeast of Partington Point (lat. 36°12'50" N, long. 121°35'30" W; near S line sec. 1, T 20 S, R 3 E). Altitude 4535 feet. Named on Tassajara Hot Springs (1956) 7.5'

quadrangle.

Black Hill [SAN LUIS OBISPO]: *hill,* 2.25 miles east-southeast of Morro Rock (lat. 35°21'30" N, long. 120°49'50" W; sec. 31, T 29 S, R 11 E). Altitude 661 feet. Named on Morro Bay South (1965) 7.5' quadrangle.

Black Lake [SAN LUIS OBISPO]: *lake,* 1300 feet long, 4.5 miles south-southwest of downtown Arroyo Grande near the coast (lat. 35°03'25" N, long. 120°36'10" W). Named on Oceano (1965) 7.5' quadrangle.

Black Lake Canyon [SAN LUIS OBISPO]: *canyon,* 3.5 miles long, opens into lowlands near the coast 4.5 miles south of the town of Arroyo Grande (lat. 35°03'25" N, long. 120°35'40" W); a stream flows for 0.25 mile from the mouth of the canyon to Black Lake. Named on Oceano (1965) 7.5' quadrangle.

Black Mountain [SAN BENITO]: *ridge,* northwest-trending, 1.5 miles long, 7.5 miles east of Bitterwater (lat. 36°23'15" N, long. 120°51'30" W). Named on Hernandez Reservoir (1969) 7.5' quadrangle.

Black Mountain [SAN LUIS OBISPO]:
(1) *ridge,* northwest-trending, 1.5 miles long, 4 miles southeast of Cypress Mountain (lat. 35°33'20" N, long. 120°54'20" W). Named on Cypress Mountain (1948) 7.5' quadrangle.
(2) *peak,* 6.25 miles north-northeast of Pozo (lat. 35°23'35" N, long. 120°21'05" W; sec. 15, T 29 S, R 15 E). Altitude 3622 feet. Named on Camatta Ranch (1966) 7.5' quadrangle.

Black Mountain: see **Castle Mountain** [MONTEREY].

Black Oak Mountain [SAN LUIS OBISPO]: *peak,* nearly 5 miles east-northeast of the village of San Simeon (lat. 35°40'25" N, long. 121°06'55" W). Altitude 2266 feet. Named on Pebblestone Shut-in (1959) 7.5' quadrangle.

Black Point [SANTA BARBARA]: *promontory,* 3 miles east-southeast of Fraser Point on Santa Cruz Island (lat. 34°02'15" N, long. 119°53'05" W). Named on Santa Cruz Island A (1943) 7.5' quadrangle. Called Punta Negra on Rand's (1931) map.

Black Point [SANTA CRUZ]: *promontory,* 1 mile west-northwest of Soquel Point on the coast at the west end of Santa Cruz Harbor (lat. 36°57'30" N, long. 121°59'30" W). Named on Soquel (1954) 7.5' quadrangle. The feature also had the names "Prieta Point" and "Santa Maria Point" (Clark, 1986, p. 33).

Black Rock [SAN LUIS OBISPO]: *rocks,* 1 mile east of Cayucos Point, and 1100 feet offshore (lat. 35°26'50" N, long. 120°55'25" W). Named on Cayucos (1965) 7.5' quadrangle.

Black Rock Creek [MONTEREY]: *stream,* flows 5 miles to San Clemente Creek 4 miles south of the town of Carmel Valley (lat. 36°25'20" N, long. 121°44'15" W; sec. 27, T 17 S, R 2 E). Named on Carmel Valley (1956) and Mount Carmel (1956) 7.5' quadrangles. South Fork enters from the south 0.5 mile upstream from the mouth of the main creek; it is 3.5 miles long and is named on Carmel Valley (1956) and Mount Carmel (1956) 7.5' quadrangles.

Black Rock Ridge [MONTEREY]: *ridge,* east-northeast-trending, 1.5 miles long, 5 miles south of the town of Carmel Valley (lat. 36° 24'35" N, long. 121°45'15" W); the ridge is between Black Rock Creek and South Fork Black Rock Creek. Named on Carmel Valley (1956) and Mount Carmel (1956) 7.5' quadrangles.

Black Spring [SAN LUIS OBISPO]: *spring,* 9.5 miles southeast of Shandon in Hughes Canyon (lat. 35°33'50" N, long. 120°14'45" W; near W line sec. 22, T 27 S, R 16 E). Named on Holland Canyon (1961) 7.5' quadrangle.

Black Sulphur Spring [SAN LUIS OBISPO]: *spring,* 5 miles north-northwest of Caliente Mountain (lat. 35°06'10" N, long. 119°48'05" W; near S line sec. 26, T 32 S, R 20 E). Named on Caliente Mountain (1959) 7.5' quadrangle.

Black Willow Spring [SANTA BARBARA]: *spring,* at Montgomery Potrero (lat. 34°49'50" N, long. 119°45'50" W). Named on Hurricane Deck (1964) 7.5' quadrangle.

Blair Canyon [MONTEREY]: *canyon,* 3 miles long, opens into the canyon of Pine Creek (3) 8 miles north-northeast of San Ardo (lat. 36°08'30" N, long. 120°51'45" W; sec. 35, T 20 S, R 10 E). Named on Monarch Peak (1967) 7.5' quadrangle. The name commemorates Robert A. Blair, who patented land in the neighborhood in the 1880's (Clark, 1991, p. 44).

Blanco [MONTEREY]: *locality,* 4.5 miles west of Salinas on the northeast side of Salinas River (lat. 36°40'40" N, long. 121°44'15" W). Named on Salinas (1947) 7.5' quadrangle. On Salinas (1912) 15' quadrangle, the name applies to a place situated 0.5 mile farther east along Pajaro Valley Consolidated Railroad. According to Gudde (1949, p. 33), the name is from Tom White, a sailor who deserted ship at Monterey in 1840, and who was known as Tomas Blanco—*blanco* means "white" in Spanish; White's place along Salinas River was known as Blanco Crossing. Postal authorities established Blanco post office in 1873, discontinued it for a time in 1878, discontinued it again in 1917, reestablished it in 1930, and discontinued it finally in 1941 (Frickstad, p. 106).

Blanco: see **Ernest Blanco Spring** [SANTA BARBARA].

Blanco Crossing: see **Blanco** [MONTEREY].

Blas Creek: see **San Vicente Creek** [SANTA CRUZ].

Blinn Spring [SAN LUIS OBISPO]: *spring,* 6.5 miles north-northeast of Pozo (lat. 35°23'25" N, long. 120°20'10" W; near S line sec. 14, T 29 S, R 15 E). Named on Camatta Ranch (1966) 7.5' quadrangle.

Blooms Creek [SANTA CRUZ]: *stream,* flows 3 miles to join Opal Creek and form East Waddell Creek at the south end of Big Basin (lat. 37°09'55" N, long. 122°13'25" W; near E line sec. 7, T 9 S, R 3 W). Named on Big Basin (1955) 7.5' quadrangle. The name is for Irvin T. Bloom, who acquired land along the stream in 1897 (Clark, 1986, p. 34).

Blooms Mill [SANTA CRUZ]: *locality,* 5.25 miles northwest of the town of Boulder Creek (lat 37°09'50" N, long. 122°11'55" W; sec. 9, T 9 S, R 3 W); the place is along Blooms Creek. Named on Santa Cruz (1902) 30' quadrangle. The locality also was called Old Park Mill and Park Mills (Clark, 1986, p. 34).

Blue Bank: see **Valley Anchorage** [SANTA BARBARA].

Blue Canyon [MONTEREY]: *canyon,* drained by a stream that flows 2.5 miles to Priest Valley nearly 4 miles north of Charley Mountain (lat. 36°11'15" N, long. 120°39'35" W; sec. 15, T 20 S, R 12 E). Named on Priest Valley (1969) 7.5' quadrangle.

Blue Canyon [SANTA BARBARA]: *canyon,* 5.25 miles long, opens into the canyon of Santa Ynez River 7.5 miles south-southwest of Hildreth Peak (lat. 34°30'15" N, long. 119°36'30" W). Named on Carpinteria (1952) and Hildreth Peak (1964) 7.5' quadrangles.

Blue Canyon Pass [SANTA BARBARA]: *pass,* 6.5 miles north-northwest of Carpinteria (lat. 34°29'10" N, long. 119°33'20" W; sec. 25, T 5 N, R 26 W); the pass is near the head of Blue Canyon. Named on Carpinteria (1952) 7.5' quadrangle.

Blue Canyon Pass: see **Romero Saddle** [SANTA BARBARA].

Blue Creek [MONTEREY]: *stream,* flows nearly 2 miles to Carmel River 1.5 miles north-northeast of Ventana Cone (lat. 36°18'10" N, long. 121°39'55" W; sec. 5, T 19 S, R 3 E). Named on Ventana Cones (1956) 7.5' quadrangle.

Bluefish Cove [MONTEREY]: *embayment,* 0.5 mile east of Point Lobos on the south side of Carmelo Bay (lat. 36°31'15" N, long. 121°56'35" W). Named on Monterey (1947) 7.5' quadrangle. According to Clark (1991, p. 46), the name is from blue rockfish found at the place. California Department of Parks and Recreation's map has the name "Viscaino Hill" on the east side of the cove, and has the name "Guillemot Island" for a small island at the northwest corner of the cove.

Blue Jay Splash [SAN BENITO]: *water feature,* 4 miles east-northeast of Bitterwater along San Benito River (lat. 36°24'10" N, long. 120°56'10" W; near SW cor. sec. 31, T 17 S, R 10 E). Named on Rock Spring Peak (1969) 7.5' quadrangle.

Blue Oak Spring [SAN LUIS OBISPO]: *spring,* 6.25 miles north-northeast of Pozo (lat. 35°22'50" N, long. 120°19'25" W; near W line sec. 24, T 29 S, E 15 E). Named on Camatta Ranch (1966) 7.5' quadrangle.

Blue Point [SAN LUIS OBISPO]: *peak,* 12 miles northeast of Shandon (lat. 35°46'35" N, long. 120°12'55" W; sec. 11, T 25 S, R 16 E). Named on Tent Hills (1942) 7.5' quadrangle.

Bluerock Mountain [MONTEREY]: *peak,* 12 miles north of Gonzales (lat. 36°40'55" N, long. 121°29'10" W). Altitude 2556 feet. Named on Mount Harlan (1968) 7.5' quadrangle.

Blue Rock Ridge [MONTEREY]: *ridge,* northeast-trending, 2.5 miles long, 7 miles south-southeast of the town of Carmel Valley (lat. 36°23'15" N, long. 121°41'05" W). Named on Carmel Valley (1956) 7.5' quadrangle.

Bluff: see **The Bluff** [SAN BENITO].

Bluff Campground [SANTA BARBARA]: *locality,* 2 miles south-southwest of Big Pine Mountain by Indian Creek (lat. 34°40'25" N, long. 119°39'55" W). Named on Big Pine Mountain (1964) 7.5' quadrangle. Called Bluff Camp on Big Pine Mountain (1944) 7.5' quadrangle.

Bluff Spring [SAN LUIS OBISPO]: *spring,* 4 miles west-northwest of Branch Mountain (lat. 35°12'35" N, long. 120°08'45" W). Named on Los Machos Hills (1967) 7.5' quadrangle.

Boar Peak [SAN LUIS OBISPO]: *peak,* nearly 1 mile north-northeast of Huasna Peak (lat. 35°02'50" N, long. 120°21'15" W; sec. 9, T 11 N, R 33 W). Altitude 1871 feet. Named on Huasna Peak (1967) 7.5' quadrangle.

Boat Landing: see **Ladys Harbor** [SANTA BARBARA].

Bolcoff Creek: see **Wilder Creek** [SANTA CRUZ].

Bolsa [SAN BENITO]: *valley,* the southeasternmost extension of Santa Clara Valley north and northeast of Hollister. Named on Chittenden (1955) and San Felipe (1955) 7.5' quadrangles.

Bolsa Chica Lake [SAN LUIS OBISPO]: *lake,* 1100 feet long, 4 miles south-southwest of downtown Arroyo Grande near the coast (lat. 35°04'05" N, long. 120°36'10" W). Named on Oceano (1965) 7.5' quadrangle. Called Bolsa Chico Lake on Arroyo Grande (1942) 15' quadrangle.

Bolsa de Chamisal [SAN LUIS OBISPO]: *land grant,* south of Arroyo Grande Creek along the coast. Named on Arroyo Grande NE (1965) and Oceano (1965) 7.5' quadrangles. Francisco Quijada received the land in 1837; Lewis T. Burton claimed 14,335 acres patented in 1867 (Cowan, p. 26; Cowan used the form "Bolsa de Chamizal" for the name). Angel (1883, p. 215) used the name "Bolsa de Chemisal," for the grant, but United States Board on Geographic Names (1933, p. 155) rejected the names "Bolsa de Chemisal" and "Chemisal" for it.

Bolsa de las Escorpinas [MONTEREY]: *land grant,* 6 miles north of Salinas. Named on Prunedale (1954), Salinas (1947), and San Juan Bautista (1955) 7.5' quadrangles. Salvador Espinosa received 2 leagues before 1828, and again in 1837; he claimed 6416 acres patented in 1876 (Cowan, p. 34; Cowan listed the grant under the designation "Escarpines, (or Escorpinas, or Escarpiones), Bolsa de, (or) San Miguel").

Bolsa del Moro Cojo: see **Bolsa Nueva y Moro Cojo** [MONTEREY].

Bolsa del Pajaro [SANTA CRUZ]: *land grant,* at and southwest of Watsonville in Pajaro Valley. Named on Moss Landing (1954), Watsonville East (1955), and Watsonville West (1954) 7.5' quadrangles. Sebastian Rodriguez received 2 leagues in 1837 and claimed 5497 acres patented in 1860 (Cowan, p. 56).

Bolsa del Potrero y Moro Cojo [MONTEREY]: *land grant,* 6 miles northwest of Salinas. Named on Marina (1947), Moss Landing (1954), Prunedale (1954), and Salinas (1947) 7.5' quadrangles; the maps have the name "La Sagrada Familia" as an alternate title for the grant. Jose Joaquin de la Torre received 2 leagues in 1822 and sold the land to John B.R. Cooper in 1829; Cooper claimed 6916 acres patented in 1859 (Cowan, p. 35-36).

Bolsa de San Cayetano [MONTEREY]: *land grant,* 15 miles northwest of Salinas near the coast. Named on Moss Landing (1954), Prunedale (1954), Watsonville East (1955), and Watsonville West (1954) 7.5' quadrangles. Ignacio Vincente Ferrer Vallejo received 2 leagues in 1824; Jose de Jesus Vallejo claimed 8866 acres patented in 1865 (Cowan, p. 74). According to Perez (p. 56), Jose Ignacio Vallejo was the grantee in 1834.

Bolsa de San Felipe [SAN BENITO]: *land grant,* north of Hollister. Named on San Felipe (1955) and Three Sisters (1954) 7.5' quadrangles. Francisco Perez Pacheco received 2 leagues in 1836 and 1840; he claimed 6795 acres patented in 1871 (Cowan, p. 75). *Bolsa* means "pocket" in Spanish, and this term was applied because a swamp, a willow grove, and a ravine almost enclosed the grant (Hoover, Rensch, and Rensch, p. 312).

Bolsa Knolls [MONTEREY]: *settlement,* 4 miles north-northeast of Salinas (lat. 36°44' N, long. 121°38'15" W). Named on Salinas (1947, photorevised 1968 and 1975) 7.5' quadrangle.

Bolsa Nueva y Moro Cojo [MONTEREY]: *land grant,* near Prunedale. Named on Moss Landing (1954), Prunedale (1954), and San Juan Bautista (1955) 7.5' quadrangles. According to Cowan (p. 49-50, 53), this feature is a combination of two grants: Francisco Soto received Bolsa Nueva (listed by Cowan under the name "Nueva Bolsa") in 1829 and 1836; Simeon Castro received 2 leagues, called Bolsa del Moro Cojo, in 1825, 1836-1837, and 1844, and added Bolsa Nueva to it; M. Antonia Pico de Castro and others claimed 30,901 acres patented in 1873. There is a tradition that the name "Moro Cojo" is from a lame black horse—*cojo* means "lame" in Spanish, and *moro* here has the meaning "black" rather that the more common meaning "Moor" (Hoover, Rensch, and Rensch, p. 224).

Bonanza Gulch [SAN BENITO]: *canyon,* 1.5 miles long, opens into the canyon of Bird Creek 5.5 miles south of Hollister (lat. 36°46'15" N, long. 121°24'40" W). Named on Hollister (1955) 7.5' quadrangle.

Bone Mountain [SANTA BARBARA]: *peak,* 4.5 miles southeast of Tepusquet Peak (lat. 34°51'45" N, long. 120°07'55" W). Altitude 2822 feet. Named on Foxen Canyon (1964) 7.5' quadrangle.

Bonnet Rock [SAN LUIS OBISPO]: *relief feature,* 16 miles northeast of the town of Nipomo (lat. 35°13'10" N, long. 120°18'15" W). Named on Caldwell Mesa (1967) 7.5' quadrangle.

Bonnie Doon [SANTA CRUZ]: *settlement,* 3.25 miles northeast of Davenport (lat. 37°02'30" N, long. 122°09' W). Named on Davenport (1955) 7.5' quadrangle. United States Board on Geographic Names (1933, p. 157) first rejected the form "Bonny Doon" for the name, but later (1995, p. 5) approved it. Postal authorities established Bonny Doon post office in 1887 and discontinued it in 1930; they established Waddell post office in 1890 and discontinued it in 1891, when they moved the service to Bonny Doon (Frickstad, p. 176, 177).

Bonny Brae: see **Felton** [SANTA CRUZ].

Bonny Doon: see **Bonnie Doon** [SANTA CRUZ].

Boot Canyon [SANTA BARBARA]: *canyon,* drained by a stream that flows 2.5 miles to Horse Canyon (3) 5.5 miles east-northeast of Santa Ynez Peak (lat. 34°34'05" N, long. 119°53'25" W). Named on Lake Cachuma (1959) 7.5' quadrangle.

Bootleg Spring [MONTEREY]: *spring,* 5 miles east of Lonoak (lat. 36°16'30" N, long. 120°51'15" W; sec. 14, T 19 S, R 10 E). Named on Hepsedam Peak (1969) 7.5' quadrangle.

Boronda Creek [MONTEREY]: *stream,* flows 3.25 miles to Cachagua Creek 8.5 miles southeast of the town of Carmel Valley (lat. 36°23'30" N, long. 121°37'45" W; sec. 3, T 18 S, R 3 E). Named on Carmel Valley (1956), Chews Ridge (1956), and Ventana Cones (1956) 7.5' quadrangles. The name commemorates a family of early settlers in the neighborhood (Gudde, 1949, p. 37). Clark (1991, p. 48) noted use of the name "Percys Creek" for the stream.

Borregas Creek [SANTA CRUZ]: *stream,* flows nearly 1.5 miles to the sea 3 miles east-northeast of Soquel Point (lat. 36°58'40" N, long. 121°55'40" W). Named on Soquel (1954) 7.5' quadrangle. Clark (1986, p. 39) referred to Borregas Gulch, and noted that the feature had the name "Sanjon de Borregas" or "Zanjon de Borregas" in Spanish days—*borregas* means "lamb" in Spanish

Borregas Gulch: see **Borregas Creek** [SANTA CRUZ].

Bosworth Canyon [SAN BENITO]: *canyon,* drained by a stream that flows nearly 2 miles to San Benito River 3 miles north-northwest of San Benito (lat. 36°32'50" N, long. 121°06'20" W). Named on San Benito (1968) 7.5' quadrangle.

Bottchers Gap: see **Bouchers Gap** [MONTEREY].

Bouchers Gap [MONTEREY]: *pass,* 6 miles northeast of Point Sur (lat. 36°21'15" N, long. 121°48'45" W; sec. 24, T 18 S, R 1 E). Named on Big Sur (1956) 7.5' quadrangle. United States Board on Geographic Names (1961b, p. 8) approved the name "Bottchers Gap" for the feature. Clark (1991, p. 49) noted that John Bottcher patented land in the vicinity in the 1880's.

Boulder Creek [SAN BENITO]: *stream,* flows 2 miles to Tres Pinos Creek 4.25 miles west-northwest of Panoche Pass (lat. 36°39'10" N, long. 121°04'55" W; sec. 3, T 15 S, R 8 E). Named on Panoche Pass (1968) 7.5' quadrangle.

Boulder Creek [SANTA CRUZ]:

(1) *stream,* flows 7.5 miles to San Lorenzo River in the town of Boulder Creek (lat. 37°07'35" N, long. 122°07'15" W). Named on Big Basin (1955) and Castle Rock Ridge (1955) 7.5' quadrangles.

(2) *town,* 12 miles north-northwest of Santa Cruz where Boulder Creek (1), Bear Creek, and San Lorenzo River meet (lat. 37°07'30" N, long. 122°07'15" W). Named on Castle Rock Ridge (1955), Davenport (1955), and Felton (1955) 7.5' quadrangles. The place where the three streams meet was known in the early days as the Turkey Foot (Hamman, p. 84). It was the base of operations for bull-team logging in the 1850's, and the camp there was called Boulder Creek long before 1875 (MacGregor, p. 131). A lumber mill began operations a couple of miles south of Boulder Creek (2) in 1868, and a town called Lorenzo was started near the mill in 1875 (Rowland, p. 175)—the site of the old community of Lorenzo is in the present town of Boulder Creek. Postal authorities established Boulder Creek post office in 1872, changed the name to Lorenzo in 1875, and changed it back to Boulder Creek 1877 (Frickstad, p. 176). A place called Filbert was situated along the railroad about 1 mile south of the town of Boulder Creek (MacGregor, p. 175).

Boulder Creek: see **Little Boulder Creek** [SANTA CRUZ].

Boulder Mountain: see **Mount Carmel** [MONTEREY].

Bourdieu Valley [MONTEREY]: *valley,* 1 mile west of Smith Mountain along the uppermost part of Pancho Rico Creek (lat. 36° 04'45" N, long. 120°36'30" W). Named on Smith Mountain (1969) 7.5' quadrangle. The name commemorates Ed Bourdieu, who raised cattle and sheep in the valley after 1900 (Clark, 1991, p. 50).

Bowen Point [SANTA BARBARA]: *promontory,* 5.5 miles east of Punta Arena on the south side of Santa Cruz Island (lat. 33°57'35" N, long. 119°43'15" W). Named on Santa Cruz Island B (1943) 7.5' quadrangle.

Bowman Spring [SAN LUIS OBISPO]: *spring,* 1.25 miles north-northwest of Castle Crags near the head of South Fork Willow Canyon (lat. 35°19'20" N, long. 120°12'25" W). Named on La Panza (1967) 7.5' quadrangle.

Box Spring: see **Hepsedam Spring** [SAN BENITO].

Boyer Creek [SANTA CRUZ]: *stream,* flows 3 miles to Big Creek nearly 6 miles north of Davenport (lat. 37°05'40" N, long. 122°12'20" W; near E line sec. 5, T 10 S, R 3 W). Named on Big Basin (1955) and Davenport (1955) 7.5' quadrangles. The name is for Armenia Boyea and Oliver Boyea (or Boyer), early landholders in the neighborhood (Clark, 1986, p. 41).

Bracken Brae Creek [SANTA CRUZ]: *stream,* flows 0.5 mile to Boulder Creek (1) 4.5 miles east-southeast of Big Basin (lat. 37°08'20" N, long. 122°08'40" W; sec. 24, T 9 S, R 3 W). Named on Big Basin (1955) 7.5' quadrangle. The name is from a subdivision laid out in 1904; the feature also is known as Sand Creek (Clark, 1986, p. 42).

Brackney [SANTA CRUZ]: *settlement,* 4.5 miles south-southeast of the town of Boulder Creek along San Lorenzo River (lat. 37°04'10" N, long. 122°04'50" W; near S line sec. 9, T 10 S, R 2 W). Named on Felton (1955) 7.5' quadrangle. The name commemorates Alonzo L. Brackney, an early landholder in the neighborhood (Clark, 1986, p. 42).

Bradley [MONTEREY]: *village,* 12 miles south-southeast of San Ardo along Salinas River (lat. 35°51'50" N, long. 120°48'05" W; at N line sec. 8, T 24 S, R 11 E). Named on Bradley (1949) 7.5' quadrangle. When Southern Pacific Railroad reached the site in 1886, the station there was named for Bradley V. Sargent, who owned the land (Gudde, 1949, p. 39). Postal authorities established Bradley post office in 1886 (Frickstad, p. 106). They established Nasimento post office 8 miles southwest of Bradley in 1887, changed the name to Veratina in 1888, and discontinued it in 1895 (Salley, p. 150, 230).

Bradley Canyon [SANTA BARBARA]: *canyon,* drained by a stream that flows 5 miles to Santa Maria Valley 5.5 miles east-southeast of Santa Maria (lat. 34°54'40" N, long. 120°21'10" W; sec. 28, T 10 N, R 33 W). Named on Sisquoc (1959) and Twitchell Dam (1959) 7.5' quadrangles

Bragur [SANTA BARBARA]: *locality,* 3 miles south-southeast of the town of Guadalupe along Santa Maria Valley Railroad (lat 34°56'10" N, long.

120°32'50" W). Named on Guadalupe (1959) 7.5' quadrangle.

Branch Canyon [SANTA BARBARA]: *canyon,* 8 miles long, opens into Cuyama Valley 2.25 miles south of New Cuyama (lat. 34° 55' N, long. 119°41'30" W). Named on Hurricane Deck (1964), New Cuyama (1964), and Salisbury Potrero (1964) 7.5' quadrangles.

Branch Canyon Campground [SANTA BARBARA]: *locality,* nearly 4 miles south of New Cuyama in Newsome Canyon (lat. 34°53'35" N, long. 119°42' W; sec. 6, T 9 N, R 26 W); the place is near Branch Canyon. Named on New Cuyama (1964) 7.5' quadrangle.

Branch Canyon Spring: see **Upper Branch Canyon Spring** [SANTA BARBARA].

Branch Canyon Wash [SANTA BARBARA]: *stream,* flows 4.5 miles from the mouth of Branch Canyon to Cuyama River 2.25 miles northwest of New Cuyama (lat. 34°58'25" N, long. 119°42'40" W). Named on New Cuyama (1964) 7.5' quadrangle.

Branch Creek [SAN LUIS OBISPO]: *stream,* flows 8 miles to Alamo Creek (2) 6.25 miles west-southwest of Branch Mountain (lat. 35° 08'40" N, long. 120°10'50" W); the stream heads at Branch Mountain. Named on Branch Mountain (1967) and Los Machos Hills (1967) 7.5' quadrangles

Branch Mountain [SAN LUIS OBISPO]: *peak,* 33 miles east-southeast of San Luis Obispo (lat. 35°11'05" N, long. 120°05' W; sec. 31, T 31 S, R 18 E). Altitude 3770 feet. Named on Branch Mountain (1967) 7.5' quadrangle.

Branciforte: see **Santa Cruz** [SANTA CRUZ].

Branciforte Creek [SANTA CRUZ]: *stream,* flows 9 miles to San Lorenzo River 1.5 miles north of Point Santa Cruz in Santa Cruz (lat. 36°58'25" N, long. 122°01'20" W). Named on Felton (1955), Laurel (1955), and Santa Cruz (1954) 7.5' quadrangles. The stream also has been called Arroyo de Villa and Brown's Creek (Clark, 1986, p. 44). Present Carbonera Creek has been called West Branch Branciforte Creek, West Fork Branciforte Creek, and West Branciforte Creek (Clark, 1986, p. 64-65).

Branstetter Canyon [MONTEREY]: *canyon,* drained by a stream that flows 2.5 miles to Salinas River nearly 2 miles west of King City (lat. 36°12'40" N, long. 121°09'35" W). Named on Thompson Canyon (1949) 7.5' quadrangle. The Branstetter family owned land in the canyon (Clark, 1991, p. 51).

Breaker Point [SAN LUIS OBISPO]: *promontory,* nearly 6 miles north-northwest of Piedras Blancas Point along the coast (lat. 35° 44'35" N, long. 121°19'05" W). Named on Piedras Blancas (1959) 7.5' quadrangle.

Brennans Landing: see **Pajaro River** [SANTA CRUZ].

Bridge Canyon [SAN LUIS OBISPO]: *canyon,* drained by a stream that flows nearly 2 miles to Salinas River 1 mile south of San Miguel (lat. 35°44'05" N, long. 120°41'55" W; sec. 20, T 25 S, R 12 E). Named on Paso Robles (1948) 7.5' quadrangle.

Bridge Creek [SANTA CRUZ]: *stream,* flows 2.25 miles to Aptos Creek 4.25 miles northeast of Soquel (lat. 37°01'45" N, long. 121° 54' W). Named on Laurel (1955) 7.5' quadrangle. Hamman's (1980a) map has the name "Big Tree Gulch" for a canyon that branches west from the canyon of Bridge Creek 0.5 mile north-northwest of the mouth of Bridge Creek, and shows a place called Camp No. 5 located nearly 1 mile north-northwest of the confluence of Bridge Creek and Aptos Creek at the end of a railroad spur; Camp No. 5 also was called Hoffman's Camp for the lumber company superintendent there (Hamman, p. 78). Hamman's (1980a) map shows a place called Camp No. 4 located along upper reaches of Bridge Creek between China Ridge and Hinckley Ridge—Camp No. 4 also was called Chalk Point (Hamman, p. 74).

Brinan Spring [MONTEREY]: *spring,* 7.25 miles east-northeast of San Ardo (lat. 36°04'35" N, long. 120°47'50" W; sec. 29, T 21 S, R 11 E). Named on Pancho Rico Valley (1967) 7.5' quadrangle. Called Brinnan Springs on San Ardo (1943) 15' quadrangle. The name commemorates Thomas Brinan, Sr., who settled in the neighborhood in 1886 (Clark, 1991, p. 52).

Brinnan Springs: see **Brinan Spring** [MONTEREY].

Brizziolari Creek [SAN LUIS OBISPO]: *stream,* flows 3.25 miles to Stenner Creek 1 mile north-northwest of downtown San Luis Obispo (lat. 35°17'45" N, long. 120°40' W; near SW cor. sec. 23, T 30 S, R 12 E). Named on San Luis Obispo (1965) 7.5' quadrangle.

Broadcast Peak [SANTA BARBARA]: *peak,* 1 mile east of Santa Ynez Peak (lat. 34°31'30" N, long. 119°57'30" W; sec. 7, T 5 N, R 29 W). Altitude 4028 feet. Named on Lake Cachuma (1959) 7.5' quadrangle.

Broadhurst Canyon [MONTEREY]: *canyon,* drained by a stream that flows 2 miles to lowlands 4.5 miles south of San Lucas (lat. 36°03'50" N, long. 121°01'05" W). Named on Espinosa Canyon (1949) 7.5' quadrangle.

Brock Springs [MONTEREY]: *springs,* 13 miles east of San Ardo near the head of Indian Valley (3) (lat. 36°02'50" N, long. 120°40'15" W; sec. 3, T 22 S, R 12 E). Named on Slack Canyon (1969) 7.5' quadrangle.

Brockway Point [SANTA BARBARA]: *promontory,* 6 miles west of Carrington Point on the north side of Santa Rosa Island (lat. 34°01'30" N, long. 120°08'50" W). Named on Santa Rosa Island North (1943) 7.5' quadrangle. Sunken rocks called Rodes Reef lie 1.2 miles east-northeast of Brockway Point, and 0.8 mile offshore (United States Coast and Geodetic Survey, p. 111).

Broken Bridge Creek [SAN LUIS OBISPO]: *stream,* flows 2.5 miles to San Simeon Bay 0.5 mile east of the village of San Simeon (lat. 35°38'30" N, long. 121°10'55" W). Named on San Simeon (1958) 7.5' quadrangle.

Bromela [SAN LUIS OBISPO]: *locality,* 7 miles south of the town of Arroyo Grande along Southern Pacific Railroad (lat. 35°01'05" N, long. 120°35' W). Named on Oceano (1965) 7.5' quadrangle.

Brookdale [SANTA CRUZ]: *settlement,* 1.5 miles southeast of the town of Boulder Creek along San Lorenzo River (lat. 37°06'30" N, long. 122°06'20" W; sec. 32, T 9 S, R 2 W). Named on Felton (1955) 7.5' quadrangle. John H. Logan laid out the place in 1900 at what had been known as Reed's Spur; the settlement was called Clear Creek until 1902 (Rowland, p. 186)—it is at the mouth of Clear Creek. Postal authorities established Brookdale post office in 1902, discontinued it in 1944, and reestablished it in 1945 (Frickstad, p. 176). Hamman's (1980b) map shows a place called Harris located along the railroad about 0.5 mile northwest of Brookdale

Brookshire Campground [SANTA BARBARA]: *locality,* 4.5 miles west-southwest of Miranda Pine Mountain in Pine Canyon (1) (lat. 35°01'15" N, long. 120°06'50" W). Named on Miranda Pine Mountain (1967) 7.5' quadrangle. Branch Mountain (1942) 15' quadrangle shows Plowshare Spr. at the place.

Brown: see **Davey Brown Campground** [SANTA BARBARA]; **Davey Brown Creek** [SANTA BARBARA]; **Davy Brown Canyon**, under **Fir Canyon** [SANTA BARBARA].

Brown Canyon [MONTEREY]: *canyon,* drained by a stream that flows 8 miles to Pine Creek (3) 5 miles north-northeast of San Ardo (lat. 36°05'30" N, long. 120°53'05" W; near E line sec. 21, T 21 S, R 10 E). Named on Monarch Peak (1967) and Pancho Rico Valley (1967) 7.5' quadrangles. The name is for the Brown family, early residents in the neighborhood (Clark, 1991, p. 52-53).

Brown Canyon [SAN LUIS OBISPO]: *canyon,* drained by a stream that flows 4.5 miles to Cuyama River 5 miles south of Branch Mountain (lat. 35°06'45" N, long. 120°05'40" W; sec. 30, T 32 S, R 18 E). Named on Branch Mountain (1967) and Miranda Pine Mountain (1967) 7.5' quadrangles. East Fork branches east 1.5 miles upstream from the mouth of the main canyon; it is 3.25 miles long and is named on Branch Mountain (1967) 7.5' quadrangle.

Brown Creek: see **Browns Creek** [SANTA CRUZ].

Brown Mountain [SAN LUIS OBISPO]: *peak,* nearly 5 miles south-southwest of Branch Mountain (lat. 35°07'25" N, long. 120°07'15" W). Altitude 2514 feet. Named on Miranda Pine Mountain (1967) 7.5' quadrangle.

Browns Canyon [SAN LUIS OBISPO]: *canyon,* 1.5 miles long, 9.5 miles northwest of Midway Peak on San Luis Obispo-Kern County line (lat. 35°16' N, long. 119°43' W; at N line sec. 4, T 31 S, R 21 E). Named on Reward (1951) 7.5' quadrangle.

Browns Creek [SANTA CRUZ]: *stream,* flows 4.5 miles to Corralitos Creek 0.5 mile north-northeast of Corralitos (lat. 36°59'40" N, long. 121°48'05" W). Named on Loma Prieta (1955) 7.5' quadrangle. Called Brown Creek on Watsonville West (1954) 7.5' quadrangle. The name is for Isaiah Brown, who settled in the neighborhood by 1862 (Clark, 1986, p. 48).

Brown's Creek: see **Branciforte Creek** [SANTA CRUZ].

Browns Creek: see **West Browns Creek**, under **Carbonera Creek** [SANTA CRUZ].

Browns Valley [SAN BENITO]: *valley,* 4 miles northwest of Cherry Peak along a branch of Los Muertos Creek (lat. 36°43'55" N, long. 121°11'30" W). Named on Cherry Peak (1968) 7.5' quadrangle. Henderson Brown owned land in the valley (Elliott and Moore, p. 153).

Browns Valley [SANTA CRUZ]: *valley,* 1 mile north-northeast of Corralitos (lat. 37°00'15" N, long. 121°47'45" W); the valley is drained by Browns Creek. Named on Loma Prieta (1955) and Watsonville West (1954) 7.5' quadrangles.

Brubaker Canyon [SANTA BARBARA]: *canyon,* drained by a stream that flows 1.5 miles to Ventura County 16 miles southeast of the village of Cuyama (lat. 34°44'45" N, long. 119°26'35" W). Named on Rancho Nuevo Creek (1943) 7.5' quadrangle.

Bruce Fork: see **Carmel River** [MONTEREY].

Bruce Spring [SAN LUIS OBISPO]: *spring,* 2.5 miles south-southeast of Cholame (lat. 35°41'20" N, long. 120°16'50" W; near SW cor. sec. 5, T 26 S, R 16 E). Named on Cholame (1961) 7.5' quadrangle.

Brush Lagoon [SANTA CRUZ]: *lake,* 300 feet long, 3 miles southeast of Laurel (lat. 37°04'50" N, long. 121°55'55" W). Named on Los Gatos (1919) 15' quadrangle. Called Amaya Lagoon on a map of 1881 (Clark, 1986, p. 49).

Brush Peak [SANTA BARBARA]: *ridge,* east-northeast-trending, 0.5 mile long, 2 miles west of San Marcos Pass (lat. 34°30'30" N, long. 119°51'25" W; on N line sec. 19, T 5 N, R 28 E). Named on San Marcos Pass (1959) 7.5' quadrangle.

Bryan Canyon [MONTEREY]: *canyon,* drained by a stream that flows 4 miles to Pine Creek (3) nearly 7 miles north-northeast of San Ardo (lat. 36°06'50" N, long. 120°52'25" W; sec. 10, T 21 S, R 10 E). Named on Monarch Peak (1967) and Pancho Rico Valley (1967) 7.5' quadrangles.

Bryant Canyon [MONTEREY]: *canyon,* drained by a stream that flows nearly

5 miles to lowlands 2 miles northeast of Soledad (lat. 36°26'45" N, long. 121°17'55" W; sec. 15, T 17 S, R 6 E). Named on Soledad (1955) 7.5' quadrangle.

Bryson [MONTEREY]: *settlement*, 12 miles south-southeast of Jolon (lat. 35°48'30" N, long. 121°05'15" W; near S line sec. 27, T 24 S, R 8 E). Named on Bryson (1949) 7.5' quadrangle. Postal authorities established Bryson post office in 1887, moved it 1 mile southwest in 1889, moved it 1.5 miles south in 1898, moved it 1 mile northwest in 1899, moved it 1.5 mile east in 1905, moved it 1.25 miles west in 1906, and discontinued it in 1937 (Salley, p. 28). The name is for an early settler who had a store at the site; the place first was called Sapaque (Clark, 1991, p. 54). Postal authorities established Gem post office 3 miles east of Bryson (sec. 25, T 24 S, R 8 E) in 1894 and discontinued it in 1899—the name was for the postmaster's wife (Salley, p. 83).

Buchon: see **Mount Buchon**, under **Irish Hills** [SAN LUIS OBISPO]; **Point Buchon** [SAN LUIS OBISPO].

Buchon Range: see **Irish Hills** [SAN LUIS OBISPO].

Buck Cove Spring [SANTA BARBARA]: *spring*, 6 miles west of Miranda Pine Mountain (lat. 35°02'10" N, long. 120°08'20" W). Named on Chimney Canyon (1967) 7.5' quadrangle.

Buck Creek [MONTEREY]: *stream*, flows about 2 miles to the sea 10 miles southeast of Partington Point (lat. 36°08'05" N, long. 121° 38'55" W; sec. 5, T 21 S, R 3 E). Named on Partington Ridge (1956) 7.5' quadrangle.

Buckeye Camp [SAN LUIS OBISPO]: *locality*, 16 miles north-northeast of the town of Nipomo (lat. 35°14'50" N, long. 120°20'40" W; sec. 11, T 31 S, R 15 E). Named on Caldwell Mesa (1967) 7.5' quadrangle. The name is from a lone buckeye tree at the place (Clark, 1991, p. 55).

Buckeye Canyon [MONTEREY]: *canyon*, drained by a stream that flows 3.25 miles to Carmel Valley (1) 7 miles east of the mouth of the Carmel River (lat. 36°31'20" N, long. 121°48'20" W). Named on Seaside (1947) 7.5' quadrangle.

Buckeye Hill [MONTEREY]: *peak*, 3 miles east-northeast of Jamesburg (lat. 36°23'20" N, long. 121°32'20" W; on W line sec. 3, T 18 S, R 4 E). Altitude 2541 feet. Named on Rana Creek (1956) 7.5' quadrangle.

Buckeye Ridge [MONTEREY]: *ridge*, west-trending, 3.5 miles long, 5.5 miles east of the town of Carmel Valley (lat. 36°28'30" N, long. 121°38' W). Named on Carmel Valley (1956) and Rana Creek (1956) 7.5' quadrangles.

Buckeye Spring [MONTEREY]:

(1) *spring*, 4.25 miles west-northwest of Charley Mountain (lat. 36° 09'45" N, long. 120°44'15" W). Named on Priest Valley (1969) 7.5' quadrangle.

(2) *spring*, 12 miles east-northeast of San Ardo (lat. 36°03'15" N, long. 120°41'20" W; sec. 32, T 21 S, R 12 E). Named on Slack Canyon (1969) 7.5' quadrangle.

(3) *spring*, 6 miles southeast of Cape San Martin (lat. 35°50'25" N, long. 121°22'35" W; near S line sec. 13, T 24 S, R 5 E). Named on Cape San Martin (1921) 15' quadrangle.

Buckhorn Canyon [SAN LUIS OBISPO]: *canyon*, 2.5 miles long, opens into the canyon of San Juan Creek 2.25 miles west-southwest of Freeborn Mountain (lat. 35°16'20" N, long. 120°05'30" W; sec. 31, T 30 S, R 18 E). Named on Branch Mountain (1967) and California Valley (1966) 7.5' quadrangles. Rogers Creek drains the canyon.

Buckhorn Canyon [SANTA BARBARA]: *canyon*, drained by a stream that flows 6 miles to Cuyama River 10 miles west of Miranda Pine Mountain (lat. 35°01'20" N, long. 120°12'35" W); the canyon is west of Buckhorn ridge. Named on Chimney Canyon (1967) and Tepusquet Canyon (1964) 7.5' quadrangles.

Buckhorn Creek [SANTA BARBARA]: *stream*, flows 5 miles to Indian Creek 4 miles east-southeast of Little Pine Mountain (lat. 34°34'40" N, long. 119°40'10" W). Named on Little Pine Mountain (1964) 7.5' quadrangle.

Buckhorn Ridge [SANTA BARBARA]: *ridge*, west-northwest-trending, 6 miles long, 6.5 miles north-northeast of Tepusquet Peak (lat. 35°00' N, long. 120°09'10" W). Named on Chimney Canyon (1967), Manzanita Mountain (1964), and Tepusquet Canyon (1964) 7.5' quadrangles.

Buck Opening Spring [SANTA BARBARA]: *spring*, 1.25 miles east of McPherson Peak (lat. 34°53'25" N, long. 119°47'20" W). Named on Peak Mountain (1964) 7.5' quadrangle.

Buck Peak [SAN BENITO]: *peak*, 4.25 miles south-southwest of Panoche (lat. 36°32'40" N, long. 120°52'20" W; near NW cor. sec. 15, T 16 S, R 10 E). Altitude 3535 feet. Named on Panoche (1969) 7.5' quadrangle.

Buck Ridge [SAN BENITO]: *ridge*, northwest-trending, 7.5 miles long, 5 miles north of Bitterwater (lat. 36°27'15" N, long. 121°00'45" W). Named on Rock Spring Peak (1969) and Topo Valley (1969) 7.5' quadrangles.

Buckskin Flat Camp [MONTEREY]: *locality*, 2 miles east-southeast of Uncle Sam Mountain along Carmel River (lat. 36°19'55" N, long. 121°40'20" W; sec. 29, T 18 S, R 3 E). Named on Ventana Cones (1956) 7.5' quadrangle.

Bucks Peak [SAN BENITO]: *ridge*, northwest-trending, 0.5 mile long, 11.5 miles east-northeast of Bitterwater (lat. 36°27'30" N, long. 120°49'15" W; near SW cor. sec. 7, T 17 S, R 11 E). Named on Hernandez Reservoir (1969) 7.5' quadrangle.

Bucks Peak Spring [SAN BENITO]: *spring*, 11 miles east-northeast of Bitterwater (lat. 36°27'15" N, long. 120°49'30" W; near NE cor. sec. 13, T 17 S, R 10 E); the spring is on the southwest side of Bucks Peak. Named on Hernandez Reservoir (1969) 7.5' quadrangle.

Buck Spring [SAN BENITO]: *spring*, nearly 5 miles west-southwest of Panoche (lat. 36°34'20" N, long. 120°54'45" W; near NE cor. sec. 6, T 16 S, R 10 E). Named on Llanada (1969) 7.5' quadrangle.

Buck Spring [SAN LUIS OBISPO]: *spring*, nearly 3 miles south-southwest of Branch Mountain (lat. 35°08'50" N, long. 120°06'15" W). Named on Branch Mountain (1967) 7.5' quadrangle.

Budan Spring: see **Ontario Hot Springs** [SAN LUIS OBISPO].

Bud Canyon [SAN LUIS OBISPO]: *canyon*, drained by a stream that flows 7 miles to McMillan Canyon 2.25 miles northwest of Shandon (lat. 35°40'25" N, long. 120°24'25" W; near SW cor. sec. 7, T 26 S, R 15 E). Named on Cholame Valley (1961) and Shandon (1961) 7.5' quadrangles. Called Budd Canyon on Cholame (1917) 30' quadrangle, but United States Board on Geographic Names (1963b, p. 13) rejected the names "Budd Canyon" and "McMillan Canyon" for the feature.

Budd Canyon: see **Bud Canyon** [SAN LUIS OBISPO].

Buell: see **Buellton** [SANTA BARBARA].

Buell Reservoir [SANTA BARBARA]: *lake*, 650 feet long, 4.25 miles northwest of Carpinteria (lat. 34°26'40" N, long. 119°34'05" W). Named on Carpinteria (1952) 7.5' quadrangle.

Buellton [SANTA BARBARA]: *town*, 27 miles south-southeast of Santa Maria along Santa Ynez River (lat. 34°36'50" N, long. 120° 11'35" W); the town is on San Carlos de Jonata grant. Named on Solvang (1959) 7.5' quadrangle. Postal authorities established Buell post office in 1897, discontinued it in 1900, and reestablished it in 1920 with the name "Buellton" (Salley, p. 29). The name is from Rufus Thompson Buell and his brother Alonzo Buell, who bought San Carlos de Jonata grant in 1867 (Rife, p. 90).

Buenaventura River: see **Salinas River** [MONTEREY-SAN LUIS OBISPO].

Buena Vista [MONTEREY]:

(1) *land grant*, 6 miles south-southeast of Salinas. Named on Chualar (1947), Salinas (1947), and Spreckels (1947) 7.5' quadrangles. Jose Maria Soberanes and Joaquin Castro held the land in 1795; Santiago and Jose Mariano Estrada received 2 leagues in 1822-1823, and Mariano Malarin claimed 7726 acres patented in 1869 (Cowan, p. 20). According to Perez (p. 56), Jose S. Estrada was the grantee in 1822, and the patentee in 1869.

(2) *locality*, 8 miles south-southeast of Salinas along Pajaro Valley Consolidated Railroad (lat. 36°34'35" N, long. 121°35'10" W); the place is on Buena Vista grant. Named on Salinas (1912) 15' quadrangle. Postal authorities established Buena Vista post office for a brief time in 1959 (Salley, p. 29). California Mining Bureau's (1917b) map shows a place called Agenda along the railroad between Buena Vista (2) and Spreckels; postal authorities established Agenda post office in 1896 and discontinued it in 1907 (Frickstad, p. 106).

Buena Vista: see **San Vicente Creek** [SANTA CRUZ].

Bull Canyon [MONTEREY]:

(1) *canyon*, 5 miles long; the lower is part drained by a stream that enters Sweetwater Canyon 4.5 miles east-northeast of King City (lat. 36°14' N, long. 121°03' W; sec. 36, T 19 S, R 8 E). Named on Lonoak (1969), Nattrass Valley (1967), and San Lucas (1949) 7.5' quadrangles. A tributary to San Lorenzo Creek drains the upper part of the feature.

(2) *canyon*, drained by a stream that flows 2 miles to Nacimiento River 11 miles south-southeast of Jolon (lat. 35°48'45" N, long. 121°07'55" W; sec. 29, T 24 S, R 8 E). Named on Burnett Peak (1949) 7.5' quadrangle.

Bull Creek [SANTA CRUZ]: *stream*, flows 2 miles to San Lorenzo River 5.5 miles south-southeast of the town of Boulder Creek at Felton (lat. 37°03'10" N, long. 122°04'15"W). Named on Felton (1955) 7.5' quadrangle. The name commemorates Thomas Bull, who was in the neighborhood in the 1860's (Clark, 1986, p. 50).

Bull Ridge [SANTA BARBARA]: *ridge*, north-trending, 2.5 miles long, 2.25 miles north-northeast of Salisbury Potrero (lat. 34°51'15" N, long. 119°41'25" W). Named on Salisbury Potrero (1964) 7.5' quadrangle.

Burned Mountain [MONTEREY]: *peak*, 5.5 miles north of Jamesburg (lat. 36°27'05" N, long. 121°35'30" W). Altitude 2846 feet. Named on Rana Creek (1956) 7.5' quadrangle.

Burnett Camp [SAN LUIS OBISPO]: *locality*, 6.5 miles north of the village of San Simeon (lat. 35°44'25" N, long. 121°11'40" W); the place is along Burnett Creek. Named on San Simeon (1958) 7.5' quadrangle.

Burnett Creek [SAN LUIS OBISPO]: *stream*, flows 7.5 miles to join Marmolejo Creek and form Arroyo de la Cruz 4 miles north-northeast of the village of San Simeon (lat. 35°41'55" N, long. 121°10'15" W); the stream heads at Burnett Peak. Named on Burnett Peak (1949) and San Simeon (1958) 7.5' quadrangles. West Fork enters from the northwest 4 miles upstream from the mouth of the main creek; it is 3.25 miles long and is named on Burnett Peak (1949) and San Simeon (1958) 7.5' quadrangles.

Burnett Creek: see **Little Burnett Creek** [SAN LUIS OBISPO].

Burnett Peak [SAN LUIS OBISPO]: *peak*, 8 miles north of the village of San Simeon (lat. 35°45'25" N, long. 121°09'35" W; near E line sec. 13, T 25 S, R 7 E). Named on Burnett Peak (1949) 7.5' quadrangle.

Burns Creek [MONTEREY]: *stream*, flows nearly 1 mile to the sea 3.5 miles southeast of Partington Point (lat. 36°08'30" N, long. 121°39'15" W; at S line sec. 32, T 20 S, R 3 E). Named on Partington Ridge (1956) 7.5' quadrangle. The name commemorates John B. Burns, who settled in the neighborhood in the 1860's (Clark, 1991, p. 57).

Burns Creek [SANTA CRUZ]: *stream*, flows 2.5 miles to join Laurel Creek and form West Branch Soquel Creek at Laurel (lat. 37°07'10" N, long. 121°57'35" W). Named on Laurel (1955) and Los Gatos (1953) 7.5' quadrangles.

Burrell Creek: see **Laurel Creek** [SANTA CRUZ].

Burrito Creek [SAN LUIS OBISPO]: *stream*, flows 2 miles to Rinconada Creek 3.5 miles northeast of Lopez Mountain (lat. 35°20'15" N, long. 120°31'55" W). Named on Lopez Mountain (1965) 7.5' quadrangle.

Burro Canyon [SANTA BARBARA]: *canyon*, drained by a stream that flows 3 miles to Sisquoc River 3.25 miles west-northwest of Bald Mountain (1) (lat. 34°49'40" N, long. 119°59'25" W). Named on Bald Mountain (1964) 7.5' quadrangle.

Burro Mountain [MONTEREY]: *peak*, 11 miles east of Cape San Martin (lat. 35°52'15" N, long. 121°16'20" W; sec. 1, T 24 S, R 6 E). Altitude 2827 feet. Named on Burro Mountain (1949) 7.5' quadrangle.

Burros Creek: see **Little Burros Creek** [MONTEREY].

Burton Mesa [SANTA BARBARA]: *area*, 4.5 miles north-northeast of Surf (lat. 34°44'15" N, long. 120°34'30" W); the place is on Jesus Maria grant, for which Luis T. Burton was a claimant. Named on Casmalia (1959) and Surf (1959) 7.5' quadrangles.

Burton Mound: see **Mission Creek** [SANTA BARBARA].

Burton Mount Sulphur Springs: see **Mission Creek** [SANTA BARBARA].

Bush Gulch [SANTA CRUZ]: *canyon*, drained by a stream that flows 1.25 miles to the sea 5.25 miles east of Soquel Point (lat. 36°57'05" N, long. 121°52'50" W). Named on Soquel (1954) and Watsonville West (1954) 7.5' quadrangles. The name commemorates Conrad Bush, who bought land in the canyon in 1866 (Clark, 1986, p. 52).

Butterfly Canyon [SAN BENITO]: *canyon*, drained by a stream that flows nearly 2 miles to Johnson Canyon 8.5 miles northeast of Bitterwater (lat. 36°27'40" N, long. 120°52'55" W; sec. 9, T 17 S, R 10 E). Named on Rock Spring Peak (1969) 7.5' quadrangle.

Buttle Canyon [MONTEREY]: *canyon*, drained by a stream that flows nearly 2 miles to Hames Valley 3.5 miles west-southwest of Bradley (lat. 35°51'05" N, long. 120°51'55" W; sec. 11, T 24 S, R 10 E). Named on Bradley (1949) and Tierra Redonda Mountain (1949) 7.5' quadrangles. Members of the Buttle family owned land at the place (Clark, 1991, p. 58).

Buzzard Canyon [MONTEREY]: *canyon*, drained by a stream that flows 4.25 miles to Big Sandy Creek 13 miles northeast of Bradley (lat. 35°59'35" N, long. 120°36'20" W; sec. 30, T 22 S, R 13 E). Named on Smith Mountain (1969) 7.5' quadrangle.

Buzzard Lagoon [SANTA CRUZ]: *lake*, 175 feet long, 4.25 miles north-northwest of Corralitos (lat. 37°02'50" N, long. 121°50' W; sec. 23, T 10 S, R 1 E). Named on Loma Prieta (1955) 7.5' quadrangle.

Byles Canyon [SAN BENITO]: *canyon*, drained by a stream that flows 4 miles to Hernandez Valley 10.5 miles east of Bitterwater (lat. 36°22'10" N, long. 120°47'30" W; near S line sec. 8, T 18 S, R 11 E). Named on Hepsedam Peak (1969) and Hernandez Reservoir (1969) 7.5' quadrangles.

Bythenia Springs: see **Veronica Springs** [SANTA BARBARA].

- C -

Caballada Creek [SAN LUIS OBISPO]: *stream*, flows 1.25 miles to Little Burnett Creek 9 miles northeast of the village of San Simeon (lat. 35°44'40" N, long. 121°05'40" W; sec. 22, T 25 S, R 8 E). Named on Bryson (1949) and Pebblestone Shut-in (1959) 7.5' quadrangles.

Cabeza de Milligan: see **Mulligan Hill** [MONTEREY].

Cabezo Prieto [MONTEREY]: *ridge*, west-northwest-trending, 1 mile long, 7 miles east-southeast of Point Sur (lat. 36°17'10" N, long. 121°46'55" W; near N line sec. 18, T 19 S, R 2 E). Named on Big Sur (1956) 7.5' quadrangle.

Cable Corral Spring [SAN LUIS OBISPO]: *spring*, nearly 7 miles west-southwest of Branch Mountain along Alamo Creek (2) (lat. 35°08'20" N, long. 120°11'10" W). Named on Los Machos Hills (1967) 7.5' quadrangle.

Cabo de Galera: see **Point Conception** [SANTA BARBARA].

Cabo de Nieve: see **Cypress Point** [MONTEREY].

Cabrillo: see **Point Cabrillo**, under **Mussel Point** [MONTEREY].

Cachagua Creek [MONTEREY]: *stream*, formed by the confluence of Finch Creek and James Creek, flows 4.5 miles to Carmel River 7 miles southeast of the town of Carmel Valley (lat. 36°24'05" N, long. 121°39'30" W; near S line sec. 32, T 17 S, R 3 E). Named on Carmel Valley (1956) and Rana Creek (1956) 7.5' quadrangles. On Jamesburg (1921) 15' quadrangle, the name "Cachagua Creek" applies to present Finch Creek.

Cache Creek: see **Coche Creek** [SANTA BARBARA].

Cachuma: see **Cachuma Village** [SANTA BARBARA].

Cachuma Bay [SANTA BARBARA]: *embayment*, 5 miles north-northeast of Santa Ynez Peak (lat. 34°35'40" N, long. 119°56'30" W); the feature is along the north side of Lake Cachuma at the mouth of Cachuma Creek. Named on Lake Cachuma (1959) 7.5' quadrangle.

Cachuma Camp [SANTA BARBARA]: *locality*, 5 miles southeast of Figueroa Mountain (lat. 34°41'50" N, long. 119°54'45" W); the place is along Cachuma Creek. Named on Figueroa Mountain (1959) 7.5' quadrangle.

Cachuma Cañon: see **Cachuma Creek** [SANTA BARBARA].

Cachuma Creek [SANTA BARBARA]: *stream*, flows 9.5 miles to Lake Cachuma 6 miles north-northeast of Santa Ynez Peak (lat. 34°36'20" N, long. 119°56'10" W). Named on Figueroa Mountain (1959) and Lake Cachuma (1959) 7.5' quadrangles. Irelan (p. 537) referred to Cuchamma River, and Fairbanks (1894, p. 504) described Cachuma Cañon. The name apparently is of Indian origin (Gudde, 1949, p. 48).

Cachuma Lake: see **Lake Cachuma** [SANTA BARBARA].

Cachuma Mountain [SANTA BARBARA]: *peak*, 5 miles east-southeast of Figueroa Mountain (lat. 34°43'35" N, long. 119°54' W; sec. 35, T 8 N, R 29 W). Altitude 4696 feet. Named on Figueroa Mountain (1959) 7.5' quadrangle.

Cachuma Point [SANTA BARBARA]: *promontory*, 4.5 miles north-northeast of Santa Ynez Peak (lat. 34°35'15" N, long. 119°56'55" W); the feature is on the north side of Lake Cachuma at the mouth of Cachuma Bay. Named on Lake Cachuma (1959) 7.5' quadrangle.

Cachuma Reservoir: see **Lake Cachuma** [SANTA BARBARA].

Cachuma Village [SANTA BARBARA]: *locality*, 4 miles north of Santa Ynez Peak (lat. 34°35'10" N, long. 119°59'20" W); the place is just below the dam that forms Lake Cachuma. Named on Lake Cachuma (1959) 7.5' quadrangle. United States Board on Geographic Names (1962a, p. 6) rejected the name "Cachuma" for the place.

Cahoon Spring [MONTEREY]: *spring*, about 4 miles south-southeast of Jamesburg (lat. 36°19'40" N, long. 121°33'25" W; near SE cor. sec. 29, T 18 S, R 4 E). Named on Chews Ridge (1956) 7.5' quadrangle.

Calabazal Creek [SANTA BARBARA]: *stream*, flows 4.25 miles to Santa Ynez River 3 miles southeast of Santa Ynez (lat. 34°35'20" N, long. 120°02'20" W). Named on Santa Ynez (1959) 7.5' quadrangle. Called San Lucas Creek on Lompoc (1905) 30' quadrangle, but United States Board on Geographic Names (1961b, p. 9) rejected this name for the stream.

Calaboose Creek [MONTEREY]: *stream*, flows nearly 5 miles to Piney Creek 13 miles southwest of Soledad (lat. 36°17'45" N, long. 121°29'35" W; near E line sec. 11, T 19 S, R 4 E). Named on Chews Ridge (1956) and Sycamore Flat (1956) 7.5' quadrangles.

Caldwell Canyon [MONTEREY]: *canyon*, drained by a stream that flows 3.25 miles to Chualar Canyon 9 miles north-northeast of Gonzales (lat. 36°37'20" N, long. 121°22'05" W; sec. 13, T 15 S, R 5 E). Named on Mount Harlan (1968) and Paicines (1968) 7.5' quadrangles.

Caldwell Gulch [SANTA CRUZ]: *canyon*, drained by a stream that flows 0.5 mile to Hester Creek 3 miles south-southeast of Laurel (lat. 37°04'35" N, long. 121°56'20" W). Named on Laurel (1955) 7.5' quadrangle.

Caldwell Mesa [SAN LUIS OBISPO]: *area*, 16 miles northeast of the town of Nipomo (lat. 35°13'20" N, long. 120°18' W). Named on Caldwell Mesa (1967) 7.5' quadrangle.

Caldwell Mountain [SAN LUIS OBISPO]: *peak*, 12 miles northeast of the town of Nipomo (lat. 35°10'25" N, long. 120°20' W; sec. 2, T 32 S, R 15 E). Altitude 1812 feet. Named on Caldwell Mesa (1967) 7.5' quadrangle.

Calera Canyon [MONTEREY]: *canyon*, 6 miles long, on the upper reaches of El Toro Creek above the confluence with Watson Creek 9.5 miles south-southwest of Salinas (lat. 36°33' N, long. 121°43'55" W). Named on Spreckels (1947) 7.5' quadrangle.

Calf Canyon [SAN LUIS OBISPO]: *canyon*, drained by a stream that flows nearly 4 miles to Salinas River 3 miles northeast of Santa Margarita (lat. 35°25'15" N, long. 120°34'10" W; sec. 10, T 29 S, R 13 E). Named on Santa Margarita (1965) 7.5' quadrangle.

Caliente Canyon: see **Little Caliente Canyon** [SANTA BARBARA].

Caliente Mountain [SAN LUIS OBISPO]: *peak*, 25 miles south-southeast of Simmler (lat. 35°02'10" N, long. 119°45'35" W; sec. 16, T 11 N, R 27 W); the peak is in Caliente Range. Altitude 5106 feet. Named on Caliente Mountain (1959) 7.5' quadrangle. According to Gudde (1949, p. 50), the name "Caliente" comes from a hot spring located south of the peak in Cuyama Valley—*caliente* means "hot" in Spanish.

Caliente Range [SAN LUIS OBISPO]: *range*, between Carrizo Plain and Cuyama Valley. Named on Caliente Mountain (1959), Chimineas Ranch (1959), Cuyama (1964), Elkhorn Hills (1954), Painted Rock (1959), Taylor Canyon (1959), and Wells Ranch (1954) 7.5' quadrangles.

Caliente Spring: see **Little Caliente Spring** [SANTA BARBARA].

California Flats [MONTEREY]: *valley*, 6 miles southeast of Parkfield (lat. 35°50'45" N, long. 120°20'45" W). Named on Cholame Valley (1961) 7.5' quadrangle.

California Flats Canyon [MONTEREY]: *canyon*, drained by a stream that flows nearly 2 miles to California Flats 6 miles southeast of Parkfield (lat. 35°50'55" N, long. 120°20'55" W). Named on Cholame Valley (1961) 7.5' quadrangle.

California Valley [SAN LUIS OBISPO]: *settlement*, 3.5 miles northeast of Freeborn Mountain in Carrizo Plain (lat. 35°19'10" N, long. 120°00'20" W; near NE cor. sec. 14, T 30 S, R 18 E). Named on California Valley (1966) 7.5' quadrangle. Postal authorities established California Valley post office in 1963 and discontinued it in 1974 (Salley, p. 32). Development of the place began in 1960 (Lee and others, p. 30).

Callender [SAN LUIS OBISPO]: *locality*, nearly 5 miles south of the town of Arroyo Grande along Southern Pacific Railroad (lat. 35° 03'10" N, long. 120°35'45" W). Named on Oceano (1965) 7.5' quadrangle.

Call Mountains [SAN BENITO]: *ridge*, west-northwest- to north-northwest-trending, 5 miles long, 4 miles west of Panoche Pass (lat. 36°37'30" N, long. 121°05' W). Named on Panoche Pass (1968) and San Benito (1968) 7.5' quadrangles.

Calpaco: see **Port Watsonville** [SANTA CRUZ].

Camatta Canyon [SAN LUIS OBISPO]: *canyon*, drained by Camatta Creek, which flows 17 miles to lowlands 4.5 miles south-southeast of Shandon (lat. 35°35'50" N, long. 120°20'20" W; sec. 10, T 27 S, R 15 E). Named on Camatta Canyon (1961) and Camatta Ranch (1966) 7.5' quadrangles. Called Commatti Canyon on Cholame (1917) 30' quadrangle. Anderson and Martin (p. 49) referred to Cammatti Canyon. United States Board on Geographic Names (1962a, p. 7) rejected the names "Cammatta Canyon," "Cammatti Canyon," "Commatri Canyon," "Commatta Canyon," and "Commatti Canyon" for the feature. G.A. Waring (p. 77) listed Cameta Warm Spring, which from his description probably was in or near Camatta Canyon.

Camatta Creek [SAN LUIS OBISPO]: *stream* and *dry wash*, extends for 17 miles to lowlands 4.5 miles south-southeast of Shandon (lat. 35°35'50" N, long. 120°20'20" W; sec. 10, T 27 S, R 15 E); the feature drains Camatta Canyon. Named on Camatta Ranch (1966) 7.5' quadrangle. Called Cammatti Creek on Pozo (1922) 15' quadrangle. United States Board on Geographic Names (1962a, p. 7) rejected the names "Cammatta Creek," "Cammatti Creek," "Commatri Creek," "Commatta Creek," and "Commatti Creek" for the feature.

Cambria [SAN LUIS OBISPO]: *town*, 8.5 miles southeast of the village of San Simeon (lat. 35°33'50" N, long. 121°04'50" W). Named on Cambria (1959) 7.5' quadrangle. The place was settled in the 1860's and called Slabtown (Gudde, 1949, p. 52). Names proposed for the community included Rosaville, Santa Rosa, and San Simeon (Angel, 1883, p. 337). Postal authorities established San Simeon post office in 1864, discontinued it in 1865, reestablished it in 1867, and changed the name to Cambria in 1870 (Frickstad, p. 166). Although the townsfolk first agreed on the name "Santa Rosa" for their community—for the stream that runs by the town—postal authorities gave the name "San Simeon" to the post office there (Hamilton, p. 7). Finally the name was changed to Cambria, from the Latin name for Wales, because of the urgings of a single Welsh resident (Stewart, p. 73).

Cambria Pines [SAN LUIS OBISPO]: *district*, 7 miles southeast of San Simeon at the mouth of Santa Rosa Creek (lat. 35°34' N, long. 121°06'15" W). Named on San Simeon (1942) 15' quadrangle.

Cambria Rock [SAN LUIS OBISPO]: *rock*, 2.25 miles west of Cambria, and 2750 feet offshore (lat. 35°34'15" N, long. 121°07'20" W). Named on Cambria (1959) 7.5' quadrangle.

Camelback Hill [SANTA BARBARA]: *peak*, 4.5 miles southeast of Orcutt (lat. 34°48'55" N, long. 120°23'20" W). Named on Orcutt (1959) 7.5' quadrangle.

Camerus Valley Creek: see **Carneros Creek** [SANTA BARBARA].

Cameta Warm Spring: see **Camatta Canyon** [SAN LUIS OBISPO].

Cammatta Canyon: see **Camatta Canyon** [SAN LUIS OBISPO].

Cammatta Creek: see **Camatta Creek** [SAN LUIS OBISPO].

Cammatti Canyon: see **Camatta Canyon** [SAN LUIS OBISPO].

Cammatti Creek: see **Camatta Creek** [SAN LUIS OBISPO].

Campbell: see **Camp Campbell** [SANTA CRUZ].

Camp Ben Lomond [SANTA CRUZ]: *locality*, 4 miles southeast of Big Basin (lat. 37°07'50" N, long. 122°10'05" W); the place is on Ben Lomond Mountain. Named on Big Basin (1955) 7.5' quadrangle.

Camp Campbell [SANTA CRUZ]: *locality*, 4.5 miles east of Big Basin near San Lorenzo River (lat. 37°09'45" N, long. 122°08'10" W; sec. 12, T 9 S, R 3 W). Named on Big Basin (1955) 7.5' quadrangle. The place is a YMCA camp started in 1934 and named for George Campbell, a principal donor (Clark, 1986, p. 56).

Camp Capitola: see **Capitola** [SANTA CRUZ].

Camp Cawatre Campground [MONTEREY]: *locality*, 1.25 miles southwest of Arroyo Center (lat. 36°13'20" N, long. 121°29'15" W; sec. 1, T 20 S, R 4 E). Named on Junipero Serra (1961) 15' quadrangle. Junipero Serra (1930) 15' quadrangle has the name "Santa Lucia Ranger Sta." at the place. The name recalls Camp Cawatre, a Girl Scout facility that was abandoned in 1984; the word "Cawatre" was coined from the words "camp" (or "cabin"), "water," and "trees" (Clark, 1991, p. 66).

Camp Clayton Military Reservation: see **Fort Ord Military Reservation** [MONTEREY].

Camp Cooke Military Reservation: see **Vandenberg Air Force Base** [SANTA BARBARA].

Camp Creek [MONTEREY]: *stream*, flows 1.5 miles to Zigzag Creek 7 miles east-northeast of Partington Point (lat. 36°11'50" N, long. 121°34'35" W; sec. 18, T 20 S, R 4 E). Named on Tassajara Hot Springs (1956) 7.5' quadrangle.

Camp Drake [SANTA BARBARA]: *locality*, 2 miles northeast of Santa Ynez Peak (lat. 34°33'05" N, long. 119°57'20" W; at S line sec. 32, T 6 N, R 29 W). Named on Lake Cachuma (1959) 7.5' quadrangle.

Camp Evers [SANTA CRUZ]: *locality*, 7.5 miles southeast of the town of Boulder Creek (lat. 37°02'35" N, long. 122°01'25" W). Named on Felton (1955) 7.5' quadrangle. Postal authorities established Camp Evers post office in 1947 and discontinued it in 1951; the name "Evers" is for the proprietor of a store and lodging place (Salley, p. 34).

Camp Four: see **Camphora** [MONTEREY].

Camp Goodall: see **Palm Beach** [SANTA CRUZ].

Camp Hill [SAN LUIS OBISPO]: *peak*, at Pismo Beach 0.5 mile inland from the coast (lat. 35°38'35" N, long. 120°38'15" W). Named on Pismo Beach (1965) 7.5' quadrangle.

Camphora [MONTEREY]: *locality*, 3 miles northwest of Soledad along Southern Pacific Railroad (lat. 36°27'15" N, long. 121°22'15" W). Named on Palo Escrito Peak (1956) and Soledad (1955) 7.5' quadrangles. A railroad construction camp at the place in 1873 was called Camp Four; Mexican workers referred to the place as Camphora, and railroad officials adopted this name for their station there (Gudde, 1949, p. 53).

Camp Huffman [MONTEREY]: *locality*, 4.5 miles east of Seaside on Fort Ord Military Reservation (lat. 36°37'15" N, long. 121°46'15" W). Named on Seaside (1947) 7.5' quadrangle.

Camp Hunter Liggett Military Reservation: see **Hunter Liggett Military Reservation** [MONTEREY].

Camp Low: see **San Juan Bautista** [SAN BENITO].

Camp McCallum [MONTEREY]: *locality*, 7 miles east-southeast of Salinas (lat. 36°38'35" N, long. 121°32' W). Named on Natividad (1947) 7.5' quadrangle. Postal authorities established Camp McCallum post office in 1942 and discontinued it in 1961 (Salley, p. 35). The place began in 1942 as housing for a project sponsored by the federal government to produce rubber from guayule plants—the name was for Dr. William B. McCallum, a pioneer of guayule farming; farm workers lived at the site later (Clark, 1991, p. 67).

Camp McQuaide: see **San Andres** [SANTA CRUZ].

Camp Merriam: see **Camp San Luis Obispo** [SAN LUIS OBISPO].

Camp Nacimiento [MONTEREY]: *locality*, 9 miles north-northeast of Cape San Martin (lat. 35°59'50" N, long. 121°22'55" W; sec. 24, T 22 S, R 5 E); the place is along Nacimiento River. Named on Cape San Martin (1949) 7.5 quadrangle.

Camp Natoma [SAN LUIS OBISPO]: *locality*, 4 miles east-southeast of Lime Mountain (lat. 35°38'35" N, long. 120°56' W; sec. 30, T 26 S, R 10 E). Named on Lime Mountain (1948) 7.5' quadrangle.

Camp Number 5: see **Bridge Creek** [SANTA CRUZ].

Camp Number 4: see **Bridge Creek** [SANTA CRUZ].

Camp Number 1: see **Aptos Creek** [SANTA CRUZ].

Camp Number 3: see **Santa Rosalia Mountain** [SANTA CRUZ].

Camp Ord: see **Fort Ord Military Reservation** [MONTEREY].

Camp Ord Military Reservation: see **Fort Ord Military Reservation** [MONTEREY].

Camp Pacific [MONTEREY]: *locality*, on Fort Ord Military Reservation south of Main Garrison (lat. 36°38'55" N, long. 121°48'05" W). Named on Marina (1947) 7.5' quadrangle.

Camp Roberts: see **Camp Roberts Military Reservation** [MONTEREY-SAN LUIS OBISPO].

Camp Roberts Military Reservation [MONTEREY-SAN LUIS OBISPO]: *military installation*, on both sides of Salinas River on Monterey-San Luis Obispo County line. Named on Adelaida (1948), Bradley (1949), Paso Robles (1948), San Miguel (1948), and Valleton (1948) 7.5' quadrangles. On San Miguel (1947) 15' quadrangle, the barracks area near Salinas River has the name "Camp Roberts," and the barracks area east of the river has the name "East Garrison." The installation was established in 1940 and named for Corporal Harold W. Roberts, a World War I tank driver who received the Medal of Honor posthumously (Clark, 1991, p. 68).

Camp San Luis Obispo [SAN LUIS OBISPO]: *military installation*, 5.5 miles northwest of San Luis Obispo (lat. 35°19'30" N, long. 120°44'15" W). Named on San Luis Obispo (1965) 7.5' quadrangle. The area in which the camp sets is called Camp San Luis Obispo Military Reservation on Morro Bay South (1965) and San Luis Obispo (1965) 7.5' quadrangles, although it is called Camp San Luis Obispo on Atascadero (1965) 7.5' quadrangle. The place originally was called Camp Merriam, but it was renamed in 1940 (Lee and others, p. 33). Postal authorities established Camp San Luis Obispo post office in 1940, discontinued it in 1948, reestablished it in 1952, and discontinued it in 1957 (Salley, p. 35).

Camp San Luis Obispo Military Reservation: see **Camp San Luis Obispo** [SAN LUIS OBISPO].

Camp Stephani [MONTEREY]: *locality,* 1 mile southeast of the town of Carmel Valley along Carmel River (lat. 36°28'15" N, long. 121° 43' W). Named on Carmel Valley (1956) 7.5' quadrangle. The name commemorates Joseph Steffani, who settled at the site about 1888 and later subdivided part of his ranch for summer homes; the place also was called Eagle Camp (Clark, 1991, p. 68-69).

Camp Talaki [SAN LUIS OBISPO]: *locality,* 12 miles north of the town of Nipomo in Lopez Canyon (lat. 35°12'45" N, long. 120°28'50" W; sec. 21, T 31 S, R 14 E). Named on Tar Spring Ridge (1967) 7.5' quadrangle.

Camp Wasibo [SANTA CRUZ]: *locality,* 5.5 miles east of the town of Boulder Creek along Zayante Creek (lat. 37°07'15" N, long. 122°00'55" W; sec. 30, T 9 S, R 1 W). Named on Felton (1955) 7.5' quadrangle.

Camuesa Canyon: see **Camuesa Creek** [SANTA BARBARA].

Camuesa Creek [SANTA BARBARA]: *stream,* flows 6 miles to Gibraltar Reservoir 6.25 miles southeast of Little Pine Mountain (lat. 34°32' N, long. 119°39'50" W; sec. 12, T 5 N, R 27 W). Named on Little Pine Mountain (1964) 7.5' quadrangle. On Santa Ynez (1905) 30' quadrangle, the canyon of the stream has the name "Camuesa Canyon."

Camuesa Peak [SANTA BARBARA]: *peak,* 4.5 miles southeast of Little Pine Mountain (lat. 34°32'50" N, long. 119°41'25" W; near NE cor. sec. 3, T 5 N, R 27 W); the peak is south of Camuesa Creek. Altitude 3180 feet. Named on Little Pine Mountain (1964) 7.5' quadrangle.

Cañada Agua Vina: see **Cañada Agua Viva** [SANTA BARBARA].

Cañada Agua Viva [SANTA BARBARA]: *canyon,* drained by a stream that flows 2.5 miles to the sea 2.5 miles southwest of Tranquillon Mountain (lat. 34°33'25" N, long. 120°35'35" W). Named on Tranquillon Mountain (1959) 7.5' quadrangle. Called Canada Agua Vina on Guadalupe (1905) 30' quadrangle, but United States Board on Geographic Names (1962a, p. 7) rejected the forms "Canada Agua Vina," "Cañada Agua Vina," "Cañada Agua Viña," "Cañada Agua Vino," and "Cañada Aqua Vina" for the name.

Cañada Alcatraz [SANTA BARBARA]: *canyon,* drained by a stream that flows 1.25 miles to the sea 0.5 mile east of Gaviota (lat. 34°28'15" N, long. 120°12'15" W). Named on Gaviota (1953) 7.5' quadrangle.

Cañada Angosta: see **San Luis Obispo Creek** [SAN LUIS OBISPO].

Cañada Aqua Vina: see **Cañada Agua Viva** [SANTA BARBARA].

Cañada Arena [SANTA BARBARA]: *canyon,* drained by a stream that flows 2 miles to Cañada de los Coches 10.5 miles south of Tepusquet Peak (lat. 34°45'45" W, long. 120°13'35" W). Named on Foxen Canyon (1964) 7.5' quadrangle.

Cañada Arena: see **Cañada de los Coches** [SANTA BARBARA] (2).

Cañada Azul [SAN BENITO]: *canyon,* 2.5 miles long, along Cantua Creek 4 miles east-southeast of Idria near San Benito-Fresno County line (lat. 36°23'15" N, long. 120°36'20" W). Named on Ciervo Mountain (1969) 7.5' quadrangle.

Cañada Benito: see **San Benito River** [SAN BENITO].

Cañada Botella [SANTA BARBARA]: *canyon,* drained by a stream that flows 1.5 miles to Zaca Creek nearly 3 miles north of Buellton (lat. 34°39'15" N, long. 120°11' W). Named on Zaca Creek (1959) 7.5' quadrangle.

Cañada Cervada [SANTA BARBARA]: *canyon,* drained by a stream that flows 4.5 miles to the sea 4 miles southeast of Fraser Point on Santa Cruz Island (lat. 34°01'25" N, long. 119°52'35" W). Named on Santa Cruz Island A (1943) 7.5' quadrangle, which shows Christi ranch situated near the mouth of the canyon. Called Christy Cñ. on Bremner's (1932) map. Goodyear (1890, p. 156) stated that the name should have the form "Cañon de Cebada."

Cañada Coches Prietos: see **Coches Prietos Anchorage** [SANTA BARBARA].

Cañada Corral: see **Arlington Canyon** [SANTA BARBARA].

Cañada de Alegria [SANTA BARBARA]: *canyon,* drained by a stream that flows 3 miles to the sea 11.5 miles east of Point Conception (lat. 34°28'05" N, long. 120°16'15" W). Named on Sacate (1953) and Santa Rosa Hills (1959) 7.5' quadrangles. Called Alegria Canyon on Point Conception (1942) 15' quadrangle.

Cañada de Guillermo [SANTA BARBARA]: *canyon,* drained by a stream that flows 1.25 miles to the sea 3.5 miles east of Gaviota (lat. 34°28'25" N, long. 120°09'05" W). Named on Gaviota (1953) 7.5' quadrangle.

Cañada de Jolon: see **Jolon Valley** [MONTEREY].

Canada de la Brea: see **Cañada de las Panochas** [SANTA BARBARA].

Cañada de la Carpinteria [MONTEREY]: *land grant,* 12 miles north of Salinas. Named on Prunedale (1954) and San Juan Bautista (1955) 7.5' quadrangles. Joaquin Soto received 0.5 league in 1845 and his heirs claimed 2236 acres patented in 1873 (Cowan, p. 25). According to Perez (p. 58), the grant was made in 1835.

Cañada de la Cuarta [SANTA BARBARA]: *canyon,* drained by a stream that flows nearly 3 miles to the sea 10.5 miles east of Point Conception (lat. 34°28'10" N, long. 120°17'20" W). Named on Sacate (1953) and Santa Rosa Hills (1959) 7.5' quadrangles. Called Cuarta Canyon on Lompoc (1905) 30' quadrangle.

Cañada de la Destiladera [SANTA BARBARA]: *canyon,* drained by a stream that flows 1.5 miles to the sea 12 miles east of Gaviota (lat. 34°27'40" N, long. 120°00'25" W). Named on Tajiguas (1953) 7.5' quadrangle.

Cañada de la Gallina [SANTA BARBARA]: *canyon,* drained by a stream that flows 0.5 mile to the sea 4 miles east of Gaviota (lat. 34°28'25" N, long. 120°08'40" W). Named on Gaviota (1953) 7.5' quadrangle.

Cañada de la Gaviota [SANTA BARBARA]: *canyon,* drained by a stream that flows 6.5 miles to the sea 0.5 mile west of Gaviota (lat. 34°28'15" N, long. 120°13'30" W). Named on Gaviota (1953) and Solvang (1959) 7.5' quadrangles. Called Gaviota Canyon on Lompoc (1905) 30' quadrangle, but United States Board on Geographic Names (1978b, p. 4) rejected this name for the feature. Soldiers of the Portola expedition gave the name "Gaviota" to an Indian village at the mouth of the canyon in 1769, when they killed a seagull there—*gaviota* means "seagull" in Spanish (Wagner, H.R., p. 389). Parke (p. 16) referred to Gaviote creek.

Cañada del Agua [SANTA BARBARA]: *canyon,* drained by a stream that flows 2.25 miles to the sea 9 miles east of Point Conception (lat. 34°27'55" N, long. 120°18'50" W). Named on Sacate (1953) 7.5' quadrangle.

Cañada del Agua Amarga [SANTA BARBARA]: *canyon,* drained by a stream that flows 1.5 miles to Cañada de los Coches 10.5 miles south-southwest of Tepusquet Peak (lat. 34°45'55" N, long. 120° 13'50" W). Named on Foxen Canyon (1964) 7.5' quadrangle.

Cañada del Agua Caliente [SANTA BARBARA]: *canyon,* drained by a stream that flows 3.25 miles to the sea 13 miles east of Point Conception (lat. 34°28'05" N, long. 120°15'05" W). Named on Sacate (1953) and Santa Rosa Hills (1959) 7.5' quadrangles.

Cañada de la Huerta [SANTA BARBARA]: *canyon,* drained by a stream that flows 0.5 mile to the sea 4.5 miles east of Gaviota (lat. 34°28'25" N, long. 120°08'50" W). Named on Gaviota (1953) 7.5' quadrangle.

Cañada de la Laguna [SANTA BARBARA]: *canyon,* drained by a stream that flows 3.5 miles to lowlands nearly 2 miles west-northwest of Buellton (lat. 34°37'30" N, long. 120°13'20" W). Named on Zaca Creek (1959) 7.5' quadrangle.

Cañada del Alamo: see **Alamos Anchorage** [SANTA BARBARA].

Cañada de la Llegua [SANTA BARBARA]: *canyon,* drained by a stream that flows 2.25 miles to the sea nearly 6 miles east of Point Conception (lat. 34°27'25" N, long. 120°22'10" W). Named on Sacate (1953) 7.5' quadrangle.

Cañada de la Ordena [MONTEREY]: *canyon,* drained by a stream that flows 1.5 miles to Carmel Valley (1) 6 miles east of the mouth of Carmel River (lat. 36°32' N, long. 121°49'15" W). Named on Seaside (1947, photorevised 1968) 7.5' quadrangle.

Cañada de la Pila [SANTA BARBARA]: *canyon,* drained by a stream that flows 1.5 miles to the sea 5 miles east of Gaviota (lat. 34°28'20" N, long. 120°07'35" W). Named on Gaviota (1953) 7.5' quadrangle.

Cañada de la Posta [SANTA BARBARA]: *canyon,* drained by a stream that flows 2 miles to the sea 3.25 miles east of Gaviota (lat. 34°28'20" N, long. 120°09'35" W). Named on Gaviota (1953) 7.5' quadrangle.

Cañada de la Puente [SANTA BARBARA]: *canyon,* drained by a stream that flows 2 miles to San Antonio Creek (1) 7 miles northwest of Los Olivos (lat. 34°43'30" N, long. 120°12'55" W). Named on Zaca Creek (1959) 7.5' quadrangle. Called Cañada de la Puenta on Los Olivos (1943) 15' quadrangle.

Cañada de las Agujas [SANTA BARBARA]: *canyon,* drained by a stream that flows 2.5 miles to the sea 7.5 miles east of Point Conception (lat. 34°27'35" N, long. 120°20'20" W). Named on Sacate (1953) 7.5' quadrangle.

Cañada de la Salud: see **Waddell Creek** [SANTA CRUZ].

Cañada de las Calaveras [SANTA BARBARA]: *canyon,* drained by a stream that flows 2 miles to Los Alamos Valley at the town of Los Alamos (lat. 34°44'15" N, long. 120°16'40" W). Named on Los Alamos (1959) 7.5' quadrangle.

Cañada de las Cruces [SANTA BARBARA]: *canyon,* drained by a stream that flows 4 miles to Cañada de la Gaviota 7.5 miles south-southwest of Buellton at Las Cruces (lat. 34°30'35" N, long. 120° 13'35" W). Named on Solvang (1959) 7.5' quadrangle.

Cañada de la Segunda [MONTEREY]: *land grant,* east of Carmel By The Sea and north of Carmel River. Named on Monterey (1947) and Seaside (1947, photorevised 1968) 7.5' quadrangles. Lazaro Soto received 1 league in 1839; F.M. Haight claimed 4367 acres patented in 1859 (Cowan, p. 97).

Cañada de las Encinas [SANTA BARBARA]: *canyon,* drained by a stream that flows 2.5 miles to Santa Maria Valley nearly 4 miles southwest of Tepusquet Peak (lat. 34°51'55" N, long. 120°13'40" W). Named on Lompoc (1905) 30' quadrangle. The lower part of the canyon corresponds to present Kelly Canyon (2).

Cañada de las Flores [SANTA BARBARA]: *canyon,* drained by a stream that flows 3.5 miles to San Antonio Creek (1) 8 miles south-southwest of the village of Sisquoc (lat. 34°45'25" N, long. 120°21'20" W). Named on Sisquoc (1959) 7.5' quadrangle. Called Careaga Canyon on Lompoc (1905) 30' quadrangle, which has the name "Canada de las Flores" for present Careaga Canyon. United States Board on Geographic Names (1962a, p.

7) rejected the name "Careaga Canyon" for the feature, and rejected the form "Canada de las Flores" for the name.

Canada de las Llagas: see **Cañada del Capitan** [SANTA BARBARA].

Cañada de las Panochas [SANTA BARBARA]: *canyon,* drained by a stream that flows 2.25 miles to Cañada del Agua 9 miles east of Point Conception (lat. 34°27'55" N, long. 120°18'50" W). Named on Sacate (1953) 7.5' quadrangle. Called Canada de la Brea on Lompoc (1905) 30' quadrangle.

Cañada de las Zorrillas [SANTA BARBARA]: *canyon,* drained by a stream that flows nearly 1 mile to the sea 2 miles east of Gaviota (lat. 34°28'15" N, long. 120°10'40" W). Named on Gaviota (1953) 7.5' quadrangle.

Cañada de la Vina [SANTA BARBARA]: *canyon,* drained by a stream that flows 3 miles to lowlands 6.5 miles east-southeast of the city of Lompoc (lat. 34°36'15" N, long. 120°20'55" W). Named on Santa Rosa Hills (1959) 7.5' quadrangle.

Cañada del Barro [SANTA BARBARA]: *canyon,* drained by a stream that flows nearly 1 mile to the sea at Gaviota (lat. 34°28'15" N, long. 120°13'05" W). Named on Gaviota (1953) 7.5' quadrangle.

Cañada del Capitan [SANTA BARBARA]: *canyon,* drained by a stream that flows 5.5 miles to the sea 11 miles east of Gaviota (lat. 34°27'30" N, long. 120°01'15" W). Named on Lake Cachuma (1959) and Tajiguas (1953) 7.5' quadrangles. Called Canada de las Llagas on Lompoc (1905) 30' quadrangle, which has the name "Canada del Capitan" for present Cañada del Corral (1).

Cañada del Cementerio [SANTA BARBARA]:

(1) *canyon,* drained by a stream that flows nearly 2 miles to Cañada del Cojo 3.5 miles east-northeast of Point Conception (lat. 34°27'35" N, long. 120°24'45" W). Named on Point Conception (1953) 7.5' quadrangle.

(2) *canyon,* drained by a stream that flows 1.25 miles to the sea 0.5 mile east of Gaviota (lat. 34°28'15" N, long. 120°12'20" W). Named on Gaviota (1953) 7.5' quadrangle. Members of Anza's expedition saw an Indian burial ground at the place in 1776—*cementerio* means "graveyard" in Spanish (Bolton, p. 238).

Cañada del Chiclan [SANTA BARBARA]: *canyon,* drained by a stream that flows 1.25 miles to Arroyo San Augustin 6.5 miles east of Point Conception (lat. 34°27'50" N, long. 120°21'30" W). Named on Sacate (1953) 7.5' quadrangle.

Cañada del Chorro: see **El Chorro** [SAN LUIS OBISPO].

Cañada del Cojo [SANTA BARBARA]: *canyon,* drained by a stream that flows 2.5 miles to the sea 3.25 miles east of Point Conception (lat. 34°27'10" N, long. 120°24'55" W); the mouth of the canyon is east of Cojo Bay. Named on Point Conception (1953) 7.5' quadrangle. Members of the Portola expedition camped at the place in 1769 and called the Indian village there Rancheria del Cojo because the village chief was lame—*cojo* means "lame" or "lame man" in Spanish; A.M. Harrison of United States Coast Survey gave the name "Valley of the Coxo" to the feature in 1850 (Gudde, 1949, p. 73).

Cañada del Comasa [SANTA BARBARA]: *canyon,* drained by a stream that flows 7.5 miles to San Antonio Creek (1) 7.5 miles northwest of Los Olivos (lat. 34°43'40" N, long. 120°13'10" W). Named on Foxen Canyon (1964), Zaca Creek (1959), and Zaca Lake (1964) 7.5' quadrangles.

Cañada del Corral [SANTA BARBARA]:

(1) *canyon,* drained by a stream that flows 5.5 miles to the sea 10 miles east of Gaviota (lat. 34°27'45" N, long. 120°02'40" W). Named on Santa Ynez (1959) and Tajiguas (1953) 7.5' quadrangles. Called Canada del Capitan on Lompoc (1905) 30' quadrangle, where present Cañada del Venadito is called Canada del Corral.

(2) *land grant,* at Capitan; Cañada del Corral (1) is on the grant. Named on Dos Pueblos Canyon (1951), Santa Ynez (1959), and Tajiguas (1953) 7.5' quadrangles. Jose D. Ortega received 2 leagues in 1841 and claimed 8876 acres patented in 1866 (Cowan, p. 29).

Canada del Corral: see **Cañada del Venadito** [SANTA BARBARA].

Cañada del Coyote [SANTA BARBARA]: *canyon,* drained by a stream that flows 1.5 miles to the sea 10 miles east of Point Conception (lat. 34°28'10" N, long. 120°17'50" W). Named on Sacate (1953) 7.5' quadrangle. Called Sacate Canyon on Lompoc (1905) 30' quadrangle.

Cañada del Gato [SANTA BARBARA]: *canyon,* drained by a stream that flows nearly 2 miles to Barranca Honda 5 miles east of Point Conception at the coast (lat. 34°27'25" N, long. 120°22'55" W). Named on Point Conception (1953) 7.5' quadrangle. On Lompoc (1905) 30' quadrangle, the name applies to present Barranca Honda.

Cañada del Gato: see **Cat Canyon** [SANTA BARBARA].

Cañada del Jolloru [SANTA BARBARA]: *canyon,* drained by a stream that flows 3 miles to the sea 3.5 miles south-southeast of Tranquillon Mountain (lat. 34°32'10" N, long. 120°32'05" W). Named on Tranquillon Mountain (1959) 7.5' quadrangle. Called Canada El Jolloru on Guadalupe (1905) 30' quadrangle.

Cañada del Leon [SANTA BARBARA]: *canyon,* drained by a stream that flows 1 mile to the sea 1 mile east of Gaviota (lat. 34°28'15" N, long. 120°11'45" W). Named on Gaviota (1953) 7.5' quadrangle.

Cañada del Medio: see **Central Valley** [SANTA BARBARA].

Cañada del Molino [SANTA BARBARA]: *canyon,* drained by a stream that flows 2.5 miles to the sea nearly 3 miles east of Gaviota (lat. 34°28'10" N, long. 120°10'05" W). Named on Gaviota (1953) and Solvang (1959) 7.5' quadrangles. Called Cañada de Molino on Gaviota (1943) 15' quadrangle.

Cañada del Morida [SANTA BARBARA]: *canyon,* drained by a stream that flows 2.5 miles to the sea 2.5 miles south of Tranquillon Mountain (lat. 34°32'35" N, long. 120°33'20" W). Named on Tranquillon Mountain (1959) 7.5' quadrangle. Called Canada El Morida on Guadalupe (1905) 30' quadrangle.

Cañada de los Alisos [SANTA BARBARA]: *canyon,* drained by a stream that flows 6.25 miles to Los Alamos Valley 8.5 miles northwest of Los Olivos (lat. 34°44'20" N, long. 120°13'55" W). Named on Foxen Canyon (1964) and Zaca Creek (1959) 7.5' quadrangles.

Cañada de los Alisos: see **Clark Valley** [SAN LUIS OBISPO].

Cañada de los Coches [SANTA BARBARA]:

(1) *canyon,* drained by a stream that flows 3.5 miles to Cuyama River 8 miles east of Santa Maria (lat. 34°56'55" N, long. 120°17'35" W); the canyon heads near Los Coches Mountain. Named on Twitchell Dam (1959) 7.5' quadrangle.

(2) *canyon,* drained by a stream that flows 3.5 miles to Los Alamos Valley 8.5 miles northwest of Los Olivos (lat. 34°44'20" N, long. 120°13'55" W). Named on Foxen Canyon (1964) and Zaca Creek (1959) 7.5' quadrangles. United States Board on Geographic Names (1962a, p. 8) rejected the names "Cañada Arena," "Canada Arena," and "Canada de los Coches" for the feature, and pointed out that *Cañada de los Coches* reportedly is a Mexican provincial term meaning "Valley of the Hogs."

Cañada del Osito: see **Santa Rosa Creek** [SAN LUIS OBISPO].

Cañada de los Ladrones [SANTA BARBARA]: *canyon,* drained by a stream that flows 2 miles to the sea nearly 2 miles south-southwest of Tranquillon Mountain (lat. 34°33'10" N, long. 120°34'20" W). Named on Tranquillon Mountain (1959) 7.5' quadrangle.

Cañada de los Laureles: see **Los Laurelles** [MONTEREY] (2).

Cañada de Los Osos: see **Los Osos Valley** [SAN LUIS OBISPO].

Cañada de los Osos y Pecho y Islay [SAN LUIS OBISPO]: *land grant,* covers the west part of Los Osos Valley and the west coast of Irish Hills. Named on Morro Bay South (1965), Port San Luis (1965), and San Luis Obispo (1965) 7.5' quadrangles. Victor Linares and others received 11 leagues in 1842, 1843, and 1845; John Wilson claimed 32,430 acres patented in 1869 (Cowan, p. 55). According to Perez (p. 59), the grantees were James Scott and John Wilson in 1845.

Cañada de los Palos Blancos [SANTA BARBARA]: *canyon,* 4.5 miles long, opens into lowlands 3 miles west-northwest of Buellton (lat. 34°37'30" N, long. 120°14'35" W). Named on Los Alamos (1959) and Zaca Creek (1959) 7.5' quadrangles.

Cañada de los Pinos or College Rancho [SANTA BARBARA]: *land grant,* at and northeast of Santa Ynez. Named on Figueroa Mountain (1959), Lake Cachuma (1959), Los Olivos (1959), and Santa Ynez (1959) 7.5' quadrangles. The Catholic Church received 6 leagues in 1844 and claimed 35,499 acres patented in 1861 (Cowan, p. 92-93; Cowan listed the grant under the designation "Santa Inez (or) Cañada de los Pinos, (or) College").

Cañada de los Sauces [SANTA BARBARA]:

(1) *canyon,* drained by a stream that flows 2 miles to the sea 2.25 miles south of Tranquillon Mountain (lat. 34°33'05" N, long. 120° 34'05" W). Named on Tranquillon Mountain (1959) 7.5' quadrangle.

(2) *canyon,* drained by a stream that flows 4.5 miles to the sea 4.25 miles southeast of Fraser Point on Santa Cruz Island (lat. 34°00'45" N, long. 119°52'55" W). Named on Santa Cruz Island A (1943) 7.5' quadrangle. Called Cñ. los Sauces del Oeste on Bremner's (1932) map.

Cañada del Pecho: see **Pecho Creek** [SAN LUIS OBISPO].

Cañada del Pescado [SANTA BARBARA]: *canyon,* drained by a stream that flows 1.5 miles to Arroyo San Augustin nearly 7 miles east of Point Conception (lat. 34°27'40" N, long. 120°21'20" W). Named on Sacate (1953) 7.5' quadrangle.

Cañada del Portezuelo: see **Central Valley** [SANTA BARBARA].

Cañada del Poso: see **Cañada Posa** [SANTA BARBARA].

Canada del Puerto: see **Prisoners Harbor** [SANTA BARBARA].

Cañada del Refugio [SANTA BARBARA]: *canyon,* drained by a stream that flows 6 miles to the sea 8.5 miles east of Gaviota (lat. 34°27'45" N, long. 120°04'05" W). Named on Santa Ynez (1959) and Tajiguas (1953) 7.5' quadrangles.

Cañada del Rincon en El Rio San Lorenzo de Santa Cruz [SANTA CRUZ]: *land grant,* between Santa Cruz and Felton. Named on Felton (1955) and Santa Cruz (1954) 7.5' quadrangles. Pierre Sainsevain received 2 leagues in 1843 and claimed 5827 acres patented in 1858 (Cowan, p. 92). According to Perez (p. 60), the grant was made in 1846.

Cañada del Rodeo [SANTA BARBARA]: *canyon,* drained by a stream that flows nearly 2 miles to the sea 2 miles south-southwest of Tranquillon Mountain (lat. 34°33'25" N, long. 120°34'50" W). Named on Tranquillon Mountain (1959) 7.5' quadrangle.

Cañada del Sacate [SANTA BARBARA]: *canyon,* drained by a stream that flows 2.5 miles to the sea 10.5 miles east of Point Conception (lat. 34°28'15"

N, long. 120°17'35" W). Named on Sacate (1953) and Santa Rosa Hills (1959) 7.5' quadrangles.

Cañada del Venadito [SANTA BARBARA]: *canyon,* drained by a stream that flows 3.5 miles to the sea 9.5 miles east of Gaviota (lat. 34°27'40" N, long. 120°03'10" W). Named on Santa Ynez (1959) and Tajiguas (1953) 7.5' quadrangles. Called Canada del Corral on Lompoc (1905) 30' quadrangle.

Cañada de Na-joa-ui: see **Nojoqui Creek** [SANTA BARBARA].

Cañada de Salispuedes [SANTA BARBARA]: *land grant,* southeast of the city of Lompoc; Salispuedes Creek crosses the grant. Named on Lompoc (1959), Lompoc Hills (1959), and Santa Rosa Hills (1959) 7.5' quadrangles. Pedro Cordero received 1.5 leagues in 1844; John Keyes claimed 6656 acres patented in 1874 (Cowan, p. 71).

Cañada de San Benancio: see **San Benancio Gulch** [MONTEREY].

Cañada de Santa Anita [SANTA BARBARA]: *canyon,* drained by a stream that flows 5 miles to the sea 9.5 miles east of Point Conception (lat. 39°28' N, long. 120°18'20" W). Named on Sacate (1953) and Santa Rosa Hills (1959) 7.5' quadrangles.

Cañada de Santa Rosa [SANTA BARBARA]: *canyon,* drained by a stream that flows 2.25 miles to Los Alamos Valley 1.5 miles west of the town of Los Alamos (lat. 34°44'30" N, long. 120°18'20" W). Named on Los Alamos (1959) 7.5' quadrangle.

Cañada de Santa Rosalia: see **Surf** [SANTA BARBARA].

Cañada de Santa Ynez [SANTA BARBARA]: *canyon,* drained by a stream that flows 3.5 miles to Los Alamos Valley 1.5 miles southeast of Los Alamos (lat. 34°43'45" N, long. 120°15'30" W). Named on Los Alamos (1959) and Zaca Creek (1959) 7.5' quadrangles.

Cañada de Tequepis: see **Tequipis Canyon** [SANTA BARBARA].

Canada El Jolloru: see **Cañada del Jolloru** [SANTA BARBARA].

Canada El Morida: see **Cañada del Morida** [SANTA BARBARA].

Canada Gallion: see **Cañada Tecolote** [SANTA BARBARA].

Canada Garanon: see **Cañada Tecolote** [SANTA BARBARA].

Cañada Honda Creek [SANTA BARBARA]: *stream,* flows 9 miles to the sea 2.25 miles north-northeast of Point Arguello (lat. 34°36'30" N, long. 120°35'10" W); the stream drains La Honda Canyon. Named on Point Arguello (1959) and Tranquillon Mountain (1959) 7.5' quadrangles.

Cañada Laguna: see **Laguna Canyon** [SANTA BARBARA].

Cañada Laguna Seca [SANTA BARBARA]: *canyon,* drained by a stream that flows nearly 4 miles to Los Alamos Valley 2.5 miles west of the town of Los Alamos (lat. 34°44'50" N, long. 120°19'20" W). Named on Los Alamos (1959) 7.5' quadrangle.

Cañada La Jolla: see **Wreck Canyon** [SANTA BARBARA].

Cañada Las Sauces de los Colorados: see **Willows Anchorage** [SANTA BARBARA].

Cañada Lobos [SANTA BARBARA]: *canyon,* drained by a stream that flows 3.25 miles to the sea 3.25 miles west-southwest of Carrington Point on Santa Rosa Island (lat. 34°01'10" N, long. 120°05'45" W). Named on Santa Rosa Island North (1943) 7.5' quadrangle.

Cañada los Sauces del Oeste: see **Cañada de los Sauces** [SANTA BARBARA] (2).

Cañada Malvareal: see **Malva Real Anchorage** [SANTA BARBARA].

Canada Montosa: see **Canada Montuosa** [MONTEREY].

Canada Montuosa [MONTEREY]: *canyon,* drained by a stream that flows 3.5 miles to Powell Canyon nearly 6.5 miles north-northeast of Bradley (lat. 35°57' N, long. 120°44'50" W; near N line sec. 11, T 23 S, R 11 E). Named on Valleton (1948) 7.5' quadrangle. Called Canada Montosa on San Miguel (1919) 15' quadrangle.

Cañada Pomona: see **Valley Anchorage** [SANTA BARBARA].

Cañada Posa [SANTA BARBARA]: *canyon,* drained by a stream that flows 3 miles to the sea 6.5 miles southeast of Frazer Point on Santa Cruz Island (lat. 33°58'40" N, long. 119°51'50" W). Named on Santa Cruz Island A (1943) 7.5' quadrangle. Called Cñ. del Poso on Bremner's (1932) map.

Cañada San Onofre [SANTA BARBARA]: *canyon,* drained by a stream that flows 2.5 miles to the sea 1.5 miles east of Gaviota (lat. 34°28'10" N, long. 120°11'10" W). Named on Gaviota (1953) and Solvang (1959) 7.5' quadrangles.

Cañada Seca: see **Surf** [SANTA BARBARA].

Cañada Soledad [SANTA BARBARA]: *canyon,* drained by a stream that flows 6.5 miles to the sea 6.5 miles west of Carrington Point on Santa Rosa Island (lat. 34°01' N, long. 120°09'15" W). Named on Santa Rosa Island North (1943) 7.5' quadrangle.

Canada Tecolokita: see **Cañada Tecolote** [SANTA BARBARA].

Cañada Tecolote [SANTA BARBARA]: *canyon,* drained by a stream that flows 5 miles to the sea 3.25 miles east of Sandy Point on Santa Rosa Island (lat. 34°00'20" N, long. 120°11'35" W). Named on Santa Rosa Island North (1943) and Santa Rosa Island West (1943) 7.5' quadrangles. Orr (map on back cover) used the name "Canada Tecolokita" for a tributary that branches south near the mouth of Cañada Tecolote, used the name "Skull Gulch" for a canyon that opens to the sea 900 feet west-southwest of the mouth of Cañada Tecolote, used the name "Fox Gulch" for a canyon that opens to the sea 1500 feet west-southwest of the mouth of Cañada Tecolote, and used the name "Canada Garanon" for a canyon that opens to the sea 3000 feet west of the mouth of Cañada Tecolote. Orr's Canada Garanon is called C. Gallion on Kew's (1927) map.

Cañada Tortuga [SANTA BARBARA]: *canyon,* drained by a stream that flows 2 miles to the sea nearly 2 miles north of Surf (lat. 34° 42'35" N, long. 120°36'05" W). Named on Surf (1959) 7.5' quadrangle.

Cañada Verde [SAN BENITO]: *canyon,* drained by a stream that flows 5.25 miles to Quien Sabe Creek 7 miles south of Potrero Peak (lat. 36°45'30" N, long. 121°09'20" W). Named on Quien Sabe Valley (1968) 7.5' quadrangle. On Quien Sabe (1922) 15' quadrangle, the name "Cañada Verde" applies also to part of the canyon of present Quien Sabe Creek.

Cañada Verde [SAN LUIS OBISPO]: *canyon,* drained by a stream that flows nearly 3 miles to Pismo Creek 1.25 miles south of Edna (lat. 35°11'05" N, long. 120°36'50" W). Named on Arroyo Grande NE (1965) 7.5' quadrangle.

Cañada Verde [SANTA BARBARA]: *canyon,* drained by a stream that flows 6.25 miles to the sea 5.25 miles west of Carrington Point on Santa Rosa Island (lat. 34°01'30" N, long. 120°08' W). Named on Santa Rosa Island North (1943) 7.5' quadrangle.

Cañada Verde: see **Green Valley** [SANTA CRUZ].

Cañada y arroyo del Pecho: see **Pecho Creek** [SAN LUIS OBISPO].

Cañadita: see **Laguna Seca** [MONTEREY] (2).

Canal de Santa Barbara: see **Santa Barbara Channel** [SANTA BARBARA].

Cane Canyon [SAN BENITO]: *canyon,* drained by a stream that flows 3.25 miles to Hernandez Reservoir 10 miles east of Bitterwater (lat. 36°24' N, long. 120°49'35" W; near E line sec. 36, T 17 S, R 10 E). Named on Hernandez Reservoir (1969) 7.5' quadrangle.

Cane Canyon: see **Baker Canyon** [SAN BENITO].

Cane Mountain: see **Tucker Mountain** [SAN BENITO].

Canfield: see **San Juan Bautista** [SAN BENITO].

Cannery Point: see **Carmel Cove** [MONTEREY].

Cañon de Cebada: see **Cañada Cervada** [SANTA BARBARA].

Cañon de las Piedras: see **Stony Valley** [MONTEREY].

Canovas Canyon [SANTA BARBARA]: *canyon,* drained by a stream that flows 2.25 miles to South Fork La Brea Creek 2.25 miles west-southwest of Manzanita Mountain (lat. 34°53'05" N, long. 120°07'05" W). Named on Manzanita Mountain (1964) 7.5' quadrangle.

Can Rock [SANTA BARBARA]: *rock,* 3.5 miles northwest of Cardwell Point, and 2350 feet offshore on the north side of San Miguel Island (lat. 34°03'15" N, long. 120°20'25" W). Named on San Miguel Island East (1950) 7.5' quadrangle.

Cantinas: see **The Cantinas** [SAN LUIS OBISPO].

Cantinas Creek [SAN LUIS OBISPO]: *stream,* flows 3 miles to Nacimiento Reservoir 13 miles northeast of the village of San Simeon (lat. 35°45'40" N, long. 121°00'40" W; near S line sec. 9, T 25 S, R 9 E); the stream flows past the feature called The Cantinas. Named on Bryson (1949, photorevised 1979) 7.5' quadrangle.

Cantua Creek [SAN BENITO]: *stream,* flows nearly 4 miles to Fresno County 5 miles east-southeast of Idria (lat. 36°23'30" N, long. 120°35'50" W; at E line sec. 1, T 18 S, R 12 E). Named on Ciervo Mountain (1969) and Santa Rita Peak (1969) 7.5' quadrangles. The name commemorates a member of the Cantua family (Gudde, 1949, p. 55).

Canyon de los Alisos [SAN LUIS OBISPO]: *canyon,* drained by a stream that flows 3 miles to Tar Spring Creek 7 miles southeast of Edna (lat. 35°08'10" N, long. 120°30'50" W). Named on Arroyo Grande NE (1965) and Tar Spring Ridge (1967) 7.5' quadrangles.

Canyon del Rey [MONTEREY]: *canyons,* extend end to end for 8 miles from Seaside to an unnamed canyon 8 miles south-southwest of Salinas (lat. 36°34'45" N, long. 121°43'38" W). Named on Seaside (1947) and Spreckels (1947) 7.5' quadrangles. The stream in the eastern canyon flows to Torro Creek, and the stream in the western canyon flows toward the sea.

Canyon Number 1 [SAN LUIS OBISPO]: *canyon,* drained by a stream that flows 1.5 miles to Canyon Number 2 about 4.5 miles south of Edna (lat. 35°08'30" N, long. 120°35'55" W). Named on Arroyo Grande NE (1965) 7.5' quadrangle.

Canyon Number 2 [SAN LUIS OBISPO]: *canyon,* drained by a stream that flows 1.5 miles to Canyon Number 1 about 4.5 miles south of Edna (lat. 35°08'30" N, long. 120°35'55" W). Named on Arroyo Grande NE (1965) 7.5' quadrangle.

Canyon Secundo [MONTEREY]: *canyon,* drained by a stream that flows 2.5 miles to Carmel Valley (1) 4.25 miles east of the mouth of Carmel River (lat. 36°32'05" N, long. 121°51' W). Named on Monterey (1913) 15' quadrangle.

Canyon Spring [SAN LUIS OBISPO]: *spring,* 5 miles south of Atascadero along Hale Creek (lat. 35°25'05" N, long. 120°41'05" W; near E line sec. 9, T 29 S, R 12 E). Named on Atascadero (1965) 7.5' quadrangle.

Cape San Martin [MONTEREY]: *promontory,* 37 miles southeast of Point Sur along the coast (lat. 39°53'20" N, long. 121°27'50" W; sec. 31, T 23 S, R 5 E). Named on Cape San Martin (1949) 7.5' quadrangle. Called Punta Gorda on Blake's (1857) map, and called Pt. Gorda on Parke's (1854-

1855) map. According to H.R. Wagner (p. 411), members of United States Coast Survey applied the name to the feature because they thought that Cabrillo had given it the name "San Martin." The feature is identified by three rocks, called San Martin Rocks, that lie from 100 yards to 0.5 mile offshore; a rock 4 miles north of Cape San Martin, and 0.7 mile offshore, is called Tide Rock (United States Coast and Geodetic Survey, p. 117).

Capital Hill [SAN LUIS OBISPO]: *district,* east of Salinas River opposite Paso Robles (lat. 35°37'40" N, long. 120°40'45" W). Named on Paso Robles (1948) 7.5' quadrangle.

Capitan [SANTA BARBARA]: *locality,* 10 miles east of Gaviota along Southern Pacific Railroad (lat. 34°27'50" N, long. 120°02'40" W); the place is near the mouth of Cañada del Corral (1), which has the name "Canon del Capitan" on Lompoc (1905) 30' quadrangle. Named on Tajiguas (1953) 7.5' quadrangle.

Capitola [SANTA CRUZ]: *town,* 2 miles northeast of Soquel Point along the coast (lat. 36°58'30" N, long. 121°57' W). Named on Soquel (1954) 7.5' quadrangle. In 1869 F.A. Hihn established a campground for vacationers on flat land east of the mouth of Soquel Creek; the place was called Camp Capitola, and in 1883 Hihn began selling lots there (Lyndon and Swift, p. 21, 36). In 1868 residents of Soquel invited the State of California to move the state capitol to their community; and Hihn created the name "Capitola" from that incident (Hanna, p. 55). The name "Camp Capitola" gave way to the name "Capitola-by-the-Sea," and this finally became the name "Capitola" (Clark, 1986, p. 61). Postal authorities established Capitola post office in 1889 (Frickstad, p. 176). Soquel Landing, which was at present Capitola, had a small wharf before 1857 (Rowland, p. 130). Michael Lodge hauled lumber in the early days to the beach at Capitola, which then was known as Lodge's Beach (Burgess, p. 240).

Capitola-by-the-Sea: see **Capitola** [SANTA CRUZ].

Carbonera Creek [SANTA CRUZ]: *stream,* flows 9 miles to Branciforte Creek 2.5 miles north-northeast of Point Santa Cruz in Santa Cruz (lat. 36°59'10" N, long. 122°00'50" W). Named on Felton (1955), Laurel (1955), and Santa Cruz (1954) 7.5' quadrangles. The stream was called West Browns Creek on a map of 1881; it also was called West Branch Branciforte Creek, West Fork Branciforte Creek, and West Branciforte Creek (Clark, 1986, p. 48, 64-65).

Cardwell Point [SANTA BARBARA]: *promontory,* at the easternmost tip of San Miguel Island (lat. 34°01'20" N, long. 120°17'40" W). Named on San Miguel Island East (1950) 7.5' quadrangle.

Careaga [SANTA BARBARA]: *locality,* 5 miles west of Los Alamos along Pacific Coast Railroad (lat. 34°45'15" N, long. 120°22' W); the place is near the mouth of Careaga Canyon. Named on Lompoc (1905) 30' quadrangle. Postal authorities established Careaga post office in 1902, discontinued it in 1903, reestablished it in 1904, and discontinued it in 1909 (Salley, p. 37). The name commemorates Juan B. Careaga of the firm of Careaga and Harris, a farming enterprise that operated near Los Alamos in the early 1880's (Gudde, 1949, p. 56).

Careaga Canyon [SANTA BARBARA]: *canyon,* drained by a stream that flows 4.5 miles to San Antonio Creek (1) 8.5 miles south-southwest of the village of Sisquoc (lat. 34°45'25" N, long. 120°21'45" W). Named on Orcutt (1959) and Sisquoc (1959) 7.5' quadrangles. Called Canada de las Flores on Lompoc (1905) 30' quadrangle, which has the name "Careaga Canyon" for present Cañada de las Flores. United States Board on Geographic Names (1962a, p. 8) rejected the name "Cañada de las Flores" for present Careaga Canyon.

Carisa: see **Painted Rock** [SAN LUIS OBISPO].

Carisa Plain: see **Carrizo Plain** [SAN LUIS OBISPO].

Carisa Valley: see **Carrizo Plain** [SAN LUIS OBISPO].

Carmel: see **Carmel By The Sea** [MONTEREY]; **Carmel Valley** [MONTEREY] (2); **Mount Carmel** [MONTEREY]; **Point Carmel**, under **Pinnacle Point** [MONTEREY].

Carmel Bay [MONTEREY]: *embayment,* along the coast between Pescadero Point on the north and Carmel Point on the south (lat. 35°32'30" N, long. 121°57'15" W). Named on Monterey (1947) 7.5' quadrangle. According to Davidson (1907, p. 29), a Spanish chart made before Spanish settlement of California has the name "po de Pinos" for the bay. Forbes' (1839) map has the name "Carmel Cove" for the feature. Whitney (p. 158) referred to Carmelo Bay, and Farnham (p. 111) mentioned the bay of San Carmelo.

Carmel Beach [MONTEREY]: *beach,* on the east side of Carmel Bay at Carmel By The Sea (lat. 36°33' N, long. 121°55'40" W). Named on Monterey (1947) 7.5' quadrangle. Lawson's (1893) map has the name "Abalone Pt." for a promontory near the south end of the beach.

Carmel By The Sea [MONTEREY]: *town,* north of the mouth of Carmel River along Carmel Bay (lat. 36°33'15" N, long. 121°55'15" W). Named on Monterey (1947) 7.5' quadrangle. Called Carmel on Santa Cruz (1956) 1°x 2° quadrangle. The place began in 1903 as an artist colony (Lewis, 1977, p. 1). Postal authorities established Carmel post office in 1903 (Frickstad, p. 106), and the town incorporated in 1916. United States Board on Geographic Names (1960c, p. 16) approved the hyphenated form "Carmel-by-the-Sea" for the name.

Carmel Cove [MONTEREY]: *embayment,* less than 1 mile east of Point Lobos along the coast (lat. 36°31'15" N, long. 121°56'15" W); the embayment is on the south side of Carmel Bay. Named on Monterey (1947) 7.5' quadrangle. United States Board on Geographic Names (1974b, p. 3) decided in favor of the name "Whalers Cove" for the feature, and gave the name "Carmel Cove" as a variant. California Department of Parks and Recreation's map has the name "Coal Chute Point" for a promontory on the east side of the cove, and the name "Cannery Point" for a promontory on the west side. According to Mosier (p. 5), a coal bunker was built in 1879 at the tip of Coal Chute Point, where coal was loaded on ships; a railroad brought the coal from a mine 5 miles south of the loading place. Cannery Point was the site of an abalone cannery that ceased operation in 1928 (Clark, 1991, p. 69-70).

Carmel Cove: see **Carmel Bay** [MONTEREY].

Carmel Highlands [MONTEREY]: *settlement,* 3.5 miles south of present Carmel-by-the-Sea (lat. 36°30' N, long. 121°56' W). Named on Monterey (1947) and Soberanes Point (1956) 7.5' quadrangles. Franklin Devendorf and Frank Powers began development of the place in 1916 (Clark, 1991, p. 76). California Mining Bureau's (1917b) map shows a place called Carmelito situated along the road just north of present Carmel Highlands; the name recalls a failed land development attempt in the late nineteenth century (Clark, 1991, p. 77).

Carmelito: see **Carmel Highlands** [MONTEREY].

Carmelo: see **Point Carmelo**, under **Pinnacle Point** [MONTEREY]; **Point Carmelo**, under **Point Lobos** [MONTEREY].

Carmelo Bay: see **Carmel Bay** [MONTEREY].

Carmelo River: see **Carmel River** [MONTEREY].

Carmelo Valley: see **Carmel Valley** [MONTEREY] (1).

Carmel Point: see **Pinnacle Point** [MONTEREY].

Carmel River [MONTEREY]: *stream,* flows 38 miles to the sea at Carmel Bay (lat. 36°32'10" N, long. 121°55'40" W); the stream drains Carmel Valley (1). Named on Carmel Valley (1956), Monterey (1947), Mount Carmel (1956), Seaside (1947), and Ventana Cones (1956) 7.5' quadrangles. Vizcaino named the river in 1603, probably for three Carmelite friars who accompanied him (Wagner, H.R., p. 379). Greenhow (p. 16) mentioned River San Carmelo in 1844, Townsend (p. 98) called the stream San Carlos River in 1855, and Whitney (p. 152) referred to Carmelo River in 1865. Miller Fork enters from the east 28 miles upstream from the mouth of the river; it is 7.25 miles long and is named on Chews Ridge (1956) and Ventana Cones (1956) 7.5' quadrangles. Bruce Fork enters from the southeast 29 miles upstream from the mouth of the river; it is 2.5 miles long and is named on Ventana Cones (1956) 7.5' quadrangle. The name "Bruce Fork" commemorates members of the Bruce family, early residents in the vicinity (Clark, 1991, p. 53)

Carmel River Camp [MONTEREY]: *locality,* 3.25 miles east-northeast of Uncle Sam Mountain (lat. 36°21'05" N, long. 121°29' W; sec. 21, T 18 S, R 3 E); the place is along Carmel River. Named on Ventana Cones (1956) 7.5' quadrangle.

Carmel Valley [MONTEREY]:

(1) *valley,* extends for 12 miles inland from the coast along Carmel River. Named on Carmel Valley (1956), Monterey (1947), Mount Carmel (1956), and Seaside (1947) 7.5' quadrangles. Whitney (p. 152) referred to Carmelo Valley.

(2) *town,* 12 miles from the coast near the east end of Carmel Valley (1) (lat. 36°28'45" N, long. 121°43'45" W). Named on Carmel Valley (1956) 7.5' quadrangle. Postal authorities established Robles del Rio post office in 1941 and changed the name to Carmel Valley in 1952 (Frickstad, p. 109). California Mining Bureau's (1917b) map shows a place called Carmel located 13 miles east-southeast of Carmel by the Sea on the north side of Carmelo River. Postal authorities established Carmel post office in 1889, discontinued it in 1890, reestablished it in 1893, moved it 1 mile east in 1902, and discontinued it in 1903 (Salley, p. 38).

Carmel Woods [MONTEREY]: *district,* at the north edge of present Carmel-by-the-Sea (lat. 36°34'05" N, long. 121°54'55" W). Named on Monterey (1947) 7.5' quadrangle.

Carnasa Creek: see **Carnaza Creek** [SAN LUIS OBISPO].

Carnaza Creek [SAN LUIS OBISPO]: *stream,* flows 7.5 miles to the valley of San Juan Creek 15 miles northeast of Pozo (lat. 35°25'20" N, long. 120°09'45" W; near W line sec. 9, T 29 S, R 17 E). Named on La Panza NE (1966) and La Panza Ranch (1966) 7.5' quadrangles. United States Board on Geographic Names (1933, p. 196) rejected the form "Carnasa Creek" for the name.

Carnaza Spring [SAN LUIS OBISPO]: *spring,* 16 miles east-northeast of Pozo (lat. 35°26' N, long. 120°07'30" W; sec. 2, T 29 S, R 17 E); the spring is along Carnaza Creek. Named on La Panza NE (1966) 7.5' quadrangle.

Carneros Canyon [SAN LUIS OBISPO]: *canyon,* drained by a stream that flows 3.5 miles to Kern County 8 miles northeast of Simmler (lat. 35°25'45" N, long. 119°52'45" W; at E line sec. 1, T 29 S, R 19 E). Named on Las Yeguas Ranch (1959) 7.5' quadrangle.

Carneros Creek [SANTA BARBARA]: *stream,* flows nearly 6 miles to

Goleta Slough 1.5 miles west-southwest of downtown Goleta (lat. 34°25'35" N, long. 119°50'55" W). Named on Goleta (1950) 7.5' quadrangle. The stream drains Bartlett Canyon. Goleta (1903) 15' quadrangle has the name "Carneros Valley" for the canyon of the creek below Bartlett Canyon. United States Board on Geographic Names (1961b, p. 9) rejected the name "Camerus Valley Creek" for the stream.

Carneros Valley: see **Carneros Creek** [SANTA BARBARA].

Carpenter Canyon [SAN LUIS OBISPO]: *canyon,* drained by a stream that flows nearly 2 miles to Corbit Canyon 5 miles south-southeast of Edna (lat. 35°08'20" N, long. 120°33'55" W). Named on Arroyo Grande NE (1965) 7.5' quadrangle.

Carpenteria: see **Carpinteria** [SANTA BARBARA].

Carpenteria Creek: see **Carpinteria Creek** [SANTA BARBARA].

Carpinteria [SANTA BARBARA]: *town,* 10 miles east of Santa Barbara (lat. 34°23'50" N, long. 119°31'05" W). Named on Carpinteria (1952) 7.5' quadrangle. Postal authorities established Carpenteria post office in 1867, discontinued it in 1869, reestablished it in 1870, moved it 1 mile west to the railroad depot in 1889, and changed the name to Carpinteria in 1900 (Salley, p. 38). The town incorporated in 1965. United States Board on Geographic Names (1933, p. 197) rejected the form "Carpenteria" for the name. Members of the Portola expedition found an Indian village at or near the place in 1769 and called it La Carpinteria because an Indian was building a canoe there—*carpinteria* means "carpenter shop" in Spanish (Wagner, H.R., p. 379). California Mining Bureau's (1917c) map shows a place called Benham located along the railroad about halfway between Carpinteria and Santa Barbara-Ventura County line.

Carpinteria Creek [SANTA BARBARA]: *stream,* flows 7.5 miles to the sea at Carpinteria (lat. 34°23'25" N, long. 119°31'10" W). Named on Carpinteria (1952) and White Ledge Peak (1952) 7.5' quadrangles. United States Board on Geographic Names (1933, p. 197) rejected the form "Carpenteria Creek" for the name.

Carpinteria Lagoon: see **El Estero** [SANTA BARBARA].

Carpinteria Landing: see **Serena** [SANTA BARBARA].

Carpinteria Slough: see **El Estero** [SANTA BARBARA].

Carr [SANTA BARBARA]: *locality,* 4.5 miles southeast of the town of Guadalupe along Santa Maria Valley Railroad (lat. 34°55'50" N, long. 120°30'35" W). Named on Guadalupe (1959) 7.5' quadrangle.

Carrals Spring [MONTEREY]: *spring,* 4 miles southeast of Cone Peak (lat. 36°00'35" N, long. 121°26'30" W, sec. 20, T 22 S, R 5 E). Named on Cone Peak (1949) 7.5' quadrangle. The misspelled name is from corrals at the place (Clark, 1991, p. 88).

Carrie Creek [SAN LUIS OBISPO]: *stream,* flows 8 miles to Huasna River 4 miles north of Huasna Peak (lat. 35°05'45" N, long. 120° 21'05" W). Named on Caldwell Mesa (1967) and Huasna Peak (1967) 7.5' quadrangles. Called Aliso Creek on Nipomo (1922) 15' quadrangle, but United States Board on Geographic Names (1963b, p. 13) rejected this name.

Carrington Point [SANTA BARBARA]: *promontory,* 12 miles east-northeast of Sandy Point on the north side of Santa Rosa Island (lat. 34°02'10" N, long. 120°02'30" W). Named on Santa Rosa Island North (1943) 7.5' quadrangle. A shoal called Beacon Reef lies 0.3 mile north of Carrington Point (United States Coast and Geodetic Survey, p. 111).

Carrisa Plains: see **Carrizo Plain** [SAN LUIS OBISPO].

Carriso Plain: see **Carrizo Plain** [SAN LUIS OBISPO].

Carrizo Canyon [SAN LUIS OBISPO]: *canyon,* drained by a stream that flows 7.25 miles to Cuyama River 13 miles west of Caliente Mountain (lat. 35°04'10" N, long. 119°59'50" W). Named on Chimineas Ranch (1959) and Taylor Canyon (1959) 7.5' quadrangles.

Carrizo Creek: see **Garrizo Creek** [MONTEREY]; **San Juan Creek** [SAN LUIS OBISPO].

Carrizo Plain [SAN LUIS OBISPO]: *valley,* southwest of Temblor Range, and northeast of La Panza Range and Caliente Range. Named on Bakersfield (1962) and San Luis Obispo (1956) 1°x 2° quadrangles. The valley was called the Estero in Spanish times (Angel, 1890c, p. 568). Parke's (1854-1855) map has the name "Llano Estero" for the feature, and Hamlin's (1904) map has the name Carriso Plain. Other names applied to the valley include: Estero plain (Antisell, 1856, p. 54), Carrisa Plains (Angel, 1890c, p. 568), Carisa Plain (Fairbanks, 1895, p. 274), Carisa Valley (Anderson, F.M., p. 168), Carrizo Valley (Anderson and Martin, p. 35), and Carrizo Plains (Anderson and Martin, p. 50). California Mining Bureau's (1909b) map shows a place called Goodwin located near the southeast end of Carrizo Plain, 40 miles by stage line southeast of Simmler. Postal authorities established Goodwin post office in 1889, discontinued it in 1891, reestablished it in 1892, and discontinued it in 1899; they established Carissa Plains post office in 1916 and discontinued it the same year (Frickstad, p. 164).

Carrizo Valley: see **Carrizo Plain** [SAN LUIS OBISPO].

Carrol Canyon [SAN LUIS OBISPO]: *canyon,* drained by a stream that flows 3 miles to Town Creek 10 miles east-northeast of the village of San Simeon (lat. 35°40'35" N, long. 121°00'40" W; sec. 16, T 26 S, R 9 E). Named on Pebblestone Shut-in (1959) 7.5' quadrangle. Called Carroll Canyon on San Simeon (1959) 15' quadrangle.

Carter Spring [SANTA BARBARA]: *spring,* 1.5 miles east-southeast of Salisbury Potrero (lat. 34°48'35" N, long. 119°40'40" W). Named on Salisbury Potrero (1964) 7.5' quadrangle.

Cascade Creek [SANTA CRUZ]: *stream,* flows 1.25 miles to San Mateo County 3.5 miles north-northwest of the mouth of Waddell Creek (lat. 37°08'35" N, long. 122°18'30" W; sec. 21, T 9 S, R 4 W). Named on Franklin Point (1955) 7.5' quadrangle. The name goes back to 1863, when Cascade dairy began operating along the stream (Brown, p. 17).

Casey Gulch [MONTEREY]: *canyon,* drained by a stream that flows 1 mile to lowlands nearly 3.5 miles northwest of San Ardo (lat. 36° 03'20" N, long. 120°56'45" W). Named on San Ardo (1967) 7.5' quadrangle.

Casmale: see **Casmalia** [SANTA BARBARA] (2).

Casmalia [SANTA BARBARA]:

(1) *land grant,* mainly northwest of the village of Casmalia. Named on Casmalia (1959), Guadalupe (1959), and Point Sal (1958) 7.5' quadrangles. Antonio Olivera received 2 leagues in 1840 and claimed 8841 acres patented in 1863 (Cowan, p. 25).

(2) *village,* 9.5 miles south-southwest of Santa Maria (lat. 34°50'15" N, long. 120°31'50" W); the place is on Casmalia grant. Named on Casmalia (1959) 7.5' quadrangle. Called Casmale on Goddard's (1857) map. Postal authorities established Casmalia post office in 1896 (Frickstad, p. 170).

Casmalia Canyon [SANTA BARBARA]: *canyon,* drained by a stream that flows nearly 6 miles to Shuman Canyon less than 1 mile west-southwest of the village of Casmalia (lat. 34°49'55" N, long. 120° 32'35" W). Named on Casmalia (1959) and Guadalupe (1959) 7.5' quadrangles.

Casmalia Hills [SANTA BARBARA]: *range,* south of Santa Maria Valley between Graciosa Canyon and Point Sal. Named on Casmalia (1959), Guadalupe (1959), Orcutt (1959), and Point Sal (1958) 7.5' quadrangles.

Casserly Creek [SANTA CRUZ]: *stream,* flows 3 miles to Pajaro Valley 4.25 miles north of Watsonville (lat. 36°58'30" N, long. 121°44'30" W). Named on Watsonville East (1955) 7.5' quadrangle. The name is for Eugene Casserly, a settler of 1853 (Clark, 1986, p. 66).

Casserly Ridge [SANTA CRUZ]: *ridge,* southwest-trending, 1.5 miles long, 5 miles northeast of Watsonville (lat. 36°57'40" N, long. 121°41'05" W). Named on Watsonville East (1955) 7.5' quadrangle.

Cass' Wharf: see **Cayucos** [SAN LUIS OBISPO].

Castillo: see **Point Castillo** [SANTA BARBARA].

Castle Crags [SAN LUIS OBISPO]: *peak,* 10 miles east of Pozo (lat. 35°18'20" N, long. 120°12'05" W). Altitude 2677 feet. Named on La Panza (1967) 7.5' quadrangle.

Castle Mountain [MONTEREY]: *peak,* 6 miles east-northeast of Parkfield on Monterey-Fresno County line (lat. 35°56'20" N, long. 120°20'20" W; sec. 10, T 23 S, R 15 E). Altitude 4343 feet. Named on The Dark Hole (1961) 7.5' quadrangle. The feature also has been called Black Mountain and Castle Peak (Clark, 1991, p. 91).

Castle Peak: see **Castle Mountain** [MONTEREY].

Castle Rock [MONTEREY]: *rock,* 250 feet long, nearly 5 miles north of Point Sur, and 850 feet offshore (lat. 36°22'30" N, long. 121°54'25" W). Named on Point Sur (1956) and Soberanes Point (1956) 7.5' quadrangles.

Castle Rock [SAN BENITO]: *relief feature,* 11 miles northeast of Bitterwater (lat. 36°29'05" N, long. 120°50'55" W; sec. 2, T 17 S, R 10 E). Named on Hernandez Reservoir (1969) 7.5' quadrangle.

Castle Rock [SANTA BARBARA]: *island,* 0.25 mile long, 2 miles north-northeast of Point Bennett and 3100 feet offshore on the north side of San Miguel Island (lat. 34°03'20" N, long. 120°26'10" W). Named on San Miguel Island West (1950) 7.5' quadrangle. The feature had the local name "Flea Island" (Doran, p. 213). Bremner's (1933) map shows a place called Wescott Shoal situated less than 1 mile north of Castle Rock.

Castle Rock [SANTA CRUZ]: *relief feature,* 7.25 miles north of the town of Boulder Creek on Santa Cruz-Santa Clara County line (lat. 37°13'40" N, long. 122°05'40" W; near NE cor. sec. 20, T 8 S, R 2 W). Named on Castle Rock Ridge (1955) 7.5' quadrangle.

Castle Rock Falls [SANTA CRUZ]: *waterfall,* 7 miles north of the town of Boulder Creek (lat. 37°13'35" N, long. 122°06'20" W; sec. 20, T 8 S, R 2 W); the feature is 0.5 mile west-southwest of Castle Rock. Named on Castle Rock Ridge (1955) 7.5' quadrangle.

Castle Rock Ridge [SANTA CRUZ]: *ridge,* northwest-trending, 7 miles long, 7 miles north-northeast of the town of Boulder Creek on Santa Cruz-Santa Clara County line (lat. 37°13'30" N, long. 122°05'30" W); Castle Rock is on the ridge. Named on Castle Rock Ridge (1955) and Cupertino (1961) 7.5' quadrangles.

Castro Canyon [MONTEREY]: *canyon,* drained by a stream that flows 1.5 miles to the sea nearly 4 miles east-southeast of Pfeiffer Point (lat. 36°12'45" N, long. 121°45'15" W; sec. 9, T 20 S, R 2 E). Named on Partington Ridge (1956) and Pfeiffer Point (1956) 7.5' quadrangles. The name commemorates David Antonio Castro, who received a patent to land at the mouth of the canyon in 1883 (Clark, 1991, p. 91).

Castro Canyon [SAN LUIS OBISPO]: *canyon,* drained by a stream that flows 2.25 miles to San Luis Obispo Creek nearly 3 miles northeast of Avila Beach (lat. 35°12'25" N, long. 120°41'40" W). Named on Pismo Beach (1965) 7.5' quadrangle.

Castro Canyon [SANTA BARBARA]: *canyon,* drained by a stream that flows 6.25 miles to Cuyama Valley 3 miles south of the village of Cuyama (lat. 34°53'30" N, long. 119°37'05" W; sec. 1, T 9 N, R 26 W). Named on Cuyama (1964), Fox Mountain (1964), and Salisbury Potrero (1964) 7.5' quadrangles.

Castroville [MONTEREY]: *town,* 9 miles northwest of Salinas (lat. 36°46' N, long. 121°45' W). Named on Moss Landing (1954) and Prunedale (1954) 7.5' quadrangles. Juan B. Castro founded the town in 1864 and named it for his father, Simeon Nepomuceno Castro, owner of Bolsa Nuevo y Moro Cojo grant, where the town lies (Hanna, p. 59). Postal authorities established Castroville post office in 1867 (Frickstad, p. 106).

Cat Canyon [SAN LUIS OBISPO]: *canyon,* drained by a stream that flows 1.25 miles to Huasna River 4 miles north-northwest of Huasna Peak (lat. 35°05'30" N, long. 120°22' W). Named on Huasna Peak (1967) and Nipomo (1965) 7.5' quadrangles.

Cat Canyon [SANTA BARBARA]: *canyon,* drained by a stream that flows 10.5 miles to Santa Maria Valley at the village of Sisquoc (lat. 34°51'50" N, long. 120°17'30" W; near SW cor. sec. 7, T 9 N, R 32 W); the upper part of the canyon is north of Gato Ridge. Named on Foxen Canyon (1964) and Sisquoc (1959) 7.5' quadrangles. Called Canada del Gato on Santa Maria (1947) 15' quadrangle, but United States Board on Geographic Names (1962a, p. 9) rejected the names "Canada del Gato" and "Cañada del Gato" for the feature.

Catfish Lake [MONTEREY]: *intermittent lake,* 300 feet long, 4.5 miles north of Parkfield (lat. 35°57'50" N, long. 120°26'45" W; sec. 3, T 23 S, R 14 E). Named on Parkfield (1961) 7.5' quadrangle.

Cathedral Peak [SANTA BARBARA]: *peak,* 4.5 miles north-northwest of downtown Santa Barbara (lat. 34°29'10" N, long. 119°42'55" W; sec. 28, T 5 N, R 27 W). Altitude 3333 feet. Named on Santa Barbara (1952) 7.5' quadrangle.

Cavalry Bluff [MONTEREY]: *escarpment,* 4 miles west-southwest of Salinas (lat. 36°39'20" N, long. 121°43'45" W); the feature is at the boundary of Fort Ord Military Reservation. Named on Salinas (1947, photorevised 1968 and 1975) 7.5' quadrangle. The name is for the 11th Cavalry, stationed at Presidio of Monterey from 1919 until 1940 (Clark, 1991, p. 93).

Cave Gulch [SANTA CRUZ]: *canyon,* drained by a stream that flows 2 miles to Wilder Creek 3.5 miles northwest of Point Santa Cruz (lat. 36°59'05" N, long. 122°04'15" W). Named on Felton (1955) and Santa Cruz (1954) 7.5' quadrangles.

Cave Landing: see **Mallagh Landing** [SAN LUIS OBISPO].

Cavern Point [SANTA BARBARA]: *promontory,* 3 miles west-northwest of San Pedro Point on the north side of Santa Cruz Island (lat. 34°03'20" N, long. 119°33'45" W). Named on Santa Cruz Island D (1943) 7.5' quadrangle. Called Palo Parado on Rand's (1931) map.

Caves: see **The Caves** [MONTEREY].

Cawatre: see **Camp Cawatre Campground** [MONTEREY].

Cayucas: see **Cayucos** [SAN LUIS OBISPO].

Cayucos [SAN LUIS OBISPO]: *town,* 18 miles northwest of San Luis Obispo near the north end of Estero Bay (lat. 35°26'45" N, long. 120°53'45" W). Named on Cayucos (1965) 7.5' quadrangle. *Cayucos* means "boats" or "skiffs" in South-American Spanish (Kroeber, 1916, p. 38). The name probably came from the small boats used by Indians, and was applied first to Moro y Cayucos grant, and then to the town (Hanna, p. 59). Angel (1883, p. 323, 341-342) referred to a landing called Cayucos, where James Cass built Cass' Wharf in 1873. Present Cayucos is near the mouth of Old Creek; postal authorities established Old Creek post office in 1868, moved it 1 mile northwest and changed the name to Cayucas in 1879, and changed the name again to Cayucos in 1883 (Salley, p. 40, 160).

Cayucos Creek [SAN LUIS OBISPO]: *stream,* flows 6.5 miles to Estero Bay at Cayucos (lat. 35°26'55" N, long. 120°54'25" W). Named on Cayucos (1965) and Cypress Mountain (1948) 7.5' quadrangles. United States Board on Geographic Names (1938, p. 11) rejected the name "Estero River" for the stream. H.R. Wagner (p. 513) believed that a lagoon at the mouth of the creek might be the one that members of the Portola expedition called Estero de Santa Serafina in 1769, although he pointed out that Bolton identified present Ellysly Creek as Portola's Estero de Santa Serafina. Hamilton (p. 106-107) placed El Estero de Santa Serafina at the mouth of present Villa Creek.

Cayucos Creek: see **Little Cayucos Creek** [SAN LUIS OBISPO].

Cayucos Point [SAN LUIS OBISPO]: *promontory,* 20 miles northwest of San Luis Obispo along the coast (lat. 35°26'45" N, long. 120°56'20" W); the feature is 2 miles west of the mouth of Cayucos Creek. Named on Cayucos (1965) 7.5' quadrangle.

Cebada Canyon [SANTA BARBARA]: *canyon,* drained by a stream that flows 5.25 miles to lowlands 3.25 miles northeast of the city of Lompoc (lat. 34°39'55" N, long. 120°24'20" W). Named on Lompoc (1959) and Los Alamos (1959) 7.5' quadrangles.

Cebola Canyon: see **Chavoya Canyon** [MONTEREY].

Cedar Canyon [SAN LUIS OBISPO]: *canyon,* drained by a stream that flows nearly 2 miles to the valley of San Juan Creek 15 miles northeast of Pozo (lat. 35°27'25" N, long. 120°10'05" W; sec. 29, T 28 S, R 17 E). Named on La Panza Ranch (1966) 7.5' quadrangle. On La Panza (1935) 15' quadrangle, the stream in the canyon is called Cedar Creek.

Cedar Creek: see **Cedar Canyon** [SAN LUIS OBISPO].

Cedar Flat [SAN BENITO]: *valley,* 7.25 miles south-southeast of Panoche (lat. 36°30'35" N, long. 120°45'40" W; on E line sec. 28, T 16 S, R 11 E). Named on Panoche (1969) 7.5' quadrangle.

Cedar Flat Canyon [SAN BENITO]: *canyon,* drained by a stream that flows 7.25 miles to Panoche Creek 3.25 miles east of Panoche (lat. 36°35'25" N, long. 120°46'15" W; sec. 28, T 15 S, R 11 E); the canyon heads at Cedar Flat. Named on Panoche (1969) 7.5' quadrangle.

Cedar Spring [SAN BENITO]: *spring,* 13 miles east-southeast of Bitterwater (lat. 36°18'50" N, long. 120°46'20" W; near S line sec. 33, T 18 S, R 11 E). Named on Hepsedam Peak (1969) 7.5' quadrangle.

Cedar Spring [SAN LUIS OBISPO]: *spring,* 15 miles northeast of Pozo (lat. 35°27'30" N, long. 120°09'30" W; near E line sec. 29, T 28 S, R 17 E); the spring is in Cedar Canyon. Named on La Panza Ranch (1966) 7.5' quadrangle.

Celery Lake [SAN LUIS OBISPO]: *lake,* 0.5 mile long, 3.5 miles south-southwest of downtown Arroyo Grande near the coast (lat. 35°04'20" N, long. 120°36'10" W). Named on Oceano (1965) 7.5' quadrangle, which shows marshy places in the lake. Arroyo Grande (1952) 15' quadrangle shows an unnamed marsh instead of a lake.

Cement Trough Spring [SAN LUIS OBISPO]: *spring,* 4 miles west-southwest of Cholame (lat. 35°42'20" N, long. 120°22' W; sec. 33, T 25 S, R 15 E). Named on Cholame (1961) 7.5' quadrangle.

Centerville: see **Idria** [SAN BENITO].

Central Canyon [SANTA BARBARA]: *canyon,* drained by a stream that flows nearly 3 miles to join the stream in East Canyon and form Bitter Creek 4 miles southwest of New Cuyama (lat. 34°54'25" N, long. 119°44'10" W; sec. 35, T 10 N, R 27 W). Named on New Cuyama (1964) and Peak Mountain (1964) 7.5' quadrangles.

Central City: see **Santa Maria** [SANTA BARBARA].

Central Valley [SANTA BARBARA]: *canyon,* 7 miles long, center 4 miles south of Diablo Point in the middle of Santa Cruz Island (lat. 34°00'15" N, long. 119°44'45" W). Named on Santa Cruz Island B (1943) 7.5' quadrangle, which shows Stanton ranch near the east end of the canyon. Called Cñ. del Medio on Bremner's (1932) map, which has the name "Main Rch." for present Stanton ranch. Postal authorities established Laplaya post office at Main ranch in 1895 and discontinued it in 1903 (Salley, p. 117; Doran, p. 154). Bremner's (1932) map has the name "Cñ. del Portezuelo" for the west part of present Central Valley, and shows a place called Portezuelo there.

Cerro Alto [SAN LUIS OBISPO]: *peak,* 6.25 miles southwest of Atascadero (lat. 35°24'50" N, long. 120°44' W; sec. 7, T 29 S, R 12 E). Altitude 2624 feet. Named on Atascadero (1965) 7.5' quadrangle.

Cerro Alto: see **Hollister Peak** [SAN LUIS OBISPO].

Cerro Alto Campground [SAN LUIS OBISPO]: *locality,* 6 miles southwest of Atascadero (lat. 35°25'30" N, long. 120°44'20" W; near NE cor. sec. 12, T 29 S, R 11 E); the place is less than 1 mile north-northwest of Cerro Alto. Named on Atascadero (1965) 7.5' quadrangle.

Cerro Bonito [SAN BENITO]: *ridge,* west-northwest-trending, 3 miles long, 5.5 miles west-southwest of Panoche (lat. 36°34'15" N, long. 120°56' W). Named on Llanada (1969) 7.5' quadrangle. Called Cerros Bonito on Santa Cruz (1956) 1°x 2° quadrangle. Anderson and Pack (p. 17) referred to Cerro Bonito Ridge.

Cerro Bonito Ridge: see **Cerro Bonito** [SAN BENITO].

Cerro Cabrillo [SAN LUIS OBISPO]: *hill,* 3 miles east-southeast of Morro Rock (lat. 35°21'10" N, long. 120°49' W; near N line sec. 5, T 30 S, R 11 E). Named on Morro Bay South (1965) 7.5' quadrangle. The name honors Juan Rodriguez Cabrillo, commander of the first expedition to sail along the California coast (United States Board on Geographic Names, 1965a, p. 9).

Cerro Colorado [SAN BENITO]: *peak,* 11 miles northwest of Panoche (lat. 36°43'05" N, long. 120°57'20" W; sec. 14, T 14 S, R 9 E). Altitude 3656 feet. Named on Cerro Colorado (1969) 7.5' quadrangle.

Cerro del Venado: see **Sugarloaf** [SAN BENITO].

Cerro Romaldo: see **Cerro Romualdo** [SAN LUIS OBISPO].

Cerro Romauldo: see **Cerro Romualdo** [SAN LUIS OBISPO].

Cerro Romualdo [SAN LUIS OBISPO]: *peak,* 4.5 miles west-northwest of San Luis Obispo (lat. 35°18'50" N, long. 120°43'35" W); the peak is south of Huerta de Romualdo grant. Altitude 1307 feet. Named on San Luis Obispo (1965) 7.5' quadrangle. Called Cerro Romauldo on San Luis Obispo (1897) 15' quadrangle. Goodyear (1888, p. 99) called the peak Picacho de Romualdo. United States Board on Geographic Names (1964, p. 15) rejected the names "Cerro Romaldo" and "Cerro Romauldo" for the feature. The name commemorates Romualdo, the Indian who received Huerta Romualdo grant (Gudde, 1949, p. 62-63).

Cerro San Luis Obispo [SAN LUIS OBISPO]: *peak,* 1 mile west of downtown San Luis Obispo (lat. 35°17' N, long. 120°40'45" W; sec. 27, T 30 S, R 12 E). Altitude 1292 feet. Named on San Luis Obispo (1965) 7.5' quadrangle. Goodyear (1888, p. 99) called the feature San Luis Peak, but United

States Board on Geographic Names (1961b, p. 9) rejected this name.

Cerros Bonito: see **Cerro Bonito** [SAN BENITO].

Chalk Hill [SAN LUIS OBISPO]: *hill,* 1 mile northeast of Santa Margarita (lat. 35°24' N, long. 120°35'30" W). Named on Santa Margarita (1965) 7.5' quadrangle.

Chalk Hill [SANTA BARBARA]: *peak,* 2.5 miles east of Buellton (lat. 34°36'50" N, long. 120°08'45" W). Named on Solvang (1959) 7.5' quadrangle.

Chalk Mountain [SAN LUIS OBISPO]: *peak,* 4 miles west-southwest of Caliente Mountain at the edge of Cuyama Valley (lat. 35°01' N, long. 119°49'35" W; on W line sec. 25, T 11 N, R 28 W). Named on Caliente Mountain (1959) 7.5' quadrangle.

Chalk Mountain [SANTA CRUZ]: *peak,* 4.5 miles north of the mouth of Waddell Creek (lat. 37°09'40" N, long. 122°17'20" W); the peak is at the south end of The Chalks. Altitude 1609 feet. Named on Franklin Point (1955) 7.5' quadrangle.

Chalk Peak [MONTEREY]:

(1) *peak,* 13 miles northeast of San Ardo (lat. 36°10'35" N, long. 120°46'05" W). Altitude 2456 feet. Named on Monarch Peak (1967) 7.5' quadrangle.

(2) *peak,* 7 miles north-northeast of Cape San Martin (lat. 35°59'15" N, long. 121°25'50" W; sec. 28, T 22 S, R 5 E). Altitude 3590 feet. Named on Cape San Martin (1949) 7.5' quadrangle.

Chalk Peak Camp [MONTEREY]: *locality,* 7.5 miles north-northeast of Cape San Martin (lat. 35°59'40" N, long. 121°25'50" W; sec. 28, T 22 S, R 5 E); the site is 0.5 mile north of Chalk Peak (2). Named on Cape San Martin (1949) 7.5' quadrangle. The place also was called Apple Camp and Apple Tree Camp (Clark, 1991, p. 94). On Cape San Martin (1961) 15' quadrangle, Chalk Peak Camp is shown 0.5 mile south-southwest of Chalk Peak (2).

Chalk Point: see **Camp No. 4**, under **Bridge Creek** [SANTA CRUZ].

Chalks: see **The Chalks** [SANTA CRUZ].

Chalone: see **Metz** [MONTEREY].

Chalone Creek [MONTEREY-SAN BENITO]: *stream,* heads in San Benito County and flows 27 miles to Salinas River 2.5 miles northeast of Greenfield in Monterey County (lat. 36°20'50" N, long. 121°12'35" W; sec. 21, T 18 S, R 7 E). Named on Bickmore Canyon (1968), Greenfield (1956), Mount Johnson (1968), and North Chalone Peak (1969) 7.5' quadrangles. Whitney (p. 159) referred to Chelone Creek.

Chalone Creek Campground [SAN BENITO]: *locality,* 3.25 miles north-northeast of North Chalone Peak (lat. 36°29'30" N, long. 121°10'10" W; sec. 35, T 16 S, R 7 E); the place is along Chalone Creek. Named on North Chalone Peak (1969) 7.5' quadrangle.

Chalone Mountain: see **North Chalone Peak** [MONTEREY-SAN BENITO].

Chalone Peak: see **North Chalone Peak** [MONTEREY-SAN BENITO]; **South Chalone Peak** [MONTEREY].

Chamisal Ridge [MONTEREY]: *ridge,* northwest- to west-northwest-trending, 3.5 miles long, 5.5 miles east-northeast of Soberanes Point (lat. 36°28'45" N, long. 121°50' W). Named on Mount Carmel (1956) 7.5' quadrangle.

Chandler Lake: see **Corralitos Lagoon** [SANTA CRUZ].

Channel Islands: see **Santa Barbara Channel** [SANTA BARBARA].

Chanslor: see **McKay** [SAN LUIS OBISPO].

Chaparral Campground [SAN BENITO]: *locality,* 3.25 miles north-northwest of North Chalone Peak (lat. 36°29'35" N, long. 121°12'35" W; sec. 33, T 16 S, R 7 E). Named on North Chalone Peak (1969) 7.5' quadrangle.

Chaparral Overlook [SAN BENITO]: *locality,* 3 miles north-northwest of North Chalone Peak (lat. 36°29'20" N, long. 121°12'45" W; at S line sec. 33, T 16 S, R 7 E). Named on North Chalone Peak (1969) 7.5' quadrangle.

Charles McFadden: see **One Suerte** [MONTEREY].

Charley Creek [MONTEREY]: *stream,* flows 4.5 miles to San Lorenzo Creek 2.5 miles west-southwest of Charley Mountain (lat. 36° 07'55" N, long. 120°42'35" W; sec. 6, T 21 S, R 12 E); the stream heads at Charley Valley. Named on Priest Valley (1969) and Slack Canyon (1969) 7.5' quadrangles.

Charley Mountain [MONTEREY]: *peak,* 15 miles east-northeast of San Ardo on Monterey-Fresno County line (lat. 36°08'25" N, long. 120°39'50" W; sec. 34, T 20 S, R 12 E). Altitude 3885 feet. Named on Priest Valley (1969) 7.5' quadrangle.

Charley Valley [MONTEREY]: *valley,* 1.5 miles south of Charley Mountain (lat. 36°07'15" N, long. 120°39'50" W). Named on Priest Valley (1969) and Slack Canyon (1969) 7.5' quadrangles.

Charlie Valley [SAN LUIS OBISPO]: *valley,* 10.5 miles southwest of Branch Mountain (lat. 35°03'50" N, long. 120°11'55" W; on S line sec. 36, T 12 N, R 32 W). Named on Chimney Canyon (1967) 7.5' quadrangle.

Chase's Corners: see **Dunneville** [SAN BENITO].

Chavoya Canyon [MONTEREY]: *canyon,* drained by a stream that flows 3.25 miles to Pancho Rico Valley 8 miles east-northeast of San Ardo (lat. 36°04'10" N, long. 120°46'30" W; sec. 27, T 21 S, R 11 E). Named on Pancho Rico Valley (1967) 7.5' quadrangle. Called Cebolla Canyon on San Ardo (1943) 15' quadrangle. The name recalls the Chavoya family, early settlers in the neighborhood (Clark, 1991, p. 97-98).

Chelame Pass: see **Cholame Creek** [MONTEREY-SAN LUIS OBISPO].

Chelone: see **Mount Chelone**, under **North Chalone Peak** [MONTEREY-SAN BENITO].

Chelone Creek: see **Chalone Creek** [MONTEREY-SAN BENITO].

Chemisal: see **Bolsa de Chamisal** [SAN LUIS OBISPO].

Chemise Ridge [SAN BENITO]: *ridge,* north- to northwest-trending, 2 miles long, 3.25 miles east of Panoche Pass (lat. 36°37'45" N, long. 121°04'15" W). Named on Panoche Pass (1968) and San Benito (1968) 7.5' quadrangles.

Cherokee Spring [SANTA BARBARA]: *spring,* 3 miles east of Tepusquet Peak (lat. 34°54'25" N, long. 120°07'50" W). Named on Tepusquet Canyon (1964) 7.5' quadrangle.

Cherry Canyon [MONTEREY]:

(1) *canyon,* drained by a stream that flows 4.5 miles to San Carlos Canyon 4.5 miles east-northeast of Greenfield (lat. 36°20'15" N, long. 121°09'55" W). Named on Greenfield (1956) and Pinalito Canyon (1969) 7.5' quadrangles.

(2) *canyon,* drained by a stream that flows nearly 4 miles to Quinado Canyon 5.5 miles south of King City (lat. 36°08'05" N, long. 121°07'45" W; sec. 5, T 21 S, R 8 E). Named on Thompson Canyon (1949) 7.5' quadrangle.

Cherry Canyon [SAN BENITO]: *canyon,* drained by a stream that flows 1.25 miles to Chalone Creek 2.5 miles east-southeast of North Chalone Peak (lat. 36°25'35" N, long. 121°09'15" W; sec. 25, T 17 S, R 7 E). Named on North Chalone Peak (1969) 7.5' quadrangle.

Cherry Orchard Spring [SANTA BARBARA]: *spring,* 1 mile west-southwest of Salisbury Potrero (lat. 34°49'05" N, long. 119°42'55" W). Named on Salisbury Potrero (1964) 7.5' quadrangle.

Cherry Peak [SAN BENITO]: *peak,* 8 miles east-southeast of Paicines (lat. 36°41'35" N, long. 121°08'35" W; near NW cor. sec. 30, T 14 S, R 8 E). Altitude 2916 feet. Named on Cherry Peak (1968) 7.5' quadrangle.

Cherry Ridge [SANTA BARBARA]: *ridge,* south- to south-southwest-trending, 2 miles long, 7.5 miles south-southwest of the city of Lompoc (lat. 34°32'15" N, long. 120°29'40" W). Named on Lompoc Hills (1959) and Tranquillon Mountain (1959) 7.5' quadrangles.

Cherry Thicket [MONTEREY]: *locality,* 2.5 miles south-southeast of Jamesburg (lat. 36°20'25" N, long. 121°36' W; near N line sec. 25, T 18 S, R 3 E). Named on Chews Ridge (1956) 7.5' quadrangle.

Cherry Tree Ridge [MONTEREY]: *ridge,* north-northwest-trending, 1.5 miles long, 2.5 miles west-northwest of Fremont Peak (lat. 36° 46'10" N, long. 121°32'40" W). Named on San Juan Bautista (1955) 7.5' quadrangle.

Chester Spring [SAN LUIS OBISPO]: *spring,* 3 miles north-northwest of Castle Crags (lat. 35°20'25" N, long. 120°13'45" W). Named on La Panza (1967) 7.5' quadrangle.

Chews Creek: see **Kincannon Canyon** [MONTEREY].

Chews Ridge [MONTEREY]: *ridge,* northwest-trending, 4 miles long, 5 miles south-southeast of Jamesburg (lat. 36°19'15" N, long. 121°34'45" W). Named on Chews Ridge (1956) 7.5' quadrangle. The name commemorates Constantine Marcus Chew, who patented land on the west side of the ridge in the 1890's (Clark, 1991, p. 98).

Chibo Peak: see **Cibo Peak** [SAN BENITO].

Chicken Springs: see **Goat Rock** [SANTA BARBARA].

Childs: see **Santa Ynez** [SANTA BARBARA].

Chileno Camp [SAN LUIS OBISPO]: *locality,* 5 miles north-northwest of the village of San Simeon (lat. 35°42'20" N, long. 121°14'10" W). Named on San Simeon (1958) 7.5' quadrangle.

Chimney Canyon [SAN LUIS OBISPO]: *canyon,* 3.5 miles long, opens into the canyon of Cuyama River 14 miles southwest of Branch Mountain (lat. 35°01'30" N, long. 120°13'50" W). Named on Chimney Canyon (1967) 7.5' quadrangle.

Chimney Rock [SAN LUIS OBISPO]: *relief feature,* 5.25 miles east-northeast of Adelaida on the south side of San Marcos Creek (lat. 35°41'20" N, long. 120°47'35" W; near N line sec. 9, T 26 S, R 11 E). Named on Adelaida (1948) 7.5' quadrangle.

China Camp [MONTEREY]: *locality,* 5.5 miles south-southeast of Jamesburg (lat. 36°17'45" N, long. 121°34' W; sec. 7, T 19 S, R 4 E). Named on Chews Ridge (1956) 7.5' quadrangle. A labor camp for Chinese workers was at the site (Clark, 1991, p. 99).

China Cove [MONTEREY]: *embayment,* 1 mile southeast of Point Lobos along the coast (lat. 36°30'30" N, long. 121°56'25" W). Named on Monterey (1947) 7.5' quadrangle. California Department of Parks and Recreation's map shows a place called Hidden Beach situated on the coast about 750 feet north of China Cove.

China Gulch [MONTEREY]:

(1) *canyon,* drained by a stream that flows nearly 1.5 miles to San Antonio River 8.5 miles southeast of Junipero Serra Peak (lat. 36° 03'40" N, long. 121°18'30" W). Named on Bear Canyon (1949) 7.5' quadrangle.

(2) *canyon,* drained by a stream that flows nearly 2 miles to lowlands 4 miles south-southeast of Jolon (lat. 35°55' N, long. 121°08'45" W). Named on Jolon (1949) 7.5' quadrangle.

China Harbor [SAN LUIS OBISPO]: *embayment,* 0.5 mile east-northeast of Point Estero (lat. 35°27'45" N, long. 120°59'30" W; sec. 34, T 28 S, R 9 E). Named on Cayucos (1965) 7.5' quadrangle.

China Harbor: see **Chinese Harbor** [SANTA BARBARA].

China Ladder: see **Arroyo las Trancas** [SANTA CRUZ].

China Point: see **Mussel Point** [MONTEREY].

China Ridge [SANTA CRUZ]: *ridge*, south- to southwest-trending, 2 miles long, 6 miles northeast of Soquel (lat. 37°02'55" N, long. 121°52'50" W). Named on Laurel (1955) 7.5' quadrangle. The name is from the Chinese railroad workers who built a broad-gauge line up the canyon of Aptos Creek about 1890 (Lydon, p. 105).

Chinese Harbor [SANTA BARBARA]: *embayment*, 4.25 miles east of Prisoners Harbor on the north side of Santa Cruz Island (lat. 34° 01'35" N, long. 119°36'30" W). Named on Santa Cruz Island C (1943) 7.5' quadrangle. Called China Harbor on Bremner's (1932) map. Yankee skippers landed Chinese coolies at the place while awaiting an opportunity to smuggle them to the mainland (Gleason, p. 49).

Chittenden [SANTA CRUZ]: *settlement*, 8 miles west of Watsonville along Pajaro River (lat. 36°54'10" N, long. 121°36'20" W). Named on Chittenden (1955) 7.5' quadrangle. Postal authorities established Chittenden post office in 1893 and discontinued it in 1923; the name is for W.W. Chittenden, who purchased the site 1852 (Salley, p. 43). Chittenden's Sulphur Springs, known locally for their medicinal properties, were near the settlement (Crawford, 1896, p. 519). The springs also were known as Shale Sulphur Springs, El Pajaro Springs (Waring, G.A., p. 274-275), Chittenden Springs, and Saint Francis Springs—the last name when they were owned by the Franciscan order (Laizure, 1926, p. 89). One of the springs was called Railroad Spring because it was a favorite of railroad men; two nearby springs were called White Sulphur Springs—the water of these became milky and deposited natural sulphur after flowing for a few yards (Waring, G.A., p. 274).

Chittenden Pass [SAN BENITO-SANTA CRUZ]: *canyon*, nearly 2 miles north-northeast of Aromas along Pajaro River on San Benito-Santa Cruz County line (lat. 36°54'40" N, long. 121° 37'30" W). Named on Chittenden (1955) and Watsonville East (1955) 7.5' quadrangles. The narrow part of the canyon is called Pajaro Gap.

Chittenden Springs: see **Chittenden's Sulphur Springs**, under **Chittenden** [SANTA CRUZ].

Chittenden's Sulphur Springs: see **Chittenden** [SANTA CRUZ].

Choice Valley [SAN LUIS OBISPO]: *valley*, 11 miles east-southeast of Shandon on San Luis Obispo-Kern County line (lat. 35°37'40" N, long. 120°11'30" W). Named on Orchard Peak (1961) 7.5' quadrangle.

Chokecherry Canyon [SANTA BARBARA]: *canyon*, drained by a stream that flows 3.5 miles to Santa Barbara Canyon 3 miles north-northeast of Madulce Peak (lat. 34°44' N, long. 119°34'15" W). Named on Madulce Peak (1964) 7.5' quadrangle.

Chokecherry Spring [SANTA BARBARA]: *spring*, 2.5 miles northeast of Big Pine Mountain (lat. 34°43'30" N, long. 119°37'35" W); the spring is near the head of Chokecherry Canyon. Named on Big Pine Mountain (1964) 7.5' quadrangle.

Cholame [MONTEREY-SAN LUIS OBISPO]: *land grant*, north of the village of Cholame on Monterey-San Luis Obispo County line; the grant covers most of Cholame Valley. Named on Cholame (1961), Cholame Hills (1961), Cholame Valley (1961), Orchard Peak (1961), and Tent Hills (1942) 7.5' quadrangles. Mauricio Gonzales received 6 leagues in 1844; Ellen E. White claimed 26,622 acres patented in 1865 (Cowan, p. 27; Perez, p. 62). The name is from an Indian village located near San Miguel mission (Kroeber, 1916, p. 38). Angel (1883, p. 215) used the form "Cholamie," and Gudde (1949, p. 67) mentioned early use of the name "Cholan."

Cholame [SAN LUIS OBISPO]: *village*, 23 miles east-northeast of Paso Robles (lat. 35°43'25" N, long. 120°17'45" W; sec. 30, T 25 S, R 16 E); the place is in Cholame Valley. Named on Cholame (1961) 7.5' quadrangle. Postal authorities established Cholame post office in 1873, discontinued it in 1908, and reestablished it the same year (Salley, p. 43).

Cholame Creek [MONTEREY-SAN LUIS OBISPO]: *stream*, heads in Monterey County and flows 35 miles to join San Juan Creek and form Estrella River at Shandon in San Luis Obispo County (lat. 35°39'35" N, long. 120°22'10" W; near NW cor. sec. 21, T 26 S, R 15 E). Named on Cholame (1961), Cholame Hills (1961), Cholame Valley (1961), Parkfield (1961), and Stockdale Mountain (1948) 7.5' quadrangles. Gudde (1949, p, 67) noted that a Land Office map of 1859 has the name "Choloma Creek." Parke's (1854-1855) map has the name "Chelame Pass" for the valley of Cholame Creek between present Shandon and Cholame. On a county map of 1877, the lower part of present Cholame Creek is called Russells Creek (Clark, 1991, p. 103).

Cholame Creek: see **Little Cholame Creek** [MONTEREY].

Cholame Hills [MONTEREY-SAN LUIS OBISPO]: *range*, southwest of Cholame Valley on Monterey-San Luis Obispo County line—mainly in Monterey County. Named on Cholame (1961), Cholame Hills (1961), Cholame Valley (1961), Parkfield (1961), and Stockdale Mountain (1948) 7.5' quadrangles.

Cholame Valley [MONTEREY-SAN LUIS OBISPO]: *valley*, mainly northwest of the village of Cholame on Monterey-San Luis Obispo County line; Cholame Creek drains the valley. Named on Cholame (1961), Cholame Hills (1961) and Cholame Valley (1961) 7.5' quadrangles.

Cholame Valley: see **Little Cholame Valley**, under **Little Cholame Creek** [MONTEREY].

Cholamie: see **Cholame** [MONTEREY-SAN LUIS OBISPO].

Cholan: see **Cholame** [MONTEREY-SAN LUIS OBISPO].

Cholla Creek [SAN BENITO]: *stream*, flows nearly 4 miles to Bitterwater Creek 4.5 miles southeast of Bitterwater (lat. 36°20' N, long. 120°56'25" W; sec. 25, T 18 S, R 9 E). Named on Lonoak (1969) 7.5' quadrangle.

Choloma Creek: see **Cholame Creek** [MONTEREY-SAN LUIS OBISPO].

Chorro [SAN LUIS OBISPO]: *locality*, 3.25 miles north-northwest of downtown San Luis Obispo along Southern Pacific Railroad (lat. 35°19'35" N, long. 120°40'35" W). Named on San Luis Obispo (1965) 7.5' quadrangle.

Chorro: see **Huerta de Romualdo** [SAN LUIS OBISPO].

Chorro Creek [SAN LUIS OBISPO]: *stream*, flows 14 miles to Morro Bay 3 miles southeast of Morro Rock (lat. 35°20'25" N, long. 120° 50'25" W); the stream is partly on El Chorro grant. Named on Morro Bay South (1965) and San Luis Obispo (1965) 7.5' quadrangles. United States Board on Geographic Names (1933, p. 219) rejected the name "San Luisito Creek" for the stream.

Chorro Reservoir [SAN LUIS OBISPO]: *lake*, 1000 feet long, 4.25 miles north-northwest of San Luis Obispo (lat. 35°20'15" N, long. 120°41'10" W); the lake is along Chorro Creek. Named on San Luis Obispo (1965) 7.5' quadrangle.

Chris Flood Creek [MONTEREY-SAN LUIS OBISPO]: *stream*, heads in Monterey County and flows nearly 6 miles to San Carpoforo Creek 3.25 miles east-northeast of the mouth of that creek in San Luis Obispo County (lat. 35°47'05" N, long. 121°16'15" W; sec. 1, T 25 S, R 6 E). Named on Burnett Peak (1949) and Burro Mountain (1949) 7.5' quadrangles.

Christy Cañada: see **Cañada Cervada** [SANTA BARBARA].

Chualar [MONTEREY]:

(1) *land grant*, 11 miles southeast of Salinas around the village of Chualar. Named on Chualar (1947) and Gonzales (1955) 7.5' quadrangles. Juan Malarin received 2 leagues in 1839; Mariano Malarin, executor, claimed 8890 acres patented in 1872 (Cowan, p. 27; Cowan listed the grant under the name "Santa Rosa de Chualar"). *Chual* is an Indian word for the plant commonly called pigweed; the name "Chualar" apparently is a Spanish adaptation of the Indian word and means "place where chual grows" (Stewart, p. 97).

(2) *village*, 10 miles southeast of Salinas (lat. 36°34'15" N, long. 121°31' W); the place is on Chualar grant. Named on Chualar (1947) 7.5' quadrangle. Postal authorities established Chualar post office in 1871, discontinued it in 1873, and reestablished it in 1874 (Frickstad, p. 106).

Chualar Canyon [MONTEREY]: *canyon*, drained by a stream that flows 7.5 miles to lowlands 5 miles east-northeast of the village of Chualar (lat. 36°35'30" N, long. 121°27'30" W). Named on Gonzales (1955), Mount Johnson (1968), and Paicines (1968) 7.5' quadrangles.

Chualar Creek [MONTEREY]: *stream*, flows 5 miles from the mouth of Chualar Canyon to a point 0.5 mile south-southwest of the village of Chualar (lat. 36°33'40" N, long. 121°31'20" W). Named on Gonzales (1955) 7.5' quadrangle.

Chumash Peak [SAN LUIS OBISPO]: *peak*, 3.25 miles northwest of San Luis Obispo (lat. 35°18'25" N, long. 120°42'20" W; near N line sec. 20, T 30 S, R 12 E). Altitude 1268 feet. Named on San Luis Obispo (1965) 7.5' quadrangle. The name is for a linguistic family of California Indians (United States Board on Geographic Names, 1965a, p. 9).

Chupines Creek [MONTEREY]: *stream*, flows 8 miles to Tularcitos Creek 3 miles southeast of the town of Carmel Valley (lat. 36°27'10" N, long. 121°41'45" W). Named on Carmel Valley (1956) and Rana Creek (1956) 7.5' quadrangles.

Church Creek [MONTEREY]: *stream*, flows 4.5 miles to Tassajara Creek 1.25 miles west-northwest of Tassajara Hot Springs (lat. 36° 14'35" N, long. 121°34'35" W; near N line sec. 31, T 19 S, R 4 E). Named on Chews Ridge (1956) and Tassajara Hot Springs (1956) 7.5' quadrangles. The name commemorates the Church family, first settlers near the stream (Gudde, 1949, p. 68).

Church Creek Divide [MONTEREY]: *pass*, 6 miles south-southwest of Jamesburg (lat. 36°17'25" N, long. 121°36'40" W; sec. 11, T 19 S, R 3 E); the feature is at the head of Church Creek. Named on Chews Ridge (1956) 7.5' quadrangle.

Church Creek Rockshelter: see **The Caves** [MONTEREY].

Cibo Peak [MONTEREY]: *peak*, 4.25 miles west-southwest of Potrero Peak (lat. 36°49'40" N, long. 121°13'05" W). Altitude 2845 feet. Named on Quien Sabe Valley (1968) 7.5' quadrangle. Called Chibo Peak on California Mining Bureau's (1917b) map.

Cienega: see **Thompson Creek** [SAN BENITO].

Cienega Camp [MONTEREY]: *locality*, 5.5 miles north-northeast of Partington Point (lat. 36°14'50" N, long. 121°39'10" W; sec. 29, T 19 S, R 3 E); the place is along Cienega Creek. Named on Partington Ridge (1956)

7.5' quadrangle.

Cienega Creek [MONTEREY]: *stream,* flows 2 miles to North Fork Big Sur River 5.25 miles north-northeast of Partington Point (lat. 36°14'35" N, long. 121°39'20" W; at N line sec. 32, T 19 S, R 3 E). Named on Partington Ridge (1956) and Ventana Cones (1956) 7.5' quadrangles. The name is from marsh located 0.5 mile north of the mouth of the stream—*cienega* means "marsh" or "swamp" in Spanish (Clark, 1991, p. 105).

Cienega Creek [SAN LUIS OBISPO]: *stream,* flows nearly 4 miles to Santa Rita Creek 2 miles southwest of York Mountain (lat. 35°31'25" N, long. 120°51'05" W). Named on Cypress Mountain (1948) and York Mountain (1948) 7.5' quadrangles.

Cienega del Gabilan [MONTEREY-SAN BENITO]: *land grant,* 10 miles east-northeast of Salinas on Monterey-San Benito County line. Named on Hollister (1955), Mount Harlan (1968), Natividad (1947), Paicines (1968), San Juan Bautista (1955), and Tres Pinos (1955) 7.5' quadrangles. Antonio Chavis received the grant in 1843; Jessie D. Carr claimed 48,781 acres patented in 1867 (Cowan, p. 37—Cowan listed the grant under the designation "Cienega del Gavilan (or Gabilan)"; Perez, p. 62). United States Board on Geographic Names (1933, p. 221) rejected the form "Sienega del Gabilan" for the name.

Cienega de los Paicines [SAN BENITO]: *land grant,* around Paicines along and west of Tres Pinos Creek. Named on Paicines (1968) and Tres Pinos (1955) 7.5' quadrangles. Angel Castro and Jose Rodroguez received 2 leagues in 1842; Castro claimed 8918 acres patented in 1869 (Cowan, p. 56—Cowan listed the grant under the designation "Cienege de los Paicines (or Pajines, or Paycines)"; Perez, p. 62). According to Kroeber (1916, p. 53), the name "Paicines," or "Pajines," probably is from the designation of an Indian tribe.

Cienega Valley [SAN BENITO]: *valley,* 4 miles west-southwest of Paicines along Pescadero Creek (lat. 36°43' N, long. 121°20'50" W). Named on Paicines (1968) 7.5' quadrangle.

Cienega Valley [SAN LUIS OBISPO]: *area,* 3 miles south-southwest of downtown Arroyo Grande near the coast (lat. 35°05'10" N, long. 120°36'20" W). Named on Oceano (1965) 7.5' quadrangle.

Cieneguitas Creek [SANTA BARBARA]: *stream,* flows 3 miles to Atascadero Creek 3 miles east of downtown Goleta (lat. 34°26'05" N, long. 119°46'30" W). Named on Goleta (1950) 7.5' quadrangle.

Cierro Chalon: see **North Chalone Peak** [MONTEREY-SAN BENITO].

Ciervo Hills [SAN BENITO]: *range,* east of Tumey Gulch on San Benito-Fresno County line, mainly in Fresno County. Named on Ciervo Mountain (1969), Idria (1969), and Tumey Hills (1956) 7.5' quadrangles.

Cigarette Spring [SANTA BARBARA]: *spring,* 5 miles north-northwest of Tepusquet Peak (lat. 34°58'50" N, long. 120°12'30" W). Named on Tepusquet Canyon (1964) 7.5' quadrangle.

Cinco Canoas Canyon [MONTEREY-SAN BENITO]: *canyon,* drained by a stream that heads in San Benito County and flows nearly 8.5 miles to San Carlos Canyon 4.5 miles east-northeast of Greenfield in Monterey County (lat. 36°20'15" N, long. 121°09'55" W). Named on Greenfield (1956) and Pinalito Canyon (1969) 7.5' quadrangles.

Cinnabar: see **San Benito River** [SAN BENITO].

City of King: see **The City of King**, under **King City** [MONTEREY].

Clapboard Canyon [SAN LUIS OBISPO]: *canyon,* drained by a stream that flows 3.25 miles to Arroyo Grande Creek 10 miles north of the town of Nipomo (lat. 35°11'15" N, long. 120°27'35" W; sec. 34, T 31 S, R 14 E). Named on Tar Spring Ridge (1967) 7.5' quadrangle.

Clark Canyon [SANTA BARBARA]: *canyon,* 1.5 miles long, opens into Lake Cachuma 4.5 miles north of Santa Ynez Peak (lat. 34°35'30" N, long. 119°58'30" W). Named on Lake Cachuma (1959) 7.5' quadrangle. Water of Lake Cachuma now floods the lower part of the canyon.

Clark Colony: see **Arroyo Seco** [MONTEREY] (2).

Clarke Canyon [SAN LUIS OBISPO]: *canyon,* drained by a stream that flows 5.5 miles to lowlands along Estrella Creek 11 miles east-northeast of Paso Robles (lat. 35°40'40" N, long. 120°30'05" W; sec. 7, T 26 S, R 14 E). Named on Shandon (1961) 7.5' quadrangle.

Clarke City: see **Greenfield** [MONTEREY].

Clark Valley [SAN LUIS OBISPO]: *valley,* 7.5 miles southeast of Morro Rock along the upper part of Los Osos Creek (lat. 35°16'45" N, long. 120°47' W). Named on Morro Bay South (1965) 7.5' quadrangle. Called Cañada de los Alisos on a diseño made in 1842 of Cañada de los Osos grant (Becker, 1969).

Clayton: see **Camp Clayton Military Reservation**, under **Fort Ord Military Reservation** [MONTEREY].

Clear Creek [SAN BENITO]: *stream,* flows 8.5 miles to San Benito River 12.5 miles east of Bitterwater (lat. 36°21'20" N, long. 120° 47' W; near SE cor. sec. 17, T 18 S, R 11 E). Named on Hepsedam Peak (1969), Idria (1969), and San Benito Mountain (1969) 7.5' quadrangles.

Clear Creek [SANTA BARBARA]: *stream,* flows 4.25 miles to Cuyama River 6.5 miles northwest of Miranda Pine Mountain (lat. 35°05'50" N, long. 120°07'25" W). Named on Miranda Pine Mountain (1967) 7.5' quadrangle.

Clear Creek [SANTA CRUZ]: *stream,* flows 2.25 miles to San Lorenzo River 1.25 miles southeast of the town of Boulder Creek (lat. 37°06'35" N, long. 122°06'25" W; sec. 32, T 9 S, R 2 W). Named on Davenport (1955) and Felton (1955) 7.5' quadrangles.

Clear Creek: see **Brookdale** [SANTA CRUZ].

Clear Lake [SAN LUIS OBISPO]: *intermittent lake,* 350 feet long, 7.5 miles northeast of Santa Margarita (lat. 35°28'30" N, long. 120°31'15" W). Named on Santa Margarita (1965) 7.5' quadrangle.

Clear Ridge: see **Pfeiffer Ridge** [MONTEREY].

Clems [SANTA CRUZ]: *locality,* 2.25 miles southwest of Laurel along Southern Pacific Railroad (lat. 37°05'55" N, long. 121°59'50" W; near N line sec. 5, T 10 S, R 1 W). Named on Los Gatos (1919) 15' quadrangle. Hamman's (1980b) map shows a place called Tank Siding located nearly 1 mile northwest of Clems along the railroad.

Cleveland Rock [MONTEREY]: *peak,* 16 miles north-northeast of San Ardo on Mustang Ridge (lat. 36°14'45" N, long. 120°49'20" W; sec. 30, T 19 S, R 11 E). Altitude 2494 feet. Named on Monarch Peak (1967) 7.5' quadrangle. The name is for early settlers who owned land near the peak (Clark, 1991, p. 108).

Cliff Canyon [SANTA BARBARA]: *canyon,* drained by a stream that flows 4.5 miles to Sisquoc River 5.25 miles south-southwest of Salisbury Potrero (lat. 34°45'10" N, long. 119°44'25" W). Named on Salisbury Potrero (1964) 7.5' quadrangle.

Cliff Springs: see **Hot Springs** [SANTA BARBARA] (2).

Clipper Gulch [SANTA CRUZ]: *canyon,* drained by a stream that flows nearly 1 mile to Eureka Canyon 3 miles north-northwest of Corralitos (lat. 37°01'50" N, long. 121°49'05" W; at W line sec. 25, T 10 S, R 1 E). Named on Loma Prieta (1955) 7.5' quadrangle.

Clough Canyon [SAN BENITO]: *canyon,* drained by a stream that flows nearly 6.5 miles to Panoche Valley 1 mile west-northwest of Panoche (lat. 36°36' N, long. 120°50'55" W; sec. 26, T 15 S, R 10 E). Named on Llanada (1969) 7.5' quadrangle.

Clover Basin Camp [MONTEREY]: *locality,* 4.25 miles east of Uncle Sam Mountain (lat. 36°20'35" N, long. 121°37'45" W; near SE cor. sec. 22, T 18 S, R 3 E). Named on Ventana Cones (1956) 7.5' quadrangle.

Cluster Point [SANTA BARBARA]: *promontory,* 6.5 miles southeast of Sandy Point on the south side of Santa Rosa Island (lat. 33°55'30" N, long. 120°10'45" W). Named on Santa Rosa Island West (1943) 7.5' quadrangle.

Coal Chute Point: see **Carmel Cove** [MONTEREY].

Coal Oil Point [SANTA BARBARA]: *promontory,* 3.5 miles southwest of Goleta along the coast (lat. 34°24'25" N, long. 119°52'40" W). Named on Dos Pueblos Canyon (1951) 7.5' quadrangle. H.R. Wagner (p. 519) noted the Spanish name "Punta de Tobar" for present Coal Oil Point. Goodyear (1888, p. 91) called the feature Salinas Point, and noted that a large petroleum spring is beneath the sea about 0.5 mile off the point.

Coast: see **Santa Cruz** [SANTA CRUZ].

Coati Point [SANTA BARBARA]: *promontory,* 0.5 mile south of Carrington Point on the north side of Santa Rosa Island (lat. 34°01'40" N, long. 120°02'35" W). Named on Santa Rosa Island North (1943) 7.5' quadrangle.

Cobblestone Creek: see **Steve Creek** [MONTEREY].

Coburn [MONTEREY]: *locality,* 5.5 miles east-southeast of Greenfield along Southern Pacific Railroad (lat. 36°17'20" N, long. 121° 09'05" W). Named on Greenfield (1956) 7.5' quadrangle The name commemorates Loren Coburn, who deeded right of way at the place to the railroad in 1883 (Clark, 1991, p. 111).

Coche Campground [SANTA BARBARA]: *locality,* 4.5 miles west-southwest of Big Pine Mountain (lat. 34°40'50" N, long. 119° 44' W); the place is along Coche Creek. Named on Big Pine Mountain (1964) 7.5' quadrangle.

Coche Creek [SANTA BARBARA]: *stream,* flows 4.5 miles to West Fork Santa Cruz Creek 4.25 miles southeast of San Rafael Mountain (lat. 34°39'50" N, long. 119°45'50" W). Named on Big Pine Mountain (1964) and San Rafael Mountain (1959) 7.5' quadrangles. Called Grapevine Cr. on San Rafael Mountain (1943) 15' quadrangle, and called Cache Cr. on San Rafael Mountain (1959) 15' quadrangle.

Coche Point [SANTA BARBARA]: *promontory,* 4.5 miles east-northeast of Prisoners Harbor on the north side of Santa Cruz Island (lat. 34°02'15" N, long. 119°36'30" W). Named on Santa Cruz Island C (1943) 7.5' quadrangle.

Coches Prietos Anchorage [SANTA BARBARA]: *embayment,* nearly 4 miles south-southwest of Prisoners Harbor on the south side of Santa Cruz Island (lat. 33°58'05" N, long. 119°42'15" W). Named on Santa Cruz Island C (1943) 7.5' quadrangle. United States Board on Geographic Names (1936b, p. 18) rejected the forms "Cochies Prietos Anchorage" and "Coche Prietos Anchorage" for the name, and noted that *coches prietos* means "dark barges" or "black barges" in Spanish. Bremner's (1932) map has the name "Cñ. Coches Prietos" for the canyon that opens to the sea at present Coches Prietos Anchorage.

Cochies Prietos Anchorage: see **Coches Prietos Anchorage** [SANTA BARBARA].

Cocks: see **Henry Cocks** [MONTEREY].
Cocks'Station: see **San Bernabe** [MONTEREY].
Coja Creek: see **Majors Creek** [SANTA CRUZ].
Cojo Anchorage: see **Cojo Bay** [SANTA BARBARA].
Cojo Bay [SANTA BARBARA]: *embayment,* 1.5 miles east of Point Conception along the coast (lat. 34°26'50" N, long. 120°26'30" W); the embayment is west of the mouth of Cañada del Cojo. Named on Point Conception (1953) 7.5' quadrangle. Cabrillo called the place Puerto de Todos Santos in 1542, and Esteban Jose Martinez called it Ensenada de la Purisima Concepcion in 1782 (Wagner, H.R., p. 487, 519). United States Board on Geographic Names (1978b, p. 4) approved the name "Cojo Anchorage" for the place, and rejected the name "Cojo Bay." United States Coast and Geodetic Survey (p. 104) noted that a cove 1.7 miles east of Cojo Anchorage is known as Little Cojo or Old Cojo. Parke's (1854-1855) map has the name "Rcho. Coxo" at present Cojo Anchorage, and Eddy's (1854) map shows a place called Coxo there. The Spaniards used the name "Punta de Sanchez" for the promontory situated east of Cojo Anchorage (Wagner, H.R., p. 509). Cojo Anchorage was an important refuge that the Spaniards preferred to Santa Barbara; some nineteenth-century whaling vessels processed their catches on the beach there (Fagan, p. 96).
Cojo Creek [SANTA BARBARA]: *stream,* flows 2.5 miles to the sea 1.5 miles east of Point Conception at present Cojo Anchorage (lat. 34°27' N, long. 120°26'30" W). Named on Point Conception (1942) 15' quadrangle.
Cold Spring [MONTEREY]: *spring,* nearly 3 miles north-northeast of Partington Point (lat. 36°12'45" N, long. 121°40'45" W; sec. 7, T 20 S, R 3 E). Named on Lucia (1921) 15' quadrangle.
Cold Spring [SAN LUIS OBISPO]: *spring,* 8 miles north-northeast of the town of Nipomo (lat. 35°08'40" N, long. 120°24'50" W). Named on Tar Spring Ridge (1967) 7.5' quadrangle.
Cold Spring [SANTA BARBARA]:
(1) *spring,* 2 miles west of San Rafael Mountain (lat. 34°42'25" N, long. 119°50'40" W; near SE cor. sec. 5, T 7 N, R 28 W). Named on San Rafael Mountain (1959) 7.5' quadrangle.
(2) *locality,* 1 mile northwest of San Marcos Pass (lat. 34°31'15" N, long. 119°50'20" W); the place is in Cold Spring Canyon (1). Named on San Marcos Pass (1959) 7.5' quadrangle. San Rafael Mountain (1943) 15' quadrangle shows Cold Spring Tavern at the site, but United States Board on Geographic Names (1962a, p. 9) rejected this name for the locality.
Cold Spring Camp [MONTEREY]: *locality,* nearly 3 miles north-northeast of Partington Point (lat. 36°12'45" N, long. 121°40'45" W; sec. 7, T 20 S, R 3 E); Cold Spring is at the place. Named on Partington Ridge (1956) 7.5' quadrangle.
Cold Spring Canyon [SANTA BARBARA]:
(1) *canyon,* drained by a stream that flows 2 miles to Los Laureles Canyon 1 mile north-northwest of San Marcos Pass (lat. 34°31'40" N, long. 119°49'45" W; sec. 8, T 5 N, R 28 W); Cold Spring (2) is in the canyon. Named on San Marcos Pass (1959) 7.5' quadrangle.
(2) *canyon,* 2.5 miles long, along Montecito Creek above a point 3.25 miles northeast of downtown Santa Barbara (lat. 34°27' N, long. 119°39'10" W; at SE cor. sec. 1, T 4 N, R 27 W). Named on Santa Barbara (1952) 7.5' quadrangle. East Fork branches northeast 0.5 mile upstream from the mouth of the main canyon and is 2 miles long. West Fork branches northwest 1 mile upstream from the mouth of the main canyon and is 1.5 miles long. Both forks are named on Santa Barbara (1952) 7.5' quadrangle. United States Board on Geographic Names (1961b, p. 9) rejected the form "Cold Springs Canyon" for the name.
Cold Spring Saddle [SANTA BARBARA]: *pass,* 5.5 miles northeast of downtown Santa Barbara (lat. 34°29' N, long. 119°38'15" W; at E line sec. 30, T 5 N, R 26 W); the pass is near the head of East Fork Cold Spring Canyon (2). Named on Santa Barbara (1952) 7.5' quadrangle.
Cold Spring Tavern: see **Cold Spring** [SANTA BARBARA] (2).
Coldwater Campground [SANTA BARBARA]: *locality,* 2.5 miles south-southwest of Bald Mountain (1) along Manzana Creek (lat. 34°46'45" N, long. 119°57'25" W). Named on Bald Mountain (1964) 7.5' quadrangle.
Coleman Canyon [MONTEREY]: *canyon,* drained by a stream that flows 4.5 miles to an unnamed valley 9 miles east-southeast of Junipero Serra Peak (lat. 36°04'45" N, long. 121°16'45" W). Named on Bear Canyon (1949) 7.5' quadrangle. The name commemorates John W. Coleman, who received a patent to land near the canyon in 1891 (Clark, 1991, p. 112).
Cole Spring [SANTA BARBARA]: *spring,* 6 miles west-northwest of McPherson Peak (lat. 34°55'20" N, long. 119°54'30" W). Named on Bates Canyon (1964) 7.5' quadrangle.
Cole Spring Campground [SANTA BARBARA]: *locality,* 6 miles west-northwest of McPherson Peak (lat. 34°55'30" N, long. 119° 54'30" W); the place is 1100 feet north of Cole Spring. Named on Bates Canyon (1964) 7.5' quadrangle.
College Lake [SANTA CRUZ]: *intermittent lake,* about 1.25 miles long, 2.25 miles north of Watsonville (lat. 36°56'50" N, long. 121° 44'50" W). Named on Watsonville East (1955) and Watsonville West (1954) 7.5' quadrangles. The feature is shown as a permanent lake on San Juan Bautista (1917) 15' quadrangle. It first was called Laguna Grande and took the name "College Lake" after a Roman Catholic orphanage, known as the college, was built nearby in 1869 (Clark, 1986, p. 81).
College Rancho: see **Cañada de los Pinos or College Rancho** [SANTA BARBARA].
Colson Canyon [SANTA BARBARA]: *canyon,* drained by a stream that flows nearly 5 miles to Tepusquet Canyon 2 miles west-northwest of Tepusquet Peak (lat. 34°55'25" N, long. 120°13'10" W). Named on Tepusquet Canyon (1964) 7.5' quadrangle.
Colson Canyon Campgrounds [SANTA BARBARA]: *localities,* 2.25 miles north-northeast of Tepusquet Peak (lat. 34°56'20" N, long. 120°10'05" W); the campgrounds are in Colson Canyon. Named on Tepusquet Canyon (1964) 7.5' quadrangle.
Comings Creek: see **Pine Creek** [MONTEREY] (2).
Commatri Canyon: see **Camatta Canyon** [SAN LUIS OBISPO].
Commatri Creek: see **Camatta Creek** [SAN LUIS OBISPO].
Commatta Canyon: see **Camatta Canyon** [SAN LUIS OBISPO].
Commatta Creek: see **Camatta Creek** [SAN LUIS OBISPO].
Commatti Canyon: see **Camatta Canyon** [SAN LUIS OBISPO].
Commatti Creek: see **Camatta Creek** [SAN LUIS OBISPO].
Concepcion [SANTA BARBARA]: *locality,* 1 mile east-northeast of Point Conception along Southern Pacific Railroad (lat. 34°27'10" N, long. 120°27'15" W). Named on Point Conception (1953) 7.5' quadrangle. Postal authorities established Concepcion post office in 1902 and discontinued it in 1953 (Frickstad, p. 170).
Concepcion: see **Point Concepcion**, under **Point Conception** [SANTA BARBARA].
Conception: see **Point Conception** [SANTA BARBARA].
Condor Point [SANTA BARBARA]: *peak,* 3.5 miles east-southeast of Santa Ynez Peak (lat. 34°30'20" N, long. 119°55'25" W; sec. 21, T 5 N, R 29 W). Named on Lake Cachuma (1959) 7.5' quadrangle.
Conejo Creek [MONTEREY]: *stream,* flows 5 miles to Finch Creek 1.5 miles north of Jamesburg (lat. 36°23'20" N, long. 121°35'35" W; sec. 1, T 18 S, R 3 E). Named on Rana Creek (1956) 7.5' quadrangle.
Cone Peak [MONTEREY]: *peak,* nearly 8 miles southwest of Junipero Serra Peak (lat. 36°03'05" N, long. 121°29'45" W; sec. 2, T 22 S, R 4 E). Altitude 5155 feet. Named on Cone Peak (1949) 7.5' quadrangle. The name is from the shape of the peak (Clark, 1991, p. 114).
Confederate Corners [MONTEREY]: *locality,* 2 miles south-southwest of Salinas (lat. 36°38'40" N, long. 121°39'45" W). Named on Salinas (1947) 7.5' quadrangle. The name is from the Southerners who settled at the site in the late 1860's; place also was known as Springtown, or Spring Town (Clark, 1991, p. 115).
Conne Gulch [SANTA CRUZ]: *canyon,* 2 miles long, along Bear Creek above a point 5.5 miles northeast of the town of Boulder Creek (lat. 37°11'05" N, long. 122°03'20" W; at N line sec. 2, T 9 S, R 2 W). Named on Castle Rock Ridge (1955) 7.5' quadrangle. The misspelled name is for A.B. Conley, an early settler (Clark, 1986, p. 81).
Conroy Spring [SAN LUIS OBISPO]: *spring,* 3 miles west-southwest of Cholame (lat. 35°42'50" N, long. 120°21'05" W; sec. 34, T 25 S, R 15 E). Named on Cholame (1961) 7.5' quadrangle.
Constantine Rock [SAN LUIS OBISPO]: *rock,* 3.5 miles east-southeast of Point Estero, and 0.5 mile offshore (lat. 35°26'20" N, long. 120°56'40" W). Named on Cayucos (1965) 7.5' quadrangle.
Cook: see **Pinnacles** [SAN BENITO].
Cooke: see **Camp Cooke Military Reservation**, under **Vandenberg Air Force Base** [SANTA BARBARA].
Cookhouse Gulch [SANTA CRUZ]: *canyon,* drained by a stream that flows nearly 0.5 mile to Eureka Canyon 3.5 miles north of Corralitos (lat. 37°02'20" N, long. 121°49' W; near NW cor. sec. 25, T 10 S, R 1 E). Named on Loma Prieta (1955) 7.5' quadrangle.
Coon Creek [SAN LUIS OBISPO]: *stream,* flows 9 miles to the sea less than 0.5 mile northeast of Point Buchon (lat. 35°15'35" N, long. 120°53'35" W). Named on Morro Bay South (1965) and Port San Luis (1965) 7.5' quadrangles. United States Board on Geographic Names (1936b, p. 19) rejected the name "Valencia Creek" for the stream.
Cooper [MONTEREY]: *locality,* 4.5 miles northwest of Salinas along Southern Pacific Railroad (lat. 36°42'50" N, long. 121°43' W). Named on Salinas (1947, photorevised 1968 and 1975) 7.5' quadrangle. Called Coopers on Salinas (1947) 7.5' quadrangle.
Cooper Point [MONTEREY]: *promontory,* 1.5 miles northwest of Pfeiffer Point along the coast (lat. 36°14'55" N, long. 121°50'10" W; sec. 27, T 19 S, R 1 E). Named on Pfeiffer Point (1956) 7.5' quadrangle. The promontory is near the south end of El Sur grant, which J.B.R. Cooper owned.
Cooper Slough: see **Tembladero Slough** [MONTEREY].
Copperhead Canyon Creek: see **Copperhead Creek** [MONTEREY].
Copperhead Creek [MONTEREY]: *stream,* flows 5 miles to San Antonio River 11 miles southeast of Jolon (lat. 35°52'10" N, long. 121°00'25" W). Named on Bryson (1949) 7.5' quadrangle. Laizure (1925, p. 35) used the name "Copperhead Canyon Creek." The stream now enters San Antonio Reservoir.
Corbett Canyon: see **Corbit Canyon** [SAN LUIS OBISPO].

Corbit Canyon [SAN LUIS OBISPO]: *canyon,* drained by a stream that flows 4.5 miles to Arroyo Grande Creek nearly 6 miles south-southeast of Edna (lat. 35°07'25" N, long. 120°34'30" W). Named on Arroyo Grande NE (1965) 7.5' quadrangle. United States Board on Geographic Names (1967b, p. 7) rejected the form "Corbett Canyon" for the name.

Corcoran Lagoon [SANTA CRUZ]: *lake,* 1500 feet long, 0.5 mile northwest of Soquel Point near the coast (lat. 36°57'40" N, long. 121°58'50" W; sec. 20, 21, T 11 S, R 1 W). Named on Soquel (1954) 7.5' quadrangle. The name commemorates James Corcoran, a farmer in the neighborhood in the 1850's (Clark, 1986, p. 82).

Cormack Canyon [SAN LUIS OBISPO]: *canyon,* drained by a stream that flows nearly 6.5 miles to San Juan Creek 1 mile south-southeast of Shandon (lat. 35°38'25" N, long. 120°22'05" W; sec. 28, T 26 S, R 15 E). Named on Cholame (1917) 30' quadrangle. The lowermost part of the canyon is called Pfost Gulch on Cholame (1961) 7.5' quadrangle.

Corncob Canyon [MONTEREY]: *canyon,* drained by a stream that flows 1.25 miles to an unnamed canyon 2.25 miles southeast of Watsonville (lat. 36°53'05" N, long. 121°43'30" W). Named on Watsonville East (1955) 7.5' quadrangle. The name allegedly is from piles of corn cobs left from whiskey production at the place during Prohibition time (Clark, 1991, p. 118)

Coromar [SANTA BARBARA]: *locality,* 2.25 miles west of downtown Goleta along Southern Pacific Railroad (lat. 34°26'05" N, long. 119°52' W). Named on Goleta (1950) 7.5' quadrangle.

Corral Canyon [MONTEREY]: *canyon,* drained by a stream that flows 1.5 miles to Paloma Creek 12 miles southwest of Soledad (lat. 36°17'10" N, long. 121°27'30" W; near NE cor. sec. 18, T 19 S, R 5 E). Named on Sycamore Flat (1956) 7.5' quadrangle.

Corral Creek [SAN LUIS OBISPO]: *stream,* flows 2.5 miles to Alamo Creek (2) 10.5 miles southwest of Branch Mountain (lat. 35°05'50" N, long. 120°14'05" W; sec. 35, T 32 S, R 16 E). Named on Chimney Canyon (1967) 7.5' quadrangle.

Corral de Cuati: see **Corral de Quati** [SANTA BARBARA].

Corral de Piedra [SAN LUIS OBISPO]: *land grant,* southeast of San Luis Obispo around Edna. Named on Arroyo Grande NE (1965), Lopez Mountain (1965), and Pismo Beach (1965) 7.5' quadrangles. Jose Maria Villavicencio received 2 leagues in 1841 and 1846; he claimed 30,911 acres patented in 1867 (Cowan, p. 60).

Corral de Piedra Creek: see **East Corral de Piedra Creek** [SAN LUIS OBISPO]; **West Corral de Piedra Creek** [SAN LUIS OBISPO].

Corral de Quati [SANTA BARBARA]: *land grant,* north of Los Olivos. Named on Los Olivos (1959) and Zaca Creek (1959) 7.5' quadrangles. Agustin Davila received 3 leagues in 1845; Maria Antonia de la Guerra de Lataillade claimed 13,322 acres patented in 1876 (Cowan, p. 31; Cowan listed the grant under the designation "Cuati, (or Quate), Corral de").

Corral de Tierra [MONTEREY]: *land grant,* 11 miles south-southwest of Salinas. Named on Seaside (1947) and Spreckels (1947) 7.5' quadrangles. Guadalupe Figueroa received the land in 1836; H.D. McCobb claimed 4435 acres patented in 1876 (Cowan, p. 103).

Corral de Tierra: see **Corral de Tierra Valley** [MONTEREY].

Corral de Tierra Valley [MONTEREY]: *canyon,* 3 miles long, 10 miles south of Salinas on upper reaches of Watson Creek (lat. 36° 31'30" N, long. 121°41'15" W); the canyon is on and near Corral de Tierra grant. Named on Spreckels (1947) 7.5' quadrangle. Called Corral de Tierra on Salinas (1912) 15' quadrangle, where the name applies to the east part of the valley only. Postal authorities established Corral de Tierra post office in 1912, moved it 1 mile west from its original location (NW quarter sec. 19, T 16 S, R 3 E) in 1918, moved it 2 miles north in 1929, and discontinued it in 1931 (Clark, 1991, p. 119).

Corrales Canyon [SANTA BARBARA]: *canyon,* drained by a stream that flows about 6.5 miles to Santa Agueda Creek 5 miles east of Los Olivos (lat. 34°38'55" N, long. 120°01'30" W). Named on Figueroa Mountain (1959) and Los Olivos (1959) 7.5' quadrangles.

Corralillos Canyon: see **Corralitos Canyon** [SANTA BARBARA].

Corralitos [SANTA CRUZ]: *town,* 6 miles north-northwest of Watsonville (lat. 36°59'20" N, long. 121°48'20" W); the town is along Corralitos Creek on Los Corralitos grant. Named on Watsonville West (1954) 7.5' quadrangle. Postal authorities established Corralitos post office in 1861, discontinued it in 1862, reestablished it in 1876, discontinued it in 1923, and reestablished it in 1957 (Salley, p. 51).

Corralitos Canyon [SANTA BARBARA]: *canyon,* drained by a stream that flows 6 miles to Santa Maria Valley 2.5 miles south of the town of Guadalupe (lat. 34°56' N, long. 120°34'05" W). Named on Guadalupe (1959) 7.5' quadrangle. Called Corralillos Canyon on Point Sal (1947) 15' quadrangle, but United States Board on Geographic Names (1962c, p. 18) rejected this name.

Corralitos Creek [SANTA CRUZ]: *stream,* flows 13 miles to Salsipuedes Creek 1.5 miles north-northeast of Watsonville (lat. 36°56'05" N, long. 121°44'30" W). Named on Loma Prieta (1955), Watsonville East (1955), and Watsonville West (1954) 7.5' quadrangles. On San Juan Bautista (1917) 15' quadrangle, the name "Corralitos Creek" applies to present Salsipuedes Creek all the way to Pajaro River. Gudde (1949, p. 296) suggested that a stream called Arroyo de Salsipuedes on a Mexican map of 1836 is present Corralitos Creek.

Corralitos Lagoon [SANTA CRUZ]: *intermittent lake,* 0.5 mile long, 1.5 miles south-southwest of Corralitos (lat. 36°58' N, long. 121° 48'50" W); the lake is on Los Corralitos grant. Named on Watsonville West (1954) 7.5' quadrangle. Capitola (1914) 15' quadrangle shows marsh at the place. The feature also was called Chandler Lake for the family that owned it in the 1920's (Clark, 1986, p. 72).

Corralitos Valley [SAN LUIS OBISPO]: *canyon,* drained by a stream that flows 1.25 miles to Arroyo Grande Creek nearly 6 miles southeast of Edna (lat. 35°08'50" N, long. 120°32'05" W). Named on Arroyo Grande NE (1965) 7.5' quadrangle.

Corral Point [SANTA BARBARA]: *promontory,* 1 mile south of Carrington Point on the north side of Santa Rosa Island (lat. 34°01'20" N, long. 120°02'40" W). Named on Santa Rosa Island North (1943) 7.5' quadrangle.

Corral Viejo Canyon [MONTEREY]: *canyon,* 3.5 miles long, along Conejo Creek above a point 2 miles northeast of Jamesburg (lat. 36°23'45" N, long. 121°33'30" W). Named on Rana Creek (1956) 7.5' quadrangle.

Cosio Knob [MONTEREY]: *peak,* 8 miles north-northwest of Jolon (lat. 36°04'50" N, long. 121°14' W; sec. 29, T 21 S, R 7 E). Altitude 2530 feet. Named on Cosio Knob (1949) 7.5' quadrangle. Members of the Cosio family owned land near the feature (Clark, 1991, p. 91). Smith (p. 88-93) described a cave called La Cueva Pintada that is located less than 0.5 mile north of Cosio Knob. Padres from San Antonio mission gave this name to the cave (Clark, 1991, p. 256), which is decorated with Indian pictographs—*la cueva pintada* means "the painted cave" in Spanish.

Cottage Corners [SAN BENITO]: *locality,* 1 mile north of Hollister (lat. 36°52'10" N, long. 121°24' W). Named on Hollister (1955) 7.5' quadrangle.

Cotter Spring [SAN LUIS OBISPO]: *spring,* 3.5 miles southwest of Castle Crags (lat. 35°16'05" N, long. 120°14'40" W). Named on La Panza (1967) 7.5' quadrangle.

Cottontail Creek [SAN LUIS OBISPO]: *stream,* flows 5 miles to Whale Rock Reservoir 6 miles north of the mouth of Morro Creek (lat. 35°27'50" N, long. 120°52'15" W; sec. 26, T 28 S, R 10 E). Named on Cayucos (1965), Cypress Mountain (1948), Morro Bay North (1965), and York Mountain (1948) 7.5' quadrangles.

Cottonwood Camp [MONTEREY]: *locality,* 5 miles south-southwest of Parkfield in Keyes Canyon (lat. 35°50'15" N, long. 120°28'30" W; sec. 16, T 24 S, R 14 E). Named on Cholame Hills (1961) 7.5' quadrangle.

Cottonwood Campground [SANTA BARBARA]: *locality,* 4.25 miles northwest of Big Pine Mountain along Sisquoc River (lat. 34°44'45" N, long. 119°41'50" W). Named on Big Pine Mountain (1964) 7.5' quadrangle.

Cottonwood Canyon [SANTA BARBARA]: *canyon,* drained by a stream that flows 9.5 miles to Cuyama River 9 miles east of Miranda Pine Mountain (lat. 35°02'20" N, long. 119°52'55" W). Named on Bates Canyon (1964) and Taylor Canyon (1959) 7.5' quadrangles.

Cottonwood Creek [MONTEREY]: *stream,* flows 9 miles to Cholame Creek 8 miles southeast of Parkfield (lat. 35°48'15" N, long. 120°20'25" W). Named on Cholame Valley (1961) and The Dark Hole (1961) 7.5' quadrangles. Part of the stream was called Rector Creek when the Rector family lived along it (Clark, 1991, p. 120), but United States Board on Geographic Names (1963a, p. 6) rejected this name.

Cottonwood Gulch [SAN BENITO]: *canyon,* drained by a stream that flows nearly 2 miles to Rock Springs Creek 5.5 miles north-northeast of Bitterwater (lat. 36°27'30" N, long. 120°58' W; near N line sec. 14, T 17 S, R 9 E); the canyon heads near the west end of Cottonwood Ridge. Named on Rock Spring Peak (1969) 7.5' quadrangle.

Cottonwood Pass [SAN LUIS OBISPO]: *pass,* 13 miles northeast of Shandon at the northeasternmost corner of San Luis Obispo County (lat. 35°46'50" N, long. 120°12'25" W; sec. 1, T 25 S, R 16 E). Named on Tent Hills (1942) 7.5' quadrangle. F.M. Anderson (p. 158) noted that the feature also has the name "Estrella Pass."

Cottonwood Ridge [SAN BENITO]: *ridge,* east- to northeast-trending, 1.5 miles long, 8 miles north-northeast of Bitterwater (lat. 36° 29'40" N, long. 120°57'10" W). Named on Rock Spring Peak (1969) 7.5' quadrangle.

Cottonwood Spring [SAN LUIS OBISPO]:

(1) *spring,* 5.5 miles north-northeast of Simmler (lat. 35°26' N, long. 119°57'50" W; sec. 5, T 29 S, R 19 E). Named on Las Yeguas Ranch (1959) 7.5' quadrangle.

(2) *spring,* 3.5 miles north-northwest of Caliente Mountain (lat. 35° 05'15" N, long. 119°46'40" W; near N line sec. 32, T 12 N, R 27 W). Named on Caliente Mountain (1959) 7.5' quadrangle.

Cottonwood Springs [SAN BENITO]: *springs,* 10.5 miles east-southeast of Bitterwatrer (lat. 36°18'40" N, long. 120°49'50" W; near NW cor. sec. 6, T 19 S, R 11 E). Named on Hepsedam Peak (1969) 7.5' quadrangle.

Cottonwood Well [SAN LUIS OBISPO]: *well,* 6 miles southeast of Cholame in Palo Prieto Canyon (lat. 35°40'05" N, long. 120°14'10" W; sec. 15, T

26 S, R 16 E). Named on Orchard Peak (1961) 7.5' quadrangle.

Covington Lake [MONTEREY]: *intermittent lake,* 900 feet long, nearly 3.5 miles south-southeast of Parkfield (lat. 35°51'20" N, long. 120°24'20" W; sec. 12, T 24 S, R 14 E). Named on Cholame Hills (1961) 7.5' quadrangle. The name commemorates the Covington family, who settled in Parkfield in 1883 (Clark, 1991, p. 121).

Coward Creek [SANTA CRUZ]: *stream,* flows 3.25 miles to Pajaro Valley 3.5 miles northeast of Watsonville (lat. 36°56'50" N, long. 121°42'10" W). Named on Watsonville East (1955) 7.5' quadrangle. The name commemorates John Rawson Coward, a farmer in the neighborhood as early as 1868 (Clark, 1986, p. 84).

Cow Canyon [SANTA BARBARA]: *canyon,* drained by a stream that flows 3.25 miles to the sea nearly 4 miles west-southwest of Carrington Point on Santa Rosa Island (lat. 34°01'10" N, long. 120°06'20" W). Named on Santa Rosa Island North (1943) 7.5' quadrangle.

Cowell Beach [SANTA CRUZ]: *beach,* less than 1 mile north of Point Santa Cruz in Santa Cruz (lat. 36°57'40" N, long. 122°01'25" W). Named on Santa Cruz (1954) 7.5' quadrangle. The name recalls the Cowell family, who owned the beach (Clark, 1986, p. 84).

Cox Canyon [SANTA BARBARA]: *canyon,* drained by a stream that flows 3.5 miles to Santa Barbara Canyon 2.5 miles south-southeast of Fox Mountain (lat. 34°46'50" N, long. 119°34'25" W). Named on Fox Mountain (1964) 7.5' quadrangle.

Cox Creek: see **Valencia Creek** [SANTA CRUZ].

Cox Flat [SANTA BARBARA]: *area,* 2.5 miles southeast of Fox Mountain in Santa Barbara Canyon (lat. 34°46'55" N, long. 119° 34'15" W); the place is at the mouth of Cox Canyon. Named on Fox Mountain (1964) 7.5' quadrangle.

Coxo: see **Cojo Bay** [SANTA BARBARA].

Coyote: see **Mesa Coyote** [MONTEREY].

Coyote Canyon [MONTEREY]: *canyon,* drained by a stream that flows 5.5 miles to lowlands 6 miles north-northwest of San Ardo (lat. 36°05'55" N, long. 120°57'10" W; sec. 13, T 21 S, R 9 E). Named on Nattrass Valley (1967) and San Ardo (1967) 7.5' quadrangles. The feature also was called Doig Canyon (Clark, 1991, p. 121).

Coyote Gulch [MONTEREY]: *canyon,* drained by a stream that flows nearly 3 miles to Carmel River 7.5 miles east of the mouth of the river (lat. 36°31'10" N, long. 121°47'40" W). Named on Seaside (1947) 7.5' quadrangle.

Coyote Gulch [SANTA BARBARA]: *canyon,* drained by a stream that flows 4.25 miles to Cuyama River 7 miles north-northeast of McPherson Peak (lat. 34°59'15" N, long. 119°47' W). Named on Peak Mountain (1964) 7.5' quadrangle. United States Board on Geographic Names (1965c, p. 10) rejected the name "Wells Creek" for the feature.

Coyote Hole [SAN LUIS OBISPO]: *relief feature,* 2.5 miles south of Castle Crags at a wide place in an unnamed canyon (lat. 35°16'15" N, long. 120°12'30" W). Named on La Panza (1967) 7.5' quadrangle.

Coyote Peak [SAN BENITO]: *peak,* 6.25 miles east-northeast of Hollister (lat. 36°52'40" N, long. 121°17'45" W). Altitude 1543 feet. Named on Three Sisters (1954) 7.5' quadrangle.

Coyote Point [SAN LUIS OBISPO]: *peak,* 9 miles south-southwest of Atascadero (lat. 35°23' N, long. 120°43'55" W; near SW cor. sec. 19, T 29 S, R 12 E). Altitude 1176 feet. Named on Atascadero (1965) 7.5' quadrangle.

Coyote Valley [SAN BENITO]: *valley,* 8 miles north-northwest of Panoche Pass (lat. 36°44'15" N, long. 121°03' W). Named on Panoche Pass (1968) 7.5' quadrangle.

Crawford Canyon [SANTA BARBARA]: *canyon,* 3 miles long, opens into the canyon of Santa Rosa Creek 7.5 miles south of the town of Los Alamos (lat. 34°38'10" N, long. 120°16'45" W). Named on Los Alamos (1959) 7.5' quadrangle.

Crazy Canyon [MONTEREY]: *canyon,* drained by a stream that flows 2 miles to Quinado Canyon 8 miles south-southwest of King City (lat. 36°05'35" N, long. 121°09'40" W; sec. 24, T 21 S, R 7 E). Named on Cosio Knob (1949) 7.5' quadrangle.

Crazy Horse Canyon [MONTEREY]: *canyon,* drained by a stream that flows 3.25 miles to Gabilan Creek 8.5 miles north-northeast of Salinas (lat. 36°46'20" N, long. 121°36'05" W). Named on San Juan Bautista (1955) 7.5' quadrangle. According to legend, the name is from a horse that ate loco weed and was called *caballo loco,* which means "crazy horse" in Spanish (Clark, 1991, p. 122).

Creston [SAN LUIS OBISPO]: *village,* 12 miles southeast of Paso Robles (lat. 35°31'10" N, long. 120°31'20" W). Named on Creston (1948) 7.5' quadrangle. Messers. Adams, Amborse, Webster, and Cressy bought 40,000 acres of Huer Huero grant and laid out the townsite in 1884; they called the place Huer Huero, but the townspeople called it Creston in honor of. Mr. Cressy (Lee and others, p. 47). Postal authorities established Creston post office in 1885 (Frickstad, p. 164).

Cristo: see **Manresa** [SANTA CRUZ].

Crocker: see **Templeton** [SAN LUIS OBISPO].

Crocker Canyon [SAN LUIS OBISPO]: *canyon,* drained by a stream that flows nearly 4.5 miles to Kern County 20 miles east-southeast of Simmler (lat. 35°13'45" N, long. 119°39'55" W; at E line sec. 13, T 31 S, R 21 E). Named on Panorama Hills (1954) and Reward (1951) 7.5' quadrangles.

Crook Point [SANTA BARBARA]: *promontory,* 3.5 miles west of Cardwell Point on the south side of San Miguel Island (lat. 34°00'50" N, long. 120°21'30" W). Named on San Miguel Island East (1950) 7.5' quadrangle. United States Coast and Geodetic Survey (p. 112) listed a shoal called Wyckoff Ledge located 1.4 miles west of Crook Point and 0.5 mile offshore.

Cross Canyon [MONTEREY]: *canyon,* drained by a stream that flows nearly 1 mile to Bixby Creek 4.5 miles north-northeast of Point Sur (lat. 36°22' N, long. 121°52'20" W; sec. 16, T 18 S, R 1 E). Named on Big Sur (1956) 7.5' quadrangle.

Crowbar Canyon [SAN LUIS OBISPO]: *canyon,* 1 mile long, opens into lowlands near the coast 7.5 miles northwest of Point San Luis (lat. 35°13'35" N, long. 120°51'55" W). Named on Port San Luis (1965) 7.5' quadrangle.

Crow Canyon [MONTEREY]: *canyon,* drained by a stream that flows 0.5 mile to Miners Gulch 5.25 miles north-northeast of Greenfield (lat. 36°23'15" N, long. 121°11'45" W; sec. 3, T 18 S, R 7 E). Named on North Chalone Peak (1969) 7.5' quadrangle.

Crows Nest [SAN LUIS OBISPO]: *peak,* 3 miles north-northeast of Cambria (lat. 35°36' N, long. 121°03'30" W; sec. 12, T 27 S, R 8 E). Named on San Simeon (1919) 15' quadrangle.

Cruessville: see **San Miguel** [SAN LUIS OBISPO].

Crystal Creek [SANTA CRUZ]: *stream,* flows nearly 2 miles to Branciforte Creek 3.25 miles north-northwest of Soquel (lat. 37°01'40" N, long. 121°59'10" W; sec. 29, T 10 S, R 1 W). Named on Laurel (1955) 7.5' quadrangle.

Crystal Knob [MONTEREY]: *peak,* 11 miles south of Jolon (lat. 35° 48'35" N, long. 121°09'45" W; sec. 25, T 24 S, R 7 E). Named on Burnett Peak (1949) 7.5' quadrangle. The name is from crystalline rocks that crop out on the feature (Clark, 1991, p. 124).

Cuarta Canyon: see **Cañada de la Cuarta** [SANTA BARBARA].

Cuaslui Creek [SANTA BARBARA]: *stream,* flows nearly 4 miles to Cañada de los Alisos 11 miles south of Tepusquet Peak (lat. 34°44'55" N, long. 120°12'15" W). Named on Foxen Canyon (1964) 7.5' quadrangle. The name is of Indian origin (Gudde, 1949, p. 85).

Cuchamma River: see **Cachuma Creek** [SANTA BARBARA].

Cuchudas Canyon [SANTA BARBARA]: *canyon,* drained by a stream that flows 1 mile to South Fork La Brea Creek 3 miles east-northeast of Manzanita Mountain (lat. 34°54'20" N, long. 120°01'50" W). Named on Manzanita Mountain (1964) 7.5' quadrangle.

Cuesta [SAN LUIS OBISPO]: *locality,* 5.5 miles north-northeast of San Luis Obispo along Southern Pacific Railroad (lat. 35°21'25" N, long. 120°38'05" W; sec. 36, T 29 S, R 12 E); the place is 0.5 mile north-northwest of Cuesta Pass. Named on San Luis Obispo (1965) 7.5' quadrangle.

Cuesta-by-the-Sea [SAN LUIS OBISPO]: *village,* 2.5 miles south-southeast of Morro Rock at the south edge of Morro Bay (lat. 35° 19'05" N, long. 120°50'45" W; sec. 13, T 30 S, R 10 E). Named on Morro Bay South (1965) 7.5' quadrangle. Cayucos (1951) 15' quadrangle has the form "Cuesta-By-The-Sea" for the name. The community is called Redfield Woods on Cayucos (1943) 15' quadrangle. The place now is part of Los Osos.

Cuesta de Los Gatos: see **Santa Cruz Mountains** [SANTA CRUZ].

Cuesta Pass [SAN LUIS OBISPO]: *pass,* 5 miles north-northeast of San Luis Obispo between the head of San Luis Obispo Creek and the head of Santa Margarita Creek (lat. 35'20'55" N, long. 120°37'50" W; near W line sec. 6, T 30 S, R 13 E). Named on San Luis Obispo (1965) 7.5' quadrangle. Called Cuesto Pass on Hamlin's (1904) map. Parke (p. 2, 16) used the names "San Luis Pass" and "San Louis Pass" for the feature.

Cueva Pintada: see **La Cueva Pintada,** under **Cosio Knob** [MONTEREY]; **Painted Cave** [SANTA BARBARA] (2).

Cueva Valdaze [SANTA BARBARA]: *cave,* 3.5 miles west of Diablo Point on Santa Cruz Island (lat. 34°03'05" N, long. 119°49'05" W). Named on Santa Cruz Island B (1943) 7.5' quadrangle. Doran (p. 146) called the feature Cueva Valdez, and stated that it is at Valdez Harbor, one of the principal landing places on the island.

Cummings Canyon [SANTA CRUZ]: *canyon,* drained by a stream that flows 1.5 miles to Coward Creek 4 miles northeast of Watsonville (lat. 36°57' N, long. 121°41'50" W). Named on Watsonville East (1955) 7.5' quadrangle.

Cushing [SAN LUIS OBISPO]: *locality,* 2.25 miles north of Santa Margarita along Southern Pacific Railroad (lat. 35°25'35" N, long. 120°36'10" W). Named on Santa Margarita (1965) 7.5' quadrangle.

Cushman Hill [SAN BENITO]: *peak,* 2.5 miles south-southwest of Mount Johnson (lat. 36°34'50" N, long. 121°17'15" W; sec. 35, T 15 S, R 6 E). Altitude 2926 feet. Named on Mount Johnson (1968) 7.5' quadrangle.

Cuyama [SAN LUIS OBISPO-SANTA BARBARA]:

(1) *land grant,* at the west end of Cuyama Valley on San Luis Obispo-Santa Barbara County line. Named on Bates Canyon (1964), Miranda Pine Mountain (1967) and Taylor Canyon (1959) 7.5' quadrangles. Called Cuyama No. 1 on McKittrick (1912) 30' quadrangle and on Branch Moun-

tain (1952) 15' quadrangle. Jose Maria Rojo received 5 leagues in 1843; Maria Antonia de la Guerra de Lataillade claimed 22,193 acres patented in 1877 (Cowan, p. 32).

(2) *land grant*, in the central and east parts of Cuyama Valley on San Luis Obispo-Santa Barbara County line. Named on Ballinger Canyon (1943), Bates Canyon (1964), Caliente Mountain (1959), Cuyama (1964), New Cuyama (1964), Peak Mountain (1964), and Taylor Canyon (1959) 7.5' quadrangles. Called Cuyama No. 2 on McKittrick (1912) 30' quadrangle. Cesario Lataillade received 11 leagues in 1846 and his heirs claimed 48,828 acres patented in 1879 (Cowan, p. 32).

Cuyama [SANTA BARBARA]: *village*, 36 miles north of Santa Barbara in Cuyama Valley (lat. 34°56'05" N, long. 119°36'45" W). Named on Cuyama (1964) 7.5' quadrangle. Postal authorities established Cuyama post office in 1942 (Salley, p. 54).

Cuyama: see **New Cuyama** [SANTA BARBARA].

Cuyama Hot Springs: see **Hot Spring** [SANTA BARBARA].

Cuyama Mountains: see **Sierra Madre Mountains** [SANTA BARBARA].

Cuyama Peak [SANTA BARBARA]: *peak*, 15 miles southeast of the village of Cuyama (lat. 34°45'15" N, long. 119°28'30" W). Altitude 5875 feet. Named on Cuyama Peak (1943) 7.5' quadrangle.

Cuyama Plain: see **Cuyama Valley** [SAN LUIS OBISPO-SANTA BARBARA].

Cuyama Range: see **Sierra Madre Mountains** [SANTA BARBARA].

Cuyama River [SAN LUIS OBISPO-SANTA BARBARA]: *stream*, heads in Ventura County and flows 92 miles along and near San Luis Obispo-Santa Barbara County line to join Sisquoc River and form Santa Maria River 13 miles southeast of the town of Nipomo (lat. 34°54'10" N, long. 120°18'40" W; sec. 36, T 10 N, R 33 W); the stream flows through Cuyama Valley. Named on Caliente Mountain (1959), Chimney Canyon (1967), Cuyama (1964), Cuyama Peak (1943), Fox Mountain (1964), Huasna Peak (1967), Miranda Pine Mountain (1967), New Cuyama (1964), Peak Mountain (1964), Taylor Canyon (1959), and Twitchell Dam (1959) 7.5' quadrangles. Called Guyamas River on Goddard's (1857) map, Rio S. Maria on Parke's (1854-1855) map, R. Guaymas or Sta. Maria on Colton's (1863) map, and Santa Maria River on California Mining Bureau's (1909c) map. According to Kroeber (1916, p. 41), the term "Cuyama" is from an Indian place name.

Cuyamas Range: see **Sierra Madre Mountains** [SANTA BARBARA].

Cuyamas Valley: see **Cuyama Valley** [SAN LUIS OBISPO-SANTA BARBARA].

Cuyama Valley [SAN LUIS OBISPO-SANTA BARBARA]: *valley*, extends along the upper part of Cuyama River southwest of Caliente Range on San Luis-Obispo-Santa Barbara County line. Named on Ballinger Canyon (1943), Caliente Mountain (1959), Cuyama (1964), Cuyama Peak (1943), Fox Mountain (1964), Miranda Pine Mountain (1967), New Cuyama (1964), Peak Mountain (1964), and Taylor Canyon (1959) 7.5' quadrangles. Parke (p. 6) called the valley Cuyama plain, and Fairbanks (1895, p. 274) called it Cuyamas Valley.

Cuyler Harbor [SANTA BARBARA]: *embayment*, 3.5 miles northwest of Cardwell Point on the north side of San Miguel Island (lat. 34°03' N, long. 120°21' W). Named on San Miguel Island East (1950) 7.5' quadrangle. James Alden of United States Coast Survey named the feature in 1852 for Lieutenant R.M. Cuyler, a member of his surveying party (Gudde, 1949, p. 87).

Cypress Cove [MONTEREY]: *embayment*, east of Point Lobos on the south side of Carmel Bay (lat. 36°31'20" N, long. 121°56'55" W). Named on Monterey (1947) 7.5' quadrangle. California Department of Parks and Recreation's map has the name "North Point" for the promontory situated west of Cypress Cove.

Cypress Mountain [SAN LUIS OBISPO]: *peak*, 7.5 miles east-northeast of Cambria (lat. 35°36'05" N, long. 120°57'15" W; sec. 12, T 27 S, R 9 E). Altitude 2933 feet. Named on Cypress Mountain (1948) 7.5' quadrangle.

Cypress Point [MONTEREY]: *promontory*, 4.5 miles southwest of Point Pinos along the coast (lat. 36°34'50" N, long. 121°58'40" W). Named on Monterey (1947, photorevised 1968) 7.5' quadrangle. Called Point Cypress on Monterey (1947) 7.5' quadrangle, but United States Board on Geographic Names (1967d, p. 4) rejected this form of the name. H.R. Wagner (p. 476) tentatively identified the promontory as probably the one that Cabrillo called Cabo de Nieve in 1542. Gudde (1949, p. 87) noted that the name "La Punta de cipresses" was used in 1774. Taylor (v. 1, p. 172) recorded the name "Punta de los Cipreses" for the feature.

Cypress Point Rock [MONTEREY]: *rock*, 4.5 miles southwest of Point Pinos, and 650 feet offshore (lat. 36°34'50" N, long. 121°58'40" W); the feature is at Cypress Point. Named on Monterey (1947, photorevised 1968) 7.5' quadrangle. Called Point Cypress Rock on Monterey (1947) 7.5' quadrangle.

Cypress Ridge [SANTA BARBARA]: *ridge*, southwest-trending, 2 miles long, 3.25 miles west of Tranquillon Mountain (lat. 34°34'35" N, long. 120°37' W). Named on Point Arguello (1959) and Tranqullon Mountain (1959) 7.5' quadrangles.

- D -

Dairy Creek [SAN LUIS OBISPO]: *stream*, flows 4.5 miles to Chorro Creek 5 miles northwest of San Luis Obispo (lat. 35°19'30" N, long. 120°44' W). Named on San Luis Obispo (1965) 7.5' quadrangle.

Dairy Flat [SAN BENITO]: *valley*, drained by a stream that flows 2.25 miles to Las Aguilas Creek (1) 7 miles north of Panoche Pass (lat. 36°43'40" N, long. 121°02'05" W). Named on Panoche Pass (1968) and Ruby Canyon (1968) 7.5' quadrangles.

Dairy Gulch [MONTEREY]: *canyon*, drained by a stream that flows 0.5 mile to Bixby Creek 4.5 miles north-northeast of Point Sur (lat. 36°22'10" N, long. 121°51'55" W; sec. 16, T 18 S, R 1 E). Named on Big Sur (1956) 7.5' quadrangle.

Damond Ridge [SANTA CRUZ]: *ridge*, south-southeast-trending, 1.25 miles long, 6 miles north-northeast of the town of Boulder Creek (lat. 37°12'35" N, long. 122°05'20" W; in and near sec. 28, T 8 S, R 2 W). Named on Castle Rock Ridge (1955) 7.5' quadrangle.

Damsite Canyon [SANTA BARBARA]: *canyon*, drained by a stream that flows 3 miles to the sea 2.5 miles east of Point Conception (lat. 34°27' N, long. 120°25'30" W). Named on Point Conception (1953) 7.5' quadrangle.

Danford Canyon [SAN LUIS OBISPO]: *canyon*, drained by a stream that flows 2 miles to Suey Creek nearly 5 miles east of Nipomo (lat. 35°03'15" N, long. 120°23'35" W; near N line sec. 7, T 11 N, R 33 W). Named on Nipomo (1965) 7.5' quadrangle.

Dani Ridge [MONTEREY]: *ridge*, west-trending, 2 miles long, 4 miles east-northeast of Point Sur (lat. 36°19'20" N, long. 121° 50' W). Named on Big Sur (1956) 7.5' quadrangle. The name is for the Dani family, pioneers of the neighborhood (Clark, 1991, p. 128).

Dani Ridge: see **Pfeiffer Ridge** [MONTEREY].

Dani's Beach: see **Pfeffer Beach** [MONTEREY].

Danish Creek [MONTEREY]: *stream*, flows 6.25 miles to Carmel River 3.25 miles northeast of Uncle Sam Mountain (lat. 36°22'20" N, long. 121°39'45" W; near NW cor. sec. 16, T 18 S, R 3 E). Named on Carmel Valley (1956) and Ventana Cones (1956) 7.5' quadrangles.

Dark Range Peak [SAN LUIS OBISPO]: *peak*, 6.5 miles northeast of the mouth of Morro Creek (lat. 35°26'50" N, long. 120°47'20" W; sec. 33, T 28 S, R 11 E). Altitude 2005 feet. Named on Morro Bay North (1965) 7.5' quadrangle.

Davenport [SANTA CRUZ]: *village*, 10 miles west-northwest of Santa Cruz near the coast (lat. 37°00'40" N, long. 122°11'35" W). Named on Davenport (1955) 7.5' quadrangle. The name is from nearby Davenport Landing (Gudde, 1949, p. 89). Postal authorities established Davenport post office in 1906; a previous Davenport post office was located at Davenport Landing (Salley, p. 55). California Mining Bureau's (1917a) map shows a place called Lagos located along the railroad between Davenport and Godola (present Gordola).

Davenport Creek [SAN LUIS OBISPO]: *stream*, flows nearly 6 miles to San Luis Obispo Creek 3.5 miles northeast of Avila Beach (lat. 35°13'20" N, long. 120°41'20" W). Named on Arroyo Grande NE (1965) and Pismo Beach (1965) 7.5' quadrangles.

Davenport Landing [SANTA CRUZ]: *locality*, 1.5 miles northwest of Davenport along the coast (lat. 37°01'30" N, long. 122°12'55" W). Named on Davenport (1955) 7.5' quadrangle. Captain John P. Davenport began a whaling station at the place in the 1850's and built a wharf there 450 feet long; a stage station was at the landing in 1872, and a stage station called Berry Falls was between Davenport Landing and present Swanton (Hoover, Rensch, and Rensch, p. 475, 478). Postal authorities established Davenport post office at Davenport Landing in 1874 and discontinued it in 1889; they established another Davenport post office later at the village of Davenport (Salley, p. 55).

Davey Brown Campground [SANTA BARBARA]: *locality*, 4 miles south-southwest of Bald Mountain (1) in Munch Canyon (lat. 34° 45'25" N, long. 119°57'05" W); the place is near Davey Brown Creek. Named on Bald Mountain (1964) 7.5' quadrangle.

Davey Brown Creek [SANTA BARBARA]: *stream*, flows 4.5 miles to Manzana Creek nearly 3 miles south of Bald Mountain (1) (lat. 34°46'20" N, long. 119°56'35" W). Named on Bald Mountain (1964) 7.5' quadrangle. The name recalls an early settler who lived near the creek in the 1880's (Rife, p. 119). The stream drains Fir Canyon.

Davis: see **Lonnie Davis Campground** [SANTA BARBARA].

Davis Canyon [MONTEREY]:

(1) *canyon*, 1 mile long, along San Carpoforo Creek above a point 12 miles east-southeast of Cape San Martin (lat. 35°49'10" N, long. 121°16'25" W; sec. 25, T 24 S, R 6 E). Named on Burro Mountain (1949) 7.5' quadrangle. Called Devils Canyon on Cape San Martin (1921) 15' quadrangle.

(2) *canyon*, 3.5 miles long, opens into lowlands 3.5 miles east-northeast of Jolon (lat. 35°59'25" N, long. 121°07'15" W). Named on Espinosa Canyon (1949) 7.5' quadrangle. The name commemorates members of the Davis family who received patents to land in and near the canyon in the 1890's and in 1905 (Clark, 1991, p. 129).

Davis Canyon [SAN LUIS OBISPO]: *canyon,* drained by a stream that flows 3 miles to See Canyon 2.25 miles north of Avila Beach (lat. 35°12'45" N, long. 120°43'25" W; sec. 19, T 31 S, R 12 E). Named on Pismo Beach (1965) and Port San Luis (1965) 7.5' quadrangles.

Davis Canyon [SANTA BARBARA]: *canyon,* drained by a stream that flows nearly 4 miles to Green Canyon 4 miles north of McPherson Peak (lat. 34°56'55" N, long. 119°49'15" W). Named on Peak Mountain (1964) 7.5' quadrangle.

Davy Brown Canyon: see **Fir Canyon** [SANTA BARBARA].

Day Valley [SANTA CRUZ]: *valley,* 2.5 miles west of Corralitos (lat. 36°59'40" N, long. 121°51'15" W). Named on Watsonville West (1954) 7.5' quadrangle. The name is for Darius Washington Day and his wife, who bought land at the place in 1862 (Clark, 1986, p. 92).

Deadman Canyon [SANTA BARBARA]:

(1) *canyon,* drained by a stream that flows 5.25 miles to Cuyama Valley 7.5 miles north of McPherson Peak (lat. 34°59'50" N, long. 119°49'50" W). Named on Peak Mountain (1964) 7.5' quadrangle.

(2) *canyon,* 2 miles long, along San Jose Creek above a point 0.5 mile south-southwest of San Marcos Pass (lat. 34°30'15" N, long. 119°49'45" W; near NE cor. sec. 20, T 5 N, R 28 W). Named on Goleta (1903) 15' quadrangle.

Deadman Flat [SAN LUIS OBISPO]: *area,* 12.5 miles south of Simmler (lat. 35°10'30" N, long. 119°59'30" W; near NE cor. sec. 1, T 32 S, R 18 E). Named on Chimineas Ranch (1959) 7.5' quadrangle.

Deadman Gulch [MONTEREY]: *canyon,* drained by a stream that flows 3.5 miles to Lynch Canyon 8.5 miles north-northwest of Bradley (lat. 35°58'55" N, long. 120°51' W; sec. 25, T 22 S, R 10 E). Named on Wunpost (1949) 7.5' quadrangle, where the name extends into a north branch that is called Dry Gulch on Pancho Rico Valley (1967) 7.5' quadrangle.

Deadman Gulch [SANTA CRUZ]: *canyon,* drained by a stream that flows 2.5 miles to Big Creek 6 miles north of Davenport (lat. 37° 06'05" N, long. 122°11'30" W). Named on Davenport (1955) 7.5' quadrangle.

De Alvarez Creek [SAN BENITO]: *stream,* flows nearly 4 miles to Bitterwater Creek 6 miles southeast of Bitterwater (lat. 36°19' N, long. 120°55'35" W; sec. 31, T 18 S, R 10 E). Named on Lonoak (1969) 7.5' quadrangle.

Dean [MONTEREY]: *locality,* 1.25 miles northwest of Gonzales along Southern Pacific Railroad (lat. 36°31'35" N, long. 121°27'40" W). Named on Gonzales (1921) 15' quadrangle.

Deer Canyon [MONTEREY]: *canyon,* drained by a stream that flows 7.5 miles to Portuguese Canyon (2) 8.5 miles east-southeast of Bradley (lat. 35°50' N, long. 120°39'20" W; near NE cor. sec. 22, T 24 S, R 12 E). Named on San Miguel (1948) and Valleton (1948) 7.5' quadrangles.

Deer Canyon [SAN LUIS OBISPO]:

(1) *canyon,* drained by a stream that flows 1 mile to the sea 3.5 miles northwest of Point San Luis (lat. 35°11'20" N, long. 120°48'40" W). Named on Port San Luis (1965) 7.5' quadrangle. United States Board on Geographic Names (1967c, p. 2) approved the name "Little Irish Canyon" for the feature.

(2) *canyon,* drained by a stream that flows 1 mile to Corbit Canyon 4.25 miles southeast of Edna (lat. 35°09'35" N, long. 120°33'25" W). Named on Arroyo Grande NE (1965) 7.5' quadrangle. Called Bee Canyon on Arroyo Grande (1897) 15' quadrangle, where present Bee Canyon is called Deer Canyon.

(3) *canyon,* drained by a stream that flows 2 miles to Huasna River 4 miles north-northwest of Huasna Peak (lat. 35°05'35" N, long. 120°21'45" W). Named on Huasna Peak (1967) 7.5' quadrangle. Called Bear Canyon on Nipomo (1922) 15' quadrangle, but United States Board on Geographic Names (1963b, p. 14) rejected this name for the feature.

Deer Creek [MONTEREY]: *stream,* flows 5 miles to San Antonio River 8.5 miles southeast of Jolon (lat. 35°53'20" N, long. 121°03'05" W). Named on Bryson (1949) and Williams Hill (1949) 7.5' quadrangles.

Deer Creek [SANTA CRUZ]: *stream,* flows nearly 4 miles to Bear Creek 4 miles northeast of the town of Boulder Creek (lat. 37°10'15" N, long. 122°04'25" W; near SW cor. sec. 3, T 9 S, R 2 W). Named on Castle Rock Ridge (1955) 7.5' quadrangle.

Deer Flat [SAN LUIS OBISPO]: *area,* 11.5 miles east-northeast of the village of San Simeon (lat. 35°41'45" N, long. 121°00'05" W; sec. 4, 9, T 26 S, R 9 E). Named on Pebblestone Shut-in (1959) 7.5' quadrangle.

Deer Park Canyon [SANTA BARBARA]: *canyon,* drained by a stream that heads in Ventura County and flows nearly 5 miles to Cuyama Valley 9.5 miles east-southeast of the village of Cuyama (lat. 34°51'50" N, long. 119°28'45" W; sec. 18, T 9 N, R 25 W). Named on Cuyama Peak (1943) 7.5' quadrangle.

Deer Pasture [MONTEREY]: *area,* 4.25 miles south of Tassajara Hot Springs (lat. 36°10'25" N, long. 121°32'20" W; sec. 21, T 20 S, R 4 E). Named on Tassajara Hot Springs (1956) 7.5' quadrangle.

Deer Ridge [SANTA CRUZ]: *ridge,* south-southwest-trending, 1 mile long, 6.5 miles north-northeast of the town of Boulder Creek (lat. 37°12'50" N, long. 122°04'45" W; sec. 21, 28, T 8 S, R 2 W). Named on Castle Rock Ridge (1955) 7.5' quadrangle.

Deer Spring [SAN LUIS OBISPO]: *spring,* 4 miles south of Wilson Corner (lat. 35°24'40" N, long. 120°23'05" W; sec. 8, T 29 S, R 15 E). Named on Wilson Corner (1966) 7.5' quadrangle.

Deer Spring [SANTA BARBARA]: *spring,* 1200 feet north-northwest of the top of McPherson Peak (lat. 34°53'30" N, long. 119°47'45" W). Named on Peak Mountain (1964) 7.5' quadrangle.

Deer Valley [SANTA CRUZ]: *canyon,* 1 mile long, opens into lowlands 3.25 miles west-northwest of Corralitos (lat. 37°00'30" N, long. 121°51'45" W). Named on Loma Prieta (1955) 7.5' quadrangle.

Defiance: see **Mount Defiance** [SAN BENITO].

De la Guerra Camp [SANTA BARBARA]: *locality,* 5.25 miles southeast of Figueroa Mountain (lat. 34°40'55" N, long. 119°55'30" W; sec. 15, T 7 N, R 29 W). Named on Figueroa Mountain (1959) 7.5' quadrangle.

De la Guerra Gulch: see **Placer Creek** [SAN LUIS OBISPO].

De la Questa Canyon [SANTA BARBARA]: *canyon,* drained by a stream that flows nearly 2 miles to lowlands 1 mile south of Buellton (lat. 34°35'55" N, long. 120°11'40" W). Named on Solvang (1959) 7.5' quadrangle.

Deleissigues Creek [SAN LUIS OBISPO]: *stream,* flows 2.5 miles to Nipomo Creek 0.5 mile west-southwest of the town of Nipomo (lat. 35°02'25" N, long. 120°28'55" W). Named on Nipomo (1965) 7.5' quadrangle.

Del Mar Heights: see **Morro Bay** [SAN LUIS OBISPO] (2).

Delmonte [MONTEREY]: *locality,* east of Monterey along Southern Pacific Railroad (lat. 36°36'05" N, long. 121°52'10" W). Named on Seaside (1947, photorevised 1968) 7.5' quadrangle. Called Del Monte on Seaside (1947) 7.5' quadrangle. Monterey (1913) 15' quadrangle shows Hotel Del Monte just south of the place. Charles Crocker named the hotel (Gudde, 1949, p. 92). Postal authorities established Delmonte post office in 1882 and discontinued it in 1883; they established Del Monte post office in 1901, discontinued it for a time in 1911, and discontinued it finally in 1952 (Frickstad, p. 106).

Del Monte Heights [MONTEREY]: *district,* 1 mile east of downtown Seaside (lat. 36°36'45" N, long. 121°50' W). Named on Seaside (1947) 7.5' quadrangle. George W. Phelps and F.M. Hilby laid out the place in 1909—now it is a residential district in Seaside (Clark, 1991, p. 133).

Del Monte Junction [MONTEREY]: *locality,* east of Castroville along Southern Pacific Railroad (lat. 38°45'30" N, long. 121°44'30" W). Named on San Juan Bautista (1917) 15' quadrangle. Prunedale (1954) 7.5' quadrangle shows the place as part of Castroville.

Del Monte Lake [MONTEREY]: *lake,* 1150 feet long, at Del Monte (lat. 36°35'55" N, long. 121°52'10" W). Named on Seaside (1947) 7.5' quadrangle.

Del Rey Oaks [MONTEREY]: *town,* southeast of Seaside (lat. 36°35'30" N, long. 121°50' W). Named on Seaside (1947, photorevised 1968) 7.5' quadrangle. The town incorporated in 1953. Before incorporation, the place was known as Del Rey Woods (Clark, 1991, p. 135). Postal authorities established Del Rey Oaks post office in 1968 (Salley, p. 57).

Del Rey Woods: see **Del Rey Oaks** [MONTEREY].

Demesio Spring [SANTA BARBARA]: *spring,* 5.5 miles south of Santa Cruz Mountain (lat. 34°37'50" N, long. 119°49'35" W). Named on San Rafael Mountain (1959) 7.5' quadrangle.

Demijohn Spring [SANTA BARBARA]: *spring,* 2.5 miles south of Salisbury Potrero (lat. 34°47'10" N, long. 119°42'05" W). Named on Salisbury Potrero (1964) 7.5' quadrangle.

De Redwood: see **Redwood Lodge** [SANTA CRUZ].

Destroyer Rock [SANTA BARBARA]: *rock,* nearly 2 miles north of Point Arguello, and 700 feet offshore (lat. 34°36'10" N, long. 120° 38'40" W). Named on Point Arguello (1959) 7.5' quadrangle.

De Vaul Canyon [SANTA BARBARA]: *canyon,* drained by a stream that flows 2.5 miles to Lake Cachuma 4 miles northeast of Santa Ynez Peak (lat. 34°33'35" N, long. 119°55' W). Named on Lake Cachuma (1959) 7.5' quadrangle. Called Bear Canyon on Santa Ynez (1905) 30' quadrangle.

Devil Hill [MONTEREY]: *peak,* 2.5 miles south of Monterey (lat. 36° 34' N, long. 121°53'45" W). Named on Monterey (1947) 7.5' quadrangle. Called Devils Hill on Monterey (1913) 15' quadrangle.

Devils Canyon [MONTEREY]: *canyon,* drained by a stream that flows 2.5 miles to Big Creek (2) 4.5 miles north-northwest of Lopez Point (lat. 36°04'35" N, long. 121°35'40" W; near W line sec. 25, T 21 S, R 3 E). Named on Lopez Point (1956) 7.5' quadrangle. The canyon divides at the head to form Middle Fork and South Fork. Middle Fork is 4 miles long and South Fork is nearly 4 miles long. North Fork branches off less than 2 miles from the mouth of the main canyon and is 2.5 miles long. All the forks are named on Lopez Point (1956) 7.5' quadrangle.

Devils Canyon [SAN BENITO]: *canyon,* drained by a stream that flows nearly 4 miles to San Benito River 3.5 miles north-northeast of Bitterwater (lat. 36°25'35" N, long. 120°58'05" W). Named on Rock Spring Peak (1969) 7.5' quadrangle.

Devils Canyon [SANTA BARBARA]: *canyon,* drained by a stream that flows 2.5 miles to Santa Ynez River 6 miles south-southeast of Little Pine Mountain (lat. 34°31'20" N, long. 119°41'15" W; at SE cor. sec. 10, T 5 N, R 27 W). Named on Little Pine Mountain (1964) 7.5' quadrangle.

Devils Canyon: see **Davis Canyon** [MONTEREY] (1).

Devils Caudron [MONTEREY]: *water feature,* rocky place in the sea just south of Point Lobos (lat. 36°31'05" N, long. 121°57'15" W). Named on Monterey (1947) 7.5' quadrangle.

Devils Gap [SAN LUIS OBISPO]: *narrows*, 4.5 miles west-southwest of Atascadero (2) along Morro Creek (lat. 35°27'40" N, long. 120° 44'20" W). Named on Atascadero (1965) 7.5' quadrangle.

Devils Hill: see **Devil Hill** [MONTEREY].

Devils Peak [MONTEREY]: *peak*, 8 miles northeast of Point Sur (lat. 36°22'35" N, long. 121°47'05" W). Altitude 4158 feet. Named on Mount Carmel (1956) 7.5' quadrangle.

Devil's Peak: see **Diablo Point** [SANTA BARBARA].

Devon [SANTA BARBARA]: *locality*, less than 1 mile east-northeast of Casmalia (2) along Southern Pacific Railroad (lat. 34°50'30" N, long. 120°31'05" W). Named on Casmalia (1959) 7.5' quadrangle.

Diablo Anchorage [SANTA BARBARA]: *embayment*, less than 0.5 mile west of Diablo Point on the north side of Santa Cruz Island (lat. 34°03'25" N, long. 119°45'50" W). Named on Santa Cruz Island B (1943) 7.5' quadrangle.

Diablo Canyon [SAN LUIS OBISPO]: *canyon*, drained by a stream that flows 5 miles to the sea 6.5 miles northwest of Point San Luis (lat. 35°12'45" N, long. 120°51'25" W). Named on Port San Luis (1965) 7.5' quadrangle.

Diablo Canyon [SANTA BARBARA]: *canyon*, drained by a stream that flows 6.25 miles to Agua Caliente Canyon 3.5 miles south of Hildreth Peak (lat. 34°32'50" N, long. 119°33'30" W). Named on Hildreth Peak (1964) and Old Man Mountain (1943) 7.5' quadrangles. East Fork branches southeast 2 miles upstream from the mouth of the main canyon; it is 2.25 miles long and is named on Hildreth Peak (1964) 7.5' quadrangle.

Diablo Canyon: see **Lauro Canyon** [SANTA BARBARA].

Diablo Gulch [SANTA BARBARA]: *canyon*, drained by a stream that flows 1.5 miles to Corralitos Creek 4.5 miles north of Corralitos (lat. 37°03'05" N, long. 121°49'15" W; sec. 23, T 10 S, R 1 E). Named on Loma Prieta (1955) 7.5' quadrangle.

Diablo Point [SANTA BARBARA]: *promontory*, 10 miles east of Fraser Point on the north side of Santa Cruz Island (lat. 34°03'30" N, long. 119°45'30" W). Named on Santa Cruz Island B (1943) 7.5' quadrangle. The feature is called Punta Diablo on Bremner's (1932) map, which shows a peak called Picacho Diablo located about 2.5 miles southwest of Diablo Point. Goodyear (1890, p. 156) called the same peak Picacho del Diablo, and Loew (p. 215) called it Devil's Peak.

Diablo Range [MONTEREY-SAN BENITO]: *range*, extends from Carquinez Strait in Contra Costa County southeast to Antelope Valley in Kern County; the east part of San Benito County and the southeasternmost part of Monterey County are in the range. Named on Santa Cruz (1956) and San Luis Obispo (1956) 1°x 2° quadrangles. Mount Diablo is near the northwest end of the range in Contra Costa County. Called Sierra del Monte Diablo on Parke's (1854-1855) map. Whitney (p. 2) called it Monte Diablo Range and stated that it "is so called from the conspicuous point of that name." United States Board on Geographic Names (1933, p. 264) rejected the names "Monte Diablo Range," "Mount Diablo Range," and "Sierra del Monte Diablo" for the feature.

Dibblee Hill [SANTA BARBARA]: *peak*, 1 mile south of downtown Santa Barbara and northwest of Punta del Castillo (present Point Castillo) (lat. 34°24'20" N, long. 119°41'50" W). Named on Santa Barbara (1944) 7.5' quadrangle.

Dicks Harbor: see **Platts Harbor** [SANTA BARBARA].

Difficult Spring [SANTA BARBARA]: *spring*, 2.25 miles east-southeast of Tepusquet Peak (lat. 34°54' N, long. 120°08'45" W). Named on Tepusquet Canyon (1964) 7.5' quadrangle.

Dinsmore Canyon: see **San Ysidro Canyon** [SANTA BARBARA].

Dip Creek [SAN LUIS OBISPO]: *stream*, flows 10 miles to Nacimiento River 6.5 miles northeast of Lime Mountain (lat. 35°44'30" N, long. 120°54'35" W; sec. 20, T 25 S, R 10 E). Named on Adelaida (1948) and Lime Mountain (1948) 7.5' quadrangles. The stream now enters an arm of Nacimiento Reservoir

Divide [SANTA BARBARA]: *locality*, 8.5 miles south of Santa Maria along Pacific Coast Railroad (lat. 34°49'40" N, long. 120°27' W); the place is at the divide between Graciosa Canyon and Harris Canyon. Named on Lompoc (1905) 30' quadrangle.

Divide Camp [MONTEREY]: *locality*, 6 miles south-southwest of Jamesburg (lat. 36°17'25" N, long. 121°37' W; near W line sec. 11, T 19 S, R 3 E); the place is less than 0.5 mile west of Church Creek Divide. Named on Chews Ridge (1956) 7.5' quadrangle.

Divide Canyon [MONTEREY]: *canyon*, drained by a stream that flows 3 miles to Miners Gulch 3.25 miles south of North Chalone Peak (lat. 36°24' N, long. 121°12'25" W; near NE cor. sec. 4, T 18 S, R 7 E). Named on North Chalone Peak (1969) 7.5' quadrangle.

Divide Peak [SANTA BARBARA]: *peak*, 7.5 miles north-northeast of Rincon Point (lat. 34°28'35" N, long. 119°26'40" W; sec. 36, T 5 N, R 25 W). Altitude 4690 feet. Named on White Ledge Peak (1952) 7.5' quadrangle.

Division Knoll [MONTEREY]: *peak*, 5 miles north of Point Sur near the coast (lat. 36°22'30" N, long. 121°54'05" W; sec. 7, T 18 S, R 1 E). Named on Point Sur (1956) and Soberanes Point (1956) 7.5' quadrangles.

Dixon Canyon [SAN BENITO]: *canyon*, drained by a stream that flows nearly 4 miles to Tully Creek 3.5 miles southeast of Bitterwater (lat. 36°20'50" N, long. 120°56'55" W; sec. 24, T 18 S, R 9 E). Named on Lonoak (1969) 7.5' quadrangle.

Dixon Spring [SAN BENITO]: *spring*, 15 miles east-northeast of Bitterwater along Los Pinos Creek (lat. 36°28'35" N, long. 120°46'20" W; sec. 4, T 17 S, R 11 E). Named on Hernandez Reservoir (1969) 7.5' quadrangle, where a windmill symbol marks the feature.

Docas [MONTEREY]: *locality*, 5 miles north-northwest of San Ardo along Southern Pacific Railroad (lat. 36°05' N, long. 120°56'50" W; sec. 24, T 21 S, R 9 E). Named on San Ardo (1956) 15' quadrangle. Docas is between San Ar<u>do</u> and San Lu<u>cas</u>; the name was coined from the last letters of the names of these two places (Gudde, 1949, p. 96).

Docs Spring Campground [SANTA BARBARA]: *locality*, 7 miles west-northwest of McPherson Peak (lat. 34°56'05" N, long. 119° 54'50" W). Named on Bates Canyon (1964) 7.5' quadrangle.

Doig Canyon: see **Coyote Canyon** [MONTEREY].

Dolan Canyon [MONTEREY]: *canyon*, drained by a stream that flows nearly 2 miles to the sea 6.25 miles southeast of Partington Point (lat. 36°06'20" N, long. 121°37'30" W; sec. 15, T 21 S, R 3 E). Named on Lopez Point (1956) 7.5' quadrangle. Fink (p. 209) associated the name with Phil Dolan, an early settler in the neighborhood.

Dolan Rock [MONTEREY]: *rock*, 150 feet long, 8 miles southeast of Partington Point, and 75 feet offshore (lat. 36°05'05" N, long. 121° 37' W); the feature is 1.5 miles south-southeast of the mouth of Dolan Canyon. Named on Lopez Point (1956) 7.5' quadrangle.

Dolans Hot Spring: see **Big Creek** [MONTEREY] (2).

Dolan's Hot Sulphur Spring: see **Big Creek** [MONTEREY] (2).

Dolores Creek [MONTEREY]: *stream*, flows nearly 1 mile to Big Sur River 1.5 miles south-southwest of Ventana Cone (lat. 36°15'05" N, long. 121°41'35" W; sec. 25, T 19 S, R 2 E). Named on Partington Ridge (1956) 7.5' quadrangle.

Don Victor Campground [SANTA BARBARA]: *locality*, 4.25 miles east-southeast of Madulce Peak along Mono Creek (lat. 34°40'10" N, long. 119°31' W); the place is in Don Victor Valley. Named on Madulce Peak (1964) 7.5' quadrangle.

Don Victor Canyon [SANTA BARBARA]: *canyon*, 4 miles long, along Mono Creek above a point 4.25 miles east-southeast of Madulce Peak (lat. 34°40'20" N, long. 119°31'15" W). Named on Madulce Peak (1964) 7.5' quadrangle.

Don Victor Valley [SANTA BARBARA]: *valley*, 4.25 miles east-southeast of Madulce Peak along Mono Creek (lat. 34°40'20" N, long. 119°31'05" W); the valley is at the mouth of Don Victor Canyon. Named on Madulce Peak (1964) 7.5' quadrangle. The name commemorates Don Victor, a tuberculosis sufferer who homesteaded at the place early in the 1900's and lived a long life (Gagnon, p. 77).

Doolans Hole Creek [MONTEREY]: *stream*, flows 1.5 miles to Ventana Creek (2) 4 miles west-southwest of Ventana Cone (lat. 36°15'55" N, long. 121°44'35" W; sec. 21, T 19 S, R 2 E). Named on Big Sur (1956) and Ventana Cones (1956) 7.5' quadrangles.

Dos Pueblos Canyon [SANTA BARBARA]: *canyon*, drained by a stream that flows nearly 7 miles to the sea 5.5 miles west-northwest of Coal Oil Point (lat. 34°26'25" N, long. 119°57'50" W). Named on Dos Pueblos Canyon (1951) and Lake Cachuma (1959) 7.5' quadrangles. The name is from two Indian villages situated at the mouth of the canyon—*dos pueblos* means "two towns" in Spanish (Gudde, 1949, p. 98).

Double Corral Canyon [SAN LUIS OBISPO]: *canyon*, 4 miles long, opens into the canyon of Carrie Creek 12.5 miles northeast of the town of Nipomo (lat. 35°38'30" N, long. 120°17'30" W; sec. 17, T 32 S, R 16 E). Named on Caldwell Mesa (1967) and Los Machos Hills (1967) 7.5' quadrangles.

Double Rock [SAN LUIS OBISPO]: *rock*, 100 feet long, 3.5 miles west-northwest of Point San Luis, and 550 feet offshore (lat. 35°11'15" N, long. 120°48'50" W). Named on Port San Luis (1965) 7.5' quadrangle.

Double Springs [SAN LUIS OBISPO]: *springs*, two, nearly 6 miles southwest of Branch Mountain (lat. 35°07'35" N, long. 120°09'05" W). Named on Los Machos Hills (1967) 7.5' quadrangle.

Double Summit: see **Ventana Double Cone** [MONTEREY].

Doud Creek [MONTEREY]: *stream*, flows 4 miles to the sea 8 miles north of Point Sur (lat. 36°25'20" N, long. 121°54'50" W). Named on Mount Carmel (1956) and Soberanes Point (1956) 7.5' quadrangles. The name is for Francis Doud, who had extensive land holdings in Monterey County; on some old maps the stream has the name "Sozers Creek" (Clark, 1991, p. 144).

Dougherty's Mill Number 2: see **Riverside Grove** [SANTA CRUZ].

Douglas Canyon [SAN LUIS OBISPO]: *canyon*, drained by a stream that flows 3 miles to the Salinas River 4.5 miles east-southeast of Pozo (lat. 35°16'35" N, long. 120°17'55" W). Named on Pozo Summit (1967) 7.5' quadrangle.

Douglas Spring [SAN LUIS OBISPO]: *spring*, 5 miles east of Pozo (lat. 35°17'25" N, long. 120°17'10" W); the spring is in Douglas Canyon. Named on Pozo Summit (1967) 7.5' quadrangle.

Douty: see **Point Douty**, under **Sunset Point** [MONTEREY].

Dove [SAN LUIS OBISPO]: *locality,* 3.25 miles southeast of present downtown Atascadero (lat. 35°27' N, long. 120°38' W). Named on San Luis Obispo (1897) 15' quadrangle. Postal authorities established Dove post office in 1889 and discontinued it in 1915 (Frickstad, p. 164).

Dove Canyon [SAN LUIS OBISPO]: *canyon,* 1.5 miles long, drained by a stream that joins a branch of Jack Creek nearly 3 miles north-northwest of York Mountain (lat. 35°34'55" N, long. 120°50'20" W). Named on York Mountain (1948) 7.5' quadrangle.

Doyle Gulch: see **Rodeo Creek Gulch** [SANTA CRUZ].

Drake [SANTA BARBARA]: *locality,* 9.5 miles east of Point Conception along Southern Pacific Railroad (lat. 34°28'15" N, long. 120° 18'10" W); the place is near the mouth of Cañada de Santa Anita. Named on Sacate (1953) 7.5' quadrangle. Called Santa Anita on Lompoc (1905) 30' quadrangle.

Drake: see **Camp Drake** [SANTA BARBARA].

Drew Lake [SANTA CRUZ]: *lake,* 0.5 mile long, 2 miles northeast of Watsonville in Pajaro Valley (lat. 36°56'10" N, long. 121°43'50" W). Named on Watsonville East (1955) 7.5' quadrangle.

Dripping Spring [SANTA BARBARA]: *spring,* 9.5 miles northwest of McPherson Peak (lat. 34°59'25" N, long. 119°55'20" W). Named on McPherson Peak (1943) 15' quadrangle.

Drum Canyon [SANTA BARBARA]: *canyon,* 5.25 miles long, along Santa Rosa Creek above a point 7.5 miles south of the town of Los Alamos (lat. 34°38'10" N, long. 120°17' W). Named on Los Alamos (1959) 7.5' quadrangle.

Dry Canyon [SAN LUIS OBISPO]:
(1) *canyon,* nearly 2 miles long, 8 miles southwest of Shandon (lat. 35°35'20" N, long. 120°29'15" W). Named on Shedd Canyon (1961) 7.5' quadrangle.
(2) *canyon,* drained by a stream that flows 1.25 miles to Railpen Canyon 1.5 miles north-northeast of Huasna Peak (lat. 35°04' N, long. 120°19'30" W). Named on Huasna Peak (1967) 7.5' quadrangle.

Dry Canyon [SANTA BARBARA]:
(1) *canyon,* drained by a stream that flows 4.5 miles to Santa Barbara Canyon 2.5 miles southeast of Fox Mountain (lat. 34°47'10" N, long. 119°34'05" W). Named on Fox Mountain (1964) 7.5' quadrangle.
(2) *canyon,* drained by a stream that flows 4 miles to the sea 6.25 miles west of Carrington Point on Santa Rosa Island (lat. 34°01'05" N, long. 120°09' W). Named on Santa Rosa Island North (1943) 7.5' quadrangle.

Dry Creek [SAN LUIS OBISPO]:
(1) *stream,* flows 15 miles to Huerhuero Creek 3.5 miles east-northeast of Paso Robles (lat. 35°39'10" N, long. 120°38'20" W; at W line sec. 24, T 26 S, R 12 E). Named on Creston (1948) and Estrella (1948) 7.5' quadrangles. Shedd Canyon (1961) 7.5' quadrangle shows Dry Canyon (1) along the uppermost part of the watercourse.
(2) *stream,* flows nearly 4 miles to Huffs Hole Creek 12 miles north of the town of Nipomo (lat. 35°13'05" N, long. 120°26'35" W; sec. 23, T 31 S, R 14 E). Named on Tar Spring Ridge (1967) 7.5' quadrangle.

Dry Creek [SANTA BARBARA]:
(1) *stream,* flows 2.25 miles to Manzana Creek 2.5 miles northeast of Zaca Lake (lat. 34°48'10" N, long. 120°00'15" W). Named on Zaca Lake (1964) 7.5' quadrangle.
(2) *stream* and *dry wash,* flows 4.25 miles to Zaca Creek nearly 2 miles north-northeast of Buellton (lat. 34°38'15" N, long. 120° 11' W). Named on Zaca Creek (1959) 7.5' quadrangle.
(3) *stream,* flows 1 mile to Bartlett Canyon nearly 3 miles northwest of downtown Goleta (lat. 34°28'05" N, long. 119°51'25" W; sec. 31, T 5 N, R 28 W). Named on Goleta (1950) 7.5' quadrangle.

Dry Gulch [MONTEREY]: *canyon,* drained by a stream that flows nearly 6 miles to Deadman Gulch 8.5 miles north of Bradley (lat. 35°59'10" N, long. 120°50' W; near E line sec. 25, T 22 S, R 10 E). Named on Bradley (1961) 15' quadrangle, and on Pancho Rico Valley (1967) 7.5' quadrangle. Shown as part of Deadman Gulch on San Ardo (1956) 15' quadrangle, and on Wunpost (1949) 7.5' quadrangle.

Dry Lake [SAN BENITO]:
(1) *intermittent lake,* 1 mile long, 8 miles north-northwest of Bitterwater (lat. 36°28'45" N, long. 121°04'20" W; sec. 2, T 17 S, R 8 E). Named on Topo Valley (1969) 7.5' quadrangle.
(2) *intermittent lake,* 350 feet long, 9.5 miles east-southeast of Bitterwater (lat. 36°19'15" N, long. 120°50'50" W; sec. 36, T 18 S, R 10 E). Named on Hepsedam Peak (1969) 7.5' quadrangle.

Dry Lake: see **Soda Lake** [SAN LUIS OBISPO]; **The Dry Lake** [MONTEREY].

Dry Lake Valley [SAN BENITO]: *valley,* 8 miles north-northwest of Bitterwater (lat. 36°29' N, long. 121°04'15" W); Dry Lake (1) is in the valley. Named on Topo Valley (1969) 7.5' quadrangle.

Dughi Spring [SAN LUIS OBISPO]: *spring,* 6 miles north-northwest of San Luis Obispo (lat. 35°21'50" N, long. 120°41'20" W; sec. 33, T 29 S, R 12 E). Named on San Luis Obispo (1965) 7.5' quadrangle.

Dunbar: see **Dunbarton** [MONTEREY].

Dunbarton [MONTEREY]: *locality,* 2.25 miles south of Aromas (lat. 36°51'25" N, long. 121°39' W). Named on San Juan Bautista (1917) 15' quadrangle. Called Dunbar on California Mining Bureau's (1917b) map. Postal authorities established Dunbarton post office in 1900 and discontinued it in 1909 (Frickstad, p. 107)

Dunham Canyon [SAN BENITO]: *canyon,* drained by a stream that flows 2.5 miles to North Fork Lewis Creek 10 miles south-southwest of Idria (lat. 36°17'05" N, long. 120°44'05" W; near S line sec. 11, T 19 S, R 11 E). Named on Hepsedam Peak (1969) and San Benito Mountain (1969) 7.5' quadrangles.

Dunham Spring [SAN BENITO]: *spring,* 15 miles east-southeast of Bitterwater (lat. 36°18'05" N, long. 120°45'30" W; sec. 3, T 19 S, R 11 E); the spring is in Dunham Canyon. Named on Hepsedam Peak (1969) 7.5' quadrangle.

Dunn Canyon [MONTEREY]: *canyon,* drained by a stream that flows 4.5 miles to an unnamed canyon 7 miles east-northeast of Salinas (lat. 36°42'05" N, long. 121°32'05" W). Named on Mount Harlan (1968) and Natividad (1947, photorevised 1968) 7.5' quadrangles.

Dunne Ridge [SAN BENITO]: *ridge,* north-trending, mainly in Santa Clara County, but extends south into San Benito County 8 miles north-northeast of Hollister (lat. 36°57'30" N, long. 121°21'15" W). Named on Three Sisters (1954) 7.5' quadrangle.

Dunneville [SAN BENITO]: *locality,* 6 miles north of Hollister (lat. 36°56'25" N, long. 121°24'35" W). Named on San Felipe (1955) 7.5' quadrangle. A small community called Dunneville, situated on the ranch of the Dunne family, failed to develop (Shumate, p. 23-24). Postal authorities established Dunneville post office in 1874 and discontinued it in 1875 (Salley, p. 62). The place also was called Chase's Corners for a man who operated a bar there (Pierce, p. 96).

Duri [SAN BENITO]: *locality,* 1 mile north-northwest of Hollister along Southern Pacific Railroad (lat. 36°52' N, long. 121°24'30" W). Named on Hollister (1921) 15' quadrangle.

Dutch Henry Canyon [MONTEREY]: *canyon,* drained by a stream that flows nearly 4 miles to Portugee Canyon 5.5 miles northeast of San Ardo (lat. 36°05'20" N, long. 120°50'45" W; sec. 24, T 21 S, R 10 E). Named on Pancho Rico Valley (1967) 7.5' quadrangle. On San Ardo (1956) 15' quadrangle, present Redhead Canyon is called Dutch Henry Canyon.

Dutchman Spring [SAN LUIS OBISPO]: *spring,* 2.25 miles south-southeast of Branch Mountain (lat. 35°09'20" N, long. 120°04'05" W). Named on Branch Mountain (1967) 7.5' quadrangle.

Dutch Oven Campground [SANTA BARBARA]: *locality,* 1.5 miles south of Madulce Peak in Alamar Canyon (lat. 34°40'15" N, long. 119°35'35" W). Named on Madulce Peak (1964) 7.5' quadrangle.

Dutra Creek [MONTEREY]: *stream,* flows 3.25 miles to San Carpoforo Creek 11 miles east-southeast of Cape San Martin (lat. 35°48'05" N, long. 121°16'55" W; sec. 35, T 24 S, R 6 E). Named on Burro Mountain (1949) 7.5' quadrangle. The name commemorates Manuel Dutra, who settled by the stream about 1885 (Clark, 1991, p. 146). A place called Pear Orchard is situated along Dutra Creek where an ancient pear tree survived into modern times; the name of the place traditionally dates from mission days, when workers at a silver mine farther up Dutra Creek supposedly lived there (Hoover, Rensch, and Rensch, p. 237-238).

- E -

Eagle: see **Valleton** [MONTEREY].

Eagle Camp: see **Camp Stephani** [MONTEREY].

Eagle Canyon [SANTA BARBARA]: *canyon,* drained by a stream that flows 4.5 miles to the sea 3.5 miles west-northwest of Coal Oil Point (lat. 34°26'05" N, long. 119°55'40" W). Named on Dos Pueblos Canyon (1951) 7.5' quadrangle. The Spaniards called the feature Arroyo de Agalia—*agalia* means "eagle" in Spanish (Gudde, 1949, p. 102).

Eagle Cliff: see **Bay Point** [SANTA BARBARA].

Eagle Creek [SAN LUIS OBISPO]: *stream,* flows 2 miles to Atascadero Creek nearly 4 miles south-southwest of Atascadero (lat. 35° 26'15" N, long. 120°41'35" W); the stream heads east of Eagle Peak. Named on Atascadero (1965) 7.5' quadrangle.

Eagle Dell Peak [SANTA CRUZ]: *peak,* 3.5 miles east-southeast of the town of Boulder Creek (lat. 37°06'20" N, long. 122°03'35" W; sec. 34, T 9 S, R 2 W). Named on Felton (1955) 7.5' quadrangle.

Eagle Hills [SAN LUIS OBISPO]: *range,* 6 miles north of Shandon on the northwest side of McMillan Canyon (lat. 35°44'30" N, long. 120°22' W). Named on Cholame (1943) 7.5' quadrangle. Cholame (1917) 30' quadrangle shows Eagle school located about 1 mile northwest of the range.

Eagle Mountain [SAN BENITO]: *peak,* 5 miles southeast of Bitterwater (lat. 36°19'25" N, long. 120°57' W; sec. 36, T 18 S, R 9 E). Altitude 2494 feet. Named on Lonoak (1969) 7.5' quadrangle.

Eagle Peak [SAN LUIS OBISPO]: *peak,* 4.5 miles south of Atascadero (lat. 35°25'35" N, long. 120°41'10" W; near S line sec. 4, T 29 S, R 12 E). Altitude 2182 feet. Named on Atascadero (1965) 7.5' quadrangle.

Eagle Peak: see **Eagle Rock** [SANTA CRUZ].

Eagle Rock [MONTEREY]: *relief feature,* 2 miles south-southwest of Smith Mountain (lat. 36°03'25" N, long. 120°36'35" W; sec. 31, T 21 S, R 13 E). Named on Smith Mountain (1969) 7.5' quadrangle.

Eagle Rock [SAN LUIS OBISPO]: *peak,* 10.5 miles east of the village of San Simeon (lat. 35°40' N, long. 121°00'25" W; sec. 16, T 26 S, R 9 E). Named on Pebblestone Shut-in (1959) 7.5' quadrangle.

Eagle Rock [SANTA CRUZ]: *peak,* 2 miles southeast of Big Basin (lat. 37°08'50" N, long. 122°11'40" W; sec. 16, T 9 S, R 3 W). Altitude 2488 feet. Named on Big Basin (1955) 7.5' quadrangle. Called Eagle Pk. on California Mining Bureau's (1917a) map.

Eaglet: see **Have** [SAN LUIS OBISPO].

East Beach [SANTA BARBARA]: *beach,* 2 miles east of downtown Santa Barbara along the coast (lat. 34°25' N, long. 119°40' W). Named on Santa Barbara (1952) 7.5' quadrangle.

East Canyon [SANTA BARBARA]: *canyon,* drained by a stream that flows nearly 2 miles to join the stream in Central Canyon and form Bitter Creek 4 miles southwest of New Cuyama (lat. 34°54'25" N, long. 119°44'10" W; sec. 35, T 10 N, R 27 W). Named on New Cuyama (1964) 7.5' quadrangle.

East Corral de Piedra Creek [SAN LUIS OBISPO]: *stream,* flows 6 miles to join West Corral de Piedra Creek and form Pismo Creek nearly 0.5 mile south-southeast of Edna (lat. 35°11'50" N, long. 120°36'35" W); the stream is on Corral de Piedra grant. Named on Arroyo Grande NE (1965) 7.5' quadrangle.

East End Anchorage: see **Scorpion Anchorage** [SANTA BARBARA].

East Garrison: see **Camp Roberts Military Reservation** [MONTEREY-SAN LUIS OBISPO]; **Fort Ord Military Reservation** [MONTEREY].

East Mine Canyon Spring [SANTA BARBARA]: *spring,* 1.5 miles west-northwest of Montgomery Potrero (lat. 34°50'35" N, long. 119°46'35" W); the spring is 1 mile east-southeast of North Mine Canyon Spring in Mine Canyon (3). Named on Hurricane Deck (1964) 7.5' quadrangle.

East Monterey: see **Seaside** [MONTEREY].

Easton Spring [MONTEREY]: *spring,* 7 miles south-southwest of Charlie Mountain (lat. 36°02'20" N, long. 120°42'35" W; near SE cor. sec. 6, T 22 S, R 12 E). Named on Slack Canyon (1969) 7.5' quadrangle.

East Pinery [SANTA BARBARA]: *area,* 2 miles east-southeast of Figueroa Mountain (lat. 34°44' N, long. 119°57'15" W; on S line sec. 29, T 8 N, R 29 W). Named on Figueroa Mountain (1959) 7.5' quadrangle.

East Point [SANTA BARBARA]: *promontory,* at the easternmost tip of Santa Rosa Island (lat. 33°56'35" N, long. 119°58' W). Named on Santa Rosa Island East (1943) 7.5' quadrangle.

East Salinas: see **Alisal** [MONTEREY].

East Tuley Springs [SAN LUIS OBISPO]: *springs,* two, 850 feet apart, 5 miles north-northwest of Shandon (lat. 35°43'05" N, long. 120°25'15" W; sec. 25, T 25 S, R 14 E); the springs are 0.5 mile east of West Tuley Springs. Named on Shandon (1961) 7.5' quadrangle.

East Waddell Creek [SANTA CRUZ]: *stream,* formed by the confluence of Opal Creek and Blooms Creek, flows 3.5 miles to join West Waddell Creek and form Waddell Creek 2.5 miles north-northwest of the mouth of Waddell Creek (lat. 36°08' N, long. 122°16' W; near S line sec. 23, T 9 S, R 4 W). Named on Big Basin (1955) and Franklin Point (1955) 7.5' quadrangles.

Eblen Spring [MONTEREY]: *spring,* 3 miles south-southeast of Charley Mountain (lat. 36°05'45" N, long. 120°39'15" W; near NE cor. sec. 22, T 21 S, R 12 E). Named on Slack Canyon (1969) 7.5' quadrangle.

Eblis: see **Santa Cruz** [SANTA CRUZ].

Eccles [SANTA CRUZ]: *locality,* 5 miles southeast of the town of Boulder Creek along the railroad that extends up Zayante Creek (lat. 37°04'55" N, long. 122°03' W; near N line sec. 11, T 10 S, R 2 W). Named on Santa Cruz (1902) 30' quadrangle. The name commemorates John Sanderson Eccles, who deeded right of way to South Pacific Coast Railroad in 1878 (Clark, 1986, p. 104). Postal authorities established Eccles post office in 1893 and changed the name to Olympia in 1915 (Frickstad, p. 176). Clark (1986, p. 171-172) listed a railroad stop called Kenville that was located between Eccles and Meehan; the name was for Joseph Kenville, who came to Santa Cruz in 1865 and established the first express company there.

Echo Valley [MONTEREY]: *canyon,* drained by a stream that flows 1.5 miles to San Miguel Canyon 3 miles north of Prunedale (lat. 36°49'15" N, long. 121°40'15" W). Named on Prunedale (1954) 7.5' quadrangle.

Eckart Canyon [SANTA BARBARA]: *canyon,* drained by a stream that flows 3 miles to Moon Canyon 9.5 miles northwest of McPherson Peak (lat. 34°59'10" N, long. 119°55'45" W; at N line sec. 1, T 10 N, R 29 W). Named on Bates Canyon (1964) 7.5' quadrangle.

Eddys Camp [SAN LUIS OBISPO]: *locality,* 8 miles southwest of Shandon (lat. 35°33'40" N, long. 120°27'50" W; near E line sec. 21, T 27 S, R 14 E). Named on Shedd Canyon (1961) 7.5' quadrangle.

Edna [SAN LUIS OBISPO]: *village,* 6 miles south-southeast of San Luis Obispo (lat. 35°12'15" N, long. 120°36'45" W). Named on Arroyo Grande NE (1965) 7.5' quadrangle. Postal authorities established Edna post office in 1887 and discontinued it in 1920 (Frickstad, p. 164).

El Alisal [MONTEREY]:

(1) *land grant,* 4 miles east of Salinas. Named on Natividad (1947) 7.5' quadrangle. Feliciano Soberanes received the land in 1823 and 1834, and Manuel Butron received it in 1828; Basilio Bernal claimed 5941 acres patented in 1866 (Cowan, p. 14).

(2) *land grant,* 6 miles east-southeast of Salinas. Named on Natividad (1947) 7.5' quadrangle. William E. Hartnell received 0.75 league in 1834; Maria Teresa de la Guerra de Hartnell claimed 2971 acres patented in 1882 (Cowan, p. 14-15; Cowan gave the name "Patrocino" as an alternate).

El Arroyo de San Marcos: see **San Marcos Creek** [SAN LUIS OBISPO].

El Cabo de Martin: see **Point Pinos** [MONTEREY].

El Cabo de San Martin: see **Point Pinos** [MONTEREY].

El Callejon Creek [SANTA BARBARA]: *stream,* flows 2.5 miles to El Jaro Creek 12.5 miles southeast of the city of Lompoc (lat. 34° 31'35" N, long. 120°17'20" W). Named on Santa Rosa Hills (1959) 7.5' quadrangle.

El Cantil: see **San Simeon Creek** [SAN LUIS OBISPO].

El Capitan Beach [SANTA BARBARA]: *beach,* 10.5 miles east of Gaviota along the coast (lat. 34°27'30" N, long. 120°01'35" W); the feature is west of the mouth of Cañada del Capitan. Named on Gaviota (1943) 15' quadrangle.

El Capitan Lodge [SANTA BARBARA]: *locality,* 6.25 miles south-southeast of Santa Ynez (lat. 34°32'15" N, long. 120°01'15" W). Named on Los Olivos (1943) 15' quadrangle.

El Chamisal [MONTEREY]: *land grant,* 6 miles southwest of Salinas. Named on Salinas (1947), Seaside (1947), and Spreckels (1947) 7.5' quadrangles. Felipe Vasquez received 1 league in 1835 and his heirs claimed 2737 acres patented in 1877 (Cowan, p. 26; Cowan gave both the forms "El Chamizal" and "El Chamisal" for the name). According to Gudde (1949, p. 261-262), a place called Pilarcitos was located on the grant.

El Chorro [SAN LUIS OBISPO]: *land grant,* 4 miles northwest of San Luis Obispo; Chorro Creek is a boundary of the grant. Named on San Luis Obispo (1965) 7.5' quadrangle. James Scott and John Wilson received 1 league in 1845; Wilson claimed 3167 acres patented in 1861 (Cowan, p. 27—Cowan used the name "Cañada del Chorro" for the grant; Perez, p. 60).

Elder Spring [SAN LUIS OBISPO]: *spring,* nearly 4 miles west-northwest of Cholame in McMillan Canyon (lat. 35°44'45" N, long. 120°21'30" W; near N line sec. 21, T 25 S, R 15 E). Named on Cholame (1961) 7.5' quadrangle.

Eldorado Creek [SANTA BARBARA]: *stream,* flows 3.5 miles to join Steer Creek and form Gobernador Creek 3.5 miles north of Rincon Point (lat. 34°25'30" N, long. 119°28'25" W; sec. 14, T 4 N, R 25 W). Named on White Ledge Peak (1952) 7.5' quadrangle.

Elephant Mountain [MONTEREY]: *peak,* 1 mile east-northeast of Uncle Sam Mountain (lat. 36°20'55" N, long. 121°41'20" W; sec. 19, T 18 S, R 3 E). Named on Ventana Cones (1956) 7.5' quadrangle.

El Estero [MONTEREY]: *lake,* 4000 feet long, near the coast in Monterey (lat. 36°35'55" N, long. 121°53'05" W). Named on Monterey (1947, photorevised 1968) 7.5' quadrangle. The lake was part of an estuary before 1874, when construction of Monterey and Salinas Valley Railroad separated the lake from the sea (Clark, 1991, p. 153).

El Estero [SANTA BARBARA]: *marsh,* west of Carpinteria along the coast (lat. 34°24' N, long. 119°32' W). Named on Carpinteria (1952) 7.5' quadrangle. United States Board on Geographic Names (1961b, p. 10) rejected the names "Carpinteria Lagoon" and "Carpinteria Slough" for the feature.

El Jarro: see **Agua Puerca y las Trancas** [SANTA CRUZ].

El Jaro Creek [SANTA BARBARA]: *stream,* flows 11.5 miles to Salsipuedes Creek 4.5 miles southeast of the city of Lompoc (lat. 34°35'05" N, long. 120°24'25" W). Named on Lompoc Hills (1959) and Santa Rosa Hills (1959) 7.5' quadrangles.

El Jarro Point [SANTA CRUZ]: *promontory,* 2 miles west-northwest of Davenport along the coast (lat. 37°01'30" N, long. 122°13'20" W). Named on Davenport (1955) 7.5' quadrangle. The promontory is on Agua Puerca y las Trancas grant, which formerly had the name "El Jarro" (Cowan, p. 13).

Elkhorn [MONTEREY]: *locality,* 13 miles northwest of Prunedale along Southern Pacific Railroad (lat. 36°49'25" N, long. 121°44'20" W); the place is on the east side of Elkhorn Slough. Named on Prunedale (1954) 7.5' quadrangle.

Elkhorn Ferry: see **Pauls Ferry**, under **Pauls Island** [MONTEREY].

Elkhorn Hills [SAN LUIS OBISPO]: *range,* southwest of the southeast end of Temblor Range at the southeast end of Carrizo Plain (lat. 35°02'30" N, long. 119°32'30" W). Named on Elkhorn Hills (1954) and Maricopa (1951) 7.5' quadrangles. Arnold and Johnson (1910, p. 20) proposed the name.

Elkhorn Plain [SAN LUIS OBISPO]: *valley,* between Temblor Range on the northeast and Panorama Hills and Elkhorn Hills on the southwest. Named on Elkhorn Hills (1954), Maricopa (1951), Painted Rock (1959), Panorama Hills (1954), and Wells Ranch (1954) 7.5' quadrangles. Called Elkhorn Valley on Mendenhall's (1908) map.

Elkhorn Scarp [SAN LUIS OBISPO]: *escarpment,* northwest-trending, 18 miles long, on the northeast side of Carrizo Plain southwest of Panorama Hills and Elkhorn Hills. Named on Elkhorn Hills (1954), Panorama Hills

(1954), and Wells Ranch (1954) 7.5' quadrangles. Arnold and Johnson (1910, p. 20) proposed the name and noted that the term "scarp" is appropriate because the feature is along San Andreas fault.

Elkhorn Slough [MONTEREY]: *water feature*, 7 miles long, enters the sea at Moss Landing (lat. 36°48'30" N, long. 121°47'15" W). Named on Moss Landing (1954) and Prunedale (1954) 7.5' quadrangles. According to Elliott and Moore (p. 74), the crookedness of the slough inspired the name. The feature also has the names "Estero Grande," "Estero Vallejo" or "Vallejo Slough," "Estero Viejo," and "Roadhouse Slough"—the last for Joseph Truman Roadhouse, who lived near the slough (Clark, 1991, p. 154-155).

Elkhorn Spring [SAN BENITO]: *spring*, 4 miles northwest of present Idria along Larious Creek (lat. 36°27' N, long. 120°43'55" W; sec. 14, T 17 S, R 11 E). Named on New Idria (1943) 15' quadrangle.

Elkhorn Valley: see **Elkhorn Plain** [SAN LUIS OBISPO].

Ellicott [SANTA CRUZ]: *locality*, 4.5 miles west of Watsonville along Southern Pacific Railroad (lat. 36°55'15" N, long. 121°50'10" W). Named on Watsonville West (1954) 7.5' quadrangle.

Elliot Creek [SANTA CRUZ]: *stream*, flows 1.5 miles to San Mateo County 1.5 miles north-northwest of the mouth of Waddell Creek (lat. 37°06'55" N, long. 122°17'25" W; sec. 27, T 9 S, R 4 W). Named on Año Nuevo (1955) and Franklin Point (1955) 7.5' quadrangles.

Elliott Hill [MONTEREY]: *peak*, 6.25 miles west-southwest of Salinas (lat. 36°37'45" N, long. 121°45'15" W). Named on Marina (1947) 7.5' quadrangle. Salinas (1947) 7.5' quadrangle has the form "Elliot Hill" for the name.

Ellis Canyon [MONTEREY]: *canyon*, drained by a stream that flows 2 miles to Chualar Canyon 9 miles east-northeast of Chualar (lat. 36°37'20" N, long. 121°22' W; sec. 13, T 15 S, R 5 E). Named on Mount Johnson (1968) 7.5' quadrangle. Called Loudon Gulch on Gonzales (1921) 15' quadrangle.

El Llanito de San Francisquito: see **San Francisquito Flat** [MONTEREY].

El Lobo: see **Lion Rock** [SAN LUIS OBISPO].

Ell Peak [MONTEREY]: *peak*, 7.5 miles southwest of Soledad (lat. 36°21'55" N, long. 121°26'05" W; sec. 16, T 18 S, R 5 E). Named on Sycamore Flat (1956) 7.5' quadrangle.

Ellwood [SANTA BARBARA]: *locality*, nearly 2 miles north-northwest of Coal Oil Point along Southern Pacific Railroad (lat. 34°25'55" N, long. 119°53'15" W); the place is near the mouth of Ellwood Canyon. Named on Dos Pueblos Canyon (1951) 7.5' quadrangle. California Mining Bureau's (1917c) map shows a place called Vilo located along the railroad about 2 miles west of Ellwood.

Ellwood Canyon [SANTA BARBARA]: *canyon*, drained by a stream that flows 5.5 miles to Bell Canyon 2.5 miles north-northwest of Coal Oil Point (lat. 34°26'30" N, long. 119°53'50" W). Named on Dos Pueblos Canyon (1951) and Lake Cachuma (1959) 7.5' quadrangles. United States Board on Geographic Names (1962a, p. 11) rejected the form "Elwood Canyon" for the name, which is from Ellwood Cooper, a horticulturist who had a ranch in the canyon (Tompkins and Ruiz, p. 67).

Ellysly Creek [SAN LUIS OBISPO]: *stream*, flows nearly 4 miles to Villa Creek 2.5 miles northwest of Cayucos Point (lat. 35°28'05" N, long. 120°58'35" W; sec. 26, T 28 S. R 9 E). Named on Cayucos (1965) 7.5' quadrangle.

El Moro: see **Baywood Park** [SAN LUIS OBISPO].

El Morro: see **Morro Rock** [SAN LUIS OBISPO].

El Morro Creek: see **Morro Creek** [SAN LUIS OBISPO].

El Morro Rock: see **Morro Rock** [SAN LUIS OBISPO].

El Pajaro Springs: see **Chittenden's Sulphur Springs**, under **Chittenden** [SANTA CRUZ].

El Paso de Robles: see **Paso Robles** [SAN LUIS OBISPO].

El Pescadero [MONTEREY]: *land grant*, north of Carmel Bay. Named on Monterey (1947) 7.5' quadrangle. Fabian Barreto received 1 league in 1836; David Jacks claimed 4426 acres patented in 1868 (Cowan, p. 59). The name is from fishing activities at the site—*el pescadero* means "the place where fishing is done" in Spanish (Hoover, Rensch, and Rensch, p. 231).

El Piojo [MONTEREY]: *land grant*, 5 miles south of Jolon. Named on Alder Peak (1949), Burnett Peak (1949), and Jolon (1949) 7.5' quadrangles. Joaquin Soto received 3 leagues in 1842 and his heirs claimed 13,329 acres patented in 1866 (Cowan, p. 61). Irelan (p. 405) used the name "Pyojo" for the grant.

El Piojo Creek [MONTEREY]: *stream*, flows nearly 7 miles to Nacimiento River 10 miles south of Jolon (lat. 35°49'50" N, long. 121° 08'50" W; sec. 19, T 24 S, R 8 E); the stream is partly on El Piojo grant. Named on Burnett Peak (1949) and Jolon (1949) 7.5' quadrangles.

El Pizmo: see **Pismo Beach** [SAN LUIS OBISPO].

El Potrero de San Carlos [MONTEREY]: *land grant*, south of Carmel River and 2.5 miles from the coast. Named on Monterey (1947), Mount Carmel (1956), and Seaside (1947) 7.5' quadrangles. Fructuso Real received 1 league in 1837; Joaquin Guiterrez, Estefana Guiterrez, and Maria Guiterrez claimed 4307 acres patented in 1862 (Cowan, p. 74; Perez, p. 82).

El Puerto de Monte-Rey: see **Monterey Bay** [MONTEREY].

El Rincon [SANTA BARBARA]: *land grant*, at Rincon Point on Santa Barbara-Ventura County line. Named on Carpinteria (1952) and White Ledge Peak (1952) 7.5' quadrangles. Teodoro Arellanes received 1 league in 1835 and claimed 4460 acres patented in 1872 (Cowan, p. 67-68).

El Rio Grande del Sur: see **Big Sur River** [MONTEREY].

Elsa [MONTEREY]: *locality*, 2.5 miles north-northwest of King City along Southern Pacific Railroad (lat. 36°15' N, long. 121°08'15" W). Named on Greenfield (1956) 7.5' quadrangle.

El Sueno [SANTA BARBARA]: *locality*, 3.25 miles east of downtown Goleta (lat. 34°26'35" N, long. 119°46'10" W). Named on Goleta (1950) 7.5' quadrangle.

El Sur [MONTEREY]: *land grant*, along the coast at Point Sur. Named on Big Sur (1956) and Point Sur (1956) 7.5' quadrangles. Juan Bautista Alvarado received 2 leagues in 1834; John B.R. Cooper claimed 8949 acres patented in 1866 (Cowan, p. 100).

El Toro [MONTEREY]: *land grant*, 6 miles south-southwest of Salinas. Named on Salinas (1947), Seaside (1947), and Spreckels (1947) 7.5' quadrangles. Jose Ramon Estrada received 1.5 leagues in 1835; Charles Wolters claimed 5668 acres patented in 1862 (Cowan, p. 104). According to Clark (1991, p. 158), the grant was named for El Toro Creek.

El Toro Creek [MONTEREY]: *stream*, flows 14 miles to Salinas River 3.5 miles south-southwest of Salinas (lat. 36°37'45" N, long. 121°41'15" W). Named on Spreckels (1947) 7.5' quadrangle. Called Toro Creek on Salinas (1947) 7.5' quadrangle.

El Toro Lake [MONTEREY]: *intermittent lake*, 1150 feet long, 9.5 miles south-southeast of Salinas (lat. 36°33'25" N, long. 121°44'10" W); the feature is on El Toro grant. Named on Spreckels (1947) 7.5' quadrangle.

El Tranquillon: see **Tranquillon Mountain** [SANTA BARBARA].

El Tranquillon Mountain: see **Tranquillon Mountain** [SANTA BARBARA].

El Tucho [MONTEREY]: *land grant*, 4.5 miles west of Salinas. Named on Salinas (1947) 7.5' quadrangle. Jose Manuel Boronda received the land about 1795; Boronda and Blas Martinez received it in 1835; Simon Castro received 800 varas in 1841 and his heirs claimed 113 acres patented in 1867; David Jacks claimed 400 acres patented in 1876 (Cowan, p. 105).

Elvina: see **Paicines** [SAN BENITO].

Elwood Canyon: see **Ellwood Canyon** [SANTA BARBARA].

Emmett: see **Emmett Station** [SAN BENITO].

Emmett Station [SAN BENITO]: *locality*, 12 miles north-northwest of San Benito along Tres Pinos Creek (lat. 36°39'45" N, long. 121° 10' W; sec. 2, T 15 S, R 7 E). Named on San Benito (1919) 15' quadrangle. Postal authorities established Emmett post office in 1873 and discontinued it in 1908; they established Beckett post office 8 miles east of Emmett in 1886 and discontinued it in 1887—the name was for Thomas J. Beckett, first postmaster (Salley, p. 17, 69).

Encinal y Buena Esperanza [MONTEREY]: *land grant*, 9 miles east-southeast of Salinas. Named on Chualar (1947), Gonzales (1955), Mount Harlan (1968), and Natividad (1947) 7.5' quadrangles. David Spence received 3 leagues in 1834 and 1839; he claimed 13,391 acres patented in 1862 (Cowan, p. 33). Perez (p. 65) gave the size of the grant as 13,351.65 acres.

Enright: see **Majors** [SANTA CRUZ].

Ensenada de Abrigo: see **San Luis Obispo Bay** [SAN LUIS OBISPO].

Ensenada de Buchon: see **San Luis Obispo Bay** [SAN LUIS OBISPO].

Ensenada de la Purisima Concepcion: see **Cojo Bay** [SANTA BARBARA].

Ensenada del Roque: see **Estero Bay** [SAN LUIS OBISPO].

Entrance Rock: see **North Entrance Rock** [SAN LUIS OBISPO].

Erie: see **Hernandez** [SAN BENITO].

Ernest Blanco Spring [SANTA BARBARA]: *spring*, 5.5 miles west-northwest of Montgomery Potrero (lat. 34°52'15" N, long. 119°50'35" W). Named on Hurricane Deck (1964) 7.5' quadrangle.

Esalen Institute: see **Slates Hot Springs** [MONTEREY].

Escalona Gulch [SANTA CRUZ]: *canyon*, drained by a stream that flows 0.5 mile to the sea 2 miles northeast of Soquel Point (lat. 36° 58'35" N, long. 121°56'35" W). Named on Soquel (1954) 7.5' quadrangle.

Escondido Camp Ground [MONTEREY]: *locality*, 4 miles west of Junipero Serra Peak (lat. 36°08'25" N, long. 121°29'35" W; near NE cor. sec. 2, T 21 S, R 4 E). Named on Junipero Serra Peak (1949) 7.5' quadrangle. Called Escondido Camp on Junipero Serra (1948) 15' quadrangle, and called Escondido Campground on Junipero Serra (1961) 15' quadrangle. Junipero Serra (1930) 15' quadrangle has the name "Rancho Escondido" at or near the site.

Escondido Canyon [SANTA BARBARA]: *canyon*, drained by a stream that flows 2 miles to Blue Canyon nearly 7 miles north-northwest of Carpinteria (lat. 34°29'10" N, long. 119°34' W; near E line sec. 26, T 5 N, R 26 W). Named on Carpinteria (1952) 7.5' quadrangle.

Escondido Creek [SANTA BARBARA]: *stream*, flows 4 miles to Jalama Creek 8.5 miles south of the city of Lompoc (lat. 34°30'50" N, long. 120°27'15" W). Named on Lompoc Hills (1959) 7.5' quadrangle.

Espada: see **The Espada** [SANTA BARBARA].

Espada Bluff [SANTA BARBARA]: *relief feature*, 4.25 miles south-southeast of Tranquillon Mountain along the coast (lat. 34°31'55" N, long.

120°31'20" W); the feature is near The Espada. Named on Tranquillon Mountain (1959) 7.5' quadrangle. The Railway (1903) map shows a place called Espada Ldg. situated along the coast at or near present Espada Bluff.

Espada Creek [SANTA BARBARA]: *stream,* flows 5 miles to Jalama Creek 9 miles south of the city of Lompoc (lat. 34°30'40" N, long. 120°29'25" W). Named on Lompoc Hills (1959) 7.5' quadrangle. Members of the Portola expedition gave the name "Espada" to an Indian village in the neighborhood in 1769 because a soldier recovered a sword there that had been stolen from him—*espada* means "sword" in Spanish (Wagner, H.R., p. 386).

Espada Landing: see **Espada Bluff** [SANTA BARBARA].

Espinosa Canyon [MONTEREY]:

(1) *canyon,* drained by a stream that flows 2.25 miles to Chualar Canyon 8 miles east-northeast of Gonzales (lat. 36°36'55" N, long. 121°23' W; sec. 23, T 15 S, R 5 E). Named on Gonzales (1955) and Mount Harlan (1968) 7.5' quadrangles.

(2) *canyon,* drained by a discontinuous stream that extends for nearly 5 miles to lowlands 4 miles south of San Lucas (lat. 36°04'25" N, long. 121°02' W). Named on Espinosa Canyon (1949) 7.5' quadrangle. The name commemorates Loridon (or Loredan) Espinosa (or Espinoza), who patented land in the canyon in 1892 (Clark, 1991, p. 28, 160).

Espinosa Lake [MONTEREY]: *marsh,* 1.25 miles long, 5.5 miles north-northwest of Salinas (lat. 36°44'30" N, long. 121°42'30" W); the feature is on Bolsa de las Escorpinas grant, which belonged to Salvador Espinosa. Named on Salinas (1947) 7.5' quadrangle. Salinas (1912) 15' quadrangle shows the feature as a lake, which has the designation "Laguna" on the diseño that accompanied Espinosa's petition for the grant (Becker, 1969). According to H.R. Wagner (p. 460, 509), this probably is the feature that soldiers of the Portola expedition called Laguna de las Grullas in 1769 for the numerous cranes seen there—*grulla* means "crane" in Spanish—and that Crespi at the same time named Laguna Santa Brigida for the saint on whose day the expedition visited the place. This feature and Merritt Lake together are called Lagunas de la Herba de los Mansos on a diseño of Bolsa del Potrero y Moro Cojo grant (Becker, 1964).

Esteras Bay: see **Estero Bay** [SAN LUIS OBISPO].

Estero: see **Carrizo Plain** [SAN LUIS OBISPO]; **Point Estero** [SAN LUIS OBISPO].

Estero Bay [SAN LUIS OBISPO]: *embayment,* on the coast between Point Estero and Point Buchon. Named on Cayucos (1965), Morro Bay North (1965), and Morro Bay South (1965) 7.5' quadrangles. Called Ensenada del Roque on an early Spanish map (Wagner, H.R., p. 386), called Bay de los Esteros on Colton's (1855) map, and called Esteras Bay on Rogers and Johnston's (1857) map. United States Board on Geographic Names (1933, p. 293) rejected the forms "Esteros Bay" and "Estros Bay" for the name.

Estero de Santa Serafina: see **Cayucos Creek** [SAN LUIS OBISPO].

Estero Grande: see **Elkhorn Slough** [MONTEREY].

Estero Plain: see **Carrizo Plain** [SAN LUIS OBISPO].

Estero River: see **Cayucos Creek** [SAN LUIS OBISPO].

Esteros Bay: see **Estero Bay** [SAN LUIS OBISPO].

Estero Valllejo: see **Elkhorn Slough** [MONTEREY].

Estero Viejo: see **Elkhorn Slough** [MONTEREY].

Estrada Creek [SAN LUIS OBISPO]: *stream,* flows 4 miles to San Carpoforo Creek 3 miles east of the mouth of that stream (lat. 35° 46'20" N, long. 121°16'25" W; sec. 12, T 25 S, R 6 E). Named on Burnett Peak (1949) and Burro Mountain (1949) 7.5' quadrangles.

Estrada Ridge [SAN LUIS OBISPO]: *ridge,* north-northwest-trending, 0.5 mile long, nearly 3 miles southeast of Cambria (lat. 35°31'50" N, long. 121°03'05" W). Named on Cambria (1959, photorevised 1979) 7.5' quadrangle. The name is for Julian Estrada, owner of Santa Rosa grant, who built his home on the east slope of the ridge (United States Board on Geographic Names, 1974a, p. 2).

Estrella [SAN LUIS OBISPO]: *village,* 7 miles northeast of Paso Robles (lat. 35°42'20" N, long. 120°36'35" W; sec. 31, T 25 S, R 13 E); the village is north of Estrella Creek. Named on Estrella (1948) 7.5' quadrangle. Derby (p. 5) described a place called Estrella, apparently located a few miles east of present Estrella, where four valleys diverge, and stated: "The peculiarity of the divergence of these four valleys, and their corresponding ridges from this point resembling the rays of a star, has given it its very appropriate name—Estrella." *Estrella* means "star" in Spanish. Postal authorities established Estrella post office in 1886 and discontinued it in 1918 (Frickstad, p. 164).

Estrella Creek [SAN LUIS OBISPO]: *stream,* formed by the confluence of San Juan Creek and Cholame Creek at Shandon, flows 28 miles to Salinas River less than 1 mile south of San Miguel (lat. 35°44'30" N, long. 120°41'30" W; sec. 21, T 25 S, R 12 E). Named on Estrella (1948) and Paso Robles (1948) 7.5' quadrangles. Called Estrella River on Cholame (1961) and Shandon (1961) 7.5' quadrangles; United States Board on Geographic Names (1963b, p. 14) approved this name for the stream. Called Rio de la Estrella on Parke's (1854-1855) map. Antisell (1856, p. 93) considered Estrella Creek and San Juan Creek to be one stream, and referred to "San Juan or Estrella river." Antisell (1855, p. 35) earlier called the stream Rio Estrello and Estrella River. Trask (p. 21) used the name "Estella," Parke (p. 8) mentioned Estrella valley, and Goodyear (1888, p. 87) referred to La Estrella Creek.

Estrella Pass: see **Cottonwood Pass** [SAN LUIS OBISPO].

Estrella River: see **Estrella Creek** [SAN LUIS OBISPO].

Estrella Valley: see **Estrella Creek** [SAN LUIS OBISPO].

Estros Bay: see **Estero Bay** [SAN LUIS OBISPO].

Eto Lake [SAN LUIS OBISPO]: *lakes,* three connected, largest 400 feet long, 5 miles southeast of Morro Rock in Los Osos Valley (lat. 35°19' N, long. 120°48'50" W). Named on Morro Bay South (1965) 7.5' quadrangle.

Eugene Well [SAN BENITO]: *well,* 14 miles east-northeast of Bitterwater in Vallecitos (lat. 36°28'50" N, long. 120°47'05" W; sec. 5, T 17 S, R 11 E). Named on Hernandez Reservoir (1969) 7.5' quadrangle, where a windmill symbol marks the feature. On Priest Valley (1915) 30' quadrangle, a spring symbol marks it.

Eureka Canyon [SANTA CRUZ]: *canyon,* nearly 6 miles long, drained by Corralitos Creek above a point 0.5 mile north-northeast of Corralitos (lat. 36°59'45" N, long. 121°48'10" W). Named on Loma Prieta (1955) and Watsonville West (1954) 7.5' quadrangles.

Eureka Gulch [SANTA CRUZ]: *canyon,* drained by a stream that flows 1.5 miles to Eureka Canyon 3.25 miles north-northwest of Corralitos (lat. 37°02'10" N, long. 121°49'05" W; near E line sec. 26, T 10 S, R 1 E). Named on Loma Prieta (1955) 7.5' quadrangle.

Evers: see **Camp Evers** [SANTA CRUZ].

Ewing: see **Grant Ewing Ridge** [MONTEREY].

Ex Mission Soledad [MONTEREY]: *land grant,* 3 miles west-southwest of Soledad; includes the site of Soledad mission. Named on Palo Escrito Peak (1956), Paraiso Springs (1956), and Soledad (1955) 7.5' quadrangles. Feliciano Soberanes purchased the land in 1846 and claimed 8900 acres patented in 1874; the Catholic Church claimed 34 acres patented in 1859 (Cowan, p. 99; Cowan listed the grant under the name "Mision Nuestra Señora de la Soledad"). According to Perez (p. 66), Feliciano Soberanes was the grantee in 1846.

- F -

Fairbank Point [SAN LUIS OBISPO]: *promontory,* nearly 2 miles southeast of Morro Rock on the east side of Morro Bay (lat. 35°21'05" N, long. 120°50'40" W; sec. 1, T 30 S, R 10 E). Named on Morro Bay South (1965) 7.5' quadrangle. The name commemorates Dr. and Mrs. Charles Oliver Fairbank, who lived near the feature (United States Board on Geographic Names, 1963a, p. 6).

Fairoaks: see **Oaks** [SAN LUIS OBISPO].

Fairview: see **Twin Lakes** [SANTA CRUZ].

Fall Canyon [SANTA BARBARA]: *canyon,* drained by a stream that flows 4 miles to Sisquoc River nearly 6 miles northwest of Big Pine Mountain (lat. 34°45' N, long. 119°43'55" W); Sisquoc Falls is in the canyon. Named on Big Pine Mountain (1964) 7.5' quadrangle.

Fall Creek [SANTA CRUZ]: *stream,* flows 5 miles to San Lorenzo River 5 miles south-southeast of the town of Boulder Creek (lat. 37°03'35" N, long. 122°04'40" W). Named on Davenport (1955) and Felton (1955) 7.5' quadrangles.

Falls: see **The Falls** [MONTEREY]:

False Point Sur [MONTEREY]: *hill,* 1 mile southeast of Point Sur (lat. 36°17'45" N, long. 121°52'45" W). Altitude 209 feet. Named on Point Sur (1956) 7.5' quadrangle. United States Board on Geographic Names (1960c, p. 16) approved the name "False Sur" for the feature.

False Sur: see **False Point Sur** [MONTEREY].

Fan Shell Beach [MONTEREY]: *beach,* 0.5 mile east of Cypress Point (lat. 36°34'55" N, long. 121°58'05" W). Named on Monterey (1947) 7.5' quadrangle.

Farallon de Lobos: see **Richardson Rock** [SANTA BARBARA].

Faris: see **Bill Faris Campground** [SANTA BARBARA].

Farley [SANTA CRUZ]: *locality,* 0.5 mile southeast of Aptos along Southern Pacific Railroad in present Del Mar (lat. 36°58'10" N, long. 121°53'35" W). Named on Capitola (1914) 15' quadrangle.

Fat Buck Ridge [SANTA CRUZ]: *ridge,* south- to west-trending, nearly 2 miles long, 5 miles north-northeast of the town of Boulder Creek (lat. 37°11'55" N, long. 122°05'45" W). Named on Castle Rock Ridge (1955) 7.5' quadrangle.

Fauntleroy Canyon [SAN LUIS OBISPO]: *canyon,* drained by a stream that flows nearly 1 mile to Danford Canyon 4.5 miles east of the town of Nipomo (lat. 35°03'20" N, long. 120°23'40" W; near S line sec. 6, T 11 N, R 33 W). Named on Nipomo (1965) 7.5' quadrangle.

Fawn Lake [SAN BENITO]: *lake,* 200 feet long, 6 miles south of Idria (lat. 36°20' N, long. 120°40'25" W; near W line sec. 28, T 18 S, R 12 E); the lake is 500 feet south of Fawn Spring. Named on San Benito Mountain (1969) 7.5' quadrangle.

Fawn Spring [SAN BENITO]: *spring,* 6 miles south of Idria (lat. 36°20'05" N, long. 120°40'25" W; sec. 28, T 18 S, R 12 E); the spring is 500 feet north of Fawn Lake. Named on San Benito Mountain (1969) 7.5' quadrangle.

Feeder Creek: see **San Lorenzo Park** [SANTA CRUZ].

Felipe: see **Point Felipe**, under **Santa Barbara Point** [SANTA BARBARA].

Feliz Canyon [MONTEREY]: *canyon*, drained by a stream that flows nearly 4 miles to an unnamed stream 5 miles southwest of San Lucas (lat. 36°04'40" N, long. 121°04'40" W; sec. 26, T 21 S, R 8 E). Named on Espinosa Canyon (1949) 7.5' quadrangle. The name is for Vincente Feliz, who patented land in the canyon in 1892 (Clark, 1991, p. 165).

Felton [SANTA CRUZ]: *town*, 5.5 miles south-southeast of the town of Boulder Creek along San Lorenzo River (lat. 37°03' N, long. 122°04'30" W). Named on Felton (1955) 7.5' quadrangle. Edward Stanley laid out the town in 1868 at a place that had been a lumbering center since 1843, when Isaac Graham moved his mill to San Lorenzo River there opposite Fall Creek; the name commemorates Stanley's attorney, Charles N. Felton, who became a senator from California (Rowland, p. 169). Postal authorities established Felton post office in 1870 (Salley, p. 73). South Pacific Coast Railroad had a depot serving Felton situated 0.5 mile west of the town just south of the rail crossing of Zayante Creek; the depot sometimes was called New Felton and the town was called Old Felton (MacGregor, p. 127, 152). Santa Cruz (1902) 30' quadrangle has the name "Station" at the depot site, which is in present Mount Hermon (lat. 37°02'45" N, long. 122°03'55" W). Hamman's (1980b) map shows a place called Felton Junction located 1.5 miles south-southeast of Felton, where a branch line to Felton left the main rail line, and shows a place called Bonny Brae situated along the branch line on the northeast side of San Lorenzo River near the north edge of present Felton.

Felton Junction: see **Felton** [SANTA CRUZ].

Fep [SAN BENITO]: *locality*, 9 miles northwest of Hollister along Southern Pacific Railroad (lat. 36°56'45" N, long. 121°30'25" W). Named on San Juan Bautista (1917) 15' quadrangle.

Ferini: see **Orcutt** [SANTA BARBARA].

Fernald Point [SANTA BARBARA]: *promontory*, 6 miles west-northwest of Carpinteria along the coast (lat. 34°25'05" N, long. 119°37'10" W). Named on Carpinteria (1952) 7.5' quadrangle.

Fernandez Creek [SAN LUIS OBISPO]: *stream*, flows 6.5 miles to Shell Creek 2.5 miles east-southeast of Wilson Corner (lat. 35°27'30" N, long. 120°20' W; sec. 26, T 28 S, R 15 E). Named on Camatta Ranch (1966) 7.5' quadrangle. United States Board on Geographic Names (1968b, p. 7) rejected the name "Fernando Creek" for the stream.

Fernandez Spring [SAN LUIS OBISPO]: *spring*, 9.5 miles north of Pozo (lat. 35°26'25" N, long. 120°21'50" W; near NE cor. sec. 4, T 29 S, R 15 E). Named on Camatta Ranch (1966) 7.5' quadrangle.

Fernando Creek: see **Fernandez Creek** [SAN LUIS OBISPO].

Fern Canyon [SAN LUIS OBISPO]:

(1) *canyon*, drained by a stream that flows nearly 2 miles to lowlands at Paso Robles (lat. 35°37'40" N, long. 120°42'05" W). Named on Paso Robles (1948) 7.5' quadrangle.

(2) *canyon*, drained by a stream that flows 1 mile to Lopez Canyon 4.25 miles southeast of Lopez Mountain (lat. 35°15'50" N, long. 120°31'15" W; near SW cor. sec. 31, T 30 S, R 14 E). Named on Lopez Mountain (1965) 7.5' quadrangle.

Fern Canyon [SANTA CRUZ]: *canyon*, drained by a stream that flows nearly 1.5 miles to Coward Creek 4.5 miles east-northeast of Watsonville (lat. 36°56'50" N, long. 121°40'45" W). Named on Watsonville East (1955) 7.5' quadrangle. United States Board on Geographic Names (1992, p. 4) approved the name "Mill Canyon" for the feature.

Fern Gulch [SANTA CRUZ]: *canyon*, nearly 1 mile long, opens into the canyon of Soquel Creek 7 miles north-northeast of Soquel (lat. 37°05' N, long. 121°54'30" W). Named on Laurel (1955) 7.5' quadrangle.

Ficay Creek: see **Picay Creek** [SANTA BARBARA].

Figueroa Camp [SANTA BARBARA]: *locality*, 0.5 mile south-southwest of Figueroa Mountain (lat. 34°44'05" N, long. 119°59'20" W; near S line sec. 25, T 8 N, R 30 W). Named on Figueroa Mountain (1959) 7.5' quadrangle.

Figueroa Creek [SANTA BARBARA]: *stream*, flows 5.5 miles to Santa Agueda Creek nearly 5 miles east of Los Olivos (lat. 34° 40'05" N, long. 120°01'45" W). Named on Los Olivos (1959) 7.5' quadrangle. United States Board on Geographic Names (1961b, p. 10) rejected the form "Figuero Creek" for the name.

Figueroa Mountain [SANTA BARBARA]: *peak*, 10 miles west-northwest of San Rafael Mountain (lat. 34°44'35" N, long. 119° 59' W; at E line sec. 25, T 8 N, R 30 W). Altitude 4528 feet. Named on Figueroa Mountain (1959) 7.5' quadrangle.

Figueroa Station [SANTA BARBARA]: *locality*, 8 miles northeast of Los Olivos (lat. 34°44'10" N, long. 120°00'20" W; at S line sec. 26, T 8 N, R 30 W). Named on Los Olivos (1959) 7.5' quadrangle.

Filbert: see **Boulder Creek** [SANTA CRUZ] (2).

Finch Creek [MONTEREY]: *stream*, flows 8 miles to join James Creek and form Cachagua Creek 1 mile north-northwest of Jamesburg (lat. 36°23'20" N, long. 121°35'35" W; sec. 1, T 18 S, R 3 E). Named on Chews Ridge (1956) and Rana Creek (1956) 7.5' quadrangles. Called Cachagua Creek on Jamesburg (1921) 15' quadrangle. The name is for brothers Charles Finch and James Finch, ranchers in the neighborhood (Clark, 1991, p. 166).

Fine Spring [SANTA BARBARA]: *spring*, less than 1 mile south of Figueroa Mountain (lat. 34°43'55" N, long. 119°59'05" W; near NE cor. sec. 36, T 8 N, R 30 W). Named on Figueroa Mountain (1959) 7.5' quadrangle.

Fingers: see **The Fingers** [SAN BENITO].

Finney Creek [SANTA CRUZ]: *stream*, flows nearly 1 mile to San Mateo County 2 miles north-northeast of the mouth of Waddell Creek (lat. 37°07'10" N, long. 122°17'30" W; sec. 27, T 9 S, R 4 W). Named on Año Nuevo (1955) and Franklin Point (1955) 7.5' quadrangles. Called Finny Creek on Año Nuevo (1948) 15' quadrangle. Seldon J. Finney had a ranch along the stream from the 1860's until the 1880's (Brown, p. 33-34).

Finny Creek: see **Finney Creek** [SANTA CRUZ].

Fir Canyon [SANTA BARBARA]: *canyon*, 4.5 miles long, opens into the canyon of Manzanita Creek nearly 3 miles south of Bald Mountain (1) (lat. 34°46'20" N, long. 119°56'35" W). Named on Bald Mountain (1964) and Figueroa Mountain (1959) 7.5' quadrangles. The canyon is drained by Davy Brown Creek, and is called Davy Brown Canyon on Santa Ynez (1905) 30' quadrangle, but United States Board on Geographic Names (1962b, p. 16) rejected this name for the feature. Davy Brown built a cabin in the canyon in 1884 (Rife, p. 120).

Fiscalini Creek [SAN LUIS OBISPO]: *stream*, flows 1 mile to Perry Creek 2 miles southeast of Cambria (lat. 35°32'30" N, long. 121° 03'15" W). Named on Cambria (1959) 7.5' quadrangle.

Fish Creek [SAN LUIS OBISPO]: *stream*, flows 5.25 miles to Alamo Creek 10 miles southwest of Branch Mountain (lat. 35°05'40" N, long. 120°14'25" W; near SW cor. sec. 35, T 32 S, R 16 E). Named on Chimney Canyon (1967) 7.5' quadrangle.

Fish Creek [SANTA BARBARA]: *stream*, flows 4 miles to Manzana Creek 4 miles south-southeast of Bald Mountain (1) (lat. 34°45'35" N, long. 119°54'05" W). Named on Bald Mountain (1964) and Figueroa Mountain (1959) 7.5' quadrangles. East Fork enters nearly 1 mile upstream from the mouth of the main creek; it is 1.5 miles long and is named on Bald Mountain (1964) and Figueroa Mountain (1959) 7.5' quadrangles. United States Board on Geographic Names (1962a, p. 10) rejected the name "Fish Creek" for present East Fork.

Fish Creek Campground [SANTA BARBARA]: *locality*, nearly 4 miles south-southeast of Bald Mountain (1) along Manzana Creek (lat. 34°45'45" N, long. 119°54'15" W); the place is near the mouth of Fish Creek. Named on Bald Mountain (1964) 7.5' quadrangle.

Fish Head Hill [MONTEREY]: *peak*, nearly 2 miles northeast of Mount Carmel (lat. 36°24'15" N, long. 121°45'55" W; near SW cor. sec. 33, T 17 S, R 2 E). Named on Mount Carmel (1956) 7.5' quadrangle.

Fitzpatrick Spring [SAN BENITO]: *spring*, 6 miles south of Idria (lat. 36°19'50" N, long. 120°40'45" W; sec. 29, T 18 S, R 12 E). Named on San Benito Mountain (1969) 7.5' quadrangle.

Five Willow Spring [SAN LUIS OBISPO]: *spring*, 19 miles southeast of Simmler near the southwest edge of Carrizo Plain (lat. 35°07'45" N, long. 119°50' W; sec. 21, T 32 S, R 20 E). Named on Painted Rock (1959) 7.5' quadrangle. McKittrick (1912) 30' quadrangle shows the spring located about 1 mile farther southeast (near W line sec. 27, T 32 S, R 20 E).

Flea Island: see **Castle Rock** [SANTA BARBARA].

Fletcher Canyon [MONTEREY]: *canyon*, drained by a stream that flows 3.5 miles to lowlands 6 miles west of Chualar (lat. 36°34'30" N, long. 121°36'20" W). Named on Chualar (1947) 7.5' quadrangle.

Flint Hills [SAN BENITO]: *range*, 4 miles west-northwest of Hollister (lat. 35°52'30" N, long. 121°28' W). Named on Hollister (1955) and San Felipe (1955) 7.5' quadrangles. The range is on San Justo grant; Thomas Flint and Benjamin Flint, along with their cousin Llewelyn Bixby, bought the grant in 1855 (Pierce, p. 49).

Flood: see **Chris Flood Creek** [MONTEREY-SAN LUIS OBISPO].

Flores Camp [SANTA BARBARA]: *locality*, nearly 5 miles southeast of San Rafael Mountain along West Fork Santa Cruz Creek (lat. 34°39'30" N, long. 119°45'30" W; near NE cor. sec. 30, T 7 N, R 27 W). Named on San Rafael Mountain (1959) 7.5' quadrangle. Gagnon (p. 80) called the site Flores Flat, and stated that the name commemorates Jose Flores, who according to local legend built a cabin there at the turn of the century.

Flores Canyon [SANTA BARBARA]: *canyon*, drained by a stream that flows 5 miles to join the stream in Roque Canyon and form North Fork La Brea Creek 5.5 miles north-northeast of Manzanita Mountain (lat. 34°58'10" N, long. 120°03'05" W). Named on Manzanita Mountain (1964) and Miranda Pine Mountain (1967) 7.5' quadrangles.

Flores Flat [SANTA BARBARA]: *area*, 4.5 miles north of downtown Santa Barbara (lat. 34°29' N, long. 119°40'45" W; sec. 26, T 5 N, R 27 W). Named on Santa Barbara (1952) 7.5' quadrangle.

Flores Flat: see **Flores Camp** [SANTA BARBARA].

Folger: see **Swanton** [SANTA CRUZ].

Folger Wye: see **Swanton** [SANTA CRUZ].

Fontenay Villa [SANTA CRUZ]: *locality*, 2.5 miles south of Laurel (lat.

37°04'55" N, long. 121°58'25" W; near N line sec. 9, T 10 S, R 1 W). Named on Los Gatos (1919) 15' quadrangle.

Forbush Canyon [SANTA BARBARA]: *canyon,* drained by a stream that flows 1.5 miles to Blue Canyon 8.5 miles northwest of Carpinteria (lat. 34°29'45" N, long. 119°36'40" W; sec. 21, T 5 N, R 26 W); the canyon heads at Forbush Flat. Named on Carpinteria (1952) and Santa Barbara (1952) 7.5' quadrangles.

Forbush Flat [SANTA BARBARA]: *area,* 6.25 miles north-northeast of downtown Santa Barbara (lat. 34°29'50" N, long. 119°38'15" W; on W line sec. 20, T 5 N, R 26 W). Named on Santa Barbara (1952) 7.5' quadrangle. Fred Forbush, a turn-of-the-century homesteader, lived at the place (Gagnon, p. 81).

Force Canyon [MONTEREY]: *canyon,* drained by a stream that flows 2 miles to lowlands 6 miles west of Greenfield (lat. 36°19'20" N, long. 121°20' W; near E line sec. 32, T 18 S, R 6 E). Named on Paraiso Springs (1956) 7.5' quadrangle.

Ford Point [SANTA BARBARA]: *promontory,* 4 miles east-northeast of South Point on the south side of Santa Rosa Island (lat. 33°54'55" N, long. 120°02'50" W). Named on Santa Rosa Island South (1943) 7.5' quadrangle.

Foreman Creek [SANTA CRUZ]: *stream,* flows 1.25 miles to Boulder Creek (1) 5.5 miles east-southeast of Big Basin (lat. 37° 07'50" N, long. 122°08' W; near SW cor. sec. 19, T 9 S, R 2 W). Named on Big Basin (1955) and Davenport (1955) 7.5' quadrangles.

Forest Creek [MONTEREY]: *stream,* flows nearly 4 miles to San Antonio River 8 miles southeast of Junipero Serra Peak (lat. 36° 04' N, long. 121°18'45" W). Named on Bear Canyon (1949) 7.5' quadrangle.

Foresters Leap Canyon [SANTA BARBARA]: *canyon,* drained by a stream that flows 6 miles to Sisquoc River 4 miles south-southwest of Montgomery Potrero (lat. 34°47'05" N, long. 119°47'30" W). Named on Hurricane Deck (1964) and Salisbury Potrero (1964) 7.5' quadrangles.

Forest Lake [MONTEREY]: *lake,* 1200 feet long, 3 miles south-southwest of Point Pinos (lat. 36°35'30" N, long. 121°56'30" W). Named on Monterey (1947) 7.5' quadrangle. Pacific Improvement Company created the reservoir in 1888 (Clark, 1991, p. 169).

Forest Park [SANTA CRUZ]: *settlement,* 5 miles east-southeast of Big Basin along Boulder Creek (1) (lat. 37°08'05" N, long. 122°08'20" W; sec. 24, T 9 S, R 3 W). Named on Big Basin (1955) 7.5' quadrangle.

Forest Springs [SANTA CRUZ]: *settlement,* about 4.5 miles east-southeast of Big Basin (lat. 37°08'20" N, long. 122°08'50" W; sec. 24, T 9 S, R 3 W). Named on Big Basin (1955) 7.5' quadrangle.

Forney Cove [SANTA BARBARA]: *embayment,* 0.5 mile east of Fraser Point at the west end of Santa Cruz Island (lat. 34°03'25" N, long. 119°55' W). Named on Santa Cruz Island A (1943) 7.5' quadrangle. Called Forneys Cove on Bremner's (1932) map.

Fort Halleck: see **Presidio of Monterey** [MONTEREY].

Fort Hunter Liggett: see **Hunter Liggett Military Reservation** [MONTEREY].

Fort Mervine: see **Presidio of Monterey** [MONTEREY].

Fort Ord: see **Fort Ord Military Reservation** [MONTEREY].

Fort Ord Military Reservation [MONTEREY]: *military installation,* between Marina and Seaside along the coast, and extends inland nearly to Salinas. Named on Marina (1947), Salinas (1947), Seaside (1947), and Spreckels (1947) 7.5' quadrangles. Marina (1947) 7.5' quadrangle has the name "Main Garrison" for a cluster of buildings located on the installation 1.5 miles south of Marina. Monterey (1940) 15' quadrangle has the name "Camp Clayton Military Reservation" for the same cluster of buildings, and the has name "Camp Ord Military Reservation" for the entire installation. Salinas (1947) 7.5' quadrangle has the names "Fort Ord" and "East Garrison" for a cluster of buildings situated near Salinas River 4.5 miles west-southwest of Salinas. Salinas (1940) 15' quadrangle has the name "Camp Ord" at the same place. The federal government purchased about 15,000 acres from David Jacks Corporation in 1917 near present East Garrison, and used the land for training troops stationed at Presidio of Monterey; the place first was called Gigling Reservation, for the Gigling family, who had lived on a bluff overlooking Salinas River, and in 1933 the name was changed to Camp Ord; the facility was used only as a summer training ground until 1938, when WPA workers started building what eventually became East Garrison; Camp Ord was combined with Camp Clayton in 1940, and the whole was named Fort Ord—the name "Ord" is for Major General Edward Otho Cresap Ord, who as a Lieutenant was stationed at Monterey in 1847 (Clark, 1991, p. 171; *San Jose Mercury-News,* February 7, 1965).

Fort Ord Village [MONTEREY]: *district,* north of Seaside (lat. 36° 37'30" N, long. 121°50' W); the place is on Fort Ord Military Reservation. Named on Marina (1947) and Seaside (1947) 7.5' quadrangles. Postal authorities established Ord Village post office in 1942 and discontinued it in 1954 (Salley, p. 162).

Fort Romie [MONTEREY]: *settlement,* 2 miles south-southwest of Soledad (lat. 36°24' N, long. 121°20'45" W). Named on Soledad (1955) 7.5' quadrangle. Postal authorities established Romie post office in 1898 and discontinued it in 1900 (Frickstad, p. 109). Salvation Army officials started the place in 1898 as an agricultural commune on a 600-acre tract purchased from Charles Romie, but the endeavor was unsuccessful (Fink, p. 163-164).

Fort Stockton: see **Presidio of Monterey** [MONTEREY].

Fossil Point [SAN LUIS OBISPO]: *promontory,* 0.5 mile southeast of Avila Beach along the coast (lat. 35°10'25" N, long. 120°43'25" W). Named on Pismo Beach (1965) 7.5' quadrangle. On Arroyo Grande (1942) 15' quadrangle, the name applies to a promontory located nearly 1 mile farther west-northwest.

Four Corners [SANTA BARBARA]: *locality,* 2.5 miles northeast of the city of Lompoc (lat. 34°39'50" N, long. 120°25'15" W). Named on Lompoc (1959) 7.5' quadrangle.

Four Corners: see **Santa Cruz** [SANTA CRUZ].

Fourth of July Spring [SAN BENITO]: *spring,* 8 miles east-southeast of Bitterwater (lat. 36°18'55" N, long. 120°52'35" W; sec. 34, T 18 S, R 10 E). Named on Lonoak (1969) 7.5' quadrangle.

Foxen: see **Sisquoc** [SANTA BARBARA] (3).

Foxen Canyon [SANTA BARBARA]: *canyon,* 10 miles long, opens into lowlands 5.25 miles south-southwest of Tepusquet Peak (lat. 34°50"55" N, long. 120°14'25" W). Named on Foxen Canyon (1964) and Zaca Lake (1964) 7.5' quadrangles. The name is for Benjamin Foxen, an English sailor who came to California in 1828 and later received Tinaquaic grant (Gudde, 1949, p. 120).

Fox Gulch: see **Cañada Tecolote** [SANTA BARBARA].

Fox Mountain [SANTA BARBARA]: *peak,* 8.5 miles south of the village of Cuyama (lat. 34°48'50" N, long. 119°35'55" W). Altitude 5167 feet. Named on Fox Mountain (1964) 7.5' quadrangle.

Fox Spring [SAN BENITO]: *spring,* 7 miles east-southeast of Bitterwater (lat. 36°21'15" N, long. 120°53'10" W; near E line sec. 21, T 18 S, R 10 E). Named on Lonoak (1969) 7.5' quadrangle.

Fox Spring [SAN LUIS OBISPO]: *spring,* 6 miles north-northeast of Pozo (lat. 35°23'20" N, long. 120°21'05" W; near N line sec. 22, T 29 S, R 15 E). Named on Camatta Ranch (1966) 7.5' quadrangle.

Frames Peak [MONTEREY]: *peak,* 4.25 miles southeast of Smith Mountain (lat. 36°02'10" N, long. 120°32'30" W; sec. 11, T 22 S, R 13 E). Altitude 3602 feet. Named on Smith Mountain (1969) 7.5' quadrangle.

Franciscan Creek [SAN LUIS OBISPO]: *stream,* flows 1.5 miles to Kern County 14 miles east-southeast of Shandon (lat. 35°36'50" N, long. 120°07'30" W; at N line sec. 3, T 27 S, R 17 E). Named on Holland Canyon (1961) 7.5' quadrangle.

Franklin Canyon [SANTA BARBARA]: *canyon,* 1 mile long, along present Franklin Creek above a point 1.5 miles north-northeast of downtown Carpinteria (lat. 34°24'55" N, long. 119°30'30" W). Named on Santa Barbara (1903) 15' quadrangle.

Franklin Creek [SAN LUIS OBISPO]: *stream,* flows 7.25 miles to Las Tablas Creek 3 miles east-northeast of Lime Mountain (lat. 35°41'25" N, long. 120°56'45" W; near NE cor. sec. 12, T 26 S, R 9 E). Named on Lime Mountain (1948) 7.5' quadrangle. The stream now enters Nacimiento Reservoir.

Franklin Creek [SANTA BARBARA]: *stream,* flows 3.25 miles to the sea 0.5 mile west-southwest of downtown Carpinteria (lat. 34° 23'45" N, long. 119°31'40" W). Named on Carpinteria (1952) 7.5' quadrangle.

Fraser Canyon [SAN LUIS OBISPO]: *canyon,* nearly 3.5 miles long, opens into lowlands 3.25 miles east-northeast of Pozo (lat. 35° 19' N, long. 120°19' W; near N line sec. 13, T 30 S, R 15 E). Named on Pozo Summit (1967) 7.5' quadrangle. Pozo (1922) 15' quadrangle shows the canyon 1 mile farther west at present Bean Canyon.

Fraser Point [SANTA BARBARA]: *promontory,* at the west end of Santa Cruz Island (lat. 34°03'35" N, long. 119°55'45" W). Named on Santa Cruz Island A (1943) 7.5' quadrangle.

Freeborn Mountain [SAN LUIS OBISPO]: *peak,* 18 miles east of Pozo (lat. 35°17'05" N, long. 120°03'10" W; sec. 28, T 30 S, R 18 E). Altitude 3312 feet. Named on California Valley (1966) 7.5' quadrangle.

Freedom [SANTA CRUZ]: *town,* 1.5 miles northwest of Watsonville (lat. 36°56'05" N, long. 121°46'20" W). Named on Watsonville West (1954) 7.5' quadrangle. Postal authorities established Freedom post office in 1940 (Salley, p. 80). The name is from a saloon at the site; the saloon displayed an American flag and a sign with the legend "Flag of Freedom" (Stewart, p. 172). The place first was known as Whiskey Hill (Chase, p. 228).

Freeman Canyon: see **Mason Canyon** [SAN LUIS OBISPO].

Fremont Campground [SANTA BARBARA]: *locality,* 2 miles north of San Marcos Pass along Santa Ynez River (lat. 34°32'35" N, long. 119°49'30" W). Named on San Marcos Pass (1959) 7.5' quadrangle.

Fremont Peak [MONTEREY-SAN BENITO]: *peak,* 10 miles northeast of Salinas on Monterey-San Benito County line (lat. 36°45'25" N, long. 121°30'10" W); the peak is near the north end of Gabilan Range. Altitude 3171 feet. Named on San Juan Bautista (1955) 7.5' quadrangle. Called Gabilan Pk. on San Juan Bautista (1917) 15' quadrangle, and called Picacho de Gavilan on Parke's (1854-1855) map. Talbot (p. 41) called the feature La Natividad Mt., and Whitney (p. 159) called it Gavilan Peak—*gabilan* or *gavilan* means "hawk" in Spanish, and the feature sometimes is called Hawks Peak (Hanna, p. 116). United States Board on Geographic Names (1933, p. 315) approved the name "Gabilan Peak" for the feature, and rejected the names "Fremont Peak" and "Gavilan Peak," but later the Board (1960c, p. 16-17) reversed the decision and approved the name "Fremont Peak" while rejecting the names "Gabilan Peak" and "Gavilan Peak." The name "Fremont" commemorates John Charles Fremont, who built a fort near the peak in 1846 (Spence and Jackson, p. 123).

French Camp [SAN LUIS OBISPO]: *locality,* 9 miles east of Wilson Corner near Navajo Creek (lat. 35°29'30" N, long. 120°12'45" W; sec. 14, T 28 S, R 16 E). Named on La Panza Ranch (1966) 7.5' quadrangle. The place was a placer-mining settlement as late as the 1890's (Dillon, 1960, p. 8).

French Canyon [MONTEREY-SAN BENITO]: *canyon,* drained by a stream that heads in San Benito County and flows nearly 1 mile to Towne Creek 4.5 miles northwest of Fremont Peak in Monterey County (lat. 36°48'20" N, long. 121°33'40" W). Named on San Juan Bautista (1955) 7.5' quadrangle.

Frenchs Pass [SAN BENITO]: *pass,* 1.5 miles southwest of Mariposa Peak on San Benito-Merced County line (lat. 36°56'25" N, long. 121°13'40" W; sec. 32, T 11 S, R 7 E). Named on Mariposa Peak (1969) 7.5' quadrangle, which shows French ranch situated 0.5 mile northwest of the pass.

Friar's Harbor: see **Frys Harbor** [SANTA BARBARA].

Friis Campground [SAN LUIS OBISPO]: *locality,* 6 miles north-northeast of Pozo (lat. 35°22'55" N, long. 120°19'40" W; sec. 23, T 29 S, R 15 E). Named on Camatta Ranch (1966) 7.5' quadrangle.

Fritch Creek [SANTA CRUZ]: *stream,* flows 1 mile to Love Creek 2 miles east-southeast of the town of Boulder Creek (lat. 37°06'40" N, long. 122°05'20" W; sec. 33, T 9 S, R 2 W). Named on Felton (1955) 7.5' quadrangle.

Frog Canyon [SAN BENITO]: *canyon,* drained by a stream that flows 3.5 miles to Chalone Creek 3 miles northeast of North Chalone Peak (lat. 36°28'35" N, long. 121°09'20" W; sec. 1, T 17 S, R 7 E). Named on North Chalone Peak (1969) 7.5' quadrangle.

Frog Pond Mountain [SAN LUIS OBISPO]: *ridge,* northwest-trending, 2 miles long, 4 miles southwest of Atascadero (lat. 35°26'45" N, long. 120°43' W). Named on Atascadero (1965) 7.5' quadrangle.

Froom Creek [SAN LUIS OBISPO]: *stream,* flows 3.5 miles to San Luis Obispo Creek 2.5 miles south-southwest of downtown San Luis Obispo (lat. 35°14'30" N, long. 120°40'55" W). Named on Pismo Beach (1965) and San Luis Obispo (1965) 7.5' quadrangles.

Frys Harbor [SANTA BARBARA]: *embayment,* 0.5 mile southeast of Diablo Point on the north side of Santa Cruz Island (lat. 34°03'10" N, long. 119°45'10" W). Named on Santa Cruz Island B (1943) 7.5' quadrangle. The place also is called Friar's Harbor and Fry's Harbor (Doran, p. 147).

Fulger Point [SANTA BARBARA]: *promontory,* 7.5 miles east-southeast of Santa Maria along Santa Maria River opposite the confluence of Cuyama River and Sisquoc River (lat. 34°54'20" N, long. 120°19'05" W; sec. 35, T 10 N, R 33 W). Named on Twitchell Dam (1959) 7.5' quadrangle. Hobson (p. 600) called the feature Fulger's Point.

- G -

Gabilan [MONTEREY]: *locality,* 4 miles northwest of Gonzales along Southern Pacific Railroad (lat. 36°32'45" N, long. 121°29'30" W). Named on Gonzales (1921) 15' quadrangle.

Gabilan: see **Alisal** [MONTEREY].

Gabilan Acres [MONTEREY]: *settlement,* 6.5 miles west of Fremont Peak (lat. 36°45'15" N, long. 121°37' W); the place is along Gabilan Creek (1). Named on San Juan Bautista (1955) 7.5' quadrangle.

Gabilan Creek [MONTEREY]:

(1) *stream,* flows 17 miles to marsh 2.5 miles northeast of Salinas (lat. 36°42'20" N, long. 121°37'15" W); the stream heads in Gabilan Range. Named on Hollister (1955), Mount Harlan (1968), Natividad (1947), and San Juan Bautista (1955) 7.5' quadrangles. Natividad (1947, photorevised 1968) 7.5' quadrangle does not show the marsh, but it does show the end of the stream at about the same place.

(2) *stream,* flows 6 miles to Nacimiento River 6.5 miles southwest of Jolon (lat. 35°53'50" N, long. 121°14'20" W). Named on Jolon (1949) 7.5' quadrangle. Called Agua del Gavilan on a diseño of El Piojo grant (Becker, 1964).

Gabilan Hills: see **Gabilan Range** [MONTEREY-SAN BENITO].

Gabilan Mountains: see **Gabilan Range** [MONTEREY-SAN BENITO].

Gabilan Peak: see **Fremont Peak** [MONTEREY-SAN BENITO].

Gabilan Range [MONTEREY-SAN BENITO]: *range,* east of Salinas River from near Salinas to Greenfield on Monterey-San Benito County line. Named on Santa Cruz (1956) 1°x 2° quadrangle. Called Sierra de Gavilan on Parke's (1854-1855) map. Blake (1856, p. 378) noted that the north part of the feature was called San Juan range, and farther south it sometimes was called Gavilan or Salinas range. Brewer (p. 128) referred to Gabilan hills, and Irelan (p. 483) mentioned Gabilan Mountains. Elliott and Moore (p. 95) described a mining camp called Rootville that was situated 6 miles northeast of Soledad in Gabilan Range; the place was named for Mr. Root, who discovered gold there about 1870.

Gaffey Creek [SANTA CRUZ]: *stream,* flows 1.5 miles to Casserly Creek 5.25 miles north-northeast of Watsonville (lat. 36°59'25" N, long. 121°44'05" W). Named on Watsonville East (1955) 7.5' quadrangle. The name commemorates Judge William Vincent Gaffey, who lived in Watsonville in the 1870's and 1880's (Clark, 1986, p. 128).

Galen Creek: see **Pancho Rico Creek** [MONTEREY].

Galligan Slough [SANTA CRUZ]: *stream,* flows 3 miles to Harkins Slough 3 miles west-southwest of Watsonville (lat. 36°54'20" N, long. 121°48'15" W). Named on Watsonville West (1954) 7.5' quadrangle. The name commemorates Bartley Galligan, who had land near the stream (Clark, 1986, p. 128).

Gamboa Point [MONTEREY]: *promontory,* 2.5 miles northwest of Lopez Point along the coast (lat. 36°03' N, long. 121°35'25" W; sec. 1, T 22 S, R 3 E). Named on Lopez Point (1956) 7.5' quadrangle. The Gamboa family homesteaded in the neighborhood (Howard, p. 65).

Gamecock Canyon [SANTA CRUZ]: *canyon,* drained by a stream that flows 2.25 miles to Browns Creek 3 miles northeast of Corralitos (lat. 37°01'30" N, long. 121°46'25" W). Named on Loma Prieta (1955) 7.5' quadrangle. The name is from a sawmill called Gamecock Mill (Clark, 1986, p. 128).

Garcia Creek [SAN BENITO]: *stream,* flows 3 miles to Lewis Creek 11.5 miles southeast of Bitterwater (lat. 36°16'30" N, long. 120°50'20" W; sec. 13, T 19 S, R 10 E). Named on Hepsedam Peak (1969) 7.5' quadrangle. The name commemorates Joaquín García, who settled along Lewis Creek in 1871 (Clark, 1991, p. 181).

Garcia Mountain [SAN LUIS OBISPO]: *ridge,* west-northwest-trending, 10 miles long, 6 miles southeast of Pozo (lat. 35°14'45" N, long. 120°18' W); the ridge is between Salinas River and Trout Creek (2). Named on Caldwell Mesa (1967), Los Machos Hills (1967), Pozo Summit (1967), and Santa Margarita Lake (1967) 7.5' quadrangles.

Garcia Potrero Spring [SAN LUIS OBISPO]: *spring,* 9 miles west of Branch Mountain along Stony Creek (lat. 35°11'55" N, long. 120° 14'30" W). Named on Los Machos Hills (1967) 7.5' quadrangle. Branch Mountain (1952) 15' quadrangle shows the spring located 1.5 miles farther east-southeast (near N line sec. 36, T 31 S, R 16 E).

Garcia Valley: see **Pozo** [SAN LUIS OBISPO].

Garden Farms [SAN LUIS OBISPO]: *settlement,* nearly 2 miles north of Santa Margarita (lat. 35°25'10" N, long. 120°36'20" W). Named on Santa Margarita (1965) 7.5' quadrangle

Garey [SANTA BARBARA]: *village,* 8 miles east-southeast of Santa Maria (lat. 34°53'20" N, long. 120°18'50" W; sec. 2, T 9 N, R 33 W). Named on Twitchell Dam (1959) 7.5' quadrangle. Called Gary on Lompoc (1905) 30' quadrangle. Postal authorities established Garey post office in 1889 and discontinued it in 1902 (Frickstad, p. 170). The name commemorates Thomas A. Garey, a nurseryman and horticulturist whose specialty was citrus fruit (Gudde, 1949, p. 124).

Garrapata Creek [MONTEREY]: *stream,* flows 7.5 miles to the sea 8 miles north of Point Sur (lat. 36°25'05" N, long. 121°54'55" W). Named on Mount Carmel (1956) and Soberanes Point (1956) 7.5' quadrangles. According to Gudde (1949, p. 124), the name "Arroyo de las Garrapatas" appeared on a map as early as 1835. *Garrapata* means "sheep tick" or "cattle tick" in Spanish (Hanna, p. 117).

Garrapata Creek [SANTA BARBARA]: *stream,* flows 0.5 mile to Torro Canyon Creek 4 miles northwest of Carpinteria (lat. 34° 26' N, long. 119°34'15" W). Named on Carpinteria (1952, photorevised 1967) 7.5' quadrangle. On Carpinteria (1952) 7.5' quadrangle, the name applies to present Torro Canyon Creek.

Garrissere Canyon [MONTEREY]: *canyon,* drained by a stream that flows 6 miles to lowlands 2.25 miles west of San Ardo (lat. 36°01'30" N, long. 120°56'35" W). Named on Hames Valley (1949) and San Ardo (1967) 7.5' quadrangles. English (p. 245) used the name "Garrissere Gulch." The Garrissere family owned land in or near the canyon (Clark, 1991, p. 183).

Garrissere Gulch: see **Garrissere Canyon** [MONTEREY].

Garrity Peak [SAN LUIS OBISPO]: *peak,* 5.25 miles north-northwest of San Simeon (lat. 35°43'10" N, long. 121°12'35" W). Altitude 2397 feet. Named on San Simeon (1958) 7.5' quadrangle.

Garrizo Creek [MONTEREY]: *stream,* flows 2.5 miles to North Fork San Antonio River nearly 4 miles south of Junipero Serra Peak (lat. 36°05'30" N, long. 121°26' W). Named on Cone Peak (1949) 7.5' quadrangle. Called Carrizo Creek on Junipero Serra (1930) 15' quadrangle.

Gary: see **Garey** [SANTA BARBARA].

Gasper Creek [SANTA BARBARA]: *stream,* flows 4.25 miles to Jalama Creek 8.5 miles south of the city of Lompoc (lat. 34°30'45" N, long. 120°28'30" W). Named on Lompoc Hills (1959) 7.5' quadrangle.

Gates [SANTA BARBARA]: *locality,* 5 miles east-southeast of Santa Maria along Santa Maria Valley Railroad (lat. 34°55'30" N, long. 120°21'20" W). Named on Twitchell Dam (1959) 7.5' quadrangle.

Gato [SANTA BARBARA]: *locality,* 5.5 miles east of Point Conception along

Southern Pacific Railroad (lat. 34°27'25" N, long. 120° 22'30" W); the place is less than 0.5 mile east of the mouth of Cañada del Gato. Named on Point Conception (1953) and Sacate (1953) 7.5' quadrangles. California Division of Highways' (1934) map shows a place called Anacapa located less than 1 mile west of Gato along the railroad.

Gato Canyon [SANTA BARBARA]: *canyon,* drained by a stream that flows 6 miles to the sea 7 miles west-northwest of Coal Oil Point (lat. 34°27' N, long. 119°59'15" W). Named on Dos Pueblos Canyon (1951) and Lake Cachuma (1959) 7.5' quadrangles.

Gato Ridge [MONTEREY]: *ridge,* generally northwest-trending, 2.5 miles long, 9 miles south-southwest of Tepusquet Peak (lat. 34° 47' N, long. 120°14'30" W). Named on Foxen Canyon (1964) and Sisquoc (1959) 7.5' quadrangles.

Gaudalupe: see **Guadalupe** [SAN LUIS OBISPO-SANTA BARBARA]; **Guadalupe** [SANTA BARBARA].

Gavilan House: see **Lagunita Lake** [MONTEREY].

Gavilan Peak: see **Fremont Peak** [MONTEREY-SAN BENITO].

Gavilan Range: see **Gabilan Range** [MONTEREY-SAN BENITO].

Gaviota [SANTA BARBARA]: *village,* 29 miles west of Santa Barbara (lat. 34°28'15" N, long. 120°12'55" W); the place is 0.5 mile east of the mouth of Cañada de la Gaviota. Named on Gaviota (1953) 7.5' quadrangle. Postal authorities established Gaviota post office in 1896, discontinued it for a time in 1901, moved it 0.25 mile west in 1937, discontinued it in 1957, and reestablished it the same year (Salley, p. 83). California Division of Highways' (1934) map shows a place called Seagirt located 1 mile east of Gaviota along Southern Pacific Railroad.

Gaviota Beach [SANTA BARBARA]: *beach,* 0.5 mile west of Gaviota along the coast (lat. 34°28'15" N, long. 120°13'30" W); the feature is at the mouth of Gaviota Canyon (present Cañada de la Gaviota). Named on Gaviota (1943) 15' quadrangle.

Gaviota Canyon: see **Cañada de la Gaviota** [SANTA BARBARA].

Gaviota Creek: see **Pancho Rico Creek** [MONTEREY].

Gaviota Gorge: see **Gaviota Pass** [SANTA BARBARA].

Gaviota Hot Springs: see **Hot Springs** [SANTA BARBARA] (1).

Gaviota Pass [SANTA BARBARA]: *narrows,* 1.25 miles north-northwest of Gaviota in Cañada de la Gaviota (lat. 34°29'20" N, long. 120°13'30" W). Named on Gaviota (1953) 7.5' quadrangle. Called Gaviota Gorge on Gaviota (1943) 15' quadrangle.

Gaviota Pass: see **Nojoqui Summit** [SANTA BARBARA].

Gaviota Peak [SANTA BARBARA]: *peak,* 8 miles south of Buellton (lat. 34°30'05" N, long. 120°11'50" W; sec. 23, T 5 N, R 32 W); the peak is east of Cañada de la Gaviota. Altitude 2458 feet. Named on Solvang (1959) 7.5' quadrangle.

Gaviota Wharf: see **Port Orford** [SANTA BARBARA].

Gaviote Creek: see **Cañada de la Gaviota** [SANTA BARBARA].

Gaviotito Creek [SANTA BARBARA]: *stream,* flows 1.25 miles to El Jaro Creek 12 miles southeast of the town of Lompoc (lat. 34°30'55" N, long. 120°18'55" W). Named on Santa Rosa Hills (1959) 7.5' quadrangle.

Gay Mountain [SAN LUIS OBISPO]: *peak,* 1.25 miles southeast of Lopez Mountain (lat. 35°17'20" N, long. 120°33'45" W; sec. 27, T 30 S, R 13 E). Altitude 2859 feet. Named on Lopez Mountain (1965) 7.5' quadrangle.

Gem: see **Bryson** [MONTEREY].

George Hansen Canyon [SAN BENITO]: *canyon,* drained by a stream that flows nearly 4 miles to Rosas Canyon 3.25 miles east of North Chalone Peak (lat. 36°27'05" N, long. 121°08'05" W; near E line sec. 18, T 17 S, R 8 E). Named on North Chalone Peak (1969) and Topo Valley (1969) 7.5' quadrangles.

Getty: see **Getty Siding** [MONTEREY].

Getty Siding [MONTEREY]: *locality,* 8.5 miles north-northwest of Bradley along Southern Pacific Railroad (lat. 35°58'25" N, long. 120°52'25" W). Named on Wunpost (1949) 7.5' quadrangle. Called Getty on California Mining Bureau's (1917b) map.

Gibbons: see **Adelaida** [SAN LUIS OBISPO].

Gibbs [SANTA CRUZ]: *locality,* 5 miles east-southeast of the town of Boulder Creek along the rail line that follows Zayante Creek (lat. 37°05'30" N, long. 122°02'30" W; near W line sec. 1, T 10 S, R 2 W). Named on Santa Cruz (1902) 30' quadrangle. Postal authorities established Gibbs post office in 1900, discontinued it in 1906, reestablished it in 1907, and discontinued it in 1916; the name is for Albert W.J. Gibbs, a member of a pioneer family (Salley, p. 84).

Gibraltar Reservoir [SANTA BARBARA]: *lake,* behind a dam on Santa Ynez River 6 miles south-southeast of Little Pine Mountain (lat. 34°31'35" N, long. 119°41'10" W; near W line sec. 11, T 5 N, R 27 W). Named on Little Pine Mountain (1964) 7.5' quadrangle, which shows Gibraltar mine located just south of the lake. Called Santa Barbara Reservoir on Little Pine Mountain (1944) 7.5' quadrangle, but United States Board on Geographic Names (1965d, p. 9) rejected this name for the feature.

Gibson Beach: see **Sandy Beach** [MONTEREY].

Gibson Creek [MONTEREY]: *stream,* flows 2.25 miles to the sea 1.25 miles south-southeast of Point Lobos (lat. 36°30'25" N, long. 121°56'15" W). Named on Monterey (1947) and Soberanes Point (1956) 7.5' quadrangles. The name is for George Martin Gibson, a lumberman who took redwood posts from the canyon; earlier the stream was called Redwood Creek, and then Prader Creek for a man who reportedly cut trees near the stream (Clark, 1991, p. 186).

Gidney Creek [SANTA BARBARA]: *stream,* flows 3.5 miles to Gibraltar Reservoir nearly 7 miles southeast of Little Pine Mountain (lat. 34°31'10" N, long. 119°40'10" W). Named on Little Pine Mountain (1964) 7.5' quadrangle.

Gifford Spring [SAN LUIS OBISPO]: *spring,* 5 miles south-southeast of Branch Mountain (lat. 35°07'20" N, long. 120°02'25" W; on N line sec. 27, T 32 S, R 18 E). Named on Miranda Pine Mountain (1967) 7.5' quadrangle, which shows Gifford ranch situated 0.5 mile south-southwest of the spring.

Gigling: see **Gigling Siding** [MONTEREY].

Gigling Reservation: see **Fort Ord Military Reservation** [MONTEREY].

Gigling Siding [MONTEREY]: *locality,* 2.5 miles south-southwest of Marina along Southern Pacific Railroad on Fort Ord Military Reservation (lat. 36°39' N, long. 121°49' W). Named on Marina (1947) 7.5' quadrangle. Called Gigling on Monterey (1913) 15' quadrangle. The name commemorates the Gigling family, who owned land at the place (Gudde, 1949, p. 127).

Gillam Spring [SAN LUIS OBISPO]: *spring,* 4.5 miles southeast of Branch Mountain (lat. 35°08'35" N, long. 120°01'35" W). Named on Branch Mountain (1967) 7.5' quadrangle.

Gillis Canyon [SAN LUIS OBISPO]: *canyon,* drained by a stream that flows nearly 7 miles to San Juan Creek 4.5 miles south-southeast of Shandon (lat. 35°36'05" N, long. 120°19'55" W; near N line sec. 11, T 27 S, R 15 E). Named on Camatta Canyon (1961), Cholame (1961), and Orchard Peak (1961) 7.5' quadrangles.

Gipsy Peak: see **Antimony Peak** [SAN BENITO].

Glau Canyon [MONTEREY]: *canyon,* 3.5 miles long, opens into lowlands nearly 7 miles east of Jolon (lat. 35°57'15" N, long. 121° 03'20" W; sec. 1, T 23 S, R 8 E). Named on Williams Hill (1949) 7.5' quadrangle. The name commemorates the Glau family, who settled in the neighborhood in the late 1880's (Clark, 1991, p. 189).

Glaucophane Ridge [SAN BENITO]: *ridge,* northwest-trending, 6.5 miles long, 5 miles north-northwest of Panoche on the northeast side of Panoche Valley (lat. 36°40' N, long. 120°52' W). Named on Cerro Colorado (1969) and Mercey Hot Springs (1969) 7.5' quadrangles.

Glen Annie Canyon [SANTA BARBARA]: *canyon,* 3.25 miles long, drained by Tecolotito Creek above a point 2.5 miles west of downtown Goleta (lat. 34°26'10" N, long. 119°52'15" W). Named on Dos Pueblos Canyon (1951) and Goleta (1950) 7.5' quadrangles. Called Glen Anne Canyon on Goleta (1903) 15' quadrangle. West Fork branches north-northwest 4 miles north of Coal Oil Point; it is 2 miles long and is named on Dos Pueblos Canyon (1951) 7.5' quadrangle. In 1869 W.W. Hollister bought land that included the canyon, which he renamed for his wife; previously the feature was called Tecolotito Canyon (Tompkins and Ruiz, p. 88).

Glen Annie Reservoir [SANTA BARBARA]: *lake,* 1700 feet long, 4.5 miles north of Coal Oil Point (lat. 34°28'20" N, long. 119°52'50" W); the lake is in West Fork Glen Annie Canyon. Named on Dos Pueblos Canyon (1951) 7.5' quadrangle.

Glen Arbor [SANTA CRUZ]: *settlement,* 4 miles south-southeast of the town of Boulder Creek along San Lorenzo River (lat. 37°04'30" N, long. 122°04'50" W; sec. 9, T 10 S, R 2 W). Named on Felton (1955) 7.5' quadrangle. Postal authorities established Glen Arbor post office in 1914 and discontinued it in 1915 (Frickstad, p. 176).

Glenecho: see **Aptos** [SANTA CRUZ] (2).

Glen Haven: see **Grover Gulch** [SANTA CRUZ].

Glenrose Spring [SAN LUIS OBISPO]: *spring,* 5.25 miles north-northwest of Point San Luis along Coon Creek (lat. 35°14'35" N, long. 120°48'05" W; sec. 9, T 31 S, R 11 E). Named on Port San Luis (1965) 7.5' quadrangle.

Glenwood [SANTA CRUZ]: *settlement,* 8.5 miles north of Soquel along Bean Creek (lat. 37°06'30" N, long. 121°59'10" W; near E line sec. 32, T 9 S, R 1 W). Named on Laurel (1955) 7.5' quadrangle. Postal authorities established Glenwood post office in 1880 and discontinued it in 1954 (Frickstad, p. 176). The place was called Bean Hollow in the 1850's for the Bean family of Bean Creek (Clark, 1986, p. 21).

Glenwood Basin [SANTA CRUZ]: *valley,* 7 miles north of Soquel along West Branch Soquel Creek (lat. 37°05'20" N, long. 121°57'40" W); the feature is 2 miles southeast of Glenwood. Named on Laurel (1955) 7.5' quadrangle.

Glenwood Magnetic Springs: see **Magnetic Spring** [SANTA CRUZ].

Glines Canyon [SANTA BARBARA]: *canyon,* drained by a stream that flows 2 miles to Cuyama River 7 miles west-northwest of Miranda Pine Mountain (lat. 35°05'25" N, long. 120°08'20" W; near NW cor. sec. 28, T 12 N, R 31 W). Named on Chimney Canyon (1967) 7.5' quadrangle. United States Board on Geographic Names (1968c, p. 5) rejected the form "Gline Canyon" for the name.

Gloria Lake [SAN BENITO]: *intermittent lake,* 0.25 mile long, 7 miles south-

southeast of Mount Johnson along Chalone Creek (lat. 36°30'45" N, long. 121°16'40" W; sec. 26, T 16 S, R 6 E); the feature is in Gloria Valley. Named on Mount Johnson (1968) 7.5' quadrangle.

Gloria Valley [SAN BENITO]: *valley*, 7 miles south-southeast of Mount Johnson at the head of Chalone Creek (lat. 36°31' N, long. 121°16'45" W). Named on Mount Johnson (1968) 7.5' quadrangle.

Goat Camp [MONTEREY]: *locality*, about 7 miles south-southwest of San Lucas in Espinosa Canyon (2) (lat. 36°02'30" N, long. 121° 04'50" W; near W line sec. 2, T 22 S, T 8 E). Named on King City (1919) 15' quadrangle.

Goat Camp [SAN LUIS OBISPO]: *locality*, 8.5 miles east of the village of San Simeon (lat. 35°39'30" N, long. 121°02'30" W; sec. 19, T 26 S, R 9 E). Named on San Simeon (1919) 15' quadrangle.

Goat Mountain [SAN BENITO]: *peak*, 5.5 miles southwest of Idria (lat. 36°21'05" N, long. 120°44'05" W); sec. 23, T 18 S, R 11 E). Altitude 4085 feet. Named on San Benito Mountain (1969) 7.5' quadrangle.

Goat Rock [SANTA BARBARA]: *peak*, 4 south-southeast of Figueroa Mountain (lat. 34°41'30" N, long. 119°57'10" W; at N line sec. 17, T 7 N, R 29 W). Named on Figueroa Mountain (1959) 7.5' quadrangle. United States Board on Geographic Names (1981b, p. 3) approved the name "Chicken Springs" for springs located 2 miles southeast of Goat Rock (lat. 34°40'53" N, long. 119°55'05" W; sec. 15, T 7 N, R 29 W), and (p. 4) approved the name "Soldiers Home Spring" for a spring located 1.4 miles north-northwest of Chicken Springs (lat. 34°42'00" N, long. 119°55'32" W; sec. 10, T 7 N, R 29 W)—Soldiers Home Spring was named for Civil War veterans who homesteaded in the neighborhood.

Goat Rock [SANTA CRUZ]: *relief feature*, 7 miles north of the town of Boulder Creek (lat. 37°13'40" N, long. 122°06'25" W; near N line sec. 20, T 8 S, R 2 W). Named on Castle Rock Ridge (1955) 7.5' quadrangle.

Goat Spring [SAN LUIS OBISPO]: *spring*, 3.25 miles north-northwest of Caliente Mountain (lat. 32°04'45" N, long. 119°46'55" W; sec. 32, T 12 N, R 27 W). Named on Caliente Mountain (1959) 7.5' quadrangle.

Gobernador Creek [SANTA BARBARA]: *stream*, formed by the confluence of Eldorado Creek and Steer Creek, flows nearly 3.5 miles to Carpinteria Creek 2 miles north-northwest of Rincon Point (lat. 34°24'05" N, long. 119°29'05" W). Named on White Ledge Peak (1952) 7.5' quadrangle.

Godola: see **Gordola** [SANTA CRUZ].

Golden Hill [SAN LUIS OBISPO]: *peak*, 6.25 miles east of Adelaida (lat. 35°38'15" N, long. 120°45'45" W; sec. 26, T 26 S, R 11 E). Named on Adelaida (1961) 15' quadrangle.

Gold Gulch [SANTA CRUZ]: *canyon*, drained by a stream that flows 2.5 miles to San Lorenzo River 6.5 miles south-southeast of the town of Boulder Creek (lat. 37°02'25" N, long. 122°04'05" W). Named on Felton (1955) 7.5' quadrangle. John Hines discovered gold in the canyon in 1853 (Hamman, p. 83).

Gold Hill [MONTEREY]: *ridge*, northwest-trending, 1 mile long, 6.5 miles southeast of Parkfield on the northeast side of Cholame Valley (lat. 35°49'50" N, long. 120°21' W). Named on Cholame Valley (1961) 7.5' quadrangle.

Goldtree [SAN LUIS OBISPO]: *locality*, 3 miles north-northwest of San Luis Obispo along Southern Pacific Railroad (lat. 35°19'20" N, long. 120°40'55" W). Named on San Luis Obispo (1965) 7.5' quadrangle. According to Gudde (1969, p. 123), the name is an Americanization of the surname of Morris Goldbaum, who settled at the place in the 1890's—*baum* means "tree" in German. California Mining Bureau's (1917c) map has the name "Hathaway" at the place.

Goleta [SANTA BARBARA]: *town*, 8 miles west of Santa Barbara (lat. 34°26'10" N, long. 119°49'35" W). Named on Goleta (1950) 7.5' quadrangle. Postal authorities established Goleta post office in 1875 (Frickstad, p. 170). They established Los Alisos post office less than 2 miles north-northeast of present downtown Goleta (N half sec. 4, T 4 N, R 28 W) in 1870 and discontinued it in 1871 (Salley, p. 126-127). They established Inez post office 11 miles west of Goleta in 1881 and discontinued it the same year (Salley, p. 104).

Goleta Landing [SANTA BARBARA]: *locality*, 1.5 miles southeast of present downtown Goleta along the coast (lat. 34°24'55" N, long. 119°48'50" W). Named on Goleta (1903) 15' quadrangle.

Goleta Point [SANTA BARBARA]: *promontory*, 2.25 miles south-southwest of downtown Goleta along the coast (lat. 34°24'15" N, long. 118°50'35" W). Named on Goleta (1950) 7.5' quadrangle. United States Board on Geographic Names (1933, p. 329) rejected the name "Pelican Point" for the feature. H.R. Wagner (p. 481) noted that the promontory had the name "Punta de Pantoja" in Spanish times.

Goleta Slough [SANTA BARBARA]: *marsh*, 1.25 miles southwest of downtown Goleta (lat. 34°25'15" N, long. 119°50'30" W). Named on Goleta (1950) 7.5' quadrangle.

Gomez's Pass: see **Mud Creek** [MONTEREY].

Gonzales [MONTEREY]: *town*, 16 miles southeast of Salinas (lat. 36°30'30" N, long. 121°26'40" W). Named on Gonzales (1955) 7.5' quadrangle. Postal authorities established Gonzales post office in 1873 (Frickstad, p. 107), and the town incorporated in 1947. The name commemorates the Gonzales family, owner of Ricon de la Puente del Monte grant where the town lies (Hoover, Rensch, and Rensch, p. 229).

Goodall: see **Camp Goodall**, under **Palm Beach** [SANTA BARBARA].

Goode Canyon [SANTA BARBARA]: *canyon*, drained by a stream that flows 3.5 miles to Cuyama Valley 4 miles southeast of the village of Cuyama (lat. 34°53'15" N, long. 119°34'35" W; sec. 5, T 9 N, R 25 W). Named on Cuyama (1964) and Fox Mountain (1964) 7.5' quadrangles.

Goode Spring [SANTA BARBARA]: *spring*, 2.25 miles north of Fox Mountain (lat. 34°50'50" N, long. 119°35'40" W); the spring is near the head of Goode Canyon. Named on Fox Mountain (1964) 7.5' quadrangle.

Goodwin: see **Carrizo Plain** [SAN LUIS OBISPO].

Gorda [MONTEREY]: *locality*, 3 miles north of Cape San Martin near the coast (lat. 35°56' N, long. 121°28' W; sec. 18, T 23 S, R 5 E). Named on Cape San Martin (1949) 7.5' quadrangle. Cape San Martin (1921) 15' quadrangle has the name "Gorda P.O." at the place. Postal authorities established Gorda post office in 1893, moved it 1 mile north in 1910, and discontinued it in 1923 (Salley, p. 87).

Gorda: see **Point Gorda**, under **Cape San Martin** [MONTEREY].

Gordola [SANTA CRUZ]: *locality*, 6.25 miles west-northwest of Point Santa Cruz along Southern Pacific Railroad (lat. 36°58'30" N, long. 122°08' W). Named on Santa Cruz (1954) 7.5' quadrangle. Called Godola on California Mining Bureau's (1917a) map. Pio Scaroni moved to the vicinity in 1868 and named the site for his birthplace in Switzerland (Clark, 1986, p. 137).

Gorge: see **The Gorge** [SAN BENITO].

Gorge Creek [SAN BENITO]: *stream*, flows 2.5 miles to Red Mountain Creek nearly 6 miles east-northeast of Bitterwater (lat. 36°25'15" N, long. 120°54'25" W; sec. 29, T 17 S, R 10 E). Named on Rock Spring Peak (1969) 7.5' quadrangle.

Gould Creek [SAN LUIS OBISPO]: *stream*, flows nearly 5 miles to Little Burnett Creek 9.5 miles northeast of the village of San Simeon (lat. 35°44'50" N, long. 121°04'40" W; at S line sec. 14, T 25 S, R 8 E). Named on Bryson (1949) and Pebblestone Shut-in (1959) 7.5' quadrangles.

Government Point [SANTA BARBARA]: *promontory*, 1 mile east-southeast of Point Conception along the coast (lat. 34°26'30" N, long. 120°27'05" W); the feature is west of Cojo Bay. Named on Point Conception (1953) 7.5' quadrangle. H.R. Wagner (p. 449) noted that Esteban Jose Martinez gave the name "Punta de Echevarria" to the promontory in 1782 to honor Agustin de Echevarria, the captain of a vessel under the command of Martinez. H.R. Wagner (p. 523) also mentioned that the promontory west of Cojo Bay was called Punta de Villaverde by the Spaniards to honor Jose Villaverde, chaplain of the Martinez expedition in 1782.

Graciosa [SANTA BARBARA]: *locality*, 6.5 miles south of Santa Maria along Pacific Coast Railroad (lat. 34°51'30" N, long. 120°27'05" W); the place is in Graciosa Canyon. Named on Lompoc (1905) 30' quadrangle.

Graciosa Canyon [SANTA BARBARA]: *canyon*, 2 miles long, opens into the canyon of Orcutt Creek 0.25 mile west of Orcutt (lat. 34° 51'50" N, long. 120°27' W); the canyon heads west of Graciosa Ridge. Named on Orcutt (1959) 7.5' quadrangle. The name "Graciosa" in the region dates from the time of the Portola expedition in 1769 (Gudde, 1949, p. 132). Postal authorities established La Graciosa post office 9 miles south of Santa Maria in 1872, moved it 1 mile north in 1880, and discontinued it in 1889—the name was for the canyon (Salley, p. 114).

Graciosa Ridge [SANTA BARBARA]: *ridge*, generally west-trending, 2 miles long, 3 miles southeast of Orcutt (lat. 34°50' N, long. 120°24'20" W); the ridge is east of Graciosa Canyon. Named on Orcutt (1959) 7.5' quadrangle. United States Board on Geographic Names (1978b, p. 4) rejected the form "Gracioso Ridge" for the name.

Gragg Canyon [SAN LUIS OBISPO]: *canyon*, drained by a stream that flows 3 miles to the canyon of San Luis Obispo Creek 1.5 miles east of Avila Beach (lat. 35°10'50" N, long. 120°42'10" W). Named on Pismo Beach (1965) 7.5' quadrangle. United States Board on Geographic Names (1992, p. 4) rejected the form "Gregg Canyon" for the name, and noted that George Gragg settled at the place.

Grahams: see **Zayanta** [SANTA CRUZ].

Grand Central Sulphur Spring: see **Paso Robles** [SAN LUIS OBISPO].

Grande Canyon: see **Llano Grande Canyon** [MONTEREY].

Grandmas Flat [MONTEREY]: *area*, 9 miles west-southwest of Greenfield on the south side of Arroyo Seco (1) (lat. 36°15'40" N, long. 121°23'10" W; sec. 23, 24, T 19 S, R 5 E). Named on Sycamore Flat (1956) 7.5' quadrangle.

Grand Spring [SANTA BARBARA]: *spring*, 4.5 miles southwest of San Rafael Mountain (lat. 34°39'50" N, long. 119°52'05" W; sec. 19, T 7 N, R 28 W). Named on San Rafael Mountain (1959) 7.5' quadrangle.

Granger Spring [SAN LUIS OBISPO]: *spring*, 2.5 miles southwest of Cholame (lat. 35°42'25" N, long. 120°20' W; sec. 35, T 25 S, R 15 E). Named on Cholame (1961) 7.5' quadrangle.

Grangeville: see **Santa Maria** [SANTA BARBARA].

Granite Canyon [MONTEREY]: *canyon*, drained by a stream that flows 3 miles to the sea 9 miles north of Point Sur (lat. 36°26'10" N, long. 121°55'05" W). Named on Soberanes Point (1956) 7.5' quadrangle.

Granite Creek [SANTA CRUZ]: *stream*, flows 2.5 miles to Branciforte Creek 7 miles south-southwest of Laurel (lat. 37°01'05" N, long. 121°59'45" W; sec. 32, T 10 S, R 1 W). Named on Laurel (1955) 7.5' quadrangle. The canyon of the stream has been called both Bachelder Gulch and Waddell Gulch (Clark, 1986, p. 139).

Granite Point [MONTEREY]: *promontory*, 1 mile east of Point Lobos on the south side of Carmel Bay (lat. 36°31'25" N, long. 121°56'10" W). Named on Monterey (1947) 7.5' quadrangle.

Granite Ridge [SAN LUIS OBISPO]: *ridge*, west-northwest-trending, 1.25 miles long, 5 miles north-northeast of Santa Margarita (lat. 35°27'20" N, long. 120°34'10" W). Named on Santa Margarita (1965) 7.5' quadrangle.

Grant Ewing Ridge [MONTEREY]: *ridge*, west-northwest-trending, 0.5 mile long, 4 miles south of Marina (lat. 36°37'45" N, long. 121°47'10" W). Named on Marina (1947) 7.5' quadrangle.

Grant Lake [SAN LUIS OBISPO]: *lake*, 800 feet long, 13 miles east-southeast of Shandon in Palo Prieto Pass (lat. 35°35'45" N, long. 120°09' W; sec. 9, T 27 S, R 17 E). Named on Cholame (1917) 30' quadrangle. Holland Canyon (1961) 7.5' quadrangle does not show the lake.

Grapevine Campground: see **Lower Grapevine Campground** [SANTA BARBARA].

Grapevine Creek [SANTA BARBARA]: *stream*, flows 4 miles to East Fork Santa Cruz Creek 4.5 miles southwest of Big Pine Mountain (lat. 34°39'30" N, long. 119°43'05" W). Named on Big Pine Mountain (1964) 7.5' quadrangle.

Grapevine Creek: see **Coche Creek** [SANTA BARBARA].

Grass Valley [SAN BENITO]: *valley*, 5.5 miles west of Paicines along Pescadero Creek (lat. 36°43'45" N, long. 121°22'30" W). Named on Mount Harlan (1968) and Paicines (1968) 7.5' quadrangles.

Grassy Canyon [SAN BENITO]: *canyon*, drained by a stream that flows nearly 2 miles to Chalone Creek 3 miles northeast of North Chalone Peak (lat. 36°28'30" N, long. 121°09'05" W; near SE cor. sec. 1, T 17 S, R 7 E). Named on North Chalone Peak (1969) 7.5' quadrangle.

Graves [MONTEREY]: *locality*, 2.5 miles west-northwest of Salinas along Southern Pacific Railroad (lat. 36°41'45" N, long. 121°41'50" W). Named on Salinas (1947) 7.5' quadrangle.

Graves: see **Ben Graves Canyon** [MONTEREY].

Graves Canyon [MONTEREY]: *canyon*, drained by a stream that flows 1.5 miles to Mule Canyon Creek 4.25 miles east-southeast of Pfeiffer Point (lat. 36°13'10" N, long. 121°45'30" W; sec. 5, T 20 S, R 2 E). Named on Partington Ridge (1956) and Pfeiffer Point (1956) 7.5' quadrangles. The name is from graves in a small Castro-family cemetery in the canyon (Clark, 1991, p. 195).

Graves Creek [SAN LUIS OBISPO]: *stream*, flows 10.5 miles to Salinas River 7 miles south of Paso Robles (lat. 35°31'50" N, long. 120°42'10" W). Named on Atascadero (1965), Morro Bay North (1965), and Templeton (1948) 7.5' quadrangles.

Green Canyon [SAN LUIS OBISPO]: *canyon*, drained by a stream that flows 3.5 miles to Arroyo de la Cruz nearly 5 miles north-northwest of the village of San Simeon (lat. 35°42'10" N, long. 121°13'55" W). Named on San Simeon (1958) 7.5' quadrangle.

Green Canyon [SANTA BARBARA]: *canyon*, drained by a stream that flows 7 miles to Cuyama Valley 7 miles north of McPherson Peak (lat. 34°59'25" N, long. 119°48'55" W). Named on Peak Mountain (1964) 7.5' quadrangle.

Greenfield [MONTEREY]: *town*, 33 miles southeast of Salinas (lat. 36°19'15" N, long. 121°14'30" W). Named on Greenfield (1956) and Paraiso Springs (1956) 7.5' quadrangles. Promoters laid out the town between 1902 and 1905; first it was called Clarke City for John S. Clarke, one of the promoters, but when postal authorities rejected the name "Clarke City," the town was renamed Greenfield (Gudde, 1949, p. 135). Postal authorities established Greenfield post office in 1905 (Frickstad, p. 107), and the town incorporated in 1947.

Green Mountain [SANTA BARBARA]: *ridge*, south-southeast-trending, 1 mile long, 4 miles east of Point Bennett on San Miguel Island (lat. 34°02'10" N, long. 120°23'05" W). Named on San Miguel Island West (1950) 7.5' quadrangle.

Green Oaks Creek [SANTA CRUZ]: *stream*, flows 1 mile to San Mateo County 3.25 miles north-northwest of the mouth of Waddell Creek (lat. 37°08'20" N, long. 122°18'20" W; sec. 21, T 9 S, R 4 W). Named on Franklin Point (1955) 7.5' quadrangle. Santa Cruz (1902) 30' quadrangle has the form "Greenoaks Cr." for the name, which is from the Green Oaks dairy ranch that was started along the stream in 1863 (Brown, p. 37).

Green Peak [SAN LUIS OBISPO]: *peak*, 5 miles northwest of Point San Luis (lat. 35°12'20" N, long. 120°49'35" W). Altitude 1414 feet. Named on Port San Luis (1965) 7.5' quadrangle.

Greentree Spring [SAN BENITO]: *spring*, 6.25 miles east-southeast of Bitterwater along Cholla Creek (lat. 36°20'15" N, long. 120°54'05" W; near W line sec. 28, T 18 S, R 10 E). Named on Lonoak (1969) 7.5' quadrangle.

Green Valley [MONTEREY]: *canyon*, nearly 3 miles long, opens into Long Valley 9 miles east-northeast of San Lucas (lat. 36°10' N, long. 120°53'10" W; near NE cor. sec. 28, T 20 S, R 10 E). Named on Monarch Peak (1967) and Nattrass Valley (1967) 7.5' quadrangles.

Green Valley [SAN LUIS OBISPO]: *valley*, 2.5 miles long, 4 miles southeast of Cambria (lat. 35°32' N, long. 121°01' W). Named on Cambria (1959) 7.5' quadrangle.

Green Valley [SANTA CRUZ]: *valley*, 1.5 miles east of Corralitos (lat. 36°59'30" N, long. 121°46'35" W). Named on Loma Prieta (1955) and Watsonville West (1954) 7.5' quadrangles. Gudde (1949, p. 134-135) noted that the valley is called Cañada Verde on a Mexican map of 1844. The stream in the valley is called Green Valley Cr. on Alexander's (1953) map.

Green Valley Creek [SAN LUIS OBISPO]: *stream*, flows 7.25 miles to Perry Creek 3 miles southeast of Cambria (lat. 35°31'55" N, long. 121°02'55" W); the stream drains Green Valley. Named on Cambria (1959) and Cypress Mountain (1948, photorevised 1979) 7.5' quadrangles.

Green Valley Creek: see **Green Valley** [SANTA CRUZ].

Gregg Canyon: see **Gragg Canyon** [SAN LUIS OBISPO].

Grey Canyon [SANTA BARBARA]: *canyon*, 2.25 miles long, opens to the sea 1.5 miles north-northeast of Point Arguello (lat. 34°35'40" N, long. 120°38'20" W). Named on Point Arguello (1959) and Tranquillon Mountain (1959) 7.5' quadrangles.

Grey Eagle Terrace: see **Seaside** [MONTEREY].

Greyhound Rock [SANTA CRUZ]: *promontory*, 1.25 miles south-southeast of the mouth of Waddell Creek along the coast (lat. 37° 04'40" N, long. 122°16' W). Named on Año Nuevo (1955) 7.5' quadrangle.

Grimes Canyon [MONTEREY]: *canyon*, drained by a stream that flows nearly 1.5 miles to the sea 3 miles northwest of Point Sur (lat. 36°12'20" N, long. 121°44'20" W; near W line sec. 10, T 20 S, R 2 E). Named on Partington Ridge (1956) 7.5' quadrangle.

Grimes Point [MONTEREY]: *promontory*, 3 miles northwest of Point Sur along the coast (lat. 36°12'20" N, long. 121°44'10" W; at W line sec. 10, T 20 S, R 2 E); the feature is just south of the mouth of Grimes Canyon. Named on Partington Ridge (1956) 7.5' quadrangle.

Griswold: see **San Lucas** [MONTEREY] (2).

Griswold Canyon [MONTEREY]: *canyon*, 2.25 miles long, branches north from Long Valley 9.5 miles east-northeast of San Lucas (lat. 36°10' N, long. 120°52'05" W; near NE cor. sec. 27, T 20 S, R 10 E). Named on Monarch Peak (1967) 7.5' quadrangle. The name is for William E. Griswold, who owned land at and near the mouth of the canyon (Clark, 1991, p. 198).

Griswold Canyon [SAN BENITO]: *canyon*, 3.5 miles long, 3.5 miles south of Panoche between Panoche Valley and Vallecitos (lat. 36° 32'30" N, long. 120°50' W); the canyon is at the west end of Griswold Hills along Griswold Creek. Named on Panoche (1969) 7.5' quadrangle. According to Anderson and Pack (p. 18), "the canyon has been termed variously Griswold, Grizzly, and Lyon Canyon, but Griswold is believed to be the original name." United States Board on Geographic Names (1972a, p. 1) listed the names "Grizzly Canyon" and "Lyon Canyon" as variants.

Griswold Creek [SAN BENITO]: *stream*, formed by the confluence of Vallecitos Creek and Pimental Creek, flows 6.5 miles to Panoche Creek 1.5 miles southeast of Panoche (lat. 36°35' N, long. 120°48'35" W; sec. 31, T 15 S, R 11 E). Named on Panoche (1969) 7.5' quadrangle. The name is for an early rancher (Hoover, Rensch, and Rensch, p. 314).

Griswold Creek: see **Vallecitos Creek** [SAN BENITO].

Griswold Hills [SAN BENITO]: *range*, 4.5 miles south-southeast of Panoche between Panoche Valley on the north, Vallecitos on the south, Griswold Creek on the west, and Silver Creek on the east (lat. 36°32'30" N, long. 120°47'30" W). Named on Idria (1969), Panoche (1969), and Tumey Hills (1956) 7.5' quadrangles.

Griswolds [SAN BENITO]: *locality*, 8 miles northwest of Idria near present Syncline Divide (lat. 36°28'50" N, long. 120°47'15" W; sec. 5, T 17 S, R 11 E). Named on Priest Valley (1915) 30' quadrangle. Whitney (p. 56) referred to Griswold's as a ranch house, and added, "But what the inducements could be to live in such a place it was beyond our power to determine."

Grizzly Bend [SAN LUIS OBISPO]: *bend*, 10 miles northeast of the village of San Simeon along Nacimiento River (lat. 35°45' N, long. 121°03'15" W; near E line sec. 13, 24, T 25 S, R 8 E). Named on Bryson (1949) and Pebblestone Shut-in (1959) 7.5' quadrangles.

Grizzly Bend Creek: see **North Grizzly Bend Creek** [SAN LUIS OBISPO].

Grizzly Canyon: see **Griswold Canyon** [SAN BENITO].

Grizzly Flat [SANTA BARBARA]: *area*, nearly 4 miles north of Corralitos (lat. 37°02'35" N, long. 121°47'40" W; sec. 19, T 10 S, R 2 E). Named on Loma Prieta (1955) 7.5' quadrangle.

Grizzly Mountain: see **Grizzly Rock** [SANTA CRUZ].

Grizzly Rock [SANTA CRUZ]: *relief feature*, 6 miles north-northeast of the town of Boulder Creek (lat. 37°12' N, long. 122°04' W; near S line sec. 27, T 8 S, R 2 W). Altitude 2716 feet. Named on Castle Rock Ridge (1955) 7.5' quadrangle. Called Grizzly Mt. on Hubbard's (1943) map.

Grizzly Spring [SAN LUIS OBISPO]: *spring*, 1 mile east of Branch Mountain (lat. 35°11'05" N, long. 120°03'50" W; sec. 32, T 31 S, R 18 E). Named on Branch Mountain (1967) 7.5' quadrangle.

Grogan: see **Paicines** [SAN BENITO].

Grover: see **Grover City** [SAN LUIS OBISPO].

Grover City [SAN LUIS OBISPO]: *town*, 2 miles west of downtown Arroyo Grande (lat. 35°07'15" N, long. 120°37'15" W). Named on Arroyo Grande NE (1965), Oceano (1965), and Pismo Beach (1965) 7.5' quadrangles. Called Grover on Arroyo Grande (1942) 15' quadrangle. W.A. Grover founded the town in 1890 (Lee and others, p. 64). Postal authorities established Grover City post office in 1947 (Frickstad, p. 164), and the town incorporated in 1959. According to Gudde (1969, p. 129), the town was named Grover in 1892 for Henry Grover; H.V. Bagwell renamed the place Grover City in 1937.

Grover Gulch [SANTA CRUZ]: *canyon*, drained by a stream that flows 2.5 miles to Bates Creek 2 miles northeast of Soquel (lat. 37° 00'35" N, long. 121°56'05" W). Named on Laurel (1955) 7.5' quadrangle. According to Clark (1986, p. 133), the feature now is called Glen Haven.

Gruenhagen Flat [SAN LUIS OBISPO]: *area*, 6.25 miles west of Shandon on the north side of Estrella River (lat. 35°39' N, long. 120°29'15" W). Named on Shandon (1961) 7.5' quadrangle.

Guadaloupe: see **Guadalupe** [SAN LUIS OBISPO-SANTA BARBARA]; **Guadalupe** [SANTA BARBARA].

Guadalupe [SAN LUIS OBISPO-SANTA BARBARA]: *land grant*, at and near the town of Guadalupe on San Luis Obispo-Santa Barbara County line in Santa Maria Valley. Named on Guadalupe (1959), Oceano (1965), Point Sal (1958), and Santa Maria (1959) 7.5' quadrangles. Diego Olivera and Teodoro Arellanes received the land in 1840 and claimed 43,682 acres patented in 1870 (Cowan, p. 38). United States Board on Geographic Names (1933, p. 342) rejected the forms "Gaudalupe," "Guadaloupe," and "Guadelupe" for the name.

Guadalupe [SANTA BARBARA]: *town*, 8 miles west of Santa Maria (lat. 34°58'20" N, long. 120°34'15" W). Named on Guadalupe (1959) 7.5' quadrangle. Postal authorities established Guadaloupe post office in 1873 and changed the name to Guadalupe in 1915 (Frickstad, p. 171). The town incorporated in 1946. United States Board on Geographic Names (1933, p. 342) rejected the forms "Gaudalupe," "Guadaloupe," and "Guadelupe" for the name.

Guadalupe Lake [SANTA BARBARA]: *intermittent lake*, 1.5 miles long, 4.5 miles south-southeast of the town of Guadalupe (lat. 34° 54'35" N, long. 120°32'05" W). Named on Point Sal (1947) 15' quadrangle. Guadalupe (1905) 30' quadrangle shows a permanent lake. H.R. Wagner (p. 498) identified the lake as the one that members of the Portola expedition called Laguna Grande de San Daniel in 1769, and noted that Portola also called the feature Laguna Larga.

Guadalupe Largo: see **Santa Maria Valley** [SAN LUIS OBISPO-SANTA BARBARA].

Guadalupe y Llanitos de los Correos [MONTEREY]: *land grant*, 2.5 miles southwest of Chualar. Named on Chualar (1947), Gonzales (1955), Palo Escrito Peak (1956), and Rana Creek (1956) 7.5' quadrangles. Juan Malarin received 2 leagues in 1833; Mariano Malarin, executor, claimed 8859 acres patented in 1865 (Cowan, p. 38). Perez (p. 68) gave 1835 as the date of the grant.

Guadelupe: see **Guadalupe** [SAN LUIS OBISPO-SANTA BARBARA]; **Guadalupe** [SANTA BARBARA].

Guaya Canyon [SAN LUIS OBISPO]: *canyon*, 2.5 miles long, opens into Arroyo Grande Valley 1.5 miles east of downtown Arroyo Grande (lat. 35°07'15" N, long. 120°33'25" W). Named on Oceano (1965) 7.5' quadrangles.

Guaymas River: see **San Antonio Creek** [SANTA BARBARA] (1).

Guillemot Island: see **Bluefish Cove** [MONTEREY].

Gulch House Creek [MONTEREY]: *stream*, flows 2.5 miles to Sapaque Creek 13 miles south-southeast of Jolon (lat. 35°47'50" N, long. 121°05'35" W; sec. 34, T 24 S, R 8 E). Named on Bryson (1949) 7.5' quadrangle. The name is from a place called The Gulch House that Job Wood owned in Sapaque Valley (Clark, 1991, p. 198).

Gull Island [SANTA BARBARA]: *island*, 550 feet long, 4000 feet south-southwest of Punta Arena off Santa Cruz Island (lat. 33° 57' N, long. 119°49'30" W). Named on Santa Cruz Island B (1943) 7.5' quadrangle.

Gull Island: see **Sutil Island** [SANTA BARBARA].

Gull Neck Rock [MONTEREY]: *relief feature*, 18 miles north of San Ardo on Mustang Ridge (lat. 36°16'55" N, long. 120°51'50" W; sec. 14, T 19 S, R 10 E). Named on Hepsedam Peak (1969) 7.5' quadrangle.

Gum [SANTA BARBARA]: *locality*, 4.5 miles southeast of the town of Guadalupe along Santa Maria Valley Railroad (lat. 34°55'15" N, long. 120°31'20" W). Named on Guadalupe (1959) 7.5' quadrangle.

Guyamas River: see **Cuyama River** [SAN LUIS OBISPO-SANTA BARBARA].

Gypsum Canyon [SAN LUIS OBISPO]: *canyon*, drained by a stream that flows 3.5 miles to Cuyama River 6.5 miles south of Branch Mountain (lat. 35°05'40" N, long. 120°03'35" W; sec. 33, T 32 S, R 18 E). Named on Branch Mountain (1967) and Miranda Pine Mountain (1967) 7.5' quadrangles.

- H -

Hadley [SAN LUIS OBISPO]: *locality*, 1 mile south of Etna along Southern Pacific Railroad (lat. 35°11'15" N, long. 120°36'40" W). Named on Arroyo Grande (1952) 15' quadrangle. Called Hadley Tower on Arroyo Grande (1942) 15' quadrangle, which shows Pacific Coast Railroad crossing Southern Pacific Railroad at the place.

Hadley Tower: see **Hadley** [SAN LUIS OBISPO].

Haelleck Canyon [MONTEREY]: *canyon*, drained by a stream that flows 1 mile to James Creek at Jamesburg (lat. 36°22'10" N, long. 121°35'20" W; sec. 18, T 18 S, R 4 E). Named on Chews Ridge (1956) 7.5' quadrangle. Clark (1991, p. 200) associated the name with the Hallock family, who owned land in or near the canyon.

Hains Point [MONTEREY]: *ridge*, east-trending, nearly 0.5 mile long, 4 miles southwest of Salinas (lat. 36°38'15" N, long. 121°42'45" W). Named on Salinas (1947) 7.5' quadrangle.

Halcyon [SAN LUIS OBISPO]: *village*, 1.5 miles south-southwest of downtown Arroyo Grande (lat. 35°06'10" N, long. 120°35'35" W). Named on Oceano (1965) 7.5' quadrangle. In 1904 Dr. William H. Dower and Mrs. Francia A. La Due opened a sanatorium at the place that grew into a cooperative theosophical colony (Hoover, Rensch, and Rensch, p. 386). Postal authorities established Halcyon post office in 1908 (Frickstad, p. 164).

Hale Creek [SAN LUIS OBISPO]: *stream*, flows nearly 3 miles to Atascadero Creek 5 miles south-southwest of Atascadero (lat. 35° 25'25" N, long. 120°41'50" W; sec. 9, T 29 S, R 12 E). Named on Atascadero (1965) 7.5' quadrangle.

Hale McLeod Canyon [SAN LUIS OBISPO]: *canyon*, drained by a stream that flows nearly 3 miles to Kern County 28 miles east-southeast of Simmler (lat. 35°08'55" N, long. 119°33'20" W; at E line sec. 12, T 32 S, R 22 E). Named on Fellows (1951) 7.5' quadrangle. Rintoul (p. 92) noted that Hale-McLeod Oil Company operated in the neighborhood.

Halfway House: see **Salinas** [MONTEREY].

Hall [MONTEREY]: *settlement*, 7 miles north-northwest of Prunedale (lat. 36°51'50" N, long. 121°44' W). Named on Prunedale (1954) 7.5' quadrangle. The name is from a pioneer family (Clark, 1991, p. 200). United States Board on Geographic Names (1994, p. 5) approved the name "Las Lomas" for the place.

Hall Canyon [MONTEREY]: *canyon*, 4.5 miles long, opens into lowlands 3.5 miles east of Jolon (lat. 35°58'45" W, long. 121°06'35" W; sec. 33, T 22 S, R 8 E). Named on Espinosa Canyon (1949) and Williams Hill (1949) 7.5' quadrangles. The name commemorates Wilson Hall, who lived in the canyon (Clark, 1991, p. 200).

Halleck: see **Fort Halleck**, under **Presidio of Monterey** [MONTEREY].

Hall's Natural Bridge: see **Moore Creek** [SANTA CRUZ].

Hames: see **Hames Valley** [MONTEREY].

Hames Creek [MONTEREY]: *stream*, flows 14 miles to Salinas River 2 miles west-northwest of Bradley (lat. 35°52'40" N, long. 120°50' W; near NE cor. sec. 1, T 24 S, R 10 E); the stream drains Hames Valley. Named on Hames Valley (1949) and Tierra Redonda Mountain (1949) 7.5' quadrangles.

Hames Valley [MONTEREY]: *valley*, 4.5 miles west of Bradley (lat. 35°52'30" N, long. 120°53' W). Named on Bradley (1949), Hames Valley (1949), and Tierra Redonda Mountain (1949) 7.5' quadrangles. California Mining Bureau's (1909a) map shows a place called Hames located 6 miles by stage line west of Bradley. Postal authorities established Hames post office in Hames Valley in 1889, moved it 1.25 miles northeast in 1892, and discontinued it in 1914 (Salley, p. 92). The name is for John Hames, a landowner in the valley (Clark, 1991, p. 201).

Hamilton Canyon [MONTEREY]: *canyon*, drained by a stream that flows 5 miles to lowlands 3.25 miles north-northwest of San Lucas (lat. 36°10'35" N, long. 121°02' W; sec. 19, T 20 S, R 9 E). Named on Nattrass Valley (1967) and San Lucas (1949) 7.5' quadrangles. The name is for Samuel Hamilton, John Steinbeck's maternal grandfather, who patented land in the canyon in 1891 (Clark, 1991, p. 201-202).

Hammond Spring [SAN LUIS OBISPO]: *spring*, 3 miles west-northwest of Cholame (lat. 35°44'15" N, long. 120°20'55" W; sec. 22, T 25 S, R 15 E). Named on Cholame (1961) 7.5' quadrangle.

Hampton Canyon [SAN LUIS OBISPO]: *canyon*, drained by a stream that flows 1.5 miles to Reservoir Canyon 2.25 miles southwest of Lopez Mountain (lat. 35°16'40" N, long. 120°36'15" W; sec. 32, T 30 S, R 13 E). Named on Lopez Mountain (1965) 7.5' quadrangle.

Handley Canyon [MONTEREY]: *canyon*, drained by a stream that flows 0.5 mile to the canyon of Chalone Creek 4 miles northeast of Greenfield (lat. 36°21'50" N, long. 121°11'45" W). Named on Greenfield (1956) 7.5' quadrangle.

Hanlon: see **Jacques Hanlon Creek** [MONTEREY]; **Mount Hanlon**, under **Mount Harlan** [SAN BENITO].

Hansen: see **George Hansen Canyon** [SAN BENITO].

Hanson Slough [SANTA CRUZ]: *stream*, flows 1 mile in an artificial watercourse to Watsonville Slough 2.5 miles west-southwest of Watsonville (lat. 36°53'50" N, long. 121°47'25" W). Named on Watsonville West (1954) 7.5' quadrangle.

Happy Canyon [SANTA BARBARA]: *canyon,* drained by a stream that flows 9 miles to Santa Agueda Creek 3.5 miles east-southeast of Santa Ynez (lat. 34°36'05" N, long. 120°01'10" W). Named on Figueroa Mountain (1959), Lake Cachuma (1959), and Santa Ynez (1959) 7.5' quadrangles.

Happy Hunting Ground Campground [SANTA BARBARA]: *locality,* 7 miles southwest of Montgomery Potrero (lat. 34°45'05"N, long. 119°49'20" W). Named on Hurricane Deck (1964) 7.5' quadrangle.

Happy Valley [MONTEREY]: *canyon,* drained by a stream that flows 1.5 miles to an unnamed valley 0.5 mile east of Paraiso Springs (lat. 36°20' N, long. 121°21'25" W; sec. 30, T 18 S, R 8 E). Named on Paraiso Springs (1956) 7.5' quadrangle.

Harbor of Saint Simeon: see **San Simeon Bay** [SAN LUIS OBISPO].

Hare Canyon [MONTEREY]:

(1) *canyon,* drained by a stream that flows 3.5 miles to Limekiln Creek nearly 3 miles east-southeast of Lopez Point (lat. 36°00'40" N, long. 121°31' W; near S line sec. 15, T 22 S, R 4 E). Named on Cone Peak (1949) and Lopez Point (1956) 7.5' quadrangles. According to Clark (1991, p. 203), Lou G. Hare, the surveyor who produced the official map of Monterey County in 1898, named the feature for himself.

(2) *canyon,* drained by a stream that flows 6 miles to Salinas River 2 miles east of Bradley (lat. 35°51'30" N, long. 120°46' W; sec. 10, T 24 S, R 11 E). Named on Bradley (1949) and Valleton (1948) 7.5' quadrangles.

Hare Creek [SANTA CRUZ]: *stream,* flows 1.5 miles to Boulder Creek (1) 3.5 miles east-southeast of Big Basin (lat. 37°09'10" N, long. 122°09'40" W; sec. 14, T 9 S, R 3 W). Named on Big Basin (1955) 7.5' quadrangle.

Hare Rock [SANTA BARBARA]: *rock,* 4.5 miles northwest of Cardwell Point, and 600 feet offshore on the north side of San Miguel Island (lat. 34°03'55" N, long. 120°21'15" W). Named on San Miguel Island East (1950) 7.5' quadrangle.

Harford: see **Port Harford**, under **Port San Luis** [SAN LUIS OBISPO].

Harford Canyon [SAN LUIS OBISPO]: *canyon,* drained by a stream that flows 2.5 miles to San Luis Obispo Creek 0.5 mile west-northwest of Avila Beach (lat. 35°10'50" N, long. 120°44'20" W). Named on Pismo Beach (1965) 7.5' quadrangle. Called Hartford Canyon on Arroyo Grande (1942) 15' quadrangle, but United States Board on Geographic Names (1967a, p. 9) rejected this name.

Harkins Slough [SANTA CRUZ]: *stream,* flows 7.25 miles to Watsonville Slough 3 miles west-southwest of Watsonville (lat. 36°53'25" N, long. 121°48'05" W). Named on Watsonville West (1954) 7.5' quadrangle.

Harlan: see **Mount Harlan** [SAN BENITO].

Harlan Creek [SAN BENITO]: *stream,* flows 2.5 miles to Indian Canyon 5.25 miles west-southwest of Paicines (lat. 36°42'20" N, long. 121°22'05" W; near N line sec. 24, T 14 S, R 5 E); the stream heads near Mount Harlan. Named on Mount Harlan (1968) and Paicines (1968) 7.5' quadrangles.

Harlan Rock [MONTEREY]: *rock,* 100 feet long, 2 miles east of Lopez Point, and 0.25 mile offshore (lat. 36°00'40" N, long. 121° 32'05" W). Named on Lopez Point (1956) 7.5' quadrangle.

Harlan Spring [MONTEREY]: *spring,* 6 miles south of Parkfield (lat. 35°48'50" N, long. 120°26'50" W; sec. 27, T 24 S, R 14 E). Named on Cholame Hills (1961) 7.5' quadrangle. The name is for a member the Harlan family who came to Cholame Valley in 1869 (Clark, 1991, p. 205).

Harlech Castle Rock [SAN LUIS OBISPO]: *rock,* nearly 2 miles north-northwest of Piedras Blancas Point, and 3500 feet offshore (lat. 35°41'10" N, long. 121°18' W). Named on Piedras Blancas (1959) 7.5' quadrangle.

Harlem [MONTEREY]: *locality,* 4.25 miles east-southeast of Soledad along Southern Pacific Railroad (lat. 36°24' N, long. 121°15'15" W; sec. 6, T 18 S, R 7 E). Named on Soledad (1955) 7.5' quadrangle.

Harmony [SAN LUIS OBISPO]: *locality,* 5 miles southeast of Cambria (lat. 35°30'30" N, long. 121°01'20" W). Named on Cambria (1959) 7.5' quadrangle. A Swiss named Salmina started a community at the place about 1910 as a center for a thriving dairy industry (Lee and others, p. 67). Postal authorities established Harmony post office in 1915 (Frickstad, p. 164).

Harmony Valley [SAN LUIS OBISPO]: *valley,* 5 miles southeast of Cambria along Perry Creek (lat. 35°30'45" N, long. 121°01' W); Harmony is in the valley. Named on Cambria (1959) 7.5' quadrangle.

Harper Creek [MONTEREY]: *stream,* flows 3.25 miles to San Benancio Gulch 8 miles south-southwest of Salinas (lat. 36°34'10" N, long. 121°42'25" W). Named on Spreckels (1947) 7.5' quadrangle.

Harris [SANTA BARBARA]: *locality,* 7 miles south of Orcutt (lat. 34°46' N, long. 120°25'25" W); the place is near the mouth of Harris Canyon. Named on Santa Maria (1947) 15' quadrangle. California Mining Bureau's (1917c) map shows a place called Orby located at or near the site of Harris. Postal authorities established Orby post office in 1909, changed the name to Harriston in 1924, and discontinued it in 1934 (Frickstad, p. 171).

Harris: see **Brookdale** [SANTA CRUZ].

Harris Canyon [SANTA BARBARA]: *canyon,* 4.5 miles long, opens into the canyon of San Antonio Creek (1) 6.5 miles south of Orcutt (lat. 34°46'15" N, long. 120°25'45" W). Named on Orcutt (1959) 7.5' quadrangle.

Harris Creek [MONTEREY]: *stream,* flows 8.5 miles to San Antonio River 8 miles west-southwest of Bradley (lat. 35°48'45" N, long. 120°55'40" W); the stream heads in Harris Valley. Named on Bryson (1949) and Tierra Redonda Mountain (1949) 7.5' quadrangles.

Harris Point [SANTA BARBARA]: *promontory,* 5.5 miles northwest of Cardwell Point at the northernmost tip of San Miguel Island (lat. 34°04'35" N, long. 120°22' W). Named on San Miguel Island East (1950) 7.5' quadrangle. Doran (p. 214) noted that a feature called Wilson Rock, locally known as West Rock, lies 2.25 miles northwest of Point Harris.

Harriston: see **Harris** [SANTA BARBARA].

Harris Valley [MONTEREY]: *valley,* 14 miles southeast of Jolon (lat. 35°49'30" N, long. 121°00'30" W); the valley is along upper reaches of Harris Creek. Named on Bryson (1949) and Tierra Redonda Mountain (1949) 7.5' quadrangles. E.S. Harris farmed in the valley in 1875 (Clark, 1991, p. 207).

Hartford: see **Port Hartford**, under **Port San Luis** [SAN LUIS OBISPO].

Hartford Canyon: see **Harford Canyon** [SAN LUIS OBISPO].

Hasbrouck: see **Mount Hasbrouck**, under **Big Baldy** [SAN LUIS OBISPO].

Hathaway: see **Goldtree** [SAN LUIS OBISPO].

Hatton Canyon [MONTEREY]: *canyon,* drained by a stream that flows 2 miles to Carmel Valley 1.5 miles east-northeast of the mouth of Carmel River (lat. 36°32'35" N, long. 121°54'20" W). Named on Monterey (1947) 7.5' quadrangle. The name is for the Hatton family, who owned land at the place (Clark, 1991, p. 210).

Have [SAN LUIS OBISPO]: *locality,* 3 miles southeast of present Atascadero along Southern Pacific Railroad (lat. 35°27'30" N, long. 120°37'45" W). Named on San Luis Obispo (1897) 15' quadrangle. Diller and others' (1915) map shows a place called Eaglet located along the railroad at or near this place.

Hawkins Lake [SAN BENITO]: *lake,* 0.5 mile long, behind a dam in Little Peak Canyon 9 miles north-northeast of Hollister (lat. 36°57'20" N, long. 121°18'35" W). Named on Three Sisters (1954) 7.5' quadrangle, which shows Hawkins ranch 3.5 miles downstream from the lake.

Hawkins Peak [SAN BENITO]: *peak,* nearly 3 miles north of North Chalone Peak (lat. 36°29'15" N, long. 121°11'45" W; on S line sec. 34, T 16 S, R 7 E). Named on North Chalone Peak (1969) 7.5' quadrangle.

Hawks Peak: see **Fremont Peak** [MONTEREY-SAN BENITO].

Hay Canyon [SAN LUIS OBISPO]: *canyon,* drained by a stream that flows nearly 6 miles to San Juan Creek 4 miles east-northeast of Castle Crags (lat. 35°19'15" N, long. 120°08' W; near N line sec. 15, T 30 S, R 17 E). Named on La Panza (1967) 7.5' quadrangle. On La Panza (1935) 15' quadrangle, present Willow Canyon and North Fork Willow Canyon are called Hay Canyon, and present Hay Canyon is called Martinez Canyon, but United States Board on Geographic Names (1968c, p. 5) rejected the name "Martinez Canyon" and approved the name "Hay Canyon" for present Hay Canyon. Angel (1883, p, 249) referred to Haystock Cañon. According to Dillon (1960, p. 7), present Hay Canyon was called Haystack Canyon.

Hay Canyon: see **Willow Canyon** [SAN LUIS OBISPO].

Haystack Canyon [SAN LUIS OBISPO]: *canyon,* drained by a stream that flows 6.5 miles to Stephens Canyon 3.5 miles north-northeast of Huasna Peak (lat. 35°05'20" N, long. 120°19'55" W; sec. 27, T 12 N, R 33 E). Named on Caldwell Mesa (1967), Huasna Peak (1967), and Los Machos Hills (1967) 7.5' quadrangles.

Haystack Canyon: see **Hay Canyon** [SAN LUIS OBISPO].

Haystack Hill [MONTEREY]: *peak,* 2 miles northeast of Jamesburg (lat. 36°23'05" N, long. 121°33'40" W; near N line sec. 8, T 18 S, R 4 E). Altitude 2100 feet. Named on Rana Creek (1956) 7.5' quadrangle.

Haystock Cañon: see **Hay Canyon** [SAN LUIS OBISPO].

Hazard Canyon [SAN LUIS OBISPO]: *canyon,* drained by a stream that flows 3 miles to the sea 5.5 miles south of Morro Rock (lat. 35°17'20" N, long. 120°52'55" W; sec. 27, T 30 S, R 10 E). Named on Morro Bay South (1965) 7.5' quadrangle.

Headland Cove [MONTEREY]: *embayment,* 2.5 miles southwest of present Carmel-by-the-Sea along the coast on the south side of Point Lobos (lat. 36°31'10" N, long. 121°57'05" W). Named on Monterey (1947) 7.5' quadrangle. The feature first was called Point Cove after Point Lobos (Clark, 1991, p. 211).

Headland Meadow [MONTEREY]: *area,* 2.5 miles southwest of present Carmel-by-the-Sea (lat. 36°31'05" N, long. 121°56'50" W); the place is less than 0.5 mile southeast of Headland Cove. Named on Monterey (1947) 7.5' quadrangle.

Heath Campground [SANTA BARBARA]: *locality,* 3.25 miles north-northwest of Big Pine Mountain along Sisquoc River (lat. 34°44'15" N, long. 119°40'55" W). Named on Big Pine Mountain (1964) 7.5' quadrangle. The place was a favorite hunting and fishing spot for Jim Heath (Gagnon, p. 84).

Heath Spring [SANTA BARBARA]: *spring,* 3 miles north-northwest of

McPherson Peak in Green Canyon (lat. 34°55'30" N, long. 119° 50'15" W). Named on Peak Mountain (1964) 7.5' quadrangle.

Hecker Pass [SANTA CRUZ]: *pass,* 6 miles north-northeast of Watsonville on Santa Cruz-Santa Clara County line (lat. 36°59'45" N, long. 121°43' W). Named on Watsonville East (1955) 7.5' quadrangle. The name honors Henry Hecker, who was a Santa Clara County supervisor when the road over the pass was completed in 1928 (Rambo, p. 36). A change made in the county line in 1971 left the pass entirely in Santa Clara County (Clark, 1986, p. 149).

Heins Lake [MONTEREY]: *lake,* 1 mile long, 3 miles east-southeast of Salinas (lat. 36°39'15" N, long. 121°36'15" W). Named on Salinas (1912) 15' quadrangle. The name commemorates a farmer who settled at the place before 1868 (Gudde, 1949, p. 145).

Hell Hole [SAN BENITO]: *canyon,* drained by a stream that flows nearly 1 mile to Peak Canyon 6.25 miles southwest of Hollister (lat. 36°47'40" N, long. 121°29'20" W). Named on Hollister (1955) 7.5' quadrangle.

Hells Gate: see **Aptos Creek** [SANTA CRUZ].

Hells Half Acre [SANTA BARBARA]: *area,* 6 miles east-southeast of Figueroa Mountain (lat. 34°42'40" N, long. 119°53'05" W; sec. 1, T 7 N, R 29 W). Named on Figueroa Mountain (1959) 7.5' quadrangle.

Hendrys Beach [SANTA BARBARA]: *beach,* 2.5 miles southwest of downtown Santa Barbara along the coast (lat. 34°24'05" N, long. 119°44'20" W). Named on Santa Barbara (1944) 7.5' quadrangle.

Hennicksons Ridge [MONTEREY]: *ridge,* northwest-trending, 2.5 miles long, 4 miles east-northeast of Uncle Sam Mountain (lat. 36° 22'15" N, long. 121°38'30" W). Named on Carmel Valley (1956) and Ventana Cones (1956) 7.5' quadrangles. According to Clark (1991, p. 212), the corrupted name is from the Henningsen family, early settlers in the neighborhood.

Henrietta Peak [SAN BENITO]: *peak,* nearly 4 miles south-southwest of Mariposa Peak (lat. 36°54'15" N, long. 121°13'55" W; sec. 8, T 12 S, R 7 E). Altitude 3626 feet. Named on Mariposa Peak (1969) 7.5' quadrangle.

Henry [SAN LUIS OBISPO]: *locality,* 1.25 miles east of downtown Atascadero along Southern Pacific Railroad (lat. 35°29'20" N, long. 120°38'50" W). Named on Atascadero (1965) 7.5' quadrangle. San Luis Obispo (1897) 15' quadrangle has the name "Atascadero" at this spot, and has the name "Henry" at a place situated 1.5 miles farther northwest.

Henry Ashurst Spring: see **Ashurst Spring** [SAN BENITO].

Henry Cocks [MONTEREY]: *land grant,* 2.5 miles west of Salinas. Named on Salinas (1947) 7.5' quadrangle. Esteban Espinosa received 0.25 league in 1840; Henry Cocks claimed 1106 acres patented in 1870 (Cowan, p. 112).

Henry Creek [SANTA CRUZ]: *stream,* flows 1.25 miles to West Waddell Creek 4.5 miles north of the mouth of Waddell Creek (lat. 37°09'40" N, long. 122°16'20" W; near S line sec. 11, T 9 S, R 4 W). Named on Franklin Point (1955) 7.5' quadrangle. Año Nuevo (1948) 15' quadrangle has the name "Henry Creek" for a stream that joins Berry Creek (1) 0.5 mile northeast of the confluence of present Henry Creek and West Waddell Creek.

Henry Sands Canyon [MONTEREY]: *canyon,* drained by a stream that flows 4.25 miles to lowlands 5 miles east of Gonzales (lat. 36° 30'30" N, long. 121°21'15" W; sec. 30, T 16 S, R 6 E). Named on Mount Johnson (1968) 7.5' quadrangle.

Hepsedam Creek [SAN BENITO]: *stream,* flows 4 miles to Lewis Creek 9.5 miles southeast of Bitterwater (lat. 36°17'35" N, long. 120°52'15" W; sec. 10, T 19 S, R 10 E); the stream is west of Hepsedam Peak. Named on Hepsedam Peak (1969) 7.5' quadrangle.

Hepsedam Peak [SAN BENITO]: *peak,* 11 miles east-southeast of Bitterwater (lat. 36°18'50" N, long. 120°49'25" W; near S line sec. 31, T 18 S, R 11 E). Altitude 4487 feet. Named on Hepsedam Peak (1969) 7.5' quadrangle.

Hepsedam Spring [SAN BENITO]: *spring,* 11.5 miles east-southeast of Bitterwater (lat. 36°18'20" N, long. 120°49'05" W; sec. 6, T 19 S, R 11 E); the spring is 3500 feet south-southeast of the summit of Hepsedam Peak. Named on Hepsedam Peak (1969) 7.5' quadrangle. Called Box Spring on Hernandez Valley (1943) 15' quadrangle.

Hermon: see **Mount Hermon** [SANTA CRUZ].

Hernandez [SAN BENITO]: *locality,* 11 miles east of Bitterwater (lat. 36°22'30" N, long. 120°48' W; near W line sec. 8, T 18 S, R 11 E); the place is in Hernandez Valley. Named on Priest Valley (1915) 30' quadrangle. Postal authorities established Erie post office in 1874, moved it 1.5 miles northwest and changed the name to Hernandez in 1892; they moved it 1.5 miles southeast in 1896, moved it 1 mile north in 1904, and discontinued it in 1936—the name "Hernandez" commemorates Rafael Hernandez and Jesus Hernandez, farmers in the region in the 1870's (Salley, p. 70, 96). The name "Erie" was from Erie school district, where the post office was situated (Elliott and Moore, p. 153). Postal authorities established Rex post office 11.5 miles northwest of Erie post office in 1892 and discontinued in 1900 (Salley, p. 184).

Hernandez Reservoir [SAN BENITO]: *lake,* behind a dam on San Benito River 9 miles east of Bitterwater (lat. 36°23'45" N, long. 120°50'10" W; near N line sec. 1, T 18 S, R 10 E). Named on Hepsedam Peak (1969) and Hernandez Reservoir (1969) 7.5' quadrangles.

Hernandez Valley [SAN BENITO]: *valley,* 11.5 miles east of Bitterwater along San Benito River (lat. 36°22' N, long. 120°48' W). Named on Hernandez Valley (1957) 15' quadrangle. Water of Hernandez Reservoir now covers most of the valley.

Hester Creek [SANTA CRUZ]: *stream,* flows 4 miles to West Branch Soquel Creek 5 miles north-northeast of Soquel (lat. 37°03'20" N, long. 121°56'25" W; sec. 14, T 10 S, R 1 W). Named on Laurel (1955) 7.5' quadrangle. The name commemorates Craven P. Hester, a landowner in the neighborhood in the 1850's (Clark, 1986, p. 151).

Hewitt Valley [MONTEREY]: *valley,* drained by a stream that flows 1.5 miles to Lynch Canyon 9 miles east-northeast of San Ardo (lat. 36°03' N, long. 120°44'35" W; near W line sec. 1, T 22 S, R 11 E). Named on Slack Canyon (1969) 7.5' quadrangle.

Hiawatha Campground [SANTA BARBARA]: *locality,* 11 miles west-northwest of McPherson Peak along South Fork La Brea Creek (lat. 34°56'15" N, long. 120°00' W). Named on Bates Canyon (1964) 7.5' quadrangle.

Hicks' Ford: see **Ben Lomond** [SANTA CRUZ].

Hidalgo Canyon [MONTEREY]: *canyon,* drained by a stream that flows 2.5 miles to Peachtree Canyon 10 miles east-northeast of San Ardo (lat. 36°05'45" N, long. 120°45'25" W; near S line sec. 14, T 21 S, R 11 E). Named on Monarch Peak (1967) and Pancho Rico Valley (1967) 7.5' quadrangles.

Hidden Beach: see **China Cove** [MONTEREY].

Hidden Potrero [SANTA BARBARA]: *area,* 2.5 miles south of Little Pine Mountain (lat. 34°33'50" N, long. 119°44'30" W). Named on Little Pine Mountain (1964) 7.5' quadrangle.

Hidden Spring [SAN BENITO]: *spring,* 6.5 miles east-southeast of Bitterwater (lat. 36°20'35" N, long. 120°53'25" W; sec. 21, T 18 S, R 10 E). Named on Lonoak (1969) 7.5' quadrangle.

Hidden Spring [SANTA BARBARA]: *spring,* 4.25 miles west of McPherson Peak (lat. 34°54'10" N, long. 119°53'10" W). Named on Bates Canyon (1964) 7.5' quadrangle.

Hidden Valley [MONTEREY]: *valley,* 18 miles east of San Ardo on upper reaches of Wayland Creek (lat. 36°02' N, long. 120°34'45" W). Named on Smith Mountain (1969) 7.5' quadrangle.

Hidden Valley Hot Springs: see **Ontario Hot Springs** [SAN LUIS OBISPO].

Hiding Canyon [MONTEREY]: *canyon,* drained by a stream that flows nearly 2 miles to Carmel River 2 miles north of Ventana Cone (lat. 36°18'50" N, long. 121°40'40" W; near S line sec. 32, T 18 S, R 3 E). Named on Ventana Cones (1956) 7.5' quadrangle.

Hiding Canyon Camp [MONTEREY]: *locality,* 2.5 miles north of Ventana Cone along Carmel River (lat. 36°19'15" N, long. 121°41'05" W; sec. 31, T 18 S, R 3 W); the place is less than 1 mile northwest of the mouth of Hiding Canyon. Named on Ventana Cones (1956) 7.5' quadrangle.

Higgins Camp [MONTEREY]: *locality,* 8 miles southwest of Tassajara Hot Springs (lat. 36°10'45" N, long. 121°36'15" W; sec. 23, T 20 S, R 3 E); the place is along an upper branch of Higgins Creek. Named on Tassajara Hot Springs (1956) 7.5' quadrangle.

Higgins Creek [MONTEREY]: *stream,* flows nearly 5 miles to Lost Valley Creek 5.25 miles south of Tassajara Hot Springs (lat. 36° 09'25" N, long. 121°33'35" W; sec. 29, T 20 S, R 4 E). Named on Tassajara Hot Springs (1956) 7.5' quadrangle.

Highland: see **Laurel** [SANTA CRUZ].

Higuera: see **Juan Higuera Creek** [MONTEREY].

Hihn Mill: see **Logan Creek** [SANTA CRUZ].

Hihn Spur: see **Aptos Creek** [SANTA CRUZ].

Hildreth Peak [SANTA BARBARA]: *peak,* 10.5 miles east of Little Pine Mountain (lat. 34°36' N, long. 119°33'05" W). Altitude 5065 feet. Named on Hildreth Peak (1964) 7.5' quadrangle.

Hill: see **Mary Hill Mineral Well**, under **Paso Robles** [SAN LUIS OBISPO]; **Wayland Creek** [MONTEREY].

Hilltown: see **Old Hilltown** [MONTEREY].

Hilton Canyon [SANTA BARBARA]: *canyon,* drained by a stream that flows 4 miles to Santa Ynez River 4 miles north of Santa Ynez Peak (lat. 34°35'15" N, long. 119°59'10" W). Named on Lake Cachuma (1959) 7.5' quadrangle. Called Rock Canyon on Santa Ynez (1905) 30' quadrangle, but United States Board on Geographic Names (1962a, p. 12) rejected this name for the feature.

Hi Mountain [SAN LUIS OBISPO]: *peak,* 4 miles southwest of Pozo (lat. 35°15'35" N, long. 120°25'25" W; near N line sec. 1, T 31 S, R 14 E). Altitude 3198 feet. Named on Santa Margarita Lake (1967) 7.5' quadrangle.

Hi Mountain Campground [SAN LUIS OBISPO]: *locality,* 3.5 miles southwest of Pozo (lat. 35°15'40" N, long. 120°24'50" W; near S line sec. 31, T 30 S, R 15 E); the place is 0.5 mile east of Hi Mountain. Named on Santa Margarita Lake (1967) 7.5' quadrangle.

Hi Mountain Potrero [SAN LUIS OBISPO]: *area,* 4 miles southwest of Pozo (lat. 35°16'05" N, long. 120°25'45" W; sec. 36, T 30 S, R 14 E); the place is 0.5 mile north-northwest of Hi Mountain. Named on Santa Margarita Lake (1967) 7.5' quadrangle.

Hi Mountain Spring [SAN LUIS OBISPO]: *spring,* nearly 4 miles southwest of Pozo (lat. 35°15'35" N, long. 120°24'50" W; near N line sec. 6, T 31 S, R 15 E); the spring is 0.5 mile east of Hi Mountain. Named on Santa Margarita Lake (1967) 7.5' quadrangle.

Hinckley Creek [SANTA CRUZ]: *stream,* flows 4 miles to Soquel Creek 5 miles north-northeast of Soquel (lat. 37°03'20" N, long. 121°55'20" W); the stream is north of Hinckley Ridge. Named on Laurel (1955) and Loma Prieta (1955) 7.5' quadrangles. The name commemorates Roger Gibson Hinkley, who settled in the neighborhood about 1854 (Clark, 1986, p. 156-157).

Hinckley Ridge [SANTA CRUZ]: *ridge,* west- to west-southwest-trending, 2.5 miles long, 5.5 miles northeast of Soquel (lat. 37°03'15" N, long. 121°53'45" W); the ridge is south of Hinckley Creek. Named on Laurel (1955) 7.5' quadrangle.

Hinns Sulphur Spring: see **Olive Springs** [SANTA CRUZ].

Hitchcock Canyon [MONTEREY]: *canyon,* drained by a stream that flows 3.5 miles to Carmel River at the town of Carmel Valley (lat. 36°28'25" N, long. 121°43'30" W). Named on Carmel Valley (1956) and Mount Carmel (1956) 7.5' quadrangles. The name commemorates Joe Hitchcock, who lived in the canyon (Fink, p. 199).

Hi Valley [SAN LUIS OBISPO]: *valley,* 5 miles southeast of Pozo (lat. 35°15' N, long. 120°25' W; on E line sec. 1, T 31 S, R 14 E); the valley is less than 1 mile south-southeast of Hi Mountain. Named on Santa Margarita Lake (1967) and Tar Spring Ridge (1967) 7.5' quadrangles.

Hoffman's Camp: see **Camp No. 5**, under **Bridge Creek** [SANTA CRUZ].

Hog Canyon [MONTEREY]:

(1) *canyon,* drained by a stream that flows 5 miles to Paris Valley 3.5 miles west-northwest of San Ardo (lat. 36°02' N, long. 120°58'10" W; sec. 11, T 22 S, R 9 E). Named on San Ardo (1967) 7.5' quadrangle.

(2) *canyon,* drained by a stream that flows 3.25 miles to Sargent Canyon 8 miles east of San Ardo (lat. 36°00'05" N, long. 120°45'30" W; sec. 23, T 22 S, R 11 E). Named on Pancho Rico Valley (1967) and Slack Canyon (1969) 7.5' quadrangles.

Hog Canyon [MONTEREY-SAN LUIS OBISPO]: *canyon,* drained by a stream that heads in Monterey County and flows 15 miles to Estrella Creek 7.5 miles northeast of Paso Robles in San Luis Obispo County (lat. 35°42'10" N long. 120°36'10" W; at NW cor. sec. 5, T 26 S, R 13 E). Named on Cholame Hills (1961) Estrella (1948), and Ranchito Canyon (1948) 7.5' quadrangles. Stanley (map on p. 18) called the feature Pleasant Valley.

Hog Hole [SAN BENITO]: *relief feature,* 14 miles east-southeast of Bitterwater (lat. 36°18'05" N, long. 120°46'25" W; sec. 4, T 19 S, R 11 E). Named on Hepsedam Peak (1969) 7.5' quadrangle, which shows two small intermittent lakes at the place.

Hog Pen Spring [SANTA BARBARA]: *spring,* 1.5 miles east-southeast of McPherson Peak (lat. 34°52'45" N, long. 119°47'10" W). Named on Peak Mountain (1964) 7.5' quadrangle.

Hog Pen Spring: see **Upper Hog Pen Spring** [SANTA BARBARA].

Hog's Back: see **Paradise Park** [SANTA CRUZ].

Hogs Canyon [MONTEREY]: *canyon,* drained by a stream that flows nearly 1 mile to lowlands 5 miles west of Greenfield (lat. 36°18'55" N, long. 121°19'45" W). Named on Paraiso Springs (1956) 7.5' quadrangle.

Hole: see **The Hole** [SAN BENITO].

Holland Canyon [SAN LUIS OBISPO]: *canyon,* drained by a stream that flows 5 miles to San Juan Valley 10.5 miles southeast of Shandon (lat. 35°32'55" N, long. 120°14'10" W; sec. 27, T 27 S, R 16 E). Named on Holland Canyon (1961) 7.5' quadrangle.

Hollins Hot Springs: see **Dolans Hot Spring**, under **Big Creek** [MONTEREY] (2).

Hollister [SAN BENITO]: *town,* near the northwest end of San Benito County (lat. 36°51'05" N, long. 121°24'05" W). Named on Hollister (1955) 7.5' quadrangle. San Justo Homestead Association bought 21,000 acres of San Justo grant from W.W. Hollister in 1868 and laid out a town that they named for the former owner of the land (Pierce, p. 103). Postal authorities established Hollister post office in 1869 (Frickstad, p. 136), and the town incorporated in 1874.

Hollister Peak [SAN LUIS OBISPO]: *peak,* 5 miles east-southeast of Morro Rock (lat. 35°20'40" N, long. 120°47'10" W). Named on Morro Bay South (1965) 7.5' quadrangle. United States Coast Survey personnel gave the name in 1884 for the Hollister family, ranchers at the base of the peak, which also was known as Cerro Alto and Morro Twin (Gudde, 1949, p. 151).

Honda [SANTA BARBARA]: *locality,* 3 miles north-northeast of Point Arguello along Southern Pacific Railroad (lat. 34°36'55" N, long. 120°37'55" W); the place is 0.5 mile north-northeast of the mouth of La Honda Canyon. Named on Point Arguello (1959) 7.5' quadrangle.

Honda Valley [SANTA BARBARA]: *canyon,* 1.25 miles long, 1 mile south-southwest of downtown Santa Barbara (lat. 34°24'20" N, long. 119°42'20" W). Named on Santa Barbara (1952) 7.5' quadrangle.

Honeymoon Flat [SANTA BARBARA]: *area,* 4 miles west-northwest of Zaca Lake (lat. 34°47'50" N, long. 120°06'30" W). Named on Zaca Lake (1964) 7.5' quadrangle.

Hope Ranch [SANTA BARBARA]:

(1) *locality,* 4 miles east of Goleta along Southern Pacific Railroad (lat. 34°26'15" N, long. 119°45'15" W); the place is at the north edge of Hope Ranch district. Named on Goleta (1950) 7.5' quadrangle. Called Irma on Goleta (1903) 15' quadrangle.

(2) *district,* 4 miles west of downtown Santa Barbara (lat. 34°25'20" N, long. 119°46' W). Named on Goleta (1950) 7.5' quadrangle. Thomas W. Hope bought part of Las Positas y La Calera grant in 1870 and called the property Hope Ranch; Hope's heirs subdivided the land (Gudde, 1949, p. 153).

Hopkins Gulch [SANTA CRUZ]: *canyon,* drained by a stream that flows 1 mile to Bear Creek 1.5 miles east-northeast of the town of Boulder Creek (lat. 37°08'10" N, long. 122°05'55" W; sec. 20, T 9 S, R 2 W). Named on Castle Rock Ridge (1955) 7.5' quadrangle.

Hopkins Ridge [MONTEREY]: *ridge,* west-southwest-trending, 1 mile long, 7 miles east-southeast of Point Sur (lat. 36°16'05" N, long. 121°46'45" W). Named on Big Sur (1956) 7.5' quadrangle.

Hopper Canyon [SAN LUIS OBISPO]: *canyon,* drained by a stream that flows 2.5 miles to lowlands along Estrella River nearly 1 mile north-northwest of Shandon (lat. 35°40' N, long. 120°22'15" W; near W line sec. 16, T 26 S, R 15 E). Named on Cholame (1961) 7.5' quadrangle.

Horse Canyon [MONTEREY]: *canyon,* drained by Horse Creek, which flows 7.5 miles to Arroyo Seco (1) 11 miles west-southwest of Greenfield (lat. 36°15'10" N, long. 121°24'55" W; sec. 27, T 19 S, R 5 E). Named on Junipero Serra Peak (1949) and Reliz Canyon (1949) 7.5' quadrangles. Clark (1991, p. 222) reported an account that attributed the name to stolen horses left in the canyon by Tiburcio Vasquez, the outlaw.

Horse Canyon [SAN LUIS OBISPO]: *canyon,* drained by a stream that flows 4.25 miles to Cuyama Valley 2.5 miles north of New Cuyama [SANTA BARBARA] (lat. 34°58'55" N, long. 119°41'10" W; sec. 5, T 10 N, R 26 W). Named on New Cuyama (1964) 7.5' quadrangle.

Horse Canyon [SANTA BARBARA]:

(1) *canyon,* drained by a stream that flows 10.5 miles to Sisquoc River 4 miles north-northeast of Zaca Lake (lat. 34°50'05" N, long. 120°01'05" W). Named on Bald Mountain (1964), Bates Canyon (1964), and Zaca Lake (1964) 7.5' quadrangles. Called Horse Gulch on Lompoc (1905) 30' quadrangle.

(2) *canyon,* drained by a stream that flows 2.5 miles to Santa Ynez River 6.25 miles south-southwest of Hildreth Peak (lat. 34°30'50" N, long. 119°35'25" W). Named on Hildreth Peak (1964) 7.5' quadrangle.

(3) *canyon,* drained by a stream that flows nearly 7 miles to Lake Cachuma 5.25 miles east-northeast of Santa Ynez Peak (lat. 34° 33'55" N, long. 119°53'45" W). Named on Lake Cachuma (1959) and San Marcos Pass (1959) 7.5' quadrangles.

Horse Canyon: see **Upper Horse Canyon** [SANTA BARBARA].

Horse Creek [MONTEREY]: *stream,* flows 7.5 miles to Arroyo Seco (1) 11 miles west-southwest of Greenfield (lat. 36°15'10" N, long. 121°24'55" W; sec. 27, T 19 S, R 5 E); the stream drains Horse Canyon. Named on Sycamore Flat (1956) 7.5' quadrangle.

Horse Gulch: see **Horse Canyon** [SANTA BARBARA] (1).

Horse Mesa [SAN LUIS OBISPO]: *area,* 2 miles southwest of Pozo (lat. 35°17'10" N, long. 120°24'10" W; sec. 30, T 30 S, R 15 E). Named on Santa Margarita Lake (1967) 7.5' quadrangle.

Horse Pasture: see **Horse Pasture Camp** [MONTEREY].

Horse Pasture Camp [MONTEREY]: *locality,* nearly 1 mile northeast of Tassajara Hot Springs (lat. 36°14'25" N, long. 121°32'30" W; sec. 33, T 19 S, R 4 E). Named on Tassajara Hot Springs (1956) 7.5' quadrangle. Lucia (1921) 15' quadrangle has the name "Horse Pasture" at the place. A fenced horse pasture was at the site originally (Clark, 1991, p. 222).

Horse Potrero [SANTA BARBARA]: *area,* 3 miles east of Salisbury Potrero (lat. 34°49'40" N, long. 119°38'40" W). Named on Salisbury Potrero (1964) 7.5' quadrangle.

Horse Run [MONTEREY]: *stream,* flows 2.25 miles to Arroyo Seco (1) 6.25 miles north-northwest of Junipero Serra Peak (lat. 36° 14' N, long. 121°27'10" W; sec. 32, T 19 S, R 5 E). Named on Junipero Serra Peak (1949) 7.5' quadrangle.

Horseshoe Canyon [SANTA BARBARA]: *canyon,* drained by a stream that flows 2.25 miles to Pine Canyon (1) 5.5 miles west-southwest of Miranda Pine Mountain (lat. 35°00'10" N, long. 120° 07'50" W). Named on Manzanita Mountain (1964) 7.5' quadrangle.

Horseshoe Spring [SANTA BARBARA]: *spring,* 7.5 miles north-northwest of Manzanita Mountain (lat. 34°59'50" N, long. 120°07'05" W); the spring is in Horseshoe Canyon. Named on Manzanita Mountain (1964) 7.5' quadrangle.

Hospital Lake [SAN LUIS OBISPO]: *lake,* 1850 feet long, nearly 4 miles south-southwest of downtown Arroyo Grande near the coast (lat. 35°04'20" N, long. 120°36'40" W). Named on Oceano (1965) 7.5' quadrangle.

Hot Spring [SANTA BARBARA]: *spring,* 5.5 miles east of Santa Ynez Peak (lat. 34°32'15" N, long. 119°52'50" W; near SE cor. sec. 2, T 5 N, R 29 W). Named on Lake Cachuma (1959) 7.5' quadrangle. Berkstresser (p. A-

16) called the feature San Marcos Hot Springs, and gave the names "Mountain Glen Hot Springs" and "Cuyama Hot Springs" as alternates.

Hot Spring Canyon [SANTA BARBARA]: *canyon,* drained by a stream that flows 3 miles to Santa Ynez River 6 miles east-northeast of Santa Ynez Peak (lat. 34°33'20" N, long. 119°52'45" W); Hot Spring is in the canyon. Named on Lake Cachuma (1959) 7.5' quadrangle.

Hot Spring Canyon: see **Hot Springs Canyon** [SANTA BARBARA].

Hot Springs [SANTA BARBARA]:

(1) *spring,* 8 miles south of Buellton (lat. 34°30'10" N, long. 120° 13'05" W); the feature is 0.5 mile southeast of Las Cruces (2). Named on Solvang (1959) 7.5' quadrangle. Berkstresser (p. A-16) called the feature Gaviota Hot Springs, and gave the names "Las Cruces Hot Springs" and "Las Cruces Sulphur Springs" as alternates.

(2) *springs,* 4.5 miles northeast of downtown Santa Barbara (lat. 34°27'45" N, long. 119°38'20" W; near NE cor. sec. 6, T 4 N, R 26 W). Named on Santa Barbara (1952) 7.5' quadrangle. Berkstresser (p. A-15) called the feature Montecito Hot Springs, gave the name "Santa Barbara Hot Springs" as an alternate, and listed the names "Lower Barn Springs," "Upper Barn Springs," "Arsenic Springs," and "Cliff Springs" for elements of the group. Crawford (1896, p. 517) called the place Santa Barbara Hot Sulphur Springs.

Hot Springs: see **Paso Robles** [SAN LUIS OBISPO].

Hot Springs Canyon [MONTEREY]: *canyon,* drained by a stream that flows 3 miles to the sea 8 miles north-northwest of Lopez Point (lat. 36°07'25" N, long. 121°38'20" W; sec. 9, T 21 S, R 3 E); the mouth of the canyon is 850 feet northwest of Slates Hot Springs. Named on Partington Ridge (1956) and Tassajara Hot Springs (1956) 7.5' quadrangles.

Hot Springs Canyon [SANTA BARBARA]: *canyon,* drained by a stream that flows 2 miles to Montecito Creek 3 miles east-northeast of downtown Santa Barbara (lat. 34°26'35" N, long. 119°39' W); Hot Springs (2) are in the canyon. Named on Santa Barbara (1952) 7.5' quadrangle. Called Hot Spring Canyon on Santa Barbara (1903) 15' quadrangle, but United States Board on Geographic Names (1961b, p. 10) rejected this form for the name.

Hot Springs Creek [SANTA BARBARA]: *stream,* flows 1 mile to Las Canovas Creek 7.5 miles south of Buellton (lat. 34°30'20" N, long. 120°13'20" W); Hot Springs (1) is along the stream. Named on Solvang (1959) 7.5' quadrangle.

Hot Springs Landing: see **Andersen Landing** [MONTEREY].

Howard Canyon [SANTA BARBARA]: *canyon,* drained by a stream that flows 3.5 miles to Los Alamos Valley 7 miles south of the village of Sisquoc (lat. 34°45'45" N, long. 120°17'35" W). Named on Sisquoc (1959) 7.5' quadrangle.

Howell Rock [SAN LUIS OBISPO]: *shoal,* 1.5 miles south of Avila Beach in San Luis Obispo Bay (lat. 35°09'30" N, long. 120°43'35" W). Named on Pismo Beach (1965) 7.5' quadrangle.

Huasna [SAN LUIS OBISPO]:

(1) *land grant,* 20 miles southeast of San Luis Obispo; covers Huasna Valley and much of the drainage areas of Huasna River and Huasna Creek. Named on Caldwell Mesa (1967), Huasna Peak (1967), Nipomo (1965), and Tar Spring Ridge (1967) 7.5' quadrangles. Isaac J. Sparks received 5 leagues in 1843 and claimed 22,153 acres patented in 1879 (Cowan, p. 40). The name apparently is from the designation of an Indian village (Kroeber, 1916, p. 43).

(2) *locality,* 7.25 miles northeast of the town of Nipomo (lat. 35°07'20" N, long. 120°23'35" W); the place is along Huasna Creek on Huasna grant. Named on Nipomo (1965) 7.5' quadrangle. Postal authorities established Huasna post office in 1889 and discontinued it in 1910 (Salley, p. 101).

Huasna Creek [SAN LUIS OBISPO]: *stream,* flows 7.5 miles to Huasna River 3 miles north-northwest of Huasna Peak (lat. 35°04'50" N, long. 120°22'15" W). Named on Huasna Peak (1967), Nipomo (1965), and Tar Spring Ridge (1967) 7.5' quadrangles. The stream now enters Twitchell Reservoir.

Huasna Peak [SAN LUIS OBISPO]: *peak,* 7.5 miles east of Nipomo (lat. 35°02'10" N, long. 120°20'50" W; near W line sec. 15, T 11 N, R 33 W). Altitude 1902 feet. Named on Huasna Peak (1967) 7.5' quadrangle.

Huasna River [SAN LUIS OBISPO]: *stream,* formed by the confluence of Trout Creek (2) and Stony Creek, flows 18 miles to Cuyama River 9 miles east of the town of Nipomo (lat. 35° 00'55" N, long. 120°19'40" W). Named on Caldwell Mesa (1967) and Huasna Peak (1967) 7.5' quadrangles. Called Rio Wasna on Parke's (1854-1855) map. Parke (p. 6) also used the name "Wasna creek." Gudde (1949, p. 155) noted that the name "Arroyo del Huasna" appears on an early map. The stream now enters Twitchell Reservoir.

Huasna Valley [SAN LUIS OBISPO]: *valley,* 3 miles north-northwest of Huasna Peak along Huasna Creek and the lower part of Huasna River (lat. 35°05' N, long. 120°22' W). Named on Huasna Peak (1967) and Nipomo (1965) 7.5' quadrangles. Water of Twitchell Reservoir now floods part of the valley.

Hubbard Gulch [SANTA CRUZ]: *canyon,* drained by Marshall Creek, which flows 1.5 miles to San Lorenzo River 2.5 miles south-southeast of the town of Boulder Creek (lat. 37°05'30" N, long. 122°05'35" W; near W line sec. 4, T 10 S, R 2 W). Named on Felton (1955) 7.5' quadrangle.

Hubbard Hill [SAN LUIS OBISPO]: *peak,* nearly 4 miles northwest of Freeborn Mountain (lat. 35°19'30" N, long. 120°06'05" W; sec. 12, T 30 S, R 17 E). Altitude 1966 feet. Named on California Valley (1966) 7.5' quadrangle.

Huckleberry Hill [MONTEREY]:

(1) *hill,* 3.5 miles south of Point Pinos (lat. 36°35'10" N, long. 121° 55'15" W). Named on Monterey (1947) 7.5' quadrangle.

(2) *peak,* 2 miles east-southeast of Point Lobos (lat. 36°30'40" N, long. 121°55'10" W; sec. 25, T 16 S, R 1 W). Altitude 932 feet. Named on Monterey (1947) 7.5' quadrangle.

Hudson Canyon [SANTA BARBARA]: *canyon,* drained by a stream that flows 3 miles to Tepusquet Canyon 2.5 miles west of Tepusquet Peak (lat. 34°54'15" N, long. 120°13'45" W). Named on Tepusquet Canyon (1964) 7.5' quadrangle.

Huerfano: see **Huerhuero** [SAN LUIS OBISPO].

Huer Huero: see **Creston** [SAN LUIS OBISPO]; **Huerhuero** [SAN LUIS OBISPO].

Huerhuero [SAN LUIS OBISPO]: *land grant,* 12 miles southeast of Paso Robles along Huerhuero Creek. Named on Creston (1948), Santa Margarita (1965), Shedd Canyon (1961), and Wilson Corner (1966) 7.5' quadrangles. Jose Mariano Bonilla received 1 league in 1842 and 1844; Francis Z. Branch claimed 15,685 acres patented in 1866 (Cowan, p. 40; Cowan gave the name "Huerfano" as an alternate). Angel (1883, p. 215) used the form "Huer-Huero" for the name, but United States Board on Geographic Names (1933, p. 377) rejected the forms "Huer Huero," "Huer-Huero," and "Huero Huero." According to Gudde (1949, p. 156), the name may be from a place called Huergüero as early as 1843, and may be related to *huero,* which means "putrid," or "rotten," in Mexican Spanish—perhaps referring to the odor of sulphur water.

Huer-Huero Creek: see **Huerhuero Creek** [SAN LUIS OBISPO].

Huerhuero Creek [SAN LUIS OBISPO]: *stream,* formed by the confluence of East Branch and Middle Branch at Creston, flows 21 miles to Salinas River 3 miles north of Paso Robles (lat. 35°40'30" N, long. 120°41'10" W; sec. 9, T 26 S, R 12 E). Named on Creston (1948), Estrella (1948), and Paso Robles (1948) 7.5' quadrangles. Called Rio de la Sta. Isabel on Parke's (1854-1855) map. Franke (p. 457) mentioned Huer-Huero creek. United States Board on Geographic Names (1933, p. 377) rejected the forms "Huer-Huero Creek," "Huer Huero Creek," and "Huero Huero Creek" for the name. East Branch is 10.5 miles long and Middle Branch is 15 miles long; both branches are named on Creston (1948), Santa Margarita (1965), and Wilson Corner (1966) 7.5' quadrangles. West Branch enters 18 miles upstream from the mouth of the main creek; it is 8.5 miles long and is named on Creston (1948) and Santa Margarita (1965) 7.5' quadrangles.

Huer Huero Springs: see **Iron Spring** [SAN LUIS OBISPO] (1)

Huero Huero: see **Huerhuero** [SAN LUIS OBISPO].

Huero Huero Creek: see **Huerhuero Creek** [SAN LUIS OBISPO].

Huerta de la Nacion: see **Noche Buena** [MONTEREY].

Huerta de Romaldo: see **Huerta de Romualdo** [SAN LUIS OBISPO].

Huerta de Romualdo [SAN LUIS OBISPO]: *land grant,* 4.5 miles northwest of downtown San Luis Obispo along Chorro Creek. Named on San Luis Obispo (1965) 7.5' quadrangle. Romaldo, an Indian, received 0.1 league in 1842; John Wilson claimed 117 acres patented in 1871 (Cowan, p. 27; Cowan listed the grant under the designation "Chorro (or) Huerta de Romaldo"). Perez (p. 69) gave 1846 as the date of the grant.

Huffman: see **Camp Huffman** [MONTEREY].

Huffs Hole [SAN LUIS OBISPO]: *relief feature,* 15 miles north of the town of Nipomo (lat. 35°14'50" N, long. 120°26' W; near NW cor. sec. 12, T 31 S, R 14 E). Named on Tar Spring Ridge (1967) 7.5' quadrangle.

Huffs Hole Creek [SAN LUIS OBISPO]: *stream,* flows nearly 5 miles to Wittenberg Creek 12 miles north of the town of Nipomo (lat. 35°12'50" N, long. 120°27'25" W; sec. 22, T 31 S, R 14 E); one branch of the stream heads at Huffs Hole. Named on Tar Spring Ridge (1967) 7.5' quadrangle.

Hughes Canyon [SAN LUIS OBISPO]: *canyon,* drained by a stream that flows 5.5 miles to San Juan Valley 10 miles southeast of Shandon (lat. 35°33'25" N, long. 120°15'20" W; near N line sec. 28, T 27 S, R 16 E). Named on Camatta Canyon (1961) and Holland Canyon (1961) 7.5' quadrangles.

Hughes Creek [SANTA CRUZ]: *stream,* flows 2.25 miles to Pajaro Valley 4 miles north-northeast of Watsonville (lat. 36°58'25" N, long. 121°44'05" W). Named on Watsonville East (1955) 7.5' quadrangle.

Hughes Spring [SAN LUIS OBISPO]: *spring,* 8 miles east-southeast of Shandon (lat. 35°37' N, long. 120°14'05" W; sec. 34, T 26 S, R 16 E); the spring is in the upper part of Hughes Canyon. Named on Holland Canyon (1961) 7.5' quadrangle.

Hungry Flats: see **Lockwood** [MONTEREY].

Hungryman Gulch [SANTA BARBARA]: *canyon,* less than 0.5 mile long, 0.5 mile west of San Pedro Point at the east end of Santa Cruz Island (lat. 34°02' N, long. 119°31'35" W). Named on Santa Cruz Island D (1943) 7.5' quadrangle.

Hunter Liggett Military Reservation [MONTEREY]: *military installation,* covers a large area in and near Santa Lucia Range southwest of King City, mainly in the upper San Antonio River drainage area. Named on San Luis Obispo (1956) and Santa Cruz (1956) 1°x 2° quadrangles. Called Camp Hunter Liggett Military Reservation on Bryson (1942) 15' quadrangle. The installation, which started in 1941, now is called Fort Hunter Liggett; the name honors Major General Hunter Liggett, who commanded a corps in World War I (Clark, 1991, p. 170).

Hunter Spring [SAN LUIS OBISPO]: *spring,* 6.25 miles north-northeast of Pozo (lat. 35°23' N, long. 120°19'20" W; sec. 24, T 29 S, R 15 E). Named on Camatta Ranch (1966) 7.5' quadrangle.

Hunter Spring [SANTA BARBARA]: *spring,* 6.5 miles north of Zaca Lake in Alkali Canyon (lat. 34°52'15" N, long. 120°03'45" W). Named on Zaca Lake (1964) 7.5' quadrangle.

Hunt Spring [SAN LUIS OBISPO]: *spring,* 3 miles south-southeast of Branch Mountain (lat. 39°09'05" N, long. 120°04'05" W). Named on Branch Mountain (1967) 7.5' quadrangle.

Hurricane Deck [SANTA BARBARA]: *ridge,* west-northwest-trending, 4 miles long, 6 miles southwest of Montgomery Potrero (lat. 34°46' N, long. 119°49' W). Named on Hurricane Deck (1964) 7.5' quadrangle. The name is from high winds that are common on the ridge (Gudde, 1949, p. 157).

Hurricane Point [MONTEREY]: *promontory,* 3.5 miles north of Point Sur along the coast (lat. 36°21'25" N, long. 121°54'20" W; sec. 19, T 18 S, R 1 E). Named on Point Sur (1956) 7.5' quadrangle. The name is from strong winds at the place (Lussier, p. 16).

- I -

Idlewild: see **Little Sur River** [MONTEREY].

Idria [SAN BENITO]: *village,* 18 miles east of Bitterwater along San Carlos Creek (lat. 36°25' N, long. 120°40'20" W; sec. 29, T 17 S, R 12 E); New Idria mine is at the place. Named on Idria (1969) 7.5' quadrangle. New Idria (1943) 15' quadrangle has the names "New Idria" and "Idria P.O." at the site. United States Board on Geographic Names (1964, p. 14) rejected the name "New Idria," but noted that the place was named for New Idria quicksilver mine. Stewart (p. 218) pointed out that the name "Idria" is from the Italian form of the name of a city in former Yugoslavia that is famous for its quicksilver production. Postal authorities established New Idria post office in 1869 and discontinued it in 1894; they established Idria post office in 1894, discontinued it in 1934, reestablished it in 1938, and discontinued it in 1974 (Salley, p. 103). Brewer (p. 138-139) noted that a cluster of miners' tents and cabins called Centerville was situated south of Idria between New Idria mine and San Carlos mine.

Idria Peak [SAN BENITO]: *peak,* 1.5 miles south-southwest of Idria (lat. 36°23'50" N, long. 120°41'15" W; near SE cor. sec. 31, T 17 S, R 12 E). Altitude 4655 feet. Named on Idria (1969) 7.5' quadrangle.

Impossible Canyon [MONTEREY]: *canyon,* 2.5 miles long, 5 miles east of Seaside (lat. 36°36'30" N, long. 121°45'40" W); the canyon is west of Impossible Ridge. Named on Seaside (1947) 7.5' quadrangle.

Impossible Ridge [MONTEREY]: *ridge,* north- to northeast-trending, nearly 1 mile long, 6 miles east of Seaside (lat. 36°36'20" N, long. 121°45'20" W); the ridge is east of Impossible Canyon. Named on Seaside (1947) 7.5' quadrangle.

Imusdale: see **Parkfield** [MONTEREY].

Indian Canyon [SAN BENITO]: *canyon,* drained by a stream that flows 1.5 miles to Grass Valley 5 miles west of Paicines (lat. 36° 43'10" N, long. 121°22' W). Named on Paicines (1968) 7.5' quadrangle.

Indian Creek [SAN LUIS OBISPO]:

(1) *stream,* flows nearly 3 miles to Estrella River 6 miles west of Shandon (lat. 35°38'45" N, long. 120°28'45" W; near SE cor. sec. 20, T 26 S, R 14 E). Named on Shandon (1961) and Shedd Canyon (1961) 7.5' quadrangles.

(2) *stream,* flows 10 miles to Shedd Canyon 9 miles south of Shandon (lat. 35°31'45" N, long. 120°24'25" W; sec. 31, T 27 S, R 15 E). Named on Shedd Canyon (1961) and Wilson Corner (1966) 7.5' quadrangles.

Indian Creek [SANTA BARBARA]: *stream,* flows 16 miles to Mono Creek 7.5 miles southeast of Little Pine Mountain (lat. 34°32' N, long. 119°37'55" W). Named on Big Pine Mountain (1964) and Little Pine Mountain (1964) 7.5' quadrangles.

Indian Creek: see **San Antonio River, North Fork** [MONTEREY].

Indian Creek Campground [SANTA BARBARA]: *locality,* 3.5 miles east of Little Pine Mountain (lat. 34°36'40" N, long. 119°40'25" W); the place is along Indian Creek. Named on Little Pine Mountain (1964) 7.5' quadrangle.

Indian Head Beach [MONTEREY]: *beach,* between Seaside and Marina along the coast (lat. 36°40' N, long. 121°49'10" W). Named on Marina (1947) 7.5' quadrangle.

Indian Head Rock [SANTA BARBARA]: *rock,* at Point Conception (lat. 34°26'55" N, long. 120°28'10" W). Named on Point Conception (1953) 7.5' quadrangle.

Indian Knob [SAN LUIS OBISPO]: *peak,* 4.25 miles east-northeast of Avila Beach (lat. 35°11'55" N, long. 120°39'30" W). Altitude 887 feet. Named on Pismo Beach (1965) 7.5' quadrangle.

Indians: see **The Indians** [MONTEREY].

Indian Spring [MONTEREY]: *spring,* 1.5 miles east-northeast of the center of Priest Valley (lat. 36°11'50" N, long. 120°40'10" W; near NW cor. sec. 15, T 20 S, R 12 E). Named on Priest Valley (1969) 7.5' quadrangle.

Indian Valley [MONTEREY]:

(1) *area,* 5.25 miles southwest of Tassajara Hot Springs on upper reaches of Higgins Creek (lat. 36°10'50" N, long. 121°37'10" W; sec. 22, T 20 S, R 3 E). Named on Tassajara Hot Springs (1956) 7.5' quadrangle.

(2) *area,* 7 miles west of Greenfield at Paraiso Springs (lat. 36° 20' N, long. 121°22' W; near W line sec. 30, T 18 S, R 6 E). Named on Paraiso Springs (1956) 7.5' quadrangle.

(3) *canyon,* 20 miles long, lower part drained by Big Sandy Creek, which reaches Salinas River 6.5 miles southeast of Bradley (lat. 35°47'30" N, long. 120°43'30" W; near SW cor. sec. 31, T 24 S, R 12 E). Named on San Miguel (1948), Slack Canyon (1969), and Valleton (1948) 7.5' quadrangles. The upper part of the canyon is drained by a tributary of Big Sandy Creek. California Mining Bureau's (1917b) map shows a place called Pope located along a railroad about 10 miles northeast of Bradley where Big Sandy Creek enters Indian Valley.

Indian Valley [SAN BENITO]: *valley,* 4 miles northeast of Panoche on San Benito-Fresno County line (lat. 36°37'55" N, long. 120° 47' W; around SE cor. sec. 8, T 15 S, R 4 E). Named on Mercey Hot Springs (1969) 7.5' quadrangle.

Indian Valley Creek: see **Big Sandy Creek** [MONTEREY].

Inez: see **Goleta** [SANTA BARBARA].

Ingalls Station: see **Swanton** [SANTA CRUZ].

Inspiration Point [SANTA CRUZ]: *locality,* 9.5 miles north of Soquel (lat. 37°07'20" N, long. 121°58'20" W). Named on Laurel (1955) 7.5' quadrangle.

Inspiration Point: see **Rincon** [SANTA CRUZ].

Intermediate Point: see **Point Joe** [MONTEREY].

Ionata: see **Solvang** [SANTA BARBARA].

Iremel [SANTA BARBARA]: *locality,* 4.25 miles southeast of the town of Guadalupe along Santa Maria Valley Railroad (lat. 34°55'25" N, long. 120°31'35" W). Named on Guadalupe (1959) 7.5' quadrangle.

Irish Canyon: see **Little Irish Canyon**, under **Deer Canyon** [SAN LUIS OBISPO] (1); **Vineyard Canyon** [SAN LUIS OBISPO].

Irish Hills [SAN LUIS OBISPO]: *range,* west of San Luis Obispo Creek between Los Osos Valley and the sea. Named on Morro Bay South (1965), Pismo Beach (1965), Port San Luis (1965), and San Luis Obispo (1965) 7.5' quadrangles. Called San Luis Range on Cayucos (1897) 15' quadrangle. H.R. Wagner (p. 378) noted the early names "Monte de Buchon" and "Sierra de Buchon" for the range. Vancouver (p. 142) in 1793 referred to Mountain del Buchon and Mount del Buchon. Angel (1883, p. 323) mentioned the names "Monte de Buchon" and "Mount Buchon," and later (1890c, p. 570) considered the name "Buchon Range" as appropriate. Harder (p. 20) referred to "the San Luis Range or Los Osos Mountains." United States Coast and Geodetic Survey (p. 115) called the range Mount Buchon, and described it as "a rugged mountain mass between San Luis Obispo Bay, Estero Bay, and the valley of San Luis Obispo." United States Board on Geographic Names (1995, p. 5) rejected both the names "Mount Buchon" and "San Luis Range" for the feature.

Irma: see **Hope Ranch** [SANTA BARBARA] (1).

Iron Spring [SAN LUIS OBISPO]:

(1) *spring:* 7 miles northeast of Santa Margarita (lat. 35°27'55" N, long. 120°31'20" W; sec. 25, T 28 S, R 13 E). Named on Santa Margarita (1965) 7.5' quadrangle. G.A. Waring (p. 277) described this spring under the name "New Springs," and described another spring located about 2 miles farther north under the name "Old Spring"; he noted that New Spring was used by campers and that the area around Old Spring was used as a summer campground—Old Spring also was the site of Keunard German settlement. Waring referred to the two springs collectively as Huer Huero Springs.

(2) *spring,* 0.5 mile west-northwest of Branch Mountain (lat. 35° 11'15" N, long. 120°05'35" W; near W line sec. 31, T 31 S, R 18 E). Named on Branch Mountain (1967) 7.5' quadrangle.

Iron Springs [MONTEREY]: *springs,* 8 miles east of San Ardo in Lynch Canyon (lat. 36°02'40" N, long. 120°45'40" W; sec. 3, T 22 S, R 11 E). Named on Pancho Rico Valley (1967) 7.5' quadrangle.

Isla Capitana: see **San Miguel Island** [SANTA BARBARA].

Isla de Baxos: see **Richardson Rock** [SANTA BARBARA].

Isla de Gente Barbudo: see **Santa Cruz Island** [SANTA BARBARA].

Isla de Juan Rodrigues: see **San Miguel Island** [SANTA BARBARA].

Isla de Lobos: see **Richardson Rock** [SANTA BARBARA].

Island: see **The Island**, under **Aptos Creek** [SANTA CRUZ].

Island Mountain [MONTEREY]: *peak,* nearly 3 miles west-southwest of Ventana Cone (lat. 36°15'55" N, long. 121°43'25" W; near E line sec. 22, T 19 S, R 2 E). Named on Ventana Cones (1956) 7.5' quadrangle.

Isla Posesion: see **San Miguel Island** [SANTA BARBARA].

Isla San Ambrosio: see **Santa Rosa Island** [SANTA BARBARA].

Isla San Sebastian: see **Santa Cruz Island** [SANTA BARBARA].

Islas de San Lucas: see **San Miguel Island** [SANTA BARBARA]; **Santa Cruz Island** [SANTA BARBARA]; **Santa Rosa Island** [SANTA BARBARA].

Islay Creek [SAN LUIS OBISPO]: *stream*, flows 7.5 miles to the sea 6.5 miles south of Morro Rock (lat. 35°16'35" N, long. 120°53'15" W). Named on Morro Bay South (1965) 7.5' quadrangle. The name is from an Indian word for the so-called hollyleaf cherry (Gudde, 1949, p. 162). G.A. Waring (p. 69) described Pecho Warm Springs, two springs located in the canyon of Islay Creek about 2 miles from the coast; the warm sulphureted water of the springs was used for drinking and bathing

Islay Hill [SAN LUIS OBISPO]: *hill*, 3 miles north of Edna (lat. 35° 14'45" N, long. 120°37'15" W). Named on Arroyo Grande NE (1965) 7.5' quadrangle.

Italian Flat [MONTEREY]: *area*, 8 miles south-southwest of Jolon (lat. 35°51'10" N, long. 121°13' W; on S line sec. 9, T 24 S, R 7 E). Named on Burnett Peak (1949) 7.5' quadrangle.

- J -

Jackass Canyon [MONTEREY]: *canyon*, drained by a stream that flows 2.25 miles to Divide Canyon 6.25 miles north-northeast of Greenfield (lat. 36°24'40" N, long. 121°12'25" W; near E line sec. 33, T 17 S, R 7 E). Named on North Chalone Peak (1969) 7.5' quadrangle.

Jack Canyon [SAN LUIS OBISPO]: *canyon*, 2 miles long, 5 miles east of Cholame on San Luis Obispo-Kern County line (lat. 35°42'30" N, long. 120°11'45" W). Named on Orchard Peak (1961) 7.5' quadrangle.

Jack Creek [SAN LUIS OBISPO]: *stream*, flows 8 miles to Paso Robles Creek 2.25 miles east of York Mountain (lat. 35°32'55" N, long. 120°47'30" W). Named on York Mountain (1948) 7.5' quadrangle.

Jack Lake [SAN LUIS OBISPO]: *intermittent lake*, 100 feet long, nearly 6 miles south of the town of Arroyo Grande near the coast (lat. 35°02'20" N, long. 120°36'10" W). Named on Oceano (1965) 7.5' quadrangle.

Jackrabbit Flat [SANTA BARBARA]: *area*, 4.5 miles west-southwest of Big Pine Mountain (lat. 34°40'35" N, long. 119°43'35" W). Named on Big Pine Mountain (1964) 7.5' quadrangle. On Big Pine Mountain (1944) 7.5' quadrangle, the name applies to a place located about 1 mile farther south-southeast along lower reaches of Grapevine Creek.

Jacks Hill [SAN BENITO]: *peak*, 2 miles west of Mariposa Peak (lat. 36°57'05" N, long. 121°14'40" W; sec. 30, T 11 S, R 7 E). Altitude 2297 feet. Named on Mariposa Peak (1969) 7.5' quadrangle.

Jackson Camp [MONTEREY]: *locality*, 6.5 miles east of Point Sur along Little Sur River (lat. 36°19'35" N, long. 121°47' W). Named on Big Sur (1956) 7.5' quadrangle.

Jackson Creek: see **Ventana Creek** [MONTEREY] (1).

Jackson Hill [MONTEREY]: *peak*, nearly 7 miles southeast of Jolon (lat. 35°54'40" N, long. 121°04'45" W; sec. 23, T 23 S, R 8 E). Altitude 1283 feet. Named on Williams Hill (1949) 7.5' quadrangle. The name is for Milligan Jackson, who settled in Tule Canyon in the early 1900's (Clark, 1991, p. 235).

Jackson Spring [SANTA BARBARA]: *spring*, 1.25 miles west of Montgomery Potrero (lat. 34°50' N, long. 119°46'35" W). Named on Hurricane Deck (1964) 7.5' quadrangle.

Jack Spring [SAN LUIS OBISPO]: *spring*, 2.5 miles south-southeast of Branch Mountain (lat. 35°09'05" N, long. 120°04'05" W). Named on Branch Mountain (1967) 7.5' quadrangle.

Jacques Hanlon Creek [MONTEREY]: *stream*, flows 3.25 miles to Quail Creek 10 miles north of Gonzales (lat. 36°39' N, long. 121° 27'30" W). Named on Mount Harlan (1968) 7.5' quadrangle.

Jade Cove: see **Plaskett** [MONTEREY].

Jalama [SANTA BARBARA]: *locality*, 3.5 miles north-northwest of Point Conception along Southern Pacific Railroad (lat. 34°29'50" N, long. 120°29'35" W); the place is 1 mile south-southeast of the mouth of Jalama Creek. Named on Point Conception (1953) 7.5' quadrangle.

Jalama Creek [SANTA BARBARA]: *stream*, flows 9.5 miles to the sea 6 miles southeast of Tranquillon Mountain (lat. 34°30'40" N, long. 120°30'05" W). Named on Lompoc Hills (1959) 7.5' quadrangle. The name is from the designation of an Indian village (Kroeber, 1916, p. 44).

Jamesburg [MONTEREY]: *settlement*, 7.5 miles northeast of Ventana Cone (lat. 36°22'10" N, long. 121°35'20" W; sec. 18, T 18 S, R 4 E); the place is along James Creek. Named on Chews Ridge (1956) 7.5' quadrangle. Jamesburg (1921) 15' quadrangle shows the place situated 0.5 mile farther north. The name commemorates John James, who founded the settlement in 1867 (Gudde, 1949, p. 164). Postal authorities established Jamesburgh post office in 1886, changed the name to Jamesburg in 1894, and discontinued it in 1935 (Frickstad, p. 107).

James Canyon [SAN BENITO]: *canyon*, drained by a stream that flows 3 miles to Lewis Creek 13 miles southeast of Bitterwater (lat. 36°15'35" N, long. 120°49'40" W; near W line sec. 19, T 19 S, R 11 E). Named on Hepsedam Peak (1969) 7.5' quadrangle.

James Creek [MONTEREY]: *stream*, flows 4.5 miles to join Finch Creek and form Cachagua Creek 1 mile north-northwest of Jamesburg (lat. 36°23'20" N, long. 121°35'35" W; sec. 1, T 18 S, R 3 E). Named on Chews Ridge (1956) and Rana Creek (1956) 7.5' quadrangles.

James Creek [SAN BENITO]: *stream*, flows 4.5 miles to San Benito River 4 miles east of Bitterwater (lat. 36°23'25" N, long. 120°55'50" W; sec. 6, T 18 S, R 10 E). Named on Rock Spring Peak (1969) 7.5' quadrangle.

James Meadows [MONTEREY]: *land grant*, 6 miles east of the mouth of Carmel River on the north side of Carmel Valley (1). Named on Seaside (1947) 7.5' quadrangle. Called Meadows Tract on Santa Cruz (1956) 1°x 2° quadrangle. Antonio Romero received 1 league in 1840; James Meadows claimed 4592 acres patented in 1866 (Cowan, p. 112).

Jameson Lake [SANTA BARBARA]: *lake*, behind a dam on Santa Ynez River 6.5 miles north of Carpinteria (lat. 34°29'30" N, long. 119°30'25" W; sec. 28, T 5 N, R 25 W). Named on Carpinteria (1952) and White Ledge Peak (1952) 7.5' quadrangles.

James Spring [SANTA BARBARA]: *spring*, 1.5 miles west of Salisbury Potrero (lat. 34°49'20" N, long. 119°43'35" W). Named on Salisbury Potrero (1964) 7.5' quadrangle.

Jamieson Creek [SAN BENITO]: *stream*, flows 2.5 miles to Pescadero Creek 10 miles west of Paicines (lat. 36°41'55" N, long. 121° 26'55" W; sec. 20, T 14 S, R 5 E). Named on Mount Harlan (1968) 7.5' quadrangle.

Jamison Creek [SANTA CRUZ]: *stream*, flows 2.25 mile to Boulder Creek (1) 4 miles east-southeast of Big Basin (lat. 37°08'45" N, long. 122°09'20" W; sec. 14, T 9 S, R 3 W). Named on Big Basin (1955) 7.5' quadrangle.

Jenks Spring [SAN LUIS OBISPO]: *spring*, 20 miles southeast of Shandon (lat. 35°27'50" N, long. 120°05'50" W; sec. 25, T 28 S, R 17 E). Named on La Panza NE (1966) 7.5' quadrangle.

Jespersen Spring [SAN LUIS OBISPO]: *spring*, 0.5 mile north of Cholame (lat. 35°43'55" N, long. 120°17'50" W; sec. 19, T 25 S, R 16 E). Named on Cholame (1961) 7.5' quadrangle.

Jesse Campground [SANTA BARBARA]: *locality*, 4 miles north-northwest of Manzanita Mountain along North Fork La Brea Creek (lat. 34°56'45" N, long. 120°06'20" W). Named on Manzanita Mountain (1964) 7.5' quadrangle.

Jesse Canyon: see **Jesus Canyon** [SANTA BARBARA].

Jesus Canyon [SANTA BARBARA]: *canyon*, drained by a stream that flows 3.25 miles to Foxen Canyon 4 miles west of Zaca Lake (lat. 34°46'30" N, long. 120°06'30" W). Named on Zaca Lake (1964) 7.5' quadrangle. United States Board on Geographic Names (1978b, p. 4) rejected the name "Jesse Canyon" for the feature.

Jesus Maria [SANTA BARBARA]: *land grant*, at and east of Purisima Point. Named on Casmalia (1959), Lompoc (1959), Orcutt (1959), and Surf (1959) 7.5' quadrangles. Lucas Olivera and others received 11 leagues in 1837; Luis T. Burton and others claimed 42,185 acres patented in 1871 (Cowan, p. 42).

Jesus Maria River: see **San Antonio Creek** [SANTA BARBARA] (1).

Jim Lawson Gulch [MONTEREY]: *canyon*, drained by a stream that flows 4.25 miles to lowlands nearly 2 miles north-northwest of San Ardo (lat. 36°02'45" N, long. 120°54'45" W; sec. 5, T 22 S, R 10 E). Named on Pancho Rico Valley (1967) and San Ardo (1967) 7.5' quadrangles.

Jim Lowe's: see **Mansfield Canyon** [MONTEREY].

Joaquin Canyon [MONTEREY]: *canyon*, drained by a stream that flows 9 miles to Little Cholame Creek 1 mile north of Parkfield (lat. 35°55' N, long. 120°26'05" W). Named on Parkfield (1961) and The Dark Hole (1961) 7.5' quadrangles.

Joaquin Canyon [SAN LUIS OBISPO]: *canyon*, drained by a stream that flows 2.5 miles to Huasna River 13 miles northeast of the town of Nipomo (lat. 35°11'30" N, long. 120°20'45" W; near NW cor. sec. 35, T 31 S, R 15 E). Named on Caldwell Mesa (1967) 7.5' quadrangle.

Joaquin's Valley: see **Priest Valley** [MONTEREY-SAN BENITO].

Joe: see **Point Joe** [MONTEREY].

Joe's Point: see **Point Joe** [MONTEREY].

Johnson: see **Mount Johnson** [SAN BENITO].

Johnson Canyon [SAN BENITO]: *canyon*, drained by a stream that flows nearly 4 miles to McCoy Creek 9 miles east-northeast of Bitterwater (lat. 36°26'25" N, long. 120°51'35" W; near NW cor. sec. 23, T 17 S, R 10 E). Named on Hernandez Reservoir (1969) and Rock Spring Peak (1969) 7.5' quadrangles. On Hernandez Valley (1957) 15' quadrangle, the name "Johnson Canyon" applies to a canyon that branches north-northeast from McCoy Creek 0.5 mile upstream from the mouth of present Johnson Canyon

Johnson Canyon [MONTEREY]: *canyon*, 3 miles long, 5.5 miles northeast of Gonzales (lat. 36°34' N, long. 121°23' W). Named on Gonzales (1955) and Mount Johnson (1968) 7.5' quadrangles. The name is from an early settler (Clark, 1991, p. 242).

Johnson Canyon [SANTA BARBARA]: *canyon*, 2 miles long, opens into Lake Cachuma 4 miles north of Santa Ynez Peak (lat. 34°35'35" N, long. 119°57'45" W). Named on Lake Cachuma (1959) 7.5' quadrangle. Water of Lake Cachuma now floods the lower part of the canyon.

Johnson Corner [SANTA CRUZ]: *locality,* nearly 3 miles east-northeast of Watsonville in Pajaro Valley (lat. 36°55'45" N, long. 121° 42'20" W). Named on Watsonville East (1955) 7.5' quadrangle.

Johnson Creek [MONTEREY]: *stream,* heads at the mouth of Johnson Canyon and flows 5.5 miles, partly in an artificial watercourse, to a point near Gonzales (lat. 36°31' N, long. 121°26'45" W). Named on Gonzales (1955) 7.5' quadrangle.

Johnsons Lee [SANTA BARBARA]: *anchorage,* 0.5 mile northeast of South Point on Santa Rosa Island (lat. 33°54' N, long. 120°06'25" W). Named on Santa Rosa Island South (1943) 7.5' quadrangle.

Johnson Surprise Spring [SANTA BARBARA]: *spring,* 3 miles west-southwest of Miranda Pine Mountain (lat. 35°01'05" N, long. 120°05'10" W). Named on Miranda Pine Mountain (1967) 7.5' quadrangle.

Johnston Canyon [SANTA BARBARA]: *canyon,* drained by a stream that flows 1.25 miles to the sea 8 miles southeast of Fraser Point on Santa Cruz Island (lat. 33°58'10" N, long. 119°50'35" W). Named on Santa Cruz Island A (1943) 7.5' quadrangle. Bremner's (1932) map shows an anchorage called Johnston Lee situated off the mouth of present Johnston Canyon.

Johnston Lee: see **Johnston Canyon** [SANTA BARBARA].

Johnston Spring [SANTA BARBARA]: *spring,* 1.5 miles east-southeast of McPherson Peak (lat. 34°52'50" N, long. 119°48'45" W). Named on Peak Mountain (1964) 7.5' quadrangle.

Jolla Vista Canyon [SANTA BARBARA]: *canyon,* drained by a stream that flows nearly 4 miles to the sea 2.5 miles east-northeast of South Point on Santa Rosa Island (lat. 33°54'35" N, long. 120° 04'25" W). Named on Santa Rosa Island South (1943) 7.5' quadrangle.

Jollo Creek [SAN LUIS OBISPO]: *stream,* flows 5 miles to Alamo Creek 4.5 miles east-northeast of Huasna Peak (lat. 35°04'20" N, long. 120°16'50" W; sec. 31, T 12 N, R 32 W). Named on Chimney Canyon (1967) and Huasna Peak (1967) 7.5' quadrangles.

Jollo Creek: see **Little Jolo Creek** [SAN LUIS OBISPO].

Jolon [MONTEREY]: *village,* 17 miles south of King City in the valley of San Antonio River (lat. 35°58'15" N, long. 121°10'30" W). Named on Bryson (1961) 15' quadrangle. Antonio Ramirez built an adobe inn at the site in 1850 (Clark, 1991, p. 242), and postal authorities established Jolon post office in 1872 (Frickstad, p. 107). Kroeber (1925, p. 895) considered the name "Jolon" as probably Indian in origin.

Jolon Creek [MONTEREY]: *stream,* flows 10 miles to San Antonio River 2.25 miles south-southeast of Jolon (lat. 35°56'20" N, long. 121°09'55" W). Named on Cosio Knob (1949) and Jolon (1949) 7.5' quadrangles. The name is from the village of Jolon (Clark, 1991, p. 244).

Jolon Valley [MONTEREY]: *valley,* 4 miles north of Jolon (lat. 36° 01'45" N, long. 121°10'15" W); the valley is along upper reaches of Jolon Creek. Named on Cosio Knob (1949) 7.5' quadrangle. According to Gudde (1949, p. 168), the name "Cañada de Jolon" is recorded as early as 1842. The Jolon Valley neighborhood was called Argyle District, a name given by teacher Allen McLean for his favorite Scottish statesman (Howard, p. 56). King City (1919) 15' quadrangle shows Argyle school in Jolon Valley, and later maps show Argyle Road there.

Jones: see **Sam Jones Canyon** [MONTEREY].

Jones Mountain [MONTEREY]: *peak,* 13 miles east-southeast of Cape San Martin (lat. 35°48'25" N, long. 121°15'15" W; sec. 31, T 24 S, R 7 E). Named on Burro Mountain (1949) 7.5' quadrangle. The name is for homesteaders who lived near the peak (Clark, 1991, p. 245).

Josephine: see **Adelaida** [SAN LUIS OBISPO].

Joshua Creek [MONTEREY]: *stream,* flows nearly 3.5 miles to Garrapata Creek 7.5 miles north of Point Sur (lat. 36°24'55" N, long. 121°54'15" W; sec. 31, T 17 S, R 1 E). Named on Mount Carmel (1956) and Soberanes Point (1956) 7.5' quadrangles.

Juan de Matte Canyon [MONTEREY]: *canyon,* drained by a stream that flows nearly 2 miles to Carmel River 9 miles east of the mouth of that river (lat. 36°30'35" N, long. 121°45'55" W). Named on Seaside (1947) 7.5' quadrangle. The name is for Juan de Mata Boronda, son of José Manuel Boronda, grantee of Los Laureles grant where the canyon lies (Clark, 1991, p. 245).

Juan Higuera Creek [MONTEREY]: *stream,* flows 2 miles to Big Sur River 3.5 miles east-southeast of the mouth of that river (lat. 36°15'50" N, long. 121°47'55" W; sec. 24, T 19 S, R 1 E). Named on Big Sur (1956) 7.5' quadrangle. The name is for Juan Nepomuceno Higuera, a vaquero who began working on Sur grant in 1866 (Clark, 1991, p. 245).

Juan Spring [SANTA BARBARA]: *spring,* 1.5 miles south of Salisbury Potrero (lat. 34°47'50" N, long. 119°41'55" W). Named on Salisbury Potrero (1964) 7.5' quadrangle.

Judell Canyon [SANTA BARBARA]: *canyon,* drained by a stream that flows 4.25 miles to Sisquoc River 3.5 miles north-northwest of Big Pine Mountain (lat. 34°44'20" N, long. 119°41'05" W). Named on Big Pine Mountain (1964) and Salisbury Potrero (1964) 7.5' quadrangles.

Judge Rock [SANTA BARBARA]: *rock,* 4 miles west-northwest of Cardwell Point, and 450 feet offshore in Cuyler Harbor on the north side of San Miguel Island (lat. 34°03' N, long. 120°21'15" W). Named on San Miguel Island East (1950) 7.5' quadrangle.

Judith Rock [SANTA BARBARA]: *rock,* nearly 2 miles east of Point Bennett, and 100 feet offshore on the south side of San Miguel Island (lat. 34°01'30" N, long. 120°25'15" W). Named on San Miguel Island West (1950) 7.5' quadrangle.

Juncal Campground [SANTA BARBARA]: *locality,* 6.5 miles north of Carpinteria along Santa Ynez River (lat. 34°29'15" N, long. 119°32'15" W; sec. 30, T 5 N, R 25 W). Named on Carpinteria (1952) 7.5' quadrangle.

Juncal Canyon [SANTA BARBARA]: *canyon,* 2.5 miles long, along Santa Ynez River above a point 8 miles north of Rincon Point (lat. 34°29'15" N, long. 119°29'30" W). Named on White Ledge Peak (1952) 7.5' quadrangle.

Juncal Creek, North Fork [SANTA BARBARA]: *stream,* flows 5.25 miles to Jameson Lake nearly 7 miles north of Carpinteria (lat. 34° 29'40" N, long. 119°30'05" W; at N line sec. 28, T 5 N, R 25 W). Named on Carpinteria (1952), Hildreth Peak (1964), and Old Man Mountain (1943) 7.5' quadrangles.

Junction Camp [SANTA BARBARA]: *locality,* nearly 1 mile south-southeast of Figueroa Mountain (lat. 34°43'55" N, long. 119°58'45" W). Named on Figueroa Mountain (1959) 7.5' quadrangle.

Junipero Serra Peak [MONTEREY]: *peak,* 17 miles west-southwest of King City (lat. 36°08'45" N, long. 121°25'05" W; sec. 34, T 20 S, R 5 E). Altitude 5862 feet. Named on Junipero Serra Peak (1949) 7.5' quadrangle. Davidson (1887, p. 210) called the peak Santa Lucia Mountain. United States Board on Geographic Names (1933, p. 403) rejected the name "Santa Lucia Peak" for the feature.

Juniper Spring [SAN LUIS OBISPO]: *spring,* nearly 3 miles north-northwest of New Cuyama [SANTA BARBARA] (lat. 34°59'05" N, long. 119°42'20" W; sec. 6, T 10 N, R 26 W). Named on New Cuyama (1964) 7.5' quadrangle.

- K -

Kalte Canyon [MONTEREY]: *canyon,* drained by a stream that flows 2 miles to Pine Canyon (1) 6.5 miles south-southeast of Salinas (lat. 36°34'15" N, long. 121°37'35" W; sec. 3, T 16 S, R 3 E). Named on Spreckels (1947) 7.5' quadrangle.

Kasler Point [MONTEREY]: *promontory,* 7.5 miles north of Point Sur along the coast (lat. 36°24'40" N, long. 121°54'55"). Named on Soberanes Point (1956) 7.5' quadrangle. Clark (1991, p. 249) associated the name with Charles Kasler, who lived near the promontory in 1877.

Kathleen Valley [SAN LUIS OBISPO]: *valley,* 5 miles south of the town of Atascadero (lat. 35°24'45" N, long. 120°40'20" W; near S line sec. 10, T 29 S, R 12 E). Named on Atascadero (1965) 7.5' quadrangle.

Kavanaugh Creek [MONTEREY-SAN LUIS OBISPO]: *stream,* heads in Monterey County and flows 6 miles to an arm of Nacimiento Reservoir 4 miles west of Tierra Redonda Mountain in San Luis Obispo County (lat. 35°46'05" N, long. 121°00'15" W; sec. 9, T 25 S, R 9 E). Named on Bryson (1949, photorevised 1979) 7.5' quadrangle. The misspelled name commemorates John Kavanagh, who settled near the stream in the 1880's (Clark, 1991, p. 249).

Kelly Canyon [SANTA BARBARA]:

(1) *canyon,* drained by a stream that flows 6.5 miles to Cuyama Valley 5.25 miles east of Miranda Pine Mountain (lat. 35°02'55" N, long. 119°56'50" W). Named on Bates Canyon (1964) and Taylor Canyon (1959) 7.5' quadrangles.

(2) *canyon,* drained by a stream that flows 3 miles to Sisquoc River 4.5 miles south-southwest of Tepusquet Peak (lat. 34°51'15" N, long. 120°14' W). Named on Foxen Canyon (1964) and Tepusquet Canyon (1964) 7.5' quadrangles.

Kelly Creek [SANTA BARBARA]: *stream,* flows 4 miles to Santa Ynez River 3 miles northwest of San Marcos Pass (lat. 34°32'35" N, long. 119°51'30" W). Named on San Marcos Pass (1959) 7.5' quadrangle. The stream drains Los Laureles Canyon.

Kelly Creek [SANTA CRUZ]: *stream,* flows nearly 1 mile to West Waddell Creek 1.5 miles west of Big Basin (lat. 37°10'20" N, long. 122°15' W; sec. 12, T 9 S, R 4 W). Named on Big Basin (1955) 7.5' quadrangle. The name commemorates Dr. Thomas Kelly, who took up a timber claim in the neighborhood in the 1870's (Clark, 1986, p. 171).

Kelly Lake [SANTA CRUZ]: *lake,* 0.5 mile long, 2 miles north-northeast of Watsonville in Pajaro Valley (lat. 36°56'25" N, long. 121°44' W). Named on Watsonville East (1955) 7.5' quadrangle. The name is for Edward Kelly, an early landowner in the neighborhood; the feature also was called White Lake for W.F. White, who owned part of it (Clark, 1986, p. 171, 400).

Kelsey Canyon [SANTA BARBARA]: *canyon,* drained by a stream that flows 5 miles to join the stream in Moon Canyon 10 miles northwest of McPherson Peak (lat. 34°59'45" N, long. 119°55'25" W; at W line sec. 31, T 11 N, R 28 W). Named on Bates Canyon (1964) 7.5' quadrangle.

Kemp Canyon [MONTEREY]: *canyon,* 2 miles long, opens into lowlands along San Antonio River 5.5 miles southwest of Bradley (lat. 35°48' N, long. 120°51'45" W; sec. 35, T 24 S, R 10 E). Named on Bradley (1949) and Tierra Redonda Mountain (1949) 7.5' quadrangles.

Kendall Spring [SANTA BARBARA]: *spring*, 2 miles south-southeast of Fox Mountain (lat. 34°47'20" N, long. 119°35'15" W). Named on Fox Mountain (1964) 7.5' quadrangle.

Kennel Creek [SAN LUIS OBISPO]: *stream*, flows 6.5 miles to Aliso Creek 5.25 miles west of Branch Mountain (lat. 35°11' N, long. 120°10'40" W). Named on Branch Mountain (1967) and Los Machos Hills (1967) 7.5' quadrangles.

Kenner Lake [MONTEREY]: *lake*, 600 feet long, 5.25 miles east of Lonoak (lat. 36°16'05" N, long. 120°50'55" W; on W line sec. 24, T 19 S, R 10 E). Named on Hepsedam Peak (1969) 7.5' quadrangle.

Kennolyn Camp [SANTA CRUZ]: *locality*, 3.5 miles north-northeast of Soquel (lat. 37°02'10" N, long. 121°55'50" W). Named on Laurel (1955) 7.5' quadrangle. The name is from syllables in the names of Kenneth and Carolyn, children of the owners and founders of the private summer camp, which began in 1946 (Clark, 1986, p. 171).

Kent Canyon: see **Quinado Canyon** [MONTEREY].

Kenville: see **Eccles** [SANTA CRUZ].

Kerr Lake [SAN LUIS OBISPO]: *intermittent lake*, 1100 feet long, 8.5 miles north of Shandon in Cholame Hills near the head of White Canyon (lat. 35°46'35" N, long. 120°21'35" W; on S line sec. 4, T 25 S, R 15 E). Named on Cholame Valley (1961) 7.5' quadrangle.

Kerr Spring [SAN LUIS OBISPO]: *spring*, 7.5 miles north of Shandon (lat. 35°45'45" N, long. 120°21'20" W; near SE cor. sec. 9, T 25 S, R 15 E); the spring is 1 mile south of Kerr Lake. Named on Cholame Valley (1961) 7.5' quadrangle.

Kerry Canyon [SANTA BARBARA]: *canyon*, drained by a stream that flows 5.5 miles to North Fork La Brea Creek 5.25 miles north of Manzanita Mountain (lat. 34°58'15" N, long. 120°04'40" W). Named on Manzanita Mountain (1964) and Miranda Pine Mountain (1967) 7.5' quadrangles.

Kerry Canyon Campground [SANTA BARBARA]: *locality*, 7.25 miles north of Manzanita Mountain (lat. 34°59'55" N, long. 120° 03'45" W); the place is situated in Kerry Canyon. Named on Manzanita Mountain (1964) 7.5' quadrangle.

Keunard German Settlement: see **Iron Spring** [SAN LUIS OBISPO] (1).

Keyes Canyon [MONTEREY-SAN LUIS OBISPO]: *canyon*, drained by a stream that heads in Monterey County and flows 14 miles to Estrella Creek 8.5 miles northeast of Paso Robles in San Luis Obispo County (lat. 35°41'50" N, long. 120°34'05" W; at W line sec. 3, T 26 S, R 13 E). Named on Cholame Hills (1961), Estrella (1948), and Ranchito Canyon (1948) 7.5' quadrangles. Cholame (1917) 30' quadrangle has the form "Keys Canyon" for the name.

Keys Canyon: see **Keyes Canyon** [MONTEREY-SAN LUIS OBISPO].

Kid Rock [SANTA BARBARA]: *rock*, 100 feet off of Prince Island at the east end of San Miguel Island (lat. 34°03'35" N, long. 120°19'50" W). Named on San Miguel Island East (1950) 7.5' quadrangle.

Kiler Canyon [SAN LUIS OBISPO]: *canyon*, drained by a stream that flows nearly 1 mile to lowlands along Salinas River near the south edge of Paso Robles (lat. 35°36'50" N, long. 120°41'20" W). Named on Templeton (1948) 7.5' quadrangle.

Kincannon Canyon [MONTEREY]: *canyon*, on upper reaches of James Creek above a point 2.25 miles from the head of the creek (lat. 36°20'50" N, long. 121°35'45" W). Named on Chews Ridge (1956) 7.5' quadrangle. The name commemorates Elgin W. Kincannon, who homesteaded in 1913 or 1914 along Chews Creek, an early name for the stream in present Kincannon Canyon (Clark, 1991, p. 250).

King Camp [MONTEREY]: *locality*, 6.5 miles west-southwest of Jolon (lat. 35°55'50" N, long. 121°17' W). Named on Cape San Martin (1921) 15' quadrangle.

King City [MONTEREY]: *town*, 21 miles southeast of Salinas along Salinas River (lat. 36°12'45" N, long. 121°07'30" W). Named on San Lucas (1949) and Thompson Canyon (1949) 7.5' quadrangles. The name commemorates C.H. King, who laid out the town on his San Lorenzo (2) grant when the railroad reached the place in 1886 (Gudde, 1949, p. 174). Postal authorities established King City post office in 1887 (Frickstad, p. 107), and the town incorporated under the name "The City of King" in 1911. Crawford (1894, p. 29) called the place Kings City.

King David Spring [SAN LUIS OBISPO]: *spring*, 2.5 miles north of Castle Crags in North Fork Willow Canyon (lat. 35°20'25" N, long. 120°12'35" W). Named on La Panza (1967) 7.5' quadrangle.

Kings City: see **King City** [MONTEREY].

Kings Creek [SANTA CRUZ]: *stream*, flows 6.5 miles to San Lorenzo River 5 miles east of Big Basin (lat. 37°09'20" N, long. 122° 08' W; near W line sec. 18, T 9 S, R 2 W). Named on Big Basin (1955) and Castle Rock Ridge (1955) 7.5' quadrangles. The name commemorates James King, who had a ranch near the mouth of the stream (Clark, 1986, p. 172).

Kinky Canyon: see **Mill Canyon** [SANTA CRUZ].

Kinton Point [SANTA BARBARA]: *promontory*, 4.25 miles southeast of Fraser Point on Santa Cruz Island (lat. 34°00'30" N, long. 119° 53'10" W). Named on Santa Cruz Island A (1943) 7.5' quadrangle.

Kirk Canyon [MONTEREY]: *canyon*, drained by a stream that flows 2.5 miles to Jolon Valley 5.5 miles north of Jolon (lat. 36°02'40" N, long. 121°10'25" W; sec. 2, T 22 S, R 7 E). Named on Cosio Knob (1949) 7.5' quadrangle. The name commemorates Edward William Kirk and his family, who lived at the place (Clark, 1991, p. 253).

Kirk Creek [MONTEREY]: *stream*, flows 2.5 miles to the sea 7 miles north-northwest of Cape San Martin (lat. 35°59'15" N, long. 121°29'40" W; sec. 26, T 22 S, R 4 E). Named on Cape San Martin (1949) 7.5' quadrangle.

Klau [SAN LUIS OBISPO]: *locality*, 6.5 miles east-southeast of Lime Mountain (lat. 35°37'30" N, long. 120°53'30" W; near E line sec. 33, T 26 S, R 10 E). Named on Lime Mountain (1948) 7.5' quadrangle. Postal authorities established Klau post office in 1901 and discontinued it in 1924 (Frickstad, p. 165).

Klondike Canyon [MONTEREY]: *canyon*, drained by a stream that flows nearly 3 miles to Carmel River 1 mile southeast of the town of Carmel Valley (lat. 36°28'10" N, long. 121°42'50" W). Named on Carmel Valley (1956) 7.5' quadrangle.

- L -

Laboratory Point: see **Lovers Point** [MONTEREY].

La Brea Creek [SANTA BARBARA]: *stream*, formed by the confluence of North Fork and South Fork, flows 6.25 miles to Sisquoc River 4.25 miles south-southwest of Tepusquet Peak (lat. 34°51' N, long. 120°12' W). Named on Foxen Canyon (1964) and Tepusquet Canyon (1964) 7.5' quadrangles. Called Labrea Creek on Lompoc (1905) 30' quadrangle, but United States Board on Geographic Names (1961b, p. 10) rejected this form of the name. North Fork is formed by the confluence of streams in Flores Canyon and Roque Canyon; it is 11 miles long and is named on Manzanita Mountain (1964) and Tepusquet Canyon (1964) 7.5' quadrangles. United States Board on Geographic Names (1961b, p. 12) approved the name "North Fork La Brea Creek" and rejected the forms "North Fork Labrea Creek" and "North Fork of La Brea Creek" for the name. South Fork is 15 miles long and is named on Bates Canyon (1964), Manzanita Mountain (1964), and Tepusquet Canyon (1964) 7.5' quadrangles. United States Board on Geographic Names (1961b, p. 16) rejected the names "South Fork Labrea Creek" and "La Brea Creek" for present South Fork La Brea Creek.

La Cañada de San Luis Beltran: see **Waddell Creek** [SANTA CRUZ].

La Carbonera [SANTA CRUZ]: *land grant*, extends north from Santa Cruz into Santa Cruz Mountains. Named on Felton (1955) and Santa Cruz (1954) 7.5' quadrangles. William Buckle received 0.5 league in 1838 and claimed 2225 acres patented in 1873 (Cowan, p. 24). Perez (p. 61) gave the grant date as 1839.

La Carpa Potrero [SANTA BARBARA]: *area*, 6 miles north-northwest of Old Man Mountain (1) (lat. 34°35'55" N, long. 119°29'20" W). Named on Old Man Mountain (1943) 7.5' quadrangle. United States Board on Geographic Names (1981b, p. 4) approved the name "Three Sisters" for a relief feature described as "rocks" located 1.6 miles east-northeast of La Carpa Potrero at the head of Agua Caliente Canyon (lat. 34°36'16" N, long. 119°27'45" W).

La Carpa Spring [SANTA BARBARA]: *spring*, about 6 miles north-northwest of Old Man Mountain (1) (lat. 34°36' N, long. 119°29'25" W); the spring is at La Carpa Potrero. Named on Old Man Mountain (1943) 7.5' quadrangle.

La Corona [SANTA CRUZ]: *peak*, 2.5 miles northwest of Soquel (lat. 37°00'25" N, long. 121°59'45" W; sec. 5, T 11 S, R 1 W). Altitude 456 feet. Named on Laurel (1955) 7.5' quadrangle. Jose Vincent De Laveaga named the peak about 1880—*la corona* means "the crown" in Spanish (Clark, 1986, p. 173).

Lacosca Creek [SANTA BARBARA]: *stream*, flows 4 miles to Mono Creek 6 miles southeast of Madulce Peak (lat. 34°37'50" N, long. 119°30'35" W). Named on Madulce Peak (1964) and Rancho Nuevo Creek (1943) 7.5' quadrangles.

La Cruz Rock [SAN LUIS OBISPO]: *rock*, 550 feet long, nearly 3.5 miles north-northeast of Piedras Blancas Point, and 800 feet offshore (lat. 35°42'25" N, long. 121°18'40" W); the rock is at the mouth of Arroyo de la Cruz. Named on Piedras Blancas (1959) 7.5' quadrangle.

La Cueva Pintada: see **Cosio Knob** [MONTEREY].

La Cumbre Peak [SANTA BARBARA]: *peak*, 5 miles north of downtown Santa Barbara (lat. 34°29'40" N, long. 119°42'40" W; at S line sec. 21, T 5 N, R 27 W). Altitude 3985 feet. Named on Santa Barbara (1952) 7.5' quadrangle. Called simply La Cumbre on California Mining Bureau's (1917c) map.

Ladies Harbor: see **Ladys Harbor** [SANTA BARBARA].

Ladys Harbor [SANTA BARBARA]: *embayment*, 1.5 miles west of Diablo Point on the north side of Santa Cruz Island (lat. 34°03'20" N, long. 119°47'15" W). Named on Santa Cruz Island B (1943) 7.5' quadrangle. Called Ladies Hbr. on Rand's (1931) map. Doran (p. 146) noted that Lady's Harbor also is called Boat Landing.

La Estrella Creek: see **Estrella Creek** [SAN LUIS OBISPO].

Lafler Canyon [MONTEREY]: *canyon,* drained by a stream that flows 1.5 miles to the sea 2.25 miles northwest of Point Sur (lat. 36°12' N, long. 121°43'35" W; sec. 15, T 20 S, R 2 E). Named on Partington Ridge (1956) 7.5' quadrangle. The name commemorates Harry Lafler, poet and editor (Clark, 1991, p. 256).

Lafler Rock [MONTEREY]: *rock,* 100 feet long, 2.25 miles northwest of Point Sur, and 250 feet offshore (lat. 36°11'55" N, long. 121°43'35" W); the feature is opposite the mouth of Lafler Creek. Named on Partington Ridge (1956) 7.5' quadrangle.

La Goleta [SANTA BARBARA]: *land grant,* at Goleta. Named on Goleta (1950) 7.5' quadrangle. Daniel Hill received 1 league in 1846 and claimed 4426 acres patented in 1865 (Cowan, p. 37).

Lagos: see **Davenport** [SANTA CRUZ].

La Graciosa: see **Graciosa Canyon** [SANTA BARBARA].

Laguna [SAN LUIS OBISPO]: *land grant,* 2.5 miles southwest of downtown San Luis Obispo in Los Osos Valley around Laguna Lake. Named on Pismo Beach (1965) and San Luis Obispo (1965) 7.5' quadrangles. The grant originally was part of the mission lands; the Catholic Church claimed 4157 acres patented in 1859 (Cowan, p. 43-44). Angel (1883, p. 215) used the form "La Laguna" for the name.

Laguna: see **Nuga** [SANTA CRUZ].

Laguna Blanca [SANTA BARBARA]: *lake,* 1450 feet long, 4 miles east of Goleta (lat. 34°25'55" N, long. 119°45'30" W). Named on Goleta (1950) 7.5' quadrangle.

Laguna Canyon [MONTEREY]: *canyon,* drained by a stream that flows 1.25 miles to lowlands along San Antonio River 10 miles southeast of Jolon (lat. 35°53'10" N, long. 121°01'35" W). Named on Williams Hill (1949) 7.5' quadrangle. The name is from the Laguna family (Clark, 1991, p. 257).

Laguna Canyon [SANTA BARBARA]: *canyon,* drained by a stream on Santa Cruz Island that flows nearly 4 miles to the sea 1.25 miles east of Punta Arena (lat. 33°57'45" N, long. 119°47'45" W). Named on Santa Cruz Island B (1943) 7.5' quadrangle. Called Cñ. Laguna on Bremner's (1932) map.

Laguna Creek [SAN BENITO]: *stream,* flows 8 miles to Hernandez Reservoir 9.5 miles east of Bitterwater (lat. 36°22'35" N, long. 120°50' W; sec. 12, T 18 S, R 10 E). Named on Hepsedam Peak (1969) and Hernandez Reservoir (1969) 7.5' quadrangles.

Laguna Creek [SANTA CRUZ]: *stream,* flows 8.5 miles to the sea 7.5 miles west-northwest of Point Santa Cruz (lat. 36°58'55" N, long. 122°09'15" W); the stream forms the east boundary of Arroyo de la Laguna grant near the coast. Named on Davenport (1955) and Santa Cruz (1954) 7.5' quadrangles. The Mexicans used the names "Laguna de Pala" and "Arroyo de la Laguna" for the stream (Hoover, Rensch, and Rensch, p. 472, 473).

Laguna de las Calabasas [SANTA CRUZ]: *land grant,* 2 miles southwest of Corralitos. Named on Watsonville West (1954) 7.5' quadrangle. Felipe Hernandez received 2 leagues in 1833; Felipe Hernandez and C. Morse claimed 2305 acres patented in 1868 (Cowan, p. 21-22; Cowan used the form "Laguna de las Calabazas" for the name).

Laguna de las Grullas: see **Espinosa Lake** [MONTEREY].

Laguna de las Trancas: see **Arroyo las Trancas** [SANTA CRUZ].

Laguna del Rey [MONTEREY]: *lake,* 0.5 mile long, in Seaside (lat. 36°36'20" N, long. 121°51'20" W). Named on Seaside (1947) 7.5' quadrangle. The feature is connected to the sea and a highway bisects it.

Laguna de Pala: see **Laguna Creek** [SANTA CRUZ].

Laguna Grande: see **College Lake** [SANTA CRUZ].

Laguna Grande de San Daniel: see **Guadalupe Lake** [SANTA BARBARA].

Laguna Harbor [SANTA BARBARA]: *embayment,* 1.25 miles east of Punta Arena on the south side of Santa Cruz Island (lat. 33°57'40" N, long. 119°47'45" W); the embayment is at the mouth of Laguna Canyon. Named on Santa Cruz Island B (1943) 7.5' quadrangle.

Laguna Lake [SAN BENITO]: *lake,* 400 feet long, 12 miles east-southeast of Bitterwater (lat. 36°18'35" N, long. 120°48'25" W; sec. 6, T 19 S, R 11 E). Named on Hepsedam Peak (1969) 7.5' quadrangle.

Laguna Lake [SAN LUIS OBISPO]: *lake,* 1 mile long, 2 miles west-southwest of downtown San Luis Obispo in Los Osos Valley (lat. 35°15'55" N, long. 120°41'25" W); the lake is on Laguna grant. Named on San Luis Obispo (1965) 7.5' quadrangle.

Laguna Larga: see **Guadalupe Lake** [SANTA BARBARA].

Laguna Mountain [SAN BENITO]: *peak,* 11 miles east-southeast of Bitterwater (lat. 36°20'20" N, long. 120°48'30" W; sec. 30, T 18 S, R 11 E); the peak is east of Laguna Creek. Altitude 4512 feet. Named on Hepsedam Peak (1969) 7.5' quadrangle.

Laguna Santa Bridida: see **Espinosa Lake** [MONTEREY].

Lagunas de la Herba de los Mansos: see **Merritt Lake** [MONTEREY].

Lagua Seca [MONTEREY]:

(1) *intermittent lake,* 1800 feet long, 5.5 miles east-southeast of Seaside (lat. 36°35' N, long. 121°45'15" W); the feature is on Laguna Seca grant. Named on Seaside (1947) 7.5' quadrangle.

(2) *land grant,* 5 miles east-southeast of Seaside. Named on Seaside (1947) 7.5' quadrangle. Catalina Manzaneli de Munras received the land in 1833 and 1834, and claimed 2179 acres patented in 1865 (Cowan, p. 44; Cowan gave the alternate name "Cañadita" for the grant). The name is from Laguna Seca (1).

Lagunita Lake [MONTEREY]: *intermittent lake,* 600 feet long, 8 miles north-northeast of Salinas (lat. 36°46'30" N, long. 121°36'05" W). Named on San Juan Bautista (1955) 7.5' quadrangle. According to Clark (1991, p. 259), both a travelers stop called Gavilan House and the first location of Natividad post office were at the place.

La Honda Canyon [SANTA BARBARA]: *canyon,* drained by Cañada Honda Creek, which flows 9 miles to the sea 2.25 miles north-northeast of Point Arguello (lat. 34°36'30" N, long. 120°38'10" W). Named on Point Arguello (1959) and Tranquillon Mountain (1959) 7.5' quadrangles.

La Hoya Creek [SANTA BARBARA]: *stream,* flows 4.25 miles to Salsipuedes Creek 5 miles southeast of the city of Lompoc (lat. 34° 34'50" N, long. 120°24'30" W). Named on Lompoc Hills (1959) 7.5' quadrangle.

La Jolla Basin [SANTA BARBARA]: *area,* 5 miles southwest of San Rafael Mountain (lat. 34°39'15" N, long. 119°52'15" W). Named on Figueroa Mountain (1959) and San Rafael Mountain (1959) 7.5' quadrangles.

La Jolla Spring [SANTA BARBARA]:

(1) *spring,* 3 miles north-northwest of Salisbury Potrero (lat. 34°51'50" N, long. 119°42'45" W). Named on Salisbury Potero (1964) 7.5' quadrangle.

(2) *spring,* 2 miles southeast of Zaca Lake (lat. 34°45'25" N, long. 120°00'40" W). Named on Zaca Lake (1964) 7.5' quadrangle.

Lake Cachuma [SANTA BARBARA]: *lake,* behind a dam on Santa Ynez River 4 miles north of Santa Ynez Peak (lat. 34°35'15" N, long. 119°58'50" W). Named on Lake Cachuma (1959) 7.5' quadrangle. United States Board on Geographic Names (1961b, p. 9) rejected the names "Cachuma Lake" and "Cachuma Reservoir" for the feature.

Lake Canyon [SANTA BARBARA]: *canyon,* 2.5 miles long, opens into Santa Lucia Canyon 5.25 miles north-northwest of the city of Lompoc (lat. 34°42'30" N, long. 120°29'25" W). Named on Lompoc (1959) and Surf (1959) 7.5' quadrangles.

Lake Nacimiento: see **Nacimiento Reservoir** [SAN LUIS OBISPO].

Lake Pajaro: see **Watsonville** [SANTA CRUZ].

Lakes: see **The Lakes** [MONTEREY].

Lake San Antonio: see **San Antonio Reservoir** [MONTEREY].

Lake Spring [SAN BENITO]: *spring,* 12.5 miles east-southeast of Bitterwater (lat. 36°18'05" N, long. 120°48' W; near E line sec. 6, T 19 S, R 11 E). Named on Hepsedam Peak (1969) 7.5' quadrangle.

Lake Tanganyika [SAN BENITO]: *intermittent lake,* 275 feet long, 6 miles east-southeast of Bitterwater (lat. 36°21'15" N, long. 120°53'50" W; sec. 21, T 18 S, R 10 E). Named on Lonoak (1969) 7.5' quadrangle.

Lake Tynan [SANTA CRUZ]: *lake,* partly intermittent, 0.5 mile long, 1.5 miles east-northeast of Watsonville (lat. 36°55'45" N, long. 121°43'40" W). Named on Watsonville East (1955) 7.5' quadrangle. The name is for James Tynan, who owned land by the lake (Clark, 1986, p. 177).

Lake View [SANTA BARBARA]: *locality,* 4 miles south of Santa Maria along Pacific Coast Railroad (lat. 34°53'40" N, long. 120°26'45" W). Named on Lompoc (1905) 30' quadrangle. Called Lakeview on California Mining Bureau's (1917a) map, which shows a place called Union located along the railroad about 2 miles north of Lakeview.

Lake Watsonville: see **Watsonville** [SANTA CRUZ].

Lake Ysabel [SAN LUIS OBISPO]: *lake,* 200 feet long, 3 miles south-southeast of Paso Robles (lat. 35°35'20" N, long. 120°40'30" W); the lake is on Santa Ysabel grant. Named on Paso Robles (1919) 15' quadrangle.

La Laguna [SANTA BARBARA]: *land grant,* northeast of Los Olivos. Named on Figueroa Mountain (1959), Foxen Canyon (1964), Los Alamos (1959), Los Olivos (1959), Sisquoc (1959), Zaca Creek (1959), and Zaca Lake (1964) 7.5' quadrangles. Octaviano Gutierrez received 4 leagues in 1845 and claimed 48,704 acres patented in 1867 (Cowan, p. 43).

La Laguna: see **Laguna** [SAN LUIS OBISPO].

Lambert Flats [MONTEREY]: *area,* 1 mile east-southeast of Jamesburg (lat. 36°21'50" N, long. 121°34'15" W; sec. 17, T 18 S, R 4 E). Named on Chews Ridge (1956) 7.5' quadrangle. The name is for the Lambert family, early residents of the neighborhood (Clark, 1991, p. 261).

La Mesa [SANTA BARBARA]: *area,* 1.5 miles south-southwest of downtown Santa Barbara (lat. 34°23'55" N, long. 119°42'40" W). Named on Santa Barbara (1952) 7.5' quadrangle.

La Mission Vieja de la Purisima [SANTA BARBARA]: *land grant,* extends south-southwest from La Purisima Concepcion mission past the city of Lompoc. Named on Lompoc (1959) and Lompoc Hills (1959) 7.5' quadrangles. Joaquin Carrillo and Jose Antonio Carrillo received 1 league in 1845 and claimed 4414 acres patented in 1873 (Cowan, p. 65).

La Natividad [MONTEREY]: *land grant,* 6 miles north-northeast of Salinas. Named on Natividad (1947), Salinas (1947), and San Juan Bautista (1955) 7.5' quadrangles. Manuel Butron and Nicolas Alviso received 2 leagues about 1830 and in 1837; Ramon Butron and others claimed 8642 acres patented in 1874 (Cowan, p. 51).

La Natividad de la Nuestra Señora: see **Los Osos Valley** [SAN LUIS OBISPO].

La Natividad Mountain: see **Fremont Peak** [MONTEREY-SAN BENITO].

Lang Canyon [MONTEREY]:
(1) *canyon*, drained by a stream that flows 2.5 miles to Sargent Canyon 9 miles north of Bradley (lat. 35°59'30" N, long. 120°46'35" W; sec. 27, T 22 S, R 11 E). Named on Pancho Rico Valley (1967) 7.5' quadrangle.
(2) *canyon*, drained by a stream that flows 2.25 miles to Cholame Creek 2.5 miles west of Parkfield (lat. 35°54'25" N, long. 120°28'25" W; near NW cor. sec. 28, T 23 S, R 14 E). Named on Parkfield (1961) 7.5' quadrangle. The name commemorates members of the Lang family, who homesteaded at the place as early as 1887 (Clark, 1991, p. 262).

Langley Canyon [MONTEREY]: *canyon*, 1.5 miles long, opens into San Miguel Canyon 2 miles north of Prunedale (lat. 36°48'15" N, long. 121°40' W). Named on Prunedale (1954) 7.5' quadrangle. The name commemorates Charles F. Langley, who settled in the neighborhood as early as the 1860's (Clark, 1991, p. 262).

Lankford Flat [SAN BENITO]: *valley*, opens into the canyon of Las Aguilas Creek (1) 5.5 miles north-northwest of Panoche Pass (lat. 36°42'15" N, long. 121°02'50" W). Named on Panoche Pass (1968) 7.5' quadrangle.

Lansing Rock [SAN LUIS OBISPO]: *shoal*, east of Point San Luis, and 0.5 mile offshore in San Luis Obispo Bay (lat. 35°09'45" N, long. 120°44'45" W). Named on Pismo Beach (1965) 7.5' quadrangle.

La Olla [SANTA BARBARA]: *canyon*, drained by a stream that flows 1.25 miles to Cañada del Cojo 4.25 miles northeast of Point Conception (lat. 34°28'55" N, long. 120°24'30" W). Named on Point Conception (1953) 7.5' quadrangle.

La Pansa: see **La Panza** [SAN LUIS OBISPO].

La Panza [SAN LUIS OBISPO]: *locality*, 4 miles north of Castle Crags (lat. 35°21'40" N, long. 120°12'50" W; sec. 36, T 29 S, R 16 E); the place is in La Panza Range. Named on La Panza (1967) 7.5' quadrangle. A settlement developed at the place after discovery of gold at nearby Placer Creek in 1878 (Lee and others, p. 81). Postal authorities established Lapanza post office in 1879, changed the name to La Panza in 1905, discontinued it in 1908, reestablished it in 1911, and discontinued it in 1935 (Salley, p. 117). United States Board on Geographic Names (1968c, p. 5) rejected the names "La Pansa" and "McLean" for the place. *La panza* means "the paunch" in Spanish, and recalls the use of the paunch of slaughtered cattle as bait for grizzly bears (Dillon, 1960, p. 4). Gudde (1969, p. 172) noted that the name was used in the neighborhood as early as 1828.

La Panza Campground [SAN LUIS OBISPO]: *locality*, 7.25 miles east-northeast of Pozo (lat. 35°21'15" N, long. 120°15'45" W; near S line sec. 33, T 29 S, R 16 E); the place is in La Panza Range. Named on Pozo Summit (1967) 7.5' quadrangle.

La Panza Canyon [SAN LUIS OBISPO]: *canyon*, drained by a stream that flows 3 miles to San Juan Creek 6 miles northeast of Castle Crags (lat. 35°22'20" N, long. 120°08'30" W; sec. 27, T 29 S, R 17 E); the canyon is in La Panza Range. Named on La Panza (1967) 7.5' quadrangle.

La Panza Range [SAN LUIS OBISPO]: *range*, northeast of Santa Lucia Range and southwest of the northwest end of Carrizo Plain. Named on San Luis Obispo (1956) 1°x 2° quadrangle. Antisell (1855, p. 35) used the name "Panza hills," and later he (1856, p. 47) used the names "Sierra San Jose" and "San Jose mountains" for the range "between the upper waters of the Salinas river and the valley of Panza and Cariso." Fairbanks (1893, p. 72) used the term "San Jose range" for the feature.

La Panza Summit [SAN LUIS OBISPO]: *locality*, 8 miles east-northeast of Pozo (lat. 35°21'20" N, long. 120°15'05" W; sec. 34, T 29 S, R 16 E); the place is in La Panza Range. Named on Pozo Summit (1967) 7.5' quadrangle.

La Patera [SANTA BARBARA]: *locality*, 1 mile west of downtown Goleta along Southern Pacific Railroad (lat. 34°26'15" N, long. 119°50'25" W). Named on Goleta (1950) 7.5' quadrangle.

La Piedra Pintada: see **Painted Rock** [SAN LUIS OBISPO].

Lapis Siding [MONTEREY]: *locality*, 2.25 miles north-northeast of Marina along Southern Pacific Railroad (lat. 36°42'55" N, long. 121°47'30" W). Named on Marina (1947) 7.5' quadrangle.

La Playa: see **Avila Beach** [SAN LUIS OBISPO]

Laplaya: see **Central Valley** [SANTA BARBARA].

La Punta de Cipreses: see **Cypress Point** [MONTEREY].

La Punta de Pinos: see **Point Pinos** [MONTEREY].

La Purisima: see **Lompoc** [SANTA BARBARA] (2); **Mission La Purisima** [SANTA BARBARA].

Larious Canyon [SAN BENITO]: *canyon*, 6.5 miles long, opens into Vallecitos 4 miles northwest of Idria (lat. 36°27'15" N, long. 120° 43'45" W; sec. 14, T 17 S, R 11 E); the canyon is along Larious Creek. Named on Idria (1969) 7.5' quadrangle.

Larious Creek [SAN BENITO]: *stream*, flows 10 miles to join San Carlos Creek and form Silver Creek 3.5 miles north of Idria (lat. 36°28'05" N, long. 120°41'05" W; near W line sec. 8, T 17 S, R 12 E). Named on Idria (1969) 7.5' quadrangle.

Larious Spring [SAN BENITO]: *spring*, 4 miles west-northwest of Idria (lat. 36°26'25" N, long. 120°44'20" W; sec. 23, T 17 S, R 11 E); the spring is along Larious Creek. Named on Idria (1969) 7.5' quadrangle.

Larkins Valley [SANTA CRUZ]: *valley*, 3 miles south-southwest of Corralitos (lat. 36°56'50" N, long. 121°49'15" W). Named on Watsonville West (1954) 7.5' quadrangle. Capitola (1914) 15' quadrangle has the form "Larkin Valley" for the name.

La Saca: see **La Zaca** [SANTA BARBARA].

La Sagrada Familia: see **Bolsa del Potrero y Morro Cojo** [MONTEREY].

Las Aguilas Canyon [SAN BENITO]: *canyon*, drained by Las Aguilas Creek (2), or a branch of that creek, which flows nearly 3.5 miles in the canyon to a point 7 miles west-northwest of Panoche (lat. 36°38'50" N, long. 120°56'15" W; sec. 1, T 15 S, R 9 E). Named on Cerro Colorado (1969) 7.5' quadrangle.

Las Aguilas Creek [SAN BENITO]:
(1) *stream*, flows 12.5 miles to Tres Pinos Creek 5.5 miles west-northwest of Panoche Pass (lat. 36°39'45" N, long. 121°06' W; sec. 4, T 15 S, R 8 E); the stream is largely on Real de las Aguilas grant. Named on Panoche Pass (1968) 7.5' quadrangle.
(2) *stream*, flows 9 miles to Panoche Creek nearly 2 miles north-northwest of Panoche in Panoche Valley (lat. 36°37'10" N, long. 120°50'55" W; sec. 14, T 15 S, R 10 E); the stream heads on a ridge east of Real de las Aguilas grant. Named on Cerro Colorado (1969), Mercey Hot Springs (1969), and Panoche (1969) 7.5' quadrangles.

Las Aguilas Mountains [SAN BENITO]: *ridge*, northeast-trending, 4 miles long, 7.5 miles north of Panoche Pass (lat. 36°44'19" N, long. 121°00'30" W); the feature is southeast of Las Aguilas Valley. Named on Cerro Colorado (1969), Ortigalita Peak (1969), and Panoche Pass (1968) 7.5' quadrangles.

Las Aguilas Valley [SAN BENITO]: *valley*, 7.5 miles north of Panoche Pass (lat. 36°44'30" N, long. 121°01' W); the valley is along upper reaches of Las Aguilas Creek (1). Named on Panoche Pass (1968) and Ruby Canyon (1968) 7.5' quadrangles.

Las Alamos Creek: see **San Antonio Creek** [SANTA BARBARA] (1).

La Salle [SANTA BARBARA]: *locality*, 5 miles east-southeast of Surf along Southern Pacific Railroad (lat. 34°38'50" N, long. 120°31'30" W); the place is near the mouth of La Salle Canyon. Named on Surf (1959) 7.5' quadrangle. California Division of Highways' (1934) map shows a place called Murray located along the railroad 1 mile east-southeast of La Salle.

La Salle Canyon [SANTA BARBARA]: *canyon*, drained by a stream that flows 2.5 miles to lowlands 5.5 miles east-southeast of Surf (lat. 34°38'30" N, long. 120°31'25" W). Named on Surf (1959) and Tranquillon Mountain (1959) 7.5' quadrangles.

Las Animas Creek [SANTA BARBARA]: *stream*, flows 2.5 miles to the sea 1.5 miles north of Point Conception (lat. 34°28'25" N, long. 120°28'30" W). Named on Point Conception (1942) 15' quadrangle. The stream drains present Black Canyon (2).

Las Animas Spring [SANTA BARBARA]: *spring*, 2.5 miles north-northeast of Point Conception (lat. 34°29' N, long. 120°27'10" W). Named on Point Conception (1953) 7.5' quadrangle.

Las Aromitas y Agua Caliente [SAN BENITO]: *land grant*, in the northwesternmost part of San Benito County near Aromas. Named on Chittenden (1955), Prunedale (1954), San Juan Bautista (1955), and Watsonville East (1955) 7.5' quadrangles. Juan M. Ansar received 3 leagues in 1835; F.A. McDougall and others claimed 8660 acres patented in 1862 (Cowan, p. 16).

Las Canovas Creek [SANTA BARBARA]: *stream*, flows 1.25 miles to Cañada de la Gaviota 8 miles south-southwest of Buellton (lat. 34°30'15" N, long. 120°13'35" W). Named on Solvang (1959) 7.5' quadrangle.

Las Chiches [SAN LUIS OBISPO]: *peak*, 5.25 miles northeast of Pozo (lat. 35°21'20" N, long. 120°18'30" W; near E line sec. 36, T 29 S, R 15 E). Altitude 3141 feet. Named on Pozo Summit (1967) 7.5' quadrangle.

Las Cruces [SANTA BARBARA]:
(1) *land grant*, at and north of Las Cruces (2) along Cañada de las Cruces. Named on Gaviota (1953), Santa Rosa Hills (1959), and Solvang (1959) 7.5' quadrangles. Miguel Cordero received the land in 1836 and claimed 8888 acres patented in 1883 (Cowan, p. 31). Perez gave the grant date as 1837, and gave the grant size as 8512.81 acres. The name goes back to the late eighteenth century, when Franciscan missionaries discovered many Indian grave mounds in the neighborhood and marked each with a cross—*las cruces* means "the crosses" in Spanish (Rife, p. 103).
(2) *locality*, 7.5 miles south-southwest of Buellton (lat. 34°30'25" N, long. 120°13'35" W); at the mouth of Cañada de las Cruces on Las Cruces grant. Named on Solvang (1959) 7.5' quadrangle. Postal authorities established Las Cruces post office in 1869 and discontinued it in 1887 (Frickstad, p. 171). They established Nojoqui post office 4 miles north of Las Cruces in 1887 and discontinued it in 1898 (Salley, p. 155).

Las Cruces Hot Springs: see **Hot Springs** [SANTA BARBARA] (1).

Las Cruces Sulphur Springs: see **Hot Springs** [SANTA BARBARA] (1).

La Selva Beach [SANTA CRUZ]: *town*, 6.25 miles west-northwest of Watsonville near the coast (lat. 36°56'15" N, long. 121°51'30" W). Named on Watsonville East (1955) 7.5' quadrangle. Postal authorities established La Selva Beach post office in 1952 (Salley, p. 118). The train station at the place was called Manresa before 1922, when promoters began Rob Roy real-estate development and changed the station name to Rob Roy; the name became La Selva Beach after the development changed hands in 1935 (Hamman, p. 268).

Las Flores Canyon [SANTA BARBARA]: *canyon,* drained by a stream that flows 2.5 miles to Cañada del Corral 10 miles east of Gaviota (lat. 34°28'45" N, long. 120°02'30" W). Named on Santa Ynez (1959) and Tajiguas (1953) 7.5' quadrangles.

Las Gazas Creek [MONTEREY]: *stream,* flows 7.5 miles to Carmel River 2.25 miles northwest of the town of Carmel Valley (lat. 36° 29'30" N, long. 121°45' W). Named on Mount Carmel (1956) 7.5' quadrangle.

Lasher Canyon [MONTEREY]: *canyon,* drained by a stream that flows nearly 1 mile to lowlands 4.25 miles south-southwest of Soledad (lat. 36°21'55" N, long. 121°21'10" W; sec. 18, T 18 S, R 6 E). Named on Paraiso Springs (1956) 7.5' quadrangle.

Las Llagas Canyon [SANTA BARBARA]: *canyon,* drained by a stream that flows nearly 4 miles to the sea 8 miles west-northwest of Coal Oil Point (lat. 34°27'30" N, long. 120°00'05" W). Named on Dos Pueblos Canyon (1951) 7.5' quadrangle. Called Las Yeguas Canyon on Goleta (1903) 15' quadrangle.

Las Lomas: see **Hall** [MONTEREY].

Las Mesas del Potrero [MONTEREY]: *area,* 6.5 miles east-southeast of the mouth of Carmel River (lat. 36°30'10" N, long. 121°49' W; near N line sec. 35, T 16 S, R 1 E). Named on Monterey (1913) 15' quadrangle.

Las Muertas Canyon [MONTEREY-SAN BENITO]: *canyon,* drained by a stream that heads in San Benito County and flows nearly 5 miles to Cinco Canoas Canyon 6.5 miles east of Greenfield in Monterey County (lat. 36°20'20" N, long. 121°07'45" W). Named on Greenfield (1956) and Pinalito Canyon (1969) 7.5' quadrangles.

Las Piedras Canyon [MONTEREY]: *canyon,* drained by Rocky Creek (1), which flows 6 miles to the sea 5 miles north of Point Sur (lat. 36°22'45" N, long. 121°54'05" W; sec. 7, T 18 S, R 1 E). Named on Mount Carmel (1956) and Soberanes Point (1956) 7.5' quadrangles.

Las Positas y la Calera [SANTA BARBARA]: *land grant,* west of Santa Barbara along the coast. Named on Goleta (1950) and Santa Barbara (1952) 7.5' quadrangles. Narcisco Fabregat and Thomas M. Robbins received the land in 1843 and 1846; Manuela Carrillo de Jones and Robbins claimed 3282 acres patented in 1870 (Cowan, p. 22; Perez, p. 82).

Las Pozas: see **San Miguel** [SAN LUIS OBISPO].

Las Salinas [MONTEREY]: *land grant,* 7 miles west-northwest of Salinas. Named on Marina (1947) and Salinas (1947) 7.5' quadrangles. Gabriel Espinosa received 1 league in 1836 and his heirs claimed 4414 acres patented in 1867 (Cowan, p. 70).

Las Sierras de San Martin: see **Santa Lucia Range** [MONTEREY-SAN LUIS OBISPO].

Las Tablas Creek [SAN LUIS OBISPO]: *stream,* flows 20 miles to Nacimiento River 5.25 miles north-northeast of Lime Mountain (lat. 35°44'35" N, long. 120°57'25" W; sec. 24, T 15 S, R 9 E). Named on Adelaida (1948), Cypress Mountain (1948), and Lime Mountain (1948) 7.5' quadrangles. The stream now enters an arm of Nacimiento Reservoir.

Last Chance Creek [SANTA CRUZ]: *stream,* flows 1.25 miles to East Waddell Creek nearly 3 miles north-northeast of the mouth of Waddell Creek (lat. 37°08'20" N, long. 122°15'30" W; sec. 24, T 9 S, R 4 W). Named on Big Basin (1955) and Franklin Point (1955) 7.5' quadrangles.

Las Varas Canyon [SANTA BARBARA]: *canyon,* drained by a stream that flows 4 miles to the sea 6 miles west-northwest of Coal Oil Point (lat. 34°26'40" N, long. 119°58'15" W). Named on Dos Pueblos Canyon (1951) 7.5' quadrangle.

Las Vegas Creek [SANTA BARBARA]: *stream,* flows 3 miles to San Pedro Creek near downtown Goleta (lat. 34°26'10" N, long. 119° 49'50" W). Named on Goleta (1950) 7.5' quadrangle.

Las Yeguas Canyon: see **Las Llagas Canyon** [SANTA BARBARA].

Latigo Canyon [SANTA BARBARA]: *canyon,* 5.5 miles long, along Santa Agueda Creek above a point nearly 5 miles east of Los Olivos (lat. 34°40' N, long. 120°01'45" W). Named on Los Olivos (1959) 7.5' quadrangle.

La Tinta Basin [SANTA BARBARA]: *area,* 6 miles south of the city of Lompoc along Gasper Creek (lat. 34°33'05" N, long. 120° 28' W); the place is 2 miles south-southeast of La Tinta Hill. Named on Lompoc Hills (1959) 7.5' quadrangle.

La Tinta Hill [SANTA BARBARA]: *peak,* 4.5 miles south-southwest of the city of Lompoc (lat. 34°34'45" N, long. 120°29'15" W). Named on Lompoc Hills (1959) 7.5' quadrangle.

Launtz Creek [MONTEREY]: *stream,* flows nearly 1.5 miles to South Fork Little Sur River 6 miles east of Point Sur (lat. 36°18'35" N, long. 121°47'30" W; at E line sec. 1, T 19 S, R 1 E); the stream is south of Launtz Ridge. Named on Big Sur (1956) 7.5' quadrangle.

Launtz Ridge [MONTEREY]: *ridge,* northwest- to west-trending, 2.5 miles long, 7 miles east of Point Sur (lat. 36°18'55" N, long. 121° 46'30" W). Named on Big Sur (1956) 7.5' quadrangle. The name commemorates the Launtz family (Clark, 1991, p. 265).

Laurel [SANTA CRUZ]: *settlement,* 9 miles north of Soquel (lat. 37° 07'05" N, long. 121°57'45" W). Named on Laurel (1955) 7.5' quadrangle. Postal authorities established Laurel post office in 1882 and discontinued it in 1953 (Frickstad, p. 176). The place first was called Highland, but after it became a construction site for South Pacific Coast Railroad, the name was changed to Laurel (Clark, 1986, p. 180).

Laurel Canyon: see **Lauro Canyon** [SANTA BARBARA].

Laurel Creek [SANTA CRUZ]: *stream,* flows 3 miles to join Burns Creek and form West Branch Soquel Creek 9 miles north of Soquel at Laurel (lat. 37°07'10" N, long. 121°57'35" W). Named on Laurel (1955) 7.5' quadrangle. The stream first was called Burrell Creek; the name "Laurel" is from the settlement of Laurel (Clark, 1986, p. 180).

Laurel Grove: see **Swanton** [SANTA CRUZ].

Laurel Spring [SAN LUIS OBISPO]: *spring,* 9.5 miles north-northeast of the mouth of Morro Creek (lat. 35°29'25" N, long. 120°45'55" W). Named on Morro Bay North (1965) 7.5' quadrangle.

Laurel Springs [SANTA BARBARA]: *springs,* 1.5 miles east of San Marcos Pass (lat. 34°30'40" N, long. 119°47'45" W; sec. 15, T 5 N, R 28 W). Named on San Marcos Pass (1959) 7.5' quadrangle. San Rafael Mountain (1943) 15' quadrangle shows Laurel Springs Lodge at the site.

Lauro Canyon [SANTA BARBARA]: *canyon,* drained by a stream that flows 1.25 miles to lowlands 2.5 miles northwest of downtown Santa Barbara (lat. 34°27' N, long. 119°43'45" W; at S line sec. 5, T 4 N, R 27 W). Named on Santa Barbara (1952) 7.5' quadrangle. Called Diablo Canyon on Santa Barbara (1944) 7.5' quadrangle, but United States Board on Geographic Names (1961b, p. 11) rejected the names "Diablo Canyon" and "Laurel Canyon" for the feature.

Lavega Peak [SAN BENITO]: *peak,* 5 miles south-southeast of Mariposa Peak on San Benito-Merced County line (lat. 36°53'25" N, long. 121°10'35" W; sec. 14, T 12 S, R 7 E). Altitude 3801 feet. Named on Mariposa Peak (1969) 7.5' quadrangle.

Lavigia Hill [SANTA BARBARA]: *peak,* 1.5 miles southwest of downtown Santa Barbara (lat. 34°24'15" N, long. 119°42'50" W). Altitude 459 feet. Named on Santa Barbara (1952) 7.5' quadrangle.

Lawson: see **Jim Lawson Gulch** [MONTEREY].

Lawson Canyon [MONTEREY]: *canyon,* drained by a stream that flows 3 miles to Portugee Canyon 5.5 miles northeast of San Ardo (lat. 36°05'15" N, long. 120°50'45" W; sec. 24, T 21 S, R 10 E). Named on Pancho Rico Valley (1967) 7.5' quadrangle.

Lawson Spring [SAN LUIS OBISPO]: *spring,* 30 miles southeast of Simmler (lat. 35°01' N, long. 119°36'45" W; near NW cor. sec. 25, T 11 N, R 26 W). Named on Elkhorn Hills (1954) 7.5' quadrangle.

La Zaca [SANTA BARBARA]: *land grant,* 9 miles east of Los Alamos. Named on Foxen Canyon (1964), Los Olivos (1959), Zaca Creek (1959), and Zaca Lake (1964) 7.5' quadrangles. Antonio, possibly an Indian, received the land in 1838; Maria Antonio de la Guerra de Lataillade claimed 4458 acres patented in 1876 (Cowan, p. 69; Cowan gave the form "La Saca" as an alternate).

La Zaca Creek: see **Zaca Creek** [SANTA BARBARA].

Lazaro Canyon [SANTA BARBARA]: *canyon,* drained by a stream that flows 6.5 miles to Cachuma Creek 7.5 miles south-southeast of Figueroa Mountain (lat. 34°38'50" N, long. 119°55'10" W). Named on Figueroa Mountain (1959) and San Rafael Mountain (1959) 7.5' quadrangles.

Lazy Campground [SANTA BARBARA]: *locality,* 4.5 miles north of Manzanita Mountain along North Fork La Brea Creek (lat. 34°57'45" N, long. 120°05'10" W). Named on Manzanita Mountain (1964) 7.5' quadrangle.

Leaf Spring [SAN LUIS OBISPO]: *spring,* 8 miles northeast of Pozo (lat. 35°22'55" N, long. 120°16'10" W; near SW cor. sec. 21, T 29 S, R 16 E). Named on Camatta Ranch (1966) 7.5' quadrangle.

Leary Hill [MONTEREY]: *peak,* 4.5 miles south-southeast of Marina (lat. 36°37'35" N, long. 121°45'25" W). Named on Marina (1947) 7.5' quadrangle.

Lee Canyon [MONTEREY]: *canyon,* drained by a stream that flows 2.25 miles to lowlands along Cholame Creek 1.25 miles southwest of Parkfield (lat. 35°53'20" N, long. 120°26'50" W; sec. 34, T 23 S, R 14 E). Named on Parkfield (1961) 7.5' quadrangle.

Leffingwell Creek [SAN LUIS OBISPO]: *stream,* flows 2 miles to the sea 2.5 miles west-northwest of Cambria (lat. 35°34'50" N, long. 121°07'05" W; near S line sec. 16, T 27 S, R 8 E). Named on Cambria (1959) 7.5' quadrangle.

Leffingwell Landing [SAN LUIS OBISPO]: *locality,* 2.5 miles west-northwest of Cambria along the coast (lat. 35°34'50" N, long. 121°07'10" W; near S line sec. 16, T 27 S, R 8 E); the place is at the mouth of present Leffingwell Creek. Named on San Simeon (1919) 15' quadrangle. William Leffingwell, Sr., settled in 1858 on the coast between San Simeon and Santa Rosa grants, where he established a beach landing known as Leffingwell Landing; in 1874 Leffingwell and J.C. Baker purchased land a little farther south at the mouth of present Leffingwell Creek and constructed a pier there that was called Leffingwell Landing, Leffingwell Pier, and Leffingwell Wharf (Hamilton, p. 122, 124-125). The indentation in the coast at the mouth of Leffingwell Creek was known as Rickard's Cove in the early days for Warren C. Rickard and William C. Rickard, who had a store there (Hamilton, p. 182).

Leffingwell Pier: see **Leffingwell Landing** [SAN LUIS OBISPO].

Leffingwell Wharf: see **Leffingwell Landing** [SAN LUIS OBISPO].

Lento [SANTA BARBARA]: *locality*, 3.25 miles east of Gaviota along Southern Pacific Railroad (lat. 34°28'20" N, long. 120°09'35" W). Named on Gaviota (1953) 7.5' quadrangle.

Leonard [SANTA CRUZ]: *locality*, 6.5 miles west-northwest of Watsonville along Southern Pacific Railroad (lat. 36°56'45" N, long. 121°52'15" W). Named on Capitola (1914) 15' quadrangle. Postal authorities established Leonard post office 7 miles west of Watsonville in 1883 and discontinued it that year—the name was for John Leonard, first postmaster (Salley, p. 121).

Leon Canyon [SANTA BARBARA]: *canyon*, drained by a stream that flows 1.5 miles to Tajiguas Creek 7 miles east of Gaviota (lat. 34°28'45" N, long. 120°05'40" W). Named on Tajiguas (1953) 7.5' quadrangle.

Lettuce Lake [SAN LUIS OBISPO]: *lake*, 600 feet long, 6 miles south-southwest of the town of Arroyo Grande near the coast (lat. 35°02'10" N, long. 120°36'30" W). Named on Arroyo Grande (1952) 15' quadrangle. Oceano (1965) 7.5' quadrangle shows a dry lake.

Lewis Canyon [SANTA BARBARA]: *canyon*, drained by a stream that flows 1.5 miles to Santa Ynez River 3 miles northeast of San Marcos Pass (lat. 34°32'35" N, long. 119°47' W). Named on San Marcos Pass (1959) 7.5' quadrangle.

Lewis Creek [MONTEREY-SAN BENITO]: *stream*, heads in Monterey County and flows 29 miles, partly in San Benito County, to San Lorenzo Creek 10 miles east-northeast of King City (lat. 36°16'50" N, long. 120°57'45" W; sec. 14, T 19 S, R 9 E). Named on Hepsedam Peak (1969), Lonoak (1969), Monarch Peak (1967), and Priest Valley (1969) 7.5' quadrangles. Frank De Alvarez and E.C. Tully named the stream for Dutch Lewis, a cattleman in the region; the stream was called Priest Valley Creek on an early survey (Clark, 1991, p. 267). North Fork enters from the north 24 miles upstream from the mouth of the main creek; it is 9 miles long and is named on Priest Valley (1969) and San Benito Mountain (1969) 7.5' quadrangles. East Fork enters North Fork 4.5 miles upstream from the mouth of North Fork; it is 3.25 miles long and is named on San Benito Mountain (1969) 7.5' quadrangle. Monterey-San Benito County line follows Lewis Creek from San Lorenzo Creek to North Fork, and then follows North Fork.

Lewis Flat [SAN BENITO]: *area*, 7 miles south-southwest of Idria along San Benito River (lat. 36°19'45" N, long. 120°44' W; sec. 26, T 18 S, R 11 E). Named on San Benito Mountain (1969) 7.5' quadrangle.

Liddell Creek [SANTA CRUZ]: *stream*, flows 3 miles to the sea 1 mile southeast of Davenport (lat. 37°00' N, long. 122°10'50" W). Named on Davenport (1955) 7.5' quadrangle. The name commemorates George Liddell, who started a sawmill along the stream in 1851 (Clark, 1986, p. 183). East Branch enters from the east-northeast 1 mile upstream from the mouth of the main creek; it is nearly 2 miles long and is named on Davenport (1955) 7.5' quadrangle.

Liddell Creek: see **West Liddell Creek** [SANTA CRUZ].

Liebe Canyon [SANTA BARBARA]: *canyon*, drained by a stream that flows 1.25 miles to Zaca Creek 2.25 miles west-northwest of Zaca Lake (lat. 34°47'15" N, long. 120°04'35" W). Named on Zaca Lake (1964) 7.5' quadrangle.

Liggett: see **Hunter Liggett Military Reservation** [MONTEREY].

Lighthouse Point: see **Point Pinos** [MONTEREY]; **Point Santa Cruz** [SANTA CRUZ].

Ligs Spring [SAN BENITO]: *spring*, 4.5 miles southeast of Bitterwater (lat. 36°20'35" N, long. 120°56'10" W; near SW cor. sec. 19, T 18 S, R 10 E). Named on Lonoak (1969) 7.5' quadrangle.

Lime Creek [MONTEREY]: *stream*, flows 1.5 miles to the sea 0.25 mile south-southeast of Slates Hot Springs (lat. 36°07'10" N, long. 121°37'55" W; sec. 9, T 21 S, R 3 E). Named on Lopez Point (1956) 7.5' quadrangle.

Limekiln [MONTEREY]: *locality*, nearly 5 miles north-northeast of Point Sur near the junction of Dairy Gulch and Bixby Creek (lat. 36°22'15" N, long. 121°52'05" W; sec. 16, T 18 S, R 1 E). Named on Point Sur (1925) 15' quadrangle. Monterey Lime Company had kilns at the place (Clark, 1991, p. 268).

Limekiln Creek [MONTEREY]:

(1) *stream*, flows 5 miles to Salinas River 3 miles south of Chualar (lat. 36°31'30" N, long. 121°31' W). Named on Chualar (1947) 7.5' quadrangle. A limekiln operated at the place at one time (Hart, E.W., p. 78).

(2) *stream*, flows 2.5 miles to the sea nearly 3 miles east-southeast of Lopez Point at Rockland Landing (lat. 36°00'30" N, long. 121° 31'05" W; sec. 22, T 22 S, R 4 E). Named on Lopez Point (1956) 7.5' quadrangle. Rockland Cement Company operated limekilns in the canyon in the 1880's, and shipped lime from Rockland Landing (Lussier, p. 35). The canyon of the stream was known as Redwood Cañon in the early days (Clark, 1991, p. 268). West Fork enters from the northwest 0.5 mile upstream from the mouth of the main creek; it is 4 miles long and is named on Lopez Point (1956) 7.5' quadrangle.

Lime Mountain [SAN LUIS OBISPO]: *peak*, 17 miles west of Paso Robles (lat. 35°40'20" N, long. 120°59'35" W; sec. 15, T 26 S, R 9 E). Altitude 2230 feet. Named on Lime Mountain (1948) 7.5' quadrangle. A limestone quarry is at the summit of the peak (Hart, E.W., p. 87).

Lime Rock Spring [SANTA BARBARA]: *spring*, 2.5 miles north of Salisbury Potrero (lat. 34°51'35" N, long. 119°41'35" W). Named on Salisbury Potrero (1964) 7.5' quadrangle.

Lingo Canyon [SAN LUIS OBISPO]: *canyon*, drained by a stream that flows 1.25 miles to McGinnis Creek 6 miles northeast of Pozo (lat. 35°22'10" N, long. 120°18'25" W). Named on Pozo Summit (1967) 7.5' quadrangle.

Linne [SAN LUIS OBISPO]: *locality*, 4.5 miles north-northwest of Creston (lat. 35°34'20" N, long. 120°34' W; near SW cor. sec. 15, T 27 S, R 13 E). Named on Creston (1948) 7.5' quadrangle. Postal authorities established Linné post office in 1889 and discontinued it in 1925 (Frickstad, p. 165). The place was a Swedish community (Lee and others, p. 47).

Lion Canyon [SANTA BARBARA]:

(1) *canyon*, drained by a stream that flows 2.25 miles to Cachuma Creek 4.5 miles southeast of Figueroa Mountain (lat. 34°42'10" N, long. 119°55' W; sec. 10, T 7 N, R 29 W). Named on Figueroa Mountain (1959) 7.5' quadrangle.

(2) *canyon*, drained by a stream that flows 3 miles to Sisquoc River 4 miles north-northeast of Zaca Lake (lat. 34°50' N, long. 120°00'35" W). Named on Zaca Lake (1964) 7.5' quadrangle.

(3) *canyon*, drained by a stream that flows 2.5 miles to South Fork La Brea Creek 1.5 miles east-northeast of Manzanita Mountain (lat. 34°54'20" N, long. 120°03'20" W). Named on Manzanita Mountain (1964) 7.5' quadrangle.

(4) *canyon*, drained by a stream that flows 5.5 miles to Newsome Canyon 3.5 miles north of Salisbury Potrero (lat. 34°52'20" N, long. 119°42'30" W; sec. 7, T 9 N, R 26 W). Named on Salisbury Potrero (1964) 7.5' quadrangle.

Lion Creek [MONTEREY]: *stream*, flows 3.25 miles to Big Sur River 2.5 miles south-southwest of Ventana Cone (lat. 36°15'05" N, long. 121°41'40" W; sec. 25, T 19 S, R 2 E). Named on Ventana Cones (1956) 7.5' quadrangle. The name is from the two mountain lions that Joseph William Post, Jr., killed by the creek in 1920 (Clark, 1991, p. 269).

Lion Creek: see **McWay Canyon** [MONTEREY]; **Rogers Creek** [SANTA CRUZ].

Lion Gulch: see **McWay Canyon** [MONTEREY].

Lion Peak [MONTEREY]: *peak*, 8.5 miles east-southeast of Cape San Martin (lat. 35°51'05" N, long. 121°19'10" W; near NE cor. sec. 16, T 24 S, R 6 E). Altitude 3499 feet. Named on Burro Mountain (1949) 7.5' quadrangle.

Lion Rock [SAN LUIS OBISPO]: *rock*, 600 feet long, 7.5 miles west-northwest of Point San Luis, and 850 feet offshore (lat. 35°13'05" N, long. 120°52'30" W). Named on Port San Luis (1965) 7.5' quadrangle. The name is from the sea lions at the place; in early days the rock was called El Lobo—*el lobo* means "the wolf," or here "the sea wolf," in Spanish (Gudde, 1949, p. 189)

Lion Rock [SANTA BARBARA]: *rock*, 7.5 miles southwest of Guadalupe, 2000 feet southeast of Point Sal, and 600 feet offshore (lat. 34°53'55" N, long. 120°39'55" W). Named on Point Sal (1958) 7.5' quadrangle. Called Seal Rock on Guadalupe (1905) 30' quadrangle, but United States Board on Geographic Names (1960c, p. 17) rejected this name for the feature.

Lions Head [SANTA BARBARA]: *promontory*, 5.25 miles west-northwest of the village of Casmalia (lat. 34°52'15" N, long. 120° 36'50" W). Named on Casmalia (1959) 7.5' quadrangle. Called Lion's Head on Fairbanks' (1896) map, which shows a promontory called Pt. Morrito located nearly 1 mile west-northwest of Lion's Head along the coast. Postal authorities established Morritto post office near Point Morrito in 1881 and discontinued it in 1884 (Salley, p. 146).

Lion Spring: see **Lower Lion Spring** [SANTA BARBARA].

Lisque Creek [SANTA BARBARA]: *stream* and *dry wash*, flows 4 miles to Figueroa Creek 4.5 miles east-northeast of Los Olivos (lat. 34°41'15" N; long. 120°02'10" W). Named on Los Olivos (1959) 7.5' quadrangle.

Little Basin [SANTA CRUZ]: *valley*, 1.25 miles southeast of Big Basin (lat. 37°09'30" N, long. 122°12'10" W; near NW cor. sec. 16, T 9 S, R 3 W). Named on Big Basin (1955) 7.5' quadrangle.

Little Bear Trap [MONTEREY]: *locality*, 4.5 miles east-northeast of Uncle Sam Mountain (lat. 36°21'30" N, long. 121°37'45" W; near SE cor. sec. 15, T 18 S, R 3 E). Named on Ventana Cones (1956) 7.5' quadrangle.

Little Bitterwater Canyon [MONTEREY]: *canyon*, drained by a stream that flows 3.25 miles to Pancho Rico Creek 11 miles east-northeast of San Ardo (lat. 36°04'40" N, long. 120°43'20" W; sec. 30, T 21 S, R 12 E). Named on Slack Canyon (1969) 7.5' quadrangle.

Little Bitterwater Spring [MONTEREY]: *spring*, 12.5 miles east-northeast of San Ardo (lat. 36°04'20" N, long. 120°41'15" W; near W line sec. 28, T 21 S, R 12 E); the spring is in Little Bitterwater Canyon. Named on Slack Canyon (1969) 7.5' quadrangle.

Little Boulder Creek [SANTA CRUZ]: *stream*, flows nearly 1 mile to San Mateo County 3.5 miles north-northeast of Big Basin (lat. 37°12'55" N, long. 122°11'40" W; at N line sec. 28, T 8 S, R 3 W). Named on Big Basin (1955) 7.5' quadrangle.

Little Burnett Creek [SAN LUIS OBISPO]: *stream*, flows 9 miles to

Nacimiento River 10 miles northeast of the village of San Simeon (lat. 35°44'55" N, long. 121°04'10" W; near N line sec. 23, T 25 S, R 8 E); the stream heads near Burnett Peak. Named on Bryson (1949), Burnett Peak (1949), and Pebblestone Shut-in (1959) 7.5' quadrangles.

Little Burros Creek [MONTEREY]: *stream,* flows nearly 3 miles to Los Burros Creek 0.5 mile south-southeast of Burro Mountain (lat. 35°51'50" N, long. 121°16'05" W; sec. 12, T 24 S, R 6 E). Named on Burro Mountain (1949) 7.5' quadrangle.

Little Caliente Canyon [SANTA BARBARA]: *canyon,* drained by a stream that flows 3 miles to Mono Creek 7.5 miles southeast of Little Pine Mountain (lat. 34°32'05" N, long. 119°37'45" W). Named on Hildreth Peak (1964) 7.5' quadrangle.

Little Caliente Spring [SANTA BARBARA]: *spring,* 5.5 miles southwest of Hildreth Peak (lat. 34°32'25" N, long. 119°37'10" W); the spring is in a branch of Little Caliente Canyon. Named on Hildreth Peak (1964) 7.5' quadrangle.

Little Cayucos Creek [SAN LUIS OBISPO]: *stream,* flows 3 miles to Estero Bay 0.25 mile east-southeast of the mouth of Cayucos Creek at Cayucos (lat. 35°26'40" N, long. 120°54'10" W). Named on Cayucos (1965) 7.5' quadrangle. Called Little Creek on San Luis (1903) 30' quadrangle.

Little Cholame Creek [MONTEREY]: *stream,* flows 10 miles to Cholame Creek 1 mile south of Parkfield (lat. 35°53' N, long. 120° 25' W; sec. 35, T 23 S, R 14 E). Named on Parkfield (1961) and Stockdale Mountain (1948) 7.5' quadrangles. Goodyear (1888, p. 87) referred to the valley of the stream as Little Cholame Valley.

Little Cholame Valley: see **Little Cholame Creek** [MONTEREY].

Little Cojo: see **Cojo Bay** [SANTA BARBARA].

Little Creek [SANTA CRUZ]: *stream,* flows 3 miles to Scott Creek 4 miles north-northwest of Davenport (lat. 37°03'50" N, long. 122° 13'40" W). Named on Davenport (1955) 7.5' quadrangle.

Little Creek: see **Little Cayucos Creek** [SAN LUIS OBISPO].

Little Falls Canyon: see **Big Falls Canyon** [SAN LUIS OBISPO].

Little Falls Creek [SAN LUIS OBISPO]: *stream,* flows 2.5 miles to Lopez Canyon 14 miles north of the town of Nipomo (lat. 35°14'45" N, long. 120°29'10" W; near W line sec. 9, T 31 S, R 14 E). Named on Santa Margarita Lake (1967) and Tar Spring Ridge (1967) 7.5' quadrangles.

Little Falls Spring [SAN LUIS OBISPO]: *spring,* 6 miles west-southwest of Pozo (lat. 35°16'35" N, long. 120°28'35" W); the spring is at the head of Little Falls Creek. Named on Santa Margarita Lake (1967) 7.5' quadrangle.

Little Irish Canyon: see **Deer Canyon** [SAN LUIS OBISPO] (1).

Little Jollo Creek [SAN LUIS OBISPO]: *stream,* flows nearly 3 miles to Alamo Creek (2) 8.5 miles west-southwest of Branch Mountain (lat. 35°07'20" N, long. 120°12'40" W; near S line sec. 24, T 32 S, R 16 E). Named on Chimney Canyon (1967) and Los Machos Hills (1967) 7.5' quadrangles.

Little Morro Creek [SAN LUIS OBISPO]: *stream,* flows 7.25 miles to Morro Creek 3700 feet east-northeast of the mouth of that creek (lat. 35°22'45" N, long. 120°51'05" W). Named on Morro Bay North (1965) 7.5' quadrangle.

Little Oak Flat [MONTEREY]: *area,* 9 miles south of Jolon near Nacimiento River (lat. 35°50'35" N, long. 121°10'10" W; near W line sec. 13, T 24 S, R 7 E). Named on Bryson (1929) 15' quadrangle.

Little Oso Flaco Lake [SAN LUIS OBISPO]: *lake,* 0.5 mile long, 6.5 miles south of the town of Arroyo Grande (lat. 35°01'55" N, long. 120°36'30" W); the feature is east of Oso Flaco Lake. Named on Oceano (1965) 7.5' quadrangle.

Little Panoche Creek [SAN BENITO]: *stream,* flows 1.5 miles to Fresno County 7.5 miles north-northwest of Panoche (lat. 36°42'05" N, long. 120°52'05" W; sec. 22, T 14 S, R 10 E). Named on Cerro Colorado (1969) and Mercey Hot Springs (1969) 7.5' quadrangles. United States Board on Geographic Names (1933, p. 466) ruled against the name "Panochita Creek" for the stream. South Fork heads in San Benito County and flows 5 miles to join the main stream in Fresno County; it is named on Mercey Hot Springs (1969) 7.5' quadrangle.

Little Panoche Valley [SAN BENITO]: *valley,* mainly in Fresno County, but extends south into San Benito County 6 miles north of Panoche (lat. 36°41' N, long. 120°51' W); Little Panoche Creek and South Fork Little Panoche Creek drain the valley. Named on Mercey Hot Springs (1969) 7.5' quadrangle. United States Board on Geographic Names (1933, p. 466) ruled against the name "Panochita Valley" for the feature.

Little Peak Canyon [SAN BENITO]: *canyon,* drained by a stream that heads in Santa Clara County and flows nearly 3 miles to Arroyo de las Viboras 8.5 miles north-northeast of Hollister (lat. 36°57'15" N, long. 121°18'55" W. Named on Three Sisters (1954) 7.5' quadrangle.

Little Pico Creek [SAN LUIS OBISPO]: *stream,* flows 5 miles to the sea 1.5 miles east-southeast of the village of San Simeon (lat. 35° 38' N, long. 121°09'45" W); the mouth of the stream is 1.5 miles north-northwest of the mouth of Pico Creek. Named on San Simeon (1958) 7.5' quadrangle.

Little Pine Mountain [SANTA BARBARA]: *peak,* 13 miles north-northwest of Santa Barbara (lat. 34°36' N, long. 119°44'15" W). Named on Little Pine Mountain (1964) 7.5' quadrangle.

Little Pines [MONTEREY]: *locality,* 1.5 miles northwest of Uncle Sam Mountain (lat. 36°21'25" N, long. 121°43'20" W). Named on Ventana Cones (1956) 7.5' quadrangle.

Little Pines Camp [MONTEREY]: *locality,* 1.25 miles northwest of Uncle Sam Mountain (lat. 36°21'10" N, long. 121°43'25" W); the place is 1700 feet south of Little Pines. Named on Ventana Cones (1956) 7.5' quadrangle.

Little Pine Spring [SANTA BARBARA]: *spring,* 8 miles north-northeast of San Marcos Pass (lat. 34°36'30" N, long. 119°45'05" W); the spring is 1 mile northwest of Little Pine Mountain. Named on San Marcos Pass (1959) 7.5' quadrangle.

Little Pinnacles [SAN BENITO]: *relief feature,* 2 miles north-northeast of North Chalone Peak (lat. 36°28'20" N, long. 121°10'40" W); the feature is 1.5 miles southeast of Pinnacle Rocks. Named on North Chalone Peak (1969) 7.5' quadrangle.

Little Quien Sabe Valley [SAN BENITO]: *valley,* 4 miles west-southwest of Potrero Peak (lat. 36°50'30" N, long. 121°13'15" W); the valley is west of the center of Quien Sabe Valley. Named on Quien Sabe Valley (1968) 7.5' quadrangle.

Little Rabbit Valley [SAN BENITO]: *valley,* opens into the north end of Topo Valley 5.25 miles north-northwest of Bitterwater (lat. 36°26'50" N, long. 121°02'45" W); the valley is northwest of Rabbit Valley. Named on Topo Valley (1969) 7.5' quadrangle.

Little Rabbit Valley: see **Rabbit Valley** [SAN BENITO].

Little River: see **Little Sur River** [MONTEREY].

Little River Hill [MONTEREY]: *peak,* nearly 2 miles east-northeast of Point Sur (lat. 36°19' N, long. 121°52'15" W). Altitude 1214 feet. Named on Big Sur (1956) 7.5' quadrangle.

Little Salmon Creek: see **Salmon Creek** [MONTEREY] (2).

Little Sand Creek [MONTEREY]: *stream,* flows nearly 2 miles to Paloma Creek 11.5 miles southeast of Soledad (lat. 36°20'15" N, long. 121°29'50" W; sec. 25, T 18 S, R 4 E). Named on Sycamore Flat (1956) 7.5' quadrangle. The stream is subparallel to and about 1 mile northwest of Big Sand Creek, which is called Little Sand Creek on Soledad (1915) 15' quadrangle.

Little Scorpion: see **Scorpion Anchorage** [SANTA BARBARA].

Little Slate Rock [MONTEREY]: *rock,* 0.5 mile west of Slates Hot Springs, and 1600 feet offshore (lat. 36°07'25" N, long. 121°38'45" W); the feature is 1400 feet southeast of Slate Rock. Named on Lucia (1921) 15' quadrangle.

Little Spring [SANTA BARBARA]: *spring,* 5 miles northwest of McPherson Peak (lat. 34°55'45" N, long. 119°52'45" W); the feature is 850 feet north of Big Spring (1). Named on Bates Canyon (1964) 7.5' quadrangle.

Little Spring Canyon [SANTA BARBARA]: *canyon,* drained by a stream that flows less than 0.5 mile to Big Spring Canyon 5 miles northwest of McPherson Peak (lat. 34°55'45" N, long. 119°52'40" W); Little Spring is in the canyon. Named on Bates Canyon (1964) 7.5' quadrangle.

Little Sulphur Spring [SANTA BARBARA]: *spring,* 1.25 miles west of Salisbury Potrero (lat. 34°49'10" N, long. 119°43'15" W). Named on Salisbury Potrero (1964) 7.5' quadrangle.

Little Sur River [MONTEREY]: *stream,* flows 14 miles to the sea 2 miles north of Point Sur (lat. 36°20'05" N, long. 121°53'35" W; sec. 29, T 18 S, R 1 E). Named on Big Sur (1956), Point Sur (1956), and Ventana Cones (1956) 7.5' quadrangles. According to Lussier (p. 4, 16), the early Spaniards at Carmel mission called the wilderness to the south *El Pais Grande del Sur,* which means "the big country to the south" in Spanish, and called the smaller of two major streams there *El Rio Chiqauito del Sur,* which means "the little river to the south"—eventually the stream took the partial translation "Little Sur River" for a name, although early residents called it simply Little River. South Fork enters from the south nearly 2 miles upstream from the mouth of the main river. It is 10.5 miles long and is named on Big Sur (1956) 7.5' quadrangle. A resort town called Idlewild flourished about 1900 along the stream approximately 1 mile above the present highway bridge (Lussier, p. 17).

Little Tiger Spring [MONTEREY]: *spring,* 10 miles east-southeast of Parkfield (lat. 35°51'55" N, long. 120°15'45" W; sec. 5, T 24 S, R 16 E). Named on Cholame Valley (1961) 7.5' quadrangle.

Live Oak Spring [MONTEREY]:

(1) *spring,* 15 miles east-northeast of San Ardo (lat. 36°05'35" N, long. 120°38'15" W; sec. 23, T 21 S, R 12 E). Named on Slack Canyon (1969) 7.5' quadrangle.

(2) *spring,* 10 miles east-northeast of San Ardo (lat. 36°03'45" N, long. 120°43'05" W; sec. 31, T 21 S, R 12 E). Named on Slack Canyon (1969) 7.5' quadrangle.

Live Oak Spring [SAN LUIS OBISPO]: *spring,* about 1 mile east of Branch Mountain (lat. 35°11'15" N, long. 120°03'55" W; sec. 32, T 31 S, R 18 E). Named on Branch Mountain (1967) 7.5' quadrangle.

Live Oak Spring [SANTA BARBARA]:

(1) *spring,* 6 miles west of Montgomery Potrero (lat. 34°50'15" N, long. 119°51'35" W). Named on Hurricane Deck (1964) 7.5' quadrangle.

(2) *spring*, 5.5 miles south-southwest of San Rafael Mountain (lat. 34°38'20" N, long. 119°51'35" W). Named on San Rafael Mountain (1959) 7.5' quadrangle.

Lizard Head [SANTA BARBARA]: *peak*, 18 miles south-southeast of the village of Cuyama (lat. 34°41'55" N, long. 119°28' W). Named on Rancho Nuevo Creek (1943) 7.5' quadrangle.

Llanada [SAN BENITO]: *locality*, nearly 5 miles west of Panoche in Panoche Valley (lat. 36°36'35" N, long. 120°54'55" W; sec. 19, T 15 S, R 10 E). Named on Llanada (1969) 7.5' quadrangle. Postal authorities established Llanada post office in 1891 and discontinued it in 1929 (Frickstad, p. 136). According to Gudde (1949, p. 190), the name was given because of the wide expanse of Panoche Valley—*llanada* means "plain" or "level ground" in Spanish.

Llanito Creek [SANTA BARBARA]: *stream*, flows 2.25 miles to El Callejon Creek 12.5 miles southeast of the city of Lompoc (lat. 34° 31'55" N, long. 120°17'05" W). Named on Santa Rosa Hills (1959) 7.5' quadrangle.

Llano de Buena Vista [MONTEREY]: *land grant*, 2.5 miles south-southeast of Salinas. Named on Chualar (1947), Natividad (1947), Salinas (1947), and Spreckels (1947) 7.5' quadrangles. Santiago Estrada and Jose Mariano Estrada received 2 leagues in 1822 and 1823; David Spence claimed 8446 acres patented in 1860 (Cowan, p. 20-21).

Llano del Tequisquita [SAN BENITO]: *land grant*, 9 miles northwest of Hollister between Pajaro River and Lomerias Muertas (1); a small part of the grant is in Santa Clara County. Named on Chittenden (1955) and San Felipe (1955) 7.5' quadrangles. Jose Maria Sanchez received the land in 1835; Vincent Sanchez and others claimed 16,016 acres patented in 1871 (Cowan, p. 102; Cowan listed the grant under the name "Tequisquite"). Arbuckle (p. 23) used the name "Llano del Tequesquite" for the grant. The word "tequesquite" is from an Aztec term for the saline or alkaline deposit found at the bed of a dry lake (Becker, 1969).

Llano Estero: see **Carrizo Plain** [SAN LUIS OBISPO].

Llano Grande Canyon [MONTEREY-SAN BENITO]: *canyon*, drained by a stream that heads in San Benito County and flows 8 miles to lowlands 9 miles east-southeast of Greenfield in Monterey County (lat. 36°15'35" N, long. 121°06'20" W). Named on Pinalito Canyon (1969) 7.5' quadrangle. United States Board on Geographic Names (1972b, p. 4) gave the name "Grande Canyon" as a variant.

Llomas Muertas: see **Lomerias Muertas** [SAN BENITO] (1).

Loanoke: see **Lonoak** [MONTEREY].

Lobos: see **Point Lobos** [MONTEREY].

Lobos Rocks [MONTEREY]: *rocks*, largest 250 feet long, 0.5 mile northwest of Soberanes Point, and 2000 feet offshore (lat. 36°27'20" N, long. 121°56'10" W). Named on Soberanes Point (1956) 7.5' quadrangle. The rocks also were known as Piedras de los Lobos, Piedra de Lobos, and Twin Seal Rocks (Clark, 1991, p. 274).

Loch Lomond [SANTA CRUZ]: *lake*, 2.25 miles long, behind a dam on Newell Creek 3 miles east-southeast of the town of Boulder Creek (lat. 37°06'10" N, long. 122°04'20" W; sec. 34, T 9 S, R 2 W); the lake is 1.5 miles upstream from Ben Lomond. Named on Castle Rock Ridge (1955, photorevised 1968) and Felton (1955, photorevised 1980) 7.5' quadrangles. The lake first was called Newell Creek Reservoir and Newell Lake (Clark, 1986, p. 187).

Lockhart Gulch [SANTA CRUZ]: *canyon*, drained by a stream that flows nearly 3 miles to Bean Creek 6.5 miles southeast of the town of Boulder Creek (lat. 37°03'25" N, long. 122°01'55" W). Named on Felton (1955) 7.5' quadrangle. The name commemorates Samuel Lockhart, who lived in the canyon about 1865 (Clark, 1986. p. 188).

Lockwood [MONTEREY]: *settlement*, 6 miles east-southeast of Jolon (lat. 35°56'40" N, long. 121°04'50" W; sec. 10, 11, T 23 S, R 8 E). Named on Williams Hill (1949) 7.5' quadrangle. Postal authorities established Lockwood post office in 1888—the name commemorates Belva Lockwood, Equal Rights Party candidate for president in 1884 and 1888; the place also was known as Hungry Flats (Salley, p. 124). The area around Lockwood has the informal name "Lockwood Valley."

Lockwood Valley: see **Lockwood** [MONTEREY].

Lodge's Beach: see **Capitola** [SANTA CRUZ].

Loeb: see **Point Loeb**, under **Point Alones** [MONTEREY].

Loeber Canyon [MONTEREY]: *canyon*, drained by a stream that flows 3 miles to lowlands 7.5 miles east-southeast of Jolon (lat. 35° 56'40" N, long. 121°02'35" W; sec. 7, T 23 S, R 9 E). Named on Williams Hill (1949) 7.5' quadrangle. The name commemorates Henry F. Loeber, who ran the store at Lockwood (Clark, 1991, p. 275).

Logan [SAN BENITO]: *locality*, 1.5 miles north-northeast of Aromas along Southern Pacific Railroad (lat. 36°54'30" N, long. 121°37'50" W). Named on Watsonville East (1955) 7.5' quadrangle.

Logan Canyon [SANTA BARBARA]: *canyon*, drained by a stream that flows 4 miles to Sisquoc River 4.5 miles northwest of Big Pine Mountain (lat. 34°44'45" N, long. 119°42'10" W). Named on Big Pine Mountain (1964) and Salisbury Potrero (1964) 7.5' quadrangles.,

Logan Creek [SAN LUIS OBISPO]: *stream*, flows 2.25 miles to Branch Creek 5 miles southwest of Branch Mountain (lat. 35°08'25" N, long. 120°09'15" W); the stream is northeast of Logan Ridge. Named on Chimney Canyon (1967) and Los Machos Hills (1967) 7.5' quadrangles.

Logan Creek [SANTA CRUZ]: *stream*, flows 1.5 miles to Kings Creek 4 miles north of the town of Boulder Creek (lat. 37°11'05" N, long. 122°07'20" W; sec. 6, T 9 S, R 2 W). Named on Castle Rock Ridge (1955) 7.5' quadrangle. Hamman's (1980b) map shows a place called Hihn Mill located along Kings Creek just north of the junction with Logan Creek.

Logan Potrero [SANTA BARBARA]: *area*, 4 miles south-southeast of Salisbury Potrero (lat. 34°46'15" N, long. 119°40'10" W); the place is near the head of Logan Canyon. Named on Salisbury Potrero (1964) 7.5' quadrangle.

Logan Ridge [SAN LUIS OBISPO]: *ridge*, northwest-trending, 2.5 miles long, 6 miles southwest of Branch Mountain (lat. 35°07'45" N, long. 120°09'35" W); the ridge is southwest of Logan Creek. Named on Chimney Canyon (1967) and Los Machos Hills (1967) 7.5' quadrangles.

Logan Spring [SANTA BARBARA]: *spring*, 4.25 miles south-southeast of Salisbury Potrero (lat. 34°46'35" N, long. 119°40'30" W); the spring is in Logan Canyon. Named on Salisbury Potrero (1964) 7.5' quadrangle.

Log Cabin Canyon [SAN BENITO]: *canyon*, drained by a stream that flows 2 miles to Pimental Creek 6.25 miles southwest of Panoche (lat. 36°31'20" N, long. 120°53'35" W; near E line sec. 20, T 16 S, R 10 E). Named on Llanada (1969) 7.5' quadrangle.

Log Cabin Spring [MONTEREY]: *spring*, 3.5 miles northwest of Charley Mountain (lat. 36°10'20" N, long. 120°43' W; sec. 19, T 20 S, R 12 E). Named on Priest Valley (1969) 7.5' quadrangle.

Logwood Creek [MONTEREY]: *stream*, flows 4.25 miles to Big Sur River 5.25 miles north-northwest of Partington Point (lat. 36°15' N, long. 121°43' W; sec. 26, T 19 S, R 2 E); the stream is southwest of Logwood Ridge. Named on Partington Ridge (1956) 7.5' quadrangle.

Logwood Ridge [MONTEREY]: *ridge*, north-northwest-trending, 2 miles long, 4 miles north of Partington Point (lat. 36°13'45" N, long. 121°41'30" W). Named on Partington Ridge (1956) 7.5' quadrangle. The name is from an early settler named Logwood (Clark, 1991, p. 276).

Loma Alta [MONTEREY]: *peak*, 3.25 miles east-northeast of the mouth of Carmel River (lat. 36°33'45" N, long. 121°52'30" W). Named on Monterey (1913) 15' quadrangle.

Loma Alta [SANTA BARBARA]: *peak*, nearly 5 miles north of San Marcos Pass (lat. 34°34'50" N, long. 119°49'40" W). Altitude 2758 feet. Named on San Marcos Pass (1959) 7.5' quadrangle.

Loma Alta Spring [SANTA BARBARA]: *spring*, 5.25 miles north-northwest of San Marcos Pass (lat. 34°35'15" N, long. 119°50'40" W); the spring is 1 mile west-northwest of Loma Alta. Named on San Marcos Pass (1959) 7.5' quadrangle.

Loma Pelona [SAN LUIS OBISPO]: *peak*, 4.5 miles north-northeast of the town of Nipomo (lat. 35°06' N, long. 120°26'10" W; sec. 35, T 32 S, R 14 E). Altitude 1784 feet. Named on Nipomo (1965) 7.5' quadrangle.

Loma Pelona [SANTA BARBARA]: *peak*, 3.5 miles south-southwest of Madulce Peak (lat. 34°38'35" N, long. 119°36'55" W). Altitude 4453 feet. Named on Madulce Peak (1964) 7.5' quadrangle.

Loma Prieta: see **Aptos Creek** [SANTA BARBARA].

Lomas de La Purificacion [SANTA BARBARA]: *land grant*, southeast of Santa Ynez. Named on Lake Cachuma (1959) and Santa Ynez (1959) 7.5' quadrangles. Agustin Janssens received 3 leagues in 1844 and claimed 13,341 acres patented in 1871 (Cowan, p. 65).

Lomerias del Espiritu Santo: see **Lomerias Muertas** [SAN BENITO] (2).

Lomerias Muertas [SAN BENITO]:

(1) *range*, 4 miles north of San Juan Bautista between San Juan Valley and Santa Clara Valley (lat. 36°54'20" N, long. 121°31'15" W). Named on Chittenden (1955) and San Felipe (1955) 7.5' quadrangles. Antisell (1856, p. 36) used the form "Llomas Muertas" for the name, which is from the lack of trees on the range—*lomerias muertas* means "dead hills" in Spanish (Gudde, 1949, p. 192).

(2) *land grant*, at San Juan Bautista; includes Lomerias Muertas (1). Named on Chittenden (1955), San Felipe (1955), and San Juan Bautista (1955) 7.5' quadrangles. Jose Antonio Castro received 1.5 leagues in 1842; the heirs of Vicente Sanchez claimed 6659 acres patented in 1866 (Cowan, p. 45—Cowan gave the name "Lomerias del Espiritu Santo" as an alternate; Perez, p. 72).

Lomita [SANTA CRUZ]: *peak*, 4 miles east of Laurel on Santa Cruz-Santa Clara County line (lat. 37°06'40" N, long. 121°53'40" W). Named on Laurel (1955) 7.5' quadrangle.

Lompico [SANTA CRUZ]: *settlement*, 4 miles east-southeast of the town of Boulder Creek (lat. 37°06'15" N, long. 122°03' W; sec. 35, T 9 S, R 2 W); the settlement is along Lompico Creek. Named on Felton (1955) 7.5' quadrangle.

Lompico Creek [SANTA CRUZ]: *stream*, flows 4.5 miles to Zayante Creek 5 miles southeast of the town of Boulder Creek (lat. 37°04'55" N, long. 122°03' W; sec. 11, T 10 S, R 2 W). Named on Castle Rock Ridge (1955) and Felton (1955) 7.5' quadrangles. Hamman's (1980b) map shows a place called Meehan located along the railroad near the mouth of Lompico Creek.

Lompoc [SANTA BARBARA]:

(1) *land grant*, at and near the city of Lompoc. Named on Lompoc (1959), Lompoc Hills (1959), Point Arguello (1959), Surf (1959), and Tranquillon Mountain (1959) 7.5' quadrangles. Joaquin Carrillo and Jose Antonio Carrillo received the land in 1837 and claimed 42,085 acres patented in 1873 (Cowan, p. 46). The name is from an Indian village (Kroeber, 1916, p. 46).

(2) *city*, 21 miles south of Santa Maria (lat. 34°38'20" N, long. 120° 27'25" W); the place is mainly on Lompoc grant. Named on Lompoc (1959) 7.5' quadrangle. Postal authorities established Lompoc post office in 1875 (Frickstad, p. 171), and the city incorporated in 1888. Parke (p. 9) used the name "La Purisima" for the part of the valley of Santa Ynez River around the present city of Lompoc. United States Board on Geographic Names (1988, p. 3) approved the name "Lompoc Valley" for the tract that extends for 19 miles inland along the river from the sea, and that has Lompoc near the center. Postal authorities established Stuart post office 9.5 miles northeast of Lompoc in 1885 and discontinued it in 1902 (Salley, p. 214).

Lompoc Beach: see **Surf** [SANTA BARBARA].

Lompoc Canyon [SANTA BARBARA]: *canyon*, drained by a stream that flows 4.5 miles to the valley of Santa Ynez River 3 miles east-southeast of Surf (lat. 34°40'05" N, long. 120°33'30" W). Named on Surf (1959) 7.5' quadrangle.

Lompoc Hills [SANTA BARBARA]: *range*, 4 miles south of the city of Lompoc (lat. 34°35' N, long. 120°27'30" W). Named on Lompoc Hills (1959) 7.5' quadrangle.

Lompoc Junction: see **Surf** [SANTA BARBARA].

Lompoc Landing [SANTA BARBARA]: *locality*, 2.5 miles north of Surf along the coast (lat. 34°43'15" N, long. 120°36'30" W); the place is 10 miles northwest of the city of Lompoc. Site named on Surf (1959) 7.5' quadrangle.

Lompoc Terrace [SANTA BARBARA]: *area*, 2.5 miles south-southeast of Surf (lat. 34°39' N, long. 120°35'15" W); the place is 7 miles west of the city of Lompoc. Named on Surf (1959) 7.5' quadrangle.

Lompoc Valley: see **Lompoc** [SANTA BARBARA] (2).

Lone Black Rock [SAN LUIS OBISPO]: *shoal*, 0.5 mile west of Point San Luis, and 0.25 mile offshore (lat. 35°09'35" N, long. 120°46'15" W). Named on Port San Luis (1965) 7.5' quadrangle.

Lone Oak: see **Lonoak** [MONTEREY].

Lone Pine Camp [MONTEREY]: *locality*, 1.5 miles south-southwest of Uncle Sam Mountain (lat. 36°19'20" N, long. 121°43' W). Named on Ventana Cones (1956) 7.5' quadrangle.

Lone Rock [SAN LUIS OBISPO]: *rock*, nearly 1 mile southeast of Avila Beach, and 650 feet offshore in San Luis Obispo Bay (lat. 35°10'25" N, long. 120°43'10" W). Named on Pismo Beach (1965) 7.5' quadrangle.

Lone Tree: see **Mariposa Peak** [SAN BENITO].

Lonetree: see **Mariposa Peak** [SAN BENITO].

Lone Tree Creek [SAN BENITO]: *stream*, flows 2.5 miles to Arroyo Dos Picachos nearly 7 miles east-northeast of Hollister (lat. 36° 53'15" N, long. 121°17'15" W; sec. 14, T 12 S, R 6 E). Named on Three Sisters (1954) 7.5' quadrangle.

Lone Tree Hill [SAN LUIS OBISPO]: *peak*, 3 miles north-northeast of the village of San Simeon (lat. 35°41'10" N, long. 121°10'40" W). Named on San Simeon (1958) 7.5' quadrangle.

Long Canyon [MONTEREY]:

(1) *canyon*, drained by a stream that flows nearly 3 miles to marsh along Elkhorn Slough 4.25 miles northwest of Prunedale (lat. 36° 48'50" N, long. 121°43'45" W). Named on Prunedale (1954) 7.5' quadrangle.

(2) *canyon*, drained by a stream that flows nearly 3 miles to Quail Creek 9.5 miles north of Gonzales (lat. 36°38'45" N, long. 121° 28' W). Named on Mount Harlan (1968) 7.5' quadrangle.

(3) *canyon*, nearly 2 miles long, opens into the canyon of Paloma Creek 12 miles west-southwest of Greenfield (lat. 36°16'30" N, long. 121°27' W; sec. 17, T 19 S, R 5 E). Named on Sycamore Flat (1956) 7.5' quadrangle.

Long Canyon [SAN BENITO]: *canyon*, drained by a stream that flows 2 miles to the canyon of San Benito River 5.25 miles east of Bitterwater (lat. 36°23' N, long. 120°54'15" W; near NE cor. sec. 8, T 18 S, R 10 E). Named on Rock Spring Peak (1969) 7.5' quadrangle.

Long Canyon [SAN LUIS OBISPO]:

(1) *canyon*, drained by a stream that flows 3 miles to Arroyo de la Cruz 3.5 miles north of the village of San Simeon (lat. 35°41'55" N, long. 121°11'30" W). Named on San Simeon (1958) 7.5' quadrangle.

(2) *canyon*, 8 miles long, opens into San Juan Valley 12.5 miles southeast of Shandon (lat. 35°31'05" N, long. 120°13'40" W; sec. 2, T 28 S, R 16 E). Named on Camatta Ranch (1966), Holland Canyon (1961), and La Panza Ranch (1966) 7.5' quadrangles.

(3) *canyon*, 3.25 miles long, opens into the canyon of Huasna Creek 7.5 miles northeast of the town of Nipomo (lat. 35°07'40" N, long. 120°23'50" W). Named on Caldwell Mesa (1967) and Tar Spring Ridge (1967) 7.5' quadrangles.

(4) *canyon*, drained by a stream that flows 2.5 miles to an unnamed canyon 2.5 miles northeast of Huasna Peak (lat. 35°03'30" N, long. 120°18'50" W). Named on Huasna Peak (1967) 7.5' quadrangle.

Long Canyon [SANTA BARBARA]:

(1) *canyon*, 2.5 miles long, opens into Harris Valley 5.5 miles south of Orcutt (lat. 34°47'05" N, long. 120°25'30" W). Named on Orcutt (1959) 7.5' quadrangle.

(2) *canyon*, drained by a stream that flows 3 miles to Santa Maria Valley 1 mile southeast of the village of Sisquoc (lat. 34°51'25" N, long. 120°16'35" W; at E line sec. 18, T 9 N, R 32 W). Named on Sisquoc (1959) 7.5' quadrangle.

(3) *canyon*, drained by a stream that flows about 3 miles to La Brea Creek 3.5 miles south of Tepusquet Peak (lat. 34°51'35" N, long. 120°10'30" W). Named on Foxen Canyon (1964) and Tepusquet Canyon (1964) 7.5' quadrangles. Called Rattlesnake Canyon on Lompoc (1905) 30' quadrangle.

(4) *canyon*, 2 miles long, opens into the canyon of Jaro Creek 5.5 miles southeast of the city of Lompoc (lat. 34°35' N, long. 120° 23' W). Named on Lompoc Hills (1959) and Santa Rosa Hills (1959) 7.5' quadrangles.

Long Gulch [SAN BENITO]: *canyon*, drained by a stream that flows 2.25 miles to Pescadero Creek 9 miles west of Paicines (lat. 36°42'30" N, long. 121°26'25" W; sec. 17, T 14 S, R 5 E). Named on Mount Harlan (1968) 7.5' quadrangle.

Long Gulch: see **Aptos Creek** [SANTA CRUZ].

Long Horn Canyon [SANTA BARBARA]: *canyon*, drained by a stream that flows 2 miles to lowlands along the coast 4.5 miles southeast of Tranquillon Mountain (lat. 34°31'45" N, long. 120° 31' W). Named on Tranquillon Mountain (1959) 7.5' quadrangle.

Long Lake [SAN LUIS OBISPO]: *intermittent lake*, 900 feet long, 4.5 miles southeast of Cholame (lat. 35°40'50" N, long. 120°13'55" W; sec. 10, T 26 S, R 16 E). Named on Orchard Peak (1961) 7.5' quadrangle.

Long Ridge [MONTEREY]:

(1) *ridge*, west- to northwest-trending, 3 miles long, 3 miles south of the town of Carmel Valley (lat. 36°26'15" N, long. 121°43' W). Named on Carmel Valley (1956) and Mount Carmel (1956) 7.5' quadrangles.

(2) *ridge*, west-trending, 4 miles long, 5.5 miles north-northeast of Point Sur (lat. 36°22'30" N, long. 121°51'30" W). Named on Big Sur (1956), Mount Carmel (1956), and Point Sur (1956) 7.5' quadrangles.

Long Ridge [SAN LUIS OBISPO]: *ridge*, east-trending, 1.25 miles long, 1.5 miles southeast of Branch Mountain (lat. 35°10'05" N, long. 120°03'50" W). Named on Branch Mountain (1967) 7.5' quadrangle.

Long Ridge [SANTA CRUZ]: *ridge*, southwest-trending, 1.25 miles long, 5 miles east-northeast of Watsonville (lat. 36°57'20" N, long. 121°40'30" W). Named on Watsonville East (1955) 7.5' quadrangle. United States Board on Geographic Names (1992, p. 4) approved the name "Mill Ridge" for the feature.

Long Valley [MONTEREY]: *canyon*, 14 miles long, opens into lowlands east of San Lucas (lat. 36°07'40" N, long. 121°00'50" W). Named on Monarch Peak (1967), Nattrass Valley (1967), and San Lucas (1949) 7.5' quadrangles.

Long Valley [SAN LUIS OBISPO]: *valley*, drained by a stream that flows 1.5 miles to Graves Creek 1.5 miles west of the town of Atascadero (lat. 35°29'20" N, long. 120°41'50" W). Named on Atascadero (1965) 7.5' quadrangle.

Long Valley [SANTA CRUZ]: *canyon*, 1 mile long, opens into lowlands 3.25 miles west-northwest of Corralitos (lat. 37°00' N, long. 121°51'50" W). Named on Loma Prieta (1955) 7.5' quadrangle.

Lonnie Davis Campground [SANTA BARBARA]: *locality*, 5.5 miles south-southwest of Montgomery Potrero along South Fork Sisquoc River (lat. 34°45'20" N, long. 119°46'35" W). Named on Hurricane Deck (1964) 7.5' quadrangle. The name commemorates the head of a pioneer family that settled by Sisquoc River in the late nineteenth century (Gagnon, p. 89).

Lonoak [MONTEREY]: *locality*, 11 miles east-northeast of King City (lat. 36°16'35" N, long. 120°56'35" W; sec. 13, T 19 S, R 9 E). Named on Lonoak (1969) 7.5' quadrangle. Postal authorities established Lonoak post office in 1885 and discontinued it in 1954 (Frickstad, p. 136). Fairbanks (1894, p. 522) called the place Lone Oak, and Vander Leck (p. 229) called it Loanoke.

Lookout Mountain [SANTA BARBARA]: *peak*, 1.5 miles west of Zaca Lake (lat. 34°46'45" N, long. 120°03'55" W). Named on Zaca Lake (1964) 7.5' quadrangle.

Lookout Peak [SAN BENITO]: *peak*, 5.5 miles northeast of Bitterwater near the southeast end of Squire Ridge (lat. 36°25'40" N, long. 120°55'15" W; sec. 30, T 17 S, R 10 E). Altitude 2986 feet. Named on Rock Spring Peak (1969) 7.5' quadrangle.

Lookout Ridge [MONTEREY]: *ridge*, north-trending, 0.5 mile long, 6 miles southwest of Salinas (lat. 36°36'15" N, long. 121°44'20" W). Named on Spreckels (1947) 7.5' quadrangle.

Loon Point [SANTA BARBARA]: *promontory*, 3.5 miles west-northwest of Carpinteria along the coast (lat. 34°24'45" N, long. 119°34'30" W). Named on Carpinteria (1952) 7.5' quadrangle.

Lopez Campground: see **Upper Lopez Campground** [MONTEREY].

Lopez Canyon [MONTEREY]: *canyon*, drained by a stream that flows 2 miles to an unnamed canyon 10.5 miles north of Greenfield (lat. 36°28'35" N, long. 121°14'50" W; sec. 6, T 17 S, R 7 E). Named on North Chalone Peak (1969) 7.5' quadrangle.

Lopez Canyon [SAN LUIS OBISPO]: *canyon*, drained by a stream that flows 16 miles to Arroyo Grande Creek 10 miles north of the town of Nipomo (lat. 35°11'20" N, long. 120°29'05" W; sec. 33, T 31 S, R 14 E). Named on Lopez Mountain (1965), Santa Margarita Lake (1967), and Tar Spring Ridge (1967) 7.5' quadrangles. A dam on Arroyo Grande Creek near the mouth of Lopez Canyon (lat. 35°11'15" N, long. 120°29'15" W) forms a lake called Lopez Lake, or Lopez Reservoir, that extends into Lopez Canyon (United States Board on Geographic Names, 1975, p. 4).

Lopez Creek [SAN BENITO]: *stream*, flows 5.5 miles to Los Pinos Creek 4 miles northwest of Idria in Vallecitos (lat. 36°27'40" N, long. 120°43'05" W; sec. 12, T 17 S, R 11 E). Named on Hernandez Reservoir (1969) and Idria (1969) 7.5' quadrangles.

Lopez Lake: see **Lopez Canyon** [SAN LUIS OBISPO].

Lopez Mountain [SAN LUIS OBISPO]: *peak*, 5 miles east-northeast of San Luis Obispo (lat. 35°18'05" N, long. 120°34'40" W; near E line sec. 21, T 30 S, R 13 E). Altitude 2868 feet. Named on Lopez Mountain (1965) 7.5' quadrangle.

Lopez Point [MONTEREY]: *promontory*, 27 miles southeast of Point Sur along the coast (lat. 36°01'10" N, long. 121°34' W; sec. 18, T 22 S, R 4 E). Named on Lopez Point (1956) 7.5' quadrangle. Clark (1991, p. 279) attributed the name to the Lopez family, pioneers in the region.

Lopez Reservoir: see **Lopez Canyon** [SAN LUIS OBISPO].

Lopez Rock [MONTEREY]: *rock*, 150 feet long, less than 1 mile west-northwest of Lopez Point, and 0.25 mile offshore (lat. 36°01'35" N, long. 121°34'45" W). Named on Lopez Point (1956) 7.5' quadrangle.

Lorenzo: see **Boulder Creek** [SANTA CRUZ] (2).

Lorenzo Creek: see **San Lorenzo Creek** [MONTEREY-SAN BENITO].

Lorenzo Vasquez Canyon [SAN BENITO]: *canyon*, drained by a stream that flows 3.5 miles to San Benito River nearly 6 miles east of Bitterwater (lat. 36°22'45" N, long. 120°53'50" W; sec. 9, T 18 S, R 10 E). Named on Hepsedam Peak (1969), Lonoak (1969), and Rock Spring Peak (1969) 7.5' quadrangles. On Priest Valley (1915) 30' quadrangle, the stream in the canyon has the name "San Lorenzo Cr."

Loridon Canyon [MONTEREY]: *canyon*, drained by a stream that flows 1.25 miles to Espinosa Canyon (2) 7 miles south-southwest of San Lucas (lat. 36°02'25" N, long. 121°04'45" W; sec. 2, T 22 S, R 8 E). Named on Espinosa Canyon (1949) 7.5' quadrangle. The misspelled name is for Loredan Espinoza, who patented land in the canyon in 1892 (Clark, 1991, p. 28).

Los Alamos [SANTA BARBARA]:

(1) *land grant*, at and west of the town of Los Alamos. Named on Lompoc (1959), Los Alamos (1959), Orcutt (1959), and Sisquoc (1959) 7.5' quadrangles. Jose Antonio de la Guerra received the land in 1839 and claimed 48,803 acres patented in 1872 (Cowan, p. 14). According to Perez (p. 53), Jose A. Carrillo was the grantee and patentee.

(2) *town*, 12.5 miles northeast of the city of Lompoc (lat. 34°44'40" N, long. 120°15'40" W); the town is in Los Alamos Valley on Los Alamos grant. Named on Los Alamos (1959) 7.5' quadrangle. Postal authorities established Los Alamos post office in 1877 (Frickstad, p. 171). California Mining Bureau's (1917c) map shows a place called Wigmore located along the railroad about 4 miles east of Los Alamos. Postal authorities established Wickham post office, 13 miles north of Los Alamos in 1898 and discontinued it in 1899—the name was for Frederick Wickenden, first postmaster (Salley, p. 240).

Los Alamos Valley [SANTA BARBARA]: *valley*, along San Antonio Creek (1) above a point 7 miles south of Orcutt (lat. 34°46' N, long. 120°25'45" W); the valley is on Los Alamos grant. Named on Los Alamos (1959), Orcutt (1959), Sisquoc (1959), and Zaca Creek (1959) 7.5' quadrangles.

Los Alisos: see **Goleta** [SANTA BARBARA].

Los Amoles Creek [SANTA BARBARA]: *stream*, flows 4.5 miles to El Jaro Creek 7.5 miles southeast of the city of Lompoc (lat. 34°33'40" N, long. 120°21'50" W). Named on Santa Rosa Hills (1959) 7.5' quadrangle.

Los Banos Creek, South Fork [SAN BENITO]: *stream*, flows 3.25 miles to Merced County 6 miles east-southeast of Potrero Peak (lat. 36°48'15" N, long. 121°03'40" W; sec. 14, T 13 S, R 8 E). Named on Ruby Canyon (1968) 7.5' quadrangle. South Fork joins North Fork in Merced County to form Los Banos Creek.

Los Berros: see **Berros** [SAN LUIS OBISPO].

Los Berros Canyon [SAN LUIS OBISPO]: *canyon*, 8 miles long, along Los Berros Creek above a point 4.5 miles southeast of downtown Arroyo Grande (lat. 35°04'40" N, long. 120°37'30" W). Named on Nipomo (1965) and Oceano (1965) 7.5' quadrangles.

Los Berros Creek [SAN LUIS OBISPO]: *stream*, flows 12.5 miles to Arroyo Grande Valley 1.25 miles south of downtown Arroyo Grande (lat. 35°06'10" N, long. 120°34'40" W); the stream drains Los Berros Canyon. Named on Oceano (1965) 7.5' quadrangle.

Los Bueyes Creek [MONTEREY]: *stream*, flows 4 miles to Los Burros Creek 7 miles south-southwest of Jolon (lat. 35°52'35" N, long. 121°13'50" W). Named on Alder Peak (1949) and Jolon (1949) 7.5' quadrangles.

Los Burros: see **Alder Creek** [MONTEREY].

Los Burros Creek [MONTEREY]: *stream*, flows 10 miles to Nacimiento River 7 miles south-southwest of Jolon (lat. 35°52'30" N, long. 121°13' W). Named on Alder Peak (1949), Burnett Peak (1949), Burro Mountain (1949), and Jolon (1949) 7.5' quadrangles. North Fork enters from the north 6.25 miles upstream from the mouth of the main creek; it is 4.5 miles long and is named on Alder Peak (1949) 7.5' quadrangle.

Los Carneros [MONTEREY]:

(1) *land grant*, 6 miles north-northwest of Prunedale. Named on Moss Landing (1954) and Prunedale (1954) 7.5' quadrangles. David Littlejohn received 1 league in 1834 and his heirs claimed 4482 acres patented in 1866 (Cowan, p. 24).

(2) *land grant*, 11 miles north-northeast of Salinas. Named on San Juan Bautista (1955) 7.5' quadrangle. Maria Antonia Linares received 1 league in 1842; F.A. McDougall and others claimed 1629 acres patented in 1862 (Cowan, p. 24). According to Perez (p. 61), Maria A. Anzar was the patentee.

Los Coches [MONTEREY]: *land grant*, 3.5 miles south-southeast of Soledad. Named on Paraiso Springs (1956) and Soledad (1955) 7.5' quadrangles. Josefa Soberanes received 2.25 leagues in 1841 and claimed 8794 acres patented in 1917 (Cowan, p. 28; Perez, p. 62).

Los Coches Mountain [SANTA BARBARA]: *peak*, 10.5 miles east-northeast of Santa Maria (lat. 34°59' N, long. 120°15'25" W); the peak is near the head of Cañada de los Coches (1). Altitude 3016 feet. Named on Twitchell Dam (1959) 7.5' quadrangle.

Los Corralitos [SANTA CRUZ]: *land grant*, north and northwest of Watsonville. Named on Loma Prieta (1955), Watsonville East (1955), and Watsonville West (1954) 7.5' quadrangles. Jose Amesti received 4 leagues in 1844 and his heirs claimed 15,440 acres patented in 1861 (Cowan, p. 30).

Los Dos Pueblos [SANTA BARBARA]: *land grant*, west of Goleta along the coast; includes the lower part of Dos Pueblos Canyon. Named on Dos Pueblos Canyon (1951) and Goleta (1950) 7.5' quadrangles. Nicholas A. Den received 3 leagues in 1842 and claimed 15,535 acres patented in 1877 (Cowan, p. 33).

Los Gatos [MONTEREY]: *land grant*, 4 miles north-northwest of Salinas. Named on Salinas (1947, photorevised 1968 and 1975) 7.5' quadrangle, which gives the name "Santa Rita" as an alternate. Trinidad Espinosa received 1 league in 1820 and 1837; Fermina E. Perez and Domingo Perez claimed 4424 acres patented in 1870 (Cowan, p. 37; Perez, p. 67).

Los Laureles [MONTEREY]:

(1) *land grant*, 8.5 miles east of the mouth of Carmel River on the north side of Carmel Valley (1). Named on Seaside (1947) 7.5' quadrangle. Jose Agricia received 2000 varas in 1844; L. Ransom claimed 718 acres patented in 1871 (Cowan, p. 44-45; Cowan listed the grant under the name "Rincon de los Laureles").

(2) *land grant*, 10 miles east-southeast of the mouth of Carmel River in Carmel Valley (1). Named on Carmel Valley (1956), Mount Carmel (1956), Seaside (1947), and Spreckels (1947) 7.5' quadrangles. Jose Antonio Romero received 1.5 leagues in 1835; Jose Boronda and others received the land in 1839 and claimed 6625 acres patented in 1866 (Cowan, p. 44; Cowan gave the name "Cañada de los Laureles" as an alternate).

Los Laureles Canyon [SANTA BARBARA]: *canyon*, drained by Kelly Creek, which flows 4 miles to Santa Ynez River 3 miles northwest of San Marcos Pass (lat. 34°32'35" N, long. 119° 51'30" W). Named on San Marcos Pass (1959) 7.5' quadrangle.

Los Lobos Spring [MONTEREY]: *spring*, 9 miles northwest of Bradley (lat. 35°57'35" N, long. 120°54'35" W; sec. 5, T 23 S, R 10 E). Named on Hames Valley (1949) 7.5' quadrangle.

Los Machos Creek [SAN LUIS OBISPO]: *stream*, flows 3.25 miles to Kennel Creek 4 miles west of Branch Mountain (lat. 35°11'05" N, long. 120°09'15" W). Named on Los Machos Hills (1967) 7.5' quadrangle.

Los Machos Hills [SAN LUIS OBISPO]: *ridge*, west-trending, 3 miles long, 4 miles west of Branch Mountain (lat. 35°10'40" N, long. 120°09' W); the feature is south of the confluence of Los Machos Creek and Kennel Creek. Named on Los Machos Hills (1967) 7.5' quadrangle.

Los Muertos Creek [SAN BENITO]: *stream*, flows 11 miles to Tres Pinos Creek 5 miles west of Cherry Peak (lat. 36°42' N, long. 121° 13'45" W; sec. 20, T 14 S, R 7 E); the stream heads in Los Muertos Valley. Named on Cherry Peak (1968) and Panoche Pass (1968) 7.5' quadrangles.

Los Muertos Valley [SAN BENITO]: *valley*, 9.25 miles north-northwest of Panoche Pass (lat. 36°44'45" N, long. 121°05'30" W); the valley is at the head of Los Muertos Creek. Named on Panoche Pass (1968) and Ruby Canyon (1968) 7.5' quadrangles. Pierce (p. 145) attributed the name to a story about three men found hanging from a tree in the valley in the early days—*los muertos* means "the dead ones" in Spanish.

Los Ojitos [MONTEREY]: *land grant*, 5 miles southeast of Jolon. Named on Jolon (1949) and Williams Hill (1949) 7.5' quadrangles. Mariano Soberanes received 2 leagues in 1842 and claimed 8900 acres patented in 1871 (Cowan, p. 54). The name refers to a pair of natural seepages near

Quail Top that are believed to have been a watering place for mission cattle during the dry season; the seepages have the appearance of two eyes from a distance—*los ojitos* means "the little eyes" in Spanish (Howard, p. 85). Howard (p. 86) noted that a building on the grant may have housed San Antonio post office, which opened in 1858 and moved to Jolon in 1872. According to Frickstad (p. 109), postal authorities established San Antonio post office in 1858 and discontinued it in 1887, when they moved the service to King City. Postal Route (1884) map shows San Antonio post office situated south of present King City, apparently near the mouth of present Quinado Canyon, and not on Los Ojitos grant. According to Clark (1991, p. 499), San Antonio post office was situated at the junction of Mansfield Canyon and Quinado Canyon (SE quarter sec. 18, T 21 S, R 8 E).

Los Olivos [SANTA BARBARA]: *village*, 4 miles north-northwest of Santa Ynez (lat. 34°40' N, long. 120°06'50" W; at S line sec. 23, T 7 N, R 31 W). Named on Los Olivos (1959) 7.5' quadrangle. Postal authorities established Los Olivos post office in 1887 (Frickstad, p. 171). The name is from trees left after an attempt to start an olive industry at the place (Rife, p. 78).

Los Osos [SAN LUIS OBISPO]: *town*, 4.5 miles south-southwest of Morro Rock (lat. 35°18'40" N, long. 120°49'55" W); the place is in Los Osos Valley on Cañada de los Osos y Pecho grant. Named on Morro Bay South (1965) 7.5' quadrangle. Postal authorities established Los Osos post office in 1954 and discontinued it in 1969; they combined part of Los Osos post office with Baywood Park post office in 1967 to form a new post office called Bay-Osos, which they discontinued in 1974, when they reestablished Los Osos post office (Salley, p. 16, 128).

Los Osos Creek [SAN LUIS OBISPO]: *stream*, flows 10 miles to Morro Bay 3 miles southeast of Morro Rock (lat. 35°20'20" N, long. 120°49'40" W). Named on Morro Bay South (1965) 7.5' quadrangle.

Los Osos Mountains: see **Irish Hills** [SAN LUIS OBISPO].

Los Osos Valley [SAN LUIS OBISPO]: *valley*, extends 10 miles east-southeast from Morro Bay to San Luis Obispo; partly on Cañada de los Osos y Pecho grant. Named on Morro Bay South (1965) and San Luis Obispo (1965) 7.5' quadrangles. The east part of the valley is called San Luis Valley on San Luis Obispo (1897) 15' quadrangle. According to Whitney (p. 139), the Valley of San Luis Obispo extends southeast from Estero Bay nearly to Arroyo Grande (2), and "embraces the San Luis Valley, so called, and the Cañada de los Osos." United States Board on Geographic Names (1964, p. 15) rejected the name "San Luis Valley," and later the Board (1966, p. 5) rejected the name "Valley of the Bears" for Los Osos Valley. Soldiers of the Portola expedition in 1769 named a valley, perhaps this one, Cañada de Los Osos because they had a fight with bears there; Crespi gave the same place the name "La Natividad de la Nuestra Señora" (Wagner, H.R., p. 401).

Los Padres Post Office [SAN LUIS OBISPO]: *locality*, 3.5 miles northwest of downtown San Luis Obispo at California Mens Colony (lat. 35°19'30" N, long. 120°42' W). Named on San Luis Obispo (1965) 7.5' quadrangle. Postal authorities established the post office in 1956 and discontinued it in 1969 (Salley, p. 128).

Lospe: see **Mount Lospe** [SANTA BARBARA].

Los Pelados [SAN LUIS OBISPO]: *peak*, 6.25 miles northwest of Branch Mountain (lat. 35°14'35" N, long. 120°09'55" W). Altitude 3305 feet. Named on Los Machos Hills (1967) 7.5' quadrangle.

Lospie: see **Point Lospie**, under **Point Sal** [SANTA BARBARA].

Los Pinos Creek [SAN BENITO]: *stream*, flows 6.5 miles to Larious Creek 3.5 miles northwest of Idria in Vallecitos (lat. 36°27'30" N, long. 120°42'35" W; near S line sec. 12, T 17 S, R 11 E). Named on Hernandez Reservoir (1969) and Idria (1969) 7.5' quadrangles.

Los Prietos Campground [SANTA BARBARA]: *locality*, 2.25 miles north-northeast of San Marcos Pass (lat. 34°32'25" N, long. 119° 48' W; sec. 3, T 5 N, R 28 W). Named on San Marcos Pass (1959) 7.5' quadrangle.

Los Prietos y Najalayegua [SANTA BARBARA]: *land grant*, along the upper part of Santa Ynez River. Named on Carpinteria (1952), Hildreth Peak (1964), Little Pine Mountain (1964), Old Man Mountain (1943), San Marcos Pass (1959), and White Ledge Peak (1952) 7.5' quadrangles. Jose Dominguez received the land in 1845 and claimed 48,729 acres patented in 1875 (Cowan, p. 64).

Los Sauces: see **Willows Anchorage** [SANTA BARBARA].

Lost Knife Spring [SANTA BARBARA]: *spring*, 5 miles west-northwest of Montgomery Potrero (lat. 34°52' N, long. 119°50'05" W). Named on Hurricane Deck (1964) 7.5' quadrangle.

Los Tularcitos [MONTEREY]: *land grant*, 14 miles south of Salinas. Named on Carmel Valley (1956), Chualar (1947), Rana Creek (1956), and Spreckels (1947) 7.5' quadrangles. Rafael Gomez received 6 leagues in 1834 and his heirs claimed 26,581 acres patented in 1866 (Cowan, p. 105). The name refers to a tule-bordered lake on the grant—*los tularcitos* means "the little tules" in Spanish (Hoover, Rensch, and Rensch, p. 232).

Lost Valley [MONTEREY]: *canyon*, 1 mile long, 5.5 miles south of Tassajara Hot Springs along Higgins Creek (lat. 36°09'20" N, long. 121°34' W); the valley is near the confluence of Lost Valley Creek and Higgins Creek. Named on Tassajara Hot Springs (1956) 7.5' quadrangle.

Lost Valley Creek [MONTEREY]: *stream*, flows 6.5 miles to Arroyo Seco (1) 5 miles south-southeast of Tassajara Hot Springs (lat. 36° 10'10" N, long. 121°30'50" W; near N line sec. 27, T 20 S, R 4 E). Named on Tassajara Hot Springs (1956) 7.5' quadrangle.

Los Vaqueros Creek: see **Vaqueros Creek** [MONTEREY].

Los Vaqueros Valley: see **Vaqueros Creek** [MONTEREY].

Los Vergeles [MONTEREY-SAN BENITO]: *land grant*, 10 miles north-northeast of Salinas on Monterey-San Benito County line. Named on San Juan Bautista (1955) 7.5' quadrangle. Jose Joaquin Gomez received 2 leagues in 1835; James C. Stokes claimed 8760 acres patented in 1875 (Cowan p. 107; Cowan gave the form "Verjeles" as an alternate). *Vergel* means "flower and fruit garden" in Spanish (Gudde, 1949, p. 378).

Los Yeguas Creek: see **Yeguas Creek** [SAN LUIS OBISPO].

Loudon Gulch: see **Ellis Canyon** [MONTEREY].

Love Creek [SANTA CRUZ]: *stream*, flows nearly 4 miles to San Lorenzo River 3 miles southeast of the town of Boulder Creek at Ben Lomond (lat. 37°05'20" N, long. 122°05'10" W). Named on Castle Rock Ridge (1955) and Felton (1955) 7.5' quadrangles. The name commemorates Harry Love, who had a sawmill at the confluence of Love Creek and San Lorenzo River (Hoover, Rensch, and Rensch, p. 480).

Love Gulch: see **Aptos Creek** [SANTA CRUZ].

Lovers of Jesus Point: see **Lovers Point** [MONTEREY].

Lovers Point [MONTEREY]: *promontory*, 1.25 miles southeast of Point Pinos along the coast (lat. 36°37'35" N, long. 121°54'50" W). Named on Monterey (1947) 7.5' quadrangle. Called Pt. Aulon on Monterey (1913) 15' quadrangle, but United States Board on Geographic Names (1961b, p. 11) rejected this name for the feature. According to Fink (p. 167), the name "Lovers Point" dates from 1875, when the place was called Lovers of Jesus Point because of outdoor prayer sessions held there. Clark (1991, p. 284-285) gave evidence that this origin of the name is fanciful, and noted that the feature also had the names "Laboratory Point" for Hopkins Seaside Laboratory there, and "Organ Point" from the noise of breaking waves.

Low: see **Camp Low**, under **San Juan Bautista** [SAN BENITO].

Lowder Canyon [MONTEREY]: *canyon*, drained by a stream that flows 1.5 miles to lowlands nearly 5 miles west of Greenfield (lat. 36°18'15" N, long. 121°19'30" W). Named on Paraiso Springs (1956) 7.5' quadrangle. The name commemorates John Ellis Lowder, who patented land nearby in 1908 (Clark, 1991, p. 186).

Lowe: see **Jim Lowe's**, under **Mansfield Canyon** [MONTEREY]; **Mount Lowe** [SAN LUIS OBISPO].

Lowe Canyon [MONTEREY]: *canyon*, 3.25 miles long, opens into Long Valley from the northeast 3.5 miles east-northeast of San Lucas (lat. 36°09' N, long. 120°58' W; sec. 35, T 20 S, R 9 E). Named on Nattrass Valley (1967) 7.5' quadrangle.

Lower Alamar Campground [SANTA BARBARA]: *locality*, about 4 miles south of Madulce Peak (lat. 34°37'55" N, long. 119°35'05" W); the place is in Alamar Canyon. Named on Madulce Peak (1964) 7.5' quadrangle.

Lower Barn Springs: see **Hot Springs** [SANTA BARBARA] (2).

Lower Bear Campground [SANTA BARBARA]: *locality*, 1 mile northeast of Big Pine Mountain along Sisquoc River (lat. 34°42'30" N, long. 119°38'25" W); the place is 0.5 mile downstream from Bear Campground. Named on Big Pine Mountain (1964) 7.5' quadrangle.

Lower Bee Camp [MONTEREY]: *locality*, 3 miles east of Slates Hot Springs along North Fork Big Creek (lat. 36°07'25" N, long. 121° 35' W; sec. 12, T 21 S, R 3 E); the place is less than 1 mile south of Bee Camp. Named on Lopez Point (1956) 7.5' quadrangle.

Lower Berry Creek Falls: see **Berry Creek Falls** [SANTA CRUZ].

Lower Grapevine Campground [SANTA BARBARA]: *locality*, nearly 4 miles west-southwest of Big Pine Mountain (lat. 34°41' N, long. 119°43'05" W); the place is along Grapevine Creek. Named on Big Pine Mountain (1964) 7.5' quadrangle.

Lower Lion Spring [SANTA BARBARA]: *spring*, 4 miles north-northwest of Salisbury Potrero (lat. 34°52'25" N long. 119°43'15" W); the spring is in Lion Canyon (4). Named on Salisbury Potrero (1964) 7.5' quadrangle.

Lower Newsome Spring [SANTA BARBARA]: *spring*, 2.5 miles north of Salisbury Potrero (lat. 34°51'25" N, long. 119°42' W); the spring is in Newsome Canyon 3600 feet north of Upper Newsome Spring. Named on Salisbury Potrero (1964) 7.5' quadrangle.

Lower Oso Campground [SANTA BARBARA]: *locality*, 3.5 miles north-east of San Marcos Pass along Santa Ynez River (lat. 34°32'50" N, long. 119°46'30" W); the place is less than 1 mile south-southwest of Upper Oso Campground near the mouth of Oso Canyon. Named on San Marcos Pass (1959) 7.5' quadrangle.

Lower Piletas Canyon [SAN LUIS OBISPO]: *canyon*, drained by a stream that heads at Upper Piletas Canyon and flows 2 miles to San Juan Creek 4 miles west-northwest of Freeborn Mountain (lat. 35° 18'15" N, long. 120°07'15" W; sec. 23, T 30 S, R 17 E). Named on California Valley (1966) 7.5' quadrangle. Upper Piletas Canyon and Lower Piletas Canyon together are called simply Piletas Canyon on La Panza (1935) 15' quadrangle, but United States Board on Geographic Names (1968c, p. 5, 7) rejected this name.

Lower Sand Spring [SANTA BARBARA]: *spring,* 3.5 miles south of Salisbury Potrero (lat. 34°46'10" N, long. 119°41'20" W). Named on Salisbury Potrero (1964) 7.5' quadrangle.

Lowes Canyon [MONTEREY-SAN LUIS OBISPO]: *canyon,* drained by San Jacinto Creek, which heads in Monterey County and flows 16 miles to Estrella Creek nearly 3 miles southeast of San Miguel in San Luis Obispo County (lat. 35°43'40" N, long. 120°39'25" W; near W line sec. 26, T 25 S, R 12 E). Named on Paso Robles (1948), Ranchito Canyon (1948), and San Miguel (1948) 7.5' quadrangles. Called San Vicente Canyon on English and Kew's (1916) map. According to Stanley (p. 112), Frank E. Lowe took a farm in 1865 in what was called San Jacinto Canyon, but which later was renamed Lowe's Canyon. Stanley (p. 18) used the name "San Vicenta Valley" for present Lowes Canyon on his map.

Lucas: see **Santa Cruz** [SANTA CRUZ].

Lucas Point [MONTEREY]: *promontory,* 0.5 mile east-southeast of Point Pinos along the coast (lat. 36°38'10" N, long. 121°55'25" W). Named on Monterey (1947) 7.5' quadrangle. Clark (1991, p. 287) suggested that the name commemorates Captain Allen Luce, keeper of the lighthouse at Point Pinos in the 1870's.

Lucia [MONTEREY]: *settlement,* 1 mile east of Lopez Point near the coast (lat. 36°01'15" N, long. 121°33' W; sec. 17, T 22 S, R 4 E). Named on Lopez Point (1956) 7.5' quadrangle. Postal authorities established Lucia post office in 1900, moved it 1 mile southwest in 1906, discontinued it in 1933, reestablished it in 1936, and discontinued it in 1938 (Salley, p. 129). The name was for the postmaster, Lucia Dani, who had been named for Santa Lucia Range (Lussier, p. 35).

Lugo Canyon [MONTEREY]: *canyon,* drained by a stream that flows 5 miles to San Antonio River 2.5 miles south-southeast of Jolon (lat. 35°56'05" N, long. 121°09'45" W). Named on Jolon (1949) 7.5' quadrangle. The name is for Antonio Lugo, who served as an altar boy for Junipero Serra (Clark, 1991, p. 288).

Lumber Canyon [MONTEREY]: *canyon,* drained by a stream that flows 5 miles to Chalone Creek 4.5 miles northeast of Greenfield (lat. 36°22'20" N, long. 121°11'20" W). Named on Greenfield (1956) and Pinalito Canyon (1969) 7.5' quadrangles.

Lyda Spring [SAN LUIS OBISPO]: *spring,* 7.5 miles east-northeast of Pozo (lat. 35°21'05" N, long. 120°15'25" W). Named on Pozo Summit (1967) 7.5' quadrangle.

Lynch: see **Tierra Redonda Mountain** [SAN LUIS OBISPO].

Lynch Canyon [MONTEREY]: *canyon,* drained by a stream that flows 10.5 miles to lowlands 9 miles north-northwest of San Ardo (lat. 35°58'35" N, long. 120°51'45" W; sec. 35, T 22 S, R 10 E). Named on Pancho Rico Valley (1967), Slack Canyon (1969), and Wunpost (1949) 7.5' quadrangles. The name commemorates Thomas Lynch, who received a patent to land in the canyon in 1892 (Clark, 1991, p. 289).

Lynch's Creek: see **Bee Rock Canyon** [MONTEREY-SAN LUIS OBISPO].

Lynch's Mountain: see **Tierra Redonda Mountain** [SAN LUIS OBISPO].

Lyon Canyon: see **Griswold Canyon** [SAN BENITO].

Lyon Spring [SAN LUIS OBISPO]: *spring,* 7 miles west-northwest of Shandon in Wolf Canyon (lat. 35°42'20" N, long. 120°28'55" W; sec. 32, T 25 S, R 14 E). Named on Shandon (1961) 7.5' quadrangle.

- M -

Machesna Mountain [SAN LUIS OBISPO]: *peak,* 2.5 miles southwest of Castle Crags (lat. 35°16'45" N, long. 120°13'50" W). Altitude 4063 feet. Named on La Panza (1967) 7.5' quadrangle. Called McChesney Mountain on La Panza (1935) 15' quadrangle, but United States Board on Geographic Names (1962a, p. 13) ruled against this name for the feature.

Machesna Potrero [SAN LUIS OBISPO]: *area,* 1.5 miles south of Castle Crags (lat. 35°16'50" N, long. 120°12'10" W); the place is 1.5 miles east of Machesna Mountain. Named on La Panza (1967) 7.5' quadrangle.

Machesna Spring [SAN LUIS OBISPO]: *spring,* 8.5 miles west-northwest of Branch Mountain (lat. 35°14'10" N, long. 120°13'05" W). Named on Los Machos Hills (1967) 7.5' quadrangle.

Machete Ridge [SAN BENITO]: *peak,* 3.5 miles north of North Chalone Peak (lat. 36°29'50" N, long. 121°12' W; sec. 34, T 16 S, R 7 E). Named on North Chalone Peak (1969) 7.5' quadrangle.

Machine Gun Flats [MONTEREY]: *area,* 5.5 miles west-southwest of Salinas (lat. 36°38'10" N, long. 121°44'30" W); the place is on Fort Ord Military Reservation. Named on Salinas (1947) 7.5' quadrangle.

Mackenzie Creek [SANTA CRUZ]: *stream,* flows 1.5 miles to Bean Creek 7 miles east-southeast of the town of Boulder Creek (lat. 37° 04'20" N, long. 122°00'55" W; sec. 7, T 10 S, R 1 W). Named on Felton (1955) 7.5' quadrangle.

Maddocks Creek [SANTA CRUZ]: *stream,* flows nearly 1 mile to Opal Creek 1 mile north of Big Basin (lat. 37°11'05" N, long. 122° 13'05" W; sec. 5, T 9 S, R 3 E). Named on Big Basin (1955) 7.5' quadrangle. The name commemorates Thomas Maddock, who arrived in the neighborhood in 1882 and built a squatter's cabin along Opal Creek (Clark, 1986, p. 194).

Madrona Canyon [MONTEREY]: *canyon,* 4 miles long, drained by Big Creek (1) above a point 2.5 miles east-northeast of Jamesburg (lat. 36°23'10" N, long. 121°33' W; near S line sec. 4, T 18 S, R 4 E). Named on Rana Creek (1956) 7.5' quadrangle.

Madulce Peak [SANTA BARBARA]: *peak,* 10.5 miles northeast of Little Pine Mountain (lat. 34°41'25" N, long. 119°35'25" W). Altitude 6536 feet. Named on Madulce Peak (1964) 7.5' quadrangle. United States Board on Geographic Names (1939, p. 23) rejected the name "Strawberry Peak" for the feature.

Magetti Flats [SAN LUIS OBISPO]: *area,* 4.25 miles northwest of Pozo in Parola Canyon (lat. 35°20'50" N, long. 120°25'50" W; sec. 1, T 30 S, R 14 E). Named on Santa Margarita Lake (1967) 7.5' quadrangle.

Magnetic Spring [SANTA CRUZ]: *locality,* 3.5 miles south-southwest of Laurel (lat. 37°04'15" N, long. 121°59'10" W). Named on Los Gatos (1919) 15' quadrangle. Clark (1986, p. 136) noted that a resort called Glenwood Magnetic Springs was at the place as early as 1875.

Mahoney Canyon [MONTEREY-SAN LUIS OBISPO]: *canyon,* drained by a stream that heads in Monterey County and flows 9.5 miles to Salinas River 1 mile north-northeast of San Miguel in San Luis Obispo County (lat. 35°45'55" N, long. 120°41'15" W; sec. 9, T 25 S, R 12 E). Named on San Miguel (1948) 7.5' quadrangle. Stanley (p. 1) called the feature Mahoney's Canyon.

Mail Camp: see **San Miguel Creek** [MONTEREY].

Mail Trail Pond [SAN BENITO]: *lake,* 850 feet long, 12 miles east-southeast of Bitterwater (lat. 36°20'40" N, long. 120°47'35" W; sec. 20, T 18 S, R 11 E). Named on Hepsedam Peak (1969) 7.5' quadrangle, which shows the lake near a route that has the label "Mail Trail."

Main Sulphur Spring: see **Paso Robles** [SAN LUIS OBISPO].

Majors [SANTA CRUZ]: *settlement,* 7 miles west-northwest of Point Santa Cruz (lat. 36°59' N, long. 122°08'40" W); the place is near the mouth of Majors Creek. Named on Santa Cruz (1954) 7.5' quadrangle. It first was called Enright (Clark, 1986, p. 195).

Majors Creek [SANTA CRUZ]: *stream,* flows 5.5 miles to the sea 6.5 miles west-northwest of Point Santa Cruz (lat. 36°58'35" N, long. 122°08'25" W). Named on Felton (1955) and Santa Cruz (1954) 7.5' quadrangles. The stream flows through Refugio grant, part of which belonged to Joseph L. Majors. Hubbard's (1943) map has the name "Coja Cr." for the stream

Mallagh Landing [SAN LUIS OBISPO]: *locality,* 1 mile east-southeast of Avila Beach at the end of a promontory that extends into San Luis Obispo Bay (lat. 35°10'25" N, long. 120°42'55" W). Named on Pismo Beach (1965) 7.5' quadrangle. The place was called Cave Landing before about 1860, when David Mallagh, an Irish sea captain, built a warehouse on the cliff there and had a wooden chute down to the water; the name "Cave Landing" is from a nearby cave called Robbers' Cave because it had been a hiding place for bandits' loot (Hoover, Rensch, and Rensch, p. 380).

Malosky Creek [SANTA CRUZ]: *stream,* flows nearly 1 mile to San Lorenzo River near the south edge of the town of Boulder Creek (lat. 37°06'50" N, long. 122°07' W; near SE cor. sec. 30, T 9 S, R 2 W). Named on Davenport (1955) and Felton (1955) 7.5' quadrangles. Clark (1986, p. 211) used the form "Molasky Creek" for the name.

Malpaso Creek [MONTEREY]: *stream,* flows 4.25 miles to the sea nearly 1 mile south-southeast of Yankee Point (lat. 36°28'50" N, long. 121°56'15" W). Named on Mount Carmel (1956) and Soberanes Point (1956) 7.5' quadrangles. The name probably is from difficulty that horses had crossing the creek—*malpaso* means "bad crossing" in Spanish (Lussier, p. 12).

Malva Real Anchorage [SANTA BARBARA]: *anchorage,* just east of Punta Arena on the south side of Santa Cruz Island (lat. 33°57'40" N, long. 119°48'45" W). Named on Santa Cruz Island B (1943) 7.5' quadrangle. Bremner's (1932) map has the name "Cñ.. Malvareal" for a canyon that opens to the sea just west of present Malva Real Anchorage.

Manchester: see **Alder Creek** [MONTEREY].

Mangels Creek: see **Mangles Gulch** [SANTA CRUZ].

Mangels Gulch: see **Mangles Gulch** [SANTA CRUZ].

Mangles Gulch [SANTA CRUZ]: *canyon,* drained by a stream that flows 2 miles to Aptos Creek 4.25 miles east-northeast of Soquel Point (lat. 36°58'50" N, long. 121°54'10" W). Named on Laurel (1955) and Soquel (1954) 7.5' quadrangles. Called Mangels Gulch on Soquel (1954, photorevised 1968) 7.5' quadrangle. United States Board on Geographic Names (1972c, p. 3) noted that the name is for Claus Mangels, a former landowner at the place; the Board gave the name "Mangels Creek" as a variant.

Mann Canyon [MONTEREY]: *canyon,* 1.25 miles long, opens into Shirttail Gulch 7.5 miles north of Greenfield (lat. 36°25'50" N, long. 121°13'45" W; near S line sec. 20, T 17 S, R 7 E). Named on North Chalone Peak (1969) 7.5' quadrangle.

Manresa [SANTA CRUZ]: *locality,* 6.25 miles west-northwest of Watsonville at present La Selva Beach (lat. 36°56'10" N, long. 121°51'50" W). Named on Capitola (1914) 15' quadrangle. Manresa was the train station for Villa

Manresa, a Catholic Church retreat named for Manresa, Spain, where Saint Ignatius of Loyola conceived the idea for the Jesuit order (Clark, 1986, p. 197). Hubbard's (1943) map shows a place called Cristo located along the railroad at about the site of present Manresa.

Manresa: see **La Selva Beach** [SANTA CRUZ].

Mansfield: see **Alder Creek** [MONTEREY].

Mansfield Canyon [MONTEREY]: *canyon*, drained by a stream that flows 2.25 miles to Quinado Canyon 7 miles west-southwest of San Lucas (lat. 36°05'50" N, long. 121°08'50" W; near N line sec. 19, T 21 S, R 8 E). Named on Cosio Knob (1949) 7.5' quadrangle. Howard (p. 65) noted that a roadhouse called Jim Lowe's was located near the mouth of Mansfield Canyon.

Manson Creek [SANTA CRUZ]: *stream*, flows 1 mile to San Lorenzo River 4.25 miles south-southeast of the town of Boulder Creek (lat. 37°04'10" N, long. 122°05' W; near S line sec. 9, T 10 S, R 2 W). Named on Felton (1955) 7.5' quadrangle.

Manuel Peak [MONTEREY]: *peak*, 7.5 miles east-southeast of Point Sur (lat. 36°16'25" N, long. 121°46'10" W; near S line sec. 17, T 19 S, R 2 E). Named on Big Sur (1956) 7.5' quadrangle. The name is for Manuel Innocenti, a Santa Barbara mission Indian who settled in the region in the mid-nineteenth century (Lussier, p. 23; Lussier called the feature Mount Manuel).

Manzana Camp [SANTA CRUZ]: *locality*, 4 miles west-northwest of San Rafael Mountain (lat. 34°44'05" N, long. 119°52'25" W); the place is along Manzana Creek. Named on San Rafael Mountain (1959) 7.5' quadrangle.

Manzana Campground [SANTA BARBARA]: *locality*, 3.5 miles west-northwest of Bald Mountain (1) (lat. 34°49'30" N, long. 119° 59'35" W); the place is near the mouth of Manzana Creek. Named on Bald Mountain (1964) 7.5' quadrangle.

Manzana Canyon: see **Manzana Creek** [SANTA BARBARA].

Manzana Creek [SANTA BARBARA]: *stream*, flows 21 miles to Sisquoc River 3.5 miles west-northwest of Bald Mountain (1) (lat. 34°49'35" N, long. 119°59'35" W). Named on Bald Mountain (1964), Figueroa Mountain (1959), San Rafael Mountain (1959), and Zaca Lake (1964) 7.5' quadrangles. The canyon of the stream is called Manzana Canyon on Santa Ynez (1905) 30' quadrangle. The name was given in the 1870's for a large apple orchard situated near the stream—*manzana* means "apple" in Spanish (Gudde, 1949, p. 203).

Manzana Narrows Camp [SANTA BARBARA]: *locality*, 3.5 miles west-northwest of San Rafael Mountain (lat. 34°44'15" N, long. 119°51'55" W); the place is along Manzana Creek. Named on San Rafael Mountain (1959) 7.5' quadrangle.

Manzanita Canyon [MONTEREY-SAN LUIS OBISPO]: *canyon*, drained by a stream that heads in Monterey County and flows nearly 5 miles to Shimmin Canyon 6 miles north-northwest of Shandon in San Luis Obispo County (lat. 35°44'15" N, long. 120° 25'05" W; sec. 24, T 25 S, R 14 E). Named on Cholame Hills (1961) and Shandon (1961) 7.5' quadrangles.

Manzanita Mountain [SANTA BARBARA]: *peak*, 20 miles east of Santa Maria (lat. 34°53'40" N, long. 120°04'45" W). Altitude 3193 feet. Named on Manzanita Mountain (1964) 7.5' quadrangle.

Marble Peak [MONTEREY]: *peak*, 4 miles east of Partington Point (lat. 36°10'25" N, long. 121°37'35" W; sec. 22, T 20 S, R 3 E). Altitude 4031 feet. Named on Partington Ridge (1956) 7.5' quadrangle. The name is from limestone and marble at the place (Clark, 1991, p. 295).

March Rock [SANTA BARBARA]: *rock*, 5.5 miles northwest of Cardwell Point, and 200 feet offshore at the northeast end of Simonton Cove on San Miguel Island (lat. 34°04'25" N, long. 120° 22'05" W). Named on San Miguel Island East (1950) 7.5' quadrangle.

Mare Spring [SAN LUIS OBISPO]: *spring*, 9 miles northeast of Pozo (lat. 35°23'30" N, long. 120°15'50" W; sec. 21, T 29 S, R 16 E). Named on Camatta Ranch (1966) 7.5' quadrangle.

Mariana Creek [SAN LUIS OBISPO]: *stream*, flows 1.5 miles to Navajo Creek nearly 6.5 miles east-northeast of Pozo (lat. 35°21'25" N, long. 120°16'30" W; sec. 32, T 29 S, R 16 E). Named on Pozo Summit (1967) 7.5' quadrangle.

Maria Ygnacio Creek [SANTA BARBARA]: *stream*, flows nearly 7 miles to Atascadero Creek 1.25 miles southeast of downtown Goleta (lat. 34°25'30" N, long. 119°48'35" W). Named on Goleta (1950) and San Marcos Pass (1959) 7.5' quadrangles. East Fork enters from the northeast nearly 3 miles upstream from the mouth of the main creek; it is 2 miles long and is named on Goleta (1950) 7.5' quadrangle.

Marina [MONTEREY]: *town*, 8 miles west of Salinas near the coast (lat. 36°41' N, long. 121°48' W). Named on Marina (1947) 7.5' quadrangle. Postal authorities established Marina post office in 1916 (Frickstad, p. 107), and the town incorporated in 1975. William Locke-Paddon bought 1500 acres of land and had the town laid out in 1913 (Clark, 1991, p. 295).

Mariposa Peak [SAN BENITO]: *peak*, 12.5 miles east-northeast of Hollister on San Benito-Merced County line (lat. 36°57'25" N, long. 121°12'40" W; near S line sec. 21, T 11 S, R 7 E). Altitude 3448 feet. Named on Mariposa Peak (1969) 7.5' quadrangle. California Mining Bureau's (1917b) map shows a place called Lone Tree located nearly 5 miles south-southwest of Mariposa Peak. California Mining Bureau's (1909a) map has the form "Lonetree" for the name. Postal authorities established Lonetree post office in 1900 and discontinued it in 1911 (Frickstad, p. 136).

Marmolejo Creek [SAN LUIS OBISPO]: *stream*, flows 5 miles to join Burnett Creek and form Arroyo de la Cruz 4 miles north-northeast of the village of San Simeon (lat. 35°41'55" N, long. 121° 10'15" W). Named on Pebblestone Shut-in (1959) and San Simeon (1958) 7.5' quadrangles.

Marmolejo Flats [SAN LUIS OBISPO]: *area*, 5 miles east-northeast of the village of San Simeon (lat. 35°41'05" N, long. 121°06'55" W); the place is along Marmolejo Creek. Named on Pebblestone Shut-in (1959) 7.5' quadrangle.

Marre Canyon [SANTA BARBARA]: *canyon*, drained by a stream that flows 5.25 miles to Santa Agueda Creek 6 miles east-southeast of Los Olivos (lat. 34°37'40" N, long. 120°01'10" W). Named on Figueroa Mountain (1959) and Los Olivos (1959) 7.5' quadrangles. Figueroa Mountain (1959) 7.5' quadrangle shows Marre ranch near the head of the canyon. Called Morey Canyon on Santa Ynez (1905) 30' quadrangle, but United States Board on Geographic Names (1961b, p. 11) rejected this name for the feature.

Mars: see **Mount Mars** [MONTEREY].

Marshall Creek [SANTA CRUZ]: *stream*, flows 1.5 miles to San Lorenzo River 2.5 miles south-southeast of the town of Boulder Creek (lat. 37°05'30" N, long. 122°05'35" W; near W line sec. 4, T 10 S, R 2 W). Named on Felton (1955) 7.5' quadrangle. The name is for J.D. Marshall, who came from Texas in 1852 and settled along the stream (Rowland, p. 184).

Martin Canyon [MONTEREY]: *canyon*, drained by a stream that flows 1.5 miles to Carmel Valley (1) 2.5 miles east of the mouth of Carmel River (lat. 36°32'35" N, long. 121°53' W). Named on Monterey (1947) 7.5' quadrangle. The name commemorates John Martin, who settled in the canyon (Clark, 1991, p. 297).

Martinez Canyon [SAN LUIS OBISPO]: *canyon*, drained by a stream that flows nearly 3 miles to the canyon of San Juan Creek 4.5 miles east of Castle Crags (lat. 35°18'35" N, long. 120°07'20" W; near S line sec. 14, T 30 S, R 17 E). Named on La Panza (1967) 7.5' quadrangle. On La Panza (1935) 15' quadrangle, present Hay Canyon has the name "Martinez Canyon."

Martin Station: see **Neponset** [MONTEREY].

Martinus Corner [MONTEREY]: *locality*, 4 miles east-southeast of Jolon (lat. 35°56'25" N, long. 121°07'05" W; near E line sec. 8, T 23 S, R 8 E). Named on Williams Hill (1949) 7.5' quadrangle. The name commemorates Jan Henry Martinus, who patented land near place in 1891 (Clark, 1991, p. 298).

Mary Hill Mineral Well: see **Paso Robles** [SAN LUIS OBISPO].

Mason Canyon [MONTEREY-SAN LUIS OBISPO]: *canyon*, drained by a stream that heads in Monterey County and flows 10 miles to Estrella Creek 10 miles east-northeast of Paso Robles in San Luis Obispo County (lat. 35°41'15" N, long. 120°31'55" W; near NW cor. sec. 12, T 26 S, R 13 E). Named on Cholame Hills (1961) 7.5' quadrangle. Called Freeman Canyon on Estrella (1948) 7.5' quadrangle. On Cholame (1917) 30' quadrangle, the name "Mason Canyon" applies to present Willow Springs Canyon.

Matarana Gulch [MONTEREY]: *canyon*, drained by a stream that flows 2.5 miles to Chualar Canyon 10 miles north-northeast of Gonzales (lat. 36°38'05" N, long. 121°21'10" W; near N line sec. 18, T 15 S, R 6 E). Named on Mount Johnson (1968) and Paicines (1968) 7.5' quadrangles. The misspelled name is for Jesús Maturano, who patented land in the canyon in 1900 (Clark, 1991, p. 299).

Mattos Gulch [SANTA CRUZ]: *canyon*, 1 mile long, opens into Pajaro Valley 4.5 miles east of Watsonville (lat. 36°55'30" N, long. 121°40'15" W). Named on Watsonville East (1955) 7.5' quadrangle.

Maxwellton [SAN LUIS OBISPO]: *locality*, nearly 0.25 mile southwest of Edna along Pacific Coast Railroad and Southern Pacific Railroad (lat. 35°12' N, long. 120°37' W). Named on Arroyo Grande (1897) 15' quadrangle.

Maymens Flat [SANTA CRUZ]: *area*, 6.5 miles north of Corralitos (lat. 37°04'55" N, long. 121°49'15" W; near NE cor. sec. 11, T 10 S, R 1 E). Named on Loma Prieta (1955) 7.5' quadrangle. Charles Maymen and James Maymen homesteaded at the place in the 1890's (Young, p. 64).

McCabe Canyon [SAN BENITO]: *canyon*, drained by a stream that flows 3.25 miles to Bear Valley 4 miles northeast of North Chalone Peak (lat. 36°29'30" N, long. 121°08'55" W; sec. 31, T 16 S, R 8 E). Named on Bickmore Canyon (1968) and North Chalone Peak (1969) 7.5' quadrangles.

McCallum: see **Camp McCallum** [MONTEREY].

McChesney Mountain: see **Machesna Mountain** [SAN LUIS OBISPO].

McClappin Spring [SAN LUIS OBISPO]: *spring*, 3.5 miles southwest of Atascadero (lat. 35°26'55" N, long. 120°42'30" W). Named on Atascadero (1965) 7.5' quadrangle.

McClusky Slough [MONTEREY]: *water feature*, lakes and marsh near the coast south of the mouth of Pajaro River (lat. 36°50'25" N, long. 121°47'40"

W). Named on Moss Landing (1954) 7.5' quadrangle. Capitola (1914) 15' quadrangle has the name for three connected lakes.

McConnell Canyon [MONTEREY]: *canyon,* drained by a stream that flows about 2 miles to Espinosa Canyon (2) 6 miles south-southwest of San Lucas (lat. 36°02'50" N, long. 121°03'50" W; sec. 1, T 22 S, R 8 E). Named on Espinosa Canyon (1949) 7.5' quadrangle. The name commemorates William S. McConnell, who owned land at the place (Clark, 1991, p. 301).

McCoy Canyon [MONTEREY]: *canyon,* 5.5 miles long, opens into lowlands 4.5 miles east-northeast of Gonzales (lat. 36°31'45" N, long. 121°21'45" W; near W line sec. 19, T 16 S, R 6 E); McCoy Creek drains the canyon. Named on Mount Johnson (1968) 7.5' quadrangle. The name commemorates Thomas A. McCoy, who patented land at the place in 1884 and 1892 (Clark, 1991, p. 301-302).

McCoy Canyon [SANTA BARBARA]: *canyon,* drained by a stream that flows 2.25 miles to Glen Annie Canyon 3.5 miles northwest of Goleta (lat. 34°28'15" N, long. 119°52'30" W; sec. 36, T 5 N, R 29 W). Named on Goleta (1950) 7.5' quadrangle.

McCoy Creek [MONTEREY]: *stream,* flows 8 miles before ending in lowlands 5.5 miles northwest of Soledad (lat. 36°29'35" N, long. 121°23' W; sec. 35, T 16 S, R 5 E); the stream flows through McCoy Canyon. Named on Gonzales (1955), Mount Johnson (1968), and Palo Escrito Peak (1956) 7.5' quadrangles.

McCoy Creek [SAN BENITO]: *stream,* flows nearly 7 miles to San Benito River 8.5 miles east-northeast of Bitterwater (lat. 36°24'30" N, long. 120°51' W; sec. 35, T 17 S, R 10 E). Named on Hernandez Reservoir (1969) 7.5' quadrangle.

McDonald Canyon [SAN LUIS OBISPO]: *canyon,* drained by a stream that flows 6.5 miles to San Juan Valley 4 miles south-southeast of Shandon (lat. 35°36'10" N, long. 120°21'20" W; sec. 4, T 27 S, R 15 E). Named on Camatta Canyon (1961) 7.5' quadrangle.

McDonald Gulch [SANTA CRUZ]: *canyon,* 1 mile long, along Kings Creek above a point 6.25 miles north of the town of Boulder Creek (lat. 37°13' N, long. 122°07'15" W; near S line sec. 19, T 8 S, R 2 W). Named on Castle Rock Ridge (1955) 7.5' quadrangle.

McFadden: see **Chas. McFadden**, under **One Suerte** [MONTEREY].

McGaffigan's Switch: see **San Lorenzo Park** [SANTA CRUZ].

McGinnis Creek [SAN LUIS OBISPO]: *stream,* flows nearly 3 miles to Navajo Creek 7.5 miles northeast of Pozo (lat. 35°22'50" N, long. 120°16'50" W; near S line sec. 20, T 29 S, R 16 E). Named on Camatta Ranch (1966) and Pozo Summit (1967) 7.5' quadrangles.

McGowan Canyon [MONTEREY]: *canyon,* nearly 2 miles long, opens into lowlands 8.5 miles southeast of Jolon (lat. 35°53'45" N, long. 121°03'05" W). Named on Williams Hill (1949) 7.5' quadrangle.

McKay [SAN LUIS OBISPO]: *locality,* 3.5 miles northwest of San Miguel along Southern Pacific Railroad at Camp Roberts Military Reservation (lat. 35°47' N, long. 120°43'30" W; sec. 6, T 25 S, R 12 E). Named on San Miguel (1948) 7.5' quadrangle. California Mining Bureau's (1909b) map has the name "Chanslor" for a place located at or near present McKay.

McKenna Canyon [SAN BENITO]: *canyon,* drained by a stream that flows 3.5 miles to Los Muertos Creek 2.25 miles west-northwest of Cherry Peak (lat. 36°42'05" N, long. 121°10'50" W; sec. 23, T 14 S, R 7 E). Named on Cherry Peak (1968) 7.5' quadrangle.

McKinley Mountain [SANTA BARBARA]: *peak,* 2 miles west-southwest of San Rafael Mountain (lat. 34°42'05" N, long. 119°50'40" W; at E line sec. 8, T 7 N, R 28 W). Named on San Rafael Mountain (1959) 7.5' quadrangle.

McLain Spring [SAN LUIS OBISPO]:

(1) *spring,* 5.25 miles south of Atascadero in Kathleen Valley (lat. 35°24'45" N, long. 120°40'10" W; near S line sec. 10, T 29 S, R 12 E). Named on Atascadero (1965) 7.5' quadrangle.

(2) *spring,* 5.5 miles northeast of Simmler (lat. 35°24'30" N, long. 119°54'50" W; near NW cor. sec. 14, T 29 S, R 10 E). Named on Las Yeguas Ranch (1959) 7.5' quadrangle.

McLaughlin Canyon [SAN LUIS OBISPO]: *canyon,* drained by a stream that flows 2.25 miles to Town Creek 11 miles east-northeast of the village of San Simeon (lat. 35°41' N, long. 121°00' W; sec. 9, T 26 S, R 9 E). Named on Pebblestone Shut-in (1959) 7.5' quadrangle.

McLean: see **La Panza** [SAN LUIS OBISPO].

McLeod: see **Hale McLeod Canyon** [SAN LUIS OBISPO].

McMillan Canyon [SAN LUIS OBISPO]: *canyon,* drained by a stream that flows 8 miles to Estrella River 2 miles west of Shandon (lat. 35°39'15" N, long. 120°24'40" W; sec. 24, T 26 S, R 14 E). Named on Cholame (1961), Cholame Valley (1961), and Shandon (1961) 7.5' quadrangles.

McMillan Canyon: see **Bud Canyon** [SAN LUIS OBISPO].

McMillan Spring [MONTEREY]: *spring,* 14 miles east-northeast of San Ardo along Pancho Rico Creek (lat. 36°05'15" N, long. 120° 40' W; sec. 22, T 21 S, R 12 E). Named on Slack Canyon (1969) 7.5' quadrangle.

McNeil Spring [SAN LUIS OBISPO]: *spring,* 2.5 miles southwest of Pozo (lat. 35°16'25" N, long. 120°24'10" W; near S line sec. 30, T 30 S, R 15 E). Named on Santa Margarita Lake (1967) 7.5' quadrangle.

McPhails Peak [MONTEREY-SAN BENITO]: *peak,* 11 miles north-northeast of Gonzales on Monterey-San Benito County line (lat. 36°39'25" N, long. 121°21'55" W; sec. 1, T 15 S, R 5 E). Altitude 3353 feet. Named on Paicines (1968) 7.5' quadrangle.

McPherson: see **Mount McPherson**, under **Bielawski Mountain** [SANTA CRUZ].

McPherson Peak [SANTA BARBARA]: *peak,* 33 miles north-northwest of Santa Barbara (lat. 34°53'20" N, long. 119°48'45" W). Altitude 5749 feet. Named on Peak Mountain (1964) 7.5' quadrangle.

McQuaide: see **Camp McQuaide**, under **San Andres** [SANTA CRUZ].

McWay Canyon [MONTEREY]: *canyon,* drained by a stream that flows 2.5 miles to the sea 2 miles southeast of Partington Point (lat. 36°09'30" N, long. 121°40'15" W; sec. 30, T 20 S, R 3 E). Named on Partington Ridge (1956) 7.5' quadrangle. The McWay family homesteaded in the neighborhood before 1900 (Fink, p. 210). The feature also was called Lion Gulch, and the stream in it was called Lion Creek (Clark, 1991, p. 304).

McWay Rocks [MONTEREY]: *rocks,* largest 225 feet long, 1.5 miles southeast of Partington Point, and 400 to 900 feet offshore (lat. 36° 09'45" N, long. 121°40'40" W); the rocks are 0.5 mile northwest of the mouth of McWay Canyon . Named on Partington Ridge (1956) 7.5' quadrangle.

Meadow Creek [SAN LUIS OBISPO]: *stream,* flows 2.5 miles from Pismo Lake south through marsh and lakes situated near the coast to Arroyo Grande Creek 3 miles west-southwest of downtown Arroyo Grande (lat. 35°06' N, long. 120°37'45" W). Named on Oceano (1965) and Pismo Beach (1965) 7.5' quadrangles.

Meadows: see **James Meadows** [MONTEREY].

Meadows Canyon [MONTEREY]: *canyon,* drained by a stream that flows 2.25 miles to Carmel Valley (1) 7.5 miles east of the mouth of Carmel River (lat. 36°31'30" N, long. 121°47'35" W); the canyon is near the east edge of James Meadows grant. Named on Seaside (1947) 7.5' quadrangle.

Meadows Tract: see **James Meadows** [MONTEREY].

Meder Creek: see **Peasley Gulch** [SANTA CRUZ]; **Wilder Creek** [SANTA CRUZ].

Medford Valley [MONTEREY]: *valley,* opens into Indian Valley (3) 13 miles northeast of Bradley (lat. 35°59'50" N, long. 120°38'45" W; sec. 23, T 22 S, R 12 E). Named on Slack Canyon (1969) 7.5' quadrangle.

Meehan: see **Lompico Creek** [SANTA CRUZ].

Mehlscaw Creek: see **Mehlschau Creek** [SAN LUIS OBISPO].

Mehlschau Creek [SAN LUIS OBISPO]: *stream,* flows 2.5 miles to Nipomo Creek nearly 2 miles west-northwest of the town of Nipomo (lat. 35°03'25" N, long. 120°30' W). Named on Nipomo (1965) 7.5' quadrangle. Called Mehlscaw Creek on Nipomo (1922) 15' quadrangle.

Mercey Creek [SAN BENITO]: *stream,* heads just inside Merced County and flows 6 miles through San Benito County to Fresno County 10 miles north-northwest of Panoche (lat. 36°43'50" N, long. 121°54'25" W; near N line sec. 8, T 14 S, R 10 E). Named on Cerro Colorado (1969) and Ortigalita Peak (1969) 7.5' quadrangles. Called Mercy Creek on Panoche Valley (1944) 15' quadrangle. South Fork enters from the southwest 2.5 miles upstream from the entrance of the main creek into Fresno County; it is nearly 2 miles long and is named on Cerro Colorado (1969) 7.5' quadrangle.

Mercy Creek: see **Mercey Creek** [SAN BENITO].

Merriam: see **Camp Merriam**, under **Camp San Luis Obispo** [SAN LUIS OBISPO].

Merrilis Hill [MONTEREY]: *peak,* 5 miles east of Seaside (lat. 36° 37'10" N, long. 121°45'45" W). Named on Seaside (1947) 7.5' quadrangle. Clark (1991, p. 306) used the form "Merrillis Hill" for the name.

Merrill Lake [SAN BENITO]: *lake,* 225 feet long, 11.5 miles east-northeast of Bitterwater (lat. 36°26'20" N, long. 120°48'25" W; sec. 19, T 17 S, R 11 E). Named on Hernandez Reservoir (1969) 7.5' quadrangle.

Merritt Lake [MONTEREY]: *valley,* drained by an artificial watercourse that reaches Tembladero Slough 4 miles west-southwest of Prunedale (lat. 36°45'05" N, long. 121°44'15" W). Named on Prunedale (1954) 7.5' quadrangle. San Juan Bautista (1917) 15' quadrangle shows marsh and lakes along the valley. This place and Espinosa Lake together are called Lagunas de la Herba de los Mansos on a diseño of Bolsa del Potrero y Moro Cojo grant (Becker, 1964). The name "Merritt" is for Josiah Merritt, who came to Monterey in 1850 (Clark, 1991, p. 307).

Mervine: see **Fort Mervine**, under **Presidio of Monterey** [MONTEREY].

Mesa: see **The Mesa** [MONTEREY]; **The Mesa**, under **Nipomo Mesa** [SAN LUIS OBISPO].

Mesa Coyote [MONTEREY]: *area,* 4.5 miles south-southwest of Jolon (lat. 35°54'25" N, long. 121°11'45" W). Named on Jolon (1949) 7.5' quadrangle.

Mesa de Ojo de Agua [SANTA CRUZ]: *land grant,* 2.25 miles north-northwest of Point Santa Cruz in Santa Cruz. Named on Santa Cruz (1954) 7.5' quadrangle.

Mesa Grande [MONTEREY]: *area,* 5 miles east-southeast of the mouth of Carmel River (lat. 36°30'25" N, long. 121°50'45" W). Named on Monterey (1913) 15' quadrangle.

Mescal Island: see **Mescalitan Island** [SANTA BARBARA].

Mescalitan Island [SANTA BARBARA]: *hill,* 1 mile south-southwest of downtown Goleta (lat. 34°25'15" N, long. 119°49'55" W). Named on Goleta (1950) 7.5' quadrangle. Called Mescal I. on Goleta (1903) 15' quadrangle, which shows the feature surrounded by water and marsh. In 1769 members of the Portola expedition gave the name "Mescalitan" to the island, a name derived from a similar island in a lake near modern Mazatlan, Mexico (Tompkins and Ruiz, p. 10).

Mescal Ridge [MONTEREY]: *ridge*, west-trending, 4 miles long, 4.5 miles northeast of Point Sur (lat. 36°21'20" N, long. 121°51' W). Named on Big Sur (1956) and Point Sur (1956) 7.5' quadrangles.

Messenger Canyon [SANTA BARBARA]: *canyon*, drained by a stream that flows 4 miles to Wells Creek 3.5 miles north-northeast of McPherson Peak (lat. 34°56'20" N, long. 119°47'50" W). Named on Peak Mountain (1964) 7.5' quadrangle.

Messenger Canyon: see **Wells Creek** [SANTA BARBARA].

Messic Mountain [SAN BENITO]: *peak*, 9 miles northeast of Hollister (lat. 36°57' N, long. 121°17'45" W). Altitude 1814 feet. Named on Three Sisters (1954) 7.5' quadrangle.

Metz [MONTEREY]: *locality*, 3 miles northeast of Greenfield along Southern Pacific Railroad (lat. 36°21'20" N, long. 121°12'40" W; sec. 21, T 18 S, R 7 E). Named on Greenfield (1956) 7.5' quadrangle. Postal authorities established Metz post office in 1888 and discontinued it in 1933 (Frickstad, p. 107). The railroad reached the place in 1886 and the station was called Chalone, for nearby North Chalone Peak and South Chalone Peak, but when the post office opened there it was called it Metz, for W.H.H. Metz, first postmaster (Gudde, 1949, p. 213).

Meyers Peak [SAN BENITO]: *peak*, 5 miles southwest of Panoche (lat. 36°32'55" N, long. 120°54'05" W; sec. 8, T 16 S, R 10 E). Altitude 3721 feet. Named on Llanada (1969) 7.5' quadrangle.

Michaels Hill [MONTEREY]: *ridge*, northwest-trending, 1 mile long, 2.5 miles northeast of Partington Point (lat. 36°12'20" N, long. 121°40'15" W). Named on Partington Ridge (1956) 7.5' quadrangle. The feature also was known as Picks Summit (Clark, 1991, p. 310).

Midco [SANTA BARBARA]: *locality*, 2 miles southwest of downtown Santa Maria along Santa Maria Valley Railroad (lat. 34°56'10" N, long. 120°27'45" W). Named on Santa Maria (1959) 7.5' quadrangle.

Middle Anchorage [SANTA BARBARA]: *anchorage*, 3 miles southwest of San Pedro Point at the east end of Santa Cruz Island (lat. 34°00'05" N, long. 119°33' W). Named on Santa Cruz Island D (1943) 7.5' quadrangle.

Middle Canyon [SAN LUIS OBISPO]:

(1) *canyon*, drained by a stream that flows 1.5 miles to Shimmin Canyon 6.5 miles north-northwest of Shandon (lat. 35°44'40" N, long. 120°24'40" W; near N line sec. 24, T 25 S, R 14 E). Named on Cholame Hills (1961) and Shandon (1961) 7.5' quadrangles.

(2) *canyon*, drained by a stream that flows 3.5 miles to Cuyama Valley 2.5 miles north of New Cuyama [SANTA BARBARA] (lat. 34°59'10" N, long. 119°40'55" W; sec. 5, T 10 N, R 26 W). Named on New Cuyama (1964) 7.5' quadrangle.

Middle Canyon [SANTA BARBARA]: *canyon*, drained by a stream that flows 3 miles to Horse Canyon (3) 6 miles east-northeast of Santa Ynez Peak (lat. 34°34'15" N, long. 119°53' W). Named on Lake Cachuma (1959) and San Marcos Pass (1959) 7.5' quadrangles.

Middle Cove [MONTEREY]: *embayment*, at the northwest end of Point Lobos along the coast (lat. 36°31'25" N, long. 121°57'10" W). Named on Monterey (1947) 7.5' quadrangle.

Middle Fork [MONTEREY]: *stream*, flows 7.25 miles to Vineyard Canyon 12 miles east of Bradley (lat. 35°51'30" N, long. 120°35'55" W; sec. 8, T 24 S, R 13 E). Named on Ranchito Canyon (1948) and Stockdale Mountain (1948) 7.5' quadrangles.

Middle Mountain [MONTEREY]: *ridge*, northwest-trending, 8 miles long, 6 miles northwest of Parkfield (lat. 35°57'30" N, long. 120° 30' W). Named on Parkfield (1961) and Stockdale Mountain (1948) 7.5' quadrangles.

Middle Ridge [SAN LUIS OBISPO]: *ridge*, southwest-trending, 4 miles long, 5 miles east of the village of San Simeon (lat. 35°39'15" N, long. 121°06' W); the ridge is between North Fork Pico Creek and South Fork Pico Creek. Named on Pebblestone Shut-in (1959) 7.5' quadrangle.

Middle Rock [SANTA BARBARA]: *rock*, 3.5 miles northwest of Cardwell Point on the north side of San Miguel Island (lat. 34° 03'15" N, long. 120°20'40" W); the feature is in the middle of the opening to Cuyler Harbor. Named on San Miguel Island East (1950) 7.5' quadrangle.

Middle Santa Ynez Campground [SANTA BARBARA]: *locality*, 6.25 miles south-southwest of Hildreth Peak along Santa Ynez River (lat. 34°30'40" N, long. 119°34'45" W). Named on Hildreth Peak (1964) 7.5' quadrangle.

Midway Peak [SAN LUIS OBISPO]: *peak*, 25 miles east-southeast of Simmler (lat. 35°09'45" N, long. 119°37' W; sec. 4, T 32 S, R 22 E). Altitude 3662 feet. Named on Fellows (1951) 7.5' quadrangle.

Midway Point [MONTEREY]: *promontory*, 2.5 miles west-northwest of present Carmel-by-the-Sea along the coast (lat. 36°34' N, long. 121°57'45" W). Named on Monterey (1947) 7.5' quadrangle. The name is from the position of the feature about midway between Sunset Point and Pescadero Point (Clark, 1991, p. 310).

Milburn Spring [SAN LUIS OBISPO]: *spring*, 4.5 miles south of Wilson Corner (lat. 35°24'05" N, long. 120°23'30" W; sec. 17, T 29 S, R 15 E). Named on Wilson Corner (1966) 7.5' quadrangle.

Miles [SAN LUIS OBISPO]: *locality*, 1.5 miles east-northeast of Avila Beach near San Luis Obispo Creek (lat. 35°11'05" N, long. 120°42'10" W). Named on Pismo Beach (1965) 7.5' quadrangle. Arroyo Grande (1897) 15' quadrangle shows the place along Pacific Coast Railroad. California (1891) map has the label "Miles Sta. or Root P.O." at the site. Postal authorities established Root post office in 1883 and discontinued it in 1894; the name was for Oroville Root, first postmaster (Salley, p. 188).

Milindee Canyon [MONTEREY]: *canyon*, drained by a stream that flows 0.5 mile to lowlands 5 miles west of Greenfield (lat. 36°18'50" N, long. 121°19'45" W). Named on Paraiso Springs (1956) 7.5' quadrangle.

Milkcan Spring [SAN LUIS OBISPO]: *spring*, 4.5 miles south of Wilson Corner in Wilson Canyon (lat. 35°24'15" N, long. 120°22'35" W; near N line sec. 16, T 29 S, R 15 E). Named on Wilson Corner (1966) 7.5' quadrangle.

Mill Canyon [SANTA CRUZ]: *canyon*, drained by a stream that flows 1.5 miles to Coward Creek 4.25 miles east-northeast of Watsonville (lat. 36°56'50" N, long. 121°41'15" W). Named on Watsonville East (1955) 7.5' quadrangle. United States Board on Geographic Names (1992, p. 4) approved the name "Kinky Canyon" for the feature.

Mill Canyon: see **Fern Canyon** [SANTA CRUZ].

Mill Creek [MONTEREY]:

(1) *stream*, flows 3 miles to join Turner Creek and form Bixby Creek 5.5 miles north-northeast of Point Sur (lat. 36°22'20" N, long. 121°50'35" W; near NE cor. sec. 15, T 18 S, R 1 E). Named on Big Sur (1956) 7.5' quadrangle. On Point Sur (1925) 15' quadrangle, the stream is considered part of Bixby Creek. Postal authorities established Sur post office along Mill Creek (Wall, p. 53) in 1889 and discontinued it in 1913 (Salley, p. 216).

(2) *stream*, flows 3.5 miles to the sea 6.5 miles north-northwest of Cape San Martin (lat. 35°58'55" N, long. 121°29'25" W; near S line sec. 25, T 22 S, R 4 E). Named on Cape San Martin (1949) 7.5' quadrangle. The name is from a sawmill along the stream (Clark, 1991, p. 311).

Mill Creek [SANTA CRUZ]:

(1) *stream*, flows 0.5 mile to Lompico Creek 4.25 miles east-southeast of the town of Boulder Creek (lat. 37°06'40" N, long. 122°02'50" W; sec. 35, T 9 S, R 2 W). Named on Felton (1955) 7.5' quadrangle.

(2) *stream*, flows 5 miles to Scott Creek 5.25 miles north-northwest of Davenport (lat. 37°04'35" N, long. 122°14'35" W). Named on Big Basin (1955) and Davenport (1955) 7.5' quadrangles.

(3) *stream*, flows nearly 3 miles to San Vicente Creek 2.5 miles north-northeast of Davenport (lat. 37°02'30" N, long. 122°10'25" W). Named on Davenport (1955) 7.5' quadrangle. The name is from the Glassell Brothers Mill located along the stream (Clark, 1986, p. 207).

Mill Creek: see **Bixby Creek** [MONTEREY].

Mill Creek, West Fork [SANTA BARBARA]: *stream*, flows nearly 2 miles to Manzana Creek 2.5 miles northeast of Zaca Lake (lat. 34° 48'05" N, long. 120°00' W). Named on Zaca Lake (1964) 7.5' quadrangle, which fails to show a Mill Creek.

Miller Canyon [MONTEREY]: *canyon*, drained by Miller Fork Carmel River, which flows 7.25 miles through the canyon to Carmel River 3.25 miles east-northeast of Uncle Sam Mountain (lat. 36° 21'10" N, long. 121°39' W). Named on Chews Ridge (1956) and Ventana Cones (1956) 7.5' quadrangles.

Miller Canyon [SAN BENITO]: *canyon*, 1.5 miles long, 10 miles east of Bitterwater along Laguna Creek (lat. 36°21'20" N, long. 120°49'35" W). Named on Hepsedam Peak (1969) 7.5' quadrangle.

Miller Canyon [SANTA BARBARA]: *canyon*, drained by a stream that flows nearly 3 miles to Sisquoc River 3 miles east-northeast of Bald Mountain (1) (lat. 34°49'45" N, long. 119°53'15" W). Named on Bald Mountain (1964) 7.5' quadrangle.

Miller Canyon Camp [MONTEREY]: *locality*, 4.5 miles east of Uncle Sam Mountain (lat. 36°20'20" N, long. 121°37'30" W; sec. 26, T 18 S, R 3 E); the place is along Miller Fork Carmel River. Named on Chews Ridge (1956) 7.5' quadrangle.

Miller Flat [SAN LUIS OBISPO]: *area*, 1.25 miles south-southeast of Santa Margarita (lat. 35°22'30" N, long. 120°36' W). Named on Lopez Mountain (1965) and Santa Margarita (1965) 7.5' quadrangles.

Miller Flats [SAN LUIS OBISPO]: *area*, 16 miles east-southeast of Shandon (lat. 35°36' N, long. 120°06'15" W). Named on Packwood Creek (1961) 7.5' quadrangle. Arnold and Johnson (1910, p. 21) proposed the name to commemorate James Miller, an early settler in the neighborhood.

Miller Fork: see **Carmel River** [MONTEREY].

Miller Mountain [MONTEREY]: *peak*, nearly 4 miles east-southeast of Uncle Sam Mountain (lat. 36°19'10" N, long. 121°38'40" W; sec. 34, T 18 S, R 3 E). Named on Ventana Cones (1956) 7.5' quadrangle.

Miller's Landing: see **Pajaro River** [SANTA CRUZ].

Millpond Lake [SANTA CRUZ]: *lake*, 550 feet long, 5 miles south-southeast of Laurel (lat. 37°03'05" N, long. 121°55'30" W). Named on Laurel (1955) 7.5' quadrangle.

Mill Ridge: see **Long Ridge** [SANTA CRUZ].

Milpitas [MONTEREY]: *land grant,* extends for 17 miles northwest of Jolon. Named on Alder Peak (1949), Bear Canyon (1949), Cone Peak (1949), Cosio Knob (1949), and Jolon (1949) 7.5' quadrangles. Ignacio Pastor received 3 leagues in 1838 and claimed 43,281 acres patented in 1875 (Cowan, p. 48).

Mincey Canyon [MONTEREY]: *canyon,* drained by a stream that flows 3 miles to an unnamed canyon 9.5 miles west-northwest of Bradley (lat. 35°55'10" N, long. 120°57'40" W; sec. 23, T 23 S, R 9 E). Named on Hames Valley (1949) 7.5' quadrangle. On Bradley (1929) 15' quadrangle, the name "Mincey Canyon" applies also to part of the unnamed canyon. The name is for Samuel C. Mincey, who patented land in the canyon in 1911 (Clark, 1991, p. 313).

Mine Canyon [SAN BENITO]: *canyon,* drained by a stream that flows nearly 3 miles to Moody Canyon 7.5 miles west-southwest of Panoche (lat. 36°34' N, long. 120°57'40" W; sec. 2, T 16 S, R 9 E). Named on Llanada (1969) 7.5' quadrangle.

Mine Canyon [SAN LUIS OBISPO]: *canyon,* drained by a stream that flows 2.5 miles to Harford Canyon nearly 2 miles north-northwest of Avila Beach (lat. 35°12'10" N, long. 120°44'35" W; sec. 25, T 31 S, R 11 E). Named on Port San Luis (1965) 7.5' quadrangle.

Mine Canyon [SANTA BARBARA]:

(1) *canyon,* drained by a stream that flows 4.5 miles to Peachtree Canyon 5 miles south-southwest of San Rafael Mountain (lat. 34° 38'40" N, long. 119°51' W). Named on San Rafael Mountain (1959) 7.5' quadrangle. Called Peachtree Canyon on San Rafael Mountain (1943) 15' quadrangle.

(2) *canyon,* drained by a stream that flows 2 miles to San Lucas Creek 4.5 miles southeast of Santa Ynez (lat. 34°34'30" N, long. 120°00'45" W). Named on Lake Cachuma (1959) and Santa Ynez (1959) 7.5' quadrangles.

(3) *canyon,* drained by a stream that flows 5.5 miles to Sisquoc River 5 miles west-southwest of Montgomery Potrero (lat. 34°48'55" N, long. 119°50'20" W). Named on Hurricane Deck (1964) 7.5' quadrangle.

Mine Canyon Spring [SANTA BARBARA]: *spring,* 4.5 miles southwest of San Rafael Mountain (lat. 34°39'35" N, long. 119°51'35" W); the spring is near Mine Canyon (1). Named on San Rafael Mountain (1959) 7.5' quadrangle.

Mine Canyon Spring: see **East Mine Canyon Spring** [SANTA BARBARA]; **North Mine Canyon Spring** [SANTA BARBARA].

Mine Creek [SAN BENITO]: *stream,* flows 2.5 miles to James Creek 5.5 miles east-northeast of Bitterwater (lat. 36°25'10" N, long. 120° 54'40" W; sec. 29, T 17 S, R 10 E). Named on Rock Spring Peak (1969) 7.5' quadrangle, which shows Fireflex mine situated along upper reaches of the stream.

Mine Hill [SAN LUIS OBISPO]: *ridge,* northwest-trending, 1 mile long, 4 miles southwest of downtown San Luis Obispo (lat. 35°14'40" N, long. 120°42'35" W). Named on Pismo Beach (1965) 7.5' quadrangle.

Mine Mountain [MONTEREY]: *peak,* 5 miles north of Parkfield on Monterey-Fresno County line (lat. 35°58'10" N, long. 120°26' W; sec. 35, T 22 S, R 14 E). Named on Parkfield (1961) 7.5' quadrangle. The name is from mercury mines at the place (Clark, 1991, p. 313).

Miners Gulch [MONTEREY]: *canyon,* drained by a stream that flows 6.25 miles to Chalone Creek 5 miles northeast of Greenfield (lat. 36°22'35" N, long. 121°11'15" W; sec. 10, T 18 S, R 7 E). Named on North Chalone Peak (1969) 7.5' quadrangle.

Mining Ridge [MONTEREY]: *ridge,* southwest-trending, 3.5 miles long, 5 miles north of Lopez Point (lat. 36°05'30" N, long. 121° 33'45" W). Named on Lopez Point (1956) 7.5' quadrangle.

Miramar [SANTA BARBARA]: *locality,* 4 miles east of downtown Santa Barbara (lat. 34°25'10" N, long. 119°37'40" W). Named on Santa Barbara (1903) 15' quadrangle.

Miranda Canyon [SANTA BARBARA]: *canyon,* drained by a stream that flows 4 miles to Cuyama Valley 3.5 miles east-northeast of Miranda Pine Mountain (lat. 35°03'30" N, long. 120°59' W). Named on Miranda Pine Mountain (1967) and Taylor Canyon (1959) 7.5' quadrangles.

Miranda Creek: see **Pine Canyon** [SANTA BARBARA] (1).

Miranda Pine Campground [SANTA BARBARA]: *locality,* 850 feet south of the top of Miranda Pine Mountain (lat. 35°02'05" N, long. 120°02'10" W). Named on Miranda Pine Mountain (1967) 7.5' quadrangle.

Miranda Pine Creek: see **Pine Canyon** [SANTA BARBARA] (1).

Miranda Pine Mountain [SANTA BARBARA]: *peak,* 23 miles east-northeast of Santa Maria (lat. 35°02'15" N, long. 120°02'10" W). Altitude 4061 feet. Named on Miranda Pine Mountain (1967) 7.5' quadrangle.

Miranda Pine Spring [SANTA BARBARA]: *spring,* 1000 feet south-southwest of the top of Miranda Pine Mountain (lat. 35°02'05" N, long. 120°02'15" W). Named on Miranda Pine Mountain (1967) 7.5' quadrangle.

Mision Nuestra Señora de la Soledad: see **Ex Mission Soledad** [MONTEREY].

Mission Canyon [SANTA BARBARA]: *canyon,* 3.5 miles long, drained by Mission Creek above a point 2 miles north-northwest of downtown Santa Barbara (lat. 34°26'45" N, long. 119°42'25" W). Named on Santa Barbara (1952) 7.5' quadrangle.

Mission Creek [MONTEREY]: *stream,* flows 10 miles to San Antonio River 5 miles northwest of Jolon (lat. 36°00'40" N, long. 121°15'10" W); the mouth of the stream is near San Antonio mission. Named on Bear Canyon (1949) and Cosio Knob (1949) 7.5' quadrangles. Howard (p. 48) noted that an aqueduct paralleled the creek from San Miguel Spring to the mission. The stream first was called Arroyo San Miguel, and later was called San Miguel Creek and Arroyo la Mission (Clark, 1991, p. 314).

Mission Creek [SANTA BARBARA]: *stream,* flows 8.5 miles to the sea less than 1 mile southeast of downtown Santa Barbara (lat. 34° 24'45" N, long. 119°41'10" W); the stream drains Mission Canyon and flows past Santa Barbara mission. Named on Santa Barbara (1952) 7.5' quadrangle. United States Board on Geographic Names (1961b, p. 12) rejected the names "Arroyo del Pedregoso" and "Pedregoso Creek" for the feature. The landing place for the mission and for the presidio at Santa Barbara was situated west of the mouth of Mission Creek, and was east of as well as on an elevation called Burton Mound—the name "Burton" was for Lewis T. Burton, who acquired land at the landing place, including the mound, in 1860 (Hoover, Rensch, and Rensch, p. 414). Burton Mound Sulphur Springs issued along the beach there; water from one spring was utilized at a hotel that was built over it (Huguenin, p. 741).

Mission La Purisima [SANTA BARBARA]: *land grant,* north of the town of Lompoc; La Purisima Concepcion mission is on the grant. Named on Lompoc (1959) and Surf (1959) 7.5' quadrangles. Jose Ramon Malo received the land in 1845 and claimed 14,736 acres patented in 1882 (Cowan, p. 65).

Mission Pine Basin [SANTA BARBARA]: *area,* 5 miles west of Big Pine Mountain (lat. 34°42'25" N, long. 119°44'25" W). Named on Big Pine Mountain (1964) 7.5' quadrangle. The name is from the legend that pine trees at the place provided beams for the mission at Santa Barbara (Gagnon, p. 98).

Mission Pine Camp [SANTA BARBARA]: *locality,* 1 mile east-southeast of San Rafael Mountain (lat. 34°42'25" N, long. 119°47'40" W). Named on San Rafael Mountain (1959) 7.5' quadrangle.

Mission Springs [SANTA CRUZ]: *settlement,* 6.5 miles southeast of the town of Boulder Creek (lat. 37°03'50" N, long. 122°01'55" W; sec. 13, T 10 S, R 2 W). Named on Felton (1955) 7.5' quadrangle.

Mocho Camp [MONTEREY]: *locality,* 4 miles north-northeast of Partington Point (lat. 36°13'30" N, long. 121°39'45" W; sec. 5, T 20 S, R 3 E); the place is along Mocho Creek. Named on Partington Ridge (1956) 7.5' quadrangle.

Mocho Creek [MONTEREY]: *stream,* flows 1 mile to South Fork Big Sur River 4 miles north-northeast of Partington Point (lat. 36° 13'10" N, long. 121°39'45" W; sec. 5, T 20 S, R 3 E). Named on Partington Ridge (1956) 7.5' quadrangle.

Molasky Creek: see **Malosky Creek** [SANTA CRUZ].

Molino: see **Aptos Creek** [SANTA CRUZ].

Molino Creek [SANTA CRUZ]: *stream,* flows 3.5 miles to the sea 2.5 miles northwest of Davenport (lat. 37°02'10" N, long. 122°13'40" W). Named on Davenport (1955) 7.5' quadrangle. Gudde (1949, p. 220) pointed out that the stream is called Arroyo del Molino on a Mexican map of 1846—*molino* means "mill" in Spanish.

Molus [MONTEREY]: *locality,* 5 miles northwest of Soledad along Southern Pacific Railroad (lat. 36°28'05" N, long. 121°23'35" W). Named on Palo Escrito Peak (1956) 7.5' quadrangle.

Monarch Peak [MONTEREY]: *peak,* 15 miles north-northeast of San Ardo on Mustang Ridge (lat. 36°13'05" N, long. 120°48'45" W; sec. 5, T 20 S, R 11 E). Altitude 2767 feet. Named on Monarch Peak (1967) 7.5' quadrangle.

Monica Creek: see **Santa Monica Creek** [SAN BENITO].

Monjas Creek [SANTA BARBARA]: *stream,* flows 1.5 miles to Alisal Creek nearly 6 miles southeast of Buellton (lat. 34°32'45" N, long. 120°08'05" W; sec. 4, T 5 N, R 31 W). Named on Solvang (1959) 7.5' quadrangle.

Monjas Spring [SANTA BARBARA]: *spring,* 6.5 miles south-southeast of Buellton (lat. 34°31'55" N, long. 120°08'10" W; at W line sec. 9, T 5 N, R 31 W); the spring is along Monjas Creek. Named on Solvang (1959) 7.5' quadrangle.

Mono Campground [SANTA BARBARA]: *locality,* 8 miles southeast of Little Pine Mountain (lat. 34°31'45" N, long. 119°37'40" W); the place is along Mono Creek. Named on Little Pine Mountain (1964) 7.5' quadrangle. Called Mono Public Camp on Little Pine Mountain (1944) 7.5' quadrangle.

Mono Cañon: see **Mono Creek** [SANTA BARBARA].

Mono Creek [SANTA BARBARA]: *stream,* flows 25 miles to Gibraltar Reservoir 8 miles southeast of Little Pine Mountain (lat. 34°31'20" N, long. 119°37'45" W). Named on Hildreth Peak (1964), Little Pine Mountain (1964), and Madulce Peak (1964) 7.5' quadrangles. Fairbanks (1894, p. 504) referred to Mono Cañon.

Mono Creek: see **Morro Creek** [SAN LUIS OBISPO].

Mono Public Camp: see **Mono Campground** [SANTA BARBARA].

Mono Rock: see **Morro Rock** [SAN LUIS OBISPO].

Monroe Canyon [MONTEREY]: *canyon,* 4 miles long, drained by Monroe Creek, which enters lowlands 4.5 miles south-southeast of Greenfield (lat.

36°15'20" N, long. 121°13'30" W). Named on Greenfield (1956), Reliz Canyon (1949), and Thompson Canyon (1949) 7.5' quadrangles.

Monroe Creek [MONTEREY]: *stream*, flows 6.5 miles to Salinas River floodplain 5 miles southeast of Greenfield (lat. 36°16'10" N, long. 121°10'50" W); the stream drains Monroe Canyon. Named on Greenfield (1956) 7.5' quadrangle.

Monroe Lake [MONTEREY]: *intermittent lake*, 700 feet long, 3 miles west of Charley Mountain (lat. 36°08'50" N, long. 120°43'10" W; sec. 31, T 20 S, R 12 E); the feature is 0.5 mile south of Monroe Valley. Named on Priest Valley (1969) 7.5' quadrangle.

Monroe Valley [MONTEREY]: *valley*, 3.25 miles west-northwest of Charley Mountain (lat. 36°09'05" N, long. 120°43'05" W). Named on Priest Valley (1969) 7.5' quadrangle.

Monte Arido [SANTA BARBARA]: *peak*, 1.5 miles north-northwest of Old Man Mountain (1) (lat. 34°32'20" N, long. 119°27'55" W; near S line sec. 2, T 5 N, R 25 W). Altitude 6003 feet. Named on Old Man Mountain (1943) 7.5' quadrangle. Called Montecito on Mount Pinos (1903) 30' quadrangle.

Montecito [SANTA BARBARA]: *town*, 4 miles east of downtown Santa Barbara (lat. 34°25'25" N, long. 119°37'45" W). Named on Carpinteria (1952) and Santa Barbara (1952) 7.5' quadrangles. Postal authorities established Montecito post office in 1886, discontinued it in 1914, and reestablished it in 1958 (Salley, p. 145). Santa Barbara (1903) 15' quadrangle has the name "Montecito" for a community located 1.25 miles inland from the coast, and has the same name for a site along the railroad at the coast—both places are in present Montecito.

Montecito: see **Monte Arido** [SANTA BARBARA].

Montecito Creek [SANTA BARBARA]: *stream*, flows 5.5 miles to the sea 3.5 miles east of downtown Santa Barbara (lat. 34°25' N, long. 119°38' W); the mouth of the creek is in Montecito. Named on Santa Barbara (1952) 7.5' quadrangle. The stream drains Cold Spring Canyon (2). United States Board on Geographic Names (1961b, p. 12) rejected the name "Arroyo del Montecito" for the stream.

Montecito Hot Springs: see **Hot Springs** [SANTA BARBARA] (2).

Montecito Peak [SANTA BARBARA]: *peak*, 5 miles northeast of downtown Santa Barbara (lat. 34°28'20" N, long. 119°38'15" W; at E line sec. 31, T 5 N, R 26 W); the peak is 3.25 miles north of Montecito. Altitude 3214 feet. Named on Santa Barbara (1952) 7.5' quadrangle.

Monte de Buchon: see **Irish Hills** [SAN LUIS OBISPO].

Monte Diablo Range: see **Diablo Range** [MONTEREY-SAN BENITO].

Monterey [MONTEREY]: *city*, along the coast at the south end of Monterey Bay (lat. 36°36' N, long. 121°53'30" W). Named on Monterey (1947) 7.5' quadrangle. Fremont's (1845) map has the form "Monte Rey" for the name, and Emory's (1857-1858) map has the form "Montery." Postal authorities established Monterey post office 1849 (Salley, p. 145), and the city incorporated in 1889. New Monterey, a district north of Presidio of Monterey, is named on Monterey (1947) 7.5' quadrangle. Postal authorities established New Monterey post office in 1909 and discontinued it in 1913 (Salley, p. 154).

Monterey: see **East Monterey**, under **Seaside** [MONTEREY].

Monterey Bay [MONTEREY-SANTA CRUZ]: *embayment*, along the coast north of Point Pinos; extends into Santa Cruz County. Named on Santa Cruz (1956) 1°x 2° quadrangle. Cabrillo discovered the feature in 1542 and called it Bahia de los Pinos (Wagner, H.R., p. 398). Cermeño saw it in 1595 and gave it the name "Bahia de San Pedro" to honor a martyr whose day preceded the day of Cermeño's visit (Wagner, H.R., p. 506). Vizcaino anchored in the present harbor of Monterey in 1602 and gave the name "Puerto de Monterey" to his anchorage in honor of the Conde de Monterey, Viceroy of New Spain (Wagner, H.R., p. 398). According to Davidson (1907, p. 29), a Spanish chart made before the settlement of Monterey has the name "Po. de Monterey" for the north part of present Monterey Bay. Davidson (1887, p. 212) also noted that Vizcaino's name for the harbor was El Puerto de Monte-Rey.

Monte Toyon [SANTA CRUZ]: *locality*, 5.25 miles northeast of Soquel Point in Mangles Gulch (lat. 36°59'45" N, long. 121°53'40" W). Named on Soquel (1954) 7.5' quadrangle

Monte Vista: see **Aptos Creek** [SANTA CRUZ].

Montgomery Number 3 Spring [SANTA BARBARA]: *spring*, 5 miles southeast of McPherson Peak (lat. 34°49'55" N, long. 119° 45'50" W); the spring is at Montgomery Potrero 2300 feet southwest of Montgomery Spring. Named on Hurricane Deck (1964) 7.5' quadrangle.

Montgomery Number 2 Spring [SANTA BARBARA]: *spring*, 5 miles southeast of McPherson Peak (lat. 34°49'55" N, long. 119° 45'15" W); the spring is at Montgomery Potrero 1700 feet southeast of Montgomery Spring. Named on Hurricane Deck (1964) 7.5' quadrangle.

Montgomery Potrero [SANTA BARBARA]: *area*, 5 miles southeast of McPherson Peak (lat. 34°50'10" N, long. 119°45'10" W). Named on Hurricane Deck (1964) 7.5' quadrangle. Fairbanks (1894, p. 498) referred to Montgomery's Potrero.

Montgomery Spring [SANTA BARBARA]: *spring*, 5 miles southeast of McPherson Peak (lat. 34°50'10" N, long. 119°45'30" W); the spring is at Montgomery Potrero. Named on Hurricane Deck (1964) 7.5' quadrangle.

Moody Canyon [SAN BENITO]: *canyon*, drained by a stream that flows nearly 5 miles to Bitterwater Canyon 7.5 miles west of Panoche (lat. 36°35' N, long. 120°58' W; sec. 34, T 15 S, R 9 E). Named on Llanada (1969) 7.5' quadrangle.

Moody Sulphur Spring [SAN BENITO]: *spring*, 8 miles west-southwest of Panoche (lat. 36°33'05" N, long. 120°58' W; sec. 11, T 16 S, R 9 E); the spring is in Moody Canyon. Named on Llanada (1969) 7.5' quadrangle.

Moon Canyon [SANTA BARBARA]: *canyon*, drained by a stream that flows 3.5 miles to join he stream in Kelsey Canyon 10 miles northwest of McPherson Peak (lat. 34°59'45" N, long. 119°55'25" W; at W line sec. 31, T 11 N, R 28 W). Named on Bates Canyon (1964) 7.5' quadrangle.

Mooney Canyon [MONTEREY]: *canyon*, drained by a stream that flows about 4 miles to Pine Valley (2) 4.5 miles north of San Ardo (lat. 36°05'10" N, long. 120°53'55" W; sec. 21, T 21 S, R 10 E). Named on Nattrass Valley (1967) and San Ardo (1967) 7.5' quadrangles.

Moonshine Canyon [SANTA BARBARA]: *canyon*, drained by a stream that flows 2.5 miles to Nojoqui Creek 3.5 miles south of Buellton (lat. 34°33'35" N, long. 120°11'30" W). Named on Solvang (1959) 7.5' quadrangle.

Moore Creek [SANTA CRUZ]: *stream*, flows 3.5 miles, partly in a discontinuous watercourse near the coast, to the sea almost 2 miles west of Point Santa Cruz (lat. 36°57' N, long. 122°03'25" W). Named on Santa Cruz (1954) 7.5' quadrangle. The name commemorates Eli Moore, who came to Santa Cruz in 1847 and owned a ranch along the stream (Clark, 1986, p. 214). Natural Bridges Beach state park is at the mouth of Moore Creek. The first stage station on the route from Santa Cruz up the coast to San Mateo County in 1872 was called Hall's Natural Bridge (Hoover, Rensch, and Rensch, p. 478)—the name apparently referred to natural bridges at the mouth of Moore Creek.

Moores Gulch [SANTA CRUZ]: *canyon*, 1 mile long, 5.25 miles north of Soquel (lat. 37°03'45" N, long. 121°57'35" W; sec. 15, T 10 S, R 1 W). Named on Laurel (1955) 7.5' quadrangle.

Moore Spring: see **Veronica Springs** [SANTA BARBARA].

Morada: see **Rosa Morada**, under **San Joaquin** [SAN BENITO].

Morales Canyon [SAN LUIS OBISPO]: *canyon*, drained by a stream that flows 7 miles to Cuyama Valley (lat. 35°01'20" N, long. 119° 50' W; sec. 23, T 11 N, R 28 W). Named on Caliente Mountain (1959) 7.5' quadrangle.

Moran Lake [SANTA CRUZ]: *lake*, 900 feet long, 1000 feet north-northwest of Soquel Point near the coast (lat. 36°57'25" N, long. 121°58'35" W). Named on Soquel (1954) 7.5' quadrangle.

Morano Creek: see **Moreno Creek** [SAN LUIS OBISPO].

Morellini Creek [SAN BENITO]: *stream*, flows nearly 3 miles to Bitterwater Creek 2.5 miles east-southeast of Bitterwater (lat. 36° 21'50" N, long. 120°57'45" W; sec. 14, T 18 S, R 9 E). Named on Lonoak (1969) and Rock Spring Peak (1969) 7.5' quadrangles.

Moreno Creek [SAN LUIS OBISPO]: *stream*, flows 4 miles in a discontinuous watercourse to Salinas River 2.5 miles east-northeast of Santa Margarita (lat. 35°24'35" N, long. 120°34'05" W; near S line sec. 10, T 29 S, R 13 E). Named on Santa Margarita (1965) 7.5' quadrangle. Called Morano Creek on San Luis Obispo (1897) 15' quadrangle, but United States Board on Geographic Names (1967c, p. 2) rejected this name for the feature.

Morey Canyon: see **Marre Canyon** [SANTA BARBARA].

Morgenson Springs [SAN LUIS OBISPO]: *springs*, two, 0.25 mile apart, 6.5 miles northwest of Shandon (lat. 35°43'25" N, long. 120° 27'15" W; sec. 27, T 25 S, R 14 E). Named on Shandon (1961) 7.5' quadrangle.

Mormon Gulch [SANTA CRUZ]: *canyon*, drained by a stream that flows 1 mile to Corralitos Creek 1.5 miles north-northwest of Corralitos (lat. 37°00'45" N, long. 121°48'40" W; at S line sec. 36, T 10 S, R 1 E). Named on Loma Prieta (1955) 7.5' quadrangle.

Moro Cojo Slough [MONTEREY]: *water feature*, 4 miles long, joins Elkhorn Slough and Old Salinas River at Moss Landing (lat. 36° 48'15" N, long. 121°47' W); the feature is on Bolsa Nueva y Moro Cojo grant. Named on Moss Landing (1954) and Prunedale (1954) 7.5' quadrangles.

Moro Creek: see **Morro Creek** [SAN LUIS OBISPO].

Moro Rock: see **Morro Rock** [SAN LUIS OBISPO].

Moro y Cayucos [SAN LUIS OBISPO]: *land grant*, along the coast between Cayucos Creek and Morro Creek. Named on Cayucos (1965) and Morro Bay North (1965) 7.5' quadrangles. Vicente Felix and Martin Olivera received 2 leagues in 1842; James McKinley claimed 8845 acres patented in 1878 (Cowan, p. 49).

Morrito: see **Point Morrito**, under **Lions Head** [SANTA BARBARA].

Morritto: see **Lions Head** [SANTA BARBARA].

Morro: see **Morro Bay** [SAN LUIS OBISPO] (2).

Morro Bay [SAN LUIS OBISPO]:

(1) *bay*, 11 miles west-northwest of San Luis Obispo (lat. 35°22'30" N, long. 120°51' W); the bay is connected to the sea by a channel near Morro Rock. Named on Morro Bay South (1965) 7.5' quadrangle. According to H.R. Wagner (p. 503), Unamuno called the place Puerto de San Lucas on

October 18, 1587, the day of the saint. Captain William Shaler called the feature Bernard's Bay about 1805 (Hamilton, p. 116).

(2) *town*, 12 miles west-northwest of San Luis Obispo (lat. 35°21'45" N, long. 120°50'45" W); the town is at the north end of Morro Bay (1). Named on Morro Bay North (1965) and Morro Bay South (1965) 7.5' quadrangles. Called Morro on Cayucos (1897) 15' quadrangle. The part of the town north of Morro Creek is called Morro Beach on Cayucos (1951) 15' quadrangle. The community of Morro Bay began in 1870 when Franklin Riley bought and developed 160 acres of land facing Morro Rock (Lee and others, p. 94). Postal authorities established Morro post office in 1870 and changed the name to Morro Bay in 1923 (Frickstad, p. 165). The town incorporated in 1964. Postal authorities established Del Mar-Heights post office 2 miles north of Morro Bay post office in 1953, changed the name to Del Mar Heights in 1966, and discontinued it in 1972 (Salley, p. 57). United States Board on Geographic Names (1983b, p. 3) approved the name "Alva Paul Creek," and rejected the name "Pauls Creek," for a stream that flows 3 miles to Estero Bay in the town of Morro Bay (lat. 35°23'50" N, long. 120°51'57" W); the name commemorates Alva Paul, who purchased land along the creek in 1882 and lived there until 1915.

Morro Beach: see **Morro Bay** [SAN LUIS OBISPO] (2).

Morro Creek [SAN LUIS OBISPO]: *stream*, flows 13 miles to the sea at the town of Morro Bay (lat. 35°22'35" N, long. 120°51'45" W). Named on Atascadero (1965) and Morro Bay North (1965) 7.5' quadrangles. United States Board on Geographic Names (1933, p. 532) rejected the names "Mono Creek," "Moro Creek," and "El Morro Creek" for the stream. East Fork enters from the east 8 miles upstream from the mouth of the main creek; it is nearly 2 miles long and is named on Atascadero (1965) and Morro Bay North (1965) 7.5' quadrangles.

Morro Creek: see **Little Morro Creek** [SAN LUIS OBISPO].

Morro Rock [SAN LUIS OBISPO]: *relief feature*, 13 miles west-northwest of San Luis Obispo along the coast (lat. 35°22'10" N, long. 120°52' W); the feature is at the entrance to Morro Bay (1). Altitude 578 feet. Named on Morro Bay South (1965) 7.5' quadrangle. Called Moro Rock on Parke's (1854-1855) map. Angel (1883, p. 323) called it El Morro. The Portola expedition applied the term "morro redondo" to the feature in 1769—*morro* is a Spanish word for a crown-shaped hill (Wagner, H.R., p. 398). Gudde (1949, p. 225) pointed out that *moro* rather than *morro* was used in the name of the nearby Moro y Caucos grant, probably because of an assumed connection with *moro*, which means "Moor" or "blue roan horse" in Spanish. United States Board on Geographic Names (1933, p. 532) rejected the forms "Mono Rock," "Moro Rock," and "El Morro Rock" for the name.

Morro Trompo: see **Point Sur** [MONTEREY].

Morro Twin: see **Hollister Peak** [SAN LUIS OBISPO].

Morse [SAN BENITO]: *locality*, 5.25 miles west-southwest of Hollister (lat. 36°50'15" N, long. 121°29'35" W). Named on Hollister (1955) 7.5' quadrangle.

Morse Creek [SANTA BARBARA]: *stream*, flows 1 mile to Alder Creek 6 miles north of Carpinteria (lat. 34°29'05" N, long. 119°30'55" W; sec. 29, T 5 N, R 25 W). Named on Carpinteria (1952) 7.5' quadrangle.

Morse Point [SANTA BARBARA]: *promontory*, 8 miles southeast of Fraser Point on the south side of Santa Cruz Island (lat. 33°58'05" N, long. 119°50'50" W). Named on Santa Cruz Island A (1943) 7.5' quadrangle.

Moses Spring [SAN BENITO]: *spring*, 2 miles north-northeast of North Chalone Peak in Bear Gulch (1) (lat. 36°28'30" N, long. 121°11'10" W; near SW cor. sec. 2, T 17 S, R 7 E). Named on North Chalone Peak (1969) 7.5' quadrangle.

Moss: see **Moss Landing** [MONTEREY].

Moss Beach [MONTEREY]: *beach*, east of Point Joe along the coast (lat. 36°36'35" N, long. 121°56'55" W). Named on Monterey (1947) 7.5' quadrangle. On Monterey (1913) 15' quadrangle, the name also applies farther north-northeast along the coast. Reinstedt (1975, p. 85) gave the name "Asilomar Beach" as an alternate.

Moss Landing [MONTEREY]: *village*, 15 miles north-northeast of Monterey at the mouth of Elkhorn Slough (lat. 36°48'15" N, long. 121°47'10" W). Named on Moss Landing (1954) 7.5' quadrangle. The name commemorates Charles Moss, who with Cato Vierra built a wharf at the site (Fink, p. 139). The place was an important whaling station in the early days (Hoover, Rensch, and Rensch, p. 235). Capitola (1914) 15' quadrangle shows a place called Moss located along Pajaro Valley Consolidated Railroad near present Moss Landing. Postal authorities established Moss post office in 1895 and changed the name to Moss Landing in 1917 (Frickstad, p. 108).

Mountain Charlie Gulch [SANTA CRUZ]: *canyon*, drained by a stream that flows 4 miles to Zayante Creek 5.5 miles east-southeast of the town of Boulder Creek (lat. 37°06'20" N, long. 122°01'15" W; at W line sec. 31, T 9 S, R 1 W). Named on Felton (1955), Laurel (1955), and Los Gatos (1953) 7.5' quadrangles. The name commemorates Charles McKiernan, who came to the area in 1850 and was known to later arrivals by the name "Mountain Charlie" (Hoover, Rensch, and Rensch, p. 476-477).

Mountain Creek: see **Soquel Creek** [SANTA CRUZ].

Mountain del Buchon: see **Irish Hills** [SAN LUIS OBISPO].

Mountain Glen Hot Springs: see **Hot Spring** [SANTA BARBARA].

Mount Bielawski: see **Bielawski Mountain** [SANTA CRUZ].

Mount Buchon: see **Irish Hills** [SAN LUIS OBISPO].

Mount Carmel [MONTEREY]: *peak*, 8.5 miles northeast of Point Sur (lat. 36°23'10" N, long. 121°47'15" W). Altitude 4417 feet. Named on Mount Carmel (1956) 7.5' quadrangle. The peak also was called Boulder Mountain for the boulders that cover it (Clark, 1991, p. 344).

Mount Chelone: see **North Chalone Peak** [MONTEREY-SAN BENITO].

Mount Cross Camp [SANTA CRUZ]: *locality*, 4 miles south-southeast of the town of Boulder Creek (lat. 37°04'20" N, long. 122°05'10" W; sec. 9, T 10 S, R 2 W). Named on Felton (1955) 7.5' quadrangle.

Mount Defiance [SAN BENITO]: *peak*, 2 miles northeast of North Chalone Peak (lat. 36°28' N, long. 121°10'15" W; near E line sec. 11, T 17 S, R 7 E). Altitude 2657 feet. Named on North Chalone Peak (1969) 7.5' quadrangle.

Mount del Buchon: see **Irish Hills** [SAN LUIS OBISPO].

Mount Diablo Range: see **Diablo Range** [MONTEREY-SAN BENITO].

Mount Hanlon: see **Mount Harlan** [SAN BENITO].

Mount Harlan [SAN BENITO]: *peak*, 7.5 miles west-southwest of Paicines (lat. 36°41'50" N, long. 121°24'15" W; sec. 22, T 14 S, R 5 E). Altitude 3274 feet. Named on Mount Harlan (1968) 7.5' quadrangle. Called Mt. Hanlon on Gonzales (1921) 15' quadrangle.

Mount Hasbrouck: see **Big Baldy** [SAN LUIS OBISPO].

Mount Hermon [SANTA CRUZ]: *settlement*, 6.25 miles southeast of the town of Boulder Creek (lat. 37°03' N, long. 122°03'30" W). Named on Felton (1955) 7.5' quadrangle. In 1905 a Christian group purchased a resort called The Tuxedo and renamed it Mount Hermon for a peak in Palestine (Gudde, 1949, p. 226). The group then proceeded to model the place after summer religious assemblies in Massachusetts and Indiana (Rowland, p. 184). Postal authorities established Mount Hermon post office in 1908 (Frickstad, p. 177). MacGregor (p. 173) noted that a railroad station called Tuxedo was 0.5 mile north of Felton at the original resort.

Mount Johnson [SAN BENITO]: *peak*, 8.5 miles south-southwest of Paicines (lat. 36°36'40" N, long. 121°18'50" W; sec. 21, T 15 S, R 6 E). Altitude 3465 feet. Named on Mount Johnson (1968) 7.5' quadrangle.

Mount Lospe [SANTA BARBARA]: *ridge*, west-trending, 1 mile long, 5.5 miles south-southwest of the town of Guadalupe (lat. 34° 53'40" N, long. 120°36'05" W). Named on Guadalupe (1959) 7.5' quadrangle.

Mount Lowe [SAN LUIS OBISPO]: *peak*, nearly 2 miles northwest of Lopez Mountain (lat. 35°19'10" N, long. 120°36' W; sec. 17, T 30 S, R 13 E). Named on Lopez Mountain (1965) 7.5' quadrangle.

Mount Manuel: see **Manuel Peak** [MONTEREY].

Mount Mars [MONTEREY]: *peak*, 9 miles southeast of Cape San Martin (lat. 35°48'45" N, long. 121°20'20" W; sec. 29, T 24 S, R 6 E). Altitude 2674 feet. Named on Burro Mountain (1949) 7.5' quadrangle.

Mount McPherson: see **Bielawski Mountain** [SANTA CRUZ].

Mount Olds [MONTEREY]: *peak*, 9.5 miles north-northeast of Gonzales (lat. 36°38'35" N, long. 121°23'55" W; on E line sec. 10, T 15 S, R 5 E). Altitude 3010 feet. Named on Mount Harlan (1968) 7.5' quadrangle.

Mount Olmstead [MONTEREY]: *peak*, 4 miles north of Partington Point (lat. 36°14' N, long. 121°41'35" W; sec. 36, T 19 S, R 2 E). Altitude 3711 feet. Named on Partington Ridge (1956) 7.5' quadrangle.

Mount Pajaro [SANTA CRUZ]: *peak*, 7 miles east of Watsonville on Santa Cruz-Santa Clara County line (lat. 36°55'25" N, long. 121° 37'40" W). Altitude 1573 feet. Named on Watsonville East (1955) 7.5' quadrangle.

Mount Reynolds [SAN BENITO]: *peak*, nearly 3 miles southeast of Mount Johnson (lat. 36°35'05" N, long. 121°16'35" W; near E line sec. 35, T 15 S, R 6 E). Altitude 3146 feet. Named on Mount Johnson (1968) 7.5' quadrangle.

Mount Roberta [SANTA CRUZ]: *peak*, 7.5 miles north-northwest of Soquel (lat. 37°05'30" N, long. 121°59'40" W; sec. 5, T 10 S, R 1 W). Named on Laurel (1955) 7.5' quadrangle.

Mount Solomon [SANTA BARBARA]: *peak*, 4 miles east-southeast of Orcutt (lat. 34°50'05" N, long. 120°22'55" W); the peak is in Solomon Hills. Altitude 1346 feet. Named on Orcutt (1959) 7.5' quadrangle. The name is for Solomon Pico, a highwayman (Gudde, 1949, p. 338).

Mount Solomon: see **Solomon Hills** [SANTA BARBARA].

Mount Toro [MONTEREY]: *peak*, 6 miles west-southwest of Chualar (lat. 36°31'35" N, long. 121°36'30" W; sec. 23, T 16 S, R 3 E). Altitude 3560 feet. Named on Chualar (1947) 7.5' quadrangle.

Mount Torro Range: see **Sierra de Salinas** [MONTEREY].

Mouse Rock [SAN LUIS OBISPO]: *rock*, nearly 2 miles east-southeast of Cayucos Point, and 0.5 mile offshore (lat. 35°26'25" N, long. 120°54'30" W). Named on Cayucos (1965) 7.5' quadrangle.

Mucho Spring [SAN LUIS OBISPO]: *spring*, 3 miles southeast of Cholame (lat. 35°41'25" N, long. 120°15'55" W; near SE cor. sec. 5, T 26 S, R 16 E). Named on Cholame (1961) 7.5' quadrangle.

Mud Creek [MONTEREY]: *stream*, flows 6.25 miles to Gabilan Creek 8.5 miles north-northeast of Salinas (lat. 36°46'55" N, long. 121°35'05" W). Named on San Juan Bautista (1955) 7.5' quadrangle. The adobe house of

Don Joaquin Gomez was near the confluence of Mud Creek and Gabilan Creek; the route past the house and over highlands to the north was called Gomez's Pass (Pierce, p. 75).

Muddy Creek [MONTEREY]: *stream,* flows 3.5 miles to Chualar Canyon 7 miles north-northeast of Gonzales (lat. 36°36'10" N, long. 121°24'25" W). Named on Gonzales (1955) and Mount Johnson (1968) 7.5' quadrangles.

Mudhen Lake [MONTEREY]: *intermittent lake,* 850 feet long, 5.25 miles southwest of Salinas (lat. 36°37'40" N, long. 121°43'50" W). Named on Salinas (1947) 7.5' quadrangle.

Mud Lake [SAN LUIS OBISPO]: *marsh,* 4.25 miles south-southwest of downtown Arroyo Grande near the coast (lat. 35°03'45" N, long. 120°36'40" W). Named on Oceano (1965) 7.5' quadrangle. The marsh contains three lakes, the largest 800 feet long.

Mud Spring [SAN BENITO]: *spring,* 7.5 miles east-northeast of Bitterwater (lat. 36°26'20" N, long. 120°53'15" W; sec. 21, T 17 S, R 10 E). Named on Rock Spring Peak (1969) 7.5' quadrangle.

Mud Spring [SANTA BARBARA]: *spring,* 5.25 miles south of San Rafael Mountain (lat. 34°38'05" N, long. 119°49'30" W). Named on San Rafael Mountain (1959) 7.5' quadrangle.

Mud Springs Canyon [MONTEREY-SAN LUIS OBISPO]: *canyon,* drained by a stream that heads in Monterey County and flows 8 miles to Mason Canyon 10 miles north-northwest of Shandon in San Luis Obispo County (lat. 35°46'45" N, long. 120°28'05" W; sec. 4, T 25 S, R 14 E). Named on Cholame Hills (1961) 7.5' quadrangle.

Muertos Canyon [SAN BENITO]: *canyon,* drained by a stream that flows 1.25 miles to an unnamed canyon 5 miles west-northwest of San Juan Bautista (lat. 36°52'15" N, long. 121°37'10" W). Named on Chittenden (1955) and San Juan Bautista (1955) 7.5' quadrangles.

Mulberry: see **Paicines** [SAN BENITO].

Mulch Spring [MONTEREY]: *spring,* 22 miles east-northeast of King City (lat. 36°18'05" N, long. 120°44'40" W; sec. 2, T 19 S, R 11 E). Named on San Benito Mountain (1969) 7.5' quadrangle.

Mule Canyon Creek [MONTEREY]: *stream,* flows 1.25 miles to the sea 3.25 miles east-southeast of Pfeiffer Point (lat. 36°13'05" N, long. 121°45'35" W; sec. 5, T 20 S, R 2 E). Named on Pfeiffer Point (1956) 7.5' quadrangle. Clark (1991, p. 346) associated the name "Mule Canyon" with the pasturing of mules.

Mulligan Hill [MONTEREY]: *hill,* 11.5 miles north-northeast of Monterey near the mouth of Salinas River (lat. 36°44'55" N, long. 121°47'55" W). Named on Marina (1947) 7.5' quadrangle. Called Cabeza de Milligan on a diseño of Bolsa del Potrero y Moro Cojo grant (Becker, 1964). The feature for a long time was called Mulligan's Head for John Milligan, an Irish sailor who arrived in California before 1819 and became part owner of the land grant that includes the hill (Gudde, 1949, p. 228).

Mulligan's Head: see **Mulligan Hill** [MONTEREY].

Munch Canyon [SANTA CRUZ]: *canyon,* drained by a stream that flows 2.5 miles to Davey Brown Creek nearly 4 miles south-southwest of Bald Mountain (1) (lat. 34°45'35" N, long. 119°57'15" W). Named on Bald Mountain (1964) and Figueroa Mountain (1959) 7.5' quadrangles.

Mungo: see **Point Sur** [MONTEREY].

Municipal Baths Springs: see **Paso Robles** [SAN LUIS OBISPO].

Murphy Crossing [MONTEREY-SANTA CRUZ]: *locality,* 2.25 miles north-west of Aromas along Pajaro River on Monterey-Santa Cruz County line (lat. 36°54'20" N, long. 121°40'30" W). Named on Watsonville East (1955) 7.5' quadrangle.

Murphy Flat [SAN BENITO]: *area,* 7 miles west-northwest of Bitterwater (lat. 36°24'25" N, long. 121°07'15" W; sec. 32, T 17 S, R 8 E). Named on North Chalone Peak (1969) and Topo Valley (1969) 7.5' quadrangles.

Murphy Hill [SAN LUIS OBISPO]: *hill,* 2 miles west-northwest of Shandon near the mouth of McMillan Canyon (lat. 35°39'50" N, long. 120°24'35" W; sec. 13, T 26 S, R 14 E). Altitude 1268 feet. Named on Shandon (1961) 7.5' quadrangle.

Murray: see **La Salle** [SANTA BARBARA].

Murray Creek: see **Murry Creek** [MONTEREY].

Murry Creek [MONTEREY]: *stream,* flows 5 miles to Jolon Creek just east of Jolon (lat. 35°58'15" N, long. 121°10'15" W). Named on Jolon (1949) 7.5' quadrangle. On Bryson (1919) 15' quadrangle, the name "Argyle Creek" applies to present Murry Creek and to the lower part of Jolon Creek below its junction with Murry Creek. Howard (p. 75) called the stream Murray Creek, and stated that apparently it was named for brothers Carl Murray and Ernest Murray, who lived north of Jolon.

Muscio [SANTA BARBARA]: *locality,* 6 miles southeast of Santa Maria (lat. 34°54'15" N, long. 120°20'50" W; at W line sec. 34, T 10 N, R 33 W). Named on Santa Maria (1947) 15' quadrangle.

Muscle Point: see **Mussel Point** [MONTEREY].

Musick [SAN LUIS OBISPO]: *locality,* 12.5 miles north-northeast of the town of Nipomo along Arroyo Grande Creek (lat. 35°12'25" N, long. 120°23'55" W; near SW cor. sec. 20, T 31 S, R 15 E). Named on Nipomo (1922) 15' quadrangle. Postal authorities established Musick post office in 1880 and discontinued it in 1921 (Frickstad, p. 165). The name commemorates an early landowner in the neighborhood (Angel, 1883, p. 354).

Mussel Point [MONTEREY]: *promontory,* 2 miles southeast of Point Pinos along the coast (lat. 36°37'20" N, long. 121°54'15" W). Named on Monterey (1947) 7.5' quadrangle. Called Point Cabrillo on Monterey (1947, photorevised 1968) 7.5' quadrangle. Blake (1856, p. 391) referred to "Point Almeja, or Muscle Point." Davidson (1907, p. 31) mentioned that a chart of surveys made in 1851 and 1852 has the designation "Almeja or Mussel Rock" for "the principal jutting point between the presidio and Point of Pines." United States Board on Geographic Names (1936a, p. 10) approved the name "Point Cabrillo" for the feature and rejected the names "China Point" and "Mussel Point"—the name "Point Cabrillo" was given because Cabrillo is thought to have landed at the place in 1542.

Mussel Point [SANTA BARBARA]: *promontory,* 6 miles west-southwest of the town of Guadalupe along the coast (lat. 34°55'45" N, long. 120°40' W). Named on Point Sal (1958) 7.5' quadrangle.

Mussel Rock [SANTA BARBARA]: *rock,* 6 miles west-southwest of the town of Guadalupe (lat. 34°55'45" N, long. 120°39'55" W); the feature is at Mussel Point. Named on Point Sal (1958) 7.5' quadrangle.

Mussel Rock: see **Mussel Point** [MONTEREY].

Mustang Canyon [SANTA BARBARA]: *canyon,* drained by a stream that flows 5.5 miles to Cuyama Valley 4 miles east-northeast of Miranda Pine Mountain (lat. 35°03' N, long. 119°58' W). Named on Bates Canyon (1964) and Taylor Canyon (1959) 7.5' quadrangles.

Mustang Peak [MONTEREY]: *peak,* 5 miles north of Parkfield on Monterey-Fresno County line (lat. 35°58'30" N, long. 120°24'45" W; sec. 36, T 22 S, R 14 E). Named on Parkfield (1961) 7.5' quadrangle.

Mustang Ridge [MONTEREY]: *ridge,* northwest-trending, 16 miles long, northeast of Peach Tree Valley (lat. 36°13'30" N, long. 120° 48'30" W). Named on Hepsedam Peak (1969), Lonoak (1969), Monarch Peak (1967), and Priest Valley (1969) 7.5' quadrangles.

Mustang Spring [SAN LUIS OBISPO]: *spring,* 21 miles east-northeast of Pozo (lat. 35°24'30" N, long. 120°01'10" W; sec. 14, T 29 S, R 18 E). Named on La Panza NE (1966) 7.5' quadrangle.

Mustard Creek [SAN LUIS OBISPO]: *stream,* flows 4 miles to Salinas River 2.5 miles north of Paso Robles (lat. 35°39'55" N, long. 120°41'40" W; near E line sec. 17, T 26 S, R 12 E). Named on Paso Robles (1948) 7.5' quadrangle.

- N -

Nacimento River: see **Nacimiento River** [MONTEREY-SAN LUIS OBISPO].

Nacimiento [MONTEREY]: *locality,* 5 miles southeast of Bradley along Southern Pacific Railroad (lat. 35°48'35" N, long. 120° 45' W; sec. 26, T 24 S, R 11 E). Named on San Miguel (1948) 7.5' quadrangle. The railroad station at the place was named in 1905 for Nacimiento River (Gudde, 1949, p. 230).

Nacimiento: see **Camp Nacimiento** [MONTEREY].

Nacimiento Reservoir [SAN LUIS OBISPO]: *lake,* behind a dam on Nacimiento River 5.5 miles east of Tierra Redonda Mountain (lat. 35°45'30" N, long. 120°53' W; sec. 15, T 25 S, R 10 E). Named on Bryson (1949, photorevised 1979), Lime Mountain (1948, photorevised 1979), Pebblestone Shut-in (1959), and Tierra Redonda Mountain (1949, photorevised 1979) 7.5' quadrangles. United States Board on Geographic Names (1979a, p. 7) approved the name "Lake Nacimiento" for the feature.

Nacimiento River [MONTEREY-SAN LUIS OBISPO]: *stream,* heads in Monterey County and flows 70 miles, partly in San Luis Obispo County, to Salinas River 3.25 miles southeast of Bradley in Monterey County (lat. 35°50' N, long. 120°45'20" W; sec. 23, T 24 S, R 11 E). Named on Alder Peak (1949), Bradley (1949), Bryson (1949), Burnette Peak (1949), Cape San Martin (1949), Cone Peak (1949), Jolon (1949), Lime Mountain (1948), Pebblestone Shut-in (1959), and Tierra Redonda Mountain (1949) 7.5' quadrangles. Present Nacimiento River is called Nacismento R. on Goddard's (1857) map, and is called Sierra River on Diller and others' (1915) map. The river is identified as Rio de la Sierra on a diseño of San Miguelito de Trinidad grant made in 1841 (Becker, 1964). Whitney (p. 145) mentioned Nascimiento River, Fairbanks (1893, p. 72) noted Nacimento River, Nutter (p. 335) referred to Nacimiento Creek, and Trask (p. 21) used the name "Nacismiento River." According to Gudde (1949, p. 230), members of the Portola expedition camped by the stream in 1769 and Crespi described it as a very large arroyo whose source (*nacimiento* in Spanish) was nearby; later Anza saw the river and apparently believed that the stream had been given the name "Nacimiento," perhaps with the meaning "nativity." According to Smith (p. 3), the Portola expedition called the river Rio de las Truchas. United States Board on Geographic Names (1933, p. 540) rejected the names "Nacimento River" and "Sierra River" for the stream. Nigger Fork enters 58 miles upstream from the mouth of the river; it is 4 miles long and is named on Cape San Martin (1949) 7.5' quadrangle. Clark (1991, p. 356) associated the name of the fork with Mary L.C. Norman, known locally as Nigger Mary, who settled along the stream in 1919.

Nacimiento Summer Camp [MONTEREY]: *locality,* 5 miles west of Lopez Point (lat. 36°01'10" N, long. 121°28'30" W; sec. 13, T 22 S, R 4 E). Named on Junipero Serra (1940) 15' quadrangle.

Nacional [MONTEREY]: *land grant,* 2 miles southwest of Salinas. Named on Salinas (1947) 7.5' quadrangle. Vicente Cantua received 2 leagues in 1839 and claimed 6633 acres patented in 1866 (Cowan, p. 50-51).

Naples [SANTA BARBARA]: *locality,* 5 miles west-northwest of Coal Oil Point along Southern Pacific Railroad (lat. 34°26'25" N, long. 119°57'30" W). Named on Dos Pueblos Canyon (1951) 7.5' quadrangle. Postal authorities established Naples post office in 1890 and discontinued it in 1923 (Frickstad, p. 171).

Napoma: see **Nipomo** [SAN LUIS OBISPO] (1).

Napoma Ridge: see **Nipomo Valley** [SAN LUIS OBISPO].

Narlon [SANTA BARBARA]: *locality,* 4.25 miles west-southwest of the village of Casmalia along Southern Pacific Railroad (lat. 34°48'35" N, long. 120°35'50" W). Named on Casmalia (1959) 7.5' quadrangle.

Narrows: see **The Narrows** [MONTEREY]; **The Narrows** [SANTA BARBARA].

Narrows Campground [SANTA BARBARA]: *locality,* 4 miles south of Big Pine Mountain along Indian Creek (lat. 34°38'20" N, long. 119°39'05" W). Named on Big Pine Mountain (1964) 7.5' quadrangle.

Nashua [MONTEREY]: *locality,* 4.5 miles north-northeast of Marina along Southern Pacific Railroad (lat. 36°44'30" N, long. 121°45'50" W). Named on Marina (1947) 7.5' quadrangle.

Nasimento: see **Bradley** [MONTEREY].

Natividad [MONTEREY]: *settlement,* 5 miles northeast of Salinas (lat. 36°44' N, long. 121°35'45" W); the place is on La Natividad grant. Named on Natividad (1947) 7.5' quadrangle. Postal authorities established Natividad post office in 1855 and discontinued it in 1908 (Frickstad, p. 108). According to Clark (1991, p. 259), Natividad post office first was at a travellers stop called Gavilan House that was situated by Lagunita Lake. Natividad was a flourishing stage station in the 1850's before traffic was routed through Salinas (Hoover, Rensch, and Rensch, p. 225).

Natividad Creek [MONTEREY]: *stream,* flows 5 miles to an artificial watercourse at the northeast edge of Salinas (lat. 36°41'30" N, long. 121°37'05" W); the stream is mainly on La Natividad grant. Named on Natividad (1947) 7.5' quadrangle. Salinas (1912) 15' quadrangle shows the stream ending in a marsh.

Natoma: see **Camp Natoma** [SAN LUIS OBISPO].

Nattrass Valley [MONTEREY]: *canyon,* nearly 5 miles long, opens into Wildhorse Canyon from the east 12 miles north-northwest of San Ardo (lat. 36°11'30" N, long. 120°57'35" W; sec. 14, T 20 S, R 9 E). Named on Nattrass Valley (1967) 7.5' quadrangle. The name commemorates the Nattrass family, early landowners in the neighborhood (Clark, 1991, p. 354).

Navajo [SAN LUIS OBISPO]: *locality,* 7.5 miles northeast of Pozo (lat. 35°22'45" N, long. 120°16'50" W; sec. 29, T 29 S, R 16 E); the place is by Navajo Creek. Named on Pozo (1922) 15' quadrangle.

Navajoa Creek: see **Navajo Creek** [SAN LUIS OBISPO].

Navajo Campground [SAN LUIS OBISPO]: *locality,* nearly 6 miles northeast of Pozo along McGinnis Creek (lat. 35°22'10" N, long. 120°18'40" W; sec. 25, T 29 S, R 15 E). Named on Pozo Summit (1967) 7.5' quadrangle.

Navajo Creek [SAN LUIS OBISPO]: *stream,* flows 15 miles to San Juan Creek 10 miles east of Wilson Corner (lat. 35°30' N, long. 120°12' W; near S line sec. 12, T 28 S, R 16 E). Named on Camatta Ranch (1966), La Panza Ranch (1966), and Pozo Summit (1967) 7.5' quadrangles. Anderson and Martin (p. 49) used the name "Navajoa Creek" for the stream.

Neals Spring [SAN LUIS OBISPO]: *spring,* 4.5 miles south-southeast of Paso Robles (lat. 35°34'30" N, long. 120°38'50" W). Named on Templeton (1948) 7.5' quadrangle.

Nearys Lagoon [SANTA CRUZ]: *marsh,* nearly 1 mile north-northwest of Point Santa Cruz in Santa Cruz (lat. 36°57'50" N, long. 122°01'50" W). Named on Santa Cruz (1954) 7.5' quadrangle.

Needle Rock Point [SANTA CRUZ]: *relief feature,* 4.5 miles west of Point Santa Cruz along the coast (lat. 36°57'20" N, long. 122°06'20" W). Named on Santa Cruz (1954) 7.5' quadrangle. A slender pillar of rock stands a short distance seaward from the face of cliffs at the place (United States Coast and Geodetic Survey, p. 121).

Nelson Creek [MONTEREY]: *stream,* flows 5 miles to Big Sandy Creek 18 miles east of San Ardo (lat. 36°00'40" N, long. 120°34'55" W; sec. 16, T 22 S, R 13 E). Named on Smith Mountain (1969) and Stockdale Mountain (1948) 7.5' quadrangles. A map of Monterey County used about 1900 has the name "Nelson's Cr." for present Big Sandy Creek above the place that Big Sandy Creek enters Indian Valley.

Nelson Flat [MONTEREY]: *area,* nearly 7 miles south-southeast of Jolon (lat. 35°53'15" N, long. 121°06'45" W; sec. 33, T 23 S, R 8 E). Named on Williams Hill (1949) 7.5' quadrangle.

Neponset [MONTEREY]: *locality,* 8.5 miles west-northwest of Salinas along Southern Pacific Railroad (lat. 36°43'45" N, long. 121°47' W). Named on Marina (1947) 7.5' quadrangle. The place was called Martin Station before about 1900 (Gudde, 1949, p. 233). The name "Neponset" is an Indian one that was transferred from Massachusetts (Clark, 1991, p. 355).

New Cuyama [SANTA BARBARA]: *town,* 4.25 miles west of the village of Cuyama (lat. 34°56'50" N, long. 119°41'15" W); the place is in Cuyama Valley. Named on New Cuyama (1964) 7.5' quadrangle. Postal authorities established New Cuyama post office in 1953; Richfield Oil Company built the town in 1938 for their employees (Salley, p. 153).

Newell Creek [SANTA CRUZ]: *stream,* flows 7.5 miles to San Lorenzo River nearly 4 miles southeast of the town of Boulder Creek (lat. 37°04'50" N, long. 122°04'45" W; sec. 9, T 10 S, R 2 W). Named on Castle Rock Ridge (1955) and Felton (1955) 7.5' quadrangles. The name is for Addison Newell, who owned land along the stream in the 1860's (Clark, 1986, p. 228).

Newell Creek Reservoir: see **Loch Lomond** [SANTA CRUZ].

Newell Lake: see **Loch Lomond** [SANTA CRUZ].

New Felton: see **Felton** [SANTA CRUZ].

New Idria: see **Idria** [SAN BENITO].

Newlove Hill [SANTA BARBARA]: *peak,* 3 miles southeast of Orcutt on Graciosa Ridge (lat. 34°50'05" N, long. 120°24'10" W). Named on Orcutt (1959) 7.5' quadrangle.

New Mill Canyon [SAN BENITO]: *canyon,* drained by a stream that flows 2.5 miles to Topo Valley 5.5 miles northwest of Bitterwater (lat. 36°26'30" N, long. 121°04' W; sec. 23, T 17 S, R 8 E). Named on Topo Valley (1969) 7.5' quadrangle.

New Monterey: see **Monterey** [MONTEREY].

New Republic: see **Santa Rita** [MONTEREY].

New River [SAN LUIS OBISPO]: *stream,* flows 4.25 miles to Cuyama River 2 miles north-northeast of New Cuyama [SANTA BARBARA] (lat. 34°58'25" N, long. 119°40'15" W). Named on Cuyama (1964) and New Cuyama (1964) 7.5' quadrangles.

Newsom Canyon [SAN LUIS OBISPO]: *canyon,* drained by a stream that flows 2 miles to Guaya Canyon nearly 2 miles east of downtown Arroyo Grande (lat. 35°07'05" N, long. 120°33'05" W); the canyon is south of Newsom Ridge. Named on Arroyo Grande NE (1965) and Oceano (1965) 7.5' quadrangles.

Newsome Canyon [SANTA BARBARA]: *canyon,* drained by a stream that flows 6 miles to Branch Canyon 4.25 miles south of New Cuyama (lat. 34°53'50" N, long. 119°41'35" W; near NE cor. sec. 6, T 9 N, R 26 W). Named on New Cuyama (1964) and Salisbury Potrero (1964) 7.5' quadrangles.

Newsome Spring: see **Lower Newsome Spring** [SANTA BARBARA]; **Upper Newsome Spring** [SANTA BARBARA].

Newsom Ridge [SAN LUIS OBISPO]: *ridge,* west-trending, 7 miles long, 5.5 miles north of the town of Nipomo (lat. 35°07'15" N, long. 120°29'30" W). Named on Arroyo Grande NE (1965), Nipomo (1965), and Oceano (1965) 7.5' quadrangles.

Newsom's Arroyo Grande Springs: see **Newsom Springs** [SAN LUIS OBISPO].

Newsoms Arroyo Grande Warm Springs: see **Newsom Springs** [SAN LUIS OBISPO].

Newsom Springs [SAN LUIS OBISPO]: *spring,* 2 miles east of downtown Arroyo Grande (lat. 35°07'20" N, long. 120°32'35" W); the feature is in Newsom Canyon. Named on Oceano (1965) 7.5' quadrangle. D.F. Newsom homesteaded at the place in 1864; a resort called Newsom's Arroyo Grande Warm Springs used water from the spring (Logan, p. 694). Winslow Anderson (p. 207-208) referred to the resort as Newsom's Arroyo Grande Springs, and G.A. Waring (p. 68-69) referred to it as Newsoms Arroyo Grande Warm Spring.

New Springs: see **Iron Spring** [SAN LUIS OBISPO] (1).

New Town: see **Santa Ynez** [SANTA BARBARA].

New Year Creek: see **Año Nuevo Creek** [SANTA CRUZ].

Nifty Rock [SANTA BARBARA]: *rock,* 5 miles northwest of Cardwell Point, and 350 feet offshore on the north side of San Miguel Island (lat. 34°04'20" N, long. 120°21'35" W). Named on San Miguel Island East (1950) 7.5' quadrangle.

Nigger Fork: see **Nacimiento River** [MONTEREY].

Nigger Hill [MONTEREY]: *hill,* 12 miles northeast of San Ardo in Peachtree Valley (lat. 36°09'45" N, long. 120°46'40" W). Named on San Ardo (1956) 15' quadrangle. Clark (1991, p. 357) related the name to a Negro who was killed when he lost control of a loaded wagon on the hill.

Nimpomo: see **Nipomo** [SAN LUIS OBISPO] (1).

Nimrod Canyon [SAN BENITO]: *canyon,* drained by a stream that flows nearly 2 miles to San Benito River 7 miles south-southwest of Idria (lat. 36°19'50" N, long. 120°44'10" W; sec. 26, T 18 S, R 11 E). Named on Hepsedam Peak (1969) and San Benito Mountain (1969) 7.5' quadrangles.

Nineteen Oaks [SANTA BARBARA]: *locality,* nearly 6 miles northeast of San Marcos Pass (lat. 34°34'20" N, long. 119°45'10" W; at W line sec. 29, T 6 N, R 27 E). Named on San Marcos Pass (1959) 7.5' quadrangle.

Nipoma: see **Nipomo** [SAN LUIS OBISPO] (1) and (2).

Nipomo [SAN LUIS OBISPO]:

(1) *land grant,* at and around Nipomo Valley and Nipomo Mesa. Named on Guadalupe (1959), Huasna Peak (1967), Nipomo (1965), Oceamo (1965),

and Santa Maria (1959) 7.5' quadrangles. William G. Dana received 15 leagues in 1837 and claimed 37,888 acres patented in 1868 (Cowan, p. 52). Parke's (1854-1855) map has the name "Rcho. Napoma," and Whitney (p. 138) referred to Nipoma Ranch. United States Board on Geographic Names (1933, p. 554) rejected the forms "Nimpomo" and "Nipoma" for the name, which is from an Indian village (Kroeber, 1916, p. 50)—the word is said to have the meaning "foot of the mountain" (Hoover, Rensch, and Rensch, p. 386).

(2) *town,* 7.5 miles southeast of the town of Arroyo Grande (lat. 35° 02'35" N, long. 120°28'30" W); the town is in Nipomo Valley on Nipomo grant. Named on Nipomo (1965) 7.5' quadrangle. The heirs of William G. Dana had the town laid out in 1889 (Gudde, 1949, p. 237). Postal authorities established Nipoma post office in 1883, discontinued it in 1885, reestablished it in 1886, and changed the name to Nipomo in 1887 (Frickstad, p. 165).

Nipomo Creek [SAN LUIS OBISPO]: *stream,* flows 9 miles to Santa Maria River 4 miles south-southeast of the town of Nipomo (lat. 34°59'40" N, long. 120°26'20" W). Named on Nipomo (1965), Oceano (1965), and Santa Maria (1959) 7.5' quadrangles.

Nipomo Hill [SAN LUIS OBISPO]: *peak,* 1.5 miles south of downtown Arroyo Grande (lat. 35°06' N, long. 120°34'40" W); the peak is at the north end of Nipomo Mesa. Altitude 409 feet. Named on Oceano (1965) 7.5' quadrangle.

Nipomo Mesa [SAN LUIS OBISPO]: *area,* southeast of the town of Arroyo Grande between Santa Maria Valley and Nipomo Valley. Named on Nipomo (1965) and Oceano (1965) 7.5' quadrangles. Called The Mesa on Santa Maria (1959) 7.5' quadrangle, but United States Board on Geographic Names (1966, p. 5) rejected this name for the place.

Nipomo Valley [SAN LUIS OBISPO]: *valley,* at and near the town of Nipomo along Nipomo Creek. Named on Nipomo (1965) and Oceano (1965) 7.5' quadrangles. Parke (p. 6) used the name "Napoma Ridge" for the ridge situated between present Nipomo Valley and Huasna Valley; Parke's (1854-1855) map has the name "Sierra Napoma" for the same feature.

Nira Campground [SANTA BARBARA]: *locality,* 3 miles south of Bald Mountain (1) along Manzana Creek (lat. 34°46'15" N, long. 119°56'15" W). Named on Bald Mountain (1964) 7.5' quadrangle.

Noche Buena [MONTEREY]: *land grant,* at and northeast of Seaside near the coast. Named on Marina (1947) and Seaside (1947) 7.5' quadrangles. Juan Antonio Muñoz received 1 league in 1835; J. and J. de Monomany claimed 4412 acres patented in 1862 (Cowan, p. 40; Cowan gave the name "Huerta de la Nacion" as an alternate).

Nojoqui [SANTA BARBARA]: *land grant,* south of Solvang. Named on Santa Ynez 1959) and Solvang (1959) 7.5' quadrangles. Raimundo Carrillo received 3 leagues in 1843 and claimed 13,285 acres patented in 1869 (Cowan, p. 53; Cowan used the name "Nojoque" for the grant). The name seems to be of Indian origin (Kroeber, 1916, p. 50).

Nojoqui: see **Las Cruces** [SANTA BARBARA] (2).

Nojoqui Creek [SANTA BARBARA]: *stream,* flows 8.5 miles to Santa Ynez River 0.5 mile south of Buellton (lat. 34°36'20" N, long. 120°11'35" W). Named on Solvang (1959) 7.5' quadrangle. The canyon of the stream is called Cañada de Na-joa-ui on a diseño of Las Cruces grant made in 1835 (Becker, 1964).

Nojoqui Falls [SANTA BARBARA]: *waterfall,* 6 miles south of Buellton (lat. 34°31'40" N, long. 120°10'15" W; near W line sec. 7, T 5 N, R 31 W); the feature is along Nojoqui Creek. Named on Solvang (1959) 7.5' quadrangle.

Nojoqui Pass: see **Nojoqui Summit** [SANTA BARBARA].

Nojoqui Summit [SANTA BARBARA]: *pass,* 6 miles south of Buellton (lat. 34°31'40" N, long. 120°11'45" W; sec. 11, T 5 N, R 32 W). Named on Solvang (1959) 7.5' quadrangle. Called Gaviota Pass on Lompoc (1905) 30' quadrangle. Hanna (p. 213) called the feature Nojoqui Pass.

Noon Peak [SANTA BARBARA]: *peak,* 6.5 miles north of Rincon Point (lat. 34°28'10" N, long. 119°28'25" W; sec. 35, T 5 N, R 25 W). Altitude 4084 feet. Named on White Ledge Peak (1952) 7.5' quadrangle.

Norn Hill [SAN LUIS OBISPO]: *peak,* 1 mile west-northwest of downtown Paso Robles (lat. 35°38'15" N, long. 120°42'25" W). Altitude 1125 feet. Named on Paso Robles (1948) 7.5' quadrangle.

North Beach Campground [SAN LUIS OBISPO]: *locality,* 1 mile south-southeast of Pismo beach (lat. 35°07'50" N, long. 120° 38' W). Named on Pismo Beach (1965) 7.5' quadrangle.

North Canyon [SAN BENITO]: *canyon,* drained by a stream that flows 2.25 miles to Bird Creek 5.5 miles south-southwest of Hollister (lat. 36°46'25" N, long. 121°25'45" W). Named on Hollister (1955) 7.5' quadrangle.

North Chalone Peak [MONTEREY-SAN BENITO]: *peak,* 9 miles north-northeast of Greenfield on Monterey-San Benito County line (lat. 36°26'50" N, long. 121°11'40" W; sec. 15, T 17 S, R 7 E); the peak is 1 mile northwest of South Chalone Peak. Altitude 3304 feet. Named on North Chalone Peak (1969) 7.5' quadrangle. North Chalone Peak and South Chalone Peak together have the name "Chalone Mtn." on Metz (1921) 15' quadrangle. Parke's (1854-1855) map shows Mt. Chelone. The word "Chalone" is from a group of Indians who lived near the peak; an early Spanish map has the name "Cierro Chalon" (Gudde, 1949, p. 63).

North Entrance Rock [SAN LUIS OBISPO]: *rock,* 100 feet long, 0.5 mile south of the village of San Simeon, and 250 feet offshore near San Simeon Point (lat. 35°38'05" N, long. 120°11'30" W). Named on San Simeon (1958) 7.5' quadrangle.

North Grizzly Bend Creek [SAN LUIS OBISPO]: *stream,* flows 1.5 miles to present Nacimiento Reservoir 11 miles northeast of the village of San Simeon (lat. 35°45'10" N, long. 121°03'05" W; near W line sec. 18, T 25 S, R 9 E); the mouth of the creek is at Grizzly Bend. Named on Bryson (1949) 7.5' quadrangle.

North Hill [SAN BENITO]: *peak,* 1.5 miles south-southeast of Idria (lat. 36°23'50" N, long. 120°39'35" W; near N line sec. 4, T 18 S, R 12 E); the feature is 0.5 mile north-northwest of San Carlos Peak. Altitude 4658 feet. Named on Idria (1969) 7.5' quadrangle.

North Mine Canyon Spring [SANTA BARBARA]: *spring,* 2.5 miles west-northwest of Montgomery Potrero (lat. 34°51'05" N, long. 119°47'30" W); the spring is 1 mile west-northwest of East Mine Canyon Spring in a branch of Mine Canyon (3). Named on Hurricane Deck (1964) 7.5' quadrangle.

North Point: see **Cypress Cove** [MONTEREY].

North Santa Maria [SANTA BARBARA]: *locality,* in the west part of the city of Santa Maria along Santa Maria Valley Railroad (lat. 34°57'20" N, long. 120°26'35" W; sec. 10, T 10 N, R 34 W). Named on Santa Maria (1959) 7.5' quadrangle.

Northwest Anchorage [SANTA BARBARA]: *anchorage,* 1.5 miles south of Carrington Point on the north side of Santa Rosa Island in Beecher Bay (lat. 34°00'55" N, long. 120°02'50" W). Named on Santa Rosa Island North (1943) 7.5' quadrangle.

Notleys Landing [MONTEREY]: *locality,* 6.5 miles north of Point Sur near the mouth of Palo Colorado Canyon (lat. 36°23'50" N, long. 121°54'15" W; sec. 6, T 18 S, R 1 E). Named on Soberanes Point (1956) 7.5' quadrangle. A village sprang up at the place after Godfrey Notley built a landing for the shipment of tanbark and lumber (Fink, p. 210). Shipping activity at the place lasted from 1898 until 1907 (Lussier, p. 13).

Nova: see **Thyle** [SAN LUIS OBISPO].

Nuestra Señora del Refugio [SANTA BARBARA]: *land grant,* east and west of Gaviota along the coast. Named on Gaviota (1953), Point Conception (1953), Sacate (1953), Santa Rosa Hills (1959), and Tajiguas (1953) 7.5' quadrangles. Jose Francisco Ortega received 6 leagues in 1795; Antonio Maria Ortega got the land in 1834 and claimed 26,529 acres patented in 1866 (Cowan, p. 67).

- O -

Oak Canyon [SANTA BARBARA]:

(1) *canyon,* drained by a stream that flows 3.5 miles to Sisquoc River 2.5 miles northeast of Bald Mountain (1) (lat. 34°50' N, long. 119°54' W). Named on Bald Mountain (1964) 7.5' quadrangle.

(2) *canyon,* drained by a stream that flows 3.25 miles to Santa Ynez River 4.5 miles east of Surf (lat. 34°40'50" N, long. 120°31'30" W). Named on Surf (1959) 7.5' quadrangle.

Oak Creek [SANTA BARBARA]: *stream,* flows 2.5 miles to the sea 4 miles east of downtown Santa Barbara (lat. 34°25'10" N, long. 119°37'35" W). Named on Santa Barbara (1952) 7.5' quadrangle. United States Board on Geographic Names (1961b, p. 13) rejected the name "Arroyo del Tulare" for the stream.

Oak Flat [MONTEREY]: *area,* 7.5 miles south of Jolon (lat. 35°51'35" N, long. 121°11'40" W). Named on Burnett Peak (1949) 7.5' quadrangle.

Oak Flat: see **Big Oak Flat** [SAN BENITO]; **Big Sandy Creek** [MONTEREY]; **Little Oak Flat** [MONTEREY].

Oak Grove Canyon [MONTEREY]: *canyon,* 3 miles long, drained by a stream that enters California Flats 6.25 miles east-southeast of Parkfield (lat. 35°51'05" N, long. 120°20'05" W). Named on Cholame Valley (1961) 7.5' quadrangle.

Oak Knoll [SAN LUIS OBISPO]: *peak,* 3 miles west-northwest of the village of San Simeon (lat. 35°39'50" N, long. 121°14'20" W). Named on San Simeon (1958) 7.5' quadrangle.

Oak Knoll Creek [SAN LUIS OBISPO]: *stream,* flows 3.25 miles to the sea nearly 1.5 miles west-northwest of the village of San Simeon (lat. 35°39'05" N, long. 121°13'05" W). Named on San Simeon (1958) 7.5' quadrangle.

Oak Mountain [SANTA BARBARA]: *peak,* 4 miles east-southeast of Tranquillon Mountain (lat. 34°33'05" N, long. 120°30'05" W). Altitude 2014 feet. Named on Lompoc Hills (1959) and Tranquillon Mountain (1959) 7.5' quadrangles.

Oak Park [SAN LUIS OBISPO]: *district,* in the north part of Paso Robles (lat. 35°38'55" N, long. 120°41'25" W). Named on Paso Robles (1948) 7.5' quadrangle.

Oak Ridge [SAN LUIS OBISPO]: *ridge,* west-northwest-trending, nearly 1 mile long, 5 miles east-southeast of York Mountain (lat. 35°30'25" N, long. 120°45'30" W). Named on Adelaida (1961) 15' quadrangle.

Oak Ridge [SANTA CRUZ]: *ridge,* south-trending, 1.25 miles long, 6.5 miles northeast of the town of Boulder Creek (lat. 37°12' N, long. 122°03'15" W). Named on Castle Rock Ridge (1955) 7.5' quadrangle.

Oaks [SAN LUIS OBISPO]: *district,* on the west side of the town of Arroyo Grande (lat. 35°07' N, long. 120°35'45" W). Named on Oceano (1965) 7.5' quadrangle. Called Fairoaks on Arroyo Grande (1942) 15' quadrangle. Postal authorities established Oaks post office in 1949 (Salley, p. 158).

Oaks: see **The Oaks** [SAN LUIS OBISPO].

Oak Spring [SANTA BARBARA]: *spring,* 4.5 miles southeast of Salisbury Potrero (lat. 34°46'25" N, long. 119°38'55" W). Named on Salisbury Potrero (1964) 7.5' quadrangle.

Oak Tree Spring [SAN BENITO]: *spring,* 3 miles north of North Chalone Peak (lat. 36°29'20" N, long. 121°12'15" W; near SW cor. sec. 34, T 16 S, R 7 E). Named on North Chalone Peak (1969) 7.5' quadrangle.

Oat Canyon [SAN BENITO]: *canyon,* drained by a stream that flows 6 miles to Lewis Creek 16 miles southeast of Bitterwater (lat. 36°13'45" N, long. 120°47' W; sec. 33, T 19 S, R 11 E). Named on Hepsedam Peak (1969) and Monarch Peak (1967) 7.5' quadrangles. North Fork branches northwest 2.25 miles upstream from the mouth of the main canyon; it is 3 miles long and is named on Hepsedam Peak (1969) 7.5' quadrangle.

Oat Hills [MONTEREY]: *ridge,* north-trending, 1.25 miles long, 9.5 miles southwest of King City (lat. 36°05'50" N, long. 121°13'40" W). Named on Cosio Knob (1949) 7.5' quadrangle.

Obispo Peak: see **Bishop Peak** [SAN LUIS OBISPO].

O'Brien Lake [SAN LUIS OBISPO]: *intermittent lake,* 750 feet long, 5.25 miles southeast of Cholame (lat. 35°40'25" N, long. 120°13'40" W; near SW cor. sec. 11, T 26 S, R 16 E). Named on Orchard Peak (1961) 7.5' quadrangle.

Oceano [SAN LUIS OBISPO]: *town,* 2 miles southwest of downtown Arroyo Grande near the coast (lat. 35°06'10" N, long. 120°36'30" W). Named on Oceano (1965) 7.5' quadrangle. Postal authorities established Oceano post office in 1895 (Frickstad, p. 165).

Oceano Beach [SAN LUIS OBISPO]: *locality,* 0.5 mile north of the mouth of Arroyo Grande Creek (lat. 35°06'15" N, long. 120°37'45" W); the place is west of Oceano. Named on Arroyo Grande (1942) 15' quadrangle.

Ocean View Summit [SANTA CRUZ]: *peak,* 1.5 miles north-northwest of Big Basin (lat. 37°11'25" N, long. 122°14' W; sec. 31, T 8 S, R 3 W). Altitude 1685 feet. Named on Big Basin (1955) 7.5' quadrangle.

Oil Canyon [SANTA BARBARA]:

(1) *canyon,* drained by a stream that flows 2.25 miles to Horse Canyon (3) 6.5 miles east-northeast of Santa Ynez Peak (lat. 34°34'25" N, long. 119°52'35" W). Named on San Marcos Pass (1959) 7.5' quadrangle.

(2) *canyon,* drained by a stream that flows 2.25 miles to Arroyo Paredon 3 miles north-northwest of Carpinteria (lat. 34°26'05" N, long. 119°32'55" W; near NE cor. sec. 13, T 4 N, R 26 W). Named on Carpinteria (1952) 7.5' quadrangle.

Oil Creek [SANTA CRUZ]: *stream,* flows 1.25 miles to San Mateo County 9.5 miles north of the town of Boulder Creek (lat. 37°15'35" N, long. 122°09'05" W; at W line sec. 1, T 8 S, R 3 W). Named on Mindego Hill (1961) 7.5' quadrangle.

Oilport: see **San Luis Obispo Bay** [SAN LUIS OBISPO].

Oil Well Canyon [SAN LUIS OBISPO]: *canyon,* drained by a stream that flows nearly 2 miles to West Corral de Piedra Creek 3 miles south of Lopez Mountain (lat. 35°15'35" N, long. 120°35'05" W). Named on Lopez Mountain (1965) 7.5' quadrangle.

Oil Well Canyon [SANTA BARBARA]: *canyon,* drained by a stream that flows 2.5 miles to the sea 4 miles west-southwest of Tranquillon Mountain (lat. 34°33'20" N, long. 120°37'25" W). Named on Tranquillon Mountain (1959) 7.5' quadrangle.

Ojeda Canyon [SAN BENITO]: *canyon,* drained by a stream that flows 1.25 miles to an unnamed branch of South Fork Los Banos Creek 9 miles east-southeast of Potrero Peak (lat. 36°46'50" N, long. 121°00'30" W; near N line sec. 29, T 13 S, R 9 E). Named on Ruby Canyon (1968) 7.5' quadrangle.

Old Canyon [SAN LUIS OBISPO]: *canyon,* 3 miles long, opens into the canyon of San Juan Creek 5.25 miles northeast of Castle Crags (lat. 35°21'35" N, long. 120°08'15" W; sec. 34, T 29 S, R 17 E). Named on California Valley (1966) and La Panza (1967) 7.5' quadrangles.

Old Cojo: see **Cojo Bay** [SANTA BARBARA].

Old Creek [SAN LUIS OBISPO]: *stream,* flows 10 miles to the sea at Cayucos (lat. 35°26'05" N, long. 120°53'10" W). Named on Morro Bay North (1965) and York Mountain (1948) 7.5' quadrangles.

Old Creek: see **Cayucos** [SAN LUIS OBISPO].

Old Felton: see **Felton** [SANTA CRUZ].

Old Hilltown [MONTEREY]: *locality,* 3 miles south-southwest of Salinas on the north bank of Salinas River (lat. 36°37'55" N, long. 121°40'05" W). Named on Salinas (1947) 7.5' quadrangle. A ford near the site of Hill Town was called Paso del Quinto; later Hill Town had one of the first ferries on Salinas River—the ferry operated until a bridge was built in 1889 (Hoover, Rensch, and Rensch, p. 228).

Old Man Canyon [MONTEREY]: *canyon,* drained by a stream that flows 1.5 miles to Ruby Canyon 2.5 miles north-northwest of Jolon (lat. 36°00'05" N, long. 121°11'50" W). Named on Cosio Knob (1949) 7.5' quadrangle. Waring and Bradley (p. 606) used the form "Old Man's Cañon" for the name.

Old Man Mountain [SANTA BARBARA]:

(1) *peak,* 9 miles north-northeast of Carpinteria (lat. 34°31' N, long. 119°27'05" W; sec. 13, T 5 N, R 25 W). Altitude 5525 feet. Named on Old Man Mountain (1943) 7.5' quadrangle.

(2) *ridge,* west-northwest-trending, 1 mile long, 7 miles north-northeast of San Marcos Pass (lat. 34°36'20" N, long. 119°46'30" W). Named on San Marcos Pass (1959) 7.5' quadrangle.

Old Park Mill: see **Blooms Mill** [SANTA CRUZ].

Olds: see **Mount Olds** [MONTEREY].

Old Salinas River [MONTEREY]: *water feature,* extends for 5 miles from near the mouth of Salinas River to near the mouth of Elkhorn Slough at Moss Landing (lat. 36°48'15" N, long. 121°47'10" W). Named on Moss Landing (1954) 7.5' quadrangle. Salinas River followed the feature to the sea north of Moss Landing before the winter of 1909 and 1910, when the river broke through coastal dunes to reach the sea 5.5 miles farther south (Clark, 1991, p. 363).

Old Spring: see **Iron Spring** [SAN LUIS OBISPO] (1).

Old Town [SANTA BARBARA]: *locality,* less than 1 mile northwest of downtown Carpinteria (lat. 34°24'10" N, long. 119°31'50" W). Named on Carpinteria (1952) 7.5' quadrangle.

Old Wagon Cave Campground [MONTEREY]: *locality,* 4.25 miles south of Junipero Serra Peak (lat. 36°05'05" N, long. 121°24'05" W). Named on Junipero Serra (1961) 15' quadrangle.

Old Womans Creek [SANTA CRUZ]: *stream,* flows nearly 1 mile to San Mateo County 6.25 miles north-northwest of the mouth of Waddell Creek (lat. 37°10'55" N, long. 122°18'55" W; near W line sec. 4, T 9 S, R 4 W). Named on Franklin Point (1955) 7.5' quadrangle.

O'Leary: see **Tim O'Leary Canyon** [SAN LUIS OBISPO].

Olivas Canyon [SAN BENITO]: *canyon,* drained by a stream that flows 3 miles to Wildhorse Canyon 7.5 miles west-northwest of Bitterwater (lat. 36°26'20" N, long. 121°06'55" W; near W line sec. 21, T 17 S, R 8 E). Named on Topo Valley (1969) 7.5' quadrangle.

Olive Canyon [SANTA BARBARA]: *canyon,* drained by a stream that flows nearly 4 miles to Cuyama Valley 3 miles south of the village of Cuyama (lat. 34°53'25" N, long. 119°36'30" W; sec. 1, T 9 N, R 26 W). Named on Cuyama (1964) and Fox Mountain (1964) 7.5' quadrangles.

Olivera Canyon [SANTA BARBARA]: *canyon,* drained by a stream that flows 2.25 miles to Santa Maria Valley nearly 2 miles east-southeast of the village of Sisquoc (lat. 34°51'15" N, long. 120°15'55" W; sec. 17, T 9 N, R 32 W). Named on Foxen Canyon (1964) and Sisquoc (1959) 7.5' quadrangles.

Olive Spring [SANTA BARBARA]: *spring,* 2.5 miles north of Fox Mountain (lat. 34°51'10" N, long. 119°36'05" W); the spring is in Olive Canyon. Named on Fox Mountain (1964) 7.5' quadrangle.

Olive Springs [SANTA CRUZ]: *spring,* 5.5 miles north-northeast of Soquel (lat. 37°03'30" N, long. 121°55' W). Named on Laurel (1955) 7.5' quadrangle. On Los Gatos (1919) 15' quadrangle, the name applies to a group of buildings at the confluence of Soquel Creek and Hinckley Creek, 0.25 mile west-southwest of present Olive Springs. George Olive owned the place before 1897 (Clark, 1986, p. 237). Laizure (1926, p. 88) described a small unimproved cold spring called Hinns Sulphur Spring that was located near the top of Hinckley Ridge about 1 mile east of Olive Springs.

Oliviers Mountain: see **Puerta del Diablo** [MONTEREY].

Olmstead: see **Mount Olmstead** [MONTEREY].

Olson's Cave: see **Orzaba Pictograph Cave**, under **Twin Harbors** [SANTA BARBARA].

Olympia [SANTA CRUZ]: *settlement,* 5 miles southeast of the town of Boulder Creek along Zayante Creek (lat. 37°04'15" N, long. 122°03'25" W). Named on Felton (1955) 7.5' quadrangle. Postal authorities changed the name of Eccles post office to Olympia in 1915 and discontinued it in 1942 (Frickstad, p. 177).

One Suerte [MONTEREY]: *land grant,* nearly 5 miles west of Salinas; adjacent to Two Suertes grant. Named on Salinas (1947, photorevised 1968 and 1975) 7.5' quadrangle. The grant has the name "Chas. McFadden" on Salinas (1947) 7.5' quadrangle.

Ontario Hot Springs [SAN LUIS OBISPO]: *locality,* 1.5 miles east of Avila Beach (lat. 35°10'50" N, long. 120°42'10" W). Named on Pismo Beach (1965) 7.5' quadrangle. Called Hidden Valley Hot Springs on Arroyo Grande (1952) 15' quadrangle. Logan (p. 691) described a resort at the place that was called Budan Spring for the owner, Mrs. E. Budan, and noted that water at a temperature of 178° Fahrenheit flows from an artesian well drilled there in 1908.

Opal Cliffs [SANTA CRUZ]: *district,* at and northeast of Soquel Point near the coast (lat. 36°57'45" N, long. 121°57'50" W). Named on Soquel (1954) 7.5' quadrangle.

Opal Creek [SANTA CRUZ]: *stream,* flows nearly 4 miles to join Blooms Creek and form East Waddell Creek at the south end of Big Basin (lat.

37°09'55" N, long. 122°13'25" W; near E line sec. 7, T 9 S, R 3 W). Named on Big Basin (1955) 7.5' quadrangle.

Orange Flat [SAN LUIS OBISPO]: *area,* nearly 5 miles south of Atascadero (lat. 35°25'10" N, long. 120°40' W; near E line sec. 10, T 29 S, R 12 E). Named on Atascadero (1965) 7.5' quadrangle.

Orby: see **Harris** [SANTA BARBARA]; **Santa Cruz** [SANTA CRUZ].

Orcutt [SANTA BARBARA]: *town,* 6 miles south of Santa Maria (lat. 34°51'50" N, long. 120°26'40" W; on N line sec. 15, T 9 N, R 34 W). Named on Orcutt (1959) 7.5' quadrangle. Postal authorities established Orcutt post office in 1904 (Frickstad, p. 171). Officials of Union Oil Company had the town laid out in 1903 and named it for W.W. Orcutt, geologist for the company (Gudde, 1949, p. 244). California Division of Highways' (1934) map shows a place called Ferini located 1.25 miles south of Orcutt along Pacific Coast Railroad.

Orcutt Creek [SANTA BARBARA]: *stream,* flows 12 miles to end in lowlands 6 miles southeast of the town of Guadalupe (lat. 34° 54' N, long. 120°30'55" W); the stream goes through Orcutt. Named on Guadalupe (1959), Orcutt (1959), Santa Maria (1959), and Sisquoc (1959) 7.5' quadrangles.

Ord: see **Fort Ord Military Reservation** [MONTEREY].

Ord Barracks: see **Presidio of Monterey** [MONTEREY].

Ord Village: see **Fort Ord Village** [MONTEREY].

Orejano Flat [SAN BENITO]: *area,* 15 miles east-southeast of Bitterwater (lat. 36°16'35" N, long. 120°45'10" W; sec. 15, T 19 S, R 11 E). Named on Hepsedam Peak (1969) 7.5' quadrangle.

Orejano Spring [SAN BENITO]: *spring,* 15 miles east-southeast of Bitterwater (lat. 36°16'30" N, long. 120°45'10" W; sec. 15, T 19 S, R 11 E); the spring is at Orejano Flat. Named on Hepsedam Peak (1969) 7.5' quadrangle.

Orella [SANTA BARBARA]: *locality,* 9 miles east of Gaviota along Southern Pacific Railroad (lat. 34°27'40" N, long. 120°03'30" W). Named on Lompoc (1905) 30' quadrangle.

Orford: see **Port Orford** [SANTA BARBARA].

Organ Point: see **Lovers Point** [MONTEREY].

Orizaba: see **Twin Harbors** [SANTA BARBARA].

Orizaba Pictograph Cave: see **Twin Harbors** [SANTA BARBARA].

Oro Fino Canyon [MONTEREY]: *canyon,* drained by a stream that flows 3.25 miles to San Antonio River 2 miles west of Jolon (lat. 35°57'50" N, long. 121°12'35" W). Named on Jolon (1949) 7.5' quadrangle.

Oro Fino Canyon [MONTEREY-SAN LUIS OBISPO]: *canyon,* drained by a stream that heads in San Luis Obispo County and flows 2.25 miles to San Antonio River 5.5 miles southwest of Bradley in Monterey County (lat. 35°47'40" N, long. 120°51'35" W; sec. 35, T 24 S, R 10 E). Named on Bradley (1949) 7.5' quadrangle.

Ortega [SANTA BARBARA]: *locality,* 4 miles west-northwest of Carpinteria along Southern Pacific Railroad (lat. 34°25' N, long. 119°35'05" W); the place is 1.5 miles east-southeast of Ortega Hill. Named on Carpinteria (1952, photorevised 1967) 7.5' quadrangle. Called Ortega Siding on Carpinteria (1952) 7.5' quadrangle.

Ortega Creek [SAN BENITO]: *stream,* heads in Santa Clara County and flows 4.25 miles to San Felipe Lake 9.5 miles north-northwest of Hollister (lat. 36°59'05" N, long. 121°27'15" W). Named on San Felipe (1955, photorevised 1971) 7.5' quadrangle. The name commemorates Ygnacio Ortega, original owner of San Ysidro grant in Santa Clara County (United States Board on Geographic Names, 1973, p. 3).

Ortega Hill [SANTA BARBARA]: *hill,* 5.5 miles west-northwest of Carpinteria (lat. 34°25'20" N, long. 119°36'25" W). Named on Carpinteria (1952) 7.5' quadrangle.

Ortega Siding: see **Ortega** [SANTA BARBARA].

Ortega Spring [SAN LUIS OBISPO]: *spring,* 6 miles east-southeast of Cholame (lat. 35°40'50" N, long. 120°12'10" W; sec. 12, T 26 S, R 16 E). Named on Orchard Peak (1961) 7.5' quadrangle.

Osborne Ridge [MONTEREY]: *ridge,* west-trending, nearly 2 miles long, 2.5 miles south of the town of Carmel Valley (lat. 36°26'45" N, long. 121°43'30" W). Named on Carmel Valley (1956) 7.5' quadrangle.

Oso Campground: see **Lower Oso Campground** [SANTA BARBARA]; **Upper Oso Campground** [SANTA BARBARA].

Oso Canyon [SANTA BARBARA]: *canyon,* drained by a stream that flows 6 miles to Santa Ynez River 3.5 miles northeast of San Marcos Pass (lat. 34°32'45" N, long. 119°46'30" W). Named on Little Pine Mountain (1964) and San Marcos Pass (1959) 7.5' quadrangles.

Oso Creek [SAN LUIS OBISPO]: *stream,* flows 3 miles to Arroyo Seco 15 miles northeast of the town of Nipomo (lat. 35°10'25" N, long. 120°16'50" W; near E line sec. 5, T 32 S, R 16 E). Named on Caldwell Mesa (1967) 7.5' quadrangle.

Oso Flaco Creek [SAN LUIS OBISPO]: *stream,* flows 7.25 miles to the sea nearly 7 miles south-southwest of the town of Arroyo Grande (lat. 35°01'50" N, long. 120°38' W); the stream goes through Oso Flaco Lake, Little Oso Flaco Lake, and marsh. Named on Guadalupe (1959) and Oceano (1965) 7.5' quadrangles.

Oso Flaco Lake [SAN LUIS OBISPO]: *lake,* 0.5 mile long, 6.5 miles southwest of the town of Arroyo Grande near the coast (lat. 35°01'50" N, long. 120°37'15" W). Named on Oceano (1965) 7.5' quadrangle. When the Portola expedition camped by the lake in 1769, Crespi gave the place the name of the Lake of the Holy Martyrs, San Juan de Perucia and San Pedro de Sacro Terrato (Hanna, p. 221-222), but the soldiers called it Oso Flaco because they killed a very lean bear on the shore of the lake—*oso flaco* means "lean bear" in Spanish (Hoover, Rensch, and Rensch, p. 379).

Oso Flaco Lake: see **Little Oso Flaco Lake** [SAN LUIS OBISPO].

Otter Harbor: see **Simonton Cove** [SANTA BARBARA].

Outer Islet: see **Piedras Blancas Point** [SAN LUIS OBISPO].

Outlaw Camp [MONTEREY]: *locality,* 5 miles north-northwest of Partington Point along Terrace Creek (lat. 36°14'30" N, long. 121° 43'50" W; sec. 34, T 19 S, R 2 E). Named on Partington Ridge (1956) 7.5' quadrangle. The name is from the taking of redwood shakes from the place illegally (Clark,1991, p. 365).

Owl Canyon [SANTA BARBARA]: *canyon,* drained by a stream that flows 1.5 miles to South Fork La Brea Creek 3.5 miles east-northeast of Manzanita Mountain (lat. 34°54'35" N, long. 120°01'20" W). Named on Manzanita Mountain (1964) 7.5' quadrangle

- P -

Pacer [SANTA BARBARA]: *locality,* 3.25 miles west-southwest of Santa Maria along Santa Maria Valley Railroad (lat. 34°56'05" N, long. 120°29'20" W). Named on Santa Maria (1959) 7.5' quadrangle.

Pacheco Creek [SAN BENITO]: *stream,* heads in Santa Clara County and flows 5 miles in San Benito County to San Felipe Lake 6.25 miles north-northwest of Hollister (lat. 35°58'35" N, long. 121°27'35" W). Named on San Felipe (1955) and Three Sisters (1954) 7.5' quadrangles. Called Arroyo de S. Felipe on a diseño of San Joaquin grant made in 1836 (Becker, 1964). Hollister (1921) 15' quadrangle shows the stream ending at a marsh 2 miles southeast of San Felipe Lake. The name "Pacheco" commemorates Francisco Perez Pacheco, who had his ranch headquarters near the stream (Shumate, p. 12).

Pacific: see **Camp Pacific** [MONTEREY].

Pacific Grove [MONTEREY]: *town,* along the coast between Monterey and Point Pinos (lat. 36°37'15" N, long. 121°55' W). Named on Monterey (1947) 7.5' quadrangle. A group of Methodists founded the place in 1875 and modeled it after an encampment at Ocean Grove, New Jersey (Fink, p. 167). Postal authorities established Pacific Grove post office in 1886, discontinued it the same year, and reestablished it in 1887 (Frickstad, p. 108). The town incorporated in 1889.

Pacific Grove Acres [MONTEREY]: *district,* northwest of the main part of Pacific Grove (lat. 36°37'40" N, long. 121°55'50" W). Named on Monterey (1947) 7.5' quadrangle.

Pacific Mills: see **Ben Lomond** [SANTA CRUZ].

Pacific Valley: see **Plaskett** [MONTEREY].

Padrones Canyon [SAN LUIS OBISPO]: *canyon,* drained by a stream that flows 4 miles to Cuyama Valley 3 miles northeast of New Cuyama [SANTA BARBARA] (lat. 34°58'40" N, long. 119°38'40" W; sec. 3, T 10 N, R 26 W). Named on New Cuyama (1964) and Wells Ranch (1954) 7.5' quadrangles.

Padrones Spring [SAN LUIS OBISPO]: *spring,* 33 miles southeast of Simmler (lat. 35°00'10" N, long. 119°35'15" W; near N line sec. 31, T 11 N, R 25 W). Named on Elkhorn Hills (1954) 7.5' quadrangle. Called Pataroma Spring on Arnold and Johnson's (1910) map.

Paicines [SAN BENITO]: *village,* 11 miles southeast of Hollister near Tres Pinos Creek (lat. 36°43'40" N, long. 121°16'35" W); the village is on Cienega de los Paicines grant. Named on Paicines (1968) 7.5' quadrangle. The place first was called Tres Pinos for three pine trees there, but when in 1873 Southern Pacific Railroad built a branch line to a point 5 miles farther north-northwest, the name "Tres Pinos" was taken for the station at the end of the new rail line, and the older place was given the name "Paicines" for Cienega de los Paicines grant (Pierce, p. 126). Postal authorities established Tres Pinos post office in 1871, changed the name to Grogan in 1874, and changed the name to Paicines the same year (Frickstad, p. 136, 137). The name "Grogan" was for Alexander B. Grogan, owner of Cienega de los Paicines grant (Pierce, p. 139, 141). Kroeber (1916, p. 53) noted that Paicines is probably an Indian tribal name. California Mining Bureau's (1909a) map shows a place called Mulberry located 7 miles by stage line south-southeast of Paicines. Postal authorities established Elvina post office in 1885, changed the name to Mulberry in 1886, and discontinued it in 1917—the name "Mulberry" was from a failed scheme to plant mulberry trees for silkworm culture (Salley, p. 69, 149).

Painted Cave [SANTA BARBARA]:

(1) *cave,* about 2.25 miles east-southeast of San Marcos Pass (lat. 34°30'15" N, long. 119°47'10" W; sec. 23, T 5 N, R 28 W). Named on San Marcos Pass (1959) 7.5' quadrangle.

(2) *cave,* 4 miles east of Fraser Point on the north side of Santa Cruz Island (lat. 34°04'15" N, long. 119°51'30" W). Named on Santa Cruz Island A

(1943) 7.5' quadrangle. The name is from the heavy growths of red, yellow, and green lichens on rocks of the cave (Emery, p. 38). Gleason (p. 51) gave the Spanish equivalent "Cueva Pintada" as an alternate name.

Painted Rock [SAN LUIS OBISPO]: *relief feature*, 16 miles south-southeast of Simmler near the southwest edge of Carrizo Plain (lat. 35°08'45" N, long. 119°51'40" W; near NW cor. sec. 17, T 32 S, R 20 E). Named on Painted Rock (1959) 7.5' quadrangle. Early settlers called the feature La Piedra Pintada because of numerous Indian pictographs there—*la piedra pintada* means "the painted rock" in Spanish (Hoover, Rensch, and Rensch, p. 379). Postal authorities established Carisa post office in 1882, moved it and changed the name to Painted Rock in 1888, and discontinued it in 1895 (Salley, p. 37, 165).

Painted Rock Campground [SANTA BARBARA]: *locality*, 5 miles south-east of McPherson Peak in Montgomery Potrero (lat. 34°50'10" N, long. 119°45'10" W). Named on Hurricane Deck (1964) 7.5' quadrangle. The name is from pictographs in shallow sandstone caves near the place (Gagnon, p. 101).

Pajaro [MONTEREY]: *town*, 5 miles northeast of the mouth of Pajaro River on the south side (lat. 36°54'15" N, long. 121°44'50" W). Named on Watsonville East (1955) and Watsonville West (1954) 7.5' quadrangles. Postal authorities established Pajaro post office in 1872, discontinued it in 1873, reestablished it in 1882, and discontinued it in 1888 (Frickstad, p. 108).

Pajaro: see **Lake Pajaro**, under **Watsonville** [SANTA CRUZ]; **Mount Pajaro** [SANTA CRUZ]; **Watsonville Junction** [MONTEREY].

Pajaro Dunes: see **Palm Beach** [SANTA CRUZ].

Pajaro Gap [SAN BENITO-SANTA CRUZ]: *narrows*, nearly 2 miles north-northeast of Aromas along Pajaro River on San Benito-Santa Cruz County line (lat. 36°54'45" N, long. 121°37'30" W); the feature is the narrow part of Chittenden Pass. Named on Chittenden (1955) and Watsonville East (1955) 7.5' quadrangles.

Pajaro Landing: see **Pajaro River** [MONTEREY-SAN BENITO-SANTA CRUZ].

Pajaro River [MONTEREY-SAN BENITO-SANTA CRUZ]: *stream*, heads near San Felipe Lake and flows 30 miles to the sea 15 miles northwest of Salinas (lat. 36°51' N, long. 121°48'30" W; sec. 36, T 12 S, R 1 E); the stream marks San Benito-Santa Clara County line from near San Felipe Lake to beyond the mouth of San Benito River, and then defines San Benito-Santa Cruz County line and Monterey-Santa Cruz County line to the sea. Named on Chittenden (1955), Moss Landing (1954), San Felipe (1955), Watsonville East (1955), and Watsonville West (1954) 7.5' quadrangles. Called Sanjon de la Brea on a diseño of Llano de Tequisquita grant (Becker, 1969), called Payaro R. on Baker's (1855) map, and called R. Pajaros on Mitchell's (1856) map; on the last two maps the names apply also to present San Benito River. Some early maps from Spanish days had the name "Rio de San Antonio" for the stream (Clark, 1986, p. 307). Taylor (p. 175) called it Rio del Pajaro. Soldiers of the Portola expedition gave the name "Pajaro" to the feature in 1769 because the natives that they saw there had a huge stuffed bird (Wagner, H.R., p. 401)—*pajaro* means "bird" in Spanish. Clark (1991, p. 371) noted that the stream also had the names "Pigeon River," "Río de La Señora La Santa Ana," "Río del Paxaro," "Río de Santa Ana," "San Antonio River," and "Sanjon del Tequesquite." A landing place at the mouth of the river was called Pajaro Landing; the next landing place north along the coast, called Miller's Landing, was on land purchased by Captain C.F. Miller (Hoover, Rensch, and Rensch, p. 474). Another landing place near the mouth of the river was called Brennans Landing, for Captain James Brennan, and was used as early as 1856 (Clark, 1986, p. 45).

Pajaro Valley [MONTEREY-SANTA CRUZ]: *valley*, extends inland from the coast for 13 miles along Pajaro River on Monterey-Santa Cruz County line. Named on Moss Landing (1954), Watsonville East (1955), and Watsonville West (1954) 7.5' quadrangles.

Pala Prieta Valley: see **Palo Prieto Canyon** [SAN LUIS OBISPO].

Palisades: see **The Palisades** [MONTEREY].

Palm Beach [SANTA CRUZ]: *settlement*, 5 miles southwest of Watsonville near the coast (lat. 36°52'05" N, long. 121°49'05" W). Named on Moss Landing (1954) 7.5' quadrangle. Called Camp Goodall on Capitola (1914) 15' quadrangle. Camp Goodall, a shipping port for produce from Pajaro Valley, was named for Captain Goodall of Goodall Perkins & Co., steamship owners; it became a popular resort area and is the location of the present development called Pajaro Dunes (Lewis, 1976, p. 144).

Palmer [SANTA BARBARA]: *locality*, nearly 3 miles south-southwest of Sisquoc (2) (lat. 34°49'40" N, long. 120°19'10" W). Named on Santa Maria (1947) 15' quadrangle.

Palmer Flats [SAN LUIS OBISPO]: *area*, 3 miles north of Cambria along San Simeon Creek (lat. 35°36'35" N, long. 121°04'20" W). Named on Cambria (1959) 7.5' quadrangle.

Palo Alto Hill [SANTA BARBARA]: *peak*, 4.5 miles northeast of Point Conception (lat. 34°29'40" N, long. 120°25' W). Altitude 1394 feet. Named on Point Conception (1953) 7.5' quadrangle.

Palo Colorado Canyon [MONTEREY]: *canyon*, drained by a stream that flows nearly 4 miles to the sea 6.5 miles north of Point Sur (lat. 36°23'55" N, long. 121°54'15" W; sec. 6, T 18 S, R 1 E). Named on Mount Carmel (1956) and Soberanes Point (1956) 7.5' quadrangles. Gudde (1949, p. 251) noted that a Spanish map of 1835 has the name "Arroyo del palo Colorado"—*palo colorado* means "redwood tree" in Spanish, and redwood trees grow in the canyon. Some old maps have the name "Soberanes Creek" for the stream in the canyon (Clark, 1991, p. 373).

Palo Corona [MONTEREY]: *peak*, 3.5 miles east of Soberanes Point (lat. 36°27'05" N, long. 121°52'05" W; near W line sec. 16, T 17 S, R 1 E). Altitude 2972 feet. Named on Mount Carmel (1956) 7.5' quadrangle.

Palo Escrito: see **Sierra de Salinas** [MONTEREY].

Palo Escrito Peak [MONTEREY]: *peak*, 9 miles west of Soledad (lat. 36°24'20" N, long. 121°29'25" W; sec. 36, T 17 S, R 4 E). Altitude 4467 feet. Named on Palo Escrito Peak (1956) 7.5' quadrangle. According to Stewart (p. 356), *palo escrito* means "tree-inscribed" in Spanish, and the name probably originated with a tree marked with symbols.

Paloma: see **Paloma Creek** [MONTEREY].

Paloma Creek [MONTEREY]: *stream*, flows 13 miles to Piney Creek 12 miles west-southwest of Greenfield (lat. 36°16'25" N, long. 121°26'55" W; near S line sec. 17, T 19 S, R 5 E). Named on Chews Ridge (1956), Palo Escrito Peak (1956), and Sycamore Flat (1956) 7.5' quadrangles. On Soledad (1915) 15' quadrangle, the lower part of present Piney Creek—below its junction with present Paloma Creek—is called Paloma Creek. Postal authorities established Paloma post office in 1923 and discontinued it in 1933 (Salley, p. 166). The post office was along Paloma Creek (NE quarter sec. 36, T 18 S, R 4 E) and was named for the stream (Clark, 1991, p. 376).

Paloma Creek [SAN LUIS OBISPO]: *stream*, flows 4.25 miles to Salinas River 2.5 miles southeast of Atascadero (lat. 35°28' N, long. 120°37'45" W). Named on Atascadero (1965) 7.5' quadrangle.

Paloma Mountain [MONTEREY]: *peak*, 9 miles west-southwest of Soledad (lat. 36°23'15" N, long. 121°28'10" W; near S line sec. 6, T 18 S, R 5 E). Altitude 3970 feet. Named on Palo Escrito Peak (1956) 7.5' quadrangle.

Paloma Ridge [MONTEREY]: *ridge*, south-southeast-trending, 5 miles long, 7 miles southwest of Soledad (lat. 36°21' N, long. 121° 24'30" W). Named on Palo Escrito Peak (1956) and Sycamore Flat (1956) 7.5' quadrangles.

Palo Parado: see **Cavern Point** [SANTA BARBARA].

Palo Prieto: see **Palo Prieto Canyon** [SAN LUIS OBISPO].

Palo Prieto Canyon [SAN LUIS OBISPO]: *canyon*, drained by a stream that flows 6 miles to Cholame Creek nearly 1 mile south-southwest of Cholame (lat. 35°42'45" N, long. 120°18'05" W; sec. 36, T 25 S, R 15 E). Named on Cholame (1961) and Orchard Peak (1961) 7.5' quadrangles. Called Prieto Canyon on Cholame (1943) 7.5' quadrangle. Angel (1890c, p. 569) called the feature Pala Prieta Valley. Postal authorities established Palo Prieto post office in 1888 and discontinued it in 1889 (Frickstad, p. 165). The post office presumably was in or near the canyon.

Palo Prieto Canyon: see **Palo Prieto Pass** [SAN LUIS OBISPO].

Palo Prieto Pass [SAN LUIS OBISPO]: *valley*, 12 miles east-southeast of Shandon on San Luis Obispo-Kern County line (lat. 35°37'30" N, long. 120°11' W). Named on Holland Canyon (1961) and Orchard Peak (1961) 7.5' quadrangles. The valley is mainly in San Luis Obispo County southeast of the head of Palo Prieto Canyon. United States Board on Geographic Names (1968a, p. 6) rejected the names "Palo Prieto Canon" and "Palo Prieto Canyon:" for the valley, and described the feature as extending for 7 miles southeast from Palo Prieto Canyon through Choice Valley.

Palos Colorados Creek [SANTA BARBARA]: *stream*, flows 2.5 miles to El Jaro Creek 6.5 miles southeast of the city of Lompoc (lat. 34°34'20" N, long. 120°22'05" W). Named on Santa Rosa Hills (1959) 7.5' quadrangle.

Palo Scrito Hills: see **Sierra de Salinas** [MONTEREY].

Palo Serito Hills: see **Sierra de Salinas** [MONTEREY].

Pancho Rico Creek [MONTEREY]: *stream*, flows 26 miles to Salinas River at San Ardo (lat. 36°00'55" N, long. 120°54'40" W). Named on Pancho Rico Valley (1967), San Ardo (1967), Slack Canyon (1969), and Smith Mountain (1969) 7.5' quadrangles. Called Poncho Rico Creek on Priest Valley (1915) 30' quadrangle, but United States Board on Geographic Names (1961b, p. 13) rejected this form of the name. Called Gaviota Cr. on California Mining Bureau's (1917b) map. Van Winkle and Eaton (p. 75) used the names "Poncha Rica Creek" and "Gaviota Creek" for the feature. The name "Pancho Rico" commemorates Francisco Rico, who received San Lorenzo (2) grant; the stream also had the names "Galen Creek," "San Bernardo Creek," and "Williams Creek" (Clark, 1991, p. 376).

Pancho Rico Valley [MONTEREY]: *canyon*, 7.5 miles long, opens into lowlands along Salinas River at San Ardo (lat. 35°01'10" N, long. 120°53'10" W; sec. 16, T 22 S, R 10 E); Pancho Rico Creek drains the canyon. Named on Pancho Rico Valley (1967) and San Ardo (1967) 7.5' quadrangles. Kew (1920, p. 83) called the feature Pence Enrico Canyon.

Panoche [SAN BENITO]: *locality*, 15 miles east-northeast of San Benito (lat. 36°35'45" N, long. 120°50' W; sec. 25, T 15 S, R 10 E); the place is in Panoche Valley. Named on Panoche (1969) 7.5' quadrangle. Postal authorities established Panoche post office in 1870 and discontinued it in

1915 (Frickstad, p. 136). According to Hanna (p. 229), the name is a corruption of *panocha*, which is a Mexican-Spanish word for a confection of brown sugar. According to Gudde (1949, p. 252), *panoche*, or *panocha*, was the name of a sweet substance that the Indians extracted from reeds and wild fruit.

Panoche Creek [SAN BENITO]: *stream*, flows 20 miles to Fresno County 4.5 miles east of Panoche (lat. 36°36'25" N, long. 120° 45' W; sec. 22, T 15 S, R 11 E); the stream drains Panoche Valley. Named on Llanada (1969) and Panoche (1969) 7.5' quadrangles. Whitney (p. 55) referred to Big Panoche Creek, which runs through Panoche Plain.

Panoche Creek: see **Little Panoche Creek** [SAN BENITO]; **Silver Creek** [SAN BENITO].

Panoche Hills [SAN BENITO]: *range*, northeast of Panoche Valley, mainly in Fresno County. Named on Mercey Hot Springs (1969) and Panoche (1969) 7.5' quadrangles.

Panoche Pass [SAN BENITO]: *pass*, 9 miles north-northeast of San Benito (lat. 36°37'40" N, long. 121°00'45" W; sec. 17, T 15 S, R 9 E); the pass is near the head of Panoche Creek. Named on Panoche Pass (1968) 7.5' quadrangle.

Panoche Plain: see **Panoche Valley** [SAN BENITO].

Panoche Valley [SAN BENITO]: *valley*, 35 miles east-southeast of Hollister and southwest of Panoche Hills (lat. 36°37' N, long. 120° 51' W); Panoche Creek and its tributaries drain the valley. Named on Cerro Colorado (1969), Llanada (1969), Mercey Hot Springs (1969), and Panoche (1969) 7.5' quadrangles. Whitney (p. 55) referred to Panoche Plain.

Panoche Valley: see **Little Panoche Valley** [SAN BENITO].

Panochita Creek: see **Little Panoche Creek** [SAN BENITO].

Panochita Valley: see **Little Panoche Valley** [SAN BENITO].

Panorama Hills [SAN LUIS OBISPO]: *range*, 10 miles north-northeast of Caliente Mountain between Temblor Range and Carrizo Plain (lat. 35°11'30" N, long. 119°43'15" W). Named on Painted Rock (1959) and Panorama Hills (1954) 7.5' quadrangles. Arnold and Johnson (1910, p. 21) proposed the name.

Panorama Point [SAN LUIS OBISPO]: *peak*, 20 miles southeast of Simmler (lat. 35°10'45"N, long. 119°42'35" W; sec. 34, T 31 S, R 21 E); the peak is in Panorama Hills. Altitude 2521 feet. Named on Panorama Hills (1954) 7.5' quadrangle. According to Arnold and Johnson (1910, p. 22), the name was used by E.W. White, a settler in the neighborhood.

Panther Peak [SAN BENITO]: *peak*, 13 miles east-southeast of Bitterwater (lat. 36°18' N, long. 120°47'20" W; sec. 5, T 19 S, R 11 E). Altitude 4276 feet. Named on Hepsedam Peak (1969) 7.5' quadrangle.

Panza Hills: see **La Panza Range** [SAN LUIS OBISPO].

Paradise Campground [SAN LUIS OBISPO]: *locality*, 4 miles west-southwest of Branch Mountain (lat. 35°09'15" N, long. 120°08'35" W). Named on Los Machos Hills (1967) 7.5' quadrangle.

Paradise Canyon [MONTEREY]: *canyon*, 2 miles long, opens into an unnamed canyon 2.5 miles northwest of Prunedale (lat. 36°48'10" N, long. 121°42'10" W). Named on Prunedale (1954) 7.5' quadrangle.

Paradise Canyon [SANTA BARBARA]: *canyon*, drained by a stream that flows 2.5 miles to Santa Ynez River 2.25 miles north-northeast of San Marcos Pass (lat. 34°32'35" N, long. 119°48'45" W; sec. 4, T 5 N, R 28 W). Named on San Marcos Pass (1959) 7.5' quadrangle.

Paradise Park [SANTA CRUZ]: *settlement*, 9 miles south-southeast of the town of Boulder Creek along San Lorenzo River (lat. 37° 00'35" N, long. 122°02'35" W). Named on Felton (1955) 7.5' quadrangle. The settlement is at a place long known as Powder Mill Flat for a plant there that manufactured explosives from 1865 until 1916 (Hoover, Rensch, and Rensch, p. 471). A railroad siding that served the plant was called Powder Mill Siding (MacGregor, p. 130). In 1919 the place became the site of a cottage colony for members of the Masonic fraternity (Rowland, p. 216). A narrow ridge near Powder Mill Flat that is almost encircled by San Lorenzo River was called Hog's Back (Hamman, p. 85).

Paradise Valley [SAN LUIS OBISPO]: *valley*, 3 miles west of Atascadero along Graves Creek (lat. 35°29' N, long. 120°43'15" W). Named on Atascadero (1965) 7.5' quadrangle.

Paraiso Springs [MONTEREY]: *locality*, 7 miles west of Greenfield (lat. 36°19'55" N, long. 121°22' W; near E line sec. 25, T 18 S, R 5 E). Named on Paraiso Springs (1956) 7.5' quadrangle. According to Winslow Anderson (p. 219), friars at Soledad mission drank and bathed in the water, which they called Water of Paradise—*paraiso* means "paradise" in Spanish. G.A. Waring (p. 60-61) noted that at least five mineral springs rise at the place in an area of several acres where in 1908 a hotel and cottages provided accommodations for 200 guests. Postal authorities established Paraiso Springs post office in 1877, discontinued it for a time in 1899, and discontinued it finally in 1939 (Frickstad, p. 108).

Paraje de Sanchez [MONTEREY]: *land grant*, 7 miles west-northwest of Soledad. Named on Palo Escrito Peak (1956) and Rana Creek (1956) 7.5' quadrangles. Francisco Lugo received 1.5 leagues in 1839; Juana Briones de Lugo and others claimed 6584 acres patented in 1866 (Cowan, p. 58).

Parida Creek: see **Arroyo Paredon** [SANTA BARBARA].

Paris Valley [MONTEREY]: *valley*, 3.5 miles west-northwest of San Ardo (lat. 36°02'15" N, long. 120°58'10" W). Named on San Ardo (1967) 7.5' quadrangle. The name is from the large number of families of French descent that lived in the valley (Clark, 1991, p. 378).

Parker Canyon [MONTEREY]: *canyon*, drained by a stream that flows 2.5 miles to lowlands 5 miles west of Chualar (lat. 36°34'40" N, long. 121°36'20" W). Named on Chualar (1947) 7.5' quadrangle.

Parker Flats [MONTEREY]: *area*, 3.5 miles south-southeast of Marina (lat. 36°38'05" N, long. 121°47'05" W). Named on Marina (1947) 7.5' quadrangle.

Parkfield [MONTEREY]: *village*, 21 miles east of Bradley along Little Cholame Creek (lat. 35°54' N, long. 120°25'50" W; sec. 26, T 23 S, R 14 E). Named on Parkfield (1961) 7.5' quadrangle. Postal authorities established Parkfield post office in 1884 and discontinued it in 1954 (Frickstad, p. 108). According to Gudde (1949, p. 254), the place first had the name "Russelsville," but when postal officials rejected this, the postmaster selected the name "Parkfield" because the village is in a natural oak park. California Mining Bureau's (1909a) map shows a place called Imusdale located 5 miles by stage line west-northwest of Parkfield, about where Stockdale Mountain (1948) 7.5' quadrangle shows Imusdale cemetery. Postal authorities established Imusdale post office in 1875, moved it 0.5 mile north in 1899, and discontinued it in 1902; the name was for the Imus brothers, Charles, William, and Edwin, who were the first settlers in Cholame Valley (Salley, p. 103).

Park Hill [SAN BENITO]: *ridge*, north-northwest-trending, nearly 1 mile long, at the north edge of Hollister (lat. 35°51'30" N, long. 121°24'20" W). Named on Hollister (1955) 7.5' quadrangle.

Park Mills: see **Blooms Mill** [SANTA CRUZ].

Park Ridge [SAN LUIS OBISPO]: *ridge*, northwest-trending, 2 miles long, 3.5 miles east-southeast of Morro Rock (lat. 35°20'45" N, long. 120°48'30" W). Named on Morro Bay South (1965) 7.5' quadrangle.

Parks-Lead Siding [SANTA BARBARA]: *locality*, at the west edge of the city of Lompoc along Southern Pacific Railroad (lat. 34°38'40" N, long. 120°28'25" W). Named on Lompoc (1959) 7.5' quadrangle.

Parks Valley [SAN BENITO]: *canyon*, 1 mile long, 5 miles southeast of Mount Johnson (lat. 36°33'10" N, long. 121°15'25" W; on E line sec. 12, T 16 S, R 6 E). Named on Mount Johnson (1968) 7.5' quadrangle.

Parola Canyon [SAN LUIS OBISPO]: *canyon*, nearly 4 miles long, drained by Alamo Creek (1), which enters Santa Margarita Lake 4.5 miles west-northwest of Pozo (lat. 35°19'40" N, long. 120°26'20" W; sec. 11, T 30 S, R 14 E). Named on Santa Margarita Lake (1967) 7.5' quadrangle.

Parrot Spring [SAN BENITO]: *spring*, 8 miles west-southwest of Panoche (lat. 36°33'10" N, long. 120°57'50" W; sec. 11, T 16 S, R 9 E). Named on Llanada (1969) 7.5' quadrangle.

Parsons Creek [MONTEREY]: *stream*, flows 3.5 miles to Chualar Canyon 6.5 miles north of Gonzales (lat. 36°36'10" N, long. 121° 25'35" W; sec. 28, T 15 S, R 5 E). Named on Gonzales (1955) and Mount Harlan (1968) 7.5' quadrangles.

Parson Spring [MONTEREY]: *spring*, 7 miles north-northeast of Soledad (lat. 36°24'50" N, long. 121°11'35" W; sec. 34, T 17 S, R 7 E). Named on North Chalone Peak (1969) 7.5' quadrangle.

Partington Cove: see **Partington Point** [MONTEREY].

Partington Creek [MONTEREY]: *stream*, flows 2.5 miles to the sea east of Partington Point (lat. 36°10'30" N, long. 121°41'45" W; sec. 24, T 20 S, R 2 E). Named on Partington Ridge (1956) 7.5' quadrangle.

Partington Landing: see **Partington Point** [MONTEREY].

Partington Point [MONTEREY]: *promontory*, 14 miles southeast of Point Sur along the coast (lat. 36°10'30" N, long. 121°41'50" W; sec. 24, T 20 S, R 2 E). Named on Partington Ridge (1956) 7.5' quadrangle. According to Lussier (p. 28), a small embayment 700 feet east of the point, and east of the cove into which Partington Creek flows, is called Partington Cove—it was the site of Partington Landing, a shipping point for tanbark, cattle, and hides in the early days. However, United States Board on Geographic Names (1992, p. 4) approved instead the name "Partington Cove" for the embayment at the mouth of Partington Creek (lat. 36°10'30" N, long. 121°41'48" W).

Partington Ridge [MONTEREY]: *ridge*, north-trending, 2.25 miles long, north of Partington Point (lat. 36°11'30" N, long. 121°41'55" W). Named on Partington Ridge (1956) 7.5' quadrangle. John Partington and Laura Partington homesteaded at the ridge in 1874 (Lussier, p. 27).

Pasa Robles: see **Paso de Robles** [SAN LUIS OBISPO].

Pasa Robles Creek: see **Paso Robles Creek** [SAN LUIS OBISPO].

Pasatiempo [SANTA CRUZ]: *settlement*, 10 miles southeast of the town of Boulder Creek (lat. 37°00'15" N, long. 122°01'30" W). Named on Felton (1955) 7.5' quadrangle.

Paso del Quinto: see **Old Hilltown** [MONTEREY].

Paso de Robles [SAN LUIS OBISPO]: *land grant*, west of Salinas River at and southwest of Paso Robles. Named on Paso Robles (1948), Templeton (1948), and York Mountain (1948) 7.5' quadrangles. Pedro Narvaez received 6 leagues in 1844; Petronilo Rios claimed 25,993 acres patented in 1866 (Cowan, p. 68). Parke's (1854-1855) map has the name "Pasa Robles," Derby (p. 4) referred to Passo de Roblas and Paso de Roblas, and

Whitney (p. 145) used the name "Paso el Roble." *Paso de robles* means "passage through the oaks" in Spanish; the name was used as early as 1828 (Gudde, 1949, p. 255).

Paso el Roble: see **Paso de Robles** [SAN LUIS OBISPO].

Paso Robles [SAN LUIS OBISPO]: *town*, 24 miles north of San Luis Obispo along Salinas River (lat. 35°37'40" N, long. 120°41'25" W); the town is on Paso de Robles grant. Named on Paso Robles (1948) and Templeton (1948) 7.5' quadrangles. Promoters founded the town in 1886 and it incorporated under the name "El Paso de Robles" in 1889 (Gudde, 1949, p. 255). United States Board on Geographic Names (1933, p. 591) rejected the name "Paso de Robles" for the town, and approved the form "Paso Robles." Postal authorities established Hot Springs post office in 1867, discontinued it the same year, reestablished it in 1868, and moved it 3 miles south and changed the name to Paso Robles in 1870 (Salley, p. 100). Hot springs that occur at the original site of Hot Springs post office were well known to the Indians and were improved for use by Franciscan friars, possibly as early as 1797 (Hoover, Rensch, and Rensch, p. 386). These natural springs of warm water issue along the bank of Salinas River near the north edge of the present town, and provided water for what were known as Paso Robles Mud Bath Springs (Waring, G.A., p. 73). According to G.A. Waring (p. 72-73), by 1865 a spring of warm sulphureted water in the south part of the present town was cemented to form a swimming pool and covered by a large masonry dome; a hotel was built there about 1888, and later a bathhouse built adjoining the hotel was supplied with water at a temperature of 105° Fahrenheit from an artisan well known as Main Sulphur Spring. A bathhouse called Municipal Baths Springs was supplied with hot water from another artisan well, and a well called Grand Central Sulphur Spring, drilled in the center of town in 1911, supplied water to yet another bathhouse (Logan, p. 692-693). Water from Mary Hill mineral well, located about 0.25 mile west of the center of the town, was bottled for local sale (Logan, p. 690-691).

Paso Robles Creek [SAN LUIS OBISPO]: *stream*, flows 11.5 miles to Salinas River 6.5 miles south of Paso Robles (lat. 35°31'55" N, long. 120°42'20" W); the stream is mainly on Paso de Robles grant. Named on Templeton (1948) and York Mountain (1948) 7.5' quadrangles. Parke (p. 14) referred to Pasa Robles creek.

Paso Robles Mud Bath Springs: see **Paso Robles** [SAN LUIS OBISPO].

Pass of San Lorenzo: see **San Lorenzo Creek** [MONTEREY-SAN BENITO].

Pataroma Spring: see **Padrones Spring** [SAN LUIS OBISPO].

Pato Canyon [SANTA BARBARA]: *canyon*, drained by a stream that flows nearly 5 miles to Cuyama River 12 miles southeast of the village of Cuyama (lat. 34°48'55" N, long. 119°28'25" W). Named on Cuyama Peak (1943) 7.5' quadrangle.

Patrocino: see **El Alisal** [MONTEREY] (2).

Pat Springs Camp [MONTEREY]: *locality*, 2.5 miles northwest of Uncle Sam Mountain (lat. 36°21'50" N, long. 121°44'35" W). Named on Ventana Cones (1956) 7.5' quadrangle.

Paul: see **Alva Paul Creek**, under **Morro Bay** [SAN LUIS OBISPO] (2).

Pauls Creek: see **Alva Paul Creek**, under **Morro Bay** [SAN LUIS OBISPO] (2).

Pauls Island [MONTEREY]: *island*, 1 mile long, 1 mile north of Moss Landing near the junction of Elkhorn Slough and Bennett Slough (lat. 36°59' N, long. 121°47' W; sec. 7, T 13 S, R 2 E). Named on Moss Landing (1954) 7.5' quadrangle. The name commemorates Paul Lazere, who owned the island; Lazere also owned Pauls Ferry, which operated in the 1850's across Elkhorn Slough near the mouth of the slough just north of Moss Landing—the ferry also had the names "Elkhorn Ferry" and "St. Paul's Ferry" (Clark, 1991, 384-385).

Pauls Ferry: see **Pauls Island** [MONTEREY].

Payaro River: see **Pajaro River** [MONTEREY-SAN BENITO-SANTA CRUZ].

Payne Creek [SAN BENITO]: *stream*, flows 9 miles to Tres Pinos Creek 1.5 miles northwest of Panoche Pass (lat. 36°36'45" N, long. 121°01'40" W; near N line sec. 7, T 15 S, R 9 E). Named on Panoche Pass (1968) and San Benito (1968) 7.5' quadrangles.

P-Bar Flats [SANTA BARBARA]: *area*, 6.25 miles south-southwest of Hildreth Peak along Santa Ynez River (lat. 34°30'50" N, long. 119°35'20" W). Named on Hildreth Peak (1964) 7.5' quadrangle.

P-Bar Flats Campground [SANTA BARBARA]: *locality*, 6.25 miles south-southwest of Hildreth Peak along Santa Ynez River (lat. 34° 30'50" N, long. 119°35'25" W); the place is at P-Bar Flats. Named on Hildreth Peak (1964) 7.5' quadrangle.

Peach Tree: see **Peachtree Valley** [MONTEREY].

Peachtree Canyon [MONTEREY]: *canyon*, drained by a stream that flows 4.25 miles to Pancho Rico Creek 8 miles east-northeast of San Ardo (lat. 36°04'05" N, long. 120°46'30" W; sec. 27, T 21 S, R 11 E); the canyon heads southwest of Peachtree Valley. Named on Pancho Rico Valley (1967) and Slack Canyon (1969) 7.5' quadrangles. San Ardo (1943) 15' quadrangle has the form "Peach Tree Canyon" for the name.

Peachtree Canyon [SANTA BARBARA]: *canyon*, drained by a stream that flows 5.5 miles to Santa Cruz Creek 5.5 miles south-southwest of San Rafael Mountain (lat. 34°38' N, long. 119° 51' W). Named on San Rafael Mountain (1959) 7.5' quadrangle.

Peachtree Canyon: see **Mine Canyon** [SANTA BARBARA] (1).

Peachtree Creek: see **San Lorenzo Creek** [MONTEREY-SAN BENITO].

Peach Tree Spring [SANTA BARBARA]: *spring*, 3.5 miles north of Tepusquet Peak (lat. 34°57'40" N, long. 120°10'30" W). Named on Tepusquet Canyon (1964) 7.5' quadrangle.

Peachtree Valley [MONTEREY]: *valley*, 20 miles long, 10 miles east-northeast of King City along San Lorenzo Creek (lat. 36°16'50" N, long. 120°57'45" W; sec. 14, T 19 S, R 9 E). Named on Lonoak (1969), Monarch Peak (1967), Nattrass Valley (1967), Priest Valley (1969), and Slack Canyon (1969) 7.5' quadrangles. Angel (1890a, p. 345) used the form "Peach Tree Valley" for the name. The place also was called San Lorenzo Valley (Clark, 1991, p. 386). California Mining Bureau's (1909a) map shows a place called Peach Tree located 4 miles by stage line southeast of Lonoak. Postal authorities established Peach Tree post office in 1873, discontinued it for a time the same year, changed the name to Peachtree in 1897, and discontinued it in 1909 (Salley, p. 168). Elliott and Moore (p. 76) described the village of Peach Tree as "a store, saloon and post-office in one building, a hotel, blacksmith shop and another saloon."

Peachy Canyon [SAN LUIS OBISPO]: *canyon*, drained by a stream that flows nearly 3 miles to lowlands near the south edge of Paso Robles (lat. 35°37'05" N, long. 120°41'25" W). Named on Paso Robles (1948) and Templeton (1948) 7.5' quadrangles.

Peak: see **The Peak** [SANTA CRUZ].

Peak Canyon [SAN BENITO]: *canyon*, drained by a stream that flows 3 miles to San Juan Canyon 6 miles southwest of Hollister (lat. 36°48' N, long. 121°29'15" W); the canyon heads near Fremont Peak. Named on Hollister (1955) 7.5' quadrangle.

Peak Canyon: see **Little Peak Canyon** [SAN BENITO].

Peak Mountain [SANTA BARBARA]: *peak*, nearly 3 miles west-northwest of McPherson Peak (lat. 34°54'05" N, long. 119°51'30" W). Altitude 5843 feet. Named on Peak Mountain (1964) 7.5' quadrangle.

Pear Orchard: see **Dutra Creek** [MONTEREY].

Pearson Spring [SAN LUIS OBISPO]: *spring*, 8.5 miles west-northwest of Caliente Mountain (lat. 35°05'05" N, long. 119°53'50" W; near E line sec. 31, T 12 S, R 28 W). Named on Taylor Canyon (1959) 7.5' quadrangle.

Pear Spring [SAN LUIS OBISPO]: *spring*, 5 miles west-northwest of Shandon in Shimmin Canyon (lat. 35°41'35" N, long. 120°27'10" W; sec. 3, T 26 S, R 14 E). Named on Shandon (1961) 7.5' quadrangle.

Pear Tree Spring [SAN LUIS OBISPO]: *spring*, 12.5 miles southeast of Shandon near the mouth of Long Canyon (2) (lat. 35°31'05" N, long. 120°13'40" W; near W line sec. 2, T 28 S, R 16 E). Named on Holland Canyon (1961) 7.5' quadrangle.

Peartree Spring [SAN LUIS OBISPO]: *spring*, 3.5 miles west-northwest of Branch Mountain (lat. 35°12'10" N, long. 120°08'25" W). Named on Los Machos Hills (1967) 7.5' quadrangle.

Peasley Gulch [SANTA CRUZ]: *canyon*, drained by a stream that flows 3 miles to Wilder Creek 3.25 miles west-northwest of Point Santa Cruz (lat. 36°57'50" N, long. 122°04'55" W). Named on Felton (1955) and Santa Cruz (1954) 7.5' quadrangles. On Santa Cruz (1902) 30' quadrangle, the stream in the canyon is called Meder Creek—the name "Meder" is for Moses Meder, who owned part of Refugio grant, where the stream is located (Clark, 1986, p. 203-204).

Peavine Creek [SANTA CRUZ]: *stream*, flows 1 mile to Boulder Creek (1) nearly 5 miles east-southeast of Big Basin (lat. 37°08'20" N, long. 122°08'35" W; sec. 24, T 9 S, R 3 W). Named on Big Basin (1955) 7.5' quadrangle. Berkstresser (p. A-18) listed Peavine Spring, which is located 4500 feet southwest of the mouth of Peavine Creek.

Peavine Spring: see **Peavine Creek** [SANTA CRUZ].

Pebble Beach [MONTEREY]:

(1) *beach*, on the north side of Carmel Bay (lat. 36°34' N, long. 121°56'45" W). Named on Monterey (1947) 7.5' quadrangle. The name is from the pebbly nature of the beach (Clark, 1991, p. 386).

(2) *town*, north of Carmel Bay near Pebble Beach (1) (lat. 36°34'10" N, long. 121°56'30" W). Named on Monterey (1913) 15' quadrangle. Postal authorities established Pebble Beach post office in 1909 (Frickstad, p. 108).

Pebblestone Shut-in [SAN LUIS OBISPO]: *narrows*, 11 miles northeast of the village of San Simeon along Nacimiento River (lat. 35°44'45" N, long. 121°02'20" W; near N line sec. 19, T 25 S, R 9 E). Named on Pebblestone Shut-in (1959) 7.5' quadrangle.

Pebbly Beach: see **Sand Hill Cove** [MONTEREY].

Pecho Creek [SAN LUIS OBISPO]: *stream*, flows 3.25 miles to the sea 2.25 miles northwest of Point San Luis (lat. 35°10'45" N, long. 120°47'30" W); the stream is on the southeast boundary of Cañada de los Osos y Pecho y Islay grant. Named on Port San Luis (1965) 7.5' quadrangle. Called Cañada y arroyo del Pecho on the diseño of Pecho y Islay grant made in 1843 (Becker, 1969). United States Board on Geographic Names (1967a, p. 10) rejected the names "Arroyo del Pecho," and "Cañada del Pecho" for the feature. On Port Harford (1897) 15' quadrangle, Pecho Creek is shown 0.5

mile farther northwest in present Vineyard Canyon (2).

Pecho Rock [SAN LUIS OBISPO]: *rock,* 375 feet long, 3.5 miles west-northwest of Point San Luis, and 3200 feet offshore (lat. 35° 10'45" N, long. 120°48'55" W); the rock is 1.25 miles west-southwest of the mouth of Pecho Creek. Named on Port San Luis (1965) 7.5' quadrangle.

Pecho Warm Springs: see **Islay Creek** [SAN LUIS OBISPO].

Pedernales: see **Point Pedernales** [SANTA BARBARA].

Pedregoso Creek: see **Mission Creek** [SANTA BARBARA].

Pelican Bay [SANTA BARBARA]: *embayment,* nearly 1.5 miles northwest of Prisoners Harbor on the north side of Santa Cruz Island (lat. 34°02' N, long. 119°42'05" W). Named on Santa Cruz Island C (1943) 7.5' quadrangle.

Pelican Point: see **Goleta Point** [SANTA BARBARA]; **Sandy Beach** [MONTEREY].

Pelican Rock [SANTA CRUZ]: *rock,* 250 feet long, 1.5 miles south-southeast of the mouth of Waddell Creek, and 400 feet offshore (lat. 37°04'25" N, long. 122°15'50" W). Named on Año Nuevo (1955) 7.5' quadrangle.

Pence Enrico Canyon: see **Pancho Rico Valley** [MONTEREY].

Pendola Campground [SANTA BARBARA]: *locality,* 6.25 miles south of Hildreth Peak (lat. 34°30'40" N, long. 119°34'30" W). Named on Hildreth Peak (1964) 7.5' quadrangle.

Pennington Creek [SAN LUIS OBISPO]: *stream,* flows 5 miles to Chorro Creek 6 miles west-northwest of San Luis Obispo (lat. 35° 19'30" N, long. 120°45' W). Named on San Luis Obispo (1965) 7.5' quadrangle.

Penvir [MONTEREY]: *locality,* 3 miles northwest of Gonzales along Southern Pacific Railroad (lat. 36°32'20" N, long. 121°29' W). Named on Gonzales (1955) 7.5' quadrangle.

People's Wharf: see **Avila Beach** [SAN LUIS OBISPO].

Pepper Spring [SANTA BARBARA]: *spring,* nearly 3 miles south of Salisbury Potrero (lat. 34°46'50" N, long. 119°42'15" W). Named on Salisbury Potrero (1964) 7.5' quadrangle.

Percys Creek: see **Boronda Creek** [MONTEREY].

Perfumo Canyon: see **Prefumo Canyon** [SAN LUIS OBISPO].

Perry Creek [SAN LUIS OBISPO]: *stream,* flows 9 miles to Santa Rosa Creek nearly 1 mile east-northeast of Cambria (lat. 35°34'05" N, long. 121°04'10" W). Named on Cambria (1959) and Cypress Mountain (1948, photorevised 1979) 7.5' quadrangles.

Perry Ridge [MONTEREY]: *ridge,* north-trending, 0.5 mile long, 6 miles southwest of Salinas (lat. 36°37' N, long. 121°44'20" W). Named on Spreckels (1947) 7.5' quadrangle.

Pesante Canyon [MONTEREY]: *canyon,* drained by a stream that flows 3.25 miles to an unnamed canyon at Prunedale (lat. 36°46'15" N, long. 121°39'55" W). Named on Prunedale (1954) 7.5' quadrangle. The name commemorates John Pesante, an early settler (Clark, 1991, p. 388).

Pescadero Canyon [MONTEREY]: *canyon,* drained by a stream that flows 2 miles to Carmel Bay just north of Carmel-by-the-Sea (lat. 36°33'25" N, long. 121°55'50" W); the canyon is on El Pescadero grant. Named on Monterey (1947) 7.5' quadrangle.

Pescadero Creek [SAN BENITO]: *stream,* flows 14 miles to San Benito River 2.5 miles south-southwest of Paicines (lat. 36°41'40" N, long. 121°17'10" W). Named on Mount Harlan (1968) and Paicines (1968) 7.5' quadrangles. Called Sanjon del Pescadero on a diseño of Cienega de los Paicines grant (Gudde, 1949, p. 259).

Pescadero Creek [SANTA CRUZ]: *stream,* heads in San Mateo County and flows 1 mile in Santa Cruz County before reentering San Mateo County 4 miles northeast of Big Basin (lat. 37°12'55" N, long. 122°10'40" W; at N line sec. 27, T 8 S, R 3 W). Named on Big Basin (1955) 7.5' quadrangle.

Pescadero Point [MONTEREY]: *promontory,* 2 miles southeast of Cypress Point on the north side of Carmel Bay (lat. 36°33'40" N, long. 121°57'05" W); the feature is on El Pescadero grant. Named on Monterey (1947) 7.5' quadrangle. The point and nearby rocks received the name because of fishing activity carried on there in the early days—*pescadero* means "place where fishing is done" in Spanish (Hoover, Rensch, and Rensch, p. 231). United States Board on Geographic Names (1983a, p. 6) approved the name "The Pinnacles" for a reef located 0.7 mile southwest of Pescadero Point at the north entrance to Carmel Bay (lat. 36°33'23" N, long. 121°58'03" W).

Pescadero Rocks [MONTEREY]: *rocks,* 2000 feet east of Pescadero Point (lat. 36°33'40" N, long. 121°56'35" W). Named on Monterey (1947) 7.5' quadrangle.

Pesco [SANTA BARBARA]: *locality,* 2.25 miles south of downtown Santa Maria along Santa Maria Valley Railroad (lat. 34°55'15" N, long. 120°26'40" W; sec. 27, T 10 N, R 34 W). Named on Santa Maria (1959) 7.5' quadrangle.

Peters Creek [SANTA CRUZ]: *stream,* flows nearly 1 mile to San Mateo County 11 miles north of the town of Boulder Creek (lat. 37°16'55" N, long. 122°09'05" W; at W line sec. 36, T 7 S, R 3 W). Named on Mindego Hill (1961) 7.5' quadrangle.

Pettits Peak [MONTEREY]: *peak,* 5.5 miles southwest of Greenfield (lat. 36°15'50" N, long. 121°18'35" W; sec. 22, T 19 S, R 6 E). Altitude 2067 feet. Named on Paraiso Springs (1956) 7.5' quadrangle. The name is for Charles Pettit, who owned land near the feature (Clark, 1991, p. 391).

Pfeiffer Beach [MONTEREY]: *beach,* just north of Pfeiffer Point along the coast (lat. 36°14'20" N, long. 121°48'50" W; sec. 35, T 19 S, R 1 E). Named on Pfeiffer Point (1956) 7.5' quadrangle. The feature also had the names "Dani's Beach," from the Dani family who lived near it, and "Sycamore Beach" (Clark, 1991, p. 391).

Pfeiffer Falls [MONTEREY]: *waterfall,* along Pfeiffer-Redwood Creek 0.5 mile upstream from the mouth of the creek (lat. 36°15'25" N, long. 121°46'50" W; sec. 30, T 19 S, R 2 E). Named on Big Sur (1956) 7.5' quadrangle.

Pfeiffer Gulch [MONTEREY]: *canyon,* drained by a stream that flows nearly 1 mile to Post Creek 2.25 miles east-northeast of Pfeiffer Point (lat. 36°14'30" N, long. 121°46'20" W; near W line sec. 32, T 19 S, R 2 E). Named on Pfeiffer Point (1956) 7.5' quadrangle.

Pfeiffer Point [MONTEREY]: *promontory,* 7 miles southeast of Point Sur along the coast (lat. 36°14'05" N, long. 121°48'50" W; sec. 35, T 19 S, R 1 E). Named on Pfeiffer Point (1956) 7.5' quadrangle. United States Coast Survey personnel named the feature in 1885 to 1887 for Michael Pfeiffer, an early settler (Gudde, 1949, p. 260).

Pfeiffer-Redwood Creek [MONTEREY]: *stream,* flows 1.5 miles to Big Sur River 7.5 miles east-southeast of Point Sur (lat. 36°15'05" N, long. 121°47'10" W; sec. 30, T 19 S, R 2 E). Named on Big Sur (1956) 7.5' quadrangle.

Pfeiffer Ridge [MONTEREY]: *ridge,* northwest- to west-northwest-trending, 4 miles long, 5.5 miles east-southeast of Point Sur (lat. 36°15'45" N, long. 121°49' W). Named on Big Sur (1956) 7.5' quadrangle. United States Board on Geographic Names (1981c, p. 5) approved the name "Clear Ridge" for a feature that extends for 1.2 miles southeast from Pfeiffer Ridge (sec. 26, 35, T 19 S, R 1 E), and rejected the name "Dani Ridge" for it; the name "Clear Ridge" was given because this ridge commonly is clear when surrounding features are lost in fog.

Pfeiffer Rock [MONTEREY]: *rock,* 150 feet long, 0.25 mile southeast of Pfeiffer Point, and 300 feet offshore (lat. 36°13'55" N, long. 121°48'35" W). Named on Pfeiffer Point (1956) 7.5' quadrangle.

Pfost Gulch [SAN LUIS OBISPO]: *canyon,* 1 mile long, 1.5 miles east-southeast of Shandon (lat. 36°38'35" N, long. 120°21'10" W). Named on Cholame (1961) 7.5' quadrangle. Cholame (1917) 30' quadrangle shows the feature as part of Cormack Canyon.

Phelan Point: see **Point Santa Cruz** [SANTA CRUZ].

Pheneger Creek [MONTEREY]: *stream,* flows 1.25 miles to Big Sur River 5.5 miles east-southeast of Point Sur (lat. 36°16'10" N, long. 121°48'25" W; sec. 24, T 19 S, R 1 E). Named on Big Sur (1956) 7.5' quadrangle.

Phoenix Creek [SAN LUIS OBISPO]: *stream,* flows 3.25 miles to Arroyo Grande Creek 10 miles north-northeast of the town of Nipomo (lat. 35°11'05" N, long. 120°26'15" W). Named on Tar Spring Ridge (1967) 7.5' quadrangle.

Picacho [SAN LUIS OBISPO]: *peak,* nearly 3 miles east-southeast of downtown Arroyo Grande (lat. 35°06'10" N, long. 120°32'25" W; on W line sec. 36, T 32 S, R 13 E). Altitude 922 feet. Named on Oceano (1965) 7.5' quadrangle.

Picacho: see **Picacho Peak** [SAN BENITO].

Picacho Creek [SAN BENITO]: *stream,* flows nearly 3 miles to San Benito River 7 miles south-southwest of Idria (lat. 36°19'35" N, long. 120°43'15" W; at S line sec. 25, T 18 S, R 11 E); the stream heads near Picacho Peak. Named on San Benito Mountain (1969) 7.5' quadrangle.

Picacho de Gavilan: see **Fremont Peak** [MONTEREY-SAN BENITO].

Picacho del Diablo: see **Diablo Point** [SANTA BARBARA].

Picacho de Romualdo: see **Cerro Romualdo** [SAN LUIS OBISPO].

Picacho Diablo: see **Diablo Point** [SANTA BARBARA].

Picacho Peak [SAN BENITO]: *peak,* 5 miles south of Idria (lat. 36° 20'45" N, long. 120°41'15" W; sec. 20, T 18 S, R 12 E); the peak is at the southeast end of The Picachos. Altitude 4657 feet. Named on San Benito Mountain (1969) 7.5' quadrangle, which shows Picacho mine situated 1200 feet west-northwest of the peak. This mine was discovered in 1858; a settlement near the mine was called Picacho (Hoover, Rensch, and Rensch, p. 315). Postal authorities established Picacho post office in 1869, discontinued it for a time in 1876, and discontinued it finally in 1880 (Frickstad, p. 136).

Picachos: see **The Picachos** [SAN BENITO].

Picay Creek [SANTA BARBARA]: *stream,* flows 2 miles to Romero Creek 5.25 miles west-northwest of Carpinteria (lat. 34°26'05" N, long. 119°35'45" W). Named on Carpinteria (1952, photorevised 1967) 7.5' quadrangle. Called Ficay Cr. on Santa Barbara (1903) 15' quadrangle, but United States Board on Geographic Names (1961b, p. 13) rejected this name for the stream. On Carpinteria (1952) 7.5' quadrangle, the name applies to present Romero Creek below its junction with present Picay Creek.

Pick Creek [MONTEREY]: *stream,* flows nearly 3 miles to South Fork Big Sur River 4.25 miles northeast of Partington Point (lat. 36°12'35" N, long. 121°38' W; sec. 9, T 20 S, R 3 E). Named on Partington Ridge (1956) 7.5' quadrangle. The name commemorates Charles Pick, an early settler (Clark,

1991, p. 394).

Picks Summit: see **Michaels Hill** [MONTEREY].

Picnic Canyon [MONTEREY]: *canyon,* 0.5 mile long, 5.5 miles southwest of Salinas (lat. 36°37'15" N, long. 121°44' W). Named on Spreckels (1947) 7.5' quadrangle.

Picnic Gulch Creek: see **Bates Creek** [SANTA CRUZ].

Pico Blanco [MONTEREY]: *peak,* 5 miles east of Point Sur (lat. 36° 19'05" N, long. 121°48'40" W; sec. 36, T 18 S, R 1 E). Altitude 3709 feet. Named on Big Sur (1956) 7.5' quadrangle.

Pico Creek [SAN LUIS OBISPO]: *stream,* formed by the confluence of North Fork and South Fork, flows 1 mile to the sea 3 miles southeast of the village of San Simeon (lat. 35°36'55" N, long. 121°08'55" W). Named on Pico Creek (1959) 7.5' quadrangle. The name commemorates Jose de Jesus Pico, owner of Piedra Blanca grant where the creek is located (Gudde, 1949, p. 261). North Fork is 8 miles long and South Fork is nearly 6 miles long; both forks are named on Pebblestone Shut-in (1959), Pico Creek (1959), and San Simeon (1958) 7.5' quadrangles.

Pico Creek: see **Little Pico Creek** [SAN LUIS OBISPO].

Pico Rock [SAN LUIS OBISPO]: *rock,* poorly labeled on the quadrangle map, but apparently 4.25 miles southeast of the village of San Simeon, and about 1700 feet offshore (lat. 35°35'50" N, long. 121°08'10" W). Named on Pico Creek (1959) 7.5' quadrangle.

Pie Canyon [SANTA BARBARA]: *canyon,* drained by a stream that flows 5.5 miles to Mono Creek 4.25 miles west-southwest of Hildreth Peak (lat. 34°34'05" N, long. 119°37' W). Named on Hildreth Peak (1964) and Little Pine Mountain (1964) 7.5' quadrangles.

Piedra Blanca [SAN LUIS OBISPO]: *land grant,* along the coast between the mouths of Pico Creek and San Carpoforo Creek; the grant includes Piedras Blancas Point. Named on Burnett Peak (1949), Burro Mountain (1949), Pebblestone Shut-in (1959), Pico Creek (1959), Piedras Blancas (1959), and San Simeon (1958) 7.5' quadrangles. Jose de Jesus Pico received the land in 1840 and claimed 48,806 acres patented in 1876 (Cowan, p. 60). Postal authorities established Piedra Blanca post office in 1870 and discontinued it in 1871 (Frickstad, p. 165). The post office was in the adobe home of Juan Castro (Hamilton, p. 136).

Piedra Creek: see **Stony Creek** [MONTEREY].

Piedra de Lobos: see **Lobos Rocks** [MONTEREY].

Piedras Atlas [MONTEREY]: *ridge,* northwest-trending, 1 mile long, 7.25 miles south-southwest of Jolon (lat. 35°52'05" N, long. 121° 12'20" W). Named on Burnett Peak (1949) 7.5' quadrangle. Hamlin (p. 12) used the term "Sierra de las Piedras" for the range that lies between San Antonio River and Nacimiento River, including present Piedras Atlas.

Piedras Blancas [SAN LUIS OBISPO]: *rocks,* two, each about 200 feet long, 1 mile east-southeast of Piedras Blancas Point, and 1500 feet offshore (lat. 35°39'35" N, long. 121°16'05" W). Named on Piedras Blancas (1959) 7.5' quadrangle. Cabrillo named the rocks for their white color—*piedras blancas* means "white rocks" in Spanish; guano covers the rocks and was gathered in the 1880's (Hamilton, p. 163, 168).

Piedras Blancas: see **Piedras Blancas Point** [SAN LUIS OBISPO].

Piedras Blancas Point [SAN LUIS OBISPO]: *promontory,* 5.5 miles west-northwest of the village of San Simeon along the coast (lat. 35°39'55" N, long. 121°17'05" W); the feature is 1 mile west-northwest of the two rocks called Piedras Blancas. Named on Piedras Blancas (1959) 7.5' quadrangle. United States Board on Geographic Names (1961b, p. 13) approved the form "Point Piedras Blancas" for the name. A lighthouse was constructed at the place in 1874 and 1875, and a post office called Piedras Blancas operated at the construction site (Hamilton, p. 164-165). Postal authorities established Piedras Blancas post office in 1875, and discontinued it the same year (Frickstad, p. 166). A large white rock located west of the point is called Outer Islet (United States Coast and Geodetic Survey, p. 116).

Piedras de los Lobos: see **Lobos Rocks** [MONTEREY].

Pigeon Point [MONTEREY]: *peak,* 5.5 miles east-southeast of Jamesburg (lat. 36°19'35" N, long. 121°30'05" W; near NW cor. sec. 36, T 18 S, R 4 E). Named on Chews Ridge (1956) 7.5' quadrangle.

Pigeon River: see **Pajaro River** [MONTEREY-SAN BENITO-SANTA CRUZ].

Pilarcitos: see **El Chamisal** [MONTEREY].

Pilarcitos Canyon [MONTEREY]: *canyon,* drained by a stream that flows 4 miles to lowlands 4 miles southwest of Salinas (lat. 36° 38' N, long. 121°42' W). Named on Salinas (1947) and Spreckels (1947) 7.5' quadrangles.

Pilarcitos Ridge [MONTEREY]: *ridge,* east- to northeast-trending, 1 mile long, 5 miles southwest of Salinas (lat. 36°37'30" N, long. 121°43'15" W); the ridge is northwest of Pilarcitos Canyon. Named on Salinas (1947) and Spreckels (1947) 7.5' quadrangles.

Piletas Canyon: see **Lower Piletas Canyon** [SAN LUIS OBISPO]; **Upper Piletas Canyon** [SAN LUIS OBISPO].

Pilitas Creek [SAN LUIS OBISPO]: *stream,* flows 5.5 miles to Salinas River 5 miles northeast of Lopez Mountain (lat. 35°21' N, long. 120°30'40" W; sec. 6, T 30 S, R 14 E). Named on Lopez Mountain (1965) and Santa Margarita Lake (1967) 7.5' quadrangles.

Pilitas Mountain [SAN LUIS OBISPO]: *peak,* 1 mile west-northwest of Branch Mountain (lat. 35°11'35" N, long. 120°06' W). Altitude 3624 feet. Named on Branch Mountain (1967) 7.5' quadrangle.

Pillar Rock [SAN LUIS OBISPO]: *rock,* 125 feet long, 50 feet off the north end of Morro Rock (lat. 35°22'30" N, long. 120°52'05" W). Named on Morro Bay South (1965) 7.5' quadrangle.

Pimental: see **The Pimental**, under **Pimental Creek** [SAN BENITO].

Pimental Creek [SAN BENITO]: *stream,* flows 8 miles to join Vallecitos Creek and form Griswold Creek 5.5 miles south of Panoche (lat. 36°30'55" N, long. 120°50' W; near N line sec. 25, T 16 S, R 10 E). Named on Llanada (1969) and Panoche (1969) 7.5' quadrangles. Preston (1893b, p. 372) referred to Primetal Cañon, and Anderson and Pack (p. 19) described a small valley called The Pimental that forms the westward continuation of The Vallecitos. United States Board on Geographic names (1933, p. 604) approved the names "Pimental Valley" and "Pimental Creek," but rejected the name "The Pimental" for the valley drained by the Creek.

Pimental Valley: see **Pimental Creek** [SAN BENITO].

Pinal Creek [MONTEREY]: *stream,* flows 5 miles to Rattlesnake Creek (2) nearly 5 miles south-southeast of Junipero Serra Peak (lat. 36°04'50" N, long. 121°23'40" W). Named on Cone Peak (1949) 7.5' quadrangle.

Pinalito Canyon [MONTEREY-SAN BENITO]: *canyon,* drained by a stream that heads in San Benito County and flows 6.5 miles to Llano Grande Canyon 8.5 miles east-southeast of Greenfield in Monterey County (lat. 36°17'20" N, long. 121°05'40" W). Named on Pinalito Canyon (1969) 7.5' quadrangle.

Pinalito Creek [MONTEREY]: *stream,* flows 3 miles to San Antonio River 6 miles south-southwest of Junipero Serra Peak (lat. 36°04'15" N, long. 121°21'45" W); the stream is 0.5 mile east of Pinal Creek. Named on Bear Canyon (1949) and Cone Peak (1949) 7.5' quadrangles.

Pine Canyon [MONTEREY]:

(1) *canyon,* drained by a stream that flows nearly 4 miles to lowlands 5 miles west-northwest of Chualar (lat. 36°35'05" N, long. 121°36'20" W). Named on Chualar (1947) and Spreckels (1947) 7.5' quadrangles.

(2) *canyon,* drained by a stream that flows 8 miles to lowlands 2 miles south-southwest of King City (lat. 36°11' N, long. 121°08'45" W). Named on Thompson Canyon (1949) 7.5' quadrangle. Called Arroyo del Pino on a diseño of Posa de los Ositos grant made in 1839 (Becker, 1969). A map of Monterey County used about 1900 has the name "Pine Cr." for the stream in the canyon.

(3) *canyon,* 4.25 miles long, opens into lowlands 6.5 miles east-southeast of Jolon (lat. 35°57' N, long. 121°03'45" W; near NW cor. sec. 12, T 23 S, R 8 E). Named on Williams Hill (1949) 7.5' quadrangle.

(4) *canyon,* drained by a stream that flows nearly 4 miles to Little Cholame Creek 4.5 miles north-northwest of Parkfield (lat. 35° 57'20" N, long. 120°28'35" W; sec. 5, T 23 S, R 14 E). Named on Parkfield (1961) 7.5' quadrangle.

Pine Canyon [MONTEREY-SAN LUIS OBISPO]: *canyon,* drained by a stream that heads in Monterey County and flows 13 miles to lowlands along Estrella River 6.54 miles west of Shandon in San Luis Obispo County (lat. 35°39'45" N, long. 120°29'30" W; sec. 17, T 26 S, R 14 E). Named on Cholame Hills (1961) and Shandon (1961) 7.5' quadrangles. The stream below the canyon is called Pine Creek on Estrella (1948) 7.5' quadrangle.

Pine Canyon [SANTA BARBARA]:

(1) *canyon,* drained by a stream that flows 12 miles to Cuyama River 9 miles west of Miranda Pine Mountain (lat. 35°01'45" N, long. 120°11'40" W). Named on Chimney Canyon (1967) and Miranda Pine Mountain (1967) 7.5' quadrangles. The stream in the canyon is called Miranda Pine Creek on Branch Mountain (1952) 15' quadrangle, but United States Board on Geographic Names (1968c, p. 6) rejected the names "Miranda Pine Creek," "Miranda Creek," and "Pine Creek" for the feature.

(2) *canyon,* drained by a stream that flows 6.5 miles to Mono Creek 4.25 miles east-southeast of Madulce Peak (lat. 34°40'10" N, long. 119°31'05" W). Named on Madulce Peak (1964) 7.5' quadrangle.

(3) *canyon,* 1 mile long, 2.5 miles southeast of Orcutt (lat. 34°50'40" N, long. 120°24'35" W; sec. 24, T 9 N, R 34 W). Named on Orcutt (1959) 7.5' quadrangle.

(4) *canyon,* 2 miles long, opens into Santa Lucia Canyon 5.5 miles east of Surf (lat. 34°41'35" N, long. 120°30'15" W). Named on Surf (1959) 7.5' quadrangle.

(5) *canyon,* drained by a stream that flows 1.25 miles to Santa Cruz Creek 7 miles northeast of Santa Ynez Peak (lat. 34°36'15" N, long. 119°54'05" W). Named on Lake Cachuma (1959) 7.5' quadrangle.

Pine Canyon Campground [SANTA BARBARA]: *locality,* 2.5 miles east-southeast of Madulce Peak (lat. 34°40'20" N, long. 119°33'05" W); the place is in Pine Canyon (2). Named on Madulce Peak (1964) 7.5' quadrangle.

Pinecate: see **Santa Rita** [MONTEREY].

Pinecate Peak [SAN BENITO]: *peak,* 4.5 miles west-northwest of San Juan Bautista (lat. 36°51'30" N, long. 121°36'50" W). Altitude 752 feet. Named on San Juan Bautista (1955) 7.5' quadrangle.

Pine Corral Potreros [SANTA BARBARA]: *area,* 1.5 miles west of

Salisbury Potrero (lat. 34°49'25" N, long. 119°43'35" W). Named on Salisbury Potrero (1944) 7.5' quadrangle.

Pine Corral Spring [SANTA BARBARA]: *spring,* 1.5 miles west of Salisbury Potrero (lat. 34°49'30" N, long. 119°43'35" W); the spring is at Pine Corral Potreros. Named on Salisbury Potrero (1964) 7.5' quadrangle, which shows a feature called Pine Corral situated 950 feet west of the spring.

Pine Creek [MONTEREY]:

(1) *stream,* flows 7 miles to Carmel River 5.5 miles south-southeast of the town of Carmel Valley (lat. 36°24'25" N, long. 121°41'25" W; near W line sec. 31, T 17 S, R 3 E). Named on Big Sur (1956), Carmel Valley (1956), and Mount Carmel (1956) 7.5' quadrangles.

(2) *stream,* flows nearly 3 miles to Little Sur River 8 miles east of Point Sur (lat. 36°19'55" N, long. 121°45'15" W). Named on Big Sur (1956) 7.5' quadrangle. United States Board on Geographic Names (1967b, p. 6) approved the name "Comings Creek" for the stream; Big Sur (1956) 7.5' quadrangle shows Comings cabin near the head of a branch of the creek. The name "Comings" is from the family that had land along the stream from 1927 until the 1950's (Clark, 1991, p. 113).

(3) *stream,* flows 8 miles to Salinas River 3.5 miles north-northwest of San Ardo (lat. 36°03'55" N, long. 120°56'10" W); the stream drains Pine Valley (2). Named on Monarch Peak (1967), Pancho Rico Valley (1967), and San Ardo (1967) 7.5' quadrangles.

Pine Creek [SAN LUIS OBISPO]:

(1) *stream,* flows 1.25 miles to Estrella Creek 10.5 miles east of Paso Robles (lat. 35°39'15" N, long. 120°30'30" W; sec. 19, T 26 S, R 14 E). Named on Estrella (1948) 7.5' quadrangle, which shows the stream draining Pine Canyon [MONTEREY-SAN LUIS OBISPO], although the stream is unnamed in the canyon on the map.

(2) *stream,* flows 5 miles to Arroyo Seco 12.5 miles northeast of the town of Nipomo (lat. 35°09'55" N, long. 120°19'10" W; near S line sec. 1, T 32 S, R 15 E). Named on Caldwell Mesa (1967) 7.5' quadrangle.

Pine Creek: see **Pine Canyon** [MONTEREY] (2); **Pine Canyon** [SANTA BARBARA] (1).

Pine Creek Camp [MONTEREY]: *locality,* 9 miles northeast of Point Sur (lat. 36°23'05" N, long. 121°46'05" W); the place is along Pine Creek (1). Named on Mount Carmel (1956) 7.5' quadrangle.

Pine Falls [MONTEREY]: *waterfall,* 2.5 miles east-northeast of Ventana Cone (lat. 36°18' N, long. 121°38'05" W; near NW cor. sec. 10, T 19 S, R 3 E); the feature is in Pine Valley (1). Named on Ventana Cones (1956) 7.5' quadrangle.

Pine Flat [SANTA BARBARA]: *area,* 1.5 miles southwest of Miranda Pine Mountain (lat. 35°01'20" N, long. 120°03'25" W); the place is at the head of Pine Canyon (1). Named on Miranda Pine Mountain (1967) 7.5' quadrangle.

Pine Mountain [SAN BENITO]: *peak,* 7 miles northeast of Bitterwater (lat. 36°27'15" N, long. 120°55'05" W; sec. 18, T 17 S, R 10 E). Altitude 3814 feet. Named on Rock Spring Peak (1969) 7.5' quadrangle.

Pine Mountain [SAN LUIS OBISPO]:

(1) *peak,* 6.5 miles east-northeast of the village of San Simeon (lat. 35°41'25" N, long. 121°05'35" W; sec. 10, T 26 S, R 8 E). Altitude 3594 feet. Named on Pebblestone Shut-in (1959) 7.5' quadrangle.

(2) *hill,* nearly 1 mile east of downtown Atascadero (lat. 35°29'35" N, long. 120°39'20" W). Altitude 1326 feet. Named on Atascadero (1965) 7.5' quadrangle.

(3) *ridge,* west-trending, 3.5 miles long, 7.5 miles east-northeast of Pozo (lat. 35°20' N, long. 120°15' W). Named on La Panza (1967) and Pozo Summit (1967) 7.5' quadrangles.

Pine Mountain [SANTA CRUZ]: *ridge,* north-northwest-trending, 1.5 miles long, 1.5 miles south-southwest of Big Basin (lat. 37°08'50" N, long. 122°13'45" W; in and near sec. 18, 19, T 9 S, R 3 W). Named on Big Basin (1955) 7.5' quadrangle. The name is from a heavy growth of knob-cone pine trees on the summit of the feature (Clark, 1986, p. 257).

Pine Mountain: see **Big Pine Mountain** [SANTA BARBARA]; **Little Pine Mountain** [SANTA BARBARA].

Pine Mountain Springs [SAN LUIS OBISPO]: *spring,* 5 miles east of Pozo (lat. 35°18'20" N, long. 120°17' W); the spring is 1.5 miles south-southwest of the west end of Pine Mountain (3). Named on Pozo Summit (1967) 7.5' quadrangle.

Pine Ridge [MONTEREY]:

(1) *ridge,* west-trending, 0.5 mile long, nearly 1 mile southeast of Point Lobos (lat. 36°30'55" N, long. 121°56'35" W). Named on Monterey (1947) 7.5' quadrangle.

(2) *ridge,* west-northwest-trending, 1 mile long, 1.5 miles east-southeast of Ventana Cone (lat. 36°16'35" N, long. 121°38'55" W). Named on Ventana Cones (1956) 7.5' quadrangle. The ridge has a fine stand of ponderosa pine trees (Clark, 1991, p. 398).

Pine Ridge [SAN BENITO]: *ridge,* northwest-trending, 2.5 miles long, 3.5 miles northeast of San Benito (lat. 36°33' N, long. 121°02'30" W). Named on San Benito (1968) 7.5' quadrangle.

Pine Ridge [SAN LUIS OBISPO]: *ridge,* northwest-trending, 6.5 miles long, 16 miles northeast of the town of Nipomo (lat. 35°12'30" N, long. 120°16'45" W). Named on Caldwell Mesa (1967) and Los Machos Hills (1967) 7.5' quadrangles.

Pine Ridge Camp [MONTEREY]: *locality,* nearly 2 miles east-southeast of Ventana Cone (lat. 36°16'25" N, long. 121°38'55" W; sec. 16, T 19 S, R 3 E); the place is on the south side of Pine Ridge (2). Named on Ventana Cones (1956) 7.5' quadrangle.

Pine Rock [SAN BENITO]: *peak,* 5 miles northwest of San Benito (lat. 36°33'50" N, long. 121°08'05" W; near SW cor. sec. 5, T 16 S, R 8 E). Named on Bickmore Canyon (1968) 7.5' quadrangle. California Mining Bureau's (1909a) map shows a place called Pinerock located near the peak. Postal authorities established Pinerock post office in 1888, discontinued it in 1893, reestablished it in 1894, and discontinued it in 1911 (Frickstad, p. 136).

Pinerock: see **Pine Rock** [SAN BENITO].

Pinery: see **East Pinery** [SANTA BARBARA].

Pines: see **Little Pines** [MONTEREY]; **Santa Margarita** [SAN LUIS OBISPO] (2).

Pines Camp: see **Little Pines Camp** [MONTEREY].

Pines Campground: see **The Pines Campground** [SANTA BARBARA].

Pine Spring [SAN LUIS OBISPO]: *spring,* 1.25 miles south-southwest of Castle Crags (lat. 35°17'20" N, long. 120°12'25" W). Named on La Panza (1967) 7.5' quadrangle. United States Board on Geographic Names (1968c, p. 6) rejected the name "Pine Spring Number 1 and 2" for the feature.

Pine Spring: see **Little Pine Spring** [SANTA BARBARA].

Pine Spring Number 1 and 2: see **Pine Spring** [SAN LUIS OBISPO].

Pine Springs [MONTEREY]: *spring,* 9 miles east-southeast of Parkfield (lat. 35°52'20" N, long. 120°16'15" W). Named on Cholame Ranch (1943) 7.5' quadrangle.

Pine Top Mountain [SAN LUIS OBISPO]: *ridge,* northwest-trending, 1.25 miles long, 5.5 miles north-northeast of Piedras Blancas Point (lat. 35°44'40" N, long. 121°15'40" W). Named on Piedras Blancas (1959) 7.5' quadrangle.

Pine Valley [MONTEREY]:

(1) *valley,* nearly 3 miles east-northeast of Ventana Cone near the head of Carmel River (lat. 36°18'05" N, long. 121°38' W). Named on Chews Ridge (1956) and Ventana Cones (1956) 7.5' quadrangles.

(2) *valley,* opens into lowlands 4 miles north-northwest of San Ardo (lat. 36°04'25" N, long. 120°55'45" W); the valley is drained by Pine Creek (3). Named on San Ardo (1967) 7.5' quadrangle.

Piney: see **Piney Creek** [MONTEREY].

Piney Creek [MONTEREY]: *stream,* flows 10.5 miles to Arroyo Seco (1) 11 miles west-southwest of Greenfield (lat. 36°15'05" N, long. 121°25'05" W; sec. 27, T 19 S, R 5 E). Named on Chews Ridge (1956) and Sycamore Flat (1956) 7.5' quadrangles. Soledad (1915) 15' quadrangle shows Piney Creek as a tributary of Paloma Creek, and shows Paloma Creek continuing along the course of present Piney Creek to Arroyo Seco (1). Postal authorities established Piney post office, located 7 miles southwest of Paraiso Springs on the east side of Piney Creek (NE quarter sec. 28, T 19 S, R 5 E), in 1897, moved it 2.5 miles east in 1904, and discontinued it in 1905 (Salley, p. 172; Clark, 1991, p. 399).

Piney Creek Campground [MONTEREY]: *locality,* 13 miles west of Greenfield (lat. 36°17'10" N, long. 121°28'45" W; at S line sec. 12, T 19 S, R 4 E); the place is along Piney Creek. Named on Sycamore Flat (1956) 7.5' quadrangle.

Piney Ridge [SAN LUIS OBISPO]: *ridge,* west- to north-northwest-trending, 0.5 mile long, 2 miles south-southeast of Lopez Mountain (lat. 35°16'40" N, long. 120°33'45" W). Named on Lopez Mountain (1965) 7.5' quadrangle.

Pinkham's Santa Barbara Mineral Springs: see **Veronica Springs** [SANTA BARBARA].

Pinnacle: see **The Pinnacle**, under **Pinnacle Point** [MONTEREY].

Pinnacle Cove [MONTEREY]: *embayment,* near the northwest end of Point Lobos along the coast (lat. 36°31'20" N, long. 121°57'10" W); the feature is just south of Pinnacle Point. Named on Monterey (1947) 7.5' quadrangle.

Pinnacle Point [MONTEREY]: *promontory,* at the northwest end of Point Lobos along the coast (lat. 36°31'25" N, long. 121°57'10" W). Named on Monterey (1947, photorevised 1968) 7.5' quadrangle. Called Carmel Point on Monterey (1947) 7.5' quadrangle, which shows Pinnacle Point as an island off Carmel Point. On California Department of Parks and Recreation's map the island has the name "The Pinnacle." Malaspina's (1791) map has the name "Punta del Carmelo" at the place, Parke's (1854-1855) map has the name "Pt. Carmel" at the south end of Carmel Bay, and Whitney (p. 157) referred to Point Carmelo. United States Board on Geographic Names (1975, p. 4-5) gave the variant names "Carmel Point" and "Pyramid Point" for the feature. At the same time, the Board (p. 4) applied the name "Carmel Point" to a promontory on the east shore of Carmel Bay just north of the mouth of Carmel River and at the southwest end of present Carmel-by-the-Sea (lat. 36°32'37" N, long. 121°55'55" W).

Pinnacle Rocks [SAN BENITO]: *relief feature,* 2.5 miles north of North

Chalone Peak (lat. 36°29'15" N, long. 121°12' W; on N line sec. 3, T 17 S, R 7 E). Named on North Chalone Peak (1969) 7.5' quadrangle. The feature sometimes is called Vancouver's Pinnacles because English navigator George Vancouver supposedly visited the place in 1794 (Hoover, Rensch, and Rensch, p. 315).

Pinnacles [SAN BENITO]: *locality*, 4 miles west-northwest of San Benito in Bear Valley (lat. 36°32' N, long. 121°08'40" W; near NW cor. sec. 19, T 16 S, R 8 E). Named on Bickmore Canyon (1968) 7.5' quadrangle. San Benito (1919) 15' quadrangle has the name "Cook" at the site. Postal authorities established Cook post office in 1894, moved it and changed the name to Pinnacles in 1924, and discontinued it in 1953 (Salley, p. 49, 172).

Pinnacles: see **Little Pinnacles** [SAN BENITO]; **The Pinnacles** [MONTEREY]; **The Pinnacles**, under **Pescadero Point** [MONTEREY].

Pinole Spring [SAN LUIS OBISPO]: *spring*, 22 miles northeast of Pozo (lat. 35°29'50" N, long. 120°04'15" W; near NE cor. sec. 18, T 28 S, R 18 E). Named on La Panza NE (1966) 7.5' quadrangle.

Pinos: see **Point Pinos** [MONTEREY].

Pinto Lake [SANTA CRUZ]: *lake*, nearly 1 mile long, 3 miles north-northwest of Watsonville (lat. 36°57'20" N, long. 121°46'15" W). Named on Watsonville West (1954) 7.5' quadrangle. The name commemorates Rafael Pinto, a former Lieutenant in the Mexican army who lived near Watsonville (Rowland, p. 45).

Pinyon Peak [MONTEREY]:

(1) *peak*, 8.5 miles east-northeast of Soberanes Point (lat. 36°29'20" N, long. 121°47'10" W). Altitude 2249 feet. Named on Mount Carmel (1956) 7.5' quadrangle.

(2) *peak*, nearly 3 miles northeast of Junipero Serra Peak (lat. 36° 10'05" N, long. 121°22'50" W; sec. 25, T 20 S, R 5 E). Altitude 5264 feet. Named on Junipero Serra Peak (1949) 7.5' quadrangle. A map of Monterey County used about 1900 has the name "Vaquero Pk." for the feature, which is west of Vaqueros Creek.

Pionne Peak [SAN BENITO]: *peak*, 6.5 miles north-northwest of San Benito (lat. 36°35'10" N, long. 121°08'40" W; sec. 31, T 15 S, R 8 E). Altitude 2704 feet. Named on Bickmore Canyon (1968) 7.5' quadrangle.

Pipeline Lake [SAN LUIS OBISPO]: *lake*, 2050 feet long, 3.5 miles south-southwest of downtown Arroyo Grande near the coast (lat. 35°04'30" N, long. 120°36'25" W). Named on Oceano (1965) 7.5' quadrangle.

Pipin Corner [SAN LUIS OBISPO]: *locality*, 1.5 miles west-southwest of Pozo along Salinas River (lat. 35°17'55" N, long. 120°24'10" W; sec. 19, T 30 S, R 15 E). Named on Santa Margarita Lake (1967) 7.5' quadrangle.

Pismo [SAN LUIS OBISPO]: *land grant*, along the coast between Shell Beach and the mouth of Arroyo Grande Creek; the grant includes Pismo Beach. Named on Arroyo Grande NE (1965), Oceano (1965), and Pismo Beach (1965) 7.5' quadrangles. Jose Ortega received 2 leagues in 1835; Isaac J. Sparks claimed 8839 acres patented in 1866 (Cowan, p. 61). Perez (p. 81) gave 1840 as the year of the grant. According to Gudde (1949, p. 264), the name is derived from an Indian word that has the meaning "tar."

Pismo: see **Pismo Beach** [SAN LUIS OBISPO].

Pismo Beach [SAN LUIS OBISPO]: *town*, 10 miles south of San Luis Obispo (lat. 35°08'30" N, long. 120°38'20" W); the town is on Pismo grant. Named on Arroyo Grande NE (1965) and Pismo Beach (1965) 7.5' quadrangles. Called Pismo on Arroyo Grande (1897) 15' quadrangle. According to Angel (1883, p. 322), in the early days the whole coast from Point Sal [SANTA BARBARA] to Point San Luis usually was called Pismo Beach. The town was founded in 1891 and incorporated in 1946 (Lee and others, p. 119). Postal authorities established Pismo post office in 1894 and changed the name to Pismo Beach in 1923 (Frickstad, p. 166). Chase (p. 142-143) described "El Pizmo, a newly exploited beach resort."

Pismo Bench [SAN LUIS OBISPO]: *area*, nearly 1 mile northeast of the mouth of Pismo Creek (lat. 35°08'30" N, long. 120°37'40" W); the place is in the town of Pismo Beach. Named on Pismo Beach (1965) 7.5' quadrangle.

Pismo Creek [SAN LUIS OBISPO]: *stream*, formed by the confluence of East Corral de Piedra Creek and West Corral de Piedra Creek, flows 5.25 miles to the sea at Pismo Beach (lat. 35°08' N, long. 120°38'25" W). Named on Arroyo Grande NE (1965) and Pismo Beach (1965) 7.5' quadrangles.

Pismo Lake [SAN LUIS OBISPO]: *marsh*, 1 mile southeast of downtown Pismo Beach (lat. 35°07'55" N, long. 120°37'40" W). Named on Pismo Beach (1965) 7.5' quadrangle.

Pit: see **The Pit** [MONTEREY].

Pitman Canyon [MONTEREY]: *canyon*, drained by a stream that flows 4 miles to Peachtree Canyon 8.5 miles east-northeast of San Ardo (lat. 36°04'55" N, long. 120°46'15" W; near S line sec. 22, T 21 S, R 11 E). Named on Monarch Peak (1967) and Pancho Rico Valley (1967) 7.5' quadrangles. The name commemorates William Luther Pitman, who homesteaded in the canyon (Clark, 1991, p. 402).

Placer Creek [SAN LUIS OBISPO]: *stream*, flows nearly 7 miles to San Juan Creek 4.5 miles northeast of Castle Crags (lat. 35°21'05" N, long. 120°08'25" N, near N line sec. 3, T 30 S, R 17 E). Named on La Panza (1967) 7.5' quadrangle. Prospectors discovered gold along the stream in 1878 (Lee and others, p. 81). This may be the feature called De la Guerra Gulch that Angel (1883, p. 248) mentioned as the site of most of the mining done in the old La Panza placer mining district.

Plaskett [MONTEREY]: *locality*, 2 miles north of Cape San Martin along the coast (lat. 35°55' N, long. 121°28' W; sec. 19, T 23 S, R 5 E); the place is near the mouth of Plaskett Creek. Named on Cape San Martin (1949) 7.5' quadrangle, which shows Pacific Valley school situated north of Plaskett near the mouth of Plaskett Creek.. Crippen (p. 6) gave the name "Plaskett Point" to the first promontory along the coast south of the mouth of Plaskett Creek, and gave the name "Jade Cove" to the embayment south of the point, where nephrite jade is found. Lussier (p. 36) used the name "Pacific Valley" for a small community situated near Plaskett.

Plaskett Creek [MONTEREY]: *stream*, flows 2.5 miles to the sea 2.25 miles north-northwest of Cape San Martin (lat. 35°55'10" N, long. 121°28'15" W; sec. 19, T 23 S, R 5 E). Named on Cape San Martin (1949) 7.5' quadrangle. The name commemorates the Plaskett family, early residents in the neighborhood (Clark, 1991, p. 402-403).

Plaskett Point: see **Plaskett** [MONTEREY].

Plaskett Rock [MONTEREY]: *rock*, 325 feet long, 2.25 miles north-northwest of Cape San Martin, and 825 feet offshore (lat. 35°55'15" N, long. 121°28'40" W); the feature is opposite the mouth of Plaskett Creek. Named on Cape San Martin (1949) 7.5' quadrangle.

Platts Harbor [SANTA BARBARA]: *embayment*, 1.5 miles east-southeast of Diablo Point on he north side of Santa Cruz Island (lat. 34°02'50" N, long. 119°44' W). Named on Santa Cruz Island B (1943) 7.5' quadrangle. Called Dicks Harbor on Bremner's (1932) map. Doran (p. 147) referred to to the harbor as "Dick's, sometimes called Platt's."

Pleasant Valley [SANTA CRUZ]: *valley*, 1.5 miles west-northwest of Corralitos (lat. 36°59'45" N, long. 121°50' W). Named on Loma Prieta (1955) and Watsonville West (1954) 7.5' quadrangles.

Pleasant Valley: see **Hog Canyon** [MONTEREY-SAN LUIS OBISPO].

Pleito: see **Pleyto** [MONTEREY] (1) and (2).

Pleyto [MONTEREY]:

(1) *land grant*, 13 miles southeast of Jolon along San Antonio River. Named on Bryson (1949), Hames Valley (1949), Tierra Redonda Mountain (1949), and Williams Hill (1949) 7.5' quadrangles. Jose Antonio Chavez received 3 leagues in 1845; W.S. Johnson and others claimed 13,299 acres patented in 1872 (Cowan, p. 61-62; Cowan listed the grant under the names "Pleito," "Pleyto," and "San Bartolome"). The name "Pleyto" supposedly is derived from *pleito*, which means "lawsuit" in Spanish, and dates from the time that a group of Spaniards saw Indians at the place talking as if arguing legal points (Hoover, Rensch, and Rensch, p. 227).

(2) *locality*, 12.5 miles southeast of Jolon along San Antonio River (lat. 35°51'35" N, long. 120°59'35" W); the place is on Pleyto grant. Named on Tierra Redonda Mountain (1949) 7.5' quadrangle. Water of Lake San Antonio now covers the site. Postal authorities established Pleito post office in 1870, discontinued it in 1872, reestablished it in 1874, discontinued it in 1876, reestablished it in 1884, changed the name to Pleyto in 1884, and discontinued it in 1925 (Frickstad, p. 108). William Pinkerton planned the community on land he bought in 1868 (Clark, 1991, p. 404).

Plowshare Peak [SANTA BARBARA]: *peak*, 1 mile north-northwest of Miranda Pine Mountain (lat. 35°03'10" N, long. 120°02'30" W). Named on Miranda Pine Mountain (1967) 7.5' quadrangle.

Plowshare Spring [SANTA BARBARA]: *spring*, 2 miles west-northwest of Miranda Pine Mountain (lat. 35°02'45" N, long. 120° 04' W); the spring is 1.5 miles west-southwest of Plowshare Peak. Named on Miranda Pine Mountain (1967) 7.5' quadrangle. Branch Mountain (1942) 15' quadrangle shows Plowshare Spr. at the site of present Brookshire Campground.

Pocket Lake: see **Big Pocket Lake** [SAN LUIS OBISPO].

Point Almeja: see **Mussel Point** [MONTEREY].

Point Alones [MONTEREY]: *promontory*, 2.25 miles southeast of Point Pinos along the coast (lat. 37°05' N, long. 121°54' W). Named on Monterey (1947) 7.5' quadrangle. According to Clark (1991, p. 406), the name is derived from an Indian word meaning "abalone"—abalone are found at the place; the feature has the variant names "Abalone Point" and "Point Loeb," the last for Jacques Loeb, an experimental biologist who did research in the vicinity.

Point Arguelia: see **Point Arguello** [SANTA BARBARA].

Point Arguello [SANTA BARBARA]: *promontory*, 11.5 miles west-southwest of the city of Lompoc (lat. 34°34'35" N, long. 120° 39' W). Named on Point Arguello (1959) 7.5' quadrangle. United States Board on Geographic Names (1933, p. 102) rejected the name "Point Arguelia" for the feature. Vancouver named the promontory in 1792 for Jose Dario Arguello, the commandant at Monterey; soldiers of the Portola expedition called it Punta Pedernales in 1769 because they found some big flints there (Wagner, H.R., p. 373, 482)—*pedernales* means "flints" in Spanish. The name "Pedernales" now applies to a nearby promontory.

Point Aulon: see **Lovers Point** [MONTEREY].

Point Bennett [SANTA BARBARA]: *promontory*, at the westernmost tip of San Miguel Island (lat. 34°01'50" N, long. 120°27'05" W). Named on San Miguel Island West (1950) 7.5' quadrangle.

Point Buchon [SAN LUIS OBISPO]: *promontory,* 8 miles south-southwest of Morro Rock on the coast at the west extremity of Irish Hills (lat. 35°15'20" N, long. 120°53'55" W). Named on Morro Bay South (1965) 7.5' quadrangle. When members of the Portola expedition ascended present Price Canyon in 1769, they found a group of Indians whose chief had a large goiter; the soldiers called the place Buchon—*buchon* means "goiter" in Spanish—and this designation is perpetuated in the name of the point (Wagner, H.R., p. 377-378).

Point Cabrillo: see **Mussel Point** [MONTEREY].

Point Carmel: see **Pinnacle Point** [MONTEREY].

Point Carmelo: see **Pinnacle Point** [MONTEREY]; **Point Lobos** [MONTEREY].

Point Castillo [SANTA BARBARA]: *promontory,* 1.25 miles south-southeast of downtown Santa Barbara along the coast (lat. 34°24'10" N, long. 119°41'25" W). Named on Santa Barbara (1952) 7.5' quadrangle. Called Punta del Castillo on Santa Barbara (1903) 15' quadrangle, but United States Board on Geographic Names (1961b, p. 9) rejected this name for the promontory. The feature was called Punta de San Esteban in Spanish days (Wagner, H.R., p. 498).

Point Concepcion: see **Point Conception** [SANTA BARBARA].

Point Conception [SANTA BARBARA]: *promontory,* 45 miles west of Santa Barbara along the coast (lat. 34°26'55" N, long. 120°28'15" W). Named on Point Conception (1953) 7.5' quadrangle. Cabrillo called the promontory Cabo de Galera in 1542 for its galley-like shape (Wagner, H.R., p. 381). A map by Palacios that resulted from Vizcaino's voyage of 1602 has the name "Punta de la Limpia Concepcion" for the feature; Vizcaino reached the place about December 8, the day of celebration of the Purisima Concepcion (Wagner, H.R., p. 381). The promontory is called Pta. Concepcion on Parke's (1854-1855) map. United States Board on Geographic Names (1933, p. 232) rejected the form "Point Concepcion" for the name

Point Cove: see **Headland Cove** [MONTEREY].

Point Cypress: see **Cypress Point** [MONTEREY].

Point Cypress Rock: see **Cypress Point Rock** [MONTEREY].

Point Douty: see **Sunset Point** [MONTEREY].

Point Estero [SAN LUIS OBISPO]: *promontory,* 3.5 miles west-northwest of Cayucos Point along the coast (lat. 35°27'35" N, long. 121°00'05" W; sec. 33, T 28 S, R 9 E); the feature is at the north end of Estero Bay. Named on Cayucos (1965) 7.5' quadrangle. Called Punta del Estero on Costano's map that resulted from the Portola expedition (Gudde, 1949, p. 110), and called Pt. Estero on United States Coast Survey's (1854) map. Vancouver (p. 141) used the name "Punto del Esteros" in 1793. According to H.R. Wagner (p. 386), the name "Estero" evidently is from the estero at the mouth of Ellysly's Creek, or possibly from the name "Los Esteros" applied on Spanish maps to present Estero Bay.

Point Felipe: see **Santa Barbara Point** [SANTA BARBARA].

Point Gorda: see **Cape San Martin** [MONTEREY].

Point Harris: see **Harris Point** [SANTA BARBARA].

Point Joe [MONTEREY]: *promontory,* nearly 2.5 miles southwest of Point Pinos along the coast (lat. 36°36'35" N, long. 121°57'20" W). Named on Monterey (1947) 7.5' quadrangle. The feature first was called Pyramid Point; the name "Joe" is for a squatter who lived near the promontory for many years (Reinstedt, 1975, p. 94). The squatter was known as Chinaman Joe, but whether the point was named for Joe, or Joe for the point, is a question (Lydon, p. 152). Clark (1991, p. 407) gave Intermediate Point and Joe's Point as alternate names for the feature.

Point Lobos [MONTEREY]: *promontory,* 2.5 miles southwest of present Carmel-by-the-Sea along the coast on the south side of Carmel Bay (lat. 36°31'20" N, long. 121°57'10" W). Named on Monterey (1947) 7.5' quadrangle. Rogers and Johnston's (1857) map has the designation "Pta. de Lobos or Carmel" for the feature. On Lawson's (1893) map, the whole peninsula that includes Point Lobos has the name "Point Carmelo," and a promontory just south of present Sand Hill has the name "Pt. Lobos." California Department of Parks and Recreation's map has the name "Punta de los Lobos Marinos" for the next promontory northwest of the one called Pt. Lobos on Lawson's (1893) map; this point is between Headland Cove and Sea Lion Cove. Stewart (p. 261) identified the name "Lobos" with *lobo marino,* which means "seal" or "sea lion" in Spanish.

Point Loeb: see **Point Alones** [MONTEREY].

Point Lospie: see **Point Sal** [SANTA BARBARA].

Point Morrito: see **Lions Head** [SANTA BARBARA].

Point Pedernales [SANTA BARBARA]: *promontory,* 2 miles north-northeast of Point Arguello along the coast (lat. 34°36'15" N, long. 120°38'30" W). Named on Point Arguello (1959) 7.5' quadrangle. Soldiers of the Portola expedition gave the name "Punta Pedernales" to present Point Arguello in 1769 because they found some flints there (Wagner, H.R., p. 482)—*pedernales* means "flints" in Spanish. The name "Pedernales" applied to present Purisima Point in the 1850's, and was transferred to present Point Pedernales after 1900 (Gudde, 1949, p. 257).

Point Piedras Blancas: see **Piedras Blancas Point** [SAN LUIS OBISPO].

Point Pinos [MONTEREY]: *promontory,* northernmost point of land northwest of Monterey at the south end of Monterey Bay (lat. 36° 38'15" N, long. 121°55'50" W). Named on Monterey (1947) 7.5' quadrangle. Called Punta de los Pinos on Williamson's (1853) map. Davidson (1887, p. 212) identified present Point Pinos as the feature that Cabrillo and Ferrelo called El Cabo de San Martin and El Cabo de Martin in 1542, and that Vizcaino called La Punta de Pinos in 1602. Davidson (1907, p. 28) also noted that a map of 1646 has the name "C.S. Barbera," a map of 1672 has the name "P. de S. Barbera," and an atlas of 1709 has the name "P. de Carinde" for the promontory. The name "Pinos" is from pine trees at the place; the feature also was called Lighthouse Point (Clark, 1991, p. 410).

Point Pinos Range: see **Santa Lucia Range** [MONTEREY].

Point Sal [SANTA BARBARA]: *promontory,* 7.5 miles southwest of the town of Guadalupe along the coast (lat. 34°54'10" N, long. 120°40'15" W; sec. 34, T 10 N, R 36 W). Named on Point Sal (1958) 7.5' quadrangle. Called Pta. Sal on Parke's (1854-1855) map. Vancouver (p. 142) named the promontory to honor Hermenegildo Sal, Spanish commandant at San Francisco. Fairbanks' (1896) map has the name "Point Lospie" for a promontory 2.25 miles southeast of Point Sal.

Point Sal Landing [SANTA BARBARA]: *locality,* 1.5 miles east of Point Sal along the coast (lat. 34°53'50" N, long. 120°38'45" W). Named on Guadalupe (1905) 30' quadrangle.

Point Sal Ridge [SANTA BARBARA]: *ridge,* west-trending, 4.5 miles long, 6 miles southwest of the town of Guadalupe (lat. 34° 54'05" N, long. 120°38' W); Point Sal is at the west end of the ridge. Named on Guadalupe (1959) and Point Sal (1958) 7.5' quadrangles. Harold W. Fairbanks named the feature (Arnold and Anderson, 1907a, p. 16).

Point San Luis [SAN LUIS OBISPO]: *promontory,* 10 miles south-southwest of San Luis Obispo along the coast (lat. 35°09'35" N, long. 120°45'30" W); the feature is at the west end of San Luis Obispo Bay. Named on Port San Luis (1965) 7.5' quadrangle. Called Pta. St. Luis on Emory's (1857-1858) map.

Point Santa Cruz [SANTA CRUZ]: *promontory,* at the west end of Santa Cruz Harbor at Santa Cruz (lat. 36°57' N, long. 122°01'30" W). Named on Santa Cruz (1954) 7.5' quadrangle. Called Punta de Lobos on a Spanish map of 1796, and called Phelan Point in the 1920's; the feature acquired the unofficial name "Lighthouse Point" after a lighthouse was built there in 1869 (Clark, 1986, p. 183).

Point Sierra Nevada [SAN LUIS OBISPO]: *promontory,* 4 miles north-northwest of Piedras Blancas Point along the coast (lat. 35° 42'50" N, long. 121°18'55" W). Named on Piedras Blancas (1959) 7.5' quadrangle. The name commemorates the steamship *Sierra Nevada,* which was stranded on rocks northwest of the point (United States Coast and Geodetic Survey, p. 117).

Point Sur [MONTEREY]: *promontory,* 23 miles south of Point Pinos along the coast (lat. 36°18'25" N, long. 121°54'10" W); the feature is on El Sur grant. Named on Point Sur (1956) 7.5' quadrangle. The promontory had the name "Punta que Parece Isla" in Spanish times, although in 1769 the Portola expedition called it Morro Trompo, an allusion to the shape of the feature—*trompa* means "horn" or "trumpet" in Spanish (Wagner, H.R., p. 418, 521). A lighthouse was built at the point in 1889 (Fink, p. 215). Postal authorities established Point Sur post office 1 mile north of Bisby Creek at Bixby's Mill in 1883 and discontinued it the same year; they established Sur post office in 1889 and discontinued it in 1913; they established Mungo post office in 1895 and discontinued it in 1898, when they moved the service to Sur—the name "Mungo" was for Mungo McHolme, first postmaster (Salley, p. 149, 175, 216)

Poison Oak Hill [MONTEREY]: *peak,* 2.5 miles east of Jamesburg (lat. 36°22' N, long. 121°32'35" W; sec. 16, T 18 S, R 4 E); the peak is at the southeast end of Poison Oak Ridge. Altitude 2754 feet. Named on Chews Ridge (1956) 7.5' quadrangle.

Poison Oak Ridge [MONTEREY]: *ridge,* west-northwest-trending, 1 mile long, 2.25 miles east of Jamesburg (lat. 36°22'15" N, long. 121°33' W). Named on Chews Ridge (1956) 7.5' quadrangle.

Poison Spring [MONTEREY]: *spring,* 23 miles east-northeast of King City (lat. 36°17'15" N, long. 120°42'45" W; sec. 12, T 19 S, R 11 E). Named on San Benito Mountain (1969) 7.5' quadrangle.

Poison Water Pond [SAN LUIS OBISPO]: *lake,* 225 feet long, nearly 4 miles east-northeast of Cholame (lat. 35°44'30" N, long. 120° 14' W). Named on Annette (1943) 7.5' quadrangle.

Pole Canyon [MONTEREY]: *canyon,* drained by a stream that flows 3 miles to Jolon Valley 4.5 miles north-northeast of Jolon (lat. 36° 02' N, long. 121°09'35" W; sec. 12, T 22 S, R 7 E). Named on Cosio Knob (1949) 7.5' quadrangle.

Polonia Valley: see **Polonio Pass** [SAN LUIS OBISPO].

Polonio Pass [SAN LUIS OBISPO]: *valley,* 5.5 miles east of Cholame on San Luis Obispo-Kern County line (lat. 35°43'30" N, long. 120° 11'35" W). Named on Orchard Peak (1961) 7.5' quadrangle. Angel (1890c, p. 569) used the name "Polonia Valley."

Poncha Rica Creek: see **Pancho Rico Creek** [MONTEREY].

Poncho Rico Creek: see **Pancho Rico Creek** [MONTEREY].

Ponciano Ridge [MONTEREY]: *ridge,* west-trending, 3.5 miles long, 6 miles south of the town of Carmel Valley (lat. 36°23'45" N, long. 121°44'15" W). Named on Carmel Valley (1956) and Mount Carmel (1956) 7.5' quadrangles. The name commemorates Ponciano Manjares, a homesteader in the region (Clark, 1991, p. 413).

Poorman Canyon [SAN LUIS OBISPO]: *canyon,* drained by a stream that flows 1 mile to Corbit Canyon 5.25 miles south-southeast of Edna (lat. 35°08'05" N, long. 120°34'10" W). Named on Arroyo Grande NE (1965) 7.5' quadrangle.

Pope: see **Indian Valley** [MONTEREY] (3).

Poplar Campground [SANTA BARBARA]: *locality,* about 3.5 miles south-southeast of Big Pine Mountain along Indian Creek (lat. 34° 38'45" N, long. 119°38'10" W). Named on Big Pine Mountain (1964) 7.5' quadrangle.

Porta Suela [SAN LUIS OBISPO]: *pass,* 5.25 miles southeast of Cambria near Harmony (lat. 35°30'15" N, long. 121°01' W). Named on San Simeon (1919) 15' quadrangle.

Porter Gulch [SANTA CRUZ]: *canyon,* 1.5 miles long, opens into Tannery Gulch 4 miles northeast of Soquel Point (lat. 36°59'45" N, long. 121°55'20" W). Named on Laurel (1955) and Soquel (1954) 7.5' quadrangles. Ben Porter and his cousin George had a tannery in the canyon in the 1850's (Rowland, p. 71).

Porter Gulch: see **Aptos Creek** [SANTA CRUZ].

Porter Peak [SANTA BARBARA]: *peak,* 3.5 miles west-northwest of Miranda Pine Mountain (lat. 35°03'15" N, long. 120°05'55" W). Altitude 3384 feet. Named on Miranda Pine Mountain (1967) 7.5' quadrangle.

Porter's Landing: see **Soquel Creek** [SANTA CRUZ].

Porter Spring [SANTA BARBARA]: *spring,* 3.5 miles west-northwest of Miranda Pine Mountain (lat. 35°03'25" N, long. 120°05'45" W; sec. 1, T 11 N, R 31 W); the spring is 1700 feet northeast of present Porter Peak. Named on Branch Mountain (1952) 15' quadrangle.

Portezuelo: see **Central Valley** [SANTA BARBARA].

Port Harford: see **Port San Luis** [SAN LUIS OBISPO].

Port Hartford: see **Port San Luis** [SAN LUIS OBISPO].

Port Orford [SANTA BARBARA]: *locality,* 0.5 mile west of Gaviota along the coast at the mouth of Cañada de la Gaviota (lat. 34°28'15" N, long. 120°13'40" W). Site named on Gaviota (1953) 7.5' quadrangle. Farmers shipped their products from Gaviota Wharf, a 1000-foot-long pier at the place, from 1875 through the 1890's (Rife, p. 104).

Port Rogers: see **Port Watsonville** [SANTA CRUZ].

Port San Luis [SAN LUIS OBISPO]: *locality,* 1 mile north-northeast of Point San Luis along the coast (lat. 35°10'35" N, long. 120°45'10" W). Named on Port San Luis (1965) 7.5' quadrangle. Called Port Harford on Port Harford (1897) 15' quadrangle. Dr. John O'Farrell, one of the owners and managers of the railroad built to the site, gave the name "Port Harford" to the place to honor John Harford, the original owner of the wharf there (Angel, 1883, p. 350). Postal authorities established Port Harford post office in 1882, changed the name to Port San Luis in 1907, and discontinued it in 1932 (Frickstad, p. 166). United States Board on Geographic Names (1933, p. 616) rejected the name "Port Hartford" for the place.

Portugee Canyon [MONTEREY]: *canyon,* drained by a stream that flows 8 miles to Pine Creek (3) 4 miles north of San Ardo (lat. 36° 04'45" N, long. 120°54'20" W). Named on Pancho Rico Valley (1967) 7.5' quadrangle. Called Redhead Canyon on San Ardo (1956) 15' quadrangle, but United States Board on Geographic Names (1968c, p. 6) rejected this name for the feature. The name "Portugee Canyon" recalls an old homesteader known as The Portugee (Clark, 1991, p. 416).

Portuguese Canyon [MONTEREY]:

(1) *canyon,* drained by a stream that flows 9 miles to Salinas River 0.5 mile east of Bradley (lat. 35°51'40" N, long. 120°47'40" W; sec. 9, T 24 S, R 11 E). Named on Bradley (1949), Valleton (1948), and Wunpost (1949) 7.5' quadrangles. The name is from the large number of Portuguese people who settled east of Bradley in the 1860's (Clark, 1991, p. 417).

(2) *canyon,* drained by a stream that flows 12 miles to Vineyard Canyon 8.5 miles east-southeast of Bradley (lat. 35°49'15" N, long. 120°39'45" W; near S line sec. 22, T 24 S, R 12 E). Named on San Miguel (1948), Stockdale Mountain (1948), and Valleton (1948) 7.5' quadrangles.

Portuguese Ridge [MONTEREY]: *ridge,* west- to southwest-trending, 2 miles long, 2 miles east-southeast of Soberanes Point (lat. 36°26'30" N, long. 121°53'20" W). Named on Soberanes Point (1956) 7.5' quadrangle.

Port Watsonville [SANTA CRUZ]: *locality,* 4.5 miles southwest of Watsonville along the coast (lat. 36°52'30" N, long. 121°49'30" W); the place is 2 miles north-northwest of the mouth of Pajaro River. Named on Capitola (1914) 15' quadrangle. Port Watsonville began in 1903 with construction of a wharf and other facilities; at first it was called Port Rogers—W.J. Rogers was one of the promoters of the enterprise (Lewis, 1976, p. 143). Beach property at the place later was offered for sale in a subdivision called Calpaco from letters in the name "California Pacific Company" (Lewis 1976, p. 148).

Posa Anchorage [SANTA BARBARA]: *anchorage,* 6.5 miles southeast of Fraser Point at the southwest end of Santa Cruz Island (lat. 33°58'45" N, long. 119°52'05" W); the anchorage is at the mouth of Cañada Posa. Named on Santa Cruz Island A (1943) 7.5' quadrangle. Called Poso Anchorage on Bremner's (1932) map.

Posa de los Ositos [MONTEREY]: *land grant,* south of Greenfield. Named on Greenfield (1956), Paraiso Springs (1956), and Thompson Canyon (1949) 7.5' quadrangles. Carlos Espinosa received 4 leagues in 1839 and claimed 16,939 acres patented in 1865 (Cowan, p. 63; Cowan listed the grant under the name "Poza de los Ositos"). California Mining Bureau's (1917b) map shows a place called Venezuela located about 4 miles southeast of Greenfield on the grant west of Salinas River.

Poso Anchorage: see **Posa Anchorage** [SANTA BARBARA].

Poso Ortega [SAN LUIS OBISPO]: *lake,* 300 feet long, 18 miles east-southeast of Shandon (lat. 35°31'15" N, long. 120°05'40" W; sec. 1, T 28 S, R 17 E). Named on Packwood Creek (1961) 7.5' quadrangle. Called Poso Ortega Lake on Packwood (1943) 7.5' quadrangle, and called Pozo Ortegta on Arnold and Johnson's (1910) map.

Poso Ortega Lake: see **Poso Ortega** [SAN LUIS OBISPO].

Post [SANTA BARBARA]: *locality,* 4.5 miles east-southeast of Surf along Southern Pacific Railroad (lat. 34°39'15" N, long. 120°32'05" W). Named on Surf (1959) 7.5' quadrangle.

Post Canyon [SAN BENITO]: *canyon,* drained by a stream that flows 1.25 miles to Byles Canyon 13 miles east of Bitterwater (lat. 36°23'20" N, long. 120°46'20" W; sec. 4, T 18 S, R 11 E). Named on Hernandez Reservoir (1969) 7.5' quadrangle.

Post Canyon [SAN LUIS OBISPO]: *canyon,* drained by a stream that flows 5 miles to Cuyama Valley 3.5 miles southwest of Caliente Mountain (lat. 35°00'30" N, long. 119°48'45" W; sec. 25, T 11 N, R 28 W). Named on Caliente Mountain (1959) 7.5' quadrangle.

Post Creek [MONTEREY]: *stream,* flows nearly 1.5 miles to Big Sur River 2.25 miles east-northeast of Pfeiffer Point (lat. 36°14'35" N, long. 121°46'25" W; at W line sec. 32, T 19 S, R 2 E). Named on Pfeiffer Point (1956) 7.5' quadrangle.

Posts [MONTEREY]: *locality,* 3 miles east-southeast of Pfeiffer Point (lat. 36°13'40" N, long. 121°45'45" W; sec. 5, T 20 S, R 2 E); the place is along Posts Creek. Named on Pfeiffer Point (1956) 7.5' quadrangle. William Brainard Post homesteaded in the neighborhood in the late 1860's and his ranch served as a stage station (Lussier, p. 24-25). Postal authorities established Posts post office in 1889, moved it 2 miles northwest in 1905, and discontinued it in 1910 (Salley, p. 177).

Post Summit [MONTEREY]: *peak,* 6 miles east of Point Sur (lat. 36° 17'20" N, long. 121°47'25" W; near SW cor. sec. 7, T 19 S, R 2 E). Altitude 3455 feet. Named on Big Sur (1956) 7.5' quadrangle.

Potato Bay: see **Potato Harbor** [SANTA BARBARA].

Potato Harbor [SANTA BARBARA]: *embayment,* 5.5 miles east-northeast of Prisoners Harbor on the north side of Santa Cruz Island (lat. 34°02'55" N, long. 119°35'30" W). Named on Santa Cruz Island C (1943) 7.5' quadrangle. Called Potato Bay on Bremner's (1932) map. Doran (p. 143, 150) noted that the place also was called Tyler Harbor.

Potrancas Creek: see **Anthony Creek** [MONTEREY].

Potrero Canyon [MONTEREY]: *canyon,* drained by a stream that flows 5.25 miles to Carmel River 3.5 miles east of the mouth of that river (lat. 36°32'10" N, long. 121°52'10" W); the canyon is on El Potrero de San Carlos grant. Named on Mount Carmel (1956) and Seaside (1947) 7.5' quadrangles. United States Board on Geographic Names (1977, p. 3) approved the name "Saddle Mountain" for a ridge that is between Potrero Canyon and Robinson Canyon (lat. 36°30'35" N, long. 121°49'30" W, at the east end). Milton Frumkin and his wife, Marie, owners of land on the side of the ridge, named the feature for its shape (Clark, 1991, p. 485).

Potrero Creek [SAN LUIS OBISPO]:

(1) *stream,* flows 1.5 miles to Lopez Canyon 2.25 miles east-southeast of Lopez Mountain (lat. 35°17'10" N, long. 120°32'35" W; sec. 26, T 30 S, R 13 E). Named on Lopez Mountain (1965) 7.5' quadrangle.

(2) *stream,* flows 2.5 miles to Arroyo Grande Creek 10.5 miles north-northeast of the town of Nipomo (lat. 35°11'25" N, long. 120°26' W). Named on Tar Spring Ridge (1967) 7.5' quadrangle.

Potrero de San Luis Obispo [SAN LUIS OBISPO]: *land grant,* 3 miles north of downtown San Luis Obispo. Named on San Luis Obispo (1965) 7.5' quadrangle. M. Concepcion Boronda received 1 league in 1842 and claimed 3506 acres patented in 1870 (Cowan, p. 84).

Potrero Peak [SAN BENITO]: *peak,* 14 miles east of Hollister on San Benito-Merced County line (lat. 36°51'25" N, long. 121°08'55" W; sec. 25, T 12 S, R 7 E). Altitude 3742 feet. Named on Quien Sabe Valley (1968) 7.5' quadrangle.

Potreros y Rincon de San Pedro de Reglado [SANTA CRUZ]: *land grant,* 2.5 miles north-northwest of Point Santa Cruz in Santa Cruz. Named on Santa Cruz (1954) 7.5' quadrangle. Jose Arana received the land in 1842; Thomas W. Russell claimed 92 acres patented in 1885 (Cowan, p. 87). According to Perez (p. 83), Nicolas Dordero was the patentee of 176.03 acres in 1861.

Powder Mill Flat: see **Paradise Park** [SANTA CRUZ].

Powder Mill Siding: see **Paradise Park** [SANTA CRUZ].

Powell Canyon [MONTEREY]: *canyon,* drained by a stream that flows 14 miles to Sargent Creek 7 miles north-northwest of Bradley (lat. 35°57'45" N, long. 120°50' W; near E line sec. 1, T 23 S, R 10 E). Named on Slack Canyon (1969), Valleton (1948), and Wunpost (1949) 7.5' quadrangles. Called Alexander Canyon on English and Kew's (1916) map. The name commemorates George S. Powell, an early settler in the canyon (Clark, 1991, p. 420).

Powell Canyon [SANTA BARBARA]: *canyon,* drained by a stream that flows 3.5 miles to Cuyama Valley 5.5 miles east of Miranda Pine Mountain (lat. 35°02'55" N, long. 119°56'15" W). Named on Taylor Canyon (1959) 7.5' quadrangle.

Powell Spring [MONTEREY]: *spring,* 13 miles east of San Ardo (lat. 36°01'10" N, long. 120°40'40" W; sec. 16, T 22 S, R 12 E); the spring is in Powell Canyon. Named on Slack Canyon (1969) 7.5' quadrangle.

Poza de los Ositos: see **Posa de los Ositos** [MONTEREY].

Pozo [SAN LUIS OBISPO]: *village,* 16 miles east of San Luis Obispo (lat. 35°18'15" N, long. 120°22'30" W; at N line sec. 21, T 30 S, R 15 E); the village is along Pozo Creek. Named on Pozo Summit (1967) and Santa Margarita Lake (1967) 7.5' quadrangles. Postal authorities established Pozo post office in 1878 and discontinued it in 1942 (Frickstad, p. 166). The place first was called San Jose—it lies in what was known as San Jose Valley (Angel, 1883, p. 364)—and then was called Garcia Valley for one of the early families there (Lee and others, p. 124). G.W. Lingo proposed the name "Pozo" for the post office because the village is in a holelike valley—*pozo* means "well" or "hole" in Spanish (Angel, 1883, p. 366).

Pozo Creek [SAN LUIS OBISPO]: *stream,* flows 7.5 miles to Salinas River 1 mile southwest of Pozo (lat. 35°17'45" N, long. 120°23'20" W; sec. 20, T 30 S, R 15 E). Named on Pozo Summit (1967) and Santa Margarita Lake (1967) 7.5' quadrangles. The part of the stream in present Fraser Canyon is called Sycamore Creek on Pozo (1922) 15' quadrangle, but United States Board on Geographic Names (1968b, p. 8) rejected this name for the feature.

Pozo Hondo Creek [MONTEREY]: *stream,* flows nearly 4 miles to Salmon Creek 9.5 miles south of Jolon (lat. 35°50'10" N, long. 121°12'15" W; sec. 22, T 24 S, R 7 E). Named on Burnett Peak (1949) and Burro Mountain (1949) 7.5' quadrangles.

Pozo Ortega: see **Poso Ortega** [SAN LUIS OBISPO].

Pozo Summit [SAN LUIS OBISPO]: *locality,* 5.5 miles east-northeast of Pozo (lat. 35°20'50" N, long. 120°17'40" W). Named on Pozo Summit (1967) 7.5' quadrangle.

Prader Creek: see **Gibson Creek** [MONTEREY].

Prefumo Canyon [SAN LUIS OBISPO]: *canyon,* drained by a stream that flows 3.5 miles to Los Osos Valley 2.5 miles west-southwest of San Luis Obispo (lat. 35°15'40" N, long. 120°42'10" W). Named on Morro Bay South (1965) and San Luis Obispo (1965) 7.5' quadrangles. Called Perfumo Canyon on Harder's (1910) map, but United States Board on Geographic Names (1964, p. 15) rejected this name for the feature.

Prefuno Creek [SAN LUIS OBISPO]: *stream,* flows 1.25 miles to San Luis Obispo Creek 3.5 miles south-southwest of downtown San Luis Obispo (lat. 35°14'40" N, long. 120°40'50" W). Named on Pismo Beach (1965) and San Luis Obispo (1965) 7.5' quadrangles.

Prescott: see **San Juan Bautista** [SAN BENITO].

Presidio de Santa Barbara Virgen y Martir: see **Santa Barbara** [SANTA BARBARA].

Presidio of Monterey [MONTEREY]: *military installation,* adjacent to the city of Monterey (lat. 35°36'20" N, long. 121°54'30" W). Named on Monterey (1947) 7.5' quadrangle. Postal authorities established Presidio of Monterey post office in 1915 (Frickstad, p. 108). Portola founded Presidio of San Carlos Borromeo de Monterey at present Monterey in 1770, and in 1822 the Mexicans built a fort about 1 mile northwest of the original presidio; after American occupation of Monterey in 1846, Colonel Richard B. Mason had a redoubt built in 1847 about 700 feet up the hill above the Mexican installation (Frazer, p. 27). The redoubt was christened Fort Stockton to honor Commodore Stockton, but the commodore ordered that it be known as Fort Mervine (*Californian,* October 3, 1846). Finally, the installation was named Fort Halleck for Lieutenant H.W. Halleck, who laid it out (Hoover, Rensch, and Rensch, p. 218). The cantonment at the place was named Ord Barracks in 1903, and this name was changed to Presidio of Monterey in 1904 (Whiting and Whiting, p. 52).

Pretty Flat [SAN BENITO]: *area,* 17 miles southeast of Bitterwater (lat. 36°14'15" N, long. 120°44'50" W; near E line sec. 34, T 19 S, R 11 E). Named on Priest Valley (1969) 7.5' quadrangle.

Prewitt Creek [MONTEREY]: *stream,* flows 3.5 miles to the sea 3.25 miles north of Cape San Martin (lat. 35°56'05" N, long. 121° 28'30" W; sec. 18, T 23 S, R 5 E). Named on Cape San Martin (1949) 7.5' quadrangle. The name recalls Jim Prewitt, who had a cabin by the stream (Clark, 1991, p. 421). South Fork enters 1.25 miles upstream from the mouth of the creek; it is 2 miles long and is named on Cape San Martin (1949) 7.5' quadrangle.

Price Canyon [SAN LUIS OBISPO]: *canyon,* nearly 4 miles long, opens into lowlands along the coast at Pismo Beach (lat. 35°08'25" N, long. 120°38' W). Named on Arroyo Grande NE (1965) and Pismo Beach (1965) 7.5' quadrangles. Pismo Creek drains the canyon.

Priest Canyon [SAN LUIS OBISPO]: *canyon,* drained by a stream that flows 3.25 miles to Cuyama Valley 4 miles northwest of New Cuyama [SANTA BARBARA] (lat. 34°58'45" N, long. 119°44'25" W; sec. 2, T 10 N, R 27 W). Named on New Cuyama (1964) 7.5' quadrangle.

Priest's Ford: see **Ben Lomond** [SANTA CRUZ].

Priest Spring [SAN LUIS OBISPO]: *spring,* 4.5 miles northwest of New Cuyama [SANTA BARBARA] (lat. 34°59'40" N, long. 119°44'25" W; sec. 34, T 11 N, R 27 W); the spring is in Priest Canyon. Named on New Cuyama (1964) 7.5' quadrangle.

Priest Valley [MONTEREY]: *locality,* 3 miles north of Charley Mountain in Priest Valley [MONTEREY-SAN BENITO] (lat. 36°10'25" N, long. 120°40'20" W; sec. 21, T 20 S, R 12 E). Named on Priest Valley (1915) 30' quadrangle. Postal authorities established Priest Valley post office in 1882, moved it 1.5 miles east in 1897, discontinued it in 1909, reestablished it in 1910, and discontinued it in 1934 (Salley, p. 178).

Priest Valley [MONTEREY-SAN BENITO]: *valley,* 19 miles east-northeast of San Lucas on Monterey-San Benito County line, mainly in Monterey County (lat. 36°11'15" N, long. 120°41'45" W). Named on Priest Valley (1969) 7.5' quadrangle. Dillon (1966, p. 162) related a story about the name originating when some Americans found a padre and a hundred mission Indians rounding up wild horses in the valley; Dillon also noted that the place was known as Joaquin's Valley, for Joaquin Murieta, the Mexican outlaw.

Priest Valley Creek: see **Lewis Creek** [MONTEREY-SAN BENITO].

Prieta Point: see **Black Point** [SANTA CRUZ].

Prieto Canyon: see **Palo Prieto Canyon** [SAN LUIS OBISPO].

Primetal Cañon: see **Pimental Creek** [SAN BENITO].

Prince Island [SANTA BARBARA]: *island,* 2000 feet long, 3.25 miles northwest of Cardwell Point and 0.5 mile offshore on the north side of San Miguel Island (lat. 34°03'30" N, long. 120° 20' W). Named on San Miguel Island East (1950) 7.5' quadrangle. Called Princess Island on Bremner's (1933) map.

Princes Camp [MONTEREY]: *locality,* nearly 7 miles southeast of the town of Carmel Valley along Carmel River (lat. 36°24'05" N, long. 121°39'30" W; sec. 4, T 18 S, R 3 E). Named on Carmel Valley (1956) 7.5' quadrangle.

Princess Island: see **Prince Island** [SANTA BARBARA].

Prisoners Harbor [SANTA BARBARA]: *embayment,* 9 miles west of San Pedro Point on the north side of Santa Cruz Island (lat. 34° 01'15" N, long. 119°41' W). Named on Santa Cruz Island C (1943) 7.5' quadrangle. The name recalls the arrival at the place in 1830 of thirty convicts exiled from Mexico (Hanna, p. 244). Bremner's (1932) map has the name "Cn. del Puerto" for the canyon that opens to the sea at Prisoners Harbor.

Profile Point [SANTA BARBARA]: *promontory,* 4 miles east-northeast of Fraser Point on the north side of Santa Cruz Island (lat. 34° 04'15" N, long. 119°51'40" W). Named on Santa Cruz Island A (1943) 7.5' quadrangle.

Prunedale [MONTEREY]: *town,* 8 miles north of Salinas (lat. 36°46'45" N, long. 121°40'15" W). Named on Prunedale (1954) 7.5' quadrangle. Postal authorities established Prunedale post office in 1894, discontinued it in 1908, and reestablished it in 1953 (Salley, p. 178).

Puerta del Diablo [MONTEREY]: *peak,* nearly 2 miles east-southeast of Soberanes Point (lat. 36°26'15" N, long. 121°53'55" W; sec. 19, T 17 S, R 1 E). Altitude 1833 feet. Named on Soberanes Point (1956) 7.5' quadrangle. United States Board on Geographic Names (1960a, p. 16) rejected the name "Oliviers Mountain" for the feature.

Puerto de la Cañada del Sur: see **Valley Anchorage** [SANTA BARBARA].

Puerto de Monterey: see **Monterey Bay** [MONTEREY].

Puerto de San Lucas: see **Morro Bay** [SAN LUIS OBISPO] (2).

Puerto de Todos Santos: see **Cojo Bay** [SANTA BARBARA].

Puerto Suello Creek [MONTEREY]: *stream,* flows 2.25 miles to Little Sur River 2.5 miles west-southwest of Uncle Sam Mountain (lat. 36°19'45" N, long. 121°44'40" W). Named on Ventana Cones (1956) 7.5' quadrangle.

Punta Arena [SANTA BARBARA]: *promontory,* 7.5 miles south-southwest of Diablo Point on the south side of Santa Cruz Island (lat. 33°57'35" N, long. 119°49' W). Named on Santa Cruz Island B (1943) 7.5' quadrangle.

Punta Concepcion: see **Point Conception** [SANTA BARBARA].

Punta de Carmel: see **Point Lobos** [MONTEREY].

Punta de Echevarria: see **Government Point** [SANTA BARBARA].

Punta de la Concepcion [SANTA BARBARA]: *land grant,* at Point Conception. Named on Lompoc Hills (1959), Point Arguello (1959), Point Conception (1953), and Tranquillon Mountain (1959) 7.5' quadrangles. Anastacio Carrillo received 6 leagues in 1837 and claimed 24,992 acres patented in 1880 (Cowan, p. 29). According to Perez (p. 85), the patent was dated 1863.

Punta de la Laguna [SAN LUIS OBISPO-SANTA BARBARA]: *land grant,* west and southwest of Santa Maria; almost entirely in Santa Barbara County, but a small part extends across Santa Maria River into San Luis Obispo County. Named on Casmalia (1959), Guadalupe (1959), Orcutt (1959), and Santa Maria (1959) 7.5' quadrangles. Luis Arellanes and Emilio

Miguel Ortega received 6 leagues in 1844 and claimed 26,648 acres patented in 1873 (Cowan, p. 44).

Punta de la Limpia Concepcion: see **Point Conception** [SANTA BARBARA].

Punta del Carmelo: see **Pinnacle Point** [MONTEREY].

Punta del Castillo: see **Point Castillo** [SANTA BARBARA].

Punta del Estero: see **Point Estero** [SAN LUIS OBISPO].

Punta de Lobos: see **Point Lobos** [MONTEREY]; **Point Santa Cruz** [SANTA CRUZ].

Punta de los Cipreses: see **Cypress Point** [MONTEREY].

Punta de los Lobos Marinos: see **Point Lobos** [MONTEREY].

Punta de los Pinos: see **Point Pinos** [MONTEREY].

Punta de Nuestra Señora de Los Angeles: see **Sand Point** [SANTA BARBARA].

Punta de Pantoja: see **Goleta Point** [SANTA BARBARA].

Punta de Pinos [MONTEREY]: *land grant*, south-southwest of Point Pinos on the coast. Named on Monterey (1947) 7.5' quadrangle. Jose M. Armenta and Jose Abrego received 2 leagues in 1833 and 1834; H. DeGraw and others claimed 2667 acres patented in 1880 (Cowan, p. 61). According to Perez (p. 84), Jose Abrego was the grantee in 1844.

Punta de Sanchez: see **Cojo Bay** [SANTA BARBARA].

Punta de San Esteban: see **Point Castillo** [SANTA BARBARA].

Punta de Santa Marta: see **Purisima Point** [SANTA BARBARA].

Punta de Tobar: see **Coal Oil Point** [SANTA BARBARA].

Punta de Villaverde: see **Government Point** [SANTA BARBARA].

Punta Diablo: see **Diablo Point** [SANTA BARBARA].

Punta Gorda: see **Cape San Martin** [MONTEREY].

Punta Negra: see **Black Point** [SANTA BARBARA].

Punta Pedernales: see **Point Arguello** [SANTA BARBARA].

Punta Purisima: see **Purisima Point** [SANTA BARBARA].

Punta que Parece Isla: see **Point Sur** [MONTEREY].

Punta Saint Luis: see **Point San Luis** [SAN LUIS OBISPO].

Punto del Esteros: see **Point Estero** [SAN LUIS OBISPO].

Purd Camp [MONTEREY]: *locality*, 6.5 miles southwest of Soledad (lat. 36°21'10" N, long. 121°23'50" W; sec. 23, T 18 S, R 5 E). Named on Sycamore Flat (1956) 7.5' quadrangle.

Purisima Canyon [SANTA BARBARA]: *canyon*, drained by a stream that flows 5.5 miles to lowlands 3 miles northeast of the city of Lompoc at La Purisima mission (lat. 34°40'10" N, long. 120°25'15" W). Named on Lompoc (1959) 7.5' quadrangle.

Purisima Hills [SANTA BARBARA]: *range*, extends from north of the city of Lompoc to Solvang. Named on Casmalia (1959), Lompoc (1959), Los Alamos (1959), Los Olivos (1959), Orcutt (1959), Sisquoc (1959), Solvang (1959), and Zaca Creek (1959) 7.5' quadrangles.

Purisima Point [SANTA BARBARA]: *promontory*, 8 miles southwest of the village of Casmalia along the coast (lat. 34°45'20" N, long. 120°38'10" W). Named on Casmalia (1959) 7.5' quadrangle. Called Pta. Purisima on Parke's (1854-1855) map. The Spaniards called the feature Punta de Santa Marta (Wagner, H.R., p. 512). It was known in the 1850's as Point Pedernales, a name now applied to a point located 10 miles farther south (Gudde, 1949, p. 257).

Purisima River: see **Santa Ynez River** [SANTA BARBARA].

Pyojo: see **El Piojo** [MONTEREY].

Pyramid Point: see **Pinnacle Point** [MONTEREY]; **Point Joe** [MONTEREY].

- Q -

Quail Canyon [SAN LUIS OBISPO]: *canyon*, drained by a stream that flows 3.25 miles to Cuyama Valley 3.5 miles east-northeast of Cuyama [SANTA BARBARA] (lat. 34°57'20" N, long. 119°33'30" W; sec. 16, T 10 N, R 25 W). Named on Cuyama (1964) 7.5' quadrangle.

Quail Creek [MONTEREY]: *stream*, flows 5 miles to lowlands 8.5 miles north-northwest of Gonzales (lat. 36°37'30" N, long. 121°29'25" W). Named on Chualar (1947), Gonzales (1955), and Mount Harlan (1968) 7.5' quadrangles.

Quail Flat [SAN LUIS OBISPO]: *area*, 8 miles south-southwest of Atascadero (lat. 35°23'05" N, long. 120°44'05" W; near SW cor. sec. 19, T 29 S, R 12 E). Named on Atascadero (1965) 7.5' quadrangle.

Quail Knob: see **Quail Top** [MONTEREY].

Quail Spring [SAN LUIS OBISPO]: *spring*, 4.5 miles south-southwest of Branch Mountain in Brown Canyon (lat. 35°07'20" N, long. 120°06' W). Named on Miranda Pine Mountain (1967) 7.5' quadrangle.

Quail Spring Reservoir [SAN LUIS OBISPO]: *lake*, 75 feet long, 5 miles northeast of Cuyama [SANTA BARBARA] (lat. 34°59'25" N, long. 119°33'15" W; near S line sec. 33, T 11 N, R 25 W); the lake is in Quail Canyon. Named on Cuyama (1964) 7.5' quadrangle.

Quail Top [MONTEREY]: *peak*, 6.5 miles southeast of Jolon on the south side of San Antonio River (lat. 35°53'25" N, long. 121°06'45" W; sec. 33, T 23 S, R 8 E). Altitude 1146 feet. Named on Williams Hill (1949) 7.5' quadrangle. Howard (p. 85) referred to Quail Knob.

Quail Water Creek [SAN LUIS OBISPO]: *stream*, flows 7.25 miles to Indian Creek (2) 9.5 miles south of Shandon (lat. 35°31'20" N, long. 120°23'55" W; sec. 6, T 28 S, R 15 E). Named on Shedd Canyon (1961) and Wilson Corner (1966) 7.5' quadrangles. Anderson and Martin's (1914) map has the form "Quailwater Creek" for the name.

Quarry Lake [SAN BENITO]: *lake*, 400 feet long, nearly 1.5 miles northeast of Aromas (lat. 36°54'10" N, long. 121°37'30" W). Named on Chittenden (1955) and Watsonville East (1955) 7.5' quadrangles.

Quartel: see **Quatal**, under **Santa Barbara Canyon** [SANTA BARBARA].

Quatal: see **Santa Barbara Canyon** [SANTA BARBARA].

Quatal Canyon [SANTA BARBARA]: *canyon*, mainly in Ventura County, but opens into Cuyama Valley at Santa Barbara-Ventura County line 11 miles southeast of the village of Cuyama (lat. 34° 49' N, long. 119°26'30" W; near S line sec. 33, T 9 N, R 24 W). Named on Cuyama Peak (1943) 7.5' quadrangle.

Queen Bee Campground [SAN LUIS OBISPO]: *locality*, nearly 4 miles north-northwest of Castle Crags (lat. 35°21'05" N, long. 120° 14'25" W). Named on La Panza (1967) 7.5' quadrangle. Queen Bee mine was near the place (Franke, p. 421).

Queen Canyon [SAN BENITO]: *canyon*, drained by a stream that flows 0.5 mile to San Juan Canyon 3.25 miles south-southeast of San Juan Bautista (lat. 36°48'15" N, long. 121°30'15" W). Named on San Juan Bautista (1955) 7.5' quadrangle. United States Board on Geographic Names (1994, p. 5) approved the name "Quinn Canyon" for the feature.

Quesada Spring [MONTEREY]: *spring*, 22 miles east of San Ardo (lat. 36°00'25" N, long. 120°29'55" W; sec. 19, T 22 S, R 14 E). Named on Curry Mountain (1969) 7.5' quadrangle.

Quien Sabe: see **Santa Ana y Quien Sabe** [SAN BENITO].

Quien Sabe Creek [SAN BENITO]: *stream*, flows 14 miles to Los Muertos Creek 3 miles north of Cherry Peak (lat. 36°44'10" N, long. 121°08'50" W; near NE cor. sec. 12, T 14 S, R 7 E); the stream drains Quien Sabe Valley. Named on Cherry Peak (1968), Mariposa Peak (1969), and Quien Sabe Valley (1968) 7.5' quadrangles.

Quien Sabe Valley [SAN BENITO]: *valley*, 11 miles east of Hollister (lat. 36°50' N, long. 121°11'30" W); the valley is on Santa Ana y Quien Sabe grant. Named on Mariposa Peak (1969) and Quien Sabe Valley (1968) 7.5' quadrangles.

Quien Sabe Valley: see **Little Quien Sabe Valley** [SAN BENITO].

Quinado Canyon]MONTEREY]: *canyon*, nearly 7 miles long, opens into lowlands 3 miles south of King City (lat. 36°10'15" N, long. 121°07'40" W). Named on Cosio Knob (1949), Espinosa Canyon (1949), and Thompson Canyon (1949) 7.5' quadrangles. According to Gudde (1949, p. 277), the name is a Spanish version of an Indian word for "evil smelling," and refers to the odor of sulphur springs. On some earlier maps the feature was called Kent Canyon for John Tupper Kent, who patented land at the head of the canyon in 1884 (Clark, 1991, p. 429-431). United States Board on Geographic Names (1936a, p. 21) rejected the name Kent Canyon for the feature.

Quinn Canyon: see **Queen Canyon** [SAN BENITO].

Quiota Creek [SANTA BARBARA]: *stream*, flows 6.5 miles to Santa Ynez River 2.5 miles southwest of Santa Ynez (lat. 34°34'50" N, long. 120°06'35" W). Named on Santa Ynez (1959) 7.5' quadrangle. Called Ballard Creek on Lompoc (1905) 30' quadrangle, but United States Board on Geographic Names (1961b, p. 14) rejected the names "Ballard Creek" and "Refugio Creek" for the stream.

- R -

Rabbit Valley [SAN BENITO]: *valley*, 3 miles north of Bitterwater (lat. 36°25'15" N, long. 121°00'30" W). Named on Rock Spring Peak (1969) and Topo Valley (1969) 7.5' quadrangles. United States Board on Geographic Names (1972b, p. 4) gave the name "Little Rabbit Valley" as a variant.

Rabbit Valley: see **Little Rabbit Valley** [SAN BENITO].

Rafael Creek [SAN LUIS OBISPO]: *stream*, flows 5 miles to the canyon of San Juan Creek 4.5 miles north of Branch Mountain (lat. 35°15'05" N, long. 120°04'20" W; sec. 5, T 31 S, R 18 E). Named on Branch Mountain (1967) 7.5' quadrangle.

Ragged Point [SAN LUIS OBISPO]: *promontory*, nearly 0.5 mile south-southeast of the mouth of San Carpoforo Creek along the coast (lat. 35°45'35" N, long. 121°19'35" W). Named on Burro Mountain (1949) 7.5' quadrangle.

Railpen Canyon [SAN LUIS OBISPO]: *canyon*, drained by a stream that flows 2.5 miles to Twitchell Reservoir 2 miles northeast of Huasna Peak (lat. 35°03'35" N, long. 120°19'25" W). Named on Huasna Peak (1967) 7.5' quadrangle.

Railroad Spring: see **Chittenden's Sulphur Springs**, under **Chittenden** [SANTA CRUZ].

Rainbow Camp [MONTEREY]: *locality*, 7 miles north of Slates Hot Springs (lat. 36°13'20" N, long. 121°39'15" W; sec. 5, T 20 S, R 3 E). Named on Partington Ridge (1956) 7.5' quadrangle.

Rainbow Canyon [SANTA BARBARA]: *canyon,* drained by a stream that flows 1.25 miles to Santa Barbara Canyon 3 miles east-northeast of Fox Mountain (lat. 34°49'45" N, long. 119°33'05" W). Named on Fox Mountain (1964) 7.5' quadrangle.

Rainbow Lodge: see **Big Sur** [MONTEREY].

Rambo Spring [MONTEREY]: *spring,* 15 miles east-northeast of San Ardo in Slack Canyon (lat. 36°04'25" N, long. 120°38'55" W; sec. 26, T 21 S, R 12 E). Named on Slack Canyon (1969) 7.5' quadrangle.

Ramrod Canyon [SANTA BARBARA]: *canyon,* drained by a stream that flows 1 mile to South Fork La Brea Creek nearly 2 miles west-northwest of Manzanita Mountain (lat. 34°54' N, long. 120° 06'30" W). Named on Manzanita Mountain (1964) 7.5' quadrangle.

Ramsey Gulch [SANTA CRUZ]: *canyon,* drained by a stream that flows 2.25 miles to Browns Creek 3 miles north-northeast of Corralitos (lat. 37°01'35" N, long. 121°46'35" W; near N line sec. 32, T 10 S, R 2 E). Named on Loma Prieta (1955) 7.5' quadrangle.

Rana Creek [MONTEREY]: *stream,* flows 6.25 miles to Tularcitos Creek 6.5 miles east-southeast of the town of Carmel Valley (lat. 36°26'10" N, long. 121°37'50" W). Named on Carmel Valley (1956) and Rana Creek (1956) 7.5' quadrangles.

Ranchero Rock: see **Banchero Rock** [MONTEREY].

Ranchita: see **Arroyo Grande** [SAN LUIS OBISPO] (1).

Ranchita Canyon: see **Ranchito Canyon** [MONTEREY-SAN LUIS OBISPO].

Ranchita de Santa Fe [SAN LUIS OBISPO]: *land grant,* 3.25 miles south-southwest of downtown San Luis Obispo along San Luis Obispo Creek. Named on Pismo Beach (1965) 7.5' quadrangle. Vicente Linares received 1000 varas in 1842 and claimed 166 acres patented in 1866 (Cowan, p. 92)

Ranchita Valley: see **Ranchito Canyon** [MONTEREY-SAN LUIS OBISPO].

Ranchito Canyon [MONTEREY-SAN LUIS OBISPO]: *canyon,* drained by a stream that heads in Monterey County and flows 32 miles to Estrella Creek 4.25 miles southeast of San Miguel in San Luis Obispo County (lat. 35°42'55" N, long. 120°38'10" W; sec. 36, T 25 S, R 12 E). Named on Estrella (1948), Paso Robles (1948), Ranchito Canyon (1948) and Stockdale Mountain (1948) 7.5' quadrangles. Called Ranchita Canyon on English and Kew's (1916) map. Stanley (map on p. 18) called the feature Ranchita Valley.

Rancho del Mar: see **Aptos** [SANTA CRUZ] (2).

Rancho Nacional: see **San Julian** [SANTA BARBARA].

Rancho Nuevo Creek [SANTA BARBARA]: *stream,* flows 9 miles to Ventura County 20 miles south-southeast of the village of Cuyama (lat. 34°41'30" N, long. 119°26'35" W). Named on Madulce Peak (1964) and Rancho Nuevo Creek (1943) 7.5' quadrangles. The upper part of present Rancho Nuevo Creek is called Bear Creek on Santa Ynez (1905) 30' quadrangle, but United States Board on Geographic Names (1950, p. 1) rejected this name for the stream.

Ranger Canyon [SAN LUIS OBISPO]: *canyon,* drained by a stream that flows 3 miles to Arroyo Seco 12.5 miles northeast of the town of Nipomo (lat. 35°10' N, long. 120°19'05" W; sec. 1, T 32 S, R 15 E). Named on Caldwell Mesa (1967) 7.5' quadrangle.

Ranger Peak [SANTA BARBARA]: *peak,* 2.5 miles southeast of Figueroa Mountain (lat. 34°43'15" N, long. 119°56'55" W; at NE cor. sec. 5, T 7 N, R 29 W). Named on Figueroa Mountain (1959) 7.5' quadrangle.

Rapetti: see **Santa Cruz** [SANTA CRUZ].

Rat Creek [MONTEREY]: *stream,* flows 1.5 miles to the sea nearly 6 miles north-northwest of Lopez Point (lat. 36°05'30" N, long. 121°37'10" W; sec. 22, T 21 S, R 3 E). Named on Lopez Point (1956) 7.5' quadrangle.

Rat Hill [MONTEREY]: *hill,* 1 mile southeast of Point Lobos (lat. 36° 30'50" N, long. 121°56'15" W). Named on Monterey (1947) 7.5' quadrangle.

Rattlesnake Canyon [SAN LUIS OBISPO]: *canyon,* drained by a stream that flows 1.5 miles to the sea 1.5 miles northwest of Point San Luis (lat. 35°10'25" N, long. 120°46'55" W). Named on Port San Luis (1965) 7.5' quadrangle.

Rattlesnake Canyon [SANTA BARBARA]:

(1) *canyon,* drained by a stream that flows 3 miles to Sisquoc River 4.5 miles northwest of Big Pine Mountain (lat. 34°44'45" N, long. 119°42'15" W). Named on Big Pine Mountain (1964) 7.5' quadrangle.

(2) *canyon,* drained by a stream that flows 4 miles to South Fork La Brea Creek 1.25 miles north of Manzanita Mountain (lat. 34°54'35" N, long. 120°04'35" W). Named on Manzanita Mountain (1964) 7.5' quadrangle.

(3) *canyon,* drained by a stream that flows 3.5 miles to Sisquoc River 5.25 mile north-northwest of Zaca Lake (lat. 34°50'35" N, long. 120°05'15" W). Named on Manzanita Mountain (1964) and Zaca Lake (1964) 7.5' quadrangles.

(4) *canyon,* drained by a stream that flows 1.5 miles to North Fork La Brea Creek 2.25 miles east of Tepusquet Peak (lat. 34°54'50" N, long. 120°08'40" W). Named on Tepusquet Canyon (1964) 7.5' quadrangle.

(5) *canyon,* drained by a stream that flows 3.5 miles to Mission Creek 2 miles north-northwest of downtown Santa Barbara (lat. 34°26'50" N, long. 119°42'30" W). Named on Santa Barbara (1952) 7.5' quadrangle.

Rattlesnake Canyon: see **Long Canyon** [SANTA BARBARA] (3).

Rattlesnake Creek [MONTEREY]:

(1) *stream,* flows 3 miles to Danish Creek nearly 3 miles north-northeast of Uncle Sam Mountain (lat. 36°22'35" N, long. 121°41'05" W; sec. 7, T 18 S, R 3 E). Named on Ventana Cones (1956) 7.5' quadrangle.

(2) *stream,* flows 4 miles to North Fork San Antonio River 5 miles south-southeast of Junipero Serra Peak (lat. 36°04'25" N, long. 121°23'50" W; sec. 26, T 21 S, R 5 E). Named on Cone Peak (1949) 7.5' quadrangle. United States Board on Geographic Names (1981a, p. 4) approved the name "Wagon Caves" for caves and bold outcrops of rock located along North Fork San Antonio River nearly 1 mile north-northwest of the mouth of Rattlesnake Creek (2) (lat. 36°04'55" N, long. 121°24'07" W); the name is from use of the shelter by pioneers in winter.

Rattlesnake Gulch [SAN BENITO]:

(1) *canyon,* drained by a stream that flows 1.5 miles to San Benito River 7 miles east of Bitterwater (lat. 36°23'40" N, long. 120° 52'40" W; sec. 3, T 18 S, R 10 E). Named on Rock Spring Peak (1969) 7.5' quadrangle.

(2) *canyon,* drained by a stream that flows 0.5 mile to Oat Canyon 14 miles east-southeast of Bitterwater (lat. 36°17'25" N, long. 120° 46'05" W; sec. 9, T 19 S, R 11 E). Named on Hepsedam Peak (1969) 7.5' quadrangle.

Rattlesnake Gulch [SANTA CRUZ]: *canyon,* drained by a stream that flows 1.5 miles to Grizzly Flat nearly 4 miles north of Corralitos (lat. 37°02'40" N, long. 121°47'35" W; sec. 19, T 10 S, R 2 E). Named on Loma Prieta (1955) 7.5' quadrangle.

Rattlesnake Spring [SANTA BARBARA]: *spring,* 1.5 miles south-southwest of Salisbury Potrero (lat. 34°48'05" N, long. 119°42'45" W). Named on Salisbury Potrero (1964) 7.5' quadrangle.

Ready: see **Aptos Creek** [SANTA CRUZ].

Real de las Aguilas [SAN BENITO]: *land grant,* 20 miles east-southeast of Hollister. Named on Cerro Colorado (1969), Cherry Peak (1968), Panoche Pass (1968), Quien Sabe Valley (1968), and Ruby Canyon (1968) 7.5' quadrangles. Francisco Arias and Saturnino Cariaga received 7 leagues in 1844; F.A. McDougal and others claimed 31,052 acres patented in 1869 (Cowan, p. 67).

Reason Mountain [MONTEREY]: *peak,* 23 miles east of San Ardo (lat. 36°00'20" N, long. 120°29'25" W; sec. 20, T 22 S, R 14 E). Altitude 3753 feet. Named on Curry Mountain (1969) 7.5' quadrangle. The name is for George Reasons, a local rancher (Clark, 1991, p. 471).

Rector Creek: see **Cottonwood Creek** [MONTEREY].

Red Corral Spring [SAN BENITO]: *spring,* 9 miles east-northeast of Bitterwater along McCoy Creek (lat. 36°26'25" N, long. 120°51'35" W; near NW cor. sec. 23, T 17 S, R 10 E). Named on Hernandez Reservoir (1969) 7.5' quadrangle, which has the name "Red Corral" at the site.

Redfield Woods: see **Cuesta-by-the Sea** [SAN LUIS OBISPO].

Redhead Canyon [MONTEREY]: *canyon,* 3.25 miles long, opens into lowlands 2 miles north of San Ardo (lat. 36°02'55" N, long. 120° 54'40" W; sec. 5, T 22 S, R 10 E). Named on Pancho Rico Valley (1967) and San Ardo (1967) 7.5' quadrangles. Called Dutch Henry Canyon on San Ardo (1956) 15' quadrangle, and called Redwood Canyon on Priest Valley (1915) 30' quadrangle.

Redhead Canyon: see **Portugee Canyon** [MONTEREY].

Red Hill [MONTEREY]: *peak,* 4 miles east-northeast of Jamesburg (lat. 36°23'40" N, long. 121°32'50" W; sec. 4, T 18 S, R 4 E). Named on Rana Creek (1956) 7.5' quadrangle. The name is from red rocks on the peak (Clark, 1991, p. 471).

Red Hills [SAN LUIS OBISPO]: *ridge,* north- to north-northeast-trending, 3 miles long, 8 miles east-southeast of Shandon (lat. 35° 36' N, long. 120°15' W). Named on Camatta Canyon (1961) and Holland Canyon (1961) 7.5' quadrangles.

Red Mountain [SAN BENITO]: *ridge,* north-trending, 1 mile long, 7.5 miles east-northeast of Bitterwater (lat. 36°24'45" N, long. 120°52'20" W; sec. 27, 34, T 17 S, R 10 E). Named on Hernandez Reservoir (1969) 7.5' quadrangle.

Red Mountain [SAN LUIS OBISPO]: *peak,* 6.5 miles east of the village of San Simeon (lat. 35°38'35" N, long. 121°04'25" W; sec. 26, T 26 S, R 8 E). Altitude 2047 feet. Named on Pebblestone Shut-in (1959) 7.5' quadrangle.

Red Mountain Creek [SAN BENITO]: *stream,* flows almost 2 miles to Mine Creek nearly 6 miles east-northeast of Bitterwater (lat. 36°25'10" N, long. 120°54'35" W; sec. 29, T 17 S, R 10 E); the stream heads west of Red Mountain. Named on Rock Spring Peak (1969) 7.5' quadrangle.

Red Mountain Spring [SAN BENITO]: *spring,* 6.5 miles east-northeast of Bitterwater (lat. 36°25'10" N, long. 120°53'45" W; near W line sec. 28, T 17 S, R 10 E); the spring is east of Red Mountain along Red Mountain Creek. Named on Rock Spring Peak (1969) 7.5' quadrangle.

Red Rock [SAN LUIS OBISPO]: *peak,* nearly 4 miles northeast of the village of San Simeon (lat. 35°41'10" N, long. 121°08'40" W). Altitude 1653 feet. Named on San Simeon (1958) 7.5' quadrangle.

Red Rock Campground [SANTA BARBARA]: *locality,* 4.25 miles south-

southeast of Little Pine Mountain along Santa Ynez River (lat. 34°32'25" N, long. 119°43'10" W; sec. 4, T 5 N, R 27 W). Named on Little Pine Mountain (1964) 7.5' quadrangle.

Red Rock Canyon [MONTEREY]: *canyon,* drained by a stream that heads in Monterey County and flows 5 miles to Cholame Valley 9.5 miles north-northeast of Shandon in San Luis Obispo County (lat. 35°45'55" N, long. 120°16'40" W). Named on Cholame Valley (1961) and Tent Hills (1942) 7.5' quadrangles. Cholame Ranch (1943) 7.5' quadrangle has the form "Redrock Canyon" for the name.

Red Rock Canyon [SAN LUIS OBISPO]: *canyon,* drained by a stream that flows 4.25 miles to Taylor Canyon 11 miles west-northwest of Caliente Mountain (lat. 35°04'20" N, long. 119°56'40" W). Named on Taylor Canyon (1959) 7.5' quadrangle. McKittrick (1912) 30' quadrangle has the form "Redrock Canyon" for the name.

Redrock Canyon [SANTA BARBARA]: *canyon,* drained by a stream that flows nearly 6 miles to Santa Ynez River 2.5 miles north of San Marcos Pass (lat. 34°32'55" N, long. 119°49'15" W). Named on San Marcos Pass (1959) 7.5' quadrangle. An outcrop of banded jasper 300 feet high, known as the Red Rock, is at the head of the canyon (Fairbanks, 1894, p. 504).

Redrock Mountain [SANTA BARBARA]: *peak,* 3.5 miles south of the town of Los Alamos (lat. 34°41'30" N, long. 120°16' W). Altitude 1984 feet. Named on Los Alamos (1959) 7.5' quadrangle. California Mining Bureau's (1917c) map has the form "Red Rock Mt." for the name. Combustion of hydrocarbons in normally white shale has altered the color of rocks at the peak to a brilliant rose or brick red (Arnold and Anderson, 1907b, p. 750, 753).

Red Roof Canyon [SANTA BARBARA]: *canyon,* 2 miles long, opens into Grey Canyon 1.5 miles northeast of Point Arguello (lat. 34°35'35" N, long. 120°38'10" W). Named on Point Arguello (1959) and Tranquillon Mountain (1959) 7.5' quadrangles.

Redwood Camp [SANTA CRUZ]: *locality,* 3.5 miles north of the town of Boulder Creek along Kings Creek (lat. 37°10'30" N, long. 122°07'05" W; sec. 6, T 9 S, R 2 W). Named on Castle Rock Ridge (1955) 7.5' quadrangle.

Redwood Canyon [SANTA CRUZ]: *canyon,* drained by a stream that flows 1.5 miles to Browns Creek 3 miles north-northeast of Corralitos (lat. 37°01'35" N, long. 121°46'50" W; near N line sec. 32, T 10 S, R 2 E). Named on Loma Prieta (1955) 7.5' quadrangle.

Redwood Canyon: see **Limekiln Creek** [MONTEREY] (2); **Redhead Canyon** [MONTEREY].

Redwood Creek [MONTEREY]: *stream,* flow 2.5 mile to North Fork Big Sur River 5 miles north-northeast of Partington Point (lat. 36° 14'50" N, long. 121°40'30" W; sec. 30, T 19 S, R 3 E). Named on Partington Ridge (1956) and Ventana Cones (1956) 7.5' quadrangles.

Redwood Creek: see **Gibson Creek** [MONTEREY]; **San Clemente Creek** [MONTEREY].

Redwood Creek Camp [MONTEREY]: *locality,* 2 miles south-southeast of Ventana Cone (lat. 36°15'20" N, long. 121°40'05" W; near W line sec. 29, T 19 S, R 3 E); the place is along Redwood Creek. Named on Ventana Cones (1956) 7.5' quadrangle.

Redwood Glen Camp [SANTA CRUZ]: *locality,* 7 miles east-southeast of the town of Boulder Creek along Bean Creek (lat. 37°04'50" N, long. 122°00'25" W; sec. 7, T 10 S, R 1 W). Named on Felton (1955) 7.5' quadrangle.

Redwood Grove [SANTA CRUZ]: *settlement,* 5 miles east-southeast of Big Basin near San Lorenzo River (lat. 37°09'20" N, long. 122° 07'50" W; in and near sec. 18, T 9 S, R 2 W). Named on Big Basin (1955) 7.5' quadrangle. Ben Lomond (1946) 15' quadrangle has the name "Rices Junction" at the place.

Redwood Gulch [MONTEREY]: *canyon,* drained by a stream that flows 2.25 miles to the sea 5.5 miles southeast of Cape San Martin (lat. 35°50' N, long. 121°23'40" W; sec. 23, T 24 S, R 5 E). Named on Villa Creek (1949) 7.5' quadrangle.

Redwood Lodge [SANTA CRUZ]: *settlement,* 8.5 miles north of Soquel (lat. 37°06'30" N, long. 121°56'40" W). Named on Laurel (1955) 7.5' quadrangle. The name is from a summer resort at the place (Clark, 1986, p. 292). The resort first was called Hotel de Redwood (Hoover, Rensch, and Rensch, p. 478). Postal authorities established De Redwood post office in 1879 and discontinued it in 1882 (Frickstad, p. 176).

Redwood Park: see **Big Basin** [SANTA CRUZ].

Redwood Spring [MONTEREY]: *spring,* 9.5 miles south-southwest of Junipero Serra Peak (lat. 36°00'45" N, long. 121°27'30" W; near SE cor. sec. 18, T 22 S, R 5 E). Named on Cone Peak (1949) 7.5' quadrangle.

Redwood Springs [SANTA CRUZ]: *spring,* 6.25 miles southeast of the town of Boulder Creek at Mount Hermon (lat. 37°03'05" N, long. 122°03'10" W). Named on Felton (1955) 7.5' quadrangle.

Reeds [SAN LUIS OBISPO]: *locality,* 2.25 miles southeast of Edna along Pacific Coast Railroad (lat. 35°10'45" N, long. 120°35'20" W). Named on Arroyo Grande (1897) 15' quadrangle.

Reed's Spur: see **Brookdale** [SANTA CRUZ].

Refugio [SANTA CRUZ]: *land grant,* west of Santa Cruz along the coast, and inland into the highlands. Named on Davenport (1955), Felton (1955), and Santa Cruz (1954) 7.5' quadrangles. Three Castro sisters, Maria de los Angeles, Candida, and Jacinta, received 1 league in 1839, and Jose Bolcof received the grant in 1841; two sons of Jose Bolcoff, husband of Candida, claimed 12,147 acres patented in 1860; Joseph L. Majors, husband of Maria de los Angeles, later received one-third of the grant (Cowan, p. 67; Rowland, p. 42).

Refugio Beach [SANTA BARBARA]: *beach,* 8.5 miles east of Gaviota along the coast (lat. 34°27'45" N, long. 120°04'05" W); the beach is at the mouth of Cañada del Refugio. Named on Gaviota (1943) 15' quadrangle.

Refugio Creek: see **Quiota Creek** [SANTA BARBARA].

Refugio Pass [SANTA BARBARA]: *pass,* 5.5 miles south of Santa Ynez (lat. 34°32' N, long. 120°03'35" W; sec. 7, T 5 N, R 30 W); the pass is near the head of Cañada del Refugio. Named on Santa Ynez (1959) 7.5' quadrangle.

Reggiardo Creek [SANTA CRUZ]: *stream,* flows nearly 2 miles to Laguna Creek 3.5 miles east-northeast of Davenport (lat. 37°01'25" N, long. 122°07'50" W; near SW cor. sec. 30, T 10 S, R 2 W). Named on Davenport (1955) 7.5' quadrangle. Clark (1986, p. 293) associated the name with Filippo Regiardo, an Italian immigrant who had land along the stream in 1889.

Reinoso Peak [SAN BENITO]: *peak,* 2.5 miles south-southeast of Potrero Peak (lat. 36°49'20" N, long. 121°08'10" W; sec. 7, T 13 S, R 8 E). Altitude 3472 feet. Named on Quien Sabe Valley (1968) 7.5' quadrangle.

Release Canyon: see **Reliz Canyon** [MONTEREY].

Reliz: see **Reliz Canyon** [MONTEREY].

Reliz Canyon [MONTEREY]: *canyon,* 13 miles long, opens into lowlands 4.25 miles southwest of Greenfield (lat. 36°16'50" N, long. 121°18'05" W; sec. 15, T 19 S, R 6 E); Reliz Creek drains the canyon. Named on Paraiso Springs (1956) and Reliz Canyon (1949) 7.5' quadrangles. Goodyear (1888, p. 87) referred to Release Cañon, and Smith (p. 25) cited use of the name "Release Canyon." *Reliz* means "landslide" in Mexican Spanish (Stewart, p. 403). Postal authorities established Reliz post office in Reliz Canyon (NE quarter sec. 11, T 20 S, R 6 E) in 1899, moved it 2 miles west in 1900, and discontinued it in 1903 (Salley, p. 183).

Reliz Canyon Camp Ground [MONTEREY]: *locality,* 10 miles south-southwest of Greenfield (lat. 36°11' N, long. 121°17'45" W; near NE cor. sec. 22, T 20 S, R 6 E); the place is in Reliz Canyon. Named on Reliz Canyon (1949) 7.5' quadrangle. Called Reliz Canyon Camp on Junipero Serra (1948) 15' quadrangle.

Reliz Creek [MONTEREY]: *stream,* flows 16 miles to Arroyo Seco (1) nearly 3 miles west of Greenfield (lat. 36°18'50" N, long. 121° 17'35" W); the stream drains Reliz Canyon. Named on Paraiso Springs (1956) and Reliz Canyon (1949) 7.5' quadrangles.

Reservoir Canyon [SAN LUIS OBISPO]: *canyon,* drained by a stream that flows 2.5 miles to San Luis Obispo Creek 2 miles east-northeast of downtown San Luis Obispo (lat. 35°17'35" N, long. 120°37'50" W; near E line sec. 25, T 30 S, R 12 E). Named on Lopez Mountain (1965) 7.5' quadrangle.

Respini Creek: see **Yellow Bank Creek** [SANTA CRUZ].

Retreat [MONTEREY]: *locality,* along Southern Pacific Railroad in Seaside (lat. 36°36'10" N, long. 121°51'50" W). Named on Seaside (1947) 7.5' quadrangle.

Rex [SANTA BARBARA]: *locality,* 3.5 miles east of Santa Maria along Santa Maria Valley Railroad (lat. 34°56'40" N, long. 120°22'30" W). Named on Santa Maria (1959) and Twitchell Dam (1959) 7.5' quadrangles.

Rex: see **Hernandez** [SAN BENITO].

Reynolds: see **Mount Reynolds** [SAN BENITO].

Rices Junction: see **Redwood Grove** [SANTA CRUZ].

Richardson Canyon [SANTA BARBARA]: *canyon,* drained by a stream that flows nearly 6 miles to Cuyama Valley 7 miles north of McPherson Peak (lat. 34°59'25" N, long. 119°48'55" W). Named on Peak Mountain (1964) 7.5' quadrangle.

Richardson Rock [SANTA BARBARA]: *rock,* 6.5 miles northwest of the westernmost tip of San Miguel Island (lat. 34°06'30" N, long. 120°31' W). Named on Santa Maria (1956) 1°x 2° quadrangle. The feature was known in Spanish times as Isla de Baxos, Isla de Lobos, or Farallon de Lobos (Wagner, H.R., p. 405).

Richardson Spring [SANTA BARBARA]: *spring,* about 5.5 miles northwest of McPherson Peak (lat. 34°55'35" N, long. 119°51' W); the spring is in Richardson Canyon. Named on Peak Mountain (1964) 7.5' quadrangle.

Rickard's Cove: see **Leffingwell Landing** [SAN LUIS OBISPO].

Rider Creek [SANTA CRUZ]: *stream,* flows nearly 2 miles to Corralitos Creek 2 miles north-northwest of Corralitos (lat. 37° 01' N, long. 121°48'55" W; sec. 36, T 10 S, R 1 E). Named on Loma Prieta (1955) 7.5' quadrangle.

Rincon [SANTA CRUZ]: *locality,* 8.5 miles south-southeast of the town of Boulder Creek along Southern Pacific Railroad (lat. 37° 00'45" N, long. 122°03'05" W); the place is on Cañada del Rincon en el Rio San Lorenzo de Santa Cruz grant. Named on Felton (1955) 7.5' quadrangle. Hamman (p. 87) noted that Rincon first had the name "Summit," but Hamman's

(1980b) map shows a place called Summit situated southeast of Rincon at a railroad tunnel. The same map also shows a place called Inspiration Point located along the railroad nearly 1 mile north-northwest of Rincon.

Rinconada Creek [SAN LUIS OBISPO]: *stream,* flows 7.25 miles to Salinas River 5 miles north-northeast of Lopez Mountain (lat. 35° 21'40" N, long. 120°32' W; sec. 36, T 29 S, R 13 E). Named on Lopez Mountain (1965) and Santa Margarita Lake (1967) 7.5' quadrangles.

Rinconada del Zanjon: see **Rincon del Zanjon** [MONTEREY].

Rincon Creek [SANTA BARBARA]: *stream,* heads in Ventura County and flows 9.5 miles, mainly along Santa Barbara-Ventura County line, to the sea at Rincon Point (lat. 34°22'25" N, long. 119° 28'35" W). Named on White Ledge Peak (1952) 7.5' quadrangle.

Rincon de la Puente del Monte [MONTEREY]: *land grant,* at and near Gonzales. Named on Gonzales (1955), Mount Johnson (1968), and Palo Escrito Peak (1956) 7.5' quadrangles. Teodoro Gonzales received 7 leagues in 1836 and claimed 15,219 acres patented in 1866 (Cowan, p. 49; Cowan used the form "Rincon de la Puenta del Monte" for the name).

Rincon de las Salinas [MONTEREY]: *land grant,* mainly south of Salinas River near the coast. Named on Marina (1947) and Moss Landing (1954) 7.5' quadrangles. Cristina Delgado received 0.5 league in 1833; Rafael Estrada claimed 2220 acres patented in 1881 (Cowan, p. 70).

Rincon de los Laureles: see **Los Laurelles** [MONTEREY] (1).

Rincon del Zanjon [MONTEREY]: *land grant,* 3 miles northwest of Salinas. Named on Salinas (1947) 7.5' quadrangle. Jose Eusebio Boronda received 1.5 leagues in 1840 and claimed 2230 acres patented in 1860 (Cowan, p. 68; Cowan, listed the grant under the designation "Rinconada (or Rincon) del Zanjon").

Rincon Point [SANTA BARBARA]: *promontory,* 3 miles east-southeast of Carpinteria along the coast at Santa Barbara-Ventura County line (lat. 34°22'55" N, long. 119°28'35" W); the feature is at the mouth of Rincon Creek on El Rincon grant. Named on White Ledge Peak (1952) 7.5' quadrangle.

Rio Buenaventura: see **Salinas River** [MONTEREY-SAN LUIS OBISPO].

Rio de la Estrella: see **Estrella Creek** [SAN LUIS OBISPO].

Rio de la Santa Inez: see **Santa Ynez River** [SANTA BARBARA].

Rio de la Santa Isabel: see **Huerhuero Creek** [SAN LUIS OBISPO].

Rio de la Santa Maria: see **Santa Maria River** [SAN LUIS OBISPO-SANTA BARBARA].

Rio de La Señora La Santa Ana: see **Pajaro River** [MONTEREY-SAN BENITO-SANTA CRUZ].

Rio de la Sierra: see **Nacimiento River** [MONTEREY-SAN LUIS OBISPO].

Rio de las Truchas: see **Nacimiento River** [MONTEREY-SAN LUIS OBISPO].

Rio Del Mar [SANTA CRUZ]: *town,* 4.5 miles east-northeast of Soquel Point near the coast (lat. 36°58' N, long. 121°53'45" W). Named on Soquel (1954) and Watsonville West (1954) 7.5' quadrangles.

Rio del Pajaro: see **Pajaro River** [MONTEREY-SAN BENITO-SANTA CRUZ].

Río del Paxaro: see **Pajaro River** [MONTEREY-SAN BENITO-SANTA CRUZ].

Rio de Monterrey: see **Salinas River** [MONTEREY].

Rio de San Antonio: see **Pajaro River** [MONTEREY-SAN BENITO-SANTA CRUZ]; **San Antonio River** [MONTEREY]; **Salinas River** [MONTEREY-SAN LUIS OBISPO].

Rio de San Bernardo: see **Santa Ynez River** [SANTA BARBARA].

Rio de San Lorenzo: see **San Lorenzo Creek** [MONTEREY-SAN BENITO].

Río de Santa Ana: see **Pajaro River** [MONTEREY-SAN BENITO-SANTA CRUZ].

Rio de Santa Rosa: see **Santa Ynez River** [SANTA BARBARA].

Rio de San Verardo: see **Santa Ynez River** [SANTA BARBARA].

Rio Estrello: see **Estrella Creek** [SAN LUIS OBISPO].

Rio Grande: see **Arroyo Grande Creek** [SAN LUIS OBISPO].

Rio Guadalupe: see **Santa Maria River** [SAN LUIS OBISPO-SANTA BARBARA].

Rioly Run [SAN LUIS OBISPO]: *stream,* flows 0.5 mile to San Simeon Creek 3.5 miles north of Cambria (lat. 35°37' N, long. 121°04' W; near W line sec. 1, T 27 S, R 8 E). Named on Cambria (1959) 7.5' quadrangle.

Rio Pajaro: see **San Benito River** [SAN BENITO].

Rio Piedras: see **Rocky Creek** [MONTEREY] (1).

Rio Sabinos: see **Salinas River** [MONTEREY-SAN LUIS OBISPO].

Rio Salinas: see **Salinas River** [MONTEREY-SAN LUIS OBISPO].

Rio Salinas de Monterey: see **Salinas River** [MONTEREY-SAN LUIS OBISPO].

Rio San Agustine: see **San Lorenzo River** [SANTA CRUZ].

Rio San Benito: see **San Benito River** [SAN BENITO].

Rio San Buenaventura: see **Salinas River** [MONTEREY-SAN LUIS OBISPO].

Rio San Elizario: see **Salinas River** [MONTEREY].

Rio Santa Maria: see **Cuyama River** [SAN LUIS OBISPO-SANTA BARBARA]; **Santa Maria River** [SAN LUIS OBISPO-SANTA BARBARA].

Rio Selina: see **Salinas River** [MONTEREY-SAN LUIS OBISPO].

Rio Wasna: see **Huasna River** [SAN LUIS OBISPO].

River Oaks [SAN BENITO]: *settlement,* 4.5 miles northwest of San Juan Bautista on the south side of Pajaro River (lat. 36°54' N, long. 121°35'30" W). Named on Chittenden (1955) 7.5' quadrangle.

Riverside Grove [SANTA CRUZ]: *settlement,* 4.5 miles east of Big Basin near San Lorenzo River (lat. 37°10'25" N, long. 122°08'30" W; sec. 1, 12, T 9 S, R 3 W). Named on Big Basin (1955) 7.5' quadrangle. Hamman's (1980b) map shows Dougherty's Mill #2 at present Riverside Grove, and shows a place called Sinnott Switch located along the railroad a short distance north of Dougherty's Mill #2.

Roach Canyon [MONTEREY]: *canyon,* drained by a stream that flows 2 miles to Carmel Valley (1) 3.25 miles east of the mouth of Carmel River (lat. 36°32'25" N, long. 121°52' W). Named on Seaside (1947) 7.5' quadrangle.

Roadamite [SANTA BARBARA]: *locality,* 2.25 miles southwest of the village of Sisquoc (lat. 34°50'40" N, long. 120°19'25" W). Named on Santa Maria (1947) 15' quadrangle.

Roadhouse Slough: see **Elkhorn Slough** [MONTEREY].

Robbers' Cave: see **Cave Landing**, under **Mallagh Landing** [SAN LUIS OBISPO].

Roberta: see **Mount Roberta** [SANTA BARBARA].

Roberts: see **Camp Robers Military Reservation** [MONTEREY-SAN LUIS OBISPO].

Robertson Creek [MONTEREY]: *stream,* flows 3.5 miles to Finch Creek 1.5 miles east-northeast of Jamesburg (lat. 36°22'40" N, long. 121°33'45" W; sec. 8, T 18 S, R 4 E). Named on Chews Ridge (1956) and Rana Creek (1956) 7.5' quadrangles. The stream was called Smith Creek before it was called Robertson Creek—both names record early residents in the neighborhood (Clark, 1991, p. 476).

Roberts Spring [SAN LUIS OBISPO]: *spring,* nearly 4 miles south-southeast of Cholame (lat. 35°40'35" N, long. 120°15'50" W; sec. 9, T 26 S, R 16 E). Named on Cholame (1961) 7.5' quadrangle.

Robinson Canyon [MONTEREY]:

(1) *canyon,* drained by a stream that flows 3.25 miles to Carmel River 6.5 miles east of the mouth of that river (lat. 36°31'05" N, long. 121°4840" W; near N line sec. 25, T 16 S, R 1 E). Named on Mount Carmel (1956) and Seaside (1947) 7.5' quadrangles. Called Robison Canyon on Monterey (1913) and Point Sur (1925) 15' quadrangles.

(2) *canyon,* 3.5 miles long, opens into lowlands 3.5 miles northeast of Jolon (lat. 36°00'40" N, long. 121°08'10" W; sec. 18, T 22 S, R 8 E). Named on Cosio Knob (1949) and Espinosa Canyon (1949) 7.5' quadrangles.

Robison Canyon: see **Robinson Canyon** [MONTEREY] (1).

Roblar Canyon [SANTA BARBARA]: *canyon,* drained by a stream that flows 5 miles to Mono Creek 1.5 miles north-northeast of Hildreth Peak (lat. 34°37'20" N, long. 119°32'35" W). Named on Hildreth Peak (1964) and Madulce Peak (1964) 7.5' quadrangles.

Roblar Valley: see **Stony Valley** [MONTEREY].

Robla Valley: see **Stony Valley** [MONTEREY].

Roble Canyon: see **Alamar Canyon** [SANTA BARBARA].

Robles del Rio [MONTEREY]: *district,* part of the town of Carmel Valley south of Carmel River (lat. 36°28'15" N, long. 121°43'30" W). Named on Carmel Valley (1956) 7.5' quadrangle. Postal authorities established Robles del Rio post office in 1941 and changed the name to Carmel Valley in 1952 (Frickstad, p. 109). Frank Porter laid out the place in 1926 (Clark, 1991, p. 478).

Rob Roy: see **La Selva Beach** [SANTA CRUZ].

Rob Roy Junction [SANTA BARBARA]: *locality,* 4 miles west-southwest of Corralitos (lat. 36°58'15" N, long. 121°52'20" W). Named on Watsonville West (1954) 7.5' quadrangle. Rob Roy real-estate development began in 1922 at present La Selva Beach (Hamman, p. 268).

Rock Canyon: see **Hilton Canyon** [SANTA BARBARA].

Rockland: see **Rockland Landing** [MONTEREY].

Rockland Landing [MONTEREY]: *locality,* 3 miles east-southeast of Lopez Point along the coast at the mouth of Limekiln Creek (2) (lat. 36°00'30" N, long. 121°31'05" W; sec. 22, T 22 S, R 4 E). Site named on Lopez Point (1956) 7.5' quadrangle. Officials of Rockland Cement Company constructed a landing, installed three large kilns, and built houses for workmen at the place in the 1880's (Fink, p. 213). Preston (1893a, p. 260) mentioned "Rockland, on the coast," where limekilns operated formerly.

Rocks: see **The Rocks** [MONTEREY].

Rock Spring [SAN BENITO]: *spring,* 8 miles northeast of Bitterwater (lat. 36°28'20" N, long. 120°55'05" W; near NE cor. sec. 7, T 17 S, R 10 E); the spring is at the head of a tributary of Rock Springs Creek. Named on Rock Spring Peak (1969) 7.5' quadrangle.

Rock Spring [SAN LUIS OBISPO]:

(1) *spring,* 4.25 miles west of Cholame in McMillan Canyon (lat. 35°42'55" N, long. 120°22'20" W; sec. 32, T 25 S, R 15 E). Named on Cholame (1961) 7.5' quadrangle.

(2) *spring,* 4.5 miles south-southeast of Wilson Corner (lat. 35°24'20" N, long. 120°20'40" W; near SE cor. sec. 10, T 29 S, R 15 E). Named on Camatta Ranch (1966) 7.5' quadrangle.

Rock Spring Peak [SAN BENITO]: *peak,* 8 miles northeast of Bitterwater (lat. 36°28' N, long. 120°54'20" W; sec. 8, T 17 S, R 10 E); the peak is less than 1 mile east-southeast of Rock Spring. Altitude 4033 feet. Named on Rock Spring Peak (1969) 7.5' quadrangle.

Rock Springs Creek [SAN BENITO]: *stream,* flows 6 miles to San Benito River 5.5 miles north-northeast of Bitterwater (lat. 36°26'45" N, long. 120°58'40" W; sec. 15, T 17 S, R 9 E). Named on Rock Spring Peak (1969) 7.5' quadrangle.

Rocky Butte [SAN LUIS OBISPO]: *peak,* 7.5 miles east of the village of San Simeon (lat. 35°39'55" N, long. 121°03'30" W; near N line sec. 24, T 26 S, R 8 E). Altitude 3432 feet. Named on Pebblestone Shut-in (1959) 7.5' quadrangle.

Rocky Canyon [SAN LUIS OBISPO]: *canyon,* 2 miles long, opens into lowlands 5 miles north of Santa Margarita (lat. 35°27'45" N, long. 120°37'15" W). Named on Santa Margarita (1965) 7.5' quadrangle.

Rocky Canyon: see **Stephens Canyon** [SAN LUIS OBISPO].

Rocky Creek [MONTEREY]:

(1) *stream,* flows 6 miles to the sea 5 miles north of Point Sur (lat. 36°22'45" N, long. 121°54'05" W; sec. 7, T 18 S, R 1 E); the stream goes through Las Piedras Canyon. Named on Mount Carmel (1956) and Soberanes Point (1956) 7.5' quadrangles. According to Lussier (p. 13), the early Spaniards called the creek Rio Piedras, probably because of rocks in the stream—*piedras* means "stones" in Spanish.

(2) *stream,* flows 4.25 miles to Arroyo Seco (1) 7.5 miles north-northwest of Junipero Serra Peak (lat. 36°14'10" N, long. 121°29'25" W; sec. 36, T 19 S, R 4 E). Named on Chews Ridge (1956), Junipero Serra Peak (1949), and Tassajara Hot Springs (1956) 7.5' quadrangles.

Rocky Creek [SAN LUIS OBISPO]: *stream,* flows 5 miles to Santa Rita Creek 1.25 miles south of York Mountain (lat. 35°31'40" N, long. 120°50'10" W). Named on Adelaida (1961) 15' quadrangle.

Rocky Creek Camp [MONTEREY]: *locality,* 2.5 miles east-northeast of Tassajara Hot Springs (lat. 36°14'50" N, long. 121°30'15" W; sec. 26, T 19 S, R 4 E); the place is along Rocky Creek (2). Named on Tassajara Hot Springs (1956) 7.5' quadrangle.

Rocky Gorge [SAN LUIS OBISPO]: *canyon,* 1.5 miles long, 4 miles west of Atascadero along Graves Creek (lat. 35°29'20" N, long. 120°44'15" W). Named on Atascadero (1965) 7.5' quadrangle.

Rocky Point [MONTEREY]: *promontory,* 3.25 miles south-southeast of Soberanes Point along the coast (lat. 36°24'10" N, long. 121°54'50" W). Named on Soberanes Point (1956) 7.5' quadrangle.

Rocky Point [SANTA BARBARA]: *promontory,* 1 mile southeast of Point Arguello along the coast (lat. 34°33'50" N, long. 120°38'20" W). Named on Point Arguello (1959) 7.5' quadrangle.

Rocky Ridge [MONTEREY]: *ridge,* west-trending, 2 miles long, west of Fremont Peak (lat. 36°45'20" N, long. 121°31'15" W). Named on San Juan Bautista (1955) 7.5' quadrangle.

Rodeo Creek Gulch [SANTA CRUZ]: *canyon,* drained by a stream that flows 5.5 miles to Corcoran Lagoon 0.5 mile north-northwest of Soquel Point (lat. 36°57'45" N, long. 121°58'45" W); the canyon is on the west border of Arroyo del Rodeo grant. Named on Laurel (1955) and Soquel (1954) 7.5' quadrangles. Called Doyle Gulch on Los Gatos (1919) and Capitola (1914) 15' quadrangles. The name "Doyle" commemorates John Doyle, who had a farm at the place in the 1860's and 1870's (Rowland, p. 68).

Rodes Reef: see **Brockway Point** [SANTA BARBARA].

Rogers: see **Port Rogers**, under **Port Watsonville** [SANTA CRUZ].

Rogers Creek [SAN LUIS OBISPO]: *stream,* flows nearly 7 miles to San Juan Creek 2.25 miles west-southwest of Freeborn Mountain (lat. 35°16'30" N, long. 120°05'20" W; sec. 31, T 30 S, R 18 E). Named on Branch Mountain (1967) and California Valley (1966) 7.5' quadrangles.

Rogers Creek [SANTA CRUZ]: *stream,* flows less than 1 mile to Opal Creek 1.5 miles north of Big Basin (lat. 37°11'35" N, long. 122°13'05" W; sec. 32, T 8 S, R 3 W). Named on Big Basin (1955) 7.5' quadrangle. The misspelled name is for Winfield Scott Rodgers, who had tan-bark camps in the vicinity; the stream was called Lion Creek before 1895 (Clark, 1986, p. 301).

Rogue Canyon: see **Roque Canyon** [SANTA BARBARA].

Romer Canyon: see **Romero Canyon** [SANTA BARBARA].

Romero Canyon [SANTA BARBARA]: *canyon,* 2.5 miles long, along Romero Creek above a point 5.25 miles northwest of Carpinteria (lat. 34°26'40" N, long. 119°35'35" W; sec. 10, T 4 N, R 26 W). Named on Carpinteria (1952) 7.5' quadrangle. United States Board on Geographic Names (1961b, p. 14) rejected the name "Romer Canyon" for the feature.

Romero Canyon Creek [SANTA BARBARA]: see **Romero Creek** [SANTA BARBARA].

Romero Creek [SANTA BARBARA]: *stream,* flows 5 miles to the sea 6 miles west-northwest of Carpinteria and less than 1 mile west-southwest of Ortega Hill (lat. 34°25'05" N, long. 119°37'10" W); the stream drains Romero Canyon. Named on Carpinteria (1952, photorevised 1967) 7.5' quadrangle. Called Arroyo de las Ortegas on Santa Barbara (1903) 15' quadrangle, and the lower part is called Picay Creek on Carpinteria (1952) 7.5' quadrangle, but United States Board on Geographic Names (1961b, p. 14) rejected the names "Arroyo de las Ortegas," "Picay Creek," and "Romero Canyon Creek" for the stream.

Romero Reservoir [SANTA BARBARA]: *lake,* 250 feet long, 5.5 miles northwest of Carpinteria (lat. 34°26'50" N, long. 119°35'50" W). Named on Carpinteria (1952) 7.5' quadrangle.

Romero Saddle [SANTA BARBARA]: *pass,* 7 miles northwest of Carpinteria (lat. 34°28'35" N, long. 119°35'40" W); sec. 34, T 5 N, R 26 W); the pass is near the head of Romero Canyon. Named on Carpinteria (1952) 7.5' quadrangle. Called Blue Canyon Pass on Santa Barbara (1903) 15' quadrangle.

Romie: see **Fort Romie** [MONTEREY].

Roosevelt Creek [MONTEREY]: *stream,* flows 2.5 miles to Arroyo Seco (1) 3.25 miles west-southwest of Junipero Serra Peak (lat. 36°07'25" N, long. 121°28'10" W; sec. 7, T 21 S, R 5 E). Named on Cone Peak (1949) and Junipero Serra Peak (1949) 7.5' quadrangles.

Rooster Canyon [MONTEREY]: *canyon,* drained by a stream that flows nearly 2 miles to McCoy Canyon 7.5 miles northeast of Gonzales (lat. 36°34'50" N, long. 121°20'25" W; sec. 32, T 15 S, R 6 E). Named on Mount Johnson (1968) 7.5' quadrangle.

Root: see **Miles** [SAN LUIS OBISPO].

Rootville: see **Gabilan Range** [MONTEREY-SAN BENITO].

Roque Campground [SANTA BARBARA]: *locality,* 7 miles north-northeast of Manzanita Mountain (lat. 34°58'45" N, long. 120°00'50" W); the place is in Roque Canyon. Named on Manzanita Mountain (1964) 7.5' quadrangle.

Roque Canyon [SANTA BARBARA]: *canyon,* drained by a stream that flows nearly 4 miles to join the stream in Flores Canyon and form North Fork La Brea Creek 5.5 miles north-northeast of Manzanita Mountain (lat. 34°58'10" N, long. 120°03'05" W). Named on Manzanita Mountain (1964) 7.5' quadrangle. United States Board on Geographic Names (1967a, p. 10) rejected the name "Rogue Canyon" for the feature.

Rosa Morada: see **San Joaquin** [SAN BENITO].

Rosaria Creek: see **Tres Pinos Creek** [SAN BENITO].

Rosario del Serafin de Asculi: see **Soquel Creek** [SANTA CRUZ].

Rosas Canyon [SAN BENITO]: *canyon,* drained by a stream that flows 4 miles to an unnamed canyon nearly 3 miles east of North Chalone Peak (lat. 36°27'20" N, long. 121°08'45" W; sec. 18, T 17 S, R 8 E). Named on North Chalone Peak (1969) and Topo Valley (1969) 7.5' quadrangles.

Rosaville: see **Cambria** [SAN LUIS OBISPO].

Rose Canyon [SANTA BARBARA]: *canyon,* drained by a stream that flows 2 miles to Santa Ynez River 6.5 miles south-southwest of Hildreth Peak (lat. 34°30'50" N, long. 119°35'55" W). Named on Hildreth Peak (1964) 7.5' quadrangle.

Rosemary [SANTA BARBARA]: *locality,* 2.25 miles east of downtown Santa Maria along Santa Maria Valley Railroad (lat. 34°56'45" N, long. 120°23'35" W; sec. 18, T 10 N, R 33 W). Named on Santa Maria (1959) 7.5' quadrangle.

Rose Reservoir [SANTA CRUZ]: *lake,* 750 feet long, 3.5 miles north-northeast of Watsonville (lat. 36°58' N, long. 121°44'15" W). Named on Watsonville East (1955) 7.5' quadrangle.

Round Corral Canyon [SANTA BARBARA]: *canyon,* drained by a stream that flows 2 miles to Sisquoc River 6 miles south-southeast of Tepusquet Peak (lat. 34°49'50" N, long. 120°08'25" W). Named on Foxen Canyon (1964) and Zaca Lake (1964) 7.5' quadrangles.

Round Hill [SANTA BARBARA]: *hill,* 1.5 miles south of Tranquillon Mountain (lat. 34°33'30" N, long. 120°33'55" W). Named on Tranquillon Mountain (1959) 7.5' quadrangle.

Round Mountain [MONTEREY]: *peak,* 6.5 miles north of Charley Mountain on Monterey-Fresno County line (lat. 36°14'10" N, long. 120°39'55" W; sec. 34, T 19 S, R 12 E). Named on Priest Valley (1969) 7.5' quadrangle.

Round Potrero [SANTA BARBARA]: *area,* 2.5 miles east-southeast of Salisbury Potrero (lat. 34°48'10" N, long. 119°39'45" W). Named on Salisbury Potrero (1964) 7.5' quadrangle.

Round Potrero Spring [SANTA BARBARA]: *spring,* 2 miles east-southeast of Salisbury Potrero (lat. 34°48'25" N, long. 119°40'05" W); the spring is less than 0.5 mile west-northwest of Round Potrero. Named on Salisbury Potrero (1964) 7.5' quadrangle.

Round Rock Camp [MONTEREY]: *locality,* nearly 2 miles north of Ventana Cone along Carmel River (lat. 36°18'35" N, long. 121°40'35" W; sec. 6, T 19 S, R 3 E). Named on Ventana Cones (1956) 7.5' quadrangle.

Round Spring [MONTEREY]: *spring,* 7.5 miles east of Cape San Martin (lat. 35°54'45" N, long. 121°20' W; near E line sec. 20, T 23 S, R 6 E). Named on Alder Peak (1949) 7.5' quadrangle.

Round Spring Valley [SAN BENITO]: *area,* 6.5 miles southeast of Fremont Peak near the head of a branch of Jamieson Creek (lat. 36°40'35" N, long. 121°26'25" W; sec. 32, T 14 S, R 5 E). Named on Mount Harlan (1968) 7.5' quadrangle.

Round Top [SAN LUIS OBISPO]: *peak,* 6.25 miles east of Edna (lat. 35°12'45" N, long. 120°31'45" W; sec. 19, T 31 S, R 14 E). Altitude 2058 feet. Named on Arroyo Grande NE (1965) 7.5' quadrangle.

Roundtree Hill: see **Twin Peak** [MONTEREY].

Ruby Canyon [MONTEREY]: *canyon,* drained by a stream that flows nearly 4 miles to lowlands 1.25 miles northwest of Jolon (lat. 35°59' N, long. 121°11'45" W). Named on Cosio Knob (1949) and Jolon (1949) 7.5' quadrangles.

Ruda Canyon [SAN LUIS OBISPO]: *canyon,* drained by a stream that flows 2 miles to Coon Creek 7.5 miles northwest of Point San Luis (lat. 35°14'35" N, long. 120°50'45" W; sec. 12, T 31 S, R 10 E). Named on Port San Luis (1965) 7.5' quadrangle. Called Ruder Canyon on Port Harford (1897) 15' quadrangle.

Ruder Canyon: see **Ruda Canyon** [SAN LUIS OBISPO].

Rude Spring [MONTEREY]: *spring,* 15 miles east-northeast of San Ardo along Pancho Rico Creek (lat. 36°04'10" N, long. 120°37'55" W; sec. 25, T 21 S, R 12 E). Named on Slack Canyon (1969) 7.5' quadrangle.

Rudolf Canyon [SAN BENITO]: *canyon,* drained by a stream that flows 1.5 miles to San Benito River 7 miles south-southwest of Idria (lat. 36°19'50" N, long. 120°43'50" W; sec. 26, T 18 S, R 11 E). Named on San Benito Mountain (1969) 7.5' quadrangle.

Ruins Creek [SANTA CRUZ]: *stream,* flows nearly 3 miles to Bean Creek 7 miles southeast of the town of Boulder Creek (lat. 37°03'25" N, long. 122°01'50" W). Named on Felton (1955) 7.5' quadrangle.

Ruiz Canyon [SANTA BARBARA]: *canyon,* drained by a stream that flows 2.5 miles to Tepusquet Canyon 2.25 miles west of Tepusquet Peak (lat. 34°54'55" N, long. 120°13'30" W). Named on Tepusquet Canyon (1964) 7.5' quadrangle.

Russels Creek: see **Cholame Creek** [MONTEREY-SAN LUIS OBISPO].

Russelsville: see **Parkfield** [MONTEREY].

Rusty Peak [SAN LUIS OBISPO]: *peak,* 6.5 miles north-northeast of the mouth of Morro Creek (lat. 35°27'50" N, long. 120°48'55" W; near N line sec. 32, T 28 S, R 11 E). Altitude 1837 feet. Named on Morro Bay North (1965) 7.5' quadrangle.

- S -

Sacate [SANTA BARBARA]: *locality,* 10.5 miles east of Point Conception along Southern Pacific Railroad (lat. 34°28'20" N, long. 120°17'35" W); the place is near the mouth of Cañada del Sacate. Named on Sacate (1953) 7.5' quadrangle.

Sacate Canyon: see **Cañada del Coyote** [SANTA BARBARA].

Saddle Mountain: see **Potrero Canyon** [MONTEREY].

Saddle Peak [SAN LUIS OBISPO]: *peak,* nearly 5 miles north-northwest of Point San Luis (lat. 35°13'20" N, long. 120°47'30" W; near SE cor. sec. 16, T 31 S, R 11 E). Altitude 1819 feet. Named on Port San Luis (1965) 7.5' quadrangle.

Sage [MONTEREY]: *locality,* 4 miles north-northeast of Salinas (lat. 36°43'45" N, long. 121°37'30" W). Named on Salinas (1947) 7.5' quadrangle.

Sage Hill [SANTA BARBARA]: *peak,* 3.5 miles north-northeast of San Marcos Pass (lat. 34°33'20" N, long. 119°47'50" W; sec. 35, T 6 N, R 28 W). Named on San Marcos Pass (1959) 7.5' quadrangle.

Sagunto: see **Santa Ynez** [SANTA BARBARA].

Saint Francis Springs: see **Chittenden's Sulphur Springs**, under **Chittenden** [SANTA CRUZ].

Saint Paul's Ferry: see **Pauls Ferry**, under **Pauls Island** [MONTEREY].

Sal: see **Point Sal** [SANTA BARBARA].

Salina Plains: see **Salinas River** [MONTEREY].

Salinas [MONTEREY]: *city,* 10 miles east-southeast of the mouth of Salinas River (lat. 36°40'30" N, long. 121°39'15" W). Named on Salinas (1947) and Natividad (1947, photorevised 1968) 7.5' quadrangles. A tavern called Halfway House opened in 1856 at the intersection of stage routes, and a village sprang up around it; the city of Salinas was laid out at the place in 1867 and incorporated in 1874 (Bancroft, p. 524). Postal authorities established Salinas post office in 1854 (Frickstad, p. 109).

Salinas: see **East Salinas**, under **Alisal** [MONTEREY].

Salinas Mountains: see **Sierra de Salinas** [MONTEREY].

Salinas Plains: see **Salinas River** [MONTEREY].

Salinas Point: see **Coal Oil Point** [SANTA BARBARA].

Salinas Range: see **Gabilan Range** [MONTEREY-SAN BENITO].

Salinas Reservoir: see **Santa Margarita Lake** [SAN LUIS OBISPO].

Salinas River [MONTEREY-SAN LUIS OBISPO]: *stream,* heads in San Luis Obispo County and flows for about 170 miles to the sea 11 miles north-northeast of Monterey in Monterey County (lat. 36° 44'45" N, long. 121°48'15" W). Named on San Luis Obispo (1956) and Santa Cruz (1956) 1°x 2° quadrangles. Marina (1947) 7.5' quadrangle shows a bar across the mouth of the stream. Members of the Portola expedition discovered the river in 1769 near present King City, and Crespi gave it the name "Rio San Elizario" in honor of the saint whose day is September 27, the day after the discovery (Wagner, H.R., p. 498). According to Davidson (1907, p. 103), the river was called Santa Delfina—Delfina was the wife of Elizario—but H.R. Wagner (p. 498) pointed out that Crespi gave her name only to a camp near the mouth of the stream. Font in 1776 used the name "Santa Delfina Valley" for the valley of Salinas River (Bolton, p. 271). The stream is called R. de Sn. Antonio on Malaspina's (1791) map, and is called Rio de Monterrey on a diseño of Guadalupe y Llanito de los Correos in 1833 (Becker, 1969). On Greenhow's (1844) map the river has the name "Buenaventura R.," on Fremont's (1845) map it has the name "Rio San Buenaventura," and on Bartlett's (1854) map it has the name "R. Sabinos or Buenaventura." Parke's (1854-1855) map has the name "Rio Salinas de Monterey," and in his text Parke (p. 1) referred to the stream by the name "Rio Salinas." Keller (p. 38) used the name "Rio Selina" in 1851. The valley of Salinas River commonly is called Salinas Valley, but that name was unknown in Spanish times, when the feature was known as Valley of Monterey (Cerruti, p. 130). During the Mexican War, Americans used the names "Salina plains" (Carson, p. 106) and "the plains of Salinaeus" (*The California Star,* August 21, 1847). Parke's (1854-1855) map has the name "Salinas Plains" along the river north of Soledad mission. Hanna (p. 264) attributed the name "Salinas" to salt marshes near the mouth of the river, Antisell (1856, p. 43) thought that the name referred to the flavor of water in the river, and Logan (p. 721) stated that the name—from the Spanish word for "salty"—was given for saline springs located along the stream and near its source. In Spanish times two small lakes 12 miles from Monterey near the sea produced salt when they dried up (Cerruti, p. 130).

Salinas River: see **Old Salinas River** [MONTEREY].

Salinas Valley: see **Salinas River** [MONTEREY].

Salisbury Canyon [SANTA BARBARA]: *canyon,* 9 miles long, opens into Cuyama Valley 3.5 miles south-southeast of New Cuyama (lat. 34°54' N, long. 119°39'35" W); the canyon heads at Salisbury Potrero. Named on New Cuyama (1964) and Salisbury Potrero (1964) 7.5' quadrangles.

Salisbury Canyon Wash [SANTA BARBARA]: *stream,* flows 4.5 miles from the mouth of Salisbury Canyon to Branch Canyon Wash near New Cuyama (lat. 34°57'10" N, long. 119°41'40" W). Named on New Cuyama (1964) 7.5' quadrangle.

Salisbury Potrero [SANTA BARBARA]: *area,* 9 miles south-southwest of the village of Cuyama (lat. 34°49'15" N, long. 119°42' W). Named on Salisbury Potrero (1964) 7.5' quadrangle.

Salmon Cone [MONTEREY]: *peak,* 8 miles southwest of Cape San Martin (lat. 35°48'40" N, long. 121°21'50" W; sec. 30, T 24 S, R 6 E); the peak is just north of the mouth of Salmon Creek (1). Named on Burro Mountain (1949) 7.5' quadrangle. The feature also was called Salmon Peak (Clark, 1991, p. 494).

Salmon Creek [MONTEREY]:

(1) *stream,* flows 4.25 miles to the sea 8 miles southeast of Cape San Martin (lat. 35°48'30" N, long. 121°21'45" W; sec. 31, T 24 S, R 6 E). Named on Burro Mountain (1949) 7.5' quadrangle.

(2) *stream,* flows nearly 6 miles to Nacimiento River 8.5 miles south of Jolon (lat. 35°50'50" N, long. 121°11'40" W; sec. 15, T 24 S, R 7 E). Named on Burnett Peak (1949) 7.5' quadrangle. United States Board on Geographic Names (1978b, p. 5) rejected the name "Little Salmon Creek" for the stream.

Salmon Peak: see **Salmon Cone** [MONTEREY].

Salsipuedes [SANTA CRUZ]: *land grant,* north and northeast of Watsonville; extends into Santa Clara County. Named on Chittenden (1955), Loma Prieta (1955), Mount Madona (1955), Watsonville East (1955), and Watsonville West (1954) 7.5' quadrangles. Manuel Jimeno Casarin received 8 leagues in 1834 and 1840; James Blair and others claimed 31,201 acres patented in 1861 (Cowan, p. 71). The name refers to the rugged terrain on the grant—*salsipuedes* has the meaning "get out if you can" in Spanish (Arbuckle, p. 29-30).

Salsipuedes Canyon [SANTA BARBARA]: *canyon,* drained by a stream that flows 3 miles to South Fork La Brea Creek 4 miles east-northeast of Manzanita Mountain (lat. 34°55'25" N, long. 120°01'05" W). Named on Manzanita Mountain (1964) 7.5' quadrangle. United States Board on Geographic Names (1978b, p. 5) rejected the form "Salscepudes" for the name.

Salsipuedes Creek [MONTEREY]:

(1) *stream,* flows nearly 2 miles to Las Gazas Creek 4.25 miles north-northwest of Mount Carmel (lat. 36°26'50" N, long. 121°49'10" W; near S line sec. 13, T 17 S, R 1 E). Named on Mount Carmel (1956) 7.5' quadrangle.

(2) *stream,* flows 2 miles to San Antonio River 3.5 miles east of Cone Peak (lat. 36°03'35" N, long. 121°26'05" W; sec. 33, T 21 S, R 5 E). Named on Cone Peak (1949) 7.5' quadrangle, which shows Avila ranch near the stream. According to Stewart (p. 420), *salsipuedes* means literally "jump if you can" in Spanish, and is used conventionally for difficult places. Vicente Avila took his family to an isolated valley north of San Antonio mission and gave his ranch there the name "Salsipuedes" (Fink, p. 210).

Salsipuedes Creek [SAN LUIS OBISPO]: *stream,* flows 4.5 miles to Santa Margarita Lake 5.25 miles west of Pozo (lat. 35°18'55" N, long. 120°27'55" W; sec. 15, T 30 S, R 14 E). Named on Santa Margarita Lake (1967) 7.5' quadrangle.

Salsipuedes Creek [SANTA BARBARA]: *stream,* flows 9 miles to Santa Ynez River 2.5 miles east of the city of Lompoc (lat. 34° 37'55" N, long.

120°24'40" W); the stream is partly on Cañada de Salsipuedes grant. Named on Lompoc (1959) and Lompoc Hills (1959) 7.5' quadrangles. Parke (p. 16) used the form "Sal si Puedes creek" for the name.

Salsipuedes Creek [SANTA CRUZ]: *stream,* joins Pajaro River on the east side of Watsonville (lat. 36°54'35" N, long. 121°44'40" W); part of the stream is on Salsipuedes grant. Named on Watsonville East (1955) 7.5' quadrangle. On San Juan Bautista (1917) 15 quadrangle, which does not name Salsipuedes Creek, the stream is shown as part of Corralitos Creek

Salsipuedes Number Two: see **Salsipuedes Spring Number 2** [SAN LUIS OBISPO].

Salsipuedes Spring Number 1 [SAN LUIS OBISPO]: *spring,* 4.5 miles west-southwest of Pozo (lat. 35°16'35" N, long. 120°26'50" W; sec. 26, T 30 S, R 14 E); the spring is 0.5 mile northwest of Salsipuedes Spring Number 2 along a tributary of Salsipuedes Creek . Named on Santa Margarita Lake (1967) 7.5' quadrangle. United States Board on Geographic Names (1968c, p. 6) approved the name "Salsipuedes Spring Number One" for the feature, and rejected the names "Number One Salsipuedes Springs" and "Salsipuedes Spring Number Two."

Salsipuedes Spring Number 2 [SAN LUIS OBISPO]: *spring,* 4.25 miles west-southwest of Pozo (lat. 35°16'15" N, long. 120°26'20" W; sec. 35, T 30 S, R 14 E); the spring is 0.5 mile southeast of Salsipuedes Spring Number 1 along Salsipuedes Creek. Named on Santa Margarita Lake (1967) 7.5' quadrangle. United States Board on Geographic Names (1968c, p. 6) approved the name "Salsipuedes Spring Number Two" for the feature, and rejected the names "Salsipuedes Number Two," "Salsipuedes Spring Number One," and "Salsipuedes Springs Number Two."

Salt Canyon [SAN LUIS OBISPO]: *canyon,* 1.5 miles long, opens into lowlands 15 miles east-southeast of Shandon (lat. 35°34'30" N, long. 120°06'55" W; sec. 14, T 27 S, R 17 E). Named on Packwood Creek (1961) 7.5' quadrangle.

Salt Creek [SAN BENITO]: *stream,* flows 9 miles to Tres Pinos Creek 3.25 miles south-southeast of Cherry Peak (lat. 36°38'50" N, long. 121°07'35" W; sec. 8, T 15 S, R 8 E). Named on Panoche Pass (1968) and San Benito (1968) 7.5' quadrangles.

Salt Creek [SAN LUIS OBISPO]: *stream,* flows 4.5 miles to Trout Creek (2) 15 miles north-northeast of the town of Nipomo (lat. 35°13'50" N, long. 120°20'50" W; near E line sec. 15, T 31 S, R 15 E). Named on Caldwell Mesa (1967) and Tar Spring Ridge (1967) 7.5' quadrangles. According to G.A. Waring (p. 301), the stream has "notable amounts of salt that are deposited along its bed and in several other ravines near by."

Salt Lake: see **Soda Lake** [SAN LUIS OBISPO].

Saltos Canyon [SAN LUIS OBISPO]: *canyon,* drained by a stream that flows nearly 6 miles to Carrizo Canyon 14 miles west-northwest of Caliente Mountain (lat. 35°06'10" N, long. 119°59'05" W; near SW cor. sec. 30, T 32 S, R 19 E). Named on Chimineas Ranch (1959) and Taylor Canyon (1959) 7.5' quadrangles.

Sam Jones Canyon [MONTEREY]: *canyon,* drained by a stream that flows 2 miles to San Antonio River 5.25 miles south-southeast of Jolon (lat. 35°54'20" N, long. 121°07'35" W). Named on Jolon (1949) 7.5' quadrangle. The name is for an early settler in the canyon (Clark, 1991, p. 496).

Samon Peak [SANTA BARBARA]: *peak,* 2.5 miles north of Big Pine Mountain (lat. 34°44'05" N, long. 119°38'40" W). Altitude 6227 feet. Named on Big Pine Mountain (1964) 7.5' quadrangle.

Sampson Creek [SAN BENITO]: *stream,* flows 4.25 miles to Larious Creek 4 miles west-northwest of Idria (lat. 36°25'55" N, long. 120° 44'20" W; sec. 23, T 17 S, R 11 E). Named on Idria (1969) 7.5' quadrangle.

Sampson Peak [SAN BENITO]: *peak,* nearly 2 miles west-southwest of Idria (lat. 36°24'30" N, long. 120°42'10" W; near W line sec. 31, T 17 S, R 12 E). Altitude 4663 feet. Named on Idria (1969) 7.5' quadrangle. United States Board on Geographic Names (1933, p. 663) rejected the name "Venado Peak" for the feature.

San Agustine Creek: see **San Lorenzo River** [SANTA CRUZ].

San Andreas: see **San Andres** [SANTA CRUZ].

San Andres [SANTA CRUZ]: *land grant,* west of Watsonville near the coast. Named on Moss Landing (1954) and Watsonville West (1954) 7.5' quadrangles. Joaquin Castro received 2 leagues in 1833; Guadalupe Castro and others claimed 8912 acres patented in 1876 (Cowan, p. 71). The grant also was called San Andreas in late Mexican or early American times (Rowland, p. 41). Ashley's (1894) map shows a place called San Andreas located along the railroad 3 miles west-northwest of Watsonville. Camp McQuaide, a World War I army camp, was on the grant (Hoover, Rensch, and Rensch, p. 468). Postal authorities established Camp McQuaide post office in 1941 and discontinued it in 1949; the name honored Father Joseph F. McQuaide, a World War I army chaplain (Salley, p. 35).

San Antonio: see **Los Ojitos** [MONTEREY].

San Antonio Creek [SANTA BARBARA]:

(1) *stream,* flows 31 miles to the sea 5.5 miles west-southwest of the village of Casmalia (lat. 34°47'55" N, long. 120°37'10" W). Named on Casmalia (1959), Los Alamos (1959), Orcutt (1959), Sisquoc (1959), and Zaca Creek (1959) 7.5' quadrangles. Lompoc (1905) 30' quadrangle has the name "Arroyo de los Alamos" for part of the stream, but United States Board on Geographic Names (1961a, p. 12) rejected this designation. The Board (1933, p. 664) also rejected the names "Guaymas River," "Jesus Maria River," and "Las Alamos Creek" for the stream.

(2) *stream,* flows 6.25 miles to Maria Ygnacio Creek 1.25 miles east-northeast of downtown Goleta (lat. 34°26'30" N, long. 119° 48'15" W). Named on Goleta (1950) and San Marcos Pass (1959) 7.5' quadrangles.

San Antonio Creek: see **San Antonio River** [MONTEREY].

San Antonio Hills: see **San Antonio River** [MONTEREY].

San Antonio Range: see **San Antonio River** [MONTEREY].

San Antonio Reservoir [MONTEREY]: *lake,* behind a dam on San Antonio River 6.5 miles southwest of Bradley (lat. 35°47'55" N, long. 120°53' W; sec. 34, T 24 S, R 10 E). Named on Tierra Redonda Mountain (1949, photorevised 1979) 7.5' quadrangle. United States Board on Geographic Names (1979b, p. 6) approved the name "Lake San Antonio" for the feature.

San Antonio River [MONTEREY]: *stream,* flows 58 miles to Salinas River at Bradley (lat. 35°51'30" N, long. 120°48' W; sec. 8, T 24 S, R 11 E); the stream goes past San Antonio mission. Named on Bear Canyon (1949), Bradley (1949), Bryson (1949), Cone Peak (1949), Cosio Knob (1949), Jolon (1949), Tierra Redonda Mountain (1949), and Williams Hill (1949) 7.5' quadrangles. Called Rio de S. Antonio on Parke's (1854-1855) map. Irelan (p. 405) called the stream San Antonio Creek. According to Gudde (1949, p. 297), Junipero Serra named the river before he founded San Antonio mission. North Fork enters from the northwest 44 miles upstream from the mouth of the river; it is 6.25 miles long and is named on Cone Peak (1949) 7.5' quadrangle—North Fork has the name "Indian Creek" on a Forest Service map of 1908 (Clark, 1991, p. 229). According to Smith (p. 11), the valley of San Antonio River was known in early Spanish times as the valley of Los Robles. Eldridge (1903) called it San Antonio Valley. Antisell (1856, p. 41) and Whitney (p. 111) used the name "San Antonio Hills" for the range that lies between San Antonio River and Salinas River. Whitney (p. 151) also used the name "San Antonio Range" for the same feature.

San Antonio River: see **Pajaro River** [MONTEREY-SAN BENITO-SANTA CRUZ].

San Antonio Terrace [SANTA BARBARA]: *area,* 3.5 miles west-southwest of the village of Casmalia (lat. 34°49' N, long. 120°35'15" W); the place is north of the lower part of San Antonio Creek (1). Named on Casmalia (1959) 7.5' quadrangle.

San Antonio Valley [SANTA BARBARA]: *valley,* along San Antonio Creek (1) above a point 4.5 miles south-southwest of the village of Casmalia (lat. 34°46'30" N, long. 120°33'15" W). Named on Casmalia (1959) and Orcutt (1959) 7.5' quadrangles.

San Antonio Valley: see **San Antonio River** [MONTEREY].

San Aqueda Creek: see **Santa Agueda Creek** [SANTA BARBARA].

San Ardo [MONTEREY]: *town,* 18 miles southeast of King City at the mouth of Pancho Rico Valley (lat. 35°01'15" N, long. 120°54'15" W). Named on San Ardo (1967) 7.5' quadrangle. M.J. Brandenstein, owner of San Bernardo grant, laid out the town when the railroad reached the place in 1886; he called the community San Bernardo, but when postal authorities objected to this, he shortened the name to San Ardo (Gudde, 1949, p. 298). Postal authorities established San Bernardo post office in 1886 and changed the name to San Ardo in 1887 (Frickstad, p. 109).

San Augustin [SANTA CRUZ]: *land grant,* at Scotts Valley (1). Named on Felton (1955) and Laurel (1955) 7.5' quadrangles. Joseph L. Majors received 1 league in 1841 and claimed 4437 acres patented in 1866 (Cowan, p. 72).

San Augustin Canyon [SANTA BARBARA]: *canyon,* drained by a stream that flows 2.5 miles to the sea 4.5 miles west-southwest of East Point on Santa Rosa Island (lat. 33°55'15" N, long. 120°02'25" W). Named on Santa Rosa Island South (1943) 7.5' quadrangle.

San Augustine [SANTA BARBARA]: *locality,* nearly 7 miles east of Point Conception along Southern Pacific Railroad (lat. 34°27'35" N, long. 120°21'25" W); the place is near the mouth of Arroyo San Augustine. Named on Sacate (1953) 7.5' quadrangle.

San Bartolome: see **Pleyto** [MONTEREY] (1).

San Benancio Gulch [MONTEREY]: *canyon,* drained by a stream that flows 5.5 miles to El Toro Creek 7 miles south-southwest of Salinas (lat. 36°34'50" N, long. 121°43' W). Named on Spreckels (1947) 7.5' quadrangle. According to Gudde (1949, p. 298), a map of 1834 has the name "Cañada de San Benancio."

San Benito [MONTEREY]: *land grant,* along Salinas River at San Lucas. Named on Espinosa Canyon (1949) and San Lucas (1949) 7.5' quadrangles. Francisco Garcia received 1.5 leagues in 1842; James Watson claimed 6671 acres patented in 1869 (Cowan, p. 73).

San Benito [SAN BENITO]: *locality,* 18 miles southeast of Paicines (lat. 36°30'35" N, long. 121°04'50" W; on W line sec. 26, T 16 S, R 8 E); the place is near San Benito River. Named on San Benito (1968) 7.5' quadrangle. Postal authorities established San Benito post office in 1869, moved it 1 mile southeast in 1940, and discontinued it in 1968 (Salley, p. 192).

San Benito Hill [SAN BENITO]: *locality,* 5.25 miles south of Idria (lat. 36°20'35" N, long. 120°39'50" W; sec. 21, T 18 S, R 12 E); the place is along San Benito River. Site named on San Benito Mountain (1969) 7.5' quadrangle.

San Benito Mountain [SAN BENITO]: *peak,* 3.5 miles south-southeast of Idria (lat. 36°22'10" N, long. 120°38'35" W; on N line sec. 15, T 18 S, R 12 E). Altitude 5241 feet. Named on San Benito Mountain (1969) 7.5' quadrangle.

San Benito River [SAN BENITO]: *stream,* flows 105 miles to Pajaro River nearly 4 miles north-northwest of San Juan Bautista (lat. 36° 53'45" N, long. 121°33'45" W). Named on Santa Cruz (1956) 1°x 2° quadrangle. Called Rio San Benito on Parke's (1854-1855) map, called R. Pajaro on Eddy's (1854) map, and called San Juan Riv. on Holt's (1863) map. Goddard's (1857) map has the name "Cañada Benito" along upper reaches of the river. Crespi gave the name "San Benedicto" to the stream in 1772 to honor Saint Benedict, but the name later was contracted to San Benito (Bradley and Logan, p. 616). Elliott and Moore (p. 163) mentioned that Cinnabar post office was located 22 miles from Hollister on the right bank of San Benito River. Salley (p. 44) noted that postal authorities established Cinnabar post office 5 miles north of San Benito post office in 1875 and discontinued it in 1882.

San Benito Valley: see **San Juan Valley** [SAN BENITO].

San Benvenuto: see **Santa Rosa Creek** [SAN LUIS OBISPO].

San Bernabe [MONTEREY]: *land grant,* along Salinas River south and southeast of King City. Named on San Lucas (1949) and Thompson Canyon (1949) 7.5' quadrangles. Jesus Molina and Petronilo Rios received 3 leagues in 1841 and 1842; Henry Cocks claimed 13,297 acres patented in 1873 (Cowan, p. 73; Perez, p. 88). Cocks was an English marine on United States Man-of-War *Dale*; he deserted at Monterey in 1846, married a daughter of Francisco Garcia, and moved in 1853 to San Bernabe grant, where his adobe house was known as Cocks'Station (Howard, p. 90).

San Bernardino: see **San Bernardo** [MONTEREY].

San Bernardo [MONTEREY]: *land grant,* along Salinas River at San Ardo. Named on Espinosa Canyon (1949), Hames Valley (1949), San Ardo (1967), and Wunpost (1949) 7.5' quadrangles. Mariano Soberanes and Jose Soberanes received 3 leagues in 1841; Mariano Soberanes claimed 13,346 acres patented in 1874 (Cowan, p. 73—Cowan listed the grant under the name "San Bernardino"; Perez, p. 89).

San Bernardo [SAN LUIS OBISPO]: *land grant,* near the coast at the town of Morro Bay. Named on Morro Bay North (1965) and Morro Bay South (1965) 7.5' quadrangles. Vicente Cane received 1 league in 1840 and claimed 4379 acres patented in 1865 (Cowan, p. 73).

San Bernardo: see **San Ardo** [MONTEREY].

San Bernardo Creek [SAN LUIS OBISPO]: *stream,* flows nearly 7 miles to Chorro Creek 3.25 miles east-southeast of Morro Rock (lat. 35°21'25" N, long. 120°48'40" W). Named on Atascadero (1965), Morro Bay North (1965), and Morro Bay South (1965) 7.5' quadrangles.

San Bernardo Creek: see **Pancho Rico Creek** [MONTEREY].

San Buenaventura: see **Santa Rosa Creek** [SAN LUIS OBISPO].

San Carlos Bolsa [SAN BENITO]: *area,* 3 miles east of Idria (lat. 36° 24'55" N, long. 120°37'15" W); the place is on upper reaches of East Fork San Carlos Creek. Named on Ciervo Mountain (1969) and Idria (1969) 7.5' quadrangles. According to Anderson and Pack (p. 20), *bolsa* means "pocket" or "purse" in Spanish, and applies to a topographic basin.

San Carlos Canyon [MONTEREY]: *canyon,* drained by a stream that flows 1.5 miles to lowlands 3 miles east-northeast of Greenfield (lat. 36°20'05" N, long. 121°11'20" W). Named on Greenfield (1956) 7.5' quadrangle.

San Carlos Creek [SAN BENITO]: *stream,* flows 9 miles to join Larious Creek and form Silver Creek 3.5 miles north of Idria (lat. 36°28'05" N, long. 120°41'05" W; near N line sec. 8, T 17 S, R 12 E); the stream heads southeast of San Carlos Peak. Named on Idria (1969) 7.5' quadrangle. East Fork enters from the east 3 miles upstream from the mouth of the main stream; it is 9 miles long and is named on Ciervo Mountain (1969) and Idria (1969) 7.5' quadrangles.

San Carlos de Jonata [SANTA BARBARA]: *land grant,* at and north of Buellton. Named on Los Alamos (1959), Los Olivos (1959), Santa Ynez (1959), Solvang (1959), and Zaca Creek (1959) 7.5' quadrangles. Joaquin Carrillo and others received 6 leagues in 1846 and claimed 26,634 acres patented in 1872 (Cowan, p. 74). According to Perez (p. 89), Joaquin Carillo and Jose Covarrubias were the grantees in 1845 and the patentees in 1872.

San Carlos Peak [SAN BENITO]: *peak,* 2 miles south-southeast of Idria (lat. 36°23'30" N, long. 120°39'20" W; sec. 4, T 18 S, R 12 E); the peak is near San Carlos Creek and San Carlos mine. Altitude 4845 feet. Named on Idria (1969) 7.5' quadrangle.

San Carlos River: see **Carmel River** [MONTEREY].

San Carpoforo Creek [MONTEREY-SAN LUIS OBISPO]: *stream,* heads in Monterey County and flows 10.5 miles to the sea 11 miles northwest of the village of San Simeon in San Luis Obispo County (lat. 35°45'50" N, long. 121°19'25" W). Named on Burro Mountain (1949) 7.5' quadrangle. Crespi gave the name "Santa Humiliana" to the stream when the Portola expedition reached it in 1769 (Wagner, H.R., p. 511). United States Board on Geographic Names (1933, p. 664) rejected the names "San Carpojaro Creek," "San Carpojo Creek," and "San Carpovoro Creek." for the stream, and later the Board (1943, p. 12) rejected the names "Arroyo San Carpoforo," "Arroyo San Carpojo," "San Carpoforo Valley," and "San Carpojoro Creek."

San Carpoforo Valley: see **San Carpoforo Creek** [MONTEREY-SAN LUIS OBISPO].

San Carpojaro Creek: see **San Carpoforo Creek** [MONTEREY-SAN LUIS OBISPO].

San Carpojo Creek: see **San Carpoforo Creek** [MONTEREY-SAN LUIS OBISPO].

San Carpojoro Creek: see **San Carpoforo Creek** [MONTEREY-SAN LUIS OBISPO].

San Carpovoro Creek: see **San Carpoforo Creek** [MONTEREY-SAN LUIS OBISPO].

San Clemente Creek [MONTEREY]: *stream,* flows 7.5 miles to a lake 3.5 miles south-southeast of the town of Carmel Valley along Carmel River (lat. 36°25'55" N, long. 121°42'45" W; near S line sec. 23, T 17 S, R 2 E). Named on Carmel Valley (1956) and Mount Carmel (1956) 7.5' quadrangles. The stream first was called Redwood Creek (Clark, 1991, p. 505).

San Clemente Ridge [MONTEREY]: *ridge,* west-trending, nearly 2 miles long, 4.25 miles south-southwest of the town of Carmel Valley (lat. 36°25'15" N, long. 121°45'30" W); the ridge is south of San Clemente Creek. Named on Carmel Valley (1956) and Mount Carmel (1956) 7.5' quadrangles.

Sand Canyon: see **Sandy Canyon** [SAN LUIS OBISPO].

Sand City [MONTEREY]: *village,* 2 miles northeast of Monterey near the coast (lat. 36°37' N, long. 121°50'50" W). Named on Seaside (1947, photorevised 1983) 7.5' quadrangle. Postal authorities established Sand City post office in 1961 (Salley, p. 193). Sand City occupies an area 2.5 miles long and 0.5 mile wide; it incorporated in 1960 with the backing of sand companies, and is almost entirely industrial (Grant Harden in *San Jose Mercury News*, February 15, 1981).

Sand Creek [MONTEREY]: *stream,* flows 8 miles to Piney Creek 11 miles west-southwest of Greenfield (lat. 36°15'50" N, long. 121° 25'50" W; sec. 21, T 19 S, R 5 E). Named on Sycamore Flat (1956) 7.5' quadrangle.

Sand Creek: see **Big Sand Creek** [MONTEREY]; **Bracken Brae Creek** [SANTA CRUZ]; **Little Sand Creek** [MONTEREY]; **Sandy Canyon** [SAN LUIS OBISPO].

Sand Cut: see **Aromas** [MONTEREY-SAN BENITO].

Sand Hill [MONTEREY]: *hill,* 0.25 mile south of Point Lobos near the coast (lat. 36°31'05" N, long. 121°57' W). Named on Monterey (1947) 7.5' quadrangle.

Sand Hill Bluff [SANTA CRUZ]: *relief feature,* 7 miles west-northwest of Point Santa Cruz along the coast (lat. 36°58'40" N, long. 122°09' W). Named on Santa Cruz (1954) 7.5' quadrangle.

Sand Hill Cove [MONTEREY]: *embayment,* nearly 1 mile south-southeast of Point Lobos along the coast (lat. 36°31' N, long. 121° 56'55" W); the embayment is southeast of Sand Hill. Named on Monterey (1947) 7.5' quadrangle. California Department of Parks and Recreation's map shows a feature called Pebbly Beach situated 0.5 mile southeast of Sand Hill Cove, about halfway between Sand Hill Cove and China Cove; United States Board on Geographic Names (1980, p. 4) approved the name "Weston Beach" for this feature to honor photographer Edward Weston, noted for his photographs of Point Lobos and vicinity.

San Diego Creek [SAN LUIS OBISPO]: *stream,* heads in Kern County and flows 3.5 miles to Carrizo Plain 8 miles east-southeast of Simmler (lat. 35°19'20" N, long. 119°51'05" W; near N line sec. 17, T 30 S, R 20 E). Named on McKittrick Summit (1959) 7.5' quadrangle. McKittrick (1912) 30' quadrangle has the form "Sandiego Creek" for the name. United States Board on Geographic Names (1933, p. 665) first approved the form "Sandiego Creek," but later (1978d, p. 3) decided in favor of the form "San Diego Creek."

San Diego Joe's [SAN LUIS OBISPO]: *locality,* 8 miles east-southeast of Simmler along Sandiego Creek (present San Diego Creek) (lat. 35°19'45" N, long. 119°50'40" W; near E line sec. 8, T 30 S, R 20 E). Named on McKittrick (1912) 30' quadrangle.

Sand Point [SANTA BARBARA]: *promontory,* 1 mile west of downtown Carpinteria along the coast (lat. 34°23'45" N, long. 119°32'10" W). Named on Carpinteria (1952) 7.5' quadrangle. Esteban Jose Martinez gave the name "Punta de Nuestra Señora de los Angeles" to the feature in 1782 (Wagner, H.R., p. 478).

Sands: **Henry Sands Canyon** [MONTEREY].

Sand Spring: see **Lower Sand Spring** [SANTA BARBARA].

Sandstone Point [SANTA BARBARA]: *promontory,* 3.5 miles southeast of San Pedro Point at the east end of Santa Cruz Island (lat. 33°59'40" N, long. 119°33'45" W). Named on Santa Cruz Island D (1943) 7.5' quadrangle. Goodyear (1890, map following p. 156) showed Shaw Anch. [Anchorage] off present Sandstone Point. The name "Shaw" recalls Dr. Shaw, who was superintendent of Santa Cruz Island Company (Doran, p. 151).

Sandstone Ridge [MONTEREY]: *ridge,* east-northeast-trending, 1.5 miles long, 5 miles southwest of Salinas (lat. 36°38' N, long. 121° 43'30" W). Named on Salinas (1947) 7.5' quadrangle.

Sandy Beach [MONTEREY]: *beach,* 1.25 miles southeast of Point Lobos along the coast (lat. 36°30'25" N, long. 121°56'20" W). Named on Monterey (1947) 7.5' quadrangle. Called Gibson Beach on California Department of Parks and Recreation's map—the beach is by the mouth of Gibson Creek; the map has the name "Pelican Point" for the promontory at the west end of the beach.

Sandy Canyon [SAN LUIS OBISPO]: *canyon,* drained by a stream that flows 8 miles to San Juan Valley 15 miles southeast of Shandon (lat. 35°30'20" N, long. 120°11'30" W; near W line sec. 7, T 28 S, R 17 E). Named on La Panza NE (1966) and La Panza Ranch (1966) 7.5' quadrangles. Called Sand Canyon on Holland Canyon (1961) 7.5' quadrangle. The stream in the canyon is called Sand Creek on La Panza (1935) 15' quadrangle, and on Packwood Creek (1961) 7.5' quadrangle, but United States Board on Geographic Names (1968b, p. 9) rejected the names "Sand Canyon" and "Sand Creek" for the feature.

Sandy Creek: see **Big Sandy Creek** [MONTEREY].

Sandy Flat Gulch [SANTA CRUZ]: *canyon,* drained by a stream that flows 1.25 miles to the sea 3.5 miles west of Point Santa Cruz (lat. 36°57'15" N, long. 122°05'25" W). Named on Santa Cruz (1954) 7.5' quadrangle.

Sandyland [SANTA BARBARA]: *settlement,* nearly 2 miles west-northwest of Carpinteria along the coast (lat. 34°24'20" N, long. 119°32'45" W). Named on Carpinteria (1952) 7.5' quadrangle.

Sandyland Cove [SANTA BARBARA]: *embayment,* 1 mile west of downtown Carpinteria along the coast (lat. 34°23'45" N, long. 119° 32' W); the feature is 1 mile southeast of Sandyland. Named on Carpinteria (1952) 7.5' quadrangle.

Sandy Point [SANTA BARBARA]: *promontory,* at the westernmost tip of Santa Rosa Island (lat. 34°00'05" N, long. 120°14'55" W). Named on Santa Rosa Island West (1943) 7.5' quadrangle. Doran (p. 190) called the feature West Point. United States Coast and Geodetic Survey (p. 111) described Talcott Shoal, which is 1.5 miles north-northeast of Sandy Point.

San Felipe Lake [SAN BENITO]: *lake,* 3300 feet long, 9.5 miles north-northwest of Hollister (lat. 36°58'55" N, long. 121°27'35" W); the lake is connected to the head of Pajaro River by an artificial watercourse. Named on San Felipe (1955) 7.5' quadrangle. The feature also was called Soap Lake because Jose Maria Sanchez and Thomas O. Larkin had a soap-making operation there until 1848 (Hoover, Rensch, and Rensch, p. 312).

San Francisco Canyon [SAN LUIS OBISPO]: *canyon,* 1.25 miles long, drained by a stream that enters Dover Canyon 2.5 miles northwest of York Mountain (lat. 35°34'15" N, long. 120°51'45" W; sec. 23, T 27 S, R 10 E). Named on Adelaida (1961) 15' quadrangle.

San Francisco Mountain: see **Sugarloaf Mountain** [SANTA CRUZ].

San Francisquito [MONTEREY]: *land grant,* south of Carmel Valley (1) 7.5' miles east-southeast of the mouth of Carmel River. Named on Mount Carmel (1956) and Seaside (1947) 7.5' quadrangles. Catalina Manzaneli de Munras received 2 leagues in 1835; Jose Abrego and others claimed 8814 acres patented in 1862 (Cowan, p. 77).

San Francisquito Flat [MONTEREY]: *valley,* 7 miles east of Soberanes Point (lat. 36°27'25" N, long. 121°48'15" W); the valley is on San Francisquito grant. Named on Mount Carmel (1956) 7.5' quadrangle. According to Gudde (1949, p. 304), the place probably was mentioned as early as 1822 under the name "el llanito de San Francisquito."

San Geronimo [SAN LUIS OBISPO]: *land grant,* northwest of Cayucos near the coast. Named on Cambria (1959), Cayucos (1965), and Cypress Mountain (1948) 7.5' quadrangles. Rafael Villavicencio received 2 leagues in 1842 and claimed 8893 acres patented in 1876 (Cowan, p. 78). Postal authorities established Villa Creek post office on the grant in 1879 and discontinued it the same year (Salley, p. 231).

San Jacinto Canyon: see **Lowes Canyon** [MONTEREY-SAN LUIS OBISPO].

San Jacinto Creek [MONTEREY-SAN LUIS OBISPO]: *stream,* heads in Monterey County and flows 16 miles to Estrella Creek 3 miles southeast of San Miguel in San Luis Obispo County (lat. 35°43'40" N, long. 120°39'25" W; near W line sec. 26, T 25 S, R 12 E). Named on Paso Robles (1948) and San Miguel (1948) 7.5' quadrangles. The stream drains Lowes Canyon.

Sanja Cota Creek: see **Zanja de Cota Creek** [SANTA BARBARA].

San Joaquin [SAN BENITO]: *land grant,* 4.5 miles northeast of Hollister. Named on San Felipe (1955) and Three Sisters (1954) 7.5' quadrangles. Cruz Cervantes received 2 leagues in 1836 and claimed 7425 acres patented in 1874 (Cowan, p. 69; Cowan gave the alternate name "Rosa Morada" for the grant).

San Joaquin Peak [SAN BENITO]: *peak,* 8.5 miles east-northeast of Hollister (lat. 36°54'15" N, long. 121°15'40" W; sec. 12, T 12 S, R 6 E); the peak is east of San Joaquin grant. Altitude 2918 feet. Named on Three Sisters (1954) 7.5' quadrangle.

Sanjon de Borregas: see **Borregas Creek** [SANTA CRUZ].

Sanjon de la Brea: see **Pajaro River** [MONTEREY-SAN BENITO].

Sanjon del Pescadero: see **Pescadero Creek** [SAN BENITO].

Sanjon del Tembladera: see **Tembladero Slough** [MONTEREY].

Sanjon del Tequesquite: see **Pajaro River** [MONTEREY-SAN BENITO-SANTA CRUZ]; **Tequisquita Slough** [SAN BENITO].

San Jose: see **Pozo** [SAN LUIS OBISPO].

San Jose Creek [MONTEREY]: *stream,* flows 8.5 miles to Carmel Bay nearly 1 mile south of the mouth of Carmel River (lat. 36°31'35" N, long. 121°55'25" W); the stream is on San Jose y Sur Chiquito grant. Named on Monterey (1947) and Mount Carmel (1956) 7.5' quadrangles. According to Howard (p. 32), the name of the stream probably came from an Indian village called San Jose by the Spaniards and located west of the mouth of the creek. North Fork enters 1.25 miles upstream from the mouth of the creek; it is 2.25 miles long and is named on Monterey (1947) 7.5' quadrangle.

San Jose Creek [SANTA BARBARA]: *stream,* flows 10 miles to San Pedro Creek 1 mile south of downtown Goleta (lat. 34°25'15" N, long. 119°49'45" W). Named on Goleta (1950) and San Marcos Pass (1959) 7.5' quadrangles.

San Jose Mountains: see **La Panza Range** [SAN LUIS OBISPO].

San Jose Range: see **La Panza Range** [SAN LUIS OBISPO].

San Jose Valley: see **Pozo** [SAN LUIS OBISPO].

San Jose y Sur Chiquito [MONTEREY]: *land grant,* between Carmel River and Palo Colorado Canyon near the coast. Named on Monterey (1947) and Soberanes Point (1956) 7.5' quadrangles. Teodoro Gonzales received 2 leagues in 1835, and Marcelino Escobar received the land in 1839; Jose Castro claimed 8876 acres patented in 1888 (Cowan, p. 80—Cowan used the form "Chiquita" in the name; Perez, p. 92).

San Juan: see **San Juan Bautista** [SAN BENITO].

San Juan Bautista [SAN BENITO]: *town,* 7.5 miles west of Hollister (lat. 36°50'40" N, long. 121°32'10" W); the town is in San Juan Valley. Named on San Juan Bautista (1955) 7.5' quadrangle. Called S. Juan Baptista on Farnham's (1845) map, and called San Juan on Goddard's (1857) map. The town grew around San Juan Bautista mission, founded in 1797 on the feast day of Saint John the Baptist, and named for that saint (Hoover, Rensch, and Rensch, p. 309). Jose Tiburcio Castro became the civil administrator of the mission after secularization, and for a short time the town was known as San Juan de Castro (Pierce, p. 29). Postal authorities established San Juan post office in 1851 and changed the name to San Juan Bautista in 1905 (Frickstad, p. 137). The town incorporated in 1896. A military establishment at the place during the Civil War was called Camp Low for California Governor Frederick F. Low (Hoover, Rensch, and Rensch, p. 311). San Juan Bautista (1917) 15' quadrangle shows California Central Railroad extending southeast from Southern Pacific Railroad at Pajaro River and through the valley east of San Juan Bautista before continuing on up present San Juan Canyon for 3 miles. California Mining Bureau's (1917b) map shows two stations on this rail line: Prescott, located less than 2 miles north of San Juan Bautista, and Canfield, situated about halfway from Prescott to the junction with Southern Pacific Railroad.

San Juan Canyon [SAN BENITO]: *canyon,* drained by a stream that flows 4.5 miles to San Juan Valley less than 1 mile south-southeast of San Juan Bautista (lat. 36°50'05" N, long. 121°31'40" W; sec. 4, T 13 S, R 4 E). Named on Hollister (1955) and San Juan Bautista (1955) 7.5' quadrangles. The stream in the canyon is called San Juan Creek on San Juan Bautista (1917) 15' quadrangle.

San Juan Creek [SAN LUIS OBISPO]: *stream,* flows 45 miles to join Cholame Creek and form Estrella River at Shandon (lat. 35°39'35" N, long. 120°22'10" W; near NW cor. sec. 21, T 26 S, R 15 E). Named on Branch Mountain (1967), California Valley (1966), Camatta Canyon (1961), Cholame (1961), Holland Canyon (1961), La Panza (1967), La Panza Ranch (1966), and Shandon (1961) 7.5' quadrangles. Called San Juan River on Cholame (1917) 30' quadrangle. Antisell (1856, p. 93) considered San Juan Creek and Estrella Creek as one stream, referred to "San Juan or Estrella river," and stated that the upper part of this combined stream is called Carrizo Creek.

San Juan Creek: see **San Juan Canyon** [SAN BENITO].

San Juan Range: see **Gabilan Range** [MONTEREY-SAN BENITO].

San Juan River: see **San Benito River** [SAN BENITO]; **San Juan Creek** [SAN LUIS OBISPO].

San Juan Valley [SAN BENITO]: *valley,* along San Benito River from west of Hollister to Pajaro River; San Juan Bautista is in the valley. Named on Chittenden (1955), Hollister (1955), and San Juan Bautista (1955) 7.5' quadrangles. Called San Benito Valley on San Juan Bautista (1917) 15' quadrangle.

San Juan Valley [SAN LUIS OBISPO]: *valley,* opens into lowlands 2.5 miles south-southeast of Shandon (lat. 35°37' N, long. 120° 21' W); the valley is along the lower course of San Juan Creek. Named on Camatta Canyon (1961) and Holland Canyon (1961) 7.5' quadrangles.

San Julian [SANTA BARBARA]: *land grant,* southeast of the city of Lompoc. Named on Gaviota (1953), Lompoc Hills (1959), Point Conception (1953), Sacate (1953), Santa Rosa Hills (1959), and Solvang (1959) 7.5' quadrangles. George Rock, acting for Jose de la Guerra y Noriega, received 6 leagues in 1837; Jose de la Guerra y Noriega claimed 48,221 acres patented in 1873 (Cowan, p. 82). The place was called Rancho Nacional when it was established in 1817 to provide meat for soldiers at Santa Barbara (Dibblee, p. 11).

San Justo [SAN BENITO]: *land grant,* at and around Hollister. Named on Hollister (1955), San Felipe (1955), San Juan Bautista (1955), and Tres Pinos (1955) 7.5' quadrangles. Jose Castro received 4 leagues in 1839; Francisco Perez Pacheco claimed 34,620 acres patented in 1865 (Cowan, p. 82).

San Lawrence Terrace [SAN LUIS OBISPO]: *settlement,* 1 mile east-southeast of San Miguel on the east side of Salinas River (lat. 35°44'45" N, long. 120°41' W; sec. 21, T 25 S, R 12 E). Named on Paso Robles (1948) 7.5' quadrangle.

San Lorenzo [MONTEREY]:

(1) *land grant,* at and north of King City. Named on Greenfield (1956), Pinalito Canyon (1969), San Lucas (1949), and Thompson Canyon (1949) 7.5' quadrangles. Feliciano Soberanes received 5 leagues in 1841 and claimed 21,884 acres patented in 1866 (Cowan, p. 83).

(2) *land grant,* 18 miles east of King City, where it covers part of Peachtree Valley. Named on Monarch Peak (1967), Nattrass Valley (1967), and Priest Valley (1969) 7.5' quadrangles. Francisco Rico received 5 leagues in 1842; the heirs of Andrew Randall claimed 22,264 acres patented in 1870 (Cowan, p. 83).

San Lorenzo [MONTEREY-SAN BENITO]: *land grant,* 10 miles east-northeast of Greenfield on Monterey-San Benito County line. Named on Greenfield (1956), North Chalone Peak (1969), and Pinalito Canyon (1969), Rock Spring Peak (1969), and Topo Valley (1969) 7.5' quadrangles. Rafael Sanchez received 11 leagues in 1846 and claimed 48,286 acres patented in 1870 (Cowan, p. 83).

San Lorenzo Creek [MONTEREY-SAN BENITO]: *stream,* heads near Priest Valley and flows 45 miles, partly along Monterey-San Benito County line, to Salinas River at King City (lat. 36°11'50" N, long. 121°07'30" W). Named on Santa Cruz (1956) 1°x 2° quadrangle. Called Rio de San Lorenzo on Parke's (1854-1855) map. Parke (p. 13) also used the name "San Lorenzo creek" for the feature, which he stated "forms what is known as the San Lorenzo Pass" to Tulare plain. Derby's (1850) map has the name "Pass of San Lorenzo" along the creek. Gabb (p. 106) referred to San Lorenzo Valley, and Fairbanks (1894, p. 522) mentioned Lorenzo Creek. On Eldridge's (1901) map and on Hamlin's (1904) map, the part of present San Lorenzo Creek in Peachtree Valley has the name "Peachtree Cr."

San Lorenzo Creek: see **Lorenzo Vasquez Canyon** [SAN BENITO].

San Lorenzo Park [SANTA CRUZ]: *settlement,* 4.5 miles east-northeast of Big Basin near San Lorenzo River (lat. 37°11'45" N, long. 122°08'35" W; sec. 36, T 8 S, R 3 W). Named on Big Basin (1955) 7.5' quadrangle. The place also is called San Lorenzo River Park (Clark, 1986, p. 310). Hamman's (1980b) map shows a place called McGaffigan's Switch located along a railroad at about present San Lorenzo Park; it was named for Patrick J. McGaffigan, a lumber company superintendent (Hamman, p. 118). The same map shows a place called Waterman Switch located 1.5 miles up the river from present San Lorenzo Park along a railroad; it was at the end of a mile-long skid road built to bring lumber over Waterman Gap (Hamman, p. 123). The same map also shows a stream called Feeder Creek that joins San Lorenzo River 1 mile south of present San Lorenzo Park; the name is from use of water from the stream to augment the water in a V-flume that carried lumber down the canyon of San Lorenzo River to Felton (Hoover, Rensch, and Rensch, p. 479).

San Lorenzo Pass: see **San Lorenzo Creek** [MONTEREY-SAN BENITO].

San Lorenzo River [SANTA CRUZ]: *stream,* flows 30 miles to the sea 1.25 miles northeast of Point Santa Cruz in Santa Cruz (lat. 36° 57'50" N, long. 122°00'40" W). Named on Big Basin (1955), Castle Rock Ridge (1955), Cupertino (1961), Felton (1955), Mindego Hill (1961), and Santa Cruz (1954) 7.5' quadrangles. Members of the Portola expedition named the stream in 1769 (Wagner, H.R., p. 410). Goddard's (1857) map has the name "San Agustine C." for what appears to be present San Lorenzo River, and Trask (p. 24) mentioned Rio San Augustine in 1854

San Lorenzo River Park: see **San Lorenzo Park** [SANTA BARBARA].

San Lorenzo Valley: see **Peachtree Valley** [MONTEREY]; **San Lorenzo Creek** [MONTEREY].

San Louis Pass: see **Cuesta Pass** [SAN LUIS OBISPO].

San Lucas [MONTEREY]:

(1) *land grant,* south of the village of San Lucas near Salinas River. Named on Espinosa Canyon (1949) and San Ardo (1967) 7.5' quadrangles. Rafael Estrada received 2 leagues in 1842; James McKinley claimed 8875 acres patented in 1872 (Cowan, p. 83).

(2) *village,* 8 miles southeast of King City along Salinas River (lat. 36°07'45" N, long. 121°01'10" W). Named on San Lucas (1949) 7.5' quadrangle. Officials of Southern Pacific Railroad named the place in 1886 for nearby San Lucas grant (Gudde, 1949, p. 308). Postal authorities established Griswold post office, named for William Griswold, first postmaster, in Long Valley (NE quarter sec. 27, T 20 N, R 10 E) in 1884; they moved it 8.5 miles west and changed the name to San Lucas in 1887 (Salley, p. 90; Clark, 1991, p. 198). Southern Pacific Railroad's (1890) map shows a place called Upland located along the railroad less than halfway from San Lucas to San Ardo.

San Lucas Canyon [MONTEREY]: *canyon,* 4.25 miles long, opens into lowlands 2.5 miles north of Lockwood (lat. 35°58'30" N, long. 121°05' W; sec. 34, T 22 S, R 8 E). Named on Espinosa Canyon (1949) and Williams Hill (1949) 7.5' quadrangles.

San Lucas Creek [SANTA BARBARA]: *stream,* flows 5 miles to Santa Ynez River 4 miles east-southeast of Santa Ynez (lat. 34° 35'30" N, long. 120°00'55" W). Named on Santa Ynez (1959) 7.5' quadrangle. Called Wons Creek on Los Olivos (1943) 15' quadrangle, but United States Board on Geographic Names (1961b, p. 14) rejected this name for the stream.

San Lucas Creek: see **Calabazal Creek** [SANTA BARBARA].

San Luis: see **Point San Luis** [SAN LUIS OBISPO]: **Port San Luis** [SAN LUIS OBISPO].

San Luis Canyon [SAN LUIS OBISPO]: *canyon,* drained by a stream that flows nearly 4 miles to Wilkinson Canyon 13 miles southeast of Shandon (lat. 35°32' N, long. 120°11'50" W; sec. 36, T 27 S, R 16 E). Named on Holland Canyon (1961) 7.5' quadrangle.

San Luis Hill [SAN LUIS OBISPO]: *peak,* 0.5 mile north-northwest of Point San Luis (lat. 35°10'05" N, long. 120°45'50" W). Altitude 705 feet. Named on Port San Luis (1965) 7.5' quadrangle.

San Luis Hot Spring: see **Sycamore Springs** [SAN LUIS OBISPO].

San Luisito [SAN LUIS OBISPO]: *land grant,* 7 miles northwest of San Luis Obispo along San Luisito Creek and Chorro Creek. Named on Morro Bay South (1965) and San Luis Obispo (1965) 7.5' quadrangles. Guadalupe Cantua received the land in 1841 and claimed 4390 acres patented in 1860 (Cowan, p. 84).

San Luisito Creek [SAN LUIS OBISPO]: *stream,* flows 6.25 miles to Chorro Creek 4.5 miles east-southeast of Morro Rock (lat. 35°21'15" N, long. 120°47'30" W); the stream is partly on San Luisito grant. Named on Atascadero (1965), Morro Bay South (1965), and San Luis Obispo (1965) 7.5' quadrangles.

San Luisito Creek: see **Chorro Creek** [SAN LUIS OBISPO].

San Luis Obispo [SAN LUIS OBISPO]: *city,* 9 miles from the coast along San Luis Obispo Creek (lat. 35°16'45" N, long. 120°39'30" W). Named on Arroyo Grande NE (1965), Lopez Mountain (1965), Pismo Beach (1965), and San Luis Obispo (1965) 7.5' quadrangles. The mission at the place was founded in 1772 and named for Saint Louis, Bishop of Toulouse; W.R. Hutton laid out and named the city in 1850 (Gudde, 1949, p. 309). Postal authorities established San Luis Obispo post office in 1851 (Frickstad, p. 166), and the city incorporated in 1856.

San Luis Obispo: see **Camp San Luis Obispo** [SAN LUIS OBISPO].

San Luis Obispo Bay [SAN LUIS OBISPO]: *embayment,* 9 miles south-southwest of San Luis Obispo (lat. 35°10' N, long. 120° 44' W); the feature is east of Point San Luis. Named on Pismo Beach (1965) and Port San Luis (1965) 7.5' quadrangles. According to Gleason (p. 128), Cabrillo discovered the embayment and named it Todos Santos. H.R. Wagner (p. 378) noted that at one time it was called Ensenada de Buchon, and he (p. 411) identified it also as the place called Ensenada de Abrigo where Vizcaino stopped and traded with Indians. Whitney (p. 139) called the feature Bay of San Luis. Chase (p. 143) mentioned a place on the shore of the embayment called Oilport, where oil pipelines reached the coast. Postal authorities established Oilport post office in 1907 and discontinued it in 1908 (Frickstad, p. 165).

San Luis Obispo Creek [SAN LUIS OBISPO]: *stream,* flows 17 miles to San Luis Obispo Bay at the west end of Avila Beach (lat. 35°10'45" N, long. 120°44'15" W); the stream goes through San Luis Obispo. Named on Lopez Mountain (1965), Pismo Beach (1965), and San Luis Obispo (1965) 7.5' quadrangles. Soldiers of the Portola expedition gave the name "Cañada Angosta" to the valley of the creek in 1769 (Wagner, H.R. p. 426).

San Luis Pass: see **Cuesta Pass** [SAN LUIS OBISPO].

San Luis Peak: see **Cerro San Luis Obispo** [SAN LUIS OBISPO],

San Luis Range: see **Irish Hills** [SAN LUIS OBISPO].

San Luis Valley: see **Los Osos Valley** [SAN LUIS OBISPO].

San Marcos [SANTA BARBARA]: *land grant,* north of San Marcos Pass along and north of Santa Ynez River. Named on Figueroa Mountain (1959), Lake Cachuma (1959), San Marcos Pass (1959), and San Rafael Mountain (1959) 7.5' quadrangles. Richard S. Den bought the land in 1846, and Nicholas A. Den claimed 35,573 acres patented in 1869; the property was part of Santa Barbara mission lands (Cowan, p. 84). Perez (p. 94) listed Nicolas A. Den and Richard Den as both grantees and patentees.

San Marcos: see **San Miguel** [SAN LUIS OBISPO].

San Marcos Creek [SAN LUIS OBISPO]: *stream,* flows 13 miles to Salinas River 6 miles north of Paso Robles (lat. 35°43'15" N, long. 120°41'40" W; sec. 29, T 25 S, R 12 E). Named on Adelaida (1948) and Paso Robles (1948) 7.5' quadrangles. According to Gudde (1949, p. 309), the stream was mentioned under the name "El arroyo de San Marcos" as early as 1795.

San Marcos Hot Springs: see **Hot Spring** [SANTA BARBARA].

San Marcos Pass [SANTA BARBARA]: *pass,* 10 miles northwest of Santa

Barbara (lat. 34°30'45" N, long. 119°49'30" W; near W line sec. 16, T 5 N, R 28 W). Named on San Marcos Pass (1959) 7.5' quadrangle.

San Marcos Trout Club [SANTA BARBARA]: *locality,* 4 miles north-northeast of Goleta (lat. 34°29'25" N, long. 119°47'55" W; sec. 27, T 5 N, R 28 W). Named on Goleta (1950) 7.5' quadrangle.

San Martin: see **Cape San Martin** [MONTEREY].

San Martin Rocks: see **Cape San Martin** [MONTEREY].

San Martin Top [MONTEREY]: *peak,* 3.25 miles east-southeast of Cape San Martin (lat. 35°52'30" N, long. 121°24'25" W; sec. 3, T 24 S, R 5 E). Named on Cape San Martin (1949) 7.5' quadrangle. The name is from Cape San Martin (Clark, 1991, p. 509).

San Miguel [SAN LUIS OBISPO]: *town,* 8.5 miles north of Paso Robles on the west side of Salinas River (lat. 35°45'20" N, long. 120°41'45" W). Named on Paso Robles (1948) and San Miguel (1948) 7.5' quadrangles. The Franciscans founded San Miguel Arcangel mission at the place in 1797; the site was known as Las Pozas in Spanish times (Gudde, 1949, p. 272, 310). The town was started south of the mission about 1846, but it was relocated north of the mission after a fire in 1887 (Lee and others, p. 136). Postal authorities established San Miguel post office in 1860, discontinued it the same year, reestablished it in 1861, and discontinued it in 1862; they established San Marcos post office in 1864, discontinued it in 1865, reestablished it in 1869, and moved it 3 miles north when they renamed it San Miguel in 1881 (Salley, p. 196). They established Cruessville post office 8 miles north of San Miguel in Monterey County near Big Sandy Creek (NE quarter sec. 8, T 24 S, R 12 E) in 1888 and discontinued it in 1891; the name was for Frank Cruess, first postmaster (Clark, 1991, p. 123).

San Miguel: see **Bolsa de las Escorpinas** [MONTEREY].

San Miguel Canyon [MONTEREY]: *canyon,* drained by a stream that flows 5 miles to Merritt Lake 0.5 mile south of Prunedale (lat. 36°46' N, long. 121°40'10" W). Named on Prunedale (1954) 7.5' quadrangle.

San Miguel Canyon [SAN LUIS OBISPO]: *canyon,* 1.25 miles long, opens into lowlands at the south edge of San Miguel (lat. 35°44'45" N, long. 120°42' W; near N line sec. 20, T 25 S, R 12 E). Named on Paso Robles (1919) 15' quadrangle.

San Miguel Creek [MONTEREY]: *stream,* flows 8 miles to Nacimiento River 10 miles east-northeast of Cape San Martin (lat. 35°56'50" N, long. 121°18' W; sec. 10, T 23 S, R 6 E). Named on Alder Peak (1949) and Cape San Martin (1949) 7.5' quadrangles. Clark (1991, p. 291) noted that a place called Mail Camp was situated near the confluence of San Miguel Creek and Nacimiento River; a stage brought mail from King City to the place, where pack animals were kept to carry the mail on to residents along the coast.

San Miguel Creek: see **Mission Creek** [MONTEREY].

San Miguel Island [SANTA BARBARA]: *island,* 9 miles long, 45 miles southwest of Santa Barbara (lat. 34°02'30" N, long. 120°22'30" W). Named on San Miguel Island East (1950) and San Miguel Island West (1950) 7.5' quadrangles. Cabrillo discovered the island in 1542 and gave the name "Islas de San Lucas" to it and neighboring islands (Wagner, H.R., p. 503). Cabrillo later called present San Miguel Island by the name "Isla Posesion," and after Cabrillo's death the island was called Isla de Juan Rodrigues and Isla Capitana to honor him (Wagner, H.R., p. 465, 486).

San Miguelito [MONTEREY]: *land grant,* 5 miles west-southwest of Jolon. Named on Alder Peak (1949), Bear Canyon (1949), and Jolon (1949) 7.5' quadrangles. Rafael Gonzales received 5 leagues in 1841; Mariana Gonzales claimed 22,136 acres patented in 1867 (Cowan, p. 86; Cowan listed the grant under the name "San Miguelito de Trinidad"). Perez (p. 94) listed Jose R. Gonzales as both grantee and patentee.

San Miguelito [SAN LUIS OBISPO]: *land grant,* near the coast on lower reaches of San Luis Obispo Creek and at Point San Luis. Named on Pismo Beach (1965) and Port San Luis (1965) 7.5' quadrangles. Miguel Avila received 2 leagues in 1842 and 1846; he claimed 14,198 acres patented in 1877 (Cowan, p. 85-86). Perez (p. 94) gave 1839 as the date of the grant.

San Miguelito Creek [SANTA BARBARA]: *stream,* flows 6.5 miles to the valley of Santa Ynez River 0.5 mile south-southwest of downtown Lompoc (lat. 34°37'50" N, long. 120°27'35" W). Named on Lompoc (1959), Lompoc Hills (1959), and Tranquillon Mountain (1959) 7.5' quadrangles.

San Miguelito de Trinidad: see **San Miguelito** [MONTEREY].

San Miguel Passage [SANTA BARBARA]: *water feature,* strait between San Miguel Island and Santa Rosa Island (lat. 34°01' N, long. 120°16' W). Named on San Miguel Island East (1950) and Santa Rosa Island West (1943) 7.5' quadrangles.

San Miguel Spring: see **Mission Creek** [MONTEREY].

San Pedro Alcantara: see **Scott Creek** [SANTA CRUZ].

San Pedro Canyon [SANTA BARBARA]: *canyon,* 3.5 miles long, along San Pedro Creek above a point 1.5 miles northwest of downtown Goleta (lat. 34°27'15" N, long. 119°50'35" W). Named on Goleta (1950) 7.5' quadrangle.

San Pedro Creek [SANTA BARBARA]: *stream,* flows 6.5 miles to the sea 1.25 miles south of downtown Goleta (lat. 34°25'05" N, long. 119°49'45" W). Named on Goleta (1950) 7.5' quadrangle.

San Pedro Point [SANTA BARBARA]: *promontory,* at the extreme east end of Santa Cruz Island (lat. 34°02'05" N, long. 119°31'10" W). Named on Santa Cruz Island D (1943) 7.5' quadrangle.

San Rafael Mountain [SANTA BARBARA]: *peak,* 21 miles north-northwest of Santa Barbara (lat. 34°42'40" N, long. 119°48'45" W; sec. 3, T 7 N, R 28 W); the peak is in San Rafael Mountains. Altitude 6593 feet. Named on San Rafael Mountain (1959) 7.5' quadrangle.

San Rafael Mountains [SANTA BARBARA]: *range,* south of Sisquoc River. Named on Bald Mountain (1964), Big Pine Mountain (1964), Figueroa Mountain (1959), Foxen Canyon (1964), Hurricane Deck (1964), San Rafael Mountain (1959), Twitchell Dam (1959), and Zaca Lake (1964) 7.5' quadrangles. Called Sierra de San Rafael on Parke's (1854-1855) map, but United States Board on Geographic Names (1965b, p. 15) rejected the names "Sierra de San Rafael" and "Sierra Madre Mountains" for the range.

San Rafael Mountains: see **Sierra Madre Mountains** [SANTA BARBARA].

San Ramon: see **Arroyo Grande** [SAN LUIS OBISPO] (1).

San Roque Canyon [SANTA BARBARA]: *canyon,* 4 miles long, along San Roque Creek above a point 3 miles northwest of downtown Santa Barbara (lat. 34°27' N, long. 119°44' W). Named on Santa Barbara (1952) 7.5' quadrangle. United States Board on Geographic Names (1961b, p. 15) rejected the name "San Rouke Canyon" for the feature.

San Roque Creek [SANTA BARBARA]: *stream,* flows 5.25 miles to Arroyo Burro (3) 3 miles west-northwest of downtown Santa Barbara (lat. 34°26'20" N, long. 119°44'45" W). Named on Santa Barbara (1952) 7.5' quadrangle.

San Roque Creek: see **Arroyo Burro** [SANTA BARBARA] (3).

San Rouke Canyon: see **San Roque Canyon** [SANTA BARBARA].

Sans [MONTEREY]: *locality,* 9 miles northeast of Cape San Martin (lat. 35°58'25" N, long. 121°20'20" W; sec. 32, T 22 S, R 6 E). Named on Cape San Martin (1921) 15' quadrangle, where the name applies to buildings situated near Nacimiento River, including one with the label "Nacimiento School."

San Simeon [SAN LUIS OBISPO]:

(1) *land grant,* on the coast between San Simeon Creek and Pico Creek. Named on Cambria (1959), Pebblestone Shut-in (1959), Pico Creek (1959), and San Simeon (1958) 7.5' quadrangles. Jose Ramon Estrada received 1 league in 1842; Jose Miguel Gomez claimed 4469 acres patented in 1865 (Cowan, p. 88).

(2) *village,* 38 miles northwest of San Luis Obispo near the coast (lat. 35°38'40" N, long. 121°11'20" W). Named on San Simeon (1958) 7.5' quadrangle. Leopold Frankl founded and named the village in the mid-1870's (Gudde, 1949, p. 313). Postal authorities established San Simeon post office in 1873, discontinued it in 1876, and reestablished it in 1878 (Frickstad, p. 166). The place was a whaling station (Bancroft, p. 523).

San Simeon: see **Cambria** [SAN LUIS OBISPO].

San Simeon Bay [SAN LUIS OBISPO]: *embayment,* along the coast at the village of San Simeon (lat. 35°38'25" N, long. 121°11'15" W). Named on San Simeon (1958) 7.5' quadrangle. Called Harbor of St. Simeon on Colton's (1855) map. According to Hamilton (p. 150), records of San Miguel mission for 1830 record Bay of San Simeon.

San Simeon Creek [SAN LUIS OBISPO]: *stream,* formed by the confluence of North Fork and South Fork, flows 5.5 miles to the sea 3.25 miles northwest of Cambria (lat. 35°35'40" N, long. 121°07'35" W). Named on Cambria (1959) 7.5' quadrangle. North Fork is 3.5 miles long and is named on Pebblestone Shut-in (1959) 7.5' quadrangle. South Fork is 4.5 miles long and is named on Cambria (1959) and Pebblestone Shut-in (1959) 7.5' quadrangles. Crespi called the stream Arroyo de San Nicolas when the Portola expedition reached the place in 1769; soldiers of the expedition called it El Cantil, probably because of steep cliffs there—*el cantil* means "a steep rock" in Spanish (Wagner, H.R., p. 439, 506).

San Simeon Point [SAN LUIS OBISPO]: *promontory,* 0.5 mile south-southwest of the village of San Simeon along the coast (lat. 35°38'05" N, long. 121°11'35" W); the feature is at San Simeon Bay. Named on San Simeon (1958) 7.5' quadrangle.

Santa Agueda Creek [SANTA BARBARA]: *stream,* flows 12 miles to Santa Ynez River 3.25 miles east-southeast of Santa Ynez (lat. 34°35'15" N, long. 120°01'55" W). Named on Los Olivos (1959) and Santa Ynez (1959) 7.5' quadrangles. United States Board on Geographic Names (1961b, p. 15) rejected the names "San Aqueda Creek" and "Santa Aqueda Creek" for the stream.

Santa Ana Creek [SAN BENITO]: *stream,* flows 20 miles to Tequisquita Slough 5.25 miles north of Hollister (lat. 36°55'40" N, long. 121°24'50" W); the upper part of the stream is on Santa Ana y Quien Sabe grant. Named on Hollister (1955), Quien Sabe Valley (1968), San Felipe (1955), and Tres Pinos (1955) 7.5' quadrangles.

Santa Ana Mountain [SAN BENITO]: *peak,* 8 miles east-northeast of Hollister (lat. 36°52'40" N, long. 121°15'45" W); the peak is on Santa Ana y Quien Sabe grant. Altitude 3112 feet. Named on Three Sisters (1954) 7.5' quadrangle.

Santa Ana Valley [SAN BENITO]: *valley,* 6 miles east of Hollister (lat.

36°50'30" N, long. 121°17'30" W); the valley is along Santa Ana Creek on Santa Ana y Quien Sabe grant. Named on Tres Pinos (1955) 7.5' quadrangle.

Santa Ana y Quien Sabe [SAN BENITO]: *land grant,* east of Hollister Valley in Diablo Range. Named on Mariposa Peak (1969), Quien Sabe Valley (1968), Three Sisters (1954), and Tres Pinos (1955) 7.5' quadrangles. Francisco Javier Castillo Negrete received 7 leagues in 1836; the land was regranted in 1839 to Manuel Larios and Juan Maria Anzar, who claimed 48,823 acres patented in 1860 (Cowan, p. 90). According to Gudde (1949, p. 277), *quien sabe* means "who knows?" in Spanish, and probably was applied to the grant in jest when the phrase came in answer to the question of the extent or ownership of the land.

Santa Anita: see **Drake** [SANTA BARBARA].

Santa Aqueda Creek: see **Santa Agueda Creek** [SANTA BARBARA].

Santa Barbara [SANTA BARBARA]: *city,* in the southeast part of Santa Barbara County (lat. 34°25'15" N, long. 119°41'50" W); the city is along Santa Barbara Channel. Named on Santa Barbara (1952) 7.5' quadrangle. Postal authorities established Santa Barbara post office in 1850 (Frickstad, p. 171), and the city incorporated the same year. Spaniards established Presidio de Santa Barbara Virgen y Martir at the place in 1782 (Frazer, p. 31); they founded Santa Barbara mission there in 1783 and named it for Santa Barbara Channel (Wagner, H.R., p. 413). Travelers landed at Santa Barbara by boat through the surf before a pier was built in 1865 (Gleason, p. 127).

Santa Barbara Canyon [SANTA BARBARA]: *canyon,* drained by a stream that flows 15 miles to Cuyama Valley 6 miles northeast of Fox Mountain (lat. 34°52'10" N, long. 119°31'05" W). Named on Fox Mountain (1964) and Madulce Peak (1964) 7.5' quadrangles. Huguenin (p. 737) noted that a gypsum deposit was located on the east side of Santa Barbara Canyon 5 miles south of Quartel post office in Cuyama Valley—the post office apparently was near the mouth of Santa Barbara Canyon; Huguenin must have meant Quatal post office, which postal authorities established in 1896, moved 4 miles south in 1899, and discontinued in 1904 (Salley, p. 179).

Santa Barbara Channel [SANTA BARBARA]: *water feature,* between the sea coast and the islands of San Miguel, Santa Rosa, Santa Cruz, and Anacapa (Anacapa is in Ventura County). Named on Los Angeles (1955) and Santa Maria (1956) 1°x 2° quadrangles. Vizcaino gave the name "Canal de Santa Barbara" to the feature when he sailed through it in 1602 on December 4, the day of the saint (Wagner, H.R., p. 118, 413). The four islands—Anacapa, Santa Cruz, Santa Rosa, and San Miguel—located on the south side of Santa Barbara Channel are called Santa Barbara Islands, and are part of the larger group called Channel Islands (United States Coast and Geodetic Survey, p. 106).

Santa Barbara Hot Springs: see **Hot Springs** [SANTA BARBARA] (2).

Santa Barbara Hot Sulphur Springs: see **Hot Springs** [SANTA BARBARA] (2).

Santa Barbara Island [SANTA BARBARA]: *island,* 9000 feet long, 75 miles south-southeast of Santa Barbara (lat. 33°28'35" N, long. 119°02' W). Named on United States Geological Survey's (1973) map. Vizcaino named the island in 1602 (Wagner, H.R., p. 413).

Santa Barbara Islands: see **Santa Barbara Channel** [SANTA BARBARA].

Santa Barbara Mountains: see **Santa Lucia Range** [MONTEREY-SAN LUIS OBISPO]; **Santa Ynez Mountains** [SANTA BARBARA].

Santa Barbara Point [SANTA BARBARA]: *promontory,* 1.5 miles south of downtown Santa Barbara along the coast (lat. 34°23'50" N, long. 119°42'05" W). Named on Santa Barbara (1952) 7.5' quadrangle. Vancouver (p. 161) called the feature Point Felipe in 1793 to honor the commandant of Santa Barbara.

Santa Barbara Potrero [SANTA BARBARA]: *area,* 4.25 miles southeast of Salisbury Potrero (lat. 34°46'25" N, long. 119°38'25" W). Named on Salisbury Potrero (1964) 7.5' quadrangle.

Santa Barbara Reservoir: see **Gibralter Reservoir** [SANTA BARBARA].

Santa Barbara Springs: see **Veronica Springs** [SANTA BARBARA].

Santa Clara Valley [SAN BENITO]: *valley,* almost entirely in Santa Clara County, but the southeasternmost end extends into northern San Benito County northwest of Hollister. Named on Santa Cruz (1956) 1°x 2° quadrangle.

Santa Cora Creek: see **Zanja de Cota Creek** [SANTA BARBARA].

Santa Cota Creek: see **Zanja de Cota Creek** [SANTA BARBARA].

Santa Cruz [SANTA CRUZ]: *city,* on the coast around the mouth of San Lorenzo River (lat. 36°58'30" N, long. 122°01'45" W). Named on Santa Cruz (1954) and Soquel (1954) 7.5' quadrangles. Members of the Portola expedition gave the name "Santa Cruz" to a stream near the present city in 1768 (Rowland, p. 95), and the name was perpetuated by Santa Cruz mission (Hanna, p. 289), built west of the San Lorenzo River in 1791. A pueblo called Branciforte was started in 1797 across the river from the mission; the name honored the Marquis de Branciforte, Viceroy of Mexico (Hoover, Rensch, and Rensch, p. 466). After secularization of the mission, a community that grew up around the mission plaza was called Santa Cruz; the state legislature granted it a charter in 1866, and it incorporated in 1876 (Hoover, Rensch, and Rensch, p. 467). Farnham's (1845) map has both the names "S. Cruz" and "Ville de Francfort" at the site. Postal authorities established Santa Cruz post office in 1850 (Frickstad, p. 177). Branciforte became part of the city of Santa Cruz by a special election in 1907 (Hoover, Rensch, and Rensch, p. 467). Postal authorities established Rapetti post office as a branch of Santa Cruz post office in 1911 and discontinued it in 1912 (Salley, p. 181). Hamman's (1980b) map shows a place called Eblis located along the railroad 2 miles north of Point Santa Cruz in Santa Cruz. Rowland (p. 148) noted a place called Four Corners in the 1860's was located at the intersection of present Bay Street and Mission Street in Santa Cruz. California Mining Bureau's (1917a) map shows a place called Seabright located east of Santa Cruz along the railroad—United States Coast and Geodetic Survey (p. 121) referred to Seabright as a suburb of Santa Cruz. Postal authorities established Seabright post office in 1899; the place was named in 1880 after Seabright, New Jersey (Salley, p. 200). California Mining Bureau's (1909d) map shows a place called Orby located along the railroad near the west edge of present Santa Cruz, probably about 0.5 mile east of the railroad crossing of Moore Creek. Postal authorities established Coast post office 9 miles northwest of Santa Cruz in 1889 and discontinued it in 1905 (Salley, p. 46). They established Lucas post office in 1885 and discontinued it in 1886, when they moved the service to Santa Cruz; the name was for Jonathan Lucas, lumberman and pioneer of 1838 (Salley, p. 129).

Santa Cruz: see **Point Santa Cruz** [SANTA CRUZ].

Santa Cruz Bay [SANTA BARBARA]: *embayment,* 5 miles northeast of Santa Ynez Peak along the north side of Lake Cachuma (lat. 34° 34'55" N, long. 119°55'20" W); the feature is at the mouth of Santa Cruz Creek. Named on Lake Cachuma (1959) 7.5' quadrangle.

Santa Cruz Beach [SANTA CRUZ]: *beach,* 1 mile north-northeast of Point Santa Cruz and west of the mouth of San Lorenzo River (lat. 36°57'50" N, long. 122°01' W); the beach is in Santa Cruz. Named on Santa Cruz (1954) 7.5' quadrangle.

Santa Cruz Channel [SANTA BARBARA]: *water feature,* strait between Santa Cruz Island and Santa Rosa Island (lat. 33°59' N, long. 119°56' W). Named on Santa Cruz Island A (1943) and Santa Rosa Island East (1943) 7.5' quadrangles.

Santa Cruz Creek [SANTA BARBARA]: *stream,* formed by the confluence of East Fork and West Fork, flows 13 miles to Lake Cachuma 5.5 miles northeast of Santa Ynez Peak at Santa Cruz Bay (lat. 34°35'30" N, long. 119°54'50" W). Named on Lake Cachuma (1959), San Marcos Pass (1959), and San Rafael Mountain (1959) 7.5' quadrangles. East Fork is 7.25 miles long and is named on Big Pine Mountain (1964) 7.5' quadrangle. West Fork is 5.5 miles long and is named on San Rafael Mountain (1959) 7.5' quadrangle.

Santa Cruz Harbor [SANTA CRUZ]: *embayment,* along the coast between Point Santa Cruz and Black Point (lat. 36°57'30" N, long. 122°00' W). Named on Santa Cruz (1954) and Soquel (1954) 7.5' quadrangles.

Santa Cruz Island [SANTA BARBARA]: *island,* 23 miles long, 25 miles south of Santa Barbara across Santa Barbara Channel. Named on Santa Cruz Island A (1943), Santa Cruz Island B (1943), Santa Cruz Island C (1943), and Santa Cruz Island D (1943) 7.5' quadrangles. Cabrillo discovered the island in 1542 and gave the name "Islas de San Lucas" to it and neighboring islands (Wagner, H.R., p. 503). Ferrer called it Isla San Sebastian in 1543 on the day of the saint, and Vizcaino called it Isla de Gente Barbudo because one of the members of the expedition claimed that he saw bearded men there; the present name stems from an incident in 1769, when one of the friars on the ship *San Antonio* left a staff with a cross on it at the island, and Indians returned the staff (Wagner, H.R., p. 414).

Santa Cruz Mountains [SANTA CRUZ]: *range,* extends northwest from Pajaro River into San Mateo County; the east boundary of Santa Cruz County is along the crest of the range. Named on San Francisco (1956), San Jose (1962), and Santa Cruz (1956) 1°x 2° quadrangles. Called Sierra de la Santa Cruz on Parke's (1854-1855) map. Fremont (p. 30) used the designation "cuesta de los gatos (wild-cat ridge)" for the feature, and Blake (1856, p. 378) called it Santa Cruz range.

Santa Cruz Peak [SANTA BARBARA]: *peak,* 3 miles south of San Rafael Mountain (lat. 34°40'10" N, long. 119°48'40" W; near E line sec. 22, T 7 N, R 28 W); the peak is north of Santa Cruz Creek. Altitude 5570 feet. Named on San Rafael Mountain (1959) 7.5' quadrangle.

Santa Cruz Point [SANTA BARBARA]: *promontory,* 4 miles northeast of Santa Ynez Peak on the north side of Lake Cachuma (lat. 34°34'25" N, long. 119°55'55" W); the feature is at the mouth of Santa Cruz Bay. Named on Lake Cachuma (1959) 7.5' quadrangle.

Santa Cruz Range: see **Santa Cruz Mountains** [SANTA CRUZ].

Santa Delfina Valley: see **Salinas River** [MONTEREY-SAN LUIS OBISPO].

Santa Humiliana: see **San Carpoforo Creek** [MONTEREY-SAN LUIS OBISPO].

Santa Inez: see **Cañada de los Pinos or College Rancho** [SANTA BARBARA].

Santa Inez Range: see **Santa Ynez Mountains** [SANTA BARBARA].

Santa Inez River: see **Santa Ynez River** [SANTA BARBARA].

Santa Inez Valley: see **Santa Ynez Valley** [SANTA BARBARA].

Santa Isabel: see **Santa Ysabel** [SAN LUIS OBISPO].

Santa Lucia Canyon [SANTA BARBARA]: *canyon*, drained by a stream that flows 6.5 miles to Santa Ynez River 5 miles east of Surf (lat. 34°40'50" N, long. 120°31'05" W). Named on Lompoc (1959) and Surf (1959) 7.5' quadrangles.

Santa Lucia Creek [MONTEREY]:

(1) *stream*, flows 10 miles to Arroyo Seco (1) 7 miles northwest of Junipero Serra Peak (lat. 36°13'20" N, long. 121°29'45" W; sec. 2, T 20 S, R 4 E); the stream is in Santa Lucia Range. Named on Junipero Serra Peak (1949) 7.5' quadrangle. South Fork enters from the south-southeast nearly 3 miles upstream from the mouth of the main stream; it is 3 miles long and is named on Junipero Serra Peak (1949) 7.5' quadrangle.

(2) *stream*, flows 3.5 miles to North Fork San Antonio River 4.25 miles south of Junipero Serra Peak (lat. 36°05'05" N, long. 121°25'05" W); the stream is in Santa Lucia Range. Named on Cone Peak (1949) 7.5' quadrangle. Called Sycamore Creek on Junipero Serra (1948) 15' quadrangle.

Santa Lucia Mountain: see **Junipero Serra Peak** [MONTEREY].

Santa Lucia Mountains: see **Santa Lucia Range** [MONTEREY-SAN LUIS OBISPO].

Santa Lucia Peak: see **Junipero Serra Peak** [MONTEREY].

Santa Lucia Range [MONTEREY-SAN LUIS OBISPO]: *range*, extends southeast from Monterey Bay along and near the coast in Monterey and San Luis Obispo Counties. Named on San Luis Obispo (1956) and Santa Cruz (1956) 1°x 2° quadrangles. According to Davidson (1887, p. 210-211), Cabrillo and Ferrelo gave the range the name "Las Sierras de San Martin" in 1542, and Vizcaino gave it the name "Sierra de Santa Lucia" in 1602. According to H.R. Wagner (p. 414), Cabrillo used the name "Sierra Nevadas" for the range, and Vizcaino applied the name "Santa Lucia" to the north part only to honor the saint whose day is December 13, the day before Vizcaino sighted the range from northwest of Point Sur. Greenhow's (1844) map has the name "Sta. Barbara Mountains" along the coast, and Parke's (1854-1855) map has the name "Sierra de la Santa Lucia" for coastal mountains all the way from Monterey Bay to present Ventura County. Parke's (1854-1855) map also has the name "Sierra Wasna" for the part of the present Santa Lucia Range at the head of Rio Wasna (present Huasna River). Antisell (1856, p. 47) used the name "Point Pinos Range" for the north part of present Santa Lucia Range, and (p. 58) used the name "Santa Lucia Mountains" for the rest. Whitney (p. 111) used the names "Sierra Santa Lucia" and "Santa Lucia chain" for the entire range.

Santa Manuela [SAN LUIS OBISPO]: *land grant*, 5 miles east of the town of Arroyo Grande. Named on Arroyo Grande NE (1965), Nipomo (1965), Oceano (1965), and Tar Spring Ridge (1967) 7.5' quadrangles. Francis Z. Branch received the land in 1837 and claimed 16,955 acres patented in 1869 (Cowan, p. 93). Perez (p. 97) gave 1868 as the date of the patent. Branch named the grant for his wife, Manuela (Nicholson, p. 12).

Santa Margarita [SAN LUIS OBISPO]:

(1) *land grant*, around the town of Santa Margarita. Named on Atascadero (1965), Lopez Mountain (1965), San Luis Obispo (1965), Santa Margarita (1965), and Santa Margarita Lake (1967) 7.5' quadrangles. Joaquin Estrada received 4 leagues in 1841 and claimed 17,735 acres patented in 1861 (Cowan, p. 93). Rogers and Johnston's (1857) map has the name "Sta. Margarite."

(2) *town*, 8 miles north-northeast of San Luis Obispo (lat. 35°23'30" N, long. 120°36'20" W); the town is on Santa Margarita grant. Named on Santa Margarita (1965) 7.5' quadrangle. The town was laid out when Southern Pacific Railroad reached the place in 1889 (Lee and others, p. 137). Postal authorities established Santa Margarita post office in 1867, discontinued it in 1881, and reestablished it in 1889 (Frickstad, p. 166). They established Pines post office 17 miles southeast of Santa Margarita in 1893 and discontinued it the same year (Salley, p. 172).

Santa Margarita Creek [SAN LUIS OBISPO]: *stream*, flows 9 miles to Salinas River 3.5 miles north of the town of Santa Margarita (lat. 35°26'40" N, long. 120°36'20" W; sec. 31, T 28 S, R 13 E). Named on Atascadero (1965), San Luis Obispo (1965), and Santa Margarita (1965) 7.5' quadrangles.

Santa Margarita Lake [SAN LUIS OBISPO]: *lake*, behind a dam on Salinas River 5 miles east-northeast of Lopez Mountain (lat. 35°20'15" N, long. 120°30'05" W; near NW cor. sec. 8, T 30 S, R 14 E). Named on Santa Margarita Lake (1967) 7.5' quadrangle. Called Salinas Reservoir on Lopez Mountain (1965) 7.5' quadrangle, but United States Board on Geographic Names (1968c, p. 6) rejected this name for the lake.

Santa Maria [SANTA BARBARA]: *city*, 55 miles northwest of Santa Barbara (lat. 34°57'10" N, long. 120°26'05" W; around NE cor. sec. 15, T 10 N, R 34 W); the city is in Santa Maria Valley. Named on Santa Maria (1959) 7.5' quadrangle. Postal authorities established Santa Maria post office in 1869, discontinued it in 1871, and reestablished it in 1875 (Frickstad, p. 171). The city incorporated in 1905. The place first was called Grangeville and later Central City (Hoover, Rensch, and Rensch, p. 423). California Division of Highways' (1934) map shows a place called Suey Junction located along Pacific Coast Railroad 1.5 miles south-southwest of downtown Santa Maria (sec. 22, T 10 N, R 34 E), and a place called Suey situated along the railroad 4 miles east of Suey Junction (sec. 20, T 10 N, R 33 W).

Santa Maria: see **North Santa Maria** [SANTA BARBARA]; **Tepusquet** [SANTA BARBARA].

Santa Maria Canyon [SANTA BARBARA]: *canyon*, drained by a stream that flows 2.5 miles to Santa Maria Valley 11 miles east-southeast of Santa Maria (lat. 34°53'05" N, long. 120°16'15" W). Named on Twitchell Dam (1959) 7.5' quadrangle.

Santa Maria Plain: see **Santa Maria Valley** [SANTA BARBARA].

Santa Maria Point: see **Black Point** [SANTA CRUZ].

Santa Maria River [SAN LUIS OBISPO-SANTA BARBARA]: *stream*, formed by the confluence of Cuyama River and Sisquoc River, flows 24 miles along and near San Luis Obispo-Santa Barbara County line to the sea 4.5 miles west of the town of Guadalupe (lat. 34°58'15" N, long. 120°38'55" W). Named on Guadalupe (1959), Point Sal (1958), Santa Maria (1959), and Twitchell Dam (1959) 7.5' quadrangles. Called R. Guadalupe on Wilkes' (1849) map, and called Rio de la Sta. Maria on Parke's (1854-1855) map, which has the name "Rio S. Maria" for present Cuyama River. Parke (p. 2) also used the name "Rio Santa Maria" for present Santa Maria River. Present Cuyama River is called Santa Maria River on California Mining Bureau's (1909c) map, and present Sisquoc River has the name "Santa Maria R." on Goddard's (1857) map.

Santa Maria Valley [SAN LUIS OBISPO-SANTA BARBARA]: *valley*, along Santa Maria River on San Luis Obispo-Santa Barbara County line, and extends eastward along Sisquoc River in Santa Barbara County. Named on Foxen Canyon (1964), Guadalupe (1959), Nipomo (1965), Oceano (1965), Point Sal (1958), Santa Maria (1959), Sisquoc (1959), and Twitchell Dam (1959) 7.5' quadrangles. Called Guadalupe Largo on Parke's (1854-1855) map. Fairbanks (1894, p. 501) called it Santa Maria Plain.

Santa Monica Canyon [SANTA BARBARA]: *canyon*, 3.5 miles long, along Santa Monica Creek above a point 1.5 miles north-northwest of Carpinteria (lat. 34°25'10" N, long. 119°31'35" W; sec. 20, T 4 N, R 25 W). Named on Carpinteria (1952) 7.5' quadrangle.

Santa Monica Creek [SANTA BARBARA]: *stream*, flows nearly 5 miles to El Estero 0.5 mile west-northwest of downtown Carpinteria (lat. 34°24' N, long. 119°31'45" W); the stream drains Santa Monica Canyon. Named on Carpinteria (1952) 7.5' quadrangle. United States Board on Geographic Names (1978b, p. 5) rejected the name "Monica Creek" for the stream.

Santa Rita [MONTEREY]: *town*, 3.5 miles north of Salinas (lat. 36° 43'30" N, long. 121°39'15" W); the town is on Los Gatos or Santa Rita grant. Named on Salinas (1947) 7.5' quadrangle. Jose Manuel Soto bought the grant and set aside 1 square mile for a townsite that he named New Republic (Newhall, p. 31-32). Postal authorities established New Republic post office in 1870, changed the name to Santa Rita in 1874, and discontinued it in 1907 (Salley, p. 154, 198). The place also was known as Sotoville for Jose Manuel Soto, and as Pinecate for nearby Pinecate Peak [SAN BENITO] (Clark, 1991, p. 513).

Santa Rita [SANTA BARBARA]:

(1) *land grant*, east and northeast of the city of Lompoc. Named on Lompoc (1959), Lompoc Hills (1959), Los Alamos (1959), and Santa Rosa Hills (1959) 7.5' quadrangles. Jose Ramon Malo received 3 leagues in 1845 and claimed 13,316 acres patented in 1875 (Cowan, p. 94).

(2) *settlement*, 7.5 miles east of the town of Lompoc (lat. 34°40' N, long. 120°19'40" W); the place is in Santa Rita Valley. Named on Lompoc (1905) 30' quadrangle. Postal authorities established Santa Rita post office in 1909 and discontinued it in 1914 (Frickstad, p. 172).

Santa Rita: see **Los Gatos** [MONTEREY].

Santa Rita Creek [SAN LUIS OBISPO]: *stream*, flows 9 miles to Paso Robles Creek 4.5 miles east of York Mountain (lat. 35°32'10" N, long. 120°45'05" W). Named on York Mountain (1948) 7.5' quadrangle. South Fork enters from the south 4 miles upstream from the mouth of the main stream; it is 4.25 miles long and is named on Morro Bay North (1965) and York Mountain (1948) 7.5' quadrangles.

Santa Rita Hills [SANTA BARBARA]: *range*, east of the city of Lompoc between Santa Ynez River and Santa Rita Valley, on and near Santa Rita grant. Named on Lompoc (1959), Los Alamos (1959), and Santa Rosa Hills (1959) 7.5' quadrangles. Called Serro de Santa Rita on a diseño of Santa Rosa grant made in the mid-1830's (Becker, 1964).

Santa Rita Peak [SAN BENITO]: *peak*, 6.25 miles southeast of Idria (lat. 36°20'50" N, long. 120°36'05" W; sec. 24, T 18 S, R 12 E). Altitude 5165 feet. Named on Santa Rita Peak (1969) 7.5' quadrangle.

Santa Rita Valley [SANTA BARBARA]: *valley*, 6.5 miles south-southwest of the town of Los Alamos (lat. 34°39'40" N, long. 120° 20'30" W); the valley is on Santa Rita grant. Named on Los Alamos (1959) 7.5' quadrangle.

Santa Rosa [SAN LUIS OBISPO]: *land grant*, on the coast south and southeast of Cambria. Named on Cambria (1959) and Cypress Mountain (1948) 7.5' quadrangles. Julian Estrada received 3 leagues in 1841 and claimed 13,184 acres patented in 1865 (Cowan, p. 95).

Santa Rosa [SANTA BARBARA]: *land grant*, west of Buellton along Santa

Ynez River. Named on Los Alamos (1959), Santa Rosa Hills (1959), Solvang (1959), and Zaca Creek (1959) 7.5' quadrangles. Francisco Cota received 3.5 leagues in 1839; M.J. Olivera de Cota and others claimed 15,526 acres patented in 1872 (Cowan, p. 95). Perez (p. 98) gave 1845 as the date of the grant.

Santa Rosa: see **Cambria** [SAN LUIS OBISPO].

Santa Rosa Creek [SAN LUIS OBISPO]: *stream,* flows 14 miles to the sea at Cambria (lat. 35°34'05" N, long. 121°06'35" W). Named on Cambria (1959) and Cypress Mountain (1948) 7.5' quadrangles. Crespi gave the name "San Benvenuto" to the stream, or to its valley, when the Portola expedition reached the place in 1769; soldiers of the expedition called it Cañada del Osito, and on the return trip Crespi referred to the site as San Buenaventura (Wagner, H.R., p. 480, 497). Angel (1883, p. 340) used the name "Santa Rosa Valley" for the valley of the stream.

Santa Rosa Creek [SANTA BARBARA]: *stream,* flows 7.5 miles to Santa Ynez River 10 miles east-southeast of the city of Lompoc (lat. 34°36'30" N, long. 120°17'15" W); the creek is on and near Santa Rosa grant. Named on Los Alamos (1959) and Santa Rosa Hills (1959) 7.5' quadrangles.

Santa Rosa de Chualar: see **Chualar** [MONTEREY] (1).

Santa Rosa Hills [SANTA BARBARA]: *range,* 10.5 miles east-southeast of the city of Lompoc (lat. 34°34'30" N, long. 120°17'30" W); the range is south of Santa Rosa grant. Named on Santa Rosa Hills (1959) 7.5' quadrangle.

Santa Rosa Island [SANTA BARBARA]: *island,* 16 miles long, 39 miles south-southwest of Santa Barbara (lat. 33°58' N, long. 120°06' W). Named on Santa Rosa Island East (1943), Santa Rosa Island North (1943), Santa Rosa Island South (1943), and Santa Rosa Island West (1943) 7.5' quadrangles. Cabrillo discovered the island in 1542 and gave the name "Islas de San Lucas" to it and neighboring islands; later he restricted the name to present Santa Rosa Island (Wagner, H.R., p. 503). Vizcaino called the feature Isla San Ambrosio in 1602 for the saint whose day is December 7 (Wagner, H.R., p. 495).

Santa Rosalia Mountain [SANTA CRUZ]: *peak,* 6.5 miles north-northwest of Corralitos (lat. 37°04'20" N, long. 121°51'25" W). Named on Loma Prieta (1955) 7.5' quadrangle. Hamman's (1980a) map shows a place called Camp No. 3 situated about 0.5 mile north-northwest of Santa Rosalia Mountain. Hamman (p. 70) noted that Camp No. 3 also was called Sheep Camp because the meadow surrounding the place was leased for sheep grazing.

Santa Rosa Reef [SAN LUIS OBISPO]: *shoal,* 1.5 miles west of Point San Luis and 1 mile offshore (lat. 35°09'20" N, long. 120°47'20" W). Named on Port San Luis (1965) 7.5' quadrangle.

Santa Rosa Valley: see **Santa Rosa Creek** [SAN LUIS OBISPO].

Santa Ynez [SANTA BARBARA]: *town,* 6.5 miles east of Buellton on Cañada de los Pinos or College Rancho grant (lat. 34°36'45" N, long. 120°04'50" W); the town is in Santa Ynez Valley. Named on Santa Ynez (1959) 7.5' quadrangle. Postal authorities established Santa Ynez post office in 1863, discontinued it in 1868, and reestablished it in 1883 (Frickstad, p. 172). Bishop Francisco Mora opened the Church's Cañada de los Pinos grant for subdivision in 1881, and the community that started there was called New Town by residents of nearby Ballard; for a short time the community was called Sagunto, for the Spanish village where Bishop Mora was born, but it took the name "Santa Ynez" when the post office opened (Tompkins and Ruiz, p. 79). Postal Route (1884) map shows a place called Childs located 8.5 miles west of Santa Ynez. Postal authorities established Childs post office in 1881 and discontinued it in 1888—the name was for Augustus F. Childs, first postmaster (Salley, p. 42).

Santa Ynez Campground [SANTA BARBARA]: *locality,* 4.25 miles south of Little Pine Mountain (lat. 34°32'15" N, long. 119°44'30" W; near SE cor. sec. 6, T 5 N, R 27 W); the place is along Santa Ynez River. Named on Little Pine Mountain (1964) 7.5' quadrangle.

Santa Ynez Campground: see **Middle Santa Ynez Campground** [SANTA BARBARA]; **Upper Santa Ynez Campground** [SANTA BARBARA].

Santa Ynez Mountains [SANTA BARBARA]: *range,* between Santa Ynez River and the coast. Named on Los Angeles (1955) and Santa Maria (1956) 1°x 2° quadrangles. Called Sierra de la Santa Inez on Parke's (1854-1855) map. Blake (1857, p. 137) called the feature Santa Inez range, Antisell (1856, p. 65) called it Santa Barbara Mountains, and Whitney (p. 111) called it Sierra Santa Iñez.

Santa Ynez Peak [SANTA BARBARA]: *peak,* 9 miles west of San Marcos Pass (lat. 34°31'35" N, long. 119°58'40" W); the peak is in Santa Ynez Mountains. Altitude 4298 feet. Named on Lake Cachuma (1959) 7.5' quadrangle.

Santa Ynez Point [SANTA BARBARA]: *promontory,* 5 miles northeast of Santa Ynez Peak on the south side of Lake Cachuma (lat. 34°34'05" N, long. 119°54'15" W). Named on Lake Cachuma (1959) 7.5' quadrangle.

Santa Ynez River [SANTA BARBARA]: *stream,* heads just inside Ventura County and flows 90 miles to the sea 0.5 mile north of Surf (lat. 34°41'30" N, long. 120°36'10" W). Named on Los Angeles (1955) and Santa Maria (1956) 1°x 2° quadrangles. Called Rio de la Sta. Inez on Parke's (1854-1855) map, and called Santa Inez River on Ransom and Doolittle's (1863) map. H.R. Wagner (p. 403, 414) gave the names "Purisima River," "Rio de San Bernardo," "Rio de San Verardo," and "Rio de Santa Rosa" as early designations for the stream.

Santa Ynez Valley [SANTA BARBARA]: *valley,* at and north of Santa Ynez (lat. 34°38' N, long. 120°04' W). Named on Los Olivos (1959) and Santa Ynez (1959) 7.5' quadrangles. Parke (p. 9) referred to Santa Inez valley.

Santa Ysabel [SAN LUIS OBISPO]: *land grant,* east of Salinas River and southeast of Paso Robles. Named on Creston (1948), Estrella (1948), Paso Robles (1948), and Templeton (1948) 7.5' quadrangles. Francisco C. Arce received 4 leagues in 1844 and claimed 17,774 acres patented in 1866 (Cowan, p. 93; Cowan used the form "Santa Isabel" for the name).

Santa Ysabel Springs: see **Sulphur Spring** [SAN LUIS OBISPO] (1).

San Vicenta Valley: see **Lowes Canyon** [MONTEREY-SAN LUIS OBISPO].

San Vicente [MONTEREY]: *land grant,* at and northwest of Soledad. Named on Gonzales (1955), Palo Escrito Peak (1956), and Soledad (1955) 7.5' quadrangles. Francisco Esteban Munras received 2 leagues in 1835; Concepcion Munras and others claimed 19,979 acres patented in 1865 (Cowan, p. 89). According to Perez (p. 95), Stephen Munras was the grantee in 1842.

San Vicente [SANTA CRUZ]: *land grant,* extends from the coast north of Davenport into Santa Cruz Mountains. Named on Big Basin (1955) and Davenport (1955) 7.5' quadrangles. Antonio Rodriguez received 2 leagues in 1839; Blas A. Escamilla received the land in 1846 and claimed 10,803 acres patented in 1870 (Cowan, p. 89).

San Vicente Canyon: see **Lowes Canyon** [MONTEREY-SAN LUIS OBISPO].

San Vicente Creek [SANTA CRUZ]: *stream,* flows 9 miles to the sea at Davenport (lat. 37°00'35" N, long. 122°11'35" W); the stream forms the east boundary of San Vicente grant. Named on Davenport (1955) 7.5' quadrangle. The stream also was called Arroyo de San Vicente and Blas Creek; the name "Blas" was for Blas A. Escamilla, who received San Vicente grant (Clark, 1986, p. 33). Hamman's (1980c) map shows West Fork and Middle Fork entering the main creek 2 miles northwest of present Bonnie Doon; the map has the name "East Fork" for the present main stream above Middle Fork, and has the name "Bear Trap Gulch" for the canyon of Middle Fork. In the 1850's, lumber was loaded on schooners at Williams Landing, which was located at the mouth of San Vicente Creek on the edge of Arroyo de la Laguna grant; the place also was a stage station and was named for the owners of the grant (Hoover, Rensch, and Rensch, p. 473, 478). Hamman's (1980c) map shows a place called Buena Vista located along San Vicente Creek near the mouth of Mill Creek. This was a company town started by Santa Cruz Portland Cement Company about 1920 and destroyed by a landslide in 1961 (Clark, 1986, p. 50).

San Vicente Junction: see **Swanton** [SANTA CRUZ].

San Ysidro Canyon [SANTA BARBARA]: *canyon,* 2.5 miles long, along San Ysidro Creek above a point nearly 7 miles west-northwest of Carpinteria (lat. 34°26'50" N, long. 119°37'15" W). Named on Carpinteria (1952) 7.5' quadrangle. United States Board on Geographic Names (1961b, p. 15) rejected the name "Dinsmore Canyon" for the feature.

San Ysidro Creek [SANTA BARBARA]: *stream,* flows 4.5 miles to the sea 6 miles west-northwest of Carpinteria (lat. 34°25'10" N, long. 119°37'10" W); the stream drains San Ysidro Canyon. Named on Carpinteria (1952) 7.5' quadrangle. United States Board on Geographic Names (1961b, p. 15) rejected the name "Arroyo San Ysidro" for the stream.

Sapaque: see **Bryson** [MONTEREY].

Sapaque Creek [MONTEREY-SAN LUIS OBISPO]: *stream,* heads in Monterey County and flows 4 miles to Nacimiento River 11 miles north-northeast of the village of San Simeon in San Luis Obispo County (lat. 35°47'20" N, long. 121°05'25" W; sec. 3, T 25 S, R 8 E); the stream goes through Sapaque Valley. Named on Bryson (1949) 7.5' quadrangle. The stream first was called Woods Creek, for Job Wood, an early settler (Clark, 1991, p. 514).

Sapaque Valley [MONTEREY]: *valley,* 12 miles south-southeast of Jolon (lat. 35°48'20" N, long. 121°05'25" W). Named on Bryson (1949) 7.5' quadrangle. The place also was called Woods Valley, for Job Wood, a landowner there (Clark, 1991, p. 514).

Saquel: see **Soquel** [SANTA CRUZ].

Saquel Cove: see **Soquel Cove** [SANTA CRUZ].
Saquel Creek: see **Soquel Creek** [SANTA CRUZ].
Saquel Point: see **Soquel Point** [SANTA CRUZ].
Sarah Canyon [MONTEREY]: *canyon,* drained by a stream that flows 6 miles to Salinas River 2.5 miles northwest of Bradley (lat. 35°53'20" N, long. 120°50'05" W; sec. 36, T 23 S, R 10 E). Named on Wunpost (1949) 7.5' quadrangle.
Saratoga Gap [SANTA CRUZ]: *pass,* 9 miles north of the town of Boulder Creek on Santa Cruz-Santa Clara County line (lat. 37°15'30" N, long. 122°07'10" W; near S line sec. 6, T 8 S, R 2 W). Named on Cupertino (1961) 7.5' quadrangle.
Sargent Canyon [MONTEREY]: *canyon,* drained by Sargent Creek, which flows 14 miles to lowlands 7 miles north-northwest of Bradley (lat. 35°57'05" N, long. 120°51'40" W; near S line sec. 2, T 23 S, R 10 E). Named on Pancho Rico Valley (1967), Slack Canyon (1969), and Wunpost (1949) 7.5' quadrangles. Called Sargent Gulch on a map of Monterey County used about 1900. The name is for Bradley V. Sargent, who owned land at the place (Clark, 1991, p. 515).
Sargent Creek [MONTEREY]: *stream,* flows 14 miles to lowlands 7 miles north-northwest of Bradley (lat. 35°57'05" N, long. 120°51'40" W; near S line sec. 2, T 23 S, R 10 E); the stream goes through Sargent Canyon. Named on Wunpost (1949) 7.5' quadrangle.
Sargent Gulch: see **Sargent Canyon** [MONTEREY].
Saucelito Creek [SAN LUIS OBISPO]: *stream,* flows nearly 4 miles to Arroyo Grande Creek 11.5 miles north-northeast of the town of Nipomo (lat. 35°12'15" N, long. 120°25'15" W). Named on Tar Spring Ridge (1967) 7.5' quadrangle.
Saucelito Ridge [SAN LUIS OBISPO]: *ridge,* north-northwest- to north-west-trending, 2.5 miles long, 11 miles east-northeast of the town of Nipomo (lat. 35°11'30" N, long. 120°24'30" W); the ridge is southwest of Saucelito Creek. Named on Tar Spring Ridge (1967) 7.5' quadrangle.
Saucito [MONTEREY]: *land grant,* 2.5 miles south-southeast of Seaside. Named on Seaside (1947) 7.5' quadrangle. Graciano Manjares received 1.5 leagues in 1833; John Wilson and others claimed 2212 acres patented in 1862 (Cowan, p. 96).
Saucito Canyon [MONTEREY]: *canyon,* drained by a stream that flows 2.25 miles to the canyon of Chalone Creek 3.25 miles northeast of Greenfield (lat. 36°21'15" N, long. 121°12'05" W). Named on Greenfield (1956) 7.5' quadrangle.
Sauguil: see **Soquel** [SANTA CRUZ].
Sauquel: see **Soquel** [SANTA CRUZ].
Sauquel Cove: see **Soquel Cove** [SANTA CRUZ].
Sauquel Creek: see **Soquel Creek** [SANTA CRUZ].
Sauquel Point: see **Soquel Point** [SANTA CRUZ].
Sausal [MONTEREY]: *land grant,* north and northeast of Salinas. Named on Natividad (1947) and Salinas (1947) 7.5' quadrangles. Agustin Soberanes received 2 leagues in 1823, and the land was regranted to Jose Tiburcio Castro in 1834 and 1845; Jacob P. Leese claimed 10,242 acres patented in 1859 (Cowan, p. 96; Cowan listed the grant under the name "Sauzal").
Sauzal: see **Sausal** [MONTEREY].
Sawmill Basin [SANTA BARBARA]: *area,* less than 1 mile southwest of Figueroa Mountain (lat. 34°44'05" N, long. 119°59'40" W; on S line sec. 25, T 8 N, R 30 W). Named on Figueroa Mountain (1959) 7.5' quadrangle.
Sawmill Canyon [MONTEREY]: *canyon,* drained by a stream that flows 2 miles to Stone Canyon 6.5 miles southeast of Smith Mountain (lat. 36°00'35" N, long. 120°30'45" W; near E line sec. 13, T 22 S, R 13 E). Named on Curry Mountain (1969) and Smith Mountain (1969) 7.5' quadrangles. Priest Valley (1915) 30' quadrangle has the label "Old Sawmill" for a building near the mouth of the canyon.
Sawmill Creek [SAN BENITO]: *stream,* flows 3.5 miles to San Benito River 5.25 miles south of Idria (lat. 36°20'35" N, long. 120° 39'30" W; near SE cor. sec. 21, T 18 S, R 12 E). Named on San Benito Mountain (1969) and Santa Rita Peak (1969) 7.5' quadrangles.
Sawmill Flat Campground [MONTEREY]: *locality,* about 2.25 miles east-northeast of Pfeiffer Point (lat. 36°14'55" N, long. 121° 46'45" W; sec. 30, T 19 S, R 2 E). Named on Pfeiffer Point (1956) 7.5' quadrangle.
Sawmill Gulch [MONTEREY]: *canyon,* drained by a stream that flows 2 miles to the sea 2.25 miles south-southwest of Point Pinos (lat. 35°36'30" N, long. 121°57' W). Named on Monterey (1947) 7.5' quadrangle.
Sayante: see **Zayanta** [SANTA CRUZ].
Schau Peak [SAN LUIS OBISPO]: *peak,* 3 miles north of the town of Nipomo on Temettate Ridge (lat. 35°05'20" N, long. 120°28'20" W). Named on Nipomo (1965) 7.5' quadrangle.
Schillings Camp: see **Aptos Creek** [SANTA CRUZ].
Schneider Hill [MONTEREY]: *peak,* 1.25 miles south-southeast of Prunedale (lat. 36°45'40" N, long. 121°39'35" W). Named on Prunedale (1954) 7.5' quadrangle.
School Hill [MONTEREY]: *hill,* 2.25 miles east-northeast of Jamesburg (lat. 36°22'50" N, long. 121°33' W; sec. 9, T 18 S, R 4 E). Altitude 2158 feet. Named on Rana Creek (1956) 7.5' quadrangle. The name is from a private school established in 1929 and closed in 1941 (Clark, 1991, p. 517).
Schoolhouse Canyon [SANTA BARBARA]:
(1) *canyon,* drained by a stream that flows 8 miles to Cuyama River 12 miles east of Miranda Pine Mountain (lat. 35°00'15" N, long. 119°49'35" W). Named on Caliente Mountain (1959) and Peak Mountain (1964) 7.5' quadrangles.
(2) *canyon,* 2 miles long, opens into the canyon of Asphaltum Creek 8 miles south-southeast of Tepusquet Peak (lat. 34°48' N, long. 120°07'50" W). Named on Foxen Canyon (1964) and Zaca Lake (1964) 7.5' quadrangles.
Schoolhouse Ridge [SAN BENITO]: *ridge,* north-northwest-trending, about 2 miles long, 3.5 miles southwest of Potrero Peak (lat. 36°49'30" N, long. 121°11'45" W). Named on Quien Sabe Valley (1968) 7.5' quadrangle. Quien Sabe (1922) 15' quadrangle shows Quien Sabe school situated at the east base of the ridge in Quien Sabe Valley.
School Spring [SAN LUIS OBISPO]: *spring,* 4 miles east of the mouth of San Carpoforo Creek (lat. 35°46'40" N, long. 121°15'10" W; sec. 7, T 25 S, R 7 E). Named on Burro Mountain (1949) 7.5' quadrangle.
Schumann: see **Shuman** [SANTA BARBARA].
Schumann Canyon: see **Shuman Canyon** [SANTA BARBARA].
Schwan Lake: see **Schwans Lagoon** [SANTA CRUZ].
Schwans Lagoon [SANTA CRUZ]: *lake,* 0.5 mile long, 1.25 miles west-northwest of Soquel Point near the coast (lat. 36°57'55" N, long. 121°59'40" W). Named on Soquel (1954) 7.5' quadrangle. According to Clark (1986, p. 329), who called the feature Schwan Lake, the name commemorates Jacob Schwan, who came to the neighborhood before 1862; this lake and Woods Lagoon together are known as Twin Lakes. United States Board on Geographic Names (1994, p. 5) approved the name "Schwan Lagoon" for the feature, and rejected the forms "Schwan Lake," "Schwans Lagoon," "Schwans Lake," and "Swan Lake" for the name.
Scorpion: see **Little Scorpion**, under **Scorpion Anchorage** [SANTA BARBARA].
Scorpion Anchorage [SANTA BARBARA]: *embayment,* 2.25 miles west-northwest of San Pedro Point on the north side of Santa Cruz Island (lat. 34°02'55" N, long. 119°33'15" W). Named on Santa Cruz Island D (1943) 7.5' quadrangle. Called Scorpion Harbor on Bremner's (1932) map. United States Board on Geographic Names (1934, p. 16) rejected the name "East End Anchorage" for the feature. Two bold rocks near shore just east of Scorpion Anchorage form a protected place called Little Scorpion (Gleason, p. 49).
Scorpion Harbor: see **Scorpion Anchorage** [SANTA BARBARA].
Scott Creek [SANTA CRUZ]: *stream,* flows 10.5 miles to the sea nearly 3 miles northwest of Davenport (lat. 37°02'25" N, long. 122°13'40" W). Named on Año Nuevo (1955), Big Basin (1955), and Davenport (1955) 7.5' quadrangles. According to H.R. Wagner (p. 506), Crespi gave the name "San Pedro Alcantara" in 1769 to a camping place of the Portola expedition that probably was near Scott Creek. California Mining Bureau's (1909d) map shows a place called Scott Jn. located along the railroad where the line turns inland along Scott Creek to Swanton.
Scott Junction: see **Scott Creek** [SANTA CRUZ].
Scott Rock [SAN LUIS OBISPO]: *peak,* 1 mile north-northeast of Cambria (lat. 35°34'35" N, long. 121°04'25" W; sec. 23, T 27 S, R 8 E). Altitude 660 feet. Named on Cambria (1959) 7.5' quadrangle.
Scotts Valley [SANTA CRUZ]:
(1) *valley,* 7.5 miles southeast of the town of Boulder Creek along Carbonera Creek (lat. 37°03'45" N, long. 122°00'15" W). Named on Felton (1955) and Laurel (1955) 7.5' quadrangles. Called Scott Valley on Los Gatos (1919) 15' quadrangle. The name commemorates Hiram Daniel Scott, who in 1852 bought San Augustin grant where the valley is situated (Hoover, Rensch, and Rensch, p. 471).
(2) *town,* 7.5 miles southeast of the town of Boulder Creek (lat. 37° 03' N, long. 122°00'50" W); the town is in Scotts Valley (1). Named on Felton (1955) 7.5' quadrangle. Called Scott Valley on Ben Lomond (1946) 15' quadrangle. Postal authorities established Scotts Valley post office in 1951 (Salley, p. 199), and the town incorporated in 1966.
Scott Valley: see **Scotts Valley** [SANTA CRUZ] (1) and (2).

Scout Peak [SAN BENITO]: *peak,* 2.25 miles north of North Chalone Peak (lat. 26°28'45" N, long. 121°11'55" W; sec. 3, T 17 S, R 7 E). Named on North Chalone Peak (1969) 7.5' quadrangle.

Script Canyon Number 1 [SANTA BARBARA]: *canyon,* drained by a stream that flows 2 miles to South Fork La Brea Creek 1.5 miles northwest of Manzanita Mountain (lat. 34°54'30" N, long. 120°05'55" W); the feature is west of Script Canyon Number 2. Named on Manzanita Mountain (1964) 7.5' quadrangle.

Script Canyon Number 2 [SANTA BARBARA]: *canyon,* drained by a stream that flows 2.5 miles to South Fork La Brea Creek 1.25 miles north-northwest of Manzanita Mountain (lat. 34°54'35" N, long. 120°05'30" W); the feature is east of Script Canyon Number 1. Named on Manzanita Mountain (1964) 7.5' quadrangle.

Seabright: see **Santa Cruz** [SANTA CRUZ].

Seagirt: see **Gaviota** [SANTA BARBARA].

Seagull Canyon [SANTA BARBARA]: *canyon,* drained by a stream that flows 3 miles to Redrock Canyon 4.5 miles north of San Marcos Pass (lat. 34°34'40" N, long. 119°48'30" W). Named on San Marcos Pass (1959) 7.5' quadrangle.

Sea Lion Cove [MONTEREY]: *embayment,* 0.25 mile south of Point Lobos (lat. 36°31'05" N, long. 121°57'05" W). Named on Monterey (1947) 7.5' quadrangle.

Sea Lion Rocks: see **Seal Rocks** [MONTEREY].

Seal Rock [MONTEREY]: *rock,* 150 feet long, nearly 1 mile northeast of Cypress Point, and 500 feet offshore (lat. 36°35'20" N, long. 121°57'55" W). Named on Monterey (1947) 7.5' quadrangle.

Seal Rock: see **Lion Rock** [SANTA BARBARA].

Seal Rock Creek [MONTEREY]: *stream,* flows 2.25 miles to the sea 2.5 miles northeast of Cypress Point (lat. 36°35'20" N, long. 121° 57'50" W); the mouth of the stream is opposite Seal Rock. Named on Monterey (1947) 7.5' quadrangle.

Seal Rocks [MONTEREY]: *rocks,* 0.5 mile southwest of Point Lobos, and 0.25 mile offshore (lat. 36°31' N, long. 121°57'20" W). Named on Monterey (1947) 7.5' quadrangle. Called Sea Lion Rocks on California Department of Parks and Recreation's map. Monterey (1913) 15' quadrangle has the name "Whalers Rock" near present Seal Rocks.

Seaside [MONTEREY]: *city,* 2.25 miles east-northeast of Monterey near the coast (lat. 36°36'30" N, long. 121°51' W). Named on Seaside (1947) 7.5' quadrangle. Dr. J.L.D. Roberts laid out the community in 1888 and called it East Monterey; when postal authorities rejected this name, Roberts gave the place the name "Seaside" (Gudde, 1949, p. 323). Postal authorities established Seaside post office in 1891 (Salley, p. 200), and the city incorporated in 1954. According to Johnston (p. 117), an Indian named White Wolf came to Seaside about 1900, married a wealthy woman, and built Grey Eagle Terrace, a home for elderly Indians; the structure burned in 1917, but the district around the site still is known as Grey Eagle Terrace.

Seaside: see **Arroyo las Trancas** [SANTA CRUZ].

See Canyon [SAN LUIS OBISPO]: *canyon,* drained by a stream that flows nearly 6 miles to San Luis Obispo Creek 1.25 miles east-northeast of Avila Beach (lat. 35°11'15" N, long. 120°42'45" W). Named on Pismo Beach (1965) and Port San Luis (1965) 7.5' quadrangles. The name commemorates Joseph See, who came to the neighborhood in 1857 (Hanna, p. 299).

Sellars Potrero [SAN LUIS OBISPO]: *area,* 5 miles southeast of Pozo (lat. 35°15'35" N, long. 120°18'10" W). Named on Pozo Summit (1967) 7.5' quadrangle. United States Board on Geographic Names (1968b, p. 9) rejected the form "Sellers Potrero" for the name.

Semas Mountain [MONTEREY]: *peak,* nearly 2 miles northwest of Bradley (lat. 35°52'55" N, long. 120°49'15" W; sec. 31, T 23 S, R 11 E). Altitude 1225 feet. Named on Wunpost (1949) 7.5' quadrangle.

Semper Spring [SAN LUIS OBISPO]: *spring,* 27 miles southeast of Simmler (lat. 35°02'20" N, long. 119°41'45" W; sec. 18, T 11 N, R 26 W). Named on Wells Ranch (1954) 7.5' quadrangle.

Sempervirens Creek [SANTA CRUZ]: *stream,* flows 2 miles to Blooms Creek near the east end of Big Basin (lat. 37°10'05" N, long. 122°12'45" W; sec. 8, T 9 S, R 3 W). Named on Big Basin (1955) 7.5' quadrangle.

Sempervirens Reservoir [SANTA CRUZ]: *lake,* 950 feet long, behind a dam on Sempervirens Creek 1.5 miles north-northeast of Big Basin (lat. 37°11'25" N, long. 122°12'25" W; near E line sec. 32, T 8 S, R 3 W). Named on Big Basin (1955) 7.5' quadrangle.

Seneca Creek [MONTEREY]: *stream,* flows nearly 3 miles to San Jose Creek 3.5 miles southeast of the mouth of Carmel River (lat. 36°30'05" N, long. 121°52'50" W; sec. 32, T 16 S, R 1 E). Named on Mount Carmel (1956) and Soberanes Point (1956) 7.5' quadrangles.

Serena [SANTA BARBARA]: *settlement,* 2.5 miles west-northwest of Carpinteria (lat. 34°24'45" N, long. 119°33'20" W). Named on Carpinteria (1952) 7.5' quadrangle. Postal authorities established Serena post office in 1889 and discontinued it in 1900 (Frickstad, p. 172). Santa Barbara (1903) 15' quadrangle shows Carpinteria Landing at the site.

Serena Park [SANTA BARBARA]: *settlement,* 3.5 miles west-northwest of Carpinteria (lat. 34°25'05" N, long. 119°34'15" W); the place is less than 1 mile west-northwest of Serena. Named on Carpinteria (1952) 7.5' quadrangle.

Serra: see **Junipero Serra Peak** [MONTEREY].

Serra Hill: see **Sierra Hill** [MONTEREY].

Serrano [SAN LUIS OBISPO]: *locality,* 3.5 miles north of San Luis Obispo along Southern Pacific Railroad (lat. 35°20'05" N, long. 120°39'10" W). Named on San Luis Obispo (1965) 7.5' quadrangle. Postal authorities established Serrano post office in 1907 and discontinued it in 1908 (Frickstad, p. 166). Railroad officials named the place in 1893 for the Serrano family, from whom the right of way there was obtained (Gudde, 1949, p. 326).

Seven Well Canyon [MONTEREY]: *canyon,* drained by a stream that flows 2.5 miles to lowlands 4.5 miles west-southwest of San Lucas (lat. 36°05'55" N, long. 121°05'30" W; sec. 15, T 21 S, R 8 E). Named on Espinosa Canyon (1949) 7.5' quadrangle. The name reportedly is from seven wells drilled for water before the last was successful (Clark, 1991, p. 522)

Shady Lane Canyon [MONTEREY]: *canyon,* drained by a stream that flows 2.25 miles to McCoy Canyon 5.5 miles east-northeast of Gonzales (lat. 36°32'25" N, long. 121°21'05" W; sec. 18, T 16 S, R 6 E). Named on Mount Johnson (1968) 7.5' quadrangle.

Shag Rock [SANTA BARBARA]: *island,* 400 feet long, 350 feet off the north side of Santa Barbara Island (lat. 33°29'15" N, long. 119° 02'05" W). Named on United States Geological Survey's (1973) map.

Shale Sulphur Springs: see **Chittenden's Sulphur Springs**, under **Chittenden** [SANTA CRUZ].

Shandon [SAN LUIS OBISPO]: *village,* 18 miles east of Paso Robles (lat. 35°39'20" N, long. 120°22'30" W; sec. 20, T 26 S, R 15 E). Named on Cholame (1961) and Shandon (1961) 7.5' quadrangles. According to Salley (p. 202, 212), postal authorities established Starkey post office in 1885, moved it 1.5 miles northeast in 1888, and moved it 1.5 miles northeast again in 1891, when they changed the name to Shandon; the post office names were for Starkey Shandon, a pioneer settler. According to Stanley (p. 46), the townsite, first called Sunset, was surveyed in 1890 and developed by West Coast Land Company; the name was changed from Sunset to Shandon in 1891 at the suggestion of Dr. John Hughes, after Dr. Hughes had read a story called "Shandon Belle" published in *Harper's* in 1882.

Shandon Flat [SAN LUIS OBISPO]: *area,* 1.5 miles southwest of Shandon (lat. 35°38'10" N, long. 120°23'40" W). Named on Shandon (1961) 7.5' quadrangle.

Shaw Anchorage: see **Sandstone Point** [SANTA BARBARA].

Shaw Canyon [SAN LUIS OBISPO]: *canyon,* drained by a stream that flows 3.25 miles to Alamo Creek 8 miles west-southwest of Branch Mountain (lat. 35°07'30" N, long. 120°12'25" W; sec. 24, T 32 S, R 16 E). Named on Chimney Canyon (1967) 7.5' quadrangle.

Shear Creek [SANTA CRUZ]: *stream,* flows nearly 2 miles to Bear Creek 5.5 miles northeast of the town of Boulder Creek (lat. 37°11'05" N, long. 122°03'20" W; near S line sec. 35, T 8 S, R 2 W). Named on Castle Rock Ridge (1955) 7.5' quadrangle.

Shedd Canyon [SAN LUIS OBISPO]: *canyon,* 9 miles long, opens into lowlands nearly 4 miles west of Shandon (lat. 35°39'15" N, long. 120°26'30" W; sec. 23, T 26 S, R 14 E). Named on Shandon (1961) and Shedd Canyon (1961) 7.5' quadrangles.

Sheehee Spring [MONTEREY]: *spring,* 5.5 miles southwest of Smith Mountain (lat. 36°01'50" N, long. 120°40'15" W; sec. 10, T 22 S, R 12 E). Named on Slack Canyon (1969) 7.5' quadrangle.

Sheep Camp [SAN LUIS OBISPO]: *locality,* 12 miles south-southeast of Simmler (lat. 35°12' N, long. 119°52' W; sec. 30, T 31 S, R 20 E). Named on Painted Rock (1959) 7.5' quadrangle.

Sheep Camp: see **Camp No. 3**, under **Santa Rosalia Mountain** [SANTA CRUZ].

Sheep Camp Canyon [SAN LUIS OBISPO]: *canyon,* drained by a stream that flows 5 miles to lowlands along Estrella Creek 11 miles east-northeast of Paso Robles (lat. 35°41' N, long. 120°30'40" W; sec. 7, T 26 S, R 14 E). Named on Shandon (1961) 7.5' quadrangle.

Sheep Camp Creek [SANTA BARBARA]: *stream,* flows 2.5 miles to Aliso Creek 5 miles west of Miranda Pine Mountain (lat. 35°02'05" N, long. 120°07'15" W). Named on Miranda Pine Mountain (1967) 7.5' quadrangle.

Sheepcamp Creek [SAN LUIS OBISPO]: *stream,* flows nearly 6 miles to Paso Robles Creek 3.25 miles east of York Mountain (lat. 35°33'05" N, long. 120°46'30" W). Named on York Mountain (1948) 7.5' quadrangle. Adelaida (1947) 15' quadrangle has the form "Sheep Camp Creek" for the name.

Sheep Canyon [MONTEREY]: *canyon,* drained by a stream that flows 3.5 miles to Powell Canyon 5.5 miles north of Bradley (lat. 35°56'45" N, long. 120°48'10" W; sec. 8, T 23 S, R 11 E). Named on Wunpost (1949) 7.5' quadrangle.

Sheep Creek [SAN LUIS OBISPO]: *stream,* flows 4.5 miles to Alamo Creek

5.5 miles west of Branch Mountain (lat. 35°11'05" N, long. 120°10'45" W). Named on Los Machos Hills (1967) 7.5' quadrangle.

Sheffield Reservoir [SANTA BARBARA]: *lake,* 950 feet long, 1.5 miles north of downtown Santa Barbara (lat. 34°26'40" N, long. 119°41'30" W; sec. 10, T 4 N, R 27 W). Named on Santa Barbara (1952) 7.5' quadrangle.

Shell Beach [SAN LUIS OBISPO]: *district,* 2 miles west-northwest of downtown Pismo Beach along the coast (lat. 35°09'20" N, long. 120°40'15" W). Named on Pismo Beach (1965) 7.5' quadrangle. Postal authorities established Shell Beach post office in 1939 (Frickstad, p. 166). Floyd Calvert laid out the community on 41 acres of land that he bought in 1926 (Lee and others, p. 139). The place now is part of Pismo Beach.

Shell Creek [SAN LUIS OBISPO]: *stream,* flows 7.5 miles to Camatta Canyon 3 miles east-northeast of Wilson Corner (lat. 35°29' N, long. 120°19'40" W; near N line sec. 23, T 28 S, R 15 E). Named on Camatta Ranch (1966) 7.5' quadrangle.

Shell Peak [SAN LUIS OBISPO]: *peak,* 10 miles southwest of Branch Mountain (lat. 35°04'20" N, long. 120°11'20" W; near W line sec. 31, T 12 N, R 31 W). Altitude 2460 feet. Named on Chimney Canyon (1967) 7.5' quadrangle.

Shepard Mesa [SANTA BARBARA]: *ridge,* west-trending, 0.5 mile long, 2 miles north-northeast of Rincon Point (lat. 34°23'55" N, long. 119°27'55" W). Named on White Ledge Peak (1952) 7.5' quadrangle. Ventura (1941) 15' quadrangle has the name "Shepard Park" on the ridge.

Shepard Park: see **Shepard Mesa** [SANTA BARBARA].

Shepards [SANTA BARBARA]: *locality,* 2.25 miles northeast of Rincon Point (lat. 34°23'50" N, long. 119°27'10" W); the place is east of present Shepard Mesa. Named on Ventura (1904) 15' quadrangle.

Shields Canyon [SAN BENITO]: *canyon,* drained by a stream that flows nearly 4 miles to San Benito River 2.5 miles north-northwest of San Benito (lat. 36°32'30" N, long. 121°06'05" W). Named on San Benito (1968) 7.5' quadrangle.

Shimmin Canyon [SAN LUIS OBISPO]: *canyon,* drained by a stream that flows 12 miles to Estrella River 5.5 miles west of Shandon (lat. 35°39'10" N, long. 120°28'05" W; sec. 21, T 26 S, R 14 E). Named on Cholame Hills (1961) and Shandon (1961) 7.5' quadrangles. Called Simmons Canyon on Cholame (1917) 30' quadrangle.

Shingle Mill Creek [SANTA CRUZ]: *stream,* flows 1.5 miles to San Lorenzo River 6.25 miles south-southeast of the town of Boulder Creek (lat. 37°02'35" N, long. 122°04'15" W). Named on Felton (1955) 7.5' quadrangle.

Shingle Mill Gulch [SANTA CRUZ]: *canyon,* nearly 1 mile long, branches east from Eureka Canyon 4 miles north of Corralitos (lat. 37°02'40" N, long. 121°48'50" W; sec. 24, T 10 S, R 1 E). Named on Loma Prieta (1955) 7.5' quadrangle.

Shingle Springs: see **Ben Lomond** [SANTA CRUZ].

Shirttail Gulch [MONTEREY]: *canyon,* 3.5 miles long, opens into lowlands 3.5 miles east-southeast of Soledad (lat. 36°24'50" N, long. 121°15'45" W; sec. 36, T 17 S, R 6 E). Named on North Chalone Peak (1969) and Soledad (1955) 7.5' quadrangles.

Shoquel [SANTA CRUZ]: *land grant,* at and east of Soquel near the coast. Named on Soquel (1954) 7.5' quadrangle. Martina Castro received 0.5 league in 1833 and claimed 1668 acres patented in 1860 (Rowland, p. 39; Rowland listed the grant under the name "Soquel"). The name is from an Indian village (Kroeber, 1916, p. 59)

Shoquel: see **Soquel** [SANTA CRUZ].

Shoquel Augmentation [SANTA CRUZ]: *land grant,* along and east of Soquel Creek; extends a short distance over the crest of Santa Cruz Mountains into Santa Clara County. Named on Laurel (1955), Loma Prieta (1955), Los Gatos (1953), Soquel (1954), and Watsonville West (1954) 7.5' quadrangles. Arbuckle (p. 35) listed the grant under the name "Soquel Augmentacion," and noted that Martina Castro, who received the land in 1844 as an addition to her Shoquel grant, claimed 32,702 acres patented in 1860.

Shoquel Cove: see **Soquel Cove** [SANTA CRUZ].

Shoquel Creek: see **Soquel Creek** [SANTA CRUZ].

Shoquel Point: see **Soquel Point** [SANTA CRUZ].

Shovel Handle Creek [MONTEREY]: *stream,* flows nearly 1 mile to Zigzag Creek 3.25 miles southwest of Tassajara Hot Springs (lat. 36°11'45" N, long. 121°34'55" W; sec. 13, T 20 S, R 3 E). Named on Tassajara Hot Springs (1956) 7.5' quadrangle.

Shuman [SANTA BARBARA]: *locality,* 2 miles north-northeast of the village of Casmalia along Southern Pacific Railroad (lat. 34°52' N, long. 120°31'20" W); the place is near the head of Shuman Canyon. Named on Casmalia (1959) 7.5' quadrangle. Called Schumann on Guadalupe (1905) 30' quadrangle, but United States Board on Geographic Names (1949, p. 4) rejected the forms "Schumann" and "Schuman" for the name.

Shuman Canyon [SANTA BARBARA]: *canyon,* drained by a stream that flows 7.5 miles to lowlands along the coast 3.5 miles west of the village of Casmalia (lat. 34°50'45" N, long. 120°35'40" W). Named on Casmalia (1959) 7.5' quadrangle. Called Schumann Canyon on Guadalupe (1905) 30' quadrangle, but United States Board on Geographic Names (1949, p. 4) rejected this form of the name.

Shut-in: see **The Shut-in** [MONTEREY].

Sienega del Gabilan: see **Cienega del Gabilan** [MONTEREY-SAN BENITO].

Sierra Blanca [SANTA BARBARA]: *ridge,* south-southwest-trending, 0.5 mile long, 1.25 miles north of Punta Arena on Santa Cruz Island (lat. 33°58'50" N, long. 119°49'10" W). Named on Santa Cruz Island B (1943) 7.5' quadrangle.

Sierra Creek [MONTEREY]: *stream,* flows 3.25 miles to Bixby Creek 4.25 miles north-northeast of Point Sur (lat. 36°21'55" N, long. 121°53'10" W; sec. 17, T 18 S, R 1 E); the stream is northeast of Sierra Hill. Named on Big Sur (1956) and Point Sur (1956) 7.5' quadrangles.

Sierra de Buchon: see **Irish Hills** [SAN LUIS OBISPO].

Sierra de Gavilan: see **Gabilan Range** [MONTEREY-SAN BENITO].

Sierra de la Santa Cruz: see **Santa Cruz Mountains** [SANTA CRUZ].

Sierra de la Santa Inez: see **Santa Ynez Mountains** [SANTA BARBARA].

Sierra de la Santa Lucia: see **Santa Lucia Range** [MONTEREY-SAN LUIS OBISPO].

Sierra de las Piedras: see **Piedras Atlas** [MONTEREY].

Sierra del Monte Diablo: see **Diablo Range** [MONTEREY-SAN BENITO].

Sierra de Salinas [MONTEREY]: *range,* extends along the southwest side of Salinas River from near Salinas to Greenfield. Named on Santa Cruz (1956) 1°x 2° quadrangle. Whitney (p. 111) used the name "Palo Scrito Hills" for the range, Fairbanks (1894, p. 520) used the name "Soledad Hills" for the feature, Angel (1890a, p. 568) used the name "Palo Serito Hills" for it, and Reed (p. 44) mentioned the names "Palo Escrito" and "Mount Torro Range." Parke's (1854-1855) map has the name "Sierra Salinas" for highlands west of Salinas River as far south as San Antonio River, and in his text Parke (p. 6) used the name "Salinas mountains" for the same highlands.

Sierra de San Rafael: see **San Rafael Mountains** [SANTA BARBARA].

Sierra de Santa Lucia: see **Santa Lucia Range** [MONTEREY-SAN LUIS OBISPO].

Sierra Hill [MONTEREY]: *ridge,* northwest-trending, 2 miles long, 3.25 miles north-northeast of Point Sur (lat. 36°21' N, long. 121° 53' W); the ridge is southwest of Sierra Creek. Named on Point Sur (1956) 7.5' quadrangle. According to Clark (1991, p. 520-521), the feature should have the name "Serra Hill."

Sierra Madre Mountains [SANTA BARBARA]: *range,* between Cuyama Valley and Sisquoc River. Named on Los Angeles (1955) and San Luis Obispo (1956) 1°x 2° quadrangles. Called San Rafael Mountains on San Luis Obispo (1948) and Santa Maria (1956) 1°x 2° quadrangles, but United States Board on Geographic Names (1965b, p. 15) rejected this name for the feature. Parke (p. 6) called the range Cuyama mountains, Whitney (p. 112) called it Cuyamas Range, and Fairbanks (1894, p. 498) called it Cuyama range.

Sierra Madre Mountains: see **San Rafael Mountains** [SANTA BARBARA].

Sierra Napoma: see **Nipomo Valley** [SAN LUIS OBISPO].

Sierra Nevada: see **Point Sierra Nevada** [SAN LUIS OBISPO].

Sierra Nevadas: see **Santa Lucia Range** [MONTEREY-SAN LUIS OBISPO].

Sierra Pablo [SANTA BARBARA]: *ridge,* east-northeast-trending, less than 1 mile long, 3.5 miles west of East Point on Santa Rosa Island (lat. 33°56'35" N, long. 120°01'40" W). Named on Santa Rosa Island East (1943) 7.5' quadrangle.

Sierra River: see **Nacimiento River** [MONTEREY-SAN LUIS OBISPO].

Sierra Salinas: see **Sierra de Salinas** [MONTEREY].

Sierra San Jose: see **La Panza Range** [SAN LUIS OBISPO].

Sierra Santa Iñez: see **Santa Ynez Mountains** [SANTA BARBARA].

Sierra Santa Lucia: see **Santa Lucia Range** [MONTEREY-SAN LUIS OBISPO].

Sierra Wasna: see **Santa Lucia Range** [SAN LUIS OBISPO].

Silver Creek [SAN BENITO]: *stream,* formed by the confluence of San Carlos Creek and Larious Creek, flows 10 miles to Fresno County 7 miles east-southeast of Panoche (lat. 36°34'05" N, long. 120°42'05" W; sec. 6, T 16 S, R 12 E). Named on Idria (1969) and Tumey Hills (1956) 7.5' quadrangles. United States Board on Geographic Names (1933, p. 693) rejected the name "Panoche Creek" for the stream.

Silver Creek [SANTA CRUZ]: *stream,* flows 0.5 mile to Boulder Creek (1) 5 miles east-southeast of Big Basin (lat. 37°08' N, long. 122°08'20" W; sec. 24, T 9 S, R 3 W). Named on Big Basin (1955) quadrangle.

Silver Lake [SAN LUIS OBISPO]: *intermittent lake,* 500 feet long, 8 miles northeast of Santa Margarita (lat. 35°28'50" N, long. 120°31'20" W). Named on Santa Margarita (1965) 7.5' quadrangle.

Silver Peak [MONTEREY]: *peak,* 6.5 miles east-southeast of Cape San Martin (lat. 35°50'50" N, long. 121°21'30" N; sec. 18, T 24 S, R 6 E). Altitude 3590 feet. Named on Burro Mountain (1949) 7.5' quadrangle.

Simas Lake [SANTA CRUZ]: *lake,* 950 feet long, 5.5 miles north of Watsonville (lat. 36°59'50" N, long. 121°44'20" W). Named on Watsonville East (1955) 7.5' quadrangle.

Simmler [SAN LUIS OBISPO]: *settlement,* 38 miles east of San Luis Obispo in the north part of Carrizo Plain (lat. 35°21'05" N, long. 119°59'10" W; near SW cor. sec. 31, T 29 S, R 19 E). Named on Simmler (1959) 7.5' quadrangle. Postal authorities established Simmler post office in 1887 and discontinued it in 1930 (Frickstad, p. 166). The name commemorates the John J. Simmler family, who came to California in 1853 (Gudde, 1949, p. 333).

Simmons Canyon: see **Shimmin Canyon** [SAN LUIS OBISPO].

Simonton Cove [SANTA BARBARA]: *embayment,* 4 miles east-northeast of Point Bennett on the north side of San Miguel Island (lat. 34°03'20" N, long. 120°23'15" W). Named on San Miguel Island East (1950) and San Miguel Island West (1950) 7.5' quadangles. Bremner's (1933) map has the name "Otter Harbor" at the west end of the embayment.

Sinnott Switch: see **Riverside Grove** [SANTA CRUZ].

Sisquoc [SANTA BARBARA]:

(1) *land grant,* east-southeast of Santa Maria along and near Sisquoc River. Named on Foxen Canyon (1964), Manzanita Mountain (1964), Tepusquet Canyon (1964), and Zaca Lake (1964) 7.5' quadrangles. Maria Antonio Caballero received the land in 1833; James B. Huie and others claimed 35,486 acres patented in 1866 (Cowan, p. 98). Perez (p. 99) gave 1845 as the date of the grant.

(2) *village,* 10 miles southeast of Santa Maria (lat. 34°51'55" N, long. 120°17'30" W; at SW cor. sec. 7, T 9 N, R 32 W); the village is near Sisquoc River. Named on Sisquoc (1959) 7.5' quadrangle.

(3) *locality,* 6.5 miles northeast of Los Alamos in Foxen Canyon (lat. 34°47'45" N, long. 120°11'05" W). Named on Lompoc (1905) 30' quadrangle. Postal authorities established Sis Quoc post office in 1881, discontinued it in 1898, and reestablished it with the name "Sisquoc" the same year; they moved the post office 3 miles southeast in 1902, discontinued it in 1910, reestablished it in 1911, and discontinued it in 1931 (Salley, p. 205). California Mining Bureau's (1917c) map shows a place called Foxen located about 2.5 miles northwest of Sisquoc. Postal authorities established Foxen post office in 1910, when they moved Sisquoc post office to the place, and discontinued it in 1914 (Salley, p. 79). They established Asphaltea post office in 1897 and discontinued it in 1898, when they moved it 10 miles northwest to Sisquoc; the name was from nearby deposits of asphaltum (Salley, p. 11).

Sisquoc Falls [SANTA BARBARA]: *waterfall,* 5.5 miles northwest of Big Pine Mountain (lat. 34°44'35" N, long. 119°43'50" W); the feature is along a tributary of Sisquoc River. Named on Big Pine Mountain (1964) 7.5' quadrangle.

Sisquoc Grange [SANTA BARBARA]: *locality,* nearly 2 miles east-southeast of the village of Sisquoc (lat. 34°51'15" N, long. 120°15'50" W; sec. 17, T 9 N, R 32 W). Named on Sisquoc (1959) 7.5' quadrangle.

Sisquoc River [SANTA BARBARA]: *stream,* flows 55 miles to join Cuyama River and form Santa Maria River 8 miles east-southeast of Santa Maria (lat. 34°54'10" N, long. 120°18'40" W; at E line sec. 36, T 10 N, R 33 W). Named on Bald Mountain (1964), Big Pine Mountain (1964), Foxen Canyon (1964), Hurricane Deck (1964), Salisbury Potrero (1964), Sisquoc (1959), Twitchell Dam (1959), and Zaca Lake (1964) 7.5' quadrangles. Called Santa Maria R. on Goddard's (1857) map. South Fork enters from the south 5.25 miles south-southwest of Montgomery Potrero; it is 4.25 miles long and is named on Hurricane Deck (1964) and San Rafael Mountain (1959) 7.5' quadrangles.

Sixteen Spring [SAN LUIS OBISPO]: *spring,* 14 miles east-northeast of Pozo along San Juan Creek (lat. 35°24'15" N, long. 120°09'35" W; sec. 16, T 29 S, R 17 E). Named on La Panza Ranch (1966) 7.5' quadrangle.

Skinner Creek [MONTEREY]: *stream,* flows 3.5 miles to Little Sur River 6.25 miles east-northeast of Point Sur (lat. 36°19'40" N, long. 121°47'35" W); the stream is east of Skinner Ridge. Named on Big Sur (1956) 7.5' quadrangle.

Skinner Ridge [MONTEREY]: *ridge,* southeast- to south-trending, 3 miles long, 7 miles east-northeast of Point Sur (lat. 36°21'30" N, long. 121°47'30" W); the ridge is west of Skinner Creek. Named on Big Sur (1956) 7.5' quadrangle.

Skull Gulch: see **Cañada Tecolote** [SANTA BARBARA].

Skunk Campground [SANTA BARBARA]: *locality,* 5.25 miles south-southwest of Salisbury Potrero along Sisquoc River (lat. 34° 45'10" N, long. 119°44'25" W). Named on Salisbury Potrero (1964) 7.5' quadrangle.

Skunk Point [SANTA BARBARA]: *promontory,* nearly 3 mile north-northwest of East Point (lat. 33°59' N, long. 119°58'40" W). Named on Santa Rosa Island East (1943) 7.5' quadrangle.

Skyland: see **Skyland Ridge** [SANTA CRUZ].

Skyland Ridge [SANTA CRUZ]: *ridge,* east- to southeast-trending, 3 miles long, 8.5 miles north-northeast of Soquel (lat. 37°06'30" N, long. 121°55'15" W). Named on Laurel (1955) 7.5' quadrangle. California Mining Bureau's (1917a) map shows a place called Skyland located 2.5 miles east of Laurel on or near present Skyland Ridge. Postal authorities established Skyland post office in 1884, discontinued it in 1886, reestablished it in 1893, and discontinued it in 1912 (Salley, p. 206).

Slabtown: see **Cambria** [SAN LUIS OBISPO].

Slack Canyon [MONTEREY]: *valley,* 3 miles west-southwest of Smith Mountain (lat. 36°03'30" N, long. 120°38' W). Named on Slack Canyon (1969) and Smith Mountain (1969) 7.5' quadrangles. The valley is drained by Pancho Rico Creek and a tributary of that creek. J.W. Slack came to California in the 1850's and took up range land in the canyon that bears his name (Stanley, p. 126-127). Fairbanks (1894, p. 522) referred to Slack's Cañon. Postal authorities established Slack Canyon post office in 1873 about 15 miles north of Valleton (NE quarter sec. 27, T 21 S, R 12 E) and discontinued it in 1902 (Salley, p. 206).

Slacks Valley [SAN BENITO]: *valley,* drained by a stream that flows 4 miles to Las Aguilas Creek (1) 6.25 miles north-northwest of Panoche Pass (lat. 36°42'55" N, long. 121°02'20" W). Named on Cerro Colorado (1969) and Panoche Pass (1968) 7.5' quadrangles.

Slate Canyon [MONTEREY]: *canyon,* drained by a stream that flows 3.25 miles to Robertson Creek 4.25 miles east of Jamesburg (lat. 36°21'55" N, long. 121°31' W; sec. 14, T 18 S, R 4 E). Named on Chews Ridge (1956), Palo Escrito Peak (1956), and Rana Creek (1956) 7.5' quadrangles.

Slate Rock [MONTEREY]: *rock,* 125 feet long, less than 1 mile west-northwest of Slates Hot Spring, and 0.25 mile offshore (lat. 36°07'35" N, long. 121°38'55" W). Named on Partington Ridge (1956) 7.5' quadrangle.

Slate Rock: see **Little Slate Rock** [MONTEREY].

Slates Hot Springs [MONTEREY]: *spring,* 8 miles north-northwest of Lopez Point (lat. 36°07'20" N, long. 121°38'10" W; sec. 9, T 21 S, R 3 E). Named on Lopez Point (1956) 7.5' quadrangle. On Lucia (1921) 15' quadrangle, the name "Slate's Hot Springs" applies to a building. Irelan (p. 411) referred to Slate's Springs, Crawford (1894, p. 341) described Slate's Hot Sulphur Springs, and Berkstresser (p. A-9) listed the feature under the name "Big Sur Hot Springs." Thomas B. Slate settled at the place in 1868 after water from the spring there apparently cured him of arthritis; later a small resort developed at the site (Waring, G.A., p. 56; Fink, p. 209, 230). Esalen Institute is at the place now (Wall, p. 75, 142).

Sleeper Gulch [SANTA CRUZ]: *canyon,* drained by a stream that flows 1 mile to Kings Creek 5.5 miles north of the town of Boulder Creek (lat. 37°12'20" N, long. 122°07' W; sec. 30, T 8 S, R 2 W). Named on Castle Rock Ridge (1955) 7.5' quadrangle.

Sleepy Hollow [MONTEREY]: *locality,* 2.5 miles south-southeast of the town of Carmel Valley at a wide place in the canyon of Carmel River (lat. 36°26'40" N, long. 121°42'50" W; sec. 23, T 17 S, R 2 E). Named on Carmel Valley (1956) 7.5' quadrangle.

Slickrock Creek [MONTEREY]: *stream,* flows 2 miles to Nacimiento River 9 miles northeast of Cape San Martin (lat. 35°58'45" N, long. 121°21'05" W; sec. 31, T 22 S, R 6 E). Named on Alder Peak (1949) 7.5' quadrangle. Cape San Martin (1921) 15' quadrangle has the form "Slick Rock Creek" for the name.

Slide Hill [SAN LUIS OBISPO]: *peak,* nearly 6 miles east-northeast of Edna (lat. 35°13'20" N, long. 120°31'55" W; sec. 13, T 31 S, R 13 E). Altitude 2168 feet. Named on Arroyo Grande NE (1965) 7.5' quadrangle.

Sloans Canyon [SANTA BARBARA]: *canyon,* drained by a stream that flows 3.5 miles to lowlands along Santa Ynez River 6.5 miles east-southeast of Surf (lat. 34°38'10" N, long. 120°30'10" W). Named on Lompoc (1959), Surf (1959), and Tranquillon Mountain (1959) 7.5' quadrangles.

Slocum Canyon [SAN LUIS OBISPO]: *canyon,* drained by a stream that flows 3.5 miles to San Juan Valley 3 miles south-southeast of Shandon (lat. 35°37' N, long. 120°20'55" W; near S line sec. 34, T 26 S, R 15 E). Named on Camatta Canyon (1961) and Cholame (1961) 7.5' quadrangles.

Small Twin Lake [SAN LUIS OBISPO]: *lake,* 1000 feet long, nearly 4 miles south-southwest of downtown Arroyo Grande near the coast (lat. 35°04'10" N, long. 120°36'15" W); the feature is east of Big Twin Lake. Named on Oceano (1965) 7.5' quadrangle.

Smith Canyon [SANTA BARBARA]: *canyon,* drained by a stream that flows 4.5 miles to Manzanita Mountain (lat. 34°57'30" N, long. 120°05'45" W). Named on Manzanita Mountain (1964) and Miranda Pine Mountain (1967) 7.5' quadrangles.

Smith Creek [SAN LUIS OBISPO]: *stream,* flows nearly 2 miles to Toro Creek 4 miles north-northeast of the town of Morro Bay (lat. 35°26'30" N, long. 120°49'50" W). Named on Morro Bay North (1965) 7.5' quadrangle.

Smith Creek [SANTA CRUZ]: *stream,* flows nearly 1 mile to Love Creek 2.5 miles southeast of the town of Boulder Creek (lat. 37° 05'55" N, long. 122°05'05" W; at S line sec. 33, T 9 S, R 2 W). Named on Felton (1955) 7.5' quadrangle.

Smith Creek: see **Robertson Creek** [MONTEREY].

Smith Island [SAN LUIS OBISPO]: *island,* 250 feet long, 0.5 mile east-northeast of Point San Luis and 250 feet offshore (lat. 35°09'45" N, long. 120°45'15" W). Named on Port San Luis (1965) 7.5' quadrangle. The name, given in the 1880's, commemorates Joe Smith and Mattie Smith, who lived on the island (Lee and others, p. 123).

Smith Mountain [MONTEREY]: *peak,* 18 miles east-northeast of San Ardo on Monterey-Fresno County line (lat. 36°04'45" N, long. 120°35'55" W; sec. 29, T 21 S, R 13 E). Altitude 3947 feet. Named on Smith Mountain (1969) 7.5' quadrangle.

Smoker Canyon [SAN BENITO]: *canyon,* drained by a stream that flows 5.25 miles to San Benito River 8 miles north-northwest of Bitterwater (lat. 36°29'30" N, long. 121°01'45" W; sec. 31, T 16 S, R 9 E). Named on Llanada (1969), San Benito (1968), and Topo Valley (1969) 7.5' quadrangles.

Smugglers Cove [SANTA BARBARA]: *embayment,* 1.5 miles southwest of San Pedro Point at the east end of Santa Cruz Island (lat. 34°01'10" N, long. 119°32'20" W). Named on Santa Cruz Island D (1943) 7.5' quadrangle.

Snake Creek [SAN LUIS OBISPO]: *stream,* flows 7 miles to Nacimiento River 7 miles northeast of Lime Mountain (lat. 35°44'25" N, long. 120°54'25" W; near W line sec. 21, T 25 S, R 10 E). Named on Adelaida (1948) and Lime Mountain (1948) 7.5' quadrangles. The stream now enters an arm of Nacimiento Reservoir.

Snivleys Ridge [MONTEREY]: *ridge,* north- to northwest-trending, 2 miles long, 8 miles east-southeast of the mouth of Carmel River and south of Carmel Valley (1) (lat. 36°30'15" N, long. 121°47'20" W). Named on Mount Carmel (1956) and Seaside (1947) 7.5' quadrangles. The misspelled name commemorates Richard Collier Snively, who had a fruit farm and dairy near the mouth of Robinson Canyon (1) (Clark, 1991, p. 531).

Snowball Mountain [SANTA BARBARA]: *peak,* 4 miles north of Rincon Point (lat. 34°25'45" N, long. 119°28'55" W; sec. 15, T 4 N, R 25 W). Altitude 1680 feet. Named on White Ledge Peak (1952) 7.5' quadrangle.

Soap Lake: see **San Felipe Lake** [SAN BENITO].

Soberanes Creek [MONTEREY]: *stream,* flows 3.5 miles to the sea north of Soberanes Point (lat. 36°27'20" N, long. 121°55'25" W). Named on Soberanes Point (1956) 7.5' quadrangle.

Soberanes Creek: see **Palo Colorado Canyon** [MONTEREY].

Soberanes Point [MONTEREY]: *promontory,* 10 miles north of Point Sur along the coast (lat. 36°27' N, long. 121°55'40" W). Named on Soberanes Point (1956) 7.5' quadrangle. The name commemorates early settlers who homesteaded near the feature (Lussier, p. 12).

Soda Lake [SAN LUIS OBISPO]: *intermittent lake,* 5 miles long, 10 miles southeast of Simmler in Carrizo Plain (lat. 35°14' N, long. 119°53'30" W). Named on Chimineas Ranch (1959), Painted Rock (1959), and Simmler (1959) 7.5' quadrangles. According to Arnold and Johnson (1909, p. 3), the feature was known locally as Soda Lake or Salt Lake. Logan (p. 721) referred to "Soda Lake, or Dry Lake, as it is often called." United States Board on Geographic Names (1933, p. 704) rejected the name "Salt Lake" for the feature.

Soda Lake [SANTA CRUZ]: *lake,* 1600 feet long, 8 miles east of Watsonville (lat. 36°54'30" N, long. 121°36'25" W). Named on Chittenden (1955) 7.5' quadrangle. Shown as an intermittent lake on Chittenden (1955, photorevised 1968 and 1973) 7.5' quadrangle.

Soda Spring Creek [MONTEREY]: *stream,* flows nearly 1.5 miles to the sea 7 miles southeast of Cape San Martin (lat. 35°49' N, long. 121°22'35" W; sec. 25, T 24 S, R 5 E). Named on Burro Mountain (1949) 7.5' quadrangle. The name is from a soda spring found near the feature (Clark, 1991, p. 533).

Soldiers Home Spring: see **Goat Rock** [SANTA BARBARA].

Soledad [MONTEREY]: *town,* 25 miles southeast of Salinas near Salinas River (lat. 36°25'30" N, long. 121°19' W). Named on Soledad (1955) 7.5' quadrangle. Postal authorities established Soledad post office in 1869 (Frickstad, p. 109), and the town incorporated in 1921. When the Portola expedition passed the place in 1769, an Indian there responded to a question with a word that sounded like *soledad*, which means "solitude" in Spanish; later a nearby mission took the name "La Mision de Nuestra Señora de la Soledad" (Gudde, 1949, p. 338).

Soledad Hills: see **Sierra de Salinas** [MONTEREY].

Solomon: see **Mount Solomon** [SANTA BARBARA]; **Mount Solomon**, under **Solomon Hills** [SANTA BARBARA].

Solomon Canyon [SANTA BARBARA]: *canyon,* 3 miles long, along Orcutt Creek above a point 3.25 miles east-southeast of Orcutt (lat. 34°51'10" N, long. 120°23'05" W); the canyon is in Solomon Hills. Named on Orcutt (1959) and Sisquoc (1959) 7.5' quadrangles. The name commemorates Solomon Pico, a highway robber who used the canyon as a base in the 1850's (Gudde, 1949, p. 338).

Solomon Hills [SANTA BARBARA]: *range,* south of Santa Maria Valley and Sisquoc River between Graciosa Canyon and Zaca Creek. Named on Foxen Canyon (1964), Los Olivos (1959), Orcutt (1959), Sisquoc (1959), and Zaca Creek (1959) 7.5' quadrangles. United States Board on Geographic Names (1965d, p. 12) rejected the name "Mount Solomon" for the range.

Solvang [SANTA BARBARA]: *town,* 3.25 miles east-southeast of Buellton along Santa Ynez River (lat. 34°35'45" N, long. 120°08'25" W). Named on Solvang (1959) 7.5' quadrangle. Postal authorities established Solvang post office in 1912 (Frickstad, p. 172). Danish-American Corporation founded a colony at the place in 1911—*solvang* means "sun meadow" in Danish (Gudde, 1949, p. 338). Postal authorities established Ionata post office near present Solvang (SW quarter sec. 21, T 6 N, R 31 W) in 1874 and discontinued it in 1876; the name was from San Carlos de Jonata grant (Salley, p. 105).

Soqual: see **Soquel** [SANTA CRUZ].

Soque: see **Soquel** [SANTA CRUZ].

Soque Cove: see **Soquel Cove** [SANTA CRUZ].

Soque Creek: see **Soquel Creek** [SANTA CRUZ].

Soquel [SANTA CRUZ]: *town,* 2.5 miles north-northeast of Soquel Point (lat. 36°59'15" N, long. 121°57'20" W); the town is along Soquel Creek and partly on Shoquel grant. Named on Soquel (1954) 7.5' quadrangle. Called Sauguil on Rogers and Johnston's (1857) map, and called Soqual on Bancroft's (1864) map. United States Board on Geographic Names (1933, p. 706) rejected the forms "Saquel," "Sauquel," "Shoquel," and "Soque" for the name. The first general store at the place opened in 1853 (Lewis, 1977, p. 80), and postal authorities established Soquel post office in 1857 (Frickstad, p. 177).

Soquel: see **Shoquel** [SANTA CRUZ].

Soquel Augmentacion: see **Shoquel Augmentation** [SANTA CRUZ].

Soquel Cove [SANTA CRUZ]: *embayment,* east of Soquel Point (lat. 36°58' N, long. 121°56' W). Named on Soquel (1954) 7.5' quadrangle. United States Board on Geographic Names (1933, p. 706) rejected the forms "Saquel Cove," "Sauquel Cove," "Shoquel Cove," and "Soque Cove" for the name.

Soquel Creek [SANTA CRUZ]: *stream,* flows 18 miles to the sea 1.5 miles northeast of Soquel Point (lat. 36°58'20" N, long. 121°57'05" W). Named on Laurel (1955), Loma Prieta (1955), and Soquel (1954) 7.5' quadrangles. Trask (p. 24) mentioned the arroya Sogell in 1854. United States Board on Geographic Names (1933, p. 706) rejected the forms "Saquel Creek," "Sauquel Creek," "Shoquel Creek," and "Soque Creek" for the name. Members of the Portola expedition called the valley of the stream Rosario del Serafin de Asculi in 1769 because they found wild roses there that reminded them of the roses of Spain (Rowland, p. 95). West Branch enters from the north 6.5 miles upstream from the mouth of the main stream; it is formed by the confluence of Burns Creek and Laurel Creek, is 6 miles long, and is named on Laurel (1955) 7.5' quadrangle. Alexander (fig. 5) used the name "Mtn. Cr." for the next tributary to Soquel Creek south of West Branch (lat. 37°01'50" N, long. 121°56'45" W; near E line sec. 27, T 10 S, R 1 W)—Laurel (1955) 7.5' quadrangle shows Mountain school near the mouth of this tributary. A place called Porter's Landing was situated on the coast at the mouth of Soquel Creek in the early days (Hoover, Rensch, and Rensch, p. 474).

Soquel Landing: see **Capitola** [SANTA BARBARA].

Soquel Point [SANTA CRUZ]: *promontory,* 3 miles east of Point Santa Cruz along the coast (lat. 36°57'15" N, long. 121°58'30" W). Named on Soquel (1954) 7.5' quadrangle. United States Board on Geographic Names (1933, p. 706) rejected the forms "Saquel Point," "Sauquel Point," "Shoquel Point," and Soque Point" for the name.

Soque Point: see **Soquel Point** [SANTA CRUZ].

Soto Canyon [SAN LUIS OBISPO]: *canyon,* drained by a stream that flows 4 miles to Salinas River 3 miles east-southeast of Pozo (lat. 35°17'10" N, long. 120°19'20" W; near NW cor. sec. 25, T 30 S, R 15 E). Named on Pozo Summit (1967) 7.5' quadrangle.

Soto Spring [SAN LUIS OBISPO]: *spring,* 5 miles southwest of Branch Mountain along Branch Creek (lat. 35°08'20" N, long. 120° 08'50" W). Named on Los Machos Hills (1967) 7.5' quadrangle.

Sotoville: see **Santa Rita** [MONTEREY].

South Campground [MONTEREY]: *locality,* 2.25 miles east-northeast of Pfeiffer Point (lat. 36°14'35" N, long. 121°46'30" W; sec. 31, T 19 S, R 2 E). Named on Pfeiffer Point (1956) 7.5' quadrangle.

South Chalone Peak [MONTEREY]: *peak,* 8.5 miles north-northeast of Greenfield (lat. 36°26'10" N, long. 121°11'05" W; sec. 23, T 17 S, R 7 E); the peak is 1 mile southeast of North Chalone Peak. Altitude 3269 feet. Named on North Chalone Peak (1969) 7.5' quadrangle. On Metz (1921) 15' quadrangle, South Chalone Peak and North Chalone Peak together have the name "Chalone Mtn."

Southeast Anchorage [SANTA BARBARA]: *embayment,* 3.5 miles northwest of East Point on the north side of Santa Rosa Island (lat. 33°58'50" N, long. 120°00'20" W). Named on Santa Rosa Island East (1943) 7.5' quadrangle.

South Fall Creek [SANTA CRUZ]: *stream,* flows 1.5 miles to Fall Creek 5 miles south-southeast of the town of Boulder Creek (lat. 37°03'25" N, long. 122°05'30" W; sec. 16, T 10 S, R 2 W). Named on Felton (1955) 7.5' quadrangle.

South Point [MONTEREY]: *promontory,* on the west side of Point Lobos between Pinnacle Cove and Headland Cove (lat. 36°31'20" N, long. 121°57'15" W). Named on Monterey (1947, photorevised 1968) 7.5' quadrangle.

South Point [SAN LUIS OBISPO]: *promontory,* 3.5 miles east-southeast of Avila Beach along the coast at Shell Beach (lat. 35°09'10" N, long. 120°40'25" W). Named on Pismo Beach (1965) 7.5' quadrangle

South Point [SANTA BARBARA]: *promontory,* at southernmost tip of Santa Rosa Island (lat. 33°53'40" N, long. 120°07' W). Named on Santa Rosa Island South (1943) 7.5' quadrangle.

South Ventana: see **South Ventana Cone** [MONTEREY].

South Ventana Cone [MONTEREY]: *peak,* 2.5 miles east-southeast of Ventana Cone (lat. 36°16'30" N, long. 121°38'10" W; on E line sec. 16, T 19 S, R 3 E). Altitude 4965 feet. Named on Ventana Cones (1956) 7.5' quadrangle. United States Board on Geographic Names (1962a, p. 16) rejected the name "South Ventana" for the peak.

Souza Rock [SAN LUIS OBISPO]: *shoal,* 3.25 miles south of Avila Beach in San Luis Obispo Bay (lat. 35°07'50" N, long. 120°44'15" W). Named on Pismo Beach (1965) 7.5' quadrangle.

Sozers Creek: see **Doud Creek** [MONTEREY].

Spanish Bay [MONTEREY]: *embayment,* 1.5 miles south-southwest of Point Pinos along the coast (lat. 36°37' N, long. 121°56'30" W). Named on Monterey (1947) 7.5' quadrangle.

Spanish Cabin Creek [SAN LUIS OBISPO]: *stream,* flows 2 miles to Burnett Creek 5.25 miles north-northeast of San Simeon (lat. 35° 42'55" N, long. 121°09'45" W). Named on San Simeon (1958) 7.5' quadrangle.

Spanish Flats [SAN BENITO]: *area,* 9.5 miles southeast of Bitterwater (lat. 36°18' N, long. 120°51'35" N; on S line sec. 2, T 19 S, R 10 E). Named on Hepsedam Peak (1969) 7.5' quadrangle.

Spence [MONTEREY]: *locality,* 7 miles southeast of Salinas along Southern Pacific Railroad (lat. 36°36'45" N, long. 121°34' W). Named on Chualar (1947) 7.5' quadrangle. Railroad officials named the station at the place in the 1870's for David Spence, owner of Encinal y Buena Esperanza grant, where the station is situated (Gudde, 1949, p. 340).

Split Oak Spring [SAN BENITO]: *spring,* 15 miles east-southeast of Bitterwater (lat. 36°17'10" N, long. 120°45'30" W; near S line sec. 10, T 19 S, R 11 E). Named on Hepsedam Peak (1969) 7.5' quadrangle.

Split Rock [SAN BENITO]: *relief feature,* 13 miles east-southeast of Bitterwater on the east side of Horsethief Canyon (2) (lat. 36°19'05" N, long. 120°46'05" W). Named on Hepsedam Peak (1969) 7.5' quadrangle.

Splitrock Canyon [MONTEREY]: *canyon,* drained by a stream that flows 4 miles to Sargent Canyon 10 miles west-southwest of Smith Mountain (lat. 36°00'20" N, long. 120°44'55" W; sec. 23, T 22 S, R 11 E). Named on Slack Canyon (1969) 7.5' quadrangle.

Splitrock Spring [MONTEREY]: *spring,* 4.25 miles west-northwest of Smith Mountain (lat. 36°05'30" N, long. 120°40'05" W; sec. 22, T 21 S, R 12 E). Named on Slack Canyon (1969) 7.5' quadrangle.

Spoor Canyon [SANTA BARBARA]: *canyon,* drained by a stream that flows 5 miles to Kelly Canyon (1) 6 miles east of Miranda Pine Mountain (lat. 35°01' N, long. 119°56'15" W). Named on Bates Canyon (1964) and Taylor Canyon (1959) 7.5' quadrangles.

Sprague Camp [SAN LUIS OBISPO]: *locality,* 10 miles south of Shandon in Commatti (present Camatta) Canyon (lat. 35°31'10" N, long. 120°19'40" W). Named on Commatti Canyon (1943) 7.5' quadrangle.

Spreckels [MONTEREY]: *town,* 3 miles south of Salinas (lat. 36°37'25" N, long. 121°38'40" W). Named on Salinas (1947) and Spreckels (1947) 7.5' quadrangles. The name commemorates Claus Spreckels, who built a sugar refinery at the place in 1899 (Gudde, 1949, p. 341). Postal authorities established Spreckels post office in 1898 (Frickstad, p. 109).

Spreckels Junction [MONTEREY]: *locality,* in the southeast part of Salinas along Southern Pacific Railroad (lat. 36°39'30" N, long. 121°37'45" W); a rail line to Spreckels branches off at the place. Named on Salinas (1947) 7.5' quadrangle.

Spreckels Lagoon: see **Valencia Lagoon** [SANTA CRUZ].

Spring Canyon [MONTEREY]: *canyon,* drained by a stream that flows 4.5 miles to Sweetwater Canyon 6.25 miles north of San Lucas (lat. 36°13'15" N, long. 121°00'30" W; sec. 4, T 20 S, R 9 E). Named on Nattrass Valley (1967) 7.5' quadrangle.

Spring Canyon [SANTA BARBARA]: *canyon,* drained by a stream that flows 1.25 miles to lowlands along the coast 3.5 miles south of Surf (lat. 34°37'55" N, long. 120°37' W). Named on Surf (1959) and Tranquillon Mountain (1959) 7.5' quadrangles.

Spring Canyon: see **Little Spring Canyon** [SANTA BARBARA].

Spring Creek [SANTA CRUZ]: *stream,* flows 0.5 mile to San Lorenzo River 5 miles east-southeast of Big Basin (lat. 37°08'55" N, long. 122°08'10" W; sec. 13, T 9 S, R 3 W). Named on Big Basin (1955) 7.5' quadrangle.

Spring Creek: see **Aptos Creek** [SANTA CRUZ].

Spring Creek Gulch [SANTA CRUZ]: *canyon,* drained by a stream that flows 0.5 mile to San Lorenzo River near the south edge of the town of Boulder Creek (lat. 37°07' N, long. 122°06'50" W; near W line sec. 29, T 9 S, R 2 W). Named on Felton (1955) 7.5' quadrangle.

Springer: see **Betteravia Stockyards** [SANTA BARBARA].

Spring in Bush [MONTEREY]: *spring,* 8 miles east of Parkfield (lat. 35°53'35" N, long. 120°17'20" W; near S line sec. 30, T 23 S, R 16 E). Named on The Dark Hole (1961) 7.5' quadrangle.

Springs: see **Sycamore Springs** [SAN LUIS OBISPO].

Springtown: see **Confederate Corners** [MONTEREY].

Spruce Creek [MONTEREY]: *stream,* flows 1 mile to the sea 2.25 miles southeast of Cape San Martin (lat. 35°52'05" N, long. 121° 26'20" W; near SW cor. sec. 4, T 24 S, R 5 E). Named on Villa Creek (1949) 7.5' quadrangle.

Square Black Rock [MONTEREY]: *rock,* 125 feet long, nearly 2 miles northwest of Gamboa Point, and 1000 feet offshore (lat. 36° 04'20" N, long. 121°36'35" W). Named on Lopez Point (1956) 7.5' quadrangle.

Square Corral Spring [SAN LUIS OBISPO]: *spring,* 10 miles north-northwest of Shandon in Mason Canyon (lat. 35°47' N, long. 120° 27'45" W; near E line sec. 4, T 25 S, R 14 E). Named on Cholame Hills (1961) 7.5' quadrangle.

Squaw Peak [MONTEREY]: *peak,* 16 miles east of San Lucas (lat. 36°03'30" N, long. 120°36'15" W; near E line sec. 13, T 21 S, R 13 E). Altitude 2924 feet. Named on Smith Mountain (1969) 7.5' quadrangle.

Squire Canyon [SAN LUIS OBISPO]: *canyon,* drained by a stream that flows 1.5 miles to the canyon of San Luis Obispo Creek 2.25 miles east-northeast of Avila Beach (lat. 35°11'35" N, long. 120° 41'35" W). Named on Pismo Beach (1965) 7.5' quadrangle.

Squire Ridge [SAN BENITO]: *ridge,* northwest- to west-northwest-trending, 2 miles long, 5.25 miles northeast of Bitterwater (lat. 36° 26' N, long. 120°55'50" W). Named on Rock Spring Peak (1969) 7.5' quadrangle.

Squirrel Spring [MONTEREY]: *spring,* 13 miles east-northeast of Cape San Martin (lat. 35°58'25" N, long. 121°15'30" W). Named on Cape San Martin (1921) 15' quadrangle.

Stag Canyon [SANTA BARBARA]: *canyon,* drained by a stream that flows 3.25 miles to Roque Canyon 5.25 miles north-northeast of Manzanita Mountain (lat. 34°57'55" N, long. 120°02'45" W). Named on Manzanita Mountain (1964) 7.5' quadrangle.

Stanley Mountain [SAN LUIS OBISPO]: *peak,* 6 miles east-northeast of Huasna Peak (lat. 35°04'25" N, long. 120°15' W; sec. 33, T 12 N, R 32 W). Altitude 2490 feet. Named on Chimney Canyon (1967) and Huasna Peak (1967) 7.5' quadrangles.

Star Flat [MONTEREY-SAN BENITO]: *area,* 4.5 miles southeast of North Chalone Peak on Monterey-San Benito County line (lat. 36° 23'55" N, long. 121°08' W). Named on North Chalone Peak (1969) 7.5' quadrangle.

Starkey: see **Shandon** [SAN LUIS OBISPO].

Steele [SAN LUIS OBISPO]: *locality,* 1 mile north-northwest of Edna along the railroad (lat. 35°12'50" N, long. 120°37' W). Named on Arroyo Grande (1897, reprinted 1903) 15' quadrangle. Called Steeles on California Mining Bureau's (1917c) map.

Steer Creek [SANTA BARBARA]: *stream,* flows 4 miles to join El Dorado Creek and form Gobernador Creek 3.5 miles north of Rincon Point (lat. 34°25'30" N, long. 119°28'25" W; sec. 14, T 4 N, R 25 E). Named on White Ledge Peak (1952) 7.5' quadrangle.

Steinbach Canyon: see **Steinback Canyon** [SAN BENITO].

Steinback Canyon [SAN BENITO]: *canyon,* drained by a stream that flows 1.5 miles to San Juan Canyon 6.5 miles southwest of Hollister (lat. 36°48'05" N, long. 121°29'50" W). Named on Hollister (1955) 7.5' quadrangle. Called Steinbach Canyon on San Juan Bautista (1955) 7.5' quadrangle. United States Board on Geographic Names (1994, p. 5) approved the name "Steinbeck Canyon" for the feature, and rejected the forms "Steinbach Canyon" and "Steinback Canyon" for the name.

Steiner Creek [SAN LUIS OBISPO]: *stream,* flows 8 miles to San Simeon Creek 3.25 miles north of Cambria (lat. 35°36'35" N, long. 121°04'20" W). Named on Cambria (1959) and Cypress Mountain (1948) 7.5' quadrangles.

Stenner Creek [SAN LUIS OBISPO]: *stream,* flows nearly 7.25 miles to San Luis Obispo Creek 0.5 mile west-southwest of downtown San Luis Obispo (lat. 35°16'35" N, long. 120°40'05" W; sec. 34, T 30 S, R 12 E). Named on San Luis Obispo (1965) 7.5' quadrangle.

Stephani: see **Camp Stephani** [MONTEREY].

Stephens Canyon [SAN LUIS OBISPO]: *canyon,* drained by a stream that flows 5.5 miles to Carrie Creek 4 miles north of Huasna Peak (lat. 35°05'40" N, long. 120°20'05" W; sec. 35, T 32 S, R 15 E). Named on Huasna Peak (1967) 7.5' quadrangle. Called Rocky Canyon on Nipomo (1922) 15' quadrangle, but United States Board on Geographic Names (1963b, p. 15) rejected this name.

Steve Creek [MONTEREY]: *stream,* flows 3 miles to Salmon Creek 8 miles south-southwest of Jolon (lat. 35°50'40" N, long. 121°11'55" W; sec. 15, T 24 S, R 7 E). Named on Burnett Peak (1949) 7.5' quadrangle. The stream first was called Cobblestone Creek; Serafin Steve patented land near the creek in 1886 (Clark, 1991, p. 544).

Stillwater Cove [MONTEREY]: *embayment,* west of Arrowhead Point on the north side of Carmel Bay (lat. 36°33'55" N, long. 121°56'30" W). Named on Monterey (1947) 7.5' quadrangle.

Stockdale Mountain [MONTEREY]: *peak,* 15 miles northeast of Bradley (lat. 35°59'15" N, long. 120°34'50" W; near W line sec. 28, T 22 S, R 13 E). Altitude 2593 feet. Named on Stockdale Mountain (1948) 7.5' quadrangle. The name is for a member of the Stockdale family, early residents of Cholame Valley (Clark, 1991, p. 545).

Stockton [MONTEREY]: see **Fort Stockton**, under **Presidio of Monterey** [MONTEREY].

Stone Canyon [MONTEREY]:

(1) *canyon,* 5 miles long, 5 miles south-southeast of Smith Mountain along upper reaches of Big Sandy Creek (lat. 36°01' N, long. 120°33' W). Named

on Smith Mountain (1969) 7.5' quadrangle. Fairbanks (1894, p. 520) used the name "Stone's Cañon." F.M. Stone discovered coal at the place in 1870, and a coal mine operated there intermittently until 1935; a railroad built along Big Sandy Creek reached the mine in 1907 (Mosier, p. 7).

(2) *locality,* at the end of the rail line to the coal mine in Stone Canyon (1) (lat. 36°00'50" N, long. 120°32'30" W; sec. 14, T 22 S, R 13 E). Named on Priest Valley (1915) 30' quadrangle, where the name has the form "Stone Canon." Postal authorities established Stone Canon post office in 1900 and discontinued it in 1932 (Frickstad, p. 109).

Stone Canyon [SAN BENITO]: *canyon,* drained by Stone Creek, which flows 10 miles to San Benito River 6.5 miles southwest of Cherry Peak (lat. 36°38'20" N, long. 121°14'10" W; near SE cor. sec. 7, T 15 S, R 7 E). Named on Cherry Peak (1968) and Paicines (1968) 7.5' quadrangles, where the name may apply only to the part of the canyon along lower reaches of Stone Creek.

Stone Corral Canyon [MONTEREY-SAN LUIS OBISPO]: *canyon,* nearly 2 miles long, on Monterey-San Luis Obispo County line; opens into Cholame Valley 11 miles southeast of Parkfield (lat. 35° 47' N, long. 120°17'35" W). Named on Cholame Valley (1961) 7.5' quadrangle.

Stone Corral Flats [MONTEREY]: *area,* 10.5 miles southeast of Parkfield (lat. 35°48'30" N, long. 120°16'30" W). Named on Cholame Valley (1961) 7.5' quadrangle.

Stone Creek [SAN BENITO]: *stream,* flows 10 miles to San Benito River 6.5 miles southwest of Cherry Peak (lat. 36°38'20" N, long. 121°14'10" W; near SE cor. sec. 7, T 15 S, R 7 E). Named on Mount Johnson (1968) and Paicines (1968) 7.5' quadrangles.

Stonewall Canyon [MONTEREY]: *canyon,* 6 miles long, opens into lowlands 2 miles east-northeast of Soledad (lat. 36°26'25" N, long. 121°30' W; sec. 23, T 17 S, R 6 E). Named on North Chalone Peak (1969) and Soledad (1955) 7.5' quadrangles. The name is from the steep rocky sides of the canyon (Gudde, 1949, p. 344).

Stonewall Creek [MONTEREY]: *stream,* flows 8.5 miles to Salinas River 1.5 miles southeast of Soledad (lat. 36°24'30" N, long. 121° 18'20" W); the stream drains Stonewall Canyon. Named on Soledad (1955) 7.5' quadrangle.

Stony Creek [MONTEREY]: *stream,* flows 11 miles to Nacimiento River 11 miles east-northeast of Cape San Martin (lat. 35°55'40" N, long. 121°16'35" W). Named on Alder Peak (1949) and Bear Canyon (1949) 7.5' quadrangles. The stream is identified as Arroyo de las Piedras on a diseño of San Miguelito de Trinidad grant made in 1841 (Becker, 1964; Becker noted the alternate name "Piedra Creek" for the stream).

Stony Creek [SAN LUIS OBISPO]: *stream,* flows 10 miles to join Trout Creek (2) and form Huasna River 13 miles northeast of the town of Nipomo (lat. 35°12'05" N, long. 120°21' W; sec. 27, T 31 S, R 15 E). Named on Caldwell Mesa (1967) and Los Machos Hills (1967) 7.5' quadrangles.

Stony Creek Campground [SAN LUIS OBISPO]: *locality,* 17 miles northeast of the town of Nipomo (lat. 35°12'35" N, long. 120°15'30" W); the place is along Stony Creek. Named on Caldwell Mesa (1967) 7.5' quadrangle.

Stony Valley [MONTEREY]: *valley,* 11.5 miles east-northeast of Cape San Martin (lat. 35°59' N, long. 121°18' W); Stony Creek drains the valley. Named on Alder Peak (1949) 7.5' quadrangle. The place is identified as Cañon de las Piedras on a diseño of San Miguelito de Trinidad grant made in 1841 (Becker, 1964). Cozzens and Davies' (1927) map has the name "Robla Valley" along Nacimiento River for the first valley southwest of Stony Valley. Smith (p. 63) mentioned a feature called Roblar Valley located along Nacimiento River;

Stovall Canyon [SANTA BARBARA]: *canyon,* drained by a stream that flows 2 miles to Schoolhouse Canyon (1) 4.5 miles northwest of McPherson Peak (lat. 34°56'25" N, long. 119°52' W). Named on Peak Mountain (1964) 7.5' quadrangle.

Strawberry Camp [MONTEREY]: *locality,* 3.5 miles southwest of Tassajara Hot Springs (lat. 36°12'15" N, long. 121°36'05" W; sec. 11, T 20 S, R 3 E); the place is in Strawberry Valley, and Clark (1991, p. 548) called it Strawberry Valley Camp. Named on Tassajara Hot Springs (1956) 7.5' quadrangle.

Strawberry Canyon [MONTEREY]: *canyon,* drained by a stream that flows 2.5 miles to marsh along Elkhorn Slough 5 miles northwest of Prunedale (lat. 36°49'45" N, long. 121°44' W). Named on Prunedale (1954) 7.5' quadrangle.

Strawberry Peak: see **Madulce Peak** [SANTA BARBARA].

Strawberry Valley [MONTEREY]: *canyon,* 1 mile long, drained by Zigzag Creek above the confluence of Zigzag Creek and Tan Oak Creek nearly 4 miles southwest of Tassajara Hot Springs (lat. 36° 11'45" N, long. 121°35'55" W; near E line sec. 14, T 20 S, R 3 E). Named on Tassajara Hot Springs (1956) 7.5' quadrangle.

Strawberry Valley Camp: see **Strawberry Camp** [MONTEREY].

Struve Slough [SANTA CRUZ]: *stream,* flows nearly 3 miles, mainly in an artificial watercourse, to Watsonville Slough 2 miles southwest of Watsonville (lat. 36°54' N, long. 121°47' W). Named on Watsonville West (1954) 7.5' quadrangle. The name is for Hans Christian Struve, a Danish farmer who came to California in 1855 (Clark, 1986, p. 356). West Branch enters from the north-northwest 0.5 mile above the mouth of the main stream; it is 2 miles long, is partly in an artificial watercourse, and is named on Watsonville West (1954) 7.5' quadrangle.

Stuart: see **Lompoc** [SANTA BARBARA] (2).

Stuke Canyon [SANTA BARBARA]: *canyon,* drained by a stream that flows 3.5 miles to Santa Cruz Creek 8 miles northeast of Santa Ynez Mountain (lat. 34°37' N, long. 119°52'40" W). Named on Figueroa Mountain (1959), Lake Cachuma (1959), and San Rafael Mountain (1959) 7.5' quadrangles.

Sudden [SANTA BARBARA]: *locality,* 3.25 miles south-southeast of Tranquillon Mountain along Southern Pacific Railroad (lat. 34°32'25" N, long. 120°32'20" W); the place is near the mouth of Sudden Canyon. Named on Tranquillon Mountain (1959) 7.5' quadrangle. Postal authorities established Sudden post office in 1901, discontinued it for a time in 1908, and discontinued it finally in 1914 (Frickstad, p. 172). The name commemorates Robert Sudden, a ship's master who came to California in 1850 and later owned property at the site (Hanna, p. 319).

Sudden Canyon [SANTA BARBARA]: *canyon,* drained by a stream that flows 1.25 miles to the sea 3 miles south-southeast of Tranquillon Mountain (lat. 34°32'25" N, long. 120°32'35" W). Named on Tranquillon Mountain (1959) 7.5' quadrangle.

Sudden Flats [SANTA BARBARA]: *area,* 2 miles south-southwest of Tranquillon Mountain along the coast (lat. 34°33' N, long. 120°34'45" W); the place is 2.5 miles west-northwest of the mouth of Sudden Canyon. Named on Tranquillon Mountain (1959) 7.5' quadrangle.

Sudden Peak [SANTA BARBARA]: *peak,* 3.5 miles east-southeast of Tranquillon Mountain (lat. 34°33'55" N, long. 120°30' W); the peak is 3 miles northeast of the mouth of Sudden Canyon. Altitude 2122 feet. Named on Lompoc Hills (1959) and Tranquillon Mountain (1959) 7.5' quadrangles.

Suey [SAN LUIS OBISPO-SANTA BARBARA]: *land grant,* mainly east of Santa Maria along Cuyama River on San Luis Obispo-Santa Barbara County line. Named on Chimney Canyon (1967), Huasna Peak (1967), Nipomo (1965), Santa Maria (1959), Tepusquet Canyon (1964), and Twitchell Dam (1959) 7.5' quadrangles. Ramona Carrillo received the land in 1837; Ramona Carrillo de Wilson claimed 48,834 acres patented in 1865 (Cowan, p. 100). Postal authorities established Suey post office on the grant at the ranch headquarters in 1870 and discontinued it in 1875; the post office was in Santa Barbara County until a county-line change in 1872 placed it in San Luis Obispo County (Salley, p. 214).

Suey [SANTA BARBARA]: *locality,* 1.25 mile east-southeast of downtown Santa Maria along Santa Maria Valley Railroad (lat. 34° 56'45" N, long. 120°24'45" W); the place is near the boundary of Suey grant. Named on Santa Maria (1959) 7.5' quadrangle.

Suey: see **Santa Maria** [SANTA BARBARA].

Suey Canyon [SANTA BARBARA]: *canyon,* drained by a stream that flows 4 miles to Tepusquet Canyon 3.5 miles northwest of Tepusquet Peak (lat. 34°56'40" N, long. 120°13'40" W); the canyon is on Suey grant. Named on Tepusquet Canyon (1964) 7.5' quadrangle.

Suey Creek [SAN LUIS OBISPO]: *stream,* flows 9.5 miles to Santa Maria River 6.5 miles southeast of the town of Nipomo (lat. 34°58'15" N, long. 120°24' W); the stream is on Suey grant. Named on Huasna Peak (1967), Nipomo (1965), Santa Maria (1959), and Twitchell Dam (1959) 7.5' quadrangles.

Suey Junction: see **Santa Maria** [SANTA BARBARA].

Sugarloaf [MONTEREY]: *peak,* about 11 miles west-southwest of Soledad (lat. 36°21'05" N, long. 121°31'15" W; near W line sec. 23, T 18 S, R 4 E). Altitude 2706 feet. Named on Chews Ridge (1956) 7.5' quadrangle.

Sugarloaf [SAN BENITO]: *peak,* 8 miles northwest of Panoche Pass (lat. 36°42'35" N, long. 121°07' W). Altitude 2840 feet. Named on Panoche Pass (1968) 7.5' quadrangle. This may be the feature called Cerro del Venado on California Mining Bureau's (1917b) map.

Sugarloaf Mountain [SANTA CRUZ]: *peak,* 5.5 miles north-northeast of Soquel (lat. 37°03'55" N, long. 121°55'55" W). Altitude 1268 feet. Named on Laurel (1955) 7.5' quadrangle. The feature formerly was called San Francisco Mountain (Clark, 1986, p. 310).

Sugarloaf Peak [MONTEREY]: *hill,* 7.5 miles north-northeast of Salinas (lat. 36°46'05" N, long. 121°35'40" W). Altitude 954 feet. Named on San Juan Bautista (1955) 7.5' quadrangle.

Sugar Tail Spring [MONTEREY]: *spring,* 9.5 miles east of Parkfield (lat. 35°53'20" N, long. 120°15'35" W; sec. 32, T 23 S, R 16 E). Named on The Dark Hole (1961) 7.5' quadrangle.

Sullivan Canyon [MONTEREY]: *canyon,* drained by a stream that flows nearly 3 miles to lowlands 4.5 miles east of Gonzales (lat. 36°30'55" N, long. 121°21'30" W; sec. 30, T 16 S, R 6 E). Named on Mount Johnson (1968) 7.5' quadrangle. Daniel Sullivan patented land in the lower part of the canyon in 1889 (Clark, 1991, p. 549).

Sulphur Canyon [MONTEREY-SAN LUIS OBISPO]: *canyon,* drained by a stream that heads in San Luis Obispo County and flows 2.5 miles to San Antonio River 6.25 miles southwest of Bradley in Monterey County (lat. 35°47'40" N, long. 120°52'20" W; sec. 34, T 24 S, R 10 E). Named on Bradley (1949) and Tierra Redonda Mountain (1949) 7.5' quadrangles.

Sulphur Canyon [SAN BENITO]:
(1) *canyon*, drained by a stream that flows nearly 4 miles to San Benito River 3 miles west-northwest of Paicines (lat. 36°44'30" N, long. 121°19'40" W; sec. 5, T 14 S, R 6 E). Named on Paicines (1968) 7.5' quadrangle.
(2) *canyon*, 2.25 miles long, 11 miles east-southeast of Bitterwater along Laguna Creek (lat. 36°19'30" N, long. 120°49'15" W). Named on Hepsedam Peak (1969) 7.5' quadrangle.

Sulphur Canyon [SAN LUIS OBISPO]: *canyon*, drained by a stream that flows 5.5 miles to Cuyama Valley 3.5 miles northwest of New Cuyama [SANTA BARBARA] (lat. 34°58'45" N, long. 119°43'55" W; sec. 2, T 10 N, R 27 W); Sulphur Spring (3) is in the canyon. Named on New Cuyama (1964) 7.5' quadrangle.

Sulphur Creek [SAN BENITO]:
(1) *stream*, flows 3 miles to San Benito River 5.5 miles north-northwest of San Benito (lat. 36°34'25" N, long. 121°07'55" W; sec. 5, T 16 S, R 8 E). Named on Bickmore Canyon (1968) and San Benito (1968) 7.5' quadrangles.
(2) *stream*, heads in Santa Clara County and flows nearly 3 miles to Arroyo de las Vibaoras 8 miles north-northeast of Hollister (lat. 36°57'20" N, long. 121°20'25" W). Named on Three Sisters (1954) 7.5' quadrangle.

Sulphur Creek [SANTA BARBARA]: *stream*, flows 1 mile to Dry Creek (1) 2.25 miles northeast of Zaca Lake (lat. 34°48'05" N, long. 120°00'30" W); the stream heads near Sulphur Spring (2). Named on Zaca Lake (1964) 7.5' quadrangle.

Sulphuritos Creek [SAN BENITO]: *stream*, flows nearly 4 miles to Tres Pinos Creek 3.5 miles northwest of Panoche Pass (lat. 36°39'20" N, long. 121°03'50" W; sec. 2, T 15 S, R 8 E). Named on Panoche Pass (1968) 7.5' quadrangle.

Sulphur Pots [SAN LUIS OBISPO]: *springs*, 1.5 miles east-southeast of Lopez Mountain in Lopez Canyon (lat. 35°17'40" N, long. 120° 33'10" W; near S line sec. 23, T 30 S, R 13 E). Named on Lopez Mountain (1965) 7.5' quadrangle.

Sulphur Spring [MONTEREY]:
(1) *spring*, 2.5 miles east of Uncle Sam Mountain (lat. 36°20'50" N, long. 121°39'35" W; sec. 21, T 18 S, R 3 E). Named on Jamesburg (1939) 15' quadrangle.
(2) *spring*, 0.5 mile north-northwest of Smith Mountain (lat. 36°05'15" N, long. 120°36' W; sec. 20, T 21 S, R 13 E). Named on Smith Mountain (1969) 7.5' quadrangle.

Sulphur Spring [SAN BENITO]:
(1) *spring*, 6.5 miles east-southeast of Bitterwater (lat. 36°20'50" N, long. 120°53'20" W; sec. 21, T 18 S, R 10 E). Named on Lonoak (1969) 7.5' quadrangle.
(2) *spring*, 14 miles east-southeast of Bitterwater (lat. 36°17'50" N, long. 120°46'20" W; near N line sec. 9, T 19 S, R 11 E). Named on Hepsedam Peak (1969) 7.5' quadrangle.

Sulphur Spring [SAN LUIS OBISPO]:
(1) *spring*, 3.5 miles south-southeast of Paso Robles (lat. 35°34'55" N, long. 120°39'50" W). Named on Templeton (1948) 7.5' quadrangle. Berkstresser (p. A-15) identified this feature as Santa Ysabel Springs—it is on Santa Ysabel grant. According to Winslow Anderson (p. 235), Santa Ysabel Spring was used by Indians and Spaniards, who came from afar to seek cures by drinking the water and bathing in it. A resort was started at the spring in the late 1880's, but by 1908 there was only a small private bathhouse (Waring, G.A., p. 76).
(2) *spring*, 2.5 miles east-southeast of Branch Mountain (lat. 35°10'25" N, long. 120°02'30" W). Named on Branch Mountain (1967) 7.5' quadrangle.
(3) *spring*, 4.5 miles northwest of New Cuyama [SANTA BARBARA] (lat. 34°59'50" N, long. 119°44' W; sec. 35, T 11 N, R 27 W); the spring is in Sulphur Canyon. Named on New Cuyama (1964) 7.5' quadrangle.
(4) *spring*, 4.5 miles north-northwest of Caliente Mountain (lat. 35°05'40" N, long. 119°47'10" W; sec. 36, T 32 S, R 20 E). Named on Caliente Mountain (1959) 7.5' quadrangle. On Caliente Mountain (1941) 15' quadrangle, the name applies to a spring located 0.5 mile farther northwest.

Sulphur Spring [SANTA BARBARA]:
(1) *spring*, 6 miles south of the city of Lompoc along Espada Creek (lat. 34°33'10" N, long. 120°28'35" W). Named on Lompoc Hills (1959) 7.5' quadrangle.
(2) *spring*, 1.5 miles east-northeast of Zaca Lake (lat. 34°47'10" N, long. 120°00'40" W); the spring is near the head of Sulphur Creek. Named on Zaca Lake (1964) 7.5' quadrangle.
(3) *spring*, 4 miles east-southeast of Salisbury Potrero (lat. 34° 48' N, long. 119°38' W); the spring is in Sulphur Spring Canyon (1). Named on Salisbury Potrero (1964) 7.5' quadrangle.

Sulphur Spring: see **Little Sulphur Spring** [SANTA BARBARA]; **Sulphur Spring Canyon** [MONTEREY].

Sulphur Spring Canyon [MONTEREY]: *canyon*, drained by a stream that flows 6.5 miles to lowlands 4.5 miles northwest of Jolon (lat. 36°00'30" N, long. 121°14'25" W). Named on Cosio Knob (1949) 7.5' quadrangle. According to Berkstresser (p. A-9), a spring called Sulphur Spring is located less than 3 miles above the mouth of Sulphur Spring Canyon (lat. 36°02'28" long. 121°13'15" W).

Sulphur Spring Canyon [SANTA BARBARA]:
(1) *canyon*, drained by a stream that flows 5 miles to Salisbury Canyon 2 miles east-northeast of Salisbury Potrero (lat. 34°49'40" N, long. 119°40' W); Sulphur Spring (3) is in the canyon. Named on Salisbury Potrero (1964) 7.5' quadrangle.
(2) *canyon*, drained by a stream that flows 4.5 miles to Manzana Creek 4.25 miles south-southeast of Bald Mountain (1) (lat. 34°45'30" N, long. 119°53'40" W). Named on Bald Mountain (1964) and Hurricane Deck (1964) 7.5' quadrangles.

Sulphur Springs [MONTEREY]: *spring*, 7 miles north-northwest of Parkfield (lat. 35°59'45" N, long. 120°28'40" W; sec. 20, T 22 S, R 14 E). Named on Parkfield (1961) 7.5' quadrangle.

Sulphur Springs [SAN BENITO]: *springs*, 6 miles south of Bitterwater near San Lorenzo Creek (lat. 36°17'40" N, long. 120°59'05" W; sec. 10, T 19 S, R 9 E). Named on Lonoak (1969) 7.5' quadrangle.

Sulphur Springs [SANTA CRUZ]: *spring*, 8 miles north-northeast of Soquel (lat. 37°05'10" N, long. 121°53'20" W). Named on Laurel (1955) 7.5' quadrangle. On Los Gatos (1919) 15' quadrangle, the name has the singular form "Sulphur Spring."

Sulphur Springs: see **Willow Spring** [MONTEREY] (3).

Sulphur Springs Camp [MONTEREY]: *locality*, 2.5 miles east of Uncle Sam Mountain (lat. 36°20'50" N, long. 121°39'35" W; sec. 21, T 18 S, R 3 E). Named on Ventana Cones (1956) 7.5' quadrangle. Jamesburg (1939) 15' quadrangle shows Sulphur Spring (1) at the place.

Summerland [SANTA BARBARA]: *town*, 5 miles west-northwest of Carpinteria (lat. 34°25'20" N, long. 119°35'45" W). Named on Carpinteria (1952) 7.5' quadrangle. Postal authorities established Summerland post office in 1889 (Frickstad, p. 172).

Summit [SAN LUIS OBISPO]: *locality*, 3 miles northwest of the town of Nipomo along Pacific Coast Railroad (lat. 35°04'05" N, long. 120°30'40" W). Named on Arroyo Grande (1897) 15' quadrangle. Arroyo Grande (1952) 15' quadrangle has the name "Summit" at the place, although it does not show the railroad.

Summit: see **Rincon** [SANTA CRUZ].

Summit Canyon [SAN LUIS OBISPO]: *canyon*, 3.5 miles long, 5 miles north-northeast of York Mountain (lat. 35°36'45" N, long. 120°48'10" W). Named on York Mountain (1948) 7.5' quadrangle.

Summit Creek [SAN LUIS OBISPO]: *stream*, flows 5.25 miles to a branch of Jack Creek nearly 3 miles north of York Mountain (lat. 35°35'10" N, long. 120°49'55" W); the stream drains Summit Canyon. Named on Adelaida (1948) and York Mountain (1948) 7.5' quadrangles.

Sunium Point: see **Arrowhead Point** [MONTEREY].

Sunset: see **Shandon** [SAN LUIS OBISPO].

Sunset Point [MONTEREY]: *promontory*, nearly 1 mile south-southeast of Cypress Point along the coast (lat. 36°34'10" N, long. 121° 58'10" W). Named on Monterey (1947) 7.5' quadrangle. Called Pt. Douty on Monterey (1913) 15' quadrangle, but United States Board on Geographic Names (1936a, p. 23) rejected this name for the feature.

Sunset Valley [SANTA BARBARA]: *valley*, 4 miles south of Bald Mountain (1) (lat. 34°45'10" N, long. 119°56' W). Named on Bald Mountain (1964) and Figueroa Mountain (1959) 7.5' quadrangles. McPherson Peak (1943) 15' quadrangle shows the feature located about 1.5 miles farther east along Fish Creek.

Sur: see **Mill Creek** [MONTEREY] (1); **Point Sur** [MONTEREY].

Sur Breakers [MONTEREY]: *shoal*, 1.25 miles south-southeast of Point Sur and less than 1 mile offshore (lat. 36°17'20" N, long. 121°53'20" W). Named on Point Sur (1956) 7.5' quadrangle.

Sur Chiquito: see **San Jose y Sur Chiquuito** [MONREREY].

Surf [SANTA BARBARA]: *locality*, 9 miles west-northwest of the city of Lompoc along Southern Pacific Railroad near the coast (lat. 34°41'05" N, long. 120°36'10" W). Named on Surf (1959) 7.5' quadrangle. Postal authorities established Surf post office in 1897 and discontinued in 1957 (Salley, p. 216). The place first was called Lompoc Junction (Hanna, p. 320). Crespi, while with the Portola expedition in 1769, gave the name "Cañada de Santa Rosalia" to a dry creek just south of present Surf, and soldiers of the expedition called the same feature Cañada Seca (Wagner, H.R., p. 513, 515). The beach at Surf has been called Lompoc Beach (Diller and others, p. 111). California Division of Highways' (1934) map shows a place called Ajax located 1.5 miles north-northeast of Surf along Southern Pacific Railroad.

Sur River: see **Big Sur River** [MONTEREY]; **Little Sur River** [MONTEREY].

Sur Rock [MONTEREY]: *rock*, less than 2 miles south-southwest of Point Sur, and 4500 feet offshore (lat. 36°16'55" N, long. 121°53'15" W). Named on Point Sur (1956) 7.5' quadrangle. Point Sur (1925) 15' quadrangle shows the feature located much closer to shore.

Susie Spring [MONTEREY]: *spring*, 16 miles east-northeast of King City near Lewis Creek (lat. 36°17'15" N, long. 120°51'30" W; sec. 11, T 19 S, R 10 E). Named on Hepsedam Peak (1969) 7.5' quadrangle.

Sutil Island [SANTA BARBARA]: *island*, 1250 feet long, 1900 feet off the southwest end of Santa Barbara Island (lat. 33°27'50" N, long. 119°02'50" W). Named on United States Geological Survey's (1973) map. United States Board on Geographic Names (1939, p. 34) rejected the name "Gull Island" for the feature, and noted that the name "Sutil" is for one of Vizcaino's ships.

Sutton Canyon [SANTA BARBARA]: *canyon*, drained by a stream that flows 3.5 miles to Carpinteria Creek 4 miles north-northwest of Rincon Point (lat. 34°25'45" N, long. 119°29'25" W; sec. 15, T 4 N, R 25 W). Named on Carpinteria (1952) and White Ledge Peak (1952) 7.5' quadrangles.

Swain's Canyon: see **Swain Valley** [MONTEREY].

Swain Valley [MONTEREY]: *canyon*, 3.25 miles long, opens into lowlands 3 miles northwest of Bradley (lat. 35°53'30" N, long. 120°50'30" W; near N line sec. 36, T 23 S, R 10 E). Named on Hames Valley (1949) and Wunpost (1949) 7.5' quadrangles. English (p. 237) referred to Swains Canyon, and Kew (1920, p. 104) mentioned Swain's Canyon. Charles Swain and George H. Swain took up land at the place in 1891 (Clark, 1991, p. 552-553).

Swallow Rock [SAN LUIS OBISPO]: *peak*, 3 miles south-southeast of Cambria (near lat. 35°31'25" N, long. 121°03'45" W). Named on San Simeon (1919) 15' quadrangle, where the exact location is uncertain.

Swamp Creek [MONTEREY]: *stream*, flows nearly 2 miles through a series of lakes to Gabilan Creek 16 miles north of Gonzales (lat. 36°44'20" N, long. 121°28'25" W). Named on Mount Harlan (1968) 7.5' quadrangle.

Swan Lake: see **Schwans Lagoon** [SANTA CRUZ].

Swanson Bluff [SAN BENITO]: *escarpment*, northwest-trending, 3.25 miles long, 9 miles southeast of Hollister on the southwest side of Tres Pinos Creek (lat. 36°45' N, long. 121°18' W). Named on Paicines (1968) and Tres Pinos (1955) 7.5' quadrangles.

Swanton [SANTA CRUZ]: *locality*, 4 miles north-northwest of Davenport along Scott Creek (lat. 37°03'50" N, long. 122°13'35" W). Named on Davenport (1955) 7.5' quadrangle. Postal authorities established Swanton post office in 1897 and discontinued it in 1930 (Frickstad, p. 177). The name commemorates one of the builders of a power house on Big Creek; the place earlier was the site of a stage station called Laurel Grove (Hoover, Rensch, and Rensch, p. 473). Ingalls Station was a stage stop located along Scott Creek near the mouth of Big Creek in what later became Swanton; the name was for Nathan P. Ingalls, who took over Santa Cruz-Pescadero stage line in 1874 (Clark, 1986, p. 164-165). Hamman's (1980c) map shows a place called Folger Wye located along the railroad 1.25 miles south of Swanton. J.R. Wagner (p. 61) mentioned a small settlement called Folger, situated near Swanton, that served as a center for the lumber industry. The name "Folger" was for J.A. Folger, a San Francisco coffee merchant and first vice-president of Ocean Shore Railroad (Clark, 1986, p. 121). Hamman's (1980c) map also shows a place called San Vicente Junction located along the railroad just south of Swanton, where a rail line of San Vicente Lumber Company starts up Little Creek.

Sweetwater Canyon [MONTEREY]: *canyon*, 10 miles long, opens into lowlands 2.5 miles east-northeast of King City (lat. 36°13' N, long. 121°04'35" W). Named on Nattrass Valley (1967) and San Lucas (1949) 7.5' quadrangles.

Sweetwater Canyon [SANTA BARBARA]: *canyon*, drained by a stream that flows 6.5 miles to Sisquoc River 5 miles south-southwest of Montgomery Potrero (lat. 34°46'05" N, long. 119°46'55" W). Named on Hurricane Deck (1964) and Salisbury Potrero (1964) 7.5' quadrangles.

Sweetwater Creek [MONTEREY]: *stream*, flows 5.5 miles to Arroyo Seco (1) 7.5 miles west-southwest of Greenfield (lat. 36°15'45" N, long. 121°21'15" W; sec. 19, T 19 S, R 6 E). Named on Paraiso Springs (1956) and Reliz Canyon (1949) 7.5' quadrangles.

Sweetwater Creek [SANTA BARBARA]: *stream*, flows 1 mile to Lake Cachuma 3.5 miles north of Santa Ynez Peak (lat. 34°34'40" N, long. 119°58'20" W). Named on Lake Cachuma (1959) 7.5' quadrangle.

Sweetwater Spring [SAN BENITO]: *spring*, 8.5 miles east-southeast of Bitterwater (lat. 36°21'15" N, long. 120°54'05" W; near NE cor. sec. 23, T 18 S, R 10 E). Named on Hepsedam Peak (1969) 7.5' quadrangle.

Swiss Canyon [MONTEREY]:

(1) *canyon*, drained by a stream that flows nearly 2 miles to marsh along Elkhorn Slough 5 miles northwest of Salinas (lat. 36°49'45" N, long. 121°43'40" W). Named on Prunedale (1954) 7.5' quadrangle.

(2) *canyon*, drained by a stream that flows nearly 2 miles to the sea 2.25 miles southeast of Point Sur (lat. 36°17'10" N, long. 121° 52' W). Named on Big Sur (1956) 7.5' quadrangle.

Swope Canyon [MONTEREY]: *canyon*, drained by a stream that flows 2 miles to Chualar Canyon 9.5 miles north-northeast of Gonzales (lat. 36°37'50" N, long. 121°21'35" W; sec. 18, T 15 S, R 6 E). Named on Paicines (1968) 7.5' quadrangle.

Sycamore Beach: see **Pfeiffer Beach** [MONTEREY].

Sycamore Campground [SANTA BARBARA]: *locality*, 3.5 miles west-southwest of Montgomery Potrero along Sisquoc River (lat. 34°48'30" N, long. 119°48'15" W). Named on Hurricane Deck (1964) 7.5' quadrangle.

Sycamore Canyon [MONTEREY]: *canyon*, drained by a stream that flows 2 miles to the sea just north of Pfeiffer Point (lat. 36°14'15" N, long. 121°48'50" W; sec. 35, T 19 S, R 1 E). Named on Pfeiffer Point (1956) 7.5' quadrangle.

Sycamore Canyon [SAN LUIS OBISPO]:

(1) *canyon*, drained by a stream that flows 1.25 miles to Toro Creek 9 miles north-northeast of the mouth of Morro Creek (lat. 35°28'55" N, long. 120°47'05" W). Named on Morro Bay North (1965) 7.5' quadrangle.

(2) *canyon*, drained by a stream that flows 2.5 miles to Los Osos Valley 3 miles west of San Luis Obispo (lat. 35°16'25" N, long. 120°42'55" W). Named on San Luis Obispo (1965) 7.5' quadrangle.

(3) *canyon*, 1 mile long, opens into Miller Flat 4 miles north of Lopez Mountain (lat. 35°21'45" N, long. 120°35'10" W). Named on Lopez Mountain (1965) 7.5' quadrangle.

(4) *canyon*, drained by a stream that flows 2 miles to Los Berros Canyon nearly 4 miles north of the town of Nipomo (lat. 35°05'50" N, long. 120°28'20" W; sec. 33, T 32 S, R 14 E). Named on Nipomo (1965) 7.5' quadrangle.

(5) *canyon*, drained by a stream that flows nearly 2 miles to Suey Creek 5.5 miles east of the town of Nipomo (lat. 35°02'10" N, long. 120°22'25" W). Named on Nipomo (1965) 7.5' quadrangle.

Sycamore Canyon [SANTA BARBARA]:

(1) *canyon*, drained by a stream that flows 5.5 miles to Alamo Pintado Creek 3.5 miles north of Los Olivos (lat. 34°43'05" N, long. 120°06'35" W). Named on Los Olivos (1959) and Zaca Lake (1964) 7.5' quadrangles.

(2) *canyon*, 2.5 miles long, along Sycamore Creek above a point 1.25 miles east-northeast of downtown Santa Barbara (lat. 34°25'45" N, long. 119°40'35" W). Named on Santa Barbara (1952) 7.5' quadrangle. United States Board on Geographic Names (1961b, p. 17) rejected the name "Valley of Los Alisos" for the canyon.

Sycamore Canyon Creek: see **Sycamore Creek** [SANTA BARBARA].

Sycamore Creek [MONTEREY]: *stream*, flows 2.5 miles to El Piojo Creek 9 miles south of Jolon (lat. 35°50'25" N, long. 121°09'20" W; sec. 13, T 24 S, R 7 E). Named on Burnett Peak (1949) 7.5' quadrangle.

Sycamore Creek [SAN LUIS OBISPO]: *stream*, flows 3 miles to Cuyama River 7.25 miles south-southeast of Branch Mountain (lat. 35°05'20" N, long. 120°02'20" W); the creek heads on Sycamore Ridge. Named on Miranda Pine Mountain (1967) 7.5' quadrangle.

Sycamore Creek [SANTA BARBARA]: *stream*, flows nearly 4 miles to the sea 2 miles east of downtown Santa Barbara (lat. 34°25' N, long. 119°39'55" W); the stream drains Sycamore Canyon (2). Named on Santa Barbara (1952) 7.5' quadrangle. United States Board on Geographic Names (1961b, p. 17) rejected the name "Sycamore Canyon Creek" for the stream.

Sycamore Creek: see **Pozo Creek** [SAN LUIS OBISPO]; **Santa Lucia Creek** [MONTEREY] (2).

Sycamore Flat [MONTEREY]: *settlement*, 9 miles west-southwest of Greenfield along Arroyo Seco (1) (lat. 36°15'50" N, long. 121°23'30" W; sec. 23, T 19 S, R 5 E). Named on Sycamore Flat (1956) 7.5' quadrangle.

Sycamore Gulch [MONTEREY]: *canyon*, drained by a stream that flows 2.5 miles to the canyon of Tularcitos Creek 5 miles east-southeast of the town of Carmel Valley (lat. 36°26'50" N, long. 121°38'50" W). Named on Carmel Valley (1956) 7.5' quadrangle.

Sycamore Hot Sulphur Spring: see **Sycamore Springs** [SAN LUIS OBISPO].

Sycamore Ridge [SAN LUIS OBISPO]: *ridge*, northwest-trending, 3.5 miles long, 6 miles southeast of Branch Mountain (lat. 35°07'15" N, long. 120°00'15" W). Named on Branch Mountain (1967), Chimineas Ranch (1959), Miranda Pine Mountain (1967), and Taylor Canyon (1959) 7.5' quadrangles.

Sycamore Spring [MONTEREY]: *spring,* 9 miles east of Cape San Martin (lat. 35°55'10" N, long. 121°18'15" W; sec. 22, T 23 S, R 6 E). Named on Alder Peak (1949) 7.5' quadrangle.

Sycamore Spring [SAN LUIS OBISPO]: *spring,* 8 miles northeast of the town of Morro Bay (lat. 35°29'15" N, long. 120°46'35" W); the spring is on the east side of Sycamore Canyon (1). Named on Morro Bay North (1965) 7.5' quadrangle.

Sycamore Springs [SAN LUIS OBISPO]: *locality,* 1.25 miles east-northeast of Avila Beach along San Luis Obispo Creek (lat. 35° 11'10" N, long. 120°42'50" W). Named on Pismo Beach (1965) 7.5' quadrangle. Sycamore Hot Sulphur Spring, a health and pleasure resort at the place, used warm water from an artesian well drilled from 1885 to 1887 (Crawford, 1896, p. 517). G.A. Waring (p. 70) called the resort San Luis Hot Spring. Postal authorities established Springs post office, named for Sycamore Hot Springs, in 1900 and discontinued it the same year (Salley, p. 210).

Sykes Camp [MONTEREY]: *locality,* 5 miles north of Partington Point along Big Sur River (lat. 36°14'55" N, long. 121°41'05" W; sec. 30, T 19 S, R 3 E). Named on Partington Ridge (1956) 7.5' quadrangle. The name is from Sykes Hot Springs, which are situated 400 yards downstream from the camp (Clark, 1991, p. 555).

Sykes Hot Springs: see **Sykes Camp** [MONTEREY].

Sylvester Spring [SAN BENITO]: *spring,* 6.25 miles south of Idria (lat. 36°19'45" N, long. 120°41'40" W; sec. 30, T 18 S, R 12 E). Named on San Benito Mountain (1969) 7.5' quadrangle.

Syncline Divide [SAN BENITO]: *pass,* about 14 miles east-northeast of Bitterwater near the head of Vallecitos Creek (lat. 36°28'55" N, long. 120°47'25" W; sec. 5, T 17 S, R 11 E). Named on Hernandez Reservoir (1969) 7.5' quadrangle.

Syncline Hill [SAN LUIS OBISPO]: *ridge,* west-northwest-trending, 1.5 miles long, 6 miles north-northwest of Freeborn Mountain (lat. 35°21'50" N, long. 120°06'15" W). Named on California Valley (1966) 7.5' quadrangle. Arnold and Johnson (1910, p. 22) proposed the name because rocks at the place form a syncline.

- T -

Table Mountain [MONTEREY]: *ridge,* west- to northwest-trending, 10 miles long, 6 miles east of Parkfield, where Monterey County, Fresno County, and Kings County meet (lat. 35°54'30" N, long. 120°19' W). Named on Garza Peak (1953), Parkfield (1961), and The Dark Hole (1961) 7.5' quadrangles.

Table Rock [SANTA CRUZ]: *promontory,* 6 miles west of Point Santa Cruz along the coast (lat. 36°58'05" N, long. 122°08'05" W). Named on Santa Cruz (1954) 7.5' quadrangle.

Tajea Flat [SAN LUIS OBISPO]: *area,* 2 miles east-southeast of Branch Mountain (lat. 35°10'15" N, long. 120°03'10" W). Named on Branch Mountain (1967) 7.5' quadrangle.

Tajea Spring [SAN LUIS OBISPO]: *spring,* 2.5 miles southeast of Branch Mountain (lat. 35°09'45" N, long. 120°02'55" W); the spring is near the south end of Tajea Flat. Named on Branch Mountain (1967) 7.5' quadrangle.

Tajiguas [SANTA BARBARA]: *locality,* 6.25 miles east of Gaviota along Southern Pacific Railroad (lat. 34°28' N, long. 120°06'20" W); the place is west of the mouth of Tajiguas Creek. Named on Tajiguas (1953) 7.5' quadrangle.

Tajiguas Creek [SANTA BARBARA]: *stream,* flows 5.25 miles to the sea nearly 7 miles east of Gaviota (lat. 34°27'20" N, long. 120° 06' W). Named on Santa Ynez (1959) and Tajiguas (1953) 7.5' quadrangles. The name is from an Indian village (Kroeber, 1916, p. 61).

Talaki: see **Camp Talaki** [SAN LUIS OBISPO].

Talcott Shoal: see **Sandy Point** [SANTA BARBARA].

Tangair [SANTA BARBARA]: *locality,* 7.25 miles southwest of the village of Casmalia along Southern Pacific Railroad (lat. 34°45'15" N, long. 120°36'35" W). Named on Casmalia (1959) 7.5' quadrangle.

Tanganyika: see **Lake Tanganyika** [SAN BENITO].

Tank Siding: see **Clems** [SANTA BARBARA].

Tannery Gulch [SANTA CRUZ]: *canyon,* drained by a stream that flows 2.5 miles to the sea 2.5 miles northeast of Soquel Point (lat. 36°58'40" N, long. 121°56'15" W). Named on Laurel (1955) and Soquel (1954) 7.5' quadrangles. The name is from tanneries operated in the canyon as early as 1854 (Clark, 1986, p. 364).

Tan Oak Camp [MONTEREY]: *locality,* nearly 4 miles southwest of Tassajara Hot Springs (lat. 36°11'50" N, long. 121°35'55" W; sec. 14, T 20 S, R 3 E); the place is near the mouth of Tan Oak Creek. Named on Tassajara Hot Springs (1956) 7.5' quadrangle.

Tan Oak Creek [MONTEREY]: *stream,* flows nearly 1 mile to Zigzag Creek 4 miles southwest of Tassajara Hot Springs (lat. 36° 11'45" N, long. 121°35'55" W; sec. 14, T 20 S, R 3 E). Named on Tassajara Hot Springs (1956) 7.5' quadrangle.

Taro Creek: see **Toro Creek** [SAN LUIS OBISPO] (2).

Tar Spring Creek [SAN LUIS OBISPO]: *stream,* flows 9 miles to Arroyo Grande Creek 6 miles southeast of Edna (lat. 35°08' N, long. 120°33' W); the stream heads at Tar Spring Ridge. Named on Arroyo Grande NE (1965) and Tar Spring Ridge (1967) 7.5' quadrangles. Natural deposits of tar occur along the stream.

Tar Spring Ridge [SAN LUIS OBISPO]: *ridge,* east-southeast- to southeast-trending, 4.5 miles long, 8 miles north-northeast of the town of Nipomo (lat. 35°09' N, long. 120°26'30" W); the ridge is north of Tar Spring Creek. Named on Tar Spring Ridge (1967) 7.5' quadrangle.

Tash Creek [MONTEREY]: *stream,* flows 6 miles to Paloma Creek 13 miles west of Greenfield (lat. 36°18'05" N, long. 121°28'25" W; sec. 6, T 19 S, R 5 E). Named on Sycamore Flat (1956) 7.5' quadrangle. The name is from the Tash family, early residents of the neighborhood (Clark, 1991, p. 558).

Tassajara: see **Tassajara Hot Springs** [MONTEREY].

Tassajara Creek [MONTEREY]: *stream,* flows 11 miles to Arroyo Seco (1) 10 miles northeast of Slates Hot Springs (lat. 36°13'10" N, long. 121°30'05" W; sec. 2, T 20 S, R 4 E). Named on Chews Ridge (1956), Tassajara Hot Springs (1956), and Ventana Cones (1956) 7.5' quadrangles. The name is from Tassajara Hot Springs (Clark, 1991, p. 559).

Tassajara Hot Springs [MONTEREY]: *locality,* 9 miles east-northeast of Partington Point (lat. 36°14' N, long. 121°32'55" W; sec. 32, T 19 S, R 4 E); the place is along Tassajara Creek. Named on Tassajara Hot Springs (1956) 7.5' quadrangle. Postal authorities established Tassajara post office in 1892 and discontinued it in 1894; they established Tassajara Hot Springs post office in 1912 and discontinued it in 1944 (Frickstad, p. 109). A hotel was built at the springs in 1893 and 1894 (Johnston, p. 118). According to G.A. Waring (p. 57-58), about 17 thermal springs occur at the place; the name, which dates from early days of the cattle industry, is from an Indian or Mexican word that means "the place where meat is cured by drying."

Tassajera Creek [SAN LUIS OBISPO]: *stream,* flows 4 miles to Santa Margarita Creek 2 miles west-southwest of the town of Santa Margarita (lat. 35°22'45" N, long. 120°38'25" W). Named on Atascadero (1965) 7.5' quadrangle.

Taylor Canyon [MONTEREY-SAN LUIS OBISPO]: *canyon,* drained by a stream that heads in Monterey County and flows 7 miles to Shimmin Canyon 5 miles northwest of Shandon in San Luis Obispo County (lat. 35°42'25" N, long. 120°26'05" W; sec. 35, T 25 S, R 14 E). Named on Cholame Hills (1961) and Shandon (1961) 7.5' quadrangles.

Taylor Canyon [SAN LUIS OBISPO]: *canyon,* drained by a stream that flows 8 miles to Cuyama River 11 miles west of Caliente Mountain (lat. 35°03'20" N, long. 119°57'15" W). Named on Taylor Canyon (1959) 7.5' quadrangle.

Taylor Spring [MONTEREY]: *spring,* nearly 1 mile west-northwest of Smith Mountain along Pancho Rico Creek (lat. 36°04'55" N, long. 120°36'25" W; sec. 19, T 21 S, E 13 E). Named on Smith Mountain (1969) 7.5' quadrangle.

Taylor Spring [SAN LUIS OBISPO]: *spring,* 11 miles west-northwest of Caliente Mountain (lat. 35°05'40" N, long. 119°54'55" W; near W line sec. 35, T 32 S, R 19 E); the spring is in Taylor Canyon (2). Named on Taylor Canyon (1959) 7.5' quadrangle.

Taylor Well [SAN LUIS OBISPO]: *well,* 3.5 miles southeast of Branch Mountain along San Juan Creek (lat. 35° 10' N, long. 120° 01'30" W). Named on Branch Mountain (1967) 7.5' quadrangle.

Tecolito Creek: see **Tecolotito Creek** [SANTA BARBARA].

Tecolote Canyon [SANTA BARBARA]: *canyon,* drained by a stream that flows 6.5 miles to the sea 3 miles northwest of Coal Oil Point (lat. 34°25'50" N, long. 119°55' W). Named on Dos Pueblos Canyon (1951) and Lake Cachuma (1959) 7.5' quadrangles. *Tecolote* means "small owl" in Mexican Spanish (Gudde, 1949, p. 355).

Tecolotito Canyon: see **Glen Annie Canyon** [SANTA BARBARA].

Tecolotito Creek [SANTA BARBARA]: *stream,* flows 4.5 miles to Goleta Slough 1.5 miles west-southwest of downtown Goleta (lat. 34°25'35" N, long. 119°50'55" W). Named on Goleta (1950) 7.5' quadrangle. United States Board on Geographic Names (1978b, p. 5) rejected the name "Tecolito Creek" for the stream.

Tembladero Slough [MONTEREY]: *stream,* heads at a ditch that drains Merritt Lake and flows nearly 4 miles to Old Salinas River 2 miles south of Moss Landing (lat. 36°46'25" N, long. 121°47'15" W). Named on Moss Landing (1954) and Prunedale (1954) 7.5' quadrangles. Called Sanjon del Tembladera in a diseño of Bolsa del Potrero y Moro Cojo grant (Becker, 1964). United States Board on Geographic Names (1943, p. 14) rejected the name "Cooper Slough" for the feature.

Temblor Range [SAN LUIS OBISPO]: *range,* northeast of Carrizo Plain and San Juan Valley along San Luis Obispo-Kern County line. Named on Bakersfield (1962) and San Luis Obispo (1956) 1°x 2° quadrangles. Arnold and Anderson (1908, p. 13) named the feature and stated that *temblor* means "earthquake" in Spanish and is particularly suited for the range "because the great California fault line [San Andreas fault], along which earthquakes have repeatedly originated, follows the range from one end to the other," and because the well-known old Temblor ranch is on its west flank. United States Board on Geographic Names (1933, p. 748) rejected the form "Temploa Range" for the name.

Temettate Creek [SAN LUIS OBISPO]: *stream,* flows 2.25 miles to Los Berros Canyon 3.5 miles northeast of the town of Nipomo (lat. 35°04'40" N, long. 120°25'50" W); the stream heads on Temettate Ridge. Named on Nipomo (1965) 7.5' quadrangle. Gudde (1949, p. 358) traced the name to *temetate,* a Mexican word for a curved stone used as a mortar for grinding corn.

Temettate Ridge [SAN LUIS OBISPO]: *ridge,* northwest-trending, 9 miles long, 2.5 miles east-northeast of the town of Nipomo on the northeast side of Nipomo Valley (lat. 35°03'30" N, long. 120° 26' W). Named on Huasna Peak (1967) and Nipomo (1965) 7.5' quadrangles.

Templeton [SAN LUIS OBISPO]: *town,* 5.5 miles south of Paso Robles (lat. 35°33' N, long. 120°42'15" W). Named on Templeton (1948) 7.5' quadrangle. Postal authorities established Templeton post office in 1886 (Frickstad, p. 166). The town was laid out in 1886 when the railroad reached the place; first it was called Crocker and then Templeton, perhaps for Templeton Crocker, grandson of Charles Crocker of Central Pacific Railroad (Gudde, 1949, p. 358). The Templeton neighborhood was called Bethel District (Lee and others, p. 147)—Templeton (1948) 7.5' quadrangle shows the abandoned Bethel school situated 2.25 miles north-northwest of Templeton.

Temploa Range: see **Temblor Range** [SAN LUIS OBISPO].

Tennison Canyon [SANTA BARBARA]: *canyon,* drained by a stream that flows nearly 6 miles to Cuyama Valley 4.5 miles southeast of the village of Cuyama (lat. 34°53'20" N, long. 119°33'20" W). Named on Cuyama (1964) and Fox Mountain (1964) 7.5' quadrangles.

Tennison Spring [SANTA BARBARA]: *spring,* 2.25 miles north-northeast of Fox Mountain (lat. 34°50'30" N, long. 119°34'35" W); the spring is in Tennison Canyon. Named on Fox Mountain (1964) 7.5' quadrangle.

Tepusquet [SANTA BARBARA]: *land grant,* east of the confluence of Cuyama River and Sisquoc River. Named on Foxen Canyon (1964), Sisquoc (1959), Tepusquet Canyon (1964), and Twitchell Dam (1959) 7.5' quadrangles. Tomas Olivera received 2 leagues in 1837; Antonia Maria Cota and others claimed 8901 acres patented in 1871 (Cowan, p. 102). Angel (1883, p. 215) gave the alternate name "Santa Maria" for the grant.

Tepusquet Canyon [SANTA BARBARA]: *canyon,* 9 miles long, opens into Santa Maria Valley 4.5 miles southwest of Tepusquet Peak (lat. 34°52'05" N, long. 120°14'40" W); Tepusquet Creek drains the canyon. Named on Tepusquet Canyon (1964) 7.5' quadrangle. Called Arroyo de Tepusque on a diseño of Tepusquet grant made in 1837 (Becker, 1969).

Tepusquet Creek [SANTA BARBARA]: *stream,* flows 10 miles to Sisquoc River 2 miles east of the village of Sisquoc (lat. 34°51'45" N, long. 120°15'15" W). Named on Foxen Canyon (1964), Sisquoc (1959), and Tepusquet Canyon (1964) 7.5' quadrangles.

Tepusquet Peak [SANTA BARBARA]: *peak,* 15 miles east of Santa Maria (lat. 34°54'35" N, long. 120°11'05" W); the peak is east of Tepusquet Canyon. Altitude 3253 feet. Named on Tepusquet Canyon (1964) 7.5' quadrangle.

Tequepis [SANTA BARBARA]: *land grant,* along Santa Ynez River at the mouth of Cachuma Creek. Named on Lake Cachuma (1959) 7.5' quadrangle. Joaquin Villa received 2 leagues in 1843; Antonio M. Villa claimed 8919 acres patented in 1869 (Cowan, p. 102). According to Perez (p. 101), Antonio M. Villa was the grantee in 1845. The name is from an Indian village (Kroeber, 1916, p. 62).

Tequepis Canyon [SANTA BARBARA]: *canyon,* drained by a stream that flows 3.25 miles to Lake Cachuma 3.25 miles north-northeast of Santa Ynez Peak (lat. 34°34'10" N, long. 119°56'55" W); the mouth of the canyon is on Tequepis grant. Named on Lake Cachuma (1959) 7.5' quadrangle. Called Cañada de Tequepis on a diseño of Tequepis grant (Becker, 1969).

Tequepis Point [SANTA BARBARA]: *promontory,* 4 miles north-northeast of Santa Ynez Peak on the south side of Lake Cachuma (lat. 34°35'05" N, long. 119°57'25" W); the feature is on Tequepis grant. Named on Lake Cachuma (1959) 7.5' quadrangle.

Tequisquita Slough [SAN BENITO]: *stream,* formed by the confluence of Arroyo de las Viboras and Arroyo Dos Picachoes, flows nearly 7 miles, partly in an artificial watercourse, to San Felipe Lake 9 miles north-northeast of Hollister (lat. 36°58'45" N, long. 121°27'45" W). Named on San Felipe (1955) 7.5' quadrangle. Called Sanjon del Tequesquite on a diseño of Llano de Tequisquita grant made in 1834 (Becker, 1969)—the stream is partly on the grant.

Tequisquite: see **Llano del Tequisquita** [SAN BENITO].

Terminal Rock: see **Big Dome Cove** [MONTEREY].

Terrace Creek [MONTEREY]: *stream,* flows 1 mile to Big Sur River 5.25 miles north-northwest of Partington Point (lat. 36°14'55" N, long. 121°43'35" W; sec. 27, T 19 S, R 2 E). Named on Partington Ridge (1956) 7.5' quadrangle.

Terrace Creek Camp [MONTEREY]: *locality,* 5.25 miles north-northwest of Partington Point (lat. 36°14'45" N, long. 121°43'45" W; sec. 27, T 19 S, R 2 E); the place is along Terrace Creek. Named on Partington Ridge (1956) 7.5' quadrangle.

Terrace Hill [SAN LUIS OBISPO]: *hill,* 0.5 mile southeast of downtown San Luis Obispo (lat. 35°16'25" N, long. 120°39' W; near E line sec. 35, T 30 S, R 12 E). Named on San Luis Obispo (1965) 7.5' quadrangle.

Terrace Point [SANTA CRUZ]: *promontory,* 2.25 miles west of Point Santa Cruz along the coast (lat. 36°56'55" N, long. 122°03'55" W). Named on Santa Cruz (1954) 7.5' quadrangle.

The Basin [MONTEREY]: *relief feature,* 9.5 miles west of Greenfield (lat. 36°19'10" N, long. 121°24'40" W; sec. 34, T 18 S, R 5 E); the feature is on upper reaches of Basin Creek, where the canyon of the creek widens and the stream divides into four major branches. Named on Sycamore Flat (1956) 7.5' quadrangle.

The Bear Trap [MONTEREY]: *ridge,* north-northwest-trending, 1.5 miles long, 3 miles southeast of Jamesburg (lat. 36°19'45" N, long. 121°33'15" W). Named on Chews Ridge (1956) 7.5' quadrangle.

The Bluff [SAN BENITO]: *escarpment,* northeast-trending, 0.25 mile long, 5.5 miles northeast of Bitterwater (lat. 36°26'05" N, long. 120°55'40" W; sec. 19, T 17 S, R 10 E). Named on Rock Spring Peak (1969) 7.5' quadrangle.

The Cantinas [SAN LUIS OBISPO]: *relief feature,* 13 miles northeast of the village of San Simeon (lat. 35°45'55" N, long. 121°00'50" W; near W line sec. 9, T 25 S, R 9 E); the feature is along Cantinas Creek. Named on Bryson (1949) 7.5' quadrangle. On Bryson (1919) 15' quadrangle, the name applies to three small ponds situated 0.5 mile farther north-northeast in narrows along Cantinas Creek.

The Caves [MONTEREY]: *locality,* 6.5 miles south of Jamesburg (lat. 36°16'25" N, long. 121°35'05" W; sec. 13, T 19 S, R 3 E). Named on Chews Ridge (1956) 7.5' quadrangle. The name is from caves and rockshelters in sandstone at the place, which has the variant name "Church Creek Rockshelter" (Clark, 1991, p. 564).

The Chalks [SANTA CRUZ]: *area,* 5.5 miles north of the mouth of Waddell Creek (lat. 37°10'30" N, long. 122°17' W); the place is north-northeast of Chalk Mountain. Named on Franklin Point (1955) 7.5' quadrangle.

The City of King: see **King City** [MONTEREY].

The Dry Lake [MONTEREY]: *intermittent lake,* 400 feet long, 10.5 miles west-southwest of Greenfield (lat. 36°16'25" N, long. 121° 25'25" W; sec. 16, T 19 S, R 5 E). Named on Sycamore Flat (1956) 7.5' quadrangle.

The Espada [SANTA BARBARA]: *relief feature,* 4.25 miles southeast of Tranquillon Mountain (lat. 34°32' N, long. 120°31' W). Named on Tranquillon Mountain (1959) 7.5' quadrangle.

The Falls [MONTEREY]: *waterfall,* 10.5 miles northeast of Bradley in Walters Canyon (lat. 35°59'20" N, long. 120°41'50" W; sec. 29, T 22 S, R 12 E). Named on San Miguel (1919) 15' quadrangle.

The Fingers [SAN BENITO]: *relief feature,* 2.5 miles north-northwest of North Chalone Peak (lat. 36°29' N, long. 121°12'20" W; on E line sec. 4, T 17 S, R 7 E). Named on North Chalone Peak (1969) 7.5' quadrangle.

The Gorge [SAN BENITO]: *canyon,* 1 mile long, 10.5 miles east-southeast of Bitterwater along Laguna Creek (lat. 36°20'45" N, long. 120°49'15" W; sec. 19, T 18 S, R 11 E). Named on Hepsedam Peak (1969) 7.5' quadrangle.

The Hole [SAN BENITO]: *canyon,* 0.5 mile long, 7 miles north of San Benito (lat. 36°36'35" N, long. 121°05'20" W; sec. 22, T 15 S, R 8 E). Named on San Benito (1968) 7.5' quadrangle.

The Indians [MONTEREY]: *locality,* 3 miles south-southwest of Junipero Serra Peak (lat. 36°06'20" N, long. 121°26'05" W). Named on Cone Peak (1949) 7.5' quadrangle. The name is from neophytes of San Antonio mission who settled at the place after secularization of the mission (Clark, 1991, p. 566).

The Island: see **Aptos Creek** [SANTA CRUZ].

The Lakes [MONTEREY]: *lakes,* two, largest 1650 feet long, 7 miles north-northwest of Junipero Serra Peak near Arroyo Seco (1) (lat. 36°14' N, long. 121°28'55" W; near S line sec. 36, T 19 S, R 4 E). Named on Junipero Serra Peak (1949) 7.5' quadrangle.

The Mesa [MONTEREY]: *area,* nearly 6 miles east of Ventana Cone (lat. 36°16'10" N, long. 121°34'45" W; sec. 19, T 19 S, R 4 E). Named on Chews Ridge (1956) 7.5' quadrangle.

The Mesa: see **Nipomo Mesa** [SAN LUIS OBISPO].

The Narrows [MONTEREY]: *narrows,* 5.5 miles south of Stockdale Mountain along a branch of Middle Fork (lat. 35°54'35" N, long. 120°34'15" W; sec. 21, T 23 S, R 13 E). Named on Stockdale Mountain (1948) 7.5' quadrangle.

The Narrows [SANTA BARBARA]: *narrows,* 2 miles west-northwest of

Hildreth Peak (lat. 34°36'45" N, long. 119°34'45" W). Named on Hildreth Peak (1964) 7.5' quadrangle.

The Oaks [SAN LUIS OBISPO]: *locality,* 4 miles southeast of San Simeon (lat. 35°36'10" N, long. 121°08'10" W). Named on Pico Creek (1959) 7.5' quadrangle.

The Palisades [MONTEREY]: *ridge,* north-northwest-trending, 1.5 miles long, 8 miles south-southwest of Jolon (lat. 35°51'55" N, long. 121°12'40" W). Named on Burnett Peak (1949) 7.5' quadrangle.

The Peak [SANTA CRUZ]: *peak,* 7 miles north-northeast of the town of Boulder Creek on Castle Rock Ridge (lat. 37°13'10" N, long. 122°04'15" W; sec. 22, T 8 S, R 2 W). Altitude 2886 feet. Named on Castle Rock Ridge (1955) 7.5' quadrangle.

The Picachos [SAN BENITO]: *ridge,* northwest-trending, 1.25 miles long, 4.5 miles south-southwest of Idria (lat. 36°21'10" N, long. 120°41'40" W); the ridge extends northwest from Picacho Peak. Named on San Benito Mountain (1969) 7.5' quadrangle.

The Pimental: see **Pimental Creek** [SAN BENITO].

The Pines Campground [SANTA BARBARA]: *locality,* 5 miles southwest of Big Pine Mountain (lat. 34°38'30" N, long. 119°42'35" W). Named on Big Pine Mountain (1964) 7.5' quadrangle.

The Pinnacle: see **Pinnacle Point** [MONTEREY];

The Pinnacles [MONTEREY]: *peak,* 1.5 miles southeast of Smith Mountain on Monterey-Fresno County line (lat. 36°03'40" N, long. 120°34'45" W; sec. 33, T 21 S, R 13 E). Named on Smith Mountain (1969) 7.5' quadrangle.

The Pinnacles: see **Pescadero Point** [MONTEREY].

The Pit [MONTEREY]: *embayment,* less than 1 mile east of Point Lobos along the coast on the south side of Carmel Bay (lat. 36°31'15" N, long. 121°56'10" W). Named on Monterey (1947) 7.5' quadrangle. The name is from a gravel pit that was operated at the place from 1920 until 1926 (Clark, 1991, p. 569).

The Rocks [MONTEREY]:*relief feature,* bold northwest-trending sandstone outcrops 6.5 miles east of Junipero Serra Peak between Reliz Creek and Vaqueros Creek (lat. 36°09'50" N, long. 121°18'15" W; sec. 27, T 20 S, R 6 E). Named on Reliz Canyon (1949) 7.5' quadrangle.

The Shut-in [MONTEREY]: *narrows,* 10 miles south of Jolon along Nacimiento River (lat. 35°49'50" N, long. 121°09' W; sec. 19, T 24 S, R 8 E). Named on Burnett Peak (1949) 7.5' quadrangle.

The Tules [SAN BENITO]: *water feature,* three springs and two small spring-fed lakes 7.25 miles northeast of Bitterwater (lat. 36°27'25" N, long. 120°54'45" W; near NW cor. sec. 17, T 17 S, R 10 E). Named on Rock Spring Peak (1969) 7.5' quadrangle.

The Tuxedo: see **Mount Hermon** [SANTA CRUZ].

The Vallecitos: see **Vallecitos** [SAN BENITO].

The Wash [SAN LUIS OBISPO]: *stream,* flows 4.5 miles to New River 1.5 miles north-northeast of Cuyama [SANTA BARBARA] (lat. 34°57'15" N, long. 119°36'15" W). Named on Cuyama (1964) 7.5' quadrangle.

The Willows [SANTA CRUZ]: *settlement,* 8 miles north-northeast of Soquel (lat. 37°06'10" N, long. 121°55'25" W). Named on Laurel (1955) 7.5' quadrangle.

Thirtyfive Canyon [SAN LUIS OBISPO]: *canyon,* drained by a stream that flows 4.5 miles to Branch Creek 4.5 miles southwest of Branch Mountain (lat. 35°08'20" N, long. 120°08'25" W). Named on Branch Mountain (1967) and Los Machos Hills (1967) 7.5' quadrangles.

Thompson Canyon [MONTEREY]: *canyon,* drained by a stream that flows 8 miles to lowlands 3.25 miles west-southwest of King City (lat. 36°13'30" N, long. 121°10'45" W; sec. 2, T 20 S, R 7 E). Named on Thompson Canyon (1949) 7.5' quadrangle. The name commemorates Pleasant Thompson, who settled in the neighborhood in 1872 (Clark, 1991, p. 571).

Thompson Creek [SAN BENITO]: *stream,* flows 6 miles to Pescadero Creek 3 miles southwest of Paicines (lat. 36°42'05" N, long. 121°19'10" W). Named on Mount Harlan (1968) and Paicines (1968) 7.5' quadrangles. Irelan (p. 488) discussed lime manufacturing carried out at a place called Cienega that was located near present Thompson Creek (sec. 30, T 14 S, R 6 E). Paicines (1968) 7.5' quadrangle shows Limekiln Road along the creek.

Thompson Spring [SAN LUIS OBISPO]:

(1) *spring,* about 1.5 miles east of Branch Mountain (lat. 35°11'20" N, long. 120°03'25" W; sec. 33, T 31 S, R 18 E). Named on Branch Mountain (1967) 7.5' quadrangle.

(2) *spring,* nearly 1 mile northeast of Simmler (lat. 35°21'40" N, long. 119°58'40" W; sec. 31, T 29 S, R 19 E). Named on Simmler (1959) 7.5' quadrangle.

Thompson Valley [SAN BENITO]: *valley,* 8 miles southwest of Paicines (lat. 36°39'55" N, long. 121°23'20" W; on S line sec. 35, T 14 S, R 5 E); the valley is along a branch of Thompson Creek. Named on Mount Harlan (1968) 7.5' quadrangle.

Three Corners [SAN BENITO]: *locality,* 7.5 miles northeast of Bitterwater, where three ridges meet (lat. 36°27'35" N, long. 121° 54'10" W; near S line sec. 8, T 17 S, R 10 E). Named on Rock Spring Peak (1969) 7.5' quadrangle.

Three Corners Creek [SAN BENITO]: *stream,* flows nearly 2 miles to James Creek 6 miles northeast of Bitterwater (lat. 36°26'05" N, long. 120°54'50" W; near W line sec. 20, T 17 S, R 10 E); the stream heads near Three Corners. Named on Rock Spring Peak (1969) 7.5' quadrangle.

Three Mile Flat: see **Arroyo Seco** [MONTEREY] (2).

Three Peaks [MONTEREY]: *peaks,* 9 miles east-southeast of Cape San Martin (lat. 35°51' N, long. 121°18'25" W; sec. 15, T 24 S, R 6 E). Named on Burro Mountain (1949) 7.5' quadrangle.

Three Sisters [SAN BENITO]: *peaks,* on an east-trending ridge 1 mile long situated 8 miles east-northeast of Hollister (lat. 36°53'35" N, long. 121°15'45" W; sec. 13, T 12 S, R 6 E). Named on Three Sisters (1954) 7.5' quadrangle.

Three Sisters: see **La Carpa Potrero** [SANTA BARBARA].

Three Troughs [SAN LUIS OBISPO]: *water feature,* 3 miles northeast of the village of San Simeon (lat. 35°40'30" N, long. 121° 09' W). Named on San Simeon (1958) 7.5' quadrangle.

Three Troughs Canyon [SAN BENITO]: *canyon,* drained by a stream that flows nearly 2 miles to Stone Canyon 6 miles south of Paicines (lat. 36°38'45" N, long. 121°17'05" W; sec. 11, T 15 S, R 6 E). Named on Paicines (1968) 7.5' quadrangle.

Thyle [SAN LUIS OBISPO]: *locality,* 4.5 miles north-northeast of San Luis Obispo along Southern Pacific Railroad (lat. 35°20'25" N, long. 120°37'55" W). Named on San Luis Obispo (1965) 7.5' quadrangle. California Mining Bureau's (1917c) map shows a place called Nova located along the railroad about 1.5 miles south-southeast of present Thyle.

Tiber [SAN LUIS OBISPO]: *locality,* 1.5 miles south of Edna along Southern Pacific Railroad (lat. 35°10'40" N, long. 120°37'05" W); the place is near the mouth of Tiber Canyon. Named on Arroyo Grande NE (1965) 7.5' quadrangle.

Tiber Canyon [SAN LUIS OBISPO]: *canyon,* drained by a stream that flows 1 mile to Pismo Creek 1.5 miles south-southwest of Edna (lat. 35°10'45" N, long. 120°37'05" W). Named on Arroyo Grande NE (1965) 7.5' quadrangle.

Tickner Canyon [MONTEREY]: *canyon,* 1.5 miles long, opens into the valley of Pine Creek (3) 8 miles north-northeast of San Ardo (lat. 36°08'15" N, long. 120°51'45" W; sec. 2, T 21 S, R 10 E). Named on Monarch Peak (1967) 7.5' quadrangle. The name is for members of the Tickner family who had land in the neighborhood (Clark, 1991, p. 572).

Tide Rock: see **Cape San Martin** [MONTEREY].

Tie Gulch [SANTA CRUZ]: *canyon,* drained by a stream that flows nearly 1 mile to Branciforte Creek 4.5 miles north-northwest of Soquel (lat. 37°03' N, long. 121°58'50" W; sec. 21, T 10 S, R 1 W). Named on Laurel (1955) 7.5' quadrangle.

Tierra Redonda Mountain [SAN LUIS OBISPO]: *mountain,* 19 miles west-northwest of Paso Robles (lat. 35°46'15" N, long. 120°59'05" W; sec. 10, 11, T 25 S, R 9 E). Altitude 2051 feet. Named on Tierra Redonda Mountain (1949) 7.5' quadrangle. Arnold (p. 18, 70) called the feature Lynch's Mountain and Lynchs Mountain for James Lynch, who came to California in 1846 with Stevenson's New York Volunteers, and later lived near the mountain (Lynch, p. 65). Loel and Corey (p. 121) called it Tierra Redondo Mountain. California Mining Bureau's (1909b) map shows a place called Lynch located 7 miles by stage line south of Pleyto [MONTEREY] at the north base of Tierra Redonda Mountain, where James Lynch lived. Postal authorities established Lynch post office in 1894, moved it 4 miles northeast in 1910, and discontinued it in 1912; the name was for Alice C. Lynch, first postmaster (Salley, p. 129).

Tiger Spring [MONTEREY]: *spring,* 10 miles east of Parkfield (lat. 35°5245" N, long. 120°14'50" W; sec. 33, T 23 S, R 16 E). Named on Garza Peak (1953) 7.5' quadrangle.

Tiger Spring: see **Little Tiger Spring** [MONTEREY].

Timber Peak [SANTA BARBARA]: *peak,* 2 miles southeast of Miranda Pine Mountain (lat. 35°00'50" N, long. 120°00'45" W). Altitude 4764 feet. Named on Miranda Pine Mountain (1967) 7.5' quadrangle.

Timber Top [MONTEREY]: *peak,* 3 miles north-northwest of Partington Point (lat. 36°13'05" N, long. 121°42'45" W; sec. 2, T 20 S, R 2 E). Named on Partington Ridge (1956) 7.5' quadrangle.

Tim O'Leary Canyon [SAN LUIS OBISPO]: *canyon,* drained by a stream that flows 2.25 miles to Huasna Creek 6.5 miles east-northeast of the town of Nipomo (lat. 35°04'35" N, long. 120°22'10" W). Named on Nipomo (1965) 7.5' quadrangle.

Tims Creek [SANTA CRUZ]: *stream,* flows 0.5 mile to West Waddell Creek nearly 2 miles west-northwest of Big Basin (lat. 37°10'40" N, long. 122°15'05" W; sec. 1, T 9 S, R 4 W). Named on Big Basin (1955) 7.5' quadrangle. Clark (1986, p. 373) used the form "Timms" for the name, and noted that George Timm was an early resident of the neighborhood.

Tinaquaic [SANTA BARBARA]: *land grant,* at and near the west part of Foxen Canyon. Named on Foxen Canyon (1964) and Sisquoc (1959) 7.5' quadrangles. Victor Linares received 2 leagues in 1837; William D. Foxen claimed 8875 acres patented in 1872 (Cowan, p. 103; Cowan used the form "Tinaguaic" for the name, and gave the form "Tinaquaic" as an alternate).

Tin Can Canyon: see **Tin Pan Canyon** [SAN LUIS OBISPO].

Tinker's Cove: see **Twin Harbors** [SANTA BARBARA].

Tinkers Harbor: see **Twin Harbors** [SANTA BARBARA].

Tin Pan Canyon [SAN LUIS OBISPO]: *canyon*, 4 miles long, branches south-southwest from San Juan Valley 10 miles southeast of Shandon (lat. 35°32'45" N, long. 120°15'30" W; sec. 28, T 27 S, R 16 E). Named on Camatta Canyon (1961) and Camatta Ranch (1966) 7.5' quadrangles. Called Tin Can Canyon on Commatti Canyon (1943) 7.5' quadrangle.

Tinta Creek [SANTA BARBARA]: *stream*, flows 5.25 miles to Ventura County 17 miles southeast of the village of Cuyama (lat. 34°44'20" N, long. 119°26'35" W). Named on Madulce Peak (1964) and Rancho Nuevo Creek (1943) 7.5' quadrangles.

Tobacco Creek [SAN LUIS OBISPO]: *stream*, flows 5 miles to Little Burnett Creek 8.5 miles northeast of the village of San Simeon (lat. 35°44'35" N, long. 121°05'45" W; sec. 22, T 25 S, R 8 E). Named on Pebblestone Shut-in (1959) 7.5' quadrangle.

Todds Spring [MONTEREY]: *spring*, 3.5 miles south-southwest of Parkfield (lat. 35°50'55" N, long. 120°27'10" W; near S line sec. 10, T 24 S, R 14 E). Named on Cholame Hills (1961) 7.5' quadrangle. The name commemorates William Lewis Todd, who raised stock in the neighborhood in the 1870's (Clark, 1991, p. 574).

Todds Spring Canyon [MONTEREY]: *canyon*, drained by a stream that flows nearly 4 miles to Cholame Creek 3 miles south-southeast of Parkfield (lat. 35°51'45" N, long 120°24'20" W; near NE cor. sec. 12, T 24 S, R 14 E); Todds Spring is in a branch of the canyon. Named on Cholame Hills (1961) 7.5' quadrangle.

Todos Santos: see **San Luis Obispo Bay** [SAN LUIS OBISPO].

Todos Santos y San Antonio [SANTA BARBARA]: *land grant*, 10 miles south-southwest of Santa Maria. Named on Casmalia (1959), Lompoc (1959), and Orcutt (1959) 7.5' quadrangles. Salvador Osio received 5 leagues in 1841; the heirs of William E.P. Hartnell claimed 20,772 acres patented in 1876 (Cowan, p. 103). According to Perez (p. 102), Hartnell was the grantee in 1841.

Tomasini Canyon [MONTEREY]: *canyon*, drained by a stream that flows 1 mile to Carmel River 8.5 miles east of the mouth of that river (lat. 36°30'50" N, long. 121°46'25" W; sec. 29, T 16 S, R 2 E). Named on Seaside (1947) 7.5' quadrangle.

Tom Valley [MONTEREY]: *valley*, drained by a stream that flows 4.5 miles to Wildhorse Canyon 5.5 miles northeast of San Lucas (lat. 36°11'30" N, long. 120°57'35" W; sec. 14, T 20 S, R 9 E). Named on Nattrass Valley (1967) 7.5' quadrangle.

Tongue Ridge [MONTEREY]: *ridge*, east- to east-northeast-trending, nearly 1 mile long, 5.25 miles east of Seaside (lat. 36°37'10" N, long. 121°45'15" W). Named on Seaside (1947) 7.5' quadrangle.

Toomey Gulch: see **Tumey Gulch** [SAN BENITO].

Topo Creek [MONTEREY-SAN BENITO]: *stream*, heads in San Benito County and flows 12 miles to Chalone Creek 6.5 miles northeast of Greenfield in Monterey County (lat. 36°23'20" N, long. 121°09'50" W); the stream drains Topo Valley. Named on North Chalone Peak (1969) and Topo Valley (1969) 7.5' quadrangles.

Topo Valley [SAN BENITO]: *valley*, 4.5 miles northwest of Bitterwater near the southeast end of Gabilan Range (lat. 36°24'45" N, long. 121°04'15" W). Named on Topo Valley (1969) 7.5' quadrangle.

Toro: see **Mount Toro** [MONTEREY].

Toro Canyon [SANTA BARBARA]: *canyon*, 2 miles long, along Toro Canyon Creek above a point 4 miles northwest of Carpinteria (lat. 34°26' N, long. 119°34'15" W; sec. 14, T 4 N, R 26 W). Named on Carpinteria (1952, photorevised 1967) 7.5' quadrangle.

Toro Canyon Creek [SANTA BARBARA]: *stream*, flows 3.5 miles to the sea 3 miles west-northwest of Carpinteria (lat. 34°24'55" N, long. 119°33'55" W). Named on Carpinteria (1952, photorevised 1967) 7.5' quadrangle. Called Garrapata Creek on Carpinteria (1952) 7.5' quadrangle, but United States Board on Geographic Names (1962a, p. 18) rejected this name.

Toro Creek [SAN LUIS OBISPO]:

(1) *stream*, flows 11 miles to the sea 2.5 miles north-northwest of the mouth of Morro Creek (lat. 35°24'45" N, long. 120°52'20" W). Named on Morro Bay North (1965) 7.5' quadrangle.

(2) *stream*, flows 5 miles to Salinas River 3 miles west-northwest of Pozo (lat. 35°19'20" N, long. 120°25'25" W; sec. 12, T 30 S, R 14 E). Named on Pozo Summit (1967) and Santa Margarita Lake (1967) 7.5' quadrangles. United States Board on Geographic Names (1968b, p. 10) rejected the name "Taro Creek" for the stream.

Toro Creek: see **El Toro Creek** [MONTEREY].

Torre Canyon [MONTEREY]: *canyon*, drained by a stream that flows 1.5 miles to the sea 1.5 miles northwest of Partington Point (lat. 36°11'30" N, long. 121°42'50" W; sec. 14, T 20 S, R 2 E). Named on Partington Ridge (1956) 7.5' quadrangle. The name commemorates the de la Torre family, early residents of the neighborhood (Lussier, p. 27).

Town Creek [SAN LUIS OBISPO]: *stream*, flows 9 miles to Las Tablas Creek 4 miles north-northwest of Lime Mountain (lat. 35° 43'10" N, long. 120°57'20" W; near N line sec. 36, T 25 S, R 9 E). Named on Lime Mountain (1948) and Pebblestone Shut-in (1959) 7.5' quadrangles. The stream now enters an arm of Nacimiento Reservoir.

Towne Creek [MONTEREY-SAN BENITO]: *stream*, heads in San Benito County and flows nearly 4 miles to Mud Creek 10 miles north-northeast of Salinas in Monterey County (lat. 36°47'50" N, long. 121°34'05" W). Named on San Juan Bautista (1955) 7.5' quadrangle.

Town Spring [SAN LUIS OBISPO]: *spring*, 10.5 miles east-northeast of the village of San Simeon (lat. 35°40'45" N, long. 121°00'30" W; at N line sec. 16, T 26 S, R 9 E); the spring is near Town Creek. Named on Pebblestone Shut-in (1959) 7.5' quadrangle.

Trail Spring Camp [MONTEREY]: *locality*, about 4.5 miles northeast of Lopez Point (lat. 36°03'30" N, long. 121°30'05" W; sec. 35, T 21 S, R 4 E). Named on Lopez Point (1956) 7.5' quadrangle.

Trampa Canyon [MONTEREY]: *canyon*, drained by a stream that flows 2 miles to Cachagua Creek 8.5 miles southeast of the town of Carmel Valley (lat. 36°23'30" N, long. 121°37'25" W; sec. 2, T 18 S, R 13 E). Named on Carmel Valley (1956) and Rana Creek (1956) 7.5' quadrangles.

Tranquillon Mountain [SANTA BARBARA]: *peak*, 7 miles southwest of the city of Lompoc (lat. 34°34'55" N, long. 120°33'40" W). Altitude 2159 feet. Named on Tranquillon Mountain (1959) 7.5' quadrangle. Called El Tranquillon on Guadalupe (1905) 30' quadrangle, but United States Board on Geographic Names (1962a, p. 18) rejected the names "El Tranquillon," "El Tranquillon Mountain," "Arguello," and "Arguello Mountain" for the peak. William Eimbeck of United States Coast Survey named the peak formally in 1873; the name had been used locally and is of Indian origin (Gudde, 1969, p. 343).

Tranquillon Ridge [SANTA BARBARA]: *ridge*, extends for 4.5 miles west-northwest from Tranquillon Mountain (center near lat. 34°35'15" N, long. 120°35'30" W). Named on Point Arguello (1959) and Tranquillon Mountain (1959) 7.5' quadrangles.

Treasure Island: see **The Island**, under **Aptos Creek** [SANTA CRUZ].

Treplett Mountain [SANTA BARBARA]: *peak*, 2.5 miles southwest of Miranda Pine Mountain (lat. 35°00'55" N, long. 120°04'20" W). Altitude 3828 feet. Named on Miranda Pine Mountain (1967) 7.5' quadrangle.

Tres Ojos de Agua [SANTA CRUZ]: *land grant*, 2 miles north-northwest of Point Santa Cruz in Santa Cruz. Named on Santa Cruz (1954) 7.5' quadrangle. Nicolas Dodero received 1300 varas in 1844 and claimed 176 acres patented in 1866 (Cowan, p. 104-105). *Tres ojos de agua* means "three eyes of water" in Spanish, and refers to springs (Hoover, Rensch, and Rensch, p. 474).

Tres Pinos [SAN BENITO]: *village*, 6.5 miles southeast of Hollister (lat. 36°47'25" N, long. 121°19'15" W); the village is on the east side of Tres Pinos Creek. Named on Tres Pinos (1955) 7.5' quadrangle. When Southern Pacific Railroad reached the site in 1873, the name "Tres Pinos" was appropriated from present Paicines and applied to the new station (Pierce, p. 126). Postal authorities established Tres Pinos post office at the place in 1874 (Frickstad, p. 137).

Tres Pinos Creek [SAN BENITO]: *stream*, flows 30 miles to San Benito River 5 miles south-southeast of Hollister (lat. 36°47'05" N, long. 121°21'45" W; near E line sec. 24, T 13 S, R 5 E). Named on Cherry Peak (1968), Paicines (1968), Panoche Pass (1968), and Tres Pinos (1955) 7.5' quadrangles. Called Rosaria Creek on California Mining Bureau's (1917b) map. Gudde (1949, p. 368) noted that on old maps the stream has the names "Arroyo del puerto del Rosario" and "Arroyo del Rosario." Whitney (p. 53) used the name "Arroyo Joaquin Soto" for what probably is present Tres Pinos Creek.

Trough Canyon [SANTA BARBARA]: *canyon*, drained by a stream that flows 2.25 miles to Branch Canyon 4.25 miles northwest of Salisbury Potrero (lat. 34°52'20" N, long. 119°44'35" W). Named on Hurricane Deck (1964) and Salisbury Potrero (1964) 7.5' quadrangles.

Trough Canyon Spring: see **Upper Trough Canyon Spring** [SANTA BARBARA].

Trough Spring [SAN BENITO]: *spring*, 6 miles east-southeast of Bitterwater (lat. 36°20'55" N, long. 120°53'55" W; sec. 21, T 18 S, R 10 E). Named on Lonoak (1969) 7.5' quadrangle.

Trout Creek [SAN LUIS OBISPO]:

(1) *stream*, flows 10 miles to Santa Margarita Creek 3.5 miles north of Santa Margarita (lat. 35°26'30" N, long. 120°36'25" W). Named on Lopez Mountain (1965) and Santa Margarita (1965) 7.5' quadrangles.

(2) *stream*, flows 8 miles to join Stony Creek and form Huasna River 13 miles northeast of the town of Nipomo (lat. 35°12'05" N, long. 120°21' W; sec. 27, T 31 S, R 15 E). Named on Caldwell Mesa (1967), Pozo Summit (1967), and Santa Margarita (1965) 7.5' quadrangles.

Trout Creek: see **Trout Creek Gulch** [SANTA CRUZ].

Trout Creek Gulch [SANTA CRUZ]: *canyon*, drained by a stream that flows 4 miles to Valencia Creek 4.5 miles east-northeast of Soquel Point at Aptos (lat. 36°58'35" N, long. 121°53'45" W). Named on Laurel (1955) and Soquel (1954) 7.5' quadrangles. Capitola (1914) and Los Gatos (1919) 15' quadrangles show Trout Creek in the canyon.

Trujillo Creek [SAN LUIS OBISPO]: *stream*, flows nearly 4 miles to Pozo

Creek 1.5 miles east-northeast of Pozo (lat. 35°18'45" N, long. 120°20'55" W; sec. 15, T 30 S, R 15 E). Named on Pozo Summit (1967) 7.5' quadrangle.

Tucker Canyon [SAN LUIS OBISPO]: *canyon,* drained by a stream that flows 7 miles to San Juan Creek 3.5 miles south-southeast of Shandon (lat. 35°36'30" N, long. 120°21' W; sec. 3, T 27 S, R 15 E). Named on Camatta Canyon (1961) and Cholame (1961) 7.5' quadrangles.

Tucker Gulch [SAN BENITO]: *canyon,* drained by a stream that flows nearly 3 miles to San Benito River 11 miles east of Bitterwater (lat. 36°22'15" N, long. 120°48'10" W; sec. 7, T 18 S, R 11 E). Named on Hepsedam Peak (1969) and Hernandez Reservoir (1969) 7.5' quadrangles.

Tucker Mountain [SAN BENITO]: *peak,* 12.5 miles east of Bitterwater (lat. 36°24'50" N, long. 120°46'50" W; near SE cor. sec. 29, T 17 S, R 11 E). Altitude 4092 feet. Named on Hernandez Reservoir (1969) 7.5' quadrangle. Called Cane Mtn. on Hernandez Valley (1943) 15' quadrangle.

Tularcitos Creek [MONTEREY]: *stream,* flows 14 miles to Carmel River 1.5 miles southeast of the town of Carmel Valley (lat. 36°27'50" N, long. 121°42'50" W); the stream is mainly on Los Tularcitos grant. Named on Carmel Valley (1956) and Rana Creek (1956) 7.5' quadrangles.

Tularcitos Ridge [MONTEREY]: *ridge,* west-northwest-trending, 7 miles long, 6 miles southeast of the town of Carmel valley (lat. 36° 25'30" N, long. 121°39'30" W); the ridge is south of Tularcitos Creek. Named on Carmel Valley (1956) and Rana Creek (1956) 7.5' quadrangles.

Tule Canyon [MONTEREY]: *canyon,* nearly 1.5 miles long, opens into the canyon of San Antonio River 7 miles southeast of Jolon (lat. 35°54'10" N, long. 121°05'10" W). Named on Williams Hill (1949) 7.5' quadrangle.

Tules: see **The Tules** [SAN BENITO].

Tuley Springs: see **East Tuley Springs** [SAN LUIS OBISPO]: **West Tuley Springs** [SAN LUIS OBISPO].

Tully Creek [SAN BENITO]: *stream,* flows nearly 3 miles to Bitterwater Creek 4 miles southeast of Bitterwater (lat. 36°20'35" N, long. 120°56'55" W; near S line sec. 24, T 18 S, R 9 E). Named on Lonoak (1969) 7.5' quadrangle. Called Alvarez Cr. on Priest Valley (1915) 30' quadrangle.

Tully Mountain [SAN BENITO]: *peak,* 6 miles east-southeast of Bitterwater (lat. 36°21'25" N, long. 120°53'50" W; on N line sec. 21, T 18 S, R 10 E). Named on Lonoak (1969) 7.5' quadrangle.

Tumey Gulch [SAN BENITO]: *canyon,* drained by a stream that flows nearly 7 miles to Fresno County 12.5 miles east-southeast of Panoche (lat. 36°30'40" N, long. 120°37'55" W; sec. 26, T 16 S, R 12 E); the canyon is east of Tumey Hills. Named on Idria (1969) and Tumey Hills (1956) 7.5' quadrangles. According to Gudde (1969, p. 347), the name also had the form "Toomey."

Tumey Hills [SANTA BARBARA]: *range,* 9 miles east-southeast of Panoche and east of Silver Creek on San Benito-Fresno County line (lat. 36°32'30" N, long. 120°40' W). Named on Idria (1969) and Tumey Hills (1956) 7.5' quadrangles.

Tunnel Canyon [MONTEREY]: *canyon,* drained by a stream that flows 5 miles to Deer Canyon 8.5 miles east of Bradley (lat. 35° 52'20" N, long. 120°39'15" W; near E line sec. 3, T 24 S, R 12 E). Named on Valleton (1948) 7.5' quadrangle.

Tunnel Canyon [SANTA BARBARA]: *canyon,* drained by a stream that flows 4.25 miles to Sisquoc River 5 miles north of Zaca Lake (lat. 34°50'55" N, long. 120°03'20" W). Named on Manzanita Mountain (1964) and Zaca Lake (1964) 7.5' quadrangles.

Tunnel Flat [SAN LUIS OBISPO]: *area,* 2.5 miles east-southeast of Huasna Peak near the mouth of Alamo Creek (lat. 35°01'05" N, long. 120°18'30" W). Named on Huasna Peak (1967) 7.5' quadrangle. Water of Twitchell Reservoir now covers the place.

Tunnel Point [SAN LUIS OBISPO]: *promontory,* 1.25 miles north-northeast of Point San Luis along the coast near Port Harford (lat. 35°10'30" N, long. 120°45'10" W). Named on Port Harford (1897) 15' quadrangle.

Tunnel Spring [SAN LUIS OBISPO]: *spring,* 10 miles east-southeast of Shandon in Holland Canyon (lat. 35°36'05" N, long. 120°12'25" W; sec. 1, T 27 S, R 16 E). Named on Holland Canyon (1961) 7.5' quadrangle.

Tunnel Spring [SANTA BARBARA]: *spring,* nearly 6 miles north of Zaca Lake (lat. 34°51'40" N, long. 120°02'55" W); the spring is in Tunnel Canyon. Named on Zaca Lake (1964) 7.5' quadrangle.

Turkey Camp [SAN LUIS OBISPO]: *locality,* 10.5 miles south of Simmler (lat. 35°12'05" N, long. 119°58'05" W; near W line sec. 29, T 31 S, R 19 E). Named on Chimineas Ranch (1959) 7.5' quadrangle.

Turkey Camp Well [SAN LUIS OBISPO]: *well,* 10.5 miles south-southeast of Simmler (lat. 35°12'05" N, long. 119°57'05" W; near W line sec. 28, T 31 S, R 19 E); the well is 1 mile east of Turkey Camp. Named on Chimineas Ranch (1959) 7.5' quadrangle. McKittrick (1912) 30' quadrangle has the form "Turkeycamp Well" for the name.

Turkey Flat [MONTEREY]: *area,* 4.5 miles east-southeast of Parkfield (lat. 35°53' N, long,. 120°21'30" W). Named on Cholame Valley (1961), Parkfield (1961), and The Dark Hole (1961) 7.5' quadrangles. The name reportedly is from turkeys raised at the place in the early days (Clark, 1991, p. 581).

Turkey Foot: see **Boulder Creek** [SANTA CRUZ] (2).

Turkey Trap Ridge [SANTA BARBARA]: *ridge,* west-northwest-trending, 1 mile long, 1.25 miles east-northeast of New Cuyama in Cuyama Valley (lat. 34°57'25" N, long. 119°40' W). Named on New Cuyama (1964) 7.5' quadrangle.

Turner Creek [MONTEREY]: *stream,* flows nearly 3 miles to join Hill Creek (1) and form Bixby Creek 5.5 miles north-northeast of Point Sur (lat. 36°22'20" N, long. 121°50'35" W; near NE cor. sec. 15, T 18 S, R 1 E). Named on Big Sur (1956) and Mount Carmel (1956) 7.5' quadrangles.

Turner Creek Camp [MONTEREY]: *locality,* 7 miles northeast of Point Sur (lat. 36°22'40" N, long. 121°48'35" W; sec. 12, T 18 S, R 1 E); the place is along Turner Creek. Named on Mount Carmel (1956) 7.5' quadrangle. Clark (1991, p. 17) listed a place called Apple Tree Camp located along Turner Creek about 1.5 miles southeast of Turner Creek Camp (SW quarter sec. 7, T 18 S, R 2 E).

Turtle Creek [MONTEREY]: *stream,* flows nearly 4.5 miles to Nacimiento River 12.5 miles south-southeast of Jolon (lat. 35°47'55" N, long. 121°06'20" W; sec. 33, T 24 S, R 8 E). Named on Bryson (1949) 7.5' quadrangle.

Tuxedo: see **Mount Hermon** [SANTA CRUZ].

Twin Harbors [SANTA BARBARA]: *embayments,* 2.5 miles east-southeast of Diablo Point on the north side of Santa Cruz Island (lat. 34°02'35" N, long. 119°42'55" W). Named on Santa Cruz Island B (1943) 7.5' quadrangle. Goodyear (1890, map following p. 156) called the feature Tinkers Hbr., but United States Board on Geographic Names (1936b, p. 42) rejected this name for the place. Doran (p. 147) noted that the names "Twin Harbors," "Tinker's Cove," and "Orizaba" have been used interchangeably, and that Orizaba Pictograph Cave—also called Olson's Cave—is in the first draw west of the west embayment of Twin Harbors.

Twin Lake: see **Big Twin Lake** [SAN LUIS OBISPO]; **Small Twin Lake** [SAN LUIS OBISPPO].

Twin Lakes [SANTA CRUZ]: *town,* 1.5 miles west-northwest of Soquel Point near the coast (lat. 36°57'55" N, long. 121°59'50" W); the town is mainly between Woods Lagoon and Schwans Lagoon. Named on Soquel (1954) 7.5' quadrangle. The name is from the two lagoons, which are called Twin Lakes (Clark, 1986, p. 329). Ashley (plate 23) showed a place called Fairview located along the railroad at or near present Twin Lakes.

Twin Lakes: see **Schwans Lagoon** [SANTA CRUZ].

Twin Lakes Beach [SANTA CRUZ]: *beach,* 1.5 miles west-northwest of Soquel Point (lat. 36°57'45" N, long. 121°59'55" W); the beach is at the town of Twin Lakes. Named on Santa Cruz (1954) and Soquel (1954) 7.5' quadrangles.

Twin Peak [MONTEREY]: *peak,* 4 miles northeast of Lopez Point (lat. 36°03'10" N, long. 121°30'25" W; sec. 2, T 22 S, R 4 E). Altitude 4843 feet. Named on Lopez Point (1956) 7.5' quadrangle. This appears to be the feature called Roundtree Hill on Hamlin's (1904) map.

Twin Peaks [MONTEREY]:

(1) *peak,* 8 miles north-northeast of Point Sur (lat. 36°24'05" N, long. 121°49'25" W; sec. 2, T 18 S, R 1 E). Altitude 3568 feet. Named on Mount Carmel (1956) 7.5' quadrangle.

(2) *peaks,* two, 900 feet apart, 7 miles southwest of Soledad (lat. 36°22'15" N, long. 121°25'40" W; near N line sec. 16, T 18 S, R 5 E). Named on Sycamore Flat (1956) 7.5' quadrangle.

(3) *peaks,* two, 5.5 miles north of Charley Mountain on Monterey-Fresno County line (lat. 36°13'15" N, long. 120°38'40" W; sec. 2, T 20 S, R 12 E). Named on Priest Valley (1969) 7.5' quadrangle.

Twin Rocks [SAN LUIS OBISPO]: *peaks,* two, 5.5 miles south-southwest of Branch Mountain (lat. 35°06'45" N, long. 120°07'15" W; near E line sec. 26, T 32 S, R 17 E). Named on Miranda Pine Mountain (1967) 7.5' quadrangle.

Twin Seal Rocks: see **Lobos Rocks** [MONTEREY].

Twin Valley Creek [MONTEREY]: *stream,* flows 2.5 miles to El Piojo Creek 7 miles south of Jolon (lat. 35°52'10" N, long. 121°10'20" W). Named on Burnett Peak (1949) 7.5' quadrangle. The name was given because the stream heads in two separate valleys (Clark, 1991, p. 583).

Twisselmann Lake [SAN LUIS OBISPO]: *intermittent lake,* 450 feet long, 6 miles east-southeast of Cholame (lat. 35°39'40" N, long. 120°12'50" W; sec. 14, T 26 S, R 16 E). Named on Orchard Peak (1961) 7.5' quadrangle.

Twitchell Reservoir [SAN LUIS OBISPO-SANTA BARBARA]: *lake,* 8 miles long, behind a dam on Cuyama River 7 miles east-northeast of Santa Maria on San Luis Obispo-Santa Barbara County line (lat. 34°59'10" N, long. 120°19'20" W). Named on Huasna Peak (1967), Nipomo (1965), and Twitchell Dam (1959) 7.5' quadrangles. United States Board on Geographic Names (1959, p. 3) rejected the name "Vaquero Reservoir" for the lake, and noted that the name "Twitchell" honors T.A. Twitchell for his efforts in behalf of water conservation in the region.

Two Bar Creek [SANTA BARBARA]: *stream,* flows nearly 4 miles to San Lorenzo River 5.25 miles east-southeast of Big Basin (lat. 37°08'30" N, long. 122°07'55" W; near NW cor. sec. 19, T 9 S, R 2 W). Named on Big

Basin (1955) and Castle Rock Ridge (1955) 7.5' quadrangles.

Two Suertes [MONTEREY]: *land grant*, 5 miles west of Salinas. Named on Salinas (1947) 7.5' quadrangle. Gregory and Williams claimed 38 acres patented in 1872 (Cowan, p. 106).

Tyler Bight [SANTA BARBARA]: *embayment*, on the south side of San Miguel Island 2.25 miles east of Point Bennett (lat. 34°01'50" N, long. 120°24'40" W). Named on San Miguel Island West (1950) 7.5' quadrangle.

Tyler Canyon [SANTA BARBARA]: *canyon*, drained by a stream that flows 2 miles to Colson Canyon 2.25 miles north-northwest of Tepusquet Peak (lat. 34°56'30" N, long. 120°11'50" W). Named on Tepusquet Canyon (1964) 7.5' quadrangle.

Tyler Harbor: see **Potato Harbor** [SANTA BARBARA].

Tynan: see **Lake Tynan** [SANTA CRUZ].

- U -

Uncle Sam Mountain [MONTEREY]: *peak*, 4.5 miles north-northwest of Ventana Cone (lat. 36°20'30" N, long. 121°42'20" W). Altitude 4766 feet. Named on Ventana Cones (1956) 7.5' quadrangle. The name is from an early Mexican resident of the neighborhood who had the nickname "Uncle Sam" (Clark, 1991, p. 585).

Union [SAN LUIS OBISPO]: *locality*, 7.5 miles east of Paso Robles near Dry Creek (1) (lat. 35°38'15" N, long. 120°33'35" W; sec. 27, T 26 S, R 13 E). Named on Paso Robles (1919) 15' quadrangle. Postal authorities established Union post office in 1900 and discontinued it in 1924 (Frickstad, p. 166).

Union: see **Lake View** [SANTA BARBARA].

Union Creek [SANTA CRUZ]: *stream*, flows 1.5 miles to Sempervirens Creek nearly 1 mile northeast of Big Basin (lat. 37°10'30" N, long. 122°12'30" W; near NE cor. sec. 8, T 9 S, R 3 E). Named on Big Basin (1955) 7.5' quadrangle. The name is from Union Mill, built in 1895 (Clark, 1986, p. 382).

Upland: see **San Lucas** [MONTEREY] (2).

Upper Barn Springs: see **Hot Springs** [SANTA BARBARA] (2).

Upper Bee Camp: see **Bee Camp** [MONTEREY].

Upper Branch Canyon Spring [SANTA BARBARA]: *spring*, 0.5 mile north-northwest of Montgomery Potrero (lat. 34°50'45" N, long. 119°45'20" W); the spring is in Branch Canyon. Named on Hurricane Deck (1964) 7.5' quadrangle.

Upper Hog Pen Spring [SANTA BARBARA]: *spring*, 1 mile east-southeast of McPherson Peak (lat. 34°52'55" N, long. 119°47'30" W); the spring is 1300 feet northwest of Hog Pen Spring. Named on Peak Mountain (1964) 7.5' quadrangle.

Upper Horse Canyon [SANTA BARBARA]: *canyon*, drained by a stream that flows 1.5 miles to Horse Canyon (3) 6.5 miles north-northwest of San Marcos Pass (lat. 34°36'25" N, long. 119°50'55" W). Named on San Marcos Pass (1959) 7.5' quadrangle.

Upper Lopez Campground [SAN LUIS OBISPO]: *locality*, nearly 1 mile east-northeast of Lopez Mountain (lat. 35°18'20" N, long. 120°34' W; sec. 22, T 30 S, R 13 E); the place is in Lopez Canyon. Named on Lopez Mountain (1965) 7.5' quadrangle.

Upper Newsome Spring [SANTA BARBARA]: *spring*, nearly 2 miles north of Salisbury Potrero (lat. 34°50'50" N, long. 119°42' W); the spring is 3600 feet south of Lower Newsome Spring in Newsome Canyon. Named on Salisbury Potrero (1964) 7.5' quadrangle.

Upper Oso Campground [SANTA BARBARA]: *locality*, 4.5 miles north-east of San Marcos Pass (lat. 34°33'25" N, long. 119°45'10" W); the place is less than 1 mile north-northeast of Lower Oso Campground in Oso Canyon. Named on San Marcos Pass (1959) 7.5' quadrangle.

Upper Piletas Canyon [SAN LUIS OBISPO]: *canyon*, drained by a stream that flows nearly 2 miles to Lower Piletas Canyon 4.5 miles east-southeast of Castle Crags (lat. 35°16'40" N, long. 120°07'45" W; near NE cor. sec. 34, T 30 S, R 17 E). Named on La Panza (1967) 7.5' quadrangle. Upper Piletas Canyon and Lower Piletas Canyon together are called Piletas Canyon on La Panza (1935) 15' quadrangle, but United States Board on Geographic Names (1968c, p. 5) rejected the name "Piletas Canyon" for the combined features.

Upper Santa Ynez Campground [SANTA BARBARA]: *locality*, 8 miles north of Rincon Point (lat. 34°29'30" N, long. 119°27'05" W; sec. 25, T 5 N, R 25 W); the place is near the head of Santa Ynez River. Named on White Ledge Peak (1952) 7.5' quadrangle.

Upper Trough Canyon Spring [SANTA BARBARA]: *spring*, 2.5 miles north-northwest of Montgomery Potrero (lat. 34°52'15" N, long. 119°46'05" W); the spring is in Trough Canyon. Named on Hurricane Deck (1964) 7.5' quadrangle.

Upton Canyon [SAN LUIS OBISPO]: *canyon*, 6.25 miles long, opens into Shedd Canyon 9 miles south of Shandon (lat. 35°31'55" N, long. 120°24'10" W; sec. 31, T 27 S, R 15 E). Named on Camatta Canyon (1961), Camatta Ranch (1966), and Shedd Canyon (1961) 7.5' quadrangles.

- V -

Vaca Flat [SAN LUIS OBISPO]: *area*, 5.5 miles west-northwest of Pozo (lat. 35°19'25" N, long. 120°28'05" W; near W line sec. 10, T 30 S, R 14 E). Named on Santa Margarita Lake (1967) 7.5' quadrangle.

Valdez Harbor: see **Cueva Valdaze** [SANTA BARBARA].

Valencia: see **Valencia Creek** [SANTA CRUZ].

Valencia Creek [SANTA CRUZ]: *stream*, flows 7.25 miles to Aptos Creek 4.25 miles east-northeast of Soquel Point at Aptos (lat. 36° 58'30" N, long. 121°54'05" W). Named on Loma Prieta (1955) Soquel (1954), and Watsonville West (1954) 7.5' quadrangles. Hamman's (1980a) map shows a place called Valencia Creek Mill situated along the stream 2 miles east-northeast of Aptos, and a tributary called Cox Creek that joins Valencia Creek near the mill. California Mining Bureau's (1909d) map shows a place called Valencia located 3 miles by road east-northeast of Aptos. Postal authorities established Valencia post office in 1893 and discontinued it in 1909 (Frickstad, p. 177).

Valencia Creek: see **Coon Creek** [SAN LUIS OBISPO].

Valencia Creek Mill: see **Valencia Creek** [SANTA CRUZ].

Valencia Lagoon [SANTA CRUZ]: *marsh*, 5.25 miles east-northeast of Soquel Point (lat. 36°58'25" N, long. 121°52'55" W); the feature is near Valencia Creek. Named on Soquel (1954) 7.5' quadrangle. Capitola (1914) 15' quadrangle has the name for a lake. The feature was called Spreckels Lagoon in the 1880's (Clark, 1986, p. 384).

Valencia Peak [SAN LUIS OBISPO]: *peak*, 7.25 miles south of Morro Rock (lat. 35°15'50" N, long. 120°52'15" W). Altitude 1347 feet. Named on Morro Bay South (1965) 7.5' quadrangle.

Vallecitos [SAN BENITO]: *valley*, center 9 miles south-southeast of Panoche (lat. 36°29' N, long. 120°46' W); the northwest part of the valley is drained by Vallecitos Creek. Named on Hernandez Reservoir (1969), Idria (1969), and Panoche (1969) 7.5' quadrangles. Called The Vallecitos on Priest Valley (1915) 30' quadrangle.

Vallecitos Creek [SAN BENITO]: *stream*, flows 4.25 miles to join Pimental Creek and form Griswold Creek 5.5 miles south of Panoche (lat. 36°30'55" N, long. 120°50' W; near N line sec. 25, T 16 S, R 10 E); the stream drains part of Vallecitos. Named on Hernandez Reservoir (1969) and Panoche (1969) 7.5' quadrangles. Called Griswold Creek on Santa Cruz (1956) 1°x 2° quadrangle, and United States Board on Geographic Names (1972a, p. 1) listed this name as a variant.

Vallejo Slough: see **Elkhorn Slough** [MONTEREY].

Valleton [MONTEREY]: *locality*, 6 miles east-northeast of Bradley in Indian Valley (3) (lat. 35°53'20" N, long. 120°42'15" W; sec. 32, T 23 S, R 12 E). Named on Valleton (1948) 7.5' quadrangle. Postal authorities established Valleton post office in 1887, moved it 4 miles southwest in 1901, and discontinued it in 1918 (Salley, p. 229). San Miguel (1919) 15' quadrangle shows the place along Stone Canyon Railroad. California Mining Bureau's (1917b) map shows a place called Eagle located along the railroad 2.5 miles north-northeast of Valleton—San Miguel (1919) 15' quadrangle shows Eagle school in the same neighborhood.

Valley Anchorage [SANTA BARBARA]: *embayment*, nearly 3 miles south-southeast of Prisoners Harbor on the south side of Santa Cruz Island (lat. 33°59'05" N, long. 119°39'45" W); the embayment is east of the east end of Central Valley. Named on Santa Cruz Island C (1943) 7.5' quadrangle. Called Puerto de la Cañada del Sur on Rand's (1931) map. Bremner's (1932) map has the name "Blue Bank" at the place, and has the name "Cñ. Pomona" for the canyon that opens to the sea there.

Valley of Los Alisos: see **Sycamore Canyon** [SANTA BARBARA] (2).

Valley of Los Robles: see **San Antonio River** [MONTEREY].

Valley of Monterey: see **Salinas Valley**, under **Salinas River** [MONTEREY-SAN LUIS OBISPO].

Valley of San Luis Obispo: see **Los Osos Valley** [SAN LUIS OBISPO].

Valley of the Bears: see **Los Osos Valley** [SAN LUIS OBISPO].

Valley of the Coxo: see **Cañada del Cojo** [SANTA BARBARA].

Van Allen Ridge [SANTA CRUZ]: *ridge*, south-southwest-trending, 1.25 miles long, 4.5 miles east-southeast of the town of Boulder Creek (lat. 37°06'15" N, long. 122°02'30" W). Named on Felton (1955) 7.5' quadrangle.

Van Cliff Canyon [SAN BENITO]: *canyon*, drained by a stream that flows 3.25 miles to Pimental Creek 6.25 miles south-southwest of Panoche (lat. 36°30'55" N, long. 120°52'45" W; sec. 28, T 16 S, R 10 E). Named on Llanada (1969) and Rock Spring Peak (1969) 7.5' quadrangles.

Vancouver's Pinnacles: see **Pinnacle Rocks** [SAN BENITO].

Vandenberg Air Force Base [SANTA BARBARA]: *military installation*, northwest of the city of Lompoc along the coast. Named on Casmalia (1959), Guadalupe (1959), Lompoc (1959), Orcutt (1959), Point Sal (1958), and Surf (1959) 7.5' quadrangles. Called Camp Cooke Military Reservation on Point Sal (1947) 15' quadrangle, which shows Camp Cooke on the reservation. The name "Cooke" commemorated Philip St. George Cooke, who led the Mormon Battalion to California during the Mexican

War (Gudde, 1949, p. 78). The name "Vandenberg" honors General H.S. Vandenberg, who was chief of staff for United States Air Force from 1948 until 1953 (Hart, J.D., p. 461).

Van Gordon Creek [SAN LUIS OBISPO]:

(1) *stream,* flows 3.5 miles to Burnett Creek 6 miles north of the village of San Simeon (lat. 35°43'40" N, long. 121°10'25" W). Named on San Simeon (1958) 7.5' quadrangle.

(2) *stream,* flows 4.5 miles to San Simeon Creek 3 miles northwest of Cambria (lat. 35°35'40" N, long. 121°07'10" W; near NW cor. sec. 16, T 27 S, R 8 E). Named on Cambria (1959) and Pebblestone Shut-in (1959) 7.5' quadrangles.

Vanoni Peak: see **Atherton Peak** [SANTA CRUZ].

Van Winkleys Canyon [MONTEREY]: *canyon,* drained by a stream that flows 2 miles to San Jose Creek 4.5 miles northeast of Soberanes Point (lat. 36°29'10" N, long. 121°51'40" W; sec. 4, T 17 S, R 1 E). Named on Mount Carmel (1956) 7.5' quadrangle.

Vaquero Cañon: see **Vaqueros Creek** [MONTEREY].

Vaquero Creek: see **Vaqueros Creek** [MONTEREY].

Vaquero Flat [SAN LUIS OBISPO]: *area,* 1.5 miles south-southeast of Huasna Peak (lat. 35°00'50" N, long. 120°20'25" W). Named on Huasna Peak (1967) 7.5' quadrangle.

Vaquero Peak: see **Pinyon Peak** [MONTEREY] (2).

Vaquero Reservoir: see **Twitchell Reservoir** [SAN LUIS OBISPO-SANTA BARBARA].

Vaqueros Canyon: see **Vaqueros Creek** [MONTEREY].

Vaqueros Creek [MONTEREY]: *stream,* flows 10 miles to Arroyo Seco (1) 6.5 miles southwest of Greenfield (lat. 36°15'50" N, long. 121°20'10" W; sec. 20, T 19 S, R 6 E). Named on Paraiso Springs (1956) and Reliz Canyon (1949) 7.5' quadrangles. Called Vaquero Creek on Soledad (1915) 15' quadrangle. Hamlin (p. 14) used the name "Los Vaqueros Valley" for the valley along the upper part of the stream, which he (fig 11) called Los Vaqueros Cr. Goodyear (1888, p. 87) called the same valley Vaquero Cañon, and Wiedey (p. 99) called it Vaqueros Canyon.

Vasques Creek: see **Vasquez Creek** [SAN LUIS OBISPO].

Vasquez: see **Lorenzo Vasquez Canyon** [SAN BENITO].

Vasquez Creek [SAN BENITO]: *stream,* flows 5.25 miles to Fresno County 8.5 miles north-northwest of Panoche (lat. 36°42'45" N, long. 120°53' W; sec. 16, T 14 S, R 10 E). Named on Cerro Colorado (1969) 7.5' quadrangle.

Vasquez Creek [SAN LUIS OBISPO]: *stream,* flows nearly 6 miles to Lopez Canyon 11.5 miles north of the town of Nipomo (lat. 35°12'25" N, long. 120°28'55" W; sec. 21, T 31 S, R 14 E). Named on Arroyo Grande NE (1965) and Tar Spring Ridge (1967) 7.5' quadrangles. Called Basquez Creek on Arroyo Grande (1897) 15' quadrangle, but United States Board on Geographic Names (1967a, p. 10) rejected the names "Basquez Creek" and "Vasques Creek" for the stream.

Vasquez Crossing [SAN BENITO]: *locality,* 9.5 miles east-southeast of Bitterwater along Hepsedam Creek (lat. 36°19'05" N, long. 120° 51'15" W; sec. 35, T 18 S, R 10 E); the place is 1 mile southeast of Vasquez Rock. Named on Hepsedam Peak (1969) 7.5' quadrangle.

Vasquez Knob [MONTEREY]: *peak,* 9.5 miles east of Soberanes Point (lat. 36°28'10" N, long. 121°45'40" W; sec. 9, T 17 S, R 2 E). Named on Mount Carmel (1956) 7.5' quadrangle.

Vasquez Rock [SAN BENITO]: *peak,* 8 miles east-southeast of Bitterwater (lat. 36°19'35" N, long. 120°52'05" W; near NE cor. sec. 34, T 18 S, R 10 E). Altitude 3884 feet. Named on Hepsedam Peak (1969) 7.5' quadrangle.

Vega [MONTEREY]: *locality,* 2.5 miles west-northwest of Aromas along Southern Pacific Railroad (lat. 36°53'55" N, long. 121°41'20" W). Named on San Juan Bautista (1917) 15' quadrangle. The station name, given in 1871, is from Vega del Rio del Pajaro grant, where the place was located (Gudde, 1969, p. 352).

Vega del Rio del Pajaro [MONTEREY]: *land grant,* west of Aromas along Pajaro River. Named on Prunedale (1954) and Watsonville East (1955) 7.5' quadrangles. Antonio Maria Castro received the land in 1820; F.A. McDougal and others claimed 4310 acres patented in 1864 (Cowan, p. 56). Perez (p. 104) gave 1833 as the date of the grant.

Venado Peak: see **Sampson Peak** [SAN BENITO].

Venezuela: see **Posa de los Ositos** [MONTEREY].

Ventana Camp [MONTEREY]: *locality,* 4 miles west-southwest of Ventana Cone along Big Sur River (lat. 36°15'35" N, long. 121°44'30" W; sec. 21, T 19 S, R 2 E); the place is near the confluence of Big Sur River with Ventana Creek (2). Named on Ventana Cones (1956) 7.5' quadrangle.

Ventana Cone [MONTEREY]: *peak,* 12.5 miles east of Point Sur (lat. 36°17'05" N, long. 121°40'35" W; sec. 18, T 19 S, R 3 E). Altitude 4727 feet. Named on Ventana Cones (1956) 7.5' quadrangle. According to Lussier (p. 13), the name is from a windowlike gap between two peaks—*ventana* means "window" in Spanish.

Ventana Cone: see **South Ventana Cone** [MONTEREY].

Ventana Creek [MONTEREY]:

(1) *stream,* flows 2.25 miles to Little Sur River 7.5 miles east of Point Sur (lat. 36°19'35" N, long. 121°46'05" W); the stream heads near Ventana Double Cone. Named on Big Sur (1956) and Ventana Cones (1956) 7.5' quadrangles. United States Board on Geographic Names (1967b, p. 7) approved the name "Jackson Creek" for the stream. The junction of the creek with Little Sur River is 1 mile east of Jackson Camp.

(2) *stream,* flows nearly 4 miles to Big Sur River 4.25 miles west-southwest of Ventana Cone (lat. 36°15'30" N, long. 121°44'40" W; near S line sec. 21, T 19 S, R 2 E); the stream heads near Ventana Double Cone. Named on Ventana Cones (1956) 7.5' quadrangle.

Ventana Double Cone [MONTEREY]: *peaks,* two, 2.25 miles west-northwest of Ventana Cone (lat. 36°17'55" N, long. 121°42'50" W; sec. 11, T 19 S, R 2 E). Named on Ventana Cones (1956) 7.5' quadrangle. United States Board on Geographic Names (1962a, p. 18) rejected the names "Double Summit" and "Ventana Double Summit" for the peaks.

Ventana Double Summit: see **Ventana Double Cone** [MONTEREY].

Ventana Mesa Creek [MONTEREY]: *stream,* flows 2.25 miles to Carmel River 2 miles north of Ventana Cone (lat. 36°18'50" N, long. 121°40'50" W; sec. 32, T 18 S, R 3 E); the stream heads near Ventana Double Cone. Named on Ventana Cones (1956) 7.5' quadrangle.

Ventucopa [SANTA BARBARA]: *locality,* 11.5 miles southeast of the village of Cuyama (lat. 34°49'45" N, long. 119°28' W). Named on Cuyama Peak (1943) 7.5' quadrangle. Postal authorities established Ventucopa post office in 1935 and discontinued it in 1952; the coined name is from the words "Ventura" and "Maricopa" (Salley, p. 230).

Ventura Rocks [MONTEREY]: *rocks,* two, largest 75 feet long, 3.5 miles north of Point Sur, and 3000 feet offshore (lat. 36°20'35" N, long. 121°54'20" W). Named on Point Sur (1956) 7.5' quadrangle. The name commemorates the steamship *Ventura,* which was wrecked on the rocks in 1875 (Reinstedt, 1975, p. 109).

Veratina: see **Nasimento**, under **Bradley** [MONTEREY].

Verde [SAN LUIS OBISPO]: *locality,* 3.5 miles southeast of Edna in the upper part of Corbit Canyon (lat. 35°10'15" N, long. 120°33'25" W); the place is above the head of Cañada Verde. Named on Arroyo Grande NE (1965) 7.5' quadrangle. Arroyo Grande (1897) 15' quadrangle shows the place along Pacific Coast Railroad.

Veronica Springs [SANTA BARBARA]: *spring,* 2.5 miles west-southwest of downtown Santa Barbara (lat. 34°24'40" N, long. 119°44'30" W). Named on Santa Barbara (1952) 7.5' quadrangle. Huguenin (p. 743) mentioned that the springs occur on the west side of Veronica Valley. Huguenin (p. 741-742) also noted that Bythenia Springs are situated 0.5 mile northwest of Veronica Springs, Moore Spring is in Veronica Valley opposite Veronica Springs, and Pinkham's Santa Barbara Mineral Springs are near the top of a low mesa that overlooks Veronica Valley. G.A. Waring (p. 295) listed Santa Barbara Springs, which were located about 0.75 mile northeast of Veronica Springs.

Veronica Valley: see **Veronica Springs** [SANTA BARBARA].

Viboras Creek: see **Arroyo de las Viboras** [SAN BENITO].

Vicente Camp [MONTEREY]: *locality,* 1.5 miles south-southeast of Cone Peak (lat. 36°01'45" N, long. 121°29'15" W; sec. 12, T 22 S, R 4 E). Named on Cone Peak (1949) 7.5' quadrangle. Called Vicente Flat Campground on Junipero Serra (1961) 15' quadrangle. United States Board on Geographic Names (1978b, p. 5) approved the name "Vicente Flat" for the place, and rejected the names "Vicente Camp" and "Vicente Flat." The name is from Vicente Avila, who kept stock at the place and had a cabin there (Clark, 1991, p. 592).

Vicente Creek [MONTEREY]: *stream,* flows 3.25 miles to the sea 2 miles north-northwest of Lopez Point (lat. 36°02'40" N, long. 121° 35'05" W; sec. 1, T 22 S, R 3 E). Named on Lopez Point (1956) 7.5' quadrangle. The name is for Vicente Avila (Clark, 1991, p. 592).

Vicente Flat: see **Vicente Camp** [MONTEREY].

Vicente Flat Campground: see **Vicente Camp** [MONTEREY].

Vierra Canyon [MONTEREY]:

(1) *canyon,* drained by a stream that flows 2.25 miles to San Miguel Canyon at Prunedale (lat. 36°47'30" N, long. 121°40' W). Named on Prunedale (1954) 7.5' quadrangle. The name is for Roleno José Vierra, who had a summer place in the canyon (Clark, 1991, p. 594).

(2) *canyon,* drained by a stream that flows 3.25 miles to Mud Creek 8 miles north-northeast of Salinas (lat. 36°46'55" N, long. 121°35'05" W). Named on San Juan Bautista (1955) 7.5' quadrangle.

Vierras Knoll [MONTEREY]: *hill,* 1.25 miles southeast of Point Lobos (lat. 36°30'30" N, long. 121°56'20" W). Named on Monterey (1947) 7.5' quadrangle. The name commemorates Juan Vierra Pre (Clark, 1991, p. 594).

Villa Creek [MONTEREY]: *stream,* flows 4.25 miles to the sea 4 miles southeast of Cape San Martin (lat. 35°51' N, long. 121°24'30" W; sec. 17, T 24 S, R 5 E). Named on Burro Mountain (1949) and Villa Creek (1949) 7.5' quadrangles.

Villa Creek [SAN LUIS OBISPO]:

(1) *stream,* flows 12 miles to the sea nearly 2 miles east of Point Estero (lat. 35°27'35" N, long. 120°58'10" W; sec. 35, T 28 S, R 9 E). Named on Cayucos (1965) and Cypress Mountain (1948) 7.5' quadrangles.

(2) *stream,* flows 3.5 miles to East Corral de Piedra Creek 4 miles northeast of Edna (lat. 35°14'05" N, long. 120°33'20" W). Named on Arroyo Grande

NE (1965) and Lopez Mountain (1965) 7.5' quadrangles.

Villa Creek: see **San Geronimo** [SAN LUIS OBISPO].

Ville de Francfort: see **Santa Cruz** [SANTA CRUZ].

Vilo: see **Ellwood** [SANTA BARBARA].

Vincente Flat: see **Vicente Camp** [MONTEREY].

Vineyard Canyon [MONTEREY-SAN LUIS OBISPO]: *canyon*, drained by a stream that heads in Monterey County and flows 16 miles to Salinas River in 1.5 miles north-northwest of San Miguel San Luis Obispo County (lat. 35°46'30" N, long. long. 120°42'10" W; sec. 8, T 25 S, R 12 E). Named on Ranchito Canyon (1948), San Miguel (1948), and Stockdale Mountain (1948) 7.5' quadrangles. Nomland (p. 215) used the name "Vineyard Creek" for the stream in the canyon. Stanley (p. 124) mentioned Vineyard Springs that were situated "about four miles up the canyon." California Mining Bureau's (1909a) map shows a place called Apricot located in Monterey County 10 miles by stage line southwest of Imusdale. Postal authorities established Apricot post office in Vineyard Canyon 9 miles northeast of San Miguel in 1887 and discontinued it in 1900 (Salley, p. 8).

Vineyard Canyon [SAN LUIS OBISPO]: *canyon*, drained by a stream that flows 3.25 miles to the sea nearly 3 miles northwest of Point San Luis (lat. 35°11' N, long. 120°48' W). Named on Port San Luis (1965) 7.5' quadrangle. Port Harford (1897) 15' quadrangle shows Pecho Creek in the canyon. United States Board on Geographic Names (1967c, p. 2) adopted the name "Irish Canyon" for the feature, and rejected the names "Vineyard Canyon" and "Pecho Creek."

Vineyard Creek: see **Vineyard Canyon** [MONTEREY-SAN LUIS OBISPO].

Vineyard Springs: see **Vineyard Canyon** [MONTEREY]:

Vinyard [SAN BENITO]: *locality*, 7 miles south of Hollister (lat. 36° 45' N, long. 121°23'05" W). Named on Hollister (1921) 15' quadrangle. Hollister (1955) 7.5' quadrangle shows a winery at the place.

Viscaino Hill: see **Bluefish Cove** [MONTEREY].

Von Helm Rock [SAN LUIS OBISPO]: *rock*, 2.5 miles southwest of Cambria (lat. 35°32'20" N, long. 121°06'40" W). Named on Cambria (1959) 7.5' quadrangle.

Vulture Rock [SAN LUIS OBISPO]: *peak*, 9.5 miles east of the village of San Simeon (lat. 35°38'40" N, long. 121°01'05" W; sec. 29, T 26 S, R 9 E). Altitude 2849 feet. Named on Pebblestone Shut-in (1959) 7.5' quadrangle.

- W -

Waddell: see **Bonnie Doon** [SANTA CRUZ].

Waddell Creek [SANTA CRUZ]: *stream*, formed by the confluence of East Waddell Creek and West Waddell Creek, flows 3.5 miles to the sea 16 miles west-northwest of Santa Cruz (lat. 37°05'35" N, long. 122°16'30" W; near W line sec. 2, T 10 S, R 4 W). Named on Año Nuevo (1955) and Franklin Point (1955) 7.5' quadrangles. Crespi gave the name "La Cañada de San Luis Beltran" to a campsite that the Portola expedition had by the stream in 1769, but the soldiers, who rested there to recover from sickness, called the place Cañada de la Salude—*salude* means "health" in Spanish; the canyon of the stream was called Big Gulch in the early days of lumbering in the region, but the stream itself was named for William W. Waddell after he built a sawmill along it in 1862 (Hoover, Rensch, and Rensch, p. 475-476).

Waddell Creek: see **East Waddell Creek** [SANTA CRUZ]; **West Waddell Creek** [SANTA CRUZ].

Waddell Gulch: see **Granite Creek** [SANTA CRUZ].

Wagner Creek [MONTEREY]: *stream*, flows 2.5 miles to San Carpoforo Creek 12 miles east-southeast of Cape San Martin (lat. 35° 49'20" N, long. 121°16'10" W; sec. 25, T 24 S, R 6 E). Named on Burnett Peak (1949) and Burro Mountain (1949) 7.5' quadrangles.

Wagon Cave Campground: see **Old Wagon Cave Campground** [MONTEREY].

Wagon Caves: see **Rattlesnake Creek** [MONTEREY] (2).

Wagon Flat Campground [SANTA BARBARA]: *locality*, 4.5 miles north-northwest of Manzanita Mountain along North Fork La Brea Creek (lat. 34°57'25" N, long. 120°05'45" W). Named on Manzanita Mountain (1964) 7.5' quadrangle.

Waldo: see **Waldorf** [SANTA BARBARA].

Waldorf [SANTA BARBARA]: *locality*, 4.25 miles south-southeast of the town of Guadalupe along Southern Pacific Railroad (lat. 34°54'40" N, long. 120°33'15" W). Named on Guadalupe (1959) 7.5' quadrangle. Called Waldo on California Mining Bureau's (1917c) map.

Walker Canyon [MONTEREY]: *canyon*, drained by a stream that flows 7.5 miles to Sargent Creek 8 miles north of Bradley (lat. 35° 58'30" N, long. 120°47'50" W; sec. 32, T 22 S, R 11 E). Named on Slack Canyon (1969), Valleton (1948), and Wunpost (1949) 7.5' quadrangles. Members of the Walker family lived in and near the canyon (Clark, 1991, p. 598).

Walker Peak [SAN BENITO]: *peak*, 8 miles west of Panoche (lat. 36°35'50" N, long. 120°58'15" W; sec. 27, T 15 S, R 9 E). Altitude 2835 feet. Named on Llanada (1969) 7.5' quadrangle.

Waller Creek [MONTEREY]: *stream*, flows 3 miles to El Piojo Creek 9.5 miles south of Jolon (lat. 35°50'10" N, long. 121°09'10" W; near NW cor. sec. 19, T 24 S, R 8 E). Named on Bryson (1949) and Burnett Peak (1949) 7.5' quadrangles. Edward Waller patented land along the stream in 1889 (Clark, 1991, p. 598). South Fork enters 1 mile upstream from the mouth of the main stream; it is 3.25 miles long and is named on Bryson (1949) and Burnett Peak (1949) 7.5' quadrangles.

Walnut Creek [SAN LUIS OBISPO]: *stream*, heads in Kern County and flows 1 mile in San Luis Obispo County to join Yeguas Creek and form Bitterwater Creek 25 miles southeast of Shandon (lat. 35°27'30" N, long. 120°00'45" W; sec. 26, T 28 S, R 18 E). Named on La Panza NE (1966) 7.5' quadrangle.

Walters Camp [SAN LUIS OBISPO]: *locality*, 11.5 miles south-southwest of Shandon (lat. 35°30'35" N, long. 120°27'50" W). Named on Shedd Canyon (1961) 7.5' quadrangle.

Walters Canyon [MONTEREY]: *canyon*, drained by a stream that flows 5 miles to Powell Canyon 7 miles north-northeast of Bradley (lat. 35°57' N, long. 120°44'50" W; sec. 11, T 23 S, R 11 E). Named on Slack Canyon (1969) and Valleton (1948) 7.5' quadrangles.

Warden Lake [SAN LUIS OBISPO]: *marsh*, 1 mile long, 5.5 miles southeast of Morro Rock in Los Osos Valley (lat. 35°18'40" N, long. 120°47'45" W). Named on Morro Bay South (1965) 7.5' quadrangle. Cayucos (1951) 15' quadrangle shows a lake, 4300 feet long, at the place.

Warner Lake [MONTEREY]: *lake*, 1200 feet long, 5.5 miles west of Aromas in marsh (lat. 36°52'50" N, long. 121°44'30" W). Named on Watsonville East (1955) 7.5' quadrangle.

Wash: see **The Wash** [SAN LUIS OBISPO].

Washington Flat [SAN LUIS OBISPO]: *valley*, 8 miles northeast of the town of Nipomo (lat. 35°08' N, long. 120°23'30" W). Named on Nipomo (1922) 15' quadrangle.

Wasibo: see **Camp Wasibo** [SANTA CRUZ].

Wasioja [SANTA BARBARA]: *locality*, 4.5 miles north-northwest of McPherson Peak (lat. 34°56'50" N, long. 119°50'30" W). Named on Santa Ynez (1905) 30' quadrangle. Postal authorities established Wasioja post office in 1893, moved it 2 miles west in 1898, moved it 1 mile northwest in 1901, moved it 8 miles east in 1902, and discontinued it in 1933; the name is from a place in Minnesota (Salley, p. 235).

Wasna Creek: see **Huasna River** [SAN LUIS OBISPO].

Water Canyon [SAN LUIS OBISPO]: *canyon*, drained by a stream that flow nearly 3 miles to Trout Creek (1) 2.5 miles north-northwest of Lopez Mountain (lat. 35°20'20" N, long. 120°35'10" W; near S line sec. 4, T 30 S, R 13 E). Named on Lopez Mountain (1965) 7.5' quadrangle.

Water Canyon [SANTA BARBARA]:

(1) *canyon*, drained by a stream that flows 6.5 miles to Sisquoc River 2 miles north-northwest of Bald Mountain (1) (lat. 34°50'25" N, long. 119°56'35" W). Named on Bald Mountain (1964) and Bates Canyon (1964) 7.5' quadrangles. Called Wellman Canyon on Santa Ynez (1905) 30' quadrangle.

(2) *canyon*, drained by a stream that flows 2.25 miles to the sea 2.5 miles south of Tranquillon Mountain (lat. 34°32'35" N, long. 120° 33'35" W). Named on Tranquillon Mountain (1959) 7.5' quadrangle.

Water Canyon Campground [SANTA BARBARA]: *locality*, about 2.25 miles north of Bald Mountain (1) along Sisquoc River (lat. 34°50'40" N, long. 119°56'30" W); the place is near the mouth of Water Canyon (1). Named on Bald Mountain (1964) 7.5' quadrangle.

Waterdog Creek [MONTEREY]: *stream*, flows nearly 4 miles to Nacimiento River 12 miles south-southeast of Jolon (lat. 35°47'45" N, long. 121°06'15" W; sec. 33, T 24 S, R 8 E). Named on Bryson (1949) and Burnett Peak (1949) 7.5' quadrangles.

Waterman Gap [SANTA CRUZ]: *pass*, 4.5 miles northeast of Big Basin (lat. 37°12'40" N, long. 122°09'20" W; sec. 26, T 8 S, R 3 W). Named on Big Basin (1955) 7.5' quadrangle.

Waterman Switch: see **San Lorenzo Park** [SANTA CRUZ].

Watson Creek [MONTEREY]: *stream*, flows 6.5 miles to El Toro Creek 9.5 miles south-southwest of Salinas (lat. 36°33' N, long. 121°43'55" W); the stream drains Corral de Tierra Valley. Named on Spreckels (1947) 7.5' quadrangle.

Watsonville [SANTA CRUZ]: *town*, 15 miles east-southeast of Santa Cruz on the northwest side of Pajaro River (lat. 36°54'55" N, long. 121°45'10" W). Named on Watsonville East (1955) and Watsonville West (1954) 7.5' quadrangles. J.H. Watson and D.S. Gregory laid out the town in 1852 (Bancroft, p. 525). Postal authorities established Watsonville post office in 1853 (Frickstad, p. 177), and the town incorporated in 1868. Lewis (1976, p. 163) noted that a dam on Pajaro River at Watsonville formed a lake in 1907 that first was called Lake Pajaro and later was called Lake Watsonville.

Watsonville: see **Lake Watsonville**, under **Watsonville** [SANTA CRUZ]; **Port Watsonville** [SANTA CRUZ].

Watsonville Junction [MONTEREY]: *locality*, 5.5 miles west of Aromas along Southern Pacific Railroad, where the line to Watsonville branches from the main line (lat. 36°53'40" N, long. 121°44'40" W). Named on

Watsonville East (1955) 7.5' quadrangle. The place first was called Pajaro (Clark, 1991, p. 601).

Watsonville Slough [SANTA CRUZ]: *stream,* flows 7.25 miles, mainly in an artificial watercourse, to Pajaro River 5.5 miles southwest of Watsonville (lat. 36°51'10" N, long. 121°58'30" W). Named on Moss Landing (1954) and Watsonville West (1954) 7.5' quadrangles.

Wave [SANTA BARBARA]: *locality,* 1 mile northwest of Rincon Point along Southern Pacific Railroad (lat. 34°22'55" N, long. 119° 29'15" W). Named on White Ledge Peak (1952) 7.5' quadrangle.

Wayland Creek [MONTEREY]: *stream,* flows 4.5 miles to Big Sandy Creek 4.25 miles south of Smith Mountain (lat. 36°01' N, long. 120°35'25" W; sec. 17, T 22 S, R 13 E). Named on Smith Mountain (1969) 7.5' quadrangle. The name is from members of the Wayland family, landowners in the neighborhood (Clark, 1991, p. 602). California Mining Bureau's (1917b) map shows a place called Hill situated near the confluence of Wayland Creek and Big Sandy Creek along the railroad that follows Big Sandy Creek to Stone Canyon.

Weferling Canyon [MONTEREY]: *canyon,* 3 miles long, opens into lowlands nearly 6 miles east of Jolon (lat. 35°57'55" N, long. 121° 04'30" W; near W line sec. 2, T 23 S, R 8 E). Named on Williams Hill (1949) 7.5' quadrangle. The name commemorates William Weferling, who claimed 160 acres at Lockwood in the 1880's (Clark, 1991, p. 602).

Welby [MONTEREY]: *locality,* 3.5 miles east-southeast of King City along Southern Pacific Railroad (lat. 36°11'20" N, long. 121°04'15" W). Named on San Lucas (1949) 7.5' quadrangle.

Welch Ridge [MONTEREY]: *ridge,* northwest-trending, 0.5 mile long, 3.25 miles south of Marina (lat. 36°38'10" N, long. 121° 48' W). Named on Marina (1947) 7.5' quadrangle.

Wellman Canyon [SANTA BARBARA]: *canyon,* drained by a stream that flows 6.25 miles to Sisquoc River nearly 2 miles north-northeast of Bald Mountain (1) (lat. 34°50'10" N, long. 119°55'15" W). Named on Bald Mountain (1964), Bates Canyon (1964), and Peak Mountain (1964) 7.5' quadrangles.

Wellman Canyon: see **Water Canyon** [SANTA BARBARA] (1).

Wells Canyon [SAN LUIS OBISPO]: *canyon,* drained by a stream that flows 3 miles to Cuyama Valley 3 miles north-northeast of New Cuyama [SANTA BARBARA] (lat. 34°59'10" N, long. 119°40'05" W; sec. 4, T 10 N, R 26 W). Named on New Cuyama (1964) 7.5' quadrangle.

Wells Creek [SANTA BARBARA]: *stream,* flows 4.25 miles to Aliso Canyon (1) 5.5 miles north-northeast of McPherson Peak (lat. 34° 57'45" N, long. 119°46'30" W). Named on Peak Mountain (1964) 7.5' quadrangle. United States Board on Geographic Names (1965c, p. 13) rejected the name "Messenger Canyon" for the feature.

Wells Creek: see **Coyote Gulch** [SANTA BARBARA].

Wellsonia [SAN LUIS OBISPO]: *locality,* 4.5 miles north of Paso Robles (lat. 35°41'50" N, long. 120°41'35" W; sec. 4, 5, T 26 S, R 12 E). Named on Paso Robles (1948) 7.5' quadrangle. Paso Robles (1919) 15' quadrangle shows the place along Southern Pacific Railroad. Postal authorities established Wellsona post office in 1898 and discontinued it the same year (Salley, p. 236).

Wells Spring [SAN LUIS OBISPO]: *spring,* 28 miles southeast of Simmler (lat. 35°01'55" N, long. 119°41' W; near NW cor. sec. 20, T 11 N, R 26 W). Named on Wells Ranch (1954) 7.5' quadrangle.

Wescott Shoal: see **Castle Rock** [SANTA BARBARA].

Weser Spur [SANTA BARBARA]: *locality,* 1.5 miles south of Surf along Southern Pacific Railroad (lat. 34°39'40" N, long. 120°36'35" W). Named on Surf (1947) 7.5' quadrangle.

West Beach [SANTA BARBARA]: *beach,* 1.25 miles south of downtown Santa Barbara along the coast (lat. 34°24'05" N, long. 119°41'55" W). Named on Santa Barbara (1952) 7.5' quadrangle.

West Branciforte Creek: see **Carbonera Creek** [SANTA CRUZ].

West Browns Creek: see **Carbonera Creek** [SANTA CRUZ].

West Canyon [SANTA BARBARA]: *canyon,* drained by a stream that flows less than 0.5 mile to Windmill Canyon 4 miles east-northeast of McPherson Peak (lat. 34°54'45" N, long. 119°45' W; near N line sec. 34, T 10 N, R 27 W). Named on Peak Mountain (1964) 7.5' quadrangle.

West Corral de Piedra Creek [SAN LUIS OBISPO]: *stream,* flows 7 miles to join East Corral de Piedra Creek and form Pismo Creek nearly 0.5 mile south-southeast of Edna (lat. 35°11'50" N, long. 120°36'35" W); the stream is on Corral de Piedra grant. Named on Arroyo Grande NE (1965) and Lopez Mountain (1965) 7.5' quadrangles.

Westdahl Rock [SAN LUIS OBISPO]: *shoal,* 1.5 miles southwest of Point San Luis, and 1.5 miles offshore (lat. 35°08'50" N, long. 120° 46'55" W). Named on Port San Luis (1965) 7.5' quadrangle.

West Liddell Creek [SANTA CRUZ]: *stream,* flows 2.5 miles to Liddell Creek 1 mile east-southeast of Davenport (lat. 37°00'10" N, long. 122°10'35" W). Named on Davenport (1955) 7.5' quadrangle.

Weston Beach: see **Sand Hill Cove** [MONTEREY].

West Point [SANTA BARBARA]: *promontory,* 1.25 miles north-northeast of Fraser Point at the west end of Santa Cruz Island (lat. 34°04'40" N, long. 119°55'05" W). Named on Santa Cruz Island A (1943) 7.5' quadrangle.

West Point: see **Sandy Point** [SANTA BARBARA].

West Rock: see **Wilson Rock**, under **Harris Point** [SANTA BARBARA].

West Tuley Springs [SAN LUIS OBISPO]: *springs,* two, 400 feet apart, 5.5 miles northwest of Shandon (lat. 35°43'10" N, long. 120° 25'55" W; sec. 26, T 25 S, R 14 E); the springs are 0.5 mile west of East Tuley Springs. Named on Shandon (1961) 7.5' quadrangle.

West Waddell Creek [SANTA CRUZ]: *stream,* heads just inside San Mateo County and flows 6 miles to join East Waddell Creek and form Waddell Creek 2.5 miles north-northeast of the mouth of Waddell Creek (lat. 36°08' N, long. 122°16' W; near S line sec. 23, T 9 S, R 4 W). Named on Big Basin (1955) and Franklin Point (1955) 7.5' quadrangles.

Weyland Camp [MONTEREY]: *locality,* 2.5 miles east-northeast of Pfeiffer Point along Big Sur River (lat. 36°14'40" N, long. 121°46'20" W; near SW cor. sec. 29, T 19 S, R 2 E). Named on Pfeiffer Point (1956) 7.5' quadrangle. The misspelled name commemorates Dr. Charles Wayland, who started a private campground at the place in 1906 (Clark, 1991, p. 601).

Whaleboat Rock: see **Bird Rock** [MONTEREY] (2).

Whaler Island: see **Whalers Island** [SAN LUIS OBISPO].

Whale Rock [SAN LUIS OBISPO]: *rock,* 3 miles east-southeast of Cayucos Point, and 650 feet offshore (lat. 35°26'05" N, long. 120° 53'30" W). Named on Cayucos (1965) 7.5' quadrangle.

Whale Rock Reservoir [SAN LUIS OBISPO]: *lake,* 2.25 miles long, behind a dam on Old Creek 0.5 mile east-northeast of Cayucos (lat. 35°26'50" N, long. 120°53'05" W); the mouth of Old Creek is near Whale Rock. Named on Cayucos (1965) and Morro Bay North (1965) 7.5' quadrangles.

Whalers Cove: see **Carmel Cove** [MONTEREY].

Whalers Island [SAN LUIS OBISPO]: *island,* 300 feet long, 500 feet offshore at Point San Luis (lat. 35°09'35" N, long. 120°45'15" W). Named on Port San Luis (1965) 7.5' quadrangle, which shows a breakwater connecting the feature to shore. Called Whaler Id. on Port Harford (1897) 15' quadrangle, but United States Board on Geographic Names (1991, p. 7) rejected this form of the name. The place was known as Whaler's Island about 1887 because of a short-lived whaling station there that employed 29 men (Lee and others, p. 123).

Whalers Knoll [MONTEREY]: *hill,* 0.25 mile east of Point Lobos on the south side of Carmel Bay (lat. 36°31'15" N, long. 121°56'45" W). Named on Monterey (1947) 7.5' quadrangle. Whalers in the 1880's used the hill to sight whales (Clark, 1991, p. 605).

Whalers Rock: see **Seal Rocks** [MONTEREY].

Wheat Peak [SANTA BARBARA]: *peak,* 3 miles west-northwest of Bald Mountain (1) (lat. 34°49'55" N, long. 119°59' W). Altitude 2436 feet. Named on Bald Mountain (1964) 7.5' quadrangle. Hiram Preserved Wheat homesteaded near Sisquoc River in 1885 (Rife, p. 110).

Whiskey Hill: see **Freedom** [SANTA CRUZ].

Whiskey Spring [SAN LUIS OBISPO]: *spring,* 6 miles north-northwest of San Luis Obispo (lat. 35°21'45" N, long. 120°41'45" W; sec. 33, T 29 S, R 12 E). Named on San Luis Obispo (1965) 7.5' quadrangle.

White Canyon [SAN LUIS OBISPO]: *canyon,* drained by a stream that flows 5.5 miles to Cholame Creek 1 mile south-southwest of Cholame (lat. 35°42'35" N, long. 120°18'15" W; sec. 36, T 25 S, R 15 E). Named on Cholame (1961) and Cholame Valley (1961) 7.5' quadrangles.

White Hills [SANTA BARBARA]: *range,* 2.5 miles south-southeast of the city of Lompoc (lat. 34°36'15" N, long. 120°26' W). Named on Lompoc Hills (1959) 7.5' quadrangle. White strata are conspicuous in the range.

White Hills Siding [SANTA BARBARA]: *locality,* near the east edge of the city of Lompoc along Southern Pacific Railroad (lat. 34°38'35" N, long. 120°26'45" W). Named on Lompoc (1959) 7.5' quadrangle.

Whitehouse Camp [SANTA CRUZ]: *locality,* 5.5 miles north-northwest of the mouth of Waddell Creek (lat. 37°10'10" N, long. 122° 18'15" W); the place is along Whitehouse Creek. Named on Año Nuevo (1943) 15' quadrangle.

Whitehouse Creek [SANTA CRUZ]: *stream,* flows nearly 2 miles to San Mateo County 5.5 miles north-northwest of the mouth of Waddell Creek (lat. 37°10'15" N, long. 122°18'50" W; sec. 9, T 9 S, R 4 W). Named on Franklin Point (1955) 7.5' quadrangle. The name is for a white prefabricated building that was shipped around the Horn and erected near the stream in 1852; the creek was called Arroyo de Soto in the 1840's for Eugenio Soto, who lived near it, and later it had the Spanish name "Arroyo de la Casa Blanca" (Brown, p. 100-101; Brown used the form "White House Creek" for the name).

White Lake [SAN LUIS OBISPO]: *lake,* 3000 feet long, 4 miles south-southwest of downtown Arroyo Grande near the coast (lat. 35°03'55" N, long. 120°36'30" W). Named on Oceano (1965) 7.5' quadrangle.

White Lake: see **Kelly Lake** [SANTA CRUZ].

White Ledge Canyon [SANTA BARBARA]: *canyon,* drained by a stream that flows nearly 5 miles to South Fork Sisquoc River 5.5 miles south-southwest of Montgomery Potrero (lat. 34°45'25" N, long. 119°46'40" W). Named on Hurricane Deck (1964) 7.5' quadrangle.

White Oaks Camp [MONTEREY]: *locality,* 3 miles south-southeast of

Jamesburg (lat. 36°19'35" N, long. 121°34'25" W; near NW cor. sec. 32, T 18 S, R 4 E). Named on Chews Ridge (1956) 7.5' quadrangle.

White Point [SAN LUIS OBISPO]: *promontory,* 2 miles southeast of Morro Rock on the east side of Morro Bay (lat. 35°20'50" N, long. 120°50'35" W). Named on Morro Bay South (1965) 7.5' quadrangle.

White Rock [SAN LUIS OBISPO]:
(1) *rock,* 2.25 miles south of Cambria, and 750 feet offshore (lat. 35°32' N, long. 121°05'15" W). Named on Cambria (1959) 7.5' quadrangle.
(2) *rock,* 100 feet long, 1.5 miles southeast of Avila Beach in San Luis Obispo Bay, and nearly 1 mile offshore (lat. 35°09'50" N, long. 120°42'30" W). Named on Pismo Beach (1965) 7.5' quadrangle.

White Rock [SANTA CRUZ]: *relief feature,* 5.5 miles east-northeast of the town of Boulder Creek (lat. 37°09'20" N, long. 122°01'35" W). Named on Castle Rock Ridge (1955) 7.5' quadrangle.

White Rock: see **White Rock Number 1** [MONTEREY].

Whiterock Bluff [SAN LUIS OBISPO]: *escarpment,* 4 miles west-southwest of Caliente Mountain on the north side of Cuyama Valley (lat. 35°00'30" N, long. 119°49'15" W; sec. 25, T 11 N, R 28 W). Named on Caliente Mountain (1959) 7.5' quadrangle.

White Rock Canyon [SANTA BARBARA]: *canyon,* drained by a stream that flows 2 miles to Fish Creek 3.25 miles east of Figueroa Mountain (lat. 34°44'20" N, long. 119°55'35" W; sec. 27, T 8 N, R 29 W). Named on Figueroa Mountain (1959) 7.5' quadrangle.

White Rock Lake [MONTEREY]: *lake,* 700 feet long, 10 miles northeast of Point Sur (lat. 36°24'40" N, long. 121°46'20" W; sec. 32, T 17 S, R 2 E); the lake is at the east end of White Rock Ridge. Named on Mount Carmel (1956) 7.5' quadrangle.

White Rock Number 1 [MONTEREY]: *rock,* 7.5 miles southeast of Cape San Martin, and 2200 feet offshore (lat. 35°48'25" N, long. 121°22'35" W). Named on Cape San Martin (1921) 15' quadrangle. Called White Rock on Cape San Martin (1949) 15' quadrangle.

White Rock Number 2 [MONTEREY]: *rock,* 5.5 miles southeast of Cape San Martin, and 200 feet offshore (lat. 35°49'55" N, long. 121°23'50" W). Named on Cape San Martin (1921) 15' quadrangle.

White Rock Ridge [MONTEREY]: *ridge,* east-trending, 3 miles long, 9 miles north-northeast of Point Sur (lat. 36°25' N, long. 121°48'30" W). Named on Mount Carmel (1956) 7.5' quadrangle.

White's [SAN LUIS OBISPO]: *locality,* 18 miles southeast of Simmler in Elkhorn Plain (lat. 35°11'50" N, long. 119°42'50" W; sec. 27, T 31 S, R 21 E). Named on McKittrick (1912) 30' quadrangle. California Mining Bureau's (1917c) map has the form "Whites" for the name.

Whites Lagoon [SANTA CRUZ]: *lake,* 500 feet long, 6 miles northeast of Soquel on China Ridge (lat. 37°02'50" N, long. 121°52'40" W). Named on Laurel (1955) 7.5' quadrangle.

White Spring [SAN LUIS OBISPO]: *spring,* 2.5 miles west of Cholame (lat. 35°43'50" N, long. 120°20'20" W; sec. 27, T 25 S, R 15 E). Named on Cholame (1961) 7.5' quadrangle.

White Sulphur Springs: see **Chittenden's Sulphur Springs**, under **Chittenden** [SANTA CRUZ].

White Well [SAN LUIS OBISPO]: *well,* 2.5 miles west of Cholame (lat. 35°43'35" N, long. 120°20'20" W; sec. 27, T 25 S, R 15 E). Named on Cholame (1961) 7.5' quadrangle.

Whitley Gardens [SAN LUIS OBISPO]: *settlement,* 11 miles east of Paso Robles (lat. 35°39'30" N, long. 120°30'15" W). Named on Estrella (1948) and Shandon (1961) 7.5' quadrangles.

Whoop Canyon [SANTA BARBARA]: *canyon,* drained by a stream that flows 2 miles to Foxen Canyon 7 miles south of Tepusquet Peak (lat. 34°48'40" N, long. 120°12'35" W). Named on Foxen Canyon (1964) 7.5' quadrangle.

Wickham: see **Los Alamos** [SANTA BARBARA] (2).

Wigmore: see **Los Alamos** [SANTA BARBARA] (2).

Wilcox Canyon [SAN LUIS OBISPO]: *canyon,* drained by a stream that flows 2 miles to Branch Creek 4.5 miles southwest of Branch Mountain (lat. 35°08'20" N, long. 120°08'40" W). Named on Los Machos Hills (1967) 7.5' quadrangle.

Wildcat Canyon [MONTEREY]:
(1) *canyon,* drained by a stream that flows 1 mile to Impossible Canyon 5.5 miles east of Seaside (lat. 36°37'05" N, long. 121°45'10" W); the canyon is north and west of Wildcat Ridge. Named on Seaside (1947) 7.5' quadrangle.
(2) *canyon,* drained by a stream that flows nearly 4 miles to Garrapata Creek 4 miles southeast of Soberanes Point (lat. 36°24'15" N, long. 121°53'05" W; sec. 32, T 17 S, R 1 E). Named on Mount Carmel (1956) and Soberanes Point (1956) 7.5' quadrangles.
(3) *canyon,* 4 miles long, opens into lowlands 6.25 miles east of Jolon (lat. 35°57'15" N, long. 121°04'15" W; sec. 2, T 23 S, R 8 E). Named on Williams Hill (1949) 7.5' quadrangle.

Wildcat Canyon [SAN BENITO]: *canyon,* drained by a stream that flows 2 miles to Santa Clara County nearly 2 miles west of Mariposa Peak (lat. 36°57'35" N, long. 121°14'30" W; sec. 19, T 11 S, R 7 E). Named on Mariposa Peak (1969) 7.5' quadrangle.

Wildcat Creek [MONTEREY]: *stream,* flows 1.5 miles to the sea 3.5 miles north of Soberanes Point (lat. 36°29'50" N, long. 121°56'10" W). Named on Soberanes Point (1956) 7.5' quadrangle.

Wildcat Ridge [MONTEREY]: *ridge,* north-trending, 1.25 miles long, 7 miles southwest of Salinas (lat. 36°36'20" N, long. 121° 45' W). Named on Seaside (1947) and Spreckels (1947) 7.5' quadrangles.

Wild Cattle Creek [MONTEREY]: *stream,* flows nearly 2 miles to the sea 5.5 miles north-northwest of Cape San Martin (lat. 35°58'05" N, long. 121°29'05" W; near N line sec. 1, T 23 S, R 4 E). Named on Cape San Martin (1949) 7.5' quadrangle. United States Board on Geographic Names (1978b, p. 6) rejected the name "Wild Creek" for the stream.

Wild Cherry Canyon [SAN LUIS OBISPO]: *canyon,* drained by a stream that flows 3 miles to the sea nearly 1 mile west of Avila Beach (lat. 35°10'40" N, long. 120°44'45" W). Named on Pismo Beach (1965) and Port San Luis (1965) 7.5' quadrangles.

Wild Creek: see **Wild Cattle Creek** [MONTEREY].

Wilder Beach: see **Wilder Creek** [SANTA CRUZ].

Wilder Creek [SANTA CRUZ]: *stream,* flows 5 miles to the sea 3 miles west of Point Santa Cruz (lat. 36°57'10" N, long. 122°04'35" W). Named on Felton (1955) and Santa Cruz (1954) 7.5' quadrangles. The name commemorates the Wilder family, owners of land along the stream, which also was called Bolcoff Creek and Meder Creek for earlier owners of land along it; the creek reaches the sea at Wilder Beach (Clark, 1986, p. 402). Hubbard's (1943) map shows a place called Wilder Spur located along the railroad nearly 1 mile west of present Wilder Creek. California Mining Bureau's (1917a) map shows a place called Wilders situated along the coast, apparently just east of the mouth of present Wilder Creek.

Wilders: see **Wilder Creek** [SANTA CRUZ].

Wilder Spur: see **Wilder Creek** [SANTA CRUZ].

Wild Hog Creek [SAN LUIS OBISPO]: *stream,* flows nearly 3 miles to San Juan Creek 3.25 miles northeast of Branch Mountain (lat. 35°13'15" N, long. 120°02'40" W; at N line sec. 21, T 31 S, R 18 E). Named on Branch Mountain (1967) 7.5' quadrangle.

Wild Horse Canyon [SAN LUIS OBISPO]: *canyon,* drained by a stream that flows nearly 6 miles to Freeman Canyon 12 miles east-northeast of Paso Robles (lat. 35°43'20" N, long. 120°30'40" W; sec. 30, T 25 S, R 14 E). Named on Cholame Hills (1961) and Shandon (1961) 7.5' quadrangles. Estrella (1948) 7.5' quadrangle has the form "Wildhorse Canyon" for the name.

Wildhorse Canyon [MONTEREY]: *canyon,* 10 miles long, opens into lowlands 4 miles north-northwest of San Lucas (lat. 36°11'15" N, long. 121°02'30" W; sec. 18, T 20 S, R 9 E). Named on Nattrass Valley (1967) and San Lucas (1949) 7.5' quadrangle.

Wildhorse Canyon [SAN BENITO]: *canyon,* drained by a stream that flows 6 miles to Chalone Creek 3.5 miles southeast of North Chalone Peak (lat. 36°24'40" N, long. 121°08'50" W; sec. 31, T 17 S, R 8 E). Named on North Chalone Peak (1969) and Topo Valley (1969) 7.5' quadrangles.

Wildhorse Canyon [SANTA BARBARA]: *canyon,* drained by a stream that flows 4 miles to Sisquoc River 5 miles north-northwest of Zaca Lake (lat. 34°50'45" N, long. 120°04'15" W). Named on Zaca Lake (1964) 7.5' quadrangle.

Wild Horse Flat [SANTA BARBARA]: *area,* 1.5 miles west of Tranquillon Mountain (lat. 34°35'05" N, long. 120°35'25" W); the place is 0.25 mile west-southwest of Wild Horse Peak. Named on Tranquillon Mountain (1959) 7.5' quadrangle.

Wild Horse Peak [SANTA BARBARA]: *peak,* 1.5 miles west of Tranquillon Mountain (lat. 34°35'10" N, long. 120°35'05" W). Named on Tranquillon Mountain (1959) 7.5' quadrangle.

Wild Horse Spring [SAN LUIS OBISPO]: *spring,* 7 miles north of Pozo (lat. 35°24'10" N, long. 120°21'25" W; sec. 15, T 29 S, R 15 E). Named on Camatta Ranch (1966) 7.5' quadrangle.

Wild Oat Creek [SAN BENITO]: *stream,* flows 1.25 miles to Mine Creek 6.5 miles northeast of Bitterwater (lat. 36°26' N, long. 120° 54' W; sec. 20, T 17 S, R 10 E); the stream heads at Wild Oat Springs. Named on Rock Spring Peak (1969) 7.5' quadrangle.

Wild Oat Peak [SAN BENITO]: *peak,* 8 miles northeast of Bitterwater (lat. 36°27'10" N, long. 120°53'35" W; sec. 16, T 17 S, R 10 E). Altitude 3992 feet. Named on Rock Spring Peak (1969) 7.5' quadrangle.

Wild Oat Springs [SAN BENITO]: *springs,* 7.5 miles northeast of Bitterwater (lat. 36°27' N, long. 120°53'50" W; on W line sec. 16, T 17 S, R 10 E); the springs are 0.25 mile southwest of Wild Oat Peak at the head of Wild Oat Creek. Named on Rock Spring Peak (1969) 7.5' quadrangle.

Wildwood [SANTA CRUZ]: *settlement,* 5 miles east-southeast of Big Basin near San Lorenzo River (lat. 37°09'05" N, long. 122°08'05" W; near E line sec. 13, T 9 S, R 3 W). Named on Big Basin (1955) 7.5' quadrangle.

Wilkins Canyon [MONTEREY]: *canyon,* drained by a stream that flows 1.5 miles to Quinado Canyon 7.5 miles south of King City (lat. 36°06'10" N, long. 121°08'40" W; sec. 18, T 21 S, R 8 E). Named on Cosio Knob (1949) 7.5' quadrangle. The name commemorates Edward H. Wilkins, who received a patent for land at the canyon in 1892 (Clark, 1991, p. 608).

Wilkinson Canyon [SAN LUIS OBISPO]: *canyon,* drained by a stream that flows nearly 5 miles to San Juan Valley 13 miles southeast of Shandon (lat. 35°31'25" N, long. 120°12'35" W; near W line sec. 1, T 28 S, R 16 E). Named on Holland Canyon (1961) 7.5' quadrangle.

Williams Canyon [MONTEREY]:

(1) *canyon*, drained by a stream that flows 2.5 miles to San Jose Creek 4.5 miles east-northeast of Soberanes Point (lat. 36°28'50" N, long. 121°51'20" W; sec. 4, T 17 S, R 1 E). Named on Mount Carmel (1956) 7.5' quadrangle. The name commemorates Shadrack Williams, who received a patent on land at the head of the canyon in 1904 (Clark, 1991, p. 609).

(2) *canyon*, 3 miles long, opens into lowlands 9 miles east-southeast of Jolon (lat. 35°55'35" N, long. 121°01'55" W; sec. 18, T 23 S, R 9 E); the canyon heads near Williams Hill. Named on Williams Hill (1949) 7.5' quadrangle. The name commemorates Wait Williams, who had a homestead in the canyon (Clark, 1991, p. 609).

Williams Creek: see **Pancho Rico Creek** [MONTEREY].

Williams Hill [MONTEREY]: *peak*, 10 miles east of Jolon (lat. 35° 57'05" N, long. 121°00'05" W; near S line sec. 4, T 23 S, R 9 E). Named on Williams Hill (1949) 7.5' quadrangle. The name is from Williams Canyon (2) (Clark, 1991, p. 609).

Williams Hollow [SAN BENITO]: *canyon*, drained by a stream that flows 2.5 miles to San Benito River 8 miles south of Idria (lat. 36° 17'55" N, long. 120°41'35" W; near SE cor. sec. 6, T 19 S, R 12 E). Named on San Benito Mountain (1969) 7.5' quadrangle.

Williams Landing: see **San Vicente Creek** [SANTA CRUZ].

Williams Mountain [SAN BENITO]: *peak*, 11 miles south-southwest of Idria (lat. 36°15'55" N, long. 120°44'30" W; sec. 23, T 19 S, R 11 E). Altitude 4124 feet. Named on San Benito Mountain (1969) 7.5' quadrangle.

Williamson Spring [SAN LUIS OBISPO]: *spring*, 9 miles east-southeast of Shandon (lat. 35°36'10" N, long. 120°13'45" W; near E line sec. 3, T 27 S, R 16 E). Named on Holland Canyon (1961) 7.5' quadrangle

Williamson Valley [SAN BENITO]: *valley*, 5 miles south-southeast of Mount Johnson (lat. 36°32'30" N, long. 121°17'15" W). Named on Mount Johnson (1968) 7.5' quadrangle.

Willow Campground [SANTA BARBARA]: *locality*, 3 miles south-southeast of Fox Mountain in Santa Barbara Canyon (lat. 34°46'30" N, long. 119°34'20" W). Named on Fox Mountain (1964) 7.5' quadrangle.

Willow Canyon [SAN LUIS OBISPO]: *canyon*, 0.5 mile long, opens into the canyon of San Juan Creek 4 miles northeast of Castle Crags (lat. 35°20'25" N, long. 120°08'50" W; near E line sec. 4, T 30 S, R 17 E). Named on La Panza (1967) 7.5' quadrangle. The canyon divides at the head into North Fork and South Fork. North Fork is 5.25 miles long and South Fork is nearly 4 miles long; both forks are named on La Panza (1967) 7.5' quadrangle. United States Board on Geographic Names (1968c, p. 6, 7) rejected the name "Hay Canyon" for Willow Canyon, North Fork Willow Canyon, and South Fork Willow Canyon; the Board also rejected the name "Willow Canyon" for North Fork Willow Canyon.

Willow Creek [MONTEREY]:

(1) *stream*, flows 3 miles to Tassajara Creek nearly 2 miles southeast of Tassajara Hot Springs (lat. 36°12'55" N, long. 121°31'45" W; near SE cor. sec. 4, T 20 S, R 4 E). Named on Tassajara Hot Springs (1956) 7.5' quadrangle.

(2) *stream*, flows 6 miles to the sea nearly 0.5 mile north-northeast of Cape San Martin (lat. 35°53'35" N, long. 121°27'40" W; sec. 31, T 23 S, R 5 E). Named on Cape San Martin (1949) 7.5' quadrangle. North Fork enters from the northeast nearly 3 miles upstream from the mouth of the main stream, and is 4.25 miles long. South Fork enters from the southeast 1 mile upstream from the mouth of the main stream, and is 3.5 miles long. Both forks are named on Cape San Martin (1949) 7.5' quadrangle.

Willow Creek [SAN BENITO]: *stream*, flows 10 miles to San Benito River 9 miles northwest of San Benito (lat. 36°35'50" N, long. 121° 11'30" W; sec. 27, T 15 S, R 7 E). Named on Bickmore Canyon (1968) and Mount Johnson (1968) 7.5' quadrangles. South Fork enters from the south 1.25 miles upstream from the mouth of the main creek; it is 8 miles long and is named on Bickmore Canyon (1968) and Mount Johnson (1968) 7.5' quadrangles.

Willow Creek [SAN LUIS OBISPO]:

(1) *stream*, flows 4.25 miles to the sea 3.5 miles east-southeast of Cayucos Point (lat. 35°25'40" N, long. 120°52'55" W). Named on Cayucos (1965) and Morro Bay North (1965) 7.5' quadrangles.

(2) *stream*, flows nearly 5 miles to Paso Robles Creek 3.25 miles east of York Mountain (lat. 35°33'05" N, long. 120°46'25" W). Named on York Mountain (1948) 7.5' quadrangle.

Willow Creek Camp [MONTEREY]: *locality*, 2 miles south-southwest of Tassajara Hot Springs (lat. 36°12'25" N, long. 121°33'25" W; sec. 8, T 20 S, R 4 E); the place is along Willow Creek (1). Named on Tassajara Hot Springs (1956) 7.5' quadrangle.

Willow Creek Peak [SAN BENITO]: *peak*, 9.5 miles northwest of San Benito (lat. 36°35'10" N, long. 121°13'15" W; sec. 32, T 15 S, R 7 E); the peak is less than 1 mile southwest of the confluence of Willow Creek and South Fork Willow Creek. Altitude 2437 feet. Named on Bickmore Canyon (1968) 7.5' quadrangle.

Willow Lake [SAN LUIS OBISPO]: *lake*, 550 feet long, 3.5 miles south-southwest of downtown Arroyo Grande near the coast (lat. 35°04'45" N, long. 120°36'50" W). Named on Oceano (1965) 7.5' quadrangle. On Arroyo Grande (1952) 15' quadrangle, this lake, a nearby lake, and some associated marsh have the name "Willow Lake."

Willows: see **The Willows** [SANTA CRUZ].

Willows Anchorage [SANTA BARBARA]: *embayment*, 4 miles east of Punta Arena on the south side of Santa Cruz Island (lat. 33°57'45" N, long. 119°44'50" W). Named on Santa Cruz Island B (1943) 7.5' quadrangle. Bremner's (1932) map has the name "Cñ. las Sauces de los Colorados" for a canyon that opens to the sea at the west edge of present Willows Anchorage. Rand's (1931) map has the name "Los Sauces" at present Willows Anchorage.

Willow Spring [MONTEREY]:

(1) *spring*, 10 miles north-northwest of Charley Mountain (lat. 36° 16'45" N, long. 120°42'45" W; sec. 13, T 19 S, R 11 E). Named on San Benito Mountain (1969) 7.5' quadrangle.

(2) *spring*, 6.25 miles south-southwest of Parkfield (lat. 35°48'45" N, long. 120°27'55" W; sec. 28, T 24 S, R 14 E); the spring is in a branch of Willow Springs Canyon. Named on Cholame Hills (1961) 7.5' quadrangle.

(3) *spring*, 8.5 miles east-southeast of Parkfield (lat. 35°52'05" N, long. 120°17' W; sec. 6, T 24 S, R 16 E). Named on Cholame Valley (1961) 7.5' quadrangle. Called Sulphur Springs on Cholame Ranch (1943) 7.5' quadrangle, but United States Board on Geographic Names (1963a, p. 7) rejected this name.

Willow Spring [SAN BENITO]:

(1) *spring*, 5.5 miles west of San Benito (lat. 36°30'35" N, long. 121°10'50" W; sec. 26, T 16 S, R 7 E). Named on Bickmore Canyon (1968) 7.5' quadrangle.

(2) *spring*, 7 miles north-northeast of Bitterwater (lat. 36°28'05" N, long. 120°56'10" W; near NW cor. sec. 7, T 17 S, R 10 E). Named on Rock Spring Peak (1969) 7.5' quadrangle.

(3) *spring*, 5.5 miles east-southeast of Bitterwater (lat. 36°20'25" N, long. 120°54'55" W; sec. 29, T 18 S, R 10 E). Named on Lonoak (1969) 7.5' quadrangle.

(4) *spring*, 7.5 miles south of Idria (lat. 36°18'20" N, long. 120°40'35" W; near E line sec. 5, T 19 S, R 12 E). Named on San Benito Mountain (1969) 7.5' quadrangle.

Willow Spring [SAN LUIS OBISPO]:

(1) *spring*, 4.5 miles west-southwest of Atascadero (2) (lat. 35°28'20" N, long. 120°44'35" W). Named on Atascadero (1965) 7.5' quadrangle.

(2) *spring*, 4.5 miles south of Wilson Corner (lat. 35°24'05" N, long. 120°22'20" W; sec. 16, T 29 S, R 15 E). Named on Camatta Ranch (1966) 7.5' quadrangle.

(3) *spring*, 18 miles northeast of Simmler (lat. 35°29'40" N, long. 120°08'50" W; sec. 16, T 28 S, R 17 E). Named on La Panza Ranch (1966) 7.5' quadrangle.

(4) *spring*, 3.5 miles north of Cuyama [SANTA BARBARA] (lat. 34° 59'10" N, long. 119°36'05" W; near NE cor. sec. 1, T 10 N, R 26 W). Named on Cuyama (1964) 7.5' quadrangle.

Willow Spring [SANTA BARBARA]:

(1) *spring*, nearly 6 miles west-northwest of Miranda Pine Mountain (lat. 35°03'35" N, long. 120°08' W). Named on Chimney Canyon (1967) 7.5' quadrangle.

(2) *spring*, 0.5 mile east-northeast of Figueroa Mountain (lat. 34° 44'50" N, long. 119°58'25" W; near N line sec. 30, T 8 N, R 29 W. Named on Figueroa Mountain (1959) 7.5' quadrangle. On McPherson Peak (1943) 15' quadrangle, the name applies to a spring situated nearly 0.5 mile farther north.

(3) *spring*, 3.5 miles northeast of Point Conception (lat. 34°28'30" N, long. 120°24'55" W). Named on Point Conception (1953) 7.5' quadrangle.

(4) *spring*, 3.5 miles north of San Marcos Pass (lat. 34°33'50" N, long. 119°50' W). Named on San Marcos Pass (1959) 7.5' quadrangle.

Willow Spring Canyon [SANTA BARBARA]: *canyon*, drained by a stream that flows 1 mile to Fir Canyon 4.5 miles south-southwest of Bald Mountain (1) (lat. 34°45'10" N, long. 119°57'55" W); Willow Spring (2) is in the canyon. Named on Bald Mountain (1964) and Figueroa Mountain (1959) 7.5' quadrangles.

Willow Spring Creek [SAN BENITO]: *stream*, flows nearly 2 miles to Tres Pinos Creek 2.5 miles northwest of Panoche Pass (lat. 36° 39'10" N, long. 121°02'35" W; sec. 1, T 15 S, R 8 E). Named on Panoche Pass (1968) 7.5' quadrangle.

Willow Springs Canyon [MONTEREY-SAN LUIS OBISPO]: *canyon*, drained by a stream that heads in Monterey County and flows 5.25 miles to Mason Canyon 9.5 miles northwest of Shandon in San Luis Obispo County (lat. 35°46'10" N, long. 120°28'50" W; near E line. sec. 8, T 25 S, R 14 E); Willow Spring [MONTEREY] (2) is in a branch of the canyon. Named on Cholame Hills (1961) 7.5' quadrangle. Called Mason Canyon on Cholame (1917) 30' quadrangle.

Wilson Canyon [SAN LUIS OBISPO]: *canyon,* drained by a stream that flows 3.5 miles to an unnamed valley 5.25 miles south-southwest of Wilson Corner (lat. 35°23'40" N, long. 120°24'25" W; sec. 18, T 29 S, R 15 E). Named on Camatta Ranch (1966) and Wilson Corner (1966) 7.5' quadrangles.

Wilson Corner [SAN LUIS OBISPO]: *locality,* 16 miles east of Atascadero (lat. 35°28'05" N, long. 120°22'40" W; near N line sec. 29, T 28 S, R 15 E). Named on Wilson Corner (1966) 7.5' quadrangle.

Wilson Gulch [SANTA CRUZ]: *canyon,* drained by a stream that flows 0.5 mile to the sea 1.25 miles northwest of the mouth of Waddell Creek at Santa Cruz-San Mateo County line (lat. 37°06'25" N, long. 122°17'30" W; sec. 34, T 9 S, R 4 W). Named on Año Nuevo (1955) 7.5' quadrangle.

Wilson Rock: see **Harris Point** [SANTA BARBARA].

Winchester Canyon [SANTA BARBARA]: *canyon,* drained by a stream that flows 3.5 miles to Bell Canyon 3 miles north-northwest of Coal Oil Point (lat. 34°26'30" N, long. 119°54'15" W). Named on Dos Pueblos Canyon (1951) 7.5' quadrangle. The name commemorates Dr. Robert Fulton Winchester, who lived in the canyon (Tompkins and Ruiz, p. 111).

Windmill Canyon [MONTEREY]: *canyon,* drained by a stream that flows nearly 2 miles to Chavoya Canyon 8 miles east-northeast of San Ardo (lat. 36°04'45" N, long. 120°46'35" W; sec. 27, T 21 S, R 11 E). Named on Pancho Rico Valley (1967) 7.5' quadrangle.

Windmill Canyon [SANTA BARBARA]: *canyon,* drained by a stream that flows 1.25 miles to Bitter Creek 3.5 miles southwest of New Cuyama (lat. 34°54'40" N, long. 119°44'10" W; near N line sec. 35, T 10 N, R 27 W). Named on New Cuyama (1964) and Peak Mountain (1964) 7.5' quadrangles.

Windmill Creek [SAN LUIS OBISPO]: *stream,* flows 3 miles to Navajo Creek 12 miles northeast of Pozo (lat. 35°25'35" N, long. 120°13'30" W; near S line sec. 2, T 29 S, R 16 E). Named on La Panza Ranch (1966) 7.5' quadrangle.

Windsor Canyon [SANTA BARBARA]: *canyon,* drained by a stream that flows 2.5 miles to Santa Ynez River 2.5 miles north-northwest of San Marcos Pass (lat. 34°32'45" N, long. 119°50'45" W). Named on San Marcos Pass (1959) 7.5' quadrangle.

Windy Point [SAN LUIS OBISPO]: *locality,* 3.25 miles east-northeast of the mouth of San Carpoforo Creek (lat. 35°46'55" N, long. 121° 16'20" W; sec. 1, T 25 S, R 6 E). Named on Burro Mountain (1949) 7.5' quadrangle.

Winter Creek: see **Archibald Creek** [SANTA CRUZ].

Wittenberg Creek [SAN LUIS OBISPO]: *stream,* flows nearly 6 miles to Arroyo Grande Creek 11 miles north of the town of Nipomo (lat. 35°11'45" N, long. 120°28'05" W; near W line sec. 27, T 31 S, R 14 E). Named on Santa Margarita Lake (1967) and Tar Spring Ridge (1967) 7.5' quadrangles.

Wizard Gulch [MONTEREY]: *canyon,* drained by a stream that flows nearly 5 miles to San Antonio River 6 miles south of Junipero Serra Peak (lat. 36°03'35" N, long. 121°23'50" W; sec. 35, T 21 S, R 5 E). Named on Bear Canyon (1949) and Cone Peak (1949) 7.5' quadrangles.

Wolf Canyon [SAN LUIS OBISPO]: *canyon,* drained by a stream that flows 6 miles to Clarke Canyon 7 miles west-northwest of Shandon (lat. 35°41'05" N, long. 120°29'40" W; sec. 8, T 26 S, R 14 E). Named on Shandon (1961) 7.5' quadrangle.

Wolf Hill [MONTEREY]: *hill,* 5.5 miles east-southeast of Seaside (lat. 36°35'15" N, long. 121°45'30" W). Named on Seaside (1947) 7.5' quadrangle.

Wolfort's [SAN LUIS OBISPO]: *locality,* nearly 4 miles east-northeast of Simmler at the southwest base of Temblor Range (lat. 35°22'40" N, long. 119°55'40" W; sec. 27, T 29 S, R 19 E). Named on McKittrick (1912) 30' quadrangle.

Wons Creek: see **San Lucas Creek** [SANTA BARBARA].

Wood Canyon [MONTEREY]: *canyon,* drained by a stream that flows nearly 1.25 miles to lowlands 13 miles southeast of Parkfield (lat. 35°47'25" N, long. 120°14'15" W; near SE cor. sec. 33, T 24 S, R 16 E). Named on Tent Hills (1942) 7.5' quadrangle.

Wood Canyon [SAN LUIS OBISPO]: *canyon,* drained by a stream that flows 6 miles to Estrella River 2.5 miles west of Shandon (lat. 35°39'15" N, long. 120°25'15" W; sec. 24, T 26 S, R 14 E). Named on Shandon (1961) and Shedd Canyon (1961) 7.5' quadrangles.

Wood Canyon [SANTA BARBARA]: *canyon,* drained by a stream that flows 3.5 miles to the sea 1.5 miles east of Point Conception (lat. 34°27'05" N, long. 120°26'30" W). Named on Point Conception (1953) 7.5' quadrangle.

Woods Creek: see **Sapaque Creek** [MONTEREY-SAN LUIS OBISPO].

Woods Lagoon [SANTA CRUZ]: *lake,* nearly 1 mile long, 1.5 miles northeast of Point Santa Cruz near the coast (lat. 36°58' N, long. 122°00'05" W). Named on Santa Cruz (1954) and Soquel (1954) 7.5' quadrangles. The name commemorates John Woods, who had property by the lake; this lake and Schwans Lagoon together are known as Twin Lakes (Clark, 1986, p. 329, 406).

Woods Valley: see **Sapaque Valley** [MONTEREY].

Woodtick Canyon [MONTEREY]: *canyon,* drained by a stream that flows 3 miles to Arroyo Seco (1) 6.5 miles north-northwest of Junipero Serra Peak (lat. 36°14'20" N, long. 121°26'35" W; sec. 32, T 19 S, R 5 E). Named on Junipero Serra Peak (1949) 7.5' quadrangle.

Workfield Siding [MONTEREY]: *locality,* 3 miles south-southwest of Marina along Southern Pacific Railroad (lat. 36°38'40" N, long. 121°49'20" W). Named on Marina (1947) 7.5' quadrangle.

Wreck Beach [MONTEREY]: *beach,* 1 mile east of Pfeiffer Point along the coast (lat. 36°14'05" N, long. 120°47'50" W; sec. 36, T 19 S, R 1 E). Named on Pfeiffer Point (1956) 7.5' quadrangle. The name recalls shipwrecks that occurred at the place in 1909, 1916, and 1922 (Clark, 1991, p. 613).

Wreck Canyon [SANTA BARBARA]: *canyon,* drained by a stream that flows 3.5 miles to the sea nearly 3.25 miles east-northeast of South Point on Santa Rosa Island (lat. 33°54'45" N, long. 120°03'40" W). Named on Santa Rosa Island South (1943) 7.5' quadrangle. The name is from the wreck of the ship *Crown of England* near the mouth of the canyon; the feature first was called Cañada La Jolla (Doran, p. 190).

Wunpost [MONTEREY]: *locality,* 5.5 miles northwest of Bradley along Southern Pacific Railroad (lat. 35°55'45" N, long. 120°51'40" W; sec. 14, T 23 S, R 10 E). Named on Wunpost (1949) 7.5' quadrangle. According to local tradition, the name commemorates a Chinese workman killed near the place during construction of the railroad (Bruce Montgomery, personal communication, 1970).

Wyckoff Ledge: see **Crook Point** [SANTA BARBARA].

Wylie Canyon [SANTA BARBARA]: *canyon,* drained by a stream that flows nearly 1 mile to San Pedro Canyon 2.5 miles north-northwest of downtown Goleta (lat. 34°28'15" N, long. 119°50'35" W; at E line sec. 31, T 5 N, R 28 W). Named on Goleta (1950) 7.5' quadrangle.

- X - Y -

Yankee Point [MONTEREY]: *promontory,* 3 miles north-northwest of Soberanes Point along the coast (lat. 35°29'30" N, long. 121°56'40" W). Named on Soberanes Point (1956) 7.5' quadrangle.

Yankee Point Rock [MONTEREY]: *rock,* 100 feet long, 325 feet offshore at Yankee Point (lat. 36°29'25" N, long. 121°56'50" W). Named on Soberanes Point (1956) 7.5' quadrangle.

Yaqui Canyon [MONTEREY]: *canyon,* drained by a stream that flows 3.5 miles to Lewis Creek 14 miles east-northeast of King City (lat. 36°18'05" N, long. 120°54'15" W; near E line sec. 5, T 19 S, R 10 E). Named on Hepsedam Peak (1969) and Lonoak (1969) 7.5' quadrangles.

Yaro Creek [SAN LUIS OBISPO]: *stream,* flows 4.5 miles to Toro Creek (2) 3 miles north-northwest of Pozo (lat. 35°20'35" N, long. 120°23'50" W; at E line sec. 6, T 30 S, R 15 E). Named on Camatta Ranch (1966), Santa Margarita Lake (1967), and Wilson Corner (1966) 7.5' quadrangles.

Ybarra Spring [SAN LUIS OBISPO]: *spring,* 1.5 miles south-southeast of Cholame in Palo Prieto Canyon (lat. 35°42'15" N, long. 120°17'05" W; sec. 31, T 25 S, R 16 E). Named on Cholame (1961) 7.5' quadrangle.

Yeguas Creek [SAN LUIS OBISPO]: *stream,* heads in Kern County and flows 1.25 miles in San Luis Obispo County to join Walnut Creek and form Bitterwater Creek 25 miles southeast of Shandon (lat. 35°27'30" N, long. 120°00'45" W; sec. 26, T 28 S, R 18 E). Named on La Panza NE (1966) 7.5' quadrangle. The name "Los Yeguas Creek" was applied to the stream because many brood mares were pastured about its head—*yeguas* means "mares" in Spanish (Arnold and Johnson, 1910, p. 21).

Yellow Bank: see **Yellowbanks Anchorage** [SANTA BARBARA].

Yellow Bank Creek [SANTA CRUZ]: *stream,* flows nearly 3 miles to the sea 8.5 miles west-northwest of Point Santa Cruz (lat. 36°59'35" N, long. 122°10'10" W). Named on Davenport (1955) and Santa Cruz (1954) 7.5' quadrangles. Called Respini Creek on Ben Lomond (1946) 15' quadrangle. A Swiss settler named Respini lived along the stream (Hoover, Rensch, and Rensch, p. 473).

Yellowbanks Anchorage [SANTA BARBARA]: *embayment*, 2 miles southwest of San Pedro Point at the east end of Santa Cruz Island (lat. 34°00'40" N, long. 119°32'35" W). Named on Santa Cruz Island D (1943) 7.5' quadrangle. Bremner's (1932) map has the name "Yellow Bank" at the place.

Yellow Hill [SAN LUIS OBISPO]: *peak*, 4.25 miles north-northwest of Piedras Blancas Point (lat. 35°43'30" N, long. 121°18'05" W). Altitude 481 feet. Named on Piedras Blancas (1959) 7.5' quadrangle.

Yerba Buena Creek [SAN LUIS OBISPO]: *stream*, flows 5.5 miles to Santa Margarita Creek 1.5 miles north of Santa Margarita (lat. 35° 24'40" N, long. 120°36'20" W). Named on Lopez Mountain (1965) and Santa Margarita (1965) 7.5' quadrangles.

Ygnacio: see **Maria Ygnacio Creek** [SANTA BARBARA].

Yokum Bend [SAN LUIS OBISPO]: *bend*, 6.5 miles west-southwest of Shandon along Estrella River (lat. 35°38'15" N, long. 120°29'15" W; sec. 29, T 26 S, R 14 E). Named on Shandon (1961) 7.5' quadrangle.

York Mountain [SAN LUIS OBISPO]: *peak*, 9.5 miles southwest of Paso Robles (lat. 35°32'45" N, long. 120°50' W; near SW cor. sec. 30, T 27 S, R 11 E). Altitude 1658 feet. Named on York Mountain (1948) 7.5' quadrangle.

Yost Canyon [MONTEREY]: *canyon*, 5 miles long, opens into Hames Valley 8.5 miles west-northwest of Bradley (lat. 35°55' N, long. 120°56'20" W; near W line sec. 24, T 23 S, R 9 E). Named on Bradley (1961) 15' quadrangle. Hames Creek drains the lower part of the canyon.

Yridisis Creek [SANTA BARBARA]: *stream*, flows 3.25 miles to El Jaro Creek 12.5 miles southeast of the city of Lompoc (lat. 34°31'30" N, long. 120°17'50" W). Named on Santa Rosa Hills (1959) 7.5' quadrangle.

Ysabel: see **Lake Ysabel** [SAN LUIS OBISPO].

Ytias Creek [SANTA BARBARA]: *stream*, flows 4.25 miles to El Jaro Creek 8.5 miles southeast of the city of Lompoc (lat. 34°32'50" N, long. 120°21'25" W). Named on Santa Rosa Hills (1959) 7.5' quadrangle.

- Z -

Zaca [SANTA BARBARA]: *locality*, 2.5 miles northwest of Los Olivos along Pacific Coast Railroad (lat. 34°41'10" N, long. 120° 09'15" W); the place is along La Zaca (present Zaca) Creek. Named on Lompoc (1905) 30' quadrangle.

Zaca Creek [SANTA BARBARA]: *stream*, flows 18 miles to Santa Ynez River less than 1 mile southwest of Buellton (lat. 34°36'30" N, long. 120°12'15" W); the stream heads near Zaca Lake and crosses La Zaca grant. Named on Los Olivos (1959), Solvang (1959), Zaca Creek (1959), and Zaca Lake (1964) 7.5' quadrangles. Called La Zaca Creek on Lompoc (1905) 30' quadrangle, but United States Board on Geographic Names (1961b, p. 18) rejected this name for the feature, although the Board recognized that the stream is named for La Zaca grant.

Zaca Lake [SANTA BARBARA]: *lake*, 1150 feet long, 12 miles southeast of Tepusquet Peak (lat. 34°46'40" N, long. 120°02'20" W); the lake is near the head of Zaca Creek. Named on Zaca Lake (1964) 7.5' quadrangle.

Zaca Peak [SANTA BARBARA]: *peak*, 1 mile southeast of Zaca Lake (lat. 34°46'05" N, long. 120°01'20" W); the peak is on Zaca Ridge. Altitude 4341 feet. Named on Zaca Lake (1964) 7.5' quadrangle.

Zaca Ridge [SANTA BARBARA]: *ridge*, west- to northwest-trending, 4 miles long, center 0.5 mile south of Zaca Lake (lat. 34°46'05" N, long. 120°02'15" W). Named on Zaca Lake (1964) 7.5' quadrangle.

Zanja Cota Creek: see **Zanja de Cota Creek** [SANTA BARBARA].

Zanja de Cota Creek [SANTA BARBARA]: *stream*, flows 4 miles to Santa Ynez River 2.25 miles south-southwest of Santa Ynez (lat. 34°35' N, long. 120°05'45" W). Named on Los Olivos (1959) and Santa Ynez (1959) 7.5' quadrangles. Called Santa Cota Cr. on Lompoc (1905) 30' quadrangle, but United States Board on Geographic Names (1961a, p. 13) rejected the names "Santa Cota Creek," "Sanja Cota Creek," "Santa Cora Creek," and "Zanja Cota Creek" for the stream.

Zanjon de Borregas: see **Borregas Creek** [SANTA CRUZ].

Zanjones [MONTEREY]: *land grant*, south of Chualar. Named on Chualar (1947) and Gonzales (1955) 7.5' quadrangles. Gabriel de la Torre received 1.5 leagues in 1839; Mariano Malarin, executor, claimed 6714 acres patented in 1866 (Cowan, p. 109).

Zayanta [SANTA CRUZ]: *land grant*, at and north of Felton and Mount Hermon. Named on Felton (1955) 7.5' quadrangle. Joseph L. Majors received 1 league in 1841; Isaac Graham and others claimed 2658 acres patented in 1870 (Cowan, p. 97—Cowan listed the grant under the designation "Sayante (or Zayante)"; Perez, p. 104). Colton's (1863) map has the name "Grahams" for a place located within the grant.

Zayante [SANTA CRUZ]: *settlement*, 5 miles east-southeast of the town of Boulder Creek (lat. 37°05'20" N, long. 122°02'40" W; sec. 2, T 10 S, R 2 W); the place is along Zayante Creek. Named on Felton (1955) 7.5' quadrangle. Postal authorities established Zayante post office in 1916 and discontinued it in 1938 (Salley, p. 246).

Zayante: see **Zayanta** [SANTA CRUZ].

Zayante Creek [SANTA CRUZ]: *stream*, flows 10 miles to San Lorenzo River 6 miles south-southeast of the town of Boulder Creek (lat. 37°02'55" N, long. 122°04' W). Named on Castle Rock Ridge (1955) and Felton (1955) 7.5' quadrangles. According to Stewart (p. 548), the name "Zayante" is of Indian origin.

Zigzag Creek [MONTEREY]: *stream*, flows 5.5 miles to Lost Valley Creek 4.5 miles south of Tassajara Hot Springs (lat. 36°10'10" N, long. 121°32'45" W; near NE cor. sec. 29, T 20 S, R 4 E). Named on Tassajara Hot Springs (1956) 7.5' quadrangle.

Central Coast Region
Monterey, San Benito, San Luis Obispo, Santa Barbara and Santa Cruz Counties

References Cited

BOOKS AND ARTICLES

Alexander, C.S. 1953. "The marine and stream terraces of the Capitola-Watsonville area." *University of California Publications in Geography*, v. 10, no. 1, p. 1-44.

Anderson, Frank M. 1905. "A stratigraphic study in the Mount Diablo Range of California." *Proceedings of the California Academy of Sciences* (series 3), v. II, no. 2, p. 156-248.

Anderson, Frank M., and Martin, Bruce. 1914. "Neocene record in the Temblor basin, California, and Neocene deposits of the San Juan district, San Luis Obispo County." *Proceedings of the California Academy of Sciences* (series 4), v. 4, p. 15-112.

Anderson, Robert, and Pack, Robert W. 1915. *Geology and oil resources of the west border of the San Joaquin Valley north of Coalinga, California*. (United States Geological Survey Bulletin 603.) Washington: Government Printing Office, 220 p.

Anderson, Winslow. 1892. *Mineral springs and health resorts of California*. San Francisco: The Bancroft Company, 347 p.

Angel, Myron. 1883. *History of San Luis Obispo County, California, with illustrations and biographical sketches of its prominent men and pioneers*. Oakland, California: Thompson & West, 391 p.

____1890a. "Monterey County." *Tenth annual report of the State Mineralogist, for the year ending December 1, 1890*. Sacramento: California State Mining Bureau, p. 345-348.

____1890b. "San Benito County." *Tenth annual report of the State Mineralogist, for the year ending December 1, 1890*. Sacramento: California State Mining Bureau, p. 515-517.

____1890c. "San Luis Obispo County." *Tenth annual report of the State Mineralogist, for the year ending December 1, 1890*. Sacramento: California State Mining Bureau, p. 567-585.

Antisell, Thomas. 1855. [On fossiliferous beds in San Luis Obispo County, California.] *California Academy of Natural Sciences Proceedings*, v. 1, p. 34-35.

____1856. "Geological report." *Reports of explorations and surveys, to ascertain the most practicable and economical route for a railroad from the Mississippi River to the Pacific Ocean*. Volume VII, Part II. (33d Cong., 2d Sess., Sen. Ex. Doc. No. 78.) Washington: Beverley Tucker, Printer, 204 p.

Arbuckle, Clyde. 1968. *Santa Clara Co. Ranchos*. San Jose, California: The Rosicrucian Press, Ltd., 46 p.

Arnold, Ralph. 1906. *The Tertiary and Quaternary pectens of California*. (United States Geological Survey Professional Paper 47.) Washington: Government Printing Office, 264 p.

Arnold, Ralph, and Anderson, Robert. 1907a. *Geology and oil resources of the Santa Maria oil district, Santa Barbara County, California*. (United States Geological Survey Bulletin 322.) Washington: Government Printing Office, 161 p.

____1907b. "Metamorphism by combustion of the hydrocarbons in the oil-bearing shale of California." *Journal of Geology*, v. 15, no. 8, p. 750-758.

____1908. *Preliminary report on the Coalinga oil district, Fresno and Kings Counties, California*. (United States Geological Survey Bulletin 357.) Washington: Government Printing Office, 142 p.

Arnold, Ralph, and Johnson, Harry R. 1909. *Sodium sulphate in Soda Lake, Carriso Plain, San Luis Obispo County, California*. (United States Geological Survey Bulletin 380-L.) Washington: Government Printing Office, 5 p.

____1910. *Preliminary report on the McKittrick-Sunset oil region, Kern and San Luis Obispo Counties, California*. (United States Geological Survey Bulletin 406.) Washington: Government Printing Office, 225 p.

Ashley, George Hall. 1895. "The Neocene of the Santa Cruz Mountains: I—Stratigraphy." *Proceedings of the California Academy of Sciences* (series 2), v. 5, p. 273-367.

Bancroft, Hubert Howe. 1888. *History of California, Volume VI, 1848-1859*. San Francisco; The History Company, Publishers, 787 p.

Becker, Robert H. 1964. *Diseños of California ranchos*. San Francisco: The Book Club of California, (no pagination).

____1969. *Designs on the land*. San Francisco: The Book Club of California, (no pagination).

Berkstresser, C.F., Jr. 1968. *Data for springs in the Southern Coast, Transverse, and Peninsular Ranges of California*. (United States Geological Survey, Water Resources Division, Open-file report.) Menlo Park, California, 21 p. + appendices.

Blake, William P. 1856. "Observations on the physical geography and geology of the coast of California, from Bodega bay to San Diego." *United States Coast Survey, Report of the Superintendent 1855*. (34th Cong., 1st Sess., Sen. Ex. Doc. No. 22.) Appendix 65, p. 376-398.

____1857. "Geological report." *Reports of explorations and surveys, to ascertain the most practicable and economical route for a railroad from the Mississippi River to the Pacific Ocean*. Volume V, Part II. (33d Cong., 2d Sess., Sen. Ex. Doc. No. 78.) Washington: Beverley Tucker, Printer, 370 p.

Bolton, Herbert Eugene. 1931. *Outpost of empire*. New York: Alfred A Knopf, 334 p.

Bradley, Walter W., and Logan, C.A. 1919. "San Benito County." *Report XV of the State Mineralogist*. Sacramento: California State Mining Bureau, p. 617-673.

Bremner, Carl St. J. 1932. *Geology of Santa Cruz Island, Santa Barbara County, California*. (Occasional Papers Number 1.) Santa Barbara, California: Santa Barbara Museum of Natural History, 33 p.

____1933. *Geology of San Miguel Island, Santa Barbara County, California*. (Occasional Papers Number 2.) Santa Barbara, California: Santa Barbara Museum of Natural History, 23 p.

Brewer, William H. 1949. *Up and down California in 1860-1864*. Berkeley and Los Angeles: University of California Press, 583 p.

Brown, Alan K. 1975. *Place names of San Mateo County*. San Mateo, California: San Mateo County Historical Association, 118 p.

Burgess, Sherwood D. 1962. "Lumbering in Hispanic California." *The California Historical Society Quarterly*, v. 41, no. 3, p. 237-248.

California Division of Highways. 1934. *California highway transportation survey, 1934*. Sacramento: Department of Public Works, Division of Highways, 130 p. + appendices.

Carson, James H. 1950. *Recollections of the California mines*. Oakland, California: Biobooks, 113 p.

Cerruti, Henry. 1954. *Ramblings in California, The adventures of Henry Cerruti*. Berkeley, California: Friends of the Bancroft Library, 143 p.

Chase, J. Smeaton. 1913. *California coast trails*. Boston and New York: Houghton Mifflin Company, 326 p.

Clark, Donald Thomas. 1986. *Santa Cruz County place names*. Santa Cruz: Santa Cruz Historical Society, 552 p.

____1991. *Monterey County place names*. Carmel Valley, California: Kestrel Press, 737 p.

Cowan, Robert G. 1956. *Ranchos of California*. Fresno, California: Academy Library Guild, 151 p.

Coy, Owen C. 1923. *California county boundaries*. Berkeley: California Historical Survey Commission, 335 p.

Crawford, J.J. 1894. "Report of the State Mineralogist." *Twelfth report of the State Mineralogist, (Second Biennial,) two years ending September 15, 1894*. Sacramento: California State Mining Bureau, p. 8-412.

____1896. "Report of the State Mineralogist." *Thirteenth report (Third Biennial) of the State Mineralogist for the two years ending September 15, 1896*. Sacramento: California State Mining Bureau, p. 10-646.

Crippen, Richard A., Jr. 1951. *Nephrite jade and associated rocks of the Cape San Martin region, Monterey County, California*. (California Division of Mines Special Report 10-A.) San Francisco: Division of Mines, 14 p.

Davidson, George. 1887. "An examination of some of the early voyages of discovery and exploration on the northwest coast of America, from 1539 to 1603." *Report of the Superintendent of the U.S. Coast and Geodetic Survey, showing progress of the work during the fiscal year ending with June, 1886*. Appendix No. 7. Washington: Government Printing Office, p.

155-247.

_____1907. "The discovery of the Bay of San Francisco and the rediscovery of the Port of Monterey." *Transactions and Proceedings of the Geographical Society of the Pacific* (series II), v. IV, p, 1-153.

Davis, Charles H. 1912. "The Los Burros mining district." *Mining and Scientific Press,* v. 104, no. 20, p. 696-698.

Derby, Geo. H. 1852. "A report of the Tulare valley." *Report of the Secretary of War.* (32d Cong., 1st Sess., Sen. Ex. Doc. 110.) 17 p.

Dibblee, T.W., Jr. 1950. *Geology of southwestern Santa Barbara County, California.* (California Division of Mines Bulletin 150.) San Francisco: Division of Mines, 95 p.

Diller, J.S., and others. 1915. *Guidebook of the Western United States, Part D. The Shasta Route and Coast Line.* (United States Geological Survey Bulletin 614.) Washington: Government Printing Office, 142 p.

Dillon, Richard H. 1960. *La Panza.* San Francisco: Printed for private circulation by the Grabhorn Press, 12 p.

_____1966. *The legend of Grizzly Adams: California's greatest mountain man.* New York: Coward-McCann, Inc., 223 p.

Doran, Adelaide LeMert. 1980. *Pieces of eight Channel Islands, A bibliographical guide and source book.* Glendale, California: The Arthur H. Clark Company, 340 p.

Eldridge, George H. 1901. "The asphalt and bituminous rock deposits of the United States." *Twenty-second annual report of the United States Geological Survey to the Secretary of the Interior, 1900-01.* Part. I. Washington: Government Printing Office, p. 209-452.

_____1903. "Origin and distribution of asphalt and bituminous rock deposits in the United States." *Contributions to economic geology, 1902.* (United States Geological Survey Bulletin 213.) Washington: Government Printing Office, p. 296-305.

Elliott and Moore. 1881. *History of Monterey County, California.* San Francisco, California: Elliott and Moore, Publishers, 197 p.

Emery, K.O. 1954. "The Painted Cave, Santa Cruz Island." *Sea and Pacific Motorboat,* v. 46, p. 38-39, 91-92.

English, Walter A. 1918. "Geology and oil prospects of the Salinas Valley-Parkfield area, California." *Contributions to economic geology, 1918, Part II.—Mineral fuels.* (United States Geological Survey Bulletin 691-H.) Washington: Government Printing Office, p. 219-250.

Fagan, Brian M. 1981. *California coastal passages.* Santa Barbara and Anaheim, California: Capra Press and CharGuide Ltd., 159 p.

Fairbanks, Harold W. 1893. "Notes on a farther study of the pre-Cretaceous rocks of the California Coast Ranges." *American Geologist,* v. 11, no. 2, p. 69-84.

_____1894. "Geology of northern Ventura, Santa Barbara, San Luis Obispo, Monterey, and San Benito Counties." *Twelfth report of the State Mineralogist, (Second Biennial,) two years ending September 15, 1894.* Sacramento: California State Mining Bureau, p. 493-526.

_____1895. "On analcite diabase from San Luis Obispo County, California." *University, of California, Bulletin of the Department of Geology,* v. 1, no. 9, p. 273-300.

_____1896. "The geology of Point Sal." *University of California, Bulletin of the Department of Geology,* v. 2, no. 1, p. 1-92.

Farnham, Thomas Jefferson. 1947. *Travels in California.* Oakland, California: Biobooks, 166 p.

Fink, Augusta. 1972. *Monterey, The presence of the past.* San Francisco: Chronicle Books, 254 p.

Forbes, Alexander. 1839. *California, A history of Upper and Lower California, from their first discovery to the present time.* London: Smith, Elder and Co., Cornhill, 352 p.

Franke, Herbert A. 1935. "Mines and mineral resources of San Luis Obispo County." *California Journal of Mines and Geology,* v. 31, no. 4, p. 402-464.

Frazer, Robert W. 1965. *Forts of the West.* Norman: University of Oklahoma Press, 246 p.

Fremont, John Charles. 1964. *Geographical memoir upon Upper California in illustration of his map of Oregon and California, newly reprinted from the edition of 1848.* San Francisco: The Book Club of California, 65 p.

Frickstad, Walter N. 1955. *A century of California post offices, 1848 to 1954.* Oakland, California: Philatelic Research Society, 395 p.

Gabb, W.M. 1869. *Cretaceous and Tertiary fossils.* (Geological Survey of California. Palæontology, Volume II.) Published by authority of the Legislature of California, 299 p.

Gagnon, Dennis R. 1981. *Exploring the Santa Barbara backcountry.* Santa Cruz: Western Tanager Press, 151 p.

Gleason, Duncan. 1958. *The islands and ports of California.* New York: The Devin-Adair Company, 201 p.

Goodyear, W.A. 1888. "Petroleum, asphaltum, and natural gas." *Seventh annual report of the State Mineralogist, for the year ending October 1, 1887.* Sacramento: California State Mining Bureau, p. 63-114.

_____1890. "Santa Cruz Island." *Ninth Annual Report of the State Mineralogist, for the year ending December 1, 1889.* Sacramento: California State Mining Bureau, p. 155-170.

Greenhow, Robert. 1844. *The history of Oregon and California, and the other territories on the North-west coast of North America.* Boston: Charles C. Little and James Brown, 482 p.

Gudde, Erwin G. 1949. *California place names.* Berkeley and Los Angeles: University of California Press, 431 p.

_____1969. *California place names.* Berkeley and Los Angeles: University of California Press, 416 p.

Hamilton, Geneva. 1974. *Where the highway ends—Cambria, San Simeon and the ranchos.* San Luis Obispo, California: Padre Productions, 219 p.

Hamlin, Homer. 1904. *Water resources of the Salinas Valley, California.* (United States Geological Survey Water-Supply and Irrigation Paper No. 89.) Washington: Government Printing Office, 91 p.

Hamman, Rick. 1980. *California central coast railways.* Boulder, Colorado: Pruett Publishing Company, 309 p.

Hanna, Phil Towsend. 1951. *The dictionary of California land names.* Los Angeles: The Automobile Club of Southern California, 392 p.

Harder, E.C. 1910 "Some chromite deposits in western and central California." *Contributions to economic geology, 1909, Part I.—Metals and nonmetals, except fuels. Rare Metals.* (United States Geological Survey Bulletin 430-D.) Washington: Government Printing Office, p. 19-35.

Hart, Earl W. 1978. *Limestone, dolomite, and shell resources of the Coast Range Province, California.* (California Division of Mines and Geology Bulletin 197.) Sacramento, California: California Division of Mines and Geology, 103 p.

Hart, James D. 1978. *A companion to California.* New York: Oxford University Press, 504 p.

Hobson, J.B. 1890. "The Santa Maria River." *Tenth annual report of the State Mineralogist, for the year ending December 1, 1890.* Sacramento: California State Mining Bureau, p. 600-601.

Hoover, Mildred Brooke, Rensch, Hero Eugene, and Rensch, Ethel Grace. 1966. *Historic spots in California.* (Third edition, revised by William N. Abeloe.) Stanford, California: Stanford University Press, 642 p.

Howard, Don. 1973. *Lost adobes of Monterey County.* Carmel, California: Monterey County Archæological Society, 105 p.

Hubbard, Henry G. 1943. "Mines and mineral resources of Santa Cruz County." *California Journal of Mines and Geology,* v. 39, no. 1, p. 11-52.

Huguenin, Emile. 1919. "Santa Barbara County." *Report XV of the State Mineralogist.* Sacramento: California State Mining Bureau, p. 727-750.

Irelan, William, Jr. 1888. "Report of the State Mineralogist." *Eighth annual report of the State Mineralogist. For the year ending October 1, 1888.* Sacramento, California State Mining Bureau, p. 12-695.

Johnston, Robert B. 1970. *Old Monterey County, A pictorial history.* (No place): Monterey Savings and Loan Association, 119 p.

Keller, George. 1955. *A trip across the plains and life in California.* Oakland, California: Biobooks, 44 p.

Kew, William S.W. 1920. "Cretaceous and Cenozoic Echinoidea of the Pacific Coast of North America." *University of California Publications in Geology,* v. 12, no. 2, p. 23-236.

_____1927. "Geologic sketch of Santa Rosa Island, Santa Barbara County, California." *Bulletin of the Geological Society of America,* v. 38, no. 4, p. 645-653.

Kroeber, A.L. 1916. "California place names of Indian origin." *University of California Publications in American Archæology and Ethnology,* v. 12, no. 2, p. 31-69.

_____1925. *Handbook of the Indians of California.* (Smithsonian Institution, Bureau of American Ethnology Bulletin 78.) Washington: Government Printing Office, 995 p.

Laizure, C. McK. 1925. "San Francisco field division (Monterey County)." *Mining in California,* v. 21, no. 1, p. 23-57.

_____1926. "San Francisco field division (Santa Cruz County)." *Mining in California,* v. 22, no. 1, p. 68-93.

Lawson, Andrew C. 1893. "The geology of Carmelo Bay." *University of California, Bulletin of the Department of Geology,* v. 1, no. 1, p. 1-59.

Lee, Georgia, and others. 1977. *An uncommon guide to San Luis Obispo County, California.* San Luis Obispo, California: Padre Productions, 160 p.

Lewis, Betty. 1976. *Watsonville, Memories that linger.* Fresno: Valley Publishers, 220 p.

_____1977. *Monterey Bay yesterday.* Fresno: Valley Publishers, 124 p.

Loel, Wayne, and Corey, W.H. 1932. "The Vaqueros Formation, lower Miocene of California; I, Paleontology." *University of California Publications, Bulletin of the Department of Geological Sciences,* v. 22, no. 3, p. 31-410.

Loew, Oscar. 1876. "Report on the physical and agricultural features of southern California, and especially of the Mohave Desert." *Annual report upon the geographical surveys west of the one hundredth meridian, in California, Nevada, Utah, Colorado, Wyoming, New Mexico, Arizona, and Montana.* (Appendix JJ of *The Annual Report of the Chief of Engineers for 1876.*) Washington: Government Printing Office, p. 214-222.

Logan, C.A. 1917. "San Luis Obispo County." *Report XV of the State Mineralogist.* Sacramento: California State Mining Bureau, p. 674-726.

Lussier, Tomi Kay. 1979. *Big Sur, A complete history and guide*. Monterey, California: Big Sur Publications, 59 p.
Lydon, Sandy. 1985. *Chinese gold, The Chinese in the Monterey Bay region*. Capitola, California: Capitola Book Company, 550 p.
Lydon, Sandy, and Swift, Carolyn. 1978. *Soquel Landing to Capitola-by-the-Sea*. California History Center, DeAnza College, 99 p.
Lynch, James. 1970. "With Stevenson to California, 1846-1848." *The New York Volunteers in California*. Glorieta, New Mexico: The Rio Grande Press, Inc., 65 p.
MacGregor, Bruce A. 1968. *South Pacific Coast, An illustrated history of the narrow gauge South Pacific Coast Railroad*. Berkeley, California: Howell-North Books, 280 p.
Mendenhall, Walter C. 1908. *Preliminary report on the ground waters of San Joaquin Valley, California*. (United States Geological Survey Water-Supply Paper 222.) Washington: Government Printing Office, 52 p.
Mosier, Dan L. 1979. *California coal towns, coaling stations, & landings*. San Leandro, California: Mines Road Books, 8 p.
Newhall, Ruth Waldo. 1958. *The Newhall ranch*. San Marino, California: The Huntington Library, 120 p.
Nicholson, Loren. 1980. *Rails across the ranchos*. Fresno, California: Valley Publishers, 197 p.
Nomland, Jorgen O. 1917. "The Etchegoin Pliocene of middle California." *University of California Publications, Bulletin of the Department of Geology*, v. 10, no. 14, p. 191-254.
Nutter, Edward Hoit. 1901. "Sketch of the geology of the Salinas Valley, California." *Journal of Geology*, v. 9, no. 4, p. 330-336.
Orr, Phil C. 1960. *Radiocarbon dates from Santa Rosa Island, II*. (Bulletin No. 3, Department of Anthropology.) Santa Barbara: Santa Barbara Museum of Natural History, 10 p.
Parke, John G. 1857. "General report." *Reports of explorations and surveys, to ascertain the most practicable and economical route for a railroad from the Mississippi River to the Pacific Ocean*. Volume VII. (33d Cong., 2d Sess., Sen. Ex. Doc. No. 78.) Washington: Beverley Tucker, Printer, 42 p.
Perez, Crisostomo N. 1996. *Land grants in Alta California*. Rancho Cordova, California: Landmark Enterprises, 264 p.
Pierce, Marjorie. 1977. *East of the Gabilans*. Fresno: Valley Publishers, 194 p.
Preston, E.B. 1893a. "Monterey County." *Eleventh report of the State Mineralogist, (First Biennial,) Two years ending September 15, 1892*. Sacramento: California State Mining Bureau, p. 259-262.
_____1893b. "San Benito County." *Eleventh report of the State Mineralogist, (First Biennial,) Two years ending September 15, 1892*. Sacramento: California State Mining Bureau, p. 370-373.
Rambo, F. Ralph. 1964. *Almost forgotten*. (Author), 48 p.
Rand, William W. 1931. "Preliminary report of the geology of Santa Cruz Island, Santa Barbara County, California." *Mining in California*, v. 27, no. 2, p. 214-219.
Reed, Ralph D. 1933. *Geology of California*. Tulsa, Oklahoma: American Association of Petroleum Geologists, 355 p.
Reinstedt, Randall A. 1973. *Gold in the Santa Lucias*. Carmel, California: Ghost Town Publications, 96 p.
_____1975. *Shipwrecks & sea monsters of California's central coast*. Carmel, California: Ghost Town Publications, 168 p.
Rife, Joanne. 1977. *Where the light turns gold, The story of the Santa Ynez Valley*. Fresno: Valley Publishers, 167 p.
Rintoul, William. 1978. *Oildorado*. Santa Cruz, California: Valley Publishers, 241 p.
Rowland, Leon. 1980. *Santa Cruz, The early years*. Santa Cruz, California: Paper Vision Press, 273 p.
Salley, H.E. 1977. *History of California post offices, 1849-1976*. La Mesa, California: Postal History Associates, Inc., 300 p.
Shumate, Albert. 1977. *Francisco Pacheco of Pacheco Pass*. Stockton, California: University of the Pacific, 47 p.
Smith, Frances Rand. 1932. *The mission of San Antonio de Padua*. Stanford University, California: Stanford University Press, 108 p.
Spence, Mary Lee, and Jackson, Donald (editors). 1973. *The expeditions of John Charles Frémont, Volume 2, The Bear Flag revolt and the court-martial*. Urbana, Chicago, and London: University of Illinois Press, 519 p.
Stanley, Leo L. 1976. *San Miguel at the turn of the century*. Fresno: Valley Publishers, 148 p.
Stewart, George R. 1970. *American place-names, A concise and selective dictionary for the continental United States of America*. New York: Oxford University Press, 550 p.
Talbot, Theodore. 1972. *Soldier in the West, Letters of Theodore Talbot during his services in California, Mexico and Oregon, 1845-53*. Norman: University of Oklahoma Press, 210 p.
Taylor, Bayard. 1850. *Eldorado, or Adventures in the path of empire*. New York: George P. Putnam, (two volumes) 251 p. + 255 p.
Tompkins, Walker A., and Ruiz, Russell A. 1970. Historical *high lights of Santa Barbara*. (No place): Santa Barbara National Bank, 136 p.
Townsend, E.D. 1970. *The California diary of General E.D. Townsend*. Los Angeles: The Ward Ritchie Press, 184 p.
Trask, John B. 1854. *Report on the geology of the Coast Mountains, and part of the Sierra Nevada: embracing their industrial resources in agriculture and mining*. (Sen., Sess. of 1854, Doc. No. 9.) Sacramento: State Printer, 95 p.
United States Board on Geographic Names (under name "United States Geographic Board"). 1933. *Sixth report of the United States Geographic Board, 1890 to 1932*. Washington: Government Printing Office, 834 p.
_____(under name "United States Geographic Board"). 1934. *Decisions of the United States Geographic Board, No. 34—Decisions June 1933-March 1934*. Washington: Government Printing Office, 20 p.
_____(under name "United States Board on Geographical Names"). 1936a. *Decisions of the United States Board on Geographical Names, Decisions rendered between July 1, 1934, and June 30, 1935*. Washington: Government Printing Office, 26 p.
_____(under name "United States Board on Geographical Names"). 1936b. *Decisions of the United States Board on Geographical Names, Decisions rendered between July 1, 1935, and June 30, 1936*. Washington: Government Printing Office, 44 p.
_____(under name "United States Board on Geographical Names"). 1938. *Decisions of the United States Board on Geographical Names, Decisions rendered between July 1, 1937, and June 30, 1938*. Washington: Government Printing Office, 62 p.
_____(under name "United States Board on Geographical Names"). 1939. *Decisions of the United States Board on Geographical Names, Decisions rendered between July 1, 1938, and June 30, 1939*. Washington: Government Printing Office, 41 p.
_____(under name "Board on Geographical Names"). 1943. *Decisions rendered between July 1, 1941, and June 30, 1943*. Washington: Department of the Interior, 104 p.
_____1949. *Decision lists nos. 4905, 4906, May, June, 1949*. Washington: Department of the Interior, 10 p.
_____1950. *Decision lists nos. 4910, 4911, 4912, October, November, December, 1949*. Washington: Department of the Interior, 10 p.
_____1959. *Decisions on names in the United States, Puerto Rico and the Virgin Islands, Decisions rendered from April 1957 through December 1958*. (Decision list no. 5901.) Washington: Department of the Interior, 100 p.
_____1960a. *Decisions on names in the United States and Puerto Rico, Decisions rendered in May, June, July, and August, 1959*. (Decision list no. 5903.) Washington: Department of the Interior, 79 p.
_____1960b. *Decisions on names in the United States, Decisions rendered from September 1959 through December 1959*. (Decision list no. 5904.) Washington: Department of the Interior, 68 p.
_____1960c. *Decisions on names in the United States, Puerto Rico and the Virgin Islands, Decisions rendered from January through April 1960*. (Decision list no. 6001.) Washington: Department of the Interior, 79 p.
_____1961a. *Decisions on names in the United States, Decisions rendered from January through April 1961*. (Decision list no. 6101.) Washington: Department of the Interior, 74 p.
_____1961b. *Decisions on names in the United States, Decisions rendered from May through August 1961*. (Decision list no. 6102.) Washington: Department of the Interior, 81 p.
_____1962a. *Decisions on names in the United States, Decisions rendered from September through December 1961*. (Decision list no. 6103.) Washington: Department of the Interior, 75 p.
_____1962b. *Decisions on names in the United States, Decisions rendered from January through April 1962*. (Decision list no. 6201.) Washington: Department of the Interior, 72 p.
_____1962c. *Decisions on names in the United States, Decisions rendered from May through August 1962*. (Decision list no. 6202.) Washington: Department of the Interior, 81 p.
_____1963a. *Decisions on names in the United States, Decisions rendered from September through December 1962*. (Decision list no. 6203.) Washington: Department of the Interior, 59 p.
_____1963b. *Decisions on geographic names in the United States, May through August 1963*. (Decision list no. 6302.) Washington: Department of the Interior, 81 p.
_____1964. *Decisions on geographic names in the United States, May through August 1964*. (Decision List No. 6402.) Washington: Department of the Interior, 85 p.
_____1965a. *Decisions on geographic names in the United States, September through December 1964*. (Decision list no. 6403.) Washington: Department of the Interior, 66 p.
_____1965b. *Decisions on geographic names in the United States, January through March 1965*. (Decision list no. 6501.) Washington: Department of the Interior, 85 p.
_____1965c. *Decisions on geographic names in the United States, April through June 1965*. (Decision list no. 6502.) Washington: Department of

the Interior, 39 p.

_____1965d. *Decisions on geographic names in the United States, July through September 1965*. (Decision list no. 6503.) Washington: Department of the Interior, 74 p.

_____1966. *Decisions on geographic names in the United States, April through June 1966*. (Decision list no. 6602.) Washington: Department of the Interior, 36 p.

_____1967a. *Decisions on geographic names in the United States, July through September 1966*. (Decision list no. 6603.) Washington: Department of the Interior, 38 p.

_____1967b. *Decisions on geographic names in the United States, October through December 1966*. (Decision list no. 6604.) Washington: Department of the Interior, 36 p.

_____1967c. *Decisions on geographic names in the United States, January through March 1967*. (Decision list no. 6701.) Washington: Department of the Interior, 20 p.

_____1967d. *Decisions on geographic names in the United States, July through September 1967*. (Decision list no. 6703.) Washington: Department of the Interior, 29 p.

_____1968a. *Decisions on geographic names in the United States, October through December 1967*. (Decision list no. 6704.) Washington: Department of the Interior, 46 p.

_____1968b. *Decisions on geographic names in the United States, January through March 1968*. (Decision list no. 6801.) Washington: Department of the Interior, 51 p.

_____1968c. *Decisions on geographic names in the United States, April through June 1968*. (Decision list no. 6802.) Washington: Department of the Interior, 42 p.

_____1972a. *Decisions on geographic names in the United States, October through December 1971*. (Decision list no. 7104.) Washington: Department of the Interior, 20 p.

_____1972b. *Decisions on geographic names in the United States, January through March 1972*. (Decision list no. 7201.) Washington: Department of the Interior, 32 p.

_____1972c. *Decisions on geographic names in the United States, July through September 1972*. (Decision list no. 7203.) Washington: Department of the Interior, 17 p.

_____1973. *Decisions on geographic names in the United States, October through December 1972*. (Decision list no. 7204.) Washington: Department of the Interior, 15 p.

_____1974a. *Decisions on geographic names in the United States, January through March 1974*. (Decision list no. 7401.) Washington: Department of the Interior, 27 p.

_____1974b. *Decisions on geographic names in the United States, July through September 1974*. (Decision list no. 7403.) Washington: Department of the Interior, 34 p.

_____1975. *Decisions on geographic names in the United States, July through September 1975*. (Decision list no. 7503.) Washington: Department of the Interior, 33 p.

_____1977. *Decisions on geographic names in the United States, July through September 1977*. (Decision list no. 7703.) Washington: Department of the Interior, 25 p.

_____1978a. *Decisions on geographic names in the United States, January through March 1978*. (Decision list no. 7801.) Washington: Department of the Interior, 18 p.

_____1978b. *Decisions on geographic names in the United States, April through June 1978*. (Decision list no. 7802.) Washington: Department of the Interior, 30 p.

_____1978c. *Decisions on geographic names in the United States, July through September 1978*. (Decision list no. 7803.) Washington: Department of the Interior, 32 p.

_____1978d. *Decisions on geographic names in the United States, October through December 1978*. (Decision list no. 7804.) Washington: Department of the Interior, 48 p.

_____1979a. *Decisions on geographic names in the United States, April through June 1979*, (Decision list no. 7902.) Washington: Department of the Interior, 33 p.

_____1979b. *Decisions on geographic names in the United States, July through September 1979*. (Decision list no. 7903.) Washington: Department of the Interior, 38 p.

_____1980. *Decisions on geographic names in the United States, October through December 1979*. (Decision list no. 7904.) Washington: Department of the Interior, 26 p.

_____1981a. *Decisions on geographic names in the United States, January through March 1981*. (Decision list no. 8101.) Washington: Department of the Interior, 23 p.

_____1981b. *Decisions on geographic names in the United States, April through June 1981*. (Decision list no. 8102.) Washington: Department of the Interior, 28 p.

_____1981c. *Decisions on geographic names in the United States, July through September 1981*. (Decision list no. 8103.) Washington: Department of the Interior, 20 p.

_____1983a. *Decisions on geographic names in the United States, January through March 1983*. (Decision list no. 8301.) Washington: Department of the Interior, 33 p.

_____1983b. *Decisions on geographic names in the United States, July through September 1983*. (Decision list no. 8303.) Washington: Department of the Interior, 26 p.

_____1988. *Decisions on geographic names in the United States, July through September 1988*. (Decision list no. 8803.) Washington: Department of the Interior, 19 p.

_____1991. *Decisions on geographic names in the United States*. (Decision list no. 1991.) Washington: Department of the Interior, 40 p.

_____1992. *Decisions on geographic names in the United States*. (Decision list no. 1992.) Washington: Department of the Interior, 21 p.

_____1994. *Decisions on geographic names in the United States*. (Decision list no. 1994.) Washington: Department of the Interior, 17 p.

_____1995. *Decisions on geographic names in the United States*. (Decision list no. 1995.) Washington: Department of the Interior, 19 p.

United States Coast and Geodetic Survey. 1963. *United States Coast Pilot 7, Pacific Coast, California, Oregon, Washington, and Hawaii*. (Ninth edition.) Washington: United States Government Printing Office, 336 p.

United States Coast Survey. 1855. *Report of the Superintendent of the Coast Survey, showing the progress of the Survey during the year 1854*. Washington: Beverley Tucker, Public Printer.

Vancouver, George. 1953. *Vancouver in California, 1792-1794*. (The original account edited and annotated by Marguerite Eyer Wilbur.) Los Angeles: Glen Dawson, 274 p.

Vander Leck, Lawrence. 1922. "Memoranda on asphalt and bituminous sand deposits of California." *Mining in California*, v. 18, no. 5, p. 228-230.

Van Winkle, Walton, and Eaton, Frederick M. 1910. *The quality of the surface waters of California*. (United States Geological Survey Water-Supply Paper 237.) Washington: Government Printing Office, 142 p.

Wagner, Henry R. 1968. *The cartography of the Northwest coast of America to the year 1800*. (One-volume reprint of the 1937 edition.) Amsterdam: N. Israel, 543 p.

Wagner, Jack R. 1974. *The last whistle (Ocean Shore Railroad)*. Berkeley, California: Howell-North Books, 135 p.

Wall, Rosalind Sharpe. 1987. *When the coast was wild and lonely, Early settlers of The Sur*. Pacific Grove, California: The Boxwood Press, 190 p.

Waring, Clarence A., and Bradley, Walter W. 1917. "Monterey County." *Report XV of the State Mineralogist*. Sacramento: California Mining Bureau, p. 595-615.

Waring, Gerald A. 1915. *Springs of California*. (United States Geological Survey Water-Supply Paper 338.) Washington: Government Printing Office, 410 p.

Whiting, J.S., and Whiting, Richard J. 1960. *Forts of the State of California*. Seattle, Washington: (Authors), 90 p.

Whitney, J.D. 1865. *Report of progress and synopsis of the field-work from 1860 to 1864*. (Geological Survey of California, Geology, Volume I.) Published by authority of the Legislature of California, 498 p.

Wiedey, Lionel William. 1928. "Notes on the Vaqueros and Temblor Formations of the California Miocene, with descriptions of new species." *Transactions of the San Diego Society of Natural History*, v. 5, no. 10, p. 95-182.

Young, John V. 1979. *Ghost towns of the Santa Cruz Mountains*. Santa Cruz, California: Paper Vision Press, 156 p.

QUADRANGLE MAPS

(All maps published by United States Geological Survey, except as noted. Dates identify the editions of the maps. If a reprinted or revised map was used, the year of reprinting or revision is given in parentheses, unless the reprinted or revised map is cited specifically in the text.)

Adelaida 15'—1947; 1961.
7.5'—1948.
Alder Peak 7.5'—1949.
Annette 7.5' (same area as Orchard Peak 7.5')—1943.
Año Nuevo 15'—1943 (Army); 1948 (Army).
7.5'—1955.
Arroyo Grande 15'—1897; 1897, reprinted 1903; 1942; 1952.
Arroyo Grande NE 7.5'—1965.
Atascadero 7.5'—1965.
Bakersfield 1°x 2°—1962.
Bald Mountain 7.5'—1964.
Ballinger Canyon 7.5'—1943.
Bates Canyon 7.5'—1964.
Bear Canyon 7.5'—1949.
Ben Lomond 15'—1946 (Army).
Bickmore Canyon 7.5'—1968.
Big Basin 7.5'—1955.

Big Pine Mountain 7.5'—1944 (Army); 1964.
Big Sur 7.5'—1956.
Bradley 15'—1929; 1961.
7.5'—1949.
Branch Mountain 15'—1942; 1952.
7.5'—1967.
Bryson 15'—1919; 1929; 1942 (Army); 1961.
7.5'—1949; 1949, photorevised 1979.
Burnett Peak 7.5'—1949.
Burro Mountain 7.5'—1949.
Caldwell Mesa 7.5'—1967.
Caliente Mountain 15'—1941.
7.5'—1959.
California Valley 7.5'—1966.
Camatta Canyon 7.5' (same area as Commatti Canyon 7.5')—1961.
Camatta Ranch 7.5'—1966.
Cambria 7.5'—1959; 1959, photorevised 1979.
Cape San Martin 15'—1921 (reprinted 1932); 1948; 1961.
7.5'—1949.
Capitola 15'—1914 (reprinted 1947).
Carmel Valley 7.5'—1956.
Carpinteria 7.5'—1952; 1952, photorevised 1967.
Casmalia 7.5'—1959.
Castle Rock Ridge 7.5'—1955; 1955, photorevised 1968.
Cayucos 15'—1897 (reprinted 1937); 1943; 1951.
7.5'—1965.
Cerro Colorado 7.5'—1969.
Cherry Peak 7.5'—1968.
Chews Ridge 7.5'—1956.
Chimineas Ranch 7.5'—1959.
Chimney Canyon 7.5'—1967.
Chittenden 7.5'—1955; 1955, photorevised 1968 and 1973.
Cholame 30'—1917.
7.5'—1943; 1961.
Cholame Hills 7.5'—1961.
Cholame Ranch 7.5' (same area as Cholame Valley 7.5')—1943 (Army).
Cholame Valley 7.5' (same area as Cholame Ranch 7.5')—1961.
Chualar 7.5'—1947 (Army).
Ciervo Mountain 7.5'—1969.
Commatti Canyon 7.5' (same area as Camatta Canyon 7.5')—1943 (Army).
Cone Peak 7.5'—1949.
Cosio Knob 7.5'—1949.
Creston 7.5'—1948.
Cupertino 7.5'—1961.
Curry Mountain 7.5'—1969.
Cuyama 7.5' (same area as East of Cuyama Ranch 7.5')—1964.
Cuyama Peak 7.5'—1943.
Cypress Mountain 7.5'—1948; 1948, photorevised 1979.
Davenport 7.5'—1955.
Dos Pueblos Canyon 7.5'—1951.
Elkhorn Hills 7.5'—1954.
Espinosa Canyon 7.5'—1949.
Estrella 7.5'—1948.
Fellows 7.5'—1951.
Felton 7.5'—1955; 1955, photorevised 1980.
Figueroa Mountain 7.5'—1959.
Foxen Canyon 7.5'—1964.
Fox Mountain 7.5'—1964.
Franklin Point 7.5'—1955.
Garza Peak 7.5'—1953.
Gaviota 15'—1943 (Army).
7.5'—1953.
Goleta 15'—1903 (reprinted 1924).
7.5'—1950.
Gonzales 15'—1921.
7.5'—1955.
Greenfield 7.5'—1956.
Guadalupe 30'—1905 (reprinted 1913).
7.5'—1959.
Hames Valley 7.5'—1949.
Hepsedam Peak 7.5'—1969.
Hernandez Reservoir 7.5'—1969.
Hernandez Valley 15'—1943 (reprinted 1958); 1957
Hildreth Peak 7.5'—1964.
Holland Canyon 7.5' (same area as Grant Lake 7.5')—1961.
Hollister 15'—1921.
7.5'—1955.
Huasna Peak 7.5'—1967.
Hurricane Deck 7.5'—1964.
Idria 7.5'—1969.
Jamesburg 15'—1921; 1939.
Jolon 7.5'—1949.
Junipero Serra 15'—1930; 1940 (Army); 1948; 1961.
Junipero Serra Peak 7.5'—1949.
King City 15'—1919 (reprinted 1941).
Lake Cachuma 7.5'—1959.
La Panza 15'—1935.
7.5'—1967.
La Panza NE 7.5'—1966.
La Panza Ranch 7.5'—1966.
Las Yeguas Ranch 7.5'—1959.
Laurel 7.5'—1955.
Lime Mountain 7.5'—1948; 1948, photorevised 1979.
Little Pine Mountain 7.5'—1944 (Army); 1964.
Llanada 7.5'—1969.
Loma Prieta 7.5'—1955.
Lompoc 30'—1905 (reprinted 1931).
7.5'—1959.
Lompoc Hills 7.5'—1959.
Lonoak 7.5'—1969.
Lopez Mountain 7.5'—1965.
Lopez Point 7.5'—1956.
Los Alamos 7.5'—1959.
Los Angeles 1°x 2°—1955 (Army).
Los Gatos 15' (same area as New Almaden 15')—1919 (reprinted 1942).
7.5'—1953.
Los Machos Hills 7.5'—1967.
Los Olivos 15'—1943 (Army).
7.5'—1959.
Lucia 15'—1921 (reprinted 1941).
Madulce Peak 7.5' (same area as Strawberry Peak 7.5')—1964.
Manzanita Mountain 7.5'—1964.
Maricopa 7.5'—1951.
Marina 7.5'—1947 (Army).
Mariposa Peak 7.5'—1969.
McKittrick 30'—1912 (reprinted 1920).
McKittrick Summit 7.5'—1959.
McPherson Peak 15'—1943 (Army).
Mercey Hot Springs 7.5'—1969.
Metz 15' (same area as Greenfield 15')—1921.
Mindego Hill 7.5'—1961.
Miranda Pine Mountain 7.5'—1967.
Monarch Peak 7.5'—1967.
Monterey 15'—1913 (reprinted 1932); 1940.
7.5'—1947 (Army); 1947, photorevised 1968.
Morro Bay North 7.5'—1965.
Morro Bay South 7.5'—1965.
Moss Landing 7.5'—1954.
Mount Carmel 7.5'—1956.
Mount Harlan 7.5'—1968.
Mount Johnson 7.5'—1968.
Mount Madonna 7.5'—1955.
Mount Pinos 30'—1903 (reprinted 1918).
Natividad 7.5'—1947 (Army); 1947, photorevised 1968.
Nattrass Valley 7.5'—1967.
New Cuyama 7.5' (same area as Cuyama Ranch 7.5')—1964.
New Idria 15'—1943.
Nipomo 15'—1922 (reprinted 1932).
7.5'—1965.
North Chalone Peak 7.5'—1969.
Oceano 7.5'—1965.
Old Man Mountain 7.5'—1943.
Orchard Peak 7.5' (same area as Annette 7.5')—1961.
Orcutt 7.5'—1959.
Ortigalita Peak 7.5'—1969.
Packwood 7.5' (same area as Packwood Creek 7.5')—1943.
Packwood Creek 7.5' (same area as Packwood 7.5')—1961.
Paicines 7.5'—1968.
Painted Rock 7.5'—1959.
Palo Escrito Peak 7.5'—1956.
Pancho Rico Valley 7.5'—1967.
Panoche 7.5'—1969.
Panoche Pass 7.5'—1968.
Panoche Valley 15'—1944.
Panorama Hills 7.5'—1954.
Paraiso Springs 7.5'—1956.
Parkfield 7.5'—1961.
Partington Ridge 7.5'—1956.
Paso Robles 15'—1919.
7.5'—1948.
Peak Mountain 7.5'—1964.
Pebblestone Shut-in 7.5'—1959.

Pfeiffer Point 7.5'—1956.
Pico Creek 7.5'—1959.
Piedras Blancas 7.5'—1959.
Pinalito Canyon 7.5'—1969.
Pismo Beach 7.5'—1965.
Point Arguello 7.5'—1959.
Point Conception 15'—1942 (Army).
7.5'—1953.
Point Sal 15'—1947.
7.5'—1958.
Point Sur 15'—1925 (Coast and Geodetic Survey).
7.5'—1956.
Port Harford 15' (same area as Port San Luis 15')—1897.
Port San Luis 7.5'—1965.
Pozo 15'—1922 (reprinted 1940).
Pozo Summit 7.5'—1967.
Priest Valley 30'—1915.
7.5'—1969.
Prunedale 7.5'—1954.
Quien Sabe 15'—1922.
Quien Sabe Valley 7.5'—1968.
Rana Creek 7.5'—1956.
Ranchito Canyon 7.5'—1948.
Rancho Nuevo Creek 7.5' (same area as Morro Hill 7.5')—1943.
Reliz Canyon 7.5'—1949.
Reward 7.5'—1951.
Rock Spring Peak 7.5'—1969.
Ruby Canyon 7.5'—1968.
Sacate 7.5'—1953.
Salinas 15'—1912 (reprinted 1931); 1940 (U.S. Army).
7.5'—1947 (Army); 1947, photorevised 1968 and 1975.
Salisbury Potrero 7.5'—1944 (Army); 1964.
San Ardo 15'—1943; 1956.
7.5'—1967.
San Benito 15'—1919.
7.5'—1968.
San Benito Mountain 7.5'—1969.
San Felipe 7.5'—1955; 1955, photorevised 1971.
San Francisco 1·x 2°—1956 (revised 1969).
San Jose 1°x 2°—1962 (revised 1969).
San Juan Bautista 15'—1917 (reprinted 1931).
7.5'—1955.
San Lucas 7.5'—1949.
San Luis 30'—1903.
San Luis Obispo 1°x 2°—1948 (Army); 1956 (revised 1969).
15'—1897 (reprinted 1931).
7.5'—1965.
San Marcos Pass 7.5'—1959.
San Miguel 15'—1919 (reprinted 1941); 1947.
7.5'—1948.
San Miguel Island East 7.5'—1950.
San Miguel Island West 7.5'—1950.
San Rafael Mountain 15'—1943 (Army); 1959.
7.5'—1959.
San Simeon 15'—1919; 1942 (Army); 1959.
7.5'—1958.
Santa Barbara 15'—1903.
7.5'—1944 (Army); 1952.
Santa Cruz 1°x 2°—1956.
30'—1902 (reprinted 1939).
7.5'—1954.
Santa Cruz Island A 7.5'—1943.
Santa Cruz Island B 7.5'—1943.
Santa Cruz Island C 7.5'—1943.
Santa Cruz Island D 7.5'—1943.
Santa Margarita 7.5'—1965.
Santa Margarita Lake 7.5'—1967.
Santa Maria 1°x 2°—1956 (Army).
15'—1947.
7.5'—1959.
Santa Rita Peak 7.5'—1969.
Santa Rosa Hills 7.5'—1959.
Santa Rosa Island East 7.5'—1943.
Santa Rosa Island North 7.5'—1943.
Santa Rosa Island South 7.5'—1943.
Santa Rosa Island West 7.5'—1943.
Santa Ynez 30'—1905 (reprinted 1944).
7.5'—1959.
Seaside 7.5'—1947 (Army); 1947, photorevised 1968; 1947, photorevised 1983.
Shandon 7.5'—1961.
Shedd Canyon 7.5'—1961.
Simmler 7.5'—1959.
Sisquoc 7.5'—1959.
Slack Canyon 7.5'—1969.
Smith Mountain 7.5'—1969.
Soberanes Point 7.5'—1956.
Soledad 15'—1915.
7.5'—1955.
Solvang 7.5'—1959.
Soquel 7.5'—1954; 1954, photorevised 1968.
Spreckels 7.5'—1947 (Army).
Stockdale Mountain 7.5'—1948.
Strawberry Peak 7.5' (same area as Madulce Peak 7.5')—1944.
Surf 7.5'—1947 (Army); 1959.
Sycamore Flat 7.5'—1956.
Tajiguas 7.5'—1953.
Tar Spring Ridge 7.5'—1967.
Tassajara Hot Springs 7.5'—1956.
Taylor Canyon 7.5'—1959.
Templeton 7.5'—1948.
Tent Hills 7.5'—1942.
Tepusquet Canyon 7.5'—1964.
Tepusquet Peak 15'—1943 (Army).
The Dark Hole 7.5'—1961.
Thompson Canyon 7.5'—1949.
Three Sisters 7.5'—1954.
Tierra Redonda Mountain 7.5'—1949; 1949, photorevised 1979.
Topo Valley 7.5'—1969.
Tranquillon Mountain 7.5'—1959.
Tres Pinos 7.5'—1955.
Tumey Hills 7.5'—1956.
Twitchell Dam 7.5'—1959.
Valleton 7.5'—1948.
Ventana Cones 7.5'—1956.
Ventura 15'—1904 (reprinted 1946); 1941 (Army).
Villa Creek 7.5'—1949.
Watsonville East 7.5'—1955.
Watsonville West 7.5'—1954.
Wells Ranch 7.5'—1954.
White Ledge Peak 7.5'—1952.
Williams Hill 7.5'—1949.
Wilson Corner 7.5'—1966.
Wunpost 7.5'—1949.
York Mountain 7.5'—1948.
Zaca Creek 7.5'—1959.
Zaca Lake 7.5'—1964.

MISCELLANEOUS MAPS

Alexander. 1953. (Untitled map, fig. 5 *in* Alexander.)
Anderson and Martin. 1914. "Geologic map of the San Juan district, northeastern San Luis Obispo County, California." (Plate X *in* Anderson and Martin.)
Arnold and Johnson. 1910. "Preliminary geologic and structural map of the McKittrick-Sunset oil region, California." (Plate I *in* Arnold and Johnson, 1910.)
Ashley. 1894. "Sketch map of the area of the Santa Cruz Mountains." (Plate XXIII *in* Ashley.)
Baker. 1855. "Map of the mining region, of California." Drawn by Geo A. Baker.
Bancroft. 1864. "Bancroft's map of the Pacific States." Compiled by Wm. H. Knight. Published by H.H. Bancroft & Co., Booksellers and Stationers, San Francisco, Cal..
Bartlett. 1854. "General map showing the countries explored & surveyed by the United States & Mexican Boundary Commission in the years 1850, 51, 52, & 53, under the direction of John R. Bartlett, U.S. Commissioner."
Blake. 1857. "Geological map of a part of the State of California explored in 1855 by Lieut. R.S. Williamson, U.S. Top. Engr." (*Accompanies* Blake, 1857.)
Bremner. 1932. "Geologic map, Santa Cruz Island, Santa Barbara County, California." (Plate IV *in* Bremner, 1932.)
_____1933. "Geologic map, San Miguel Island, Santa Barbara County, California." (Plate IV *in* Bremner, 1933.)
California. 1891. (Map reproduced in *Early California, Southern Edition*. Corvalis, Oregon: Western Guide Publishers, p. 44-45.)
California Department of Parks and Recreation. (No date.) (Map of Point Lobos State Reserve.)
California Division of Highways. 1934. (Appendix "A" *of* California Division of Highways.)
California Mining Bureau. 1909a. "San Benito and Monterey Counties." (*In* California Mining Bureau Bulletin 56.)

_____1909b. "San Luis Obispo County." (*In* California Mining Bureau Bulletin 56.)

_____1909c. "Santa Barbara and Ventura Counties." (*In* California Mining Bureau Bulletin 56.)

_____1909d. "San Francisco, San Mateo, Contra Costa, Alameda, Santa Clara, and Santa Cruz Counties." (*In* California Mining Bureau Bulletin 56.)

_____1917a. (Untitled map *in* California Mining Bureau Bulletin 74, p. 166.)

_____1917b. (Untitled map *in* California Mining Bureau Bulletin 74, p. 172.)

_____1917c. (Untitled map *in* California Mining Bureau Bulletin 74, p. 173.)

Colton. 1855. "California." J.H. Colton & Co., New York.

_____1863. "Colton's map of California, Nevada, Utah, Colorado, Arizona, & New Mexico." Published by J.H. Colton, 172 William St., New York.

Cozzens and Davies. 1927. "Map showing location of Mission San Antonio de Padua." Compiled by H.F. Cozzens and Wm. Davies. (Plate II *in* Smith.)

Derby. 1850. "Reconnaissance of the Tulares Valley." Lieut. G.H. Derby, Topl. Engrs., April and May, 1850.

Diller and others. 1915. "Geologic and topographic map of the Coast Route from Los Angeles, California, to San Francisco, California." (*In* Diller and others.)

Eddy. 1854. "Approved and declared to be the official map of the State of California by an act of the Legislature passed March 25th 1853." Compiled by W.M. Eddy, State Surveyor General. Published for R.A. Eddy, Marysville, California, by J.H. Colton, New York.

Eldridge. 1901. "Region of San Lorenzo Creek, Cal." (Figure 45 *in* Eldridge, 1901.)

Emory. 1857-1858. "Map of the United States and their territories between the Mississippi and the Pacific Ocean, and part of Mexico." Compiled from Surveys made under the order of W.H. Emory.

English and Kew. 1916. "Geologic map of middle Salinas Valley, Cal." (Plate 27 *in* English.)

Fairbanks. 1896. "Geological map of Point Sal." (Plate I *in* Fairbanks, 1896.)

Farnham. 1845. "Map of the Californias." (*Accompanies* Farnham.)

Forbes. 1839. "The coasts of Guatimala and Mexico from Panama to Cape Mendocino, with the principal harbors in California." (*Accompanies* Forbes.)

Fremont. 1845. "Map of an exploring expedition to the Rocky Mountains in the year 1842 and to Oregon & North California in the years 1843-44." By Brevet Capt. J.C. Frémont.

Goddard. 1857. "Britton & Rey's map of the State of California." By George H. Goddard.

Greenhow. 1844. "Map of the western and middle portions of North America, to illustrate the history of California, Oregon, and other countries on the north-west coast of America." By Robert Greenhow.

Hamlin. 1904. "Map of the drainage basin of the Salinas River, showing hydrographic features." (Plate I *in* Hamlin.)

Hamman. 1980a. "Aptos Creek." (*In* Hamman, p. 38.)

_____1980b. "Santa Cruz to Los Gatos & the San Lorenzo River basin railroads." (*In* Hamman, p. 82.)

_____1980c. "Ocean Shore Southern Pacific San Vicinte Lumber Co. railroads. " (*In* Hamman, p. 168.)

Harder. 1910. "Map showing the distribution of serpentine areas and chromite mines in the San Luis Obispo district, California." (Plate I *in* Harder.)

Holt. 1863. "A new map of the State of California and Nevada Territory." Published by W. Holt, San Francisco.

Hubbard. 1943. "Map of Santa Cruz County." (Plate II *in* Hubbard.)

Kew. 1927. "Geologic map of Santa Rosa Island, Santa Barbara County, California." (Figure 1 *in* Kew, 1927).

Lawson. 1893. "Geological map of Carmelo Bay." (Plate I *in* Lawson.).

Malaspina. 1791. "Plano del Puerto y Bahie de Monterey, situado en la costa de Californ."

Mendenhall. 1908. "Artesian areas and groundwater levels in the San Joaquin Valley, California." (Plate I *in* Mendenhall.)

Mitchell. 1856. "Mitchell's new national map." Published by S. Augustus Mitchell, Philadelphia.

Parke. 1854-1855. "Map No. 1, San Francisco Bay to the plains of Los Angeles." From explorations and surveys made by Lieut. John G. Parke. Constructed and drawn by H. Custer. (In *Reports of explorations and surveys, to ascertain the most practicable and economical route for a railroad from the Mississippi River to the Pacific Ocean*. Volume XI. 1861.)

Postal Route. 1884. (Map reproduced in *Early California, Southern Edition*. Corvalis, Oregon: Western Guide Publishers, p. 34-43.)

Railway. 1903. "Commissioners official railway map of California." Approved by the Board of Railroad Commissioners, November 1st, 1903. (Map reproduced in *Early California, Southern Edition*. Corvalis, Oregon: Western Guide Publishers, p. 46-47.)

Rand. 1931. "Geologic map of Santa Cruz Island, California." (*Accompanies* Rand.)

Ransom and Doolittle. 1863. "A new map of the State of California and Nevada Territory." By Lander Ransom and A.J. Doolittle. Published by W. Holt, San Francisco.

Rogers and Johnston. 1857. "State of California." By Prof. H.D. Rogers & A. Keith Johnston.

Southern Pacific Railroad. 1890. "Map of Coast Line from San Francisco to San Luis Obispo." (Reproduced *in* Nicholson, p. 176.)

United States Coast Survey. 1854. "Sketch J, showing progress of the survey on the western coast of the United States, sections X & XI, from 1850 to 1854." (*In* United States Coast Survey.)

United States Geological Survey. 1973. "Channel Island National Monument."

Wilkes. 1849. "Map of Upper California." By the best authorities.

Williamson. 1853. "General map of explorations and surveys in California." By Lieut. R.S. Williamson, Topl. Engr., assisted by Lieut. J.G. Parke, Topl. Engr., and Mr. Isaac William Smith, Civ. Engr. (In *Reports of explorations and surveys, to ascertain the most practicable and economical route for a railroad from the Mississippi River to the Pacific Ocean*. Volume XI. 1861.)

Part Eight
South San Joaquin Valley Region

Fresno, Kern, Kings and Tulare Counties

Part Eight– South San Joaquin Valley Region

South San Joaquin Valley Region Fresno, Kern, Kings and Tulare Counties

Regional Setting

General.—This section concerns geographic features in four counties—Fresno, Kern, Kings, and Tulare—that lie in and around the south part of San Joaquin Valley. Townships (T) North and Ranges (R) West refer to San Bernardino Base and Meridian; Townships South and Ranges East refer to Mount Diablo Base and Meridian. San Joaquin Valley is the south part of the Central Valley, or Great Valley, of California, and takes its name from San Joaquin River, which drains most of it. Early Spanish explorers in the valley found a lake that they called Laguna de los Tulares because of the tules or cattails around it, and later the Spaniards called the valley itself Los Tulares (Mitchell, A.R., p. 5). The *Californian* newspaper used the name "Toolary valley" on August 22, 1846, and Carson (p. 93, 95) used the names "Tulare Valley" and "Tulare Plains" in 1852. The valley is called Tulares Valley on Derby's (1850) map. The whole Central Valley is called Buena Ventura Valley on Wilkes' (1841) map. Map makers apparently devised many names for features in and near Kettleman Hills, names that may have little or no local use.

The map on the facing page shows the location of the South San Joaquin Valley Region and the counties in it. The Sierra Nevada lies east of San Joaquin Valley. United States Board on Geographic Names (1933a, p. 692) ruled against the form "Sierra Nevadas" for the name of the range. The term "High Sierra" commonly is accepted for the part of the range that includes the high peaks (Gudde, 1949, p. 148). Garces gave the name "Sierra de San Marcos" to the present Sierra Nevada in 1776 (Boyd, p. 3), Wilkes (p. 44) called it the California Range in 1841, Lyman (p. 307) called it "Sierra Nevada, or Snowy Mountains" in 1849, and Kip (p. 46) called it Snowy Range in 1850. Whitney (p. 2) pointed out that the range was long known to the Spaniards as Sierra Nevada, or Snowy Range, because "the most distant and loftiest elevations are never entirely bare of snow, and for a large portion of the year are extensively covered with it." Diablo Range is along the west side of San Joaquin Valley from Contra Costa County to the northwest corner of Kern County. The range is called Sierra del Monte Diablo on Parke's (1854-1855) map. Whitney (p. 2) called the feature Monte Diablo Range and stated that it "is so called from the conspicuous point [Mount Diablo] of that name." United States Board on Geographic Names (1933a, p. 246) rejected the names "Monte Diablo Range," "Mount Diablo Range," and "Sierra del Monte Diablo" for the feature. The southeasternmost part of the region lies in Mojave Desert. The name "Mojave" is from the designation of Indians that lived near Colorado River at the east side of the desert (Gudde, 1949, p. 219); United States Board on Geographic Names (1934, p. 11) rejected the form "Mohave Desert" for the name, and cited local usage for the decision.

Fresno County.—Fresno County extends from the crest of the Sierra Nevada westward across San Joaquin Valley into Diablo Range. The state legislature created the county in 1856 from what previously had been the south part of Merced County and the south and east parts of Mariposa County. The original territory of Fresno County had three major reductions: the part east of the crest of Sierra Nevada went to Mono County when that county was organized in 1861; the northwest part went to San Benito County in 1887; and the north part went to form Madera County in 1893 (Coy, p. 101, 104-105). Millerton was the first county seat, but in 1874 the county government moved to Fresno, where it remains; *fresno* means "ash tree" in Spanish—early Spanish explorers used the name in the region because of the abundance of ash trees along watercourses there (Hoover, Rensch, and Rensch, p. 89).

Kern County.—Kern County extends eastward from Temblor Range across San Joaquin Valley and the Sierra Nevada into Mojave Desert. The state legislature created the county in 1866 from parts of previously organized Tulare County and Los Angeles County; the original boundaries of Kern County have had only minor changes (Coy, p. 116-119). The name is from Kern River; Havilah was the county seat until 1874, when the county government moved to Bakersfield (Hoover, Rensch, and Rensch, p. 121).

Kings County.—Kings County lies mainly in San Joaquin Valley, where it includes most of the bed of Tulare Lake, but also extends southwest from the valley across Kettleman Hills into Diablo Range. The state legislature formed Kings County in 1893 from territory of Tulare County; Kings County gained some land from Fresno County in 1909 (Coy, p. 120-121). The county name is from Kings River; Hanford is and always has been the county seat (Hoover, Rensch, and Rensch, p. 135).

Tulare County.—Tulare County extends from the crest of the Sierra Nevada westward into San Joaquin Valley. The state legislature created the county in 1852 from the south part of Mariposa County and the north part of Los Angeles County; Wood's Cabin, or Woodsville, was the first county seat, but the county government moved to Visalia in 1853, and remains there (Hoover, Rensch, and Rensch, p. 558, 561). The original Tulare County lost considerable territory with the formation of Fresno County in 1856, with the formation of Inyo and Kern Counties in 1866, and with the formation of Kings County in 1893 (Coy, p. 282-287). The name "Tulare" is from the Spanish term for the cattails, or tules, that grow in profusion at Tulare Lake, which was in the original territory of the county.

South San Joaquin Valley Region
Fresno, Kern, Kings and Tulare Counties

— A —

Abbot: see **Mount Abbot** [FRESNO].

Abbott: see **Abbott Mill** [FRESNO].

Abbott Creek [FRESNO]: *stream,* flows 4.5 miles to Mill Flat Creek 11 miles south-southeast of Balch Camp (lat. 36°46'20" N, long. 119°01' W; sec. 23, T 13 S, R 27 E). Named on Patterson Mountain (1952) and Tehipite Dome (1952) 15' quadrangles.

Abbott Mill [FRESNO]: *locality,* 3.5 miles west-southwest of Hume (lat. 36°46'15" N, long. 118°58' W; sec. 19, T 13 S, R 28 E); the place is north of Abbott Creek. Named on Tehipite (1903) 30' quadrangle. California Mining Bureau's (1917a) map has the name "Abbott" at the site. The mill was built in 1902 to handle timber cut on the Millwood side of Hoist Ridge; the place also was called Camp Three (Johnston, p. 76).

Abel Mountain: see **Cerro Noroeste** [KERN].

Abilene [TULARE]: *locality,* 4.5 miles south-southeast of Lindsay along Visalia Electric Railroad (lat. 36°08'45" N, long. 119°03'10" W; sec. 33, T 20 S, R 27 E). Named on Lindsay (1928) 7.5' quadrangle.

Academy [FRESNO]: *settlement,* 10 miles east-northeast of Clovis (lat. 36°33'15" N, long. 119°32'15" W; sec. 14, T 12 S, R 22 E). Named on Academy (1964) 7.5' quadrangle. Postal authorities established Academy post office in 1876, discontinued it in 1877, reestablished it in 1892, discontinued it in 1903, reestablished it in 1905, and discontinued it in 1951 (Salley, p. 1). The name "Academy" is from a private secondary school that was started in the neighborhood in 1872 (Hoover, Rensch, and Rensch, p. 94). Postal authorities established Big Dry Creek post office 2 miles north of Academy in 1870, moved it 2.5 miles south in 1888, and discontinued it in 1893 (Salley, p. 21).

Acrodectes Peak: see **Mount Baxter** [FRESNO].

Actis [KERN]: *locality,* 6.5 miles north of Rosamond (lat. 34°57'30" N, long. 118°08'55" W; at W line sec. 15, T 10 N, R 12 W). Named on Soledad Mountain (1973) 7.5' quadrangle. Called Gloster on Soledad Mountain (1947) 7.5' quadrangle. Thompson's (1921) map shows Runnington P.O. at present Actis. Postal authorities established Highberg post office in 1917, changed the name to Runnington in 1918, and discontinued it in 1927 (Frickstad, p. 56, 59).

Adams Flat [TULARE]: *area,* 4 miles southeast of Auckland (lat. 36°33'10" N, long. 119°02'45" W; in and near sec. 9, T 16 S, R 27 E). Named on Auckland (1966) 7.5' quadrangle.

Adams Gap [TULARE]: *pass,* 4 miles southeast of Auckland (lat. 36°32'30" N, long. 119°03'35" W; near N line sec. 17, T 16 S, R 27 E); the pass is 1 mile southwest of Adams Flat. Named on Auckland (1966) 7.5' quadrangle.

Adelaide: see **Mount Adelaide** [KERN].

Administration Point: see **Admiration Point** [TULARE].

Admiration Point [TULARE]: *relief feature,* nearly 4 miles east-southeast of Yucca Mountain (lat. 36°33'10" N, long. 118°48'15" W). Named on Giant Forest (1956) 15' quadrangle. United States Board on Geographic Names (1933a, p. 80) rejected the name "Administration Point" for the feature.

Adobe Canyon [KERN]: *canyon,* drained by a stream that flows 8.5 miles to Poso Creek 3.5 miles south-southeast of Knob Hill (lat. 35°31' N, long. 118°35'15" W; near SW cor. sec. 1, T 28 S, R 28 E). Named on Knob Hill (1965) and Pine Mountain (1965) 7.5' quadrangles.

Adobe Flat [FRESNO]: *area,* 13 miles west of Coalinga (lat. 36°15'25" N, long. 120°35'20" W; near SE cor. sec. 20, T 19 S, R 13 E). Named on Santa Rita Peak (1969) 7.5' quadrangle.

Adobe Station [KERN]: *locality,* 12 miles south of Bakersfield (lat. 35°11'45" N, long. 118°58' W; near SW cor. sec. 27, T 31 S, R 28 E). Named on Caliente (1914) 30' quadrangle. Telegraph Stage Company had a station at the place in the 1870's (Boyd, p. 42).

Advance [TULARE]: *locality,* 4.25 miles south-southwest of Yucca Mountain along North Fork Kaweah River (lat. 36°31' N, long. 118°54'10" W). Named on Giant Forest (1956) 15' quadrangle. The place was the site of the administrative center, general store, post office, and school for Kaweah Cooperative Colony, a socialistic experiment begun in 1885 and ended in 1891 (Kaiser, p. 63, 67). Postal authorities established Advance post office in 1890, changed the name to Kaweah the same year, and moved it to Kaweah in 1910 (Mitchell, A.R., p. 64).

Aerial Acres [KERN]: *locality,* 5.5 miles east-southeast of Castle Butte in Peerless Valley (lat. 35°05'20" N, long. 117°47'20" W; sec. 36, T 12 N, R 9 W). Named on North Edwards (1973) 7.5' quadrangle.

Agassiz: see **Mount Agassiz** [FRESNO].

Agassiz Col [FRESNO]: *pass,* 10.5 miles east of Mount Goddard on Fresno-Inyo County line (lat. 36°06'25" N, long. 119°31'45" W); the pass is 1600 feet south of Mount Agassiz. Named on Mount Goddard (1948) 15' quadrangle.

Agassiz Needle: see **Mount Agassiz** [FRESNO].

Agua Caliente: see **Caliente** [KERN]; **Scovern Hot Springs** [KERN].

Agua Caliente Creek: see **Caliente Creek** [KERN].

Agua de los Alamos: see **Sinks of the Tejon**, under **Tejon Creek** [KERN].

Agua Fria Spring [KERN]: *spring,* 9 miles east of Mount Adelaide (lat. 35°25' N, long. 118°35'25" W; sec. 7, T 29 S, R 32 E). Named on Breckenridge Mountain (1972) 7.5' quadrangle.

Ahart Meadow [FRESNO]: *area,* 8 miles southeast of Dinkey Dome along East Fork Deer Creek (3) (lat. 37°01'15" N, long. 119°02'30" W; near W line sec. 33, T 10 S, R 27 E). Named on Huntington Lake (1953) 15' quadrangle. The name commemorates John Ahart, who patented land at the place about 1890 (Hanna, p. 4). According to Browning (p. 2), the landowner had the name "John Earthart."

Aido Spring [KERN]: *spring,* 2 miles southeast of Orchard Peak (lat. 35°42'55" N, long. 120°06'40" W; on S line sec. 26, T 25 S, R 17 E). Named on Sawtooth Ridge (1961) 7.5' quadrangle. Two oil prospectors named the spring one hot summer day from initial letters of the phrase "all in, down and out" (Waring, p. 368).

Air Compressor Springs: see **Miracle Hot Springs** [KERN].

Airplane Flat [KERN]: *area,* 12.5 miles north of Mojave (lat. 35°13'45" N, long. 118°11'40" W; near S line sec. 14, T 31 S, R 35 E). Named on Cache Peak (1973) 7.5' quadrangle.

Alameda [KERN]: *locality,* 9 miles south of Bakersfield (lat. 35°14'15" N, long. 119°00'10" W; at SW cor. sec. 8, T 31 S, R 28 E). Named on Conner (1954) 7.5' quadrangle. A farming colony called Winter Garden was situated south of present Alameda in 1888 and 1889 (Bailey, 1962, p. 59).

Alamo Solo Spring [KERN]: *spring,* 14 miles north-northwest of present Blackwells Corner (lat. 35°46'50" N, long. 119°59'55" W; sec. 2, T 25 S, R 18 E). Named on Lost Hills (1914) 30' quadrangle. The name is for a single cottonwood tree at the spring—*alamo solo* means "lone cottonwood" in Spanish (Arnold and Johnson, p. 19). After the spring dried up, a well at the place was called Light Well for the Light family, who lived there (Latta, 1949, p. 299).

Alaska Flat [KERN]: *area,* 4.25 miles north-northwest of Claraville (lat. 35°30' N, long. 118°21'25" W; sec. 18, T 28 S, R 34 E). Named on Claraville (1972) and Woolstalf Creek (1972) 7.5' quadrangles.

Albanita Meadows [TULARE]: *area,* 5.5 miles south of Monache Mountain (lat. 36°07'40" N, long. 118°11'45" W; sec. 3, 4, T 21 S, R 35 E). Named on Monache Mountain (1956) 15' quadrangle.

Alcalde [FRESNO]: *locality,* 4.5 miles southwest of Coalinga along Warthan Creek (lat. 35°05'45" N, long. 120°25' W; near SW cor. sec. 13, T 21 S, R 14 E). Named on Coalinga (1912) 30' quadrangle, which shows the place in Alcalde Canyon. Postal authorities established Alcalde post office in 1888 and discontinued it in 1904; they established Warthan post office 10 miles west of Alcalde in 1880 and discontinued it in 1902, when they moved the service to Alcalde (Salley, p. 4, 234).

Alcalde Canyon [FRESNO]: *canyon,* drained by a stream that flows 2.5 miles to Warthan Creek 4.5 miles southwest of Coalinga (lat. 36°05'50" N, long. 120°25' W; near SW cor. sec. 13, T 21 S, R 14 E). Named on Curry Mountain (1969) 7.5' quadrangle. On Coalinga (1912) 30' quadrangle, the canyon of Wartham Creek (present Warthan Creek) has the name "Alcalde Canyon." Arnold and Anderson (1908, p. 15) applied the name "Alcalde Canyon" to only the lower part of the canyon of Warthan Creek "extending from the edge of Waltham Valley, where the stream cuts between Juniper Ridge and Curry Mountain, to Pleasant Valley."

Alcalde Creek: see **Warthan Creek** [FRESNO].

Alcalde Hills [FRESNO]: *range,* 5 miles west-northwest of Coalinga (lat. 36°10' N, long. 120°26'30" W). Named on Alcalde Hills (1969) and Curry Mountain (1969) 7.5' quadrangles. Arnold and Anderson (1908, p. 14) gave the name "Alcalde Hills" to "the foothills between Los Gatos and Waltham Creeks, east of Juniper Ridge, northwest of Alcalde and west of Coalinga."

Alder Creek [KERN]: *stream,* flows 3.25 miles to Cedar Creek 3.5 miles west of Alta Sierra (lat. 35°43'05" N, long. 118°36'50" W; sec. 26, T 25 S, R 31 E). Named on Alta Sierra (1972) 7.5' quadrangle.

Alder Creek [TULARE]:

(1) *stream,* flows 3.5 miles to Dry Meadow Creek 9 miles southeast of Camp Nelson (lat. 36°02'15" N, long. 118°30'55" W; near NW cor. sec. 10, T 22 S, R 32 E). Named on Camp Nelson (1956) 15' quadrangle.

(2) *stream,* flows 2 miles to Tyler Creek nearly 2 miles north-northeast of California Hot Springs (lat. 35°54'10" N, long. 118°39'10" W; sec. 29, T 23 S, R 31 E). Named on California Hot Springs (1958) 15' quadrangle.

Alder Creek: see **North Alder Creek** [TULARE]; **South Alder Creek** [TULARE].

Alder Creek Campground [KERN]: *locality,* 3.5 miles west of Alta Sierra (lat. 35°43'10" N, long. 118°36'40" W; near SE cor. sec. 26, T 25 S, R 31 E); the place is near the mouth of Alder Creek. Named on Alta Sierra (1972) 7.5' quadrangle.

Alder Springs [FRESNO]: *village,* 5.5 miles west-southwest of Shaver Lake Heights (present town of Shaver Lake) (lat. 37°04' N, long. 119°24' W; sec. 18, T 10 S, R 24 E). Named on Shaver Lake (1953) 15' quadrangle.

Alexander's Corner: see **Weed Patch** [KERN].

Alex Cook Spring [KERN]: *spring,* 10 miles southwest of Blackwells Corner (lat. 35°30'35" N, long. 119°59' W; sec. 12, T 28 S, R 18 E). Named on Shale Point (1953) 7.5' quadrangle.

Alfac [TULARE]: *locality,* 2 miles south of Tipton along Southern Pacific Railroad (lat. 36°01'55" N, long. 119°18'25" W; sec. 7, T 22 S, R 25 E). Named on Tipton (1928) 7.5' quadrangle.

Alfonce Well [KERN]: *well,* 11 miles southeast of Orchard Peak along Packwood Creek (lat. 35°36'25" N, long. 120°01'10" W; sec. 3, T 27 S, R 18 E). Named on Packwood Creek (1961) 7.5' quadrangle.

Alfonsos [KERN]: *locality,* 13 miles south-southeast of Orchard Peak (lat. 35°34'15" N, long. 120°00'50" W; near SW cor. sec. 14, T 27 S, R 18 E). Named on Cholame (1917) 30' quadrangle.

Algoso [KERN]: *locality,* 4.5 miles east-southeast of downtown Bakersfield along the railroad (lat. 35°21'35" N, long. 118°55'30" W; sec. 36, T 29 S, R 28 E). Named on Lamont (1954) 7.5' quadrangle. The place was called Weed Patch before the railroad reached the site; railroad officials chose the name "Algoso" for the station to avoid confusion with another place called Weed Patch—*algoso* means "weedy" in Spanish (Gudde, 1949, p. 7).

Alila: see **Earlimart** [TULARE].

Alkali City: see **Bakersfield** [KERN].

Alkali Flat [TULARE]: *area,* 8 miles south-southwest of Springville (lat. 36°01' N, long. 118°51'05" W; sec. 16, T 22 S, R 29 E). Named on Globe (1956) 7.5 quadrangle.

Allard: see **Bealville** [KERN].

Allen: see **Royal Allen Lake**, under **Little Kern Lake** [TULARE].

Allen Gap [TULARE]: *pass,* 7.5 miles northeast of Exeter (lat. 36°21'45" N, long. 119°02'10" W; sec. 15, T 18 S, R 27 E); the pass is 1 mile northwest of Allen Hill. Named on Rocky Hill (1951) 7.5' quadrangle.

Allen Hill [TULARE]: *ridge,* southwest-trending, nearly 1 mile long, 7.5 miles east-northeast of Exeter (lat. 36°21' N, long. 119°01'35" W; on E line sec. 22, T 18 S, R 27 E). Named on Rocky Hill (1951) 7.5' quadrangle.

Allen's Camp: see **Caliente** [KERN].

Allensworth [TULARE]: *village,* 6.5 miles west-southwest of Earlimart (lat. 35°51'50" N, long. 119°23'20" W; near SW cor. sec. 4, T 24 S, R 24 E). Named on Allensworth (1954) 7.5' quadrangle. The name commemorates Lieutenant Colonel Allen Allensworth, an army chaplain who was born a slave in 1842 and who started the village as a Negro colony after 1902 (Hanna, p. 7). Postal authorities established Allensworth post office in 1909 and discontinued it in 1933 (Frickstad, p. 209).

Alpaugh [TULARE]: *town,* 12 miles west of Earlimart (lat. 35°53'15" N, long. 119°29'10" W; mainly in sec. 33, T 23 S, R 23 E). Named on Alpaugh (1953) 7.5' quadrangle. Called Alspaugh on California Mining Bureau's (1917b) map. Postal authorities established Alpaugh post office in 1906 (Frickstad, p. 209). The name commemorates John Alpaugh, a founder of the community (Mitchell, A.R., p. 67). The town is on a slight elevation of the valley floor that escaped winter floods; Judge J.J. Atwell of Visalia used the land as pasture for hogs in the 1850's, and the place then became known as Atwell's Island (Hoover, Rensch, and Rensch, p. 560). It also was called Root Island and Hog Island (Mitchell, A.R., p. 67). During highest water the west end of Atwell's Island became a separate island that was called Skull Island for Indian remains found there by early settlers (Hoover, Rensch, and Rensch, p. 560).

Alpaugh: see **West Alpaugh** [TULARE].

Alphie Canyon [KERN]: *canyon,* drained by a stream that flows 9.5 miles to Jawbone Canyon 4.5 miles north-northwest of Cinco (lat. 35°19'10" N, long. 118°04'30" W; near SE cor. sec. 14, T 30 S, R 36 E). Named on Cinco (1972) and Dove Spring (1972) 7.5' quadrangles. Called Gold Canyon on Cross Mountain (1943) 15' quadrangle, and United States Board on Geographic Names (1975b, p. 8) gave this name as a variant.

Alphie Spring [KERN]: *spring,* 7.5 miles north-northwest of Cinco (lat. 35°22'05" N, long. 118°04'40" W; sec. 35, T 29 S, R 36 E); the spring is in Alphie Canyon. Named on Cinco (1972) 7.5' quadrangle.

Alpine Col [FRESNO]: *pass,* 8 miles north of Mount Goddard on Glacier Divide (lat. 37°12'55" N, long. 118°41'35" W). Named on Mount Goddard (1948) 15' quadrangle.

Alpine Creek [FRESNO]: *stream,* flows 4.5 miles to Middle Fork Kings River 10 miles west of Marion Peak (lat. 36°56'45" N, long. 118°41'35" W). Named on Marion Peak (1953) and Mount Goddard (1948) 15' quadrangles.

Alpine Creek [TULARE]: *stream,* flows 6.5 miles to Little Kern River 8 miles northeast of Camp Nelson (lat. 36°13'50" N, long. 118°30'45" W; sec. 33, T 19 S, R 32 E). Named on Camp Nelson (1956) and Mineral King (1956) 15' quadrangles.

Alpine Meadow [TULARE]: *area,* 7.5 miles north of Camp Nelson (lat. 36°14'55" N, long. 118°35'55" W; sec. 27, T 19 S, R 31 E). Named on Camp Nelson (1956) 15' quadrangle.

Alspaugh: see **Alpaugh** [TULARE].

Alta: see **Sultana** [TULARE].

Alta Meadow [TULARE]: *area,* 7 miles west of Triple Divide Peak (lat. 36°34'50" N, long. 118°39'15" W; near E line sec. 36, T 15 S, R 30 E). Named on Triple Divide Peak (1956) 15' quadrangle. Tom Witt, N.B. Witt, and W.B. Wallace named the place in 1876 for its high elevation (Hanna, p. 9).

Alta Peak [TULARE]: *peak,* 7.5 miles west of Triple Divide Peak (lat. 36°35'25" N, long. 118°39'45" W; sec. 25, T 15 S, R 30 E); the peak is 1 mile northwest of Alta Meadow. Altitude 11,204 feet. Named on Triple Divide Peak (1956) 15' quadrangle. The feature first was known as Tharps Peak for Hale Tharp, a mountaineer—Tharps Rock is at the place (Hanna, p. 9).

Alta Sierra [KERN]: *town,* 8.5 miles east of Glennville (lat. 35°43'45" N, long, 118°33' W; in and near sec. 28, T 25 S, R 32 E). Named on Alta Sierra (1972) 7.5' quadrangle.

Alum Creek [FRESNO]: *stream,* flows 1.5 miles to Deep Well Canyon 3 miles east of Smith Mountain (2) (lat. 36°04'35" N, long. 120°32'35" W; sec. 26, T 21 S, R 13 E). Named on Smith Mountain (1969) 7.5' quadrangle.

Amalie: see **Loraine** [KERN].

Amargo: see **Boron** [KERN].

Amargo Springs [KERN]: *springs,* 5 miles south of Arvin (lat. 35°08'15" N, long. 118°49'25" W). Named on Arvin (1955) 7.5' quadrangle.

Ambition Lake [FRESNO]: *lake,* 2100 feet long, 2.25 miles east of Blackcap Mountain (lat. 37°04'40" N, long. 118°45'05" W). Named on Blackcap Mountain (1953) and Mount Goddard (1948) 15' quadrangles.

Ambler [TULARE]: *settlement,* 1.5 miles south-southeast of Visalia (lat. 36°18'30" N, long. 119°16'45" W; sec. 5, T 19 S, R 25 E). Named on Visalia (1949) 7.5' quadrangle.

Ambrose Well [KERN]: *well,* 9 miles south-southeast of Orchard Peak (lat. 35°37'05" N, long. 120°03'30" W; sec. 32, T 26 S, R 18 E). Named on Packwood Creek (1961) 7.5' quadrangle.

Ames Hole [TULARE]: *relief feature,* 2.5 miles south of California Hot Springs along White River (1) (lat. 35°50'30" N, long. 118°40'10" W; sec. 18, T 24 S, R 31 E). Named on California Hot Springs (1958) 15' quadrangle.

Amphitheater Lake [FRESNO]: *lake,* 2800 feet long, 13 miles east-southeast of Mount Goddard (lat. 37°01'30" N, long. 118°30'35" W). Named on Mount Goddard (1948) 15' quadrangle. J.N. LeConte named the lake in 1902 (Farquhar, 1923, p. 382).

Amphitheater Lake [TULARE]: *lake,* 1600 feet long, 2.5 miles east of Mineral King (lat. 36°26'45" N, long. 118°33'05" W). Named on Mineral King (1956) 15' quadrangle. W.F. Dean named the feature in 1889 (Browning, p. 5).

Amphitheater Point [TULARE]: *relief feature,* 5.5 miles east-southeast of Yucca Mountain (lat. 36°32'15" N, long. 118°46'50" W). Named on Giant Forest (1956) 15' quadrangle.

Anderson Point [TULARE]: *peak,* 3 miles east of Monache Mountain (lat. 36°12'20" N, long. 118°08'40" W; near NW cor. sec. 12, T 20 S, R 35 E). Named on Monache Mountain (1956) 15' quadrangle.

Andress Spring [KERN]: *spring,* 4.5 miles north-northwest of Weldon (lat. 35°43'30" N, long. 118°19'45" W). Named on Weldon (1972) 7.5' quadrangle.

Andrews: see **Figarden** [FRESNO].

Andy Berry's Landing: see **Millwood** [FRESNO].

Angel Creek [KERN]: *stream*, flows 5.25 miles to Poso Creek 1.25 miles southwest of Glennville (lat. 35°43' N, long. 118°43'15" W; at S line sec. 26, T 25 S, R 30 E). Named on California Hot Springs (1958) 15' quadrangle, and on Glennville (1972) 7.5' quadrangle. United States Board on Geographic Names (1960a, p. 5) rejected the name "Angle Creek" for it.

Angiola [TULARE]: *village*, 13 miles west-northwest of Earlimart (lat. 35°59'25" N, long. 119°28'25" W; sec. 27, T 22 S, R 23 E). Named on Alpaugh (1953) 7.5' quadrangle. Postal authorities established Angiola post office in 1898 and discontinued it in 1927 (Frickstad, p. 209). Mr. Bacigalupi, who owned property at the place, named the village for his wife, Angela (Mitchell, A.R., p. 67).

Angle Creek: see **Angel Creek** [KERN].

Angora Creek [TULARE]: *stream*, flows 2 miles to Kern River 7.25 miles west-southwest of Kern Peak (lat. 36°16'10" N, long. 118°24'15" W); the stream heads near Angora Mountain. Named on Kern Peak (1956) 15' quadrangle.

Angora Mountain [TULARE]: *peak*, 9.5 miles west-southwest of Kern Peak on Great Western Divide (lat. 36°15'50" N, long. 118° 26'45" W). Altitude 10,202 feet. Named on Kern Peak (1956) 15' quadrangle. Called Sheep Mtn. on Olancha (1907) 30' quadrangle, but United States Board on Geographic Names (1938, p. 4) rejected this name for the feature. A sheepman named the peak for an Angora goat that led his flock (Browning, p. 5).

Anna Mills: see **Mount Anna Mills,** under **Mount Guyot** [TULARE].

Anne Lake [FRESNO]: *lake*, 2400 feet long, 12.5 miles west-northwest of Mount Abbot on the north side of Silver Divide (lat. 37°27'40" N, long. 118°59'25" W). Named on Mount Abbot (1953) 15' quadrangle.

Annette [KERN]: *locality*, 6.5 miles south-southwest of Orchard Peak (lat. 35°39'05" N, long. 120°10'40" W; sec. 19, T 26 S, R 17 E); the place is 1.5 miles northeast of Palo Prieto Pass. Named on Orchard Peak (1961) 7.5' quadrangle. The locality first was called Palo Prieto (Dillon, p. 5). Postal authorities established Annette post office in 1889, moved it 2.5 miles southwest in 1894, and discontinued it in 1930; the name was for Annette L. Jenness, first postmaster (Salley, p. 8).

Ansel [KERN]: *locality*, 3 miles north-northeast of Rosamond along Southern Pacific Railroad (lat. 34°54'20" N, long. 118°09'10" W; near N line sec. 4, T 9 N, R 12 W). Named on Soledad Mountain (1973) 7.5' quadrangle.

Ansel Lake: [TULARE]: *lake*, 600 feet long, 4 miles south of Mineral King (lat. 36°23'30" N, long. 118°35'50" W). Named on Mineral King (1956) 15' quadrangle. The name is for Ansel Franklin Hall, a ranger and later information officer at Sequoia National Park (Browning, p. 6).

Ant Canyon [TULARE]: *canyon*, drained by a stream that flows 4 miles to Kern River 3.5 miles southeast of Fairview (lat. 35°53'05" N, long. 118°27'30" W; sec. 31, T 23 S, R 33 E). Named on California Hot Springs (1958) and Kernville (1956) 15' quadrangles.

Antelope Canyon [KERN]:

(1) *canyon*, drained by a stream that flows 5 miles to Tehachapi Valley 2.25 miles south of Tehachapi (lat. 35°05'55" N, long. 118° 26'35" W; sec. 33, T 32 S, R 33 E). Named on Tehachapi South (1966) 7.5' quadrangle.

(2) *canyon*, drained by a stream that flows 3 miles to lowlands 7.5 miles south-southwest of Liebre Twins (lat. 34°51'45" N, long. 118°38'30" W; near SW cor. sec. 13, T 9 N, R 17 W). Named on La Liebre Ranch (1965) and Winters Ridge (1966) 7.5' quadrangles.

Antelope Creek [TULARE]: *stream*, flows 6.5 miles to lowlands 1.5 miles north of Woodlake (lat. 36°26'15" N, long. 119°05'45" W; sec. 19, T 17 S, R 27 E). Named on Auckland (1966) and Woodlake (1952) 7.5' quadrangles.

Antelope Hills [KERN]: *range*, 6.5 miles southeast of Blackwells Corner (lat. 35°32'30" N, long. 119°48'30" W). Named on Blackwells Corner (1953) 7.5' quadrangle. Arnold and Johnson (p. 19) proposed the name for "the group of low hills" that "are a range for the few wild antelope left in this region."

Antelope Mountain [TULARE]: *ridge*, generally west-trending, 1.25 miles long, 2 miles northeast of Woodlake (lat. 36°25'50" N, long. 119°04'15" W); the ridge is south of Antelope Valley. Named on Woodlake (1952) 7.5' quadrangle. Called Woodlake Mtn. on Lemon Cove (1928) 7.5' quadrangle.

Antelope Plain [KERN]: *valley*, southwest of the village of Lost Hills (lat. 35°38' N, long. 119°50' W). Named on Antelope Plain (1954), Avenal Gap (1954), Blackwells Corner (1953), Emigrant Hill (1953), and Shale Point (1953) 7.5' quadrangles.

Antelope Spring [KERN]: *spring*, 7.25 miles west-northwest of Carneros Rocks (lat. 35°28'45" N, long. 119°58'05" W; sec. 19, T 28 S, R 19 E). Named on Las Yeguas Ranch (1959) 7.5' quadrangle, which has a windmill symbol at the place.

Antelope Valley [KERN]:

(1) *valley*, 8 miles southeast of Orchard Peak (lat. 35°39'30" N, long. 120°01'30" W). Named on Emigrant Hill (1953), Orchard Peak (1961), Packwood Creek (1961), Sawtooth Ridge (1961), and Shale Point (1953) 7.5' quadrangles.

(2) *area*, part of Mojave Desert southeast of Tehachapi Mountains on Kern-Los Angeles County line. Named on Los Angeles (1975) and San Bernardino (1957) 1°x 2° quadrangles. Called Palma Plain on Williamson's (1853) map.

Antelope Valley [TULARE]: *valley*, 2.5 miles north-northeast of Woodlake (lat. 36°26'50" N, long. 119°04'15" W); the valley is north of Antelope Mountain. Named on Woodlake (1952) 7.5' quadrangle.

Antes [TULARE]: *locality*, 1.25 miles north-northeast of Exeter along Atchison, Topeka and Santa Fe Railroad (lat. 36°18'35" N, long. 119°07'45" W; sec. 2, T 19 S, R 26 E). Named on Exeter (1952) 15' quadrangle.

Ant Hill [KERN]: *peak*, 7.25 miles east-northeast of downtown Bakersfield (lat. 35°25'35" N, long. 118°53'10" W; at N line sec. 8, T 29 S, R 29 E). Altitude 960 feet. Named on Oil Center (1954) 7.5' quadrangle.

Anticline Canyon: see **Cooper Canyon** [FRESNO].

Anticline Ridge [FRESNO]: *ridge*, southeast-trending, 11 miles long, 6.5 miles north-northeast of Coalinga (lat. 36°14' N, long. 120°19'30" W). Named on Coalinga (1956), Guijarral Hills (1956), and Joaquin Rocks (1969) 7.5' quadrangles. The ridge "is formed by a perfect anticlinal nose" that gives the feature its name (Arnold and Anderson, 1908, p. 13)

Antimony Flat [KERN]: *valley*, 1.25 miles south of Cross Mountain (lat. 35°15'30" N, long. 118°08'15" W). Named on Cross Mountain (1972) 7.5' quadrangle.

Antimony Peak [KERN]:

(1) *peak*, 2.5 miles south-southeast of Eagle Rest Peak (lat. 34°52'35" N, long. 119°06'40" W; sec. 10, T 9 N, R 21 W). Altitude 6848 feet. Named on Pleito Hills (1958) 7.5' quadrangle. Antimony has been mined on the slopes of the peak (Troxel and Morton, p. 56).

(2) *peak*, 3 miles southwest of Loraine (lat. 35°16'50" N, long. 118° 28'35" W; sec. 31, T 30 S, R 33 E); the peak is at the north end of Antimony Ridge (1). Named on Loraine (1972) 7.5' quadrangle.

Antimony Ridge [KERN]:

(1) *ridge*, north-trending, less than 1 mile long, 3 miles southwest of Loraine (lat. 35°16'30" N, long. 118°28'30" W; sec. 31, T 30 S, R 33 E). Named on Loraine (1972) 7.5' quadrangle

(2) *ridge*, northwest-trending, 0.25 mile long, nearly 6 miles northwest of Emerald Mountain (lat. 35°19'10" N, long. 118°20'55" W; at S line sec. 17, T 30 S, R 34 E). Named on Emerald Mountain (1972) 7.5' quadrangle.

Apollo Lake [FRESNO]: *lake*, 1400 feet long, 7 miles west-southwest of Mount Abbot (lat. 37°20' N, long 118°53'25" W). Named on Mount Abbot (1953) 15' quadrangle.

Aqueduct: see **Monolith** [KERN].

Aramburu Canyon [KERN]: *canyon*, 1 mile long, 8.5 miles west of McKittrick (lat. 35°18'45" N, long. 119°46'30" W; on E line sec. 13, T 30 S, R 20 E). Named on McKittrick Summit (1959) 7.5' quadrangle. The name commemorates John L. Aramburu, a Portuguese settler who lived at the mouth of the canyon (Arnold and Johnson, p. 19).

Araujo Spring: see **Lower Araujo Spring** [KERN]; **Upper Araujo Spring** [KERN].

Arbios [FRESNO]: *locality*, 6.5 miles south-southeast of Firebaugh along Southern Pacific Railroad (lat. 36°46'35" N, long. 120°23'50" W; sec. 25, T 13 S, R 14 E). Named on Firebaugh (1956) 7.5' quadrangle.

Archer Camp [FRESNO]: *locality*, 15 miles northwest of Coalinga (lat. 36°17'55" N, long. 120°33'55" W; sec. 3, T 19 S, R 13 E); the place is nearly 1 mile southwest of Archer mine. Named on Santa Rita Peak (1969) 7.5' quadrangle.

Arch Rock [FRESNO]: *relief feature*, 12.5 miles north-northeast of Kaiser Peak (lat. 37°26'50" N, long. 119°04'20" W). Named on Kaiser Peak (1953) 15' quadrangle.

Arc Pass [TULARE]: *pass*, 2.25 miles southeast of Mount Whitney on Tulare-Inyo County line (lat. 36°33'05" N, long. 118°16'05" W). Named on Mount Whitney (1956) 15' quadrangle. Chester Versteeg proposed the descriptive name in 1936 (Browning, p. 6).

Arctic Lake [FRESNO]: *lake*, 800 feet long, 4 miles north of Blackcap Mountain (lat. 37°07'50" N, long. 118°47'45" W). Named on Blackcap Mountain (1953) 15' quadrangle.

Arctic Lake [TULARE]: *lake*, 1100 feet long, 1 mile west-northwest of Mount Whitney (lat. 36°35' N, long. 118°18'25" W). Named on Mount Whitney (1956) 15' quadrangle. Chester Versteeg proposed the name in 1953 (Browning, p. 6).

Arkansas Creek [FRESNO]: *stream*, flows nearly 2 miles to Dinkey Creek (1) 0.25 mile northeast of Dinkey Dome (lat. 37°07' N, long. 119°07'35" W; sec. 27, T 9 S, R 26 E). Named on Huntington Lake (1953) 15' quadrangle.

Arkansas Meadow [FRESNO]: *area*, 1 mile southeast of Dinkey Dome (lat. 37°06'20" N, long. 119°07'05" W; sec. 34, T 9 S, R 26 E); the place is along Arkansas Creek. Named on Huntington Lake (1953) 15' quadrangle.

Armistead [KERN]: *locality*, 9 miles southwest of Inyokern (lat. 35° 32'50" N, long. 117°55'40" W; sec. 31, T 27 S, R 38 E). Named on Freeman Junction (1972) 7.5' quadrangle.

Armitage Field [KERN]: *military installation*, 5 miles north of Ridgecrest (lat. 35°41'30" N, long. 117°41' W). Named on Ridgecrest (1953) 15' quadrangle. The place now is called Inyokern Airport (Darling, p. 62).

Armona [KINGS]: *town,* 3.5 miles west-southwest of Hanford (lat. 36°18'55" N, long. 119°42'30" W; in and near sec. 32, 33, T 18 S, R 21 E). Named on Hanford (1954) 7.5' quadrangle. The name applied to a railroad station in the 1880's, and was transferred to the present location on Southern Pacific Railroad in 1891 (Gudde, 1949, p. 15). Postal authorities established Armona post office in 1887—the name was coined by switching the first two letters of the name "Ramona" (Salley, p. 10).

Armstrong [FRESNO]: *village,* 0.5 mile southwest of Shaver Lake before the lake was enlarged; near present Rock Haven (lat. 37°07'25" N, long. 119°18'45" W; near NW cor. sec. 25, T 9 S, R 24 E). Named on Kaiser (1904) 30' quadrangle.

Army Pass [TULARE]: *pass,* 17 miles north-northwest of Olancha Peak on Tulare-Inyo County line (lat. 36°29'50" N, long. 118°14'20" W). Named on Olancha (1956) 15' quadrangle.

Army Pass: see **New Army Pass** [TULARE].

Arnett Spring [TULARE]: *spring,* 4.25 miles north of Cliff Peak (lat. 36°37'05" N, long. 119°09'35" W; near W line sec. 16, T 15 S, R 26 E). Named on Stokes Mountain (1966) 7.5' quadrangle.

Arosi: see **East Orosi** [TULARE].

Arp's Addition: see **Riverview**, under **Bakersfield** [KERN].

Arrastra Canyon [TULARE]: *canyon,* drained by a stream that flows 1.25 miles to Dry Creek (1) 4.25 miles east-northeast of Woodlake (lat. 36°25'40" N, long. 119°01'30" W; near NW cor. sec. 26, T 17 S, R 27 E). Named on Woodlake (1952) 7.5' quadrangle.

Arrastre Creek [KERN-TULARE]: *stream,* heads in Kern County and flows 8.5 miles to White River (1) 7 miles southeast of Fountain Springs at White River (2) in Tulare County (lat. 35°48'50" N, long. 118°50'40" W; sec. 28, T 24 S, R 29 E). Named on White River (1952) 15' quadrangle.

Arrojo los Gates: see **Los Gatos Creek** [FRESNO].

Arrow Creek [FRESNO]: *stream,* flows 4.5 miles to South Fork Kings River 6 miles south of Marion Peak (lat. 36°52'15" N, long. 118°30'50" W); the stream is southeast of Arrow Ridge. Named on Marion Peak (1953) and Mount Pinchot (1953) 15' quadrangles.

Arrowhead Lake [FRESNO]: *lake,* 700 feet long, 9.5 miles west-northwest of Mount Abbot (lat. 37°25'30" N, long. 118°56'50" W). Named on Mount Abbot (1953) 15' quadrangle. The outline of the lake on a map has the shape of an arrowhead.

Arrow Peak [FRESNO]: *peak,* 5 miles west-southwest of Mount Pinchot (lat. 36°55'40" N, long. 118°29'20" W). Altitude 12,958 feet. Named on Mount Pinchot (1953) 15' quadrangle. Bolton C. Brown made the first ascent of the peak and named it in 1895 (Browning, p. 7).

Arrow Ridge [FRESNO]: *ridge,* northeast-trending, 3 miles long, 3 miles south-southeast of Marion Peak (lat. 36°54'30" N, long. 118° 30'30" W); the ridge extends southwest from Arrow Peak. Named on Marion Peak (1953) and Mount Pinchot (1953) 15' quadrangles.

Arroyo Ancho [KERN]: *stream,* 2 miles long, ends 11 miles north-northwest of Blackwells Corner (lat. 35°46' N, long. 119°55'05" W; near W line sec. 10, T 25 S, R 19 E). Named on Avenal Gap (1954) 7.5' quadrangle. United States Board on Geographic Names (1933b, p. 2) noted that *ancho* means "broad" in Spanish.

Arroyo Bifido [KINGS]: *stream,* flows 2 miles to lowlands 5 miles north-northeast of Avenal (lat. 36°03'55" N, long. 120°05'10" W; near S line sec. 25, T 21 S, R 17 E). Named on La Cima (1963) 7.5' quadrangle. United States Board on Geographic Names (1933b, p. 2) noted that the name is from the two branches near the head of the stream—*bifido* means "two-forked" in Spanish.

Arroyo Chico [KINGS]: *stream,* flows less than 2 miles to Kettleman Plain 1.5 miles east-southeast of Avenal (lat. 36°00' N, long. 120° 06'15" W; sec. 23, T 22 S, R 17 E). Named on La Cima (1963) 7.5' quadrangle. United States Board on Geographic Names (1933b, p. 2) noted that the name is descriptive—*chico* means "small" in Spanish.

Arroyo Ciervo [FRESNO]: *stream,* flows 8 miles to lowlands 15 miles southwest of Tranquility (lat. 36°31' N, long. 120°27'50" W; near SE cor. sec. 20, T 16 S, R 14 E); the stream is in Ciervo Hills. Named on Ciervo Mountain (1969) 7.5' quadrangle.

Arroyo Conchoso [KINGS]: *stream,* flows nearly 3 miles to Kettleman Plain 3.5 miles east-southeast of Avenal (lat. 35°58'40" N, long. 120°04'25" W; near SW cor. sec. 30, T 22 S, R 18 E). Named on Kettleman Plain (1953) and La Cima (1963) 7.5' quadrangles. The name refers to the abundance of fossil shells at the place—*conchoso* means "shelly" in Spanish (United States Board on Geographic Names, 1933b, p. 2).

Arroyo Corto [FRESNO]: *stream,* flows 1.5 miles to Kettleman Plain 12 miles east-southeast of Coalinga (lat. 36°03'05" N, long. 120°10'35" W; near S line sec. 31, T 21 S, R 17 E). Named on Avenal (1954) 7.5' quadrangle. United States Board on Geographic Names (1933b, p. 2) noted that the name is descriptive—*corto* means "short" in Spanish

Arroyo Culebrino [KINGS]: *stream,* flows 3.25 miles to lowlands 5.5 miles south-southeast of Kettleman City (lat. 35°56' N, long. 119°55'50" W; near NW cor. sec. 16, T 23 S, R 19 E). Named on Los Viejos (1954) 7.5' quadrangle. United States Board on Geographic Names (1933b, p. 2) noted that *culebrino* means "snaky" in Spanish.

Arroyo Curvo [KINGS]: *stream,* flows nearly 2 miles to Kettleman Plain 1 mile north-northwest of Avenal (lat. 36°01'05" N, long. 120°08'10" W; sec. 16, T 22 S, R 17 E). Named on Avenal (1954) 7.5' quadrangle. United States Board on Geographic Names (1933b, p. 2) pointed out that *curvo* means "bent" in Spanish.

Arroyo Degollado [KINGS]: *stream,* flows 2.5 miles to lowlands nearly 1.5 miles west-northwest of Kettleman City (lat. 36°01' N, long. 119°59' W; near E line sec. 14, T 22 S, R 18 E). Named on Kettleman City (1963) and La Cima (1963) 7.5' quadrangles. The name refers to the apparent capture of the headwaters of the stream by Arroyo Robador—*degollado* means "beheaded" in Spanish (United States Board on Geographic Names, 1933b, p. 2).

Arroyo de las Encinas: see **Liveoak Canyon** [KERN].

Arroyo de las Uvas: see **Grapevine Creek** [KERN].

Arroyo del Camino [KINGS]: *stream,* flows 1.5 miles to Kettleman Plain at Avenal (lat. 36°00'30" N, long. 120°07'15" W; sec. 15, T 22 S, R 17 E). Named on La Cima (1963) 7.5' quadrangle. United States Board on Geographic Names (1933b, p. 4) related the name to a road that follows the stream, and pointed out that *camino* means "road" in Spanish. On Discovery Well (1930) 7.5' quadrangle, the canyon of the stream has the name "Tar Canyon."

Arroyo del Conejo [KINGS]: *stream,* flows 3 miles before ending 5.25 miles south of Kettleman City (lat. 35°55'50" N, long. 119°57'30" W; sec. 18, T 23 S, R 19 E). Named on Los Viejos (1954) 7.5' quadrangle. United States Board on Geographic Names (1933b, p. 4) pointed out that *conejo* means "rabbit" in Spanish.

Arroyo Delgado [KINGS]: *stream,* flows 2.25 miles to Kettleman Plain 5.5 miles east-southeast of Avenal (lat. 35°57'40" N, long. 120°02'50" W; sec. 5, T 23 S, R 18 E). Named on Kettleman Plain (1953) 7.5' quadrangle. United States Board on Geographic Names (1933b, p. 2-3) related the name to the narrow course of the stream—*delgado* means "slender" in Spanish.

Arroyo de los Alamos: see **Tejon Creek** [KERN].

Arroyo de los Alizos: see **Sycamore Canyon** [KERN] (1).

Arroyo de los Osos: see **Williams Canyon** [KERN].

Arroyo del Paso [KINGS]: *stream,* flows 4.25 miles to end 5 miles south of Kettleman City (lat. 35°56'45" N, long. 119°57'45" W; sec. 7, T 23 S, R 19 E). Named on Kettleman Plain (1953) and Los Viejos (1954) 7.5' quadrangles. United States Board on Geographic Names (1933b, p. 4) connected the name with the nearby pass called El Paso.

Arroyo del Tejon: see **Tejon Creek** [KERN].

Arroyo de Tecuya: see **Tecuya Creek** [KERN].

Arroyo Doblegado [KINGS]: *stream,* flows 4 miles to lowlands 6.5 miles east-northeast of Avenal (lat. 36°01'40" N, long. 120°00'45" W; sec. 10, T 22 S, R 18 E). Named on La Cima (1963) 7.5' quadrangle. United States Board on Geographic Names (1933b, p. 3) noted that the name is descriptive—*doblegado* means "twisted" in Spanish.

Arroyo Escaso [KINGS]: *dry wash,* extends for 1 mile to Kettleman Plain 8 miles southeast of Avenal (lat. 35°56'10" N, long. 120° 01' W; near S line sec. 10, T 23 S, R 18 E). Named on Kettleman Plain (1953) 7.5' quadrangle. United States Board on Geographic Names (1933b, p. 3) pointed out that *escaso* means "short" (in the sense of "scarce") in Spanish.

Arroyo Esquinado [KINGS]: *stream,* flows 2 miles to Kettleman Plain at Avenal (lat. 36°00'45" N, long. 120°07'35" W; sec. 15, T 22 S, R 17 E). Named on La Cima (1963) 7.5' quadrangle. United States Board on Geographic Names (1933b, p. 3) related the descriptive name to a sharp bend in the watercourse—*esquinado* means "angled" in Spanish.

Arroyo Estrecho [KINGS]: *stream,* flows 4.5 miles to lowlands 3.5 miles south-southeast of Kettleman City (lat. 35°57'45" N, long. 119°56'20" W; near N line sec. 5, T 23 S, R 19 E). Named on Los Viejos (1954) 7.5' quadrangle. The name is descriptive—*estrecho* means "narrow" in Spanish (United States Board on Geographic Names, 1933b, p. 3).

Arroyo Finito [KINGS]: *stream,* flows 1.5 miles to lowlands 6.25 miles east-northeast of Avenal (lat. 36°02'05" N, long. 120°01'30" W; near N line sec. 9, T 22 S, R 18 E). Named on La Cima (1963) 7.5' quadrangle. The name refers to the restricted drainage area of the stream—*finito* means "limited" in Spanish (United States Board on Geographic Names, 1933b, p. 3).

Arroyo Hondo [FRESNO]: *stream,* heads in San Benito County and flows 14 miles to lowlands 24 miles north of Coalinga (lat. 36° 28'45" N, long. 120°26' W; sec. 3, T 17 S, R 14 E). Named on Ciervo Mountain (1969) and Lillis Ranch (1956) 7.5' quadrangles. United States Board on Geographic Names (1933a, p. 104) rejected the name "Dry Creek" for the stream.

Arroyo Hondo [KINGS]: *stream,* flows 2.5 miles to lowlands 5.5 miles east-northeast of Avenal (lat. 36°02'40" N, long. 120°02'20" W; near E line sec. 5, T 22 S, R 18 E). Named on La Cima (1963) 7.5' quadrangle. United States Board on Geographic Names (1933b, p. 3) pointed out that *hondo* means "deep" or "low" in Spanish.

Arroyo Largo [FRESNO-KINGS]: *stream,* heads in Kings County and flows 5 miles to lowlands 14 miles east-southeast of Coalinga in Fresno County (lat. 36°04'45" N, long. 120°06'45" W; near N line sec. 27, T 21 S, R 17 E). Named on La Cima (1963) 7.5' quadrangle. The name is descriptive—*largo* means "long" in Spanish (United States Board on Geographic Names, 1933b, p. 3).

Arroyo Larguito [KINGS]: *stream,* heads just inside Fresno County and flows 1.25 miles to Kettleman Plain 2 miles north-northwest of Avenal (lat. 36°01'45" N, long. 120°09'45" W; sec. 8, T 22 S, R 17 E). Named on Avenal (1954) 7.5' quadrangle. United States Board on Geographic Names (1933b, p. 3) pointed out that *larguito* means "a little long" in Spanish.

Arroyo las Gatos: see **Los Gatos Creek** [FRESNO].

Arroyo Leona [FRESNO]: *stream,* flows 6.5 miles to Cantua Creek 5.5 miles south-southeast of Ciervo Mountain (lat. 36°23'40" N, long. 120°32'10" W; near E line sec. 3, T 18 S, R 13 E). Named on Ciervo Mountain (1969) and Santa Rita Peak (1969) 7.5' quadrangles.

Arroyo Mellado [KINGS]: *stream,* flows 2 miles to Kettleman Plain 2 miles east-southeast of Avenal (lat. 35°59'30" N, long. 120°05'40" W; near NE cor. sec. 26, T 22 S, R 17 E). Named on Kettleman Plain (1953) and La Cima (1963) 7.5' quadrangles. United States Board on Geographic Names (1933b, p. 3) noted that the name is descriptive—*mellado* means "jagged" in Spanish.

Arroyo Menudo [KINGS]: *stream,* flows 1.5 miles to Kettleman Plain 9 miles south of Kettleman City (lat. 35°52'30" N, long. 119° 59'45" W; near N line sec. 2, T 24 S, R 18 E). Named on Avenal Gap (1954) and Los Viejos (1954) 7.5' quadrangles. The name is descriptive—*menudo* means "small" in Spanish (United States Board on Geographic Names, 1933b, p. 3).

Arroyo Murado [KINGS]: *stream,* flows 2.5 miles to Arroyo Torcido 4.25 miles northeast of Avenal (lat. 36°02'50" N, long. 120°04'20" W; sec. 6, T 22 S, R 18 E). Named on La Cima (1963) 7.5' quadrangle. The name is descriptive—*murado* means "walled" in Spanish (United States Board on Geographic Names, 1933b, p. 3).

Arroyo Passajero: see **Los Gatos Creek** [FRESNO].

Arroyo Pastoria: see **Pastoria Creek** [KERN].

Arroyo Pequeño [KINGS]: *stream,* flows 2 miles to lowlands 5.5 miles east-northeast of Avenal (lat. 36°02'25" N, long. 120°02' W; sec. 4, T 22 S, R 18 E). Named on La Cima (1963) 7.5' quadrangle. The name is descriptive—*pequeño* means "small" in Spanish (United States Board on Geographic Names, 1933b, p. 3).

Arroyo Petreo [KINGS]: *stream,* flows 1.25 miles to Kettleman Plain 10.5 miles south of Kettleman City (lat. 35°51'10" N, long. 119°58'25" W; sec. 12, T 24 S, R 18 E). Named on Avenal Gap (1954) 7.5' quadrangle. The name refers to gravel in the stream bed—*petreo* means "stony" in Spanish (United States Board on Geographic Names, 1933b, p. 3).

Arroyo Pino [KINGS]: *stream,* flows 3 miles to lowlands 2 miles south-southeast of Kettleman City (lat. 35°58'45" N, long. 119° 57' W; near SE cor. sec. 30, T 22 S, R 19 E). Named on Los Viejos (1954) 7.5' quadrangle. United States Board on Geographic Names (1933b, p. 4) pointed out that *pino* means "steep" in Spanish.

Arroyo Pinoso [FRESNO]: *canyon,* drained by a stream that flows 5 miles to Zapato Chino Creek 4.5 miles north-northeast of Castle Mountain (lat. 36°00'05" N, long. 120°19' W; near E line sec. 23, T 22 S, R 15 E). Named on The Dark Hole (1961) 7.5' quadrangle, where the name applies to the stream in the canyon. On Cholame (1917) 30' quadrangle, and on The Dark Hole (1937) 7.5' quadrangle, the name applies to the canyon. Arnold and Anderson (1908, p. 16) called the feature Sulphur Spring Canyon "from the abundance of sulphur water that issues in it." The Dark Hole (1937) 7.5' quadrangle shows ruins of Pinoso house in the canyon (sec. 2, T 23 S, R 15 E). United States Board on Geographic Names (1964c, p. 15) rejected the names "Arroyo Piñoso," "Sulphur Spring Canyon," and "West Fork Zapato Creek" for the feature, and classified Arroyo Pinoso as a valley.

Arroyo Poso de Chane: see **Los Gatos Creek** [FRESNO].

Arroyo Ramoso [KINGS]: *stream,* flows 2.5 miles to Kettleman Plain nearly 5 miles east-southeast of Avenal (lat. 35°58' N, long. 120°03'20" W; near W line sec. 32, T 22 S, R 18 E). Named on Kettleman Plain (1953) 7.5' quadrangle.

Arroyo Raso [KINGS]: *stream,* flows 2 miles to Kettleman Plain 6.5 miles southeast of Avenal (lat. 37°57' N, long. 120°01'50" W; near S line sec. 4, T 23 S, R 18 E). Named on Kettleman Plain (1953) 7.5' quadrangle. United States Board on Geographic Names (1933b, p. 4) noted that *raso* means "open" or "unobstructed" in Spanish.

Arroyo Recodo [KINGS]: *stream,* flows 2.25 miles before ending at La Porteria 8 miles south-southeast of Kettleman City (lat. 35°53'55" N, long. 119°55'05" W; sec. 28, T 23 S, R 19 E). Named on Los Viejos (1954) 7.5' quadrangle. United States Board on Geographic Names (1933b, p. 4) noted that the name is descriptive—*recodo* means "winding" in Spanish.

Arroyo Recto [FRESNO]: *stream,* flows 1.5 miles to Kettleman Plain 10.5 miles east-southeast of Coalinga (lat. 36°04'10" N, long. 120° 11'45" W; sec. 25, T 21 S, R 16 E). Named on Avenal (1954) 7.5' quadrangle. The name is descriptive—*recto* means "straight" in Spanish (United States Board on Geographic Names, 1933b, p. 4).

Arroyo Robador [KINGS]: *stream,* flows 5 miles to lowlands 1 mile south of Kettleman City (lat. 35°59'35" N, long. 119°57'45" W; near SW cor. sec. 19, T 22 S, R 19 E). Named on Kettleman City (1963), Kettleman Plain (1953), La Cima (1963), and Los Viejos (1954) 7.5' quadrangles. The name refers to the apparent capture of the headwaters of Arroyo Degollado by Arroyo Robador—*robador* means "robber" in Spanish (United States Board on Geographic Names, 1933b, p. 4).

Arroyo San Arminio: see **San Emigdio Creek** [KERN].

Arroyo Seco [FRESNO]: *stream,* flows 2.5 miles to lowlands 11 miles east-southeast of Coalinga (lat. 36°06' N, long. 120°10' W; sec. 18, T 21 S, R 17 E). Named on Avenal (1954) 7.5' quadrangle. The name is descriptive—*seco* means "dry" in Spanish (United States Board on Geographic Names, 1933b, p. 4).

Arroyo Somero [KINGS]: *stream,* flows nearly 2 miles to Kettleman Plain 1 mile east of Avenal (lat. 36°00'05" N, long. 120°06'30" W; sec. 23, T 22 S, R 17 E). Named on La Cima (1963) 7.5' quadrangle. United States Board on Geographic Names (1933b, p. 4) pointed out that *somero* means "shallow" in Spanish.

Arroyo Torcido [KINGS]: *stream,* flows 4 miles to lowlands 5.25 miles north-east of Avenal (lat. 36°03'25" N, long. 120°03'40" W; sec. 31, T 21 S, R 18 E). Named on La Cima (1963) 7.5' quadrangle. The name is descriptive—*torcido* means "twisted" in Spanish (United States Board on Geographic Names, 1933b, p. 4).

Arroyo Tozo [KINGS]: *stream,* flows 1 mile to lowlands 13 miles south-southeast of Kettleman City (lat. 35°49'20" N, long. 119°53'30" W; sec. 23, T 24 S, R 19 E). Named on Avenal Gap (1954) 7.5' quadrangle. United States Board on Geographic Names (1933b, p. 4) pointed out that *tozo* means "small" or "dwarf" in Spanish.

Arroyo Vadoso [FRESNO]: *stream,* flows 3.5 miles to lowlands 13 miles east-southeast of Coalinga (lat. 36°05'25" N, long. 120°08'15" W; sec. 21, T 21 S, R 17 E). Named on Avenal (1954) and La Cima (1963) 7.5' quadrangles. The name is descriptive—*vadoso* means "shallow" in Spanish (United States Board on Geographic Names, 1933b, p. 4).

Arroyo Venado [FRESNO]: *stream,* flows 2.5 miles to Arroyo Leona 6 miles south-southeast of Ciervo Mountain (lat. 36°23'05" N, long. 120°32'35" W; near N line sec. 10, T 18 S, R 13 E). Named on Ciervo Mountain (1969) and Santa Rita Peak (1969) 7.5' quadrangles.

Artwell: see **Bannister** [KERN].

Arvin [KERN]: *town,* 15 miles southeast of Bakersfield (lat. 35°12'30" N, long. 118°49'45" W; in and near sec. 23, 26, T 31 S, R 29 E). Named on Arvin (1955) 7.5' quadrangle. Postal authorities established Arvin post office in 1914 (Frickstad, p. 54), and the town incorporated in 1960. The first postmaster, Mrs. Birdie Heard, named the place for Arvin Richardson, a pioneer in construction and installation of concrete irrigation pipe in the region (Hanna, p. 18).

Ashely Hot Spring [KERN]: *spring,* 5 miles north-northwest of Weldon (lat. 35°44'05" N, long. 118°18'55" W). Named on Weldon (1972) 7.5' quadrangle.

Ash Peaks [TULARE]: *peaks,* 3.25 miles south-southeast of Yucca Mountain (lat. 36°31'30" N, long. 118°51'15" W). Named on Giant Forest (1956) 15' quadrangle.

Ash Peaks Ridge [TULARE]: *ridge,* southwest-trending, 4.5 miles long, 3 miles southeast of Yucca Mountain (lat. 36°32' N, long. 118°50'10" W); Ash Peaks are at the southwest end of the ridge. Named on Giant Forest (1956) 15' quadrangle. United States Board on Geographic Names (1933a. p. 105) rejected the name "Park Road Ridge" for the feature.

Ash Spring Mountain [TULARE]: *peak,* 2 miles east of Auckland (lat. 36°35'30" N, long. 119°04'05" W; near W line sec. 29, T 15 S, R 27 E). Named on Auckland (1966) 7.5' quadrangle.

Aspen Meadow [FRESNO]: *area,* 5.5 miles west of Kaiser Peak (lat. 37°16'45" N, long. 119°17'25" W; near NW cor. sec. 31, T 7 S, R 25 E). Named on Shuteye Peak (1953) 15' quadrangle.

Asphalto: see **McKittrick** [KERN].

Aster Lake [TULARE]: *lake,* 600 feet long, 8 miles west of Triple Divide Peak (lat. 36°36'10" N, long. 118°40'40" W; sec. 24, T 15 S, R 30 E). Named on Triple Divide Peak (1956) 15' quadrangle. Colonel John R. White named the feature in the early 1920's for flowers that grow along the lake shore (Browning, p. 8).

Atwell Creek [TULARE]: *stream,* flows 1.5 miles to East Fork Kaweah River 4.25 miles west of Mineral King (lat. 36°27'20" N, long. 118°40'20" W). Named on Mineral King (1956) 15' quadrangle, which shows Atwell Mill ranger station by the stream. Atwell Mill was a sawmill built in 1879 and later owned by A.J. Atwell of Visalia (Hanna, p. 19).

Atwell Mill: see **Atwell Creek** [TULARE].

Atwell's Island: see **Alpaugh** [TULARE].

Auberry [FRESNO]: *town,* 9.5 miles east-southeast of Shaver Lake Heights (present town of Shaver Lake) along Little Sandy Creek (lat. 37°04'45" N, long. 119°29'05" W; sec. 8, T 10 S, R 23 E). Named on Shaver Lake (1953) 15' quadrangle. On Kaiser (1904) 30' quadrangle. the name "Auberry" applies to a place located 1.25 miles farther north-northwest at present New Auberry. The name "Auberry" is for Al Yarborough, but the spelling follows the common pronunciation of Yarborough's name (Gudde, 1949, p. 18). Postal authorities established Auberry post office in 1884, moved it 1.5 miles southwest in 1887, moved it 1.5 miles south in 1888, and moved it 8 miles northeast in 1906 (Salley, p. 12). They established Thermal post office 5 miles southwest of Auberry in 1889 and discontinued it in 1900—the post office was at a resort built around hot springs (Salley, p. 221).

Auberry: see **New Auberry** [FRESNO].

Auberry Valley [FRESNO]: *valley,* 2.5 miles west of Prather (lat. 37°02' N, long. 119°33'45" W). Named on Millerton Lake East (1965) 7.5' quadrangle.

Auckland [TULARE]: *locality,* 16 miles east-northeast of Dinuba along Cottonwood Creek (lat. 36°35'20" N, long. 119°06'20" W; at W line sec. 25, T 15 S, R 26 E). Named on Auckland (1966) 7.5' quadrangle. Dunlap (1944) 15' quadrangle shows Auckland ranch at the site. Settlers from Auckland, New Zealand, named the place about 1860 (Mitchell, A.R., p. 67).

Avalanche Creek [FRESNO]: *stream,* flows 3 miles to South Fork Kings River 12 miles south of Marion Peak in Kings Canyon (lat. 36°47'15" N, long. 118°33'45" W); the stream is east of Avalanche Peak. Named on Marion Peak (1953) 15' quadrangle.

Avalanche Lake [FRESNO]: *lake,* 500 feet long, 1.5 miles northeast of Kaiser Peak (lat. 37°18'35" N, long. 119°10' W). Named on Kaiser Peak (1953) 15' quadrangle.

Avalanche Pass [FRESNO]: *pass,* 20 miles east of Hume (lat. 36°44'50" N, long. 118°33'25" W); the pass is 0.5 mile east of Palmer Mountain, which originally was called Avalanche Peak. Named on Triple Divide Peak (1956) 15' quadrangle.

Avalanche Peak [FRESNO]: *peak,* 14 miles south-southwest of Marion Peak (lat. 36°46' N, long. 118°34'55" W). Altitude 10,077 feet. Named on Marion Peak (1953) 15' quadrangle. John Muir named the feature in 1891; on some maps the name applies to present Palmer Mountain, situated 1.5 miles farther southeast (United States Board on Geographic Names, 1933a, p. 108).

Avalon: see **Kaweah** [TULARE].

Avenal [KINGS]: *town,* 35 miles southwest of Hanford (lat. 36°00'20" N, long. 120°07'50" W; sec. 15, 16, 21, 22, T 22 S, R 17 E). Named on Avenal (1954), Garza Peak (1953), and La Cima (1963) 7.5' quadrangles. Postal authorities established Avenal post office in 1929 (Frickstad, p. 60), and the town incorporated in 1979. The name is from *avena,* which means "oats," usually "wild oats," in Spanish (Stewart, p. 29). United States Board on Geographic Names (1988b, p. 2) approved the name "Zwang Peak" for a feature, altitude 3078 feet, located 8 miles southwest of Avenal (lat. 35°56'48" N, long. 120°14'48" W; sec. 9, T 23 S, R 16 E); the name commemorates Jake Zwang, who came to the neighborhood in 1906 and started a cattle ranch southwest of Avenal.

Avenal Canyon [FRESNO-KINGS]: *canyon,* drained by Little Avenal Creek, which heads in Fresno County and flows 18 miles to Avenal Creek 10 miles south of Avenal in Kings County (lat. 35°51'35" N, long. 120°08'45" W; near NW cor. sec. 9, T 24 S, R 17 E). Named on Garza Peak (1953), Tent Hills (1942), and The Dark Hole (1961) 7.5' quadrangles.

Avenal Creek [KINGS]: *stream,* flows 7.5 miles to Sunflower Valley 10.5 miles south of Avenal (lat. 35°51' N, long. 120°07' W; sec. 10, T 24 S, R 17 E). Named on Pyramid Hills (1953) and Tent Hills (1942) 7.5' quadrangles. United States Board on Geographic Names (1991, p. 3) rejected the names "Avendale Creek," "Dicks Creek," and "Little Avenal Creek" for the feature.

Avenal Creek: see **Little Avenal Creek** [FRESNO-KINGS]; **Little Avenal Creek,** under **Lovel Canyon** [KINGS].

Avenal Gap [KINGS]: *pass,* 11.5 miles south of Kettleman City between Middle Dome and South Dome of Kettleman Hills (lat. 35°50'15" N, long. 119°57' W). Named on Avenal Gap (1954) 7.5' quadrangle.

Avenal Ridge [KINGS]: *ridge,* northwest-trending, 11 miles long, southeast of Lovel Canyon (lat. 35°49'30" N, long. 120°09'45" W). Named on Pyramid Hills (1953) and Tent Hills (1942) 7.5' quadrangles. Arnold and Anderson (1908, p. 14) applied the name to "the southernmost of the spurs of Diablo Range" between Avenal Creek and McLure (present Sunflower) Valley; they noted that "the name, which means a field of oats, is appropriate because the hills forming the ridge are rounded and grass grown."

Avenal Ridge: see **Bluestone Ridge** [KERN].

Avendale Creek: see **Avenal Creek** [KINGS].

Avocado [FRESNO]: *locality,* nearly 2 miles southwest of Piedra on the southeast side of Kings River (lat. 36°47'20" N, long. 119°24'10" W; sec. 19, T 13 S, R 24 E). Named on Piedra (1965) 7.5' quadrangle. Orangedale School (1923) 7.5' quadrangle shows the place along the Atchison, Topeka and Santa Fe Railroad branch line to Piedra.

Avocado Lake [FRESNO]: *lake,* 0.5 mile long, 2.25 miles southwest of Piedra on lowlands near Kings River (lat. 36°47'15" N, long. 119°24'40" W); on E line sec. 24, T 13 S, R 23 E); the lake is 0.25 mile west of Avocado. Named on Piedra (1965) 7.5' quadrangle.

Aweetasal Lake [FRESNO]: *lake,* 1100 feet long, 6.5 miles south of Mount Abbot (lat. 37°17'35" N, long. 118°48'25" W). Named on Mount Abbot (1953) 15' quadrangle. Elden H. Vestal of California Department of Fish and Game named the lake in 1951; Vestal believed that the word "aweetasal" refers to a kind of Indian back carrier for babies (Browning, p. 9).

Azalea Campground [FRESNO-TULARE]: *locality,* less than 1 mile west-northwest of Wilsonia on Tulare-Fresno County line (lat. 36° 44'30" N, long. 118°57'55" W; at S line sec. 31, T 13 S, R 28 E). Named on Giant Forest (1956) 15' quadrangle.

—B—

Babbitt: see **Camp Babbitt,** under **Visalia** [TULARE].

Baby King Canyon [KINGS]: *canyon,* 1 mile long, 6 miles southwest of Avenal (lat. 35°56'30" N, long. 120°12'25" W); the canyon is at the head of Baby King Creek. Named on Garza Peak (1953) 7.5' quadrangle.

Baby King Creek [KINGS]: *stream,* flows 5 miles to Kettleman Plain 2.5 miles south-southwest of Avenal (lat. 35°58'10" N, long. 120°08'55" W; sec. 32, T 22 S, R 17 E). Named on Garza Peak (1953) 7.5' quadrangle.

Baby Lake [FRESNO]: *lake,* 550 feet long, 15 miles northeast of Kaiser Peak (lat. 37°28'20" N, long. 119°02'15" W). Named on Kaiser Peak (1953) 15' quadrangle. The lake is one of the group called Margaret Lakes

Backbone Creek [FRESNO]: *stream,* flows 2.25 miles to San Joaquin River 8.5 miles west of Shaver Lake Heights (present town of Shaver Lake) (lat. 37°06'35" N, long. 119°28'15" W; near N line sec. 33, T 9 S, R 23 E); the stream heads east of Backbone Mountain. Named on Shaver Lake (1953) 15' quadrangle.

Backbone Creek [TULARE]: *stream,* flows 4.5 miles to North Fork Tule River 17 miles south-southeast of Kaweah (lat. 36°15'05" N, long. 118°47'40" W; at SW cor. sec. 24, T 19 S, R 29 E). Named on Kaweah (1957) and Mineral King (1956) 15' quadrangles.

Backbone Mountain [FRESNO]: *ridge,* north-northwest-trending, nearly 2 miles long, 8.5 miles west-southwest of Shaver Lake Heights (present town of Shaver Lake) (lat. 37°04'30" N, long. 119°28' W). Named on Shaver Lake (1953) 15' quadrangle. Members of United States Geological Survey applied the name in 1904 for the shape of the ridge (Gudde, 1949, p. 19).

Back Canyon [KERN]: *canyon,* 8 miles long, along Caliente Creek above a point 2.5 miles east of Loraine (lat. 35°18'40" N, long. 118°23'25" W; at N line sec. 24, T 30 S, R 33 E). Named on Emerald Mountain (1972) and Loraine (1972) 7.5' quadrangles.

Bacon Hill [TULARE]: *hill,* 5.25 miles west-northwest of Woodlake (lat. 26°27'05" N, long. 119°10'50" W; sec. 17, T 17 S, R 26 E). Named on Exeter (1952) 15' quadrangle.

Bacon Hills [KERN]: *ridge,* northwest-trending, 2.5 miles long, 3 miles northeast of Carneros Rocks (lat. 35°28'05" N, long. 119°48'30" W). Named on Carneros Rocks (1959) 7.5' quadrangle.

Bacon Meadow [TULARE]: *area,* 2.25 miles east-southeast of Wilsonia (lat. 36°43'45" N, long. 118°55' W; at S line sec. 3, T 14 S, R 28 E). Named on Giant Forest (1956) 15' quadrangle. The name commemorates Fielding Bacon, a pioneer stockman (Hanna, p. 21).

Badger [TULARE]: *locality,* 11 miles east of Tucker Mountain (lat. 36°37'55" N, long. 119°00'45" W; sec. 11, T 15 S, R 27 E); the place is along Badger Creek. Named on Miramonte (1966) 7.5' quadrangle. Postal authorities established Camp Badger post office in 1879 and changed the name to Badger in 1894 (Frickstad, p. 210). Myron Woodard, who came from the Badger State of Wisconsin, named the place in 1870 (Mitchell, A.R., p. 67).

Badger Canyon [KERN]: *canyon,* drained by Badger Creek, which flows 4.25 miles to Poso Creek 1.5 miles south-southeast of Pine Mountain (lat. 35°32'55" N, long. 118°45'35" W; at N line sec. 33, T 27 S, R 30 E). Named on Democrat Hot Springs (1972) 7.5' quadrangle.

Badger Creek [FRESNO-TULARE]: *stream,* heads in Fresno County and flows 7 miles to Dry Creek (1) 6.25 miles east-northeast of Auckland in Tulare County (lat. 36°37'10" N, long. 119°00' W; sec. 13, T 15 S, R 27 E); the stream goes past Badger. Named on Auckland (1966) and Miramonte (1966) 7.5' quadrangles.

Badger Creek [KERN]: *stream,* flows 4.25 miles to Poso Creek 1.5 miles south-southeast of Pine Mountain (lat. 35°32'35" N, long. 118°45'35" W; at N line sec. 33, T 27 S, R 30 E); the stream drains Badger Canyon. Named on Pine Mountain (1965) 7.5' quadrangle.

Badger Flat [FRESNO]: *area,* 4.5 miles east-southeast of Kaiser Peak (lat. 37°16'05" N, long. 119°06'45" W; sec. 3, T 8 S, R 26 E). Named on Kaiser Peak (1953) 15' quadrangle. Called Badger Flats on Kaiser (1904) 30' quadrangle.

Badger Gap [KERN]: *pass,* 2 miles northwest of Democrat Hot Springs (lat. 35°32'45" N, long. 118°41'25" W; near SW cor. sec. 30, T 27 S, R 31 E). Named on Democrat Hot Springs (1972) 7.5' quadrangle.

Badger Hill [KINGS]: *peak,* 12.5 miles south of Kettleman City (lat. 35°49'40" N, long. 119°55'50" W; near W line sec. 21, T 24 S, R 19 E). Named on Avenal Gap (1954) 7.5' quadrangle.

Badger Hill [TULARE]: *peak,* 2.5 miles east-northeast of Exeter (lat. 36°18'20" N, long. 119°05'25" W; sec. 6, T 19 S, R 27 E). Altitude 1152 feet. Named on Rocky Hill (1951) 7.5' quadrangle.

Bad Name Spring [KERN]: *spring,* 9.5 miles west of Liebre Twins (lat. 34°57'55" N, long. 118°44' W; sec. 7, T 10 N, R 17 W). Named on Winters Ridge (1966) 7.5' quadrangle.

Bagby Hill [TULARE]: *peak,* 8 miles south of Springville (lat. 36°00'55" N, long. 118°50'25" W; near E line sec. 16, T 22 S, R 29 E). Named on Globe (1956) 7.5' quadrangle.

Bago: see **Mount Bago** [FRESNO].

Bakeoven Meadows [TULARE]: *area,* 2 miles north of Monache Mountain (lat. 36°14' N, long, 118°12' W; near NW cor. sec. 33, T 19 S, R 35 E). Named on Monache Mountain (1956) 15' quadrangle.

Bakeoven Pass [TULARE]: *pass,* 13 miles south of Monache Mountain (lat. 36°00'40" N, long. 118°12'50" W; sec. 17, T 22 S, R 35 E). Named on Monache Mountain (1956) 15' quadrangle. The name is from a rock oven at the place (Browning, p. 10).

Baker [KERN]: *locality,* 3 miles north-northwest of Boron (lat. 35° 02'30" N, long. 117°40' W; at NW cor. sec. 19, T 11 N, R 7 W). Named on Boron (1954) 15' quadrangle, which shows Boron P.O. at the place.

Baker: see **West Baker** [KERN].

Baker Meadow [TULARE]: *area,* 8.5 miles east-southeast of California Hot Springs (lat. 35°51'15" N, long. 118°31'20" W; sec. 9, T 24 S, R 32 E); the place is 0.5 mile south-southwest of Baker Peak on Baker Ridge. Named on California Hot Springs (1958) 15' quadrangle.

Baker Peak [TULARE]: *peak,* 8.5 miles east of California Hot Springs (lat. 35°51'35" N, long. 118°31'15" W; on E line sec. 9, T 24 S, R 32 E); the peak is near the north end of Baker Ridge. Altitude 7926 feet. Named on California Hot Springs (1958) 15' quadrangle.

Baker Point [TULARE]: *peak,* 10 miles east of California Hot Springs (lat. 35°51'10" N, long. 118°30'05" W; on E line sec. 10, T 24 S, R 32 E); the feature is on the east side of Baker Ridge. Altitude 7753 feet. Named on California Hot Springs (1958) 15' quadrangle.

Baker Ridge [TULARE]: *ridge,* south- to south-southeast-trending, 5.5 miles long, 9 miles east-southeast of California Hot Springs (lat. 35°50' N, long. 118°31'20" W), Baker Peak is near the north end of the ridge. Named on California Hot Springs (1958) 15' quadrangle.

Bakersfield [KERN]: *city,* just west of the center of Kern County on the east side of San Joaquin Valley near the entrance of Kern River to the valley (lat. 35°22'30" N, long. 119°00' W). Named on Gosford (1954), Lamont (1954), Oil Center (1954), and Oildale (1954) 7.5' quadrangles. Postal authorities established Bakersfield post office in 1868 (Frickstad, p. 54). The city incorporated in 1873, disincorporated in 1876, and incorporated again in 1898 (Bailey, 1967, p. 1). The name "Bakersfield" originated with a fenced field of about 20 acres that Colonel Thomas Baker had at the place (Latta, 1976, p. 35). Early names for the site were Kern Island, given for its location between watercourses of Kern River (Hoover, Rensch, and Rensch, p. 132), and Alkali City (Bailey, 1967, p. 1). United States Geological Survey's (1906) map shows a community called Kern located 1.5 miles east of Bakersfield (lat. 35°22'40" N, long. 118°59'25" W). Officials of Southern Pacific Railroad had Kern laid out in 1874 after the railroad bypassed Bakersfield because of a dispute with the city; the railroad community first was called Sumner and later was called Kern, Kern City, and East Bakersfield (Bailey, 1967, p. 7). Postal authorities established Sumner post office in 1876, changed the name to Kern in 1893, and discontinued it in 1924; the name "Sumner" was for Joseph W. Sumner, mine owner, rancher, and judge (Salley, p. 111, 215). The community became part of Bakersfield in 1909 (Hoover, Rensch, and Rensch, p. 133). California Mining Bureau's (1917c) map shows a place called Nome located about 2 miles northwest of downtown Bakersfield along Southern Pacific Railroad. California Mining Bureau's (1909a) map shows a place called Pylema situated 10 miles south-southwest of Bakersfield by stage line. Postal authorities established Pylema post office in 1895 and discontinued it in 1905; the name was for Mary R. Pyle, a pioneer settler and later postmaster (Salley, p. 179). In 1881 Isaac Rumford started a small Utopian colony called Joyfull, officially known as Association of Brotherly Cooperation, located about 2 miles southwest of present Bakersfield; the colony disbanded in 1884 (Bailey, 1967, p. 12). Postal authorities established Joyful post office in 1883 and discontinued it in 1884 (Frickstad, p. 56). A community called Riverview is situated just north of Bakersfield across Kern River; it first was called Arp's Addition for James H. Arp, a real estate developer (Bailey, 1967, p. 23). Postal authorities established Clarkson post office 16 miles northeast of Bakersfield in 1890 and discontinued it in 1891; they established Glenburn post office 7 miles northwest of Bakersfield in 1890 and discontinued it in 1891; they established Unadilla post office 24 miles southeast of Bakersfield in 1892 and discontinued it in 1899; they established Toolwass post office 25 miles southeast of Bakersfield in 1892 and discontinued it in 1899; they established Langdon post office 16 miles southeast of Bakersfield in 1898 and discontinued it in 1900 (Salley, p. 45, 85, 117, 223, 227).

Balance Rock [TULARE]:

(1) *relief feature,* 5.25 miles south of California Hot Springs (lat. 35°48'15" N, long. 118°39'20" W; near S line sec. 29, T 24 S, R 31 E). Named on California Hot Springs (1958) 15' quadrangle.

(2) *settlement,* 5.25 miles south of California Hot Springs (lat. 35°48'20" N, long. 118°39'10" W; near S line sec. 29, T 24 S, R 31 E); the place is east of Balance Rock (1). Named on California Hot Springs (1958) 15' quadrangle. Postal authorities established Balance Rock post office in 1935 and discontinued it in 1950 (Frickstad, p. 209). Mrs. Shively named the place in 1900 for its proximity to Balance Rock (1) (Gudde, 1949, p. 20).

Balch Camp [FRESNO]: *village,* 38 miles east-northeast of Fresno near the confluence of Dinkey Creek (1) and North Fork Kings River (lat. 36°54'20" N, long. 119°07'20" W; sec. 10, T 12 S, R 26 E). Named on Patterson Mountain (1952) 15' quadrangle.

Balch Park: see **Milo** [TULARE].

Bald Eagle Peak [KERN]: *peak,* 3 miles south of Bodfish (lat. 35°32'40" N, long. 118°28'40" W; near S line sec. 30, T 27 S, R 33 E). Altitude 6181 feet. Named on Lake Isabella South (1972) 7.5' quadrangle.

Bald Hills [KERN]: *ridge,* southwest-trending, 1 mile long, 4 miles north-northeast of Glennville (lat. 35°47'10" N, long. 118°41'10" W; mainly in sec. 6, T 25 S, R 31 E). Named on California Hot Springs (1958) 15' quadrangle.

Bald Knob [TULARE]: *peak,* 5 miles west-southwest of California Hot Springs (lat. 35°50'50" N, long. 118°45' W; near NW cor. sec. 16, T 24 S, R 30 E). Altitude 2720 feet. Named on California Hot Springs (1958) 15' quadrangle.

Bald Mill Creek [FRESNO]: *stream,* flows 3.5 miles to San Joaquin River 8.5 miles west of Shaver Lake Heights (present town of Shaver Lake) (lat. 37°06'50" N, long. 119°28'05" W; sec. 28, T 9 S, R 23 E); the stream heads at Bald Mountain (1). Named on Shaver Lake (1953) 15' quadrangle. Corlew Mill was along the creek; the stream was named for the mill and for Bald Mountain (Gudde, 1949, p. 21). United States Board on Geographic Names (1978b, p. 3) rejected the name "Ball Mill Creek" for the stream.

Bald Mountain [FRESNO]:

(1) *ridge,* northwest-trending, 2 miles long, 6 miles west-southwest of Shaver Lake Heights (present town of Shaver Lake) (lat. 37° 04' N, long. 119°24'45" W). Named on Shaver Lake (1953) 15' quadrangle. United States Board on Geographic Names (1980, p. 4) rejected the name "Ball Mountain" for the ridge.

(2) *peak,* 4 miles west-southwest of Dinkey Dome (lat. 37°06'15" N, long. 119°12'15" W; near E line sec. 35, T 9 S, R 25 E). Altitude 7832 feet. Named on Huntington Lake (1953) 15' quadrangle.

(3) *peak,* 11 miles south-southwest of Balch Camp (lat. 36°46' N, long. 119°12'05" W; sec. 25, T 13 S, R 25 E). Altitude 3605 feet. Named on Patterson Mountain (1952) 15' quadrangle.

(4) *ridge,* north-northwest-trending, nearly 1 mile long, 5 miles north-northeast of Charley Mountain on Fresno-Monterey County line (lat. 36°12'25" N, long. 120°37'40" W; sec. 12, T 20 S, R 12 E). Named on Priest Valley (1969) 7.5' quadrangle.

(5) *ridge,* northwest-trending, 4 miles long, 4 miles north-northwest of Coalinga Mineral Springs (lat. 36°11'30" N, long. 120°35'30" W). Named on Sherman Peak (1969) 7.5' quadrangle.

Bald Mountain [TULARE]:

(1) *peak,* 7.5 miles southeast of Fountain Springs (lat. 35°48'40" N, long. 118°49'40" W; sec. 27, T 24 S, R 29 E). Altitude 2397 feet. Named on White River (1965) 7.5' quadrangle.

(2) *peak,* 15 miles south-southeast of Hockett Peak (lat. 36°01'15" N, long. 118°15'10" W). Altitude 9382 feet. Named on Hockett Peak (1956) and Monache Mountain (1956) 15' quadrangles.

Baldy: see **Big Baldy** [TULARE]; **Little Baldy** [TULARE].

Baldy Saddle: see **Little Baldy Saddle** [TULARE].

Balfour: see **Oilfields** [FRESNO]; **Strathmore** [TULARE].

Ball Dome [TULARE]: *peak,* 11.5 miles northwest of Triple Divide Peak (lat. 36°41'05" N, long. 118°42' W). Altitude 9357 feet. Named on Triple Divide Peak (1956) 15' quadrangle.

Ballinger Canyon [KERN]: *canyon,* drained by a stream that flows 2.25 miles to Ventura County 14 miles west of Eagle Rest Peak (lat. 34°52'50" N, long. 119°22'45" W; near W line sec. 7, T 9 N, R 23 W). Named on Ballinger Canyon (1943) and Santiago Creek (1943) 7.5' quadrangles.

Ball Meadow [TULARE]: *area,* 11.5 miles south-southeast of Monache Mountain (lat. 36°03'55" N, long. 118°04'55" W); the place is 0.5 mile east of Ball Mountain. Named on Monache Mountain (1956) 15' quadrangle.

Ball Mill Creek: see **Bald Mill Creek** [FRESNO].

Ball Mountain [KERN]:

(1) *peak,* 3 miles northwest of Democrat Hot Springs (lat. 35°33'30" N, long. 118°42'25" W; on S line sec. 24, T 27 S, R 30 E). Named on Democrat Hot Springs (1972) 7.5' quadrangle.

(2) *peak,* 2 miles east-southeast of Miracle Hot Springs (lat. 35°34'10" N, long. 118°30'10" W; sec. 23, T 27 S, R 32 E). Named on Miracle Hot Springs (1972) 7.5' quadrangle.

Ball Mountain [TULARE]: *peak,* 11.5 miles south-southeast of Monache Mountain (lat. 36°03'50" N, long. 118°05'35" W). Altitude 9256 feet. Named on Monache Mountain (1956) 15' quadrangle.

Ball Mountain: see **Bald Mountain** [FRESNO] (1).

Balsam Creek [FRESNO]: *stream,* flows 3 miles to Big Creek (1) 7 miles north-northeast of Shaver Lake Heights (present town of Shaver Lake) (lat. 37°11'45" N, long. 119°15'35" W; sec. 32, T 8 S, R 25 E). Named on Huntington Lake (1953) and Shaver Lake (1953) 15' quadrangles. Bradley (p. 456) noted a resort called Balsam Grove Springs that was located 0.25 mile from Carlson Station on San Joaquin and Eastern Railroad. From Bradley's description, the resort probably was near the mouth of Balsam Creek. Kaiser (1904) 30' quadrangle shows San Joaquin and Eastern Railroad near the mouth of the stream.

Balsam Grove Springs: see **Balsam Creek** [FRESNO].

Banada Ridge [KERN]: *ridge,* south-trending, 2 miles long, 8.5 miles north-northeast of Caliente (lat. 35°24'35" N, long. 118°34'50" W). Named on Breckenridge Mountain (1972) 7.5' quadrangle.

Bandit Rocks: see **Robbers Roost** [KERN].

Banner [KINGS]: *locality,* 3 miles north-northwest of Hanford along Atchison, Topeka and Santa Fe Railroad (lat. 36°22'30" N, long. 119°39'50" W; on N line sec. 14, T 18 S, R 21 E). Named on Hanford (1926) 7.5' quadrangle.

Bannister [KERN]: *locality,* 9.5 miles southwest of Bakersfield along Sunset Railroad (lat. 35°15'55" N, long. 119°06' W; near N line sec. 5, T 31 S, R 27 E). Named on Gosford (1954) 7.5' quadrangle. California Mining Bureau's (1917c) map shows a place called Artwell located 2.5 miles south of Bannister along the railroad.

Barbarossa Ridge [KERN]: *ridge,* east-southeast- to south-trending, 2.5 miles long, center 2.25 miles north of Loraine (lat. 35°20'05" N, long. 118°26'40" W). Named on Loraine (1972) 7.5' quadrangle, which shows Barbarossa mine on the ridge.

Barberry Spring [FRESNO]: *spring,* 5 miles northwest of Coalinga Mineral Springs (lat. 36°11'40" N, long. 120°37'15" W; sec. 13, T 20 S, R 12 E). Named on Sherman Peak (1969) 7.5' quadrangle.

Barbour: see **Camp Barbour**, under **Old Fort Miller** [FRESNO].

Barigan Stringer [TULARE]: *stream,* flows 3.5 miles to Golden Trout Creek 7.25 miles north of Kern Peak (lat. 36°24'45" N, long. 118°16'35" W; sec. 27, T 17 S, R 34 E). Named on Kern Peak (1956) 15' quadrangle.

Barillo Valley: see **Barrel Valley** [KERN].

Barker Creek [KERN]: *stream,* flows 3.5 miles to Cottonwood Creek (2) 2.25 miles south-southeast of Mount Adelaide (lat. 35° 24' N, long. 118°43'50" W; at S line sec. 14, T 29 S, R 30 E). Named on Mount Adelaide (1972) 7.5' quadrangle. Called Parker Creek on Breckenridge Mountain (1943) 15' quadrangle, and United States Board on Geographic Names (1975b, p. 8) gave this name as a variant.

Barnard: see **Mount Barnard** [TULARE].

Barn Canyon [KERN]: *canyon,* 1.5 miles long, 3.25 miles south of Alta Sierra along Stable Creek (lat. 35°40'50" N, long. 118°32'25" W; sec. 9, T 26 S, R 32 E). Named on Alta Sierra (1972) 7.5' quadrangle.

Barnes Mountain [FRESNO]: *ridge,* northwest- to north-trending, 3 miles long, 9.5 miles southwest of Dinkey Dome (lat. 37°00'30" N, long. 119°14'30" W). Named on Huntington Lake (1953), Patterson Mountain (1952), and Shaver Lake (1953) 15' quadrangles.

Barnes Settlement: see **Old River** [KERN].

Barn Spring [FRESNO]: *spring,* 9 miles northwest of Coalinga (lat. 36°13'35" N, long. 120°28'35" W; sec. 32, T 19 S, R 14 E). Named on Alcalde Hills (1969) 7.5' quadrangle.

Barrel Spring [KERN]: *spring,* 3.25 miles west-northwest of Emerald Mountain (lat. 35°16'40" N, long. 118°20' W). Named on Emerald Mountain (1972) 7.5' quadrangle.

Barrel Valley [KERN]: *valley,* 5.5 miles south of Orchard Peak (lat. 35°39'40" N, long. 120°07'30" W). Named on Orchard Peak (1961) and Sawtooth Ridge (1961) 7.5' quadrangles. Called Barril Valley on Arnold and Johnson's (1910) map, but United States Board on Geographic Names (1933a, p. 124) rejected the names "Barril Valley" and "Barillo Valley" for the feature.

Barren Ridge [KERN]: *ridge,* northeast-trending, 7 miles long, 11 miles north-northeast of Mojave (lat. 35°12'15" N, long. 118°07'45" W). Named on Cache Peak (1973) and Mojave NE (1973) 7.5' quadrangles.

Barrett Lakes [FRESNO]: *lakes,* largest 1800 feet long, 11 miles east of Mount Goddard in Palisade Basin (lat. 37°05' N, long. 118°31'30" W). Named on Mount Goddard (1948) 15' quadrangle.

Barril Valley: see **Barrel Valley** [KERN].

Barrington Spring [KERN]: *spring,* 3.5 miles southeast of Caliente (lat. 35°15'50" N, long. 118°34'35" W; sec. 6, T 31 S, R 32 E). Named on Oiler Peak (1972) 7.5' quadrangle.

Barris Hill [TULARE]: *peak,* 2.5 miles east-northeast of Dinuba at the south end of Smith Mountain (1) (lat. 36°33'30" N, long. 119° 21' W; sec. 10, T 16 S, R 24 E). Named on Orange Cove South (1966) 7.5' quadrangle. On Sultana (1923) 7.5' quadrangle, the name applies to a feature situated less than 0.5 mile farther south.

Barr Spring [FRESNO]: *spring,* 4 miles north-northeast of Coalinga Mineral Springs (lat. 36°11'50" N, long. 120°31'45" W; near N line sec. 13, T 20 S, R 13 E). Named on Sherman Peak (1969) 7.5' quadrangle.

Barstow [FRESNO]: *locality,* 3.25 miles west-southwest of Herndon (lat. 36°48'55" N, long. 119°58'10" W; near W line sec. 12, T 13 S, R 18 E). Named on Herndon (1964) 7.5' quadrangle.

Bartolas Country [KERN]: *area,* 7 miles north of Weldon (lat. 35° 46' N, long. 118°16' W); the place is on upper reaches of Bartolas Creek. Named on Kernville (1956) and Lamont Peak (1956) 15' quadrangles, and on Onyx (1972) and Weldon (1972) 7.5' quadrangles. The name commemorates a Frenchman who ran sheep in the area in the early days (Gudde, 1969, p. 22).

Bartolas Creek [KERN]: *stream,* flows 7.5 miles to South Fork Kern River 4.5 miles north-northeast of Onyx (lat. 35°44'45" N, long. 118°11'05" W). Named on Kernville (1956) and Lamont Peak (1956) 15' quadrangles, and on Onyx (1972) 7.5' quadrangle.

Barton: see **Steve Barton Point** [TULARE]; **Sunnyside** [FRESNO].

Barton Creek [TULARE]: *stream,* flows 3 miles to Roaring River 7.25 miles north-northwest of Triple Divide Peak and 2.5 miles east of Barton Peak (lat. 36°41'40" N, long. 118°33'25" W). Named on Triple Divide Peak (1956) 15' quadrangle.

Barton Hills: see **Devils Den** [KERN] (1).

Barton Peak [TULARE]: *peak,* 8 miles north-northwest of Triple Divide Peak (lat. 36°41'30" N, long. 118°35'55" W). Altitude 10,370 feet. Named on Triple Divide Peak (1956) 15' quadrangle. United States Board on Geographic Names (1933a, p. 125) rejected the name "Mount Moraine" for the peak, and noted that the Sierra Club proposed the name "Barton" to commemorate James Barton, a local stockman.

Barton Ranch: see **Kaweah** [TULARE].

Barton's: see **Mineral King** [TULARE].

Bartons: see **Devils Den** [KERN] (1).

Bartons Resort [FRESNO]: *locality,* 3 miles northeast of Hume (lat. 36°49'05" N, long. 118°53'10" W). Named on Tehipite Dome (1952) 15' quadrangle. Clyde Barton and Virginia Barton started a resort at what originally was called Burro Flat (Forest M. Clingan, personal communication, 1990).

Basin [FRESNO]: *locality,* 15 miles southwest of Kaiser Peak along San Joaquin and Eastern Railroad (lat. 37°07'30" N, long. 119°22'15" W; near NE cor. sec. 29, T 9 S, R 24 E); the place is in Jose Basin. Named on Kaiser (1904) 30' quadrangle. California Mining Bureau's (1917a) map shows a place called Webstone located along the railroad between Lodge and Duncan Mill, at or near the site of Basin.

Basin: see **Huntington Lake** [FRESNO] (2); **The Basin**, under **Huntington Lake** [FRESNO] (1)

Basin Creek [FRESNO]: *stream,* flows 2 miles to North Fork Kings River 1 mile east of Balch Camp (lat. 36°54'20" N, long. 119°06'20" W; sec. 11, T 12 S, R 26 E). Named on Patterson Mountain (1952) 15' quadrangle.

Basin Creek: see **Walker Basin Creek** [KERN].

Basket Flat [KERN]: *area,* nearly 5 miles south-southeast of Glennville (lat. 35°39'55" N, long. 118°39'55" W; sec. 17, T 26 S, R 31 E); the place is less than 2 miles west-northwest of Basket Peak. Named on Glennville (1972) 7.5' quadrangle.

Basket Pass [KERN]: *pass,* 6.5 miles southeast of Glennville (lat. 35° 39'25" N, long. 118°37'40" W; sec. 22, T 26 S, R 31 E); the pass is 0.5 mile east-northeast of Basket Peak on Basket Ridge. Named on Glennville (1972) 7.5' quadrangle.

Basket Peak [KERN]: *peak,* 6.25 miles south-southeast of Glennville (lat. 35°39'10" N, long. 118°38'20" W; sec. 22, T 26 S, R 31 E). Altitude 6122 feet. Named on Glennville (1972) 7.5' quadrangle.

Basket Ridge [KERN]: *ridge,* generally west-trending, 4 miles long, center is 6 miles south-southeast of Glennville (lat. 35°39'15" N, long. 118°39' W); Basket Peak is on the ridge. Named on Alta Sierra (1972) and Glennville (1972) 7.5' quadrangles.

Basque Encino [KERN]: *locality,* 2.5 miles southwest of Liebre Twins (lat. 34°56' N, long. 118°36'15" W; at N line sec. 19, T 10 N, R 16 W). Named on Neenach (1943) 15' quadrangle.

Bateman Ridge [TULARE]: *ridge,* north-trending, 1.5 miles long, 3 miles southwest of Camp Nelson (lat. 36°07'10" N, long. 118° 39' W). Named on Camp Nelson (1956) 15' quadrangle.

Bates Slough [TULARE]: *water feature,* discontinuous watercourse that extends for 9 miles in lowlands to a point 10 miles southwest of Tulare (lat. 36°06'50" N, long. 119°29'25" W; sec. 9, T 21 S, R 23 E). Named on Paige (1950), Taylor Wier (1950), and Tulare (1950) 7.5' quadrangles. Called Packwood Cr. on Lake View School (1927) 7.5' quadrangle, and called North Fork Deep Creek on Paige (1927) 7.5' quadrangle. On Taylor Weir (1950, photorevised 1969) 7.5' quadrangle, the feature extends to Deep Creek (2).

Bathtub Lake [FRESNO]: *lake,* 1100 feet long, 14 miles northeast of Kaiser Peak (lat. 37°27'50" N, long. 119°02'20" W). Named on Kaiser Peak (1953) 15' quadrangle. The feature is one of the group called Margaret Lakes.

Battalion Lake [FRESNO]: *lake,* 1200 feet long, 3.25 miles south-southwest of Mount Goddard (lat. 37°03'25" N, long. 118°44'25" W); the lake is 0.5 mile east-southeast of Division Lake. Named on Mount Goddard (1948) 15' quadrangle.

Battle Creek [TULARE]: *stream,* flows less than 1 mile to South Fork Kaweah River 9.5 miles southeast of Kaweah (lat. 36°21'35" N, long. 118°49' W; sec. 15, T 18 S, R 29 E). Named on Kaweah (1957) 15' quadrangle. The name stems from a battle between a mountain lion and a burro, won by the burro (United States Board on Geographic Names, 1970a, p. 2). Salley (p. 16) listed Battle Mound post office, established 25 miles northeast of Porterville in 1871, and discontinued the same year; the named was from the same incident.

Battle Creek: see **Bennett Creek** [TULARE].

Battle Mound: see **Battle Creek** [TULARE].

Battle Mountain [TULARE]: *hill,* 17 miles south-southeast of Kaweah near North Fork Tule River (lat. 36°15'10" N, long. 118° 47'15" W). Altitude 2936 feet. Named on Kaweah (1957) 15' quadrangle, and on Springville (1957) 7.5' quadrangle. The place was the site of a battle with Indians in 1856 (Gist, p. 22).

Baxter: see **Mount Baxter** [FRESNO]; **Wade Baxter Spring** [KINGS].

Baxter Creek [FRESNO]: *stream,* flows nearly 4 miles to South Fork Woods Creek 5.5 miles south of Mount Pinchot (lat. 36°51'05" N, long. 118°24'35" W); the stream heads near Baxter Pass and goes through Baxter Lakes. Named on Mount Pinchot (1953) 15' quadrangle.

Baxter Lakes [FRESNO]: *lakes,* largest 1900 feet long, 7 miles south of Mount Pinchot (lat. 36°50'50" N, long. 118°22'45" W); the lakes are southwest of Mount Baxter along Baxter Creek. Named on Mount Pinchot (1953) 15 quadrangle.

Baxter Pass [FRESNO]: *pass,* 8 miles south of Mount Pinchot on Fresno-Inyo County line (lat. 36°50'10" N, long. 118°22'30" W); the pass is 2 miles south-southwest of Mount Baxter. Named on Mount Pinchot (1953) 15' quadrangle.

Beach Creek [TULARE]: *stream,* flows 6.5 miles to Rattlesnake Creek (3) 9 miles south-southeast of Hockett Peak (lat. 36°05'40" N, long. 118°20'25" W; sec. 18, T 21 S, R 34 E); the stream goes through Beach Meadows. Named on Hockett Peak (1956) 15' quadrangle. Called Smith Cr. on Olancha (1907) 30' quadrangle.

Beach Meadows [TULARE]: *area,* 9 miles southeast of Hockett Peak (lat. 36°07'10" N, long. 118°17'40" W); the place is along Beach Creek. Named on Hockett Peak (1956) 15' quadrangle.

Beale: see **Bealville** [KERN].

Bealville [KERN]: *locality,* 1.25 miles south of Caliente along Southern Pacific Railroad (lat. 35°16'20" N, long. 118°37'30" W). Named on Bena (1972) and Oiler Peak (1972) 7.5' quadrangles. Postal authorities established Beale post office at the place in 1879 and discontinued it in 1881 (Salley, p. 17). The name commemorates Edward Fitzgerald Beale, owner of El Tejon grant (Hanna, p. 27). California Division of Highways' (1934) map shows a place called Allard located about 2 miles west-northwest of Bealville along the railroad.

Bean [KINGS]: *locality,* 3.25 miles north-northwest of Corcoran along Atchison, Topeka and Santa Fe Railroad (lat. 36°08'20" N, long. 119°35'05" W). Named on Waukena (1928) 7.5' quadrangle.

Bean Canyon [KERN]: *canyon,* drained by a stream that flows 6.25 miles to lowlands 6.5 miles northwest of the village of Willow Springs (lat. 34°57'30" N, long. 118°21'45" W; at W line sec. 15, T 10 N, R 14 W). Named on Tehachapi South (1966), Tylerhorse Canyon (1965), and Willow Springs (1965) 7.5' quadrangles.

Bean Spring [KERN]: *spring,* 1 mile west of the village of Willow Springs (lat. 34°52'55" N, long. 118°18'50" W; sec. 12, T 9 N, R 14 W). Named on Willow Springs (1965) 7.5' quadrangle. Darling (p. 10) associated the name with Charles M. Bean, who owned land in the neighborhood in the 1880's.

Bear Butte [FRESNO]: *peak,* 6.5 miles east-northeast of the town of Big Creek (lat. 37°14'30" N, long. 119°08'05" W; near S line sec. 9, T 8 S, R 26 E). Altitude 8598 feet. Named on Huntington Lake (1953) 15' quadrangle.

Bear Canyon [FRESNO]: *canyon,* drained by a stream that flows 5.5 miles to Los Gatos Creek 8 miles north-northwest of Coalinga Mineral Springs (lat. 36°14'45" N, long. 120°36'45" W; sec. 30, T 19 S, R 13 E). Named on Priest Valley (1969) and Sherman Peak (1969) 7.5' quadrangles.

Bear Canyon [KERN]:

(1) *canyon,* 2.25 miles long, along Delonegha Creek above a point 4.5 miles west of Miracle Hot Springs (lat. 35°34'25" N, long. 118° 36'50" W). Named on Democrat Hot Springs (1972) and Miracle Hot Springs (1972) 7.5' quadrangles.

(2) *canyon,* drained by a stream that flows 1.25 miles to El Paso Creek 6 miles west of Liebre Twins (lat. 34°58'20" N, long. 118° 40'35" W; sec. 3, T 10 N, R 17 W). Named on Winters Ridge (1966) 7.5' quadrangle.

(3) *canyon,* drained by a stream that heads in Los Angeles County and flows 1.5 miles to Castac Valley 1 mile southeast of Lebec (lat. 34°49'30" N, long. 118°51'15" W; near E line sec. 35, T 9 N, R 19 W). Named on Lebec (1958) 7.5' quadrangle.

Bear Canyon: see **Little Bear Canyon** [FRESNO].

Bear Creek [FRESNO]:

(1) *stream,* flows 2.25 miles to Huntington Lake (1) 3 miles south of Kaiser Peak (lat. 37°15'05" N, long. 119°10'45" W; sec. 7, T 8 S, R 26 E). Named on Kaiser Peak (1953) 15' quadrangle.

(2) *stream,* formed by the confluence of East Fork, South Fork, and West Fork, flows 10.5 miles to South Fork San Joaquin River 12.5 miles west-southwest of Mount Abbot (lat. 37°19'15" N, long. 118° 59'30" W). Named on Mount Abbot (1953) 15' quadrangle. East Fork and South Fork each are 5 miles long, and West Fork is 3.5 miles long. All three forks are named on Mount Abbot (1953) 15' quadrangle. Hilgard Branch enters 9 miles upstream from the mouth of the main stream; it heads near Bear Creek Spire, is 6.5 miles long, and is named on Mount Abbot (1953) 15' quadrangle. United States Board on Geographic Names (1983a, p. 3) rejected the name "Bear Meadow Creek" for Bear Creek (2).

(3) *stream,* flows 7.5 miles to Dinkey Creek (1) 5.5 miles south of Dinkey Dome (lat. 37°02'15" N, long. 119°08'30" W; near N line sec. 28, T 10 S, R 26 E); the stream goes past Bear Meadow (2). Named on Huntington Lake (1953) 15' quadrangle.

(4) *stream,* flows 3.5 miles to White Deer Creek 8 miles south-southwest of Balch Camp (lat 36°47'50" N, long. 119°10'30" W; sec. 17, T 13 S, R 26 E). Named on Patterson Mountain (1952) 15' quadrangle.

Bear Creek [KERN]: *stream,* flows 5 miles to Cedar Creek 4 miles east-southeast of Glennville (lat. 35°42'30" N, long. 118°38'20" W; sec. 34, T 25 S, R 31 E). Named on Alta Sierra (1972) and Glennville (1972) 7.5' quadrangles.

Bear Creek [TULARE]:

(1) *stream,* flows 7.25 miles to Dry Creek (1) 7 miles southeast of Auckland (lat. 36°31' N, long. 119°01'05" W; near E line sec. 22, T 16 S, R 27 E); the stream heads at Bear Mountain. Named on Auckland (1966) 7.5' quadrangle. United States Board on Geographic Names (1967d, p. 4) rejected the name "Murry Creek" for the feature.

(2) *stream,* flows 8.5 miles to North Fork Tule River 3.5 miles north-northeast of Springville (lat. 36°10'40" N, long. 118°47'45" W; near NW cor. sec. 24, T 20 S, R 29 E). Named on Camp Nelson (1956) and Springville (1957) 15' quadrangles.

(3) *stream,* flows 2.5 miles to South Fork of Middle Fork Tule River less than 1 mile southwest of Camp Nelson (lat. 36°07'55" N, long. 118°37'15" W; sec. 3, T 21 S, R 31 E). Named on Camp Nelson (1956) 15' quadrangle.

(4) *stream,* flows nearly 3 miles to join Double Bunk Creek and form South Creek 8 miles northeast of California Hot Springs (lat. 35°57'35" N, long. 118°34'20" W; near E line sec. 1, T 23 S, R 31 E); the stream goes through Bear Meadow (3). Named on California Hot Springs (1958) 15' quadrangle.

(5) *stream,* flows 2.5 miles to North Fork Kaweah River 5 miles south-southwest of Yucca Mountain (lat. 36°30'15" N, long. 118° 54'20" W). Named on Giant Forest (1956) and Kaweah (1957) 15' quadrangles.

(6) *stream,* flows 4.25 miles to South Fork Tule River 9.5 miles south-southwest of Camp Nelson (lat. 36°01'40" N, long. 118°42'15" W). Named on California Hot Springs (1958) and Camp Nelson (1956) 15' quadrangles.

Bear Creek: see **South Bear Creek** [TULARE].

Bear Creek Spine: see **Bear Creek Spire** [FRESNO].

Bear Creek Spire [FRESNO]: *peak,* 1.5 miles southeast of Mount Abbot on Fresno-Inyo County line (lat. 37°22'05" N, long. 118° 46' W); the peak is near the head of Hilgard Branch Bear Creek (2). Altitude 13,713 feet. Named on Mount Abbot (1953) 15' quadrangle. United States Board on Geographic Names (1933a, p. 131) rejected the name "Bear Creek Spine" for the feature.

Bear Dens [KERN]: *relief feature,* 4.5 miles northeast of Glennville (lat. 35°45'45" N, long. 118°38'15" W; near SW cor. sec. 10, T 25 S, R 31 E). Named on California Hot Springs (1958) 15' quadrangle.

Bear Dome [FRESNO]: *peak,* 10 miles west-southwest of Mount Abbot (lat. 37°19'45" N, long. 118°57' W). Altitude 9947 feet. Named on Mount Abbot (1953) 15' quadrangle.

Bear Flat [KERN]: *area,* 4.5 miles north of Caliente (lat. 35°21'20" N, long. 118°37'30" W; on S line sec. 35, T 29 S, R 31 E). Named on Bena (1972) and Oiler Peak (1972) 7.5' quadrangles.

Bear Flat [TULARE]: *area,* 3 miles east of Auckland (lat. 36°34'50" N, long. 119°03'05" W; at W line sec. 33, T 15 S, R 27 E); the place is along Bear Creek (1). Named on Auckland (1966) 7.5' quadrangle.

Bear Gulch [FRESNO]: *canyon,* drained by a stream that flows 1.25 miles to Bear Canyon 7 miles north-northwest of Coalinga Mineral Springs (lat. 36°13'45" N, long. 120°37'20" W; sec. 36, T 19 S, R 12 E). Named on Priest Valley (1969) and Sherman Peak (1969) 7.5' quadrangles.

Bear Hallow Creek: see **Bear Hollow Creek** [KERN].

Bear Hill [TULARE]: *peak,* 5.5 miles east of Yucca Mountain (lat. 36°33'40" N, long. 118°46'05" W; sec. 6, T 16 S, R 30 E). Named on Giant Forest

(1956) 15' quadrangle.

Bear Hollow [KERN]: *valley,* 2.2 miles west-southwest of Glennville (lat. 35°43'05" N, long. 118°44'40" W). Named on Glennville (1972) 7.5' quadrangle.

Bear Hollow Creek [KERN]: *stream,* flows 5.25 miles to Poso Creek 3 miles south-southwest of Glennville (lat. 35°41'35" N, long. 118°43'55" W; sec. 3, T 26 S, R 30 E); the stream goes through Bear Hollow. Named on White River (1965) and Woody (1965) 7.5' quadrangles. Called Bearwallow Creek on White River (1936) and Woody (1935) 15' quadrangles, but United States Board on Geographic Names (1966b, p. 4) rejected the names "Bearwallow Creek" and "Bear Hallow Creek" for the stream.

Bear Lake: see **Big Bear Lake** [FRESNO]; **Little Bear Lake** [FRESNO].

Bear Meadow [FRESNO]:

(1) *area,* 11 miles north-northeast of Kaiser Peak (lat. 37°26'55" N, long. 119°07'40" W). Named on Kaiser Peak (1953) 15' quadrangle.

(2) *area,* 4 miles southeast of Dinkey Dome (lat. 37°04'15" N, long. 119°04'50" W; sec. 12, T 10 S, R 26 E); the place is along Bear Creek (3). Named on Huntington Lake (1953) 15' quadrangle.

(3) *area,* 7 miles south-southwest of Dinkey Dome (lat. 37°01'05" N, long. 119°10'25" W; sec. 31, T 10 S, R 26 E). Named on Huntington Lake (1953) 15' quadrangle.

Bear Meadow [TULARE]:

(1) *area,* 10 miles north-northwest of Olancha Peak (lat. 36°24'05" N, long. 118°10' W; sec. 34, T 17 S, R 35 E). Named on Olancha (1956) 15' quadrangle.

(2) *area,* 1.5 miles north of Kern Peak (lat. 36°19'55" N, long. 118° 17'30" W; sec. 28, T 18 S, R 34 E). Named on Kern Peak (1956) 15' quadrangle.

(3) *area,* 6.5 miles northeast of California Hot Springs (lat. 35°56'45" N, long. 118°35' W; sec. 12, T 23 S, R 31 E); the place is along Bear Creek (4). Named on California Hot Springs (1958) 15' quadrangle.

Bear Meadow Creek [FRESNO]: *stream,* flows 6 miles to Dinkey Creek (1) 4 miles north-northwest of Balch Camp (lat. 36°57'20" N, long. 119°08'25" W); the stream goes through Bear Meadow (3). Named on Huntington Lake (1953) and Patterson Mountain (1952) 15' quadrangles.

Bear Meadow Creek: see **Bear Creek** [FRESNO] (2).

Bear Mountain [FRESNO]:

(1) *peak,* 2.5 miles east-southeast of Dinkey Dome (lat. 37°05'45" N, long. 119°05'35" W; near SW cor. sec. 36, T 9 S, R 26 E). Altitude 9512 feet. Named on Huntington Lake (1953) 15' quadrangle.

(2) *ridge,* northeast-trending, about 1.5 miles long, 9 miles north-northeast of Orange Cove (lat. 36°45' N, long. 119°16'35" W). Named on Orange Cove North (1966) and Pine Flat Dam (1965) 7.5' quadrangles.

Bear Mountain [KERN]: *peak,* 6 miles south of Caliente (lat. 35°12'15" N, long. 118°38'15" W; sec. 27, T 31 S, R 31 E). Altitude 6913 feet. Named on Bear Mountain (1966) 7.5' quadrangle. Called Bear Peak on Wheeler's (1875-1878) map, which shows White Wolf Spr. located 4.5 miles northwest of the peak. The name "White Wolf" is from packs of white wolves formerly found in the neighborhood (Wilke and Lawton *in* Davidson, p. 38). The name "Bear Mountain" is from the numerous bears that lived on the slopes of the peak (Bailey, 1962, p. 65). The peak also was called Livermore Mountain (Wines, p. 86).

Bear Mountain [TULARE]: *peak,* 3.25 miles east of Auckland (lat. 36°35'45" N, long. 119°02'45" W; sec. 28, T 15 S, R 27 E). Altitude 4116 feet. Named on Auckland (1966) 7.5' quadrangle.

Bearpaw Lake [FRESNO]: *lake,* 1200 feet long, nearly 4 miles south of Mount Abbot (lat. 37°19'50" N, long. 118°47'40" W). Named on Mount Abbot (1953) 15' quadrangle. Elden H. Vestal of California Department of Fish and Game named the lake in 1952; the name also has the form "Bear Paw Lake" (Browning, p. 13).

Bearpaw Meadow [TULARE]: *area,* 5.5 miles west-southwest of Triple Divide Peak (lat. 36°33'55" N, long. 118°37'20" W). Named on Triple Divide Peak (1956) 15' quadrangle. The name was given after a bear caught its foot in a trap at the place (Browning, p. 13-14).

Bearpaw Meadow: see **Little Bearpaw Meadow** [TULARE].

Bear Peak: see **Bear Mountain** [KERN].

Bear Ridge [FRESNO]: *ridge,* southwest-trending, 5 miles long, 10.5 miles west-southwest of Mount Abbot (lat. 37°21'45" N, long. 118° 57'45" W). Named on Mount Abbot (1953) 15' quadrangle.

Bearskin Creek [FRESNO-TULARE]: *stream,* heads just inside Tulare County and flows nearly 3 miles to Tenmile Creek 2 miles south-southeast of Hume in Fresno County (lat. 36°45'40" N, long. 118°53'55" W; sec. 26, T 13 S, R 28 E); the mouth of the stream is at Bearskin Meadow. Named on Giant Forest (1956) and Tehipite Dome (1952) 15' quadrangles.

Bearskin Meadow [FRESNO]: *area,* 2 miles south-southeast of Hume (lat. 36°45'35" N, long. 118°54' W; sec. 26, T 13 S, R 28 E); the place is along Bearskin Creek. Named on Tehipite Dome (1952) 15' quadrangle. The name reportedly is from the resemblance of a snow patch at the place to a bearskin (Browning, p. 14).

Bear Spring [KERN]:

(1) *spring,* 4.5 miles north of Caliente (lat. 35°21'25" N, long. 118° 36'55" W; near SE cor. sec. 35, T 29 S, R 31 E); the spring is 0.5 mile northeast of Bear Flat. Named on Oiler Peak (1972) 7.5' quadrangle.

(2) *spring,* 6 miles east-southeast of Mount Adelaide (lat. 35°23'10" N, long. 118°39' W; near SE cor. sec. 21, T 29 S, R 31 E). Named on Mount Adelaide (1972) 7.5' quadrangle.

Bear Trap Canyon [KERN]:

(1) *canyon,* drained by a stream that flows 2.5 miles to East Fork Erskine Creek 9.5 miles south-southwest of Weldon (lat. 35°32'35" N, long. 118°22'15" W). Named on Woolstalf Creek (1972) 7.5' quadrangle.

(2) *canyon,* 9.5 miles long, along Pastoria Creek above a point 6 miles northeast of Lebec (lat. 34°54'10" N, long. 118°47'50" W). Named on Pastoria Creek (1958) and Winters Ridge (1966) 7.5' quadrangles.

Bear Trap Canyon [TULARE]: *canyon,* drained by a stream that flows 1.5 miles to White River (1) 3.5 miles southwest of California Hot Springs (lat. 35°50'10" N, long. 118°42'25" W; sec. 14, T 24 S, R 30 E). Named on California Hot Springs (1958) 15' quadrangle.

Beartrap Creek [KERN]: *stream,* flows 2.5 miles to Walker Basin Creek 3.25 miles west of Piute Peak (lat. 35°26'30" N, long. 118° 26'55" W; near N line sec. 4, T 29 S, R 33 E). Named on Piute Peak (1972) 7.5' quadrangle. United States Board on Geographic Names (1975b, p. 8) gave the form "Bear Trap Creek" as a variant.

Beartrap Creek: see **Woodward Creek** [TULARE].

Beartrap Lake [FRESNO]: *lake,* 600 feet long, 3.5 miles south-southwest of Mount Abbot (lat. 37°20'30" N, long. 118°49'15" W). Named on Mount Abbot (1953) 15' quadrangle.

Bear Trap Meadow [TULARE]: *area,* 5.25 miles east-northeast of Monache Mountain (lat. 36°13'50" N, long. 118°06'25" W). Named on Monache Mountain (1956) 15' quadrangle

Beartrap Meadow [TULARE]: *area,* 3.5 miles west-southwest of Shell Mountain along Woodward Creek (lat. 36°40'30" N, long. 118°51'30" W; sec. 29, T 14 S, R 29 E). Named on Giant Forest (1956) 15' quadrangle.

Bear Trap Ridge [TULARE]: *ridge,* west- to west-northwest-trending, 1.5 miles long, 3.5 miles south-southeast of California Hot Springs (lat. 35°49'50" N, long. 118°38'45" W). Named on California Hot Springs (1958) 15' quadrangle.

Bear Trap Spring [KERN]: *spring,* 8.5 miles north of Caliente (lat. 35°24'45" N, long. 118°36'10" W; on N line sec. 13, T 29 S, R 31 E). Named on Breckenridge Mountain (1972) 7.5' quadrangle.

Bear Trap Spring [TULARE]: *spring,* 4 miles south-southeast of California Hot Springs (lat. 35°49'30" N, long. 118°38'50" W; sec. 20, T 24 S, R 31 E); the spring is south of Bear Trap Ridge. Named on California Hot Springs (1958) 15' quadrangle.

Beartrap Spring [KERN]: *spring,* 4 miles southwest of Loraine (lat. 35°16'05" N, long. 118°29'15" W; on N line sec. 1, T 31 S, R 32 E). Named on Loraine (1972) 7.5' quadrangle.

Bear Twin Lakes [FRESNO]: *lakes,* two, each 500 feet long, 6.25 miles west-southwest of Mount Abbot (lat. 37°21'10" N, long. 118° 53'10" W); the lakes are along a branch of Bear Creek (2). Named on Mount Abbot (1953) 15' quadrangle.

Bear Valley [KERN]: *valley,* 9 miles south of Caliente (lat. 35°09'45" N, long. 118°38'15" W). Named on Bear Mountain (1966) and Keene (1966) 7.5' quadrangles. The first settlers in the valley named the place for the large number of bears found there (Latta, 1976, p. 199).

Bear Wallow [FRESNO]: *area,* 3.5 miles east-southeast of Balch Camp (lat. 36°52'40" N, long. 119°0420" W; near N line sec. 19, T 12 S, R 27 E). Named on Patterson Mountain (1952) 15' quadrangle.

Bear Wallow Creek [FRESNO]: *stream,* flows nearly 3 miles to Dinkey Creek (1) 4 miles north of Balch Camp (lat. 36°57'50" N, long. 119°07'30" W). Named on Patterson Mountain (1952) 7.5' quadrangle.

Bearwallow Creek: see **Bear Hollow Creek** [KERN].

Beaver Canyon [KERN]: *canyon,* extends for 1 mile above the mouth of Delonegha Creek, which is 4.5 miles west-southwest of Miracle Hot Springs (lat. 35°33'15" N, long. 118°36'25" W). Named on Miracle Hot Springs (1972) 7.5' quadrangle.

Beck Canyon [KERN]: *canyon,* drained by a stream that flows 2.25 miles to Harper Canyon 4.25 miles northeast of Caliente (lat. 35°19'30" N, long. 118°33'50" W; near S line sec. 8, T 30 S, R 32 E). Named on Oiler Peak (1972) 7.5' quadrangle.

Becketts Backbone [TULARE]: *ridge,* southwest-trending, 4 miles long, 8 miles west-southwest of Yucca Mountain (lat. 36°31'15" N, long. 118°59'30" W). Named on Auckland (1966) 7.5' and Giant Forest (1956) 15' quadrangles.

Beck Meadows [TULARE]: *area,* 4 miles southeast of Monache Mountain (lat. 36°09'45" N, long. 119°09'45" W). Named on Monache Mountain (1956) 15' quadrangle.

Beck Spring: see **Lower Beck Spring** [KERN]; **Upper Beck Spring** [KERN].

Bee Canyon [FRESNO]: *canyon,* drained by a stream that flows nearly 2 miles to Warthan Creek 3.25 miles west of Coalinga Mineral Springs (lat. 36°08'15" N, long. 120°36'45" W; sec. 6, T 21 S, R 13 E). Named on Priest Valley (1969) and Sherman Peak (1969) 7.5' quadrangles.

Beer Keg Meadow [TULARE]: *area,* 7.5 miles east of Hockett Peak (lat.

36°14'20" N, long. 118°15'20" W). Named on Hockett Peak (1956) 15' quadrangle.

Beetlebug Lake [FRESNO]: *lake,* 1650 feet long, 16 miles northeast of Kaiser Peak at the head of Long Canyon (lat. 37°28'20" N, long. 119°00'15" W). Named on Kaiser Peak (1953) 15' quadrangle.

Bela Vista [KERN]: *locality,* 2 miles west-southwest of Weldon (lat. 35°39'10" N, long. 118°19'15" W; sec. 22, T 26 S, R 34 E). Named on Weldon (1972) 7.5' quadrangle.

Belknap Creek [TULARE]: *stream,* flows 2.5 miles to South Fork of Middle Fork Tule River 0.5 mile east of Camp Nelson (lat. 36°08'25" N, long. 118°35'50" W; sec. 34, T 20 S, R 31 E). Named on Camp Nelson (1956) 15' quadrangle. Corrington G. Belknap patented land near the stream in 1891 (Browning, p. 15).

Bell: see **Iva Bell Hot Springs**, under **Fish Creek Hot Springs** [FRESNO].

Bell Camp Meadow [TULARE]: *area,* nearly 3 miles north-northwest of Olancha Peak (lat. 36°18' N, long. 118°08'30" W; near W line sec. 1, T 19 S, R 35 E). Named on Olancha (1956) 15' quadrangle.

Belleville: see **Poplar** [TULARE].

Bellevue [KERN]: *locality,* 7.5 miles west-southwest of Bakersfield (lat. 35°20' N, long. 119°07'30" W; sec. 7, T 30 S, R 27 E). Named on Buena Vista Lake (1912) 30' quadrangle.

Beltran Creek [FRESNO]: *stream,* flows 5 miles to Zapato Chino Creek 10 miles south-southeast of Coalinga (lat. 36°00'30" N, long. 120°17'10" W; sec. 18, T 22 S, R 16 E). Named on Kreyenhagen Hills (1956) and The Dark Hole (1961) 7.5' quadrangles.

Bena [KERN]: *locality,* 7 miles west-northwest of Caliente along Southern Pacific Railroad (lat. 35°19'35" N, long. 118°44'20" W). Named on Bena (1972) 7.5' quadrangle. Called Pampa on Mendenhall's (1908) map. Postal authorities established Pampa post office in 1889, discontinued it in 1890, reestablished it in 1901, and discontinued it the same year (Frickstad, p. 58). The name "Pampa" was from Pampa Peak (Wines, p. 34). California (1891) map shows a place called Sand Cut located along the railroad about halfway between Pampa and Wade (present Edison).

Bench Lake [FRESNO]: *lake,* 3400 feet long, 3.25 miles west of Mount Pinchot (lat. 36°56'50" N, long. 118°27'40" W). Named on Mount Pinchot (1953) 15' quadrangle. J. N. LeConte named the lake in 1902 (Browning, p. 15). The name describes the topographic setting of the lake (Versteeg, p. 422).

Bench Lakes: see **Double Peak** [FRESNO].

Bench Valley [FRESNO]: *canyon,* 3 miles long, 1.5 miles northwest of Blackcap Mountain along Fall Creek (lat. 37°05'15" N, long. 118°48'45" W). Named on Blackcap Mountain (1953) 15' quadrangle.

Bender [FRESNO]: *locality,* 2 miles north of Lanare along Southern Pacific Railroad (lat. 36°27'45" N, long. 119°57'15" W; sec. 8, T 17 S, R 19 E). Named on Burrel (1927) 7.5' quadrangle.

Benight Pond [FRESNO]: *intermittent lakes,* two, largest 1300 feet long, 3.25 miles southwest of Selma (lat. 36°31'45" N, long. 119°39'10" W; sec. 23, T 16 S, R 21 E). Named on Conejo (1963) 7.5' quadrangle. On Selma (1946) 15' quadrangle, the name applies to a permanent lake and two intermittent lakes.

Benita: see **Delano** [KERN].

Benito [FRESNO]: *locality,* 2.5 miles south-southeast of Firebaugh along Southern Pacific Railroad (lat. 36°49'15" N, long. 120°26'10" W; at N line sec. 10, T 13 S, R 14 E). Named on Firebaugh (1956) 7.5' quadrangle.

Bennett Creek [TULARE]: *stream,* flows 4 miles to South Fork Kaweah River 10 miles southeast of Kaweah (lat. 36°21'25" N, long. 118°48'15" W; sec. 14, T 18 S, R 29 E). Named on Kaweah (1957) 15' quadrangle. Kaweah (1909) 30' quadrangle has the name "Battle Creek" for the lower part of present Bennett Creek, and for a west branch of present Bennett Creek. The name "Bennett" commemorates William F. Bennett, a stockman in the neighborhood in the 1870's (United States Board on Geographic Names, 1933a, p. 137).

Bennett Mill [FRESNO]: *locality,* 20 miles southwest of Kaiser Peak (lat. 37°05'30" N, long. 119°25'45" W; sec. 2, T 10 S, R 23 E). Named on Kaiser (1904) 30' quadrangle.

Benninger Canyon [KERN]: *canyon,* drained by a stream that flows 3 miles to Walker Basin Creek 6 miles north of Caliente (lat. 35° 22'25" N, long. 118°36'10" W; sec. 25, T 29 S, R 31 E). Named on Breckenridge Mountain (1972) 7.5' quadrangle.

Benson Gulch [KERN]: *canyon,* drained by a stream that flows less than 1 mile to Fremont Valley 2.5 miles northeast of Garlock (lat. 35°25'30" N, long. 117°45'10" W; near W line sec. 12, T 29 S, R 39 E). Named on Garlock (1967) 7.5' quadrangle.

Benson Well [KERN]: *well,* 6.5 miles northwest of Randsburg (lat. 35°25'30" N, long. 117°44'50" W; sec. 12, T 29 S, R 39 E). Named on El Paso Peaks (1967) 7.5' quadrangle.

Bequette Canyon [TULARE]: *canyon,* drained by a stream that flows 1 mile to Dry Creek (1) nearly 5 miles northeast of Woodlake (lat. 36°27'10" N, long. 119°27'10" W; sec. 15, T 17 S, R 27 E). Named on Woodlake (1952) 7.5' quadrangle.

Berry: see **Andy Berry's Landing**, under **Millwood** [FRESNO].

Berts Canyon [KERN]: *canyon,* drained by a stream that flows 4 miles to Canebrake Creek 5 miles north-northwest of Walker Pass (lat. 35°43'25" N, long. 118°04'25" W; near W line sec. 25, T 25 S, R 36 E). Named on Walker Pass (1972) 7.5' quadrangle. Called Indian Wells Canyon on Kernville (1908) 30' quadrangle.

Beryl Lake [FRESNO]: *lake,* 800 feet long, 4.5 miles north-northeast of Dinkey Dome (lat. 37°10'40" N, long. 119°06'20" W; sec. 2, T 9 S, R 26 E). Named on Huntington Lake (1953) 15' quadrangle.

Betty Lake [FRESNO]: *lake,* 350 feet long, 3 miles east-southeast of Dinkey Dome (lat. 37°06'15" N, long. 119°04'45" W; on E line sec. 36, T 9 S, R 26 E). Named on Huntington Lake (1953) 15' quadrangle.

Betty Spring [TULARE]: *spring,* 1 mile southeast of California Hot Springs (lat. 35°52'05" N, long. 118°39'40" W; sec. 5, T 24 S, R 31 E). Named on California Hot Springs (1958) 15' quadrangle.

Betty Waller Meadow [TULARE]: *area,* 3 miles southeast of California Hot Springs (lat. 35°51' N, long. 118°38' W; sec. 9, T 24 S, R 31 E). Named on California Hot Springs (1958) 15' quadrangle.

Beulah: see **Mineral King** [TULARE].

Beulah Camp: see **Mineral King** [TULARE].

Beverly: see **Lou Beverly Lake** [FRESNO].

Beville Lake [TULARE]: *lake,* 650 feet long, 10 miles west-northwest of Triple Divide Peak (lat. 36°39'40" N, long. 118°41'25" W). Named on Triple Divide Peak (1956) 15' quadrangle. The name commemorates a family from Visalia (Browning, p. 16).

Bickel Camp [KERN]: *locality,* 5.25 miles north of Saltdale (lat. 35° 26'10" N, long. 117°53'10" W). Named on Saltdale NW (1967) 7.5' quadrangle.

Big Arroyo [TULARE]: *stream,* flows 14 miles to Kern River 11.5 miles northwest of Kern Peak (lat. 36°26'15" N, long. 118°24'45" W). Named on Kern Peak (1956), Mineral King (1956), and Triple Divide Peak (1956) 15' quadrangles. Called The Big Arroyo on Olmsted's (1900) map. On Olancha (1907) and Tehipite (1903) 30' quadrangles, the name applies to the canyon of the stream. The canyon was called Jenny Lind Cañon in the early days when the stream itself was called Crabtree Creek—the name "Jenny Lind" was from Jenny Lind mine (Browning, p. 16).

Big Baldy [TULARE]: *peak,* 7 miles north of Yucca Mountain (lat. 36°40'20" N, long. 118°52'50" W; near SE cor. sec. 25, T 14 S, R 28 E). Altitude 8209 feet. Named on Giant Forest (1956) 15' quadrangle. The name is from the bare summit of the feature (Browning, p. 16).

Big Baldy Ridge [TULARE]: *ridge,* south-trending, 4 miles long, 7.5 miles north of Yucca Mountain (lat. 36°40'30" N, long. 118°52'45" W); the peak called Big Baldy is on the ridge. Named on Giant Forest (1956) 15' quadrangle.

Big Bear Lake [FRESNO]: *lake,* 1200 feet long, 4 miles south-southwest of Mount Abbot (lat. 37°19'55" N, long. 118°48'05" W); the feature is 600 feet upstream from Little Bear Lake. Named on Mount Abbot (1953) 15' quadrangle. Elden H. Vestal of California Department of Fish and Game named the lake in 1952 (Browning, p. 16).

Big Bend [FRESNO]: *bend,* 6.5 miles west of Prather along San Joaquin River on Fresno-Madera County line (lat. 37°01'15" N, long. 119°38' W). Named on Millerton Lake West (1965) 7.5' quadrangle. Water of Millerton Lake now covers the place.

Big Bird Lake [TULARE]: *lake,* 4000 feet long, 4 miles west-northwest of Triple Divide Peak (lat. 36°37'15" N, long. 118°35'30" W). Named on Triple Divide Peak (1956) 15' quadrangle. United States Board on Geographic Names (1962, p. 5) rejected the name "Dollar Lake" for the feature, and noted that the name "Big Bird" was given about 1902 for the tracks of a large bird found on the lake shore.

Big Blue Hills [FRESNO]: *range,* 16 miles north-northwest of Coalinga between Cantua Creek and Domengine Creek (lat. 36°22' N, long. 120°25' W). Named on Domengine Ranch (1956), Joaquin Rocks (1969), Lillis Ranch (1956), and Tres Picos Farms (1956) 7.5' quadrangles. Anderson and Pack (p. 17) named the feature because "the central and most prominent summits in the group are high, domelike hills of light-blue color formed of serpentine fragments derived from the beds locally known as the Big Blue."

Big Blue Mill [KERN]: *locality,* nearly 2 miles south of present Kernville and 1 mile north of the original site of Kernville (lat. 35° 43'45" N, long. 118°25'40" W). Named on Isabella (1943) 15' quadrangle, which shows Big Blue mine situated 0.5 mile west-southwest of the place. Lovely Rogers discovered gold about 1 mile north of the original site of Kernville in 1861, and a town to be called Rogersville was laid out there, but failed to materialize; resumption of mining at the place in 1873 resulted in a new community called Quartzburg, and a camp located 0.5 mile farther north called Burkeville for Edwin Burke, co-owner of Big Blue mine—Burkeville also was called Millville and Milltown (Hensher and Peskin, p. 11).

Big Brewer Lake [TULARE]: *lake,* 1700 feet long, 8 miles north of Triple Divide Peak (lat. 36°42'10" N, long. 118°30'30" W); the lake is along Brewer Creek. Named on Triple Divide Peak (1956) 15' quadrangle.

Big Campbell [TULARE]: *peak,* 8.5 miles east of Porterville (lat. 36° 05'35" N, long. 118°52'05" W; near N line sec. 20, T 21 S, R 29 E); the peak is southeast across Tule River from Little Campbell. Altitude 1328 feet.

Named on Globe (1956) 7.5' quadrangle.

Big Chief Lake [FRESNO]: *lake,* 2200 feet long, 8.5 miles south-southwest of Mount Abbot (lat. 37°16' N, long. 118°49'20" W). Named on Mount Abbot (1953) 15' quadrangle. Elden H. Vestal of California Department of Fish and Game named the lake in 1951 (Browning, p. 16).

Big Creek [FRESNO]:

(1) *stream,* formed by the confluence of East Fork and South Fork, flows 17 miles to San Joaquin River 7.25 miles north of Shaver Lake Heights (present town of Shaver Lake) (lat. 37°12'40" N, long. 119°19'45" W; near W line sec. 26, T 8 S, R 24 E). Named on Huntington Lake (1953) and Shaver Lake (1953) 15' quadrangles. East Fork is 4 miles long, and South Fork is 6.5 miles long; both forks are named on Huntington Lake (1953) 15' quadrangle.

(2) *stream,* flows 15 miles to Pine Flat Reservoir nearly 7 miles west of Balch Camp (lat. 36°54'30" N, long. 119°14'30" W; near NW cor. sec. 10, T 12 S, R 25 E). Named on Huntington Lake (1953), Patterson Mountain (1952), and Shaver Lake (1953) 15' quadrangles.

(3) *town,* 7 miles south-southwest of Kaiser Peak (lat. 37°12'15" N, long. 119°14'35" W; sec. 28, T 8 S, R 25 E); the town is along Big Creek (1). Named on Huntington Lake (1953) and Shaver Lake (1953) 15' quadrangles. The name is from the Big Creek project of Southern California Edison Company, started in 1911 (Hanna, p. 32). The railroad station at the place was called Cascada until 1926; the area near the present town was known as Big Creek Flats in the 1870's, and as Manzanita Park in 1902 (Redinger, p. 13, 20). Postal authorities established Big Creek post office in 1912 (Frickstad, p. 31). California Mining Bureau's (1917a) map shows a place called Portal along the railroad between Shaver and the town of Big Creek.

Big Creek, North Fork: see **Rancheria Creek** [FRESNO] (1).

Big Creek Canyon [FRESNO]: *canyon,* 7.5 miles long, along Big Creek (1) between Huntington Lake (1) and the confluence of Big Creek (1) and San Joaquin River, 7.5 miles north of Shaver Lake Heights (present town of Shaver Lake) (lat. 37°12'40" N, long. 119°19'45" W; near W line sec. 26, T 8 S, R 24 E). Named on Huntington Lake (1953) and Shaver Lake (1953) 15' quadrangles.

Big Creek Flats: see **Big Creek** [FRESNO] (3).

Big Dry Creek: see **Academy** [FRESNO]; **Dry Creek** [FRESNO].

Big Dry Meadow [TULARE]: *area,* 3.5 miles north-northwest of Olancha Peak along Dry Creek (3) (lat. 36°18'45" N, long. 118° 08' W; sec. 36, T 18 S, R 35 E). Named on Olancha (1956) 15' quadrangle.

Big Dry Meadows [TULARE]: *area,* nearly 3 miles west of Monache Mountain (lat. 36°12'35" N, long. 118°14'40" W; sec. 1, 12, T 20 S, R 34 E). Named on Monache Mountain (1956) 15' quadrangle. Called Dry Meadows on Olancha (1907) 30' quadrangle.

Big E Spring [KERN]: *spring,* 3.25 miles east-southeast of Caliente in Deer Canyon (lat. 35°16'15" N, long. 118°34'35" W; near SE cor. sec. 31, T 30 S, R 32 E). Named on Oiler Peak (1972) 7.5' quadrangle.

Big Five Lakes [TULARE]: *lakes,* five, largest 0.5 mile long, 4.5 miles east-northeast of Mineral King (lat. 36°28'50" N, long. 118° 31'15" W). Named on Mineral King (1956) 15' quadrangle. United States Board on Geographic Names (1933a, p. 142) rejected the name "The Five Lakes" for the group.

Big Hart Canyon [KERN]: *canyon,* drained by a stream that flows 2 miles to Hart Canyon 8 miles north of Emerald Mountain (lat. 35° 22'10" N, long. 118°18'50" W). Named on Claraville (1972) and Emerald Mountain (1972) 7.5' quadrangles.

Bighorn Lake [FRESNO]:

(1) *lake,* 2000 feet long, 8 miles northwest of Mount Abbot (lat. 37° 28'05" N, long. 118°52'45" W). Named on Mount Abbot (1953) 15' quadrangle.

(2) *lake,* 1100 feet long, 2 miles east of Blackcap Mountain (lat. 37° 04'05" N, long 118°45'25" W). Named on Blackcap Mountain (1953) 15' quadrangle.

Bighorn Plateau [TULARE]: *area,* 5.5 miles west-northwest of Mount Whitney (lat. 36°37' N, long. 118°22'30" W). Named on Mount Whitney (1956) 15' quadrangle. Called Sandy Plateau on Mount Whitney (1907) 30' quadrangle, but United States Board on Geographic Names (1933a, p. 142) rejected this name for the feature.

Big Last Chance Canyon [KERN]: *canyon,* drained by a stream that flows 1.5 miles to Caliente Creek 2 miles west of Loraine (lat. 35°18'05" N, long. 118°28'15" W; sec. 19, T 30 S, R 33 E); the canyon is less than 1 mile east of Little Last Chance Canyon. Named on Loraine (1972) 7.5' quadrangle.

Big Margaret Lake [FRESNO]: *lake,* 3500 feet long, 14 miles northeast of Kaiser Peak (lat. 37°27'30" N, long. 119°02' W); the feature is the largest of the group called Margaret Lakes. Named on Kaiser Peak (1953) 15' quadrangle.

Big Maxson Meadow [FRESNO]: *area,* 2.5 miles west-southwest of Blackcap Mountain along North Fork Kings River (lat. 37°03'05" N, long. 118°50' W); the place is 7.5 miles east-southeast of Maxson Meadows. Named on Blackcap Mountain (1953) 15' quadrangle.

Big Meadow [TULARE]: *area,* 9.5 miles east-southeast of Fairview (lat. 35°52'45" N, long. 118°20'15" W). Named on Kernville (1956) 15' quadrangle.

Big Meadows [TULARE]: *area,* 2.5 miles west-northwest of Shell Mountain (lat. 36°42'40" N, long. 118°50'30" W). Named on Giant Forest (1956) 15' quadrangle. Called Big Meadow on Tehipite (1903) 30' quadrangle. The name was in use by the 1860's (Browning, p. 17).

Big Meadows Creek [TULARE]: *stream,* flows 6 miles to Boulder Creek (1) 3 miles north-northeast of Shell Mountain at Tulare-Fresno County line (lat. 36°44'25" N, long. 118°47' W; at N line sec. 1, T 14 S, R 29 E); the stream goes through Big Meadows. Named on Giant Forest (1956) 15' quadrangle. Called Big Meadow Creek on Tehipite (1903) 30' quadrangle.

Big Moccasin Lake [FRESNO]: *lake,* 1000 feet long, 8 miles south of Mount Abbot (lat. 37°46'30" N, long. 118°48' W); the lake is 400 feet northeast of Little Moccasin Lake. Named on Mount Abbot (1953) 15' quadrangle.

Big Panoche Creek: see **Panoche Creek** [FRESNO].

Big Pete Meadow [FRESNO]: *area,* 6.5 miles east of Mount Goddard along Middle Fork Kings River (lat. 37°06'40" N, long. 118°36'15" W); the place is 0.5 mile upstream from Little Pete Meadow. Named on Mount Goddard (1948) 15' quadrangle.

Big Pine Meadow [TULARE]: *valley,* 10 miles north of Lamont Peak (lat. 35°56'15" N, long. 118°03'30" W). Named on Lamont Peak (1956) 15' quadrangle.

Big Sandy Bluffs [FRESNO]: *escarpment,* northwest-trending, 3.5 miles long, 7.5 miles west-southwest of Shaver Lake Heights (present town of Shaver Lake) (lat. 37°03'15" N, long. 119° 26'15" W); the feature is northeast of Big Sandy Valley. Named on Shaver Lake (1953) 15' quadrangle. United States Board on Geographic Names (1980, p. 4) approved the form "Big Sandy Bluff" for the name.

Big Sandy Creek [FRESNO]: *stream,* flows 10.5 miles to San Joaquin River 3.5 miles west-northwest of Prather (lat. 37°03'45" N, long. 119°34' W; sec. 16, T 10 S, R 22 E); the stream goes through Big Sandy Valley. Named on Shaver Lake (1953) 15' quadrangle, and on Millerton Lake East (1965) 7.5' quadrangle.

Big Sandy Valley [FRESNO]: *valley,* 9 miles west-southwest of Shaver Lake Heights (present town of Shaver Lake) (lat. 37°02'30" N, long. 119°27'30" W); the valley is along Big Sandy Creek. Named on Shaver Lake (1953) 15' quadrangle.

Big Spring [KERN]: *spring,* 8 miles west of Inyokern (lat. 35°37'30" N, long. 117°57'30" W; sec. 36, T 26 S, R 37 E). Named on Freeman Junction (1972) and Owens Peak (1972) 7.5' quadrangles.

Big Spring [TULARE]: *spring,* 11 miles southwest of Mineral King in Putnam Canyon (lat. 36°20'35" N, long. 118°44'40" W). Named on Mineral King (1956) 15' quadrangle.

Big Springs [TULARE]: *spring,* 6 miles north-northwest of Yucca Mountain in Redwood Canyon (lat. 36°39'15" N, long 118°54'15" W; sec. 2, T 15 S, R 28 E). Named on Giant Forest (1956) 15' quadrangle.

Big Sycamore Canyon [KERN]: *canyon,* drained by a stream that flows 4 miles to lowlands 10 miles southwest of Liebre Twins (lat. 34°50'35" N, long. 118°41' W; sec. 28, T 9 N, R 17 W); the mouth of this canyon is 1 mile northeast of the mouth of Little Sycamore Canyon (2). Named on La Liebre Ranch (1965) and Winters Ridge (1966) 7.5' quadrangles.

Big Tar Canyon [KINGS]: *canyon,* 3 miles long, 6 miles south-southwest of Avenal (lat. 35°55'30" N, long. 120°10' W); the canyon is on upper reaches of Big Tar Creek. Named on Garza Peak (1953) 7.5' quadrangle, which shows a tar seep in the canyon.

Big Tar Creek [KINGS]: *stream,* flows 6 miles to Kettleman Plain 4.25 miles south-southeast of Avenal (lat. 35°56'50" N, long. 120° 06'30" W; sec. 11, T 23 S, R 17 E); the stream drains Big Tar Canyon. Named on Garza Peak (1953) and Kettleman Plain (1953) 7.5' quadrangles.

Big Tenant Spring [KERN]: *spring,* 2.25 miles north of Democrat Hot Springs (lat. 35°33'35" N, long. 118°39'40" W; near SE cor. sec. 20, T 27 S, R 31 E); the spring is 0.5 mile northeast of Little Tenant Spring near the head of Tenant Creek. Named on Democrat Hot Springs (1972) 7.5' quadrangle.

Big West Meadow: see **Big Wet Meadow** [TULARE].

Big Wet Meadow [TULARE]: *area,* 5 miles north of Triple Divide Peak along Roaring River in Cloud Canyon (lat. 36°39'45" N, long. 118°31'50" W). Named on Triple Divide Peak (1956) 15' quadrangle. United States Board on Geographic Names (1968b, p. 5) rejected the name "Big West Meadow" for the feature.

Big Whitney Meadow [TULARE]: *area,* 9 miles north of Kern Peak on upper reaches of Golden Trout Creek (lat. 36°26' N, long. 118° 16' W; in and near sec. 23, T 17 S, R 34 E); the place is 6 miles northeast of Little Whitney Meadow. Named on Kern Peak (1956) 15' quadrangle. Called Whitney Meadows on Olancha (1907) 30' quadrangle. United States Board on Geographic Names (1933a, p. 816) rejected the name "Golden Trout Meadows" for the feature.

Bill Lake [FRESNO]: *lake,* 450 feet long, 1 mile west-northwest of Kaiser Peak (lat. 37°18' N, long. 119°12' W; near E line sec. 23, T 7 S, R 25 E). Named on Kaiser Peak (1953) 15' quadrangle.

Bill Moore Canyon [TULARE]: *canyon,* drained by a stream that flows about 1.5 miles to Dry Creek (1) 5 miles east-southeast of Auckland (lat. 36°34'15" N, long. 119°01'15" W; near N line sec. 3, T 16 S, R 27 E); the canyon is northeast of Bill Moore Ridge. Named on Auckland (1966) 7.5' quadrangle.

Bill Moore Ridge [TULARE]: *ridge*, east-southeast- to southeast-trending, 1.5 miles long, 4 miles east-southeast of Auckland (lat. 36°34'30" N, long. 119°02'15" W). Named on Auckland (1966) 7.5' quadrangle.

Billy Creek [FRESNO]:

(1) *stream*, flows 1 mile to Huntington Lake (1) 2.5 miles north-northeast of the town of Big Creek (lat. 37°14'15" N, long. 119°13'45" W; sec. 15, T 8 S, R 25 E). Named on Huntington Lake (1953) 15' quadrangle.

(2) *stream*, flows 2.5 miles to Pine Flat Reservoir 1 mile south of Trimmer (lat. 36°53'25" N, long. 119°17'40" W; near W line sec. 18, T 12 S, R 25 E). Named on Trimmer (1965) 7.5' quadrangle.

Billy Spring [KERN]: *spring*, 3.5 miles northwest of Caliente (lat. 35°19'35" N, long. 118°40'25" W). Named on Bena (1972) 7.5' quadrangle.

Bino Springs [KERN]: *springs*, 13 miles south-southeast of Arvin (lat. 35°00'55" N, long. 118°45'20" W; near NW cor. sec. 25, T 11 N, R 18 W). Named on Tejon Hills (1955) 7.5' quadrangle.

Biola [FRESNO]: *town*, 6 miles north-northeast of Kerman (lat. 36° 48'10" N, long. 120°01' W; sec. 16, T 13 S, R 18 E). Named on Biola (1963) 7.5' quadrangle. William Kerchoff started the town in 1912 and coined the name from initial letters of the term "Bible Institute of Los Angeles" (Gudde, 1949, p. 31). Postal authorities established Biola post office in 1915, discontinued in it 1918, and reestablished it in 1920 (Frickstad, p. 31).

Biola Junction [FRESNO]: *locality*, 5.5 miles west-northwest of downtown Fresno along Southern Pacific Railroad (lat. 36°48'05" N, long. 119°52'05" W; sec. 14, T 13 S, R 19 E). Named on Fresno North (1965) 7.5' quadrangle.

Bird Spring [KERN]: *spring*, 5.5 miles northeast of Pinyon Mountain (lat. 35°29'55" N, long. 118°04'35" W). Named on Dove Spring (1972) 7.5' quadrangle.

Bird Spring Canyon [KERN]: *canyon*, drained by a stream that flows 7.25 miles to Indian Wells Valley 7 miles east-northeast of Pinyon Mountain (lat. 35°29'40" N, long. 118°02'45" W; at E line sec. 13, T 28 S, R 36 E); Bird Spring is in the canyon. Named on Cane Canyon (1972), Dove Spring (1972), and Horse Canyon (1972) 7.5' quadrangles.

Bird Spring Pass [KERN]: *pass*, 1 mile south-southwest of Skinner Peak (lat. 35°33'10" N, long. 118°07'55" W); the pass is at the head of Bird Spring Canyon. Named on Cane Canyon (1972) 7.5' quadrangle.

Bishop Pass [FRESNO]: *pass*, 10 miles east of Mount Goddard on Fresno-Inyo County line (lat. 37°06'55" N, long. 118°32'40" W). Named on Mount Goddard (1948) 15' quadrangle.

Bissell [KERN]: *locality*, 13 miles northeast of Rosamond along Atchison, Topeka and Santa Fe Railroad (lat. 34°59'40" N, long. 118°00' W; sec. 1, T 10 N, R 11 W). Named on Bissell (1973) and Edwards (1973) 7.5' quadrangles. On Bissell (1947) 7.5' quadrangle, the name is at a site situated 2 miles farther southwest along an abandoned railroad grade (lat. 34°58'15" N, long. 118°01'20" W; near SW cor. sec. 11, T 10 N, R 11 W).

Bissell Hills [KERN]: *range*, 10 miles east-northeast of Rosamond (lat. 34°56' N, long. 118°00' W); the range is south of Bissell. Named on Bissell (1973) and Edwards (1973) 7.5' quadrangles.

Bitter Creek [KERN]: *stream*, flows 10 miles to lowlands 5 miles southeast of Maricopa (lat. 35°01'15" N, long. 119°20'25" W; near S line sec. 21, T 11 N, R 23 W). Named on Ballinger Canyon (1943), Pentland (1953), and Santiago Creek (1943) 7.5' quadrangles. The name is from the quality of water in the stream (Arnold and Johnson, p. 19).

Bitter Creek [TULARE]: *stream*, flows 3.5 miles to South Fork Kern River 12.5 miles south-southeast of Monache Mountain (lat. 36°02'05" N, long. 118°08' W; sec. 6, T 22 S, R 36 E). Named on Monache Mountain (1956) 15' quadrangle.

Bitter Creek: see **Bitterwater Creek** [KERN] (1).

Bitterwater Canyon [KERN]: *canyon*, 5 miles long, on Kern-San Luis Obispo County line along Bitterwater Creek (2) above a point 14 miles south of Orchard Peak (lat. 35°32' N, long. 120°04'45" W; sec. 31, T 27 S, R 18 E). Named on La Panza NE (1966) and Packwood Creek (1961) 7.5' quadrangles.

Bitterwater Creek [KERN]:

(1) *stream*, heads just inside San Luis Obispo County and flows 12.5 miles to end 4.5 miles northeast of Maricopa (lat. 35°06'50" N, long. 119°21' W; sec. 25, T 32 S, R 24 E). Named on Ballinger Canyon (1943), Maricopa (1951), and Pentland (1953) 7.5' quadrangles. United States Board on Geographic Names (1990, p. 6) rejected the name "Bitter Creek" for the stream.

(2) *stream*, flows 15 miles, partly in San Luis Obispo County, to Antelope Plain 6 miles west-southwest of Blackwells Corner (lat. 35°35'10" N, long. 119°58' W; at N line sec. 18, T 27 S, R 19 E); the stream drains Bitterwater Canyon and Bitterwater Valley. Named on Emigrant Hill (1953), La Panza NE (1966), Packwood Creek (1961), and Shale Point (1953) 7.5' quadrangles. Called East Palo Prieto Cr. on Mendenhall's (1908) map. The name "Bitterwater" is from the quality of water in the stream (Arnold and Johnson, p. 19).

Bitterwater Spring [KERN]:

(1) *spring*, 16 miles south-southeast of Orchard Peak (lat. 35°31'05" N, long. 120°04' W; near W line sec. 5, T 28 S, R 18 E); the spring is in Bitterwater Canyon. Named on Packwood Creek (1961) 7.5' quadrangle.

(2) *spring*, 5 miles south-southwest of Maricopa (lat. 35°00'05" N, long. 119°27'15" W; near NW cor. sec. 33, T 11 N, R 24 W); the spring is along Bitterwater Creek (1). Named on Maricopa (1951) 7.5' quadrangle.

Bitterwater Valley [KERN]: *valley*, along Bitterwater Creek (2) above the entrance of the stream into Antelope Plain 6 miles west-southwest of Blackwells Corner (lat. 35°35'10" N, long. 119° 58' W; at N line sec. 18, T 27 S, R 19 E). Named on Packwood Creek (1961) and Shale Point (1953) 7.5' quadrangles. United States Board on Geographic Names (1933a, p. 147) rejected the name "Palo Prieto Valley" for the feature.

Bitterwater Wells [KERN]: *well*, 13 miles south-southeast of Orchard Peak (lat. 35°34'20" N, long. 120°00'55" W; near SE cor. sec. 15, T 27 S, R 18 E); the feature is in Bitterwater Valley along Bitterwater Creek (2). Named on Packwood Creek (1961) 7.5' quadrangle.

Black Bear Lake [FRESNO]: *lake*, 1500 feet long, 3.25 miles south of Mount Abbot (lat. 37°20'15" N, long. 118°47'35" W). Named on Mount Abbot (1953) 15' quadrangle. Elden H. Vestal of California Department of Fish and Game named the lake in 1952 (Browning, p. 20).

Black Bill Peak [KERN]: *peak*, nearly 4 miles north-northwest of Loraine (lat. 35°21' N, long. 118°28'15" W; sec. 6, T 30 S, R 33 E); the peak is on Black Bill Ridge. Altitude 5067 feet. Named on Loraine (1972) 7.5' quadrangle.

Black Bill Ridge [KERN]: *ridge*, generally north-northeast-trending, 1 mile long, 4 miles north-northwest of Loraine (lat. 35°21'10" N, long. 118°28' W). Named on Loraine (1972) 7.5' quadrangle.

Black Bob Canyon [KERN]: *canyon*, drained by a stream that flows 5.25 miles to Salt Creek (2) 6.25 miles east of Eagle Rest Peak (lat. 34°54'35" N, long. 119°01'20" W; near NW cor. sec. 33, T 10 N, R 20 W). Named on Frazier Mountain (1958), Grapevine (1958), and Pleito Hills (1958) 7.5' quadrangles. Frazier Mountain (1958) 7.5' quadrangle shows Black Bob mine in the canyon.

Blackburn Canyon [KERN]: *canyon*, drained by a stream that flows 5.25 miles to Tehachapi Valley 3 miles southeast of Tehachapi (lat. 35°05'45" N, long. 118°24'45" W; at N line sec. 31, T 12 N, R 14 W). Named on Tehachapi South (1966) 7.5' quadrangle.

Blackcap Basin [FRESNO]: *area*, 2 miles east of Blackcap Mountain at the head of North Fork Kings River (lat. 37°04' N, long. 118° 46' W). Named on Blackcap Mountain (1953) and Mount Goddard (1948) 15' quadrangles.

Blackcap Mountain [FRESNO]: *peak*, 4.5 miles west-southwest of Mount Goddard (lat. 37°04'20" N, long. 118°47'35" W). Altitude 11,559 feet. Named on Blackcap Mountain (1953) 15' quadrangle.

Black Divide [FRESNO]: *ridge*, north-northwest- to north-trending, 7 miles long, between LeConte Canyon and Enchanted Gorge (lat. 37°04' N, long. 118°38' W); Black Giant is at the north end of the ridge. Named on Mount Goddard (1948) 15' quadrangle. George R. Davis of United States Geological Survey named the feature about 1907 (Farquhar, 1923, p. 384).

Black Giant [FRESNO]: *peak*, 4 miles east of Mount Goddard (lat. 37°06'10" N, long. 118°38'50" W); the peak is at the north end of Black Divide. Altitude 13,330 feet. Named on Mount Goddard (1948) 15' quadrangle. J.N. LeConte gave the name "Black Giant" to the peak, but members of United States Geological Survey later called it Mount Goode (Farquhar, 1923, p. 399). United States Board on Geographic Names (1933a, p. 149) rejected the name "Mount Goode" for the peak, and then (1978b, p. 3) rejected the form "Black Giant Peak" for the name.

Black Giant Peak: see **Black Giant** [FRESNO].

Black Gulch [KERN]: *canyon*, drained by a stream that flows 4.25 miles to Kern River 1.25 miles north-northeast of Miracle Hot Springs (lat. 35°35'35" N, long. 118°31'40" W). Named on Alta Sierra (1972) and Miracle Hot Springs (1972) 7.5' quadrangles.

Black Hills [KERN]: *range*, 8.5 miles north of Saltdale on the northwest side of El Paso Range (lat. 35°28'30" N, long. 117°51'30" W). Named on Garlock (1967), Inyokern SE (1972), and Saltdale NW (1967) 7.5' quadrangles.

Black Hills Well [KERN]: *well*, 9.5 miles north of Saltdale (lat. 35° 29'35" N, long. 117°55'15" W); the well is west of Black Hills. Named on Saltdale NW (1967) 7.5' quadrangle.

Black Kaweah [TULARE]: *peak*, 3.25 miles south-southeast of Triple Divide Peak (lat. 36°32'45" N, long. 118°30'55" W); the peak is on Kaweah Peaks Ridge. Altitude 13,765 feet. Named on Triple Divide Peak (1956) 15' quadrangle. United States Board on Geographic Names (1969c, p. 8) approved the name "Kaweah Queen" for a peak located less than 1 mile north-northeast of Black Kaweah on Kaweah Peaks Ridge.

Black Mountain [FRESNO]:

(1) *ridge*, west-northwest-trending, 2 miles long, 10 miles southwest of Shaver Lake Heights (present town of Shaver Lake) (lat. 37°00'30" N,

long. 119°26'45" W). Named on Shaver Lake (1953) 15' quadrangle.
(2) *peak,* 9.5 miles south of Mount Pinchot on Fresno-Inyo County line (lat. 36°48'30" N, long. 118°22'40" W). Altitude 13,289 feet. Named on Mount Pinchot (1953) 15' quadrangle. Members of the Wheeler survey named the peak in the late 1870's (Browning, p. 20).
(3) *peak,* 3 miles east-southeast of Joaquin Rocks (lat. 36°18'15" N, long. 120°24'05" W; sec. 1, T 19 S, R 14 E). Altitude 3640 feet. Named on Joaquin Rocks (1969) 7.5' quadrangle.
(4) *peak,* 9.5 miles southwest of Coalinga (lat. 36°01'40" N, long. 120°27'30" W; on W line sec. 10, T 22 S, R 14 E). Altitude 2447 feet. Named on Curry Mountain (1969) 7.5' quadrangle.
(5) *ridge,* east-trending, 4 miles long, east of Castle Mountain (lat. 35°56'30" N, long. 120°18'30" W). Named on The Dark Hole (1961) 7.5' quadrangle.

Black Mountain [KERN]:
(1) *peak,* 1.5 miles northeast of Alta Sierra (lat. 35°44'30" N, long. 118°31'25" W; sec. 22, T 25 S, R 32 E). Altitude 7438 feet. Named on Alta Sierra (1972) 7.5' quadrangle.
(2) *peak,* 4.5 miles south-southeast of Keene (lat. 35°09'50" N, long. 118°31'40" W; sec. 10, T 32 S, R 32 E). Altitude 5686 feet. Named on Keene (1966) 7.5' quadrangle.
(3) *ridge,* east- to northeast-trending, 1 mile long, 5.5 miles northwest of Garlock (lat 35°28'15" N, long. 117°50'45" W). Named on Garlock (1967) 7.5' quadrangle. The name is from the mantle of dark volcanic rock that covers the feature (Fairbanks, 1897, p. 36).

Black Mountain [TULARE]:
(1) *peak,* 7.5 miles west-southwest of Camp Nelson (lat. 36°05'50" N, long. 118°44' W; near W line sec. 15, T 21 S, R 30 E). Named on Camp Nelson (1956) 15' quadrangle.
(2) *peak,* 12.5 miles west-northwest of Lamont Peak (lat. 35°51'10" N, long. 118°14'15" W). Named on Lamont Peak (1956) 15' quadrangle.

Black Mountain Saddle [KERN]: *pass,* 1.25 miles north-northeast of Alta Sierra (lat. 35°44'35" N, long. 118°32'15" W; sec. 21, T 25 S, R 32 E); the pass is nearly 1 mile west of Black Mountain (1). Named on Alta Sierra (1972) 7.5' quadrangle.

Black Oak Flat [FRESNO]: *area,* 3.5 miles east of Dunlap (lat. 36° 44'40" N, long. 119°03'15" W; around SE cor. sec. 32, T 13 S, R 27 E). Named on Miramonte (1966) 7.5' quadrangle.

Black Pass: see **Black Rock Pass** [TULARE].

Black Peak [FRESNO]: *peak,* 6.5 miles northeast of Dinkey Dome (lat. 37°10'55" N, long. 119°03' W; sec. 5, T 9 S, R 27 E). Altitude 9771 feet. Named on Huntington Lake (1953) 15' quadrangle. United States Board on Geographic Names (1983b, p. 4) rejected the names "Potato Butte" and "Potato Mountain" for the feature.

Black Point [FRESNO]: *peak,* 10 miles north-northeast of Shaver Lake Heights (present town of Shaver Lake) (lat. 37°14'20" N, long. 119°15'30" W; sec. 17, T 8 S, R 25 E). Altitude 8111 feet. Named on Shaver Lake (1953) 15' quadrangle.

Black Rock [FRESNO]: *relief feature,* 4.25 miles east-northeast of Balch Camp (lat. 36°55'55" N, long. 119°03'10" W; sec. 32, T 11 S, R 27 E). Named on Patterson Mountain (1952) 15' quadrangle.

Black Rock Creek [FRESNO]: *stream,* flows 1 mile to North Fork Kings River 5.25 miles east of Balch Camp (lat. 36°55' N, long. 119°01'40" W; sec. 4, T 12 S, R 27 E); the stream heads near Black Rock. Named on Patterson Mountain (1952) 15' quadrangle.

Blackrock Lake [FRESNO]: *lake,* 1200 feet long, 4 miles north-northwest of Blackcap Mountain (lat. 37°07'45" N, long. 118°48'45" W). Named on Blackcap Mountain (1953) 15' quadrangle.

Blackrock Mountain [TULARE]: *peak,* 7 miles east-southeast of Hockett Peak (lat. 36°10'45" N, long. 118°16'35" W). Named on Hockett Peak (1956) 15' quadrangle. Hunters named the feature for a large black boulder at the summit (Browning, p. 21).

Black Rock Pass [TULARE]: *pass,* 3.5 miles northeast of Mineral King on Great Western Divide (lat. 36°29'05" N, long. 118°23'05" W). Named on Mineral King (1956) 15' quadrangle. The name is from a band of black rock that contrasts with red and white rocks that prevail nearby (United States Board on Geographic Names, 1933a, p. 149). The feature also was called Black Pass and Cliff Pass (Browning, p. 20).

Black Rock Reservoir [FRESNO]: *lake,* behind a dam on North Fork Kings River 5.5 miles east of Balch Camp (lat. 36°55'10" N, long. 119°01'20" W; sec. 3, T 12 S, R 27 E); the lake is 2 miles east-southeast of Black Rock. Named on Patterson Mountain (1952) 15' quadrangle.

Blackwells Corner [KERN]: *locality,* 50 miles west-northwest of Bakersfield (lat. 35°36'55" N, long. 119°52' W; at NE cor. sec. 1, T 27 S, R 19 E). Named on Blackwells Corner (1953) 7.5' quadrangle. The name commemorates George Blackwell, who started a travelers stop at the place in 1921 (Bailey, 1967, p. 2).

Blanco [TULARE]: *locality,* 7 miles south of Waukena along Atchison, Topeka and Santa Fe Railroad (lat. 36°02'10" N, long. 119°30'40" W; at N line sec. 8, T 22 S, R 23 E). Named on Corcoran (1954) 7.5' quadrangle.

Blaney Meadows [FRESNO]: *area,* 13 miles north-northwest of Blackcap Mountain along South Fork San Joaquin River (lat. 37° 14'30" N, long. 118°53'45" W; sec. 15, T 8 S, R 28 E). Named on Blackcap Mountain (1953) 15' quadrangle. United States Board on Geographic Names (1971a, p. 2) approved the name "Blayney Meadows" for the feature, and gave the names "Blaney Meadows," "Hidden Valley," "Hidden Valley Meadows," and "Lost Valley" as variants. At the same time the Board noted that the name "Blayney" commemorates William Farris Blayney, who grazed sheep in the neighborhood in the 1870's. Waring (p. 54) described Blaney Meadows Hot Springs, located "about a mile above the upper end of Blaney Meadows," where bathing pools were dug out at three or four springs.

Blaney Meadows Hot Springs: see **Blaney Meadows** [FRESNO].

Blayney Meadows: see **Blaney Meadows** [FRESNO].

Block Hill [KINGS]: *peak,* 7.5 miles east-southeast of Avenal (lat. 35°58'25" N, long. 120°00'05" W; near W line sec. 35, T 22 S, R 18 E). Named on Kettleman Plain (1953) 7.5' quadrangle. United States Board on Geographic Names (1933b, p. 5) noted that the name is descriptive

Blossom Lakes [TULARE]: *lakes,* largest 700 feet long, 5.5 miles south of Mineral King (lat. 36°22'15" N, long. 118°35'45" W). Named on Mineral King (1956) 15' quadrangle. R.B. Marshall of United States Geological Survey named the lake in 1909 for Charles W. Blossom, a ranger at Sequoia National Park (Hanna, p. 35).

Blossom Peak [TULARE]: *peak,* 3.5 miles south-southeast of Kaweah (lat. 36°25'25" N, long. 118°53'15" W; on E line sec. 25, T 17 S, R 28 E). Altitude 2539 feet. Named on Kaweah (1957) 15' quadrangle.

Blue Canyon [FRESNO]:
(1) *canyon,* 9.5 miles long, along Big Creek (2) 7.5 miles northwest of Balch Camp (lat. 35°58'30" N, long. 119°13'30" W; sec. 15, T 11 S, R 25 E). Named on Huntington Lake (1953), Patterson Mountain (1952), and Shaver Lake (1953) 15' quadrangles.
(2) *canyon,* 5 miles long, drained by Blue Canyon Creek, which joins Middle Fork Kings River 12.5 miles west of Marion Peak (lat. 36°55'50" N, long. 118°44'35" W). Named on Marion Peak (1953) and Tehipite Dome (1952) 15' quadrangles. Frank Dusy and Gustav Eisen named the canyon in the late 1870's (Browning, p. 22).

Blue Canyon [TULARE]:
(1) *canyon,* drained by a stream that flows 1.5 miles to Collier Creek nearly 4 miles south of Auckland (lat. 36°32' N, long. 119° 06' W; sec. 13, T 16 S, R 26 E). Named on Auckland (1966) 7.5' quadrangle.
(2) *canyon,* 1 mile long, opens into the canyon of Blue Creek 6 miles southeast of Springville (lat. 36°03'25" N, long. 118°45'20" W). Named on Globe (1956) 7.5' quadrangle.

Blue Canyon Creek [FRESNO]: *stream,* flows 8.5 miles to Middle Fork Kings River 12.5 miles west of Marion Peak (lat. 36°55'50" N, long. 118°44'35" W); the stream heads near Blue Canyon Peak and goes through Blue Canyon (2). Named on Mount Goddard (1948) 15' quadrangle.

Blue Canyon Falls [FRESNO]: *waterfall,* 13 miles west of Marion Peak near Middle Fork Kings River (lat. 36°55'50" N, long. 118° 44'50" W); the feature is in Blue Canyon (2). Named on Marion Peak (1953) 15' quadrangle. Frank Dusy and Gustav Eisen named the falls in the late 1870's (Browning, p. 22).

Blue Canyon Peak [FRESNO]: *peak,* 5.25 miles south of Mount Goddard (lat. 37°01'45" N, long. 118°42'30" W); the peak is near the head of Blue Canyon Creek. Altitude 11,849 feet. Named on Mount Goddard (1948) 15' quadrangle.

Blue Creek [TULARE]: *stream,* flows 4.5 miles to South Fork Tule River 7 miles south-southeast of Springville (lat. 36°02'25" N, long. 118°45'35" W). Named on Camp Nelson (1956) and Springville (1957) 15' quadrangles.

Blue Dome: see **Little Blue Dome** [TULARE].

Blue Flower Pass: see **Glen Pass** [FRESNO].

Blue Jay Lakes [FRESNO]: *lakes,* largest 600 feet long, 6.5 miles northwest of Mount Abbot (lat. 37°26'45" N, long. 118°52'30" W). Named on Mount Abbot (1953) 15' quadrangle.

Blue Mountain [KERN]: *ridge,* generally east-southeast- to south-trending, 5.5 miles long, 5.5 miles northeast of Woody (lat. 35°45'35" N, long. 118°46'10" W). Named on California Hot Springs (1958) 15' quadrangle, and on Glennville (1972), White River (1965), and Woody (1965) 7.5' quadrangles.

Blue Mountain [TULARE]: *ridge,* east- to east-southeast-trending, 2.5 miles long, 3 miles south-southeast of Auckland (lat. 36°33'10" N, long. 119°04'40" W). Named on Auckland (1966) 7.5' quadrangle.

Blue Point [KERN]: *relief feature,* nearly 5 miles north-northwest of Cinco (lat. 35°19'15" N, long. 118°04'55" W; near S line sec. 14, T 30 S, R 36 E). Named on Cinco (1972) 7.5' quadrangle.

Blue Ridge [KERN]: *ridge,* generally west-trending, 2.5 miles long, 7 miles west of Eagle Rest Peak (lat. 34°53'40" N, long. 119°15'20" W). Named on Eagle Rest Peak (1942) and Santiago Creek (1943) 7.5' quadrangles.

Blue Ridge [TULARE]: *ridge,* south-southwest- to south-trending, 4 miles long, 15 miles south-southeast of Kaweah (lat. 36°16' N, long. 118°51' W). Named on Kaweah (1957) and Springville (1957) 15' quadrangles.

Bluestone Ridge [KERN]: *ridge,* southeast- to east-trending, 8 miles long, center near Orchard Peak (lat. 35°44'15" N, long. 120° 08' W). Named on Orchard Peak (1961), Sawtooth Ridge (1961), and Tent Hills (1942) 7.5' quadrangles. Called Avenal Ridge on Sawtooth Ridge (1943) 7.5' quadrangle. Marsh (p. 41) noted that the feature has the local name "Orchard Ridge."

Board Camp Creek: see **Garfield Creek** [TULARE].

Bobby Lake [FRESNO]: *lake,* 250 feet long, 2000 feet west-northwest of Kaiser Peak (lat. 37°17'45" N, long. 119°11'25" W; near S line sec. 24, T 7 S, R 25 E). Named on Kaiser Peak (1953) 15' quadrangle.

Bobcat Point [TULARE]: *relief feature,* 6.25 miles east-southeast of Yucca Mountain (lat. 36°32'45" N, long. 118°45'30" W). Named on Giant Forest (1956) 15' quadrangle.

Bobcat Spring [KERN]: *spring,* nearly 6.5 miles east of Caliente (lat. 35°16'20" N, long. 118°31' W; sec. 35, T 30 S, R 32 E). Named on Oiler Peak (1972) 7.5' quadrangle.

Bob Rabbit Canyon [KERN]: *canyon,* 3.25 miles long, drained by Dry Meadow Creek above a point 7 miles south of Weldon (lat. 35°34'05" N, long. 118°16'20" W). Named on Woolstalf Creek (1972) 7.5' quadrangle, which shows the site of Bob Rabbit place near the mouth of the canyon. United States Board on Geographic Names (1974b, p. 2) approved the name "Bob Rabbit Place" and gave the name "Roberts" as a variant; the Board noted that Robert Roberts, known as Bob Rabbit, was an Indian who hunted cottontail rabbits in the neighborhood.

Bobs Flat [FRESNO]: *area,* 4 miles north of Trimmer (lat. 36°57'55" N, long. 119°17'40" W; near NE cor. sec. 24, T 11 S, R 24 E). Named on Trimmer (1965) 7.5' quadrangle.

Bobs Lake [FRESNO]: *lake,* 1500 feet long, 9.5 miles northwest of Mount Abbot (lat. 37°28'30" N, long. 118°55' W). Named on Mount Abbot (1953) 15' quadrangle. United States Board on Geographic Names (1969a, p. 5) approved the name "Warrior Lake" for the feature.

Bob Spring [KERN]: *spring,* 5.5 miles east-southeast of Caliente (lat. 35°15'25" N, long. 118°32'05" W; sec. 3, T 31 S, R 32 E). Named on Oiler Peak (1972) 7.5' quadrangle.

Bodfish [KERN]: *town,* 32 miles east-northeast of Bakersfield (lat. 35°35'20" N, long. 118°29'15" W; around SE cor. sec. 12, T 27 S, R 32 E). Named on Lake Isabella South (1972) 7.5' quadrangle. Called Vaughn on Kernville (1908) 30' quadrangle, which shows Bodfish P.O. at the place. Postal authorities established Bodfish post office in 1892, discontinued it in 1895, and reestablished it in 1906 (Salley, p. 24). The name Bodfish is for George Homer Bodfish, who came to California about 1867 (Hanna, p. 36). Postal authorities established Vaughn post office 5 miles south of Isabella post office in 1897 and discontinued it in 1906, when they moved it to Bodfish; they established Borel post office 2.5 miles southwest of Vaughn post office in 1904 and discontinued it in 1908—the name "Vaughn" was for Edward Vaughn, first postmaster, and the name "Borel" was from Borel Canal Construction Company (Salley, p. 25, 230).

Bodfish Canyon [KERN]: *canyon,* 6.25 miles long, drained by Bodfish Creek above a point 2 miles east-southeast of Bodfish (lat. 35° 34'50" N, long. 118°27'20" W; sec. 17, T 27 S, R 33 E). Named on Lake Isabella South (1972) 7.5' quadrangle.

Bodfish Creek [KERN]: *stream,* flows 9 miles to Kern River less than 1 mile north-northwest of Bodfish (lat. 35°36' N, long. 118° 29'45" W; near N line sec. 12, T 27 S, R 32 E); the stream drains Bodfish Canyon. Named on Lake Isabella South (1972) 7.5' quadrangle.

Bodfish Peak [KERN]: *peak,* 3.25 miles southeast of Bodfish (lat. 35°33' N, long. 118°27'10" W; sec. 29, T 27 S, R 33 E). Altitude 6038 feet. Named on Lake Isabella South (1972) 7.5' quadrangle.

Bog Creek: see **Ferguson Creek** [TULARE].

Boggs Slough [KINGS]: *water feature,* extends for 4 miles from near North Fork Kings River to Fresno Slough 10 miles northwest of Lemoore (lat. 36°23'40" N, long. 119°55'15" W; near W line sec. 4, T 18 S, R 19 E). Named on Burrel (1954) and Vanguard (1956) 7.5' quadrangles.

Boggy Meadow [FRESNO]: *area,* 11 miles east-northeast of Kaiser Peak (lat. 37°22'30" N, long. 119°00'30" W). Named on Kaiser (1904) 30' quadrangle. Water of Lake Thomas A. Edison now covers the place.

Bog Hole Spring [KERN]: *spring,* 3.25 miles north-northeast of Democrat Hot Springs (lat. 35°34' N, long. 118°38' W). Named on Democrat Hot Springs (1972) 7.5' quadrangle.

Bohna Creek [KERN]: *stream,* flows 2.5 miles to Cedar Creek 4.25 miles east-southeast of Glennville (lat. 35°42'50" N, long. 118°37'35" W; near NE cor. sec. 34, T 25 S, R 31 E). Named on Alta Sierra (1972) and Glennville (1972) 7.5' quadrangles.

Bohna Peak [KERN]: *peak,* 6.5 miles east-northeast of Glennville (lat. 35°45'35" N, long. 118°35'35" W; at N line sec. 13, T 25 S, R 31 E). Named on California Hot Springs (1958) 15' quadrangle.

Boiler Spring [KERN]: *spring,* nearly 7 miles east of Caliente (lat. 35°16'15" N, long. 118°30'30" W; sec. 35, T 30 S, R 32 E). Named on Oiler Peak (1972) 7.5' quadrangle. The name is for a small boiler that was abandoned at the place (Bailey, 1962, p. 17).

Boiler Spring: see **Lower Boiler Spring** [KERN].

Bolsillo Campground [FRESNO]: *locality,* 8 miles east of Kaiser Peak (lat. 37°18'50" N, long. 119°02'30" W); the place is along Bolsillo Creek. Named on Kaiser Peak (1953) 15' quadrangle.

Bolsillo Creek [FRESNO]: *stream,* flows 3 miles to South Fork San Joaquin River 9 miles east-northeast of Kaiser Peak (lat. 37°19'45" N, long. 119°01'55" W). Named on Kaiser Peak (1953) 15' quadrangle.

Bolton Brown: see **Mount Bolton Brown** [FRESNO].

Bonanza Gulch [KERN]: *canyon,* drained by a stream that flows 3.5 miles to Last Chance Canyon 5.25 miles north of Saltdale (lat. 35° 26' N, long. 117°53'30" W). Named on Garlock (1967) and Saltdale NW (1967) 7.5' quadrangles. The canyon had rich gold placers in 1893 (Wynn, 1963, p. 64).

Bond Creek [TULARE]: *stream,* flows 7.5 miles to South Fork Tule River 7.25 miles south-southeast of Springville (lat. 36°02'15" N, long. 118°45'25" W). Named on California Hot Springs (1958), Camp Nelson (1956), and Springville (1957) 15' quadrangles.

Bone Canyon [TULARE]: *canyon,* drained by a stream that flows 1 mile to lowlands 4.5 miles north of Woodlake (lat. 36°28'45" N, long. 119°05'30" W; sec. 6, T 17 S, R 27 E). Named on Woodlake (1952) 7.5' quadrangle.

Bone Creek [TULARE]: *stream,* flows 5 miles to Nobe Young Creek 11 miles northeast of California Hot Springs (lat. 35°59'55" N, long. 118°02'10" W; sec. 20, T 22 S, R 32 E). Named on California Hot Springs (1958) and Camp Nelson (1956) 15' quadrangles.

Bone Meadow [TULARE]: *area,* 9 miles north-northeast of California Hot Springs (lat. 35°59'45" N, long. 118°36'30" W; near NE cor. sec. 27, T 22 S, R 31 E); the place is at the head of Bone Creek. Named on California Hot Springs (1958) 15' quadrangle.

Boneyard Meadow [FRESNO]: *area,* 3 miles east of the town of Big Creek (lat. 37°12' N, long. 119°11'10" W; on S line sec. 25, T 8 S, R 25 E). Named on Huntington Lake (1953) 15' quadrangle. The name is from the bones of sheep that died at the place during a heavy spring snowstorm in the 1870's (Browning, p. 23).

Bonita Creek [TULARE]: *stream,* flows 1.5 miles to Rattlesnake Creek (3) 13 miles south-southeast of Hockett Peak (lat. 36°02'30" N, long. 118°18'10" W). Named on Hockett Peak (1956) 15' quadrangle.

Bonita Flat [TULARE]: *area,* 9 miles south-southeast of Hockett Peak (lat. 36°06' N, long. 118°20'30" W; sec. 18, T 21 S, R 34 E). Named on Hockett Peak (1956) 15' quadrangle.

Bonita Meadows [TULARE]: *area,* 13 miles south-southeast of Hockett Peak (lat. 36°02'20" N, long. 118°19'50" W); the place is at the head of Bonita Creek. Named on Hockett Peak (1956) 15' quadrangle.

Bonnie Lake [FRESNO]: *lake,* 600 feet long, 0.5 mile west-northwest of Kaiser Peak (lat. 37°17'50" N, long. 119°11'40" W; near S line sec. 24, T 7 S, R 25 E). Named on Kaiser Peak (1953) 15' quadrangle.

Bonsall Hill [TULARE]: *ridge,* west-trending, 1 mile long, 7.5 miles south-southwest of Springville (lat. 36°01'35" N, long. 118°52'05" W). Named on Globe (1956) 7.5' quadrangle.

Boone Lake: see **Pine Flat Reservoir** [FRESNO].

Boone Meadow [TULARE]: *area,* 10.5 miles east-northeast of Fairview along Trout Creek (lat. 35°59'50" N, long. 118°19'45" W; sec. 20, T 22 S, R 34 E). Named on Kernville (1956) 15' quadrangle.

Bootleg Canyon [KERN]: *canyon,* drained by a stream that flows 2 miles to Oak Creek Canyon 7.5 miles south of Tehachapi (lat. 35° 01'10" N, long. 118°25'40" W; sec. 25, T 11 N, R 15 W). Named on Tehachapi South (1966) 7.5' quadrangle.

Boreal Plateau [TULARE]: *area,* 10 miles north-northwest of Kern Peak (lat. 36°26'30" N, long. 118°21' W). Named on Kern Peak (1956) 15' quadrangle. Oliver Kehrlein suggested the name to reflect the frigid, windswept nature of the place (Browning, p. 23).

Borel: see **Bodfish** [KERN].

Borel Canyon [KERN]: *canyon,* drained by a stream that flows 5.25 miles to Adobe Canyon 2.5 miles east of Knob Hill (lat. 35°33'20" N, long. 118°54'05" W; sec. 30, T 27 S, R 29 E). Named on Knob Hill (1965) 7.5' quadrangle.

Boron [KERN]: *town,* 15 miles east-southeast of Castle Butte (lat. 35°00'05" N, long. 117°38'55" W; sec. 31, 32, T 11 N, R 7 W). Named on Boron (1973) and Leuhman Ridge (1973) 7.5' quadrangles. Postal authorities established Boron post office in 1938; the name is from the borate mines nearby (Salley, p. 25). Kramer (1942) 15' quadrangle has the name "Amargo" at the site.

Boron: see **Baker** [KERN].

Borreguero Spring [FRESNO]: *spring,* 2.5 miles south of Ciervo Mountain along Arroyo Hondo (lat. 36°25'40" N, long. 120°34'35" W; sec. 29, T 17 S, R 13 E). Named on Ciervo Mountain (1969) 7.5' quadrangle.

Borrough: see **Burrough Valley** [FRESNO].

Boulder Canyon [KERN]:

(1) *canyon,* drained by a stream that flows 6.25 miles to Sage Canyon 6 miles east of Skinner Peak (lat. 35°33'30" N, long. 118° 01'05" W). Named on Horse Canyon (1972) and Walker Pass (1972) 7.5' quadrangles.

(2) *canyon,* drained by a stream that flows 1.5 miles to Indian Wells Valley 10.5 miles north-northwest of Inyokern (lat. 35°47'10" N, long. 118°53'50" W; near SW cor. sec. 4, T 25 S, R 38 E). Named on Little Lake (1954) 15'

quadrangle.

Boulder Creek [FRESNO]: *stream,* flows 4.5 miles to Florence Lake 14 miles northwest of Blackcap Mountain (lat. 37°14'35" N, long. 118°56'45" W; sec, 18, T 8 S, R 28 E). Named on Blackcap Mountain (1953) 15' quadrangle.

Boulder Creek [FRESNO-TULARE]: *stream,* heads in Tulare County and flows 11.5 miles to South Fork Kings River 6 miles east-northeast of Hume in Fresno County (lat. 36°48'35" N, long. 118° 48'35" W). Named on Giant Forest (1956) and Tehipite Dome (1952) 15' quadrangles. The stream was called Glacier Creek in the 1860's and 1870's (Forest M. Clingan, personal communication, 1990).

Boulder Creek [TULARE]: *stream,* flows 3 miles to South Fork of Middle Fork Tule River 2 miles east of Camp Nelson (lat. 36°08'15" N, long. 118°34'25" W; near W line sec. 36, T 20 S, R 31 E). Named on Camp Nelson (1956) 15' quadrangle.

Boulder Creek: see **Little Boulder Creek** [FRESNO].

Boulder Gulch [KERN]: *canyon,* drained by a stream that flows 1.5 miles to Last Chance Canyon 5.25 miles north of Saltdale (lat. 35° 26'10" N, long. 117°53'05" W). Named on Saltdale NW (1967) 7.5' quadrangle.

Boulder Gulch Campground [KERN]: *locality,* 2.5 miles south-southwest of Wofford Heights (lat. 35°40'20" N, long. 118°28'10" W; near NE cor. sec. 18, T 26 S, R 33 E). Named on Lake Isabella North (1972) 7.5' quadrangle.

Boulder Hill [KINGS]: *peak,* 10 miles south-southeast of Kettleman City (lat. 35°51'55" N, long. 119°54'40" W; sec. 3, T 24 S, R 19 E). Named on Avenal Gap (1954) 7.5' quadrangle. The name refers to conglomerate that covers the peak (United States Board on Geographic Names, 1933b, p. 5).

Boulder Spring [KERN]: *spring,* 5.5 miles east of Skinner Peak (lat. 35°34'45" N, long. 118°01'40" W); the spring is in Boulder Canyon (1). Named on Horse Canyon (1972) 7.5' quadrangle. Called Boulder Springs on Kernville (1908) 30' quadrangle.

Boust City: see **Taft Heights** [KERN].

Bowen: see **Joe Bowen Canyon** [TULARE].

Bowerbank [KERN]: *locality,* 3.5 miles east of Buttonwillow along Southern Pacific Railroad (lat. 35°23'55" N, long. 119°24'30" W; at N line sec. 21, T 29 S, R 24 E). Named on Buttonwillow (1954) 7.5' quadrangle.

Bowles [FRESNO]: *village,* 11 miles south of downtown Fresno (lat. 36°36'10" N, long. 119°45'05" W; near NW cor. sec. 25, T 15 S, R 20 E). Named on Caruthers (1963) and Conejo (1963) 7.5' quadrangles. Postal authorities established Bowles post office in 1904 and discontinued it in 1943 (Frickstad, p. 31). The name is from a pioneer family in the region (Hanna, p. 39).

Boyden Cave [FRESNO]: *cave,* 6 miles east-northeast of Hume along South Fork Kings River (lat. 36°48'55" N, long. 118°49' W). Named on Tehipite Dome (1952) 15' quadrangle. Pete Boyden discovered the cave (Gudde, 1969, p. 36).

Bracchi Spring [KERN]: *spring,* nearly 3 miles south-southwest of Piute Peak (lat. 35°24'50" N, long. 118°24'45" W; sec. 11, T 29 S, R 33 E). Named on Piute Peak (1972) 7.5' quadrangle.

Bradford Mountain [FRESNO]: *ridge,* northwest-trending, 1 mile long, 3 miles north-northeast of Trimmer (lat. 36°56'45" N, long. 119°17'10" W; mainly in sec. 30, T 11 S, R 25 E). Named on Trimmer (1965) 7.5' quadrangle.

Bradley: see **Mount Bradley** [TULARE].

Bradley Canyon [KERN]: *canyon,* drained by a stream that flows 2.5 miles to Black Bob Canyon 7.5 miles west-northwest of Lebec (lat. 34°52'25" N, long. 118°59'30" W; near W line sec. 10, T 9 N, R 20 W). Named on Cuddy Valley (1943) and Frazier Mountain (1958) 7.5' quadrangles.

Bradshaw Creek [KERN]: *stream,* flows 5 miles to Lilly Canyon 1.5 miles west of Miracle Hot Springs (lat. 35°34'45" N, long. 118° 33'30" W). Named on Alta Sierra (1972) and Miracle Hot Springs (1972) 7.5' quadrangles.

Bradys [KERN]: *locality,* 5 miles northwest of Inyokern (lat. 35°42'05" N, long. 117°52'05" W; near E line sec. 3, T 26 S, R 38 E). Named on Inyokern (1943) 15' quadrangle.

Braitman Spring [KERN]: *spring,* 8.5 miles northwest of Cross Mountain (lat. 35°22'25" N, long. 118°14'15" W; sec. 32, T 29 S, R 35 E). Named on Cross Mountain (1972) 7.5' quadrangle.

Brave Lake [FRESNO]: *lake,* 950 feet long, 11.5 miles northwest of Mount Abbot (lat. 37°29'15" N, long. 118°56'45" W). Named on Mount Abbot (1953) 15' quadrangle.

Bravo Lake [TULARE]: *lake,* 1 mile long, at southeast edge of Woodlake (lat. 36°24'30" N, long. 119°05'30" W; sec. 31, T 17 S, R 27 E). Named on Woodlake (1952, photorevised 1969) 7.5' quadrangle. Called Wood Lake on Lemon Cove (1928) 7.5' quadrangle. According to local tradition, the name "Bravo Lake" was given by Indians who saw a fight between two Irishmen by the lake—*bravo* means "brave" in Spanish (Hanna, p. 358).

Breckenridge Campground [KERN]: *locality,* 10 miles east-northeast of Mount Adelaide (lat. 35°28' N, long. 118°34'50" W; sec. 30, T 28 S, R 32 E); the place is near the northeast end of Breckenridge Mountain. Named on Breckenridge Mountain (1972) 7.5' quadrangle.

Breckenridge Lodge: see **Breckenridge Meadows** [KERN].

Breckenridge Meadows [KERN]: *area,* about 8 miles east-northeast of Mount Adelaide (lat. 35°28' N, long. 118°36'25" W; sec. 26, T 28 S, R 31 E); the place is 1.25 miles west of Breckenridge Mountain. Named on Breckenridge Mountain (1972) 7.5' quadrangle. Breckenridge Mountain (1943) 15' quadrangle shows the abandoned Breckenridge Lodge at the place.

Breckenridge Mountain [KERN]: *ridge,* generally southwest-trending, 2.25 miles long, 9 miles east of Mount Adelaide (lat. 35°27'30" N, long. 118°35'05" W). Named on Breckenridge Mountain (1972) 7.5' quadrangle. Called Mt. Breckenridge on Olmsted's (1900) map, and called Canon Mt. on Williamson's (1853) map. The peak also was known as Cross Mountain (Wines, p. 86). The name "Breckenridge" was applied at the time of the Civil War, presumably by Southern sympathizers to honor John C. Breckenridge of Kentucky, who was a presidential candidate in the election of 1860 (Bailey, 1962, p. 74).

Bretz Mill [FRESNO]: *settlement,* 8 miles southwest of Dinkey Dome in Blue Canyon (1) (lat. 37°02'20" N, long. 119°14'30" W; near NW cor. sec. 27, T 10 S, R 25 E). Named on Huntington Lake (1953) 15' quadrangle.

Bretz Mill: see **Old Bretz Mill** [FRESNO].

Brewer: see **Mount Brewer** [TULARE].

Brewer Creek [TULARE]: *stream,* flows 4.5 miles to Roaring River 7.5 miles north-northwest of Triple Divide Peak (lat. 36°42' N, long. 118°33'35" W); the stream heads near Mount Brewer. Named on Mount Whitney (1956) and Triple Divide Peak (1956) 15' quadrangles.

Brewer Lake [FRESNO]: *lake,* 600 feet long, 3.5 miles north of Dinkey Dome (lat. 37°10' N, long. 119°07'20" W; sec. 10, T 9 S, R 26 E). Named on Huntington Lake (1953) 7.5' quadrangle.

Brewer Lake: see **Big Brewer Lake** [TULARE]; **East Lake** [TULARE].

Bridge: see **El Prado** [FRESNO] (1).

Bridge Camps [TULARE]: *locality,* 4.5 miles east of Yucca Mountain along Marble Fork Kaweah River (lat. 36°34'40" N, long. 118° 47'20" W). Named on Tehipite (1903) 30' quadrangle.

Bright Star Canyon [KERN]: *canyon,* 9 miles long, along Kelso Creek, and a branch of that creek, above a point 3.5 miles west-northwest of Pinyon Mountain (lat. 35°29' N, long. 118°12'45" W). Named on Claraville (1972), Pinyon Mountain (1972), and Woolstalf Creek (1972) 7.5' quadrangles.

Brights Valley: see **Brite Valley** [KERN].

Brin Canyon [TULARE]: *canyon,* drained by a stream that flows 2.5 miles to Kern River 1.5 miles northeast of Fairview (lat. 35°56'45" N, long. 118°28'35" W). Named on Kernville (1956) 15' quadrangle.

Brinn Canyon: see **Gold Ledge Creek** [TULARE].

Brite Creek [KERN]: *stream,* flows 10 miles to Tehachapi Creek 2.5 miles northwest of Tehachapi (lat. 35°09'25" N, long. 118°28'30" W; sec. 7, T 32 S, R 33 E). Named on Cummings Mountain (1966), Keene (1966), Tehachapi North (1966), and Tehachapi South (1966) 7.5' quadrangles.

Brite Valley [KERN]: *valley,* 5.5 miles north-northeast of Cummings Mountain (lat. 35°07' N, long. 118°32'30" W). Named on Cummings Mountain (1966) and Keene (1966) 7.5' quadrangles. Goodyear (1888a, p. 310) called the feature Brights Valley. The name "Brite" is for John M. Brite, who settled in the valley in 1857 (Boyd, p. 172).

Broad Creek [KERN]: *stream,* heads in Midway Valley and flows 9 miles to end in Buena Vista Valley 5 miles northeast of Taft (lat. 35°11'55" N, long. 119°23'50" W; sec. 28, T 31 S, R 24 E). Named on Fellows (1951) and Taft (1950) 7.5' quadrangles.

Broder Meadows [TULARE]: *area,* 3.5 miles south of Monache Mountain (lat. 36°09'15" N, long. 118°11'15" W; in and near sec. 28, T 20 S, R 35 E). Named on Monache Mountain (1956) 15' quadrangle.

Broken Hill [KINGS]: *peak,* 2.5 miles south-southwest of Kettleman City (lat. 35°58'20" N, long. 119°58'45" W; sec. 36, T 22 S, R 18 E). Altitude 715 feet. Named on Los Viejos (1954) 7.5' quadrangle. The name refers to strata that are broken by faults (United States Board on Geographic Names, 1933b, p. 6).

Bronco Canyon [KERN]:

(1) *canyon,* drained by a stream that flows 3.25 miles to lowlands 9 miles southwest of Liebre Twins (lat. 34°51'30" N, long. 118°40'20" W; sec. 22, T 9 N, R 17 W). Named on La Liebre Ranch (1965) and Winters Ridge (1966) 7.5' quadrangles.

(2) *canyon,* drained by a stream that flows 5.5 miles to El Paso Creek 7 miles west-northwest of Liebre Twins (lat. 34°59'25" N, long. 118°40'50" W; sec. 34, T 11 N, R 17 W). Named on Liebre Twins (1965) and Winters Ridge (1966) 7.5' quadrangles.

Bronge [FRESNO]: *locality,* 4.25 miles south-southeast of Clovis along Fresno Interurban Railroad (lat. 36°45'55" N, long. 119°40'55" W; near NE cor. sec. 33, T 13 S, R 21 E). Named on Clovis (1922) 7.5' quadrangle.

Brown [KERN]: *locality,* 9 miles north-northwest of Inyokern along Southern Pacific Railroad (lat. 35°46'30" N, long. 117°51' W; near E line sec. 11, T 25 S, R 38 E); the place is 8.5 miles east-northeast of Owens Peak.

Named on Little Lake (1954) 15' quadrangle. Postal authorities established Brown post office in 1909, changed the name to Mount Owen in 1948, and discontinued it in 1950 (Frickstad, p. 54, 57). The place first was called Siding 18 and was along the rail line built to carry supplies for construction of the aqueduct that takes Owens Valley water from Inyo County to Los Angeles; the name "Brown" was for George Brown, who built a hotel at the site (Hensher and Peskin, p. 32). The place also was known as Front (Wines, p. 86).

Brown: see **Mount Bolton Brown** [FRESNO].

Brown Bear Lake [FRESNO]: *lake,* 1650 feet long, 3 miles south-southwest of Mount Abbot (lat. 37°20'45" N, long. 118°48'35" W). Named on Mount Abbot (1953) 15' quadrangle. Employees of California Department of Fish and Game named the lake in the 1950's (Browning, p. 27).

Brown Butte [KERN]: *hill,* 11.5 miles northeast of Rosamond (lat. 34°59'05" N, long. 118°01'55" W; at S line sec. 3, T 10 N, R 11 W). Altitude 2906 feet. Named on Bissell (1973) 7.5' quadrangle.

Brown Canyon: see **Browns Canyon** [KERN].

Brown Cone [FRESNO]: *peak,* 8 miles north-northwest of Kaiser Peak (lat. 37°24'15" N, long. 119°13'55" W; sec. 15, T 6 S, R 25 E). Altitude 7130 feet. Named on Kaiser Peak (1953) 15' quadrangle.

Brown Cow Camp [TULARE]: *locality,* 3 miles west-northwest of Olancha Peak (lat. 36°16'30" N, long. 118°10' W; sec. 15, T 19 S, R 35 E); the place is in Brown Meadow. Named on Olancha (1956) 15' quadrangle.

Brown Flat [TULARE]: *area,* 3 miles east-southeast of Auckland (lat. 36°34'25" N, long. 119°03'20" W; sec. 32, T 15 S, R 27 E). Named on Auckland (1966) 7.5' quadrangle.

Brown Meadow [KERN]: *area,* 2.25 miles north-northwest of Piute Peak along Clear Creek (1) (lat. 35°29' N, long. 118°24'15" W; sec. 23, T 28 S, R 35 E); the place is 1 mile east of Brown Peak. Named on Piute Peak (1972) 7.5' quadrangle.

Brown Meadow [TULARE]: *area,* 3 miles west-northwest of Olancha Peak (lat. 36°17'15" N, long. 118°09'55" W); Brown Cow Camp is at the place. Named on Olancha (1956) 15' quadrangle.

Brown Mountain [TULARE]: *peak,* 3.5 miles west of Olancha Peak (lat. 36°15'35" N, long. 118°10'45" W; sec. 22, T 19 S, R 35 E). Altitude 9958 feet. Named on Olancha (1956) 15' quadrangle.

Brown Peak [FRESNO]: *peak,* 4.25 miles east of Dinkey Dome (lat. 37°07'30" N, long. 119°03'20" W; on N line sec. 29, T 9 S, R 27 E). Altitude 10,349 feet. Named on Huntington Lake (1953) 15' quadrangle.

Brown Peak [KERN]: *peak,* 3 miles northwest of Piute Peak (lat. 35° 29'05" N, long. 118°25'25" W; near N line sec. 22, T 28 S, R 33 E). Altitude 8095 feet. Named on Piute Peak (1972) 7.5' quadrangle. The name commemorates Charlie Brown, a miner who lived in the neighborhood in the early 1900's (United States Board on Geographic Names, 1975b, p. 8).

Browns Canyon [KERN]: *canyon,* 1.5 miles long, 6 miles west-southwest of McKittrick on Kern-San Luis Obispo County line (lat 35°16' N, long. 119°43' W; in and near sec. 33, T 30 S, R 21 E). Named on Reward (1951) 7.5' quadrangle. Called Brown Canyon on Arnold and Johnson's (1910) map.

Browns Mill [KERN]: *locality,* 5 miles south-southwest of Alta Sierra (lat. 35°39'25" N, long. 118°34'15" W; near NE cor. sec. 19, T 26 S, R 32 E). Site named on Alta Sierra (1972) 7.5' quadrangle.

Brown Spring [KERN]: *spring,* 4.25 miles east-southeast of Weldon (lat. 35°36'50" N, long. 118°15'10" W; near NW cor. sec. 5, T 27 S, R 35 E). Named on Woolstalf Creek (1972) 7.5' quadrangle.

Brown Valley: see **Indian Wells Valley** [KERN].

Broza Ridge [KERN]: *ridge,* generally north-northwest-trending, 1 mile long, 6.5 miles east of Caliente (lat. 35°17'30" N, long. 118° 30'55" W). Named on Oiler Peak (1972) 7.5' quadrangle.

Brush Canyon [FRESNO]: *canyon,* drained by a stream that flows 2.5 miles to Middle Fork Kings River nearly 6 miles northeast of Hume (lat. 36°51' N, long. 118°51'10" W). Named on Tehipite Dome (1952) 15' quadrangle.

Brush Creek [TULARE]: *stream,* flows 8.5 miles to Kern River 3 miles north-northeast of Fairview (lat. 35°57'55" N, long. 118°28'45" W; sec. 36, T 22 S, R 32 E). Named on Kernville (1956) 15' quadrangle.

Brush Creek: see **Little Brush Creek**, under **Cannell Creek** [KERN-TULARE].

Brush Meadow [FRESNO]: *area,* 7.5 miles south-southeast of Dinkey Dome (lat. 37°00'45" N, long. 119°04'50" W; near SE cor. sec. 36, T 10 S, R 26 E). Named on Huntington Lake (1953) 15' quadrangle.

Brush Meadow [TULARE]: *area,* 4.5 miles northeast of Monache Mountain (lat. 36°15' N, long. 118°08' W). Named on Monache Mountain (1956) and Olancha (1956) 15' quadrangles.

Brush Mountain [KERN]: *peak,* 5.5 miles west-southwest of Eagle Rest Peak (lat. 34°53'10" N, long. 119°13'35" W; at NW cor. sec. 10, T 9 N, R 22 W). Named on Eagle Rest Peak (1942) 7.5' quadrangle.

Brushy Hill [KERN]: *peak,* 5 miles south-southwest of Knob Hill (lat. 35°30'20" N, long. 118°59'55" W; sec. 7, T 28 S, R 28 E). Named on Knob Hill (1965) 7.5' quadrangle.

Bryanthus Lake: see **Bullfrog Lake** [FRESNO] (2).

Bubbs Creek [FRESNO-TULARE]: *stream,* heads in Tulare County and flows 18 miles to South Fork Kings River 12 miles south of Marion Peak in Fresno County (lat. 36°47'20" N, long. 118°33' W). Named on Mount Whitney (1907) 30' quadrangle, and on Marion Peak (1953) and Mount Pinchot (1953) 15' quadrangles. The name commemorates John Bubbs, who crossed Kearsarge Pass with a party of prospectors in 1864 (Hanna, p. 42).

Buck Canyon [TULARE]:

(1) *canyon,* 2.5 miles long, along Buck Creek above a point 6 miles west-southwest of Triple Divide Peak (lat. 36°34' N, long. 118° 38' W). Named on Triple Divide Peak (1956) 15' quadrangle.

(2) *canyon,* drained by a stream that flows 1 mile to Dry Creek (1) nearly 6 miles east-southeast of Auckland (lat. 36°33' N, long. 119°00'45" W; sec. 11, T 16 S, R 27 E). Named on Auckland (1966) 7.5' quadrangle.

Buck Creek [TULARE]: *stream,* flows 6.5 miles to Middle Fork Kaweah River 8.5 miles west-southwest of Triple Divide Peak (lat. 36°32'20" N, long. 118°40'10" W). Named on Triple Divide Peak (1956) 15' quadrangle.

Buckeye Creek [TULARE]: *stream,* flows less than 1 mile to Cottonwood Creek 0.5 mile north of Auckland (lat. 36°35'50" N, long. 119°06'15" W; near W line sec. 25, T 15 S, R 26 E). Named on Auckland (1966) 7.5' quadrangle.

Buckeye Flat [TULARE]:

(1) *area,* 7 miles east-southeast of Yucca Mountain along Middle Fork Kaweah River (lat. 36°31'15" N, long. 118°45'45" W). Named on Giant Forest (1956) 15' quadrangle.

(2) *area,* 5 miles north of Woodlake (lat. 36°29'20" N, long. 119° 05'25" W; on E line sec. 36, T 16 S, R 26 E). Named on Woodlake (1952) 7.5' quadrangle.

Buckeye Gulch [TULARE]: *canyon,* drained by a stream that flows 1.5 miles to North Fork Tule River 2.25 miles north-northeast of Springville (lat. 36°09'35" N, long. 118°48' W; sec. 26, T 20 S, R 29 E). Named on Springville (1957) 7.5' quadrangle.

Buckeye Spring [FRESNO]: *spring,* 11 miles south-southwest of Coalinga (lat. 36°00'05" N, long. 120°26'20" W; near W line sec. 23, T 22 S, R 14 E). Named on Curry Mountain (1969) 7.5' quadrangle.

Buckey Spring [KERN]: *spring,* 2 miles northeast of Caliente (lat. 35°18'50" N, long. 118°36'20" W). Named on Oiler Peak (1972) 7.5' quadrangle.

Buckhorn Lake [KERN]: *dry lake,* 4 miles south-southwest of Edwards at Kern-Los Angeles County line (lat. 34°49'45" N, long, 117°58'30" W). Named on Redman (1973) 7.5' quadrangle. Johnson's (1911) map shows Buckhorn Springs located about 2 miles east-northeast of the center of Buckhorn Lake (sec. 27, T 9 N, R 10 W).

Buckhorn Springs: see **Buckhorn Lake** [KERN].

Buck Meadow [FRESNO]: *area,* about 8.5 miles south-southeast of Dinkey Dome along Deer Creek (3) (lat. 37°00'20" N, long. 119° 03'45" W; near E line sec. 6, T 11 S, R 27 E). Named on Huntington Lake (1953) 15' quadrangle.

Buck Meadow [TULARE]: *area,* 1.5 miles west of Olancha Peak (lat. 36°16'10" N, long. 118°08'45" W). Named on Olancha (1956) 15' quadrangle.

Buck Peak [FRESNO]: *peak,* 11 miles south of Marion Peak (lat. 36° 48'15" N, long. 118°33'25" W). Altitude 8776 feet. Named on Marion Peak (1953) 15' quadrangle.

Buck Peak [TULARE]:

(1) *peak,* 5.25 miles east-northeast of Fountain Springs (lat. 35° 55'05" N, long. 118°49'35" W; near N line sec. 22, T 23 S, R 29 E). Altitude 2318 feet. Named on Gibbon Peak (1965) 7.5' quadrangle.

(2) *peak,* nearly 5 miles south-southwest of California Hot Springs (lat. 35°49'20" N, long. 118°43'10" W; near E line sec. 22, T 24 S, R 30 E). Named on California Hot Springs (1958) 15' quadrangle.

Buck Rock [TULARE]: *peak,* 4.5 miles northwest of Shell Mountain (lat. 36°44'10" N, long. 118°51'30" W; near E line sec. 6, T 14 S, R 29 E). Altitude 8500 feet. Named on Giant Forest (1956) 15' quadrangle. The feature originally was called Finger Rock or Finger Peak (Forest M. Clingan, personal communication, 1989).

Buck Rock Campground [TULARE]: *locality,* 3.25 miles west-northwest of Shell Mountain (lat. 36°43'10" N, long. 118°50'50" W; sec. 8, T 14 S, R 29 E); the place is 1.5 miles south-southeast of Buck Rock. Named on Giant Forest (1956) 15' quadrangle.

Buck Rock Creek [FRESNO]: *stream,* flows 1.5 miles to Little Boulder Creek 5.5 miles east-southeast of Hume (lat. 36°45'10" N, long. 118°49'20" W). Named on Giant Forest (1956) 15' quadrangle.

Buck Slide [TULARE]: *relief feature,* 6 miles north of California Hot Springs (lat. 35°58' N, long. 118°41' W; near E line sec. 36, T 22 S, R 30 E). Named on California Hot Springs (1958) 15' quadrangle.

Buena Ventura Valley: see "Regional setting."

Buena Vista: see **Buttonwillow** [KERN]; **Visalia** [TULARE].

Buenavista [TULARE]: *locality,* 2.5 miles southeast of Wilsonia near the head of Redwood Creek (1) (lat. 36°42'45" N, long. 118°55' W; sec. 15, T 14 S, R 28 E). Named on Tehipite (1903) 30' quadrangle.

Buena Vista Canal Slough: see **Kern River** [KERN-TULARE].

Buena Vista Canyon [KERN]: *canyon*, 2 miles long, 9 miles west-northwest of Inyokern (lat. 35°41'20" N, long. 117°57'45" W). Named on Owens Peak (1972) 7.5' quadrangle.

Buena Vista Creek [KERN]: *stream*, flows 17 miles, mainly through Buena Vista Valley, to end 6 miles northeast of Taft at Buena Vista Lake Bed (lat. 35°12'15" N, long. 119°23' W; sec. 27, T 31 S, R 24 E). Named on Fellows (1951), Panorama Hills (1954), Taft (1950), and West Elk Hills (1954) 7.5' quadrangles.

Buena Vista Creek [TULARE]: *stream*, flows 1 mile to Redwood Creek (1) 3.5 miles southeast of Wilsonia (lat. 36°42' N, long. 118° 54'40" W; near SW cor. sec. 14, T 14 S, R 28 E); the stream heads near Buena Vista Peak. Named on Giant Forest (1956) 15' quadrangle.

Buena Vista Hills [KERN]: *range*, between Buena Vista Valley and Midway Valley, center 2.5 miles north-northeast of Taft (lat. 35° 10'15" N, long. 119°26' W). Named on Fellows (1951), Mouth of Kern (1950), and Taft (1950) 7.5' quadrangles. Arnold and Johnson (p. 19) proposed the name because of the proximity of the range to Buena Vista Lake.

Buena Vista Lake: see **Buena Vista Lake Bed** [KERN].

Buena Vista Lake Bed [KERN]: *area*, dry bed of Buena Vista Lake 10 miles east-northeast of Taft (lat. 35°11'30" N, long. 119°17'30" W). Named on Mouth of Kern (1950) 7.5' quadrangle The area is called Buena Vista Lake on Millux (1954) 7.5' quadrangle. Buena Vista Lake (1912) 30' quadrangle shows a water-filled lake 8 miles long. Pedro Fages led a group into San Joaquin Valley in 1772, and gave the name "Buena Vista" to an Indian village by the lake (Boyd, p. 2). Buena Vista Lake was fed by water of Kern River, but diversion of the water in the valley and a levee built in the basin of Buena Vista Lake allowed cultivation of part of the lake bed (Mendenhall, Dole, and Stabler, p. 96).

Buena Vista Peak [TULARE]: *peak*, 3.5 miles east-southeast of Wilsonia (lat. 36°42'40" N, long. 118°53'45" W; near SE cor. sec. 14, T 14 S, R 28 E). Altitude 7603 feet. Named on Giant Forest (1956) 15' quadrangle.

Buena Vista Slough [KERN]: *water feature*, extends from near the east end of Elk Hills to Tulare County 50 miles northwest of Bakersfield. Named on Buena Vista Lake (1912) and McKittrick (1912) 30' quadrangles. The feature now is entirely confined by artificial levees, and nearly all of the water is diverted into canals (Davis, Green, Olmsted, and Brown, p. 30).

Buena Vista Valley [KERN]: *valley*, extends northwest from Buena Vista Lake Bed between Elk Hills and Buena Vista Hills. Named on Fellows (1951), Mouth of Kern (1950), Taft (1950), and West Elk Hills (1954) 7.5' quadrangles. Arnold and Johnson (p. 19) proposed the name for the proximity of the valley to Buena Vista Lake.

Bullard: see **Figarden** [FRESNO].

Bull Creek [FRESNO]: *stream*, flows 3.5 miles to Deer Creek (3) 6.5 miles north of Balch Camp (lat. 36°59'59" N, long. 119°06' W). Named on Patterson Mountain (1952) 15' quadrangle.

Bull Creek [FRESNO-TULARE]: *stream*, heads in Fresno County and flows 9 miles to Cottonwood Creek 0.5 mile north of Auckland in Tulare County (lat. 36°35'50" N, long. 119°06'25" W; sec. 26, T 15 S, R 26 E). Named on Auckland (1966), Miramonte (1966), and Tucker Mountain (1966) 7.5' quadrangles.

Bullet Lake [FRESNO]: *lake*, 450 feet long, 2.25 miles north-northeast of Blackcap Mountain (lat. 37°06'10" N, long. 118°47' W). Named on Blackcap Mountain (1953) 15' quadrangle.

Bull Flat [KERN]: *area*, 8.5 miles north-northeast of Caliente (lat. 35°24'40" N, long. 118°34'55" W; near NE cor. sec. 18, T 20 S, R 32 E). Named on Breckenridge Mountain (1972) 7.5' quadrangle.

Bullfrog Lake [FRESNO]:

(1) *lake*, 500 feet long, 5.25 miles east-northeast of Dinkey Dome (lat. 37°08'50" N, long. 119°02'25" W; sec. 16, T 9 S, R 27 E). Named on Huntington Lake (1953) 15' quadrangle.

(2) *lake*, 1400 feet long, about 12 miles south of Mount Pinchot (lat. 36°46'20" N, long. 118°24'10" W). Named on Mount Pinchot (1953) 15' quadrangle. John Muir called the feature Bryanthus Lake (Browning, p. 28).

Bullfrog Lakes [TULARE]: *lakes*, largest 900 feet long, 4.5 miles south-southeast of Mineral King (lat. 36°23'45" N, long. 118°33'15" W). Named on Mineral King (1956) 15' quadrangle.

Bullfrog Meadow [TULARE]: *area*, 11 miles north-northwest of Olancha Peak (lat. 36°24'15" N, long. 118°13' W; on E line sec. 31, T 17 S, R 35 E). Named on Olancha (1956) 15' quadrangle.

Bull Meadow [TULARE]: *area*, 2.25 miles south-southwest of Monache Mountain (lat. 36°10'30" N, long. 118°13' W; near NW cor. sec. 20, T 20 S, R 35 E). Named on Monache Mountain (1956) 15' quadrangle.

Bullpen Canyon [KINGS]: *canyon*, drained by a stream that flows nearly 2 miles to Avenal Canyon 8.5 miles southwest of Avenal (lat. 35°54'55" N, long. 120°14' W; near W line sec. 22, T 23 S, R 16 E). Named on Garza Peak (1953) 7.5' quadrangle.

Bull Run Basin [TULARE]: *relief feature*, 10 miles southeast of California Hot Springs (lat. 35°47'55" N, long. 118°31'15" W; on E line sec. 33, T 24 S, R 32 E); the feature is along Bull Run Creek. Named on California Hot Springs (1958) 15' quadrangle.

Bull Run Creek [KERN-TULARE]: *stream*, heads in Tulare County and flows 11 miles to Kern River 2.25 miles north-northwest of Kernville in Kern County (lat. 35°46'55" N, long. 118°26'40" W; sec. 4, T 25 S, R 33 E); the stream heads near Bull Run Pass. Named on California Hot Springs (1958) and Kernville (1956) 15' quadrangles. On Kernville (1908) 30' quadrangle, the name has the form "Bullrun Creek."

Bull Run Meadow [TULARE]: *area*, 6 miles east-southeast of California Hot Springs (lat. 35°50'25" N, long. 118°34'45" W; sec. 13, T 24 S, R 31 E); the place is west of Bull Run Pass. Named on California Hot Springs (1958) 15' quadrangle.

Bull Run Pass [TULARE]: *pass*, 6 miles east-southeast of California Hot Springs (lat. 35°50'20" N, long. 118°34'35" W; near E line sec. 13, T 24 S, R 31 E). Named on California Hot Springs (1958) 15' quadrangle. Joel Carver used the name "Bull Run Pass" in the early 1880's for a stock trail from Linns Valley to Bull Run Basin (Gudde, 1949, p. 292).

Bull Run Peak [TULARE]: *peak*, 6.25 miles east-southeast of California Hot Springs (lat. 35°50' N, long. 118°34'35" W; near NE cor. sec. 24, T 24 S, R 31 E); the peak is 0.5 mile south of Bull Run Pass. Altitude 8024 feet. Named on California Hot Springs (1958) 15' quadrangle.

Bull Slough [KINGS]: *water feature*, heads at a canal and extends for 2.25 miles to another canal 21 miles east-southeast of Kettleman City (lat. 35°51'45" N, long. 119°37'05" W; at N line sec. 8, T 24 S, R 22 E). Named on Hacienda Ranch (1954) 7.5' quadrangle.

Bull Spring [KERN]:

(1) *spring*, 6 miles west-northwest of Carneros Rocks (lat. 35°28'35" N, long. 119°56'40" W; near E line sec. 20, T 28 S, R 19 E). Named on Las Yeguas Ranch (1959) 7.5' quadrangle.

(2) *spring*, 6.5 miles east-southeast of Caliente (lat. 35°16'05" N, long. 118°30'45" W; near N line sec. 2, T 31 S, R 32 E). Named on Oiler Peak (1972) 7.5' quadrangle.

(3) *spring*, 1.25 miles east of Caliente (lat. 35°17'25" N, long. 118° 36'15" W). Named on Oiler Peak (1972) 7.5' quadrangle.

Bullwheel Ridge [KINGS]: *ridge*, southeast-trending, 2 miles long, nearly 3 miles southwest of Kettleman City (lat. 35°58'25" N, long. 119°59'30" W). Named on Kettleman Plain (1953) and Los Viejos (1954) 7.5' quadrangles. The name refers to a bullwheel used in oil fields that was abandoned on the ridge (United States Board on Geographic Names, 1933b, p. 6).

Bunchgrass Flat [FRESNO]: *area*, 9 miles west of Marion Peak (lat. 36°58'15" N, long. 118°40'40" W). Named on Marion Peak (1953) 15' quadrangle.

Burham Canyon [KERN]: *canyon*, drained by a stream that flows about 4.5 miles to lowlands 8.25 miles west-northwest of Willow Springs (2) (lat. 34°57' N, long. 118°25' W; near NE cor. sec. 24, T 10 N, R 15 W). Named on Tehachapi South (1966) and Tylerhorse Canyon (1965) 7.5' quadrangles.

Burke Creek: see **Mormon Canyon** [KERN].

Burke Hill [KERN]: *peak*, 6.25 miles north-northwest of Democrat Hot Springs (lat. 35°37' N, long. 118°41'45" W; near SE cor. sec. 36, T 26 S, R 30 E). Named on Democrat Hot Springs (1972) 7.5' quadrangle.

Burkeville: see **Big Blue Mill** [KERN].

Burling [TULARE]: *locality*, 1.5 miles south of downtown Tulare along Southern Pacific Railroad (lat. 36°11'05" N, long. 119°20'35" W; sec. 14, T 20 S, R 24 E). Named on Tulare (1927) 7.5' quadrangle.

Burness [FRESNO]: *locality*, 4.5 miles south-southeast of Clovis along Atchison, Topeka and Santa Fe Railroad (lat. 36°45'55" N, long. 119°39'30" W; on S line sec 26, T 13 S, R 21 E). Named on Clovis (1964) 7.5' quadrangle.

Burning Moscow Spring [KERN]: *spring*, 4.25 miles east-northeast of Claraville (lat. 35°27'40" N, long. 118°15'20" W; sec. 30, T 28 S, R 35 E); the spring is 1.5 miles south-southeast of Burning Moscow mine. Named on Claraville (1972) 7.5' quadrangle.

Burns Flat [FRESNO]: *area*, 5.5 miles east-southeast of Dunlap (lat. 36°41'50" N, long. 119°02'05" W; near NW cor. sec. 22, T 14 S, R 27 E). Named on Miramonte (1966) 7.5' quadrangle.

Burns Meadow [FRESNO]: *area*, 13 miles west-southwest of Marion Peak (lat. 36°51'05" N, long. 118°43'30" W). Named on Marion Peak (1953) 15' quadrangle. The place was the site of Burns sheep camp about 1900 (Forest M. Clingan, personal communication, 1990).

Burns Slough: see **Lonetree Channel** [FRESNO].

Burnt Camp Creek [TULARE]: *stream*, flows 1.5 miles to South Fork Kaweah River 11.5 miles southeast of Kaweah (lat. 36°21'10" N, long. 118°46'30" W; near NE cor. sec. 24, T 18 S, R 29 E). Named on Kaweah (1957) 15' quadrangle.

Burnt Canyon [KERN]: *canyon*, drained by a stream that flows 3.5 miles to Fay Creek nearly 4 miles north-northwest of Weldon (lat. 35°43'05" N, long. 118°18'20" W). Named on Weldon (1972) 7.5' quadrangle.

Burnt Corral Creek [FRESNO]: *stream*, flows 5.5 miles to Post Corral Creek 7.5 miles northwest of Blackcap Mountain (lat. 37° 08' N, long. 118°54'10" W; sec. 22, T 9 S, R 28 E); the stream goes through Burnt Corral Meadow. Named on Blackcap Mountain (1953) 15' quadrangle.

Burnt Corral Meadow [FRESNO]: *area,* 10 miles northwest of Blackcap Mountain (lat. 37°10'15" N, long. 118°55'35" W; near SW cor. sec. 4, T 9 S, R 28 E); the place is along Burnt Corral Creek. Named on Blackcap Mountain (1953) 15' quadrangle. United States Board on Geographic Names (1983d, p. 1) rejected the form "Burnt Corral Meadows" for the name.

Burnt Corral Meadows [TULARE]: *area,* 6.5 miles west of Hockett Peak (lat. 36°13'20" N, long. 118°30' W). Named on Camp Nelson (1956) and Hockett Peak (1956) 15' quadrangles. The name is from a sheep corral that burned at the place (Browning, p. 29).

Burnt House Canyon: see **Cow Canyon** [KERN].

Burnt Mountain [FRESNO]: *peak,* 11.5 miles west of Marion Peak (lat. 36°58'20" N, long. 118°43'30" W). Altitude 10,608 feet. Named on Marion Peak (1953) 15' quadrangle.

Burnt Point [TULARE]: *peak,* 2.5 miles west-northwest of Yucca Mountain (lat. 36°35' N, long. 118°54'40" W; sec. 35, T 15 S, R 28 E). Altitude 3757 feet. Named on Giant Forest (1956) 15' quadrangle.

Burnt Point Creek [TULARE]: *stream,* flows 3 miles to North Fork Kaweah River 1.5 miles west-northwest of Yucca Mountain (lat. 36°34'40" N, long. 118°53'40" W); sec. 36, T 15 S, R 28 E); the mouth of the stream is 1 mile east-southeast of Burnt Point. Named on Giant Forest (1956) 15' quadrangle. United States Board on Geographic Names (1933a, p. 177) rejected the name "Cow Creek" for the stream.

Burnt Ridge [TULARE]: *ridge,* generally east-trending, 2.5 miles long, 7.5 miles east-northeast of California Hot Springs (lat. 35°54'45" N, long. 118°32'45" W). Named on California Hot Springs (1958) 15' quadrangle.

Burnt Spring [KERN]: *spring,* 5.5 miles southeast of Glennville (lat. 35°39'50" N, long. 118°38'50" W; sec. 16, T 26 S, R 31 E). Named on Glennville (1972) 7.5' quadrangle.

Burr [TULARE]: *locality,* 3 miles north-northwest of Lindsay along Southern Pacific Railroad (lat. 36°14'40" N, long. 119°06'50" W; sec. 25, T 19 S, R 26 E). Named on Lindsay (1951) 7.5' quadrangle.

Burrel [FRESNO]: *village,* nearly 5 miles northwest of Lanare (lat. 36°29'20" N, long. 119°59' W; near S line sec. 35, T 16 S, R 18 E). Named on Burrel (1954) 7.5' quadrangle. Postal authorities established Burrel post office in 1912 (Frickstad, p. 31). The railroad station at the place was named in 1889 for Cuthbert Burrel, or Burrell, a stockman in Fresno County in the 1860's and owner of Elkhorn Ranch (Gudde, 1949, p. 45). Elkhorn Station, located 1.5 miles southeast of present Burrel, was a stop on Butterfield Overland stage line from 1856 until the stage stopped running in 1861 (Hoover, Rensch, and Rensch, p. 92).

Burre Mountain: see **Burrough Mountain** [FRESNO].

Burro Creek [TULARE]: *stream,* flows 3 miles to North Fork of Middle Fork Tule River 6 miles north-northwest of Camp Nelson (lat. 36°13'30" N, long. 118°38'45" W; sec. 32, T 19 S, R 31 E). Named on Camp Nelson (1956) 15' quadrangle.

Burro Flat: see **Bartons Resort** [FRESNO].

Burrough: see **Burrough Valley** [FRESNO].

Burrough Mountain [FRESNO]: *ridge,* northwest-trending, 2.5 miles long, 7.25 miles south-southwest of Shaver Lake Heights (present town of Shaver Lake) (lat. 37°00'30" N, long. 119°21'45" W). Named on Shaver Lake (1953) 15' quadrangle, and on Trimmer (1965) 7.5' quadrangle. Called Burre Mountain on Kaiser (1904) 30' quadrangle.

Burrough Valley [FRESNO]: *valley,* 6.5 miles northwest of Trimmer on upper reaches of Little Dry Creek (2) (lat. 36°58'30" N, long. 119°22' W). Named on Humphreys Station (1965) and Trimmer (1965) 7.5' quadrangles. Mendenhall's (1908) map shows a place called Burrough located at or near present Burrough Valley, and Lippincott's (1902) map shows Burrough P.O. there. California Division of Highways' (1934) map has the name "Borrough" for a place in present Burrough Valley (near E line sec. 17, T 11 S, R 24 E). Postal authorities established Burrough post office in 1889, moved it 0.5 mile south in 1900, and discontinued it in 1917; the name is for Colonel Henry Burrough, a resident of the neighborhood in 1858 (Salley, p. 30).

Burton Camp [TULARE]: *locality,* 5.5 miles northeast of Fairview (lat. 35°58'40" N, long. 118°25'05" W; sec. 28, T 22 S, R 33 E). Named on Kernville (1956) 15' quadrangle. Called Corral Meadow on Kernville (1908) 30' quadrangle, but United States Board on Geographic Names (1961b, p. 9) rejected this name for the place. The name "Burton" commemorates a rancher who used the site at roundup time (Browning, p. 29).

Burton Meadow [FRESNO]: *area,* 4.25 miles east-southeast of Hume (lat. 36°45'20" N, long. 118°50'40" W). Named on Tehipite Dome (1952) 15' quadrangle. The name commemorates an early-day stockman (Browning, p. 29).

Burton Mill [KERN]: *locality,* 7.5 miles southeast of Bodfish (lat. 35°30'05" N, long. 118°24'20" W; at N line sec. 14, T 28 S, R 33 E). Named on Lake Isabella South (1972) 7.5' quadrangle.

Burton Mountain: see **Burton Pass** [FRESNO].

Burton Pass [FRESNO]: *pass,* 4 miles east-southeast of Hume (lat. 36°45'15" N, long. 118°51' W); the pass is west of Burton Meadow. Named on Tehipite Dome (1952) 15' quadrangle. California Mining Bureau's (1917a) map shows Burton Mountain near present Burton Meadow and Burton Pass.

Burton's Hill: see **Tropico Hill** [KERN].

Burton's Tropico Hill: see **Tropico Hill** [KERN].

Busane Peak [FRESNO]: *peak,* 8.5 miles south-southwest of Coalinga (lat. 36°01'40" N, long. 120°25'25" W; near E line sec. 11, T 22 S, R 14 E). Altitude 2212 feet. Named on Curry Mountain (1969) 7.5' quadrangle.

Bush Spring [KERN]: *spring,* 2.25 miles south-southeast of Cummings Mountain (lat. 35°00'25" N, long. 118°33'20" W; near NW cor. sec. 35, T 11 N, R 16 W). Named on Cummings Mountain (1943b) 15' quadrangle.

Butera [TULARE]: *locality,* 5.25 miles south of Earlimart along Southern Pacific Railroad (lat. 35°48'30" N, long. 119°15'25" W; sec. 27, T 24 S, R 25 E). Named on Delano West (1954) 7.5' quadrangle.

Butler [FRESNO]: *locality,* 4 miles northeast of Malaga along Southern Pacific Railroad (lat. 36°43'20" N, long. 119°41' W; near SE cor. sec. 9, T 14 S, R 21 E). Named on Selma (1946) 15' quadrangle.

Butler Spring [KERN]: *spring,* 4.5 miles east-southeast of Woody (lat. 35°41' N, long. 118°45'10" W; sec. 9, T 26 S, R 30 E). Named on Woody (1965) 7.5' quadrangle.

Butterbread Canyon: see **Butterbredt Canyon** [KERN].

Butterbread Peak: see **Butterbredt Peak** [KERN].

Butterbread Spring: see **Butterbredt Spring** [KERN].

Butterbread Well: see **Butterbredt Well** [KERN].

Butterbredt Canyon [KERN]: *canyon,* drained by a stream that flows 8 miles to Alphie Canyon 7 miles northwest of Cinco (lat. 35°21'20" N, long. 118°05' W; sec. 2, T 30 S, R 36 E). Named on Cinco (1972), Dove Spring (1972), and Pinyon Mountain (1972) 7.5' quadrangles. Called Butterbread Canyon on Cross Mountain (1943) 15' quadrangle. United States Board on Geographic Names (1974b, p. 2) gave the name "Butterbread Canyon" as a variant.

Butterbredt Peak [KERN]: *peak,* 5.25 miles south of Pinyon Mountain (lat. 35°23' N, long. 118°09'10" W; sec. 30, T 29 S, R 36 E); the peak is southwest of Butterbredt Canyon. Altitude 5997 feet. Named on Pinyon Mountain (1972) 7.5' quadrangle. Called Butterbread Peak on Cross Mountain (1943) 15' quadrangle. United States Board on Geographic Names (1974b, p. 2) gave the name "Butterbread Peak" as a variant—the name "Butterbredt" is for Frederick Butterbredt, who settled in Kern County in the 1860's.

Butterbredt Spring [KERN]: *spring,* 6 miles south-southeast of Pinyon Mountain (lat. 35°22'55" N, long. 118°06'45" W; near E line sec. 28, T 29 S, R 36 E); the spring is in Butterbredt Canyon. Named on Dove Spring (1972) 7.5' quadrangle. Called Butterbread Spring on Cross Mountain (1943) 15' quadrangle, and United States Board on Geographic Names (1974b, p. 2) gave this name as a variant.

Butterbredt Well [KERN]: *well,* 3.5 miles south-southeast of Pinyon Mountain (lat. 35°24'20" N, long. 118°08'30" W; sec. 17, T 29 S, R 36 E); the well is in Butterbredt Canyon 2.5 miles northwest of Butterbredt Spring. Named on Pinyon Mountain (1972) 7.5' quadrangle. Called Butterbread Well on Cross Mountain (1943) 15' quadrangle, and United States Board on Geographic Names (1974b, p. 2) gave this name as a variant.

Buttonwillow [KERN]: *town,* 26 miles west of Bakersfield (lat. 35° 24' N, long. 119°28'10" W; in and near sec. 14, T 29 S, R 23 E). Named on Buttonwillow (1954) 7.5' quadrangle. Postal authorities established Buttonwillow post office in 1895 (Frickstad, p. 54). The name is from a lone tree that was a landmark in the early days; when the town was laid out in 1895 it was called Buena Vista, but the old name "Buttonwillow" prevailed (Wines, p. 42).

Buttonwillow Peak [TULARE]: *peak,* 2.5 miles east-northeast of Tucker Mountain (lat. 36°38'55" N, long. 119°09'45" W; sec. 5, T 15 S, R 26 E). Altitude 2264 feet. Named on Tucker Mountain (1966) 7.5' quadrangle.

Buttonwillow Ridge [KERN]: *ridge,* northwest-trending, 13 miles long, center 5 miles north-northwest of Buttonwillow (lat. 35°28'15" N, long. 119°29'15" W). Named on Buttonwillow (1954), Lokern (1954), and Semitropic (1954) 7.5' quadrangles.

Buzzard Ridge [KERN]: *ridge,* north- to northwest-trending, 1 mile long, 7 miles east-southeast of Caliente (lat. 35°15'45" N, long. 118°30'30" W; sec 2, T 31 S, R 32 E). Named on Oiler Peak (1972) 7.5' quadrangle.

Buzzard Roost [TULARE]: *peak,* 3.5 miles east of Auckland (lat. 36° 34'55" N, long. 119°02'30" W; sec. 33, T 15 S, R 27 E). Altitude 3082 feet. Named on Auckland (1966) 7.5' quadrangle.

Buzzard Roost: see **Ellis Mountain** [TULARE].

Buzzard Spring [KERN]: *spring,* nearly 7 miles east-southeast of Caliente (lat. 35°15'50" N, long. 118°30'40" W; sec. 2, T 31 S, R 32 E); the spring is at the north end of Buzzard Ridge. Named on Oiler Peak (1972) 7.5' quadrangle.

Buzzards' Roost: see **Waukena** [TULARE].

Byles Jamison Camp [FRESNO]: *locality,* 7.25 miles south-southwest of Dinkey Dome in Bear Meadow (3) (lat. 37°01'05" N, long. 119°10'25" W; sec. 31, T 10 S, R 26 E). Named on Huntington Lake (1953) 15' quadrangle.

Byrd Slough [FRESNO]: *water feature,* heads at a canal and extends for 9 miles to Kings River 5.5 miles south of Centerville (lat. 36° 39'05" N, long. 119°28'45" W; sec. 4, T 15 S, R 23 E). Named on Piedra (1965) and Wahtoke (1966) 7.5' quadrangles.

– C –

Cabernet: see **McFarland** [KERN].

Cabin Cove [TULARE]: *locality,* 3.5 miles west-northwest of Mineral King (lat. 36°27'55" N, long. 118°39'15" W). Named on Mineral King (1956) 15' quadrangle.

Cabin Creek [FRESNO]:

(1) *stream,* flows 1.5 miles to Rancheria Creek (3) 12 miles north of Hume (lat. 36°57'25" N, long. 118°54'15" W). Named on Tehipite Dome (1952) 15' quadrangle.

(2) *stream,* flows 2.5 miles to Kings River 6.25 miles north-northwest of Hume (lat. 36°51'40" N, long. 118°58'15" W). Named on Tehipite Dome (1952) 15' quadrangle.

Cabin Creek [TULARE]: *stream,* flows 2.5 miles to Dorst Creek 4 miles south-southwest of Shell Mountain (lat. 36°38'20" N, long. 118°48'40" W; sec. 10, T 15 S, R 29 E); the stream goes past Cabin Meadow. Named on Giant Forest (1956) 15' quadrangle.

Cabin Meadow [FRESNO]:

(1) *area,* 4 miles south-southeast of Dinkey Dome (lat. 37°03'30" N, long. 119°07' W; sec. 14, 15, T 10 S, R 26 E). Named on Huntington Lake (1953) 15' quadrangle.

(2) *area,* 5.5 miles north-northeast of Balch Camp (lat. 36°58'45" N, long. 119°05' W). Named on Patterson Mountain (1952) 15' quadrangle.

Cabin Meadow [TULARE]: *area,* 3 miles south-southwest of Shell Mountain (lat. 36°39'15" N, long. 118°48'35" W; near E line sec. 3, T 15 S, R 29 E). Named on Giant Forest (1956) 15' quadrangle. United States Board on Geographic Names (1933a, p. 180) rejected the name "Guttrie Meadow" for the place. The name "Cabin Meadow" is from a cabin built at the site by an early-day sheepherder (Browning, p. 29).

Cabin Meadow: see **Green Meadow** [TULARE].

Cable [KERN]: *locality,* 3 miles north-northwest of Tehachapi along the railroad (lat. 35°10'05" N, long. 118°28'25" W; at N line sec. 7, T 32 S, R 33 E). Named on Tehachapi North (1966) 7.5' quadrangle. California Mining Bureau's (1917c) map shows a place called Sedwell located about 1 mile west-northwest of Cable along the railroad.

Cache Creek [KERN]: *stream,* flows 19 miles to lowlands 4.5 miles north of Mojave (lat. 35°07' N, long. 118°11'30" W; sec. 26, T 32 S, R 35 E); the stream heads at Cache Peak. Named on California City North (1973), California City South (1973), Mojave (1973), Monolith (1966), Sanborn (1973), and Tehachapi NE (1966) 7.5' quadrangles. Called Tehachapi Creek on Mojave (1947) 7.5' quadrangle.

Cache Peak [KERN]: *peak,* 12.5 miles north-northwest of Mojave (lat. 35°13'20" N, long. 118°15' W; near W line sec. 20, T 31 S, R 35 E). Altitude 6698 feet. Named on Cache Peak (1973) and Tehachapi NE (1966) 7.5' quadrangles.

Cactus Creek: see **Yucca Creek** [TULARE].

Cactus Mountain: see **Yucca Mountain** [TULARE].

Cactus Point [TULARE]: *peak,* 5 miles south-southeast of Yucca Mountain (lat. 36°30'40" N, long. 118°49'10" W). Altitude 3738 feet. Named on Giant Forest (1956) 15' quadrangle. National Park Service officials named the peak for the many yuccas growing there (Browning, p. 30).

Cactus Ridge: see **Yucca Ridge** [TULARE].

Cadogan: see **Mendota** [FRESNO].

Caesar: see **Mount Julius Caesar** [FRESNO].

Cahoon Creek [TULARE]: *stream,* flows 3 miles to Horse Creek (1) 6.25 miles west-southwest of Mineral King (lat. 36°25'05" N, long. 118°42' W); the stream heads at Cahoon Meadow (2). Named on Mineral King (1956) 15' quadrangle. The name commemorates an early settler who had a cabin by the stream (United States Board on Geographic Names, 1933a, p. 183).

Cahoon Gap [TULARE]: *pass,* 12 miles west-northwest of Triple Divide Peak (lat. 36°38'35" N, long. 118°44'10" W; near SW cor. sec. 4, T 15 S, R 30 E); the pass is about 1 mile north of Cahoon Meadow (1). Named on Triple Divide Peak (1956) 15' quadrangle.

Cahoon Meadow [TULARE]:

(1) *area,* 12 miles west-northwest of Triple Divide Peak (lat. 36°37'50" N, long. 118°44' W; at W line sec. 9, T 15 S, R 30 E); the place is 1 mile south of Cahoon Gap. Named on Triple Divide Peak (1956) 15' quadrangle.

(2) *area,* 7.5 miles southwest of Mineral King (lat. 36°23' N, long. 118°42'10" W); the place is at the head of Cahoon Creek. Named on Mineral King (1956) 15' quadrangle. The name commemorates George Cahoon, an early settler who had a cabin at the place (United States Board on Geographic Names, 1933a, p. 183).

Cahoon Meadow: see **Silliman Meadow** [TULARE].

Cahoon Mountain [TULARE]: *peak,* 8.5 miles southeast of Kaweah (lat. 36°22'20" N, long. 118°49'20" W; sec. 10, T 18 S, R 29 E). Altitude 4229 feet. Named on Kaweah (1957) 15' quadrangle. The name is for George Cahoon of Cahoon Meadow (2) (Hanna, p. 48).

Cahoon Peak: see **Evelyn Lake** [TULARE].

Cahoon Rock: see **Evelyn Lake** [TULARE].

Cain Slough [KINGS]: *stream* and *dry wash,* extends south for 4.5 miles to a point nearly 6 miles west-southwest of Guernsey (lat. 36°11'30" N, long. 119°44'30" W). Named on Guernsey (1929) 7.5' quadrangle. The mostly dry watercourse is called Jacobs Slough on Guernsey (1954) 7.5' quadrangle.

Cain Spring [TULARE]: *spring,* 5 miles northwest of California Hot Springs (lat. 35°55'40" N, long. 118°44'20" W; sec. 16, T 23 S, R 30 E). Named on California Hot Springs (1958) 15' quadrangle.

Cain Spring Gap [TULARE]: *pass,* nearly 5 miles northwest of California Hot Springs (lat. 35°55'10" N, long. 118°44'30" W; near N line sec. 21, T 23 S, R 30 E); the pass is 0.5 mile south-southwest of Cain Spring. Named on California Hot Springs (1958) 15' quadrangle.

Cairns [TULARE]: *locality,* 4.25 miles west-northwest of Woodlake along Atchison, Topeka and Santa Fe Railroad (lat. 36°26' N, long. 119°10' W; at W line sec. 21, T 17 S, R 26 E). Named on Exeter (1952) 15' quadrangle.

Cairns Corner [TULARE]: *locality,* 2.5 miles west of Lindsay (lat. 36°12'40" N, long. 119°08'10" W; at SW cor. sec. 2, T 20 S, R 26 E). Named on Cairns Corner (1950) 7.5' quadrangle.

Calders Corner [KERN]: *locality,* 8 miles south of Shafter (lat. 35° 23' N, long. 119°15'05" W; at SW cor. sec. 24, T 29 S, R 25 E). Named on Rio Bravo (1954) 7.5' quadrangle.

Caldwell [FRESNO]: *locality,* 3 miles southeast of San Joaquin along Southern Pacific Railroad (lat. 36°34'40" N, long. 120°08'45" W). Named on San Joaquin (1925) 7.5' quadrangle.

Caldwell Creek [KERN]: *stream,* flows 7.25 miles to Kern River 3 miles northeast of Wofford Heights (lat. 35°44'25" N, long. 118° 24'55" W; near E line sec. 22, T 25 S, R 33 E). Named on Kernville (1956) 15' quadrangle, and on Lake Isabella North (1972) 7.5' quadrangle. Called Cowell Creek on Kernville (1908) 30' quadrangle, and Cowel Cr. on Olmstead's (1900) map.

Calfax [FRESNO]: *locality,* 20 miles northeast of Coalinga (lat. 36° 20'35" N, long. 120°06'05" W; near NW cor. sec. 26, T 18 S, R 17 E). Named on Calfax (1956) 7.5' quadrangle.

Calf Creek [KERN]: *stream,* flows 2 miles to Cow Creek 10 miles east-northeast of Glennville (lat. 35°46'15" N, long. 118°32' W; at W line sec. 10, T 25 S, R 32 E). Named on California Hot Springs (1958) 15' quadrangle, and on Alta Sierra (1972) 7.5' quadrangle.

Calgro [TULARE]: *locality,* 11 miles north of Visalia along Atchison, Topeka and Santa Fe Railroad (lat. 36°29'20" N, long. 119°17'05" W; near SW cor. sec. 32, T 16 S, R 25 E); the place is 1.5 miles west of Yettem. Named on Monson (1949) 7.5' quadrangle. Called Yettem Sta. on Monson (1927) 7.5' quadrangle. The railroad station was called Yettem from 1910 until 1936; the name "Calgro" is from the term "California Growers Wineries" (Gudde 1949, p. 49, 395). Lippincott's (1902) map shows a place called Lovell near present Calgro. Postal authorities established Lovell post office in 1912 and discontinued it in 1913 (Frickstad, p. 212).

Calico [KERN]: *locality,* 3.5 miles south-southeast of McFarland along Southern Pacific Railroad (lat. 35°38' N, long. 119°12'20" W; near SE cor. sec. 30, T 26 S, R 26 E). Named on McFarland (1954) 7.5' quadrangle.

Caliente [KERN]: *village,* 22 miles east-southeast of Bakersfield (lat. 35°17'25" N, long. 118°37'35" W); the place is along Caliente Creek. Named on Bena (1972) and Oiler Peak (1972) 7.5' quadrangles. Postal authorities established Caliente post office in 1875, discontinued it in 1883, and reestablished it in 1890 (Frickstad, p. 54). The site first was known as Agua Caliente for some nearby hot springs, then as Allen's Camp for Gabriel Allen, and finally as Caliente when Southern Pacific Railroad set up a work camp at the place in 1874 (Bailey, 1967, p. 3).

Caliente Creek [KERN]: *stream,* flows 38 miles to lowlands 5.25 miles southeast of Edison (lat. 35°16'55" N, long. 118°48'40" W; near NE cor. sec. 36, T 30 S, R 29 E). Named on Bena (1972), Edison (1954), Emerald Mountain (1972), Loraine (1972), and Oiler Peak (1972) 7.5' quadrangles. Boyd (p. 170) called the feature Agua Caliente Creek, and noted that the name is from hot springs located near the head of the stream.

Caliente Spring [KERN]: *spring,* 2.25 miles east of Caliente (lat. 35° 17'30" N, long. 118°35'15" W; sec. 30, T 30 S, R 32 E). Named on Oiler Peak (1972) 7.5' quadrangle.

California City [KERN]: *town,* desert retirement community 11 miles east-northeast of Mojave (lat. 35°07'30" N, long. 117° 59' W). Named on Boron NW (1973), California City North (1973), California City South (1973), Galileo Hill (1973), Johannesburg (1967), Mohave NE (1973), North Edwards (1973), Saltdale SE (1967), and Sanborn (1973) 7.5' quadrangles. Postal authorities established California City post office in 1960 (Salley, p. 32), and the town incorporated in 1965. California City Development Company started the planned community in 1958; the development covers 158 square miles (Bailey, 1967, p. 3).

California Hot Springs [TULARE]: *locality,* 20 miles east of Ducor (lat. 35°52'45" N, long. 118°40'15" W; sec. 31, T 23 S, R 31 E); the place is along Deer Creek (2). Named on California Hot Springs (1958) 15' quadrangle. Postal authorities established Hot Springs post office in 1900, and changed the name to California Hot Springs in 1926 (Frickstad, p. 211). Four springs with water temperatures of 120° to 126° Fahrenheit are the basis of a resort; the place first was called Deer Creek Hot Springs (Waring, p. 49).

California Range: see "Regional setting."

Callioud Spring [KERN]: *spring*, 5 miles north of Democrat Hot Springs (lat. 35°36' N, long. 118°39'15" W). Named on Democrat Hot Springs (1972) 7.5' quadrangle.

Caltech Peak [TULARE]: *peak*, 9.5 miles northwest of Mount Whitney (lat. 36°41'15" N, long. 118°23'20" W). Altitude 13,832 feet. Named on Mount Whitney (1956) 15' quadrangle. The name is for California Institute of Technology (United States Board on Geographic Names, 1962, p. 7)

Calwa [FRESNO]: *district*, 4 miles south-southeast of downtown Fresno (lat. 36°42'40" N, long. 119°45'15" W). Named on Fresno South (1963) and Malaga (1964) 7.5' quadrangles. Officials of Atchison, Topeka and Santa Fe Railroad coined the name in 1913 from letters of the term "California Wine Association"—a large winery was near the place (Hanna, p. 52). California Mining Bureau's (1917a) map has the name "Calwa City" along the railroad just southeast of Fresno. Postal authorities established Calwa City post office in 1913 and changed the name to Calwa in 1949 (Salley, p. 33).

Calwa City: see **Calwa** [FRESNO].

Cambio [KERN]: *locality*, nearly 4 miles northeast of Mojave along Southern Pacific Railroad (lat. 35°05'40" N, long. 118°08' W). Named on Mojave (1915) 30' quadrangle.

Camden [FRESNO]: *village*, 3.5 miles east of Riverdale (lat. 36°25'50" N, long. 119°47'50" W; near NW cor. sec. 27, T 17 S, R 20 E). Named on Riverdale (1954) 7.5' quadrangle. Postal authorities established Camden post office in 1903 and discontinued it in 1904 (Frickstad, p. 31).

Cameo [FRESNO]: *locality*, 4 miles south of Clovis along Atchison, Topeka and Santa Fe Railroad (lat. 36°45'50" N, long. 119°42' W; near NE cor. sec. 32, T 13 S, R 21 E). Named on Clovis (1964) 7.5' quadrangle.

Cameron [KERN]: *locality*, 9 miles east-southeast of Tehachapi along the railroad (lat. 35°05'50" N, long. 118°17'45" W; near S line sec. 35, T 32 S, R 34 E); the place is near the mouth of Cameron Canyon. Named on Monolith (1966) 7.5' quadrangle. Postal authorities established Cameron post office in 1899, discontinued it in 1922, reestablished it in 1923, and discontinued it the same year; the name commemorates George W. Cameron, an early settler (Salley, p. 33). Wheeler's (1875-1878) map shows a place called Nadeau located about 5 miles east of Cameron along the railroad.

Cameron Canyon [KERN]: *canyon*, drained by a stream that flows 3.5 miles to the canyon of Cache Creek 8.5 miles east-southeast of Tehachapi (lat. 35°05'35" N, long. 118°18'15" W; sec. 31, T 12 N, R 13 W). Named on Monolith (1966) 7.5' quadrangle. The stream in the canyon is called Cameron Creek on Tehachapi (1943) 15' quadrangle.

Cameron Creek [TULARE]: *stream*, diverges west from Deep Creek (1) and flows 27 miles to a canal 1.5 miles southwest of Waukena (lat. 36°07'40" N, long. 119°31'45" W; sec. 6, T 21 S, R 23 E). Named on Exeter (1952), Tulare (1942), and Visalia (1949) 15' quadrangles, and on Waukena (1954) 7.5' quadrangle. The name commemorates either Alexander Cameron or Monroe Cameron (Mitchell, A.R., p. 78).

Cameron Creek: see **Cameron Canyon** [KERN].

Cameron Creek Colony [TULARE]: *locality*, 4 miles west-northwest of Exeter (lat. 36°19' N, long. 119°12'15" W; sec. 31, T 18 S, R 25 E); the place is on the south side of Cameron Creek. Named on Exeter (1952) 15' quadrangle.

Cameron Slough [FRESNO]: *water feature*, diverges from Kings River 1.25 miles east-southeast of Centerville and extends for 5.5 miles before rejoining the river 5.5 miles south of Centerville (lat. 36°39'10" N, long. 119°29'45" W; sec. 5, T 15 S, R 23 E). Named on Sanger (1965) and Wahtoke (1966) 7.5' quadrangles.

Cameron Station: see **Tehachapi Valley** [KERN].

Camp Babbitt: see **Visalia** [TULARE].

Camp Badger: see **Badger** [TULARE].

Camp Barbour: see **Old Fort Miller** [FRESNO].

Campbell: see **Big Campbell** [TULARE]; **Campbell Mountain** [FRESNO]; **Little Campbell** [TULARE]; **Mount Ian Campbell**, under **Mount Givens** [FRESNO].

Campbell Creek [TULARE]: *stream*, flows 6.5 miles to Tule River 3.5 miles southwest of Springville (lat. 36°06'05" N, long. 118° 52' W; sec. 17, T 21 S, R 39 E). Named on Springville (1957) 15' quadrangle.

Campbell Mountain [FRESNO]: *mountain*, 5 miles east-southeast of Centerville (lat. 36°41'45" N, long. 119°25'15" W; in and near sec. 24, T 14 S, R 23 E). Altitude 1752 feet. Named on Wahtoke (1966) 7.5' quadrangle. The name is for William Campbell, who had a store at Poole's Ferry on Kings River (Gudde, 1969, p. 51). Eddy's (1854) map shows Campbells Ferry on Kings River, and Bancroft's (1864) map shows Mt. Campbell and a place called Campbell located on the north side of Kings River about where Eddy's (1854) map shows Campbells Ferry.

Campbells Ferry: see **Campbell Mountain** [FRESNO].

Camp Chawanakee [FRESNO]: *locality*, 1.5 miles east-northeast of Shaver Lake Heights (present town of Shaver Lake) on the south side of Shaver Lake (lat. 37°06'45" N, long. 119°17'25" W; sec. 30, T 9 S, R 25 E). Named on Shaver Lake (1953) 15' quadrangle.

Camp Condor [KERN]: *locality*, 6 miles southwest of Eagle Rest Peak (lat. 34°50'55" N, long. 119°12'25" W; on E line sec. 22, T 9 N, R 22 W). Named on Sawmill Mountain (1943) 7.5' quadrangle.

Camp Conifer [TULARE]: *locality*, 5 miles west of Mineral King (lat. 36°27'30" N, long. 118°41'15" W). Named on Mineral King (1956) 15' quadrangle.

Camp Dix [KERN]: *locality*, 18 miles west-northwest of Eagle Rest Peak (lat. 34°57'50" N, long. 119°26'40" W; sec. 9, T 10 N, R 24 W). Named on Ballinger Canyon (1943) 7.5' quadrangle.

Camp Earl-Anna [KERN]: *locality*, 6 miles south-southwest of Tehachapi (lat. 35°03'10" N, long. 118°29'50" W; at S line sec. 8, T 11 N, R 15 W). Named on Tehachapi South (1966) 7.5' quadrangle.

Campfire Lake [FRESNO]: *lake*, 300 feet long, nearly 0.5 mile northeast of Kaiser Peak (lat. 37°17'45" N, long. 119°10'40" W; at N line sec. 30, T 7 S, R 26 E). Named on Kaiser Peak (1953) 15' quadrangle.

Camp Fresno [FRESNO]: *locality*, 3.5 miles south-southwest of Dinkey Dome on the east side of Dinkey Creek (1) (lat. 37°04'10" N, long. 119°09'05" W; near SE cor. sec. 8, T 10 S, R 26 E). Named on Huntington Lake (1953) 15' quadrangle.

Camp Kanawyer: see **Kanawyers** [FRESNO].

Camp Kaweah [KERN]: *locality*, 0.25 mile west-northwest of Alta Sierra (lat. 35°43'50" N, long. 118°33'20" W; near NE cor. sec. 29, T 25 S, R 32 E). Named on Alta Sierra (1972) 7.5' quadrangle.

Camp Kemeric [KERN]: *locality*, 0.5 mile north-northwest of downtown Kernville along Kern River (lat. 35°45'50" N, long. 118°25'50" W; near SW cor. sec. 10, T 25 S, R 33 E). Named on Kernville (1956) 15' quadrangle.

Camp Leonard: see **Weldon** [KERN].

Camp Miller: see **Old Fort Miller** [FRESNO].

Camp Nelson [TULARE]: *town*, 12 miles east of Springville along South Fork of Middle Fork Tule River (lat. 36°08'30" N, long. 118°36'30" W; sec. 33, 34, T 20 S, R 31 E). Named on Camp Nelson (1956) 15' quadrangle. Called Nelson on Kaweah (1909) 30' quadrangle. Postal authorities established Camp Nelson post office in 1935 (Frickstad, p. 210). The name commemorates John M. Nelson, who homesteaded in the neighborhood in 1884 and opened a summer resort there in 1899 (Hanna, p. 208). The place also was known as Nelson Soda Springs (Waring, p. 243) and Nelson's Soda Springs (Tucker, p. 945).

Camp Nick Williams [KERN]: *locality*, 1.25 miles north-northwest of Claraville (lat. 35°27'35" N, long. 118°20'30" W; sec. 32, T 28 S, R 34 E). Named on Claraville (1972) 7.5' quadrangle.

Camp Oljato [FRESNO]: *locality*, 4 miles east-northeast of the town of Big Creek on the south side of Huntington Lake (lat. 37°14'10" N, long. 119°10'40" W; sec. 18, T 8 S, R 26 E). Named on Huntington Lake (1953) 15' quadrangle.

Camp Owens [KERN]: *locality*, 1 mile north of Kernville along Kern River (lat. 35°46'10" N, long. 118°25'35" W; sec. 10, T 25 S, R 33 E). Named on Kernville (1956) 15' quadrangle.

Camp Seven [FRESNO]: *locality*, 5 miles east of Hume (lat. 36° 47' N, long. 119°49'40" W). Site named on Tehipite Dome (1952) 15' quadrangle. Hume-Bennett Lumber Company (later called Sanger Lumber Company) built a lumber camp at the spot in 1917 (Browning, p. 30).

Camp 7-C [FRESNO]: *locality*, 4.25 miles north-northwest of Coalinga in Pleasant Valley (lat. 36°12' N, long. 120°22'45" W; sec. 7, T 20 S, R 15 E). Named on Coalinga (1956) 7.5' quadrangle.

Camp Sierra [FRESNO]: *settlement*, 7 miles north-northeast of Shaver Lake Heights (present town of Shaver Lake) (lat. 37°11'30" N, long. 119°15'30" W; sec. 32, T 8 S, R 25 E); the place is in the Sierra Nevada. Named on Shaver Lake (1953) 15' quadrangle. Postal authorities established Sierra Chautauqua post office in 1918, changed the name to Camp Sierra in 1924, and discontinued it in 1935; the name "Chautauqua" is from a place in New York State called Camp Chautauqua (Salley, p. 35, 204).

Camp 61 Campground [FRESNO]: *locality*, 6.5 miles east-northeast of Kaiser Peak (lat. 37°19'10" N, long. 119°04'10" W); the place is along Camp 61 Creek. Named on Kaiser Peak (1953) 15' quadrangle.

Camp 61 Creek [FRESNO]: *stream*, formed by the confluence of East Fork and West Fork, flows 2 miles to South Fork San Joaquin River 8 miles east-northeast of Kaiser Peak (lat. 37°20'30" N, long. 119°03'30" W). Named on Kaiser Peak (1953) 15' quadrangle. East Fork is 2.5 miles long and West Fork, which heads at Camp 61 Lake, is 1.5 miles long; both forks are named on Kaiser Peak (1953) 15' quadrangle.

Camp 61D Campground [FRESNO]: *locality*, 5 miles east-northeast of Kaiser Peak (lat. 37°19'15" N, long. 119°05'50" W; sec. 14, T 7 S, R 26 E); the place is 1.5 miles west of Camp 61 Campground. Named on Kaiser Peak (1953) 15' quadrangle.

Camp 61 Lake [FRESNO]: *lake*, 450 feet long, 5.25 miles east of Kaiser

Peak (lat. 37°18'30" N, long. 119°05'20" W; sec. 24, T 7 S, R 26 E); the lake is at the head of West Fork Camp 61 Creek. Named on Kaiser Peak (1953) 15' quadrangle.

Camp 62 Creek [FRESNO]: *stream,* flows 3.5 miles to South Fork San Joaquin River 9.5 miles east-northeast of Kaiser Peak (lat. 37° 19'35" N, long. 119°01'30" W). Named on Kaiser Peak (1953) 15' quadrangle, which shows the stream diverted into a pipeline.

Camp 35-A [FRESNO]: *locality,* 6.5 miles north-northeast of Coalinga (lat. 36°13'40" N, long. 120°19' W; sec. 35, T 19 S, R 15 E). Named on Coalinga (1956) 7.5' quadrangle.

Camp Three: see **Abbott Mill** [FRESNO].

Camp 25-D [FRESNO]: *locality,* 2.5 miles west-northwest of Coalinga (lat. 36°09'30" N, long. 120°24' W; sec. 25, T 20 S, R 14 E). Named on Coalinga (1956) 15' quadrangle.

Camp Whitsett [TULARE]: *locality,* 10.5 miles south-southeast of Camp Nelson (lat. 36°00'05" N, long. 118°32'10" W; at E line sec. 20, T 22 S, R 32 E). Named on Camp Nelson (1956) 15' quadrangle.

Camp Wishon [TULARE]: *locality,* 4.5 miles northwest of Camp Nelson (lat. 36°11'30" N, long. 118°39'50" W; at N line sec. 18, T 20 S, R 31 E). Named on Camp Nelson (1956) 15' quadrangle. The place is a summer resort named for A.G. Wishon, who was general manager of San Joaquin Power Company, manager of Fresno Water Company, and vice president and manager of Fresno City Railroad (Hanna, p. 357).

Camp Yenis Hante [KERN]: *locality,* 0.5 mile northwest of Alta Sierra (lat. 35°43'55" N, long. 118°33'20" W; at S line sec. 20, T 25 S, R 32 E). Named on Alta Sierra (1972) 7.5' quadrangle.

Canada del Agua Escondida [KERN]: *canyon,* 2.25 miles long, opens into Canyon del Gato-Montes 4.25 miles southwest of Liebre Twins (lat. 34°54'25" N, long. 118°37'10" W). Named on Liebre Twins (1965) 7.5' quadrangle.

Canada de la Oasis: see **Oso Canyon** [KERN].

Cañada de las Uvas: see **Grapevine Creek** [KERN].

Canara Springs: see **Carneros Spring** [KERN].

Canaris Spring: see **Carneros Spring** [KERN].

Canary Spring [KERN]: *spring,* 2.5 miles northwest of Democrat Hot Springs (lat. 35°33'15" N, long. 118°41'40" W; sec. 25, T 27 S, R 30 E). Named on Democrat Hot Springs (1972) 7.5' quadrangle.

Canary Spring: see **Carneros Spring** [KERN].

Cando [FRESNO]: *locality,* 6.5 miles east-northeast of Riverdale along Southern Pacific Railroad (lat. 36°28'50" N, long. 119°45'30" W; sec. 1, T 17 S, R 20 E). Named on Riverdale (1927) 7.5' quadrangle.

Canebrake [KERN]:

(1) *settlement,* 5 miles east-northeast of Onyx (lat. 35°43'40" N, long. 118°08'20" W; sec. 29, T 25 S, R 36 E); the place is along Canebrake Creek. Named on Onyx (1972) 7.5' quadrangle.

(2) *locality,* 5.5 miles north-northwest of Walker Pass (lat. 35°43'45" N, long. 118°04'30" W; near NE cor. sec. 26, T 25 S, R 36 E); the place is along Canebrake Creek. Named on Kernville (1908) 30' quadrangle.

Canebrake Creek [KERN]: *stream,* heads near Walker Pass and flows 15 miles to South Fork Valley 4 miles northeast of Onyx (lat. 35°43'45" N, long. 118°10' W). Named on Lamont Peak (1956) 15' quadrangle, and on Onyx (1972) and Walker Pass (1972) 7.5' quadrangles. Called Chay-o-poo-ya-pah, a version of the Indian name, on Williamson's (1853) map.

Canebrake Flat [KERN]: *area,* 6.5 miles northwest of Walker Pass (lat. 35°44' N, long. 118°06'30" W); the place is along Canebrake Creek. Named on Walker Pass (1972) 7.5' quadrangle.

Cane Canyon [KERN]: *canyon,* drained by a stream that flows 7.5 miles to the canyon of Kelso Creek 6.5 miles west-northwest of Skinner Peak (lat. 35°35'50" N, long. 118°14' W; near E line sec. 8, T 27 S, R 35 E). Named on Cane Canyon (1972) 7.5' quadrangle.

Cane Creek [KERN]: *stream,* flows 3.5 miles to Tillie Creek nearly 2 miles west-northwest of Wofford Heights (lat. 35°42'50" N, long. 118°29' W; at W line sec. 31, T 25 S, R 33 E). Named on Alta Sierra (1972) and Lake Isabella North (1972) 7.5' quadrangles.

Cane Meadow [KERN]: *area,* 7.25 miles east-northeast of Kernville (lat. 35°46'45" N, long. 118°18'05" W; sec. 2, T 25 S, R 34 E). Named on Kernville (1956) 15' quadrangle.

Cane Peak [KERN]: *peak,* 2.25 miles west-northwest of Wofford Heights (lat. 35°43'35" N, long. 118°20'15" W; near E line sec. 25, T 25 S, R 32 E). Altitude 4539 feet. Named on Lake Isabella North (1972) 7.5' quadrangle.

Cane Spring [KERN]:

(1) *spring,* 10.5 miles east of Glennville (lat. 35°45'10" N, long. 118°31' W; at E line sec. 15, T 25 S, R 32 E). Named on California Hot Springs (1958) 15' quadrangle.

(2) *spring,* 4.5 miles east-southeast of Wofford Heights (lat. 35°40'55" N, long. 118°22'50" W; sec. 12, T 26 S, R 33 E). Named on Lake Isabella North (1972) 7.5' quadrangle.

Cane Springs: see **Koehn Spring** [KERN].

Cane Well [KERN]: *well,* 5.5 miles west-northwest of Skinner Peak (lat. 35°35'40" N, long. 118°13' W; near W line sec. 10, T 27 S, R 35 E); the feature is in Cane Canyon. Named on Cane Canyon (1972) 7.5' quadrangle.

Canfield: see **Old River** [KERN].

Cannell Creek [KERN-TULARE]: *stream,* heads in Tulare County and flows 10.5 miles, partly in Kern County, to Kern River 9.5 miles south-southeast of Fairview at Kern-Tulare County line (lat. 35°47'35" N, long. 118°26'50" W; at S line sec. 32, T 24 S, R 33 E); the stream heads near Cannell Peak and goes through Cannell Meadow. Named on Kernville (1956) 15' quadrangle. Called Lit. Brush Cr. on Olmsted's (1900) map.

Cannell Meadow [TULARE]: *area,* 10 miles southeast of Fairview (lat. 35°49'15" N, long. 118°22' W); the place is along Cannell Creek. Named on Kernville (1956) 15' quadrangle.

Cannell Meadow: see **Little Cannel Meadow** [TULARE].

Cannell Peak [TULARE]: *peak,* 8.5 miles east-southeast of Fairview (lat. 35°51'55" N, long. 118°21'35" W; near SW cor. sec. 6, T 24 S, R 34 E). Altitude 9407 feet. Named on Kernville (1956) 15' quadrangle.

Canoas Canyon: see **Canoas Creek** [FRESNO].

Canoas Creek [FRESNO]: *stream,* flows 8 miles to Kettleman Plain 11.5 miles southeast of Coalinga (lat. 36°01'30" N, long. 120°12'05" W; near E line sec. 11, T 22 S, R 16 E). Named on Avenal (1954), Garza Peak (1953), and The Dark Hole (1961) 7.5' quadrangles. Stewart (p. 75) pointed out that *canoa,* which means "canoe" in Spanish, is used in place names in the Mexican sense to mean a trough or ditch for carrying irrigation water, and sometimes is applied to a natural stream. Arnold and Anderson (1908, p. 16) gave the name "Canoas Canyon" to the canyon at the head of Canoas Creek.

Cañon Falls: see **Chagoopa Falls** [TULARE].

Canon Mountain: see **Breckenridge Mountain** [KERN].

Cantil [KERN]: *village,* 6 miles southwest of Saltdale (lat. 35°18'30" N, long. 117°57'05" W; at E line sec. 23, T 30 S, R 37 E). Named on Cantil (1967) 7.5' quadrangle. Postal authorities established Cantil post office in 1916 (Frickstad, p. 54). The place began in 1908 or 1909 as a station on Nevada and California Railroad—*cantil* means "steep rock" in Spanish (Darling, p. 24). Desert Spring, located 1.5 miles northeast of present Cantil, was an important watering place for Indians, early explorers, prospectors, and freighters (Bailey, 1967, p. 6-7).

Can-too-oa Creek: see **Warthan Creek** [FRESNO].

Cantua: see **Cantua Creek** [FRESNO] (2).

Cantua Creek [FRESNO]:

(1) *stream,* heads in San Benito County and flows 19 miles to lowlands 19 miles north of Coalinga (lat. 36°24'40" N, long. 120° 24' W; sec. 36, T 17 S, R 14 E). Named on Ciervo Mountain (1969), Lillis Ranch (1956), and Tres Picos Farms (1956) 7.5' quadrangles. The name commemorates a member of the Cantua family (Gudde, 1949, p. 55).

(2) *settlement,* 11 miles south-southwest of Tranquillity (lat. 36°30'05" N, long. 120°18'50" W; near SW cor. sec. 26, T 16 S, R 15 E). Named on Cantua Creek (1956) 7.5' quadrangle. Postal authorities established and discontinued Cantua post office in 1888, reestablished it in 1890, and discontinued it in 1892; they established Cantua Creek post office in 1941 (Salley, p. 36).

Cantua Creek: see **Warthan Creek** [FRESNO].

Cantua Well [FRESNO]: *well,* 5.25 miles southeast of Ciervo Mountain (lat. 36°24'25" N, long. 120°31'05" W; near E line sec. 35, T 17 S, R 13 E); the well is along a branch of Cantua Creek (1). Named on Ciervo Mountain (1969) 7.5' quadrangle.

Canyon Creek: see **Wilcox Creek** [TULARE].

Canyon de la Lecheria [KERN]: *canyon,* 2.25 miles long, along Pescado Creek above a point 6.5 miles southwest of Liebre Twins (lat. 34°53'20" N, long. 118°39'05" W). Named on Winters Ridge (1966) 7.5' quadrangle.

Canyon del Gato-Montes [KERN]: *canyon,* 3 miles long, opens into lowlands 5 miles south-southwest of Liebre Twins (lat. 34°52'45" N, long. 118°36'15" W). Named on Liebre Twins (1965) and Winters Ridge (1966) 7.5' quadrangles. Called Livsey Canyon on Johnson's (1911) map.

Canyon del Secretario: see **Sacatara Creek** [KERN].

Canyon del Sectario: see **Sacatara Creek** [KERN].

Caparell Creek [KERN]: *stream,* flows 2.5 miles to end in lowlands 10.5 miles south of Arvin (lat. 35°03' N, long. 118°49'05" W; sec. 8, T 11 N, R 18 W). Named on Tejon Hills (1955) 7.5' quadrangle.

Cap Canyon [KERN]: *canyon,* drained by a stream that flows 4.5 miles to South Fork Valley 3 miles east-northeast of Onyx (lat. 35° 42'45" N, long. 118°10'15" W). Named on Onyx (1972) and Walker Pass (1972) 7.5' quadrangles. Called Horse Canyon on Onyx (1943) 15' quadrangle, and United States Board on Geographic Names (1975b, p. 9) gave this name as a variant.

Cape Horn [FRESNO]: *relief feature,* 7.5 miles west-southwest of Blackcap Mountain, where there is a steep drop from the end of a ridge into the canyon of North Fork Kings River (lat. 37°02'45" N, long. 118°55'25" W; sec. 21, T 10 S, R 28 E). Named on Blackcap Mountain (1953) 15' quadrangle.

Capinero Creek [TULARE]: *stream,* flows 6 miles to Deer Creek (2) 0.5 mile east of California Hot Springs (lat. 35°52'50" N, long. 118°39'30"

W; sec. 32, T 23 S, R 31 E). Named on California Hot Springs (1958) 15' quadrangle.

Capinero Flat: see **Pine Flat** [TULARE] (1).

Capinero Saddle [TULARE]: *pass,* 2.5 miles southeast of California Hot Springs (lat. 35°51'25" N, long. 118°37'55" W; sec. 9, T 24 S, R 31 E). Named on California Hot Springs (1958) 15' quadrangle.

Capita Canyon [FRESNO]: *canyon,* drained by a stream that flows 5 miles to lowlands 17 miles southwest of Firebaugh (lat. 36°41'50" N, long. 120°41'50" W; sec. 19, T 14 S, R 12 E). Named on Chounet Ranch (1956) and Mercey Hot Springs (1969) 7.5' quadrangles.

Capital Peak: see **Capitol Rock** [TULARE].

Capitol Rock [TULARE]: *peak,* 11 miles northeast of California Hot Springs (lat. 35°58'50" N, long. 118°31'30" W; sec. 28, T 22 S, R 32 E). Altitude 5927 feet. Named on California Hot Springs (1958) 15' quadrangle. Called Capital Peak on Olmsted's (1900) map.

Caratan [TULARE]: *locality,* 4.5 miles south of Earlimart along Southern Pacific Railroad (lat. 35°49'10" N, long. 119°15'30" W; at S line sec. 22, T 24 S, R 25 E). Named on Delano West (1954) 7.5' quadrangle.

Cardinal Lake [FRESNO]: *lake,* 2200 feet long, 4 miles north-northwest of Mount Pinchot (lat. 37°00' N, long. 118°25'40" W); the lake is 1 mile west of Cardinal Mountain. Named on Big Pine (1950) and Mount Pinchot (1953) 15' quadrangles.

Cardinal Mountain [FRESNO]: *peak,* 3.5 miles north of Mount Pinchot on Fresno-Inyo County line (lat. 36°59'55" N, long. 118° 24'45" W). Altitude 13,397 feet. Named on Mount Pinchot (1953) 15' quadrangle. George R. Davis of United States Geological Survey named the peak because the red color at the summit suggests the cap of a cardinal (Browning, p. 31).

Caric [TULARE]: *locality,* 3.5 miles south of Earlimart along Southern Pacific Railroad (lat. 35°49'55" N, long. 119°15'40" W; sec. 22, T 24 S, R 25 E). Named on Delano West (1954) 7.5' quadrangle.

Carillon: see **Mount Carillon** [TULARE].

Carlile: see **Caruthers** [FRESNO].

Carlson Station: see **Balsam Creek** [FRESNO].

Carmelita: see **Reedley** [FRESNO].

Carnaris Spring: see **Carneros Spring** [KERN].

Carnaros Spring: see **Carneros Spring** [KERN].

Carneros Canyon [KERN]: *canyon,* 6.5 miles long, on Kern-San Luis Obispo County line along Carneros Creek above a point less than 1 mile north of Carneros Rocks (lat. 35°26'45" N, long. 119° 50'35" W; sec. 32, T 28 S, R 20 E). Named on Carneros Rocks (1959) and Las Yeguas Ranch (1959) 7.5' quadrangles. United States Board on Geographic Names (1933a, p. 196) rejected the name "McLean Canyon" for the feature.

Carneros Creek [KERN]: *stream,* heads in San Luis Obispo County and flows 9 miles to Santos Creek 3.25 miles north-northeast of Carneros Rocks (lat. 35°28'55" N, long. 119°49'45" W; near NW cor. sec. 21, T 28 S, R 20 E). Named on Carneros Rocks (1959) 7.5' quadrangle.

Carneros Rocks [KERN]: *relief feature,* 15 miles northwest of McKittrick (lat. 35°26'15" N, long. 119°50'50" W; sec. 5, T 29 S, R 20 E); the feature is near the mouth of Carneros Canyon. Named on Carneros Rocks (1959) 7.5' quadrangle.

Carneros Spring [KERN]: *spring,* at Carneros Rocks (lat. 35°26'20" N, long. 119°50'45" W; sec. 5, T 29 S, R 20 E). Named on Carneros Rocks (1959) 7.5' quadrangle. Anderson (p. 169) mentioned Canara Springs. United States Board on Geographic Names (1933a, p. 196) rejected the names "Canaris Spring," "Canary Spring," "Carnaris Spring," and "Carnaros Spring" for the feature.

Carol Col: see **Humphreys Basin** [FRESNO].

Cartridge Creek [FRESNO]: *stream,* flows 6.5 miles to Middle Fork Kings River nearly 4.5 miles northwest of Marion Peak (lat. 36° 59'50" N, long. 118°35'15" W); the stream heads near Cartridge Pass. Named on Marion Peak (1953) and Mount Pinchot (1953) 15' quadrangles. Farquhar (1923, p. 386) connected the name with a story about a man who had a good shot at a deer near the creek, but who in his excitement pumped all of the cartridges out of the magazine of his rifle—this act prompted his companions to give the name "Cartridge" to the creek. South Fork enters from the south 2 miles upstream from the mouth of the main stream; it is 2.5 miles long and is named on Marion Peak (1953) 15' quadrangle.

Cartridge Pass [FRESNO]: *pass,* 5 miles west-northwest of Mount Pinchot (lat. 36°58'30" N, long. 118°29'10" W); the pass is at the head of Cartridge Creek. Named on Mount Pinchot (1953) 15' quadrangle. The feature first was called Red Pass (Versteeg, p. 423).

Caruthers [FRESNO]: *town,* 15 miles south of downtown Fresno (lat. 36°32'30" N, long. 119°50' W; sec. 18, T 16 S, R 20 E). Named on Caruthers (1963) 7.5' quadrangle. The name commemorates W.A. Caruthers, a local farmer (Gudde, 1949, p. 59). Postal authorities established Caruthers post office in 1891; they established Carlile post office 7 miles northwest of Riverdale in 1894, moved it 1.25 miles east in 1899, and discontinued it in 1905 when they moved the service to Caruthers (Salley, p. 38, 39).

Carver Camp [TULARE]: *locality,* 11 miles south-southeast of Camp Nelson (lat. 36°00'05" N, long. 118°31'25" W; sec. 21, T 22 S, R 32 E). Named on Camp Nelson (1956) 15' quadrangle.

Carver Peak [TULARE]: *peak,* 6 miles south-southwest of California Hot Springs (lat. 35°48'10" N, long. 118°42'20" W; sec. 35, T 24 S, R 30 E). Altitude 4242 feet. Named on California Hot Springs (1958) 15' quadrangle.

Carver Spring [KERN]: *spring,* 3.25 miles west-southwest of Woody (lat. 35°41' N, long. 118°53'20" W; sec. 7, T 26 S, R 29 E). Named on Sand Canyon (1965) 7.5' quadrangle.

Casa Vieja Meadows [TULARE]: *area,* 7 miles east-southeast of Hockett Peak (lat. 36°12' N, long. 118°16'10" W; mainly in sec. 11, T 20 S, R 34 E). Named on Hockett Peak (1956) 15' quadrangle. The name is from an old house or cabin at the place (Browning, p. 33).

Cascada: see **Big Creek** [FRESNO] (3).

Cascada Spring [FRESNO]: *spring,* 18 miles northwest of Coalinga (lat. 36°18' N, long. 120°37'25" W; sec. 1, T 19 S, R 12 E). Named on Santa Rita Peak (1969) 7.5' quadrangle.

Cascade Creek [TULARE]: *stream,* flows 2.25 miles to Yucca Creek 2.5 miles east-northeast of Yucca Mountain (lat. 36°35'20" N, long., 118°49'40" W; near E line sec. 28, T 15 S, R 29 E). Named on Giant Forest (1956) 15' quadrangle.

Cascade Creek: see **Cave Creek** [TULARE].

Cascade Valley [FRESNO]: *canyon,* 3.5 miles long, 5 miles west of Red Slate Mountain along Fish Creek (1) (lat. 37°30'20" N, long. 118°57'30" W). Named on Mount Abbot (1953) and Mount Morrison (1953) 15' quadrangles. J.N. LeConte and J.S. Hutchinson called the place Peninsula Meadow in 1908 for a peninsula that juts into the stream (Farquhar, 1923, p. 386).

Cascajo Hill [KERN]: *peak,* 12 miles north of Blackwells Corner (lat. 35°47' N, long. 119°55' W; near W line sec. 3, T 25 S, R 19 E). Altitude 590 feet. Named on Avenal Gap (1954) 7.5' quadrangle. United States Board on Geographic Names (1933b, p. 6) noted that the name refers to conglomerate that crops out on the peak—*cascajo* means "gravel" in Spanish.

Case Mountain [TULARE]: *peak,* 8 miles east-southeast of Kaweah at the northwest end of Salt Creek Ridge (lat. 36°24'40" N, long. 118°48'10" W). Altitude 5818 feet Named on Kaweah (1957) 15' quadrangle. The name commemorates Bill Case, who hauled shakes from the neighborhood with a team made up of a horse, a mule, a burro, and a steer (Hanna, p. 58).

Cassadys Bar: see **Old Millerton** [FRESNO].

Castac [KERN]: *land grant,* at and southeast of Grapevine. Named on Frazier Mountain (1958), Grapevine (1958), Lebec (1958), and Pastoria Creek (1958) 7.5' quadrangles. Jose Maria Covarrubias received 5 leagues in 1843 and claimed 22,178 acres patented in 1866 (Cowan, p. 25; Cowan gave the form "Castec" as an alternate). The name is of Indian origin (Kroeber, p. 37).

Castac Lake [KERN]: *lake,* 1.25 miles long, 1.25 miles east of Lebec (lat. 34°50'05" N, long. 118°50'35" W); the lake is on Castac grant. Named on Lebec (1958) 7.5' quadrangle. Called Castaic Lake on Lebec (1945) 7.5' quadrangle, but United States Board on Geographic Names (1960b, p. 16) rejected this form of the name. Blake (1857, p. 47) referred to "Salt pond, or Casteca lake (dry)."

Castac Valley [KERN]: *valley,* at and near Lebec on Castac grant; extends into Los Angeles County near the mouth of Cuddy Canyon. Named on Frazier Mountain (1958), Grapevine (1958), and Lebec (1958) 7.5' quadrangles. Called Castaic Valley on Frazier Mountain (1944) and Lebec (1945) 7.5' quadrangles, but United States Board on Geographic Names (1960b, p. 16) rejected this form of the name.

Castaic Lake: see **Castac Lake** [KERN].

Castaic Valley: see **Castac Valley** [KERN].

Castec: see **Castac** [KERN].

Castle Butte [KERN]: *peak,* 17 miles east-northeast of Mojave (lat. 35°06'50" N, long. 117°52'35" W; at SW cor. sec. 26, T 32 S, R 38 E). Altitude 3124 feet. Named on California City South (1973) 7.5' quadrangle. Called Castle Rock on California Mining Bureau's (1917c) map.

Castle Butte Well [KERN]: *well,* 14 miles north-northwest of Boron (lat. 35°11'40" N, long. 117°42'45" W; sec. 32, T 31 S, R 40 E); the well is 11 miles east-northeast of Castle Butte. Named on Boron NW (1973) 7.5' quadrangle.

Castle Creek [TULARE]: *stream,* flows 4 miles to Middle Fork Kaweah River 9.5 miles west-southwest of Triple Divide Peak (lat. 36°32'20" N, long. 118°41'10" W). Named on Mineral King (1956) and Triple Divide Peak (1956) 15' quadrangles. The stream is named from Castle Rocks (Browning, p. 34).

Castle Domes [FRESNO]: *relief feature,* 4.5 miles south-southwest of Mount Pinchot (lat. 36°52'45" N, long. 118°26'45" W). Named on Mount Pinchot (1953) 15' quadrangle.

Castle Mountain [FRESNO]: *peak,* 13 miles south of Coalinga on Fresno-Monterey County line (lat. 35°56'20" N, long. 120°20'20" W; sec. 10, T 23 S, R 15 E). Altitude 4343 feet. Named on The Dark Hole (1961) 7.5' quadrangle.

Castle Peak [FRESNO]: *peak,* 14 miles north of Hume (lat. 36°59'15" N, long. 118°51'45" W). Altitude 10,677 feet. Named on Tehipite Dome

(1952) 15' quadrangle.

Castle Rock [TULARE]:

(1) *peak,* 5 miles southwest of Hockett Peak (lat. 36°10'40" N, long. 118°27'30" W). Altitude 7740 feet. Named on Hockett Peak (1956) 15' quadrangle. The name is for the castlelike appearance of the feature (Browning, p. 34).

(2) *hill,* less than 1 mile northwest of Woodlake (lat. 36°25'25" N, long. 119°05'20" W; sec. 30, T 17 S, R 27 E). Altitude 538 feet. Named on Woodlake (1952) 7.5' quadrangle.

Castle Rock: see **Castle Butte** [KERN].

Castle Rocks [TULARE]: *relief feature,* 12 miles west-southwest of Triple Divide Peak (lat. 36°30' N, long. 118°42'45" W). Named on Mineral King (1956) and Triple Divide Peak (1956) 15' quadrangles. Professor Dean, who had a homestead at the place, named the feature for its resemblance to the medieval castles on the Rhine (Browning, p. 34).

Castro Canyon [FRESNO]: *canyon,* drained by a stream that flows 3 miles to Jacalitos Creek 9 miles southwest of Coalinga (lat. 36°02'20" N, long. 120°27'10" W; sec. 3, T 22 S, R 14 E). Named on Curry Mountain (1969) 7.5' quadrangle.

Castro Spring [FRESNO]: *spring,* 9 miles southwest of Coalinga (lat. 36°02' N, long. 120°27'40" W; sec. 9, T 22 S, R 14 E); the spring is in Castro Canyon. Named on Curry Mountain (1969) 7.5' quadrangle.

Cataract Creek [FRESNO]: *stream,* flows 3 miles to Palisade Creek 12 miles east-southeast of Mount Goddard at Deer Meadow (1) (lat. 37°03'15" N, long. 118°31'10" W). Named on Mount Goddard (1948) 15' quadrangle. J.N. LeConte and his companions named the stream (Browning, p. 34-35).

Cat Canyon [KERN]: *canyon,* 10 miles west of Liebre Twins (lat. 34°59' N, long. 118°44'50" W; on S line sec. 36, T 11 N, R 18 W). Named on Winters Ridge (1966) 7.5' quadrangle.

Cathedral Lake [FRESNO]: *lake,* 1800 feet long, 4.5 miles south-southwest of Mount Goddard (lat. 37°02'25" N, long. 118°44'25" W). Named on Mount Goddard (1948) 15' quadrangle.

Cats Head Mountain [FRESNO]: *peak,* 4.5 miles north-northeast of Trimmer (lat. 36°57'30" N, long. 119°15'05" W; sec. 21, T 11 S, R 25 E). Altitude 3460 feet. Named on Trimmer (1965) 7.5' quadrangle.

Catskin Canyon [KINGS]: *canyon,* 3 miles long, 13 miles south of Avenal (lat. 35°49'30" N, long. 120°09'30" W). Named on Tent Hills (1942) 7.5' quadrangle.

Cattle Creek: see **Pastoria Creek** [KERN].

Caughran Spring [KERN]: *spring,* 2.25 miles northwest of Democrat Hot Springs (lat. 35°33'20" N, long. 118°41'20" W; near NW cor. sec. 30, T 27 S, R 31 E). Named on Democrat Hot Springs (1972) 7.5' quadrangle.

Cave Creek [TULARE]: *stream,* flows nearly 2 miles to Yucca Creek 2.25 miles east-northeast of Yucca Mountain (lat. 36°35'05" N, long. 118°50' W; near N line sec. 33, T 15 S, R 29 E). Named on Giant Forest (1956) 15' quadrangle. United States Board on Geographic Names (1933a, p. 204) rejected the name "Cascade Creek" for the stream.

Cawelo [KERN]: *locality,* 13 miles northwest of Bakersfield along Southern Pacific Railroad (lat. 35°30' N, long. 119°09'55" W). Named on Famoso (1953) and Rosedale (1954) 7.5' quadrangles. The name was coined from letters in names of partners of Camp, West, Lowe, Farm Company (Bailey, 1967, p. 4). In 1909 Harry J. Marten promoted a colony called Martendale that was located a short distance south of Cawelo and made up of 109 Mennonite and Adventist families (Bailey, 1967, p. 16). Postal authorities established Martensdale post office in 1909 and discontinued it in 1910 (Salley, p. 134).

Cecile [FRESNO]: *locality,* 1.5 miles northeast of Malaga along Atchison, Topeka and Santa Fe Railroad (lat. 36°42' N, long. 119° 43' W; near W line sec. 20, T 14 S, R 21 E). Named on Malaga (1964) 7.5' quadrangle.

Cecile Lake [FRESNO]: *lake,* 1300 feet long, 1 mile west of Red Slate Mountain (lat. 37°30'20" N, long. 118°53'20" W). Named on Mount Morrison (1953) 15' quadrangle.

Cedarbrook [FRESNO]: *settlement,* 6.5 miles east-southeast of Dunlap (lat. 36°42'30" N, long. 119°00'20" W; sec. 14, T 14 S, R 27 E). Named on Miramonte (1966) 7.5' quadrangle.

Cedar Canyon [FRESNO]: *canyon,* drained by a stream that flows nearly 4 miles to Zapato Chino Creek 10 miles south-southeast of Coalinga (lat. 36°00'45" N, long. 120°17' W; sec. 18, T 22 S, R 16 E). Named on Kreyenhagen Hills (1956) 7.5' quadrangle.

Cedar Canyon [KERN]:

(1) *canyon,* drained by a stream that flows 6.5 miles to Bitterwater Creek (2) 13 miles south-southeast of Orchard Peak (lat. 35°33'35" N, long. 120°02'40" W; sec. 21, T 27 S, R 18 E). Named on Las Yeguas Ranch (1959), Packwood Creek (1961), and Shale Point (1953) 7.5' quadrangles.

(2) *canyon,* drained by a stream that flows 5.5 miles to Tejon Creek nearly 6 miles west of Cummings Mountain (lat. 35°02'45" N, long. 118°40'10" W). Named on Cummings Mountain (1966) and Tejon Ranch (1966) 7.5' quadrangles.

(3) *canyon,* drained by a stream that flows 1.25 miles to El Paso Creek 6.5 miles west-northwest of Liebre Twins (lat. 34°58'45" N, long. 118°40'45" W; sec. 3, T 10 N, R 17 W). Named on Winters Ridge (1966) 7.5' quadrangle.

Cedar Canyon [TULARE]: *canyon,* drained by a stream that flows 3 miles to Durrwood Creek 12 miles south-southwest of Hockett Peak (lat. 36°03'20" N, long. 118°25'55" W). Named on Hockett Peak (1956) 15' quadrangle.

Cedar Creek [KERN]: *stream,* flows 15 miles to Poso Creek 6.25 miles south-southwest of Glennville (lat. 35°38'30" N, long. 118° 44'25" W; near N line sec. 27, T 26 S, R 30 E). Named on California Hot Springs (1958) 15' quadrangle, and on Alta Sierra (1972) and Glennville (1972) 7.5' quadrangles.

Cedar Creek [TULARE]:

(1) *stream,* flows 3.25 miles to Dry Creek (1) 6.25 miles east-southeast of Auckland (lat. 36°32'25" N, long. 119°00'35" W; sec. 14, T 16 S, R 27 E). Named on Giant Forest (1956) 15' quadrangle, and on Auckland (1966) 7.5' quadrangle. Called Elder Creek on Dinuba (1924) 30' quadrangle, but United States Board on Geographic Names (1967c, p. 3) rejected this name for the stream.

(2) *stream,* flows 2.5 miles to Yucca Creek 1.5 miles south-southeast of Yucca Mountain (lat. 36°33'15" N, long. 118°51'20" W). Named on Giant Forest (1956) 15' quadrangle.

(3) *stream,* flows 4 miles to South Fork Tule River 8 miles south-southwest of Camp Nelson (lat. 36°02'20" N, long. 118°40'10" W). Named on Camp Nelson (1956) 15' quadrangle.

(4) *stream,* flows 2 miles to South Fork Kaweah River 10 miles southwest of Mineral King (lat. 36°21'20" N, long. 118°43'55" W). Named on Mineral King (1956) 15' quadrangle. United States Board on Geographic Names (1960b, p. 17) rejected the name "Squaw Creek" for the stream.

Cedar Creek Campground [KERN]: *locality,* 2.25 miles northwest of Alta Sierra (lat. 35°44'55" N, long. 118°34'55" W; sec. 18, T 25 S, R 32 E); the place is along Cedar Creek. Named on Alta Sierra (1972) 7.5' quadrangle.

Cedar Crest [FRESNO]: *town,* 3.5 miles northeast of the town of Big Creek on the north side of Huntington Lake (1) (lat. 37°15' N, long. 119°11'45" W; in and near sec. 11, 12, T 8 S, R 25 E). Named on Huntington Lake (1953) and Kaiser Peak (1953) 15' quadrangles. Postal authorities established Cedar Crest post office in 1923, discontinued it in 1955, and reestablished it in 1962 (Salley, p. 40).

Cedar Grove [FRESNO]: *locality,* 14 miles southwest of Marion Peak in Kings Canyon (lat. 36°47'30" N, long. 118°40'10" W). Named on Marion Peak (1953) 15' quadrangle. Incense-cedar trees are abundant at the place; John Muir called the spot Deer Park (Browning, p. 35).

Cedar Slope [TULARE]: *locality,* 1.5 miles east of Camp Nelson (lat. 36°08'40" N, long. 118°34'40" W; sec. 33, T 20 S, R 31 E). Named on Camp Nelson (1956) 15' quadrangle.

Cedar Spring [TULARE]: *spring,* 1.25 miles south-southwest of California Hot Springs (lat. 35°51'50" N, long. 118°41' W; sec. 1, T 24 S, R 30 E). Named on California Hot Springs (1958) 15' quadrangle.

Cedric Wright: see **Mount Cedric Wright** [FRESNO].

Cella [FRESNO]: *locality,* 3.5 miles southeast of Centerville along Atchison, Topeka and Santa Fe Railroad (lat. 36°41'30" N, long. 119°27'10" W; at S line sec. 22, T 14 S, R 23 E). Named on Wahtoke (1966) 7.5' quadrangle. Called Wahtoke Winery on Wahtoke (1923) 7.5' quadrangle.

Ceneda [KERN]: *locality,* less than 1 mile southwest of Saltdale along Southern Pacific Railroad (lat. 35°21'15" N, long. 117°53'50" W). Named on Cantil (1967) 7.5' quadrangle.

Centennial Peak: see **Colby Pass** [TULARE].

Centennial Ridge [KERN]: *ridge,* west- to west-southwest-trending, 6 miles long, center 6.25 miles east-northeast of Caliente (lat. 35° 20'10" N, long. 118°32'15" W). Named on Loraine (1972) and Oiler Peak (1972) 7.5' quadrangles.

Center Basin [TULARE]: *relief feature,* 11 miles north-northwest of Mount Whitney (lat. 36°43'30" N, long. 118°21' W); the feature is east of Center Peak. Named on Mount Whitney (1956) 15' quadrangle.

Center Basin Crags [TULARE]: *relief feature,* 11 miles north-northwest of Mount Whitney on Tulare-Inyo County line (lat. 36°44'10" N, long. 118°20'45" W); the feature is northeast of Center Basin. Named on Mount Whitney (1956) 15' quadrangle.

Center Peak [FRESNO]: *peak,* 5.5 miles northwest of Coalinga Mineral Springs (lat. 36°12'10" N, long. 120°37'20" W; sec. 12, T 20 S, R 12 E). Altitude 4536 feet. Named on Sherman Peak (1969) 7.5' quadrangle.

Center Peak [TULARE]: *peak,* 11 miles north-northwest of Mount Whitney (lat. 36°43'15" N, long. 118°21'40" W). Altitude 12,760 feet. Named on Mount Whitney (1956) 15' quadrangle. Cornelius B. Bradley and his companions named the peak in 1898 for its position in the center of a cirque (Gudde, 1949, p. 62).

Centerville [FRESNO]: *town,* 16 miles east of Fresno on the northwest side of Kings River (lat. 36°44' N, long. 119°29'50" W; sec. 8, T 14 S, R 23 E). Named on Sanger (1923) and Wahtoke (1966) 7.5' quadrangles. A village called Scottsburg started in 1854 on a knoll in the bottom lands of Kings River east of present Sanger, where in the winter of 1861 and 1862 a flood destroyed it; residents rebuilt the place at the foot of a bluff to the northeast, where in 1867 another flood engulfed it; finally the community moved to the top of the bluff and was rechristened Centerville (Hoover, Rensch, and Rensch, p. 92). Postal authorities established Scottsburgh post office in 1856, discontinued it in 1858, reestablished it in 1859, and discontinued it in 1864 (Frickstad, p. 37). Grunsky (p. 40-41) used the name "Centerville Bottoms" for bottom lands that extend for about 9 miles along Kings River near Centerville. California Mining Bureau's (1917a) map has the name "King River" for a locality near present Centerville, and Mendenhall's (1908) map has the name "Kings River" for what appears to be the same place.

Centerville Bottoms: see **Centerville** [FRESNO].

Central Fork Cottonwood Creek: see **Crystal Creek** [KERN].

Central Fork Rattlesnake Creek: see **Crystal Creek** [KERN].

Central Valley: see "Regional setting."

Cerro Alto [KINGS]: *peak,* 5.25 miles east of Avenal (lat. 35°59'25" N, long. 120°02'05" W; sec. 28, T 22 S, R 18 E). Named on Kettleman Plain (1953) 7.5' quadrangle. United States Board on Geographic Names (1933b, p. 6) noted that the name is descriptive—*cerro alto* means "high hill" in Spanish

Cerro del Sur [KERN]: *hill,* 10 miles north of Blackwells Corner (lat. 35°45'55" N, long. 119°53'20" W; sec. 11, T 25 S, R 19 E). Named on Avenal Gap (1954) 7.5' quadrangle. Altitude 475 feet. United States Board on Geographic Names (1933b, p. 6) pointed out that the feature is the southernmost hill of South Dome, Kettleman Hills.

Cerro Lodoso [KINGS]: *peak,* 2.5 miles north-northeast of Avenal (lat. 36°02'20" N, long. 120°06'45" W; sec. 3, T 22 S, R 17 E). Altitude 1242 feet. Named on La Cima (1963) 7.5' quadrangle. United States Board on Geographic Names (1933b, p. 6) noted that *cerro lodoso* means "muddy hill" in Spanish.

Cerro Noroeste [KERN]: *peak,* 6.5 miles southwest of Eagle Rest Peak (lat. 34°49'50" N, long. 119°12'10" W; near SW cor. sec. 26, T 9 N, R 22 W). Altitude 8286 feet. Named on Sawmill Mountain (1943) 7.5' quadrangle. United States Board on Geographic Names (1990, p. 9) rejected the names "Abel Mountain" and "Mount Abel" for the feature. The Board (1981c, p. 6) approved the name "Puerta del Suelo" for a pass situated 0.5 mile east-southeast of Cerro Noroeste (lat. 34°49'37" N, long. 119°11'37" W; sec. 35, T 9 N, R 22 W); the name, which has the meaning "passage" in Spanish, is from the legend that Spanish priests used the pass.

Cerro Noroeste Camp [KERN]: *locality,* 6.5 miles southwest of Eagle Rest Peak (lat. 34°49'55" N, long. 119°12'35" W; near SE cor. sec. 27, T 9 N, R 22 W); the place is on the west side of Cerro Noroeste. Named on Sawmill Mountain (1943) 7.5' quadrangle.

Cerro Ultimo [KINGS]: *peak,* 6 miles east-northeast of Avenal (lat. 35°58'45" N, long. 120°01'20" W; near SE cor. sec. 28, T 22 S, R 18 E). Named on Kettleman Plain (1953) 7.5' quadrangle. The name refers to the feature being the last high peak along the road that traverses North Dome, Kettleman Hills—*cerro ultimo* means "last hill" in Spanish (United States Board on Geographic Names, 1933b, p. 6).

Chaffee [KERN]: *locality,* 1 mile north of downtown Mojave along Southern Pacific Railroad (lat. 35°04' N, long. 118°10'15" W; near NE cor. sec. 8, T 11 N, R 12 W). Named on Mojave (1973) 7.5' quadrangle. Called Chaffe on California Mining Bureau's (1917c) map.

Chagoopa Creek [TULARE]: *stream,* flows 7 miles to Kern River 13 miles north-northwest of Kern Peak (lat. 36°28' N, long. 118° 24'30" W); Chagoopa Falls is along the stream. Named on Kern Peak (1956) and Mount Whitney (1956) 15' quadrangles.

Chagoopa Falls [TULARE]: *waterfall,* 13 miles north-northwest of Kern Peak (lat. 36°28'10" N, long. 118°24'45" W); the feature is along Chagoopa Creek. Named on Kern Peak (1956) 15' quadrangle. W.B. Wallace, J.W.A. Wright, and F.H. Wales named the feature Sha-goo-pah Falls in 1881 to commemorate an old Piute Indian (Browning, p. 36), but United States Board on Geographic Names (1933a, p. 207) rejected the form "Shagoopah Falls" for the name. The feature was called Cañon Falls on a Sequoia National Park map of 1906 (Browning, p. 36).

Chagoopa Plateau [TULARE]: *area,* 15 miles northwest of Kern Peak (lat. 36°29'15" N, long. 118°26'30" W); Chagoopa Creek crosses the area. Named on Kern Peak (1956) and Mount Whitney (1956) 15' quadrangles. William R. Dudley and his companions named the place in 1897 (Browning, p. 36).

Chain Lakes [FRESNO]: *lakes,* largest 1100 feet long, 14 miles north of Hume (lat. 36°58'50" N, long. 118°53' W). Named on Tehipite Dome (1952) 15' quadrangle.

Chalaney Creek [TULARE]: *stream,* flows 6.25 miles to White River (1) nearly 7 miles southeast of Fountain Springs (lat. 35°49'20" N, long. 118°49'50" W; sec. 22, T 24 S, R 29 E). Named on White River (1965) 7.5' quadrangle. Called Chanley Creek on White River (1936) 15' quadrangle, and called Chilean Creek on White River (1952) 15' quadrangle, but United States Board on Geographic Names (1967a, p. 9) rejected both names for the stream.

Chalk Buttes [KINGS]: *peaks,* on a ridge, nearly 4 miles long, that is 8 miles south-southwest of Avenal (lat. 35°53'30" N, long. 120°10'45" W). Named on Garza Peak (1953) 7.5' quadrangle.

Chalk Cliff [KERN]: *relief feature,* 4.25 miles east-northeast of Knob Hill (lat. 35°35'15" N, long. 118°52'50" W). Named on Knob Hill (1965) 7.5' quadrangle.

Chamberlain Lake [FRESNO]: *lake,* 1200 feet long, 10 miles southwest of Mount Abbot (lat. 37°17'20" N, long. 118°54'35" W). Named on Mount Abbot (1953) 15' quadrangle. Forest Service employees Neil Perkins and Harvey Sauter named the lake for Joel Oliver Chamberlain of Fresno, who guided a group to the site in 1947 (Browning, p. 36-37).

Chamberlains Camp [FRESNO]: *locality,* 9 miles west-northwest of Blackcap Mountain (lat. 37°07' N, long. 118°56'50" W; sec. 29, T 9 S, R 28 E). Named on Blackcap Mountain (1953) 15' quadrangle. Carl Chamberlain built a cabin at the place in 1945 when he was running cattle in the neighborhood (Browning, p. 37).

Chamberlin: see **Mount Chamberlin** [TULARE].

Champagne Spring [KERN]: *spring,* 13 miles north-northwest of Mojave (lat. 35°13'30" N, long. 118°14'40" W; near N line sec. 20, T 31 S, R 35 E). Named on Cache Peak (1973) 7.5' quadrangle.

Chanac Canyon: see **Chanac Creek** [KERN].

Chanac Creek [KERN]: *stream,* heads in Cummings Valley and flows 10.5 miles to Tejon Creek 10 miles west of Cummings Mountain (lat. 35°04'05" N, long. 118°44'45" W; sec. 1, T 11 N, R 18 E). Named on Cummings Mountain (1966) and Tejon Ranch (1966) 7.5' quadrangles. The canyon of the stream was called Chanac Canyon for François Chanac, a Frenchman who lived there (Latta, 1976, p. 171).

Chaney Ranch Canyon [FRESNO]: *canyon,* drained by a stream that flows 1.5 miles to lowlands 17 miles southwest of Firebaugh (lat. 36°42'30" N, long. 120°42' W; sec. 18, T 14 S, R 12 E). Named on Chounet Ranch (1956) 7.5' quadrangle.

Chaneys: see **Panoche Creek** [FRESNO].

Chanley Creek: see **Chalaney Creek** [TULARE].

Chanz: see **Mojave** [KERN].

Chapel Lake [FRESNO]: *lake,* 800 feet long, 4.5 miles south-southwest of Mount Goddard (lat. 37°02'45" N, long. 118°44'45" W). Named on Mount Goddard (1948) 15' quadrangle. William A. Dill of California Department of Fish and Game named the lake in 1948 for its proximity to Cathedral Lake (Browning, p. 37).

Charley Mountain [FRESNO]: *peak,* 17 miles west of Coalinga on Fresno-Monterey County line (lat. 36°08'25" N, long. 120°39'50" W; sec. 34, T 20 S, R 12 E). Altitude 3885 feet. Named on Priest Valley (1969) 7.5' quadrangle.

Charlotte Creek [FRESNO]: *stream,* flows 4 miles to Bubbs Creek 13 miles south-southwest of Mount Pinchot (lat. 36°46'20" N, long. 118°29'15" W); the stream heads at Charlotte Lake. Named on Mount Pinchot (1953) 15' quadrangle.

Charlotte Lake [FRESNO]: *lake,* 2100 feet long, 12 miles south of Mount Pinchot (lat. 36°46'35" N, long. 118°25'30" W); the lake is at the head of Charlotte Creek. Named on Mount Pinchot (1953) 15' quadrangle. In the early days the feature was called Rhoda Lake for Mrs. Charles Houle, who camped there frequently in the 1880's (Browning, p. 37).

Charybdis [FRESNO]: *peak,* 3 miles east-southeast of Mount Goddard (lat. 37°05'15" N, long. 118°40' W); the peak is southeast of Ionian Basin and 1.25 miles east-northeast of Scylla. Altitude 13,091 feet. Named on Mount Goddard (1948) 15' quadrangle. Theodore S. Solomons and Ernest C. Bonner named the peak in 1895; the feature also was called Charybdis Peak (Browning, p. 37). United States Board on Geographic Names (1964b, p. 12) rejected the form "Charybois" for the name, and noted that Charybdis is the whirlpool off the Sicilian coast that figures prominently in Greek mythology.

Charybdis Peak: see **Charybdis** [FRESNO].

Charybois: see **Charybdis** [FRESNO].

Chasm Lake [FRESNO]: *lake,* 2300 feet long, 2.5 miles east-southeast of Mount Goddard in Ionian Basin (lat. 37°05'25" N, long. 118°40'40" W). Named on Mount Goddard (1948) 15' quadrangle. Lewis Clark of the Sierra Club proposed the name (Browning, p. 37).

Chawanakee: see **Camp Chawanakee** [FRESNO].

Chawanakee Flat [FRESNO]: *area,* 7.5 miles north of Shaver Lake Heights (present town of Shaver lake) (lat. 37°13' N, long. 119°19'15" W; sec. 23, T 8 S, R 24 E). Named on Shaver Lake (1953) 15' quadrangle.

Chay-o-poo-ya-pah: see **Canebrake Creek** [KERN].

Cherokee Flat [TULARE]: *area,* 5.5 miles south of Kaweah (lat. 36° 23'35" N, long. 118°54' W; mainly in sec. 1, T 18 S, R 28 E). Named on Kaweah (1957) 15' quadrangle.

Cherokee Strip [KERN]: *locality,* 2.5 miles south-southeast of Shafter (lat. 35°28' N, long. 119°15'35" W; at W line sec. 26, T 28 S, R 25 E). Named on Rio Bravo (1954) 7.5' quadrangle.

Cherry Creek [KERN]: *stream,* flows 2.5 miles to Salt Creek (2) 6.5 miles east-southeast of Eagle Rest Peak (lat. 34°52'20" N, long. 119°01'55" W; near SE cor. sec. 7, T 9 N, R 20 W). Named on Cuddy Valley (1943) 7.5' quadrangle. United States Board on Geographic Names (1989c, p. 1) rejected the name "Salt Creek" for the stream.

Cherry Creek: see **Salt Creek** [KERN] (2).

Cherry Flat [FRESNO]: *area,* 6 miles north of Trimmer (lat. 36°59'40" N, long. 119°17'40" W; at SE cor. sec. 1, T 11 S, R 24 E). Named on Trimmer (1965) 7.5' quadrangle.

Cherry Flat [TULARE]: *area,* 4.5 miles north-northwest of Yucca Mountain (lat. 36°37'50" N, long. 118°53'50" W; near SE cor. sec. 11, T 15 S, R 28 E). Named on Giant Forest (1956) 15' quadrangle.

Cherry Gap [FRESNO]: *pass,* 2.5 miles west-southwest of Hume (lat. 36°46'35" N, long. 118°57'35" W; sec. 20, T 13 S, R 28 E). Named on Tehipite Dome (1952) 15' quadrangle.

Cherry Gap [KERN]: *pass,* 8 miles northeast of Mount Adelaide (lat. 35°29'55" N, long. 118°37'20" W; near NE cor. sec. 15, T 28 S, R 31 E). Named on Breckenridge Mountain (1972) 7.5' quadrangle.

Cherry Hill [TULARE]: *peak,* 7 miles east of Fairview (lat. 35°55'20" N, long. 118°22'20" W; sec. 13, T 23 S, R 33 E). Altitude 8833 feet. Named on Kernville (1956) 15' quadrangle.

Chickencoop Canyon [TULARE]: *canyon,* 2.25 miles long, 12.5 miles south of Kaweah (lat. 36°17'30" N, long. 118°55'30" W). Named on Kaweah (1957) 15' quadrangle.

Chicken Spring Lake [TULARE]: *lake,* 1300 feet long, 14 miles north-northwest of Olancha Peak (lat. 36°27'55" N, long. 118°13'35" W; sec. 7, T 17 S, R 35 E). Named on Olancha (1956) 15' quadrangle.

Chicken Spring Pass: see **Cottonwood Pass** [TULARE].

Chico Canyon [KERN-TULARE]: *canyon,* drained by a stream that heads in Kern County and flows 3 miles to Kern River 9 miles south-southeast of Fairview in Tulare County (lat. 35°48'10" N, long. 118°27'10" W; at E line sec. 31, T 24 S, R 33 E). Named on Kernville (1956) 15' quadrangle.

Chico Martinez Creek [KERN]: *stream,* flows 8 miles to lowlands 3.5 miles east of Carneros Rocks (lat. 35°25'50" N, long. 119°47'10" W; near E line sec. 2, T 29 S, R 20 E). Named on Belridge (1953) and Carneros Rocks (1959) 7.5' quadrangles. The stream, which also is called El Arroyo de Chico Martinez, was named for a Spanish pioneer in the neighborhood (Hoover, Rensch, and Rensch, p. 128).

Chief Lake: see **Big Chief Lake** [FRESNO]; **Warrior Lake** [FRESNO].

Chilean Creek: see **Chalaney Creek** [TULARE]:

Chimney Creek [KERN-TULARE]: *stream,* heads in Tulare County and flows 21 miles to Canebrake Creek 5.5 miles east-northeast of Onyx in Kern County (lat. 35°43'50" N, long. 118°08'15" W; sec. 29, T 25 S, R 36 E); the stream passes east of Chimney Peak. Named on Lamont Peak (1956) 15' quadrangle, and on Onyx (1972) 7.5' quadrangle.

Chimney Lake [FRESNO]: *lake,* 1000 feet long, 6.25 miles west-southwest of Blackcap Mountain (lat. 37°01'40" N, long. 118°53'25" W; sec. 26, T 10 S, R 28 E). Named on Blackcap Mountain (1953) 15' quadrangle.

Chimney Meadow [TULARE]: *area,* 4.5 miles north-northeast of Lamont Peak (lat. 35°51'20" N, long. 118°00'35" W); the place is 2 miles east-southeast of Chimney Peak along Chimney Creek. Named on Lamont Peak (1956) 15' quadrangle. Called Chimney Meadows on Olmsted's (1900) map.

Chimney Peak [TULARE]: *peak,* 5 miles north of Lamont Peak (lat. 35°52' N, long. 118°02'30" W). Altitude 7990 feet. Named on Lamont Peak (1956) 15' quadrangle.

Chimney Rock [TULARE]: *peak,* 5.5 miles north of Yucca Mountain (lat. 36°39'15" N, long. 118°52' W; sec. 6, T 15 S, R 29 E). Altitude 7711 feet. Named on Giant Forest (1956) 15' quadrangle.

Chimney Rock: see **Finger Rock** [FRESNO].

Chimney Spring [FRESNO]: *spring,* 11 miles east-northeast of Clovis (lat. 36°52' N, long. 119°30'55" W; near N line sec. 25, T 12 S, R 22 E). Named on Round Mountain (1964) 7.5' quadrangle, which has a windmill symbol at the place.

Chimney Spring [TULARE]: *spring,* 3.25 miles southeast of Auckland (lat. 36°33'20" N, long. 119°03'55" W; sec. 8, T 16 S, R 27 E). Named on Auckland (1966) 7.5' quadrangle.

Chimo Flat [KERN]: *area,* 6.25 miles north-northwest of Caliente (lat. 35°22'10" N, long. 118°40'55" W). Named on Bena (1972) 7.5' quadrangle.

China Borax Lake: see **China Lake** [KERN] (1).

China Garden [KERN]: *area,* 1.5 miles east-northeast of Democrat Hot Springs along Kern River (lat. 35°32'10" N, long. 118°38'35" W). Named on Democrat Hot Springs (1972) 7.5' quadrangle. On Glennville (1956) 15' quadrangle, the name applies to a locality.

China Lake [KERN]:

(1) *dry lake,* mainly in San Bernardino County, but extends west into Kern County 7 miles north-northeast of Ridgecrest (lat. 35° 43' N, long. 117°37'30" W). Named on Ridgecrest North (1973) 7.5' quadrangle. The feature also was called China Borax Lake; this name was from borax operations at the place, presumably carried on by Chinese labor (Gale, p. 269).

(2) *town,* 2.5 miles north-northeast of Ridgecrest on China Lake Naval Weapons Center (lat. 35°39'15" N, long. 117°38'45" W). Named on Ridgecrest North (1973) 7.5' quadrangle. Postal authorities established China Lake post office in 1948 (Frickstad, p. 54). The town took its name from the dry lake (Bailey, 1967, p. 5).

China Lake Naval Weapons Center [KERN]: *military installation,* mainly in Indian Wells Valley north of Ridgecrest, and at and near China Lake (1). Named on Inyokern (1972), Lone Butte (1973), and Ridgecrest North (1973) 7.5' quadrangles. Construction of the facility began in 1943 (Wines, p. 81).

Chinese Peak [FRESNO]: *peak,* 5 miles east of the town of Big Creek (lat. 37°13'10" N, long. 119°09'15" W; sec. 20, T 8 S, R 26 E). Altitude 8709 feet. Named on Huntington Lake (1953) 15' quadrangle.

Chinowths Corner [TULARE]: *locality,* 2.5 miles west of Visalia (lat. 36°19'35" N, long. 119°20'05" W; at N line sec. 35, T 18 S, R 24 E). Named on Visalia (1949) 7.5' quadrangle.

Chinquapin Creek [FRESNO]: *stream,* flows nearly 3 miles to Camp 62 Creek 9 miles east of Kaiser Peak (lat. 37°18'45" N, long. 119°01'30" W). Named on Kaiser Peak (1953) 15' quadrangle, which shows the water of Camp 62 Creek diverted into a pipeline above the place that Chinquapin Creek reaches the bed of Camp 62 Creek.

Chinquapin Lakes [FRESNO]: *lakes,* largest 400 feet long, 4.5 miles east of Dinkey Dome (lat. 37°06'20" N, long. 119°03'05" W; sec. 32, T 9 S, R 27 E). Named on Huntington Lake (1953) 15' quadrangle.

Chintache Lake: see **Tulare Lake** [KINGS].

Chipmunk Landing: see **Huntington Lake** [FRESNO] (1).

Choice Valley [KERN]: *valley,* 8 miles south-southwest of Orchard Peak on Kern-San Luis Obispo County line (lat. 35°37'40" N, long. 120°11'30" W). Named on Holland Canyon (1961) and Orchard Peak (1961) 7.5' quadrangles.

Choke Creek [FRESNO]: *stream,* flows 2 miles to Grizzly Creek 15 miles southwest of Marion Peak (lat. 36°49'25" N, long. 118°43'45" W). Named on Marion Peak (1953) 15' quadrangle.

Cholla Canyon [KERN]: *canyon,* drained by a stream that flows 3.5 miles to the canyon of Kelso Creek 7 miles west-northwest of Skinner Peak (lat. 35°36'45" N, long. 118°14' W; at W line sec. 4, T 27 S, R 35 E). Named on Cane Canyon (1972) 7.5' quadrangle.

Chollo Well [KERN]: *well,* 6 miles west-northwest of Skinner Peak (lat. 35°36'40" N, long. 118°13'05" W; at W line sec. 3, T 27 S, R 35 E); the well is in Cholla Canyon. Named on Cane Canyon (1972) 7.5' quadrangle.

Cholly Canyon [KERN]: *canyon,* drained by a stream that flows 3 miles to Rancheria Creek (2) 5 miles southwest of Piute Peak (lat. 35°23'45" N, long. 118°26'50" W; sec. 21, T 29 S, R 33 E). Named on Piute Peak (1972) 7.5' quadrangle.

Chrysoprase Hill [TULARE]: *hill,* 1.25 miles southeast of Lindsay (lat. 36°11'40" N, long. 119°04'05" W; on N line sec. 17, T 20 S, R 27 E). Named on Lindsay (1951) 7.5' quadrangle.

Chuck Pass [FRESNO]: *pass,* 5.5 miles southwest of Blackcap Mountain (lat. 37°00'30" N, long. 118°51'30" W; near NW cor. sec. 6, T 11 S, R 29 E); the pass is near the head of Woodchuck Creek. Named on Blackcap Mountain (1953) 15' quadrangle.

Chuckwalla Mountain [KERN]: *peak,* 3.5 miles west of Cinco (lat. 35°16'20" N, long. 118°05'40" W; near NW cor. sec. 2, T 31 S, R 36 E). Altitude 5029 feet. Named on Cinco (1972) 7.5' quadrangle.

Church Dome [TULARE]: *peak,* 13 miles east-southeast of Fairview (lat. 35°51' N, long. 118°16'15" W; near W line sec. 12, T 24 S, R 34 E). Named on Kernville (1956) 15' quadrangle.

Churchill: see **Yettem** [TULARE].

Church Rock [FRESNO]: *peak,* 9.5 miles southwest of Coalinga (lat. 36°02'05" N, long. 120°28'05" W; sec. 9, T 22 S, R 14 E). Named on Curry Mountain (1969) 7.5' quadrangle.

Chute Spring [TULARE]: *spring,* 3 miles north-northeast of California Hot Springs (lat. 35°55'10" N, long. 119°39' W; sec. 20, T 23 S, R 31 E). Named on California Hot Springs (1958) 15' quadrangle.

Cienaga Canyon [KERN]: *canyon,* drained by a stream that flows 9.5 miles to lowlands 3 miles southeast of Maricopa (lat. 35°02'05" N, long. 119°21'55" W; near SW cor. sec. 17, T 11 N, R 23 W). Named on Ballinger Canyon (1943), Pentland (1953), and Santiago Creek (1943) 7.5' quadrangles. United States Board on Geographic Names (1990, p. 6) approved the name "Cienaga Creek" for the stream that flows through Cienega Canyon and ends in the community of Pentland (sec. 8, T 11 N, R 23 W); the Board rejected the form "Cienega Creek" for the name.

Cienaga Creek: see **Cienaga Canyon** [KERN]

Ciervo Hills [FRESNO]: *range,* 28 miles south of Firebaugh on Fresno-San Benito County line between Tumey Gulch and Cantua Creek. Named on Ciervo Mountain (1969), Levis (1956), Lillis Ranch (1956), Monocline Ridge (1955), and Tumey Hills (1956) 7.5' quadrangles.

Ciervo Mountain [FRESNO]: *ridge,* north-trending, 1 mile long, 27 miles south-southwest of Firebaugh (lat. 36°28' N, long. 120°34'40" W; sec. 5, 8, T 17 S, R 13 E); the ridge is in Ciervo Hills. Named on Ciervo Mountain (1969) 7.5' quadrangle.

Ciervo Spring [FRESNO]: *spring,* 1.25 miles northeast of Ciervo Mountain (lat. 36°28'50" N, long. 120°33'25" W; sec. 4, T 17 S, R 13 E); the spring is in Ciervo Hills along Arroyo Ciervo. Named on Ciervo Mountain (1969) 7.5' quadrangle.

Cima Hill [FRESNO]: *peak,* 20 miles southwest of Firebaugh (lat. 36°38'35" N, long. 120°41'40" W; sec. 7, T 15 S, R 12 E). Altitude 1355 feet. Named on Chounet Ranch (1956) 7.5' quadrangle.

Cimarron [KINGS]: *locality,* 1.5 miles west of Lemoore along Southern Pacific Railroad (lat. 36°17'55" N, long. 119°48'45" W; near SW cor. sec. 4, T 19 S, R 20 E). Named on Lemoore (1954) 7.5' quadrangle. Called Heinlen on Lemoore (1927) 7.5' quadrangle.

Cinco [KERN]: *locality,* 6 miles east of Cross Mountain at the edge of Fremont Valley (lat. 35°15'45" N, long. 118°02'10" W; near W line sec. 5, T 31 S, R 37 E). Named on Cinco (1972) 7.5' quadrangle. The place was a construction camp for the aqueduct that takes Owens Valley water from Inyo County to Los Angeles; it was the fifth such camp from Mojave—*cinco* means "fifth" in Spanish (Bailey, 1962, p. 54). California Mining Bureau's (1909a) map shows a place called Pine situated 4.5 miles south of Cinco along the railroad, and a stopping place called 18 Mile House was located just south of present Cinco (Barras, p. 125).

Cincotta [FRESNO]: *locality,* in downtown Fresno along Atchison, Topeka and Santa Fe Railroad (lat. 36°45'40" N, long. 119°45'15" W). Named on Fresno North (1965) 7.5' quadrangle.

Cinnamon Creek [TULARE]: *stream,* flows 3.5 miles to South Fork Kaweah River 7.5 miles south-southeast of Kaweah (lat. 36°22'35" N, long. 118°51'20" W; near E line sec. 8, T 18 S, R 29 E). Named on Kaweah (1957) 15' quadrangle.

Cinnamon Gap [TULARE]: *pass,* 7 miles southeast of Kaweah (lat. 36°24'25" N, long. 118°49'40" W; sec. 33, T 17 S, R 29 E); the pass is near the head of a branch of Cinnamon Creek. Named on Kaweah (1957) 15' quadrangle.

Circle Meadow [TULARE]: *area,* 6.5 miles east of Yucca Mountain (lat. 36°33'55" N, long. 118°45'10" W; on E line sec. 6, T 16 S, R 30 E). Named on Giant Forest (1956) 15' quadrangle.

Cirque Creek [FRESNO]: *stream,* flows 2.5 miles to Bear Creek (2) 8 miles west-southwest of Mount Abbot (lat. 37°21'45" N, long. 118°55'40" W); the stream heads at Cirque Lake. Named on Mount Abbot (1953) 15' quadrangle.

Cirque Crest [FRESNO]: *ridge,* north-northeast- to northeast-trending, 7 miles long, includes Marion Peak (lat. 36°57'25" N, long. 118°31'15" W). Named on Marion Peak (1953) and Mount Pinchot (1953) 15' quadrangles.

Cirque Lake [FRESNO]: *lake,* 2250 feet long, 8 miles west-southwest of Mount Abbot (lat. 37°20' N, long. 118°54'15" W); the lake is at the head of Cirque Creek. Named on Mount Abbot (1953) 15' quadrangle. Scott M. Soule and Jack Criqui of California Department of Fish and Game named the lake in 1948 for its location in a cirque (Browning, p. 39-40).

Cirque Peak [TULARE]: *peak,* 16 miles north-northwest of Olancha Peak on Tulare-Inyo County line (lat. 36°28'40" N, long. 118°14'10" W; on W line sec. 6, T 17 S, R 35 E). Altitude 12,900 feet. Named on Olancha (1956) 15' quadrangle.

Citadel: see **The Citadel** [FRESNO].

Citro [TULARE]: *locality,* 4.25 miles east-southeast of Woodlake along Visalia Electric Railroad (lat. 36°23'35" N, long. 119°01'25" W; sec. 2, T 18 S, R 27 E). Named on Woodlake (1952) 7.5' quadrangle.

Citrus Cove [FRESNO]: *valley,* 5.5 miles northwest of the town of Orange Cove (lat. 36°42'15" N, long. 119°21' W). Named on Orange Cove North (1966) 7.5' quadrangle.

Claire Lake: see **Little Claire Lake** [TULARE].

Clarasillo: see **Claraville** [KERN].

Claraville [KERN]: *locality,* 13 miles north of Emerald Mountain (lat. 35°26'30" N, long. 118°19'45" W; sec. 4, T 29 S, R 34 E). Named on Claraville (1972) 7.5' quadrangle. Postal authorities established Claraville post office in 1940, discontinued it in 1941, reestablished it in 1949, and discontinued it in 1957 (Salley, p. 44). A mining camp called Kelso—later called Claraville for Clara Munckton, the first white girl there—developed in the 1860's, but by 1869 it was deserted; a small community, also called Claraville, grew at the place with a revival of mining in the depression years of the 1930's (Boyd, p. 165; Hensher and Peskin, p. 18). Whipple (p. 149) referred to Clarasillo.

Claraville Flat [KERN]: *area,* at Claraville (lat. 35°26'35" N, long. 118°19'35" W; near E line sec. 4, T 29 S, R 34 E). Named on Claraville (1972) 7.5' quadrangle.

Clarence King: see **Mount Clarence King** [FRESNO].

Clark Canyon [TULARE]: *canyon,* drained by a stream that flows 1.5 miles to Dry Creek (1) 6.5 miles southeast of Auckland (lat. 36°31'50" N, long. 119°00'35" W; sec. 14, T 16 S, R 27 E). Named on Giant Forest (1956) 15' quadrangle, and on Auckland (1966) 7.5' quadrangle.

Clarks Fork: see **Kings River** [KINGS].

Clark Slough [KINGS]: *stream,* flows 6 miles to a ditch 2.5 miles south-southwest of Guernsey (lat. 36°10'35" N, long. 119°39'30" W). Named on Guernsey (1929) 7.5' quadrangle. Called Melga Canal on Guernsey (1954) 7.5' quadrangle.

Clarkson: see **Bakersfield** [KERN].

Clark Valley [FRESNO]: *valley,* 9 miles north-northwest of Orange Cove along upper reaches of Wahtoke Creek (lat. 36°45' N, long. 119°22' W). Named on Orange Cove North (1966), Piedra (1965), and Pine Flat Dam (1965) 7.5' quadrangles. Called Clarks Valley on Lippincott's (1902) map.

Clavicle: see **Springville** [TULARE].

Claw Lake [FRESNO]: *lake,* 1400 feet long, nearly 5 miles south of Mount Abbot (lat. 37°19'10" N, long. 118°48' W). Named on Mount Abbot (1953) 15' quadrangle.

Clear Creek [KERN]:

(1) *stream,* flows 14 miles to Kern River less than 0.25 mile east-southeast of Miracle Hot Springs (lat. 35°34'30" N, long. 118°31'40" W; near S line sec. 15, T 27 S, R 32 E). Named on Lake Isabella South (1972), Miracle Hot Springs (1972), and Piute Peak (1972) 7.5' quadrangles.

(2) *stream,* flows 6 miles to Tehachapi Creek 0.5 mile southeast of Caliente (lat. 35°17' N, long. 118°38'10" W). Named on Bear Mountain (1966), Keene (1966), and Oiler Peak (1972) 7.5' quadrangles.

Clear Creek Hot Springs: see **Miracle Hot Springs** [KERN].

Clearing: see **The Clearing** [FRESNO].

Clicks Creek [TULARE]: *stream,* flows 5.5 miles to Little Kern River 8 miles northeast of Camp Nelson (lat. 36°13'15" N, long. 118°30'10" W; near SE cor. sec. 33, T 19 S, R 32 E). Named on Camp Nelson (1956) 15' quadrangle. The name commemorates Mark, or Martin, Click, a sheepman of 1877 (Browning, p. 41). North Fork enters 2.5 miles upstream from the mouth of the stream; it is 3.25 miles long and is named on Camp Nelson (1956) 15' quadrangle.

Cliff [KERN]: *locality,* 2 miles southeast of Caliente along Southern Pacific Railroad (lat. 35°16'05" N, long. 119°36'25" W). Named on Oiler Peak (1972) 7.5' quadrangle.

Cliff Camp [FRESNO]: *locality,* 14 miles north-northwest of Hume (lat. 36°59'15" N, long. 118°58'25" W). Named on Tehipite Dome (1952) 15' quadrangle.

Cliff Creek [TULARE]: *stream,* flows 8.5 miles to Middle Fork Kaweah River 8 miles west-southwest of Triple Divide Peak (lat. 36°32' N, long. 118°39'20" W). Named on Mineral King (1956) and Triple Divide Peak (1956) 15' quadrangles. The name is from Cliff Pass, an early designation of present Black Rock Pass (Browning, p. 41).

Cliff Lake [FRESNO]: *lake,* 1800 feet long, 5 miles east-northeast of Dinkey Dome (lat. 37°08'30" N, long. 119°02'40" W; near SE cor. sec. 17, T 9 S, R 27 E). Named on Huntington Lake (1953) 15' quadrangle.

Cliff Pass: see **Black Rock Pass** [TULARE].

Cliff Peak [TULARE]: *peak,* 12 miles east of Dinuba (lat. 36°33'25" N, long. 119°10'15" W; near N line sec. 8, T 16 S, R 26 E). Named on Stokes Mountain (1966) 7.5' quadrangle.

Clifton: see **Del Rey** [FRESNO].

Clingans Junction: see **Mill Creek** [FRESNO-TULARE].

Clint [FRESNO]: *locality,* nearly 5 miles east of Riverdale along Atchison, Topeka and Santa Fe Railroad (lat. 36°25'55" N, long. 119°46'20" W; near S line sec. 23, T 17 S, R 20 E). Named on Riverdale (1954) 7.5' quadrangle.

Clotho [FRESNO]: *locality,* 3 miles west-northwest of Sanger along Southern Pacific Railroad (lat. 36°43'15" N, long. 119°36'30" W; near NW cor. sec. 17, T 14 S, R 22 E). Named on Sanger (1965) 7.5' quadrangle. Lippincott's (1902) map has the name "Minneola" at the place, but Grunsky's (1898) map has the name "Minneola" at present Ivesta.

Cloud: see **Lemoore** [KINGS].

Cloudburst Canyon [KERN]: *canyon,* 2.5 miles long, opens into the canyon of San Emigdio Creek 1.25 miles west-southwest of Eagle Rest Peak (lat. 34°53'50" N, long. 119°09'10" W; near E line sec. 6, T 9 N, R 21 W). Named on Eagle Rest Peak (1942) 7.5' quadrangle.

Cloud Canyon [TULARE]: *canyon,* 9 miles long, along Roaring River above a point 8 miles north-northwest of Triple Divide Peak (lat. 36°42'15" N, long. 118°34'30" W). Named on Triple Divide Peak (1956) 15' quadrangle. United States Board on Geographic Names (1933a, p. 225) rejected the names "Cloudy Canyon," "Copper Canyon," and "Deadman Canyon" for the feature. In 1880 Judge W.B. Wallace gave the name "The Cloud mine" to a mining claim near the stream because clouds hung so low overhead, and named the stream at the same time (Farquhar, 1924, p. 47-48).

Cloudy Canyon: see **Cloud Canyon** [TULARE]; **Deadman Canyon** [TULARE] (1).

Clough Cave [TULARE]: *cave,* 12 miles southeast of Kaweah along South Fork Kaweah River (lat. 36°21' N, long. 118°45'40" W). Named on Kaweah (1957) 15' quadrangle. The name is for William O. Clough, who discovered the cave in 1885 (United States Board on Geographic Names, 1933a, p. 225). Goodyear (1888b, p. 647) called the feature Clough's Cave.

Clover Creek [TULARE]:

(1) *stream,* formed by the confluence of East Fork and West Fork, flows 3.5 miles to Marble Fork 12 miles west of Triple Divide Peak (lat. 36°36'10" N, long. 118°44'40" W; sec. 20, T 15 S, R 30 E). Named on Giant Forest (1956) and Triple Divide Peak (1956) 15' quadrangles. East Fork is 2.5 miles long and West Fork is 1.5 miles long; both forks are named on Triple Divide Peak (1956) 15' quadrangle. United States Board on Geographic Names (1933a, p. 225) rejected the name "East Fork" for present Clover Creek, and (1962, p. 10) rejected the name "Clover Creek" for present

East Fork.

(2) *stream,* flows nearly 3 miles to Horse Creek (1) 5.5 miles southwest of Mineral King (lat. 36°24'10" N, long. 118°40'30" W). Named on Mineral King (1956) 15' quadrangle.

Clover Meadow [TULARE]:

(1) *area,* 7.5 miles south-southeast of Monache Mountain along Crag Creek (lat. 36°06'40" N, long. 118°07'30" W). Named on Monache Mountain (1956) 15' quadrangle.

(2) *area,* 6.25 miles northeast of California Hot Springs (lat. 35°56'20" N, long. 118°35'05" W; at N line sec. 13, T 23 S, R 31 E). Named on California Hot Springs (1958) 15' quadrangle.

Clovis [FRESNO]: *city,* 6.5 miles northeast of downtown Fresno (lat. 36°49'25" N, long. 119°42' W; around SE cor. sec. 5, T 13 S, R 21 E). Named on Clovis (1964) 7.5' quadrangle. Officials of Southern Pacific Railroad named the station at the place in 1889 for Clovis Cole, owner of a large wheat ranch that the railroad crossed with a branch line in 1889 (Gudde, 1949, p. 71). Postal authorities established Clovis post office in 1895 (Frickstad, p. 32), and the city incorporated in 1912. They established Garfield post office 12 miles northeast of Fresno in 1891 and discontinued it in 1897 when they moved the service Clovis (Salley, p. 82).

Clyde: see **Norman Clyde Peak**, under **Middle Palisade** [FRESNO].

Coalinga [FRESNO]: *town,* 52 miles southwest of Fresno in Pleasant Valley (lat. 36°08'25" N, long. 120°21'35" W; in and near sec. 32, T 20 S, R 15 E). Named on Coalinga (1956) 7.5' quadrangle. The place was called Coaling Station after officials of Southern Pacific Railroad had a branch line built to the site in 1888 to carry lignitic coal from nearby mines; according to local tradition, the present name was coined when a railroad official added the letter "a" to the word "coaling" (Gudde, 1949, p. 72). Postal authorities established Coalinga post office in 1899 (Frickstad, p. 32), and the town incorporated in 1906. Called Coalingo on California (1891) map, which shows a place called Dathol located along the railroad east of present Coalinga about halfway to Huron. California Division of Highways' (1934) map shows a place called Leroy situated 3.5 miles southwest of Coalinga along Wartham (present Warthan) Creek (near E line sec. 13, T 21 S, R 14 E).

Coalinga Mineral Springs [FRESNO]: *locality,* 11 miles west of Coalinga (lat. 36°08'40" N, long. 120°33'15" W; sec. 34, T 20 S, R 13 E); the place is in Hot Spring Canyon. Named on Sherman Peak (1969) 7.5' quadrangle. Called Fresno Hot Springs on Priest Valley (1915) 30' quadrangle. About 20 springs issue from the canyon wall, and water is piped 0.5 mile from the springs to a resort (Berkstresser, p. A-5). California Mining Bureau's (1909b) map shows a place called Rogers located near present Coalinga Mineral Springs. Postal authorities established Rogers post office in 1897 and discontinued it in 1909 (Frickstad, p. 37).

Coalinga Nose [FRESNO]: *ridge,* northeast-trending, 1.5 miles long, 6 miles east-northeast of Coalinga on Anticline Ridge (lat. 36°11'15" N, long. 120°16'15" W; mainly in sec. 18, T 20 S, R 16 E). Named on Coalinga (1956) 7.5' quadrangle.

Coalinga Sulphur Baths [FRESNO]: *locality,* 2.5 miles west-southwest of Coalinga (lat. 36°07'20" N, long. 120°23'50" W; near NW cor. sec. 7, T 21 S, R 15 E). Named on Coalinga (1956) 15' quadrangle. Mineral water comes from a well that was drilled in 1906 for oil, but which tapped an artesian flow of hot sulphur water instead (Laizure, p. 320).

Coalinga Valley: see **Pleasant Valley** [FRESNO].

Coalingo: see **Coalinga** [FRESNO].

Coaling Station: see **Coalinga** [FRESNO].

Coalmine Canyon [FRESNO]: *canyon,* drained by a stream that flows 2.25 miles to Pleasant Valley 3.5 miles west-northwest of Coalinga (lat. 36°09'30" N, long. 120°24'50" W; sec. 26, T 30 S, R 14 E). Named on Alcalde Hills (1969) 7.5' quadrangle.

Coal Oil Canyon [KERN]: *canyon,* drained by a stream that flows 2.5 miles to lowlands 5 miles west-southwest of Mettler (lat. 35° 01'45" N, long. 119°02'50" W; near E line sec. 19, T 11 N, R 20 W). Named on Coal Oil Canyon (1955) 7.5' quadrangle. Buena Vista Lake (1912) 30' quadrangle has the form "Coaloil Canyon" for the name.

Coarse Gold Creek [KERN-TULARE]: *stream,* heads in Kern County and flows 4.5 miles to White River (1) 6.25 miles south-southeast of Fountain Springs in Tulare County (lat. 35°48'25" N, long. 118°52'30" W; near E line sec. 30, T 24 S, R 29 E). Named on Quincy School (1965) and White River (1965) 7.5' quadrangles.

Cobbs Island [FRESNO]: *island,* 11 miles north of downtown Fresno in San Joaquin River (lat. 36°55' N, long. 119°46' W; sec. 2, 3, T 12 S, R 20 E). Named on Herndon (1965) 15' quadrangle.

Cochran Spring [KERN]: *spring,* nearly 3 miles northwest of Skinner Peak (lat. 35°35'45" N, long. 118°09'40" W). Named on Cane Canyon (1972) 7.5' quadrangle.

Cockscomb: see **Sharktooth Peak** [FRESNO].

Code: see **Terese** [KERN].

Coffee Canyon [KERN]: *canyon,* 5 miles long, along Poso Creek above a point 3.5 miles south-southeast of Knob Hill (lat. 35°31' N, long. 118°55' W; sec. 1, T 28 S, R 28 E). Named on Knob Hill (1965) and Pine Mountain (1965) 7.5' quadrangles.

Coffee Canyon [TULARE]: *canyon,* drained by a stream that flows nearly 3 miles to Middle Fork Tule River 7.5 miles west of Camp Nelson (lat. 36°09'05" N, long. 118°44'15" W). Named on Camp Nelson (1956) 15' quadrangle.

Coffee Creek [KERN]: *stream,* flows 2.5 miles to Little Poso Creek 6 miles north of Democrat Hot Springs (lat. 35°36'55" N, long. 118°40'55" W; near N line sec. 6, T 27 S, R 31 E). Named on Democrat Hot Springs (1972) 7.5' quadrangle.

Coffee Mill Meadow [TULARE]: *area,* 3.5 miles east of Camp Nelson (lat. 36°08'20" N, long. 118°32'50" W; sec. 31, T 20 S, R 32 E). Named on Camp Nelson (1956) 15' quadrangle.

Coffeepot Canyon [TULARE]: *canyon,* drained by a stream that flows 3.25 miles to East Fork Kaweah River 9 miles east-southeast of Kaweah (lat. 36°25'30" N, long. 118°46' W; near NE cor. sec. 25, T 17 S, R 29 E). Named on Kaweah (1957) and Mineral King (1956) 15' quadrangles. The name is said to be from an old coffeepot that hunters found at the place (Browning, p. 43). United States Board on Geographic Names (1933a, p. 227) approved the name "Coffeepot Canyon Creek" for the stream in the canyon.

Coffeepot Canyon Creek: see **Coffeepot Canyon** [TULARE].

Coffin Spring [KERN]: *spring,* 2.5 miles east-southeast of Caliente (lat. 35°16'55" N, long. 118°35'05" W; at S line sec. 30, T 30 S, R 32 E). Named on Oiler Peak (1972) 7.5' quadrangle.

Coho Creek [TULARE]: *stream,* flows 8.5 miles to White River (1) 6 miles south-southeast of Fountain Springs (lat. 35°48'35" N, long. 118°52'40" W; sec. 30, T 24 S, R 29 E). Named on Gibbon Peak (1965), Quincy School (1965), and White River (1965) 7.5' quadrangles. Called Coko Creek on White River (1936) 15' quadrangle, but United States Board on Geographic Names (1966b, p. 4) rejected this name for the feature.

Coko Creek: see **Coho Creek** [TULARE].

Colby Lake [TULARE]: *lake,* 0.5 mile long, 2.5 miles north-northeast of Triple Divide Peak (lat. 36°37'40" N, long. 118°30'45" W); the lake is 1 mile northwest of Colby Pass. Named on Triple Divide Peak (1956) 15' quadrangle. The name commemorates William E. Colby of the Sierra Club; the club proposed the name in 1927 for what before that time was called Hutchinson Lake (Browning. p. 43).

Colby Meadow [FRESNO]: *area,* 5.25 miles north of Mount Goddard in Evolution Valley (lat. 37°10'45" N, long. 118°43'30" W). Named on Mount Goddard (1948) 15' quadrangle. Forest Service officials named the place in 1915 for William E. Colby of the Sierra Club (Farquhar, 1923, p. 388).

Colby Pass [TULARE]: *pass,* 2.5 miles northeast of Triple Divide Peak on Great Western Divide (lat. 36°37'05" N, long. 118°30' W). Named on Mount Whitney (1956) and Triple Divide Peak (1956) 15' quadrangles. A party from the Sierra Club discovered the route through the pass in 1912 and named the place for the leader of the group, William E. Colby (Farquhar, 1923, p. 388). United States Board on Geographic Names (1990, p. 6) approved the name "Centennial Peak" for a high point located 1 mile northeast of Colby Pass; the name commemorates the one-hundredth anniversary of Sequoia National Park.

Cold Canyon Creek: see **Cold Creek** [FRESNO].

Cold Creek [FRESNO]: *stream,* flows 8.5 miles to Lake Thomas A. Edison 12 miles east-northeast of Kaiser Peak (lat. 37°22'50" N, long. 119°00'05" W). Named on Kaiser Peak (1953) and Mount Abbot (1953) 15' quadrangles. Called Cold Canyon Creek on Lippincott's (1902) map. United States Board on Geographic Names (1959, p. 2) rejected the name "Cole Creek" for the feature.

Cold Creek [TULARE]: *stream,* flows 7 miles to Ninemile Creek 2.5 miles east-northeast of Hockett Peak (lat. 36°13'45" N, long. 118° 20'20" W); the stream goes through Cold Meadows. Named on Hockett Peak (1956) and Kern Peak (1956) 15' quadrangles.

Cold Meadows [TULARE]: *area,* nearly 2 miles south-southwest of Kern Peak (lat. 36°17'10" N, long. 118°18' W); the place is along Cold Creek. Named on Kern Peak (1956) 15' quadrangle.

Cold Spring [FRESNO]: *spring,* 3 miles east-northeast of Castle Mountain (lat. 35°57'30" N, long. 120°17'30" W; sec. 6, T 23 S, R 16 E). Named on The Dark Hole (1961) 7.5' quadrangle.

Cold Spring [KERN]:

(1) *spring,* 5 miles north of Democrat Hot Springs (lat. 35°35'55" N, long. 118°38'50" W). Named on Democrat Hot Springs (1972) 7.5' quadrangle.

(2) *spring,* 1 mile north-northwest of Piute Peak (lat. 35°28' N, long. 118°23'45" W; near E line sec. 26, T 28 S, R 33 E). Named on Piute Peak (1972) 7.5' quadrangle.

Cold Spring [TULARE]: *spring,* 7 miles southeast of California Hot Springs (lat. 35°48'30" N, long. 118°34'55" W; sec. 25, T 24 S, R 31 E). Named on California Hot Springs (1958) 15' quadrangle.

Cold Spring: see **North Cold Spring** [TULARE].

Cold Springs Canyon [KERN]: *canyon,* drained by a stream that flows 2 miles to Cuddy Canyon 6 miles west of Lebec (lat. 34°49'15" N, long. 118°58'30" W; at W line sec. 35, T 9 N, R 20 W). Named on Frazier Mountain (1958) 7.5' quadrangle.

Cold Springs Creek [TULARE]: *stream,* flows 4 miles to a presently unnamed stream—called Nigger Rube Creek on Tobias Peak (1936) 30' quadrangle—3.5 miles north-northwest of California Hot Springs (lat. 35°55'20" N, long. 118°42'10" W; sec. 14, T 23 S, R 30 E); the stream heads near Cold Springs Peak. Named on California Hot Springs (1958) 15' quadrangle. Called Cold Spring Cr. on Tobias Peak (1936) 30' quadrangle.

Cold Springs Peak [TULARE]: *peak,* 3.5 miles north-northeast of California Hot Springs (lat. 35°55'50" N, long. 118°38'50" W; sec. 17, T 23 S, R 31 E); the peak is near the head of Cold Springs Creek. Named on California Hot Springs (1958) 15' quadrangle. Called Cold Spring Pk. on Tobias Peak (1936) 30' quadrangle.

Cold Springs Saddle [TULARE]: *pass,* 4 miles north-northeast of California Hot Springs (lat. 35°56'05" N, long. 118°38'50" W; sec. 17, T 23 S, R 31 E); the pass is near the head of Cold Springs Creek. Name on California Hot Springs (1958) 15' quadrangle. Called Cold Spring Saddle on Tobias Peak (1936) 30' quadrangle.

Cold Sulfur Spring [TULARE]: *spring,* 5.25 miles east of Auckland along Dry Creek (1) (lat. 36°34'55" N, long. 119°00'35" W; near S line sec. 26, T 15 S, R 27 E). Named on Auckland (1966) 7.5' quadrangle.

Cole Creek: see **Cold Creek** [FRESNO].

Cole Slough [FRESNO-KINGS]: *water feature,* diverges from Kings River 12 miles north-northeast of Hanford in Kings County and extends for 9 miles to rejoin the river 1 mile east-southeast of Laton in Fresno County (lat. 36°25'50" N, long. 119°40'15" W; near SW cor. sec. 23, T 17 S, R 21 E). Named on Burris Park (1954) and Laton (1953) 7.5' quadrangles.

Cole Spring [FRESNO]: *spring,* 5.5 miles north of Trimmer (lat. 36° 59'05" N, long. 119°16'45" W; sec. 7, T 11 S, R 25 E). Named on Trimmer (1965) 7.5' quadrangle. On Watts Valley (1942) 15' quadrangle, the name applies to at a place located 0.5 mile farther east-northeast.

College Lake [FRESNO]: *lake,* 300 feet long, 0.5 mile east-southeast of Kaiser Peak (lat. 37°17'35" N, long. 119°10'35" W; sec. 30, T 7 S, R 26 E); the lake is 1.5 miles north of College Rock. Named on Kaiser Peak (1953) 15' quadrangle.

College Rock [FRESNO]: *relief feature,* 1.5 miles south-southeast of Kaiser Peak (lat. 37°16'20" N, long. 119°10'25" W; sec. 31, T 7 S, R 26 E). Altitude 9076 feet. Named on Kaiser Peak (1953) 15' quadrangle.

Collier Cove [TULARE]: *valley,* 4.5 miles south-southeast of Auckland (lat. 36°31'30" N, long. 119°05' W; in and near sec. 19, T 16 S, R 27 E); the valley is along Collier Creek. Named on Auckland (1966) 7.5' quadrangle.

Collier Creek [TULARE]: *stream,* flows nearly 4 miles to Cottonwood Creek 3.5 miles south of Auckland (lat. 36°32'20" N, long. 119°06'35" W; sec. 14, T 16 S, R 26 E). Named on Auckland (1966) 7.5' quadrangle.

Collins Creek [FRESNO]: *stream,* heads 1.5 miles northeast of Centerville and flows 8 miles to Kings River 2.5 miles southeast of Sanger (lat. 36°40'20" N, long. 119°31'40" W; sec. 36, T 14 S, R 22 E). Named on Sanger (1965) and Wahtoke (1966) 7.5' quadrangles.

Collins Meadow: see **Crown Valley** [FRESNO].

Collins Spring: see **Sulphur Springs** [FRESNO].

Collis: see **Kerman** [FRESNO].

Colony Meadow [TULARE]: *stream,* 3.5 miles south-southeast of Shell Mountain (lat. 36°38'35" N, long. 118°46'40" W; at S line sec. 1, T 15 S, R 29 E). Named on Giant Forest (1956) 15' quadrangle. The name recalls Kaweah Colony (Gudde, 1949, p. 75).

Colony Peak [TULARE]: *peak,* 2.5 miles east-southeast of Yucca Mountain (lat. 36°33'45" N, long. 118°48'15" W). Altitude 6132 feet. Named on Giant Forest (1956) 15' quadrangle. The name commemorates Kaweah Cooperative Commonwealth Colony, organized to cut giant redwoods for lumber in 1886 (United States Board on Geographic Names, 1933a, p. 230).

Colorado Camp [KERN]: *locality,* 3.5 miles northwest of Garlock (lat. 35°26'50" N, long. 117°49'35" W). Named on Garlock (1967) 7.5' quadrangle.

Colored Lady: see **Painted Lady** [FRESNO].

Colorful Creek: see **Salt Creek** [KERN] (2).

Colosseum Mountain [FRESNO]: *peak,* 3.25 miles southeast of Mount Pinchot on Fresno-Inyo County line (lat. 36°54'30" N, long. 118°22'10" W). Altitude 12,473 feet. Named on Mount Pinchot (1953) 15' quadrangle.

Colt Lake [FRESNO]: *lake,* 450 feet long, 1 mile north-northwest of Blackcap Mountain (lat. 37°05'10" N, long. 118°47'50" W). Named on Blackcap Mountain (1953) 15' quadrangle. William A. Dill of California Department of Fish and Game chose the name in 1948 because the outline of the lake on a map has the shape of a colt's head, and because the feature is near Horsehead Lake (Browning, p. 44).

Columbine Lake [TULARE]: *lake,* 0.5 mile long, 2.5 miles east-northeast of Mineral King (lat. 36°27'45" N, long. 118°33' W). Named on Mineral King (1956) 15' quadrangle. Joseph Palmer, a pioneer in the neighborhood, named the lake for the abundance of columbine plants growing around it (Gudde, 1949, p. 75).

Columbine Peak [FRESNO]: *peak,* 10 miles east of Mount Goddard (lat. 37°05'20" N, long. 118°32'25" W). Altitude 12,652 feet. Named on Mount Goddard (1948) 15' quadrangle. The Sierra Club proposed the name before 1939; columbine plants grow nearly to the summit of the peak (Browning, p. 44).

Colvin Mountain [TULARE]: *ridge,* south-southeast-trending, 3.5 miles long, 3.5 miles northwest of Woodlake (lat. 36°26'40" N, long. 119°08'50" W). Named on Exeter (1952) 15' quadrangle.

Colvin Ranch: see **Redbanks** [TULARE].

Comanche Creek [KERN]: *stream,* flows 13 miles to lowlands 5 miles south of Arvin (lat. 35°08'15" N, long. 118°48'45" W). Named on Arvin (1955), Tejon Hills (1955), and Tejon Ranch (1966) 7.5' quadrangles. The name commemorates a man who was known as Comanche, and who was believed to be part Comanche Indian—the man lived at a rancheria at Comanche Point (Latta, 1976, p. 199, 201).

Comanche Meadow [TULARE]: *area,* 12 miles northwest of Triple Divide Peak (lat. 36°42'45" N, long. 118°41'05" W; near N line sec. 14, T 14 S, R 30 E). Named on Triple Divide Peak (1956) 15' quadrangle.

Comanche Point [KERN]: *relief feature,* 5 miles south of Arvin at the north end of Tejon Hills (lat. 35°08' N, long. 118°49'15" W); the feature is west of lower reaches of Comanche Creek. Named on Arvin (1955) and Tejon Hills (1955) 7.5' quadrangles.

Comanche Spring [KERN]: *spring,* 5.25 miles south of Arvin (lat. 35°07'55" N, long. 118°48'45" W); the spring is along Comanche Creek. Named on Arvin (1955) 7.5' quadrangle.

Comb Creek [FRESNO]: *stream,* flows 3.5 miles to Lewis Creek (2) 12.5 miles southwest of Marion Peak (lat. 36°49'50" N, long. 118° 40'55" W); the stream heads on Comb Spur. Named on Marion Peak (1953) 15' quadrangle.

Comb Rocks [TULARE]: *relief feature,* 1 mile east-northeast of Kaweah (lat. 36°28'35" N, long. 118°54' W; sec. 1, T 17 S, R 28 E). Named on Kaweah (1957) 15' quadrangle.

Comb Spur [FRESNO]: *ridge,* southeast-trending, 2.5 miles long, 9 miles southwest of Marion Peak (lat. 36°51'15" N, long. 118°37'40" W). Named on Marion Peak (1953) 15' quadrangle.

Compressor Hot Springs: see **Miracle Hot Springs** [KERN].

Condor: see **Camp Condor** [KERN].

Condor Peak [FRESNO]: *peak,* 18 miles northwest of Coalinga (lat. 36°19' N, long. 120°37' W; sec. 36, T 18 S, R 12 E). Altitude 4970 feet. Named on Santa Rita Peak (1969) 7.5' quadrangle.

Conejo [FRESNO]: *settlement,* 7.25 miles west-southwest of Selma (lat. 36°31' N, long. 119°43'10" W; near NE cor. sec. 30, T 16 S, R 21 E). Named on Conejo (1963) 7.5' quadrangle. Postal authorities established Conejo post office in 1898 and discontinued it in 1920 (Frickstad, p. 32).

Cone River: see **Kern-Kaweah River** [TULARE].

Conifer: see **Camp Conifer** [TULARE].

Conifer Ridge [TULARE]: *ridge,* southwest-trending, 3 miles long, nearly 7 miles west of Mineral King (lat. 36°27'45" N, long. 118° 42'50" W). Named on Mineral King (1956) 15' quadrangle. H.Y. Alles suggested the name—conifers grow on the ridge (Browning, p. 44).

Connecting Slough [KERN]: *water feature,* center 2 miles southeast of Millux (lat. 35°10' N, long. 119°10' W); the feature connects Buena Vista Lake Bed to Kern Lake Bed. Named on Conner (1954) and Millux (1954) 7.5' quadrangles.

Conner [KERN]: *locality,* 4.5 miles east of Millux along Sunset Railroad (lat. 35°10'50" N, long. 119°06'55" W; at S line sec. 31, T 31 S, R 27 E). Named on Conner (1954) 7.5' quadrangle. California Mining Bureau's (1917c) map shows a place called Progress located about 2 miles north-northeast of Conner along the railroad. Postal authorities established Progress post office 1913 and discontinued it in 1915 (Frickstad, p. 58).

Connor Station: see **Porterville** [TULARE].

Converse: see **Converse Basin** [FRESNO].

Converse Basin [FRESNO]: *area,* 3 miles west-northwest of Hume (lat. 36°48' N, long. 118°58' W); the place is on upper reaches of Converse Creek southwest of Converse Mountain. Named on Tehipite Dome (1952) 15' quadrangle. The name commemorates Charles F. Converse, who claimed the area in the 1860's (Johnston, p. 58). California Mining Bureau's (1917a) map shows a place called Converse in the area.

Converse Creek [FRESNO]: *stream,* flows 6 miles to Kings River 7 miles northwest of Hume (lat. 36°51'30" N, long. 119°00' W); the stream heads in Converse Basin. Named on Tehipite Dome (1952) 15' quadrangle.

Converse Ferry: see **Friant** [FRESNO].

Converse Mountain [FRESNO]: *peak,* 3 miles northwest of Hume (lat. 36°49'10" N, long. 118°56'45" W); the peak is northeast of Converse Basin. Altitude 7208 feet. Named on Tehipite Dome (1952) 15' quadrangle.

Cook: see **Alex Cook Spring** [KERN].

Cook Peak [KERN]: *peak,* 3.5 miles northeast of Bodfish (lat. 35°37'20" N, long. 118°26'15" W; sec. 33, T 26 S, R 33 E). Altitude 5405 feet. Named on Lake Isabella South (1972) 7.5' quadrangle. Called Cook's Pt. on Wheeler's (1875-1878) map.

Cooksie Canyon [TULARE]: *canyon,* drained by a stream that flows 0.5 mile to White River (1) nearly 3 miles south of California Hot Springs (lat. 35°50'20" N, long. 118°39'55" W; sec. 18, T 24 S, R 31 E). Named on California Hot Springs (1958) 15' quadrangle.

Cooks Peak [KERN]: *peak,* 1.5 miles south of Alta Sierra (lat. 35°42'20" N, long. 118°52'50" W; near S line sec. 33, T 25 S, R 32 E). Altitude 6921 feet. Named on Alta Sierra (1972) 7.5' quadrangle.

Cook's Point: see **Cook Peak** [KERN].

Coombs: see **The Loop** [KERN].

Coon Creek [FRESNO]: *stream,* flows about 2.5 miles to Huntington Lake (1) 4.25 miles east-northeast of the town of Big Creek (lat. 37°14'05" N, long. 119°10'25" W; sec. 18, T 8 S, R 26 E). Named on Huntington Lake (1953) 15' quadrangle.

Coon Spring [TULARE]: *spring,* 6 miles southeast of Auckland (lat. 36°31'20" N, long. 119°02'25" W; sec. 21, T 16 S, R 27 E). Named on Auckland (1966) 7.5' quadrangle.

Cooper Canyon [FRESNO]: *canyon,* drained by a stream that flows 7.5 miles to Warthan Creek 3.25 miles southwest of Coalinga (lat. 36°06'20" N, long. 120°24' W; sec. 13, T 21 S, R 14 E). Named on Alcalde Hills (1969) and Curry Mountain (1969) 7.5' quadrangles. Arnold and Anderson (1908, p. 16) called the feature Anticline Canyon because "its course across sections 2, 11, 12 is practically coincident with an anticline."

Copper Canyon: see **Cloud Canyon** [TULARE]: **Deadman Canyon** [TULARE] (1).

Copper Creek [FRESNO]: *stream,* flows 5.25 miles to South Fork Kings River 12 miles south-southwest of Marion Peak in Kings Canyon (lat. 36°47'40" N, long. 118°34'45" W). Named on Marion Peak (1953) 15' quadrangle. Copper deposits were known in the neighborhood as early as the 1860's, and E.C. Winchell called the stream Malachite Creek in 1868—giving it the name of a copper mineral; the name "Copper Creek" was in use in 1890, when two men operated a small mine by the stream (Browning, p. 46).

Copper Mountain: see **Laurel Mountain** [KERN].

Corbett Lake [FRESNO]: *lake,* 700 feet long, 7.5 miles east of Kaiser Peak (lat. 37°17'25" N, long. 119°03'05" W). Named on Kaiser Peak (1953) 15' quadrangle.

Corcoran [KINGS]: *town,* 17 miles south-southeast of Hanford (lat. 36°05'50" N, long. 119°33'45" W; in and near sec. 14, 23, T 21 S, R 22 E). Named on Corcoran (1954) 7.5' quadrangle. Postal authorities established Corcoran post office in 1901; the name is for a civil engineer of Atchison, Topeka and Santa Fe Railroad (Salley, p. 50). The town incorporated in 1914.

Corcoran: see **South Corcoran** [KINGS].

Corcoran Mountain: see **Mount Corcoran** [TULARE].

Corlew Meadows [FRESNO]: *area,* 6 miles west-southwest of Shaver Lake Heights (present town of Shaver Lake) (lat. 37°04'45" N, long. 119°25'30" W; sec. 11, 12, T 10 S, R 23 E). Named on Shaver Lake (1953) 15' quadrangle. Kaiser (1904) 30' quadrangle shows Corlew Mill in Corlew Meadow.

Corlew Mill: see **Corlew Meadows** [FRESNO].

Corlew Mountain [FRESNO]: *ridge,* west-trending, 2 miles long, 3 miles southwest of Prather (lat. 37°00'10" N, long. 119°33' W; in and near sec. 2, 3, T 11 S, R 22 E). Named on Millerton Lake East (1965) 7.5' quadrangle.

Corn Camp [KERN]: *locality,* 9 miles northeast of McKittrick (lat. 35°24'30" N, long. 119°31'05" W; at E line sec. 17, T 29 S, R 23 E). Named on Lokern (1954) 7.5' quadrangle.

Corn Jack Peak [TULARE]: *peak,* nearly 3 miles east of Tucker Mountain (lat. 36°38'20" N, long. 119°09'30" W; near W line sec. 9, T 15 S, R 26 E). Altitude 2386 feet. Named on Tucker Mountain (1966) 7.5' quadrangle.

Cornwell [KINGS]: *locality,* 7 miles north of Lemoore along Atchison, Topeka and Santa Fe Railroad (lat. 36°23'55" N, long. 119°46'45" W). Named on Riverdale (1927) 7.5' quadrangle. Called Lynn on California Mining Bureau's (1917b) map. California Division of Highways' (1934) map shows Lynn located about 1 mile east of Cornwell along the railroad.

Coronet Lake [FRESNO]: *lake,* 800 feet long, 4 miles south-southwest of Mount Abbot (lat. 37°20' N, long. 118°48'50" W). Named on Mount Abbot (1953) 15' quadrangle.

Corral Canyon [KERN]: *canyon,* drained by a stream that flows 4 miles to Little Creek (1) 5 miles north-northwest of Knob Hill (lat. 35°37'35" N, long. 118°59'15" W; sec. 32, T 26 S, R 28 E). Named on Knob Hill (1965) 7.5' quadrangle.

Corral Creek [TULARE]: *stream,* flows 5.5 miles to Kern River nearly 6 miles south-southeast of Fairview (lat. 35°51' N, long. 118°27'05" W; near NW cor. sec. 17, T 24 S, R 33 E). Named on Kernville (1956) 15' quadrangle.

Corral Creek Campground [TULARE]: *locality,* 5.5 miles south-southeast of Fairview (lat. 35°51'20" N, long. 118°27' W; sec. 8, T 24 S, R 33 E); the place is near the mouth of Corral Creek. Named on Kernville (1956) 15' quadrangle.

Corral Hill [TULARE]: *peak,* 4 miles northwest of California Hot Springs on Pinnell Camp Ridge (lat. 35°55'20" N, long. 118°43'10" W; near SE cor. sec. 15, T 23 S, R 30 E). Named on California Hot Springs (1958) 15' quadrangle.

Corral Meadow [FRESNO]: *area,* south of Shaver Lake (lat. 37°06'45" N, long. 119°18'15" W; in and near sec. 25, 36, T 9 S, R 24 E). Named on Kaiser (1904) 30' quadrangle. Water of an enlarged Shaver Lake now covers the place.

Corral Meadow [TULARE]: *area,* 12.5 miles south of Hockett Peak (lat. 36°02'15" N, long. 118°22'15" W). Named on Hockett Peak (1956) 15' quadrangle.

Corral Meadow: see **Burton Camp** [TULARE].

Corral Mountain [FRESNO]: *peak,* 7.25 miles west-northwest of Blackcap Mountain (lat. 37°06'15" N, long. 118°55' W; sec. 33, T 9 S, R 28 E). Altitude 9698 feet. Named on Blackcap Mountain (1953) 15' quadrangle.

Corral Spring [KERN]: *spring,* 12 miles north-northwest of Mojave (lat. 35°12'50" N, long. 118°14'35" W; near S line sec. 20, T 31 S, R 35 E). Named on Cache Peak (1973) 7.5' quadrangle.

Cortez Canyon [KERN]: *canyon,* drained by a stream that flows 6.25 miles to the canyon of Kelso Creek 7 miles west of Skinner Peak (lat. 35°33'15" N, long. 118°14'30" W; sec. 29, T 27 S, R 35 E). Named on Cane Canyon (1972) and Woolstalf Creek (1972) 7.5' quadrangles.

Cortez Spring [KERN]: *spring,* 10 miles south of Weldon (lat. 35° 30'45" N, long. 118°17'55" W; near SW cor. sec. 11, T 28 S, R 34 E); the spring is near the head of Cortez Canyon. Named on Woolstalf Creek (1972) 7.5' quadrangle.

Cottage: see **Visalia** [TULARE].

Cotter: see **Mount Cotter** [FRESNO].

Cotton Center [TULARE]: *locality,* 3.5 miles east-southeast of Woodville (lat. 36°04'05" N, long. 119°08'35" W; near SW cor. sec. 26, T 21 S, R 26 E). Named on Woodville (1950) 7.5' quadrangle.

Cotton Lake [FRESNO]: *lake,* 800 feet long, 9 miles northwest of Mount Abbot (lat. 37°29'05" N, long. 118°53'30" W). Named on Mount Abbot (1953) 15' quadrangle.

Cottonwood Canyon [KERN]: *canyon,* 5.5 miles long, drained by Cottonwood Creek (1) above a point 3.25 miles north-northeast of Orchard Peak (lat. 35°46'55" N, long. 120°06'55" W; near W line sec. 2, T 25 S, T 17 E); the canyon heads at Cottonwood Pass in San Luis Obispo County. Named on Tent Hills (1942) 7.5' quadrangle.

Cottonwood Canyon: see **Los Alamos Creek** [KERN].

Cottonwood Creek [KERN]:

(1) *stream,* flows 4.5 miles to Kings County 4 miles north-northeast of Orchard Peak (lat. 35°47'20" N, long. 120°06'20" W; at N line sec. 2, T 25 S, R 17 E); the stream drains Cottonwood Canyon. Named on Pyramid Hills (1953) and Tent Hills (1942) 7.5' quadrangles.

(2) *stream,* formed by the confluence of North Fork and South Fork, flows 9 miles to Kern River 4.5 miles west of Mount Adelaide (lat. 35°25'30" N, long. 118°49'30" W; at W line sec. 12, T 29 S, R 29 E). Named on Mount Adelaide (1972) and Rio Bravo Ranch (1954) 7.5' quadrangles. North Fork is 8.5 miles long and is named on Mount Adelaide (1972) 7.5' quadrangle. United States Board on Geographic Names (1975b, p. 9) gave the variant names "Walkers Creek" and "North Fork Cottonwood Creek" for North Fork. South Fork is 12.5 miles long and is named on Breckenridge Mountain (1972) and Mount Adelaide (1972) 7.5' quadrangles.

(3) *stream,* flows 18 miles to Jawbone Canyon 1.5 miles north of Cross Mountain (lat. 35°18' N, long. 118°08'20" W; sec. 29, T 30 S, R 36 E). Named on Claraville (1972), Cross Mountain (1972), and Emerald Mountain (1972) 7.5' quadrangles.

(4) *stream,* flows 11.5 miles to lowlands 10.5 miles west of the village of Willow Springs (lat. 34°54'30" N, long. 118°28'15" W; sec. 33, T 10 N, R 15 W). Named on Fairmont Butte (1965), Liebre Twins (1965), and Tylerhorse Canyon (1965) 7.5' quadrangles.

Cottonwood Creek [TULARE]: *stream* and *dry wash,* extends for 38 miles to join Elbow Creek and form Cross Creek (1) 9 miles northwest of Visalia (lat. 36°25'55" N, long. 119°23'45" W; sec. 20, T 17 S, R 24 E). Named on Exeter (1952) and Visalia (1949) 15' quadrangles, and on Auckland (1966) and Stokes Mountain (1966) 7.5' quadrangles.

Cottonwood Creek, Central Fork: see **Crystal Creek** [KERN].

Cottonwood Pass [TULARE]: *pass,* 14 miles north-northwest of Olancha Peak on Tulare-Inyo County line (lat. 36°27'10" N, long. 118°12'50" W; sec. 17, T 17 S, R 35 E); the pass is at the head of a branch of a Cottonwood Creek that is in Inyo County. Named on Olancha (1956) 15' quadrangle. The feature was known locally as Chicken Spring Pass (Browning, p. 47).

Cottonwood Spring [KERN]: *spring,* 4.25 miles east-northeast of Mount Adelaide (lat. 35°27'10" N, long. 118°40'25" W; near E line sec. 31, T 28 S, R 31 E). Named on Mount Adelaide (1972) 7.5' quadrangle.

Cottonwood Springs Creek [FRESNO]: *stream,* flows 1.25 miles to Kings River 5.5 miles west-southwest of Balch Camp (lat. 36°52'15" N, long. 119°12'35" W; sec. 23, T 12 S, R 25 E). Named on Patterson Mountain (1952) 15' quadrangle.

Cottonwood Station [KERN]: *locality,* 9 miles south of Bakersfield (lat. 35°14'45" N, long. 118°59' W; at W line sec. 9, T 31 S, R 28 E). Named on Caliente (1914) 30' quadrangle.

Cougar Camp [TULARE]: *locality,* 6.25 miles north of California Hot Springs (lat. 35°58'10" N, long. 118°41' W; sec. 36, T 22 S, R 30 E).

Named on California Hot Springs (1958) 15' quadrangle.

Council Lake [FRESNO]: *lake,* 1000 feet long, 7 miles south of Mount Abbot (lat. 37°17'05" N, long. 118°48'20" W). Named on Mount Abbot (1953) 15' quadrangle.

County Line Canyon [KERN]: *canyon,* drained by a stream that flows 1 mile to Indian Wells Valley 11.5 miles north-northwest of Inyokern (lat. 35°47'45" N, long. 117°53'45" W; sec. 4, T 25 S, R 38 E); the feature is on Kern-Inyo County line. Named on Little Lake (1954) 15' quadrangle.

County Well [KERN]: *well,* 2.5 miles east of present Blackwells Corner (lat. 35°36'55" N, long. 119°49'30" W). Named on Lost Hills (1914) 30' quadrangle.

Courtright Reservoir [FRESNO]: *intermittent lake,* behind a dam on Helms Creek 10 miles west of Blackcap Mountain (lat. 37°04'45" N, long. 118°58'10" W; on E line sec. 12, T 10 S, R 27 E). Named on Blackcap Mountain (1953) 15' quadrangle. The name is for H.H. Courtright, president of San Joaquin Light and Power Corporation and general manager of Pacific Gas and Electric Company (Browning, p. 48).

Cove Canyon [TULARE]: *canyon,* drained by a stream that flows 2.25 miles to White River (1) 3 miles south-southwest of California Hot Springs (lat. 35°50'20" N, long. 118°41'35" W; sec. 13, T 24 S, R 30 E). Named on California Hot Springs (1958) 15' quadrangle.

Covel: see **Easton** [FRESNO].

Covington Mountain: see **Tylerhorse Canyon** [KERN].

Cow Canyon [KERN]: *canyon,* drained by a stream that flows 4.5 miles to Canebrake Creek 6.25 miles north-northwest of Walker Pass (lat. 35°44'35" N, long. 118°04'45" W; sec. 23, T 25 S, R 36 E). Named on Walker Pass (1972) 7.5' quadrangle. Called Burnt House Canyon on Onyx (1943) 15' quadrangle, and United States Board on Geographic Names (1975b, p. 9) gave this name as a variant.

Cow Canyon [TULARE]: *canyon,* drained by a stream that flows 3.5 miles to South Fork Kern River 3.5 miles east-southeast of Monache Mountain (lat. 36°11' N, long. 118°08'20" W; sec. 13, T 20 S, R 35 E). Named on Monache Mountain (1956) 15' quadrangle.

Cow Chip Spring [KERN]: *spring,* 7.25 miles west of Liebre Twins (lat. 34°57'20" N, long. 118°41'50" W; sec. 9, T 10 N, R 17 W). Named on Winters Ridge (1966) 7.5' quadrangle.

Cow Chip Spring: see **Lower Cow Chip Spring** [KERN].

Cow Cove [KERN]: *canyon,* drained by a stream that flows less than 1 mile to Heck Canyon 5.5 miles east-northeast of Caliente (lat. 35°19'25" N, long. 118°32'05" W; at N line sec. 15, T 30 S, R 32 E). Named on Oiler Peak (1972) 7.5' quadrangle.

Cow Cove Spring [KERN]: *spring,* 6 miles east-northeast of Caliente (lat. 35°20' N, long. 118°32'05" W; sec. 10, T 30 S, R 32 E); the spring is near the head of Cow Cove. Named on Oiler Peak (1972) 7.5' quadrangle.

Cow Creek [FRESNO]: *stream,* flows 4 miles to Dinkey Creek (1) 1.25 miles west-southwest of Dinkey Dome (lat. 37°06'30" N, long. 119°09'10" W; sec. 32, T 9 S, R 26 E). Named on Huntington Lake (1953) 15' quadrangle.

Cow Creek [KERN]: *stream,* flows 2.5 miles to Bull Run Creek 10.5 miles east-northeast of Glennville (lat. 35°46'45" N, long. 118°31'40" W; near S line sec. 3, T 25 S, R 32 E). Named on California Hot Springs (1958) 15' quadrangle.

Cow Creek: see **Burnt Point Creek** [TULARE]; **Cow Flat Creek** [KERN]; **Horse Creek** [TULARE] (1).

Cowell Creek: see **Caldwell Creek** [KERN].

Cow Flat [KERN]: *area,* 6 miles northeast of Mount Adelaide (lat. 35°29'50" N, long. 118°40'40" W). Named on Mount Adelaide (1972) 7.5' quadrangle.

Cow Flat Creek [KERN]: *stream,* flows 4 miles to Kern River 2.5 miles southwest of Democrat Hot Springs (lat. 35°30' N, long. 118° 41'35" W); the stream goes pass Cow Flat. Named on Democrat Hot Springs (1972) and Mount Adelaide (1972) 7.5' quadrangles. Called Cow Cr. on Caliente (1914) 30' quadrangle.

Cow Heaven Canyon [KERN]: *canyon,* drained by a stream that flows nearly 6 miles to Indian Wells Valley 11 miles west-southwest of Inyokern (lat. 35°34'20" N, long. 117°59'10" W; sec. 22, T 27 S, R 37 E). Named on Freeman Junction (1972), Horse Canyon (1972), and Walker Pass (1972) 7.5' quadrangles.

Cow Heaven Spring [KERN]: *spring,* 6.5 miles east-northeast of Skinner Peak (lat. 35°37'05" N, long. 118°01'30" W); the spring is in Cow Heaven Canyon. Named on Horse Canyon (1972) 7.5' quadrangle.

Cow Meadow [FRESNO]:

(1) *area,* 9 miles north of Kaiser Peak (lat. 37°25'25" N, long. 119° 12'25" W; near N line sec. 11, T 6 S, R 25 E). Named on Kaiser Peak (1953) 15' quadrangle.

(2) *area,* 11.5 miles north of Hume (lat. 36°57' N, long. 118°53'05" W). Named on Tehipite Dome (1952) 15' quadrangle.

Cow Mountain [TULARE]: *peak,* 5.25 miles south-southeast of Springville (lat. 36°03'25" N, long. 118°47'05" W). Altitude 3774 feet. Named on Globe (1956) 7.5' quadrangle.

Cow Mountain Creek [TULARE]: *stream,* flows 1.5 miles to the canyon of South Fork Tule River 7 miles south-southeast of Springville (lat. 36°01'50" N, long. 118°47'15" W); the stream heads near Cow Mountain. Named on Globe (1956) 7.5' quadrangle.

Cow Wells: see **Garlock** [KERN].

Coy Creek [TULARE]: *stream,* flows 3 miles to South Fork of Middle Fork Tule River 1 mile southwest of Camp Nelson (lat. 36° 07'55" N, long. 118°37'20" W; sec. 3, T 21 S, R 31 E); the stream goes past Coy Flat. Named on Camp Nelson (1956) 15' quadrangle.

Coy Flat [TULARE]: *area,* 1 mile south-southwest of Camp Nelson (lat. 36°07'45" N, long. 118°37'10" W; sec. 3, T 21 S, R 31 E); the place is along Coy Creek. Named on Camp Nelson (1956) 15' quadrangle.

Coyote Canyon [FRESNO]: *canyon,* drained by a stream that flows 5.5 miles to Los Gatos Creek 8 miles northwest of Coalinga (lat. 36°13'05" N, long. 120°27'30" W; sec. 4, T 20 S, R 14 E). Named on Alcalde Hills (1969) and Joaquin Rocks (1969) 7.5' quadrangles.

Coyote Creek [TULARE]: *stream,* flows 6 miles to Kern River 7 miles west-northwest of Kern Peak (lat. 36°20'35" N, long. 118°24'15" W); the stream is north of Coyote Peaks. Named on Kern Peak (1956) 15' quadrangle.

Coyote Flat [TULARE]: *area,* nearly 1 mile south-southeast of Auckland (lat. 36°34'35" N, long. 119°06' W; sec. 36, T 15 S, R 26 E). Named on Auckland (1966) 7.5' quadrangle.

Coyote Gulch [KERN]: *canyon,* drained by a stream that flows 3 miles to Rag Gulch 7.5 miles west-northwest of Woody (lat. 35°44'15" N, long. 118°57'25" W; near E line sec. 21, T 25 S, R 28 E). Named on Quincy School (1965) and Sand Canyon (1965) 7.5' quadrangles.

Coyote Holes: see **Freeman** [KERN].

Coyote Lake [FRESNO]:

(1) *lake,* 1600 feet long, 14 miles east-northeast of Kaiser Peak (lat. 37°27'50" N, long. 119°03'05" W). Named on Kaiser Peak (1953) 15' quadrangle. The lake is one of the group called Margaret Lakes

(2) *lake,* 3000 feet long, 5.5 miles north-northeast of Dinkey Dome (lat. 37°11'10" N, long. 119°05'20" W; near SE cor. sec. 35, T 8 S, R 26 E). Named on Huntington Lake (1953) 15' quadrangle.

Coyote Lakes [TULARE]: *lakes,* two, largest 1100 feet long, 9 miles west of Kern Peak (lat. 36°18'25" N, long. 118°27' W); the lakes are south of Coyote Peaks. Named on Kern Peak (1956) 15' quadrangle.

Coyote Pass [FRESNO]: *pass,* 16 miles north-northeast of Hume on Kettle Ridge (lat. 36°58'50" N, long. 118°45'45" W). Named on Tehipite Dome (1952) 15' quadrangle.

Coyote Pass [TULARE]: *pass,* 11 miles west of Kern Peak on Great Western Divide (lat. 36°20'05" N, long. 118°29' W); the pass is near the head of Coyote Creek. Named on Kern Peak (1956) 15' quadrangle.

Coyote Peaks [TULARE]: *peaks,* 9 miles west of Kern Peak (lat. 36° 18'45" N, long. 118°26'45" W); the peaks are south of Coyote Creek. Altitude of highest is 10,892 feet. Named on Kern Peak (1956) 7.5' quadrangle.

Coyote Ridge [FRESNO]: *ridge,* northwest-trending, 1 mile long, 4.5 miles west of Piedra (lat. 36°48'55" N, long. 119°28' W; sec. 9, 10, T 13 S, R 23 E). Named on Piedra (1965) 7.5' quadrangle.

Coyote Spring [KERN]:

(1) *spring,* 4.25 miles east-northeast of Mount Adelaide (lat. 35°27'10" N, long. 118°40'20" W; sec. 32, T 28 S, R 31 E). Named on Mount Adelaide (1972) 7.5' quadrangle.

(2) *spring,* 6 miles northwest of Woody (lat. 35°45'10" N, long. 118°55'10" W; near W line sec. 13, T 25 S, R 28 E); the spring is in Coyote Gulch. Named on Quincy School (1965) 7.5 quadrangle.

(3) *spring,* nearly 5 miles north-northwest of Walker Pass in Berts Canyon (lat. 35°43'45" N, long. 118°03'20" W). Named on Walker Pass (1972) 7.5' quadrangle.

(4) *spring,* 3.25 miles east of Owens Peak (lat. 35°43'50" N, long. 117°56'15" W; near W line sec. 30, T 25 S, R 38 E). Named on Owens Peak (1972) 7.5' quadrangle.

Coyote Springs: see **Freeman** [KERN].

Coyote Springs Creek [FRESNO]: *stream,* flows 1 mile to Kings River nearly 7 miles west-southwest of Balch Camp (lat. 36°52'10" N, long. 119°14' W; sec. 22, T 12 S, R 25 E). Named on Patterson Mountain (1952) 15' quadrangle.

Crabtree [FRESNO]: *locality,* nearly 5 miles south-southeast of Balch Camp along Mill Flat Creek (lat. 36°05'40" N, long. 119°05'15" W; sec. 36, T 12 S, R 26 E). Named on Patterson Mountain (1952) 15' quadrangle. The name commemorates John F. Crabtree, who homesteaded in section 36 in 1911 (Browning, p. 48).

Crabtree Creek [TULARE]: *stream,* flows 4 miles to Whitney Creek 4 miles west-southwest of Mount Whitney at Crabtree Meadow (lat. 36°33'30" N, long. 118°21'25" W); the stream goes through Crabtree Lakes. Named on Mount Whitney (1956) 15' quadrangle.

Crabtree Creek: see **Big Arroyo** [TULARE].

Crabtree Lake [FRESNO]: *lake,* 900 feet long, 2.5 miles north of Blackcap Mountain (lat. 37°06'25" N, long. 118°47'45" W). Named on Blackcap Mountain (1953) 15' quadrangle. The name, given in 1945, commemorates Rae Crabtree, a packer (Browning, p. 48).

Crabtree Lakes [TULARE]: *lakes,* largest 0.5 mile long, about 3 miles southwest of Mount Whitney (lat. 36°32'40" N, long. 118° 18' W); the lakes are along Crabtree Creek Named on Mount Whitney (1956) 15' quadrangle.

Crabtree Meadow [TULARE]: *area,* 4 miles west-southwest of Mount Whitney (lat. 36°33'10" N, long. 118°21'20" W); the place is at the mouth of Crabtree Creek. Named on Mount Whitney (1956) 15' quadrangle. The name commemorates W.N. Crabtree, who grazed cattle at the site before 1900 (Browning, p. 48).

Craft: see **Ricardo** [KERN].

Crag Creek [TULARE]: *stream,* flows 3 miles to South Fork Kern River 9 miles south-southeast of Monache Mountain (lat. 36°05'50" N, long. 118°06'50" W); the stream is east of Crag Peak. Named on Monache Mountain (1956) 15' quadrangle.

Crag Peak [TULARE]: *peak,* about 7 miles south-southeast of Monache Mountain (lat. 36°06'45" N, long. 118°09'10" W). Altitude 9455 feet. Named on Monache Mountain (1956) 15' quadrangle.

Cramer: see **Milo** [TULARE].

Crandall Hill: see **Tropico Hill** [KERN].

Crane Canyon [KERN]: *canyon,* drained by a stream that heads in Los Angeles County and flows 2 miles to Castac Lake 1.25 miles east-southeast of Lebec (lat. 34°49'35" N, long. 118°50'35" W). Named on Lebec (1958) 7.5' quadrangle.

Crane Meadow [TULARE]: *area,* 9 miles south of Camp Nelson (lat. 36°00'50" N, long. 118°36'30" W; near SE cor. sec. 15, T 22 S, R 31 E). Named on Camp Nelson (1956) 15' quadrangle.

Crater Creek [FRESNO]: *stream,* flows nearly 3.5 miles to Florence Lake 13 miles southwest of Mount Abbot (lat. 37°16'35" N, long. 118°58'15" W); the stream heads at Crater Lake. Named on Mount Abbot (1953) 15' quadrangle.

Crater Lake [FRESNO]: *lake,* 900 feet long, 10 miles east-southeast of Kaiser Peak (lat. 37°15' N, long. 119°00'25" W). Named on Huntington Lake (1953) and Kaiser Peak (1953) 15' quadrangles.

Crater Lake Meadow [FRESNO]: *area,* in a circular depression 8 miles north-northeast of Kaiser Peak (lat. 37°24'15" N, long. 119° 08'45" W). Named on Kaiser Peak (1953) 15' quadrangle.

Crater Mountain [FRESNO]: *peak,* 2 miles south-southwest of Mount Pinchot (lat. 36°55'20" N, long. 118°25'15" W). Altitude 12,874 feet. Named on Mount Pinchot (1953) 15' quadrangle.

Crawford Camp [TULARE]: *locality,* nearly 5 miles south of Camp Nelson (lat. 36°04'20" N, long. 118°36' W; sec. 26, T 21 S, R 31 E); the place is at the head of Crawford Creek. Named on Camp Nelson (1956) 15' quadrangle.

Crawford Creek [TULARE]: *stream,* flows 1.5 miles to Windy Creek (1) nearly 6 miles south of Camp Nelson (lat. 36°03'30" N, long. 118°37'15" W; sec. 34, T 21 S, R 31 E). Named on Camp Nelson (1956) 15' quadrangle.

Crazy Lake [FRESNO]: *lake,* 750 feet long, 8.5 miles southwest of Mount Abbot (lat. 37°18'05" N, long. 118°53'50" W). Named on Mount Abbot (1953) 15' quadrangle. A group from California Department of Fish and Game gave the name in 1948 because the lake is at such a desolate site that anyone who visits the place must be crazy (Browning, p. 49).

Credow Mountain: see **Quedow Mountain** [TULARE].

Crescent Creek [TULARE]: *stream,* flows 3.5 miles to Moro Creek nearly 7 miles east-southeast of Yucca Mountain (lat. 36°32'15" N, long. 118°45'25" W). Named on Giant Forest (1956) and Triple Divide Peak (1956) 15' quadrangles.

Crescent Lake [TULARE]: *lake,* 1300 feet long, 9 miles west-northwest of Triple Divide Peak (lat. 36°38'40" N, long. 118°41' W). Named on Triple Divide Peak (1956) 15' quadrangle.

Crescent Lawn: see **Horse Corral Meadow** [FRESNO].

Crescent Meadow [TULARE]: *area,* 12.5 miles west-southwest of Triple Divide Peak (lat. 36°33'25" N, long. 118°44'45" W; on S line sec. 5, T 16 S, R 30 E). Named on Triple Divide Peak (1956) 15' quadrangle.

Crew Creek [TULARE]: *stream,* flows nearly 4 miles to South Fork Tule River 6.25 miles south-southwest of Springville (lat. 36°02'55" N, long. 118°51'30" W; near E line sec. 5, T 22 S, R 29 E). Named on Globe (1956) 7.5' quadrangle.

Crocker: see **Mount Crocker** [FRESNO].

Crocker Canyon [KERN]: *canyon,* drained by a stream that heads in San Luis Obispo County and flows 5.25 miles in Kern County to Midway Valley 4.25 miles north-northwest of Fellows (lat. 35°13'45" N, long. 119°34'50" W; sec. 14, T 31 S, R 22 E). Named on Fellows (1951) and Panorama Hills (1954) 7.5' quadrangles.

Crocker Flat [KERN]: *area,* 7 miles south-southwest of McKittrick (lat. 35°12'20" N, long. 119°39'40" W; on S line sec. 19, T 31 S, R 22 E); the place is 1.5 miles south of Crocker Canyon. Named on Panorama Hills (1954) 7.5' quadrangle. Arnold and Johnson (p. 20) proposed the name.

Crocker Spring [KERN]: *spring,* 5.5 miles south-southwest of McKittrick (lat. 35°13'35" N, long. 119°40'10" W; at W line sec. 18, T 31 S, R 22 E); the spring is in Crocker Canyon. Named on McKittrick (1912) 30' quadrangle.

Crofton Spring [KERN]: *spring,* 4 miles east-southeast of Caliente (lat. 35°16' N, long. 118°33'50" W; near N line sec. 5, T 31 S, R 32 E). Named on Oiler Peak (1972) 7.5' quadrangle.

Crome [KERN]: *locality,* 12 miles west-northwest of Bakersfield along Atchison, Topeka and Santa Fe Railroad (lat. 35°26'30" N, long. 119°11'50" W; at S line sec. 32, T 28 S, R 26 E). Named on Rosedale (1954) 7.5' quadrangle.

Cromir [FRESNO]: *locality,* 4 miles south-southeast of Firebaugh along Southern Pacific Railroad (lat. 36°48'20" N, long. 120°25'20" W; near NE cor. sec. 15, T 13 S, R 14 E). Named on Firebaugh (1956) 7.5' quadrangle. On Firebaugh (1923) 7.5' quadrangle, the name applies to a place located 1 mile farther west along a former Atchison, Topeka and Santa Fe Railroad line.

Crooked Slough [KINGS]: *stream,* diverges from Kings River and flows 3 miles to South Fork Kings River 4.5 miles north-northwest of Lemoore (lat. 36°21'50" N, long. 119°48'15" W; sec. 16, T 18 S, R 20 E). Named on Lemoore (1954) and Riverdale (1954) 7.5' quadrangles.

Cross [TULARE]: *locality,* 2.5 miles south-southeast of Traver along Southern Pacific Railroad (lat. 36°25'20" N, long. 119°28' W; sec. 27, T 17 S, R 23 E); the place is 1.5 miles north-northwest of the railroad crossing of Cross Creek (1). Named on Traver (1949) 7.5' quadrangle.

Cross Creek [FRESNO-TULARE]: *stream,* heads in Tulare County and flows 3 miles to Bubbs Creek 13 miles south-southwest of Mount Pinchot in Fresno County (lat. 36°46'15" N, long. 118°28'50" W). Named on Mount Whitney (1907) 30' quadrangle, and on Mount Pinchot (1953) 15' quadrangle.

Cross Creek [KINGS-TULARE]: *stream,* formed by the confluence of Cottonwood Creek and Elbow Creek in Tulare County, flows 31 miles before it divides to form Middle Branch and West Branch 5.5 miles south of Guernsey in Kings County (lat. 36°07'50" N, long. 119°38' W; sec. 6, T 21 S, R 22 E). Named on Burris Park (1954), Guernsey (1954), Remnoy (1954), Traver (1949), and Waukena (1954) 7.5' quadrangles. Middle Branch is named on Corcoran (1954), El Rico Ranch (1954), and Guernsey (1954) 7.5' quadrangles. West Branch is named on El Rico Ranch (1954) and Guernsey (1954) 7.5' quadrangles. East Branch diverges from Cross Creek 3.5 miles northwest of Corcoran, and flows 7 miles before rejoining Cross Creek 6 miles east of Hanford. East Branch is named on Corcoran (1954), Goshen (1949), Remnoy (1954), Traver (1949), and Waukena (1954) 7.5' quadrangles.

Cross Creek: see **Traver** [TULARE].

Cross Ferry: see **Kern River** [KERN].

Cross Mountain [KERN]: *peak,* 15 miles north of Mojave (lat. 35° 16'45" N, long. 118°08'10" W; sec. 32, T 30 S, R 36 E). Altitude 5203 feet. Named on Cross Mountain (1972) 7.5' quadrangle.

Cross Mountain [TULARE]: *peak,* 10 miles north of Triple Divide Peak (lat. 36°44'10" N, long. 119°30'10" W). Altitude 12,185 feet. Named on Triple Divide Peak (1956) 15' quadrangle.

Cross Mountain: see **Breckenridge Mountain** [KERN].

Crown Basin [FRESNO]: *valley,* 3.25 miles south-southeast of Blackcap Mountain (lat. 37°01'45" N, long. 118°46'15" W); the valley is at the head of Crown Creek. Named on Blackcap Mountain (1953) 15' quadrangle.

Crown Creek [FRESNO]: *stream,* flows 12 miles to Middle Fork Kings River 11 miles northeast of Hume (lat. 36°54'30" N, long. 118°47' W); the stream heads in Crown Basin. Named on Blackcap Mountain (1953) and Tehipite Dome (1952) 15' quadrangles.

Crown Lake [FRESNO]: *lake,* 1800 feet long, 4 miles southwest of Blackcap Mountain (lat. 37°02' N, long. 118°50'50" W). Named on Blackcap Mountain (1953) 15' quadrangle.

Crown Mountain: see **Crown Rock** [FRESNO].

Crown Ridge [FRESNO]: *ridge,* southwest-trending, 2 miles long, 13 miles north of Hume (lat. 36°58' N, long. 118°52'20" W). Named on Tehipite Dome (1952) 15' quadrangle.

Crown Rock [FRESNO]: *relief feature,* 12 miles north-northeast of Hume (lat. 36°57'15" N, long. 118°52' W); the feature is between Crown Valley and Crown Ridge. Altitude 9342 feet. Named on Tehipite Dome (1952) 15' quadrangle. Called Crown Mt. on Tehipite (1903) 30' quadrangle. Frank Dusy gave the name "Crown Mountain" to the feature about 1870 because of its crownlike top (Browning, p. 50).

Crown Valley [FRESNO]: *valley,* 12 miles north-northeast of Hume (lat. 36°57' N, long. 118°50'45" W); the valley is drained by a branch of Crown Creek. Named on Tehipite Dome (1952) 15' quadrangle. Called Collins Meadow on Tehipite (1903) 30' quadrangle.

Crumville: see **Ridgecrest** [KERN].

Crunigen Creek [TULARE]: *stream,* flows 2.5 miles to East Fork Kaweah River 8 miles east-southeast of Kaweah (lat. 36°26'40" N, long. 118°46'30" W; sec. 13, T 17 S, R 29 E). Named on Kaweah (1957) 15' quadrangle. United States Board on Geographic Names (1988b, p. 1) approved the name "Grunigen Creek" for the feature, and noted that the name commemorates John Grunigen, a resident of the neighborhood after 1900.

Crystal Cave [TULARE]: *cave,* 2.5 miles east-northeast of Yucca Mountain (lat. 36°35'20" N, long. 118°49'40" W; near E line sec. 28, T 15 S, R 29 E). Named on Giant Forest (1956) 15' quadrangle. A.L. Medley and C.M.

Webster discovered the cave in 1918; Walter Fry named it (Browning, p. 50).

Crystal Creek [FRESNO]: *stream,* flows 2 miles to Middle Fork Kings River 12.5 miles northeast of Hume (lat. 36°55' N, long. 118°45'45" W). Named on Marion Peak (1953) and Tehipite Dome (1952) 15' quadrangles.

Crystal Creek [KERN]: *stream,* flows 2.5 miles to South Fork Cottonwood Creek (2) 6.5 miles east of Mount Adelaide (lat. 35° 24'55" N, long. 118°37'35" W; sec. 11, T 29 S, R 31 E). Named on Breckenridge Mountain (1972) 7.5' quadrangle. Called Central Fork [of Cottonwood Creek (2)] on Breckenridge Mountain (1943) 15' quadrangle. United States Board on Geographic Names (1975b, p. 9) gave the names "Central Fork Cottonwood Creek" and "Central Fork Rattlesnake Creek" as variants.

Crystal Creek [TULARE]: *stream,* flows 1.5 miles to East Fork Kaweah River 1 mile south-southeast of Mineral King (lat. 36°26'10" N, long. 118°35'20" W); the stream heads at Crystal Lake. Named on Mineral King (1956) 15' quadrangle. The stream first was called Silver Creek (Jackson, p. 25).

Crystal Lake [TULARE]: *lake,* 1000 feet long, 2 miles east-southeast of Mineral King (lat. 36°26'30" N, long. 118°33'40" W); the lake is at the head of Crystal Creek. Named on Mineral King (1956) 15' quadrangle. The feature first was called Silver Lake (Jackson, p. 25).

Crystal Springs Campground [FRESNO]: *locality,* 4 miles southwest of Hume (lat. 36°44'40" N, long. 118°57'35" W; sec. 32, T 13 S, R 28 E). Named on Giant Forest (1956) 15' quadrangle.

Cudahy Camp [KERN]: *locality,* 4.25 miles north-northwest of Saltdale in Last Chance Canyon (lat. 35°24'40" N, long. 117°55'30" W). Site named on Saltdale NW (1967) 7.5' quadrangle.

Cuddy Canyon [KERN]: *canyon,* 6.5 miles long, on Kern-Los Angeles County line, opens into Castac Valley 1.5 miles southwest of Lebec (lat. 34°49' N, long. 118°53'15" W; near SW cor. sec. 34, T 9 N, R 19 W). Named on Frazier Mountain (1958) 7.5' quadrangle.

Cuddy Creek [KERN]: *stream,* flows 6 miles to Cuddy Canyon 8 miles west of Lebec (lat. 34°49'05" N, long. 119°00'10" W); the stream goes through Cuddy Valley. Named on Cuddy Valley (1943) 7.5' quadrangle.

Cuddy Valley [KERN]: *valley,* 7 miles southeast of Eagle Rest Peak (lat. 34°50' N, long. 119°03'30" W); the valley is at the head of Cuddy Creek. Named on Cuddy Valley (1943) 7.5' quadrangle. Fairbanks (1894b, p. 494) referred to Cuddy's Valley. The name commemorates John Fletcher Cuddy, a hunter at Fort Tejon who built a log cabin in the valley (Latta, 1976, p. 204).

Cueva Canyon [FRESNO]: *canyon,* drained by a stream that flows 1 mile to Salt Creek (2) 7 miles south-southwest of Coalinga (lat. 36° 03' N, long. 120°24'50" W; sec. 1, T 22 S, R 14 E). Named on Curry Mountain (1969) 7.5' quadrangle.

Cuidado Mountain: see **Quedow Mountain** [TULARE].

Cuidow Mountain: see **Quedow Mountain** [TULARE].

Cummings Creek [KERN]: *stream,* flows 5.5 miles to Cummings Valley 4 miles north-northwest of Cummings Mountain (lat. 35°05'45" N, long. 118°35' W; near S line sec. 31, T 32 S, R 32 E). Named on Cummings Mountain (1966) 7.5' quadrangle.

Cummings Mountain [KERN]: *peak,* 9 miles southwest of Tehachapi (lat. 35°02'30" N, long. 118°34'15" W; sec. 15, T 11 N, R 16 W). Altitude 7725 feet. Named on Cummings Mountain (1966) 7.5' quadrangle. The name is for George Cummings of Cummings Valley (Gudde, 1949, p. 86). This appears to be the feature called Tehachapai Peak on Wheeler's (1875-1878) map.

Cummings Valley [KERN]: *valley,* 5 miles north-northwest of Cummings Mountain (lat. 35°06'30" N, long. 118°36' W). Named on Cummings Mountain (1966), Keene (1966), and Tejon Ranch (1966) 7.5' quadrangles. The name commemorates George Cummings, who bought land in the valley in the late 1850's (Boyd, p. 173).

Cuneo [KINGS]: *locality,* 4 miles north of Stratford along Southern Pacific Railroad (lat. 36°14'50" N, long. 119°50' W). Named on Stratford (1929) 7.5' quadrangle.

Cunningham Creek [TULARE]: *stream,* flows 4 miles to Roaring River 5.5 miles north of Triple Divide Peak (lat. 36°40'20" N, long. 118°32'15" W). Named on Mount Whitney (1956) and Triple Divide Peak (1956) 15' quadrangles.

Cunningham Lake [FRESNO]: *lake,* 600 feet long, 7 miles east of Kaiser Peak (lat. 37°17'10" N, long. 119°03'35" W). Named on Kaiser Peak (1953) 15' quadrangle.

Curry Mountain [FRESNO]: *ridge,* northwest-trending, 2 miles long, 7 miles southwest of Coalinga (lat. 36°05' N, long. 120°27'30" W). Named on Curry Mountain (1969) 7.5' quadrangle.

Curtis Mountain [TULARE]: *ridge,* west-trending, 2.5 miles long, 8 miles east-northeast of Dinuba (lat. 36°35'45" N, long. 119°15'45" W). Named on Orange Cove South (1966) and Stokes Mountain (1966) 7.5' quadrangles.

Cutler [TULARE]: *town,* 5.5 miles east-southeast of Dinuba (lat. 36° 31'30" N, long. 119°17'15" W; sec. 19, 20, T 16 S, R 25 E). Named on Orange Cove South (1966) 7.5' quadrangle. Postal authorities established Cutler post office in 1910 (Frickstad, p. 210). Officials of Atchison, Topeka and Santa Fe Railroad named the place in 1897 for Dr. John Cutler, a pioneer of Tulare County (Mitchell, A.R., p. 67).

Cuts Meadow: see **Cutts Meadow** [FRESNO].

Cuttens: see **Lost Hills** [KERN] (2).

Cutterbank Spring [KERN]: *spring,* 5.25 miles west-northwest of Cinco (lat. 35°17'30" N, long. 118°07'20" W; near SW cor. sec. 28, T 30 S, R 36 E). Named on Cinco (1972) 7.5' quadrangle.

Cutts Meadow [FRESNO]: *area,* 3 miles northwest of Dinkey Dome (lat. 37°08'35" N, long. 119°10'25" W; sec. 18, T 9 S, R 26 E). Named on Huntington Lake (1953) 15' quadrangle. Called Cuts Meadow on Kaiser (1904) 30' quadrangle.

Cyclamen Lake [TULARE]: *lake,* 900 feet long, 2.5 miles east-northeast of Mineral King (lat. 36°28'05" N, long. 118°33'05" W). Named on Mineral King (1956) 15' quadrangle. The name is for cyclamen plants that grow near the lake (United States Board on Geographic Names, 1933a, p. 250).

Cyclone Meadow [TULARE]: *area,* 9.5 miles south-southwest of Mineral King (lat. 36°19'05" N, long. 118°37'50" W; mainly in sec. 32, T 18 S, R 31 E). Named on Mineral King (1956) 15' quadrangle.

Cyrus Canyon [KERN]: *canyon,* drained by a stream that flows 6 miles to Isabella Lake less than 2 miles east of Wofford Heights (lat. 35°42'30" N, long. 118°25'20" W; sec. 34, T 25 S, R 33 E). Named on Lake Isabella North (1972) and Weldon (1972) 7.5' quadrangles.

Cyrus Flat [KERN]: *valley,* 2.5 miles east of Wofford Heights (lat. 35°42'25" N, long. 118°24'20" W); the valley is at the mouth of Cyrus Canyon. Named on Lake Isabella North (1972) 7.5' quadrangle.

— D —

Dabney Canyon [KERN]: *canyon,* drained by a stream that flows 5 miles to Midway Valley nearly 3 miles west-northwest of Fellows (lat. 35°11'45" N, long. 119°35'10" W; near SW cor. sec. 26, T 31 S, R 22 E). Named on Fellows (1951) and Panorama Hills (1954) 7.5' quadrangles.

Dade: see **Mount Dade** [FRESNO].

Dagany Gap [KERN]: *pass,* 7.5 miles east-northeast of Orchard Peak in Pyramid Hills (lat. 35°46'50" N, long. 120°00'30" W; on E line sec. 3, T 25 S, R 18 E). Named on Pyramid Hills (1953) 7.5' quadrangle. The name commemorates F.P. Daganey, a French stockman who lived at the place (Latta, 1949, p. 335).

Dale Lake [FRESNO]: *lake,* 900 feet long, 6 miles north-northwest of Blackcap Mountain (lat. 37°09'05" N, long. 118°49'55" W). Named on Blackcap Mountain (1953) 15' quadrangle. Employees of California Department of Fish and Game named the lake for John Dale, a packer, when the lake first was planted with fish in 1936 (Browning, p. 51).

Daley Mill [KERN]: *locality,* 3 miles west-southwest of Saltdale (lat. 35°20'20" N, long. 117°55'55" W). Ruins named on Cantil (1967) 7.5' quadrangle.

Dalton Mountain [FRESNO]: *ridge,* west-northwest-trending, 3.5 miles long, 11 miles southwest of Balch Camp (lat. 36°46'35" N, long. 119°14'30" W). Named on Patterson Mountain (1952) 15' quadrangle, and on Pine Flat Dam (1965) 7.5' quadrangle. The name is from the outlaw Dalton brothers, or from Gratton Dalton, the eldest outlaw brother who hid near the feature after he escaped from jail (Hanna, p. 81).

Damon Mill [FRESNO]: *locality,* 2.25 miles north-northwest of the present town of Shaver Lake (formerly Shaver Lake Heights) (lat. 37°08'20" N, long. 119°19'40" W; near NW cor. sec. 23, T 9 S, R 24 E); the place is near the head of Mill Creek (2). Named on Kaiser (1904) 30' quadrangle. Called Duncan Mill on California Mining Bureau's (1917a) map.

Danner Meadow [TULARE]: *area,* 11.5 miles south of Hockett Peak (lat. 36°03'25" N, long. 118°21'40" W). Named on Hockett Peak (1956) 15' quadrangle.

Darby Pond [FRESNO]: *lake,* 1500 feet long, 3.5 miles west-northwest of Selma (lat. 36°34'55" N, long. 119°40'15" W; sec. 34, T 15 S, R 21 E). Named on Selma (1946) 15' quadrangle. Conejo (1963) 7.5' quadrangle has the name for a dry depression.

Dark Canyon [TULARE]:

(1) *canyon,* drained by a stream that flows 3.25 miles to Trout Creek 14 miles east-northeast of Fairview (lat. 35°58'45" N, long. 118°15'35" W; sec. 25, T 22 S, R 34 E). Named on Hockett Peak (1956) and Kernville (1956) 15' quadrangles.

(2) *canyon,* drained by a stream that flows 1.25 miles to White River (1) 3 miles southeast of California Hot Springs (lat. 35° 50'40" N, long. 118°38'15" W; sec. 16, T 24 S, R 31 E). Named on California Hot Springs (1958) 15' quadrangle.

(3) *canyon,* drained by a stream that flows 2 miles to Chico Canyon 9 miles south-southeast of Fairview (lat. 35°48'10" N, long. 118° 27'30" W; sec. 31, T 24 S, R 33 E). Named on Kernville (1956) 15' quadrangle.

Dark Hole: see **The Dark Hole** [FRESNO-KINGS].

Darwin: see **Mount Darwin** [FRESNO]; **Reedley** [FRESNO].

Darwin Canyon [FRESNO]: *canyon,* 2 miles long, 6 miles north-northeast of Mount Goddard (lat. 37°11'15" N, long. 118°41' W); the feature is 1.5 miles north-northwest of Mount Darwin. Named on Mount Goddard (1948) 15' quadrangle.

Darwin Glacier [FRESNO]: *glacier,* 5.5 miles north-northeast of Mount Goddard (lat. 37°10'20" N, long. 118°40'30" W); the glacier is 0.25 mile north of Mount Darwin. Named on Mount Goddard (1948) 15' quadrangle.

Dathol: see **Coalinga** [FRESNO].

Daulton Creek [FRESNO]: *stream,* flows 4 miles to Mammoth Pool Reservoir on San Joaquin River 8 miles west-northwest of Kaiser Peak (lat. 37°19'25" N, long. 119°18'50" W; near N line sec. 14, T 7 S, R 24 E). Named on Shuteye Peak (1953) 15' quadrangle. The name commemorates H.C. Daulton, an early stockman in the neighborhood (Browning, p. 52).

Daulton Station [FRESNO]: *locality,* 6 miles west-northwest of Kaiser Peak (lat. 35°20'05" N, long. 119°17'05" W; sec. 7, T 7 S, R 25 E). Named on Shuteye Peak (1953) 15' quadrangle. Kaiser (1904) 30' quadrangle shows Daulton ranger station at the site.

Daunt: see **Springville** [TULARE].

Davis: see **Scarlet and Davis Canyon** [TULARE].

Davis Campground [KERN]: *locality,* 5.25 miles west-northwest of Miracle Hot Springs (lat. 35°36'55" N, long. 118°36'50" W). Named on Miracle Hot Springs (1972) 7.5' quadrangle.

Davis Creek [FRESNO]: *stream,* flows 2.5 miles to Mill Flat Creek nearly 5 miles south-southeast of Balch Camp (lat. 36°50'35" N, long. 119°05'15" W; sec. 36, T 12 S, R 26 E); the stream heads near Davis Flat. Named on Patterson Mountain (1952) 15' quadrangle.

Davis Flat [FRESNO]: *area,* 6 miles south-southeast of Balch Camp (lat. 36°49'15" N, long. 119°05'15" W; near SW cor. sec. 6, T 13 S, R 27 E). Named on Patterson Mountain (1952) 15' quadrangle.

Davis Lake [FRESNO]:

(1) *lake,* 1600 feet long, nearly 7 miles north-northwest of Blackcap Mountain (lat. 37°09'55" N, long. 118°04'45" W). Named on Blackcap Mountain (1953) 15' quadrangle.

(2) *lakes,* two joined, 1.5 miles long together, 2 miles north of Mount Goddard (lat. 37°07'45" N, long. 118°43'30" W). Named on Mount Goddard (1948) 15' quadrangle. The name commemorates George R. Davis of United States Geological Survey (United States Board on Geographic Names, 1933a, p. 256).

Davis Mountain [FRESNO]: *ridge,* west-northwest-trending, 1 mile long, nearly 6 miles north of Trimmer (lat. 36°59'15" N, long. 119° 17'50" W; on E line sec. 12, T 11 S, R 24 E). Named on Trimmer (1965) 7.5' quadrangle.

Davis Mountain [TULARE]: *ridge,* west-southwest-trending, about 1.5 miles long, 4.5 miles northeast of Woodlake (lat. 36°28' N, long. 119°02'45" W). Named on Woodlake (1952) 7.5' quadrangle.

Dead Horse Canyon [KERN]: *canyon,* drained by a stream that flows 1.5 miles to Oiler Canyon 3.5 miles northeast of Caliente (lat. 35°19'50" N, long. 118°35'20" W; sec. 7, T 30 S, R 32 E). Named on Oiler Peak (1972) 7.5' quadrangle.

Dead Horse Meadow [TULARE]: *area,* 4.5 miles east of California Hot Springs (lat. 35°52'25" N, long. 118°35'15" W; sec. 1, T 24 S, R 31 E). Named on California Hot Springs (1958) 15' quadrangle.

Dead Horse Slough [TULARE]: *water feature,* dry watercourse 2 miles long that heads 3.5 miles west-northwest of Porterville (lat. 36°05'40" N, long. 119°04'25" W; near SE cor. sec. 17, T 21 S, R 27 E). Named on Porterville (1929) 7.5' quadrangle.

Dead Horse Spring [KERN]: *spring,* nearly 4 miles north-northeast of Caliente (lat. 35°20'20" N, long. 118°35'40" W; near SW cor. sec. 6, T 30 S, R 32 E); the spring is in Dead Horse Canyon. Named on Oiler Peak (1972) 7.5' quadrangle.

Deadman Canyon [FRESNO]: *canyon,* drained by a stream that flows 3.5 miles to Jacalitos Creek 6.25 miles south of Coalinga (lat. 36°03' N, long. 120°21'55" W; near N line sec. 4, T 22 S, R 15 E). Named on Kreyenhagen Hills (1956) 7.5' quadrangle.

Deadman Canyon [TULARE]:

(1) *canyon,* drained by a stream that flows 8 miles to Roaring River 8.5 miles north-northwest of Triple Divide Peak (lat. 36°42'25" N, long. 118°34'45" W). Named on Triple Divide Peak (1956) 15' quadrangle. The grave of a sheepherder is at the lower end of the canyon (Browning, p. 53). United States Board on Geographic Names (1933a, p. 257) rejected the names "Cloudy Canyon" and "Copper Canyon" for the feature.

(2) *canyon,* drained by a stream that flows 1.5 miles to Kern River 4.5 miles south of Hockett Peak (lat. 36°09'10" N, long. 118°23'55" W). Named on Hockett Peak (1956) 15' quadrangle.

Deadman Canyon: see **Cloud Canyon** [TULARE].

Deadman Creek [KERN]: *stream,* flows 3.25 miles to Tecuya Creek 3.5 miles southwest of Grapevine (lat. 34°53'10" N, long. 118° 58' W; sec, 2, T 9 N, R 20 W). Named on Grapevine (1958) and Frazier Mountain (1958) 7.5' quadrangles. On Frazier Mountain (1944) and Tecuya Creek (1945) 7.5' quadrangles, the name has the form "Dead Man Creek."

Deadman Creek [TULARE]: *stream,* flows 3 miles to South Fork of Middle Fork Tule River 2.5 miles west of Camp Nelson (lat. 36°08'55" N, long. 118°39'10" W). Named on Camp Nelson (1956) 15' quadrangle.

Deadman Gap [KINGS]: *pass,* 12.5 miles south-southeast of Avenal in Pyramid Hills (lat. 35°50'05" N, long. 120°02'45" W; sec. 17, T 24 S, R 18 E). Named on Pyramid Hills (1953) 7.5' quadrangle.

Deadmans Corners [FRESNO]: *locality,* 27 miles northeast of Coalinga (lat. 36°29'15" N, long. 120°05'50" W; at SW cor. sec. 35, T 16 S, R 17 E). Named on Five Points (1956) 7.5' quadrangle.

Dead Mule Saddle [TULARE]: *pass,* 2.5 miles north-northeast of California Hot Springs (lat. 35°55' N, long. 118°39'15" W; sec. 20, T 23 S, R 31 E). Named on California Hot Springs (1958) 15' quadrangle.

Dead Ox Creek [KERN]: *stream,* flows 9 miles to Willow Spring Creek (1) 4.5 miles west-southwest of Woody (lat. 35°40'40" N, long. 118°54'35" W; sec. 12, T 26 S, R 28 E). Named on Sand Canyon (1965) and Woody (1965) 7.5' quadrangles. Called Rabbit Creek on Woody (1935) 15' quadrangle, where present Five Dog Creek is called Dead Ox Creek, but United States Board on Geographic Names (1966b, p. 4) rejected the name "Rabbit Creek" for present Dead Ox Creek.

Dead Ox Spring [KERN]: *spring,* 3.5 miles south of Woody (lat. 35° 39'20" N, long. 118°50'25" W; sec. 22, T 26 S, R 29 E); the spring is along Dead Ox Creek. Named on Woody (1965) 7.5' quadrangle.

Dead Pine Ridge [FRESNO]: *ridge,* north-trending, 5 miles long, 7.5 miles west-southwest of Marion Peak (lat. 36°54'30" N, long. 118° 38'45" W). Named on Marion Peak (1953) 15' quadrangle.

Deadwood Meadow [TULARE]: *area,* 8 miles east of Fairview (lat. 35°55'35" N, long. 118°21'15" W; sec. 18, T 23 S, R 34 E). Named on Kernville (1956) 15' quadrangle.

Death Canyon [TULARE]: *canyon,* drained by a stream that flows 3 miles to Dry Creek (3) 4 miles north-northwest of Olancha Peak (lat. 36°19'10" N, long. 118°08' W). Named on Olancha (1956) 15' quadrangle.

Deep Canyon [TULARE]:

(1) *canyon,* 1.5 miles long, opens into the canyon of Middle Fork Tule River 2.5 miles east of Springville (lat. 36°07'55" N, long. 118°46'10" W; sec. 5, T 21 S, R 30 E). Named on Springville (1957) 15' quadrangle.

(2) *canyon,* 3.5 miles long, along the lower part of Marble Fork above a point 5.25 miles southeast of Yucca Mountain (lat. 36°31'20" N, long. 118°47'50" W). Named on Giant Forest (1956) 15' quadrangle.

Deep Creek [FRESNO]: *stream,* flows 4.5 miles to Big Creek (2) 7 miles west-northwest of Balch Camp (lat. 36°56' N, long. 119°14'40" W; sec. 33, T 11 S, R 25 E). Named on Patterson Mountain (1952) and Trimmer (1965) 7.5' quadrangles.

Deep Creek [KERN-TULARE]: *stream,* heads in Tulare County and flows 6.5 miles to Cow Creek 10.5 miles east-northeast of Glennville in Kern County (lat. 35°46'35" N, long. 118°31'50" W; at S line sec. 3, T 25 S, R 32 E). Named on California Hot Springs (1958) 15' quadrangle.

Deep Creek [TULARE]:

(1) *stream,* diverges southwest from Kaweah River and flows 11.5 miles to a ditch 5.5 miles south of Visalia (lat. 36°15'05" N, long. 119°16'55" W; sec. 29, T 19 S, R 25 E). Named on Exeter (1952) and Visalia (1949) 15' quadrangles.

(2) *stream,* heads 11 miles southwest of Tulare and flows 5 miles to Tule River 6 miles south of Waukena (lat. 36°03'10" N, long. 119° 30'05" W; sec. 32, T 21 S, R 23 E). Named on Corcoran (1954) and Taylor Weir (1950) 7.5' quadrangles. Lake View School (1927) 7.5' quadrangle shows North Fork, Middle Fork, and South Fork joining to form the stream, but Taylor Weir (1950, photorevised 1969) 7.5' quadrangle fails to name the forks, and has the name "Deep Creek" along the North Fork of the older map.

(3) *stream,* flows 5 miles to Little Kern River 4.5 miles west-southwest of Hockett Peak (lat. 36°12'20" N, long. 118°27'40" W). Named on Hockett Peak (1956) and Kern Peak (1956) 15' quadrangles.

Deep Creek, North Fork: see **Bates Slough** [TULARE].

Deep Creek Cave [TULARE]: *cave,* 8 miles southeast of California Hot Springs (lat. 35°48'40" N, long. 118°33'45" W; sec. 30, T 24 S, R 32 E); the cave is near Deep Creek [KERN-TULARE]. Named on California Hot Springs (1958) 15' quadrangle.

Deep Lake: see **Little Deep Lake**, under **Fingerbowl Lake** [FRESNO].

Deep Meadow [TULARE]: *area,* 3.5 miles east-northeast of Camp Nelson along Boulder Creek (2) (lat. 36°09'05" N, long. 118°32'45" W; sec. 30, T 20 S, R 32 E). Named on Camp Nelson (1956) 15' quadrangle.

Deep Well Canyon [FRESNO]: *canyon,* drained by a stream that flows 3.25 miles to Warthan Creek 3.25 miles east-northeast of Smith Mountain (2) (lat. 36°05'15" N, long. 120°32'15" W; sec. 23, T 21 S, R 13 E). Named on Smith Mountain (1969) 7.5' quadrangle.

Deer Canyon [FRESNO]: *canyon,* drained by a stream that flows 5.5 miles to Middle Fork Kings River 4.5 miles north-northeast of Hume (lat. 36°50'25" N, long. 118°52'10" W); the canyon is east of Deer Ridge. Named on Tehipite Dome (1952) 15' quadrangle.

Deer Canyon [KERN]: *canyon,* drained by a stream that flows 1.25 miles to Tehachapi Creek 2.5 miles east-southeast of Caliente (lat. 35°16'10" N, long. 118°35'30" W). Named on Oiler Peak (1972) 7.5' quadrangle.

Deer Cove [FRESNO]: *area,* 14 miles southwest of Marion Peak (lat. 36°49'

N, long. 118°43' W). Named on Marion Peak (1953) 15' quadrangle.

Deer Cove Creek [FRESNO]: *stream,* flows 2.5 miles to South Fork Kings River 15 miles southwest of Marion Peak (lat. 36°48'15" N, long. 118°43'15" W); the stream drains Deer Cove. Named on Marion Peak (1953) 15' quadrangle. United States Board on Geographic Names (1989a, p. 3) rejected the name "Deer Creek" for the feature.

Deer Creek [FRESNO]:

(1) *stream,* flows 5.5 miles to Fish Creek (1) 1.5 miles north of Double Peak (lat. 37°32'40" N, long. 119°02'20" W); the stream heads at Deer Lakes. Named on Devils Postpile (1953) and Mount Morrison (1953) 15' quadrangles.

(2) *stream,* flows 2 miles to Huntington Lake (1) 3 miles south of Kaiser Peak (lat. 37°15'05" N, long. 119°10'30" W; sec. 7, T 8 S, R 26 E). Named on Kaiser Peak (1953) 15' quadrangle.

(3) *stream,* flows 10 miles to Dinkey Creek (1) 6 miles south-southeast of the village of Dinkey Creek (lat. 37°00'05" N, long. 119°07'10" W). Named on Huntington Lake (1953) and Patterson Mountain (1952) 15' quadrangles. East Fork enters from the southeast 3.5 miles upstream from the mouth of the main creek; it is 4 miles long and is named on Huntington Lake (1953) and Patterson Mountain (1952) 15' quadrangles.

(4) *stream,* flows 3 miles to Pine Flat Reservoir 5 miles north-northeast of Tivy Mountain (lat. 36°52'05" N, long. 119°20'10" W; sac. 22, T 12 S, R 24 E). Named on Pine Flat Dam (1965) and Trimmer (1965) 7.5' quadrangles.

Deer Creek [TULARE]:

(1) *stream,* flows 2 miles to East Fork Kaweah River 4.25 miles west of Mineral King (lat. 36°27'20" N, long. 118°40'10" W). Named on Mineral King (1956) 15' quadrangle.

(2) *stream,* flows 35 miles to lowlands 6.25 miles north of Ducor (lat. 35°58'55" N, long. 119°02'45" W; sec. 27, T 22 S, R 27 E). Named on California Hot Springs (1958), Springville (1957), and White River (1952) 15' quadrangles, and on Alpaugh (1953), Ducor (1952), Pixley (1954), and Sausalito School (1954) 7.5' quadrangles. Ducor (1952) and Porterville (1951) 7.5' quadrangles show Old Deer Creek Channel, which diverges northwest from Deer Creek (2) near the entrance of the creek to lowlands.

Deer Creek: see **Deer Cove Creek** [FRESNO]; **Hamilton Creek** [TULARE]; **Little Deer Creek** [TULARE]; **Timber Gap Creek** [TULARE].

Deer Creek Campground [FRESNO]: *locality,* 3 miles south of Kaiser Peak on the north shore of Huntington Lake (1) (lat. 37°15'10" N, long. 119°10'35" W; sec. 7, T 8 S, R 26 E); the place is near the mouth of Deer Creek (2). Named on Kaiser Peak (1953) 15' quadrangle.

Deer Creek Colony [TULARE]: *settlement,* 7.5 miles northwest of Fountain Springs (lat. 35°58'45" N, long. 118°59'55" W; around NW cor. sec. 31, T 22 S, R 28 E); the place is near Deer Creek (2). Named on Ducor (1929) and Fountain Springs (1965) 7.5' quadrangles.

Deer Creek Hot Springs: see **California Hot Springs** [TULARE].

Deer Creek Slough [TULARE]: *water feature,* 5.5 miles long, ends 8 miles north-northwest of Earlimart (lat. 35°59'15" N, long. 19°20'40" W; sec. 26, T 22 S, R 24 E). Named on Pixley (1929) and Tipton (1928) 7.5' quadrangles.

Deer Creek Switch: see **Terra Bella** [TULARE].

Deer Crossing [FRESNO]: *settlement,* 5 miles southeast of Dunlap (lat. 36°41'25" N, long. 119°02'50" W; sec. 21, T 14 S, R 27 E). Named on Miramonte (1966) 7.5' quadrangle.

Deerhorn Mountain [TULARE]: *peak,* 11.5 miles northwest of Mount Whitney (lat. 36°42'45" N, long. 118°24'30" W). Altitude 13,265 feet. Named on Mount Whitney (1956) 15' quadrangle. J.N. LeConte named the peak in 1895 for the resemblance of its double summit to a pair of horns (Browning, p. 54).

Deer Island [TULARE]: *hill,* 2.5 miles east-southeast of Monache Mountain (lat. 36°11'30" N, long. 118°09' W; on N line sec. 14, T 20 S, R 35 E). Named on Monache Mountain (1956) 15' quadrangle.

Deer Lake [FRESNO]: *lake,* 400 feet long, 5 miles east of Kaiser Peak (lat. 37°17'10" N, long. 119°05'35" W; sec. 26, T 7 S, R 26 E). Named on Kaiser Peak (1953) 15' quadrangle.

Deer Lakes [FRESNO]: *lakes,* largest 1000 feet long, 7.5 miles west-northwest of Red Slate Mountain (lat. 33°37'40" N, long. 118°59'15" W); the lakes are at the head of Deer Creek (1). Named on Mount Morrison (1953) 15' quadrangle.

Deer Meadow [FRESNO]:

(1) *area,* 11.5 miles east-southeast of Mount Goddard along Palisade Creek (lat. 37°03'20" N, long. 118°31'20" W). Named on Mount Goddard (1948) 15' quadrangle.

(2) *area,* 8.5 miles east of Hume (lat. 36°46'35" N, long. 118°45'40" W). Named on Tehipite Dome (1952) 15' quadrangle.

(3) *area,* 5.5 miles east-southeast of Dinkey Mountain (lat. 37°00'50" N, long. 119°04' W; sec. 31, T 10 S, R 27 E); the place is along Deer Creek (3). Named on Kaiser (1904) 30' quadrangle.

Deer Mountain [TULARE]: *peak,* 5.5 miles southeast of Monache Mountain (lat. 36°09' N, long. 118°07'20" W; near S line sec. 30, T 20 S, R 36 E). Altitude 9410 feet. Named on Monache Mountain (1956) 15' quadrangle.

Deer Park: see **Cedar Grove** [FRESNO].

Deer Ridge [FRESNO]: *ridge,* south- to southeast-trending, 4.5 miles long, 6 miles north of Hume (lat. 36°52' N, long. 118°53'30" W); the ridge is west of Deer Canyon. Named on Tehipite Dome (1952) 15' quadrangle.

Deer Ridge [TULARE]: *ridge,* southwest-trending, 1.25 miles long, 5 miles east-southeast of Yucca Mountain (lat. 36°32'40" N, long. 118°47'05" W). Named on Giant Forest (1956) 15' quadrangle.

Deer Spring [KERN]: *spring,* 3.25 miles east-southeast of Caliente (lat. 35°16'15" N, long. 118°34'35" W; near SE cor. sec. 31, T 30 S, R 32 E); the spring is in Deer Canyon. Named on Oiler Peak (1972) 7.5' quadrangle.

Deer Spring [TULARE]: *spring,* 12 miles north of Lamont Peak (lat. 35°58' N, long. 118°01'35" W). Named on Lamont Peak (1956) 15' quadrangle.

Delano [KERN]: *town,* 31 miles north-northwest of Bakersfield (lat. 35°46'15" N, long. 119°14'5" W; in and near sec. 11, T 25 S, R 25 E). Named on Delano East (1953) and Delano West (1954) 7.5' quadrangles. Postal authorities established Delano post office in 1874 (Frickstad, p. 55), and the town incorporated in 1915. Officials of Southern Pacific Railroad named their station at the place in 1873 for Secretary of the Interior Columbus Delano, who headed his department from 1870 until 1875 (Bailey, 1967, p. 6). Postal authorities established Shamrock post office 12 miles south of Delano in 1880 and discontinued it in 1881; they established Benita post office 31 miles southwest of Delano in 1888 and discontinued it in 1889; they established Gyle post office 23.5 miles southwest of Delano in 1888 and discontinued it in 1889 (Salley, p. 19, 91, 202).

Delft Colony [TULARE]: *village,* 4 miles west-southwest of Dinuba (lat. 36°30'40" N, long. 119°26'45" W; sec. 26, T 16 S, R 23 E). Named on Reedley (1966) 7.5' quadrangle.

Delkern: see **Greenfield** [KERN].

Delonegha Creek [KERN]: *stream,* flows 3.5 miles to Kern River 4.5 miles west-southwest of Miracle Hot Springs (lat. 35°33'25" N, long. 118°36'25" W). Named on Democrat Hot Springs (1972) and Miracle Hot Springs (1972) 7.5' quadrangles.

Delonegha Hot Springs [KERN]: *springs,* 4.5 miles west-southwest of Miracle Hot Springs along Kern River (lat. 35°33'25" N, long. 118°36'40" W); the springs are near the mouth of Delonegha Creek. Named on Miracle Hot Springs (1972) 7.5' quadrangle. Called Delonegha Springs on Glennville (1956) 15' quadrangle, and United States Board on Geographic Names (1975b, p. 9) gave this name as a variant. The springs supported a small resort in 1908 (Waring, p. 51). The name "Delonegha" is from a gold-mining settlement of the 1830's in Georgia; a mining place of 1866 situated along Kern River near the springs was called Hot Springs Bar (Boyd, p. 57).

Delonegha Springs: see **Delonegha Hot Springs** [KERN].

Delpiedra: see **Piedra** [FRESNO].

Del Rey [FRESNO]: *town,* 3.5 miles south-southwest of Sanger (lat. 36°39'30" N, long. 119°35'35" W; near E line sec. 5, T 15 S, R 22 E). Named on Sanger (1965) 7.5' quadrangle. The place first was called Clifton, but when the railroad reached the site in 1898 the name was changed to Del Rey because the station was on Rio del Rey ranch (Gudde, 1949, p. 92). Postal authorities established Clifton post office in 1885 and changed the name to Del Rey in 1898; the name "Clifton" was for Clift Wilkinson, founder of the town (Salley, p. 46).

Democrat Hot Springs [KERN]: *locality,* 14 miles south of Glennville along Kern River (lat. 35°31'40" N, long. 118°40' W). Named on Democrat Hot Springs (1972) 7.5' quadrangle. Called Democrat Springs on Glennville (1956) 15' quadrangle, and United States Board on Geographic Names (1975a, p. 4) gave this name as a variant. Dell Hill started a health resort at the site in 1905 (Bailey, 1967, p. 6).

Democrat Spring [KERN]: *spring,* 1.5 miles south-southwest of Democrat Hot Springs (lat. 35°30'25" N, long. 118°40'40" W). Named on Democrat Hot Springs (1972) 7.5' quadrangle.

Democrat Springs: see **Democrat Hot Springs** [KERN].

Den Lake [FRESNO]: *lake,* 1000 feet long, 4.5 miles south of Mount Abbot (lat. 37°19'20" N, long. 118°47'35" W). Named on Mount Abbot (1953) 15' quadrangle. Employees of California Department of Fish and Game named the lake in 1952 (Browning, p. 54).

Dennison Mountain [TULARE]: *peak,* 12.5 miles southwest of Mineral King (lat. 36°19'05" N, long. 118°44'45" W); the peak is at the west end of Dennison Ridge. Altitude 8650 feet. Named on Mineral King (1956) 15' quadrangle.

Dennison Peak [TULARE]: *peak,* 15 miles southeast of Kaweah (lat. 36°17'50" N, long. 118°45'30" W); the peak is 1.5 miles south-southwest of Dennison Mountain. Altitude 7290 feet. Named on Kaweah (1957) 15' quadrangle.

Dennison Ridge [TULARE]: *ridge,* southwest- to west-trending, 4.5 miles long, 10.5 miles southwest of Mineral King (lat. 36°19'30" N, long. 118°42' W). Named on Mineral King (1956) 15' quadrangle. The name is for a pioneer who built a trail from the foothills to the high part of the Sierra Nevada in the 1860's (Browning, p. 54).

Dent: see **Nellie Dent Creek** [KERN].

Depot Flat [TULARE]: *area,* 10.5 miles east of Tucker Mountain (lat. 36°38'10" N, long. 119°01'10" W; near W line sec. 11, T 15 S, R 27 E). Named on Miramonte (1966) 7.5' quadrangle.

Depressed Lake [FRESNO]: *lake,* 900 feet long, 8 miles west-southwest of Mount Abbot (lat. 37°19'40" N, long. 118°54'55" W). Named on Mount Abbot (1953) 15' quadrangle. Jack Criqui and Scott M. Soule of California Department of Fish and Game named the lake in 1948 for its position in a depression (Browning, p. 54).

Derby Acres [KERN]: *village,* 5.5 miles north-northwest of Fellows (lat. 35°14'50" N, long. 119°35'40" W; sec. 10, T 31 S, R 22 E). Named on Fellows (1951) and West Elk Hills (1954) 7.5' quadrangles. The community began in the 1930's (Bailey, 1967, p. 6).

Deseret: see **Wildflower** [FRESNO].

Desert Butte [KERN]: *hill,* 4 miles west-southwest of Castle Butte (lat. 35°05'10" N, long. 117°56'20" W; near NE cor. sec. 4, T 11 N, R 10 W). Altitude 2849 feet. Named on California City South (1973) 7.5' quadrangle. The feature is one of Twin Buttes.

Desert Lake [KERN]: *village,* 2.5 miles west of Boron (lat. 35°00'15" N, long. 117°42' W; sec. 35, T 11 N, R 8 W). Named on Boron (1973) 7.5' quadrangle.

Desert Lake: see **Koehn Lake** [KERN].

Desert Spring: see **Cantil** [KERN].

Desert Springs: see **Koehn Spring** [KERN].

Desert Springs Valley: see **Fremont Valley** [KERN].

Desert Wells [KERN]: *wells,* 3.5 miles west-northwest of Castle Butte (lat. 35°08'15" N, long. 117°56' W). Named on Searles Lake (1915) 1° quadrangle.

Desolation Lake [FRESNO]: *lake,* 1 mile long, 2 miles west of Mount Humphreys in Humphreys Basin (lat. 37°16'25" N, long. 118°42'15" W); the lake is 0.5 mile north of Lower Desolation Lake. Named on Mount Tom (1949) 15' quadrangle. J.N. LeConte named the lake in 1898 (Farquhar, 1923, p. 391).

Desolation Lake: see **Lower Desolation Lake** [FRESNO].

De Stazo Hill [KERN]: *hill,* 10.5 miles north-northeast of Rosamond (lat. 34°59'35" N, long. 118°04'30" W; near W line sec. 5, T 10 N, R 11 W). Altitude 2976 feet. Named on Bissell (1973) 7.5' quadrangle. Rosamond (1956) 15' quadrangle shows De Stazo ranch at the place.

Devel: see **Joe Devel Peak** [TULARE].

Devil Canyon [KERN]: *canyon,* drained by a stream that flows 4.5 miles to Caliente Creek 6 miles east-northeast of Caliente (lat. 35° 18'50" N, long. 118°31'45" W; sec. 15, T 30 S, R 32 E); the canyon is east of Devils Backbone. Named on Oiler Peak (1972) 7.5' quadrangle.

Devils Backbone [KERN]: *ridge,* generally north-trending, 3 miles long, center 5.25 miles east of Caliente (lat. 35°17'15" N, long. 118°32'05" W); the ridge is west of Devil Canyon. Named on Oiler Peak (1972) 7.5' quadrangle.

Devils Bathtub [FRESNO]: *lake,* 3200 feet long, 12 miles west-northwest of Mount Abbot (lat. 37°26' N, long. 118°59'50" W). Named on Mount Abbot (1953) 15' quadrangle. George R. Davis of United States Geological Survey named the lake about 1907 (Farquhar, 1923, p. 391).

Devils Canyon [KERN]: *canyon,* 10 miles west of Liebre Twins (lat. 34°58'45" N, long. 118°44'25" W). Named on Winters Ridge (1966) 7.5' quadrangle.

Devils Canyon [TULARE]: *canyon,* drained by a stream that flows nearly 3 miles to South Fork Kaweah River 10.5 miles southeast of Kaweah (lat. 36°21'10" N, long. 118°47'50" W; near N line sec. 23, T 18 S, R 29 E). Named on Kaweah (1957) 15' quadrangle.

Devils Crags [FRESNO]: *relief feature,* 7.5 miles southeast of Mount Goddard on a northwest-trending ridge 1 mile long (lat. 37°02'10" N, long. 118°36'30" W). Named on Mount Goddard (1948) 15' quadrangle. J.N. LeConte named the feature in 1906 (Farquhar, 1923, p. 391).

Devils Den [KERN]:

(1) *relief feature,* 5 miles east of Orchard Peak (lat. 35°44'15" N, long. 120°02'45" W; at E line sec. 20, T 25 S, R 18 E). Named on Sawtooth Ridge (1961) 7.5' quadrangle. The place was called The Devil's Glen on some old maps (Latta, 1949, p. 296). Arnold and Johnson's (1910) map has the name "Barton Hills" for the range southeast of Devils Den (1), and has the name "Bartons" for a place located 2.5 miles east of Devils Den (1) (near N line sec. 23, T 25 S, R 18 E). According to Arnold and Johnson (p. 19), the name "Barton's" applied to a group of buildings, including the cabin of Orlando D. Barton, an old settler.

(2) *village,* 12 miles north-northwest of Blackwells Corner (lat. 35°45'55" N, long. 119°58'25" W; at W line sec. 7, T 25 S, R 19 E); the village is 4.5 miles east-northeast of Devils Den (1). Named on Avenal Gap (1954) 7.5' quadrangle. Postal authorities established Devils Den post office in 1946 and discontinued it in 1948 (Frickstad, p. 55). The name applied first to a community located 2 miles south of the present village site (Bailey, 1967, p. 7).

Devils Den [TULARE]: *relief feature,* 6.25 miles north-northwest of California Hot Springs near the head of North Fork Gordon Creek (lat. 35°58' N, long. 118°42'15" W; sec. 35, T 22 S, R 30 E). Named on California Hot Springs (1958) 15' quadrangle.

Devils Den: see **Devils Gate** [FRESNO] (2).

Devils Elbow [KERN]: *bend,* 6 miles east-northeast of Caliente along Caliente Creek (lat. 35°18'50" N, long. 118°31'40" W; sec. 15, T 30 S, R 32 E); the feature is near the mouth of Devil Canyon. Named on Oiler Peak (1972) 7.5' quadrangle.

Devils Gate [FRESNO]:

(1) *narrows,* 4.5 miles northwest of Coalinga Mineral Springs in Hans Grieve Canyon (lat. 36°11' N, long. 120°37'15" W; near N line sec. 24, T 20 S, R 12 E). Named on Sherman Peak (1969) 7.5' quadrangle.

(2) *narrows,* 9 miles south-southwest of Coalinga along Jasper Creek (lat. 36°01'20" N, long. 120°25' W; near N line sec. 13, T 22 S, R 14 E). Named on Curry Mountain (1969) 7.5' quadrangle. Called Devils Den on Coalinga (1956) 15' quadrangle.

Devil's Glen: see **The Devil's Glen**, under **Devils Den** [KERN] (1).

Devils Gulch [KERN]: *canyon,* 4 miles long, opens into lowlands 1 mile south-southwest of Maricopa (lat. 35°03' N, long. 119°24'30" W). Named on Maricopa (1951) 7.5' quadrangle.

Devils Kitchen [KERN]: *canyon,* 2 miles long, along San Emigdio Creek above a point 2.5 miles west-northwest of Eagle Rest Peak (lat. 34°55'15" N, long. 119°10'30" W). Named on Eagle Rest Peak (1942) 7.5' quadrangle.

Devils Kitchen [TULARE]: *area,* nearly 4 miles south-southwest of California Hot Springs in Bear Trap Canyon (lat. 35°49'55" N, long. 118°42'25" W; at N line sec. 23, T 24 S, R 30 E). Named on California Hot Springs (1958) 15' quadrangle.

Devils Punchbowl [FRESNO]: *lake,* 2000 feet long, 4.25 miles north-northwest of Blackcap Mountain (lat. 37°07'30" N, long. 118°49'50" W). Named on Blackcap Mountain (1953) 15' quadrangle.

Devils Spring [KERN]: *spring,* 6 miles east of Caliente (lat. 35°16'55" N, long. 118°31'15" W; near NW cor. sec. 35, T 30 S, R 32 E); the spring is in Devil Canyon. Named on Oiler Peak (1972) 7.5' quadrangle.

Devils Table [FRESNO]: *ridge,* northwest-trending, 0.25 mile long, 9 miles east-northeast of Kaiser Peak (lat. 37°20'15" N, long. 119°01'40" W). Named on Kaiser Peak (1953) 15' quadrangle.

Devils Thumb [TULARE]: *peak,* 5.25 miles north-northwest of California Hot Springs (lat. 35°56'50" N, long. 118°42'40" W; sec. 11, T 23 S, R 30 E). Named on California Hot Springs (1958) 15' quadrangle.

Devils Top [FRESNO]: *peak,* 1 mile northeast of Double Peak (lat. 37°31'20" N, long. 119°01'45" W). Altitude 9931 feet. Named on Devils Postpile (1953) 15' quadrangle.

Devils Washbowl [FRESNO]: *water feature,* 10 miles southeast of Mount Goddard along Middle Fork Kings River (lat. 37°01' N, long. 118°35' W). Named on Mount Goddard (1948) 15' quadrangle.

Devilwater Creek [KERN]: *stream,* flows 4.5 miles to Antelope Plain 6.5 miles south-southwest of Blackwells Corner (lat. 35°31'15" N, long. 119°53'45" W; sec. 2, T 28 S, R 19 E). Named on Las Yeguas Ranch (1959) and Shale Point (1953) 7.5' quadrangles. United States Board on Geographic Names (1933a, p. 264) rejected the form "Devil Water Creek" for the name.

Dewey: see **Wasco** [KERN].

Deweyville: see **Wasco** [KERN].

Dewolf: see **Wolf** [FRESNO].

Diablo Range: see "Regional setting."

Diamond Mesa [TULARE]: *area,* 8 miles north-northwest of Mount Whitney (lat. 36°40'30" N, long. 118°22'10" W). Named on Mount Whitney (1956) 15' quadrangle. Sheepmen named the feature for its shape (Browning, p. 56).

Diamond Peak [FRESNO]: *peak,* 8.5 miles south of Mount Pinchot on Fresno-Inyo County line (lat. 36°49'35" N, long. 118°23'20" W). Altitude 13,126 feet. Named on Mount Pinchot (1953) 15' quadrangle.

Diamond-X Lake [FRESNO]: *lake,* 800 feet long, 6.25 miles north-northwest of Blackcap Mountain (lat. 37°09'40" N, long. 118°49'20" W). Named on Blackcap Mountain (1953) 15' quadrangle. William A. Dill of California Department of Fish and Game named the lake in 1947 for Diamond-X pack train (Browning, p. 56).

Diaz Canyon [FRESNO]: *canyon,* drained by a stream that flows 8.5 miles to White Creek 6.5 miles north-northeast of Coalinga Mineral Springs (lat. 36°13'40" N, long. 120°30'05" W; sec. 31, T 19 S, R 14 E). Named on Alcalde Hills (1969), Joaquin Rocks (1969), Santa Rita Peak (1969), and Sherman Peak (1969) 7.5' quadrangles.

Dickerson: see **Raco** [FRESNO].

Dicks Creek: see **Avenal Creek** [KINGS].

Dick Wright Spring [FRESNO]: *spring,* 16 miles northwest of Coalinga (lat. 36°19' N, long. 120°32'20" W; sec. 34, T 18 S, R 13 E); the feature is nearly 1 mile south-southwest of Wright Mountain. Named on Santa Rita Peak (1969) 7.5' quadrangle.

Di Giorgio [KERN]: *village,* 6.5 miles south of Edison (lat. 35°15'10" N, long. 118°50'45" W). Named on Arvin (1955) and Edison (1954) 7.5' quadrangles. Postal authorities established Di Giorgio post office in 1944 (Frickstad, p. 55). The name commemorates Joseph Di Giorgio, founder of a huge agricultural enterprise (Hanna, p. 87).

Dillon Canyon [TULARE]: *canyon,* drained by a stream that flows 2 miles to North Fork Tule River 13 miles south-southwest of Mineral King (lat. 36°17'30" N, long. 118°43'15" W; sec. 9, T 19 S, R 30 E); Dillon Mill was situated in the canyon. Named on Mineral King (1956) 15' quadrangle.

Dillon Mill [TULARE]: *locality,* 12 miles south-southwest of Mineral King (lat. 36°18'10" N, long. 118°42'55" W). Named on Kaweah (1909) 30' quadrangle. Nathan P. Dillon started a sawmill at the place in the late 1870's (Browning, p. 56).

Dillons Point: see **Steve Barton Point** [TULARE].

Dinkey Creek [FRESNO]:

(1) *stream,* flows 27 miles to North Fork Kings River at Balch Camp (lat. 36°54'10" N, long. 119°07'15" W; sec. 10, T 12 S, R 26 E); the stream heads at Second Dinkey Lake. Named on Huntington Lake (1953) and Patterson Mountain (1952) 15' quadrangles. Four hunters named the creek in 1863 for their dog, who was injured in a fight with a grizzly bear (Gudde, 1949, p. 95).

(2) *village,* 2.5 miles southwest of Dinkey Dome (lat. 37°05'10" N, long. 119°09'20" W; sec. 5, T 10 S, R 26 E); the village is along Dinkey Creek (1). Named on Huntington Lake (1953) 15' quadrangle. Postal authorities established Dinkey Creek post office in 1925 and discontinued it in 1972 (Salley, p. 59).

Dinkey Dome [FRESNO]: *peak,* 13 miles south-southeast of Kaiser Peak (lat. 37°06'55" N, long. 119°07'50" W; near E line sec. 28, T 9 S, R 26 E); the peak is near Dinkey Creek (1). Altitude 7697 feet. Named on Huntington Lake (1953) 15' quadrangle.

Dinkey Lake: see **First Dinkey Lake** [FRESNO]; **Second Dinkey Lake** [FRESNO].

Dinkey Meadow [FRESNO]: *area,* 5 miles south-southwest of Dinkey Dome (lat. 37°02'45" N, long. 119°09'45" W; sec. 20, T 10 S, R 26 E). Named on Huntington Lake (1953) 15' quadrangle.

Dinkey Meadow Creek [FRESNO]: *stream,* flows 1 mile to Dinkey Creek (1) nearly 5 miles south-southwest of Dinkey Dome (lat. 37°02'55" N, long. 119°09'25" W; sec. 20, T 10 S, R 26 E); the stream goes through Dinkey Meadow. Named on Huntington Lake (1953) 15' quadrangle.

Dinkey Mountain [FRESNO]: *peak,* 6 miles south-southwest of Dinkey Dome (lat. 37°01'45" N, long. 119°09'45" W; sec. 29, T 10 S, R 26 E); the peak is 1 mile south of Dinkey Meadow. Altitude 6697 feet. Named on Huntington Lake (1953) 15' quadrangle. California Mining Bureau's (1917a) map shows a place called Peterson located a mile northwest of Dinkey Mountain.

Dinuba [TULARE]: *town,* 15 miles north-northwest of Visalia (lat. 36°32'35" N, long. 119°23'10" W; in and near sec. 8, 17, T 16 S, R 24 E). Named on Orange Cove South (1966) and Reedley (1966) 7.5' quadrangles. Postal authorities established Dinuba post office in 1889 (Frickstad, p. 210), and the town incorporated in 1906. The promoters who laid out the townsite in 1888 called the place Sibleyville to honor James Sibley, a landowner there, but officials of Southern Pacific Railroad gave the name "Dinuba" to their station at the site—they coined the name from the first syllables of the names of two teamsters, Dinsmore and Uballis, who hauled grain to the railroad (Hanna, p. 87).

Dinuba: see **North Dinuba** [TULARE].

Dirty Spring [KINGS]: *spring,* 7 miles west-southwest of Avenal (lat. 35°57'50" N, long. 120°14'30" W; near N line sec. 4, T 23 S, R 16 E). Named on Garza Peak (1953) 7.5' quadrangle.

Disappearing Creek [FRESNO]: *stream,* flows 4 miles to Goddard Creek 7 miles south-southeast of Mount Goddard (lat. 37°00'55" N, long. 118°39'35" W). Named on Mount Goddard (1948) 15' quadrangle. Theodore S. Solomons named the stream in 1895 (Farquhar, 1923, p. 392).

Disappointment Lake [FRESNO]: *lake,* 1300 feet long, 5 miles north-northwest of Blackcap Mountain (lat. 37°08'25" N, long. 118°49' W). Named on Blackcap Mountain (1953) 15' quadrangle. Tourists reportedly named the lake after they had poor luck fishing (Browning, p. 57).

Disappointment Peak [FRESNO]: *peak,* 2 miles northwest of Mount Bolton Brown on Fresno-Inyo County line (lat. 37°04'05" N, long. 118°28' W). Altitude 13,917 feet. Named on Big Pine (1950) 15' quadrangle. J. Milton Davis, A.L. Jordan, and H.H. Bliss gave the name "Peak Disappointment" to the feature in 1919, when they made the first ascent and found to their disappointment that it is not the highest point on Middle Palisade (Browning, p. 57).

Discovery Pinnacle [TULARE]: *peak,* 1.5 miles south of Mount Whitney on Tulare-Inyo County line (lat. 36°33'30" N, long. 118° 17'25" W). Named on Mount Whitney (1956) 15' quadrangle. Chester Versteeg suggested the name in 1953 (Browning, p. 57).

Discovery Ridge [KINGS]: *ridge,* northeast-trending, 0.5 mile long, 3 miles northeast of Avenal (lat. 36°02'15" N, long. 120°05'35" W). Named on La Cima (1963) 7.5' quadrangle. La Cima (1934) 7.5' quadrangle shows Discovery Well on the ridge—the name of the ridge is from the well (United States Board on Geographic Names, 1933b, p. 8).

Division Lake [FRESNO]: *lake,* 1800 feet long, 2.5 miles east-southeast of Blackcap Mountain (lat. 37°03'40" N, long. 118°45'05" W); the lake is 0.5 mile west-northwest of Battalion Lake. Named on Blackcap Mountain (1953) and Mount Goddard (1948) 15' quadrangles.

Dix: **Camp Dix** [KERN].

Dixie: see **Little Dixie** [KERN].

Dixie Wash: see **Little Dixie Wash** [KERN].

Dobie Spring [KERN]: *spring,* 5.5 miles east of Mount Adelaide (lat. 35°25'35" N, long. 118°38'40" W; near N line sec. 10, T 29 S, R 31 E). Named on Mount Adelaide (1972) 7.5' quadrangle.

Doctor Williams Canyon: see **Williams Canyon** [KERN]

Doc Williams Canyon: see **Williams Canyon** [KERN].

Dodge Hill [FRESNO]: *peak,* 2 miles west-southwest of Coalinga (lat. 36°07'55" N, long. 120°23'40" W; near W line sec. 6, T 21 S, R 15 E). Altitude 1085 feet. Named on Alcalde Hills (1969) 7.5' quadrangle.

Doe Lake [FRESNO]: *lake,* 800 feet long, 13 miles east-southeast of Mount Goddard (lat. 37°02'35" N, long. 118°30'05" W). Named on Mount Goddard (1948) 15' quadrangle.

Doe Meadow [TULARE]: *area,* 2.5 miles south of Hockett Peak (lat. 36°11'10" N, long. 118°23'15" W). Named on Hockett Peak (1956) 15' quadrangle.

Dog Creek [FRESNO]:

(1) *stream,* flows 18 miles to Redbank Slough 4.5 miles southeast of Clovis (lat. 36°46'40" N, long. 119°38'20" W; sec. 25, T 13 S, R 21 E). Named on Academy (1964), Clovis (1964), Humphreys Station (1965), and Round Mountain (1964) 7.5' quadrangles.

(2) *stream,* flows 3.5 miles to Middle Fork Kings River 9.5 miles west of Marion Peak (lat. 36°56'45" N, long. 118°41'20" W). Named on Marion Peak (1953) 15' quadrangle.

Dogtooth Peak [FRESNO]: *peak,* nearly 6 miles east-northeast of Dinkey Dome (lat. 37°09'15" N, long. 119°02'20" W; near NW cor. sec. 16, T 9 S, R 27 E). Altitude 10,311 feet. Named on Huntington Lake (1953) 15' quadrangle.

Dog Town: see **Mineral King** [TULARE].

Dogtown: see **White River** [TULARE] (2).

Dogwood Canyon [FRESNO]: *canyon,* drained by a stream that flows nearly 3 miles to Warthan Creek 3 miles west-southwest of Coalinga Mineral Springs (lat. 36°07'05" N, long. 120°36'10" W; near W line sec. 5, T 21 S, R 13 E). Named on Sherman Peak (1969) and Smith Mountain (1969) 7.5' quadrangles.

Dollar Lake: see **Big Bird Lake** [TULARE].

Dome Creek [TULARE]:

(1) *stream,* flows 3 miles to Middle Fork Kaweah River 12 miles west-southwest of Triple Divide Peak (lat. 36°31'50" N, long. 118° 43'45" W). Named on Triple Divide Peak (1956) 15' quadrangle.

(2) *stream,* flows 2 miles to Dry Meadow Creek 7.25 miles south-southeast of Camp Nelson (lat. 36°03'15" N, long. 118°32'05" W; near NW cor. sec. 4, T 22 S, R 32 E); the stream is west of Dome Rock (1). Named on Camp Nelson (1956) 15' quadrangle.

Dome Land [TULARE]: *area,* 15 miles northwest of Lamont Peak (lat. 35°56' N, long. 118°14'30" W). Named on Kernville (1956) and Lamont Peak (1956) 15' quadrangles.

Domengine Creek [FRESNO]: *stream,* flows 11.5 miles to lowlands 14 miles north-northeast of Coalinga (lat. 36°20'30" N, long. 120° 18'45" W; near S line sec. 23, T 18 S, R 15 E). Named on Domengine Ranch (1956) and Joaquin Rocks (1969) 7.5' quadrangles. The name commemorates Adolf Domengine, an early settler in the neighborhood (Anderson and Pack, p. 18).

Domengine Spring [FRESNO]: *spring,* 2.5 miles east-northeast of Joaquin Rocks (lat. 36°19'55" N, long. 120°24'05" W; sec. 25, T 18 S, R 14 E); the spring is along Domengine Creek. Named on Joaquin Rocks (1969) 7.5' quadrangle.

Dome Rock [TULARE]:

(1) *peak,* nearly 7 miles southeast of Camp Nelson (lat. 36°04' N, long. 118°31'45" W; near N line sec. 33, T 21 S, R 32 E). Altitude 7221 feet. Named on Camp Nelson (1956) 15' quadrangle.

(2) *peak,* 8.5 miles northeast of California Hot Springs (lat. 35° 58' N, long. 118°33'50" W). Named on Tobias Peak (1936) 30' quadrangle.

Domino: see **Willow Springs** [KERN] (2).

Doney Gulch [KERN]: *canyon,* drained by a stream that flows 3.5 miles to Rag Gulch 1.5 miles north-northeast of Woody (lat. 35°43'25" N, long. 118°49'15" W; sec. 26, T 25 S, R 29 E). Named on Woody (1965) 7.5' quadrangle.

Doney Hill [KERN]: *peak,* 3.25 miles northeast of Woody (lat. 35° 43'40" N, long. 118°47'05" W; sec. 30, T 25 S, R 30 E); the peak is north of Doney Gulch. Altitude 2862 feet. Named on Woody (1965) 7.5' quadrangle.

Donut Rock [FRESNO]: *peak,* 3.5 miles south-southeast of Joaquin Rocks (lat. 36°16'25" N, long. 120°25'20" W; sec. 14, T 19 S, R 14 E). Altitude 3062 feet. Named on Joaquin Rocks (1969) 7.5' quadrangle.

Dora Belle [FRESNO]: *settlement,* at the north edge of Shaver Lake Heights (present town of Shaver Lake) (lat. 37°06'40" N, long. 119°18'50" W; near N line sec. 35, T 9 S, R 24 E). Named on Shaver Lake (1953) 15' quadrangle.

Doris Lake [FRESNO]: *lake,* 1450 feet long, 10 miles east-northeast of Kaiser Peak (lat. 37°20'15" N, long. 119°00'50" W). Named on Kaiser Peak (1953) 15' quadrangle. Ruby Rouch and her daughter Alva planted fish in the lake in 1928 and named the feature for Alva's daughter (Browning, p. 58).

Doris Lake: see **Little Doris Lake** [FRESNO].

Dorst Campground [TULARE]: *locality,* 4.25 miles south-southwest of Shell Mountain (lat. 36°38'10" N, long. 118°48'35" W; near E line sec. 10, T 15 S, R 29 E); the place is near Dorst Creek. Named on Giant Forest (1956) 15' quadrangle. Called Dorst Camp on Tehipite (1903) 30' quadrangle.

Dorst Creek [TULARE]: *stream,* flows 6.5 miles to join Stony Creek and form North Fork Kaweah River 4.5 miles southwest of Shell Mountain (lat. 36°38'35" N, long. 118°50'40" W; near SW cor. sec. 4, T 15 S, R 29 E). Named on Giant Forest (1956) 15' quadrangle. The name commemorates Captain J.H. Dorst, first acting superintendent of Sequoia National Park in 1891 and 1892 (United States Board on Geographic Names, 1933a, p. 270).

Dosados Canyon [FRESNO]: *canyon,* drained by a stream that flows 2.25 miles to lowlands 19 miles southwest of Firebaugh (lat. 36° 39'35" N, long. 120°41'35" W; sec. 6, T 15 S, R 12 E). Named on Chounet Ranch (1956) 7.5' quadrangle.

Dos Palos Slough [FRESNO]: *stream,* flows 10 miles to Merced County 6 miles northwest of Oxalis (lat. 36°58' N, long. 120°38'10" W; at NW cor. sec. 23, T 11 S, R 12 E). Named on Panoche (1913) 30' quadrangle.

Double Bunk Creek [TULARE]: *stream,* flows 2.5 miles to join Bear Creek (4) and form South Creek 8 miles northeast of California Hot Springs (lat. 35°57'35" N, long. 118°34'20" W; near E line sec. 1, T 23 S, R 31 E); the stream goes through Double Bunk Meadow. Named on California Hot Springs (1958) 15' quadrangle.

Double Bunk Meadow [TULARE]: *area,* 6.25 miles northeast of California Hot Springs (lat. 35°57'10" N, long. 118°36'05" W; on N line sec. 11, T 23 S, R 31 E); the place is along Double Bunk Creek. Named on California Hot Springs (1958) 15' quadrangle.

Double Hill [KINGS]: *peaks,* two, 3.25 miles north-northeast of Avenal (lat. 36°02'45" N, long. 120°05'55" W; sec. 2, T 22 S, R 17 E). Named on La Cima (1963) 7.5' quadrangle.

Double Meadow [FRESNO]: *area,* 14 miles north-northwest of Blackcap Mountain (lat. 37°14'55" N, long. 118°54'50" W; sec. 9, 16, T 8 S, R 28 E). Named on Blackcap Mountain (1953) and Mount Abbot (1953) 15' quadrangles.

Double Mountain [KERN]: *peaks,* two, 600 feet apart, 7 miles south-southwest of Tehachapi (lat. 35°02' N, long. 118°29'05" W; on E line sec. 20, T 11 N, R 15 W). Altitude of each peak is 7981 feet. Named on Tehachapi South (1966) 7.5' quadrangle. Called Double Pk. on Wheeler's (1875-1878) map.

Double Peak [FRESNO]: *peaks,* two, 0.25 mile apart, 17 miles north-northeast of Kaiser Peak (lat. 37°30'35" N, long. 119°02'15" W). Altitudes 10,644 and 10,621 feet. Named on Devils Postpile (1953) 15' quadrangle. United States Board on Geographic Names (1971a, p. 2) approved the name "Bench Lakes" for four lakes, largest 650 feet long, situated 1.4 miles east-southeast of Double Peak (lat. 37°30'32" N, long. 119°00'52" W).

Double Peak: see **Double Mountain** [KERN].

Double Spring [KINGS]: *spring,* 10.5 miles southwest of Avenal (lat. 35°52'55" N, long. 120°14'30" W; sec. 33, T 23 S, R 16 E). Named on Garza Peak (1953) 7.5' quadrangle.

Double Trough Spring [FRESNO]: *spring,* 2.25 miles north-northeast of Joaquin Rocks (lat. 36°21'05" N, long. 120°26'05" W; sec. 22, T 18 S, R 14 E). Named on Joaquin Rocks (1969) 7.5' quadrangle.

Double Trough Spring [TULARE]: *spring,* 3.25 miles east-southeast of Auckland (lat. 36°33'50" N, long. 119°03'20" W; sec. 5, T 16 S, R 27 E). Named on Auckland (1966) 7.5' quadrangle.

Dougherty Canyon [KERN]: *canyon,* drained by a stream that flows 1.5 miles to Harper Canyon 6 miles northeast of Caliente (lat. 35° 20'30" N, long. 118°32'25" W; sec. 3, T 30 S, R 32 E). Named on Oiler Peak (1972) 7.5' quadrangle.

Dougherty Creek [FRESNO]: *stream,* formed by the confluence of East Fork and West Fork, flows 3 miles to Middle Fork Kings River 6.5 miles west of Marion Peak (lat. 36°57'45" N, long. 118° 38'30" W). Named on Marion Peak (1953) 15' quadrangle. The name commemorates Bill Dougherty and Bob Dougherty, pioneer sheepmen in the neighborhood (Hanna, p. 89). East Fork heads near Dougherty Peak and is 4.5 miles long. West Fork is 5.25 miles long. Middle Fork is 4 miles long and enters West Fork 0.25 mile upstream from the junction of East Fork and West Fork. All three forks are named on Marion Peak (1953) 15' quadrangle.

Dougherty Creek [KERN]: *stream,* flows 2.5 miles to Kern River 3.5 miles north-northeast of Mount Adelaide (lat. 35°28'20" N, long. 118°42'45" W). Named on Mount Adelaide (1972) 7.5' quadrangle.

Dougherty Flat [KERN]: *area,* nearly 6 miles northeast of Caliente (lat. 35°21'15" N, long. 118°33'40" W; at NW cor. sec. 4, T 30 S, R 32 E); the place is at the head of Dougherty Canyon. Named on Oiler Peak (1972) 7.5' quadrangle.

Dougherty Meadow [FRESNO]: *area,* 4 miles west-southwest of Marion Peak (lat. 36°55'35" N, long. 118°35'15" W); the place is along East Fork Dougherty Creek. Named on Marion Peak (1953) 15' quadrangle. The name commemorates Bill Dougherty and Bob Dougherty of Dougherty Creek (Hanna, p. 89).

Dougherty Meadow: see **Simpson Meadow** [FRESNO].

Dougherty Peak [FRESNO]: *peak,* 2.5 miles south-southwest of Marion Peak (lat. 36°55'15" N, long. 118°32'45" W). Altitude 12,244 feet. Named on Marion Peak (1953) 15' quadrangle.

Dougherty Spring [KERN]: *spring,* 6 miles northwest of Caliente (lat. 35°21'15" N, long. 118°33'05" W; near N line sec. 4, T 30 S, R 32 E); the spring is in Dougherty Canyon. Named on Oiler Peak (1972) 7.5' quadrangle.

Dove Spring [KERN]: *spring,* 3.25 miles east of Pinyon Mountain (lat. 35°27'10" N, long. 118°05'55" W). Named on Dove Spring (1972) 7.5' quadrangle.

Dove Spring Canyon [KERN]: *canyon,* drained by a stream that flows 7 miles to lowlands 9 miles east-southeast of Pinyon Mountain (lat. 35°26'35" N, long. 118°03'20" W; sec. 6, T 29 S, R 37 E); Dove Spring is in the canyon. Named on Dove Spring (1972) and Pinyon Mountain (1972) 7.5' quadrangles. Called Redrock Canyon on Mojave (1915) 30' quadrangle.

Dove Spring Mill [KERN]: *locality,* 3.25 miles east of Pinyon Mountain (lat. 35°27'10" N, long. 118°05'55" W); the place is at Dove Spring. Named on Cross Mountain (1943) 15' quadrangle.

Dove Well [KERN]: *well,* 2 miles east of Pinyon Mountain (lat. 35° 27'30" N, long. 118°07'15" W); the well is in Dove Spring Canyon 1.25 miles west-northwest of Dove Spring. Named on Dove Spring (1972) 7.5' quadrangle.

Dow: see **Minter Village** [KERN].

Dragon Lake [FRESNO]: *lake,* 1800 feet long, 10 miles south of Mount Pinchot (lat. 36°48'05" N, long. 118°23'05" W); the lake is 1 mile northwest of Dragon Peak. Named on Mount Pinchot (1953) 15' quadrangle.

Dragon Peak [FRESNO]: *peak,* 11 miles south of Mount Pinchot on Fresno-Inyo County line (lat. 36°47'30" N, long. 118°22'30" W). Altitude 12,995 feet. Named on Mount Pinchot (1953) 15' quadrangle. The outline of the peak, as seen from Rae Lakes, resembles a dragon (Browning, p. 59).

Drapersville: see **Kingsburg** [FRESNO].

Drillers Ridge [KINGS]: *ridge,* southeast-trending, 1.25 miles long, 7 miles east-southeast of Avenal (lat. 35°58'25" N, long. 120°00'30" W; in and near sec. 34, T 22 S, R 18 E). Named on Kettleman Plain (1953) 7.5' quadrangle. United States Board on Geographic Names (1933b, p. 8) associated the new name with the oil industry.

Dripping Spring [FRESNO]: *spring,* 8 miles west-southwest of Coalinga (lat. 36°06'55" N, long. 120°29'40" W; sec. 7, T 21 S, R 14 E). Named on Curry Mountain (1969) 7.5' quadrangle.

Dripping Spring [KERN]: *spring,* 2.25 miles south-southeast of Mount Adelaide at the mouth of Barker Creek (lat. 35°24' N, long. 118°43'50" W; at S line sec. 14, T 29 S, R 30 E). Named on Mount Adelaide (1972) 7.5' quadrangle.

Drum Valley [TULARE]: *valley,* 4 miles east of Tucker Mountain, partly along Bull Creek (lat. 36°38'30" N, long. 119°08' W). Named on Miramonte (1966) and Tucker Mountain (1966) 7.5' quadrangles. Called Drums Valley on Mendenhall's (1908) map. Postal authorities established Drum Valley post office in 1877 and discontinued it in 1879 (Frickstad, p. 210).

Dry Canyon [KERN]: *canyon,* drained by a stream that flows 2.5 miles to lowlands 6.25 miles south of Weldon (lat. 35°34'40" N, long. 118°16'20" W). Named on Woolstalf Creek (1972) 7.5' quadrangle.

Dry Creek [FRESNO]: *stream,* flows 22 miles to lowlands 6.5 miles east-northeast of Clovis (lat. 36°52'10" N, long. 119°35'40" W; sec. 20, T 12 S, R 22 E). Named on Shaver Lake (1953) 15' quadrangle, and on Academy (1964), Clovis (1964), Fresno North (1965), Humphreys Station (1965), and Round Mountain (1964) 7.5' quadrangles. Called Big Dry Cr. on Friant (1922) 7.5' quadrangle, and called Tollhouse Cr. on Kaiser (1904) 30' quadrangle—the stream flows through the village of Tollhouse.

Dry Creek [TULARE]:

(1) *stream,* flows 25 miles to Kaweah River 4.25 miles east of Woodlake and 1 mile west of Limekiln Hill (lat. 36°24'25" N, long. 119°01'20" W; sec. 35, T 17 S, R 27 E). Named on Giant Forest (1956) 15' quadrangle, and on Auckland (1966) and Woodlake (1952, photorevised 1969) 7.5' quadrangles. Called Limekiln Creek on Lemon Cove (1928) 7.5' quadrangle. East Fork enters 8 miles southeast of Auckland. It is 4 miles long and is named on Giant Forest (1956) 15' quadrangle, and on Auckland (1966) 7.5' quadrangle.

(2) *stream,* flows 7 miles to lowlands 5.25 miles northeast of Exeter (lat. 36°20'25" N, long. 119°03'40" W; near SW cor. sec. 21, T 18 S, R 27 E). Named on Exeter (1952) and Kaweah (1957) 15' quadrangles.

(3) *stream,* flows 4.5 miles to South Fork Kern River 5.25 miles northwest of Olancha Peak (lat. 36°19' N, long. 118°11'05" W; sec. 33, T 18 S, R 35 E). Named on Olancha (1956) 15' quadrangle.

Dry Creek: see **Arroyo Hondo** [FRESNO]; **Big Dry Creek**, under **Academy** [FRESNO]; **Dry Meadow Creek** [TULARE]; **Little Dry Creek** [FRESNO]; **Spring Mountain Gulch** [KERN]; **Willow Spring Creek** [KERN] (1).

Dry Meadow [TULARE]: *area,* 7.5 miles east-southeast of California Hot Springs (lat. 35°50'30" N, long. 118°32'45" W; sec. 17, T 24 S, R 32 E). Named on California Hot Springs (1958) 15' quadrangle.

Dry Meadow: see **Big Dry Meadow** [TULARE]; **Little Dry Meadow** [KERN]; **Little Dry Meadow** [TULARE].

Dry Meadow Creek [KERN]: *stream,* flows 5 miles to Woolstalf Creek 6.5 miles south of Weldon (lat. 35°34'15" N, long. 118° 16' W; near N line sec. 19, T 27 S, R 35 E); the stream heads at Dry Meadows. Named on Woolstalf Creek (1972) 7.5' quadrangle.

Dry Meadow Creek [TULARE]: *stream,* flows 8 miles to Kern River 4.5 miles north of Fairview (lat. 35°59'35" N, long. 118°28'55" W; near SE cor. sec. 23, T 22 S, R 32 E). Named on Camp Nelson (1956) and Kernville (1956) 15' quadrangles. Called Dry Creek on Kaweah (1909) and Kernville (1908) 30' quadrangles.

Dry Meadows [KERN]: *area,* 7.5 miles south-southwest of Weldon (lat. 35°33'45" N, long. 118°20'10" W). Named on Woolstalf Creek (1972) 7.5' quadrangle.

Dry Meadows [TULARE]: *area,* 7.5 miles east of Hockett Peak along Lost Trout Creek (lat. 36°12'50" N, long. 118°15'10" W; on W line sec. 1, T 20 S, R 34 E). Named on Hockett Peak (1956) 15' quadrangle. United States Board on Geographic Names (1962, p. 10) rejected the name "Lost Trout Meadow" for the place.

Dry Meadows: see **Big Dry Meadows** [TULARE].

Dry Valley [TULARE]: *valley,* along Dry Creek (1) above a point nearly 6 miles east-northeast of Auckland (lat. 36°36'45" N, long. 119°00'20" W; near SE cor. sec. 14, T 15 S, R 27 E). Named on Giant Forest (1956) 15' quadrangle, and on Auckland (1966) 7.5' quadrangle.

Duck Lake [FRESNO]:

(1) *lake,* 1 mile long, 6 miles west-northwest of Red Slate Mountain (lat. 37°33' N, long. 118°57'40" W). Named on Mount Morrison (1953) 15' quadrangle. One account of the name concerns ducks found frozen in ice on the lake; another account attributes the name to a patch of snow that at certain times resembles the word "DUK" (Smith, Genny, p. 49).

(2) *lake,* 700 feet long, 14 miles north of Hume (lat. 36°59'35" N, long. 118°53'30" W). Named on Tehipite Dome (1952) 15' quadrangle. Rae Crabtree and Bill White named the lake after they saw a duck on it (Browning, p. 59).

Duckworth Canyon [FRESNO]: *canyon,* drained by a stream that flows 3.25 miles to Los Gatos Creek 18 miles west-northwest of Coalinga (lat. 36°16'40" N, long. 120°38'40" W; sec. 14, T 19 S, R 12 E). Named on San Benito Mountain (1969) 7.5' quadrangle.

Ducor [TULARE]: *village,* 12 miles south of Porterville (lat. 35°53'30" N, long. 119°02'50" W; on N line sec. 34, T 23 S, R 27 E). Named on Ducor (1952) 7.5' quadrangle. The place first was called Dutch Corners because four Germans homesteaded there, but when the railroad reached the site in 1889, railroad officials shortened the old name and called their station Ducor (Mitchell, A.R., p. 67). Postal authorities established Ducor post office in 1907 (Frickstad, p. 210).

Dudley [KINGS]: *locality,* 13 miles south-southeast of Avenal in McLure (present Sunflower) Valley (lat. 35°49'40" N, long. 120° 03'25" W; at E line sec. 19, T 24 S, R 18 E). Named on Cholame (1917) 30' quadrangle. Postal authorities established Dudley post office in 1887 and discontinued it in 1918; the name was for Edmund R. Dudley and Benjamin B. Dudley, who developed oil fields in the region (Salley, p. 62). California Mining Bureau's (1909a) map shows a place called Esperanza located 15 miles by stage line north of Dudley. Postal authorities established Esperanza post office in 1889, moved it 5.5 miles northwest in 1893, moved it 1.5 miles northwest in 1896, moved it 4.5 miles southwest in 1900, and discontinued it in 1901 (Salley, p. 70).

Dudley Pond [FRESNO]: *lake,* 1500 feet long, 1.5 miles southwest of Selma (lat. 36°33'25" N, long. 119°37'50" W; sec. 12, T 16 S, R 21 E). Named on Selma (1946) 15' quadrangle. On Conejo (1963) 7.5' quadrangle, the name applies to a dry depression.

Dudley Ridge [KINGS]: *ridge,* west-northwest-trending, 5 miles long, 9 miles southeast of Kettleman City at the south edge of Tulare Lake Bed (lat. 35°55'30" N, long. 119°49'15" W). Named on Dudley Ridge (1954) 7.5' quadrangle.

Dudley Spring [TULARE]: *spring,* 4.5 miles south of Auckland (lat. 36°31'20" N, long. 119°06'05" W; sec. 24, T 16 S, R 26 E). Named on Auckland (1966) 7.5' quadrangle.

Duff Creek [FRESNO]: *stream,* flows 2.5 miles to Big Creek (2) in Blue Canyon (1) 8.5 miles southwest of Dinkey Dome (lat. 37°01'15" N, long. 119°13'35" W; sec. 34, T 10 S, R 25 E). Named on Huntington Lake (1953) 15' quadrangle.

Dumbell Lakes [FRESNO]: *lakes,* two, each 2400 feet long, located 13 miles east-southeast of Mount Goddard (lat. 37°00'30" N, long. 118°30'40" W). Named on Mount Goddard (1948) 15' quadrangle. The outline of the lakes has a dumbell shape on the map.

Dumtah [TULARE]: *locality,* 6 miles east of Exeter (lat. 36°18'20" N, long. 119°01'50" W; sec. 3, T 19 S, R 27 E). Named on Rocky Hill (1951) 7.5' quadrangle, which has the notation "Indian Camp Ground site" at the place.

Duncan Canyon [FRESNO]: *canyon,* drained by a stream that flows 1 mile to Burrough Valley nearly 7 miles northwest of Trimmer (lat. 36°59'05" N, long. 119°22' W; near E line sec. 8, T 11 S, R 24 E). Named on Trimmer (1965) 7.5' quadrangle.

Duncan Canyon [TULARE]: *canyon,* drained by a stream that flows 1.5 miles to South Fork Tule River 7 miles south-southeast of Springville (lat. 36°02'25" N, long. 118°45'50" W). Named on Globe (1956) 7.5' quadrangle.

Duncan Mill: see **Damon Mill** [FRESNO].

Dunlap [FRESNO]: *settlement,* 13 miles northeast of Orange Cove (lat. 36°44'15" N, long. 119°07'10" W; sec. 2, T 14 S, R 26 E). Named on Miramonte (1966) 7.5' quadrangle. The name commemorates George Dunlap Moss, a school teacher who helped get a post office for the settlement (Hanna, p. 92). Postal authorities established Dunlap post office in 1882, discontinued it for a time in 1885, and moved it 2.5 miles northeast in 1898 (Salley, p. 62).

Dunlap Meadow [TULARE]: *area,* 7 miles east of California Hot Springs (lat. 35°51'45" N, long. 118°32'45" W; sec. 5, 8, T 24 S, R 32 E). Named on California Hot Springs (1958) 15' quadrangle.

Durkas Flat [TULARE]: *area,* 5.5 miles south-southeast of California Hot Springs (lat. 35°48'10" N, long. 118°38'50" W; near NE cor. sec. 32, T 24 S, R 31 E). Named on California Hot Springs (1958) 15' quadrangle.

Durrwood Camp [TULARE]: *locality,* 12 miles south-southwest of Hockett Peak (lat. 36°03'35" N, long. 118°28' W); the place is along Kern River near the mouth of Durrwood Creek. Named on Hockett Peak (1956) 15' quadrangle.

Durrwood Creek [TULARE]: *stream,* flows 6.5 miles to Kern River 12 miles south-southwest of Hockett Peak (lat. 36°03'40" N, long. 118°27'55" W). Named on Hockett Peak (1956) 15' quadrangle. The name commemorates Billy Durwood (Mitchell, A.R., p. 78; Mitchell gave the name with one "r"). Called Tibbetts Cr. on Olmsted's (1900) map.

Durrwood Meadows [TULARE]: *area,* 8 miles east-northeast of Fairview (lat. 35°59' N, long. 118°22' W; sec. 25, T 22 S, R 33 E). Named on Kernville (1956) 15' quadrangle.

Dustin Acres [KERN]: *settlement,* 6.5 miles north-northeast of Taft (lat. 35°13'10" N, long. 119°23'20" W; sec. 22, T 31 S, R 24 E). Named on Taft (1950) 7.5' quadrangle.

Dusy Basin [KERN]: *area,* 9.5 miles east of Mount Goddard (lat. 37° 05'45" N, long. 118°33' W); the place is at the head of Dusy Branch. Named on Mount Goddard (1948) 15' quadrangle. Lakes in the area are called Dusy Lakes on Mount Goddard (1912) 30' quadrangle.

Dusy Branch [KERN]: *stream,* flows 4 miles to Middle Fork Kings River 7 miles east of Mount Goddard in LeConte Canyon (lat. 37° 05'30" N, long. 118°35'35" W); the stream heads in Dusy Basin. Named on Mount Goddard (1948) 15' quadrangle. L. A. Winchell named the stream in 1879 for Frank Dusy, a stockman in the region as early as 1869 (Farquhar, 1923, p. 392-393).

Dusy Creek [FRESNO]: *stream,* flows 6.5 miles to Helms Creek 10.5 miles west-northwest of Blackcap Mountain in Courtright Reservoir (lat. 37°06'30" N, long. 118°58'20" W; sec. 36, T 9 S, R 27 E). Named on Blackcap Mountain (1953) 15' quadrangle.

Dusy Lakes: see **Dusy Basin** [FRESNO].

Dusy Meadow [FRESNO]: *area,* 10.5 miles west-southwest of Blackcap Mountain along North Fork Kings River (lat. 37°00'45" N, long. 118°58' W; near S line sec. 31, T 10 S, R 28 E). Named on Mount Goddard (1912) 30' quadrangle. Water of Wishon Reservoir now covers the place

Dusy Meadows [FRESNO]: *area,* 11 miles west-northwest of Blackcap Mountain (lat. 37°08'45" N, long. 118°57'40" W; in and near sec. 18, 19, T 9 S, R 28 E); the place is along Dusy Creek. Named on Blackcap Mountain (1953) 15' quadrangle.

Dutch Bar: see **Gordons Ferry** [KERN].

Dutch Corners: see **Ducor** [TULARE].

Dutch Flat [KERN]: *area,* 4.5 miles southwest of Wofford Heights (lat. 35°39'20" N, long. 118°30' W; sec. 24, T 26 S, R 32 E). Named on Alta Sierra (1972) and Lake Isabella North (1972) 7.5' quadrangles.

Dutch John Cut [KINGS]: *water feature,* diverges from Cole Slough and extends for 2.5 miles to Kings River 7 miles north of Hanford (lat. 36°25'50" N, long. 119°38'25" W; near N line sec. 25, T 17 S, R 21 E). Named on Burris Park (1954) and Laton (1953) 7.5' quadrangles.

Dutch John Flat [TULARE]: *area,* 7 miles southeast of Monache Mountain (lat. 36°08'10" N, long. 118°06' W; sec. 32, T 20 S, R 36 E). Named on Monache Mountain (1956) 15' quadrangle.

Dutch Lake [FRESNO]: *lake,* 1000 feet long, 14 miles southwest of Mount Abbot (lat. 37°15'15" N, long. 118°59'15" W). Named on Mount Abbot

(1953) 15' quadrangle.

Dutchman Canyon [FRESNO]: *canyon,* drained by a stream that flows 1 mile to Hot Springs Canyon 2.25 miles southeast of Coalinga Mineral Springs (lat. 36°07'30" N, long. 120°31'20" W; near S line sec. 1, T 21 S, R 13 E). Named on Sherman Peak (1969) 7.5' quadrangle.

Dutchman Prospect Spring [KERN]: *spring,* 6.5 miles north of Caliente along Placeritas Creek (lat. 35°23'15" N, long. 118°37'20" W; sec. 23, T 29 S, R 31 E). Named on Breckenridge Mountain (1972) 7.5' quadrangle.

Dutch Oven Meadow [FRESNO]: *area,* 15 miles northwest of Blackcap Mountain (lat. 37°13'30" N, long. 118°59'45" W). Named on Blackcap Mountain (1953) 15' quadrangle.

Dyer Creek [KERN]: *stream,* flows 9.5 miles to lowlands 4.5 miles east-northeast of McFarland (lat. 35°41'40" N, long. 119°09'10" W; near E line sec. 3, T 26 S, R 26 E). Named on Deepwell Ranch (1952) and McFarland (1954) 7.5' quadrangles.

Dyke Ridge: see **Monarch Divide** [FRESNO].

— E —

Eagle Creek [TULARE]:

(1) *stream,* flows nearly 2 miles to East Fork Kaweah River 1 mile south-southeast of Mineral King (lat. 36°26'20" N, long. 118°35'30" W); the stream heads at Eagle Lake. Named on Mineral King (1956) 15' quadrangle. United States Board on Geographic Names (1960b, p. 18) rejected the name "Spring Creek" for the stream.

(2) *stream,* flows 4 miles to Kessing Creek 9.5 miles south-southwest of Camp Nelson (lat. 36°01' N, long. 118°40'50" W). Named on California Hot Springs (1958) and Camp Nelson (1956) 15' quadrangles.

Eagle Hotel [TULARE]: *relief feature,* 2.5 miles northeast of California Hot Springs (lat. 35°54'30" N, long. 118°38'35" W; near W line sec. 21, T 23 S, R 31 E). Named on California Hot Springs (1958) 15' quadrangle.

Eagle Lake [TULARE]: *lake,* 1700 feet long, 2.5 miles south-southwest of Mineral King (lat. 36°24'55" N, long. 118°36'20" W; sec. 28, T 17 S, R 31 E); the lake is at the head of Eagle Creek (1). Named on Mineral King (1956) 15' quadrangle.

Eagle Peak [FRESNO]:

(1) *peak,* 6.5 miles east-southeast of Dinkey Dome (lat. 37°05'20" N, long. 119°01' W; sec. 3, T 10 S, R 27 E). Altitude 10,318 feet. Named on Huntington Lake (1953) 15' quadrangle.

(2) *peak,* 2.5 miles north-northeast of Trimmer (lat. 36°56'25" N, long. 119°16'35" W; near SW cor. sec. 29, T 11 S, R 25 E). Altitude 3272 feet. Named on Trimmer (1965) 7.5' quadrangle.

Eagle Peak [KERN]: *peak,* 4 miles south-southwest of Loraine (lat. 35°15'10" N, long. 118°28'30" W; near N line sec. 7, T 31 S, R 33 E). Named on Loraine (1972) 7.5' quadrangle.

Eagle Peaks [FRESNO]: *peaks,* 9.5 miles east-northeast of Hume (lat. 36°50'55" N, long. 118°45'40" W); the peaks are at the southeast end of Eagle Spur. Named on Tehipite Dome (1952) 15' quadrangle.

Eagle Rest Peak [KERN]: *peak,* 16 miles west-northwest of Lebec (lat. 34°54'25" N, long. 119°08' W; near SW cor. sec. 33, T 10 N, R 21 W). Altitude 5955 feet. Named on Eagle Rest Peak (1942) 7.5' quadrangle.

Eagle Rock [FRESNO]: *peak,* 10 miles southwest of Coalinga (lat. 36°01'50" N, long. 120°28'10" W; sec. 9, T 22 S, R 14 E). Named on Curry Mountain (1969) 7.5' quadrangle.

Eagle Scout Creek [TULARE]: *stream,* flows 4.25 miles to Middle Fork Kaweah River 7.25 miles west-southwest of Triple Divide Peak (lat. 36°32'20" N, long. 118°38'20" W); the stream heads near Eagle Scout Peak. Named on Triple Divide Peak (1956) 15' quadrangle. United States Board on Geographic Names (1933a, p. 279) rejected the name "North Fork" for the stream.

Eagle Scout Peak [TULARE]: *peak,* 3.5 miles south-southwest of Triple Divide Peak on Great Western Divide (lat. 36°32'45" N, long. 118°33'45" W). Altitude 12,040 feet. Named on Triple Divide Peak (1956) 15' quadrangle. Francis P. Farquhar and three eagle scouts made the first ascent of the peak in 1926 (United States Board on Geographic Names, 1933a, p. 279). United States Board on Geographic Names (1976b, p. 4) approved the name "Lawson Peak" for a feature located 2.8 miles east-northeast of Eagle Scout Peak on Kaweah Peaks Ridge (lat. 36°33'40" N, long. 118°30'50" W); the name commemorates Andrew C. Lawson, professor of geology at University of California.

Eagles Nest [KERN]: *ridge,* northeast-trending, 0.25 mile long, south of Loraine (lat. 35°17'05" N, long. 118°26'25" W; at S line sec. 28, T 30 S, R 33 E). Named on Loraine (1972) 7.5' quadrangle.

Eagle Spring [KERN]: *spring,* 7 miles north-northwest of Mojave (lat. 35°08'45" N, long. 118°13'40" W; sec. 16, T 32 S, R 35 E). Named on Cache Peak (1973) 7.5' quadrangle.

Eagle Spur [FRESNO]: *ridge,* northwest-trending, 3 miles long, 9 miles northeast of Hume (lat. 36°52' N, long. 118°47' W); Eagle Peaks are at the southeast end of the ridge. Named on Tehipite Dome (1952) 15' quadrangle.

Eaires [KERN]: *locality,* nearly 5 miles north of Rosamond (lat. 34° 55'50" N, long. 118°08'55" W; at E line sec. 28, T 10 N, R 12 W). Named on Soledad Mountain (1947) 7.5' quadrangle.

Earl-Anna: see **Camp Earl-Anna** [KERN].

Earlimart [TULARE]: *town,* 19 miles southwest of Porterville (lat. 35°53' N, long. 119°16'10" W; mainly in sec. 33, T 23 S, R 25 E). Named on Pixley (1954) 7.5' quadrangle. The place first was called Alila, which means "land of flowers," but promoters of the town changed the name to Earlimart to indicate that crops ripen early at the place (Mitchell, A.R., p. 68). Postal authorities established Alila post office in 1885, discontinued it in 1893, reestablished it in 1896, and discontinued it in 1899; they established Earlimart post office in 1907 (Frickstad, p. 209, 210).

Earthquake Spring [KERN]: *spring,* 5.25 miles north-northeast of Caliente (lat. 35°21'50" N, long. 118°36'10" W; sec. 36, T 29 S, R 31 E). Named on Oiler Peak (1972) 7.5' quadrangle.

East Bakersfield: see **Kern**, under **Bakersfield** [KERN].

East Creek [FRESNO-TULARE]: *stream,* heads in Tulare County and flows 12 miles to Bubbs Creek 13 miles south of Mount Pinchot in Fresno County (lat. 36°45'15" N, long. 118°26'25" W); East Lake [TULARE] is along the stream. Named on Mount Whitney (1907) 30' quadrangle, and on Mount Pinchot (1953) 15' quadrangle.

Eastern Brook Lake [FRESNO]: *lake,* 500 feet long, 3.5 miles northeast of Dinkey Dome (lat. 37°09'10" N, long. 199°05'10" W; sec. 13, T 9 S, R 26 E); the lake is 900 feet west of Rainbow Lake (2). Named on Huntington Lake (1953) 15' quadrangle.

East Farmersville [TULARE]: *locality,* 3.25 miles west of Exeter (lat. 36°18'05" N, long. 119°11'40" W; sec. 6, T 19 S, R 26 E); the place is 0.5 mile east of Farmersville. Named on Exeter (1952) 15' quadrangle.

East Fork Spring [TULARE]: *spring,* 2.25 miles southeast of California Hot Springs (lat. 35°51'25" N, long. 118°38'35" W; near W line sec. 9, T 24 S, R 31 E). Named on California Hot Springs (1958) 15' quadrangle.

East Horse Meadow [TULARE]: *area,* 7.5 miles east of California Hot Springs (lat. 35°52'15" N, long. 118°32'25" W; near E line sec. 5, T 24 S, R 32 E). Named on California Hot Springs (1958) 15' quadrangle.

East Kennedy Lake [FRESNO]: *lake,* 900 feet long, 9 miles southwest of Marion Peak (lat. 36°52'35" N, long. 118°39'05" W); the lake is at the head of Kennedy Creek. Named on Marion Peak (1953) 15' quadrangle.

East Lake [FRESNO]: *lake,* 600 feet long, 7.25 miles northeast of Dinkey Dome (lat. 37°10'45" N, long. 119°01'35" W; sec. 4, T 9 S, R 27 E). Named on Huntington Lake (1953) 15' quadrangle.

East Lake [TULARE]: *lake,* 2000 feet long, 13 miles northwest of Mount Whitney (lat. 36°43'30" N, long. 118°26'30" W); the lake is along East Creek. Named on Mount Whitney (1956) 15' quadrangle. State Hydrographic Survey employees named the lake about 1881 for Thomas Benton East, a hunter, trapper, and cattleman of Eshom Valley (Hanna, p. 94). The feature was called Brewer Lake on a map of 1896 (Browning, p. 61).

Easton [FRESNO]: *town,* 7.5 miles south of downtown Fresno (lat. 36°39' N, long. 119°47'20" W; around SW cor. sec. 3, T 15 S, R 30 E). Named on Fresno South (1963) 7.5' quadrangle. Called Covel on Fresno (1923) 7.5' quadrangle. Postal authorities established Easton post office in 1881, moved it 0.5 mile northwest in 1883, discontinued it in 1902, and reestablished it in 1952; the name commemorates O.W. Easton, a land agent (Salley, p. 64).

East Orosi [TULARE]: *village,* 7 miles east of Dinuba (lat. 36°32'55" N, long. 119°15'40" W; sec. 9, T 16 S, R 25 E); the village is 1.5 miles east of Orosi. Named on Orange Cove South (1966) 7.5' quadrangle. Sultana (1923) 7.5' quadrangle shows the place along Atchison, Topeka and Santa Fe Railroad, and the map has the alternate name "Orosi Sta." at the site. Called Arosi on California Mining Bureau's (1917b) map.

East Palo Prieto Creek: see **Bitterwater Creek** [KERN] (2).

East Pinnacles Creek [FRESNO]: *stream,* flows nearly 3 miles to Piute Creek about 9 miles south of Mount Abbot (lat. 37°15'30" N, long. 118°47'45" W); the stream is east of The Pinnacles (1). Named on Mount Abbot (1953) 15' quadrangle.

East Potholes [TULARE]: *area,* 6.5 miles north-northwest of Olancha Peak (lat. 36°21'20" N, long. 118°08'45" W). Named on Olancha (1956) 15' quadrangle. United States Board on Geographic Names (1989a, p. 3) rejected the name "East Potholes Meadow" for the feature.

East Potholes Meadow: see **East Potholes** [TULARE].

East Spur [TULARE]: *ridge,* north-trending, 3 miles long, 12 miles north-northwest of Mount Whitney (lat. 36°43'45" N, long. 118°23'50" W); the ridge is 1 mile east across Vidette Creek from West Spur. Named on Mount Whitney (1956) 15' quadrangle

East Twin Creek: see **Santiago Creek** [KERN].

East Vidette [TULARE]: *peak,* 13 miles north-northwest of Mount Whitney (lat. 36°44'40" N, long. 118°24' W); the peak is 1.25 miles northeast of West Vidette. Altitude 12,350 feet. Named on Mount Whitney (1956) 15' quadrangle.

Echo Canyon [FRESNO]: *canyon,* drained by a stream that flows nearly 3 miles to Warthan Creek 2.5 miles north-northeast of Smith Mountain (2) (lat. 36°07' N, long. 120°34'50" W; sec. 9, T 21 S, R 13 E). Named on Sherman Peak (1969) and Smith Mountain (1969) 7.5' quadrangles.

Eclipse Hill [TULARE]: *peak,* 7.5 miles south-southeast of Fountain Springs near Kern-Tulare County line (lat. 35°47'30" N, long. 118° 52'05" W; near S line sec. 32, T 24 S, R 29 E). Altitude 1922 feet. Named on White River (1965) 7.5' quadrangle.

Eden Creek [TULARE]: *stream,* flows 2 miles to East Fork Kaweah River 8 miles west of Mineral King (lat. 36°25'45" N, long. 118° 44' W). Named on Mineral King (1956) 15' quadrangle.

Edgemont Acres: see **North Edwards** [KERN].

Edison [KERN]: *town,* 7.5 miles east-southeast of Bakersfield (lat. 35°20'50" N, long. 118°52'10" W; sec. 4, T 30 S, R 29 E). Named on Edison (1954) 7.5' quadrangle. Postal authorities established Edison post office in 1903, discontinued it in 1929, and reestablished it in 1946 (Frickstad, p. 55). Edison Electric Company constructed a substation at the place in 1902; Southern Pacific Railroad built a station called Wade at the site in 1903, but changed the name to Edison the same year (Bailey, 1967, p. 7).

Edison: see **Lake Thomas A. Edison** [FRESNO].

Edmiston [FRESNO]: *locality,* 9 miles east-southeast of Clovis (lat. 36°46'40" N, long. 119°32'20" W; near NE cor. sec. 26, T 13 S, R 22 E). Named on Round Mountain (1964) 7.5' quadrangle.

Edmundson Acres [KERN]: *locality,* 1.25 miles north-northeast of Arvin (lat. 35°13'40" N, long. 118°49'20" W; at W line sec. 13, T 31 S, R 29 E). Named on Arvin (1955) 7.5' quadrangle.

Edwards [KERN]: *town,* 16 miles east-southeast of Mojave (lat. 34° 55'30" N, long. 117°56'15" W; around NE cor. sec. 33, T 10 N, R 10 W); the place is on Edwards Air Force Base. Named on Edwards (1973) 7.5' quadrangle. Rogers Lake (1956) 15' quadrangle has the designation "Wherry Housing (Edwards P.O.)" for the place. Postal authorities established Edwards post office in 1951 when they changed the post office name "Muroc" to "Edwards" (Frickstad, p. 55, 57).

Edwards: see **North Edwards** [KERN].

Edwards Air Force Base [KERN]: *military installation,* 11 miles east-southeast of Mojave in Mojave Desert. Named on Los Angeles (1975), San Bernardino (1957), and Trona (1957) 1°x 2° quadrangles. The installation includes more than 301,000 acres (Bailey, 1967, p. 8). The Army Air Corps used Muroc Dry Lake (present Rogers Lake) for bombing practice in 1933; the facility was called Muroc Army Air Field until 1946, when it became Muroc Air Force Base; it was renamed Edwards Air Force Base in 1950 to honor Captain Glen W. Edwards, a test pilot who was fatally injured at the place in 1948 (Wines, p. 145).

Edwards Siding [KERN]: *locality,* 7.5 miles south of Castle Butte along Atchison, Topeka and Santa Fe Railroad (lat. 35°00'20" N, long. 117°53' W; sec. 36, T 11 N, R 10 W). Named on California City South (1973) and North Edwards (1973) 7.5' quadrangles. Called Edwards Station on Castle Butte (1956) 15' quadrangle.

Edwards Station: see **Edwards Siding** [KERN].

Eighteen-mile House: see **Cinco** [KERN]; **Porterville** [TULARE].

Eisen: see **Mount Eisen** [TULARE].

El Arco [KERN-KINGS]: *ridge,* south-southeast-trending, 2.25 miles long, 12 miles north of Blackwells Corner on Kern-Kings County line (lat. 35°47'20" N, long. 119°55'15" W). Named on Avenal Gap (1954) 7.5' quadrangle. The name is descriptive and means "bow" in Spanish (United States Board on Geographic Names, 1933b, p. 9).

El Arroyo de Chico Martinez: see **Chico Martinez Creek** [KERN].

El Arroyo de Jacalitos: see **Jacalitos Creek** [FRESNO].

Elba [TULARE]: *locality,* 2.5 miles northeast of Tulare (lat. 36°13'55" N, long. 119°18'45" W; at E line sec. 36, T 19 S, R 24 E). Named on Tulare (1927) 7.5' quadrangle.

Elbow: see **Old Millerton** [FRESNO].

Elbow Creek [TULARE]: *stream,* flows 11.5 miles to join Cottonwood Creek and form Cross Creek (1) 9 miles northwest of Visalia (lat. 36°25'55" N, long. 119°23'45" W; sec. 20, T 17 S, R 24 E). Named on Exeter (1952) and Visalia (1949) 15' quadrangles. On Traver (1949, photorevised 1969) 7.5' quadrangle, Elbow Creek ends before it reaches Cottonwood Creek.

El Bulto [KINGS]: *peak,* 5.5 miles south-southwest of Kettleman City (lat. 35°56'05" N, long. 119°59'50" W; near N line sec. 14, T 23 S, R 18 E). Altitude 1005 feet. Named on Los Viejos (1954) 7.5' quadrangle. The name is descriptive and means "the bulk" in Spanish (United States Board on Geographic Names, 1933b, p. 9).

El Caballete [KINGS]: *ridge,* north-northwest-trending, 4 miles long, 8.5 miles south of Kettleman City (lat. 35°53' N, long. 119°58' W). Named on Avenal Gap (1954) and Los Viejos (1954) 7.5' quadrangles. *El Caballete* means "ridge" in Spanish (United States Board on Geographic Names, 1933b, p. 9)

El Campo [KINGS]: *ridge,* north-trending, less than 0.5 mile long, 7 miles east-southeast of Avenal (lat. 35°59'05" N, long. 120°00'25" W; sec. 27, T 22 S, R 18 E). Named on Kettleman Plain (1953) 7.5' quadrangle. *El Campo* means "field" in Spanish (United States Board on Geographic Names, 1933b, p. 9)

El Chichon [KINGS]: *peak,* 2.5 miles east-northeast of Avenal (lat. 36°01'15" N, long. 120°05'15" W; sec. 13, T 22 S, R 17 E). Named on La Cima (1963) 7.5' quadrangle. The name is descriptive; *El Chichon* means "knob" or "lump on the head" in Spanish (United States Board on Geographic Names, 1933b, p. 9).

El Collado [KINGS]: *peak,* 3.5 miles south-southwest of Kettleman City (lat. 35°57'25" N, long. 119°59'50" W; near S line sec. 35, T 22 S, R 18 E). Named on Los Viejos (1954) 7.5' quadrangle. *El Collado* means "small hill" in Spanish (United States Board on Geographic Names, 1933b, p. 9).

Elderberry Springs [KERN]: *springs,* two, 1500 feet apart, 9.5 miles west-southwest of Liebre Twins (lat. 34°55'05" N, long. 118° 44' W). Named on Winters Ridge (1966) 7.5' quadrangle.

Elder Creek: see **Cedar Creek** [TULARE] (1).

Elderwood [TULARE]: *settlement,* 4 miles north-northwest of Woodlake (lat. 36°28'20" N, long. 119°07'15" W; on S line sec. 2, T 17 S, R 26 E). Named on Woodlake (1952) 7.5' quadrangle.

Elderwood Station [TULARE]: *locality,* 4.5 miles north-northwest of Woodlake at the end of Visalia Electric Railroad (lat. 36°28'45" N, long. 119°06'55" W, at E line sec. 2, T 17 S, R 26 E); the place is 0.5 mile northeast of Elderwood. Named on Woodlake (1952) 7.5' quadrangle. Lemon Cove (1928) 7.5' quadrangle has the name "Elderwood" at the place.

El Dombo [KINGS]: *peak,* 3 miles east of Avenal (lat. 35°59'50" N, long. 120°04'40" W; sec. 24, T 22 S, R 17 E). Altitude 1109 feet. Named on Kettleman Plain (1953) 7.5' quadrangle. The name is descriptive and means "dome" in Spanish (United States Board on Geographic Names, 1933b, p. 9).

El Dorado Camp: see **Sageland** [KERN].

Elephant Back [TULARE]: *ridge,* south-southeast-trending, 2 miles long, 2.5 miles northeast of Lindsay (lat. 36°13'40" N, long. 119° 03'10" W). Named on Lindsay (1951) 7.5' quadrangle.

Elephant Butte: see **Standard Hill** [KERN].

Elephant Ear: see **Elephant Knob** [TULARE].

Elephant Hill [FRESNO]: *peak,* 13 miles east-southeast of Coalinga (lat. 36°03'55" N, long. 120°08'25" W; at N line sec. 33, T 21 S, R 17 E). Named on Avenal (1954) 7.5' quadrangle. The name is from discovery of fossil elephant remains on top of the hill (United States Board on Geographic Names, 1933b, p. 9).

Elephant Knob [TULARE]: *peak,* 12 miles northeast of California Hot Springs (lat. 35°59'50" N, long. 118°30'40" W; sec. 22, T 22 S, R 32 E). Altitude 5090 feet. Named on California Hot Springs (1958) 15' quadrangle. Called Elephant Ear on Tobias Peak (1936) 30' quadrangle, but United States Board on Geographic Names (1960a, p. 8) rejected this name for the feature.

El Hocico [FRESNO]: *relief feature,* 10 miles east-southeast of Coalinga (lat. 36°05'40" N, long. 120°11'25" W). Named on Avenal (1954) 7.5' quadrangle. The name is descriptive; *El Hocico* means "the snout" in Spanish—the feature is the snoutlike protrusion of the northwest end of Kettleman Hills (United States Board on Geographic Names, 1933b, p. 9).

Elizabeth Lake [FRESNO]: *lake,* 300 feet long, 15 miles north-northeast of Hume (lat. 36°59'15" N, long. 118°50'30" W). Named on Tehipite Dome (1952) 15' quadrangle.

Elizabeth Pass [TULARE]: *pass,* 2.5 miles west of Triple Divide Peak (lat. 36°35'55" N, long. 118°34'30" W). Named on Triple Divide Peak (1956) 15' quadrangle. Stewart Edward White named the pass in 1906 for his wife (United States Board on Geographic Names, 1933a, p. 286). The feature also was called Turtle Pass for a large rock that resembles a turtle (Browning, p. 64).

Elk [FRESNO]: *locality,* 7.25 miles southwest of Piedra along Atchison, Topeka and Santa Fe Railroad (lat. 36°45' N, long., 119°29'25" W; near S line sec. 32, T 13 S, R 23 E). Named on Piedra (1965) 7.5' quadrangle. Called Elk Siding on Watts Valley (1942) 15' quadrangle.

Elk Bayou [TULARE]: *stream,* formed by the confluence of Inside Creek and Outside Creek, flows 12 miles to Tule River 8 miles south-southwest of Tulare (lat. 36°05'40" N, long. 119°24'15" W; near N line sec. 20, T 21 S, R 24 E). Named on Taylor Weir (1950, photorevised 1969), Tipton (1950, photorevised 1969), and Tulare (1950, photorevised 1969) 7.5' quadrangles.

Elk Creek [TULARE]: *stream,* flows 2.5 miles to Kaweah River 5.5 miles southeast of Yucca Mountain (lat. 36°30'50" N, long. 118° 48'05" W). Named on Giant Forest (1956) 15' quadrangle.

Elk Hills [KERN]: *range,* center 10 miles north of Taft (lat. 35° 18' N, long. 119°28' W). Named on East Elk Hills (1954), Mouth of Kern (1950), Taft (1950), Tupman (1954), and West Elk Hills (1954) 7.5' quadrangles. Arnold and Johnson (p. 20) proposed the name and noted that "the few remaining elk in this region are said to range in these hills."

Elkhorn Station: see **Burrel** [FRESNO].

Elk Siding: see **Elk** [FRESNO].

El Leon [KINGS]: *peak,* 4.25 miles east of Avenal (lat. 36°00' N, long. 120°03' W; sec. 20, T 22 S, R 18 E). Named on La Cima (1963) 7.5' quadrangle. United States Board on Geographic Names (1933b, p. 9) pointed out that the name means "lion" in Spanish.

Ellings Spring [KERN]: *spring,* 5.25 miles southwest of Orchard Peak (lat.

35°40'35" N, long. 120°11'30" W; near W line sec. 7, T 26 S, T 17 E). Named on Orchard Peak (1961) 7.5' quadrangle.

Elliot Spring [FRESNO]: *spring,* 3.5 miles north-northeast of Coalinga Mineral Springs (lat. 36°11'25" N, long. 120°31'20" W; sec. 13, T 20 S, R 13 E). Named on Sherman Peak (1969) 7.5' quadrangle.

Ellis Meadow [TULARE]: *area,* 10 miles northwest of Triple Divide Peak (lat. 36°42'25" N, long. 118°38'20" W). Named on Triple Divide Peak (1956) 15' quadrangle. The name is for Sam L.N. Ellis, forest ranger and Tulare County supervisor (Gudde, 1949, p. 106).

Ellis Mountain [TULARE]: *peak,* 5.5 miles southeast of Auckland (lat. 36°32'40" N, long. 119°01'15" W; near S line sec. 10, T 16 S, R 27 E). Altitude 2503 feet. Named on Auckland (1966) 7.5' quadrangle. Called Buzzard Roost on Dinuba (1924) 30' quadrangle.

El Lobo [KINGS]: *peak,* 5 miles east of Avenal (lat. 35°59'40" N, long. 120°02'15" W; near SW cor. sec. 21, T 22 S, R 18 E). Altitude 1225 feet. Named on Kettleman Plain (1953) 7.5' quadrangle. United States Board on Geographic Names (1933b, p. 9) pointed out that the name means "wolf" in Spanish.

El Loro [KINGS]: *peak,* nearly 5 miles east of Avenal (lat. 35°59'50" N, long. 120°02'35" W; sec. 20, T 22 S, R 18 E). Named on Kettleman Plain (1953) 7.5' quadrangle. United States Board on Geographic Names (1933b, p. 10) noted that the name means "parrot" in Spanish.

Elmco [TULARE]: *locality,* 7 miles north of Ducor along Southern Pacific Railroad (lat. 35°59'35" N, long. 119°02'30" W; at N line sec. 27, T 22 S, R 27 E). Named on Ducor (1952) 7.5' quadrangle.

Elmer: see **Granite Station** [KERN].

El Mirador [KINGS]: *peak,* 8 miles east-southeast of Avenal (lat. 35°56'40" N, long. 120°00'05" W; sec. 11, T 23 S, R 18 E). Named on Kettleman Plain (1953) 7.5' quadrangle. The name refers to the outstanding location of the feature—it means "watchman" or "balcony" in Spanish (United States Board on Geographic Names, 1933b, p. 10).

El Mirador [TULARE]: *locality,* 4.5 miles east-southeast of Lindsay (lat. 36°10'40" N, long. 119°01'05" W; sec. 23, T 20 S, R 27 E). Named on Lindsay (1951) 7.5' quadrangle. On Lindsay (1928) 7.5' quadrangle, the name applied to a place situated 0.25 mile farther west along Visalia Electric Railroad.

Elmo [KERN]: *locality,* 5.5 miles north of Wasco along Atchison, Topeka and Santa Fe Railroad (lat. 35°40'45" N, long. 119°19'45" W; on W line sec. 7, T 26 S, R 25 E). Named on Pond (1953) 7.5' quadrangle.

El Monte de las Avilas: see **Wheeler Ridge** [KERN] (1).

Elm View [FRESNO]: *village,* 15 miles south of downtown Fresno (lat. 36°32'50" N, long. 119°47'20" W; at NW cor. sec. 15, T 16 S, R 20 E). Named on Caruthers (1963) 7.5' quadrangle.

El Pajaro [KINGS]: *peak,* 2 miles east of Avenal (lat. 36°00'15" N, long. 120°05'40" W; sec. 23, T 22 S, R 18 E). Altitude 1112 feet. Named on La Cima (1963) 7.5' quadrangle. United States Board on Geographic Names (1933b, p. 10) noted that the name means "bird" in Spanish.

El Paso [KINGS]: *pass,* 8 miles east-southeast of Avenal (lat. 35°56'55" N, long. 120°00'10" W; at NW cor. sec. 11, T 23 S, R 18 E). Named on Kettleman Plain (1953) 7.5' quadrangle. United States Board on Geographic Names (1933b, p. 10) pointed out that the feature is the main pass along the road through Kettleman Hills.

El Paso City: see **Laurel Mountain** [KERN].

El Paso Creek [KERN]: *stream,* flows 18 miles to end 11.5 miles south of Arvin (lat. 35°02'30" N, long. 118°50'55" W; sec. 13, T 11 N, R 19 W). Named on Liebre Twins (1965), Tejon Hills (1955), Tejon Ranch (1966), and Winters Ridge (1966) 7.5' quadrangles.

El Paso Mountains [KERN]: *range,* south of Indian Wells Valley and north of Fremont Valley (center near lat. 35°27' N, long. 117° 50' W). Named on Cantil (1967), El Paso Peaks (1967), Garlock (1967), Inyokern SE (1972), and Saltdale NW (1967) 7.5' quadrangles.

El Paso Peaks [KERN]: *peaks,* 8 miles north-northwest of Randsburg (lat. 35°28'30" N, long. 117°42'30" W; sec. 30, T 28 S, R 40 E); the peaks are at the east end of El Paso Mountains. Altitude of highest peak is 4578 feet. Named on El Paso Peaks (1967) 7.5' quadrangle.

El Perno [KINGS]: *peak,* 4.5 miles east-northeast of Avenal (lat. 36° 01'25" N, long. 120°03'15" W; sec. 8, T 22 S, R 18 E). Named on La Cima (1963) 7.5' quadrangle. The name is descriptive and means "spike" in Spanish (United States Board on Geographic Names, 1933b, p. 10).

El Perro [KINGS]: *peak,* 2.5 miles north of Avenal (lat. 36°02'25" N, long. 120°08'10" W; sec. 4, T 22 S, R 17 E). Named on Avenal (1954) 7.5' quadrangle. United States Board on Geographic Names (1933b, p. 10) noted that the name means "dog" in Spanish.

El Piso [KERN]: *area,* nearly 4 miles east of Avenal (lat. 36°00'10" N, long. 120°03'35" W; sec. 19, T 22 S, R 18 E). Named on La Cima (1963) 7.5' quadrangle. The name refers to slabs of limestone that pave the area—*el piso* means "floor" in Spanish (United States Board on Geographic Names, 1933b, p. 10).

El Piton [FRESNO]: *peak,* 14 miles east-southeast of Coalinga (lat. 36°02'35" N, long. 120°08'40" W; near W line sec. 4, T 22 S, R 17 E). Named on Avenal (1954) 7.5' quadrangle. The name is descriptive and means "protuberance" in Spanish (United States Board on Geographic Names, 1933b, p. 10).

El Portillo [KINGS]: *canyon,* less than 1 mile long, 6.25 miles south-southeast of Kettleman City (lat. 35°55'10" N, long. 119°56'05" W; near NE cor. sec. 20, T 23 S, R 19 E). Named on Los Viejos (1954) 7.5' quadrangle. United States Board on Geographic Names (1933b, p. 10) noted that the name means "gap" or "open pass between hills" in Spanish.

El Prado [FRESNO]:

(1) *locality,* 6 miles north-northwest of Clovis at the junction of Southern Pacific Railroad and San Joaquin and Eastern Railroad (lat. 36°54'20" N, long. 119°43'50" W; near E line sec. 12, T 12 S, R 20 E). Named on Friant (1922) 7.5' quadrangle. California Mining Bureau's (1917a) map shows a place called Bridge located along San Joaquin River west-southwest of El Prado. Postal authorities established Bridge post office, named for Lanes Bridge, in 1902 and discontinued it in 1907 (Salley, p. 26). Lanes Bridge (1922) 7.5' quadrangle shows Lanes Bridge across San Joaquin River 3.5 miles west-southwest of El Prado (1) (lat. 36°53'35" N, long. 119°47'15" W; near N line sec. 16, T 12 S, R 20 E).

(2) *ridge,* northwest-trending, 1.5 miles long, 12.5 miles east-southeast of Coalinga (lat. 36°03'45" N, long. 120°09'20" W). Named on Avenal (1954) 7.5' quadrangle.

El Pulgar [KINGS]: *peak,* 3 miles east-northeast of Avenal (lat. 36° 01'10" N, long. 120°04'15" W; sec. 18, T 22 S, R 18 E). Named on La Cima (1963) 7.5' quadrangle. The name means "thumb" in Spanish (United States Board on Geographic Names, 1933b, p. 10)

El Rabo [KINGS]: *ridge,* southeast-trending, 1 mile long, 11 miles south of Kettleman City (lat. 35°51' N, long. 119°56'10" W). Named on Avenal Gap (1954) 7.5' quadrangle. The name is for the position of the ridge at the end of the most prominent part of Kettleman Hills—it means "tail" in Spanish (United States Board on Geographic Names, 1933b, p. 10).

El Rascador [KINGS]: *peak,* 5 miles east of Avenal (lat. 36°01'10" N, long. 120°02'30" W; sec. 17, T 22 S, R 18 E). Named on La Cima (1963) 7.5' quadrangle. The name is descriptive and means "scraper" in Spanish (United States Board on Geographic Names, 1933b, p. 10).

El Rico [KINGS]: *locality,* 6 miles south-southwest of Corcoran along Kings Lake Shore Railroad (lat. 36°01'25" N, long. 119° 37' W). Named on Corcoran (1928) 7.5' quadrangle.

El Rincon [KINGS]: *area,* 12.5 miles south of Kettleman City (lat. 35°49'30" N, long. 119°55'30" W; sec. 21, T 24 S, R 19 E). Named on Avenal Gap (1954) 7.5' quadrangle. The name means "corner" in Spanish (United States Board on Geographic Names, 1933b, p. 10).

El Rio de los Santos Reyes: see **Kings River** [FRESNO-KINGS-TULARE].

El Rita: see **Keene** [KERN].

El Serrijon [KINGS]: *ridge,* west-northwest-trending, 0.5 mile long, 3.5 miles east-northeast of Avenal (lat. 36°01'35" N, long. 120°04'15" W; mainly in sec. 7, T 22 S, R 18 E). Named on La Cima (1963) 7.5' quadrangle. United States Board on Geographic Names (1933b, p. 10) pointed out that the name means "small hill" in Spanish.

Elsie: see **Lake Elsie**, under **Fingerbowl Lake** [FRESNO].

El Taco [KINGS]: *peak,* 3.5 miles northeast of Avenal (lat. 36°02'15" N, long. 120°04'55" W; near S line sec. 1, T 22 S, R 17 E). Named on La Cima (1963) 7.5' quadrangle. The name means "stopper" in Spanish (United States Board on Geographic Names, 1933b, p. 10).

El Tejon [KERN]: *land grant,* southeast of Arvin. Named on Arvin (1955), Bear Mountain (1966), Bena (1972), Edison (1954), Pastoria Creek (1958), Tejon Hills (1955), Tejon Ranch (1966), and Winters Ridge (1966) 7.5' quadrangles. Jose Antonio Aguirre and Ignacio del Valle received 22 leagues in 1843 and claimed 97,617 acres patented in 1863 (Cowan, p. 101). The name originated with a dead badger found by early Spanish explorers—it means "badger" in Spanish (Latta, 1976, p. 226).

El Tolete [KINGS]: *peak,* nearly 4 miles east-northeast of Avenal (lat. 36°01'30" N, long. 120°03'50" W; sec. 7, T 22 S, R 18 E). Altitude 1212 feet. Named on La Cima (1963) 7.5' quadrangle. The name is descriptive and means "club" or "cudgel" in Spanish (United States Board on Geographic Names, 1933b, p. 11).

El Vallejo [KERN]: *valley,* 11.5 miles north of Blackwells Corner (lat. 35°46'25" N, long. 119°54'45" W; on N line sec. 10, T 25 S, R 19 E). Named on Avenal Gap (1954) 7.5' quadrangle. The name is descriptive and means "the small valley" in Spanish (United States Board on Geographic Names, 1933b, p. 11).

El Vejon [KERN]: *peak,* 11.5 miles north of Blackwells Corner (lat. 35°46'55" N, long. 119°53'30" W; sec. 2, T 25 S, R 19 E). Altitude 542 feet. Named on Avenal Gap (1954) 7.5 quadrangle. United States Board on Geographic Names (1933b, p. 11) noted that the feature is physiographically old—*vejon* means "very old man" in Spanish.

Ely Creek: see **Ely Meadow** [FRESNO].

Ely Meadow [FRESNO]: *area,* 5 miles north-northeast of Shaver Lake Heights (present town of Shaver Lake) (lat. 37°10'15" N, long. 119°17' W; on S line sec. 6, T 9 S, R 25 E); the place is 1 mile northwest of Ely Mountain. Named on Shaver Lake (1953) 15' quadrangle. United States Board on Geographic Names (1983a, p. 3) approved the name "Ely Creek" for a stream that heads at Ely Meadow and flows 2 miles north to Big Creek (1) 3 miles north of Shaver Lake (lat. 37°11'46" N, long. 119°17'02" W; sec. 31, T 8 S, R 25 E).

Ely Mountain [FRESNO]: *peak,* 4.5 miles northeast of Shaver Lake Heights (present town of Shaver Lake) (lat. 37°09'30" N, long. 119°16'20" W; sec. 8, T 9 S, R 25 E). Altitude 6886 feet. Named on Shaver Lake (1953) 15' quadrangle.

Emerald Lake [TULARE]: *lake,* 800 feet long, 8 miles west of Triple Divide Peak (lat. 36°35'50" N, long. 118°40'30" W; sec. 25, T 15 S, R 30 E). Named on Triple Divide Peak (1956) 15' quadrangle. Superintendent John R. White of Sequoia National Park named the feature in 1925 (Browning, p. 65).

Emerald Mountain [KERN]: *peak,* 12 miles northeast of Tehachapi (lat. 35°15'20" N, long. 118°17' W; near SW cor. sec. 1, T 31 S, R 34 E). Altitude 4990 feet. Named on Emerald Mountain (1972) 7.5' quadrangle.

Emerald Peak [FRESNO]: *peak,* nearly 7 miles north-northeast of Blackcap Mountain (lat. 37°09'55" N, long. 118°45'45" W). Altitude 12,543 feet. Named on Blackcap Mountain (1953) 15' quadrangle. Theodore S. Solomons named the peak in 1895 for its color (Farquhar, 1923, p. 394).

Emigrant Hill [KERN]: *hill,* 10.5 miles northwest of Blackwells Corner (lat. 35°44'20" N, long. 119°58'55" W; sec. 24, T 25 S, R 18 E). Named on Emigrant Hill (1953) 7.5' quadrangle. On Emigrant Hill (1943) 7.5' quadrangle, the name applies to a hill located 0.5 mile farther northeast. The feature is said to have been a landmark for early travelers in the neighborhood (Arnold and Johnson, p. 20).

Empire Mountain [TULARE]: *peak,* 1.5 miles northeast of Mineral King (lat. 36°28' N, long. 118°34'30" W). Altitude 11,509 feet. Named on Mineral King (1956) 15' quadrangle.

Enchanted Gorge [FRESNO]: *canyon,* 5.5 miles long, drained by Disappearing Creek, which joins Goddard Creek 7 miles south-southeast of Mount Goddard (lat. 37°00'55" N, long. 118°39'35" W). Named on Mount Goddard (1948) 15' quadrangle. Theodore S. Solomons named the canyon in 1895 (Farquhar, 1923, p. 394).

Engineer Point [KERN]: *peninsula,* 4 miles south of Wofford Heights along Isabella Lake just north of the dam that forms the lake (lat. 35°39'05" N, long. 118°28'05" W; on E line sec. 19, T 26 S, R 33 E). Named on Lake Isabella North (1972) 7.5' quadrangle.

Engle: see **Lake Engle** [KERN].

Enson [TULARE]: *locality,* 1.25 miles north-northeast of Dinuba along Atchison, Topeka and Santa Fe Railroad (lat. 36°33'30" N, long. 119°22'25" W; near NW cor. sec. 9, T 16 S, R 24 E). Named on Orange Cove South (1966) 7.5' quadrangle. Called Giffen on Sultana (1923) 7.5' quadrangle.

Ercil Lake [KERN]: *lake,* 600 feet long, 3.25 miles southwest of Glennville (lat. 35°41'55" N, long. 118°44'45" W; at E line sec. 4, T 26 S, R 30 E). Named on Glennville (1972) 7.5' quadrangle.

Eric [KERN]: *locality,* 7 miles east of Tehachapi along the railroad (lat. 35°06'35" N, long. 118°19'30" W; at SE cor. sec. 28, T 32 S, R 34 E). Named on Monolith (1966) 7.5' quadrangle.

Eric Spring [FRESNO]: *spring,* 0.5 mile northeast of Smith Mountain (2) (lat. 36°05'05" N, long. 120°35'20" W; sec. 20, T 21 S, R 13 E). Named on Smith Mountain (1969) 7.5' quadrangle.

Ericsson: see **Mount Ericsson** [TULARE].

Ericsson Crags [TULARE]: *relief feature,* 11 miles northwest of Mount Whitney (lat. 36°42'10" N, long. 118°25' W); the feature is north of Mount Ericsson. Named on Mount Whitney (1956) 15' quadrangle.

Erin Lake [TULARE]: *lake,* 1700 feet long, 4.5 miles south of Mount Whitney (lat. 36°30'55" N, long. 118°17'10" W). Named on Mount Whitney (1956) 15' quadrangle. Chester Versteeg suggested the name because the outline of the lake on a map resembles the shape of Ireland on a map (Browning, p. 66).

Ershim Lake [FRESNO]: *lake,* 1500 feet long, 8 miles north-northeast of Dinkey Dome (lat. 37°12'50" N, long. 119°03'20" W). Named on Huntington Lake (1953) 15' quadrangle.

Erskine Creek [KERN]: *stream,* formed by the confluence of East Fork and Middle Fork, flows 8 miles to Kern River 1.5 miles north of Bodfish (lat. 35°36'40" N, long. 118°29'25" W; sec. 1, T 27 S, R 32 E). Named on Lake Isabella South (1972) 7.5' quadrangle. Whipple (p. 149) referred to Erskine's Creek. East Fork is 3 miles long and Middle Fork is 2.25 miles long; both forks are named on Lake Isabella South (1972) and Woolstalf Creek (1972) 7.5' quadrangles. South Fork, which enters from the south just below the confluence of East Fork and Middle Fork, is 6.5 miles long and is named on Lake Isabella South (1972) and Piute Peak (1972) 7.5' quadrangles.

Erskine Creek Cave [KERN]: *cave,* 2 miles east of Bodfish (lat. 35° 35'40" N, long. 118°27'05" W; sec. 8, T 27 S, R 33 E); the cave is above Erskine Creek. Named on Lake Isabella South (1972) 7.5' quadrangle.

Escarpado Canyon [FRESNO]: *canyon,* drained by a stream that flows 2 miles to lowlands 19 miles southwest of Firebaugh (lat. 36°38'30" N, long. 120°40'30" W; near W line sec. 9, T 15 S, R 12 E). Named on Chounet Ranch (1956) 7.5' quadrangle.

Eshel [FRESNO]: *locality,* 3 miles north-northeast of Malaga along Southern Pacific Railroad (lat. 36°43'20" N, long. 119°42'30" W; at S line sec. 8, T 14 S, R 21 E). Named on Malaga (1923) 7.5' quadrangle.

Eshom Creek [TULARE]: *stream,* flows 11 miles to North Fork Kaweah River 3 miles west-northwest of Yucca Mountain (lat. 36° 35'45" N, long. 118°55' W; sec. 27, T 15 S, R 28 E); the stream goes through Eshom Valley. Named on Giant Forest (1956) 15' quadrangle.

Eshom Point [TULARE]: *peak,* 6 miles northwest of Yucca Mountain (lat. 36°38' N, long. 118°56'20" W; sec. 9, T 15 S, R 28 E); the peak is 1.5 miles northeast of Eshom Valley. Named on Giant Forest (1956) 15' quadrangle.

Eshom Valley [TULARE]: *valley,* 6 miles northwest of Yucca Mountain (lat. 36°37'15" N, long. 119°57'45" W); the feature is along Eshom Creek. Named on Giant Forest (1956) 15' quadrangle. John Perry Eshom homesteaded in the valley (Browning, p. 66).

Esperanza: see **Dudley** [KINGS].

Esperanza Canyon [KERN]: *canyon,* drained by a stream that flows 1.25 miles to Kelso Valley 4.5 miles east-southeast of Claraville (lat. 35°25'05" N, long. 118°15'15" W; near E line sec. 18, T 29 S, R 35 E). Named on Claraville (1972) 7.5' quadrangle.

Etheda Springs [FRESNO]: *settlement,* 7 miles east-southeast of Dunlap (lat. 36°41'40" N, long. 119°00'25" W; sec. 23, T 14 S, R 27 E). Named on Miramonte (1966) 7.5' quadrangle.

Eugeneville: see **Garlock** [KERN].

Evans Creek [FRESNO]: *stream,* flows 2.5 miles to Boulder Creek (1) 6.5 miles east of Hume (lat. 36°48'10" N, long. 118°48'05" W). Named on Tehipite Dome (1952) 15' quadrangle. The name commemorates John Evans, who lived near Evans Grove and protected the trees there from fire (Browning, p. 67).

Evans Flat [KERN]: *area,* 6 miles south-southwest of Alta Sierra along Greenhorn Creek (lat. 35°38'45" N, long. 118°35'20" W; near SE cor. sec. 24, T 26 S, R 31 E). Named on Alta Sierra (1972) 7.5' quadrangle.

Evans Flat Campground [KERN]: *locality,* 6.25 miles south-southwest of Alta Sierra (lat. 35°38'30" N, long. 118°35'15" W; near NW cor. sec. 30, T 26 S, R 32 E); the place is near present Evans Flat. Named on Glennville (1956) 15' quadrangle.

Evelyn Lake [TULARE]: *lake,* 750 feet long, 7 miles southwest of Mineral King (lat. 36°23'05" N, long. 118°41' W). Named on Mineral King (1956) 15' quadrangle. The name commemorates Evelyn Clough, sister of William O. Clough of Clough Cave (United States Board on Geographic Names, 1933a, p. 294). United States Board on Geographic Names (1989b, p. 2) approved the name "Cahoon Rock" for a peak located 0.5 mile southwest of Evelyn Lake (lat. 36°22'43" N, long. 118°41'23" W), and rejected the name "Cahoon Peak" for the same feature.

Everts: see **Raco** [FRESNO].

Evolution Basin [FRESNO]: *canyon,* 3.5 miles long, 2 miles northeast of Mount Goddard (lat. 37°08' N, long. 118°41'45" W); the canyon is at the head of Evolution Creek. Named on Mount Goddard (1948) 15' quadrangle.

Evolution Creek [FRESNO]: *stream,* flows 11 miles to South Fork San Joaquin River 9 miles north of Blackcap Mountain (lat. 37°11'45" N, long. 118°47'45" W); the stream heads in Evolution Basin and goes through Evolution Valley. Named on Mount Goddard (1948) 15' quadrangle. Called Middle Branch on Lippincott's (1902) map. In 1895 Theodore S. Solomons named the peaks at the head of the stream (which then was called The Middle Fork of the South Fork of the San Joaquin River) for Darwin, Wallace, Huxley, Haeckel, Spencer, and Fiske—known as the evolution group of philosophers; he gave the name "Evolution Lake" to the lake at the foot of Mount Darwin, and the name was extended to the creek (Farquhar, 1923, p. 395).

Evolution Lake [FRESNO]: *lake,* nearly 1 mile long, 4.5 miles north-northeast of Mount Goddard (lat. 37°10' N, long. 118°41'40" W); the lake is along Evolution Creek 1.25 miles west of Mount Darwin. Named on Mount Goddard (1948) 15' quadrangle. Theodore S. Solomons named the lake in 1895 (Farquhar, 1923, p. 395).

Evolution Meadow [FRESNO]: *area,* 8.5 miles north of Blackcap Mountain (lat. 37°11'45" N, long. 118°46'35" W); the place is near the west end of Evolution Valley. Named on Blackcap Mountain (1953) 15' quadrangle.

Evolution Valley [FRESNO]: *valley,* 6 miles north-northwest of Mount Goddard (lat. 37°11'20" N, long. 118°45' W); Evolution Creek drains the valley. Named on Blackcap Mountain (1953) and Mount Goddard (1948) 15' quadrangles.

Ewe Lake [FRESNO]: *lake,* 500 feet long, 3 miles south-southwest of Mount Goddard (lat. 37°03'50" N, long, 118°44'50" W); the lake is situated next to Ram Lake (2). Named on Mount Goddard (1948) 15' quadrangle. William A. Dill of California Department of Fish and Game named the lake in 1948 for its proximity to Bighorn Lake (2) (Browning, p. 67).

Exchequer Creek [FRESNO]: *stream,* flows 4 miles to Dinkey Creek (1) 4.25 miles south-southwest of Dinkey Dome (lat. 37°03'30" N, long. 119°09'30" W; sec. 17, T 10 S, R 26 E); the stream goes through Exchequer Meadow. Named on Huntington Lake (1953) 15' quadrangle.

Exchequer Meadow [FRESNO]: *area,* 3 miles south-southeast of Dinkey

Dome (lat. 37°04'20" N, long. 119°06'45" W; on W line sec. 11, T 10 S, R 26 E); the place is along Exchequer Creek. Named on Huntington Lake (1953) 15' quadrangle.

Exeter [TULARE]: *town,* 9 miles east-southeast of Visalia (lat. 36° 17'45" N, long. 119°08'15" W; around NE cor. sec. 10, T 19 S, R 26 E). Named on Exeter (1952) 15' quadrangle. D.W. Parkhurst, land agent for Southern Pacific Railroad, named the town in 1888 for his home at Exeter, England; previously the place was called Firebaugh, for John Firebaugh, an owner of the townsite (Mitchell, A.R., p. 68). Postal authorities established Exeter post office in 1889 (Frickstad, p. 210), and the town incorporated in 1911. California Mining Bureau's (1917b) map shows a place called Orangehurst located along the railroad between Exeter and Lindsay. Postal authorities established Orangehurst post office in 1908 and discontinued it in 1916 (Frickstad, p. 212). California Mining Bureau's (1917b) map also shows a place called Kaweah located along the railroad about 4 miles north-northwest of Exeter, and shows a place called Velma situated about 2 miles northwest of Kaweah along the same railroad. Postal authorities established Velma post office 7 miles northwest of Exeter (NW quarter of sec. 21, T 18 S, R 26 E) in 1911 and it discontinued in 1913; the name "Velma" was for the postmaster's wife (Salley, p. 230).

— F —

Failing: see **Smith and Failing Meadow** [TULARE].

Faires [KERN]: *locality,* 5 miles north of Rosamond (lat. 34°55'50" N, long. 118°09' W). Named on Rosamond (1943) 15' quadrangle.

Fairview [FRESNO]: *locality,* 9 miles east-southeast of Clovis along Atchison, Topeka and Santa Fe Railroad (lat. 36°45'50" N, long. 119°33'20" W; near NE cor. sec. 34, T 13 S, R 22 E). Named on Round Mountain (1964) 7.5' quadrangle.

Fairview [TULARE]: *locality,* 11 miles east-northeast of California Hot Springs along Kern River (lat. 35°55'30" N, long. 118°29'40" W). Named on Kernville (1956) 15' quadrangle. Called Roads End on Bakersfield (1956) 1°x 2° quadrangle. Postal authorities established Roads End post office in 1936 and discontinued it in 1955; the road north along Kern River formerly ended at the site (Salley, p. 186).

Fairy Gulch [KERN]: *canyon,* 0.25 mile long, 5 miles north of Randsburg near Teagle (lat. 35°26'25" N, long. 117°38'20" W; sec. 1, T 29 S, R 40 E). Named on Randsburg (1911) 15' quadrangle.

Fall Creek [FRESNO]: *stream,* flows 5.5 miles to North Fork Kings River 2.5 miles west of Blackcap Mountain (lat. 37°04'30" N, long. 118°50'30" W). Named on Blackcap Mountain (1953) 15' quadrangle.

Falls Canyon [KINGS]: *canyon,* drained by a stream that flows 1.5 miles to Avenal Canyon 9.5 miles south-southwest of Avenal (lat. 35°52'55" N, long. 120°12'25" W; sec. 35, T 23 S, R 16 E). Named on Garza Peak (1953) 7.5' quadrangle.

Falls Creek [KERN]: *stream,* flows nearly 2 miles to Jawbone Canyon 4 miles west-southwest of Cross Mountain (lat. 35°15'05" N, long. 118°11'50" W; sec. 11, T 31 S, R 35 E). Named on Cache Peak (1973) and Cross Mountain (1972) 7.5' quadrangles.

Famoso [KERN]: *village,* 5.5 miles south-southeast of McFarland along Poso Creek (lat. 35°35'50" N, long. 119°12'20" W; near E line sec. 7, T 27 S, R 26 E). Named on Famoso (1953) 7.5' quadrangle. Wheeler's (1875-1878) map shows a place called Poso at the site. Postal authorities established Spottiswood post office in 1888, changed the name to Famoso in 1895, closed it for a time in 1919, moved it 0.5 mile northwest in 1940, and discontinued it in 1946 (Salley, p. 73, 210). Officials of Southern Pacific Railroad called their station at the site Poso, for Poso Creek, when the rail line reached the place in the 1870's, but postal authorities refused to accept the name (Gudde, 1949, p. 113). California Mining Bureau's (1917c) map shows a place called Page located about 5 miles south of Famoso along the railroad.

Fancher Creek [FRESNO]: *stream,* flows 13 miles to flat lands 9 miles east of Clovis (lat. 36°48' N, long. 119°32'10" W; near W line sec. 13, T 13 S, R 22 E). Named on Humphreys Station (1965), Piedra (1965), and Round Mountain (1964) 7.5' quadrangles. Called Fancy Creek on Round Mountain (1922) 7.5' quadrangle. Grunsky (p. 71) gave the name "Fanshaw Creek" as an alternate.

Fancy Creek: see **Fancher Creek** [FRESNO].

Fane [TULARE]: *locality,* 5.25 miles north of Exeter along Atchison, Topeka and Santa Fe Railroad (lat. 36°22'15" N, long. 119°08' W; near SW cor. sec. 11, T 18 S, R 26 E). Named on Exeter (1952) 15' quadrangle.

Fanshaw Creek: see **Fancher Creek** [FRESNO].

Farewell Canyon [TULARE]: *canyon,* 2 miles long, 3 miles south-southeast of Mineral King at the head of East Fork Kaweah River (lat. 36°24'45" N, long. 118°34'30" W); the canyon heads at Farewell Gap. Named on Mineral King (1956) 15' quadrangle.

Farewell Gap [TULARE]: *pass,* nearly 4 miles south-southeast of Mineral King (lat. 36°24' N, long. 118°34'10" W); the pass is at the head of Farewell Canyon. Named on Mineral King (1956) 15' quadrangle. Miners named the feature about 1872 (Browning, p. 68).

Fargo [FRESNO]: *locality,* 5.25 miles south-southeast of Sanger along Southern Pacific Railroad (lat. 36°38'10" N, long. 119°30'45" W; sec. 7, T 15 S, R 23 E). Named on Selma (1946) 15' quadrangle. Called Fortuna on Grunsky's (1898) map.

Farmersville [TULARE]: *town,* 4 miles west of Exeter (lat. 36° 18' N, long. 119°12'25" W; around SE cor. sec. 1, T 19 S, R 25 E). Named on Exeter (1952) 15' quadrangle. Postal authorities established Farmersville post office in 1868 and moved it 0.5 mile north in 1900 (Salley, p. 73). The town incorporated in 1960. Settlers named the place about 1860 (Mitchell, A.R., p. 68).

Farmersville: see **East Farmersville** [TULARE].

Farquhar: see **Mount Farquhar**, under **Mount Brewer** [TULARE].

Fat Cow Meadow [TULARE]: *area,* 5.5 miles west-northwest of Olancha Peak (lat. 36°17'45" N, long. 118°12'30" W; sec. 5, 8, T 19 S, R 35 E). Named on Olancha (1956) 15' quadrangle.

Faull Slough [KINGS]: *stream,* flows nearly 2 miles to North Fork Kings River 7.5 miles northwest of Lemoore (lat. 36°22'25" N, long. 119°53'05" W; near SW cor. sec. 11, T 18 S, R 19 E). Named on Burrel (1954), Riverdale (1954), and Vanguard (1956) 7.5' quadrangles. Called N. Fk. Kings River on Riverdale (1927) 7.5' quadrangle, where present North Fork Kings River is called Fresno Slough.

Faust Mill [KERN]: *locality,* 6.5 miles southeast of Bodfish (lat. 35° 30'55" N, long. 118°24'30" W; at S line sec. 2, T 28 S, R 33 E). Ruins of the place are named on Lake Isabella South (1972) 7.5' quadrangle.

Fawn Meadow [FRESNO]: *area,* 10.5 miles north-northeast of Kaiser Peak (lat. 37°26'20" N, long. 119°07'20" W). Named on Kaiser Peak (1953) 15' quadrangle.

Faxon: see **Goshen** [TULARE].

Fay Creek [KERN-TULARE]: *stream,* heads in Tulare County and flows 12.5 miles to South Fork Valley 2 miles north-northwest of Weldon in Kern County (lat. 35°41'35" N, long. 118°18'05" W; sec. 2, T 26 S, R 34 E). Named on Kernville (1956) 15' quadrangle, and on Weldon (1972) 7.5' quadrangle. Called Fay Ranch Cr. on Olmsted's (1900) map.

Fayette [TULARE]: *locality,* 1.5 miles east-southeast of Lindsay along Visalia Electric Railroad (lat. 36°12'05" N, long. 119°03'50" W; sec. 8, T 20 S, R 27 E). Named on Lindsay (1951) 7.5' quadrangle.

Fay Ranch Creek: see **Fay Creek** [KERN-TULARE].

Feather Lake: see **Vermillion Lake** [FRESNO].

Fellows [KERN]: *town,* 5 miles west-northwest of Taft (lat. 35°10'40" N, long. 119°32'25" W; near N line sec. 6, T 32 S, R 23 E). Named on Fellows (1951) 7.5' quadrangle. Postal authorities established Fellows post office in 1910 (Frickstad, p. 55). The name commemorates Charles A. Fellows, a contractor for Sunset Western Railroad (Bailey, 1967, p. 8). California Mining Bureau's (1917c) map shows a place called Vernette located about 1 mile north-northwest of Fellows along the railroad, and a place called Shale situated 1 mile northwest of Vernette along the railroad. Postal authorities established Shale post office in 1912 and discontinued it in 1923 (Frickstad, p. 59). California Mining Bureau's (1909a) map shows a place called Midway located at or near present Fellows.

Fence Camp Flat [KERN]: *area,* 5.25 miles north of Caliente along Walker Basin Creek (lat. 35°21'55" N, long. 118°36'55" W; at E line sec. 35, T 29 S, R 31 E); the place is 0.25 mile northwest of Fence Camp Spring. Named on Oiler Peak (1972) 7.5' quadrangle.

Fence Camp Spring [KERN]: *spring,* 5 miles north or Caliente (lat. 35°21'40" N, long. 118°36'40" W; sec. 36, T 29 S, R 31 E). Named on Oiler Peak (1972) 7.5' quadrangle.

Fence Meadow [FRESNO]: *area,* 5.5 miles north-northwest of Balch Camp (lat. 36°58'25" N, long. 119°10'20" W). Named on Patterson Mountain (1952) 15' quadrangle.

Ferguson Creek [TULARE]: *stream,* flows 8.5 miles to Sugarloaf Creek just inside Fresno County 11.5 miles north-northwest of Triple Divide Peak (lat. 36°44'25" N, long. 118°37'35" W). Named on Triple Divide Peak (1956) 15' quadrangle. S.L.N. Ellis named the creek in the early 1920's for Andrew D. Ferguson, who in 1916 was appointed field agent for California Department of Fish and Game; earlier the stream was called Bog Creek (Browning, p. 69). West Fork enters from the south-southwest 2.5 miles upstream from the mouth of the main stream; it is 5.5 miles long and is named on Triple Divide Peak (1956) 15' quadrangle.

Ferguson Meadow [TULARE]: *area,* 6 miles northwest of Triple Divide Peak (lat. 36°39'15" N, long. 118°36'35" W); the place is along Ferguson Creek. Named on Triple Divide Peak (1956) 15' quadrangle. United States Board on Geographic Names (1938, p. 20) rejected the name "Long Meadow" for the feature.

Fern Lake [FRESNO]: *lake,* 750 feet long, 14 miles northeast of Kaiser Peak (lat. 37°27'25" N, long. 119°02'30" W). Named on Kaiser Peak (1953) 15' quadrangle. The feature is one of the group called Margaret Lakes.

Fiddler Gulch [KERN]: *canyon,* drained by a stream that flows 5.5 miles to Fremont Valley 4.5 miles northwest of Randsburg (lat. 35° 24'20" N, long. 117°43' W; near N line sec. 20, T 29 S, R 40 E). Named on El Paso Peaks (1967) and Johannesburg (1967) 7.5' quadrangles. The name is from the fiddlers who made music at the place in the evenings (Wynn, 1963, p. 97).

Figarden [FRESNO]: *village,* 6 miles northwest of downtown Fresno (lat. 36°49'25" N, long. 119°51'35" W; near SW cor. sec. 1, T 13 S, R 19 E). Named on Fresno North (1965) 7.5' quadrangle. Called Bullard on Bullard (1923) 7.5' quadrangle. Postal authorities established Figarden post office in 1925, moved it 0.25 mile east in 1939, discontinued it in 1944, reestablished it in 1947, discontinued it in 1951, and reestablished it in 1952 with the name "Fig Garden Village" (Salley, p. 74). The name "Figarden" was given because of a large fig orchard at the place (Stewart, p. 165). California Mining Bureau's (1917a) map shows a place called Andrews located along the railroad between Fresno and Bullard about 4 miles southeast of Figarden in present Fresno.

Fig Garden Village: see **Figarden** [FRESNO].

Fig Orchard [KERN]: *locality,* nearly 3 miles east-northeast of Caliente along Caliente Creek (lat. 35°18'30" N, long. 118°35' W; near N line sec. 19, T 30 S, R 32 E). Named on Oiler Peak (1972) 7.5' quadrangle.

Fig Spring [FRESNO]: *spring,* 7.25 miles northwest of Coalinga in Post Canyon (lat. 36°11'55" N, long. 120°28' W; sec. 8, T 20 S, R 14 E). Named on Alcalde Hills (1969) 7.5' quadrangle.

Fig Tree Spring [KERN]:

(1) *spring,* nearly 2 miles southwest of Orchard Peak (lat. 34°43'05" N, long. 120°09'20" W; sec. 29, T 25 S, R 17 E). Named on Orchard Peak (1961) 7.5' quadrangle.

(2) *spring,* 6 miles north-northwest of Caliente (lat. 35°22'10" N, long. 118°40'20" W; near N line sec. 32, T 29 S, R 31 E). Named on Bena (1972) 7.5' quadrangle.

Filly Lake [FRESNO]: *lake,* 700 feet long, 1.25 miles north of Blackcap Mountain (lat. 37°05'30" N, long. 118°47'30" W). Named on Blackcap Mountain (1953) 15' quadrangle.

Filo: see **Strathmore** [TULARE].

Finch: see **Rosy Finch Lake** [FRESNO].

Fin Dome [FRESNO]: *peak,* 9 miles south of Mount Pinchot (lat. 36° 48'50" N, long. 118°24'40" W). Altitude 11,693 feet. Named on Mount Pinchot (1953) 15' quadrangle. Bolton C. Brown named the peak in 1899 for the fancied resemblance of the feature to the fin on the back of a sea serpent (Browning, p. 69).

Fine Spring [KERN]: *spring,* nearly 4 miles east of Woody (lat. 35° 42'20" N, long. 118°45'55" W; near SE cor. sec. 32, T 25 S, R 30 E). Named on Woody (1965) 7.5' quadrangle.

Fingerbowl Lake [FRESNO]: *lake,* 400 feet long, 4.25 miles northeast of Dinkey Dome (lat. 37°09' N, long. 119°04'05" W; sec. 18, T 9 S, R 27 E). Named on Huntington Lake (1953) 15' quadrangle. The feature also was called Lake Elsie and Little Deep Lake (Browning, p. 69).

Finger Peak [FRESNO]: *peak,* 5 miles south of Mount Goddard (lat. 37°01'50" N, long. 118°43'45" W). Altitude 12,404 feet. Named on Mount Goddard (1948) 15' quadrangle.

Finger Peak: see **Buck Rock** [TULARE].

Finger Rock [FRESNO]: *relief feature,* 14 miles north of Hume (lat. 36°59'30" N, long. 118°54'35" W). Altitude 9606 feet. Named on Tehipite Dome (1952) 15' quadrangle. The feature originally was called Chimney Rock (Forest Clingan, personal communication, 1989).

Finger Rock [TULARE]: *peak,* 6 miles south-southeast of Monache Mountain (lat. 36°07'15" N, long. 118°10' W; near S line sec. 2, T 21 S, R 35 E). Altitude 9145 feet. Named on Monache Mountain (1956) 15' quadrangle.

Finger Rock: see **Buck Rock** [TULARE].

Fir Camp Saddle [TULARE]: *pass,* nearly 6 miles southeast of California Hot Springs (lat. 35°49'45" N, long. 118°35'20" W; sec. 24, T 24 S, R 31 E). Named on California Hot Springs (1958) 15' quadrangle.

Firebaugh [FRESNO]: *town,* 38 miles west of Fresno on the west side of San Joaquin River (lat. 36°51'30" N, long. 120°27'15" W; in and near sec. 28, 29, T 12 S, R 14 E). Named on Firebaugh (1956) 7.5' quadrangle. A.D. Fierbaugh established a trading post and ferry across San Joaquin River in 1854; the misspelled name "Firebaugh's Ferry" was used as early as 1856 (Gudde, 1949, p. 116). Postal authorities established Firebaugh's Ferry post office in 1860 and discontinued it in 1862; they established Firebaugh post office in 1865 (Frickstad, p. 33). The town incorporated in 1914. The place was a station on Butterfield Overland stage line (Ormsby, p. 120-121).

Firebaugh: see **Exeter** [TULARE].

Firebaugh's Ferry: see **Firebaugh** [FRESNO].

First Dinkey Lake [FRESNO]: *lake,* 1500 feet long, 5 miles northeast of Dinkey Dome (lat. 37°09'50" N, long. 119°04' W; sec. 7, T 9 S, R 27 E); the feature is along upper reaches of Dinkey Creek 1 mile downstream from Second Dinkey Lake. Named on Huntington Lake (1953) 15' quadrangle. Called Dinkey Lake on Kaiser (1904) 30' quadrangle.

First Recess [FRESNO]: *canyon,* drained by a stream that flows 2.5 miles to Mono Creek 5.25 miles west-northwest of Mount Abbot (lat. 37°25'10" N, long. 118°52'10" W); the feature is the first major canyon east of Lake Thomas A. Edison on the south side of Mono Creek. Named on Mount Abbot (1953) 15' quadrangle. Theodore S. Solomons discovered and named the canyon in 1894 (Farquhar, 1925, p. 127).

First Recess Lakes [FRESNO]: *lakes,* two, each about 500 feet long, 4.25 miles west of Mount Abbot (lat. 37°23'40" N, long. 118°51'30" W); the lakes are near the head of First Recess. Named on Mount Abbot (1953) 15' quadrangle.

Fish Camp [FRESNO]: *locality,* nearly 5 miles northwest of Mount Abbot along Mono Creek (lat. 37°25'35" N, long. 118°51'15" W). Named on Mount Abbot (1953) 15' quadrangle.

Fish Canyon: see **Pescado Creek** [KERN].

Fish Creek [FRESNO]:

(1) *stream,* flows 16 miles to Madera County 3.25 miles west-northwest of Double Peak (lat. 37°31'50" N, long. 119°05'25" W). Named on Devils Postpile (1953), Mount Abbot (1953), and Mount Morrison (1953) 15' quadrangles.

(2) *stream,* flows nearly 6 miles to Kings River 2 miles southwest of Piedra (lat. 36°47'35" N, long. 119°24'40" W; near NE cor. sec. 24, T 13 S, R 23 E). Named on Piedra (1965) 7.5' quadrangle.

Fish Creek [TULARE]:

(1) *stream,* flows 5.5 miles to Little Kern River 4.25 miles west-southwest of Hockett Peak (lat. 36°12'15" N, long. 118°27'30" W). Named on Camp Nelson (1956) and Hockett Peak (1956) 15' quadrangles.

(2) *stream,* flows 19 miles to South Fork Kern River 13 miles north-northwest of Lamont Peak (lat. 35°57'10" N, long. 118°09'50" W; near W line sec. 1, T 23 S, R 35 E). Named on Hockett Peak (1956), Lamont Peak (1956), and Monache Mountain (1956) 15' quadrangles.

Fish Creek Hot Springs [FRESNO]: *spring,* 1.5 miles north-northeast of Double Peak along Sharktooth Creek (lat. 37°31'55" N, long. 119°01'30" W); the spring is 1 mile upstream from Fish Creek (1). Named on Devils Postpile (1953) 15' quadrangle. United States Board on Geographic Names (1984a, p. 2) approved the name "Iva Bell Hot Springs" for the feature to commemorate a woman who was born at the site.

Fish Creek Meadow [TULARE]: *area,* 11 miles south of Monache Mountain (lat. 36°03' N, long. 118°12' W; sec. 33, T 21 S, R 35 E); the place is along Fish Creek (2). Named on Monache Mountain (1956) 15' quadrangle. United States Board on Geographic Names (1988a, p. 2) approved the name "Rodeo Flat" for the feature.

Fisher Flat [TULARE]: *area,* 3.5 miles north of Cliff Peak (lat. 36° 36'35" N, long. 119°10'05" W; sec. 20, T 15 S, R 26 E). Named on Stokes Mountain (1966) 7.5' quadrangle.

Fisher Flat: see **Mankins Flat** [TULARE] (1).

Fish Slough [FRESNO]: *water feature,* extends for 2 miles from Fresno Slough to James Bypass 2 miles north of Helm (lat. 36°33'45" N, long. 120°05'30" W). Named on Helm (1963) 7.5' quadrangle.

Fish Valley [FRESNO]: *canyon,* 3 miles long, 2 miles northwest of Double Peak (lat. 37°32' N, long. 119°03'45" W); the canyon is along Fish Creek (1). Named on Devils Postpile (1953) 15' quadrangle.

Fiske: see **Mount Fiske** [FRESNO].

Fiss Hill [KERN]: *hill,* 4 miles northwest of Rosamond (lat. 34° 54' N, long. 118°13' W; near W line sec. 1, T 9 N, R 13 W). Named on Rosamond (1956) 15' quadrangle.

Five Dog Creek [KERN]: *stream,* flows 25 miles to Rag Gulch 12.5 miles east of Delano (lat. 35°45'50" N, long. 119°01'45" W; near SE cor. sec. 11, T 25 S, R 27 E). Named on Deepwell Ranch (1952), Knob Hill (1965), Pine Mountain (1965), Richgrove (1952), Sand Canyon (1965), and Woody (1965) 7.5' quadrangles. Called Dead Ox Creek on Woody (1935) 15' quadrangle, but United States Board on Geographic Names (1966b, p. 4) rejected this name for the stream. Boyd (p. 159) noted that the name "Five Dogs Gulch" is from five dogs at a mining camp of the 1860's.

Five Dogs: see **Granite Station** [KERN].

Five Dogs Gulch: see **Five Dog Creek** [KERN].

Five Fingers [KERN]: *relief features,* 6.25 miles west-northwest of Inyokern (lat. 35°41'15" N, long. 117°54'25" W; sec. 8, T 26 S, R 38 E). Named on Owens Peak (1972) 7.5' quadrangle.

Five Lakes: see **Big Five Lakes** [TULARE]; **Little Five Lakes** [TULARE].

Five Points [FRESNO]: *settlement,* 25 miles northeast of Coalinga (lat. 35°25'45" N, long. 120°06'05" W; near SW cor. sec. 23, T 17 S, R 17 E); five roads meet at the place. Named on Five Points (1956) 7.5' quadrangle. Postal authorities established Five Points post office in 1944 (Frickstad, p 33).

Five Points [KERN]: *locality,* 3.5 miles east of Cummings Mountain (lat. 35°03'05" N, long. 118°30'40" W; at N line sec. 18, T 11 N, R 15 W); five roads meet at the site. Named on Cummings Mountain (1966) 7.5' quadrangle.

Five Springs [FRESNO]: *spring,* 4 miles east-southeast of Tivy Mountain (lat. 36°46'10" N, long. 119°17'35" W; sec. 30, T 13 S, R 25 E). Named on Pine Flat Dam (1965) 7.5' quadrangle.

Flag Peak [FRESNO]: *peak,* 2.5 miles north-northeast of Coalinga Mineral Springs on Juniper Ridge (lat. 36°10'40" N, long. 120°31'50" W; near W line sec. 24, T 20 S, R 13 E). Altitude 3966 feet. Named on Sherman Peak (1969) 7.5' quadrangle. Called Sherman Peak on Priest Valley (1915) 30' quadrangle.

Flatiron [TULARE]: *relief feature,* 4 miles south-southwest of Hockett Peak between Kern River and Little Kern River (lat. 36° 10' N, long. 118°25' W). Named on Hockett Peak (1956) 15' quadrangle.

Flat Note Lake [FRESNO]: *lake,* 700 feet long, 7.5 miles south-southwest of Mount Abbot (lat. 37°17'40" N, long. 118°51'10" W); less than 1 mile north of Sharp Note Lake. Named on Mount Abbot (1953) 15' quadrangle.

Flattop [KINGS]: *peak,* 5.5 miles south-southwest of Avenal on Reef Ridge (lat. 35°55'40" N, long. 120°09'15" W; sec. 17, T 23 S, R 17 E). Altitude 2205 feet. Named on Garza Peak (1953) 7.5' quadrangle.

Fleming Creek [FRESNO]: *stream,* flows 7.5 miles to North Fork Kings River 4.25 miles west-northwest of Blackcap Mountain (lat. 37°05'10" N, long. 118°52'05" W; sec. 1, T 10 S, R 28 E). Named on Blackcap Mountain (1953) 15' quadrangle.

Fleming Lake [FRESNO]: *lake,* 700 feet long, 6 miles north-northwest of Blackcap Mountain (lat. 37°08'45" N, long. 118°51' W); the lake is along Fleming Creek 1 mile south-southeast of Fleming Mountain. Named on Blackcap Mountain (1953) 15' quadrangle.

Fleming Mountain [FRESNO]: *peak,* 7 miles north-northwest of Blackcap Mountain (lat. 37°09'30" N, long. 118°51'25" W); the peak is west of Fleming Creek. Altitude 10,796 feet. Named on Blackcap Mountain (1953) 15' quadrangle.

Fleta [KERN]: *locality,* 3.5 miles south-southeast of Mojave along Southern Pacific Railroad (lat. 35°00'15" N, long. 118°09'25" W; sec. 33, T 11 N, R 12 W). Named on Mojave (1973) and Soledad Mountain (1973) 7.5' quadrangles.

Florence Lake [FRESNO]: *lake,* behind a dam on South Fork San Joaquin River 13 miles southwest of Mount Abbot (lat. 37°16'20" N, long. 118°58' W). Named on Blackcap Mountain (1953) and Mount Abbot (1953) 15' quadrangles. Mount Goddard (1912) 30' quadrangle has the name "Lake Florence" for a natural lake in the upper part of the basin of present Florence Lake; Walter H. Starr and his companions camped by this lake in 1896 and named it for Walter's sister (Farquhar, 1923, p. 395-396). United States Board on Geographic Names (1965b, p. 13) rejected the name "Lake Florence" for the present lake.

Florence Peak [TULARE]: *peak,* 4 miles southeast of Mineral King on Great Western Divide (lat. 36°24'20" N, long. 118°33' W). Altitude 12,432 feet. Named on Mineral King (1956) 15' quadrangle. United States Board on Geographic Names (1933a, p. 305) once approved the name "Mount Florence" for the feature, and rejected the name "Mount Needham."

Floyd [FRESNO]: *locality,* 11 miles west of downtown Fresno along Southern Pacific Railroad (lat. 36°44'05" N, long. 119°59'30" W; at N line sec. 10, T 14 S, R 18 E). Named on Kearney Park (1923) 7.5' quadrangle.

Fluhr [KERN]: *locality,* 2 miles north-northwest of present Edwards along Atchison, Topeka and Santa Fe Railroad (lat. 34°56'45" N, long. 117°57' W; at W line sec. 21, T 10 N, R 10 W). Named on Rogers Lake (1942) 15' quadrangle. The name commemorates C.G. Fluhr, a superintendent of the railroad (Hanna, p. 108).

Flume Peak [FRESNO]: *peak,* 2.5 miles north-northwest of Shaver Lake Heights (present town of Shaver Lake) (lat. 37°08'40" N, long. 119°20' W; near E line sec. 15, T 9 S, R 24 E). Altitude 5979 feet. Named on Shaver Lake (1953) 15' quadrangle. Kaiser (1904) 30' quadrangle shows a flume belonging to Fresno Flume and Irrigation Co. west of the peak.

Fly Creek [TULARE]: *stream,* flows 2 miles to Bear Creek (1) 6 miles southeast of Auckland (lat. 36°31'35" N, long. 119°01'35" W; sec. 22, T 16 S, R 27 E). Named on Auckland (1966) 7.5' quadrangle.

Flying Dutchman Creek [KERN]: *stream,* flows nearly 3 miles to Havilah Canyon 15 miles north-northeast of Caliente (lat. 35°29'10" N, long. 118°31'30" W; at N line sec. 22, T 28 S, R 32 E). Named on Breckenridge Mountain (1972) 7.5' quadrangle.

Flynn Canyon [TULARE]: *canyon,* flows 3 miles to Tobias Creek 10 miles east-northeast of California Hot Springs (lat. 35°55'05" N, long. 118°30' W; near W line sec. 23, T 23 S, R 32 E). Named on California Hot Springs (1958) 15' quadrangle.

Foolish Lake [FRESNO]: *lake,* 400 feet long, 8.5 miles southwest of Mount Abbot (lat. 37°18'15" N, long. 118°54' W). Named on Mount Abbot (1953) 15' quadrangle. Employees of California Department of Fish and Game gave the name to the lake in 1948 because they thought that it would be foolish for anyone to revisit the place (Browning, p. 72).

Footman Canyon [FRESNO]: *canyon,* drained by a stream that flows 1.25 miles to Boulder Creek (1) 6.5 miles east of Hume (lat. 36°46'45" N, long. 118°46'45" W). Named on Tehipite Dome (1952) 15' quadrangle.

Ford City [KERN]: *town,* 1 mile north of downtown Taft (lat. 35°09'20" N, long. 119°27'30" W; sec. 12, T 32 S, R 23 E). Named on Taft (1950) 7.5' quadrangle. The name is from the abundance of Model-T Ford cars at the place when it was an oil-boom tent city (Hanna, p. 108).

Ford's Camp: see **Mineral King** [TULARE].

Forester Pass [TULARE]: *pass,* 9 miles north-northwest of Mount Whitney on Kings-Kern Divide (lat. 36°41'40" N, long. 118°22'15" W). Named on Mount Whitney (1956) 15' quadrangle. Frank Cunningham, supervisor of Sequoia National Forest, named the pass in 1929 for the foresters—including himself—who discovered it (Browning, p. 73).

Forgotten Canyon [TULARE]: *canyon,* drained by a stream that flows 2.5 miles to Rock Creek 13 miles north-northwest of Kern Peak (lat. 36°29'30" N, long. 118°20'30" W). Named on Kern Peak (1956) 15' quadrangle.

Forked Meadow Creek [FRESNO]: *stream,* flows 1 mile to Dinkey Creek (1) 4 miles south-southwest of Dinkey Dome (lat. 37°03'30" N, long. 119°09'30" W; sec. 17, T 10 S, R 26 E). Named on Huntington Lake (1953) 15' quadrangle.

Fort Camp: see **Forthcamp** [FRESNO].

Forthcamp [FRESNO]: *locality,* 4.25 miles south-southeast of Clovis along Atchison, Topeka and Santa Fe Railroad (lat. 36°45'50" N, long. 119°40'20" W; at N line sec. 34, T 13 S, R 21 E). Named on Clovis (1946) 15' quadrangle. Called Fort Camp on Clovis (1922) 7.5' quadrangle, which shows the place along Fresno Interurban Railroad.

Fort Hill: see **Keyesville** [KERN].

Fort Keysville: see **Keyesville** [KERN].

Fort Miller: see **Old Fort Miller** [FRESNO]; **Old Millerton** [FRESNO].

Fort Tejon: see **Old Fort Tejon** [KERN].

Fortuna: see **Fargo** [FRESNO].

Fort Washington: see **Old Fort Miller** [FRESNO].

Foster Ridge [FRESNO]: *ridge,* northeast-trending, 2.5 miles long, 3 miles north-northwest of Dinkey Dome (lat. 37°09'25" N, long. 119°08'30" W). Named on Huntington Lake (1953) 15' quadrangle.

Fountain Spring: see **Fountain Springs** [TULARE].

Fountain Springs [TULARE]: *locality,* 7 miles east of Ducor (lat. 35°53'25" N, long. 118°54'50" W; near N line sec. 35, T 23 S, R 28 E). Named on Fountain Springs (1965) 7.5' quadrangle. Postal authorities established Fountain Springs post office in 1875, discontinued it for a time in 1878, discontinued it in 1879, reestablished it in 1887, and discontinued it in 1888 (Frickstad, p. 210). A spring at the place called Fountain Spring was long known and used (Waring, p. 336). Officials of Butterfield Overland stage line had one of their stations built at the site in 1858 (Hanna, p. 110).

Fountain Springs Gulch [TULARE]: *canyon,* drained by a stream that flows 22 miles to Deer Creek (2) 6 miles north of Ducor (lat. 35°58'55" N, long. 119°02'35" W; sec. 27, T 22 S, R 27 E); the place called Fountain Springs is in the canyon. Named on Fountain Springs (1965), Gibbon Peak (1965), and Quincy School (1965) 7.5' quadrangles.

Four Canyons [TULARE]: *relief feature,* 5.5 miles north-northwest of Olancha Peak (lat. 36°20'30" N, long. 118°09'20" W). Named on Olancha (1956) 15' quadrangle. United States Board on Geographic Names (1989a, p. 4) rejected the name "Four Canyons Meadow" for the feature.

Four Canyons Meadow: see **Four Canyons** [TULARE].

Four Creek Country: see **Kaweah River** [TULARE].

Four Forks Creek [FRESNO]: *stream,* flows 5.5 miles to South Fork San Joaquin River 8 miles north-northeast of Mount Tom (lat. 37° 24'15" N, long. 119°07'45" W). Named on Kaiser Peak (1953) 15' quadrangle.

Four Gables [FRESNO]: *peak,* nearly 3 miles north-northwest of Mount Humphreys on Fresno-Inyo County line (lat. 37°18'25" N, long. 118°41'35" W; near SW cor. sec. 28, T 7 S, R 30 E). Named on Mount Tom (1949) 15' quadrangle.

Four Springs Gulch [KERN]: *canyon,* drained by a stream that flows nearly 4 miles to Dead Ox Creek 3.5 miles southwest of Woody (lat. 35°40' N, long. 118°52'45" W; sec. 17, T 26 S, R 29 E). Named on Sand Canyon (1965) and Woody (1965) 7.5' quadrangles.

Fourth Home Extension Colony: see **Wasco** [KERN].

Fourth Recess [FRESNO]: *canyon,* drained by a stream that flows 3.5 miles to Golden Creek 4.25 miles north of Mount Abbot (lat. 37°26'55" N, long. 118°47'25" W); the feature is the fourth large canyon east of Lake Thomas A. Edison on the south side of Mono Creek. Named on Mount Abbot (1953) 15' quadrangle. Theodore S. Solomons discovered and named the feature in 1894 (Farquhar, 1925, p. 127).

Fourth Recess Lake [FRESNO]: *lake,* 3300 feet long, 3.5 miles north of Mount Abbot (lat. 37°26'15" N, long. 118°47'05" W); the lake is in Fourth Recess. Named on Mount Abbot (1953) 15' quadrangle.

Fowler [FRESNO]: *town,* 11 miles southeast of downtown Fresno (lat. 36°37'50" N, long. 119°40'35" W; in and near sec. 15, T 15 S, R 21 E). Named on Conejo (1963) and Malaga (1964) 7.5' quadrangles. Postal authorities established Fowler post office in 1882 (Frickstad, p. 33), and the town incorporated in 1908. The name commemorates Thomas Fowler, cattle rancher and California state senator, who shipped cattle from a corral at the site (Hanna, p. 110).

Fox Canyon [FRESNO]: *canyon,* drained by a stream that flows nearly 2 miles to Kings River 6 miles east-southeast of Balch Camp (lat. 36°51'35" N, long. 119°00'55" W; sec. 27, T 12 S, R 27 E). Named on Patterson Mountain (1952) 15' quadrangle.

Fox Canyon [KERN]: *canyon,* drained by a stream that flows 4 miles to Indian Creek 2 miles west-northwest of Emerald Mountain (lat. 35°15'50" N, long. 118°19' W; sec. 3, T 31 S, R 34 E). Named on Emerald Mountain (1972) and Tehachapi NE (1966) 7.5' quadrangles.

Fox Creek: see **Hotel Creek** [FRESNO]; **Sheep Creek** [FRESNO].

Fox Flat [TULARE]: *area,* 6 miles west-northwest of Yucca Mountain (lat. 36°35'15" N, long. 118°58'15" W; sec. 30, T 15 S, R 28 E). Named on Giant Forest (1956) 15' quadrangle.

Fox Meadow [TULARE]: *area,* 1.5 miles northwest of Shell Mountain (lat. 36°42'30" N, long. 118°49' W; sec. 15, T 14 S, R 29 E). Named on Giant Forest (1956) 15' quadrangle. The name commemorates John Fox, a packer, hunter, and guide in the Kings River neighborhood (Hanna, p. 110).

Fox Spring [FRESNO]: *spring,* 10 miles south-southeast of Balch Camp (lat. 36°46'15" N, long. 119°04'45" W; at N line sec. 30, T 13 S, R 27 E). Named on Patterson Mountain (1952) 15' quadrangle.

Fram [KERN]: *locality,* 3 miles north-northwest of Mojave along Southern Pacific Railroad (lat. 35°05'50" N, long. 118°11'10" W; near SE cor. sec. 35, T 32 S, R 35 E). Named on Mojave (1915) 30' quadrangle. California Mining Bureau's (1917c) map shows a place called Reservoir located about 1 mile south-southeast of Fram along the railroad.

Franciscan Creek [KERN]: *stream,* heads in San Luis Obispo County and flows 6 miles to Antelope Valley (1) 6 miles south-southeast of Orchard Peak (lat. 35°39'25" N, long. 120°05'30" W; sec. 24, T 26 S, R 17 E). Named on Holland Canyon (1961), Packwood Creek (1961), and Sawtooth Ridge (1961) 7.5' quadrangles. Arnold and Johnson (p. 20) proposed the name because rocks of the Franciscan Formation crop out along the stream.

Francis Flat [TULARE]: *area,* 3.5 miles south-southeast of Auckland (lat. 36°32'15" N, long. 119°05'10" W; near W line sec. 18, T 16 S, R 27 E). Named on Auckland (1966) 7.5' quadrangle.

Frank Canyon [FRESNO]: *canyon,* drained by a stream that flows nearly 1 mile to Salt Creek (2) 7 miles south-southwest of Coalinga (lat. 36°03'05" N, long. 120°25' W; near N line sec. 1, T 22 S, R 14 E). Named on Curry Mountain (1969) 7.5' quadrangle.

Franklin Canyon [TULARE]: *canyon,* 2 miles long, 12.5 miles south of Kaweah (lat. 36°17'30" N, long. 118°57'30" W). Named on Kaweah (1957) 15' quadrangle.

Franklin Creek [TULARE]: *stream,* flows 2.25 miles to East Fork Kaweah River 2 miles south-southeast of Mineral King (lat. 36°25'40" N, long. 118°35' W); the stream heads at Franklin Lakes. Named on Mineral King (1956) 15' quadrangle. United States Board on Geographic Names (1968b, p. 7) rejected the name "East Fork Kaweah River" for the stream.

Franklin Lake [FRESNO]: *lake,* 1400 feet long, 3 miles northwest of Red Slate Mountain at the head of Purple Creek (lat. 37°32' N, long. 118°54'45" W). Named on Mount Morrison (1953) 15' quadrangle.

Franklin Lakes [TULARE]: *lakes,* largest 2200 feet long, 3.25 miles southeast of Mineral King (lat. 36°25' N, long. 118°33'25" W); the lakes are at the head of Franklin Creek. Named on Mineral King (1956) 15' quadrangle. The name is from Lady Franklin mine (United States Board on Geographic Names, 1933a, p. 310), which in turn was named for the widow of Sir John Franklin, the lost English Arctic explorer (Adler, p. 24). Tucker (p. 951) noted that Lady Franklin mine is 1.5 miles southeast of Mineral King on the ridge south of Lady Franklin Cañon. Present Franklin Lakes originally were called Silver Lakes (Browning, p. 74).

Franklin Pass [TULARE]: *pass,* 4 miles southeast of Mineral King on Great Western Divide (lat. 36°24'50" N, long. 118°32'35" W); the pass is near the head of Franklin Creek. Named on Mineral King (1956) 15' quadrangle.

Frazer Spring [KERN]: *spring,* 5 miles west-northwest of McKittrick (lat. 35°20'45" N, long. 119°41'40" W; at W line sec. 2, T 30 S, R 21 E). Named on Reward (1951) 7.5' quadrangle. Called Frazers Spring on Arnold and Johnson's (1910) map.

Frazer Valley [KERN]: *valley,* 5 miles west-northwest of McKittrick (lat. 35°20'25" N, long. 119°42' W; in and near sec. 3, T 30 S, R 21 E); Frazer Spring is in the valley. Named on Reward (1951) 7.5' quadrangle. Arnold and Johnson (p. 20) proposed the name.

Frazier [TULARE]: *locality,* 7 miles west-southwest of Springville (lat. 36°06'45" N, long. 118°56'45" W; near W line sec. 10, T 21 S, R 28 E); the place is in Frazier Valley. Named on Kaweah (1909) 30' quadrangle. Postal authorities established Frazier post office in 1882 and discontinued it in 1904 (Frickstad, p. 210). They established Rosedale post office 7.5 miles east of Frazier (NE quarter of sec. 15, T 21 S, R 29 E) in 1883 and discontinued it the same year (Salley, p. 189).

Frazier Creek [TULARE]: *stream,* flows 5.5 miles to lowlands 5.25 miles north-northeast of Porterville (lat. 36°08'35" N, long. 118°59'30" W; near E line sec. 36, T 20 S, R 27 E); the stream drains Frazier Valley. Named on Frazier Valley (1957) and Lindsay (1951) 7.5' quadrangles.

Frazier Park [KERN]: *town,* 5 miles west of Lebec in Cuddy Canyon (lat. 34°49'20" N, long. 118°57' W); the town is 3.5 miles north-northeast of Frazier Mountain, which is in Ventura County. Named on Frazier Mountain (1958) 7.5' quadrangle. Postal authorities established Frazier Park post office in 1927 (Frickstad, p. 55). Harry McBain founded the community in 1925 and named it in 1926 for nearby Frazier Mountain (Bailey, 1967, p. 9).

Frazier Valley [TULARE]: *valley,* 5 miles northeast of Porterville (lat. 36°08' N, long. 118°58' W); the valley is along Frazier Creek. Named on Frazier Valley (1957) and Lindsay (1951) 7.5' quadrangles.

Freckles Meadow [TULARE]: *area,* 8 miles north-northwest of Olancha Peak (lat. 36°22' N, long. 118°10'30" W). Named on Olancha (1956) 15' quadrangle.

Freeman [KERN]: *locality,* 7 miles west-southwest of Inyokern (lat. 35°36' N, long. 117°55'30" W); the place is about 1.25 miles west of present Freeman Junction at the mouth of Freeman Canyon. Named on Searles Lake (1915) 1° quadrangle. Postal authorities established Freeman post office in 1889 and discontinued it in 1909 (Frickstad, p. 55). Freeman S. Raymond started a stage station at a site in 1874 (Bailey, 1967, p. 9). The place first was known as Coyote Holes because water was obtained from shallow pits excavated where coyotes had dug a short distance to water (Waring, p. 340). It also was known as Coyote Springs (Latta, 1976, p. 254).

Freeman Canyon [KERN]: *canyon,* drained by a stream that heads at Walker Pass and flows 7.25 miles to Indian Wells Valley 7 miles west-southwest of Inyokern (lat. 35°36' N, long. 117°55'30" W; sec. 7, T 27 S, R 38 E). Named on Freeman Junction (1972), Owens Peak (1972), and Walker Pass (1972) 7.5' quadrangles.

Freeman Creek [KERN]: *stream,* flows 3 miles to Greenhorn Creek 4.25 miles west of Miracle Hot Springs (lat. 35°35'20" N, long. 118°36'25" W). Named on Democrat Hot Springs (1972) and Miracle Hot Springs (1972) 7.5' quadrangles.

Freeman Creek [TULARE]: *stream,* flows 7.25 miles to Kern River 9 miles south-southwest of Hockett Peak (lat. 36°06'30" N, long. 118°27'15" W). Named on Camp Nelson (1956) and Hockett Peak (1956) 15' quadrangles. Tucker (p. 944) used the form "Freeman's Creek" for the name.

Freeman Gulch [KERN]: *gully,* extends for 4.5 miles from the mouth of Freeman Canyon to Little Dixie Wash 7.5 miles south-southwest of Inyokern (lat. 35°33' N, long. 117°52'30" W; at S line sec. 27, T 27 S, R 38 E). Named on Freeman Junction (1972) 7.5' quadrangle.

Freeman Junction [KERN]: *locality,* 6 miles west-southwest of Inyo Kern (lat. 35°36'05" N, long. 117°45'10" W; near E line sec. 8, T 27 S, R 38 E); the place is near the mouth of Freeman Canyon. Named on Freeman Junction (1972) 7.5' quadrangle.

Freeman Wash Well [KERN]: *well,* 8 miles south-southwest of Inyokern (lat. 35°33' N, long. 117°52'55" W; at SW cor. sec. 27, T 27 S, R 38 E); the well is along Freeman Gulch. Named on Freeman Junction (1972) 7.5' quadrangle.

Freeman Well [KERN]: *well,* 1 mile southeast of Walker Pass (lat. 35°39'05" N, long. 118°00'45" W; sec. 21, T 26 S, R 37 E); the well is in Freeman Canyon. Named on Walker Pass (1972) 7.5' quadrangle.

Freezeout Meadow [TULARE]: *area,* 5.5 miles south-southeast of Camp Nelson (lat. 36°04' N, long. 118°34'40" W; sec. 36, T 21 S, R 31 E). Named on Camp Nelson (1956) 15' quadrangle.

Freitas Spring [FRESNO]: *spring,* 3.25 miles northeast of Coalinga Mineral Springs (lat. 36°10'55" N, long. 120°31'10" W; near N line sec. 24, T 20 S, R 13 E). Named on Sherman Peak (1969) 7.5' quadrangle.

Frémont's Pass: see **Oak Creek Pass** [KERN].

Fremont Valley [KERN]: *area,* east of the south end of the Sierra Nevada and southeast of El Paso Mountains. Named on Bakersfield (1962, revised 1971) and Trona (1957) 1°x 2° quadrangles. Fairbanks (1894a, p. 456) called the area Desert Springs Valley.

French Canyon [FRESNO]: *canyon,* drained by a stream that flows 5 miles to Piute Creek 8.5 miles south of Mount Abbot (lat. 37°15'55" N, long. 118°46'40" W); the canyon heads at French Lake. Named on Mount Abbot (1953) and Mount Tom (1949) 15' quadrangles.

French Gulch [KERN]:

(1) *canyon,* drained by a stream that flows 7 miles to Isabella Lake 4 miles south-southwest of Wofford Heights (lat. 35°39'30" N, long. 118°29'05" W; near NW cor. sec. 19, T 26 S, R 33 E). Named on Alta Sierra (1972) and Lake Isabella North (1972) 7.5' quadrangles.

(2) *canyon,* drained by a stream that flows 4.25 miles to Kelso Creek less than 1 mile north-northeast of Claraville (lat. 35°27'05" N, long. 118°19'15" W; at S line sec. 33, T 28 S, R 34 E); French Meadow is in the canyon. Named on Claraville (1972) 7.5' quadrangle. United States Board on Geographic Names (1975b, p. 9) gave the name "French Meadow Gulch" as a variant.

French Gulch: see **French Ranch Gulch** [KERN].

French Joe Meadow [TULARE]: *area,* 7 miles northeast of California Hot Springs (lat. 35°56'30" N, long. 118°34'30" W; near SE cor. sec. 12, T 23 S, R 31 E). Named on California Hot Springs (1958) 15' quadrangle.

French Lake [FRESNO]: *lake,* 2800 feet long, 4 miles northwest of Mount Humphreys (lat. 37°18'50" N, long. 118°43' W; sec. 30, T 7 S, R 30 E); the lake is at the head of French Canyon. Named on Mount Tom (1949) 15' quadrangle.

French Meadow [KERN]: *area,* 1.5 miles north-northwest of Claraville (lat. 34°27'45" N, long. 118°20'40" W; sec. 32, T 28 S, R 34 E); the place is in French Gulch (2). Named on Claraville (1972) 7.5' quadrangle. Called Weldon Meadow on Emerald Mountain (1943) 15' quadrangle, where present Weldon Meadow is called French Meadow.

French Meadow Gulch: see **French Gulch** [KERN] (2).

French Ranch Gulch [KERN]: *canyon,* drained by a stream that flows 3.5 miles to Little Poso Creek 4.25 miles northwest of Democrat Hot Springs (lat. 35°34'50" N, long. 118°42'30" W; near W line sec. 13, T 27 S, R 30

E). Named on Democrat Hot Springs (1972) 7.5' quadrangle, which shows French ranch in the canyon. Called French Gulch on Glennville (1956) 15' quadrangle, and United States Board on Geographic Names (1975a, p. 4) gave this name as a variant.

Fresno [FRESNO]: *city,* near the east side of San Joaquin Valley between San Joaquin River and Kings River (lat. 36°46' N, long. 119°47' W). Named on Clovis (1964), Fresno North (1965), Fresno South (1963), and Malaga (1964) 7.5' quadrangles. Postal authorities established Fresno City post office in 1872 and changed the name to Fresno in 1889 (Frickstad, p. 33). The city incorporated in 1885. *Fresno* means "ash tree" in Spanish; the name was applied first to a river because of ash trees along it, and later it was transferred to the city (Stewart, p. 173). Postal authorities established Temperance post office, named for the Christian Temperance Union, 6.5 miles northeast of Fresno in 1881 and discontinued it in 1886; they established Kelso post office, named for Napolean B. Kelso, first postmaster, 10 miles northeast of Fresno in 1891 and discontinued it in 1893; they established Fruitvale post office 5 miles northeast of Fresno City post office in 1883, discontinued it for a time in 1888, and discontinued it finally in 1892 (Salley, p. 81, 110, 219).

Fresno: see **Camp Fresno** [FRESNO]; **Pueblo de las Juntas**, under **Mendota** [FRESNO].

Fresno Beach: see **Scout Island** [FRESNO].

Fresno Branch San Joaquin River: see **Fresno Slough** [FRESNO].

Fresno City: see **Fresno** [FRESNO]; **Tranquillity** [FRESNO].

Fresno Hot Springs: see **Coalinga Mineral Springs** [FRESNO].

Fresno Slough [FRESNO-KINGS]: *stream,* diverges from North Fork Kings River in Kings County and flows 46 miles to San Joaquin River 7 miles southeast of Firebaugh in Fresno County (lat. 36° 47' N, long. 120°22'05" W; near E line sec. 19, T 13 S, R 15 E). Named on Burrel (1954), Five Points (1956), Helm (1963), Jamesan (1963), Mendota Dam (1956), San Joaquin (1963) and Tranquillity (1956) 7.5' quadrangles. Called Tulare Lake Slough on Coalinga (1912) 30' quadrangle, and called Kings River Slough on Jamesan (1924), Mendota (1924), and Tranquillity (1924) 7.5' quadrangles. The stream also is called South Branch or Fresno Branch San Joaquin River (Hoover, Rensch, and Rensch, p. 92). Present North Fork Kings River is called Fresno Slough on Riverdale (1927) 7.5' quadrangle, where present Faull Slough is called N. Fk. Kings River.

Fresno Slough By-Pass: see **James Bypass** [FRESNO].

Fresno Springs Canyon: see **Hot Springs Canyon** [FRESNO].

Friant [FRESNO]: *village,* 11.5 miles north of Clovis near San Joaquin River (lat. 36°59'15" N, long. 119°42'35" W; sec. 7, T 11 S, R 21 E). Named on Friant (1964) 7.5' quadrangle. The place was known first as Converse Ferry, for Charles Converse, who established a ferry there in 1852, and later it was called Jones Ferry; when Southern Pacific Railroad reached the site in 1891, the station was called Pollasky for Marcus Pollasky, a railroad agent, and in the early 1920's the village was renamed for Thomas Friant of White-Friant Lumber Company (Gudde, 1949, p. 122). The place also was called Hamptonville (Hanna, p. 114). Postal authorities established Hamptonville post office, named for William R. Hampton, first postmaster, in 1881, changed the name to Pollasky in 1891, and moved it and changed the name to Friant in 1910 (Salley, p. 92, 175). J.R. Jones had a store on the south bank of San Joaquin River just below Converse Ferry that was a noted supply point for many years (Wright, p. 45).

Fridley Canyon [TULARE]: *canyon,* drained by a stream that flows 0.5 mile to Dry Creek (1) 6 miles northeast of Woodlake (lat. 36° 28'35" N, long. 119°01'10" W; sec. 2, T 17 S, R 27 E). Named on Exeter (1952) 15' quadrangle.

Frog Creek [KERN]: *stream,* flows 4 miles to Kelso Creek 6 miles southwest of Skinner Peak (lat. 35°30'20" N, long. 118°12'20" W; sec. 10, T 28 S, R 35 E). Named on Cane Canyon (1972) 7.5' quadrangle.

Frog Lake [FRESNO]:

(1) *lake,* 900 feet long, 13 miles north-northeast of Kaiser Peak (lat. 37°27'25" N, long. 119°03'40" W). Named on Kaiser Peak (1953) 15' quadrangle. The feature is one of the group called Margaret Lakes.

(2) *lake,* 700 feet long, 3.5 miles northwest of Mount Abbot (lat. 37°25'25" N, long. 118°49'35" W). Named on Mount Abbot (1953) 15' quadrangle.

Frog Lakes [TULARE]: *lakes,* two, largest 500 feet long, 11.5 miles south of Mineral King (lat. 36°17'15" N, long. 118°37'15" W). Named on Mineral King (1956) 15' quadrangle.

Frog Meadow [TULARE]: *area,* 5.25 miles east of California Hot Springs (lat. 35°52'25" N, long. 118°34'30" W; on E line sec. 1, T 24 S, R 31 E). Named on California Hot Springs (1958) 15' quadrangle.

Frog Spring [KERN]: *spring,* 5.5 miles southwest of Skinner Peak (lat. 35°30'25" N, long. 118°11'35" W; near NE cor. sec. 10, T 28 S, E 35 E); the spring is along Frog Creek. Named on Cane Canyon (1972) 7.5' quadrangle.

Front: see **Brown** [KERN].

Fruitvale [KERN]: *settlement,* 4.5 miles west of Bakersfield (lat. 35° 23' N, long. 119°05' W; on S line sec. 21, T 29 S, R 27 E). Named on Oildale (1954) 7.5' quadrangle. The community began in 1891 (Bailey, 1967, p. 9).

Fruitvale: see **Fresno** [FRESNO].

Frypan Meadow [FRESNO]: *area,* 12 miles southwest of Marion Peak (lat. 36°51'10" N, long. 118°41'35" W). Named on Marion Peak (1953) 15' quadrangle.

Frys Point [TULARE]: *peak,* 4.5 miles south-southeast of Yucca Mountain (lat. 36°30'30" N, long. 118°50'30" W). Altitude 4504 feet. Named on Giant Forest (1956) 15' quadrangle. R. B. Marshall of United States Geological Survey named the peak in 1909 for Walter Fry, who was superintendent of Sequoia and General Grant National Parks from 1914 until 1920 (Hanna, p. 114). United States Board on Geographic Names (1933a, p. 313) rejected the form "Fry's Point" for the name, and noted that Walter Fry entered the first protest against cutting down the big redwood trees after he counted 2000 rings on a stump.

Fuller Acres [KERN]: *locality,* 7.25 miles southeast of downtown Bakersfield (lat. 35°17'55" N, long. 118°54'45" W; near SW cor. sec. 19, T 30 S, R 29 E). Named on Lamont (1954, photorevised 1968) 7.5' quadrangle.

Fulton Creek [KERN]: stream, formed by the confluence of McFarland Creek and Peyton Creek, flows nearly 3 miles to Cedar Creek 2.5 miles southeast of Glennville (lat. 35°42' N, long. 118°40'15" W; near N line sec. 5, T 26 S, R 31 E). Named on Glennville (1972) 7.5' quadrangle.

Fulton Peak [KERN]: *peak,* 2.5 miles east of Glennville (lat. 35°43'20" N, long. 118°39'40" W; near E line sec. 29, T 25 S, R 31 E). Altitude 4786 feet. Named on Glennville (1972) 7.5' quadrangle.

Funston Camp: see **Funston Meadow** [TULARE].

Funston Creek [TULARE]: *stream,* flows nearly 3 miles to Kern River 12.5 miles northwest of Kern Peak (lat. 36°27'20" N, long. 118°24'45" W); the mouth of the stream is at Upper Funston Meadow. Named on Kern Peak (1956) 15' quadrangle. The name is for James Funston, who ran sheep near the stream in 1870 (United States Board on Geographic Names, 1933a, p. 314).

Funston Lake [TULARE]: *lake,* 2100 feet long, 10.5 miles north-northwest of Kern Peak (lat. 36°26'55" N, long. 118°20'50" W). Named on Kern Peak (1956) 15' quadrangle.

Funston Meadow [TULARE]: *area,* 8.5 miles northwest of Kern Peak in Kern Canyon (lat. 36°23' N, long. 118°24'15" W). Named on Kern Peak (1956) 15' quadrangle. Called Lower Funston Meadow on Olancha (1907) 30' quadrangle. California Mining Bureau's (1917b) map shows a place called Funston Camp located at or near present Funston Meadow.

Funston Meadow: see **Upper Funston Meadow** [TULARE]; **Upper Funston Meadow,** under **Sky Parlor Meadow** [TULARE].

Funstons: see **Upper Funston Meadow** [TULARE].

— G —

Gabb: see **Mount Gabb** [FRESNO].

Gail Spring [KERN]: *spring,* 6.5 miles northeast of Caliente (lat. 35° 21'30" N, long. 118°32'40" W; at E line sec. 33, T 29 S, R 32 E). Named on Oiler Peak (1972) 7.5' quadrangle.

Gains: see **Visalia** [TULARE].

Galena Creek [TULARE]: *stream,* flows 1.5 miles to North Fork of Middle Fork Tule River 7.5 miles north-northwest of Camp Nelson (lat. 36°14'30" N, long. 118°39'15" W). Named on Mineral King (1956) 15' quadrangle.

Gale Spring [KERN]: *spring,* 6 miles east-southeast of Caliente (lat. 35°15'15" N, long. 118°31'55" W; at S line sec. 3, T 31 S, R 32 E). Named on Oiler Peak (1972) 7.5' quadrangle.

Galileo Hill [KERN]: *hill,* 10 miles northeast of Castle Butte (lat. 35° 12'45" N, long. 117°45'10" W; at NW cor. sec. 25, T 31 S, R 39 E). Altitude 3310 feet. Named on Galileo Hill (1973) 7.5' quadrangle.

Gallats Lake [TULARE]: *lake,* 1000 feet long, 10.5 miles west of Mount Whitney along Kern-Kaweah River (lat. 36°35'45" N, long. 118°28'25" W). Named on Mount Whitney (1956) 15' quadrangle.

Galley Mountain [TULARE]: *peak,* 6 miles east of Fountain Springs (lat. 35°54'20" N, long. 118°48'35" W; near S line sec. 23, T 23 S, R 39 E). Altitude 2852 feet. Named on Gibbon Peak (1965) 7.5' quadrangle.

Gamba: see **Mojave** [KERN].

Gamble Spring Canyon [KERN]: *canyon,* drained by a stream that flows 4 miles to lowlands 9 miles west-northwest of the village of Willow Springs (lat. 34°57'15" N, long. 118°25'30" W; near S line sec. 13, T 10 N, R 15 W). Named on Tehachapi South (1966) and Tylerhorse Canyon (1965) 7.5' quadrangles.

Garcia Canyon [FRESNO]:

(1) *canyon,* drained by a stream that flows 2.5 miles to Los Gatos Creek 20 miles west-northwest of Coalinga (lat. 36°17'10" N, long. 120°39'35" W; near S line sec. 10, T 19 S, R 12 E). Named on San Benito Mountain (1969) 7.5' quadrangle.

(2) *canyon,* drained by a stream that flows 4 miles to Zapato Chino Creek 9.5 miles southeast of Coalinga (lat. 36°01'40" N, long. 120° 15'45" W; sec. 8, T 22 S, R 16 E). Named on Kreyenhagen Hills (1956) 7.5' quadrangle.

Garden City Station [KERN]: *locality,* 9 miles north of Randsburg along Trona Railroad (lat. 35°29'40" N, long. 117°38'20" W; at N line sec. 23, T

28 S, R 40 E). Named on El Paso Peaks (1967) 7.5' quadrangle.

Gardiner: see **Mount Gardiner** [FRESNO].

Gardiner Basin [FRESNO]: *valley,* 9.5 miles south-southwest of Mount Pinchot (lat. 36°49' N, long. 118°27'30" W); the valley is at the head of Gardiner Creek. Named on Mount Pinchot (1953) 15' quadrangle.

Gardiner Creek [FRESNO]: *stream,* flows 6.25 miles to South Fork Kings River 10 miles south of Marion Peak (lat. 36°48'45" N, long. 118°32'50" W); the stream heads in Gardiner Basin. Named on Marion Peak (1953) and Mount Pinchot (1953) 15' quadrangles.

Gardiner Lakes [FRESNO]: *lakes,* 9.5 miles south-southwest of Mount Pinchot (lat. 36°49' N, long. 118°27' W); the lakes are in Gardiner Basin. Named on Mount Pinchot (1953) 15' quadrangle.

Gardiner Pass [FRESNO]: *pass,* 11 miles south-southwest of Mount Pinchot (lat. 36°48' N, long. 118°28'45" W). Named on Mount Pinchot (1953) 15' quadrangle.

Gardner Field [KERN]: *military installation,* 6 miles east-northeast of Maricopa (lat. 35°06'15" N, long. 119°18'30" W). Named on Pentland (1945) 7.5' quadrangle.

Garfield: see **Clovis** [FRESNO].

Garfield Creek [TULARE]: *stream,* flows 3 miles to South Fork Kaweah River 11 miles southwest of Mineral King (lat. 36°20'50" N, long. 118°44'10" W). Named on Mineral King (1956) 15' quadrangle. United States Board on Geographic Names (1933a, p. 318) rejected the name "Board Camp Creek" for the feature. The stream is north of Garfield grove of redwood trees, which R.B. Marshall of United States Geological Survey named for President James A. Garfield (Hanna, p. 117).

Garlic Falls [FRESNO]: *waterfall,* 5.5 miles north-northwest of Hume (lat. 36°51'40" N, long. 118°57' W); the feature is along Garlic Meadow Creek. Named on Tehipite Dome (1952) 15' quadrangle.

Garlic Meadow [FRESNO]: *area,* 9 miles north of Hume (lat. 36°55'05" N, long. 118°55'25" W). Named on Tehipite Dome (1952) 15' quadrangle. Called Garlic Meadows on Lippincott's (1902) map.

Garlic Meadow Creek [FRESNO]: *stream,* flows 4.5 miles to Kings River 5.5 miles north-northwest of Hume (lat. 36°51'35" N, long. 118°57'05" W); the stream heads 1.5 miles west of Garlic Meadow. Named on Tehipite Dome (1952) 15' quadrangle.

Garlic Spur [FRESNO]: *ridge,* south-southeast-trending, 3.5 miles long. 7.5 miles north-northwest of Hume (lat. 36°53'15" N, long. 118°57'45" W); the ridge is west of Garlic Meadow Creek. Named on Tehipite Dome (1952) 15' quadrangle.

Garlock [KERN]: *locality,* 6.25 miles east-northeast of Saltdale (lat. 35°24'15" N, long. 117°47'20" W; at NW cor. sec. 22, T 29 S, R 39 E). Named on Garlock (1967) 7.5' quadrangle. Postal authorities established Garlock post office in 1896, discontinued it in 1904, reestablished it in 1923, and discontinued it in 1926 (Frickstad, p. 55). The name commemorates Eugene Garlock, who built a stamp mill at a watering place called Cow Wells; Garlock called the establishment Eugeneville, but later the site took his surname (Barras, p. 39).

Garlock: see **Old Garlock** [KERN].

Garlock Station [KERN]: *locality,* 1 mile south-southwest of Garlock along Southern Pacific Railroad (lat. 35°23'30" N, long. 117° 47'50" W; sec. 21, T 29 S, R 39 E). Named on Saltdale (1943a) 15' quadrangle.

Garrison Canyon [FRESNO]: *canyon,* drained by a stream that flows 2 miles to Los Gatos Creek 18 miles west-northwest of Coalinga (lat. 36°16'35" N, long. 120°39' W; sec. 14, T 19 S, R 12 E). Named on San Benito Mountain (1969) 7.5' quadrangle.

Garza Creek [FRESNO-KINGS]: *stream,* heads in Kings County and flows 7 miles to Kettleman Plain 12.5 miles southeast of Coalinga in Fresno County (lat. 36°00'30" N, long. 120°11'35" W; near N line sec. 24, T 22 S, R 16 E). Named on Avenal (1954) 7.5' quadrangle. United States Board on Geographic Names (1933a, p. 319) rejected the name "Las Garzas Creek" for the feature.

Garza Peak [KINGS]: *peak,* 6.25 miles southwest of Avenal (lat. 35° 56' N, long. 120°11'55" W; near W line sec. 13, T 23 S, R 16 E). Altitude 2698 feet. Named on Garza Peak (1953) 7.5' quadrangle.

Gassenberg Spring [TULARE]: *spring,* 7.5 miles east of Exeter (lat. 36°17'50" N, long. 119°00'15" W; at S line sec. 1, T 19 S, R 27 E). Named on Rocky Hill (1951) 7.5' quadrangle.

Gates Lake [FRESNO]: *intermittent lake,* 1.25 miles long, 4 miles north of Clovis (lat. 36°53' N, long. 119°41'30" W). Named on Friant (1922) 7.5' quadrangle.

Gautche Point [KERN]: *promontory,* 4.5 miles south-southeast of Wofford Heights along Isabella Lake (lat. 35°39'05" N, long. 118° 25' W; sec. 22, T 26 S, R 33 E). Named on Lake Isabella North (1972) 7.5' quadrangle.

Gautche Springs [KERN]: *springs,* 5 miles east of Bodfish (lat. 35° 36'15" N, long. 118°24'05" W; sec. 2, T 27 S, R 33 E). Named on Lake Isabella South (1972) 7.5' quadrangle.

Gavilan Ridge [FRESNO]: *ridge,* northeast-trending, 1 mile long, 10 miles southwest of Coalinga (lat. 36°01'05" N, long. 120°27'45" W; sec. 16, T 22 S, R 14 E). Named on Curry Mountain (1969) 7.5' quadrangle.

Gavilan Rock [FRESNO]: *peak,* 10 miles south-southwest of Coalinga (lat. 36°01'10" N, long. 120°27'45" W; sec. 15, T 22 S, R 14 E); the feature is on Gavilan Ridge. Named on Curry Mountain (1969) 7.5' quadrangle.

Geghus Ridge [KERN]: *ridge,* west-southwest-trending, 1.25 miles long, 10.5 miles west-southwest of Liebre Twins (lat. 34°54'15" N, long. 118°44'30" W). Named on Winters Ridge (1966) 7.5' quadrangle.

Gem Hill [KERN]: *peak,* 5.5 miles northwest of Rosamond (lat. 34° 55'30" N, long. 118°13'15" W). Named on Soledad Mountain (1973) 7.5' quadrangle.

Gemini [FRESNO]: *peak,* 6.5 miles south-southwest of Mount Abbot (lat. 37°17'45" N, long. 118°49' W). Altitude 12,866 feet. Named on Mount Abbot (1953) 15' quadrangle. Chester Versteeg proposed the name for the double peak (Gudde, 1969, p. 118).

General Canyon [TULARE]: *canyon,* drained by a stream that flows 1 mile to Dry Creek (1) 6.5 miles northeast of Woodlake (lat. 36° 29'05" N, long. 119°00'55" W; near N line sec. 2, T 17 S, R 27 E). Named on Woodlake (1952) 7.5' quadrangle.

General Canyon: see **Liveoak Canyon** [TULARE].

Geneva: see **Mount Geneva**, under **Mount Genevra** [TULARE].

Genevra: see **Mount Genevra** [TULARE].

George Lake [FRESNO]: *lake,* 900 feet long, nearly 1 mile east-southeast of Kaiser Peak (lat. 37°17'25" N, long. 119°10'15" W; sec. 30, T 7 S, R 26 E). Named on Kaiser Peak (1953) 15' quadrangle.

Gepford [KINGS]: *locality,* 7 miles north-northwest of Lemoore along Atchison, Topeka and Santa Fe Railroad (lat. 36°23'55" N, long. 119°48'35" W; sec. 4, T 18 S, R 20 E). Named on Riverdale (1954) 7.5' quadrangle.

Geraldine Lakes [FRESNO]: *lakes,* largest 900 feet long, 9 miles northnortheast of Hume (lat. 36°54'50" N, long. 118°52'45" W). Named on Tehipite Dome (1952) 15' quadrangle.

Gerbracht Camp [KERN]: *locality,* 3.5 miles northwest of Garlock (lat. 35°26'15" N, long. 117°50'20" W). Named on Garlock (1967) 7.5' quadrangle.

Giant Forest: see **Kaweah Camp** [TULARE].

Giant Oak [TULARE]: *locality,* 2.5 miles west-northwest of Exeter along Southern Pacific Railroad (lat. 36°18'20" N, long. 119°11'15" W; near W line sec. 5, T 19 S, R 26 E). Named on Exeter (1926) 7.5' quadrangle.

Gibbon Canyon: see **Gibbon Creek** [TULARE].

Gibbon Creek [TULARE]: *stream,* flows 6.25 miles to South Fork Tule River 7.25 miles south of Springville (lat. 36°01'35" N, long. 118°47'35" W); the stream heads near Gibbon Peak. Named on Globe (1956) 7.5' quadrangle. Gibbon Peak (1965) 7.5' quadrangle has the name "Gibbon Canyon" for the canyon of the stream, but fails to name the stream itself.

Gibbon Peak [TULARE]: *peak,* 9.5 miles east-southeast of Fountain Springs (lat. 35°57'20" N, long. 118°45'50" W; sec. 5, T 23 S, R 30 E). Altitude 4512 feet. Named on Gibbon Peak (1965) 7.5' quadrangle.

Gibonney Canyon [KERN]: *canyon,* drained by a stream that flows 2 miles to South Fork Valley 2.5 miles north-northeast of Weldon (lat. 35°41'55" N, long. 118°15'55" W; sec. 6, T 26 S, R 35 E). Named on Weldon (1972) 7.5' quadrangle.

Giffen [KERN]: *locality,* 2.5 miles northeast of Arvin along the railroad (lat. 35°14'20" N, long. 118°47'55" W; at S line sec. 7, T 31 S, R 30 E). Named on Arvin (1933) 7.5' quadrangle. California Division of Highways' (1934) map shows a place called Giffen Jct. located 1.5 miles west of Giffen along the railroad.

Giffen: see **Enson** [TULARE].

Giffen Junction: see **Giffen** [KERN].

Gilbert: see **Mount Gilbert** [FRESNO].

Gilbert Campground [KERN]: *locality,* less then 1 mile north of downtown Kernville along Kern River (lat. 35°46' N, long. 118°25'30" W; sec. 10, T 25 S, R 33 E). Named on Kernville (1956) 15' quadrangle.

Gillette [TULARE]: *locality,* 3.5 miles southeast of Lindsay along Atchison, Topeka and Santa Fe Railroad (lat. 36°10'25" N, long. 119°02'10" W; sec. 22, T 20 S, R 27 E). Named on Lindsay (1951) 7.5' quadrangle. On Lindsay (1928) 7.5' quadrangle, the name applies to a place located nearly 1 mile farther west at the end of a spur line of Visalia Electric Railroad (sec. 21, T 20 S, R 27 E). The name commemorates King C. Gillette of safety-razor fame, who owned a citrus orchard at the place (Gudde, 1949, p. 127).

Girard: see **Keene** [KERN].

Giraud Peak [FRESNO]: *peak,* 9 miles east of Mount Goddard (lat. 37°04'40" N, long. 118°33'50" W). Altitude 12,585 feet. Named on Mount Goddard (1948) 15' quadrangle. Called Giroud Pk. on Mount Goddard (1912) 30' quadrangle. The name commemorates Alfred R. Giroud, a sheepman of Inyo County (Farquhar, 1923, p. 398).

Giroud Peak: see **Giraud Peak** [FRESNO].

Givens: see **Mount Givens** [FRESNO].

Glacier Brook: see **Glacier Creek** [FRESNO] (1).

Glacier Creek [FRESNO]:

(1) *stream,* flows 1.5 miles to Palisade Creek 11 miles east-southeast of Mount Goddard (lat. 37°03'15" N, long. 118°31'10" W). Named on Mount Goddard (1948) 15' quadrangle. J.N. LeConte and his companions gave the name "Glacier Brook" to the stream in 1903 (Browning, p. 81).

(2) *stream,* flows 2.25 miles to South Fork Kings River 11 miles south of Marion Peak (lat. 36°48' N, long. 118°32'45" W); the stream heads near Glacier Monument. Named on Marion Peak (1953) 15' quadrangle.

Glacier Creek: see **Boulder Creek** [FRESNO-TULARE].

Glacier Divide [FRESNO]: *ridge,* west-trending, 9 miles long, 11 miles north-northeast of Blackcap Mountain between Muriel Peak and Pavilion Dome (lat. 37°13'30" N, long. 118°45' W). Named on Blackcap Mountain (1953) and Mount Goddard (1948) 15' quadrangles. United States Board on Geographic Names (1972b, p. 3) approved the name "Matthes Glaciers" for features on Glacier Divide 2.2 miles east of Pavilion Dome; the name honors geologist François E. Matthes, who studied glaciers in the Sierra Nevada.

Glacier Lake [TULARE]: *lake,* 850 feet long, 0.25 mile northwest of Triple Divide Peak (lat. 36°35'45" N, long. 118°32' W). Named on Triple Divide Peak (1956) 15' quadrangle.

Glacier Lakes [FRESNO]: *lakes,* 5 miles southwest of Marion Peak (lat. 36°54' N, long. 18°35' W). Named on Marion Peak (1953) 15' quadrangle.

Glacier Monument [FRESNO]: *peak,* 11 miles south of Marion Peak (lat. 36°47'55" N, long. 118°30'15" W). Altitude 11,165 feet. Named on Marion Peak (1953) 15' quadrangle.

Glacier Pass: see **Sawtooth Pass** [TULARE].

Glacier Ridge [TULARE]: *ridge,* north-trending, 5.5 miles long, 3 miles north-northwest of Triple Divide Peak between Deadman Canyon and Cloud Canyon (lat. 36°38' N, long. 118°33'15" W). Named on Triple Divide Peak (1956) 15' quadrangle.

Glacier Valley [FRESNO]: *canyon,* drained by a stream that heads at Glacier Lakes and flows 1.5 miles to East Fork Dougherty Creek 4 miles southwest of Marion Peak (lat. 36°55'20" N, long. 118° 35' W). Named on Marion Peak (1953) 15' quadrangle.

Glenburn: see **Bakersfield** [KERN].

Glen Lake [FRESNO]: *lake,* 800 feet long, 4 miles west-northwest of Red Slate Mountain on upper reaches of Purple Creek (lat. 37°32'25" N, long. 118°55'45" W). Named on Mount Morrison (1953) 15' quadrangle.

Glen Meadow [FRESNO]: *area,* 4 miles southwest of Dinkey Dome (lat. 37°04'30" N, long. 119°11' W; near W line sec. 7, T 10 S, R 26 E). Named on Huntington Lake (1953) 15' quadrangle.

Glen Meadow Creek [FRESNO]: *stream,* flows 2.5 miles to Dinkey Creek (1) 3.5 miles south-southwest of Dinkey Dome (lat. 37°03'55" N, long. 119°09'20" W; sec. 17, T 10 S, R 26 E); the stream heads near Glen Meadow. Named on Huntington Lake (1953) 15' quadrangle.

Glennette Lake [FRESNO]: *lake,* 700 feet long, 4 miles west-northwest of Red Slate Mountain on upper reaches of Purple Creek (lat. 37°32'10" N, long. 118°55'45" W); the feature is 750 feet south of Glen Lake. Named on Mount Morrison (1953) 15' quadrangle.

Glennville [KERN]: *village,* 30 miles north-northeast of Bakersfield (lat. 35°43'54" N, long. 118°42'10" W; sec. 25, T 25 S, R 30 E). Named on Glennville (1972) 7.5' quadrangle. Called Glenville on Mendenhall's (1909) map. Postal authorities established Linn's Valley post office in 1860, changed the name to Glenville in 1872, discontinued it in 1874, and reestablished it the same year with the name "Glennville" (Salley, p. 86, 123). The name "Glennville" commemorates James M. Glenn, who had his home and a blacksmith shop at the place (Boyd, p. 156). David Lavers settled in 1858 at a spot situated a mile west-northwest of present Glennville near Poso Creek; the community that grew there was called Lavers' Crossing, and was the trading center for Linns Valley for a decade before Glennville assumed that role (Boyd, p. 153, 156; Hoover, Rensch, and Rensch, p. 130).

Glen Pass [FRESNO]: *pass,* 11 miles south of Mount Pinchot (lat. 36°47'25" N, long. 118°24'40" W). Named on Mount Pinchot (1953) 15' quadrangle. The name (misspelled "Glenn" on early maps) commemorates Glen H. Crow, an assistant with United States Geological Survey in 1905, and later a Forest Service ranger; Bolton C. Brown called the feature Blue Flower Pass in 1899 (Browning, p. 82).

Glenville: see **Glennville** [KERN].

Globe [TULARE]: *settlement,* 2.25 miles south-southwest of Springville (lat. 36°06'05" N, long. 118°49'40" W; sec. 15, T 21 S, R 29 E). Named on Globe (1956) 7.5' quadrangle. Postal authorities established Globe post office in 1890 and discontinued it in 1915 (Frickstad, p. 211).

Gloria Meadow [FRESNO]: *area,* 2 miles west-northwest of Kaiser Peak (lat. 37°18'30" N, long. 119°13' W; near NW cor. sec. 23, T 7 S, R 25 E). Named on Kaiser Peak (1953) 15' quadrangle.

Glorietta [FRESNO]: *locality,* 1 mile north-northwest of Clovis along Southern Pacific Railroad (lat. 36°50'20" N, long 119°42'30" W; near SW cor. sec. 32, T 12 S, R 21 E). Named on Clovis (1964) 7.5' quadrangle.

Gloster: see **Actis** [KERN].

Gnat Meadow [FRESNO]: *area,* 10.5 miles north-northeast of Hume (lat. 36°54'45" N, long. 118°48'40" W). Named on Tehipite Dome (1952) 15' quadrangle. United States Board on Geographic Names (1988a, p. 2) approved the name "Hay Meadow" for the feature, and gave the name "Gnat Meadow" to a nearby area (lat. 36°54'30" N, long. 118°49'17" W).

Goat Crest [FRESNO]: *ridge,* northwest-trending, 1.5 miles long, 6 miles southwest of Marion Peak (lat. 36°53'10" N, long. 118° 35' W). Named on Marion Peak (1953) 15' quadrangle.

Goat Hill [TULARE]: *peak,* 3.5 miles northeast of Auckland (lat. 36° 37'05" N, long. 119°03'15" W; near SE cor. sec. 17, T 15 S, R 27 E). Altitude 2439 feet. Named on Auckland (1966) 7.5' quadrangle.

Goat Mountain [FRESNO]:

(1) *peak,* nearly 7 miles south-southwest of Marion Peak (lat. 36°52'10" N, long. 118°34'25" W); the peak is near the southeast end of Goat Crest. Altitude 12,207 feet. Named on Marion Peak (1953) 15' quadrangle. United States Board on Geographic Names (1978a, p. 4) approved the name "Munger Peak" for a peak located 0.5 mile northwest of Goat Mountain (1) (lat. 36°52'27" N, long. 118°34'45" W); the name honors Maynard Munger, who was instrumental in preserving Kings Canyon, Sequoia, and Yosemite National Parks.

(2) *peak,* 5.25 miles northwest of Coalinga Mineral Springs (lat. 36° 12'30" N, long. 120°36'30" W; sec. 7, T 20 S, R 13 E). Altitude 3721 feet. Named on Sherman Peak (1969) 7.5' quadrangle.

Goat Peak [KERN]: *peak,* nearly 6 miles south-southeast of Glennville (lat. 35°39'10" N, long. 118°39'40" W; sec. 20, T 26 S, R 31 E). Altitude 5286 feet. Named on Glennville (1972) 7.5' quadrangle.

Goat Ranch Canyon [KERN]: *canyon,* drained by a stream that flows 2.5 miles to lowlands 5.5 miles southwest of Weldon (lat. 35°37'15" N, long. 118°22'15" W; sec. 31, T 26 S, R 34 E). Named on Woolstalf Creek (1972) 7.5' quadrangle.

Goat Spring [FRESNO]: *spring,* 4 miles north of Coalinga Mineral Springs (lat. 36°12'15" N, long. 120°33'10" W; sec. 10, T 20 S, R 13 E). Named on Sherman Peak (1969) 7.5' quadrangle.

Goddard: see **Mount Goddard** [FRESNO].

Goddard Canyon [FRESNO]: *canyon,* 10 miles long, along South Fork San Joaquin River above the confluence of Piute Creek with South Fork 11 miles north-northwest of Blackcap Mountain (lat. 37°13'25" N, long. 118°50' W); the canyon is northwest of Mount Goddard. Named on Blackcap Mountain (1953) 15' quadrangle.

Goddard Creek [FRESNO]: *stream,* flows 10.5 miles to Middle Fork Kings River 6 miles west-northwest of Marion Peak (lat. 36° 58'50" N, long. 118°37'30" W); the stream heads near Mount Goddard. Named on Marion Peak (1953) and Mount Goddard (1948) 15' quadrangles.

Goddard Creek: see **North Goddard Creek** [FRESNO].

Goddard Divide [FRESNO]: *ridge,* extends 5.5 miles east and northeast from Mount Goddard (lat. 37°06'45" N, long. 118°40'15" W). Named on Mount Goddard (1948) 15' quadrangle.

Goethe: see **Mount Goethe** [FRESNO].

Goethe Cirque: see **Goethe Glacier** [FRESNO].

Goethe Glacier [FRESNO]: *glacier,* 7.25 miles north of Mount Goddard on Glacier Divide (lat. 37°12'35" N, long. 118°42'30" W); the feature is west-northwest of Mount Goethe. Named on Mount Goddard (1948) 15' quadrangle. United States Board on Geographic Names (1949b, p. 4) approved the name "Goethe Cirque" for the cirque on the north side of Mount Goethe that encompasses Goethe Glacier and Goethe Lake.

Goethe Lake [FRESNO]: *lake,* 0.5 mile long, 8 miles north of Mount Goddard (lat. 37°13'15" N, long. 118°42'10" W); the lake is 1 mile north of Mount Goethe. Named on Mount Goddard (1948) 15' quadrangle.

Gold Canyon [KERN]: *canyon,* drained by a stream that flows 2 miles to Indian Wells Canyon 6 miles west-northwest of Inyokern (lat. 35°40'50" N, long. 117°54'55" W; near SW cor. sec. 8, T 26 S, R 38 E). Named on Owens Peak (1972) 7.5' quadrangle.

Gold Canyon: see **Alphie Canyon** [KERN].

Golden Bear Lake [TULARE]: *lake,* 1700 feet long, 11 miles north-northwest of Mount Whitney in Center Basin (lat. 36°43'35" N, long. 118°21'15" W). Named on Mount Whitney (1956) 15' quadrangle.

Golden Creek [FRESNO]: *stream,* flows 3 miles to Mono Creek 4.25 miles north of Mount Abbot (lat. 37°26'50" N, long. 118°47'35" W). Named on Mount Abbot (1953) 15' quadrangle.

Golden Lake [FRESNO]: *lake,* 1700 feet long, 4.5 miles north-northeast of Mount Abbot (lat. 37°27' N, long. 118°45'55" W); the lake is along Golden Creek. Named on Mount Abbot (1953) 15' quadrangle.

Golden Oaks Spring [KERN]: *spring,* 12.5 miles north-northwest of Mojave (lat. 35°13'30" N, long. 118°14' W; near NW cor. sec. 21, T 31 S, R 35 E). Named on Cache Peak (1973) 7.5' quadrangle.

Golden Trout Creek [TULARE]: *stream,* flows 16 miles to Kern River 7.25 miles west-northwest of Kern Peak (lat. 36°21' N, long. 118°24'15" W). Named on Kern Peak (1956) 15' quadrangle. United States Board on Geographic Names (1933a, p. 328) rejected the names "Volcano Creek" and "Whitney Creek" for the stream.

Golden Trout Creek: see **Stokes Stringer** [TULARE].

Golden Trout Lake [FRESNO]: *lake,* 1800 feet long, about 9.5 miles north of Mount Goddard along Piute Creek (lat. 37°14'25" N, long. 118°43'10" W). Named on Mount Goddard (1948) 15' quadrangle.

Golden Trout Meadows: see **Big Whitney Meadow** [TULARE].

Goldleaf [FRESNO]: *locality,* 3 miles north-northeast of Malaga along Southern Pacific Railroad (lat. 36°43'20" N, long. 119°43'05" W; near SE cor.

sec. 7, T 14 S, R 21 E). Named on Malaga (1964) 7.5' quadrangle.

Gold Ledge Campground [TULARE]: *locality,* 4 miles south-southeast of Fairview along Kern River (lat. 35°52'40" N, long. 118°27'20" W; sec. 6, T 24 S, R 33 E); the place is near the mouth of Gold Ledge Creek. Named on Kernville (1956) 15' quadrangle.

Gold Ledge Creek [TULARE]: *stream,* flows 3.5 miles to Kern River 4 miles south-southeast of Fairview (lat. 35°52'40" N, long. 118°27'20" W; sec. 6, T 24 S, R 33 E). Named on Kernville (1956) 15' quadrangle. The canyon of the stream is called Brinn Canyon on Olmsted's (1900) map.

Goldpan Canyon [KERN]: *canyon,* drained by a stream that flows 2.5 miles to Caliente Creek 7.25 miles east-northeast of Caliente (lat. 35°18'50" N, long. 118°30'10" W; near SW cor. sec. 13, T 30 S, R 32 E). Named on Loraine (1972) and Oiler Peak (1972) 7.5' quadrangles.

Gold Peak [KERN]: *peak,* 1 mile south-southeast of Pinyon Mountain (lat. 35°26'40" N, long. 118°09'05" W; sec. 6, T 29 S, R 36 E). Altitude 5963 feet. Named on Pinyon Mountain (1972) 7.5' quadrangle.

Gold Peak Well [KERN]: *well,* 5.5 miles east of Pinyon Mountain in Dove Spring Canyon (lat. 35°26'40" N, long. 118°03'30" W; near NE cor. sec. 1, T 29 S, R 36 E). Named on Dove Spring (1972) 7.5' quadrangle.

Goldstein Peak [TULARE]: *peak,* 3 miles east-southeast of Tucker Mountain (lat. 36°37'45" N, long. 119°09'30" W; near NW cor. sec. 16, T 15 S, R 26 E). Altitude 2821 feet. Named on Tucker Mountain (1966) 7.5' quadrangle. The name commemorates Ike Goldstein of Visalia, who ran hogs near the peak (Gudde, 1949, p. 130).

Gold Town [KERN]: *locality,* 9.5 miles north of Rosamond (lat. 34° 59'55" N, long. 118°10'30" W). Named on Mojave (1943) and Rosamond (1943) 15' quadrangles.

Goler [KERN]: *locality,* 7 miles west-northwest of Randsburg along Southern Pacific Railroad (lat. 35°24'40" N, long. 117°45'30" W); the place is southwest of the mouth of present Goler Gulch. Named on Searles Lake (1915) 1° quadrangle.

Goler Gulch [KERN]: *canyon,* 3.25 miles long, opens into Fremont Valley 6.5 miles northwest of Randsburg (lat. 35°25'45" N, long. 117°44'50" W; sec. 12, T 29 S, R 39 E). Named on El Paso Peaks (1967) and Garlock (1967) 7.5' quadrangles. The name commemorates John Goler (or Goller, or Galler), a forty-niner who reported making a rich gold discovery on his trip out of Death Valley (Gudde, 1969, p. 123-124).

Goler Heights [KERN]: *locality,* 6.5 miles northwest of Randsburg (lat. 35°25'35" N, long. 117°44'40" W; sec. 12, T 29 S, R 39 E); the place is near the mouth of Goler Canyon. Named on El Paso Peaks (1967) 7.5' quadrangle.

Golf Meadow [KERN]:
(1) *area,* 8 miles east-northeast of Mount Adelaide (lat. 35°29'15" N, long. 118°37'20" W; at SW cor. sec. 15, T 28 S, R 31 E). Named on Breckenridge Mountain (1972) 7.5' quadrangle.
(2) *area,* nearly 3 miles south of Hobo (present Miracle) Hot Springs (lat. 35°32' N, long. 118°31'55" W; sec. 34, T 27 S, R 32 E). Named on Glennville (1956) 15' quadrangle. Miracle Hot Springs (1972) 7.5' quadrangle shows Goff ranch at the place.

Gomez Meadow [TULARE]: *area,* 2.5 miles north of Olancha Peak on Tulare-Inyo County line (lat. 36°18'10" N, long. 118°07'10" W). Named on Olancha (1956) 15' quadrangle.

Goodale [TULARE]: *locality,* 4 miles southeast of Woodlake along Visalia Electric Railroad (lat. 36°22'40" N, long. 119°02'35" W; at W line sec. 10, T 18 S, R 28 E). Named on Woodlake (1952) 7.5' quadrangle.

Goodale Pass: see **Silver Pass** [FRESNO].

Goode: see **Mount Goode** [FRESNO]; **Mount Goode**, under **Black Giant** [FRESNO].

Goodmill [FRESNO]: *locality,* 10 miles south-southeast of Balch Camp along Mill Flat Creek (lat. 36°46'50" N, long. 119°01'20" W; sec. 22, T 13 S, R 27 E). Site named on Patterson Mountain (1952) 15' quadrangle.

Goodwater Spring [KERN]: *spring,* 12.5 miles east-northeast of Tehachapi (lat. 35°12'35" N, long. 118°15'05" W; near NW cor. sec. 29, T 31 S, R 35 E). Named on Tehachapi NE (1966) 7.5' quadrangle.

Gooseberry Campground [TULARE]: *locality,* 6.5 miles southeast of California Hot Springs (lat. 35°49'10" N, long. 118°34'55" W; near S line sec. 24, T 24 S, R 31 E). Named on California Hot Springs (1958) 15' quadrangle.

Goose Lake Bed [KERN]: *area,* 9 miles east-southeast of the village of Lost Hills between Semitropic Ridge and Buttonwillow Ridge (lat. 35°33'45" N, long. 119°32'30" W). Named on Semitropic (1954) 7.5' quadrangle. Watts' (1894) map shows Goose Lake at the place.

Goose Lake Slough [KERN]: *stream,* branches west from Kern River 7.25 miles west of Bakersfield (lat. 35°21'15" N, long. 119° 07'35" W; near SE cor. sec. 36, T 29 S, R 26 E). Named on Stevens (1954) and Tupman (1954) 7.5' quadrangles. On Buttonwillow (1942) 15' quadrangle, the name applies to present Jerry Slough.

Goose Slough: see **Jerry Slough** [KERN].

Gordon [FRESNO]: *locality,* 5.25 miles north-northwest of Clovis along Southern Pacific Railroad (lat. 36°53'45" N, long. 119°43'45" W; near NW cor. sec. 18, T 12 S, R 21 E). Named on Friant (1964) 7.5' quadrangle. Called Gordon Siding on Friant (1922) 7.5' quadrangle.

Gordon Creek [TULARE]: *stream,* formed by the confluence of North Fork and South Fork, flows 2.5 miles to Deer Creek (2) 8.5 miles east of Fountain Springs (lat. 35°54'35" N, long. 118°45'55" W; sec. 20, T 23 S, R 30 E). Named on California Hot Springs (1958) and White River (1952) 15' quadrangles. North Fork is 3 miles long and South Fork is 3.5 miles long; both forks are named on California Hot Springs (1958) 15' quadrangle.

Gordon Gulch [KERN]: *canyon,* drained by a stream that flows 8.5 miles to Rag Gulch 5.25 miles west of Woody (lat. 35°43'10" N, long. 118°55'35" W; near S line sec. 26, T 25 S, R 28 E). Named on Sand Canyon (1965), White River (1965), and Woody (1965) 7.5' quadrangles. The name is for John Gordon, a miner and businessman (Boyd, p. 159).

Gordon Hills [TULARE]: *ridge,* west-trending, 1.25 miles long, 7 miles north-northwest of California Hot Springs (lat. 35°58'10" N, long. 118°43'25" W; mainly in sec. 34, T 22 S, R 30 E). Named on California Hot Springs (1958) 15' quadrangle.

Gordon Lake [FRESNO]: *lake,* 900 feet long. 9 miles southwest of Mount Abbot (lat. 37°18'25" N, long. 118°55' W). Named on Mount Abbot (1953) 15' quadrangle. The name is for Gordon Bartholomew, who was damkeeper at Florence Lake (Browning, p. 84).

Gordons Ferry [KERN]: *locality,* 4 miles north-northeast of downtown Bakersfield along Kern River (lat. 35°25'30" N, long. 118° 58' W; near NE cor. sec. 9, T 29 S, R 28 E). Site named on Oil Center (1954) 7.5' quadrangle. Aneas B. Gordon operated a ferry at the place from 1853 until 1859 (Bailey, 1967, p. 10), and Butterfield Overland stage line had a station there (Ormsby, p. 118). Goddard's (1857) map shows a place called Dutch Bar situated on the south side of Kern River about 12 miles east of Gordons Ferry.

Gordon Siding: see **Gordon** [FRESNO].

Gorge: see **The Gorge** [FRESNO].

Gorge of Despair [FRESNO]: *canyon,* 3 miles long, opens into Tehipite Valley 11.5 miles northeast of Hume (lat. 36°54'30" N, long. 118°46'30" W). Named on Marion Peak (1953) and Tehipite Dome (1952) 15' quadrangles. L.A. Winchell named the canyon in 1879 (Browning, p. 84).

Gosford [KERN]: *locality,* 7 miles southwest of Bakersfield along Southern Pacific Railroad (lat. 35°18'40" N, long. 119°05'45" W; at S line sec. 17, T 30 S, R 27 E). Named on Gosford (1954) 7.5' quadrangle. Southern Pacific Railroad officials started a community at the place in 1893 and named it for the Earl of Gosford, who once owned the property (Bailey, 1967, p. 10).

Goshen [TULARE]: *town,* 7.5 miles west of Visalia (lat. 36°20'55" N, long. 119°25'15" W; on W line sec. 19, T 18 S, R 24 E). Named on Goshen (1949) 7.5' quadrangle. Officials of Southern Pacific Railroad named the place in 1872; the site also was called Goshen Junction (Mitchell, A.R., p. 68). California Mining Bureau's (1917b) map shows a place called Faxon situated along a rail line between Goshen and Visalia.

Goshen Junction: see **Goshen** [TULARE].

Gould: see **Mount Gould** [FRESNO].

Gould Hill [KERN]: *peak,* nearly 5 miles east-southeast of Carneros Rocks (lat. 35°24'50" N, long. 119°45'55" W; near SW cor. sec. 12, T 29 S, R 21 E). Altitude 1402 feet. Named on Carneros Rocks (1959) 7.5' quadrangle.

Government Peak [KERN]: *peak,* 1.5 miles southwest of Randsburg (lat. 35°21'05" N, long. 117°40'20" W; sec. 3, T 30 S, R 40 E). Altitude 4741 feet. Named on Johannesburg (1967) 7.5' quadrangle.

Grabast Canyon [FRESNO]: *canyon,* drained by a stream that flows 2 miles to Hot Springs Canyon 1.5 miles north-northwest of Coalinga Mineral Springs (lat. 36°10' N, long. 120°33'45" W; sec. 27, T 20 S, R 13 E). Named on Sherman Peak (1969) 7.5' quadrangle.

Grabners: see **Marshall Station** [FRESNO].

Graham Creek [TULARE]: *stream,* flows 5.5 miles to Tule River 2.5 miles south-southwest of Springville (lat. 36°05'45" N, long. 118°49'55" W; sec. 15, T 21 S, R 29 E). Named on Globe (1956) 7.5' quadrangle.

Grahamton: see **San Joaquin** [FRESNO].

Grand Bluff [FRESNO]: *escarpment,* northwest-trending, 0.5 mile long, 6.25 miles west-southwest of Dinkey Dome (lat. 37°04' N, long. 119°13'30" W; near NE cor. sec. 15, T 10 S, R 25 E). Named on Huntington Lake (1953) 15' quadrangle.

Grand Dike [FRESNO]: *ridge,* southeast-trending, 2 miles long, 15 miles west-southwest of Marion Peak (lat. 36°50'15" N, long. 118° 44'50" W). Named on Marion Peak (1953) and Tehipite Dome (1952) 15' quadrangles.

Grand Sentinel [FRESNO]: *peak,* 12.5 miles south-southwest of Marion Peak (lat. 36°47' N, long. 118°35' W). Altitude 8504 feet. Named on Marion Peak (1953) 15' quadrangle.

Grandview: see **Traver** [TULARE].

Grangeville [KINGS]: *village,* 3.5 miles west-northwest of Hanford (lat. 36°20'40" N, long. 119°42'35" W; on E line sec. 20, T 18 S, R 21 E). Named on Hanford (1954) 7.5' quadrangle. Postal authorities established Grangeville post office in 1874 and discontinued it in 1920 (Frickstad, p. 61).

Granite: see **Granite Station** [KERN].

Granite Canyon [KERN]: *canyon,* drained by a stream that flows 6.5 miles to Poso Creek 2.5 miles south-southwest of Knob Hill (lat. 35°31'50" N, long. 118°57'50" W; at S line sec. 33, T 27 S, R 28 E). Named on Knob Hill (1965) 7.5' quadrangle.

Granite Creek [FRESNO]: *stream,* flows 6.5 miles to South Fork Kings River 12.5 miles south-southwest of Marion Peak in Kings Canyon (lat. 36°47'30" N, long. 118°36'05" W); the feature heads near Granite Pass. Named on Marion Peak (1953) 15' quadrangle. J.N. LeConte called the stream Kellogg Creek (Browning, p. 85).

Granite Creek [TULARE]: *stream,* flows 4.5 miles to Eagle Scout Creek 7 miles west-southwest of Triple Divide Peak (lat. 36°32'25" N, long. 118°38' W). Named on Triple Divide Peak (1956) 15' quadrangle.

Granite Gorge [FRESNO]: *canyon,* 1.5 miles long, 14 miles north-northwest of Hume along North Fork Kings River (lat. 36°58'45" N, long. 118°59' W). Named on Tehipite Dome (1952) 15' quadrangle.

Granite Hill [FRESNO]: *ridge,* northwest- to north-trending, 1.5 miles long, 5.25 miles north-northwest of Orange Cove (lat. 36°41'20" N, long. 119°21'45" W). Named on Orange Cove North (1966) 7.5' quadrangle.

Granite Knob [TULARE]: *peak,* 4 miles south-southwest of Monache Mountain (lat. 36°09'10" N, long. 118°13'25" W; sec. 30, T 20 S, R 35 E). Altitude 9050 feet. Named on Monache Mountain (1956) 15' quadrangle.

Granite Lake [FRESNO]: *lake,* 2400 feet long, 8.5 miles southwest of Marion Peak (lat. 36°51'50" N, long. 118°37'05" W); the lake is near the head of Granite Creek. Named on Marion Peak (1953) 15' quadrangle.

Granite Pass [FRESNO]: *pass,* 7.5 miles southwest of Marion Peak on Monarch Divide (lat. 36°52'40" N, long. 118°36'35" W). Named on Marion Peak (1953) 15' quadrangle.

Granite Ridge [FRESNO]: *ridge,* northwest-trending, 1.5 miles long, about 4 miles west-southwest of Trimmer (lat. 36°52'50" N, long. 119°21'35" W). Named on Pine Flat Dam (1965) and Trimmer (1965) 7.5' quadrangles.

Granite Station [KERN]: *locality,* 6.25 miles west-northwest of Pine Mountain along Five Dog Creek (lat. 35°36'50" N, long. 118°51'30" W; near N line sec. 4, T 27 S, R 29 E). Named on Pine Mountain (1965) 7.5' quadrangle. Postal authorities established Granite post office at the site in 1875 and discontinued it in 1876; they established Elmer post office, named for Elmer Bohana, there in 1890, discontinued it in 1892, reestablished it in 1900, and discontinued it in 1914—the place also was called Five Dogs (Salley, p. 68, 88).

Grant Wells [KERN]: *wells,* 9.5 miles south-southeast of Orchard Peak (lat. 35°37'55" N, long. 120°02'40" W; near W line sec. 33, T 26 S, R 18 E). Named on Packwood Creek (1961) 7.5' quadrangle.

Granz: see **Sunnyside** [FRESNO].

Grapes Spring: see **Lower Grapes Spring** [KERN]; **Upper Grapes Spring** [KERN].

Grapevine [KERN]: *village,* 7 miles north-northwest of Lebec (lat. 34°55'40" N, long. 118°56' W); the village is located near the entrance of Grapevine Creek to lowlands. Named on Grapevine (1958) 7.5' quadrangle. Postal authorities established Grapevine post office in 1923 and discontinued it in 1960 (Salley, p. 88). United States Board on Geographic Names (1982a, p. 3) approved the name "Metralla Canyon" for a feature, 1.2 miles long, that opens into lowlands 1 mile west of Grapevine (lat. 34°55'50" N, long. 118°56'43" W).

Grapevine Canyon [KERN]: *canyon,* drained by a stream that flows 7 miles to lowlands 7.5 miles northwest of Inyokern (lat. 35°44' N, long. 117°53'30" W; sec. 28, T 25 S, R 38 E). Named on Little Lake (1954) 15' quadrangle, and on Owens Peak (1972) 7.5' quadrangle.

Grapevine Canyon: see **Grapevine Creek** [KERN].

Grapevine Creek [KERN]: *stream,* flows 8 miles to lowlands at Grapevine (lat. 34°55'45" N, long. 118°55'35" W). Named on Frazier Mountain (1958), Grapevine (1958), Lebec (1958), and Mettler (1955) 7.5' quadrangles. Called Arroyo de las Uvas on Williamson's (1853) map. The canyon of the stream is called Canada de las Uvas on Parke's (1854-1855) map. Cullimore (p. 12) called the feature Grapevine Canyon, and noted that when Pedro Fages traversed it in 1771 he called it Pass of Cortes. Francisco Ruiz went through the defile in 1806 and named it *Cañada de las Uvas,* which means "Canyon of the Grapes" in Spanish (Hanna, p. 125).

Grapevine Creek [TULARE]:

(1) *stream,* flows 3 miles to Cottonwood Creek 3 miles southeast of Cliff Peak (lat. 36°31'45" N, long. 119°07'35" W; at S line sec. 15, T 16 S, R 26 E); the stream heads near Grapevine Peak. Named on Auckland (1966) and Stokes Mountain (1966) 7.5' quadrangles.

(2) *stream,* flows 2 miles to Morgan Canyon 2 miles southeast of Auckland (lat. 36°34' N, long. 119°05'10" W; sec. 6, T 16 S, R 27 E). Named on Auckland (1966) 7.5' quadrangle.

Grapevine Peak [KERN]: *peak,* 2 miles southeast of Grapevine (lat. 34°54'10" N, long. 118°54'10" W). Named on Grapevine (1958) 7.5' quadrangle.

Grapevine Peak [TULARE]: *peak,* 2 miles south-southwest of Auckland (lat. 36°33'50" N, long. 119°07'15" W; sec. 2, T 16 S, R 26 E); the peak is near the head of Grapevine Creek (1). Altitude 1935 feet. Named on Auckland (1966) 7.5' quadrangle.

Grasshopper Creek [TULARE]: *stream,* flows 3.5 miles to Kern River 7 miles west-southwest of Kern Peak (lat. 36°16'35" N, long. 118°24'20" W); the mouth of the stream is at Grasshopper Flat. Named on Kern Peak (1956) 15' quadrangle.

Grasshopper Flat [TULARE]: *area,* 7 miles west-southwest of Kern Peak along Kern River (lat. 36°17' N, long. 118°24'20" W); the placed is at the mouth of Grasshopper Creek. Named on Kern Peak (1956) 15' quadrangle.

Grassy Canyon [TULARE]: *canyon,* drained by a stream that flows 2 miles to White River (1) 4.25 miles southwest of California Hot Springs (lat. 35°50'15" N, long. 118°43'30" W; sec. 15, T 24 S, R 30 E). Named on California Hot Springs (1958) 15' quadrangle.

Grassy Lake [FRESNO]: *lake,* 950 feet long, 12 miles northwest of Mount Abbot (lat. 37°28'55" N, long. 118°57'40" W). Named on Mount Abbot (1953) 15' quadrangle.

Gravelly Flat [FRESNO]: *area,* 3 miles northwest of Coalinga Mineral Springs (lat. 36°10'25" N, long. 120°35'35" W; sec. 20, T 20 S, R 13 E). Named on Sherman Peak (1969) 7.5' quadrangle.

Gravesboro [FRESNO]: *settlement,* 3 miles southwest of Piedra on the southeast side of Kings River (lat. 36°46'20" N, long. 119°24'45" W; sec. 25, T 13 S, R 23 E). Named on Piedra (1965) 7.5' quadrangle. Orangedale School (1923) 7.5' quadrangle shows the place along the Atchison, Topeka and Santa Fe Railroad branch line to Piedra.

Graveyard Lakes [FRESNO]: *lakes,* largest 1400 feet long, 11.5 miles west-northwest of Mount Abbot (lat. 37°27' N, long. 118°58'20" W); the lakes are nearly 1 mile east of Graveyard Peak. Named on Mount Abbot (1953) 15' quadrangle.

Graveyard Meadow: see **Upper Graveyard Meadow** [FRESNO].

Graveyard Meadows [FRESNO]: *area,* 10 miles west of Mount Abbot along Cold Creek (lat. 37°24'50" N, long. 118°57'35" W). Named on Mount Abbot (1953) 15' quadrangle. Sheepmen named the place for graves there of two murdered men (Farquhar, 1923, p. 400).

Graveyard Peak [FRESNO]: *peak,* 12 miles west-northwest of Mount Abbot (lat. 37°27' N, long. 118°59'15" W); the peak is 3 miles north-northwest of Graveyard Meadows. Altitude 11,494 feet. Named on Mount Abbot (1953) 15' quadrangle.

Gray: see **Jim Gray Creek** [TULARE].

Greasy Creek [TULARE]: *stream,* flows 3.5 miles to Lake Kaweah 5 miles southwest of Kaweah (lat. 36°25'35" N, long. 118°59'30" W; near SW cor. sec. 19, T 17 S, R 28 E). Named on Kaweah (1957) 15' quadrangle.

Great Cliffs [FRESNO]: *relief feature,* 9 miles southeast of Mount Goddard (lat. 37°01' N, long. 118°35'45" W). Named on Mount Goddard (1948) 15' quadrangle.

Great Valley: see "Regional setting."

Great Western Divide [TULARE]: *ridge,* 38 miles long, separates the drainage basin of Kern River from the drainage basins of Tulare River and Kings River. Named on Kern Peak (1956), Mineral King (1956), Mount Whitney (1956), and Triple Divide Peak (1956) 15' quadrangles.

Greenacres [KERN]: *town,* 6.25 miles west of Bakersfield (lat. 35° 22'55" N, long. 119°06'45" W; mainly in sec. 30, T 29 S, R 27 E). Named on Oildale (1954) 7.5' quadrangle. Called Green Acres on Bakersfield West (1942) 15' quadrangle. The town began in 1930 (Bailey, 1967, p. 11).

Greenfield [KERN]: *town,* 7 miles south of Bakersfield (lat. 35°16'15" N, long. 119°00'10" W). Named on Gosford (1954) 7.5' quadrangle. Postal authorities established Delkern post office at the place in 1949; the name was coined from letters in the term "Kern Delta," an early designation of the neighborhood (Salley, p. 57).

Greenhorn: see **Petersburg** [KERN].

Greenhorn Cave [KERN]: *cave,* 3.25 miles west of Miracle Hot Springs (lat. 35°34'15" N, long. 118°35'25" W); the cave is along Greenhorn Creek. Named on Miracle Hot Springs (1972) 7.5' quadrangle.

Greenhorn Creek [KERN]: *stream,* flows 8 miles to Kern River 3 miles west-southwest of Miracle Hot Springs (lat. 35°34' N, long. 118°35' W); the stream is in Greenhorn Mountains. Named on Alta Sierra (1972) and Miracle Hot Springs (1972) 7.5' quadrangles.

Greenhorn Mountains [KERN-TULARE]: *range,* north and west of Kern River on Kern-Tulare County line, mainly in Kern County. Named on Bakersfield (1962, revised 1971) 1°x 2° quadrangle. Whipple (p. 149) used the form "Green Horn Mountains" for the name. According to local legend, the name commemorates two novice gold miners—called greenhorns—who were sent into the range to seek gold where gold was thought not to occur, but they found it there anyway (Hanna, p. 126).

Greenhorn Summit [KERN]: *pass,* less than 1 mile north-northwest of Alta Sierra (lat. 35°44'15" N, long. 118°33'20" W; sec. 20, T 25 S, R 32 E); the pass is in Greenhorn Mountains. Named on Alta Sierra (1972) 7.5' quadrangle. Tobias Peak (1943) 30' quadrangle shows Summit store at the place.

Green Meadow [TULARE]: *area,* 7.5 miles south of Mineral King at the head of South Fork Kaweah River (lat. 36°20'25" N, long. 118° 36' W). Named on Mineral King (1956) 15' quadrangle. United States Board on Geographic Names (1938, p. 23) rejected the name "Cabin Meadow" for the feature.

Green Mountain [FRESNO]: *peak,* 2.25 miles east-northeast of Humphreys

Station (lat. 36°58'15" N, long. 119°24'25" W; sec. 13, T 11 S, R 23 E). Altitude 3110 feet. Named on Humphreys Station (1965) 7.5' quadrangle.

Green Slough [KINGS]: *stream,* flows 5 miles to South Fork Kings River 3.5 miles north-northwest of Lemoore (lat. 36°20'50" N. long. 119°49'05" W; sec. 20, T 18 S, R 20 E). Named on Lemoore (1954) 7.5' quadrangle.

Green Spring [KERN]: *spring,* 5.5 miles southwest of Pinyon Mountain in Kelso Valley (lat. 35°23'50" N, long. 118°13'15" W; sec. 21, T 29 S, R 35 E). Named on Pinyon Mountain (1972) 7.5' quadrangle.

Green Spring [TULARE]: *spring,* 3 miles south of Auckland (lat. 36° 32'35" N, long. 119°06'20" W; at NW cor. sec. 13, T 16 S, R 26 E). Named on Auckland (1966) 7.5' quadrangle.

Green Water Spring [FRESNO]: *spring,* 17 miles north-northwest of Coalinga (lat. 36°22'45" N, long. 120°28'40" W; sec. 8, T 18 S, R 14 E). Named on Lillis Ranch (1956) 7.5' quadrangle.

Greenwich: see **Tehachapi** [KERN].

Gregorys Monument [TULARE]: *peak,* 10 miles northwest of Mount Whitney (lat. 36°42'05" N, long. 118°23'40" W). Named on Mount Whitney (1956) 15' quadrangle. Bolton C. Brown named the feature in 1896 (Browning, p. 88).

Gres Canyon [FRESNO]: *canyon,* drained by a stream that flows 1 mile to lowlands 17 miles west-southwest of Firebaugh (lat. 36°43'50" N, long. 120°42'50" W; sec. 12, T 14 S, R 11 E). Named on Chounet Ranch (1956) 7.5' quadrangle.

Grey Meadow [TULARE]: *area,* 7.5 miles northeast of Camp Nelson (lat. 36°12'35" N, long. 118°30'10" W; at E line sec. 4, T 20 S, R 32 E). Named on Camp Nelson (1956) 15' quadrangle.

Grey Rocks [TULARE]: *locality,* 2.5 miles southeast of Exeter along Visalia Electric Railroad (lat. 36°16'05" N, long. 119°06'15" W; at S line sec. 13, T 19 S, R 26 E). Named on Rocky Hill (1927) 7.5' quadrangle.

Grieve: see **Hans Grieve Canyon** [FRESNO].

Grimaud Creek [KERN]: *stream,* flows 7.25 miles to Monotti Creek 5.5 miles west-northwest of Pine Mountain (lat. 35°35' N, long. 118°52' W; sec. 16, T 27 S, R 29 E). Named on Pine Mountain (1965) 7.5' quadrangle. Called Grimoud Creek on Woody (1935) 15' quadrangle.

Grinnell Lake [FRESNO]: *lake,* 1 mile long, 6.5 miles north-northwest of Mount Abbot (lat. 37°28' N, long. 118°50'55" W). Named on Mount Abbot (1953) 15' quadrangle. Leon A. Talbot of California Department of Fish and Game named the lake in 1946 in memory of Joseph Grinnell, professor of zoology and director of Museum of Vertebrate Zoology at University of California (Gudde, 1949, p. 136; Gudde used the form "Lake Joseph Grinnell" for the name).

Grinnell Lake: see **Little Grinnell Lake** [FRESNO].

Grist Mill Peak [TULARE]: *peak,* 5.5 miles south-southwest of California Hot Springs (lat. 35°48'05" N, long. 118°41'25" W; sec. 36, T 24 S, R 30 E). Named on California Hot Springs (1958) 15' quadrangle.

Grizzly Creek [FRESNO]: *stream,* flows 5 miles to South Fork Kings River 16 miles southwest of Marion Peak (lat. 36°48'15" N, long. 118°44'35" W); the stream heads at Grizzly Lakes. Named on Marion Peak (1953) 15' quadrangle. East Fork enters from the northeast 2 miles upstream from the mouth of the main stream; it is 4 miles long and is named on Marion Peak (1953) 15' quadrangle. Tehipite (1903) 30' quadrangle shows the main stream following present East Fork, and has the name "West Fork" on the present main stream above its confluence with present East Fork.

Grizzly Gulch [KERN-TULARE]: *canyon,* drained by a stream that heads in Kern County and flows 9.5 miles to White River (1) 7 miles south of Fountain Springs in Tulare County (lat. 35°48'03" N, long. 118°54'20" W; sec. 36, T 24 S, R 28 E). Named on Quincy School (1965) and White River (1965) 7.5' quadrangles.

Grizzly Lakes [FRESNO]: *lakes,* largest 300 feet long. 13 miles west-southwest of Marion Peak (lat. 36°51'50" N, long. 118°43'10" W); the lakes are at the head of Grizzly Creek. Named on Marion Peak (1953) 15' quadrangle.

Groundhog Meadow [TULARE]: *area,* 4.25 miles north-northwest of Kern Peak near Golden Trout Creek (lat. 36°22' N, long. 118°18'25" W; around NW cor. sec. 16, T 18 S, R 34 E). Named on Kern Peak (1956) 15' quadrangle. United States Board on Geographic Names (1933a, p. 342) rejected the name "Volcano Meadow" for the feature. Miners named the place for marmots found there, which the miners misidentified as groundhogs (Adler, p. 22).

Grouse Canyon [TULARE]: *canyon,* drained by a stream that flows 2 miles to Kern River 2.25 miles south-southeast of Hockett Peak (lat. 36°11'30" N, long. 118°22' W). Named on Hockett Peak (1956) 15' quadrangle.

Grouse Creek [FRESNO]: *stream,* flows 1.5 miles to Big Creek (1) 2 miles east-northeast of the town of Big Creek (lat. 37°13'10" N, long. 119°12'50" W; sec. 23, T 8 S, R 25 E). Named on Huntington Lake (1953) 15' quadrangle.

Grouse Creek [TULARE]: *stream,* flows 6.5 miles to South Fork Kaweah River 8 miles south-southeast of Kaweah (lat. 36°22'10" N, long. 118°51'10" W; near NW cor. sec. 16, T 18 S, R 29 E); the stream heads at Upper Grouse Valley and goes through Grouse Valley. Named on Kaweah (1957) 15' quadrangle.

Grouse Lake [FRESNO]:

(1) *lake,* 700 feet long, 3.5 miles east of Dinkey Dome (lat. 37°07'10" N, long. 119°04'15" W; sec. 30, T 9 S, R 27 E). Named on Huntington Lake (1953) 15' quadrangle.

(2) *lake,* 1400 feet long, 8 miles south-southwest of Marion Peak (lat. 36°51'30" N, long. 118°35'15" W). Named on Marion Peak (1953) 15' quadrangle.

Grouse Meadow [KERN]: *area,* 2.25 miles south of Claraville (lat. 35°24'35" N, long. 118°20'05" W). Named on Claraville (1972) 7.5' quadrangle.

Grouse Meadow [TULARE]:

(1) *area,* 2 miles south of Wilsonia along Dry Creek (1) (lat. 36°42'15" N, long. 118°57'20" W; sec. 17, T 14 S, R 28 E). Named on Giant Forest (1956) 15' quadrangle. According to United States Board on Geographic Names (1987b, p. 1), Grouse Meadow is 2.7 miles south-southwest of Wilsonia (lat. 36°41'50" N, long. 118°58'10" W; sec. 19, T 14 S, R 28 E).

(2) *area,* 5 miles north-northwest of Olancha Peak (lat. 36°20'10" N, long. 118°08'40" W). Named on Olancha (1956) 15' quadrangle.

Grouse Meadows [FRESNO]: *area,* 8 miles east-southeast of Mount Goddard along Middle Fork Kings River (lat. 37°03'35" N, long. 118°35'05" W). Named on Mount Goddard (1948) 15' quadrangle. L.A. Winchell named the feature in 1879; the name now has the singular form "Grouse Meadow" (Browning, p. 88).

Grouse Peak [TULARE]: *peak,* 11 miles south-southeast of Kaweah (lat. 36°20' N, long. 118°49'05" W; sec. 27, T 18 S, R 29 E); the peak is northeast of Grouse Valley. Altitude 5317 feet. Named on Kaweah (1957) 15' quadrangle.

Grouse Valley [TULARE]: *valley,* 11.5 miles south-southeast of Kaweah (lat. 36°19' N, long. 118°50' W); the valley is on upper reaches of Grouse Creek. Named on Kaweah (1957) 15' quadrangle.

Grouse Valley: see **Upper Grouse Valley** [TULARE].

Grubtree Creek: see **Whitney Creek** [TULARE].

Gruff Lake [FRESNO]: *lake,* 300 feet long, 5 miles south of Mount Abbot (lat. 37°18'59" N, long. 118°47'45" W). Named on Mount Abbot (1953) 15' quadrangle. Employees of California Department of Fish and Game named the lake in 1952 (Browning, p. 89).

Grunigen Creek: see **Crunigen Creek** [TULARE].

Guernsey [KINGS]: *locality,* 9 miles north-northwest of Corcoran along Atchison, Topeka and Santa Fe Railroad (lat. 36°12'45" N, long. 119°38'25" W; sec. 1, T 20 S, R 21 E). Named on Guernsey (1954) 7.5' quadrangle. Postal authorities established Guernsey post office in 1898 and discontinued it in 1918 (Frickstad, p. 61). The name is for James Guernsey, who owned land at the place (Gudde, 1949, p. 138).

Guernsey Mill [TULARE]: *locality,* 4.5 miles southeast of California Hot Springs (lat. 35°50' N, long. 118°36'50" W; near S line sec. 15, T 24 S, R 31 E). Named on California Hot Springs (1958) 15' quadrangle.

Guernsey Slough [KINGS]: *stream,* flows 12 miles to a point nearly 3 miles south of Guernsey (lat. 36°10'20" N, long. 119°38'20" W). Named on Guernsey (1929), Remnoy (1927), and Waukena (1928) 7.5' quadrangles. Remnoy (1954) and Waukena (1954) 7.5' quadrangles have the name on a watercourse that is mainly dry.

Guest Lake [FRESNO]: *lake,* 1300 feet long, nearly 0.5 mile north-northwest of Blackcap Mountain (lat. 37°04'40" N, long. 118°47'50" W). Named on Blackcap Mountain (1953) 15' quadrangle.

Guijarral Hills [FRESNO]: *range,* 8 miles east of Coalinga (lat. 36° 09' N, long. 120°13'30" W). Named on Guijarral Hills (1956) 7.5' quadrangle. Arnold and Anderson (1908, p. 15) named the range, described it as "a small low group of gravelly hills," and noted that *guijarral* means "a heap of pebbles" or "a place abounding in pebbles" in Spanish.

Gulf [KERN]: *locality,* 2 miles east of Millux along Sunset Railroad (lat. 35°10'50" N, long. 119°09'35" W). Named on Millux (1954) 7.5' quadrangle.

Guttrie Meadow: see **Cabin Meadow** [TULARE].

Guyot: see **Mount Guyot** [TULARE].

Guyot Creek [TULARE]: *stream,* flows 32 miles to Rock Creek 13 miles north-northwest of Kern Peak (lat. 36°29'30" N, long. 118° 21' W); the stream is east of Mount Guyot. Named on Kern Peak (1956) and Mount Whitney (1956) 15' quadrangles.

Guyot Flat [TULARE]: *area,* 5.25 miles southwest of Mount Whitney (lat. 36°31'25" N, long. 118°21' W). Named on Mount Whitney (1956) 15' quadrangle. The place also was called Sand Flat (Browning, p. 89).

Gyle: see **Delano** [KERN].

Gypsite [KERN]: *locality,* 3 miles southwest of Saltdale (lat. 35°19'50" N, long. 117°55'50" W). Named on Cantil (1967) 7.5' quadrangle. Postal authorities established Gypsite post office in 1911 and discontinued it in 1912; the name was from a gypsum mine (Salley, p. 91).

—H—

Hacker Mountain [FRESNO]: *peak,* 0.5 mile north-northeast of Trimmer (lat. 36°54'55" N, long. 119°17'35" W; near W line sec. 6, T 12 S, R 25 E).

Altitude 2331 feet. Named on Trimmer (1965) 7.5' quadrangle.

Haeckel: see **Mount Haeckel** [FRESNO].

Haggin Well [KERN]: *well,* 9.5 miles north-northwest of Randsburg (lat. 35°29'55" N, long. 117°42'25" W; sec. 18, T 28 S, R 40 E). Named on El Paso Peaks (1967) 7.5' quadrangle. Called Higgins Well on Searles Lake (1915) 1° quadrangle.

Haight Canyon [KERN]: *canyon,* drained by a stream that flows 6.25 miles to Havilah Canyon 4.25 miles south-southwest of Miracle Hot Springs (lat. 35°30'50" N, long. 118°31' W; near NW cor. sec. 11, T 28 S, R 32 E). Named on Breckenridge Mountain (1972), Miracle Hot Springs (1972), and Piute Peak (1972) 7.5' quadrangles.

Haiwee Pass [TULARE]: *pass,* 8.5 miles southeast of Monache Mountain on Tulare-Inyo County line (lat. 36°08'05" N, long. 118° 04'15" W); the pass is near the head of Haiwee Creek, which is in Inyo County. Named on Monache Mountain (1956) 15' quadrangle.

Hale: see **Mount Hale** [TULARE].

Hale McLeod Canyon [KERN]: *canyon,* drained by a stream that heads in San Luis Obispo County and flows 4.5 miles to Midway Valley 1 mile south-southeast of Fellows (lat. 35°09'50" N, long. 119°31'50" W; near N line sec. 8, T 32 S, R 23 E). Named on Fellows (1951) 7.5' quadrangle. The name recalls Hale-McLeod Oil Company, which operated in the neighborhood (Rintoul, p. 92).

Half Corral Meadow [FRESNO]: *area,* 5.25 miles north-northeast of Kaiser Peak (lat. 37°22'05" N, long. 119°09'25" W). Named on Kaiser Peak (1953) 15' quadrangle.

Halfmoon Lake [FRESNO]: *lake,* 2300 feet long, 3.5 miles west-southwest of Blackcap Mountain (lat. 37°03' N, long. 118°50'50" W). Named on Blackcap Mountain (1953) 15' quadrangle.

Halfway House [KERN]: *locality,* nearly 2 miles north-northwest of Knob Hill (lat. 35°35'20" N, long. 118°57'35" W; near SE cor. sec. 9, T 27 S, R 28 E). Named on Knob Hill (1965) 7.5' quadrangle.

Hall Meadow [FRESNO]: *area,* 9 miles southeast of Dinkey Dome (lat. 37°01' N, long. 119°01'15" W; sec. 34, T 10 S, R 27 E); the place is 1.5 miles south of Hall Mountain. Named on Huntington Lake (1953) 15' quadrangle. Called House Meadow on Kaiser (1904) 30' quadrangle. The name "Hall" is for a sheepman and cattle rancher who settled at the place about 1870 (Browning, p. 91).

Hall Mountain [FRESNO]: *ridge,* northwest-trending, 2 miles long. 8.5 miles southeast of Dinkey Dome (lat. 37°02'15" N, long. 119° 01' W; in and near sec. 22, 27, T 10 S, R 27 E). Named on Huntington Lake (1953) 15' quadrangle.

Halls Corner [KINGS]: *locality,* about 3 miles north-northwest of Lemoore (lat. 36°20'35" N, long. 119°48'25" W; at N line sec. 28, T 18 S, R 20 E). Named on Lemoore (1954) 7.5' quadrangle.

Halstead Creek [TULARE]: *stream,* flows 3.5 miles to Marble Fork 5 miles east of Yucca Mountain (lat. 36°34'55" N, long. 118° 47' W; sec. 36, T 15 S, R 29 E); the stream goes through Halstead Meadow. Named on Giant Forest (1956) 15' quadrangle. United States Board on Geographic Names (1933a, p. 349) rejected the name "Suwanee River" for the stream.

Halstead Meadow [TULARE]: *area,* nearly 5.5 miles northeast of Yucca Mountain (lat. 36°37' N, long. 118°47' W; sec. 13, T 15 S, R 29 E); the place is along Halstead Creek. Named on Giant Forest (1956) 15' quadrangle. The name commemorates Sam Halstead, who pastured horses in the neighborhood (United States Board on Geographic Names, 1933a, p. 349).

Hamblin [KINGS]: *settlement,* 2 miles east of Hanford (lat. 36°19'45" N, long. 119°36'30" W; near S line sec. 29, T 18 S, R 22 E). Named on Remnoy (1954) 7.5' quadrangle.

Hambright Canyon [TULARE]: *canyon,* drained by a stream that flows about 0.5 mile to Dry Creek (1) 7 miles northeast of Woodlake (lat. 36°29'30" N, long. 119°01' W; sec. 35, T 16 S, R 27 E). Named on Woodlake (1952) 7.5' quadrangle.

Hamilton Creek [TULARE]: *stream,* flows 3.5 miles to join Lone Pine Creek and form Middle Fork Kaweah River 4.5 miles west-southwest of Triple Divide Peak (lat. 36°33'50" N, long. 118°36'05" W); Hamilton Lakes are along the creek. Named on Triple Divide Peak (1956) 15' quadrangle. United States Board on Geographic Names (1968b, p. 7) rejected the name "Deer Creek" for the stream.

Hamilton Hill: see **Tropico Hill** [KERN].

Hamilton Lake: see **Precipice Lake** [TULARE].

Hamilton Lakes [TULARE]: *lakes,* two, largest 2400 feet long, 3.25 miles southwest of Triple Divide Peak (lat. 36°33'45" N, long. 118°34'30" W); the lakes are along Hamilton Creek. Named on Triple Divide Peak (1956) 15' quadrangle. The name is for James Hamilton, who stocked the lakes with fish that he packed on his back from Big Arroyo (Browning, p. 91).

Hammond [FRESNO]: *locality,* in Fresno where a rail line branches east from the main line of Atchison, Topeka and Santa Fe Railroad (lat. 36°45'35" N, long. 119°47'10" W). Named on Fresno North (1965) 7.5' quadrangle.

Hammond [TULARE]: *locality,* 3.25 miles east of Kaweah along Kaweah River (lat. 36°27'55" N, long. 118°51'40" W; sec. 8, T 17 S, R 29 E). Named on Kaweah (1957) 15' quadrangle. Postal authorities established Hammond post office in 1905 and discontinued it in 1928 (Frickstad, p. 211).

Hamptonville: see **Friant** [FRESNO].

Hamp Williams Pass [KERN]: *pass,* 5.5 miles north of Emerald Mountain (lat. 35°20'10" N, long. 118°17'10" W). Named on Emerald Mountain (1972) 7.5' quadrangle.

Hanford [KINGS]: *town,* in the north part of Kings County (lat. 36° 20' N, long. 119°38'45" W; in and near sec. 25, T 18 S, R 21 E). Named on Hanford (1954) 7.5' quadrangle. Postal authorities established Hanford post office in 1877 (Frickstad, p. 61), and the town incorporated in 1891. Officials of Central Pacific Railroad named the place for James Hanford, treasurer of the railroad (Hart, J.D., p. 176).

Hanning Flat [KERN]: *valley,* 4.5 miles west-northwest of Weldon (lat. 35°41'15" N, long. 118°21'50" W). Named on Weldon (1972) 7.5' quadrangle.

Hans Grieve Canyon [FRESNO]: *canyon,* drained by a stream that flows 5.25 miles to Warthan Creek 3 miles west-southwest of Coalinga Mineral Springs (lat. 36°07'50" N, long. 120°36'15" W; near E line sec. 6, T 21 S, R 13 E). Named on Priest Valley (1969) and Sherman Peak (1969) 7.5' quadrangles.

Hante: see **Camp Yenis Hante** [KERN].

Happy Gap [FRESNO]:

(1) *pass,* 10 miles east-northeast of Hume (lat. 36°51' N, long. 118° 45'05" W). Named on Tehipite Dome (1952) 15' quadrangle. According to Browning (p. 91), the name describes the feelings of anyone who manages to get a pack train to the place.

(2) *pass,* 6.25 miles southwest of Hume (lat. 36°43'25" N, long. 118°59'30" W; sec. 12, T 14 S, R 27 E). Named on Giant Forest (1956) 15' quadrangle. Early teamsters named the feature (Forest M. Clingan, personal communication, 1990).

Hardcash Gulch [KERN]: *canyon,* less than 1 mile long, 5 miles north of Randsburg (lat. 35°26'35" N, long. 117°38'55" W; on W line sec. 1, T 29 S, R 40 E). Named on El Paso Peaks (1967) 7.5' quadrangle.

Hardwick [KINGS]: *village,* 6.5 miles northwest of Hanford (lat. 36°24'10" N, long. 119°43'10" W; near S line sec. 32, T 17 S, R 21 E). Named on Laton (1953) 7.5' quadrangle. Postal authorities established Hardwick post office in 1895, discontinued it in 1904, reestablished it in 1909, and discontinued it in 1942; the name commemorates an official of Southern Pacific Railroad (Salley, p. 93). A place called Kingston was founded in 1856 on the south bank of Kings River at Whitmore's Ferry, 8.5 miles northwest of present Hanford; L.A. Whitmore started the ferry there in 1854 (Hoover, Rensch, and Rensch, p. 136). Laton (1953) 7.5' quadrangle shows Kingston historical marker 2 miles northeast of Hardwick on the south side of Kings River. Postal authorities established Joneso post office 11 miles southeast of Kingston (NW quarter sec. 14, T 18 S, R 22 E) in 1874 and discontinued it in 1879 (Salley, p. 108).

Harlow: see **Shirley** [KINGS].

Harmon Peak [FRESNO]: *peak,* 2 miles east-southeast of Tivy Mountain (lat. 36°47'05" N, long. 119°19'25" W; sec. 23, T 13 S, R 24 E). Altitude 2190 feet. Named on Pine Flat Dam (1965) 7.5' quadrangle.

Harney: see **Mike Harney Canyon** [KERN].

Harper Canyon [KERN]: *canyon,* drained by a stream that flows 9 miles to Caliente Creek 3.25 miles east-northeast of Caliente (lat. 35°18'30" N, long. 118°34'35" W; near NE cor. sec. 19, T 30 S, R 32 E). Named on Loraine (1972) and Oiler Peak (1972) 7.5' quadrangles.

Harper Peak [KERN]: *peak,* 5.5 miles northwest of Loraine (lat. 35° 22'15" N, long. 118°29'35" W; near SE cor. sec. 25, T 29 S, R 32 E). Altitude 5804 feet. Named on Loraine (1972) 7.5' quadrangle.

Harpertown [KERN]: *locality,* 7 miles southeast of downtown Bakersfield along the railroad (lat. 35°17'40" N, long. 118°55'20" W; at N line sec. 25, T 30 S, R 28 E). Named on Lamont (1954) 7.5' quadrangle.

Harrington: see **Mount Harrington** [FRESNO].

Harris Creek: see **Rattlesnake Creek** [TULARE] (3).

Harris Grade Spring [KERN]: *spring,* 3.5 miles east-northeast of Claraville (lat. 35°27'35" N, long. 118°16'15" W; sec. 36, T 28 S, R 34 E). Named on Claraville (1972) 7.5' quadrangle.

Harrison Pass [TULARE]: *pass,* 10.5 miles northwest of Mount Whitney (lat. 36°41'55" N, long. 118°24' W). Named on Mount Whitney (1956) 15' quadrangle. Called Harrisons Pass on Olmsted's (1900) map. The name commemorates Ben Harrison, a sheepherder who built a monument at the pass in the 1880's (Hanna, p. 134).

Harris Spring [FRESNO]: *spring,* 7 miles south-southeast of Ciervo Mountain (lat. 36°22'50" N, long. 120°31'15" W; sec. 11, T 18 S, R 13 E). Named on Ciervo Mountain (1969) 7.5' quadrangle.

Harry Payne Spring [KERN]: *spring,* 6.5 miles east-southeast of Caliente (lat. 35°15'35" N, long. 118°31' W; sec. 2, T 31 S, R 32 E). Named on Oiler Peak (1972) 7.5' quadrangle.

Harry's Bend: see **Mineral King** [TULARE].

Hart: see **Jack Hart Spring** [FRESNO].

Hart Canyon [KERN]. *canyon,* drained by a stream that flows 2.5 miles to

Weaver Creek 7.5 miles north-northwest of Emerald Mountain (lat. 35°21' N, long. 118°21' W; near S line sec. 5, T 30 S, R 34 E); the canyon splits at the head to form Big Hart Canyon and Little Hart Canyon. Named on Emerald Mountain (1972) 7.5' quadrangle.

Hartland [TULARE]: *locality,* 5.5 miles south of Wilsonia (lat. 36° 39'10" N, long. 118°57'25" W; sec. 5, T 15 S, R 28 E). Named on Giant Forest (1956) 15' quadrangle. The name commemorates William Hart, who operated a sawmill near Badger (Browning, p. 93).

Hart Meadow [TULARE]: *area,* 3.5 miles east-southeast of Wilsonia (lat. 36°42'25" N, long. 118°54'05" W; sec. 14, T 14 S, R 28 E). Named on Giant Forest (1956) 15' quadrangle. Mitchel Hart patented land in section 14 in 1890 (Browning, p. 93).

Harts Place [KERN]: *locality,* 13 miles southwest of Inyokern (lat. 35°30'05" N, long. 117°56'50" W; sec. 13, T 28 S, R 37 E). Named on Freeman Junction (1972) 7.5' quadrangle.

Hart Station: see **Old Hart Station** [KERN].

Harvester [KINGS]: *locality,* 18 miles east of Kettleman City along Kings Lake Shore Railroad (lat. 35°58'50" N, long. 119°38'30" W). Named on Harvester (1935) 7.5' quadrangle.

Harvey Lake [FRESNO]: *lake,* 800 feet long, 9 miles southwest of Mount Abbot (lat. 37°18'20" N, long. 118°54'45" W). Named on Mount Abbot (1953) 15' quadrangle. Employees of California Department of Fish and Game named the lake in 1947 for Harvey Sauter of High Sierra Pack Station (Browning, p. 93).

Haslett Basin [FRESNO]: *area,* 7 miles northwest of Balch Camp (lat. 36°58' N, long. 119°12'40" W; near SE cor. sec. 14, T 11 S, R 25 E). Named on Patterson Mountain (1952) 15' quadrangle.

Hatchet Peak [TULARE]:

(1) *peak,* 1.5 miles north-northwest of Springville (lat. 36°09' N, long. 118°49'45" W; near SW cor. sec. 27, T 20 S, R 29 E). Altitude 3286 feet. Named on Springville (1957) 7.5' quadrangle.

(2) *peak,* 4.25 miles north-northeast of California Hot Springs (lat. 35°56'30" N, long. 118°39'20" W; sec. 8, T 23 S, R 31 E). Altitude 6385 feet. Named on California Hot Springs (1958) 15' quadrangle.

Hatch Lake [FRESNO]: *lake,* 1100 feet long, 4 miles east-southeast of Dinkey Dome (lat. 37°05'30" N, long. 119°03'45" W; sec. 6, T 10 S, R 27 E). Named on Huntington Lake (1953) 15' quadrangle.

Havala Spring [KERN]: *spring,* 5.25 miles west-southwest of Cummings Mountain (lat. 35°00'40" N, long. 118°39'15" W; near NE cor. sec. 26, T 11 N, R 17 W). Named on Tejon Ranch (1966) 7.5' quadrangle.

Havilah [KERN]: *village,* 4 miles south-southeast of Miracle Hot Springs (lat. 35°31' N, long. 118°31' W). Named on Miracle Hot Springs (1972) 7.5' quadrangle. Postal authorities established Havilah post office in 1866 and discontinued it in 1918 (Frickstad, p. 56). The community was the first county seat of Kern County. Asbury Harpending (p. 102-103) claimed that he named the place for a biblical country rich in gold.

Havilah Canyon [KERN]: *canyon,* drained by a stream that flows 5.5 miles to Clear Creek (1) 3 miles south-southeast of Miracle Hot Springs (lat. 35°32'05" N, long. 118°30'45" W; sec. 35, T 27 S, R 32 E); Havilah is in the canyon. Named on Breckenridge Mountain (1972) and Miracle Hot Springs (1972) 7.5' quadrangles. On Glennville (1956) 15' quadrangle, the stream in the canyon is called Havilah Creek.

Havilah Creek: see **Havilah Canyon** [KERN].

Hawkins [TULARE]: *locality,* 1.5 miles northeast of Lindsay along Visalia Electric Railroad (lat. 36°13'15" N, long. 119°04'05" W; sec. 5, T 20 S, R 27 E). Named on Lindsay (1928) 7.5' quadrangle.

Hawthorne's Station: see **San Joaquin** [FRESNO].

Hay Corral Ridge [KERN]: *ridge,* generally west-southwest-trending, 2.5 miles long, the center is 2.5 miles east of Caliente (lat. 35°17'25" N, long. 118°34'45" W). Named on Oiler Peak (1972) 7.5' quadrangle.

Hayes: see **Mendota** [FRESNO].

Hayes Canyon [KERN]: *canyon,* drained by a stream that flows 2.5 miles to Winters Canyon 9 miles west-northwest of Liebre Twins (lat. 34°59'25" N, long. 118°43'05" W; sec. 32, T 11 N, R 17 W). Named on Winters Ridge (1966) 7.5' quadrangle.

Hay Flat [KINGS]: *valley,* 8.5 miles south of Avenal (lat. 35°52'50" N, long. 120°08'45" W). Named on Garza Peak (1953) and Tent Hills (1942) 7.5' quadrangles.

Hay Meadow: see **Gnat Meadow** [FRESNO].

Haypress Canyon [KERN]: *canyon,* drained by a stream that flows 2 miles to the canyon of Caliente Creek nearly 4 miles west-northwest of Caliente (lat. 35°18'25" N, long. 118°41'30" W). Named on Bena (1972) 7.5' quadrangle. The name recalls an unsuccessful attempt to haul a hay press through the canyon (Bailey, 1962, p. 43).

Haypress Spring [KERN]: *spring,* 4 miles west of Caliente (lat. 35° 17'40" N, long. 118°41'40" W); the spring is in Haypress Canyon. Named on Bena (1972) 7.5' quadrangle.

Hazelton [KERN]: *locality,* 1.5 miles southeast of Maricopa along Sunset Railroad (lat. 35°02'35" N, long. 119°33' W; on W line sec. 18, T 11 N, R 23 W). Named on Maricopa (1951) 7.5' quadrangle. The place first was called Sunset or Sunset Camp before the railroad reached the site; a locality 2.5 miles farther east (sec. 21, T 11 N, R 23 W) that originally was called Sunset became known as Old Sunset (Latta, 1949, p. 78, 102). Judge Lovejoy gave the name "Sunset" to Old Sunset because of the beautiful sunsets seen there; the name "Hazelton" is for Hazelton Blodget, son of Hugh A. Blodget, a pioneer oilman (Latta, 1949, p. 84, 91).

Hazen: see **Mount Hazen,** under **Table Mountain** [TULARE] (2).

Heald Peak [KERN]: *peak,* 5.25 miles south-southwest of Weldon (lat. 35°35'30" N, long. 118°18'30" W). Altitude 6901 feet. Named on Woolstalf Creek (1972) 7.5' quadrangle. The name commemorates Weldon F. Heald, writer, consultant to Secretary of the Interior, and leader in conservation projects in California (United States Board on Geographic Names, 1974a, p. 3).

Heart Lake [FRESNO]: *lake,* 950 feet long, 9 miles southwest of Mount Abbot (lat. 37°16'55" N, long. 118°52'30" W); the lake has a somewhat heart-shaped outline on a map. Named on Mount Abbot (1953) 15' quadrangle.

Heart Meadow [TULARE]: *area,* 2.5 miles north-northwest of Shell Mountain (lat. 36°43'40" N, long. 118°48'45" W; near N line sec. 10, T 14 S, R 29 E). Named on Giant Forest (1956) 15' quadrangle.

Heather Lake [TULARE]: *lake,* 700 feet long, 9 miles west of Triple Divide Peak (lat. 36°36'05" N, long. 118°41'10" W; near S line sec. 23, T 15 S, R 30 E). Named on Triple Divide Peak (1956) 15' quadrangle. Superintendent White of Sequoia National Park named the feature in 1925 (United States Board on Geographic Names, 1933a, p. 359).

Heather Meadow: see **Lone Pine Meadow** [TULARE].

Heck Canyon [KERN]: *canyon,* drained by a stream that flows 2 miles to Caliente Creek 5.25 miles east-northeast of Caliente (lat. 35°19' N, long. 118°32'10" W; sec. 15, T 30 S, R 32 E). Named on Oiler Peak (1972) 7.5' quadrangle.

Hedrick Meadow [FRESNO]: *area,* 11.5 miles northeast of Kaiser Peak (lat. 37°25'55" N, long. 119°04'05" W). Named on Kaiser Peak (1953) 15' quadrangle.

Heid: see **Redbanks** [TULARE].

Heinlen: see **Cimarron** [KINGS].

Helen Lake [FRESNO]:

(1) *lake,* 600 feet long, 10 miles northwest of Mount Abbot (lat. 37° 28'40" N, long. 118°55'20" W). Named on Mount Abbot (1953) 15' quadrangle. United States Board on Geographic Names (1969a, p. 5) approved the name "Squaw Lake" for the feature.

(2) *lake,* 3000 feet long, 3.25 miles east-northeast of Mount Goddard (lat. 37°07'10" N, long. 118°39'50" W); the lake is northeast of Muir Pass. Named on Mount Goddard (1948) 15' quadrangle. Helen Lake and Wanda Lake, on opposite sides of Muir Pass, were named for daughters of John Muir—this one for Mrs. Helen Muir Funk (Farquhar, 1923, p. 402).

Hell For Sure [TULARE]: *area,* 6.25 miles west-southwest of Kern Peak on the east side of Kern River (lat. 36°16'40" N, long. 118°23'30" W). Named on Kern Peak (1956) 15' quadrangle.

Hell for Sure Lake [FRESNO]: *lake,* 0.5 mile long, 4.5 miles north of Blackcap Mountain (lat. 37°08'20" N, long. 118°48' W); the lake is 0.25 mile southwest of Hell for Sure Pass. Named on Blackcap Mountain (1953) 15' quadrangle.

Hell for Sure Pass [FRESNO]: *pass,* 5 miles north of Blackcap Mountain (lat. 37°08'45" N, long. 118°47'45" W). Named on Blackcap Mountain (1953) 15' quadrangle. J.N. LeConte named the pass in 1904 (Farquhar, 1923, p. 403).

Hell Hole Meadow [FRESNO]: *area,* 12 miles west-southwest of Mount Abbot (lat. 37°18'30" N, long. 118°58'30" W). Named on Mount Abbot (1953) 15' quadrangle.

Hells Hole [TULARE]: *area,* 6.25 miles southwest of Kern Peak (lat. 36°15' N, long. 118°22' W). Named on Hockett Peak (1956) and Kern Peak (1956) 15' quadrangles.

Helm [FRESNO]: *village,* 13 miles south of Kerman (lat. 36°31'55" N, long. 120°05'45" W; near SW cor. sec. 14, T 16 S, R 17 E). Named on Helm (1963) 7.5' quadrangle. Postal authorities established Helm post office in 1913 (Frickstad, p. 33). The name commemorates William Helm, a sheepman who came to California in 1859 (Gudde, 1949, p. 146).

Helm Corner [KINGS]: *locality,* 4.5 miles west of Corcoran (lat. 36° 05'50" N, long. 119°38'35" W; at W line sec. 18, T 21 S, R 22 E). Named on El Rico Ranch (1954) 7.5' quadrangle.

Helmke Pond [FRESNO]: *intermittent lake,* 1150 feet long, 5 miles west of Selma (lat. 36°34'15" N, long. 119°41'50" W; sec. 4, T 16 S, R 21 E). Named on Conejo (1963) 7.5' quadrangle. Called Ralmke Pond on Selma (1946) 15' quadrangle, which shows a lake 3000 feet long.

Helms Creek [FRESNO]: *stream,* flows 12 miles to North Fork Kings River about 8.5 miles west of Blackcap Mountain (lat. 37° 03' N, long. 118°56'35" W; sec. 20, T 10 S, R 28 E). Named on Blackcap Mountain (1953) and Huntington Lake (1953) 15' quadrangles. This apparently is the stream called West Branch on Lippincott's (1902) map.

Helms Meadow [FRESNO]: *area,* 12.5 miles west-northwest of Blackcap Mountain (lat. 37°08'40" N, long. 119°00' W; mainly in sec. 14, 15, T 9 S, R 27 E); the place is along Helms Creek. Named on Blackcap Mountain

(1953) and Huntington Lake (1953) 15' quadrangles. The name commemorates William Helm, an early sheepman (Farquhar, 1923, p. 403).

Hengst Peak: see **Mineral King** [TULARE].

Henry: see **Mount Henry** [FRESNO].

Hermit: see **The Hermit** [FRESNO].

Herndon [FRESNO]: *town,* 9 miles northwest of downtown Fresno (lat. 36°50'15" N, long. 119°55' W; on S line sec. 32, T 12 S, R 19 E). Named on Herndon (1964) 7.5' quadrangle. Postal authorities established Herndon post office in 1887, discontinued it in 1893, and reestablished it in 1907 (Frickstad, p. 33). The place was called Sycamore in 1872, when the railroad crossing of San Joaquin River was there; later it was renamed Herndon for a relative of an irrigation promoter (Gudde, 1949, p. 147).

Herrick's Cross: see **Tulare** [TULARE].

Hessian Meadow [TULARE]: *area,* 2.5 miles northeast of Monache Mountain (lat. 36°14'10" N, long. 118°09'55" W; sec. 27, 34, T 19 S, R 35 E). Named on Monache Mountain (1956) 15' quadrangle. Olancha (1907) 30' quadrangle has the form "Hessian Meadows" for the name.

Hester Lake: see **Langille Peak** [FRESNO].

Hewey Valley [TULARE]: *valley,* 2 miles north-northeast of Fountain Springs (lat. 35°55' N, long. 118°54'10" W). Named on Fountain Springs (1965) 7.5' quadrangle. Called Huey Valley on White River (1936) 15' quadrangle, but United States Board on Geographic Names (1967a, p. 9) rejected this form of the name.

Hickman Creek [TULARE]: *stream,* flows 2.5 miles to North Fork Tule River 3.5 miles north-northeast of Springville (lat. 36°10'50" N, long. 118°47'50" W; near SE cor. sec. 14, T 20 S, R 29 E). Named on Springville (1957) 7.5' quadrangle.

Hicko: see **Hiko**, under **Visalia** [TULARE].

Hicks: see **Hiko**, under **Visalia** [TULARE].

Hico: see **Hiko**, under **Visalia** [TULARE].

Hidden Lake [FRESNO]:

(1) *lake,* 850 feet long, 2.5 miles west of Kaiser Peak (lat. 37°18' N, long. 119°14' W; sec. 22, T 7 S, R 25 E). Named on Kaiser Peak (1953) 15' quadrangle.

(2) *lake,* 800 feet long, 16 miles northwest of Blackcap Mountain (lat. 37°15' N, long. 118°59' W). Named on Blackcap Mountain (1953) and Mount Abbot (1953) 15' quadrangles.

Hidden Lake [TULARE]: *lake,* 300 feet long, 9.5 miles south of Mineral King (lat. 36°18'45" N, long. 118°36'15" W). Named on Mineral King (1956) 15' quadrangle.

Hidden Spring [TULARE]: *spring,* 2.25 miles north-northeast of Yucca Mountain (lat. 36°36'15" N, long. 118°51'30" W; near W line sec. 20, T 15 S, R 29 E). Named on Giant Forest (1956) 15' quadrangle.

Hidden Valley [KERN]: *valley,* 3 miles north-northwest of Rosamond (lat. 34°54'10" N, long. 118°11'30" W; sec. 6, T 9 N, R 12 W). Named on Soledad Mountain (1973) 7.5' quadrangle.

Hidden Valley: see **Blaney Meadows** [FRESNO].

Hidden Valley Meadows: see **Blaney Meadows** [FRESNO].

Higby [TULARE]: *locality,* 3 miles south of Visalia along Atchison, Topeka and Santa Fe Railroad (lat. 36°17'05" N, long. 119°17'10" W; at N line sec. 17, T 19 S, R 25 E). Named on Visalia (1949) 7.5' quadrangle.

Higgins Well: see **Haggin Well** [KERN].

Highberg: see **Actis** [KERN].

High Mountain: see **Pine Top Mountain** [TULARE].

Hights Corner [KERN]: *locality,* 12.5 miles west-northwest of Bakersfield (lat. 35°26'35" N, long. 119°12'10" W; at S line sec. 32, T 28 S, R 26 E). Named on Rosedale (1954) 7.5' quadrangle.

High Sierra: see "Regional setting."

Highway City [FRESNO]: *town,* 2.5 miles southeast of Herndon (lat. 36°48'40" N, long. 119°53'05" W; near SE cor. sec. 10, T 13 S, R 19 E). Named on Herndon (1965) 15' quadrangle. Postal authorities established Highway City post office in 1951 (Salley, p. 97).

Hiko: see **Visalia** [TULARE].

Hilgard: see **Mount Hilgard** [FRESNO].

Hilgard Branch: see **Bear Creek** [FRESNO] (2).

Hilgard Lake [FRESNO]: *lake,* 1100 feet long, 3.25 miles west-southwest of Mount Abbot (lat. 37°22' N, long. 118°50'20" W); the lake is 1 mile northwest of Mount Hilgard at the head of a fork of Hilgard Branch Bear Creek (2). Named on Mount Abbot (1953) 15' quadrangle.

Hill Canyon [KERN]: *canyon,* drained by a stream that flows 1 mile to Oiler Canyon 3 miles northeast of Caliente (lat. 35°19'20" N, long. 118°35'25" W; near NW cor. sec. 18, T 30 S, R 32 E). Named on Oiler Peak (1972) 7.5' quadrangle.

Hillcrest Point [KERN]: *peak,* 6.5 miles east of McKitrick in Elk Hills (lat. 35°17'15" N, long 119°30'35" W; sec. 28, T 30 S, R 23 E). Altitude 1551 feet. Named on West Elk Hills (1954) 7.5' quadrangle.

Hillmaid [TULARE]: *locality,* 2 miles west of Woodlake along Atchison, Topeka and Santa Fe Railroad and Visalia Electric Railroad (lat. 36°24'50" N, long. 119°08' W; at SW cor. sec. 26, T 17 S, R 26 E). Named on Exeter (1952) 15' quadrangle. Ivanhoe (1926) 7.5' quadrangle has the name "Redbanks" as an alternate

Hills Valley [FRESNO]: *valley,* 5 miles north of Orange Cove (lat. 36°41'45" N, long. 119°18'15" W). Named on Orange Cove North (1966) 7.5' quadrangle.

Hillvale Canyon [KERN]: *canyon,* drained by a stream that flows 4.25 miles to Poso Creek 4.25 miles southeast of Knob Hill (lat. 35°30'55" N, long. 118°54'15" W; near SW cor. sec. 6, T 28 S, R 29 E). Named on Knob Hill (1965) and Pine Mountain (1965) 7.5' quadrangles.

Hitchcock: see **Mount Hitchcock** [TULARE].

Hitchcock Lakes [TULARE]: *lakes,* two, largest 3000 feet long, 1.5 miles southwest of Mount Whitney (lat. 36°33'35" N, long. 118°18'30" W); the lakes are northeast of Mount Hitchcock. Named on Mount Whitney (1956) 15' quadrangle. Called Twin Lakes on Mount Whitney (1907) 30' quadrangle, but United States Board on Geographic Names (1933a, p. 367) rejected this name for the pair.

Hitchcock Meadow [TULARE]: *area,* 1.25 miles southwest of Wilsonia (lat. 36°43'25" N, long. 118°58'30" W; sec. 7, T 14 S, R 28 E). Named on Giant Forest (1956) 15' quadrangle.

Hobler Lake [FRESNO]: *lake,* 900 feet long, 9 miles west-northwest of Mount Shinn (lat. 37°08' N, long. 118°56'10" W; sec. 20, T 9 S, R 28 E). Named on Blackcap Mountain (1953) 15' quadrangle. The name reportedly commemorates Sig Hobler, a cattleman (Browning, p. 97).

Hobo Campground [KERN]: *locality,* less than 0.5 mile east of Miracle (formerly Hobo) Hot Springs along Kern River (lat. 35°34'30" N, long. 118°31'30" W; near S line sec. 15, T 27 S, R 32 E). Named on Miracle Hot Springs (1972) 7.5' quadrangle.

Hobo Hot Springs: see **Miracle Hot Springs** [KERN].

Hobo Ridge [KERN]: *ridge,* north-trending, 3 miles long, center 3.5 miles south-southwest of Miracle Hot Springs (formerly Hobo Hot Springs) (lat. 35°32' N, long. 118°33'30" W). Named on Miracle Hot Springs (1972) 7.5' quadrangle.

Hockett Lakes [TULARE]: *lakes,* largest 1200 feet long, 7.5 miles south-southwest of Mineral King (lat. 36°21'25" N, long. 118° 40' W). Named on Mineral King (1956) 15' quadrangle. The name commemorates John B. Hockett, a pioneer of 1849 and a trail builder (United States Board on Geographic Names, 1933a, p. 368).

Hockett Meadows [TULARE]:

(1) *area,* 6.25 miles south-southwest of Mineral King (lat. 36°22'30" N, long. 118°39'15" W). Named on Mineral King (1956) 15' quadrangle.

(2) *area,* less than 1 mile west-northwest of Hockett Peak (lat. 36° 13'30" N, long. 118°23'50" W). Named on Hockett Peak (1956) 15' quadrangle.

Hockett Peak [TULARE]: *peak,* 15 miles west of Olancha Peak (lat. 36°13'15" N, long. 118°23'05" W). Altitude 8551 feet. Named on Hockett Peak (1956) 15' quadrangle.

Hockett Peak Creek [TULARE]: *stream,* flows 2 miles to Kern River 2.25 miles south-southeast of Hockett Peak (lat. 36°11'30" N, long. 118°22'05" W); the stream heads near Hockett Peak. Named on Hockett Peak (1956) 15' quadrangle.

Hockett Well [KERN]: *well,* 6.5 miles northwest of Woody (lat. 35° 46' N, long. 118°55'20" W; near E line sec. 11, T 25 S, R 28 E). Named on Quincy School (1965) 7.5' quadrangle.

Hodges Canyon [KERN]: *canyon,* drained by a stream that flows 2.25 miles to Barrel Valley 5 miles south of Orchard Peak (lat. 35° 40'05" N, long. 120°08'40" W; sec. 16, T 26 S, R 17 E). Named on Orchard Peak (1961) 7.5' quadrangle.

Hoffman Canyon [KERN]: *canyon,* drained by a stream that flows 6 miles to Jawbone Canyon 5 miles northwest of Cinco (lat. 35°18'35" N, long. 118°06'10" W; sec. 22, T 30 S, R 36 E). Named on Cinco (1972) and Cross Mountain (1972) 7.5' quadrangles.

Hoffman Creek [FRESNO]: *stream,* flows 3.5 miles to South Fork San Joaquin River 10 miles north of Kaiser Peak (lat. 37°16' N, long. 119°10'15" W); the stream goes through Hoffman Meadow. Named on Kaiser Peak (1953) 15' quadrangle.

Hoffman Meadow [FRESNO]: *area,* 7.5 miles north of Kaiser Peak (lat. 37°24' N, long. 119°11'20" W; sec. 13, T 6 S, R 25 E); the place is on upper reaches of Hoffman Creek. Named on Kaiser Peak (1953) 15' quadrangle.

Hoffman Mountain [FRESNO]: *ridge,* west-southwest-trending, 1.5 miles long, 14 miles north of Hume (lat. 36°59'30" N, long. 118° 55'10" W). Named on Tehipite Dome (1952) 15' quadrangle.

Hoffman Point [FRESNO]: *peak,* 5.5 miles southwest of Dunlap (lat. 36°41'30" N, long. 119°11'45" W; near E line sec. 24, T 14 S, R 25 E). Altitude 1525 feet. Named on Tucker Mountain (1966) 7.5' quadrangle.

Hoffman Summit [KERN]: *pass,* 6.5 miles north-northwest of Cross Mountain (lat. 35°22'20" N, long. 118°09'45" W; on E line sec. 36, T 29 S, R 35 E); the pass is near the head of Hoffman Canyon. Named on Cross Mountain (1972) 7.5' quadrangle.

Hoffman Well [KERN]: *well,* 8 miles north-northwest of Cinco (lat. 35°21'35" N, long. 118°06'35" W; near NE cor. sec. 4, T 30 S, R 36 E). Named on Cinco (1972) 7.5' quadrangle.

Hogback Peak [FRESNO]: *peak,* 12 miles west-southwest of Marion Peak on Monarch Divide (lat. 36°52'35" N, long. 118°42'35" W). Altitude 11,077 feet. Named on Marion Peak (1953) 15' quadrangle.

Hog Camp [KERN]: *locality,* nearly 2 miles north-northwest of Caliente (lat. 35°18'50" N, long. 118°38'20" W). Named on Bena (1972) 7.5' quadrangle.

Hog Camp Spring [KERN]: *spring,* 2 miles north-northwest of Caliente (lat. 35°19'05" N, long. 118°38'15" W); the spring is 0.25 mile north-northeast of Hog Camp. Named on Bena (1972) 7.5' quadrangle.

Hog Camp Spring: see **Lower Hog Camp Spring** [KERN].

Hog Canyon [FRESNO]: *canyon,* drained by a stream that flows 2 miles to Warthan Creek 3 miles north of Smith Mountain (2) (lat. 36°07'25" N, long. 120°35'45" W; sec. 8, T 21 S, R 13 E). Named on Sherman Peak (1969) 7.5' quadrangle.

Hog Canyon [KERN]: *canyon,* drained by a stream that flows 5.5 miles to Indian Creek 1 mile southeast of Loraine (lat. 35°17'35" N, long. 118°25'15" W; sec. 27, T 30 S, R 33 E). Named on Loraine (1972) and Tehachapi North (1966) 7.5' quadrangles. The stream in the canyon is called Hog Creek on Mojave (1915) 30' quadrangle.

Hog Creek [FRESNO]: *stream,* flows 5.5 miles to Fancher Creek 9.5 miles east of Clovis (lat. 36°49'20" N, long. 119°31'45" W; near N line sec. 12, T 13 S, R 22 E). Named on Piedra (1965) and Round Mountain (1964) 7.5' quadrangles.

Hog Creek: see **Hog Canyon** [KERN].

Hogeye: see **Keyesville** [KERN].

Hogeye Gulch [KERN]: *canyon,* drained by a stream that flows 3.25 miles to Kern River 5.5 miles south-southwest of Wofford Heights (lat. 35°37'55" N, long. 118°29'25" W; near S line sec. 25, T 26 S, R 32 E). Named on Alta Sierra (1972) and Lake Isabella North (1972) 7.5' quadrangles.

Hog Island: see **Alpaugh** [TULARE].

Hog Mountain [FRESNO]: *ridge,* west- to northwest-trending, 1 mile long, nearly 2 miles southwest of Trimmer (lat. 36°53'15" N, long. 119°19' W). Named on Trimmer (1965) 7.5' quadrangle.

Hog Spring [KERN]:

(1) *spring,* 5.5 miles north-northeast of Caliente (lat. 35°21'45" N, long. 118°35'10" W; sec. 31, T 29 S, R 32 E). Named on Oiler Peak (1972) 7.5' quadrangle.

(2) *spring,* 9 miles west of Liebre Twins (lat. 34°57'05" N, long. 118°43'55" W). Named on Winters Ridge (1966) 7.5' quadrangle.

Hog Spring Canyon [TULARE]: *canyon,* drained by a stream that flows 0.5 mile to Dry Creek (1) 7 miles northeast of Woodlake (lat. 36°29'35" N, long. 119°01' W; sec. 35, T 16 S, R 27 E). Named on Woodlake (1952) 7.5' quadrangle. Lemon Cove (1928) 7.5' quadrangle shows Hog Spring Creek in the canyon.

Hog Spring Creek: see **Hog Spring Canyon** [TULARE].

Hoist Ridge [FRESNO]: *ridge,* north-northwest- to northwest-trending, 5 miles long, 4 miles west of Hume (lat. 36°48' N, long. 118° 59'30" W). Named on Patterson Mountain (1952) and Tehipite Dome (1952) 15' quadrangles. Donkey steam engines hoisted logs to the ridge crest, from which place the logs were lowered to a rail line (Browning, p. 99).

Holby Meadow [TULARE]: *area,* 5 miles southeast of Camp Nelson (lat. 36°06'10" N, long. 118°32'10" W; near E line sec. 17, T 21 S, R 32 E). Named on Camp Nelson (1956) 15' quadrangle.

Hole-in-the-Ground [TULARE]: *area,* 7.5 miles west-southwest of Kern Peak along Kern River (lat. 36°15' N, long. 118°24' W). Named on Hockett Peak (1956) and Kern Peak (1956) 15' quadrangles.

Hole in the Mountain [KERN]: *relief feature,* 8.5 miles east of Mount Adelaide (lat. 35°26'05" N, long. 118°35'45" W; at W line sec. 6, T 29 S, R 32 E). Named on Breckenridge Mountain (1972) 7.5' quadrangle.

Holey Meadow [TULARE]: *area,* 6 miles north-northeast of California Hot Springs (lat. 35°57'15" N, long. 118°36'55" W; at S line sec. 3, T 23 S, R 31 E). Named on California Hot Springs (1958) 15' quadrangle.

Holland Camp [KERN]: *locality,* 4 miles north of Garlock (lat. 35° 27'45" N, long. 117°47'40" W). Named on Garlock (1967) 7.5' quadrangle.

Holland Creek [FRESNO]: *stream,* flows 9 miles to Kings River 3.5 miles southwest of Piedra (lat. 36°46'30" N, long. 119°25'45" W; sec. 26, T 13 S, R 23 E). Named on Piedra (1965) 7.5' quadrangle.

Hollis [KERN]: *locality,* 2.25 miles east-southeast of McFarland along Southern Pacific Railroad (lat. 35°40' N, long. 119°11'25" W; sec. 17, T 26 S, R 26 E). Named on McFarland (1954) 7.5' quadrangle.

Holloway Camp [KERN]: *locality,* 3.5 miles northwest of Saltdale in Last Chance Canyon (lat. 35°24'10" N, long. 117°55'20" W; near N line sec. 20, T 29 S, R 38 E). Named on Saltdale (1943a) 15' quadrangle.

Holly Camp [KERN]: *locality,* 6 miles north of Saltdale (lat. 35°26'50" N, long. 117°53'45" W; at SW cor. sec. 33, T 28 S, R 38 E). Named on Saltdale (1943a) 15' quadrangle. A quarry at the place provided material for Holly-brand cleanser (Schumacher, p. 18).

Hollyhock Spring [FRESNO]: *spring,* 4.5 miles north of Coalinga Mineral Springs (lat. 36°12'40" N, long. 120°33'50" W; near NW cor. sec. 10, T 20 S, R 13 E). Named on Sherman Peak (1969) 7.5' quadrangle.

Holman Mill [FRESNO]: *locality,* 16 miles northwest of Coalinga along White Creek (lat. 36°17'55" N, long. 120°34'45" W; sec. 4, T 19 S, R 13 E). Site named on Santa Rita Peak (1969) 7.5' quadrangle.

Holster Lake [FRESNO]: *lake,* 800 feet long, 2.5 miles north-northeast of Blackcap Mountain (lat. 37°06'25" N, long. 118°47' W). Named on Blackcap Mountain (1953) 15' quadrangle.

Home Camp Creek [FRESNO]: *stream,* flows 4 miles to the west end of Huntington Lake (1) at the village of Huntington Lake (lat. 37°14'10" N, long. 119°14'10" W; near E line sec. 16, T 8 S, R 25 E). Named on Huntington Lake (1953), Kaiser Peak (1953), and Shaver Lake (1953) 15' quadrangles.

Homer Cove [TULARE]: *relief feature,* 7.5 miles northeast of Woodlake (lat. 36°27'40" N, long. 119°00'30" W; sec. 35, T 16 S, R 27 E). Named on Woodlake (1952) 7.5' quadrangle. On Lemon Cove (1928) 7.5' quadrangle, the name "Homer Cove" applies to the lower part of present Indian Canyon.

Homers Nose [TULARE]: *peak,* 9 miles west-southwest of Mineral King (lat. 36°23'05" N, long. 118°44'15" W). Named on Mineral King (1956) 15' quadrangle. The name, given in 1872, commemorates John Homer, a pioneer of 1853 (United States Board on Geographic Names, 1933a, p. 370).

Home Spring [FRESNO]: *spring,* 11 miles east-northeast of Clovis (lat. 36°52'25" N, long. 119°30'35" W; sec. 19, T 12 S, R 23 E). Named on Round Mountain (1964) 7.5' quadrangle.

Home Spring [KERN]: *spring,* 8 miles north-northeast of Caliente (lat. 35°24'15" N, long. 118°34'30" W; sec. 17, T 29 S, R 32 E). Named on Breckenridge Mountain (1972) 7.5' quadrangle.

Homestead: see **Indian Wells** [KERN].

Homestead Spring [FRESNO]: *spring,* 4.25 miles east-northeast of Joaquin Rocks (lat. 36°20'50" N, long. 120°22'45" W; sec. 19, T 18 S, R 15 E). Named on Joaquin Rocks (1969) 7.5' quadrangle.

Honeybee Creek [TULARE]: *stream,* flows 3 miles to South Fork Kern River 7.5 miles southeast of Monache Mountain (lat. 36°08'40" N, long. 118°05'15" W). Named on Monache Mountain (1956) 15' quadrangle.

Honeymoon Lake: see **Lower Honeymoon Lake** [FRESNO]; **Upper Honeymoon Lake** [FRESNO].

Hooker Meadow [TULARE]: *area,* about 7 miles south of Monache Mountain (lat. 36°06'20" N, long. 118°11'45" W; near SE cor. sec. 9, T 21 S, R 35 E). Named on Monache Mountain (1956) 15' quadrangle.

Hoopah Lake [FRESNO]: *lake,* 450 feet long, 8 miles south-southwest of Mount Abbot (lat. 37°16'20" N, long. 118°49'10" W). Named on Mount Abbot (1953) 15' quadrangle. Elden H. Vestal of California Department of Fish and Game named the lake in 1951 using a word that he believed was the Indian name for a type of woven carrier for water (Browning, p. 99).

Hooper: see **Mount Hooper** [FRESNO].

Hooper Creek [FRESNO]: *stream,* flows 3.5 miles to the canyon of South Fork San Joaquin River 11 miles west-southwest of Mount Abbot, where it is diverted into a pipeline (lat. 37°18'20" N, long. 118°57' W); the stream heads northwest of Mount Hooper. Named on Mount Abbot (1953) 15' quadrangle.

Hooper Creek: see **San Joaquin River** [FRESNO], **South Fork**.

Hooper Hill [KERN]: *peak,* 1.25 miles east-southeast of Miracle Hot Springs (lat. 35°34' N, long. 118°30'45" W; sec. 23, T 17 S, R 32 E). Altitude 4462 feet. Named on Miracle Hot Springs (1972) 7.5' quadrangle.

Hooper Lake [FRESNO]: *lake,* 750 feet long, 9 miles southwest of Mount Abbot (lat. 37°18' N, long. 118°54'30" W); the lake is 1 mile northwest of Mount Hooper at the head of a branch of Hooper Creek. Named on Mount Abbot (1953) 15' quadrangle.

Hoosier Flat [KERN]: *area,* 4.5 miles east of Mount Adelaide (lat. 35°26'40" N, long. 118°40'05" W; sec. 32, T 28 S, R 31 E). Named on Mount Adelaide (1972) 7.5' quadrangle.

Hopkins: see **Mount Hopkins** [FRESNO].

Hopkins Creek [FRESNO]: *stream,* flows 3 miles to Mono Creek 4.25 miles north-northwest of Mount Abbot (lat. 37°26'25" N, long. 118°49'25" W); the stream heads at Upper Hopkins Lakes near Hopkins Pass. Named on Mount Abbot (1953) 15' quadrangle.

Hopkins Lake: see **Lower Hopkins Lake** [FRESNO]; **Upper Hopkins Lakes** [FRESNO].

Hopkins Pass [FRESNO]: *pass,* 7.25 miles north-northwest of Mount Abbot on Fresno-Mono County line (lat. 37°28'50" N, long. 118° 50'30" W); the pass is near the head of Hopkins Creek. Named on Mount Abbot (1953) 15' quadrangle.

Horned Toad Hills [KERN]: *area,* 3.5 miles northwest of Mojave (lat. 35°05'45" N, long. 118°12'30" W). Named on Mojave (1973) 7.5' quadrangle.

Horn Mountain [TULARE]: *peak,* 6.5 miles southeast of Kaweah (lat. 36°24' N, long. 118°50'30" W). Altitude 4450 feet. Named on Kaweah (1957) 15' quadrangle.

Horse Canyon [KERN]:

(1) *canyon,* drained by a stream that flows 3 miles to Willow Spring Creek (1) 5 miles west-southwest of Woody (lat. 35°40'30" N, long. 118°54'40" W; at N line sec. 13, T 26 S, R 28 E). Named on Sand Canyon (1965) 7.5' quadrangle.

(2) *canyon,* drained by a stream that flows 4 miles to Cache Creek 9.5 miles east-northeast of Tehachapi (lat. 39°10'50" N, long. 118° 17'30" W; near NE cor. sec. 2, T 32 S, R 34 E). Named on Tehachapi NE (1966) 7.5' quadrangle. The name is from fossil bones of horses found in the neighborhood in the early 1900's (Barras, p. 46).

(3) *canyon,* drained by a stream that flows 6.5 miles to lowlands 5.5 miles east-southeast of Skinner Peak (lat. 35°32'50" N, long. 118° 01'35" W). Named on Horse Canyon (1972) 7.5' quadrangle.

Horse Canyon [KINGS]: *canyon,* drained by a stream that flows less than 1 mile to Kettleman Plain at Avenal (lat. 36°00'40" N, long. 120°07'25" W; sec. 15, T 22 S, R 17 E). Named on La Cima (1963) 7.5' quadrangle.

Horse Canyon [TULARE]: *canyon,* 2 miles long, 6.5 miles south-southeast of Camp Nelson on upper reaches of Dry Meadow Creek (lat. 36°03'30" N, long. 118°33'15" W). Named on Camp Nelson (1956) 15' quadrangle.

Horse Canyon: see **Cap Canyon** [KERN].

Horse Canyon Spring [KERN]: *spring,* 2.5 miles east-northeast of Skinner Peak (lat. 35°34'35" N, long. 118°05' W); the spring is in a branch of Horse Canyon (3). Named on Horse Canyon (1972) 7.5' quadrangle.

Horse Canyon Well [KERN]: *well,* 5.25 miles east of Skinner Peak (lat. 35°33'25" N, long. 118°02' W); the well is in Horse Canyon (3). Named on Horse Canyon (1972) 7.5' quadrangle.

Horse Corral Creek [FRESNO]: *stream,* flows 3.5 miles to Boulder Creek (1) 8 miles east-southeast of Hume (lat. 36°44'25" N, long. 118°47' W); the stream passes through Horse Corral Meadow. Named on Giant Forest (1956) 15' quadrangle.

Horse Corral Meadow [FRESNO]: *area,* 8.5 miles east-southeast of Hume (lat. 36°44'50" N, long. 118°45'05" W). Named on Giant Forest (1956) and Triple Divide Peak (1956) 15' quadrangles. The name is from a corral that Jasper H. Harrell built for horses at the site in 1877 (Browning, p. 100). Winchell (p. 241) called the place Crescent Lawn in 1868.

Horse Creek [TULARE]:

(1) *stream,* flows 8.5 miles to East Fork Kaweah River 7.5 miles west of Mineral King (lat. 36°25'50" N, long. 118°43'30" W). Named on Mineral King (1956) 15' quadrangle. United States Board on Geographic Names (1933a, p. 373) rejected the name "Cow Creek" for the stream.

(2) *stream,* flows 4.5 miles to Lake Kaweah 6 miles south-southwest of Kaweah (lat. 36°23'05" N, long. 118°56'30" W; sec. 4, T 18 S, R 28 E). Named on Kaweah (1957) 15' quadrangle.

Horsehead Lake [FRESNO]: *lake,* 1800 feet long, 1.25 miles north-northwest of Blackcap Mountain (lat. 37°05'25" N, long. 118°47'55" W); the outline of the lake on a map suggests the head and body of a horse. Named on Blackcap Mountain (1953) 15' quadrangle. William A. Dill and Jack Criqui of California Department of Fish and Game named the lake in 1948 (Browning, p. 100).

Horse Heaven [FRESNO]: *area,* 10.5 miles northwest of Mount Abbot along Fish Creek (1) (lat. 37°29'45" N, long. 118°54'45" W). Named on Mount Abbot (1953) 15' quadrangle.

Horse Meadow [FRESNO]: *area,* 9 miles south-southeast of Dinkey Dome along East Fork Deer Creek (3) (lat. 37°00'05" N, long. 119°02'45" W; sec. 5, T 11 S, R 27 E). Named on Huntington Lake (1953) 15' quadrangle.

Horse Meadow [TULARE]:

(1) *area,* 7 miles north-northeast of California Hot Springs (lat. 35° 58'15" N, long. 118°37'15" W; near SW cor. sec. 34, T 22 S, R 31 E). Named on California Hot Springs (1958) 15' quadrangle.

(2) *area,* 7 miles east-southeast of Fairview along Salmon Creek (lat. 35°54'10" N, long. 118°22'35" W; sec. 25, T 23 S, R 33 E). Named on Kernville (1956) 15' quadrangle.

Horse Meadow: see **East Horse Meadow** [TULARE].

Horse Meadow Creek [TULARE]: *stream,* flows 2 miles to Parker Meadow Creek 6.5 miles north-northeast of California Hot Springs (lat. 35°57'50" N, long. 118°37'05" W; sec. 3, T 23 S, R 31 E); the stream goes through Horse Meadow (1). Named on California Hot Springs (1958) 15' quadrangle.

Horse Meadows: see **Little Horse Meadows** [TULARE].

Horseshoe: see **The Horseshoe** [KERN].

Horseshoe Bend [FRESNO]:

(1) *bend,* 9 miles west of Shaver Lake Heights (present town of Shaver Lake) along San Joaquin River on Fresno-Madera County line (lat. 37°06'40" N, long. 119°28'15" W). Named on Shaver Lake (1953) 15' quadrangle.

(2) *bend,* 5.5 miles east-northeast of Hume along South Fork Kings River (lat. 36°49'15" N, long. 118°49'45" W). Named on Tehipite Dome (1952) 15' quadrangle.

Horseshoe Creek [FRESNO]: *stream,* flows 4.5 miles to Middle Fork Kings River 6.5 miles west of Marion Peak (lat. 36°58'10" N, long. 118°38'05" W); the stream heads at Horseshoe Lakes. Named on Marion Peak (1953) 15' quadrangle.

Horseshoe Lake [FRESNO]: *lake,* 1600 feet long, 4.25 miles north of Blackcap Mountain (lat. 37°08' N, long. 118°48'15" W); the outline of the lake on a map has the crude shape of a horseshoe. Named on Blackcap Mountain (1953) 15' quadrangle.

Horseshoe Lakes [FRESNO]: *lakes,* largest 1250 feet long, 3 miles west-southwest of Marion Peak (lat. 36°56'45" N, long. 118°34'15" W); the lakes are near the head of Horseshoe Creek. Named on Marion Peak (1953) 15' quadrangle.

Horseshoe Meadows [FRESNO]: *area,* 3.5 miles west of Marion Peak (lat. 36°57' N, long. 118°34'50" W); the place is near Horseshoe Lakes. Named on Marion Peak (1953) 15' quadrangle.

Horsethief Canyon [FRESNO]: *canyon,* drained by a stream that flows 1 mile to Salt Creek (1) 4.25 miles north-northwest of Joaquin Rocks (lat. 36°22'20" N, long. 120°29' W; near SE cor. sec. 7, T 18 S, R 14 E). Named on Joaquin Rocks (1969) 7.5' quadrangle.

Horsethief Canyon [KERN]: *canyon,* drained by a stream that flows 2.5 miles to Oak Creek 8 miles south of Tehachapi (lat. 35°00'50" N, long. 118°26'20" W; sec. 26, T 11 N, R 15 W). Named on Tehachapi South (1966) 7.5' quadrangle.

Horsethief Flat [KERN]: *area,* 9.5 miles northwest of Cummings Mountain (lat. 35°07'25" N, long. 118°42'10" W; on S line sec. 24, T 32 S, R 30 E). Named on Bear Mountain (1966) and Tejon Ranch (1966) 7.5' quadrangles.

Horsethief Lake: see **Lower Horsethief Lake** [FRESNO]; **Upper Horsethief Lake** [FRESNO].

Horsethief Mountain [KERN]: *peak,* 10 miles west-northwest of Cummings Mountain (lat. 35°06'45" N, long. 118°43'20" W; sec. 26, T 32 S, R 30 E). Altitude 3170 feet. Named on Tejon Ranch (1966) 7.5' quadrangle.

Hortense Lake [FRESNO]: *lake,* 1200 feet long, 10 miles northwest of Mount Abbot (lat. 37°29'30" N, long. 118°54'55" W). Named on Mount Abbot (1953) 15' quadrangle.

Hossack Creek [TULARE]: *stream,* flows 2 miles to North Fork of Middle Fork Tule River 4.5 miles northwest of Camp Nelson (lat. 36°11'20" N, long. 118°39'45" W; near N line sec. 18, T 20 S, R 30 E); the stream heads at Hossack Meadow. Named on Camp Nelson (1956) 15' quadrangle.

Hossack Meadow [TULARE]: *area,* 2.5 miles north-northwest of Camp Nelson (lat. 36°10'35" N, long. 118°37'45" W; near NW cor. sec. 21, T 20 S, R 31 E); the place is at the head of Hossack Creek. Named on Camp Nelson (1956) 15' quadrangle. The name commemorates John Hossack, a pioneer stockman (Browning, p. 101).

Hotel Creek [FRESNO]: *stream,* flows 4 miles to South Fork Kings River 14 miles southwest of Marion Peak in Kings Canyon (lat. 36°47'30" N, long. 118°40'10" W). Named on Marion Peak (1953) 15' quadrangle. The name recalls a log hotel that Hugh Robinson built at Cedar Grove in 1897; J.N. LeConte called the stream Fox Creek in 1890 (Browning, p. 101).

Hot Springs [KERN]: *springs,* 3 miles east-northeast of Wofford Heights (lat. 35°43'45" N, long. 118°24'30" W; sec. 26, T 25 S, R 33 E). Named on Lake Isabella North (1972) 7.5' quadrangle. Wheeler's (1875-1878) map shows Hot Sprs. Stage Sta. at or near the place.

Hot Springs: see **California Hot Springs** [TULARE].

Hot Springs Bar: see **Delonegha Hot Springs** [KERN].

Hot Springs Canyon [FRESNO]: *canyon,* drained by a stream that flows 10.5 miles to Warthan Creek nearly 4 miles east of Smith Mountain (1) (lat. 36°05'05" N, long. 120°31'35" W; sec. 24, T 21 S, R 13 E); Coalinga Mineral Springs is in the canyon. Named on Sherman Peak (1969) and Smith Mountain (1969) 7.5' quadrangles. Called Fresno Springs Canyon on Priest Valley (1915) 30' quadrangle, which has the name "Fresno Hot Springs" for present Coalinga Mineral Springs.

Hot Springs Pass [FRESNO]: *pass,* 14 miles northwest of Blackcap Mountain (lat. 37°11'55" N, long. 118°59'40" W). Named on Blackcap Mountain (1953) 15' quadrangle.

Hot Springs Stage Station: see **Hot Springs** [KERN].

Hot Spring Valley [KERN]: *valley,* along Kern River at the town of Lake Isabella (lat. 35°37'30" N, long. 118°28'30" W). Named on Lake Isabella North (1972) and Lake Isabella South (1972) 7.5' quadrangles. The name is from springs of hot water in the valley (Boyd, p. 162).

House Meadow: see **Hall Meadow** [FRESNO].

Houser Camp [KINGS]: *locality,* 12 miles east-southeast of Kettleman City (lat. 35°56' N, long. 119°45'10" W; at NE cor. sec. 13, T 23 S, R 20 E). Named on Dudley Ridge (1954) 7.5' quadrangle.

House Spring [KERN]: *spring,* 1.5 miles north-northeast of Caliente (lat. 35°18'45" N, long. 118°36'50" W). Named on Oiler Peak (1972) 7.5' quadrangle.

House Spring [TULARE]: *spring,* 4.25 miles south-southeast of Auckland (lat. 36°31'35" N, long. 119°07'20" W; sec. 23, T 16 S, R 26 E). Named on Auckland (1966) 7.5' quadrangle.

Howling Gulch [KERN]: *canyon,* drained by a stream that flows 5 miles to Spring Mountain Gulch 0.25 mile west of Woody (lat. 35°42'10" N, long. 118°50'20" W; at N line sec. 3, T 26 S, R 29 E). Named on Woody (1965) 7.5' quadrangle. United States Board on Geographic Names (1966b, p. 5) rejected the name "Wildcat Creek" for the feature.

Howton: see **Success** [TULARE].

Hub [FRESNO-KINGS]: *locality,* 7.25 miles north-northwest of Lemoore on Fresno-Kings County line (lat. 36°24'05" N, long. 119°48'30" W; on N line sec. 4, T 18 S, R 20 E). Named on Riverdale (1954) 7.5' quadrangle.

Riverdale (1927) 7.5' quadrangle shows Hub located along Southern Pacific Railroad, which on the map appears to be just inside Kings County.

Huckleberry Creek: see **Huntington Lake** [FRESNO] (1).

Huckleberry Meadow [FRESNO]: *area*, 2 miles southwest of Hume (lat. 36°46' N, long. 118°56'20" W; sec. 28, T 13 S, R 28 E). Named on Tehipite Dome (1952) 15' quadrangle. Called Huckleberry Valley on Tehipite (1903) 30' quadrangle.

Huckleberry Meadow [TULARE]: *area*, 6.5 miles east of Yucca Mountain (lat. 36°33'20" N, long. 118°45'15" W; near SE cor. sec. 6, T 16 S, R 30 E). Named on Giant Forest (1956) 15' quadrangle.

Huckleberry Valley: see **Huckleberry Meadow** [FRESNO].

Hudson Station: see **Rose Station** [KERN].

Huey Valley: see **Hewey Valley** [TULARE].

Hughes Creek [FRESNO]: *stream*, formed by the confluence of North Fork and West Fork, flows 5 miles to Kings River 0.5 mile north-northeast of Piedra (lat. 36°49'10" N, long. 119°22'45" W; sec. 8, T 13 S, R 24 E). Named on Piedra (1965) and Pine Flat Dam (1965) 7.5' quadrangles. North Fork is 2.5 miles long and is named on Humphreys Station (1965) and Trimmer (1965) 7.5' quadrangles. West Fork also is 2.5 miles long and is named on Humphreys Station (1965) and Piedra (1965) 7.5' quadrangles.

Hughes Mountain [FRESNO]: *ridge*, northwest-trending, 1.5 miles long, 3.25 miles north-northeast of Tivy Mountain (lat. 36°50'40" N, long. 119°20'25" W; in and near sec. 34, T 12 S, R 24 E). Named on Pine Flat Dam (1965) 7.5' quadrangle. The name commemorates John R. Hughes, an early settler (Gudde, 1949, p. 156).

Hugh Mann Canyon [KERN]: *canyon*, drained by a stream that flows 4.25 miles to Weaver Creek 7 miles northwest of Emerald Mountain (lat. 35°20'15" N, long. 118°21'25" W; near W line sec. 8, T 30 S, R 34 E). Named on Emerald Mountain (1972) 7.5' quadrangle.

Hume [FRESNO]: *settlement*, 50 miles east of Fresno (lat. 36°47'10" N, long. 118°54'45" W; in and near sec. 14, 15, T 13 S, R 28 E); the place is near Hume Lake. Named on Tehipite Dome (1952) 15' quadrangle. Postal authorities established Hume post office in 1908, discontinued it in 1924, and reestablished it in 1938 (Frickstad, p. 34).

Hume Lake [FRESNO]: *lake*, 1 mile long, behind a dam on Tenmile Creek 1 mile northeast of Hume (lat. 36°47'40" N, long. 118°54'05" W; sec. 14, T 13 S, R 28 E). Named on Tehipite Dome (1952) 15' quadrangle. The name commemorates Thomas A. Hume, who started a sawmill at the place in 1908 and built the dam that formed the lake in 1909 (Hanna, p. 144).

Hum-pah-ya-mup: see **Kelso Creek** [KERN].

Hum-pah-ya-mup Pass: see **Walker Pass** [KERN].

Humphreys: see **Humphreys Station** [FRESNO]; **Mount Humphreys** [FRESNO].

Humphreys Basin [FRESNO]: *area*, 10 miles north of Mount Goddard (lat. 37°15' N, long. 118°42'30" W); the place is west-southwest of Mount Humphreys. Named on Mount Goddard (1948) and Mount Tom (1949) 15' quadrangles. United States Board on Geographic Names (1978a, p. 3) approved the name "Carol Col" for a pass on the northwest rim of Humphreys Basin 2.9 miles west-northwest of Mount Humphreys (lat. 37°16'42" N, long. 118°43'19" W); the name honors Carol Kassler Ransford, hiker and climber, who spent many summers with youth groups in the neighborhood, and who led a group over the pass in 1973.

Humphreys Lakes [FRESNO]: *lakes*, largest 1400 feet long, 1 mile west-southwest of Mount Humphreys (lat. 37°16' N, long. 118°41'15" W); the lakes are in Humphreys Basin. Named on Mount Tom (1949) 15' quadrangle.

Humphreys Station [FRESNO]: *locality*, 23 miles northwest of Fresno (lat. 36°57'40" N, long. 119°26'40" W; sec. 22, T 11 S, R 23 E). Named on Humphreys Station (1965) 7.5' quadrangle. Called Humphreys on Dinuba (1924) 30' quadrangle. The name commemorates John W. Humphreys, pioneer lumberman and stockman (Gudde, 1969, p. 148).

Hungry Gulch Campground [KERN]: *locality*, 2.5 miles south-southwest of Wofford Heights (lat. 35°40'20" N, long. 118°28'20" W; near NE cor. sec. 18, T 26 S, R 33 E). Named on Lake Isabella North (1972) 7.5' quadrangle.

Hungry Hollow [TULARE]: *valley*, 6 miles north of Fountain Springs (lat. 35°58'30" N, long. 118°55'45" W). Named on Fountain Springs (1965) 7.5' quadrangle.

Hungry Spring [KERN]: *spring*, 11 miles north-northwest of Mojave (lat. 35°12'15" N, long. 118°13'25" W; sec. 28, T 31 S, R 35 E). Named on Cache Peak (1973) 7.5' quadrangle.

Hunsaker: see **Tulare** [TULARE].

Hunt: see **McFarland** [KERN].

Hunter Creek [TULARE]: *stream*, flows 4.25 miles to South Fork Kaweah River 8 miles south-southwest of Mineral King (lat. 36° 20'25" N, long. 118°38' W; sec. 20, T 18 S, R 31 E). Named on Mineral King (1956) 15' quadrangle. United States Board on Geographic Names (1968b, p. 7) rejected the name "South Fork Kaweah River" for the stream.

Huntington: see **Mount Huntington** [FRESNO].

Huntington Lake [FRESNO]:

(1) *lake*, 4.5 miles long, behind a dam on Big Creek (1) 2.5 miles northeast of the town of Big Creek (lat. 37°14' N, long. 119°12'45" W; sec. 14, T 8 S, R 25 E). Named on Huntington Lake (1953) and Kaiser Peak (1953) 15' quadrangles. Pacific Light and Power Company created the reservoir in 1912 and named it for the company president, Henry E. Huntington (Hart, J.D., p. 199). The place that now holds the lake had the name "The Basin" before the lake formed; a landing place on the lake shore was known as Chipmunk Landing for the abundance of chipmunks there (Redinger, p. 19, 99). United States Board on Geographic Names (1987a, p. 1) approved the name "Huckleberry Creek" for a stream that flows 1.5 miles to Huntington Lake (1) 3.3 miles northeast of the town of Big Creek (lat. 37°14'24" N, long. 119°12'25" W; sec. 14, T 8 S, R 25 E); huckleberry bushes grow along the creek.

(2) *village*, 2 miles north of the town of Big Creek (lat. 37°13'50" N, long. 119°14'10" W; in and near sec. 16, T 8 S, R 25 E); the village is at the west end of Huntington Lake (1). Named on Huntington Lake (1953) 15' quadrangle. Postal authorities established Basin post office in 1913 and changed the name to Huntington Lake in 1916 (Frickstad, p. 31).

Huron [FRESNO]: *town*, 15 miles east-northeast of Coalinga (lat. 36°12'15" N, long. 120°05'55" W; sec. 10, 11, T 20 S, R 17 E). Named on Huron (1956) 7.5' quadrangle. Postal authorities established Huron post office in 1877, discontinued it in 1883, and reestablished it in 1886 (Frickstad, p. 34). The town incorporated in 1951. Postal authorities established Last post office 14 miles southwest of Huron in 1890 and discontinued it in 1895 (Salley, p. 119).

Hutchings: see **Mount Hutchings** [FRESNO].

Hutchins [FRESNO]: *locality*, 19 miles southwest of Kaiser Peak along San Joaquin and Eastern Railroad (lat. 37°06'30" N, long. 119°27' W; near N line sec. 34, T 9 S, R 23 E). Named on Kaiser (1904) 30' quadrangle.

Hutchinson Lake: see **Colby Lake** [TULARE].

Hutchinson Meadow [FRESNO]: *area*, 8 miles south of Mount Abbot in Piute Canyon (lat. 37°16'05" N, long. 118°46'50" W). Named on Mount Abbot (1953) 15' quadrangle. The name commemorates James S. Hutchinson, who climbed and explored in the Sierra Nevada for many years (Gudde, 1949, p. 158).

Hutton: see **Mount Hutton**, under **Red Mountain** [FRESNO] (2).

Huxley: see **Mount Huxley** [FRESNO].

Hydril [KINGS]: *locality*, less than 2 miles east-northeast of Avenal (lat. 36°00'50" N, long. 120°06'50" W; sec. 14, T 22 S, R 17 E). Named on La Cima (1963) 7.5' quadrangle.

Hydril Hill [KINGS]: *peak*, 1.5 miles east-northeast of Avenal (lat. 36°00'40" N, long. 120°06'05" W; sec. 14, T 22 S, R 17 E); the peak is 0.25 mile west-southwest of Hydril. Named on La Cima (1963) 7.5' quadrangle. According to United States Board on Geographic Names (1933b, p. 14), the name is in common use locally and was derived from the term "high drill."

— I —

Ian Campbell: see **Mount Ian Campbell**, under **Mount Givens** [FRESNO].

Ice Creek [TULARE]: *stream*, flows 1 mile to Alder Creek (1) 8.5 miles south-southeast of Camp Nelson (lat. 36°01'50" N, long. 118°32'40" W; sec. 8, T 22 S, R 32 E). Named on Camp Nelson (1956) 15' quadrangle.

Ice House: see **Ice House Creek** [KERN].

Ice House Creek [KERN]: *stream*, flows nearly 2 miles to Shirley Creek 1.25 miles east-southeast of Alta Sierra (lat. 35°43'15" N, long. 118°31'45" W; sec. 27, T 25 S, R 32 E). Named on Alta Sierra (1972) 7.5' quadrangle. California Division of Highways' (1934) map shows a place called Ice House located near present Ice House Creek (sec. 21, T 25 S, R 32 E).

Ickes: see **Mount Ickes** [FRESNO].

Idaho Lake [FRESNO]: *lake*, 650 feet long, 3 miles east of Kaiser Peak (lat. 37°17'35" N, long. 119°07'45" W; sec. 28, T 7 S, R 26 E). Named on Kaiser Peak (1953) 15' quadrangle.

Ida Lake [TULARE]: *lake*, 1000 feet long, behind a dam on Nobe Young Creek 11.5 miles northeast of California Hot Springs (lat. 35°59'55" N, long. 118°31'50" W). Named on California Hot Springs (1958) 15' quadrangle.

Idlewild [TULARE]: *settlement*, 4.5 miles south of California Hot Springs (lat. 35°48'45" N, long. 118°40'10" W; sec. 30, T 24 S, R 31 E). Named on California Hot Springs (1958) 15' quadrangle.

Illinois Mills: see **Visalia** [TULARE].

Ilmon [KERN]: *locality*, 5 miles west-northwest of Caliente along Southern Pacific Railroad (lat. 35°18'45" N, long. 118°41'35" W). Named on Bena (1972) 7.5' quadrangle.

Imhoff [TULARE]: *locality*, 1 mile east-northeast of downtown Tulare along Atchison, Topeka and Santa Fe Railroad (lat. 36°12'55" N, long. 119°19'50" W; at W line sec. 1, T 20 S, R 24 E). Named on Tulare (1927) 7.5' quadrangle.

Indian Basin [FRESNO]: *area*, 2 miles west-northwest of Hume (lat. 36°48' N, long. 118°56'30" W; on S line sec. 9, T 13 S, R 28 E); Indian Creek drains the place. Named on Tehipite Dome (1952) 15' quadrangle.

Indian Canyon [TULARE]: *canyon,* drained by a stream that flows 1.5 miles to Dry Creek (1) 6.5 miles northeast of Woodlake (lat. 36°28'50" N, long. 119°01'05" W; sec. 2, T 17 S, R 27 E). Named on Exeter (1952) and Kaweah (1957) 15' quadrangles. The lower part of Indian Canyon is called Homer Cove on Lemon Cove (1928) 7.5' quadrangle, which has the name "Indian Canyon" for a presently unnamed canyon 2 miles farther south.

Indian Creek [FRESNO]: *stream,* flows 5.25 miles to Tenmile Creek 2.5 miles northeast of Hume (lat. 36°49' N, long. 118°53'15" W); the stream goes through Indian Basin. Named on Tehipite Dome (1952) 15' quadrangle.

Indian Creek [FRESNO-TULARE]: *stream,* heads in Fresno County and flows 6.5 miles to Murry Creek (1) 3 miles northeast of Auckland in Tulare County (lat. 36°37'15" N, long, 119°03'55" W; sec. 17, T 15 S, R 27 E). Named on Auckland (1966) and Miramonte (1966) 7.5' quadrangles.

Indian Creek [KERN]: *stream,* flows 14 miles to Caliente Creek at Loraine (lat. 35°18'20" N, long. 118°26'15" W; sec. 21, T 30 S, R 33 E). Named on Emerald Mountain (1972), Loraine (1972), and Tehachapi NE (1966) 7.5' quadrangles.

Indian Head [TULARE]: *relief feature,* nearly 3 miles south of Kern Peak (lat. 36°16'10" N, long. 118°17' W). Named on Kern Peak (1956) 15' quadrangle.

Indian Hill [TULARE]: *peak,* 8 miles east of Tucker Mountain (lat. 36°38'05" N, long. 119°03'30" W; sec. 8, T 15 S, R 27 E); the peak is east of Indian Creek. Altitude 2740 feet. Named on Miramonte (1966) 7.5' quadrangle.

Indian John Spring [KERN]: *spring,* 4.5 miles south-southwest of Tehachapi (lat. 35°04'10" N, long. 118°28'30" W; near S line sec. 4, T 11 N, R 15 E). Named on Tehachapi South (1966) 7.5' quadrangle.

Indian Lake: see **Lower Indian Lake** [FRESNO]; **Upper Indian Lake** [FRESNO].

Indian Painting Spring [TULARE]: *spring,* 6 miles south-southeast of Auckland (lat. 36°30'20" N, long. 119°03'50" W; sec. 29, T 16 S, R 27 E). Named on Auckland (1966) 7.5' quadrangle.

Indian Rock [FRESNO]: *peak,* 2.5 miles north-northeast of Balch Camp (lat. 36°56'10" N, long. 119°06'15" W). Named on Patterson Mountain (1952) 15' quadrangle.

Indian Rocks [KERN]: *relief feature,* 2.5 miles east-northeast of Orchard Peak (lat. 35°45'10" N, long. 120°05'20" W; sec. 13, T 25 S, R 17 E). Named on Pyramid Hills (1953) 7.5' quadrangle.

Indian Spring [KERN]: *spring,* nearly 4 miles south-southwest of Orchard Peak (lat. 35°41'05" N, long. 120°09'15" W; near NE cor. sec. 8, T 26 S, R 17 E). Named on Orchard Peak (1961) 7.5' quadrangle.

Indian Spring [TULARE]: *spring,* 5.25 miles south-southeast of Auckland (lat. 36°30'55" N, long. 119°04'30" W; sec. 19, T 16 S, R 27 E). Named on Auckland (1966) 7.5' quadrangle.

Indian Springs [FRESNO]:

(1) *spring,* 7 miles southwest of Blackcap Mountain (lat. 37°00'15" N, long. 118°53' W; sec. 2, T 11 S, R 28 E). Named on Blackcap Mountain (1953) 15' quadrangle.

(2) *spring,* 8 miles northwest of Coalinga (lat. 36°13'10" N, long. 120°27'30" W; sec. 4, T 20 S, R 14 E). Named on Alcalde Hills (1969) 7.5' quadrangle. Called Nunez Spr. on Coalinga (1944) 15' quadrangle.

Indian Springs: see **Rosamond** [KERN].

Indian Valley [FRESNO]: *valley,* 6.5 miles southeast of Mercey Hot Springs on Fresno-San Benito County line (lat. 36°37'55" N, long. 120°47' W; around SE cor. sec. 8, T 15 S, R 11 E). Named on Mercey Hot Springs (1969) 7.5' quadrangle.

Indian Wells [KERN]: *locality,* 3.5 miles west-northwest of Inyokern (lat. 35°40'05" N, long. 117°52'20" W; near S line sec. 15, T 26 S, R 38 E); the place is at the west edge of Indian Wells Valley. Named on Inyokern (1972) 7.5' quadrangle. Called Homestead on Inyokern (1943) 15' quadrangle. Searles Lake (1915) 1° quadrangle shows a watering place called Indian Wells at the site.

Indian Wells Canyon [KERN]: *canyon,* drained by a stream that flows 8.5 miles to Indian Wells Valley 3.5 miles west-northwest of Inyokern near Indian Wells (lat. 35°40'20" N, long. 117°52'05" W; sec. 15, T 26 S, R 38 E). Named on Owens Peak (1972) 7.5' quadrangle.

Indian Wells Canyon: see **Berts Canyon** [KERN].

Indian Wells Valley [KERN]: *valley,* east of the Sierra Nevada and north of El Paso Mountains at the northeast corner of Kern County; extends into Inyo County and San Bernardino County. Named on Trona (1957) 1°x 2° quadrangle. Called Salt Wells Valley on Wheeler's (1871-1878) map. The feature also was called Inyo-kern Valley and Brown Valley (Thompson, D.G., 1929, p. 144). United States Board on Geographic Names (1933a, p. 388) rejected the names "Salt Wells Valley," "Inyokern Valley," "Inyo-Kern Valley," and "Brown Valley" for the place.

Infant Buttes [FRESNO]: *relief features,* 9.5 miles west-southwest of Mount Abbot (lat. 37°19'30" N, long. 118°56'25" W). Named on Mount Abbot (1953) 15' quadrangle. Theodore S. Solomons gave the name (Farquhar, 1923, p. 406).

Ingle [FRESNO]: *locality,* 7.25 miles east-southeast of Mendota along Southern Pacific Railroad (lat. 36°43'15" N, long. 120°15'25" W; near SW cor. sec. 8, T 14 S, R 16 E). Named on Tranquillity (1956) 7.5' quadrangle.

Ingram Canyon [FRESNO]: *canyon,* drained by a stream that flows 2 miles to Lavrock Canyon 7 miles south of Orchard Peak (lat. 35° 38'20" N, long. 120°08'45" W; sec. 28, T 26 S, R 17 E). Named on Orchard Peak (1961) 7.5' quadrangle.

Injun Flats: see **Jackass Meadow** [FRESNO].

Inside Creek [TULARE]: *stream,* diverges from Outside Creek and flows 4 miles to rejoin Outside Creek and form Elk Bayou 5 miles east-southeast of Tulare (lat. 36°11'30" N, long. 119°15'20" W; sec. 15, T 20 S, R 25 E). Named on Cairns Corner (1950, photorevised 1969) and Tulare (1950) 7.5' quadrangles.

Inspiration Point [KERN]: *peak,* 11.5 miles south-southwest of Weldon (lat. 35°30'45" N, long. 118°21'25" W; near SE cor. sec. 7, T 28 S, R 34 E). Altitude 7835 feet. Named on Woolstalf Creek (1972) 7.5' quadrangle.

Inyokern [KERN]: *village,* 8 miles west of Ridgecrest (lat. 35°38'50" N, long. 117°48'45" W; on E line sec. 30, T 26 S, R 39 E). Named on Inyokern (1972) 7.5' quadrangle. Postal authorities established Inyokern post office in 1910 (Frickstad, p. 56). The place started during construction of the aqueduct that takes Owens Valley water from Inyo County to Los Angeles; it was called Siding 16 and Magnolia before 1913, when Robert Thompson, Sr., a resident, suggested the name "Inyokern" for the location near Kern-Inyo County line (Bailey, 1967, p. 11).

Inyo-Kern Valley: see **Indian Wells Valley** [KERN].

Inyo Well [KERN]: *well,* 3.5 miles south of Inyokern along Little Dixie Wash (lat. 35°35'45" N, long. 117°48'55" W; near SE cor. sec. 7, T 27 S, R 30 E). Named on Inyokern SE (1972) 7.5' quadrangle.

Ionian Basin [FRESNO]: *area,* 2.25 miles east-southeast of Mount Goddard (lat. 37°05'40" N, long. 118°40'45" W); the place is near Scylla and Charybdis. Named on Mount Goddard (1948) 15' quadrangle. Lewis Clark of the Sierra Club proposed the name to carry out the Greek theme begun with the names "Scylla" and "Charybdis" (Browning, p. 107).

Iridescent Lake [TULARE]: *lake,* 1500 feet long, 3.5 miles south-southeast of Mount Whitney (lat. 36°32'05" N, long. 118°15'30" W). Named on Mount Whitney (1956) 15' quadrangle.

Iron Canyon [KERN]: *canyon,* drained by a stream that flows 1.5 miles to Fremont Valley 2 miles northeast of Garlock (lat. 35°25'15" N, long. 117°45'50" W). Named on Garlock (1967) 7.5' quadrangle.

Iron Mountain [KERN]: *peak,* 1.5 miles south-southwest of Woody (lat. 35°41'15" N, long. 118°50'55" W; near NW cor. sec. 10, T 26 S, R 29 E). Altitude 2486 feet. Named on Woody (1965) 7.5' quadrangle.

Iron Spring [FRESNO]:

(1) *spring,* 6.25 miles southeast of Smith Mountain (2) (lat. 36°01'35" N, long. 120°30'10" W; sec. 7, T 22 S, R 14 E). Named on Smith Mountain (1969) 7.5' quadrangle.

(2) *spring,* 11 miles southwest of Coalinga (lat. 36°00'35" N, long. 120°28'25" W; near SW cor. sec. 16, T 22 S, R 14 E). Named on Curry Mountain (1969) 7.5' quadrangle.

Iron Spring [TULARE]: *spring,* 5 miles west of Olancha Peak (lat. 36°16'25" N, long. 118°12'20" W; sec. 17, T 19 S, R 35 E). Named on Olancha (1956) 15' quadrangle.

Isabella [KERN]: *locality,* 4.5 miles north-northeast of Bodfish along Kern River at the mouth of South Fork (lat. 35°39'25" N, long. 118°27'35" W). Named on Isabella (1943) 15' quadrangle. Postal authorities established Isabella post office in 1896, moved it 1.5 miles south in 1953, and changed the name to Lake Isabella in 1957 (Salley, p. 115). Steven Barton founded the town and named it for Queen Isabella of Spain in 1893, the year of the Columbian Exposition celebrating the quadricentennial of the discovery of America (Gudde, 1949, p. 162). Water of Isabella Lake now covers the site.

Isabella: see **Lake Isabella** [KERN].

Isabella Lake [KERN]: *lake,* behind a dam on Kern River 4.5 miles south-southwest of Wofford Heights (lat. 35°38'45" N, long. 118° 28'50" W; near SW cor. sec. 19, T 26 S, R 33 E); water of the lake covers the site of the former town of Isabella. Named on Lake Isabella North (1972) and Weldon (1972) 7.5' quadrangles. Called Isabella Reservoir on Isabella (1943) 15' quadrangle. United States Board on Geographic Names (1972a, p. 4) gave the names "Lake Isabella" and "Isabella Reservoir" as variants. The dam that forms the lake was completed in 1953 (Wines, p. 131).

Isabella Reservoir: see **Isabella Lake** [KERN].

Isham Hill [KERN]: *peak,* 4 miles north-northwest of Woody (lat. 35°45'45" N, long. 118°51' W; near SE cor. sec. 9, T 25 S, R 29 E). Altitude 2196 feet. Named on White River (1965) 7.5' quadrangle.

Island Crossing [FRESNO]: *locality,* 2.25 miles northwest of Double Peak along Fish Creek (1) (lat. 37°32'05" N, long. 119°04' W). Named on Devils Postpile (1953) 15' quadrangle.

Island Lake [FRESNO]: *lake,* 1100 feet long, 4.5 miles east-northeast of Dinkey Dome (lat. 37°09'05" N, long. 119°03'40" W; sec. 18, T 9 S, R 27 E); the lake contains five islands. Named on Huntington Lake (1953) 15' quadrangle.

Island Number 1 [FRESNO]: *island,* 11 miles north of downtown Fresno in San Joaquin River (lat. 36°55'10" N, long. 119°45'25" W; sec. 2, T 12 S,

R 20 E). Named on Herndon (1965) 15' quadrangle.

Isosceles Peak [FRESNO]: *peak,* 10 miles east of Mount Goddard (lat. 37°05'40" N, long. 118°32'15" W). Named on Mount Goddard (1948) 15' quadrangle. Lewis Clark and Nathan Clark named the peak about 1939 for its appearance from Dusy Basin (Browning, p. 108).

Italian Bar [FRESNO]: *locality,* 9 miles northwest of Shaver Lake Heights (present town of Shaver Lake) along San Joaquin River on Fresno-Madera County line (lat. 37°09'25" N, long. 119°24'15" W; near SW cor. sec. 7, T 9 S, R 24 E). Named on Shaver Lake (1953) 15' quadrangle.

Italian Creek [FRESNO]: *stream,* flows nearly 3 miles to San Joaquin River 5.5 miles west-northwest of Shaver Lake Heights (present town of Shaver Lake) (lat. 37°08'55" N, long. 119°23'55" W; sec. 18, T 9 S, R 24 E); the stream enters San Joaquin River near Italian Bar. Named on Shaver Lake (1953) 15' quadrangle.

Italy: see **Lake Italy** [FRESNO].

Italy Pass [FRESNO]: *pass,* 2.5 miles south of Mount Abbot on Fresno-Inyo County line (lat. 37°21'05" N, long. 118°47' W); the pass is 1 mile east-southeast of Lake Italy. Named on Mount Abbot (1953) 15' quadrangle.

Iva Bell Hot Springs: see **Fish Creek Hot Springs** [FRESNO].

Ivanhoe [TULARE]: *town,* 7 miles west-southwest of Woodlake (lat. 36°23'15" N, long. 119°13' W; mainly in sec. 1, T 18 S, R 25 E). Named on Exeter (1952) 15' quadrangle. The place was called Klink, for George T. Klink, a railroad auditor, before Mrs. Ellen Boas, a schoolboard member, suggested the name "Ivanhoe" from Ivanhoe school district (Mitchell, A.R., p. 68). Postal authorities established Ivanhoe post office first in 1895 and discontinued it in 1896; they established Klink post office in 1910 and changed the name to Ivanhoe in 1924 (Salley, p. 105, 113). They established Orange Heights post office 12 miles northeast of Visalia in 1910 and discontinued it in 1912, when they moved the service to Klink (Salley, p. 162).

Ive: see **Ivesta** [FRESNO].

Ivesta [FRESNO]: *locality,* 6 miles east-northeast of Malaga along Southern Pacific Railroad (lat. 36°43'20" N, long. 119°38'10" W; on S line sec. 12, T 14 S, R 21 E). Named on Malaga (1964) 7.5' quadrangle. Called Ive on Malaga (1923) 7.5' quadrangle, and called Minneola on Grunsky's (1898) map.

Ivory [TULARE]: *locality,* nearly 3 miles northwest of Dinuba along Southern Pacific Railroad (lat. 36°34'05" N, long. 119°25'25" W; sec. 1, T 16 S, R 23 E). Named on Reedley (1966) 7.5' quadrangle.

Ivy [KERN]: *locality,* 3 miles south of Wasco along Atchison, Topeka and Santa Fe Railroad (lat. 35°33' N, long. 119°19'30" W; sec. 30, T 27 S, R 25 E). Named on Wasco (1953) 7.5' quadrangle.

Izaak Walton: see **Mount Izaak Walton** [FRESNO].

Izaak Walton Lake [FRESNO]: *lake,* 1100 feet long, 9.5 miles southwest of Mount Abbot (lat. 37°29'05" N, long. 118°54' W); the lake is 1 mile north-northwest of Mount Izaak Walton. Named on Mount Abbot (1953) 15' quadrangle.

—J—

Jacalitos Creek [FRESNO]: *stream,* flows 27 miles to Los Gatos Creek 5.5 miles east of Coalinga (lat. 36°08'50" N, long. 120°15'45" W; near W line sec. 32, T 20 S, R 16 E). Named on Coalinga (1956), Curry Mountain (1969), Kreyenhagen Hills (1956), and Smith Mountain (1969) 7.5' quadrangles. Spaniards called the stream El Arroyo de Jacalitos for the many Indian dwellings found near it (Hoover, Rensch, and Rensch, p. 89). *Jacalitos* means "little huts" in Mexican Spanish, with special reference to Indian dwellings (Stewart, p. 225).

Jacalitos Hills [FRESNO]: *range,* 4 miles south of Coalinga between Jacalitos Creek and Warthan Creek (lat. 36°05' N, long. 120°22'30" W). Named on Curry Mountain (1969) and Kreyenhagen Hills (1956) 7.5' quadrangles.

Jackass Creek [TULARE]: *stream,* flows 4.5 miles to Fish Creek (2) 10 miles south of Monache Mountain (lat. 36°03'50" N, long. 118° 13'05" W; sec. 29, T 21 S, R 35 E); the stream heads near Jackass Peak and goes through Jackass Meadows. Named on Monache Mountain (1956) 15' quadrangle.

Jackass Dike [FRESNO]: *ridge,* north-northwest-trending, 1.25 miles long, 11.5 miles west-southwest of Mount Abbot (lat. 37°18' N, long. 118°57'40" W); the ridge is 1 mile north of Jackass Meadow. Named on Mount Abbot (1953) 15' quadrangle.

Jackass Flat: see **Jackass Meadow** [FRESNO].

Jackass Meadow [FRESNO]: *area,* 12.5 miles southwest of Mount Abbot along South Fork San Joaquin River (lat. 37°16'55" N, long. 118°57'45" W); the place is 1 mile south of Jackass Dike. Named on Mount Abbot (1953) 15' quadrangle. Called Jackass Flat on Lippincott's (1902) map. The place first was called Injun Flats (Browning, p. 109).

Jackass Meadows [TULARE]: *area,* 8 miles southwest of Monache Mountain (lat. 36°05'40" N, long. 118°13'35" W; sec. 17, T 21 S, R 35 E): the place is along Jackass Creek. Named on Monache Mountain (1956) 15' quadrangle.

Jackass Peak [TULARE]: *peak,* nearly 5 miles south of Monache Mountain (lat. 36°08'15" N, long. 118°12'20" W; sec. 32, T 20 S, R 35 E). Altitude 9245 feet. Named on Monache Mountain (1956) 15' quadrangle.

Jack Canyon [KERN]: *canyon,* 2 miles long, 4 miles southwest of Orchard Peak on Kern-San Luis Obispo County line (lat. 35°42'30" N, long. 120°11'45" W). Named on Orchard Peak (1961) 7.5' quadrangle.

Jack Hart Spring [FRESNO]: *spring,* 3.5 miles northeast of Coalinga Mineral Springs (lat. 36°10'45" N, long. 120°30'45" W; near NW cor. sec. 19, T 20 S, R 14 E). Named on Sherman Peak (1969) 7.5' quadrangle.

Jackrabbit Hill [KERN]: *hill,* 11.5 miles south-southwest of Boron (lat. 34°50'20" N, long. 117°42'10" W; near SE cor. sec. 27, T 9 N, R 8 W). Altitude 2881 feet. Named on Jackrabbit Hill (1973) 7.5' quadrangle.

Jacks Camp [KERN]: *locality,* 7.5 miles northwest of Cummings Mountain (lat. 35°06'40" N, long. 118°40'20" W; near S line sec. 29, T 32 S, R 31 E). Named on Tejon Ranch (1966) 7.5' quadrangle.

Jacks Creek [KERN]: *stream,* flows 5 miles to Canebrake Creek 2 miles northwest of Walker Pass (lat. 35°41'05" N, long. 118°03'05" W; sec. 7, T 26 S, R 37 E). Named on Walker Pass (1972) 7.5' quadrangle.

Jackson Meadow [FRESNO]: *area,* 13 miles northwest of Mount Abbot (lat. 37°29'45" N, long. 118°58'10" W). Named on Mount Abbot (1953) 15' quadrangle.

Jacksons Hole [KERN]: *relief feature,* 2.5 miles west-southwest of Claraville (lat. 35°25'50" N, long. 118°22'30" W). Named on Claraville (1972) and Piute Peak (1972) 7.5' quadrangles.

Jack Spring [FRESNO]: *spring,* 3.5 miles south-southwest of Coalinga (lat. 36°05'40" N, long. 120°23'05" W; sec. 18, T 21 S, R 15 E). Named on Curry Mountain (1969) 7.5' quadrangle. Called Jack Springs on Coalinga (1956) 15' quadrangle.

Jack Spring [KERN]: *spring,* 4 miles southwest of Orchard Peak (lat. 35°42'05" N, long. 120°11'20" W; near NW cor. sec. 6, T 26 S, R 17 E); the spring is in Jack Canyon. Named on Orchard Peak (1961) 7.5' quadrangle.

Jacks Station [KERN]: *locality,* 2 miles northwest of Walkers Pass (lat. 35°41' N, long. 118°03' W; sec. 7, T 26 S, R 37 E). Named on Kernville (1908) 30' quadrangle.

Jacobsen Meadow [TULARE]: *area,* 6 miles north of Camp Nelson (lat. 36°13'45" N, long. 118°36'10" W; sec. 34, T 19 S, R 31 E); the place is near the head of Jacobson Creek. Named on Camp Nelson (1956) 15' quadrangle.

Jacobson Creek [TULARE]: *stream,* flows nearly 2 miles to South Mountaineer Creek 6.5 miles north-northeast of Camp Nelson (lat. 36°13'50" N, long. 118°34'05" W; sec. 36, T 19 S, R 31 E). Named on Camp Nelson (1956) 15' quadrangle.

Jacobs Slough: see **Cain Slough** [KINGS].

Jamesan [FRESNO]: *locality,* 8 miles west of Kerman along Southern Pacific Railroad (lat. 36°43'10" N, long. 120°12'35" W; at S line sec. 10, T 14 S, R 16 E). Named on Jamesan (1963) 7.5' quadrangle. Called Jamison on Mendenhall's (1908) map. Postal authorities established Jamison post office in 1893, changed the name to Jameson in 1911, and discontinued it in 1912—the name was for J.G. James, first postmaster (Salley, p. 106).

James Bypass [FRESNO]: *water feature,* artificial watercourse that extends for 14 miles from Fish Slough to Fresno Slough 8 miles southeast of Mendota (lat. 36°40'35" N, long. 120°16' W; sec. 30, T 14 S, R 16 E). Named on Helm (1963), Jamesan (1963), San Joaquin (1963), and Tranquillity (1956) 7.5' quadrangles. Called Main Bypass on San Joaquin (1925) 7.5' quadrangle, and called Fresno Slough By-Pass on Tranquillity (1946) 15' quadrangle.

Jameson: see **Jamesan** [FRESNO].

Jamison: see **Byles Jamison Camp** [FRESNO]; **Jamesan** [FRESNO].

Jasmin [KERN]: *locality,* 6.5 miles northeast of McFarland along Southern Pacific Railroad (lat. 35°44'35" N, long. 119°08'40" W; sec. 23, T 25 S, R 26 E). Named on McFarland (1954) 7.5' quadrangle. Postal authorities established Jasmine (with the final "e") post office at Jasmin in 1913 and discontinued it in 1923 (Salley, p. 106).

Jasmine: see **Jasmin** [KERN].

Jasper Canyon: see **Jasper Creek** [FRESNO].

Jasper Creek [FRESNO]: *stream,* flows nearly 6 miles to Jacalitos Creek 7.5 miles south-southwest of Coalinga (lat. 36°02'10" N, long. 120°24'05" W; near NW cor. sec. 7, T 22 S, R 15 E). Named on Curry Mountain (1969) and Parkfield (1961) 7.5' quadrangles. The canyon of the stream is called Jasper Canyon on Coalinga (1912) 30' quadrangle. Arnold and Anderson (1908, p. 16) named the stream "from the picturesque and brilliant colored buttes of jasper that surround its upper portion," and applied the name "Jasper Canyon" to the gorge that the stream cut across the northwest end of Reef Ridge.

Jastro [KERN]: *locality,* 4 miles west of Bakersfield along Atchison, Topeka and Santa Fe Railroad (lat. 35°22'35" N, long. 119°04'15" W; near W line sec. 27, T 29 S, R 7 E). Named on Oildale (1954) 7.5' quadrangle.

Jawbone Canyon [KERN]: *canyon,* 16 miles long, opens into Fremont Valley 3 miles northeast of Cinco (lat. 35°18' N, long. 118° 00'20" W; near N line sec. 28, T 30 S, R 37 E). Named on Cache Peak (1973), Cinco (1972), and Cross Mountain (1972) 7.5' quadrangles. The name reportedly is from the discovery of the jawbone of a fossil mammal (Bailey, 1963, p. 13).

Jawbone Canyon: see **Little Jawbone Canyon** [KERN].

Jawbone Lake [FRESNO]: *lake,* 1100 feet long, 7 miles south of Mount Abbot (lat. 37°17'15" N, long. 118°48' W). Named on Mount Abbot (1953) 15' quadrangle.

Jawbone Well [KERN]: *well,* 5.25 miles west-northwest of Cinco (lat. 35°18'05" N, long. 118°07' W; sec. 28, T 30 S, R 36 E); the well is in Jawbone Canyon. Named on Cinco (1972) 7.5' quadrangle.

Jenkins: see **Mount Jenkins**, under **Morris Peak** [KERN].

Jennie Lake [TULARE]: *lake,* 1500 feet long, 2 miles east-southeast of Shell Mountain (lat. 36°40'50" N, long. 118°45'50" W; sec. 30, T 14 S, R 30 E). Named on Giant Forest (1956) 15' quadrangle. S.L.N. Ellis named the lake in 1897 for his wife (Browning, p. 110).

Jenny Creek [TULARE]: *stream,* flows 2.5 miles to North Fork Tule River 14 miles south-southwest of Mineral King (lat. 36°16'45" N, long. 118°44'10" W). Named on Mineral King (1956) 15' quadrangle.

Jenny Lind Cañon: see **Big Arroyo** [TULARE].

Jenny Lind Canyon [KERN]: *canyon,* drained by a stream that flows 2 miles to Clear Creek (1) 4.5 miles south of Miracle Hot Springs (lat. 35°30'50"N, long. 118°31'05" W; near E line sec. 10, T 28 S, R 32 E). Named on Miracle Hot Springs (1972) 7.5' quadrangle.

Jepson: see **Mount Jepson**, under **Mount Sill** [FRESNO].

Jerkey Meadows [TULARE]: *area,* 6.25 miles west-southwest of Hockett Peak (lat. 36°11'05" N, long. 118°29'15" W). Named on Hockett Peak (1956) 15' quadrangle. United States Board on Geographic Names (1988b, p. 2) approved the singular form "Jerkey Meadow" for the name, and rejected the forms "Jerkey Meadows" and "Jerky Meadow."

Jerry Slough [KERN]: *stream,* flows 7.25 miles to Goose Lake Bed 10.5 miles east-southeast of the village of Lost Hills (lat. 35°33' N, long. 119°31'15" W). Named on Buttonwillow (1954), Semitropic (1954), and Wasco SW (1953) 7.5' quadrangles. Called Goose Slough on Watts' (1894) map. On Buttonwillow (1942) 15' quadrangle, Jerry Slough extends to present Goose Lake Slough; the map has the name "Jerry Slough" for both features.

Jesse Morrow Mountain [FRESNO]: *ridge,* southwest-trending, 3 miles long, 5 miles east of Centerville (lat. 36°44'10" N, long. 119° 24'30" W). Named on Wahtoke (1966) 7.5' quadrangle.

Jewel Lake [FRESNO]: *lake,* 300 feet long, 1200 feet east of Kaiser Peak (lat. 37°17'40" N, long. 119°10'45" W; on W line sec. 30, T 7 S, R 26 E). Named on Kaiser Peak (1953) 15' quadrangle.

Jewetta: see **Saco** [KERN].

Jim Gray Creek [TULARE]: *stream,* flows about 4 miles to Horse Creek (2) 9 miles south-southwest of Kaweah (lat. 36°20'35" N, long. 118°57' W; sec. 21, T 18 S, R 28 E). Named on Kaweah (1957) 15' quadrangle.

Joaquin Flat [KERN]: *area,* 7 miles west of Cummings Mountain (lat. 35°01'40" N, long. 118°41'30" W; near SE cor. sec. 16, T 11 N, R 17 W). Named on Tejon Ranch (1966) 7.5' quadrangle.

Joaquin Flat [TULARE]: *area,* 5.5 miles south-southeast of Springville (lat. 36°03'15" N, long. 118°47'30" W; sec. 36, T 21 S, R 29 E). Named on Springville (1957) 15' quadrangle.

Joaquin Mill [FRESNO]: *locality,* 16 miles northwest of Coalinga along White Creek (lat. 36°16'20" N, long. 120°35'30" W; sec. 17, T 19 S, R 13 E). Site named on Santa Rita Peak (1969) 7.5' quadrangle.

Joaquin Ridge [FRESNO]: *ridge,* west-trending, 10 miles long, 14 miles north-northwest of Coalinga (lat. 36°19'30" N, long. 120°29'30" W). Named on Joaquin Rocks (1969) and Santa Rita Peak (1969) 7.5' quadrangles. Arnold and Anderson (1908, p. 13) named the ridge and pointed out that the feature called Joaquin Rocks is on it.

Joaquin River: see **San Joaquin River** [FRESNO].

Joaquin Rocks [FRESNO]: *relief feature,* 13 miles north-northwest of Coalinga (lat. 36°19'10" N, long. 120°26'50" W; near E line sec. 33, T 18 S, R 14 E). Named on Joaquin Rocks (1969) 7.5' quadrangle. United States Board on Geographic Names (1933a, p. 399) rejected the name "Tres Piedras" for the feature—Joaquin Rocks has three prominent outcrops.

Joaquin Spring [FRESNO]: *spring,* 0.25 mile southwest of Joaquin Rocks (lat. 36°18'55" N, long. 120°27'10" W; sec. 33, T 18 S, R 14 E). Named on Joaquin Rocks (1969) 7.5' quadrangle.

Joe Bowen Canyon [TULARE]: *canyon,* nearly 3 miles long, 6.5 miles south-southwest of California Hot Springs (lat. 35°48'10" N, long. 118°44'15" W). Named on California Hot Springs (1958) 15' and White River (1965) 7.5' quadrangles.

Joe Devel Peak [TULARE]: *peak,* 4.25 miles south of Mount Whitney (lat. 36°31' N, long. 118°17'45" W). Altitude 13,325 feet. Named on Mount Whitney (1956) 15' quadrangle. Owen L. Williams of the Sierra Club named the peak in 1937 for Joseph Devel, a member of the Wheeler survey (Browning, p. 111).

Joe Walker Town: see **Walker Basin** [KERN].

Johannesburg [KERN]: *village,* 1 mile east-northeast of Randsburg (lat. 35°22'20" N, long. 117°38' W; sec. 36, T 29 S, R 40 E). Named on Johannesburg (1967) 7.5' quadrangle. Postal authorities established Johannesburg post office in 1897 (Frickstad, p. 56). The name is from the mining center of Johannesburg in South Africa (Wines, p. 40).

Johnnycakes Lake [KERN]: *lake,* 250 feet long, 3 miles southwest of Glennville (lat. 35°41'45" N, long. 118°44'25" W; sec. 3, T 26 S, R 30 E). Named on Glennville (1972) 7.5' quadrangle.

Johnson: see **Mount Johnson** [FRESNO].

Johnson Canyon [KERN]:

(1) *canyon,* drained by a stream that flows 2.5 miles to Walker Basin 11 miles north-northeast of Caliente (lat. 35°26' N, long. 118°32'10" W; sec. 3, T 29 S, R 32 E). Named on Breckenridge Mountain (1972) 7.5' quadrangle.

(2) *canyon,* drained by a stream that flows 2.5 miles to Castac Valley 3.5 miles south-southeast of Grapevine (lat. 34°52'45" N, long. 118°54'05" W). Named on Frazier Mountain (1958) and Grapevine (1958) 7.5' quadrangles.

Johnson Creek [TULARE]: *stream,* flows 6 miles to Golden Trout Creek 5.5 miles northwest of Kern Peak in Little Whitney Meadow (lat. 36°22'30" N, long. 118°20'40" W); the stream heads at Johnson Lake. Named on Kern Peak (1956) 15' quadrangle.

Johnsondale [TULARE]: *village,* 10 miles northeast of California Hot Springs (lat. 35°58'25" N, long. 118°32'20" W; sec. 32, T 22 S, R 32 E). Named on California Hot Springs (1958) 15' quadrangle. Postal authorities established Johnsondale post office in 1939 (Frickstad, p. 211). The name, given in 1938 by Mount Whitney Lumber Company, commemorates Walter Johnson, an officer of the company (Mitchell, A.R., p. 68).

Johnson Flat [FRESNO]: *area,* 4 miles east-southeast of Dunlap (lat. 36°43' N, long. 119°03'20" W). Named on Miramonte (1966) 7.5' quadrangle.

Johnson Lake [TULARE]: *lake,* 1200 feet long, 9 miles north-northwest of Kern Peak (lat. 36°26' N, long. 118°20'10" W); the lake is less than 1 mile north of Johnson Peak at the head of Johnson Creek. Named on Kern Peak (1956) 15' quadrangle.

Johnson Peak [KINGS]: *peak,* 14 miles south of Avenal (lat. 38° 48' N, long. 120°09'10" W; sec. 32, T 24 S, R 17 E). Named on Tent Hills (1942) 7.5' quadrangle.

Johnson Peak [TULARE]: *peak,* 8 miles north-northwest of Kern Peak (lat. 36°25'10" N, long. 118°20' W; sec. 30, T 17 S, R 34 E). Altitude 11,371 feet. Named on Kern Peak (1956) 15' quadrangle.

Johnson Point [FRESNO]: *peak,* 4 miles southeast of Dunlap (lat. 36°42' N, long. 119°04' W; near NW cor. sec. 20, T 14 S, R 27 E); the feature is 1.5 miles south-southwest of present Johnson Flat. Named on Dinuba (1924) 30' quadrangle.

Johnson Slough [TULARE]: *water feature,* 3 miles north-northwest of Exeter (lat. 36°20' N, long. 119°09'30" W). Named on Exeter (1952) 15' quadrangle. The feature is part of the Kaweah River distributary system.

Johnson Spring [KERN]: *spring,* 12.5 miles north-northeast of Caliente (lat. 35°27'35" N, long. 118°32'40" W; sec. 28, T 28 S, R 32 E); the spring is in Johnson Canyon (1). Named on Breckenridge Mountain (1972) 7.5' quadrangle.

Johns Peak [KERN]: *peak,* 5 miles west-southwest of Piute Peak (lat. 35°24'55" N, long. 118°28' W; near S line sec. 8, T 29 S, R 33 E). Altitude 4917 feet. Named on Piute Peak (1972) 7.5' quadrangle.

Jo Lake: see **Little Jo Lake** [FRESNO].

Jones Corner [TULARE]: *locality,* 5 miles west of Porterville (lat. 36°03'25" N, long. 119°06'25" W; at SW cor. sec. 30, T 21 S, R 27 E). Named on Porterville (1951) 7.5' quadrangle.

Jones Ferry: see **Friant** [FRESNO].

Joneso: see **Hardwick** [KINGS].

Jon Hill [TULARE]: *ridge,* south-southwest-trending, 1 mile long, 4.5 miles west-northwest of California Hot Springs (lat. 35°54'45" N, long. 118°44'40" W; mainly in sec. 21, T 23 S, R 30 E). Named on California Hot Springs (1958) 15' quadrangle.

J.O. Pass [TULARE]: *pass,* 13 miles west-northwest of Triple Divide Peak (lat. 36°40'30" N, long. 118°44'35" W; sec. 29, T 14 S, R 30 E). Named on Triple Divide Peak (1956) 15' quadrangle. The name is from the initials "J.O." carved on a tree in the early days (United States Board on Geographic Names, 1933a, p. 399).

Jordan: see **Mount Jordan** [TULARE]; **Mount Jordan**, under **North Palisade** [FRESNO]; **Springville** [TULARE].

Jordan Flat [TULARE]: *area,* 9 miles south-southwest of Kaweah (lat. 36°21' N, long. 118°58'30" W; on E line sec. 19, T 18 S, R 28 E). Named on Kaweah (1957) 15' quadrangle.

Jordan Hot Springs [TULARE]: *springs,* 4.5 miles east of Hockett Peak along Ninemile Creek (lat. 36°13'45" N, long. 118°18'05" W). Named on Hockett Peak (1956) 15' quadrangle. According to Waring (p. 53), about 14 springs issue in a little flat along Ninemile Creek and are named for Mr. Jordan, who first blazed a trail through the neighborhood.

Jordan Peak [TULARE]: *peak,* nearly 3 miles north-northeast of Camp Nelson (lat. 36°10'50" N, long. 118°35'50" W; near SE cor. sec. 15, T 20 S, R 31 E). Altitude 9115 feet. Named on Camp Nelson (1956) 15' quadrangle. Browning (p. 112-113) associated thc name with John J. Jordan, who built a trail across the Sierra Nevada from Yokohl Valley in 1861.

Jose Basin [FRESNO]: *area,* 3.5 miles west of Shaver Lake Heights (present town of Shaver Lake) (lat. 37°06' N, long. 119°23' W); Jose Creek drains the feature. Named on Shaver Lake (1953) 15' quadrangle.

Jose Creek [FRESNO]: *stream,* flows 7 miles to San Joaquin River nearly 5 miles northwest of Shaver Lake Heights (present town of Shaver Lake) (lat. 37°08'55" N, long. 119°23'15" W; sec. 18, T 9 S, R 24 E). Named on Shaver Lake (1953) 15' quadrangle.

Joseph Grinnell: see **Lake Joseph Grinnell**, under **Grinnell Lake** [FRESNO].

Josephine Lake [TULARE]: *lake,* 1800 feet long, nearly 5 miles north-northwest of Triple Divide Peak (lat. 36°39'45" N, long. 118° 33' W). Named on Triple Divide Peak (1956) 15' quadrangle. S.L.N. Ellis named the lake for Josephine Perkins (Browning, p. 113).

Joughin Cove [KERN]: *embayment,* 5.5 miles southeast of Wofford Heights along Isabella Lake (lat. 35°38'45" N, long. 118°23'35" W; near NW cor. sec. 25, T 26 S, R 33 E). Named on Lake Isabella North (1972) 7.5' quadrangle.

Jovista [TULARE]: *locality,* 10 miles southwest of Ducor along Southern Pacific Railroad (lat. 35°47'50" N, long. 119°10'50" W; sec. 32, T 24 S, R 26 E). Named on Delano East (1953) 7.5' quadrangle, which shows Sierra Vista ranch at the place. Railroad officials coined the name about 1920 by combining the first two letters of Joseph Di Giorgio's given name with the word "vista" (Gudde, 1949, p. 168).

Joyful: see **Bakersfield** [KERN].

Juan Yaqui Spring [KERN]: *spring,* 6.25 miles west-southwest of Liebre Twins (lat. 34°55'45" N, long. 118°40'20" W). Named on Winters Ridge (1966) 7.5' quadrangle.

Jug Spring [TULARE]: *spring,* 5 miles west-southwest of Hockett Peak (lat. 36°11'45" N, long. 118°28' W). Named on Hockett Peak (1956) 15' quadrangle.

Julia Lake [KERN]: *lake,* 450 feet long, 8 miles north-northeast of Caliente along Walker Basin Creek (lat. 35°23'10" N, long. 118° 33'10" W; near S line sec. 21, T 29 S, R 32 E). Named on Breckenridge Mountain (1972) 7.5' quadrangle.

Julius Caesar: see **Mount Julius Caesar** [FRESNO].

Jumble Lake [FRESNO]: *lake,* 1800 feet long, 2.5 miles south-southwest of Mount Abbot (lat. 37°21' N, long. 118°47'45" W). Named on Mount Abbot (1953) 15' quadrangle. Employees of California Department of Fish and Game named the lake in 1952; it first was called Jumble Moraine Lake for the jumble of boulders in a nearby moraine (Browning, p. 113).

Jumble Moraine Lake: see **Jumble Lake** [FRESNO].

Junction Meadow [FRESNO]: *area,* 13 miles south of Mount Pinchot along Bubbs Creek (lat. 36°45'15" N, long. 118°26'30" W). Named on Mount Pinchot (1953) 15' quadrangle.

Junction Meadow [TULARE]:
(1) *area,* 7 miles west of Mount Whitney (lat. 36°34'50" N, long. 118°25' W); the place is at the confluence of Kern River and Kern-Kaweah River. Named on Mount Whitney (1956) 15' quadrangle.
(2) *area,* 4.5 miles northeast of Camp Nelson (lat. 36°10'45" N, long. 118°32'40" W; sec. 18, T 20 S, R 32 E). Named on Camp Nelson (1956) 15' quadrangle.

Junction Meadow: see **Log Cabin Meadow** [TULARE].

Junction Pass [TULARE]: *pass,* 9 miles north-northwest of Mount Whitney on Tulare-Inyo County line (lat. 36°41'45" N, long. 118° 21'20" W); the pass is 0.5 mile east-northeast of Junction Peak, for which it is named (United States Board on Geographic Names, 1933a, p. 403). Named on Mount Whitney (1956) 15' quadrangle.

Junction Peak [TULARE]: *peak,* 9 miles north-northwest of Mount Whitney on Tulare-Inyo County line (lat. 36°41'30" N, long. 118° 21'55" W). Altitude 13,888 feet. Named on Mount Whitney (1956) 15' quadrangle. J.N. LeConte named the peak in 1896; the feature is at the junction of Kings-Kern Divide with the crest of the Sierra Nevada (Farquhar, 1923, p. 407).

Junction Ridge [FRESNO]: *ridge,* west-trending, 6 miles long, 7 miles east-northeast of Hume (lat. 36°50'05" N, long. 118°48'15" W); the ridge is the part of Monarch Divide east of the junction of South Fork Kings River and Middle Fork Kings River. Named on Tehipite Dome (1952) 15' quadrangle.

Juniper Ridge [FRESNO]: *ridge,* northwest-trending, 14 miles long, 2.5 miles northeast of Coalinga Mineral Springs (lat. 36°10' N, long. 120°31' W). Named on Alcalde Hills (1969), Curry Mountain (1969), and Sherman Peak (1969) 7.5' quadrangles. Arnold and Anderson (1908, p. 14) named the ridge for its characteristic vegetation.

– K –

Kaiser Campground: see **West Kaiser Campground** [FRESNO].

Kaiser Creek [FRESNO]: *stream,* flows 13 miles to Mammoth Pool Reservoir 7.5 miles west-northwest of Kaiser Peak (lat. 37°21'20" N, long. 119°17'30" W; near SE cor. sec. 36, T 6 S, R 24 E); the stream heads near Kaiser Pass. Named on Kaiser Peak (1953) and Shuteye Peak (1953) 15' quadrangles. The name commemorates Fred Kaiser, who started to mine along San Joaquin River in 1852 (Gudde, 1975, p. 181).

Kaiser Creek: see **West Kaiser Creek** [FRESNO].

Kaiser Creek Diggings [FRESNO]: *locality,* 5.5 miles northwest of Kaiser Peak (lat. 37°21'30" N, long. 119°14'40" W; near N line sec. 4, T 7 S, R 25 E); the place is along Kaiser Creek. Named on Kaiser (1904) 30' quadrangle.

Kaiser Crest: see **Kaiser Ridge** [FRESNO].

Kaiser Pass [FRESNO]: *pass,* 4.5 miles east of Kaiser Peak (lat. 37° 17'25" N, long. 119°06'05" W; sec. 26, T 7 S, R 26 E); the pass is on Kaiser Ridge near the head of Kaiser Creek. Named on Kaiser Peak (1953) 15' quadrangle. Farquhar (1924, p. 49) noted that the forms "Kaiser Pass" and "Keyser Pass" both are used locally for the name.

Kaiser Pass Meadow [FRESNO]: *area,* 4.5 miles east of Kaiser Peak (lat. 37°17'40" N, long. 119°06'10" W; on N line sec. 26, T 7 S, R 26 E); the place is 0.25 mile north of Kaiser Pass. Named on Kaiser Peak (1953) 15' quadrangle.

Kaiser Peak [FRESNO]: *peak,* 3 miles north-northwest of the east end of Huntington Lake (1) (lat. 37°17'40" N, long. 119°11'05" W; near NE cor. sec. 25, T 7 S, R 25 E); the peak is on Kaiser Ridge. Altitude 10,320 feet. Named on Kaiser Peak (1953) 15' quadrangle. Farquhar (1924, p. 49) noted that the forms "Kaiser Peak" and "Keyser Peak" both are used locally for the name.

Kaiser Peak Meadows [FRESNO]: *area,* nearly 4 miles east-northeast of Kaiser Peak (lat. 37°18'35" N, long. 119°07'10" W; on N line sec. 22, T 7 S, R 26 E). Named on Kaiser Peak (1953) 15' quadrangle.

Kaiser Ridge [FRESNO]: *ridge,* mainly west-trending, 15 miles long, center 2 miles north of the east end of Huntington Lake (1) (lat. 37°17'15" N, long. 119°09' W). Named on Kaiser Peak (1953) and Shuteye Peak (1953) 15' quadrangles. United States Board on Geographic Names (1981a, p. 2) rejected the designation "Kaiser Crest" for the ridge.

Kaktus Korner [FRESNO]: *locality,* 6.5 miles north-northwest of Orange Cove (lat. 36°42'55" N, long. 119°20'50" W; sec. 15, T 14 S, R 24 E). Named on Orange Cove North (1966) 7.5' quadrangle.

Kanawyers [FRESNO]: *locality,* 12 miles south-southwest of Marion Peak in Kings Canyon (lat. 36°47'45" N, long. 118°34'45" W). Named on Marion Peak (1953) 15' quadrangle. Called Kanawyer on California Mining Bureau's (1917a) map. Postal authorities established Kanawyer post office in 1908 and discontinued it in 1914 (Salley, p. 109). According to Forest M. Clingan (personal communication, 1987), Peter Apoleon ("Pole") Kanawyer started Camp Kanawyer in 1908; a son, Ione Napoleon ("Poley") Kanawyer, helped his mother run the place after the death of the elder Kanawyer, and another son, Thomas Izy Kanawyer, was the first postmaster of Kanawyer post office.

Kane: see **Koehn Spring** [KERN].

Kane Dry Lake: see **Koehn Lake** [KERN].

Kane Lake: see **Koehn Lake** [KERN].

Kane Springs: see **Koehn Spring** [KERN].

Kaweah [TULARE]: *settlement,* 24 miles north-northwest of Springville along North Fork Kaweah River (lat. 36°28'15" N, long. 118° 55' W; near N line sec. 11, T 17 S, R 28 E). Named on Kaweah (1957) 15' quadrangle. The place was a townsite of Kaweah Cooperative Colony, founded in 1886 (Kaiser, p. 67). Postal authorities changed the name of Advance post office to Kaweah in 1890 and moved it to present Kaweah in 1910 (Mitchell, A.R., p. 64). They discontinued the post office in 1925 and reestablished it in 1926 (Frickstad, p. 211). Kaiser (fig. 1) showed a place called Avalon, a townsite of Kaweah Cooperative Colony, located southeast of Kaweah on the north side of Kaweah River a mile or less upstream from the mouth of North Fork, and a place called Barton Ranch, another townsite of the colony, located on the west side of Kaweah River about halfway from Kaweah to Three Rivers.

Kaweah: see **Black Kaweah** [TULARE]; **Camp Kaweah** [KERN]; **Exeter** [TULARE]; **Lake Kaweah** [TULARE]; **Mount Kaweah** [TULARE].

Kaweah Basin [TULARE]: *relief feature,* 11 miles west-southwest of Mount Whitney (lat. 36°32'30" N, long. 118°29' W); the feature is north of Mount Kaweah. Named on Mount Whitney (1956) 15' quadrangle.

Kaweah Camp [TULARE]: *locality,* 5.25 miles east of Yucca Mountain (lat. 36°33'55" N, long. 118°46'25" W). Named on Giant Forest (1956) 15' quadrangle, which also has the designation "Sequoia National Park (P.O.)" at the site. California Mining Bureau's (1909a) map shows a place called Ranger located 27 miles by stage line northeast of Kaweah. Postal authorities established Ranger post office at Sequoia National Park ranger headquarters in 1907, changed the name to Giant Forest in 1915, and moved it when they changed the name to Sequoia National Park in 1918 (Salley, p. 84, 181). The name "Giant Forest" is from huge redwood trees at the place; Hale Tharp discovered the trees in 1858, and John Muir gave them the name "Giant Forest" in 1875 (Hanna, p. 120).

Kaweah Gap [TULARE]: *pass,* 2.5 miles south-southwest of Triple Divide Peak (lat. 36°33'25" N, long. 118°33' W). Named on Triple Divide Peak (1956) 15' quadrangle.

Kaweah Hills: see **Venice Hills** [TULARE].

Kaweah Peaks: see **Kaweah Peaks Ridge** [TULARE].

Kaweah Peaks Ridge [TULARE]: *ridge,* south-southeast-trending, 7 miles long, center 3 miles south-southeast of Triple Divide Peak (lat. 36°33'15" N, long. 118°30'45" W); Black Kaweah, Red Kaweah, and Mount Kaweah are on the ridge. Named on Mount Whitney (1956) and Triple Divide Peak (1956) 15' quadrangles. Mount Whitney (1907) 30' quadrangle has the name "Kaweah Peaks" at the ridge.

Kaweah Queen: see **Black Kaweah** [TULARE].

Kaweah River [TULARE]: *stream,* formed by the confluence of Marble Fork and Middle Fork, flows 32 miles to where it divides 5.5 miles west-northwest of Exeter to form Mill Creek (2) and Packwood Creek (lat. 36°20'10" N, long. 119°13'20" W; sec. 25, T 18 S, R 25 E). Named on Exeter (1952), Giant Forest (1956), and Kaweah (1957) 15' quadrangles. Gabriel Moraga discovered the river in 1806 and called it San Gabriel (Brooks *in* Smith, J.S., p. 142). Derby's (1850) map has the designation "River Francis or San Gabriel" for the stream. Williamson (p. 13) referred to "the Pi-pi-yu-na, or Kah-wée-ya, and very commonly known as Four Creeks," and Blake (1856, p. 367) mentioned "Caweea or Four creeks." The name "Kaweah" is from a tribe of Indians that lived near the spot that the river emerges from the foothills (Kroeber, p. 44). In the early days the river debouched from highlands into a swamp, where it divided into four streams—St. Johns River, Mill Creek (1), Packwood Creek, and Outside Creek; except at times of great freshets, water in the streams sank into the ground before reaching the middle of San Joaquin Valley (Angel, 1890b, p. 728). According to Grunsky (p. 11), four overflow streams gave the name "Four Creek Country" to the neighborhood of Visalia. East Fork enters from the southeast 4.5 miles east of Kaweah; it is 21 miles long and is named on Kaweah (1957) and Mineral King (1956) 15' quadrangles. United States Board on Geographic Names (1968b, p. 7) rejected the name "East Fork of Kaweah River" for East Fork. Marble Fork is 16 miles long and is named on Giant Forest (1956) and Triple Divide Peak (1956) 15' quadrangles. United States Board on Geographic Names (1962, p. 13) rejected the names "Marble Fork Creek" and "Marble Fork of Kaweah River" for Marble Fork. Middle Fork is formed by the confluence of Hamilton Creek and Lone Pine Creek; it is 14 miles long and is named on Giant Forest (1956) and Triple Divide Peak (1956) 15' quadrangles. United States Board on Geographic Names (1968b, p. 8) rejected the names "Kaweah River," and "Middle Fork of Kaweah River" for Middle Fork, and rejected the name "Middle Fork Kaweah River" for present Lone Pine Creek [TULARE]. North Fork, formed by the confluence of Stony Creek and Durst Creek, flows 20 miles to join the main stream from the north 2 miles south-southeast of Kaweah; it is named on Giant Forest (1956) and Kaweah (1957) 15' quadrangles. United States Board on Geographic Names (1968b, p. 8) rejected the name "North Fork of Kaweah River" for North Fork. South Fork enters from the southeast 3.25 miles south of Kaweah; it is 23 miles long and is named on Kaweah (1957) and Mineral King (1956) 15' quadrangles. United States Board on Geographic Names (1968b, p. 9) rejected the name "South Fork of Kaweah River" for South Fork.

Kayandee [KERN]: *locality,* 2 miles south of downtown Bakersfield along Southern Pacific Railroad (lat. 35°20'50" N, long. 118°59'40" W; sec. 5, T 30 S, R 28 E). Named on Lamont (1954) 7.5' quadrangle.

Kearney [FRESNO]: *locality,* 7.5 miles west of downtown Fresno along Southern Pacific Railroad (lat. 36°44'45" N, long. 119°55'20" W; sec. 5, T 14 S, R 19 E); a rail line to Kearney Park branched south at the spot. Named on Kearney Park (1923) 7.5' quadrangle. The name "Kearney" for the county park commemorates Martin Theodore Kearney, a rich landholder who came to Fresno County about 1877 (Hanna, p. 159). Postal authorities established Kearney Park post office in 1901 and discontinued it in 1935 (Frickstad, p. 34).

Kearney Park: see **Kearney** [FRESNO].

Kearsarge Lakes [FRESNO]: *lakes,* largest 1600 feet long, 13 miles south of Mount Pinchot (lat. 36°45'45" N, long. 118°23'15" W). Named on Mount Pinchot (1953) 15' quadrangle.

Kearsarge Pass [FRESNO]: *pass,* 12 miles south of Mount Pinchot on Fresno-Inyo County line (lat. 36°46'25" N, long. 118°22'35" W). Named on Mount Pinchot (1953) 15' quadrangle. The name is from Kearsarge mine, which is situated east of the pass in Inyo County (Farquhar, 1924, p. 49).

Kearsarge Pinnacles [FRESNO]: *relief features,* 13 miles south of Mount Pinchot along a northwest-trending ridge 2 miles long (lat. 36°45'35" N, long. 118°23'05" W); the features are southwest of Kearsarge Lakes. Named on Mount Pinchot (1953) 15' quadrangle.

Kecks Corner [KERN]: *locality,* about 5.5 miles south-southeast of Orchard Peak in Antelope Valley (1) (lat. 35°40'15" N, long. 120° 04'50" W; near NE cor. sec. 13, T 26 S, R 17 E). Named on Sawtooth Ridge (1961) 7.5' quadrangle. Called Kecks Corners on Sawtooth Ridge (1943) 7.5' quadrangle, and called Keck's Corner on California Division of Highways' (1934) map.

Keehn Well: see **Koehn Spring** [KERN].

Keeler Needle [TULARE]: *relief feature,* 1000 feet south of Mount Whitney on Tulare-Inyo County line (lat. 36°34'30" N, long. 118° 17'30" W). Named on Mount Whitney (1956) 7.5' quadrangle. The name commemorates James Edward Keeler, who accompanied S.P. Langley on an expedition to Mount Whitney in 1881, and who later was director of Lick Observatory (Farquhar, 1924, p. 50).

Keene [KERN]: *village,* 8.5 miles northwest of Tehachapi (lat. 35°13'25" N, long. 118°33'50" W; near N line sec. 20, T 31 S, R 32 E). Named on Keene (1966) 7.5' quadrangle, which shows Keene P.O. located 0.5 mile farther southeast at or near Woodford. Postal authorities established Keene post office in 1879, discontinued it in 1881, and reestablished it in 1885 (Frickstad, p. 56). The community began in 1876 as a railroad camp; the station at the place first was called Wells, for Madison P. Wells, a local cattleman, but later was renamed for James R. Keene, a San Francisco financier; the station and village also were called Woodford for a time (Barras, p. 132). Cummings Mountain (1943a) 15' quadrangle shows a place called El Rita situated near present Keene post office, and California (1891) map shows a place called Girard located along the railroad about halfway between Keene and Tehachapi.

Keeneysburg: see **White River** [TULARE] (2).

Keith: see **Mount Keith** [TULARE].

Keller Valley [KERN]: *valley,* 3.5 miles south of Keene (lat. 35°10'25" N, long. 118°33'15" W; on E line sec. 5, T 32 S, R 32 E). Named on Keene (1966) 7.5' quadrangle.

Kelley Canyon: see **Kelly Canyon** [KERN].

Kellogg Creek: see **Granite Creek** [FRESNO].

Kelly Canyon [KERN]: *canyon,* drained by a stream that flows 1.5 miles to Poso Creek 3.25 miles south-southeast of Knob Hill (lat. 35°31'10" N, long. 118°55'40" W; sec. 2, T 28 S, R 28 E). Named on Knob Hill (1965) 7.5' quadrangle. Called Kelley Canyon on Woody (1952) 15' quadrangle.

Kelso: see **Claraville** [KERN]; **Fresno** [FRESNO].

Kelso Creek [KERN]: *stream,* flows 27 miles to South Fork Valley 2.25 miles southeast of Weldon (lat. 35°38'45" N, long. 118°15'15" W; near SE cor. sec. 19, T 26 S, R 35 E). Named on Cane Canyon (1972), Claraville (1972), Onyx (1972), Pinyon Mountain (1972), Weldon (1972), and Woolstalf Creek (1972) 7.5' quadrangles. Called Hum-pah-ya-mup on Williamson's (1853) map.

Kelso Peak [KERN]: *peak,* 6.5 miles west-southwest of Skinner Peak (lat. 35°31' N, long. 118°13'25" W; sec. 4, T 28 S, R 35 E); the peak is west of Kelso Creek. Named on Cane Canyon (1972) 7.5' quadrangle.

Kelso Valley [KERN]: *valley,* about 5.5 miles southwest of Pinyon Mountain (lat. 35°24' N, long. 118°13'30" W). Named on Cross Mountain (1972) and Pinyon Mountain (1972) 7.5' quadrangles. The name commemorates John W. Kelso, a freighter and trader (Boyd, p. 166).

Kemeric: see **Camp Kemeric** [KERN].

Kennedy Canyon [FRESNO]: *canyon,* drained by Kennedy Creek, which flows 4.5 miles to Slide Creek 8.5 miles west of Marion Peak (lat. 36°56'10" N, long. 118°40'10" W). Named on Marion Peak (1953) 15' quadrangle.

Kennedy Creek [FRESNO]: *stream,* flows 4.5 miles to Slide Creek 8.5 miles west of Marion Peak (lat. 36°56'10" N, long. 118°40'10" W); the stream heads at East Kennedy Lake near Kennedy Pass. Named on Marion Peak (1953) 15' quadrangle. West Fork enters from the southwest 3.25 miles upstream from the mouth of the main stream; it is 1 mile long, goes through West Kennedy Lake, and is named on Marion Peak (1953) 15' quadrangle.

Kennedy Lake: see **East Kennedy Lake** [FRESNO]; **West Kennedy Lake** [FRESNO].

Kennedy Meadow [FRESNO]: *area,* 4.5 miles east-southeast of Hume (lat. 36°46'15" N, long. 118°50' W). Named on Tehipite Dome (1952) 15' quadrangle.

Kennedy Meadows [TULARE]: *area,* 15 miles north-northwest of Lamont Peak along South Fork Kern River (lat. 36°00' N, long. 118°07' W); the place is north of Kennedy Peak. Named on Lamont Peak (1956) and Monache Mountain (1956) 15' quadrangles.

Kennedy Meadows Camp [TULARE]: *locality,* 11 miles south-southeast of Monache Mountain along South Fork Kern River (lat. 36°03'10" N, long. 118°07'50" W); the place is at the north end of Kennedy Meadows. Named on Monache Mountain (1956) 15' quadrangle.

Kennedy Mountain [FRESNO]: *peak,* 10 miles southwest of Marion Peak (lat. 36°52'45" N, long. 118°40' W). Altitude 11,433 feet. Named on Marion Peak (1953) 15' quadrangle.

Kennedy Pass [FRESNO]: *pass,* 9.5 miles southwest of Marion Peak on Monarch Divide (lat. 36°52'30" N, long. 118°39'35" W); the pass is near the head of Kennedy Creek. Named on Marion Peak (1953) 15' quadrangle.

Kennedy Peak [TULARE]: *peak,* 14 miles north-northwest of Lamont Peak (lat. 36°59'05" N, long. 118°07' W; near N line sec. 29, T 22 S, R 36 E). Named on Lamont Peak (1956) 15' quadrangle.

Kennedy Pond [FRESNO]: *intermittent lake,* 450 feet long, 6 miles west-northwest of Selma (lat. 36°35'25" N, long. 119°43' W; near NW cor. sec. 32, T 15 S, R 21 E). Named on Conejo (1963) 7.5' quadrangle. Selma (1946) 15' quadrangle shows a permanent lake 1600 feet long.

Kennedy Spring [KERN]: *spring,* 5 miles south of Piute Peak (lat. 35°22'50"

N, long. 118°22'40" W). Named on Piute Peak (1972) 7.5' quadrangle.

Kenyon: see **Pine Ridge** [FRESNO] (3).

Kerckhoff Dome [FRESNO]: *peak,* 0.5 mile east-northeast of the town of Big Creek (lat. 37°12'40" N, long. 119°13'55" W; sec. 27, T 8 S., R 25 E). Named on Huntington Lake (1953) 15' quadrangle. John S. Eastwood, an engineer who made early surveys for power development on San Joaquin River, named the feature to honor William G. Kerckhoff of Kerckhoff Lake (Redinger, p. 8). United States Board on Geographic Names (1983a, p. 4) rejected the form "Kerkhoff Dome" for the name.

Kerckhoff Lake [FRESNO]: *lake,* behind a dam on San Joaquin River 6.25 miles north of Prather on Fresno-Madera County line (lat. 37°07'40" N, long. 119°31'30" W; near S line sec. 24, T 9 S, R 22 E). Named on North Fork (1965) 7.5' quadrangle. The name is from Kerckhoff electric power plant, put into operation in 1920 and named for William G. Kerckhoff, one of the organizers of the company that operated the plant (Gudde, 1949, p. 173).

Kerkhoff Dome: see **Kerckhoff Dome** [FRESNO].

Kerman [FRESNO]: *town,* 15 miles west of Fresno (lat. 36°43'30" N, long. 120°03'30" W). Named on Kerman (1963) 7.5' quadrangle. Postal authorities established Collis post office at the place in 1894, discontinued it in 1899, reestablished it in 1904, and changed the name to Kerman in 1906 (Frickstad, p. 32). The town incorporated in 1946. The Southern Pacific Railroad station built at the site in 1895 was called Collis, for Collis P. Huntington; W.G. Kerckhoff and Jacob Mansar promoted a colony of Germans and Scandinavians from the Middle West at the place in 1906, and called the settlement and station Kerman, a name coined from the first three letters of each promoter's surname (Gudde, 1949, p. 173).

Kern: see **Bakersfield** [KERN].

Kern Canyon [TULARE]: *canyon,* 30 miles long, along Kern River above a point about 7.5 miles west-southwest of Kern Peak (lat. 36°15' N, long. 118°24' W). Named on Kern Peak (1956) and Mount Whitney (1956) 15' quadrangles.

Kern City [KERN]: *locality,* 4 miles west-southwest of downtown Bakersfield (lat. 35°21' N, long. 119°04'15" W). Named on Bakersfield (1962, revised 1971) 1°x 2° quadrangle. Postal authorities established Kern City post office in 1962 and discontinued it in 1976 (Salley, p. 111). The place is a planned retirement community begun in 1961 on 349 acres (Bailey, 1967, p. 13).

Kern City: see **Bakersfield** [KERN].

Kernell [KERN]: *locality,* 5.5 miles west of Delano along Atchison, Topeka and Santa Fe Railroad (lat. 35°45'30" N, long. 119°20'35" W; sec. 13, T 25 S, R 24 E). Named on Delano West (1954) and Pond (1953) 7.5' quadrangles.

Kern Flat [TULARE]: *area,* 3 miles south-southeast of Hockett Peak (lat. 36°10'45" N, long. 118°22'15" W); the place is along Kern River. Named on Hockett Peak (1956) 15' quadrangle.

Kern Hot Spring [TULARE]: *spring,* 13 miles north-northwest of Kern Peak (lat. 36°28'40" N, long. 118°24'15" W); the spring is along Kern River. Named on Kern Peak (1956) 15' quadrangle.

Kern Island: see **Bakersfield** [KERN]; **Kern Lake Bed** [KERN].

Kern-Kaweah River [TULARE]: *stream,* flows 8 miles to Kern River 7.25 miles west of Mount Whitney (lat. 36°34'50" N, long. 118°25'10" W). Named on Mount Whitney (1956) and Triple Divide Peak (1956) 15' quadrangles. Called Kern Kaweah (without the hyphen) River on Mount Whitney (1907) and Tehipite (1903) 30' quadrangles. United States Board on Geographic Names (1933a, p. 424) rejected the name "Cone River" for the stream.

Kern Lake [KERN]: *locality,* 7.5 miles east-southeast of Millux (lat. 35°08'25" N, long. 119°04'30" W; near SE cor. sec. 16, T 32 S, R 27 E); the place is in Kern Lake Bed. Named on Conner (1954) 7.5' quadrangle.

Kern Lake [TULARE]: *lake,* 2400 feet long, 6.5 miles west of Kern Peak along Kern River (lat. 36°19' N, long. 118°24'15" W). Named on Kern Peak (1956) 15' quadrangle. United States Board on Geographic Names (1938, p. 28) rejected the name "Soda Spring Lake" for the feature. Little Yosemite Soda Spring is situated about 2.25 miles north of the lake near Kern River; according to Waring (p. 244), the name probably is from the resemblance of the canyon near the spring to Yosemite Valley.

Kern Lake: see **Kern Lake Bed** [KERN]; **Little Kern Lake** [TULARE].

Kern Lake Bed [KERN]: *area,* 16 miles south-southwest of Bakersfield (lat. 35°08'30" N, long. 119°04' W). Named on Coal Oil Canyon (1955), Conner (1954), and Weed Patch (1955) 7.5' quadrangles. Called Kern Island on Coal Oil Canyon (1934) and Conner (1933) 7.5' quadrangles, but United States Board on Geographic Names (1937, p. 16) rejected this name for the feature. Blake (1857, p. 44) used the name "Posuncula" for the lake, as well as for Kern River (p. 35). Wheeler's (1875-1878) map shows Kern Lake. Buena Vista Lake (1912) 30' quadrangle shows a small Kern Lake near the east end of present Kern Lake Bed.

Kern Lake Creek: see **Little Kern Lake Creek** [TULARE].

Kern Mesa [KERN]: *area,* 16 miles east-southeast of Bakersfield (lat. 35°15' N; long. 118°45' W). Named on Breckenridge Mountain (1943) and Cummings Mountain (1943b) 15' quadrangles.

Kern Peak [TULARE]: *peak,* 18 miles south of Mount Whitney (lat. 36°18'30" N, long. 118°17'10" W; at S line sec. 34, T 18 S, R 34 E). Altitude 11,510 feet. Named on Kern Peak (1956) 15' quadrangle.

Kern Peak Stringer [TULARE]: *stream,* flows 2.5 miles to South Fork Kern River 3.5 miles north-northeast of Kern Peak in Ramshaw Meadows (lat. 36°21'20" N, long. 118°16'05" W; sec. 14, T 18 S, R 34 E); the stream heads near Kern Peak. Named on Kern Peak (1956) 15' quadrangle.

Kern Point [TULARE]: *peak,* 8.5 miles west of Mount Whitney (lat. 36°35'50" N, long. 118°26'35" W); the peak is at the southeast end of Kern Ridge. Altitude 12,789 feet. Named on Mount Whitney (1956) 15' quadrangle.

Kern Ridge [TULARE]: *ridge,* southeast-trending, 4 miles long, 10 miles west-northwest of Mount Whitney (lat. 36°36'45" N, long. 118°27'45" W). Named on Mount Whitney (1956) 15' quadrangle.

Kern River [KERN-TULARE]: *stream,* heads in Tulare County and flows 137 miles to lowlands 2.5 miles north of downtown Bakersfield in Kern County (lat. 35°24'45" N, long. 119°00' W). Named on Bakersfield (1962, revised 1971) and Fresno (1962) 1°x 2° quadrangles. Williamson's (1853) map has the name "Po-sun-co-la or Kern River" for the stream, and Goddard's (1857) map has the designation "Kern or Porsiuncula R." Garces called the stream Rio de San Felipe in 1776, and Padre Zalvidea named it La Porciuncula in 1804; John C. Fremont gave it the name "Kern" to honor his topographer, Edward M. Kern, but the Mexicans called it Rio Bravo (Wines, p. 86). After reaching lowlands, the river forms distributaries; the principal distributary extends for 21 miles to a canal (formerly Buena Vista Slough) near Elk Hills. Wood and Dale (fig. 4) included a sketch map showing Kern River distributaries during pioneer stages of irrigation development, and (p. 21, 23) described Kern River distributaries as follows:

> Near Bakersfield, the river leaves the hills and flows southwestward for 20 mile in a shallow bed ranging in width from 200 to 800 feet to a point near the east tip of Elk Hills, where it branches into two main distributaries, the lesser of which, called Buena Vista Slough, flows northward toward Tulare Lake bed and the other southward into Buena Vista Lake bed. Before irrigation projects changed the natural drainage, the river changed its course many times, after leaving the hills. New channels were formed during floods, because old channels and distributaries had become choked with alluvial debris during low stages. The principal known channels were: Old South Fork, which flowed southward from its head, 2 miles northeast of Bakersfield, to its outfall into Kern Lake; Old River, which flowed southwestward from its head, 1.5 miles west of Bakersfield, toward a point between Kern and Buena Vista Lakes; and Buena Vista Canal Slough, which left the present channel of Kern River 2 miles below the head of Old River and flowed southwestward toward Buena Vista Lake. Of these channels Old South Fork was the main waterway until the flood of 1862. Old River then became the main channel and remained so until the present Kern River channel was formed by the floods of 1867-68. Since that time, the river has been controlled in one main channel, and many of the distributaries have been modified for use as irrigation canals.

South Fork Kern River heads in Tulare County and flows 90 miles to join the main stream 3.5 miles south of Wofford Heights at Isabella Lake in Kern County (lat. 35°39'35" N, long. 118°27'50" W). South Fork is named on Bakersfield (1962, revised 1971) and Fresno (1962) 1°x 2° quadrangles. Olmstead's (1900) map has the name "North Fork" for present Kern River above the junction with South Fork. A community called Solitaire was located along Kern River in the mid-1850's just above the junction with South Fork (Boyd, p. 51); Cross Ferry, built by James Cross in 1868, was situated along Kern River just below the junction with South Fork (Bailey, 1967, p. 5).

Kern River: see **Little Kern River** [TULARE].

Kern River, East Fork: see **Wallace Creek** [TULARE]; **Wright Creek** [TULARE].

Kern River Channel [KERN-KINGS]: *stream,* flows from Kern River Flood Canal in Kern County north into Kings County 12.5 miles north-northwest of the village of Lost Hills (lat. 35°47'25" N, long. 119°43' W; at N line sec. 4, T 25 S, R 21 E). Named on Lone Tree Well (1954), Lost Hills (1953), and Lost Hills NW (1954) 7.5' quadrangles.

Kern River Slough: see **Lamont** [KERN].

Kernvale: see **Lake Isabella** [KERN].

Kernville [KERN]: *town,* 42 miles northeast of Bakersfield (lat. 35° 45'20" N, long. 118°25'30" W; in and near sec. 15, T 25 S, R 33 E); the town is along Kern River. Named on Kernville (1956) 15' quadrangle. Kernville (1908) 30' quadrangle shows the place along the river 3 miles farther south (lat. 35°42'40" N, long. 118° 26'15" W; sec. 33, T 25 S, R 33 E); the formation of Isabella Lake in 1951 forced removal of the town from its original site to the present place (Bailey, 1967, p. 13). Postal authorities established Kernville post office in 1868 (Frickstad, p. 56). A mining camp called Williamsburg started at the original site of Kernville in 1863; the place also was known as Whiskey Flat for Adam Hamilton's saloon, but in 1864 it became Kernville (Bailey, 1967, p. 13). Kernville Hot Springs were located 2 miles northeast of the first site of Kernville (sec. 34, T 25 S, R 33 E) (Brown, p. 521)—Lake Isabella North (1972) 7.5' quadrangle shows numerous hot springs in that neighborhood.

Kernville Hot Springs: see **Kernville** [KERN].

Kerto [KERN]: *locality,* 1.5 miles northeast of Maricopa along Sunset Railroad (lat. 35°04'45" N, long. 119°22'45" W; near SW cor. sec. 31, T 12 N, R 23 W). Named on Maricopa (1951) 7.5' quadrangle. Postal authorities established Kerto post office in 1912 and discontinued it in 1923; the name was coined from the term "Kern Trading and Oil Company" (Salley, p. 111). California Mining Bureau's (1917c) map shows a place called Signa located about 3 miles northwest of Kerto along the railroad.

Kessing Creek [TULARE]: *stream,* flows 5.5 miles to South Fork Tule River 9 miles south-southwest of Camp Nelson (lat. 36°01'30" N, long. 118°41'25" W). Named on Camp Nelson (1956) 15' quadrangle.

Kettle Dome [FRESNO]: *peak,* 13 miles north-northeast of Hume (lat. 36°56'50" N, long. 118°47' W); the peak is at the southwest end of Kettle Ridge. Altitude 9446 feet. Named on Tehipite Dome (1952) 15' quadrangle.

Kettle Lake: see **Seville Lake** [TULARE].

Kettleman City [KINGS]: *town,* 28 miles southwest of Hanford (lat. 36°00'30" N, long. 119°57'45" W; near S line sec. 18, T 22 S, R 19 E); the place is near the northeast base of Kettleman Hills. Named on Kettleman City (1963) 7.5' quadrangle. A. Mansford Brown laid out the town in 1929 to serve the nearby oil field (Gudde, 1949, p. 174), and postal authorities established Kettleman City post office the same year (Frickstad, p. 61).

Kettleman Hills [FRESNO-KERN-KINGS]: *range,* extends along the southwest side of San Joaquin Valley from Fresno County through Kings County into Kern County. Named on Avenal (1954), Avenal Gap (1954), Emigrant Hill (1953), Kettleman City (1963), Kettleman Plain (1953), La Cima (1963), and Los Viejos (1954) 7.5' quadrangles. The name commemorates David Kettleman, who came to California in 1849 and later pastured cattle in the range (Gudde, 1949, p. 174). United States Board on Geographic Names (1933a, p. 425) rejected the form "Kittleman Hills" for the name. The range has three geographic divisions: North Dome at the north end on Kings-Fresno County line, Middle Dome in the central part, and South Dome at the south end on Kings-Kern County line; the divisions are based on geologic structure, but are applied to geographic units (Woodring, Stewart, and Richards, p. 9). North Dome is named on Avenal (1954), Kettleman Plain (1953), La Cima (1963), and Los Viejos (1954) 7.5' quadrangles.

Middle Dome is named on Avenal Gap (1954) and Los Viejos (1954) 7.5' quadrangles. South Dome is named on Avenal Gap (1954) 7.5' quadrangle.

Kettleman Plain [FRESNO-KINGS]: *valley,* between Kettleman Hills and Diablo Range on Fresno-Kings County line, mainly in Kings County. Named on Avenal (1954), Avenal Gap (1954), Garza Peak (1953), Kettleman Plain (1953), La Cima (1963), and Pyramid Hills (1953) 7.5' quadrangles. United States Board on Geographic Names (1933a, p. 425) rejected the form "Kittleman Plain" for the name.

Kettleman Station [FRESNO]: *locality,* 11 miles southeast of Coalinga (lat. 36°02'55" N, long. 120°11'50" W; near NW cor. sec. 1, T 22 S, R 16 E); the place is in Kettleman Plain. Named on Avenal (1954) 7.5' quadrangle.

Kettleman Station [KINGS]: *locality,* 0.5 mile south of Kettleman City (lat. 35°59'55" N, long. 119°57'45" W; sec. 19, T 22 S, R 19 E); the place is at the east base of Kettleman Hills. Named on Los Viejos (1954) 7.5' quadrangle.

Kettle Peak [TULARE]: *peak,* 12.5 miles west-northwest of Triple Divide Peak (lat. 36°40'25" N, long. 118°43'55" W; near S line sec. 28, T 14 S, R 30 E). Altitude 10,041 feet. Named on Triple Divide Peak (1956) 15' quadrangle.

Kettle Ridge [FRESNO]: *ridge,* southwest-trending, 7 miles long, 17 miles north-northeast of Hume (lat. 37°00' N, long. 118°45'30" W); Kettle Dome is at the southwest end of the ridge. Named on Blackcap Mountain (1953), Mount Goddard (1948), and Tehipite Dome (1952) 15' quadrangles.

Keyes: see **Sally Keyes Lakes** [FRESNO].

Keyes Gulch: see **Keyesville** [KERN].

Keyesville [KERN]: *locality,* 7.25 miles south-southeast of Alta Sierra (lat. 35°37'35" N, long. 118°30'40" W; sec. 35, T 26 S, R 32 E); the place is in Hogeye Gulch. Named on Alta Sierra (1972) 7.5' quadrangle. Called Keysville on Glennville (1956) 15' quadrangle, and United States Board on Geographic Names (1975b, p. 10) gave this name as a variant. Richard Keyes discovered a rich quartz vein in what became known as Keyes Gulch; the town that grew there first was called Hogeye, and later Keyesville (Wines, p. 23). Miners built an earthen fort on a hill outside the community in 1855 or 1856 in anticipation of trouble with Indians; the place was called Fort Hill and Fort Keysville (Whiting and Whiting, p. 32).

Keyhole: see **The Keyhole** [FRESNO].

Keyser Pass: see **Kaiser Pass** [FRESNO].

Keyser Peak: see **Kaiser Peak** [FRESNO].

Keys Mountain [FRESNO]: *ridge,* north- to east-trending, 1.25 miles long, 2 miles west-southwest of Humphreys Station (lat. 36°57'10" N, long. 119°28'55" W). Named on Humphreys Station (1965) 7.5' quadrangle.

Keysville: see **Keyesville** [KERN].

Kiavah Mountains: see **Scodie Mountains** [KERN].

Kid Creek [FRESNO]: *stream,* flows 3 miles to South Fork Kings River 4.5 miles south of Marion Peak (lat. 36°53'40" N, long. 118° 31'55" W); the stream heads at Kid Lakes. Named on Marion Peak (1953) 15' quadrangle. North Fork enters 0.5 mile upstream from the mouth of the main stream; it is 2.25 miles long and is named on Marion Peak (1953) 15' quadrangle.

Kid Lakes [FRESNO]: *lakes,* 6 miles south-southwest of Marion Peak (lat. 36°52'45" N, long. 118°33'30" W); the lakes are on upper reaches of Kid Creek. Named on Marion Peak (1953) 15' quadrangle.

Kid Peak [FRESNO]: *peak,* 5.5 miles south-southwest of Marion Peak (lat. 36°52'40" N, long. 118°33' W). Altitude 11,458 feet. Named on Marion Peak (1953) 15' quadrangle.

Kilmer Spring [KERN]: *spring,* 3.25 miles east of Orchard Peak (lat. 35°44'50" N, long. 120°04'40" W; near SW cor. sec. 18, T 25 S, R 18 E). Named on Sawtooth Ridge (1961) 7.5' quadrangle.

Kilowatt [KERN]: *locality,* 1 mile east of Buttonwillow along Southern Pacific Railroad (lat. 35°23'55" N, long. 119°27' W; near SE cor. sec. 13, T 29 S, R 23 E). Named on Buttonwillow (1954) 7.5' quadrangle.

Kimberlina [KERN]: *locality,* 10.5 miles south of McFarland (lat. 35°31'50" N, long. 119°11'50" W; at S line sec. 32, T 27 S, R 26 E). Named on Famoso (1930) 7.5' quadrangle. The name commemorates J.M. Kimberlin and O.B. Kimberlin, who had a way station at the place in the 1890's (Bailey, 1962, p. 73).

Kimble [KINGS]: *locality,* nearly 5 miles northwest of Hanford along Southern Pacific Railroad (lat. 36°22'05" N, long. 119°43' W; sec. 17, T 18 S, R 21 E). Named on Hanford (1926) 7.5' quadrangle.

King: see **Mount Clarence King** [FRESNO].

King Canyon [KERN]: *canyon,* drained by a stream that flows 2.5 miles to Antelope Valley (1) 3.25 miles south of Orchard Peak (lat. 35°41'25" N, long. 120°08'30" W; near S line sec. 4, T 26 S, R 17 E). Named on Orchard Peak (1961) 7.5' quadrangle.

Kingfisher Ridge [TULARE]: *ridge,* south-trending, 5 miles long, 2.5 miles northwest of Monache Mountain (lat. 36°13'45" N, long. 118°14' W). Named on Monache Mountain (1956) and Olancha (1956) 15' quadrangles.

Kingfisher Stringer [TULARE]: *stream,* flows 2 miles to Soda Creek (2) 1.5 miles northwest of Monache Mountain (lat. 36°13'10" N, long. 118°12'50" W; near N line sec. 5, T 20 S, R 35 E); the stream is east of Kingfisher Ridge. Named on Monache Mountain (1956) 15' quadrangle.

King George Peak [TULARE]: *peak,* 4 miles west of California Hot Springs (lat. 35°52'15" N, long. 118°44'30" W; sec. 4, T 24 S, R 30 E); the peak is on King George Ridge. Altitude 4377 feet. Named on California Hot Springs (1958) 15' quadrangle.

King George Ridge [TULARE]: *ridge,* west-southwest- to west-trending, 3 miles long, 4.5 miles west of California Hot Springs (lat. 35°52'15" N, long. 118°45' W); King George Peak is on the ridge. Named on California Hot Springs (1958) and White River (1952) 15' quadrangles.

King River: see **Centerville** [FRESNO]; **Kings River** [FRESNO-KINGS-TULARE].

Kingriver: see **Reedley** [FRESNO].

Kingsburg [FRESNO]: *town,* 5 miles southeast of Selma (lat. 36° 31' N, long. 119°33' W); the town is 1.5 miles from Kings River. Named on Selma (1964) 7.5' quadrangle. The place first was called Kings River Switch, then Drapersville, and later Wheatville; Josiah Draper founded the town in the 1870's (Hanna, p. 162). Postal authorities established Wheatville post office in 1874, changed the name to Kingsburgh in 1875, and changed it to Kingsburg in 1876 (Salley, p. 112, 238). The town incorporated in 1908. Postal authorities established Sanders post office 8 miles northeast of Kingsburg in 1879 and discontinued it in 1894; the name was for Charlotte E. Sanders, first postmaster (Salley, p. 193).

Kings Canyon [FRESNO]: *canyon,* 10 miles long, 13 miles south-southwest of Marion Peak (lat. 36°47' N, long. 118°37'30" W); the canyon is along South Fork Kings River. Named on Marion Peak (1953) 15' quadrangle. Called Kings River Canyon on Tehipite (1903) 30' quadrangle.

Kings-Kern Divide [TULARE]: *ridge,* generally west- to southwest-trending, 7 miles long, 11 miles northwest of Mount Whitney (lat. 36°41'30" N, long. 118°25'45" W); the ridge separates Kern River drainage basin from Kings River drainage basin. Named on Mount Whitney (1956) 15' quadrangle.

King Solomons Ridge [KERN]: *ridge,* east- to southeast-trending, nearly 5 miles long, the center is 3.5 miles northwest of Piute Peak (lat. 35°29'30" N, long. 118°25'30" W). Named on Lake Isabella South (1972) and Piute Peak (1972) 7.5' quadrangles.

King Spur [FRESNO]: *ridge,* north-trending, 5 miles long, 8 miles south-southwest of Mount Pinchot (lat. 36°50'15" N, long. 118°26'45" W); Mount Clarence King is near the center of the ridge. Named on Mount Pinchot (1953) 15' quadrangle.

Kings River [FRESNO-KINGS-TULARE]: *stream,* formed in Fresno County by the confluence of Middle Fork and South Fork, flows 125 miles, partly in Tulare County, to Tulare Lake Bed south of Stratford in Kings County.

Named on Fresno (1962) 1°x 2° quadrangle. Early Spanish explorers gave the name "El Rio de los Santos Reyes" to present Kings River to honor the Three Wise Men—*El Rio de los Santos Reyes* means "The River of the Holy Kings" in Spanish (Hoover, Rensch, and Rensch, p. 89). Called Lake Fork on Fremont's (1848) map. The stream also was known as the Wilmilche in the early days of American occupation (Preston, p. 14). The name has the form "King River" on Hamlin's (1904) map, and Williamson (p. 13) used the form "King's river," but United States Board on Geographic Names (1933a, p. 428) rejected both forms. Middle Fork is 35 miles long and is named on Marion Peak (1953), Mount Goddard (1948), and Tehipite Dome (1952) 15' quadrangles. South Fork is 42 miles long and is named on Big Pine (1950), Marion Peak (1953), Mount Pinchot (1953), and Tehipite Dome (1952) 15' quadrangles. North Fork enters from the north 51 miles upstream from the entrance of the main stream into Tulare County; it is 35 miles long and is named on Blackcap Mountain (1953), Patterson Mountain (1952), and Tehipiate Dome (1952) 15' quadrangles. Stratford (1942) 15' quadrangle shows Kings River reaching an artificially confined Tulare Lake 10 miles south of Stratford through an artificial watercourse, and Stratford SE (1954) 7.5' quadrangle shows Kings River in an artificial watercourse in Tulare Lake Bed. Kings River splits 6 miles north of Lemoore into a second set of North and South Forks; these forks then join to reform Kings River nearly 5 miles west of Lemoore. The second North Fork is 11 miles long and is named on Burrel (1954), Lemoore (1954), Riverdale (1954), and Vanguard (1956) 7.5' quadrangles; it is called Fresno Slough on Riverdale (1927) 7.5' quadrangle. The second South Fork is 9.5 miles long and is named on Lemoore (1954) and Riverdale (1954) 7.5' quadrangles. Clarks Fork diverges from the second South Fork and flows 5.5 miles to rejoin second North Fork 6 miles west-northwest of Lemoore; it is named on Lemoore (1954) and Vanguard (1956) 7.5' quadrangles.

King's River: see **Kings River** [FRESNO-KINGS-TULARE]; **Reedley** [FRESNO].

Kings River: see **Centerville** [FRESNO].

Kings River Canyon: see **Kings Canyon** [FRESNO].

Kings River Slough: see **Fresno Slough** [FRESNO-KINGS].

Kings River Switch: see **Kingsburg** [FRESNO].

Kingston: see **Hardwick** [KINGS]; **Laton** [FRESNO].

Kip Camp [FRESNO]: *locality,* 6.25 miles west-southwest of Mount Abbot along Bear Creek (2) (lat. 37°22'05" N, long. 118°53'35" W). Named on Mount Abbot (1953) 15' quadrangle.

Kip Slough: see **Lonetree Channel** [FRESNO].

Kirch Flat [FRESNO]: *area,* 2.25 miles west-southwest of Balch Camp along Kings River (lat. 36°53'15" N, long. 119°09'15" W; near E line sec. 17, T 12 S, R 26 E). Named on Patterson Mountain (1952) 15' quadrangle.

Kirkman Hill [FRESNO]: *ridge,* west-southwest-trending, 1 mile long, 7.5 miles west-southwest of Piedra (lat. 36°45'50" N, long. 119°30'10" W). Named on Piedra (1965) and Round Mountain (1964) 7.5' quadrangles.

Kissack Bay [KERN]: *embayment,* 5 miles southeast of Wofford Heights along Isabella Lake (lat. 35°39' N, long. 118°24'15" W). Named on Lake Isabella North (1972) 7.5' quadrangle.

Kissack Cove [KERN]: *embayment,* 4.5 miles south-southeast of Wofford Heights along Isabella Lake (lat. 35°38'55" N, long. 118° 24'55" W; near SE cor. sec. 22, T 26 S, R 33 E); the feature is at the west end of Kissack Bay. Named on Lake Isabella North (1972) 7.5' quadrangle.

Kittleman Hills: see **Kettleman Hills** [FRESNO-KERN-KINGS-].

Kittleman Plain: see **Kettleman Plain** [FRESNO-KINGS].

Klink: see **Ivanhoe** [TULARE].

Knapsack Pass [FRESNO]: *pass,* 10 miles east of Mount Goddard (lat. 37°05' N, long. 118°32'30" W). Named on Mount Goddard (1948) 15' quadrangle. A.L. Jordan discovered the pass in 1917, and Chester Versteeg suggested the name in 1935 (Browning, p. 121).

Knecht: see **Twin Lakes** [KERN] (1).

Knight Camp: see **Qualls Camp** [FRESNO].

Knob Hill [KERN]: *peak,* 12.5 miles south-southwest of Woody (lat. 35°33'50" N, long. 118°56'55" W; sec. 22, T 27 S, R 28 E). Altitude 1161 feet. Named on Knob Hill (1965) 7.5' quadrangle.

Knob Lake [FRESNO]: *lake,* 950 feet long, 4.25 miles west of Mount Humphreys in Humphreys Basin (lat. 37°16' N, long. 118°44'50" W). Named on Mount Tom (1949) 15' quadrangle. The name is from a knoblike rock tower on the shore of the lake (Browning, p. 121).

Koehn: see **Koehn Spring** [KERN].

Koehn Dry Lake: see **Koehn Lake** [KERN].

Koehn Lake [KERN]: *dry lake,* south of Saltdale in Fremont Valley (lat. 35°19'55" N, long. 117°52'55" W). Named on Cantil (1967) and Saltdale SE (1967) 7.5' quadrangles. Called Koehn Dry Lake on Saltdale (1943a) 15' quadrangle, and Kane Lake on Baker's (1911) map. The feature also was called Kane Dry Lake, Desert Lake, and Salt Lake (Wynn, 1963, p. 29, 32).

Koehn Spring [KERN]: *locality,* 3.25 miles northeast of Cantil (lat. 35°20'30" N, long. 117°55' W); the place is near present Koehn Lake. Named on Searles Lake (1915) 1° quadrangle. Called Kane on Baker's (1911) map. Postal authorities established Koehn post office in 1893 and discontinued it in 1898; the name was for Charles A. Koehn, first postmaster (Salley, p. 113), who homesteaded at the place and operated a store as well as the post office (Wynn, 1963, p. 60). Koehn Spring was known also as Cane Springs, Kane Springs, Mesquite Springs, Desert Springs (Brown, p. 477), and Keehn Well (Mendenhall, 1909, p. 50).

Kolingo Creek [FRESNO]: *stream,* flows 2.25 miles to Cooper Canyon 3.25 miles west-southwest of Coalinga (lat. 36°07' N, long. 120°24'40" W; sec. 12, T 21 S, R 14 E). Named on Alcalde Hills (1969) and Curry Mountain (1969) 7.5' quadrangles.

Kramer Creek [TULARE]: *stream,* flows 5 miles to Backbone Creek 16 miles south-southeast of Kaweah (lat. 36°15'35" N, long. 118° 47'05" W; sec. 24, T 19 S, R 29 E). Named on Kaweah (1957) 15' quadrangle.

Kramer Meadow [TULARE]: *area,* 5.5 miles east-southeast of Camp Nelson (lat. 36°06'10" N, long. 118°31'15" W; sec. 16, T 21 S, R 32 E). Named on Camp Nelson (1956) 15' quadrangle.

Kreyenhagen Hills [FRESNO-KINGS]: *range,* southwest of Kettleman Plain on Fresno-Kings County line. Named on Avenal (1954), Curry Mountain (1969), Garza Peak (1953), Kettleman Plain (1953), Kreyenhagen Hills (1956), and The Dark Hole (1961) 7.5' quadrangles. Arnold and Anderson (1908, p. 14) named the range for three families named Kreyenhagen who owned large tracts of land there, and stated that "they [the Kreyenhagens] are early settlers and practically the only inhabitants, and the region is generally known as the Kreyenhagen country or Kreyenhagen's."

Kreyenhagen Peak [FRESNO]: *peak,* 1 mile north-northeast of Coalinga Mineral Springs (lat. 36°09'30" N, long. 120°32'50" W; near W line sec. 26, T 20 S, R 13 E). Altitude 3561 feet. Named on Sherman Peak (1969) 7.5' quadrangle.

Kurth: see **Porterville** [TULARE].

Kyan [KERN]: *locality,* 11.5 miles east of Taft along Sunset Railroad (lat. 35°07'30" N, long. 119°15'40" W; sec. 23, T 32 S, R 25 E). Named on Mouth of Kern (1932) 7.5' quadrangle.

—L—

La Aleta [KINGS]: *ridge,* east-southeast-trending, 0.5 mile long. 4.5 miles east of Avenal (lat. 36°00'30" N, long. 120°02'40" W; near S line sec. 17, T 22 S, R 18 E). Named on La Cima (1963) 7.5' quadrangle. The descriptive name refers to the curved shape of the feature—*aleta* means "wing" in Spanish (United States Board on Geographic Names, 1933b, p. 15).

La Arena [KERN]: *area,* 11 miles north of Blackwells Corner (lat. 35°46'25" N, long. 119°54'05" W; around NW cor. sec. 11, T 25 S, R 19 E). Named on Avanal Gap (1954) 7.5' quadrangle.

La Bajada [KINGS]: *area,* 5.5 miles south of Kettleman City (lat. 35°55'30" N, long. 119°58'30" W; in and near sec. 13, T 23 S, R 18 E). Named on Los Viejos (1954) 7.5' quadrangle. United States Board on Geographic Names (1933b, p. 15-16) pointed out that *bajada* means "slope" or "descent" in Spanish.

La Brecha [KINGS]: *pass,* 8 miles south of Kettleman City (lat. 35° 53'40" N, long. 119°58'35" W; sec. 25, T 23 S, R 18 E). Named on Los Viejos (1954) 7.5' quadrangle. *Brecha* means "breach" in Spanish (United States Board on Geographic Names, 1933b, p. 16).

La Caldera [KINGS]: *canyon,* 0.5 mile long, 7.5 miles east-southeast of Avenal (lat. 35°57'30" N, long. 120°00'20" W; on E line sec. 3, T 23 S, R 18 E). Named on Kettleman Plain (1953) 7.5' quadrangle. The name is descriptive—*caldera* means "caldron" in Spanish (United States Board on Geographic Names, 1933b, p. 16).

La Cañada Simada [FRESNO]: *canyon,* drained by a stream that flows 1.5 miles to Kettleman Plain 12.5 miles east-southeast of Coalinga (lat. 36°02'25" N, long. 120°09'50" W; near W line sec. 5, T 22 S, R 17 E). Named on Avenal (1954) 7.5' quadrangle. The name is descriptive and means "deep ravine" in Spanish (United States Board on Geographic Names, 1933b, p. 16).

La Ceja [FRESNO-KINGS]: *ridge,* west-northwest-trending, 3.5 miles long, 4.5 miles north-northeast of Avenal on Kings-Fresno County line (lat. 36°04' N, long. 120°06'15" W). Named on La Cima (1963) 7.5' quadrangle. The name is descriptive and means "summit" in Spanish (United States Board on Geographic Names, 1933b, p. 16).

La Cima [KINGS]: *peak,* 4 miles east of Avenal (lat. 36°00'15" N, long. 120°03'20" W; near W line sec. 20, T 22 S, R 18 E). Altitude 1365 feet. Named on La Cima (1963) 7.5' quadrangle. The name is descriptive and means "summit" in Spanish (United States Board on Geographic Names, 1933b, p. 16).

Lacjac [FRESNO]: *locality,* 2 miles west-northwest of Reedley along Atchison, Topeka and Santa Fe Railroad (lat. 36°36'40" N, long. 119°28'55" W; near W line sec. 21, T 15 S, R 23 E). Named on Reedley (1966) 7.5' quadrangle. Daniel J. Ellis, who built a winery and distillery at the place for the firm of Lachman & Jacobi, coined the name in 1899 from the title of the firm (Gudde, 1949, p. 178).

La Clavija [KINGS]: *peak,* 3.25 miles northeast of Avenal (lat. 36° 02'05" N, long. 120°05' W; sec. 12, T 22 S, R 17 E). Named on La Cima (1963) 7.5' quadrangle. The name is descriptive and means "pin" or "peg" in Spanish (United States Board on Geographic Names, 1933b, p. 16).

La Cuba [KINGS]: *peak,* 4 miles south-southwest of Kettleman City (lat. 35°57'05" N, long. 119°59'05" W; sec. 1, T 23 S, R 18 E). Named on Los Viejos (1954) 7.5' quadrangle. The name is descriptive and means "cask" in Spanish (United States Board on Geographic Names, 1933b, p. 16).

La Cuesta [KINGS]: *peak,* nearly 4 miles east-northeast of Avenal (lat. 36°01'35" N, long. 120°04' W; sec. 7, T 22 S, R 18 E). Named on La Cima (1963) 7.5' quadrangle. United States Board on Geographic Names (1933b, p. 16) pointed out that the name means "hill" or "slope" in Spanish.

La Cumbre [KINGS]: *peak,* 2.5 miles north of Avenal (lat. 36°02'25" N, long. 120°07'15" W; sec. 3, T 22 S, R 17 E). Named on La Cima (1963) 7.5' quadrangle. The name was given because the peak is one of the highest points in Kettleman Hills—*cumbre* means "crest" in Spanish (United States Board on Geographic Names, 1933b, p. 16).

La Cuna [KINGS]: *area,* 4 miles east-northeast of Avenal (lat. 36° 01'10" N, long. 120°03'40" W; sec. 18, T 22 S, R 18 E). Named on La Cima (1963) 7.5' quadrangle. The name is descriptive—*cuna* means "cradle" in Spanish (United States Board on Geographic Names, 1933b, p. 16).

Ladder Lake [FRESNO]: *lake,* 2300 feet long, 6 miles east-southeast of Mount Goddard (lat. 37°04'10" N, long. 118°37'10" W). Named on Mount Goddard (1948) 15' quadrangle.

Lady Franklin Cañon: see **Franklin Lakes** [TULARE].

La Escudilla [KINGS]: *area,* 7 miles south of Kettleman City (lat. 35°54'25" N, long. 119°57'20" W; near S line sec. 19, T 23 S, R 19 E). Named on Los Viejos (1954) 7.5' quadrangle. United States Board on Geographic Names (1933b, p. 16) pointed out that *escudilla* means "bowl" or "soup plate" in Spanish.

Lagoon Lake [FRESNO]: *lake,* 450 feet long, 12.5 miles northwest of Mount Abbot (lat. 37°29'40" N, long. 118°57'55" W). Named on Mount Abbot (1953) 15' quadrangle.

Laguna de los Tulares: see "Regional setting."

Laguna de Tache [FRESNO-KINGS]: *land grant,* north of Hanford on Fresno-Kings County line, mainly in Kings County. Named on Burrel (1954), Burris Park (1954), Laton (1953), Lemoore (1954), Riverdale (1954), and Vanguard (1956) 7.5' quadrangles. Manuel de Jesus Castro received the land in 1846 and claimed 48,801 acres patented in 1866 (Cowan, p. 101). The name "Tache" is from the Tachi Indians, who lived in the region (Kroeber, p. 60).

Lairds Corner [TULARE]: *locality,* 3.5 miles south-southwest of Woodville (lat. 36°03'05" N, long. 119°13'55" W; at NE cor. sec. 2, T 22 S, R 25 E). Named on Woodville (1950) 7.5' quadrangle.

La Jolla Creek [FRESNO]: *stream,* flows 1.25 miles to Beltran Creek nearly 4 miles northeast of Castle Mountain (lat. 35°58'35" N, long. 120°17'25" W; sec. 31, T 22 S, R 16 E). Named on The Dark Hole (1961) 7.5' quadrangle.

Lake Basin [FRESNO]: *valley,* 2 miles north-northeast of Marion Peak along Cartridge Creek (lat. 36°59' N, long. 118°30' W). Named on Marion Peak (1953) and Mount Pinchot (1953) 15' quadrangles. J.N. LeConte used the name descriptively in 1902 (Browning, p. 122).

Lakecamp Lake [FRESNO]: *lake,* 700 feet long, 8 miles east-southeast of Kaiser Peak (lat. 37°15'25" N, long. 119°03'10" W). Named on Kaiser Peak (1953) 15' quadrangle.

Lake Elsie: see **Fingerbowl Lake** [FRESNO].

Lake Engle [KERN]: *lake,* 450 feet long, 7.25 miles south-southeast of Glennville along Little Poso Creek (lat. 35°38' N, long. 118°38'45" W; near S line sec. 28, T 26 S, R 31 E). Named on Glennville (1972) 7.5' quadrangle.

Lake Florence: see **Florence Lake** [FRESNO].

Lake Fork: see **Kings River** [FRESNO-KINGS-TULARE].

Lake Isabella [KERN]: *town,* 35 miles east-northeast of Bakersfield along Kern River in Hot Spring Valley (lat. 35°37'30" N, long. 118°28'30" W); the town is below Isabella Lake. Named on Lake Isabella North (1972) and Lake Isabella South (1972) 7.5' quadrangles. Called Isabella on Bakersfield (1962, revised 1971) 1°x 2° quadrangle, which shows a place called Kernvale situated 1.25 miles farther south-southwest. Formation of Isabella Lake forced removal of the original community of Isabella to a site 1.5 miles farther south below the dam that forms the lake. Isabella post office operated at the new site from 1953 until its name was changed to Lake Isabella in 1957 (Salley, p. 115). United States Board on Geographic Names (1975b, p. 10) gave the variant names "Isabella" and "Kernvale" for the town.

Lake Isabella: see **Isabella Lake** [KERN].

Lake Italy [FRESNO]: *lake,* 1.5 miles long, 2.25 miles south-southwest of Mount Abbot (lat. 37°21'30" N, long. 118°48'15" W). Named on Mount Abbot (1953) 15' quadrangle. Members of United States Geological Survey named the feature about 1907 for the resemblance of the outline of the lake on a map to the bootlike shape of Italy on a map (Farquhar, 1923, p. 407).

Lake Joseph Grinnell: see **Grinnell Lake** [FRESNO].

Lake Kaweah [TULARE]: *lake,* behind a dam on Kaweah River 5.25 miles east of Woodlake (lat. 36°25' N, long. 119°00'10" W; sec. 25, T 17 S, R 27 E). Named on Kaweah (1957) 15' quadrangle, and on Woodlake (1952, photorevised 1969) 7.5' quadrangle.

Lake Los Nietos [FRESNO]: *lake,* with three parts, the largest part 250 feet long, located 7 miles northeast of Coalinga (lat. 36°12'40" N, long. 120°16' W; sec. 6, T 20 S, R 16 E). Named on Coalinga (1956) 7.5' quadrangle.

Lake Marion [KERN]: *lake,* 500 feet long, 7 miles south-southeast of Glennville along Little Poso Creek (lat. 35°37'55" N, long. 118° 39'55" W; near S line sec. 29, T 26 S, R 31 E). Named on Glennville (1972) 7.5' quadrangle.

Lake Marjorie [FRESNO]: *lake,* 1800 feet long, 1.5 miles west of Mount Pinchot (lat. 36°56'40" N, long. 118°25'45" W). Named on Mount Pinchot (1953) 15' quadrangle. Browning (p. 137) associated the name with Marjorie Mott, daughter of Ernest J. Mott of Mott Lake.

Lake McDermand: see **Mount Goddard** [FRESNO].

Lake Ming [KERN]: *lake,* nearly 1 mile long, 9 miles east-northeast of Bakersfield along Kern River (lat. 35°26'20" N, long. 118°51'50" W). Named on Bakersfield (1962, revised 1971) 1°x 2° quadrangle. The artificial lake was dedicated in 1959 and named for Floyd Ming, a former district supervisor of Kern County (Bailey, 1967, p. 14).

Lake of the Fallen Moon [FRESNO]: *lake,* 900 feet long, nearly 6 miles west-southwest of Marion Peak (lat. 36°54'50" N, long. 118° 36'50" W). Named on Marion Peak (1953) 15' quadrangle. The author of a poem with the title "Lake of the Fallen Moon" named the feature (Stewart, p. 162).

Lake of the Lone Indian [FRESNO]: *lake,* 1300 feet long, 10.5 miles northwest of Mount Abbot (lat. 37°28'35" N, long. 118°56'10" W). Named on Mount Abbot (1953) 15' quadrangle. The distinct profile of an Indian face and feathered headdress on the slope above the lake suggested the name (Farquhar, 1924, p. 55).

Lake of the Woods [KERN]: *lake,* 550 feet long, 7.5 miles west of Lebec near the head of Cuddy Canyon (lat. 34°49'05" N, long. 118°59'55" W; sec. 33, T 9 N, R 20 W). Named on Frazier Mountain (1958) 7.5' quadrangle.

Lake Paulina [KERN]: *intermittent lake,* 700 feet long, 4.5 miles south-southwest of Weed Patch (lat. 35°10'45" N, long. 118°57'05" W; near NE cor. sec. 3, T 32 S, R 28 E). Named on Weed Patch (1955) 7.5' quadrangle.

Lake Reflection [TULARE]: *lake,* 3500 feet long, 12 miles northwest of Mount Whitney along East Creek (lat. 36°42' N, long. 118°26'40" W). Named on Mount Whitney (1956) 15' quadrangle. Howard Longley and his companions named the lake in 1894 (Browning, p. 181).

Lakeshore [FRESNO]: *village,* nearly 3 miles south-southeast of Kaiser Peak (lat. 37°15'10" N, long. 119°10'25" W; sec. 6, 7, T 8 S, R 26 E); the village is on the north shore of Huntington Lake (1). Named on Kaiser Peak (1953) 15' quadrangle. Postal authorities established Lakeshore post office in 1924 (Frickstad, p. 34).

Lake South America [TULARE]: *lake,* 2000 feet long, 9 miles northwest of Mount Whitney (lat. 36°40'45" N, long. 118°24' W). Named on Mount Whitney (1956) 15' quadrangle. Called South American Lake on Mount Whitney (1907) 30' quadrangle, but United States Board on Geographic Names (1933a, p. 707) rejected this form of the name, and noted that Professor Bolton C. Brown of Stanford University named the feature in 1896 for the resemblance of its outline on a map to the outline of South America on a map.

Lake Stockton [KERN]: *lake,* 300 feet long, 7.25 miles south-southeast of Glennville along Little Poso Creek (lat. 35°37'55" N, long. 118°39'05" W; near S line sec. 28, T 26 S, R 31 E). Named on Glennville (1972) 7.5' quadrangle.

Lake Success [TULARE]: *lake,* behind a dam on Tule River 5.5 miles east of Porterville (lat. 36°03'35" N, long. 118°55'05" W; sec. 35, T 21 S, R 28 E); the lake is near the site of the village of Success. Named on Success Dam (1956) 7.5' quadrangle. United States Board on Geographic Names (1962, p. 17) rejected the name "Success Reservoir" for the lake.

Lake Thomas A. Edison [FRESNO]: *lake,* behind a dam on Mono Creek 11.5 miles west of Mount Abbot (lat. 37°22'10" N, long. 118°59'15" W). Named on Kaiser Peak (1953) and Mount Abbot (1953) 15' quadrangles. The name was given in the early 1950's (Browning, p. 62) to the lake that occupies Vermilion Valley.

Lake Tulare: see **Tulare Lake** [KINGS].

Lakeview [KERN]: *locality;* 8.5 miles west-northwest of Mettler (lat. 35°05'40" N, long. 119°06'30" W; at SW cor. sec. 32, T 32 S, R 27 E); the place is southwest of Kern Lake Bed. Named on Coal Oil Canyon (1955) 7.5' quadrangle.

Lake Virginia [FRESNO]: *lake,* 3700 feet long, 3.5 miles west of Red Slate Mountain (lat. 37°30'40" N, long. 118°56' W). Named on Mount Morrison (1953) 15' quadrangle.

Lake Woollomes [KERN]: *lake,* 2 miles long, 5 miles north-northeast of McFarland (lat. 35°44'20" N, long. 119°10'40" W). Named on McFarland (1954, photorevised 1969) 7.5' quadrangle. The name, given in 1959, is for W.R. Woollomes, a former district supervisor of Kern County (Bailey, 1967, p. 15).

La Liebra [KERN]: *land grant,* on the southeast side of Tehachapi Mountains; extends south into Los Angeles County. Named on La Liebra Ranch (1965), Lebec (1958), Liebre Twins (1965), Neenach School (1965), Tylerhorse Canyon (1965), and Winters Ridge (1966) 7.5' quadrangles. Jose M. Flores received 11 leagues in 1846 and claimed 48,800 acres patented in 1875 (Cowan, p. 45).

La Llanura [KINGS]: *valley,* 5.5 miles south of Kettleman City (lat. 35°55'30" N, long. 119°57'10" W; in and near sec. 18, T 23 S, R 19 E). Named on Los Viejos (1954) 7.5' quadrangle. The name is descriptive and means "flatness" or "plain" in Spanish (United States Board on Geographic Names, 1933b, p. 16).

La Loba [KINGS]: *ridge,* northwest-trending, 0.25 mile long, 3 miles east-northeast of Avenal (lat. 36°01'35" N, long. 120°04'45" W; sec. 12, T 22 S, R 17 E). Named on La Cima (1963) 7.5' quadrangle. United States Board on Geographic Names (1933b, p. 16) noted that *loba* means "ridge" in Spanish.

La Lomera [FRESNO]: *ridge,* north-trending, nearly 1 mile long, 13 miles east-southeast of Coalinga (lat. 36°03'25" N, long. 120°08'20" W; sec. 33, T 21 S, R 17 E). Named on Avenal (1954) 7.5' quadrangle. The United States Board on Geographic Names (1933b, p. 17) noted that *la lomera* means "the ridge of a house" in Spanish

La Lomica [KINGS]: *peak,* 4 miles south of Kettleman City (lat. 35° 56'55" N, long. 119°57'30" W; on S line sec. 6, T 23 S, R 19 E). Altitude 580 feet. Named on Los Viejos (1954) 7.5' quadrangle. United States Board on Geographic Names (1933b, p. 17) pointed out that *lomica* means "very little hill" in Spanish.

La Luneta [FRESNO]: *peak,* 10.5 miles east-southeast of Coalinga (lat. 36°04'35" N, long. 120°11'10" W; sec. 25, T 21 S, R 16 E). Altitude 999 feet. Named on Avenal (1954) 7.5' quadrangle. The descriptive name refers to the semicircular erosion of the west slope—it means "half moon" in Spanish (United States Board on Geographic Names, 1933b, p. 17).

Lamarck: see **Mount Lamarck** [FRESNO].

Lamarck Col [FRESNO]: *pass,* 6.5 miles north-northeast of Mount Goddard on Fresno-Inyo County line (lat. 37°11'25" N, long. 118° 40' W); the pass is 0.25 mile south-southeast of Mount Lamarck. Named on Mount Goddard (1948) 15' quadrangle. Art Schober built a trail to the place, which he and his brother John named Schober's Pass in 1939; David Brower suggested the present name, which was in use as early as 1942 (Browning, p. 122).

La Marmita [KINGS]: *relief feature,* closed depression 6.5 miles east of Avenal (lat. 36°00'55" N, long. 120°00'35" W; sec. 15, T 22 S, R 18 E). Named on La Cima (1963) 7.5' quadrangle. La Cima (1934) 7.5' quadrangle shows an intermittent Lake, 350 feet long, in the depression. United States Board on Geographic Names (1933b, p. 17) pointed out that *marmita* means "pot" or "kettle" in Spanish

La Meseta [KINGS]: *peak,* 4.25 miles east of Avenal (lat. 36°00'05" N, long. 120°03' W; sec. 20, T 22 S, R 18 E). Named on La Cima (1963) 7.5' quadrangle. The name refers to the position of the peak about halfway up the north slope of El Leon—*meseta* means "landing place of a staircase" in Spanish (United States Board on Geographic Names, 1933b, p. 17).

Lamont [KERN]: *town,* 9 miles south-southeast of downtown Bakersfield (lat. 35°15'35" N, long. 118°54'45" W; on W line sec. 6, T 31 S, R 29 E). Named on Lamont (1954) and Weed Patch (1955) 7.5' quadrangles. Postal authorities established Lamont post office in 1947 (Frickstad, p. 56). Promoters started the town in 1923, and Arthur S. McFadden named it for the Scottish clan of his family (Bailey, 1967, p. 15). A station on Butterfield Overland stage line of 1858 to 1861 was located 3 miles west of present Lamont; the station had the name "Kern River Slough" (Bailey, 1967, p. 13).

Lamont Meadow [TULARE]: *area,* about 2 miles north of Lamont Peak along Chimney Creek (lat. 35°49'15" N, long. 118°02'45" W). Named on Lamont Peak (1956) 15' quadrangle. Called La Motte Meadows on Olmsted's (1900) map.

Lamont Peak [TULARE]: *peak,* 37 miles east of California Hot Springs (lat. 35°47'35" N, long. 118°02'35" W). Altitude 7430 feet. Named on Lamont Peak (1956) 15' quadrangle.

La Morra [KINGS]: *peak,* 6.25 miles south-southwest of Kettleman City (lat. 35°55'05" N, long. 119°59'35" W; sec. 23, T 23 S, R 18 E). Altitude 941 feet. Named on Los Viejos (1954) 7.5' quadrangle. The name is descriptive—*morra* means "head" or "top" in Spanish (United States Board on Geographic Names, 1933b, p. 19).

La Motte Meadows: see **Lamont Meadow** [TULARE].

La Muralla [KINGS]: *ridge,* west- to north-northwest-trending, 1 mile long, 5.5 miles east of Avenal (lat. 36°00' N, long. 120°01'35" W). Named on Kettleman Plain (1953) and La Cima (1963) 7.5' quadrangles. The name is descriptive—*muralla* means "wall" or "rampart" in Spanish (United States Board on Geographic Names, 1933b, p. 17).

Lanare [FRESNO]: *village,* 24 miles south-southwest of Fresno (lat. 36°25'55" N, long. 119°55'50" W; near S line sec. 20, T 17 S, R 19 E). Named on Burrel (1954) 7.5' quadrangle. Postal authorities established Lanare post office in 1912 and discontinued it in 1925 (Frickstad, p. 34). The name is from the initials and surname of <u>L</u>lewellyn <u>A</u>. <u>Nares</u>, who with Charles A. Laton purchased a large part of Laguna de Tache grant in 1896 (Hanna, p. 166-167); the name was applied when Laton and Western Railway was built in 1911 (Gudde, 1949, p. 181).

Landco [KERN]: *locality,* 3.5 miles west of Bakersfield along Atchison, Topeka and Santa Fe Railroad (lat. 35°22'50" N, long. 119°03'40" W; sec. 27, T 29 S, R 27 E). Named on Oildale (1954) 7.5' quadrangle.

Land Company Spring [KERN]: *spring,* 5.5 mile east-southeast of Caliente (lat. 35°15'40" N, long. 118°32' W; sec. 3, T 31 S, R 32 E). Named on Oiler Peak (1972) 7.5' quadrangle.

Landers Creek [KERN]: *stream,* flows 2.25 miles to Kelso Creek less than 1 mile east of Claraville (lat. 35°26'40" N, long. 118°18'55" W; sec. 3, T 29 S, R 34 E). Named on Claraville (1972) 7.5' quadrangle.

Landers Meadow [KERN]: *area,* 2 miles east of Claraville along Kelso Creek (lat. 35°26'50" N, long. 118°17'45" W); the place is above the mouth of Landers Creek. Named on Claraville (1972) 7.5' quadrangle.

Landslide Creek [FRESNO]: *stream,* flows 2.5 miles to Tenmile Creek 1.5 miles southeast of Hume (lat. 36°46'15" N, long. 118°53'35" W; near SE cor. sec. 23, T 13 S, R 28 E). Named on Tehipite Dome (1952) 15' quadrangle.

Lane Slough [TULARE]: *stream,* diverges southwest from St. Johns River and flows 2.5 miles to Kaweah River 4.25 miles north of Exeter (lat. 36°21'30" N, long. 119°08'15" W; sec. 15, T 18 S, R 26 E). Named on Exeter (1952) 15' quadrangle.

Lane Spring [FRESNO]: *spring,* 10.5 miles northwest of Coalinga (lat. 36°14'25" N, long. 120°29'45" W; sec. 30, T 19 S, R 14 E). Named on Alcalde Hills (1969) 7.5' quadrangle.

Langdon: see **Bakersfield** [KERN].

Langille Peak [FRESNO]: *peak,* 6 miles east of Mount Goddard (lat. 37°06' N, long. 118°36'35" W). Altitude 11,991 feet. Named on Mount Goddard (1948) 15' quadrangle. Charles H. Shinn suggested the name to honor Harold Douglas Langille, who visited the region in 1904 as forest inspector of General Land Office (Hanna, p. 167). United States Board on Geographic Names (1961a, p. 18) approved the name "Hester Lake" for a feature, about 1300 feet long, situated 0.8 mile southwest of Langille Peak (lat. 37°05'35" N, long. 118°37'25" W); the name honors both Robert M. Hester, co-pilot of a B-24 bomber that crashed at the lake in 1943 and was found in 1960, and the co-pilot's father, Clinton Hester, who searched for his son's body for more than 14 years.

Langley: see **Mount Langley** [TULARE]; **Mount Langley**, under **Mount Corcoran** [TULARE].

Lang Pond [FRESNO]: *intermittent lake,* 750 feet long, 2.5 miles southwest of Selma (lat. 36°32'35" N, long. 119°38'15" W; sec. 13, T 16 S, R 21 E). Named on Conejo (1963) 7.5' quadrangle. Selma (1946) 15' quadrangle shows a permanent lake 2100 feet long.

La Oveja [KINGS]: *peak,* 4 miles east-southeast of Avenal (lat. 35° 59'05" N, long. 120°03'45" W; sec. 30, T 22 S, R 18 E). Altitude 1063 feet. Named on Kettleman Plain (1953) 7.5' quadrangle. The name refers to the raising of sheep in Kettleman Hills—*oveja* means "sheep" in Spanish (United States Board on Geographic Names, 1933b, p. 17).

La Palomera [KINGS]: *peak,* nearly 6 miles east of Avenal (lat. 36° 00'25" N, long. 120°01'35" W; near N line sec. 21, T 22 S, R 18 E). Altitude 1069 feet. Named on La Cima (1963) 7.5' quadrangle. The name is descriptive—*palomera* means "dove cot" in Spanish (United States Board on Geographic Names, 1933b, p. 17).

La Porciuncula: see **Kern River** [KERN-TULARE].

La Porteria [KINGS]: *pass,* 8 miles south-southeast of Kettleman City (lat. 35°53'55" N, long. 119°55'05" W; sec. 28, T 23 S, R 19 E). Named on Los Viejos (1954) 7.5' quadrangle. The pass is the principal entrance to the interior of Middle Dome Kettleman Hills— *porteria* means "principal opening of a large building" in Spanish (United States Board on Geographic Names, 1933b, p. 17).

La Rambla [KINGS]: *area,* 5 miles southeast of Kettleman City (lat. 35°57'05" N, long. 119°54'35" W). Named on Los Viejos (1954) 7.5' quadrangle. The place is a former beach of Tulare Lake—*rambla* means "sandy place" in Spanish (United States Board on Geographic Names, 1933b, p. 17).

Large Meadow [FRESNO]: *area,* 15 miles north-northeast of Hume (lat. 37°00' N, long. 118°51' W). Named on Blackcap Mountain (1953) and Tehipite Dome (1952) 15' quadrangles.

Larione's Ferry: see **Old Fort Miller** [FRESNO].

La Rose [KERN]: *locality,* nearly 3 miles northwest of Mojave along Southern Pacific Railroad (lat. 35°06'30" N, long. 118°14'45" W; near N line sec. 32, T 32 S, R 35 E). Named on Mojave (1915) 30' quadrangle.

La Rose Creek [KERN]: *stream,* flows 4.5 miles to Cache Creek 10.5 miles east of Tehachapi (lat. 35°06'15" N, long. 118°16'15" W; near W line sec. 31, T 32 S, R 35 E). Named on Monolith (1966) and Tehachapi NE (1966) 7.5' quadrangles.

La Salida [KINGS]: *pass,* 5.5 miles south-southeast of Kettleman City (lat.

35°55'50" N, long. 119°56'15" W; sec. 17, T 23 S, R 19 E). Named on Los Viejos (1954) 7.5' quadrangle. United States Board on Geographic Names (1933b, p. 17) pointed out that *salida* means "exit" or "outlet" in Spanish.

Las Alturas [KINGS]: *ridge,* north-northwest-trending, 9 miles long, 7 miles south of Kettleman City (lat. 35°54' N, long. 119°59' W). Named on Avenal Gap (1954), Kettleman Plain (1953), and Los Viejos (1954) 7.5' quadrangles. The name is descriptive—*las alturas* means "the heights" or "summits" in Spanish (United States Board on Geographic Names, 1933b, p. 18).

Las Colinas [KINGS]: *ridge,* north-trending, 3.5 miles long, 13 miles south of Kettleman City (lat. 35°48'45" N, long. 119°56'30" W). Named on Avenal Gap (1954) 7.5' quadrangle. *Colinas* means "hills" in Spanish (United States Board on Geographic Names, 1933b, p. 18).

Las Garzas Creek: see **Garza Creek** [FRESNO-KINGS].

Las Gatas Creek: see **Los Gatos Creek** [FRESNO].

Las Juntas: see **Pueblo de las Juntas**, under **Mendota** [FRESNO].

Las Lomas [KINGS]: *peaks,* 15 miles south of Kettleman City (lat. 35°48' N, long. 119°54'40" W; in and near sec. 34, T 24 S, R 19 E). Named on Avenal Gap (1954) 7.5' quadrangle. United States Board on Geographic Names (1933b, p. 18) pointed out that *las lomas* means "the little hills" in Spanish.

Las Palmas [FRESNO]: *locality,* 4.5 miles south of Clovis along Southern Pacific Railroad (lat. 36°45'30" N, long. 119°42' W; at W line sec. 33, T 13 S, R 21 E). Named on Clovis (1964) 7.5' quadrangle. Called Los Palmas on California Mining Bureau's (1917a) map. Postal authorities established Womack post office in 1909, changed the name to Las Palmas in 1910, and discontinued it in 1913; the name "Womack" was for D. Donald Womack, first postmaster (Salley, p. 118, 242).

Las Paredes [KINGS]: *ridge,* northwest-trending, 0.5 mile long, 4.5 miles east-northeast of Avenal (lat. 36°01'10" N, long. 120°03'05" W; on N line sec. 17, T 22 S, R 18 E). Named on La Cima (1963) 7.5' quadrangle. The name refers to the precipitous southwest side of the feature—*las paredes* means "the walls" in Spanish (United States Board on Geographic Names, 1933b, p. 18).

Las Perillas [KINGS]: *ridge,* north-northeast-trending, 1 mile long. 12 miles south-southeast of Kettleman City (lat. 35°50'05" N, long. 119°54'30" W; sec. 15, 22, T 24 S, R 29 E). Named on Avenal Gap (1954) 7.5' quadrangle. The name is descriptive; *las perillas* means "knob" or "small pear" in Spanish (United States Board on Geographic Names, 1933b, p. 18).

Last: see **Huron** [FRESNO].

Last Chance Canyon [KERN]: *canyon,* drained by a stream that flows 11.5 miles to Fremont Valley 1.5 miles west-northwest of Saltdale (lat. 35°22'15" N, long. 117°54'25" W). Named on Garlock (1967) and Saltdale NW (1967) 7.5' quadrangles.

Last Chance Canyon: see **Big Last Chance Canyon** [KERN]; **Little Last Chance Canyon** [KERN].

Last Chance Meadow [TULARE]: *area,* 10 miles south-southeast of Camp Nelson (lat. 36°00'15" N, long. 118°34' W; sec. 19, T 22 S, R 32 E). Named on Camp Nelson (1956) 15' quadrangle.

Las Tiendas: see **Tent Hills** [KINGS].

Las Tinajas de los Indios: see **Point of Rocks** [KERN].

Latache: see **Lemoore** [KINGS].

Laton [FRESNO]: *town,* 23 miles south-southeast of Fresno (lat. 36° 26'05" N, long. 119°41'05" W; sec. 21, 22, T 17 S, R 21 E). Named on Laton (1953) 7.5' quadrangle. The name commemorates Charles A Laton, who with L.A. Nares acquired part of Laguna de Tache grant in the 1890's (Gudde, 1949, p. 184). Postal authorities established Kingston post office in 1859, discontinued it in 1862, reestablished it in 1866, and moved it 1.5 miles in 1890 when they changed the name to Sans Tache; they changed the name to Lillis in 1891, and moved the post office 1 mile east in 1900 when they and changed the name to Laton (Salley, p. 112, 119, 122, 197). The name "Lillis" was for Simon C. Lillis, superintendent of Laguna de Tache cattle ranch before 1917 (Gudde, 1949, p. 188). California Mining Bureau's (1917a) map has the name "Lillis" for a place located along the railroad about 2 miles west of Laton.

La Tusa [KINGS]: *ridge,* northwest-trending, 0.5 mile long, 3 miles east-northeast of Avenal (lat. 36°01'25" N, long. 120°04'55" W; near S line sec. 12, T 22 S, R 17 E). Named on La Cima (1963) 7.5' quadrangle. The name is descriptive and means "corncob" in Spanish (United States Board on Geographic Names, 1933b, p. 17).

Lauhman Ridge: see **Leuhman Ridge** [KERN].

Laura Peak [KERN]: *peak,* 6 miles east-southeast of Bodfish (lat. 35°34' N, long. 118°23' W; sec. 24, T 27 S, R 33 E). Altitude 5254 feet. Named on Lake Isabella South (1972) 7.5' quadrangle.

Laurel Creek [FRESNO]:

(1) *stream,* flows 2.5 miles to Mono Creek nearly 5 miles northwest of Mount Abbot (lat. 37°25'45" N, long. 118°51' W). Named on Mount Abbot (1953) 15' quadrangle.

(2) *stream,* flows 4 miles to Bear Creek (3) 5 miles south of Dinkey Dome (lat. 37°02'30" N, long. 119°07'45" W; sec. 22, T 10 S, R 26 E). Named on Huntington Lake (1953) 15' quadrangle

Laurel Creek [TULARE]: *stream,* flows 5.5 miles to Kern River 8.5 miles northwest of Kern Peak (lat. 36°23' N, long. 118°23' W). Named on Kern Peak (1956) 15' quadrangle.

Laurel Lake [FRESNO]: *lake,* 700 feet long, 6.5 miles northwest of Mouth Abbot (lat. 37°27'40" N, long. 118°51'30" W); the lake is at the head of a branch of Laurel Creek (1). Named on Mount Abbot (1953) 15' quadrangle.

Laurel Mountain [KERN]: *peak,* 8 miles north of Randsburg (lat. 35°28'45" N, long. 117°41' W; at NE cor. sec. 29, T 28 S, R 40 E). Named on El Paso Peaks (1967) 7.5' quadrangle. The feature also was known as Copper Mountain (Hess, p. 25). A mining camp called El Paso City was located near Laurel Mountain in the 1860's (Bailey, 1967, p. 8).

Lava Butte [FRESNO]: *peak,* 2.5 miles southeast of Hume (lat. 36° 45'35" N, long. 118°53'15" W; sec. 25, T 13 S, R 28 E). Altitude 6122 feet. Named on Tehipite Dome (1952) 15' quadrangle.

Lava Rock Canyon: see **Lavrock Canyon** [KERN].

La Vega [KINGS]: *area,* 4 miles northeast of Avenal (lat. 37°03'15" N, long. 120°05'10" W; sec. 36, T 21 S, R 17 E). Named on La Cima (1963) 7.5' quadrangle. United States Board on Geographic Names (1933b, p. 17) noted that *la vega* means "the meadow" in Spanish.

Lavers' Crossing: see **Glennville** [KERN].

Lavrock Canyon [KERN]: *canyon,* drained by a stream that flows 2 miles to Still Canyon 7 miles south of Orchard Peak (lat. 35°38'15" N, long. 120°08'35" W; sec. 28, T 26 S, R 17 E). Named on Orchard Peak (1961) 7.5' quadrangle. Called Lava Rock Canyon on Annette (1943) 7.5' quadrangle.

Lawson Peak: see **Eagle Scout Peak** [TULARE].

La Zanja [KINGS]: *relief feature,* a line of topographic depressions 9 miles south of Kettleman City (lat. 35°52'30" N, long. 119°57'45" W). Named on Avenal Gap (1954) and Los Viejos (1954) 7.5' quadrangles. The name is descriptive; *la zanja* means "trench" or "furrow" in Spanish (United States Board on Geographic Names, 1933b, p. 17).

Leavis Flat Campground [TULARE]: *locality,* at California Hot Springs (lat. 35°52'45" N, long. 118°40'30" W; sec. 31, T 23 S, R 31 E). Named on California Hot Springs (1958) 15' quadrangle.

Lebec [KERN]: *village,* 38 miles south of Bakersfield (lat. 34°50'05" N, long. 118°51'50" W; sec. 26, T 9 N, R 19 W). Named on Lebec (1958) 7.5' quadrangle. Postal authorities established Tejon post office in 1895; they moved it 3 miles south and changed the name to Lebec the same year (Salley, p. 219). The name "Lebec" commemorates Peter Lebeck, or Lebecque, who probably was a trapper; according to an epitaph carved on an oak tree at Old Fort Tejon, Lebeck was killed by a bear in 1837 (Cullimore, p. 15-16).

Lecheria Creek: see **Pescado Creek** [KERN].

LeConte: see **Mount LeConte** [TULARE].

LeConte Canyon [FRESNO]: *canyon,* 6 miles long, 7 miles east-southeast of Mount Goddard along Middle Fork Kings River above Palisade Creek (lat. 37°05' N, long. 118°35'40" W). Named on Mount Goddard (1948) 15' quadrangle. The name honors Joseph N. LeConte, professor of engineering mechanics at University of California and president of the Sierra Club (Farquhar, 1924, p. 54). United States Board on Geographic Names (1933a, p. 453) rejected the form "Leconte Canyon" for the name.

LeConte Divide [FRESNO]: *ridge,* 12 miles long, mainly between Mount Henry and Mount Reinstein; center 5 miles north of Blackcap Mountain (lat. 37°09' N, long. 118°48' W). Named on Blackcap Mountain (1953) and Mount Goddard (1948) 15' quadrangles. The name is for Joseph N. LeConte of LeConte Canyon (Farquhar, 1924, p. 53). United States Board on Geographic Names (1933a, p. 453) rejected the form "Leconte Divide" for the name.

Lee Lake [FRESNO]: *lake,* 1800 feet long, 1 mile west-southwest of Red Slate Mountain (lat. 37°30'05" N, long. 118°53'15" W). Named on Mount Abbot (1953) and Mount Morrison (1953) 15' quadrangles.

Lefever Creek [FRESNO]: *stream,* flows 5.25 miles to Pine Flat Reservoir 7 miles northeast of Tivy Mountain (lat. 36°51'30" N, long. 119°15'15" W; sec. 28, T 12 S, R 25 E). Named on Patterson Mountain (1952) 15' quadrangle, and on Pine Flat Dam (1965) 7.5' quadrangle.

Left Stringer [TULARE]: *stream,* flows 3.5 miles to Right Stringer 4 miles north-northwest of Kern Peak (lat. 36°21'25" N, long, 118° 19'35" W). Named on Kern Peak (1956) 15' quadrangle.

Leggett Creek [TULARE]: *stream,* flows 2.5 miles to Kern River 7 miles west-southwest of Kern Peak (lat. 36°16'30" N, long. 118°24'20" W). Named on Kern Peak (1956) 15' quadrangle.

Leliter [KERN]: *locality,* 4.5 miles north-northwest of Inyokern along Southern Pacific Railroad (lat. 35°42'35" N, long. 117°49'45" W; at NW cor. sec. 6, T 26 S, R 39 E). Named on Inyokern (1943) 15' quadrangle. Searles Lake (1915) 1° quadrangle has the names "Muerto" and "Leliter P.O." at the place. Postal authorities established Leliter post office in 1910 and discontinued it in 1927 (Frickstad, p. 57).

Lemon: see **Lemoncove** [TULARE].

Lemoncove [TULARE]: *village,* 4.5 miles east-southeast of Woodlake (lat. 36°23' N, long. 119°01'30" W; around SW cor. sec. 2, T 18 S, R 27 E); the village is 2 miles south-southwest of Limekiln Hill. Named on Woodlake

(1952) 7.5' quadrangle. Called Lemon Cove on Lemon Cove (1928) 7.5' quadrangle, and called Lemon on Mendenhall's (1908) map. J.W.C. Pogue founded the village on his ranch and named it in 1870 (Mitchell, A.R., p. 68). California Mining Bureau's (1909a) map shows a place called Lime Kiln located 2 miles east of Lemoncove along a rail line. Postal authorities established Lime Kiln post office in 1879, moved it 1.25 miles southwest in 1890, and changed the name to Lemoncove in 1898; the name "Lime Kiln" was for a kiln used to produce lime from limestone at the place (Salley, p. 122).

Lemoore [KINGS]: *town,* 7.5 miles west-southwest of Hanford (lat. 36°18'05" N, long. 119°47' W; in and near sec. 3, T 19 S, R 20 E). Named on Lemoore (1954) 7.5' quadrangle. Postal authorities established Lemoore post office in 1875 (Frickstad, p. 61), and the town incorporated in 1900. John Kurtz settled at the place in 1859; Dr. Lovern Lee Moore arrived in 1871 and called the community there Latache, but when Dr. Moore requested a post office, the post office name was coined from his name (Gudde, 1969, p. 176). Postal authorities established Watertown post office 10 miles west of Lemoore in 1896 and discontinued it in 1900; they established Cloud post office 35 miles southwest of Lemoore (SE quarter sec. 26, T 23 S, R 19 E) in 1913 and discontinued it in 1921 (Salley, p. 46, 235).

Lempon [TULARE]: *locality,* 8.5 miles north-northwest of Fountain Springs along Atchison, Topeka and Santa Fe Railroad (lat. 35°59'55" N, long. 118°59'35" W; sec. 19, T 22 S, R 28 E). Named on White River (1936) 15' quadrangle. The name was coined in 1917 from letters in the words "lemon" and "pomegranate" (Gudde, 1949, p. 186; Gudde used the form "Lempom" for the name).

Leonard: see **Camp Leonard**, under **Weldon** [KERN].

Leonards [KERN]: *locality,* 5 miles southwest of Wasco (lat. 35°33'05" N, long. 119°24'10" W; at E line sec. 29, T 27 S, R 24 E). Named on Leonards (1930) 7.5' quadrangle.

Leppy Spring [KERN]: *spring,* 5 miles east of Caliente (lat. 35°16'35" N, long. 118°32'25" W; sec. 33, T 30 S, R 32 E). Named on Oiler Peak (1972) 7.5' quadrangle.

Lerdo [KERN]: *locality,* 12 miles northwest of Bakersfield along Southern Pacific Railroad (lat. 35°29'25" N, long. 119°09'05" W; at W line sec. 14, T 28 S, R 26 E). Named on Rosedale (1954) 7.5' quadrangle. Postal authorities established Lerdo post office in 1890 and discontinued it in 1894 (Frickstad, p. 57).

Lerona [FRESNO]: *locality,* 6.5 miles west-northwest of Shaver Lake Heights (present town of Shaver Lake) (lat. 37°07'45" N, long. 119°25'50" W; sec. 23, T 9 S, R 23 E). Named on Shaver Lake (1953) 15' quadrangle.

Leroy: see **Coalinga** [FRESNO].

Letcher [FRESNO]: *locality,* 12 miles east-northeast of Clovis (lat. 36°54'30" N, long. 119°31' W; sec. 12, T 12 S, R 22 E). Named on Clovis (1946) 15' quadrangle. Postal authorities established Letcher post office in 1886 and discontinued it in 1915; the name commemorates F.F. Letcher, who was a county supervisor (Salley, p. 121).

Lethent [KINGS]: *locality,* 6 miles west of Lemoore along Southern Pacific Railroad (lat. 36°17'10" N, long. 119°53' W; near SW cor. sec. 11, T 19 S, R 19 E). Named on Lethent (1926) 7.5' quadrangle.

Leuhman Ridge [KERN]: *ridge,* northeast-trending, 3 miles long, 4.5 miles south-southwest of Boron (lat. 34°56'30" N, long. 117° 41'20" W). Named on Leuhman Ridge (1973) 7.5' quadrangle. Called Lauhman Ridge on Kramer (1956) 15' quadrangle.

Levee: see **Levee Spur** [KERN].

Levee Spur [KERN]: *locality,* nearly 3 miles southwest of Millux along Sunset Railroad (lat. 35°09'15" N, long. 119°14'05" W; near SE cor. sec. 12, T 32 S, R 25 E). Named on Millux (1954) 7.5' quadrangle. Millux (1933) 7.5' quadrangle shows a place called Levee located 1.5 miles farther north along the railroad.

Levis [KERN]: *locality,* 9 miles west-southwest of Tranquillity (lat. 36°37'25" N, long. 120°24'20" W; near E line sec. 14, T 15 S, R 14 E). Named on Levis (1956) 7.5' quadrangle.

Lewis: see **Sam Lewis Camp** [TULARE].

Lewis Creek [FRESNO]:

(1) *stream,* flows 2.5 miles to Holland Creek 3 miles west-southwest of Piedra (lat. 36°48' N, long. 119°26'05" W; sec. 14, T 13 S, R 23 E). Named on Piedra (1965) 7.5' quadrangle.

(2) *stream,* flows 6.5 miles to South Fork Kings River 14 miles southwest of Marion Peak (lat. 36°48'05" N, long. 118°41'45" W); the stream heads at Lewis Lake. Named on Marion Peak (1953) 15' quadrangle. The name commemorates brothers Frank M Lewis and Jeff Lewis, pioneer prospectors and stockmen of the region (Hanna, p. 171). East Fork enters from the northeast 3.5 miles upstream from the mouth of the main stream; it is 3 miles long and is named on Marion Peak (1953) 15' quadrangle.

Lewis Creek [TULARE]: *stream,* flows 9.5 miles to lowlands 8 miles north of Porterville (lat. 36°11'05" N, long. 119°00' W; sec. 13, T 20 S, R 27 E). Named on Cairns Corner (1927), Frazier Valley (1957), Lindsay (1951), and Springville (1957) 7.5' quadrangles. The name commemorates either Frank Lewis or Jeff Lewis (Mitchell, A.R., p. 78).

Lewis Hill [TULARE]: *peak,* 2.5 miles north of Porterville (lat. 36° 06'20" N, long. 119°00'40" W). Altitude 1028 feet. Named on Porterville (1951) 7.5' quadrangle.

Lewis Lake [FRESNO]: *lake,* 600 feet long, 10 miles west-southwest of Marion Peak (lat. 36°52'50" N, long. 118°40'35" W); the lake is at the head of Lewis Creek (2). Named on Marion Peak (1953) 15' quadrangle.

Lewis Stringer [TULARE]: *stream,* flows 3.25 miles to South Fork Kern River 8 miles northwest of Olancha Peak in Templeton Meadows (lat. 36°20'05" N, long. 118°13'55" W; sec. 30, T 18 S, R 35 E). Named on Kern Peak (1956) and Olancha (1956) 15' quadrangles.

Liberty [TULARE]: *settlement,* 4.25 miles south-southwest of Visalia (lat. 36°16'15" N, long. 119°18'50" W; near SE cor. sec. 13, T 19 S, R 24 E). Named on Visalia (1949) 15' quadrangle.

Liberty: see **Tonyville** [TULARE].

Liberty Settlement: see **Riverdale** [FRESNO].

Liebel Peak [KERN]: *peak,* 7.5 miles southeast of Bodfish (lat. 35° 30'25" N, long. 118°23'50" W; near E line sec. 11, T 28 S, R 33 E). Altitude 3085 feet. Named on Lake Isabella South (1972) 7.5' quadrangle. The name, given in the 1930's, commemorates Michael Otto Liebel, who came to the region in 1876 and settled near the peak (Gudde, 1949, p. 187).

Liebre Twins [KERN]: *peak,* 24 miles west-northwest of Rosamond (lat. 34°57'20" N, long. 118°34'20" W; near SW cor. sec. 15, T 10 N, R 16 W). Altitude 6413 feet. Named on Liebre Twins (1965) 7.5' quadrangle.

Lieva Springs [KERN]: *springs,* 9.5 miles east of Tehachapi (lat. 35°07'20" N, long. 118°16'55" W; near N line sec. 25, T 32 S, R 34 E). Named on Monolith (1966) 7.5' quadrangle.

Lightner Peak [KERN]: *peak,* 3.5 miles south-southwest of Miracle Hot Springs (lat. 35°31'45" N, long. 118°33'45" W); the peak is 2 miles north of Lightners Flat. Altitude 6430 feet. Named on Miracle Hot Springs (1972) 7.5' quadrangle.

Lightners Flat [KERN]: *area,* 5.25 miles south-southwest of Miracle Hot Springs (lat. 35°30'05" N, long. 118°33'35" W; at S line sec 8, T 28 S, R 32 E); the place is 2 miles south of Lightner Peak. Named on Miracle Hot Springs (1972) 7.5' quadrangle.

Lightning Creek [FRESNO]: *stream,* flows 4 miles to South Fork Kings River 16 miles southwest of Marion Peak (lat. 36°48'10" N, long. 118°44' W). Named on Marion Peak (1953) 15' quadrangle.

Light Well: see **Alamo Solo Spring** [KERN].

Likely Mill: see **Old Likely Mill** [KERN].

Lillis: see **Laton** [FRESNO].

Lilly Canyon [KERN]: *canyon,* drained by a stream that flows nearly 3 miles to Kern River 1.25 miles west of Miracle Hot Springs (lat. 35°34'40" N, long. 118°33'25" W). Named on Miracle Hot Springs (1972) 7.5' quadrangle.

Lime Dyke [KERN]: *relief feature,* 4.25 miles east-southeast of Wofford Heights along Isabella Lake (lat. 35°40'15" N, long. 118° 23'30" W; sec. 13, T 26 S, R 33 E). Named on Lake Isabella North (1972) 7.5' quadrangle.

Lime Kiln: see **Lemoncove** [TULARE].

Limekiln Creek: see **Dry Creek** [TULARE] (1)

Limekiln Hill [TULARE]: *hill,* 5.25 miles east of Woodlake (lat. 36° 24'50" N, long. 119°00'15" W; mainly in sec. 36, T 17 S, R 27 E). Altitude 986 feet. Named on Woodlake (1952) 7.5' quadrangle.

Lime Point [KERN]: *promontory,* 5 miles southeast of Wofford Heights (lat. 35°39'15" N, long. 118°23'30" W; sec. 24, T 26 S, R 33 E). Named on Lake Isabella North (1972) 7.5' quadrangle.

Limestone Cliff Campground [TULARE]: *locality,* 2.5 miles north-northeast of Fairview along Kern River (lat. 35°57'45" N, long. 118°28'45" W). Named on Kernville (1956) 15' quadrangle.

Lind: see **Jenny Lind Cañon**, under **Big Arroyo** [TULARE]; **Jenny Lind Canyon** [KERN].

Lindcove [TULARE]: *village,* 6 miles northeast of Exeter (lat. 36°21'30" N, long. 119°03'45" W; near E line sec. 17, T 18 S, R 27 E). Named on Rocky Hill (1951) 7.5' quadrangle. Rocky Hill (1927) 7.5' quadrangle shows a place called Lind Cove located along Visalia Electric Railroad 0.5 mile south of present Lindcove.

Lindsay [TULARE]: *town,* 10.5 miles north-northwest of Porterville (lat. 36°12'20" N, long. 119°05'20" W; in and near sec 7, T 20 S, R 27 E). Named on Lindsay (1951) 7.5' quadrangle. Postal authorities established Lindsay post office in 1889 (Frickstad, p. 212), and the town incorporated in 1910. Arthur J. Hutchinson, an owner of Lindsay Land Company, gave his wife's maiden name to the town in 1888 (Mitchell, A.R., p. 68).

Lindsay Peak [TULARE]: *peak,* 3 miles north-northeast of Lindsay (lat. 36°14'40" N, long. 119°03'35" W; sec. 28, T 19 S, R 27 E). Altitude 1434 feet. Named on Lindsay (1951) 7.5' quadrangle.

Line Creek [FRESNO]: *stream,* flows 4.25 miles to Huntington Lake (1) nearly 4 miles south of Kaiser Peak (lat. 37°14'25" N, long. 119°12'30" W; sec. 14, T 8 S, R 25 E). Named on Huntington Lake (1953) and Kaiser Peak (1953) 15' quadrangles.

Line Creek Lake [FRESNO]: *lake,* 400 feet long, 0.5 mile west-southwest of Kaiser Peak (lat. 37°17'35" N, long. 119°11'30" W; sec. 25, T 7 S, R 25 E); the lake is near the head of Line Creek. Named on Kaiser Peak (1953)

15' quadrangle.

Linnell Post Office [TULARE]: *locality,* 5 miles west-northwest of Exeter (lat. 36°18'40" N, long. 119°13'25" W; near NW cor. sec. 1, T 19 S, R 25 E). Named on Exeter (1952) 15' quadrangle. Postal authorities established Linnell post office in 1942 (Frickstad, p. 212).

Linn's Valley: see **Glennville** [KERN]; **Linns Valley** [KERN-TULARE].

Linns Valley [KERN-TULARE]: *valley,* on Kern-Tulare County line, mainly in Kern County, 6 miles long, along Poso Creek above a point 1.5 miles south-southwest of Glennville (lat. 35°42'30" N, long. 118°43' W). Named on California Hot Springs (1958) 15' and Glennville (1972) 7.5' quadrangles. Called Lynn Valley on Tobias Peak (1943) 30' quadrangle, but United States Board on Geographic Names (1960a, p. 8) rejected the names "Lynn Valley" and "Lynns Valley" for the feature. Whitney (p. 221) mentioned Linn's Valley. The name commemorates W.P. Linn, who settled at the place in the 1850's (Barker, p. 2-3).

Lion Canyon [TULARE]: *canyon,* drained by a stream that flows 1 mile to Cedar Creek (1) 6.25 miles east-southeast of Auckland (lat. 36°32'30" N, long. 119°00'25" W; sec. 14, T 16 S, R 27 E). Named on Giant Forest (1956) 15' quadrangle, and on Auckland (1966) 7.5' quadrangle.

Lion Creek [TULARE]:

(1) *stream,* flows 4 miles to Little Kern River 14 miles south-southeast of Mineral King (lat. 36°15'30" N, long. 118°30'55" W; sec. 21, T 19 S, R 32 E); the stream goes through Lion Meadows (1). Named on Kern Peak (1956) and Mineral King (1956) 15' quadrangles.

(2) *stream,* flows 2 miles to Beach Creek 9 miles south-southeast of Hockett Peak (lat. 36°06' N, long. 118°20' W; sec. 17, T 21 S, R 34 E). Named on Hockett Peak (1956) 15' quadrangle.

Lion Flat [KERN]: *area,* 5.25 miles east-southeast of Caliente (lat. 35°15'40" N, long. 118°32'25" W; sec. 4, T 31 S, R 32 E). Named on Oiler Peak (1972) 7.5' quadrangle.

Lion Lake [TULARE]: *lake,* 2400 feet long, 0.5 mile west-southwest of Triple Divide Peak (lat. 36°35'20" N, long. 118°32'20" W); the lake is less than 0.5 mile north-northeast of Lion Rock. Named on Triple Divide Peak (1956) 15' quadrangle.

Lion Meadows [TULARE]:

(1) *area,* 12.5 miles west-southwest of Kern Peak (lat. 36°16' N, long. 118°30' W); the place is along Lion Creek (1). Named on Kern Peak (1956) and Mineral King (1956) 15' quadrangles.

(2) *area,* 7 miles south-southeast of Hockett Peak (lat. 36°07'40" N, long. 118°20'05" W; near W line sec. 5, T 21 S, R 34 E). Named on Hockett Peak (1956) 15' quadrangle.

Lion Ridge [TULARE]: *ridge,* southwest- to west-trending, 4 miles long, 4 miles east-northeast of California Hot Springs (lat. 35° 54' N, long. 118°36' W). Named on California Hot Springs (1958) 15' quadrangle.

Lion Rock [TULARE]: *peak,* 1 mile southwest of Triple Divide Peak (lat. 36°35' N, long. 118°32'30" W). Named on Triple Divide Peak (1956) 15' quadrangle. The name, given in 1896, is for the fancied resemblance of the feature to the front of a couchant lion (Browning, p. 127).

Lion Spring [KERN]: *spring,* 5 miles east-southeast of Caliente (lat. 35°16' N, long. 118°32'30" W; near N line sec 4, T 31 S, R 32 E); the spring is less than 0.5 mile north of Lion Flat. Named on Oiler Peak (1972) 7.5' quadrangle.

Lippincott Mountain [TULARE]: *peak,* 5.25 miles south-southwest of Triple Divide Peak on Great Western Divide (lat. 36°31'15" N, long. 118°33'45" W). Altitude 12,260 feet. Named on Triple Divide Peak (1956) 15' quadrangle. The name is for Joseph Barlow Lippincott, hydrographer for United States Geological Survey and the Reclamation Service (Hanna, p. 172), who allegedly was involved in the acquisition of Owens Valley water by the City of Los Angeles (Kahrl, p. 124-127).

Lisko [TULARE]: *locality,* 2 miles north-northwest of Porterville along Southern Pacific Railroad (lat. 36°05'50" N, long. 119°02'10" W; sec. 15, T 21 S, R 27 E). Named on Porterville (1951) 7.5' quadrangle.

List [TULARE]: *locality,* 1.5 miles south-southeast of Exeter along Atchison, Topeka and Santa Fe Railroad (lat. 36°16'35" N, long. 119°07'35" W; sec. 14, T 19 S, R 26 E). Named on Exeter (1952) 15' quadrangle.

Lithmore: see **Zante** [TULARE].

Little Avenal Creek [FRESNO-KINGS]: *stream,* heads in Fresno County and flows 15 miles to Avenal Creek 10 miles south of Avenal in Kings County (lat. 35°51'35" N, long. 120°08'45" W; near NW cor. sec. 9, T 24 S, R 17 E). Named on Tent Hills (1942) 7.5' quadrangle.

Little Avenal Creek: see **Avenal Creek** [KINGS]; **Lovel Canyon** [KINGS].

Little Baldy [TULARE]: *peak,* 4.5 miles northeast of Yucca Mountain (lat. 36°36'50" N, long. 118°48'15" W; near S line sec. 14, T 15 S, R 29 E); the peak is 6 miles southeast of Big Baldy. Altitude 8044 feet. Named on Giant Forest (1956) 15' quadrangle.

Little Baldy Saddle [TULARE]: *pass,* 4.5 miles northeast of Yucca Mountain (lat. 36°37'10" N, long. 118°48'30" W; at W line sec. 14, T 15 S, R 29 E); the pass is less than 0.5 mile northwest of Little Baldy. Named on Giant Forest (1956) 15' quadrangle.

Little Bear Canyon [FRESNO]: *canyon,* drained by a stream that flows nearly 3 miles to Bear Canyon 7.25 miles north-northeast of Charley Mountain (lat. 36°14'30" N, long. 120°37'45" W; sec. 36, T 19 S, R 12 E). Named on Priest Valley (1969) 7.5' quadrangle.

Little Bear Lake [FRESNO]: *lake,* 1400 feet long, 4 miles south-southwest of Mount Abbot (lat. 37°19'50" N, long. 118°48'30" W); the lake is 600 feet downstream from Big Bear Lake. Named on Mount Abbot (1953) 15' quadrangle.

Little Bearpaw Meadow [TULARE]: *area,* 6.25 miles west-southwest of Triple Divide Peak (lat. 36°33'15" N, long. 118°37'50" W); the place is 1 mile south-southwest of Bearpaw Meadow. Named on Triple Divide Peak (1956) 15' quadrangle. United States Board on Geographic Names (1938, p. 31) rejected the name "Wet Meadow" for the feature.

Little Blue Dome [TULARE]: *peak,* 7.5 miles west-southwest of Triple Divide Peak (lat. 36°33'50" N, long. 118°39'25" W). Altitude 7315 feet. Named on Triple Divide Peak (1956) 15' quadrangle.

Little Boulder Creek [FRESNO]: *stream,* flows 3.25 miles to Boulder Creek (1) 6.5 miles east-southeast of Hume (lat. 36°45'55" N, long. 118°47'55" W). Named on Tehipite Dome (1952) 15' quadrangle.

Little Brush Creek: see **Cannell Creek** [KERN-TULARE].

Little Campbell [TULARE]: *hill,* 8 miles east-northeast of Porterville (lat. 36°06'05" N, long. 118°52'35" W; sec. 18, T 21 S, R 29 E); the feature is northwest across Tule River from Big Campbell. Named on Success Dam (1956) 7.5' quadrangle.

Little Cannell Meadow [TULARE]: *area,* 13 miles southeast of Fairview (lat. 35°47'30" N, long. 118°19'50" W; sec. 32, T 24 S, R 34 E); the place is 3 miles southeast of Cannell Meadow. Named on Kernville (1956) 15' quadrangle.

Little Claire Lake [TULARE]: *lake,* 1100 feet long, 4.5 miles east-southeast of Mineral King (lat. 36°25'20" N, long. 118°31'15" W). Named on Mineral King (1956) 15' quadrangle. Ralph Hopping and his companions named the lake in 1900 for Hopping's little daughter (United States Board on Geographic Names, 1933a, p. 464).

Little Creek [KERN]:

(1) *stream,* flows 12 miles to the canyon of Poso Creek 6.5 miles east-southeast of Famoso (lat. 35°33'20" N, long. 119°06'25" W; sec. 30, T 27 S, R 27 E). Named on Knob Hill (1965), North of Oildale (1954), and Sand Canyon (1965) 7.5' quadrangles.

(2) *stream,* flows 1.5 miles to Kern River nearly 3 miles west of Miracle Hot Springs (lat. 35°34'05" N, long. 118°34'55" W). Named on Miracle Hot Springs (1972) 7.5' quadrangle.

Little Deep Lake: see **Fingerbowl Lake** [FRESNO].

Little Deer Creek [TULARE]: *stream,* flows 2 miles to Marble Fork 4.5 miles east of Yucca Mountain (lat. 36°34'30" N, long. 118°47'05" W; sec. 36, T 15 S, R 29 E). Named on Giant Forest (1956) 15' quadrangle. United States Board on Geographic Names (1938, p. 31) rejected the name "Deer Creek" for the feature.

Little Dixie [KERN]: *locality,* 17 miles north-northeast of Cross Mountain (lat. 35°29'50" N, long. 118°00'05" W; sec. 16, T 28 S, R 37 E); the place is along Little Dixie Wash. Named on Mojave (1915) 30' quadrangle.

Little Dixie Wash [KERN]: *stream,* flows for 27 miles from the mouth of Bird Spring Canyon before ending 5.5 miles north-northeast of Inyokern (lat. 35°43' N, long. 117°45'30" W; near W line sec. 35, T 25 S, R 39 E). Named on Dove Spring (1972), Freeman Junction (1972), Inyokern (1972), Inyokern SE (1972), and Saltdale NW (1967) 7.5' quadrangles. On Mojave (1915) 30' quadrangle, the name "Little Dixie Wash" extends up present Bird Spring Canyon.

Little Doris Lake [FRESNO]: *lake,* 400 feet long, nearly 4 miles east-northeast of Dinkey Dome (lat. 37°07'40" N, long. 119°03'50" W; sec. 19, T 9 S, R 27 E). Named on Huntington Lake (1953) 15' quadrangle.

Little Dry Creek [FRESNO]:

(1) *stream,* flows 19 miles to flatlands along San Joaquin River 8 miles north-northwest of Clovis (lat. 36°56'05" N, long. 119°44'45" W; near W line sec. 31, T 11 S, R 21 E). Named on Shaver Lake (1953) 15' quadrangle, and on Academy (1964), Friant (1964), and Humphreys Station (1965) 7.5' quadrangles. Called Dry Creek on Kaiser (1904) 30' quadrangle. North Fork enters from the north 9 miles upstream from the place that the creek reaches flatlands along San Joaquin River; it is 7.5 miles long and is named on Academy (1964) and Millerton Lake East (1965) 7.5' quadrangles.

(2) *stream,* flows 6 miles to Watts Creek nearly 2 miles northwest of Trimmer (lat. 36°55'25" N, long. 119°19'10" W; near S line sec. 35, T 11 S, R 24 E). Named on Trimmer (1965) 7.5' quadrangle.

Little Dry Meadow [KERN]: *area,* 7 miles southwest of Weldon (lat. 35°35' N, long. 118°21'45" W); the place is 2 miles northwest of Dry Meadows. Named on Woolstalf Creek (1972) 7.5' quadrangle.

Little Dry Meadow [TULARE]: *area,* 2.25 miles west-southwest of Monache Mountain (lat. 36°11'40" N, long. 118°14'05" W; near SW cor. sec. 7, T 20 S, R 35 E); the place is 1.25 miles south-southeast of Big Dry Meadows. Named on Monache Mountain (1956) 15' quadrangle.

Littlefield Mill [FRESNO]: *locality,* 17 miles south-southeast of Kaiser Peak (lat. 37°04'50" N, long. 119°20' W; near NE cor. sec. 10, T 10 S, R 24 E). Named on Kaiser (1904) 30' quadrangle.

Little Five Lakes [TULARE]: *lakes,* 6.5 miles south of Triple Divide Peak (lat. 36°30' N, long. 118°32'45" W); the lakes are northwest of Big Five Lakes. Named on Mineral King (1956) and Triple Divide Peak (1956) 15' quadrangles.

Little Grinnell Lake [FRESNO]: *lake,* 700 feet long, 7.5 miles northwest of Mount Abbot (lat. 37°28'30" N, long. 118°51'40" W); the lake is 1300 feet west-northwest of Grinnell Lake. Named on Mount Abbot (1953) 15' quadrangle.

Little Hart Canyon [KERN]: *canyon,* drained by a stream that flows 1.5 miles to Hart Canyon 8 miles north of Emerald Mountain (lat. 35°22'10" N, long. 118°18'50" W). Named on Claraville (1972) and Emerald Mountain (1972) 7.5' quadrangles.

Little Horse Meadows [TULARE]: *area,* 7 miles southeast of Hockett Peak (lat. 36°08'45" N, long. 118°18'15" W; sec. 33, T 20 S, R 34 E). Named on Hockett Peak (1956) 15' quadrangle.

Little Jawbone Canyon [KERN]: *canyon,* drained by a stream that flows 4.5 miles to Jawbone Canyon nearly 1.5 miles northwest of Cross Mountain (lat. 35°17'35" N, long. 118°09'10" W; sec. 30, T 30 S, R 36 E). Named on Cross Mountain (1972) 7.5' quadrangle.

Little Jo Lake [FRESNO]: *lake,* 1150 feet long, 1.25 miles north-northeast of Blackcap Mountain (lat. 37°05'15" N, long. 118° 47' W). Named on Blackcap Mountain (1953) 15' quadrangle.

Little Kern: see **Little Kern River** [TULARE].

Little Kern Lake [TULARE]: *lake,* 1100 feet long, 6.5 miles west of Kern Peak (lat. 36°18'25" N, long. 118°24'15" W); the lake is less than 0.5 mile south of Kern Lake. Named on Kern Peak (1956) 15' quadrangle. Called Little Lake on Olancha (1907) 30' quadrangle, but United States Board on Geographic Names (1938, p. 31) rejected this name for the feature. Called Royal Allen L. on Olmsted's (1900) map.

Little Kern Lake Creek [TULARE]: *stream,* flows 3 miles to Kern River 6.5 miles west of Kern Peak near Little Kern Lake (lat. 36° 18'10" N, long. 118°24'15" W). Named on Kern Peak (1956) 15' quadrangle.

Little Kern River [TULARE]: *stream,* flows 23 miles to Kern River 7 miles south-southwest of Hockett Peak (lat. 36°08' N, long. 118° 26'10" W). Named on Camp Nelson (1956), Hockett Peak (1956), and Mineral King (1956) 15' quadrangles. Called Little Kern on Olmsted's (1900) map.

Little Lake [FRESNO]: *lake,* 1000 feet long, 5.5 miles east-northeast of Dinkey Dome (lat. 37°09'30" N, long. 119°02'35" W; sec. 8, T 9 S, R 27 E). Named on Huntington Lake (1953) 15' quadrangle.

Little Lake: see **Little Kern Lake** [TULARE]; **Little Lakes** [TULARE].

Little Lakes [TULARE]: *lakes,* two, largest 550 feet long, 10.5 miles west-northwest of Triple Divide Peak (lat. 36°38'50" N, long, 118° 42'15" W). Named on Triple Divide Peak (1956) 15' quadrangle. Called Little Lake on Tehipite (1903) 30' quadrangle, but United States Board on Geographic Names (1989b, p. 2) rejected this form of the name.

Little Last Chance Canyon [KERN]: *canyon,* drained by a stream that flows less than 1 mile to Caliente Creek nearly 3 miles west of Loraine (lat. 35°18'20" N, long. 118°29'05" W; near W line sec. 19, T 30 S, R 33 E); the canyon is less than 1 mile west of Big Last Chance Canyon. Named on Loraine (1972) 7.5' quadrangle.

Little Matterhorn: see **Mineral Peak** [TULARE].

Little Moccasin Lake [FRESNO]: *lake,* 400 feet long, 8 miles south of Mount Abbot (lat. 37°16'25" N, long. 118°48'05" W); the lake is 400 feet southwest of Big Moccasin Lake. Named on Mount Abbot (1953) 15' quadrangle.

Little Oak Canyon [KERN]: *canyon,* drained by a stream that flows 2.5 miles to lowlands 2.25 miles east-southeast of Liebre Twins (lat. 34°56'20" N, long. 118°32'15" W). Named on Liebre Twins (1965) 7.5' quadrangle. Johnson's (1911) map has the name "Little Oak Creek" for the stream in the canyon.

Little Oak Creek: see **Little Oak Canyon** [KERN].

Little Oak Flat [FRESNO]: *area,* nearly 2 miles northeast of Coalinga Mineral Springs (lat. 36°09'55" N, long. 120°32'10" W; sec. 23, 26, T 20 S, R 13 E). Named on Sherman Peak (1969) 7.5' quadrangle. Called Oak Flat on Priest Valley (1944) 15' quadrangle.

Little Oak Flat [KERN]: *area,* 3.5 miles northeast of Caliente (lat. 35°19'50" N, long. 118°35'05" W; sec. 7, T 30 S, R 32 E). Named on Oiler Peak (1972) 7.5' quadrangle.

Little Oak Flat [TULARE]: *area,* 7 miles south of Kaweah (lat. 36° 22'10" N, long. 118°55'40" W; on N line sec. 15, T 18 S, R 28 E); the place is north of Oak Flat (1). Named on Kaweah (1957) 15' quadrangle.

Little Oak Spring [FRESNO]: *spring,* 3.5 miles east-northeast of Joaquin Rocks in Ragged Valley (lat. 36°20'05" N, long. 120°23'15" W; sec. 30, T 18 S, R 15 E). Named on Joaquin Rocks (1969) 7.5' quadrangle.

Little Panoche Creek [FRESNO]: *stream,* heads in San Benito County and flows 13 miles to lowlands 18 miles west-southwest of Firebaugh (lat. 36°47'30" N, long. 120°45'40" W; sec. 22, T 13 S, R 11 E). Named on Hammond Ranch (1956), Laguna Seca Ranch (1956), and Mercey Hot Springs (1969) 7.5' quadrangles. United States Board on Geographic Names (1933a, p. 466) rejected the name "Panochita Creek" for the feature. South Fork enters from the south 11 miles above the place that the main stream reaches lowlands; it heads in San Benito County, is 5 miles long, and is named on Mercey Hot Springs (1969) 7.5' quadrangle.

Little Panoche Valley [FRESNO]: *valley,* along Little Panoche Creek and South Fork Little Panoche Creek; partly in Merced and San Benito Counties (lat. 36°43'30" N, long. 120°52' W). Named on Cerro Colorado (1969), Laguna Seca Ranch (1956), Mercey Hot Springs (1969), and Ortigalita Peak (1969) 7.5' quadrangles. United States Board on Geographic Names (1933a, p. 466) rejected the name "Panochita Valley" for the feature.

Little Pete Meadow [FRESNO]: *area,* 6.5 miles east of Mount Goddard along Middle Fork Kings River (lat. 37°06'10" N, long. 118° 35'50" W); the place is 0.5 mile downstream from Big Pete Meadow. Named on Mount Goddard (1948) 15' quadrangle. According to Hanna (p. 120-121), the name probably commemorates Pierre "Little Pete" Giraud.

Little Posé Flat: see **Poso Flat** [KERN].

Little Poso Creek [KERN]: *stream,* flows 12 miles to Poso Creek 4.5 miles northwest of Democrat Hot Springs (lat. 35°34'20" N, long. 118°43'45" W; near SW cor. sec. 14, T 27 S, R 30 E). Named on Alta Sierra (1972), Democrat Hot Springs (1972), and Glennville (1972) 7.5' quadrangles.

Little Rancheria Creek [FRESNO]: *stream,* flows 5 miles to Rancheria Creek (3) 12 miles north-northwest of Hume (lat. 36°57'20" N, long. 118°57'30" W). Named on Tehipite Dome (1952) 15' quadrangle. Called North Fork on Tehipite (1903) 30' quadrangle.

Little Sand Meadow [TULARE]: *area,* 9.5 miles southwest of Triple Divide Peak (lat. 36°30'15" N, long. 118°39'25" W). Named on Triple Divide Peak (1956) 15' quadrangle. United States Board on Geographic Names (1938, p. 32) rejected the name "Sand Meadow" for the place.

Little Sandy Creek [FRESNO]: *stream,* flows 4.5 miles to Big Sandy Creek nearly 1 mile east-northeast of Prather (lat. 37°02'30" N, long. 119°30'05" W; sec. 19, T 10 S, R 23 E). Named on Millerton Lake East (1965) 7.5' quadrangle.

Little Santa Maria Valley [KERN]: *valley,* center 5 miles west of McKittrick (lat. 35°18'35" N, long. 119°42'45" W). Named on Reward (1951) 7.5' quadrangle. Called Santa Maria Valley on McKittrick Summit (1959) and Olig (1943) 7.5' quadrangles. United States Board on Geographic Names (1970b, p. 2) listed the variant names "Santa Maria Valley" and "Santa Marie Valley" for the feature.

Little Signal Hills [KERN]: *area,* 3 miles northwest of Maricopa (lat. 35°05'35" N, long. 119°26'35" W). Named on Maricopa (1951) 7.5' quadrangle.

Little Spanish Lake [FRESNO]: *lake,* 600 feet long, 10 miles north of Hume (lat. 36°55'40" N, long. 118°54'25" W); the lake is 1750 feet west of Spanish Lake (1). Named on Tehipite Dome (1952) 15' quadrangle.

Little Sycamore Canyon [KERN]:

(1) *canyon,* drained by a stream that flows 6.25 miles to lowlands 3.5 miles southeast of Arvin (lat. 35°10' N, long. 118°47'20" W; near SE cor. sec. 6, T 32 S, R 30 E); the canyon opens into lowlands 3 miles southwest of the mouth of Sycamore Canyon (1). Named on Arvin (1955) and Bear Mountain (1966) 7.5' quadrangles.

(2) *canyon,* drained by a stream that flows 4 miles to lowlands 11 miles southwest of Liebre Twins (lat. 34°50'10" N, long. 118°41'50" W; near E line sec. 29, T 9 N, R 17 W); the canyon opens into lowlands nearly 1 mile west-southwest of the mouth of Big Sycamore Canyon. Named on La Liebre Ranch (1965) 7.5' quadrangle.

Little Tar Canyon [KINGS]: *canyon,* drained by a stream that flows 0.5 mile to Sunflower Valley 7.5 miles south of Avenal (lat. 35° 53'35" N, long. 120°07'05" W; sec. 27, T 23 S, R 17 E). Named on Kettleman Plain (1953) 7.5' quadrangle.

Little Tar Canyon: see **Sulphur Spring Canyon** [KINGS] (2).

Little Tehipite Valley [FRESNO]: *valley,* 10 miles northeast of Hume along Middle Fork Kings River (lat. 36°53'15" N, long. 118° 47'45" W); the place is 1.5 miles south-southwest of Tehipite Valley. Named on Tehipite Dome (1952) 15' quadrangle.

Little Tenant Spring [KERN]: *spring,* 2 miles north of Democrat Hot Springs (lat. 35°33'20" N, long. 118°40'05" W; near N line sec. 29, T 27 S, R 31 E); the spring is 0.5 mile southwest of Big Tenant Spring in a branch of Tenant Creek. Named on Democrat Hot Springs (1972) 7.5' quadrangle.

Little Trout Creek [TULARE]: *stream,* flows 4.5 miles to Trout Creek 12.5 miles east-northeast of Fairview (lat. 35°58'40" N, long. 118°17' W; near W line sec. 26, T 22 S, R 34 E). Named on Kernville (1956) 15' quadrangle.

Little Troy Meadow [TULARE]: *area,* 10.5 miles south-southwest of Monache Mountain along Mahogany Creek (lat. 36°03'35" N, long. 118°14'10" W; sec. 31, T 21 S, R 35 E); the place is 1 mile south of Troy Meadows. Named on Monache Mountain (1956) 15' quadrangle.

Little White Deer Creek: see **Mill Creek** [FRESNO-TULARE].

Little White Deer Valley: see **Mill Creek** [FRESNO-TULARE].

Little Whitney Meadow [TULARE]: *area,* 5.5 miles northwest of Kern Peak along Golden Trout Creek (lat. 36°22'20" N, long. 118° 20'45" W; on W line sec. 7, T 18 S, R 34 E); the place is 6 miles southwest of Big Whitney Meadow. Named on Kern Peak (1956) 15' quadrangle. Called Long Meadow on Olancha (1907) 30' quadrangle, but United States Board on

Geographic Names (1938, p. 32) rejected this name for the feature.
Little Yosemite Soda Spring: see **Kern Lake** [TULARE].
Live Oak Campground [KERN]: *locality,* 0.5 mile southwest of the center of Wofford Heights (lat. 35°42'10" N, long. 118°27'35" W; near N line sec. 5, T 26 S, R 33 E). Named on Lake Isabella North (1972) 7.5' quadrangle.
Live Oak Canyon [KERN]: *canyon,* drained by a stream that flows 2 miles to Cummings Valley 4 miles northwest of Cummings Mountain (lat. 35°04'50" N, long. 118°37'15" W; near N line sec. 6, T 11 N, R 16 W). Named on Cummings Mountain (1966) 7.5' quadrangle.
Liveoak Canyon [KERN]: *canyon,* drained by a stream that flows 6 miles to lowlands 2.5 miles east of Grapevine (lat. 34°56' N, long. 118°52'50" W). Named on Grapevine (1958), Lebec (1958), and Pastoria Creek (1958) 7.5' quadrangles. The stream in the canyon was called Arroyo de las Encinas in the early days (Latta, 1976, p. 205).
Liveoak Canyon [TULARE]: *canyon,* drained by a stream that flows 1.5 miles to Dry Creek (1) 5.5 miles northeast of Woodlake (lat. 36°27'55" N, long. 119°01'30" W; near W line sec. 11, T 17 S, R 27 E). Named on Woodlake (1952) 7.5' quadrangle. Called General Canyon on Lemon Cove (1928) 7.5' quadrangle.
Liveoak Canyon: see **Ragle Canyon** [TULARE].
Live Oak Gulch [TULARE]: *canyon,* drained by a stream that flows 2.5 miles to North Fork Kaweah River 3 miles west-northwest of Yucca Mountain (lat. 36°35'35" N, long. 118°54'45" W; near W line sec. 26, T 15 S, R 28 E). Named on Giant Forest (1956) 15' quadrangle.
Live Oak Pass [TULARE]: *pass,* 4.5 miles west of Yucca Mountain (lat. 36°34'15" N, long. 118°57'05" W; at S line sec. 32, T 15 S, R 28 E); the pass is near the head of Live Oak Gulch. Named on Giant Forest (1956) 15' quadrangle.
Live Oak Spring [FRESNO]: *spring,* 4.5 miles northwest of Coalinga Mineral Springs (lat. 36°11'40" N, long. 120°36'40" W; sec. 18, T 20 S, R 13 E). Named on Sherman Peak (1969) 7.5' quadrangle.
Livermore Mountain: see **Bear Mountain** [KERN].
Livsey Canyon: see **Canyon del Gato-Montes** [KERN].
L Lake [FRESNO]: *lake,* 2400 feet long, 3.25 miles west-northwest of Mount Humphreys (lat. 37°17'45" N, long. 118°43'15" W; sec. 31, T 7 S, R 30 E). Named on Mount Tom (1949) 15' quadrangle, where the outline of the lake on the map resembles a backward letter "L."
Lloyd: see **Lloyd Meadows** [TULARE].
Lloyd Meadows [TULARE]: *area,* 7.5 miles southwest of Hockett Peak (lat. 36°08'40" N, long. 118°28'40" W). Named on Hockett Peak (1956) 15' quadrangle. Olancha (1907) 30' quadrangle has the name "Llyd" at or near the place. According to Gudde (1949, p. 196), the name is for John W. Loyd, who ran sheep at the place in the 1870's. Tucker (p. 944) used the name "Lloyd Meadows Springs" for springs in the area.
Lloyd Meadows Creek [TULARE]: *stream,* flows 3.5 miles to Freeman Creek 8 miles southwest of Hockett Peak (lat. 36°08'15" N, long. 118°28'35" W); the stream goes through Lloyd Meadows. Named on Hockett Peak (1956) 15' quadrangle.
Lloyd Meadows Springs: see **Lloyd Meadows** [TULARE].
Lobe Lakes [FRESNO]: *lakes,* largest 1200 feet long, 12 miles north of Blackcap Mountain (lat. 37°14'35" N, long. 118°45'20" W). Named on Blackcap Mountain (1953) 15' quadrangle.
Locans [FRESNO]: *locality,* nearly 5 miles northeast of Malaga along Southern Pacific Railroad (lat. 36°43'20" N, long. 119°39'45" W; near SW cor. sec. 11, T 14 S, R 21 E). Named on Malaga (1964) 7.5' quadrangle. Called Logan on Malaga (1923) 7.5' quadrangle.
Locked Gate Gulch [KERN]: *canyon,* drained by a stream that flows 5.5 miles to Rag Gulch 13 miles east of Delano (lat. 35°45'40" N, long. 119°00'50" W; near N line sec. 13, T 25 S, R 27 E). Named on Sand Canyon (1965) 7.5' quadrangle.
Lockwood Creek [FRESNO]: *stream,* flows 3 miles to South Fork Kings River 4.25 miles northeast of Hume (lat. 36°50'10" N, long. 118°52'10" W). Named on Tehipite Dome (1952) 15' quadrangle.
Loco Bill Canyon [KERN]: *canyon,* 4.5 miles long, along Rancheria Creek (2) above a point 4.5 miles south of Piute Peak (lat. 35°23'10" N, long. 118°23'15" W; sec. 24, T 29 S, R 33 E). Named on Claraville (1972) and Piute Peak (1972) 7.5' quadrangles.
Lodge [FRESNO]: *locality,* 24 miles southwest of Kaiser Peak along Big Creek (2) (lat. 37°02'35" N, long. 119°29'45" W; sec. 19, T 10 S, R 23 E). Named on Kaiser (1904) 30' quadrangle. Postal authorities established Lodge post office in 1888, discontinued it in 1899, reestablished in it 1902, moved it 3 miles north in 1903, and discontinued it in 1904 (Salley, p. 124).
Lodgepole [TULARE]: *locality,* 11 miles west of Triple Divide Peak along Marble Fork (lat. 36°36'15" N, long. 118°43'20" W; sec. 21, T 15 S, R 30 E). Named on Triple Divide Peak (1956) 15' quadrangle.
Logan: see **Locans** [FRESNO].
Log Bridge Campground [TULARE]: *locality,* 11 miles west of Triple Divide Peak along Marble Fork (lat. 36°36'20" N, long. 118°43'15" W; sec. 21, T 15 S, R 30 E). Named on Triple Divide Peak (1956) 15' quadrangle.
Log Cabin Meadow [TULARE]: *area,* 3.5 miles northeast of Camp Nelson (lat. 36°10'20" N, long. 118°33'40" W; sec. 24, T 20 S, R 31 E). Named on Camp Nelson (1956) 15' quadrangle. United States Board on Geographic Names (1967a, p. 9) rejected the name "Junction Meadow" for the place.
Log Corral Meadow [TULARE]: *area,* 1.25 miles east-southeast of Wilsonia (lat. 36°43'45" N, long. 118°56' W; near S line sec. 4, T 14 S, R 28 E). Named on Giant Forest (1956) 15' quadrangle.
Logger Point [FRESNO]: *ridge,* west-trending, 0.5 mile long, 7 miles east-southeast of Dunlap (lat. 36°42' N, long. 119°00' W). Named on Giant Forest (1956) 15' quadrangle, and on Miramonte (1966) 7.5' quadrangle.
Loggy Meadows [TULARE]: *area,* 5 miles northeast of Camp Nelson along Fish Creek (1) (lat. 36°11'10" N, long. 118°32'10" W; sec. 17, T 20 S, R 32 E). Named on Camp Nelson (1956) 15' quadrangle. United States Board on Geographic Names (1967a, p. 9) rejected the singular form "Loggy Meadow" for the name.
Log Meadow [TULARE]: *area,* 12 miles west-southwest of Triple Divide Peak (lat. 36°33'30" N, long. 118°44'30" W; sec. 5, T 16 S, R 30 E). Named on Triple Divide Peak (1956) 15' quadrangle. Tharps Log, a log made into a dwelling, is in the meadow. United States Board on Geographic Names (1933a, p. 469) rejected the names "Tharpe Meadow," "Tharpe's Log Meadow," and "Wolverton Meadow" for the place. The name "Wolverton" is from James Wolverton, the hunter who named General Sherman tree (Hanna, p. 357).
Lois [TULARE]: *locality,* 3.5 miles south of Porterville along Southern Pacific Railroad (lat. 36°01'05" N, long. 119°01'35" W; sec. 14, T 22 S, R 27 E). Named on Porterville (1951) 7.5' quadrangle.
Lokern [KERN]: *locality,* 8 miles north-northeast of McKittrick along Southern Pacific Railroad (lat. 35°24' N, long. 119°32'30" W; near S line sec. 18, T 29 S, R 23 E). Named on Lokern (1954) 7.5' quadrangle.
Loma [TULARE]: *locality,* 5 miles south of Visalia along Atchison, Topeka and Santa Fe Railroad (lat. 36°15'25" N, long. 119°17'10" W; at S line sec. 20, T 19 S, R 25 E). Named on Visalia (1949) 7.5' quadrangle.
Loma Atravesada [FRESNO]: *ridge,* west- to northwest-trending, 2 miles long, 18 miles north-northwest of Coalinga (lat. 36°21'20" N, long. 120°31'45" W). Named on Santa Rita Peak (1969) 7.5' quadrangle. The peak called Three Sisters (2) is on the ridge, but United States Board on Geographic Names (1933a, p. 470) rejected the name "Three Sisters" for the ridge itself.
Lomar Meadow [KERN]: *area,* near Claraville (lat. 35°26'40" N, long. 118°19'35" W; near E line sec. 4, T 29 S, R 34 E). Named on Claraville (1972) 7.5' quadrangle.
London [TULARE]: *town,* 2.5 miles east-northeast of Traver (lat. 36°28'30" N, long. 119°26'30" W; sec. 2, T 17 S, R 23 E). Named on Traver (1949, photorevised 1969) 7.5' quadrangle. Called New London on Visalia (1949) 15' quadrangle.
Lone Doe Lake [FRESNO]: *lake,* 550 feet long, 2 miles north-northwest of Blackcap Mountain (lat. 37°06' N, long. 118°48' W). Named on Blackcap Mountain (1953) 15' quadrangle.
Lone Oak Mountain [TULARE]: *peak,* 3 miles north of Woodlake (lat. 36°27'25" N, long. 119°06'05" W; near N line sec. 13, T 17 S, R 26 E). Altitude 1107 feet. Named on Woodlake (1952) 7.5' quadrangle.
Lone Oak Slough [KINGS]: *stream,* heads near Hanford and flows south 7.5 miles to a point 3 miles west of Guernsey (lat. 36°12'55" N, long. 119°41'45" W). Named on Guernsey (1929) and Hanford (1926) 7.5' quadrangles. Guernsey (1954) and Hanford (1954) 7.5' quadrangles have the name on a dry watercourse.
Lone Pine: see **McFarland** [KERN].
Lone Pine Canyon [FRESNO]: *canyon,* 1 mile long, drained by a stream that joins Kings River 5.5 miles west-southwest of Balch Camp (lat. 36°52'15" N, long. 119°12'40" W; sec. 23, T 12 S, R 25 E). Named on Patterson Mountain (1952) 15' quadrangle.
Lone Pine Canyon [TULARE]: *canyon,* drained by a stream that flows 1 mile to White River (1) 3 miles south-southwest of California Hot Springs (lat. 35°50'20" N, long. 118°41'45" W; sec. 13, T 24 S, R 30 E). Named on California Hot Springs (1958) 15' quadrangle.
Lone Pine Creek [TULARE]: *stream,* flows 4.5 miles to join Hamilton Creek and form Middle Fork Kaweah River 4.5 miles west-southwest of Triple Divide Peak (lat. 36°33'50" N, long. 118°36'05" W); the stream goes through Lone Pine Meadow. Named on Triple Divide Peak (1956) 15' quadrangle. United States Board on Geographic Names (1968b, p. 8) rejected the name "Middle Fork Kaweah River" for the stream.
Lone Pine Meadow [TULARE]: *area,* 2.5 miles west-southwest of Triple Divide Peak (lat. 36°35' N, long. 118°34'15" W); the place is along Lone Pine Creek. Named on Triple Divide Peak (1956) 15' quadrangle. William R. Dudley called the feature Heather Meadow in 1896; the name "Lone Pine" also has the form "Lonepine" (Browning, p. 130).
Lone Pine Mountain [TULARE]: *peak,* 7.25 miles north-northwest of California Hot Springs (lat. 35°58'10" N, long. 118°44'10" W; near E line sec. 33, T 22 S, R 30 E). Altitude 5072 feet. Named on California Hot Springs (1958) 15' quadrangle.

Lone Star [FRESNO]: *locality,* 3.25 miles east-northeast of Malaga along Atchison, Topeka and Santa Fe Railroad (lat. 36°42' N, long. 119°40'45" W; near W line sec. 22, T 14 S, R 21 E). Named on Malaga (1964) 7.5' quadrangle. Called Lonestar on California Mining Bureau's (1909b) map. Postal authorities established Lonestar post office in 1891, discontinued it in 1895, reestablished it in 1900, and discontinued it in 1910; settlers at the place came from the Lone Star State of Texas (Salley, p. 125).

Lone Tree Canyon: see **Pine Tree Canyon** [KERN].

Lonetree Channel [FRESNO]: *water feature,* diverges from Fowler Switch Canal and extends for 7 miles to a ditch 1.5 miles south of Sanger (lat. 36°40'40" N, long. 119°33'35" W). Named on Sanger (1965) 7.5' quadrangle. Grunsky (p. 71) called the feature Lone Tree Slough, and gave the name "Kip Slough" as an alternate; he noted that it was a natural watercourse that became an important distributary of water from a canal system. The name is from a foothill white oak that grew on the west bank of the feature northeast of present Sanger (about on N line sec. 14, T 14 S, R 22 E) (Teilman and Shafer, p. 36). Grunsky (p. 71) mentioned a natural watercourse called Burns Slough that was a tributary of Kip Slough (present Lonetree Channel).

Lone Tree Slough: see **Lonetree Channel** [FRESNO].

Lone Tree Well [KERN]: *well,* 9.5 miles north of the village of Lost Hills (lat. 35°45'10" N, long. 119°39'20" W; sec. 13, T 25 S, R 21 E). Named on Lone Tree Well (1954) 7.5' quadrangle.

Long Branch [TULARE]: *stream,* flows 5 miles to South Fork Tule River 7.25 miles south-southwest of Springville (lat. 36°01'40" N, long. 118°50'50" W; sec. 9, T 22 S, R 29 E). Named on Globe (1956) 7.5' quadrangle.

Long Canyon [FRESNO]: *canyon,* 3 miles long, opens into an unnamed valley 6.5 miles west of Red Slate Mountain (lat. 37°30'20" N, long. 118°59'05" W). Named on Kaiser Peak (1953), Mount Abbot (1953), and Mount Morrison (1953) 15' quadrangles.

Long Canyon [KERN]: *canyon,* drained by a stream that flows 3.25 miles to lowlands 4 miles southwest of Weldon (lat. 35°37'15" N, long. 118°20'20" W). Named on Woolstalf Creek (1972) 7.5' quadrangle.

Long Canyon [TULARE]:

(1) *canyon,* 2 miles long, along Long Canyon Creek above a point 3.25 miles northwest of Monache Mountain (lat. 36°14' N, long. 118°14'30" W; sec. 36, T 19 S, R 34 E). Named on Monache Mountain (1956) and Olancha (1956) 15' quadrangles.

(2) *canyon,* drained by a stream that flows nearly 5 miles to Middle Fork Tule River 3.25 miles east-northeast of Springville (lat. 36° 08'35" N, long. 118°45'30" W; sec. 32, T 20 S, R 30 E). Named on Camp Nelson (1956) and Springville (1957) 15' quadrangles.

(3) *canyon,* drained by a stream that flows 7 miles to Sacatar Meadow 14 miles north of Lamont Peak (lat. 35°59'40" N, long. 118°04'45" W). Named on Monache Mountain (1956) 15' quadrangle.

Long Canyon: see **Long Hollow** [FRESNO].

Long Canyon Creek [TULARE]: *stream,* flows 5 miles to Ninemile Creek 6 miles east of Hockett Peak (lat. 36°13'15" N, long. 118°16'50" W; at N line sec. 3, T 20 S, R 34 E); the stream drains Long Canyon (1). Named on Hockett Peak (1956) 15' quadrangle.

Long Creek [TULARE]: *stream,* flows 7.25 miles to lowlands 2 miles west of Cliff Peak (lat. 36°33'35" N, long. 119°12'35" W; sec. 1, T 16 S, R 25 E); the stream is in Long Valley (1). Named on Stokes Mountain (1966) and Tucker Mountain (1966) 7.5' quadrangles.

Long Hollow [FRESNO]: *canyon,* drained by a stream that flows 6.5 miles to Warthan Creek 7.5 miles west-southwest of Coalinga (lat. 36°05'05" N, long. 120°28'40" W; sec. 20, T 21 S, R 14 E). Named on Alcalde Hills (1969), Curry Mountain (1969), and Sherman Peak (1969) 7.5' quadrangles. Called Long Canyon on Coalinga (1912) 30' quadrangle.

Long Lake [FRESNO]: *lake,* 1400 feet long, 1 mile north-northeast of Kaiser Peak (lat. 37°18'30" N, long. 119°10'40" W; sec. 19, T 7 S, R 26 E). Named on Kaiser Peak (1953) 15' quadrangle.

Longley Pass [TULARE]: *pass,* 13 miles northwest of Mount Whitney on Great Western Divide (lat. 36°41'20" N, long. 118°28'45" W). Named on Mount Whitney (1956) 15' quadrangle. The name, given in 1895, commemorates Howard Longley, leader of the group that discovered the pass (United States Board on Geographic Names, 1933a, p. 472).

Long Meadow [FRESNO]:

(1) *area,* 8 miles northeast of Dinkey Dome (lat. 37°12' N, long. 119°02' W). Named on Huntington Lake (1953) 15' quadrangle.

(2) *area,* 9 miles west-northwest of Blackcap Mountain (lat. 37°07'45" N, long. 118°55'10" W; sec. 21, T 9 S, R 28 E). Named on Blackcap Mountain (1953) 15' quadrangle. On Mount Goddard (1912) 30' quadrangle, the name has the plural form "Long Meadows."

(3) *area,* at and southwest of Hume (lat. 36°46'45" N, long. 118°55'25" W; in and near sec. 22, T 13 S, R 28 E). Named on Tehipite Dome (1952) 15' quadrangle.

Long Meadow [TULARE]:

(1) *area,* 13 miles south-southwest of Mineral King along North Fork of Middle Fork Tule River (lat. 36°16'30" N, long. 118° 40' W). Named on Mineral King (1956) 15' quadrangle.

(2) *area,* 11 miles west of Triple Divide Peak (lat. 36°35'30" N, long. 118°44'10" W; on E line sec. 29, T 15 S, R 30 E). Named on Triple Divide Peak (1956) 15' quadrangle.

(3) *area,* 8.5 miles northeast of California Hot Springs (lat. 35° 58'45" N, long. 118°34'55" W; mainly in sec. 36, T 22 S, R 31 E). Named on California Hot Springs (1958) 15' quadrangle.

(4) *area,* 11 miles southeast of Fairview along Fay Creek (lat. 35° 49'30" N, long. 118°20'20" W; sec. 20, T 24 S, R 34 E). Named on Kernville (1956) 15' quadrangle.

Long Meadow: see **Ferguson Meadow** [TULARE]; **Little Whitney Meadow** [TULARE]; **Long Meadow Creek** [FRESNO]; **Rock Meadow** [FRESNO].

Long Meadow Creek [FRESNO]: *stream,* flows 2.5 miles to North Fork Kings River 14 miles north-northwest of Hume (lat. 36°58'10" N, long. 118°59'30" W). Named on Patterson Mountain (1952) and Tehipite Dome (1952) 15' quadrangles. Dinuba (1924) 30' quadrangle shows the stream in a valley called Long Meadow. West Fork enters from the west nearly 1 mile upstream from the mouth of the main stream; it is 1.5 miles long and is named on Patterson Mountain (1952) 15' quadrangle.

Long Meadow Creek [TULARE]: *stream,* flows 2.5 miles to Bone Creek 11 miles northeast of California Hot Springs (lat. 35°59'55" N, long. 118°32'30" W; sec. 20, T 22 S, R 32 E); the stream heads at Long Meadow (3). Named on California Hot Springs (1958) 15' quadrangle.

Long Mountain [TULARE]: *ridge,* south-trending, 6 miles long, 6 miles south-southeast of Auckland (lat. 36°30' N, long. 119°02'50" W). Named on Auckland (1966) and Woodlake (1952) 7.5' quadrangles.

Long Stringer [TULARE]:

(1) *stream,* flows 1.5 miles to an unnamed stream 2.5 miles north-northwest of Olancha Peak (lat. 36°18'10" N, long. 118°07'55" W; sec. 1, T 19 S, R 35 E). Named on Olancha (1956) 15' quadrangle.

(2) *stream,* flows 3 miles to Long Canyon Creek 6.5 miles east of Hockett Peak (lat. 36°13'55" N, long. 118°16'20" W). Named on Hockett Peak (1956) and Kern Peak (1956) 15' quadrangles.

Long Tom: see **Long Tom Gulch** [KERN].

Long Tom Gulch [KERN]: *canyon,* drained by a stream that flows 6.5 miles to Poso Creek nearly 5 miles west-southwest of Pine Mountain (lat. 35°31'40" N, long. 118°50'30" W; near N line sec. 3, T 28 S, R 29 E). Named on Pine Mountain (1965) 7.5' quadrangle. The stream in the canyon is called Pine Mountain Creek on Woody (1952) 15' quadrangle, which has the name "Long Tom Gulch" for a branch of present Long Tom Gulch (in sec. 26, T 27 S, R 29 E). United States Board on Geographic Names (1966b, p. 5) rejected the names "Pine Mountain Creek" and "Mountain Creek" for present Long Tom Gulch. A mining camp called Long Tom was situated along Pine Mountain Creek about 1.5 miles north of Poso Creek (Boyd, p. 159).

Long Top [FRESNO]: *ridge,* north-northeast-trending, 2 miles long, 8.5 miles west-northwest of Blackcap Mountain (lat. 37°06' N, long. 118°56'15" W). Named on Blackcap Mountain (1953) 15' quadrangle.

Long Valley [TULARE]:

(1) *valley,* along Long Creek above a point 3.25 miles north-northeast of Cliff Peak (lat. 36°36' N, long. 119°11'20" W; at S line sec. 19, T 15 S, R 26 E). Named on Stokes Mountain (1966) and Tucker Mountain (1966) 7.5' quadrangles.

(2) *valley,* 4 miles long, 7 miles northwest of Lamont Peak (lat. 35° 51'30" N, long. 118°08' W). Named on Lamont Peak (1956) 15' quadrangle.

Lonsmith [KERN]: *locality,* 5 miles east-southeast of downtown Bakersfield along the railroad (lat. 35°20'25" N, long. 118°55'20" W; at S line sec. 1, T 30 S, R 28 E). Named on Lamont (1954) 7.5' quadrangle.

Lookout Hill [KERN]: *hill,* 9 miles north-northeast of Rosamond (lat. 34°59' N, long. 118°05'45" W; at SE cor. sec. 1, T 10 N, R 12 W). Altitude 2744 feet. Named on Bissell (1973) 7.5' quadrangle.

Lookout Mountain [TULARE]: *peak,* 11.5 miles south of Hockett Peak (lat. 36°03'30" N, long. 118°22'30" W). Altitude 9722 feet. Named on Hockett Peak (1956) 15' quadrangle.

Lookout Peak [FRESNO]: *peak,* 17 miles southwest of Marion Peak (lat. 36°46'25" N, long. 118°42'55" W). Altitude 8531 feet. Named on Marion Peak (1953) 15' quadrangle. E.C. Winchell called the feature Winchell's Peak in 1868 for his cousin, Alexander Winchell, State Geologist of Michigan; later L.A. Winchell gave the name "Mount Winchell" to another feature, and the name "Winchell" was lost to present Lookout Peak (Browning, p. 131).

Loop: see **The Loop** [KERN].

Loper Peak [FRESNO]: *peak,* nearly 7 miles west-southwest of Blackcap Mountain (lat. 37°02'20" N, long. 118°54'20" W; on S line sec. 22, T 10 S, R 28 E). Altitude 10,059 feet. Named on Blackcap Mountain (1953) 15' quadrangle. The name commemorates John W. Loper, a cattleman who came to Fresno County in 1883 (Browning, p. 131).

Lopez Flats [KERN]: *area,* 3.5 miles west-southwest of Liebre Twins (lat. 34°56'20" N, long. 118°37'50" W; on S line sec. 19, T 10 N, R 16 E). Named on Winters Ridge (1966) 7.5' quadrangle.

Loraine [KERN]: *village,* 12 miles north of Tehachapi (lat. 35°18'15" N, long. 118°26'05" W; sec. 21, T 30 S, R 33 E). Named on Loraine (1972) 7.5' quadrangle. Emerald Mountain (1943) 15' quadrangle shows the place situated nearly 1 mile west of the present site (sec. 20, T 30 S, R 33 E). Postal authorities established Paris post office in 1903, changed the name to Loraine in 1912, discontinued it in 1918, reestablished it in 1922, and discontinued it in 1926 (Frickstad, p. 57, 58). United States Board on Geographic Names (1975b, p. 10) listed the names "Paris" and "Paris-Loraine" as variants. French and Alsatian miners gave the names "Paris" and "Loraine" to the place (Bailey, 1962, p. 50). California Mining Bureau's (1917c) map shows a place called Amalie located 2.5 miles southwest of Loraine. Postal authorities established Amalie post office in 1894, moved it 2 miles south in 1902, moved it 1.25 miles southeast in 1906, and discontinued it in 1908; the name was from Amalie mine (Salley, p. 6), which Loraine (1972) 7.5' quadrangle shows situated less than 1 mile northeast of Loraine.

Lort [TULARE]: *locality,* 3.5 miles north-northwest of Exeter along Southern Pacific Railroad (lat. 36°20'30" N, long. 119°09'10" W; near SE cor. sec. 21, T 18 S, R 26 E). Named on Exeter (1952) 15' quadrangle.

Los Alamitos: see **Sinks of the Tejon**, under **Tejon Creek** [KERN].

Los Alamos Creek [KERN]: *stream,* flows 3.5 miles to lowlands 11.5 miles southwest of Liebre Twins (lat. 34°50' N, long. 118°42'40" W; near SW cor. sec. 29, T 9 N, R 17 W). Named on La Liebre Ranch (1965) 7.5' quadrangle. The canyon of the stream is called Cottonwood Canyon on Neenach (1943) 15' quadrangle.

Los Alamos y Agua Caliente [KERN]: *land grant,* in southwest part of Tehachapi Mountains. Named on Lebec (1958), Pastoria Creek (1958), and Winters Ridge (1966) 7.5' quadrangles. Francisco Lopez and others received 6 leagues in 1846; Agustin Olivera and others claimed 26,626 acres patented in 1866 (Cowan, p. 14).

Los Gatos Creek [FRESNO]: *stream,* flows 26 miles to Pleasant Valley 5.5 miles northwest of Coalinga (lat. 36°11'45" N, long. 120°25'45" W; sec. 10, T 20 S, R 14 E). Named on Alcalde Hills (1969), Coalinga (1956), Guijarral Hills (1956), San Benito Mountain (1969), Santa Rita Peak (1969), and Sherman Peak (1969) 7.5' quadrangles. Called Las Gatas Creek on Parke's (1854-1855) map, and called Arrojo los Gates on Goddard's (1857) map. The coarse of the stream in San Joaquin Valley is called Arroyo Passajero on Guijarral Hills (1936) 7.5' quadrangle. United States Board on Geographic Names (1933a, p. 475) rejected the names "Arroyo las Gatos," "Las Gatas Creek," and "Polvodero Creek" for the stream, and later (1964c, p. 15) rejected the names "Arroyo Passajero" and "Arroyo Poso de Chane" as well.

Los Jinetes [KINGS]: *peaks,* 3 miles east-northeast of Avenal (lat. 36°01' N, long. 120°04'45" W; sec. 13, T 22 S, R 17 E). Named on La Cima (1963) 7.5' quadrangle.

Los Lobos Creek [KERN]: *stream,* flows 8 miles to lowlands 7.5 miles northwest of Eagle Rest Peak (lat. 34°59'05" N, long. 119° 13'35" W; sec. 4, T 10 N, R 22 W). Named on Conner SW (1955) and Eagle Rest Peak (1942) 7.5' quadrangles.

Los Medanos [KINGS]: *ridge,* southeast-trending, 0.5 mile long, 2 miles south of Kettleman City (lat. 35°58'50" N, long. 119°57'55" W). Named on Los Viejos (1954) 7.5' quadrangle. Sand dunes that cover the side of the ridge account for the name (United States Board on Geographic Names, 1933b, p. 18)—*medanos* means "sand banks" or "dunes" in Spanish.

Los Morones [KERN]: *ridge,* southeast-trending, less than 1 mile long, 11 miles north-northwest of Blackwells Corner (lat. 35°45'55" N, long. 119°54'40" W; sec. 10, T 25 S, R 19 E). Named on Avenal Gap (1954) 7.5' quadrangle. United States Board on Geographic Names (1933b, p. 18-19) noted that *los morones* means "little hills" in Spanish.

Los Nietos: see **Lake Los Nietos** [FRESNO].

Los Palmas: see **Las Palmas** [FRESNO].

Los Piramidos: see **Pyramid Hills** [KERN-KINGS].

Lost Canyon [FRESNO]:

(1) *canyon,* 2.5 miles long, 10 miles west of Blackcap Mountain (lat. 37°03'15" N, long. 118°58'20" W); the canyon is 1 mile west of Lost Peak. Named on Blackcap Mountain (1953) 15' quadrangle.

(2) *canyon,* 1.5 miles long, drained by a stream that joins Middle Fork Kings River 11 miles west of Marion Peak (lat. 36°56'25" N, long. 118°43'05" W). Named on Marion Peak (1953) 15' quadrangle.

Lost Canyon [KERN]: *canyon,* drained by a stream that flows 4.5 miles to Pleito Creek 3 miles east-northeast of Eagle Rest Peak (lat. 34°56' N, long. 119°05'20" W; near N line sec. 26, T 10 N, R 21 W). Named on Pleito Hills (1958) 7.5' quadrangle.

Lost Canyon [TULARE]: *canyon,* drained by a stream that flows 4.5 miles to Big Arroyo 14 miles northwest of Kern Peak (lat. 36°27'35" N, long. 118°28'10" W). Named on Kern Peak (1956) and Mineral King (1956) 15' quadrangles. A sheepherder and his sheep were lost in the canyon for six days (Browning, p. 132).

Lost Creek [FRESNO]: *stream,* flows 3.5 miles to Big Creek (2) 9 miles south-southwest of Dinkey Dome (lat. 37°00'20" N, long. 119°13'10" W; sec. 2, T 11 S, R 25 E); the stream heads in Lost Meadow (1). Named on Huntington Lake (1953) 15' quadrangle.

Lost Creek [TULARE]: *stream,* flows 8.5 miles to South Fork Kern River 10.5 miles south-southeast of Monache Mountain (lat. 36°03'40" N, long. 118°07'50" W). Named on Monache Mountain (1956) 15' quadrangle.

Lost Hills [KERN]:

(1) *ridge,* southeast-trending, 12 miles long, center 7.5 miles west-northwest of the village of Lost Hills (lat. 35°40' N, long. 119°46'15" W). Named on Antelope Plain (1954), Lost Hills (1953), and Lost Hills NW (1954) 7.5' quadrangles. According to one account, the name is from the apparent disappearance of the ridge as it is approached (Hanna, p. 176).

(2) *village,* 42 miles west-northwest of Bakersfield (lat. 35°36'55" N, long. 119°41'20" W; at NE cor. sec. 3, T 27 S, R 21 E); the village is east of the ridge of the same name. Named on Lost Hills (1953) 7.5' quadrangle. Postal authorities established Lost Hills post office in 1911, discontinued it in 1912, reestablished it in 1913, and moved it 0.5 mile mile west in 1937 (Salley, p. 128). They established Cuttens post office, named for Charles R. Cuttens, first postmaster, in 1911 and discontinued it in 1913, when they moved it 10 miles east and reestablished it as Lost Hills post office (Salley, p. 54).

Lost Keys Lakes [FRESNO]: *lakes,* three, each about 750 feet long, 2 miles east of Double Peak (lat. 37°30'50" N, long. 119°00'20" W). Named on Devils Postpile (1953) 15' quadrangle. The group comprises Lower Lost Keyes Lake, Middle Lost Keyes Lake, and Upper Lost Keys Lake (United States Board on Geographic Names, 1971a, p. 2).

Lost Lake [FRESNO]:

(1) *lake,* 850 feet long, 12.5 miles northwest of Blackcap Mountain (lat. 37°12'10" N, long. 118°56'45" W; sec. 31, T 8 S, R 28 E). Named on Blackcap Mountain (1953) 15' quadrangle.

(2) *lake,* nearly 0.5 mile long, 7 miles north-northwest of Clovis near San Joaquin River (lat. 36°58' N, long. 119°44'10" W). Named on Friant (1964) 7.5' quadrangle.

Lost Lake [TULARE]: *lake,* 1000 feet long, 11.5 miles west-northwest of Triple Divide Peak (lat. 36°40'25" N, long. 118°42'15" W). Named on Triple Divide Peak (1956) 15' quadrangle.

Lost Lakes [FRESNO]: *lakes,* largest 1000 feet long, 8.5 miles north-northeast of Mount Goddard (lat. 37°13'25" N, long. 118°41'15" W). Named on Mount Goddard (1948) 15' quadrangle. Art Schober chose the name because the lakes are so well hidden (Browning, p. 132).

Lost Meadow [FRESNO]:

(1) *area,* 6.5 miles south-southwest of Dinkey Dome (lat. 37°02' N, long. 119°11'05" W; on W line sec. 30, T 10 S, R 26 E); the place is near the head of Lost Creek. Named on Huntington Lake (1953) 15' quadrangle.

(2) *area,* 11 miles north of Hume (lat. 36°56'35" N, long. 118°56'10" W). Named on Tehipite Dome (1952) 15' quadrangle.

(3) *area,* 8 miles east-southeast of Hume (lat. 36°45'10" N, long. 118°46'50" W). Named on Tehipite Dome (1952) 15' quadrangle.

Lost Meadows [TULARE]: *area,* about 4.5 miles south-southeast of Monache Mountain (lat. 36°08'30" N, long. 118°10'15" W; mainly in sec. 34, T 20 S, R 35 E). Named on Monache Mountain (1956) 15' quadrangle.

Lost Peak [FRESNO]: *peak,* 9.5 miles west of Blackcap Mountain (lat. 37°02'50" N, long. 118°57'40" W; sec. 19, T 10 S, R 28 E); the peak is nearly 1 mile east of Lost Canyon (1). Altitude 8476 feet. Named on Blackcap Mountain (1953) 15' quadrangle.

Lost Trout Creek [TULARE]: *stream,* flows 1.5 miles to Long Canyon Creek 7 miles east of Hockett Peak (lat. 36°13'35" N, long. 118°15'35" W). Named on Hockett Peak (1956) 15' quadrangle.

Lost Trout Meadow: see **Dry Meadows** [TULARE].

Los Tulares: see "Regional setting"; **Tulare Lake** [KINGS].

Lost Valley: see **Blaney Meadows** [FRESNO].

Los Viejos [KINGS]: *ridge,* south-southeast-trending, 4 miles long, 5 miles south of Kettleman City (lat. 35°56' N, long. 119°56'45" W). Named on Los Viejos (1954) 7.5' quadrangle. The name refers to the ridge being physiographically older than nearby hills—*los viejos* means "the old men" in Spanish (United States Board on Geographic Names, 1933b, p. 19).

Los Yeguas Creek: see **Yeguas Creek** [KERN].

Lou Beverly Lake [FRESNO]: *lake,* 900 feet long. 6.5 miles southwest of Mount Abbot along South Fork Bear Creek (2) (lat. 37° 19' N, long. 118°51'35" W). Named on Mount Abbot (1953) 15' quadrangle.

Lousy Spring [FRESNO]: *spring,* 4 miles east of Balch Camp (lat. 36°53'45" N, long. 119°02'40" W; near SE cor. sec. 8, T 12 S, R 27 E). Named on Patterson Mountain (1952) 15' quadrangle.

Lovejoy Lake: see **Packsaddle Lake** [FRESNO].

Lovel Canyon [KINGS]: *canyon,* drained by a stream that flows 5 miles to Avenal Canyon 10 miles south-southwest of Avenal (lat. 35°51'40" N, long. 120°11' W; near NE cor. sec. 12, T 24 S, R 16 E). Named on Tent Hills (1942) 7.5' quadrangle. On Cholame (1917) 30' quadrangle, the stream in the canyon is called Little Avenal Creek.

Lovell: see **Calgro** [TULARE].

Lower Araujo Spring [KERN]: *spring,* nearly 6 miles west-southwest of Liebre Twins (lat. 34°55'55" N, long. 118°40'10" W); the spring is 1550 feet west-southwest of Upper Araujo Spring. Named on Winters Ridge

(1966) 7.5' quadrangle.

Lower Beck Spring [KERN]: *spring,* 4.5 miles northeast of Caliente (lat. 35°20'15" N, long. 118°34' W; near N line sec. 8, T 30 S, R 32 E); the spring is in Beck Canyon 0.5 mile south of Upper Beck Spring. Named on Oiler Peak (1972) 7.5' quadrangle.

Lower Boiler Spring [KERN]: *spring,* nearly 7 miles east of Caliente (lat. 35°16'40" N, long. 118°30'45" W; sec. 35, T 30 S, R 32 E); the spring is 0.5 mile north-northwest of Boiler Spring. Named on Oiler Peak (1972) 7.5' quadrangle.

Lower Cow Chip Spring [KERN]: *spring,* 7.25 miles west of Liebre Twins (lat. 34°57'10" N, long. 118°41'45" W; at S line sec. 9, T 10 N, R 17 W); the spring is 1150 feet south-southeast of Cow Chip Spring. Named on Winters Ridge (1966) 7.5' quadrangle.

Lower Desolation Lake [FRESNO]: *lake,* 1750 feet long, 2 miles west-southwest of Mount Humphreys in Humphreys Basin (lat. 37° 15'35" N, long. 118°42'25" W); the lake is 0.5 mile south of Desolation Lake. Named on Mount Tom (1949) 15' quadrangle.

Lower Funston Meadow: see **Funston Meadow** [TULARE].

Lower Grapes Spring [KERN]: *spring,* 7 miles east of Caliente (lat. 35°17' N, long. 118°30'05" W; near NW cor. sec. 36, T 30 S, R 32 E); the spring is 0.25 mile east-southeast of Upper Grapes Spring. Named on Oiler Peak (1972) 7.5' quadrangle.

Lower Hog Camp Spring [KERN]: *spring,* nearly 2 miles north-northwest of Caliente (lat. 35°18'45" N, long. 118°38'35" W); the spring is 0.5 mile south-southwest of Hog Camp Spring. Named on Bena (1972) 7.5' quadrangle.

Lower Honeymoon Lake [FRESNO]: *lake,* 1150 feet long, 9.5 miles south of Mount Abbot (lat. 37°15'05" N, long. 118°45'55" W); the lake is 0.25 mile north of Upper Honeymoon Lake. Named on Mount Abbot (1953) 15' quadrangle.

Lower Hopkins Lake [FRESNO]: *lake,* 900 feet long, 5.25 miles north-northwest of Mount Abbot (lat. 35°27'20" N, long. 118°49'40" W); the lake is 1.5 miles south-southeast of Upper Hopkins Lakes at the head of a fork of Hopkins Creek. Named on Mount Abbot (1953) 15' quadrangle.

Lower Horsethief Lake [FRESNO]: *lake,* 450 feet long, 4.5 miles west of Kaiser Peak (lat. 37°17'15" N, long. 119°16'15" W; sec. 29, T 7 S, R 25 E); the lake is 0.25 mile northwest of Upper Horsethief Lake. Named on Shuteye Peak (1953) 15' quadrangle.

Lower Hot Springs: see **Mono Hot Springs** [FRESNO].

Lower Indian Lake [FRESNO]: *lake,* 1700 feet long, nearly 7 miles north-northwest of Blackcap Mountain (lat. 37°09'45" N, long. 118°50'40" W); the lake is 1.5 miles south-southeast of Upper Indian Lake. Named on Blackcap Mountain (1953) 15' quadrangle.

Lower Lost Keys Lake: see **Lost Keys Lakes** [FRESNO].

Lower Mills Creek Lake [FRESNO]: *lake,* 1300 feet long, 1.5 miles west-northwest of Mount Abbot (lat. 37°23'55" N, long. 118°48'35" W); the lake is along Mills Creek 0.5 mile downstream from Upper Mills Creek Lake. Named on Mount Abbot (1953) 15' quadrangle.

Lower Mineral Hot Springs: see **Mono Hot Springs** [FRESNO].

Lower Mineral Public Camp: see **Mono Hot Springs** [FRESNO].

Lower Rancheria Creek [FRESNO]: *stream,* flows 5 miles to Kings River 3.25 miles west-southwest of Balch Camp (lat. 36°52'55" N, long. 119°10'25" W; near SE cor. sec. 18, T 12 S, R 26 E). Named on Patterson Mountain (1952) 15' quadrangle.

Lower Springhill Campground [TULARE]: *locality,* 5.25 miles south-southeast of Fairview along Kern River (lat. 35°51'40" N, long. 118°26'50" W; sec. 8, T 24 S, R 33 E); the place is 0.25 mile south of Upper Springhill Campground. Named on Kernville (1956) 15' quadrangle.

Lower Tent Meadow [FRESNO]: *area,* 9.5 miles south-southwest of Marion Peak (lat. 36°49'30" N, long. 118°34'30" W); the place is nearly 1 mile south-southeast of Upper Tent Meadow. Named on Marion Peak (1953) 15' quadrangle. A large block of granite in the meadow resembles a white tent from a distance (Browning, p. 214).

Lower Tobias Meadow [TULARE]: *area,* 7 miles east of California Hot Springs (lat. 35°52'45" N, long. 118°32'45" W; sec. 32, T 23 S, R 32 E); the place is along Tobias Creek 1.5 miles northeast of Tobias Meadow. Named on California Hot Springs (1958) 15' quadrangle.

Lower Turret Lake [FRESNO]: *lake,* 1700 feet long, 9.5 miles south-southwest of Mount Abbot (lat. 37°15'20" N, long. 118° 50' W); the lake is 0.5 mile south of Middle Turret Lakes along Turret Creek. Named on Mount Abbot (1953) 15' quadrangle.

Lower Twin Lake [FRESNO]: *lake,* 1000 feet long, nearly 2 miles east of Kaiser Peak (lat. 37°17'40" N, long. 119°09'10" W; sec. 29, T 7 S, R 26 E); the lake is 1100 feet east-southeast of Upper Twin Lake. Named on Kaiser Peak (1953) 15' quadrangle. On Kaiser (1904) 30' quadrangle, present Lower Twin Lake and present Upper Twin Lake together are called Twin Lakes.

Lowes Corner [TULARE]: *locality,* 1.5 miles west of Woodville (lat. 36°05'40" N, long. 119°13'55" W; at SW cor. sec. 13, T 21 S, R 25 E). Named on Woodville (1950) 7.5' quadrangle.

Lucas Creek [KERN]: *stream,* flows 7.25 miles to Kern River 4 miles northeast of Mount Adelaide (lat. 35°29' N, long. 118° 42'35" W). Named on Breckenridge Mountain (1972) and Mount Adelaide (1972) 7.5' quadrangles.

Lucca [TULARE]: *locality,* 2.5 miles north of Lindsay along Atchison, Topeka and Santa Fe Railroad (lat. 36°14'45" N, long. 119°05'25" W; sec. 30, T 19 S, R 27 E). Named on Lindsay (1951) 7.5' quadrangle.

Lucerne [KINGS]: *locality,* 3.5 miles north of Hanford along Atchison, Topeka and Santa Fe Railroad (lat. 36°22'50" N, long. 119° 39'45" W; sec. 11, T 18 S, R 21 E). Named on Laton (1953) 7.5' quadrangle. The place is in a neighborhood named for Mussel Slough, but in 1887 it received the name "Lucerne Valley" from Lucerne in Europe (Gudde, 1949, p. 197).

Lucerne Valley: see **Mussel Slough** [KINGS].

Luckett Mountain [FRESNO]: *peak,* 8 miles south-southwest of Balch Camp (lat. 36°48'35" N, long. 119°11'30" W; sec. 7, T 13 S, R 26 E). Altitude 3181 feet. Named on Patterson Mountain (1952) 15' quadrangle.

Luck Point [FRESNO]: *peak,* 5 miles east of Kaiser Peak (lat. 37° 18' N, long. 119°05'50" W; sec. 23, T 7 S, R 26 E). Named on Kaiser Peak (1953) 15' quadrangle.

Lucky Canyon [TULARE]: *canyon,* drained by a stream that flows 1.25 miles to Dry Creek (1) 6.5 miles southeast of Auckland (lat. 36°32'05" N, long. 119°00'35" W; sec. 14, T 16 S, R 27 E). Named on Giant Forest (1956) 15' quadrangle, and on Auckland (1966) 7.5' quadrangle.

Lucy Runyon Canyon [TULARE]: *canyon,* drained by a stream that flows 1.5 miles to Dry Creek (1) 5 miles east-southeast of Auckland (lat. 36°34'15" N, long. 119°01'15" W; near N line sec. 3, T 16 S, R 27 E). Named on Auckland (1966) 7.5' quadrangle.

Lucys Foot Pass [TULARE]: *pass,* 11 miles northwest of Mount Whitney on Kings-Kern Divide (lat. 36°41'45" N, long. 118°25'15" W). Named on Mount Whitney (1956) 15' quadrangle. Browning (p. 133) associated the name with Lucy Fletcher Brown (Mrs. Bolton C. Brown), who crossed the pass in 1896.

Lumer [TULARE]: *locality,* 2.5 miles south-southeast of Porterville along Atchison, Topeka and Santa Fe Railroad (lat. 36°02'15" N, long. 118°59'25" W; at S line sec. 6, T 22 S, R 28 E). Named on Success Dam (1956) 7.5' quadrangle.

Lumreau Creek [KERN]: *stream,* flows 6.5 miles to Cedar Creek 3 miles south-southeast of Glennville (lat. 35°41'20" N, long. 118° 41'15" W; near S line sec. 6, T 26 S, R 31 E). Named on Alta Sierra (1972) and Glennville (1972) 7.5' quadrangles.

Lumreau Mountain [TULARE]: *peak,* 3 miles northeast of Springville (lat. 36°09'55" N, long. 118°46'55" W; near SE cor. sec. 24, T 20 S, R 29 E). Altitude 3085 feet. Named on Springville (1957) 7.5' quadrangle.

Luna [TULARE]: *locality,* 1.5 miles west-northwest of Exeter along Southern Pacific Railroad (lat. 36°18'20" N, long. 119°10'15" W; at W line sec. 4, T 19 S, R 26 E). Named on Exeter (1926) 7.5' quadrangle.

Lunch Meadow [TULARE]: *area,* 17 miles northwest of Lamont Peak (lat. 35°59'20" N, long. 118°13' W; sec. 20, T 22 S, R 35 E). Named on Lamont Peak (1956) 15' quadrangle.

Lurline Wells [KERN]: *wells,* 11 miles northwest of Wasco (lat. 35° 42'45" N, long. 119°27'45" W; sec. 35, T 25 S, R 23 E). Named on Wasco NW (1953) 7.5' quadrangle.

Lynch Canyon [KERN]: *canyon,* drained by a stream that flows 2 miles to lowlands 5 miles east-northeast of Bodfish (lat. 35°36'45" N, long. 118°24'30" W; sec. 2, T 27 S, R 33 E). Named on Lake Isabella South (1972) 7.5' quadrangle.

Lynn: see **Cornwell** [KINGS].

Lynns Valley: see **Linns Valley** [KERN-TULARE].

— M —

Mace Lake [FRESNO]: *lake,* 600 feet long, 10 miles northwest of Mount Abbot (lat. 37°29'05" N, long. 118°54'30" W). Named on Mount Abbot (1953) 15' quadrangle.

Mace Meadow [KERN]: *area,* about 2.5 miles south-southeast of Claraville along Cottonwood Creek (3) (lat. 35°24'20" N, long. 118°18'50" W). Named on Claraville (1972) 7.5' quadrangle.

Machine Creek [TULARE]: *stream,* flows 2.5 miles to Little Trout Creek 12 miles east-northeast of Fairview (lat. 35°58'05" N, long. 118°17'35" W; sec. 34, T 22 S, R 34 E). Named on Kernville (1956) 15' quadrangle.

Mack Meadow [KERN]: *area,* 11 miles south-southwest of Weldon (lat. 35°30'20" N, long. 118°20'45" W; sec. 17, T 28 S, R 34 E). Named on Woolstalf Creek (1972) 7.5' quadrangle.

Maddox: see **Mount Maddox** [TULARE].

Maddox Canyon [KERN]: *canyon,* nearly 2 miles long, 5.5 miles west-southwest of McKittrick (lat. 35°16'40" N, long. 119°43'50" W). Named on Olig (1943) 7.5' quadrangle.

Maggie Lakes [TULARE]: *lakes,* largest 800 feet long, 12 miles south of Mineral King (lat. 36°16'35" N, long. 118°37'15" W); the lakes are 1 mile north of Maggie Mountain. Named on Mineral King (1956) 15' quadrangle.

Maggie Mountain [TULARE]: *peak,* 13 miles south of Mineral King (lat.

36°15'50" N, long. 118°37'05" W). Altitude 10,042 feet. Named on Mineral King (1956) 15' quadrangle. Frank Knowles named the peak in the 1870's to commemorates Maggie Kincaid, a school teacher in Tulare County (Gudde, 1949, p. 201; Gudde used the name "Mount Maggie.")

Magnesite: see **Success** [TULARE].

Magnesite Junction: see **Success** [TULARE].

Magnolia [TULARE]: *locality,* 3.5 miles south-southeast of Porterville along Atchison, Topeka and Santa Fe Railroad (lat. 36°01'20" N, long. 118°59'35" W; at S line sec. 7, T 22 S, R 28 E). Named on Success Dam (1956) 7.5' quadrangle.

Magnolia: see **Inyokern** [KERN].

Magunden [KERN]: *locality,* 4 miles east of downtown Bakersfield (lat. 35°21'45" N, long. 118°55'50" W; at E line sec. 35, T 29 S, R 28 E). Named on Lamont (1954) 7.5' quadrangle.

Mahogany Creek [TULARE]: *stream,* flows 4 miles to Fish Creek (2) 10.5 miles south of Monache Mountain (lat. 36°03'15" N, long. 118°12'30" W; sec. 33, T 21 S, R 35 E). Named on Hockett Peak (1956) and Monache Mountain (1956) 15' quadrangles.

Mahogany Flat [TULARE]: *area,* 3 miles west-northwest of Camp Nelson along South Fork of Middle Fork Tule River (lat. 36°09'05" N, long. 118°39'20" W). Named on Camp Nelson (1956) 15' quadrangle.

Main Bypass: see **James Bypass** [FRESNO].

Major General: see **The Major General** [TULARE].

Malachite Creek: see **Copper Creek** [FRESNO].

Malaga [FRESNO]: *town,* 6 miles south-southeast of downtown Fresno (lat. 36°41' N, long. 119°44' W; mainly in sec. 30, T 14 S, R 21 E). Named on Malaga (1964) 7.5' quadrangle. Postal authorities established Tokay post office in 1886, changed the name to Malaga later the same year, discontinued it in 1964, and reestablished it in 1965 (Salley, p. 131, 222) The place, named for the popular malaga grape, was the site of a development called The Malaga Colony (Hanna, p. 183).

Malaga Colony: see **The Malaga Colony**, under **Malaga** [FRESNO].

Mallard Lake [FRESNO]: *lake,* 600 feet long, 8 miles east-southeast of Kaiser Peak (lat. 37°15'20" N, long. 119°02'35" W). Named on Kaiser Peak (1953) 15' quadrangle.

Mallory: see **Mount Mallory** [TULARE].

Malpais [TULARE]: *area,* 5 miles northwest of Kern Peak near Golden Trout Creek (lat. 36°22' N, long. 118°20'24" W). Named on Kern Peak (1956) 15' quadrangle.

Malta: see **Maltha** [KERN].

Maltermoro: see **Sunnyside** [FRESNO].

Maltha [KERN]: *locality,* 3.25 miles north of downtown Bakersfield along Southern Pacific Railroad in Kern River oil field (lat. 35°25'20" N, long. 118°59'45" W; sec. 8, T 29 S, R 28 E). Named on Oil Center (1954) 7.5' quadrangle. Called Malta on Oil Center (1940) 7.5' quadrangle. Maltha is a soft form of native asphalt.

Mama Pottinger Canyon [KERN]: *canyon,* 2.25 miles long, opens into Santa Maria Valley (present Little Santa Maria Valley) 5.5 miles west of McKittrick (lat. 35°18' N, long. 119°43'10" W); the canyon is 1 mile east of present Pottinger Canyon. Named on Olig (1943) 7.5' quadrangle.

Mammoth Crest [FRESNO]: *ridge,* 7 miles long, at and southeast of the place that Fresno County, Madera County, and Mono County meet (lat. 37°34'15" N, long. 119°00' W). Named on Devils Postpile (1953) and Mount Morrison (1953) 15' quadrangles.

Mammoth Pool Reservoir [FRESNO]: *lake,* behind a dam on San Joaquin River 8 miles west-northwest of Kaiser Peak on Fresno-Madera County line (lat. 37°19'25" N, long. 119°18'55" W; near N line sec. 14, T 7 S, R 24 E). Named on Shuteye Peak (1953) 15' quadrangle.

Mankins Creek [TULARE]: *stream,* flows 4 miles to North Fork Kaweah River 0.5 mile southeast of Kaweah (lat. 36°27'50" N, long. 118°54'40" W; sec. 11, T 17 S, R 28 E); the stream heads at Mankins Flat (2). Named on Kaweah (1957) 15' quadrangle. Called Mankin Cr. on Kaweah (1909) 30' quadrangle, but United States Board on Geographic Names (1968b, p. 8) rejected the form "Mankin" for the name. According to A.R. Mitchell (p. 78), the name is misspelled and commemorates James Manikin.

Mankins Flat [TULARE]:

(1) *area,* 3.25 miles north of Cliff Peak along Moore Creek (lat. 36° 36'10" N, long. 119°09'50" W; at S line sec. 20, T 15 S, R 26 E). Named on Stokes Mountain (1966) 7.5' quadrangle. Called Fisher Flat on Dunlap (1944) 15' quadrangle, but United States Board on Geographic Names (1967d, p. 5) rejected the names "Fisher Flat" and "Mankin Flat" for the name.

(2) *area,* 3 miles west-northwest of Kaweah (lat. 36°29'30" N, long. 118°57'45" W); the place is near the head of Mankins Creek. Named on Kaweah (1957) 15' quadrangle. Called Mankin Flat on Kaweah (1909) 30' quadrangle, but United States Board on Geographic Names (1968b, p. 8) rejected this form of the name.

Mankins Spring [TULARE]: *spring,* 3 miles north of Cliff Peak along Moore Creek (lat. 36°36' N, long. 119°09'50" W; near N line sec. 29, T 15 S, R 26 E); the spring is at the south end of Mankins Flat (1). Named on Stokes Mountain (1966) 7.5' quadrangle. United States Board on Geographic Names (1968b, p. 8) rejected the form "Mankin Springs" for the name.

Mann: see **Hugh Mann Canyon** [KERN].

Mannot Creek: see **Monotti Creek** [KERN].

Manse Meadow [FRESNO]: *area,* 11 miles east-southeast of Kaiser Peak (lat. 37°15'35" N, long. 118°55'55" W). Named on Kaiser Peak (1953) and Mount Abbot (1953) 15' quadrangles.

Manter Creek [TULARE]: *stream,* flows 8 miles to South Fork Kern River 10.5 miles west-northwest of Lamont Peak (lat. 35°50'45" N, long. 118°12'50" W); the stream goes through Manter Meadow. Named on Kernville (1956) and Lamont Peak (1956) 15' quadrangles. Called Manter Meadow Cr. on Olmsted's (1900) map. The name is for John Manter and Hiram Manter (Mitchell, A.R., p. 78).

Manter Meadow [TULARE]: *area,* 12.5 miles east-southeast of Fairview (lat. 35°53' N, long. 118°17' W; mainly in sec. 35, T 23 S, R 34 E); the place is along Manter Creek. Named on Kernville (1956) 15' quadrangle.

Manter Meadow Creek: see **Manter Creek** [TULARE].

Mantes Canyon [FRESNO]: *canyon,* drained by a stream that flows 2.5 miles to the canyon of Zapato Chino Creek 9.5 miles southeast of Coalinga (lat. 36°02'15" N, long. 120°15'05" W; near SW cor. sec. 4, T 22 S, R 16 E). Named on Kreyenhagen Hills (1956) 7.5' quadrangle.

Manuel Canyon [KERN]: *canyon,* less than 1 mile long, 10 miles west-northwest of Inyokern (lat. 35°42'05" N, long. 117°58'20" W; on N line sec. 2, T 26 S, R 37 E). Named on Owens Peak (1972) 7.5' quadrangle.

Manzanita: see **Milo** [TULARE].

Manzanita Canyon [TULARE]: *canyon,* drained by a stream that flows 2.5 miles to Kern River 2 miles east-southeast of Hockett Peak (lat. 36°12'40" N, long. 118°21'15" W); the canyon heads near Manzanita Knob. Named on Hockett Peak (1956) 15' quadrangle.

Manzanita Knob [TULARE]: *peak,* 4.5 miles east-southeast of Hockett Peak (lat. 36°12'30" N, long. 118°18'30" W; near SW cor. sec. 4, T 20 S, R 34 E). Altitude 9121 feet. Named on Hockett Peak (1956) 15' quadrangle.

Manzanita Park: see **Big Creek** [FRESNO] (3).

Manzanita Ridge [KERN]: *ridge,* generally west-trending, 1.5 miles long, center nearly 3 miles east-northeast of Caliente (lat. 35°16'45" N, long. 118°34'45" W). Named on Oiler Peak (1972) 7.5' quadrangle.

Maple Creek [TULARE]: *stream,* flows 1.5 miles to Yucca Creek 1.5 miles south-southeast of Yucca Mountain (lat. 36°33' N, long. 118°51'45" W). Named on Giant Forest (1956) 15' quadrangle.

Marble Canyon [TULARE]: *canyon,* drained by a stream that flows 0.5 mile to Dry Creek (1) 6 miles east-southeast of Auckland (lat. 36°32'50" N, long. 119°00'35" W; sec. 11, T 16 S, R 27 E). Named on Auckland (1966) 7.5' quadrangle.

Marble Cave [TULARE]: *cave,* 4.5 miles east of Yucca Mountain (lat. 36°33'30" N, long. 118°47'30" W); the cave is along Marble Fork near Marble Falls. Named on Tehipite (1903) 30' quadrangle.

Marble Falls [TULARE]: *waterfall,* 4.5 miles east-southeast of Yucca Mountain along Marble Fork (lat. 36°33'20" N, long. 118° 47'30" W). Named on Giant Forest (1956) 15' quadrangle.

Marble Fork: see **Kaweah River** [TULARE].

Marble Fork Creek: see **Marble Fork**, under **Kaweah River** [TULARE].

Marble Point [FRESNO]: *peak,* 1.5 miles east-southeast of Dinkey Dome (lat. 37°06'35" N, long. 119°06'20" W; sec. 35, T 9 S, R 26 E). Altitude 8858 feet. Named on Huntington Lake (1953) 15' quadrangle.

Marble Spring Canyon [KERN]: *canyon,* less than 1 mile long, 7.25 miles west-southwest of Liebre Twins (lat. 34°54'30" N, long. 118° 41' W). Named on Winters Ridge (1966) 7.5' quadrangle.

Marca Canyon [FRESNO]: *canyon,* drained by a stream that flows 3.5 miles to lowlands 17 miles southwest of Firebaugh (lat. 36° 43' N, long. 120°42'15" W; sec. 18, T 14 S, R 12 E). Named on Chounet Ranch (1956) 7.5' quadrangle.

Marcel [KERN]: *locality,* 3.5 miles southeast of Keene along the railroad (lat. 35°11'25" N, long. 118°31' W; sec. 35, T 31 S, R 32 E). Named on Keene (1966) 7.5' quadrangle.

Marcelin Spring [FRESNO]: *spring,* 11 miles southwest of Coalinga (lat. 36°01'05" N, long. 120°28'50" W; sec. 17, T 22 S, R 14 E). Named on Curry Mountain (1969) 7.5' quadrangle.

Marcella Lake [FRESNO]: *lake,* 650 feet long, 7.5 miles west-southwest of Mount Abbot (lat. 37°20'50" N, long. 118°54'50" W). Named on Mount Abbot (1953) 15' quadrangle.

Mare Spring [FRESNO]: *spring,* 3 miles north-northeast of Joaquin Rocks (lat. 36°21'35" N, long. 120°25'25" W; sec. 14, T 18 S, R 14 E). Named on Joaquin Rocks (1969) 7.5' quadrangle.

Margaret Lake: see **Big Margaret Lake** [FRESNO].

Margaret Lakes [FRESNO]: *lakes,* 14 miles north-northeast of Kaiser Peak (lat. 37°27'45" N, long. 119°02'45" W); Big Margaret Lake is the largest of the group. Named on Kaiser Peak (1953) 15' quadrangle.

Maricopa [KERN]: *town,* 6.5 miles south-southeast of Taft (lat. 35° 03'45" N, long. 119°24' W; around NW cor. sec. 12, T 11 N, R 24 W). Named on Maricopa (1951) 7.5' quadrangle. Postal authorities established Maricopa post office in 1901 (Frickstad, p. 57), and the town incorporated in 1911.

Maricopa Flat [KERN]: *area,* center 5 miles east-northeast of Maricopa (lat. 35°04'30" N, long. 119°18'15" W). Named on Pentland (1953) 7.5' quadrangle.

Maricopa Valley: see **Sunset Valley** [KERN].

Marie Lake [FRESNO]: *lake,* 1 mile long, 7.5 miles southeast of Mount Abbot (lat. 37°18' N, long. 118°52' W). Named on Mount Abbot (1953) 15' quadrangle. R.B. Marshall of United States Geological Survey named the lake for Mary Hooper, daughter of Major William B. Hooper (Gudde, 1949, p. 204); the name of nearby Mount Hooper commemorates the major.

Marilyn Lake: see **Peter Pande Lake** [FRESNO].

Marino Canyon [KERN]: *canyon,* drained by a stream that flows 2.5 miles to lowlands 4.25 miles east of Claraville (lat. 35°26' N, long. 118°15'05" W; near W line sec. 8, T 29 S, R 35 E). Named on Claraville (1972) 7.5' quadrangle.

Marion: see **Lake Marion** [KERN].

Marion Lake [FRESNO]: *lake,* 1300 feet long, 1.25 miles north-northeast of Marion Peak (lat. 36°58'25" N, long. 118°31' W). Named on Marion Peak (1953) 15' quadrangle. J.N. LeConte named the lake in 1902 for his wife, Helen Marion Gompertz LeConte (Hanna, p. 185).

Marion Peak [FRESNO]: *peak,* 24 miles east-northeast of Hume on Cirque Crest (lat. 36°57'25" N, long. 118°31'15" W). Altitude 12,719 feet. Named on Marion Peak (1953) 15' quadrangle. The name commemorates Mrs. J.N. LeConte (Hanna, p. 185).

Marjorie: see **Lake Marjorie** [FRESNO].

Markland Canyon [FRESNO]: *canyon,* drained by a stream that flows 2.5 miles to Hot Springs Canyon nearly 2 miles east-southeast of Coalinga Mineral Springs (lat. 36°07'55" N, long. 120° 32' W; sec. 1, T 21 S, R 13 E). Named on Sherman Peak (1969) 7.5' quadrangle.

Markwood Creek [FRESNO]: *stream,* flows 2.5 miles to Stevenson Creek 6.5 miles west of Dinkey Dome (lat. 37°06'20" N, long. 119°15' W; sec. 33, T 9 S, R 25 E); the stream goes through Markwood Meadow. Named on Huntington Lake (1953) 15' quadrangle.

Markwood Meadow [FRESNO]: *area,* nearly 6 miles west-southwest of Dinkey Dome (lat. 37°05'30" N, long. 119°13'55" W; sec. 3, T 10 S, R 25 E); the place is along Markwood Creek. Named on Huntington Lake (1953) 15' quadrangle. The name commemorates William Markwood, a sheepman of the 1870's (Gudde, 1949, p. 206).

Marmot Lake [FRESNO]: *lake,* 1200 feet long, 1 mile southwest of Mount Humphreys in Humphreys Basin (lat. 37°15'35" N, long. 118°40'55" W). Named on Mount Tom (1949) 15' quadrangle.

Marsala [KINGS]: *locality,* 2.25 miles north-northwest of Stratford along Southern Pacific Railroad (lat. 37°13'15" N, long. 119° 50' W). Named on Stratford (1929) 7.5' quadrangle.

Marshall Hill [FRESNO]: *hill,* 3.5 miles west-southwest of Prather (lat. 37°01'10" N, long. 119°34'25" W; sec. 33, T 10 S, R 22 E); the feature is 0.5 mile northwest of Marshall Station. Named on Millerton Lake East (1965) 7.5' quadrangle.

Marshall Lake [FRESNO]: *lake,* 1000 feet long, 8 miles southwest of Mount Abbot (lat. 37°18'05" N, long. 118°52'30" W). Named on Mount Abbot (1953) 15' quadrangle. Elden H. Vestal named the lake in 1942 (Browning, p. 138).

Marshall Meadow [TULARE]: *area,* 6.5 miles southeast of California Hot Springs (lat. 35°48'10" N, long. 118°36'10" W; near W line sec. 35, T 24 S, R 31 E). Named on California Hot Springs (1958) 15' quadrangle.

Marshall Station [FRESNO]: *locality,* 3.5 miles west-southwest of Prather near the south end of Auberry Valley (lat. 37°00'50" N, long. 119°34'05" W; sec. 33, T 10 S, R 22 E). Named on Millerton Lake East (1965) 7.5' quadrangle. Called Grabners on Millerton Lake (1945) 15' quadrangle, but United States Board on Geographic Names (1967a, p. 9) rejected this name. Postal authorities established Grabners post office in 1914, discontinued it in 1933, reestablished it in 1939, and discontinued it in 1951; the name was for a landowner at the place (Salley, p. 87).

Marsh Lake [FRESNO]:

(1) *lake,* 900 feet long, 6 miles west of Red Slate Mountain (lat. 37° 30'25" N, long. 118°58'45" W). Named on Mount Morrison (1953) 15' quadrangle.

(2) *lake,* 700 feet long, 6 miles west-southwest of Blackcap Mountain (lat. 37°01'55" N, long. 118°53'25" W; sec. 26, T 10 S, R 28 E). Named on Blackcap Mountain (1953) 15' quadrangle.

Martensdale: see **Cawelo** [KERN].

Martha Lake [FRESNO]: *lake,* 3600 feet long, 1 mile west-southwest of Mount Goddard (lat. 37°05'40" N, long. 118°44'15" W). Named on Mount Goddard (1948) 15' quadrangle. George R. Davis of United States Geological Survey named the lake in 1907 for his mother (Farquhar, 1924, p. 57).

Martina Spring [KERN]: *spring,* 6.25 miles southeast of Arvin (lat. 35°07'55" N, long. 118°46'05" W; near W line sec. 21, T 32 S, R 30 E). Named on Arvin (1955) 7.5' quadrangle.

Martinez: see **Chico Martinez Creek** [KERN].

Martinez Creek [FRESNO]: *stream,* flows 8 miles to lowlands 15 miles north of Coalinga (lat. 36°21'45" N, long. 120°21'15" W; near W line sec. 16, T 18 S, R 15 E). Named on Domengine Ranch (1956) and Joaquin Rocks (1969) 7.5' quadrangles.

Martinez Spring [FRESNO]: *spring,* 2.25 miles northeast of Joaquin Rocks (lat. 36°20'25" N, long. 120°24'55" W; sec. 26, T 18 S, R 14 E); the feature is along a branch of Martinez Creek. Named on Joaquin Rocks (1969) 7.5' quadrangle.

Martin Hill [TULARE]: *hill,* 2 miles south-southeast of Porterville (lat. 36°02'45" N, long. 118°59'45" W; sec. 6, T 22 S, R 28 E). Named on Success Dam (1956) 7.5' quadrangle.

Martin Pond [FRESNO]: *intermittent lake,* 800 feet long, 5.25 miles west of Selma (lat. 36°33'55" N, long. 119°42'10" W; sec. 5, T 16 S, R 21 E). Named on Conejo (1963) 7.5' quadrangle. Selma (1946) 15' quadrangle shows a permanent lake 1900 feet long.

Marvin Pass [TULARE]: *pass,* 15 miles northwest of Triple Divide Peak (lat. 36°43'50" N, long. 118°44'05" W; near SW cor. sec. 4, T 14 S, R 30 E). Named on Triple Divide Peak (1956) 15' quadrangle.

Marys Meadow [FRESNO]: *area,* 3 miles southwest of Kaiser Peak (lat. 37°15'40" N, long. 119°13'20" W; sec. 3, T 8 S, R 25 E). Named on Kaiser Peak (1953) 15' quadrangle.

Matchin [TULARE]: *locality,* 2.25 miles north-northeast of Exeter along Atchison, Topeka and Santa Fe Railroad (lat. 36°19'30" N, long. 119°07'45" W; near N line sec. 35, T 18 S, R 26 E). Named on Exeter (1952) 15' quadrangle.

Mather Pass [FRESNO]: *pass,* 1.5 miles southwest of Mount Bolton Brown (lat. 37°01'50" N, long. 118°27'35" W). Named on Big Pine (1950) 15' quadrangle. Mr. and Mrs. Chauncey J. Hamlin and their companions named the pass in 1921 for Stephen T. Mather, National Park Service director (Farquhar, 1924, p. 57).

Mathews Mill [FRESNO]: *locality,* 3 miles west-northwest of Shaver Lake Heights (present town of Shaver Lake) (lat. 37°07'25" N, long. 119°22'15" W; sec. 29, T 9 S, R 24 E). Named on Shaver Lake (1953) 15' quadrangle.

Mattei [FRESNO]: *locality,* 2.5 miles east-northeast of Malaga along Atchison, Topeka and Santa Fe Railroad (lat. 36°42' N, long. 119° 41'30" W; sec. 21, T 14 S, R 21 E). Named on Malaga (1964) 7.5' quadrangle.

Matterhorn: see **Little Matterhorn**, under **Mineral Peak** [TULARE].

Matthes Glaciers: see **Glacier Divide** [FRESNO].

Maxson Dome [FRESNO]: *peak,* 9.5 miles west-northwest of Blackcap Mountain (lat. 37°07'20" N, long. 118°57'15" W; sec. 30, T 9 S, R 28 E). Altitude 9547 feet. Named on Blackcap Mountain (1953) 15' quadrangles.

Maxson Lake [FRESNO]: *lake,* 450 feet long, 3 miles south-southwest of Blackcap Mountain (lat. 37°01'50" N, long. 118°48'45" W). Named on Blackcap Mountain (1953) 15' quadrangle.

Maxson Meadow: see **Big Maxson Meadow** [FRESNO].

Maxson Meadows [FRESNO]: *area,* 9.5 miles west-northwest of Blackcap Mountain (lat. 37°06'10" N, long. 118°57'20" W; sec. 31, T 9 S, R 28 E); the place is 1.5 miles south of Maxson Dome. Named on Blackcap Mountain (1953) 15' quadrangle. The name commemorates an early stockman (Browning, p. 140).

May: see **Wilbur May Lake** [FRESNO].

Mayan Peak [KERN]: *peak,* 2 miles west of Pinyon Mountain (lat. 35°27'50" N, long. 118°11'40" W; near NE cor. sec. 27, T 28 S, R 35 E). Altitude 6108 feet. Named on Pinyon Mountain (1972) 7.5' quadrangle.

Mayfair [KERN]: *locality,* 5.5 miles east-southeast of downtown Bakersfield (lat. 35°20'10" N, long. 118°54'50" W; sec. 12, T 30 S, R 28 E). Named on Lamont (1954, photorevised 1968) 7.5' quadrangle.

Mayville: see **Visalia** [TULARE].

McAdie: see **Mount McAdie** [TULARE].

McClure Flat [TULARE]: *area,* 5.5 miles southeast of Auckland (lat. 36°31'25" N, long. 119°02'45" W; sec. 21, T 16 S, R 27 E). Named on Auckland (1966) 7.5' quadrangle.

McClure Meadow [FRESNO]: *area,* 6 miles north-northwest of Mount Goddard in Evolution Valley (lat. 37°11'15" N, long. 118° 44'45" W). Named on Mount Goddard (1948) 15' quadrangle. The name honors Wilbur F. McClure, state engineer of California, for his assistance in building John Muir Trail (Farquhar, 1924, p. 57).

McClure Spring [TULARE]: *spring,* 5.5 miles southeast of Auckland (lat. 36°31'25" N, long. 119°02'40" W; sec. 21, R 16 S, R 27 E); the spring is at McClure Flat. Named on Auckland (1966) 7.5' quadrangle.

McClures Valley: see **Sunflower Valley** [KERN-KINGS].

McConnel Meadow [TULARE]: *area,* 10.5 miles northwest of Olancha Peak (lat. 36°23' N, long. 118°14'25" W; near SE cor. sec. 1, T 18 S, R 34 E). Named on Olancha (1956) 15' quadrangle.

McDermand: see **Lake McDermand**, under **Mount Goddard** [FRESNO].

McDermott Camp [TULARE]: *locality,* 7.5 miles north-northwest of California Hot Springs (lat. 35°58'55" N, long. 118°42'40" W). Named on California Hot Springs (1958) 15' quadrangle.

McDoogle: see **Mount McDoogle**, under **Mount Cedric Wright** [FRESNO].

McDuffie: see **Mount McDuffie** [FRESNO].

McFarland [KERN]: *town,* 6.5 miles south of Delano (lat. 35°40'40" N, long. 119°13'40" W; in and near sec. 12, T 26 S, R 25 E). Named on McFarland (1954) 7.5' quadrangle. Postal authorities established McFarland post office in 1908 (Frickstad, p. 57), and the town incorporated in 1957. The name is for J.B. McFarland, a founder of the community (Gudde, 1949, p. 199). The place first was known as Hunt, and later as Lone Pine (Wines, p. 86). Darling (p. 19) listed a place called Cabernet located along Southern Pacific Railroad 3 miles south of McFarland.

McFarland Creek [KERN]: *stream,* flows nearly 5 miles to join Peyton Creek and form Fulton Creek 2 miles east-northeast of Glennville (lat. 35°44'05" N, long. 118°40' W; sec. 20, T 25 S, R 31 E). Named on California Hot Springs (1958) 15' quadrangle, and on Alta Sierra (1972) and Glennville (1972) 7.5' quadrangles.

McGee: see **Mount McGee** [FRESNO].

McGee Canyon [FRESNO]: *canyon,* 1.5 miles long, drained by a stream that heads at McGee Lakes and flows to Evolution Creek 5 miles north of Mount Goddard (lat. 37°10'40" N, long. 118°43'15" W). Named on Mount Goddard (1948) 15' quadrangle.

McGee Lakes [FRESNO]: *lakes,* largest 2500 feet long, 3 miles north of Mount Goddard (lat. 37°08'55" N, long. 118°43'10" W); the lakes are 1.25 miles northeast of Mount McGee on upper reaches of McGee Creek. Named on Mount Goddard (1948) 15' quadrangle.

McGee Pass [FRESNO]: *pass,* 3500 feet southeast of Red Slate Mountain on Fresno-Mono County line (lat. 37°30'05" N, long. 118°51'35" W); the pass is near the head of McGee Creek, which is in Mono County. Named on Mount Morrison (1953) 15' quadrangle.

McGovern Gap [KERN]: *narrows,* 3.25 miles south of Orchard Peak (lat. 35°41'20" N, long. 120°08'30" W; near S line sec. 4, T 26 S, R 17 E) Named on Orchard Peak (1961) 7.5' quadrangle. A settler named McGovern lived near the place (Arnold and Johnson, p. 21).

McGuire Lake [FRESNO]: *lake,* 900 feet long, nearly 1 mile west-northwest of Blackcap Mountain (lat. 37°04'40" N, long. 118°48'20" W). Named on Blackcap Mountain (1953) 15' quadrangle. United States Board on Geographic Names (1983a, p. 4) approved the name "McGuire Lakes" for this and a nearby lake together.

McIntyre Creek [TULARE]: *stream,* flows 2.5 miles to South Fork of Middle Fork Tule River 1.25 miles east of Camp Nelson (lat. 36°08'20" N, long. 118°35'15" W; sec. 33, T 20 S, R 31 E). Named on Camp Nelson (1956) 15' quadrangle. The name commemorates Thomas McIntyre, who ran sheep in the neighborhood in the 1880's (Gudde, 1949, p. 199).

McIvers Spring [KERN]: *spring,* 5 miles northeast of Skinner Peak (lat. 35°37'15" N, long. 118°04'20" W). Named on Horse Canyon (1972) 7.5' quadrangle, which shows McIvers cabin at the place. Called Melvers Spring on Onyx (1943) 15' quadrangle. United States Board on Geographic Names (1975b, p. 10) gave the name "Melvers Spring" as a variant.

McKays Point [TULARE]: *relief feature,* 3.25 miles east-southeast of Woodlake where Saint Johns River diverges from Kaweah River (lat. 36°23'20" N, long. 119°02'45" W; near E line sec. 4, T 18 S, R 27 E). Named on Woodlake (1952) 7.5' quadrangle.

McKee Canyon [TULARE]: *canyon,* drained by a stream that flows less than 1 mile to Dry Creek (1) 4.25 miles east-northeast of Woodlake (lat. 36°26'25" N, long. 119°01'20" W; near E line sec. 22, T 17 S, R 27 E). Named on Woodlake (1952, photorevised 1969) 7.5' quadrangle.

McKenzie Fire Camp [FRESNO]: *locality,* 12 miles north-northeast of Clovis (lat. 36°58'55" N, long. 119°36'40" W; near S line sec. 7, T 11 S, R 22 E). Named on Clovis (1946) 15' quadrangle.

McKenzie Ridge [FRESNO]: *ridge,* northwest-trending, 7.5 miles long, 11 miles south-southeast of Balch Camp (lat. 36°45'45" N, long. 119°02'30" W). Named on Giant Forest (1956) and Patterson Mountain (1952) 15' quadrangles, and on Miramonte (1966) 7.5' quadrangle.

McKittrick [KERN]: *village,* 14 miles northwest of Taft (lat. 35°18'20" N, long. 119°37'20" W; on W line sec. 21, T 30 S, R 22 E). Named on Reward (1951) and West Elk Hills (1954) 7.5' quadrangles. Postal authorities established McKittrick post office in 1900 (Salley, p. 136). The name commemorates Captain William McKittrick, a local landowner and cattleman; the community incorporated in 1911 (Bailey, 1967, p. 17). California Mining Bureau's (1917c) map shows a place called Asphalto located about 3 miles northeast of McKittrick along a rail line. Postal authorities established Asphalto post office in 1893, discontinued it in 1894, reestablished it in 1898, and moved it 2 miles southwest in 1900 when they renamed it McKittrick (Salley, p. 11). At least three different places had the name "Asphalto" (Wines, p. 47), which was from deposits of asphaltum nearby (Bailey, 1967, p. 17).

McKittrick Summit [KERN]: *peak,* 8 miles west of McKittrick (lat. 35°17'25" N, long. 119°45'45" W; near N line sec. 30, T 30 S, R 21 E). Altitude 4332 feet. Named on McKittrick Summit (1959) 7.5' quadrangle. Arnold and Johnson (p. 21) proposed the name.

McKittrick Valley [KERN]: *valley,* northwest of and east-southeast of McKittrick (center near lat. 35°17'45" N, long. 119°35'45" W). Named on Reward (1951) and West Elk Hills (1954) 7.5' quadrangles. Arnold and Johnson (p. 21) proposed the name.

McLean Canyon: see **Carneros Canyon** [KERN].

McLeod: see **Hale McLeod Canyon** [KERN].

McLure Valley: see **Sunflower Valley** [KERN-KINGS].

McMillin [FRESNO]: *locality,* 12.5 miles southwest of downtown Fresno along Southern Pacific Railroad (lat. 36°39'20" N, long. 119°58' W; sec. 1, T 15 S, R 18 E). Named on Kearney Park (1923) 7.5' quadrangle.

Meadow Brook [FRESNO]: *stream,* flows 3 miles to North Fork Kings River 3.25 miles west of Blackcap Mountain (lat. 37°04'50" N, long. 118°51'10" W). Named on Blackcap Mountain (1953) 15' quadrangle.

Meadow Creek [TULARE]: *stream,* flows 1.5 miles to North Fork of Middle Fork Tule River 4.5 miles northwest of Camp Nelson (lat. 36°11'15" N, long. 118°40'10" W). Named on Camp Nelson (1956) 15' quadrangle.

Meadow Flat [TULARE]: *area,* 3.5 miles south of Wilsonia along Eshom Creek (lat. 36°41'10" N, long. 118°57' W; at SE cor. sec. 20, T 14 S, R 28 E). Named on Giant Forest (1956) 15' quadrangle.

Meadow Lakes [FRESNO]: *village,* 6.5 miles west-southwest of Shaver Lake Heights (present town of Shaver Lake) in Corlew Meadows (lat. 37°04'50" N, long. 119°25'45" W; sec. 11, T 10 S, R 23 E). Named on Shaver Lake (1953) 15' quadrangle. Postal authorities established Meadow Lakes post office in 1930, discontinued it for a time in 1932, and discontinued it finally in 1933 (Frickstad, p. 35).

Meadows Ridge [TULARE]: *ridge,* south-trending, 1 mile long, 9.5 miles east of Tucker Mountain (lat. 36°39' N, long. 119°02'10" W; on W line sec. 3, T 15 S, R 27 E). Named on Miramonte (1966) 7.5' quadrangle.

Measels Spring [KERN]: *spring,* 6.5 miles southwest of Pinyon Mountain (lat. 35°24' N, long. 118°14'55" W; sec. 20, T 29 S, R 35 E). Named on Pinyon Mountain (1972) 7.5' quadrangle.

Media Agua Creek [KERN]: *stream,* flows 8.5 miles to Antelope Plain 7 miles south of Blackwells Corner (lat. 35°30'55" N, long. 119°53'20" W; sec. 2, T 28 S, R 19 E). Named on Las Yeguas Ranch (1959) and Shale Point (1953) 7.5' quadrangles. The name is from the location of the stream halfway between Carneros Spring and a well at Point of Rocks—*media agua* means "middle water" in Spanish (Arnold and Johnson, p. 21).

Medley Lake [FRESNO]: *lake,* 1250 feet long, 7 miles south-southwest of Mount Abbot along South Fork Bear Creek (2) (lat. 37°18'10" N, long. 118°51'05" W). Named on Mount Abbot (1953) 15' quadrangle. William A. Dill of California Department of Fish and Game named the lake in 1942 (Browning, p. 143).

Megs Mud Spring [KERN]: *spring,* 11.5 miles north-northwest of Mojave (lat. 35°12'45" N, long. 118°13'25" W; near S line sec. 21, T 31 S, R 35 E). Named on Cache Peak (1973) 7.5' quadrangle.

Mehrten Creek [TULARE]: *stream,* flows 3.5 miles to Middle Fork Kaweah River 10 miles west-southwest of Triple Divide Peak (lat. 36°32'15" N, long. 118°41'30" W). Named on Triple Divide Peak (1956) 15' quadrangle. The name "Mehrten" commemorates James Mehrten, a pioneer cattleman of Three Rivers (Browning, p. 143). United States Board on Geographic Names (1938, p. 34) rejected the form "Merten Creek" for the name.

Mehrten Meadow [TULARE]: *area,* 8.5 miles west of Triple Divide Peak (lat. 36°35' N, long. 118°41' W; at E line sec. 35, T 15 S, R 30 E); the place is near the head of Mehrten Creek. Named on Triple Divide Peak (1956) 15' quadrangle. United States Board on Geographic Names (1938, p. 35) rejected the form "Merten Meadow" for the name.

Melvers Spring: see **McIvers Spring** [KERN].

Melvin [FRESNO]: *locality,* 1 mile south of the center of Clovis along Southern Pacific Railroad (lat. 36°48'25" N, long. 119°41'55" W; near NW cor. sec. 16, T 13 S, R 21 E). Named on Clovis (1964) 7.5' quadrangle.

Menagerie Canyon [KERN]: *canyon,* drained by a stream that flows 4 miles to Caliente Creek 3.25 miles west of Loraine (lat. 35°18'25" N, long. 118°29'35" W; sec. 24, T 30 S, R 32 E). Named on Loraine (1972) 7.5' quadrangle.

Mendel: see **Mount Mendel** [FRESNO].

Mendiburu Canyon [KERN]: *canyon,* drained by a stream that flows 4.25 miles to Tehachapi Valley 3.5 miles southeast of Tehachapi (lat. 35°05'40" N, long. 118°24'10" W; at N line sec. 31, T 12 N, R 14 W). Named on Tehachapi South (1966) 7.5' quadrangle.

Mendota [FRESNO]: *town,* 8.5 miles south-southeast of Firebaugh (lat. 36°45'15" N, long. 120°22'45" W; in and near sec. 31, T 13 S, R 15 E). Named on Coit Ranch (1956), Firebaugh (1956), Mendota Dam (1956), and Tranquillity (1956) 7.5' quadrangles. Postal authorities established Mendota post office in 1892; officials of Southern Pacific Railroad named the place for Mendota, Illinois (Salley, p. 138). The town incorporated in 1942. Postal authorities established Hayes post office, named for William J. Hayes, first postmaster, 18 miles southwest of Mendota in 1893 and discontinued it in 1902; they established Cadogan post office, named for James J. Cadogan, first postmaster, 20 miles south of Mendota in 1894 and discontinued it in 1895 (Salley, p. 31, 95). A place called Pueblo de las Juntas, located at the confluence of San Joaquin River and Fresno Slough (about 2 miles north of present Mendota), was one of the first places in San Joaquin Valley settled by Spaniards—*las juntas,* which means "junction" or "meeting place" in Spanish, may have referred to the location of the site at the confluence of waterways, or to the place being a rendezvous for refugees; the locality also was called Fresno for two large ash trees that grew there on the bank of the river (Hoover, Rensch, and Rensch, p. 91) Derby's (1850) map shows a place called Warsaw situated at about this same site. A place called Rancho de los Californios was located farther east on high ground near the south bank of San Joaquin River (Charles W. Clough, personal communication, 1985); notorious horse thieves hid from Spanish authorities at the locality, which continued as a den of outlaws well into the American period (Hoover, Rensch, and Rensch, p. 91).

Mendota Pool [FRESNO]: *water feature,* behind a dam on San Joaquin River 7 miles southeast of Firebaugh on Fresno-Madera County line (lat. 36°47'15" N, long. 120°22'15" W; sec. 19, T 13 S, R 15 E); the feature is 2.25 miles north of Mendota at the confluence of San Joaquin River and Fresno Slough. Named on Mendota Dam (1956) 7.5' quadrangle.

Mendota Station: see **Tranquillity** [FRESNO].

Mercey Creek [FRESNO]: *stream,* heads just inside Merced County and flows 8 miles, partly in San Benito County, to Little Panoche Creek 2 miles north-northwest of Mercey Hot Springs in Fresno County (lat. 36°44' N, long. 120°52'10" W; sec. 3, T 14 S, R 10 E). Named on Cerro Colorado (1969) and Mercey Hot Springs (1969) 7.5' quadrangles. Called Mercy Creek on Panoche Valley (1944) 15' quadrangle.

Mercey Hot Springs [FRESNO]: *locality,* 25 miles west-southwest of Firebaugh in Little Panoche Valley (lat. 36°42'15" N, long. 120° 51'30" W; near SE cor. sec. 15, T 14 S, R 10 E). Named on Mercey Hot Springs (1969) 7.5' quadrangle. Called Mercy Hot Sprs. on Panoche Valley (1944) 15' quadrangle. The name commemorates J.N. Mercy, an early stockman in the neighborhood (Stewart, p. 291). The springs were known as early as 1848, and were utilized for a health resort after about 1900 (Laizure, p. 322).

Mercy Creek: see **Mercey Creek** [FRESNO].

Mercy Hot Springs: see **Mercey Hot Springs** [FRESNO].

Meridian [KERN]: *locality,* 4.5 miles northeast of Mettler (lat. 35°06'25" N, long. 118°54'50" W; at SE cor. sec. 25, T 32 S, R 28 E). Named on Mettler (1955) 7.5' quadrangle.

Merriam Lake [FRESNO]: *lake,* 1600 feet long, 6.5 miles south of Mount Abbot (lat. 37°17'40" N, long. 118°47'30" W); the lake is 1.5 miles southwest of Merriam Peak. Named on Mount Abbot (1953) 15' quadrangle.

Merriam Peak [FRESNO]: *peak,* 5.5 miles south of Mount Abbot (lat. 37°18'35" N, long. 118°45'55" W). Altitude 13,077 feet. Named on Mount Abbot (1953) 15' quadrangle. California State Geographic Board proposed the name to honor C. Hart Merriam, chief of United States Biological Survey from 1885 until 1910, and chairman of United States Geographic Board from 1914 until 1925 (United States Board on Geographic Names, 1933a, p. 514). United States Board on Geographic Names (1983a, p. 4) rejected the name "Mount Merriam" for the feature.

Merrill: see **Pete Merrill Canyon** [FRESNO].

Merrill Pools [FRESNO]: *water feature,* 10.5 miles south-southwest of Coalinga on upper reaches of Taylor Creek (2) (lat. 36°00'25" N, long. 120°27'15" W; sec. 22, T 22 S, R 14 E). Named on Curry Mountain (1969) 7.5' quadrangle.

Merry Camp [TULARE]: *locality,* 2.5 miles north of California Hot Springs (lat. 35°55' N, long. 118°40'05" W; sec. 19, T 23 S, R 31 E); the place is along Merry Creek. Named on California Hot Springs (1958) 15' quadrangle.

Merry Creek [TULARE]: *stream,* flows 2.5 miles to Tyler Creek 1.25 miles north-northwest of California Hot Springs (lat. 35°53'50" N, long. 118°40'40" W; sec. 30, T 23 S, R 31 E). Named on California Hot Springs (1958) 15' quadrangle.

Merryman [TULARE]: *locality,* 3 miles northeast of Exeter along Visalia Electric Railroad (lat. 36°19'30" N, long. 119°06'20" W; at W line sec. 36, T 18 S, R 26 E). Named on Rocky Hill (1951) 7.5' quadrangle.

Merten Creek: see **Mehrten Creek** [TULARE].

Merten Meadow: see **Mehrten Meadow** [TULARE].

Mesa Lake [FRESNO]: *lake,* 1500 feet long, 2.5 miles west of Mount Humphreys in Humphreys Basin (lat. 37°16'05" N, long. 118°43'10" W). Named on Mount Tom (1949) 15' quadrangle.

Mesa Roida [KINGS]: *area,* 6 miles east of Avenal (lat. 35°59'25" N, long. 120°01'20" W; near NE cor. sec. 28, T 22 S, R 18 E). Named on Kettleman Plain (1953) 7.5' quadrangle. The name is descriptive—*roida* means "eroded" in Spanish (United States Board on Geographic Names, 1933b, p. 20).

Mesa Spring [KERN]: *spring,* 5.25 miles west-northwest of Garlock (lat. 35°26'35" N, long. 117°52'10" W). Named on Garlock (1967) 7.5' quadrangle.

Mesquite Canyon [KERN]: *canyon,* drained by a stream that flows nearly 4 miles to Fremont Valley 1.5 miles west-southwest of Garlock (lat. 35°23'35" N, long. 117°48'55" W). Named on Garlock (1967) 7.5' quadrangle.

Mesquite Springs [KERN]: *springs,* 1.5 miles southwest of Garlock (lat. 35°23'25" N, long. 117°48'45" W; at N line sec. 29, T 29 S, R 39 E); the springs are near the mouth of Mesquite Canyon. Named on Garlock (1967) 7.5' quadrangle.

Mesquite Springs: see **Koehn Spring** [KERN].

Metralla Canyon: see **Grapevine** [KERN].

Mettler [KERN]: *village,* 21 miles south of Bakersfield (lat. 35°03'50" N, long. 118°58'10" W; on S line sec. 1, T 11 N, R 20 W). Named on Mettler (1955) 7.5' quadrangle. The village was started in 1941 and named for W. H. Mettler, a local agriculturalist (Bailey, 1967, p. 17).

Mexican Colony [KERN]: *locality,* 2 miles south of Shafter (lat. 35° 28'05" N, long. 119°16'05" W; near N line sec. 27, T 28 S, R 25 E). Named on Rio Bravo (1954) 7.5' quadrangle.

Meyer: see **Oscar Meyer Spring** [KERN].

Middle Creek [TULARE]: *stream,* flows less than 1 mile to Alder Creek (1) 8.5 miles south-southeast of Camp Nelson (lat. 36°01'50" N, long. 118°32'50" W; sec. 8, T 22 S, R 32 E). Named on Camp Nelson (1956) 15' quadrangle.

Middle Dome: see **Kettleman Hills** [FRESNO-KERN-KINGS].

Middle Fork Spring [TULARE]: *spring,* 2.25 miles southeast of California Hot Springs (lat. 35°51'20" N, long. 118°38'45" W; near E line sec. 8, T 24 S, R 31 E). Named on California Hot Springs (1958) 15' quadrangle.

Middle Knob [KERN]: *ridge,* east-northeast-trending, 1 mile long, 8 miles north-northwest of Mojave (lat. 35°09'40" N, long. 118°13'15" W). Named on Cache Peak (1973) 7.5' quadrangle.

Middle Lost Keys Lake: see **Lost Keys Lakes** [FRESNO].

Middle Palisade [FRESNO]: *peak,* 2.5 miles northwest of Mount Bolton Brown on Fresno-Inyo County line (lat. 37°04'15" N, long. 118°28'05" W). Altitude 14,040 feet. Named on Big Pine (1950) 15' quadrangle. A peak 0.5 mile northwest of Middle Palisade is called Norman Clyde Peak for Norman A. Clyde, a mountaineer who made the first ascent of the feature in 1930 (United States Board on Geographic Names, 1974b, p. 3).

Middle Ridge [KERN]: *ridge,* west-northwest-trending, 3 miles long, 5 miles west-northwest of Liebre Twins (lat. 34°58'15" N, long. 118°39'15" W). Named on Winters Ridge (1966) 7.5' quadrangle.

Middle Spring [FRESNO]: *spring,* 4.25 miles north of Coalinga Mineral Springs (lat. 36°12'25" N, long. 120°33'30" W; sec. 10, T 20 S, R 13 E). Named on Sherman Peak (1969) 7.5' quadrangle.

Middle Turret Lakes [FRESNO]: *lakes,* two, largest 700 feet long, 8.5 miles south-southwest of Mount Abbot (lat. 37°16'05" N, long. 118°49'55" W); the lakes are between Lower Turret Lake and Upper Turret Lakes at the head of Turret Creek. Named on Mount Abbot (1953) 15' quadrangle.

Midge Creek [FRESNO]: *stream,* flows nearly 2 miles to Rancheria Creek (1) 3.5 miles southeast of Kaiser Peak (lat. 37°15'25" N, long. 119°08'30" W; sec. 4, T 8 S, R 26 E). Named on Kaiser Peak (1953) 15' quadrangle.

Midge Lake [FRESNO]: *lake,* 600 feet long, 16 miles northeast of Kaiser Peak (lat. 37°29' N, long. 119°00'40" W). Named on Kaiser Peak (1953) 15' quadrangle.

Midland: see **Midoil** [KERN].

Midoil [KERN]: *locality,* nearly 2 miles southeast of Fellows (lat. 35°09'30" N, long. 119°31'20" W; sec. 8, R 32 S, E 23 E). Named on Fellows (1951) 7.5' quadrangle. McKittrick (1912) 30' quadrangle shows Midland P.O. at the place. Postal authorities established Midland post office in 1908 and discontinued it in 1914 (Frickstad, p. 57).

Mid Ridge [KINGS]: *ridge,* east-southeast-trending, 0.5 mile long, 3.25 miles southwest of Kettleman City (lat. 35°58'10" N, long. 119°59'45" W; sec. 35, T 22 S, R 18 E). Named on Los Viejos (1954) 7.5' quadrangle.

Mid Valley [TULARE]: *locality,* 4 miles south-southeast of Goshen along Southern Pacific Railroad (lat. 36°17'50" N, long. 119°23'05" W; at NE cor. sec. 8, T 19 S, R 24 E). Named on Goshen (1949) 7.5' quadrangle.

Midway: see **Fellows** [KERN].

Midway Lake [FRESNO]: *lake,* 1200 feet long, 3.25 miles southeast of Blackcap Mountain (lat. 37°02'30" N, long. 118°45' W). Named on Blackcap Mountain (1953) 15' quadrangle.

Midway Mountain [TULARE]: *peak,* 12 miles west-northwest of Mount Whitney on Great Western Divide (lat. 36°38'35" N, long. 118°28'55" W). Altitude 13,666 feet. Named on Mount Whitney (1956) 15' quadrangle.

Midway Valley [KERN]: *valley,* southwest of Buena Vista Hills; center near Taft (lat. 35°09' N, long. 119°26' W). Named on Fellows (1951), Taft (1950), and West Elk Hills (1954) 7.5' quadrangles. The name is for the proximity of the place to Midway oil field (Arnold and Johnson, p. 21).

Mike Harney Canyon [KERN]: *canyon,* drained by a stream that flows 1.25 miles to French Ranch Gulch 3.5 miles north of Democrat Hot Springs (lat. 35°34'45" N, long. 118°40'15" W; sec. 17, T 27 S, R 31 E). Named on Democrat Hot Springs (1972) 7.5' quadrangle.

Milestone Bow: see **Milestone Bowl** [TULARE].

Milestone Bowl [TULARE]: *relief feature,* 11.5 miles west-northwest of Mount Whitney (lat. 36°37'30" N, long. 118°29' W); the feature is south of Milestone Mountain. Named on Mount Whitney (1956) 15' quadrangle. Called Milestone Bow on Mount Whitney (1907) 30' quadrangle, but United States Board on Geographic Names (1933a, p. 519) rejected this name.

Milestone Creek [TULARE]: *stream,* flows 3.5 miles to Kern River 9 miles west-northwest of Mount Whitney (lat. 36°38'25" N, long. 118°25'30" W); the stream heads near Milestone Mountain. Named on Mount Whitney (1956) 15' quadrangle.

Milestone Mountain [TULARE]: *peak,* 11.5 miles west-northwest of Mount

Whitney on Great Western Divide (lat. 36°38'05" N, long. 118°29' W). Altitude 13,641 feet. Named on Mount Whitney (1956) 15' quadrangle.

Miley [FRESNO]: *locality,* 5 miles northeast of Selma along Atchison, Topeka and Santa Fe Railroad (lat. 36°37'20" N, long. 119°32'45" W; sec. 14, T 15 S, R 22 E). Named on Selma (1964) 7.5' quadrangle. Postal authorities established Miley post office in 1899 and discontinued it in 1902; the name commemorates Julian J. Miley, first postmaster (Salley, p. 140).

Milham City [KINGS]: *locality,* 3 miles northwest of Kettleman City (lat. 36°02'15" N, long. 120°00' W; near SW cor. sec. 2, T 22 S, R 18 E). Named on Kettleman City (1937) and La Cima (1934) 7.5' quadrangles.

Milk Canyon [TULARE]: *canyon,* drained by a stream that flows 1.5 miles to North Fork of Middle Fork Tule River 5.5 miles west-northwest of Camp Nelson (lat. 36°10'05" N, long. 118°42'10" W). Named on Camp Nelson (1956) 15' quadrangle.

Milk Ranch Canyon [FRESNO]: *canyon,* drained by a stream that flows 6 miles to Mill Creek (3) 2 miles southeast of Dunlap (lat. 36°43'05" N, long. 119°05'35" W; sec. 12, T 14 S, R 26 E). Named on Miramonte (1966) 7.5' quadrangle.

Milk Ranch Peak [TULARE]: *peak,* 8 miles east of Kaweah (lat. 36° 29' N, long. 118°46'50" W; sec. 1, T 17 S, R 29 E); the peak is west of Paradise Ridge. Altitude 6250 feet. Named on Kaweah (1957) 15' quadrangle. United States Board on Geographic Names (1946, p. 2) rejected the name "Paradise Peak" for the feature.

Milk Ranch Peak: see **Paradise Peak** [TULARE].

Mill Creek [FRESNO]:

(1) *stream,* flows 5 miles to Mammoth Pool Reservoir 7.5 miles northwest of Kaiser Peak (lat. 37°21'45" N, long. 119°17'35" W; near E line sec. 36, T 6 S, R 24 E). Named on Kaiser Peak (1953) and Shuteye Peak (1953) 15' quadrangles.

(2) *stream,* flows 2.5 miles to Jose Creek 4 miles northwest of Shaver Lake Heights (present town of Shaver Lake) (lat. 37°08'20" N, long. 119°22'35" W; near N line sec. 20, T 9 S, R 24 E). Named on Shaver Lake (1953) 15' quadrangle. Kaiser (1904) 30' quadrangle shows Damon Mill situated near the headwaters of the stream.

Mill Creek [FRESNO-TULARE]: *stream,* heads in Tulare County and flows 30 miles to Kings River 1.5 miles north-northeast of Tivy Mountain in Fresno County (lat. 36°49'10" N, long. 119°21' W; near N line sec. 10, T 13 S, R 24 E). Named on Giant Forest (1956) and Patterson Mountain (1952) 15' quadrangles, and on Miramonte (1966), Pine Flat Dam (1965), and Tucker Mountain (1966) 7.5' quadrangles. United States Board on Geographic Names (1981b, p. 4) approved the name "Little White Deer Creek" for a stream that flows 4 miles to Mill Creek 2.5 miles west of Dunlap (lat. 36°44'32" N, long. 119°09'45" W; sec. 5, T 14 S, R 26 E). The Board at the same time approved the name "Little White Deer Valley" for a valley, 2.5 miles long, that is drained by Little White Deer Creek, and (p. 3) approved the name "Clingans Junction" for a locality situated in Little White Deer Valley 3 miles northwest of Dunlap (lat. 36°45'16" N, long. 119°10'10" W; sec. 32, T 13 S, R 25 E)—this name is for William Melrose Clingan, who established the first business at the place in 1946.

Mill Creek [KERN]:

(1) *stream,* flows 2.25 miles to Lumreau Creek 4.25 miles southeast of Glennville (lat. 35°40'45" N, long. 118°39'25" W; sec. 9, T 26 S, R 31 E). Named on Glennville (1972) 7.5' quadrangle.

(2) *stream,* flows 8 miles to Kern River 5.25 miles west-southwest of Miracle Hot Springs (lat. 35°32'35" N, long. 118°37'05" W). Named on Breckenridge Mountain (1972) and Miracle Hot Springs (1972) 7.5' quadrangles.

Mill Creek [KINGS]: *stream,* flows 4 miles to Cross Creek 6.5 miles southeast of Hanford (lat. 36°15'50" N, long. 119°33'35" W; sec. 23, T 19 S, R 22 E). Named on Remnoy (1927) 7.5' quadrangle. On Remnoy (1954) 7.5' quadrangle, the stream is mainly in an artificial watercourse. On Goshen (1926) 7.5' quadrangle, the name applies to a nearby stream that heads in Tulare County.

Mill Creek [TULARE]:

(1) *stream,* heads at Kaweah River and flows 16 miles to Kings County 10.5 miles west-southwest of Visalia (lat. 36°17'15" N, long. 119°28'25" W; at W line sec. 10, T 19 S, R 23 E). Named on Exeter (1952) and Visalia (1949) 15' quadrangles. Grunsky (p. 11) referred to "Visalia or Mill Creek" as a major high-water channel of Kaweah River. East Fork enters from the east 4.5 miles south-southwest of Goshen; it is 4.25 miles long and is named on Goshen (1926) 7.5' quadrangle.

(2) *stream,* flows 2 miles to South Creek 9.5 miles northeast of California Hot Springs near Johnsondale (lat. 35°58'05" N, long. 118°32'25" W; sec. 32, T 22 S, R 32 E). Named on California Hot Springs (1958) 15' quadrangle.

Mill Creek: see **Peel Mill Creek** [TULARE].

Miller: see **Camp Miller** and **Fort Miller**, under **Old Fort Miller** [FRESNO].

Miller Spring [KERN]: *spring,* 5.5 miles north of Caliente (lat. 35° 22'20" N, long. 118°39' W; near E line sec. 28, T 29 S, R 31 E). Named on Bena (1972) 7.5' quadrangle.

Miller Springs [KERN]: *springs,* 3.5 miles north of Emerald Mountain (lat. 35°18'20" N, long. 118°16'50" W). Named on Emerald Mountain (1972) 7.5' quadrangle.

Millersville [KERN]: *locality,* 1.25 miles west of Loraine along Caliente Creek (lat. 35°18'10" N, long. 118°27'20" W; sec. 20, T 30 S, R 33 E). Named on Loraine (1972) 7.5' quadrangle. The place was a mining camp that Bailey (1962, p. 50) called Millerville.

Millerton: see **Old Millerton** [FRESNO].

Millerton Lake [FRESNO]: *lake,* behind a dam on San Joaquin River 11 miles west-southwest of Prather on Fresno-Madera County line (lat. 37°00' N, long. 119°42'15" W; sec. 5, T 11 S, R 21 E). Named on Friant (1964), Millerton Lake East (1965), and Millerton Lake West (1965) 7.5' quadrangles.

Millerton Spring: see **Sulphur Springs** [FRESNO].

Millertown: see **Old Millerton** [FRESNO].

Millerville: see **Millersville** [KERN].

Mill Flat [FRESNO]: *area,* 3.5 miles south-southeast of Balch Camp along Kings River (lat. 36°51'25" N, long. 119°05'30" W; sec. 25, T 12 S, R 26 E). Named on Patterson Mountain (1952) 15' quadrangle.

Mill Flat Creek [FRESNO]: *stream,* flows 12.5 miles to Kings River 3.5 miles south-southeast of Balch Camp at Mill Flat (lat. 36°51'25" N, long. 119°05'40" W; sec. 25, T 12 S, R 26 E). Named on Giant Forest (1956) and Patterson Mountain (1952) 15' quadrangles, and on Miramonte (1966) 7.5' quadrangle.

Mill Potrero [KERN]: *marsh,* 4 miles south-southwest of Eagle Rest Peak (lat. 34°51'10" N, long. 119°10' W; sec. 19, T 9 N, R 21 W). Named on Sawmill Mountain (1943) 7.5' quadrangle. The first steam sawmill in the neighborhood was at the site (Hoover, Rensch, and Rensch, p. 127).

Mills: see **Mount Anna Mills**, under **Mount Guyot** [TULARE]; **Mount Mills** [FRESNO].

Mills Creek [FRESNO]: *stream,* flows 2.25 miles to Second Recess 3.25 miles west-northwest of Mount Abbot (lat. 37°24'15" N, long. 118°50' W); the stream heads at Upper Mills Creek Lake nearly 1 mile west-southwest of Mount Mills. Named on Mount Abbot (1953) 15' quadrangle.

Mills Creek Lake: see **Lower Mills Creek Lake** [FRESNO]; **Upper Mills Creek Lake** [FRESNO].

Mills Spring [FRESNO]: *spring,* 8 miles west of Coalinga (lat. 36°09'25" N, long. 120°29'50" W; sec. 30, T 20 S, R 14 E). Named on Alcalde Hills (1969) 7.5' quadrangle.

Milltown: see **Big Blue Mill** [KERN].

Millux [KERN]: *locality,* 15 miles east-northeast of Taft along Sunset Railroad (lat. 35°10'50" N, long. 119°11'45" W). Named on Millux (1954) 7.5' quadrangle. The name was coined in 1901 from the name of the stock-raising firm of Miller and Lux (Gudde, 1949, p. 216).

Millville: see **Big Blue Mill** [KERN].

Millwood [FRESNO]: *locality,* 6.5 miles east of Dunlap along Mill Flat Creek (lat. 36°44'40" N, long. 119°00'10" W; sec. 35, T 13 S, R 27 E). Site named on Miramonte (1966) 7.5' quadrangle. Postal authorities established Millwood post office in 1894 and discontinued it in 1909 (Frickstad, p. 35). The place was called Sequoia Mills before the post office was established (Forest M. Clingan, personal communication, 1990). Johnston (p. 54) noted a place called Andy Berry's Landing that was located between Millwood and Hoist Ridge—the Berry brothers had a log landing at the site.

Millys Foot Pass [TULARE]: *pass,* 11 miles northwest of Mount Whitney on Kings-Kern Divide (lat. 36°41'10" N, long. 118°25'45" W). Named on Mount Whitney (1956) 15' quadrangle. The name recalls Mildred Jentsch, who with Sylvia Kershaw made the first crossing of the pass in 1953 (Browning, p. 147).

Milo [TULARE]: *locality,* 6 miles north of Springville (lat. 36°13'10" N, long. 118°48'55" W; near NE cor. sec. 3, T 20 S, R 29 E). Named on Springville (1957) 7.5' quadrangle. Postal authorities established Milo post office in 1888 and discontinued it in 1922 (Salley, p. 141). The name was selected from a list that Henry Murphy submitted; Milo also was known as Mountain View (Mitchell, A.R., p. 68). Postal authorities established Manzanita post office in 1882 and changed the name the same year to Cramer, for Eleanor A. Cramer, first postmaster; they moved Cramer post office 1.5 miles south in 1887, and discontinued it in 1891 when they moved the service to Milo (Salley, p. 52, 132). Thompson's (1892) map shows both Milo P.O. (sec. 2, T 20 S, R 29 E) and Cramer P.O. (sec. 14, T 20 S, R 29 E). Postal authorities established Summerhouse post office in 1890, and discontinued it the same year when they moved the service to Cramer; the post office was at a summer campsite that Andrew J. Doty started in 1885 (Salley, p. 215). California Division of Highways' (1934) map shows a locality called Balch Park situated 8 miles east of Milo (near SE cor. sec. 25, T 19 S, R 30 E).

Mine Creek [FRESNO]: *stream,* heads in Merced County and flows 8 miles to Little Panoche Creek nearly 3 miles north of Mercey Hot Springs in Fresno County (lat. 36°44'45" N, long. 120°51'35" W; sec. 3, T 14 S, R 10 E). Named on Cerro Colorado (1969), Mercey Hot Springs (1969), and Ortigalita Peak (1969) 7.5' quadrangles.

Mine Hill [TULARE]: *peak,* 7 miles east of Porterville (lat. 36°03'25" N, long. 118°53'35" W). Altitude 1784 feet. Named on Success Dam (1956) 7.5' quadrangle.

Mine Mountain [FRESNO]: *peak,* 6 miles west-northwest of Castle Mountain on Fresno-Monterey County line (lat. 35°58'10" N, long. 120°26' W; sec. 35, T 22 S, R 14 E). Named on Parkfield (1961) 7.5' quadrangle.

Mineral Creek [TULARE]: *stream,* flows 2 miles to East Fork Kaweah River 1.5 miles west of Mineral King (lat. 36°27'05" N, long. 118°57'10" W; sec. 17, T 17 S, R 31 E); the stream heads at Mineral Lakes. Named on Mineral King (1956) 15' quadrangle. Elden H. Vestal of California Department of Fish and Game named the stream in 1956 (Browning, p. 148).

Mineral Hot Springs: see **Lower Mineral Hot Springs**, under **Mono Hot Springs** [FRESNO].

Mineral King [TULARE]: *locality,* 25 miles north-northeast of Springville along East Fork Kaweah River (lat. 36°27' N, long. 118°35'40" W). Named on Mineral King (1956) 15' quadrangle. In 1874 Harry Parole discovered the valley that contains present Mineral King and set up a camp at a bend in the river there; the place became known as Harry's Bend, and later as Sunny Slope before the dogs attracted to a butcher shop at the site gave it the name "Dog Town" (Jackson, p. 1, 48). The mining district organized in the valley in 1873 took the name "Mineral King," and the settlement there first had the biblical name "Beulah," for the land of promise (Jackson, p. 18). In 1879 the mining district contained separate settlements called Barton's, Ford's Camp, Beulah Camp, and Dog Town, but the whole place was called Mineral King (Jackson, p. 42). Postal authorities established Mineralking post office in 1877, discontinued it in 1882, reestablished it in 1897, and discontinued in it 1969 (Salley, p. 141). They established Redfield post office 6 miles west of Mineral King in 1880 and discontinued it in 1881; the name was for B. Redfield, first postmaster (Salley, p. 182). United States Board on Geographic Names (1980, p. 4) approved the name "Hengst Peak" for a feature, altitude 11,127 feet, situated 3 miles south-southwest of Mineral King (lat. 36°24'38" N, long. 118°37'15" W; sec. 32, T 17 S, R 31 E)—the name commemorates Albert Alfred Hengst of Three Rivers, who built trails and transplanted golden trout in the Sierra Nevada.

Mineral Lakes [TULARE]: *lakes,* largest 450 feet long, 2.25 miles southwest of Mineral King (lat. 36°25'40" N, long. 118°37'25" W; sec. 20, 29, T 17 S, R 31 E); the lakes are at the head of Mineral Creek. Named on Mineral King (1956) 15' quadrangle. Elden H. Vestal of California Department of Fish and Game named the lakes in 1956 (Browning, p. 148).

Mineral Peak [TULARE]: *peak,* nearly 2 miles east-southeast of Mineral King (lat. 36°26'45" N, long. 118°33'50" W). Altitude 11,550 feet. Named on Mineral King (1956) 15' quadrangle. The feature first was called Little Matterhorn for its resemblance to the peak in Switzerland called The Matterhorn (Jackson, p. 24).

Mineral Public Camp: see **Lower Mineral Public Camp**, under **Mono Hot Springs** [FRESNO].

Miner Creek [TULARE]: *stream,* flows 2.5 miles to South Fork Tule River 5 miles south-southwest of Camp Nelson (lat. 36°04'30" N, long. 118°38'30" W). Named on Camp Nelson (1956) 15' quadrangle. Browning (p. 148) associated the name with James L. Miner, who patented land in the neighborhood in 1888.

Miner's Peak: see **Sawtooth Peak** [TULARE] (1).

Ming: see **Lake Ming** [KERN].

Miningtown Meadow [FRESNO]: *area,* 3 miles northeast of Dinkey Dome (lat. 37°08'30" N, long. 119°04'45" W; near SE cor. sec. 13, T 9 S, R 26 E). Named on Huntington Lake (1953) 15' quadrangle. The name is from a proposed silver-mining town that Thomas Edward Bacon laid out in 1879, but that failed to develop (Browning, p. 148).

Minkler [FRESNO]: *village,* 2.25 miles east-southeast of Centerville (lat. 36°43'25" N, long. 119°27'20" W; sec. 10, T 14 S, R 23 E). Named on Wahtoke (1966) 7.5' quadrangle. According to Gudde (1949, p. 216), the name probably commemorates Charles O. Minkler, a farmer at nearby Sanger, or a member of his family.

Minnehaha Creek [TULARE]: *stream,* flows 2.5 miles to Cottonwood Creek 5 miles north-northwest of Woodlake (lat. 36°29'05" N, long. 119°07'10" W; near S line sec. 35, T 16 S, R 26 E). Named on Auckland (1966) and Woodlake (1952) 7.5' quadrangles.

Minneola: see **Clotho** [FRESNO]; **Ivesta** [FRESNO].

Minnie Lake [FRESNO]: *lake,* 700 feet long, 12.5 miles west-northwest of Mount Abbot (lat. 37°28' N, long. 118°59'15" W). Named on Mount Abbot (1953) 15' quadrangle. William A. Dill of California Department of Fish and Game named the lake in 1943; the name "Minnie" for the small lake is the diminutive of the word "minnow" (Browning, p. 148).

Minnow Creek [FRESNO]: *stream,* flows 4.5 miles to Fish Creek (1) 6 miles west of Red Slate Mountain in Cascade Valley (lat. 37°30'40" N, long. 118°58'15" W). Named on Mount Abbot (1953) and Mount Morrison (1953) 15' quadrangles.

Minster: see **The Minster** [TULARE].

Minter Field: see **Minter Village** [KERN].

Minter Village [KERN]: *locality,* 13 miles northwest of Bakersfield (lat. 35°30'15" N, long. 119°10'30" W). Named on Famoso (1953) 7.5' quadrangle. The name is from Minter Field, an Army Air Corps facility at the place during World War II; Minter Village was started at the site following the war (Bailey, 1967, p. 17). Postal authorities established Minter Field post office in 1942 and discontinued it in 1949; they established Minter Village post office in 1948 and discontinued it in 1961—the name "Minter Field" honored Lieutenant Hugh C. Minter, who was killed in an air crash in 1932 (Salley p. 142). Famoso (1930) 7.5' quadrangle shows a place called Dow located at the site of present Minter Village.

Miracle Hot Springs [KERN]: *village,* 14 miles southeast of Glennville along Kern River (lat. 35°34'35" N, long. 118°32' W; near SW cor. sec. 15, T 27 S, R 32 E); the village is less than 0.25 mile west-northwest of the mouth of Clear Creek (1). Named on Miracle Hot Springs (1972) 7.5' quadrangle. Called Hobo Hot Springs on Glennville (1956) 15' quadrangle. Postal authorities established Hobo Hot Springs post office in 1932 and changed the name to Miracle Hot Springs in 1947 (Frickstad, p. 56). The name "Hobo" recalls workmen on a compressor at the place—local ranchers called them hobos because they stole sheep and cattle (Bailey, 1967, p. 17-18). The place also was called Clear Creek Hot Springs (Waring, p. 51), Air Compressor Springs (Brown, p. 520), and Compressor Hot Springs (Bailey, 1967, p. 17).

Mirador [TULARE]: *locality,* 4 miles southeast of Lindsay along Atchison, Topeka and Santa Fe Railroad (lat. 36°10' N, long. 119° 02'05" W; near N line sec. 27, T 20 S, R 27 E). Named on Lindsay (1951) 7.5' quadrangle. The place was named in 1923 (Gudde, 1949, p. 217). California Division of Highways' (1934) map shows a locality called Strathmore Jct. along the railroad 1 mile south of Mirador (near N line sec. 34, T 20 S, R 27 E); the site is 1.25 miles east-northeast of Strathmore.

Miramonte [FRESNO]: *settlement,* 5 miles southeast of Dunlap along Mill Creek (3) (lat. 36°41'35" N, long. 119°03' W; sec. 21, T 14 S, R 27 E). Named on Miramonte (1966) 7.5' quadrangle. Postal authorities established Miramonte post office in 1909, discontinued in 1912 and reestablished it in 1923 (Frickstad, p. 35).

Miramonte: see **Semitropic** [KERN].

Mirror Lake [FRESNO]: *lake,* 800 feet long, 6.5 miles east of the town of Big Creek (lat. 37°12'55" N, long. 119°07'25" W; at SW cor. sec. 22, T 8 S, R 26 E). Named on Huntington Lake (1953) 15' quadrangle.

Mirror Lake [KERN]: *dry lake,* 2 miles northeast of downtown Ridgecrest on Kern-San Bernardino County line (lat. 35°38'45" N, long. 117°38'15" W; on E line sec. 26, T 26 S, R 40 E). Named on Ridgecrest North (1973) 7.5' quadrangle.

Missouri Triangle [KERN]: *locality,* 10 miles north of McKittrick (lat. 35°26'15" N, long. 119°41'20" W; sec. 2, T 29 S, R 21 E). Named on Belridge (1953) 7.5' quadrangle.

Mist Falls [FRESNO]: *waterfall,* 10 miles south of Marion Peak along South Fork Kings River (lat. 36°48'45" N, long. 118°32'55" W). Named on Marion Peak (1953) 15' quadrangle.

Mist Lake [FRESNO]: *lake,* 950 feet long, 3 miles west of Mount Abbot (lat. 37°22'55" N, long. 118°50'05" W). Named on Mount Abbot (1953) 15' quadrangle. Bob Ehlers of California Department of Fish and Game named the lake in 1952 (Browning, p. 149).

Mitchell Canyon [TULARE]: *canyon,* drained by a stream that flows less than 1 mile to Dry Creek (1) 7 miles southeast of Auckland (lat. 36°31'20" N, long. 119°00'40" W; sec. 23, T 16 S, R 27 E). Named on Auckland (1966) 7.5' quadrangle.

Mitchell Corner [TULARE]: *locality,* 4.25 miles west-northwest of Exeter (lat. 36°19'35" N, long. 119°12'20" W; at SW cor. sec. 30, T 18 S, R 26 E). Named on Exeter (1952) 15' quadrangle.

Mitchell Meadow [TULARE]: *area,* 7 miles south-southwest of Mineral King (lat. 36°21'20" N; long. 118°38'25" W; sec. 17, T 18 S, R 31 E). Named on Mineral King (1956) 15' quadrangle. The name commemorates Hyman Mitchell of White River (2) (Gudde, 1949, p. 218).

Mitchell Peak [FRESNO]: *peak,* 4.5 miles south-southeast of Dunlap (lat. 36°40'55" N, long. 119°04'25" W; sec. 30, T 14 S, R 27 E). Altitude 3574 feet. Named on Miramonte (1966) 7.5' quadrangle.

Mitchell Peak [TULARE]: *peak,* 14 miles northwest of Triple Divide Peak (lat. 36°43'55" N, long. 118°42'50" W; near W line sec. 3, T 14 S, R 30 E). Altitude 10,365 feet. Named on Triple Divide Peak (1956) 15' quadrangle. The name commemorates Susman Mitchell, banker, merchant, postmaster of Visalia (Hanna, p. 196), and son of Hyman Mitchell of Mitchell Meadow (Gudde, 1949, p. 218).

Mitchells Corner [KERN]: *locality,* 1.25 miles north-northwest of Arvin (lat. 35°13'25" N, long. 118°50'30" W; at SE cor. sec. 15, T 31 S, R 29 E). Named on Arvin (1955) 7.5' quadrangle.

Mitchell Slough [TULARE]: *stream,* flows 4.25 miles before ending 1.25 miles north-northeast of Tipton (lat. 36°04'40" N, long. 119° 18'10" W; at E line sec. 29, T 21 S, R 25 E). Named on Tipton (1950) and Woodville (1950, photorevised 1969) 7.5' quadrangles.

Miter: see **The Miter** [TULARE].

Moccasin Lake: see **Big Moccasin Lake** [FRESNO]; **Little Moccasin Lake** [FRESNO].

Mohave: see **Mojave** [KERN].

Mohave Desert: see "Regional setting."

Mojave [KERN]: *town,* 50 miles east-southeast of Bakersfield (lat. 35°03'10" N, long. 118°10'20" W; in and near sec. 8, 17, T 11 N, R 12 W); the town is in Mojave Desert. Named on Mojave (1973) 7.5' quadrangle. Called Mohave on Mendenhall's (1909) map, but United States Board on Geographic Names (1934, p. 11) rejected this form of the name. Postal authorities established Mojave post office in 1876 (Frickstad, p. 57). California Mining Bureau's (1909a) map shows a place called Chanz located 37 miles by stage line north of Mojave. Postal authorities established Chanz post office, named for George A. Chanz, first postmaster, in 1906 and discontinued it in 1909 (Salley, p. 42). Mendenhall's (1909) map shows a place called Water Station located 7.5 miles northeast of Mohave (present Mojave); it was a well-known road ranch and stage station (Mendenhall, 1909, p. 57). Thompson's (1921) map shows a place called Gamba located 4.5 miles southeast of Mojave along Atchison, Topeka and Santa Fe Railroad.

Mojave Desert: see "Regional setting."

Monache Creek [TULARE]: *stream,* flows 4.25 miles to South Fork Kern River 1.5 miles northeast of Monache Mountain in Monache Meadows (lat. 36°13'10" N, long. 118°10'15" W; sec. 3, T 20 S, R 35 E). Named on Monache Mountain (1956) and Olancha (1956) 15' quadrangles. Members of United States Geological Survey gave the name to the stream in 1905 (Gudde, 1949, p. 221).

Monache Meadows [TULARE]: *area,* east of Monache Mountain along South Fork Kern River (lat. 36°12'30" N, long. 118°10' W). Named on Monache Mountain (1956) 15' quadrangle.

Monache Mountain [TULARE]: *peak,* 6 miles southwest of Olancha Peak (lat. 36°12'20" N, long. 118°11'40" W; near N line sec. 9, T 20 S, R 35 E). Altitude 9410 feet. Named on Monache Mountain (1956) 15' quadrangle. Members of United States Geological Survey named the peak in 1905 for Monachi Indians, usually called Mono Indians (Gudde, 1949, p. 221).

Monarch [KERN]: *locality,* nearly 1 mile north of downtown Maricopa at the end of a spur of Sunset Railroad (lat. 35°04'35" N, long. 119°24'20" W; at N line sec. 2, T 11 N, R 24 W). Named on Buena Vista Lake (1912) 30' quadrangle.

Monarch Creek [TULARE]: *stream,* flows 2 miles to East Fork Kaweah River at Mineral King (lat. 36°27'10" N, long. 118°35'50" W); the stream heads at Monarch Lakes. Named on Mineral King (1956) 15' quadrangle.

Monarch Divide [FRESNO]: *ridge,* west-trending, 17 miles long, between South Fork Kings River and Middle Fork Kings River. Named on Marion Peak (1953) and Tehipite Dome (1952) 15' quadrangles. Members of the Whitney survey called the feature Dyke Ridge (Browning, p. 151).

Monarch Lakes [TULARE]: *lakes,* two, largest 2000 feet long, nearly 2 miles east of Mineral King (lat. 36°27'05" N, long. 118° 33'45" W); the lakes are at the head of Monarch Creek. Named on Mineral King (1956) 15' quadrangle.

Mon Bluff [KERN]: *relief feature,* nearly 3 miles south of Knob Hill on the south side of Poso Creek (lat. 35°31'30" N, long. 118°57'25" W; at W line sec. 3, T 28 S, R 28 E); the feature is 1 mile east of the mouth of Mon Canyon. Named on Knob Hill (1965) 7.5' quadrangle.

Mon Canyon [KERN]: *canyon,* drained by a stream that flows 2.5 miles to Poso Creek nearly 3 miles south-southwest of Knob Hill (lat. 35°31'45" N, long. 118°58'25" W; near NW cor. sec. 4, T 28 S, R 28 E). Named on Knob Hill (1965) 7.5' quadrangle.

Monmouth [FRESNO]: *village,* 7.25 miles west of Selma (lat. 36°33'55" N, long. 119°44'20" W; sec. 1, T 16 S, R 20 E). Named on Conejo (1963) 7.5' quadrangle. Officials of Atchison, Topeka and Santa Fe Railroad named the place in the 1890's for Monmouth, Illinois, former home of a settler in the village (Gudde, 1949, p. 221). Postal authorities established Monmouth post office in 1908 and discontinued it in 1919 (Frickstad, p. 35).

Monnotti Creek: see **Monotti Creek** [KERN].

Monocline Ridge [FRESNO]: *ridge,* northwest-trending, 12 miles long, 23 miles south-southwest of Firebaugh (lat. 36°32'30" N, long. 120°34' W). Named on Ciervo Mountain (1969), Lillis Ranch (1956), and Moncline Ridge (1955) 7.5' quadrangles. Anderson and Pack (p. 19) proposed the name because of the monoclinal structure of strata at the ridge.

Mono Creek [FRESNO]: *stream,* flows 20 miles to South Fork San Joaquin River 7.5 miles northeast of Kaiser Peak (lat. 37°21'20" N, long. 119°04'15" W). Named on Kaiser Peak (1953) and Mount Abbot (1953) 15' quadrangles.

Mono Creek Campground [FRESNO]: *locality,* 12 miles west of Mount Abbot along Mono Creek below Lake Thomas A. Edison (lat. 37°21'30" N, long. 118°59'50" W). Named on Mount Abbot (1953) 15' quadrangle.

Mono Crossing [FRESNO]: *locality,* 8 miles east-northeast of Kaiser Peak along South Fork San Joaquin River (lat. 37°20'30" N, long. 119°03'25" W); the place is 1.5 miles upstream from the mouth of Mono Creek. Named on Kaiser Peak (1953) 15' quadrangle.

Mono Divide [FRESNO]: *ridge,* extends for 7.5 miles southwest and then northwest from Mount Abbot (center near lat. 37°22'30" N, long. 118°50'30" W); the feature separates the drainage basin of Mono Creek from the drainage basin of Bear Creek (2). Named on Mount Abbot (1953) 15' quadrangle.

Mono Hot Springs [FRESNO]: *locality,* 9.5 miles east-northeast of Kaiser Peak (lat. 37°19'35" N, long. 119°01' W). Named on Kaiser Peak (1953) 15' quadrangle. Called Lower Hot Springs on Kaiser (1904) 30' quadrangle. Postal authorities established Mono Hot Springs post office in 1945 (Frickstad, p. 35). Laizure (p. 322) gave the alternate name "Lower Mineral Hot Springs" for the place, and mentioned that Lower Mineral Public Camp was at the site. Bradley (p. 457) noted that six springs occur at the place, the hottest with water temperature of 112° Fahrenheit.

Monolith [KERN]: *village,* 4.5 miles east of Tehachapi (lat. 35°07'15" N, long. 118°22'20" W; sec. 30, T 32 S, R 34 E). Named on Monolith (1966) 7.5' quadrangle. Postal authorities established Aqueduct post office in 1908 and changed the name to Monolith in 1910 (Salley, p. 9). The place began as a camp for workmen at a plant that supplied cement for construction of the aqueduct that takes Owens Valley water from Inyo County to Los Angeles; William Mulholland, who directed construction of the aqueduct, gave the name "Monolith" (Bailey, 1967, p. 18), which comes from the monolithic body of limestone that provided material for the cement plant (Barras, p. 59). California Mining Bureau's (1917c) map shows a place called Proctor located about 1 mile east of Monolith along the railroad near present Proctor Lake.

Mono Meadow [FRESNO]: *area,* 10 miles east-northeast of Kaiser Peak (lat. 37°20'45" N, long. 119°00'45" W); the place is along Mono Creek. Named on Kaiser Peak (1953) 15' quadrangle.

Mono Pass [FRESNO]: *pass,* 2.5 miles north-northeast of Mount Abbot on Fresno-Inyo County line (lat. 37°25'30" N, long. 118°46'20" W); the pass is at the head of the drainage basin of Mono Creek. Named on Mount Abbot (1953) 15' quadrangle.

Mono Rock [FRESNO]: *peak,* 3.5 miles north of Mount Abbot (lat. 37°26'20" N, long. 118°47'40" W); the feature is near Mono Creek. Altitude 11,555 feet. Named on Mount Abbot (1953) 15' quadrangle.

Monotti Creek [KERN]: *stream,* flows 3 miles to Adobe Canyon 4 miles east of Knob Hill (lat. 35°34'30" N, long. 118°52'40" W; near S line sec. 17, T 27 S, R 29 E). Named on Knob Hill (1965) and Pine Mountain (1965) 7.5' quadrangles. Called Mannot Creek on Woody (1935) 15' quadrangle, but United States Board on Geographic Names (1966a, p. 6) rejected the forms "Mannot Creek" and "Monnotti Creek" for the name.

Monson [TULARE]: *village,* 11.5 miles north-northwest of Visalia (lat. 36°29'35" N, long. 119°20'10" W; sec. 35, T 16 S, R 24 E). Named on Monson (1949) 7.5' quadrangle. Postal authorities established Monson post office in 1889 and discontinued it in 1920 (Frickstad, p. 212).

Monte Diablo Range: see "Regional setting."

Monterio: see **Rosamond** [KERN].

Montgomery Canyon [KERN]: *canyon,* drained by a stream that flows 4.5 miles to Caliente Creek 4.25 miles east-northeast of Caliente (lat. 35°18'45" N, long. 118°33'25" W; near SW cor. sec. 16, T 30 S, R 32 E). Named on Oiler Peak (1972) 7.5' quadrangle.

Montgomery Spring [KERN]: *spring,* 4.5 miles east of Caliente (lat. 35°17'05" N, long. 118°32'55" W; sec. 28, T 30 S, R 32 E); the spring is east of Montgomery Canyon. Named on Oiler Peak (1972) 7.5' quadrangle.

Monument Hill [TULARE]: *ridge,* southeast- to southwest-trending, 2 miles long, 6.5 miles east of Exeter (lat. 36°17'15" N, long. 119° 01'25" W). Named on Rocky Hill (1951) 7.5' quadrangle.

Moon Lake [FRESNO]: *lake,* 1400 feet long, 3.5 miles west-northwest of Mount Humphreys (lat. 37°17'35" N, long. 118°43'45" W; sec. 31, T 7 S, R 30 E). Named on Mount Tom (1949) 15' quadrangle.

Moonshine Spring [FRESNO]: *spring,* 3.5 miles northeast of Coalinga Mineral Springs (lat. 36°11'15" N, long. 120°31'05" W; sec. 13, T 20 S, R 13 E). Named on Sherman Peak (1969) 7.5' quadrangle.

Moore: see **Bill Moore Canyon** [TULARE]; **Bill Moore Ridge** [TULARE].

Moore Canyon: see **Sycamore Canyon** [KERN] (2).

Moore Creek [TULARE]: *stream,* flows 3.5 miles to Wilcox Creek 1 mile northeast of Cliff Peak (lat. 36°34'05" N, long. 119°09'15" W; sec. 4, T 16 S, R 26 E). Named on Stokes Mountain (1966) 7.5' quadrangle. Called Wilcox Cr. on Dinuba (1924) 30' quadrangle. Blake (1857, p. 28) referred to Moore's Creek.

Moorehouse Creek [TULARE]: *stream,* flows 2 miles to South Fork of Middle Fork Tule River 3 miles west-northwest of Camp Nelson (lat. 36°09'05" N, long. 118°39'10" W). Named on Camp Nelson (1956) 15' quadrangle. The name commemorates Gus Moorehouse, an early prospector (Gudde, 1949, p. 224).

Moore Mill [FRESNO]: *locality,* 6 miles south-southwest of Shaver Lake (lat. 37°03'05" N, long. 119°20' W; near N line sec. 22, T 10 S, R 24 E). Named on Kaiser (1904) 30' quadrangle.

Moose Lake [TULARE]: *lake,* 3300 feet long, 6 miles west of Triple Divide Peak (lat. 36°36' N, long. 118°38'15" W). Named on Triple Divide Peak (1956) 15' quadrangle. Hale Tharp named the lake (Browning, p. 153).

Moraine: see **Mount Moraine**, under **Barton Peak** [TULARE].

Moraine Creek [TULARE]: *stream,* flows 5.5 miles to Roaring River 10.5

miles north-northwest of Triple Divide Peak (lat. 36°43'50" N, long. 118°35'25" W); the stream goes through Moraine Meadows. Named on Triple Divide Peak (1956) 15' quadrangle.

Moraine Lake [TULARE]: *lake*, 1900 feet long, 14 miles northeast of Kern Peak (lat. 36°27'45" N, long. 118°27'20" W). Named on Kern Peak (1956) 15' quadrangle.

Moraine Meadows [TULARE]: *area*, 9 miles north-northwest of Triple Divide Peak (lat. 36°43'10" N, long. 118°34'20" W); the place is northeast of Moraine Ridge along Moraine Creek. Named on Triple Divide Peak (1956) 15' quadrangle. Called Moraine Meadow on Tehipite (1903) 30' quadrangle.

Moraine Ridge [TULARE]: *ridge*, northwest-trending, 3 miles long, 9 miles north-northwest of Triple Divide Peak (lat. 36°42'45" N, long. 118°34'30" W). Named on Triple Divide Peak (1956) 15' quadrangle.

Moreno Gulch [FRESNO]: *canyon*, drained by a stream that flows 4.25 miles to lowlands 17 miles west-southwest of Firebaugh (lat. 36°44'30" N, long. 120°43'30" W; sec. 1, T 14 S, R 11 E). Named on Chounet Ranch (1956) 7.5' quadrangle. Anderson and Pack (p. 19) remarked that the name is appropriate because some of the rocks in the canyon are brown—*moreno* means "brown" in Spanish.

Morgan Canyon [TULARE]: *canyon*, drained by a stream that flows 2.5 miles to Cottonwood Creek 2 miles south of Auckland (lat. 36° 33'35" N, long. 119°06'35" W; sec. 2, T 16 S, R 26 E). Named on Auckland (1966) 7.5' quadrangle.

Morlar Flat [FRESNO]: *area*, 2.5 miles southeast of Dunlap (lat. 36°42'10" N, long. 119°06'05" W; near SW cor. sec. 13, T 14 S, R 26 E). Named on Miramonte (1966) 7.5' quadrangle.

Mormon Canyon [KERN]: *canyon*, drained by a stream that flows 3 miles to Poso Flat 7 miles north-northwest of Democrat Hot Springs, and 1.5 miles west of Burke Hill (lat. 35°37'05" N, long. 118°43'35" W; near SW cor. sec. 35, T 26 S, R 30 E). Named on Democrat Hot Springs (1972) and Glennville (1972) 7.5' quadrangles. The stream in the canyon, and in a branch of the canyon, is called Burke Creek on Glennville (1956) 15' quadrangle. United States Board on Geographic Names (1975a, p. 4) approved the name "Mormon Canyon" for the feature, and gave the name "Burke Creek" as a variant.

Mormon Flat [KERN]: *area*, 3.5 miles north of Garlock (lat. 35°27'15" N, long. 117°47' W); the place is at the head of Mormon Gulch. Named on Garlock (1967) 7.5' quadrangle.

Mormon Gulch [KERN]: *canyon*, 1.5 miles long, opens into Goler Gulch 3.5 miles north-northeast of Garlock (lat. 35°27'05" N, long. 117°45'45" W). Named on Garlock (1967) 7.5' quadrangle.

Moro: see **Taft** [KERN].

Moro Creek [TULARE]: *stream*, flows 1.5 miles to Middle Fork Kaweah River 7.5 miles east-southeast of Yucca Mountain (lat. 36° 31'35" N, long. 118°45' W); the stream heads near Moro Rock. Named on Giant Forest (1956) 15' quadrangle.

Moron: see **Taft** [KERN].

Moro Rock [TULARE]: *peak*, 6 miles east-southeast of Yucca Mountain (lat. 36°32'40" N, long. 118°45'50" W). Altitude 6725 feet. Named on Giant Forest (1956) 15' quadrangle. The name is from a blue-roan mustang that ranged near the feature in the 1860's—*moro* is the Mexican term for the color of the animal (Browning, p. 154).

Morris Canyon [KERN]: *canyon*, drained by a stream that flows 2 miles to Indian Wells Canyon 9 miles west-northwest of Inyokern (lat. 35°42'30" N, long. 117°57'05" W). Named on Owens Peak (1972) 7.5' quadrangle.

Morris Peak [KERN]: *peak*, 10 miles west-northwest of Inyokern (lat. 35°41'25" N, long. 117°59'10" W; near SE cor. sec. 3, T 26 S, R 37 E). Altitude 7215 feet. Named on Owens Peak (1972) 7.5' quadrangle. United States Board on Geographic Names (1984b, p. 2) approved the name "Mount Jenkins" for a peak, altitude 7921 feet, situated 1.3 miles north of Morris Peak (lat. 35°42'33" N, long. 117°59'30" W); the name commemorates James Charles Jenkins, authority on the flora, fauna, and history of the southern Sierra Nevada.

Morrow: see **Jesse Morrow Mountain** [FRESNO].

Morton Flat [TULARE]: *area*, 8 miles east of Fountain Springs (lat. 35°54'15" N, long. 118°46'15" W; near NE cor. sec. 30, T 23 S, R 30 E). Named on Gibbon Peak (1965) 7.5' quadrangle.

Moseman Stage Station: see **Walker Basin** [KERN].

Moses Mountain [TULARE]: *peak*, 13 miles south-southwest of Mineral King (lat. 36°16'45" N, long. 118°40'45" W). Altitude 9331 feet. Named on Mineral King (1956) 15' quadrangle. Frank Knowles named the peak in the 1870's for an elderly fisherman who had the nickname "Moses" (Gudde, 1949, p. 226; Gudde used the form "Mount Moses" for the name).

Mosquito Creek [KINGS]: *stream*, flows 4 miles to Cross Creek 6 miles east-southeast of Hanford (lat. 36°17'35" N, long. 119°32'50" W; sec. 11, T 19 S, R 22 E). Named on Goshen (1949) and Remnoy (1954) 7.5' quadrangles.

Mosquito Creek [TULARE]: *stream*, flows 1.5 miles to East Fork Kaweah River 1.25 miles west of Mineral King (lat. 36°27'05" N, long. 118°37' W; near W line sec. 16, T 17 S, R 31 E); the stream heads below Mosquito Lakes. Named on Mineral King (1956) 15' quadrangle.

Mosquito Lakes [TULARE]: *lakes*, largest 1200 feet long, 2.25 miles south-southwest of Mineral King (lat. 36°25'20" N, long. 118°36'45" W); the lakes are above the head of Mosquito Creek. Named on Mineral King (1956) 15' quadrangle.

Mosquito Meadow [TULARE]: *area*, 8 miles east-northeast of Fairview (lat. 35°57'10" N, long. 118°21'15" W; sec. 6, T 23 S, R 34 E). Named on Kernville (1956) 15' quadrangle.

Mosquito Pass [FRESNO]: *pass*, 8.5 miles north-northwest of Blackcap Mountain (lat. 37°11'15" N, long. 118°51'10" W). Named on Blackcap Mountain (1953) 15' quadrangle.

Motte Canyon [FRESNO]: *canyon*, drained by a stream that flows 2.5 miles to Jasper Creek 9 miles south-southwest of Coalinga (lat. 36°01'15" N, long. 120°25' W; sec. 13, T 22 S, R 14 E). Named on Curry Mountain (1969) 7.5' quadrangle.

Mott Lake [FRESNO]: *lake*, 1300 feet long, 7 miles northwest of Mount Abbot (lat. 37°27'15" N, long. 118°52'55" W). Named on Mount Abbot (1953) 15' quadrangle. The name is for Ernest Julian Mott, a mountain explorer (United States Board on Geographic Names, 1933a, p. 533).

Mound [KERN]: *hill*, 3 miles south-southwest of Boron (lat. 34°57'55" N, long. 117°40'40" W; sec. 13, T 10 N, R 8 W). Altitude 2955 feet. Named on Leuhman Ridge (1973) 7.5' quadrangle.

Mount Abbot [FRESNO]: *peak*, 20 miles north of Mount Goddard on Fresno-Inyo County line (lat. 37°23'15" N, long. 118°47'05" W). Altitude 13,715 feet. Named on Mount Abbot (1953) 15' quadrangle. Members of the Whitney survey named the peak in 1864 for Henry Larcom Abbot, a captain of army engineers at the time (Farquhar, 1923, p. 381). United States Board on Geographic Names (1933a, p. 78) rejected the form "Mount Abbott" for the name.

Mount Abel: see **Cerro Noroeste** [KERN].

Mount Adelaide [KERN]: *peak*, 14 miles east-northeast of Bakersfield (lat. 35°25'50" N, long. 118°44'35" W; sec. 3, T 29 S, R 30 E). Altitude 3430 feet. Named on Mount Adelaide (1972) 7.5' quadrangle.

Mount Agassiz [FRESNO]: *peak*, 10.5 miles east of Mount Goddard on Fresno-Inyo County line (lat. 37°06'45" N, long. 118°31'50" W). Altitude 13,891 feet. Named on Mount Goddard (1948) 15' quadrangle. Called Agassiz Needle on Mount Goddard (1912) 30' quadrangle, a name that L.A. Winchell gave in 1879 to honor professor Louis Agassiz of Harvard University (Farquhar, 1923, p. 382).

Mountain Creek: see **Long Tom Gulch** [KERN].

Mountaineer Creek [TULARE]: *stream*, flows 5 miles to Alpine Creek 8 miles northeast of Camp Nelson (lat. 36°14'05" N, long. 118°30'10" W; at NW cor. sec. 33, T 19 S, R 32 E). Named on Camp Nelson (1956) 15' quadrangle.

Mountaineer Creek: see **South Mountaineer Creek** [TULARE].

Mountain Home [TULARE]: *locality*, 8 miles northwest of Camp Nelson (lat. 36°14' N, long. 118°41'35" W; sec. 35, T 19 S, R 30 E). Named on Camp Nelson (1956) 15' quadrangle.

Mountain House Station: see **Willow Springs Station**, under **Willow Spring** [KERN] (2).

Mountain Meadow [FRESNO]: *area*, 16 miles north-northeast of Hume (lat. 36°59'15" N, long. 118°46'45" W). Named on Tehipite Dome (1952) 15' quadrangle.

Mountain Mesa [KERN]: *locality*, 5.5 miles south-southeast of Wofford Heights near Isabella Lake (lat. 35°38'15" N, long. 118° 24'15" W; sec. 26, T 26 S, R 33 E). Named on Lake Isabella North (1972) 7.5' quadrangle.

Mountain Oak Spring [KERN]: *spring*, 5.25 miles east-southeast of Caliente (lat. 35°16'05" N, long. 118°32'25" W; near NE cor. sec. 4, T 31 S, R 32 E). Named on Oiler Peak (1972) 7.5' quadrangle.

Mountain Rest: see **Tollhouse** [FRESNO].

Mountain View: see **Milo** [TULARE].

Mount Anna Mills: see **Mount Guyot** [TULARE].

Mount Bago [FRESNO]: *peak*, 12.5 miles south of Mount Pinchot (lat. 36°46'15" N, long. 118°26'15" W). Altitude 11,868 feet. Named on Mount Pinchot (1953) 15' quadrangle.

Mount Barnard [TULARE]: *peak*, nearly 4 miles north-northwest of Mount Whitney on Tulare-Inyo County line (lat. 36°37'40" N, long. 118°19'15" W). Altitude 13,990 feet. Named on Mount Whitney (1956) 15' quadrangle. The name commemorates astronomer Edward E. Barnard (United States Board on Geographic Names, 1933a, p. 124).

Mount Baxter [FRESNO]: *peak*, 6.25 miles south-southeast of Mount Pinchot on Fresno-Inyo County line (lat. 36°51'45" N, long. 118°21'50" W). Altitude 13,125 feet. Named on Mount Pinchot (1953) 15' quadrangle. George R. Davis of United States Geological Survey made the first ascent of the peak and named it in 1905 for John Baxter, a rancher of Owens Valley in Inyo County (Browning, p. 12). United States Board on Geographic Names (1969c, p. 8) approved the name "Acrodectes Peak" for a feature situated about 0.5 mile west of Mount Baxter (lat. 36°51'40" N, long. 118°22'26" W).

Mount Bolton Brown [FRESNO]: *peak*, 20 miles east of Blackcap Mountain on Fresno-Inyo County line (lat. 37°02'45" N, long. 118° 26'20" W).

Altitude 13,538 feet. Named on Big Pine (1950) 15' quadrangle. Chester Versteeg and his companions climbed the peak in 1922 and named it to honor Bolton C. Brown of the Sierra Club (Versteeg, p. 426).

Mount Bradley [TULARE]: *peak,* 10.5 miles north-northwest of Mount Whitney on Tulare-Inyo County line (lat. 36°43'45" N, long. 118°20'15" W). Altitude 13,289 feet. Named on Mount Whitney (1956) 15' quadrangle. The name, given in 1898, commemorates Cornelius Beach Bradley, professor of rhetoric at University of California, and a charter member of the Sierra Club (Browning, p. 24).

Mount Breckenridge: see **Breckenridge Mountain** [KERN].

Mount Brewer [TULARE]: *peak,* 14 miles northwest of Mount Whitney on Great Western Divide (lat. 36°42'30" N, long. 118° 29' W). Altitude 13,570 feet. Named on Mount Whitney (1956) 15' quadrangle. The name commemorates William H. Brewer of the Whitney survey (Hanna, p. 40), who climbed the peak with Hoffmann and Gardner on July 4, 1864 (Whitney, p. 383). United States Board on Geographic Names (1989a, p. 4) approved the name "Mount Farquhar" for a peak, elevation 12,893 feet, located 1.6 miles northwest of Mount Brewer (lat. 36°43'43" N, long. 118° 29'53" W); the name commemorates Francis P. Farquhar, conservationist and writer, who was instrumental in creation of Kings Canyon National Park.

Mount Campbell: see **Campbell Mountain** [FRESNO].

Mount Carillon [TULARE]: *peak,* 1.25 miles northeast of Mount Whitney on Tulare-Inyo County line (lat. 36°35'30" N, long. 118° 16'40" W). Altitude 13,552 feet. Named on Mount Whitney (1956) 15' quadrangle. Chester Versteeg proposed the name for the resemblance of the feature to a bell tower (Browning, p. 31).

Mount Cedric Wright [FRESNO]: *peak,* 3.25 miles south-southeast of Mount Pinchot (lat. 36°54'15" N, long. 118°23'15" W). Altitude 12,372 feet. Named on Mount Pinchot (1953) 15' quadrangle. United States Board on Geographic Names (1962, p. 9) rejected the name "Mount McDoogle" for the peak, and noted that the name "Cedric Wright" honors photographer George Cedric Wright.

Mount Chamberlin [TULARE]: *peak,* 3.25 miles south-southwest of Mount Whitney (lat. 36°32' N, long. 118°18'35" W). Altitude 13,169 feet. Named on Mount Whitney (1956) 15' quadrangle. Members of the Sierra Club proposed the name to honor geologist Thomas Crowder Chamberlin (Browning, p. 37).

Mount Clarence King [FRESNO]: *peak,* 8 miles south-southwest of Mount Pinchot (lat. 36°50' N, long. 118°26'45" W). Altitude 12,905 feet. Named on Mount Pinchot (1953) 15' quadrangle. Called Mt. King on Mount Whitney (1907) 30' quadrangle. Members of the Whitney survey named the peak in 1864 for Clarence King of the survey (Hanna, p. 65).

Mount Corcoran [TULARE]: *peak,* 4 miles southeast of Mount Whitney on Tulare-Inyo County line (lat. 36°32'10" N, long. 118° 14'50" W). Named on Lone Pine (1958) 15' quadrangle. The name, given about 1868, commemorates philanthropist William Wilson Corcoran (United States Board on Geographic Names, 1968b, p. 6). United States Board on Geographic Names (1933a, p. 236) rejected the names "Mount Langley," "Mount Whitney No. 1," "Old Mount Whitney," and "Sheep Rock" for the peak, and later (1968b, p. 6) rejected the name "Corcoran Mountain" as well. The name "Sheep Rock" was from the large number of mountain sheep found near the peak (Whitney, p. 390).

Mount Cotter [FRESNO]: *peak,* 9 miles south-southwest of Mount Pinchot (lat. 36°49'05" N, long. 118°26'20" W). Altitude 12,721 feet. Named on Mount Pinchot (1953) 15' quadrangle. The name commemorates Richard Cotter, a member of the Whitney survey (United States Board on Geographic Names, 1938, p. 15).

Mount Crocker [FRESNO]: *peak,* 7 miles north-northwest of Mount Abbot on Fresno-Mono County line (lat. 37°29' N, long. 118°49'30" W). Altitude 12,457 feet. Named on Mount Abbot (1953) 15' quadrangle. R.B. Marshall of United States Geological Survey named the peak in memory of Charles Crocker, one of the "Big Four" of Central Pacific Railroad (Gudde, 1949, p. 84); nearby Mount Hopkins, Mount Huntington, and Mount Stanford commemorate the other three railroad magnates. The four peaks surround Pioneer Basin and are called Pioneer Peaks (Gudde, 1949, p. 264; Hanna, p. 237).

Mount Dade [FRESNO]: *peak,* 0.5 mile southeast of Mount Abbot on Fresno-Inyo County line (lat. 37°22'55" N, long. 118°46'45" W). Named on Mount Abbot (1953) 15' quadrangle.

Mount Darwin [FRESNO]: *peak,* 5 miles north-northeast of Mount Goddard on Fresno-Inyo County line (lat. 37°10' N, long. 118°40'15" W); the peak is east of Evolution Lake and Evolution Valley. Altitude 13,830 feet. Named on Mount Goddard (1948) 15' quadrangle. Theodore S. Solomons named the peak in 1895 to honor Charles Darwin (Farquhar, 1923, p. 390).

Mount Diablo Range: see "Regional setting."

Mount Eisen [TULARE]: *peak,* nearly 7 miles south-southwest of Triple Divide Peak on Great Western Divide (lat. 36°29'55" N, long. 118°34' W). Altitude 12,160 feet. Named on Mineral King (1956) and Triple Divide Peak (1956) 15' quadrangles. The name, given in 1941, commemorates Gustavus A. Eisen, a Swedish scientist who came to the United States in 1872 and was one of the first advocates of a park to protect groves of redwood trees (Hanna, p. 95).

Mount Ericsson [TULARE]: *peak,* 11 miles northwest of Mount Whitney on Kings-Kern Divide (lat. 36°41'50" N, long. 118°24'45" W). Altitude 13,608 feet. Named on Mount Whitney (1956) 15' quadrangle. Bolton C. Brown and his wife named the peak in 1896 for John Ericsson, inventor of the Union ironclad ship *Monitor* (Farquhar, 1923, p. 394).

Mount Farquhar: see **Mount Brewer** [TULARE].

Mount Fiske [FRESNO]: *peak,* 3.5 miles northeast of Mount Goddard on Goddard Divide (lat. 37°08'15" N, long. 118°40' W). Altitude 13,524 feet. Named on Mount Goddard (1948) 15' quadrangle. Theodore S. Solomons named the peak in 1895 for John Fiske, historian and philosopher (Farquhar, 1923, p. 395).

Mount Florence: see **Florence Peak** [TULARE].

Mount Gabb [FRESNO]: *peak,* 1.25 miles southwest of Mount Abbot (lat. 37°22'40" N, long. 118°48'10" W). Altitude 13,711 feet. Named on Mount Abbot (1953) 15' quadrangle. Members of the Whitney survey named the peak—or a nearby one—to honor William More Gabb, paleontologist of the survey (Farquhar, 1923, p. 396-397).

Mount Gardiner [FRESNO]: *peak,* 10 miles south-southwest of Mount Pinchot (lat. 36°48'20" N, long. 118°27'30" W). Altitude 12,907 feet. Named on Mount Pinchot (1953) 15' quadrangle. Members of the Whitney survey named the peak in 1865 for James Terry Gardiner (or Gardner), who served with the survey from 1864 until 1867 (Hanna, p. 117).

Mount Geneva: see **Mount Genevra** [TULARE].

Mount Genevra [TULARE]: *peak,* 11 miles northwest of Mount Whitney on Kings-Kern Divide (lat. 36°41' N, long. 118°26' W). Altitude 13,055 feet. Named on Mount Whitney (1956) 15' quadrangle. Helen M. Gompertz and J N. LeConte named the peak in 1899 for Genevra Magee after they had climbed to the top of Mount Brewer with Mrs. Magee (Hanna, p. 119). Called Mt. Geneva on Olmsted's (1900) map.

Mount Gilbert [FRESNO]: *peak,* 7 miles east-northeast of Mount Goddard on Fresno-Inyo County line (lat. 37°08'15" N, long. 118° 35'45" W; sec. 28, T 9 S, R 31 E). Altitude 13,103 feet. Named on Mount Goddard (1948) 15' quadrangle. The name commemorates geologist Grove Karl Gilbert (Farquhar, 1923, p. 398).

Mount Givens [FRESNO]: *peak,* 7.5 miles east of Kaiser Peak on Kaiser Ridge (lat. 37°16'45" N, long. 119°03'15" W). Altitude 10,648 feet. Named on Kaiser Peak (1953) 15' quadrangle. United States Board on Geographic Names (1982b, p. 3) approved the name "Mount Ian Campbell" for a peak situated 2.3 miles southeast of Mount Givens at the east end of Kaiser Ridge (lat. 37°15'43" N, long. 119°01'11" W); the name commemorates Ian Campbell, who was chief of California Division of Mines and Geology, and first chairman of California Advisory Committee on Geographic Names—Dr. Campbell did geologic work near the peak.

Mount Goddard [FRESNO]: *peak,* 33 miles east of Shaver Lake Heights (present town of Shaver Lake) (lat. 37°06'15" N, long. 118°43'05" W); the peak is at the head of Goddard Creek on Goddard Divide. Altitude 13,568 feet. Named on Mount Goddard (1948) 15' quadrangle. Members of the Whitney survey named the peak for George Henry Goddard, civil engineer and California map maker (Whitney, p. 382). United States Board on Geographic Names (1968c, p. 6) approved the name "Mount Solomons" for a peak situated 2.5 miles east of Mount Goddard; the name commemorates Theodore S. Solomons, who explored and mapped in the Sierra Nevada. The Board (1968a, p. 5) also approved the name "Lake McDermand" for a lake, 0.3 miles long, located 2.5 miles northeast of Mount Goddard; the name is for Charles K. McDermand, outdoorsman, writer, and authority on fishing for golden trout in the High Sierra.

Mount Goethe [FRESNO]: *peak,* 7.25 miles north of Mount Goddard on Glacier Divide (lat. 37°12'25" N, long. 118°42'15" W). Named on Mount Goddard (1948) 15' quadrangle. The name is for Johann Wolfgang Goethe and was given in commemoration of the bicentennial of Goethe's birth (United States Board on Geographic Names, 1949a, p. 3).

Mount Goode [FRESNO]: *peak,* 8.5 miles east of Mount Goddard on Fresno-Inyo County line (lat. 37°07'25" N, long. 118°34'05" W; on W line sec. 35, T 9 S, R 31 E). Altitude 13,092 feet. Named on Mount Goddard (1948) 15' quadrangle. The name commemorates topographer Richard Urquhart Goode of United States Geological Survey (Farquhar, 1923, p. 399).

Mount Goode: see **Black Giant** [FRESNO].

Mount Gould [FRESNO]: *peak,* 12 miles south of Mount Pinchot on Fresno-Inyo County line (lat. 36°46'50" N, long. 118°22'35" W). Altitude 13,005 feet. Named on Mount Pinchot (1953) 15' quadrangle. The name is for Wilson S. Gould of Oakland, who climbed the peak with J.N. LeConte in 1896; LeConte and some companions had called the feature University Peak in 1890, but that name was transferred to another place (Farquhar, 1923, p. 399).

Mount Guyot [TULARE]: *peak,* 6.25 miles southwest of Mount Whitney (lat. 36°30'30" N, long. 118°21'45" W). Altitude 12,300 feet. Named on Mount Whitney (1956) 15' quadrangle. The name commemorates Arnold H. Guyot, Swiss geologist and geographer (United States Board on Geographic Names, 1933a, p. 345). United States Board on Geographic Names

(1985b, p. 1) approved the name "Mount Anna Mills" for a peak located 2.5 miles south of Mount Guyot (lat. 36°28'30" N, long. 118°20'55" W); the name commemorates Anna Mills Johnston, one of the first women to climb Mount Whitney.

Mount Haeckel [FRESNO]: *peak,* 4.5 miles northeast of Mount Goddard on Fresno-Inyo County line (lat. 37°09' N, long. 118°39'35" W). Altitude 13,435 feet. Named on Mount Goddard (1948) 15' quadrangle. Theodore S. Solomons named the peak in 1895 for Ernest Heinrich Haeckel, professor of zoology at University of Jena (Farquhar, 1923, p. 401).

Mount Hale [TULARE]: *peak,* 1.5 miles west-northwest of Mount Whitney (lat. 36°35'15" N, long. 118°18'50" W). Named on Mount Whitney (1956) 15' quadrangle. Sierra Club officials suggested the name to commemorate astronomer George Ellery Hale (Browning, p. 90).

Mount Harrington [FRESNO]: *peak,* 13 miles west-southwest of Marion Peak (lat. 36°52'10" N, long. 118°43'55" W). Altitude 11,005 feet. Named on Marion Peak (1953) 15' quadrangle.

Mount Hazen: see **Table Mountain** [TULARE] (2).

Mount Henry [FRESNO]: *peak,* 8 miles north-northwest of Blackcap Mountain on LeConte Divide (lat. 37°11' N, long. 118°49'35" W). Altitude 12,196 feet. Named on Blackcap Mountain (1953) 15' quadrangle. J.N. LeConte named the peak for physicist Joseph Henry of Smithsonian Institution and National Academy of Sciences (Farquhar, 1923, p. 403).

Mount Hilgard [FRESNO]: *peak,* 3 miles southwest of Mount Abbot (lat. 37°21'40" N, long. 118°49'35" W). Altitude 13,361 feet. Named on Mount Abbot (1953) 15' quadrangle. Ernest C. Bonner suggested the name to honor E.W. Hilgard of University of California; apparently Bonner meant the name for present Recess Peak (Farquhar, 1923, p. 404).

Mount Hitchcock [TULARE]: *peak,* 2 miles southwest of Mount Whitney (lat. 36°33'15" N, long. 118°18'40" W). Altitude 13,184 feet. Named on Mount Whitney (1956) 15' quadrangle. The Reverend F.H. Wales of Tulare named the peak in 1881 to honor Charles Henry Hitchcock, professor of geology at Dartmouth College (Hanna, p. 139).

Mount Hooper [FRESNO]: *peak,* 9 miles southwest of Mount Abbot (lat. 37°17'30" N, long. 118°53'40" W). Altitude 12,349 feet. Named on Mount Abbot (1953) 15' quadrangle. R.B. Marshall of United States Geological Survey named the peak in memory of Major William B. Hooper (Gudde, 1949, p. 153).

Mount Hopkins [FRESNO]: *peak,* 5.5 miles north-northwest of Mount Abbot (lat. 37°27'50" N, long. 118°48'45" W); the peak is 2 miles southeast of Hopkins Pass. Altitude 12,302 feet. Named on Mount Abbot (1953) 15' quadrangle. R.B. Marshall of United States Geological Survey named the peak to commemorate Mark Hopkins, one of the "Big Four" of Central Pacific Railroad (Hanna, p. 141-142); nearby Mount Crocker, Mount Huntington, and Mount Stanford commemorate the other three railroad magnates. The four peaks surround Pioneer Basin and are called Pioneer Peaks (Gudde, 1949, p. 264; Hanna, p. 237).

Mount Humphreys [FRESNO]: *peak,* 12 miles north of Mount Goddard on Fresno-Inyo County line (lat. 37°16'15" N, long. 118° 40'15" W). Altitude 13,986 feet. Named on Mount Tom (1949) 15' quadrangle. Members of the Whitney survey named the peak in 1864 to honor General Andrew Atkinson Humphreys (Farquhar, 1923, p. 405-406).

Mount Huntington [FRESNO]: *peak,* nearly 6 miles north of Mount Abbot on Fresno-Mono County line (lat. 37°28'10" N, long. 118° 46'35" W). Altitude 12,405 feet. Named on Mount Abbot (1953) 15' quadrangle. R.B. Marshall of United States Geological Survey named the peak to honor Collis P. Huntington, one of the "Big Four" of Central Pacific Railroad (Hanna, p. 145); nearby Mount Crocker, Mount Hopkins, and Mount Stanford commemorate the other three railroad magnates. The four peaks surround Pioneer Basin and are called Pioneer Peaks (Gudde, 1949, p. 264; Hanna, p. 237).

Mount Hutchings [FRESNO]: *peak,* 9.5 miles south-southwest of Marion Peak (lat. 36°50' N, long. 118°36' W). Altitude 10,785 feet. Named on Marion Peak (1953) 15' quadrangle. The name commemorates J.M. Hutchings, pioneer of the Yosemite region and publisher of *Hutchings' California Magazine* (Farquhar, 1923, p. 406).

Mount Hutton: see **Red Mountain** [FRESNO] (2).

Mount Huxley [FRESNO]: *peak,* 3 miles northeast of Mount Goddard (lat. 37°08'15" N, long. 118°40'55" W). Altitude 13,117 feet. Named on Mount Goddard (1948) 15' quadrangle. Theodore S. Solomons named the peak in 1895 for Thomas Henry Huxley (Farquhar, 1923, p. 406). United States Board on Geographic Names (1969b, p. 4) approved the name "Mount Warlow" for a peak located 0.7 mile southeast of Mount Huxley; the name commemorates Chester H. Warlow, who helped in the creation of Kings Canyon National Park.

Mount Ian Campbell: see **Mount Givens** [FRESNO].

Mount Ickes [FRESNO]: *peak,* 2 miles west-southwest of Mount Pinchot (lat. 36°56' N, long. 118°26'20" W). Altitude 12,968 feet. Named on Mount Pinchot (1953) 15' quadrangle. 'The name commemorates Harold L. Ickes, Secretary of the Interior from 1933 until 1946 (United States Board on Geographic Names, 1964b, p. 13).

Mount Izaak Walton [FRESNO]: *peak,* 8 miles northwest of Mount Abbot (lat. 37°28'15" N, long. 118°53'20" W). Altitude 12,099 feet. Named on Mount Abbot (1953) 15' quadrangle. Francis P. Farquhar proposed the name in 1919 to honor the author of *The Compleat Angler* (Gudde, 1949, p. 163).

Mount Jenkins: see **Morris Peak** [KERN].

Mount Jepson: see **Mount Sill** [FRESNO].

Mount Johnson [FRESNO]: *peak,* 7.5 miles east-northeast of Mount Goddard on Fresno-Inyo County line (lat. 37°07'45" N, long. 118° 35'05" W; on E line sec. 33, T 9 S, R 31 E). Altitude 12,868 feet. Named on Mount Goddard (1948) 15' quadrangle. The name honors Willard D. Johnson of United States Geological Survey (United States Board on Geographic Names, 1933a, p. 401).

Mount Jordan [TULARE]: *peak,* 11.5 miles northwest of Mount Whitney on Kings-Kern Divide (lat. 36°41' N, long. 118°26'50" W). Altitude 13,344 feet. Named on Mount Whitney (1956) 15' quadrangle. The name commemorates David Starr Jordan, who was president of Stanford University (United States Board on Geographic Names, 1933a, p. 401).

Mount Jordan: see **North Palisade** [FRESNO].

Mount Julius Caesar [FRESNO]: *peak,* 2 miles south of Mount Abbot on Fresno-Inyo County line (lat. 37°21'20" N, long. 118°46'50" W); the peak is 1 mile east of Lake Italy. Altitude 13,196 feet. Named on Mount Abbot (1953) 15' quadrangle. Alfred H. Prater and Myrtle Prater made the first ascent of the peak in 1928; they named it for Julius Caesar because of its proximity to Lake Italy (Browning, p. 113). United States Board on Geographic Names (1978b, p. 4) rejected the form "Mount Julius Cesar" for the name.

Mount Kaweah [TULARE]: *peak,* 11 miles west-southwest of Mount Whitney (lat. 36°31'35" N, long. 118°28'40" W); the peak is at the southeast end of Kaweah Peaks Ridge. Altitude 13,802 feet. Named on Mount Whitney (1956) 15' quadrangle.

Mount Keith [TULARE]: *peak,* 9 miles north-northwest of Mount Whitney on Tulare-Inyo County line (lat. 36°42' N, long. 118°20'30" W). Altitude 13,977 feet. Named on Mount Whitney (1956) 15' quadrangle. Helen M. Gompertz named the peak in 1896 to honor landscape-painter William Keith (Hanna, p. 159).

Mount King: see **Mount Clarence King** [FRESNO].

Mount Lamarck [FRESNO]: *peak,* 7 miles north-northeast of Mount Goddard on Fresno-Inyo County line (lat. 37°11'40" N, long. 118° 40'10" W). Altitude 13,417 feet. Named on Mount Goddard (1948) 15' quadrangle. The name commemorates the French evolutionist Jean Baptiste Pierre Antoine de Monet de Lamarck (Browning, p. 122).

Mount Langley [TULARE]: *peak,* nearly 5 miles southeast of Mount Whitney on Tulare-Inyo County line (lat. 36°31'25" N, long. 118° 14'20" W). Altitude 14,042 feet. Named on Lone Pine (1958) 15' quadrangle. The name commemorates Samuel Pierpont Langley, secretary of Smithsonian Institution from 1877 until 1906, who led an expedition to Mount Whitney in 1881 to study solar heat (Farquhar, 1924, p. 52).

Mount Langley: see **Mount Cocoran** [TULARE].

Mount LeConte [TULARE]: *peak,* 3.5 miles southeast of Mount Whitney on Tulare-Inyo County line (lat. 36°32'30" N, long. 118° 15'05" W). Altitude 13,960 feet. Named on Mount Whitney (1956) 15' quadrangle. The name commemorates Joseph LeConte, professor of geology and natural history at University of California (Farquhar, 1924, p. 53).

Mount Maddox [TULARE]: *peak,* 15.miles northwest of Triple Divide Peak (lat. 36°43'40" N, long. 118°44'45" W; sec. 8, T 14 S, R 30 E). Named on Triple Divide Peak (1956) 15' quadrangle.

Mount Maggie: see **Maggie Mountain** [TULARE].

Mount Mallory [TULARE]: *peak,* 2.5 miles southeast of Mount Whitney on Tulare-Inyo County line (lat. 36°33' N, long. 118°15'45" W). Altitude 13,850 feet. Named on Mount Whitney (1956) 15' quadrangle. Norman Clyde, who climbed the peak in 1925, proposed the name to honor the climber who died on Mount Everest in 1924 (Farquhar, 1926, p. 306).

Mount McAdie [TULARE]: *peak,* 2.25 miles south-southeast of Mount Whitney on Tulare-Inyo County line (lat. 36°33' N, long. 118°16'30" W). Named on Mount Whitney (1956) 15' quadrangle. The name is for meteorologist Alexander G. McAdie (Browning, p. 140-141).

Mount McDoogle: see **Mount Cedric Wright** [FRESNO].

Mount McDuffie [FRESNO]: *peak,* 4.5 miles east-southeast of Mount Goddard on Black Divide (lat. 37°04'25" N, long. 118° 38'35" W). Altitude 13,271 feet. Named on Mount Goddard (1948) 15' quadrangle. The name honors Duncan McDuffie for his interest in national parks and work as a conservationist (United States Board on Geographic Names, 1954, p. 3).

Mount McGee [FRESNO]: *peak,* 2.5 miles north-northwest of Mount Goddard (lat. 37°08'20" N, long. 118°44'15" W). Altitude 12,969 feet. Named on Mount Goddard (1948) 15' quadrangle. The name commemorates William John McGee, who was with United States Geological Survey and Bureau of American Ethnology (Browning, p. 142).

Mount Mendel [FRESNO]: *peak,* 5.25 miles north-northeast of Mount Goddard (lat. 37°10'30" N, long. 118°40'50" W). Altitude 13,691 feet. Named on Mount Goddard (1948) 15' quadrangle. Sierra Club officials proposed the name before 1942 to honor Johann Gregor Mendel, Austrian geneticist; the peak was called Mt. Wallace on some maps (Browning, p. 143-144).

Mount Merriam: see **Merriam Peak** [FRESNO].

Mount Mills [FRESNO]: *peak,* 0.5 mile north-northwest of Mount Abbot on Fresno-Inyo County line (lat. 37°23'40" N, long. 118°47'20" W); the peak is near the head of Mills Creek. Altitude 13,468 feet. Named on Mount Abbot (1953) 15' quadrangle. The name commemorates Darius Ogden Mills, California banker, railroad man, and mountaineer (Hanna, p. 193)

Mount Moraine: see **Barton Peak** [TULARE].

Mount Moses: see **Moses Mountain** [TULARE].

Mount Muir [TULARE]: *peak,* 1 mile south of Mount Whitney on Tulare-Inyo County line (lat. 36°33'50" N, long. 118°17'25" W). Altitude 14,015 feet. Named on Mount Whitney (1956) 15' quadrangle. Professor Alexander G. McAdie named the peak for naturalist John Muir (Farquhar, 1924, p. 60).

Mount Needham: see **Florence Peak** [TULARE].

Mount Newcomb [TULARE]: *peak,* 2.5 miles south of Mount Whitney (lat. 36°32'25" N, long. 118°17'35" W). Altitude 13,410 feet. Named on Mount Whitney (1956) 15' quadrangle. Sierra Club officials proposed the name to honor astronomer and political economist Simon Newcomb (Browning, p. 158).

Mount Olive [FRESNO]: *hill,* 3 miles west of Orange Cove (lat. 36° 37'40" N, long. 119°22' W; sec. 16, T 15 S, R 24 E). Named on Orange Cove North (1966) 7.5' quadrangle.

Mount Owen: see **Brown** [KERN].

Mount Perkins [FRESNO]: *peak,* 2 miles southeast of Mount Pinchot on Fresno-Inyo County line (lat. 36°55'40" N, long. 118°22'50" W). Altitude 12,591 feet. Named on Mount Pinchot (1953) 15' quadrangle. Robert D. Pike named the peak in 1906 for George Perkins, governor of California from 1880 until 1883, and senator from 1893 until 1915 (Hanna, p. 233).

Mount Pheasant [KERN]: *peak,* 5.25 miles south-southeast of Woody (lat. 35°38'25" N, long. 118°47'05" W; near NE cor. sec. 30, T 26 S, R 30 E). Altitude 3629 feet. Named on Woody (1965) 7.5' quadrangle.

Mount Pickering [TULARE]: *peak,* 3.5 miles south of Mount Whitney (lat. 36°31'40" N, long. 118°17'30" W). Altitude 13,485 feet. Named on Mount Whitney (1956) 15' quadrangle. Sierra Club officials proposed the name to honor astronomer Edward Charles Pickering (Browning, p. 169).

Mount Pinchot [FRESNO]: *peak,* 6.5 miles east of Marion Peak (lat. 36°56'45" N, long. 118°24'15" W). Altitude 13,495 feet. Named on Mount Pinchot (1953) 15' quadrangle. J.N. LeConte named the peak in 1896 for conservationist Gifford Pinchot, Forest Service chief from 1898 until 1910 (Hanna, p. 236).

Mount Poso [KERN]: *peak,* 14 miles east-southeast of McFarland (lat. 35°35'35" N, long. 119°00'10" W; sec. 7, T 27 S, R 28 E); the peak is north of Poso Creek. Altitude 1215 feet. Named on North of Oildale (1954) 7.5' quadrangle.

Mount Powell [KERN]: *peak,* 5.5 miles east-northeast of Mount Goddard on Fresno-Inyo County line (lat. 37°08'15" N, long. 118° 37'40" W; sec. 30, T 9 S, R 31 E). Named on Mount Goddard (1948) 15' quadrangle. According to Farquhar (1924, p. 64), the name presumably commemorates John Wesley Powell.

Mount Prater [FRESNO]: *peak,* 3500 feet south-southeast of Mount Bolton Brown on Fresno-Inyo County line (lat. 37°02'15" N, long. 118°26' W). Altitude 13,329 feet. Named on Big Pine (1950) 15' quadrangle. The name commemorates Alfred Prater, who with his wife ascended the peak in 1928 (United States Board on Geographic Names, 1933a, p. 618).

Mount Reinstein [FRESNO]: *peak,* 2 miles southwest of Mount Goddard (lat. 37°04'45" N, long. 118°44'15" W). Altitude 12,604 feet. Named on Mount Goddard (1948) 15' quadrangle. R.B. Marshall of United States Geological Survey named the peak for Jacob B. Reinstein, a regent of University of California from 1897 until 1912 (Farquhar, 1925, p. 128).

Mount Rixford [FRESNO]: *peak,* 11 miles south of Mount Pinchot (lat. 36°47'05" N, long. 118°23'55" W). Altitude 12,890 feet. Named on Mount Pinchot (1953) 15' quadrangle. Vernon L. Kellogg named the peak in 1899 for Dr. Emmet Rixford, who was the first to climb the feature (Hanna, p. 257).

Mount Royce: see **Royce Peak** [FRESNO].

Mount Ruskin [FRESNO]: *peak,* 4.25 miles west-northwest of Mount Pinchot (lat. 36°58'45" N, long. 118°28'20" W). Altitude 12,920 feet. Named on Mount Pinchot (1953) 15' quadrangle. Bolton C. Brown named the peak in 1895 for English writer John Ruskin (Hanna, p. 261).

Mount Russell [TULARE]: *peak,* less than 1 mile north-northeast of Mount Whitney on Tulare-Inyo County line (lat. 36°35'25" N, long. 118°17'15" W). Altitude 14,086 feet. Named on Mount Whitney (1956) 15' quadrangle. The name commemorates geologist Israel C. Russell (Hanna, p. 261).

Mount Senger [FRESNO]: *peak,* 8.5 miles south-southwest of Mount Abbot (lat. 37°16'40" N, long. 118°51'25" W). Altitude 12,271 feet. Named on Mount Abbot (1953) 15' quadrangle. Theodore S. Solomons named the peak in 1894 for J. Henry Senger, professor of German at University of California and a founder of the Sierra Club (Farquhar, 1925, p. 132).

Mount Shakspere [FRESNO]: *peak,* 11.5 miles east-southeast of Mount Goddard (lat. 37°02'10" N, long. 118°31'55" W). Altitude 12,151 feet. Named on Mount Goddard (1948) 15' quadrangle.

Mount Shinn [FRESNO]: *peak,* 12 miles northwest of Blackcap Mountain (lat. 37°12'45" N, long. 118°55'05" W; sec. 28, T 8 S, R 28 E). Altitude 11,020 feet. Named on Blackcap Mountain (1953) 15' quadrangle. The name is for Charles Howard Shinn, who was supervisor of Sierra National Forest (United States Board on Geographic Names, 1933a, p. 689).

Mount Shinn Lake [FRESNO]: *lake,* 500 feet long, 12 miles northwest of Blackcap Mountain (lat. 37°12'25" N, long. 118°55'25" W; sec. 29, T 8 S, R 28 E); the lake is 0.5 mile southwest of Mount Shinn. Named on Blackcap Mountain (1953) 15' quadrangle.

Mount Sill [FRESNO]: *peak,* 12 miles east of Mount Goddard on Fresno-Inyo County line (lat. 37°05'45" N, long. 118°30'10" W). Altitude 14,162 feet. Named on Mount Goddard (1948) 15' quadrangle. J.N. LeConte named the peak in 1896 for Edward Rowland Sill, professor of literature at University of California from 1874 until 1882 (Farquhar, 1925, p. 133). United States Board on Geographic Names (1971b, p. 2) approved the name "Mount Jepson" for a peak situated 0.7 mile southeast of Mount Sill; the name honors Willis Linn Jepson, professor of botany at University of California from 1899 until 1937. The Board at the same time noted the variant name "Pine Martin Peak" for present Mount Jepson.

Mount Silliman [TULARE]: *peak,* 10 miles west-northwest of Triple Divide Peak (lat. 36°38'40" N, long. 118°41'50" W). Altitude 11,188 feet. Named on Triple Divide Peak (1956) 15' quadrangle. William H. Brewer and other members of the Whitney survey named the peak in 1864 for Professor Benjamin Silliman, Jr., of Yale University (Brewer, p. 523).

Mount Solomons: see **Mount Goddard** [FRESNO].

Mount Spencer [FRESNO]: *peak,* 4 miles north-northeast of Mount Goddard (lat. 37°09'20" N, long. 118°40'50" W). Named on Mount Goddard (1948) 15' quadrangle. Theodore S. Solomons named the peak in 1895 for Herbert Spencer, author of *Principles of Philosophy* (Farquhar, 1925, p. 134).

Mount Stanford [FRESNO]: *peak,* 7 miles north of Mount Abbot on Fresno-Inyo County line (lat. 37°29'25" N, long. 118°47'45" W). Altitude 12,851 feet. Named on Mount Abbot (1953) 15' quadrangle. R.B. Marshall of United States Geological Survey named the peak for Leland Stanford (Farquhar, 1925, p. 135), one of the "Big Four" of Central Pacific Railroad; nearby Mount Crocker, Mount Hopkins, and Mount Huntington commemorate the other three railroad magnates. The four peaks surround Pioneer Basin and are called Pioneer Peaks (Gudde, 1949, p. 264; Hanna, p. 237). United States Board on Geographic Names (1983a, p. 5) rejected the name "Stanford Peak" for Mount Stanford.

Mount Stanford [TULARE]: *peak,* 10.5 miles north-northwest of Mount Whitney (lat. 36°42'10" N, long. 118°23'40" W). Altitude 13,963 feet. Named on Mount Whitney (1956) 15' quadrangle. Bolton C. Brown named the peak in 1896 for Stanford University (Farquhar, 1925, p. 135).

Mount Starr [FRESNO]: *peak,* 3 miles north-northeast of Mount Abbot on Fresno-Inyo County line (lat. 37°25'40" N, long, 118°45'55" W). Altitude 12,870 feet. Named on Mount Abbot (1953) 15' quadrangle. Sierra Club officials named the peak to honor Walter A. Starr, Jr., mountain climber and author of *Guide to the John Muir Trail and the High Sierra Region* (United States Board on Geographic Names, 1939, p. 33).

Mount Stevenson [FRESNO]: *ridge,* north-northeast-trending, 3 miles long, 1.25 miles north-northwest of Shaver Lake Heights (present town of Shaver Lake) (lat. 37°07'20" N, long. 119°19'40" W); the ridge is south of Stevenson Creek. Named on Shaver Lake (1953) 15' quadrangle.

Mount Stewart [TULARE]: *peak,* 2 miles southwest of Triple Divide Peak on Great Western Divide (lat. 36°34'10" N, long. 118°33'15" W). Altitude 12,205 feet. Named on Triple Divide Peak (1956) 15' quadrangle. United States Board on Geographic Names (1938, p. 52) rejected the form "Stewart Mountain" for the name, and noted that California State Geographical Board named the feature in 1929 to honor Colonel George W. Stewart of Visalia, who was instrumental in creation of Sequoia National Park.

Mount Thompson [FRESNO]: *peak,* 6.5 miles east-northeast of Mount Goddard on Fresno-Inyo County line (lat. 37°08'35" N, long. 118°36'45" W; sec. 29, T 9 S, R 31 E); the peak is 1 mile east-northeast of Mount Powell. Named on Mount Goddard (1948) 15' quadrangle. R.B. Marshall of United States Geological Survey named the peak for Almon Harris Thompson, geographer with the Survey from 1882 until 1906 (Farquhar, 1925, p. 138).

Mount Tom [FRESNO]: *peak,* 5.5 miles north of Kaiser Peak (lat. 37°22'35" N, long. 119°10'40" W). Altitude 9018 feet. Named on Kaiser Peak (1953) 15' quadrangle.

Mount Tyndall [TULARE]: *peak,* 6 miles north-northwest of Mount Whitney on Tulare-Inyo County line (lat. 36°39'20" N, long. 18° 20'10" W). Altitude 14,018 feet. Named on Mount Whitney (1956) 15' quadrangle. Clarence King and Richard Cotter climbed the peak in 1864; King named the feature for John Tyndall, professor of natural philosophy at Royal Institution, London (Farquhar, 1925, p. 140).

Mount Vernon [KERN]: *hill,* 7.5 miles northwest of Blackwells Corner (lat. 35°41'50" N, long. 119°57'55" W; sec. 6, T 26 S, R 19 E). Named on Emigrant Hill (1953) 7.5' quadrangle. Called Wagon Wheel Mt. on Emigrant Hill (1943) 7.5' quadrangle.

Mount Versteeg [TULARE]: *peak,* 5 miles north-northwest of Mount Whitney on Tulare-Inyo County line (lat. 36°38'50" N, long. 118° 19'25" W). Altitude 13,470 feet. Named on Mount Whitney (1956) 15' quadrangle. The name honors Chester Versteeg, who did much to further interest in the Sierra Nevada (United States Board on Geographic Names, 1965a, p. 10-11).

Mount Wallace [FRESNO]: *peak,* 1.5 miles northeast of Mount Goddard on Fresno-Inyo County line (lat. 37°08'45" N, long. 118° 39'20" W). Altitude 13,377 feet. Named on Mount Goddard (1948) 15' quadrangle. Theodore S. Solomons named the peak in 1895 for Alfred Russell Wallace, English scientist and friend of Charles Darwin (Farquhar, 1925, p. 142).

Mount Wallace: see **Mount Mendel** [FRESNO].

Mount Warlow: see **Mount Huxley** [FRESNO].

Mount Whitney [TULARE]: *peak,* 58 miles east-northeast of Visalia on Tulare-Inyo County line (lat. 36°34'45" N, long. 118°17'30" W). Altitude 14,494 feet. Named on Mount Whitney (1956) 15' quadrangle. A field party of the Whitney survey saw the peak in 1864 and named it for their chief, Josiah Dwight Whitney (Whitney, p. 382).

Mount Whitney: see **Old Mount Whitney**, under **Mount Corcoran** [TULARE].

Mount Whitney Number 1: see **Mount Corcoran** [TULARE].

Mount Winchell [FRESNO]: *peak,* 11 miles east of Mount Goddard on Fresno-Inyo County line (lat. 37°06'15" N, long. 118°31'30" W). Altitude 13,768 feet. Named on Mount Goddard (1948) 15' quadrangle. The name honors Alexander Winchell, professor of physics, and later professor of geology at University of Michigan (Farquhar, 1925, p. 144-145).

Mount Woodworth [FRESNO]: *peak,* 6.5 miles east-southeast of Mount Goddard (lat. 37°01'35" N, long. 118°36'55" W). Altitude 12,219 feet. Named on Mount Goddard (1948) 15' quadrangle. The name commemorates Benjamin P. Woodworth, who camped in Simpson Meadow about 1888 (Farquhar, 1925, p. 145).

Mount Wynne [FRESNO]: *peak,* 0.5 mile south-southeast of Mount Pinchot (lat. 36°56'20" N, long. 118°24'10" W). Altitude 13,179 feet. Named on Mount Pinchot (1953) 15' quadrangle. The name honors Sedman W. Wynne, who lost his life while working as supervisor of Sequoia National Forest (United States Board on Geographic Names, 1933a, p. 826).

Mount Young [TULARE]: *peak,* 2 miles west of Mount Whitney (lat. 36°45'50" N, long. 118°19'35" W). Altitude 13,177 feet. Named on Mount Whitney (1956) 15' quadrangle. F.H. Wales made the first ascent of the peak in 1881 and named it for Charles Augustus Young of Western Reserve, Dartmouth, and Princeton Universities (Hanna, p. 362).

Movie Stringer [TULARE]: *stream,* flows 2.5 miles to South Fork Kern River 7.5 miles northwest of Olancha Peak in Templeton Meadows (lat. 36°19'50" N, long. 118°13'30" W; sec. 30, T 18 S, R 35 E). Named on Olancha (1956) 15' quadrangle.

Mowery Meadow [TULARE]: *area,* 7 miles north of Camp Nelson (lat. 36°14'30" N, long. 118°55'45" W; sec. 27, T 19 S, R 31 E). Named on Camp Nelson (1956) 15' quadrangle.

Mowry Lake [FRESNO]: *intermittent lake,* 2200 feet long, 4 miles east-northeast of Mendota (lat. 36°46'25" N, long. 120°18'55" W; on E line sec. 27, T 13 S, R 15 E). Named on Firebaugh (1946) 15' quadrangle.

Mud Creek [FRESNO]: *stream,* flows 5.5 miles to a canal 11 miles east-southeast of Clovis (lat. 36°46'05" N, long. 119°31'20" W; sec. 25, T 13 S, R 22 E). Named on Round Mountain (1964) 7.5' quadrangle.

Muddy Creek [KERN]: *stream,* flows 4 miles to lowlands 8 miles north-west of Eagle Rest Peak (lat. 34°59' N, long. 119°15' W; sec. 5, T 10 N, R 22 W). Named on Conner SW (1955), Eagle Rest Peak (1942), and Santiago Creek (1943) 7.5' quadrangles.

Mud Hen Creek [KERN]: *stream,* flows 1.5 miles to French Gulch (1) 4.25 miles south of Alta Sierra (lat. 35°40' N, long. 118°33' W; near W line sec. 16, T 26 S, R 32 E). Named on Alta Sierra (1972) 7.5' quadrangle.

Mud Lakes [FRESNO]: *lakes,* two, each 650 feet long, 3.25 miles east of Dinkey Dome (lat. 37°06'15" N, long. 119°04'25" W; near S line sec. 30, T 9 S, R 27 E). Named on Huntington Lake (1953) 15' quadrangle.

Mud Run [FRESNO]: *stream,* flows nearly 4 miles to Los Gatos Creek 6 miles north-northeast of Coalinga Mineral Springs (lat. 36° 13'35" N, long. 120°31'05" W; near NE cor. sec. 1, T 20 S, R 13 E). Named on Sherman Peak (1969) 7.5' quadrangle.

Mud Spring [KERN]: *spring,* 7.25 miles east-northeast of Caliente (lat. 35°20'40" N, long. 118°31'05" W; sec. 2, T 30 S, R 32 E). Named on Oiler Peak (1972) 7.5' quadrangle.

Mud Spring [TULARE]: *spring,* 3.5 miles north-northeast of California Hot Springs (lat. 35°55'45" N, long. 118°38'30" W; at W line sec. 16, T 23 S, R 31 E). Named on California Hot Springs (1958) 15' quadrangle.

Mud Spring Gap [TULARE]: *pass,* 5 miles north-northwest of Woodlake (lat. 36°28'20" N, long. 119°08'40" W; at N line sec. 10, T 17 S, R 26 E). Named on Exeter (1952) 15' quadrangle.

Mud Springs [KERN]: *springs,* 8.5 miles northwest of Emerald Mountain (lat. 35°21'30" N, long. 118°22'15" W; sec. 6, T 30 S, R 34 E). Named on Emerald Mountain (1972) 7.5' quadrangle.

Muerto: see **Leliter** [KERN].

Muir: see **Mount Muir** [TULARE].

Muir Pass [FRESNO]: *pass,* 2.5 miles east-northeast of Mount Goddard on Goddard Divide (lat. 37°06'45" N, long. 118°40'15" W); the pass is along John Muir Trail. Named on Mount Goddard (1948) 15' quadrangle. William E. Colby named the pass for John Muir (Farquhar, 1924, p. 61).

Mulch Canyon [FRESNO]: *canyon,* drained by a stream that flows 2.5 miles to Warthan Creek 2 miles east-northeast of Charley Mountain (lat. 36°09'20" N, long. 120°38'10" W; near SE cor. sec. 26, T 20 S, R 12 E). Named on Priest Valley (1969) 7.5' quadrangle.

Mule Creek [FRESNO]: *stream,* flows 2 miles to North Fork Kings River nearly 7 miles east-northeast of Balch Camp (lat. 36°55'50" N, long. 119°00'20" W; at E line sec. 34, T 11 S, R 27 E). Named on Patterson Mountain (1952) and Tehipite Dome (1952) 15' quadrangles.

Mule Meadow [TULARE]: *area,* 8.5 miles south of Camp Nelson (lat. 36°01'15" N, long. 118°35'35" W; sec. 14, T 22 S, R 31 E); the place is 1.25 miles east-northeast of Mule Peak. Named on Camp Nelson (1956) 15' quadrangle.

Mule Peak [TULARE]: *peak,* 8.5 miles south of Camp Nelson (lat. 36°01' N, long. 118°36'50" W; sec. 15, T 22 S, R 31 E); the peak is 1.25 miles west-southwest of Mule Meadow. Altitude 8142 feet. Named on Camp Nelson (1956) 15' quadrangle.

Muley Hole [FRESNO]: *locality,* 7 miles south of Dinkey Dome along Dinkey Creek (1) (lat. 37°00'50" N, long. 119°07'10" W; sec. 34, T 10 S, R 26 E). Named on Huntington Lake (1953) 15' quadrangle. Horses and mules feed at the place (Browning, p. 155).

Mulkey Creek [TULARE]: *stream,* flows 10.5 miles to South Fork Kern River 6.5 miles northwest of Olancha Peak (lat. 36°20'10" N, long. 118°11'50" W; sec. 28, T 18 S, R 35 E); the stream heads near Mulkey Pass. Named on Olancha (1956) 15' quadrangle.

Mulkey Meadows [TULARE]: *area,* 10.5 miles north-northwest of Olancha Peak (lat. 36°24'15" N, long. 118°12'15" W); the place is along Mulkey Creek. Named on Olancha (1956) 15' quadrangle. The name is for Cyrus Mulkey, Inyo County sheriff in the 1870's (Hanna, p. 204).

Mulkey Pass [TULARE]: *pass,* 12 miles north-northwest of Olancha Peak on Tulare-Inyo County line (lat. 36°25'45" N, long. 118°09'55" W; near E line sec. 22, T 17 S, R 35 E); the pass is near the head of Mulkey Creek. Named on Olancha (1956) 15' quadrangle. The feature also is called "old" Mulkey Pass—Trail Pass is called "new" Mulkey Pass (Schumacher, p. 80).

Mundgi Flat [KERN]: *area,* 5 miles north of Caliente along Walker Basin Creek (lat. 35°21'35" N, long. 118°38'15" W; sec. 34, T 29 S, R 31 E). Named on Bena (1972) 7.5' quadrangle.

Munger Peak: see **Goat Mountain** [FRESNO] (1).

Munn Camp [KERN]: *locality,* 5.25 miles east-northeast of Glennville (lat. 35°45'40" N, long. 118°37'15" W; near SW cor. sec. 11, T 25 S, R 31 E). Named on California Hot Springs (1958) 15' quadrangle.

Munzer Meadow [KERN]: *area,* 8 miles east-northeast of Mount Adelaide (lat. 35°27'40" N, long. 118°36'50" W; sec. 26, T 28 S, R 31 E). Named on Breckenridge Mountain (1972) 7.5' quadrangle.

Muriel Lake [FRESNO]: *lake,* 3200 feet long, 9 miles north of Mount Goddard (lat. 37°14' N, long. 118°41'45" W); the lake is 1 mile north of Muriel Peak. Named on Mount Goddard (1948) 15' quadrangle.

Muriel Peak [FRESNO]: *peak,* 6 miles north-northeast of Mount Goddard (lat. 37°13'05" N, long. 118°41'30" W). Altitude 12,942 feet. Named on Mount Goddard (1948) 15' quadrangle.

Muro Blanco [FRESNO]: *relief feature,* 2.5 miles south-southeast of Marion Peak on the southeast side of South Fork Kings River (lat. 36°55' N, long. 118°30'30" W). Named on Marion Peak (1953) and Mount Pinchot (1953) 15' quadrangles. The side of the canyon there resembles a solid white wall—*muro blanco* means "white wall" in Spanish (Gudde, 1969, p. 215).

Muroc [KERN]: *locality,* 3 miles east of present Edwards at the edge of Rogers Lake (lat. 34°55'30" N, long. 117°52'20" W; at N line sec. 31, T 10 N, R 9 W); the site now is on Edwards Air Force Base. Named on Rogers Lake (1942) 7.5' quadrangle. Postal authorities established Muroc post office in 1910 and discontinued it in 1951, when they changed the name to Edwards (Frickstad, p. 57). Called Yucca on Campbell's (1902) map, and called Rodriguez on Johnson's (1911) map. The place also had the names "Rogers" and "Rod" (Wines, p. 86). The name "Muroc" is the surname "Corum" spelled backward; Ralph Corum and Clifford Corum were early settlers at the place (Hoover, Rensch, and Rensch, p. 134). California Mining Bureau's (1917c) map shows a place called Neil located less than 1 mile north-northwest of Muroc at the edge of present Rogers Lake.

Muroc: see **North Muroc** [KERN]; **North Muroc**, under **North Edwards** [KERN].

Muroc Air Force Base: see **Edwards Air Force Base** [KERN].

Muroc Army Air Field: see **Edwards Air Force Base** [KERN].

Muroc Dry Lake: see **Rogers Lake** [KERN].
Muroc Junction [KERN]: *locality,* 7.25 miles south of Castle Butte (lat. 35°00'35" N, long. 117°52'45" W; at E line sec. 36, T 11 N, R 10 W). Named on Castle Butte (1956) 15' quadrangle.
Murphy Slough [FRESNO]: *water feature,* diverges from Cole Slough near Laton and extends for 22 miles to Fresno Slough 4.5 miles northwest of Lanare (lat. 36°28'10" N, long. 119°59'50" W; sec. 10, T 17 S, R 18 E). Named on Burrel (1954), Laton (1953), and Riverdale (1954) 7.5' quadrangles.
Murphy Spring [KERN]: *spring,* 12 miles east-northeast of Mount Adelaide (lat. 35°28'50" N, long. 118°32'30" W; sec. 21, T 28 S, R 32 E). Named on Breckenridge Mountain (1972) 7.5' quadrangle.
Murray [KINGS]: *locality,* 9 miles northeast of Avenal (lat. 36°05'35" N, long. 120°00'10" W; near NW cor. sec. 23, T 21 S, R 18 E). Named on La Cima (1963) 7.5' quadrangle. Postal authorities established Murray post office in 1920, discontinued it in 1929, reestablished it in 1938, and discontinued it in 1944 (Frickstad, p. 61). The name commemorates David Murray, a leader in the introduction of olive culture to the neighborhood (Gudde, 1949, p. 229).
Murry Creek [TULARE]:
(1) *stream,* flows 6.5 miles to Cottonwood Creek 1.5 miles north-northeast of Auckland (lat. 36°36'40" N, long. 119°05'45" W; sec. 24, T 15 S, R 26 E). Named on Auckland (1966) and Miramonte (1966) 7.5' quadrangles.
(2) *stream,* flows 1.5 miles to Bear Creek (1) 5.25 miles southeast of Auckland at Murry Flat (lat. 36°32'20" N, long. 119°02' W; near W line sec. 15, T 16 S, R 27 E). Named on Auckland (1966) 7.5' quadrangle.
Murry Creek: see **Bear Creek** [TULARE] (1).
Murry Flat [TULARE]: *area,* 5.25 miles southeast of Auckland (lat. 36°32'20" N, long. 119°01'55" W; in and near sec. 15, T 16 S, R 27 E). Named on Auckland (1966) 7.5' quadrangle. Called Shadley Flat on Dinuba (1924) 30' quadrangle.
Murry Gulch [TULARE]: *canyon,* drained by a stream that flows less than 1 mile to Murry Creek (1) 4.5 miles northeast of Auckland (lat. 36°37'20" N, long. 119°02'05" W; sec. 15, T 15 S, R 27 E). Named on Auckland (1966) 7.5' quadrangle.
Murry Hill [TULARE]: *hill,* less than 1 mile southeast of Porterville (lat. 36°03'50" N, long. 119°00'15" W; near W line sec. 36, T 21 S, R 27 E. Named on Porterville (1951) 7.5' quadrangle.
Muscatel [FRESNO]: *locality,* 4.5 miles west-northwest of downtown Fresno along Southern Pacific Railroad (lat. 36°47'35" N, long. 119°51'30" W; near NW cor. sec. 24, T 13 S, R 19 E). Named on Fresno North (1965) 7.5' quadrangle.
Mushroom Rock [FRESNO]: *relief feature,* 9 miles north-northeast of Shaver Lake Heights (present town of Shaver Lake) (lat. 37°13'55" N, long. 119°17' W; sec. 18, T 8 S, R 25 E). Named on Shaver Lake (1953) 15' quadrangle.
Musick Creek [FRESNO]: *stream,* flows 4.5 miles to Jose Creek 3.5 miles west-southwest of Shaver Lake Heights (present town of Shaver Lake) (lat. 37°05'30" N, long. 119°22'50" W; sec. 5, T 10 S, R 24 E). Named on Shaver Lake (1953) 15' quadrangle.
Musick Mountain [FRESNO]: *peak,* 4.5 miles north of Shaver Lake Heights (present town of Shaver Lake) (lat. 37°10'10" N, long. 119°18'30" W; sec. 1, 12, T 9 S, R 24 E). Altitude 6807 feet. Named on Shaver Lake (1953) 15' quadrangle. Called Music Pk. on Kaiser (1904) 30' quadrangle. The name "Musick" commemorates either Charles Musick or Henry Musick, both of whom were connected with a sawmill at Shaver Lake (Redinger, p. 79).
Music Peak: see **Musick Mountain** [FRESNO].
Musk [TULARE]: *locality,* 2.5 miles north-northwest of Exeter along Southern Pacific Railroad (lat. 36°19'40" N, long. 119°09' W; near SW cor. sec. 27, T 18 S, R 26 E). Named on Exeter (1926) 7.5' quadrangle.
Mussel Slough [KINGS]: *stream,* flows 20 miles to a ditch 2.5 miles east-northeast of Stratford (lat. 36°12'30" N, long. 19°46'15" W). Named on Burris Park (1926), Guernsey (1929), Hanford (1926), and Stratford (1929) 7.5' quadrangles. On Guernsey (1954) and Stratford (1954) 7.5' quadrangles, the name applies to a watercourse that is mainly dry. Grunsky (p. 87) noted in 1898 that "All of the Kings River delta south of the main channel of the river and west of Cross Creek is commonly known as the Mussel Slough country," and "Many water courses, locally called sloughs, former channels of Kings River, course through this region from the north to south." The name "Mussel Slough" is associated with the bloody conflict in 1880 between hirelings of Southern Pacific Railroad and settlers; after this tragedy, the neighborhood was renamed Lucerne Valley (Hart, J.D., p. 292).
Mustang Hill [KINGS]: *peak,* 2.25 miles southwest of Kettleman City (lat. 35°58'55" N, long. 119°59'05" W; at W line sec. 25, T 22 S, R 18 E). Altitude 738 feet. Named on Los Viejos (1954) 7.5' quadrangle.
Mustang Peak [FRESNO]: *peak,* 5 miles west-northwest of Castle Mountain on Fresno-Monterey County line (lat. 35°58'30" N, long. 120°24'45" W; sec. 36, T 22 S, R 14 E). Named on Parkfield (1961) 7.5' quadrangle.
Mustang Spring [FRESNO]: *spring,* 7.25 miles west-northwest of Coalinga (lat. 36°10'25" N, long. 120°28'35" W; sec. 20, T 20 S, R 14 E). Named on Alcalde Hills (1969) 7.5' quadrangle.
Mustang Spring [KERN]: *spring,* 4 miles southwest of Skinner Peak (lat. 35°31'25" N, long. 118°10'35" W; sec. 2, T 28 S, R 35 E). Named on Cane Canyon (1972) 7.5' quadrangle.
Myers Canyon [KERN]: *canyon,* drained by a stream that flows 4 miles to Bodfish Creek less than 1 mile east of Bodfish (lat. 35° 35'15" N, long. 118°28'20" W; at S line sec. 7, T 27 S, R 33 E). Named on Lake Isabella South (1972) 7.5' quadrangle.
Myricks Corner [KERN]: *locality,* 1.25 miles northwest of Shafter (lat. 35°30'55" N, long. 119°17'20" W; at S line sec. 4, T 28 S, R 25 E). Named on Wasco (1953) 7.5' quadrangle.
Mystery Lake [FRESNO]: *lake,* 1400 feet long, nearly 4 miles northeast of Dinkey Dome (lat. 37°09'35" N, long. 119°05'15" W; sec. 12, T 9 S, R 26 E). Named on Huntington Lake (1953) 15' quadrangle.

–N–

Nadeau: see **Cameron** [KERN].
Nagel Canyon [KERN]: *canyon,* drained by a stream that flows 1.5 miles to Weaver Creek 8 miles north-northwest of Emerald Mountain (lat. 35°21'20" N, long. 118°21' W; sec. 5, T 30 S, R 34 E). Named on Emerald Mountain (1972) 7.5' quadrangle.
Nanceville [TULARE]: *locality,* 3 miles west of Porterville (lat. 36° 04'10" N, long. 119°04'20" W; sec. 29, T 21 S, R 27 E). Named on Porterville (1951) 7.5' quadrangle.
Napoleon Spring [KERN]: *spring,* 10 miles southwest of Blackwells Corner (lat. 35°30'15" N, long. 119°58'40" W; near W line sec. 7, T 28 S, R 19 E). Named on Shale Point (1953) 7.5' quadrangle.
Naranjo [TULARE]: *locality,* 2 miles east-southeast of Woodlake along Visalia Electric Railroad (lat. 36°24'15" N, long. 119°23'40" W; near W line sec. 33, T 17 S, R 27 E). Named on Woodlake (1952) 7.5' quadrangle. Harry Brown and Senator Harding, landowners there, named the place in 1898 (Mitchell, A.R., p. 69). The locality is in a citrus-growing neighborhood—*naranjo* means "orange tree" in Spanish (Gudde, 1949, p. 231). Postal authorities established Naranjo post office in 1901, discontinued it in 1913, reestablished it in 1914, and discontinued it in 1918 (Frickstad, p. 212).
Narboe Lake: see **Proctor Lake** [KERN].
Nares [FRESNO]: *locality,* 0.5 mile northwest of Helm along Southern Pacific Railroad (lat. 36°32'15" N, long. 120°06' W). Named on Helm (1925) 7.5' quadrangle.
Narrows: see **The Narrows** [KERN].
Navelencia [FRESNO]: *village,* 7 miles east-southeast of Centerville (lat. 36°41' N, long. 119°23' W; sec. 29, T 14 S, R 24 E). Named on Wahtoke (1966) 7.5' quadrangle. Postal authorities established Navelencia post office in 1915 and discontinued it in 1931 (Frickstad, p. 36). The place is in a citrus-growing neighborhood, and the name was coined from the words "navel" and "valencia," two kinds of oranges (Gudde, 1949, p. 232).
Neasons Flat [KERN]: *area,* 3 miles east of Eagle Rest Peak along Pleito Creek (lat. 34°54'45" N, long. 119°04'45" W; near W line sec. 36, T 10 N, R 21 W). Named on Pleito Hills (1958) 7.5' quadrangle.
Needham: see **Mount Needham**, under **Florence Peak** [TULARE].
Needham Mountain [TULARE]: *peak,* 3.25 miles east of Mineral King (lat. 36°27'15" N, long. 118°32'10" W). Altitude 12,467 feet. Named on Mineral King (1956) 15' quadrangle. W.F. Dean named the peak for James Carson Needham, a congressman (Hanna, p. 208).
Needle Camp [TULARE]: *locality,* 10 miles south-southwest of Hockett Peak (lat. 36°05'25" N, long. 118°27'50" W); the place is near the mouth of Needlerock Creek. Named on Hockett Peak (1956) 15' quadrangle.
Needlerock Creek [TULARE]: *stream,* flows 3.5 miles to Kern River 10 miles south-southwest of Hockett Peak (lat. 36°05'20" N, long. 118°27'55" W); the stream is south of The Needles. Named on Camp Nelson (1956) and Hockett Peak (1956) 15' quadrangles.
Needles: see **The Needles** [TULARE].
Neelle Lake [FRESNO]: *lake,* 500 feet long, 3.5 miles north of Mount Abbot (lat. 37°26'10" N, long. 118°46'25" W). Named on Mount Abbot (1953) 15' quadrangle.
Neff Mills: see **Pinehurst** [FRESNO].
Neffs Camp [FRESNO]: *settlement,* nearly 7 miles east-southeast of Dunlap (lat. 36°42'15" N, long. 119°00'10" W; sec. 14, T 14 S, R 27 E). Named on Miramonte (1966) 7.5' quadrangle. Dinuba (1924) 30' quadrangle shows a place called Neff Mills located about 1 mile southwest of present Neffs Camp (near W line sec. 23, T 14 S, R 27 E).
Negit Lake [FRESNO]: *lake,* 1200 feet long, 7.5 miles south of Mount Abbot (lat. 37°16'55" N, long. 118°48'15" W). Named on Mount Abbot (1953) 15' quadrangle. Elden H. Vestal of California Department of Fish and Game named the lake in 1951 using a word that he thought has the meaning "night" or "darkness" in the Piute Indian language (Browning, p. 157).
Negro Creek [TULARE]: *stream,* flows 3.25 miles to lowlands 3.5 miles

west-northwest of Cliff Peak (lat. 36°35' N, long. 119°13'40" W; sec. 35, T 15 S, R 25 E). Named on Stokes Mountain (1966) 7.5' quadrangle. Called Niggerhead Cr. on Dinuba (1924) 30' quadrangle.

Negro Rube Creek: see **Nigger Rube Creek** [TULARE].

Ne Hi Canyon [FRESNO]: *canyon,* drained by a stream that flows 3 miles to Diaz Canyon nearly 3 miles southwest of Joaquin Rocks (lat. 36°17'25" N, long. 120°28'55" W; sec. 7, T 19 S, R 14 E). Named on Joaquin Rocks (1969) 7.5' quadrangle.

Neil: see **Muroc** [KERN].

Neil Lake [FRESNO]: *lake,* 800 feet long, 9 miles southwest of Mount Abbot (lat. 37°17'55" N, long. 118°54'25" W). Named on Mount Abbot (1953) 15' quadrangle. Scott M. Soule and Jack Criqui of California Department of Fish and Game named the lake in 1948 for Neil Perkins, a Forest Service ranger (Browning, p. 157).

Neill's Hot Springs: see **Scovern Hot Springs** [KERN].

Nellie Dent Creek [KERN]: *stream,* flows nearly 4 miles to Isabella Lake at Wofford Heights (lat. 35°42'20" N, long. 118°26'50" W; near SW cor. sec. 33, T 25 S, R 33 E). Named on Lake Isabella North (1972) 7.5' quadrangle.

Nellie Lake [FRESNO]: *lake,* 1200 feet long, 3.5 miles west-southwest of Kaiser Peak (lat. 37°16'50" N, long. 119°14'45" W; on S line sec. 28, T 7 S, R 25 E). Named on Kaiser Peak (1953) 15' quadrangle.

Nellies Nipple [KERN]: *peak,* 4 miles southeast of Loraine (lat. 35° 15'25" N, long. 118°23'30" W; near SW cor. sec. 1, T 31 S, R 33 E). Named on Loraine (1972) 7.5' quadrangle.

Nelson: see **Camp Nelson** [TULARE].

Nelson Creek [TULARE]: *stream,* flows 2 miles to South Fork of Middle Fork Tule River at Camp Nelson (lat. 36°08'10" N, long. 118°36'35" W; near S line sec. 33, T 20 S, R 31 E). Named on Camp Nelson (1956) 15' quadrangle. The name commemorates John M. Nelson of Camp Nelson (Browning, p. 157).

Nelson Lakes [FRESNO]: *lakes,* largest 1300 feet long, 5 miles east of Dinkey Dome (lat. 37°06'30" N, long. 119°02'20" W; in and near sec. 28, 33, T 9 S, R 27 E). Named on Huntington Lake (1953) 15' quadrangle.

Nelson Mountain [FRESNO]: *peak,* 5 miles east-southeast of Dinkey Dome (lat. 37°05'25" N, long. 119°02'55" W; sec. 5, T 10 S, R 27 E). Altitude 10,218 feet. Named on Huntington Lake (1953) 15' quadrangle. The name commemorates Thomas P. Nelson, a sheepman in the early days (Browning, p. 158).

Nelson's Hot Springs: see **Scovern Hot Springs** [KERN].

Nelson Soda Springs: see **Camp Nelson** [TULARE].

Neufeld [KERN]: *locality,* nearly 2 miles north of Wasco along Atchison, Topeka and Santa Fe Railroad (lat. 35°37'10" N, long. 119°19'50" W; on E line sec. 36, T 26 S, R 24 E). Named on Wasco (1953) 7.5' quadrangle.

Neuralia [KERN]: *locality,* 12 miles northeast of Mojave along Southern Pacific Railroad (lat. 35°11'50" N, long. 118°02'45" W; near N line sec. 31, T 31 S, R 37 E). Named on Mojave (1956) 15' quadrangle. Postal authorities established Neuralia post office in 1914 and discontinued it in 1916; the name is from the term "new railroad" (Salley, p. 153).

Nevills [FRESNO]: *locality,* 6.5 miles west of downtown Fresno along Southern Pacific Railroad (lat. 36°44'45" N, long. 119°54'10" W; sec. 4, T 14 S, R 19 E). Named on Kearney Park (1923) 7.5' quadrangle.

New Army Pass [TULARE]: *pass,* 17 miles north-northwest of Olancha Peak on Tulare-Inyo County line (lat. 36°29'25" N, long. 118°14'25" W); the feature is 0.5 mile south of Army Pass. Named on Olancha (1956) 15' quadrangle. The pass is along a trail built in 1955 to bypass the route through Army Pass (Browning, p. 158).

New Auberry [FRESNO]: *village,* 10 miles west of Shaver Lake Heights (present town of Shaver Lake) (lat. 37°05'40" N, long. 119°29'45" W; near NE cor. sec. 6, T 10 S, R 23 E). Named on Shaver Lake (1953) 15' quadrangle. Called Auberry on Kaiser (1904) 30' quadrangle.

Newcomb: see **Mount Newcomb** [TULARE].

New London: see **London** [TULARE].

Nichols Canyon [FRESNO]: *canyon,* drained by a stream that flows 2 miles to North Fork Kings River nearly 4 miles west of Blackcap Mountain (lat. 37°04'20" N, long. 118°51'35" W). Named on Blackcap Mountain (1953) 15' quadrangle.

Nichols Peak: see **Nicolls Peak** [KERN].

Nick Williams: see **Camp Nick Williams** [KERN].

Nicolls Peak [KERN]: *peak,* 3 miles south of Weldon (lat. 35°37'10" N, long. 118°17'50" W; sec. 35, T 26 S, R 34 E). Named on Woolstalf Creek (1972) 7.5' quadrangle. Called Nichols Peak on Isabella (1943) 15' quadrangle. United States Board on Geographic Names (1974b, p. 3) gave the form "Nichols Peak" as a variant; the name "Nicolls Peak" commemorates John Nicoll, who homesteaded near the peak in 1856.

Nicoll Spring [KERN]: *spring,* 2.25 miles south-southeast of Weldon (lat. 35°38' N, long. 118°16'45" W; sec. 25, T 26 S, R 34 E). Named on Weldon (1972) 7.5' quadrangle.

Niggerhead Creek: see **Negro Creek** [TULARE].

Nigger Rube Creek [TULARE]: *stream,* flows 7.5 miles to Deer Creek (2) 4 miles west-northwest of California Hot Springs (lat. 35°53'50" N, long. 118°30'10" W; near E line sec. 28, T 23 S, R 30 E). Named on Tobias Peak (1936) 30' quadrangle. United States Board on Geographic Names (1988a, p. 3) approved the name "Rube Creek" for the stream, and rejected the names "Nigger Rube Creek" and "Negro Rube Creek" for it.

Nigger Slough [TULARE]: *stream,* flows 6.5 miles to Inside Creek 8.5 miles west of Lindsay (lat. 36°12'10" N, long. 119°14'35" W; near E line sec. 10, T 20 S, R 25 E). Named on Cairns Corner (1927) and Exeter (1926) 7.5' quadrangles.

Nightingale Gulch [KERN]: *canyon,* drained by a stream that flows 7 miles to Five Dog Creek 6 miles southwest of Woody (lat. 35°38'05" N, long. 118°53'40" W; sec. 30, T 26 S, R 29 E). Named on Sand Canyon (1965) and Woody (1965) 7.5' quadrangles.

Nine Lake Basin [TULARE]: *area,* 2 miles south-southwest of Triple Divide Peak at the head of Big Arroyo (lat. 36°33'45" N, long. 118°32'15" W). Named on Triple Divide Peak (1956) 15' quadrangle.

Ninemile Creek [TULARE]: *stream,* flows 8.5 miles to Kern River 2 miles east of Hockett Peak (lat. 36°13'15" N, long. 118°21'05" W). Named on Hockett Peak (1956) 15' quadrangle.

Nobe Young Creek [TULARE]: *stream,* flows 7.5 miles to Dry Meadow Creek 11 miles south-southeast of Camp Nelson (lat. 36° 00'15" N, long. 118°30'05" W; sec. 22, T 22 S, R 32 E); the stream goes through Nobe Young Meadow. Named on California Hot Springs (1958) and Camp Nelson (1956) 15' quadrangles.

Nobe Young Meadow [TULARE]: *area,* 8 miles south-southeast of Camp Nelson (lat. 36°01'40" N, long. 118°34'30" W; sec. 12, T 22 S, R 31 E); the place is along Nobe Young Creek. Named on Camp Nelson (1956) 15' quadrangle.

Noble: see **Stony Flat** [FRESNO].

Nome: see **Bakersfield** [KERN].

Nonada Hill [FRESNO]: *peak,* 18 miles southwest of Firebaugh (lat. 36°42' N, long. 120°43' W; sec. 24, T 14 S, R 11 E). Altitude 1288 feet. Named on Chounet Ranch (1956) 7.5' quadrangle.

No Name Creek: see **Sheep Creek** [TULARE] (1).

Noradell: see **Tipton** [TULARE].

Norman Clyde Peak: see **Middle Palisade** [FRESNO].

North Alder Creek [TULARE]: *stream,* flows 3 miles to South Alder Creek 4.5 miles north-northwest of Camp Nelson (lat. 36°12'05" N, long. 118°38'45" W; sec. 8, T 20 S, R 31 E). Named on Camp Nelson (1956) 15' quadrangle.

North Cold Spring [TULARE]: *spring,* nearly 7 miles north of California Hot Springs at the head of Bond Creek (lat. 35°58'30" N, long. 118°41'40" W). Named on California Hot Springs (1958) 15' quadrangle.

North Cold Spring Peak [TULARE]: *peak,* 6.5 miles north of California Hot Springs (lat. 35°58'25" N, long. 118°41'15" W); the peak is 0.25 mile east-southeast of North Cold Spring. Altitude 6730 feet. Named on California Hot Springs (1958) 15' quadrangle.

North Dinuba [TULARE]: *locality,* less than 2 miles north-northwest of Dinuba along Atchison, Topeka and Santa Fe Railroad (lat. 36° 34' N, long. 119°23'30" W; at W line sec. 5, T 16 S, R 24 E). Named on Reedley (1966) 7.5' quadrangle.

North Dome [FRESNO]: *peak,* 11 miles south-southwest of Marion Peak (lat. 36°48'25" N, long. 118°35'45" W). Altitude 8717 feet. Named on Marion Peak (1953) 15' quadrangle. John Muir named the peak in 1875 (Browning, p. 159).

North Dome: see **Kettleman Hills** [FRESNO-KERN-KINGS].

North Edwards [KERN]: *town,* 7.25 miles south-southeast of Castle Butte (lat. 35°01' N, long. 117°49'45" W; sec. 27, 28, T 11 N, R 9 W); the town is north of Edwards Air Force Base. Named on North Edwards (1973) 7.5' quadrangle. Called Edgemont Acres on Castle Butte (1956) 15' quadrangle. United States Board on Geographic Names (1975c, p. 4) gave the names "Edgemont Acres" and "North Muroc" as variants.

North Goddard Creek [FRESNO]: *stream,* flows 5 miles to South Fork San Joaquin River 4.5 miles north-northeast of Blackcap Mountain in Goddard Canyon (lat. 37°08'05" N, long. 118°45'55" W); the stream heads north of Mount Goddard. Named on Blackcap Mountain (1953) and Mount Goddard (1948) 15' quadrangles.

North Guard [TULARE]: *peak,* 14 miles northwest of Mount Whitney on Great Western Divide (lat. 36°43' N, long. 118°29'15" W); the peak is 1.5 miles north of South Guard. Altitude 13,327 feet. Named on Mount Whitney (1956) 15' quadrangle. Lieutenant Milton F. Davis named the peak on a map in 1896 (Browning, p. 160).

North Guard Creek [FRESNO-TULARE]: *stream,* heads in Tulare County and flows 5.5 miles to Bubbs Creek 13 miles south-southwest of Mount Pinchot in Fresno County (lat. 36°46'05" N, long. 118°28'15" W). Named on Mount Whitney (1907) 30' quadrangle, and on Mount Pinchot (1953) 15' quadrangle.

North Guard Lake [TULARE]: *lake,* 1900 feet long, 15 miles northwest of Mount Whitney (lat. 36°44'35" N, long. 118°28'30" W); the lake is 2 miles north-northeast of North Guard along North Guard Creek. Named on Mount Whitney (1956) 15' quadrangle. J. Hoganson of United States Geological Survey named the lake in 1956 (Browning, p. 160).

North Meadow [TULARE]: *area,* 14 miles south of Hockett Peak (lat. 36°01' N, long. 118°24'15" W). Named on Hockett Peak (1956) 15' quadrangle.

North Meadow Creek [TULARE]: *stream,* flows 4 miles to Brush Creek 4.5 miles northeast of Fairview (lat. 35°58'15" N, long. 118° 26'10" W; sec. 32, T 22 S, R 33 E); the stream heads at North Meadow. Named on Hockett Peak (1956) and Kernville (1956) 15' quadrangles.

North Mountain [FRESNO]: *peak,* 12 miles south-southwest of Marion Peak (lat. 36°48'20" N, long. 118°37'50" W). Altitude 8632 feet. Named on Marion Peak (1953) 15' quadrangle.

North Muroc [KERN]: *locality,* 8 miles south-southeast of Castle Butte (lat. 35°00'20" N, long. 117°49' W; sec. 34, T 11 N, R 9 W). Named on Castle Butte (1956) 7.5' quadrangle.

North Muroc: see **North Edwards** [KERN].

North Palisade [FRESNO]: *peak,* 11.5 miles east of Mount Goddard on Fresno-Inyo County line (lat. 37°05'40" N, long. 118°30'50" W). Altitude 14,242 feet. Named on Mount Goddard (1948) 15' quadrangle. Called Mt. Jordan on Lippincott's (1902) map. The name "North Palisade" is from the Whitney survey (Farquhar, 1924, p. 62). Members of the Wheeler survey called the feature Northwest Palisade (Browning, p. 164). United States Board on Geographic Names (1985a, p. 3) approved the name "Polemonium Peak" for a feature 0.2 mile southeast of North Palisade on Fresno-Inyo County line (lat. 37°05'37" N, long. 118°30'40" W).

North Shafter [KERN]: *locality,* 1 mile northwest of Shafter (lat. 35° 30'40" N, long. 119°17'05" W; sec. 9, T 28 S, R 25 E). Named on Wasco (1953) 7.5' quadrangle.

North Side: see **Oildale** [KERN].

North Tule: see **Porterville** [TULARE].

Northwest Palisade: see **North Palisade** [FRESNO].

Noyer Canyon [KERN]: *canyon,* drained by a stream that flows nearly 2 miles to Kern River 3.5 miles north-northeast of Wofford Heights (lat. 35°45'05" N, long. 118°25'20" W; sec. 15, T 25 S, R 33 E). Named on Lake Isabella North (1972) 7.5' quadrangle.

Number 7 Spring [FRESNO]: *spring,* 4 miles east of Castle Mountain near the head of Canoas Creek (lat. 35°56'50" N, long. 120°16'20" W; near NE cor. sec. 7, T 23 S, R 16 E). Named on The Dark Hole (1961) 7.5' quadrangle.

Nunez Canyon [FRESNO]: *canyon,* drained by a stream that flows 5 miles to Coyote Canyon 8 miles northwest of Coalinga (lat. 36°13'15" N, long. 120°27'30" W; sec. 4, T 20 S, R 14 E). Named on Alcalde Hills (1969) and Joaquin Rocks (1969) 7.5' quadrangles.

Nunez Spring: see **Indian Springs** [FRESNO] (2).

Nutmeg Creek [FRESNO]: *stream,* flows 5.5 miles to Big Creek (2) 7 miles west-northwest of Balch Camp (lat. 36°57'30" N, long. 119°13'40" W; sec. 22, T 11 S, R 25 E); the stream heads at Nutmeg Glen. Named on Huntington Lake (1953) and Patterson Mountain (1952) 15' quadrangles.

Nutmeg Glen [FRESNO]: *locality,* 8 miles south-southwest of Dinkey Dome (lat. 37°00'30" N, long. 119°11'15" W; near SW cor. sec. 31, T 10 S, R 26 E); the place is at the head of Nutmeg Creek. Named on Huntington Lake (1953) 15' quadrangle.

—O—

Oak Canyon: see **Little Oak Canyon** [KERN].

Oak Creek [KERN]: *stream,* flows 10 miles to lowlands 10 miles southeast of Tehachapi (lat. 35°02'25" N, long. 118°18'30" W; near SW cor. sec. 18, T 11 N, R 13 W). Named on Monolith (1966), Tehachapi South (1966), and Willow Springs (1965) 7.5' quadrangles.

Oak Creek: see **Little Oak Creek**, under **Little Oak Canyon** [KERN].

Oak Creek Canyon [KERN]: *canyon,* 8 miles long, along Oak Creek above a point 10 miles southeast of Tehachapi (lat. 35°02'25" N, long. 118°18'30" W; near SW cor. sec. 18, T 11 N, R 13 W). Named on Monolith (1966) and Tehachapi South (1966) 7.5' quadrangles.

Oak Creek Pass [KERN]: *pass,* 6 miles southeast of Tehachapi (lat. 35°03'40" N, long. 118°23'15" W; sec. 8, T 11 N, R 14 W). Named on Tehachapi South (1966) 7.5' quadrangle. The feature was called Tehachapi Pass before the coming of the railroad in 1876, when the name "Tehachapi" was transferred to present Tehachapi Pass (Hoover, Rensch, and Rensch, p. 127). Whitney (p. 216) used the name "Frémont's Pass" for present Oak Creek Pass, and noted that John C. Frémont traversed the feature in 1844.

Oak Flat [FRESNO]:

(1) *area,* 5.25 miles north-northwest of Balch Camp (lat. 36°58'45" N, long. 119°08'50" W). Named on Patterson Mountain (1952) 15' quadrangle.

(2) *area,* 7.25 miles west of Coalinga (lat. 36°09'20" N, long. 120° 29'05" W; sec. 30, T 20 S, R 14 E). Named on Alcalde Hills (1969) 7.5' quadrangle.

(3) *valley,* 5 miles east-northeast of Castle Mountain (lat. 35°58'45" N, long. 120°15'45" W). Named on The Dark Hole (1961) 7.5' quadrangle.

Oak Flat [KERN]:

(1) *area,* nearly 4.5 miles northeast of Caliente (lat. 35°20'20" N, long. 118°34'40" W; at SW cor. sec. 5, T 30 S, R 32 E). Named on Oiler Peak (1972) 7.5' quadrangle.

(2) *area,* 3 miles west of Democrat Hot Springs (lat. 35°31'55" N, long. 118°43' W; sec. 35, T 27 S, R 30 E). Named on Democrat Hot Springs (1972) 7.5' quadrangle.

(3) *area,* 7.25 miles northwest of Cummings Mountain (lat. 35°07'30" N, long. 118°38'50" W). Named on Bear Mountain (1966) and Tejon Ranch (1966) 7.5' quadrangles.

Oak Flat [TULARE]:

(1) *area,* 9 miles south of Kaweah (lat. 36°20'30" N, long. 118°55'30" W). Named on Kaweah (1957) 15' quadrangle.

(2) *area,* 5.5 miles southwest of California Hot Springs (lat. 35° 49' N, long. 118°43'50" W; sec. 27, T 24 S, R 30 E). Named on California Hot Springs (1958) 15' quadrangle.

(3) *area,* 8 miles south-southeast of Springville (lat. 36°01'10" N, long. 118°46'10" W). Named on Globe (1956) 7.5' quadrangle.

Oak Flat: see **Little Oak Flat** [FRESNO]; **Little Oak Flat** [KERN]; **Little Oak Flat** [TULARE].

Oak Flat Canyon [FRESNO]: *canyon,* drained by a stream that flows 8.5 miles to Warthan Creek 5 miles southwest of Coalinga (lat. 36° 05'40" N, long. 120°25'45" W; sec. 23, T 21 S, R 14 E); Oak Flat (2) is in the canyon. Named on Alcalde Hills (1969), Curry Mountain (1969), and Sherman Peak (1969) 7.5' quadrangles.

Oak Flat Peak [TULARE]: *peak,* 8 miles south-southeast of Springville (lat. 36°01'10" N, long. 118°46'35" W); the peak is west of Oak Flat (3). Altitude 2734 feet. Named on Globe (1956) 7.5' quadrangle.

Oak Grove [TULARE]: *locality,* 7.25 miles east of Kaweah along East Fork Kaweah River (lat. 36°27'05" N, long. 118°47'25" W; near E line sec. 15, T 17 S, R 29 E). Named on Kaweah (1957) 15' quadrangle. Called Oakgrove on Kaweah (1909) 30' quadrangle.

Oakhurst [FRESNO]: *locality,* 5.25 miles southwest of Piedra along Atchison, Topeka and Santa Fe Railroad (lat. 36°45' N, long. 119° 26'25" W; near S line sec. 35, T 13 S, R 23 E). Named on Watts Valley (1942) 15' quadrangle.

Oak Ridge [KERN]: *ridge,* south-southwest-trending, 1.5 miles long, 4 miles south-southwest of Alta Sierra (lat. 35°40'35" N, long. 118°35'10" W). Named on Alta Sierra (1972) 7.5' quadrangle.

Oak Spring: see **Little Oak Spring** [FRESNO].

Oat Canyon [TULARE]: *canyon,* drained by a stream that flows 4.25 miles to Lewis Creek 8 miles north-northeast of Porterville (lat. 36°11' N, long. 118°58'20" W; near SW cor. sec. 17, T 20 S, R 28 E). Named on Frazier Valley (1957) 7.5' quadrangle.

Oat Knob [TULARE]: *peak,* 6 miles northeast of Woodlake (lat. 36° 29'05" N, long. 119°01'45" W; near NE cor. sec. 3, T 17 S, R 27 E). Named on Woodlake (1952) 7.5' quadrangle.

Oat Knob Canyon [TULARE]: *canyon,* drained by a stream that flows less than 1 mile to Dry Creek (1) 6.5 miles northeast of Woodlake (lat. 36°29' N, long. 119°01' W; sec. 2, T 17 S, R 27 E); the canyon heads near Oat Knob. Named on Woodlake (1952) 7.5' quadrangle.

Oat Mountain [FRESNO]: *ridge,* generally west-trending, 7 miles long, 7 miles southwest of Balch Camp (lat. 36°51' N, long. 119° 12' W). Named on Patterson Mountain (1952) and Watts Valley (1942) 15' quadrangles.

Oat Mountain [TULARE]: *peak,* 9 miles south of Springville (lat. 36°00' N, long. 118°47'55" W). Altitude 3519 feet. Named on Springville (1957) and White River (1952) 15' quadrangles.

Obelisk [FRESNO]: *relief feature,* 9 miles north-northeast of Hume (lat. 36°54'30" N, long. 118°51'10" W). Altitude 9700 feet. Named on Tehipite Dome (1952) 15' quadrangle. Members of United States Geological Survey applied the name in 1903 for the shape of the feature (Gudde, 1949, p. 240).

O'Brien Hill [KERN]: *peak,* 3.5 miles south of Miracle Hot Springs (lat. 35°31'25" N, long. 118°31'55" W; sec. 3, T 28 S, R 32 E); the peak is 1 mile east-northeast of O'Brien Spring. Named on Miracle Hot Springs (1972) 7.5' quadrangle.

O'Brien Spring [KERN]: *spring,* 4 miles south-southwest of Miracle Hot Springs (lat. 35°31'10" N, long. 118°32'55" W; sec. 4, T 28 S, R 32 E); the spring is 1 mile west-southwest of O'Brien Hill. Named on Miracle Hot Springs (1972) 7.5' quadrangle.

Observation Peak [FRESNO]: *peak,* 12 miles east-southeast of Mount Goddard (lat. 37°01'25" N, long. 118°31'20" W). Altitude 12,322 feet. Named on Mount Goddard (1948) 15' quadrangle. J.N. LeConte, who named the peak in 1902, also called it Panorama Point (Browning, p. 160).

Occoya Creek: see **Poso Creek** [KERN-TULARE].

Ockenden [FRESNO]: *locality,* 1.25 miles south of Shaver Lake Heights (present town of Shaver Lake) (lat. 37°05'20" N, long. 119°18'55" W; sec. 2, T 10 S, R 24 E). Named on Shaver Lake (1953) 15' quadrangle. Postal authorities established Ockenden post office in 1893 and discontinued it in 1918; the name is for Thomas J. Ockenden, first postmaster (Salley, p. 159).

O-co-ya Creek: see **Poso Creek** [KERN-TULARE].

Octol [TULARE]: *locality,* 4.5 miles north-northwest of Tipton along Southern Pacific Railroad (lat. 36°07'25" N, long. 119°19'40" W; at N line sec.

12, T 21 S, R 24 E). Named on Tipton (1950) 7.5' quadrangle.

Odessa [KINGS]: *locality,* 4 miles south of Hanford along Atchison, Topeka and Santa Fe Railroad (lat. 36°16'15" N, long. 119°38'40" W; near S line sec. 13, T 19 S, R 21 E). Named on Hanford (1926) 7.5' quadrangle.

Oil Canyon [FRESNO]: *canyon,* drained by Oil Creek, which flows 6 miles to Pleasant Valley 6 miles north of Coalinga (lat. 36°13'25" N, long. 120°21'15" W; near NE cor. sec. 5, T 20 S, R 15 E). Named on Domengine Ranch (1956) and Joaquin Rocks (1969) 7.5' quadrangles. Arnold and Anderson (1908, p. 16) named the canyon, which the road to Oil City follows.

Oil Canyon [KERN]: *canyon,* drained by a stream that flows 3.25 miles to Cache Creek 8 miles east of Tehachapi (lat. 35°09'05" N, long. 118°18'25" W; near NE cor. sec. 15, T 32 S, R 34 E). Named on Tehachapi NE (1966) 7.5' quadrangle. The name is from wells that were drilled for oil in the neighborhood in the early 1900's (Barras, p. 42).

Oil Center [KERN]: *locality,* 4.5 miles north of downtown Bakersfield (lat. 35°26'20" N, long. 118°59'15" W; near NE cor. sec. 5, T 29 S, R 28 E); the place is in Kern River oil field. Named on Oil Center (1954) 7.5' quadrangle. Postal authorities established Oilcenter post office in 1901 and discontinued it in 1937 (Frickstad, p. 58).

Oil City [FRESNO]: *locality,* 9 miles north of Coalinga (lat. 36° 16' N, long. 120°21'50" W; sec. 20, T 19 S, R 15 E); the place is in Oil Canyon. Named on Coalinga (1912) 30' quadrangle. William Youle, a pioneer oil man, named the place for Oil City, Pennsylvania (Latta, 1949, p. 139).

Oil City [KERN]: *locality,* 4.25 miles north-northeast of downtown Bakersfield along Kern River (lat. 35°25'35" N, long. 118°57'30" W; at N line sec. 10, T 29 S, R 28 E). Named on Oil Center (1954) 7.5' quadrangle.

Oil Creek [FRESNO]: *stream,* flows nearly 6 miles through Oil Canyon to Pleasant Valley 6 miles north of Coalinga (lat. 36°13'25" N, long. 120°21'15" W; near NE cor. sec. 5, T 20 S, R 15 E). Named on Coalinga (1956) 7.5' quadrangle.

Oildale [KERN]: *town,* 3.5 miles north-northwest of downtown Bakersfield on the north side of Kern River (lat. 35°25'10" N, long. 119°01'45" W; sec. 12, T 29 S, R 27 E). Named on Oildale (1954) 7.5' quadrangle. Postal authorities established Oildale post office in 1916; the name is from oil tanks at the site (Salley, p. 160). The place first was called North Side (Wines, p. 86). Samuel Dickinson subdivided 10 acres in 1909 to start the town (Bailey, 1967, p. 20).

Oiler Canyon [KERN]: *canyon,* drained by a stream that flows 3.25 miles to the canyon of Caliente Creek 2.5 miles east-northeast of Caliente (lat. 35°18'30" N, long. 118°35' W; near N line sec. 19, T 30 S, R 32 E); the canyon heads near Oiler Peak. Named on Oiler Peak (1972) 7.5' quadrangle.

Oiler Peak [KERN]: *peak,* nearly 5 miles north-northeast of Caliente (lat. 35°21'10" N, long. 118°35'10" W; near N line sec. 6, T 30 S, R 32 E). Altitude 4323 feet. Named on Oiler Peak (1972) 7.5' quadrangle.

Oilfields [FRESNO]: *settlement,* 7.5 miles north-northeast of Coalinga (lat. 36°14'45" N, long. 120°18'50" W; sec. 26, T 19 S, R 15 E). Named on Coalinga (1956) 7.5' quadrangle. Postal authorities established Oilfields post office in 1908 and discontinued it in 1951 (Frickstad, p. 36). The place originally was called Balfour from the firm of Balfour, Williamson & Company, of London, England, an investor in oil of the region, and later the name was changed to Oilfields, from California Oilfields, Ltd., also a British Company; by 1908 the "model oil town" was functioning (Franks and Lambert, p. 133).

Oil Junction [KERN]: *locality,* 4.5 miles northwest of downtown Bakersfield along Southern Pacific Railroad (lat. 35°25'10" N, long. 119°03'25" W; near E line sec. 10, T 29 S, R 27 E). Named on Oildale (1954) 7.5' quadrangle.

Oil Well Canyon [FRESNO]: *canyon,* drained by a stream that flows 1.25 miles to Salt Creek (2) 7 miles south-southwest of Coalinga (lat. 36°03'05" N, long. 120°25'20" W; near NE cor. sec. 2, T 22 S, R 14 E). Named on Curry Mountain (1969) 7.5' quadrangle.

Olancha Pass [TULARE]: *pass,* 5.25 miles east of Monache Mountain on Tulare-Inyo County line (lat. 36°12'45" N, long. 118°06'15" W; sec. 5, T 20 S, R 36 E); the pass is 4 miles south of Olancha Peak. Named on Monache Mountain (1956) 15' quadrangle.

Olancha Peak [TULARE]: *peak,* 24 miles south-southeast of Mount Whitney on Tulare-Inyo County line (lat. 36°15'55" N, long. 118° 07' W); the peak is above the village of Olancha, which is in Inyo County. Altitude 12,123 feet. Named on Olancha (1956) 15' quadrangle.

Old Bretz Mill [FRESNO]: *settlement,* 2 miles south-southeast of Shaver Lake Heights (present town of Shaver Lake) (lat. 37°04'55" N, long. 119°18' W; near SE cor. sec. 1, T 10 S, R 24 E). Named on Shaver Lake (1953) 15' quadrangle. Kaiser (1904) 30' quadrangle shows a place called Peteras Mill located near the site.

Old Deer Creek Channel: see **Deer Creek** [TULARE] (2).

Old Fort Miller [FRESNO]: *locality,* 8.5 miles west-southwest of Prather on the south side of San Joaquin River (lat. 37°00'35" N, long. 119°39'45" W; near N line sec. 3, T 11 S, R 21 E); water of Millerton Lake now covers the site. Named on Sulphur Springs (1919) 7.5' quadrangle. Members of the Mariposa Battalion built a post along the river in 1851 and called it Camp Barbour for Indian Commissioner George W. Barbour; later the same year the army built a post at or near the site and called it Camp Miller for Major Albert S. Miller; the name was changed to Fort Miller in 1852, and the post was abandoned in 1858, reoccupied in 1863, and abandoned again in 1864 (Frazer, p. 26-27). Crampton (*in* Eccleston, p. 78) noted that Camp Barbour was along San Joaquin River opposite Larione's ferry, and stated that Larione's corral (which presumably was located near the ferry) was on the south side of the river about 1 mile south of old Fort Washington, which in turn was about 10 miles below Fort Miller. The only evidence of Fort Washington on modern maps is Fort Washington school shown located 11 miles north of downtown Fresno on Herndon (1965) 15' quadrangle (lat. 36°53'45" N, long. 119°45'50" W), and nearby Fort Washington country club. Eddy's (1854) map and Baker's (1855) map both show Washington City below Fort Miller along San Joaquin River, and Rogers and Johnston's (1857) map has the name "Washington" in the same neighborhood.

Old Fort Tejon [KERN]: *locality,* 3.25 miles north-northwest of Lebec (lat. 34°52'25" N, long. 118°53'35" W). Named on Frazier Mountain (1958) 7.5' quadrangle. Fort Tejon was started in 1854, and in 1858 it became a station on Butterfield Overland stage line; the post was evacuated in 1861, reoccupied in 1863 by California volunteer troops, and abandoned in 1864 (Frazer, p. 32). Postal authorities established Fort Tejon post office in 1859, discontinued it in 1862, reestablished it in 1892, and discontinued it the same year (Salley, p. 78).

Old Garlock [KERN]: *locality,* 3 miles southwest of Garlock (lat. 35°22'30" N, long. 117°49'30" W). Named on Saltdale (1943b) 15' quadrangle.

Old Hart Station [KERN]: *locality,* 2.5 miles east of the village of Lost Hills (lat. 35°37' N, long. 119°38'45" W). Named on Hart Station (1942) 15' quadrangle.

Old Likely Mill [KERN]: *locality,* nearly 5 miles southwest of Alta Sierra (lat. 35°40'35" N, long. 118°36'25" W; near SE cor. sec. 12, T 26 S, R 31 E). Site named on Alta Sierra (1972) 7.5' quadrangle.

Old Millerton [FRESNO]: *locality,* 9.5 miles west-southwest of Prather on the south side of San Joaquin River (lat. 37°00'35" N, long. 119°40'40" W; near N line sec. 4, T 11 S, R 21 E). Named on Sulphur Springs (1919) 7.5' quadrangle, which shows Old Fort Miller located 1 mile east of Old Millerton. The place began in 1850 as a mining town called Rootville, and became the county seat when Fresno County was organized in 1856 (Hoover, Rensch, and Rensch, p. 92). By 1853 or 1854 the name "Rootville" was changed to Millerton, for nearby Fort Miller; the place also was called Millertown (Gudde, 1975, p. 295). The leading inhabitants of the town moved to Fresno after 1872 (Bancroft, p. 517). Water of Millerton Lake now covers the site of Old Millerton. Postal authorities established Millerton post office in 1853, discontinued it in 1863, reestablished it in 1864, changed the name to Fort Miller in 1874, and discontinued it in 1876 (Frickstad, p. 33, 35). They established Elbow post office 27 miles southeast of Millerton in 1866 and discontinued it in 1868; the name "Elbow" was from a bend in Kings River (Salley, p. 66). Rich placer-gold deposits were reported in 1850 from San Joaquin River above Millerton at a place called Cassadys Bar (Gudde, 1975, p. 63).

Old Mount Whitney: see **Mount Corcoran** [TULARE].

Old Panama: see **Panama** [KERN].

Old Pipe Lake [FRESNO]: *lake,* 700 feet long, 4.25 miles west-southwest of Blackcap Mountain (lat. 37°03'40" N, long. 118° 52' W; sec. 13, T 10 S, R 28 E). Named on Blackcap Mountain (1953) 15' quadrangle.

Old River [KERN]: *village,* 9.5 miles southwest of Bakersfield (lat. 35°16' N, long. 119°06'30" W; at NW cor. sec. 5, T 31 S, R 27 E). Named on Gosford (1954) 7.5' quadrangle. The place began in the 1870's and took its name from an old channel of Kern River (Bailey, 1967, p. 20). Thomas Barnes laid out a small community in 1859 called Barnes Settlement that was situated on his homestead a short distance west of the present Old River; Charles W. Canfield laid out a townsite in 1874 near the same site and called it Canfield (Bailey, 1967, p. 2).

Old River: see **Kern River** [KERN-TULARE].

Old South Fork: see **Kern River** [KERN-TULARE].

Old Squaw Lake [FRESNO]: *lake,* 1000 feet long, 8 miles south-southwest of Mount Abbot (lat. 37°16'25" N, long. 118°49'40" W). Named on Mount Abbot (1953) 15' quadrangle.

Old Sunset: see **Hazelton** [KERN].

Old Town [KERN]: *locality,* 3 miles west-northwest of Tehachapi (lat. 35°08'35" N, long. 118°29'40" W; sec. 13, T 32 S, R 32 E). Named on Tehachapi North (1966) 7.5' quadrangle. Cummings Mountain (1943b) 15' quadrangle shows the place situated 1.25 miles farther southwest (lat. 35°07'40" N, long. 118°30'20" W; sec. 23, T 32 S, R 32 E). The community first was called Williamsburg for James E. Williams, an early businessman there (Boyd, p. 175). Postal authorities established Tehichipa post office near Oak Creek Pass in 1869, moved it in 1877 to present Old Town, and discontinued it in 1885 (Boyd, p. 176; Salley, p. 219). Gray's (1873) map has the name "Tehichipa" along the railroad.

Oleander [FRESNO]:

(1) *locality,* 9 miles south-southeast of downtown Fresno (lat. 36° 38' N, long. 119°45'15" W; at NE cor. sec. 14, T 15 S, R 20 E). Named on Fresno South (1963) 7.5' quadrangle. Postal authorities established Oleander post office in 1881, moved it 1 mile northeast in 1899, and discontinued it in 1935; the post office name was the middle name of the first postmaster, William O. Johnson (Salley, p. 160).

(2) *locality,* 2.5 miles south-southwest of Malaga along Atchison, Topeka and Santa Fe Railroad (lat. 36°38'40" N, long. 119°45' W; sec. 12, T 15 S, R 20 E); the place is 0.25 mile east of Oleander (1). Named on Selma (1946) 15' quadrangle.

Olig [KERN]: *locality,* 2 miles northwest of McKittrick (lat. 35°19'20" N, long. 119°39'15" W; at N line sec. 18, T 30 S, R 22 E). Named on McKittrick (1912) 30' quadrangle.

Olive: see **Mount Olive** [FRESNO].

Olive Lake [FRESNO]: *lake,* 2000 feet long, 13 miles north-northwest of Mount Abbot (lat. 37°28'25" N, long. 118°59'10" W). Named on Mount Abbot (1953) 15' quadrangle.

Oliver Rock [FRESNO]: *peak,* 10 miles south-southwest of Coalinga (lat. 36°00'35" N, long. 120°26'20" W; near SW cor. sec. 14, T 22 S, R 14 E). Named on Curry Mountain (1969) 7.5' quadrangle.

Oljato: see **Camp Oljato** [FRESNO].

O'Neil Canyon [KERN]: *canyon,* drained by a stream that flows 3.25 miles to Castac Valley 2 miles north-northwest of Lebec (lat. 34° 51'50" N, long. 118°52'50" W). Named on Frazier Mountain (1958) 7.5' quadrangle.

Onion Meadow [TULARE]: *area,* 7.5 miles south of Camp Nelson (lat. 36°02' N, long. 118°36' W; sec. 11, T 22 S, R 31 E). Named on Camp Nelson (1956) 15' quadrangle.

Onion Meadow Peak [TULARE]: *peak,* 8 miles south of Camp Nelson (lat. 36°01'40" N, long. 118°36'05" W; near S line sec. 11, T 22 S, R 31 E); the peak is south-southwest of Onion Meadow. Named on Camp Nelson (1956) 15' quadrangle.

Onion Spring Meadow [FRESNO]: *area,* 10 miles northeast of Kaiser Peak (lat. 37°24' N, long. 119°04'10" W). Named on Kaiser Peak (1953) 15' quadrangle.

Onyx [KERN]: *village,* 3.5 miles east-northeast of Weldon (lat. 35° 41'25" N, long. 118°13'10" W; sec. 4, T 26 S, R 35 E); the place is at the mouth of Scodie Canyon. Named on Onyx (1972) 7.5' quadrangle. Postal authorities established Onyx post office in 1889 (Frickstad, p. 58). The village first was called Scodie, for William Scodie, who opened a store there in 1861 (Bailey, 1967, p. 20).

Onyx Peak [KERN]: *peak,* 2.25 miles south of Onyx (lat. 35°39'25" N, long. 118°13'30" W; near N line sec. 21, T 26 S, R 35 E). Altitude 5244 feet. Named on Onyx (1972) 7.5' quadrangle.

O'Quinn Meadow [TULARE]: *area,* 3.5 miles east-southeast of California Hot Springs (lat. 35°51'10" N, long. 118°37' W; sec. 10, T 24 S, R 31 E). Named on California Hot Springs (1958) 15' quadrangle.

Ora [FRESNO]: *locality,* 2 miles east-northeast of Coalinga along Southern Pacific Railroad (lat. 36°09'05" N, long. 120°19'30" W; near S line sec. 27, T 20 S, R 15 E). Named on Coalinga (1956) 7.5' quadrangle.

Orange Cove [FRESNO]: *town,* 8 miles east-northeast of Reedley (lat. 36°37'30" N, long. 119°18'45" W; sec. 13, T 15 S, R 24 E). Named on Orange Cove North (1966) and Orange Cove South (1966) 7.5' quadrangles. Postal authorities established Orange Cove post office in 1914 (Frickstad, p. 36), and the town incorporated in 1948. Elmer M. Sheridan founded and named the town in 1914 before the neighborhood became a large producer of citrus (Hanna, p. 219).

Orange Heights: see **Ivanhoe** [TULARE].

Orangehurst: see **Exeter** [TULARE].

Orchard Peak [KERN]: *peak,* 34 miles west-northwest of Bakersfield (lat. 35°44'15" N, long. 120°08' W; near W line sec. 22, T 25 S, R 17 E). Altitude 3125 feet. Named on Orchard Peak (1961) 7.5' quadrangle. Arnold and Johnson (p. 21) proposed the name to commemorate Joseph E. Orchard, an old resident of McLure Valley (present Sunflower Valley).

Orchard Ridge: see **Bluestone Ridge** [KERN].

Orchid Lake [FRESNO]: *lake,* 750 feet long, 7.25 miles southwest of Mount Abbot (lat. 37°19'35" N, long. 118°53'25" W). Named on Mount Abbot (1953) 15' quadrangle.

Ordinance Creek [FRESNO]: *stream,* flows 3.25 miles to Big Creek (1) 6.5 miles north of Shaver Lake Heights (present town of Shaver Lake) (lat. 37°12' N, long. 119°18'10" W; sec. 25, T 8 S, R 24 E). Named on Shaver Lake (1953) 15' quadrangle.

Orejano Canyon [KERN]:

(1) *canyon,* drained by a stream that flows nearly 3 miles to Caliente Creek 5 miles northwest of Emerald Mountain (lat. 35°18'50" N, long. 118°20'05" W). Named on Emerald Mountain (1972) 7.5' quadrangle.

(2) *canyon,* drained by a stream that flows 4 miles to Tehachapi Creek nearly 3 miles southeast of Caliente (lat. 35°15'50" N, long. 118°35'25" W; at W line sec. 6, T 31 S, R 32 E); the canyon is south of Orejano Ridge. Named on Oiler Peak (1972) 7.5' quadrangle.

Orejano Ridge [KERN]: *ridge,* generally west-trending, 5 miles long, center 5 miles east-southeast of Caliente (lat. 35°15'50" N, long. 118°32'50" W); the ridge is north of Orejano Canyon (2). Named on Oiler Peak (1972) 7.5' quadrangle.

Oren [FRESNO]: *village,* 20 miles southwest of Kaiser Peak (lat. 37° 05'15" N, long. 119°25'40" W; sec. 2, T 10 S, R 23 E). Named on Kaiser (1904) 30' quadrangle. Postal authorities established Oren post office in 1899 and discontinued it in 1905 (Frickstad, p. 36). Called Oro on California Mining Bureau's (1917a) map.

Oriole Lake [TULARE]: *lake,* 400 feet long, 8 miles west of Mineral King (lat. 36°27'35" N, long. 118°44'10" W; sec. 8, T 17 S, R 30 E). Named on Mineral King (1956) 15' quadrangle.

Orion [KINGS]: *locality,* 5.25 miles west-southwest of Hanford along Southern Pacific Railroad (lat. 38°18'40" N, long. 119°44'20" W; sec. 6, T 19 S, R 21 E). Named on Hanford (1926) 7.5' quadrangle.

Orlem [TULARE]: *locality,* 2.25 miles east-southeast of Lindsay along Visalia Electric Railroad (lat. 36°11'30" N, long. 119°03' W; sec. 16, T 20 S, R 27 E). Named on Lindsay (1928) 7.5' quadrangle.

Oro: see **Oren** [FRESNO].

Oro Loma [FRESNO]: *locality,* 13 miles west of Firebaugh (lat. 36° 53'25" N, long. 120°41' W; sec. 17, T 12 S, R 12 E). Named on Dos Palos (1956) 7.5' quadrangle. Postal authorities established Oro Loma post office in 1914 and discontinued it in 1929 (Frickstad, p. 36).

Orosi [TULARE]: *town,* 5.5 miles east of Dinuba (lat. 36°32'40" N, long. 118°17'10" W; around SE cor. sec. 7, T 16 S, R 25 E). Named on Orange Cove South (1966) 7.5' quadrangle. Neal McCallum named the place in 1888, supposedly for golden poppies in the neighborhood—*oro* means "gold" in Spanish (Mitchell, A.R., p. 69). Postal authorities established Orosi post office in 1888 (Frickstad, p. 213).

Orosi: see **East Orosi** [TULARE].

Orosi Station: see **East Orosi** [TULARE].

Orris [TULARE]: *locality,* 2.5 miles south-southwest of Ducor along Southern Pacific Railroad (lat. 35°51'15" N, long. 119°03'40" W; sec. 9, T 24 S, R 27 E). Named on Richgrove (1952) 7.5' quadrangle.

Osa Creek [TULARE]: *stream,* flows 4.5 miles to Kern River 4 miles south of Hockett Peak (lat. 36°09'45" N, long. 118°22'40" W); the stream heads at Osa Meadows. Named on Hockett Peak (1956) 15' quadrangle.

Osa Meadows [TULARE]: *area,* 5.25 miles east-southeast of Hockett Peak (lat. 36°10'55" N, long. 118°18'20" W). Named on Hockett Peak (1956) 15' quadrangle.

Oscar Meyer Spring [KERN]: *spring,* 1 mile south-southwest of Democrat Hot Springs (lat. 35°30'55" N, long. 118°40'15" W). Named on Democrat Hot Springs (1972) 7.5' quadrangle.

Oso Canyon [KERN]: *canyon,* drained by a stream that flows 1 mile to Los Angeles County 4.25 miles east-southeast of Lebec (lat. 34° 49'05" N, long. 118°47'40" W). Named on Lebec (1958) 7.5' quadrangle. United States Board on Geographic Names (1967c, p. 4) rejected the name "Canada de la Oasis" for the feature.

Ousel Creek: see **Ouzel Creek** [TULARE].

Outside Creek [TULARE]: *stream,* diverges southwest from Johnson Slough 3 miles northwest of Exeter and flows for 12 miles to join Inside Creek and form Elk Bayou 5 miles east-southeast of Tulare (lat. 36°11'30" N, long. 119°15'20" W; sec. 15, T 20 S, R 25 E). Named on Exeter (1952) 15' quadrangle, and on Cairns Corner (1950, photorevised 1969) and Tulare (1950) 7.5' quadrangles. The name is from the location of the stream on the outside edge of marsh formed by the fan of Kaweah River and Saint Johns River (Gudde, 1949, p. 247).

Ouzel Creek [TULARE]: *stream,* flows 2.25 miles to East Lake 13 miles northwest of Mount Whitney (lat. 36°43'30" N, long. 118°26'40" W). Named on Mount Whitney (1956) 15' quadrangle. United States Board on Geographic Names (1933a, p. 578) rejected the form "Ousel Creek" for the name. David Starr Jordan gave the name to the stream in 1899 because John Muir had studied the water ouzel along it (Ristow, p. 424).

Overholster Meadow [TULARE]: *area,* 9 miles north-northwest of Olancha Peak along Mulkey Creek (lat. 36°22'25" N, long. 118°12'15" W; sec. 8, T 18 S, R 35 E). Named on Olancha (1956) 15' quadrangle.

Owen: see **Mount Owen**, under **Brown** [KERN].

Owens: see **Camp Owens** [KERN].

Owens Camp [KERN]: *locality,* 5.25 miles west-northwest of Garlock (lat. 35°26'35" N, long. 117°52'10" W). Named on Garlock (1967) 7.5' quadrangle.

Owens Mountain [FRESNO]: *ridge,* west-northwest-trending, 2 miles long, 8 miles north-northeast of Clovis (lat. 36°55'50" N, long. 119°38'30" W). Named on Friant (1964) 7.5' quadrangle. According to Gudde (1949, p. 247), the name probably commemorates George W. Owens, who came to California in 1862 and had a stock ranch in the foothills in the 1870's.

Owens Peak [KERN]: *peak,* 12 miles west-northwest of Inyokern (lat. 35°44'15" N, long. 117°59'45" W). Altitude 8453 feet. Named on Owens Peak (1972) 7.5' quadrangle. Birnie (p. 131) referred to Owen's Peak. The name honors Richard Owens, who was with Fremont's exploring expedition in 1845 (Hanna, p. 222, 223).

Owl Mountain [FRESNO]: *peak,* 2.5 miles southeast of Trimmer (lat. 36°52'50" N, long. 119°15'35" W; near SE cor. sec. 17, T 12 S., R 25 E).

Altitude 2181 feet. Named on Trimmer (1965) 7.5' quadrangle.

Owl Peak [TULARE]: *peak,* 1.25 miles south-southeast of Auckland (lat. 36°34'20" N, long. 119°05'40" W; near S line sec. 36, T 15 S, R 26 E). Altitude 2417 feet. Named on Auckland (1966) 7.5' quadrangle.

Oxalis [FRESNO]: *locality,* 6.5 miles northwest of Firebaugh along Southern Pacific Railroad (lat. 36°54'45" N, long. 120°32'55" W; sec. 4, T 12 S, R 13 E). Named on Oxalis (1956) 7.5' quadrangle. Railroad officials gave their station at the place the botanical name for wood sorrel (Gudde, 1949, p. 247).

Oyster Hill [KINGS]: *peak,* 13 miles south of Kettleman City (lat. 35°49'05" N, long. 119°54'50" W; near NE cor. sec. 28, T 24 S, R 19 E). Named on Avenal Gap (1954) 7.5' quadrangle.

— P —

Packsaddle Canyon [TULARE]: *canyon,* drained by a stream that flows 3.5 miles to Kern River 1.5 miles northeast of Fairview (lat. 35°56'40" N, long. 118°28'35" W). Named on Kernville (1956) 15' quadrangle.

Packsaddle Cave [TULARE]: *cave,* 2 miles east-northeast of Fairview (lat. 35°56'15" N, long. 118°27'45" W); the cave is in Packsaddle Canyon. Named on Kernville (1956) 15' quadrangle.

Packsaddle Creek [TULARE]: *stream,* flows 1.5 miles to Bear Creek (4) 6.5 miles northeast of California Hot Springs (lat. 35°56'40" N, long. 118°35' W; sec. 12, T 23 S, R 31 E); the stream heads near Packsaddle Meadow. Named on California Hot Springs (1958) 15' quadrangle.

Packsaddle Lake [FRESNO]: *lake,* 2000 feet long, 9.5 miles north of Mount Goddard in Humphreys Basin (lat. 37°14'10" N, long. 118° 44'20" W). Named on Mount Goddard (1948) 15' quadrangle. Sierra Club officials named the feature; Toby Way, a packer, called it Lovejoy Lake in 1928 or 1929, when he stocked it with fish (Browning, p. 163).

Packsaddle Meadow [TULARE]: *area,* 5 miles northeast of California Hot Springs (lat. 35°55'30" N, long. 118°35'50" W); the place is at the head of Packsaddle Creek. Named on California Hot Springs (1958) 15' quadrangle.

Packwood [KERN]: *locality,* 11 miles south-southeast of Orchard Peak (lat. 35°35'15" N, long. 120°03'35" W); the place is near the head of Packwood Creek. Named on Packwood (1943) 7.5' quadrangle. Called Packwood's on Arnold and Johnson's (1910) map.

Packwood Creek [KERN]: *stream,* flows 6.25 miles to Antelope Valley (1) 7.5 miles west of Blackwells Corner (lat. 35°37'15" N, long. 119°59'55" W; sec. 35, T 26 S, R 18 E); the stream heads near Packwood. Named on Emigrant Hill (1953), Packwood Creek (1961), Sawtooth Ridge (1961), and Shale Point (1953) 7.5' quadrangles.

Packwood Creek [TULARE]: *stream,* heads at Kaweah River and flows 15 miles to ditches 9 miles west-southwest of Visalia (lat. 36°15'45" N, long. 119°25'55" W; sec. 24, T 19 S, R 23 E). Named on Exeter (1952) and Visalia (1949) 15' quadrangles. The name commemorates Elisha Packwood (Mitchell, A.R., p. 78).

Packwood Creek: see **Bates Slough** [TULARE].

Page: see **Famoso** [KERN].

Pagliarulo [TULARE]: *locality,* 3 miles south of Earlimart along Southern Pacific Railroad (lat. 35°50'20" N, long. 119°15'50" W; sec. 15, T 24 S, R 25 E). Named on Delano West (1954) 7.5' quadrangle. Called Stone on Earlimart (1942) 15' quadrangle.

Pahute Peak: see **Piute Peak** [KERN].

Paige [TULARE]: *locality,* 4.25 miles west-southwest of Tulare along Atchison, Topeka and Santa Fe Railroad (lat. 36°10'55" N, long. 119°25'10" W; near NW cor. sec. 19, T 20 S, R 24 E). Named on Paige (1950) 7.5' quadrangle. The named was given in the 1890's for landowner Timothy Paige (Gudde, 1949, p. 248). Postal authorities established Paige post office in 1908 and discontinued it in 1914 (Frickstad, p. 213).

Paine Lake [FRESNO]: *lake,* 2250 feet long, 9 miles north of Mount Goddard in Humphreys Basin (lat. 37°13'55" N, long. 118°43'45" W). Named on Mount Goddard (1948) 15' quadrangle. United States Board on Geographic Names (1986, p. 4) approved the form "Payne Lake" for the name, which commemorates Edgar Alwin Payne, painter of scenes in the Sierra Nevada, including a view of this lake. John Schober named the feature (Browning, p. 163).

Painted Lady [FRESNO]: *peak,* 10.5 miles south of Mount Pinchot (lat. 36°47'35" N, long. 118°23'55" W). Altitude 12,126 feet. Named on Mount Pinchot (1953) 15' quadrangle. Bolton C. Brown gave the name "The Pyramid" to the feature in 1899; the peak also was known as Colored Lady (Browning, p. 163).

Painted Rock [FRESNO]: *relief feature,* 12 miles northeast of Hume in Tehipite Valley (lat. 36°54'50" N, long. 118°46'30" W). Named on Tehipite Dome (1952) 15' quadrangle.

Paiute Peak: see **Piute Peak** [KERN].

Pajuela Peak [KERN]: *peak,* 8.5 miles east of Tehachapi (lat. 35°07'15" N, long. 118°17'35" W; sec. 26, T 32 S, R 34 E). Altitude 5764 feet. Named on Monolith (1966) 7.5' quadrangle.

Palisade Basin [FRESNO]: *area,* 11 miles east of Mount Goddard (lat. 37°05' N, long. 118°31'30" W); the place is southwest of North Palisade. Named on Mount Goddard (1948) 15' quadrangle.

Palisade Creek [FRESNO]: *stream,* flows 7.5 miles to Middle Fork Kings River 8.5 miles east-southeast of Mount Goddard (lat. 37°03'10" N, long. 118°34'45" W); the stream heads near Middle Palisade and goes through Palisade Lakes. Named on Big Pine (1950) and Mount Goddard (1948) 15' quadrangles. L.A. Winchell named the stream (Browning, p. 164).

Palisade Crest [FRESNO]: *peak,* 3.5 miles northwest of Mount Bolton Brown on Fresno-Inyo County line (lat. 37°04'40" N, long. 118°29'10" W). Named on Big Pine (1950) 15' quadrangle.

Palisade Lakes [FRESNO]: *lakes,* two, largest 2400 feet long, 2 miles west-northwest of Mount Bolton Brown (lat. 37°03'20" N, long. 118°28'45" W); the lakes are along Palisade Creek. Named on Big Pine (1950) 15' quadrangle.

Palma Plain: see **Antelope Valley** [KERN] (2).

Palmer Cave [TULARE]: *cave,* 11 miles southeast of Kaweah (lat. 36°22'30" N, long. 118°45'35" W). Named on Kaweah (1957) 15' quadrangle. Joseph L. Palmer discovered the cave in 1872 and named it for himself (Browning, p. 164-165).

Palmer Mountain [FRESNO]: *peak,* 19 miles east of Hume (lat. 36° 44'50" N, long. 118°34'05" W). Altitude 11,250 feet. Named on Triple Divide Peak (1956) 15' quadrangle. The name commemorates Joe Palmer, an early prospector in the neighborhood (United States Board on Geographic Names, 1933a, p. 583). The name originally was applied to present Avalanche Peak (Hanna, p. 227).

Palmer Spring [KERN]: *spring,* 2 miles north-northeast of Caliente (lat. 35°19'10" N, long. 118°36'45" W). Named on Oiler Peak (1972) 7.5' quadrangle.

Palmo [KERN]: *locality,* 2.5 miles south of Wasco along Atchison, Topeka and Santa Fe Railroad (lat. 35°33'30" N, long. 119°19'45" W; near SW cor. sec. 19, T 27 S, R 25 E). Named on Wasco (1953) 7.5' quadrangle.

Paloma [KERN]: *locality,* 2 miles east-southeast of Millux (lat. 35° 10'20" N, long. 119°09'50" W). Named on Millux (1933) 7.5' quadrangle.

Paloma Meadows [TULARE]: *area,* 14 miles south-southeast of Hockett Peak (lat. 36°01'20" N, long. 118°19'15" W). Named on Hockett Peak (1956) 15' quadrangle.

Palo Prieto: see **Annette** [KERN].

Palo Prieto Canyon: see **Palo Prieto Pass** [KERN].

Palo Prieto Creek: see **East Palo Prieto Creek**, under **Bitterwater Creek** [KERN] (2).

Palo Prieto Pass [KERN]: *valley,* 6 miles long, 8.5 miles south-southeast of Orchard Peak on Kern-San Luis Obispo County line (lat. 35°37'30" N, long. 120°11' W). Named on Holland Canyon (1961) and Orchard Peak (1961) 7.5' quadrangles. United States Board on Geographic Names (1968a, p. 6) rejected the names "Palo Prieto Canon" and "Palo Prieto Canyon" for the feature.

Palo Prieto Valley: see **Bitterwater Valley** [KERN].

Pampa: see **Bena** [KERN].

Pampa Peak [KERN]: *peak,* 7 miles northwest of Caliente (lat. 35° 21'55" N, long. 118°42'40" W; sec. 36, T 29 S, R 30 E); the peak is 3 miles north-northeast of Bena, which formerly was called Pampa. Altitude 3176 feet. Named on Bena (1972) 7.5' quadrangle.

Panama [KERN]: *village,* 8 miles south-southwest of Bakersfield (lat. 35°16' N, long. 119°03'20" W; at SE cor. sec. 34, T 30 S, R 27 E). Named on Gosford (1954) 7.5' quadrangle. Postal authorities established Panama post office in 1874 and discontinued it in 1876 (Frickstad, p. 58). A Mexican settlement called Rio Bravo, from an early name for Kern River, was started in 1849 about 2 miles north of present Panama; later the settlement of Rio Bravo was called Panama, and later still the name "Panama" was transferred to present Panama, while the site first called Rio Bravo became known as Old Panama (Bailey, 1967, p. 21). The name "Panama" was from a comparison of the place to the low-lying, swampy, mosquito-infested lands of the Isthmus of Panama (Boyd, p. 98).

Panama Slough [KERN]: *water feature,* 2 miles southwest of Panama (lat. 35°15' N, long. 119°04'55" W). Named on Conner (1954) and Gosford (1954) 7.5' quadrangles. Gosford (1932) 7.5' quadrangle shows Panama Slough diverging from Kern River 2.5 miles west of downtown Bakersfield, and Buena Vista Lake (1912) 30' quadrangle shows it extending to Kern Lake Bed 1.25 miles east of Conner.

Pande: see **Peter Pande Lake** [FRESNO].

Panoche Creek [FRESNO]: *stream,* heads in San Benito County and flows 30 miles to lowlands 19 miles southwest of Firebaugh (lat. 36°38' N, long. 120°39'10" W; near N line sec. 15, T 15 S, R 12 E). Named on Chaney Ranch (1955), Chounet Ranch (1956), and Tumey Hills (1956) 7.5' quadrangles. Whitney (p. 55) referred to Big Panoche Creek. Anderson and Pack (p. 19) noted that the lower 3-mile reach of the stream sometimes incorrectly is termed Silver Creek, and United States Board on Geographic Names (1933a, p. 586) rejected the name "Silver Creek" for present Panoche Creek. Mendenhall's (1908) map shows a place called Schunemanns situated on the southeast side of Panoche Creek about 1 mile southwest of the entrance of the stream into lowlands (sec. 16, T 15 S, R 12 E). California Mining Bureau's (1917a) map shows a place called Chaneys located south of Panoche Creek and about 3 miles east of the entrance of Panoche Creek into lowlands—Chaney Ranch (1955) 7.5' quadrangle shows Chaney ranch at about the same site.

Panoche Creek: see **Little Panoche Creek** [FRESNO]; **Silver Creek** [FRESNO] (2).

Panoche Hills [FRESNO]: *range,* 20 miles west-southwest of Firebaugh between Panoche Creek and Little Panoche Creek (lat. 36° 42' N, long. 120°45' W). Named on Chounet Ranch (1956), Hammond Ranch (1956), Laguna Seca Ranch (1956), Mercey Hot Springs (1969), Panoche (1969), and Tumey Hills (1956) 7.5' quadrangles.

Panoche Junction [FRESNO]: *locality,* 15 miles west-southwest of Tranquillity (lat. 36°32'45" N, long. 120°29'15" W; at N line sec. 18, T 16 S, R 14 E). Named on Levis (1956) 7.5' quadrangle.

Panoche Mountain [FRESNO]: *peak,* 5.5 miles east-northeast of Mercey Hot Springs (lat. 36°43'30" N, long. 120°45'50" W; on E line sec. 9, T 14 S, R 11 E). Altitude 2091 feet. Named on Mercey Hot Springs (1969) 7.5' quadrangle.

Panoche Valley: see **Little Panoche Valley** [FRESNO].

Panochita Creek: see **Little Panoche Creek** [FRESNO].

Panochita Valley: see **Little Panoche Valley** [FRESNO].

Panorama Campground [TULARE]: *locality,* 7.5 miles southeast of California Hot Springs (lat. 35°48'35" N, long. 118°34'15" W; sec. 30, T 24 S, R 32 E). Named on California Hot Springs (1958) 15' quadrangle. Called Panorama Camp on Tobias Peak (1936) 30' quadrangle.

Panorama Heights [TULARE]: *settlement,* 5.5 miles south-southeast of California Hot Springs (lat. 35°48'20" N, long. 118°37'45" W; near SE cor. sec. 28, T 24 S, R 31 E). Named on California Hot Springs (1958) 15' quadrangle.

Panorama Point [TULARE]: *peak,* 4 miles southeast of Yucca Mountain (lat. 36°32'15" N, long. 118°48'40" W). Named on Giant Forest (1956) 15' quadrangle.

Panorama Point: see **Observation Peak** [FRESNO].

Panther Creek [TULARE]: *stream,* flows 3.25 miles to Middle Fork Kaweah River 11 miles west-southwest of Triple Divide Peak (lat. 36°32'20" N, long. 118°43'05" W); the stream heads near Panther Peak. Named on Triple Divide Peak (1956) 15' quadrangle. The name is from a mountain lion that Hale Tharp killed near the feature (Browning, p. 165).

Panther Gap [TULARE]: *pass,* 10 miles west of Triple Divide Peak (lat. 36°35' N, long. 118°42'15" W; near N line sec. 34, T 15 S, R 30 E); the pass is 0.5 mile east of Panther Peak. Named on Triple Divide Peak (1956) 15' quadrangle.

Panther Meadow [TULARE]: *area,* 10.5 miles west of Triple Divide Peak (lat. 36°35'10" N, long. 118°42'50" W; near SW cor. sec. 27, T 15 S, R 30 E); the place is north of Panther Peak. Named on Triple Divide Peak (1956) 15' quadrangle.

Panther Peak [TULARE]: *peak,* 10.5 miles west of Triple Divide Peak (lat. 36°35' N, long. 118°42'50" W; near NW cor. sec. 34, T 15 S, R 30 E). Altitude 9046 feet. Named on Triple Divide Peak (1956) 15' quadrangle.

Paoha Lake [FRESNO]: *lake,* 200 feet long, 7.5 miles south of Mount Abbot (lat. 37°16'55" N, long. 118°48'30" W). Named on Mount Abbot (1953) 15' quadrangle. Elden H. Vestal of California Department of Fish and Game named the lake in 1951; Vestal believed that the word "paoha" has the meaning "white" or "daylight" in the Piute Indian language, and therefore has a meaning opposite to that of the name of nearby Negit Lake (Browning, p. 165).

Papoose Lake [FRESNO]: *lake,* 550 feet long, 10 miles northwest of Mount Abbot (lat. 37°28'15" N, long. 118°55'55" W); the lake is between Warrior Lake and Lake of the Lone Indian. Named on Mount Abbot (1953) 15' quadrangle.

Paradise Canyon [TULARE]: *canyon,* 1.5 miles long, 9 miles south of Kaweah along the lower part of Jim Grey Creek (lat. 36°20'10" N, long. 118°56'15" W). Named on Kaweah (1957) 15' quadrangle.

Paradise Cave [TULARE]: *cave,* 9 miles east of Kaweah (lat. 36°28'45" N, long. 118°45'40" W; sec. 6, T 17 S, R 30 E); the cave is on the south side of Paradise Ridge. Named on Kaweah (1957) 15' quadrangle. H.R. Harmon discovered the cave in 1901; Charles W. Blossom and Walter Fry, rangers of Sequoia National Park, named it in 1906 (Browning, p. 166).

Paradise Cove [KERN]: *embayment,* 4.25 miles south-southeast of Wofford Heights along Isabella Lake (lat. 35°39'10" N, long. 118° 25'30" W; sec. 22, T 26 S, R 33 E). Named on Lake Isabella North (1972) 7.5' quadrangle.

Paradise Cove Campground [KERN]: *locality,* 4.5 miles south-southeast of Wofford Heights (lat. 35°38'55" N, long. 118°25'30" W; sec. 22, T 26 S, R 33 E); the place is at Paradise Cove. Named on Lake Isabella North (1972) 7.5' quadrangle.

Paradise Creek [TULARE]: *stream,* flows 4.5 miles to Middle Fork Kaweah River 7 miles east-southeast of Yucca Mountain (lat. 36° 31'15" N, long. 118°45'45" W). Named on Giant Forest (1956) and Mineral King (1956) 15' quadrangles.

Paradise Peak [TULARE]: *peak,* 6 miles west-northwest of Mineral King (lat. 36°28'35" N, long. 118°41'50" W); the peak is at the east end of Paradise Ridge. Altitude 9362 feet. Named on Mineral King (1956) 15' quadrangle. United States Board on Geographic Names (1933a, p. 588) rejected the name "Milk Ranch Peak" for the feature, and later (1938, p. 40) rejected the name "Paradise Peak Lookout."

Paradise Peak: see **Milk Ranch Peak** [TULARE].

Paradise Peak Lookout: see **Paradise Peak** [TULARE].

Paradise Ridge [TULARE]: *ridge,* west-trending, 4 miles long, 8 miles west-northwest of Mineral King (lat. 36°28'30" N, long. 118° 44' W); the ridge extends west from Paradise Peak. Named on Kaweah (1957) and Mineral King (1956) 15' quadrangles.

Paradise Valley [FRESNO]: *valley,* 7.5 miles south of Marion Peak along South Fork Kings River (lat. 36°51' N, long. 118°32' W). Named on Marion Peak (1953) 15' quadrangle.

Paradise Valley [KERN]: *valley,* 6 miles south-southwest of Tehachapi along Brite Creek (lat. 35°03'15" N, long. 118°30' W). Named on Cummings Mountain (1966) and Tehachapi South (1966) 7.5' quadrangles.

Parejo Hill [KINGS]: *peak,* 7.5 miles south of Kettleman City (lat. 35°54'05" N, long. 119°56'20" W; sec. 29, T 23 S, R 19 E). Altitude 553 feet. Named on Los Viejos (1954) 7.5' quadrangle. The name is descriptive—*parejo* means "even" in Spanish (United States Board on Geographic Names, 1933b, p. 22).

Paris: see **Loraine** [KERN].

Paris-Loraine: see **Loraine** [KERN].

Park: see **The Park**, under **Walker Basin** [KERN].

Parker Bluffs [TULARE]: *relief feature,* 9.5 miles northeast of California Hot Springs (lat. 35°59' N, long. 118°33'30" W); the feature is north of Parker Meadow Creek. Named on California Hot Springs (1958) 15' quadrangle.

Parker Creek: see **Barker Creek** [KERN]; **Parker Meadow Creek** [TULARE].

Parker Meadow [TULARE]: *area,* 6 miles north-northeast of California Hot Springs (lat. 35°57'40" N, long. 118°37'45" W; sec. 4, T 23 S, R 31 E). Named on California Hot Springs (1958) 15' quadrangle.

Parker Meadow: see **Upper Parker Meadow** [TULARE].

Parker Meadow Creek [TULARE]: *stream,* flows 7.25 miles to South Creek 9.5 miles northeast of California Hot Springs near Johnsondale (lat. 35°58'10" N, long. 118°32'15" W; sec. 32, T 22 S, R 32 E); the stream goes through Parker Meadow. Named on California Hot Springs (1958) 15' quadrangle. United States Board on Geographic Names (1960a, p. 9) rejected the name "Parker Creek" for the stream.

Parker Pass [TULARE]: *pass,* nearly 6 miles north-northeast of California Hot Springs (lat. 35°57'10" N, long. 118°37'25" W; near SW cor. sec. 3, T 23 S, R 31 E); the pass is 0.5 mile southeast of Parker Meadow. Named on California Hot Springs (1958) 15' quadrangle.

Parker Peak [TULARE]: *peak,* 6.5 miles north-northeast of California Hot Springs (lat. 35°58'20" N, long. 118°38'45" W; sec. 32, T 22 S, R 31 E). Altitude 7578 feet. Named on California Hot Springs (1958) 15' quadrangle.

Parkfield Junction [FRESNO]: *locality,* 8 miles west-southwest of Coalinga (lat. 36°04'55" N, long. 120°28'45" W; at S line sec. 20, T 21 S, R 14 E). Named on Curry Mountain (1969) 7.5' quadrangle.

Park Ridge [FRESNO-TULARE]: *ridge,* north- to northeast-trending, 7 miles long, 1.5 miles west of Hume on Fresno-Tulare County line, mainly in Fresno County (lat. 36°47' N, long. 118°56'45" W). Named on Giant Forest (1956) and Tehipite Dome (1952) 15' quadrangles.

Park Road Ridge: see **Ash Peaks Ridge** [TULARE].

Parlier [FRESNO]: *town,* 5.5 miles east-northeast of Selma (lat. 36° 36'35" N, long. 119°31'30" W; mainly in sec. 24, T 15 S, R 22 E). Named on Selma (1964) 7.5' quadrangle. Postal authorities established Parlier post office in 1898 and named it for I. N. Parlier, first postmaster (Salley, p. 167), who came to the neighborhood in the 1870's (Hanna, p. 230). The town incorporated in 1921.

Parsons: see **Wible Orchard** [KERN].

Parsons Canyon [FRESNO]: *canyon,* drained by a stream that flows 3.25 miles to Oak Flat Canyon 5.5 miles west of Coalinga (lat. 36° 07'35" N, long. 120°27'20" W; sec. 4, T 21 S, R 14 E). Named on Alcalde Hills (1969) 7.5' quadrangle.

Paso Slough: see **Poso Slough** [FRESNO].

Pass Creek: see **Tehachapi Creek** [KERN].

Pastoria Creek [KERN]: *stream,* flows 13 miles to lowlands 7 miles north of Lebec (lat. 34°56'20" N long. 118°50'30" W). Named on Pastoria Creek (1958), Tejon Hills (1955), and Winters Ridge (1966) 7.5' quadrangles. Whitney (p. 191) mentioned Arroyo Pastoria. The name was given because the stream passes through land used in the 1850's as pasture for the Indian reservation on El Tejon grant (Gudde, 1949, p. 255)—*pastoria* means "pastoral life" in Spanish. United States Board on Geographic Names (1982b, p. 2) approved the name "Cattle Creek" for a stream that flows 4.3 miles to Pastoria Creek 1.5 miles north-northwest of the entrance of Pastoria Creek into lowlands (lat. 34°57'38" N, long. 118°51'05"

W).

Patch [KERN]: *locality,* 10 miles southeast of Bakersfield along the railroad (lat. 35°15'10" N, long. 118°53'40" W; at SW cor. sec. 5, T 31 S, R 29 E). Named on Lamont (1954) 7.5' quadrangle. The site first was known as Weedpatch from the abundance of weeds there, but railroad officials abbreviated the name for their siding (Gudde, 1949, p. 255).

Pattee Rocks [TULARE]: *peak,* 4.5 miles west of Yucca Mountain (lat. 36°33'45" N, long. 118°56'50" W). Altitude 4284 feet. Named on Giant Forest (1956) 15' quadrangle.

Patterson Bend [FRESNO]: *bend,* 7.5 miles north-northwest of Prather along San Joaquin River on Fresno-Madera County line (lat. 37°08'40" N, long. 119°33'15" W). Named on North Fork (1965) 7.5' quadrangle.

Patterson Bluffs [FRESNO]: *escarpment,* west-northwest-trending, 3 miles long, 2.5 miles east-northeast of Balch Camp (lat. 36°55'15" N, long. 119°04'45" W). Named on Patterson Mountain (1952) 15' quadrangle.

Patterson Creek [FRESNO]: *stream,* flows 2.5 miles to North Fork Kings River 2.25 miles east of Balch Camp (lat. 36°54'30" N, long. 119°05' W; near NE cor. sec. 12, T 12 S, R 26 E). Named on Patterson Mountain (1952) 15' quadrangle.

Patterson Mountain [FRESNO]: *ridge,* north-northwest-trending, 4.5 miles long, 6 miles northeast of Balch Camp (lat. 36°58' N, long. 119°03' W). Named on Patterson Mountain (1952) 15' quadrangle. The name commemorates John A. Patterson and Elisha Patterson, who pastured sheep at the place (Browning, p. 167).

Pattiway [KERN]: *locality,* 15 miles west of Eagle Rest Peak (lat. 34°55'40" N, long. 119°23'55" W; at S line sec. 24, T 10 N, R 24 W). Named on Mount Pinos (1903) 30' quadrangle. Postal authorities established Pattiway post office in 1891, moved it 1 mile east in 1903, and discontinued it in 1936; the name is from the Patti family, pioneers at the place (Salley, p. 168).

Paulina: see **Lake Paulina** [KERN].

Pavilion Dome [FRESNO]: *peak,* 11 miles north of Blackcap Mountain at the west end of Glacier Divide (lat. 37°13'50" N, long. 118° 48'30" W). Altitude 11,846 feet. Named on Blackcap Mountain (1953) 15' quadrangle. L.A. Winchell named the peak in 1879 (Browning, p. 167).

Payne: see **Harry Payne Spring** [KERN].

Payne Lake: see **Paine Lake** [FRESNO].

Peak Disappointment: see **Disappointment Peak** [FRESNO].

Pear Lake [TULARE]: *lake,* 1600 feet long, 7.5 miles west of Triple Divide Peak (lat. 36°36'05" N, long. 118°40' W; on S line sec. 24, T 15 S, R 30 E). Named on Triple Divide Peak (1956) 15' quadrangle. Colonel White named the lake in the early 1920's for its pearlike shape (Browning, p. 167).

Pearl Lake [FRESNO]: *lakes,* two connected, largest 2300 feet long, nearly 4 miles south-southwest of Mount Goddard (lat. 37°03'10" N, long. 118°44'55" W). Named on Blackcap Mountain (1953) and Mount Goddard (1948) 15' quadrangles.

Pechacho Creek [KERN]: *stream,* flows 2.5 miles to Kern River nearly 3 miles north of Mount Adelaide (lat. 35°28'15" N, long. 118°45' W). Named on Mount Adelaide (1972) 7.5' quadrangle.

Pecks Canyon [TULARE]: *canyon,* drained by a stream that flows 5 miles to Alpine Creek 13 miles south of Mineral King (lat. 36°15'50" N, long. 118°33'10" W). Named on Mineral King (1956) 15' quadrangle. The name commemorates a man who ran sheep in the neighborhood about 1870 (Gudde, 1949, p. 256).

Peel Creek: see **Peel Mill Creek** [TULARE].

Peel Mill Creek [TULARE]: *stream,* flows 4.5 miles to Poso Creek 5.25 miles south of California Hot Springs (lat. 35°48'15" N, long. 118°39'50" W; near SE cor. sec. 30, T 24 S, R 31 E); the stream heads near Peel Peak. Named on California Hot Springs (1958) 15' quadrangle. United States Board on Geographic Names (1960a, p. 10) rejected the names "Mill Creek," "Peel Creek," and "Pell Mell Creek" for the stream.

Peel Peak [TULARE]: *peak,* 6.5 miles southeast of California Hot Springs (lat. 35°48'20" N, long. 118°36'10" W; sec. 26, T 24 S, R 31 E); the peak is on Peel Ridge. Altitude 6788 feet. Named on California Hot Springs (1958) 15' quadrangle.

Peel Ridge [TULARE]: *ridge,* west-southwest-trending, 2.5 miles long, 6.5 miles south-southeast of California Hot Springs (lat. 35° 47'45" N, long. 118°37'10" W); Peel Peak is near the northeast end of the ridge. Named on California Hot Springs (1958) 15' quadrangle.

Peeping Tom Spring [KERN]: *spring,* 13 miles north of Mojave (lat. 35°14'55" N, long. 118°10' W; near E line sec. 12, T 31 S, R 35 E). Named on Cache Peak (1973) 7.5' quadrangle.

Peerless Valley [KERN]: *valley,* center 4.5 miles east of Castle Butte (lat. 35°06' N, long. 117°48' W). Named on Galileo Hill (1973) and North Edwards (1973) 7.5' quadrangles.

Pelican Island [KERN]: *hill,* 12 miles east-northeast of Taft in Buena Vista Lake Bed (lat. 35°12'40" N, long. 119°16' W). Named on Mouth of Kern (1950) 7.5' quadrangle.

Pelican Island [KINGS]: *area,* 14 miles east-southeast of Kettleman City in Tulare Lake Bed (lat. 35°57' N, long. 119°43'15" W; sec. 4, 5, 8, 9, T 23 S, R 21 E). Named on Hacienda Ranch NW (1954) 7.5' quadrangle.

Pell Mell Creek: see **Peel Mill Creek** [TULARE].

Pemmican Lake [FRESNO]: *lake,* 500 feet long, 9 miles south-southwest of Mount Abbot (lat. 37°15'35" N, long. 118°48'50" W). Named on Mount Abbot (1953) 15' quadrangle.

Penasco Rock [FRESNO]: *peak,* 9.5 miles south-southwest of Coalinga (lat. 36°00'30" N, long. 120°24'50" W; near N line sec. 24, T 22 S, R 14 E); the peak is 800 feet south of Penasco Spring. Named on Curry Mountain (1969) 7.5' quadrangle.

Penasco Spring [FRESNO]: *spring,* 9.5 miles south-southwest of Coalinga (lat. 36°00'35" N, long. 120°24'50" W; sec. 13, T 22 S, R 14 E); the spring is 800 feet north of Penasco Rock. Named on Curry Mountain (1969) 7.5' quadrangle.

Pendant Lake [FRESNO]: *lake,* 1700 feet long, 9 miles south-southwest of Mount Abbot (lat. 37°15'35" N, long. 118°49'15" W). Named on Mount Abbot (1953) 15' quadrangle. Elden H. Vestal of California Department of Fish and Game named the lake in 1951 for its pendantlike shape (Browning, p. 168).

Peninsula Meadow: see **Cascade Valley** [FRESNO].

Pentland [KERN]: *locality,* 2.5 miles east of Maricopa along Sunset Railroad (lat. 35°03'30" N, long. 119°21'15" W; near N line sec. 8, T 11 N, R 23 W). Named on Pentland (1953) 7.5' quadrangle. Called Pentland Junction on Buena Vista Lake (1912) 30' quadrangle.

Pentland Junction: see **Pentland** [KERN].

Peppergrass Flat [FRESNO]: *area,* 1.5 miles east of Ciervo Mountain (lat. 36°27'55" N, long. 120°33' W; sec. 9, 10, T 17 S, R 13 E). Named on Ciervo Mountain (1969) 7.5' quadrangle.

Pepper Grass Valley [KINGS]: *valley,* 9.5 miles south of Kettleman City (lat. 35°52' N, long. 119°56'45" W). Named on Avenal Gap (1954) and Los Viejos (1954) 7.5' quadrangles.

Peppermint Creek [TULARE]: *stream,* flows 7.5 miles to Kern River 13 miles south-southwest of Hockett Peak (lat. 36°02'50" N, long. 118°28' W). Named on Camp Nelson (1956) and Hockett Peak (1956) 15' quadrangles.

Peppermint Meadows [TULARE]: *area,* 12.5 miles south-southwest of Hockett Peak (lat. 36°04' N, long. 118°30' W); the place is along a branch of Peppermint Creek. Named on Camp Nelson (1956) and Hockett Peak (1956) 15' quadrangles.

Peral [TULARE]: *locality,* 6.5 miles north of Visalia along Atchison, Topeka and Santa Fe Railroad (lat. 36°25'35" N, long. 119°17'10" W; sec. 29, T 17 S, R 25 E). Named on Monson (1949) 7.5' quadrangle. Railroad officials gave the name about 1895—*peral* means "pear tree" in Spanish (Gudde, 1949, p. 258).

Perkins: see **Mount Perkins** [FRESNO].

Pernu: see **Porterville** [TULARE].

Pernu Junction: see **Porterville** [TULARE].

Perrin Creek [TULARE]: *stream,* flows 3 miles to Rock Creek 13 miles north of Kern Peak (lat. 36°29'50" N, long. 118°19'45" W). Named on Kern Peak (1956) and Mount Whitney (1956) 15' quadrangles. G.H. Perrin, who surveyed for General Land Office in 1884, named the stream for himself (Browning, p. 168).

Persian Creek [FRESNO-TULARE]: *stream,* heads in Fresno County and flows 5 miles to Murry Creek (1) nearly 3 miles northeast of Auckland in Tulare County (lat. 36°37'15" N, long. 119°04'30" W; sec. 18, T 15 S, R 27 E). Named on Auckland (1966) and Miramonte (1966) 7.5' quadrangles.

Pescado Creek [KERN]: *stream,* flows nearly 5 miles to lowlands 9 miles southwest of Liebre Twins (lat. 34°51'30" N, long. 118°40'15" W; sec. 22, T 9 N, R 17 W). Named on La Liebre Ranch (1965) and Winters Ridge (1966) 7.5' quadrangles. United States Board on Geographic Names (1967c, p. 4) rejected the name "Lecheria Creek" for the stream. Johnson's (1911) map has the name "Fish Canyon" for the canyon of the creek.

Pete Meadow: see **Big Pete Meadow** [FRESNO]; **Little Pete Meadow** [FRESNO].

Pete Merrill Canyon [FRESNO]: *canyon,* drained by a stream that flows 2.25 miles to Jacalitos Creek 5.5 miles south-southeast of Coalinga (lat. 36°03'45" N, long. 120°20'10" W; sec. 34, T 21 S, R 15 E). Named on Kreyenhagen Hills (1956) 7.5' quadrangle.

Peteras Mill: see **Old Bretz Mill** [FRESNO].

Peter Pande Lake [FRESNO]: *lake,* 3100 feet long, 12 miles west-northwest of Mount Abbot (lat. 37°28'05" N, long. 118°58'50" W). Named on Mount Abbot (1953) 15' quadrangle. United States Board on Geographic Names (1961b, p. 11) rejected the name "Marilyn Lake" for the feature.

Peter Peak [FRESNO]: *peak,* 3.25 miles north-northwest of Mount Goddard (lat. 37°08'45" N, long. 118°44'45" W). Altitude 12,543 feet. Named on Mount Goddard (1948) 15' quadrangle. Officials of Sierra Club named the feature for Peter Grubb, who made the first ascent of the peak in 1936 (Browning, p. 169).

Petersburg [KERN]: *locality,* 4.5 miles west-northwest of Miracle Hot Springs along Greenhorn Creek (lat. 35°36'10" N, long. 118° 36'10" W; near SW cor. sec. 1, T 27 S, R 31 E). Site named on Glennville (1956) 15' quadrangle. Postal authorities established Petersburgh (with a terminal "h") post office in 1858 and discontinued it in 1863 (Salley, p. 170). The name is for Peter Gardett, who opened a store at the place in the early 1850's; the community also was known as Greenhorn (Bailey, 1962, p. 9, 13).

Peterson: see **Dinkey Mountain** [FRESNO].

Peterson Mill [FRESNO]: *locality,* 18 miles south-southwest of Kaiser Peak along Rush Creek (lat. 37°02'30" N, long. 119°17'20" W; sec. 19, T 10 S, R 25 E). Named on Kaiser (1904) 30' quadrangle.

Petro [KERN]: *locality,* 7.25 miles north of Wasco along Atchison, Topeka and Santa Fe Railroad (lat. 35°41'45" N, long. 119°19'50" W). Named on Pond (1930) 7.5' quadrangle.

Peyrone Camp [TULARE]: *locality,* 7.5 miles south of Camp Nelson (lat. 36°02' N, long. 118°36'40" W; sec. 10, T 22 S, R 31 E). Named on Camp Nelson (1956) 15' quadrangle.

Peyton Creek [KERN]: *stream,* flows 2.5 miles to join McFarland Creek and form Fulton Creek 2 miles east-northeast of Glennville (lat. 35°44'05" N, long. 118°40' W; sec. 20, T 25 S, R 31 E). Named on California Hot Springs (1958) 15' quadrangle, and on Glennville (1972) 7.5' quadrangle.

Pheasant: see **Mount Pheasant** [KERN].

Phoenix Gulch [KERN]: *canyon,* 0.5 mile long, 5.25 miles north of Randsburg (lat. 35°26'35" N, long. 117°38'15" W; sec. 1, T 29 S, R 40 E). Named on El Paso Peaks (1967) 7.5' quadrangle.

Picacho Rock [FRESNO]: *relief feature,* 2.5 miles east-northeast of Castle Mountain (lat. 35°57'40" N, long. 120°17'55" W; sec. 1, T 23 S, R 15 E). Named on The Dark Hole (1961) 7.5' quadrangle.

Pickering: see **Mount Pickering** [TULARE].

Picket Creek [TULARE]: *stream,* flows nearly 4.5 miles to Kern-Kaweah River 8.5 miles west of Mount Whitney (lat. 36°34'35" N, long. 118°26'30" W). Named on Mount Whitney (1956) 15' quadrangle.

Picket Guard Peak [TULARE]: *peak,* 10 miles west of Mount Whitney (lat. 36°34'35" N, long. 118°28'15" W); the peak is north of Picket Creek. Altitude 12,302 feet. Named on Mount Whitney (1956) 15' quadrangle.

Piedra [FRESNO]: *locality,* 23 miles east of Fresno on the south side of Kings River (lat. 36°48'35" N, long. 119°22'55" W; sec. 8, T 13 S, R 24 E). Named on Piedra (1965) 7.5' quadrangle. Watts Valley (1942) 15' quadrangle has both the names "Piedra" and "Delpiedra P.O." at the place, and Pine Flat Dam (1965) 7.5' quadrangle has the name "Piedra P.O." at a site located about 1.25 miles east-northeast of Piedra (lat. 36°49'20" N, long. 119°21'50" W; near S line sec. 4, T 13 S, R 24 E). When Atchison, Topeka and Santa Fe Railroad built a branch line in 1911 to handle rock from a quarry, the siding near the quarry was called Piedra—*piedra* means "rock" or "stone" in Spanish (Gudde, 1949, p. 261). Postal authorities established Delpiedra post office at the place in 1920 and discontinued it in 1943; they established Piedra post office in 1949 (Frickstad, p. 32, 36).

Pierce Creek [TULARE]: *stream,* flows 6 miles to North Fork Kaweah River 3.5 miles northwest of Yucca Mountain (lat. 36°36'10" N, long. 118°55' W; sec. 22, T 15 S, R 28 E); the stream goes through Pierce Valley. Named on Giant Forest (1956) 15' quadrangle.

Pierce Valley [TULARE]: *area,* 7.25 miles northwest of Yucca Mountain (lat. 36°39'30" N, long. 118°56'40" W; on N line sec. 4, T 15 S, R 28 E); the place is along Pierce Creek. Named on Giant Forest (1956) 15' quadrangle.

Pieto Creek: see **Pleito Creek** [KERN].

Pigeon Creek [TULARE]:

(1) *stream,* flows 1 mile to South Fork Kaweah River 12.5 miles southeast of Kaweah (lat. 36°20'50" N, long. 118°45'15" W). Named on Kaweah (1957) 15' quadrangle.

(2) *stream,* flows 4.25 miles to South Fork Tule River 10 miles southwest of Camp Nelson (lat. 36°02'35" N, long. 118°44'30" W). Named on Camp Nelson (1956) 15' quadrangle.

Pigeon Creek: see **Squaw Creek** [TULARE].

Pigpen Spring [KERN]: *spring,* nearly 7 miles northeast of Mount Adelaide along Flat Creek (lat. 35°29'50" N, long. 118°39'50" W; sec. 16, T 28 S, R 31 E). Named on Mount Adelaide (1972) 7.5' quadrangle.

Pika Lake [FRESNO]: *lake,* 1600 feet long, 5.5 miles west-northwest of Red Slate Mountain (lat. 37°33'05" N, long. 118°57'05" W). Named on Mount Morrison (1953) 15' quadrangle. The name is for the rabbitlike animals called pikas that live near the lake (Smith, Genny, p. 49).

Pilot Knob [FRESNO]: *peak,* 8 miles south of Mount Abbot (lat. 37° 16'25" N, long. 118°45'25" W). Altitude 12,245 feet. Named on Mount Abbot (1953) 15' quadrangle.

Pilot Knob [KERN]: *peak,* 2.5 miles north of Onyx (lat. 35°43'45" N, long. 118°12'40" W). Named on Onyx (1972) 7.5' quadrangle.

Pinchot: see **Mount Pinchot** [FRESNO].

Pinchot Pass [FRESNO]: *pass,* nearly 1 mile south-southwest of Mount Pinchot (lat. 36°56'10" N, long. 118°24'45" W). Named on Mount Pinchot (1953) 15' quadrangle.

Pincushion Mountain [FRESNO]: *peak,* 7.25 miles west of Prather on a peninsula in Millerton Lake (lat. 37°01'55" N, long. 119°38'35" W; sec. 26, T 10 S, R 21 E). Altitude 1582 feet. Named on Millerton Lake West (1965) 7.5' quadrangle.

Pincushion Peak [FRESNO]: *peak,* 13 miles north-northeast of Kaiser Peak (lat. 37°28'20" N, long. 119°06'30" W). Altitude 9819 feet. Named on Kaiser Peak (1953) 15' quadrangle. The name is for the fancied resemblance of the feature to a pincushion (Gudde, 1949, p. 262).

Pine: see **Cinco** [KERN].

Pine Canyon [FRESNO]: *canyon,* drained by a stream that flows 6.5 miles to White Creek 7 miles north-northeast of Coalinga Mineral Springs (lat. 36°14'20" N, long. 120°30'35" W; near S line sec. 30, T 19 S, R 14 E). Named on Santa Rita Peak (1969) and Sherman Peak (1969) 7.5' quadrangles.

Pine Cove [KERN]: *relief feature,* less than 1 mile east-northeast of Claraville (lat. 35°26'45" N, long. 118°19' W; sec. 3, T 29 S, R 34 E). Named on Claraville (1972) 7.5' quadrangle.

Pine Creek [TULARE]: *stream,* flows 4.5 miles to North Fork Tule River 16.miles south-southeast of Kaweah (lat. 36°16'10" N, long. 118°45'40" W; near E line sec. 18, T 19 S, R 30 E). Named on Kaweah (1957) and Mineral King (1956) 15' quadrangles.

Pine Creek Pass [FRESNO]: *pass,* 5 miles northwest of Mount Humphreys on Fresno-Inyo County line (lat. 37°19'05" N, long. 118°44'05" W; near N line sec. 30, T 7 S, R 30 E); the pass is at the head of Pine Creek, which is in Inyo County. Named on Mount Tom (1949) 15' quadrangle.

Pinedale [FRESNO]:

(1) *town,* 5.5 miles north of downtown Fresno (lat. 36°50'30" N, long. 119°47'45" W; in and near sec. 33, T 12 S, R 20 E). Named on Fresno North (1965) 7.5' quadrangle. Postal authorities established Pinedale post office in 1923 (Frickstad, p. 36).

(2) *locality,* 3.5 miles north-northwest of Clovis along Southern Pacific Railroad (lat. 36°52' N, long. 119°43'45" W; near NE cor. sec. 25, T 12 S, R 20 E). Named on Clovis (1946) 15' quadrangle. Called Setch on Clovis (1922) 7.5' quadrangle, and called Pinedale Siding on Clovis (1964) 7.5' quadrangle.

Pinedale Siding: see **Pinedale** [FRESNO] (2).

Pine Flat [FRESNO]: *area,* 5 miles northeast of Piedra along Kings River (lat. 36°51'20" N, long. 119°18'40" W; sec. 25, 26, 35, 36, T 12 S, R 24 E). Named on Watts Valley (1942) 15' quadrangle. Water of Pine Flat Lake now covers the place.

Pine Flat [KERN]: *area,* 6.25 miles east-northeast of Mount Adelaide (lat. 35°28'35" N, long. 118°38'50" W; sec. 21, T 28 S, R 31 E). Named on Mount Adelaide (1972) 7.5' quadrangle.

Pine Flat [TULARE]:

(1) *area,* 12 miles southeast of Fairview (lat. 35°47'45" N, long. 118°21'15" W; sec. 31, T 24 S, R 34 E). Named on Kernville (1956) 15' quadrangle. The place also is called Capinero Flat (Wells, p. 21).

(2) *settlement,* 1.25 miles east-southeast of California Hot Springs (lat. 35°52'30" N, long. 118°39' W; in and near sec. 5, T 24 S, R 31 E). Named on California Hot Springs (1958) 15' quadrangle.

Pine Flat Lake: see **Pine Flat Reservoir** [FRESNO].

Pine Flat Reservoir [FRESNO]: *lake,* behind a dam on Kings River 3 miles northeast of Tivy Mountain (lat. 36°49'55" N, long. 119°19'30" W; sec. 2, T 13 S, R 24 E). Named on Patterson Mountain (1952) 15' quadrangle, and on Pine Flat Dam (1965) and Trimmer (1965) 7.5' quadrangles. United States Board on Geographic Names (1972a, p. 4) approved the name "Pine Flat Lake," for the feature, and gave the names "Boone Lake" and "Pine Flat Reservoir" as variants.

Pinehurst [FRESNO]: *settlement,* 6.5 miles east-southeast of Dunlap (lat. 36°41'40" N, long. 119°00'55" W; sec. 23, T 14 S, R 27 E). Named on Miramonte (1966) 7.5' quadrangle. Dinuba (1924) 30' quadrangle shows a place called Neff Mills located at or near the site.

Pine Logging Camp [FRESNO]: *settlement,* 4 miles south-southwest of Dinkey Dome (lat. 37°03'50" N, long. 119°09'40" W; sec. 17, T 10 S, R 26 E). Named on Huntington Lake (1953) 15' quadrangle.

Pine Martin Peak: see **Mount Jepson**, under **Mount Sill** [FRESNO].

Pine Meadow: see **Big Pine Meadow** [TULARE].

Pine Mountain [KERN]: *peak,* 10.5 miles south-southeast of Woody (lat. 35°33'45" N, long. 118°46'05" W; sec. 20, T 27 S, R 30 E). Named on Pine Mountain (1965) 7.5' quadrangle.

Pine Mountain [TULARE]:

(1) *peak,* 13 miles south of Monache Mountain (lat. 36°01'15" N, long. 118°11'10" W). Named on Monache Mountain (1956) 15' quadrangle.

(2) *peak,* 2 miles southeast of California Hot Springs (lat. 35°51'25" N, long. 118°39'10" W; sec. 8, T 24 S, R 31 E). Altitude 5214 feet. Named on California Hot Springs (1958) 15' quadrangle.

Pine Mountain Creek: see **Long Tom Gulch** [KERN].

Pine Point [KERN]: *promontory,* 3.5 miles south of Wofford Heights along Isabella Lake (lat. 35°39'25" N, long. 118°26'55" W; at W line sec. 21, T 26 S, R 33 E). Named on Lake Isabella North (1972) 7.5' quadrangle.

Pine Ridge [FRESNO]:

(1) *ridge,* east-northeast- to east-trending, 8 miles long, 3 miles southeast of Shaver Lake Heights (present town of Shaver Lake) (lat. 37°05' N, long. 119°17'30" W). Named on Huntington Lake (1953) and Shaver Lake (1953) 15' quadrangles.

(2) *ridge,* north-northwest-trending, 7 miles long, 8 miles south of Balch Camp (lat. 36°47'30" N, long. 119°07' W). Named on Patterson Mountain (1952) 15' quadrangle.

(3) *village,* 4 miles southwest of Shaver Lake Heights (present town of Shaver Lake) (lat. 37°03'45" N, long. 119°21'30" W; sec. 16, T 10 S, R 24 E); the village is at the west end of Pine Ridge (1). Named on Shaver Lake (1953) 15' quadrangle. California Mining Bureau's (1909b) map has the form "Pineridge" for the name. Postal authorities established Kenyon post office in 1890, changed the name to Pine Ridge in 1892, changed it to Pineridge in 1895, and discontinued it in 1944; the name "Kenyon" was for Silas W. Kenyon, first postmaster (Salley, p. 111, 172).

Pine Ridge [TULARE]: *ridge,* generally west- and west-southwest-trending, 6 miles long, 3 miles north-northeast of Yucca Mountain (lat. 36°36'45" N, long. 118°50'30" W). Named on Giant Forest (1956) 15' quadrangle.

Pine Spring [KERN]:

(1) *spring,* nearly 4 miles southeast of Caliente (lat. 35°15'25" N, long. 118°34'25" W; near SE cor. sec. 6, T 31 S, R 32 E). Named on Oiler Peak (1972) 7.5' quadrangle.

(2) *spring,* 1.5 miles northeast of Emerald Mountain (lat. 35°16'05" N, long. 118°15'40" W; sec. 6, T 31 S, R 35 E). Named on Emerald Mountain (1972) 7.5' quadrangle.

Pine Top Mountain [TULARE]: *peak,* 7 miles west of Mineral King (lat. 36°28'05" N, long 118°43'05" W). Altitude 7915 feet. Named on Mineral King (1956) 15' quadrangle. United States Board on Geographic Names (1933a, p. 605) rejected the name "High Mountain" for the peak.

Pine Tree Canyon [KERN]: *canyon,* 13 miles long, opens into Fremont Valley 14 miles north-northeast of Mojave (lat. 35°13'50" N, long. 118°03'45" W; sec. 13, T 31 S, R 36 E). Named on Cache Peak (1973) and Mojave NE (1973) 7.5' quadrangles. Called Lone Tree Canyon on Mojave (1956) 15' quadrangle, and United States Board on Geographic Names (1975c, p. 4) gave this name as a variant. North Fork branches northwest 7.5 miles above the mouth of the main canyon; it is 4 miles long and is named on Cache Peak (1973) 7.5' quadrangle.

Pinewood Camp [TULARE]: *locality,* nearly 6 miles east of Yucca Mountain (lat. 36°34'25" N, long. 118°45'55" W; sec. 31, T 15 S, R 30 E). Named on Giant Forest (1956) 15' quadrangle.

Pinnacles: see **The Pinnacles** [FRESNO].

Pinnacles Creek: see **East Pinnacles Creek** [FRESNO]; **West Pinnacles Creek** [FRESNO].

Pinnell Camp Ridge [TULARE]: *ridge,* generally west-trending, 1 mile long, 4.25 miles northwest of California Hot Springs (lat. 35° 55'20" N, long. 118°43'30" W). Named on California Hot Springs (1958) 15' quadrangle.

Pintojo Ridge [KINGS]: *ridge,* southeast-trending, 1 mile long. 9.5 miles south of Kettleman City (lat. 35°52'10" N, long. 119°56' W). Named on Avenal Gap (1954) 7.5' quadrangle. The name refers to the appearance of strata that crop out on the ridge—*pintojo* means "spotted" in Spanish (United States Board on Geographic Names, 1933b, p. 23).

Pinto Lake [TULARE]: *lake,* 300 feet long, 2.5 miles north-northeast of Mineral King (lat. 36°29'10" N, long. 118°34'45" W). Named on Mineral King (1956) 15' quadrangle.

Pinyon Creek [KERN]: *stream,* flows 5 miles to Kelso Creek 5 miles west-southwest of Skinner Peak (lat. 35°32'50" N, long. 118°12'35" W; sec. 27, T 27 S, R 35 E). Named on Cane Canyon (1972) 7.5' quadrangle.

Pinyon Mountain [KERN]: *peak,* 28 miles north-northeast of Tehachapi (lat. 35°27'30" N, long. 118°09'25" W; at E line sec. 25, T 28 S, R 35 E). Altitude 6182 feet. Named on Pinyon Mountain (1972) 7.5' quadrangle.

Pinyon Peak [KERN]: *peak,* nearly 4 miles west-northwest of Walker Pass (lat. 35°40'55" N, long. 118°05'20" W). Altitude 6805 feet. Named on Walker Pass (1972) 7.5' quadrangle.

Pinyon Well [KERN]: *well,* 3.25 miles west of Skinner Peak (lat. 35° 33'30" N, long. 118°10'55" W; near SW cor. sec. 24, T 27 S, R 35 E); the well is along Pinyon Creek. Named on Cane Canyon (1972) 7.5' quadrangle.

Piojo Spring [KERN]: *spring,* 6.5 miles east of Mount Adelaide (lat. 35°26'55" N, long. 118°28'40" W; sec. 34, T 28 S, R 31 E). Named on Mount Adelaide (1972) 7.5' quadrangle.

Pioneer [KERN]: *locality,* 2 miles south-southeast of Maricopa (lat. 35°02'20" N, long. 119°23'05" W; near E line sec. 13, T 11 N, R 24 W). Named on Buena Vista Lake (1912) 30' quadrangle. Postal authorities established Pioneer post office in 1901 and discontinued it in 1909; the first settlers, who considered themselves pioneers, named their community (Salley, p. 172).

Pioneer Basin [KERN]: *valley,* 6 miles north of Mount Abbot (lat. 37°28'45" N, long. 118°48' W). Named on Mount Abbot (1953) 15' quadrangle. Mount Crocker, Mount Hopkins, Mount Huntington, and Mount Stanford, which are called Pioneer Peaks, surround the valley (Hanna, p. 237)—R.B. Marshall of United States Geological Survey named the four peaks for pioneer railroad builders, and also named the valley (Gudde, 1949, p. 264).

Pioneer Basin Lakes [FRESNO]: *lakes,* largest 3200 feet long, 6 miles north of Mount Abbot (lat. 37°28'45" N, long. 118°48' W); the lakes are in Pioneer Basin. Named on Mount Abbot (1953) 15' quadrangle.

Pioneer Peaks: see **Pioneer Basin** [FRESNO].

Pioneer Point [KERN]: *promontory,* 4.25 miles south-southwest of Wofford Heights along Isabella Lake (lat. 35°39'05" N, long. 118° 29' W; near W line sec. 19, T 26 S, R 33 E). Named on Lake Isabella North (1972) 7.5' quadrangle.

Pioneer Point Campground [KERN]: *locality,* 4.25 miles south-southwest of Wofford Heights along Isabella Lake (lat. 35°39'05" N, long. 118°29'10" W; on E line sec. 24, T 26 S, R 32 E); the place is just west of Pioneer Point. Named on Lake Isabella North (1972) 7.5' quadrangle.

Pipe Hill [KINGS]: *peak,* 3.5 miles south-southwest of Kettleman City (lat. 35°57'50" N, long. 119°59'30" W; at N line sec. 2, T 23 S, R 18 E). Named on Los Viejos (1954) 7.5' quadrangle. The name refers to a pipeline across the feature (United States Board on Geographic Names, 1933b, p. 23).

Pipe Lake: see **Old Pipe Lake** [FRESNO].

Pipeline Canyon [TULARE]: *canyon,* drained by a stream that flows 1.25 miles to Capinero Creek 2 miles east-southeast of California Hot Springs (lat. 35°52'15" N, long. 118°38'20" W; sec. 4, T 24 S, R 31 E). Named on California Hot Springs (1958) 15' quadrangle.

Pippin Flat [TULARE]: *area,* 4 miles east-northeast of Auckland (lat. 36°36'30" N, long. 119°02'05" W; near W line sec. 22, T 15 S, R 27 E). Named on Auckland (1966) 7.5' quadrangle.

Pistol Creek [TULARE]: *stream,* flows 1.5 miles to Shotgun Creek 8 miles south-southeast of Mineral King (lat. 36°20'45" N, long. 118°32' W). Named on Mineral King (1956) 15' quadrangle.

Pitco [KINGS]: *locality,* 2 miles north-northwest of Hanford along Atchison, Topeka and Santa Fe Railroad (lat. 36°21'25" N, long. 119°39'45" W; near N line sec. 23, T 18 S, R 21 E). Named on Hanford (1954) 7.5' quadrangle.

Pitman Creek [FRESNO]: *stream,* formed by the confluence of Tamarack Creek and South Fork Tamarack Creek, flows 2.25 miles to Big Creek (1) east of the town of Big Creek (lat. 37°12'15" N, long. 119°14'15" W; sec. 28, T 8 S, R 25 E). Named on Huntington Lake (1953) 15' quadrangle. Called Pittman Cr. on Lippincott's (1902) map. The name commemorates Elias Pitman, who had a hunting cabin by the stream (Gudde, 1949, p. 264).

Pitney Canyon [KERN]: *canyon,* drained by a stream that flows 1 mile to Oak Creek 7.5 miles south-southeast of Tehachapi (lat. 35°01'20" N, long. 118°24'50" W; near NW cor. sec. 30, T 11 N, R 14 W). Named on Tehachapi South (1966) 7.5' quadrangle.

Piute [KERN]: *locality,* 5.25 miles north-northeast of Paris (present Loraine) (lat. 35°21'55" N, long. 118°22'50" W); the place is 6 miles south of present Piute Peak. Named on Mohave (1915) 30' quadrangle. Postal authorities established Piute post office in 1875, discontinued it in 1876, reestablished it in 1894, and discontinued it in 1918 (Frickstad, p. 58).

Piute Branch: see **Piute Creek** [KERN].

Piute Canyon [KERN]: *canyon,* 7.5 miles long, drained by lower Piute Creek, which joins South Fork San Joaquin River 11 miles north-northwest of Blackcap Mountain (lat. 37°13'25" N, long. 118°50' W). Named on Blackcap Mountain (1953) and Mount Abbot (1953) 15' quadrangles.

Piute Creek [KERN]: *stream,* flows 11.5 miles to South Fork San Joaquin River 11 miles north-northwest of Blackcap Mountain (lat. 37°13'25" N, long. 118°50' W); the stream heads near Piute Pass. Named on Mount Abbot (1953), Mount Goddard (1948), and Mount Tom (1949) 15' quadrangles. Called North Branch on Lippincott's (1902) map. J.N. LeConte called the stream Piute Branch in 1904 to avoid the name "North Branch of South Fork San Joaquin River"—the name "Piute" is from Piute Pass (Browning, p. 171; Farquhar, 1924, p. 64).

Piute Mountains [KERN]: *range,* 32 miles north-northeast of Tehachapi (lat. 35°35' N, long. 118°18' W). Named on Emerald Mountain (1972), Weldon (1972), and Woolstalf Creek (1972) 7.5' quadrangles.

Piute Pass [FRESNO]: *pass,* 9.5 miles north-northeast of Mount Goddard on Fresno-Inyo County line (lat. 37°14'20" N, long. 118° 41' W); the pass is at the head of Piute Creek. Named on Mount Goddard (1948) 15' quadrangle. J.N. LeConte named the pass for Indians, commonly called Piutes, that used it (Gudde, 1949, p. 266).

Piute Peak [KERN]: *peak,* 22 miles north of Tehachapi (lat. 35°27'05" N, long. 118°23'25" W; sec. 36, T 28 S, R 33 E). Altitude 8417 feet. Named on Piute Peak (1972) 7.5' quadrangle. Called Pahute Pk. on Wheeler's (1875-1878) map, but United States Board on Geographic Names (1933a, p. 607) rejected the forms "Pahute Peak," "Pah-ute Peak," and "Paiute Peak" for the name.

Piute Spring [KERN]: *spring,* 0.25 mile south-southeast of Piute Peak (lat. 35°26'50" N, long. 118°23'20" W; sec. 36, T 28 S, R 33 E). Named on Piute Peak (1972) 7.5' quadrangle. United States Board on Geographic Names (1975b, p. 11) gave the name "Piute Springs" as a variant.

Pixley [TULARE]: *town,* 6 miles north-northwest of Earlimart (lat. 35°58'05" N, long. 119°17'25" W; mainly in sec. 32, T 22 S, R 25 E). Named on Pixley (1954) 7.5' quadrangle. Postal authorities established Pixley post office in 1887 (Frickstad, p. 213). The name is for Frank Pixley, a writer and member of the company that owned the townsite (Mitchell, A.R., p. 69).

Placeritas Creek [KERN]: *stream,* flows 4.25 miles to Walker Basin Creek

4.25 miles north-northeast of Caliente (lat. 35°21'15" N, long. 118°39'20" W). Named on Bena (1972), Breckenridge Mountain (1972), and Mount Adelaide (1972) 7.5' quadrangles.

Placeritas Spring [KERN]: *spring,* 5.25 miles north-northwest of Caliente (lat. 35°21'50" N, long. 118°39'20" W; sec. 33, T 29 S, R 31 E); the spring is along Placeritas Creek. Named on Bena (1972) 7.5' quadrangle.

Plainview [TULARE]: *village,* 5 miles south-southwest of Lindsay (lat. 36°08'40" N, long. 119°07'55" W; on W line sec. 35, T 20 S, R 26 E). Named on Cairns Corner (1950) 7.5' quadrangle.

Plano [TULARE]: *locality,* 2 miles south-southeast of Porterville (lat. 36°02'40" N, long. 119°00'25" W; sec. 1, T 22 S, R 27 E). Named on Porterville (1951) 7.5' quadrangle. Postal authorities established Plano post office in 1871 and discontinued it in 1915 (Frickstad, p. 213). A.J. Adams, the postmaster, selected the name (Mitchell, A.R., p. 69).

Plano: see **Sanborn** [KERN].

Plata Creek: see **Pleito Creek** [KERN].

Plato Creek: see **Pleito Creek** [KERN].

Plaza [TULARE]: *locality,* 2 miles southeast of Goshen (lat. 36°19'35" N, long. 119°24' W; near SW cor. sec. 29, T 18 S, R 24 E). Named on Goshen (1949) 7.5' quadrangle.

Pleasant Valley [FRESNO]: *valley,* around and east of Coalinga (lat. 36°08' N, long. 120°17' W). Named on Alcalde Hills (1969), Avenal (1954), Coalinga (1956), Guijarral Hills (1956), and Kreyenhagen Hills (1956) 7.5' quadrangles. Called Coalinga Valley on Mendenhall's (1908) map. Arnold and Anderson (1908, p. 15) noted that at least part of the valley at the mouth of Los Gatos Creek was known as Pleasant Valley, and suggested that the name be applied to the entire lowland around Coalinga.

Pleasant Valley [TULARE]: *valley,* 3 miles west-southwest of Springville (lat. 36°06'30" N, long. 118°51'30" W). Named on Springville (1957) 15' quadrangle.

Pleasant View [TULARE]: *locality,* 5.5 miles south-southeast of California Hot Springs along Von Hellum Creek (lat. 35°48'15" N, long. 118°38'20" W; near S line sec. 28, T 24 S, R 31 E). Named on California Hot Springs (1958) 15' quadrangle.

Pleitito Creek [KERN]: *stream,* flows 7 miles to lowlands 9 miles west-southwest of Mettler (lat. 35°00'30" N, long. 119°07'40" W; sec. 28, T 11 N, R 21 W). Named on Coal Oil Canyon (1955), Conner SW (1955), Eagle Rest Peak (1942), and Pleito Hills (1958) 7.5' quadrangles. The name is from nearby Pleito Creek (Latta, 1976, p. 215).

Pleito Creek [KERN]: *stream,* flows 13 miles to lowlands 9.5 miles west-southwest of Mettler (lat. 35°00'30" N, long. 119°06'45" W; sec. 27, T 11 N, R 21 W). Named on Coal Oil Canyon (1955), Cuddy Valley (1943), and Pleito Hills (1958) 7.5' quadrangles. The name has been attributed to arguments that Indians of the neighborhood had with the Spanish priests who wanted to take the Indians to Santa Barbara mission—*pleito* means "argument" or "debate" in Spanish (Latta, 1976, p. 215). Jp (p. 51) called the stream Plato Creek, but United States Board on Geographic Names (1933a, p. 609) rejected the forms "Plato Creek," "Plata Creek," and "Pieto Creek" for the name.

Pleito Hills [KERN]: *range,* 5 miles east-northeast of Eagle Rest Peak (lat. 34°56'15" N, long. 119°03' W); the range is east of Pleito Creek. Named on Pleito Hills (1958) 7.5' quadrangle.

Pocket Lake [FRESNO]: *lake,* 550 feet long, 16 miles northeast of Kaiser Peak (lat. 37°28'55" N, long. 119°01' W). Named on Kaiser Peak (1953) 15 quadrangle.

Pocket Meadow [FRESNO]: *area,* 7.5 miles west-northwest of Mount Abbot along North Fork Mono Creek (lat. 37°26'05" N, long. 118°54'30" W). Named on Mount Abbot (1953) 15' quadrangle.

Pogue Canyon [TULARE]: *canyon,* drained by a stream that flows 1.25 miles to Dry Creek (1) 4.25 miles east of Woodlake (lat. 36° 25'35" N, long. 119°01'20" W; sec. 26, T 17 S, R 27 E). Named on Woodlake (1952) 7.5' quadrangle.

Point of Rocks [KERN]: *ridge,* southeast-trending, 1 mile long, 8 miles east-southeast of Orchard Peak (lat. 35°41'35" N, long. 120° 00'15" W). Named on Emigrant Hill (1953) and Sawtooth Ridge (1961) 7.5' quadrangles. Spaniards called the ridge Las Tinajas de los Indios; it has natural holes that hold water from winter rains, and apparently it was an important Indian camp—*tinajas* means "tanks" in Spanish (Hoover, Rensch, and Rensch, p. 128).

Poison Meadow [FRESNO]: *area,* 11 miles west-southwest of Mount Abbot along South Fork San Joaquin River (lat. 37°19' N, long. 118°58'35" W). Named on Mount Abbot (1953) 15' quadrangle.

Poison Meadow [TULARE]:

(1) *area,* on the northwest side of Shell Mountain (lat. 36°41'50" N, long. 118°47'50" W; mainly in sec. 23, T 14 S, R 29 E). Named on Giant Forest (1956) 15' quadrangle. According to United States Board on Geographic Names (1987b, p. 2), Poison Meadow is at the west base of Shell Mountain (lat. 36°41'50" N, long. 118°48'30" W; sec. 22, T 14 S, R 29 E).

(2) *area,* 6.25 miles east of Fairview (lat. 35°55'30" N, long. 118° 23'10" W; sec. 14, T 23 S, R 33 E). Named on Kernville (1956) 15' quadrangle.

(3) *area,* 6 miles east-southeast of California Hot Springs (lat. 35° 50'50" N, long. 118°34'30" W; near NE cor. sec. 13, T 24 S, R 31 E). Named on California Hot Springs (1958) 15' quadrangle.

Poison Meadow Creek [TULARE]: *stream,* flows 4 miles to Brush Creek 5 miles northeast of Fairview (lat. 35°57'55" N, long. 118° 25'15" W; sec. 33, T 22 S, R 33 E); the stream heads at Poison Meadow (2). Named on Kernville (1956) 15' quadrangle.

Poison Oak Canyon [KINGS]: *canyon,* drained by a stream that flows 1 mile to Falls Canyon 9.5 miles south-southwest of Avenal (lat. 35°52'50" N, long. 120°12'30" W; sec. 35, T 23 S, R 16 E). Named on Garza Peak (1953) and Tent Hills (1942) 7.5' quadrangles.

Poison Oak Spring [KERN]:

(1) *spring,* 2.25 miles north-northeast of Caliente (lat. 35°19'15" N, long. 118°37' W). Named on Oiler Peak (1972) 7.5' quadrangle.

(2) *spring,* nearly 4 miles east-southeast of Caliente (lat. 35°16'15" N, long. 118°33'55" W; sec. 32, T 30 S, R 32 E). Named on Oiler Peak (1972) 7.5' quadrangle.

Poison Oak Spring [TULARE]: *spring,* 3.5 miles northwest of California Hot Springs (lat. 35°54'40" N, long. 118°43'20" W; sec. 22, T 23 S, R 30 E). Named on California Hot Springs (1958) 15' quadrangle.

Poison Ridge [FRESNO]: *ridge,* west-northwest-trending, 2 miles long, 3.25 miles north-northeast of Balch Camp (lat. 36°57' N, long. 119°06' W). Named on Patterson Mountain (1952) 15' quadrangle.

Poison Spring [KERN]: *spring,* 3 miles west-southwest of Garlock (lat. 35°23'40" N, long. 117°50'15" W). Named on Garlock (1967) 7.5' quadrangle.

Poleline Canyon [KERN]: *canyon,* drained by a stream that flows 2.5 miles to Jawbone Canyon 3.5 miles north of Cinco (lat. 35°18'45" N, long. 118°01'45" W; sec. 20, T 30 S, R 37 E). Named on Cinco (1972) 7.5' quadrangle.

Polemonium Peak: see **North Palisade** [FRESNO].

Pollasky: see **Friant** [FRESNO].

Polonia Valley: see **Polonio Pass** [KERN].

Polonio Pass [KERN]: *valley,* 3.5 miles west-southwest of Orchard Peak on Kern-San Luis Obispo County line (lat. 35°43'30" N, long. 120°11'35" W). Named on Orchard Peak (1961) 7.5' quadrangle. Angel (1890a, p. 569) mentioned Polonia Valley.

Polvadero Gap [FRESNO]: *pass,* 9 miles east of Coalinga between Guijarral Hills and Kettleman Hills (lat. 36°07'15" N, long. 120°11'45" W). Named on Avenal (1954) and Guijarral Hills (1956) 7.5' quadrangles. Arnold and Anderson (1908, p. 15) attributed the name to dust storms common at the place, and noted the incorrect form "Pulvero" for the name. *Polvadera* and *polvadero* are dialectal variations of *polvareda,* which means "dust storm" or "cloud of dust" in Spanish (Stewart, p. 380). Postal authorities established Pulvadera post office 8 miles southwest of Huron in 1880 and discontinued it in 1882 (Salley, p. 178).

Polvodero Creek: see **Los Gatos Creek** [FRESNO].

Ponca [TULARE]: *locality,* 2 miles south of Porterville along Southern Pacific Railroad (lat. 36°02'30" N, long. 119°01' W; at W line sec. 1, T 22 S, R 27 E). Named on Porterville (1951) 7.5' quadrangle.

Pond [KERN]: *village,* 8.5 miles north of Wasco (lat. 35°43'05" N, long. 119°19'40" W; at NW cor. sec. 31, T 25 S, R 25 E). Named on Pond (1953) 7.5' quadrangle, which shows Pondham school located 1 mile to the east. The community began about 1889 (Bailey, 1967, p. 21). Postal authorities established Pond post office in 1912; the name is from the word "Pondham" (Salley, p. 176). California Mining Bureau's (1917c) map shows a place called Smyrna located 8 miles west of Pond. Postal authorities established Smyrna post office in 1888 and discontinued it in 1889; the name was for Smyrna, Turkey, the source of imported fig trees planted at the place (Salley, p. 207).

Pond Meadow [TULARE]: *area,* 13 miles northwest of Triple Divide Peak (lat. 36°43' N, long. 118°43' W; near SE cor. sec. 9, T 14 S, R 30 E). Named on Triple Divide Peak (1956) 15' quadrangle. United States Board on Geographic Names (1933a, p. 613) rejected the name "Tamarack Meadow" for the feature.

Pool's Ferry: see **Reedley** [FRESNO].

Pool's Fort: see **Reedley** [FRESNO].

Poop Out Pass [TULARE]: *pass,* 1 mile east-southeast of Shell Mountain (lat. 36°41'15" N, long. 118°46'50" W; sec. 24, T 14 S, R 29 E). Named on Giant Forest (1956) 15' quadrangle.

Popes Valley: see **Watts Valley** [FRESNO].

Poplar [TULARE]: *town,* 4 miles southeast of Woodville (lat. 36°03'20" N, long. 119°08'35" W; on E line sec. 34, T 21 S, R 26 E). Named on Woodville (1950) 7.5' quadrangle. Postal authorities established Poplar post office in 1880 and discontinued it in 1907 (Frickstad, p. 213). Arthur Carpenter named the place in 1879 for poplar trees around his home (Mitchell, A.R., p. 69). Postal authorities established Belleville post office 10 miles southwest of Poplar in 1882, moved it 4.5 miles northeast in 1889, and discontinued it in 1892 (Salley, p. 17).

Porque: see **Treadwell** [KERN].

Porsiuncula River: see **Kern River** [KERN-TULARE].

Portal: see **Big Creek** [FRESNO] (3).

Portal Lake [FRESNO]: *lake,* 500 feet long, nearly 3 miles southeast of Blackcap Mountain (lat. 37°02'35" N, long. 118°45'25" W). Named on Blackcap Mountain (1953) 15' quadrangle.

Porter Slough [TULARE]: *water feature,* heads at Tule River 4 miles east-southeast of downtown Porterville, and extends through Porterville into lowlands. Named on Porterville (1951, photorevised 1969), Success Dam (1956), and Woodville (1950) 7.5' quadrangles, which show a partly dry watercourse. Called Porters Slough on Cairns Corner (1927) 7.5' quadrangle.

Porters Trading Post: see **Porterville** [TULARE].

Porterville [TULARE]: *city,* 24 miles southeast of Visalia where Tule River enters lowlands (lat. 36°04'15" N, long. 119°01' W). Named on Porterville (1951) and Success Dam (1956) 7.5' quadrangles. Tule River station of Butterfield Overland stage line was at the site, and after Royal Porter Putnam started a hotel and trading post there, the place was known as Porters Trading Post, Porterville, and Putnamville (Hanna, p. 241). Postal authorities established Tule post office in 1859, changed the name to Portersville in 1871, and to Porterville in 1915 (Frickstad, p. 213, 214). The city incorporated in 1902. Postal authorities established North Tule post office 23 miles northeast of Porterville (SE quarter sec. 14, T 20 S, R 29 E) in 1874 and discontinued it the same year (Salley, p. 157). Goodyear (1888b, p. 649) noted that a place called Connor Station, or Eighteen-mile House, was located about 17 miles from Visalia on the road to Porterville, and a place called Vandalia was located on the left bank of Tule River at a ford about a mile beyond Porterville and 10.5 miles from Connor Station. California Mining Bureau's (1917b) map shows a place called Kurth located along the railroad just north of Porterville. California Division of Highways' (1934) map shows a place called Pernu located at the end of a rail line 3 miles east of Porterville (near S line sec. 28, T 21 S, R 28 E), a place called Pernu Jct. situated along Southern Pacific Railroad 1 mile farther south (near S line sec. 33, T 21 S, R 28 E), and a place called Tandy located along the railroad 3.5 miles east of Porterville between Pernu Junction and Pernu (sec. 33, T 21 S, R 28 E).

Portex [TULARE]: *locality,* 5.5 miles southeast of Lindsay along Visalia Electric Railroad (lat. 36°08'45" N, long. 119°01'30" W; near W line sec. 35, T 20 S, R 27 E). Named on Lindsay (1928) 7.5' quadrangle.

Portuguese Canyon [FRESNO]: *canyon,* drained by a stream that flows 1.25 miles to enter an unnamed canyon 2 miles west-southwest of Joaquin Rocks (lat. 36°18'35" N, long. 120°29' W; sec. 6, T 19 S, R 14 E). Named on Joaquin Rocks (1969) 7.5' quadrangle.

Portuguese Meadow [TULARE]: *area,* 8 miles southeast of California Hot Springs (lat. 35°48' N, long. 118°34'30" W; near E line sec. 36, T 24 S, R 31 E). Named on California Hot Springs (1958) 15' quadrangle.

Portuguese Pass [TULARE]: *pass,* 7.5 miles southeast of California Hot Springs (lat. 35°48' N, long. 118°34'50" W; sec. 36, T 24 S, R 31 E); the pass is less than 1 mile north-northeast of Portuguese Peak. Named on California Hot Springs (1958) 15' quadrangle.

Portuguese Peak [TULARE]: *peak,* 8 miles southeast of California Hot Springs (lat. 35°47'30" N, long. 118°35'05" W; near S line sec. 36, T 24 S, R 31 E). Altitude 7914 feet. Named on California Hot Springs (1958) 15' quadrangle.

Posa Creek: see **Poso Creek** [KERN-TULARE].

Pose Creek: see **Poso Creek** [KERN-TULARE].

Posé Flat: see **Poso Flat** [KERN].

Posey [TULARE]: *village,* 5.25 miles south of California Hot Springs (lat. 35°48'20" N, long. 118°40'50" W; around SE cor. sec. 25, T 24 S, R 30 E). Named on California Hot Springs (1958) 15' quadrangle. Postal authorities established Posey post office in 1915 (Frickstad, p. 213).

Posey Creek: see **Poso Creek** [KERN-TULARE].

Posey Flats: see **Poso Flat** [KERN].

Posey Station: see **Poso Creek** [KERN-TULARE].

Poso: see **Famoso** [KERN]; **Mount Poso** [KERN].

Poso Camp: see **Poso Park** [TULARE].

Poso Creek [KERN-TULARE]: *stream,* formed by the confluence of Van Hellum Creek and Spear Creek in Tulare County, flows 60 miles to lowlands 1.5 miles east-southeast of Famoso in Kern County (lat. 35°35' N, long. 119°10'55" W; near NW cor. sec. 16, T 27 S, R 26 E). Named on California Hot Springs (1958) 15' quadrangle, and on Allensworth (1954), Democrat Hot Springs (1972), Famoso (1953), Glennville (1972), Knob Hill (1965), McFarland (1954), North of Oildale (1954), Pine Mountain (1965), and Pond (1953) 7.5' quadrangles. Called Pose Cr. on Blake's (1857) map. Goddard's (1857) map has the designation "Occoya or Posa C." for the stream, and Williamson (p. 14) used the form "O-co-ya Creek" for the name. The stream also was called Posey Creek (Wines, p. 86). The name "Poso" is descriptive of pools found along the stream during the dry season—*posa* means "pool" and *poso* means "well" in Spanish (Boyd, p. 153). Posey Station was a stop at Poso Creek for Butterfield Overland stage line from 1858 to 1861 (Bailey, 1967, p. 21).

Poso Creek: see **Little Poso Creek** [KERN].

Poso Drain 1 [FRESNO]: *water feature,* extends for 3.5 miles to Poso Slough 6.5 miles north-northwest of Firebaugh (lat. 36°57'05" N, long. 120°29'40" W; sec. 25, T 11 S, R 13 E). Named on Poso Farm (1962) 7.5' quadrangle. The feature now is considered to carry the lower reach of Poso Slough (United States Board on Geographic Names, 1964a, p. 13).

Poso Drain 2 [FRESNO]: *water feature,* extends for 2.5 miles to Poso Drain 1 about 6 miles north-northwest of Firebaugh (lat. 36° 56'20" N, long. 120°29'15" W; sec. 30, T 11 S, R 14 E). Named on Poso Farm (1962) 7.5' quadrangle.

Poso Flat [KERN]: *valley,* along Poso Creek above a point 5 miles northwest of Democrat Hot Springs (lat. 35°34'45" N, long. 118° 43'35" W). Named on Democrat Hot Springs (1972), Glennville (1972), Pine Mountain (1965), and Woody (1965) 7.5' quadrangles. Whitney (p. 221) mentioned Posé Flat and Little Posé Flat. The feature also was called Posey Flats (Wines, p. 86). Postal authorities established Pozo Flat post office 9 miles east of Elmer post office at or near present Poso Flat in 1891 and discontinued it the same year (Salley, p. 177).

Poso Park [TULARE]: *settlement,* 5.25 miles south-southeast of California Hot Springs along Spear Creek (lat. 35°48'40" N, long. 118°38'05" W; sec. 28, T 24 S, R 31 E). Named on California Hot Springs (1958) 15' quadrangle. Called Poso Camp on Tobias Peak (1943) 30' quadrangle.

Poso Slough [TULARE]: *water feature,* extends for 8 miles from near San Joaquin River to Merced County 6.5 miles north-northwest of Oxalis (lat. 37°00'20" N, long. 120°35'20" W; sec. 6, T 11 S, R 13 E). Named on Santa Rita Park (1962) 15' quadrangle, and on Oxalis (1956) and Poso Farm (1962) 7.5' quadrangles. United States Board on Geographic Names (1964a, p. 13) rejected the names "Paso Slough" and "Poso Drain 1" for the feature; by this decision the former Poso Drain 1 is considered to be part of Poso Slough.

Post Canyon [FRESNO]: *canyon,* drained by a stream that flows 4.5 miles to Los Gatos Creek 6.5 miles northwest of Coalinga (lat. 36° 12'15" N, long. 120°26'20" W; sec. 10, T 20 S, R 14 E). Named on Alcalde Hills (1969) and Sherman Peak (1969) 7.5' quadrangles.

Post Corral Creek [FRESNO]: *stream,* flows 9 miles to North Fork Kings River 6.25 miles west of Blackcap Mountain (lat. 37°05'05" N, long. 118°54'15" W; sec. 3, T 10 S, R 28 E); the stream goes through Post Corral Meadows. Named on Blackcap Mountain (1953) 15' quadrangle.

Post Corral Meadows [FRESNO]: *area,* 7.5 miles northwest of Blackcap Mountain (lat. 37°08' N, long. 118°54' W; sec. 22, T 9 S, R 28 E). Named on Blackcap Mountain (1953) 15' quadrangle.

Po-sun-co-la River: see **Kern River** [KERN-TULARE].

Posuncula Lake: see **Kern Lake Bed** [KERN].

Potato Butte: see **Black Peak** [FRESNO].

Potato Hill [TULARE]: *peak,* 10.5 miles south of Kaweah (lat. 36° 19'10" N, long. 118°56'35" W; sec. 33, T 18 S, R 28 E). Altitude 2878 feet. Named on Kaweah (1957) 15' quadrangle.

Potato Mountain: see **Black Peak** [FRESNO].

Potato Patch [KERN]:

(1) *area,* nearly 5 miles east of Kernville along Caldwell Creek (lat. 35°45'40" N, long. 118°20'30" W; near NE cor. sec. 17, T 25 S, R 34 E). Named on Kernville (1956) 15' quadrangle.

(2) *area,* 3 miles south of Alta Sierra (lat. 35°41'05" N, long. 118° 33'20" W; sec. 8, T 26 S, R 32 E). Named on Alta Sierra (1972) 7.5' quadrangle.

Pothole: see **The Pothole** [TULARE].

Pothole Creek [TULARE]: *stream,* flows 3 miles to Deer Creek (2) 6.5 miles northeast of Fountain Springs (lat. 35°57'15" N, long. 118°49'35" W; sec. 3, T 23 S, R 29 E); the stream heads at The Pothole. Named on Gibbon Peak (1965) 7.5' quadrangle.

Potholes: see **East Potholes** [TULARE].

Potholes Meadow: see **East Potholes Meadow**, under **East Potholes** [TULARE].

Potter Creek [FRESNO]: *stream,* flows 2.5 miles to Rancheria Creek (1) 3 miles south-southeast of Kaiser Peak (lat. 37°15'20" N, long. 119°09'35" W; sec. 5, T 8 S, R 26 E). Named on Kaiser Peak (1953) 15' quadrangle.

Potter Pass [FRESNO]: *pass,* 2.5 miles east of Kaiser Peak (lat. 37° 17'15" N, long. 119°08'25" W; sec. 28, T 7 S, R 26 E); the pass is near the head of Potter Creek. Named on Kaiser Peak (1953) 15' quadrangle.

Pottinger: see **Mama Pottinger Canyon** [KERN].

Pottinger Canyon [KERN]: *canyon,* 2.5 miles long, opens into Little Santa Maria Valley 6.5 miles west of McKittrick (lat. 35°18'30" N, long. 119°44'10" W; near S line sec. 17, T 30 S, R 21 E). Named on McKittrick Summit (1959) and Reward (1951) 7.5' quadrangles.

Potwisha [TULARE]: *locality,* 5.5 miles southeast of Yucca Mountain near the confluence of Middle Fork Kaweah River and Marble Fork Kaweah River (lat. 36°30'05" N, long. 118°48' W). Named on Giant Forest (1956) 15' quadrangle. Tehipite (1903) 30' quadrangle shows Potwisha Camp at the place. The name commemorates an Indian tribe that lived in the neighborhood (United States Board on Geographic Names, 1933a, p. 617).

Potwisha Camp: see **Potwisha** [TULARE].

Powder Horn Meadow [TULARE]: *area,* 5.5 miles northeast of California Hot Springs (lat. 35°56'25" N, long. 118°36'15" W; near SW cor. sec. 11, T 23 S, R 31 E). Named on California Hot Springs (1958) 15' quadrangle.

Powell: see **Mount Powell** [FRESNO].

Powell Meadow [TULARE]: *area,* 4.5 miles southwest of Monache Mountain (lat. 36°09'15" N, long. 118°14'50" W; sec. 25, T 20 S, R 34 E). Named on Monache Mountain (1956) 15' quadrangle. Called Powell Meadows on Olancha (1907) 30' quadrangle, but United States Board on Geographic Names (1988b, p. 2) rejected the names "Powell Meadows" and "Powers Meadow" for the place.

Powers Meadow: see **Powell Meadow** [TULARE].

Powers Well [KERN]: *well,* 6 miles west-northwest of Inyokern in Indian Wells Canyon (lat. 35°40'40" N, long. 117°54'45" W; sec. 17, T 26 S, R 38 E). Named on Owens Peak (1972) 7.5' quadrangle.

Pozo Flat: see **Poso Flat** [KERN].

Prater: see **Mount Prater** [FRESNO].

Prather [FRESNO]: *settlement,* 25 miles northwest of Fresno (lat. 37°02'15" N, long. 119°30'45" W; near NE cor. sec. 25, T 10 S, R 22 E). Named on Millerton Lake East (1965) 7.5' quadrangle. Postal authorities established Prather post office in 1914, discontinued it in 1935, reestablished it in 1936, and moved it 1.25 miles southwest in 1939 (Salley, p. 177). The name is for Joseph L. Prather, who came to California in 1872 and eventually settled on a ranch at the site where the later settlement is located (Hanna, p. 243-244).

Prather Pond [FRESNO]: *intermittent lake,* 1000 feet long, 8 miles west of Selma (lat. 36°33'05" N, long. 119°45' W; sec. 12, T 16 S, R 20 E). Named on Caruthers (1963) and Conejo (1963) 7.5' quadrangles. Selma (1946) 15' quadrangle shows a permanent lake.

Pratton [FRESNO]: *locality,* 6 miles west of downtown Fresno along Southern Pacific Railroad (lat. 36°44'45" N, long. 119°53'30" W; sec. 3, T 14 S, R 19 E). Named on Kearney Park (1963) 7.5' quadrangle.

Precipice Lake [TULARE]: *lake,* 1000 feet long, 3.25 miles south-southwest of Triple Divide Peak along Hamilton Creek (lat. 36°33'05" N, long. 118°33'35" W). Named on Triple Divide Peak (1956) 15' quadrangle. United States Board on Geographic Names (1968b, p. 9) rejected the name "Hamilton Lake" for the feature.

Prefedio Creek [KERN]: *stream,* flows 2.5 miles to Kern River near Democrat Hot Springs (lat. 35°31'50" N, long. 118°39'55" W; at S line sec. 32, T 27 S, R 31 E). Named on Democrat Hot Springs (1972) 7.5' quadrangle.

Prefedio Spring [KERN]: *spring,* 1.5 miles north-northwest of Democrat Hot Springs (lat. 35°32'45" N, long. 118°40'50" W; near SE cor. sec. 30, T 27 S, R 31 E); the spring is along Prefedio Creek. Named on Democrat Hot Springs (1972) 7.5' quadrangle. Glennville (1956) 15' quadrangle has the plural form "Prefedio Springs" for the name.

Prewit [TULARE]: *locality,* 5 miles southeast of Lindsay along Visalia Electric Railroad (lat. 36°09'30" N, long. 119°01'20" W; sec. 26, T 20 S, R 27 E). Named on Lindsay (1928) 7.5' quadrangle.

Prices Camp [FRESNO]: *locality,* 16 miles northeast of Piedra along Dinkey Creek (lat. 36°57'20" N, long. 19°08'35" W). Named on Dinuba (1924) 30' quadrangle.

Primero [TULARE]: *locality,* 7 miles northeast of Dinuba along Atchison, Topeka and Santa Fe Railroad (lat. 36°36' N, long. 119° 17'05" W; near NW cor. sec. 29, T 15 S, R 25 E). Named on Sultana (1923) 7.5' quadrangle. The place is the first station north of Orosi on the railroad branch line to Porterville—*primero* means "first" in Spanish (Gudde, 1949, p. 273).

Primrose Lake [TULARE]: *lake,* 1200 feet long, 4 miles south-southeast of Mount Whitney (lat. 36°31'15" N, long. 118°16'30" W). Named on Mount Whitney (1956) 15' quadrangle. Chester Versteeg proposed the name (Browning, p. 175), which is for the abundance of wild primroses on the shore of the lake (United States Board on Geographic Names, 1938, p. 43).

Proctor: see **Monolith** [KERN].

Proctor Lake [KERN]: *lake,* 6900 feet long, 6 miles east of Tehachapi (lat. 35°07' N, long. 118°20'45" W; sec. 27, 29, T 32 S, R 34 E). Named on Tehachapi (1943) 15' quadrangle. On Monolith (1966) 7.5' quadrangle, the name applies to a dry lake. John Narbo collected salt in the 1860's at the shallow lake, which he called Narboe Lake (Barras, p. 10-11); the feature also was called Salt Lake (Barras, p. 52) and Tehachapi Lake (Bailey, 1962, p. 43).

Profile View [TULARE]: *relief feature,* 14 miles west-northwest of Triple Divide Peak (lat. 36°42' N, long. 118°44'30" W; near N line sec. 20, T 14 S, R 30 E). Named on Triple Divide Peak (1956) 15' quadrangle.

Progress: see **Conner** [KERN].

Prospero [KERN]: *locality,* 10 miles northwest of Bakersfield along Southern Pacific Railroad (lat. 35°28'15" N, long. 119°07'30" W; at S line sec. 24, T 28 S, R 26 E). Named on Oildale (1954) and Rosedale (1954) 7.5' quadrangles.

Providence Creek [FRESNO]: *stream,* flows about 2.5 miles to Big Creek (2) 8 miles southwest of Dinkey Dome (lat. 37°02'15" N, long. 119°14'35" W; near NE cor. sec. 28, T 10 S, R 25 E). Named on Huntington Lake (1953) 15' quadrangle. Kaiser (1904) 30' quadrangle shows Providence mine near the head of the stream.

Pueblo de las Juntas: see **Mendota** [FRESNO].

Puerta del Suelo: see **Cerro Noroeste** [KERN].

Pulvadera: see **Polvadero Gap** [FRESNO].

Pumice Butte [FRESNO]: *peak,* 3 miles north-northwest of Double Peak (lat. 37°33'10" N, long. 119°03'35" W). Altitude 9533 feet. Named on Devils Postpile (1953) 15' quadrangle.

Pumpkin Canyon [TULARE]: *canyon,* drained by a stream that flows 2 miles to White River (1) 4.25 miles southwest of California Hot Springs (lat. 35°50'15" N, long. 118°43'25" W; sec. 15, T 24 S, R 30 E). Named on California Hot Springs (1958) 15' quadrangle.

Pumpkin Center [KERN]: *town,* 7.5 miles south-southwest of Bakersfield (lat. 35°16' N, long. 119°02' W; on S line sec. 36, T 30 S, R 27 E). Named on Gosford (1954) 7.5' quadrangle. Postal authorities established Pumpkin Center post office in 1945 (Salley, p. 178). The name originated with a crop of pumpkins grown near the place in 1932 (Bailey, 1967, p. 22).

Pup Meadow [TULARE]: *area,* 5.25 miles east-northeast of California Hot Springs (lat. 35°53'45" N, long. 118°34'45" W; sec. 25, T 23 S, R 31 E). Named on California Hot Springs (1958) 15' quadrangle.

Puppet Lake [FRESNO]: *lake,* 3300 feet long, 3.5 miles west-northwest of Mount Humphreys (lat. 37°17'10" N, long. 118°44' W). Named on Mount Tom (1949) 15' quadrangle.

Purdie Canyon Spring [KERN]: *spring,* 6 miles west-southwest of Liebre Twins (lat. 34°56'10" N, long. 118°40'20" W); the spring is near the west end of Purdie Ridge. Named on Winters Ridge (1966) 7.5' quadrangle.

Purdie Ridge [KERN]: *ridge,* west-southwest of Liebre Twins (lat. 34°56'10" N, long. 118°39'45" W; at N line sec. 23, T 10 N, R 17 W). Named on Winters Ridge (1966) 7.5' quadrangle.

Purdie Spring [KERN]: *spring,* 5 miles west-southwest of Liebre Twins (lat. 34°56'10" N, long. 118°39'30" W; near N line sec. 23, T 10 N, R 17 W). Named on Winters Ridge (1966) 7.5' quadrangle.

Purple Creek [FRESNO]: *stream,* flows 5.5 miles to Fish Creek (1) 5.5 miles west of Red Slate Mountain in Cascade Valley (lat. 37° 30'40" N, long. 118°58'15" W); Purple Lake is along the stream. Named on Mount Morrison (1953) 15' quadrangle.

Purple Lake [FRESNO]: *lake,* 0.5 mile long, 4.5 miles west-northwest of Red Slate Mountain (lat. 37°31'45" N, long. 118°56'45" W). Named on Mount Morrison (1953) 15' quadrangle. The name is for the purple tint of water in the lake at certain times (Smith, Genny, p. 49).

Putman Canyon: see **Snowslide Canyon** [TULARE].

Putnam Canyon [TULARE]: *canyon,* drained by a stream that flows 1.5 miles to South Fork Kaweah River 11.5 miles southwest of Mineral King (lat. 36°20'50" N, long. 118°45'05" W). Named on Mineral King (1956) 15' quadrangle. Called Snowslide Canyon on Kaweah (1909) 30' quadrangle, where present Snowslide Canyon is called Putman Canyon. United States Board on Geographic Names (1960b, p. 20) rejected the name "Snowslide Canyon" for present Putnam Canyon, and listed the name "Putnam Creek" for the stream in the canyon.

Putnam Creek: see **Putnam Canyon** [TULARE].

Putnamville: see **Porterville** [TULARE].

Pylema: see **Bakersfield** [KERN].

Pyles Camp [TULARE]: *locality,* 8 miles southwest of Hockett Peak along Freeman Creek (lat. 36°08'20" N, long. 118°28'35" W). Named on Hockett Peak (1956) 15' quadrangle.

Pyramid: see **The Pyramid**, under **Painted Lady** [FRESNO].

Pyramid Hill [KERN]: *ridge,* east-southeast-trending, 1.5 miles long, 6.5 miles northwest of Mount Adelaide (lat. 35°29'30" N, long. 118°49'45" W). Named on Rio Bravo Ranch (1954) 7.5' quadrangle.

Pyramid Hills [KERN-KINGS]: *ridge,* north-northwest- to northwest-trending, 6.5 miles long, 14 miles south-southeast of Avenal on Kern-Kings County line, mainly in Kings County (lat. 35°50' N, long. 120°02'30" W). Named on Pyramid Hills (1953) 7.5' quadrangle. Arnold and Anderson (1908, p. 14) named the feature because it is "capped by a succession of conical hills, which when viewed from the east appear like isolated pyramids." United States Board on Geographic Names (1933a, p. 627) rejected the names "Los Piramidos" and "The Pyramids" for the ridge.

Pyramid Peak [FRESNO]: *peak,* 4.25 miles southwest of Mount Pinchot (lat. 36°54'20" N, long. 118°27'40" W). Altitude 12,777 feet. Named on Mount Pinchot (1953) 15' quadrangle.

Pyramids: see **The Pyramids**, under **Pyramid Hills** [KERN-KINGS].

—Q—

Quail [TULARE]: *locality,* 3.5 miles south of Tipton along Southern Pacific Railroad (lat. 36°00'35" N, long. 119°18'10" W; near SW cor. sec. 17, T 22 S, R 25 E). Named on Tipton (1950) 7.5' quadrangle. Postal authorities established Quail post office in 1912 and discontinued it in 1914 (Frickstad, p. 213).

Quail Canyon [KERN]: *canyon,* drained by a stream that flows 1.25 miles to Oak Creek Canyon 7.5 miles south of Tehachapi (lat. 35°01'25" N, long. 118°25'20" W; near S line sec. 24, T 11 N, R 15 W). Named on Tehachapi South (1966) 7.5' quadrangle.

Quail Flat [TULARE]:

(1) *area,* 3 miles east-southeast of Wilsonia (lat. 36°43'20" N, long. 118°54'25" W; sec. 11, T 14 S, R 28 E). Named on Giant Forest (1956) 15' quadrangle.
(2) *valley,* 5.5 miles south-southeast of Auckland (lat. 36°30'55" N, long. 119°03'45" W; sec. 20, 29, T 16 S, R 27 E). Named on Auckland (1966) 7.5' quadrangle. Called Quail Valley on Dunlap (1944) 15' quadrangle.

Quail Meadows [FRESNO]: *areas,* two, 8 miles west-northwest of Mount Abbot along Mono Creek (lat. 37°24'45" N, long. 118°55'45" W). Named on Mount Abbot (1953) 15' quadrangle.

Quail Spring [KERN]:
(1) *spring,* 6.5 miles southwest of Pinyon Mountain (lat. 35°23'15" N, long. 118°14'10" W; near E line sec. 29, T 29 S, R 35 E). Named on Pinyon Mountain (1972) 7.5' quadrangle.
(2) *spring,* 12 miles north of Mojave (lat. 35°13'30" N, long. 118° 10'45" W; near N line sec. 24, T 31 S, R 35 E). Named on Cache Peak (1973) 7.5' quadrangle.

Quail Trap Canyon [TULARE]: *canyon,* 1 mile long, 5.5 miles south-southwest of California Hot Springs (lat. 35°48'20" N, long. 118°42'30" W; sec. 26, 35, T 24 S, R 30 E). Named on California Hot Springs (1958) 15' quadrangle.

Quail Valley: see **Quail Flat** [TULARE] (2).

Quaker Meadow [TULARE]: *locality,* nearly 4 miles southeast of Camp Nelson (lat. 36°06'35" N, long. 118°33'10" W; near NE cor. sec. 18, T 21 S, R 32 E). Named on Camp Nelson (1956) 15' quadrangle.

Quaking Aspen Camp: see **Quaking Aspen Meadow** [TULARE].

Quaking Aspen Meadow [TULARE]: *area,* 4 miles east-southeast of Camp Nelson (lat. 36°07'10" N, long. 118°32'40" W; sec. 8, T 21 S, R 32 E). Named on Camp Nelson (1956) 15' quadrangle. California Division of Highways' (1934) map shows a place called Quaking Aspen Camp situated at or near the site (near E line sec. 5, T 21 S, R 32 E).

Quality [KERN]: *locality,* 7.5 miles east of Delano along Southern Pacific Railroad (lat. 35°47' N, long. 119°07'10" W; sec. 1, T 25 S, R 26 E). Named on Richgrove (1952) 7.5' quadrangle.

Qualls Camp [FRESNO]: *locality,* 7.25 miles northeast of Dinkey Dome (lat. 37°11'15" N, long. 119°02'20" W). Named on Huntington Lake (1953) 15' quadrangle. United States Board on Geographic Names (1983c, p. 6) rejected the name "Knight Camp" for the place. Wesley Qualls had a cow camp there in the 1920's, and Walter Knight used it later (Browning, p. 176).

Quartzburg: see **Big Blue Mill** [KERN].

Quartz Mountain [KERN]: *peak,* 3.5 miles west-northwest of Miracle Hot Springs (lat. 35°35'45" N, long. 118°35'30" W). Altitude 5223 feet. Named on Miracle Hot Springs (1972) 7.5' quadrangle.

Quatro Osos Canyon: see **Williams Canyon** [KERN].

Quedow Mountain [TULARE]: *ridge,* northwest-trending, 1.25 miles long, 4 miles north-northeast of Fountain Springs (lat. 35°56'30" N, long. 118°53' W). Named on Fountain Springs (1965) 7.5' quadrangle. Called Credow Mountain on White River (1936) 15' quadrangle, and called Cuidado Mtn. on White River (1952) 15' quadrangle, but United States Board on Geographic Names (1967a, p. 10) rejected the names "Credow Mountain," "Cuidado Mountain," and "Cuidow Mountain" for the feature.

Quinn Peak [TULARE]: *peak,* about 8 miles south of Mineral King (lat. 36°20'05" N, long. 118°35'15" W). Altitude 10,168 feet. Named on Mineral King (1956) 15' quadrangle. The name commemorates Harry Quinn, who settled in California in 1868 (United States Board on Geographic Names, 1933a, p. 629).

— R —

Rabbit Creek: see **Dead Ox Creek** [KERN].

Rabbit Gulch [KERN]: *canyon,* drained by a stream that flows 1.5 miles to Dead Ox Creek 3.5 miles south-southeast of Woody (lat. 35°39'30" N, long. 118°48'15" W; near N line sec. 24, T 26 S, R 29 E). Named on Woody (1965) 7.5' quadrangle.

Rabbit Island [KERN]: *island,* 450 feet long, 4.5 miles west of Weldon in Isabella Lake (lat. 35°40'20" N, long. 118°22'20" W; near N line sec. 18, T 26 S, R 34 E). Named on Weldon (1972) 7.5' quadrangle.

Rabbit Meadow [TULARE]: *area,* 4.5 miles east-southeast of Wilsonia (lat. 36°42'45" N, long. 118°52'35" W; near NW cor. sec. 18, T 14 S, R 29 E). Named on Giant Forest (1956) 15' quadrangle.

Raco [FRESNO]: *locality,* 4.25 miles southwest of Herndon along Southern Pacific Railroad (lat. 36°48' N, long. 119°58'40" W; sec. 14, T 13 S, R 18 E). Named on Herndon (1964) 7.5' quadrangle. Called Dickerson on Herndon (1923) 7.5' quadrangle. California Mining Bureau's (1917a) map shows a place called Everts located at or just east of present Raco.

Rademacher: see **Rademacher Siding** [KERN].

Rademacher Siding [KERN]: *locality,* 11.5 miles north of Randsburg along Southern Pacific Railroad (lat. 35°32' N, long. 117° 41' W). Named on Searles Lake (1915) 1° quadrangle. Called Rademacher on California Division of Highways' (1934) map.

Radnor [TULARE]: *locality,* nearly 4 miles south of Earlimart along Southern Pacific Railroad (lat. 35°49'50" N, long. 119°15'40" W; sec. 22, T 24 S, R 25 E). Named on Delano West (1954) 7.5' quadrangle.

Rae Lake [FRESNO]: *lake,* 1000 feet long, 6.5 miles north-northwest of Blackcap Mountain (lat. 37°09'05" N, long. 118°50'55" W). Named on Blackcap Mountain (1953) 15' quadrangle. The name commemorates Rae Crabtree, a packer (Browning, p. 177).

Rae Lakes [FRESNO]: *lakes,* largest 3000 feet long, 9.5 miles south of Mount Pinchot at the head of South Fork Woods Creek (lat. 36° 48'30" N, long. 118°24' W). Named on Mount Pnchot (1953) 15' quadrangle. R.B. Marshall of United States Geological Survey named one of the lakes in 1906 for Rachel Colby, wife of William E. Colby (Browning, p. 177).

Ragged Spur [FRESNO]: *ridge,* south-southeast-trending, 4.5 miles long, 4 miles southeast of Mount Goddard (lat. 37°03' N, long. 118°40'30" W). Named on Mount Goddard (1948) 15' quadrangle.

Ragged Top [KINGS]: *peak,* 6 miles south of Avenal on Reef Ridge (lat. 35°54'55" N, long. 120°08'10" W; sec. 21, T 23 S, R 17 E). Altitude 2025 feet. Named on Garza Peak (1953) 7.5' quadrangle.

Ragged Valley [FRESNO]: *valley,* 3 miles east-northeast of Joaquin Rocks (lat. 36°20'15" N, long. 120°23'45" W). Named on Domengine Ranch (1956) and Joaquin Rocks (1969) 7.5' quadrangles.

Rag Gulch [KERN]: *canyon,* drained by a stream that flows 28 miles to a ditch on Kern-Tulare County line 7.5 miles east of Delano (lat. 35°47'25" N, long. 119°06'40" W; at N line sec. 6, T 25 S, R 27 E). Named on Delano East (1953), Quincy School (1965), Richgrove (1952), Sand Canyon (1965), White River (1965), and Woody (1965) 7.5' quadrangles. According to legend, the name is from stew, or ragout, made by French miners (Boyd, p. 159).

Ragle Canyon [TULARE]: *canyon,* drained by a stream that flows 1.5 miles to Dry Creek (1) 4.25 miles east-northeast of Woodlake (lat. 36°26'05" N, long. 119°01'30" W; near W line sec. 23, T 17 S, R 27 E). Named on Woodlake (1952) 7.5' quadrangle. Called Liveoak Canyon on Lemon Cove (1928) 7.5' quadrangle.

Rail Flat [TULARE]: *area,* 5.25 miles southwest of California Hot Springs (lat. 35°49'35" N, long. 118°44'15" W; sec. 21, T 24 S, R 30 E). Named on California Hot Springs (1958) 7.5' quadrangle.

Rail Flat Ridge [TULARE]: *ridge,* generally west-trending, 1.5 miles long, 6 miles southwest of California Hot Springs (lat. 35°49'20" N, long. 118°44'45" W); the ridge is south of Rail Flat. Named on California Hot Springs (1958) 15' quadrangle, and on White River (1965) 7.5' quadrangle.

Railroad Canyon [TULARE]: *canyon,* drained by a stream that flows 1.25 miles to White River (1) 5 miles southwest of California Hot Springs (lat. 35°50'10" N, long. 118°44'30" W; sec. 16, T 24 S, R 30 E). Named on California Hot Springs (1958) 15' quadrangle.

Railroad Spring [KERN]:
(1) *spring,* 0.5 mile southwest of Orchard Peak (lat. 35°44' N, long. 120°08'25" W; sec. 21, T 25 S, R 17 E). Named on Orchard Peak (1961) 7.5' quadrangle.
(2) *spring,* 3 miles northwest of Caliente (lat. 35°19' N, long. 118° 40' W). Named on Bena (1972) 7.5' quadrangle.

Rainbow Lake [FRESNO]:
(1) *lake,* 0.5 mile long, 15 miles north-northeast of Kaiser Peak (lat. 37°28'35" N, long. 119° 02' W); the lake is one of the group called Margaret Lakes. Named on Kaiser Peak (1953) 15' quadrangle.
(2) *lake,* 500 feet long, 3.5 miles northeast of Dinkey Dome (lat. 37° 09'10" N, long. 119°05' W; sec. 13, T 9 S, R 26 E); the lake is 900 feet east of Eastern Brook Lake. Named on Huntington Lake (1953) 15' quadrangle.
(3) *lake,* 1150 feet long, nearly 2 miles east-northeast of Blackcap Mountain (lat. 37°05'05" N, long. 118°45'50" W). Named on Blackcap Mountain (1953) 15' quadrangle.

Rainbow Lakes [FRESNO]: *lakes,* largest 1400 feet long, 8.5 miles east of Mount Goddard (lat. 37°05'15" N, long. 118°34' W). Named on Mount Goddard (1948) 15' quadrangle. Mr. Halladay, an early-day packer, named the lakes (Browning, p. 178).

Rainbow Mountain [TULARE]: *peak,* 3.25 miles southeast of Mineral King on Great Western Divide (lat. 36°25'25" N, long. 118°33' W). Named on Mineral King (1956) 15' quadrangle. The name is from the colored rocks at the peak and the shape of the crest (Browning, p. 178).

Raisin: see **Raisin City** [FRESNO].

Raisin City [FRESNO]: *village,* 13 miles south-southwest of downtown Fresno (lat. 36°36'05" N, long. 119°54'10" W; sec. 28, T 15 S, R 19 E). Named on Raisin (1963) 7.5' quadrangle, which also shows Raisin P.O. at the place. The village is called Raisin on Raisin (1925) 7.5' quadrangle. Postal authorities established Raisin post office in 1907 (Frickstad, p. 37).

Raljon Lake [KERN]: *lake,* 800 feet long, 2.5 miles southwest of Glennville (lat. 35°42'25" N, long. 118°44'10" W; sec. 34, T 25 S, R 30 E). Named on Glennville (1972) 7.5' quadrangle, which shows Raljon ranch at the lake.

Ralmke Pond: see **Helmke Pond** [FRESNO].

Rambaud Creek [FRESNO]: *stream,* flows 2 miles to Middle Fork Kings River 9 miles east-southeast of Mount Goddard (lat. 37°02'50" N, long.

118°34'50" W). Named on Mount Goddard (1948) 15' quadrangle.

Rambaud Peak [FRESNO]: *peak,* 8 miles east-southeast of Mount Goddard (lat. 37°02'20" N, long. 118°35'50" W); the peak is south of Rambaud Creek. Named on Mount Goddard (1948) 15' quadrangle. The name commemorates Pete Rambaud, a Basque sheepman who brought the first sheep into the neighborhood from Inyo County in 1877 (Farquhar, 1925, p. 127).

Ram Lake [FRESNO]:
(1) *lake,* 1100 feet long, 4 miles northwest of Red Slate Mountain on upper reaches of Purple Creek (lat. 37°32'35" N, long. 118°55'35" W). Named on Mount Morrison (1953) 15' quadrangle.
(2) *lake,* 750 feet long, 2.5 miles east-southeast of Blackcap Mountain (lat. 37°03'50" N, long. 118°45' W); the feature is next to Ewe Lake. Named on Blackcap Mountain (1953) 15' quadrangle. William A. Dill of California Department of Fish and Game named the lake in 1948 because of its proximity to Bighorn Lake (Browning, p. 178).

Ramona Lake [FRESNO]: *lake,* 0.5 mile long, 12.5 miles north of Blackcap Mountain (lat. 37°15' N, long. 118°47' W). Named on Blackcap Mountain (1953) and Mount Abbot (1953) 15' quadrangles.

Rampart Pass: see **Siberian Pass** [TULARE].

Ramshaw Meadows [TULARE]: *area,* 3.5 miles northeast of Kern Peak along South Fork Kern River (lat. 36°21' N, long. 118° 15' W). Named on Kern Peak (1956) and Olancha (1956) 15' quadrangles. The name commemorates Peter Ramshaw, a stockman in the neighborhood from 1861 until 1880 (Gudde, 1949, p. 279).

Rancheria [FRESNO]: *locality,* 6 miles southeast of Balch Camp (lat. 36°50'05" N, long. 119°03'30" W; sec. 5, T 13 S, R 27 E). Site named on Patterson Mountain (1952) 15' quadrangle.

Rancheria Campground [FRESNO]: *locality,* 3 miles south-southeast of Kaiser Peak on the north side of Huntington Lake (1) (lat. 37°15'10" N, long. 119°10' W; near NE cor. sec. 7, T 8 S, R 26 E); the place is near the mouth of Rancheria Creek (1). Named on Kaiser Peak (1953) 15' quadrangle.

Rancheria Canyon [KERN]: *canyon,* drained by a stream that flows 2.5 miles to Rattlesnake Creek (3) nearly 4 miles south of Pine Mountain (lat. 35°30'25" N, long. 118°45'45" W; near W line sec. 9, T 28 S, R 30 E). Named on Democrat Hot Springs (1972) 7.5' quadrangle.

Rancheria Canyon [TULARE]: *canyon,* drained by a stream that flows 1.25 miles to Dry Creek (1) nearly 5 miles east-southeast of Auckland at Rancheria Flat (lat. 36°33'45" N, long. 119°01'25" W; sec. 3, T 16 S, R 27 E). Named on Auckland (1966) 7.5' quadrangle.

Rancheria Creek [FRESNO]:
(1) *stream,* flows 6 miles to Huntington Lake (1) 3 miles south-southeast of Kaiser Peak (lat. 37°15'20" N, long. 119°09'40" W; sec. 5, T 8 S, R 26 E). Named on Kaiser Peak (1953) 15' quadrangle. Called North Fork [of Big Creek (1)] on Kaiser (1904) 30' quadrangle.
(2) *stream,* flows 2.5 miles to White Deer Creek 9 miles southwest of Balch Camp (lat. 36°47'55" N, long. 119°12'30" W; sec. 13, T 13 S, R 25 E). Named on Patterson Mountain (1952) 15' quadrangle.
(3) *stream,* flows 8 miles to North Fork Kings River 7.25 miles east-northeast of Balch Camp (lat. 36°56'45" N, long. 119°00'05" W; sec. 26, T 11 S, R 27 E). Named on Tehipite Dome (1952) 15' quadrangle. On Tehipite (1903) 30' quadrangle, present Little Rancheria Creek is called North Fork [Rancheria Creek (3)].

Rancheria Creek [KERN]:
(1) *stream,* flows 5.25 miles to Rattlesnake Creek (3) 5.25 miles southwest of Pine Mountain (lat. 35°30'50" N, long. 118°50'15" W; near NE cor. sec. 10, T 28 S, R 29 E). Named on Pine Mountain (1965) and Rio Bravo Ranch (1954) 7.5' quadrangles.
(2) *stream,* flows 12.5 miles to Walker Basin Creek 10.5 miles northeast of Caliente in Walker Basin (lat. 35°24'25" N, long. 118° 30'35" W; near E line sec. 14, T 29 S, R 32 E). Named on Breckenridge Mountain (1972), Claraville (1972), and Piute Peak (1972) 7.5' quadrangles. Called Williams Cr. on Wheeler's (1875-1878) map.

Rancheria Creek [TULARE]: *stream,* flows 5.5 miles to Bear Creek (2) nearly 6 miles north-northeast of Springville (lat. 36°12'05" N, long. 118°45'40" W; near E line sec. 7, T 20 S, R 30 E). Named on Camp Nelson (1956) and Springville (1957) 15' quadrangles.

Rancheria Creek: see **Little Rancheria Creek** [FRESNO]; **Lower Rancheria Creek** [FRESNO].

Rancheria Flat [TULARE]: *area,* nearly 5 miles east-southeast of Auckland along Dry Creek (1) (lat. 36°33'50" N, long. 119°01'25" W; sec. 3, T 16 S, R 27 E); the place is at the mouth of Rancheria Canyon. Named on Auckland (1966) 7.5' quadrangle.

Rancho de los Californios: see **Mendota** [FRESNO].

Rancho Seco [KERN]: *locality,* 2 miles south-southwest of Cantil (lat. 35°17' N, long. 117°59'20" W). Named on Cantil (1967) 7.5' quadrangle.

Rand [KERN]: *locality,* 4.25 miles north-northwest of Randsburg along Southern Pacific Railroad (lat. 35°25'20" N, long. 117°41'30" W). Named on El Paso Peaks (1967) 7.5' quadrangle.

Rand Camp: see **Randsburg** [KERN].

Rand Mountains [KERN]: *range,* extends southwest from Randsburg (center near lat. 35°20' N, long. 117°43' W). Named on California City North (1973), Cantil (1967), Johannesburg (1967), and Saltdale SE (1967) 7.5' quadrangles.

Randsburg [KERN]: *village,* 17 miles south of Ridgecrest (lat. 35° 22'05" N, long. 117°39'10" W; sec. 35, T 29 S, R 40 E). Named on Johannesburg (1967) 7.5' quadrangle. Postal authorities established Randsburg post office in 1896 (Frickstad, p. 58). Prospectors found gold in 1895 at Rand mine, named for the gold-producing Rand district of South Africa; the camp that grew there first was called Rand Camp, and later Randsburg (Neal, p. 14-15).

Ranger: see **Kaweah Camp** [TULARE].

Ranger Lakes [TULARE]: *lakes,* two, largest 900 feet long, 10.5 miles west-northwest of Triple Divide Peak (lat. 36°40' N, long. 118°41'30" W). Named on Triple Divide Peak (1956) 15' quadrangle. United States Board on Geographic Names (1989b, p. 2) approved the name "Ranger Lake" for one of the lakes (lat. 36°39'57" N, long. 118°41'42" W).

Ranger Meadow [TULARE]: *area,* about 5 miles northwest of Triple Divide Peak in Deadman Canyon (1) (lat. 36°38'55" N, long. 118°35' W). Named on Triple Divide Peak (1956) 15' quadrangle.

Rankin Peak [KERN]: *peak,* 3 miles south of Miracle Hot Springs (lat. 35°32' N, long. 118°31'25" W; sec. 34, T 27 S, R 32 E). Altitude 4278 feet. Named on Miracle Hot Springs (1972) 7.5' quadrangle.

Rattlesnake Creek [FRESNO]:
(1) *stream,* flows 2.5 miles to South Fork San Joaquin River 7 miles northeast of Kaiser Peak (lat. 37°21'45" N, long. 119°05'50" W). Named on Kaiser Peak (1953) 15' quadrangle.
(2) *stream,* flows 2 miles to Boulder Creek (1) 6.5 miles east of Hume (lat. 36°47'05" N, long. 118°47'50" W). Named on Tehipite Dome (1952) 15' quadrangle.
(3) *stream,* flows 3.25 miles to Middle Fork Kings River 10.5 miles west of Marion Peak (lat. 36°56'25" N, long. 118°42'40" W). Named on Marion Peak (1953) 15' quadrangle.

Rattlesnake Creek [KERN]:
(1) *stream,* flows 4.5 miles to Isabella Lake 0.5 mile south-southwest of Wofford Heights (lat. 35°41'55" N, long. 118°27'25" W; sec. 5, T 26 S, R 33 E). Named on Alta Sierra (1972) and Lake Isabella North (1972) 7.5' quadrangles.
(2) *stream,* flows 5 miles to South Fork Cottonwood Creek (2) 4 miles east-southeast of Mount Adelaide (lat. 35°24'10" N, long. 118°40'45" W; sec. 17, T 29 S, R 31 E). Named on Mount Adelaide (1972) 7.5' quadrangle.
(3) *stream,* flows 10 miles to Poso Creek 6 miles west-southwest of Pine Mountain (lat. 35°31'05" N, long. 118°51'20" W; near E line sec. 4, T 28 S, R 29 E). Named on Democrat Hot Springs (1972) and Pine Mountain (1965) 7.5' quadrangles.

Rattlesnake Creek [TULARE]:
(1) *stream,* flows 3.5 miles to Cottonwood Creek 1 mile west of Auckland (lat. 36°35'10" N, long. 119°07'15" W; near NW cor. sec. 35, T 15 S, R 26 E). Named on Auckland (1966) and Stokes Mountain (1966) 7.5' quadrangles.
(2) *stream,* flows 8.5 miles to Kern River 10 miles northwest of Kern Peak (lat. 36°25' N, long. 118°24'45" W). Named on Kern Peak (1956) and Mineral King (1956) 15' quadrangles.
(3) *stream,* flows 13 miles to Kern River 5.5 miles south of Hockett Peak (lat. 36°08'30" N, long. 118°24'05" W). Named on Hockett Peak (1956) 15' quadrangle. This appears to be the stream called Harris Creek on Olmsted's (1900) map.

Rattlesnake Creek, Central Fork: see **Crystal Creek** [KERN].

Rattlesnake Meadow [TULARE]: *area,* 15 miles east-southeast of Fairview (lat. 35°48'40" N, long. 118°16'15" W; near W line sec. 25, T 24 S, R 34 E). Named on Kernville (1956) 15' quadrangle.

Rattlesnake Ridge [TULARE]: *ridge,* southwest-trending, 1.5 miles long, 7 miles northwest of California Hot Springs (lat. 35°57'35" N, long. 118°44'35" W; on N line sec. 4, T 23 S, R 30 E). Named on California Hot Springs (1958) 15' quadrangle.

Rattlesnake Spring [FRESNO]: *spring,* 4 miles north-northwest of Joaquin Rocks (lat. 36°22'25" N, long. 120°28'30" W; sec. 8, T 18 S, R 14 E). Named on Joaquin Rocks (1969) 7.5' quadrangle.

Rattlesnake Spring [KERN]:
(1) *spring,* 4.25 miles east-southeast of Mount Adelaide (lat. 35°24'45" N, long. 118°40'20" W; near N line sec. 17, T 29 S, R 31 E); the feature is along Rattlesnake Creek (2). Named on Mount Adelaide (1972) 7.5' quadrangle.
(2) *spring,* 4.5 miles northwest of Caliente (lat. 35°20'15" N, long. 118°40'55" W). Named on Bena (1972) 7.5' quadrangle.

Rattlesnake Spring [TULARE]:
(1) *spring,* 4 miles north of Cliff Peak (lat. 36°37' N, long. 119°09'55" W; near S line sec. 17, T 15 S, R 26 E); the spring is above the head of Rattlesnake Creek (1). Named on Stokes Mountain (1966) 7.5' quadrangle.
(2) *spring,* 6.25 miles south-southeast of Auckland (lat. 36°30'30" N, long. 119°03'05" W; sec. 28, T 16 S, R 27 E). Named on Auckland (1966) 7.5' quadrangle.

Raven Pass [KERN]: *pass,* 8 miles south-southeast of Orchard Peak (lat. 35°38' N, long. 120°04'15" W; sec. 30, T 26 S, R 18 E). Named on Sawtooth Ridge (1961) 7.5' quadrangle.

Rayo [TULARE]: *locality,* 5.5 miles west-northwest of Woodlake along Atchison, Topeka and Santa Fe Railroad (lat. 36°26'50" N, long. 119°11'05" W; near W line sec. 17, T 17 S, R 26 E). Named on Exeter (1952) 15' quadrangle.

Reader Flat [KERN]: *area,* 4 miles northwest of Caliente (lat. 35° 20'20" N, long. 118°40'05" W). Named on Bena (1972) 7.5' quadrangle.

Recess Peak [FRESNO]: *peak,* 4 miles west of Mount Abbot on Mono Divide (lat. 37°23' N, long. 118°51'15" W); the peak is near the head of First Recess. Altitude 12,836 feet. Named on Mount Abbot (1953) 15' quadrangle. Theodore S. Solomons named the peak for its proximity to First Recess (Browning, p. 179).

Rector [TULARE]: *locality,* 6 miles west of Exeter along Southern Pacific Railroad (lat. 36°18'20" N, long. 119°14'30" W; on W line sec. 2, T 19 S, R 25 E). Named on Exeter (1952) 15' quadrangle.

Red and White Lake [FRESNO]: *lake,* 1800 feet long, 8 miles northwest of Mount Abbot (lat. 37°29'05" N, long. 118°52'05" W); the lake is 0.5 mile west-northwest of Red and White Mountain. Named on Mount Abbot (1953) 15' quadrangle.

Red and White Mountain [FRESNO]: *peak,* 7.5 miles north-northwest of Mount Abbot on Fresno-Mono County line (lat. 37°28'50" N, long. 118°51'25" W). Altitude 12,850 feet. Named on Mount Abbot (1953) 15' quadrangle. Theodore S. Solomons named the peak in 1894 for red and white rocks exposed on it (Farquhar, 1925, p. 127).

Red Bank Creek: see **Redbank Slough** [FRESNO].

Redbanks [TULARE]: *locality,* 2.5 miles west-northwest of Woodlake along Atchison, Topeka and Santa Fe Railroad, and along Visalia Electric Railroad (lat. 36°25'20" N, long. 119°08'35" W; sec. 27, T 17 S, R 26 E). Named on Exeter (1952) 15' quadrangle. Called Colvin Ranch on Ivanhoe (1926) 7.5' quadrangle, which has the name "Redbanks" as an alternate designation for present Hillmaid. Railroad officials named the place in 1914 for Redbanks Orchard Company, which itself had been named for the red soil in the neighborhood (Gudde, 1949, p. 282). California Mining Bureau's (1917b) map shows a place called Heid located along the railroad between Redbanks and Seville.

Redbank Slough [FRESNO]: *water feature,* extends for 13 miles to an artificial watercourse 4.5 miles southeast of Clovis (lat. 36°46'15" N, long. 119°39'05" W; sec. 26, T 13 S, R 21 E). Named on Clovis (1964) and Round Mountain (1964) 7.5' quadrangles. Grunsky (p. 71) used the name "Red Bank Creek" for the feature.

Red Buttes [KERN]: *ridge,* south-trending, 2.25 miles long, 4.5 miles north-northwest of Saltdale (lat. 35°25'15" N, long. 118°54'45" W). Named on Saltdale NW (1967) 7.5' quadrangle. On Saltdale (1943a) 15' quadrangle, the name applies to a ridge located 2 miles farther west across Last Chance Canyon.

Redfield: see **Mineral King** [TULARE].

Red Fir Meadow [TULARE]: *area,* 11 miles west of Triple Divide Peak (lat. 36°35'10" N, long. 118°43'20" W; near S line sec. 28, T 15 S, R 30 E). Named on Triple Divide Peak (1956) 15' quadrangle.

Red Hill [KERN]:

(1) *ridge,* west-southwest-trending, 2 miles long, 2.5 miles north-northeast of Glennville (lat. 35°45'35" N, long. 118°41'25" W). Named on California Hot Springs (1958) 15' quadrangle.

(2) *peak,* 4 miles northeast of Knob Hill (lat. 35°35'40" N, long. 118°53'05" W; near W line sec. 8, T 27 S, R 29 E). Altitude 1789 feet. Named on Knob Hill (1965) 7.5' quadrangle.

(3) *peak,* 2.5 miles east of Rosamond (lat. 34°52'10" N, long. 118° 07' W; near SE cor. sec. 14, T 9 N, R 12 W). Altitude 2743 feet. Named on Rosamond Lake (1973) 7.5' quadrangle.

Red Hill [TULARE]:

(1) *peak,* 4.25 miles east of Kaweah (lat. 36°28'20" N, long. 118°50'20" W; at S line sec. 4, T 17 S, R 29 E). Named on Kaweah (1957) 15' quadrangle.

(2) *peak,* 5.25 miles south of Camp Nelson (lat. 36°04' N, long. 118°37'30" W). Altitude 6292 feet. Named on Camp Nelson (1956) 15' quadrangle.

Red Hill: see **Tropico Hill** [KERN].

Red Kaweah [TULARE]: *peak,* nearly 4 miles south-southeast of Triple Divide Peak (lat. 36°32'25" N, long., 118°30'15" W); the peak is on Kaweah Peaks Ridge. Named on Triple Divide Peak (1956) 15' quadrangle.

Red Lake [FRESNO]: *lake,* 1600 feet long, 5.5 miles north of Dinkey Dome (lat. 37°11'30" N, long. 119°06'35" W; sec. 34, T 8 S, R 26 E); the lake is 0.5 mile south-southeast of the top of Red Mountain (1). Named on Huntington Lake (1953) 15' quadrangle.

Red Mountain [FRESNO]:

(1) *peak,* nearly 6 miles north of Dinkey Dome (lat. 37°11'50" N, long. 119°06'50" W; sec. 34, T 8 S, R 26 E). Altitude 9874 feet. Named on Huntington Lake (1953) 15' quadrangle.

(2) *peak,* nearly 5.5 miles north of Blackcap Mountain on LeConte Divide (lat. 37°09' N, long. 118°48' W). Altitude 11,951 feet. Named on Blackcap Mountain (1953) 15' quadrangle. United States Board on Geographic Names (1973a, p. 3) approved the name "Mount Hutton" for a peak located less than 2 miles south of Red Mountain (2) (lat. 37°07'34" N, long. 118°47'52" W); the name honors Scottish geologist James Hutton.

(3) *peak,* nearly 2 miles east of Humphreys Station (lat. 36°57'40" N, long. 119°24'50" W; sec. 24, T 11 S, R 23 E). Altitude 2804 feet. Named on Humphreys Station (1965) 7.5' quadrangle.

(4) *ridge,* north-northwest-trending, 2.5 miles long, 3 miles north-northwest of Piedra (lat. 36°51'30" N, long. 119°23'40" W). Named on Piedra (1965) 7.5' quadrangle.

Red Mountain [KERN]:

(1) *ridge,* generally west- to southwest-trending, 4.5 miles long, center 6 miles west of Piute Peak (lat. 35°28'05" N, long. 118°29'35" W). Named on Breckenridge Mountain (1972) and Piute Peak (1972) 7.5' quadrangles.

(2) *peak,* 4 miles west-southwest of Alta Sierra (lat. 35°41'55" N, long. 118°36'45" W; sec. 2, T 26 S, R 31 E). Altitude 5828 feet. Named on Alta Sierra (1972) 7.5' quadrangle.

(3) *peak,* 10 miles east of Tehachapi (lat. 35°08'55" N, long. 118° 16'20" W; at W line sec. 18, T 32 S, R 35 E). Altitude 5729 feet. Named on Tehachapi NE (1966) 7.5' quadrangle.

Red Mountain [TULARE]: *peak,* 5.25 miles south of Auckland (lat. 36°30'45" N, long. 119°05'55" W; near N line sec. 25, T 16 S, R 26 E). Altitude 2326 feet. Named on Auckland (1966) 7.5' quadrangle.

Red Mountain Basin [FRESNO]: *relief feature,* 4.5 miles north-northwest of Blackcap Mountain (lat. 37°08'10" N, long. 118° 49' W); the feature is 1.25 miles southwest of Red Mountain (2). Named on Blackcap Mountain (1953) 15' quadrangle.

Redoak Creek [FRESNO]: *stream,* flows 2.5 miles to Kings River 3.5 miles west-southwest of Balch Camp (lat. 36°52'45" N, long. 119°10'45" W; sec. 19, T 12 S, R 26 E). Named on Patterson Mountain (1952) 15' quadrangle.

Red Pass: see **Cartridge Pass** [FRESNO].

Red Point [FRESNO]: *peak,* 4600 feet north-northwest of Marion Peak (lat. 36°58'10" N, long. 118°31'35" W). Named on Marion Peak (1953) 15' quadrangle.

Redrock [KERN]:

(1) *locality,* 2.5 miles north of Cantil near the mouth of Redrock (present Red Rock) Canyon (lat. 35°20'40" N, long. 117°58'10" W; near N line sec. 11, T 30 S, R 37 E). Named on Saltdale (1943a) 15' quadrangle.

(2) *locality,* at Cantil along Southern Pacific Railroad (lat. 35°18'30" N, long. 117°58'30" W; at E line sec. 23, T 30 S, R 37 E). Named on Saltdale (1943a) 15' quadrangle.

Red Rock Canyon [KERN]: *canyon,* 4 miles long, opens into Fremont Valley 2.5 miles north of Cantil (lat. 35°20'45" N, long. 117° 58'10" W; near N line sec. 11, T 30 S, R 37 E). Named on Cantil (1967) and Saltdale NW (1967) 7.5' quadrangles. Saltdale (1943a) 15' quadrangle has the form "Redrock Canyon" for the name.

Redrock Canyon: see **Dove Spring Canyon** [KERN].

Redrock Creek [TULARE]: *stream,* flows 5.5 miles to Ninemile Creek 4.5 miles east of Hockett Peak (lat. 36°13'45" N, long. 118° 18'15" W); the stream drains Redrock Meadows. Named on Hockett Peak (1956) and Kern Peak (1956) 15' quadrangles.

Redrock Meadows [TULARE]: *area,* 3 miles south-southeast of Kern Peak (lat. 36°16'10" N, long. 118°16'15" W); the place is along upper reaches of Redrock Creek. Named on Kern Peak (1956) 15' quadrangle.

Red Slate Mountain [FRESNO]: *peak,* 23 miles northeast of Kaiser Peak on Fresno-Mono County line (lat. 37°30'30" N, long. 118°52'10" W). Altitude 13,163 feet. Named on Mount Morrison (1953) 15' quadrangle. Members of the Whitney survey named the peak in 1864 (Browning, p. 180).

Red Spring [KERN]: *spring,* 6 miles east-southeast of Caliente (lat. 35°16'10" N, long. 118°31'20" W; near SE cor. sec. 34, T 30 S, R 32 E). Named on Oiler Peak (1972) 7.5' quadrangle.

Red Spur [TULARE]: *ridge,* generally southeast-trending, 2 miles long, 8.5 miles west-southwest of Mount Whitney (lat. 36°32' N, long. 118°26' W). Named on Mount Whitney (1956) 15' quadrangle.

Red Spur Creek [TULARE]: *stream,* flows 3.5 miles to Kern River 15 miles north-northwest of Kern Peak (lat. 36°29'50" N, long. 118°24'15" W); the stream heads near Red Spur. Named on Kern Peak (1956) and Mount Whitney (1956) 15' quadrangles.

Redwood Camp [TULARE]: *locality,* 4.5 miles west-southwest of Camp Nelson (lat. 36°06'50" N, long. 118°41'10" W; sec. 12, T 21 S, R 30 E). Named on Camp Nelson (1956) 15' quadrangle.

Redwood Canyon [TULARE]: *canyon,* drained by Redwood Creek (1), which flows 7.5 miles to North Fork Kaweah River 3.5 miles north-northwest of Yucca Mountain (lat. 36°37'20" N, long. 118° 53'35" W; sec. 13, T 15 S, R 28 E). Named on Giant Forest (1956) 15' quadrangle.

Redwood Corral [TULARE]: *locality,* 7 miles north of California Hot Springs (lat. 35°58'55" N, long. 118°39'40" W); the place is near the head of Redwood Creek (2). Named on California Hot Springs (1958) 15' quadrangle.

Redwood Creek [FRESNO]: *stream,* flows 2.5 miles to South Fork Kings

River 5 miles east-northeast of Hume (lat. 36°49' N, long. 118°50'05" W). Named on Tehipite Dome (1952) 15' quadrangle.

Redwood Creek [TULARE]:

(1) *stream,* flows 7.5 miles to North Fork Kaweah River 3.5 miles north-northwest of Yucca Mountain (lat. 36°37'20" N, long. 118° 53'35" W; sec. 13, T 15 S, R 28 E); the stream is east of Redwood Mountain. Named on Giant Forest (1956) 15' quadrangle. East Fork enters from the east 5.5 miles upstream from the mouth of the main stream; it is 1.5 miles long and is named on Giant Forest (1956) 15' quadrangle.

(2) *stream,* flows 1.5 miles to Eagle Creek (2) 8 miles north of California Hot Springs (lat. 35°59'55" N, long. 118°39'55" W). Named on California Hot Springs (1958) 15' quadrangle.

(3) *stream,* flows 2 miles to East Fork Kaweah River 6 miles west of Mineral King (lat. 36°26'15" N, long. 118°41'50" W). Named on Mineral King (1956) 15' quadrangle.

Redwood Meadow [TULARE]:

(1) *area,* 7.25 miles southwest of Triple Divide Peak (lat. 36°30'50" N, long. 118°38'05" W). Named on Triple Divide Peak (1956) 15' quadrangle. William B. Wallace and his companions named the place in 1887 (United States Board on Geographic Names, 1933a, p. 638).

(2) *area,* 8 miles north-northeast of California Hot Springs (lat. 35° 58'30" N, long. 118°35'40" W; sec. 35, T 22 S, R 31 E). Named on California Hot Springs (1958) 15' quadrangle.

Redwood Mountain [TULARE]: *ridge,* south-trending, 5 miles long, 5.25 miles south-southeast of Wilsonia (lat. 36°40' N, long. 118° 55' W); the ridge is west of Redwood Canyon and Redwood Creek (1). Named on Giant Forest (1956) 15' quadrangle.

Redwood Saddle [TULARE]: *pass,* 2.5 miles southeast of Wilsonia (lat. 36°42'25" N, long. 118°55'15" W; sec. 15, T 14 S, R 28 E). Named on Giant Forest (1956) 15' quadrangle.

Reed Canyon [KERN]: *canyon,* drained by a stream that flows 3.5 miles to Sacramento Canyon 5 miles north-northeast of downtown Bakersfield (lat. 35°26'35" N, long. 118°58'45" W; near S line sec. 32, T 28 S, R 28 E). Named on Oil Center (1954) 7.5' quadrangle.

Reed Canyon: see **Tecuya Creek** [KERN].

Reedley [FRESNO]: *town,* 22 miles east-southeast of Fresno (lat. 36° 35'45" N, long. 119°27' W). Named on Reedley (1966) 7.5' quadrangle. Postal authorities established Reedley post office in 1888 and named to honor Thomas L. Reed, landowner at the place; the suffix was added because Reed objected to use of his name (Salley, p. 183). The town incorporated in 1913. California Mining Bureau's (1917a) map shows a place called Darwin located along the railroad north of Reedley and south of the rail crossing of Wahtoke Creek. The same map shows a locality called Vino situated north of Reedley just north of the rail crossing of Wahtoke Creek. A place called Pool's Ferry was settled as early as 1850 or 1851 along Kings River 2.25 miles north-northwest of present Reedley (Hoover, Rensch, and Rensch, p. 91). A map of 1863 shows Pool's Fort near the confluence of Kings River and Wahtoke Creek, at or near the site of Pool's Ferry (Whiting and Whiting, p. 63). Smith's Ferry superseded Pool's Ferry; James Smith started it in 1855 near the southwest edge of present Reedley, and it lasted until 1874 (Hoover, Rensch, and Rensch, p. 91-92). Postal authorities established Smith's Ferry post office 7 miles northeast of Sanger in 1865, changed the name to King's River in 1866, changed it to Kingriver in 1895, and discontinued it in 1905; they had established an earlier King's River post office 7 miles northeast of Sanger in 1856 and discontinued it in 1859 (Salley, p. 112, 206). Postal authorities established Carmelita post office 8.5 miles north of Reedley in 1899 and discontinued it in 1900 (Salley, p. 38).

Reedwater Canyon [FRESNO]: *canyon,* drained by a stream that flows 3 miles to Zapato Chino Canyon 4.25 miles north-northwest of Castle Mountain (lat. 35°59'55" N, long. 120°21'45" W; sec. 21, T 22 S, R 15 E). Named on The Dark Hole (1961) 7.5' quadrangle.

Reefer City [KERN]: *locality,* 3.25 miles south-southwest of Mojave (lat. 35°00'25" N, long. 118°11' W; near NW cor. sec. 32, T 11 N, R 12 W). Named on Mohave (1947) 7.5' quadrangle.

Reef Lake [FRESNO]: *lake,* 600 feet long, 16 miles northeast of Kaiser Peak (lat. 37°29' N, long. 119°01'10" W). Named on Kaiser Peak (1953) 15' quadrangle.

Reef Ridge [FRESNO-KINGS]: *ridge,* generally northwest-trending, 18 miles long, on Fresno-Kings County line northwest of Sulphur Spring Canyon [KINGS] (2). Named on Garza Peak (1953), Kettleman Plain (1953), Pyramid Hills (1953), and The Dark Hole (1961) 7.5' quadrangles. Arnold and Anderson (1908, p. 14) noted that the ridge "is formed by the prominent lower Miocene fossiliferous strata termed 'Reef beds,' which dip at a high angle and, owing to their resistance to erosion, rise high above the softer sand hills on the northeast."

Reef Station [KINGS]: *locality,* 8 miles south-southeast of Avenal in Kettleman Plain (lat. 35°54'05" N, long. 120°03'15" W; sec. 29, T 23 S, R 18 E); the place is 2.5 miles east-northeast of Reef Ridge. Named on Kettleman Plain (1953) 7.5' quadrangle.

Reese Canyon [FRESNO]: *canyon,* drained by a stream that flows 1.5 miles to Oak Flat nearly 5 miles northeast of Castle Mountain (lat. 35°58'50" N, long. 120°16'20" W; near SE cor. sec. 30, T 22 S, R 16 E). Named on The Dark Hole (1961) 7.5' quadrangle.

Reese Creek [FRESNO]: *stream,* flows 2 miles to Dinkey Creek (1) 2.5 miles south-southwest of Dinkey Dome (lat. 37°05'05" N, long. 119°09'15" W; sec. 5, T 10 S, R 26 E). Named on Huntington Lake (1953) 15' quadrangle.

Reflection: see **Lake Reflection** [TULARE].

Reinstein: see **Mount Reinstein** [FRESNO].

Reka [FRESNO]: *locality,* 1 mile south-southeast of Sanger along Southern Pacific Railroad (lat. 36°41'20" N, long. 119°33'05" W; sec. 26, T 14 S, R 22 E). Named on Sanger (1923) 7.5' quadrangle.

Remnoy [KINGS]: *locality,* 5 miles east of Hanford along Southern Pacific Railroad (lat. 36°20'20" N, long. 119°33'15" W; sec. 26, T 18 S, R 22 E). Named on Remnoy (1954) 7.5' quadrangle.

Reservoir: see **Fram** [KERN].

Reward [KERN]: *locality,* 3.5 miles west-northwest of McKittrick (lat. 35°19'15" N, long. 119°40'30" W; near NW cor. sec. 13, T 30 S, R 21 E). Named on Reward (1951) 7.5' quadrangle. Postal authorities established Reward post office in 1909 and discontinued it in 1937 (Frickstad, p. 58). The small oil-field community began in 1907 (Bailey, 1967, p. 22).

Reynolds [TULARE]: *locality,* nearly 2 miles north-northeast of Lindsay along Visalia Electric Railroad (lat. 36°13'40" N, long. 119°04'20" W; sec. 32, T 19 S, R 27 E). Named on Lindsay (1928) 7.5' quadrangle.

Rhoda Lake: see **Charlotte Lake** [FRESNO].

Rhymes Campground [KERN]: *locality,* 3 miles south-southwest of Alta Sierra (lat. 35°41'10" N, long. 118°34'25" W; sec. 7, T 26 S, R 32 E). Named on Alta Sierra (1972) 7.5' quadrangle.

Rhymes Flat [KERN]: *area,* 6 miles north-northeast of Caliente (lat. 35°21'45" N, long. 118°33'50" W; near E line sec. 32, T 29 S, R 32 E). Named on Oiler Peak (1972) 7.5' quadrangle.

Rhymes Spring [KERN]: *spring,* 6 miles north-northeast of Caliente (lat. 35°21'45" N, long. 118°34' W; sec. 32, T 29 S, R 32 E); the spring is at Rhymes Flat. Named on Oiler Peak (1972) 7.5' quadrangle.

Ribier [KERN]: *locality,* 11 miles southeast of Bakersfield along the railroad (lat. 35°15'10" N, long. 118°52'45" W; at SE cor. sec. 5, T 31 S, R 29 E). Named on Lamont (1954) 7.5' quadrangle.

Ricardo [KERN]: *locality,* nearly 5 miles north-northwest of Cantil in Red Rock Canyon (lat. 35°22'30" N, long. 117°59'20" W; near N line sec. 34, T 29 S, R 37 E). Site named on Cantil (1967) 7.5' quadrangle. Postal authorities established Ricardo post office in 1898, discontinued it in 1907, reestablished it in 1908, discontinued it in 1912, reestablished it in 1913, and discontinued it in 1917 (Frickstad, p. 58). Rudolf Hagen operated a station that he named Ricardo for his son, Richard; the station occupied two sites (Bailey, 1967, p. 23). Postal authorities established Craft post office 7 miles south of Ricardo in 1909 and discontinued it in 1911 (Salley, p. 52).

Rich [KERN]: *locality,* nearly 5 miles west-southwest of Boron along the railroad (lat. 34°58'35" N, long. 117°43'35" W; sec. 9, T 10 N, R 8 W). Named on Leuhman Ridge (1973) 7.5' quadrangle.

Richgrove [TULARE]: *town,* 7.5 miles south-southwest of Ducor (lat. 35°47'50" N, long. 119°06'25" W; on E line sec. 36, T 24 S, R 26 E). Named on Richgrove (1952) 7.5' quadrangle. Officers of Richgrove Land and Development Company named the town in 1909; the place also was known as Wildflower, for Wildflower school district (Mitchell, A.R., p. 69). Postal authorities established Richgrove post office in 1911 (Frickstad, p. 213). California Mining Bureau's (1917b) map has the form "Rich Grove" for the name.

Ridenhour Creek [TULARE]: *stream,* flows about 3 miles to Dry Creek (1) 5.5 miles northeast of Woodlake (lat. 36°28' N, long. 119°01'30" W; sec. 11, R 17 S, E 27 E). Named on Auckland (1966) and Woodlake (1952) 7.5' quadrangles.

Ridgecrest [KERN]: *town,* 48 miles north-northeast of Mojave at the edge of China Lake Naval Weapons Center (lat. 35°37'25" N, long. 117°40'15" W). Named on Ridgecrest North (1973) and Ridgecrest South (1973) 7.5' quadrangles. Postal authorities established Ridgecrest post office in 1941 (Frickstad, p. 58), and the town incorporated in 1963. The community began in 1912, when it was called Crumville for Robert Crum and James Crum, who ran a dairy (Bailey, 1967, p. 23).

Rifle Creek [TULARE]: *stream,* flows 3 miles to Little Kern River 10 miles south-southeast of Mineral King (lat. 36°19'20" N, long. 118°31'40" W); the stream is near Pistol Creek and Shotgun Creek. Named on Mineral King (1956) 15' quadrangle.

Right Angle Canyon [FRESNO]: *canyon,* drained by a stream that flows 4 miles to Panoche Creek 21 miles southwest of Firebaugh (lat. 36°36'35" N, long. 120°40'55" W; sec. 20, T 15 S, R 12 E). Named on Chounet Ranch (1956) 7.5' quadrangle.

Right Stringer [TULARE]: *stream,* flows 2.5 miles to Left Stringer 4 miles north-northwest of Kern Peak (lat. 36°21'25" N, long. 118° 19'35" W). Named on Kern Peak (1956) 15' quadrangle.

Rinaldis Well [KERN]: *well,* 9 miles north-northwest of Randsburg (lat.

35°29'30" N, long. 117°42'20" W; sec. 19, T 28 S, R 40 E). Named on El Paso Peaks (1967) 7.5' quadrangle.

Rincon [TULARE]: *area,* east of Kern River between Fairview and The Needles (center near lat. 36°02'30" N, long. 118°27' W). Named on Hockett Peak (1956) and Kernville (1956) 15' quadrangles.

Rio Bravo [KERN]: *locality,* 7.25 miles south of Shafter along Southern Pacific Railroad (lat. 35°23'50" N, long. 119°17'25" W; near NE cor. sec. 21, T 29 S, R 25 E). Named on Rio Bravo (1954) 7.5' quadrangle. Postal authorities established Rio Bravo post office in 1912 and discontinued it in 1919 (Frickstad, p. 58).

Rio Bravo: see **Kern River** [KERN-TULARE]; **Panama** [KERN].

Rio de San Felipe: see **Kern River** [KERN-TULARE].

Rio San Joaquin: see **San Joaquin River** [FRESNO].

Rio Tulare: see **San Joaquin River** [FRESNO].

Riverbend [FRESNO]: *locality,* 11.5 miles east-southeast of Clovis along Atchison, Topeka and Santa Fe Railroad (lat. 36°45'25" N, long. 119°30'40" W; sec. 31, T 13 S, R 23 E). Named on Round Mountain (1964) 7.5' quadrangle.

Riverdale [FRESNO]: *town,* 23 miles south of Fresno (lat. 36°25'55" N, long. 119°51'30" W; sec. 24, 25, T 17 S, R 19 E). Named on Riverdale (1954) 7.5' quadrangle. Postal authorities established Riverdale post office in 1875 (Frickstad, p. 37). The place first was called Liberty Settlement; the newer name is for the proximity of Kings River to the town (Gudde, 1949, p. 287).

River Hill [TULARE]: *peak,* 5.5 miles east of Kaweah (lat. 36°27'45" N, long. 118°49'10" W; sec. 10, T 17 S, R 29 E). Altitude 2767 feet. Named on Kaweah (1957) 15' quadrangle.

River Spring [TULARE]: *spring,* 4 miles south of Kern Peak (lat. 36°15'15" N, long. 118°16'40" W). Named on Kern Peak (1956) 15' quadrangle.

River Valley [TULARE]: *canyon,* 2.5 miles long, 5.5 miles west-southwest of Triple Divide Peak along Middle Fork Kaweah River (lat. 36°33'30" N, long. 118°37' W). Named on Triple Divide Peak (1956) 15' quadrangle.

Riverview: see **Bakersfield** [KERN].

Rixford: see **Mount Rixford** [FRESNO].

Roach Canyon [FRESNO]: *canyon,* drained by a stream that flows 3.5 miles to Los Gatos Creek 16 miles west-northwest of Coalinga (lat. 36°15'15" N, long. 120°36'55" W; near NW cor. sec. 30, T 19 S, R 13 E). Named on San Benito Mountain (1969) and Santa Rita Peak (1969) 7.5' quadrangles.

Roads End: see **Fairview** [TULARE].

Road Well [KERN]: *well,* 5.25 miles south-southwest of Pinyon Mountain in Kelso Valley (lat. 35°23'30" N, long. 118°11'50" W; near NW cor. sec. 26, T 29 S, R 35 E). Named on Pinyon Mountain (1972) 7.5' quadrangle.

Roaring River [FRESNO-TULARE]: *stream,* heads in Tulare County and flows 16 miles to South Fork Kings River 13 miles south-southwest of Marion Peak in Fresno County (lat. 36°47'05" N, long. 118°37'30" W). Named on Marion Peak (1953) and Triple Divide Peak (1956) 15' quadrangles. Frank M. Lewis named the stream in the 1870's (Browning, p. 184).

Roaring River Falls [FRESNO]: *waterfall,* 13 miles south-southwest of Marion Peak (lat. 36°46'50" N, long. 118°37'15" W); the feature is along Roaring River. Named on Marion Peak (1953) 15' quadrangle.

Robbers Canyon [FRESNO]: *canyon,* drained by a stream that flows nearly 2 miles to Bear Canyon 6.5 miles north-northwest of Coalinga Mineral Springs (lat. 36°13'25" N, long. 120°36'50" W; sec. 6, T 20 S, R 13 E). Named on Sherman Peak (1969) 7.5' quadrangle.

Robbers Roost [KERN]: *relief feature,* 8.5 miles west-southwest of Inyokern (lat. 35°35'30" N, long. 117°56'55" W; near N line sec. 13, T 27 S, R 37 E). Named on Freeman Junction (1972) 7.5' quadrangle. Outlaws hid at the place, which also was called Bandit Rocks (Wines, p. 36).

Roberts: see **Bob Rabbit Place**, under **Bob Rabbit Canyon** [KERN].

Robinson [KINGS]: *locality,* 8 miles north-northwest of Lemoore along Southern Pacific Railroad (lat. 36°24'05" N, long. 119°50'35" W). Named on Riverdale (1927) 7.5' quadrangle. California Division of Highways' (1934) map shows a lake called Summit Lake located 5.25 miles west-southwest of Robinson (NW quarter sec. 17, T 18 S, R 19 E).

Robinson Bay [KERN]: *embayment,* 4 miles east-southeast of Wofford Heights along Isabella Lake (lat. 35°40'25" N, long. 118°23'35" W; near NW cor. sec. 13, T 26 S, R 33 E); the embayment is east of Robinson Point. Named on Lake Isabella North (1972) 7.5' quadrangle.

Robinson Point [KERN]: *promontory,* nearly 4 miles southeast of Wofford Heights along Isabella Lake (lat. 35°40'25" N, long. 118° 24' W; on S line sec. 11, T 26 S, R 33 E). Named on Lake Isabella North (1972) 7.5' quadrangle.

Robla: see **Tulare** [TULARE].

Rock Corral Spring [KERN]: *spring,* 2.5 miles south-southeast of Glennville (lat. 35°41'50" N, long. 118°40'45" W; sec. 6, T 26 S, R 31 E). Named on Glennville (1972) 7.5' quadrangle.

Rock Creek [FRESNO]:

(1) *stream,* flows 5.5 miles to Four Forks Creek 8 miles north-northeast of Kaiser Peak (lat. 37°24'10" N, long. 119°07'20" W). Named on Kaiser Peak (1953) 15' quadrangle.

(2) *stream,* flows 5 miles to Dinkey Creek (1) 2.25 miles southwest of Dinkey Dome at the village of Dinkey Creek (lat. 37°05'15" N, long. 119°09'20" W; sec. 5, T 10 S, R 26 E). Named on Huntington Lake (1953) 15' quadrangle.

Rock Creek [TULARE]: *stream,* flows 12 miles to Kern River 13 miles north-northwest of Kern Peak (lat. 36°28'45" N, long. 118° 24'20" W). Named on Kern Peak (1956) and Mount Whitney (1956) 15' quadrangles. Present Siberian Pass Creek was called South Fork Rock Creek (Browning, p. 198).

Rock Creek Lake [FRESNO]: *lake,* 800 feet long, 13 miles north-northeast of Kaiser Peak (lat. 37°28'10" N, long. 119°04'50" W); the lake is near the head of Rock Creek (1). Named on Kaiser Peak (1953) 15' quadrangle.

Rock Haven [FRESNO]: *settlement,* 1.5 miles north of Shaver Lake Heights (present town of Shaver Lake) (lat. 37°07'40" N, long. 119°19' W; sec. 23, 26, T 9 S, R 24 E). Named on Shaver Lake (1953) 15' quadrangle.

Rockhouse Basin [TULARE]: *valley,* 12.5 miles northwest of Lamont Peak along South Fork Kern River (lat. 35°56'30" N, long. 118°09'45" W). Named on Lamont Peak (1956) 15' quadrangle.

Rockhouse Meadow [TULARE]: *area,* 11 miles northwest of Lamont Peak along South Fork Kern River (lat. 35°53'30" N, long. 118°11'15" W; on S line sec. 27, T 23 S, R 35 E). Named on Lamont Peak (1956) 15' quadrangle. Olmsted's (1900) map has the form "Rock House Meadows" for the name.

Rock Lake [FRESNO]: *lake,* 900 feet long, 5 miles east-northeast of Dinkey Dome (lat. 37°09'10" N, long. 119°03'05" W; sec. 17, T 9 S, R 27 E). Named on Huntington Lake (1953) 15' quadrangle.

Rock Meadow [FRESNO]: *area,* 7 miles northeast of Dinkey Dome (lat. 37°11'45" N, long. 119°03'35" W). Named on Huntington Lake (1953) 15' quadrangle. Called Long Meadow on Kaiser (1904) 30' quadrangle, which has the name "Rock Meadow" for a place situated 2 miles farther east.

Rock Mountain [FRESNO]: *peak,* 4.5 miles north of Prather (lat. 37° 06'15" N, long. 119°31'05" W; sec. 36, T 9 S, R 22 E). Altitude 2869 feet. Named on Millerton Lake East (1965) 7.5' quadrangle.

Rock Pile [KERN]: *hill,* 8.5 miles southeast of Edison (lat. 35°15'40" N, long. 118°45'25" W; sec. 4, T 31 S, R 30 E). Named on Edison (1931) 7.5' quadrangle.

Rockslide Lake [TULARE]: *lake,* 900 feet long, 8.5 miles west of Mount Whitney along Kern-Kaweah River (lat. 36°34'35" N, long. 118°26'30" W). Named on Mount Whitney (1956) 15' quadrangle.

Rock Spring [FRESNO]: *spring,* 8.5 miles east-northeast of Clovis (lat. 36°51' N, long. 119°33' W; near NE cor. sec. 34, T 12 S, R 22 E). Named on Round Mountain (1964) 7.5' quadrangle.

Rock Spring [KERN]:

(1) *spring,* 5 miles north-northeast of Glennville (lat. 35°47'10" N, long. 118°39'15" W; sec. 4, T 25 S, R 31 E). Named on California Hot Springs (1958) 15' quadrangle.

(2) *spring,* 0.5 mile south-southeast of Mount Adelaide (lat. 35° 25'20" N, long. 118°44'25" W; sec. 10, T 29 S, R 30 E). Named on Mount Adelaide (1972) 7.5' quadrangle. Caliente (1914) 30' quadrangle shows a locality called Rock Springs at the site.

(3) *spring,* 3 miles south-southwest of Loraine (lat. 35°15'45" N, long. 118°27'15" W; sec. 5, T 31 S, R 33 E). Named on Loraine (1972) 7.5' quadrangle.

Rock Spring [TULARE]: *spring,* 3.5 miles southeast of Auckland (lat. 36°33' N, long. 119°03'55" W; sec. 8, T 16 S, R 17 E). Named on Auckland (1966) 7.5' quadrangle.

Rock Springs: see **Rock Spring** [KERN] (2).

Rockwell Pond [FRESNO]: *lake,* 1.25 miles long, 2.25 miles west-northwest of Selma (lat. 36°34'50" N, long. 119°38'45" W; sec. 35, 36, T 15 S, R 21 E). Named on Selma (1946) 15' quadrangle. On Conejo (1963) 7.5' quadrangle, the name applies to a dry depression.

Rocky Basin Lakes [TULARE]: *lakes,* largest 1900 feet long, 10 miles north of Kern Peak (lat. 36°26'45" N, long. 118°19'15" W). Named on Kern Peak (1956) 15' quadrangle.

Rocky Creek [TULARE]: *stream,* flows 6.5 miles to South Fork Tule River 7.25 miles south-southeast of Springville (lat. 36°02'15" N, long. 118°45'20" W). Named on Camp Nelson (1956) and Springville (1957) 15' quadrangles.

Rocky Gulch [KERN]: *canyon,* drained by a stream that flows 2.5 miles to French Gulch (1) 5 miles southeast of Alta Sierra (lat. 35° 40'15" N, long. 118°30' W; near NW cor. sec. 13, T 26 S, R 32 E). Named on Alta Sierra (1972) 7.5' quadrangle.

Rocky Hill [TULARE]:

(1) *ridge,* west-trending, 2 miles long, 3 miles east-northeast of Porterville (lat. 36°05'10" N, long. 118°57'30" W). Named on Success Dam (1956) 7.5' quadrangle.

(2) *peak,* 3 miles east of Exeter (lat. 36°17'15" N, long. 119°05'05" W; sec. 7, T 19 S, R 27 E). Altitude 1580 feet. Named on Rocky Hill (1951) 7.5' quadrangle.

(3) *locality,* 1.25 miles east-northeast of Exeter along Visalia Electric Rail-

road (lat. 36°18'05" N, long. 119°07'05" W; near E line sec. 2, T 19 S, R 26 E); the place is 2 miles west-northwest of Rocky Hill (2). Named on Rocky Hill (1951) 7.5' quadrangle.

Rocky Hills [TULARE]: *range,* 10 miles north of Porterville (lat. 36° 12'30" N, long. 119°00' W). Named on Lindsay (1951) and Frazier Valley (1957) 7.5' quadrangles.

Rocky Point [KERN]:

(1) *promontory,* 2.5 miles south-southeast of Wofford Heights along Isabella Lake (lat. 35°40'25" N, long. 118°26'35" W; on S line sec. 9, T 26 S, R 33 E). Named on Lake Isabella North (1972) 7.5' quadrangle.

(2) *relief feature,* 4.5 miles southeast of Bodfish (lat. 35°32'05" N, long. 118°26'30" W; sec. 33, T 27 S, R 33 E). Named on Lake Isabella South (1972) 7.5' quadrangle.

(3) *peak,* 6.25 miles west of Skinner Peak (lat. 35°34'30" N, long. 118°14'20" W; at SE cor. sec. 17, T 27 S, R 35 E). Named on Cane Canyon (1972) 7.5' quadrangle.

Rocky Point Bay [KERN]: *embayment,* 2.5 miles southeast of Wofford Heights on the north side of Isabella Lake (lat. 35°40'45" N, long. 118°25'40" W; sec. 9, 10, T 26 S, R 33 E); the embayment is east of Rocky Point (1). Named on Lake Isabella North (1972) 7.5' quadrangle.

Rod: see **Muroc** [KERN].

Rodecker Flat [KERN]: *area,* 1.5 miles northwest of Inyokern in South Fork Sand Canyon (2) (lat. 35°46'05" N, long. 117°57'30" W). Named on Little Lake (1954) 15' quadrangle.

Rodeo Canyon [KERN]: *canyon,* drained by a stream that flows 2.5 miles to Caliente Creek 2.5 miles west of Caliente (lat. 35°17'45" N, long. 118°40'10" W). Named on Bena (1972) 7.5' quadrangle.

Rodeo Flat: see **Fish Creek Meadow** [TULARE].

Rodeo Ridge [KERN]: *ridge,* south-trending, 1.5 miles long, 3.25 miles northwest of Loraine (lat. 35°20' N, long. 118°29' W). Named on Loraine (1972) 7.5' quadrangle.

Rodeo Spring [KERN]: *spring,* 3 miles west of Caliente (lat. 35°17'10" N, long. 118°40'40" W); the spring is in Rodeo Canyon. Named on Bena (1972) 7.5' quadrangle.

Rodgers Creek [FRESNO]: see **Rogers Creek** [FRESNO].

Rodgers Crossing [FRESNO]: *locality,* 3 miles south of Balch Camp along Kings River (lat. 36°51'45" N, long. 119°07'20" W; sec. 27, T 12 S, R 26 E); the place is near the east end of Rodgers Ridge. Named on Patterson Mountain (1952) 15' quadrangle.

Rodgers Ridge [FRESNO]: *ridge,* west-trending, 14 miles long, 7 miles east of Balch Camp (lat. 36°54' N, long. 119°00' W). Named on Patterson Mountain (1952) and Tehipite Dome (1952) 15' quadrangles.

Rodrigues Lake: see **Rogers Lake** [KERN].

Rodriguez: see **Muroc** [KERN].

Rogers: see **Coalinga Mineral Springs** [FRESNO]; **Muroc** [KERN].

Rogers Camp [TULARE]: *locality,* 2.5 miles southwest of Camp Nelson (lat. 36°06'30" N, long. 118°38'10" W; near N line sec. 9, T 21 S, R 31 E). Named on Camp Nelson (1956) 15' quadrangle.

Rogers Creek [FRESNO]: *stream,* flows 5.5 miles to Crown Creek 12 miles north-northeast of Hume (lat. 36°55'50" N, long. 118°48'30" W); the stream heads near the east end of Rodgers Ridge. Named on Tehipite Dome (1952) 15' quadrangle. United States Board on Geographic Names (1987b, p. 2) approved the name "Rodgers Creek" for the stream, and noted that the name commemorates John Rodgers, an early stockman in the neighborhood.

Rogers Lake [KERN]: *dry lake,* 21 miles east-southeast of Mojave (lat. 34°54'30" N, long. 117°49'30" W). Named on Edwards (1973), Redman (1973), Rogers Lake North (1973), and Rogers Lake South (1973) 7.5' quadrangles. The feature also was known as Muroc Dry Lake and as Rodrigues Lake (Hoover, Rensch, and Rensch, p. 134).

Rogersville: see **Big Blue Mill** [KERN].

Rolinda [FRESNO]: *settlement,* 10 miles west of downtown Fresno (lat. 36°44'05" N, long. 119°57'40" W; at S line sec. 1, T 14 S, R 18 E). Named on Kearney Park (1963) 7.5' quadrangle. On Kearney Park (1923) 7.5' quadrangle, the name applies to a place situated 0.5 mile farther north along Southern Pacific Railroad. Postal authorities established Rolinda post office in 1895 and discontinued it in 1902 (Frickstad, p. 37).

Roman Four Lake [FRESNO]: *lake,* 450 feet long, 1.5 miles north of Blackcap Mountain (lat. 37°05'40" N, long. 118°47'45" W). Named on Blackcap Mountain (1953) 15' quadrangle. William A. Dill of California Department of Fish and Game named the lake in 1948 because he thought that its outline on a map resembles the Roman numeral "IV" (Browning, p. 187).

Roof Spring [KINGS]: *spring,* 6.5 miles south of Avenal (lat. 35°54'45" N, long. 120°08'40" W; sec. 21, T 23 S, R 17 E). Named on Garza Peak (1953) 7.5' quadrangle.

Root Island: see **Alpaugh** [TULARE].

Rootville: see **Old Millerton** [FRESNO].

Rosamond [KERN]: *town,* 13 miles south of Mohave (lat. 34°51'40" N, long. 118°09'45" W; in and near sec. 21, T 9 N, R 12 W). Named on Rosamond (1973) 7.5' quadrangle. Postal authorities established Rosamond post office in 1885, discontinued it in 1887, and reestablished it in 1888 (Frickstad, p. 58). Officials of Southern Pacific Railroad founded the town in 1876 and named it for the daughter of a railroad official (Wines, p. 80). Baker's (1911) map shows a place called Monterio located about 20 miles west-northwest of Rosamond. Postal authorities established Monterio post office in 1895 and discontinued it in 1899 (Salley, p. 145). Johnson's (1911) map shows some springs, called Indian Springs, situat ed 2.5 miles east of Rosamond (at SE cor. sec. 14, T 9 N, R 12 W).

Rosamond Dry Lake: see **Rosamond Lake** [KERN].

Rosamond Hills [KERN]: *range,* center 5 miles northeast of Rosamond (lat. 34°55' N, long. 118°06'30" W). Named on Bissell (1973), Edwards (1973), and Soledad Mountain (1973) 7.5' quadrangles.

Rosamond Lake [KERN]: *dry lake,* 6 miles east-southeast of Rosamond on Kern-Los Angeles County line (lat. 34°50' N, long. 118° 04' W). Named on Rosamond Lake (1973) 7.5' quadrangle. Called Rosamond Dry Lake on Rosamond (1943) 15' quadrangle.

Rosebud Lake [FRESNO]: *lake,* 700 feet long, 8 miles southwest of Mount Abbot (lat. 37°18'35" N, long. 118°53'30" W). Named on Mount Abbot (1953) 15' quadrangle.

Rose Crossing [FRESNO]: *locality,* 6 miles north of Balch Camp along Dinkey Creek (1) (lat. 36°59'15" N, long. 119°07'30" W). Named on Patterson Mountain (1952) 15' quadrangle.

Rosedale [KERN]: *town,* 8 miles west of Bakersfield (lat. 35°23' N, long. 119°08'30" W; on S line sec. 24, T 29 S, R 26 E). Named on Rosedale (1954) 7.5' quadrangle. Rosedale post office was established in 1891 and discontinued in 1913 (Frickstad, p. 58). The place preserves the name of a failed colony of English farmers started in 1891 (Bailey, 1967, p. 23-24).

Rosedale: see **Frazier** [TULARE].

Rosedale Station [KERN]: *locality,* 9 miles west-northwest of Bakersfield along Atchison, Topeka and Santa Fe Railroad 1.5 miles north-northwest of Rosedale (lat. 35°24'10" N, long. 119°09'05" W; sec. 14, T 29 S, R 26 E). Named on Rosedale (1954) 7.5' quadrangle.

Rose Lake [FRESNO]: *lake,* 3000 feet long, 8 miles southwest of Mount Abbot (lat. 37°18'30" N, long. 118°53' W). Named on Mount Abbot (1953) 15' quadrangle. R.B. Marshall of United States Geological Survey named the lake for Rosa Hooper, sister of Selden S. Hooper, a Survey assistant (Farquhar, 1925, p. 130).

Rosemarie Meadow [FRESNO]: *area,* 7 miles southwest of Mount Abbot (lat. 37°19'05" N, long. 118°52'20" W); the place is near Rose Lake and Marie Lake. Named on Mount Abbot (1953) 15' quadrangle.

Rosemarr Spring [KERN]: *spring,* 4.25 miles southwest of Cummings Mountain (lat. 35°00'05" N, long. 118°37'35" W; sec. 31, T 11 N, R 16 W). Named on Tejon Ranch (1966) 7.5' quadrangle.

Rose's Station: see **Rose Station** [KERN].

Rose Station [KERN]: *locality,* 2.5 miles north of Grapevine along Grapevine Creek (lat. 34°57'50" N, long. 118°55' W). Site named on Grapevine (1958) 7.5' quadrangle. Called Rose's Store on Wheeler's (1875-1878) map, and called Roses Station on Mendenhall's (1908) map. Postal authorities established Tejon post office in 1875, moved it 6 miles north and changed the name to Rose's Station in 1877, and discontinued it in 1883 (Salley, p. 189, 219). William W. Hudson and James V. Rosemyre had a sheep ranch at the site in the 1870's and opened a stopping place there called Hudson Station; the place was renamed Rose Station after William B. Rose acquired it (Boyd, p. 42).

Ross Creek [FRESNO]:

(1) *stream,* flows 4.5 miles to Dinkey Creek (1) 4 miles north of Balch Camp (lat. 36°57'50" N, long. 119°07'20" W). Named on Patterson Mountain (1952) 15' quadrangle.

(2) *stream,* flows 2 miles to Big Creek (2) 7 miles west-northwest of Balch Camp (lat. 36°55'30" N, long. 119°14'35" W; near E line sec. 33, T 11 S, R 25 E). Named on Patterson Mountain (1952) 15' quadrangle.

Rossi [KERN]: *locality,* nearly 3 miles west of Lemoore along Southern Pacific Railroad (lat. 36°17'45" N, long. 119°49'55" W; near W line sec. 8, T 19 S, R 20 E). Named on Lemoore (1954) 7.5' quadrangle.

Ross Meadow [FRESNO]: *area,* 4.5 miles northeast of Balch Camp (lat. 36°57'10" N, long. 119°04' W; near S line sec. 19, T 11 S, R 27 E); the place is near the head of Ross Creek (1). Named on Patterson Mountain (1952) 15' quadrangle.

Rosy Finch Lake [FRESNO]: *lake,* 1850 feet long, 7.25 miles northwest of Mount Abbot (lat. 37°27'55" N, long. 118°52'15" W). Named on Mount Abbot (1953) 15' quadrangle. William A. Dill of California Department of Fish and Game named the lake in 1943 (Browning, p. 187).

Roth: see **Strathmore** [TULARE].

Roth Spur: see **Strathmore** [TULARE].

Rough and Ready Mountain [KERN]: *peak,* 5.25 miles west-northwest of Miracle Hot Springs (lat. 35°36'40" N, long. 118°36'55" W). Named on Miracle Hot Springs (1972) 7.5' quadrangle.

Rough Creek [FRESNO]: *stream,* flows 4.5 miles to Kings River 5.25 miles north-northwest of Hume (lat. 36°51'30" N, long. 118° 56'40" W); the stream is east of Rough Spur. Named on Tehipite Dome (1952) 15' quadrangle.

Rough Spur [FRESNO]: *ridge,* south-southwest- to south-trending, 4 miles long, 7.5 miles north-northwest of Hume (lat. 36°53'45" N, long. 118°56'15" W). Named on Tehipite Dome (1952) 15' quadrangle.

Round Corral Meadow [FRESNO]: *area,* 8 miles southwest of Blackcap Mountain (lat. 37°00' N, long. 118°54'45" W; sec. 3, T 11 S, R 28 E). Named on Blackcap Mountain (1953) and Tehipite Dome (1952) 15' quadrangles.

Round Meadow [FRESNO]:
(1) *area,* 2 miles east of Kaiser Peak (lat. 37°17'45" N, long. 119° 08'55" W; on S line sec. 20, T 7 S, R 26 E). Named on Kaiser Peak (1953) 15' quadrangle.
(2) *area,* 3.5 miles south-southwest of Kaiser Peak on the north side of Huntington Lake (1) (lat. 37°14'45" N, long. 119°12'30" W; near N line sec. 14, T 8 S, R 25 E). Named on Kaiser (1904) 30' quadrangle.

Round Meadow [TULARE]:
(1) *area,* 6.5 miles south of Camp Nelson (lat. 36°02'40" N, long. 118°35'45" W; sec. 2, T 22 S, R 31 E). Named on Camp Nelson (1956) 15' quadrangle.
(2) *area,* 8 miles east-northeast of Fairview (lat. 35°57'55" N, long. 118°21'30" W; sec. 36, T 22 S, R 33 E). Named on Kernville (1956) 15' quadrangle.
(3) *area,* 5.25 miles west of Hockett Peak (lat. 36°13'10" N, long. 118°28'35" W). Named on Hockett Peak (1956) 15' quadrangle.
(4) *area,* 5.5 miles east of Yucca Mountain (lat. 36°34'05" N, long. 118°46' W; sec. 6, T 16 S, R 30 E). Named on Giant Forest (1956) 15' quadrangle.

Round Mountain [FRESNO]:
(1) *hill,* 11 miles east of Clovis (lat. 36°49'10" N, long. 119°30'35" W; sec. 7, T 13 S, R 23 E). Altitude 869 feet. Named on Round Mountain (1964) 7.5' quadrangle.
(2) *peak,* 6.5 miles north of Charley Mountain on Fresno-Monterey County line (lat. 36°14'10" N, long. 120°39'55" W; sec. 34, T 19 S, R 12 E). Named on Priest Valley (1969) 7.5' quadrangle.

Round Mountain [KERN]:
(1) *peak,* 5 miles south-southeast of Woody (lat. 35°37'55" N, long. 118°48'40" W; near S line sec. 25, T 26 S, R 29 E). Altitude 2961 feet. Named on Woody (1965) 7.5' quadrangle.
(2) *peak,* 10 miles northeast of Bakersfield (lat. 35°29'10" N, long. 118°53'20" W; near SE cor. sec. 18, T 28 S, R 29 E). Named on Oil Center (1954) 7.5' quadrangle. A ridge known as Sharktooth Hill is located 2.5 miles southwest of the peak; rocks exposed there contain fossils of Miocene marine vertebrates, including the teeth of sharks (Mitchell, Edward, p. III, 11).

Round Mountain [TULARE]: *peak,* 7 miles east of Monache Mountain on Tulare-Inyo County line (lat. 36°11'25" N, long. 118° 04'25" W). Altitude 9884 feet. Named on Monache Mountain (1956) 15' quadrangle.

Round Mountain Stringer [TULARE]: *stream,* flows 2.5 miles to South Fork Kern River 1.25 miles east-southeast of Monache Mountain (lat. 36°12'05" N, long. 118°10'25" W; sec. 10, T 20 S, R 35 E). Named on Monache Mountain (1956) 15' quadrangle.

Roundtop [KINGS]: *peak,* nearly 6 miles southwest of Avenal on Reef Ridge (lat. 35°56'20" N, long. 120°11'35" W; sec. 12, T 23 S, R 16 E). Named on Garza Peak (1953) 7.5' quadrangle.

Round Valley [TULARE]: *valley,* 3.5 miles east-northeast of Lindsay (lat. 36°13'05" N, long. 119°01'20" W). Named on Lindsay (1951) 7.5' quadrangle.

Rowell Meadow [TULARE]: *area,* 14 miles northwest of Triple Divide Peak (lat. 36°43' N, long. 118°44'15" W; near SE cor. sec. 8, T 14 S, R 30 E). Named on Triple Divide Peak (1956) 15' quadrangle. The name commemorates Chester Rowell and George Rowell, who ran sheep in the area (Gudde, 1949, p. 291).

Rowen [KERN]: *locality,* 1.5 miles northwest of Keene along the railroad (lat. 35°14'25" N, long. 118°34'35" W; near S line sec. 7, T 31 S, R 32 E). Named on Keene (1966) 7.5' quadrangle. Postal authorities established Rowen post office in 1906 and discontinued it in 1908 (Frickstad, p. 59).

Roy [KINGS]: *locality,* 8 miles north-northwest of Lemoore along Atchison, Topeka and Santa Fe Railroad (lat. 36°23'50" N, long. 119°51' W; at E line sec. 1, T 18 S, R 19 E). Named on Riverdale (1954) 7.5' quadrangle.

Royal Allen Lake: see **Little Kern Lake** [TULARE].

Royce Lakes [FRESNO]: *lakes,* largest 2400 feet long, 4.5 miles south-southeast of Mount Abbot (lat. 37°19'15" N, long. 118°45'45" W); the lakes are north and east of Royce Peak. Named on Mount Abbot (1953) 15' quadrangle.

Royce Peak [FRESNO]: *peak,* 4.5 miles south of Mount Abbot (lat. 37°19'10" N, long. 118°46'10" W). Altitude 13,253 feet. Named on Mount Abbot (1953) 15' quadrangle. United States Board on Geographic Names (1983a, p. 4) rejected the name "Mount Royce" for the feature, and noted that California State Geographic Board proposed the name in 1929 to honor Josiah Royce

Rube Creek [FRESNO]: *stream,* flows 5.5 miles to South Fork San Joaquin River 11 miles north of Kaiser Peak (lat. 37°27'10" N, long. 119°10'30" W); the stream heads near Rube Meadow. Named on Kaiser Peak (1953) 15' quadrangle.

Rube Creek: see **Nigger Rube Creek** [TULARE].

Rube Meadow [FRESNO]: *area,* 14 miles north-northeast of Kaiser Peak (lat. 37°29'20" N, long. 119°07'20" W). Named on Kaiser Peak (1953) 15' quadrangle.

Ruby Creek [FRESNO]: *stream,* flows 2.5 miles to Bear Creek (3) 4 miles southeast of Dinkey Dome in Bear Meadow (2) (lat. 37°04'15" N, long. 119°05'10" W; sec. 12, T 10 S, R 26 E). Named on Huntington Lake (1953) 15' quadrangle.

Rucker Spring [FRESNO]: *spring,* 16 miles northwest of Coalinga (lat. 36°18'45" N, long. 120°32'30" W; near S line sec. 34, T 18 S, R 13 E). Named on Santa Rita Peak (1969) 7.5' quadrangle.

Rugg [FRESNO]: *locality,* 3 miles east-northeast of Kerman along Southern Pacific Railroad (lat. 36°43'55" N, long. 120°00'10" W; near W line sec. 10, T 14 S, R 18 E). Named on Kerman (1922) 7.5' quadrangle.

Ruiz Canyon [FRESNO]: *canyon,* drained by a stream that flows nearly 2 miles to Pete Merrill Canyon 6 miles south-southeast of Coalinga (lat. 36°03'25" N, long. 120°19'55" W; sec. 34, T 21 S, R 15 E). Named on Kreyenhagen Hills (1956) 7.5' quadrangle.

Runnington: see **Actis** [KERN].

Runyon: see **Lucy Runyon Creek** [TULARE].

Runyon Spring [KERN]: *spring,* 2 miles northeast of Glennville (lat. 35°45'05" N, long. 118°40'50" W; sec. 18, T 25 S, R 31 E). Named on California Hot Springs (1958) 15' quadrangle.

Rusconi [FRESNO]: *locality,* 2 miles south of Sanger along Southern Pacific Railroad (lat. 36°40'35" N, long. 119°32'55" W; near N line sec. 35, T 14 S, R 22 E). Named on Selma (1946) 15' quadrangle.

Rush Creek [FRESNO]: *stream,* flows 10.5 miles to Big Creek (2) 8 miles northwest of Balch Camp (lat. 36°58'15" N, long. 119°14' W; sec. 15, T 11 S, R 25 E). Named on Patterson Mountain (1952) and Shaver Lake (1953) 15' quadrangles, and on Trimmer (1965) 7.5' quadrangle.

Ruskin: see **Mount Ruskin** [FRESNO].

Russell: see **Mount Russell** [TULARE].

Russells Camp [FRESNO]: *locality,* 17 miles south of Kaiser Peak (lat. 37°02'45" N, long. 119°07'50" W; sec. 22, T 10 S, R 26 E). Named on Kaiser (1904) 30' quadrangle.

Russian Charley Creek [FRESNO]: *stream,* flows nearly 2 miles to Pine Flat Reservoir 5.25 miles northeast of Tivy Mountain (lat. 36° 51'05" N, long. 119°17'15" W, near N line sec. 31, T 12 S, R 25 E). Named on Pine Flat Dam (1965) 7.5' quadrangle.

Rutan Rock [FRESNO]: *peak,* 10 miles south-southwest of Coalinga (lat. 36°00'40" N, long. 120°25'45" W; sec. 14, T 22 S, R 14 E). Named on Curry Mountain (1969) 7.5' quadrangle.

Ruth Camp Spring [KERN]: *spring,* 11 miles north of Mojave in North Fork Pine Tree Canyon (lat. 35°12'45" N, long. 118°12'25" W; near S line sec. 22, T 31 S, R 35 E). Named on Cache Peak (1973) 7.5' quadrangle.

Ruth Hill [FRESNO]: *peak,* 4 miles west of Dunlap (lat. 36°43'50" N, long. 119°11'30" W; near NW cor. sec. 7, T 14 S, R 26 E). Altitude 2731 feet. Named on Tucker Mountain (1966) 7.5' quadrangle.

—S—

Sacata Creek [FRESNO]: *stream,* flows nearly 3 miles to Kings River 6.5 miles west-southwest of Balch Camp (lat. 36°53' N, long. 119°13'55" W; sec. 15, T 12 S, R 25 E). Named on Patterson Mountain (1952) 15' quadrangle. United States Board on Geographic Names (1978c, p. 5) approved the name "Sacate Creek" for the feature, and rejected the names "Sacata Creek" and "Secata Creek."

Sacatara Creek [KERN]: *stream,* flows 3.5 miles to lowlands nearly 3 miles south-southeast of Liebre Twins (lat. 34°55' N, long. 118° 33'15" W). Named on Liebre Twins (1965) 7.5' quadrangle. The canyon of the stream is called Tierra Seca on Johnson's (1911) map, and it is called Canyon del Secretario on Neenach (1943) 15' quadrangle. United States Board on Geographic Names (1967c, p. 4) rejected the names "Canyon del Secretario" and "Canyon del Sectario" for the feature.

Sacatar Canyon [TULARE]: *canyon,* 3.5 miles long, 12.5 miles north of Lamont Peak (lat. 35°58'30" N, long. 119°02'30" W). Named on Lamont Peak (1956) 15' quadrangle.

Sacata Ridge [FRESNO]: *ridge,* south-southwest- to southwest-trending, 2.5 miles long, 6 miles west of Balch Camp (lat. 36° 54' N, long. 119°13'30" W). Named on Patterson Mountain (1952) 15' quadrangle. United States Board on Geographic Names (1978c, p. 5) approved the name "Sacate Ridge" for the feature, and rejected the forms "Sacata Ridge" and "Secata Ridge."

Sacatar Meadow [TULARE]: *area,* 14 miles north of Lamont Peak (lat. 35°59'30" N, long. 118°04'40" W; in and near sec. 22, T 22 S, R 36 E); the place is at the mouth of Sacatar Canyon. Named on Lamont Peak (1956) 15' quadrangle. *Sacatar* is the Spanish word for a place that bunchgrass called sacaton grows (Browning, p. 190).

Sacate Creek: see **Sacata Creek** [FRESNO].

Sacate Ridge: see **Sacata Ridge** [FRESNO]:

Saco [KERN]: *locality,* 7 miles northwest of Bakersfield along Southern Pacific Railroad (lat. 35°26'40" N, long. 119°05'25" W; sec. 32. T 28 S, R 27 E). Named on Oildale (1954) 7.5' quadrangle. Called Jewetta on Oildale (1935) 7.5' quadrangle. Postal authorities established Jewetta post office in 1893, discontinued it in 1896, reestablished it in 1898, and discontinued it in 1903; the name was for Solomon Jewett and Philo D. Jewett, pioneers at the place (Salley, p. 107).

Sacramento Gulch [KERN]: *canyon,* 1 mile long, opens into the canyon of Kern River 4 miles north-northeast of downtown Bakersfield (lat. 35°25'40" N, long. 118°58'25" W; near S line sec. 4, T 29 S, R 28 E). Named on Oil Center (1954) 7.5' quadrangle.

Sacratone Flat [TULARE]: *area,* 5 miles south of Hockett Peak (lat. 36°09' N, long. 118°22'45" W). Named on Hockett Peak (1956) 15' quadrangle.

Saddle [FRESNO]: *village,* 19 miles south-southwest of Kaiser Peak (lat. 37°03'35" N, long. 119°21'55" W; near W line sec. 16, T 10 S, R 24 E). Named on Kaiser (1904) 30' quadrangle.

Saddle Mountain [FRESNO]: *peak,* 13 miles northeast of Kaiser Peak (lat. 37°26'20" N, long. 119°02'40" W). Altitude 11,192 feet. Named on Kaiser Peak (1953) 15' quadrangle.

Saddle Spring [KERN]:

(1) *spring,* 3.5 miles northwest of Emerald Mountain in Orejano Canyon (1) (lat. 35°17'15" N, long. 118°19'50" W). Named on Emerald Mountain (1972) 7.5' quadrangle.

(2) *spring,* 6.5 miles southeast of Bodfish (lat. 35°31'10" N, long. 118°24'40" W; sec. 2, T 28 S, R 33 E). Named on Lake Isabella South (1972) 7.5' quadrangle.

Sage [KERN]: *locality,* 1 mile north-northwest of downtown Mojave along Southern Pacific Railroad (lat. 35°04' N, long. 118°10'40" W; at S line sec. 5, T 11 N, R 12 W). Named on Mojave (1915) 30' quadrangle.

Sagebrush Gulch [TULARE]: *canyon,* drained by a stream that flows 2 miles to Little Kern River 8 miles northeast of Camp Nelson (lat. 36°13'50" N, long. 118°30'45" W; sec. 33, T 19 S, R 32 E). Named on Camp Nelson (1956) and Hockett Peak (1956) 15' quadrangles.

Sage Canyon [KERN]: *canyon,* drained by a stream that flows 7 miles to lowlands 6.25 miles east of Skinner Peak (lat. 35°33'20" N, long. 118°00'55" W; sec. 29, T 27 S, R 37 E). Named on Freeman Junction (1972) and Horse Canyon (1972) 7.5' quadrangles.

Sageland [KERN]: *locality,* 3.5 miles west-northwest of Pinyon Mountain near Kelso Creek (lat. 35°28'45" N, long. 118°12'45" W; at NE cor. sec. 21, T 28 S, R 35 E). Named on Pinyon Mountain (1972) 7.5' quadrangle. A place called El Dorado Camp started at the site in 1866 and it was renamed Sageland the next year (Boyd, p. 166). California Mining Bureau's (1917c) map shows a place called Sorrell's located about 8 miles south of Sageland.

Saint John Ridge [KERN]: *ridge,* generally west-trending, 2.5 miles long, 4.25 miles east of Claraville (lat. 35°27'15" N, long. 118°15'30" W); Saint John mine is near the east end of the ridge. Named on Claraville (1972) and Pinyon Mountain (1972) 7.5' quadrangles. Several structures were moved south from Sageland to Saint John mine in 1872, and the name "St. Johnville" was proposed for the community at the mine (Boyd, p. 166).

Saint Johns [TULARE]: *settlement,* 2 miles south of Woodlake (lat. 36°23'05" N, long. 119°05'55" W; at SE cor. sec. 1, T 18 S, R 26 E). Named on Woodlake (1952) 7.5' quadrangle.

Saint Johns River [TULARE]: *stream,* diverges from Kaweah River 3.5 miles east-southeast of Woodlake and flows 25 miles to Cross Creek (1) 9.5 miles northwest of Visalia (lat. 36°25'20" N, long. 119°24'50" W). Named on Exeter (1952) and Visalia (1949) 15' quadrangles. Monson (1949, photorevised 1969), Traver (1949, photorevised 1969), Visalia (1949, photorevised 1969), and Woodlake (1952, photorevised 1969) 7.5' quadrangles show the stream in an artificial watercourse. The name commemorates Loomis St. Johns, an early settler in the neighborhood (Hoover, Rensch, and Rensch, p. 561). Freshets of 1861 and 1862 established the stream permanently (Grunsky, p. 12).

Saint Johnville: see **Saint John Ridge** [KERN].

Sales Creek [FRESNO]: *stream,* flows 8.5 miles to Dog Creek 10 miles east-northeast of Clovis (lat. 36°53'25" N, long. 119°32'25" W; sec. 14, T 12 S, R 22 E). Named on Academy (1964) and Humphreys Station (1965) 7.5' quadrangles.

Sallie Keyes Creek: see **Sally Keyes Lakes** [FRESNO]

Sallie Keyes Lakes: see **Sally Keyes Lakes** [FRESNO].

Sally Keyes Creek: see **Sallie Keyes Creek**, under **Sally Keyes Lakes** [FRESNO].

Sally Keyes Lakes [FRESNO]: *lakes,* three, each about 1400 feet long, 9.5 miles south-southwest of Mount Abbot (lat. 37°16'20" N, long. 118°52'30" W). Named on Mount Abbot (1953) 15' quadrangle. United States Board on Geographic Names (1983d, p. 2) approved the name "Sallie Keyes Lakes" for the features, and noted that the name commemorates Sallie Keyes Shipp, whose family members were the principal owners of Blaney Meadows from the 1890's until 1940. The Board at the same time approved the name "Sallie Keyes Creek" for the stream that flows 1.7 miles from Sallie Keyes Lakes to South Fork San Joaquin River at Blaney Meadows (lat. 37°14'26" N, long. 118°53'20" W), and rejected the names "Sally Keyes Creek" and "Senger Creek" for this stream.

Salmon Creek [TULARE]: *stream,* flows 11 miles to Kern River 2.5 miles southeast of Fairview (lat. 35°53'45" N, long. 118°28' W; near N line sec. 31, T 23 S, R 33 E). Named on Kernville (1956) 15' quadrangle.

Salmon Creek Falls [TULARE]: *waterfall,* 3.5 miles east-southeast of Fairview (lat. 35°54'35" N, long. 118°26'05" W); the feature is along Salmon Creek. Named on Kernville (1956) 15' quadrangle. United States Board on Geographic Names (1961b, p. 12) rejected the name "Salmon Falls" for the feature.

Salmon Falls: see **Salmon Creek Falls** [TULARE].

Salt Canyon [FRESNO]:

(1) *canyon,* drained by a stream that heads in Merced County and flows nearly 3 miles in Fresno County to Little Panoche Creek 20 miles west-southwest of Firebaugh (lat. 36°46'50" N, long. 120°48'10" W; near SE cor. sec. 19, T 13 S, R 11 E). Named on Laguna Seca Ranch (1956) 7.5' quadrangle.

(2) *canyon,* drained by a stream that flows 2.5 miles to Los Gatos Creek 6 miles northwest of Coalinga (lat. 36°12' N, long. 120°26'10" W; sec. 10, T 20 S, R 14 E). Named on Alcalde Hills (1969) 7.5' quadrangle.

(3) *canyon,* drained by a stream that flows 2.5 miles to Dogwood Canyon 3.25 miles north-northwest of Smith Mountain (2) (lat. 36° 07'50" N, long. 120°36'45" W; sec. 7, T 21 S, R 13 E). Named on Slack Canyon (1969) and Smith Mountain (1969) 7.5' quadrangles.

Salt Creek [FRESNO]:

(1) *stream,* flows 10.5 miles to lowlands 17 miles north of Coalinga (lat. 36°26'35" N, long. 120°23'30" W; near W line sec. 6, T 18 S, R 15 E). Named on Ciervo Mountain (1969), Joaquin Rocks (1969), Lillis Ranch (1956), Santa Rita Peak (1969), and Tres Picos Farms (1956) 7.5' quadrangles.

(2) *stream,* flows nearly 6 miles to Jacalitos Creek 6 miles south-southwest of Coalinga (lat. 36°02'55" N, long. 120°22'45" W; near E line sec. 31, T 21 S, R 15 E). Named on Curry Mountain (1969) 7.5' quadrangle.

Salt Creek [KERN]:

(1) *stream,* flows 7.25 miles to Temblor Valley 5.5 miles southeast of Carneros Rocks (lat. 35°23'25" N, long. 119°45'55" W; at W line sec. 19, T 29 S, R 21 E). Named on Belridge (1953, photorevised 1973), Carneros Rocks (1959), and McKittrick Summit (1959) 7.5' quadrangles. Called Temblor Creek on Belridge (1953) 7.5' quadrangle, but United States Board on Geographic Names (1968a, p. 7) rejected this name for the stream.

(2) *stream,* flows 10 miles to lowlands 4 miles west-northwest of Grapevine (lat. 34°56'50" N, long. 118°59'20" W; near E line sec. 15, T 10 N, R 20 W). Named on Cuddy Valley (1943), Grapevine (1958), and Pleito Hills (1958) 7.5' quadrangles. United States Board on Geographic Names (1989c, p. 1) rejected the name "Cherry Creek" for the feature. The Board (1982b, p. 2) approved the name "Colorful Creek" for a stream that joins Salt Creek (2) 1 mile south-southwest of the mouth of that creek (lat. 34°56'03" N, long. 118°59'59" W; sec. 22, T 10 N, R 20 W)—the name is from colorful rocks along the stream.

Salt Creek [TULARE]: *stream,* flows 5 miles to Kaweah River 2.5 miles east-southeast of Kaweah (lat. 36°27'35" N, long. 118°52'15" W; near SE cor. sec. 7, T 17 S, R 29 E). Named on Kaweah (1957) 15' quadrangle.

Salt Creek: see **Cherry Creek** [KERN].

Salt Creek Ridge [TULARE]: *ridge,* east-southeast-trending, 4 miles long, 9.5 miles southeast of Kaweah (lat. 36°23'45" N, long. 118° 46'45" W). Named on Kaweah (1957) and Mineral King (1956) 15' quadrangles.

Saltdale [KERN]: *village,* 21 miles south-southwest of Ridgecrest near Koehn Lake (lat. 35°21'35" N, long. 117°53'15" W). Named on Cantil (1967) 7.5' quadrangle. Postal authorities established Saltdale post office in 1916 and discontinued it in 1950 (Frickstad, p. 59). The village began when salt production started at Koehn Lake in 1914 (Bailey, 1967, p. 24).

Salt Lake: see **Koehn Lake** [KERN]; **Proctor Lake** [KERN].

Salt Lick Meadow [TULARE]: *area,* 6.5 miles north-northwest of Kern Peak (lat. 36°23'30" N, long. 118°20'05" W; sec. 6, T 18 S, R 34 E). Named on Kern Peak (1956) 15' quadrangle.

Salt Lick Spring [KERN]: *spring,* 4.5 miles east-southeast of Caliente (lat. 35°15'30" N, long. 118°33'25" W; near E line sec. 5, T 31 S, R 32 E). Named on Oiler Peak (1972) 7.5' quadrangle.

Salt Lick Spring: see **Upper Salt Lick Spring** [KERN].

Salt Wells Valley: see **Indian Wells Valley** [KERN].

Sam Lewis Camp [TULARE]: *locality,* 10.5 miles south-southwest of Monache Mountain (lat. 36°03'35" N, long. 118°14'20" W; near N line sec. 31, T 21 S, R 35 E). Named on Monache Mountain (1956) 15' quadrangle.

Sample Meadows [FRESNO]: *area,* 3.25 miles northeast of Kaiser Peak (lat. 37°20' N, long. 119°09' W; sec. 8, 9, T 7 S, R 26 E). Named on Kaiser Peak (1953) 15' quadrangle. Called Sample Meadow on Kaiser (1904) 30' quadrangle. Browning (p. 191) associated the name with D.C. Sample, an early-day sheepman in the neighborhood.

Sampson Creek [FRESNO]: *stream,* flows 4.5 miles to Mill Flat Creek 7.5

miles south-southeast of Balch Camp (lat. 36°48'50" N, long. 119°03'10" W; near NW cor. sec. 9, T 13 S, R 27 E); the stream goes through Sampson Flat. Named on Patterson Mountain (1952) 15' quadrangle. United States Board on Geographic Names (1967a, p. 10) rejected the form "Samson Creek" for the name.

Sampson Flat [FRESNO]: *area,* 8 miles south-southeast of Balch Camp (lat. 36°47'30" N, long. 119°05' W; on W line sec. 18, T 13 S, R 27 E). Named on Patterson Mountain (1952) 15' quadrangle. United States Board on Geographic Names (1967a, p. 10) rejected the form "Samson Flat" for the name. An Indian called Sampson led a party across the Sierra Nevada in 1858, and later his name was given to Sampson's Flats (Chalfant, p. 124).

Samson Creek: see **Sampson Creek** [FRESNO].

Samson Flat: see **Sampson Flat** [FRESNO].

Sam Spring [KERN]: *spring,* 3 miles northeast of Caliente (lat. 35° 19'10" N, long. 118°35'05" W; sec. 18, T 30 S, R 32 E). Named on Oiler Peak (1972) 7.5' quadrangle.

Sam Spring [TULARE]: *spring,* 12 miles south of Hockett Peak along Durrwood Creek (lat. 36°03' N, long. 118°24' W). Named on Hockett Peak (1956) 15' quadrangle.

Sanborn [KERN]: *locality,* 5.5 miles southeast of Mojave along Atchison, Topeka and Santa Fe Railroad (lat. 35°00' N, long. 118° 06'15" W). Named on Bissell (1973) and Sanborn (1973) 7.5' quadrangles. Called Plano on Elizabeth Lake (1917) and Mojave (1915) 30' quadrangles.

Sanborn Hill [KERN]: *hill,* 5.5 miles southeast of Mojave (lat. 35° 00'30" N, long. 118°06' W; sec 36, T 11 N, R 12 W); the feature is 0.5 mile north of Sanborn. Named on Sanborn (1973) 7.5' quadrangle.

Sandberg Lodge [KERN]: *locality,* 3 miles west of Liebre Twins (lat. 34°57' N, long. 118°37'30" W; at N line sec. 19, T 10 N, R 16 W). Named on Neenach (1943) 15' quadrangle.

Sand Canyon [KERN]:

(1) *canyon,* drained by a stream that flows 4.5 miles to Rag Gulch 5.25 miles west of Woody (lat. 35°43'05" N, long. 118°55'35" W; at S line sec. 26, T 25 S, R 28 E). Named on Sand Canyon (1965) 7.5' quadrangle.

(2) *canyon,* drained by a stream that heads in Inyo County and flows 3.5 miles in Kern County to Indian Wells Valley 10 miles north-northwest of Inyokern (lat. 35°46'40" N, long. 117°53'45" W; sec. 9, T 25 S, R 38 E). Named on Little Lake (1954) 15' quadrangle. South Fork branches southwest 3 miles above the mouth of the main canyon; it is 4 miles long and is named on Little Lake (1954) 15' quadrangle.

(3) *canyon,* drained by a stream that flows 6.5 miles to Caliente Creek 1 mile east-northeast of Loraine (lat. 35°18'35" N, long. 118°25' W; sec. 22, T 30 S, R 33 E). Named on Loraine (1972) 7.5' quadrangle. West Fork branches northwest 1.25 miles north of the mouth of the canyon; it is 4.25 miles long and is named on Loraine (1972) 7.5' quadrangle.

(4) *canyon,* 10.5 miles long, along Cache Creek above a point 8.5 miles east-southeast of Tehachapi (lat. 35°05'45" N, long. 118°18'15" W; near SW cor. sec. 35, T 32 S, R 34 E). Named on Monolith (1966) and Tehachapi NE (1966) 7.5' quadrangles. The name "Sand Canyon" also applies to the canyon of Sand Creek above the confluence of Sand Creek and Cache Creek.

(5) *locality,* 0.5 mile northeast of present Loraine along Caliente Creek (lat. 35°18'25" N, long. 118°25'40" W; at W line sec. 22, T 30 S, R 33 E); the place is below the mouth of Sand Canyon (3). Named on Emerald Mountain (1943) 15' quadrangle.

Sand Creek [FRESNO]: *stream,* flows 2.5 miles to Dry Creek 1.25 miles west-northwest of Humphreys Station (lat. 36°58' N, long. 119°27'55" W; near N line sec. 21, T 11 S, R 23 E). Named on Humphreys Station (1965) 7.5' quadrangle.

Sand Creek [FRESNO-TULARE]: *stream,* heads in Fresno County and flows 12.5 miles to lowlands 6.5 miles east-northeast of Dinuba in Tulare County (lat. 36°35'45" N, long. 119°17'10" W; near W line sec. 29, T 15 S, R 25 E). Named on Orange Cove South (1966), Stokes Mountain (1966), and Tucker Mountain (1966) 7.5' quadrangles.

Sand Creek [KERN]: *stream,* flows 6.25 miles to Cache Creek 8 miles east of Tehachapi (lat. 35°08'55" N, long. 118°18'30" W; near E line sec. 15, T 32 S, R 34 E); the stream drains the upper part of Sand Canyon (4). Named on Tehachapi NE (1966) 7.5' quadrangle.

Sand Cut: see **Bena** [KERN].

Sanders: see **Kingsburg** [FRESNO].

Sand Flat [KERN-TULARE]: *area,* 4.25 miles north of Glennville along Poso Creek on Kern-Tulare County line (lat. 35°47'20" N, long. 118°42'15" W; on N line sec. 1, T 25 S, R 30 E). Named on California Hot Springs (1958) 15' quadrangle.

Sand Flat [TULARE]: *area,* 5.5 miles east of California Hot Springs (lat. 35°53' N, long. 118°34'30" W; near E line sec. 36, T 23 S, R 31 E). Named on California Hot Springs (1958) 15' quadrangle.

Sand Flat: see **Guyot Flat** [TULARE].

Sand Gulch [KERN]: *canyon,* less than 1 mile long, opens into Goler Gulch 3 miles northeast of Garlock (lat. 35°26'20" N, long. 117°45'10" W). Named on Garlock (1967) 7.5' quadrangle.

Sand Hill Ridge [TULARE]: *ridge,* west- to northwest-trending, 3 miles long, 14 miles south-southwest of Hockett Peak (lat. 36°02'35" N, long. 118°29'50" W). Named on Camp Nelson (1956) and Hockett Peak (1956) 15' quadrangles.

San Diego Creek [KERN]: *stream,* flows 1 mile to San Luis Obispo County 13 miles west-northwest of McKittrick (lat. 35°21'05" N, long. 119°50'30" W; at S line sec. 32, T 29 S, R 20 E). Named on McKittrick Summit (1959) 7.5' quadrangle. On McKittrick (1912) 30' quadrangle, the name has the form "Sandiego Creek." United States Board on Geographic Names (1933a, p. 665) once approved this form for the name, but later the Board (1978d, p. 3) reversed this decision.

Sand Lake [FRESNO]: *lake,* 400 feet long, 16 miles northeast of Kaiser Peak (lat. 37°28'50" N, long. 119°01'05" W). Named on Kaiser Peak (1953) 15' quadrangle.

Sand Meadow: see **Little Sand Meadow** [TULARE].

Sand Meadows [FRESNO]: *area,* 10 miles west of Blackcap Mountain (lat. 37°05'55" N, long. 118°58'15" W; near S line sec. 36, T 9 S, R 27 E). Named on Mount Goddard (1912) 30' quadrangle. Water of Courtright Reservoir now covers the place.

Sand Meadows [TULARE]: *area,* 7 miles south-southwest of Mineral King (lat. 36°21'30" N, long. 118°39'15" W; sec. 18, T 18 S, R 31 E). Named on Mineral King (1956) 15' quadrangle.

Sand Meadows: see **Sandy Meadow** [TULARE].

Sandpiper Lake [FRESNO]: *lake,* 1300 feet long, 6.5 miles southwest of Mount Abbot along South Fork Bear Creek (2) (lat. 37°18'30" N, long. 118°51'05" W). Named on Mount Abbot (1953) 15' quadrangle. Employees of California Department of Fish and Game named the lake in 1942 for sandpipers that nest near South Fork Bear Creek (2) (Browning, p. 191).

Sand Ridge [KINGS]: *ridge,* west-southwest- to west-trending, 12.5 miles long, 20 miles southeast of Kettleman City (lat. 35°50'40" N, long. 119°39' W). Named on Hacienda Ranch (1954), Lone Tree Well (1954), and West Camp (1954) 7.5' quadrangles.

Sand Slough [KINGS]:

(1) *stream,* diverges from North Fork Kings River 7 miles northwest of Lemoore (lat. 36°22'55" N, long. 119°51'45" W; sec. 12, T 18 S, R 19 E) and flows nearly 2 miles to Faull Slough. Named on Burrel (1954) and Riverdale (1954) 7.5' quadrangles.

(2) *stream,* heads near Hanford and flows 9 miles to a ditch 2.25 miles west-southwest of Guernsey (lat. 36°12'10" N, long. 119°40'50" W; sec. 10, T 20 S, R 21 E). Named on Guernsey (1929) and Hanford (1926) 7.5' quadrangles. On Guernsey (1954) and Hanford (1954) 7.5' quadrangles, the name applies to a mainly dry watercourse.

Sandspur [TULARE]: *locality,* nearly 4 miles east-southeast of Woodlake along Visalia Electric Railroad (lat. 36°23'55" N, long. 119°02' W; near N line sec. 3, T 18 S, R 27 E). Named on Lemon Cove (1928) 7.5' quadrangle.

Sandy Bluffs: see **Big Sandy Bluffs** [FRESNO].

Sandy Creek [KERN]:

(1) *stream,* flows 6.25 miles to Poso Creek nearly 3 miles north of Glennville in Linns Valley (lat. 35°46'10" N, long. 118°42'45" W; sec. 11, T 25 S, R 30 E). Named on California Hot Springs (1958) 15' quadrangle.

(2) *stream,* flows 14 miles to end 6.5 miles east of Taft near Buena Vista Lake Bed (lat. 35°08'05" N, long. 119°20'35" W; near NE cor. sec. 24, T 32 S, R 24 E). Named on Mouth of Kern (1950) and Taft (1950) 7.5' quadrangles.

Sandy Creek: see **Big Sandy Creek** [FRESNO]; **Little Sandy Creek** [FRESNO].

Sandy Creek Spring [KERN]: *spring,* 4.25 miles northeast of Glennville (lat. 35°46'25" N, long. 118°39'05" W; at N line sec. 9, T 25 S, R 31 E); the spring is along Sandy Creek (1). Named on California Hot Springs (1958) 15' quadrangle.

Sandy Meadow [TULARE]: *area,* 4.5 miles west of Mount Whitney (lat. 36°34' N, long. 118°22'15" W). Named on Mount Whitney (1956) 15' quadrangle. Called Sand Meadows on Mount Whitney (1907) 30' quadrangle, but United States Board on Geographic Names (1938, p. 47) rejected this name for the feature.

Sandy Plateau: see **Bighorn Plateau** [TULARE].

Sandy Valley: see **Big Sandy Valley** [FRESNO].

San Emedio: see **San Emidio** [KERN] (1).

San Emedio Creek: see **San Emigdio Creek** [KERN].

San Emedio Mountain: see **San Emigdio Mountain** [KERN].

San Emedio Range: see **San Emigdio Mountains** [KERN].

San Emidio [KERN]:

(1) *land grant,* at and south of the mouth of San Emigdio Creek, mainly between San Emigdio Creek and Santiago Creek. Named on Eagle Rest Peak (1942), Pleito Hills (1958), and Santiago Creek (1943) 7.5' quadrangles. United States Board on Geographic Names (1933a, p. 665) approved the form "San Emigdio" for the name, and rejected the forms "San Emidio," "San Emedio," and "San Emidion." Jose Antonio Dominguez received 4 leagues in 1842; Francisco Dominguez and others claimed

17,710 acres patented in 1866 (Cowan, p. 75).
(2) *locality,* 6 miles east-northeast of Maricopa along Sunset Railroad (lat. 34°05'35" N, long. 119°18'15" W; sec. 26, T 12 N, R 23 W). Named on Pentland (1953) 7.5' quadrangle.

San Emidio Creek: see **San Emigdio Creek** [KERN].

San Emidio Mountain: see **San Emigdio Mountain** [KERN].

San Emidio Mountains: see **San Emigdio Mountains** [KERN].

San Emidion: see **San Emidio** [KERN] (1).

San Emidion Creek: see **San Emigdio Creek** [KERN].

San Emidion Mountain: see **San Emigdio Mountain** [KERN].

San Emigdio: see **San Emidio** [KERN] (1); **San Emigdio Creek** [KERN].

San Emigdio Creek [KERN]: *stream,* flows 13 miles to lowlands 6.5 miles north-northwest of Eagle Rest Peak (lat. 34°59'20" N, long. 119°11'05" W; near N line sec. 1, T 10 N, R 22 W). Named on Conner SW (1955), Cuddy Valley (1943), Eagle Rest Peak (1942), and Sawmill Mountain (1943) 7.5' quadrangles. Called Arroyo San Arminio on Williamson's (1853) map. Joy (p. 51) mentioned San Emigio Cañon, Whitney (p. 186) wrote of San Emidio Cañon, and Fairbanks (1894b, p. 495) described San Emedio Cañon. United States Board on Geographic Names (1933a, p. 665) rejected the forms "San Emedio Creek," "San Emidio Creek," and "San Emidion Creek " for the name. Mendenhall's (1908) map shows a place called San Emigdio situated at the entrance of San Emigdio Creek to the lowlands; Eagle Rest Peak (1942) 7.5' quadrangle shows the headquarters of San Emigdio ranch at the same place. About 3 miles farther north along San Emigdio Creek is the site of a Mexican community that was called San Emigdio (Hoover, Rensch, and Rensch, p. 127). The Mexican place was started before 1824 and was the first white community in Kern County; it was abandoned in the 1890's (Bailey, 1967, p. 24). Postal authorities established San Emigdio post office 25 miles southwest of Bakersfield in 1881 and discontinued it in 1886 (Salley, p. 193).

San Emigdio Mountain [KERN]: *peak,* 3.5 miles southwest of Eagle Rest Peak (lat. 34°52'25" N, long. 119°10'45" W; near S line sec. 12, T 9 N, R 22 W). Altitude 7495 feet. Named on Sawmill Mountain (1943) 7.5' quadrangle. United States Board on Geographic Names (1933a, p. 665) rejected the forms "San Emedio Mountain," "San Emidio Mountain," and "San Emidion Mountain" for the name.

San Emigdio Mountains [KERN]: *range,* south of San Joaquin Valley and west of Grapevine Creek. Named on Los Angeles (1975) 1°x 2° quadrangle. Joy (p. 51) called the range San Emidio Mountains, and Fairbanks (1894b, p. 493) called it San Emedio Range. United States Board on Geographic Names (1973b, p. 3) gave the name "San Emidio Mountains" as a variant.

Sanger [FRESNO]: *town,* 13 miles east-southeast of downtown Fresno (lat. 36°42'15" N, long. 119°33'30" W; around NE cor. sec. 22, T 14 S, R 22 E). Named on Sanger (1965) 7.5' quadrangle. Postal authorities established Sanger post office in 1888 (Frickstad, p. 37), and the town incorporated in 1911. The name honors Joseph Sanger, Jr., who came to San Francisco in 1887 to attend the annual convention of the Railroad Yardmasters Association, of which he was secretary-treasurer (Johnston, p. 27). California Mining Bureau's (1917a) map shows a place called Tarn about 4 miles south-southeast of Sanger along Southern Pacific Railroad.

San Joaquin [FRESNO]: *town,* 11 miles southwest of Kerman (lat. 36°36'30" N, long. 120°11'15" W; mainly in sec. 23, 24, T 15 S, R 16 E). Named on San Joaquin (1963) 7.5' quadrangle. Postal authorities established San Joaquin post office in 1913; at first it was intended to call the post office Grahamton for an early settler (Salley, p. 87, 195). The town incorporated in 1920. A place called Hawthorne's Station was about 1 mile southeast of present San Joaquin along Butterfield Overland stage line from 1858 until 1861 (Hoover, Rensch, and Rensch, p. 92).

San Joaquin River [FRESNO]: *stream,* heads in Madera County and flows 130 miles, generally along Fresno-Madera County line, to Merced County 13 miles north-northwest of Firebaugh (lat. 37°02'40" N, long. 120°32'30" W). Named on Fresno (1962), Mariposa (1957), San Jose (1962), and Santa Cruz (1958) 1°x 2° quadrangles. Called R. San Joachim on Wilkes' (1841) map, Rio San Joaquin on Fremont's (1848) map, San Joaquin R. on Wilkes' (1849) map, Joaquin River on Jefferson's (1849) map, River San Joarquin on Derby's (1850) map, and Rio Tulare or San Joaquin on Sage's (1846) map. Gabriel Moraga named the river about 1805 for St. Joachim, father of the Virgin Mary (Hart, J.D., p. 379). South Fork flows 43 miles to Madera County 11.5 miles north of Kaiser Peak, and joins the main stream in Madera County; it is named on Blackcap Mountain (1953), Kaiser Peak (1953), and Mount Abbot (1953) 15' quadrangles. United States Board on Geographic Names (1965c, p. 12) rejected the name "Hooper Creek" for South Fork San Joaquin River.

San Joaquin Valley: see "Regional setting."

Sanjon de San Jose: see **Tulare Lake** [KINGS].

San Pedro: see **Tule River** [KINGS-TULARE].

Sans Tache: see **Laton** [FRESNO].

Santa Maria Valley: see **Little Santa Maria Valley** [KERN].

Santa Rita Slough [FRESNO]: *water feature,* diverges from San Joaquin River and extends for 1 mile to Merced County 8 miles north of Oxalis (lat. 37°02' N, long. 120°33'20" W; near W line sec. 27, T 10 S, R 13 E). Named on Santa Rita Bridge (1922) 7.5' quadrangle.

Santiago Creek [KERN]: *stream,* flows 11 miles to lowlands 9 miles west-northwest of Eagle Rest Peak (lat. 34°58'10" N, long. 119°16'55" W; sec. 12, T 10 N, R 23 W). Named on Apache Canyon (1943), Pentland (1953), Santiago Creek (1943), and Sawmill Mountain (1943) 7.5' quadrangles. United States Board on Geographic Names (1982b, p. 3) approved the name "East Twin Creek" for a stream, 2 miles long, that joins Santiago Creek from the southeast about 2.5 miles upstream from the entrance of Santiago Creek into lowlands (lat. 34°56'02" N, long. 119°18'10" W; sec. 23, T 10 N, R 23 W). The Board at the same time approved the name "West Twin Creek" for a stream, 1.6 miles long, that enters Santiago Creek from the southwest 450 feet upstream from the mouth of East Twin Creek (lat. 34°55'57" N, long. 119°18'12" W; sec. 23, T 10 N, R 23 W).

Santos: see **Strathmore** [TULARE].

Santos Creek [KERN]: *stream,* heads in San Luis Obispo County and flows 4 miles to lowlands 2 miles north-northwest of Carneros Rocks (lat. 35°27'55" N, long. 119°51'25" W; sec. 30, T 28 S, R 20 E). Named on Carneros Rocks (1959) and Las Yeguas Ranch (1959) 7.5' quadrangles. The name commemorates Joe Santos, a settler (Arnold and Johnson, p. 22).

Sapphire Lake [FRESNO]: *lake,* 3000 feet long, 3.5 miles north-northeast of Mount Goddard in Evolution Basin (lat. 37°08'55" N, long. 118°41'40" W). Named on Mount Goddard (1948) 15' quadrangle.

Satellite Lake [KERN]: *playa,* 2 miles east of downtown Ridgecrest on Kern-San Bernardino County line (lat. 35°37'40" N, long. 117° 38'05" W; on E line sec. 35, T 26 S, R 40 E). Named on Ridgecrest North (1973) 7.5' quadrangle.

Saturday Peak [KERN]: *peak,* 3.5 miles west-southwest of Democrat Hot Springs (lat. 35°30'25" N, long. 118°43'20" W). Altitude 4143 feet. Named on Democrat Hot Springs (1972) 7.5' quadrangle.

Saturday Spring [KERN]: *spring,* 3 miles west-southwest of Democrat Hot Springs (lat. 35°30'30" N, long. 118°42'45" W); the spring is 0.5 mile east of Saturday Peak. Named on Democrat Hot Springs (1972) 7.5' quadrangle.

Saturday Spring Creek [KERN]: *stream,* flows 2.25 miles to Kern River 1.5 miles southwest of Democrat Hot Springs (lat. 35°30'45" N, long. 118°41'25" W). Named on Democrat Hot Springs (1972) 7.5' quadrangle.

Sawmill Canyon [KERN]: *canyon,* drained by a stream that flows nearly 4 miles to Oak Creek 8 miles south of Tehachapi (lat. 35° 01' N, long. 118°25'50" W; near W line sec. 25, T 11 N, R 15 W). Named on Tehachapi South (1966) 7.5' quadrangle.

Sawmill Flat [FRESNO]: *locality,* 7.5 miles northeast of Balch Camp (lat. 36°58'15" N, long. 119°01' W; sec. 15, T 11 S, R 27 E). Site named on Patterson Mountain (1952) 15' quadrangle.

Sawmill Mountain [KERN]: *peak,* 6.5 miles south-southwest of Eagle Rest Peak on Kern-Ventura County line (lat. 34°48'50" N, long. 119°10' W; on S line sec. 31, T 9 N, R 21 W). Named on Sawmill Mountain (1943) 7.5' quadrangle.

Sawmill Pass [FRESNO]: *pass,* 5 miles south-southeast of Mount Pinchot on Fresno-Inyo County line (lat. 36°53' N, long. 118°21'45" W); the pass is near the head of Sawmill Creek, which is in Inyo County. Named on Mount Pinchot (1953) 15' quadrangle.

Sawtooth Pass [TULARE]: *pass,* 2 miles east-northeast of Mineral King on Great Western Divide (lat. 36°27'10" N, long. 118°33'40" W); the pass is 0.5 mile northwest of Sawtooth Peak. Named on Mineral King (1956) 15' quadrangle. Called Glacier Pass on Kaweah (1909) 30' quadrangle, but United States Board on Geographic Names (1960b, p. 20) rejected this name for the feature.

Sawtooth Peak [TULARE]:
(1) *peak,* 2.25 miles east of Mineral King on Great Western Divide (lat. 36°27'20" N, long. 118°33'15" W). Named on Mineral King (1956) 15' quadrangle. United States Board on Geographic Names (1933a, p. 675) rejected the name "Miner's Peak" for the feature. The name "Sawtooth" is from the shape of the peak (Browning, p. 193).
(2) *peak,* 28 miles south-southeast of Monache Mountain on Tulare-Inyo County line (lat. 35°49'25" N, long. 117°59'50" W). Altitude 7970 feet. Named on Little Lake (1954) 15' quadrangle.

Sawtooth Ridge [KERN]: *ridge,* east-southeast-trending, 1.25 miles long, 3.5 miles southeast of Orchard Peak (lat. 35°41'55" N, long. 120°05'30" W). Named on Sawtooth Ridge (1961) 7.5' quadrangle. Arnold and Johnson (p. 22) gave the name for the jagged appearance of the ridge.

Sawyer: see **Tom Sawyer Lake** [KERN].

Sawyer Peak [TULARE]: *peak,* nearly 3 miles north of Cliff Peak (lat. 36°35'50" N, long. 119°10'10" W; sec. 29, T 15 S, R 26 E). Altitude 2403 feet. Named on Stokes Mountain (1966) 7.5' quadrangle.

Scaffold Meadows [TULARE]: *area,* 9 miles north-northwest of Triple Divide Peak along Roaring River (lat. 36°42'45" N, long. 118°35' W). Named on Triple Divide Peak (1956) 15' quadrangle. Called Scaffold Meadow on Tehipite (1903) 30' quadrangle. Sheepherders built a scaffold at the place to keep food out of the reach of animals (Browning, p. 193).

Scarab Lake [FRESNO]: *lake,* 700 feet long, 16 miles northeast of Kaiser Peak (lat. 37°28'50" N, long. 119°00'50" W). Named on Kaiser Peak (1953) 15' quadrangle.

Scarlet and Davis Canyon [TULARE]: *canyon,* drained by a stream that flows 2 miles to Tobias Creek 7.25 miles east of California Hot Springs (lat. 35°53'15" N, long. 118°32'30" W; sec. 32, T 23 S, R 32 E). Named on California Hot Springs (1958) 15' quadrangle.

Scarlett and Davis Canyon: see **Speas Creek** [TULARE] (1).

Scenic Heights [TULARE]: *ridge,* south-southeast-trending, about 1 mile long, 1.25 miles north-northwest of Porterville (lat. 36°05'20" N, long. 119°01'20" W). Named on Porterville (1951) 7.5' quadrangle.

Scenic Meadow [TULARE]: *area,* 7.25 miles north-northwest of Triple Divide Peak (lat. 36°41' N, long. 118°35'45" W). Named on Triple Divide Peak (1956) 15' quadrangle.

Scepter Creek [FRESNO]: *stream,* flows 7.25 miles to Crown Creek 13 miles north-northeast of Hume (lat. 36°57'05" N, long. 118°48'30" W); the stream heads near Scepter Pass. Named on Blackcap Mountain (1953) and Tehipite Dome (1952) 15' quadrangles.

Scepter Lake [FRESNO]: *lake,* 850 feet long, 3.5 miles southwest of Blackcap Mountain (lat. 37°01'50" N, long. 118°50'05" W); the lake is located along Scepter Creek. Named on Blackcap Mountain (1953) 15' quadrangle.

Scepter Pass [FRESNO]: *pass,* nearly 3 miles southwest of Blackcap Mountain (lat. 37°02'50" N, long. 118°50' W); the pass is at the head of Scepter Creek. Named on Blackcap Mountain (1953) 15' quadrangle.

Schaeffer Meadow [TULARE]:

(1) *area,* 5 miles west-northwest of Olancha Peak (lat. 36°17'15" N, long. 118°12' W; sec. 8, 9, T 19 S, R 35 E). Named on Olancha (1956) 15' quadrangle.

(2) *area,* 11.5 miles south of Hockett Peak (lat. 36°03'20" N, long. 118°24'25" W); the place is 1.5 miles south-southwest of Schaeffer Mountain. Named on Hockett Peak (1956) 15' quadrangle.

Schaeffer Mountain [TULARE]: *peak,* 10 miles south of Hockett Peak (lat. 36°04'30" N, long. 118°23'45" W). Altitude 9292 feet. Named on Hockett Peak (1956) 15' quadrangle.

Schaeffer Stringer [TULARE]: *stream,* flows 2 miles to South Fork Kern River 4.25 miles west of Olancha Peak (lat. 36°16'20" N, long. 118°11'40" W; sec. 16, T 19 S, R 35 E). Named on Olancha (1956) 15' quadrangle.

Schilling [FRESNO]: *locality,* nearly 2 miles south-southeast of Lanare along Atchison, Topeka and Santa Fe Railroad (lat. 36°24'30" N, long. 119°54'45" W; sec. 33, T 17 S, R 19 E). Named on Burrel (1954) 7.5' quadrangle.

Schmidt Camp [KERN]: *locality,* nearly 5 miles west of Garlock (lat. 35°24'40" N, long. 117°52'25" W). Named on Garlock (1967) 7.5' quadrangle.

Schober's Pass: see **Lamarck Col** [FRESNO].

Schoolhouse Spring [TULARE]: *spring,* 4.5 miles south-southeast of Auckland (lat. 36°31'45" N, long. 119°04'15" W; near SE cor. sec. 18, T 16 S, R 27 E). Named on Auckland (1966) 7.5' quadrangle.

Schoolhouse Well [KERN]: *well,* 8 miles northwest of Cross Mountain in Kelso Valley (lat. 35°22'15" N, long. 118°13' W; near E line sec. 33, T 29 S, R 35 E). Named on Cross Mountain (1972) 7.5' quadrangle.

Schoolmarm Lake [FRESNO]: *lake,* 1050 feet long, 2.5 miles north of Blackcap Mountain (lat. 37°06'35" N, long. 118°47'50" W). Named on Blackcap Mountain (1953) 15' quadrangle.

Schultz Creek [TULARE]: *stream,* flows 3 miles to Bull Run Creek 9.5 miles southeast of California Hot Springs (lat. 35°48'05" N, long. 118°32' W; sec. 33, T 24 S, R 32 E). Named on California Hot Springs (1958) 15' quadrangle.

Schunemanns: see **Panoche Creek** [FRESNO].

Scodie: see **Onyx** [KERN].

Scodie Canyon [KERN]: *canyon,* drained by a stream that flows 8.5 miles to South Fork Valley near Onyx (lat. 35°40'55" N, long. 118° 12'55" W; sec. 10, T 26 S, R 35 E). Named on Cane Canyon (1972) and Onyx (1972) 7.5' quadrangles.

Scodie Meadow [TULARE]: *area,* 7 miles north-northeast of Lamont Peak along Chimney Creek (lat. 35°53'25" N, long. 118°00'10" W). Named on Lamont Peak (1956) 15' quadrangle.

Scodie Mountains [KERN]: *range,* center 9 miles east of Weldon and west of Walker Pass (lat. 35°38' N, long. 118°08' W). Named on Bakersfield (1962, revised 1971) 1°x 2° quadrangle. Called Kiavah Mountains on Onyx (1943) 15' quadrangle, but United States Board on Geographic Names (1963, p. 16) rejected the names "Kiavah Mountains" and "Kiavah Mountain" for the feature, and noted that the name "Scodie" commemorates William Scodie, who opened a store at the mouth of Scodie Canyon in the 1860's.

Scodie Spring [KERN]: *spring,* nearly 4 miles south-southeast of Onyx (lat. 35°38'30" N, long. 118°11'10" W; sec. 26, T 26 S, R 35 E); the spring is in Scodie Canyon. Named on Onyx (1972) 7.5' quadrangle.

Scoop Lake [FRESNO]: *lake,* 600 feet long, 7 miles west of Red Slate Mountain (lat. 37°31'05" N, long. 118°59'40" W). Named on Mount Morrison (1953) 15' quadrangle.

Scott Canyon [FRESNO]: *canyon,* drained by a stream that flows 2 miles to Oak Flat Canyon 7.25 miles west of Coalinga (lat. 36°09'20" N, long. 120°29'10" W; sec. 30, T 20 S, R 14 E). Named on Alcalde Hills (1969) 7.5' quadrangle.

Scottsburg: see **Centerville** [FRESNO].

Scout Island [FRESNO]: *area,* 7.5 miles north-northwest of downtown Fresno on the south side of San Joaquin River (lat. 36°51'30" N, long. 119°50'30" W; sec. 25, T 12 S, R 19 E). Named on Fresno North (1965) 7.5' quadrangle. Bullard (1923) 7.5' quadrangle has the name "Fresno Beach" at the place, which it shows at the end of Fresno Beach Electric Railroad.

Scovern Hot Springs [KERN]: *springs,* 2.25 miles north-northeast of Bodfish (lat. 35°37'15" N, long. 118°28'25" W; sec. 31, T 27 S, R 33 E); the springs are in Hot Spring Valley. Named on Lake Isabella South (1972) 7.5' quadrangle. Spanish settlers called the springs Agua Caliente (Waring, p. 51). Isabella (1943) 15' quadrangle has the name for a resort at the springs; the resort also was called Neill's Hot Springs, Nelson's Hot Springs, and Walser Hot Springs (Bailey, 1962, p. 52; Bailey, 1967, p. 25).

Scraper Canyon [KERN]: *canyon,* drained by a stream that flows 4 miles to Caliente Creek 2.5 miles west-northwest of Caliente (lat. 35°18'10" N, long. 118°40'25" W). Named on Bena (1972) 7.5' quadrangle.

Scraper Spring [KERN]: *spring,* 2.5 miles north-northwest of Caliente (lat. 35°19'20" N, long. 118°38'50" W); the spring is in Scraper Canyon. Named on Bena (1972) 7.5' quadrangle.

Scratch Hill [TULARE]: *peak,* 12 miles southeast of Kaweah (lat. 36°20'45" N, long. 118°46'15" W). Named on Kaweah (1957) 15' quadrangle.

Scylla [FRESNO]: *peak,* 2.25 miles southeast of Mount Goddard (lat. 37°04'50" N, long. 118°41'20" W); the peak is 1.25 miles west-southwest of Charybdis. Altitude 12,939 feet. Named on Mount Goddard (1948) 15' quadrangle. Theodore S. Solomons named the peak in 1895 (Hanna, p. 61). United States Board on Geographic Names (1964b, p. 14) rejected the name "Scylla Peak" for the feature, and noted that the name is from the rock off the Sicilian coast that figures in Greek mythology. At the same time the Board approved the name "The Three Sirens" for three peaks located between Scylla and Charybdis.

Scylla Peak: see **Scylla** [FRESNO].

Searles [KERN]: *locality,* 8 miles north of Randsburg along Southern Pacific Railroad (lat. 35°29' N, long. 117°38'05" W; near W line sec. 23, T 28 S, R 40 E). Named on El Paso Peaks (1967) 7.5' quadrangle. Called Searles Sta. on Searles Lake (1915) 1° quadrangle.

Searles Station: see **Searles** [KERN].

Searles Valley [KERN]: *valley,* mainly in San Bernardino County, but the westernmost end of the feature extends into Kern County 8.5 miles south-southeast of Ridgecrest (lat. 35°30'30" N, long. 117°37'45" W). Named on Ridgecrest South (1973) 7.5' quadrangle. United States Board on Geographic Names (1961b, p. 12) rejected the name "Spangler Valley" for the feature.

Secata Creek: see **Sacata Creek** [FRESNO].

Secata Ridge: see **Sacata Ridge** [FRESNO].

Second Crossing [FRESNO]: *locality,* 2 miles northeast of Double Peak along Fish Creek (1) (lat. 37°32' N, long. 119°00'40" W); the place is 3.5 miles upstream from Island Crossing. Named on Devils Postpile (1953) 15' quadrangle.

Second Dinkey Lake [FRESNO]: *lake,* 600 feet long, 5 miles northeast of Dinkey Dome on upper reaches of Dinkey Creek (lat. 37° 09'20" N, long. 119°03'20" W; on S line sec. 8, T 9 S, R 27 E); the lake is 1 mile upstream from First Dinkey Lake. Named on Huntington Lake (1953) 15' quadrangle.

Second Recess [FRESNO]: *canyon,* drained by a stream that flows 4 miles to Mono Creek 4.5 miles west-northwest of Mount Abbot (lat. 37°25'25" N, long. 118°51'25" W); the feature is the second large canyon east of Lake Thomas A. Edison on the south side of Mono Creek. Named on Mount Abbot (1953) 15' quadrangle. Theodore S. Solomons discovered and named the canyon in 1894 (Farquhar, 1925, p. 127).

Sedge Lake [FRESNO]: *lake,* 500 feet long, 15 miles northeast of Kaiser Peak (lat. 37°28'25" N, long. 119°01'35" W). Named on Kaiser Peak (1953) 15' quadrangle. The lake is one of the group called Margaret Lakes.

Sedwell: see **Cable** [KERN].

Seguro [KERN]: *locality,* 3.25 miles north-northwest of downtown Bakersfield along Southern Pacific Railroad (lat. 35°25'10" N, long. 119°01' W). Named on Oildale (1954) 7.5' quadrangle. Buena Vista Lake (1912) 30' quadrangle has the name "Waits" at or near present Seguro.

Selden Pass [FRESNO]: *pass,* 8.5 miles southwest of Mount Abbot (lat. 37°17'20" N, long. 118°52'20" W). Named on Mount Abbot (1953) 15' quadrangle. R.B. Marshall of United States Geological Survey named the pass for Selden S. Hooper, who was with the Survey from 1891 until 1898 (Farquhar, 1925, p. 131); nearby Mount Hooper was named for Selden's father, and Rose Lake was named for his sister. United States Board on Geographic Names (1933a, p. 680) rejected the form "Seldon Pass" for the name.

Selma [FRESNO]: *town,* 16 miles southeast of Fresno (lat. 36°34'15" N, long. 119°36'30" W). Named on Selma (1964) 7.5' quadrangle. Postal authorities established Selma post office in 1880 and named it for the daughter of Max Gruenberg, an early settler (Salley, p. 201). The town incorporated in 1893.

Semitropic [KERN]: *locality,* 10.5 miles east of the village of Lost Hills (lat. 35°36'05" N, long. 119°30'25" W; at SW cor. sec. 4, T 27 S, R 23 E). Named on Semitropic (1954) 7.5' quadrangle. California Mining Bureau's (1917c) map has the form "Semi Tropic" for the name. Postal authorities established Semitropic post office in 1893, moved it 2 miles west in 1904, moved it 3.5 miles southeast in 1905, and discontinued it in 1913; the name was for Semitropic Fruit Company (Salley, p. 201). California Mining Bureau's (1917c) map shows a place called Mira Monte located about 5 miles north of Semi Tropic. Postal authorities established Miramonte post office in 1889 and discontinued it in 1902, when they moved the service to Semitropic (Frickstad, p. 57).

Semitropic Ridge [KERN]: *ridge,* southeast-trending, 17 miles long, center 1.5 miles south-southwest of Semitropic (lat. 35°34'45" N, long. 119°31'15" W). Named on Lost Hills NE (1954), Semitropic (1954), and Wasco SW (1953) 7.5' quadrangles.

Seneca Spring [KERN]: *spring,* 3.5 miles west-southwest of Loraine (lat. 35°16'40" N, long. 118°29'35" W; sec. 36, T 30 S, R 32 E). Named on Loraine (1972) 7.5' quadrangle.

Senger: see **Mount Senger** [FRESNO].

Senger Creek [FRESNO]: *stream,* flows 4 miles to an unnamed stream 13 miles north-northwest of Blackcap Mountain (lat. 37°14'30" N, long. 118°53'10" W; at E line sec. 15, T 8 S, R 28 E); the stream heads near Mount Senger. Named on Blackcap Mountain (1953) and Mount Abbot (1953) 15' quadrangles. United States Board on Geographic Names (1983d, p. 2) approved the name "Sallie Keyes Creek" for the previously unnamed stream that Senger Creek joins, and noted (p. 3) that T.S. Solomons named Senger Creek in 1894 to honor professor Joachim H. Senger of University of California, a founder of the Sierra Club.

Senger Creek: see **Sallie Keyes Creek**, under **Sally Keyes Lakes** [FRESNO].

Sentinel [FRESNO]: *locality,* 2.5 miles west of present Humphreys Station (lat. 36°57'50" N, long. 119°29'30" W; near NE cor. sec. 19, T 11 S, R 23 E). Named on Dinuba (1924) 30' quadrangle. Postal authorities established Sentinel post office in 1880, discontinued it in 1883, reestablished it in 1888, discontinued it in 1897, reestablished it in 1905, and discontinued it in 1910; the name is from the way Keys Mountain acts as a sentinel by the place (Salley, p. 201).

Sentinel Butte [TULARE]: *hill,* 2.5 miles north-northwest of Woodlake (lat. 36°26'50" N, long. 119°06'36" W; sec. 13, T 17 S, R 26 E). Altitude 737 feet. Named on Woodlake (1952) 7.5' quadrangle.

Sentinel Dome [FRESNO]: *peak,* 15 miles south-southwest of Marion Peak (lat. 36°45'35" N, long. 118°38'35" W); the peak is on Sentinel Ridge. Altitude 9115 feet. Named on Marion Peak (1953) 15' quadrangle.

Sentinel Peak [TULARE]: *peak,* 10 miles south-southeast of Camp Nelson (lat. 36°01' N, long. 118°31'35" W; sec. 16, T 22 S, R 32 E). Altitude 6159 feet. Named on Camp Nelson (1956) 15' quadrangle.

Sentinel Ridge [FRESNO]: *ridge,* east-northeast-trending, 5 miles long, 16 miles south-southwest of Marion Peak (lat. 36°45'10" N, long. 118°39'45" W). Named on Marion Peak (1953) and Triple Divide Peak (1956) 15' quadrangles.

Sequoia Creek [FRESNO-TULARE]: *stream,* heads in Tulare County and flows 3.5 miles to Sequoia Lake 6 miles southwest of Hume in Fresno County (lat. 36°44'15" N, long. 118°59'15" W; sec. 1, T 14 S, R 27 E). Named on Giant Forest (1956) 15' quadrangle.

Sequoia Lake [FRESNO]: *lake,* 0.5 mile long, 6 miles southwest of Hume (lat. 36°43'55" N, long. 118°59'25" W; sec. 1, T 14 S, R 27 E). Named on Giant Forest (1956) 15' quadrangle.

Sequoia Mills: see **Millwood** [FRESNO].

Sequoia National Park Post Office: see **Kaweah Camp** [TULARE].

Serefin Spring [KERN]: *spring,* 3.5 miles north-northwest of Caliente (lat. 35°19'30" N, long. 118°38'10" W). Named on Bena (1972) 7.5' quadrangle.

Setch: see **Pinedale** [FRESNO] (2).

Set Creek: see **Setimo Creek** [KERN].

Setimo Creek [KERN]: *stream,* flows about 3.5 miles to Rancheria Creek (2) 4.25 miles south of Piute Peak (lat. 35°23'20" N, long. 118°24'10" W; at E line sec. 23, T 29 S, R 33 E). Named on Piute Peak (1972) 7.5' quadrangle. Called Set Creek on Emerald Mountain (1943) 15' quadrangle. United States Board on Geographic Names (1975b, p. 11) gave the names "Set Creek" and "Setino Creek" as variants.

Seven Gables [FRESNO]: *peak,* 6 miles south-southwest of Mount Abbot (lat. 37°48'45" N, long. 118°50' W). Altitude 13,075 feet. Named on Mount Abbot (1953) 15' quadrangle. Theodore S. Solomons and Leigh Bierce climbed the peak in 1894 and gave it the name suggested by its shape (Farquhar, 1925, p. 132).

Seven Gables Lakes [FRESNO]: *lakes,* largest about 1200 feet long, 5.5 miles south-southwest of Mount Abbot (lat. 37°18'45" N, long. 118°48'45" W); the lakes are 1 mile east of Seven Gables. Named on Mount Abbot (1953) 15' quadrangle.

Sevenmile Hill [TULARE]: *ridge,* south-southwest-trending, 3 miles long, 10 miles west-southwest of Triple Divide Peak (lat. 36°33'45" N, long. 118°42' W). Named on Triple Divide Peak (1956) 15' quadrangle.

Seventeen Canyon [KERN]: *canyon,* drained by a stream that flows 4 miles to Midway Valley 2.25 miles southeast of Fellows (lat. 35° 09'35" N, long. 119°30'30" W; sec. 9, T 32 S, R 23 E); the canyon is partly in section 17. Named on Fellows (1951) 7.5' quadrangle.

Seville [TULARE]: *village,* 8.5 miles northwest of Woodlake (lat. 36° 29' N, long. 119°13'30" W; near NE cor. sec. 2, T 17 S, R 25 E). Named on Exeter (1952) 15' quadrangle. Postal authorities established Seville post office in 1915 and discontinued it in 1931 (Frickstad, p. 213). Officials of Atchison, Topeka and Santa Fe Railroad named the place in 1913 (Mitchell, A.R., p. 70).

Seville Lake [TULARE]: *lake,* 1000 feet long, 12 miles west-northwest of Triple Divide Peak (lat. 36°41' N, long. 118°43' W; on E line sec. 28, T 14 S, R 30 E). Named on Triple Divide Peak (1956) 15' quadrangle. Called Kettle Lake on a map of 1874 (Forest M. Clingan, personal communication, 1990).

Shadequarter Mountain [TULARE]: *ridge,* south-southwest- to west-trending, 2 miles long, 5.5 miles west of Yucca Mountain (lat. 36°33'45" N, long. 118°58' W). Named on Giant Forest (1956) 15' quadrangle.

Shadley Creek [TULARE]: *stream,* flows nearly 2 miles to Warm Sulphur Spring 5 miles east of Auckland (lat. 36°35'20" N, long. 119°00'50" W; sec. 26, T 15 S, R 27 E). Named on Auckland (1966) 7.5' quadrangle. Dinuba (1924) 30' quadrangle shows the stream continuing on to Dry Creek (1).

Shadley Flat: see **Murry Flat** [TULARE].

Shafter [KERN]: *town,* 18 miles west-northwest of Bakersfield (lat. 35°30'05" N, long. 119°16'20" W; in and near sec. 10, T 28 S, R 25 E). Named on Rio Bravo (1954) and Wasco (1953) 7.5' quadrangles. Postal authorities established Shafter post office in 1898, moved it 1.25 miles west in 1902, discontinued it in 1905, and reestablished it in 1914 (Salley, p. 202). The town incorporated in 1938. A railroad loading station was at the site in 1898, and a 7100-acre subdivision was placed on sale there in 1914 (Bailey, 1967, p. 25). The name honors General William Shafter, commander of United States forces in Cuba during the Spanish-American War, who lived on his ranch near Bakersfield after retirement in 1901 (Gudde, 1949, p. 326).

Shafter: see **North Shafter** [KERN].

Shagoopah Falls: see **Chagoopa Falls** [TULARE].

Shakspere: see **Mount Shakspere** [FRESNO].

Shale: see **Fellows** [KERN].

Shale Hills [KERN]: *range,* 11 miles southeast of Orchard Peak (lat. 35°37' N, long. 112°01' W). Named on Packwood Creek (1961), Sawtooth Ridge (1961), and Shale Point (1953) 7.5' quadrangles. Arnold and Johnson (p. 22) proposed the name.

Shale Point [KERN]: *ridge,* east-southeast-trending, 1 mile long, 5.5 miles west of Blackwells Corner (lat. 35°35'45" N, long. 119°57'45" W); the ridge is at the east end of Shale Hills. Named on Shale Point (1953) 7.5' quadrangle. Arnold and Johnson (p. 22) proposed the name.

Shamrock: see **Delano** [KERN].

Shannon Valley [FRESNO]: *area,* 6 miles west-southwest of Dunlap (lat. 36°42'15" N, long. 119°13' W). Named on Tucker Mountain (1966) 7.5' quadrangle.

Sharknose Ridge [TULARE]: *ridge,* west-northwest-trending, 1.5 miles long, 9.5 miles north-northwest of Olancha Peak (lat. 36°23'35" N, long. 118°10'20" W). Named on Olancha (1956) 15' quadrangle.

Sharktooth Creek [FRESNO]: *stream,* flows nearly 4 miles to Fish Creek (1) 2 miles north of Double Peak in Fish Valley (lat. 37°32'10" N, long. 119°02'35" W); the stream heads near Sharktooth Lake. Named on Devils Postpile (1953) 15' quadrangle.

Sharktooth Hill: see **Round Mountain** [KERN] (2).

Sharktooth Lake [FRESNO]: *lake,* 1100 feet long, 16 miles north-northeast of Kaiser Peak (lat. 37°29'55" N, long. 119°01'50" W); the lake is near the head of Sharktooth Creek. Named on Kaiser Peak (1953) 15' quadrangle.

Sharktooth Peak [FRESNO]: *peak,* 15 miles north-northeast of Kaiser Peak (lat. 37°29' N, long. 119°01'30" W). Altitude 11,630 feet. Named on Kaiser (1904) 30' quadrangle. Theodore S. Solomons named the peak in 1892 (Farquhar, 1925, p. 132). On Kaiser Peak (1953) 15' quadrangle, the name applies to a feature located 1.5 miles farther south-southwest (lat. 37°27'45" N, long. 119°02'35" W), but United States Board on Geographic Names (1969a, p. 4) approved the name "Cockscomb" for this second peak.

Sharp Creek: see **Wishon Reservoir** [FRESNO].

Sharp Note Lake [FRESNO]: *lake,* 600 feet long, 8.5 miles south-southwest of Mount Abbot (lat. 37°17'05" N, long. 118°51'20" W); the lake is less than 1 mile south of Flat Note Lake. Named on Mount Abbot (1953) 15' quadrangle.

Sharpville: see **Shipp** [FRESNO].

Shaver [FRESNO]: *village,* 12 miles south-southwest of Kaiser Peak at the north end of Shaver Lake (lat. 37°08'35" N, long. 119°17'50" W; near SE cor. sec. 13, T 9 S, R 24 E). Named on Kaiser (1904) 30' quadrangle. Postal authorities established Shaver post office in 1896 and discontinued it in 1925 (Frickstad, p. 37). Water of an enlarged Shaver Lake now covers the site.

Shaver Crossing [FRESNO]: *locality,* 9 miles south-southwest of Kaiser Peak along San Joaquin and Eastern Railroad (lat. 37°11'10" N, long. 119°16'40" W; near NE cor. sec. 6, T 9 S, R 25 E). Named on Kaiser (1904) 30' quadrangle.

Shaver Lake [FRESNO]: *lake,* behind a dam on Stevenson Creek nearly 3 miles north-northeast of Shaver Lake Heights (present town of Shaver Lake) (lat. 37°08'40" N, long. 119°18'10" W; sec. 13, T 9 S, R 24 E). Named on Shaver Lake (1953) 15' quadrangle. The name commemorates C.B. Shaver, co-founder of Fresno Flume and Irrigation Company; officials of this company had the dam built that forms the lake in what had been known as Stevenson Basin and Stevenson Meadows (Redinger, p. 77).

Shaver Lake: see **Shaver Lake Heights** [FRESNO].

Shaver Lake Heights [FRESNO]: *town,* 14 miles south-southwest of Kaiser Peak (lat. 37°06'25" N, long. 119°19'15" W; in and near sec. 35, T 9 S, R 24 E); the town is at the southwest end of Shaver Lake. Named on Shaver Lake (1953) 15' quadrangle, which also has the name "Shaver Lake P.O." at the place. Postal authorities established Shaver Lake post office in 1928 (Frickstad, p. 37). United States Board on Geographic Names (1983a, p. 4) approved the name "Shaver Lake" for the town.

Shaver Lake Point [FRESNO]: *promontory,* 2.25 miles north-northeast of Shaver Lake Heights (present town of Shaver Lake) (lat. 37°08'15" N, long. 119°18'15" W; sec. 24, T 9 S, R 24 E); the feature is on the west side of Shaver Lake. Named on Shaver Lake (1953) 15' quadrangle.

Sheep Creek [FRESNO]: *stream,* flows 5 miles to South Fork Kings River 14 miles southwest of Marion Peak in Kings Canyon (lat. 36°47'35" N, long. 118°40'25" W). Named on Marion Peak (1953) and Triple Divide Peak (1956) 15' quadrangles. A sheep trail followed the creek in the early days; the stream had the name Fox Creek on a map of 1896 (Forest M. Clingan, personal communication, 1990).

Sheep Creek [TULARE]:

(1) *stream,* flows 2.25 miles to Willow Creek (2) 12 miles west of Kern Peak (lat. 36°17'15" N, long. 118°30' W). Named on Kern Peak (1956) 15' quadrangle. United States Board on Geographic Names (1986, p. 4) approved the designation "No Name Creek" for the stream; at the same time the Board approved the name "Sheep Creek" for a stream that heads 2.2 miles south-southwest of Coyote Peaks and flows for 2.5 miles to Willow Creek (2) 3.5 miles northwest of Angora Mountain (lat. 36°16'47" N, long. 118°30'30" W).

(2) *stream,* flows 4 miles to North Fork Kaweah River 5.25 miles south-southwest of Yucca Mountain (lat. 36°30'10" N, long. 118° 54'40" W); the stream is southwest of Sheep Ridge. Named on Giant Forest (1956) 15' quadrangle.

Sheep Mountain [TULARE]: *peak,* 10 miles south of Mineral King (lat. 36°18'30" N, long. 118°37'25" W). Named on Mineral King (1956) 15' quadrangle.

Sheep Mountain: see **Angora Mountain** [TULARE].

Sheep Pass: see **Vacation Pass** [TULARE].

Sheep Ridge [TULARE]: *ridge,* southeast-trending, 3 miles long, 3 miles west-southwest of Yucca Peak (lat. 36°33'10" N, long. 118° 55'15" W); the ridge is northeast of Sheep Creek (2). Named on Giant Forest (1956) 15' quadrangle.

Sheep Rock: see **Mount Corcoran** [TULARE].

Sheep Spring [KERN]: *spring,* 6.5 miles north of Garlock (lat. 35° 29'50" N, long. 117°48'15" W). Named on Garlock (1967) 7.5' quadrangle.

Sheep Springs: see **Willow Springs** [KERN] (1).

Sheep Troughs Spring [KERN]: *spring,* 7.5 miles northeast of Mount Adelaide (lat. 35°29'50" N, long. 118°38'10" W; sec. 15, T 28 S, R 31 E). Named on Mount Adelaide (1972) 7.5' quadrangle.

Shelf Lake [FRESNO]: *lake,* 300 feet long, 10 miles west-northwest of Mount Abbot (lat. 37°25'55" N, long. 118°57'30" W). Named on Mount Abbot (1953) 15' quadrangle. Charles K. Fisher of California Department of Fish and Game gave the name in 1949 for the position of the lake on a topographic shelf above Cold Creek (Browning, p. 197).

Shell [KINGS]: *locality,* 1 mile east-southeast of Hanford along Southern Pacific Railroad lat. 36°19'40" N, long. 119°37'10" W; at S line sec. 30, T 18 S, R 22 E). Named on Remnoy (1954) 7.5' quadrangle.

Shell Mountain [TULARE]: *peak,* 9.5 miles north-northeast of Yucca Mountain (lat. 36°41'45" N, long. 118°47'45" W; sec. 23, T 14 S, R 29 E). Altitude 9594 feet. Named on Giant Forest (1956) 15' quadrangle.

Shepherd Cove [TULARE]: *relief feature,* wide place in the canyon of Kaweah River 3.5 miles east of Kaweah (lat. 36°28'30" N, long. 118°51'25" W; in and near sec. 5, T 17 S, R 29 E); the feature is 1.5 miles southeast of Shepherd Peak. Named on Kaweah (1957) 15' quadrangle.

Shepherd Pass [TULARE]: *pass,* 7.25 miles north-northwest of Mount Whitney on Tulare-Inyo County line (lat. 36°40'20" N, long. 118°20'35" W). Named on Mount Whitney (1956) 15' quadrangle. The name commemorates the pioneer Shepherd families of Inyo County (United States Board on Geographic Names, 1933a, p. 687).

Shepherd Peak [TULARE]: *peak,* 2.5 miles east-northeast of Kaweah (lat. 36°29'30" N, long. 118°52'35" W). Altitude 3570 feet. Named on Kaweah (1957) 15' quadrangle.

Sherman Creek [TULARE]: *stream,* flows 1.5 miles to Marble Fork 5.5 miles east of Yucca Mountain (lat. 36°34'55" N, long. 118°46'05" W; sec. 31, T 15 S, R 30 E); the stream is near General Sherman redwood tree. Named on Giant Forest (1956) 15' quadrangle.

Sherman Peak [FRESNO]: *peak,* 4 miles north of Coalinga Mineral Springs (lat. 36°12'05" N, long. 120°33'40" W; sec. 10, T 20 S, R 13 E). Altitude 3857 feet. Named on Sherman Peak (1969) 7.5' quadrangle.

Sherman Peak [TULARE]: *peak,* 14 miles south of Hockett Peak (lat. 36°00'40" N, long. 118°23'25" W). Altitude 9909 feet. Named on Hockett Peak (1956) 15' quadrangle.

Sherman Peak: see **Flag Peak** [FRESNO].

Shinn: see **Mount Shinn** [FRESNO].

Shipp [FRESNO]: *locality,* 8.5 miles north of Clovis along San Joaquin and Eastern Railroad (lat. 36°56'40" N, long. 119°40'30" W; near E line sec. 28, T 11 S, R 21 E). Named on Friant (1922) 7.5' quadrangle. California Mining Bureau's (1917a) map shows a place called Sharpville located along the railroad 4 miles east-northeast of Shipp.

Shirley [KINGS]: *locality,* 4.5 miles north of Hanford along Atchison, Topeka and Santa Fe Railroad (lat. 36°23'55" N, long. 119°39'45" W; sec. 2, T 18 S, R 21 E). Named on Laton (1953) 7.5' quadrangle. Called Harlow on Laton (1927) 7.5' quadrangle.

Shirley Creek [KERN]: *stream,* flows 4 miles to Tillie Creek 2.25 miles west of Wofford Heights (lat. 35°42'55" N, long. 118°29'35" W; sec. 36, T 25 S, R 32 E); the stream heads at Shirley Peak. Named on Alta Sierra (1972) and Lake Isabella North (1972) 7.5' quadrangles.

Shirley Meadow Campground [KERN]: *locality,* 1.25 miles south-southwest of Alta Sierra (lat. 35°42'45" N, long. 118°33'35" W; sec. 32, T 25 S, R 32 E); the place is 0.25 mile north of Shirley Peak. Named on Glennville (1956) 15' quadrangle.

Shirley Meadows [KERN]: *locality,* 1.25 miles south-southwest of Alta Sierra (lat. 35°42'35" N, long. 118°33'20" W; sec. 32, T 25 S, R 32 E); the place is 0.25 mile northeast of Shirley Peak along Shirley Creek. Named on Alta Sierra (1972) 7.5' quadrangle.

Shirley Peak [KERN]: *peak,* 1.25 miles south-southwest of Alta Sierra (lat. 35°42'25" N, long. 118°33'35" W; sec. 32, T 25 S, R 32 E); the peak is at the head of Shirley Creek. Altitude 7091 feet. Named on Alta Sierra (1972) 7.5' quadrangle.

Shoemaker Spring [KERN]: *spring,* 5 miles south-southwest of Skinner Peak (lat. 35°30'10" N, long. 118°09'55" W; sec. 12, T 28 S, R 35 E). Named on Cane Canyon (1972) 7.5' quadrangle.

Short Canyon [KERN]:

(1) *valley,* 3.5 miles south of Onyx (lat. 35°38'15" N, long. 118°13'30" W). Named on Onyx (1972) 7.5' quadrangle.

(2) *canyon,* drained by a stream that flows 3 miles to Caldwell Creek nearly 2 miles east of Kernville (lat. 35°45'05" N, long. 118°23'30" W; near W line sec. 13, T 25 S, R 33 E). Named on Lake Isabella North (1972) and Weldon (1972) 7.5' quadrangles.

(3) *canyon,* 2 miles long, opens into lowlands nearly 6 miles northwest of Inyokern (lat. 35°42'25" N, long. 117°53'20" W; sec. 4, T 26 S, R 38 E). Named on Owens Peak (1972) 7.5' quadrangle.

Short Canyon Well [KERN]: *well,* 3.5 miles south-southwest of Onyx (lat. 35°38'20" N, long. 118°14' W; near W line sec. 28, T 26 S, R 35 E); the well is in Short Canyon (1). Named on Onyx (1972) 7.5' quadrangle.

Short Hair Creek [FRESNO]: *stream,* flows 5.5 miles to North Fork Kings River at Wishon Reservoir 10.5 miles west-southwest of Blackcap Mountain (lat. 37°01'15" N, long. 118°58'10" W; at W line sec. 31, T 10 S, R 28 E); the stream goes through Short Hair Meadow. Named on Blackcap Mountain (1953) and Huntington Lake (1953) 15' quadrangles.

Short Hair Meadow [FRESNO]: *area,* 8 miles east-southeast of Dinkey Dome (lat. 37°03'30" N, long. 119°00'25" W; near E line sec. 15, T 10 S, R 27 E); the place is along Short Hair Creek. Named on Huntington Lake (1953) 15' quadrangle.

Shorty Lake [FRESNO]: *lake,* 500 feet long, 15 miles northeast of Kaiser Peak (lat. 37°28'30" N, long. 119°01'40" W); the feature is one of the group called Margaret Lakes. Named on Kaiser Peak (1953) 15' quadrangle.

Shotgun Creek [TULARE]: *stream,* flows 4.5 miles to Little Kern River about 9 miles south-southeast of Mineral King (lat. 36°20'05" N, long. 118°32' W); the stream heads near Shotgun Pass. Named on Mineral King (1956) 15' quadrangle.

Shotgun Pass [TULARE]: *pass,* 5.5 miles southeast of Mineral King (lat. 36°23'20" N, long. 118°32'10" W); the pass is near the head of Shotgun Creek. Named on Mineral King (1956) 15' quadrangle.

Siberian Outpost [TULARE]: *area,* 11.5 miles north of Kern Peak along Siberian Pass Creek (lat. 36°28'15" N, long. 118°18'15" W). Named on Kern Peak (1956) 15' quadrangle.

Siberian Outpost Creek: see **Siberian Pass Creek** [TULARE].

Siberian Pass [TULARE]: *pass,* 11 miles north of Kern Peak (lat. 36° 28'10" N, long. 118°16'15" W; near NW cor. sec. 11, T 17 S, R 34 E). Named on Kern Peak (1956) 15' quadrangle. United States Board on Geographic Names (1933a, p. 691) rejected the name "Rampart Pass" for the feature.

Siberian Pass Creek [TULARE]: *stream,* flows 5.25 miles to Rock Creek 13 miles north-northwest of Kern Peak (lat. 36°29'40" N, long. 118°20'10" W). Named on Kern Peak (1956) 15' quadrangle. Called Siberian Outpost Cr. on Olmsted's (1900) map. The stream also was called South Fork Rock Creek (Browning, p. 198).

Sibleyville: see **Dinuba** [TULARE].

Sidehill Meadow [TULARE]: *area,* 4 miles southwest of Kern Peak (lat. 36°16'10" N, long. 118°20'10" W). Named on Kern Peak (1956) 15' quadrangle.

Sides [TULARE]: *locality,* 3.5 miles southeast of Exeter along Atchison, Topeka and Santa Fe Railroad (lat. 36°15'10" N, long. 119°05'55" W; near NW cor. sec. 30, T 19 S, R 27 E). Named on Rocky Hill (1927) 7.5' quadrangle.

Siding 18: see **Brown** [KERN].

Siding Number Two: see **Taft** [KERN].

Siding 16: see **Inyokern** [KERN].

Sidney Peak [KERN]: *peak,* 4 miles southwest of Randsburg (lat. 35°19'30" N, long. 117°42' W; near W line sec. 16, T 30 S, R 40 E). Altitude 4372 feet. Named on Johannesburg (1967) 7.5' quadrangle.

Sieretta Peak: see **Sirretta Peak** [TULARE].

Sierra: see **Camp Sierra** [FRESNO]; **High Sierra**, under "Regional setting."

Sierra Chautauqua: see **Camp Sierra** [FRESNO].

Sierra del Monte Diablo: see "Regional setting."

Sierra de San Marcos: see "Regional setting."

Sierra Glen [TULARE]: *locality,* 8.5 miles west-northwest of Yucca Mountain (lat. 36°38'20" N, long. 118°59'55" W; sec. 12, T 15 S, R 27 E). Named on Giant Forest (1956) 15' quadrangle.

Sierra Heights [TULARE]: *locality,* 2 miles southeast of Lindsay along Atchison, Topeka and Santa Fe Railroad (lat. 36°11'10" N, long. 119°03'40" W; near W line sec. 16, T 20 S, R 27 E). Named on Lindsay (1951) 7.5' quadrangle.

Sierra Nevada: see "Regional setting."

Sierra Sky Park [FRESNO]: *locality,* 7 miles northwest of downtown Fresno (lat. 36°50'25" N, long. 119°51'50" W; sec. 35, T 12 S, R 19 E). Named on Fresno North (1965) 7.5' quadrangle.

Signa: see **Kerto** [KERN].

Signal Hills: see **Little Signal Hills** [KERN].

Silaxo Drain [FRESNO]: *water feature,* extends for 10 miles, partly as an artificial watercourse, to Poso Slough nearly 5 miles north of Oxalis (lat. 36°58'55" N, long. 120°33'25" W; at N line sec. 16, T 11 S, R 13 E). Named on Oxalis (1956) and Poso Farm (1962) 7.5' quadrangles. Oxalis (1956) 7.5' quadrangle shows a place called Silaxo Oil Pumping Sta. located 1.5 miles east-southeast of Oxalis along Southern Pacific Railroad. The name "Silaxo" is the word "oxalis" spelled backwards (Gudde, 1949, p. 247).

Silaxo Drain 1 [FRESNO]: *water feature,* extends for 3.5 miles to Silaxo Drain about 2.5 miles east-southeast of Oxalis (lat. 36°54'15" N, long. 120°30'15" W; sec. 12, T 12 S, R 13 E. Named on Poso Farm (1962) 7.5' quadrangle.

Sill: see **Mount Sill** [FRESNO].

Silliman: see **Mount Silliman** [TULARE].

Silliman Creek [TULARE]: *stream,* flows 4 miles to Marble Fork 12 miles west of Triple Divide Peak (lat. 36°36'10" N, long. 118°44'15" W; sec. 20, T 15 S, R 30 E); the stream heads near Mount Silliman. Named on Triple Divide Peak (1956) 15' quadrangle.

Silliman Crest [TULARE]: *ridge,* generally north-northwest-trending, 2.5 miles long, 11 miles west-northwest of Triple Divide Peak (lat. 36°39'30" N, long. 118°42'20" W); Mount Silliman is at the south end of the ridge. Named on Triple Divide Peak (1956) 15' quadrangle.

Silliman Lake [TULARE]: *lake,* 700 feet long, 10 miles west-northwest of Triple Divide Peak (lat. 36°38'10" N, long. 118°42' W); the lake is 0.5 mile south-southwest of Mount Silliman at the head of a branch of Silliman Creek. Named on Triple Divide Peak (1956) 15' quadrangle.

Silliman Meadow [TULARE]: *area,* 11 miles west-northwest of Triple Divide Peak (lat. 36°37'50" N, long. 118°43'15" W; sec. 9, T 15 S, R 30 E); the place is along Silliman Creek. Named on Triple Divide Peak (1956) 15' quadrangle. United States Board on Geographic Names (1938, p. 49) rejected the name "Cahoon Meadow" for the feature.

Silliman Pass [TULARE]: *pass,* 11 miles west-northwest of Triple Divide Peak (lat. 36°39'45" N, long. 118°42'20" W); the pass is 1.5 miles north-northwest of Mount Silliman on Silliman Crest. Named on Triple Divide Peak (1956) 15' quadrangle.

Silver City [TULARE]: *locality,* 3 miles west-northwest of Mineral King (lat. 36°28' N, long. 118°38'45" W). Named on Mineral King (1956) 15' quadrangle. Miners on the way to Mineral King started a camp at the site in 1874 (Browning, p. 199).

Silver Creek [FRESNO]:

(1) *stream,* flows 6.5 miles to Fish Creek (1) 3.25 miles west-northwest of Double Peak (lat. 37°31'50" N, long. 119°05'25" W); the stream heads on Silver Divide. Named on Devils Postpile (1953) and Kaiser Peak (1953) 15' quadrangles. Theodore S. Solomons named the creek in 1892 for its silvery appearance (Farquhar, 1925, p. 133-134).

(2) *stream,* heads in San Benito County and flows 13 miles to Panoche Creek 23 miles southwest of Firebaugh (lat. 36°36'30" N, long. 120°41'10" W; sec. 20, T 15 S, R 12 E). Named on Tumey Hills (1956) 7.5' quadrangle. United States Board on Geographic Names (1933a, p. 693) rejected the name "Panoche Creek" for the stream.

(3) *stream,* flows 4 miles to Middle Fork Kings River 9.5 miles northeast of Hume (lat. 36°53'05" N, long. 118°47'40" W); the stream is south of Silver Spur. Named on Tehipite Dome (1952) 15' quadrangle.

Silver Creek [KERN]: *stream,* flows 1.5 miles to Indian Creek 5 miles west-northwest of Emerald Mountain (lat. 35°16'20" N, long. 118°22'15" W; near N line sec. 6, T 31 S, R 34 E). Named on Emerald Mountain (1972) 7.5' quadrangle.

Silver Creek [TULARE]: *stream,* flows 2.5 miles to North Fork of Middle Fork Tule River 7 miles north-northwest of Camp Nelson (lat. 36°14'10" N, long. 118°39'05" W; near SE cor. sec. 30, T 19 S, R 31 E). Named on Camp Nelson (1956) and Mineral King (1956) 15' quadrangles.

Silver Creek: see **Crystal Creek** [TULARE]; **Panoche Creek** [FRESNO].

Silver Divide [FRESNO]: *ridge,* generally west- and northwest-trending, 13 miles long, between the drainage areas of South Fork San Joaquin River and Middle Fork San Joaquin River. Named on Devils Postpile (1953), Kaiser Peak (1953), and Mount Abbot (1953) 15' quadrangles.

Silver Lake [TULARE]: *lake,* 700 feet long, nearly 6 miles southeast of Mineral King along Shotgun Creek (lat. 36°22'55" N, long. 118° 31'55" W). Named on Mineral King (1956) 15' quadrangle.

Silver Lake: see **Crystal Lake** [TULARE].

Silver Lakes: see **Franklin Lakes** [TULARE].

Silver Pass [FRESNO]: *pass,* 9.5 miles northwest of Mount Abbot (lat. 37°28'05" N, long. 118°55'20" W); the pass is on Silver Divide. Named on Mount Abbot (1953) 15' quadrangle. United States Board on Geographic Names (1982b, p. 3) approved the name "Goodale Pass" for a place located west of Silver Pass (lat. 37°27'50" N, long. 118°56'18" W).

Silver Pass Creek [FRESNO]: *stream,* flows 2 miles to North Fork Mono Creek 8 miles west-northwest of Mount Abbot (lat. 37°26'15" N, long. 118°54'30" W); the stream heads at Silver Pass Lake. Named on Mount Abbot (1953) 15' quadrangle.

Silver Pass Lake [FRESNO]: *lake,* 2200 feet long, 9 miles west-northwest of Mount Abbot (lat. 37°27'35" N, long. 118°55'20" W); the lake is 0.5 mile south of Silver Pass. Named on Mount Abbot (1953) 15' quadrangle.

Silver Peak [FRESNO]: *peak,* 15 miles northeast of Kaiser Peak (lat. 37°28'15" N, long. 119°01'15" W); the peak is on Silver Divide. Altitude 11,878 feet. Named on Kaiser Peak (1953) 15' quadrangle. Theodore S. Solomons named the peak in 1892 for nearby Silver Creek (1) (Farquhar, 1925, p. 134).

Silver Spray Falls [FRESNO]: *waterfall,* 11.5 miles northeast of Hume along Crown Creek (lat. 36°54'50" N, long. 118°47'15" W). Named on Tehipite Dome (1952) 15' quadrangle.

Silver Spur [FRESNO]: *ridge,* west-trending, 3 miles long, 11 miles northeast of Hume (lat. 36°53' N, long. 118°46' W). Named on Marion Peak (1953) and Tehipite Dome (1952) 15' quadrangles.

Simmons Post Camp [TULARE]: *locality,* 3.5 miles southwest of Camp Nelson (lat. 36°06'40" N, long. 118°39'45" W; sec. 7, T 21 S, R 31 E). Named on Camp Nelson (1956) 15' quadrangle.

Simpson Meadow [FRESNO]: *area,* 6.5 miles west of Marion Peak along Middle Fork Kings River (lat. 36°58' N, long. 118°38'10" W). Named on Marion Peak (1953) 15' quadrangle. Called Simpson Meadows on Lippincott's (1902) map. The Simpson family ran sheep at the place in the 1880's and patented the land in 1900; the area first was called Dougherty Meadow for Bill Dougherty and Bob Dougherty, who pastured horses there (Browning, p. 201).

Sink: see **Tejon Creek** [KERN].

Sinks of Tehachapa: see **Tehachapi Valley** [KERN].

Sinks of the Tejon: see **Tejon Creek** [KERN].

Siphon Canyon [TULARE]: *canyon,* drained by a stream that flows 2 miles to Middle Fork Tule River 2.5 miles east of Springville (lat. 36°08'05" N, long. 118°46'10" W; near N line sec. 5, T 21 S, R 30 E). Named on Springville (1957) 7.5' quadrangle, which shows a siphon in the canyon.

Sirretta Meadows [TULARE]: *areas,* 10 miles east of Fairview (lat. 35°56'30" N, long. 118°19'15" W); the meadows are 1.5 miles north-northeast of Sirretta Peak. Named on Kernville (1956) 15' quadrangle.

Sirretta Peak [TULARE]: *peak,* 9 miles east of Fairview (lat. 35°50'30" N, long. 118°20' W; sec. 17, T 23 S, R 34 E). Altitude 9977 feet. Named on Kernville (1956) 15' quadrangle. California Mining Bureau's (1917b) map has the name "Sieretta Pk."

Sivert [KERN]: *locality,* 5 miles east-southeast of Edison along Southern Pacific Railroad (lat. 35°19'40" N, long. 118°47'15" W). Named on Edison (1931) 7.5' quadrangle. Called Treves on Caliente (1914) 30' quadrangle.

Six Shooter Lake [FRESNO]: *lake,* 800 feet long, 2.5 miles north of Blackcap Mountain (lat. 37°06'35" N, long. 118°47'10" W). Named on Blackcap Mountain (1953) 15' quadrangle.

Sixty Lake Basin [FRESNO]: *valley,* 9 miles south of Mount Pinchot at the head of a branch of South Fork Woods Creek (lat. 36°49' N, long. 118°25'30" W). Named on Mount Pinchot (1953) 15' quadrangle.

Skeleton Spring [FRESNO]: *spring,* 4.25 miles north-northeast of Coalinga Mineral Springs (lat. 36°12'20" N, long. 120°32'15" W; sec. 11, T 20 S, R 13 E). Named on Sherman Peak (1969) 7.5' quadrangle.

Skinner Flat [KERN]: *area,* 3 miles south-southwest of Piute Peak (lat. 35°24'55" N, long. 118°25' W; near SW cor. sec. 11, T 29 S, R 33 E). Named on Piute Peak (1972) 7.5' quadrangle.

Skinner Peak [KERN]: *peak,* 10 miles south-southeast of Onyx (lat. 35°34' N, long. 118°07'35" W). Altitude 7120 feet. Named on Cane Canyon (1972) and Horse Canyon (1972) 7.5' quadrangles.

Skull Island: see **Alpaugh** [TULARE].

Skull Spring [KERN]: *spring,* nearly 4 miles north of Caliente in Tollhouse Canyon (lat. 35°20'40" N, long. 118°38'25" W). Named on Bena (1972) 7.5' quadrangle.

Skunk Canyon [FRESNO]: *canyon,* drained by a stream that flows 1.5 miles to Salt Canyon (3) 3 miles north-northwest of Smith Mountain (2) (lat. 36°07'10" N, long. 120°37'20" W; sec. 12, T 21 S, R 12 E). Named on Slack Canyon (1969) and Smith Mountain (1969) 7.5' quadrangles.

Skunk Hollow [FRESNO]: *area,* 10.5 miles north-northeast of Coalinga (lat. 36°16'50" N, long. 120°18' W; near NE cor. sec. 14, T 19 S, R 15 E). Named on Domengine Ranch (1956) 7.5' quadrangle.

Skunk Spring [TULARE]: *spring,* 4.25 miles north-northwest of California Hot Springs (lat. 35°56' N, long. 118°42'40" W; near N line sec. 14, T 23 S, R 30 E). Named on California Hot Springs (1958) 15' quadrangle.

Skunk Spring Saddle [TULARE]: *pass,* 4.5 miles northwest of California Hot Springs (lat. 35°56'05" N, long. 118°43' W; near SW cor. sec. 11, T 23 S, R 30 E); the pass is 0.25 mile west-northwest of Skunk Spring. Named on California Hot Springs (1958) 15' quadrangle.

Sky-Blue Lake [TULARE]: *lake,* 2000 feet long, 3.25 miles south-southeast of Mount Whitney (lat. 36°32' N, long. 118°16'20" W). Named on Mount Whitney (1956) 15' quadrangle.

Sky Parlor Meadow [TULARE]: *area,* 14 miles northwest of Kern Peak along Funston Creek (lat. 36°27'40" N, long. 118°26'30" W). Named on Kern Peak (1956) 15' quadrangle. United States Board on Geographic Names (1933a, p. 699) rejected the name "Upper Funston Meadow" for the feature.

Slapjack Creek [TULARE]: *stream,* flows 1 mile to East Fork Kaweah River 6.5 miles west of Mineral King (lat. 36°26' N, long. 118°42'45" W). Named on Mineral King (1956) 15' quadrangle.

Slate Mountain [TULARE]: *ridge,* north-trending, 6 miles long, 4.25 miles south-southeast of Camp Nelson (lat. 36°05' N, long. 118°34'30" W). Named on Camp Nelson (1956) 15' quadrangle.

Slater [KERN]: *locality,* 3 miles south of Famoso along Southern Pacific Railroad (lat. 35°32'55" N, long. 119°11'45" W; sec. 29, T 27 S, R 26 E). Named on Famoso (1953) 7.5' quadrangle.

Slickrock Canyon [TULARE]: *canyon,* 3.25 miles long, along Cottonwood Creek above a point 1.5 miles north-northeast of Auckland (lat. 36°36'40" N, long. 119°05'45" W; sec. 24, T 15 S, R 26 E). Named on Auckland (1966) and Miramonte (1966) 7.5' quadrangles.

Slick Rock Creek [KERN]: *stream,* flows 2.5 miles to Cedar Creek 2.5 miles west of Alta Sierra (lat. 35°43'55" N, long. 118°35'35" W; near SE cor. sec. 24, T 25 S, R 31 E). Named on Alta Sierra (1972) 7.5' quadrangle.

Slide Bluffs [FRESNO]: *relief feature,* 8.5 miles west of Marion Peak on the south side of the canyon of Middle Fork Kings River (lat. 36°56'15" N, long. 118°40'45" W). Named on Marion Peak (1953) 15' quadrangle.

Slide Canyon: see **Snowslide Canyon** [TULARE].

Slide Creek [FRESNO]: *stream,* flows 4.5 miles to Middle Fork Kings River 8.5 miles west of Marion Peak (lat. 36°56'50" N, long. 118°40'15" W); the stream heads at Slide Lakes and joins Middle Fork Kings River at the base of Slide Bluffs. Named on Marion Peak (1953) 15' quadrangle.

Slide Lakes [FRESNO]: *lakes,* largest 600 feet long, 10 miles west-southwest of Marion Peak (lat. 36°53'30" N, long. 118°41' W); the lakes are at the head of Slide Creek. Named on Marion Peak (1953) 15' quadrangle.

Slide Peak [FRESNO]: *peak,* 10 miles west-southwest of Marion Peak (lat. 36°54' N, long. 118°41'25" W). Altitude 10,915 feet. Named on Marion Peak (1953) 15' quadrangle.

Smith and Failing Meadow [TULARE]: *area,* 3 miles east-northeast of Camp Nelson (lat. 36°09'25" N, long. 118°33'20" W; at W line sec. 30, T 20 S, R 32 E). Named on Camp Nelson (1956) 15' quadrangle.

Smith Canyon [KERN]:

(1) *canyon,* drained by a stream that flows 8.5 miles to South Fork Valley near Onyx (lat. 35°41'20" N, long. 118°12'55" W; near SW cor. sec. 3, T 26 S, R 35 E). Named on Onyx (1972) and Walker Pass (1972) 7.5' quadrangles.

(2) *canyon,* drained by a stream that flows 2.5 miles to Nagel Canyon 8 miles north-northwest of Emerald Mountain (lat. 35° 22' N, long. 118°19'55" W). Named on Claraville (1972) and Emerald Mountain (1972) 7.5' quadrangles.

Smith Corner [KERN]: *locality,* 1.5 miles south of Shafter (lat. 35° 28'45" N, long. 119°16'40" W; on E line sec. 21, T 28 S, R 25 E). Named on Rio Bravo (1954) 7.5' quadrangle.

Smith Creek: see **Beach Creek** [TULARE].

Smith Meadow [FRESNO]: *area,* 10.5 miles north-northwest of Hume (lat. 36°56' N, long. 118°58' W). Named on Tehipite Dome (1952) 15' quadrangle.

Smith Meadow [TULARE]: *area,* 16 miles northwest of Lamont Peak (lat. 35°57'50" N, long. 118°13'40" W; on W line sec. 32, T 22 S, R 35 E). Named on Lamont Peak (1956) 15' quadrangle.

Smith Meadows [TULARE]: *area,* 5 miles south-southwest of Monache Mountain (lat. 36°08'35" N, long. 118°14'30" W; sec. 36, T 20 S, R 34 E); the place is 1.5 miles northwest of Smith Mountain (2). Named on Monache Mountain (1956) 15' quadrangle.

Smith Mill [TULARE]: *locality,* 4.5 miles southwest of Camp Nelson (lat. 36°05'25" N, long. 118°39'30" W; near NW cor. sec. 20, T 21 S, R 31 E). Named on Camp Nelson (1956) 15' quadrangle.

Smith Mountain [FRESNO]: *peak,* 14 miles west-southwest of Coalinga (lat. 36°04'45" N, long. 120°35'40" W; sec. 29, T 21 S, R 13 E). Altitude 3947 feet. Named on Smith Mountain (1969) 7.5' quadrangle.

Smith Mountain [FRESNO-TULARE]: *ridge,* south-trending, 3 miles long, 3.5 miles northeast of Dinuba on Fresno-Tulare County line (lat. 37°34'55" N, long. 119°20'45" W). Named on Orange Cove South (1966) 7.5' quadrangle.

Smith Mountain [TULARE]: *peak,* 5.5 miles south-southwest of Monache Mountain (lat. 36°07'35" N, long. 118°13'25" W; sec. 5, T 21 S, R 35 E). Altitude 9515 feet. Named on Monache Mountain (1956) 15' quadrangle.

Smith's Ferry: see **Reedley** [FRESNO].

Smyrna [TULARE]: *locality,* 2.25 miles south-southeast of Dinuba along Southern Pacific Railroad (lat. 36°31' N, long. 119°23'50" W; at S line sec. 21, T 16 S, R 24 E). Named on Sultana (1923) 7.5' quadrangle.

Smyrna: see **Pond** [KERN].

Snail Head [TULARE]: *peak,* 0.5 mile south-southeast of Springville (lat. 36°07'15" N, long. 118°48'40" W; near N line sec. 11, T 21 S, R 29 E). Altitude 1901 feet. Named on Globe (1956) 7.5' quadrangle.

Snake Creek [TULARE]: *stream,* flows 6 miles to South Fork Kern River 3 miles southeast of Monache Mountain (lat. 36°10'45" N, long. 118°09'20" W; near S line sec. 14, T 20 S, R 35 E). Named on Monache Mountain (1956) 15' quadrangle.

Snow Bend [FRESNO]: *locality,* nearly 4 miles east-southeast of Kaiser Peak (lat. 37°16'05" N, long. 119°07'25" W; near W line sec. 3, T 8 S, R 26 E). Named on Kaiser Peak (1953) 15' quadrangle.

Snow Corral Creek [FRESNO]: *stream,* flows 2.25 miles to Deer Creek (3) 8 miles south-southeast of Dinkey Dome (lat. 37°00'40" N, long. 119°03'55" W; sec. 31, T 10 S, R 27 E); the stream heads near Snow Corral Meadow. Named on Huntington Lake (1953) 15' quadrangle.

Snow Corral Meadow [FRESNO]: *area,* 7 miles south-southeast of Dinkey Dome (lat. 37°01'40" N, long. 119°04'20" W; sec. 30, T 10 S, R 27 E). Named on Huntington Lake (1953) 15' quadrangle.

Snow Creek [TULARE]: *stream,* flows 3 miles to Little Trout Creek 12 miles east-northeast of Fairview (lat. 35°58' N, long. 118°17'35" W; sec. 34, T 22 S, R 34 E). Named on Kernville (1956) 15' quadrangle.

Snow Lakes [FRESNO]: *lakes,* two, each 1400 feet long, 2 miles north of Mount Abbot in Fourth Recess (lat. 37°25' N, long. 118° 47'25" W). Named on Mount Abbot (1953) 15' quadrangle.

Snowslide Canyon [TULARE]: *canyon,* drained by a stream that flows 1.5 miles to Garfield Creek 10.5 miles southwest of Mineral King (lat. 36°20'50" N, long. 118°40'05" W). Named on Mineral King (1956) 15' quadrangle. Called Putman Can. on Kaweah (1909) 30' quadrangle, where present Putnam Canyon is called Snowslide Canyon. United States Board on Geographic Names (1967b, p. 2) rejected the names "Putman Canyon" and "Slide Canyon" for present Snowslide Canyon.

Snowslide Creek [FRESNO]: *stream,* flows 1 mile to Pittman Creek just east of the town of Big Creek (lat. 37°12'10" N, long. 119°14'10" W; sec. 28, T 8 S, R 25 E). Named on Huntington Lake (1953) 15' quadrangle.

Snowy Mountains: see "Regional setting."

Snowy Range: see "Regional setting."

Soaproot Flat [FRESNO]: *area,* 7 miles south-southeast of Shaver Lake Heights (present town of Shaver Lake) (lat. 37°01'10" N, long. 119°15'50" W; sec. 32, T 10 S, R 25 E); the place is west-southwest of Soaproot Saddle. Named on Shaver Lake (1953) 15' quadrangle.

Soaproot Saddle [FRESNO]: *pass,* 7 miles south-southeast of Shaver Lake Heights (present town of Shaver Lake) (lat. 37°01'30" N, long. 119°15'05" W; near S line sec. 28, T 10 S, R 25 E); the pass is east-northeast of Soaproot Flat. Named on Shaver Lake (1953) 15' quadrangle.

Soda Butte [TULARE]: *peak,* 9 miles south of Mineral King (lat. 36° 19'20" N, long. 118°34'15" W); the peak is near the head of Soda Spring Creek.

Named on Mineral King (1956) 15' quadrangle.

Soda Creek [TULARE]:

(1) *stream,* flows 1.5 miles to South Fork of Middle Fork Tule River 3.25 miles west-northwest of Camp Nelson (lat. 36°09'15" N, long. 118°39'50" W). Named on Camp Nelson (1956) 15' quadrangle.

(2) *stream,* flows 3 miles to South Fork Kern River 1.25 miles east of Monache Mountain near Soda Springs (1) (lat. 36°12'35" N, long. 118°10'30" W; sec. 3, T 20 S, R 35 E); the stream joins South Fork near Soda Springs (1). Named on Monache Mountain (1956) 15' quadrangle.

(3) *stream,* flows 6 miles to Big Arroyo 14 miles northwest of Kern Peak (lat. 36°27'30" N, long. 118°28'05" W). Named on Kern Peak (1956) and Mineral King (1956) 15' quadrangles.

(4) *stream,* flows 3.5 miles to Kern River 4.25 miles south of Hockett Peak (lat. 36°09'30" N, long. 118°23' W). Named on Hockett Peak (1956) 15' quadrangle.

Soda Flat [TULARE]: *area,* 2.5 miles east of Hockett Peak along Ninemile Creek (lat. 36°13'40" N, long. 118°20'20" W). Named on Hockett Peak (1956) 15' quadrangle.

Soda Spring [FRESNO]: *spring,* 1.5 miles north of Double Peak along Fish Creek (1) (lat. 37°32'15" N, long. 119°02'50" W). Named on Mount Lyell (1901) 30' quadrangle.

Soda Spring [TULARE]:

(1) *spring,* 7.25 miles west-northwest of Kern Peak in Kern Canyon (lat. 36°20'45" N, long. 118°24'25" W). Named on Kern Peak (1956) 15' quadrangle. A group of campers named the spring in 1873 (Browning, p. 204).

(2) *spring,* 7.5 miles southwest of Hockett Peak (lat. 36°08'10" N, long. 118°28'30" W). Named on Hockett Peak (1956) 15' quadrangle.

(3) *spring,* on the west side of Tule River at Springville (lat. 36°07'45" N, long. 118°48'55" W; sec. 2, T 21 S, R 29 E). Named on Springville (1957) 7.5' quadrangle.

Soda Spring: see **Upper Funston Meadow** [TULARE].

Soda Spring Creek [TULARE]: *stream,* flows 8 miles to Little Kern River 14 miles south-southeast of Mineral King (lat. 36°15'15" N, long. 118°31' W; sec. 21, T 19 S, R 32 E); the stream heads near Soda Butte. Named on Mineral King (1956) 15' quadrangle.

Soda Spring Lake: see **Kern Lake** [TULARE].

Soda Springs [KERN]: *spring,* 3 miles west-northwest of Emerald Mountain along Indian Creek (lat. 35°16'05" N, long. 118°19'55" W; sec. 4, T 31 S, R 34 E). Named on Emerald Mountain (1972) 7.5' quadrangle.

Soda Springs [TULARE]:

(1) *spring,* 1 mile east-northeast of Monache Mountain in Monache Meadows (lat. 36°12'35" N, long. 118°10'30" W; sec. 3, T 20 S, R 35 E). Named on Monache Mountain (1956) 15' quadrangle.

(2) *locality,* 7 miles south-southeast of Springville along South Fork Tule River (lat. 36°02'20" N, long. 118°45'25" W). Named on Globe (1956) 7.5' quadrangle.

Soldier Meadow [TULARE]: *area,* 7 miles north-northeast of California Hot Springs (lat. 35°58'40" N, long. 118°37'45" W; sec. 33, T 22 S, R 31 E). Named on California Hot Springs (1958) 15' quadrangle.

Soldier Wells [KERN]: *springs,* 7.5 miles west-southwest of Inyokern in Freeman Canyon (lat. 35°36'40" N, long. 117°56'20" W; near SE cor. sec. 1, T 27 S, R 37 E). Named on Freeman Junction (1972) 7.5' quadrangle.

Soledad Mountain [KERN]: *range,* 8.5 miles north of Rosamond (lat. 34°58'55" N, long. 118°11'15" W). Named on Soledad Mountain (1973) 7.5' quadrangle.

Solitaire: see **Kern River** [KERN-TULARE].

Solomons: see **Mount Solomons**, under **Mount Goddard** [FRESNO].

Solon [KERN]: *locality,* 8 miles east-northeast of present Edwards along Atchison, Topeka and Santa Fe Railroad (lat. 34°57'10" N, long. 117°47'50" W; near N line sec. 23, T 10 N, R 9 W). Named on Rogers Lake (1942) 15' quadrangle.

Solo Peak [TULARE]: *peak,* 4.5 miles southwest of Camp Nelson (lat. 36°06'15" N, long. 118°40'15" W; sec. 18, T 21 S, R 31 E). Altitude 7310 feet. Named on Camp Nelson (1956) 15' quadrangle.

Sontag Point [FRESNO]: *peak,* 2.5 miles east-northeast of Dunlap (lat. 36°44'50" N, long. 119°04'30" W; sec. 31, T 13 S, R 27 E). Altitude 4223 feet. Named on Miramonte (1966) 7.5' quadrangle. The name commemorates John Sontag, an outlaw of the 1890's, who with his partner, Chris Evans, had a shoot-out with a posse at a cabin situated about 0.5 mile north of the place (Forest M. Clingan, personal communication, 1989).

Sorrell Peak [KERN]: *peak,* 3 miles southeast of Claraville (lat. 35° 25'05" N, long. 118°17'20" W). Altitude 7704 feet. Named on Claraville (1972) 7.5' quadrangle. Called Sorell Peak on Emerald Mountain (1943) 15' quadrangle. United States Board on Geographic Names (1975b, p. 11) gave the forms "Sorell Peak" and "Sorrel Peak" as variants, and noted that the name "Sorrell" commemorates Hiram H. Sorrell, a homesteader in Kelso Valley.

Sorrell's: see **Sageland** [KERN].

South Alder Creek [TULARE]: *stream,* flows 3.5 miles to North Fork of Middle Fork Tule River 5 miles north-northwest of Camp Nelson (lat. 36°12'10" N, long. 118°39' W; near W line sec. 8, T 20 S, R 31 E). Named on Camp Nelson (1956) 15' quadrangle.

South American Lake: see **Lake South America** [TULARE].

South Bear Creek [TULARE]: *stream,* flows 2.25 miles to Bear Creek (2) 6 miles northeast of Springville (lat. 36°12'05" N, long. 118°45'25" W). Named on Camp Nelson (1956) and Springville (1957) 15' quadrangles.

South Corcoran [KINGS]: *locality,* 0.5 mile south-southeast of Corcoran along Atchison, Topeka and Santa Fe Railroad (lat. 36°05'30" N, long. 119°33'15" W; on E line sec. 23, T 21 S, R 22 E). Named on Corcoran (1928) 7.5' quadrangle.

South Creek [TULARE]: *stream,* formed by the confluence of Double Bunk Creek and Bear Creek (4), flows 6 miles to Kern River 3 miles north of Fairview (lat. 35°58'05" N, long. 118°29'10" W; sec. 35, T 22 S, R 32 E). Named on California Hot Springs (1958) and Kernville (1956) 15' quadrangles. Called Wade Cr. on Olmsted's (1900) map.

South Creek Falls [TULARE]: *waterfall,* 3.25 miles north of Fairview (lat. 35°58'15" N, long. 118°29'30" W; sec. 35, T 22 S, R 32 E); the waterfall is along South Creek. Named on Kernville (1956) 15' quadrangle.

South Dome: see **Kettleman Hills** [FRESNO-KERN-KINGS].

Southeast Palisade: see **Split Mountain** [FRESNO].

South Fork Meadows [TULARE]:

(1) *area,* 8 miles south-southwest of Mineral King (lat. 36°20'50" N, long. 118°38'30" W; sec. 20, T 18 S, R 31 E); the place is along South Fork Kaweah River. Named on Mineral King (1956) 15' quadrangle.

(2) *area,* 12.5 miles northwest of Olancha Peak (lat. 36°24'45" N, long. 118°14'35" W; on S line sec. 25, T 17 S, R 34 E); the place is along South Fork Kern River. Named on Olancha (1956) 15' quadrangle.

South Fork Meadows: see **Tunnel Meadow** [TULARE].

Southfork Pass [FRESNO]: *pass,* 1.5 miles north-northwest of Mount Bolton Brown on Fresno-Inyo County line (lat. 37°04'05" N, long. 118°27'05" W); the pass is at the head of a branch of South Fork Big Pine Creek, which is in Inyo County. Named on Big Pine (1950) 15' quadrangle.

South Fork Valley [KERN]: *valley,* extends for 11 miles along South Fork Kern River above Isabella Lake. Named on Onyx (1972) and Weldon (1972) 7.5' quadrangles.

South Guard [TULARE]: *peak,* 13 miles northwest of Mount Whitney on Great Western Divide (lat. 36°41'40" N, long. 118°29' W); the peak is 1.5 miles south of North Guard. Altitude 13,224 feet. Named on Mount Whitney (1956) 15' quadrangle. Lieutenant Milton F. Davis named the feature (Browning, p. 205).

South Guard Lake [TULARE]: *lake,* 2100 feet long, 14 miles northwest of Mount Whitney (lat. 36°41'30" N, long. 118°29'40" W); the lake is 0.5 mile west of South Guard. Named on Mount Whitney (1956) 15' quadrangle.

South Lake [FRESNO]: *lake,* 1200 feet long, 4.5 miles northeast of Dinkey Dome (lat. 37°09'30" N, long. 119°03'35" W; sec. 7, T 9 S, R 27 E). Named on Huntington Lake (1953) 15' quadrangle.

South Lake [KERN]: *settlement,* 4.5 miles west-southwest of Weldon (lat. 35°38'15" N, long. 118°21'45" W; mainly in sec. 30, T 26 S, R 34 E); the place is south of the east end of Isabella Lake. Named on Weldon (1972) 7.5' quadrangle.

South Mountaineer Creek [TULARE]: *stream,* flows 3 miles to Mountaineer Creek nearly 7 miles north-northeast of Camp Nelson (lat. 36°13'55" N, long. 118°33'50" W; sec. 36, T 19 S, R 31 E). Named on Camp Nelson (1956) 15' quadrangle.

South Palisade: see **Split Mountain** [FRESNO].

South Taft [KERN]: *district,* 0.5 mile south of downtown Taft (lat. 35°08' N, long. 119°27'20" W; near N line sec. 24, T 32 S, R 23 E). Named on Taft (1950) 7.5' quadrangle.

Spa [TULARE]: *locality,* 10.5 miles west-northwest of Earlimart along Atchison, Topeka and Santa Fe Railroad (lat. 35°56'35" N, long. 119°26'30" W; sec. 12, T 23 S, R 23 E). Named on Alpaugh (1929) 7.5' quadrangle. Postal authorities established Spa post office in 1911 and discontinued it in 1920 (Frickstad, p. 213).

Spangler Valley: see **Searles Valley** [KERN].

Spanish Camp [TULARE]: *locality,* 11.5 miles north-northeast of Porterville (lat. 36°12'35" N, long. 118°54'40" W; near S line sec. 2, T 20 S, R 28 E). Named on Frazier Valley (1957) 7.5' quadrangle.

Spanish Lake [FRESNO]:

(1) *lake,* 1300 feet long, 10 miles north of Hume (lat. 36°55'50" N, long. 118°53'55" W); the lake is 1.5 miles north-northwest of Spanish Mountain. Named on Tehipite Dome (1952) 15' quadrangle.

(2) *lake,* 700 feet long, 18 miles northwest of Coalinga (lat. 36° 19'50" N, long. 120°34'30" W; sec. 29, T 18 S, R 13 E). Named on Santa Rita Peak (1969) 7.5' quadrangle.

Spanish Lake: see **Little Spanish Lake** [FRESNO].

Spanish Meadow [FRESNO]: *area,* 10 miles north of Hume (lat. 36° 55'55" N, long. 118°54'20" W); the place is nearly 2 miles north-northwest of Spanish Mountain. Named on Tehipite Dome (1952) 15' quadrangle.

Spanish Mountain [FRESNO]: *peak,* 9 miles north of Hume (lat. 36° 54'30" N, long. 118°53'25" W). Altitude 10,051 feet. Named on Tehipite Dome (1952) 15' quadrangle.

Spanish Needle Creek [KERN]: *stream,* flows 5.5 miles to Canebreak Creek 3.5 miles north-northwest of Walker Pass (lat. 35°45'05" N, long. 118°40'40" W). Named on Lamont Peak (1956) 7.5' quadrangle.

Spear Creek [TULARE]: *stream,* flows 4.5 miles to join Von Hellum Creek and form Poso Creek 5.25 miles south of California Hot Springs (lat. 35°48'15" N, long. 118°39'10" W; near S line sec. 29, T 24 S, R 31 E). Named on California Hot Springs (1958) 15' quadrangle.

Spear Creek Summer Home Tract [TULARE]: *locality,* 6 miles southeast of California Hot Springs (lat. 35°49'10" N, long. 118° 35'35" W; near SE cor. sec. 23, T 24 S, R 31 E); the place is near Spear Creek. Named on California Hot Springs (1958) 15' quadrangle.

Spearpoint Lake [FRESNO]: *lake,* 2250 feet long, 9 miles south-southwest of Mount Abbot (lat. 37°15'45" N, long. 118°49'05" W). Named on Mount Abbot (1953) 15' quadrangle. Elden H. Vestal of California Department of Fish and Game named the lake in 1951 for its shape (Browning, p. 206).

Speas Creek [TULARE]:

(1) *stream,* flows 3.5 miles to Tobias Creek 9 miles east of California Hot Springs (lat. 35°54'10" N, long. 118°31' W; sec. 27, T 23 S, R 32 E). Named on California Hot Springs (1958) 15' quadrangle. On Tobias Peak (1936) 30' quadrangle, the canyon of the stream is called Scarlett and Davis Can., but United States Board on Geographic Names (1960a, p. 10) rejected this name for the feature.

(2) *stream,* flows 2.5 miles to White River (1) 4.5 miles southwest of California Hot Springs (lat. 35°50'20" N, long. 118°43'45" W; sec. 15, T 24 S, R 30 E). Named on California Hot Springs (1958) 15' quadrangle.

Speas Dirty Camp [TULARE]: *locality,* 6.5 miles east-northeast of California Hot Springs (lat. 35°55'30" N, long. 118°33'55" W; sec. 18, T 23 S, R 32 E); the place is in Speas Meadow. Named on California Hot Springs (1958) 15' quadrangle.

Speas Meadow [TULARE]: *area,* about 7 miles east-northeast of California Hot Springs (lat. 35°55'35" N, long. 118°33'45" W; sec. 18, T 23 S, R 32 E); the place is near the head of Speas Creek (1). Named on California Hot Springs (1958) 15' quadrangle.

Speas Ridge [TULARE]: *ridge,* northeast- to east-trending, 5 miles long, 9 miles east-northeast of California Hot Springs (lat. 35° 57' N, long. 118°32' W). Named on California Hot Springs (1958) 15' quadrangle.

Speck Spring [FRESNO]: *spring,* 5.25 miles west-southwest of Coalinga in Oak Flat Canyon (lat. 36°07'10" N, long. 120°27' W; near W line sec. 10, T 21 S, R 14 E). Named on Curry Mountain (1969) 7.5' quadrangle.

Spellacy [KERN]: *locality,* 5.25 miles northwest of Maricopa (lat. 35°06'45" N, long. 119°28'15" W; sec. 26, T 32 S, R 23 E). Named on Maricopa (1951) 7.5' quadrangle.

Spellacy Hill [KERN]: *ridge,* northwest-trending, 1 mile long, 1.5 miles west-southwest of Taft (lat. 35°07'45" N, long. 119°29' W; on E line sec. 22, T 32 S, R 23 E). Named on Taft (1950) 7.5' quadrangle. Arnold and Johnson (p. 22) proposed the name to commemorate the Spellacy brothers, early investors in oil development of the neighborhood.

Spencer: see **Mount Spencer** [FRESNO]:

Sphinx: see **The Sphinx** [FRESNO].

Sphinx Creek [FRESNO-TULARE]: *stream,* heads at Sphinx Lakes in Tulare County and flows 8 miles to Bubbs Creek 12 miles south of Marion Peak in Fresno County (lat. 36°46'50" N, long. 118°32'15" W). Named on Marion Peak (1953) and Triple Divide Peak (1956) 15' quadrangles.

Sphinx Crest [TULARE]: *ridge,* northwest-trending, 3 miles long, 9 miles north of Triple Divide Peak (lat. 36°43'40" N, long. 118° 32' W). Named on Triple Divide Peak (1956) 15' quadrangle.

Sphinx Lakes [TULARE]: *lakes,* largest 2000 feet long, 9.5 miles north of Triple Divide Peak (lat. 36°44' N, long. 118°31' W); the lakes are northeast of Sphinx Crest on upper reaches of Sphinx Creek. Named on Triple Divide Peak (1956) 15' quadrangle.

Spicer City [KERN]: *locality,* 9 miles south-southeast of the village of Lost Hills (lat. 35°30'05" N, long. 119°36'10" W). Named on Semitropic (1954) 7.5' quadrangle.

Spinks Corner [TULARE]: *locality,* 8 miles west of Lindsay (lat. 36° 12'40" N, long. 119°13'55" W; at N line sec. 11, T 20 S, R 25 E). Named on Cairns Corner (1950) 7.5' quadrangle.

Split Mountain [FRESNO]: *peak,* 2 miles south-southeast of Mount Bolton Brown on Fresno-Inyo County line (lat. 37°01'15" N, long. 118°25'15" W). Altitude 14,058 feet. Named on Big Pine (1950) 15' quadrangle. Bolton C. Brown named the peak for its double summit; members of the Wheeler survey called the feature Southeast Palisade in 1876—it also was known as South Palisade (Farquhar, 1925, p. 135).

Split Mountain [KERN]: *ridge,* generally east-trending, 1.25 miles long, 3 miles west of Kernville (lat. 35°45'05" N, long. 118°28'30" W). Named on Kernville (1956) 15' quadrangle, and on Lake Isabella North (1972) 7.5' quadrangle.

Sportsman Lake [FRESNO]: *lake,* 900 feet long, 4.5 miles east-southeast of Dinkey Dome (lat. 37°05'45" N, long. 119°03'20" W; near N line sec. 5, T 10 S, R 27 E). Named on Huntington Lake (1953) 15' quadrangle.

Spottiswood: see **Famoso** [KERN].

Spout Spring [KERN]: *spring,* 8 miles east-northeast of Glennville (lat. 35°45'05" N, long. 118°33'30" W; sec. 17, T 25 S, R 32 E). Named on California Hot Springs (1958) 15' quadrangle.

Spring Canyon [KERN]: *canyon,* drained by a stream that flows 1.5 miles to Canebreak Flat 6 miles northwest of Walker Pass (lat. 35° 43'15" N, long. 118°06'25" W; near SW cor. sec. 27, T 25 S, R 36 E). Named on Walker Pass (1972) 7.5' quadrangle.

Spring Creek [FRESNO]:

(1) *stream,* flows 1 mile to Huntington Lake 3 miles south of Kaiser Peak (lat. 37°15'05" N, long. 119°10'45" W; sec. 7, T 8 S, R 26 E). Named on Kaiser Peak (1953) 15' quadrangle.

(2) *stream,* flows 3.5 miles to Kings River 6.5 miles northwest of Hume (lat. 36°51'45" N, long. 118°58'55" W). Named on Tehipite Dome (1952) 15' quadrangle.

Spring Creek: see **Eagle Creek** [TULARE] (1).

Springfield Spring [KERN]: *spring,* 11 miles north-northwest of Mojave (lat. 35°12'25" N, long. 119°12'40" W; sec. 27, T 31 S, R 35 E). Named on Cache Peak (1973) 7.5' quadrangle.

Spring Gulch [KERN]: *canyon,* 1 mile long, opens into the canyon of Erskine Creek 4.25 miles east of Bodfish (lat. 35°34'30" N, long. 118°24'45" W; near SW cor. sec. 14, T 27 S, R 33 E). Named on Lake Isabella South (1972) 7.5' quadrangle.

Springhill Campground: see **Lower Springhill Campground** [TULARE]; **Upper Springhill Campground** [TULARE].

Spring Lake [TULARE]: *lake,* 1400 feet long, 2.5 miles east-northeast of Mineral King (lat. 36°28'15" N, long. 118°33'25" W). Named on Mineral King (1956) 15' quadrangle.

Spring Mountain Creek: see **Spring Mountain Gulch** [KERN].

Spring Mountain Gulch [KERN]: *canyon,* drained by a stream that flows 3.5 miles to Rag Gulch 0.5 mile west of Woody (lat. 35° 42'10" N, long. 118°50'45" W; near S line sec. 34, T 25 S, R 29 E). Named on Woody (1965) 7.5' quadrangle. United States Board on Geographic Names (1966b, p. 6) rejected the names "Dry Creek" and "Spring Mountain Creek" for the feature.

Springville [TULARE]: *town,* 12 miles east-northeast of Porterville along Tule River (lat. 36°07'55" N, long. 118°49' W; in and near sec. 2, T 21 S, R 29 E). Named on Globe (1956) and Springville (1957) 7.5' quadrangles. A.M. Coburn, a lumberman who had mills at the place, founded the town in 1889; it first was called Daunt, for William G. Daunt, a settler of the 1860's, and later was named for Soda Spring (3) (Hanna, p. 314). Postal authorities established Daunt post office in 1886 and changed the name to Springville in 1911 (Frickstad, p. 210). California Division of Highways' (1934) map shows a place called Clavicle located 2 miles south of Springville along Southern Pacific Railroad (near E line sec. 15, T 21 S, R 29 E). Postal authorities established Jordan post office 11 miles northeast of Springville in 1951 and discontinued it in 1952 (Salley, p. 108).

Square Lake [FRESNO]: *lake,* 650 feet long, 3 miles west of Mount Humphreys in Humphreys Basin (lat. 37°16' N, long. 118°43'35" W). Named on Mount Tom (1949) 15' quadrangle.

Squaw Creek [TULARE]: *stream,* flows 2.5 miles to South Fork Kaweah River 12.5 miles southeast of Kaweah (lat. 36°20'50" N, long. 118°45'05" W). Named on Kaweah (1957) and Mineral King (1956) 15' quadrangles. United States Board on Geographic Names (1960b, p. 21) rejected the name "Pigeon Creek" for the stream. The name "Squaw Creek" was given about sixty years after a Mexican murdered his wife near the stream (Browning, p. 207).

Squaw Creek: see **Cedar Creek** [TULARE] (4).

Squaw Lake: see **Helen Lake** [FRESNO] (1); **Old Squaw Lake** [FRESNO].

Squaw Leap [FRESNO]: *peak,* nearly 3 miles northwest of Prather (lat. 37°04'10" N, long. 119°32'45" W; near SW cor. sec. 11, T 10 S, R 22 E). Named on Millerton Lake East (1965) 7.5' quadrangle.

Squaw Valley [FRESNO]:

(1) *valley,* 6.5 miles west of Dunlap (lat. 36°44' N, long. 119° 14' W). Named on Orange Cove North (1966) and Tucker Mountain (1966) 7.5' quadrangles.

(2) *locality,* 7 miles west of Dunlap (lat. 36°44'25" N, long. 119°14'40" W; sec. 3, T 14 S, R 25 E); the place is in Squaw Valley (1). Named on Tucker Mountain (1966) 7.5' quadrangle. Postal authorities established Squaw Valley post office in 1879, changed the name to Squawvalley in 1895, discontinued it in 1918, reestablished it in 1923, changed the name back to Squaw Valley in 1932, discontinued the post office in 1945, and reestablished it in 1960 (Salley, p. 211). United States Board on Geographic Names (1959, p. 2) rejected the form "Squawvalley" for the name.

Squirrel Creek [TULARE]: *stream,* flows 4 miles to East Fork Kaweah River 8.5 miles east-southeast of Kaweah (lat. 36°26'25" N, long. 118°46'15" W; at S line sec. 13, T 17 S, R 29 E). Named on Kaweah (1957) and Mineral King (1956) 15' quadrangles.

Squirrel Meadow [KERN]: *area,* 10 miles east-northeast of Mount Adelaide (lat. 35°28'30" N, long. 118°34'35" W; sec. 19, T 28 S, R 32 E). Named on Breckenridge Mountain (1972) 7.5' quadrangle.

Squirrel Mountain Valley [KERN]: *settlement,* 5 miles northeast of Bodfish (lat. 38°37'30" N, long. 118°24'30" W; sec. 35, T 26 S, R 33 E). Named on Lake Isabella North (1972) and Lake Isabella South (1972) 7.5' quadrangles.

Stable Creek [KERN]: *stream,* flows nearly 3 miles to French Gulch (1) 4.5 miles south-southeast of Alta Sierra (lat. 35°39'55" N, long. 118°31'15" W; sec. 15, T 26 S, R 32 E). Named on Alta Sierra (1972) 7.5' quadrangle.

Stag Canyon [KERN]: *canyon,* drained by a stream that flows 1.25 miles to Montgomery Canyon 4.25 miles east of Caliente (lat. 35° 17'35" N, long. 118°33'10" W; sec. 28, T 30 S, R 32 E). Named on Oiler Peak (1972) 7.5' quadrangle.

Stag Dome [FRESNO]: *peak,* 14 miles southwest of Marion Peak (lat. 36°49'15" N, long. 118°42' W). Altitude 7710 feet. Named on Marion Peak (1953) 15' quadrangle.

Stag Saddle [KERN]: *pass,* 5.25 miles east of Caliente on Devils Backbone (lat. 35°17'15" N, long. 118°32'05" W; sec. 27, T 30 S, R 32 E); the pass is near the head of Stag Canyon. Named on Oiler Peak (1972) 7.5' quadrangle.

Stag Spring [KERN]: *spring,* 4 miles southwest of Cummings Mountain (lat. 35°00'20" N, long. 118°37'20" W; sec. 31, T 11 N, R 16 W). Named on Cummings Mountain (1966) 7.5' quadrangle.

Stag Thicket Spring [KERN]: *spring,* 5.5 miles east of Caliente (lat. 35°17'15" N, long. 118°31'35" W; sec. 27, T 30 S, R 32 E). Named on Oiler Peak (1972) 7.5' quadrangle.

Stalf Creek: see **Woolstalf Creek** [KERN].

Standard Hill [KERN]: *hill,* 3 miles south of Mojave (lat. 35°00'25" N, long. 118°10'25" W; sec. 32, T 11 N, R 12 W). Altitude 3128 feet. Named on Mojave (1973) 7.5' quadrangle. Called Elephant Butte on Mojave (1947) 7.5' quadrangle, and United States Board on Geographic Names (1975c, p. 5) gave this name as a variant.

Stanford: see **Mount Stanford** [FRESNO]; **Mount Stanford** [TULARE].

Stanford Peak: see **Mount Stanford** [FRESNO].

Stanley: see **Turk** [FRESNO].

Stark Creek [KERN]: *stream,* flows 6.5 miles to Kern River 3.25 miles north-northeast of Mount Adelaide (lat. 35°28'35" N, long. 118°43'25" W). Named on Mount Adelaide (1972) 7.5' quadrangle. Called Stork Creek on Breckenridge Mountain (1943) 15' quadrangle, and United States Board on Geographic Names (1975b, p. 12) gave this name as a variant.

Starr: see **Mount Starr** [FRESNO].

Starvation Creek [TULARE]: *stream,* flows 4 miles to Tyler Creek 2 miles northeast of California Hot Springs (lat. 35°54'10" N, long. 118°38'50" W; sec. 29, T 23 S, T 31 E). Named on California Hot Springs (1958) 15' quadrangle.

State Lakes [FRESNO]: *lakes,* 2 miles southwest of Marion Peak (lat. 36°55'50" N, long. 118°33'30" W); the lakes are about 1 mile west of State Peak. Named on Marion Peak (1953) 15' quadrangle.

State Peak [FRESNO]: *peak,* 2 miles southwest of Marion Peak (lat. 36°55'55" N, long. 118°32'40" W). Altitude 12,620 feet. Named on Marion Peak (1953) 15' quadrangle.

Statham Creek: see **Statum Creek** [FRESNO].

Statham Meadow: see **Statum Meadow** [FRESNO].

Statum Creek [FRESNO]: *stream,* flows about 4 miles to Rancheria Creek (3) 12 miles north of Hume (lat. 36°57'15" N, long. 118°56'10" W). Named on Tehipite Dome (1952) 15' quadrangle. United States Board on Geographic Names (1987b, p. 2) approved the name "Statham Creek" for the stream, and pointed out that the name commemorates Albert Statham, an early-day sheepman in the neighborhood.

Statum Meadow [FRESNO]: *area,* 11 miles north of Hume (lat. 36° 56'40" N, long. 118°54'50" W); the place is along Statum (present Statham) Creek. Named on Tehipite Dome (1952) 15' quadrangle. United States Board on Geographic Names (1987b, p. 2) approved the name "Statham Meadow" for the feature.

Steelhead Lake [FRESNO]: *lake,* 2600 feet long, 3 miles northwest of Mount Humphreys (lat. 37°18'05" N, long. 118°42'40" W; near NW cor. sec. 32, T 7 S, R 30 E). Named on Mount Tom (1949) 15' quadrangle.

Stephenson Hill [FRESNO]: *peak,* 6.25 miles northwest of Piedra (lat. 36°52'15" N, long. 119°27'45" W; sec. 21, T 12 S, R 23 E). Altitude 1059 feet. Named on Piedra (1965) 7.5' quadrangle.

Steve Barton Point [TULARE]: *peak,* 4 miles east of Woodlake (lat. 36°24'15" N, long. 119°01'45" W; sec. 34, T 17 S, R 27 E). Altitude 859 feet. Named on Woodlake (1952) 7.5' quadrangle. Grunsky (p. 11) called the feature Dillons Point.

Stevens [KERN]: *locality,* 11.5 miles west-southwest of Bakersfield along Southern Pacific Railroad (lat. 35°18'50" N, long. 119°11'20" W; sec. 16, T 30 S, R 26 E). Named on Stevens (1954) 7.5' quadrangle.

Stevens Creek: see **Stevenson Creek** [FRESNO].

Stevenson: see **Mount Stevenson** [FRESNO].

Stevenson Basin: see **Shaver Lake** [FRESNO].

Stevenson Creek [FRESNO]: *stream,* flows 12 miles, including through Shaver Lake, to San Joaquin River 5 miles north-northwest of Shaver Lake Heights (present town of Shaver Lake) (lat. 37°10'15" N, long. 119°21'35" W; at N line sec. 9, T 9 S, R 24 E). Named on Huntington Lake (1953) and Shaver Lake (1953) 15' quadrangles. United States Board on Geographic Names (1933a, p. 721) rejected the names "Stevens Creek" and "Stevensons Creek" for the stream. North Fork enters Shaver Lake 3.5 miles east-northeast of Shaver Lake Heights (present town of Shaver Lake); it is 3.5 miles long and is named on Huntington Lake (1953) and Shaver Lake (1953) 15' quadrangles.

Stevenson Creek [KERN]: *stream,* flows 4.5 miles to Indian Creek 4 miles east-southeast of Loraine (lat. 35°16'20" N, long. 118°22'30" W; near NW cor. sec. 6, T 31 S, R 34 E); the stream is located 1 mile south-southeast of Stevenson Peak. Named on Emerald Mountain (1972), Loraine (1972), and Tehachapi NE (1966) 7.5' quadrangles.

Stevenson Gulch [TULARE]: *canyon,* drained by a stream that flows 2 miles to South Fork of Middle Fork Tule River 4.5 miles west-northwest of Camp Nelson (lat. 36°09'30" N, long. 118°41'15" W). Named on Camp Nelson (1956) 15' quadrangle.

Stevenson Meadows: see **Shaver Lake** [FRESNO].

Stevenson Peak [KERN]: *peak,* 3 miles east-southeast of Loraine (lat. 35°17'10" N, long. 118°23' W; sec. 25, T 30 S, R 33 E). Altitude 5026 feet. Named on Loraine (1972) 7.5' quadrangle.

Stevensons Creek: see **Stevenson Creek** [FRESNO].

Steve Spring [KERN]: *spring,* 11 miles south-southwest of Weldon (lat. 35°30'45" N, long. 118°20'05" W; at E line sec. 8, T 28 S, R 34 E). Named on Woolstaff Creek (1972) 7.5' quadrangle.

Stewart Mountain: see **Mount Stewart** [TULARE].

Still Canyon [KERN]: *canyon,* drained by a stream that flows 3.5 miles to Barrel Valley nearly 6 miles south of Orchard Peak (lat. 35°39'10" N, long. 120°07'45" W; sec. 22, T 26 S, R 17 E). Named on Orchard Peak (1961) 7.5' quadrangle.

Still Lake [KERN]: *intermittent lake,* about 600 feet long, 7.5 miles south-southwest of Orchard Peak (lat. 35°38'10" N, long. 120°11'20" W; sec. 30, T 26 S, R 17 E). Named on Orchard Peak (1961) 7.5' quadrangle.

Stine Cove [KERN]: *embayment,* 3.25 miles southeast of Wofford Heights on the north side of Isabella Lake (lat. 35°40'40" N, long. 118°24'30" W; sec. 11, T 26 S, R 33 E). Named on Lake Isabella North (1972) 7.5' quadrangle.

Stine Point [KERN]: *promontory,* 3.25 miles southeast of Wofford Heights along Isabella Lake (lat. 35°40'35" N, long. 118°24'50" W; near SE cor. sec. 10, T 26 S, R 33 E). Named on Lake Isabella North (1972) 7.5' quadrangle.

Stocking Lake [FRESNO]: *lake,* 1800 feet long, 5.5 miles south-southeast of Mount Pinchot (lat. 36°52'15" N, long. 118°22'15" W). Named on Mount Pinchot (1953) 15' quadrangle.

Stockton: see **Lake Stockton** [KERN].

Stoil [TULARE]: *locality,* 9 miles west-northwest of Earlimart along Atchison, Topeka and Santa Fe Railroad (lat. 35°55'05" N, long. 119°25'25" W; sec. 19, T 23 S, R 24 E). Named on Alpaugh (1953) 7.5' quadrangle. The name is an abbreviated form of the term "Standard Oil"—Standard Oil Company had a pumping station at the place (Gudde, 1949, p. 344).

Stoker Canyon [KERN-KINGS]: *canyon,* drained by a stream that heads in Kings County and flows 3.5 miles to Cottonwood Canyon 3.5 miles north-west of Orchard Peak in Kern County (lat. 35°46'25" N, long. 120°10'25" W; near N line sec. 7, T 25 S, R 17 E). Named on Tent Hills (1942) 7.5' quadrangle.

Stokes Mountain [TULARE]: *ridge,* south-southwest- to west-trending, 5 miles long, 10 miles east of Dinuba (lat. 36°31' N, long. 119° 11'45" W). Named on Stokes Mountain (1966) 7.5' quadrangle.

Stokes Stringer [TULARE]: *stream,* flows 3 miles to Golden Trout Creek 9 miles north of Kern Peak in Big Whitney Meadow (lat. 36°26'05" N, long. 118°15'35" W; sec. 23, T 17 S, R 34 E). Named on Kern Peak (1956) and Olancha (1956) 15' quadrangles. United States Board on Geographic Names (1989a, p. 4) rejected the name "Golden Trout Creek" for the feature.

Stone: see **Pagliarulo** [TULARE].

Stone Corral Canyon [TULARE]: *canyon,* drained by a stream that flows 1 mile to lowlands 3 miles south of Cliff Peak (lat. 36°30'40" N, long. 119°10'45" W; sec. 30, T 16 S, R 26 E). Named on Stokes Mountain (1966) 7.5' quadrangle.

Stoney Point [FRESNO]: *peak,* 4.5 miles west-northwest of Piedra (lat. 36°50'15" N, long. 119°27'10" W; near SW cor. sec. 34, T 12 S, R 23 E). Named on Piedra (1965) 7.5' quadrangle.

Stony Creek [TULARE]: *stream,* flows 4.5 miles to join Dorst Creek and form North Fork Kaweah River 4.5 miles southwest of Shell Mountain (lat. 36°38'35" N, long. 118°50'40" W; near SW cor. sec. 4, T 15 S, R 29 E). Named on Giant Forest (1956) 15' quadrangle.

Stony Creek Campground [TULARE]: *locality,* 3 miles southwest of Shell Mountain (lat. 36°39'50" N, long. 118°50' W; sec. 33, T 14 S, R 28 E); the place is along Stony Creek. Named on Giant Forest (1956) 15' quadrangle. Called Stony Creek Camp on Tehipite (1903) 30' quadrangle.

Stony Flat [FRESNO]: *area,* 5 miles east-southeast of Dunlap (lat. 36°42'55" N, long. 119°01'50" W). Named on Miramonte (1966) 7.5' quadrangle. Postal authorities established Noble post office at the place in 1892 (Forest M. Clingan, personal communication, 1990). They moved it 2 miles north in 1896, moved it 1.5 miles northwest the same year, and discontinued it in 1902 (Salley, p. 154).

Stony Meadow [TULARE]: *area,* 10 miles south of Hockett Peak (lat. 36°04'40" N, long. 118°24' W). Named on Hockett Peak (1956) 15' quadrangle.

Stork Creek: see **Stark Creek** [KERN].

Stormy Canyon [KERN]: *canyon,* drained by a stream that flows 3.5 miles to South Fork Valley less than 1 mile north-northwest of Onyx (lat. 35°42'15" N, long. 118°13'35" W; sec. 4, T 26 S, R 35 E). Named on Onyx (1972) 7.5' quadrangle.

Stormy Canyon [TULARE]: *canyon,* drained by a stream that flows 4 miles to Kern River 8 miles south-southeast of Fairview (lat. 35° 49'05" N, long. 118°27'30" W; sec. 30, T 24 S, R 33 E). Named on California Hot Springs (1958) and Kernville (1956) 15' quadrangles.

Story Creek [TULARE]: *stream,* flows nearly 3 miles to Long Creek 2 miles west of Cliff Peak (lat. 36°33'40" N, long. 119°12'25" W; sec. 1, T 16 S, R 25 E). Named on Stokes Mountain (1966) 7.5' quadrangle.

Stout [TULARE]: *locality,* 1.5 miles south-southeast of Lindsay along Southern Pacific Railroad (lat. 36°10'55" N, long. 119°04'50" W; near SW cor. sec. 17, T 20 S, R 27 E). Named on Lindsay (1951) 7.5' quadrangle.

Stove Canyon [FRESNO]: *canyon,* drained by a stream that flows 1 mile to Hot Springs Canyon 3 miles north-northwest of Coalinga Mineral Springs (lat. 36°11'10" N, long. 120°34'15" W; sec. 16, T 20 S, R 13 E). Named on Sherman Peak (1969) 7.5' quadrangle.

Stove Ridge [FRESNO]: *ridge,* north- to north-northeast-trending, 1 mile long, 4 miles north of Coalinga Mineral Springs (lat. 36° 12' N, long. 120°32'45" W; in and near sec. 11, T 20 S, R 13 E); the ridge is east of Stove Spring. Named on Sherman Peak (1969) 7.5' quadrangle.

Stove Spring [FRESNO]: *spring,* 4.25 miles north of Coalinga Mineral Springs (lat. 36°12'20" N, long. 120°32'45" W; sec. 11, T 20 S, R 13 E). Named on Sherman Peak (1969) 7.5' quadrangle.

Strader: see **Wible Orchard** [KERN].

Strand [KERN]: *locality,* 13 miles west of Bakersfield along Southern Pacific Railroad (lat. 35°20'30" N, long. 119°13'20" W; near S line sec. 6, T 30 S, R 26 E). Named on Stevens (1932) 7.5' quadrangle.

Stratford [KINGS]: *town,* 14 miles southwest of Hanford (lat. 36°11'20" N, long. 119°49'20" W; sec. 17, T 20 S, R 20 E). Named on Stratford (1954) 7.5' quadrangle. Called Stratton on California Mining Bureau's (1909a) map. The place was named Stratton in 1901 for William Stratton of Empire Land and Water Company, which operated in the neighborhood; the name was changed to Stratford in 1906 through the efforts of the local woman's club (Hanna, p. 318). Postal authorities established Stratford post office in 1910 (Frickstad, p. 61).

Strathmore [TULARE]: *town,* 4.25 miles south-southeast of Lindsay (lat. 36°08'50" N, long. 119°03'35" W; sec. 32, 33, T 20 S, R 27 E). Named on Lindsay (1951) 7.5' quadrangle. Mary Burness named the town in 1906 with the word that she said means "beautiful valley" in her native Scotland; the place also was called Balfour, Roth Spur, and Filo—the name "Balfour" was for Balfour-Guthrie Company, owner of land at the site, and the name "Roth" was for the Roth family, pioneer grain farmers (Mitchell, A.R., p. 69). The place also was called Santos (Gudde, 1949, p. 345). Postal authorities established Strathroth post office in 1896 and discontinued it in 1899; they established Strathmore post office in 1907 (Frickstad, p. 213).

Strathmore Junction: see **Mirador** [TULARE].

Stratton: see **Stratford** [KINGS].

Stratton Canyon [KERN]: *canyon,* drained by a stream that flows about 2.5 miles to Bronco Canyon (2) 4.5 miles west-northwest of Liebre Twins (lat. 34°58'50" N, long. 118°38'45" W; at N line sec. 1, T 10 N, R 17 W). Named on Liebre Twins (1965) and Winters Ridge (1966) 7.5' quadrangles.

Strawberry Creek [TULARE]: *stream,* flows 3.25 miles to South Fork Kern River 4 miles west-northwest of Olancha Peak (lat. 36° 17'50" N, long. 118°10'45" W; sec. 3, T 19 S, R 35 E); the mouth of the stream is in Strawberry Meadows. Named on Olancha (1956) 15' quadrangle.

Strawberry Lake [FRESNO]: *lake,* 600 feet long, 7.25 miles east of the town of Big Creek (lat. 37°12'15" N, long. 119°06'45" W; sec. 27, T 8 S, R 26 E). Named on Huntington Lake (1953) 15' quadrangle.

Strawberry Meadow Creek [FRESNO]: *stream,* flows nearly 1 mile to Dinkey Creek (1) 5 miles south of Dinkey Dome (lat. 37°02'35" N, long. 119°08'50" W; sec. 21, T 10 S, R 26 E). Named on Huntington Lake (1953) 15' quadrangle.

Strawberry Meadows [TULARE]: *area,* 4.5 miles northwest of Olancha Peak (lat. 36°18' N, long. 118°11' W). Named on Olancha (1956) 15' quadrangle. Called Templeton Meadows on Olancha (1907) 30' quadrangle, but United States Board on Geographic Names (1961b, p. 12) rejected the names "Templeton Meadow" and "Templeton Meadows" for the feature.

Street Canyon [TULARE]: *canyon,* drained by a stream that flows 2 miles to Gibbon Creek 9 miles south-southeast of Springville (lat. 36°00'10" N, long. 118°46'35" W). Named on Springville (1957) and White River (1952) 15' quadrangles.

Stringer District [KERN]: *locality,* 2 miles south of Randsburg (lat. 35°20'30" N, long. 117°39'15" W; sec. 11, 12, T 30 S, R 40 E). Named on Randsburg (1911) 15' quadrangle.

String Meadows [FRESNO]: *areas,* two, 3.5 miles west-southwest of Double Peak (lat. 37°30' N, long. 119°06'15" W). Named on Devils Postpile (1953) and Kaiser Peak (1953) 15' quadrangles. United States Board on Geographic Names (1985c, p. 3) rejected the singular form "String Meadow" for the name.

Striped Mountain [FRESNO]: *peak,* 1.25 miles north of Mount Pinchot on Fresno-Inyo County line (lat. 36°57'55" N, long. 118°24'10" W). Named on Mount Pinchot (1953) 15' quadrangle. Bolton C. Brown named the feature in 1895 for its appearance (Browning, p. 210).

Stub Lake [FRESNO]: *lake,* 900 feet long, 5.25 miles south-southwest of Mount Abbot (lat. 37°19' N, long. 118°49'15" W). Named on Mount Abbot (1953) 15' quadrangle.

Studebaker Flat [KERN]: *area,* 4 miles south-southeast of Bodfish (lat. 35°32'10" N, long. 118°27'05" W; near E line sec. 32, T 27 S, R 33 E). Named on Lake Isabella South (1972) 7.5' quadrangle.

Studhorse Canyon [FRESNO]: *canyon,* drained by a stream that flows 3 miles to Los Gatos Creek 5.5 miles north-northeast of Coalinga Mineral Springs (lat. 36°13'25" N, long. 120°31'40" W; sec. 1, T 20 S, R 13 E). Named on Sherman Peak (1969) 7.5' quadrangle.

Studhorse Canyon [KERN]: *canyon,* drained by a stream that flows 4.25 miles to Caliente Creek 1 mile west of Loraine (lat. 35°18'05" N, long. 118°27'20" W; sec. 20, T 30 S, R 33 E). Named on Loraine (1972) 7.5' quadrangle. The stream in the canyon is called Studhorse Creek on Mojave (1915) 30' quadrangle.

Studhorse Creek: see **Studhorse Canyon** [KERN].

Success [TULARE]: *village,* 5 miles southwest of Springville (lat. 36°04'40" N, long. 118°52'45" W; sec. 30, T 21 S, R 29 E). Named on Kaweah (1909) 30' quadrangle. Postal authorities established Success post office in 1903 and discontinued it in 1912 (Frickstad, p. 213). California Division of Highways' (1934) map shows a place called Magnesite located 2 miles east-southeast of Success along Southern Pacific Railroad (near S line sec. 30, T 21 S, R 29 E), a place called Magnesite Jct. situated nearly 1 mile south-southwest of Success along the railroad (sec. 26, T 21 S, R 28 E), and a place called Howton located nearly 3 miles east-southeast of Success at the end of a rail line (sec. 32, T 21 S, R 29 E).

Success: see **Lake Success** [TULARE].

Success Reservoir: see **Lake Success** [TULARE].

Sugarbowl Dome [TULARE]: *peak,* 7.25 miles west-southwest of Triple Divide Peak (lat. 36°33'15" N, long. 118°38'50" W). Named on Triple Divide Peak (1956) 15' quadrangle. The name is descriptive; a depression in the top of the feature holds snow most of the summer and suggests a sugar-filled bowl (Browning, p. 210).

Sugarloaf [KERN]: *peak,* 5.25 miles north of Cinco (lat. 35°20'20" N, long. 118°02'45" W; sec. 7, T 30 S, R 37 E). Altitude 4132 feet. Named on Cinco (1972) 7.5' quadrangle.

Sugarloaf [TULARE]:

(1) *peak,* 12 miles northwest of Triple Divide Peak (lat. 36°43'50" N, long. 118°39'30" W). Altitude 8002 feet. Named on Triple Divide Peak (1956) 15' quadrangle. A field party of the Whitney survey led by William H. Brewer gave the name "Sugar Loaf Rock" to the feature in 1864 (Browning, p. 210).

(2) *peak,* 2.5 miles southeast of Auckland (lat. 36°33'50" N, long. 119°04' W; sec. 5, T 16 S, R 27 E). Altitude 2653 feet. Named on Auckland (1966) 7.5' quadrangle.

Sugarloaf Creek [FRESNO-TULARE]: *stream,* heads in Tulare County and flows 9 miles to Roaring River 15 miles south-southwest of Marion Peak in Fresno County (lat. 36°45'10" N, long. 118°36'50" W); the stream goes past Suglarloaf [TULARE] (1). Named on Triple Divide Peak (1956) 15' quadrangle. South Fork enters from the south 12 miles northwest of Triple Divide Peak and is 5 miles long. East Fork enters 1 mile east-northeast of the mouth of South Fork and is 6.25 miles long. Both forks are named on Triple Divide Peak (1956) 15' quadrangle.

Sugarloaf Hill [FRESNO]: *peak,* 4.25 miles west-northwest of Shaver Lake Heights (present town of Shaver Lake) (lat. 37°07'15" N, long. 119°23'35" W; sec. 30, T 9 S, R 24 E). Altitude 3580 feet. Named on Shaver Lake (1953) 15' quadrangle.

Sugarloaf Meadow [TULARE]: *area,* 12 miles northwest of Triple Divide Peak (lat. 36°43'30" N, long. 118°39'50" W; near E line sec. 12, T 14 S, R 30 E); the place is about 0.5 mile southwest of Sugarloaf (1). Named on Triple Divide Peak (1956) 15' quadrangle.

Sugarloaf Mountain [KERN]: *peak,* 8.5 miles northeast of Tehachapi (lat. 35°13' N, long. 118°20'20" W; at W line sec. 21, T 31 S, R 34 E). Altitude 6244 feet. Named on Tehachapi NE (1966) 7.5' quadrangle.

Sugarloaf Mountain Park [TULARE]: *locality,* 4.5 miles southeast of California Hot Springs (lat. 35°50'15" N, long. 118°36'10" W; sec. 14, T 24 S, R 31 E); the place is 1 mile northeast of Sugarloaf Peak. Named on California Hot Springs (1958) 15' quadrangle.

Sugarloaf Park [KERN]: *area,* 4.5 miles north of Cinco (lat. 35°19'40" N, long. 118°01'55" W; near W line sec. 17, T 30 S, R 37 E); the place is 1 mile southeast of Sugarloaf. Named on Cinco (1972) 7.5' quadrangle.

Sugarloaf Peak [TULARE]: *peak,* 4.5 miles southeast of California Hot Springs (lat. 35°49'40" N, long. 118°37' W; sec. 22, T 24 S, R 31 E). Altitude 6265 feet. Named on California Hot Springs (1958) 15' quadrangle.

Sugar Loaf Rock: see **Sugarloaf** [TULARE] (1).

Sugarloaf Valley [FRESNO-TULARE]: *valley,* 12 miles north-northwest of Triple Divide Peak on Fresno-Tulare County line (lat. 36° 44'15" N, long. 118°38' W); the valley is along Sugarloaf Creek [FRESNO-TULARE] east of Sugarloaf [TULARE] (1). Named on Triple Divide Peak (1956) 7.5' quadrangle.

Sugarpine Hill [FRESNO]: *peak,* 12.5 miles north-northwest of Hume (lat. 36°57'15" N, long. 118°58'55" W). Altitude 7027 feet. Named on Tehipite Dome (1952) 15' quadrangle.

Sulfur Spring [KERN]: *spring,* 5 miles south of Orchard Peak (lat. 35°40' N, long. 120°08'55" W; sec. 16, T 26 S, R 17 E). Named on Orchard Peak (1961) 7.5' quadrangle.

Sullivan [KERN]: *locality,* 2.5 miles east of Tehachapi along Southern Pacific Railroad (lat. 35°07'30" N, long. 118°24'05" W). Named on Mojave (1915) 30' quadrangle.

Sulphur Creek [FRESNO]: *stream,* flows 3.5 miles to Warthan Creek 3.25 miles east-northeast of Smith Mountain (2) (lat. 36°05'45" N, long. 120°32'30" W; near N line sec. 23, T 21 S, R 13 E). Named on Smith Mountain (1969) 7.5' quadrangle.

Sulphur Flat [FRESNO]: *area,* 4 miles east of Joaquin Rocks (lat. 36°19'35" N, long. 120°22'35" W; near NE cor. sec. 31, T 18 S, R 15 E). Named on Joaquin Rocks (1969) 7.5' quadrangle.

Sulphur Flat Spring [FRESNO]: *spring,* nearly 4 miles east of Joaquin Rocks (lat. 36°19'20" N, long. 120°22'50" W; sec. 31, T 18 S, R 15 E); the spring is 0.25 mile southwest of Sulphur Flat. Named on Joaquin Rocks (1969) 7.5' quadrangle.

Sulphur Meadow [FRESNO]: *area,* 12 miles south-southwest of Kaiser Peak on the northeast side of Shaver Lake (lat. 37°08'20" N, long. 119°17'30" W). Named on Kaiser (1904) 30' quadrangle. Water of an enlarged Shaver Lake now covers the place.

Sulphur Ridge [TULARE]: *ridge,* west- to southwest-trending, 1.5 miles long, 3.5 miles west of Kaweah (lat. 36°28'35" N, long. 118° 59' W). Named on Kaweah (1957) 15' quadrangle.

Sulphur Spring [FRESNO]:

(1) *spring,* 16 miles north-northwest of Coalinga along Salt Creek (1) (lat. 36°22'30" N, long. 120°25'50" W; sec. 10, T 18 S, R 14 E). Named on Lillis Ranch (1956) 7.5' quadrangle.

(2) *spring,* 9 miles south-southwest of Coalinga (lat. 36°01'45" N, long. 120°26'15" W; sec. 11, T 22 S, R 14 E). Named on Coalinga (1956) 15' quadrangle.

(3) *spring,* 9 miles south of Coalinga (lat. 36°00'55" N, long. 120° 23'20" W; sec. 18, T 22 S, R 15 E). Named on Coalinga (1956) 15' quadrangle.

Sulphur Spring [KERN]:

(1) *spring,* 11 miles south-southeast of Orchard Peak along Packwood Creek (lat. 35°35'15" N, long. 120°03'25" W; sec. 8, T 27 S, R 18 E). Named on Packwood Creek (1961) 7.5' quadrangle.

(2) *spring,* 3.5 miles west of McKittrick (lat. 35°18'35" N, long. 119°41' W; sec. 14, T 30 S, R 21 E). Named on Reward (1951) 7.5' quadrangle.

Sulphur Spring [KINGS]: *spring,* 6.5 miles west-southwest of Avenal (lat. 35°57'25" N, long. 120°13'40" W; sec. 3, T 23 S, R 16 E). Named on Garza Peak (1953) 7.5' quadrangle.

Sulphur Spring Canyon [KINGS]:

(1) *canyon,* drained by a stream that flows 2.25 miles to Willow Spring Canyon 8 miles south-southwest of Avenal (lat. 35°54'20" N, long. 120°12'35" W; near N line sec. 26, T 23 S, R 16 E). Named on Garza Peak (1953) 7.5' quadrangle.

(2) *canyon,* drained by a stream that flows 3.5 miles to lowlands 10 miles south-southeast of Avenal (lat. 35°52'15" N, long. 120°03'50" W; sec. 6, T 24 S, R 18 E). Named on Kettleman Plain (1953) and Pyramid Hills (1953) 7.5' quadrangles. Called Little Tar Canyon on Cholame (1917) 30' quadrangle.

Sulphur Spring Canyon: see **Arroyo Pinoso** [FRESNO].

Sulphur Springs [FRESNO]: *locality,* 10 miles west-southwest of Prather on the south side of San Joaquin River (lat. 37°00'40" N, long. 119°41'15" W; near NW cor. sec. 4, T 11 S, R 21 E). Named on Sulphur Springs (1919) 7.5' quadrangle. Water of Millerton Lake now covers the site. Bradley (p. 457-458) noted that a spring at the place was called Millerton Spring, or locally Collins Spring for an owner; it was known as early as 1856 and the water was used by a resort after 1907.

Sultana [TULARE]: *village,* 2.5 miles east of Dinuba (lat. 36°32'40" N, long. 119°20'20" W; around SW cor. sec. 11, T 16 S, R 24 E). Named on Orange Cove South (1966) 7.5' quadrangle. Postal authorities established Sultana post office in 1900 (Frickstad, p. 214). Officials of Atchison, Topeka and Santa Fe Railroad named the place in 1897 for Sultana grapes grown in the neighborhood; the railroad station also had the name "Alta" (Mitchell, A.R., p. 70).

Summerhouse: see **Milo** [TULARE].

Summers Ridge [TULARE]: *ridge,* east-trending, 1.5 miles long, 1.5 miles south-southeast of Monache Mountain (lat. 36°11'15" N, long. 118°11' W). Named on Monache Mountain (1956) 15' quadrangle.

Summit [KERN]: *locality,* 2 miles east of Tehachapi along the railroad (lat. 35°07'40" N, long. 118°24'50" W; near E line sec. 22, T 32 S, R 33 E). Named on Tehachapi North (1966) 7.5' quadrangle. Called Summit Switch on California Division of Highways' (1934) map.

Summit Creek [FRESNO]: *stream,* flows 4.25 miles to Big Creek (2) 5 miles southeast of Shaver Lake Heights (present town of Shaver Lake) (lat. 37°03'30" N, long. 119°15'15" W; sec. 16, T 10 S, R 25 E); one branch of the stream heads at Summit Meadow (1). Named on Huntington Lake (1953) and Shaver Lake (1953) 15' quadrangles.

Summit Creek [TULARE]: *stream,* flows 5 miles to South Fork Kern River 6 miles east-southeast of Monache Mountain (lat. 36° 10'10" N, long. 118°06'10" W; sec. 20, T 20 S, R 36 E); the stream goes through Summit Meadows. Named on Monache Mountain (1956) 15' quadrangle.

Summit Lake [FRESNO]:

(1) *lake,* 900 feet long, 3.25 miles north-northeast of Mount Abbot (lat. 37°25'55" N, long. 118°46'05" W). Named on Mount Abbot (1953) 15' quadrangle.

(2) *lake,* 1100 feet long, 14 miles northwest of Blackcap Mountain (lat. 37°12'15" N, long. 118°59'25" W). Named on Blackcap Mountain (1953) 15' quadrangle.

(3) *lake,* 700 feet long, 9.5 miles north of Mount Goddard (lat. 37° 14'20" N, long. 118°41'20" W). Named on Mount Goddard (1948) 15' quadrangle.

Summit Lake [TULARE]: *lake,* 700 feet long, 10 miles south-southwest of Mineral King (lat. 36°18'35" N, long. 118°38'10" W; near S line sec. 32, T 18 S, R 31 E). Named on Mineral King (1956) 15' quadrangle.

Summit Lake: see **Robinson** [KINGS].

Summit Meadow [FRESNO]:

(1) *area,* 5 miles west-southwest of Dinkey Dome (lat. 37°04'55" N, long. 119°12'25" W; near NE cor. sec. 11, T 10 S, R 25 E); the place is near the head of Summit Creek. Named on Huntington Lake (1953) 15' quadrangle.

(2) *area,* 17 miles southwest of Marion Peak (lat. 36°46'10" N, long. 118°43'05" W). Named on Marion Peak (1953) 15' quadrangle.

Summit Meadow [TULARE]: *area,* 10 miles south-southwest of Mineral King (lat. 36°19'45" N, long. 118°41' W). Named on Mineral King (1956) 15' quadrangle.

Summit Meadows [TULARE]: *area,* 4.5 miles east of Monache Mountain (lat. 36°13' N, long. 118°06'45" W; in and near sec. 5, 6, T 20 S, R 36 E); the place is along Summit Creek. Named on Monache Mountain (1956) 15' quadrangle.

Summit Range [KERN]: *range,* mainly in San Bernardino County, but extends west into Kern County 6 miles north of Randsburg (lat. 35°27' N, long. 117°38' W). Named on El Paso Peaks (1967) 7.5' quadrangle. A branch line of Southern Pacific Railroad reaches its highest point in the range, which accounts for the name (Gudde, 1949, p. 347).

Summit Station: see **Tehachapi** [KERN].

Summit Switch: see **Summit** [KERN].

Sumner: see **Bakersfield** [KERN].

Sumner's [KERN]: *locality,* 15 miles south of Orchard Peak along Bitterwater Creek (2) (lat. 35°31'55" N, long. 120°05'10" W; near W line sec. 31, T 27 S, R 18 E). Named on Cholame (1917) 30' quadrangle.

Sunday Peak [KERN]: *peak,* 8 miles east-northeast of Glennville (lat. 35°46'55" N, long. 118°35' W; sec. 6, T 25 S, R 32 E). Altitude 8295 feet. Named on California Hot Springs (1958) 15' quadrangle.

Sunflower Valley [KERN-KINGS]: *valley,* 12 miles south-southeast of Avenal on Kern-Kings County line. Named on Garza Peak (1953), Kettleman Plain (1953), Pyramid Hills (1953), Sawtooth Ridge (1961), and Tent Hills (1942) 7.5' quadrangles. Called McLure Valley on Kettleman Plain (1933), Pyramid Hills (1943), and Reef Ridge (1937) 7.5' quadrangles, but United States Board on Geographic Names (1968b, p. 9) rejected the names "McLure Valley," "McLures Valley," and "McClures Valley" for the feature. The name "McLure" was for an early settler, and the name "Sunflower" is for the abundant growth of wild sunflowers at the place (Arnold and Anderson, 1908, p. 15).

Sunland [TULARE]: *locality,* 3.5 miles south-southeast of Porterville at the end of a spur of Atchison, Topeka and Santa Fe Railroad (lat. 36°01'25" N, long. 118°58'50" W; at SW cor. sec. 8, T 22 S, R 28 E). Named on Springville (1957) 15' quadrangle.

Sunnyside [FRESNO]: *locality,* 5 miles north-northeast of Malaga along Southern Pacific Railroad (lat. 36°44'55" N, long. 119°41'55" W; near NW cor. sec. 4, T 14 S, R 21 E). Named on Malaga (1964) 7.5' quadrangle. Called Granz on Selma (1946) 15' quadrangle, and called Maltermoro on Mendenhall's (1908) map. Postal authorities established Maltermoro post office in 1894 and discontinued it in 1913; the name was coined using the surname of postmaster George H. Malter (Salley, p. 131). California Mining Bureau's (1917a) map shows a place called Barton located along the railroad between present Sunnyside and Fresno. Postal authorities established Barton post office in 1949 (Salley, p. 15).

Sunny Slope: see **Mineral King** [TULARE].

Sunset: see **Hazelton** [KERN].

Sunset Camp: see **Hazelton** [KERN].

Sunset Campground [TULARE]: *locality,* 0.5 mile west-northwest of Wilsonia (lat. 36°44'15" N, long. 118°57'50" W; near E line sec. 6, T 14 S, R 28 E). Named on Giant Forest (1956) 15' quadrangle.

Sunset Meadow [TULARE]: *area,* 3 miles north-northwest of Shell Mountain (lat. 36°44' N, long. 118°46'15" W; near W line sec. 6, T 14 S, R 30 E). Named on Giant Forest (1956) 15' quadrangle.

Sunset Point [FRESNO]: *peak,* 1 mile north-northeast of the town of Big Creek (lat. 37°13' N, long. 119°14'20" W; sec. 21, T 8 S, R 25 E). Altitude 7264 feet. Named on Huntington Lake (1953) 15' quadrangle.

Sunset Point [KERN]: *peak,* 6 miles southeast of Bodfish (lat. 35°31'35" N, long. 118°24'50" W; near NE cor. sec. 3, T 28 S, R 33 E). Named on Lake Isabella South (1972) 7.5' quadrangle.

Sunset Rock [TULARE]: *relief feature,* 5.25 miles east of Yucca Mountain (lat. 36°34'40" N, long. 118°46'30" W; sec. 36, T 15 S, R 29 E). Named on Giant Forest (1956) 15' quadrangle.

Sunset Valley [KERN]: *valley,* southwest of Maricopa along Bitterwater Creek (1) (center near lat. 35°03' N, long. 119°25'30" W). Named on Maricopa (1943) 7.5' quadrangle. Arnold and Johnson (p. 21) proposed the name "Maricopa Valley" for the feature.

Surprise Arroyo [FRESNO]: *stream,* flows 1.5 miles to Arroyo Vadoso 13 miles east-southeast of Coalinga (lat. 36°04'50" N, long. 120°08'25" W; near S line sec. 21, T 21 S, R 17 E). Named on Avenal (1954) 7.5' quadrangle. The name is from the surprising discovery of oil in a well at the place, which is considerably north of other producing oil wells (United States Board on Geographic Names, 1933b, p. 26).

Suwanee Creek [TULARE]: *stream,* flows 2.5 miles to Marble Fork nearly 5 miles east of Yucca Mountain (lat. 36°34'50" N, long. 118°47' W; sec. 36, T 15 S, R 29 E). Named on Giant Forest (1956) 15' quadrangle.

Suwanee River: see **Halstead Creek** [TULARE].

Swale Campground [TULARE]: *locality,* 1 mile west-northwest of Wilsonia (lat. 36°44'25" N, long. 118°58'25" W; near N line sec. 6, T 14 S, R 28 E). Named on Giant Forest (1956) 15' quadrangle.

Swall [TULARE]: *locality,* 4 miles northeast of Tulare along Atchison, Topeka and Santa Fe Railroad (lat. 36°14'25" N, long. 119°17'10" W; at S line sec. 29, T 19 S, R 25 E). Named on Tulare (1950) 7.5' quadrangle.

Swallow Rock [FRESNO]: *relief feature,* 10 miles southwest of Coalinga (lat. 36°01'55" N, long. 120°28'35" W; near E line sec. 8, T 22 S, R 14 E). Named on Curry Mountain (1969) 7.5' quadrangle.

Swamp Creek [FRESNO]: *stream,* flows about 2.5 miles to Dinkey Creek (1) 1.5 miles east-northeast of Dinkey Dome (lat. 37°07'30" N, long. 119°06'15" W; near N line sec. 26, T 9 S, R 26 E); one branch of the stream heads at Swamp Lake and goes through Swamp Meadow. Named on Huntington Lake (1953) 15' quadrangle.

Swamp Lake [FRESNO]: *lake,* 1200 feet long, 3.5 miles east-northeast of Dinkey Dome (lat. 37°07'45" N, long. 119°04'05" W; sec. 19, T 9 S, R 27 E); the lake is at the head of Swamp Creek. Named on Huntington Lake (1953) 15' quadrangle.

Swamp Lakes [FRESNO]: *lakes,* largest 2750 feet long, 11 miles west-southwest of Marion Peak (lat. 36°53'30" N, long. 118°42'30" W). Named on Marion Peak (1953) 15' quadrangle.

Swamp Meadow [FRESNO]: *area,* 3.5 miles east-northeast of Dinkey Dome (lat. 37°08'10" N, long. 119°04'20" W; sec. 19, T 9 S, R 27 E); the place is along Swamp Creek. Named on Huntington Lake (1953) 15' quadrangle.

Swede Lake [FRESNO]: *lake,* 1100 feet long, 4.25 miles northeast of Dinkey Dome (lat. 37°09'25" N, long. 119°04'35" W; sec. 7, T 9 S, R 27 E). Named on Huntington Lake (1953) 15' quadrangle.

Sweet Ridge [KERN]: *ridge,* generally south-trending, 1.5 miles long, 11.5 miles north-northwest of Mojave (lat. 35°12'10" N, long. 118°14'05" W). Named on Cache Peak (1973) 7.5' quadrangle.

Sweetwater Spring [KERN]: *spring,* 9 miles east of Tehachapi (lat. 35°08'45" N, long. 118°17'20" W; on W line sec. 13, T 32 S, R 34 E). Named on Tehachapi NE (1966) 7.5' quadrangle.

Switchback Peak [TULARE]: *peak,* 5 miles east-southeast of Yucca Mountain (lat. 36°32'20" N, long. 118°47'25" W). Altitude 5016 feet. Named on Giant Forest (1956) 15' quadrangle. The name is from a zigzag trail, and later a road, on the east slope of the feature (United States Board on Geographic Names, 1933a, p. 734).

Sycamore: see **Herndon** [FRESNO].

Sycamore Canyon [KERN]:

(1) *canyon,* drained by a stream that flows 10 miles to lowlands 4 miles east of Arvin (lat. 35°12' N, long. 118°45'30" W; sec. 28, T 31 S, R 30 E). Named on Arvin (1955) and Bear Mountain (1966) 7.5' quadrangles. Called Arroyo de los Alizos on Williamson's (1853) map.

(2) *canyon,* drained by a stream that flows 7.25 miles to Poso Creek 5.5 miles southeast of Knob Hill (lat. 35°30'25" N, long. 118° 53' W; sec. 8, T 28 S, R 29 E). Named on Knob Hill (1965) and Pine Mountain (1965) 7.5' quadrangles. Called Moore Canyon on Woody (1952) 15' quadrangle.

(3) *canyon,* drained by a stream that flows 2.5 miles to Tehachapi Creek 2 miles southeast of Caliente (lat. 35°16'25" N, long. 118° 35'50" W). Named on Oiler Peak (1972) 7.5' quadrangle.

(4) *canyon,* drained by a stream that flows 2 miles to Caliente Creek 1.5 miles west of Loraine (lat. 35°18'15" N, long. 118°27'35" W; sec. 20, T 30 S, R 33 E). Named on Loraine (1972) 7.5' quadrangle. Emerald Mountain (1943) 15' quadrangle has the name "Sycamore Creek" for the stream in the canyon.

Sycamore Canyon: see **Big Sycamore Canyon** [KERN]; **Little Sycamore Canyon** [KERN].

Sycamore Creek [FRESNO]:

(1) *stream,* flows 14 miles to Pine Flat Reservoir 1.5 miles northeast of Trimmer (lat. 36°55'10" N, long. 119°16'40" W; near E line sec. 6, T 12 S, R 25 E). Named on Shaver Lake (1953) 15' quadrangle, and on Trimmer (1965) 7.5' quadrangle. North Fork enters from the north-northeast 9.5 miles upstream from the mouth of the main stream; it is 2.5 miles long and is named on Shaver Lake (1953) 15' quadrangle.

(2) *stream,* flows 2 miles to Mill Creek (3) 10 miles southwest of Balch Camp (lat. 36°47'30" N, long. 119°14'10" W; sec. 15, T 13 S, R 25 E). Named on Patterson Mountain (1952) 15' quadrangle.

Sycamore Creek [KERN]: *stream,* flows 2.25 miles to Kern River 5 miles west-southwest of Miracle Hot Springs (lat. 35°33'05" N, long. 118°36'50" W). Named on Democrat Hot Springs (1972) and Miracle Hot Springs (1972) 7.5' quadrangles.

Sycamore Creek [TULARE]: *stream,* flows 5 miles to North Fork Tule River 4 miles north-northeast of Springville (lat. 36°11'10" N, long. 118°47'50" W; near E line sec. 14, T 20 S, R 29 E). Named on Springville (1957) 7.5' quadrangle.

Sycamore Creek: see **Sycamore Canyon** [KERN] (4).

Sycamore Flat 1 Campground [FRESNO]: *locality,* 2.25 miles east of Trimmer near Pine Flat Reservoir (lat. 36°54'10" N, long. 119° 15'25" W; sec. 9, T 12 S, R 25 E). Named on Trimmer (1965) 7.5' quadrangle.

Sycamore Flat 2 Campground [FRESNO]: *locality,* 2 miles east of Trimmer near Pine Flat Reservoir (lat. 36°54'05" N, long. 119°15'30" W; sec. 9, T 12 S, R 25 E). Named on Trimmer (1965) 7.5' quadrangle.

Sycamore Gap [TULARE]: *pass,* 3 miles west-northwest of California Hot Springs (lat. 35°53'35" N, long. 118°43'15" W; near SE cor. sec. 27, T 23 S, R 30 E). Named on California Hot Springs (1958) 15' quadrangle.

Sycamore Spring [KERN]: *spring,* 2.5 miles east-southeast of Caliente (lat. 35°17' N, long. 118°34'45" W; at S line sec. 30, T 30 S, R 32 E); the spring is in Sycamore Canyon (3). Named on Oiler Peak (1972) 7.5' quadrangle.

Sycamore Spring [TULARE]: *spring,* 2 miles north-northeast of California Hot Springs (lat. 35°54'20" N, long. 118°39'40" W; near SW cor. sec. 20, T 23 S, R 31 E). Named on California Hot Springs (1958) 15' quadrangle.

Sycamore Springs [FRESNO]: *spring,* 2 miles west-northwest of Balch Camp (lat. 36°55' N, long. 119°09' W; sec. 4, T 12 S, R 26 E). Named on Patterson Mountain (1952) 15' quadrangle.

Sycamore Springs Creek [FRESNO]: *stream,* flows 2.5 miles to Kings River 2.5 miles west-southwest of Balch Camp (lat. 36°53'15" N, long. 119°09'30" W; sec. 17, T 12 S, R 26 E); the stream heads near Sycamore Springs. Named on Patterson Mountain (1952) 15' quadrangle.

— T —

Table Creek [TULARE]: *stream,* flows 3.25 miles to Roaring River 4 miles north of Triple Divide Peak (lat. 36°39'10" N, long. 118° 32' W); the stream heads near Table Mountain (2). Named on Mount Whitney (1956) and Triple Divide Peak (1956) 15' quadrangles.

Tableland [TULARE]: *area,* 5.5 miles west-northwest of Triple Divide Peak (lat. 36°37'30" N, long. 118°37' W). Named on Triple Divide Peak (1956) 15' quadrangle.

Table Meadow Creek [TULARE]: *stream,* flows 3 miles to the Little Kern River nearly 15 miles south of Mineral King (lat. 36°15' N, long. 118°30'55" W; at N line sec. 28, T 19 S, R 32 E). Named on Kern Peak (1956) and Mineral King (1956) 15' quadrangles.

Table Meadows [TULARE]: *area,* 6.25 miles west-northwest of Triple Divide Peak (lat. 36°37' N, long. 118°38' W); the place is west of Tableland. Named on Triple Divide Peak (1956) 15' quadrangle.

Table Mountain [FRESNO]: *ridge,* northeast- to north-trending, 2.5 miles long, 13 miles north-northeast of Clovis (lat. 37°00' N, long. 119°36'15" W). Named on Academy (1964) and Millerton Lake East (1965) 7.5' quadrangles.

Table Mountain [FRESNO-KINGS]: *ridge,* east- to southeast-trending, 10 miles long, 12 miles southwest of Avenal, where Fresno County, Kings County, and Monterey County meet at a point (lat. 35°54'30" N, long. 120°19' W). Named on Garza Peak (1953) and The Dark Hole (1961) 7.5' quadrangles.

Table Mountain [TULARE]:

(1) *peak,* 8.5 miles north-northeast of California Hot Springs (lat. 35°59'20"

N, long. 118°36'10" W; sec. 26, T 22 S, R 31 E). Named on California Hot Springs (1958) 15' quadrangle.

(2) *peak,* 11.5 miles west-northwest of Mount Whitney on Great Western Divide (lat. 36°39'35" N, long. 118°28'20" W). Altitude 13,630 feet. Named on Mount Whitney (1956) 15' quadrangle. Captain Michaelis, who commanded the signal service on a scientific expedition to Mount Whitney, named the peak Mount Hazen in 1881 to honor General Hazon, chief signal officer of the army (Browning, p. 211).

Taboose Pass [FRESNO]: *pass,* 2.5 miles north of Mount Pinchot on Fresno-Inyo County line (lat. 36°59'05" N, long. 118°24'45" W); the pass is at the head of Taboose Creek, which is in Inyo County. Named on Mount Pinchot (1953) 15' quadrangle.

Tache Lake: see **Tulare Lake** [KINGS].

Taft [KERN]: *town,* 30 miles west-southwest of Bakersfield (lat. 35° 08'25" N, long. 119°27'25" W; sec. 13, T 32 S, R 23 E). Named on Taft (1950) 7.5' quadrangle. Buena Vista Lake (1912) 30' quadrangle has both the names "Moron" and "Taft P.O." at the place. Postal authorities established Taft post office in 1909 (Frickstad, p. 59), and the town incorporated in 1910. The place began as Siding Number Two along Sunset Railroad, but the cluster of businesses that sprang up there was called Moro; the name "Moro" was changed to Moron to avoid confusion with the name "Morro," but postal authorities rejected the name "Moron" because a place in Colorado already had that name—the community was renamed Taft for newly elected President William Howard Taft (Wines, p. 54).

Taft: see **South Taft** [KERN].

Taft Heights [KERN]: *town,* 1 mile west-southwest of downtown Taft (lat. 35°08'05" N, long. 119°28'15" W; near N line sec. 23, T 32 S, R 23 E). Named on Taft (1950) 7.5' quadrangle. The place first was called Boust City for E.J. Boust, an oil pioneer who started the community (Bailey, 1967, p. 2).

Tagus [TULARE]: *locality,* 6 miles southwest of Visalia along Southern Pacific Railroad (lat. 36°16'15" N, long. 119°22' W; near SE cor. sec. 16, T 19 S, R 24 E). Named on Visalia (1949) 7.5' quadrangle. Called Tagus Ranch on California Division of Highways' (1934) map. Railroad officials named the place in 1872 (Gudde, 1949, p. 351).

Tagus Ranch: see **Tagus** [TULARE].

Tah-ee-chay-pah Pass: see **Tehachapi Pass** [KERN].

Tailholt: see **White River** [TULARE] (2).

Talus Lake [TULARE]: *lake,* 800 feet long, 4.25 miles north-northeast of Triple Divide Peak (lat. 36°38'55" N, long. 118°30'05" W). Named on Triple Divide Peak (1956) 15' quadrangle.

Tamarack Creek [FRESNO]: *stream,* flows 7 miles to join South Fork Tamarack Creek and form Pitman Creek 2.5 miles east-southeast of the town of Big Creek (lat. 37°11'30" N, long. 119°12'10" W; sec. 35, T 8 S, R 25 E). Named on Huntington Lake (1953) 15' quadrangle. South Fork is 5 miles long and is named on Huntington Lake (1953) 15' quadrangle.

Tamarack Creek [TULARE]: *stream,* flows nearly 4 miles to Little Kern River 11 miles south-southeast of Mineral King (lat. 36°18'05" N, long. 118°31'05" W). Named on Kern Peak (1956) and Mineral King (1956) 15' quadrangles.

Tamarack Lake [TULARE]: *lake,* 1600 feet long, 2 miles west-southwest of Triple Divide Peak along Lone Pine Creek (lat. 36°34'50" N, long. 118°33'50" W). Named on Triple Divide Peak (1956) 15' quadrangle.

Tamarack Meadow [FRESNO]: *area,* 4 miles northwest of Dinkey Dome (lat. 37°09'15" N, long. 119°11'05" W; near NW cor. sec. 18, T 9 S, R 26 E); the place is 2.5 miles southeast of Tamarack Mountain. Named on Huntington Lake (1953) 15' quadrangle. Called Tamarack Meadows on Kaiser (1904) 30' quadrangle.

Tamarack Meadow: see **Pond Meadow** [TULARE].

Tamarack Mountain [FRESNO]: *ridge,* north-northeast-trending, 1.5 miles long, 2.25 miles southeast of the town of Big Creek (lat. 37°10'40" N, long. 119°13'15" W; in and near sec. 2, 3, T 9 S, R 25 E). Named on Huntington Lake (1953) 15' quadrangle.

Tandy: see **Porterville** [TULARE].

Tarbel Pocket [TULARE]: *relief feature,* 4.5 miles west-northwest of Yucca Mountain along Eshom Creek (lat. 36°36'15" N, long. 118°56'25" W; sec. 21, T 15 S, R 28 E). Named on Giant Forest (1956) 15' quadrangle.

Tar Canyon: see **Arroyo del Camino** [KINGS]; **Big Tar Canyon** [KINGS]; **Little Tar Canyon**, under **Sulphur Spring Canyon** [KINGS] (2).

Tar Creek: see **Big Tar Creek** [KINGS].

Tar Gap [TULARE]: *pass,* 3.5 miles southwest of Mineral King (lat. 36°25'20" N, long. 118°38'35" W; sec. 30, T 17 S, R 31 E). Named on Mineral King (1956) 15' quadrangle.

Tarn: see **Sanger** [FRESNO].

Tar Peak [KINGS]: *peak,* 5.5 miles south-southwest of Avenal on Reef Ridge (lat. 35°56'05" N, long. 120°10'40" W; near N line sec. 18, T 23 S, R 17 E); the peak is west of Big Tar Canyon. Named on Garza Peak (1953) 7.5' quadrangle.

Tarpey [FRESNO]: *locality,* 2.25 miles south of Clovis along Southern Pacific Railroad (lat. 36°47'15" N, long. 119°41'55" W; near W line sec. 21, T 13 S, R 21 E). Named on Clovis (1964) 7.5' quadrangle. Postal authorities established Tarpey post office in 1892, discontinued it in 1914, reestablished it in 1958, and discontinued it in 1961; the named was for Arthur B. Tarpey (Salley, p. 218).

Tarpey Village [FRESNO]: *district,* 2 miles south of Clovis (lat. 36° 47'45" N, long. 119°42' W); the place is at and near Tarpey. Named on Clovis (1964) 7.5' quadrangle.

Taurusa [TULARE]: *locality,* 6.5 miles north-northeast of Visalia along Southern Pacific Railroad (lat. 36°25' N, long. 119°15'05" W; sec. 27, T 17 S, R 25 E). Named on Monson (1949) 7.5' quadrangle. California Mining Bureau's (1917b) map shows a place called Venice Hill located along the railroad between Taurusa and Klink, about 1 mile northwest of Klink.

Tawny Boy: see **Tawny Point** [TULARE].

Tawny Point [TULARE]: *peak,* 6 miles northwest of Mount Whitney (lat. 36°37'40" N, long. 118°22'30" W). Altitude 12,332 feet. Named on Mount Whitney (1956) 15' quadrangle. Chester Versteeg suggested the name "Tawny Boy" for the feature in 1953 (Browning, p. 213).

Taylor Canyon: see **Taylor Creek** [FRESNO] (2).

Taylor Creek [FRESNO]:

(1) *stream,* flows 2 miles to Rush Creek 4 miles south-southeast of Shaver Lake Heights (present town of Shaver Lake) (lat. 37°03'10" N, long. 119°18' W; near N line sec. 24, T 10 S, R 24 E). Named on Shaver Lake (1953) 15' quadrangle.

(2) *stream,* flows 3.25 miles to Jacalitos Creek 9 miles southwest of Coalinga (lat. 36°02'05" N, long. 120°27' W; sec. 10, T 22 S, R 14 E). Named on Curry Mountain (1969) 7.5' quadrangle. Coalinga (1912) 30' quadrangle shows the stream in Taylor Canyon.

Taylor Creek [TULARE]: *stream,* flows 6.5 miles to South Fork Kern River 10 miles west-northwest of Lamont Peak (lat. 35°50'05" N, long. 118°12'55" W). Named on Kernville (1956) and Lamont Peak (1956) 15' quadrangles. The name commemorates Charlie Taylor (Browning, p. 213).

Taylor Meadow [TULARE]: *area,* 13 miles east-southeast of Fairview (lat. 35°59'50" N, long. 118°17'30" W; on E line sec. 22, T 24 S, R 34 E); the place is along Taylor Creek. Named on Kernville (1956) 15' quadrangle.

Taylor Spring [KERN]: *spring,* 5.5 miles west-northwest of Carneros Rocks (lat. 35°27'45" N, long. 119°56'20" W; sec. 28, T 28 S, R 19 E). Named on Las Yeguas Ranch (1959) 7.5' quadrangle.

Teagle [KERN]: *locality,* 5 miles north of Randsburg along Southern Pacific Railroad (lat. 35°26'15" N, long. 117°38'20" W; near S line sec. 1, T 29 S, R 40 E). Named on Randsburg (1911) 15' quadrangle. Called Teague on California Mining Bureau's (1917c) map.

Teagle Wash [KERN]: *stream,* flows nearly 2 miles to San Bernardino County 8 miles south-southeast of Ridgecrest in Searles Valley (lat. 35°30'30" N, long. 117°37'45" W; near NE cor. sec. 14, T 28 S, R 40 E). Named on Ridgecrest South (1973) 7.5' quadrangle.

Teague: see **Teagle** [KERN].

Teakettle Creek [FRESNO]: *stream,* flows 3.5 miles to North Fork Kings River 7.25 miles east-northeast of Balch Camp (lat. 36°56'45" N, long. 119°00'10" W; sec. 26, T 11 S, R 27 E). Named on Patterson Mountain (1952) 15' quadrangle.

Tecuya Creek [KERN]: *stream,* flows 7.5 miles to lowlands 2 miles west of Grapevine (lat. 34°55'45" N, long. 118°57'25" W); the stream heads near Tecuya Mountain. Named on Coal Oil Canyon (1955), Frazier Mountain (1958), Grapevine (1958), and Mettler (1955) 7.5' quadrangles. Kroeber (p. 61) stated that the word "Tecuya" is from the name by which Indians of the neighborhood were known to other Indians. Latta (1976, p. 211) used the name "Arroyo de Tecuya," and attributed the word "Tecuya" to the Indian term for a large white rock at the mouth of the canyon of the stream. United States Board on Geographic Names (1982a, p. 3) approved the name "Reed Canyon" for a feature, 2.5 miles long, that opens into lowlands less than 0.25 mile east of the place that Tecuya Creek reaches lowlands (lat. 34°55'40" N, long. 118°57'15" W).

Tecuya Mountain [KERN]: *peak,* 6.5 miles west of Lebec (lat. 34°50'30" N, long. 118°58'50" W; near SE cor. sec. 22, T 9 N, R 20 W); the peak is near the head of Tecuya Creek. Altitude 7155 feet. Named on Frazier Mountain (1958) 7.5' quadrangle. United States Board on Geographic Names (1989c, p. 2) approved the name "Tecuya Ridge" for a feature that extends west for 10.5 miles from O'Neil Canyon to a point 1 mile south of Antimony Peak—Tecuya Mountain is the high point on the ridge. The Board at the same time attributed the name "Tecuya" to Chief Tecuya, the Indian leader whose tribe worked the so-called lost Los Padres mine in the nineteenth century.

Tecuya Ridge: see **Tecuya Mountain** [KERN].

Teddy Bear Lake [FRESNO]: *lake,* 700 feet long, 3 miles south-southwest of Mount Abbot (lat. 37°20'45" N, long. 118°48'50" W). Named on Mount Abbot (1953) 15' quadrangle.

Tehachapai Pass: see **Tehachapi Pass** [KERN].

Tehachapai Peak: see **Cummings Mountain** [KERN].

Tehachapai Station: see **Tehachapi** [KERN].

Tehachapi [KERN]: *town,* 35 miles east-southeast of Bakersfield (lat. 35°07'50" N, long. 118°26'45" W; in and near sec. 20, 21, T 32 S, R 33 E); the town is in Tehachapi Valley. Named on Tehachapi North (1966) and

Tehachapi South (1966) 7.5' quadrangles. Called Tehachapai Sta. on Wheeler's (1875-1878) map, but United States Board on Geographic Names (1933a, p. 747) rejected the form "Tehachapai" for the name. Tehachapi incorporated in 1909. Peter D. Greene founded a place in the 1870's called Greenwich that was located about 3 miles east of Old Town; in 1876 officials of Southern Pacific Railroad laid out another community situated by the railroad about a mile northeast of Greenwich, gave it the name Summit Station, and later called it Tehachapi (Boyd, p. 177). Postal authorities established Greenwich post office in 1875 and discontinued it in 1893, when they moved it to Tehachapi (Salley, p. 90, 219).

Tehachapi Creek [KERN]: *stream,* flows 22 miles to Caliente Creek near Caliente (lat. 35°17'20" N, long. 118°37'40" W); the stream heads at Tehachapi Valley. Named on Keene (1966), Oiler Peak (1972), and Tehachapi North (1966) 7.5' quadrangles. Fremont used the name "Pass Creek" for the stream (Williamson, p. 19).

Tehachapi Creek: see **Cache Creek** [KERN].

Tehachapi Lake: see **Proctor Lake** [KERN].

Tehachapi Mountain [KERN]: *peak,* 6 miles south-southwest of Tehachapi (lat. 35°02'50" N, long. 118°29' W; at W line sec. 16, T 11 N, R 15 W). Named on Tehachapi South (1966) 7.5' quadrangle.

Tehachapi Mountains [KERN]: *range,* between Tehachapi Pass and Grapevine Creek. Named on Bakersfield (1962, revised 1971) and Los Angeles (1975) 1°x 2° quadrangles.

Tehachapi Pass [KERN]: *canyon,* 2.5 miles long, along Cache Creek 9.5 miles east-southeast of Tehachapi (lat. 35°06'05" N, long. 118° 17' W). Named on Monolith (1966) 7.5' quadrangle. Called Tah-ee-chay-pah Pass on Williamson's (1853) map. United States Board on Geographic Names (1933a, p. 747) rejected the form "Tehachapai Pass" for the name, which is of Indian origin (Kroeber, p. 61).

Tehachapi Pass: see **Oak Creek Pass** [KERN].

Tehachapi Valley [KERN]: *valley,* at and near Tehachapi (center near lat. 35°07' N, long. 118°25' W). Named on Cummings Mountain (1966), Keene (1966), Monolith (1966), Tehachapi North (1966), and Tehachapi South (1966) 7.5' quadrangles. Alexander M. Cameron and George W. Cameron lived in the east part of the valley in the early days at what was known as Cameron Station (Boyd, p. 173). Cameron Station was called Sinks of Tehachapa in the late 1860's (Barras, p. 125).

Tehichipa: see **Old Town** [KERN].

Tehipite Dome [FRESNO]: *peak,* 12 miles northeast of Hume (lat. 36°55'10" N, long. 118°46'45" W). Altitude 7708 feet. Named on Tehipite Dome (1952) 15' quadrangle.

Tehipite Valley [FRESNO]: *valley,* 11.5 miles northeast of Hume along Middle Fork Kings River (lat. 36°54'30" N, long. 118°46'45" W); the valley is 0.5 mile south of Tehipite Dome. Named on Tehipite Dome (1952) 15' quadrangle. The word "Tehipite" is of Indian origin (Kroeber, p. 62)

Tehipite Valley: see **Little Tehipite Valley** [FRESNO].

Tejon: see **Lebec** [KERN]; **Old Fort Tejon** [KERN]; **Rose Station** [KERN].

Tejon Canyon [KERN]: *canyon,* 11 miles long, along Tejon Creek above a point 4.25 miles west of Cummings Mountain (lat. 35°02'25" N, long. 118°39'15" W). Named on Cummings Mountain (1966), Tehachapi South (1966), and Tejon Ranch (1966) 7.5' quadrangles. Parke's (1854-1855) map has the name "Tejon Pass" for the feature.

Tejon Creek [KERN]: *stream,* flows 23 miles to lowlands 8 miles south of Arvin (lat. 35°05'30" N, long. 118°49' W; sec. 29, T 12 N, R 18 W); the stream drains Tejon Canyon. Named on Arvin (1955), Tejon Hills (1955), Tejon Ranch (1966), and Weed Patch (1955) 7.5' quadrangles. The feature was known to Mexicans by the names "Arroyo del Tejon" and "Arroyo de los Alamos" (Latta, 1976, p. 201). Water of Tejon Creek sinks into sand in lowlands at a place called Sinks of the Tejon; Mexicans called the site Agua de los Alamos, or Los Alamitos, because of a spring there—the place was a gathering spot for Indians before it became an important station on Butterfield Overland stage line from 1858 until 1861 (Hoover, Rensch, and Rensch, p. 129). Postal authorities established Sink post office there in 1859 and discontinued it in 1861 (Salley, p. 205).

Tejon Hills [KERN]: *ridge,* west- to northwest-trending, 9 miles long, between Comanche Creek and Tejon Creek, center 9 miles south-southeast of Arvin (lat. 35°05'30" N, long. 118°46'45" W). Named on Arvin (1955), Tejon Hills (1955), and Tejon Ranch (1966) 7.5' quadrangles.

Tejon Pass: see **Tejon Canyon** [KERN].

Tejon Reservoir Number 1 [KERN]: *lake,* 600 feet long, 10 miles west of Cummings Mountain (lat. 35°02'05" N, long. 118°44'40" W; sec. 13, T 11 N, R 18 W); the lake is nearly 2 miles west-northwest of Tejon Reservoir Number 2. Named on Tejon Ranch (1966) 7.5' quadrangle.

Tejon Reservoir Number 2 [KERN]: *lake,* 2000 feet long, 8.5 miles west of Cummings Mountain (lat. 35°01'20" N, long. 118°43' W); the lake is nearly 2 miles east-southeast of Tejon Reservoir Number 1. Named on Tejon Ranch (1966) 7.5' quadrangle.

Telegraph Flat [TULARE]: *area,* 5.5 miles south of Fountain Springs (lat. 35°48'40" N, long. 118°55'55" W; sec. 27, T 24 S, R 28 E). Named on Quincy School (1965) 7.5' quadrangle.

Telephone Canyon [KERN]: *canyon,* drained by a stream that flows 2.5 miles to the canyon of Caliente Creek at Caliente (lat. 35°17'30" N, long. 118°37'40" W). Named on Bena (1972) and Oiler Peak (1972) 7.5' quadrangles.

Telephone Canyon Spring [KERN]: *spring,* 2 miles north of Caliente (lat. 35°19'10" N, long. 118°37'30" W); the spring is near the head of Telephone Canyon. Named on Bena (1972) 7.5' quadrangle.

Telephone Hills [KERN]: *range,* 3.5 miles south of McKittrick (lat. 35°15' N, long. 119°38' W). Named on Fellows (1951), Panorama Hills (1954), and Reward (1951) 7.5' quadrangles.

Telephone Ridge [KERN-TULARE]: *ridge,* west-trending, 5 miles long, 5.5 miles northeast of Glennville on Kern-Tulare County line (lat. 35°47'15" N, long. 118°38'15" W). Named on California Hot Springs (1958) 15' quadrangle.

Temblor Creek [KERN]: *stream,* flows 6 miles to Salt Creek (1) 5.5 miles southeast of Carneros Rocks in Temblor Valley (lat. 35°23'25" N, long. 119°45'55" W; near W line sec. 19, T 29 S, R 21 E). Named on Carneros Rocks (1959) and McKittrick Summit (1959) 7.5' quadrangles. Present Salt Creek (1) is called Temblor Creek on Belridge (1953) 7.5' quadrangle, but United States Board on Geographic Names (1968a, p. 7) rejected this name for it.

Temblor Range [KERN]: *range,* southwest of the San Joaquin Valley on Kern-San Luis Obispo County line. Named on Bakersfield (1962, revised 1971) and San Luis Obispo (1956, revised 1969) 1°x 2° quadrangles. Arnold and Anderson (1908, p. 13) applied the name—*temblor* means "earthquake" in Spanish—and stated that it is particularly suited to the range "because the great California fault line [San Andreas fault], along which earthquakes have repeatedly originated, follows the range from one end to the other," and because the well-known old Temblor ranch is on the west flank of the range. United States Board on Geographic Names (1933a, p. 748) rejected the form "Temploa Range" for the name.

Temblor Valley [KERN]: *valley,* 9.5 miles northwest of McKittrick (lat. 35°23' N, long. 119°46' W); the valley is near the northeast base of Temblor Range. Named on Belridge (1953), Carneros Rocks (1959), and Reward (1950, photorevised 1973) 7.5' quadrangles.

Temperance: see **Fresno** [FRESNO].

Temperance Flat [FRESNO]: *area,* 4 miles west-northwest of Prather (lat. 37°03'35" N, long. 119°35' W; sec. 16, 17, T 10 S, R 22 E). Named on Millerton Lake East (1965) 7.5' quadrangle.

Temple Slough [FRESNO]: *water feature,* mainly an artificial watercourse that diverges west-northwest from San Joaquin River 5.5 miles north-northeast of Oxalis (lat. 36°59' N, long. 120°30' W). Named on Oxalis (1922) 7.5' quadrangle. Oxalis (1956) 7.5' quadrangle shows the feature as the route of a canal.

Templeton Meadows [TULARE]: *area,* 7.5 miles northwest of Olancha Peak along South Fork Kern River (lat. 36°20' N, long. 118°13' W); the place is northwest of Templeton Mountain. Named on Olancha (1956) 15' quadrangle. The name is for Benjamin S. Templeton, a sheepman (Gudde, 1949, p. 358). United States Board on Geographic Names (1961b, p. 12) rejected the singular form "Templeton Meadow" for the name.

Templeton Meadows: see **Strawberry Meadows** [TULARE].

Templeton Mountain [TULARE]: *peak,* 6 miles northwest of Olancha Peak (lat. 36°18'50" N, long. 118°12'20" W); the peak is southeast of Templeton Meadows. Named on Olancha (1956) 15' quadrangle.

Temploa Range: see **Temblor Range** [KERN].

Tenant Creek [KERN]: *stream,* flows 2.5 miles to Kern River 0.5 mile east-northeast of Democrat Hot Springs (lat. 35°31'55" N, long. 118°39'20" W). Named on Democrat Hot Springs (1972) 7.5' quadrangle. Called Tenant Mine Cr. on Glennville (1956) 15' quadrangle, and United States Board on Geographic Names (1975a, p. 4) gave this name as a variant.

Tenant Mine Creek: see **Tenant Creek** [KERN].

Tenant Spring: see **Big Tenant Spring** [KERN]; **Little Tenant Spring** [KERN].

Tenmile Creek [FRESNO-TULARE]: *stream,* heads in Tulare County and flows 11.5 miles to Kings River 4.25 miles north-northeast of Hume in Fresno County (lat. 36°50'20" N, long. 118°52'45" W). Named on Giant Forest (1956) and Tehipite Dome (1952) 15' quadrangles.

Tennessee Knob [TULARE]: *peak,* 6.5 miles north-northwest of Fountain Springs (lat. 35°58'45" N, long. 118°57'15" W; near S line sec. 28, T 22 S, R 28 E); the peak is on Tennessee Ridge. Altitude 1406 feet. Named on Fountain Springs (1965) 7.5' quadrangle.

Tennessee Point [FRESNO]: *peak,* 6 miles east-northeast of Kaiser Peak (lat. 37°19'45" N, long. 119°05'10" W; sec. 12, T 7 S, R 26 E). Named on Kaiser Peak (1953) 15' quadrangle.

Tennessee Ridge [TULARE]: *ridge,* northwest- to north-trending, 4 miles long, 5 miles north-northwest of Fountain Springs (lat. 35° 57'30" N, long. 118°56'40" W); Tennessee Knob is on the ridge. Named on Fountain Springs (1965) 7.5' quadrangle.

Tent Hills [KINGS]: *peaks,* 11 miles south of Avenal along a northwest-trending ridge 3.25 miles long (lat. 35°50'45" N, long. 120° 09' W). Named on Tent Hills (1942) 7.5' quadrangle. Arnold and Anderson (1908, p. 14) named the feature for "the resemblance of the individual hills to tents."

United States Board on Geographic Names (1933a, p. 749) rejected the names "Las Tiendas" and "The Tents" for the peaks.

Tent Meadow: see **Lower Tent Meadow** [FRESNO]; **Upper Tent Meadow** [FRESNO].

Tents: see **The Tents**, under **Tent Hills** [KINGS].

Terese [KERN]: *locality,* 6 miles south-southeast of Inyokern along Southern Pacific Railroad (lat. 35°34'10" N, long. 117°46'45" W; sec. 21, T 27 S, R 39 E). Named on Inyokern (1943) 15' quadrangle. Searles Lake (1915) 1° quadrangle shows Terese Siding situated about 2.5 miles south-southeast of present Terese along the railroad, and Lee's (1912) map has the name "Code" for a place located 4 miles south-southeast of Terese along the railroad (sec. 2, T 28 S, R 39 E).

Terese Siding: see **Terese** [KERN].

Terminus [TULARE]: *locality,* 4.5 miles east of Woodlake (lat. 36° 24'45" N, long. 119°00'50" W; near N line sec. 35, T 17 S, R 27 E). Site named on Woodlake (1952) 7.5' quadrangle. Lemon Cove (1928) 7.5' quadrangle shows the place at the end of a spur line of Visalia Electric Railroad.

Terra Bella [TULARE]: *town,* nearly 5 miles north of Ducor (lat. 35° 57'40" N, long. 119°02'30" W; sec. 3, T 23 S, R 27 E). Named on Ducor (1952) 7.5' quadrangle. Postal authorities established Terrabella post office in 1891, discontinued it the same year, and reestablished it with the name "Terra Bella" in 1909 (Salley, p. 220). The place first was called Deer Creek Switch; officials of Edward Silent Real Estate Company gave the new name in 1908 (Mitchell, A.R., p. 70).

Tether Lake [FRESNO]: *lake,* 450 feet long, 8 miles south-southwest of Mount Abbot (lat. 37°16'30" N, long. 118°49'25" W). Named on Mount Abbot (1953) 15' quadrangle. Elden H. Vestal of California Department of Fish and Game chose the name because the lake is tied, or tethered, by water to two adjacent lakes (Browning, p. 214).

Tharpe Meadow: see **Log Meadow** [TULARE].

Tharpe's Log Meadow: see **Log Meadow** [TULARE].

Tharps Peak [TULARE]: *peak,* 5.25 miles south of Kaweah (lat. 36° 23'40" N, long. 118°55'50" W; sec. 3, T 18 S, R 28 E). Altitude 2760 feet. Named on Kaweah (1957) 15' quadrangle. United States Board on Geographic Names (1968b, p. 10) rejected the form "Thorps Peak" for the name.

Tharps Peak: see **Alta Peak** [TULARE].

Tharps Rock [TULARE]: *relief feature,* 8 miles west of Triple Divide Peak (lat. 36°35'05" N, long. 118°40' W; at S line sec. 25, T 15 S, R 30 E). Named on Triple Divide Peak (1956) 15' quadrangle. The name applies to a boulder, about 1100 feet high, named to honor Hale D. Tharp, first explorer in the vicinity (United States Board on Geographic Names, 1933a, p. 751).

The Basin: see **Huntington Lake** [FRESNO] (1).

The Big Arroyo: see **Big Arroyo** [TULARE].

The Citadel [FRESNO]: *peak,* 6.5 miles east-southeast of Mount Goddard (lat. 37°04' N, long. 118°36'30" W). Altitude 11,744 feet. Named on Mount Goddard (1948) 15' quadrangle. The Sierra Club proposed the name in 1941 (Browning, p. 40).

The Clearing [FRESNO]: *area,* 1.5 miles east of Joaquin Rocks (lat. 36°19' N, long. 120°25'15" W; in and near sec. 35, T 18 S, R 14 E). Named on Joaquin Rocks (1969) 7.5' quadrangle.

The Dark Hole [FRESNO-KINGS]: *canyon,* drained by a stream that heads in Fresno County and flows 3.25 miles to Avenal Canyon 10 miles southwest of Avenal in Kings County (lat. 35°55'30" N, long. 120°16'15" W; at W line sec. 17, T 23 S, R 16 E). Named on The Dark Hole (1961) 7.5' quadrangle.

The Devil's Glen: see **Devils Den** [KERN] (1).

The Five Lakes: see **Big Five Lakes** [TULARE].

The Gorge [FRESNO]: *canyon,* drained by a stream that flows 1.5 miles to Bear Canyon 5.5 miles north-northwest of Coalinga Mineral Springs (lat. 36°13' N, long. 120°36'05" W; sec. 5, T 20 S, R 13 E). Named on Sherman Peak (1969) 7.5' quadrangle.

The Hermit [FRESNO]: *peak,* 4 miles north of Mount Goddard (lat. 37°09'50" N, long. 118°43' W). Altitude 12,360 feet. Named on Mount Goddard (1948) 15' quadrangle.

The Horseshoe [KERN]: *locality;* bend in the road nearly 4 miles northeast of Caliente (lat. 35°19'55" N, long. 118°34'55" W; sec. 7, T 30 S, R 32 E). Named on Oiler Peak (1972) 7.5' quadrangle.

The Keyhole [FRESNO]: *relief feature,* 8 miles north-northwest of Mount Goddard (lat. 37°12'55" N, long. 118°40'50" W). Named on Mount Goddard (1948) 15' quadrangle. Climbers from the Sierra Club applied the name to a notch in Glacier Divide (Browning, p. 119).

The Loop [KERN]: *locality,* 2 miles southeast of Keene (lat. 35°12'05" N, long. 118°32'10" W; at W line sec. 27, T 31 S, R 32 E). Named on Keene (1966) 7.5' quadrangle. The name applies to the place that the railroad makes a loop to gain elevation and thereby crosses over itself. Wheeler's (1875-1878) map shows a place called Coombs located near the site.

The Major General [TULARE]: *peak,* 5 miles south-southeast of Mount Whitney (lat. 36°30'45" N, long. 118°30' W). Named on Mount Whitney (1956) 15' quadrangle. Chester Versteeg suggested the name in 1939 (Browning, p. 135).

The Malaga Colony: see **Malaga** [FRESNO].

The Minster [TULARE]: *peak,* 12 miles northwest of Mount Whitney (lat. 36°42'55" N, long. 118°25'15" W). Named on Mount Whitney (1956) 15' quadrangle. David Starr Jordan named the peak in 1899 (Browning, p. 148).

The Miter [TULARE]: *peak,* 3.5 miles south-southeast of Mount Whitney (lat. 36°32'05" N, long. 118°15'50" W). Altitude 12,770 feet. Named on Mount Whitney (1956) 15' quadrangle. The name is from the shape of the peak (United States Board on Geographic Names, 1938, p. 36).

The Narrows [KERN]: *narrows,* 3.5 miles north-northeast of Garlock in Goler Gulch (lat. 35°27' N, long. 117°45'45" W). Named on Garlock (1967) 7.5' quadrangle.

The Needles [TULARE]: *relief features,* 9.5 miles southwest of Hockett Peak (lat. 36°06'30" N, long. 118°28'45" W). Named on Hockett Peak (1956) 15' quadrangle.

The Park: see **Walker Basin** [KERN].

The Pinnacles [FRESNO]:

(1) *relief feature,* 7.5 miles south-southwest of Mount Abbot along a south-trending ridge, 1.5 miles long, situated between the head of East Pinnacles Creek and the head of West Pinnacles Creek (lat. 38°16'40" N, long. 118°48'45" W). Named on Mount Abbot (1953) 15' quadrangle.

(2) *peak,* 1.5 miles southeast of Smith Mountain (2) on Fresno-Monterey County line (lat. 36°03'40" N, long. 120°34'45" W; sec. 33, T 21 S, R 13 E). Named on Smith Mountain (1969) 7.5' quadrangle.

The Pothole [TULARE]: *relief feature,* 9 miles northeast of Fountain Springs (lat. 35°58'40" N, long. 118°47'45" W); the feature is near the head of Pothole Creek. Named on Gibbon Peak (1965) 7.5' quadrangle.

The Pyramid: see **Painted Lady** [FRESNO].

The Pyramids: see **Pyramid Hills** [KERN-KINGS].

Thermal: see **Auberry** [FRESNO].

The Sphinx [FRESNO]: *peak,* 13 miles south of Marion Peak (lat. 36°45'15" N, long. 118°32'55" W); the peak is west of Sphinx Creek. Altitude 9146 feet. Named on Marion Peak (1953) 15' quadrangle. John Muir named the peak in 1891; Hutchings called it The Watch Tower in 1875 (Browning, p. 206).

The Tents: see **Tent Hills** [KINGS].

The Three Sirens: see **Scylla** [FRESNO].

The Thumb [FRESNO]: *peak,* 4.5 miles north of Double Peak (lat. 37°34'35" N, long. 119°01'30" W). Altitude 10,285 feet. Named on Devils Postpile (1953) 15' quadrangle.

The Tombstone [FRESNO]: *relief feature,* 11 miles southwest of Mount Abbot (lat. 37°16'10" N, long. 118°54'55" W; sec. 4, T 8 S, R 28 E). Named on Mount Abbot (1953) 15' quadrangle. The shape of the feature suggested the name (Gudde, 1949, p. 365).

The Tunnel [TULARE]: *locality,* 4 miles north of Kern Peak (lat. 36° 22' N, long. 118°17'20" W; near NW cor. sec. 15, T 18 S, R 34 E). Named on Olancha (1907) 30' quadrangle. The name recalls a tunnel dug in the 1880's to divert water from Golden Trout Creek to meadows on South Fork Kern River (Browning, p. 226).

The Turtle Hole [KINGS]: *canyon,* 0.25 mile long, opens into Avenal Canyon from the southwest 8.5 miles southwest of Avenal (lat. 35°54'55" N, long. 120°14'15" W; sec. 21, T 23 S, R 16 E). Named on Garza Peak (1953) 7.5' quadrangle.

The Washboard [FRESNO]: *area,* 12.5 miles east of Coalinga (lat. 36°07' N, long. 120°08' W). Named on Avenal (1954), Guijarral Hills (1956), and La Cima (1963) 7.5' quadrangles. The name describes the series of parallel ridges and depressions in the area (United States Board on Geographic Names, 1933b, p. 28).

The Watch Tower: see **The Sphinx** [FRESNO].

The Wye [TULARE]: *locality;* road junction less than 1 mile south of Wilsonia (lat. 36°43'25" N, long. 118°57'15" W; sec. 8, T 14 S, R 28 E). Named on Giant Forest (1956) 15' quadrangle.

Third Recess [FRESNO]: *canyon,* drained by a stream that flows 2.5 miles to Mono Creek 4 miles north-northwest of Mount Abbot (lat. 37°26'35" N, long. 118°48'20" W); the feature is the third large canyon east of Lake Thomas A. Edison on south side of Mono Creek. Named on Mount Abbot (1953) 15' quadrangle. Theodore S. Solomons discovered and named the feature in 1894 (Farquhar, 1925, p. 127).

Third Recess Lake [FRESNO]: *lake,* 1300 feet long, 2.5 miles north-northwest of Mount Abbot (lat. 37°25'20" N, long. 118°48'10" W); the lake is in Third Recess. Named on Mount Abbot (1953) 15' quadrangle.

Thomas A. Edison: see **Lake Thomas A. Edison** [FRESNO].

Thomas Lane [KERN]: *locality,* 1.25 miles south-southwest of Shafter (lat. 35°29'15" N, long. 119°17' W; near S line sec. 16, T 28 S, R 25 E). Named on Rio Bravo (1954) 7.5' quadrangle.

Thompson: see **Mount Thompson** [FRESNO].

Thompson Camp [TULARE]: *locality,* 3.5 miles northwest of California Hot Springs (lat. 35°55'15" N, long. 118°42'30" W; at S line sec. 14, T 23 S, R 30 E); the place is near the south end of Thompson Ridge. Named on California Hot Springs (1958) 15' quadrangle.

Thompson Camp Spring [TULARE]: *spring,* 8 miles northeast of California Hot Springs (lat. 35°57'35" N, long. 118°34'15" W; near W line sec. 6, T 23 S, R 32 E). Named on California Hot Springs (1958) 15' quadrangle.

Thompson Creek [KERN]: *stream,* flows 4.5 miles to Walker Basin Creek 3.5 miles west of Piute Peak (lat. 35°26'25" N, long. 118°27'10" W; near NW cor. sec. 4, T 29 S, R 33 E). Named on Piute Peak (1972) 7.5' quadrangle.

Thompson Creek: see **Walker Basin Creek** [KERN].

Thompson Lake: see **Thomson Lake** [FRESNO].

Thompson Peak [TULARE]: *peak,* 4.5 miles north-northwest of California Hot Springs (lat. 35°56'15" N, long. 118°42'25" W; sec. 11, T 23 S, R 30 E); the peak is on Thompson Ridge. Altitude 4322 feet. Named on California Hot Springs (1958) 15' quadrangle.

Thompson Ridge [TULARE]: *ridge,* southwest- to south-trending, 2.5 miles long, 4.5 miles north-northwest of California Hot Springs (lat. 35°56'15" N, long. 118°42'30" W); Thompson Peak is on the ridge. Named on California Hot Springs (1958) 15' quadrangle.

Thompson Spring [KERN]: *spring,* 3 miles west-southwest of Piute Peak (lat. 35°26'05" N, long. 118°26'30" W; sec. 4, T 29 S, R 33 E); the spring is near Thompson Creek. Named on Piute Peak (1972) 7.5' quadrangle.

Thomson Lake [FRESNO]: *lake,* 900 feet long, 13 miles northwest of Blackcap Mountain (lat. 37°12'10" N, long. 118°57'25" W; near NW cor. sec. 31, T 8 S, R 28 E). Named on Blackcap Mountain (1953) 15' quadrangle. United States Board on Geographic Names (1978c, p. 5) approved the name "Thompson Lake" for the feature and rejected the names "Thomson Lake" and "Tompson Lake."

Thornton Meadow [KERN]: *area,* 4.5 miles south-southeast of Claraville in Big Hart Canyon (lat. 35°22'45" N, long. 118°18'35" W). Named on Claraville (1972) 7.5' quadrangle.

Thorps Peak: see **Tharps Peak** [TULARE].

Three Corners [FRESNO]: *locality,* 2.5 miles north of Coalinga (lat. 36°10'50" N, long. 120°21'15" W; at NW cor. sec. 21, T 20 S, R 15 E); three roads join at the place. Named on Coalinga (1956) 7.5' quadrangle.

Three Island Lake [FRESNO]: *lake,* 4000 feet long, 7.5 miles south-southwest of Mount Abbot (lat. 37°17'25" N, long. 118°50'50" W). Named on Mount Abbot (1953) 15' quadrangle, which shows four islands in the lake. A survey party led by William A. Dill of California Department of Fish and Game named the lake in 1942 (Browning, p. 216).

Three Peaks [KINGS]: *peaks,* 14 miles south of Avenal (lat. 35°48'10" N, long. 120°10' W; near NE cor. sec. 31, T 24 S, R 17 E). Named on Tent Hills (1942) 7.5' quadrangle.

Three Pines Canyon [KERN]: *canyon,* drained by a stream that flows 4.5 miles to Canebrake Creek 3 miles northwest of Walker Pass (lat. 35°41'50" N, long. 118°03'25" W; near W line sec. 6, T 26 S, R 37 E). Named on Owens Peak (1972) and Walker Pass (1972) 7.5' quadrangles.

Three Rivers [TULARE]: *settlement,* 2.25 miles south-southeast of Kaweah along Kaweah River (lat. 36°26'20" N, long. 118°54'15" W; in and near sec. 24, T 17 S, R 28 E). Named on Kaweah (1957) 15' quadrangle. Mrs. Louisa Rockwell named the place in 1879 for the three forks of Kaweah River (Mitchell, A.R., p. 70). Postal authorities established Three Rivers post office in 1879, changed the name to Threerivers in 1895, changed it back to Three Rivers in 1932, and moved the post office 0.5 mile north in 1940 (Salley, p. 221).

Three Sirens: see **The Three Sirens**, under **Scylla** [FRESNO].

Three Sisters [FRESNO]:

(1) *peak,* 4.5 miles east-northeast of Dinkey Dome (lat. 37°08'30" N, long. 119°03'35" W; near SE cor. sec. 18, T 9 S, R 27 E). Altitude 10,619 feet. Named on Huntington Lake (1953) 15' quadrangle.

(2) *peak,* 18 miles north-northwest of Coalinga on Loma Atravesada (lat. 36°21'25" N, long. 120°32'05" W; near SW cor. sec. 14, T 18 S, R 13 E). Altitude 4220 feet. Named on Santa Rita Peak (1969) 7.5' quadrangle.

Three Sisters: see **Loma Atravesada** [FRESNO].

Three Springs [FRESNO]: *springs,* 12 miles north of Hume (lat. 36° 57'35" N, long. 118°56'30" W). Named on Tehipite Dome (1952) 15' quadrangle, which shows two springs. Bradley (p. 459) reported three large perennial springs at the place.

Thumb: see **The Thumb** [FRESNO].

Thunderbolt Peak [FRESNO]: *peak,* 11 miles east of Mount Goddard on Fresno-Inyo County line (lat. 37°05'50" N, long. 118° 31' W). Named on Mount Goddard (1948) 15' quadrangle. Francis P. Farquhar and six companions made the first ascent of the peak in 1931; they named it after they experienced a violent thunder storm there (Browning, p. 216-217).

Thunder Mountain [TULARE]: *peak,* 12 miles west-northwest of Mount Whitney on Great Western Divide (lat. 36°40'10" N, long. 118°28'30" W). Altitude 13,588 feet. Named on Mount Whitney (1956) 15' quadrangle. George R. Davis of United States Geological Survey named the feature when he made the first ascent in 1905 (Browning, p. 216).

Tibbets Creek [TULARE]: *stream,* flows 5.5 miles to South Fork Kern River 12 miles northwest of Lamont Peak in Rockhouse Basin (lat. 35°55'45" N, long. 118°10' W; near E line sec. 14, T 23 S, R 35 E). Named on Lamont Peak (1956) 15' quadrangle.

Tibbetts Creek: see **Durrwood Creek** [TULARE].

Tierra Seca: see **Sacatara Creek** [KERN].

Tiffin [TULARE]: *locality,* 4 miles east-southeast of Lindsay along Visalia Electric Railroad (lat. 36°11' N, long. 119°01'30" W; near SW cor. sec. 14, T 20 S, R 27 E). Named on Lindsay (1928) 7.5' quadrangle.

Tiger Flat: see **Tiger Flat Campground** [KERN].

Tiger Flat Campground [KERN]: *locality,* 8.5 miles east-northeast of Glennville (lat. 35°46'40" N, long. 118°34' W; near SW cor. sec. 5, T 25 S, R 32 E). Named on California Hot Springs (1958) 15' quadrangle. Tobias Peak (1943) 30' quadrangle shows Tiger Flat at or near the site.

Tillie Creek [KERN]: *stream,* flows 5 miles to Isabella Lake 0.5 mile south of the center of Wofford Heights (lat. 35°42'05" N, long. 118°27'15" W; sec. 5, T 26 S, R 33 E). Named on Alta Sierra (1972) and Lake Isabella North (1972) 7.5' quadrangles. Called Tilly Cr. on Olmsted's (1900) map.

Tillie Creek Campground [KERN]: *locality,* 0.5 mile south of the center of Wofford Heights (lat. 35°42'05" N, long. 118°27'20" W; sec. 5, T 26 S, R 33 E); the place is near the mouth of Tillie Creek. Named on Lake Isabella North (1972) 7.5' quadrangle.

Tilly Creek: see **Tillie Creek** [KERN].

Timber Gap [TULARE]: *pass,* 1 mile north of Mineral King (lat. 36° 28'05" N, long. 118°35'50" W). Named on Mineral King (1956) 15' quadrangle.

Timber Gap Creek [TULARE]: *stream,* flows 2 miles to Cliff Creek 3.5 miles north-northwest of Mineral King (lat. 36°29'55" N, long. 118°36'55" W); the stream heads near Timber Gap. Named on Mineral King (1956) 15' quadrangle. United States Board on Geographic Names (1933a, p. 757) rejected the name "Deer Creek" for the stream.

Tipton [TULARE]: *town,* 10.5 miles south of Tulare (lat. 36°03'35" N, long. 119°18'40" W; sec. 31, T 21 S, R 25 E). Named on Tipton (1950) 7.5' quadrangle. Postal authorities established Tipton post office in 1873 (Frickstad, p. 214). According to A.R. Mitchell (p. 70), the place first was called Tip Town because it was at the tip of the railroad when construction halted there for several months. According to Hanna (p. 330), the name commemorates John Tipton, the first white child born in the neighborhood. Postal authorities established Noradell post office about 9 miles southeast of Tipton in 1879 and discontinued it in 1881; the name "Noradell" was coined from the given names of Mrs. Dellia Carey, first postmaster, and a member of her family called Nora (Salley, p. 155).

Tip Town: see **Tipton** [TULARE].

Tivy Mountain [FRESNO]: *peak,* 24 miles east of Fresno (lat. 36° 48' N, long. 119°21'30" W; near E line sec. 16, T 13 S, R 24 E); the peak is 3 miles northeast of Tivy Valley. Altitude 2848 feet. Named on Pine Flat Dam (1965) 7.5' quadrangle. On Watts Valley (1942) 15' quadrangle, the name applies to the ridge on which the peak is the high point.

Tivy Valley [FRESNO]: *valley,* 3 miles south-southwest of Piedra (lat. 36°46'15" N, long. 119°24'15" W; in and near sec. 30, T 13 S, R 24 E). Named on Piedra (1965) 7.5' quadrangle.

Tobias Creek [TULARE]: *stream,* flows 6.5 miles to Kern River 0.5 mile south-southeast of Fairview (lat. 35°55'05" N, long. 118°29'30" W; sec. 23, T 23 S, R 32 E). Named on California Hot Springs (1958) and Kernville (1956) 15' quadrangles. The name commemorates Tobias Minter (Mitchell, A.R., p. 78).

Tobias Meadow [TULARE]: *area,* 5.5 miles east-southeast of California Hot Springs (lat. 35°51'50" N, long. 118°34'15" W; on S line sec. 6, T 24 S, R 32 E); the place is at the head of Tobias Creek. Named on California Hot Springs (1958) 15' quadrangle.

Tobias Meadow: see **Lower Tobias Meadow** [TULARE].

Tobias Pass [TULARE]: *pass,* 5.5 miles east-southeast of California Hot Springs (lat. 35°51'30" N, long. 118°43'30" W; near E line sec. 12, T 24 S, R 31 E); the pass is 0.5 mile north-northwest of Tobias Peak near the head of Tobias Creek. Named on California Hot Springs (1958) 15' quadrangle.

Tobias Peak [TULARE]: *peak,* 6 miles east-southeast of California Hot Springs (lat. 35°51' N, long. 118°34'20" W; near SW cor. sec. 7, T 24 S, R 32 E); the peak is near the head of Tobias Creek. Altitude 8284 feet. Named on California Hot Springs (1958) 15' quadrangle. John Minter and Tobe Minter named the peak in 1884 in memory of their father, Tobias Minter, who homesteaded near the feature (Gudde, 1949, p. 363).

Toby [KERN]: *locality,* 2.25 miles east-northeast of Saltdale (lat. 35° 22'30" N, long. 117°51' W). Named on Saltdale (1943b) 15' quadrangle.

Tocher Lake [FRESNO]: *lake,* 900 feet long, nearly 4 miles north-northeast of Dinkey Dome (lat. 37°10'10" N, long. 119°06'40" W; near NW cor. sec. 11, T 9 S, R 26 E). Named on Huntington Lake (1953) 15' quadrangle. The name commemorates Dr. Lloyd Tocher of Fresno (Browning, p. 218).

Todds Hill [TULARE]: *ridge,* south-trending, 1 mile long, 1.25 miles north-northeast of Lindsay (lat. 36°13'25" N, long. 119°04'55" W). Named on Lindsay (1951) 7.5' quadrangle. Called Wards Hill on Porterville (1942) 15' quadrangle.

Toe Lake [FRESNO]: *lake,* 1100 feet long, 1.5 miles south-southwest of Mount Abbot (lat. 37°21'45" N, long. 118°47'25" W); the lake is near the northeast or "toe" end of boot-shaped Lake Italy. Named on Mount Abbot (1953) 15' quadrangle.

Tokay [TULARE]: *locality,* nearly 2 miles east-northeast of Dinuba along

Atchison, Topeka and Santa Fe Railroad (lat. 36°33'05" N, long. 119°21'20" W; near W line sec. 10, T 16 S, R 24 E). Named on Orange Cove South (1966) 7.5' quadrangle.

Tokay: see **Malaga** [FRESNO].

Tokopah Falls [TULARE]: *waterfall,* 9 miles west of Triple Divide Peak on Marble Fork (lat. 36°36'30" N, long. 118°41'20" W; sec. 23, T 15 S, R 30 E); the feature is above Tokopah Valley. Named on Triple Divide Peak (1956) 15' quadrangle.

Tokopah Valley [TULARE]: *canyon,* 1.5 miles long, 10 miles west of Triple Divide Peak along Marble Fork (lat. 36°36'40" N, long. 118°42'15" W; sec. 22, 23, T 15 S, R 30 E). Named on Triple Divide Peak (1956) 15' quadrangle. The name is from an Indian word that has the meaning "high" (United States Board on Geographic Names, 1933a, p. 760).

Tollgate Canyon [KERN]: *canyon,* drained by a stream that flows 6.25 miles to Indian Creek 2 miles southeast of Loraine (lat. 35°17'05" N, long. 118°24'45" W; near SW cor. sec. 26, T 30 S, R 33 E). Named on Loraine (1972) and Tehachapi North (1966) 7.5' quadrangles.

Tollhouse [FRESNO]: *village,* 7.5 miles southwest of Shaver Lake Heights (present town of Shaver Lake) (lat. 37°01'10" N, long. 119°24' W; sec. 31, T 10 S, R 24 E). Named on Shaver Lake (1953) 15' quadrangle. Lippincott's (1902) map shows Toll House P.O. at the place. Postal authorities established Toll House post office in 1876, discontinued it in 1884, reestablished it in 1885, and changed the name to Tollhouse in 1894 (Salley, p. 222). The village began in 1867 when a building was constructed where toll was levied on vehicles passing up or down a 10-mile road that led to mills near Shaver Lake; toll was collected until 1878 (Hoover, Rensch, and Rensch, p. 94). Postal authorities established Mountain Rest post office 6 miles north of Tollhouse in 1945, discontinued it in 1947, reestablished it in 1948, and discontinued it in 1953 (Salley, p. 147).

Tollhouse Canyon [KERN]: *canyon,* drained by a stream that flows 4 miles to Walker Basin Creek 4.25 miles north-northwest of Caliente (lat. 35°20'55" N, long. 118°39'25" W). Named on Bena (1972) and Oiler Peak (1972) 7.5' quadrangles—the last-named map shows a tollhouse in the canyon.

Tollhouse Creek [FRESNO]: *stream,* flows 1.5 miles to Dry Creek 6.5 miles southwest of Shaver Lake Heights (present town of Shaver Lake) (lat. 37°02'25" N, long. 119°23'50" W; sec. 19, T 10 S, R 24 E); the stream is 1.5 miles north of Tollhouse. Named on Shaver Lake (1953) 15' quadrangle. On Kaiser (1904) 30' quadrangle, Dry Creek and this tributary together are called Tollhouse Cr.

Tollhouse Flat [KERN]: *area,* 3.25 miles north of Caliente (lat. 35° 20'20" N, long. 118°37'55" W); the place is in Tollhouse Canyon. Named on Bena (1972) 7.5' quadrangle.

Tolly Spring [KERN]: *spring,* 12 miles north of Mojave (lat. 35°13'20" N, long. 118°09'10" W; sec. 19, T 31 S, R 36 E). Named on Cache Peak (1973) 7.5' quadrangle.

Tom: see **Mount Tom** [FRESNO].

Tomahawk Lake [FRESNO]: *lake,* 1900 feet long, 3 miles west-southwest of Mount Humphreys in Humphreys Basin (lat. 37°15'25" N, long. 118°43'35" W). Named on Mount Tom (1949) 15' quadrangle.

Tombstone: see **The Tombstone** [FRESNO].

Tombstone Creek [FRESNO]:

(1) *stream,* flows 2 miles to South Fork San Joaquin River 12 miles southwest of Mount Abbot (lat. 37°16'45" N, long. 118°57'35" W); the stream heads near the feature called The Tombstone. Named on Mount Abbot (1953) 15' quadrangle.

(2) *stream,* flows 4 miles to Middle Fork Kings River 7.5 miles northeast of Hume (lat. 36°52' N, long. 118°49'30" W). Named on Tehipite Dome (1952) 15' quadrangle.

Tombstone Ridge [FRESNO]: *ridge,* southeast-trending, 3 miles long, 9.5 miles north-northeast of Hume (lat. 36°53'45" N, long. 118°49' W). Named on Tehipite Dome (1952) 15' quadrangle.

Tompson Lake: see **Thomson Lake** [FRESNO].

Tom Sawyer Lake [KERN]: *lake,* 1250 feet long, 3 miles west-northwest of Tehachapi along Brite Creek (lat. 35°09'05" N, long. 118°29'30" W; sec. 13, T 32 S, R 32 E). Named on Tehachapi North (1966) 7.5' quadrangle.

Toms Hill [KERN]: *peak,* 4.25 miles north-northwest of Cross Mountain (lat. 35°20'15" N, long. 118°09'40" W; at W line sec. 7, T 30 S, R 36 E). Altitude 5048 feet. Named on Cross Mountain (1972) 7.5' quadrangle. On Cross Mountain (1943) 15' quadrangle, the name applies to a peak located 1 mile farther north (near SW cor. sec. 6, T 30 S, R 36 E).

Ton Tache: see **Tulare Lake** [KINGS].

Tonyville [TULARE]: *locality,* 3 miles north of Lindsay (lat. 36°14'55" N, long. 119°05'25" W; sec. 30, T 19 S, R 27 E). Named on Lindsay (1951) 7.5' quadrangle. Called Liberty on Lindsay (1928) 7.5' quadrangle, which shows the place along Visalia Electric Railroad.

Toolville [TULARE]: *locality,* 1.5 miles east-southeast of Exeter (lat. 36°17'10" N, long. 119°06'55" W; at W line sec. 12, T 19 S, R 26 E). Named on Rocky Hill (1951) 7.5' quadrangle.

Toolwass: see **Bakersfield** [KERN].

Toomey Gulch: see **Tumey Gulch** [FRESNO].

Tooth Lake [FRESNO]: *lake,* 700 feet long, 5 miles south of Mount Abbot (lat. 37°19' N, long. 118°47'55" W). Named on Mount Abbot (1953) 15' quadrangle.

Toowa Range [TULARE]: *ridge,* east-southeast- to southeast-trending, 5.5 miles long; Kern Peak is near the center (lat. 36°18'30" N, long. 118°17'10" W). Named on Kern Peak (1956) and Olancha (1956) 15' quadrangles. Called Too-wa Range on Olmsted's (1900) map.

Tornado Creek [FRESNO]: *stream,* flows 3.5 miles to Tenmile Creek 1.5 miles northeast of Hume (lat. 36°48' N, long. 118°53'30" W); the stream heads at Tornado Meadow. Named on Tehipite Dome (1952) 15' quadrangle.

Tornado Meadow [FRESNO]: *area,* 3.5 miles east of Hume (lat. 36° 46'45" N, long. 118°50'45" W). Named on Tehipite Dome (1952) 15' quadrangle. The name is from a tangle of trees felled by a windstorm (Forest M. Clingan, personal communication, 1990).

Tower Rock [TULARE]: *peak,* 6.5 miles west-northwest of Kern Peak (lat. 36°20'20" N, long. 118°23'50" W). Altitude 8469 feet. Named on Kern Peak (1956) 15' quadrangle.

Towne: see **Towne Oil Station** [FRESNO].

Town Oil Station [FRESNO]: *locality,* 26 miles north-northeast of Coalinga (lat. 36°28'20" N, long. 120°08'45" W; near N line sec. 8, T 17 S, R 17 E). Abandoned site named on Westside (1956) 7.5' quadrangle. Mendenhall's (1908) map has the name "Towne" at the place.

Townsend: see **Yettem** [TULARE].

Trail Crest [TULARE]: *locality,* 1.5 miles south of Mount Whitney on Tulare-Inyo County line (lat. 36°33'35" N, long. 118°17'30" W); the trail to Mount Whitney reaches the crest of the Sierra Nevada at the spot. Named on Mount Whitney (1956) 15' quadrangle.

Trail Lakes [FRESNO]: *lakes,* two, largest 700 feet long, 3.5 miles north of Mount Abbot (lat. 37°26'25" N, long. 118°46'30" W). Named on Mount Abbot (1953) 15' quadrangle.

Trail Pass [TULARE]: *pass,* 12 miles north-northwest of Olancha Peak on Tulare-Inyo County line (lat. 36°25'40" N, long. 118°10'30" W; sec. 22, T 17 S, R 35 E). Named on Olancha (1956) 15' quadrangle. Trail Pass has been called "new" Mulkey Pass, and Mulkey Pass has been called "old" Mulkey Pass (Schumacher, p. 80).

Trail Peak [TULARE]: *peak,* 12 miles north-northwest of Olancha Peak on Tulare-Inyo County line (lat. 36°25'40" N, long. 118°11'20" W; sec. 21, T 17 S, R 35 E); the peak is less than 1 mile west of Trail Pass. Altitude 11,623 feet. Named on Olancha (1956) 15' quadrangle.

Trail Spring [KERN]: *spring,* 13 miles north of Mojave (lat. 35°14'20" N, long. 118°11'25" W; near N line sec. 14, T 31 S, R 35 E). Named on Cache Peak (1973) 7.5' quadrangle.

Tranquillity [FRESNO]: *town,* 10 miles southeast of Mendota (lat. 36°38'50" N, long. 120°15' W; sec. 5, 8, T 15 S, R 16 E). Named on Jamesan (1963) and Tranquillity (1956) 7.5' quadrangles. Postal authorities established Tranquillity post office in 1910 (Frickstad, p. 38). A place called Fresno City was begun about 1855 at the head of navigation on Fresno Slough, less than 2 miles north and slightly west of present Tranquillity; Fresno City was practically abandoned by 1865 (Hoover, Rensch, and Rensch, p. 92). Postal authorities established Fresno City post office in 1860 and discontinued it in 1863 (Frickstad, p. 33). Mendenhall's (1908) map shows a place called Mendota Station located 3.5 miles west-southwest of present Tranquillity.

Traver [TULARE]: *village,* 14 miles northwest of Visalia (lat. 36°27'15" N, long. 119°29'05" W; sec. 16, T 17 S, R 23 E). Named on Traver (1949) 7.5' quadrangle. The name, given in 1884, commemorates Charles Traver, a member of 76 Land and Water Company (Mitchell, A.R., p. 70). Postal authorities established Cross Creek post office in 1874, changed the name to Grandview in 1876, and changed it to Traver in 1884 (Frickstad, p. 210, 211).

Travers Creek [FRESNO-TULARE]: *stream,* heads in Fresno County and flows 11 miles to a canal 2.5 miles west of Dinuba in Tulare County (lat. 36°32'45" N, long. 119°25'40" N; near SW cor. sec. 12, T 16 S, R 23 E). Named on Reedley (1966) 7.5' quadrangle.

Treadwell [KERN]: *locality,* 4 miles north-northwest of downtown Bakersfield along Southern Pacific Railroad (lat. 35°25'40" N, long. 118°58'20" W; near S line sec. 4, T 29 S, R 28 E). Named on Oil Center (1954) 7.5' quadrangle. California Mining Bureau's (1917c) map shows a place called Porque located about 3 miles north of Treadwell along a railroad.

Trescope [KERN]: *locality,* 8 miles northeast of Mojave along Southern Pacific Railroad (lat. 35°08'30" N, long. 118°04'30" W; near SW cor. sec. 13, T 32 S, R 36 E). Named on Mojave (1915) 30' quadrangle. Called Trescape on Mojave (1943) 15' quadrangle.

Tres Piedras: see **Joaquin Rocks** [FRESNO].

Tretten Canyon [FRESNO]: *canyon,* drained by a stream that flows 3.5 miles to Mill Creek (3) nearly 4 miles east-southeast of Tivy Mountain (lat. 36°47'15" N, long. 119°17'35" W; sec. 19, T 13 S, R 25 E). Named on Pine Flat Dam (1965) 7.5' quadrangle.

Treves: see **Sivert** [KERN].

Trimmer [FRESNO]: *locality,* 8 miles north-northeast of Piedra (lat.

36°54'20" N, long. 119°17'45" W; on E line sec. 12, T 12 S, R 24 E). Named on Trimmer (1965) 7.5' quadrangle. Watts Valley (1942) 15' quadrangle shows Trimmer situated 0.5 mile farther southeast within the limits of present Pine Flat Reservoir (near center of sec. 7, T 12 S, R 25 E). Postal authorities established Trimmer post office in 1889, discontinued it in 1890, reestablished it in 1892, moved it 1 mile south in 1894, moved it 1 mile northwest in 1895, and discontinued it in 1919 (Salley, p. 224). A resort called Trimmer Springs, for owner Morris Trimmer (Hanna, p. 333), operated before 1911 along Kings River (sec. 18, T 12 S, R 25 E) less than 1 mile south of Trimmer post office (Bradley, p. 459)—water of Pine Flat Reservoir now covers the site.

Trimmer Springs: see **Trimmer** [FRESNO].

Triple Divide Peak [TULARE]: *peak,* 13 miles west of Mount Whitney on Great Western Divide (lat. 36°35'35" N, long. 118°31'50" W). Altitude 12,634 feet. Named on Triple Divide Peak (1956) 15' quadrangle.

Triple Falls [FRESNO]: *waterfall,* 2.5 miles northwest of Marion Peak along Cartridge Creek (lat. 36°59'05" N, long. 118°33'15" W). Named on Marion Peak (1953) 15' quadrangle.

Trocha [TULARE]: *locality,* 8.5 miles southwest of Ducor along Southern Pacific Railroad (lat. 35°47'50" N, long. 119°08'45" W; sec. 34, T 24 S, R 26 E). Named on Delano East (1953) 7.5' quadrangle.

Tropico Hill [KERN]: *hill,* 4 miles west-northwest of Rosamond (lat. 34°52'45" N, long. 118°13'55" W). Named on Soledad Mountain (1973) 7.5' quadrangle. The feature also was known as Red Hill, Crandall Hill, Hamilton Hill, Burton's Hill, and Burton's Tropico Hill (Settle, p. 58, 62; Wynn, 1951, p. 16). The name "Hamilton" was for Ezra Hamilton, who recognized gold in rock at the hill; the name "Burton" was for the Burton brothers, who erected a mill at the place (Wynn, 1951, p. 16).

Trout Creek [TULARE]: *stream,* flows 15 miles to South Fork Kern River 12.5 miles northwest of Lamont Peak (lat. 35°56'35" N, long. 118°10' W; sec. 11, T 23 S, R 35 E). Named on Hockett Peak (1956), Kernville (1956), and Lamont Peak (1956) 15' quadrangles.

Trout Creek: see **Little Trout Creek** [TULARE].

Trout Meadows [TULARE]: *area,* 2 miles west-southwest of Hockett Peak (lat. 36°12'45" N, long. 118°25'10" W). Named on Hockett Peak (1956) 15' quadrangle.

Troy Meadow: see **Little Troy Meadow** [TULARE].

Troy Meadows [TULARE]: *area,* 9.5 miles south-southwest of Monache Mountain along Fish Creek (2) (lat. 36°04'20" N, long. 118°14'15" W; in and near sec. 30, T 21 S, R 35 E). Named on Monache Mountain (1956) 15' quadrangle.

True Meadow [TULARE]: *area,* 14 miles southeast of Fairview (lat. 35°48'10" N, long. 118°18'25" W; near NW cor. sec. 34, T 24 S, R 34 E). Named on Kernville (1956) 15' quadrangle. Browning (p. 221) associated the name with Henry B. True, who patented land in the neighborhood in 1891.

Tucker Creek [KERN]: *stream,* flows 2.5 miles to Kern River 2.25 miles east-northeast of Democrat Hot Springs (lat. 35°32'20" N, long. 118°37'40" W). Named on Democrat Hot Springs (1972) 7.5' quadrangle.

Tucker Mountain [TULARE]: *peak,* 12 miles northeast of Dinuba (lat. 36°38'20" N, long. 119°12'30" W; sec. 12, T 15 S, R 25 E). Altitude 2611 feet. Named on Tucker Mountain (1966) 7.5' quadrangle. The name is for a homesteader east of the peak (Gudde, 1949, p. 370).

Tulainyo Lake [TULARE]: *lake,* 0.5 mile long, 1.5 miles north-northeast of Mount Whitney (lat. 36°35'50" N, long. 118°16'46" W); the lake is near Tulare-Inyo County line. Named on Mount Whitney (1956) 15' quadrangle. R.B. Marshall of United States Geological Survey coined the name in 1917 from the words "Tulare" and "Inyo" (United States Board on Geographic Names, 1933a, p. 771).

Tula Lake: see **Tulare Lake** [KINGS].

Tulare [TULARE]: *city,* 8.5 miles south-southwest of Visalia (lat. 36°12'30" N, long. 119°20'50" W). Named on Tulare (1950) 7.5' quadrangle. Postal authorities established Tulare post office in 1872 (Frickstad, p. 214), and the city incorporated in 1888. Officials of Southern Pacific Railroad named the city in 1872 (Mitchell, A.R., p. 70). California Mining Bureau's (1917b) map shows a place called Robla located along the railroad about halfway between Tulare and Paige. Postal authorities established Hunsaker post office 10.5 miles southeast of Tulare in 1872 and discontinued it in 1884; the name was for Henry Hunsaker, a pioneer settler (Salley, p. 101). They established Herrick's Cross post office 14 miles southeast of Tulare in 1878 and discontinued it in 1882; the place was at a crossroads named for the local landowner (Salley, p. 96).

Tulare Lake [KINGS]: *lake,* south of Lemoore. Named on La Rambla (1942) and Stratford (1942) 15' quadrangles, which show the lake confined within artificial banks. Wilkes' (1841) map has the name "L. Chintache," and Wilkes (p. 47) in his report referred to Tula Lake, "called by the Indians, Chintache Lake." Fremont's (1848) map has the name "L. d. l. Tulares." Derby's (1850) map has the name "Tache Lake" and the designation "Bed of the Ton Tache" for marsh south of the lake. Eddy's (1854) map has the designation "Tulare or Tache Lake," Parke's (1854-1855) map has the name "Tulare Lake," and Rogers and Johnston's (1857) map has the name "L. Tulare." Pedro Fages discovered the lake in 1772 and gave the name "Los Tulares" to marshlands of San Joaquin Valley—*los tulares* means "the place of rushes" in Spanish (Hoover, Rensch, and Rensch, p. 135). *Tule* means "reed" or "bullrush" in American Spanish, and a place where reeds grow should be called *Tular,* but a new American term was derived from the plural form *Tulares*, apparently by simply dropping the final letter (Stewart, p. 497). According to Derby (p. 13), water overflowed north from the lake to San Joaquin River through a slough known as Sanjon de San Jose, but the lake has not overflowed to San Joaquin River since 1878, chiefly because water is diverted from Kings River for irrigation (Davis, Green, Olmsted, and Brown, p. 29). During reclamation of the lake bed for agriculture, dikes and levees restricted the lake to the northwest part of its old bed (Davis, Green, Olmsted, and Brown, p. 29), and the most recent maps show no lake at all. Tulare Lake Bed is named on Corcoran (1954), Dudley Ridge (1954), El Rico Ranch (1954), Hacienda Ranch NE (1954), Hacienda Ranch NW (1954), Kettleman City (1963), Los Viejos (1954), Stratford (1954), Stratford SE (1954), and Westhaven (1956) 7.5' quadrangles.

Tulare Lake Bed: see **Tulare Lake** [KINGS].

Tulare Lake Slough: see **Fresno Slough** [FRESNO].

Tulare Peak [TULARE]: *peak,* 3.25 miles southeast of Mineral King (lat. 36°24'45" N, long. 118°33'45" W). Altitude 11,588 feet. Named on Mineral King (1956) 15' quadrangle.

Tulare Plains: see "Regional setting."

Tulare Valley: see "Regional setting."

Tule: see **North Tule**, under **Porterville** [TULARE]; **Porterville** [TULARE].

Tule Lake [FRESNO]: *lake,* 900 feet long. 9.5 miles east-northeast of Kaiser Peak (lat. 37°20'30" N, long. 119°01'20" W). Named on Kaiser Peak (1953) 15' quadrangle.

Tule Meadow [FRESNO]:

(1) *area,* 8 miles north-northeast of Kaiser Peak (lat. 37°23'30" N, long. 119°07' W). Named on Kaiser Peak (1953) 15' quadrangle.

(2) *area,* 10 miles southeast of Dinkey Dome (lat. 37°00' N, long. 119°01'45" W; sec. 4, T 11 S, R 27 E). Named on Huntington Lake (1953) and Patterson Mountain (1952) 15' quadrangles.

Tule River [KINGS-TULARE]: *stream,* formed by the confluence of North Fork and Middle Fork in Tulare County, flows 38 miles to Kings County 7.25 miles south-southwest of Waukena (lat. 36°02'05" N, long. 119°32'05" W); in Kings County the stream flows through Tulare Lake Bed in an artificial watercourse. Named on Corcoran (1954), El Rico Ranch (1954), Globe (1956), Porterville (1951, photorevised 1969), Springville (1957), Stratford SE (1954), Success Dam (1956), Taylor Weir (1950, photorevised 1969), Tipton (1950, photorevised 1969), and Woodville (1950, photorevised 1969) 7.5' quadrangles. Derby's (1850) map has the designation "Tule River or San Pedro" for the stream. Middle Fork Tule River is formed 5.5 miles west-northwest of Camp Nelson by the confluence of North Fork of Middle Fork and South Fork of Middle Fork; it is 7 miles long and is named on Camp Nelson (1956) and Springville (1957) 15' quadrangles. North Fork of Middle Fork is 14 miles long and is named on Camp Nelson (1956) and Mineral King (1956) 15' quadrangles. South Fork of Middle Fork is 11.5 miles long and is named on Camp Nelson (1956) 15' quadrangle; it also is called East Fork of Middle Fork (Waring, p. 243). North Fork Tule River is 18 miles long and is named on Kaweah (1957), Mineral King (1956), and Springville (1957) 15' quadrangles. South Fork Tule River joins Tule River 6 miles east of Porterville in Lake Success; it is 22 miles long and is named on Camp Nelson (1956) and Springville (1957) 15' quadrangles. Tule River splits 3.25 miles east of Woodville to form North Branch and South Branch. North Branch flows 13 miles before it joins South Branch to reform Tule River 3 miles north-northwest of Tipton; it is named on Cairns Corner (1950, photorevised 1969), Tipton (1950, photorevised 1969), Tulare (1950, photorevised 1969), and Woodville (1950, photorevised 1969) 7.5' quadrangles. South Branch is 11.5 miles long and is named on Tipton (1950, photorevised 1969) and Woodville (1950, photorevised 1969) 7.5' quadrangles. North Branch is unnamed on Tipton (1928) 7.5' quadrangle, which has the name "Tule River" for present South Branch. Middle Branch diverges from South Branch 1 mile north-northeast of Woodville and flows 4.5 miles before it rejoins South Branch; it is named on Woodville (1950, photorevised 1969) 7.5' quadrangle. Lake View School (1927) 7.5' quadrangle shows Tule River situated 1 to 2 miles farther south in a watercourse called Old Channel Tule River on Taylor Wier (1950, photorevised 1969) 7.5' quadrangle.

Tule River: see **Porterville** [TULARE].

Tule Spring [FRESNO]: *spring,* 4 miles north-northwest of Coalinga Mineral Springs (lat. 36°11'10" N, long. 120°36' W; sec. 17, T 20 S, R 13 E). Named on Sherman Peak (1969) 7.5' quadrangle.

Tule Spring [KERN]: *spring,* 10 miles west of Liebre Twins in Devils Canyon (lat. 34°56'45" N, long. 118°44'25" W; at W line sec. 6, T 10 N, R 17 W). Named on Winters Ridge (1966) 7.5' quadrangle.

Tully Hole [FRESNO]: *relief feature,* 3 miles west of Red Slate Mountain (lat. 37°31'10" N, long. 118°55'15" W). Named on Mount Morrison (1953) 15' quadrangle. The feature contains marsh. Gene Tully, a Forest Service ranger, used the place to rest his stock when he was on patrol in the neighborhood (Browning, p. 222).

Tully Lake [FRESNO]: *lake,* 1350 feet long, 9 miles northwest of Mount Abbot (lat. 37°29'15" N, long. 118°53' W). Named on Mount Abbot (1953) 15' quadrangle.

Tumey Gulch [FRESNO]: *canyon,* drained by a stream that heads in San Benito County and flows 14 miles to lowlands 20 miles south-southwest of Firebaugh (lat. 36°35' N, long. 120°36' W; sec. 31, T 15 S, R 13 E). Named on Monocline Ridge (1955) and Tumey Hills (1956) 7.5' quadrangles. The name also had the form "Toomey Gulch" (Gudde, 1969, p. 347).

Tumey Hills [FRESNO]: *range,* 25 miles south-southwest of Firebaugh on Fresno-San Benito County line (lat. 36°33' N, long. 120° 39' W); the range is west of Tumey Gulch. Named on Monocline Ridge (1955) and Tumey Hills (1956) 7.5' quadrangles.

Tunemah Lake [FRESNO]: *lake,* 2000 feet long, 6 miles south of Mount Goddard (lat. 37°00'55" N, long. 118°42'10" W). Named on Mount Goddard (1948) 15' quadrangle.

Tunemah Pass [FRESNO]: *pass,* 8 miles west of Marion Peak (lat. 36°58'45" N, long. 118°40' W); the pass is 2 miles southeast of Tunemah Peak. Named on Tehipite (1903) 30' quadrangle. The name originated with a curse vented by Chinese cooks who accompanied sheepmen through the pass (Hanna, p. 336).

Tunemah Peak [FRESNO]: *peak,* 10 miles west-northwest of Marion Peak (lat. 36°59'45" N, long. 118°41'51" W). Altitude 11,894 feet. Named on Marion Peak (1953) 15' quadrangle. The name is from Tunemah Pass (Hanna, p. 336).

Tunis Creek [KERN]: *stream,* flows 15 miles to El Paso Creek 12.5 miles south of Arvin (lat. 35°01'40" N, long. 118°49'25" W; sec. 20, T 11 N, R 18 W). Named on Pastoria Creek (1958), Tejon Hills (1955), and Winters Ridge (1966) 7.5' quadrangles.

Tunnabora Peak [TULARE]: *peak,* 2 miles north-northeast of Mount Whitney on Tulare-Inyo County line (lat. 36°36'15" N, long. 118°16'50" W). Altitude 13,565 feet. Named on Mount Whitney (1956) 15' quadrangle.

Tunnel: see **The Tunnel** [TULARE].

Tunnel Air Camp [TULARE]: *locality,* 5 miles north-northeast of Kern Peak (lat. 36°22'50" N, long. 118°15'50" W; at N line sec. 11, T 18 S, R 34 E); the place is in Tunnel Meadow. Named on Kern Peak (1956) 15' quadrangle.

Tunnel Meadow [TULARE]: *area,* 5 miles north-northeast of Kern Peak along South Fork Kern River (lat. 36°22'40" N, long. 118° 16' W; mainly in sec. 10, 11, T 18 S, R 34 E); the place is northeast of The Tunnel. Named on Kern Peak (1956) 15' quadrangle. Called South Fork Meadows on Olancha (1907) 30' quadrangle, but United States Board on Geographic Names (1938, p. 56) rejected this name for the place.

Tunnel Spring [KERN]:

(1) *spring,* 2.25 miles northeast of Kernville (lat. 35°46'30" N, long. 118°23'40" W; near NW cor. sec. 12, T 25 S, R 33 E). Named on Kernville (1956) 15' quadrangle.

(2) *spring,* 3.5 miles west-northwest of Pinyon Mountain (lat. 35° 28'50" N, long. 118°12'45" W; near SE cor. sec. 16, T 28 S, R 35 E). Named on Pinyon Mountain (1972) 7.5' quadrangle.

(3) *spring,* nearly 3 miles northeast of Mount Adelaide along Stark Creek (lat. 35°27'40" N, long. 118°42'45" W). Named on Mount Adelaide (1972) 7.5' quadrangle.

Tuohy Creek [TULARE]: *stream,* flows 1.5 miles to South Fork Kaweah River 8 miles south-southwest of Mineral King (lat. 36° 20'50" N, long. 118°40'15" W); the stream goes through Tuohy Meadow. Named on Mineral King (1956) 15' quadrangle.

Tuohy Meadow [TULARE]: *area,* 9 miles south-southwest of Mineral King (lat. 36°20'15" N, long. 118°40'10" W). Named on Mineral King (1956) 15' quadrangle.

Tupman [KERN]: *village,* 20 miles west-southwest of Bakersfield (lat. 35°17'50" N, long. 119°21' W; at S line sec. 24, T 30 S, R 24 E). Named on Tupman (1954) 7.5' quadrangle. Postal authorities established Tupman post office in 1921 (Frickstad, p. 59). The name, given at a public meeting in 1920, commemorates H.V. Tupman, from whom Standard Oil Company purchased the land at the place (Gudde, 1949, p. 372).

Turf Lakes [FRESNO]: *lakes,* largest 500 feet long, 7.5 miles north-northwest of Blackcap Mountain (lat. 37°10'30" N, long. 118°49'55" W). Named on Blackcap Mountain (1953) 15' quadrangle.

Turk [FRESNO]: *locality,* 8 miles east-northeast of Coalinga along Southern Pacific Railroad (lat. 36°10'15" N, long. 120°13'15" W; sec. 22, T 20 S, R 16 E). Named on Guijarral Hills (1956) 7.5' quadrangle. Called Stanley on Arnold and Anderson's (1910) map.

Turman Spring [KERN]: *spring,* 2.5 miles north-northeast of Caliente (lat. 35°19'15" N, long. 118°36'15" W). Named on Oiler Peak (1972) 7.5' quadrangle.

Turnbull [TULARE]: *locality,* 6.25 miles south of Waukena along Atchison, Topeka and Santa Fe Railroad (lat. 36°02'55" N, long. 119°31'10" W; near NE cor. sec. 6, T 22 S, R 23 E). Named on Corcoran (1928) 7.5' quadrangle.

Turner Flat [TULARE]: *area,* 4.5 miles southwest of California Hot Springs (lat. 35°50'30" N, long. 118°44'30" W; sec. 16, T 24 S, R 30 E); the place is 1.25 miles south of Turner Peak. Named on California Hot Springs (1958) 15' quadrangle.

Turner Peak [TULARE]: *peak,* 4.25 miles west-southwest of California Hot Springs (lat. 35°51'30" N, long. 118°44'30" W; sec. 9, T 24 S, R 30 E). Altitude 3731 feet. Named on California Hot Springs (1958) 15' quadrangle.

Turret Creek [FRESNO]: *stream,* flows 2.5 miles to Piute Canyon 12 miles north of Blackcap Mountain (lat. 37°14'20" N, long. 118° 49'30" W); the stream heads near Turret Peak. Named on Blackcap Mountain (1953) 15' quadrangle.

Turret Lake: see **Lower Turret Lake** [FRESNO]; **Middle Turret Lakes** [FRESNO]; **Upper Turret Lakes** [FRESNO].

Turret Peak [FRESNO]: *peak,* 9 miles south-southwest of Mount Abbot (lat. 37°15'50" N, long. 118°50'30" W). Named on Mount Abbot (1953) 15' quadrangle.

Turtle Creek [FRESNO]: *stream,* flows 2.5 miles to Ross Creek (1) 4 miles north of Balch Camp (lat. 36°57'45" N, long. 119°07'15" W). Named on Patterson Mountain (1952) 15' quadrangle.

Turtle Hole: see **The Turtle Hole** [KINGS].

Turtle Pass: see **Elizabeth Pass** [TULARE].

Tweedy Creek [KERN]: *stream,* flows 9 miles to Tehachapi Creek 0.5 mile north-northwest of Keene (lat. 35°13'55" N, long. 118° 34' W; sec. 17, T 31 S, R 32 E). Named on Keene (1966) and Tehachapi North (1966) 7.5' quadrangles.

Twentyfive Canyon [FRESNO]: *canyon,* drained by a stream that flows nearly 5 miles to Salt Creek (1) 3.5 miles north of Joaquin Rocks (lat. 36°22'20"N, long. 120°27'35" W; near S line sec. 9, T 18 S, R 14 E). Named on Joaquin Rocks (1969) 7.5' quadrangle. Joaquin Rocks (1943) 15' quadrangle has the form "Twenty Five Canyon" for the name.

25 Hill [KERN]: *ridge,* southeast- to east-trending, 1 mile long, 5.25 miles northwest of Maricopa (lat. 35°06'50" N, long. 119°28' W; sec. 25, 26, T 32 S, R 23 E). Named on Maricopa (1951) 7.5' quadrangle.

Twentyfive Spring [FRESNO]: *spring,* 2.5 miles west-northwest of Joaquin Rocks (lat. 36°19'40" N, long. 120°29'35" W; near S line sec. 30, T 18 S, R 14 E); the spring is near the head of Twentyfive Canyon. Named on Joaquin Rocks (1969) 7.5' quadrangle. Joaquin Rocks (1943) 15' quadrangle has the form "Twenty Five Spr." for the name.

Twentyone Canyon [KERN]: *canyon,* drained by a stream that flows 4.5 miles to Midway Valley 3.5 miles southeast of Fellows (lat. 35°08'25" N, long. 119°30' W; near E line sec. 9, T 32 S, R 23 E); the canyon is in section 21. Named on Elkhorn Hills (1954) and Fellows (1950, photorevised 1973) 7.5' quadrangles.

Twentysix Camp [FRESNO]: *locality,* 3.5 miles east-northeast of Castle Mountain (lat. 35°57'15" N, long. 120°16'50" W; sec. 6, T 23 S, R 16 E). Named on The Dark Hole (1937) 7.5' quadrangle.

Twin Buck Lakes [FRESNO]: *lakes,* two, largest 900 feet long, 2 miles north of Blackcap Mountain (lat. 37°06'10" N, long. 118° 48' W). Named on Blackcap Mountain (1953) 15' quadrangle.

Twin Buttes [KERN]: *hills,* two, 1 mile apart, 4 miles southwest of Castle Butte (lat. 35°05'10" N, long. 117°56'20" W; and lat. 35°04'20" N, long. 117°55'35" W). Named on California City South (1973) 7.5' quadrangle; the northwesternmost of the two hills is called Desert Butte.

Twin Buttes [TULARE]:

(1) *hills,* two, 5.5 miles west of Woodlake (lat. 36°25'35" N long. 119°11'50" W; sec. 30, T 17 S, R 26 E). Altitudes 584 and 651 feet. Named on Exeter (1952) 15' quadrangle.

(2) *locality,* 7 miles west-northwest of Woodlake along Atchison, Topeka and Santa Fe Railroad (lat. 36°28' N, long. 119°12'15" W; at E line sec. 12, T 17 S, R 25 E); the place is 2.5 miles north of Twin Buttes (1). Named on Exeter (1952) 15' quadrangle.

Twin Creek: see **East Twin Creek** and **West Twin Creek**, under **Santiago Creek** [KERN].

Twinky Spring [KERN]: *spring,* 5.5 miles east-southeast of Caliente (lat. 35°15'15" N, long. 118°32'15" W; at SE cor. sec. 4, T 31 S, R 32 E). Named on Oiler Peak (1972) 7.5' quadrangle.

Twin Lake: see **Lower Twin Lake** [FRESNO]; **Upper Twin Lake** [FRESNO].

Twin Lakes [FRESNO]:

(1) *lakes,* two, largest 450 feet long, 9.5 miles north of Hume (lat. 36°55'15" N, long. 118°53'50" W). Named on Tehipite Dome (1952) 15' quadrangle.

(2) *lakes,* two, largest 1100 feet long, 2.5 miles south-southeast of Mount Pinchot (lat. 36°54'35" N, long. 118°23'30" W). Named on Mount Pinchot (1953) 15' quadrangle.

Twin Lakes [KERN]:

(1) *lakes,* two, largest 1000 feet long, 4.25 miles east-northeast of Liebre Twins (lat. 34°59'10" N, long. 118°30'20" W; at E line sec. 6, T 10 N, R 15 W). Named on Neenach (1943) 15' quadrangle. Johnson's (1911) map

shows a place called Knecht located 1.25 miles south of the lakes.
(2) *locality,* 4 miles east-northeast of Liebre Twins (lat. 34°59'15" N, long. 118°30'45" W; sec. 6, T 10 N, R 15 W); the place is at Twin Lakes (1). Named on Liebre Twins (1965) 7.5' quadrangle.

Twin Lakes [TULARE]:
(1) *lakes,* two, largest 1000 feet long, 11 miles west-northwest of Triple Divide Peak (lat. 36°39'30" N, long. 118°42'50" W). Named on Triple Divide Peak (1956) 15' quadrangle.
(2) *lakes,* two, largest 400 feet long, 10.5 miles south of Mineral King (lat. 36°18' N, long. 118°37'10" W). Named on Mineral King (1956) 15' quadrangle.

Twin Lakes: see **Hitchcock Lakes** [TULARE]; **Lower Twin Lake** [FRESNO].

Twin Meadows [FRESNO]: *areas,* two, 13 miles northeast of Kaiser Peak (lat. 37°24'30" N, long. 119°00'20" W). Named on Kaiser Peak (1953) 15' quadrangle.

Twin Oaks [KERN]: *locality,* 1.5 miles east-northeast of Loraine (lat. 35°18'45" N, long. 118°24'30" W; on S line sec. 14, T 30 S, R 33 E). Named on Loraine (1972) 7.5' quadrangle. Postal authorities established Twin Oaks post office in 1926 and discontinued it in 1931 (Salley, p. 226).

Twin Peak [TULARE]: *peak,* 5.5 miles south-southwest of California Hot Springs (lat. 35°48'35" N, long. 118°42'50" W; near W line sec. 26, T 24 S, R 30 E). Altitude 4168 feet. Named on California Hot Springs (1958) 15' quadrangle.

Twin Peaks [FRESNO]: *peaks,* two, 5.5 miles north of Charley Mountain on Fresno-Monterey County line (lat. 36°13'15" N, long. 120°38'40" W; sec. 2, T 20 S, R 12 E). Named on Priest Valley (1969) 7.5' quadrangle.

Twin Peaks [TULARE]: *peaks,* two, 11 miles west-northwest of Triple Divide Peak on Silliman Crest (lat. 36°39'55" N, long. 118° 42'25" W). Altitude of highest is 10,485 feet. Named on Triple Divide Peak (1956) 15' quadrangle.

Twin Springs [TULARE]: *spring,* 3 miles south of California Hot Springs (lat. 35°50'10" N, long. 118°40'15" W; sec. 18, T 24 S, R 31 E). Named on California Hot Springs (1958) 15' quadrangle.

Twisselmann Well [KERN]: *well,* 10 miles south-southeast of Orchard Peak (lat. 35°36'10" N, long. 120°03'25" W; sec. 5, T 27 S, R 18 E). Named on Packwood Creek (1961) 7.5' quadrangle.

Tyler Creek [TULARE]: *stream,* flows 8 miles to Deer Creek (2) 2 miles west of California Hot Springs (lat. 35°53' N, long. 118°42'25" W; sec. 35, T 23 S, R 30 E). Named on California Hot Springs (1958) 15' quadrangle. The name is for J.D. Tyler (Mitchell, A.R., p. 78).

Tyler Gulch [TULARE]: *canyon,* drained by a stream that flows 2 miles to White River (1) 5.25 miles south of Fountain Springs (lat. 35°48'50" N, long. 118°55'35" W; sec. 26, T 24 S, R 28 E). Named on Quincy School (1965) 7.5' quadrangle.

Tylerhorse Canyon [KERN]: *canyon,* drained by a stream that flows 5.5 miles to lowlands 10 miles west-northwest of the village of Willow Springs (lat. 34°57'10" N, long. 118°27' W; near SW cor. sec. 14, T 10 N, R 15 W). Named on Tehachapi South (1966) and Tylerhorse Canyon (1965) 7.5' quadrangles. United States Board on Geographic Names (1983c, p. 4) approved the name "Covington Mountain" for a peak, altitude 7877 feet, located 8 miles south-southwest of Tehachapi at the head of Tylerhorse Canyon (lat. 35°00'53" N, long. 118°28'25" W; sec. 28, T 11 N, R 15 W); the name is for John D. Covington, an early resident of the neighborhood.

Tyler Meadow [TULARE]: *area,* 7.5 miles east-southeast of California Hot Springs (lat. 35°50' N, long. 118°33'15" W; at NW cor. sec. 20, T 24 S, R 32 E). Named on California Hot Springs (1958) 15' quadrangle.

Tyler Peak [TULARE]: *peak,* 2 miles west-northwest of California Hot Springs (lat. 35°53'45" N, long. 118°42' W; sec. 26, T 23 S, R 30 E); the peak is northwest of Tyler Creek. Altitude 3885 feet. Named on California Hot Springs (1958) 15' quadrangle.

Tyndall: see **Mount Tyndall** [TULARE].

Tyndall Creek [TULARE]: *stream,* flows 7.5 miles to Kern River 7.25 miles west-northwest of Mount Whitney (lat. 36°36'15" N, long. 118°25' W); the stream heads near Mount Tyndall. Named on Mount Whitney (1956) 15' quadrangle.

– U –

Uhl Hill [TULARE]: *peak,* 2.5 miles west-southwest of California Hot Springs (lat. 35°52' N, long. 118°42'45" W; near W line sec. 2, T 24 S, R 30 E). Named on California Hot Springs (1958) 15' quadrangle.

Uhl Pocket [TULARE]: *relief feature,* 1.25 miles south-southwest of California Hot Springs (lat. 35°51'50" N, long. 118°40'45" W; on E line sec. 1, T 24 S, R 30 E). Named on California Hot Springs (1958) 15' quadrangle.

Uhl Station [TULARE]: *locality,* 1.5 miles east-northeast of California Hot Springs (lat. 35°53'10" N, long. 118°38'45" W; near E line sec. 32, T 23 S, R 31 E). Named on California Hot Springs (1958) 15' quadrangle.

Ultra [TULARE]: *locality,* 7 miles northwest of Fountain Springs along Atchison, Topeka and Santa Fe Railroad (lat. 35°57'55" N, long. 118°59'50" W; near SW cor. sec. 31, T 22 S, R 28 E). Named on Fountain Springs (1965) 7.5' quadrangle.

Una [KERN]: *locality,* 10.5 miles west-northwest of Bakersfield along Atchison, Topeka and Santa Fe Railroad (lat. 35°25'25" N, long. 119°10'35" W; sec. 10, T 29 S, R 26 E). Named on Rosedale (1954) 7.5' quadrangle. Rosedale (1933) 7.5' quadrangle shows Una Siding situated 2 miles farther northwest along the railroad (sec. 31, T 28 S, R 26 E).

Unadilla: see **Bakersfield** [KERN].

Una Siding: see **Una** [KERN].

University Peak [FRESNO-TULARE]: *peak,* 12.5 miles north-northwest of Mount Whitney at the spot that Fresno County, Tulare County, and Inyo County meet (lat. 36°44'50" N, long. 118°21'40" W). Altitude 13,632 feet. Named on Mount Whitney (1956) 15' quadrangle. J.N. LeConte and his party made the first ascent of the peak in 1896 and named it for University of California (Browning, p. 226).

University Peak: see **Mount Gould** [FRESNO].

Upper Araujo Spring [KERN]: *spring,* 5.5 miles west-southwest of Liebre Twins (lat. 34°56' N, long. 118°39'50" W; sec. 23, T 10 N, R 17 W); the spring is 1550 feet east-northeast of Lower Araujo Spring. Named on Winters Ridge (1966) 7.5' quadrangle.

Upper Basin [FRESNO]: *area,* 2.5 miles south-southwest of Mount Bolton Brown (lat. 37°01' N, long. 118°27'30" W). Named on Big Pine (1950) and Mount Pinchot (1953) 15' quadrangles.

Upper Beck Spring [KERN]: *spring,* 5 miles northeast of Caliente (lat. 35°20'35" N, long. 118°34'05" W; sec. 5, T 30 S, R 32 E); the feature is in Beck Canyon 0.5 mile north of Lower Beck Spring. Named on Oiler Peak (1972) 7.5' quadrangle.

Upper Funston Meadow [TULARE]: *area,* 12 miles northwest of Kern Peak in Kern Canyon (lat. 36°27' N, long. 118°24'40" W); the place is 4.5 miles north of Funston Meadow at the mouth of Funston Creek. Named on Kern Peak (1956) 15' quadrangle. Olmsted's (1900) map shows a place called Funstons at or near the place. Tucker (p. 946) listed a feature called Soda Spring, located in Upper Funston Meadow between two branches of Kern River.

Upper Funston Meadow: see **Sky Parlor Meadow** [TULARE].

Upper Grapes Spring [KERN]: *spring,* 7 miles east of Caliente (lat. 35°17'05" N, long. 118°30'15" W; near SE cor. sec. 26, T 30 S, R 32 E); the spring is 0.25 mile west-northwest of Lower Grapes Spring. Named on Oiler Peak (1972) 7.5' quadrangle.

Upper Graveyard Meadow [FRESNO]: *area,* 10.5 miles west-northwest of Mount Abbot (lat. 37°26'30" N, long. 118°57'35" W); the place is 1.5 miles upstream along Cold Creek from Graveyard Meadows. Named on Mount Abbot (1953) 15' quadrangle.

Upper Grouse Valley [TULARE]: *valley,* 13 miles south-southeast of Kaweah (lat. 36°18' N, long. 118°48'45" W); the valley is 2 miles southeast of Grouse Valley at the head of Grouse Creek. Named on Kaweah (1957) 15' quadrangle.

Upper Honeymoon Lake [FRESNO]: *lake,* 1200 feet long, 12 miles north of Blackcap Mountain (lat. 37°14'45" N, long. 118°01'05" W); the lake is 0.25 mile south of Lower Honeymoon Lake. Named on Blackcap Mountain (1953) 15' quadrangle.

Upper Hopkins Lakes [FRESNO]: *lakes,* three, largest 950 feet long, 10 miles north-northwest of Mount Abbot (lat. 37°28'30" N, long. 118°50'30" W); the lakes are 1.5 miles north-northwest of Lower Hopkins Lake at the head of Hopkins Creek. Named on Mount Abbot (1953) 15' quadrangle.

Upper Horsethief Lake [FRESNO]: *lake,* 500 feet long, 4.25 miles west of Kaiser Peak (lat. 37°17' N, long. 119°16' W; sec. 29, T 7 S, R 25 E); the lake is 0.25 mile southeast of Lower Horsethief Lake. Named on Shuteye Peak (1953) 15' quadrangle.

Upper Indian Lake [FRESNO]: *lake,* 1200 feet long, 8.5 miles north-northwest of Blackcap Mountain (lat. 37°11'05" N, long. 118°51'05" W); the lake is 1.5 miles north-northwest of Lower Indian Lake. Named on Blackcap Mountain (1953) 15' quadrangle.

Upper Lost Keys Lake: see **Lost Keys Lakes** [FRESNO].

Upper Mills Creek Lake [FRESNO]: *lake,* 1300 feet long, 1 mile west-northwest of Mount Abbot (lat. 37°23'25" N, long. 118°48'10" W); the lake is 0.5 mile upstream from Lower Mills Creek Lake at the head of Mills Creek. Named on Mount Abbot (1953) 7.5' quadrangle.

Upper Parker Meadow [TULARE]: *area,* 6.25 miles north-northeast of California Hot Springs (lat. 35°58' N, long, 118°38'05" W; on N line sec. 4, T 23 S, R 31 E); the place is 0.5 mile northwest of Parker Meadow along Parker Meadow Creek. Named on California Hot Springs (1958) 15' quadrangle.

Upper Salt Lick Spring [KERN]: *spring,* 4.5 miles east-southeast of Caliente (lat. 35°15'35" N, long. 118°33'25" W; near E line sec. 5, T 31 S, R 32 E); the spring is 250 feet north-northeast of Salt Lick Spring. Named on Oiler Peak (1972) 7.5' quadrangle.

Upper Springhill Campground [TULARE]: *locality,* 5 miles south-southeast of Fairview along Kern River (lat. 35°51'55" N, long. 118°26'50" W; near N line sec. 8, T 24 S, R 33 E); the place is 0.25 mile north of Lower

Springhill Campground. Named on Kernville (1956) 15' quadrangle.

Upper Tent Meadow [FRESNO]: *area,* 9 miles south-southwest of Marion Peak (lat. 36°50'05" N, long. 118°35' W); the place is nearly 1 mile north-northwest of Lower Tent Meadow. Named on Marion Peak (1953) 15' quadrangle. Called Tent Meadow on Tehipite (1903) 30' quadrangle.

Upper Turret Lakes [FRESNO]: *lakes,* largest 500 feet long, 8 miles south-southwest of Mount Abbot (lat. 37°16'30" N, long. 118° 50' W); the lakes are 0.5 mile north of Middle Turret Lakes, and 1 mile north-northeast of Turret Peak. Named on Mount Abbot (1953) 15' quadrangle.

Upper Twin Lake [FRESNO]: *lake,* 1400 feet long, 1.25 miles east of Kaiser Peak (lat. 37°17'45" N, long. 119°09'35" W; on S line sec. 20, T 7 S, R 26 E); the lake is 1100 feet west-northwest of Lower Twin Lake. Named on Kaiser Peak (1953) 15' quadrangle. This lake and Lower Twin Lake together are called Twin Lakes on Kaiser (1904) 30' quadrangle.

Urcado Springs [KERN]: *springs,* two, 1500 feet apart, 9 miles west-southwest of Liebre Twins (lat. 34°55'15" N, long. 118°43'15" W). Named on Winters Ridge (1966) 7.5' quadrangle.

Urruttia Canyon [FRESNO]: *canyon,* drained by a stream that flows nearly 5 miles to Salt Creek (1) 3.5 miles north of Joaquin Rocks (lat. 36°22'10" N, long. 120°26'30" W; near N line sec. 15, T 18 S, R 14 E). Named on Joaquin Rocks (1969) 7.5' quadrangle.

Ursa Lake [FRESNO]: *lake,* 900 feet long, nearly 4 miles south-southwest of Mount Abbot (lat. 37°19'55" N, long. 118°47'50" W); the lake is between Big Bear Lake and Bearpaw Lake. Named on Mount Abbot (1953) 15' quadrangle. Elden H. Vestal of California Department of Fish and Game named the lake in 1952 (Browning, p. 226).

Uva [FRESNO]: *locality,* 2.5 miles northwest of Reedley along Southern Pacific Railroad (lat. 36°37'10" N, long. 119°29'20" W; near S line sec. 17, T 15 S, R 23 E). Named on Reedley (1966) 7.5' quadrangle.

– V –

Vacation Pass [TULARE]: *pass,* 2.5 miles north-northwest of Mount Whitney on Tulare-Inyo County line (lat. 36°36'45" N, long. 118° 18' W). Named on Mount Whitney (1956) 15' quadrangle. Called Sheep Pass on Mount Whitney (1907) 30' quadrangle.

Vaccaro [KERN]: *locality,* 1.25 miles south-southeast of Arvin along the railroad (lat. 35°11'40" N, long. 118°48'50" W; at N line sec. 36, T 31 S, R 29 E). Named on Arvin (1933) 7.5' quadrangle.

Valhalla [TULARE]: *locality,* 3.5 miles west-southwest of Triple Divide Peak (lat. 36°34'05" N, long. 118°35' W). Named on Triple Divide Peak (1956) 15' quadrangle.

Valley Acres [KERN]: *settlement,* 5.25 miles north-northeast of Taft (lat. 35°12'20" N, long. 119°24'20" W; sec. 28, T 31 S, R 24 E). Named on Taft (1950) 7.5' quadrangle. The subdivision community began in 1937 (Bailey, 1967, p. 27).

Valor Lake [FRESNO]: *lake,* 1000 feet long, 2 miles southwest of Mount Goddard (lat. 37°04'55" N, long. 118°44'40" W). Named on Mount Goddard (1948) 15' quadrangle. William A. Dill of California Department of Fish and Game named the lake in 1948 (Browning, p. 226).

Vance [TULARE]: *locality,* 1.5 miles north-northwest of Lindsay along Southern Pacific Railroad (lat. 36°13'25" N, long. 119°06'10" W; near SE cor. sec. 36, T 19 S, R 26 E). Named on Lindsay (1951) 7.5' quadrangle.

Vandalia: see **Porterville** [TULARE].

Vandever Mountain [TULARE]: *peak,* 3 miles south-southeast of Mineral King (lat. 36°23'50" N, long. 118°34'50" W). Altitude 11,947 feet. Named on Mineral King (1956) 15' quadrangleThe name commemorates William Vandever, the congressman who introduced the bills that established Yosemite, Sequoia, and General Grant National Parks in 1890; the *Visalia Delta* newspaper proposed the name on September 4, 1890 (Hanna, p. 343).

Van Gordon Creek [TULARE]: *stream,* flows 7.25 miles to Yokohl Creek 14 miles south of Kaweah (lat. 36°16'15" N, long. 118°55'30" W; sec. 15, T 19 S, R 28 E). Named on Kaweah (1957) 15' quadrangle.

Vanguard [KINGS]: *locality,* 10 miles west-southwest of Lemoore (lat. 36°15'20" N, long. 119°57'15" W; sec. 30, T 19 S, R 19 E). Named on Vanguard (1956) 7.5' quadrangle.

Van Ness Slough [FRESNO]: *stream,* flows 2.25 miles to Murphy Slough nearly 2 miles northwest of Riverdale (lat. 36°27'10" N, long. 119°52'30" W; sec. 14, T 17 S, R 19 E). Named on Riverdale (1954) 7.5' quadrangle.

Vanris [FRESNO]: *locality,* 3.25 miles south of Clovis along Southern Pacific Railroad (lat. 36°46'30" N, long. 119°42' W; on W line sec. 28, T 13 S, R 21 E). Named on Clovis (1922) 7.5' quadrangle.

Vaquero Spring [KINGS]: *spring,* 10 miles southwest of Avenal (lat. 35°54'10" N, long. 120°15'25" W; sec. 29, T 23 S, E 16 E). Named on The Dark Hole (1961) 7.5' quadrangle.

Vasquez Creek [FRESNO]: *stream,* heads in San Benito County and flows 6.5 miles to Mercey Creek 2 miles northwest of Mercey Hot Springs in Fresno County (lat. 36°43'45" N, long. 120°53' W; sec. 9, T 14 S, R 10 E). Named on Cerro Colorado (1969) 7.5' quadrangle.

Vaughn: see **Bodfish** [KERN].

Vee Lake [FRESNO]: *lake,* 3400 feet long, 4.5 miles south-southwest of Mount Abbot (lat. 37°19'20" N, long. 118°48'30" W). Named on Mount Abbot (1953) 15' quadrangle, where the outline of the lake on the map resembles the letter "V."

Velma: see **Exeter** [TULARE].

Venice Cove [TULARE]: *relief feature,* re-entrant into Venice Hills 6 miles west-southwest of Woodlake (lat. 36°22'15" N, long. 119°11'20" W; at SE cor. sec. 7, T 18 S, R 26 E). Named on Exeter (1952) 15' quadrangle.

Venice Hill: see **Taurusa** [TULARE].

Venice Hills [TULARE]: *range,* 5 miles west-southwest of Woodlake (lat. 36°22'45" N, long. 119°10'30" W). Named on Exeter (1952) 15' quadrangle. Early pioneers knew the feature as Kaweah Hills (Hoover, Rensch, and Rensch, p. 561).

Venida [TULARE]: *locality,* 2.5 miles north-northeast of Exeter along Atchison, Topeka and Santa Fe Railroad (lat. 36°19'55" N, long. 119°07'45" W; sec. 26, T 18 S, R 26 E). Named on Exeter (1952) 15' quadrangle. On Exeter (1926) 7.5' quadrangle, the name applies to a place located 0.25 mile farther west at a crossroad.

Venida: see **West Venida** [TULARE].

Vennacher Needle [FRESNO]: *peak,* 5.25 miles northwest of Mount Pinchot (lat. 36°59'55" N, long. 118°28'25" W). Altitude 12,996 feet. Named on Mount Pinchot (1953) 15' quadrangle.

Venola [KERN]: *locality,* 5.25 miles south-southwest of Bakersfield along Southern Pacific Railroad (lat. 35°18'40" N, long. 119°03'15" W; near SW cor. sec. 14, T 30 S, R 27 E). Named on Gosford (1954) 7.5' quadrangle.

Vermilion Cliffs [FRESNO]: *escarpment,* east-northeast-trending, 2 miles long, 8.5 miles west-northwest of Mount Abbot (lat. 37°25'30" N, long. 118°55'30" W); the feature is northeast of the east end of Vermilion Valley. Named on Mount Abbot (1953) 15' quadrangle. United States Board on Geographic Names (1978b, p. 5) ruled against the form "Vermillion Cliffs" for the name. Theodore S. Solomons named the feature in 1894 (Browning, p. 226).

Vermilion Lake [FRESNO]: *lake,* 500 feet long, 8.5 miles west-northwest of Mount Abbot (lat. 37°25'50" N, long. 118°55'35" W); the lake is north of Vermilion Cliffs. Named on Mount Abbot (1953) 15' quadrangle. United States Board on Geographic Names (1965d, p. 8) approved the name "Feather Lak" for a feature situated 3400 feet northwest of Vermilion Lake (lat. 37°26'15" N, long. 118°56'15" W), and rejected the name "Vermilion Lake" for this second feature.

Vermilion Valley [FRESNO]: *valley,* 10 miles west of Mount Abbot along Mono Creek (lat. 37°23' N, long. 118°58' W). Named on Mount Goddard (1912) 30' quadrangle. Water of Lake Thomas A. Edison now covers most of the valley, which Theodore S. Solomons named in 1894 (Farquhar *in* Brewer, p. 548).

Vernette: see **Fellows** [KERN].

Vernon: see **Mount Vernon** [KERN].

Verplank Creek [FRESNO]: *stream,* flows 4.5 miles to Kings River nearly 6 miles east-southeast of Balch Camp (lat. 36°51'35" N, long. 119°02' W; sec. 28, T 12 S, R 27 E); the stream is northeast of Verplank Ridge. Named on Patterson Mountain (1952) 15' quadrangle.

Verplank Ridge [FRESNO]: *ridge,* northwest-trending, 4 miles long, 9 miles southeast of Balch Camp (lat. 36°48'45" N, long. 119° 01' W). Named on Patterson Mountain (1952) and Tehipite Dome (1952) 15' quadrangles.

Verplank Saddle [FRESNO]: *pass,* nearly 7 miles southeast of Balch Camp (lat. 36°50'10" N, long. 119°02'10" W; near NE cor. sec. 4, T 13 S, R 27 E); the pass is at the northwest end of Verplank Ridge. Named on Patterson Mountain (1952) 15' quadrangle.

Versteeg: see **Mount Versteeg** [TULARE].

Vestal [TULARE]: *locality,* 4 miles south-southwest of Ducor (lat. 35°50'25" N, long. 119°05'05" W; sec. 17, T 24 S, R 27 E). Named on Richgrove (1952) 7.5' quadrangle. Officials of California Edison Company named the place in 1919 for the virgin priestesses who tended the sacred fire of Vesta, Roman goddess of the hearth; the company had a substation at the site (Gudde, 1949, p. 379).

Vidette: see **East Vidette** [TULARE]; **West Vidette** [TULARE].

Vidette Creek [FRESNO-TULARE]: *stream,* heads in Tulare County and flows 5.25 miles to Bubbs Creek 13 miles south of Mount Pinchot in Fresno County (lat. 36°45'15" N, long. 118°24'10" W). Named on Mount Whitney (1907) 30' quadrangle, and on Mount Pinchot (1953) 15' quadrangle.

Vidette Lakes [TULARE]: *lakes,* about 1300 feet long, 13 miles north-northwest of Mount Whitney (lat. 36°44'30" N, long. 118°24'30" W); the lakes are along Vidette Creek. Named on Mount Whitney (1956) 15' quadrangle.

Vidette Meadow [FRESNO]: *area,* 13 miles south of Mount Pinchot (lat. 36°45'20" N, long. 118°24'05" W); the place is at the confluence of Vidette Creek and Bubbs Creek. Named on Mount Pinchot (1953) 15' quadrangle.

Vincent Meadow [TULARE]: *area,* nearly 7 miles east of California Hot Springs (lat. 35°52'35" N, long. 118°33' W; near N line sec. 5, T 24 S, R 32 E). Named on California Hot Springs (1958) 15' quadrangle.

Vinland [KERN]: *locality,* 2.5 miles north of McFarland along Southern Pacific Railroad (lat. 35°42'50" N, long. 119°14'05" W; sec. 36, T 25 S, R 25 E). Named on McFarland (1954) 7.5' quadrangle.

Vino: see **Reedley** [FRESNO].

Virginia: see **Lake Virginia** [FRESNO].

Virginia Lake [FRESNO]: *lake,* 1000 feet long, 2.5 miles east-southeast of Dinkey Dome (lat. 37°06'15" N, long. 119°05'15" W; sec. 36, T 9 S, R 26 E). Named on Huntington Lake (1953) 15' quadrangle.

Visalia [TULARE]: *city,* in the northwest part of Tulare County (lat. 36°19'50" N, long. 119°17'30" W). Named on Visalia (1949) 7.5' quadrangle. In 1852 Nathaniel Vise led a group of settlers to the site, which then was known as Buena Vista; the community that grew there was named Visalia, probably by Vise himself (Hoover, Rensch, and Rensch, p. 561-562). According to Barker (p. 1), the name originally had the spelling "Viceälia," and the place is called "Visaija" on Goddard's (1857) map. The area east of Visalia that was subject to overflow by Kaweah River generally was referred to as Visalia Swamp (Grunsky, p. 11). After the county seat moved to Visalia in 1853, the supervisors changed the name of the community to Buena Vista, but changed the name back to Visalia in 1854 (Gudde, 1949, p. 380). Postal authorities established Visalia post office in 1855 (Frickstad, p. 214), and the city incorporated in 1874. In 1862 Lieutenant Colonel George S. Evans selected a site 1 mile north of the center of Visalia for a post called Camp Babbitt, named to honor Lieutenant Colonel E.B. Babbitt, deputy quartermaster general, Department of the Pacific; the camp was set up to help control Southern sympathizers during the Civil War (Hart, H.M., p. 44). When the state legislature created Tulare County in 1852, it placed the seat of justice at a cabin built by John Wood and his companions in late 1849 or early 1850 about 7 miles east of present Visalia on the south side of Kaweah River, and provided that the county seat be called Woodsville (Hoover, Rensch, and Rensch, p. 561). Postal authorities established Woodville post office at the place in 1853 and discontinued it in 1855 (Salley, p. 243). Later they authorized a number of other post offices in the neighborhood of Visalia. They established Illinois Mills post office 8 miles east of Visalia (SW quarter sec. 28, T 18 S, R 26 E) in 1867 and discontinued it in 1868; the operator of a grain mill at the place came from Illinois (Salley, p. 103). They established Wambat post office 35 miles east of Visalia in 1874 and discontinued it in 1876; the name was from badgers that were misidentified as wombats, animals of Australia (Salley, p. 234). They established Mayville post office 12.5 miles northeast of Visalia (NW quarter of sec. 18, T 18 S, R 27 E) in 1878 and discontinued it the same year; the name was from the given name of the postmaster's wife (Salley, p. 135). They established Hiko post office 6 miles east of Visalia in 1880 and discontinued it in 1881; the name was from Hicks Company, a dairy operated by Benjamin Hicks—the place also was known as Hico, Hicko, and Hicks (Salley, p. 97). They established Cottage post office 12 miles east of Visalia in 1885 and discontinued it in 1886; the name was from the location of the post office in a cottage (Salley, p. 51). Thompson's (1892) map shows Gains P.O. located about 15 miles northeast of Visalia (sec. 35, T 16 S, R 26 E). Postal authorities established Gains post office in 1890 and discontinued it in 1891; the name was for Thomas Gains, first postmaster (Salley, p. 82).

Visalia Creek: see **Mill Creek** [TULARE] (1).

Visalia Swamp: see **Visalia** [TULARE].

Volcan [KERN]: *locality,* 3.25 miles north of downtown Bakersfield along Southern Pacific Railroad (lat. 35°25'20" N, long. 118°59'20" W; sec. 8, T 29 S, R 28 E). Named on Oil Center (1954) 7.5' quadrangle.

Volcanic Cone [FRESNO]: *peak,* 14 miles north-northeast of Hume (lat. 36°58'35" N, long. 118°50' W). Altitude 9177 feet. Named on Tehipite Dome (1952) 15' quadrangle.

Volcanic Falls: see **Volcano Falls** [TULARE].

Volcanic Knob [FRESNO]: *peak,* 6 miles west of Mount Abbot (lat. 37°23'50" N, long. 118°53'20" W). Altitude 11,168 feet. Named on Mount Abbot (1953) 15' quadrangle. Theodore S. Solomons named the peak in 1894 (Farquhar, 1925, p. 141).

Volcanic Lakes [FRESNO]: *lakes,* largest 0.5 mile long, 8 miles southwest of Marion Peak (lat. 36°53'15" N, long. 118°37'50" W). Named on Marion Peak (1953) 15' quadrangle.

Volcano Creek: see **Golden Trout Creek** [TULARE].

Volcano Falls [TULARE]: *waterfall,* 6.5 miles west-northwest of Kern Peak along Golden Trout Creek (lat. 36°21'10" N, long. 118° 23'30" W). Named on Kern Peak (1956) 15' quadrangle. United States Board on Geographic Names (1933a, p. 792) rejected the name "Volanic Falls" for the feature.

Volcano Meadow [TULARE]: *area,* 3.5 miles north-northwest of Kern Peak (lat. 36°21'10" N, long. 118°19'20" W; at SW cor. sec. 17, T 18 S, R 34 E). Named on Kern Peak (1956) 15' quadrangle.

Volcano Meadow: see **Groundhog Meadow** [TULARE].

Von Hellum Creek [TULARE]: *stream,* flows 3 miles to join Spear Creek and form Poso Creek 5.25 miles south of California Hot Springs (lat. 35°48'15" N, long. 118°39'10" W; near S line sec. 29, T 24 S, R 31 E). Named on California Hot Springs (1958) 15' quadrangle.

— W —

Wade: see **Edison** [KERN].

Wade Baxter Spring [KINGS]: *spring,* 4.25 miles southwest of Avenal (lat. 35°57'15" N, long. 120°10'20" W; sec. 6, T 23 S, R 17 E). Named on Garza Peak (1953) 7.5' quadrangle.

Wade Creek: see **South Creek** [TULARE].

Wagonshed Creek [TULARE]: *stream,* flows 1 mile to East Fork Dry Creek (1) 8 miles southeast of Auckland (lat. 36°30'15" N, long. 119°00'40" W; sec. 26, T 16 S, R 27 E). Named on Auckland (1966) 7.5' quadrangle.

Wagon Wheel Mountain [KERN]: *hill,* 9.5 miles northwest of Blackwells Corner (lat. 35°42'35" N, long. 119°59'10" W; sec. 36, T 25 S, R 18 E). Named on Emigrant Hill (1953) 7.5' quadrangle. On Emigrant Hill (1943) 7.5' quadrangle, the name applies to present Mount Vernon. Lost Hills (1914) 30' quadrangle has the form "Wagonwheel Mountain" for the name.

Wagy Flat [KERN]: *area,* 4.5 miles south of Alta Sierra in French Gulch (1) (lat. 35°39'55" N, long. 118°32'05" W; on E line sec. 16, T 26 S, R 32 E). Named on Alta Sierra (1972) 7.5' quadrangle.

Wah Hoo Lake [FRESNO]: *lake,* 350 feet long, 2.5 miles north of Blackcap Mountain (lat. 37°06'30" N, long. 118°47' W). Named on Blackcap Mountain (1953) 15' quadrangle.

Wahoo Lakes [FRESNO]: *lakes,* largest 1100 feet long, 9 miles north of Mount Goddard (lat. 37°13'45" N, long. 118°42'45" W). Named on Mount Goddard (1948) 15' quadrangle. Art Schober named the lakes for exclamations made by a fisherman (Browning, p. 229).

Wahtoka: see **Wahtoke** [FRESNO].

Wahtoke [FRESNO]: *locality,* 4.5 miles south-southeast of Centerville along Atchison, Topeka and Santa Fe Railroad (lat. 36°40'35" N, long. 119°27'20" W; near N line sec. 34, T 14 S, R 23 E). Named on Wahtoke (1966) 7.5' quadrangle. Postal authorities established Wahtoka (with the final "a") post office in 1905 and discontinued it in 1916 (Frickstad, p. 38). Kroeber (p. 66) identified the name as of Indian origin.

Wahtoke Creek [FRESNO]: *stream,* flows 20 miles to Kings River 1.5 miles north-northwest of Reedley (lat. 36°36'55" N, long. 119° 27'55" W; near W line sec. 22, T 15 S, R 23 E). Named on Orange Cove North (1966), Pine Flat Dam (1965), and Wahtoke (1966) 7.5' quadrangles. Mendenhall's (1908) map has the form "Wah to ke" for the name.

Wahtoke Lake [FRESNO]: *lake,* 4000 feet long, behind a dam on Wahtoke Creek 6.5 miles southeast of Centerville (lat. 36°40'45" N, long. 119°24'10" W; sec. 30, T 14 S, R 24 E). Named on Wahtoke (1966) 7.5' quadrangle.

Wahtoke Winery: see **Cella** [FRESNO].

Waits: see **Seguro** [KERN].

Wales Lake [TULARE]: *lake,* 4000 feet long, 2 miles northwest of Mount Whitney (lat. 36°36' N, long. 118°18'50" W). Named on Mount Whitney (1956) 15' quadrangle. The name commemorates the Reverend F.H. Wales, who visited Mount Whitney in 1881 (United States Board on Geographic Names, 1933a, p. 799).

Walker: see **Joe Walker Town**, under **Walker Basin** [KERN].

Walker Basin [KERN]: *valley,* 10 miles northeast of Caliente (lat. 35°24'30" N, long. 118°31' W). Named on Breckenridge Mountain (1972) 7.5' quadrangle, and on Piute Peak (1972) 7.5' quadrangle, which shows Joe Walker mine at the east edge of the valley (lat. 35°25'20" N, long. 118°29'35" W; near E line sec. 12, T 29 S, R 32 E). The valley is called The Park on Williamson's (1853) map. Joe Walker mine was named for the mountain man for whom Walker Pass was named; a settlement at the mine in the 1870's was called Joe Walker Town (Boyd, p. 168, 170). Wheeler's (1875-1878) map shows a place called Moseman Stage Sta. situated along Basin (present Walker Basin) Creek near the place that the stream leaves Walker Basin. Waring (p. 52) referred to a group of small thermal springs at the north edge of Walker Basin as Williams Hot Springs—they were on Williams ranch.

Walker Basin Creek [KERN]: *stream,* flows 25 miles to the canyon of Caliente Creek 6.5 miles west-northwest of Caliente (lat. 35°19'45" N, long. 118°44'15" W); the stream goes through Walker Basin. Named on Bena (1972), Breckenridge Mountain (1972), Oiler Peak (1972), and Piute Peak (1972) 7.5' quadrangles. Called Basin Creek on Emerald Mountain (1943) 15' quadrangle, and United States Board on Geographic Names (1975b, p. 12) gave the names "Basin Creek" and "Thompson Creek" as variants. North Fork enters from the northeast 5 miles west of Piute Peak; it is 5 miles long and is named on Piute Peak (1972) 7.5' quadrangle.

Walker Pass [KERN]: *pass,* 11.5 miles east of Onyx (lat. 35°39'45" N, long. 118°01'35" W; near SE cor. sec. 17, T 26 S, R 37 E). Named on Walker Pass (1972) 7.5' quadrangle. Called Walker's Pass on Williamson's (1853) map, which has the name "Hum-pah-ya-mup Pass" for a feature located about 6 miles farther south, apparently at the head of present Kelso Creek. Fremont (p. 248) named Walker Pass in 1844 for Joseph Walker, the mountain man who discovered it.

Walkers Creek: see **North Fork**, under **Cottonwood Creek** [KERN] (2).

Walker Well [KERN]: *well,* 9 miles west of Inyokern (lat. 35°39'15" N, long. 117°58'20" W; sec. 23, T 26 S, R 37 E). Named on Owens Peak

(1972) 7.5' quadrangle.

Wallace: see **Mount Wallace** [FRESNO]; **Mount Wallace**, under **Mount Mendel** [FRESNO].

Wallace Center [KERN]: *locality,* 2 miles north-northwest of Taft (lat. 35°10'05" N, long. 119°27'50" W; on W line sec. 1, T 32 S, R 23 E). Named on Taft (1950) 7.5' quadrangle.

Wallace Creek [TULARE]: *stream,* flows 7 miles to Kern River nearly 7 miles west of Mount Whitney (lat. 36°34'35" N, long. 118°24'45" W). Named on Mount Whitney (1956) 15' quadrangle. Called East Fork [of Kern River] on Mount Whitney (1907) 30' quadrangle, but United States Board on Geographic Names (1933a, p. 799) rejected this name, and noted that the name "Wallace" is for Judge William R. Wallace, a pioneer of the Kaweah neighborhood.

Wallace Lake [TULARE]: *lake,* 3600 feet long, 2.5 miles north-northwest of Mount Whitney (lat. 36°36'40" N, long. 118°18'35" W); the lake is situated along Wallace Creek. Named on Mount Whitney (1956) 15' quadrangle.

Waller: see **Betty Waller Meadow** [TULARE].

Walling Lake [FRESNO]: *lake,* 600 feet long, 1 mile northeast of Kaiser Peak (lat. 37°18'10" N, long. 119°10'20" W; sec. 19, T 7 S, R 26 E). Named on Kaiser Peak (1953) 15' quadrangle.

Walnut Creek [KERN]: *stream,* flows 2.25 miles to San Luis Obispo County 8.5 miles west-northwest of Carneros Rocks (lat. 35°27'55" N, long. 119°59'45" W; at W line sec. 25, T 28 S, R 18 E). Named on Las Yeguas Ranch (1959) 7.5' quadrangle.

Walnut Spring [KERN]: *spring,* 7.5 miles west-northwest of Carneros Rocks (lat. 35°28'35" N, long. 119°58'20" W; sec. 19, T 28 S, R 19 E); the spring is at the head of a branch of Walnut Creek. Named on Las Yeguas Ranch (1959) 7.5' quadrangle.

Walong [KERN]: *locality,* 2.25 miles southeast of Keene along the railroad (lat. 35°11'55" N, long. 118°32'15" W; near SE cor. sec. 28, T 31 S, R 32 E). Named on Keene (1966) 7.5' quadrangle. The designation, a contraction of the name of W.A. Long, a Southern Pacific Railroad trainmaster, was given in 1876 (Gudde, 1949, p. 383).

Walser Hot Springs: see **Scovern Hot Springs** [KERN].

Walsh Mill [FRESNO]: *locality,* 17 miles south-southwest of Kaiser Peak near Pine Ridge (3) (lat. 37°04'15" N, long. 119°20'30" W; sec. 10, T 10 S, R 24 E). Named on Kaiser (1904) 30' quadrangle.

Waltham Creek: see **Warthan Creek** [FRESNO].

Waltham Valley: see **Warthan Creek** [FRESNO].

Walton: see **Izaak Walton Lake** [FRESNO]; **Mount Izaak Walton** [FRESNO].

Wambat: see **Visalia** [TULARE].

Wampum Lake [FRESNO]: *lake,* 1000 feet long, 8 miles south-southwest of Mount Abbot (lat. 37°16'10" N, long. 118°49'30" W). Named on Mount Abbot (1953) 15' quadrangle. Elden H. Vestal of California Department of Fish and Game named the lake in 1951 (Browning, p. 231).

Wanda Lake [FRESNO]: *lake,* 1 mile long, 2 miles northeast of Mount Goddard in Evolution Basin (lat. 37°07'15" N, long. 118° 41'30" W); the lake is 1 mile west-northwest of Muir Pass. Named on Mount Goddard (1948) 15' quadrangle. R.B. Marshall named the lake for a daughter of John Muir (Browning, p. 231)—Helen Lake (2), on the other side of Muir Pass, is named for another of Muir's daughters.

Ward Canyon [TULARE]: *canyon,* 1.5 miles long, opens into the canyon of Middle Fork Tule River 2.5 miles east of Springville (lat. 36°07'30" N, long. 118°46'15" W; near E line sec. 6, T 21 S, R 30 E). Named on Springville (1957) 15' quadrangle.

Ward Lake [FRESNO]: *lake,* 900 feet long, 13 miles west-southwest of Mount Abbot (lat. 37°18'05" N, long. 118°59'15" W). Named on Mount Abbot (1953) 15' quadrangle. The name commemorates Dr. George C. Ward, of Ward Mountain (Browning, p. 231).

Ward Mountain [FRESNO]: *peak,* 12 miles north-northwest of Blackcap Mountain (lat. 37°13'15" N, long. 118°53'40" W; near S line sec. 22, T 8 S, R 28 E). Altitude 10,862 feet. Named on Blackcap Mountain (1953) 15' quadrangle. The name honors Dr. George Clinton Ward, who directed hydroelectric power development in the region (United States Board on Geographic Names, 1936, p. 25).

Ward Mountain Lake [FRESNO]: *lake,* 1100 feet long, 12 miles north-northwest of Blackcap Mountain (lat. 37°13'25" N, long. 118°54' W; sec. 22, T 8 S, R 28 E); the lake is 0.25 mile west of Ward Mountain. Named on Blackcap Mountain (1953) 15' quadrangle.

Wards Hill: see **Todds Hill** [TULARE].

Ward Spring [TULARE]: *spring,* 2.5 miles east-southeast of Springville (lat. 36°07' N, long. 118°46'30" W; sec. 7, T 21 S, R 30 E); the spring is in Ward Canyon. Named on Globe (1956) 7.5' quadrangle.

Warlow: see **Mount Warlow**, under **Mount Huxley** [FRESNO].

Warm Creek [FRESNO]: *stream,* flows 6 miles to South Fork San Joaquin River 7.5 miles northeast of Kaiser Peak (lat. 37°21'45" N, long 119°04'35" W). Named on Kaiser Peak (1953) 15' quadrangle.

Warm Creek Meadow [FRESNO]: *area,* 11 miles northeast of Kaiser Peak near the west end of Lake Thomas A. Edison (lat. 37° 22'45" N, long. 119°01'30" W); the place is along Warm Creek. Named on Kaiser Peak (1953) 15' quadrangle.

Warm Spring [KERN]: *spring,* 5 miles south-southeast of Arvin (lat. 35°08'50" N, long. 118°47' W; sec. 17, T 32 S, R 30 E). Named on Arvin (1955) 7.5' quadrangle.

Warm Sulfur Spring [TULARE]: *spring,* 5 miles east of Auckland (lat. 36°35'20" N, long. 119°00'50" W; sec. 26, T 15 S, R 27 E). Named on Auckland (1966) 7.5' quadrangle.

Warren [KERN]:

(1) *locality,* 1.25 miles southeast of Fellows along Sunset Railroad (lat. 35°10' N, long. 119°31'25" W; near S line sec. 5, T 32 S, R 23 E). Named on McKittrick (1912) 30' quadrangle.

(2) *locality,* 4 miles north-northwest of Mojave along the railroad (lat. 35°06'50" N, long. 118°12'10" W; sec. 27, T 32 S, R 35 E). Named on Mojave (1956) 15' quadrangle.

Warrior Lake [FRESNO]: *lake,* 1200 feet long, 10 miles northwest of Mount Abbot (lat. 37°28'15" N, long. 118°55'35" W). Named on Mount Abbot (1953) 15' quadrangle. United States Board on Geographic Names (1969a, p. 4) approved the name "Chief Lake" for the feature.

Warrior Lake: see **Bobs Lake** [FRESNO].

Warsaw: see **Pueblo de las Juntas**, under **Mendota** [FRESNO].

Wartham Creek: see **Warthan Creek** [FRESNO].

Warthan: see **Alcalde** [FRESNO].

Warthan Creek [FRESNO]: *stream,* flows 30 miles to Los Gatos Creek nearly 1.25 miles east-northeast of Coalinga (lat. 36°08'40" N, long. 120°20'10" W; near E line sec. 33, T 20 S, R 15 E). Named on Coalinga (1956), Curry Mountain (1969), Kreyenhagen Hills (1956), Priest Valley (1969), Sherman Peak (1969), and Smith Mountain (1969) 7.5' quadrangles. Called Waltham Creek on Coalinga (1912) and Priest Valley (1915) 30' quadrangles. Arnold and Anderson (1908, p. 15) used the form "Waltham Creek" for the name, and noted that the stream was known as Wartham Creek, Warthan Creek, Waltham Creek, and Alcalde Creek; they also pointed out that the stream heads in a valley known as Waltham Valley. United States Board on Geographic Names (1933a, p. 800) rejected the names "Alcalde Creek," "Can-too-oa Creek," "Canuta Creek," and "Wartham Creek" for the stream. The name "Warthan" is from a pioneer rancher (Salley, p. 234).

Wasco [KERN]: *town,* 24 miles northwest of Bakersfield (lat. 35°35'35" N, long. 119°20'05" W; in and near sec. 12, T 27 S, R 24 E). Named on Wasco (1953) 7.5' quadrangle. The place first was called Dewey, and then Deweyville (Bailey, 1967, p. 27). Postal authorities established Deweyville post office, named for Admiral George Dewey of Spanish-American War fame, in 1899 and changed the name to Wasco in 1900 (Salley, p. 58). The town incorporated in 1945. According to Hanna (p. 349), the name "Wasco" was coined from the title "Western American Sugar Company." According to Bailey (1967, p. 27), a former resident of Wasco County, Oregon, named the town. Officials of California Home Extension Association founded Fourth Home Extension Colony at the place in 1907 (Hanna, p. 349).

Washapie Mountain [TULARE]: *peak,* 3 miles east-northeast of Tucker Mountain near Fresno-Tulare County line (lat. 36°39'30" N, long. 119°09'20" W; near N line sec. 4, T 15 S, R 26 E). Named on Tucker Mountain (1966) 7.5' quadrangle. The name is from an Indian village in Drum Valley (Gudde, 1949, p. 383).

Washboard: see **The Washboard** [FRESNO].

Washburn Cove [TULARE]: *relief feature,* wide place in the canyon of Kaweah River 2 miles east-southeast of Kaweah (lat. 36°27'40" N, long. 118°53' W; in and near sec. 7, T 17 S, R 29 E). Named on Kaweah (1957) 15' quadrangle.

Washington: see **Fort Washington**, under **Old Fort Miller** [FRESNO].

Washington City: see **Old Fort Miller** [FRESNO].

Watch Tower: see **The Watch Tower**, under **The Sphinx** [FRESNO].

Water Canyon [KERN]:

(1) *canyon,* drained by a stream that flows 2 miles to Kelso Valley 5 miles east-southeast of Claraville (lat. 35°24'45" N, long. 118°15'10" W; at E line sec. 18, T 29 S, R 35 E). Named on Claraville (1972) 7.5' quadrangle.

(2) *canyon,* drained by a stream that flows 4 miles to Jawbone Canyon 3 miles north of Cinco (lat. 35°18'20" N, long. 118°01'25" W; near S line sec. 20, T 30 S, R 37 E). Named on Cinco (1972) 7.5' quadrangle.

(3) *canyon,* drained by a stream that flows nearly 4 miles to Tehachapi Valley 3 miles southwest of Tehachapi (lat. 35°06'25" N, long. 118°29'30" W; near N line sec. 36, T 32 S, R 32 E). Named on Tehachapi South (1966) 7.5' quadrangle.

(4) *canyon,* drained by a stream that flows 1.25 miles to Cummings Creek 2 miles north of Cummings Mountain (lat. 35°04'15" N, long. 118°34' W). Named on Cummings Mountain (1966) 7.5' quadrangle.

Water Canyon Creek [KERN]: *stream,* flows 3.5 miles to Tehachapi Creek 0.5 mile southeast of Keene near Keene post office (lat. 35°13'10" N, long. 118°33'20" W; near E line sec. 20, T 31 S, R 32 E). Named on Keene (1966) 7.5' quadrangle.

Waterfall Canyon [KERN]: *canyon,* drained by La Rose Creek, which flows

4.5 miles to Cache Creek 10 miles east of Tehachapi (lat. 35°06'15" N, long. 118°16'15" W; near W line sec. 31, T 32 S, R 35 E). Named on Monolith (1966) and Tehachapi NE (1966) 7.5' quadrangles.

Water Gap Spring [KERN]: *spring,* 8 miles northeast of Glennville (lat. 35°47'20" N, long. 118°35'10" W; near NW cor. sec. 6, T 25 S, R 32 E). Named on California Hot Springs (1958) 15' quadrangle.

Waterhole Mine Spring [KERN]: *spring,* 1 mile east-southeast of Claraville (lat. 35°26'20" N, long. 118°18'40" W; near SE cor. sec. 3, T 29 S, R 34 E). Named on Claraville (1972) 7.5' quadrangle. Emerald Mountain (1943) 15' quadrangle shows Waterhole mine at the place.

Water Station: see **Mojave** [KERN].

Watertown: see **Lemoore** [KINGS].

Watts Creek [FRESNO]: *stream,* flows about 7.5 miles to Sycamore Creek (1) 1.25 miles northwest of Trimmer (lat. 36°55'15" N, long. 119°18'35" W; sec. 1, T 12 S, R 24 E). Named on Humphreys Station (1965) and Trimmer (1965) 7.5' quadrangles.

Watts Valley [FRESNO]: *valley,* 4 miles west-northwest of Trimmer (lat. 36°56' N, long. 119°22' W); Watts Creek drains the valley. Named on Humphreys Station (1965) and Trimmer (1965) 7.5' quadrangles. Postal authorities established Watt's Valley post office in 1912 and discontinued it in 1919 (Frickstad, p. 39). The name commemorates C.B. Watts, who settled at what was known as Popes Valley before Watts' arrival (Gudde, 1949, p. 385).

Wauken: see **Waukena** [TULARE].

Waukena [TULARE]: *village,* 10 miles west-southwest of Tulare (lat. 36°08'20" N, long. 119°30'30" W; near SW cor. sec. 32, T 20 S, R 23 E). Named on Waukena (1954) 7.5' quadrangle. Postal authorities established Waukena post office in 1889, discontinued it in 1901, and reestablished it in 1904 (Frickstad, p. 214). The name may be a corruption of the word "Joaquin"—the place also was known as Wauken and Buzzards' Roost (Mitchell, A.R., p. 70).

Weaver Creek [KERN]: *stream,* flows 9.5 miles to Caliente Creek 2.5 miles east of Loraine (lat. 35°18'45" N, long. 118°23'30" W; near SW cor. sec. 13, T 30 S, R 33 E). Named on Claraville (1972), Emerald Mountain (1972), and Loraine (1972) 7.5' quadrangles.

Weaver Creek [TULARE]: *stream,* flows 1 mile to Meadows Creek 2 miles north-northwest of Shell Mountain (lat. 36°43'30" N, long. 118°48'20" W; near W line sec. 11, T 14 S, R 29 E). Named on Giant Forest (1956) 15' quadrangle.

Weaver Lake [TULARE]: *lake,* 1000 feet long, 0.5 mile north-northwest of Shell Mountain (lat. 36°42'10" N, long. 118°47'50" W; sec. 14, T 14 S, R 29 E). Named on Giant Forest (1956) 15' quadrangle.

Webstone: see **Basin** [FRESNO].

Wedge Lake [FRESNO]: *lake,* 800 feet long, 2.25 miles west of Mount Humphreys in Humphreys Basin (lat. 37°16'20" N, long. 118°42'45" W). Named on Mount Tom (1949) 15' quadrangle, which shows that the lake has a wedge-shaped outline.

Weed Patch [KERN]: *town,* 10 miles south-southeast of Bakersfield (lat. 35°14'15" N, long. 118°54'50" W; at SE cor. sec. 12, T 31 S, R 28 E). Named on Weed Patch (1955) 7.5' quadrangle. The town was founded in 1922 (Wines, p. 85). The name was given to the site as early as 1874 because of the abundance of weeds there; the community also was called Alexander's Corner for Cal Alexander, a resident of the place (Bailey, 1967, p. 27).

Weedpatch: see **Algoso** [KERN]; **Patch** [KERN].

Weir Creek [FRESNO]: *stream,* flows 1.5 miles to North Fork Kings River 4 miles east of Balch Camp (lat. 36°54'10" N, long. 119° 03' W; sec. 8, T 12 S, R 27 E). Named on Patterson Mountain (1952) 15' quadrangle.

Weiss Canyon [KERN]: *canyon,* 2.25 miles long, along South Fork Cottonwood Creek (2) above a point 8 miles east of Mount Adelaide (lat. 35°25'10" N, long. 118°36'10" W; sec. 12, T 29 S, R 31 E). Named on Breckenridge Mountain (1972) 7.5' quadrangle.

Welcome Valley [KERN]: *valley,* 8 miles northwest of Blackwells Corner (lat. 35°41'15" N, long. 119°58'45" W). Named on Emigrant Hill (1953) 7.5' quadrangle.

Weldon [KERN]: *village,* 9 miles east-southeast of Wofford Heights in South Fork Valley (lat. 35°40' N, long. 118°17'20" W; on W line sec. 13, T 26 S, R 34 E). Named on Weldon (1972) 7.5' quadrangle. Postal authorities established Weldon post office in 1871 and moved it 0.5 mile east in 1938 (Salley, p. 236); the name commemorates William B. Weldon, a pioneer cattleman in the neighborhood (Bailey, 1962, p. 78). A temporary army post called Camp Leonard was set up near present Weldon in 1863 (Bailey, 1967, p. 3).

Weldon Meadow [KERN]: *area,* 3 miles north of Claraville (lat. 35° 29' N, long. 118°20'15" W; near SE cor. sec. 20, T 28 S, R 34 E). Named on Claraville (1972) 7.5' quadrangle. Called French Meadow on Emerald Mountain (1943) 15' quadrangle, where present French Meadow is called Weldon Meadow. United States Board on Geographic Names (1975b, p. 12) gave the name "French Meadow" as a variant.

Weldon Peak [KERN]: *peak,* 7 miles north of Emerald Mountain (lat. 35°21'25" N, long. 118°17'20" W). Named on Emerald Mountain (1972) 7.5' quadrangle.

Weldon Pond [KERN]: *lake,* 100 feet long. 12.5 miles northwest of Mojave (lat. 35°13'25" N, long. 118°13'45" W; near N line sec. 21, T 31 S, R 35 E). Named on Cache Peak (1973) 7.5' quadrangle.

Wells: see **Keene** [KERN].

Wells Creek [TULARE]: *stream,* flows 2.5 miles to Jim Gray Creek 9 miles south of Kaweah in Oak Flat (1) (lat. 36°20'30" N, long. 118°55'40" W; at N line sec. 27, T 18 S, R 28 E). Named on Kaweah (1957) 15' quadrangle.

Welport [KERN]: *locality,* 6 miles north-northwest of McKittrick (lat. 35°22'35" N, long. 119°40'45" W). Named on Belridge (1943) 7.5' quadrangle.

Weringdale: see **Woody** [KERN].

West Alpaugh [TULARE]: *locality,* 13 miles west of Earlimart (lat. 35°53'20" N, long. 119°30'30" W; sec. 32, T 23 S, R 23 E); the place is 1 mile west of Alpaugh. Named on West Alpaugh (1929) 7.5' quadrangle.

West Baker [KERN]: *locality,* nearly 4 miles northwest of Boron (lat. 35°02'35" N, long. 117°41'25" W; at S line sec. 14, T 11 N, R 8 W); the place is 1.25 miles west of Baker. Named on Boron (1954) 15' quadrangle.

West Camp [KERN]: *locality,* 12 miles north of Blackwells Corner (lat. 35°47'20" N, long. 119°49'20" W; near N line sec. 4, T 25 S, R 20 E). Named on West Camp (1954) 7.5' quadrangle.

Western Creek: see **Woodward Creek** [TULARE].

Westfall Creek [FRESNO]: *stream,* flows 4.5 miles to Kaiser Creek 5.5 miles northwest of Kaiser Peak (lat. 37°20'40" N, long. 119°16'10" W; sec. 5, T 7 S, R 25 E). Named on Kaiser Peak (1953) and Shuteye Peak (1953) 15' quadrangles. The name commemorates Eldridge Westfall, one of the first forest rangers in the region (Browning, p. 234).

Westhaven [FRESNO]: *settlement,* 16 miles south-southwest of Riverdale (lat. 36°13'35" N, long. 119°59'35" W; near SE cor. sec. 35, T 19 S, R 18 E). Named on Westhaven (1956) 7.5' quadrangle. Postal authorities established Westhaven post office in 1918 and discontinued it in 1958 (Salley, p. 237).

Westhaven Siding [FRESNO]: *locality,* 15 miles south-southwest of Riverdale along Southern Pacific Railroad (lat. 36°14'40"N, long. 119°59'35" W; near W line sec. 26, T 19 S, R 18 E); the place is 1.25 miles north of Westhaven. Named on Westhaven (1956) 7.5' quadrangle. Called Westhaven Station on Westhaven (1929) 7.5' quadrangle.

Westhaven Station: see **Westhaven Siding** [FRESNO].

West Kaiser Campground [FRESNO]: *locality,* 4.5 miles northwest of Kaiser Peak (lat. 37°20'40" N, long. 119°14'20" W; sec. 4, T 7 S, R 25 E); the place is along West Kaiser Creek. Named on Kaiser Peak (1953) 15' quadrangle.

West Kaiser Creek [FRESNO]: *stream,* flows 5.5 miles to Kaiser Creek 5.25 miles northwest of Kaiser Peak (lat. 37°20'55" N, long. 119°15' W; sec. 4, T 7 S, R 25 E). Named on Kaiser Peak (1953) 15' quadrangle.

West Kennedy Lake [FRESNO]: *lake,* 2000 feet long, 9 miles west-southwest of Marion Peak (lat. 36°53'20" N, long. 118°39'45" W); the lake is at the head of West Fork Kennedy Creek. Named on Marion Peak (1953) 15' quadrangle.

West Lake [FRESNO]: *lake,* 800 feet long, 6.25 miles east of the town of Big Creek (lat. 37°12' N, long. 119°07'45" W; near S line sec. 28, T 8 S, R 26 E). Named on Huntington Lake (1953) 15' quadrangle.

West Meadow: see **Big West Meadow**, under **Big Wet Meadow** [TULARE].

Weston Meadow [TULARE]: *area,* 4 miles east-southeast of Wilsonia (lat. 36°43'20" N, long. 118°53'15" W; sec. 12, T 14 S, R 28 E). Named on Giant Forest (1956) 15' quadrangle. The name commemorates Austin Weston of Visalia, who used the place as his headquarters for summer stock grazing (Gudde, 1949, p. 387).

West Park [FRESNO]: *settlement,* 5 miles southwest of downtown Fresno (lat. 36°42'35" N, long. 119°51'10" W; sec. 13, T 14 S, R 19 E). Named on Fresno South (1963) 7.5' quadrangle.

West Pinnacles Creek [FRESNO]: *stream,* flows 3.5 miles to Piute Canyon 12 miles north of Blackcap Mountain (lat. 37°14'40" N, long. 118°49' W); the stream heads west of The Pinnacles (1). Named on Blackcap Mountain (1953) and Mount Abbot (1953) 15' quadrangles.

West Shore Gulch [KERN]: *canyon,* drained by a stream that flows 4.5 miles to the canyon of Kern River 3 miles north of downtown Bakersfield (lat. 35°25'40" N, long. 118°59'15" W; at S line sec. 5, T 29 S, R 28 E). Named on Oil Center (1954) 7.5' quadrangle.

Westside [FRESNO]: *settlement,* 22 miles northeast of Coalinga (lat. 36°24' N, long. 120°08'20" W; near NE cor. sec. 5, T 18 S, R 17 E). Named on Westside (1956) 7.5' quadrangle.

West Spring [FRESNO]: *spring,* 4.5 miles north of Coalinga Mineral Springs (lat. 36°12'35" N, long. 120°33'50" W; sec. 10, T 20 S, R 13 E). Named on Sherman Peak (1969) 7.5' quadrangle.

West Spur [TULARE]: *ridge,* generally north-trending, 3 miles long, 12.5 miles northwest of Mount Whitney (lat. 36°43'30" N, long. 118°25'10" W); the ridge is 1 mile west across Vidett Creek from East Spur. Named on Mount Whitney (1956) 15' quadrangle.

West Stringer [TULARE]: *stream,* flows 3.5 miles to Cold Creek 4.25 miles southwest of Kern Peak (lat. 36°15'40" N, long. 118° 20'10" W). Named on Kern Peak (1956) 15' quadrangle.

West Stringer Saddle [TULARE]: *pass,* 2 miles west of Kern Peak (lat. 36°18'45" N, long. 118°19'20" W; sec. 32, T 18 S, R 34 E); the pass is near the head of West Stringer. Named on Kern Peak (1956) 15' quadrangle.

West Twin Creek: see **Santiago Creek** [KERN].

West Venida [TULARE]: *locality,* 3.25 miles north of Exeter along Atchison, Topeka and Santa Fe Railroad (lat. 36°20'30" N, long. 119°07'45" W; at S line sec. 23, T 18 S, R 26 E); the place is 0.5 mile north of Venida. Named on Exeter (1952) 15' quadrangle.

West Vidette [TULARE]: *peak,* 13 miles north-northwest of Mount Whitney (lat. 36°44' N, long. 118°25'10" W); the peak is 1.25 miles southwest of East Vidette on West Spur. Named on Mount Whitney (1956) 15' quadrangle.

Wet Meadow [FRESNO]: *area,* 12 miles north of Hume (lat. 36° 57' N, long. 118°52'25" W). Named on Tehipite Dome (1952) 15' quadrangle.

Wet Meadow: see **Big Wet Meadow** [TULARE]; **Little Bearpaw Meadow** [TULARE].

Wet Meadows [TULARE]: *area,* 7 miles south of Mineral King (lat. 36°21'10" N, long. 118°34'50" W). Named on Mineral King (1956) 15' quadrangle.

Whaleback [TULARE]: *ridge,* generally north-trending, 3 miles long, center 2 miles north of Triple Divide Peak (lat. 36°37'20" N, long. 118°31'55" W). Named on Triple Divide Peak (1956) 15' quadrangle.

Wheat Camp [TULARE]: *locality,* 7 miles south of Waukena (lat. 36°02'35" N, long. 119°31'35" W; sec. 6, T 22 S, R 23 E). Named on Corcoran (1954) 7.5' quadrangle.

Wheatville [FRESNO]: *locality,* 29 miles northeast of Coalinga (lat. 36°27'35" N, long. 120°02'05" W; near SW cor. sec. 9, T 17 S, R 18 E). The place is named on Wheatville (1931) 7.5' quadrangle, and the site is named on Five Points (1956) 7.5' quadrangle. Postal authorities established Wheatville post office in 1891 and discontinued it in 1920 (Salley, p. 239).

Wheatville: see **Kingsburg** [FRESNO].

Wheeler Ridge [KERN]:

(1) *ridge,* generally southeast- to east-trending, 5 miles long, 4 miles south-southwest of Mettler (lat. 35°00'40" N, long. 119°00'45" W). Named on Coal Oil Canyon (1955), Mettler (1955), and Pleito Hills (1958) 7.5' quadrangles. The name commemorates the driller of an unsuccessful oil well on the ridge, which earlier was called El Monte de las Avilas for Danurio Avila and his son, Ignacio, who ran horses and cattle there (Latta, 1976, p. 213, 215).

(2) *village,* 4.25 miles south-southeast of Mettler (lat. 35°00'15" N, long. 118°56'55" W; at S line sec. 30, T 11 N, R 19 W); the village is west of Wheeler Ridge (1). Named on Mettler (1955) 7.5' quadrangle. Postal authorities established Wheeler Ridge post office in 1923 and discontinued it in 1972 (Salley, p. 239).

Wheel Mountain [FRESNO]: *peak,* 6.5 miles southeast of Mount Goddard on Black Divide (lat. 37°02'45" N, long. 118°37'45" W). Altitude 12,781 feet. Named on Mount Goddard (1948) 15' quadrangle. Lewis Clark, Marjory Bridge, John Poindexter, and John Cahill made the first ascent of the peak in 1933 and named it for the configuration of the summit, which reminded them of the spokes of a wheel (Browning, p. 235).

Wherry Housing: see **Edwards** [KERN].

Whiskey Flat: see **Kernville** [KERN].

White Bear Lake [FRESNO]: *lake,* 850 feet long, 3.5 miles south-southwest of Mount Abbot (lat. 37°20'20" N, long. 118°48' W). Named on Mount Abbot (1953) 15' quadrangle.

White Chief Lake [TULARE]: *lake,* 500 feet long, 3 miles south of Mineral King (lat. 36°24'30" N, long. 118°35'55" W); the lake is 0.25 mile north-northwest of White Chief Peak. Named on Mineral King (1956) 15' quadrangle.

White Chief Peak [TULARE]: *peak,* 3 miles south of Mineral King (lat. 36°24'20" N, long. 118°35'50" W). Named on Mineral King (1956) 15' quadrangle.

White City Canyon [KERN]: *canyon,* drained by a stream that flows 4 miles to Sunflower Valley 3.5 miles east of Orchard Peak (lat. 35°44'15" N, long. 120°04'15" W). Named on Sawtooth Ridge (1961) 7.5' quadrangle. The name is for the white tents of a camp known as White City that J.D. Spreckels put up in 1900 when he drilled for oil in the canyon (Marsh, p. 41).

White Cow Canyon [KERN]: *canyon,* drained by a stream that flows 2.25 miles to Tejon Canyon 4 miles west of Cummings Mountain (lat. 35°02'10" N, long. 118°38'15" W). Named on Cummings Mountain (1966) and Tejon Ranch (1966) 7.5' quadrangles.

White Creek [FRESNO]: *stream,* flows 14 miles to Los Gatos Creek 10 miles northwest of Coalinga (lat. 36°13'15" N, long. 120°29'50" W; sec. 6, T 20 S, R 14 E). Named on Alcalde Hills (1969), Santa Rita Peak (1969), and Sherman Peak (1969) 7.5' quadrangles.

White Deer Creek [FRESNO]: *stream,* flows 7.5 miles to Mill Creek (3) 10 miles southwest of Balch Camp (lat. 36°47'25" N, long. 119°13'35" W; near SW cor. sec. 14, T 13 S, R 25 E); the stream goes through White Deer Flat. Named on Patterson Mountain (1952) 15' quadrangle.

White Deer Creek: see **Little White Deer Creek**, under **Mill Creek** [FRESNO-TULARE].

White Deer Flat [FRESNO]: *area,* 6 miles south-southwest of Balch Camp (lat. 36°49'35" N, long. 119°10' W; sec. 4, 5, 6, T 13 S, R 26 E). Named on Patterson Mountain (1952) 15' quadrangle. The name is from an albino deer seen by early settlers (Forest M. Clingan, personal communication, 1990).

White Deer Saddle [FRESNO]: *pass,* 4.5 miles south-southwest of Balch Camp (lat. 36°50'35" N, long. 119°08'50" W; sec. 33, T 12 S, R 26 E); the pass is near the head of White Deer Creek. Named on Patterson Mountain (1952) 15' quadrangle.

White Deer Valley: see **Little White Deer Valley**, under **Mill Creek** [FRESNO-TULARE].

White Divide [FRESNO]: *ridge,* north-northwest-trending, 8.5 miles long, 5 miles south of Mount Goddard (lat. 37°02' N, long. 118° 44' W). Named on Marion Peak (1953) and Mount Goddard (1948) 15' quadrangles.

White Dome [TULARE]: *peak,* 11 miles west-northwest of Lamont Peak (lat. 35°51'50" N, long. 118°12'45" W). Altitude 7555 feet. Named on Lamont Peak (1956) 15' quadrangle.

White Fork: see **Woods Creek** [FRESNO].

White Meadow [TULARE]: *area,* 4.25 miles north-northeast of Camp Nelson (lat. 36°11'40" N, long. 118°34'10" W; near S line sec. 12, T 20 S, R 31 E). Named on Camp Nelson (1956) 15' quadrangle.

White Mountain [KERN]: *peak,* 1 mile north-northwest of Cross Mountain (lat. 35°17'40" N, long. 118°08'40" W; on E line sec. 30, T 30 S, R 36 E). Named on Cross Mountain (1972) 7.5' quadrangle.

White Mountain [TULARE]: *peak,* 11 miles west-southwest of Kern Peak (lat. 36°15'30" N, long. 118°28'30" W). Named on Kern Peak (1956) 15' quadrangle.

White Oak Lodge [KERN]: *locality,* 4 miles northwest of Liebre Twins at present Twin Lakes (2) (lat. 34°59'15" N, long. 118°30'45" W; sec. 6, T 10 S, R 15 W). Named on Neenach (1943) 15' quadrangle. Postal authorities established White Oak Lodge post office in 1930 and discontinued it in 1932 (Frickstad, p. 60).

White River [TULARE]:

(1) *stream,* flows 33 miles to lowlands 3 miles southwest of Ducor (lat. 35°51'30" N, long. 119°05'20" W; near W line sec. 8, T 24 S, R 27 E). Named on California Hot Springs (1958) and White River (1952) 15' quadrangles, and on Delano East (1953), Delano West (1954), and Richgrove (1952) 7.5' quadrangles.

(2) *locality,* 7 miles southeast of Fountain Springs (lat. 35°48'40" N, long. 118°50'35" W; sec. 28, T 24 S, R 29 E); the place is along White River (1). Named on White River (1965) 7.5' quadrangle. A mining camp called Dogtown was situated about 2 miles east of present White River (2) in Coarse Gold Gulch; when the first road built into Linns Valley bypassed Dogtown, a new settlement, also called Dogtown, grew at the site of present White River (2) (Hoover, Rensch, and Rensch, p. 563). Later the new settlement was called Tailholt, perhaps either because a miner used a cow's tail as a handle for the door to his cabin (Gudde, 1975, p. 345), or because a lady stagecoach passenger caught her dog by the tail as the dog jumped from a coach at the place (Hoover, Rensch, and Rensch, p. 563). Postal authorities established White River post office in 1862, discontinued it in 1864, reestablished it in 1866, discontinued it in 1868, reestablished it in 1873, and discontinued it in 1933 (Frickstad, p. 214). Levi Mitchell substituted the name "White River" for the name "Tailholt" when the post office was established (Gudde, 1949, p. 388). A place called Keeneysburg was the center of trading in the neighborhood before Tailholt, or White River, replaced it (Hensher and Peskin, p. 9). Postal authorities established Keeneysburgh post office, named for Mr. Keeney, owner of a trading post, in 1859 and discontinued it in 1860; the post-office site now is in Kern County (Salley, p. 110).

White River Camp: see **White River Summer Home Tract** [TULARE].

White River Summer Home Tract [TULARE]: *locality,* 3.25 miles southeast of California Hot Springs (lat. 35°50'55" N, long. 118° 37'30" W; near SW cor. sec. 10, T 24 S, R 31 E); the place is along White River (1). Named on California Hot Springs (1958) 15' quadrangle. Called White River Camp on Tobias Peak (1936) 30' quadrangle.

Whiterock Creek [KERN]: *stream,* flows 5.25 miles to Tehachapi Valley 4 miles east of Tehachapi (lat. 35°08'30" N, long. 118°22'40" W; near SW cor. sec. 18, T 32 S, R 34 E). Named on Tehachapi North (1966) 7.5' quadrangle. Wheeler's (1875-1878) map has the form "White Rock Creek" for the name. Whitney (p. 216) noted the occurrence of beds of white rock along the stream.

Whites Bridge [FRESNO]: *locality,* 2.5 miles east-southeast of Mendota along Fresno Slough (lat. 36°44' N, long. 120°20'30" W; sec. 9, T 14 S, R 15 E). Named on Tranquillity (1956) 7.5' quadrangle. Postal authorities established White's Bridge post office in 1879 and discontinued it in 1893; the name commemorates James R. White, first postmaster, who built the bridge across San Joaquin River at Fresno Slough (Salley, p. 239).

White Tank Spring [FRESNO]: *spring,* 1.5 miles south of Piedra (lat. 36°47'10" N, long. 119°23'10" W; sec. 20, T 13 S, R 24 E). Named on Piedra (1965) 7.5' quadrangle.

White Wolf Spring: see **Bear Mountain** [KERN].

Whitman Creek [TULARE]: *stream,* flows 5.25 miles to Horse Creek (1) 5.5 miles southwest of Mineral King (lat. 36°23'45" N, long. 118°39'55" W). Named on Mineral King (1956) 15' quadrangle. Soldiers named the stream for their commanding officer, Captain William Whitman, acting superintendent of Sequoia National Park in 1912 (Browning, p. 236).

Whitmore's Ferry: see **Kingston**, under **Hardwick** [KINGS].

Whitney: see **Mount Whitney** [TULARE]; **Mount Whitney Number 1** and **Old Mount Whitney**, under **Mount Corcoran** [TULARE].

Whitney Creek [TULARE]: *stream,* flows 7.5 miles to Kern River 6.5 miles west-southwest of Mount Whitney (lat. 36°33'10" N, long. 118°24'10" W); the stream heads near Mount Whitney. Named on Mount Whitney (1956) 15' quadrangle. Called Grubtree Cr. on Olmsted's (1900) map.

Whitney Creek: see **Golden Trout Creek** [TULARE].

Whitney Meadow: see **Big Whitney Meadow** [TULARE]; **Little Whitney Meadow** [TULARE].

Whitney Meadows: see **Big Whitney Meadow** [TULARE].

Whitney Pass [TULARE]: *pass,* less than 2 miles south-southeast of Mount Whitney on Tulare-Inyo County line (lat. 36°33'15" N, long. 118°16'40" W). Named on Mount Whitney (1956) 15' quadrangle.

Whitney Well [KERN]: *well,* 5 miles west-southwest of Pinyon Mountain (lat. 35°25'50" N, long. 118°14'25" W; sec. 8, T 29 S, R 35 E). Named on Pinyon Mountain (1972) 7.5' quadrangle.

Whitsett: see **Camp Whitsett** [TULARE].

Whitton Spring [KERN]: *spring,* 6.25 miles east-southeast of Caliente (lat. 35°15'20" N, long. 118°31'35" W; near S line sec. 3, T 31 S, R 32 E). Named on Oiler Peak (1972) 7.5' quadrangle.

Wible: see **Wible Orchard** [KERN].

Wible Orchard [KERN]: *locality,* 4.25 miles south-southwest of Bakersfield along Southern Pacific Railroad (lat. 35°19' N, long. 119°01'35" W; sec. 13, T 30 S, R 27 E). Named on Gosford (1954) 7.5' quadrangle, and called Wible on Gosford (1932) 7.5' quadrangle. The name commemorates Simon William Wible, who came to Kern County in 1874 (Wines, p. 16). The place is called Wible Orchards on California Division of Highways' (1934) map, which shows a locality called Strader situated 2 miles farther northeast along the railroad (near NE cor. sec. 7, T 30 S, R 28 E). California Mining Bureau's (1917c) map shows a place called Parsons located about 4 miles northeast of Wible along the railroad.

Wiesman Spring [FRESNO]: *spring,* 6 miles east of Balch Camp (lat. 36°53'45" N, long. 119°00'50" W; near S line sec. 10, T 12 S, R 27 E). Named on Patterson Mountain (1952) 15' quadrangle.

Wiggletail [TULARE]: *stream,* flows 1.5 miles to the canyon of Deer Creek (2) 7 miles north-northeast of Fountain Springs (lat. 35°59'10" N, long. 118°53'15" W; sec. 30, T 22 S, R 29 E). Named on White River (1952) 15' quadrangle.

Wik Spring [KERN]: *spring,* 4.25 miles northeast of Caliente (lat. 35°20'30" N, long. 118°34'55" W; sec. 6, T 30 S, R 32 E). Named on Oiler Peak (1972) 7.5' quadrangle.

Wilbur May Lake [FRESNO]: *lake,* 1900 feet long, 11 miles west-northwest of Mount Abbot (lat. 37°28' N, long. 118°57'15" W). Named on Mount Abbot (1953) 15' quadrangle.

Wilcox Canyon [TULARE]: *canyon,* drained by a stream that flows less than 1 mile to Wilcox Creek 1 mile east-northeast of Cliff Peak (lat. 36°33'35" N, long. 119°09'25" W; sec. 4, T 16 S, R 26 E). Named on Stokes Mountain (1966) 7.5' quadrangle.

Wilcox Creek [TULARE]: *stream,* flows 5.5 miles to Cottonwood Creek 3.5 miles southeast of Cliff Peak (lat. 36°30'50" N, long. 119°07'55" W; at S line sec. 22, T 16 S, R 26 E). Named on Stokes Mountain (1966) 7.5' quadrangle. Called Canyon Creek on Dinuba (1924) 30' quadrangle.

Wilcox Creek: see **Moore Creek** [TULARE].

Wildcat Canyon [FRESNO]: *canyon,* drained by a stream that heads in Merced County and flows 6 miles to lowlands 18 miles west of Firebaugh (lat. 36°49'45" N, long. 120°46'15" W; sec. 4, T 13 S, R 11 E). Named on Laguna Seca Ranch (1956) 7.5' quadrangle.

Wildcat Creek [FRESNO]: *stream,* flows 3 miles to Fancher Creek 5.5 miles south of Humphreys Station (lat. 36°52'50" N, long. 119° 27'30" W; near NE cor. sec. 21, T 12 S, R 23 E); the stream heads near Wildcat Mountain. Named on Humphreys Station (1965) and Piedra (1965) 7.5' quadrangles.

Wildcat Creek [KERN]: *stream,* flows 3 miles to Howling Gulch 0.5 mile south-southwest of Woody (lat. 35°41'50" N, long. 118°50'15" W; sec. 3, T 26 S, R 29 E). Named on Woody (1965) 7.5' quadrangle.

Wildcat Creek: see **Howling Gulch** [KERN].

Wildcat Mountain [FRESNO]: *peak,* 5.5 miles south of Humphreys Station (lat. 36°53' N, long. 119°25'45" W; sec. 14, T 12 S, R 23 E). Altitude 2227 feet. Named on Humphreys Station (1965) 7.5' quadrangle.

Wildcat Rock [FRESNO]: *peak,* 9 miles southwest of Coalinga (lat. 36°02'20" N, long. 120°28'05" W; near S line sec. 4, T 22 S, R 14 E). Named on Curry Mountain (1969) 7.5' quadrangle.

Wildflower [FRESNO]: *locality,* 6 miles southwest of Selma (lat. 36° 30'10" N, long. 119°40'55" W; near NE cor. sec. 33, T 16 S, R 21 E). Named on Conejo (1963) 7.5' quadrangle. Postal authorities established Wild Flower post office in 1878 and discontinued it in 1898; they established Deseret post office 6 miles west of Wild Flower in 1887 and discontinued it in 1890—Deseret was a Mormon farm community (Salley, p. 58, 240).

Wildflower: see **Richgrove** [TULARE].

Wild Hog Canyon [FRESNO-TULARE]: *canyon,* on Fresno-Tulare County line, drained by a stream that flows 2 miles to Wooley Canyon 8.5 miles east of Tucker Mountain [TULARE] (lat. 36°38'40" N, long. 119°03' W; sec. 4, T 15 S, R 27 E). Named on Miramonte (1966) 7.5' quadrangle.

Wildman Meadow [FRESNO]: *area,* 13 miles southwest of Marion Peak (lat. 36°50'45" N, long. 118°42'20" W). Named on Marion Peak (1953) 15' quadrangle. Frank Lewis and Jeff Lewis named the place about 1881 because the noise that an owl made there resembled the cries of a wild man (Browning, p. 238).

Williams: see **Camp Nick Williams** [KERN]; **Hamp Williams Pass** [KERN].

Williamsburg: see **Kernville** [KERN]; **Old Town** [KERN].

Williams Canyon [KERN]: *canyon,* drained by a stream that flows 4.25 miles to San Emigdio Creek 2.5 miles west-northwest of Eagle Rest Peak (lat. 34°55'25" N, long. 119°10'35" W). Named on Eagle Rest Peak (1942) 7.5' quadrangle. United States Board on Geographic Names (1990, p. 7) approved the name "Doc Williams Canyon" for this feature, and rejected the names "Williams Canyon," "Arroyo de los Osos," "Doctor Williams Canyon," and "Quatro Osos Canyon."

Williams Creek [FRESNO]: *stream,* flows 2.5 miles to Black Rock Reservoir nearly 6 miles east-northeast of Balch Camp (lat. 36°55'20" N, long. 119°01'10" W; near N line sec. 3, T 12 S, R 27 E). Named on Patterson Mountain (1952) 15' quadrangle.

Williams Creek: see **Rancheria Creek** [KERN] (2).

Williams Hot Springs: see **Walker Basin** [KERN].

Williams Meadow [TULARE]: *area,* 13 miles northwest of Triple Divide Peak (lat. 36°43'45" N, long. 118°41'10" W; on S line sec. 2, T 14 S, R 30 E). Named on Triple Divide Peak (1956) 15' quadrangle.

Willow Creek [FRESNO]: *stream,* flows 2.5 miles to a ditch 3.5 miles east-northeast of Reedley (lat. 36°36'55" N, long. 119°23'35" W; near W line sec. 20, T 15 S, R 24 E). Named on Orange Cove North (1966), Reedley (1966), and Wahtoke (1966) 7.5' quadrangles. On Reedley (1924) 7.5' quadrangle, the stream extends to Travers Creek.

Willow Creek [TULARE]:

(1) *stream,* flows 2.5 miles to Big Arroyo 13 miles northwest of Kern Peak (lat. 36°26'45" N, long. 118°27' W). Named on Kern Peak (1956) 15' quadrangle.

(2) *stream,* flows 4.5 miles to Little Kern River 13 miles south-southeast of Mineral King (lat. 36°16'30" N, long. 118°31' W; sec. 16, T 19 S, R 32 E). Named on Kern Peak (1956) and Mineral King (1956) 15' quadrangles.

Willow Flat [KERN]: *area,* 3 miles southwest of Wofford Heights (lat. 35°40'30" N, long. 118°29'30" W; on S line sec. 12, T 26 S, R 32 E). Named on Lake Isabella North (1972) 7.5' quadrangle.

Willow Gulch [KERN]: *canyon,* drained by a stream that flows 3.25 miles to Erskine Creek 5.25 miles east-southeast of Bodfish (lat. 35°34' N, long. 118°23'50" W; sec. 23, T 27 S, R 33 E). Named on Lake Isabella South (1972) and Woolstalf Creek (1972) 7.5' quadrangles.

Willow Lake [FRESNO]: *intermittent lake,* 0.25 mile long, 6.25 miles west of Selma (lat. 36°33'35" N, long. 119°43'20" W; sec. 7, T 16 S, R 21 E). Named on Conejo (1963) 7.5' quadrangle. Selma (1946) 15' quadrangle shows a permanent lake 4000 feet long.

Willow Meadow [FRESNO]: *area,* 2.5 miles north-northeast of Dinkey Dome (lat. 37°09' N, long. 119°06'45" W; on E line sec. 15, T 9 S, R 26 E). Named on Huntington Lake (1953) 15' quadrangle.

Willow Meadow [TULARE]: *area,* 11.5 miles west of Triple Divide Peak along Silliman Creek (lat. 36°36'55" N, long. 118°44'05" W; near SW cor. sec. 16, T 15 S, R 30 E). Named on Triple Divide Peak (1956) 15' quadrangle.

Willow Meadows Campground [TULARE]: *locality,* nearly 2 miles west-northwest of Hockett Peak (lat. 36°13'55" N, long. 118°24'50" W). Named on Hockett Peak (1956) 15' quadrangle.

Willow Spring [FRESNO]:

(1) *spring,* 3.5 miles northwest of Coalinga Mineral Springs (lat. 36°11'10" N, long. 120°35'40" W; sec. 17, T 20 S, R 13 E). Named on Sherman Peak (1969) 7.5' quadrangle.

(2) *spring,* 7 miles west of Coalinga (lat. 36°09'05" N, long. 120°29'55" W; sec. 30, T 20 S, R 14 E); the feature is at the head of Willow Springs Canyon. Named on Alcalde Hills (1969) 7.5' quadrangle.

(3) *spring,* 6.5 miles east-northeast of Castle Mountain (lat. 35°58'40" N, long. 120°14'05" W; near NW cor. sec. 34, T 22 S, R 16 E). Named on Garza Peak (1953) 7.5' quadrangle.

Willow Spring [KERN]:

(1) *spring,* 2.25 miles north-northeast of Caliente (lat. 35°19'15" N, long. 118°36'25" W). Named on Oiler Peak (1972) 7.5' quadrangle.

(2) *spring,* nearly 5 miles west of Woody (lat. 35°41'35" N, long. 119°55' W; near SW cor. sec. 1, T 26 S, R 28 E); the spring is along Willow Spring Creek (1). Named on Sand Canyon (1965) 7.5' quadrangle. On Woody (1952) 15' quadrangle, the name applies to a spring located 2000 feet

farther southeast (near N line sec. 12, T 26 S, R 28 E). On Mendenhall's (1908) map, the name applies to a locality. Boyd (p. 158) mentioned Willow Springs Station, apparently located at this place, and noted the alternate name "Mountain House Station" for the place.
(3) *spring,* 2 miles north-northwest of Skinner Peak (lat. 35°35'30" N, long. 118°08'20" W). Named on Cane Canyon (1972) 7.5' quadrangle.
(4) *spring,* 2.5 miles west-southwest of Democrat Hot Springs (lat. 35°31'15" N, long. 118°42'30" W). Named on Democrat Hot Springs (1972) 7.5' quadrangle.
(5) *spring,* 1.5 miles northwest of Pinyon Mountain (lat. 35°28'25" N, long. 118°10'25" W; near W line sec. 24, T 28 S, R 35 E). Named on Pinyon Mountain (1972) 7.5' quadrangle.
(6) *spring,* 2.5 miles east-southeast of Caliente (lat. 35°16'25" N, long. 118°35'15" W; sec. 31, T 30 S, R 32 E). Named on Oiler Peak (1972) 7.5' quadrangle.

Willow Spring [KINGS]: *spring,* 7.5 miles south-southwest of Avenal (lat. 35°54'45" N, long. 120°12'15" W; sec. 23, T 23 S, R 16 E); the spring is in Willow Spring Canyon. Named on Garza Peak (1953) 7.5' quadrangle.

Willow Spring: see **Willow Spring Well** [KERN].

Willow Spring Canyon [KINGS]: *canyon,* drained by a stream that flows 2.5 miles to Avenal Canyon 9 miles south-southwest of Avenal (lat. 35°53'20" N, long. 120°12'45" W; sec. 35, T 23 S, R 16 E); Willow Spring is in the canyon. Named on Garza Peak (1953) 7.5' quadrangle.

Willow Spring Creek [KERN]:
(1) *stream,* flows 8 miles to Rag Gulch 5.25 miles west of Woody (lat. 35°43'05" N, long. 118°55'30" W; at N line sec. 35, T 25 S, R 28 E); Willow Spring (2) is along the stream. Named on Sand Canyon (1965) and Woody (1965) 7.5' quadrangles. United States Board on Geographic Names (1966b, p. 6) rejected the name "Dry Creek" for the stream.
(2) *stream,* flows nearly 2 miles to Kern River 0.5 mile west-southwest of Democrat Hot Springs (lat. 35°31'35" N, long. 118°40'30" W). Named on Democrat Hot Springs (1972) 7.5' quadrangle.

Willow Springs [KERN]:
(1) *spring,* 7 miles west-northwest of McKittrick (lat. 35°20'45" N, long. 119°44'05" W; sec. 5, T 30 S, R 21 E); the spring is just north of Willow Springs Valley. Named on Reward (1951) 7.5' quadrangle. Called Sheep Springs on McKittrick (1912) 30' quadrangle.
(2) *village,* 7.5 miles west of Rosamond (lat. 34°52'45" N, long. 118°17'40" W; at S line sec. 7, T 9 N, R 13 W). Named on Willow Springs (1965) 7.5' quadrangle. Postal authorities established Willow Springs post office in 1909 and discontinued it in 1918 (Frickstad, p. 60). Springs at the site provided water for Indians and early travelers in the neighborhood; the place was an important stop on stage and freight lines—Ezra Hamilton built most of the stone buildings at the community about 1900 (Bailey, 1967, p. 28). Thompson's (1921) map shows a place called Domino located 8 miles west-southwest of the village of Willow Springs. Postal authorities established Domino post office in 1913 and discontinued it in 1929 (Frickstad, p. 55).

Willow Springs Butte [KERN]: *ridge,* west-trending, 1.5 miles long, east of the village of Willow Springs (lat. 34°53' N, long. 118°16'30" W). Named on Willow Springs (1965) 7.5' quadrangle.

Willow Springs Canyon [FRESNO]: *canyon,* drained by a stream that flows nearly 5 miles to Oak Flat Canyon 5 miles west-southwest of Coalinga (lat. 36°06'35" N, long. 120°26'30" W; near N line sec. 15, T 21 S, R 14 E); the canyon heads at Willow Spring (2). Named on Alcalde Hills (1969) and Curry Mountain (1969) 7.5' quadrangles.

Willow Springs Station: see **Willow Spring** [KERN] (2).

Willow Springs Valley [KERN]: *valley,* 7.25 miles west-northwest of McKittrick (lat. 35°20'30" N, long. 119°44'30" W); Willow Springs (1) is near the valley. Named on McKittrick Summit (1959) and Reward (1951) 7.5' quadrangles.

Willow Spring Well [KERN]: *well,* 8.5 miles north-northwest of Randsburg (lat. 35°28'55" N, long. 117°41'45" W; near S line sec. 20, T 28 S, R 40 E). Named on El Paso Peaks (1967) 7.5' quadrangle. Called Willow Spring on Randsburg (1911) 15' quadrangle.

Wilmilche: see **Kings River** [FRESNO-KINGS-TULARE].

Wilson Creek [TULARE]: *stream,* flows 2.5 miles to South Fork of Middle Fork Tule River nearly 2 miles west of Camp Nelson (lat. 36°08'25" N, long. 118°38'30" W). Named on Camp Nelson (1956) 15' quadrangle.

Wilsonia [TULARE]: *village,* 12.5 miles north-northwest of Yucca Mountain (lat. 36°44'05" N, long. 118°57'20" W; sec. 5, T 14 S, R 28 E). Named on Giant Forest (1956) 15' quadrangle.

Wimp [TULARE]: *locality,* 5.5 miles southwest of Cliff Peak along Atchison, Topeka and Santa Fe Railroad (lat. 36°30'05" N, long. 119°14'35" W; at S line sec. 27, T 16 S, R 25 E). Named on Stokes Mountain (1966) 7.5' quadrangle.

Winchell: see **Mount Winchell** [FRESNO].

Winchell Bay [FRESNO]: *embayment,* 8.5 miles west-southwest of Prather on the south side of Millerton Lake (lat. 37°00' N, long. 119°39'30" W); the embayment occupies the lower part of the canyon of Winchell Creek. Named on Friant (1964) and Millerton Lake West (1965) 7.5' quadrangles.

Winchell Creek [FRESNO]: *stream,* flows nearly 3 miles to Millerton Lake 12.5 miles north-northeast of Clovis (lat. 36°59'50" N, long. 119°38'55" W; sec. 2, T 11 S, R 21 E). Named on Friant (1964) and Millerton Lake East (1965) 7.5' quadrangles.

Winchell's Peak: see **Lookout Peak** [FRESNO].

Windmill Tree Peak [KERN]: *peak,* 5.5 miles south of Glennville (lat. 35°39' N, long. 118°41'55" W; sec. 24, T 26 S, R 30 E). Altitude 4587 feet. Named on Glennville (1972) 7.5' quadrangle.

Window Cliffs [TULARE]: *relief feature,* precipice 8 miles northwest of Kern Peak (lat. 36°23'50" N, long. 118°22'20" W). Named on Kern Peak (1956) 15' quadrangle. The name is from a windowlike opening at the place (United States Board on Geographic Names, 1933a, p. 821).

Window Peak [FRESNO]: *peak,* 5 miles southwest of Mount Pinchot (lat. 36°53'25" N, long. 118°27'25" W). Altitude 12,085 feet. Named on Mount Pinchot (1953) 15' quadrangle.

Windy Canyon [FRESNO]: *canyon,* drained by a stream that flows 3 miles to Middle Fork Kings River 5 miles west-northwest of Marion Peak (lat. 36°59'25" N, long. 118°35'55" W); the canyon is east of Windy Peak and west of Windy Ridge. Named on Marion Peak (1953) 15' quadrangle.

Windy Cliff [FRESNO]: *relief feature,* 11 miles southeast of Mount Goddard (lat. 37°00'20" N, long. 118°33'40" W). Named on Mount Goddard (1948) 15' quadrangle.

Windy Cliffs [FRESNO]: *relief feature,* 6 miles east-northeast of Hume on the south side of South Fork Kings River (lat. 36°48'35" N, long. 118°48'55" W); the feature is east of the mouth of Windy Gulch. Named on Tehipite Dome (1952) 15' quadrangle.

Windy Creek [TULARE]:
(1) *stream,* flows 4 miles to South Fork Tule River 6 miles south-southwest of Camp Nelson (lat. 36°03'40" N, long. 118°38'45" W); the stream heads near Windy Gap (2). Named on Camp Nelson (1956) 15' quadrangle.
(2) *stream,* flows 1.25 miles to Packsaddle Creek 6.25 miles northeast of California Hot Springs (lat. 35°56'20" N, long. 118°35'10" W; near NW cor. sec. 13, T 23 S, R 31 E). Named on California Hot Springs (1958) 15' quadrangle.

Windy Gap [TULARE]:
(1) *pass,* 8 miles south of Mineral King (lat. 36°19'50" N, long. 118°36'05" W); the feature is on Windy Ridge. Named on Mineral King (1956) 15' quadrangle.
(2) *pass,* 7 miles south of Camp Nelson (lat. 36°02'40" N, long. 118°35'10" W; near W line sec. 1, T 22 S, R 31 E). Named on Camp Nelson (1956) 15' quadrangle.

Windy Gulch [FRESNO]: *canyon,* drained by a stream that flows 2.5 miles to South Fork Kings River 6 miles east-northeast of Hume (lat. 35°48'45" N, long. 118°48'55" W); the mouth of the canyon is near Windy Cliffs. Named on Tehipite Dome (1952) 15' quadrangle.

Windy Peak [FRESNO]: *peak,* 5 miles west-northwest of Marion Peak (lat. 36°58'20" N, long. 118°36'35" W). Altitude 8867 feet. Named on Marion Peak (1953) 15' quadrangle.

Windy Point [KERN]: *relief feature,* 4 miles northeast of Caliente (lat. 35°20'10" N, long. 118°34'30" W; near NW cor. sec. 8, T 30 S, R 32 E). Named on Oiler Peak (1972) 7.5' quadrangle.

Windy Ridge [FRESNO]: *ridge,* northwest-trending, 4 miles long, 2.5 miles west of Marion Peak (lat. 36°57'30" N, long. 118°33'45" W). Named on Marion Peak (1953) 15' quadrangle.

Windy Ridge [TULARE]: *ridge,* northeast-trending, 4.5 miles long, 8.5 miles south of Mineral King (lat. 36°19'45" N, long. 118°36'15" W). Named on Mineral King (1956) 15' quadrangle.

Windy Springs [TULARE]: *spring,* 13 miles south-southeast of Monache Mountain (lat. 36°01'30" N, long. 118°06'10" W; sec. 9, T 22 S, R 36 E). Named on Monache Mountain (1956) 15' quadrangle.

Wineland [FRESNO]: *locality,* 2.25 miles southeast of Selma along Southern Pacific Railroad (lat. 36°32'35" N, long. 119°35'05" W; sec. 16, T 16 S, R 22 E). Named on Selma (1964) 7.5' quadrangle.

Winter Garden: see **Alameda** [KERN].

Winters Canyon [KERN]: *canyon,* drained by a stream that flows 3.5 miles to El Paso Creek 8.5 miles west-southwest of Cummings Mountain (lat. 35°00'40" N, long. 118°42'40" W). Named on Tejon Ranch (1966) and Winters Ridge (1966) 7.5' quadrangles.

Winters Ridge [KERN]: *ridge,* east- to east-southeast-trending, 3.5 miles long, 7.5 miles west of Liebre Twins (lat. 34°57'30" N, long. 118°42' W). Named on Winters Ridge (1966) 7.5' quadrangle.

Wirts [TULARE]: *locality,* 1 mile east-northeast of Exeter along Visalia Electric Railroad (lat. 36°18'05" N, long. 119°07'25" W; sec. 2, T 19 S, R 26 E). Named on Rocky Hill (1927) 7.5' quadrangle.

Wisdom Well [FRESNO]: *locality,* 9 miles southwest of Firebaugh (lat. 36°45'25" N, long. 120°34'35" W; sec. 33, T 13 S, R 13 E). Named on Wisdom Well (1923) 7.5' quadrangle.

Wishon: see **Camp Wishon** [TULARE].

Wishon Reservoir [FRESNO]: *intermittent lake,* behind a dam on North Fork Kings River 11 miles west-southwest of Blackcap Mountain (lat. 37°00'15" N, long. 118°58' W; sec. 6, T 11 S, R 28 E). Named on Blackcap Mountain (1953) and Tehipite Dome (1952) 15' quadrangles. Tehipite Dome (1952) 15' quadrangle shows a permanent lake, and Mount Goddard (1912) 30' quadrangle shows Dusy Meadow along the river where the lake is now. United States Board on Geographic Names (1976a, p. 5) approved the name "Sharp Creek" for a stream that flows 0.6 mile to Wishon Reservoir 10.5 miles west-southwest of Blackcap Mountain; the name commemorates Kenneth Sharp, a Pacific Gas and Electric Company civil engineer who died in an accident in 1972.

Witch Creek [KERN]: *stream,* flows 1.25 miles to El Paso Creek 5.25 miles west of Liebre Twins (lat. 34°57'45" N, long. 118°39'50" W; sec. 11, T 10 N, R 17 W). Named on Winters Ridge (1966) 7.5' quadrangle.

W-K Hill [FRESNO]: *ridge,* northwest-trending, 0.5 mile long, 6 miles north-northeast of Coalinga on Anticline Ridge (lat. 36°13'25" N, long. 120°19'30" W; on N line sec. 3, T 20 S, R 15 E). Named on Coalinga (1956) 7.5' quadrangle.

Wofford Heights [KERN]: *town,* 3.5 miles south-southwest of Kernville (lat. 35°42'30" N, long. 118°27'15" W; in and near sec. 32, T 25 S, R 33 E). Named on Lake Isabella North (1972) 7.5' quadrangle. Postal authorities established Wofford Heights post office in 1953 (Frickstad, p. 60). The name is for I.L. Wofford, who started the resort community in 1948 (Bailey, 1967, p. 28).

Wolf [FRESNO]: *locality,* 5.5 miles east of Malaga along Atchison, Topeka and Santa Fe Railroad (lat. 36°41'40" N, long. 119°38'15" W; sec. 24, T 14 S, R 21 E). Named on Malaga (1964) 7.5' quadrangle. Called Dewolf on Lippincott's (1902) map, and called DeWolf on Mendenhall's (1908) map.

Wolverton Creek [TULARE]: *stream,* flows 3.25 miles to Marble Fork 6.5 miles east-northeast of Yucca Mountain (lat. 36°35'50" N, long. 118°45'10" W; near W line sec. 29, T 15 S, R 30 E). Named on Triple Divide Peak (1956) 15' quadrangle. Browning (p. 240) associated the name with James Wolverton, who discovered and named General Sherman tree in 1879.

Wolverton Meadow: see **Log Meadow** [TULARE].

Womack: see **Las Palmas** [FRESNO].

Wood Canyon [KERN]: *canyon,* 2 miles long, opens into Santa Maria Valley (present Little Santa Maria Valley) 7.5 miles west of McKitttrick (lat. 35°18'45" N, long. 119°45'10" W; sec. 18, T 30 S, R 21 E). Named on McKittrick Summit (1959) and Reward (1951) 7.5' quadrangles.

Woodchoppers Canyon [KERN]: *canyon,* 1 mile long, opens into Canada del Agua Escondido 4 miles southwest of Liebre Twins (lat. 34°54'45" N, long. 118°37'10" W; sec. 31, T 10 N, R 16 W). Named on Liebre Twins (1965) and Winters Ridge (1966) 7.5' quadrangles.

Woodchopper Spring [KERN]: *spring,* 7.5 miles northeast of Caliente (lat. 35°22'20" N, long. 118°32'25" W; sec. 27, T 29 S, R 32 E). Named on Oiler Peak (1972) 7.5' quadrangle.

Woodchuck Country [FRESNO]: *area,* 6.5 miles southwest of Blackcap Mountain (lat. 37°01' N, long. 118°53'30" W); the place is drained by Woodchuck Creek. Named on Blackcap Mountain (1953) 15' quadrangle.

Woodchuck Creek [FRESNO]: *stream,* flows nearly 7 miles to North Fork Kings River 10.5 miles west-southwest of Blackcap Mountain in Wishon Reservoir (lat. 37°00'50" N, long. 118°58' W; sec. 31, T 10 S, R 28 E); the stream heads near Chuck Pass and goes through Woodchuck Country. Named on Blackcap Mountain (1953) 15' quadrangle.

Woodchuck Lake [FRESNO]: *lake,* 2200 feet long, 5.25 miles west-southwest of Blackcap Mountain (lat. 37°02'30" N, long. 118°52'50" W; on E line sec. 23, T 10 S, R 28 E). Named on Blackcap Mountain (1953) 15' quadrangle.

Woodcock Meadow [TULARE]: *area,* 4 miles east-southeast of Wilsonia (lat. 36°42'45" N, long. 118°53'20" W; sec. 13, T 14 S, R 28 E). Named on Giant Forest (1956) 15' quadrangle.

Woodford [KERN]: *locality,* nearly 1 mile southeast of Keene along the railroad (lat. 35°12'45" N, long. 118°33'05" W; near W line sec. 21, T 31 S, R 32 E). Named on Keene (1966) 7.5' quadrangle. Cummings Mountain (1943b) 15' quadrangle has the designation "Woodford (Keene P.O.)" at or near the place.

Wood Lake: see **Bravo Lake** [TULARE].

Woodlake [TULARE]: *town,* 12 miles east-northeast of Visalia (lat. 36°24'50" N, long. 119°05'50" W; around SE cor. sec. 25, T 17 S, R 26 E). Named on Woodlake (1952) 7.5' quadrangle. Gilbert F. Stevenson developed the townsite in 1907, and named the town for nearby Wood Lake (present Bravo Lake) (Hanna, p. 358). Postal authorities established Woodlake post office in 1908 (Frickstad, p. 214), and the town incorporated in 1941.

Woodlake Junction [TULARE]: *locality,* 1 mile west of Woodlake along Visalia Electric Railroad (lat. 36°24'50" N, long. 119°06'55" W; at SW cor. sec. 25, T 17 S, R 26 E). Named on Woodlake (1952) 7.5' quadrangle.

Woodlake Mountain: see **Antelope Mountain** [TULARE].

Woodlake Valley [TULARE]: *valley,* 3.5 miles southeast of Cliff Peak along Cottonwood Creek (lat. 36°30'45" N, long. 119°08' W). Named on Dinuba (1924) 30' quadrangle.

Woodpecker Meadow [TULARE]: *area,* 14 miles east-northeast of Fairview (lat. 35°58'45" N, long. 118°15'40" W; sec. 25, T 22 S, R 34 E). Named on Kernville (1956) 15' quadrangle.

Woods Canyon [KERN]: *canyon,* drained by a stream that flows 3.25 miles to Antelope Valley (1) 3.25 miles south of Orchard Peak (lat. 35°41'25" N, long. 120°08'30" W; near S line sec. 4, T 26 S, R 17 E). Named on Orchard Peak (1961) 7.5' quadrangle.

Woods Creek [FRESNO]: *stream,* flows 11 miles to South Fork Kings River 6.25 miles south of Marion Peak (lat. 36°52' N, long. 118°31'10" W). Named on Marion Peak (1953) and Mount Pinchot (1953) 15' quadrangles. J.N. LeConte named the stream for Robert Martin Woods, a sheepman in the vicinity of Kings River (Browning, p. 241). South Fork enters from the southeast 5 miles upstream from the mouth of the main stream and is 9 miles long. White Fork enters 6 miles upstream from the mouth of the main stream and is 3.25 miles long. Both forks are named on Mount Pinchot (1953) 15' quadrangle.

Woods Lake [FRESNO]: *lake,* 0.5 mile long, 4.25 miles south-southeast of Mount Pinchot (lat. 36°53'05" N, long. 118°22'55" W); the lake is near the head of a branch of Woods Creek. Named on Mount Pinchot (1953) 15' quadrangle. J.N. LeConte named the feature for Robert Martin Woods of Woods Creek (Browning, p. 241)

Woodsville: see **Visalia** [TULARE].

Woodville [TULARE]: *town,* 10 miles west of Porterville (lat. 36°05'35" N, long. 119°12' W; near sec. 19, T 21 S, R 26 E). Named on Woodville (1950) 7.5' quadrangle. Postal authorities established Woodville post office in 1871, discontinued it in 1908, and reestablished it in 1949 (Salley, p. 243).

Woodville: see **Visalia** [TULARE].

Woodward Creek [KERN]: *stream,* flows about 2.5 miles to French Gulch (1) 4.25 miles south of Alta Sierra (lat. 35°39'25" N, long. 118°32'45" W; sec. 16, T 26 S, R 32 E). Named on Alta Sierra (1972) 7.5' quadrangle.

Woodward Creek [TULARE]: *stream,* flows 4 miles to Stony Creek nearly 4 miles southwest of Shell Mountain (lat. 36°39'25" N, long. 118°50'40" W; near NE cor. sec. 5, T 15 S, R 29 E). Named on Giant Forest (1956) 15' quadrangle. The feature also had the names "Western Creek" and "Beartrap Creek" (Forest M. Clingan, personal communication, 1990).

Woodward Peak [KERN]: *peak,* 6 miles south-southwest of Alta Sierra (lat. 35°38'40" N, long. 118°34'50" W; near N line sec. 30, T 26 S, R 32 E). Named on Alta Sierra (1972) 7.5' quadrangle.

Woodworth: see **Mount Woodworth** [FRESNO].

Woody [KERN]: *village,* 25 miles north-northeast of Bakersfield (lat. 35°42'15" N, long. 118°50' W; near SE cor. sec. 34, T 25 S, R 29 E). Named on Woody (1965) 7.5' quadrangle. Postal authorities established Woody post office in 1889 (Frickstad, p. 60). The name commemorates Dr. Sparrell Walter Woody, a pioneer in the neighborhood (Bailey, 1967, p. 28). Joseph Weringer laid out a community at present Woody in 1891 and called the place Weringdale, but that name did not last (Bailey, 1962, p. 41-42).

Woody Flats [KERN]: *area,* 5.25 miles northeast of Woody along Bear Hollow Creek (lat. 35°44'40" N, long. 118°45'20" W; near NW cor. sec. 21, T 25 S, R 30 E). Named on Woody (1952) 15' quadrangle.

Wooley Canyon [FRESNO-TULARE]: *canyon,* drained by a stream that heads in Fresno County and flows about 4.5 miles to Murry Creek (1) 4 miles northeast of Auckland in Tulare County (lat. 36°37'25" N, long. 119°03'05" W; near W line sec. 16, T 15 S, R 27 E). Named on Miramonte (1966) 7.5' quadrangle.

Woollomes: see **Lake Woollomes** [KERN].

Woolstalf Creek [KERN]: *stream,* flows 7.25 miles to Kelso Creek nearly 7 miles south-southeast of Weldon (lat. 35°34'35" N, long. 118°15'05" W; sec. 17, T 27 S, R 35 E); Woolstalf Meadow is along upper reaches of the stream. Named on Woolstalf Creek (1972) 7.5' quadrangle. Called Stalf Creek on Kernville (1908) 30' quadrangle.

Woolstalf Meadow [KERN]: *area,* 10 miles south of Weldon (lat. 35°31'35" N, long. 118°19' W; on E line sec. 4, T 28 S, R 34 E). Named on Woolstalf Creek (1972) 7.5' quadrangle.

Wooten Creek [FRESNO-TULARE]: *stream,* heads in Fresno County and flows 3.5 miles to Tulare County 3 miles northeast of Orange Cove (lat. 36°39'35" N, long. 119°17' W; at S line sec. 32, T 14 S, R 25 E). The stream flows less than 2 miles in Tulare County before it reenters Fresno County near Orange Cove in an artificial watercourse. Named on Orange Cove North (1966) 7.5' quadrangle.

Worth [TULARE]: *locality,* 4.5 miles east-southeast of Porterville near an old railroad grade (lat. 36°03'10" N, long. 118°56'10" W; near S line sec. 34, T 21 S, R 28 E). Named on Success Dam (1956) 7.5' quadrangle.

Worthing [TULARE]: *locality,* 1.25 miles south-southeast of Lindsay along Southern Pacific Railroad (lat. 36°11'10" N, long. 119° 04'55" W; sec. 18, T 20 S, R 27 E). Named on Lindsay (1928) 7.5' quadrangle.

Wren Creek [FRESNO]:

(1) *stream,* flows 2.5 miles to Middle Fork Kings River 8.5 miles northeast of Hume (lat. 36°52'30" N, long. 118°48'20" W); the stream heads near Wren Peak. Named on Tehipite Dome (1952) 15' quadrangle.

(2) *stream,* flows 2.5 miles to Grizzly Creek 15 miles southwest of Marion Peak (lat. 36°49' N, long. 118°44'15" W). Named on Marion Peak (1953) and Tehipite Dome (1952) 15' quadrangles.

Wren Peak [FRESNO]: *peak,* 8 miles east-northeast of Hume (lat. 36°50'20" N, long. 118°47'30" W). Altitude 9450 feet. Named on Tehipite Dome (1952) 15' quadrangle.

Wright: see **Dick Wright Spring** [FRESNO]; **Mount Cedric Wright** [FRESNO].

Wright Creek [TULARE]: *stream,* flows 5.5 miles to Wallace Creek 5.5 miles west of Mount Whitney (lat. 36°35'20" N, long. 118°23'15" W). Named on Mount Whitney (1956) 15' quadrangle. United States Board on

Geographic Names (1933a, p. 825) rejected the name "East Fork, Kern River" for the stream, and noted that the name "Wright" commemorates Captain J.W.A. Wright, who in 1881 visited Mount Whitney with Judge William R. Wallace, for whom Wallace Creek is named.

Wright Lakes [TULARE]: *lakes,* 5 miles northwest of Mount Whitney (lat. 36°37'45" N, long. 118°21'30" W); the lakes are at the head of Wright Creek. Named on Mount Whitney (1956) 15' quadrangle. The name commemorates Captain J.W.A. Wright of Wright Creek (United States Board on Geographic Names, 1933a, p. 825).

Wright Mountain [FRESNO]: *peak,* 16 miles northwest of Coalinga (lat. 36°19'40" N, long. 120°32'10" W; near SE cor. sec. 27, T 18 S, R 13 E). Altitude 4566 feet. Named on Santa Rita Peak (1969) 7.5' quadrangle.

Wutchumna Hill [TULARE]: *hill,* 4 miles east-southeast of Woodlake (lat. 36°23'15" N, long. 119°01'55" W; sec. 3, T 18 S, R 27 E). Altitude 928 feet. Named on Woodlake (1952) 7.5' quadrangle.

Wye: see **The Wye** [TULARE].

Wyeth [TULARE]: *locality,* 7 miles east-southeast of Dinuba along Atchison, Topeka and Santa Fe Railroad (lat. 36°31'10" N, long. 119°15'50" W; sec. 21, T 16 S, R 25 E). Named on Orange Cove South (1966) 7.5' quadrangle. The name, applied in 1913 and 1914, is from the term "wye" for a place that railroad tracks join in the configuration of a letter "Y" (Gudde, 1949, p. 394).

Wygal Spring [KERN]: *spring,* 4.5 miles west of Carneros Rocks (lat. 35°27' N, long. 119°55'45" W; sec. 33, T 28 S, R 19 E). Named on Las Yeguas Ranch (1959) 7.5' quadrangle.

Wyleys Knob [KERN]: *peak,* 2.25 miles south-southwest of Skinner Peak (lat. 35°32'10" N, long. 118°08'20" W). Named on Cane Canyon (1972) 7.5' quadrangle.

Wynne: see **Mount Wynne** [FRESNO].

—X-Y—

Yankee Canyon [KERN]: *canyon,* drained by a stream that flows 1.25 miles to Isabella Lake 3.5 miles south of Wofford Heights (lat. 35°39'30" N, long. 118°26'25" W; near N line sec. 21, T 26 S, R 33 E). Named on Lake Isabella North (1972) 7.5' quadrangle.

Yaqui: see **Juan Yaqui Spring** [KERN].

Yates Hot Springs [KERN]: *springs,* 5.25 miles west-southwest of Piute Peak near Walker Basin Creek (lat. 35°25'55" N, long. 118° 28'55" W; sec. 6, T 29 S, R 33 E). Named on Piute Peak (1972) 7.5' quadrangle. Called Yates Hot Spring on Emerald Mountain (1943) 15' quadrangle. United States Board on Geographic Names (1975b, p. 12) gave the singular form "Yates Hot Spring" as a variant name.

Yeguas Creek [KERN]: *stream,* heads in San Luis Obispo County and flows 4.25 miles in Kern County before reentering San Luis Obispo County 8.5 miles west of Carneros Rocks (lat. 35°27' N, long. 119°59'45" W; at W line sec. 36, T 28 S, R 18 E). Named on Las Yeguas Ranch (1959) 7.5' quadrangle. Arnold and Johnson (p. 21) called the feature Los Yeguas Creek, and noted that many brood mares were pastured about the head of the stream—*yeguas* means "mares" in Spanish.

Yeguas Mountain [KERN]: *ridge,* generally southeast-trending, 4.5 miles long, 17 miles south-southeast of Orchard Peak (lat. 35°30'30" N, long. 120°01'30" W). Named on La Panza NE (1966) and Packwood Creek (1961) 7.5' quadrangles.

Yellow Aster Mill [KERN]: *locality,* 6.25 miles northwest of Randsburg near the mouth of Goler Canyon (lat. 35°25'15" N, long. 117° 44'50" W; near S line sec. 12, T 29 S, R 39 E). Ruins named on El Paso Peaks (1967) 7.5' quadrangle.

Yellow Jacket Canyon [TULARE]: *canyon,* drained by a stream that flows 1.25 miles to Bear Trap Canyon nearly 4 miles south-southwest of California Hot Springs (lat. 35°49'55" N, long. 118°42'25" W; at N line sec. 23, T 24 S, R 30 E). Named on California Hot Springs (1958) 15' quadrangle.

Yellow Jacket Spring [KERN]: *spring,* 2 miles north of Skinner Peak (lat. 35°35'40" N, long. 118°07'35" W). Named on Cane Canyon (1972) 7.5' quadrangle.

Yenis Hante: see **Camp Yenis Hante** [KERN].

Yettem [TULARE]: *settlement,* 11 miles north of Visalia (lat. 36°29'10" N, long. 119°15'30" W; on S line sec. 33, T 16 S, R 25 E). Named on Monson (1949) 7.5' quadrangle. The Reverend Jenanyan gave the name in 1902 to an Armenian settlement—*yettem* means "paradise" in Armenian (Gudde, 1949, p. 395). Postal authorities established Yettem post office in 1905 (Frickstad, p. 214). The place is in what has been called the Churchill district (Mitchell, A.R., p. 71). Postal authorities established Churchill post office, named for Enos Churchill, first postmaster, in 1881 and discontinued it in 1887 (Salley, p. 43-44). They established Townsend post office 8 miles southeast of Churchill post office in 1879 and discontinued it in 1887; the name was for Homer C. Townsend, first postmaster (Salley, p. 223-224).

Yettem Station: see **Calgro** [TULARE].

Yokohl [TULARE]: *locality,* 4 miles northeast of Exeter along Visalia Electric Railroad (lat. 36°19'30" N, long. 119°04'50" W; at SE cor. sec. 30, T 18 S, R 27 E); the place is near the rail crossing of Yokohl Creek. Named on Rocky Hill (1951) 7.5' quadrangle.

Yokohl Creek [TULARE]: *stream,* flows 17 miles to lowlands 4 miles east-northeast of Exeter (lat. 36°19'30" N, long. 119°04'45" W; near NW cor. sec. 32, T 18 S, R 27 E); the stream goes through Yokohl Valley. Named on Exeter (1952), Kaweah (1957), and Springville (1957) 15' quadrangles.

Yokohl Valley [TULARE]: *valley,* 5 miles east of Exeter (lat. 36° 16' N, long. 119°01'30" W); the valley is along lower reaches of Yokohl Creek. Named on Exeter (1952), Kaweah (1957), and Springville (1957) 15' quadrangles. The name is from an Indian tribe of the region (Kroeber, p. 67).

Yosemite Soda Spring: see **Little Yosemite Soda Spring**, under **Kern Lake** [TULARE].

Young: see **Mount Young** [TULARE]; **Nobe Young Creek** [TULARE]; **Nobe Young Meadow** [TULARE].

Yucca: see **Muroc** [KERN].

Yucca Creek [TULARE]: *stream,* flows 8 miles to North Fork Kaweah River 2.5 miles southwest of Yucca Mountain (lat. 36°32'45" N, long. 118°53'45" W; sec. 12, T 16 S, R 28 E). Named on Giant Forest (1956) 15' quadrangle. United States Board on Geographic Names (1933a, p. 831) rejected the name "Cactus Creek" for the stream.

Yucca Mountain [TULARE]: *peak,* 29 miles northeast of Visalia (lat. 36°34'15" N, long. 118°52'10" W; near S line sec. 31, T 15 S, R 29 E); the peak is at the southwest end of Yucca Ridge. Altitude 4927 feet. Named on Giant Forest (1956) 15' quadrangle. United States Board on Geographic Names (1933a, p. 831) rejected the name "Cactus Mountain" for the feature.

Yucca Point [FRESNO]: *relief feature,* 3.5 miles northeast of Hume (lat. 36°49'30" N, long. 118°52'20" W). Named on Tehipite Dome (1952) 15' quadrangle.

Yucca Ridge [TULARE]: *ridge,* extends 3 miles northeast and north from Yucca Mountain (lat. 36°35' N, long. 118°51'15" W). Named on Giant Forest (1956) 15' quadrangle. United States Board on Geographic Names (1933a, p. 831) rejected the name "Cactus Ridge" for the feature.

—Z—

Zante [TULARE]: *locality,* 3.5 miles north-northwest of Porterville along Southern Pacific Railroad (lat. 36°06'55" N, long. 119°02'40" W; sec. 10, T 21 S, R 27 E). Named on Porterville (1951) 7.5' quadrangle. California Mining Bureau's (1917b) map shows a place called Lithmore located along the railroad about halfway from Zante to Kurth.

Zapato Canyon: see **Zapato Chino Canyon** [FRESNO].

Zapato Chino Canyon [FRESNO]: *canyon,* 14 miles long, drained by Zapato Chino Creek, which enters lowlands 9 miles east-southeast of Coalinga (lat. 36°04'10" N, long. 120°13'45" W). Named on Kreyenhagen Hills (1956), Parkfield (1961), and The Dark Hole (1961) 7.5' quadrangles. Called Zapato Canyon on Cholame (1917) and Coalinga (1912) 30' quadrangles, but United States Board on Geographic Names (1964c, p. 16) rejected the names "Zapato Canyon" and "Zapatos Canyon" for the feature.

Zapato Chino Creek [FRESNO]: *stream,* flows 14 miles to lowlands 9 miles east-southeast of Coalinga (lat. 36°04'10" N, long. 120°13'45" W; sec. 27, T 21 S, R 16 E). Named on Avenal (1954), Guijarral Hills (1956), Kreyenhagen Hills (1956), and The Dark Hole (1961) 7.5' quadrangles. Called Zapato Creek on Coalinga (1912) 30' quadrangle, but United States Board on Geographic Names (1964c, p. 17) rejected the names "Zapato Creek" and "Zapatos Creek."

Zapato Creek: see **Zapato Chino Creek** [FRESNO].

Zapato Creek, West Fork: see **Arroyo Pinoso** [FRESNO].

Zapatos Canyon: see **Zapato Chino Canyon** [FRESNO].

Zapatos Creek: see **Zapato Chino Creek** [FRESNO]

Zebe Creek [FRESNO]: *stream,* flows 3.5 miles to Pine Flat Reservoir 4.25 miles northeast of Tivy Mountain (lat. 36°50'20" N, long. 119°18'05" W; near S line sec. 36, T 12 S, R 24 E). Named on Pine Flat Dam (1965) 7.5' quadrangle.

Zediker [FRESNO]: *locality,* 11 miles east-southeast of Clovis along Atchison, Topeka and Santa Fe Railroad (lat. 36°45'25" N, long. 119°31'15" W; near E line sec. 36, T 13 S, R 22 E). Named on Round Mountain (1964) 7.5' quadrangle.

Zemorra Creek [KERN]: *stream,* flows 2.5 miles to Chico Martinez Creek 2 miles southeast of Carneros Rocks (lat. 35°25'10" N, long. 119°49' W; sec. 10, T 29 S, R 20 E). Named on Carneros Rocks (1959) 7.5' quadrangle.

Zentner [KERN]: *locality,* 3.5 miles east-northeast of McFarland along Southern Pacific Railroad (lat. 35°42'10" N, long. 119°10'05" W; at NE cor. sec. 4, T 26 S, R 26 E). Named on McFarland (1954) 7.5' quadrangle.

Zumwalt Meadows [FRESNO]: *area,* 12 miles south-southwest of Marion Peak in Kings Canyon (lat. 36°47'30" N, long. 118°35'40" W). Named on Marion Peak (1953) 15' quadrangle. The name is for Daniel Kindle Zumwalt, former owner of the place and a conservation leader in the creation of Sequoia and General Grant National Parks (Hanna, p. 364).

Zwang Peak: see **Avenal** [KINGS]

South San Joaquin Valley Region
Fresno, Kern, Kings and Tulare Counties

References Cited

BOOKS AND ARTICLES

Alder, Pat. 1963. *Mineral King guide.* Glendale, California: La Siesta Press, 36 p.

Anderson, Frank M. 1905. "A stratigraphic study in the Mount Diablo Range of California." *Proceedings of the California Academy of Sciences* (series 3), v. II, no. 2, p. 156-248.

Anderson, Robert, and Pack, Robert W. 1915. *Geology and oil resources of the west border of the San Joaquin Valley north of Coalinga, California.* (United States Geological Survey Bulletin 603.) Washington: Government Printing Office, 220 p.

Angel, Myron. 1890a. "San Luis Obispo County." *Tenth annual report of the State Mineralogist, for the year ending December 1, 1890.* Sacramento: California State Mining Bureau, p. 567-585.

_____1890b. "Tulare County." *Tenth annual report of the State Mineralogist, for the year ending December 1, 1890.* Sacramento: California State Mining Bureau, p. 728-733.

Arnold, Ralph, and Anderson, Robert. 1908. *Preliminary report on the Coalinga oil district, Fresno and Kings Counties, California.* (United States Geological Survey Bulletin 357.) Washington: Government Printing Office, 142 p.

_____1910. *Geology and oil resources of the Coalinga district, California.* (United States Geological Survey Bulletin 398.) Washington: Government Printing Office, 354 p.

Arnold, Ralph, and Johnson, Harry R. 1910. *Preliminary report on the McKittrick-Sunset oil region, Kern and San Luis Obispo Counties, California.* (United States Geological Survey Bulletin 406.) Washington: Government Printing Office, 225 p.

Bailey, Richard C. 1962. *Explorations in Kern.* Bakersfield, California: Kern County Historical Society, 81 p.

_____1963. "To Claraville and the Burning Moscow mine." *Desert Magazine*, v. 26, no. 7, p. 12-15, 137.

_____1967. *Kern County place names.* Bakersfield, California: Kern County Historical Society, 28 p.

Baker, Charles Laurence. 1911. "Notes on the later Cenozoic history of the Mohave Desert region in southeastern California." *University of California Publications, Bulletin of the Department of Geology,* v. 6, no. 15, p. 333-383.

Bancroft, Hubert Howe. 1888. *History of California, Volume VI, 1848-1859.* San Francisco: The History Company, Publishers, 787 p.

Barker, John. 1955. *San Joaquin vignettes, The reminiscences of Captain John Barker.* Bakersfield, California: Kern County Historical Society, 111 p.

Barras, Judy. 1976. *The long road to Tehachapi.* Tehachapi, California: (Author), 231 p.

Berkstresser, C.F., Jr. 1968. *Data for springs in the Southern Coast, Transverse, and Peninsular Ranges of California.* (United States Geological Survey, Water Resources Division, Open-file report.) Menlo Park, California, 21 p. + appendices.

Birnie, R., Jr. 1876. "Executive report of Lieutenant R. Birnie, Jr., Thirteenth United States Infantry, on the operations of party no. 2, California section, field-season of 1875." *Annual report upon the geographical surveys west of the one hundredth meridian, in California, Nevada, Utah, Colorado, Wyoming, New Mexico, Arizona, and Montana.* (Appendix JJ of *The Annual Report of the Chief of Engineers for 1876.*) Washington: Government Printing Office, p. 130-135.

Blake, William P. 1856. "On the rate of evaporation on the Tulare Lakes of California." *American Journal of Science and Arts* (series 2), v. 21, no. 63, p. 365-368.

_____1857. "Geological report." *Reports of explorations and surveys, to ascertain the most practicable and economical route for a railroad from the Mississippi River to the Pacific Ocean.* Volume V, Part II. (33d Cong., 2d Sess., Sen. Ex. Doc. No. 78.) Washington: Beverley Tucker, Printer, 370 p.

Boyd, William Harland. 1972. *A California middle border; The Kern River country, 1772-1880.* Richardson, Texas: The Havilah Press, 226 p.

Bradley, Walter W. 1915. "Fresno County." *Report XIV of the State Mineralogist.* Sacramento: California State Mining Bureau, p. 429-470.

Brewer, William H. 1949. *Up and down California in 1860-1864.* (Edited by Francis P. Farquhar.) Berkeley and Los Angeles: University of California Press, 583 p.

Brown, G. Chester. 1915. "Kern County." *Report XIV of the State Mineralogist.* Sacramento, California: California State Mining Bureau, p. 471-523.

Browning, Peter. 1986. *Place names of the Sierra Nevada.* Berkeley: Wilderness Press, 253 p.

California Division of Highways. 1934. *California highway transportation survey, 1934.* Sacramento: Department of Public Works, Division of Highways, 130 p. + appendices.

Campbell, Marius R. 1902. *Reconnaissance of the borax deposits of Death Valley and Mohave Desert..* (United States Geological Survey Bulletin 200.) Washington: Government Printing Office, 23 p.

Carson, James H. 1950. *Recollections of the California mines.* Oakland, California: Biobooks, 113 p.

Chalfant, W.A.. 1933. *The story of Inyo.* (Revised edition.) (Author), 430 p.

Cowan, Robert G. 1956. *Ranchos of California.* Fresno, California: Academy Library Guild, 151 p.

Coy, Owen C. 1923. *California county boundaries.* Berkeley: California Historical Survey Commission, 335 p.

Cullimore, Clarence. 1949. *Old adobes of forgotten Fort Tejon.* (Second printing, revised and enlarged.) Bakersfield, California: Kern County Historical Society, 93 p.

Darling, Curtis. 1988. *Kern County place names.* (No place): Kern County Historical Society, 135 p.

Davidson, J.W. 1976. *The expedition of Capt. J.W. Davidson from Fort Tejon to the Owens Valley in 1859.* (Edited by Philip J. Wilke and Harry W. Lawton.) Socorro, New Mexico: Ballena Press, 55 p.

Davis, G.H., Green, J.H., Olmsted, F.H., and Brown, D.W. 1959. *Ground-water conditions and storage capacity in the San Joaquin Valley, California.* (United States Geological Survey Water-Supply Paper 1469.) Washington: Government Printing Office, 287 p.

Derby, Geo. H. 1852. "A report of the Tulare valley." *Report of the Secretary of War.* (32d Cong., 1st Sess., Sen. Ex. Doc. 110.) 17 p.

Dillon, Richard H. 1960. *La Panza.* San Francisco: Printed for private circulation by the Grabhorn Press, 12 p.

Eccleston, Robert. 1957. *The Mariposa Indian War, 1850-1851.* (Edited by C. Gregory Crampton.) Salt Lake City: University of Utah Press, 168 p.

Fairbanks, Harold W. 1894a. "Red Rock, Goler, and Summit mining districts, in Kern County." *Twelfth report of the State Mineralogist, (Second Biennial,) two years ending September 15, 1894.* Sacramento: California State Mining Bureau, p. 456-458.

_____1894b. "Geology of northern Ventura, Santa Barbara, San Luis Obispo, Monterey, and San Benito Counties." *Twelfth report of the State Mineralogist, (Second Biennial,) two years ending September 15, 1894.* Sacramento: California State Mining Bureau, p. 493-526.

_____1897. "An interesting case of contact metamorphism." *American Journal of Science* (series 4), v. 4, no. 19, p. 36-38.

Farquhar, Francis P. 1923. "Place names of the High Sierra [Part I]." *Sierra Club Bulletin*, v. 11, no. 4, p. 380-407.

_____1924. "Place names of the High Sierra, Part II." *Sierra Club Bulletin*, v. 12, no. 1, p. 47-64.

_____1925. "Place names of the High Sierra, Part III." *Sierra Club Bulletin*, v. 12, no. 2, p. 126-147.

_____1926. "Mountaineering notes." *Sierra Club Bulletin*, v. 12, no. 3, p. 304-307.

Franks, Kenny A., and Lambert, Paul F. 1985. *Early California oil, A photographic history, 1865-1940.* College Station: Texas A&M University Press, 243 p.

Frazer, Robert W. 1965 *Forts of the West.* Norman: University of Oklahoma Press, 246 p.

Fremont, J.C. 1845. *Report of the exploring expedition to the Rocky Moun-*

tains in the year 1842, and to Oregon and North California in the years 1843-'44. Washington: Blair and Rives, Printers, 583 p.

Frickstad, Walter N. 1955. *A century of California post offices, 1848 to 1954.* Oakland, California: Philatelic Research Society, 395 p.

Gale, Hoyt S. 1914. "Salines in the Owens, Searles, and Panamint basins, southeastern California." *Contributions to economic geology, 1913.* (United States Geological Survey Bulletin 580-L.) Washington: Government Printing Office, p. 251-323.

Gist, Brooks D. 1976. *Empire out of the tules.* Tulare, California: (Author), 234 p.

Goodyear, W.A. 1888a. "Kern County." *Eighth annual report of the State Mineralogist, for the year ending October 1, 1888.* Sacramento: California State Mining Bureau, p. 309-324.

_____1888b. "Tulare County." *Eighth annual report of the State Mineralogist, for the year ending October 1, 1888.* Sacramento: California State Mining Bureau, p. 643-652.

Grunsky, Carl Ewald. 1898. *Irrigation near Fresno, California.* (United States Geological Survey Water-Supply and Irrigation Papers No. 18.) Washington: Government Printing Office, 94 p.

Gudde, Erwin G. 1949. *California place names.* Berkeley and Los Angeles: University of California Press, 431 p.

_____1969. *California place names.* Berkeley and Los Angeles: University of California Press, 416 p.

_____1975. *California gold camps.* Berkeley, Los Angeles, London: University of California Press, 467 p.

Hamlin, Homer. 1904. *Water resources of the Salinas Valley, California.* (United States Geological Survey Water-Supply and Irrigation Paper No. 89.) Washington: Government Printing Office, 91 p.

Hanna, Phil Townsend. 1951. *The dictionary of California land names.* Los Angeles: The Automobile Club of Southern California, 392 p.

Harpending, Asbury. 1913. *The great diamond hoax and other stirring incidents in the life of Asbury Harpending.* San Francisco: The James H. Berry Co., 283 p.

Hart, Herbert M. 1965. *Old forts of the Far West.* New York: Bonanza Books, 192 p.

Hart, James D. 1978. *A companion to California.* New York: Oxford University Press, 504 p.

Hensher, Alan, and Peskin, Jack. 1980. *Ghost towns of the Kern and eastern Sierra, A concise guide.* Los Angeles: (Authors), 32 p.

Hess, Frank L. 1910. "Gold mining in the Randsburg quadrangle, California." *Contributions to economic geology, 1911.* (United States Geological Survey Bulletin 430-A.) Washington: Government Printing Office, p. 23-47.

Hoover, Mildred Brooke, Rensch, Hero Eugene, and Rensch, Ethel Grace. 1966. *Historic spots in California.* (Third edition, revised by William N. Abeloe.) Stanford, California: Stanford University Press, 642 p.

Jackson, Louise A. 1988. *Beulah, A biography of the Mineral King Valley of California.* Tucson, Arizona: Westernlore Press, 179 p.

Johnson, Harry R. 1911. *Water resources of Antelope Valley, California.* (United States Geological Survey Water-Supply Paper 278.) Washington: Government Printing Office, 92 p.

Johnston, Hank. 1966. *They felled the redwoods.* Corona del Mar, California: Trans-Anglo Books, 160 p.

Joy, Douglas A. 1876. "San Emidio district, California." *Annual report upon the geographical surveys west of the one hundredth meridian, in California, Nevada, Utah, Colorado, Wyoming, New Mexico, Arizona, and Montana.* (Appendix JJ of *The Annual Report of the Chief of Engineers for 1876.*) Washington: Government Printing Office, p. 51-52.

Kahrl, William L. 1982. *Water and power, The conflict over Los Angeles' water supply in the Owens Valley.* Berkeley, Los Angeles, London: University of California Press, 583 p.

Kaiser, William. 1977. "The Kaweah co-operative colony—A geographical appraisal of nineteenth century socialism in the mountains." *The California Geographer,* v. 17, p. 63-72.

Kip, Leonard. 1946. *California sketches, with recollections of the gold mines.* Los Angeles: N.A. Kovach, 58 p.

Kroeber, A.L. 1916. "California place names of Indian origin." *University of California Publications in American Archæology and Ethnology,* v. 12, no. 2, p. 31-69.

Laizure, C. McK. 1929. "San Francisco field division (Fresno and Lake Counties)." *Mining in California,* v. 25, no. 3, p. 301-365.

Latta, Frank F. 1949. *Black gold in the Joaquin.* Caldwell, Idaho: The Caxton Printers, 344 p.

_____1976. *Saga of Rancho El Tejon.* Santa Cruz, California: Bear State Books, 293 p.

Lee, Charles H. 1912. "Ground water resources of Indian Wells Valley, California." *Report of the Conservation Commission of the State of California to the Governor and Legislature of California.* Sacramento, California: Superintendent of State Printing, p. 401-429.

Lippincott, Joseph Barlow. 1902. *Storage of water on Kings River, California.* (United States Geological Survey Water-Supply and Irrigation Paper No. 58.) Washington: Government Printing Office, 101 p.

Lyman, C.S. 1849. "Observations on California." *American Journal of Science and Arts* (series 2), v. 7, no. 20, p. 290-292, 305-309.

Marsh, Owen T. 1960. *Geology of the Orchard Peak area, California.* (California Division of Mines Special Report 62.) San Francisco: California Division of Mines, 42 p.

Mendenhall, Walter C. 1908. *Preliminary report on the ground waters of San Joaquin Valley, California.* (United States Geological Survey Water-Supply Paper 222.) Washington: Government Printing Office, 52 p.

_____1909. *Some desert watering places in southeastern California and southwestern Nevada.* (United States Geological Survey Water-Supply Paper 224.) Washington: Government Printing Office, 98 p.

Mendenhall, W.C., Dole, R.B., and Stabler, Herman. 1916. *Ground water in San Joaquin Valley, California.* (United States Geological Survey Water-Supply Paper 398.) Washington: Government Printing Office, 310 p.

Mitchell, Annie R. 1972. *Land of the tules.* Fresno, California: Valley Publishers, 80 p.

Mitchell, Edward. 1965. *History of research at Sharktooth Hill, Kern County, California.* Bakersfield, California: Kern County Historical Society, 48 p.

Neal, Howard. 1974. "The mines of Rand." *Desert,* v. 37, no. 5, p. 12-15, 34-35.

Olmsted, Frank H. 1901. "Physical characteristics of Kern River, California, with special reference to electric power development." *Reconnaissance of Kern and Yuba Rivers, California.* (United States Geological Survey Water-Supply and Irrigation Paper No. 46.) Washington: Government Printing Office, p. 11-38.

Ormsby, Waterman L. 1968. *The Butterfield Overland Mail.* San Marino, California: The Huntington Library, 179 p.

Preston, William L. 1981. *Vanishing landscapes, Land and life in the Tulare Lake basin.* Berkeley, Los Angeles, London: University of California Press, 278 p.

Redinger, David H. 1949. *The story of Big Creek.* Los Angeles, California: Angelus Press, 182 p.

Rintoul, William. 1978. *Oildorado.* Santa Cruz, California: Valley Publishers, 241 p.

Ristow, Walter N. 1970. "A covey of names." *Surveying and Mapping,* v. 30, no. 3, p. 419-426.

Salley, H.E. 1977. *History of California post offices, 1849-1976.* La Mesa, California: Postal History Associates, Inc., 300 p.

Schumacher, Genny (editor). 1962. *Deepest Valley.* San Francisco: Sierra Club, 206 p.

Settle, Glen A. 1963. *Here roamed the antelope.* Rosamond, California: The Kern-Antelope Historical Society, Inc., 64 p.

Smith, Jedediah S. 1977. *The southwest expedition of Jedediah S. Smith, His personal account of the journey to California, 1826-1827.* (Edited by George R. Brooks.) Glendale, California: The Arthur H. Clark Company, 259 p.

Smith, Genny (editor). 1976. *Mammoth Lakes Sierra.* (Fourth edition.) Palo Alto, California: Genny Smith Books, 147 p.

Stewart, George R. 1970. *American place-names, A concise and selective dictionary for the continental United States of America.* New York: Oxford University Press, 550 p.

Teilman, I., and Shafer, W.H. 1943. *The historical story of irrigation in Fresno and Kings Counties in central California.* Fresno, California: (Authors), 55 p.

Thompson, David G. 1921. *Routes to desert watering places in the Mohave Desert region, California.* (United States Geological Survey Water-Supply Paper 490-B.) Washington: Government Printing Office, p. 87-269.

_____1929. *The Mohave Desert region, California.* (United States Geological Survey Water-Supply Paper 578.) Washington: Government Printing Office, 759 p.

Thompson, Thomas H. 1892. *Official historical atlas of Tulare County:* Tulare, California: Thos. H. Thompson, 147 p. (Reprinted in 1973 by Limited Editions of Visalia, Inc.)

Troxel, B.W., and Morton, P.K. 1962. *Mines and mineral resources of Kern County, California.* (California Division of Mines and Geology County Report 1.) San Francisco: California Division of Mines and Geology, 370 p.

Tucker, W. Burling. 1919. "Tulare County." *Report XV of the State Mineralogist.* Sacramento: California State Mining Bureau, p. 900-954.

United States Board on Geographic Names (under name "United States Geographic Board"). 1933a. *Sixth report of the United States Geographic Board, 1890 to 1932.* Washington: Government Printing Office, 834 p.

_____(under name "United States Geographic Board"). 1933b. *Decisions of the United States Geographic Board, No. 20—Decisions October 5, 1932.* Washington: Government Printing Office, 29 p.

____ (under name "United States Geographic Board"). 1934. *Decisions of the United States Geographic Board, No. 34—Decisions June 1933-March 1934.* Washington: Government Printing Office, 20 p.

_____ (under name "United States Board on Geographical Names"). 1936. *Decisions of the United States Board on Geographical Names, Decisions rendered between July 1, 1934, and June 30, 1935*. Washington: Government Printing Office, 26 p.

_____(under name "United States Board on Geographical Names"). 1937. *Decisions of the United States Board on Geographical Names, Decisions rendered between July 1, 1936, and June 30, 1937*. Washington: Government Printing Office, 33 p.

_____(under name "United States Board on Geographical Names"). 1938. *Decisions of the United States Board on Geographical Names, Decisions rendered between July 1, 1937, and June 30, 1938*. Washington: Government Printing Office, 62 p.

_____(under name "United States Board on Geographical Names"). 1939. *Decisions of the United States Board on Geographical Names, Decisions rendered between July 1, 1938, and June 30, 1939*. Washington: Government Printing Office, 41 p.

_____1946 (under name "United States Board on Geographical Names"). *Decision lists nos. 4604, 4605, 4606, April, May, June, 1946*. Washington: Department of the Interior, 9 p.

_____1949a. *Decision lists nos. 4905, 4906, May, June, 1949*. Washington: Department of the Interior, 10 p.

_____1949b. *Decision lists nos. 4907, 4908, 4909, July, August, September, 1949*. Washington: Department of the Interior, 24 p.

_____1954. *Decisions on names in the United States, Alaska and Puerto Rico, Decisions rendered from July 1950 to May 1954*. (Decision list no. 5401.) Washington: Department of the Interior, 115 p.

_____1959. *Decisions on names in the United States, Puerto Rico and the Virgin Islands, Decisions rendered from April 1957 through December 1958*. (Decision list no. 5901.) Washington: Department of the Interior, 100 p.

_____1960a. *Decisions on names in the United States, Decisions rendered from September 1959 through December 1959*. (Decision list no. 5904.) Washington: Department of the Interior, 68 p.

_____1960b. *Decisions on names in the United States and the Virgin Islands, Decisions rendered from May 1960 through August 1960*. (Decision list no. 6002.) Washington: Department of the Interior, 77 p.

_____1961a. *Decisions on names in the United States, Decisions rendered from September through December 1960*. (Decision list no. 6003.) Washington: Department of the Interior, 73 p.

_____1961b. *Decisions on names in the United States, Decisions rendered from January through April 1961*. (Decision list no. 6101.) Washington: Department of the Interior, 74 p.

_____1962. *Decisions on names in the United States, Decisions rendered from September through December 1961*. (Decision list no. 6103.) Washington: Department of the Interior, 75 p.

_____1963. *Decisions on geographic names in the United States, January through April 1963*. (Decision list no. 6301.) Washington: Department of the Interior, 78 p.

_____1964a. *Decisions on geographic names in the United States, September through December 1963*. (Decision list no. 6303.) Washington: Department of the Interior, 66 p.

_____1964b. *Decisions on geographic names in the United States, January through April 1964*. (Decision list no. 6401.) Washington: Department of the Interior, 74 p.

_____1964c. *Decisions on geographic names in the United States, May through August 1964*. (Decision list no. 6402.) Washington: Department of the Interior, 85 p.

_____1965a. *Decisions on geographic names in the United States, September through December 1964*. (Decision list no. 6403.) Washington: Department of the Interior, 66 p.

_____1965b. *Decisions on geographic names in the United States, January through March 1965*. (Decision list no. 6501.) Washington: Department of the Interior, 85 p.

_____1965c. *Decisions on geographic names in the United States, April through June 1965*. (Decision list no. 6502.) Washington: Department of the Interior, 39 p.

_____1965d. *Decisions on geographic names in the United States, July through September 1965*. (Decision list no. 6503.) Washington: Department of the Interior, 74 p.

_____1966a. *Decisions on geographic names in the United States, January through March 1966*. (Decision list no. 6601.) Washington: Department of the Interior, 44 p.

_____1966b. *Decisions on geographic names in the United States, April through June 1966*. (Decision list no. 6602.) Washington: Department of the Interior, 36 p.

_____1967a. *Decisions on geographic names in the United States, July through September 1966*. (Decision list no. 6603.) Washington: Department of the Interior, 38 p.

_____1967b. *Decisions on geographic names in the United States, January through March 1967*. (Decision list no. 6701.) Washington: Department of the Interior, 20 p.

_____1967c. *Decisions on geographic names in the United States, April through June 1967*. (Decision list no. 6702.) Washington: Department of the Interior, 26 p.

_____1967d. *Decisions on geographic names in the United States, July through September 1967*. (Decision list no. 6703.) Washington: Department of the Interior, 29 p.

_____1968a. *Decisions on geographic names in the United States, October through December 1967*. (Decision list no. 6704.) Washington: Department of the Interior, 46 p.

_____1968b. *Decisions on geographic names in the United States, January through March 1968*. (Decision list no. 6801.) Washington: Department of the Interior, 51 p.

_____1968c. *Decisions on geographic names in the United States, April through June 1968*. (Decision list no. 6802.) Washington: Department of the Interior, 42 p.

_____1969a. *Decisions on geographic names in the United States, January through March 1969*. (Decision list no. 6901.) Washington: Department of the Interior, 31 p.

_____1969b. *Decisions on geographic names in the United States, April through June 1969*. (Decision list no. 6902.) Washington: Department of the Interior, 28 p.

_____1969c. *Decisions on geographic names in the United States, July through September 1969*. (Decision list no. 6903.) Washington: Department of the Interior, 36 p.

_____1970a. *Decisions on geographic names in the United States, April through June 1970*. (Decision list no. 7002.) Washington: Department of the Interior, 20 p.

_____1970b. *Decisions on geographic names in the United States, July through September 1970*. (Decision list no. 7003.) Washington: Department of the Interior, 15 p.

_____1971a. *Decisions on geographic names in the United States, October through December, 1970*. (Decision list no. 7004.) Washington: Department of the Interior, 28 p.

_____1971b. *Decisions on geographic names in the United States, July through September 1971*. (Decision list no. 7103.) Washington: Department of the Interior, 18 p.

_____1972a. *Decisions on geographic names in the United States, January through March 1972*. (Decision list no. 7201.) Washington: Department of the Interior, 32 p.

_____1972b. *Decisions on geographic names in the United States, July through September 1972*. (Decision list no. 7203.) Washington: Department of the Interior, 17 p.

_____1973a. *Decisions on geographic names in the United States, April through June 1973*. (Decision list no. 7302.) Washington: Department of the Interior, 16 p.

_____1973b. *Decisions on geographic names in the United States, July through September 1973*. (Decision list no. 7303.) Washington: Department of the Interior, 14 p.

_____1974a. *Decisions on geographic names in the United States, October through December 1973*. (Decision list no. 7304.) Washington: Department of the Interior, 15 p.

_____1974b. *Decisions on geographic names in the United States, July through September 1974*. (Decision list no. 7403.) Washington: Department of the Interior, 34 p.

_____1975a. *Decisions on geographic names in the United States, October through December 1974*. (Decision list no. 7404.) Washington: Department of the Interior, 32 p.

_____1975b. *Decisions on geographic names in the United States, January through March 1975*. (Decision list no. 7501.) Washington: Department of the Interior, 36 p.

_____1975c. *Decisions on geographic names in the United States, July through September 1975*. (Decision list no. 7503.) Washington: Department of the Interior, 33 p.

_____1976a. *Decisions on geographic names in the United States, October through December, 1975*. (Decision list no. 7504.) Washington: Department of the Interior, 45 p.

_____1976b. *Decisions on geographic names in the United States, July through September 1976*. (Decision list no. 7603.) Washington: Department of the Interior, 25 p.

_____1978a. *Decisions on geographic names in the United States, January through March 1978*. (Decision list no. 7801.) Washington: Department of the Interior, 18 p.

_____1978b. *Decisions on geographic names in the United States, April through June 1978*. (Decision list no. 7802.) Washington: Department of the Interior, 30 p.

_____1978c. *Decisions on geographic names in the United States, July through September 1978*. (Decision list no. 7803.) Washington: Department of the Interior, 32 p.

_____1978d. *Decisions on geographic names in the United States, October through December 1978*. (Decision list no. 7804.) Washington: Department of the Interior, 48 p.

_____1980. *Decisions on geographic names in the United States, April through June 1980*. (Decision list no. 8002.) Washington: Department of

the Interior, 33 p.

_____1981a. *Decisions on geographic names in the United States, October through December 1980.* (Decision list no. 8004.) Washington: Department of the Interior, 21 p.

_____1981b. *Decisions on geographic names in the United States, January through March 1981.* (Decision list no. 8101.) Washington: Department of the Interior, 23 p.

_____1981c. *Decisions on geographic names in the United States, July through September 1981.* (Decision list no. 8103.) Washington: Department of the Interior, 20 p.

_____1982a. *Decisions on geographic names in the United States, October through December 1981.* (Decision list no. 8104.) Washington: Department of the Interior, 26 p.

_____1982b. *Decisions on geographic names in the United States, January through March 1982.* (Decision list no. 8201.) Washington: Department of the Interior, 17 p.

_____1983a. *Decisions on geographic names in the United States, July through September 1982.* (Decision list no. 8203.) Washington: Department of the Interior, 25 p.

_____1983b. *Decisions on geographic names in the United States, January through March 1983.* (Decision list no. 8301.) Washington: Department of the Interior, 33 p.

_____1983c. *Decisions on geographic names in the United States, April through June 1983.* (Decision list no. 8302.) Washington: Department of the Interior, 29 p.

_____1983d. *Decisions on geographic names in the United States, October through December 1983.* (Decision list no. 8304.) Washington: Department of the Interior, 20 p.

_____1984a. *Decisions on geographic names in the United States, July through September 1984.* (Decision list no. 8403.) Washington: Department of the Interior, 10 p.

_____1984b. *Decisions on geographic names in the United States, October through December 1984.* (Decision list no. 8404.) Washington: Department of the Interior, 18 p.

_____1985a. *Decisions on geographic names in the United States, January through March 1985.* (Decision list no. 8501.) Washington: Department of the Interior, 18 p.

_____1985b. *Decisions on geographic names in the United States, April through June 1985.* (Decision list no. 8502.) Washington: Department of the Interior, 12 p.

_____1985c. *Decisions on geographic names in the United States, October through December 1985.* (Decision list no. 8504.) Washington: Department of the Interior, 12 p.

_____1986. *Decisions on geographic names in the United States, October through December 1986.* (Decision list no. 8604.) Washington: Department of the Interior, 22 p.

_____1987a. *Decisions on geographic names in the United States, April through June 1987.* (Decision list no. 8702.) Washington: Department of the Interior, 17 p.

_____1987b. *Decisions on geographic names in the United States, October through December 1987.* (Decision list no. 8704.) Washington: Department of the Interior, 15 p.

_____1988a. *Decisions on geographic names in the United States, January through March 1988.* (Decision list no. 8801.) Washington: Department of the Interior, 16 p.

_____1988b. *Decisions on geographic names in the United States, April through June 1988.* (Decision list no. 8802.) Washington: Department of the Interior, 19 p.

_____1989a. *Decisions on geographic names in the United States, January through March 1989.* (Decision list no. 8901.) Washington: Department of the Interior, 9 p.

_____1989b. *Decisions on geographic names in the United States, July through September 1989.* (Decision list no. 8903.) Washington: Department of the Interior, 10 p.

_____1989c. *Decisions on geographic names in the United States, October through December 1989.* (Decision list no. 8904.) Washington: Department of the Interior, 9 p.

_____1990. *Decisions on geographic names in the United States.* (Decision list 1990.) Washington: Department of the Interior, 35 p.

_____1991. *Decisions on geographic names in the United States.* (Decision list 1991.) Washington: Department of the Interior, 40 p.

Versteeg, Chester. 1923. "The peaks and passes of the Upper Basin, South Fork of the Kings River." *Sierra Club Bulletin*, v. 11, no. 4, p. 421-426.

Waring, Gerald A. 1915. *Springs of California.* (United States Geological Survey Water-Supply Paper 338.) Washington: Government Printing Office, 410 p.

Watts, W.L. 1894 *The gas and petroleum yielding formations of the Central Valley of California.* (California State Mining Bureau Bulletin 3.) Sacramento: California State Mining Bureau, 100 p.

Wells, Harry L. 1938. *California names.* Los Angeles, California: Kellaway-Ide Co., 88 p.

Whipple, C.W. 1876. "Executive report of Lieutenant C.W. Whipple, Ordnance Corps, on the operations of special party, California section, field-season of 1875." *Annual report upon the geographical surveys west of the one hundredth meridian, in California, Nevada, Utah, Colorado, Wyoming, New Mexico, Arizona, and Montana.* (Appendix JJ of *The Annual report of the Chief of Engineers for 1876.*) Washington: Government Printing Office, p. 147-150.

Whiting, J.S., and Whiting, Richard J. 1960. *Forts of the State of California.* (Authors), 90 p.

Whitney, J.D. 1865. *Report of progress and synopsis of the field-work from 1860 to 1864.* (Geological Survey of California, Geology, Volume I.) Published by authority of the Legislature of California, 498 p.

Wilkes, Charles. 1958. *Columbia River to the Sacramento.* Oakland, California: Biobooks, 140 p.

Williamson, R.S. 1855. "Report." *Reports of explorations and surveys, to ascertain the most practicable and economical route for a railroad from the Mississippi River to the Pacific Ocean.* Volume V, part I. (33d Cong., 2d Sess., Sen. Ex. Doc. No. 78.) Washington: Beverley Tucker, Printer, 43 p.

Winchell, E.C. 1926. "Kings River Cañon in 1868." *Sierra Club Bulletin*, v. 12, no. 3, p. 237-251.

Wines, Howie (editor). 1966. *Kern County centennial almanac.* Bakersfield, California: Kern County Centennial Observance Committee, 176 p.

Wood, P.R., and Dale, R.H. 1964. *Geology and ground-water features of the Edison-Maricopa area, Kern County, California.* (United States Geological Survey Water-Supply Paper 1656.) Washington: Government Printing Office, 108 p.

Woodring, W.P., Stewart, Ralph, and Richards, R.W. 1940. *Geology of the Kettleman Hills Oil Field, California.* (United States Geological Survey Professional Paper 195.) Washington: Government Printing Office, 170 p.

Wright, James W.A. 1984. *The Lost Cement mine.* (Edited by Genny Smith.) Mammoth Lakes, California: Genny Smith Books, 95 p.

Wynn, Marcia Rittenhouse 1951. "When Ezra Hamilton found gold at Willow Springs." *Desert Magazine*, v. 14, no. 13, p. 15-18.

_____1963. *Desert bonanza, The story of early Randsburg, Mojave Desert mining camp.* Glendale, California: The Arthur H. Clark Company, 275 p.

QUADRANGLE MAPS

(All maps published by United States Geological Survey, except as noted. Dates identify the editions of the maps. If a reprinted or revised map was used, the year of reprinting or revision is given in parentheses, unless the reprinted or revised map is cited specifically in the text.)

Academy 7.5'—1964.
Alcalde Hills 7.5'—1969.
Allensworth 7.5'—1954.
Alpaugh 7.5' (same area as Angiola 7.5')—1929; 1953.
Alta Sierra 7.5'—1972.
Annette 7.5' (same area as Orchard Peak 7.5')—1943 (Army).
Antelope Plain 7.5'—1954.
Apache Canyon 7.5'—1943.
Arvin 7.5'—1933 (reprinted 1943); 1955 (photorevised 1968).
Auckland 7.5'—1966.
Avenal 7.5' (same area as Canoas Creek 7.5')—1954.
Avenal Gap 7.5'—1954.
Bakersfield 1°x 2°—1956 (Army); 1962, revised 1971.
Bakersfield West 15'—1942 (Army).
Ballinger Canyon 7.5'—1943.
Bear Mountain 7.5'—1966.
Belridge 7.5'—1943; 1953; 1953, photorevised 1973.
Bena 7.5'—1972.
Big Pine 15'—1950 (minor corrections 1958).
Biola 7.5'—1963.
Bissell 7.5'—1947 (Army); 1973.
Blackcap Mountain 15'—1953 (minor corrections 1962).
Blackwells Corner 7.5'—1953.
Boron 15'—1954.
7.5'—1973.
Boron NW 7.5'—1973.
Breckenridge Mountain 15'—1943.
7.5'—1972.
Buena Vista Lake 30'—1912 (reprinted 1939).
Bullard 7.5' (same area as Fresno North 7.5')—1923.
Burrel 7.5'—1927 (reprinted 1942); 1954.
Burris Park 7.5'—1926 (reprinted 1942); 1954.
Buttonwillow 15'—1942 (Army).
7.5'—1954.
Cache Peak 7.5'—1973.
Cairns Corner 7.5'—1927; 1950; 1950, photorevised 1969.
Calfax 7.5' (same area as West of Lethent 7.5')—1956.

Caliente 30'—1914 (reprinted 1929).
California City North 7.5'—1973.
California City South 7.5'—1973.
California Hot Springs 15'—1958.
Camp Nelson 15'—1956.
Cane Canyon 7.5'—1972.
Cantil 7.5'—1967.
Cantua Creek 7.5' (same area as Englebrecht Ranch 7.5')—1956.
Carneros Rocks 7.5'—1959.
Caruthers 7.5'—1963.
Castle Butte 15'—1956.
Cerro Colorado 7.5'—1969.
Chaney Ranch 7.5'—1955.
Cholame 30'—1917.
Chounet Ranch 7.5' (same area as Tierra Lomas School 7.5')—1956.
Ciervo Mountain 7.5'—1969.
Cinco 7.5'—1972.
Claraville 7.5'—1972.
Clovis 15'—1946.
7.5'—1922; 1964 (photorevised 1972).
Coalinga 30'—1912 (reprinted 1939).
15'—1944; 1956.
7.5'—1956.
Coal Oil Canyon 7.5'—1934; 1955.
Coit Ranch 7.5' (same area as Tufts Ranch 7.5')—1956.
Conejo 7.5'—1963.
Conner 7.5'—1933; 1954.
Conner SW 7.5'—1955.
Corcoran 7.5'—1928 (reprinted 1942); 1954.
Cross Mountain 15'—1943.
7.5'—1972.
Cuddy Valley 7.5'—1943.
Cummings Mountain 15'—1943a (Army); 1943b.
7.5'—1966.
Curry Mountain 7.5'—1969.
Deepwell Ranch 7.5'—1952.
Delano East 7.5' (same area as Delano 7.5')—1953.
Delano West 7.5'—(same area as Stone 7.5')—1954.
Democrat Hot Springs 7.5'—1972.
Devils Postpile 15'—1953.
Dinuba 30'—1924 (reprinted 1947).
Discovery Well 7.5' (same area as La Cima 7.5')—1930.
Domengine Ranch 7.5'—1956.
Dos Palos 7.5'—1956.
Dove Spring 7.5'—1972.
Ducor 7.5'—1929; 1952.
Dudley Ridge 7.5'—1954.
Dunlap 15'—1944.
Eagle Rest Peak 7.5'—1942.
Earlimart 15'—1942 (Army).
East Elk Hills 7.5'—1954.
Edison 7.5'—1931 (reprinted 1941); 1954 (photorevised 1968).
Edwards 7.5'—1973.
Elizabeth Lake 30'—1917 (reprinted 1941).
Elkhorn Hills 7.5'—1954.
El Paso Peaks 7.5'—1967.
El Rico Ranch 7.5'—1954.
Emerald Mountain 15'—1943.
7.5'—1972.
Emigrant Hill 7.5'—1943 (Army); 1953.
Exeter 15'—1952.
7.5'—1926 (reprinted 1944).
Fairmont Butte 7.5'—1965.
Famoso 7.5'—1930 (reprinted 1940); 1953.
Fellows 7.5'—1950, photorevised 1973; 1951.
Firebaugh 15'—1946.
7.5'—1923; 1956.
Five Points 7.5' (same area as Wheatville 7.5')—1956.
Fountain Springs 7.5'—1965.
Frazier Mountain 7.5'—1944 (Army); 1958.
Frazier Valley 7.5'—1957.
Freeman Junction 7.5'—1972.
Fresno 1°x 2°—1962 (limited revision 1967).
7.5' (same area as Fresno South 7.5')—1923.
Fresno North 7.5' (same area as Bullard 7.5')—1965 (photorevised 1972).
Fresno South 7.5' (same area as Fresno 7.5')—1963 (photorevised 1972).
Friant 7.5'—1922; 1964.
Galileo Hill 7.5'—1973.
Garlock 7.5'—1967.
Garza Peak 7.5' (same area as Reef Ridge 7.5')—1953.
Giant Forest 15'—1956 (limited revision 1967).
Gibbon Peak 7.5'—1965.
Glennville 15'—1956.
7.5'—1972.
Globe 7.5'—1956.
Gosford 7.5'—1932 (reprinted 1941); 1954.
Goshen 7.5'—1926 (reprinted 1930); 1949.
Grapevine 7.5' (same area as Tecuya Creek 7.5')—1958.
Guernsey 7.5'—1929; 1954.
Guijarral Hills 7.5'—1936 (reprinted 1947); 1956.
Hacienda Ranch 7.5'—1954.
Hacienda Ranch NE 7.5' (same area as West Alpaugh 7.5')—1954..
Hacienda Ranch NW 7.5' (same area as Harvester 7.5')—1954.
Hammond Ranch 7.5' (same area as Little Panoche 7.5')—1956.
Hanford 7.5'—1926 (reprinted 1947); 1954.
Hart Station 15'—1942 (Army).
Harvester 7.5' (same area as Hacienda Ranch NW 7.5')—1935 (reprinted 1943).
Helm 7.5'—1925; 1963.
Herndon 15'—1965.
7.5'—1923; 1964.
Hockett Peak 15'—1956.
Holland Canyon 7.5'—1961.
Horse Canyon 7.5'—1972.
Humphreys Station 7.5'—1965.
Huntington Lake 15'—1953.
Huron 7.5'—1956.
Inyokern 15'—1943.
7.5'—1972.
Inyokern SE 7.5'—1972.
Isabella 15'—1943.
Ivanhoe 7.5'—1926.
Jackrabbit Hill 7.5'—1973.
Jamesan 7.5'—1924; 1963.
Joaquin Rocks 15'—1943.
7.5'—1969.
Johannesburg 7.5'—1967.
Kaiser 30'—1904 (reprinted 1945).
Kaiser Peak 15'—1953.
Kaweah 30'—1909 (revised 1937, reprinted 1948).
15'—1957 (limited revision 1967).
Kearney Park 7.5'—1923; 1963.
Keene 7.5'—1966.
Kerman 7.5'—1922; 1963.
Kern Peak 15'—1956.
Kernville 30'—1908 (reprinted 1934).
15'—1956.
Kettleman City 7.5'—1937; 1963.
Kettleman Plain 7.5'—1933; 1953.
Knob Hill 7.5'—1965.
Kramer 15'—1942 (reprinted 1947); 1956.
Kreyenhagen Hills 7.5'—1956.
La Cima 7.5' (same area as Discovery Well 7.5')—1934; 1963.
Laguna Seca Ranch 7.5'—1956.
Lake Isabella North 7.5'—1972.
Lake Isabella South 7.5'—1972.
Lake View School 7.5 (same area as Taylor Weir 7.5')—1927
La Liebre Ranch 7.5'—1965.
Lamont 7.5' (same area as Fairfax School 7.5')—1954; 1954, photorevised 1968.
Lamont Peak 15'—1956.
Lanes Bridge 7.5'—1922.
La Panza NE 7.5'—1966.
La Rambla 15'—1942 (Army).
Las Yeguas Ranch 7.5'—1959.
Laton 7.5'—1927 (reprinted 1947); 1953.
Lebec 7.5'—1945 (Army); 1958.
Lemon Cove 7.5' (same area as Woodlake 7.5')—1928.
Lemoore 7.5'—1927 (reprinted 1942); 1954.
Leonards 7.5' (same area as Wasco SW 7.5')—1930 (reprinted 1943).
Lethent 7.5' (same area as Vanguard 7.5')—1926 (reprinted 1938).
Leuhman Ridge 7.5'—1973.
Levis 7.5'—1956.
Liebre Twins 7.5'—1965.
Lillis Ranch 7.5'—1956.
Lindsay 7.5'—1928; 1951 (photorevised 1969).
Little Lake 15'—1954.
Lokern 7.5'—1954.
Lone Butte 7.5'—1973.
Lone Pine 15'—1958.
Lone Tree Well 7.5'—1954.
Loraine 7.5'—1972.

Los Angeles 1°x 2°—1975.
Lost Hills 30'—1914 (reprinted 1947).
7.5' (same area as West of Goose Lake 7.5')—1953.
Lost Hills NE 7.5' (same area as Miramonte Ranch 7.5')—1954.
Lost Hills NW 7.5'—1954.
Los Viejos 7.5' (same area as Los Viejos Hills 7.5')—1954.
Malaga 7.5'—1923; 1964 (photorevised 1972).
Maricopa 7.5'—1943 (Army); 1951.
Marion Peak 15'—1953 (limited revision 1967).
Mariposa 1°x 2°—1957 (revised 1970).
McFarland 7.5'—1954; 1954, photorevised 1969.
McKittrick 30'—1912 (reprinted 1920).
McKittrick Summit 7.5'—1959.
Mendota 7.5' (same area as Mendota Dam 7.5')—1924.
Mendota Dam 7.5' (same area as Mendota 7.5')—1956.
Mercey Hot Springs 7.5'—1969.
Mettler 7.5' (same area as West of Tejon Hills 7.5')—1955.
Millerton Lake 15'—1945.
Millerton Lake East 7.5'—1965.
Millerton Lake West 7.5' (same area as Sulphur Springs 7.5')—1965.
Millux 7.5'—1933 (reprinted 1943); 1954.
Mineral King 15'—1956 (limited revision 1967).
Miracle Hot Springs 7.5'—1972.
Miramonte 7.5'—1966.
Mojave 30'—1915.
15'—1943 (Army); 1956.
7.5'—1947 (Army); 1973.
Mojave NE 7.5'—1973.
Monache Mountain 15'—1956.
Monocline Ridge 7.5'—1955.
Monolith 7.5'—1966.
Monson 7.5'—1927; 1949; 1949, photorevised 1969.
Mount Abbot 15'—1953.
Mount Adelaide 7.5'—1972.
Mount Goddard 30'—1912 (reprinted 1940).
15'—1948 (minor corrections 1957).
Mount Lyell 30'—1901 (reprinted 1948).
Mount Morrison 15'—1953.
Mount Pinos 30'—1903 (reprinted 1918).
Mount Pinchot 15'—1953.
Mount Tom 15'—1949.
Mount Whitney 30'—1907 (reprinted 1910).
15'—1956 (limited revision 1967).
Mouth of Kern 7.5'—1932 (reprinted 1948); 1950.
Neenach 15'—1943.
Neenach School 7.5'—1965.
North Edwards 7.5'—1973.
North Fork 7.5'—1965.
North of Oildale 7.5'—1954.
Oil Center 7.5'—1940; 1954 (photorevised 1968).
Oildale 7.5'—1935 (reprinted 1947); 1954.
Oiler Peak 7.5'—1972.
Olancha 30'—1907 (reprinted 1931).
15'—1956.
Olig 7.5' (same area as Reward 7.5')—1943 (Army).
Onyx 15'—1943.
7.5'—1972.
Orange Cove North 7.5' (same area as Citrus Cove 7.5')—1966.
Orange Cove South 7.5' (same area as Sultana 7.5')—1966.
Orangedale School 7.5' (same area as Piedra 7.5')—1923 (reprinted 1943).
Orchard Peak 7.5' (same area as Annette 7.5')—1961.
Ortigalita Peak 7.5'—1969.
Oxalis 7.5'—1922 (reprinted 1936); 1956.
Owens Peak 7.5'—1972.
Packwood 7.5' (same area as Packwood Creek 7.5')—1943.
Packwood Creek 7.5' (same area as Packwood 7.5')—1961.
Paige 7.5'—1927; 1950 (photorevised 1969).
Panoche 30'—1913 (reprinted 1948).
7.5'—1969.
Panoche Valley 15'—1944.
Panorama Hills 7.5'—1954.
Parkfield 7.5'—1961.
Pastoria Creek 7.5'—1958.
Patterson Mountain 15'—1952.
Pentland 7.5'—1945 (Army); 1953.
Piedra 7.5' (same area as Orangedale School 7.5')—1965.
Pine Flat Dam 7.5'—1965.
Pine Mountain 7.5'—1965.
Pinyon Mountain 7.5'—1972.
Piute Peak 7.5'—1972.
Pixley 7.5'—1929; 1954.
Pleito Hills 7.5'—1958.
Pond 7.5'—1930; 1953.
Porterville 15'—1942 (Army).
7.5'—1929; 1951; 1951, photorevised 1969.
Poso Farm 7.5' (same area as Pozo Farm 7.5')—1962.
Priest Valley 30'—1915.
15'—1944.
7.5'—1969.
Pyramid Hills 7.5'—1943 (Army); 1953.
Quincy School 7.5'—1965.
Raisin 7.5'—1925 (reprinted 1942); 1963.
Randsburg 15'—1911.
Redman 7.5'—1973.
Reedley 7.5'—1924; 1966.
Reef Ridge 7.5'—(same area as Garza Peak 7.5')—1937.
Remnoy 7.5'—1927 (reprinted 1947); 1954.
Reward 7.5' (same area as Olig 7.5')—1950, photorevised 1973; 1951.
Richgrove 7.5'—1952.
Ridgecrest 15'—1953.
Ridgecrest North 7.5'—1973.
Ridgecrest South 7.5'—1973.
Rio Bravo 7.5'—1954.
Rio Bravo Ranch 7.5'—1954 (photorevised 1968).
Riverdale 7.5'—1927 (reprinted 1942); 1954.
Rocky Hill 7.5'—1927 (reprinted 1947); 1951 (photorevised 1969).
Rogers Lake 15'—1942 (reprinted 1948); 1956.
Rogers Lake North 7.5'—1973.
Rogers Lake South 7.5'—1973.
Rosamond 15'—1943 (Army); 1956.
7.5'—1973.
Rosamond Lake 7.5'—1973.
Rosedale 7.5'—1933 (reprinted 1941); 1954.
Round Mountain 7.5'—1922; 1964.
Saltdale 15'—1943a; 1943b (Army).
Saltdale NW 7.5'—1967.
Saltdale SE 7.5'—1967.
San Benito Mountain 7.5'—1969.
San Bernardino 1°x 2°—1957.
Sanborn 7.5'—1973.
Sand Canyon 7.5'—1965.
Sanger 7.5'—1923; 1965.
San Joaquin 7.5'—1925; 1963.
San Jose 1°x 2°—1962 (revised 1969).
San Luis Obispo 1°x 2°—1956, revised 1969.
Santa Cruz 1°x 2°—1958.
Santa Rita Bridge 7.5'—1922.
Santa Rita Park 15'—1962.
Santa Rita Peak 7.5'—1969.
Santiago Creek 7.5'—1943.
Saucalito School 7.5'—1954.
Sawmill Mountain 7.5'—1943.
Sawtooth Ridge 7.5'—1943 (Army); 1961.
Searles Lake 1°—1915 (reprinted 1946).
Selma 15'—1946.
7.5'—1964.
Semitropic 7.5'—1954.
Shale Point 7.5'—1953.
Shaver Lake 15'—1953.
Sherman Peak 7.5'—1969.
Shuteye Peak 15'—1953 (limited revision 1965).
Slack Canyon 7.5'—1969.
Smith Mountain 7.5'—1969.
Soledad Mountain 7.5'—1947 (Army); 1973.
Springville 15'—1957.
7.5'—1957.
Stevens 7.5'—1932 (reprinted 1940); 1954.
Stokes Mountain 7.5'—1966.
Stratford 15'—1942 (Army).
7.5'—1929 (reprinted 1942); 1954.
Stratford SE 7.5' (same area as Chatom Ranch 7.5')—1954.
Success Dam 7.5'—1956 (minor corrections 1961).
Sulphur Springs 7.5' (same area as Millerton Lake West 7.5')—1919 (reprinted 1922).
Sultana 7.5' (same area as Orange Cove South 7.5')—1923.
Taft 7.5'—1950.
Taylor Weir 7.5' (same area as Lake View School 7.5')—1950; 1950, photorevised 1969.
Tecuya Creek 7.5' (same area as Grapevine 7.5')—1945 (Army).
Tehachapi 15'—1943.
Tehachapi North 7.5'—1966.
Tehachapi NE 7.5'—1966.

Tehachapi South 7.5'—1966.
Tehipite 30'—1903 (minor revisions 1937).
Tehipite Dome 15'—1952 (limited revision 1967).
Tejon Hills 7.5'—1955 (photorevised 1968).
Tejon Ranch 7.5'—1966.
Tent Hills 7.5'—1942.
The Dark Hole 7.5'—1937; 1961.
Tipton 7.5'—1928; 1950; 1950, photorevised 1969.
Tobias Peak 30'—1936; 1943.
Tranquillity 15'—1946.
 7.5'—1924; 1956.
Traver 7.5'—1949; 1949, photorevised 1969.
Tres Picos Farms 7.5' (same area as Mouth of Cantua Creek 7.5')—1956.
Trimmer 7.5'—1965.
Triple Divide Peak 15'—1956 (limited revision 1967).
Trona 1°x 2°—1957 (limited revision 1963).
Tucker Mountain 7.5'—1966.
Tulare 15'—1942 (Army).
 7.5'—1927 (reprinted 1943); 1950; 1950, photorevised 1969.
Tumey Hills 7.5'—1956.
Tupman 7.5'—1954.
Tylerhorse Canyon 7.5'—1965.
Vanguard 7.5'—1956.
Visalia 15'—1949.
 7.5'—1949; 1949, photorevised 1969.
Wahtoke 7.5'—1923; 1966.
Walker Pass 7.5'—1972.
Wasco 7.5'—1953.
Wasco NW 7.5' (same area as Hamlin School 7.5')—1953.
Wasco SW 7.5' (same area as Leonards 7.5')—1953.
Watts Valley 15'—1942.
Waukena 7.5'—1928; 1954.
Weed Patch 7.5'—1955 (photorevised 1968).
Weldon 7.5'—1972.
West Alpaugh 7.5' (same area as Hacienda Ranch NE 7.5')—1929.
West Camp 7.5'—1954.
West Elk Hills 7.5'—1954.
Westhaven 7.5'—1929 (reprinted 1943); 1956.
Westside 7.5' (same area as Towne Oil Station 7.5')—1956.
Wheatville 7.5' (same area as Five Points 7.5')—1931.
White River 15'—1936 (reprinted 1947); 1952.
 7.5'—1965.
Willow Springs 7.5'—1965.
Winters Ridge 7.5'—1966.
Wisdom Well 7.5' (same area as Broadview Farms 7.5')—1923 (reprinted 1947).
Woodlake 7.5' (same area as Lemon Cove 7.5')—1952; 1952, photorevised 1969.
Woodville 7.5'—1950; 1950, photorevised 1969.
Woody 15'—1935 (reprinted 1947); 1952.
 7.5'—1965.
Woolstalf Creek 7.5'—1972.

MISCELLANEOUS MAPS

Arnold and Anderson. 1910. "Geologic and structural map of the Coalinga district, California." (Plate I *in* Arnold and Anderson, 1910.)

Arnold and Johnson. 1910. "Preliminary geologic and structural map of the McKittrick-Sunset oil region, California." (Plate I *in* Arnold and Johnson.)

Baker. 1855. "Map of the mining region, of California." Drawn by Geo. A. Baker.

Baker. 1911. (Untitled map. Plate 34 *in* Baker.)

Bancroft. 1864. "Bancroft's map of the Pacific States." Compiled by Wm. H. Knight. Published by H.H. Bancroft & Co., Booksellers and Stationers, San Francisco, Cal.

Blake. 1857. "Geological map of a part of the State of California explored in 1855 by Lieut. R.S. Williamson, U.S. Top. Engr." (*Accompanies* Blake, 1857.)

California. 1891. (Map reproduced in *Early California, Southern Edition.* Corvalis, Oregon: Western Guide Publishers, p. 44-45.)

California Division of Highways. 1934. (Appendix "A" *of* California Division of Highways.)

California Mining Bureau. 1909a. "Kings, Tulare, and Kern Counties." (*In* California Mining Bureau Bulletin 56.)

_____1909b. "Madera and Fresno Counties." (*In* California Mining Bureau Bulletin 56.)

_____1917a. (Untitled map *in* California Mining Bureau Bulletin 74, p. 168.)

_____1917b. (Untitled map *in* California Mining Bureau Bulletin 74, p. 169.)

_____1917c. (Untitled map *in* California Mining Bureau Bulletin 74, p. 171.)

Campbell. 1902. "Sketch map of Mohave Desert and Death Valley." (Plate I *in* Campbell.)

Derby. 1850. "Reconnaissance of the Tulares Valley." Lieut. G.H. Derby, Topl. Engrs., April and May, 1850.

Eddy. 1854. "Approved and declared to be the official map of the State of California by an act of the Legislature passed March 25th 1853." Compiled by W.M. Eddy, State Surveyor General. Published for R.A. Eddy, Marysville, California, by J.H. Colton, New York.

Fremont. 1848. "Map of Oregon and Upper California from the surveys of John Charles Frémont and other authorities." Drawn by Charles Preuss. Washington City.

Goddard. 1857. "Britton & Rey's map of the State of California." By George H. Goddard.

Gray. 1873. "Gray's Atlas, New rail road and county map of the States of Oregon, California and Nevada." Compiled and drawn by Frank A. Gray. Published by O.W. Gray. Philadelphia.

Grunsky. 1898. "Map of East side of San Joaquin Valley, from Kings River to Fresno River." (Plate IV *in* Grunsky.)

Hamlin. 1904. "Map of the drainage basin of the Salinas River, showing hydrographic features." (Plate I *in* Hamlin.)

Jefferson. 1849. "Map of the emigrant road from Independence Mo. to St. Francisco, California." By T.H. Jefferson.

Johnson. 1911. "Reconnaissance hydrographic map of Antelope Valley region, California." (Plate VI *in* Johnson, H.R.)

Lee. 1912. "Map of Indian Wells Valley, California, showing China Dry Lake, approximate surface contours and location of wells." (Plate II *in* Lee.)

Lippincott. 1902. "Map of drainage basin of Kings River, California, showing route traversed by exploring parties." [Plate I *in* Lippincott.)

Mendenhall. 1908. "Artesian areas and groundwater levels in the San Joaquin Valley, California." (Plate I *in* Mendenhall, 1908.)

_____1909. "General map showing approximate location of better known springs and wells in the Mohave and adjacent deserts, southeastern California and southwestern Nevada." (Plate I *in* Mendenhall, 1909.)

Olmstead. 1900. "Map of upper Kern River." (Plate III *in* Olmstead.)

Parke. 1854-1855. "Map No. 1, San Francisco Bay to the plains of Los Angeles." From explorations and surveys made by Lieut. John C. Parke. Constructed and drawn by H. Custer. (In *Reports of explorations and surveys, to ascertain the most practicable and economical route for a railroad from the Mississippi River to the Pacific Ocean.* Volume XI. 1861.)

Rogers and Johnston. 1857. "State of California." By Prof. H.D. Rogers & A. Keith Johnston.

Sage. 1846. "Map of Oregon, California, New Mexico, N.W. Texas, & the proposed Territory of Ne-Bras-ka." By Rufus B. Sage.

Thompson. 1892. "Map of Tulare County, California." (*Accompanies* Thompson, T.H.)

Thompson. 1921. "Relief map of part of Mohave Desert region, California, showing desert watering places." (Plates IX-XIII *in* Thompson, D.G.)

United States Geological Survey. 1906. "Bakersfield Special." Scale 1:62,500.

Watts. 1894. "Map of the Great Central Valley of California." (*Accompanies* Watts.)

Wheeler. 1871-1878. "Part of southern California." (Atlas Sheet No. 73.) Expeditions of 1871, 1875-'76 & 1878 under the command of 1st Lieut. Geo. M. Wheeler.

_____1875-1878. "Part of southern California." (Atlas Sheet No. 83A.) Expeditions of 1875 & 1878 under the command of 1st Lieut. Geo. M. Wheeler.

Wilkes. 1841. "Map of Upper California." By the U.S. Ex. Ex. and best authorities.

_____1849. "Map of Upper California." By the best authorities.

Williamson. 1853. "Map of passes in the Sierra Nevada from Walker's Pass to the Coast Range." By Lieut. R.S. Williamson, Topl. Engr., assisted by Lieut. J.G. Parke, Topl. Engr., and Mr. Isaac William Smith, Civ. Engr. (In *Reports of explorations and surveys, to ascertain the most practicable and economical route for a railroad from the Mississippi River to the Pacific Ocean,.* Volume XI. 1861.)

Part Nine
East Sierra Region

Alpine, Inyo and Mono Counties

Part Nine–East Sierra Region

East Sierra Region
Alpine, Inyo and Mono Counties

Regional Setting

General.—This section concerns geographic features in three counties—Alpine, Inyo, and Mono—that lie almost entirely east of the crest of the Sierra Nevada, which passes through Alpine County and forms the west boundary of Inyo County and Mono County. Townships (T) South and Townships less than 13 North refer to Mount Diablo Base and Meridian; Townships greater than 19 North refer to San Bernardino Base and Meridian. United States Board on Geographic Names (1933, p. 692) ruled against the name "Sierra Nevadas" for the range. The name "High Sierra" commonly is accepted for the part of the Sierra Nevada that includes the high peaks (Gudde, 1949, p. 148). Garces called the range Sierra de San Marcos in 1776 (Boyd, p. 3), Jedediah Smith (p. 149) named it "St Joseph in honor of one of the best of men father Joseph Sances of St Gabriel" in 1827, Wilkes (p. 44) called it California Range in 1841, Lyman (p. 307) called it "Sierra Nevada, or Snowy Mountains" in 1849, and Kip (p. 46) called it Snowy Range in 1850. Whitney (1865, p. 2) pointed out that the feature was long known to the Spaniards as Sierra Nevada, or Snowy Range, because "the most distant and loftiest elevations are never entirely bare of snow, and for a large portion of the year are extensively covered with it." All streams east of the crest of the Sierra Nevada belong to the drainage of the Great Basin province, and their waters never reach the sea. The region is sparsely settled. Mining, lumbering, ranching, and recreation are the principal industries. The map on the facing page shows the location of the East Sierra Region and the counties in it.

Alpine *County.*—Alpine County lies on the crest of the Sierra Nevada and extends eastward to the State of Nevada. The state legislature created it in 1864 from parts of Amador, Calaveras, El Dorado, Mono, and Tuolumne Counties; the original county boundaries are unchanged (Coy, p. 65). The county seat first was at Silver Mountain, and since 1875 it has been at Markleeville; the county name reflects the alpinelike setting of the place (Hoover, Rensch, and Rensch, p. 24).

Inyo County.—Inyo County extends eastward from the crest of the Sierra Nevada to the California-Nevada State line. It contains numerous ranges and intervening valleys, and includes both the highest (Mount Whitney) and the lowest (Death Valley) places in the conterminous United States. An act of the state legislature created the county in 1866; large additions of territory were made to the county in 1870 when Inyo-Mono County line was shifted north, and in 1923 when the south boundary was changed (Coy, p. 114-115). Independence is and always has been the county seat (Hoover, Rensch, and Rensch, p. 116). The name "Inyo" is said to be of Indian origin, but this is uncertain (Kroeber, p. 43).

Mono County.—Mono County extends eastward from the crest of the Sierra Nevada to the State of Nevada. The state legislature created Mono County in 1861 from parts of Fresno County and Calaveras County; Mono County lost territory to Alpine County when that county was created in 1864, and lost territory to Inyo County when that county was formed in 1866; the Mono-Inyo County line was modified in 1870 (Coy, p. 182-183). The first county seat was Aurora, Nevada, before survey of the California-Nevada State line revealed that Aurora is in Nevada; Bridgeport became the county seat in 1863 (Hoover, Rensch, and Rensch, p. 210). The name "Mono" is from the designation of a widespread division of Shoshonean Indians that lived in the region (Kroeber, p. 48).

East Sierra Region
Alpine, Inyo and Mono Counties

— A —

Abbot: see **Mount Abbot** [INYO].

Aberdeen [INYO]:

(1) *locality,* 13 miles north of Independence along Southern Pacific Railroad (lat. 36°59'30" N, long. 118°12'40" W; sec. 13, T 11 S, R 34 E). Named on Independence (1951) 15' quadrangle. The place first was called Tibbets for the family that owned a nearby ranch (Hungerford, p. 11). A mining camp called Chrysopolis flourished briefly in the 1860's on the east side of Owens River south of Aberdeen (1) (Hoover, Rensch, and Rensch, p. 117-118). Postal authorities established Chrysopolis post office in 1866 and discontinued it in 1867 (Frickstad, p. 50). California Mining Bureau's (1917b) map shows a place called Intake located 1 mile south of Aberdeen (1) where the aqueduct that takes Owens Valley water to Los Angeles begins.

(2) *village,* 12.5 miles north-northwest of Independence (lat. 36°58'40" N, long. 118°15'15" W; near E line sec. 21, T 11 S, R 34 E); the place is 2.5 miles west-southwest of Aberdeen (1). Named on Mount Pinchot (1953) 15' quadrangle. The name is from Aberdeen (1) (Schumacher, p. 46). Postal authorities established Tibbotts post office in 1895, moved it 2 miles north and changed the name to Aberdeen in 1896, discontinued it in 1898, reestablished it in 1921, and discontinued it in 1934 (Salley, p. 1, 221).

A Canyon [INYO]: *canyon,* 3 miles long, opens into lowlands 3.5 miles south-southwest of Emigrant Pass (1) (lat. 36°17'30" N, long. 117°10'15" W). Named on Emigrant Canyon (1952) 15' quadrangle.

Acorn Canyon [ALPINE]: *canyon,* drained by a stream that flows 1 mile to West Fork Carson River 1 mile west-southwest of Woodfords (lat. 38°46'05" N, long. 119°50'25" W; sec. 34, T 11 N, R 19 E). Named on Woodfords (1979) 7.5' quadrangle.

Addie Canyon [INYO]: *canyon,* drained by a stream that flows 3 miles to Lead Canyon 5.5 miles north-northwest of the mouth of Paiute Canyon (lat. 36°55'10" N, long. 118°57'40" W). Named on Waucoba Wash (1951) 15' quadrangle.

Adobe Creek [MONO]: *stream,* flows 8 miles to Adobe Valley 10 miles north of Glass Mountain (lat. 37°55' N, long. 118°41'45" W; sec. 29, T 1 N, R 30 E). Named on Glass Mountain (1962) 15' quadrangle.

Adobe Hills [MONO]: *range,* 15 miles north-northeast of Glass Mountain (lat. 37°59'45" N, long. 118°39'15" W); the range is north of Adobe Valley. Named on Glass Mountain (1962) 15' quadrangle.

Adobe Lake [MONO]: *dry lake,* 1.25 miles long, 14 miles north-northeast of Glass Mountain (lat. 37°58' N, long. 118°38'30" W; mainly in sec. 2, 11, T 1 N, R 30 E); the feature is in Adobe Valley. Named on Glass Mountain (1962) 15' quadrangle.

Adobe Meadows: see **Adobe Valley** [MONO].

Adobe Reservoir [MONO]: *lake,* 1300 feet long, behind a dam on Dexter Creek 7 miles north of Glass Mountain near the confluence of Dexter Creek and Adobe Creek (lat. 37°52'35" N, long. 118°43'50" W; sec. 12, T 1 S, R 29 E). Named on Glass Mountain (1962) 15' quadrangle.

Adobe Valley [MONO]: *valley,* 10 miles north-northeast of Glass Mountain (lat. 37°55' N, long. 118°38' W); the valley is south of Adobe Hills. Named on Glass Mountain (1962) 15' quadrangle. Called Adobe Meadows on Wheeler's (1871) map. Colton's (1863) map shows a place called Whiskey Flat located at or near present Adobe Valley.

Aeolian Buttes [MONO]: *relief feature,* 8 miles south-southeast of Lee Vining at the south end of Pumice Valley (lat. 37°51'15" N, long. 119°03'30" W). Named on Mono Craters (1953) 15' quadrangle.

Agassiz: see **Mount Agassiz** [INYO].

Agassiz Col [INYO]: *relief feature,* 9 miles east-southeast of Mount Darwin (lat. 37°06'25" N, long. 118°31'45" W); the feature is 2000 feet south-southeast of Mount Agassiz. Named on Mount Goddard (1948) 15' quadrangle.

Agassiz Needle: see **Mount Agassiz** [INYO].

Aggie: see **Mount Aggie** [MONO].

Agnew Lake [MONO]: *lake,* 0.5 mile long, behind a dam on Rush Creek 14 miles south of Lee Vining (lat. 37°45'30" N, long. 119°07'50" W; sec. 20, T 2 S, R 26 E). Named on Mono Craters (1953) 15' quadrangle.

Agnew Pass [MONO]: *pass,* 9.5 miles northwest of Mammoth Mountain on Mono-Madera County line (lat. 37°44'05" N, long. 119°08'35" W; sec. 31, T 2 S, R 26 E). Named on Devils Postpile (1953) 15' quadrangle.

Agua de Hernandez: see **Resting Spring** [INYO].

Aguereberry Point [INYO]: *locality,* viewpoint that overlooks central Death Valley 5.5 miles east-northeast of Emigrant Pass (1) (lat. 36°21'30" N, long. 117°02'50" W). Named on Emigrant Canyon (1952) 15' quadrangle. United States Board on Geographic Names (1967, p. 6) rejected the form "Aguerreberry Point" for the name, which commemorates "French Pete" Aguereberry, who with "Shorty" Harris opened Harrisburg mine in 1906. Aguereberry laid out the first road to the point (Federal Writers' Project, p. 50).

Aiken: see **Perry Aiken Creek** [MONO]; **Perry Aiken Flat** [MONO].

Airola Peak [ALPINE]: *peak,* nearly 5 miles northeast of Dardanelles Cone (lat. 38°27'25" N, long. 119°48'50" W). Altitude 9942 feet. Named on Dardanelles Cone (1979) 7.5' quadrangle.

Airport Lake [INYO]: *dry lake,* 4.5 miles long, 10 miles east-southeast of the village of Little Lake in Coso Basin (lat. 35°54'20" N, long. 117°44'10" W). Named on Little Lake (1954) and Mountain Springs Canyon (1953) 15' quadrangles.

Alabama Cañon: see **Alabama Hills** [INYO].

Alabama Hills [INYO]: *range,* center 1.5 miles west of Lone Pine (lat. 36°36'30" N, long. 118°05'30" W). Named on Lone Pine (1958) 15' quadrangle. Southern sympathizers named the feature during the Civil War for the Confederate privateer *Alabama* (Chalfant, 1933, p. 235-236). Goodyear (p. 243) used the name "Lone Pine Hills" for the range, and on a sketch map he showed Alabama Cañon located near the north end of the hills.

Alameda Well [MONO]: *well,* 12.5 miles southeast of Bodie (lat. 38°06'20" N, long. 118°49'45" W; near W line sec. 19, T 3 N, R 29 E). Named on Trench Canyon (1958) 15' quadrangle.

Alexander Hills: see **Sperry Hills** [INYO].

Alger Creek [MONO]: *stream,* flows nearly 5 miles to Silver Lake 12 miles south of Lee Vining (lat. 37°46'50" N, long. 119°07'35" W; near N line sec. 17, T 2 S, R 26 E). Named on Mono Craters (1953) 15' quadrangle.

Alger Lakes [MONO]: *lakes,* two, largest 4300 feet long, 11.5 miles south-southwest of Lee Vining (lat. 37°47'45" N, long. 119°10'45" W); the lakes are along a branch of Alger Creek. Named on Mono Craters (1953) 15' quadrangle. The lower of the two lakes is called Alger Lake on Mount Lyell (1901) 30' quadrangle. Gudde (1949, p. 7) noted that R.B. Marshall named Lake Alger in 1909 for John Alger, a packer for United States Geological Survey.

Alice: see **Mount Alice** [INYO].

Alico [INYO]: *locality,* 5.5 miles south-southwest of New York Butte along Southern Pacific Railroad (lat. 36°34'10" N, long. 117°57'45" W; sec. 4, T 16 S, R 37 E). Named on New York Butte (1950) 15' quadrangle.

Alkali Flat [INYO]: *area,* 4.5 miles southeast of Death Valley Junction along Amargosa River (lat. 36°15' N, long. 116°22' W). Named on Ash Meadows (1952) and Eagle Mountain (1951) 15' quadrangles.

Alkali Lake: see **Big Alkali Lake** [MONO]; **Little Alkali Lake** [MONO]; **Topaz Lake** [MONO].

Alkali Valley [MONO]: *valley,* mainly in the State of Nevada, but extends 1 mile into California 8 miles east of Bodie around Larkin Lake (lat. 38°12' N, long. 118°51'50" W). Named on Trench Canyon (1958) 15' quadrangle. Called Aurora Valley on Russell's (1889) map; Russell (p. 272) named the valley for the mining town of Aurora, Nevada, but United States Board on Geographic Names (1960c, p. 15) rejected this name.

Allens Well [INYO]: *well,* 2 miles east-northeast of present Death Valley Junction (lat. 36°18'35" N, long. 116°23' W). Named on Furnace Creek (1910) 1° quadrangle. Palmer (p. 5) referred to Allen's Well, and noted that it is "named for one, Allen."

Alpers Canyon [MONO]: *canyon,* drained by a stream that flows 3.5 miles to Owens River nearly 10 miles south-southeast of the site of Mono Mills (lat. 37°45' N, long. 118°55'05" W; sec. 30, T 2 S, R 28 E). Named on

Cowtrack Mountain (1962) 15' quadrangle.

Alpine: see **Lake Alpine** [ALPINE].

Alpine Lake [MONO]: *lake,* 850 feet long, 1 mile east-southeast of Mount Conness (lat. 37°57'45" N, long. 119°18'10" W). Named on Tuolumne Meadows (1956) 15' quadrangle.

Alpine Station [ALPINE]: *locality,* 2.5 miles south of Mount Reba (lat. 38°28'25" N, long. 120°01'35" W; sec. 8, T 7 N, R 18 E). Named on Tamarack (1979) 7.5' quadrangle.

Al Rose Canyon [INYO]: *canyon,* 3.25 miles long, opens into Masourka Canyon 10 miles northeast of Independence (lat. 36° 55' N, long. 118°05' W). Named on Independence (1951) 15' quadrangle. United States Board on Geographic Names (1983b, p. 1) rejected the name "Rose Canyon" for the feature.

Alvord: see **Zurich** [INYO].

Amargosa: see **Death Valley Junction** [INYO].

Amargosa Desert [INYO]: *area,* along Amargosa River north of Death Valley Junction and northeast of Funeral Mountains; mainly in the State of Nevada. Named on Death Valley (1954) 1°x 2° quadrangle. Fremont named the feature for Amargosa River (Palmer, p. 6).

Amargosa Desert: see **Death Valley** [INYO].

Amargosa Range [INYO]: *range,* east of Death Valley and west of Amargosa Desert; comprises Black Mountains, Funeral Mountains, and Grapevine Mountains. Named on Death Valley (1954) 1°x 2° quadrangle.

Amargosa River [INYO]: *stream,* heads in the State of Nevada and flows 135 miles in California—partly in San Bernardino County—to its sink near Badwater in Death Valley. Named on Death Valley (1954) and Trona (1957) 1°x 2° quadrangles. Antonio Armijo called the stream Rio de los Payuches in 1830 (Lingenfelter, p. 25). Fremont (p. 264) noted that the river "is called by the Spaniards *Amargosa*—the bitter water of the desert."

Anderson Peak [MONO]: *peak,* 3.25 miles south of Benton on Blind Spring Hill (lat. 37°46'20" N, long. 118°29'10" W; sec. 18, T 2 S, R 32 E). Named on Benton (1962) 15' quadrangle.

Andreas Mountain [INYO]: *peak,* 5.5 miles northwest of Waucoba Mountain (lat. 37°04'35" N, long. 118°04'55" W; sec. 18, T 10 S, R 36 E). Altitude 9460 feet. Named on Waucoba Mountain (1951) 15' quadrangle.

Anna Lake [MONO]: *lake,* 2600 feet long, 5.5 miles north-northeast of Tower Peak (lat. 38°13'10" N, long. 119°30'20" W). Named on Tower Peak (1956) 15' quadrangle. The name presumably commemorates Anna Mack, whose parents had a house near the lake in the 1870's (Gudde, 1949, p. 108).

Anna Peak: see **Silver Mountain** [ALPINE].

Antelope: see **Antelope Spring** [INYO]; **Camp Antelope** [MONO].

Antelope Lake [MONO]: *intermittent lake,* 1 mile long, 11 miles northeast of Glass Mountain (lat. 37°53'30" N, long. 118°34'10" W; mainly in sec. 4, T 1 S, R 31 E); the feature is less than 1 mile west of Antelope Mountain. Named on Glass Mountain (1962) 15' quadrangle.

Antelope Mountain [MONO]: *peak,* 12 miles northeast of Glass Mountain (lat. 37°53'30" N, long. 118°33'10" W; on E line sec. 4, T 1 S, R 31 E); the peak is less than 1 mile east of Antelope Lake. Altitude 7617 feet. Named on Glass Mountain (1962) 15' quadrangle.

Antelope Peak [ALPINE-MONO]: *peak,* 10 miles east of Disaster Peak on Alpine-Mono County line (lat. 38°28'10" N, long. 119°33'20" W; near NW cor. sec. 10, T 7 N, R 22 E). Altitude 10,241 feet. Named on Lost Cannon Peak (1954) 7.5' quadrangle. Wheeler's (1876-1877) map has the name "Little Antelope Pk." for a feature situated about 2.5 miles north of Antelope Peak on present Alpine-Mono County line.

Antelope Spring [INYO]: *spring,* 4.25 miles northeast of Westgard Pass (lat. 37°20'10" N, long. 118°05'20" W; sec. 13, T 7 S, R 35 E). Named on Blanco Mountain (1951) 15' quadrangle. United States Board on Geographic Names (1975, p. 11) approved the name "Sams Spring" for this feature, and (p. 8) approved the name "Antelope Spring" for a spring situated 0.5 mile farther south (NW quarter sec. 24, T 7 S, R 35 E). Waring and Huguenin (p. 34) referred to Antelope Springs located at the southwest edge of Deep Springs Valley. Goodyear (p. 236) mentioned a place called Antelope found "at the foot of the mountains, on the northwest side of Deep Spring Valley, where there is a spring of good water."

Antelope Spring [MONO]: *spring,* 7.5 miles east-northeast of Toms Place in Chidago Canyon (lat. 37°36'55" N, long. 118°33'45" W; sec. 9, T 4 S, R 31 E). Named on Casa Diablo Mountain (1953) 15' quadrangle.

Antelope Spring: see **Little Antelope Valley** [MONO] (2).

Antelope Valley [MONO]: *valley,* 30 miles north-northwest of Bridgeport along West Walker River on California-Nevada State line (lat. 38°38' N, long. 119°28' W). Named on Desert Creek Peak (1956) and Topaz Lake (1956) 15' quadrangles.

Antelope Valley: see **Little Antelope Valley** [MONO].

Anthony's Camp: see **Pleasant Canyon** [INYO].

Antimony Spring: see **Wildrose Canyon** [INYO].

Anton: see **Grover Anton Spring** [INYO].

Anvil Camp [INYO]: *locality,* 8 miles north-northwest of Mount Whitney (1) (lat. 36°41'30" N, long. 118°19'30" W). Named on Mount Whitney (1956) 15' quadrangle.

Anvil Spring [INYO]: *spring,* 2 miles east-northeast of Manly Peak at the west edge of Butte Valley (lat. 35°55'20" N, long. 117° 05' W). Named on Manly Peak (1950) 15' quadrangle. Palmer (p. 7) noted that Sergeant Neale found an anvil at the place in 1867.

Anvil Spring Canyon [INYO]: *canyon,* 13 miles long, opens into Death Valley 6 miles northeast of Sugarloaf Peak (lat. 35°56'50" N, long. 116°51'30" W); the canyon heads across Butte Valley from Anvil Spring. Named on Manly Peak (1950) and Wingate Wash (1950) 15' quadrangles.

Aperture Peak: see **Mount Agassiz** [INYO].

Arab Canon: see **Centennial Canyon** [INYO].

Arab Spring: see **Lower Centennial Spring** [INYO].

Arcane Meadows [INYO]: *area,* 3 miles north of Telescope Peak between Bennett Peak and Rogers Peak (lat. 36°12'45" N, long. 117°05'35" W; sec. 10, T 20 S, R 45 E). Named on Telescope Peak (1952) 15' quadrangle. National Park Service officials named the place in memory of J.B. Arcane, one of the Bennett-Manly emigrant party of 1849 (Gudde, 1949, p. 13).

Arcane Peak: see **Sugarloaf Peak** [INYO].

Archilette: see **Resting Spring** [INYO].

Arc Pass [INYO]: *pass,* 2.25 miles southeast of Mount Whitney (1) on Inyo-Tulare County line (lat. 36°33'05" N, long. 118°16'05" W). Named on Mount Whitney (1956) 15' quadrangle.

Argus: see **Indian Wells Valley** [INYO].

Argus Cañon: see **Great Falls Basin** [INYO].

Argus Peak [INYO]: *peak,* 26 miles east-southeast of the village of Little Lake (lat. 35°51'10" N, long. 117°26'45" W; near N line sec. 16, T 24 S, R 42 E); the peak is in Argus Range. Altitude 6562 feet. Named on Trona (1949) 15' quadrangle.

Argus Range [INYO]: *range,* west of Panamint Valley and Searles Valley; the south end is in San Bernardino County. Named on Death Valley (1954) and Trona (1957) 1°x 2° quadrangles. The name appears on Wheeler's (1877) map, where the valley west of the north part of the range and south of Darwin is called Coso Valley. The name "Argus" is from Argus mining district; Lieutenant D.A. Lyle called the range Tortoise Mountains in 1871, and others called it Darwin Range in the early days (Palmer, p. 8, 22).

Argus Springs: see **Great Falls Basin** [INYO].

Armstrong Canyon [INYO]: *canyon,* 3.5 miles long, opens into lowlands 13 miles northwest of Independence (lat. 36°57'35" N, long. 118°20' W). Named on Mount Pinchot (1953) 15' quadrangle.

Armstrong Pass [ALPINE]: *pass,* nearly 2 miles south-southwest of Freel Peak on Alpine-El Dorado County line (lat. 38°49'55" N, long. 119°54'40" W; sec. 1, T 11 N, R 18 E). Named on Freel Peak (1955) 7.5' quadrangle.

Army Pass [INYO]: *pass,* 20 miles northwest of Olancha on Inyo-Tulare County line (lat. 36°29'50" N, long. 118°14'20" W). Named on Olancha (1956) 15' quadrangle.

Army Pass: see **New Army Pass** [INYO].

Arnot Creek [ALPINE]: *stream,* flows 7.5 miles to Clark Fork 4 miles east of Dardanelles Cone at Sand Flat (lat. 38°24'05" N, long. 119°47'55" W). Named on Dardanelles Cone (1979) 7.5' quadrangle.

Arnot Peak [ALPINE]: *peak,* 7.5 miles northeast of Dardanelles Cone (lat. 38°28'20" N, long. 119°45'30" W). Altitude 10,054 feet. Named on Dardanelles Cone (1979) 7.5' quadrangle. The name commemorates Nathaniel D. Arnot, superior judge of Alpine County from 1879 to 1904 (Gudde, 1949, p. 15).

Arrastre Spring [INYO]: *spring,* 11 miles south-southeast of Telescope Peak (lat. 36°00'50" N, long. 117°01'45" W). Named on Telescope Peak (1952) 15' quadrangle.

Arrowhead Lake [MONO]: *lake,* 1000 feet long, nearly 7 miles west-northwest of Mount Morrison along Mammoth Creek (lat. 37°35' N, long. 118°58'40" W); the outline of the lake on a map resembles an arrowhead. Named on Mount Morrison (1953) 15' quadrangle.

Artists Palette [INYO]: *relief feature,* 6.5 miles south-southeast of Furnace Creek Inn at the west edge of Black Mountains (lat. 36° 22' N, long. 116°48' W; sec. 19, T 26 N, R 2 E). Named on Furnace Creek (1952) 15' quadrangle.

Asa Lake [ALPINE]: *lake,* 400 feet long, 3.5 miles southeast of Ebbetts Pass (lat. 38°30'10" N, long. 119°46'10" W; sec. 34, T 8 N, R 20 E). Named on Ebbetts Pass (1979) 7.5' quadrangle.

Ash Creek [INYO]: *stream,* flows 9 miles to Owens Lake 7 miles north of Olancha (lat. 36°22'45" N, long. 118°00'30" W). Named on Olancha (1956) 15' quadrangle. South Fork enters from the west-southwest 3 miles upstream from the mouth of the main stream; it is 4.5 miles long and is named on Olancha (1956) 15' quadrangle.

Ashford Canyon [INYO]: *canyon,* 2.25 miles long, opens into Death Valley 8 miles west of Epaulet Peak (lat. 35°57'15" N, long. 116° 39'50" W). Named on Confidence Hills (1950) 15' quadrangle, which shows Ashford mine situated near the head of the canyon. The name is from Ashford Mill (Palmer, p. 8-9).

Ashford Junction [INYO]: *locality,* 9.5 miles west-southwest of Epaulet peak in Death Valley (lat. 35°54'35" N, long. 116°40'15" W; sec. 20, T 21 N, R 3 E); the place is 1 mile southeast of the ruins of Ashford Mill. Named on Confidence Hills (1950) 15' quadrangle.

Ashford Mill [INYO]: *locality,* 10 miles west-southwest of Epaulet Peak in Death Valley (lat. 35°57'15" N, long. 116°39'50" W); the place is located 2.5 miles south-southwest of the mouth of Ashford Canyon. Ruins named on Confidence Hills (1950) 15' quadrangle. The Ashford brothers built the mill in 1914 (Federal Writers' Project, p. 39).

Ash Hill [INYO]: *ridge,* north-trending, 6 miles long, on the west side of Panamint Valley 12.5 miles south-southwest of Panamint Butte (lat. 36°15'30" N, long. 117°24'45" W). Named on Maturango Peak (1951) and Panamint Butte (1951) 15' quadrangles.

Ash Meadow [INYO]: *area,* 11 miles northwest of Olancha (lat. 36° 23'30" N, long. 118°08'30" W); the place is at the head of Ash Creek. Named on Olancha (1956) 15' quadrangle.

Atastra Creek [MONO]: *stream,* flows nearly 3 miles to Rough Creek 11 miles east of Bridgeport (lat. 38°16'20" N, long. 119°01'20" W; near S line sec. 20, T 5 N, R 27 E). Named on Bodie (1958) and Bridgeport (1958) 15' quadrangles.

Aurora Canyon [MONO]: *canyon,* drained by a stream that flows 8 miles to East Walker River at Bridgeport (lat. 38°15'25" N, long. 119°13'20" W). Named on Bridgeport (1958) 15' quadrangle. The feature also was called Long Canyon (Wedertz, p. 65).

Aurora Valley: see **Alkali Valley** [MONO].

Austin: see **Mount Mary Austin** [INYO].

Avalanche Lake [MONO]: *lake,* 600 feet long, 1.5 miles north-northwest of Matterhorn Peak (lat. 38°06'55" N, long. 119°23'25" W). Named on Matterhorn Peak (1956) 15' quadrangle.

Avalanche Meadow [ALPINE]: *area,* nearly 4 miles west of Pacific Grade Summit (lat. 38°30'40" N, long. 119°58'40" W; sec. 27, T 8 N, R 18 E). Named on Pacific Valley (1979) 7.5' quadrangle.

Avena: see **Bishop** [INYO].

— B —

Baboon Lakes [INYO]: *lakes,* largest 1400 feet long, nearly 3 miles east of Mount Darwin (lat. 37°10' N, long. 118°37'15" W). Named on Mount Goddard (1948) 15' quadrangle. Art Schober, a packer, named the lakes in the 1930's for the fancied resemblance of some badly sunburned CCC workers at the place to baboons (Schumacher, p. 95).

Bacon Gulch [MONO]: *canyon,* drained by a stream that flows 2 miles to Mono Valley 12 miles southwest of Bodie (lat. 38°04'30" N, long. 119°09' W; sec. 31, T 3 N, R 26 E). Named on Bodie (1958) 15' quadrangle.

Badaraco Camp [ALPINE]: *locality,* 2.5 miles north of Fourth of July Peak (lat. 38°41'45" N, long. 120°01'35" W; sec. 20, T 10 N, R 18 E). Named on Caples Lake (1979) 7.5' quadrangle.

Badger Flat [INYO]: *area,* 13 miles north-northeast of Independence (lat. 36°58'20" N, long. 118°05'50" W; on S line sec. 24, T 11 S, R 35 E). Named on Independence (1951) 15' quadrangle.

Badwater [INYO]: *locality,* 7 miles northeast of Bennetts Well in Death Valley (lat. 36°13'50" N, long. 116°46' W). Named on Bennetts Well (1952) 15' quadrangle. Furnace Creek (1910) 1° quadrangle shows a lake at the place, and has the notation "bad water" there in parentheses—Palmer (p. 10) attributed the present name "Badwater" to this notation.

Badwater Springs [INYO]: *springs,* three, 4.25 miles south-southeast of the mouth of Paiute Canyon at the west edge of Saline Valley (lat. 36°47'20" N, long. 117°53'50" W). Named on Waucoba Wash (1951) 15' quadrangle.

Bagley Valley [ALPINE]: *valley,* 6.5 miles southeast of Mogul Peak (lat. 38°36'45" N, long. 119°38'50" W). Named on Heenan Lake (1979) and Wolf Creek (1979) 7.5' quadrangles.

Bainter Canyon [INYO]: *canyon,* drained by a stream that flows 1 mile to Searles Valley 4.5 miles east of Argus Peak (lat. 35°50'25" N, long. 117°21'45" W; near SW cor. sec. 17, T 24 S, R 43 E). Named on Trona (1949) 15' quadrangle.

Bainter Spring [INYO]: *spring,* nearly 4 miles east of Argus Peak (lat. 35°50'35" N, long. 117°22'50" W; sec. 18, T 24 S, R 43 E); the spring is near the head of Bainter Canyon. Named on Trona (1949) 15' quadrangle.

Bairs Creek [INYO]: *stream,* flows 3 miles to lowlands 11 miles west-northwest of Lone Pine (lat. 36°40'45" N, long. 118°14'30" W); the stream discharges into the aqueduct that takes Owens Valley water to Los Angeles. Named on Lone Pine (1958) and Mount Whitney (1956) 15' quadrangles. North Fork flows 3 miles to lowlands 12 miles west-northwest of Lone Pine (lat. 36°41'40" N, long. 118°14'50" W; near N line sec. 26, T 14 S, R 34 E), and joins Bairs Creek in the lowlands; North Fork is named on Lone Pine (1958) and Mount Whitney (1956) 15' quadrangles.

Baker Creek [INYO]: *stream,* flows 12.5 miles to lowlands 1 mile northwest of Big Pine (lat. 37°10'25" N, long. 118°18'20" W; near NW cor. sec. 18, T 9 S, R 34 E); the stream heads at Baker Lake. Named on Big Pine (1950) 15' quadrangle. On Mount Goddard (1948) 15' quadrangle, the name "Baker Creek" applies to a nearby stream that flows less than 2 miles from Thunder and Lightning Lake to Hidden Lake (1).

Baker Lake [INYO]: *lake,* 1250 feet long, 11 miles west of Big Pine (lat. 37°09'40" N, long. 118°29'40" W; near SE cor. sec. 17, T 9 S, R 32 W); the lake is at the head of Baker Creek. Named on Big Pine (1950) 15' quadrangle.

Bald Mountain [MONO]: *ridge,* northwest-trending, 2 miles long, 8.5 miles south-southeast of the site of Mono Mills (lat. 37°46'45" N, long. 118°53'30" W). Named on Cowtrack Mountain (1962) 15' quadrangle.

Bald Mountain Spring [MONO]: *spring,* 8 miles southeast of the site of Mono Mills (lat. 37°47'30" N, long. 118°52'50" W; near W line sec. 10, T 2 S, R 28 E); the spring is 1 mile northeast of Bald Mountain. Named on Cowtrack Mountain (1962) 15' quadrangle.

Bald Peak [INYO]: *peak,* 3.5 miles southeast of Emigrant Pass (1) in Panamint Range (lat. 36°18'05" N, long. 117°05'25" W; sec. 10, T 19 S, R 45 E). Named on Emigrant Canyon (1952) 15' quadrangle.

Baldwin: see **Mount Baldwin** [MONO].

Baldy: see **Rogers Peak** [INYO].

Ballarat [INYO]: *locality,* 11 miles southwest of Telescope Peak near the west base of Panamint Range (lat. 36°02'55" N, long. 117° 13'25" W; on E line sec. 4, T 22 S, R 44 E). Named on Telescope Peak (1952) 15' quadrangle. Postal authorities established Ballarat post office in 1897 and discontinued it in 1917 (Frickstad, p. 50). The town founded at the place in 1897 was named for the gold-mining camp of Ballarat in Australia (Hubbard, Bray, and Pipkin, p. 18, 20). The place served as a supply center for nearby mines (Federal Writers' Project, p. 53).

Banner Ridge [MONO]: *ridge,* north-trending, 4 miles long, 11 miles north-northeast of Toms Place (lat. 37°41'45" N, long. 118°34'35" W). Named on Casa Diablo Mountain (1953) 15' quadrangle. The name is from Banner mine (Gudde, 1969, p. 21).

Banner Springs [MONO]: *springs,* two, 10 miles north-northeast of Toms Place (lat. 37°41'05" N, long. 118°35'30" W; sec. 18, T 3 S, R 31 E); the springs are west of Banner Ridge. Named on Casa Diablo Mountain (1953) 15' quadrangle. Mount Morrison (1914) 30' quadrangle has the singular form "Banner Spring" for the name.

Barasco Gulch [MONO]: *canyon,* drained by a stream that flows 0.5 mile to lowlands 2 miles south of Benton (lat. 37°47'15" N, long. 118°28'30" W; sec. 8, T 2 S, R 32 E). Named on Benton (1962) 15' quadrangle

Barber Creek [ALPINE]: *stream,* flows 1.25 miles to the State of Nevada nearly 4 miles northeast of Freel Peak (lat. 38°53'35" N, long. 119°50'40" W; sec. 21, T 12 N, R 19 E). Named on Minden (1968) 7.5' quadrangle.

Barcroft: see **Mount Barcroft** [MONO].

Barnard: see **Mount Barnard** [INYO].

Barney Lake [MONO]:

(1) *lake,* 1400 feet long, 4.5 miles northwest of Matterhorn Peak along Robinson Creek (lat. 38°08'25" N, long. 119°26'15" W); the lake is 2 miles northeast of Peeler Lake. Named on Matterhorn Peak (1956) 15' quadrangle. The name commemorates Barney Peeler, a pioneer resident of Bridgeport (Hanna, p. 25).

(2) *lake,* 1100 feet long, 6 miles west of Mount Morrison (lat. 37° 33'55" N, long. 118°58'05" W). Named on Mount Morrison (1953) 15' quadrangle.

Barney Riley [ALPINE]: *locality,* 8.5 miles east of Woodfords along Bryant Creek (1) (lat. 38°45'50" N, long. 119°39'55" W; near NW cor. sec. 3, T 10 N, R 21 E). Site named on Mount Siegel (1957) 15' quadrangle. Called Rileys on Markleeville (1889) 30' quadrangle.

Barney Riley Creek [ALPINE]: *stream,* flows 4 miles to Bryant Creek (1) 9 miles east of Woodfords (lat. 38°45'30" N, long. 119° 39'30" W; sec. 3, T 10 N, R 21 E); the mouth of the stream is 0.5 mile southeast of the site of Barney Riley. Named on Mount Siegel (1957) and Topaz Lake (1956) 15' quadrangles.

Barrel Springs [INYO]: *spring,* 9 miles northeast of Independence in Water Canyon (1) (lat. 36°53'30" N, long. 118°04'25" W). Named on Independence (1951) 15' quadrangle.

Barrett: see **Lake Barrett** [MONO].

Bartlett [INYO]: *locality,* 13 miles north of Olancha along Southern Pacific Railroad (lat. 36°28'40" N, long. 118°01'50" W; near N line sec. 12, T 17 S, R 36 E); the place is 1 mile southwest of Point Bartlett. Named on Olancha (1956) 15' quadrangle. The name commemorates Frank J. Bartlett, treasurer of Clark Chemical Company (Palmer, p. 10). Postal authorities established Bartlett post office in 1926 and discontinued it in 1964 (Salley, p. 15).

Bartlett: see **Point Bartlett** [INYO].

Basin Mountain [INYO]: *peak,* nearly 3 miles south of Mount Tom (lat. 37°17'50" N, long. 118°39'39" W; near W line sec. 35, T 7 S, R 30 E). Altitude 13,240 feet. Named on Mount Tom (1949) 15' quadrangle.

Baxter: see **Mount Baxter** [INYO].

Baxter Pass [INYO]: *pass,* 10 miles west-northwest of Independence on Inyo-Fresno County line (lat. 36°50'10" N, long. 118°22'30" W); the pass is 2 miles south-southwest of Mount Baxter. Named on Mount Pinchot (1953) 15' quadrangle.

Baxter Spring [MONO]: *spring,* nearly 7 miles east of the site of Mono Mills (lat. 37°53'10" N, long. 118°50'10" W; sec. 1, T 1 S, R 28 E). Named on Cowtrack Mountain (1962) 15' quadrangle.

Bear Creek [ALPINE]: *stream,* flows 2.5 miles to Calaveras County 4 miles south-southwest of Mount Reba (lat. 38°27'05" N, long. 120°02'40" W);

the stream goes through the settlement of Bear Valley. Named on Tamarack (1979) 7.5' quadrangle.

Bear Creek [INYO]: *stream,* flows 5 miles to Deep Springs Valley 8 miles east-northeast of Westgard Pass (lat. 37°21'40" N, long. 118° 01'55" W; sec. 9, T 7 S, R 36 E). Named on Blanco Mountain (1951) 15' quadrangle.

Bear Creek Spine: see **Bear Creek Spire** [INYO].

Bear Creek Spire [INYO]: *peak,* 1.5 miles southeast of Mount Abbot on Inyo-Fresno County line (lat. 37°22'05" N, long. 118° 46' W). Altitude 13,713 feet. Named on Mount Abbot (1953) 15' quadrangle. United States Board on Geographic Names (1933, p. 131) rejected the name "Bear Creek Spine" for the feature.

Bear Lake [ALPINE]: *lake,* 1850 feet long, 2.5 miles south-southwest of Mount Reba (lat. 38°28'25" N, long. 120°02'40" W); the feature is along Bear Creek. Named on Tamarack (1979) 7.5' quadrangle.

Bear Lake [INYO]: *lake,* 900 feet long, 4.5 miles west-northwest of Mount Tom (lat. 37°22'20" N, long. 118°43'50" W; sec. 6, T 7 S, R 30 E). Named on Mount Tom (1949) 15' quadrangle.

Beartrack Canyon: see **Mount Dana** [MONO].

Beartrack Creek: see **Williams Butte** [MONO].

Beartrap Lake [MONO]: *lake,* 800 feet long, 3.5 miles north-northeast of Tower Peak (lat. 38°11'25" N, long. 119°30'45" W). Named on Tower Peak (1956) 15' quadrangle.

Bear Tree Meadow [ALPINE]: *area,* 3.25 miles south-southeast of Ebbetts Pass (lat. 38°30' N, long. 119°47'15" W). Named on Dardanelles Cone (1979) and Ebbetts Pass (1979) 7.5' quadrangles.

Bear Valley [ALPINE]: *settlement,* 3 miles south-southwest of Mount Reba along Bear Creek (lat. 38°28' N, long. 120°02'30" W). Named on Tamarack (1979) 7.5' quadrangle. Postal authorities established Bear Valley post office in 1967 (Salley, p. 17).

Bear Valley: see **Bloods Meadow** [ALPINE].

Beatty Junction [INYO]: *locality,* 9 miles east-southeast of Stovepipe Wells in Death Valley (lat. 36°35'20" N, long. 116°56'30" W; sec. 2, T 16 S, R 46 E). Named on Chloride Cliff (1952) 15' quadrangle. A road from Beatty, Nevada, joins a road in Death Valley at the place.

Beauty Peak [MONO]: *peak,* 14 miles east of Bridgeport on California-Nevada State line (lat. 38°17'10" N, long. 118°58'30" W; near NW cor. sec. 23, T 5 N, R 27 E). Altitude 9018 feet. Named on Aurora (1956) 15' quadrangle.

Beaver Meadow [ALPINE]: *area,* 3.25 miles west of Ebbetts Pass along Grouse Creek (2) (lat. 38°32'05" N, long. 119°52'20" W; sec. 22, T 8 N, R 19 E). Named on Ebbetts Pass (1979) 7.5' quadrangle.

Beebe Lake [ALPINE]: *lake,* 1000 feet long, 7 miles north-northwest of Mount Reba (lat. 38°36'20" N, long. 120°03'30" W). Named on Mokelumne Peak (1979) 7.5' quadrangle.

Beebe Lake: see **Lower Beebe Lake** [ALPINE].

Bee Gulch [ALPINE]: *canyon,* drained by a stream that flows 1.5 miles to Lake Alpine (1) 9 miles northwest of Dardanelles Cone (lat. 38°28'50" N, long. 119°59'50" W; near S line sec. 4, T 7 N, R 18 E). Named on Mokelumne Peak (1979), Spicer Meadow Reservoir (1979), and Tamarack (1979) 7.5' quadrangles.

Bee Springs [INYO]: *spring,* 7.5 miles east of Independence (lat. 36° 48'35" N, long. 118°03'40" W). Named on Independence (1951) 15' quadrangle.

Bee Springs Canyon [INYO]: *canyon,* drained by a stream that flows 4 miles to lowlands 7 miles east of Independence (lat. 36°48'20" N, long. 118°04'10" W); the canyon contains Bee Springs. Named on Independence (1951) 15' quadrangle.

Beiton Range: see **Benton Range** [MONO].

Belfort [MONO]: *locality,* 8.5 miles east-northeast of Fales Hot Springs (lat. 38°25' N, long. 119°16' W; sec. 31, T 7 N, R 25 E). Named on Fales Hot Springs (1956) 15' quadrangle. The place was a mining camp in the 1880's (Gudde, 1975, p. 31).

Belmont Camp: see **Cerro Gordo Peak** [INYO].

Bench Lake [INYO]: *lake,* 1000 feet long, 9.5 miles west-southwest of Independence (lat. 36°45'45" N, long. 118°21'40" W). Named on Mount Pinchot (1953) 15' quadrangle.

Bend City: see **Kearsarge** [INYO].

Bendere's Cañon: see **Water Canyon** [INYO] (4).

Bendire Canyon [INYO]: *canyon,* 7.5 miles long, opens into Panamint Valley 6 miles east-southeast of Maturango Peak (lat. 36° 05' N, long. 117°23'40" W; sec. 25, T 21 S, R 42 E). Named on Maturango Peak (1951) 15' quadrangle. The name commemorates Lieutenant Charles Emil Bendire, who commanded the first military expedition to Death Valley, and who passed through the canyon in 1867 (Hanna, p. 29).

Benko Spring [INYO]: *spring,* 3.25 miles north-northeast of Argus Peak (lat. 35°53'45" N, long. 117°25'20" W; near E line sec. 34, T 23 S, R 42 E). Named on Trona (1949) 15' quadrangle.

Bennett City: see **Bennettville** [MONO].

Bennett Peak [INYO]: *peak,* 2.5 miles north of Telescope Peak in Panamint Range (lat. 36°12'25" N, long. 117°05'30" W; sec. 10, T 20 S, R 45 E). Altitude 9980 feet. Named on Telescope Peak (1952) 15' quadrangle. According to Gudde (1949, p. 203), National Park officials applied the name "Rogers Peak" to this feature in 1936 to honor John Rogers, who with W.L. Manly led an emigrant party of 1849 out of Death Valley.

Bennett's Holes: see **Bennetts Well** [INYO].

Bennett's Spring: see **Bennetts Well** [INYO].

Bennetts Well [INYO]: *well,* 20 miles south of Furnace Creek Inn in Death Valley (lat. 36°10' N, long. 116°51'40" W). Named on Bennetts Well (1952) 15' quadrangle. Called Bennett's Wells on Wheeler's (1877) map. The feature consists of springs that were dug out and protected by barrels (Mendenhall, p. 38). Dr. Darwin French found toys and castaway clothing in 1860 at a place that he called Bennett's Holes because he thought it must have been the camping place of Asa Bennett, one of the emigrants of 1849, but identification of French's site with present Bennetts Well is uncertain (Federal Writers' Project, p. 42). Charles Bennett had a rest camp and watering station for his mules at the well when he freighted borax (Federal Writers' Project, p. 41). Palmer (p. 11) gave the name "Bennett's Spring" as an alternate.

Bennettville [MONO]: *locality,* 4 miles east-southeast of Mount Conness along Mine Creek (lat. 37°56'15" N, long. 119°15'30" W; sec. 19, T 1 N, R 25 E). Named on Tuolumne Meadows (1956) 15' quadrangle. Called Tioga on Mount Lyell (1901) 30' quadrangle. Bennettville, first called Bennett City, was named for Thomas Bennett, president of a mining company (Hubbard). A mine discovered at the place in 1860 was renamed Tioga mine when Great Sierra Consolidated Mining Company organized Tioga mining district in 1878; Bennettville was headquarters for the company (Hoover, Rensch, and Rensch, p. 214). Postal authorities established Tioga post office in 1880 and discontinued it in 1881; they established Bennettville post office in 1882 and discontinued it in 1884 (Frickstad, p. 104, 105).

Benton [MONO]: *village,* 36 miles east-southeast of Lee Vining (lat. 37°49'05" N, long. 118°28'30" W; sec. 32, T 1 S, R 32 E); the village is in Benton Valley. Named on Benton (1962) 15' quadrangle. Called Benton Sta. on White Mountain (1917) 30' quadrangle, but United States Board on Geographic Names (1964a, p. 8) rejected this name for the place. The village began in 1883 as a stop on Carson and Colorado Railroad (Myrick, p. 174). California Mining Bureau's (1917b) map shows a place called State Line located 6 miles north-northeast of Benton at California-Nevada State line.

Benton: see **Benton Hot Springs** [MONO].

Benton Crossing [MONO]: *locality,* 11 miles north-northeast of Mount Morrison along Owens River (lat. 37°41'55" N, long. 118° 45'45" W; sec. 10, T 3 S, R 29 E). Named on Mount Morrison (1953) 15' quadrangle.

Benton Hot Spring: see **Benton Hot Springs** [MONO].

Benton Hot Springs [MONO]: *village,* 10 miles east of Glass Mountain in Blind Spring Valley (lat. 37°48' N, long. 118°31'45" W; sec. 2, T 2 S, R 31 E); the village is 3 miles west-southwest of Benton. Named on Glass Mountain (1962) 15' quadrangle. Called Benton on Mount Morrison (1914) 30' quadrangle, which shows a hot spring near the place. The village was known as Hot Springs before it became Benton (Chalfant, 1933, p. 152). The name "Benton" commemorates Senator Thomas Hart Benton of Missouri (Hanna, p. 30). Postal authorities established Benton post office at the site in 1886 (Frickstad, p. 104). The village was a supply center for nearby mines, which had their greatest activity from 1862 until 1889 (DeDecker, p. 27). After the turn of the century, the place became known as Benton Hot Springs, or locally as Old Benton (Mitchell, 1978, p. 9). United States Board on Geographic Names (1964a, p. 8) rejected the names "Benton" and "Old Benton" for present Benton Hot Springs. The name "Benton" eventually was transferred to nearby Benton Station. Waring (p. 136) described Benton Hot Spring, a feature located 300 yards northwest of the village; water there at a temperature of 135° Fahrenheit had domestic and irrigation use, and in the early days it powered a small stamp mill. Wheeler's (1871) map shows Paert's Hot Spr. located near present Benton Hot Springs. Chalfant (1933, p. 152) mentioned Taylor Springs, located a mile or more northeast of present Benton Hot Springs and named for E.S. Taylor, a prospector who lived there. United States Board on Geographic Names (1978b, p. 4) approved the name "Trafton Mountain" for a peak situated 4 miles north-northwest of Benton Hot Springs in Benton Range (lat. 37°51'05" N, long. 119°34' W; sec. 21, T 1 S, R 31 E); the name commemorates George G. Trafton, who lived in the neighborhood for 40 years.

Benton Range [MONO]: *range,* center 8 miles east of Glass Mountain (lat. 37°45'45" N, long. 118°34' W); the north part of the range is 5 miles west of Benton. Named on Casa Diablo Mountain (1953) and Glass Mountain (1962) 15' quadrangles. United States Board on Geographic Names (1986, p. 2) rejected the name "Beiton Range" for the feature.

Benton Station: see **Benton** [MONO].

Benton Valley [MONO]: *valley,* west of the north end of White Mountains, and east of both Benton Range and Blind Spring Hill; Benton is in the valley. Named on Benton (1962) and Glass Mountain (1962) 15' quadrangles. Present Benton Valley and Queen Valley together are called Spring Valley on Wheeler's (1871) map.

Bergona Lake [MONO]: *lake,* 700 feet long, 2.5 miles east of Matterhorn

Peak (lat. 38°05'30" N, long. 119°19'55" W). Named on Matterhorn Peak (1956) 15' quadrangle.

Berry [ALPINE]: *locality,* 8.5 miles southeast of Markleeville in present Wolf Creek Meadows (lat. 38°35'30" N, long. 119°41'30" W) Named on Markleeville (1889) 30' quadrangle.

Beveridge: see **Beveridge Canyon** [INYO].

Beveridge Canyon [INYO]: *canyon,* drained by a stream that flows 6.5 miles to Saline Valley 6.5 miles northeast of New York Butte (lat. 36°43'30" N, long. 117°51'40" W). Named on New York Butte (1950) 15' quadrangle. The feature first was called Hahn's Canyon (DeDecker, p. 50). Postal authorities established Beveridge post office in 1881 and discontinued it in 1882 (Frickstad, p. 50). Beveridge mining district was named for John Beveridge (Chalfant, 1933, p. 294).

Biedeman: see **Mount Biedeman** [MONO].

Big Alkali [MONO]: *valley,* 8 miles west of Bodie (lat. 38°13' N, long. 119°09'15" W). Named on Bodie (1958) 15' quadrangle, which shows several intermittent lakes in the valley. Called Warm Spring Flat on Bridgeport (1909) 30' quadrangle, which shows a large intermittent lake and several small permanent lakes in the valley, but United States Board on Geographic Names (1960b, p. 16) rejected this name for the feature.

Big Alkali Lake [MONO]: *lake,* 2300 feet long, 9 miles north-northeast of Mount Morrison (lat. 37°40'40" N, long. 118°47'10" W; on N line sec. 21, T 3 S, R 29 E); the feature is 1 mile north-northeast of Little Alkali Lake. Named on Mount Morrison (1953) 15' quadrangle.

Big Cactus Flat: see **Upper Cactus Flat** [INYO].

Big Canyon: see **West Carson Canyon** [ALPINE].

Big Dodd Spring [INYO]: *spring,* 7.25 miles south of Ubehebe Peak (lat. 36°35'10" N, long. 117°34'20" W); the spring is less than 0.5 mile north-northwest of Little Dodd Spring. Named on Ubehebe Peak (1950) 15' quadrangle. Palmer (p. 44) called the feature Big Dodds Spring. On Ballarat (1913) 1° quadrangle, the name "Dodds Spring" applies to a spring situated a little way north of the site of present Big Dodd Spring. Waring and Huguenin (p. 34) listed Dodd's Springs, located 7 miles south of Ubehebe Peak.

Bigelow [INYO]: *locality,* 5 miles east-southeast of Bishop along Southern Pacific Railroad (lat. 37°20' N, long. 118°18'45" W; near SE cor. sec. 14, T 7 S, R 33 E). Named on Bishop (1949) 15' quadrangle.

Big Horn Canyon [INYO]: *canyon,* drained by a stream that flows 7 miles to Panamint Valley 5.5 miles northwest of Manly Peak (lat. 35°57'40" N, long. 117°11'45" W). Named on Manly Peak (1950) 15' quadrangle.

Big Horn Gorge [INYO]: *canyon,* 5 miles long, opens into Death Valley 4.25 miles east of Tin Mountain (lat. 36°53'50" N, long. 117°22'45" W). Named on Tin Mountain (1957) 15' quadrangle.

Big Horn Lake [MONO]: *lake,* 900 feet long, 1.5 miles southeast of Mount Conness (lat. 37°57' N, long. 119°17'50" W). Named on Tuolumne Meadows (1956) 15' quadrangle.

Bighorn Lake [MONO]: *lake,* 1100 feet long, 2.5 miles south-southwest of Mount Morrison on upper reaches of a branch of Convict Creek (lat. 37°31'45" N, long. 118°52'45" W). Named on Mount Morrison (1953) 15' quadrangle.

Big Horn Park [INYO]: *area,* 2 miles east of Mount Whitney (1) along Lone Pine Creek (lat. 36°34'20" N, long. 118°15'20" W). Named on Mount Whitney (1956) 15' quadrangle.

Big McGee Lake [MONO]: *lake,* 2000 feet long, 5 miles south of Mount Morrison (lat. 37°29'20" N, long. 118°50'20" W); the lake is less than 0.5 mile east-southeast of Little McGee Lake at the head of McGee Creek (2). Named on Mount Abbot (1953) 15' quadrangle. The name commemorates Alney McGee, a pioneer in Long Valley (2) (Hanna, p. 181).

Big Meadow [MONO]: *area,* 8 miles north-northwest of Matterhorn Peak along Buckeye Creek (lat. 38°12'30" N, long. 119°25' W; in and near sec. 11, T 4 N, R 23 E). Named on Matterhorn Peak (1956) 15' quadrangle. Called Big Meadows on Sampson's (1940) map.

Big Meadows: see **Big Meadow** [MONO]; **Bridgeport Valley** [MONO].

Big Owens Lake: see **Owens Lake** [INYO].

Big Pine [INYO]: *town,* 15 miles south-southeast of Bishop (lat. 37° 09'50" N, long. 118°17'30" W). Named on Big Pine (1950) 15' quadrangle, which has both the names "Big Pine" and "Bigpine P.O." at the place. Postal authorities established Big Pine post office in 1870, discontinued it for a time in 1877; changed the name to Bigpine in 1895, and changed it back to Big Pine in 1962 (Salley, p. 21). United States Board on Geographic Names (1962a, p. 5) rejected the form "Bigpine" for the name.

Big Pine Creek [INYO]: *stream,* formed by the confluence of North Fork and South Fork, flows 11.5 miles to Owens River 2 miles east-northeast of Big Pine (lat. 37°10'20" N, long. 118°15'30" W; near N line sec. 16, T 9 S, R 34 E); the stream goes through Big Pine. Named on Big Pine (1950) 15' quadrangle. North Fork is 6.5 miles long and is named on Big Pine (1950) 15' quadrangle; it is called Big Pine Creek on Mount Goddard (1948) 15' quadrangle, but United States Board on Geographic Names (1983d, p. 6) rejected this name for North Fork. South Fork is 3.5 miles long and is named on Big Pine (1950) 15' quadrangle.

Big Pine Lakes [INYO]: *lakes,* 11 miles west-southwest of Big Pine (lat. 37°07'30" N, long. 118°29'15" W); the lakes are along North Fork Big Pine Creek. Named on Big Pine (1950) 15' quadrangle.

Big Pine Spring [INYO]: *spring,* 4.25 miles west of Big Pine (lat. 37°10'05" N, long. 118°22'05" W; near E line sec. 16, T 9 S, R 33 E). Named on Big Pine (1950) 15' quadrangle.

Big Pothole Lake [INYO]: *lake,* 800 feet long, 10 miles west-southwest of Independence (lat. 36°46'15" N, long. 118°22'20" W); the lake is 1.25 miles west of Little Pothole Lake. Named on Mount Pinchot (1953) 15' quadrangle. Called Pothole Lake on Mount Whitney (1907) 30' quadrangle.

Big Prospector Meadow [MONO]: *area,* 7 miles south-southeast of Mount Barcroft (lat. 37°29'20" N, long. 118°10'45" W). Named on Blanco Mountain (1951) 15' quadrangle.

Big Sand Flat [MONO]: *area,* 3.5 miles east of the site of Mono Mills (lat. 37°52'45" N, long. 118°53'30" W); the place is 4.5 miles northeast of Little Sand Flat. Named on Cowtrack Mountain (1962) 15' quadrangle. Called Sand Flat on Mount Morrison (1914) 30' quadrangle, but United States Board on Geographic Names (1964b, p. 11) rejected this name for the place.

Big Seeley Spring [INYO]: *spring,* 10.5 miles south-southeast of Big Pine near Owens River (lat. 37°01'15" N, long. 118°13'30" W; sec. 2, T 11 S, R 34 E); the spring is 0.25 mile north-northwest of Little Seeley Spring. Named on Waucoba Mountain (1951) 15' quadrangle.

Big Slough [MONO]: *stream,* a distributary that diverges from West Walker River 4 miles south-southeast of Coleville in Antelope Valley (lat. 38°31'10" N, long. 119°28'20" W; sec. 20, T 8 N, R 23 E). Named on Desert Creek Peak (1956) 15' quadrangle.

Big Spring [ALPINE]: *spring,* 6.5 miles east of Mogul Peak (lat. 38°41'25" N, long. 119°35'50" W; near NE cor. sec. 30, T 10 N, R 22 E). Named on Topaz Lake (1956) 15' quadrangle.

Big Spring Campground [MONO]: *locality,* 14 miles north-northwest of Mount Morrison (lat. 37°44'55" N, long. 118°56'15" W; sec. 25, T 2 S, R 27 E); the place is near Big Springs. Named on Mount Morrison (1953) 15' quadrangle.

Big Springs [MONO]: *springs,* two, 14 miles north-northwest of Mount Morrison near the confluence of Deadman Creek and Owens River (lat. 37°45' N, long. 118°56'20" W; near NE cor. sec. 25, T 2 S, R 27 E). Named on Cowtrack Mountain (1962) 15' quadrangle.

Billy Lake [MONO]: *lake,* 300 feet long, 15 miles south of Lee Vining (lat. 37°45'15" N, long. 119°09'45" W). Named on Mono Craters (1953) 15' quadrangle.

Birch: see **Harry Birch Springs** [INYO].

Birch Creek [INYO]:

(1) *stream,* flows 13 miles to lowlands 5 miles west of Bishop (lat. 37°21' N, long. 118°29'20" W; sec. 8, T 7 S, R 32 E). Named on Bishop (1949) and Mount Tom (1949) 15' quadrangles.

(2) *stream,* formed by the confluence of North Fork and South Fork, flows 4.5 miles to Deep Springs Valley 6.25 miles east-northeast of Westgard Pass (lat. 37°20'15" N, long. 118°03' W; sec. 17, T 7 S, R 36 E). Named on Blanco Mountain (1951) 15' quadrangle. North Fork is 4 miles long and South Fork is 5 miles long; both forks are named on Blanco Mountain (1951) 15' quadrangle.

(3) *stream,* flows 8.5 miles to Tinemaha Creek 7 miles south-southeast of Big Pine (lat. 37°04' N, long. 118°15'50" W; sec. 21, T 10 S, R 34 E); the stream heads near Birch Mountain. Named on Big Pine (1950) 15' quadrangle.

Birch Creek [MONO]:

(1) *stream,* flows 3.5 miles to Rock Creek (3) 3.25 miles southeast of Toms Place (lat. 37°31'45" N, long. 118°38'15" W; near W line sec. 12, T 5 S, R 30 E). Named on Casa Diablo Mountain (1953) 15' quadrangle.

(2) *stream,* flows 8 miles before entering a ditch 8 miles west-northwest of White Mountain Peak in Hammil Valley (lat. 37° 41' N, long. 118°23' W; sec. 18, T 3 S, R 33 E). Named on White Mountain Peak (1962) 15' quadrangle.

Birchim Canyon [INYO]: *canyon,* nearly 1 mile long, 8.5 miles northeast of Mount Tom along Rock Creek above the confluence of Rock Creek [INYO-MONO] and Owens River (lat. 37°26'10" N, long. 118°33'15" W; sec. 10, T 6 S, R 31 E). Named on Mount Tom (1949) 15' quadrangle.

Birchim Lake [INYO]: *lake,* 500 feet long, 4.5 miles west of Mount Tom (lat. 37°20'50" N, long. 118°44'15" W; near SW cor. sec. 7, T 7 S, R 30 E). Named on Mount Tom (1949) 15' quadrangle.

Birch Lake [INYO]: *lake,* 2000 feet long, 10 miles southwest of Big Pine (lat. 37°04'25" N, long. 118°25'40" W); the lake is less than 1 mile north-west of Birch Mountain. Named on Big Pine (1950) 15' quadrangle.

Birch Mountain [INYO]: *peak,* 10 miles southwest of Big Pine (lat. 37°03'50" N, long. 118°25'05" W). Altitude 13,665 feet. Named on Big Pine (1950) 15' quadrangle.

Birch Spring [INYO]: *spring,* 1.5 miles north-northwest of Telescope Peak in Jail Canyon (lat. 36°11'30" N, long. 117°06'05" W; sec. 16, T 20 S, R 45 E). Named on Telescope Peak (1952) 15' quadrangle. The name is from birch trees that grow at the place (Palmer, p. 11).

Bird Spring: see **Lee Pump** [INYO].

Bishop [INYO]: *town,* near the north end of Owens Valley (lat. 37° 21'45" N, long. 118°23'45" W; sec. 6, 7, T 7 S, R 33 E). Named on Bishop (1949) 15' quadrangle. The town, which is along Bishop Creek, first had the name "Bishop Creek" (Chalfant, 1933, p. 233). Postal authorities established Bishop Creek post office in 1870; they moved it 5 miles northeast in 1889, when they changed the name to Bishop; they reestablished Bishop Creek post office in 1935 and discontinued it in 1938 (Salley, p. 22). Postal Route (1884) map shows a place called Avena located about halfway between present Bishop and Round Valley post office. Postal authorities established Avena post office in 1880 and discontinued it in 1885 (Frickstad, p. 50).

Bishop Creek [INYO]: *stream,* formed by the confluence of Middle Fork and South Fork (1), flows 9.5 miles to Owens Valley 5 miles west-southwest of Bishop (lat. 37°20' N, long. 118°28'50" W; near N line sec. 20, T 7 S, R 32 E). Named on Bishop (1949) and Mount Tom (1949) 15' quadrangles. Whitney (1865, p. 458) called the stream Bishop's Creek. The name commemorates Samuel A. Bishop, who came to the neighborhood in 1861 and built a camp at what he called San Francis ranch, which was situated about 3 miles southwest of present Bishop (Chalfant, 1933, p. 142). Middle Fork is 10 miles long and is named on Mount Goddard (1948) 15' quadrangle. North Fork (1) enters Middle Fork 3.5 miles upstream from the confluence of Middle Fork and South Fork (1); it is 5 miles long and is named on Mount Goddard (1948) 15' quadrangle. South Fork (1) is 10.5 miles long and is named on Mount Goddard (1948) and Mount Tom (1949) 15' quadrangles. Bishop Creek divides 3.5 miles west of Bishop into two forks: North Fork (2), which flows 7.5 miles to Owens River, and South Fork (2), which enters ditches near Bishop. North Fork (2) and South Fork (2) both are named on Bishop (1949) 15' quadrangle.

Bishop Creek: see **Bishop** [INYO].

Bishop Depot: see **Laws** [INYO].

Bishop Lake [INYO]: *lake,* 1000 feet long, 7.5 miles east-southeast of Mount Darwin (lat. 37°07'20" N, long. 118°33'10" W; sec. 35, T 9 S, R 31 E). Named on Mount Goddard (1948) 15' quadrangle.

Bishop Park [INYO]: *area,* nearly 7 miles northeast of Mount Darwin (lat. 37°14'30" N, long. 118°35'30" W; sec. 20, T 8 S, R 31 E); the place is along Middle Fork Bishop Creek. Named on Mount Goddard (1948) 15' quadrangle.

Bishop Pass [INYO]: *pass,* 8 miles east-southeast of Mount Darwin on Inyo-Fresno County line (lat. 37°06'55" N, long. 118°32'40" W). Named on Mount Goddard (1948) 15' quadrangle.

Bishop's Creek: see **Bishop Creek** [INYO].

Bishop Station: see **Laws** [INYO].

Black Birch Canyon [INYO-MONO]: *canyon,* drained by a stream that heads in Inyo County and flows 1.5 miles to Cottonwood Creek [INYO-MONO] 15 miles east-southeast of Mount Barcroft in Mono County (lat. 37°28' N, long. 118°00'50" W; sec. 34, T 5 S, R 36 E). Named on Blanco Mountain (1951) 15' quadrangle.

Black Butte [ALPINE]: *peak,* 1.5 miles north of Fourth of July Peak (lat. 38°41' N, long. 120°01'20" W; sec. 29, T 10 N, R 18 E). Altitude 9031 feet. Named on Caples Lake (1979) 7.5' quadrangle.

Black Canyon [INYO]:

(1) *canyon,* 9 miles long, opens into lowlands 8.5 miles southeast of Bishop (lat. 37°17'25" N, long. 118°16'20" W; near S line sec. 32, T 7 S, R 34 E). Named on Bishop (1949) and Blanco Mountain (1951) 15' quadrangles. California Mining Bureau's (1917b) map shows a locality called Black Canyon situated along the railroad opposite the mouth of this canyon.

(2) *canyon,* drained by a stream that flows 2.5 miles to lowlands 7.25 miles northwest of Independence (lat. 36°52'20" N, long. 118° 17'20" W; near W line sec. 29, T 12 S, R 34 E). Named on Mount Pinchot (1953) 15' quadrangle.

(3) *canyon,* 3 miles long, opens into lowlands 13 miles south of Coso Peak (lat. 36°00'30" N, long. 117°44'05" W; sec. 23, T 22 S, R 39 E). Named on Coso Peak (1951) 15' quadrangle.

Black Canyon [MONO]: *canyon,* 4 miles long, drained by Wet Fork above the confluence of Wet Fork and Dry Fork 6 miles north-northeast of Glass Mountain (lat. 37°50'45" N, long. 118°38'50" W; sec. 22, T 1 S, R 30 E); the canyon is west of Black Mountain (2). Named on Glass Mountain (1962) 15' quadrangle.

Black Canyon Spring [INYO]: *springs,* two, 5.25 miles north-northwest of Westgard Pass (lat. 37°21'55" N, long. 118°12'15" W; near E line sec. 2, T 7 S, R 34 E); the springs are in Black Canyon (1). Named on Blanco Mountain (1951) 15' quadrangle.

Black Dome [ALPINE]: *peak,* 2 miles west-southwest of Ebbetts Pass (lat. 38°31'50" N, long. 119°50'40" W; near W line sec. 24, T 8 N, R 19 E). Altitude 9112 feet. Named on Ebbetts Pass (1979) 7.5' quadrangle.

Black Islands: see **Lake Hill** [INYO].

Black Lake [INYO]: *lake,* 850 feet long, 11.5 miles west of Big Pine (lat. 37°07'55" N, long. 118°29'40" W; near SE cor. sec. 29, T 9 S, R 32 E). Named on Big Pine (1950) 15' quadrangle.

Black Lake [MONO]: *lake,* 1.5 miles long, 8 miles east-northeast of Glass Mountain (lat. 37°49' N, long. 118°34'40" W; in and near sec. 32, T 1 S, R 31 E). Named on Glass Mountain (1962) 15' quadrangle. According to Loew (1876b, p. 191), the name is "on account of the dark color if its water—a coloration due to its containing organic matter in solution." A number of springs, called Black Lake Springs, occur south of the lake (Waring, p. 336-337)

Black Lake Springs: see **Black Lake** [MONO].

Black Mountain [INYO]:

(1) *peak,* 4.5 miles west-southwest of Westgard Pass (lat. 37°16' N, long. 118°13'30" W; sec. 10, T 8 S, R 34 E). Altitude 9083 feet. Named on Blanco Mountain (1951) 15' quadrangle.

(2) *peak,* 10 miles west of Independence on Inyo-Fresno County line (lat. 36°48'30" N, long. 118°22'40" W). Altitude 13,289 feet. Named on Mount Pinchot (1953) 15' quadrangle.

Black Mountain [MONO]:

(1) *peak,* 7 miles southeast of Matterhorn Peak (lat. 38°02'20" N, long. 119°16'40" W; sec. 12, T 2 N, R 24 E). Named on Matterhorn Peak (1956) 15' quadrangle.

(2) *ridge,* north-trending, 2.5 miles long, 5.5 miles northeast of Glass Mountain (lat. 37°49'45" N, long. 118°38' W). Named on Glass Mountain (1962) 15' quadrangle.

Black Mountains [INYO]: *range,* west of Greenwater Valley and east of Death Valley south of Furnace Creek Inn; the feature is part of Amargosa Range. Named on Death Valley (1954) and Trona (1957) 1°x 2° quadrangles. The name is from the dark color of rocks on top of the range (Federal Writers' Project, p. 35).

Black Peak: see **Black Point** [MONO].

Black Point [INYO]: *promontory,* 11 miles southwest of Stovepipe Wells at the west base of Tucki Mountain (lat. 36°32'30" N, long. 117°12'15" W). Named on Stovepipe Wells (1952) 15' quadrangle.

Black Point [MONO]: *hill,* 5 miles north of Lee Vining on the north side of Mono Lake (lat. 38°01'40" N, long. 119°05'45" W; in and near sec. 15, T 2 N, R 26 E). Altitude 6958 feet. Named on Bodie (1958) 15' quadrangle. Called Black Pk. on Sampson's (1940) map.

Black Point: see **Hells Gate** [INYO].

Black Rock Canyon [INYO]: *canyon,* 2.5 miles long, opens into Lower Centennial Flat 7.5 miles west of Darwin (lat. 36°16' N, long. 117°43'30" W). Named on Coso Peak (1951) and Darwin (1950) 15' quadrangles.

Black Rock Lake [ALPINE]: *lake,* 650 feet long, 6.25 miles north-northwest of Mount Reba on Alpine-Amador County line (lat. 38° 35'30" N, long. 120°04'20" W). Named on Mokelumne Peak (1979) 7.5' quadrangle.

Black Rock Spring: see **Black Spring** [INYO].

Blackrock Spring: see **Little Blackrock Spring** [INYO].

Blackrock Springs [INYO]: *spring,* 9 miles north-northwest of Independence (lat. 36°55'45" N, long. 118°14' W; near SW cor. sec. 2, T 12 S, R 34 E). Named on Independence (1951) 15' quadrangle.

Blackrock Well [INYO]: *well,* 12 miles south-southwest of Ubehebe Peak on the south side of Nelson Range (lat. 36°31'20" N, long. 117°37'50" W). Named on Ubehebe Peak (1950) 15' quadrangle. The name is from dark colored rock near the well (Palmer, p. 12).

Blacksmith Creek [MONO]: *stream,* flows 3 miles to Robinson Creek 3.5 miles north of Matterhorn Peak (lat. 38°08'40" N, long. 119°22'40" W; sec. 6, T 3 N, R 24 E). Named on Matterhorn Peak (1956) 15' quadrangle.

Black Spring [INYO]: *spring,* 3.5 miles north-northwest of Coso Peak (lat. 36°14'55" N, long. 117°43'50" W); the spring is in Black Rock Canyon. Named on Coso Peak (1951) 15' quadrangle. Wheeler's (1877) map has the name "Black Rock Spr." for either this spring or for Black Springs—these two features are 1100 feet apart in Black Rock Canyon.

Black Springs [INYO]: *spring,* 8 miles west of Darwin (lat. 36°15'05" N, long. 117°43'50" W); the spring is in Black Rock Canyon. Named on Darwin (1950) 15' quadrangle. Wheeler's (1877) map has the name "Black Rock Spr." for either this spring or for Black Spring—these two features are 1100 feet apart in Black Rock Canyon.

Blacktop Peak [MONO]: *peak,* 12 miles south-southwest of Lee Vining (lat. 37°47'35" N, long. 119°11'40" W). Altitude 12,710 feet. Named on Mono Craters (1953) 15' quadrangle.

Blackwater Spring [INYO]: *spring,* nearly 7 miles east-northeast of Emigrant Pass (1) (lat. 36°23'15" N, long. 117°02'20" W); the spring is near Wet Fork Blackwater Wash. Named on Emigrant Canyon (1952) 15' quadrangle.

Blackwater Wash [INYO]: *stream,* formed by the confluence of Dry Fork and Wet Fork, flows 4.5 miles to Death Valley 7 miles west-southwest of Furnace Creek Inn (lat. 36°24'55" N, long. 116° 58' W). Named on Emigrant Canyon (1952) and Furnace Creek (1952) 15' quadrangles. Called Dry Canyon on Furnace Creek (1910) 1° quadrangle. Dry Fork is 3.5 miles long and Wet Fork is 2.5 miles long; both forks are named on Emigrant Canyon (1952) 15' quadrangle.

Blackwell Canyon [MONO]: *canyon,* 5.25 miles long, opens into lowlands 3 miles northeast of Coleville (lat. 38°35'30" N, long. 119°27'35" W; sec. 28, T 9 N, R 23 E). Named on Desert Creek Peak (1956) 15' quadrangle.

Blanco Mountain [MONO]: *peak,* 9 miles south-southeast of Mount Barcroft near Mono-Inyo County line (lat. 37°28' N, long. 118°09'45" W). Altitude 11,278 feet. Named on Blanco Mountain (1951) 15' quadrangle.

Called Blank Mountain on Sampson's (1940) map.

Blank Mountain: see **Blanco Mountain** [MONO].

Blind Spring: see **Blind Spring Valley** [MONO].

Blind Spring Hill [MONO]: *range,* center 3.5 miles south of Benton (lat. 37°46' N, long. 118°29' W); the feature is east of Blind Spring Valley. Named on Benton (1962), Glass Mountain (1962), and White Mountain Peak (1962) 15' quadrangles. Wheeler (1876, p. 47) called the range Blind Spring Mountains. A mining camp named Partzwick, for Julius Partz, was in or near the range in the late 1860's (Gudde, 1975, p. 260).

Blind Spring Mountains: see **Blind Spring Hill** [MONO].

Blind Spring Valley [MONO]: *valley,* 10.5 miles east of Glass Mountain (lat. 37°47' N, long. 118°31' W). Named on Glass Mountain (1962) 15' quadrangle. Waring (p. 323) noted that Blind Spring is located in the valley "about 3 miles east of south from Benton" (present Benton Hot Springs); he attributed the name to the lack of vegetation near the spring to indicate the presence of water there.

Bloods Creek [ALPINE]: *stream,* flows 3.5 miles to Calaveras County 4 miles south of Mount Reba (lat. 38°26'55" N, long. 120° 02'25" W); the watercourse has been altered near Bear Valley. Named on Tamarack (1979) 7.5' quadrangle. Called Blood's Cr. on Wheeler's (1876-1877) map.

Bloods Meadow [ALPINE]: *area,* 3.5 miles south-southwest of Mount Reba (lat. 38°27'30" N, long. 120°02'45" W; on W line sec. 18, T 7 N, R 18 E); the place is west of Bloods Creek. Named on Tamarack (1979) 7.5' quadrangle. Called Bear Valley on Big Meadow (1956) 15' quadrangle, which shows the site of Bloods Toll Station at the place. Powers (p. 188) called the feature Grizzly Bear Valley.

Bloods Point [ALPINE]: *promontory,* 3 miles south-southwest of Mount Reba (lat. 38°27'55" N, long. 120°03'10" W; on N line sec. 13, T 7 N, R 17 E); the feature is at the south end of Bloods Ridge. Named on Tamarack (1979) 7.5' quadrangle.

Bloods Ridge [ALPINE]: *ridge,* south-southwest- to south-southeast-trending, nearly 2 miles long, 2.5 miles southwest of Mount Reba (lat. 38°28'45" N, long. 120°03'20" W); the ridge is west of Bloods Creek. Named on Tamarack (1979) 7.5' quadrangle.

Bloods Toll Station [ALPINE]: *locality,* 3 miles south-southwest of Mount Reba (lat. 38°27'45" N, long. 120°02'35" W; sec. 18, T 7 N, R 18 E); the place is in present Bloods Meadow. Site named on Big Meadow (1956) 15' quadrangle. Called Bloods Toll on Big Trees (1891) 30' quadrangle. Wheeler (1879, p. 178) referred to Blood's Station, a "Toll-house and cattle ranch."

Bloody Canyon [MONO]: *canyon,* 6 miles long, along Walker Creek, opens into lowlands 4.25 miles south of Lee Vining (lat. 37°53'40" N, long. 119°07'15" W; near SW cor. sec. 33, T 1 N, R 26 E). Named on Mono Craters (1953) 15' quadrangle. Brewer (p. 416) attributed the name to the blood left by horses that were cut by sharp rocks on the trail through the canyon. Gudde (1975, p. 40) attributed the name to the red color of rocks in the canyon. Mike King built King's Station at the mouth of Bloody Canyon in 1880 (Fletcher, p. 57).

Bloody Lake [MONO]: *lake,* 900 feet long, 3.25 miles west of Mount Morrison at the head of Laurel Creek (lat. 37°33'35" N, long. 118° 55'05" W; near E line sec. 31, T 4 S, R 28 E); the lake is 0.5 mile west of Bloody Mountain. Named on Mount Morrison (1953) 15' quadrangle.

Bloody Mountain [MONO]: *peak,* 2.5 miles west of Mount Morrison (lat. 37°33'40" N, long. 118°54'20" W; sec. 32, T 4 S, R 28 E); the peak is 0.5 mile east of Bloody Lake. Altitude 12,544 feet. Named on Mount Morrison (1953) 15' quadrangle. The name originated with a bloody fight that took place between escaped convicts and a posse near the peak in 1871 (Gudde, 1949, p. 34).

Bloomfield Campground [ALPINE]: *locality,* less than 1 mile west-southwest of Ebbetts Pass along North Fork Mokelumne River (lat. 38°32'15" N, long. 119°49'30" W); the place is 0.5 mile northwest of Bloomfield Meadow. Named on Ebbetts Pass (1979) 7.5' quadrangle.

Bloomfield Meadow [ALPINE]: *area,* less than 1 mile south-southwest of Ebbetts Pass along North Fork Mokelumne River (lat. 38° 32' N, long. 119°49'05" W; sec. 19, T 8 N, R 20 E). Named on Ebbetts Pass (1979) 7.5' quadrangle.

Blue Creek [ALPINE]: *stream,* flows nearly 3 miles from Lower Blue Lake to Deer Creek 4 miles north of Pacific Grade Summit in Deer Valley (lat. 38°34'30" N, long. 119°54'35" W; sec. 5, T 8 N, R 19 E). Named on Pacific Valley (1979) 7.5' quadrangle.

Blue Heaven Lake [INYO]: *lake,* nearly 0.5 mile long, 3500 feet east of Mount Darwin (lat. 37°10'10" N, long. 118°39'35" W). Named on Mount Goddard (1948) 15' quadrangle.

Blue Lake [INYO]: *lake,* 2200 feet long, 3 miles east-northeast of Mount Darwin (lat. 37°11' N, long. 118°37'10" W; near W line sec. 8, T 9 S, R 31 E). Named on Mount Goddard (1948) 15' quadrangle.

Blue Lake [MONO]:

(1) *lake,* 950 feet long, nearly 7 miles east-southeast of Matterhorn Peak (lat. 38°03'05" N, long. 119°16'10" W; on E line sec. 1, T 2 N, R 24 E). Named on Matterhorn Peak (1956) 15' quadrangle. The lake is one of the group called Virginia Lakes.

(2) *lake,* 400 feet long, about 7.5 miles west-northwest of Lee Vining along South Fork Mill Creek (2) in Lake Canyon (lat. 38° 00'15" N, long. 119°14'45" W; sec. 29, T 2 N, R 25 E). Named on Bodie (1958) 15' quadrangle.

Blue Lake: see **Lower Blue Lake** [ALPINE]; **Upper Blue Lake** [ALPINE].

Blue Lake Peak: see **Upper Blue Lake** [ALPINE].

Blue Lakes: see **Lower Blue Lake** [ALPINE].

Bluff Lake [INYO]: *lake,* 400 feet long, nearly 7 miles east of Mount Darwin (lat. 37°10'40" N, long. 118°32'55" W; on E line sec. 11, T 9 S, R 31 E). Named on Mount Goddard (1948) 15' quadrangle.

Bodie [MONO]: *locality,* 12 miles east-southeast of Bridgeport (lat. 38°12'45" N, long. 119°00'40" W; near NE cor. sec. 17, T 4 N, R 27 E). Named on Bodie (1958) 15' quadrangle. The name commemorates William S. Bodey, who with three companions discovered placer gold near the site in 1859; Bodey froze to death after the gold discovery, but later his name—in altered form—was applied to the mining camp (Cain, 1956, p. 1, 5, 10). Postal authorities established Bodie post office in 1877 and discontinued it in 1942 (Frickstad, p. 104).

Bodie Bluff [MONO]: *relief feature,* 0.5 mile northeast of Bodie on the southeast side of Bodie Creek (lat. 38°13'15" N, long. 119°00'15" W; sec. 9, T 4 N, R 27 E). Named on Bodie (1958) 15' quadrangle.

Bodie Creek [MONO]: *stream,* flows 9.5 miles to the State of Nevada 15 miles east of Bridgeport (lat. 38°16'05" N, long. 118° 56'55" W; sec. 25, T 5 N, R 27 E); the stream goes through Bodie. Named on Aurora (1956), Bodie (1958), and Trench Canyon (1958) 15' quadrangles. A stage station called Sunshine was situated along Bodie Creek at California-Nevada State line (Hoover, Rensch, and Rensch, p. 214).

Bodie Hills [MONO]: *range,* extends northwesterly from Mono Valley to East Walker River; Bodie is near the southeast end. Named on Bodie (1958) and Bridgeport (1958) 15' quadrangles.

Bodie Mountain [MONO]: *peak,* 3.25 miles west-northwest of Bodie (lat. 38°13'35" N, long. 119°04'10" W; near NE cor. sec. 11, T 4 N, R 26 E); the peak is in Bodie Hills. Named on Bodie (1958) 15' quadrangle.

Bogards Camp [MONO]: *locality,* 6 miles west-southwest of Bridgeport along Robinson Creek (lat. 38°12'40" N, long. 119°19'05" W; sec. 15, T 4 N, R 24 E). Named on Matterhorn Peak (1956) 15' quadrangle.

Bog Mound Springs: see **Deep Springs Lake** [INYO].

Bohler Canyon [MONO]: *canyon,* drained by a stream that flows 3 miles to lowlands 3.5 miles south of Lee Vining (lat. 37°54'10" N, long. 119°07'20" W; near W line sec. 33, T 1 N, R 26 E). Named on Mono Craters (1953) 15' quadrangle.

Bolton Brown: see **Mount Bolton Brown** [INYO].

Bonanza Gulch [INYO]: *canyon,* drained by a stream that flows 1 mile to Mazourka Canyon 9 miles northeast of Independence (lat. 36°53'30" N, long. 118°04'55" W). Named on Independence (1951) 15' quadrangle. The name is from placer gold in the canyon (DeDecker, p. 46).

Bonner Spring: see **Grapevine Springs** [INYO].

Bonnie Lake [MONO]: *lake,* 1400 feet long, 3.5 miles north-northwest of Tower Peak (lat. 38°11'20" N, long. 119°34'35" W). Named on Tower Peak (1956) 15' quadrangle.

Boone Canyon [MONO]: *canyon,* drained by a stream that flows 3.5 miles to Bridgeport Reservoir 4 miles north of Bridgeport (lat. 38° 18'55" N, long. 119°13'10" W; near S line sec. 4, T 5 N, R 25 E). Named on Bridgeport (1958) and Fales Hot Springs (1956) 15' quadrangles.

Bootleg Canyon [MONO]: *canyon,* drained by a stream that flows 1.5 miles to the canyon of West Walker River 5.5 miles north-northwest of Fales Hot Springs (lat. 38°25'15" N, long. 119°27'05" W; sec. 28, T 7 N, R 23 E). Named on Chris Flat (1954) 7.5' quadrangle.

Borax Well: see **Zabriskie** [INYO].

Border Ruffian: see **Border Ruffian Flat** [ALPINE].

Border Ruffian Flat [ALPINE]: *area,* 6 miles southeast of Carson Pass (lat. 38°37'55" N, long. 119°54'45" W; sec. 17, T 9 N, R 19 E). Named on Carson Pass (1979) 7.5' quadrangle. Markleeville (1889) 30' quadrangle has the name "Border Ruffian" at or near the area.

Boron Springs [INYO]: *springs,* two, 4 miles west of Independence (lat. 36°47'30" N, long. 118°16'15" W; sec. 22, T 13 S, R 34 E). Named on Mount Pinchot (1953) 15' quadrangle.

Bottleneck Lake [INYO]: *lake,* 1150 feet long, 2 miles northeast of Mount Darwin (lat. 37°11'05" N, long. 118°38'40" W). Named on Mount Goddard (1948) 15' quadrangle.

Boulder Creek [ALPINE]: *stream,* flows 3 miles to Clark Fork 2.5 miles south-southeast of Disaster Peak (lat. 38°25'05" N, long. 119°42'35" W); the stream heads near Boulder Peak. Named on Disaster Peak (1979) 7.5' quadrangle.

Boulder Flat [MONO]: *area,* 8.5 miles east-northeast of Fales Hot Springs (lat. 38°25'10" N, long. 119°15'55" W; sec. 31, T 7 N, R 25 E). Named on Fales Hot Springs (1956) 15' quadrangle.

Boulder Hill: see **Silver Mountain** [ALPINE].

Boulder Lake [ALPINE]: *lake,* 600 feet long, 2 miles east-southeast of Disaster Peak (lat. 38°26' N, long. 119°42' W); the feature is along a branch of Boulder Creek. Named on Disaster Peak (1979) 7.5' quadrangle.

Boulder Peak [ALPINE]: *peak,* 2.5 miles east of Disaster Peak (lat. 38°26'50" N, long. 119°41'15" W; sec. 17, T 7 N, R 21 E). Altitude 9393 feet. Named on Disaster Peak (1979) 7.5' quadrangle.

Boulder Peak [INYO]: *peak,* 9.5 miles south of the village of Little Lake (lat. 35°47'55" N, long. 117°55'35" W). Altitude 6266 feet. Named on Little Lake (1954) 15' quadrangle.

Boundary Canyon [INYO]: *canyon,* 6.5 miles long, between Grapevine Mountains and Funeral Mountains, opens into Death Valley 9.5 miles north-northwest of Beatty Junction (lat. 36°43'20" N, long. 116°58'35" W; sec. 21, T 14 S, R 46 E); the canyon heads at Daylight Pass near California-Nevada State line. Named on Bullfrog (1954) and Chloride Cliff (1952) 15' quadrangles. The feature first was called Farley Pass, for Minard H. Farley, a member of the Darwin French expedition of 1860 (Palmer, p. 27).

Box Lake [INYO]: *lake,* 1600 feet long, 2.5 miles northeast of Mount Abbot in Little Lakes Valley (lat. 37°24'55" N, long. 118°45'10" W). Named on Mount Abbot (1953) 15' quadrangle.

Boy Scout Lake: see **Lower Boy Scout Lake** [INYO]; **Upper Boy Scout Lake** [INYO].

Bradbury Wash [INYO]: *stream,* flows 6 miles to Rhodes Wash nearly 4 miles south of Epaulet Peak (lat. 35°55'10" N, long. 116° 32'05" W). Named on Shoshone (1951) 15' quadrangle.

Bradbury Well [INYO]: *well,* nearly 4 miles south of Epaulet Peak (lat. 35°55' N, long. 116°31'30" W); the well is along Bradbury Wash. Named on Confidence Hills (1950) 15' quadrangle. The name commemorates an early prospector (Palmer, p. 12).

Bradford Siding: see **Death Valley Junction** [INYO].

Bradley: see **Mount Bradley** [INYO].

Brainard Lake [INYO]: *lake,* 800 feet long, 10.5 miles west-southwest of Big Pine (lat. 37°05'25" N, long. 118°27'25" W). Named on Big Pine (1950) 15' quadrangle. United States Board on Geographic Names (1985c, p. 2) approved the form "Brainerd Lake" for the name, which commemorates Lawson Brainerd, White Mountain district ranger for the Forest Service from 1924 until 1929.

Brainerd Lake: see **Brainard Lake** [INYO].

Braley Creek [INYO]: *stream,* flows 4 miles to lowlands 4.25 miles north-northwest of Olancha (lat. 36°20'15" N, long. 118°02'10" W). Named on Olancha (1956) 15' quadrangle. The stream now discharges into the aqueduct that takes Owens Valley water to Los Angeles.

Braley Peaks: see **Brawley Peaks** [MONO].

Braly: see **Mount Braly**, under **Brawley Peaks** [MONO].

Braly Mountain: see **Brawley Peaks** [MONO].

Brannan Springs: see **Woodfords** [ALPINE].

Brawley Peaks [MONO]: *peaks,* 5.5 miles east-northeast of Bodie on California-Nevada State line (lat. 38°15' N, long. 118°55'20" W). Named on Aurora (1956) and Trench Canyon (1958) 15' quadrangles. Called Braley Pks. on Wheeler's (1871) map, and called Mt. Braly on Bancroft's (1864) map. The name "Brawley Peaks" commemorates James M. Brawley, a prospector of the 1860's; the feature also was called Braly Mountain (Gudde, 1949, p. 39).

Breakfast Canyon [INYO]: *canyon,* 0.5 mile long, opens into Death Valley 0.5 mile south of Furnace Creek Inn (lat. 36°26'25" N, long. 116°51' W). Named on Furnace Creek (1952) 15' quadrangle. T.J. Williams, former chief ranger at Death Valley, and Charles Summers named the canyon about 1938 for its popularity as a picnic place for parties from Furnace Creek Inn (Palmer, p. 13).

Brewery Spring [INYO]: *spring,* 4.25 miles south-southwest of Telescope Peak in Surprise Canyon (lat. 36°07' N, long. 117°07'45" W). Named on Telescope Peak (1952) 15' quadrangle. A brewery operated at the spring during the boom days of Panamint (Palmer, p. 13).

Breyfogle Buttes: see **Death Valley Buttes** [INYO].

Breyfogle Canyon: see **Indian Pass** [INYO].

Breyfogle Pass: see **Indian Pass** [INYO].

Bridgeport [MONO]: *town,* along East Walker River in Bridgeport Valley (lat. 38°15'20" N, long. 119°13'45" W; in and near sec. 33, T 5 N, R 25 E). Named on Bridgeport (1958) 15' quadrangle. Wedertz (p. 72) attributed the name to a bridge built across East Walker River at the site, and to the influence of many New Englanders who lived at the place. Postal authorities established Bridgeport post office in 1864 (Frickstad, p. 104).

Bridgeport Canyon [MONO]: *canyon,* drained by a stream that flows 4.25 miles to lowlands 8 miles south-southwest of Bodie (lat. 38°06'10" N, long. 119°03'30" W; sec. 24, T 3 N, R 26 E). Named on Bodie (1958) 15' quadrangle.

Bridgeport Reservoir [MONO]: *lake,* 4.5 miles long, behind a dam on East Walker River 5 miles north of Bridgeport (lat. 38°19'35" N, long. 119°12'45" W; sec. 34, T 6 N, R 25 E); the lake is in Bridgeport Valley. Named on Bridgeport (1958) and Fales Hot Springs (1956) 15' quadrangles. United States Board on Geographic Names (1960c, p. 16) rejected the name "East Walker River Reservoir" for the feature.

Bridgeport Valley [MONO]: *valley,* at and around Bridgeport. Named on Bodie (1958), Bridgeport (1958), and Matterhorn Peak (1956) 15' quadrangles. The valley first was called Big Meadows, but soon after 1864 and the growth of Bridgeport the feature became known as Bridgeport Valley (Wedertz, p. 72).

Brier [INYO]: *locality,* 11.5 miles north of Olancha along Southern Pacific Railroad (lat. 36°26'50" N, long. 118°01'45" W; near N line sec. 24, T 17 S, R 36 E). Named on Olancha (1907) 30' quadrangle. The name commemorates J.W. Brier and his family, who crossed Death Valley with the emigrants of 1849 (Gudde, 1949, p. 40).

Bright Dot Lake [MONO]: *lake,* 1500 feet long, 1 mile south of Mount Morrison at the head of a branch of Convict Creek (lat. 37° 32'45" N, long. 118°51'40" W). Named on Mount Morrison (1953) 15' quadrangle.

Brockmans Corner [INYO]: *locality,* 2.25 miles west-northwest of Bishop (lat. 37°22'35" N, long. 118°25'50" W; on S line sec. 35, T 6 S, R 32 E). Named on Bishop (1949) 15' quadrangle.

Broken Finger Peak: see **Mount Morgan** [INYO].

Brown: see **Mount Bolton Brown** [INYO].

Brown Canyon [INYO]: *canyon,* drained by a stream that flows 1.5 miles to lowlands 2 miles south of the village of Little Lake (lat. 35°54'30" N, long. 117°54'15" W; near W line sec. 29, T 23 S, R 38 E). Named on Little Lake (1954) 15' quadrangle.

Brownie Creek [MONO]: *stream,* flows 3 miles to West Walker River 4.5 miles east of Sonora Pass (lat. 38°19'55" N, long. 119°33'05" W; near S line sec. 27, T 6 N, R 22 E). Named on Pickel Meadow (1954) 7.5' quadrangle.

Brown Lake [INYO]: *lake,* 600 feet long, 7.25 miles east of Mount Darwin (lat. 37°10'15" N, long. 118°32'30" W; sec. 13, T 9 S, R 31 E). Named on Mount Goddard (1948) 15' quadrangle.

Brown Peak [INYO]: *peak,* nearly 7 miles south-southwest of Eagle Mountain in Greenwater Range (lat. 36°06'55" N, long. 116°23'05" W; near E line sec. 24, T 23 N, R 5 E). Altitude 4947 feet. Named on Eagle Mountain (1951) 15' quadrangle. The name probably is for Charles G. Brown, a county supervisor, who built the road to Dante's View (Palmer, p. 13).

Brown's Creek: see **Dog Creek** [MONO].

Browns Pass: see **Tioga Pass** [MONO].

Browns Spring [INYO]: *spring,* nearly 2 miles south of Funeral Peak (lat. 36°04'50" N, long. 116°37'15" W). Named on Furnace Creek (1910) 1° quadrangle. Called Brown's Sp. on Tucker and Sampson's (1938) map. The feature probably was named for Charles G. Brown of Brown Peak (Palmer, p. 14).

Brownsville: see **Tecopa** [INYO].

Brown Valley: see **Indian Wells Valley** [INYO].

Bruce Canyon [INYO]: *canyon,* drained by a stream that flows 5 miles to Searles Valley 6.5 miles northeast of Argus Peak (lat. 35° 55'10" N, long. 117°21'20" W; sec. 20, T 23 S, R 43 E). Named on Trona (1949) 15' quadrangle. The name probably commemorates Jim Bruce, a personality of the Panamint boom days (Palmer, p. 14). Thompson's (1921) map shows Cabin Spring, Middle Spring, and Peach Spring in Bruce Canyon; it also shows Dripping Spring in a tributary of the canyon.

Bryant Creek [ALPINE]:

(1) *stream,* formed by the confluence of Leviathan Creek and Mountaineer Creek, flows 3.25 miles to the State of Nevada 8.5 miles east of Woodfords (lat. 38°46'10" N, long. 119°40' W; sec. 31, T 11 N, R 21 E). Named on Mount Siegel (1957) and Topaz Lake (1956) 15' quadrangles.

(2) *stream,* flows 2.25 miles to East Fork Carson River 11 miles south-southeast of Mogul Peak (lat. 38°32'35" N, long. 119°39'05" W; sec. 15, T 8 N, R 21 E). Named on Wolf Creek (1979) 7.5' quadrangle.

Buchanan Well [INYO]: *well,* 18 miles east-southeast of present Death Valley Junction in Stewart Valley (lat. 36°10' N, long. 116° 07'50" W). Named on Furnace Creek (1910) 1° quadrangle.

Buck Creek [ALPINE]: *stream,* flows about 2 miles to Hot Springs Creek 3.25 miles west of Markleeville (lat. 38°41'55" N, long. 119° 50'30" W; sec. 24, T 10 N, R 19 E). Named on Markleeville (1979) 7.5' quadrangle.

Buckeye Creek [MONO]: *stream,* formed by the confluence of North Fork and South Fork, flows 16 miles to Bridgeport Reservoir 2 miles northwest of Bridgeport (lat. 38°16'40" N, long. 119°15'15" W; sec. 19, T 5 N, R 25 E). Named on Fales Hot Springs (1956) and Matterhorn Peak (1956) 15' quadrangles. The name is from Buckeye Mill, which operated in the 1860's (Sowaal, p. 109). North Fork is nearly 3 miles long and South Fork is 4.5 miles long; both forks are named on Matterhorn Peak (1956) 15' quadrangle.

Buckeye Hot Spring [MONO]: *spring,* 5.5 miles west-southwest of Bridgeport (lat. 38°14'20" N, long. 119°19'30" W; sec. 4, T 4 N, R 24 E); the spring is along Buckeye Creek. Named on Matterhorn Peak (1956) 15' quadrangle. The owners of the spring built a bathhouse at the place in 1885 (Wedertz, p. 118).

Buckeye Pass [MONO]: *pass,* 6 miles west-northwest of Matterhorn Peak on Mono-Tuolumne County line (lat. 38°07'50" N, long. 119° 28'40" W); the pass is near the head of South Fork Buckeye Creek. Named on Matterhorn Peak (1956) 15' quadrangle.

Buckeye Peak: see **Eagle Peak** [MONO].

Buckeye Ridge [MONO]: *ridge,* northeast-trending, 7 miles long, 6.5 miles north of Matterhorn Peak (lat. 38°11' N, long. 119°24'30" W); the ridge is southeast of Buckeye Creek. Named on Matterhorn Peak (1956) 15' quadrangle.

Buckhorn Springs [INYO]: *springs,* 7 miles east-southeast of Westgard Pass near the south end of Deep Springs Valley (lat. 37°15'40" N, long. 118°02' W; sec. 9, T 8 S, R 36 E). Named on Blanco Mountain (1951) 15' quadrangle. Called Buckhorn Spring on Bishop (1913) 30' quadrangle. Mendenhall (p. 31) noted that large flowing springs at the south end of Deep Springs Valley are called Deep Springs, and Waring (p. 322) mentioned that the largest group of these springs is sometimes known as Buckhorn Springs. United States Board on Geographic Names (1964b, p. 12) approved the name "Corral Springs" for a group of springs located 1.5 miles northeast of Buckhorn Springs (sec. 3, 4, T 8 S, R 36 E).

Buck Lake [INYO]: *lake,* 800 feet long, nearly 6 miles north-northwest of Mount Tom (lat. 37°24'35" N, long. 118°42'25" W). Named on Mount Tom (1949) 15' quadrangle.

Buck Peak: see **Bucks Peak** [MONO].

Bucks Peak [MONO]: *peak,* 9 miles southeast of Mount Barcroft (lat. 37°28'50" N, long. 118°08'05" W). Named on Blanco Mountain (1951) 15' quadrangle. Called Buck Pk. on Sampson's (1940) map.

Buck Springs [MONO]: *spring,* 5 miles south of Fales Hot Springs (lat. 38°16'50" N, long. 119°24' W; sec. 13, T 5 N, R 23 E). Named on Fales Hot Springs (1954) 7.5' quadrangle.

Buckwheat Wash [INYO]: *dry wash,* between Black Mountains and Ibex Hills, extends for 4 miles to San Bernardino County 16 miles southwest of Shoshone (lat. 35°47'40" N, long. 116°26'30" W). Named on Shoshone (1951) 15' quadrangle.

Buena Vista Mountain: see **Inyo Mountains** [INYO].

Buena Vista Peak: see **Cerro Gordo Peak** [INYO].

Bull Canyon [ALPINE]:

(1) *canyon,* drained by a stream that flows 2.5 miles to Wolf Creek 12 miles south of Mogul Peak (lat. 38°31'05" N, long. 119°43'40" W). Named on Ebbetts Pass (1979) and Wolf Creek (1979) 7.5' quadrangles.

(2) *canyon,* drained by a stream that flows 3 miles to Silver King Creek 7.25 miles east of Disaster Peak in Upper Fish Valley (lat. 38°27'10" N, long. 119°35'55" W; sec. 18, T 7 N, R 22 E). Named on Disaster Peak (1979) and Lost Cannon Peak (1954) 7.5' quadrangles.

Bull Creek [MONO]: *stream,* flows less than 1 mile to Huntoon Creek (1) 4 miles south-southeast of Fales Hot Springs (lat. 35°18'05" N, long. 119°21'45" W; near SE cor. sec. 7, T 5 N, R 24 E). Named on Fales Hot Springs (1956) 15' quadrangle.

Bullion: see **Mount Bullion** [ALPINE].

Bullionae: see **Mount Buillion** [ALPINE].

Bull Lake [ALPINE]: *lake,* 750 feet long, 3.5 miles east-southeast of Ebbetts Pass (lat. 38°31'05" N, long. 119°45'10" W); the lake is south of Bull Canyon (1). Named on Ebbetts Pass (1979) 7.5' quadrangle.

Bull Lake [INYO]: *lake,* 1000 feet long, 6.5 miles east of Mount Darwin (lat. 37°09' N, long. 118°33'15" W; sec. 23, T 9 S, R 31 E). Named on Mount Goddard (1948) 15' quadrangle.

Bullona: see **Mount Bullion** [ALPINE].

Bull Run Creek [ALPINE]: *stream,* flows 3 miles to Highland Creek 2.5 miles north-northwest of Dardanelles Cone (lat. 38°26'15" N, long. 119°53'50" W); the stream heads east of Bull Run Peak. Named on Spicer Meadow Reservoir (1979) 7.5' quadrangle.

Bull Run Lake [ALPINE]: *lake,* 800 feet long, nearly 6 miles north-northwest of Dardanelles Cone (lat. 38°28'50" N, long. 119°54'50" W; on S line sec. 5, T 7 N, R 19 E); the lake is 1.25 miles west-northwest of Bull Run Peak. Named on Spicer Meadow Reservoir (1979) 7.5' quadrangle.

Bull Run Peak [ALPINE]: *peak,* 5 miles north-northwest of Dardanelles Cone (lat. 38°28'35" N, long. 119°53'25" W). Altitude 9495 feet. Named on Spicer Meadow Reservoir (1979) 7.5' quadrangle.

Bundy Canyon [INYO]: *canyon,* drained by a stream that flows 3.5 miles to Searles Valley 9.5 miles east of Argus Peak (lat. 35°50' N, long. 117°16'45" W; sec. 24, T 24 S, R 43 E). Named on Trona (1949) 15' quadrangle.

Bunker Hill Canyon [INYO]: *canyon,* 3.5 miles long, opens into lowlands 5.5 miles north-northwest of the mouth of Paiute Canyon (lat. 36°55'15" N, long. 117°56'45" W); Bunker Hill mine is in the canyon. Named on Waucoba Wash (1951) 15' quadrangle.

Bunny Lake [MONO]: *lake,* 400 feet long, 2.5 miles southwest of Mount Morrison at the head of a branch of Convict Creek (lat. 37° 32'20" N, long. 118°53'50" W). Named on Mount Morrison (1953) 15' quadrangle.

Burcham Creek [MONO]: *stream,* flows 4.5 miles to West Walker River 3.5 miles northwest of Fales Hot Springs (lat. 38°23' N, long. 119°27' W; sec. 9, T 6 N, R 23 E); the stream passes north of Burcham Flat. Named on Chris Flat (1954) 7.5' quadrangle.

Burcham Flat [MONO]: *area,* 2.25 miles northwest of Fales Hot Springs (lat. 38°22' N, long. 119°25'45" W). Named on Chris Flat (1954) and Fales Hot Springs (1954) 7.5' quadrangles. The name commemorates James Burcham, who grazed cattle at the place in the 1860's (Gudde, 1949, p. 45).

Burgess Well [INYO]: *well,* nearly 2 miles south-southeast of New York Butte (lat. 36°37'25" N, long. 117°55'05" W). Named on New York Butte (1950) 15' quadrangle.

Burnside Lake [ALPINE]: *lake,* 1250 feet long, 5.5 miles east-northeast of Carson Pass along Hot Springs Creek (lat. 38°42'45" N, long. 119°53'20" W; sec. 16, T 10 N, R 19 E). Named on Carson Pass (1979) 7.5' quadrangle. According to local tradition, the name commemorates General Ambrose E. Burnside of Civil War fame (Long, p. 47).

Burns Spring [INYO]: *spring,* 5 miles north-northwest of Emigrant Pass (1) (lat. 36°23'45" N, long. 117°11'15" W). Named on Emigrant Canyon (1952) 15' quadrangle.

Burnt Hill Spring [MONO]: *spring,* 10 miles northeast of Bridgeport near Masonic (lat. 38°22'15" N, long. 119°06'50" W; sec. 15, T 6 N, R 26 E). Named on Bridgeport (1958) 15' quadrangle.

Burnt Wagons: see **Death Valley Junction** [INYO].

Burro Canyon [INYO]: *canyon,* drained by a stream that heads in San Bernardino County and flows 7.5 miles to Indian Wells Valley 9.5 miles south of the mouth of Mountain Springs Canyon (lat. 35° 47'55" N, long. 117°34'30" W; sec. 32, T 24 S, R 41 E). Named on Mountain Springs Canyon (1953) and Trona (1949) 15' quadrangles.

Burro Lake [MONO]: *lake,* 950 feet long, nearly 7 miles southeast of Matterhorn Peak (lat. 38°01'55" N, long. 119°17'10" W; near W line sec. 12, T 2 N, R 24 E). Named on Matterhorn Peak (1956) 15' quadrangle.

Burro Spring [INYO]:

(1) *spring,* 6.5 miles south of Tin Mountain (lat. 36°47'25" N, long. 117°27' W). Named on Tin Mountain (1957) 15' quadrangle.

(2) *spring,* 5.5 miles north-northwest of Emigrant Pass (1) (lat. 36° 24'15" N, long. 117°11'15" W). Named on Emigrant Canyon (1952) 15' quadrangle.

Burt Canyon [MONO]: *canyon,* 4 miles long, along Little Walker River above a point 7.5 miles south-southwest of Fales Hot Springs (lat. 38°15'30" N, long. 119°27'45" W; near NE cor. sec. 29, T 5 N, R 23 E). Named on Fales Hot Springs (1956) and Matterhorn Peak (1956) 15' quadrangles. The name is for C.H. Burt, who herded sheep in the canyon (Gudde, 1949, p. 46).

Buscones Peak [MONO]: *peak,* 3 miles south-southwest of Benton on Blind Spring Hill (lat. 37°46'40" N, long. 118°29'30" W; sec. 18, T 2 S, R 32 E). Named on Benton (1962) 15' quadrangle.

Busher Creek [MONO]: *stream,* flows 5.25 miles to the State of Nevada 7.5 miles east-northeast of White Mountain Peak (lat. 37° 41'15" N, long. 118°08'15" W). Named on Mount Barcroft (1962) 15' quadrangle.

Bush Mountain [MONO]: *peak,* 2 miles south of Fales Hot Springs (lat. 38°19'25" N, long. 119°23'35" W; near E line sec. 36, T 6 N, R 23 E). Altitude 8848 feet. Named on Fales Hot Springs (1954) 7.5' quadrangle.

Butte: see **The Butte**, under **Striped Butte** [INYO].

Buttermilk Country [INYO]: *area,* 4 miles southeast of Mount Tom along McGee Creek (lat. 37°17'45" N, long. 118°36'20" W). Named on Mount Tom (1949) 15' quadrangle.

Butte Valley [INYO]: *valley,* 4.5 miles northeast of Manly Peak (lat. 35°57'30" N, long. 117°03'30" W); Striped Butte is in the valley. Named on Manly Peak (1950) 15' quadrangle.

Butte Valley: see **Hidden Valley** [INYO].

Buzztail Spring [MONO]: *spring,* 2.5 miles east-southeast of Mount Morrison near McGee Creek (2) (lat. 37°33' N, long. 118°48'55" W). Named on Mount Morrison (1953) 15' quadrangle.

By-Day Creek [MONO]: *stream,* flows 4.5 miles to Bridgeport Valley 3.5 miles west-northwest of Bridgeport (lat. 38°15'50" N, long. 119°17'40" W; sec. 26, T 5 N, R 24 E). Named on Fales Hot Springs (1956) 15' quadrangle.

— C —

Cabin Creek [MONO]: *stream,* flows 5.5 miles to Leidy Creek 5.5 miles north-northeast of White Mountain Peak (lat. 37°42'15" N, long. 118°12'35" W). Named on Mount Barcroft (1962) and White Mountain Peak (1962) 15' quadrangles.

Cabin Creek: see **Poison Creek** [MONO] (1).

Cabin Spring: see **Bruce Canyon** [INYO].

Cache Creek [ALPINE]: *stream,* flows 3 miles to North Fork Mokelumne River 4 miles northwest of Pacific Grade Summit (lat. 38°33'20" N, long. 119°57'35" W). Named on Pacific Valley (1979) 7.5' quadrangle.

Cactus Flat [INYO]: *area,* 11 miles north-northeast of Coso Junction (lat. 36°11'30" N, long. 117°53' W). Named on Haiwee Reservoir (1951) 15' quadrangle. United States Board on Geographic Names (1983f, p. 2) rejected the name "Little Cactus Flat" for the place.

Cactus Flat: see **Upper Cactus Flat** [INYO].

Cactus Peak [INYO]: *hill,* 8 miles east-northeast of Coso Junction (lat. 36°04'45" N, long. 117°49' W; on E line sec. 25, T 21 S, R 38 E); the feature is 2.5 miles south of Upper Cactus Flat. Named on Haiwee Reservoir (1951) 15' quadrangle.

Caesar: see **Mount Julius Caesar** [INYO].

Calico Peaks [INYO]: *peaks,* 12 miles west of Shoshone in Black Mountains (lat. 35°59' N, long. 116°28'30" W). Named on Shoshone (1951) 15' quadrangle. The name is from the varicolored rocks on the peaks (Palmer, p. 15).

Calico Range: see **Pinto Peak** [INYO].

California Creek [MONO]: *stream,* flows nearly 2 miles to Topaz Lake 8 miles north-northwest of Coleville (lat. 38°41' N, long. 119°32'45" W; sec. 27, T 10 N, R 22 E). Named on Topaz Lake (1956) 15' quadrangle.

California Range: see **Sierra Nevada**, under "Regional setting."

California Valley [INYO]: *valley,* between Nopah Range and Kingston Range; extends south into San Bernardino County. Named on Horse Thief Springs (1956) and Tecopa (1950) 15' quadrangles.

Cameron: see **Monte Cristo** [MONO].

Cameron Canyon [MONO]: *canyon,* drained by a stream that flows 2.25 miles to Summers Creek 8 miles east-northeast of Matterhorn Peak (lat. 38°09'20" N, long. 119°15'25" W; at N line sec. 6, T 3 N, R 25 E). Named on Matterhorn Peak (1956) 15' quadrangle. The name is for Robert A. Cameron, who mined in the canyon from 1897 until 1900 (Gudde, 1975, p. 57).

Camiaca Peak [MONO]: *peak,* 4 miles southeast of Matterhorn Peak on Mono-Tuolumne County line (lat. 38°03'35" N, long. 119°19'25" W). Altitude 11,739 feet. Named on Matterhorn Peak (1956) 15' quadrangle.

Camp Antelope [MONO]: *locality,* 4.5 miles southeast of Coleville (lat. 38°31'30" N, long. 119°26'30" W; sec. 22, T 8 N, R 23 E); the place is on the east side of Antelope Valley. Named on Desert Creek Peak (1956) 15' quadrangle.

Camp Egbert: see **Round Valley** [INYO-MONO].

Camp High Sierra [MONO]: *locality,* 9 miles northwest of Mount Morrison (lat. 37°38'15" N, long. 118°59'30" W; near SE cor. sec. 33, T 3 S, R 27 E); the place is in the Sierra Nevada. Named on Mount Morrison (1953) 15' quadrangle.

Camp Independence: see **Independence** [INYO].

Camp Irene [ALPINE]: *locality,* 3 miles north of Mount Reba along North Fork Mokelumne River (lat. 38°33' N, long. 120°02'15" W). Name on Mokelumne Peak (1979) 7.5' quadrangle.

Campito Meadow [MONO]: *area,* 9.5 miles south-southeast of White Mountain Peak (lat. 37°30'20" N, long. 118°12'15" W); the place is 0.5 mile northwest of Campito Mountain. Named on Mount Barcroft (1962) 15' quadrangle.

Campito Mountain [MONO]: *peak,* 6 miles south-southeast of Mount Barcroft (lat. 37°29'55" N, long. 116°12' W); the peak is 0.5 mile southeast of Campito Meadow. Altitude 11,543 feet. Named on Blanco Mountain (1951) and Mount Barcroft (1962) 15' quadrangles.

Camp Sabrina [INYO]: *locality,* 5.25 miles northeast of Mount Darwin along Middle Fork Bishop Creek (lat. 37°13'15" N, long. 118°36'20" W). Named on Mount Goddard (1948) 15' quadrangle. W.T. Scheld and Ray Wass started a resort at the place in 1922 and named it for nearby Lake Sabrina (Hanna, p. 263).

Cannon Canyon [INYO]: *canyon,* drained by a stream that flows 1.5 miles to Surprise Canyon 4 miles south-southwest of Telescope Peak (lat. 36°06'55" N, long. 117°07'05" W). Named on Telescope Peak (1952) 15' quadrangle.

Canyon Spring [INYO]: *spring,* 5.5 miles north-northwest of Emigrant Pass (1) (lat. 36°24'15" N, long. 117°11'25" W). Named on Emigrant Canyon (1952) 15' quadrangle.

Cape Horn [ALPINE]: *locality,* 8 miles northwest of Dardanelles Cone (lat. 38°29'25" N, long. 119°57'55" W; sec. 2, T 7 N, R 18 E). Named on Spicer Meadow Reservoir (1979) 7.5' quadrangle.

Caples Lake [ALPINE]: *lake,* 2 miles long, behind a dam on Caples Creek 3.5 miles north-northwest of Fourth of July Peak (lat. 38°42'25" N, long. 120°02'55" W; sec. 18, T 10 N, R 18 E). Named on Caples Lake (1979) 7.5' quadrangle. Silver Lake (1956) 15' quadrangle shows Twin Lakes Reservoir at the place, and Pyramid Peak (1896) 30' quadrangle shows two connected lakes—called Twin Lakes—and adjacent marsh there. According to Paden (*in* Moorman, p. 128), in the early days the site had only one lake, called Mountain Lake or Nevada Lake. United States Board on Geographic Names (1968b, p. 4-5) rejected the names "Clear Lake," "Summit Lake," and "Twin Lakes Reservoir" for present Caples Lake, and noted that the name "Caples Lake" is for Dr. James Caples, who built a station near the feature in the 1850's—his place became a stop on a wagon road into California.

Caples Lake Campground [ALPINE]: *locality,* 3.5 miles north-northwest of Fourth of July Peak (lat. 38°42'20" N, long. 120°03'15" W; sec. 23, T 10 N, R 17 E); the place is on the north shore of Caples Lake. Named on Caples Lake (1979) 7.5' quadrangle.

Cardinal Mountain [INYO]: *peak,* 18 miles northwest of Independence on Inyo-Fresno County line (lat. 36°59'55" N, long. 118°24'40" W). Altitude 13,397 feet. Named on Mount Pinchot (1953) 15' quadrangle.

Carey's Mills: see **Woodfords** [ALPINE].

Carillon: see **Mount Carillon** [INYO].

Carmen Lake: see **Kirman Lake** [MONO].

Carricut Lake [INYO]: *dry lake,* 2400 feet long, 5.5 miles south of Maturango Peak in Etcheron Valley (lat. 36°02'20" N, long. 117° 29'55" W; sec. 12, T 22 S, R 41 E). Named on Coso Peak (1951) and Maturango Peak (1951) 15' quadrangles. The misspelled name commemorates John Carricart, an early-day sheep rancher in the region (Koenig, p. 140).

Carroll [INYO]: *locality,* 15 miles north of Olancha along Southern Pacific Railroad (lat. 36°29'45" N, long. 118°01'50" W). Named on Olancha (1907) 30' quadrangle.

Carroll Creek [INYO]: *stream,* flows 7 miles to Owens Lake 14 miles north of Olancha (lat. 36°29' N, long. 118°01'30" W; sec. 1, T 17 S, R 36 E). Named on Lone Pine (1958) and Olancha (1956) 15' quadrangles. The name honors A.W. de la Cour Carroll of Lone Pine, a charter member of the Sierra Club (Gudde, 1949, p. 58).

Carson: see **Kit Carson Campground** [ALPINE].

Carson Camp: see **Silver Lake** [MONO].

Carson Canyon: see **West Carson Canyon** [ALPINE].

Carson Falls [ALPINE]: *waterfall,* 4 miles northeast of Disaster Peak along East Fork Carson River (lat. 38°29'20" N, long. 119°40'55" W). Named on Disaster Peak (1979) 7.5' quadrangle.

Carson Pass [ALPINE]: *pass,* 11.5 miles west of Markleeville (lat. 38°41'40" N, long. 119°59'15" W; sec. 22, T 10 N, R 18 E). Named on Carson Pass (1979) 7.5' quadrangle. Kit Carson led the Fremont exploring party through the pass in February, 1844; thereafter the place was known as Kit Carson Pass (Hoover, Rensch, and Rensch, p. 25).

Carson Peak [MONO]: *peak,* 9.5 miles north-northwest of Mammoth Mountain (lat. 37°44'50" N, long. 119°07'25" W; sec. 29, T 2 S, R 26 E). Altitude 10,909 feet. Named on Devils Postpile (1953) 15' quadrangle. Frank Lewis and his son climbed the peak in 1921 and named it for Roy Carson and Nancy Carson, operators of Carson Camp at Silver Lake (Bean, p. 16).

Carson Range [ALPINE]: *range,* extends north-northeast from Carson Pass to the State of Nevada, largely on Alpine-El Dorado County line. Named on Freel Peak (1956) and Markleeville (1956) 15' quadrangles. United States Board on Geographic Names (1939, p. 9) rejected he name "Rose Mountain Range" for the feature.

Carson River, East Fork [ALPINE]: *stream,* flows 42 miles to the State of Nevada 7 miles east of Woodfords (lat. 38°47'20" N, long. 119°41'40" W; near W line sec. 25, T 11 N, R 20 E). Named on Markleeville (1956), Mount Siegel (1957), Sonora Pass (1956), and Topaz Lake (1956) 15' quadrangles. Called East Carson River on Dardanelles (1898) 30' quadrangle. Fremont named the stream for his guide, Kit Carson (Gudde, 1949, p. 58). Eakel (p. 7) used the name "East Carson Cañon" for the canyon of the stream above Markleeville.

Carson River, Middle Fork: see **Markleeville Creek** [ALPINE].

Carson River, West Fork [ALPINE]: *stream,* flows 24 miles to the State of Nevada 5.25 miles northeast of Woodfords (lat. 38°50'15" N, long. 119°45'50" W; near N line sec. 8, T 11 N, R 20 E). Named on Carson Pass (1979), Freel Peak (1955), and Woodfords (1979) 7.5' quadrangles. The stream also was called West Carson River (Eakel, p. 7) and Pass Creek (Decker, p. 140).

Carsons Camp: see **Silver Lake** [MONO].

Carson Slough [INYO]: *stream,* heads in the State of Nevada and flows 8 miles in California to Amargosa River nearly 4 miles south-southeast of Death Valley Junction (lat. 36°15'20" N, long. 116°22'50" W). Named on Ash Meadows (1952) 15' quadrangle.

Carson Valley [ALPINE]: *valley,* mainly in the State of Nevada, but extends southwest into Alpine County along West Fork Carson River northeast of Woodfords. Named on Woodfords (1979) 7.5' quadrangle.

Cartago [INYO]: *settlement,* 3 miles north-northwest of Olancha on the west side of Owens Lake (lat. 36°19'30" N, long. 118°01'30" W). Named on Olancha (1956) 15' quadrangle. Postal authorities established Cartago post office in 1918 (Frickstad, p. 50). The name is the Spanish designation for the ancient city of Carthage—a nearby settlement was called Carthage (Gudde, 1949, p. 58). Daneri's Landing at the place served steamboats that in the 1870's carried cordwood across the lake for Cerro Gordo mine, and carried ore back from the mine (DeDecker, p. 61). Recovery of soda and other chemicals from Owens Lake started at Cartago in 1872 (Hanna, p. 57).

Cartago Creek [INYO]: *stream,* flows 3.5 miles to lowlands 3 miles northwest of Olancha (lat. 36°18'25" N, long. 118°03' W; sec. 2, T 19 S, R 36 E). Named on Olancha (1956) 15' quadrangle. Called Carthage Creek on Olancha (1907) 30' quadrangle, but United States Board on Geographic Names (1961b, p. 10) rejected this name for the feature. The stream now discharges into the aqueduct that takes Owens Valley water to Los Angeles.

Carthage [INYO]: *settlement,* 2.5 miles north-northwest of Olancha (lat. 36°19' N, long. 118°01'20" W; sec. 1, T 19 S, R 36 E). Named on Olancha (1907) 30' quadrangle.

Carthage Creek: see **Cartago Creek** [INYO].

Cary Canyon [ALPINE]: *canyon,* drained by a stream that flows 1.5 miles to West Fork Carson River at Woodfords (lat. 38°46'25" N, long. 119°49'25"

W); the canyon heads north of Cary Peak. Named on Woodfords (1979) 7.5' quadrangle.

Cary Peak [ALPINE]: *peak,* 1.5 miles west of Woodfords (lat. 38°46'45" N, long. 119°50'50" W; near N line sec. 33, T 11 N, R 19 E). Altitude 8726 feet. Named on Woodfords (1979) 7.5' quadrangle. Macomb (1878, p. 141) referred to Cary's Peak, and Long (p. 4) used the designation "Cary's (Woodfords) Peak." The name "Cary Peak" commemorates the Carey (or Cary) brothers, who settled in the neighborhood in the early 1850's (Gudde, 1949, p. 59). Present Hawkins Peak is called Cary Pk. on Wheeler's (1876-1877) map.

Cary's Mills: see **Woodfords** [ALPINE].

Casa Diablo: see **Casa Diablo Hot Springs** [MONO].

Casa Diablo Hot Springs [MONO]: *locality,* 6.5 miles north-northwest of Mount Morrison (lat. 37°38'45" N, long. 118°54'50" W; sec. 32, T 3 S, R 28 E). Named on Mount Morrison (1953) 15' quadrangle. On Mount Morrison (1914) 30' quadrangle, the name applies to a spring at the site. Waring (p. 146) noted that Indians and Americans used the hot water there to relieve rheumatism. Sampson's (1940) map has the name "Casa Diablo" at the place, and has the name "Hot Cr. Geyser" for a feature situated along Hot Creek (2) about 5 miles east-northeast of present Casa Diablo Hot Springs. California Mining Bureau's (1917b) map shows a place called Thompsons located about where Mount Morrison (1914) 30' quadrangle shows Thompson ranch 7 miles north of Casa Diablo Hot Springs. The same California Mining Bureau map shows a place called Fords located about where Mount Morrison (1914) 30' quadrangle shows Ford ranch 8 miles northeast of Casa Diablo Hot Springs near Owens River. Tucker (p. 403) noted that springs called Warner Hot Springs for their owner, P.A. Warner, are situated 1 mile northeast of Casa Diablo Hot Springs.

Casa Diablo Lake [MONO]: *lake,* 3200 feet long, 7 miles north-northwest of Mount Morrison (lat. 37°39'10" N, long. 118°55'15" W; mainly in sec. 30, T 3 S, R 28 E); the lake is north-northwest of Casa Diablo Hot Springs. Named on Mount Morrison (1914) 30' quadrangle.

Casa Diablo Mountain [MONO]: *peak,* 7.25 miles east of Toms Place (lat. 37°34'45" N, long. 118°33' W; near NW cor. sec. 27, T 4 S, R 31 E). Altitude 7912 feet. Named on Casa Diablo Mountain (1953) 15' quadrangle. The name is from Casa Diablo mine (Gudde, 1949, p. 59), discovered in 1895 and worked for gold and silver (Eakel and McLaughlin, p. 172-173).

Cascade Creek [MONO]: *stream,* flows 4 miles to West Walker River 4.25 miles north of Tower Peak (lat. 38°12'20" N, long. 119° 33'05" W). Named on Tower Peak (1956) 15' quadrangle.

Cascade Lake [MONO]: *lake,* 1100 feet long, 1.5 miles north-northeast of Mount Conness along Mill Creek (2) (lat. 37°59'25" N, long. 119°18'20" W; near SE cor. sec. 27, T 2 N, R 24 E). Named on Tuolumne Meadows (1956) 15' quadrangle.

Castle Peak: see **Dunderberg Peak** [MONO]; **Tower Peak** [MONO].

Cattle Creek [MONO]: *stream,* flows 4.5 miles to Twin Lakes (1) nearly 4 miles north of Matterhorn Peak (lat. 38°08'45" N, long. 119°22' W; sec. 6, T 3 N, R 24 E). Named on Matterhorn Peak (1956) 15' quadrangle.

Cat Valley [ALPINE]: *canyon,* drained by a stream that flows 2.5 miles to North Fork Mokelumne River 5.25 miles northwest of Pacific Grade Summit (lat. 38°33'55" N, long. 119°59'05" W). Named on Pacific Valley (1979) 7.5' quadrangle.

Cedar Camp [ALPINE]: *locality,* 2.25 miles northwest of Mount Reba along North Fork Mokelumne River (lat. 38°32'05" N, long. 120°03'10" W). Named on Mokelumne Peak (1979) 7.5' quadrangle.

Cedar Flat [INYO]: *area,* 1 mile south of Westgard Pass (lat. 37° 17' N, long. 118°09' W). Named on Blanco Mountain (1951) 15' quadrangle.

Cedar Hill [MONO]: *mountain,* 9.5 miles east-southeast of Bodie on California-Nevada State line (lat. 38°11' N, long. 118°50'30" W). Altitude 8457 feet. Named on Trench Canyon (1958) 15' quadrangle.

Cedar Spring [INYO]: *spring,* 9.5 miles north of Westgard Pass (lat. 37°26'30" N, long. 118°08'45" W; sec. 9, T 6 S, R 35 E). Named on Blanco Mountain (1951) 15' quadrangle.

Centennial Bluff [MONO]: *escarpment,* north-trending, 0.5 mile long, 1.25 miles south of Coleville on the west side of Antelope Valley (lat. 38°33' N, long. 119°30'20" W; sec. 12, T 8 N, R 22 E). Named on Topaz Lake (1956) 15' quadrangle.

Centennial Canyon [INYO]: *canyon,* 2 miles long, opens into an unnamed canyon 16 miles south-southeast of Keeler (lat. 36°16' N, long. 117°45'55" W); the canyon is between Upper Centennial Flat and Lower Centennial Flat. Named on Haiwee Reservoir (1951) and Keeler (1951) 15' quadrangles. Woodward (p. 63) called the feature Arab canon—Lower Centennial Spring, also known as Arab Spring, is in the canyon.

Centennial Flat: see **Lower Centennial Flat** [INYO]; **Upper Centennial Flat** [INYO].

Centennial Spring: see **Lower Centennial Spring** [INYO]; **Upper Centennial Spring** [INYO].

Center Basin Crags [INYO]: *relief feature,* 11 miles north-northwest of Mount Whitney (1) on Inyo-Tulare County line (lat. 36°44'10" N, long. 118°20'45" W). Named on Mount Whitney (1956) 15' quadrangle.

Center Mountain [MONO]: *peak,* 7 miles west-northwest of Matterhorn Peak on Mono-Tuolumne County line (lat. 38°08'40" N, long. 119°29'20" W). Altitude 11,273 feet. Named on Matterhorn Peak (1956) 15' quadrangle.

Centerville Flat [ALPINE]: *area,* nearly 4 miles south of Mogul Peak along East Fork Carson River (lat. 38°37'55" N, long. 119°43'20" W; on S line sec. 12, T 9 N, R 20 E). Named on Heenan Lake (1979) 7.5' quadrangle.

Centreville: see **Wolf Creek** [ALPINE].

Cerro Gordo: see **Cerro Gordo Peak** [INYO].

Cerro Gordo Landing: see **Keeler** [INYO].

Cerro Gordo Mountains: see **Inyo Mountains** [INYO].

Cerro Gordo Peak [INYO]: *peak,* 11 miles southeast of New York Butte (lat. 36°32'15" N, long. 117°47'10" W). Altitude 9184 feet. Named on New York Butte (1950) 15' quadrangle. Called Cerro Gordo on Ballarat (1913) 1° quadrangle—*cerro gordo* means "big mountain" in Spanish (Gudde, 1975, p. 66). The feature first was called Buena Vista Peak (DeDecker, p. 67). Cerro Gordo mine is located 2000 feet west-northwest of the top of the peak, and a group of buildings 0.5 mile west of the peak represents the mining camp of Cerro Gordo. Postal authorities established Cerro Gordo post office in 1869, discontinued it in 1887, reestablished it in 1889, and discontinued it in 1895 (Frickstad, p. 50). A settlement called Belmont Camp, for Belmont mine, was situated 1 mile east-southeast of Cerro Gordo Peak (DeDecker, p. 67).

Chain of Lakes [MONO]: *lakes,* four, largest 1000 feet long, 6.5 miles north of Tower Peak (lat. 38°14'20" N, long. 119°33'45" W; sec. 33, T 5 N, R 22 E). Named on Tower Peak (1956) 15' quadrangle.

Chalfant [MONO]: *locality,* 22 miles south-southeast of Benton Station (present Benton) along Southern Pacific Railroad (lat. 37° 30'35" N, long. 118°21'45" W; sec. 16, T 5 S, R 33 E); the place is in present Chalfant Valley. Named on White Mountain (1917) 30' quadrangle. Postal authorities established Chalfant post office in 1913 and discontinued it in 1928; the name is for Arthur Chalfant, a newspaper publisher, who settled at the place in 1870 (Salley, p. 41).

Chalfant Lakes [INYO]: *lakes,* largest 1050 feet long, 3 miles south-southeast of Mount Abbot (lat. 37°20'50" N, long. 118°45'30" W). Named on Mount Abbot (1953) 15' quadrangle.

Chalfant Valley [MONO]: *valley,* 9.5 miles southwest of White Mountain Peak; west of White Mountains and south of Hammil Valley (lat. 37°32'30" N, long. 118°22'30" W). Named on White Mountain Peak (1962) 15' quadrangle. Shown as part of Owens River Valley on Wheeler's (1871) map.

Champion Canyon [ALPINE]: *canyon,* drained by a stream that flows 1.5 miles to Highland Creek 3 miles north-northeast of Dardanelles Cone (lat. 38°26'50" N, long. 119°51'20" W). Named on Dardanelles Cone (1979) 7.5' quadrangle. Called Hiram Canyon on Dardanelles Cone (1956) 15' quadrangle, but United States Board on Geographic Names (1979b, p. 5) rejected this name for the feature.

Champion Canyon: see **Poison Canyon** [ALPINE] (2).

Chango Lake [MONO]: *lake,* 500 feet long, 4.5 miles northeast of Sonora Pass (lat. 38°22'40" N, long. 119°35'10" W; sec. 8, T 6 N, R 22 E). Named on Lost Cannon Peak (1954) 7.5' quadrangle.

Chappo Spring [INYO]: *spring,* 7.25 miles north-northeast of Tecopa (lat. 35°56'50" N, long. 116°11'15" W; sec. 2, T 21 N, R 7 E). Named on Tecopa (1950) 15' quadrangle.

Charity Valley [ALPINE]: *valley,* 4.5 miles east-southeast of Carson Pass (lat. 38°40' N, long. 119°54'45" W; in and near sec. 32, T 10 N, R 19 E). Named on Carson Pass (1979) 7.5' quadrangle.

Charity Valley Creek [ALPINE]: *stream,* flows 6 miles to Hot Springs Creek 5 miles west of Markleeville (lat. 38°42' N, long. 119°52'25" W; sec. 22, T 10 N, R 19 E); the stream goes through Charity Valley. Named on Carson Pass (1979) 7.5' quadrangle.

Charley's Butte: see **Charlies Butte** [INYO].

Charlie Canyon [INYO]: *canyon,* drained by a stream that flows 1.5 miles to an unnamed canyon 6.5 miles west-northwest of Independence (lat. 36°49'45" N, long. 118°18'25" W). Named on Mount Pinchot (1953) 15' quadrangle.

Charlies Butte [INYO]: *hill,* 11 miles south-southeast of Big Pine on the west side of Owens River (lat. 37°01'05" N, long. 118°13'30" W; sec. 2, T 11 S, R 34 E). Named on Waucoba Mountain (1951) 15' quadrangle. Indians killed Charley Tyler near the hill in 1863; since that time the feature has been known as Charley's Butte (Chalfant, 1933, p. 180).

Chiatovich Creek [MONO]: *stream,* North Fork flows 2.5 miles to the State of Nevada 10 miles east of Benton (lat. 37°48'20" N, long. 118°18' W); South Fork flows 3 miles to the State of Nevada 11 miles east of Benton (lat. 37°47'35" N, long. 118°17' W). The forks, which join in the State of Nevada, are named on Benton (1962) 15' quadrangle. United States Board on Geographic Names (1965a, p. 10) rejected the name "Chiatovich Creek" for North Fork. The name is for the John Chiatovich family, pioneers in Fish Lake Valley (Carlson, p. 75).

Chiatovich Flats [MONO]: *area,* 5.5 miles north of White Mountain Peak along Cabin Creek (lat. 37°42'45" N, long. 118°15'45" W). Named on

Mount Barcroft (1962) and White Mountain Peak (1962) 15' quadrangles.

Chicago Valley [INYO]: *valley,* between Resting Spring Range and Nopah Range. Named on Stewart Valley (1958) and Tecopa (1950) 15' quadrangles. The name is said to be from investors in Chicago who backed mining activity in the neighborhood (Palmer, p. 16).

Chickenfoot Lake [INYO]: *lake,* 1700 feet long, 2 miles east-northeast of Mount Abbot in Little Lakes Valley (lat. 37°24' N, long. 118°45'05" W). Named on Mount Abbot (1953) and Mount Tom (1949) 15' quadrangles.

Chidago Canyon [MONO]: *canyon,* 12 miles long, opens into Chalfant Valley 10 miles west-southwest of White Mountain Peak (lat. 37°33'30" N, long. 118°25'20" W; sec. 26, T 4 S, R 32 E). Named on Casa Diablo Mountain (1953) and White Mountain Peak (1962) 15' quadrangles.

Chidago Flat [MONO]: *area,* 9.5 miles northeast of Toms Place (lat. 37°38'35" N, long. 118°33'40" W; sec. 34, T 3 S, R 31 E); the place is north of Chidago Canyon. Named on Casa Diablo Mountain (1953) 15' quadrangle.

China Garden [MONO]: *locality,* 9.5 miles north-northwest of Fales Hot Springs along West Walker River (lat. 38°28'40" N, long. 119° 27'35" W; sec. 4, T 7 N, R 23 E). Named on Chris Flat (1954) 7.5' quadrangle.

China Gardens: see **China Gardnes Spring** [INYO].

China Garden Spring [INYO]: *spring,* 4.5 miles northeast of Darwin in Darwin Canyon (lat. 36°18'50" N, long. 117°31'50" W; sec. 4, T 19 S, R 41 E). Named on Darwin (1950) 15' quadrangle. Called Willow Spring on Wheeler's (1877) map.

China Gardens Spring [INYO]: *spring,* 6 miles east of Coso Peak (lat. 36°12'05" N, long. 117°36'20" W; near N line sec. 14, T 20 S, R 40 E). Named on Coso Peak (1951) 15' quadrangle. This appears to be the feature called McGuinnes Spr. on Wheeler's (1877) map. United States Board on Geographic Names (1985b, p. 2) rejected the names "China Gardens," "China Garden Spring," and "Chinese Garden Spring" for the feature.

China Peak [MONO]: *peak,* 2.5 miles south of Benton on Blind Spring Hill (lat. 37°46'50" N, long. 118°29' W; near NE cor. sec. 18, T 2 S, R 32 E). Named on Benton (1962) 15' quadrangle.

China Ranch Springs: see **Willow Spring** [INYO] (5).

Chinese Garden Spring: see **China Gardens Spring** [INYO].

Chloride City [INYO]: *locality,* 8.5 miles north-northeast of Beatty Junction in Funeral Mountains (lat. 36°42'20" N, long. 116°52'50" W; near NW cor. sec. 28, T 30 N, R 1 E); the place is less than 1 mile north-northwest of Chloride Cliff. Named on Chloride Cliff (1952) 15' quadrangle.

Chloride Cliff [INYO]: *relief feature,* 8 miles north-northeast of Beatty Junction in Funeral Mountains (lat. 36°41'40" N, long. 116° 52'40" W; sec. 28, T 30 N, R 1 E). Named on Chloride Cliff (1952) 15' quadrangle. The name is from the chloride mineral found at the place (Palmer, p. 16).

Chocolate Lakes [INYO]: *lakes,* three, largest 950 feet long, 7 miles east-southeast of Mount Darwin (lat. 37°08'50" N, long. 118°32'45" W; sec. 24, T 9 S, R 31 E); the lakes are 0.25 mile northeast of Chocolate Peak. Named on Mount Goddard (1948) 15' quadrangle.

Chocolate Mountain: see **Piper Mountain** [INYO].

Chocolate Peak [INYO]: *peak,* 7 miles east-southeast of Mount Darwin (lat. 37°08'45" N, long. 118°32'55" W; at NW cor. sec. 25, T 9 S, R 31 E). Altitude 11,658 feet. Named on Mount Goddard (1948) 15' quadrangle.

Chris Flat [MONO]: *area,* 4.25 miles northwest of Fales Hot Springs along West Walker River (lat. 38°23'40" N, long. 119°27'05" W; sec. 4, T 6 N, R 23 E). Named on Chris Flat (1954) 7.5' quadrangle.

Chris Wicht Camp [INYO]: *locality,* 6.25 miles southwest of Telescope Peak in Surprise Canyon (lat. 36°06'45" N, long. 117°10'30" W). Named on Telescope Peak (1952) 15' quadrangle.

Chrysopolis: see **Aberdeen** [INYO] (1).

Chuckwalla Canyon [INYO]: *canyon,* drained by a stream that flows 5.25 miles to Death Valley 6.25 miles northwest of Bennetts Well (lat. 36°13'45" N, long. 116°56'30" W). Named on Bennetts Well (1952) and Telescope Peak (1952) 15' quadrangles.

Chung Up Mountains: see **Nopah Range** [INYO].

Cienega Mirth [INYO]: *area,* 9.5 miles west-southwest of Big Pine (lat. 37°08'10" N, long. 118°27'40" W; sec. 27, T 9 S, R 32 E). Named on Big Pine (1950) 15' quadrangle. According to one account, some campers had such a good time at the place that they named it Camp Mirth (Schumacher, p. 90).

Cinder Hill [INYO]: *hill,* 12 miles west of Epaulet Peak in Death Valley (lat. 35°56'25" N, long. 116°44'05" W; sec. 11, T 21 N, R 2 E). Named on Confidence Hills (1950) 15' quadrangle.

Cinder Hill: see **Red Hill** [INYO].

Cinko Lake [MONO]: *lake,* 1000 feet long, nearly 5 miles north-northwest of Tower Peak (lat. 38°12'15" N, long. 119°35'10" W). Named on Tower Peak (1956) 15' quadrangle.

Cinnabar Canyon [MONO]: *canyon,* 1.5 miles long, opens into the canyon of Clearwater Creek 8 miles west-southwest of Bodie (lat. 38°09'50" N, long. 119°09' W; sec. 31, T 4 N, R 26 E). Named on Bodie (1958) 15' quadrangle.

Cinnamon Cut: see **Sinnamon Cut** [MONO].

Cirque Lake [INYO]: *lake,* 800 feet long, 18 miles northwest of Olancha (lat. 36°28'35" N, long. 118°13'05" W; near E line sec. 6, T 17 S, R 35 E); the lake is 1 mile east of Cirque Peak. Named on Olancha (1956) 15' quadrangle.

Cirque Mountain [MONO]: *peak,* 5 miles west-northwest of Matterhorn Peak (lat. 38°07'55" N, long. 119°27'30" W). Altitude 10,714 feet. Named on Matterhorn Peak (1956) 15' quadrangle.

Cirque Peak [INYO]: *peak,* 18 miles northwest of Olancha on Inyo-Tulare County line (lat. 36°28'40" N, long. 118°14'10" W; on W line sec. 6, T 17 S, R 35 E). Altitude 12,900 feet. Named on Olancha (1956) 15' quadrangle.

Citrus: see **Kearsarge** [INYO].

Clair Camp [INYO]: *locality,* 10 miles south-southwest of Telescope Peak in Pleasant Canyon (lat. 36°02' N, long. 117°08' W). Named on Telescope Peak (1952) 15' quadrangle. The name is for W.D. Clair and his family, local mine owners (Hubbard, Bray, and Pipkin, p. 38). United States Board on Geographic Names (1969, p. 5) approved the name "Slims Peak" for a feature located 1 mile south of Clair Camp (lat. 36°01'02" N, long. 117°07'50" W; altitude 7112 feet); the name commemorates Charles "Seldom Seen Slim" Ferge, a lone resident of nearby Ballarat for 50 years.

Clark: see **Furnace** [INYO].

Clark Canyon [MONO]:

(1) *canyon,* drained by a stream that flows 5 miles to Aurora Canyon 2 miles east-northeast of Bridgeport (lat. 38°16'10" N, long. 119°11'30" W; near NW cor. sec. 26, T 5 N, R 25 E). Named on Bodie (1958) and Bridgeport (1958) 15' quadrangles.

(2) *canyon,* 1.5 miles long, opens into an unnamed canyon nearly 9 miles south-southeast of the site of Mono Mills (lat. 37°46' N, long. 118°54'45" W). Named on Cowtrack Mountain (1962) 15' quadrangle.

Clark Fork [ALPINE]: *stream,* flows 18 miles to Middle Fork Stanislaus River 3 miles south of Dardanelles Cone (lat. 38°21'40" N, long. 119°52'40" W). Named on Dardanelle (1979), Dardanelles Cone (1979), Disaster Peak (1979), and Sonora Pass (1979) 7.5' quadrangles. Called Clark's Fork Stanislaus River on Wheeler's (1876-1877) map. Alpine-Tuolumne County line follows the stream approximately.

Clark Fork Campground [ALPINE]: *locality,* nearly 4 miles east of Dardanelles Cone on Alpine-Tuolumne County line (lat. 38°23'45" N, long. 119°48' W); the place is along Clark Fork. Named on Dardanelles Cone (1979) 7.5' quadrangle.

Clark Fork Meadow [ALPINE]: *area,* 3 miles northwest of Sonora Pass (lat. 38°21'40" N, long. 119°40'30" W); the place is along Clark Fork. Named on Sonora Pass (1979) 7.5' quadrangle.

Clark Lakes [MONO]: *lakes,* largest 1200 feet long, 10 miles northwest of Mammoth Mountain (lat. 37°44'15" N, long. 119°08'45" W; sec. 30, 31, T 2 S, R 26 E). Named on Devils Postpile (1953) 15' quadrangle.

Clarks: see **Sherwin Summit** [MONO].

Clark's Fork Stanislaus River: see **Clark Fork** [ALPINE].

Clear Lake: see **Caples Lake** [ALPINE].

Clearwater Creek [MONO]: *stream,* flows 12 miles to Virginia Creek 6 miles south-southeast of Bridgeport (lat. 38°10'30" N, long. 119°11'40" W; near W line sec. 26, T 4 N, R 25 E). Named on Bodie (1958) 15' quadrangle.

Cleaver: see **The Cleaver** [MONO].

Cliff Meadow [ALPINE]: *area,* 3.25 miles west of Pacific Grade Summit (lat. 38°30'45" N, long. 119°58'05" W; sec. 26, T 8 N, R 18 E). Named on Pacific Valley (1979) 7.5' quadrangle, which shows marsh in the area.

Clinton: see **Ferris Canyon** [MONO].

Clinton Spring [MONO]: *spring,* 13 miles north of Bridgeport on the north side of Ferris Canyon (lat. 38°26'30" N, long. 119°14'15" W; sec. 30, T 7 N, R 25 E). Named on Bridgeport (1958) 15' quadrangle.

Cloudburst Canyon [ALPINE]: *canyon,* drained by a stream that flows 1.5 miles to West Fork Carson River 2 miles west-southwest of Woodfords (lat. 38°45'55" N, long. 119°51'20" W). Named on Markleeville (1979) and Woodfords (1979) 7.5' quadrangles.

Cloudburst Creek [ALPINE]: *stream,* flows nearly 1.5 miles to Clark Fork in Tuolumne County 2.5 miles south-southeast of Dardanelles Cone (lat. 38°22' N, long. 119°51'35" W). Named on Dardanelle (1979) and Dardanelles Cone (1979) 7.5' quadrangles.

Cloudburst Creek [MONO]: *stream,* flows 2 miles to West Walker River 5.5 miles east-northeast of Sonora Pass (lat. 38°20'35" N, long. 119°32'25" W; sec. 27, T 6 N, R 22 E). Named on Pickel Meadow (1954) 7.5' quadrangle.

Cloverleaf Lake [MONO]: *lake,* 1300 feet long, 2.25 miles west-southwest of Mount Morrison along a branch of Convict Creek (lat. 37°32'55" N, long. 118°53'45" W); the lake has three major arms. Named on Mount Morrison (1953) 15' quadrangle.

Clover Patch [MONO]: *area,* 10 miles north-northeast of Toms Place (lat. 37°41'55" N, long. 118°37'40" W; near SE cor. sec. 11, T 3 S, R 30 E). Named on Casa Diablo Mountain (1953) 15' quadrangle.

Clover Valley [ALPINE]: *valley,* 5 miles north of Pacific Grade Summit along Blue Creek (lat. 38°35'30" N, long. 119°55' W; on W line sec. 32, T

9 N, R 19 E). Named on Pacific Valley (1979) 7.5' quadrangle.

Clyde: see **Norman Clyde Glacier** and **Norman Clyde Peak**, under **Middle Palisade** [INYO].

Clyde Meadow [INYO]: *area*, 1.5 miles east of Mount Whitney (1) along North Fork Lone Pine Creek (lat. 36°34'50" N, long. 118°15'55" W). Named on Mount Whitney (1956) 15' quadrangle.

Coats Meadow [INYO]: *area*, 8 miles northeast of Mount Darwin along South Fork (1) Bishop Creek (lat. 37°14'20" N, long. 118°33'50" W; sec. 22, T 8 S, R 31 E). Named on Mount Goddard (1948) 15' quadrangle.

Coffin Canyon [INYO]: *canyon*, 7 miles long, opens into Death Valley 5.5 miles east of Bennetts Well (lat. 36°09'10" N, long. 116°46' W); the canyon heads near Coffin Peak. Named on Bennetts Well (1952) and Funeral Peak (1951) 15' quadrangles. Palmer (p. 17) applied the name to upper reaches of nearby Copper Canyon (2), and noted that the name conforms with the morbid nomenclature in the Death Valley neighborhood.

Coffin Mountains: see **Funeral Mountains** [INYO].

Coffin Peak [INYO]: *peak*, 9 miles north-northwest of Funeral Peak in Black Mountains (lat. 36°12'50" N, long. 116°42'15" W). Altitude 5503 feet. Named on Funeral Peak (1951) 15' quadrangle.

Cold Spring: see **Coles Spring** [INYO].

Coldwater Canyon [MONO]: *canyon*, 7 miles long, opens into lowlands 11.5 miles south-southwest of White Mountain Peak (lat. 37° 28'35" N, long. 118°19'30" W; near N line sec. 35, T 5 S, R 33 E). Named on Bishop (1949) and Blanco Mountain (1951) 15' quadrangles.

Cold Water Creek [MONO]: *stream*, flows 2.5 miles to Lake Mary 8 miles west-northwest of Mount Morrison (lat. 37°36' N, long. 118°59'50" W; sec. 16, T 4 S, R 27 E). Named on Mount Morrison (1953) 15' quadrangle.

Coldwater Spring [INYO]: *spring*, 7.5 miles north of Westgard Pass (lat. 37°24'25" N, long. 118°10'20" W; sec. 19, T 6 S, R 35 E). Named on Blanco Mountain (1951) 15' quadrangle.

Coleman: see **Furnace Creek Ranch** [INYO].

Coleman Borax Works: see **Harmony Borax Works** [INYO].

Colemanite [INYO]: *locality*, 1.5 miles north-northeast of present Ryan (2) along Death Valley Railroad (lat. 36°20'20" N, long. 116° 39'45" W). Named on Furnace Creek (1910) 1° quadrangle. The place is named for the borate mineral mined there.

Coleman Springs: see **Furnace Creek Wash** [INYO].

Coles Flat [INYO]: *valley*, 6 miles southeast of Coso Peak (lat. 36° 08'30" N, long. 117°38' W). Named on Coso Peak (1951) 15' quadrangle.

Coles Spring [INYO]: *spring*, 4.25 miles southeast of Coso Peak (lat. 36°09' N, long. 117°40'10" W; near W line sec. 32, T 20 S, R 40 E). Named on Coso Peak (1951) 15' quadrangle. Called Cold Spring on Ballarat (1913) 1° quadrangle.

Coleville [MONO]: *village*, 26 miles northwest of Bridgeport along West Walker River in Antelope Valley (lat. 38°34' N, long. 119° 30'25" W; sec. 1, T 8 N, R 22 E). Named on Topaz Lake (1956) 15' quadrangle. Postal authorities established Coleville post office in 1868; the name commemorates Cornelius Cole, a congressman from 1863 until 1867, and a senator from 1867 until 1873 (Salley, p. 47).

Colorado Hill [ALPINE]: *peak*, 1.25 miles south-southeast of Mogul Peak (lat. 38°40'15" N, long. 119°42'30" W; sec. 31, T 10 N, R 21 E). Altitude 7482 feet. Named on Heenan Lake (1979) 7.5' quadrangle. Eakle (p. 8) referred to a peak located to the east across Loope Canyon from Colorado Hill as Morning Star Hill; the name "Morning Star Hill" recalls Morning Star mine, one of the most famous mines in Alpine County.

Colosseum Mountain [INYO]: *peak*, 12 miles northwest of Independence on Inyo-Frenso County line (lat. 36°54'30" N, long. 118°22'10" W). Altitude 12,473 feet. Named on Mount Pinchot (1953) 15' quadrangle.

Colter Spring [INYO]: *spring*, 5.5 miles north-northwest of Manly Peak in South Park Canyon (lat. 35°59'40" N, long. 117°08'20" W). Named on Manly Peak (1950) 15' quadrangle.

Comanche Gulch [MONO]: *canyon*, 1 mile long, opens into Blind Spring Valley 11 miles east of Glass Mountain (lat. 37°46'30" N, long. 118°30'30" W; sec. 13, T 2 S, R 31 E). Named on Benton (1962) and Glass Mountain (1962) 15' quadrangles.

Company Meadows [ALPINE]: *area*, 5.5 miles east-southeast of Mogul Peak (lat. 38°39'35" N, long. 119°37'15" W; sec. 1, T 9 N, R 21 E). Named on Topaz Lake (1956) 15' quadrangle.

Confidence Hills [INYO]: *range*, 10 miles southwest of Epaulet Peak on the southwest side of Death Valley (lat. 35°51'30" N, long. 116°38'30" W). Named on Confidence Hills (1950) 15' quadrangle.

Confidence Mill [INYO]: *locality*, 9.5 miles south-southwest of Epaulet Peak (lat. 35°50'20" N, long. 116°33'45" W; sec. 9, T 20 N, R 4 E); the place is opposite the southeast end of Confidence Hills. Site named on Confidence Hills (1950) 15' quadrangle. The name probably reflects the owner's confidence that nearby claims would produce enough ore to keep the mill in operation (Palmer, p. 18). Mendenhall (p. 39) used the name "Confidence Springs" for some springs located about 7 miles north of the mill site.

Confidence Springs: see **Confidence Mill** [INYO].

Confidence Wash [INYO]: *stream*, flows 7 miles to Death Valley 8 miles south-southwest of Epaulet Peak (lat. 35°51'45" N, long. 116°33'15" W); the mouth of the wash is 2 miles north-northeast of the site of Confidence Mill. Named on Confidence Hills (1950) and Shoshone (1951) 15' quadrangles.

Conglomerate Mesa [INYO]: *area*, 15 miles southeast of New York Butte (lat. 36°30' N, long. 117°45' W). Named on Keeler (1951), New York Butte (1950), and Ubehebe Peak (1950) 15' quadrangles. The name is from resistant limestone conglomerate that underlies the area (United States Board on Geographic Names, 1960c, p. 17).

Connell: see **Virgil Connell Spring** [MONO].

Connels Cow Camp [ALPINE]: *locality*, 7.25 miles east of Disaster Peak in Upper Fish Valley (lat. 38°27'10" N, long. 119°36' W; sec. 18, T 7 N, R 22 E). Named on Lost Cannon Peak (1954) 7.5' quadrangle.

Conness: see **Mount Conness** [MONO].

Conness Glacier [MONO]: *glacier*, on the northeast side of Mount Conness (lat. 37°58'10" N, long. 119°19'05" W). Named on Tuolumne Meadows (1956) 15' quadrangle.

Conness Lakes [MONO]: *lakes*, largest 1000 feet long, 1 mile northeast of Mount Conness (lat. 37°58'40" N, long. 119°18'20" W; in and near sec. 34, 35, T 2 N, R 24 E). Named on Tuolumne Meadows (1956) 15' quadrangle.

Constance Lake [MONO]: *lake*, 0.5 mile long, 3 miles south of Mount Morrison on upper reaches of Convict Creek (lat. 37°31'05" N, long. 118°52' W). Named on Mount Morrison (1953) 15' quadrangle.

Consultation Lake [INYO]: *lake*, 200 feet long, 1.5 miles southeast of Mount Whitney (1) near the head of Lone Pine Creek (lat. 36° 33'45" N, long. 118°16'20" W). Named on Mount Whitney (1956) 15' quadrangle. The men who laid out the first trail from the east to the summit of Mount Whitney named the lake about 1904; they consulted there about the direction the trail should take (United States Board on Geographic Names, 1938, p. 15).

Contact Canyon [INYO]: *canyon*, drained by a stream that flows 5 miles to Death Valley 11.5 miles southwest of Epaulet Peak (lat. 35°50'50" N, long. 116°39'30" W). Named on Confidence Hills (1950) 15' quadrangle.

Contact Pass [INYO]: *pass*, 11.5 miles west-southwest of Big Pine (lat. 37°06'30" N, long. 118°29'05" W). Named on Big Pine (1950) 15' quadrangle.

Convict Creek [MONO]: *stream*, flows 13 miles to Lake Crowley 5.5 miles northeast of Mount Morrison (lat. 37°36'30" N, long. 118°46'30" W; near N line sec. 16, T 4 S, R 29 E). Named on Mount Morrison (1953) 15' quadrangle. The name is from a gun battle that took place between escaped convicts and a posse near the creek in 1871 (Hoover, Rensch, and Rensch, p. 215). The stream first was known as Monte Diablo Creek (Chalfant, 1933, p. 252).

Convict Lake [MONO]: *lake*, 1 mile long, 2 miles north of Mount Morrison (lat. 37°35'20" N, long. 118°51'25" W; mainly in sec. 23, T 4 S, R 28 E); the lake is along Convict Creek. Named on Mount Morrison (1953) 15' quadrangle.

Conway Summit [MONO]: *locality*, 12 miles south-southeast of Bridgeport (lat. 38°05'15" N, long. 119°10'50" W; sec. 26, T 3 N, R 25 E). Named on Bodie (1958) 15' quadrangle. The name is for John Andrew Conway, who settled near the place in 1880 (Smith, Genny, p. 33).

Cooney Lake [MONO]: *lake*, 800 feet long, 6.5 miles east-southeast of Matterhorn Peak (lat. 38°02'55" N, long. 119°16'35" W; sec. 1, T 2 N, R 24 E). Named on Matterhorn Peak (1956) 15' quadrangle. The lake is one of the group called Virginia Lakes.

Copper Canyon [INYO]:

(1) *canyon*, 3 miles long, heads in the State of Nevada and opens into Last Chance Canyon 3 miles northeast of Last Chance Mountain (lat. 37°18'30" N, long. 117°39'40" W). Named on Magruder Mountain (1957) 15' quadrangle.

(2) *canyon*, 6.25 miles long, opens into Death Valley 6.5 miles east-southeast of Bennetts Well (lat. 36°07'45" N, long. 116°45'10" W). Named on Bennetts Well (1952) and Funeral Peak (1951) 15' quadrangles.

Copperfield: see **Furnace** [INYO].

Copper Mountain [MONO]: *peak*, 15 miles south of Bridgeport (lat. 38°02'45" N, long. 119°11'40" W; near W line sec. 11, T 2 N, R 25 E). Altitude 9468 feet. Named on Bodie (1958) 15' quadrangle. The name is from copper ore found at the place (Calhoun, p. 103). A mining community, first called Copper Mountain and then called Jordan after the post office opened, was located east of the base of Copper Mountain at the edge of Mono Valley (Calhoun, p. 103). Jordan mining district, organized in 1879, was most active in the 1890's (Gudde, 1975, p. 179). Postal authorities established Jordan post office in 1891, discontinued it in 1893, reestablished it in 1896, and discontinued it in 1903 (Frickstad, p. 104). An avalanche destroyed Jordan in 1911 (La Braque, p. 44).

Copper Queen Canyon [INYO]: *canyon*, drained by a stream that flows 4 miles to Searles Valley in San Bernardino County 11 miles east-southeast of Argus Peak (lat. 35°47' N, long. 117°16' W). Named on Manly Peak (1950) and Trona (1949) 15' quadrangles.

Cora Lake [MONO]: *lake*, 700 feet long, nearly 3 miles north-northwest of

Tower Peak along Cascade Creek (lat. 38°10'55" N, long. 119°33'55" W). Named on Tower Peak (1956) 15' quadrangle.

Corcoran Mountain: see **Mount Corcoran** [INYO].

Corkscrew Canyon [INYO]: *canyon,* 1.25 miles long, opens into lowlands 7.25 miles southeast of Furnace Creek Inn (lat. 36°22'30" N, long. 116°45'45" W; sec. 16, T 26 S, R 2 E). Named on Furnace Creek (1952) 15' quadrangle. Officials of Pacific Coast Borax Company named the canyon for its meandering course (Palmer, p. 18).

Corkscrew Peak [INYO]: *peak,* 10 miles east-southeast of the mouth of Titus Canyon (lat. 36°46'15" N, long. 117°00'10" W; near W line sec. 5, T 14 S, R 46 E). Altitude 5804 feet. Named on Grapevine Peak (1957) 15' quadrangle. Don Curry, naturalist of Death Valley National Monument, suggested the name in 1936 for folded rocks that give the peak somewhat the appearance of a corkscrew (Gudde, 1949, p. 78-79).

Corner Lake: see **Kirman Lake** [MONO].

Cornfield: see **Devils Cornfield** [INYO].

Corral Gulch [ALPINE]: *canyon,* drained by a stream that flows nearly 2 miles to Bloods Meadow 3.5 miles south-southwest of Mount Reba (lat. 38°27'25" N, long. 120°03'05" W; sec. 13, T 7 N, R 17 E). Named on Tamarack (1979) 7.5' quadrangle.

Corral Springs: see **Buckhorn Springs** [INYO].

Corral Valley [ALPINE]: *valley,* 9 miles east-northeast of Disaster Peak (lat. 38°29'30" N, long. 119°34'15" W; sec. 33, T 8 N, R 22 E). Named on Lost Cannon Peak (1954) 7.5' quadrangle.

Corral Valley Creek [ALPINE]: *stream,* flows 3.25 miles to Silver King Creek 8 miles east-northeast of Disaster Peak (lat. 38°29'55" N, long. 119°36'15" W; sec. 31, T 8 N, R 22 E); the stream goes through Corral Valley. Named on Lost Cannon Peak (1954) 7.5' quadrangle.

Corrie Lochan [ALPINE]: *lake,* 400 feet long, 0.5 mile south of Fourth of July Peak (lat. 38°39' N, long. 120°01'25" W). Named on Caples Lake (1979) 7.5' quadrangle.

Coso [INYO]:

(1) *locality,* 4 miles east-southeast of Coso Peak (lat. 36°10'40" N, long. 117°38'45" W; sec. 21, T 20 S, R 40 E); the place is in Coso Range. Named on Coso Peak (1951) 15' quadrangle. Dr. Darwin French found ore at the site and named the camp there in 1860 (Chalfant, 1933, p. 129, 131). According to Kroeber (p. 40), the name "Coso" apparently is from the designation of a group of Indians; originally the name may have applied to a place, and only later to the Indians. The spot was called Granite Springs in 1860 (Iroquois Research Institute, p. 117). Waring and Huguenin (p. 34) referred to Coso Well at Coso.

(2) *locality,* 3 miles north-northwest of the village of Little Lake along Southern Pacific Railroad (lat. 35°58'45" N, long. 117°55'45" W; sec. 36, T 22 S, R 37 E). Named on Little Lake (1954) 15' quadrangle.

Coso: see **Coso Junction** [INYO].

Coso Basin [INYO]: *valley,* 9.5 miles east of the village of Little Lake (lat. 35°56' N, long. 117°44' W); the valley is south of Coso Range. Named on Little Lake (1954) and Mountain Springs Canyon (1953) 15' quadrangles. Thompson (1929, p. 144) suggested the name.

Coso Hot Springs [INYO]: *spring,* 10 miles east of Coso Junction (lat. 36°02'45" N, long. 117°46'10" W; sec. 4, T 22 S, R 39 E). Named on Haiwee Reservoir (1951) 15' quadrangle. Wheeler's (1877) map has the term "Hot spr's." at the site, and gives the valley in which the springs occur the name "Hot springs Valley." The place first was a camping spot for people afflicted with rheumatism (Waring, p. 150), and later it had more permanent resort facilities (Iroquois Research Institute, p. 95).

Coso Junction [INYO]: *locality,* 30 miles south of Keeler in Rose Valley (lat. 36°02'40" N, long. 117°56'45" W; sec. 2, T 22 S, R 37 E). Named on Haiwee Reservoir (1951) 15' quadrangle. The place first was called Gill's Oasis, for Ray Gill, who homesteaded there in 1926 and planted cottonwood trees (Iroquois Research Institute, p. 96, 130). Postal authorities established Coso Junction post office in 1925, discontinued it in 1930, reestablished it in 1941 when they moved Dunmovin post office to the site, and discontinued it in 1965 (Salley, p. 51). United States Board on Geographic Names (1950, p. 4) rejected the name "Coso" for the place.

Coso Mountains: see **Coso Range** [INYO].

Coso Peak [INYO]: *peak,* 21 miles south-southeast of Keeler (lat. 36°12'10" N, long. 117°42'45" W; on S line sec. 11, T 20 S, R 39 E). Altitude 8160 feet. Named on Coso Peak (1951) 15' quadrangle.

Coso Range [INYO]: *range,* southeast of the south end of Owens Lake and north of Indian Wells Valley. Named on Death Valley (1954) 1°x 2° quadrangle. Called Coso Mts. on Wheeler's (1877) map. The name is from Coso mining district (Palmer, p. 19).

Coso Springs [INYO]: *springs,* two, 5 miles east-southeast of Coso Peak (lat. 36°10'45" N, long. 117°37'35" W; sec. 22, T 20 S, R 40 E). Named on Coso Peak (1951) 15' quadrangle. The feature also was called Darwin Springs (Iroquois Research Institute, p. 94).

Coso Valley: see **Argus Range** [INYO].

Coso Wash [INYO]: *stream,* flows 17 miles to Coso Basin 9.5 miles east-northeast of the village of Little Lake (lat. 35°59'30" N, long. 117°44'55" W; sec. 27, T 22 S, R 39 E); the stream heads in Coso Range. Named on Little Lake (1954) and Mountain Springs Canyon (1953) 15' quadrangles.

Coso Well: see **Coso** [INYO] (1).

Cottonball Basin: see **Sulphur Spring** [INYO].

Cottonball Marsh: see **Sulphur Spring** [INYO].

Cottonwood [INYO]: *locality,* 8.5 miles north of Olancha (lat. 36°24'15" N, long. 118°01' W); the place is less than 3 miles southeast of the mouth of Cottonwood Creek (3). Named on Olancha (1907) 30' quadrangle.

Cottonwood Basin [MONO]: *area,* 8 miles southeast of White Mountain Peak (lat. 37°32'40" N, long. 118°09'45" W); the place is between Cottonwood Creek (3) and South Fork Cottonwood Creek (3). Named on Mount Barcroft (1962) 15' quadrangle.

Cottonwood Canyon [ALPINE]: *canyon,* drained by a stream that flows 4.5 miles to East Fork Carson River 5.5 miles east of Woodfords (lat. 38°46'05" N, long. 119°43'15" W; sec. 34, T 11 N, R 20 E). Named on Mount Siegel (1957) and Topaz Lake (1956) 15' quadrangles.

Cottonwood Canyon [INYO]: *canyon,* 15 miles long, opens into Marble Canyon (3) 12.5 miles from the mouth of that canyon (lat. 36°37'50" N, long. 117°17'45" W); the canyon is in Cottonwood Mountains. Named on Marble Canyon (1951) 15' quadrangle. The name is from the large number of cottonwood trees in the upper part of the canyon (Palmer, p. 19).

Cottonwood Canyon [MONO]:

(1) *canyon,* drained by a stream that flows 2 miles to the State of Nevada 15 miles north of Bridgeport (lat. 38°28' N, long. 119°13'50" W; sec. 18, T 7 N, R 25 E). Named on Bridgeport (1958) and Fales Hot Springs (1956) 15' quadrangles.

(2) *canyon,* 5 miles long, opens into Mono Valley 5.5 miles south of Bodie (lat. 38°07'45" N, long. 119°01'20" W; sec. 8, T 3 N, R 27 E). Named on Bodie (1958) 15' quadrangle.

(3) *canyon,* 4 miles long, opens into Hammil Valley 5 miles west-northwest of White Mountain Peak (lat. 37°39'40" N, long. 118°20'40" W). Named on White Mountain Peak (1962) 15' quadrangle. Sampson's (1940) map has the name "Headley Creek" for the stream in Cottonwood Canyon (3)—the stream heads south of Headley Peak.

Cottonwood Canyon: see **Little Cottonwood Canyon** [ALPINE].

Cottonwood Creek [ALPINE]: *stream,* flows 1.5 miles to Clark Fork 3 miles east-southeast of Dardanelles Cone (lat. 38°22'55" N, long. 119°49'25" W). Named on Dardanelles Cone (1979) 7.5' quadrangle. On Dardanelles Cone (1956) 15' quadrangle, the name applies to the next stream to the east.

Cottonwood Creek [INYO]:

(1) *stream,* heads in the State of Nevada and flows 2.5 miles in Inyo County to the north end of Death Valley 6 miles east of Last Chance Mountain (lat. 37°16'30" N, long. 117°35'30" W). Named on Last Chance Range (1958) and Magruder Mountain (1957) 15' quadrangles.

(2) *stream,* flows 15 miles to Owens Lake 9 miles north of Olancha (lat. 36°24'45" N, long. 118°00'30" W); the stream heads at Cottonwood Lakes. Named on Olancha (1956) 15' quadrangle. South Fork enters 11.5 miles upstream from the mouth of the main stream; it heads at South Fork Lakes, is 3.5 miles long, and is named on Olancha (1956) 15' quadrangle.

Cottonwood Creek [INYO-MONO]: *stream,* flows 25 miles to Fish Lake Valley 20 miles east-southeast of Mount Barcroft (lat. 37°28'30" N, long. 117°55'15" W). Named on Blanco Mountain (1951), Mount Barcroft (1962), and Soldier Pass (1958) 15' quadrangles. The stream is on Inyo-Mono County line. South Fork enters 9.5 miles southeast of White Mountain Peak; it is nearly 4 miles long and is named on Mount Barcroft (1962) 15' quadrangle. Chalfant (1933, p. 214) mentioned a place called Roachville that was situated along Cottonwood Creek in the 1860's—its proprietor, William Roach, named it.

Cottonwood Creek [MONO]: *stream,* formed by the confluence of North Fork and South Fork, flows nearly 3 miles to Deep Creek 7.5 miles north-northwest of Fales Hot Springs (lat. 38°27'05" N, long. 119°26'25" W; sec. 15, T 7 N, R 23 E); the stream goes through Cottonwood Meadows. Named on Fales Hot Springs (1956) 15' quadrangle. North Fork is 3 miles long and South Fork is 3.5 miles long; both forks are named on Fales Hot Springs (1956) 15' quadrangle.

Cottonwood Creek: see **Little Cottonwood Creek** [INYO].

Cottonwood Creek Meadows: see **Cottonwood Meadows** [MONO].

Cottonwood Lakes [INYO]: *lakes,* 19 miles northwest of Olancha (lat. 36°29'40" N, long. 118°12'45" W); the lakes are at the head of Cottonwood Creek (2). Named on Lone Pine (1958) and Olancha (1956) 15' quadrangles.

Cottonwood Meadows [MONO]: *area,* 6.25 miles north-northwest of Fales Hot Springs (lat. 38°26'20" N, long. 119°25'20" W; sec. 23, T 7 N, R 23 E); the place is along Cottonwood Creek. Named on Fales Hot Springs (1956) 15' quadrangle. Called Cottonwood Creek Meadows on Chris Flat (1954) 7.5' quadrangle.

Cottonwood Mountains [INYO]: *range,*the name applies to the part of Panamint Range that lies north of Towne Pass and west of the north end of Death Valley. Named on Marble Canyon (1951), Panamint Butte (1951), and Tin Mountain (1957) 15' quadrangles. Palmer (p. 20) referred to the feature as Cottonwood Range, but noted that the term "North Panamints" also is used; he stated that the name "Cottonwood" is from Cottonwood Canyon.

Cottonwood Pass [INYO]: *pass,* 16 miles northwest of Olancha on Inyo-Tulare County line (lat. 36°27'10" N, long. 118°12'50" W; sec. 17, T 17 S, R 35 E); the pass is near the head of a branch of South Fork Cottonwood Creek (2). Named on Olancha (1956) 15' quadrangle.

Cottonwood Range: see **Cottonwood Mountains** [INYO].

Cottonwood Springs [INYO]: *spring,* about 11 miles south-southwest of the mouth of Marble Canyon (3) (lat. 36°30'50" N, long. 117°22'35" W); the spring is in Cottonwood Canyon. Named on Marble Canyon (1951) 15' quadrangle.

County Line Canyon [INYO]: *canyon,* drained by a stream that flows 1 mile to Indian Wells Valley in Kern County nearly 10 miles south of the village of Little Lake (lat. 35°47'45" N, long. 117°53'45" W; sec. 4, T 25 S, R 38 E); the canyon is on and near Inyo-Kern County line. Named on Little Lake (1954) 15' quadrangle.

County Line Hill [MONO]: *peak,* 8 miles south-southeast of Mount Barcroft (lat. 38°28'30" N, long. 118°11' W); the peak is less than 1 mile north of Inyo-Mono County line. Altitude 11,229 feet. Named on Blanco Mountain (1951) 15' quadrangle.

Covered Wagon Peak [ALPINE]: *peak,* 1.25 miles west of Fourth of July Peak (lat. 38°39'25" N, long. 120°02'50" W; sec. 6, T 9 N, R 18 E). Altitude 9565 feet. Named on Caples Lake (1979) 7.5' quadrangle.

Cove Spring [INYO]: *spring,* 4 miles north of New York Butte (lat. 36°42'30" N, long. 117°55'40" W). Named on New York Butte (1950) 15' quadrangle.

Coville Ridge: see **Rogers Peak** [INYO].

Cowan Station: see **Dunmovin** [INYO].

Cowcamp Creek [MONO]: *stream,* flows 3.25 miles to Little Walker River 3 miles west-southwest of Fales Hot Springs (lat. 38°20'05" N, long. 119°26'55" W; sec. 28, T 6 N, R 23 E); the mouth of the creek is near Little Walker Cowcamp. Named on Fales Hot Springs (1956) 15' quadrangle.

Cow Creek [INYO]:

(1) *stream,* flows 2 miles to Baker Creek 8 miles west of Big Pine (lat. 37°10' N, long. 118°26'20" W; near E line sec. 14, T 9 S, R 32 E). Named on Big Pine (1950) 15' quadrangle.

(2) *stream,* on the east side of Death Valley; flows 2.5 miles to a point 3.5 miles north-northwest of Furnace Creek Inn (lat. 36° 30' N, long. 116°52'10" W; sec. 4, T 27 N, R 1 E). Named on Chloride Cliff (1952) and Furnace Creek (1952) 15' quadrangles. The name recalls the loss of a number of cows in the stream during a cattle drive (Gudde, 1949, p. 82).

Cowhorn Valley [INYO]: *valley,* 9 miles north of Waucoba Mountain (lat. 37°09' N, long. 118°00' W). Named on Waucoba Mountain (1951) and Waucoba Spring (1958) 15' quadrangles.

Cowhorn Valley: see **Little Cowhorn Valley** [INYO].

Cowtrack Mountain [MONO]: *ridge,* north- to northeast-trending, 8 miles long, 8 miles northeast of the site of Mono Mills (lat. 37° 57' N, long. 119°50' W). Named on Cowtrack Mountain (1962) 15' quadrangle. Sampson's (1940) map has the name "Horse Mountain" for a peak at the northeast end of the ridge.

Cowtrack Spring [MONO]: *spring,* 10.5 miles northeast of the site of Mono Mills (lat. 37°59'15" N, long. 118°48'50" W; sec. 31, T 2 N, R 29 E); the spring is near the north end of Cowtrack Mountain. Named on Cowtrack Mountain (1962) 15' quadrangle. Mount Morrison (1914) 30' quadrangle has the name for a spring situated nearly 3 miles farther south.

Coyote Canyon [INYO]:

(1) *canyon,* drained by a stream that flows 3.5 miles to lowlands 7.25 miles east of Independence (lat. 36°47'20" N, long. 118°04'15" W). Named on Independence (1951) 15' quadrangle.

(2) *canyon,* 6.5 miles long, opens into lowlands 4 miles southwest of Manly Peak (lat. 35°52'25" N, long. 117°09'50" W). Named on Manly Peak (1950) 15' quadrangle.

Coyote Creek [INYO]: *stream,* formed by the confluence of East Fork and West Fork, flows 5.5 miles to Bishop Creek 8.5 miles east-southeast of Mount Tom (lat. 37°18'50" N, long. 118°30'35" W; sec. 30, T 7 S, R 32 E). Named on Bishop (1949) and Mount Tom (1949) 15' quadrangles. East Fork is 4.5 miles long and is named on Big Pine (1950) quadrangle; it is called Coyote Creek on Bishop (1913) 30' quadrangle. West Fork, which heads on Coyote Ridge, is 4.5 miles long and is named on Big Pine (1950) and Mount Goddard (1948) 15' quadrangles.

Coyote Creek [MONO]: *stream,* flows 4 miles to Desert Creek 10 miles east-southeast of Coleville (lat. 38°32'05" N, long. 119°19'45" W). Named on Desert Creek Peak (1956) and Fales Hot Springs (1956) 15' quadrangles.

Coyote Flat [INYO]: *area,* 10 miles west-northwest of Big Pine (lat. 37°12' N, long. 118°28' W); the place is near the head of East Fork Coyote Creek. Named on Big Pine (1950) 15' quadrangle. Called Coyote Valley on Lippincott's (1902) map.

Coyote Lake [INYO]: *lake,* 800 feet long, 9 miles east-northeast of Mount Darwin (lat. 37°12'35" N, long. 118°31'10" W; sec. 36, T 8 S, R 31 E); the lake is near the head of West Fork Coyote Creek. Named on Mount Goddard (1948) 15' quadrangle.

Coyote Ridge [INYO]: *ridge,* north-northwest- to north-northeast-trending, 5.5 miles long, 8 miles east-northeast of Mount Darwin (lat. 37°12'30" N, long. 118°32'15" W). Named on Mount Goddard (1948) 15' quadrangle.

Coyote Spring [INYO]: *spring,* 8 miles east of Independence (lat. 36°47'10" N, long. 118°03'30" W); the spring is near Coyote Canyon (1). Named on Independence (1951) 15' quadrangle.

Coyote Spring [MONO]: *spring,* 7.5 miles southwest of Bodie in Bridgeport Canyon (lat. 38°07'15" N, long. 119°05' W; near W line sec. 14, T 3 N, R 26 E). Named on Bodie (1958) 15' quadrangle.

Coyote Valley [ALPINE]: *valley,* 8 miles east of Disaster Peak (lat. 38°28'20" N, long. 119°35'15" W). Named on Lost Cannon Peak (1954) 7.5' quadrangle.

Coyote Valley: see **Coyote Flat** [INYO].

Crags View: see **Twin Lakes Campground** [MONO].

Crag View Camp: see **Twin Lakes Campground** [MONO].

Craig Canyon [INYO]: *canyon,* drained by a stream that flows 6 miles to Saline Valley nearly 6 miles east-northeast of New York Butte (lat. 36°40'30" N, long. 117°50' W). Named on New York Butte (1950) 15' quadrangle.

Crater [INYO]: *locality,* 19 miles northwest of Ubehebe Crater in Last Chance Range (lat. 37°13' N, long. 117°41'15" W; on S line sec. 27, T 8 S, R 39 E). Named on Last Chance Range (1958) 15' quadrangle.

Crater [MONO]: *locality,* 2.25 miles south-southeast of present Lee Vining (lat. 37°55'40" N, long. 119°06'10" W; sec. 22, T 1 N, R 26 E); the place is 3 miles west of the north end of Mono Craters. Named on Mount Lyell (1901) 30' quadrangle. Postal authorities established Crater post office in 1899 and discontinued it in 1911 (Frickstad, p. 104).

Crater Crest [MONO]: *ridge,* north- to north-northwest-trending, 2 miles long, 3.25 miles northeast of Matterhorn Peak (lat. 38°07'15" N, long. 119°20' W). Named on Matterhorn Peak (1956) 15' quadrangle.

Crater Lake [ALPINE]: *lake,* 975 feet long, 2 miles north-northeast of Carson Pass (lat. 38°43'25" N, long. 119°58'30" W; sec. 11, T 10 N, R 18 E). Named on Carson Pass (1979) 7.5' quadrangle.

Crater Mountain [INYO]: *mountain,* 3.5 miles south of Big Pine (lat. 37°06'45" N, long. 118°17'50" W). Altitude 6055 feet. Named on Big Pine (1950) 15' quadrangle.

Crater Mountain [MONO]: *crater,* 8.5 miles southeast of Lee Vining (lat. 37°52'45" N, long. 119°00'20" W); the feature is one of the group called Mono Craters. Named on Mono Craters (1953) 15' quadrangle.

Crest Creek [MONO]: *stream,* flows 3 miles to Gem Lake 14 miles south of Lee Vining (lat. 37°45'30" N, long. 119°09'30" W; near W line sec. 19, T 2 S, R 26 E); the stream heads near Koip Crest. Named on Mono Craters (1953) 15' quadrangle.

Crestview [MONO]: *locality,* 9.5 miles south of the site of Mono Mills (lat. 37°45'10" N, long. 118°59' W; near S line sec. 22, T 2 S, R 27 E). Named on Cowtrack Mountain (1962) 15' quadrangle. Clarence Wilson started a resort called Crestview Lodge at the place in 1927 (Hanna, p. 77). Sampson's (1940) map has the form "Crest View" for the name.

Crocker: see **Mount Crocker** [MONO].

Crocker Lake [MONO]: *lake,* 950 feet long, 5.25 miles south-southeast of Mount Morrison (lat. 37°29'15" N, long. 118°49'45" W); the lake is less than 0.5 mile northwest of Mount Crocker. Named on Mount Abbot (1953) 15' quadrangle.

Crocker Peak: see **Mount Crocker** [MONO].

Crooked Creek [INYO-MONO]: *stream,* formed by the confluence of North Fork and South Fork in Mono County, flows 10.5 miles to Wyman Creek 11.5 miles northeast of Westgard Pass in Inyo County (lat. 37°24'50" N, long. 118°00'15" W; on E line sec. 22, T 6 S, R 36 E). Named on Blanco Mountain (1951) 15' quadrangle. North Fork is 4 miles long and is named on Blanco Mountain (1951) and Mount Barcroft (1962) 15' quadrangles. South Fork is 1 mile long and is named on Blanco Mountain (1951) 15' quadrangle.

Crooked Creek [MONO]: *stream,* flows 2.5 miles to an arm of Lake Crowley 2 miles west-northwest of Toms Place (lat. 37°34'20" N, long. 118°42'45" W; sec. 30, T 4 S, R 30 E). Named on Casa Diablo Mountain (1953) 15' quadrangle.

Crooked Meadows [MONO]: *area,* 8 miles southeast of the site of Mono Mills (lat. 37°49'15" N, long. 118°50'35" W; near N line sec. 36, T 1 S, R 28 E). Named on Cowtrack Mountain (1962) 15' quadrangle. Called Crooked Meadow on Mount Morrison (1914) 30' quadrangle.

Crooked Road Canyon [INYO]: *canyon,* drained by a stream that flows 10 miles to an unnamed canyon 5.5 miles east of Big Pine (lat. 37°10'10" N, long. 118°11'15" W; sec. 18, T 9 S, R 35 E). Named on Waucoba Mountain (1951) 15' quadrangle.

Crow Canyon [INYO]: *canyon,* 5 miles long, opens into Homewood Canyon 4.5 miles northeast of Argus Peak (lat. 35°53'35" N, long. 117°23' W; sec. 31, T 23 S, R 43 E). Named on Trona (1949) 15' quadrangle.

Crowley Lake: see **Lake Crowley** [MONO].

Crown Lake [MONO]: *lake,* 1200 feet long, 3.5 miles west-northwest of Matterhorn Peak (lat. 38°06'45" N, long. 119°26'35" W); the lake is less than 1 mile east of Crown Point. Named on Matterhorn Peak (1956) 15' quadrangle.

Crown Peak: see **Crown Point** [MONO].

Crown Point [MONO]: *peak,* 4.25 miles west-northwest of Matterhorn Peak on Mono-Tuolumne County line (lat. 38°06'40" N, long. 119°27'25" W). Altitude 11,346 feet. Named on Matterhorn Peak (1956) 15' quadrangle. Called Crown Pk. on Sampson's (1940) map.

Crystal Crag [MONO]: *peak,* 3 miles south-southeast of Mammoth Mountain (lat. 37°35'25" N, long. 119°00'50" W). Altitude 10,364 feet. Named on Devils Postpile (1953) 15' quadrangle.

Crystal Lake [MONO]:
(1) *lake,* 900 feet long, 18 miles south of Bridgeport along South Fork Mill Creek (2) in Lake Canyon (lat. 38°00' N, long. 119°14'45" W; sec. 29, T 2 N, R 25 E). Named on Bodie (1958) and Mono Craters (1953) 15' quadrangles.
(2) *lake,* 1200 feet long, 2.5 miles south-southeast of Mammoth Mountain (lat. 37°35'35" N, long. 119°01' W). Named on Devils Postpile (1953) 15' quadrangle. The lake is one of the group called Mammoth Lakes.

Crystal Spring [INYO]:
(1) *spring,* 1.5 miles east-northeast of Coso Peak (lat. 36°12'50" N, long. 117°41'20" W; near E line sec. 12, T 20 S, R 39 E). Named on Coso Peak (1951) 15' quadrangle. The name is from the purity of the water (Palmer, p. 21).
(2) *spring,* 15 miles east-southeast of Tecopa in Kingston Range (lat. 35°47'40" N, long. 115°57'40" W). Named on Horse Thief Springs (1956) 15' quadrangle.

Crystal Springs Campground [ALPINE]: *locality,* 1.5 miles west-southwest of Woodfords in West Carson Canyon (lat. 38°45'55" N, long. 119°50'40" W). Named on Woodfords (1979) 7.5' quadrangle.

Cucomungo Canyon [INYO]: *canyon,* 9.5 miles long, heads in the State of Nevada and opens into Eureka Valley 12 miles east-southeast of Deep Springs (lat. 37°19'30" N, long. 117°46'30" W). Named on Magruder Mountain (1957) and Soldier Pass (1958) 15' quadrangles. The canyon is drained by Willow Creek (1).

Cuña Spring: see **Deep Springs Lake** [INYO].

Curious Butte: see **Striped Butte** [INYO].

Curtz Lake [ALPINE]: *lake,* 800 feet long, 2.25 miles north of Markleeville (lat. 38°43'30" N, long. 119°47'15" W; sec. 9, T 10 N, R 20 E). Named on Markleeville (1979) 7.5' quadrangle.

—D—

Dade: see **Mount Dade** [INYO].

Dade Lake [INYO]: *lake,* 1000 feet long, 1.25 miles east-southeast of Mount Abbot (lat. 37°22'45" N, long. 118°45'50" W); the feature is 1 mile east of Mount Dade. Named on Mount Abbot (1953) 15' quadrangle.

Daisy Canyon [INYO]: *canyon,* drained by a stream that flows 6 miles to Saline Valley 6.5 miles east of New York Butte (lat. 36° 39'30" N, long. 117°48'50" W). Named on New York Butte (1950) 15' quadrangle.

Damsite Campground [ALPINE]: *locality,* 5.25 miles south-southeast of Carson Pass by Upper Blue Lake (lat. 38°37'45" N, long. 119°56'20" W; sec. 18, T 9 N, R 19 E); the place is near the dam that forms Upper Blue Lake. Named on Carson Pass (1979) 7.5' quadrangle.

Dana: see **Mount Dana** [MONO]; **Mount Dana Glacier**, under **Glacier Canyon** [MONO].

Dana Lake [MONO]: *lake,* 1750 feet long, 6.5 miles west-southwest of Lee Vining (lat. 37°54'30" N, long. 119°13'10" W); the lake is 0.5 mile north of Mount Dana. Named on Mono Craters (1953) 15' quadrangle.

Dana Plateau [MONO]: *relief feature,* 6 miles west-southwest of Lee Vining (lat. 37°55' N, long. 119°13' W); the feature is 1.25 miles north of Mount Dana. Named on Mono Craters (1953) 15' quadrangle.

Danberg Camp [ALPINE]: *locality,* 4.5 miles south-southwest of Freel Peak in Hope Valley (lat. 38°47'30" N, long. 119°55'20" W; near N line sec. 24, T 11 N, R 18 E). Named on Freel Peak (1955) 7.5' quadrangle.

Danburg Beach [MONO]: *beach,* 4 miles north of Lee Vining along Mono Lake (lat. 38°00'50" N, long. 119°08' W; in and near sec. 20, T 2 N, R 26 E). Named on Bodie (1958) 15' quadrangle. The place had the name "Fisher Meadow" in the early days (Calhoun, p. 34).

Daneri's Landing: see **Cartago** [INYO].

Dantes View [INYO]: *locality,* 10 miles northwest of Funeral Peak (lat. 36°13'15" N, long. 116°43'30" W); the place overlooks Death Valley and Greenwater Valley. Named on Funeral Peak (1951) 15' quadrangle. Officials of Pacific Coast Borax Company named the place; Dante's description of Purgatory is said to have inspired name (Palmer, p. 21).

Dardanelles: see **The Dardanelles** [ALPINE].

Dardanelles Cone [ALPINE]: *peak,* 20 miles south-southwest of Markleeville (lat. 38°24'15" N, long. 119°52'15" W); the peak is on the ridge called The Dardanelles. Altitude 9525 feet. Named on Dardanelles Cone (1979) 7.5' quadrangle.

Dardanelles Creek [ALPINE]: *stream,* flows 1 mile to Tuolumne County 3.5 miles west-southwest of Dardanelles Cone (lat. 38°23'25" N, long. 119°56'10" W; near W line sec. 7, T 6 N, R 19 E); the stream heads west of The Dardanelles. Named on Spicer Meadow Reservoir (1979) 7.5' quadrangle.

Dardanelles Mountain: see **The Dardanelles** [ALPINE].

Dart Lake: see **Heart Lake** [MONO].

Darwin [INYO]: *village,* 22 miles southeast of Keeler (lat. 36°16'10" N, long. 117°35'30" W; sec. 24, T 19 S, R 40 E). Named on Darwin (1950) 15' quadrangle. The mining camp that sprang up after discovery of lead and silver at the place in 1875 was named for Darwin Wash (Federal Writers' Project, p. 34). Postal authorities established Darwin post office in 1875 and discontinued it briefly in 1902 (Frickstad, p. 50). United States Board on Geographic Names (1960c, p. 17) approved the name "Darwin Hills" for a range located east of Darwin between Lucky Jim Wash and Darwin Wash; the Board at the same time approved the name "Darwin Plateau" for an area that extends north for about 11 miles from Darwin Hills to Lee Flat, and (1960c, p. 21) approved the name "Talc City Hills" for a range located 6 miles northeast of Darwin where talc mines occur. Federal Writers' Project (p. 58) mentioned an elevation situated 0.5 mile northeast of Darwin that is crossed by a road to Lane mine and is called Lane Hill.

Darwin: see **Mount Darwin** [INYO].

Darwin Canyon [INYO]: *canyon,* 7.5 miles long, opens into Panamint Valley 9.5 miles southwest of Panamint Butte near Panamint Springs (lat. 36°20'10" N, long. 117°28'20" W; sec. 30, T 18 S, R 42 E); Darwin Wash drains the canyon. Named on Darwin (1950) and Panamint Butte (1951) 15' quadrangles. The name is said to commemorate Dr. Darwin French, who led a prospecting party to the neighborhood in 1860 in search of silver (Knopf, 1914, p. 3).

Darwin Falls [INYO]: *waterfall,* 5.25 miles northeast of Darwin in Darwin Canyon (lat. 36°19'15" N, long. 117°31'20" W; sec. 34, T 18 S, R 41 E). Named on Darwin (1950) 15' quadrangle. The name commemorates Dr. Darwin French, who carved his name above the feature in 1860 (Palmer, p. 21). Called Egan Fall on Wheeler's (1877) map; Lieutenant D.A. Lyle gave this name to commemorate Mr. Egan, a civilian guide for the Lyle party of the Wheeler survey who died on the way to Death Valley in 1871 (Palmer, p. 26).

Darwin Hills: see **Darwin** [INYO].

Darwin Plateau: see **Darwin** [INYO].

Darwin Range: see **Argus Range** [INYO].

Darwin Springs: see **Coso Springs** [INYO].

Darwin Wash [INYO]: *stream,* flows 26 miles to Panamint Valley 9.5 miles southwest of Panamint Butte near Panamint Springs (lat. 36°20'10" N, long. 117°28'20" W; sec. 30, T 18 S, R 42 E); the lower part of the watercourse is in Darwin Canyon. Named on Coso Peak (1951), Darwin (1950), and Panamint Butte (1951) 15' quadrangles. The name is for Dr. Darwin French (Hanks, p. 34).

Davis: see **Jeff Davis Creek** [ALPINE]; **Jeff Davis Peak** [ALPINE]; **Mount Davis** [MONO].

Davis Creek [MONO]: *stream,* flows 3 miles to the State of Nevada 11.5 miles east-southeast of Benton (lat. 37°46'55" N, long. 118° 16'10" W). Named on Benton (1962) 15' quadrangle.

Davis Lake [MONO]: *lake,* 3100 feet long, 7 miles southeast of Mount Morrison along Hilton Creek (lat. 37°30'10" N, long. 118° 45'30" W). Named on Mount Abbot (1953) and Mount Morrison (1953) 15' quadrangles.

Davis Lakes [MONO]: *lakes,* two, largest 1900 feet long, 12.5 miles northwest of Mammoth Mountain (lat. 37°43'40" N, long. 119° 13' W); the lakes are 1 mile north of Mount Davis. Named on Devils Postpile (1953) 15' quadrangle.

Davis Well [INYO]: *well,* 10 miles east of Tecopa in California Valley (lat. 36°51'30" N, long. 116°02'55" W). Named on Tecopa (1950) 15' quadrangle.

Daylight Pass [INYO]: *pass,* 14 miles north of Beatty Junction at the head of Boundary Canyon (lat. 36°47'20" N, long. 116°55'50" W; sec. 36, T 13 S, R 46 E); the pass is 0.25 mile east-southeast of Daylight Spring. Named on Bullfrog (1954) 15' quadrangle.

Daylight Spring [INYO]: *spring,* 14 miles north of Beatty Junction in Grapevine Mountains (lat. 36°47'25" N, long. 116°56'10" W; near N line sec. 35, T 13 S, R 46 E). Named on Bullfrog (1954) 15' quadrangle. The name first was Delightful Spring, then it was shortened to Delight Spring, and finally it became Daylight Spring (Federal Writers' Project, p. 44).

Deadfoot Canyon [INYO]: *canyon,* drained by a stream that flows 5 miles to Indian Wells Valley 5.5 miles south of the village of Little Lake (lat. 35°51'25" N, long. 117°54'10" W; near NW cor. sec. 17, T 24 S, R 38 E). Named on Little Lake (1954) 15' quadrangle.

Dead Horse Canyon [INYO]: *canyon,* drained by a stream that flows 3.5 miles to Marble Canyon (3) 7 miles southwest of the mouth of that canyon (lat. 36°35' N, long. 117°22'15" W). Named on Marble Canyon (1951) 15' quadrangle.

Dead Horse Canyon: see **Greenwater Canyon** [INYO].

Dead Horse Meadow [INYO]: *area*, 11.5 miles north-northeast of Westgard Pass (lat. 37°26'45" N, long. 118°03' W; sec. 8, T 6 S, R 36 E). Named on Blanco Mountain (1951) 15' quadrangle.

Deadman Canyon [INYO]:

(1) *canyon*, drained by a stream that flows 4 miles to an unnamed canyon 10.5 miles northwest of Waucoba Mountain (lat. 37°08'35" N, long. 118°07'20" W; near N line sec. 26, T 9 S, R 35 E). Named on Waucoba Mountain (1951) 15' quadrangle.

(2) *canyon*, drained by a stream that flows 4.25 miles to Indian Wells Valley 8 miles south of the mouth of Mountain Springs Canyon (lat. 35°49'25" N, long. 117°35'30" W; sec. 30, T 24 S, R 41 E). Named on Mountain Springs Canyon (1953) 15' quadrangle.

Deadman Creek [MONO]: *stream*, flows 11 miles to Owens River 14 miles north-northwest of Mount Morrison (lat. 37°45' N, long. 118°56'15" W; near NE cor. sec. 25, T 2 S, R 27 E); the stream heads near Deadman Pass. Named on Cowtrack Mountain (1962), Devils Postpile (1953), and Mount Morrison (1953) 15' quadrangles. The name is from the body of a murdered miner, Mr. Hume, found near the stream in 1861; the spot where the body was found was called Hume's Crossing, and the stream was called Murderer's Creek (Wright, p. 30).

Deadman Pass [INYO]: *pass*, 9 miles south-southwest of Eagle Mountain in Greenwater Range (lat. 36°05'55" N, long. 116°26'40" W; sec. 28, T 23 N, R 5 E). Named on Eagle Mountain (1951) 15' quadrangle. National Park Service officials proposed the name "Dead Man Pass" for the place because the body of a man was found there about 1905 (Palmer, p. 22).

Deadman Pass [MONO]: *pass*, 4.5 miles north-northwest of Mammoth Mountain on Mono-Madera County line (lat. 37°41'20" N, long. 119°04'10" W); the pass is near the head of Deadman Creek. Named on Devils Postpile (1953) 15' quadrangle.

Deadwood Canyon [ALPINE]: *canyon*, drained by a stream that flows 2.5 miles to North Fork Mokelumne River 5 miles north-northeast of Mount Reba (lat. 38°34'50" N, long. 120°00'15" W). Named on Mokelumne Peak (1979) and Pacific Valley (1979) 7.5' quadrangles.

Deadwood Canyon: see **Devils Corral** [ALPINE].

Deadwood Lake [ALPINE]: *lake*, 400 feet long, 7.25 miles northwest of Pacific Grade Summit (lat. 38°36'05" N, long. 119°59'25" W; sec. 27, T 9 N, R 18 E). Named on Pacific Valley (1979) 7.5' quadrangle.

Deadwood Peak: see **Upper Blue Lake** [ALPINE].

Death Valley [INYO]: *valley*, extends south and southeast for 130 miles from California-Nevada State line into San Bernardino County; generally lies between Panamint Range to the west and Amargosa Range to the east. Named on Death Valley (1954), Goldfield (1954), and Trona (1957) 1°x 2° quadrangles. Manly (p. 221) claimed that he and the party of emigrants of 1849 that he led out of the valley bestowed the name "Death Valley." Gudde (1949, p. 90) noted that the earliest written mention of the name was made by a member of the Boundary Commission in 1861. Palmer (p. 45) gave the names "Lost Valley," "Mesquite Valley," and "Northwest Arm" for the part of Death Valley north of the neighborhood of Stovepipe Wells; Palmer noted that Lieutenant D.A. Lyle bestowed the name "Lost Valley," evidently to commemorate the loss of his two guides in 1871. Palmer (p. 51) also mentioned that the north end of Death Valley, north of Mesquite Flat, was called Mound Spring Valley for a spring there. United States Board on Geographic Names (1933, p. 258) rejected the names "Amargosa Desert" and "Lost Valley" for present Death Valley. T.H. Means gave the name "Lake Manly" to the lake that occupied Death Valley in Pleistocene time—the name commemorates W.L. Manly (Blackwelder, p. 464).

Death Valley: see **Death Valley Junction** [INYO]; **Furnace Creek Ranch** [INYO].

Death Valley, Northwest Arm: see **Mesquite Flat** [INYO].

Death Valley Buttes [INYO]: *ridge*, west-southwest-trending, 3 miles long, 5.5 miles northeast of Stovepipe Wells on the northeast side of Death Valley (lat. 36°42'45" N, long. 117°00'30" W). Named on Chloride Cliff (1952) and Stovepipe Wells (1952) 15' quadrangles. Palmer (p. 13) noted the name "Breyfogle Buttes" as an alternate—this name commemorates Jacob Breyfogle, who discovered Breyfogle mine.

Death Valley Canyon [INYO]: *canyon*, drained by a stream that flows 6 miles to Death Valley nearly 15 miles south-southwest of Furnace Creek Inn (lat. 36°15'15" N, long. 116°57'30" W). Named on Emigrant Canyon (1952) and Furnace Creek (1952) 15' quadrangles. Palmer (p. 23) thought that the name probably was given because members of the Wheeler survey passed through the canyon on the way to Death Valley in 1871.

Death Valley Junction [INYO]: *village*, 27 miles east-southeast of Furnace Creek Inn in Amargosa Desert (lat. 36°18'10" N, long. 116°24'50" W; sec. 14, T 25 S, R 5 E). Named on Ash Meadows (1952) 15' quadrangle, which also has the name "Death Valley P.O." at the site. Called Death Valley on Furnace Creek (1910) 1° quadrangle, where the place is at the junction of Tonopah and Tidewater Railroad and Death Valley Railroad. Death Valley (1954) 1°x 2° quadrangle has both the names "Amargosa" and "Death Valley Junction" at the spot. United States Board on Geographic Names (1968b, p. 5) noted that Amargosa rural station post office is at the site, but rejected the name "Amargosa" for the community. Postal authorities established Amargosa post office in 1962 and changed the name to Death Valley Junction in 1968 (Salley, p. 6). They established Death Valley post office at present Death Valley Junction in 1908 and moved it to Furnace Creek Ranch in 1961, where it kept the name "Death Valley" (Salley, p. 56). Myrick (p. 608) noted that when Death Valley Railroad began operations in 1914 it used Tonopah and Tidewater Railroad tracks for 3.19 miles east-southeast of Death Valley Junction to a place called Horton, where the Death Valley rail line branched off; the name "Horton" was for Ben Horton, who was gang foreman and later roadmaster for Death Valley Railroad. Myrick (p. 610) also noted that a narrow-gauge rail line branched from the Tonopah and Tidewater Railroad main line at a place called Bradford Siding, and ran from there to a clay mine near Ash Meadows in the State of Nevada; Johnnie Bradford hauled clay over a dirt road to the railroad at the siding before the branch line was built—this apparently is the place that Ash Meadows (1952) 15' quadrangle shows a rail line branching from Tonopah and Tidewater Railroad 6 miles north-northwest of Death Valley Junction; the branch line extends for nearly 4 miles northeast into Nevada to a place called Clay Camp. Palmer (p. 14) mentioned a site called Burnt Wagons located about 7 miles northwest of Death Valley Junction; emigrants of 1849 are said to have abandoned and burned several wagons at the place.

Death Valley Wash [INYO]: *stream* and *dry wash*, extends for 50 miles from the north end of Death Valley to a point 4.5 miles northwest of Stovepipe Wells (lat. 36°42'30" N, long. 116°08' W). Named on Grapevine Peak (1957), Last Chance Range (1958), Stovepipe Wells (1952), Tin Mountain (1957), and Ubehebe Crater (1957) 15' quadrangles.

Dechambeau Creek [MONO]: *stream*, flows 3 miles to Mono Lake 4 miles north-northwest of Lee Vining (lat. 38°00'45" N, long. 119° 08'50" W; sec. 19, T 2 N, R 26 E). Named on Bodie (1958) 15' quadrangle, which shows Dechambeau ranch located 4 miles northeast of the mouth of the stream.

Dedeckera Canyon: see **Scottys Castle** [INYO].

Deep Canyon [ALPINE]: *canyon*, drained by a stream that flows 1.5 miles to West Fork Carson River 2.5 miles west-southwest of Woodfords (lat. 38°46'05" N, long. 119°52'10" W; sec. 32, T 11 N, R 19 E). Named on Woodfords (1979) 7.5' quadrangle.

Deep Canyon [INYO]: *canyon*, drained by a stream that flows 3.5 miles to lowlands 8 miles east of Mount Tom (lat. 37°21'45" N, long. 118°30'35" W; near SW cor. sec. 6, T 7 S, R 32 E). Named on Mount Tom (1949) 15' quadrangle.

Deep Canyon [MONO]: *canyon*, drained by a stream that flows 2.5 miles to Summers Creek 7.25 miles northeast of Matterhorn Peak (lat. 38°09'15" N, long. 119°16'30" W; sec. 1, T 3 N, R 24 E). Named on Matterhorn Peak (1956) 15' quadrangle.

Deep Creek [MONO]: *stream*, flows 9 miles to West Walker River 8 miles north-northwest of Fales Hot Springs (lat. 38°27'15" N, long. 119°27'30" W; sec. 16, T 7 N, R 23 E). Named on Fales Hot Springs (1956) 15' quadrangle.

Deep Creek: see **Little Deep Creek** [MONO].

Deep Springs [INYO]: *settlement*, 22 miles east of Bishop in Deep Springs Valley (lat. 37°22'15" N, long. 117°59' W; sec. 1, T 7 S, R 36 E). Named on Soldier Pass (1958) 15' quadrangle. The name of the settlement is from springs now called Buckhorn Springs, but earlier called Deep Springs (Mendenhall, p. 31). Postal authorities established Deep Spring post office in 1881 and discontinued it in 1883; they established Deep Springs post office in 1920 and discontinued it in 1953 (Frickstad, p. 51). United States Board on Geographic Names (1960c, p. 18) rejected the form "Deep Spring" for the name. Lida (1913) 1° quadrangle shows Stewarts ranch at the site, and California Mining Bureau's (1917b) map has the name "Stewarts" at or near the same place.

Deep Springs: see **Buckhorn Springs** [INYO].

Deep Springs Cow Camp [MONO]: *locality*, 12 miles southeast of White Mountain Peak (lat. 37°30'15" N, long. 118°06'25" W). Named on Mount Barcroft (1962) 15' quadrangle.

Deep Springs Lake [INYO]: *intermittent lake*, 1.5 miles long, 6.25 miles east-southeast of Westgard Pass (lat. 37°16'30" N, long. 118° 02'30" W); the feature is near the southwest end of Deep Springs Valley. Named on Blanco Mountain (1951) 15' quadrangle. Called Deep Spring Lake on Bishop (1913) 30' quadrangle, which shows an intermittent lake with a permanent lake in the east part, but United States Board on Geographic Names (1960c, p. 18) rejected this form of the name. The Board (1964b, p. 11) approved the name "Bog Mound Springs" for a group of springs located about 1 mile north of Deep Springs Lake (sec. 32, 33, T 7 S, R 36 E). The Board (1975, p. 9) also approved the name "Cuña Spring" for a feature situated 5 miles north-northwest of Deep Springs Lake near the base of White Mountains (lat. 37°20'40" N, long. 118°04'07" W; NW quarter sec. 18, T 7 S, R 36 E).

Deep Springs Valley [INYO]: *valley*, 8 miles east-northeast of Westgard Pass (lat. 37°19'30" N, long. 118°01' W); the settlement called Deep Springs is in the valley. Named on Blanco Mountain (1951) and Soldier Pass (1958) 15' quadrangles. Called Deep Spring Valley on Bishop (1913) 30' quadrangle, but United States Board on Geographic Names (1960c, p. 18) rejected this form of the name.

Deep Wash Canyon [MONO]: *canyon,* drained by a stream that flows 2 miles to Molybdenite Creek 5.5 miles south-southwest of Fales Hot Springs (lat. 38°16'30" N, long. 119°25'35" W; sec. 15, T 5 N, R 23 E). Named on Fales Hot Springs (1954) 7.5' quadrangle.

Deep Wells [MONO]: *well,* 16 miles southeast of Bodie (lat. 38°04'35" N, long. 118°45'35" W; sec. 34, T 3 N, R 29 E). Named on Trench Canyon (1958) 15' quadrangle. Wheeler's (1871) map has the name "Dexter's Well" at or near present Deep Wells.

Deer Creek [ALPINE]: *stream,* flows 5.5 miles to North Fork Mokelumne River 2.25 miles north-northwest of Pacific Grade Summit (lat. 38°32'30" N, long. 119°55'50" W; sec. 18, T 8 N, R 19 E); the stream goes through Deer Valley. Named on Pacific Valley (1979) 7.5' quadrangle.

Deer Mountain [MONO]: *peak,* nearly 5 miles north-northeast of Mammoth Mountain (lat. 37°41'55" N, long. 119°00'45" W; sec. 8, T 3 S, R 27 E). Altitude 8796 feet. Named on Devils Postpile (1953) 15' quadrangle.

Deer Spring [MONO]: *spring,* 8 miles north-northeast of Toms Place (lat. 37°40'20" N, long. 118°37'20" W; sec. 24, T 3 S, R 30 E). Named on Casa Diablo Mountain (1953) 15' quadrangle.

Deer Valley [ALPINE]: *valley,* 4 miles north of Pacific Grade Summit (lat. 38°34'30" N, long. 119°54'30" W; sec. 5, T 8 N, R 19 E). Named on Pacific Valley (1979) 7.5' quadrangle.

Delightful Spring: see **Daylight Spring** [INYO].

Delight Spring: see **Daylight Spring** [INYO].

Desert Creek [MONO]: *stream,* heads at Lobdell Lake and flows 7.5 miles to the State of Nevada 10 miles east-southeast of Coleville (lat. 38°32'10" N, long. 119°19'45" W). Named on Desert Creek Peak (1956) and Fales Hot Springs (1956) 15' quadrangles. East Fork enters from the east 4.5 miles upstream from California-Nevada State line; it is 4 miles long and is named on Fales Hot Springs (1956) 15' quadrangle.

Desert Spring: see **Sand Spring** [INYO].

Desolation Canyon [INYO]: *canyon,* 0.5 mile long, opens into Death Valley nearly 4 miles south of Furnace Creek Inn (lat. 36°23'40" N, long. 116°50'15" W; sec. 11, T 26 N, R 1 E). Named on Furnace Creek (1952) 15' quadrangle. Hanna (p. 85-86) suggested the name in 1949, when a centennial observation of the Manly-Jayhawker crossing of Death Valley was held in the canyon.

Devair: see **Ryan** [INYO] (2).

Devils Cornfield [INYO]: *area,* nearly 3 miles south-southeast of Stovepipe Wells in Death Valley (lat. 36°37'15" N, long. 117°03'20" W; sec. 26, T 15 S, R 45 E). Named on Stovepipe Wells (1952) 15' quadrangle. Federal Writers' Project (p. 31) referred to the place as Devil's Cornfield, and noted that arrowweed growing there resembles shocks of corn tied about the middle. Bourke Lee (p. 13) used the name "Cornfield" for the same place.

Devils Corral [ALPINE]: *canyon,* less than 1 mile long, nearly 4 miles south of Carson Pass (lat. 38°38'15" N, long. 119°59' W). Named on Carson Pass (1979) 7.5' quadrangle. Called Deadwood Canyon on Markleeville (1889) 30' quadrangle.

Devils Corral Creek [ALPINE]: *stream,* flows 2 miles to Summit City Creek 3.5 miles south of Carson Pass (lat. 38°38'40" N, long. 119°59'10" W; sec. 10, T 9 N, R 18 E); the stream goes through Devils Corral. Named on Carson Pass (1979) 7.5' quadrangle. A tributary that joins the stream near its mouth is called Grouse Creek on Markleeville (1889) 30' quadrangle.

Devils Gate [INYO]: *narrows,* 10.5 miles northwest of Waucoba Mountain (lat. 37°08'35" N, long. 118°07'25" W; near NW cor. sec. 26, T 9 S, R 35 E). Named on Waucoba Mountain (1951) 15' quadrangle.

Devils Gate [MONO]:

(1) *narrows,* 1.25 miles east of Fales Hot Springs (lat. 38°21' N, long. 119°22'35" W; sec. 19, T 6 N, R 24 E). Named on Fales Hot Springs (1954) 7.5' quadrangle.

(2) *narrows,* 11.5 miles north-northeast of Bridgeport along East Walker River (lat. 38°24'50" N, long. 119°10' W; at N line sec. 31, T 7 N, R 26 E). Named on Bridgeport (1958) 15' quadrangle.

Devils Golf Course [INYO]: *area,* 9 miles south of Furnace Creek Inn in Death Valley (lat. 36°19' N, long. 116°51' W). Named on Furnace Creek (1952) 15' quadrangle. The fanciful name suggests that only a fiend could play golf on the rough surface of crystallized salt at the place (Federal Writers' Project, p. 38).

Devils Kitchen [INYO]: *area,* 8 miles east of Coso Junction (lat. 36° 02'20" N, long. 117°48'05" W; near NE cor. sec. 7, T 22 S, R 39 E). Named on Haiwee Reservoir (1951) 15' quadrangle.

Devils Speedway [INYO]: *area,* 9 miles south of Furnace Creek Inn in Death Valley (lat. 36°19'30" N, long. 116°52'40" W). Named on Furnace Creek (1952) 15' quadrangle. The place was used for testing automobiles, and the name was given for advertising purposes (Palmer, p. 24).

Dexter Canyon [MONO]: *canyon,* 5.5 miles long, along Dexter Creek above a point 7 miles north of Glass Mountain (lat. 37°52'30" N, long. 118°44' W). Named on Cowtrack Mountain (1962) 15' quadrangle.

Dexter Creek [MONO]: *stream,* flows 9 miles to Adobe Creek 7.25 miles north of Glass Mountain (lat. 37°52'40" N, long. 119°43'50" W; sec. 12, T 1 S, R 29 E). Named on Glass Mountain (1962) 15' quadrangle.

Dexter's Well: see **Deep Wells** [MONO].

Diamond Peak [INYO]: *peak,* 11 miles west of Independence on Inyo-Fresno County line (lat. 36°49'35" N, long. 118°23'20" W). Altitude 13,126 feet. Named on Mount Pinchot (1953) 15' quadrangle.

Diamond Valley [ALPINE]: *valley,* 1.5 miles east of Woodfords (lat. 38°46'20" N, long. 119°47'30" W). Named on Woodfords (1979) 7.5' quadrangle.

Diana Gulch [MONO]: *canyon,* drained by a stream that flows 1 mile to Comanche Gulch 3.5 miles south-southwest of Benton (lat. 37° 46'15" N, long. 118°30'05" W; sec. 13, T 2 S, R 31 E); the canyon heads near Diana Peak. Named on Benton (1962) 15' quadrangle.

Diana Peak [MONO]: *peak,* 3.5 miles south of Benton on Blind Spring Hill (lat. 37°46'05" N, long. 118°29'15" W; on S line sec. 18, T 2 S, R 32 E). Named on Benton (1962) 15' quadrangle.

Diaz [INYO]: *locality,* nearly 4 miles south-southeast of Lone Pine along Southern Pacific Railroad (lat. 36°33'15" N, long. 118°02'15" W); the place is 1 mile east-southeast of present Diaz Lake. Named on Mount Whitney (1937) 30' quadrangle. Tucker and Sampson's (1938) map shows a place called Skinner located about 2.5 miles south of Diaz along the railroad.

Diaz Creek [INYO]:

(1) *stream,* flows 10 miles to Diaz Lake 3 miles south of Lone Pine (lat. 36°33'55" N, long. 118°03'20" W; near NW cor. sec. 10, T 16 S, R 36 E). Named on Lone Pine (1958) 15' quadrangle. Called Diez Creek on Mount Whitney (1907) 30' quadrangle. The name "Diaz" is for the Diaz brothers, who had a cattle ranch in the neighborhood in the 1860's (Hanna, p. 87).

(2) *stream,* flows 6.5 miles to Cottonwood Creek (2) 11 miles north-northwest of Olancha (lat. 36°26'25" N, long. 118°04'55" W). Named on Olancha (1956) 15' quadrangle.

Diaz Lake [INYO]: *lake,* 3250 feet long, 3 miles south of Lone Pine (lat. 36°33'45" N, long. 118°03'15" W; sec. 3, 10, T 16 S, R 36 E); Diaz Creek (1) flows to the lake. Named on Lone Pine (1958) 15' quadrangle.

Diez Creek: see **Diaz Creek** [INYO] (1).

Dingleberry Lake [INYO]: *lake,* 650 feet long, 2.25 miles east-northeast of Mount Darwin (lat. 37°10'55" N, long. 118°38'10" W; sec. 7, T 9 S, R 31 E). Named on Mount Goddard (1948) 15' quadrangle.

Dirty Socks [INYO]: *well,* 12 miles south-southwest of Keeler at the edge of Owens Lake (lat. 36°19'45" N, long. 117°56'55" W; near NE cor. sec. 34, T 18 S, R 37 E). Named on Keeler (1951) 15' quadrangle. A well drilled at the place in 1917 produced artisan hot water and was abandoned; reportedly, the name came from socks left by prospectors who did their laundry at the place—efforts to change the name to Olancha Wells or to Olancha Warm Springs failed (Jenkins, p. 27).

Disappointment Peak [INYO]: *peak,* nearly 12 miles southwest of Big Pine on Inyo-Fresno County line (lat. 37°04'05" N, long. 118° 28' W). Altitude 13,917 feet. Named on Big Pine (1950) 15' quadrangle.

Disaster Creek [ALPINE]: *stream,* flows nearly 5 miles to Clark Fork 6.5 miles east of Dardanelles Cone (lat. 38°25' N, long. 119° 45' W). Named on Dardanelles Cone (1979) 7.5' quadrangle. Lieutenant M.M. Macomb named the stream at the same time that he named Disaster Peak (Gudde, 1949, p. 96).

Disaster Peak [ALPINE]: *peak,* 17 miles south of Markleeville (lat. 38°26'55" N, long. 119°44' W). Altitude 10,047 feet. Named on Disaster Peak (1979) 7.5' quadrangle. Lieutenant Macomb of the Wheeler survey gave the name in 1877 after his topographer, W.A. Cowles, was severely injured when he accidentally dislodged a boulder—previously the feature was called King's Peak (Gudde, 1949, p. 96).

Discovery Pinnacle [INYO]: *peak,* 1.5 miles south of Mount Whitney (1) on Inyo-Tulare County line (lat. 36°33'30" N, long. 118°17'25" W). Named on Mount Whitney (1956) 15' quadrangle.

Division Creek [INYO]: *stream,* flows 3.5 miles to lowlands 11.5 miles northwest of Independence (lat. 36°56'05" N, long. 118°18'50" W). Named on Mount Pinchot (1953) 15' quadrangle.

Dixon Canyon [ALPINE]: *canyon,* drained by a stream that flows less than 1 mile to Upper Truckee River 4.5 miles north of Fourth of July Peak (lat. 38°43'40" N, long. 120°01'05" W; sec. 8, T 10 N, R 18 E). Named on Silver Lake (1956) 15' quadrangle.

Dixon Creek [ALPINE]: *stream,* flows 3.5 miles to Wolf Creek 9 miles south of Mogul Peak (lat. 38°33'40" N, long. 119°42'15" W; sec. 6, T 8 N, R 21 E). Named on Ebbetts Pass (1979) and Wolf Creek (1979) 7.5' quadrangles.

Dodd Spring: see **Big Dodd Spring** [INYO]; **Little Dodd Spring** [INYO].

Dodds Spring: see **Big Dodd Spring** [INYO].

Doe Canyon [MONO]: *canyon,* drained by a stream that flows 2.5 miles to Molybdenite Creek 4.5 miles south-southwest of Fales Hot Springs (lat. 38°17'25" N, long. 119°26'10" W; sec. 10, T 5 N, R 23 E). Named on Fales Hot Springs (1954) 7.5' quadrangle.

Dog Creek [MONO]: *stream,* flows 7 miles to Virginia Creek 6.5 miles south-southeast of Bridgeport (lat. 38°10' N, long. 119°11'40" W; near W line sec. 35, T 4 N, R 25 E). Named on Bodie (1958) 15' quadrangle. Wheeler's

(1871) map shows a place called Dogtown situated along present Dog Creek. In 1857 Mormons in Nevada heard that a young German, Cord Norst, and his Indian wife were taking a considerable amount of placer gold from a stream that Norst called Dogtown Creek; by 1859 a mining camp called Dogtown had developed along the stream (Cain, 1961, p. 4). Miners commonly used the name "Dogtown" to indicate a mining camp with extremely primitive living conditions (Calhoun, p. 73). Irelan (p. 366) referred to "Dogtown Diggings, along a creek of the same name." The stream also was known also as Brown's Creek (Smith, Genny, p. 133).

Dogtown: see **Dog Creek** [MONO].

Dogtown Creek: see **Dog Creek** [MONO].

Dogtown Diggins: see **Dog Creek** [MONO].

Dolomite [INYO]: *locality,* 6.5 miles south of New York Butte along Southern Pacific Railroad (lat. 36°33'15" N, long. 117°56'40" W). Named on New York Butte (1950) 15' quadrangle. The place was a siding on Carson and Colorado Railroad in 1883; a camp developed at the site when Inyo Marble Company opened a quarry there in 1885 (Strong, p. 24).

Dolomite Canyon [INYO]: *canyon,* drained by a stream that flows 4.5 miles to Panamint Valley 4.25 miles south of Panamint Butte (lat. 36°22'25" N, long. 117°20'45" W). Named on Panamint Butte (1951) 15' quadrangle.

Dome Hill [MONO]: *peak,* 10.5 miles northeast of Bridgeport near California-Nevada State line (lat. 38°21'50" N, long. 119°05'10" W; sec. 14, T 6 N, R 26 E). Altitude 8014 feet. Named on Bridgeport (1958) 15' quadrangle.

Donkey Lake [INYO]: *lake,* 1400 feet long, 3 miles east of Mount Darwin (lat. 37°10'20" N, long. 118°37' W; on N line sec. 17, T 9 S, R 31 E). Named on Mount Goddard (1948) 15' quadrangle. Art Schober named the lake in the 1930's for a burro (Schumacher, p. 95).

Donohue Pass [MONO]: *pass,* 15 miles south-southwest of Lee Vining on Mono-Tuolumne County line (lat. 37°45'40" N, long. 119°14'50" W). Named on Mono Craters (1953) 15' quadrangle. Lieutenant N.F. McClure named the pass in 1895 for a sergeant in his detachment (United States Board on Geographic Names, 1934, p. 7).

Donohue Peak [MONO]: *peak,* 14 miles south-southwest of Lee Vining on Mono-Tuolumne County line (lat. 37°46'30" N, long. 119°13'45" W); the peak is 1.5 miles northeast of Donohue Pass. Altitude 12,023 feet. Named on Mono Craters (1953) 15' quadrangle.

Dore Cliff [MONO]: *relief feature,* 3.5 miles northeast of Mount Conness (lat. 37°59'45" N, long. 119°16' W; on E line sec. 25, T 2 N, R 24 E); the feature is 0.5 mile north-northwest of Dore Pass. Named on Tuolumne Meadows (1956) 15' quadrangle.

Dore Pass [MONO]: *pass,* 3.5 miles east-northeast of Mount Conness on Tioga Crest (lat. 37°59'10" N, long. 119°15'40" W; sec. 31, T 2 N, R 25 E). Named on Tuolumne Meadows (1956) 15' quadrangle. I.C. Russell named the feature about 1882 for Louis Auguste Gustave Dore, French painter and illustrator (Hanna, p. 89).

Dorothy: see **Lake Dorothy** [MONO].

Dorothy Lake [ALPINE]: *lake,* 350 feet long, 0.5 mile northwest of Ebbetts Pass (lat. 38°32'55" N, long. 119°49'10" W; sec. 18, T 8 N, R 20 E). Named on Ebbetts Pass (1979) 7.5' quadrangle.

Dorothy Lake [INYO]: *lake,* 800 feet long, 8 miles north-northwest of Mount Tom (lat. 37°26'45" N, long. 118°42'20" W). Named on Mount Tom (1949) 15' quadrangle. According to Genny Smith (p. 37), the name is applied incorrectly on the map to a lake south of the one known locally as Dorothy Lake. United States Board on Geographic Names (1983c, p. 5) gave the location of Dorothy Lake as 1.2 miles southwest of Round Valley Peak along East Fork Rock Creek (lat. 37°26'20" N, long. 118°41'54" W).

Dorothy Lake Pass [MONO]: *pass,* 3.25 miles northwest of Tower Peak on Mono-Tuolumne County line (lat. 38°10'50" N, long. 119° 34'50" W); the pass is northeast of a Dorothy Lake located in Tuolumne County. Named on Tower Peak (1956) 15' quadrangle.

Double Canyon [INYO]: *canyon,* 0.5 mile long, opens into lowlands nearly 3 miles south of the village of Little Lake (lat. 35°53'45" N, long. 117°54'15" W; near W line sec. 32, T 23 S, R 38 E); the canyon divides at the upper end into North Fork and South Fork, each 1 mile long. The canyon and its forks are named on Little Lake (1954) 15' quadrangle.

Double Head: see **Snow Canyon** [INYO].

Dragon Peak [INYO]: *peak,* 10 miles west of Independence on Inyo-Fresno County line (lat. 36°47'30" N, long. 118°22'30" W). Altitude 12,995 feet. Named on Mount Pinchot (1953) 15' quadrangle.

Drew Creek [ALPINE]: *stream,* flows 3.5 miles to Middle Fork Stanislaus River in Tuolumne County 3.25 miles south-southwest of Dardanelles Cone (lat. 38°21'30" N, long. 119°53'15" W). Named on Dardanelles Cone (1979), Donnell Lake (1979), and Spicer Meadow Reservoir (1979) 7.5' quadrangles.

Dripping Spring: see **Bruce Canyon** [INYO].

Driveway Creek [MONO]: *stream,* flows nearly 3 miles to West Walker River 3.5 miles northwest of Fales Hot Springs (lat. 38°23'05" N, long. 119°27'05" W; sec. 9, T 6 N, R 23 E). Named on Chris Flat (1954) 7.5' quadrangle.

Drunken Sailor Lake: see **Sailor Lake** [INYO].

Dry Bone Canyon [INYO]: *canyon,* drained by a stream that flows 8 miles to an arm of Death Valley 10 miles southeast of Tin Mountain (lat. 36°46'20" N, long. 117°20' W). Named on Tin Mountain (1957) 15' quadrangle.

Dry Canyon [ALPINE]: *canyon,* drained by a stream that flows 2.25 miles to Carson Valley 3.5 miles north-northeast of Woodfords (lat. 38°49'25" N, long. 119°47'55" W; near S line sec. 12, T 11 N, R 19 E). Named on Woodfords (1979) 7.5' quadrangle.

Dry Canyon: see **Blackwater Wash** [INYO].

Dry Creek [MONO]:

(1) *stream,* flows 1.25 miles to Molybdenite Creek 4.5 miles south-southwest of Fales Hot Springs (lat. 38°17'30" N, long. 119°26'15" W; sec. 10, T 5 N, R 23 E). Named on Fales Hot Springs (1956) 15' quadrangle.

(2) *stream* and *dry wash,* extends for 12 miles to Owens River 13 miles north-northwest of Mount Morrison (lat. 37°45' N, long. 118°54'40" W; sec. 29, T 2 S, R 28 E). Named on Devils Postpile (1953) and Mount Morrison (1953) 15' quadrangles.

(3) *stream,* flows 10.5 miles to Mono Basin 4.25 miles north-northeast of the site of Mono Mills (lat. 37°56'45" N, long. 118°56'30" W; sec. 13, T 1 N, R 27 E). Named on Cowtrack Mountain (1962) 15' quadrangle.

Dry Creek: see **Hogback Creek** [INYO] (1).

Dry Creek Knoll: see **Lookout Mountain** [MONO].

Dry Fork [MONO]: *stream,* flows 6.5 miles to join Wet Fork and form Blackwater Wash 6 miles north-northeast of Glass Mountain (lat. 37°50'45" N, long. 118°38'50" W; sec. 22, T 1 S, R 30 E). Named on Glass Mountain (1962) 15' quadrangle. United States Board on Geographic Names (1964c, p. 14) rejected the name "Dry Fork Creek" for the stream.

Dry Fork Creek: see **Dry Fork** [MONO].

Dry Lake [ALPINE]: *intermittent lake,* 850 feet long, nearly 3 miles north of Mogul Peak (lat. 38°43'45" N, long. 119°43'40" W; sec. 12, T 10 N, R 20 E). Named on Heenan Lake (1979) 7.5' quadrangle.

Dry Lakes [INYO]: *dry lakes,* two, largest 2400 feet long, 12 miles southwest of the mouth of Mountain Springs Canyon in Indian Wells Valley (lat. 35°48' N, long. 117°44'45" W; sec. 27, 34, T 24 S, R 39 E). Named on Mountain Springs Canyon (1953) 15' quadrangle.

Dry Mountain [INYO]: *peak,* 38 miles north of Panamint Springs (lat. 36°54'30" N, long. 117°35'50" W). Altitude 8674 feet. Named on Dry Mountain (1957) 15' quadrangle.

Dublin Hills [INYO]: *range,* 2.5 miles west-southwest of Shoshone (lat. 35°57' N, long. 116°18'30" W). Named on Shoshone (1951) 15' quadrangle.

Dubois: see **Mount Dubois** [MONO].

Duck Creek [ALPINE]: *stream,* flows 3.25 miles to North Fork Stanislaus River 7.5 miles west-northwest of Dardanelles Cone (lat. 38°26'35" N, long. 120°00' W). Named on Spicer Meadow Reservoir (1979) 7.5' quadrangle.

Duck Lake [ALPINE]: *lake,* 1400 feet long, 7.5 miles northwest of Dardanelles Cone (lat. 38°28'30" N, long. 119°58'20" W). Named on Spicer Meadow Reservoir (1979) 7.5' quadrangle.

Duck Lake [INYO]: *intermittent lake,* 1400 feet long, 4 miles north of Independence (lat. 36°51'35" N, long. 118°11'15" W; sec. 31, T 12 S, R 35 E). Named on Independence (1951) 15' quadrangle.

Duffields Valley: see **Pickel Meadow** [MONO].

Dumont's Camp: see **Dumonts Meadows** [ALPINE].

Dumonts Meadows [ALPINE]: *area,* 13 miles south-southeast of Mogul Peak along East Fork Carson River (lat. 38°30'40" N, long. 119°39'15" W). Named on Wolf Creek (1979) 7.5' quadrangle. The name commemorates a French-Canadian woodcutter who provided timbers for Comstock mines in the 1870's (Gudde, 1949, p. 100). Wheeler (1878, p. 66) referred to Dumont's Meadow, located 3.01 miles from Dumont's Camp.

Dump Canyon [ALPINE]: *canyon,* 1 mile long, opens into Bagley Valley 7.25 miles southeast of Mogul Peak (lat. 38°36'20" N, long. 119°38'15" W; near N line sec. 26, T 9 N, R 21 E). Named on Topaz Lake (1956) 15' quadrangle.

Dunderberg Creek [MONO]: *stream,* flows 4 miles to Dog Creek 9 miles south of Bridgeport (lat. 38°07'30" N, long. 119°12'45" W; near W line sec. 15, T 3 N, R 25 E); the stream heads near Dunderberg Peak. Named on Bodie (1958) and Matterhorn Peak (1956) 15' quadrangles.

Dunderberg Mill [MONO]: *locality,* 10.5 miles south of Bridgeport (lat. 38°06'15" N, long. 119°15' W; near W line sec. 20, T 3 N, R 25 E); the place is along Dunderberg Creek. Named on Bodie (1958) 15' quadrangle. Bridgeport (1909) 30' quadrangle shows Dunderberg mine at the site. Gudde (1949, p. 101) thought that the mine probably was named for the Union man-of-war *Dunderberg.* Dr. George Munckton and others formed a mining company and developed a camp called Munckton that was active near Dunderberg mine in the early 1870's (Wedertz, p. 139). Postal authorities established Monckton post office—with the misspelled name—at Munckton in 1870 and discontinued it in 1872 (Salley, p. 144).

Dunderberg Peak [MONO]: *peak,* 6.25 miles east-southeast of Matterhorn Peak (lat. 38°03'50" N, long. 119°16'25" W; sec. 36, T 3 N, R 24 E); the peak is near the head of Dunderberg Creek. Altitude 12,374 feet. Named on Matterhorn Peak (1956) 15' quadrangle. Called Castle Peak on

Wheeler's (1871) map. Lieutenant M.M. Macomb (1879, p. 255) of the Wheeler survey gave the name "Dunderberg" to the feature for "the mines of that name upon its northerly slope, desiring to avoid duplicating the name [Castle Peak] which we had already given to the castellated volcanic mass north of Central Pacific Railroad near Summit Station." A mining camp called Ward, for Thomas Ward, was situated on the northeast side of the peak in the early 1890's (Wedertz, p. 137).

Dunes: see **The Dunes** [INYO].

Dunmovin [INYO]: *locality,* 3 miles north-northwest of Coso Junction in Rose Valley (lat. 36°05'15" N, long. 117°57'40" W; near SW cor. sec. 23, T 21 S, R 37 E). Named on Haiwee Reservoir (1951) 15' quadrangle. Postal authorities established Dunmovin post office in 1938 and discontinued it in 1941 (Frickstad, p. 51). The place first was called Cowan Station for James Cowan, who homesteaded there; Charles King and Hilda King bought out Cowan in 1936 and changed the name to Dunmovin (Iroquois Research Institute, p. 130-131).

Dutch Johns Meadow [INYO]: *area,* 5.5 miles southeast of Mount Tom (lat. 37°17'15" N, long. 118°34'30" W; near N line sec. 4, T 8 S, R 31 E). Named on Mount Tom (1949) 15' quadrangle.

Dutch Meadow [INYO]: *area,* 13 miles northwest of Olancha (lat. 36°25'45" N, long. 118°08'30" W; sec. 24, T 17 S, R 35 E). Named on Olancha (1956) 15' quadrangle.

Dutch Valley [ALPINE]: *canyon,* 3 miles long, drained by Indian Creek (1) above a point 6 miles east-northeast of Woodfords near California-Nevada State line (lat. 38°49' N, long. 119°43'20" W; sec. 15, T 11 N, R 20 E). Named on Freel Peak (1956) and Mount Siegel (1957) 15' quadrangles.

Dynamo Pond [MONO]: *lake,* about 1000 feet long, 7.5 miles south of Bridgeport along Green Creek (2) (lat. 38°08'55" N, long. 119° 13'20" W; sec. 4, T 3 N, R 25 E). Named on Bodie (1958) 15' quadrangle. The lake formed when the creek was dammed to provide water to generate electricity for a power line to Bodie that was completed in 1892 (Billeb, p. 153).

— E —

Eagle Borax Spring [INYO]: *spring,* nearly 2.5 miles north of Bennetts Well (lat. 36°12' N, long. 116°51'55" W). Named on Bennetts Well (1952) 15' quadrangle. Furnace Creek (1910) 1° quadrangle shows Eagle Borax Works at the place; this plant operated in 1882 and 1883 (Paher, p. 9). Wheeler's (1877) map has the name "Emigrant Spr." at or near the site.

Eagle Borax Works: see **Eagle Borax Spring** [INYO].

Eagle Creek [ALPINE]: *stream,* flows nearly 2 miles to Raymond Meadows Creek 2.5 miles north of Ebbetts Pass (lat. 38°35'05" N, long. 119°48'20" W). Named on Ebbetts Pass (1979) 7.5' quadrangle.

Eagle Creek [MONO]: *stream,* flows 6.5 miles to Buckeye Creek 6 miles west-southwest of Bridgeport (lat. 38°14'15" N, long. 119° 20'10" W; sec. 4, T 4 N, R 24 E); the stream heads near Eagle Peak. Named on Matterhorn Peak (1956) 15' quadrangle.

Eagle Gulch [ALPINE]: *canyon,* drained by a stream that flows 1 mile to East Fork Carson River 1.5 miles south-southwest of Mogul Peak (lat. 38°40'05" N, long. 119°43'35" W). Named on Heenan Lake (1979) 7.5' quadrangle.

Eagle Mountain [INYO]: *mountain,* 7 miles south-southeast of Death Valley Junction (lat. 36°12'45" N, long. 116°21'20" W). Altitude 3806 feet. Named on Eagle Mountain (1951) 15' quadrangle.

Eagle Peak [MONO]: *peak,* 6.25 miles north-northwest of Matterhorn Peak on Buckeye Ridge (lat. 38°10'50" N, long. 119°24'30" W; on W line sec. 24, T 4 N, R 23 E). Altitude 11,845 feet. Named on Matterhorn Peak (1956) 15' quadrangle. This apparently is the feature called Buckeye Pk. on Wheeler's (1876-1877) map.

Eagle Spring [INYO]: *spring,* nearly 1 mile north of Telescope Peak (lat. 36°10'50" N, long. 117°05'20" W; sec. 22, T 20 S, R 45 E). Named on Telescope Peak (1952) 15' quadrangle. Local Indians named the feature (Palmer, p. 25).

Earthquake Dome: see **Lookout Mountain** [MONO].

East Canyon [MONO]: *canyon,* drained by a stream that flows 1.5 miles to the State of Nevada 11 miles northeast of Bridgeport (lat. 38°21'20" N, long. 119°04'25" W; sec. 24, T 6 N, R 26 E). Named on Bridgeport (1958) 15' quadrangle.

East Carson Cañon: see **Carson River, East Fork** [ALPINE].

East Carson River: see **Carson River, East Fork** [ALPINE].

East Craters Sand Flat [MONO]: *area,* 3.5 miles south-southwest of the site of Mono Mills (lat. 37°50'30" N, long. 118°59'15" W); the place is east of Mono Craters. Named on Cowtrack Mountain (1962) 15' quadrangle.

Easter Bowl: see **Stovepipe Wells** [INYO].

Eastern Brook Lakes [INYO]: *lakes,* largest 1200 feet long, 8 miles northwest of Mount Tom in Little Lakes Valley (lat. 37°26' N, long. 118°44'30" W). Named on Mount Tom (1949) 15' quadrangle.

East Lake [MONO]: *lake,* 3900 feet long, 4.5 miles east-southeast of Matterhorn Peak (lat. 38°04'15" N, long. 119°18' W); the feature is 1.5 miles southeast of West Lake. Named on Matterhorn Peak (1956) 15' quadrangle.

East Palisade: see **The Thumb** [INYO].

East Slough [MONO]: *stream,* flows 8 miles to West Walker River 4.5 miles north of Coleville in Antelope Valley (lat. 38°38'10" N, long. 119°30'25" W; sec. 12, T 9 N, R 22 E). Named on Desert Creek Peak (1956) and Topaz Lake (1956) 15' quadrangles.

East Walker River [MONO]: *stream,* flows 18 miles to the State of Nevada 12 miles north-northeast of Bridgeport (lat. 38°25' N, long. 119°09'35" W; sec. 35, T 7 N, R 25 E). Named on Bodie (1958) and Bridgeport (1958) 15' quadrangles. Called East Fork or Rio Ida on Bancroft's (1864) map. Wedertz (p. 31) noted that the river had the early name "Vaughn's Creek." The stream is a major branch of Walker River, which is in the State of Nevada—Fremont named Walker River in 1844 for his guide, Joseph R. Walker (Gudde, 1949, p. 382).

East Walker River Reservoir: see **Bridgeport Reservoir** [MONO].

Ebbetts Pass [ALPINE]: *pass,* 10.5 miles south of Markleeville (lat. 38°32'40" N, long. 119°48'40" W). Named on Ebbetts Pass (1979) 7.5' quadrangle. Called Ebbet Pass on Markleeville (1889) 30' quadrangle, but United States Board on Geographic Names (1959, p. 6) rejected the names "Ebbet Pass" and "Ebbets Pass" for the feature. The name commemorates John A. Ebbetts, who led a group over the pass in April of 1850 and recommended the route for a railroad crossing of the Sierra Nevada (Long, p. 7).

Ebbetts Peak [ALPINE]: *peak,* 0.25 mile north-northwest of Ebbetts Pass (lat. 38°32'50" N, long. 119°48'50" W; sec. 18, T 8 N, R 20 E). Named on Ebbetts Pass (1979) 7.5' quadrangle.

Echo: see **Schwaub** [INYO].

Echo Canyon [INYO]: *canyon,* 10.5 miles long, opens into lowlands 4.5 miles east of Furnace Creek Inn (lat. 36°27'25" N, long. 116° 46'30" W; near NW cor. sec. 21, T 27 N, R 2 E). Named on Big Dune (1952), Furnace Creek (1952), and Ryan (1952) 15' quadrangles. Palmer (p. 79) noted that a peculiar feature in the canyon is called Window Rock because of a hole eroded in it.

Echo Lake [INYO]: *lake,* 1950 feet long, 2.25 miles southeast of Mount Darwin (lat. 37°08'45" N, long. 118°38'30" W; at SW cor. sec. 19, T 9 S, R 31 E). Named on Mount Goddard (1948) 15' quadrangle.

Echo Mountain: see **Winters Peak** [INYO].

Edith Lake [MONO]: *lake,* 1100 feet long, 2 miles west-southwest of Mount Morrison on a branch of Convict Creek (lat. 37°33'15" N, long. 118°53'30" W; sec. 33, T 4 S, R 28 E). Named on Mount Morrison (1953) 15' quadrangle.

Egan Fall: see **Darwin Falls** [INYO].

Egbert: see **Camp Egbert**, under **Round Valley** [INYO-MONO[.

Egypt Creek [INYO]: *stream,* flows 4.25 miles to Bishop Creek 7.25 miles east-southeast of Mount Tom (lat. 37°18' N, long. 118° 32' W; sec. 35, T 7 S, R 31 E). Named on Mount Tom (1949) 15' quadrangle.

Ehrenbeck Peak [MONO]: *peak,* less than 2 miles east-southeast of Tower Peak on Mono-Tuolumne County line (lat. 38°08'15" N, long. 119°30'50" W). Altitude 11,240 feet. Named on Tower Peak (1956) 15' quadrangle.

Elbow: see **The Elbow** [ALPINE].

Elbow Creek [ALPINE]: *stream,* flows 2.5 miles to North Fork Mokelumne River 2.25 miles west of Ebbetts Pass (lat. 38°32'40" N, long. 119°51'10" W; sec. 14, T 8 N, R 19 E); the stream goes past The Elbow. Named on Ebbetts Pass (1979) 7.5' quadrangle.

Elderberry Canyon [INYO]: *canyon,* drained by a stream that flows 2.5 miles to Round Valley (1) 3.25 miles north-northeast of Mount Tom (lat. 37°23' N, long. 118°37'45" W; sec. 36, T 6 S, R 30 E). Named on Mount Tom (1949) 15' quadrangle. Called Huckleberry Canyon on Mount Goddard (1912) 30' quadrangle.

Elder Creek [ALPINE]: *stream,* flows nearly 2 miles to Wolf Creek 3.5 miles north of Disaster Peak (lat. 38°30' N, long. 119°44'20" W). Named on Dardanelles Cone (1979), Disaster Peak (1979), and Ebbetts Pass (1979) 7.5' quadrangles.

Elephant Rock [ALPINE]: *peak,* 6 miles west-northwest of Dardanelles Cone (lat. 38°26'50" N, long. 119°58'10" W). Altitude 7425 feet. Named on Spicer Meadow Reservoir (1979) 7.5' quadrangle.

Elephant Rock Lake [ALPINE]: *lake,* 1350 feet long, 6.25 miles west-northwest of Dardanelles Cone (lat. 38°26'30" N, long. 119° 58'30" W); the lake is 0.5 mile southwest of Elephant Rock. Named on Spicer Meadow Reservoir (1979) 7.5' quadrangle.

Elephants Back [ALPINE]: *peak,* 1 mile south-southeast of Carson Pass (lat. 38°40'45" N, long. 119°58'55" W; sec. 27, T 10 N, R 18 E). Altitude 9585 feet. Named on Carson Pass (1979) 7.5' quadrangle. Called Elephant's Back on Wheeler's (1876-1877) map.

Elinore Lake [INYO]: *lake,* 850 feet long, 11.5 miles west-southwest of Big Pine (lat. 37°05'45" N, long. 118°28'45" W). Named on Big Pine (1950) 15' quadrangle.

Ellery Lake [MONO]: *lake,* 3500 feet long, behind a dam on Lee Vining Creek 6.5 miles west-southwest of Lee Vining (lat. 37°56'05" N, long. 119°13'50" W; near E line sec. 20, T 1 N, R 25 E). Named on Mono

Craters (1953) 15' quadrangle. Called Rhinedollar Reservoir on Sampson's (1940) map. The name "Ellery Lake" is for Nathaniel Ellery, the state engineer who had charge of building the road from Tioga Pass to Mono Lake in 1909 (Gudde, 1949, p. 106).

Elna [INYO]: *locality,* 6.5 miles southeast of Big Pine along Southern Pacific Railroad (lat. 37°05'40" N, long. 118°13'30" W; sec. 11, T 10 S, R 34 E). Named on Bishop (1913) 30' quadrangle.

Emerald Lake [MONO]: *lake,* 500 feet long, 8 miles west-northwest of Mount Morrison (lat. 37°35' N, long. 118°59'45" W). Named on Mount Morrison (1953) 15' quadrangle.

Emerald Lake: see **Way Lake** [MONO].

Emerald Lakes [INYO]: *lakes,* largest 500 feet long, 2.5 miles east-northeast of Mount Darwin (lat. 37°10'50" N, long. 118°37'45" W; sec. 7, T 9 S, R 31 E). Named on Mount Goddard (1948) 15' quadrangle.

Emerson: see **Mount Emerson** [INYO].

Emerson Lake [INYO]: *lake,* 1050 feet long, 4.25 miles north of Mount Darwin (lat. 37°13'50" N, long. 118°40' W); the lake is 1 mile southwest of Mount Emerson. Named on Mount Goddard (1948) 15' quadrangle.

Emigrant Canyon [INYO]: *canyon,* 8 miles long, opens into lowlands 10.5 miles north-northwest of Emigrant Pass (1) (lat. 36°28'35" N, long. 117°12'45" W). Named on Emigrant Canyon (1952) 15' quadrangle.

Emigrant Canyon: see **Redlands Canyon** [INYO]; **West Carson Canyon** [ALPINE].

Emigrant Creek [ALPINE]: *stream,* flows 1.5 miles to Caples Lake 2 miles north-northwest of Fourth of July Peak (lat. 38°41'05" N, long. 120°02'10" W; sec. 30, T 10 N, R 18 E); the stream heads at Emigrant Lake. Named on Caples Lake (1979) 7.5' quadrangle.

Emigrant Lake [ALPINE]: *lake,* 1550 feet long, less than 1 mile west of Fourth of July Peak (lat. 38°39'40" N, long. 120°02'15" W; on S line sec. 31, T 10 N, R 18 E); the lake is at the head of Emigrant Creek. Named on Caples Lake (1979) 7.5' quadrangle.

Emigrant Pass [INYO]:
(1) *pass,* 23 miles south of Stovepipe Wells in Panamint Range (lat. 36°20'10" N, long. 117°08'25" W). Altitude 5318 feet. Named on Emigrant Canyon (1952) 15' quadrangle. The name reflects the belief that emigrants of 1849 left Death Valley through the pass (Palmer, p. 26).
(2) *pass,* nearly 10 miles east-northeast of Tecopa in Nopah Range between California Valley and Chicago Valley along the Old Spanish Trail (lat. 35°53' N, long. 116°03'35" W; near NW cor. sec. 31, T 21 N, R 9 E). Named on Tecopa (1950) 15' quadrangle.

Emigrant Pass [MONO]: *pass,* 6 miles northwest of Tower Peak on Mono-Tuolumne County line (lat. 38°12' N, long. 119°37'50" W); the pass is east of Emigrant Meadow, which is in Tuolumne County. Named on Tower Peak (1956) 15' quadrangle.

Emigrant Spring [INYO]: *spring,* 7.5 miles north-northwest of Emigrant Pass (1) (lat. 36°26' N, long. 117°11'35" W); the spring is in Emigrant Canyon. Named on Emigrant Canyon (1952) 15' quadrangle. According to Mendenhall (p. 35), early emigrants from Salt Lake City used water from the spring.

Emigrant Spring: see **Eagle Borax Spring** [INYO]; **Upper Emigrant Spring** [INYO].

Emigrant Valley [ALPINE]: *area,* 1.5 miles northwest of Fourth of July Peak (lat. 38°40'15" N, long. 120°02'35" W; sec. 31, T 10 N, R 18 E); the place is less than 1 mile north-northwest of Emigrant Lake near Emigrant Creek. Named on Caples Lake (1979) 7.5' quadrangle.

Emigrant Wash [INYO]: *stream,* flows 9.5 miles from the mouth of Emigrant Canyon north to a point 7 miles southwest of Stovepipe Wells in Death Valley (lat. 36°36' N, long. 117°11' W). Named on Emigrant Canyon (1952) and Stovepipe Wells (1952) 15' quadrangles. The name commemorates the emigrants of 1849 who followed the feature on the way out of Death Valley (Federal Writers' Project, p. 32).

Emma: see **Mount Emma** [MONO].

Emma Lake [MONO]: *lake,* 900 feet long, 6.5 miles southwest of Fales Hot Springs (lat. 38°16'50" N, long. 119°28'55" W; sec. 18, T 5 N, R 23 E); the lake is nearly 0.5 mile northwest of Mount Emma. Named on Fales Hot Springs (1954) 7.5' quadrangle. The name presumably is for Emma Mack, whose parents had a house at the lake in the 1870's (Gudde, 1949, p. 108).

English Meadow [ALPINE]: *area,* 5.5 miles north-northeast of Ebbetts Pass (lat. 38°37'10" N, long. 119°46'05" W; near SW cor. sec. 15, T 9 N, R 20 E). Named on Ebbetts Pass (1979) 7.5' quadrangle.

Epaulet Peak [INYO]: *peak,* 33 miles east of Manly Peak in Black Mountains (lat. 35°58'20" N, long. 116°31'25" W). Altitude 4706 feet. Named on Confidence Hills (1950) 15' quadrangle. L.P. Noble named the peak for the fancied resemblance of outcrops there to an epaulet on the shoulder of a uniform (Palmer, p. 26).

Epidote Peak [MONO]: *peak,* 5 miles east-southeast of Matterhorn Peak (lat. 38°03'35" N, long. 119°18'15" W). Named on Matterhorn Peak (1956) 15' quadrangle.

Esha Canyon [MONO]: *canyon,* 2.5 miles long, opens into the canyon of McGee Creek (2) 3.5 miles east-southeast of Mount Morrison (lat. 37°33' N, long. 118°47'45" W). Named on Mount Morrison (1953) 15' quadrangle.

Etcharren Valley: see **Etcheron Valley** [INYO].

Etcheron Valley [INYO]: *valley,* 17 miles southeast of Coso Peak and west of Argus Range (lat. 36°02' N, long. 117°30' W). Named on Coso Peak (1951), Maturango Peak (1951), and Mountain Springs Canyon (1953) 15' quadrangles. United States Board on Geographic Names (1983f, p. 2) approved the name "Etcharren Valley" for the feature. The misspelled name commemorates Domingo Etcharron, an early-day sheep rancher (Koenig, p. 140).

Eureka Peak: see **Marble Canyon** [INYO] (2).

Eureka Valley [INYO]: *valley,* southwest of Last Chance Range and northeast of Inyo Mountains and Saline Range (lat. 37°13' N, long. 117°49' W). Named on Last Chance Range (1958), Magruder Mountain (1957), Soldier Pass (1958), and Waucoba Spring (1958) 15' quadrangles. Lieutenant D.A. Lyle of the Wheeler survey called the feature Termination Valley in 1871 (Palmer, p. 27).

Evelyn [INYO]: *locality,* 5 miles south-southeast of Eagle Mountain near Amargosa River (lat. 36°08'45" N, long. 116°19' W; sec. 10, T 23 N, R 6 E). Named on Eagle Mountain (1951) 15' quadrangle. The place was a station on Tonopah and Tidewater Railroad named in 1907 for the wife of J.M. "Borax" Smith (Palmer, p. 27). California Mining Bureau's (1917b) map shows a place called Jay located along the railroad 3 miles south of Evelyn.

Evergreen Lake [ALPINE]: *lake,* 650 feet long, 7 miles north-northwest of Pacific Grade Summit (lat. 38°36'50" N, long. 119°57'15" W). Named on Pacific Valley (1979) 7.5' quadrangle.

Excelsior Mountain [MONO]: *peak,* 6.25 miles southeast of Matterhorn Peak on Mono-Tuolumne County line (lat. 38°01'25" N, long. 119°18'15" W; near W line sec. 14, T 2 N, R 24 E). Altitude 12,446 feet. Named on Matterhorn Peak (1956) 15' quadrangle.

— F —

Faith Valley [ALPINE]: *valley,* 3.25 miles east-southeast of Carson Pass along West Fork Carson River (lat. 38°41' N, long. 119°55'45" W; sec. 30, 31, T 10 N, R 19 E); the feature is between Hope Valley and Charity Valley. Named on Carson Pass (1979) 7.5' quadrangle. Explorers named the valley in 1855 (Noyes, p. 327).

Fales: see **Fales Hot Springs** [MONO].

Fales Hot Springs [MONO]: *locality,* 11 miles northwest of Bridgeport (lat. 38°21'05" N, long. 119°23'55" W; sec. 24, T 6 N, R 23 E); the place is along Hot Creek (1). Named on Fales Hot Springs (1954) 7.5' quadrangle. Samuel Fales developed hot springs at the site in 1877 (Gudde, 1949, p. 112). Postal authorities established Fales post office in 1881 and discontinued it the same year (Frickstad, p. 104). The place had a stage station and road house in 1908, as well as a plunge and tub baths that used the hot water (Waring, p. 132).

Fall Canyon [INYO]: *canyon,* drained by a stream that flows 10 miles to Death Valley 0.5 mile north of the mouth of Titus Canyon (lat. 36°49'50" N, long. 117°10'20" W). Named on Grapevine Peak (1957) 15' quadrangle.

Fall Creek: see **Queen Dicks Canyon** [MONO].

Falls Canyon [MONO]: *canyon,* drained by a stream that flows 3.5 miles to Hammil Valley 10 miles northwest of White Mountain Peak (lat. 37°44'20" N, long. 118°22'55" W). Named on Benton (1962) and White Mountain Peak (1962) 15' quadrangles—the last-named quadrangle shows a waterfall in the canyon.

Falls Creek [INYO]: *stream,* flows nearly 2.5 miles to Walker Creek 4 miles southwest of Olancha (lat. 36°14'35" N, long. 118°03'25" W). Named on Monache Mountain (1956) and Olancha (1956) 15' quadrangles.

Falls Creek [MONO]: *stream,* flows 2.5 miles to West Fork West Walker River nearly 6 miles east-southeast of Sonora Pass (lat. 38° 17'15" N, long. 119°32'40" W; near N line sec. 15, T 5 N, R 22 E). Named on Pickel Meadow (1954) 7.5' quadrangle.

Falls Meadows [ALPINE]: *area,* 4.25 miles northeast of Disaster Peak along East Fork Carson River (lat. 38°29'45" N, long. 119° 41' W); the place is below Carson Falls. Named on Disaster Peak (1979) 7.5' quadrangle.

Fantail Lake [MONO]: *lake,* 1200 feet long, 3 miles east-southeast of Mount Conness (lat. 37°56'50" N, long. 119°16'15" W). Named on Tuolumne Meadows (1956) 15' quadrangle.

Farley Pass: see **Boundary Canyon** [INYO].

Farm Well: see **The Tanks** [INYO].

Fays Camp: see **Silver Creek** [ALPINE] (3).

Fence Creek [ALPINE]: *stream,* flows 1.5 miles to Clark Fork nearly 3 miles south of Dardanelles Cone in Tuolumne County (lat. 38° 21'50" N, long. 119°52'30" W). Named on Donnell Lake (1979) and Spicer Meadow Reservoir (1979) 7.5' quadrangles.

Ferguson's Landing: see **Owens Lake** [INYO].

Fern Creek [MONO]: *stream,* flows 2.5 miles to Reversed Creek 13 miles south of Lee Vining (lat. 37°45'45" N, long. 119°06'40" W; sec. 21, T 2 S,

R 26 E); the stream goes through Fern Lake. Named on Devils Postpile (1953) and Mono Craters (1953) 15' quadrangles.

Fern Lake [MONO]: *lake,* 800 feet long, 9 miles north-northwest of Mammoth Mountain (lat. 37°44'45" N, long. 119°06'45" W; sec. 28, T 2 S, R 26 E); the lake is along Fern Creek. Named on Devils Postpile (1953) 15' quadrangle.

Ferris Canyon [MONO]: *canyon,* drained by a stream that flows 6 miles to the State of Nevada 13 miles north of Bridgeport (lat. 38°27' N, long. 119°12'25" W; sec. 20, T 7 N, R 25 E). Named on Bridgeport (1958) and Fales Hot Springs (1956) 15' quadrangles. The name is for Andrew Ferris, who owned land in the neighborhood (Gudde, 1949, p. 115). Fales Hot Springs (1956) 15' quadrangle shows Kentuck mine on the north side of Ferris Canyon (sec. 30, T 7 N, R 25 E)—a mining settlement called Kentuck Camp was near the mine (Shannon, p. 44). Irelan (p. 358) noted that a place called Clinton was in Ferris Canyon. Postal authorities established Clinton post office in 1882 and discontinued it in 1894 (Frickstad, p. 104).

Fifth Lake [INYO]: *lake,* 0.25 mile long, 9.5 miles east-southeast of Mount Darwin along Big Pine Creek (lat. 37°07'55" N, long. 118° 30'25" W; on S line sec. 29, T 9 S, R 32 E); the feature is between Fourth Lake and Sixth Lake. Named on Mount Goddard (1948) 15' quadrangle.

Finch Lake [INYO]: *lake,* 600 feet long, 5 miles west-northwest of Mount Tom (lat. 37°22'35" N, long. 118°44'05" W; on N line sec. 6, T 7 S, R 30 E). Named on Mount Tom (1949) 15' quadrangle.

Finger Lake [INYO]: *lake,* 1900 feet long, 11 miles west-southwest of Big Pine (lat. 37°05'10" N, long. 118°27'35" W). Named on Big Pine (1950) 15' quadrangle.

Finger Lake [MONO]: *lake,* 1000 feet long, 2 miles southeast of Mount Conness (lat. 37°56'55" N, long. 119°17'35" W). Named on Tuolumne Meadows (1956) 15' quadrangle.

First Falls [INYO]: *waterfall,* 8.5 miles west-southwest of Big Pine on North Fork Big Pine Creek (lat. 37°07'30" N, long. 118°26'30" W; sec. 35, T 9 S, R 32 E); the feature is 1 mile downstream from Second Falls. Named on Big Pine (1950) 15' quadrangle.

First Lake [INYO]: *lake,* 900 feet long, 11 miles west-southwest of Big Pine along North Fork Big Pine Creek (lat. 37°07'35" N, long. 118°29' W; sec. 33, T 9 S, R 32 E); the lake is situated downstream from Second Lake. Named on Big Pine (1950) 15' quadrangle. The lake is one of the group called Big Pine Lakes.

Fish Canyon [INYO]: *canyon,* drained by a stream that flows 2.5 miles to Panamint Valley 7.25 miles west of Manly Peak (lat. 35° 53'50" N, long. 117°14'40" W). Named on Trona (1949) 15' quadrangle.

Fisherman's Peak: see **Mount Whitney** [INYO] (1).

Fisher Meadow: see **Danburg Beach** [MONO].

Fishgut Lakes [INYO]: *lakes,* largest 1100 feet long, 2.5 miles northeast of Mount Darwin (lat. 37°11'30" N, long. 118°38'30" W). Named on Mount Goddard (1948) 15' quadrangle.

Fish Lake Valley [INYO-MONO]: *valley,* east of White Mountains; mainly in the State of Nevada, but extends into Mono County and Inyo County. Named on Mount Barcroft (1962), Piper Peak (1963), and Soldier Pass (1958) 15' quadrangles.

Fish Lake Valley Wash [MONO]: *stream,* flows 7 miles to the State of Nevada 19 miles east-southeast of White Mountain Peak (lat. 37°32'30" N, long. 117°56'15" W; sec. 5, T 5 S, R 37 E); the stream is in Fish Lake Valley. Named on Piper Peak (1963) and Soldier Pass (1958) 15' quadrangles.

Fish Slough [INYO-MONO]: *stream,* heads in Mono County and flows 7.5 miles to Owens River 3.5 miles north of Bishop in Inyo County (lat. 37°24'50" N, long. 118°24' W; sec. 19, T 6 S, R 33 E). Named on Bishop (1949) 15' quadrangle. White Mountain Peak (1962) 15' quadrangle has the form "Fish Slu" for the name. The stream first was called Sand Springs Creek for some sandy-bottomed springs found along it (Schumacher, p. 64).

Fish Springs [INYO]:

(1) *springs,* three, 5 miles south-southeast of Big Pine at the west edge of Owens Valley (lat. 37°05'55" N, long. 118°15'30" W; sec. 9, T 10 S, R 34 E). Named on Big Pine (1950) 15' quadrangle.

(2) *locality,* 6.5 miles south-southeast of Big Pine (lat. 37°04'30" N, long. 118°15'05" W; near W line sec. 15, T 10 S, R 34 E); the place is 1.5 miles south-southwest of Fish Springs (1). Named on Big Pine (1950) 15' quadrangle. Postal authorities established Fish Springs post office in 1866, discontinued it the same year, reestablished it in 1868, and discontinued it in 1876 (Salley, p. 75). Called Tinemaha P.O. on Lippincott's (1902) map. Postal authorities established Tinnemaha post office in 1895 and discontinued it in 1910 (Frickstad, p. 53). The name "Tinemaha" is for a legendary Piute Indian (Gudde, 1975, p. 350).

Fish Springs Hill [INYO]: *ridge,* southeast-trending, 1 mile long, 5 miles south of Big Pine (lat. 37°05'25" N, long. 118°17'30" W); the ridge is 2 miles west-southwest of Fish Springs (1). Named on Big Pine (1950) 15' quadrangle. Bishop (1913) 30' quadrangle has the form "Fish Spring Hill" for the name.

Fish Valley: see **Lower Fish Valley** [ALPINE]; **Upper Fish Valley** [ALPINE].

Fish Valley Peak [ALPINE-MONO]: *peak,* 8 miles north-northeast of Sonora Pass on Alpine-Mono County line (lat. 38°26'05" N, long. 119°34'10" W; sec. 21, T 7 N, R 22 E); the peak is southeast of Upper Fish Valley [ALPINE]. Altitude 10,571 feet. Named on Lost Cannon Peak (1954) 7.5' quadrangle.

Five Bridges [INYO]: *locality,* 3.5 miles north of Bishop at a crossing of Owens River (lat. 37°24'45" N, long. 118°24'15" W; near E line sec. 24, T 6 S, R 32 E). Named on Bishop (1949) 15' quadrangle.

Fivemile Canyon [INYO]: *canyon,* drained by a stream that flows 6 miles to Indian Wells Valley 4.25 miles south of the village of Little Lake (lat. 35°52'30" N, long. 117°53'30" W; sec. 5, T 24 S, R 38 E). Named on Little Lake (1954) 15' quadrangle. Tucker and Sampson's (1938) map has the form "Five Mile Canyon" for the name.

Fivemile Spring [INYO]: *spring,* 5.5 miles east of Manly Peak (lat. 35°55'25" N, long. 117°01'10" W). Named on Manly Peak (1950) 15' quadrangle.

Flatiron Butte [MONO]: *peak,* 9.5 miles northwest of Matterhorn Peak (lat. 38°11'40" N, long. 119°29'35" W); the feature is at the southwest end of Flatiron Ridge. Named on Matterhorn Peak (1956) 15' quadrangle.

Flatiron Ridge [MONO]: *ridge,* generally northeast-trending, 7 miles long, 9 miles north-northwest of Matterhorn Peak (lat. 38°13' N, long. 119°26'30" W); Flatiron Butte is at the southwest end of the ridge. Named on Fales Hot Springs (1956) and Matterhorn Peak (1956) 15' quadrangles.

Flower Lake [INYO]: *lake,* 700 feet long, 9 miles west-southwest of Independence (lat. 36°46'05" N, long. 118°21'35" W). Named on Mount Pinchot (1953) 15' quadrangle.

Fly Valley [ALPINE]: *valley,* 7 miles east of Disaster Peak (lat. 38° 25'50" N, long. 119°36'40" W). Named on Lost Cannon Peak (1954) 7.5' quadrangle.

Folger Peak [ALPINE]: *peak,* 7 miles north-northeast of Dardanelles Cone (lat. 38°29'45" N, long. 119°48'55" W). Named on Dardanelles Cone (1979) 7.5' quadrangle. Called Folger's Pk. on Wheeler's (1876-1877) map. The name commemorates either Robert M. Folger, proprietor of the Alpine *Chronicle,* or his brother, Alexander M. Folger, postmaster at Markleeville (Gudde, 1949, p. 117).

Ford Flat [INYO]: *area,* 11 miles west-northwest of Big Pine (lat. 37°14'20" N, long. 118°28'10" W; sec. 21, T 8 S, R 32 E). Named on Big Pine (1950) 15' quadrangle.

Fords: see **Casa Diablo Hot Springs** [MONO].

Ford Spring [MONO]: *spring,* 10 miles southeast of the site of Mono Mills (lat. 37°46'45" N, long. 118°50'25" W; sec. 13, T 2 S, R 28 E). Named on Cowtrack Mountain (1962) 15' quadrangle.

Forest City Flat [ALPINE]: *area,* 1 mile southeast of Mogul Peak near the head of Smiths Creek (lat. 38°40'40" N, long. 119°42'20" W). Named on Heenan Lake (1979) 7.5' quadrangle.

Forestdale Creek [ALPINE]: *stream,* flows nearly 3 miles to West Fork Carson River 3 miles east-southeast of Carson Pass (lat. 38° 40'30" N, long. 119°56'10" W; near N line sec. 31, T 10 N, R 19 E). Named on Carson Pass (1979) 7.5' quadrangle.

Forestdale Divide [ALPINE]: *ridge,* north-northeast-trending, less than 1 mile long, 2.5 miles south-southeast of Carson Pass (lat. 38° 39'40" N, long. 119°58' W; on N line sec. 2, T 9 N, R 18 E); the ridge is near the head of Forestdale Creek. Named on Carson Pass (1979) 7.5' quadrangle.

Fountain Springs: see **Furnace Creek Wash** [INYO].

Four Gables [INYO]: *peak,* 3 miles southwest of Mount Tom on Inyo-Fresno County line (lat. 37°18'25" N, long. 118°41'35" W). Named on Mount Tom (1949) 15' quadrangle.

Four Mile Canyon [ALPINE]: *canyon,* drained by a stream that flows nearly 3 miles to Silver King Creek 7.5 miles east of Disaster Peak (lat. 38°26'40" N, long. 119°35'35" W). Named on Lost Cannon Peak (1954) 7.5' quadrangle. Sonora Pass (1956) 15' quadrangle has the form "Fourmile Canyon" for the name.

Fourth Lake [INYO]: *lake,* 850 feet long, 10 miles east-southeast of Mount Darwin (lat. 37°07'50" N, long. 118°30'05" W; on S line sec. 29, T 9 S, R 32 E); the feature is between Third Lake and Fifth Lake. Named on Mount Goddard (1948) 15' quadrangle.

Fourth of July Canyon [ALPINE]: *canyon,* drained by a stream that heads in Amador County and flows 2.25 miles to North Fork Mokelumne River 2.5 miles north-northwest of Mount Reba (lat. 38°32'15" N, long. 120°03' W). Named on Mokelumne Peak (1979) 7.5' quadrangle.

Fourth of July Lake [ALPINE]: *lake,* 1200 feet long, less than 1 mile south-southeast of Fourth of July Peak (lat. 38°39' N, long. 120°01' W). Named on Caples Lake (1979) 7.5' quadrangle.

Fourth of July Peak [ALPINE]: *peak,* 3 miles southwest of Carson Pass (lat. 38°39'35" N, long. 120°01'20" W; sec. 5, T 9 N, R 18 E); the peak is less than 1 mile north-northwest of Fourth of July Lake. Altitude 9536 feet. Named on Caples Lake (1979) 7.5' quadrangle.

Fourth of July Spring [MONO]: *spring,* 8.5 miles east-southeast of Coleville (lat. 38°32'40" N, long. 119°21'20" W). Named on Desert Creek Peak (1956) 15' quadrangle.

Frances: see **Lake Frances** [MONO].

Francis: see **Manzanar** [INYO].

Francis Lake [INYO]: *lake,* 500 feet long, 7.5 miles north-northwest of Mount Tom (lat. 37°26' N, long. 118°43' W). Named on Mount Tom (1949) 15' quadrangle.

Franklin Well [INYO]: *well,* 9 miles north-northwest of Death Valley Junction along Amargosa River (lat. 36°25'30" N, long. 116°27'45" W; sec. 5, T 26 S, R 5 E). Named on Ash Meadows (1952) 15' quadrangle. The name probably commemorates Thomas Franklin, an Indian fighter who was in the neighborhood of Death Valley about 1865 (Palmer, p. 28).

Frazier Canyon [MONO]: *canyon,* drained by a stream that flows 3 miles to lowlands 7 miles east of Glass Mountain (lat. 37°46'50" N, long. 118°34'45" W; near N line sec. 17, T 2 S, R 31 E). Named on Glass Mountain (1962) 15' quadrangle.

Fredericksburg [ALPINE]: *locality,* 4 miles north-northeast of Woodfords (lat. 38°49'45" N, long. 119°47'10" W; sec. 7, T 11 N, R 20 E); the site is near the mouth of Fredericksburg Canyon. Named on Woodfords (1979) 7.5' quadrangle. The place developed in the 1860's; the name may have come from nearby Fredericksburg ranch (Long, p. 22). Postal authorities established Fredericksburg post office in 1898 and discontinued it in 1911 (Frickstad, p. 4).

Fredericksburg Canyon [ALPINE]: *canyon,* drained by a stream that flows 4.25 miles to Carson Valley 4 miles north-northeast of Woodfords (lat. 38°49'50" N, long. 119°47'40" W; sec. 12, T 11 N, R 19 E); Fredericksburg is near the mouth of the canyon. Named on Woodfords (1979) 7.5' quadrangle.

Freel Peak [ALPINE]: *peak,* 13 miles north-northwest of Markleeville on Alpine-El Dorado County line (lat. 38°51'25" N, long. 119°53'55" W; on W line sec. 31, T 12 N, R 19 E). Altitude 10,881 feet. Named on Freel Peak (1955) 7.5' quadrangle. The name commemorates James Freel, who lived at the foot of the peak; William Eimbeck of the Coast Survey gave the name "Freel Peak" in 1874 to the highest of what were known as Jobs Peaks (Gudde, 1969, p. 114).

Freeman Creek [INYO]: *stream,* flows 3.5 miles to lowlands 7.25 miles northwest of Big Pine (lat. 37°14'40" N, long. 118°22'30" W; sec. 20, T 8 S, R 33 E). Named on Big Pine (1950) 15' quadrangle.

Fremont Lake [MONO]: *lake,* 3000 feet long, 7 miles southeast of Sonora Pass (lat. 38°15'15" N, long. 119°32'50" W; sec. 27, 28, T 5 N, R 22 E). Named on Pickel Meadow (1954) 7.5' quadrangle.

French Madam Spring [INYO]: *spring,* 8 miles north of Maturango Peak (lat. 36°14'10" N, long. 117°28'25" W). Named on Maturango Peak (1951) 15' quadrangle.

Frenchmans Canyon [INYO]: *canyon,* 1.5 miles long, opens into Surprise Canyon 3.5 miles south of Telescope Peak (lat. 36°07'10" N, long. 117°05'15" W). Named on Telescope Peak (1952) 15' quadrangle.

Frenchman's Station: see **Mill Creek** [MONO] (2).

French Spring [INYO]: *spring,* 4 miles west-northwest of New York Butte (lat. 36°40'30" N, long. 117°59'45" W). Named on New York Butte (1950) 15' quadrangle.

Frog Lake [ALPINE]:

(1) *lake,* 700 feet long, 0.5 mile south-southeast of Carson Pass (lat. 38°41'15" N, long. 119°59'05" W; sec. 27, T 10 N, R 18 E). Named on Carson Pass (1979) 7.5' quadrangle.

(2) *lake,* 400 feet long, 3 miles north-northeast of Mount Reba (lat. 38°32'50" N, long. 120°00'10" W). Named on Mokelumne Peak (1979) 7.5' quadrangle.

Frog Lakes [MONO]: *lakes,* 6.25 miles east-southeast of Matterhorn Peak (lat. 38°02'55" N, long. 119°16'50" W; sec. 1, T 2 N, R 24 E). Named on Matterhorn Peak (1956) 15' quadrangle. The lakes belong to the group called Virginia Lakes.

Fryingpan Canyon [MONO]: *canyon,* 4 miles long, drained by Fryingpan Creek above a point 10.5 miles north of Bridgeport (lat. 38°24'30" N, long. 119°13'30" W; sec. 31, T 7 N, R 25 E). Named on Bridgeport (1958) and Fales Hot Springs (1956) 15' quadrangles. Irelan (p. 358) used the form "Frying-pan Cañon" for the name.

Fryingpan Canyon: see **Little Fryingpan Canyon** [MONO].

Fryingpan Creek [MONO]: *stream,* flows 8 miles to East Walker River 11 miles north-northeast of Bridgeport (lat. 38°24'30" N, long. 119°10'05" W; sec. 31, T 7 N, R 26 E). Named on Bridgeport (1958) 15' quadrangle. Wheeler (1879, p. 174) used the form "Frying Pan Creek" for the name, and Irelan (p. 359) used the form "Frying-pan Creek."

Fuller Creek [INYO]: *stream,* flows 5.25 miles to Tinemaha Creek 8 miles south of Big Pine (lat. 37°03' N, long. 118°18' W; sec. 30, T 10 S, R 34 E). Named on Big Pine (1950) 15' quadrangle.

Funeral Mountains [INYO]: *range,* northeast of Death Valley and southwest of Amargosa Desert; the feature is the part of Amargosa Range that lies between Boundary Canyon and Furnace Creek Wash. Named on Death Valley (1954) 1°x 2° quadrangle. Palmer (p. 17) noted that W.L. Manly used the name "Coffin Mountains" for the range, and (p. 28) that members of the Blasdel expedition in 1866 used the name "Funeral Mountains." Gudde (1949, p. 123) cited a passage that attributes the name "Funeral" to the appearance of natural mourning given to the range by black debris that resembles a fringe of crepe. Hanna (p. 115) stated that the name commemorates the death and burial in the range of four members of the Jayhawker party of emigrants of 1849, and attributed the name to J.B. Colton, a member of the party.

Funeral Peak [INYO]: *peak,* 26 miles south-southeast of Furnace Creek Inn in Black Mountains (lat. 36°06'10" N, long. 116°37'20" W). Altitude 6384 feet. Named on Funeral Peak (1951) 15' quadrangle. According to Palmer (p. 51), this probably is the feature that J.J. McGillivray called Mount LeConte in the 1880's to honor Professor Joseph LeConte.

Funnel Lake [INYO]: *lake,* 850 feet long, 9 miles east-northeast of Mount Darwin (lat. 37°12' N, long. 118°30'40" W; on W line sec. 5, T 9 S, R 32 E). Named on Mount Goddard (1948) 15' quadrangle.

Furnace [INYO]: *locality,* 6.5 miles north-northwest of Funeral Peak at the southwest edge of Greenwater Valley (lat. 36°11'25" N, long. 116°39'50" W). Site named on Funeral Peak (1951) 15' quadrangle. Patrick "Patsy" Clark's Furnace Creek Copper Company operated at the place, which is just north of a townsite called Clark that never was settled formally (Myrick, p. 603). Furnace boomed in 1905 and was deserted by 1907 (Murbarger, p. 276). Postal authorities established Furnace post office in 1907 and discontinued it in 1908 (Salley, p. 82). A mining camp called Copperfield was situated halfway between Furnace and Greenwater in the early 1900's (Lingenfelter, p. 317).

Furnace Creek [MONO]: *stream,* flows 6.5 miles to Fish Lake Valley 14 miles east-southeast of White Mountain Peak (lat. 37° 33'50" N, long. 118°00'50" W; sec. 33, T 4 S, R 36 E). Named on Mount Barcroft (1962) 15' quadrangle.

Furnace Creek: see **Furnace Creek Wash** [INYO].

Furnace Creek Inn [INYO]: *locality,* 20 miles southeast of Stovepipe Wells on the east side of Death Valley (lat. 36°27' N, long. 116°51'05" W; sec. 22, T 27 N, R 1 E); the place is near the mouth of Furnace Creek Wash. Named on Furnace Creek (1952) 15' quadrangle.

Furnace Creek Pass: see **Pyramid Peak** [INYO].

Furnace Creek Ranch [INYO]: *locality,* 1 mile west-northwest of Furnace Creek Inn on the east side of Death Valley (lat. 36°27'20" N, long. 116°52' W); the place is near the mouth of Furnace Creek Wash. Named on Furnace Creek (1952) 15' quadrangle. "Bellerin Tex" Bennett settled at the site in 1870; later the owners of Harmony Borax Works took over the place, which they called Greenland, to grow alfalfa for their mules—officials of Pacific Coast Borax Company gave it the name "Furnace Creek Ranch" later (Federal Writers' Project, p. 30). The place also was called Greenland Ranch, apparently for the green alfalfa fields, and Coleman, for William T. Coleman (Palmer, p. 17, 33). Postal authorities moved Death Valley post office to Furnace Creek Ranch from Death Valley Junction in 1961 (Salley, p. 56). United States Board on Geographic Names (1995, p. 5) approved the name "Mars Hill" for a remnant of a basaltic lava flow located 5.9 miles south of Furnace Creek Ranch on the floor of Death Valley (lat. 36°22'54" N, long. 116°51'07" W; sec. 15, T 26 N, R 1 E); the name recognizes the unusual similarity of the feature to the surface of Mars, and commemorates the testing in May 1992 of the Russian Marsokhod Rover at the site in preparation for a 1997 Mars landing.

Furnace Creek Springs: see **Furnace Creek Wash** [INYO].

Furnace Creek Valley: see **Furnace Creek Wash** [INYO].

Furnace Creek Wash [INYO]: *stream,* flows 30 miles to Death Valley at Furnace Creek Inn (lat. 36°27' N, long. 116°51'05" W; sec. 22, T 27 N, R 1 E). Named on Furnace Creek (1952) and Ryan (1952) 15' quadrangles. The flow of water in the stream now is diverted at a point 3.5 miles upstream from Furnace Creek Inn and sent through Gower Gulch to Death Valley. The valley of the stream is called Furnace Creek Valley on Wheeler's (1877) map. According to Hanks (p. 31), members of a prospecting party headed by Dr. Darwin French found the feature in 1860 and named it Furnace Creek for the ruins that they found near it of lead furnaces used by some Mormons in 1857. Paher (p. 7) attributed the name to an assay furnace built about 1860 by Mexican prospectors. Federal Writers' Project (p. 19) stated that members of Dr. French's party gave the name "Furnace" because they found the stream during the hot season. Mendenhall (p. 36) described Coleman Springs, located at the mouth of Furnace Creek; they provided water to irrigate alfalfa at Greenland Ranch—Waring and Huguenin (p. 34) used the name "Furnace Creek Springs" for the same springs. Mendenhall (p. 35) described Fountain Springs, located 6 miles north of Coleman (present Furnace Creek Ranch).

— G —

Gabbert: see Gabbott Meadow [ALPINE].

Gabbott Meadow [ALPINE] *area,* 2.5 miles northwest of Dardanelles Cone along Highland Creek (lat. 38°25'50" N, long. 119°54'25" W; sec. 29, T 7 N, R 19 E). Named on Spicer Meadow Reservoir (1979) 7.5' quadrangle. Called Gabbot Mdw. on Dardanelles Cone (1956) 15' quadrangle, but United States Board on Geographic Names (1978b, p. 2) rejected this form of the name. Wheeler's (1876-1877) map shows a place called Gabbert at or near the place.

Gabbro Peak [MONO]: *peak,* 4 miles east-southeast of Matterhorn Peak (lat. 38°04'30" N, long. 119°18'45" W). Named on Matterhorn Peak (1956) 15' quadrangle.

Gable Creek [INYO]: *stream,* flows 3.5 miles to Pine Creek 2.5 miles northwest of Mount Tom (lat. 37°21'50" N, long. 118°41'20" W; sec. 4, T 7 S, R 30 E); the stream heads at Gable Lakes. Named on Mount Tom (1949) 15' quadrangle.

Gable Lakes [INYO]: *lakes,* largest 1000 feet long, 2 miles west-southwest of Mount Tom (lat. 37°19'45" N, long. 118°41'20" W; sec. 21, T 7 S, R 30 E); the lakes are at the head of Gable Creek. Named on Mount Tom (1949) 15' quadrangle.

Galena Canyon [INYO]: *canyon,* drained by a stream that flows 3.5 miles to Death Valley 10 miles south-southwest of Bennetts Well (lat. 36°01'20" N, long. 116°54'15" W; near W line sec. 8, T 22 N, R 1 E). Named on Bennetts Well (1952) 15' quadrangle. National Park Service officials named the canyon for deposits of galena found there (Palmer, p. 29).

Gardisky Lake [MONO]: *lake,* 1600 feet long, 7.25 miles west of Lee Vining (lat. 37°57'20" N, long. 119°15' W; at NW cor. sec. 17, T 1 N, R 25 E). Named on Mono Craters (1953) and Tuolumne Meadows (1956) 15' quadrangles.

Gardner Meadow: see **Lower Gardner Meadow** [ALPINE]; **Upper Gardner Meadow** [ALPINE].

Gaspipe Spring [MONO]: *spring,* 6.25 miles east of the site of Mono Mills (lat. 37°53'30" N, long. 118°50'50" W; near W line sec. 1, T 1 S, R 28 E). Named on Cowtrack Mountain (1962) 15' quadrangle. Frank Pellissur named the feature for a gas pipe used to bring water to a trough (La Braque, p. 108).

Gayley: see **Mount Gayley** [INYO].

Gaylor Peak [MONO]: *peak,* 4.5 miles southwest of Mount Conness on Mono-Tuolumne County line (lat. 37°55'10" N, long. 119°15'50" W; sec. 30, T 1 N, R 25 E). Altitude 11,004 feet. Named on Tuolumne Meadows (1956) 15' quadrangle. Hubbard used the name "Tioga Hill" for the feature.

Gem Lake [MONO]: *lake,* 5800 feet long, behind a dam on Rush Creek 15 miles south of Lee Vining (lat. 37°45'05" N, long. 119° 08'25" W; near N line sec. 30, T 2 S, R 26 E). Named on Devils Postpile (1953) and Mono Craters (1953) 15' quadrangles. Tom Agnew called the lake Gem-o'-the-Mountains, and the present name is from that one (Smith, Genny, p. 67).

Gem Lakes [INYO]: *lakes,* four, largest 1050 feet long, 1.5 miles east of Mount Abbot (lat. 37°23'25" N, long. 118°45'20" W). Named on Mount Abbot (1953) 15' quadrangle.

Gem-o'-the-Mountains: see **Gem Lake** [MONO].

Gem Pass [MONO]: pass, 13 miles south of Lee Vining (lat. 37°46'30" N, long. 119°09'30" W; near W line sec. 18, T 2 S, R 26 E); the pass is 1 mile north of Gem Lake. Named on Mono Craters (1953) 15' quadrangle.

Genevieve: see **Lake Genevieve** [MONO].

George: see **Lake George** [MONO].

George Creek [INYO]: stream, flows 5 miles to lowlands 10 miles west-northwest of Lone Pine (lat. 36°39' N, long. 118°14' W; near NW cor. sec. 12, T 15 S, R 34 E). Named on Lone Pine (1958) and Mount Whitney (1956) 15' quadrangles. The stream now discharges into the aqueduct that takes Owens Valley water to Los Angeles. The name is for George, an Indian leader who lived by the stream (Gudde, 1949, p. 126). Called George's Cr. on Holt's (1864) map, and called Georges Creek on Olmstead's (1900) map. The area of farm land situated between George Creek and Shepherd Creek had the name "George's Creek" in the early days (Schumacher, p. 33). Postal Route (1884) map shows a post office called George's Cr. located between Lone Pine and Independence. Postal authorities established George's Creek post office in 1875 and discontinued it in 1879 (Frickstad, p. 51).

George Lake [INYO]: *lake,* 1100 feet long, 4 miles east-northeast of Mount Darwin (lat. 37°11'05" N, long. 118°36'10" W; on W line sec. 9, T 9 S, R 31 E). Named on Mount Goddard (1948) 15' quadrangle.

George's Creek: see **George Creek** [INYO].

Gerstley: see **Shoshone** [INYO].

Gibbs: see **Mount Gibbs** [MONO].

Gibbs Canyon [MONO]: *canyon,* drained by a stream that flows 3.5 miles to Lee Vining Creek nearly 3 miles southwest of Lee Vining (lat. 37°55'40" N, long. 119°09'20" W; sec. 19, T 1 N, R 26 E). Named on Mono Craters (1953) 15' quadrangle.

Gibbs Lake [MONO]: *lake,* 850 feet long, 5.25 miles southwest of Lee Vining (lat. 37°54' N, long. 119°10'55" W); the lake is in Gibbs Canyon. Named on Mono Craters (1953) 15' quadrangle.

Gibson: see **Mollie Gibson Canyon** [INYO].

Gilbert: see **Mount Gilbert** [INYO].

Gilbert Lake [INYO]: *lake,* 550 feet long, 9 miles west-southwest of Independence (lat. 36°46'10" N, long. 118°21'15" W). Named on Mount Pinchot (1953) 15' quadrangle. The name commemorates a pioneer resident of Independence who tried to obtain water rights to the lake for an irrigation project (Schumacher, p. 87-88).

Gilbert Peak: see **Lookout Mountain** [MONO].

Gilcrest Peak [MONO]: *peak,* 7 miles west-northwest of Lee Vining (lat. 38°00'40" N, long. 119°13'45" W; near NW cor. sec. 28, T 2 N, R 25 E). Named on Bodie (1958) 15' quadrangle.

Gill's Oasis: see **Coso Junction** [INYO].

Gilman Lake [MONO]: *lake,* 1350 feet long, 5.25 miles east-southeast of Matterhorn Peak (lat. 38°03'50" N, long. 119°17'30" W). Named on Matterhorn Peak (1956) 15' quadrangle. An engineer of Standard Consolidated Mining Company named the lake in 1905 for Robert Gilman Brown, vice-president and general manager of the company (Gudde, 1949, p. 127).

Given's Mountain: see **Panamint Range** [INYO].

Glacier Camp [INYO]: *locality,* 10 miles east-southeast of Mount Darwin (lat. 37°07'55" N, long. 118°30'05" W; sec. 29, T 9 S, R 32 E). Named on Mount Goddard (1948) 15' quadrangle.

Glacier Canyon [MONO]: *canyon,* drained by a stream that flows 2 miles to Tioga Lake 5 miles southeast of Lee Vining (lat. 37°55'15" N, long. 119°15'05" W). Named on Mono Craters (1953) 15' quadrangle. Russell (p. 324-325) gave the name "Mt. Dana Glacier" to a small glacier located at the head of the canyon.

Glacier Lake [MONO]: *lake,* 1200 feet long, 2 miles northwest of Matterhorn Peak on upper reaches of Blacksmith Creek (lat. 38°06'55" N, long. 119°24'10" W). Named on Matterhorn Peak (1956) 15' quadrangle.

Glacier Lodge [INYO]: *locality,* 8 miles west-southwest of Big Pine along Big Pine Creek (lat. 37°07'30" N, long. 118°26' W; sec. 36, T 9 S, R 32 E). Named on Big Pine (1950) 15' quadrangle. George W. Hall of Big Pine started the place in 1923 and named it for its proximity to Palisade Glacier (Hanna, p. 121).

Glass Creek [MONO]: *stream,* flows 5.5 miles to Deadman Creek nearly 15 miles north-northwest of Mount Morrison (lat. 37°44'50" N, long. 118°54'10" W; sec. 27, T 2 S, R 27 E). Named on Cowtrack Mountain (1962), Devils Postpile (1953), and Mono Craters (1953) 15' quadrangles.

Glass Creek Meadow [MONO]: *area,* 7.5 miles north of Mammoth Mountain (lat. 37°44'20" N, long. 119°03' W); the place is along Glass Creek. Named on Devils Postpile (1953) 15' quadrangle.

Glass Mountain [MONO]: *peak,* 26 miles east-southeast of Lee Vining (lat. 37°46'30" N, long. 118°42'30" W; sec. 18, T 2 S, R 30 E). Altitude 11,123 feet. Named on Glass Mountain (1962) 15' quadrangle.

Glass Mountain Ridge [MONO]: *ridge,* extends 3 miles south and southeast from Glass Mountain (lat. 37°45' N, long, 118°41'45" W). Named on Casa Diablo Mountain (1953) and Glass Mountain (1962) 15' quadrangles.

Glenberry Lake [MONO]: *lake,* 400 feet long, 2.25 miles east of Matterhorn Peak (lat. 38°05'55" N, long. 119°20'30" W). Named on Matterhorn Peak (1956) 15' quadrangle.

Glen Mary: see **Laws** [INYO].

Glines Canyon [MONO]: *canyon,* nearly 2 miles long, along West Fork Green Creek (2) above the entrance of that stream into Green Lake (lat. 38°05' N, long. 119°18'35" W). Named on Matterhorn Peak (1956) 15' quadrangle. Gudde (1975, p. 131) associated the name with Charles Glines, who with others built a mill and a mining camp in the canyon in 1896.

Goat Ranch: see **Haiwee Reservoir** [INYO]; **Hector Station** [MONO].

Goat Spring [INYO]: *spring,* 8.5 miles north-northwest of Westgard Pass (lat. 37°25'20" N, long. 118°10'55" W; sec. 18, T 6 S, R 35 E). Named on Blanco Mountain (1951) 15' quadrangle.

Goff Canyon [INYO]: *canyon,* drained by a stream that flows 2.5 miles to Searles Valley 9.5 miles east of Argus Peak (lat. 35°50'50" N, long. 117°16'40" W; sec. 13, T 24 S, R 43 E). Named on Trona (1949) 15' quadrangle.

Goldbelt Spring [INYO]: *spring,* 10 miles west-southwest of the mouth of Marble Canyon (3) (lat. 36°35'50" N, long. 117°26'50" W). Named on Marble Canyon (1951) 15' quadrangle. The name is from Gold Belt mining district of the early 1900's (Lingenfelter, p. 284).

Golden Canyon [ALPINE]: *canyon,* drained by a stream that flows 3.5 miles to East Fork Carson River 3.5 miles east-northeast of Disaster Peak (lat. 38°28'25" N, long. 119°40'35" W). Named on Disaster Peak (1979) 7.5' quadrangle.

Golden Canyon [INYO]: *canyon,* 1 mile long, opens into Death Valley 2 miles south of Furnace Creek Inn (lat. 36°25'15" N, long. 116°50'45" W; near W line sec. 35, T 27 N, R 1 E). Named on Furnace Creek (1952) 15' quadrangle. Officials of Pacific Coast Borax Company named the canyon for the color of the rocks there, and for the peculiar golden glow seen in the neighborhood in the afternoon (Palmer, p. 31). A sharp peak at the head of the canyon was called Manly Beacon because it was thought that W.L. Manly used it as a landmark (Palmer, p. 46).

Golden Lake [ALPINE]: *lake,* 150 feet long, 0.5 mile east of Disaster Peak (lat. 38°26'50" N, long. 119°43'15" W); the lake is near the head of Golden Canyon. Named on Disaster Peak (1979) 7.5' quadrangle.

Golden Lake [INYO]: *lake,* 450 feet long, 5 miles west of Mount Tom (lat. 37°20'05" N, long. 118°44'50" W). Named on Mount Tom (1949) 15' quadrangle.

Golden Lake [MONO]: *lake,* 800 feet long, 5 miles south-southeast of Mount Morrison (lat. 37°29'40" N, long. 118°49'25" W). Named on Mount Abbot (1953) 15' quadrangle.

Golden Trout Camp [INYO]: *locality,* about 17 miles northwest of Olancha along Cottonwood Creek (3) (lat. 36°29' N, long. 118°10'30" W; near N line sec. 3, T 17 S, R 35 E). Named on Olancha (1956) 15' quadrangle.

Golden Trout Lake [INYO]: *lake,* 850 feet long, 9.5 miles west of Independence (lat. 36°46'50" N, long. 118°22' W). Named on Mount Pinchot (1953) 15' quadrangle.

Gold Hill [INYO]: *peak,* 12.5 miles south-southwest of Bennetts Well (lat. 36°00'45" N, long. 116°58'25" W). Altitude 5492 feet. Named on Bennetts Well (1952) 15' quadrangle.

Gold Mountain: see **Old Mammoth** [MONO].

Gold Valley [INYO]: *valley,* 4.25 miles south-southwest of Funeral Peak (lat. 36°02'45" N, long. 116°39' W). Named on Funeral Peak (1951) 15' quadrangle. Salley (p. 87) noted that a mining camp called Goldvalley was situated in the valley in 1908.

Goler Canyon: see **Goler Wash** [INYO].

Goler Meadow [INYO]: *area,* 6.5 miles west of Olancha on Inyo-Tulare County line (lat. 36°18'10" N, long. 118°07'10" W). Named on Olancha (1956) 15' quadrangle.

Goler Wash [INYO]: *stream,* flows 6 miles to Panamint Valley 4.5 miles south-southwest of Manly Peak (lat. 35°51'30" N, long. 117° 09'15" W). Named on Manly Peak (1950) 15' quadrangle. Searles Lake (1915) 1° quadrangle has the name "Goler Can.," and United States Board on Geographic Names (1933, p. 329) once favored this designation. The name "Goler" commemorates John Goler (Palmer, p. 31).

Goodale Creek [INYO]: *stream,* flows 5 miles to lowlands 14 miles north-northwest of Independence (lat. 36°58'30" N, long. 118°18'40" W; sec. 24, T 11 S, R 33 E). Named on Mount Pinchot (1953) 15' quadrangle. The name is for Ezra Goodale and Thomas Goodale, who settled in the neighborhood in the 1870's (Gudde, 1949, p. 131).

Goodale Mountain [INYO]: *peak,* 16 miles northwest of Independence (lat. 36°58'20" N, long. 118°23'05" W); the peak is near the head of Goodale Creek. Altitude 12,790 feet. Named on Mount Pinchot (1953) 15' quadrangle.

Goode: see **Mount Goode** [INYO].

Goodwin Spring [INYO]: see **Hummingbird Spring** [INYO].

Goose Lake [INYO]: *lake,* 700 feet long, 6 miles north of Independence (lat. 36°53'15" N, long. 118°10'50" W; near W line sec. 20, T 12 S, R 35 E). Named on Independence (1951) 15' quadrangle.

Goose Lake: see **Silver Lake** [MONO].

Goskey Canyon [ALPINE]: *canyon,* drained by a stream that flows 2.25 miles to Monitor Creek 2 miles southeast of Mogul Peak (lat. 38°39'55" N, long. 119°41'35" W; sec. 32, T 10 N, R 21 E). Named on Heenan Lake (1979) 7.5' quadrangle. United States Board on Geographic Names (1959, p. 6) rejected the name "Mogul Canyon" for the feature.

Gould: see **Mount Gould** [INYO].

Gower Gulch [INYO]: *canyon,* 2 miles long, opens into Death Valley nearly 3 miles south-southeast of Furnace Creek Inn (lat. 36°24'40" N, long. 116°50'20" W; sec. 2, T 26 N, R 1 E). Named on Furnace Creek (1952) 15' quadrangle. The name commemorates George Truman Gower, father of the superintendent of Pacific Coast Borax Company (Palmer, p. 31).

Graham and Jones Canyon: see **Homewood Canyon** [INYO].

Graham Spring [INYO]: *spring,* 5.25 miles east-northeast of Big Pine (lat. 37°11'20" N, long. 118°12' W; near NW cor. sec. 7, T 9 S, R 35 E). Named on Bishop (1913) 30' quadrangle.

Graham Spring: see **Homewood Canyon** [INYO].

Grand Island: see **Paoha Island** [MONO].

Grandstand: see **The Grandstand** [INYO].

Granite Basin [MONO]: *valley,* 9 miles east of the site of Mono Mills (lat. 37°54'35" N, long. 118°47'45" W); the valley is southwest of Granite Mountain. Named on Cowtrack Mountain (1962) 15' quadrangle.

Granite Canyon [INYO]: *canyon,* drained by a stream that flows 3 miles to Death Valley 12 miles south-southwest of Epaulet Peak (lat. 35°49'10" N, long. 116°37' W). Named on Confidence Hills (1950) 15' quadrangle.

Granite Lake [ALPINE]: *lake,* 950 feet long, 7.5 miles north-northwest of Pacific Grade Summit (lat. 38°37'10" N, long. 119°57'40" W). Named on Pacific Valley (1979) 7.5' quadrangle.

Granite Lake [INYO]: *lake,* 1100 feet long, 2.5 miles north-northeast of Mount Darwin (lat. 37°11'55" N, long. 118°38'55" W). Named on Mount Goddard (1948) 15' quadrangle.

Granite Lake: see **Gull Lake** [MONO].

Granite Meadow [MONO]: *area,* 8 miles southeast of White Mountain Peak (lat. 37°32'30" N, long. 118°10'30" W). Named on Mount Barcroft (1962) 15' quadrangle.

Granite Mountain [MONO]: *ridge,* west-northwest-trending, 3.5 miles long, 11 miles east-northeast of the site of Mono Mills (lat. 37°55'30" N, long. 118°45'45" W). Named on Cowtrack Mountain (1962) and Glass Mountain (1962) 15' quadrangles.

Granite Park [INYO]: *area,* 3 miles south-southeast of Mount Abbot (lat. 37°20'40" N, long. 118°46' W). Named on Mount Abbot (1953) 15' quadrangle.

Granite Peak: see **Manly Peak** [INYO].

Granite Springs: see **Coso** [INYO] (1).

Grant Lake [MONO]: *lake,* 3.5 miles long, behind a dam on Rush Creek 6.5 miles south of Lee Vining (lat. 37°51'45" N, long. 119° 06'10" W; near W line sec. 15, T 1 S, R 26 E). Named on Mono Craters (1953) 15' quadrangle.

Grapevine Canyon [INYO]:

(1) *canyon,* drained by a stream that heads in the State of Nevada and flows 7 miles to Death Valley nearly 5 miles east of Ubehebe Crater (lat. 37°00' N, long. 117°21'50" W). Named on Ubehebe Crater (1957) 15' quadrangle.

(2) *canyon,* 5.5 miles long, opens into the southeast end of Saline Valley 7 miles south of Ubehebe Peak (lat. 36°35'15" N, long. 117°35'40" W). Named on Ubehebe Peak (1950) 15' quadrangle.

Grapevine Creek: see **Little Grapevine Creek** [INYO].

Grapevine Mountains [INYO]: *range,* northeast of Death Valley on California-Nevada State line; the range is the part of Amargosa Range that lies between Grapevine Canyon (1) and Boundary Canyon. Named on Death Valley (1954) and Goldfield (1954) 1°x 2° quadrangles. Sinclair (p. 303) called the feature Grape Vine Mountains. Palmer (p. 32) referred to it as Grapevine Range, and noted that the name is for wild grapes that grow at the place.

Grapevine Range: see **Grapevine Mountains** [INYO].

Grapevine Springs [INYO]: *springs,* 4 miles east-northeast of Ubehebe Crater (lat. 37°01'45" N, long. 117°23' W); the springs are 2.5 miles north-northwest of the mouth of Grapevine Canyon (1). Named on Ubehebe Crater (1957) 15' quadrangle. Palmer (p. 32-33) noted that the name is for the occurrence of wild grapes at the spring. Palmer (p. 12) also mentioned a spring, first known as Bonner Spring, and later called Scotty's Grapevine Spring, that is located 2 miles north of the mouth of Grapevine Canyon.

Grass Lake [INYO]: *lake,* 700 feet long, 4 miles northeast of Mount Darwin (lat. 37°13' N, long. 118°37'50" W). Named on Mount Goddard (1948) 15' quadrangle.

Grass Lake [MONO]: *lake,* 500 feet long, 4.5 miles south-southeast of Mount Morrison along a branch of McGee Creek (2) (lat. 37°30'25" N, long. 118°48'55" W). Named on Mount Morrison (1953) 15' quadrangle.

Gravel Well [INYO]: *water feature,* 5.25 miles south of Bennetts Well (lat. 36°05'20" N, long. 116°51' W). Named on Bennetts Well (1952) 15' quadrangle, which lacks a symbol for the feature.

Gray Hills [MONO]: *range,* mainly in the State of Nevada, but extends into Mono County 7 miles north of Coleville near Topaz Lake (lat. 38°40'15" N, long. 119°31'15" W). Named on Topaz Lake (1956) 15' quadrangle.

Gray Mill [MONO]: *locality,* 1.5 miles east-northeast of Bodie along Bodie Creek (lat. 38°13'05" N, long. 118°59'05" W; sec. 10, T 4 N, R 27 E). Named on Trench Canyon (1958) 15' quadrangle.

Grays Crossing [ALPINE]: *locality,* 7.5 miles south-southeast of Mogul Peak along East Fork Carson River (lat. 38°35'30" N, long. 119°39'20" W; near S line sec. 27, T 9 N, R 21 E). Named on Wolf Creek (1979) 7.5' quadrangle. Long (p. 29) mentioned a place called Gray's Landing that was situated between Centreville and Silver King Valley; according to this location, Gray's Landing was at or near present Grays Crossing.

Gray's Landing: see **Grays Crossing** [ALPINE].

Grays Meadow [INYO]: *area,* 5 miles west-southwest of Independence along Independence Creek (lat. 36°46'55" N, long. 118°17'10" W; on S line sec. 21, T 13 S, R 34 E). Named on Mount Pinchot (1953) 15' quadrangle. Chalfant (1933, p. 235) noted that the place called Gray's Meadows was long known as Todd's Meadows, and mentioned that workmen there produced lumber by whipsaw. DeDecker (p. 53) pointed out that the place also was called Hill's Meadows, for one of the woodcutters.

Greater View Spring [INYO]: *spring,* 1.5 miles east of Manly Peak on the west side of Butte Valley (lat. 35°55' N, long. 117°05'10" W). Named on Manly Peak (1950) 15' quadrangle. The name is for the view eastward from the spring over Funeral Mountains (Federal Writers' Project, p. 62).

Great Falls Basin [INYO]: *canyon,* 3 miles long, opens into Searles Valley 4 miles east of Argus Peak (lat. 35°51'25" N, long. 117°22'15" W; sec. 7, T 24 S, R 43 E). Named on Trona (1949) 15' quadrangle. Thompson (1929, p. 180) referred to the feature as Great Falls Canyon, and noted a spring there called Argus Springs. Waring and Huguenin (p. 37) mentioned Argus Cañon, which by their description probably is present Great Falls Basin.

Great Falls Canyon: see **Great Falls Basin** [INYO].

Green Creek [MONO]:

(1) *stream,* flows 4 miles to the State of Nevada 13 miles north of Bridgeport (lat. 38°26'50" N, long. 119°12'15" W; near E line sec. 20, T 7 N, R 25 E). Named on Bridgeport (1958) and Fales Hot Springs (1956) 15' quadrangles. Wedertz (p. 43) associated the name with George Albert Green and his father, Amos Green, who built a sawmill on Green Creek at the base of Sweetwater Mountains.

(2) *stream,* formed by the confluence of East Fork and West Fork, flows 8.5 miles to Bridgeport Valley 5 miles south of Bridgeport (lat. 38°10'50" N, long. 119°14'25" W; sec. 29, T 4 N, R 25 E). Named on Bodie (1958) and

Matterhorn Peak (1956) 15' quadrangles. East Fork is 5 miles long and West Fork is 3.5 miles long; both forks are named on Matterhorn Peak (1956) 15' quadrangles.

Green Creek Campground [MONO]: *locality,* 6 miles east-northeast of Matterhorn Peak (lat. 38°06'35" N, long. 119°16'30" W; sec. 13, T 3 N, R 24 E); the place is along Green Creek (2). Named on Matterhorn Peak (1956) 15' quadrangle. Called Green Lake Camp on California Division of Highways' (1934) map.

Green Lake [INYO]: *lake,* 1400 feet long, 8 miles east of Mount Darwin (lat. 37°10'10" N, long. 118°31'50" W; on E line sec. 13, T 9 S, R 31 E). Named on Mount Goddard (1948) 15' quadrangle.

Green Lake [MONO]: *lake,* 0.5 mile long, 4 miles east of Matterhorn Peak (lat. 38°05'05" N, long. 119°18'30" W); the lake is along West Fork Green Creek (2). Named on Matterhorn Peak (1956) 15' quadrangle.

Green Lake Camp: see **Green Creek Campground** [MONO].

Greenland: see **Furnace Creek Ranch** [INYO].

Greenland Ranch: see **Furnace Creek Ranch** [INYO].

Greenly's Valley: see **Round Valley** [INYO-MONO].

Green Mountain: see **Sylvania Mountains** [INYO].

Green's: see **Pickett Peak** [ALPINE].

Greenstone Lake [MONO]: *lake,* 1800 feet long, nearly 2 miles east-northeast of Mount Conness (lat. 37°58'50" N, long. 119°17'20" W; sec. 35, T 2 N, R 24 E). Named on Tuolumne Meadows (1956) 15' quadrangle.

Green Treble Lake [MONO]: *lake,* 800 feet long, 2 miles east-southeast of Mount Conness (lat. 37°57'10" N, long. 119°17'25" W). Named on Tuolumne Meadows (1956) 15' quadrangle.

Greenwater [INYO]: *locality,* 5.5 miles north of Funeral Peak (lat. 36°10'45" N, long. 116°36'55" W); the place is in Greenwater Valley. Site named on Funeral Peak (1951) 15' quadrangle. After discovery of copper ore in the Greenwater neighborhood in 1904, Arthur Kunze platted a townsite and gave it the name "Kunze" for himself, but everyone else called it Greenwater; the place was in a narrow canyon, and eventually the residents of Kunze moved about 2 miles farther east to another townsite, this one called Ramsey, which eventually took the name "Greenwater" (Myrick, p. 599, 602). Postal authorities established Greenwater post office in 1906 and discontinued it in 1908 (Frickstad, p. 51). Greenwater declined in 1907 because copper could not be found in commercial quantities (Paher, p. 14).

Greenwater Canyon [INYO]: *canyon,* 4 miles long, opens into lowlands 11 miles north-northeast of Funeral Peak (lat. 36°15' N, long. 116°32'50" W); the canyon is in Greenwater Range. Named on Funeral Peak (1951) 15' quadrangle. Palmer (p. 33) mentioned that the feature was called Dead Horse Canyon during the boom days of Greenwater.

Greenwater Range [INYO]: *range,* northeast of Greenwater Valley. Named on Eagle Mountain (1951), Funeral Peak (1951), Ryan (1952), and Shoshone (1951) 15' quadrangles.

Greenwater Spring [INYO]: *spring,* 3.25 miles north of Funeral Peak near the northeast edge of Black Mountains (lat. 36°09'05" N, long. 116°37'25" W); the spring is 2 miles south-southwest of the site of Greenwater. Named on Funeral Peak (1951) 15' quadrangle. The name is for the color of water at the spring (Palmer, p. 33).

Greenwater Valley [INYO]: *valley,* between Black Mountains and Greenwater Range. Named on Eagle Mountain (1951), Funeral Peak (1951), Ryan (1952), and Shoshone (1951) 15' quadrangles.

Greer Spring [INYO]: *spring,* 6 miles north-northwest of Emigrant Pass (lat. 36°24'20" N, long. 117°11'50" W). Named on Emigrant Canyon (1952) 15' quadrangle.

Grey Haired Johnnys Corral [MONO]: *locality,* 5 miles south-southeast of White Mountain Peak (lat. 37°34'20" N, long. 118°12'20" W). Named on White Mountain (1917) 30' quadrangle.

Greyhound Canyon: see **Scottys Canyon** [INYO].

Grimshaw Lake [INYO]: *lake,* 1300 feet long, 0.25 mile north of Tecopa (lat. 35°51'10" N, long. 116°13'40" W; sec. 9, T 20 N, R 7 E). Named on Tecopa (1950) 15' quadrangle.

Grizzly Bear Valley: see **Bloods Meadow** [ALPINE].

Grizzly Lake [MONO]: *lake,* 700 feet long, nearly 5 miles northwest of Tower Peak (lat. 38°11'45" N, long. 119°36'10" W); the lake is 1 mile east-northeast of Grizzly Peak. Named on Tower Peak (1956) 15' quadrangle.

Grizzly Peak [MONO]: *peak,* 6.25 miles northwest of Tower Peak on Mono-Tuolumne County line (lat. 38°11'35" N, long. 119°37'15" W). Named on Tower Peak (1956) 15' quadrangle.

Grotto Canyon [INYO]: *canyon,* drained by a stream that flows 2 miles to Death Valley 5 miles south-southwest of Stovepipe Wells (lat. 36°35'30" N, long. 117°06'45" W; sec. 5, T 16 S, R 45 E). Named on Stovepipe Wells (1952) 15' quadrangle. Pacific Coast Borax Company employees named the feature for water-carved grottoes in limestone there (Palmer, p. 34).

Grouse Creek [ALPINE]:

(1) *stream,* flows 2.5 miles to Summit City Creek 7 miles north of Mount Reba (lat. 38°36'45" N, long. 120°01'55" W). Named on Mokelumne Peak (1979) 7.5' quadrangle.

(2) *stream,* flows 3.5 miles to North Fork Mokelumne River 2.25 miles northeast of Pacific Grade Summit (lat. 38°32'25" N, long. 119°52'45" W; sec. 15, T 8 N, R 19 E). Named on Ebbetts Pass (1979) and Pacific Valley (1979) 7.5' quadrangles.

Grouse Creek [MONO]: *stream,* flows 2 miles to West Walker River 4 miles northwest of Fales Hot Springs at Chris Flat (lat. 38°23'40" N, long. 119°27'05" W; sec. 4, T 6 N, R 23 E); the stream heads at Grouse Meadows. Named on Chris Flat (1954) 7.5' quadrangle.

Grouse Creek [ALPINE]: **Devils Corral Creek** [ALPINE].

Grouse Lake [ALPINE]: *lake,* 650 feet long, 8 miles north of Mount Reba (lat. 38°37'20" N, long. 120°00'25" W). Named on Mokelumne Peak (1979) 7.5' quadrangle.

Grouse Meadows [MONO]: *area,* 6 miles northwest of Fales Hot Springs (lat. 38°24'15" N, long. 119°29' W; near SW cor. sec. 32, T 7 N, R 23 E). Named on Chris Flat (1954) 7.5' quadrangle.

Grouse Mountain [INYO]: *peak,* 4.5 miles east-southeast of Mount Tom (lat. 37°18'25" N, long. 118°35'15" W; near SE cor. sec. 29, T 7 S, R 31 E). Altitude 8067 feet. Named on Mount Tom (1949) 15' quadrangle.

Grouse Mountain [MONO]: *peak,* 7.5 miles northwest of Matterhorn Peak (lat. 38°09'45" N, long. 119°29'20" W). Altitude 10,775 feet. Named on Matterhorn Peak (1956) 15' quadrangle.

Grouse Spring [INYO]: *spring,* 9 miles west of Big Pine (lat. 37°08'30" N, long. 118°26'55" W; sec. 26, T 9 S, R 32 E). Named on Big Pine (1950) 15' quadrangle.

Grouse Valley [ALPINE]: *valley,* 2 miles west-southwest of Mount Reba (lat. 38°29'50" N, long. 120°03'50" W). Named on Tamarack (1979) 7.5' quadrangle.

Grover: see **Grover Hot Springs** [ALPINE].

Grover Anton Spring [INYO]: *spring,* 7.5 miles northwest of Independence (lat. 36°53' N, long. 118°17'15" W; near S line sec. 20, T 12 S, R 34 E). Named on Mount Pinchot (1953) 15' quadrangle.

Grover Hot Springs [ALPINE]: *springs,* two, 3.25 miles west of Markleeville (lat. 38°41'45" N, long. 119°50'35" W); the springs are near Hot Springs Creek. Named on Markleeville (1979) 7.5' quadrangle. The Grover family, who had a hotel at Markleeville, obtained an interest in the springs in 1878 and used them in connection with their hotel (Long, p. 54). The resort at the springs is called Grovers Springs on Markleeville (1889) 30' quadrangle, and is called Grovers Hot Springs on Markleeville (1956) 15' quadrangle. Eakel (p. 27) referred to Grover's Hot Springs. United States Board on Geographic Names (1979b, p. 6) rejected the form "Grovers Hot Springs" for the name. California Mining Bureau's (1917a) map has the name "Grover" for a place situated west of Markleeville.

Grovers Hot Springs: see **Grover Hot Springs** [ALPINE].

Grovers Springs: see **Grovers Hot Springs** [ALPINE].

Gull Lake [MONO]: *lake,* 2500 feet long, nearly 13 miles south of Lee Vining along Reversed Creek (lat. 37°46'30" N, long. 119°04'55" W; sec. 14, 15, T 2 S, R 26 E). Named on Mono Craters (1953) 15' quadrangle. The name is from gulls that come to the lake from their nesting place at Mono Lake (Smith, Genny, p. 24). The feature was called Granite Lake about 1880 (Bean, p. 4).

Gunn: see **Jack Gunn Spring** [INYO].

Gunter Creek [INYO]: *stream* and *dry wash,* extends for 6 miles to lowlands 6.5 miles northeast of Bishop (lat. 37°26'35" N, long. 118°19' W; sec. 11, T 6 S, R 33 E). Named on Bishop (1949) and Blanco Mountain (1951) 15' quadrangles. The lower part of the watercourse is shown without a stream on Bishop (1949) 15' quadrangle, but Bishop (1913) 30' quadrangle shows the stream extending all the way to the lowlands.

– H –

Hadley Spring: see **Travertine Springs** [INYO].

Haeckel: see **Mount Haeckel** [INYO].

Hahn's Canyon: see **Beveridge Canyon** [INYO].

Haiwai Meadows: see **Haiwee Reservoir** [INYO].

Haiwee [INYO]: *locality,* 24 miles south-southwest of Keeler along Southern Pacific Railroad (lat. 36°08'45" N, long. 117°58' W). Named on Ballarat (1913) 1° quadrangle. Water of Haiwee Reservoir now covers the site. Ballarat (1913) 1° quadrangle shows Haiwee P.O. located about 2 miles north-northeast of Haiwee, and less than 1 mile east of the railroad. Postal authorities established Haiwee post office in 1906, moved it 1.5 miles southwest in 1909, and discontinued it in 1913 (Salley, p. 92). Campbell's (1902) map shows a place called Hawaii at or near the site of Haiwee. Tucker and Sampson's (1938) map shows a place called Haiwee situated along the railroad west of the Haiwee Reservoir (at S line sec. 33, T 20 S, R 37 E). Goodyear (p. 239) used the name "Hayways."

Haiwee Canyon: see **Haiwee Creek** [INYO].

Haiwee Creek [INYO]: *stream,* flows 8.5 mile to Rose Valley 4.5 miles north of Coso Junction (lat. 36°06'40" N, long. 117°57'20" W). Named on Haiwee Reservoir (1951) and Monache Mountain (1956) 15' quadrangles.

Called Haiwee Cn. on Tucker and Sampson's (1938) map.

Haiwee Meadows: see **Haiwee Reservoir** [INYO].

Haiwee Pass [INYO]: *pass,* nearly 11 miles south-southwest of Olancha on Inyo-Tulare County line (lat. 36°08'05" N, long. 118° 04'15" W). Named on Monache Mountain (1956) 15' quadrangle.

Haiwee Reservoir [INYO]: *lake,* 7 miles long, behind a dam 6.25 miles north of Coso Junction (lat. 36°08'15" N, long. 117°57' W). Named on Haiwee Reservoir (1951) 15' quadrangle. The reservoir, which stores water for the aqueduct that takes Owens Valley water to Los Angeles, covers land formerly called Haiwai Meadows (Chalfant, 1933, p. 219). United States Board on Geographic Names (1933, p. 356) once approved the name "Haway Meadows" and rejected the name "Hawai Meadows" for the area—the name "Haiwee Meadows" now is used. Bart Bellows filed a pre-emptive claim on Haiwee Meadows in 1870, and after he imported 8000 Angora goats, the place became known as Goat Ranch; the area was rich with bunchgrass—*haiwee* is an Indian word for Indian ricegrass, or sand bunch grass, and has a secondary meaning "dove" (Iroquois Research Institute, p. 122-123). United States Board on Geographic Names (1978b, p. 2) approved the name "Haiwee Ridge" for the north-trending ridge, 7 miles long, that lies just east of the reservoir.

Haiwee Ridge: see **Haiwee Reservoir** [INYO].

Haiwee Spring [INYO]: *spring,* 12 miles east-northeast of Coso Junction (lat. 36°07' N, long. 117°45'20" W; sec. 10, T 21 S, R 39 E). Named on Haiwee Reservoir (1951) 15' quadrangle. Called Hawai Spr. on Wheeler's (1877) map.

Half Moon Lake [ALPINE]: *lake,* 1000 feet long, 8 miles northeast of Dardanelles Cone (lat. 38°29'25" N, long. 119°46'35" W). Named on Dardanelles Cone (1979) 7.5' quadrangle.

Halfway Camp [MONO]: *locality,* 10.5 miles east-northeast of Bridgeport (lat. 38°18'30" N, long. 119°02'35" W; sec. 7, T 5 N, R 27 E). Named on Bridgeport (1958) 15' quadrangle.

Hall Canyon [INYO]: *canyon,* drained by a stream that flows 7 miles to Panamint Valley 6.5 miles west of Telescope Peak (lat. 36°09'05" N, long. 117°12'10" W). Named on Telescope Peak (1952) 15' quadrangle. Called Narboe Cañon on Wheeler's (1877) map. The name "Hall Canyon" is for Ed Hall, who had a blacksmith shop in the neighborhood (Lingenfelter, p. 129).

Hammil [MONO]: *locality,* 9 miles west-northwest of White Mountain Peak (lat. 37°40'50" N, long. 118°24'15" W; near N line sec. 24, T 3 S, R 32 E). Named on White Mountain Peak (1962) 15' quadrangle. William Hammil, Hugh Hammil, and Robert Hammil homesteaded at the place in 1870; when Carson and Colorado Railroad reached the site in 1883, a station was named for the family (Hanna, p. 133). White Mountain (1917) 30' quadrangle shows Mocalno P.O. situated less than 1 mile east-northeast of Hammil. Postal authorities established Mocalno post office in 1915 and discontinued it in 1937; the name was coined by inserting the abbreviation "cal," for California, into the county name "Mono" (Salley, p. 143).

Hammil Lake [MONO]: *lake,* 650 feet long, 8 miles west of Mount Morrison (lat. 37°34'35" N, long. 118°59'50" W). Named on Mount Morrison (1953) 15' quadrangle.

Hammil Valley [MONO]: *valley,* west of White Mountains between Benton Valley and Chalfant Valley; 8 miles west of White Mountain Peak (lat. 37°39' N, long. 118°24' W); Hammil is in the valley. Named on White Mountain Peak (1962) 15' quadrangle. Shown as the northernmost part of Owens River Valley on Wheeler's (1871) map.

Hammond's: see **Tioga Lodge** [MONO].

Hammond Station: see **Tioga Lodge** [MONO].

Hanaupah Canyon [INYO]: *canyon,* drained by a stream that flows 4 miles to Death Valley 5.5 miles northwest of Bennetts Well (lat. 36°12'40" N, long. 116°56'30" W). Named on Bennetts Well (1952) 15' quadrangle. The canyon divides at the head to form Middle Fork and North Fork; each fork is 4.5 miles long, and each is named on Telescope Peak (1952) 15' quadrangle. South Fork branches southwest 2.25 miles upstream from the mouth of the main canyon; it is 7.25 miles long and is named on Bennetts Well (1952) and Telescope Peak (1952) 15' quadrangles.

Hanaupah Spring [INYO]: *spring,* 3.5 miles east-northeast of Telescope Peak (lat. 36°11'10" N, long. 117°01'45" W); the spring is in South Fork Hanaupah Canyon. Named on Telescope Peak (1952) 15' quadrangle. Belden (p. 55) associated the name with Hanaupah Jack, a burro that belonged to Alexander "Shorty" Borden—Borden had a mine at the spring.

Hanging Rock Canyon [INYO]: *canyon,* 4 miles long, opens into Eureka Valley 22 miles northwest of Ubehebe Crater (lat. 37°13'20" N, long. 117°29'50" W; near W line sec. 30, T 8 S, R 39 E). Named on Last Chance Range (1958) 15' quadrangle.

Hanging Valley Ridge [MONO]: *ridge,* northeast-trending, 4.5 miles long, 9 miles south-southwest of Fales Hot Springs (lat. 38°14'30" N, long. 119°27'15" W). Named on Fales Hot Springs (1956) and Matterhorn Peak (1956) 15' quadrangles.

Hanna Mountain [MONO]: *peak,* 9 miles northwest of Matterhorn Peak (lat. 38°11'20" N, long. 119°29'05" W). Altitude 11,486 feet. Named on Matterhorn Peak (1956) 15' quadrangle. The name commemorates Thomas R. Hanna, who owned May Lundy mine from 1920 until 1940 (Sowaal, p. 111).

Hans Lof's: see **Toms Place** [MONO].

Happy Canyon [INYO]: *canyon,* drained by a stream that flows 8 miles to Panamint Valley 9 miles southwest of Telescope Peak (lat. 36°03'50" N, long. 117°11'20" W). Named on Telescope Peak (1952) 15' quadrangle. Called Happy Vy. Cañon on Wheeler's (1877) map.

Happy Valley Cañon: see **Happy Canyon** [INYO].

Hardy: see **Hardy Station** [MONO].

Hardy Station [MONO]: *locality,* 3 miles west of Fales Hot Springs (lat. 38°20'40" N, long. 119°27'05" W; near S line sec. 21, T 6 N, R 23 E). Named on Fales Hot Springs (1954) 7.5' quadrangle. Called Hardy on California Mining Bureau's (1917b) map.

Harkless Flat [INYO]: *area,* 9.5 miles northwest of Waucoba Mountain (lat. 37°06' N, long. 118°08'45" W). Named on Waucoba Mountain (1951) 15' quadrangle. The name commemorates a pioneer rancher who cut and sold wood at the place (Gudde, 1949, p. 142).

Harmonial City: see **Upper Blue Lake** [ALPINE].

Harmony Borax Works [INYO]: *locality,* 2.5 miles north-northwest of Furnace Creek Inn (lat. 36°28'50" N, long. 116°52'25" W; sec. 9, T 27 N, R 1 E). Named on Furnace Creek (1952) 15' quadrangle. The facility first was known as Coleman Borax Works (Palmer, p. 17). William T. Coleman had the place built in the winter of 1882, and operations there continued until 1888 (Paher, p. 7-8). The name "Harmony" supposedly is from the collaboration of former borax business rivals Coleman and F.M. Smith (Hildebrand, p. 282).

Harriet: see **Lake Harriet** [MONO].

Harris: see **Shorty Harris Canyon** [INYO].

Harrisberry: see **Harrisburg** [INYO].

Harrisburg [INYO]: *locality,* about 2.5 miles northeast of Emigrant Pass (1) (lat. 36°21'45" N, long. 117°06'50" W). Named on Emigrant Canyon (1952) 15' quadrangle. The place was a tent camp named for "Shorty" Harris, who with Pete Auguerreberry found gold nearby in 1905 (Federal Writers' Project, p. 50). It first was called Harrisberry, for the two discoverers of gold (Weight, p. 26).

Harrisburg Flats [INYO]: *valley,* north of Emigrant Pass (1) (lat. 36°22'30" N, long. 117°08' W); Harrisburg is on the east side of the valley. Named on Emigrant Canyon (1952) 15' quadrangle. National Park Service officials named the valley for Harrisburg; C. Hart Merriam called the place Perognathus Flat in 1891 because of the unusual abundance there of pocket mice of the genus *Perognathus* (Palmer, p. 35, 57).

Harris Hill [INYO]: *peak,* 10 miles west-southwest of the mouth of Marble Canyon (3) (lat. 36°35'20" N, long. 117°26' W). Altitude 5738 feet. Named on Marble Canyon (1951) 15' quadrangle.

Harry Birch Springs [INYO]: *springs,* two, 9 miles northwest of Independence (lat. 36°54'30" N, long. 118°17'10" W; sec. 17, T 12 S, R 34 E). Named on Mount Pinchot (1953) 15' quadrangle.

Hartley Springs [MONO]: *spring,* 14 miles south-southeast of Lee Vining (lat. 37°46' N, long. 119°02'25" W; at S line sec. 18, T 2 S, R 27 E). Named on Mono Craters (1953) 15' quadrangle. Bert "Bear-Bait" Hartley lived in the vicinity in the early 1940's (Bean, p. 54).

Harvey Creek [MONO]: *stream,* flows 4.25 miles to Swauger Creek 5.5 miles east-southeast of Fales Hot Springs in Huntoon Valley (lat. 38°18'45" N, long. 119°18'30" W; sec. 10, T 5 N, R 24 E). Named on Fales Hot Springs (1956) 15' quadrangle.

Hawaii: see **Haiwee** [INYO].

Hawai Meadows: see **Haiwee Reservoir** [INYO].

Hawai Spring: see **Haiwee Spring** [INYO].

Haway Meadows: see **Haiwee Reservoir** [INYO].

Hawkins Creek [ALPINE]: *stream,* flows 3 miles to West Fork Carson River 4.25 miles northeast of Carson Pass in Hope Valley (lat. 38°44'15" N, long. 119°55'50" W; sec. 6, T 10 N, R 19 E); the stream heads near Hawkins Peak. Named on Carson Pass (1979) 7.5' quadrangle.

Hawkins Peak [ALPINE]: *peak,* 6 miles northwest of Markleeville (lat. 38°44'20" N, long. 119°52'15" W; sec. 3, T 10 N, R 19 E). Altitude 10,024 feet. Named on Markleeville (1979) 7.5' quadrangle. Called Cary Pk. on Wheeler's (1876-1877) map. The name "Hawkins Peak" commemorates John Hawkins, who took up land east of the peak by squatter's rights in 1858 (Gudde, 1949, p. 144).

Hawksbeak Peak [MONO]: *peak,* 2.5 miles east-northeast of Tower Peak on Mono-Tuolumne County line (lat. 38°09'30" N, long. 119° 30'10" W). Named on Tower Peak (1956) 15' quadrangle.

Haypress Flat [ALPINE]: *area,* 2 miles northeast of Mogul Peak (lat. 38°42'45" N, long. 119°41'50" W; sec. 17, T 10 N, R 21 E). Named on Heenan Lake (1979) 7.5' quadrangle.

Hayways: see **Haiwee** [INYO].

Headache Spring [INYO]: see **Poison Spring** [INYO].

Headley Creek: see **Cottonwood Canyon** [MONO] (3).

Headley Peak [MONO]: *peak,* 4 miles north-northwest of White Mountain Peak (lat. 37°41'15" N, long., 118°17'10" W). Altitude 12,676 feet. Named on White Mountain Peak (1962) 15' quadrangle.

Heart Lake [INYO]:

(1) *lake,* 300 feet long, nearly 3 miles northeast of Mount Abbot in Little Lakes Valley (lat. 37°25'05" N, long. 118°45'10" W). Named on Mount Abbot (1953) 15' quadrangle.

(2) *lake,* 800 feet long, 9.5 miles west-southwest of Independence (lat. 36°46'10" N, long. 118°21'55" W). Named on Mount Pinchot (1953) 15' quadrangle.

Heart Lake [MONO]: *lake,* 400 feet long, 7 miles west-northwest of Mount Morrison (lat. 37°35'20" N, long. 118°58'40" W); the outline of the lake on a map is somewhat heart shaped. Named on Mount Morrison (1953) 15' quadrangle. The feature also was called Dart Lake for a prospector who had claims near it (Smith, Genny, p. 48).

Hebe Crater: see **Little Hebe Crater** [INYO].

Hector Station [MONO]: *locality,* 10 miles south-southwest of Bodie at the north edge of Mono Valley (lat. 38°05' N, long. 119°04'55" W; near SE cor. sec. 26, T 3 N, R 26 E). Site named on Bodie (1958) 15' quadrangle. Fletcher (fig. 8, p. 53) showed a place called Goat Ranch located 3 miles northeast of Hector Station along a toll road between Bodie and Lundy.

Heenan Creek [ALPINE]: *stream,* flows 2.25 miles to Heenan Lake 4.25 miles southeast of Mogul Peak (lat. 38°39'05" N, long. 119° 39'10" W). Named on Topaz Lake (1956) 15' quadrangle.

Heenan Creek: see **Monitor Creek** [ALPINE].

Heenan Lake [ALPINE]: *lake,* 3900 feet long, 4 miles southeast of Mogul Peak (lat. 38°39' N, long. 119°39'30" W; sec. 3, 10, T 9 N, R 21 E). Named on Heenan Lake (1979) 7.5' quadrangle. Named, but shown as marsh, on Markleeville (1889) 30' quadrangle. United States Board on Geographic Names (1979a, p. 3) rejected the name "Heenan Reservoir" for the feature. The name "Heenan Lake" probably commemorates a worker in nearby Leviathan mine who was killed in the 1860's by a blast (Gudde, 1949, p. 145).

Heenan Reservoir: see **Heenan Lake** [ALPINE].

Heiser Lake [ALPINE]: *lake,* 800 feet long, 6.5 miles north-northwest of Dardanelles Cone (lat. 38°29'40" N, long. 119°54'20" W; on S line sec. 32, T 8 N, R 19 E). Named on Spicer Meadow Reservoir (1979) 7.5' quadrangle. On Markleeville (1956) 15' quadrangle, the name applies to a small lake located nearly 1 mile farther north.

Helen: see **Lake Helen** [MONO].

Helen of Troy: see **Lake Helen of Troy** [INYO].

Hell Diver Lakes [INYO]: *lakes,* largest 600 feet long, 1 mile east-northeast of Mount Darwin (lat. 37°10'25" N, long. 118°39'15" W). Named on Mount Goddard (1948) 15' quadrangle.

Hellhole Lake [ALPINE]: *lake,* 550 feet long, 7 miles north of Pacific Grade Summit (lat. 38°37' N, long. 119°53' W; sec. 22, T 9 N, R 19 E). Named on Pacific Valley (1979) 7.5' quadrangle.

Hells Gate [INYO]: *locality,* 9.5 miles north-northwest of Beatty Junction at the mouth of Boundary Canyon (lat. 36°43'20" N, long. 116°58'40" W; sec. 21, T 14 S, R 46 E); the place is at the edge of Death Valley. Named on Chloride Cliff (1952) 15' quadrangle. Called Hell Gate on California Division of Highways' (1934) map. The place was named Hell's Gate in 1905 because of the way teams leaving Boundary Canyon to enter Death Valley reacted to the heat (Federal Writers' Project, p. 43). The place first was called Black Point (Palmer, p. 12).

Hennerville Peak: see **Hunewill Peak** [MONO].

Henry Peak [ALPINE]: *peak,* nearly 6 miles north of Dardanelles Cone (lat. 38°29'15" N, long. 119°52'45" W). Altitude 9354 feet. Named on Spicer Meadow Reservoir (1979) 7.5' quadrangle.

Hermit Valley [ALPINE]: *valley,* 2 miles northeast of Pacific Grade Summit along North Fork Mokelumne River (lat. 38°32'20" N, long. 119°53'10" W; on S line sec. 16, T 8 N, R 19 E). Named on Pacific Valley (1979) 7.5' quadrangle. Wheeler's (1876-1877) map has the name "Slater" for a place near the west end of Hermit Valley.

Hidden Canyon [ALPINE]: *canyon,* drained by a stream that flows 2.5 miles to West Fork Carson River nearly 3 miles west of Woodfords (lat. 38°46'25" N, long. 119°52'35" W; sec. 32, T 11 N, R 19 E). Named on Woodfords (1979) 7.5' quadrangle.

Hidden Lake [INYO]:

(1) *lake,* 1100 feet long, 11 miles west of Big Pine (lat. 37°09'30" N, long. 118°29'20" W; sec. 21, T 9 S, R 32 E). Named on Big Pine (1950) 15' quadrangle.

(2) *lake,* 1100 feet long, 18 miles northwest of Olancha (lat. 36°29'45" N, long. 118°11'50" W). Named on Olancha (1956) 15' quadrangle.

Hidden Lake [MONO]: *lake,* 600 feet long, 7.25 miles southeast of Sonora Pass (lat. 38°15'40" N, long. 119°32'05" W; sec. 22, T 5 N, T 22 E). Named on Pickel Meadow (1954) 7.5' quadrangle.

Hidden Lakes [INYO]: *lakes,* 7.5 miles northwest of Mount Tom in Little Lakes Valley (lat. 37°25'10" N, long. 118°45' W). Named on Mount Tom (1949) 15' quadrangle.

Hidden Spring [INYO]: *spring,* 2.25 miles south-southeast of Funeral Peak (lat. 36°04'40" N, long. 116°36'20" W). Named on Furnace Creek (1910) 1° quadrangle.

Hidden Spring: see **Klare Spring** [INYO].

Hidden Valley [INYO]: *valley,* 5 miles east of Ubehebe Peak (lat. 36°42' N, long. 117°29'45" W). Named on Marble Canyon (1951) and Ubehebe Peak (1950) 15' quadrangles. National Park Service officials proposed the name because the presence of the valley is unsuspected by persons approaching it from either side; the place also is called Butte Valley (Palmer, p. 36).

Higgins Lake [INYO]: *lake,* 300 feet long, 6 miles west of Olancha (lat. 36°17'15" N, long. 118°06'45" W). Named on Olancha (1956) 15' quadrangle.

High Lake [INYO]: *lake,* 800 feet long, 19 miles northwest of Olancha (lat. 36°29'20" N, long. 118°13'55" W). Named on Olancha (1956) 15' quadrangle.

Highland City: see **Highland Lakes** [ALPINE].

Highland Creek [ALPINE]: *stream,* flows 11.5 miles to Tuolumne County 4.5 miles west of Dardanelles Cone (lat. 38°24'15" N, long. 119°57'30" W). Named on Dardanelles Cone (1979) and Spicer Meadow Reservoir (1979) 7.5' quadrangles. The name is from Highland City (Gudde, 1949, p. 148).

Highland Lakes [ALPINE]: *lakes,* two, largest 2000 feet long, 7 miles north-northeast of Dardanelles Cone (lat. 38°29'30" N, long. 119°48'10" W). Named on Dardanelles Cone (1979) 7.5' quadrangle. The largest lake is at the head of North Fork Mokelumne River, and the smallest one is at the head of a branch of Highland Creek. The largest lake is called Highland L. on Wheeler's (1876-1877) map, which has the designation "Highland City (ab'd)" at a site located south of the largest lake and east of the smallest one.

Highland Lakes Campground [ALPINE]: *locality,* nearly 7 miles north-northeast of Dardanelles Cone (lat. 38°29'20" N, long. 119° 48'25" W); the place is by Highland Lakes. Named on Dardanelles Cone (1979) 7.5' quadrangle.

Highland Mountain: see **Highland Peak** [ALPINE].

Highland Peak [ALPINE]: *peak,* 3 miles east of Ebbetts Pass (lat. 38°32'40" N, long. 119°45'15" W). Altitude 10,935 feet. Named on Ebbetts Pass (1979) 7.5' quadrangle. Called Highland Mt. on California Mining Bureau's (1917a) map. The name is from Highland City (Gudde, 1949, p. 148).

Highland Reservoir: see **Union Reservoir** [ALPINE].

High Meadows [INYO]: *area,* 8.5 miles west of Big Pine (lat. 37°09'25" N, long. 118°26'45" W; sec. 23, T 9 S, R 32 E). Named on Big Pine (1950) 15' quadrangle.

High Peak [ALPINE]: *peak,* 5 miles east-northeast of Mogul Peak (lat. 38°42'25" N, long. 119°37'35" W; near S line sec. 13, T 10 N, R 21 E). Altitude 8519 feet. Named on Heenan Lake (1979) 7.5' quadrangle.

High Peak: see **Mount Tom** [INYO].

High Sierra: see **Camp High Sierra** [MONO]; **Sierra Nevada**, under "Regional setting."

Hill's Meadows: see **Grays Meadow** [INYO].

Hilton Creek [MONO]: *stream,* flows 9 miles to Lake Crowley 3.5 miles west-northwest of Toms Place (lat. 37°34'50" N, long. 118° 44'25" W; near S line sec. 23, T 4 S, R 29 E). Named on Casa Diablo Mountain (1953), Mount Abbot (1953), and Mount Morrison (1953) 15' quadrangles. Richard Hilton had a milk ranch near the creek from the 1870's until the turn of the century (Smith, Genny, p. 3).

Hilton Creek Lakes [MONO]: *lakes,* largest 2150 feet long, 8 miles southeast of Mount Morrison (lat. 37°28'30" N, long. 118°45'40" W); the lakes are along upper reaches of Hilton Creek. Named on Mount Abbot (1953) 15' quadrangle.

Hines Slough [INYO]: *stream,* flows 3 miles to an unnamed lake 9 miles north of Independence (lat. 36°56'30" N, long. 118°13'40" W; sec. 2, T 12 S, R 34 E); the stream heads at Hines Spring. Named on Mount Whitney (1907) 30' quadrangle.

Hines Spring [INYO]: *spring,* 12 miles north of Independence (lat. 36°58'45" N, long. 118°13'40" W; sec. 23, T 11 S, R 34 E). Named on Independence (1951) 15' quadrangle.

Hiram Canyon [ALPINE]: *canyon,* drained by a stream that flows 1.25 miles to Highland Creek 2.5 miles north of Dardanelles Cone (lat. 38°26'35" N, long. 119°51'40" W). Named on Dardanelles Cone (1979) 7.5' quadrangle. Called Jenkins Canyon on Dardanelles Cone (1956) 15' quadrangle, but United States Board on Geographic Names (1979b, p. 6) rejected this name.

Hiram Canyon: see **Champion Canyon** [ALPINE].

Hiram Meadow [ALPINE]: *area,* 2.5 miles north of Dardanelles Cone along Highland Creek (lat. 38°26'30" N, long. 119°51'50" W); the area is near the mouth of Hiram Canyon. Named on Dardanelles Cone (1979) 7.5' quadrangle.

Hiram Peak [ALPINE]: *ridge,* west-northwest-trending, 0.5 mile long, 6.25 miles northeast of Dardanelles Cone (lat. 38°28'40" N, long. 119°48'05" W). Named on Dardanelles Cone (1979) 7.5' quadrangle.

Hitchens Spring: see **Jayhawker Spring** [INYO].

Hobart Creek [ALPINE]: *stream,* flows 1.25 miles to Tuolumne County 6.25 miles west of Dardanelles Cone (lat. 38°25' N, long. 119°59' W). Named on Spicer Meadow Reservoir (1979) 7.5' quadrangle.

Hogback Creek [INYO]:
(1) *stream,* flows 3 miles to lowlands 9 miles west of Lone Pine (lat. 36°37'20" N, long. 118°13'30" W). Named on Lone Pine (1958) and Mount Whitney (1956) 15' quadrangles. Called Dry Cr. on Olmsted's (1900) map.
(2) *stream,* flows 3.5 miles to lowlands 6 miles south of Olancha (lat. 36°11'40" N, long. 118°01' W; sec. 18, T 20 S, R 37 E). Named on Haiwee Reservoir (1951) and Monache Mountain (1956) 15' quadrangles. The stream ends at Haiwee Reservoir, where its water joins the Owens Valley water taken by aqueduct to Los Angeles.
Hogsback: see **The Hogsback** [INYO].
Hogue: see **Mount Hogue** [MONO].
Hole-in-the-Rock Spring [INYO]: *spring,* 11 miles north of Beatty Junction in Boundary Canyon (lat. 36°44'35" N, long. 116°58' W; sec. 15, T 14 S, R 46 E). Named on Chloride Cliff (1952) 15' quadrangle. Called Hole in the Rock Spring (without the hyphens) on Furnace Creek (1910) 1° quadrangle. Mendenhall (p. 34) noted that the feature is a seep in a hole that may contain 6 or 8 gallons of water.
Hole in the Wall [INYO]: *narrows,* 7 miles north-northwest of Ryan (lat. 36°24'50" N, long. 116°43'20" W; on N line sec. 2, T 26 N, R 2 E). Named on Ryan (1952) 15' quadrangle.
Homer: see **Wasson**, under **Lake Canyon** [MONO].
Homewood Canyon [INYO]: *canyon,* drained by a stream that flows 8 miles to Searles Valley 5.5 miles east-northeast of Argus Peak (lat. 35°53'30" N, long. 117°21'15" W; sec. 32, T 23 S, R 43 E). Named on Trona (1949) 15' quadrangle. This seems to be the feature that Thompson (1929, p. 180) called Graham & Jones Canyon; Thompson's (1921) map shows Graham and Jones mine in the upper part of the canyon, and shows Graham Spring near the mine. Waring and Huguenin (p. 37) mentioned Parson's Cañon, which probably is the name that they used for present Homewood Canyon. Wheeler's (1877) map shows a place called Summit Sta. located in present Searles Valley opposite the mouth of Homewood Canyon
Honeymoon Flat Campground [MONO]: *locality,* 6.25 miles southwest of Bridgeport along Robinson Creek (lat. 38°12'05" N, long. 119°19'15" W; near SW cor. sec. 15, T 4 N, R 24 E). Named on Matterhorn Peak (1956) 15' quadrangle.
Honeymoon Lake [INYO]: *lake,* 1100 feet long, nearly 5 miles west of Mount Tom (lat. 37°20'20" N, long. 118°44'35" W). Named on Mount Tom (1949) 15' quadrangle.
Hoover Lakes [MONO]: *lakes,* two, largest 1000 feet long, 5.25 miles east-southeast of Matterhorn Peak (lat. 38°03'20" N, long. 119°17'55" W; near N line sec. 2, T 2 N, R 24 E). Named on Matterhorn Peak (1956) 15' quadrangle. An engineer of Standard Consolidated Mining Company named the lakes in 1905 for Theodore J. Hoover, manager of the company at Bodie, and brother of Herbert Hoover, the future president (Gudde, 1949, p. 153).
Hope Valley [ALPINE]: *valley,* 6.5 miles south-southwest of Freel Peak along West Fork Carson River above West Carson Canyon (lat. 38°46' N, long. 119°56' W). Named on Carson Pass (1979) and Freel Peak (1955) 7.5' quadrangles. A party of Mormons crossed the Sierra Nevada in 1848 on their way to Salt Lake City and gave the name to the valley because it was there that they began to have hope for the success of their journey (Gudde, 1969, p. 145). Postal authorities established Hope Valley post office 12 miles northwest of Markleeville in 1864, discontinued it in 1868; and reestablished it in 1963; Daniel L. Peck was the first postmaster (Salley, p. 100). Long (map, p. 28) showed both Hope Valley P.O. and a place called Pecks situated together south of Hope Valley near present Red Lake.
Hope Valley Campground [ALPINE]: *locality,* 4 miles northeast of Carson Pass (lat. 38°43'50" N, long. 119°55'40" W); the place is at the south end of Hope Valley. Named on Carson Pass (1979) 7.5' quadrangle.
Hopkins Pass [MONO]: *pass,* 5.5 miles south of Mount Morrison on Mono-Fresno County line (lat. 37°28'50" N, long. 118°50'30" W); the pass is near the head of Hopkins Creek, which is in Fresno County. Named on Mount Abbot (1953) 15' quadrangle.
Horse Camp: see **Moscow Spring** [INYO].
Horse Canyon [ALPINE]:
(1) *canyon,* drained by a stream that flows 1.5 miles to Summit City Creek 2.25 miles south of Fourth of July Peak (lat. 38°37'35" N, long. 120°01'50" W). Named on Caples Lake (1979) 7.5' quadrangle.
(2) *valley,* less than 1 mile west-southwest of Mount Reba (lat. 38° 30'15" N, long. 120°02'30" W). Named on Mokelumne Peak (1979) 7.5' quadrangle. Called Horse Valley on Silver Lake (1956) 15' quadrangle.
Horse Creek [MONO]: *stream,* flows 4.5 miles to Robinson Creek 3.5 miles north of Matterhorn Peak (lat. 38°08'40" N, long. 119°22'40" W; sec. 6, T 3 N, R 24 E). Named on Matterhorn Peak (1956) 15' quadrangle.
Horse Meadow [ALPINE]: *area,* 1.5 miles south-southeast of Freel Peak along Willow Creek (lat. 38°50'20" N, long. 119°53'30" W; sec. 6, 7, T 11 N, R 19 E). Named on Freel Peak (1955) 7.5' quadrangle.
Horse Meadow: see **Lower Horse Meadow** [MONO]; **Upper Horse Meadow** [MONO].
Horse Mountain: see **Cowtrack Mountain** [MONO].
Horseshoe Lake [MONO]: *lake,* 0.5 mile long, 1.5 miles south-southeast of Mammoth Mountain (lat. 37°36'30" N, long. 119°01'10" W; on S line sec. 8, T 4 S, R 27 E). Named on Devils Postpile (1953) 15' quadrangle. The feature is one of the group called Mammoth Lakes.
Horseshoe Meadow [INYO]: *area,* 15 miles northwest of Olancha (lat. 36°26'40" N, long. 118°10'45" W). Named on Olancha (1956) 15' quadrangle.
Horsetail Falls [MONO]: *waterfall,* 2.25 miles southeast of Mount Morrison along a branch of McGee Creek (lat. 37°32'15" N, long. 118°49'45" W). Named on Mount Morrison (1953) 15' quadrangle.
Horse Thief Canyon [INYO]: *canyon,* extends for 2.5 miles from Fish Lake Valley to Eureka Valley 8 miles east of Deep Springs (lat. 37°20'45" N, long. 117°50' W; sec. 17, T 7 S, R 38 E). Named on Soldier Pass (1958) 15' quadrangle.
Horsethief Canyon [ALPINE]: *canyon,* drained by a stream that flows nearly 3 miles to West Fork Carson River 5.5 miles south of Freel Peak (lat. 38°46'35" N, long. 119°52'50" W; near W line sec. 32, T 11 N, R 19 E). Named on Freel Peak (1955) and Woodfords (1979) 7.5' quadrangles. Thieves supposedly used the place to fatten stolen horses (Long, p. 47).
Horse Valley: see **Horse Canyon** [ALPINE] (2).
Horton: see **Death Valley Junction** [INYO].
Horton Creek [INYO]: *stream,* flows 16 miles to Owens River 5.25 miles northwest of Bishop (lat. 37°24'30" N, long. 118°28'30" W; near W line sec. 21, T 6 S, R 32 E). Named on Bishop (1949) and Mount Tom (1949) 15' quadrangles. The name commemorates William Horton, who settled in Round Valley (1) in 1864 (Gudde, 1949, p. 155).
Horton Lake [INYO]: *lake,* 2100 feet long, 1.5 miles south-southwest of Mount Tom (lat. 37°19' N, long. 118°39'55" W; near N line sec. 27, T 7 S, R 30 E); the lake is along Horton Creek. Named on Mount Tom (1949) 15' quadrangle.
Horton Lakes: see **Upper Horton Lakes** [INYO].
Hot Creek [MONO]:
(1) *stream,* flows 4.5 miles to Little Walker River nearly 3 miles west of Fales Hot Springs (lat. 38°20'35" N, long. 119°27' W; near N line sec. 28, T 6 N, R 23 E); the stream goes past Fales Hot Springs. Named on Fales Hot Springs (1954) 7.5' quadrangle.
(2) *stream,* flows 12 miles before dividing to form distributaries in Long Valley (2) 8.5 miles north-northwest of Mount Morrison (lat. 37°40'45" N, long. 118°48'25" W; near NW cor. sec. 20, T 3 S, R 29 E); several hot springs contribute water to the creek. Named on Mount Morrison (1953) 15' quadrangle—application of the name on upper reaches of the stream is unclear on the map. Hot Creek (2) and Mammoth Creek together are called S. Branch [Owens River] on Lee's (1906) map—distributaries of Hot Creek (2) join Owens River.
Hot Creek: see **Little Hot Creek** [MONO].
Hot Creek Geyser: see **Casa Diablo Hot Springs** [MONO].
Hot Spring Cove: see **Paoha Island** [MONO].
Hot Springs: see **Benton Hot Springs** [MONO]; **The Hot Springs** [MONO].
Hot Springs Canyon [MONO]: *canyon,* drained by a stream that flows 3 miles to lowlands 2 miles south-southeast of Bridgeport (lat. 38°13'40" N, long. 119°13'15" W; near N line sec. 9, T 4 N, R 25 E); the group of springs known as The Hot Springs is near the mouth of the canyon. Named on Bodie (1958) 15' quadrangle.
Hot Springs Creek [ALPINE]: *stream,* flows 7.5 miles to join Pleasant Valley Creek and form Markleeville Creek 0.5 mile west-southwest of Markleeville (lat. 38°41'30" N, long. 119°47'20" W; near N line sec. 28, T 10 N, R 20 E); the stream goes past Grover Hot Springs. Named on Markleeville (1979) 7.5' quadrangle. United States Board on Geographic Names (1957, p. 2) rejected the name "Markleeville Creek" for the stream.
Hot Springs Valley [ALPINE]: *valley,* 3 miles west of Markleeville along Hot Springs Creek (lat. 38°42' N, long. 119°50'30" W); Grover Hot Springs are in the valley. Named on Markleeville (1956) 15' quadrangle.
Hot Springs Valley: see **Coso Hot Springs** [INYO].
Hoveck: see **Skidoo** [INYO].
Huckleberry Canyon: see **Elderberry Canyon** [INYO].
Hume's Crossing: see **Deadman Creek** [MONO].
Hummingbird Canyon: see **Hummingbird Spring** [INYO].
Hummingbird Lake [MONO]: *lake,* 700 feet long, 2.5 miles northeast of Mount Conness (lat. 37°59'20" N, long. 119°17'05" W; near SW cor. sec. 25, T 2 N, R 24 E). Named on Tuolumne Meadows (1956) 15' quadrangle.
Hummingbird Spring [INYO]: *spring,* 4 miles north-northwest of Telescope Peak (lat. 36°13'15" N, long. 117°06'25" W; sec. 4, T 20 S, R 45 E). Named on Telescope Peak (1952) 15' quadrangle. Palmer (p. 31) noted the name "Goodwin Spring" for the feature; this name was for Theodore Raymond Goodwin, superintendent of Death Valley National Monument. Palmer (p. 36) also referred to a canyon that leads to the spring as Hummingbird Canyon.
Humphreys: see **Mount Humphreys** [INYO].
Hunchback: see **The Hunchback** [INYO].
Hunewill Hills [MONO]: *ridge,* east-southeast-trending, 3 miles long, 7.25 miles northeast of Matterhorn Peak (lat. 38°10' N, long. 119°17'30" W).

Named on Matterhorn Peak (1956) 15' quadrangle.

Hunewill Lake [MONO]: *lake,* 800 feet long, 3.5 miles east-northeast of Matterhorn Peak along Tamarack Creek (lat. 38°06'45" N, long. 119°19' W). Named on Matterhorn Peak (1956) 15' quadrangle.

Hunewill Peak [MONO]: *peak,* nearly 6 miles northwest of Matterhorn Peak (lat. 38°09'20" N, long. 119°26'50" W). Altitude 11,713 feet. Named on Matterhorn Peak (1956) 15' quadrangle. Called Hennerville Pk. on Bridgeport (1909) 30' quadrangle, but United States Board on Geographic Names (1962b, p. 19) rejected this name for the feature, and pointed out that the name "Hunewill" is for N.B. Hunewill, who operated a sawmill in the neighborhood in the 1860's.

Hungry Packer Lake [INYO]: *lake,* 0.5 mile long, 1.5 miles east-southeast of Mount Darwin (lat. 37°09'30" N, long. 118°38'35" W; at NW cor. sec. 19, T 9 S, R 31 E). Named on Mount Goddard (1948) 15' quadrangle. Art Schober, a packer, named the lake in the 1930's for another packer who had to spend the night there without blankets or food (Schumacher, p. 95-96). United States Board on Geographic Names (1965b, p. 10) ruled that the name "Hungry Packer Lake" does not apply to Moonlight Lake.

Hunter Canyon [INYO]: *canyon,* drained by a stream that flows 6.5 miles to Saline Valley 6 miles northeast of New York Butte (lat. 36°42' N, long. 117°50'50" W). Named on New York Butte (1950) 15' quadrangle. The name commemorates W.L. Hunter, who built three arrastras in the canyon (DeDecker, p. 50).

Hunter Flat: see **Whitney Portal** [INYO].

Hunter Mountain [INYO]: *area,* an upland area of several square miles located 11 miles south-southeast of Ubehebe Peak (lat. 36° 32'40" N, long. 117°30' W). Named on Marble Canyon (1951) and Ubehebe Peak (1950) 15' quadrangles. The name commemorates Zeb Hunter, an early settler and cattleman in the neighborhood (Hanna, p. 144).

Huntington Peak: see **Mount Huntington** [MONO].

Huntoon Camp [MONO]: *locality,* 4.5 miles west-northwest of Bridgeport along Swauger Creek (lat. 38°17'15" N, long. 119°18'05" W; near SW cor. sec. 14, T 5 N, R 24 E); the place is south of Huntoon Valley. Named on Fales Hot Springs (1956) 15' quadrangle.

Huntoon Creek [MONO]:

(1) *stream,* flows nearly 4 miles to Long Valley Creek 3.5 miles southeast of Fales Hot Springs (lat. 38°18'35" N, long. 119°21'20" W; sec. 8, T 5 N, R 24 E). Named on Fales Hot Springs (1956) 15' quadrangle.

(2) *stream,* flows 5 miles to the State of Nevada 21 miles east-southeast of Bodie (lat. 38°03'20" N, long. 118°39' W; sec. 3, T 2 N, R 30 E). Named on Huntoon Valley (1958) 15' quadrangle.

Huntoon Station: see **Huntoon Valley** [MONO].

Huntoon Valley [MONO]: *valley,* 5.25 miles east-southeast of Fales Hot Springs along Swauger Creek (lat. 38°19'15" N, long. 119°18'45" W). Named on Fales Hot Springs (1956) 15' quadrangle. Almond Huntoon moved a hotel from Bodie to the valley in 1883, and operated Huntoon Station on the stage route there (Wedertz, p. 93).

Hurd Lake [INYO]: *lake,* 400 feet long, 6 miles east of Mount Darwin (lat. 37°09'20" N, long. 118°33'45" W; sec. 23, T 9 S, R 31 E); the lake is 1 mile north of Hurd Peak. Named on Mount Goddard (1948) 15' quadrangle.

Hurd Peak [INYO]: *peak,* 6 miles east-southeast of Mount Darwin (lat. 37°08'30" N, long. 118°33'55" W; near S line sec. 26, T 9 S, R 31 E). Altitude 12,219 feet. Named on Mount Goddard (1948) 15' quadrangle. The name honors H.C. Hurd, an engineer who made the first known ascent of the peak in 1906 (Gudde, 1949, p. 157).

— I —

Ibex Hills [INYO]: *range,* between Black Mountains and the south end of Greenwater Valley (lat. 35°49'30" N, long. 116°24'15" W); the south part of the range is in San Bernardino County. Named on Shoshone (1951) 15' quadrangle. According to Palmer (p. 37), the name is for mountain sheep, locally known as ibex, found at the place. According to Lingenfelter (p. 144), the name of the hills, pass, and peak is from Ibex Mining Company of Chicago, which operated in the neighborhood in the 1880's.

Ibex Pass [INYO]: *pass,* 13 miles south-southwest of Shoshone in Sperry Hills on the Inyo-San Bernardino County line (lat. 35°37'40" N, long. 116°20'10" W). Named on Shoshone (1951) 15' quadrangle.

Ibex Peak [INYO]: *peak,* 10.5 miles southwest of Shoshone (lat. 35° 52'45" N, long. 116°25' W); the peak is in Ibex Hills. Altitude 4752 feet. Named on Shoshone (1951) 15' quadrangle.

Iceberg: see **The Iceberg** [ALPINE].

Iceberg Lake [INYO]: *lake,* 900 feet long, nearly 0.5 mile east-northeast of Mount Whitney (1) (lat. 36°34'55" N, long. 118°17'05" W). Named on Mount Whitney (1956) 15' quadrangle.

Iceberg Meadow [ALPINE]: *area,* 2.25 miles south-southwest of Disaster Peak along Clark Fork on Alpine-Tuolumne County line (lat. 38°25'05" N, long. 119°44'50" W); the place is 0.5 mile south-southwest of The Iceberg. Named on Disaster Peak (1979) 7.5' quadrangle. The name is from the feature called The Iceberg (Gudde, 1949, p. 158).

Iceberg Peak [ALPINE]: *peak,* 4 miles northeast of Dardanelles Cone (lat. 38°27' N, long. 119°49'20" W). Altitude 9781 feet. Named on Dardanelles Cone (1979) 7.5' quadrangle. The name is from the feature called The Iceberg (Gudde, 1949, p. 158).

Ice Lake [MONO]: *lake,* 800 feet long, 2.5 miles northwest of Matterhorn Peak (lat. 38°06'50" N, long. 119°25'20" W). Named on Matterhorn Peak (1956) 15' quadrangle.

Inconsolable Range [INYO]: *ridge,* north-trending, 4 miles long, 8 miles east-southeast of Mount Darwin (lat. 37°08'30" N, long. 118° 32' W). Named on Mount Goddard (1948) 15' quadrangle.

Independence [INYO]: *town,* 40 miles south-southeast of Bishop in Owens Valley (lat. 36°48'10" N, long. 118°11'55" W; sec. 17, 18, T 13 S, R 35 E). Named on Independence (1951) 15' quadrangle. In 1861 Charles Putnam built a stone trading post at the place, which first was called Putnam's or Little Pine from nearby Little Pine Creek (present Independence Creek) (Hoover, Rensch, and Rensch, p. 116). The name of the town was changed to Independence, for Camp Independence, in 1866 when the place became the county seat (Schumacher, p. 41). Postal authorities established Independence post office in 1866 (Frickstad, p. 51). On July 4, 1862, Lieutenant Colonel George S. Evans and 201 men of the Second Cavalry, California Volunteers, started a military post at a site 2 miles north of present Independence; they named it Camp Independence in honor of the day—the post was abandoned in 1877 (Hoover, Rensch, and Rensch, p. 116). Mount Whitney (1907) 30' quadrangle has the name "Old Camp Independence" at the site of the camp, and Independence (1951) 15' quadrangle shows Fort Independence Indian reservation there. DeDecker (p. 46) noted that a mining camp of the 1860's called San Carlos was situated on the east bank of Owens River 4 miles east of present Independence.

Independence Creek [INYO]: *stream,* flows 6.5 miles to lowlands 4 miles west-southwest of Independence (lat. 36°46'45" N, long. 118°16' W; sec. 27, T 13 S, R 34 E). Named on Independence (1951) and Mount Pinchot (1953) 15' quadrangles. The stream first was called Little Pine Creek, and later was named for nearby Camp Independence (Hoover, Rensch, and Rensch, p. 116). The creek now discharges into the aqueduct that takes Owens Valley water to Los Angeles.

Independence Peak [INYO]: *peak,* 8 miles west-southwest of Independence (lat. 36°45'40" N, long. 118°19'50" W). Altitude 11,744 feet. Named on Mount Pinchot (1953) 15' quadrangle.

Indiana Summit [MONO]: *locality,* 6 miles south-southeast of the site of Mono Mills (lat. 37°48'20" N, long. 118°56' W; sec. 6, T 2 S, R 28 E). Named on Cowtrack Mountain (1962) 15' quadrangle.

Indian Creek [ALPINE]:

(1) *stream,* flows 10 miles to the State of Nevada 6 miles east-northeast of Woodfords (lat. 38°48'40" N, long. 119°43'35" W; sec. 15, T 11 N, R 20 E). Named on Freel Peak (1956), Markleeville (1956), and Mount Siegel (1957) 15' quadrangles.

(2) *stream,* flows nearly 5 miles to East Fork Carson River 1 mile east-southeast of Markleeville (lat. 38°41'20" N, long. 119°45'50" W; sec. 27, T 10 N, R 20 E). Named on Markleeville (1979) 7.5' quadrangle.

Indian Creek [MONO]: *stream,* flows 3 miles to the State of Nevada 13 miles east-southeast of White Mountain Peak (lat. 37°45'50" N, long. 118°14'35" W; at N line sec. 20, T 2 S, R 34 E). Named on Benton (1962), Davis Mountain (1963), and White Mountain Peak (1962) 15' quadrangles.

Indian Creek Reservoir [ALPINE]: *lake,* 4200 feet long, behind a dam on a tributary of Indian Creek (1) 3 miles southeast of Woodfords (lat. 38°45'05" N, long. 119°46'35" W; on E line sec. 4, T 10 N, R 20 E). Named on Markleeville (1979) and Woodfords (1979) 7.5' quadrangles.

Indian Flat [MONO]: *area,* 4.5 miles east of Coleville (lat. 38°33'50" N, long. 119°25'35" W; near W line sec. 2, T 8 N, R 23 E); the place is 0.5 mile north of Indian Valley. Named on Desert Creek Peak (1956) 15' quadrangle.

Indian Garden Creek [MONO]: *stream,* flows 5 miles to Fish Lake Valley 17 miles east-southeast of White Mountain Peak (lat. 37°30'55" N, long. 117°58'30" W; sec. 13, T 5 S, R 36 E). Named on Mount Barcroft (1962) and Piper Peak (1963) 15' quadrangles.

Indian Gardens Spring [INYO]: *spring,* 4.5 miles east of Coso Peak (lat. 36°12'15" N, long. 117°37'40" W; near S line sec. 10, T 20 S, R 40 E). Named on Coso Peak (1951) 15' quadrangle. Indians came each year from Darwin to plant a garden near the spring (Iroquois Research Institute, p. 133).

Indian Joe Canyon [INYO]: *canyon,* drained by a stream that flows 1.25 miles to Searles Valley 4.15 miles east-southeast of Argus Peak (lat. 35°49'15" N, long. 117°23' W; near W line sec. 30, T 24 S, R 43 E). Named on Trona (1949) 15' quadrangle.

Indian Joe Spring [INYO]: *spring,* 3 miles east-southeast of Argus Peak (lat. 35°49'55" N, long. 117°23'50" W; sec. 24, T 24 S, R 42 E); the spring is at the head of Indian Joe Canyon. Named on Trona (1949) 15' quadrangle. An Indian known as Joe lived at the spring before the Searles brothers took the water for their borax operation (Belden and Walker, p. 9). Thompson (1929, p. 180) referred to a spring, called Searles Spring, "which comes from tunnels in Indian Joe Canyon."

Indian Meadows [MONO]: *area,* 9.5 miles north of Glass Mountain along Adobe Creek (lat. 37°54'35" N, long. 118°42' W; near SE cor. sec. 30, T 1 N, R 30 E). Named on Glass Mountain (1962) 15' quadrangle.

Indian Pass [INYO]: *locality,* 9 miles east of Beatty Junction in Funeral Mountains (lat. 36°36'30" N, long. 116°46'30" W). Named on Chloride Cliff (1952) 15' quadrangle. Palmer (p. 13) mentioned that present Indian Pass also was known as Breyfogle Canyon or Breyfogle Pass for Jacob Breyfogle, a prospector who discovered Breyfogle mine about 1864.

Indian Peak [MONO]: *peak,* 5 miles northwest of White Mountain Peak (lat. 37°41'30" N, long. 118°18'45" W). Altitude 11,297 feet. Named on White Mountain Peak (1962) 15' quadrangle.

Indian Spring [ALPINE]: *spring,* 7.25 miles east of Mogul Peak (lat. 38°42'40" N, long. 119°35'10" W; sec. 17, T 10 N, R 22 E). Named on Topaz Lake (1956) 15' quadrangle.

Indian Spring [MONO]: *spring,* 7 miles northeast of the site of Mono Mills (lat. 37°56'45" N, long. 118°51'35" W). Named on Cowtrack Mountain (1962) 15' quadrangle.

Indian Spring: see **Mesquite Spring**, under **Mesquite Spring Campground** [INYO].

Indian Valley [ALPINE]: *valley,* 4.5 miles northwest of Ebbetts Pass (lat. 38°35'30" N, long. 119°52'20" W; mainly in sec. 34, T 9 N, R 19 E). Named on Ebbetts Pass (1979) 7.5' quadrangle. George H. Goddard apparently named the valley about 1859 after hearing an account of Indian girls who were rescued there from Murietta's gang of outlaws (Long, p. 47).

Indian Valley [MONO]: *valley,* 4.5 miles east-southeast of Coleville (lat. 38°33'15" N, long. 119°25'30" W; near W line sec. 11, T 8 N, R 23 E); the valley is 0.5 mile south of Indian Flat. Named on Desert Creek Peak (1956) 15' quadrangle.

Indian Valley: see **Leavitt Meadow** [MONO]; **Little Indian Valley** [ALPINE].

Indian Wells Valley [INYO]: *valley,* between the Sierra Nevada and Argus Range south of Coso Range; mainly in Kern and San Bernardino Counties. Named on Little Lake (1954) and Mountain Springs Canyon (1953) 15' quadrangles. Called Salt Wells Valley on Wheeler's (1877) map. United States Board on Geographic Names (1933, p. 388) rejected the names "Brown Valley," "Inyo-Kern Valley," "Inyokern Valley," and "Salt Wells Valley" for the feature. California Mining Bureau's (1917b) map shows a place called Kelley located in the north part of the valley, and a place called Argus situated in the valley north-northeast of Kelley. Postal authorities established Argus post office in 1897 and discontinued it in 1899 (Frickstad, p. 50).

Ink Rocks [MONO]: *relief feature,* 9 miles northwest of Matterhorn Peak (lat. 38°11'35" N, long. 119°28'35" W). Named on Matterhorn Peak (1956) 15' quadrangle.

Inspiration Point [ALPINE]: *peak,* 8 miles northwest of Dardanelles Cone (lat. 38°28'25" N, long. 119°59'10" W; sec. 10, T 7 N, R 18 E). Named on Spicer Meadow Reservoir (1979) 7.5' quadrangle.

Intake: see **Aberdeen** [INYO] (1).

Inyo: see **Keeler** [INYO]; **Mount Inyo** [INYO].

Inyo Crater Lakes [MONO]: *lakes,* two, largest 300 feet long, 4.5 miles north-northeast of Mammoth Mountain (lat. 37°41'35" N, long. 119°00'40" W; near NE cor. sec. 17, T 3 S, R 27 E); the lakes occupy small craters. Named on Devils Postpile (1953) 15' quadrangle.

Inyo Creek [INYO]: *stream,* flows 3 miles to Lone Pine Creek 6.5 miles west of Lone Pine (lat. 36°35'55" N, long. 118°10'45" W; sec. 28, T 15 S, R 35 E). Named on Lone Pine (1958) 15' quadrangle.

Inyo Hill [INYO]: *hill,* 15 miles northeast of Coso Junction (lat. 36° 12'25" N, long. 117°45'15" W; near W line sec. 9, T 20 S, R 39 E). Named on Haiwee Reservoir (1951) 15' quadrangle.

Inyo-Kern Valley: see **Indian Wells Valley** [INYO].

Inyokern Valley: see **Indian Wells Valley** [INYO].

Inyo Mountains [INYO]: *range,* east of Owens Valley south of Westgard Pass. Named on Death Valley (1954), Fresno (1962), and Mariposa (1957) 1°x 2° quadrangles. According to Chalfant (1933, p. 140), Indians told early white settlers in Owens Valley in 1860 that the range to the east has the name "Inyo," meaning something like "dwelling place of a great spirit." Loew (1876a, p. 179) noted that the part of the range where the mining town of Cerro Gordo is located has the name "Buena Vista Mountain." Wheeler used the name "Cerro Gordo Mountains" for the same part of the range in 1871 (Gudde, 1949, p. 132).

Irene: see **Camp Irene** [ALPINE].

Iron Creek [MONO]: *stream,* flows 6 miles to Fish Lake Valley 11 miles east of White Mountain Peak (lat. 37°36'15" N, long. 118°03'45" W). Named on Mount Barcroft (1962) 15' quadrangle.

Iron Mountain [MONO]: *peak,* 11.5 miles east-southeast of Mount Barcroft (lat. 37°29'20" N, long. 118°04'15" W; sec. 30, T 5 S, R 36 E). Altitude 9530 feet. Named on Blanco Mountain (1951) 15' quadrangle.

Irvine: see **Mount Irvine** [INYO].

Isham Canyon [INYO]: *canyon,* drained by a stream that flows 1 mile to Searles Valley 9 miles east of Argus Peak (lat. 35°51'50" N, long. 117°17'30" W; sec. 12, T 24 S, R 43 E). Named on Trona (1949) 15' quadrangle.

Island Pass [MONO]: *pass,* 11.5 miles northwest of Mammoth Mountain on Mono-Madera County line (lat. 37°44'10" N, long. 119°11'35" W); the pass is north of Thousand Island Lake, which is in Madera County. Named on Devils Postpile (1953) 15' quadrangle.

Italy Pass [INYO]: *pass,* 2.5 miles south of Mount Abbot on Inyo-Fresno County line (lat. 37°21'05" N, long. 118°47' W); the pass is 1 mile east-southeast of Lake Italy, which is in Fresno County. Named on Mount Abbot (1953) 15' quadrangle.

I X L Canyon [ALPINE]: *canyon,* drained by a stream that flows 1.5 miles to Silver Creek (1) 5 miles north-northeast of Ebbetts Pass (lat. 38°36'35" N, long. 119°45'50" W; sec. 22, T 9 N, R 20 E). Named on Ebbetts Pass (1979) 7.5' quadrangle. The name is for I X L mine, which is situated near the head of the canyon (Long, p. 43). The name of the mine is from the phrase "I excel" (Eno, p. 163).

— J —

Jackass Canyon [ALPINE]: *canyon,* drained by a stream that flows 1.25 miles to North Fork Mokelumne River 4.5 miles north of Mount Reba (lat. 38°34'20" N, long. 120°01'05" W). Named on Mokelumne Peak (1979) 7.5' quadrangle.

Jackass Canyon [INYO]:

(1) *canyon,* drained by a stream that flows 2.5 miles to Grapevine Canyon (2) 10.5 miles south of Ubehebe Peak (lat. 36°32'25" N, long. 117°33'35" W). Named on Ubehebe Peak (1950) 15' quadrangle.

(2) *canyon,* 0.5 mile long, opens into Marble Canyon (2) 6 miles northeast of Waucoba Mountain (lat. 37°05'25" N, long. 117°56'35" W); Jackass Flats is at the head of the canyon. Named on Waucoba Spring (1958) 15' quadrangle.

Jackass Canyon: see **Jackson Canyon** [ALPINE].

Jackass Creek [MONO]: *stream,* flows 1 mile to the State of Nevada 8 miles east of Coleville (lat. 38°33'25" N, long. 119°21'35" W); the stream heads at Jackass Spring. Named on Desert Creek Peak (1956) 15' quadrangle.

Jackass Flat [MONO]: *area,* 8 miles east-southeast of Coleville (lat. 38°32' N, long. 119°22'20" W); the place is 1.25 miles south of Jackass Spring. Named on Desert Creek Peak (1956) 15' quadrangle.

Jackass Flats [INYO]: *valley,* 5.5 miles east-northeast of Waucoba Mountain (lat. 37°03'30" N, long. 117°55'15" W). Named on Waucoba Spring (1958) 15' quadrangle.

Jackass Spring [INYO]: *spring,* 11 miles south-southeast of Ubehebe Peak (lat. 36°32'30" N, long. 117°31'05" W); the spring is near the head of Jackass Canyon (1). Named on Ubehebe Peak (1950) 15' quadrangle. Palmer (p. 39) noted that Lieutenant Birnie reported a mule ranch at the place in 1875.

Jackass Spring [MONO]: *spring,* 7.5 miles east of Coleville (lat. 38° 33' N, long. 119°22'20" W); the spring is 1.25 miles north of Jackass Flat at the head of Jackass Creek. Named on Desert Creek Peak (1956) 15' quadrangle.

Jack Gunn Spring [INYO]: *spring,* 8 miles north of Maturango Peak (lat. 36°14'20" N, long. 117°28'10" W). Named on Maturango Peak (1951) 15' quadrangle.

Jackpot Canyon [INYO]: *canyon,* 2.5 miles long, opens into Panamint Valley 10.5 miles southwest of Telescope Peak (lat. 36°03' N, long. 117°12' W). Named on Telescope Peak (1952) 15' quadrangle.

Jackson: see **Mount Jackson** [MONO].

Jackson Canyon [ALPINE]: *canyon,* drained by a stream that flows 3 miles to North Fork Mokelumne River 4.25 miles northwest of Pacific Grade Summit (lat. 38°33'25" N, long. 119°58'05" W). Named on Pacific Valley (1979) 7.5' quadrangle. United States Board on Geographic Names (1970, p. 3) gave the name "Jackass Canyon" as a variant.

Jail Canyon [INYO]: *canyon,* drained by a stream that flows 8 miles to Panamint Valley 7 miles west of Telescope Peak (lat. 36°11'20" N, long. 117°12'45" W). Named on Telescope Peak (1952) 15' quadrangle.

Jail Spring [INYO]: *spring,* 1.5 miles north-northwest of Telescope Peak (lat. 36°11'30" N, long. 117°05'45" W; sec. 15, T 20 S, R 45 E); the spring is near the head of Jail Canyon. Named on Telescope Peak (1952) 15' quadrangle.

Jarvis: see **Musser and Jarvis Creek** [ALPINE].

Jay: see **Evelyn** [INYO].

Jayhawker Canyon [INYO]: *canyon,* 2.5 miles long, opens into lowlands 9.5 miles north-northwest of Emigrant Pass (1) (lat. 36°27'15" N, long. 117°13'20" W); Jayhawker Spring is in the canyon. Named on Emigrant Canyon (1952) 15' quadrangle. At least one group of the Jayhawker emigrant party of 1849 passed through the canyon (Lingenfelter, p. 43).

Jayhawker Spring [INYO]: *spring,* 8.5 miles north-northwest of Emigrant Pass (1) (lat. 36°26'10" N, long. 117°13'15" W). Named on Emigrant Canyon (1952) 15' quadrangle. The California state mineralogist gave the name

"Hitchens Spring" to the feature in 1883 to honor James Hitchens, a member of the Darwin French party of 1860 (Hanna, p. 153). The name was changed to Jayhawker Spring in 1936 after employees of Death Valley National Monument found names and dates on a rock by the spring that recorded the passing of the Jayhawker emigrant party in 1849 (Federal Writers' Project, p. 33).

Jayhawker Well: see **McLean Spring** [INYO].

Jeff Davis Creek [ALPINE]: *stream*, flows nearly 3 miles to Pleasant Valley Creek 6 miles southwest of Markleeville (lat. 38°38'05" N, long. 119°51'40" W; sec. 14, T 9 N, R 19 E); the stream is east of Jeff Davis Peak. Named on Carson Pass (1979) and Markleeville (1979) 7.5' quadrangles. United States Board on Geographic Names (1979b, p. 6) rejected the name "Pleasant Valley Creek" for the stream.

Jeff Davis Peak [ALPINE]: *peak*, 6.25 miles southeast of Carson Pass (lat. 38°38'10" N, long. 119°53'45" W; sec. 16, T 9 N, R 19 E). Altitude 9065 feet. Named on Carson Pass (1979) 7.5' quadrangle. Called Sentinel Rock on Wheeler's (1876-1877) map.

Jeffrey Mine Canyon [MONO]: *canyon*, drained by a stream that flows 4.25 miles to Hammil Valley 5.5 miles west of White Mountain Peak (lat. 37°37'20" N, long. 118°21'10" W; near SE cor. sec. 5, T 4 S, R 33 E). Named on White Mountain Peak (1962) 15' quadrangle, which shows Jeffrey mine in the canyon.

Jenkins Canyon [ALPINE]: *canyon*, drained by a stream that flows 2.25 miles to Highland Creek 2 miles north of Dardanelles Cone (lat. 38°25'55" N, long. 119°52'40" W). Named on Dardanelles Cone (1979) 7.5' quadrangle. Called Slaughter Canyon on Dardanelles Cone (1956) 15' quadrangle, but United States Board on Geographic Names (1979b, p. 7) rejected this name.

Jenkins Canyon: see **Hiram Canyon** [ALPINE].

Jepson: see **Mount Jepson**, under **Mount Sill** [INYO].

Jessie: see **Lake Jessie**, under **Tioga Lake** [MONO].

Jessie Montrose: see **Lake Jessie Montrose**, under **Tioga Lake** [MONO].

Jigsaw Pass [INYO]: *pass*, 8 miles east-southeast of Mount Darwin (lat. 37°07'15" N, long. 118°32' W; sec. 36, T 9 S, R 31 E). Named on Mount Goddard (1948) 15' quadrangle.

Jobs Canyon [ALPINE]: *canyon*, drained by a stream that flows nearly 3 miles to the State of Nevada 4 miles east-northeast of Freels Peak (lat. 38°53'20" N, long. 119°50'20" W; sec. 22, T 12 N, R 19 E); the canyon is north of Jobs Peak. Named on Minden (1968) and Woodfords (1979) 7.5' quadrangles.

Job's East Peak: see **Jobs Peak** [ALPINE].

Jobs Peak [ALPINE]: *peak*, 6 miles north-northwest of Woodfords (lat. 38°51'30" N, long. 119°51'35" W; near W line sec. 33, T 12 N, R 19 E). Altitude 10,633 feet. Named on Woodfords (1979) 7.5' quadrangle. Called Job's Pk. on California Mining Bureau's (1917a) map. The name commemorates Moses Job, who opened a store in the early 1850's near the base of the feature; present Jobs Peak, Jobs Sister, and Freel Peak together were known as Job's Peaks (Gudde, 1949, p. 166-167). Goddard (p. 108) referred to Job's East Peak, meaning present Jobs Peak, and (p. 141) to Job's Group of Mountains.

Job's Peaks: see **Jobs Peak** [ALPINE].

Jobs Sister [ALPINE]: *peak*, 1 mile east-northeast of Freel Peak on Alpine-El Dorado County line (lat. 38°51'45" N, long. 119°53' W; sec. 31, T 12 N, R 19 E). Altitude 10,823 feet. Named on Freel Peak (1955) 7.5' quadrangle. Present Jobs Sister, Jobs Peak, and Freel Peak together once were known as Job's Peaks (Gudde, 1949, p. 166-167).

Johnny Meadow [MONO]: *area*, 9 miles east-southeast of the site of Mono Mills (lat. 37°50'10" N, long. 118°48'15" W; near N line sec. 29, T 1 S, R 29 E). Named on Cowtrack Mountain (1962) 15' quadrangle.

Johnson: see **Mount Johnson** [INYO]; **Mount Johnson**, under **Mount Lewis** [MONO].

Johnson Canyon [INYO]:

(1) *canyon*, drained by a stream that flows 4 miles to Rose Valley 3.5 miles north-northwest of Coso Junction (lat. 36°05'35" N, long. 118°57'45" W; near E line sec. 22, T 21 S, R 37 E). Named on Haiwee Reservoir (1951) and Monache Mountain (1956) 15' quadrangles.

(2) *canyon*, 9.5 miles long, opens into Death Valley 6 miles southwest of Bennetts Well (lat. 36°05'45" N, long. 116°55'30" W). Named on Bennetts Well (1952) and Telescope Peak (1952) 15' quadrangles. The name commemorates William Johnson, who had a truck garden in the canyon to supply miners at Panamint in the 1870's (Lingenfelter, p. 20). South Fork branches southwest 4.5 miles upstream from the mouth of the main canyon; it is 4 miles long and is named on Bennetts Well (1952) and Telescope Peak (1952) 15' quadrangles.

Johnson Spring [INYO]: *spring*, 10 miles northeast of Independence (lat. 36°54'30" N, long. 118°04'45" W). Named on Independence (1951) 15' quadrangle.

Jones: see **Graham and Jones Canyon**, under **Homewood Canyon** [INYO].

Jones Canyon [ALPINE]: *canyon*, drained by a stream that flows nearly 2.5 miles to East Fork Carson River 11 miles south-southeast of Mogul Peak (lat. 38°32'20" N, long. 119°39'20" W). Named on Wolf Creek (1979) 7.5' quadrangle.

Jordan: see **Copper Mountain** [MONO].

Joshua Flat [INYO]: *area*, 15 miles south-southeast of Keeler (lat. 36°16'20" N, long. 117°48'45" W). Named on Keeler (1951) 15' quadrangle.

Joshua Flats [INYO]: *valley*, 14 miles north of Waucoba Mountain (lat. 37°13'30" N, long. 117°59'15" W). Named on Waucoba Spring (1958) 15' quadrangle.

Jubilee Mountain [INYO]: *mountain*, 6 miles south-southwest of Epaulet Peak near the southwest edge of Black Mountains (lat. 35° 53'50" N, long. 116°35' W); the feature is 1 mile south-southwest of Jubilee Pass. Altitude 2527 feet. Named on Confidence Hills (1950) 15' quadrangle. The name is from Jubilee Pass (Palmer, p. 40).

Jubilee Pass [INYO]: *pass*, 5.25 miles southwest of Epaulet Peak in Black Mountains (lat. 35°54'40" N, long. 116°34'40" W). Named on Confidence Hills (1950) 15' quadrangle. The feature also was called Suicide Pass because a young miner committed suicide near there; the present name probably is from Jubilee mine (Palmer, p. 40, 70).

Julius Caesar: see **Mount Julius Caesar** [INYO].

Jumpoff: see **The Jumpoff** [MONO].

Junction Creek [MONO]: *stream*, flows nearly 4 miles to Little Walker River 2.5 miles west of Fales Hot Springs (lat. 38°21'25" N, long. 119°26'50" W; near W line sec. 22, T 6 N, R 23 E); the stream is 0.5 mile north-northeast of Sonora Junction. Named on Fales Hot Springs (1954) 7.5' quadrangle.

Junction House: see **The Junction House**, under **Sonora Junction** [MONO].

Junction Pass [INYO]: *pass*, 9 miles north-northwest of Mount Whitney (1) on Inyo-Tulare County line (lat. 36°41'45" N, long. 118°21'20" W). Named on Mount Whitney (1956) 15' quadrangle. The name is from Junction Peak (United States Board on Geographic Names, 1933, p. 403).

Junction Peak [INYO]: *peak*, 9 miles north-northwest of Mount Whitney (1) on Inyo-Tulare County line (lat. 36°41'30" N, long. 118°21'55" W). Altitude 13,888 feet. Named on Mount Whitney (1956) 15' quadrangle. J.N. LeConte named the peak in 1896 for its position at the junction of Kings-Kern Divide, which is in Tulare County, with the main crest of Sierra Nevada (Farquhar, 1923, p. 407).

Junction Reservoir [MONO]: *lake*, 1500 feet long, 4.5 miles west-southwest of Fales Hot Springs (lat. 38°20'10" N, long. 119°28'35" W; sec. 29, T 6 N, R 23 E); the lake is along Junction Creek. Named on Fales Hot Springs (1954) 7.5' quadrangle.

June Lake [MONO]:

(1) *lake*, 6000 feet long, 12 miles south-southeast of Lee Vining at the head of Reversed Creek (lat. 37°47'15" N, long. 119°04'20" W; sec. 11, 12, T 2 S, R 26 E). Named on Mono Craters (1953) 15' quadrangle. The lake was called Summit Lake about 1880 (Bean, p. 4).

(2) *settlement*, 12.5 miles south of Lee Vining on the south side of June Lake (1) (lat. 37°46'45" N, long. 119°04'30" W; sec. 11, 14, T 2 S, R 26 E). Named on Mono Craters (1953) 15' quadrangle. Postal authorities established June Lake post office in 1927 (Frickstad, p. 104).

June Lake Junction [MONO]: *locality*, 11 miles south-southeast of Lee Vining (lat. 37°48'45" N, long. 119°03'10" W; sec. 36, T 1 S, R 26 E); the road to June Lake (1) leaves the main highway at the place. Named on Mono Craters (1953) 15' quadrangle.

Juniper Mountain [MONO]: *peak*, 7 miles east-northeast of White Mountain Peak (lat. 37°40'20" N, long. 118°08'25" W). Altitude 7862 feet. Named on Mount Barcroft (1962) 15' quadrangle.

– K –

Kasson: see **Tecopa** [INYO].

Kavanaugh Ridge [MONO]: *ridge*, north-trending, 1.5 miles long, nearly 6 miles east of Matterhorn Peak (lat. 38°05'05" N, long. 119°16'30" W; sec. 24, 25, T 3 N, R 24 E). Named on Matterhorn Peak (1956) 15' quadrangle. The name commemorates Steve Kavanaugh, who had mining claims in the neighborhood about 1900 (Wedertz, p. 137).

Keane Spring [INYO]: *spring*, 11 miles north-northeast of Beatty Junction (lat. 36°44'40" N, long. 116°54'05" W; near W line sec. 8, T 30 N, R 1 E). Named on Chloride Cliff (1952) 15' quadrangle. The name commemorates Jack Keane, who discovered Keane Wonder mine (Hanna, p. 159), which is located 4.25 miles south of the spring. The mine operated from 1908 until 1916 (Tucker and Sampson, p. 402). Postal authorities established Keane Wonder post office in 1912 and discontinued it in 1914 (Frickstad, p. 51).

Keane Wonder: see **Keane Spring** [INYO].

Kearsarge [INYO]: *locality*, 4.5 miles east of Independence along Southern Pacific Railroad (lat. 36°48'25" N, long. 118°07' W; sec. 13, T 13 S, R 35 E). Named on Independence (1951) 15' quadrangle. Called Citrus on Mount Whitney (1907) 30' quadrangle. Postal authorities established Citrus post office in 1888, discontinued it in 1905, reestablished it in 1907, and discontinued it in 1910 (Frickstad, p. 50). A mining camp called Bend City sprang up in the 1860's near present Kearsarge; the first county bridge across Owens River was at Bend City, but the earthquake of 1872 changed the course of the river and left the already deserted townsite by a dry ravine (Hoover, Rensch, and Rensch, p. 117).

Kearsarge: see **Kearsarge Peak** [INYO].

Kearsarge Pass [INYO]: *pass,* 10 miles west of Independence on Inyo-Fresno County line (lat. 36°46'25" N, long. 118°22'35" W). Named on Mount Pinchot (1953) 15' quadrangle. The name is from Kearsarge mine, which is located east of the pass (Farquhar, 1924, p. 49).

Kearsarge Peak [INYO]: *peak,* 8 miles west of Independence (lat. 36°47'20" N, long. 118°20'45" W). Altitude 12,598 feet. Named on Mount Pinchot (1953) 15' quadrangle. The men who found the first mine on the slopes of the peak named their claim in 1864 for the Union ship *Kearsarge,* victor over the Confederate raider *Alabama,* for which Alabama Hills had been named; the peak name is from the mine (Chalfant, 1933, p. 235-236). A mining camp called Kearsarge was at the south base of the peak, but after an avalanche nearly destroyed the place in 1867, the miners moved to a safer location (Hoover, Rensch, and Rensch, p. 118).

Keeler [INYO]: *village,* 11.5 miles south-southeast of New York Butte at the east edge of Owens Lake (lat. 36°29'15" N, long. 117° 52'15" W; sec. 4, 5, T 17 S, R 38 E). Named on Keeler (1951) 15' quadrangle. Officials of Carson and Colorado Railroad named their station at the place in 1882 for J.M. Keeler, manager of Inyo County marble quarry (Gudde, 1969, p. 162). Postal authorities established Keeler post office in 1883 and discontinued it for a time in 1898 (Frickstad, p. 51). Wheeler's (1877) map shows a place called Cerro Gordo Landing located on the west shore of Owens Lake about 1 mile south-southeast of present Keeler; the map also has the name "Tule Sta." for a place situated 2 miles farther south-southeast. Postal authorities established Inyo post office 5 miles north of Keeler in 1876, discontinued it in 1880, reestablished it in 1891, and discontinued it in 1907 (Salley, p. 104). California Division of Highways' (1934) map shows a place called Tramway located 5.25 miles northwest of Keeler along Southern Pacific Railroad.

Keeler Needle [INYO]: *relief feature,* 1000 feet south of Mount Whitney (1) on Inyo-Tulare County line (lat. 36°34'30" N, long. 118°17'30" W). Named on Mount Whitney (1956) 15' quadrangle. The name is for James Edward Keeler, director of Lick Observatory from 1898 until 1900, who accompanied S.P. Langley on an expedition to Mount Whitney in 1881 (Farquhar, 1924, p. 50).

Keith: see **Mount Keith** [INYO].

Kelley: see **Indian Wells Valley** [INYO].

Kelley's Station: see **Renegade Canyon** [INYO].

Kelley's Upper Well: see **Kelleys Well** [INYO].

Kelleys Well [INYO]: *well,* 3.25 miles north-northwest of Death Valley Junction (lat. 36°20'50" N, long. 116°25'35" W; sec. 34, T 26 N R 5 E). Named on Ash Meadows (1952) 15' quadrangle. Called Kelley's Well on Furnace Creek (1910) 1° quadrangle, which shows another Kelley's Well located 3 miles to the north, and a third well, called Kelley's Upper Well, located 1.5 miles south-southwest of the first. California Mining Bureau's (1917b) map has the name "Kelley Well" for present Kelleys Well.

Kelty Canyon [MONO]: *canyon,* drained by a stream that flows 3 miles to an unnamed canyon 6.25 miles east of Glass Mountain (lat. 37°45'30" N, long. 118°35'35" W; sec. 19, T 2 S, R 31 E); the canyon heads south of Kelty Meadows. Named on Glass Mountain (1962) 15' quadrangle.

Kelty Meadows [MONO]: *area,* 3.5 miles east of Glass Mountain (lat. 37°46' N, long. 118°38'30" W); the place is north of the head of Kelty Canyon. Named on Glass Mountain (1962) 15' quadrangle. Called Kelty Meadow on Mount Morrison (1914) 30' quadrangle, but United States Board on Geographic Names (1986, p. 2) rejected the singular form for the name.

Kennedy Canyon [MONO]: *canyon,* drained by a stream that flows 3 miles to West Fork West Walker River 7.25 miles north of Tower Peak (lat. 38°14'45" N, long. 119°34'15" W; near SE cor. sec. 29, T 5 N, R 22 E). Named on Sonora Pass (1956) and Tower Peak (1956) 15' quadrangles.

Kenneth Lake [INYO]: *lake,* 1000 feet long, 8 miles north-northwest of Mount Tom (lat. 37°26'35" N, long. 118°42'45" W). Named on Mount Tom (1949) 15' quadrangle.

Kentuck Camp: see **Ferris Canyon** [MONO].

Keough Hot Springs [INYO]: *locality,* 7.5 miles south of Bishop near the west edge of Owens Valley (lat. 37°15'20" N, long. 118° 22'35" W; sec. 17, T 8 S, R 33 E). Named on Bishop (1949) 15' quadrangle. Philip P. Keough of Bishop opened a resort at the spot in 1919 (Hanna, p. 160).

Kerrick Gulch [MONO]: *canyon,* drained by a stream that flows 0.25 mile to Comanche Gulch 3.25 miles south-southwest of Benton (lat. 37°46'20" N, long. 118°29'35" W; sec. 18, T 2 S, R 32 E). Named on Benton (1962) 15' quadrangle.

Kettle Peak [MONO]: *peak,* 3.5 miles northwest of Matterhorn Peak (lat. 38°07'20" N, long. 119°25'45" W). Altitude 11,010 feet. Named on Matterhorn Peak (1956) 15' quadrangle.

Keyes: see **Pat Keyes Canyon** [INYO]; **Pat Keyes Spring** [INYO].

Keynot Canyon [INYO]: *canyon,* drained by a stream that flows 5.5 miles to Saline Valley 7 miles north-northeast of New York Butte (lat. 36°44'10" N, long. 117°52' W); the canyon heads at Keynot Peak. Named on New York Butte (1950) 15' quadrangle. Keynot mineral claims are on the ridge north of the canyon (DeDecker, p. 50).

Keynot Peak [INYO]: *peak,* 4.5 miles north-northwest of New York Butte (lat. 36°42'30" N, long. 117°57'40" W). Altitude 11,101 feet. Named on New York Butte (1950) 15' quadrangle.

Kid Mountain [INYO]: *peak,* 9 miles west-southwest of Big Pine (lat. 37°06' N, long. 118°25'45" W). Altitude 11,896 feet. Named on Big Pine (1950) 15' quadrangle.

Kidney Lake [MONO]: *lake,* 1250 feet long, 6 miles southwest of Lee Vining (lat. 37°53'50" N, long. 119°11'50" W); the outline of the lake on a map is somewhat kidney shaped. Named on Mono Craters (1953) 15' quadrangle.

Kings Mill [MONO]: *locality,* 10 miles northeast of Toms Place (lat. 37°39'40" N, long. 118°32'50" W; sec. 27, T 3 S, R 31 E). Site named on Casa Diablo Mountain (1953) 15' quadrangle.

King's Peak: see **Disaster Peak** [ALPINE].

King's Station: see **Bloody Canyon** [MONO].

Kingston: see **Kingston Range** [INYO].

Kingston Range [INYO]: *range,* south of the southeast end of Pahrump Valley, mainly in San Bernardino County. Named on Horse Thief Springs (1956) 15' quadrangle. California Mining Bureau's (1917b) map shows a place called Kingston located near the extreme southeast corner of Inyo County, apparently north of Kingston Range in Pahrump Valley.

Kinney Creek [ALPINE]: *stream,* flows 2.5 miles to Silver Creek (1) 2 miles north of Ebbetts Pass (lat. 38°34'25" N, long. 119°48'20" W). Named on Ebbetts Pass (1979) 7.5' quadrangle.

Kinney Lake: see **Lower Kinney Lake** [ALPINE]; **Upper Kinney Lake** [ALPINE].

Kinney Lakes: see **Lower Kinney Lake** [ALPINE].

Kinney Reservoir [ALPINE]: *lake,* 2250 feet long, 0.5 mile north of Ebbetts Pass along Kinney Creek (lat. 38°33'15" N, long. 119°48'35" W). Named on Ebbetts Pass (1979) 7.5' quadrangle.

Kirk: see **Kirkwood** [ALPINE].

Kirkwood [ALPINE]: *locality,* 4 miles northwest of Fourth of July Peak (lat. 38°42'10" N, long. 120°04'15" W; sec. 22, T 10 N, R 17 E). Named on Caples Lake (1979) 7.5' quadrangle. Called Kirk on Wheeler's (1876-1877) map, and Wheeler in his text (1878, p. 61) referred to Kirkwood's. Zack Kirkwood built a stage station and inn at the site in 1864; Alpine County, El Dorado County, and Amador County meet at a common point in the barroom of the inn, which housed Roundtop post office (Hoover, Rensch, and Rensch, p. 29)—the post office, named for a nearby peak, was listed in Amador County (Salley, p. 190).

Kirkwood Creek [ALPINE]: *stream,* flows less than 2 miles to El Dorado County 3.5 miles northwest of Fourth of July Peak (lat. 38° 41'35" N, long. 120°04'20" W; sec. 27, T 10 N, R 17 E); the stream goes through Kirkwood Meadows. Named on Caples Lake (1979) 7.5' quadrangle.

Kirkwood Creek [MONO]: *stream,* flows 2.5 miles to West Walker River 2.5 miles north-northeast of Tower Peak (lat. 38°10'55" N, long. 119°31'50" W); the stream heads at Kirkwood Lake. Named on Tower Peak (1956) 15' quadrangle.

Kirkwood Lake [MONO]: *lake,* 1000 feet long, 2.25 miles east-northeast of Tower Peak (lat. 38°09'20" N, long. 119°30'25" W); the lake is at the head of Kirkwood Creek. Named on Tower Peak (1956) 15' quadrangle.

Kirkwood Meadows [ALPINE]: *valley,* 3.5 miles northwest of Fourth of July Peak on Alpine-Amador County line (lat. 38°41'30" N, long. 120°04'15" W); the valley is south of Kirkwood along Kirkwood Creek. Named on Caples Lake (1979) 7.5' quadrangle.

Kirkwood Spring [MONO]: *spring,* 6 miles south-southeast of Bodie in Mono Valley (lat. 38°08' N, long. 118°58'40" W; sec. 10, T 3 N, R 27 E). Named on Trench Canyon (1958) 15' quadrangle. Billeb (p. 45) noted that a place called Lime Kiln Station was situated 12 miles by rail line from Bodie; Trench Canyon (1958) 15' quadrangle shows a lime kiln located 1.5 miles east-northeast of Kirkwood Spring at the north edge of Mono Valley near an old railroad grade.

Kirman Lake [MONO]: *lake,* 1800 feet long, 5.5 miles west of Fales Hot Springs (lat. 38°20'25" N, long. 119°29'55" W; sec. 30, T 6 N, R 23 E). Named on Fales Hot Springs (1954) and Pickel Meadow (1954) 7.5' quadrangles. Called Carmen Lake on Bridgeport (1909) 30' quadrangle, but United States Board on Geographic Names (1939, p. 20) rejected the names "Carmen Lake" and "Corner Lake" for the feature. The name "Kirman Lake" commemorates Richard Kirman, an early settler in the neighborhood (Wedertz, p. 178).

Kit Carson Campground [ALPINE]: *locality,* 5.5 miles south of Freel Peak along West Fork Carson River (lat. 38°46'35" N, long. 119°53'45" W; sec. 31, T 11 N, R 19 E). Named on Freel Peak (1955) 7.5' quadrangle.

Kit Carson Pass: see **Carson Pass** [ALPINE].

Klare Spring [INYO]: *spring,* 5 miles east-northeast of the mouth of Titus Canyon in that canyon (lat. 36°50'30" N, long. 117°05'20" W). Named on Grapevine Peak (1957) 15' quadrangle. The feature also was called Hidden Spring for its concealed location in a tunnel (Palmer, p. 41).

Klondike Canyon [MONO]: *canyon,* drained by a stream that flows 3.5 miles to Adobe Valley 8 miles northeast of Glass Mountain (lat. 37°51'40"

N, long. 118°36'40" W; near E line sec. 13, T 1 S, R 30 E). Named on Glass Mountain (1962) 15' quadrangle.

Klondike Lake [INYO] *intermittent lake,* 4500 feet long, 3 miles north-northwest of Big Pine (lat. 37°12'30" N, long. 118°18'10" W; sec. 36, T 8 S, R 33 E). Named on Big Pine (1950) 15' quadrangle. Bishop (1913) 30' quadrangle shows a permanent lake in marsh.

Knight Canyon [INYO]: *canyon,* drained by a stream that flows 7 miles to Panamint Valley 6.5 miles east of Maturango Peak (lat. 36°06'20" N, long. 117°22'50" W; sec. 18, T 21 S, R 43 E). Named on Maturango Peak (1951) 15' quadrangle. Waring and Huguenin (p. 37) called the feature Knights Cañon.

Koenig Lake [MONO]: *lake,* 800 feet long, 3.25 miles south of Sonora Pass (lat. 38°16'50" N, long. 119°37'40" W). Named on Pickel Meadow (1954) and Sonora Pass (1979) 7.5' quadrangles.

Koip Crest [MONO]: *ridge,* generally south- to southeast-trending, 3.5 miles long, 12.5 miles south-southwest of Lee Vining, partly on Mono-Tuolumne County line (lat. 37°47'30" N, long. 119°12'15" W). Named on Mono Craters (1953) 15' quadrangle. United States Board on Geographic Names (1988, p. 4) rejected the names "Koip Ridge" and "Ko-it Ridge" for the feature.

Koip Peak [MONO]: *peak,* 11 miles south-southwest of Lee Vining (lat. 37°48'45" N, long. 119°12' W); the peak is near the north end of Koip Crest. Altitude 12,979 feet. Named on Mono Craters (1953) 15' quadrangle. United States Board on Geographic Names (1933, p. 434) rejected the name "Ko-it Peak" for the feature. The name probably is of Indian origin (Kroeber, p. 45).

Koip Ridge: see **Koip Crest** [MONO].

Ko-it Peak: see **Koip Peak** [MONO].

Ko-it Ridge: see **Koip Crest** [MONO].

Köngsberg: see **Silver Mountain** [ALPINE].

Konigsberg: see **Silver Mountain** [ALPINE].

Konigs Peak: see **Snodgrass Creek** [ALPINE].

Krum's Creek: see **Raymond Canyon Creek** [ALPINE].

Kuna Peak [MONO]: *peak,* 11 miles south-southwest of Lee Vining on Mono-Tuolumne County line (lat. 37°48'35" N, long. 119°12'40" W); the peak is at the southeast end of Kuna Crest, which is in Tuolumne County. Named on Mono Craters (1953) 15' quadrangle. W.D. Johnson of United States Geological Survey named the peak about 1883 (United States Board on Geographic Names, 1934, p. 13). The name probably is of Indian origin (Kroeber (p. 45).

Kunze: see **Greenwater** [INYO].

—L—

Labrosse Creek [MONO]: *stream,* flows 2 miles to Robinson Creek 6.25 miles southwest of Bridgeport (lat. 38°12'10" N, long. 119°19'20" W; near W line sec. 15, T 4 N, R 24 E). Named on Matterhorn Peak (1956) 15' quadrangle.

Lagunita: see **Little Lake** [INYO] (1).

Lake Alger: see **Alger Lakes** [MONO].

Lake Alpine [ALPINE]:

(1) *lake,* 1.25 miles long, behind a dam on Silver Creek (2) nearly 3 miles south-southeast of Mount Reba (lat. 38°28'20" N, long. 120° 00'10" W; sec. 9, T 7 N, R 18 E). Named on Spicer Meadow Reservoir (1979) and Tamarack (1979) 7.5' quadrangles.

(2) *settlement,* 2.5 miles southeast of Mount Reba (lat. 38°28'45" N, long. 120°00' W; sec. 4, 9, T 7 N, R 18 E); the place is on the north side of Lake Alpine (1). Named on Spicer Meadow Reservoir (1979) and Tamarack (1979) 7.5' quadrangles. Postal authorities established Lake Alpine post office in 1927 and discontinued it in 1972 (Salley, p. 115).

Lake Barrett [MONO]: *lake,* 700 feet long, nearly 3 miles south-southeast of Mammoth Mountain (lat. 37°35'45" N, long. 119°00'20" W; sec. 16, T 4 S, R 27 E). Named on Devils Postpile (1953) 15' quadrangle. The name commemorates Lou Barrett, an early forester (Smith, Genny, p. 51). The lake is one of the group called Mammoth Lakes.

Lake Canyon [MONO]: *canyon,* 3 miles long, opens into Lundy Canyon 8 miles northwest of Lee Vining (lat. 38°01'30" N, long. 119°14'30" W; near N line sec. 20, T 2 N, R 25 E); Blue Lake (2), Crystal Lake (1), and Oneida Lake are in the canyon. Named on Bodie (1958) and Tuolumne Meadows (1956) 15' quadrangles. A mining camp called Wasson was located in the canyon near Crystal Lake (1) (Smith, Genny, p. 32). Wasson began in 1879 at the site of William Wasson's homestead at Emigrant Flat 2 miles upstream from Lundy Lake, and next to the mines of Homer Mill and Mining Company; it remained a small company town that eventually was called Homer (Fletcher, p. 59-60).

Lake Creek: see **Rush Creek** [MONO].

Lake Crowley [INYO]: *lake,* 7.5 miles long, behind a dam on Owens River 2.25 miles northwest of Toms Place in Long Valley (2) (lat. 37°35'15" N, long. 118°42'20" W; sec. 19, T 4 S, R 30 E). Named on Casa Diablo Mountain (1953) and Mount Morrison (1953) 15' quadrangles. Mount Morrison (1953) 15' quadrangle also has the form "Crowley Lake" for the name. The dam that forms the lake was completed in 1941; the name "Crowley" commemorates Father J.J. Crowley, called the Desert Padre, who died in an automobile accident in 1940 (Smith, Genny, p. 4). Postal authorities established Crowley Lake post office in 1973 (Salley, p. 53).

Lake Dorothy [MONO]: *lake,* 1 mile long, 2 miles southwest of Mount Morrison along a branch of Convict Creek (lat. 37°32'20" N, long. 118°52'50" W). Name on Mount Morrison (1953) 15' quadrangle. The name is for Dorothy Forsyth, daughter of Major W.W. Forsyth; the major was acting superintendent of Yosemite National Park from 1909 until 1912 (Sowaal, p. 52-53).

Lake Frances [MONO]: *lake,* 400 feet long, 1.5 miles east of Matterhorn Peak (lat. 38°05'50" N, long. 119°21'10" W). Named on Matterhorn Peak (1956) 15' quadrangle.

Lake Genevieve [MONO]: *lake,* 2500 feet long, 1.5 miles west of Mount Morrison along a branch of Convict Creek (lat. 37°33'30" N, long. 118°53' W; sec. 33, T 4 S, R 28 E). Named on Mount Morrison (1953) 15' quadrangle.

Lake George [MONO]: *lake,* 1800 feet long, 2.25 miles south-southeast of Mammoth Mountain (lat. 37°36' N long. 119°00'40" W; on W line sec. 16, T 4 S, R 27 E). Named on Devils Postpile (1953) 15' quadrangle. According to one account, English owners of Mammoth mine named the lake for King George, and named nearby Lake Mary for Queen Mary of England (Smith, Genny, p. 143). The lake is one of the group called Mammoth Lakes.

Lake Harriet [MONO]: *lake,* 0.25 mile long, 3 miles north-northwest of Tower Peak along Cascade Creek (lat. 38°11'15" N, long. 119° 34'05" W). Named on Tower Peak (1956) 15' quadrangle.

Lake Helen [MONO]:

(1) *lake,* 0.25 mile long, 2.25 miles north-northwest of Tower Peak (lat. 38°10'25" N, long. 119°33'55" W). Named on Tower Peak (1956) 15' quadrangle.

(2) *lake,* 950 feet long, 8 miles southeast of Matterhorn Peak on upper reaches of Mill Creek (2) (lat. 38°00'05" N, long. 119°17'30" W; on S line sec. 23, T 2 N, R 24 E). Named on Matterhorn Peak (1956) 15' quadrangle.

Lake Helen of Troy [INYO]: *lake,* 1600 feet long, 5 miles north-northwest of Mount Whitney (1) (lat. 36°38'50" N, long. 118°19'10" W); the lake is less than 0.5 mile northwest of Trojan Peak. Named on Mount Whitney (1956) 15' quadrangle.

Lake Hill [INYO]: *ridge,* north-northwest-trending, 1 mile long, 4.25 miles southwest of Panamint Butte in Panamint Valley (lat. 36°23'05" N, long. 117°24'10" W; on W line sec. 11, T 18 S, R 42 E). Named on Panamint Butte (1951) 15' quadrangle. The ridge appears to be the southernmost of two features called Black Islands on Wheeler's (1877) map.

Lake Jessie: see **Tioga Lake** [MONO].

Lake Jessie Montrose: see **Tioga Lake** [MONO].

Lake Mamie [MONO]: *lake,* 1600 feet long, 2 miles southeast of Mammoth Mountain (lat. 37°36'30" N, long. 119°00'35" W; at SE cor. sec. 8, T 4 S, R 27 E). Named on Devils Postpile (1953) 15' quadrangle. According to one account, the name is for a dancehall girl in Bodie (Smith, Genny, p. 143). The lake is one of the group called Mammoth Lakes.

Lake Manly: see **Death Valley** [INYO].

Lake Mary [MONO]: *lake,* 3600 feet long, 2.5 miles southeast of Mammoth Mountain (lat. 37°36'10" N, long. 119°00'10" W; sec. 16, T 4 S, R 27 E). Named on Devils Postpile (1953) and Mount Morrison (1953) 15' quadrangles. The feature first was called Summit Lake (Chalfant, 1947, p. 97). According to one account, the name "Mary" commemorates Queen Mary of England, and nearby Lake George commemorates her husband, King George; according to another account, Lake Mary was named for a dancehall girl from Bodie (Smith, Genny, p. 143). The lake is one of the group called Mammoth Lakes. A place on the southeast side of the lake (sec. 9, 16, T 4 S, R 27 E) had the name "Lake Mary" (United States Board on Geographic Names, 1950, p. 5). Postal authorities established Wildyrie post office at a resort by Lake Mamie in 1930 and moved it 1 mile east and changed the name to Lake Mary in 1944; they discontinued the post office in 1968 (Salley, p. 115, 240).

Lake Mono: see **Mono Lake** [MONO].

Lake Ruth [MONO]: *lake,* 1250 feet long, 2.5 miles northwest of Tower Peak (lat. 38°10'25" N, long. 119°34'30" W). Named on Tower Peak (1956) 15' quadrangle.

Lake Sabrina [INYO]: *lake,* 1 mile long, behind a dam on Middle Fork Bishop Creek 4.5 miles northeast of Mount Darwin (lat. 37° 12'45" N, long. 118°36'45" W). Named on Mount Goddard (1948) 15' quadrangle. The name commemorates Mrs. Sabrina Hobbs, wife of C.M. Hobbs, first general manager of the power company that built the dam and formed the lake in 1907 and 1908 (Farquhar, 1925, p. 130). United States Board on Geographic Names (1933, p. 655) rejected the form "Lake Sebrina" for the name.

Lake Sebrina: see **Lake Sabrina** [INYO].

Lake Valley [ALPINE]: *valley,* 0.5 mile north of Mount Reba (lat. 38°31' N, long. 120°01'35" W). Named on Mokelumne Peak (1979) 7.5' quadrangle.

Lakeview: see **Lee Vining** [MONO].

Lakeview Spring [MONO]: *spring,* 8.5 miles northeast of Bridgeport (lat. 38°21'30" N, long. 119°08'30" W; near N line sec. 20, T 6 N, R 26 E). Named on Bridgeport (1958) 15' quadrangle.

Lake Wit-so-nah-pah [MONO]: *lake,* 650 feet long, 2.5 miles south-southwest of Mount Morrison along Convict Creek (lat. 37°31'30" N, long. 118°52'30" W). Named on Mount Morrison (1953) 15' quadrangle.

Lamarch Mountain: see **Mount Lamarck** [INYO].

Lamarck: see **Mount Lamarck** [INYO].

Lamarck Col [INYO]: *relief feature,* 1.5 miles north of Mount Darwin (lat. 37°11'30" N, long. 118°40' W); the feature is 0.25 mile southeast of Mount Lamarck. Named on Mount Goddard (1948) 15' quadrangle.

Lamarck Creek [INYO]: *stream,* flows 4 miles to North Fork (1) Bishop Creek 5 miles northeast of Mount Darwin (lat. 37°13'45" N, long. 118°37'15" W); the stream heads near Mount Lamarck. Named on Mount Goddard (1948) 15' quadrangle.

Lamarck Lake: see **Lower Lamarck Lake** [INYO]; **Upper Lamarck Lake** [INYO].

Lamb Camp [MONO]: *locality,* 5.5 miles south-southeast of White Mountain Peak (lat. 37°33'20" N, long. 118°13'45" W). Named on Mount Barcroft (1962) 15' quadrangle.

La Motte Spring [INYO]: *spring,* 9.5 miles north of Argus Peak (lat. 35°59'05" N, long. 117°28'45" W; near NE cor. sec. 31, T 22 S, R 42 E). Named on Trona (1949) 15' quadrangle. On Searles Lake (1915) 1° quadrangle, the name has the form "Lamotte Spr."

Lane Hill: see **Darwin** [INYO].

Lane Lake [MONO]: *lake,* 950 feet long, nearly 6 miles east-southeast of Sonora Pass (lat. 38°17'35" N, long. 119°32'25" W; sec. 10, T 5 N, R 22 E). Named on Pickel Meadow (1954) 7.5' quadrangle.

Langley: see **Mount Langley** [INYO]; **Mount Langley**, under **Mount Corcoran** [INYO].

Larkin Lake [MONO]: *dry lake,* 3500 feet long, 8 miles east of Bodie at the northeast end of Trench Canyon (lat. 38°12' N, long. 118°51'50" W; around SW cor. sec. 14, T 4 N, R 28 E). Named on Trench Canyon (1958) 15' quadrangle.

Larson Canyon [ALPINE]: *canyon,* drained by a stream that flows 2 miles to Carson Valley 2.25 miles north-northeast of Woodfords (lat. 38°48'20" N, long. 119°48'25" W; sec. 23, T 11 N, R 19 E). Named on Woodfords (1979) 7.5' quadrangle.

Last Chance Canyon [INYO]: *canyon,* 5.5 miles long, opens into the north end of Death Valley 4.5 miles east of Last Chance Mountain (lat. 37°31' N, long. 117°37' W). Named on Magruder Mountain (1957) 15' quadrangle.

Last Chance Gulch [MONO]: *canyon,* drained by a stream that flows 1 mile to Benton Valley 2.5 miles south of Benton (lat. 37° 46'50" N, long. 118°28'10" W; sec. 17, T 2 S, R 32 E). Named on Benton (1962) 15' quadrangle.

Last Chance Meadow [INYO]: *area,* 14 miles northwest of Olancha (lat. 36°27'15" N, long. 118°08'50" W; near NE cor. sec. 14, T 17 S, R 35 E). Named on Olancha (1956) 15' quadrangle.

Last Chance Mountain [INYO]: *peak,* 17 miles east-southeast of Deep Springs (lat. 37°16'50" N, long. 117°41'55" W; sec. 4, T 8 S, R 39 E); the peak is in Last Chance Range. Altitude 8456 feet. Named on Magruder Mountain (1957) 15' quadrangle.

Last Chance Range [INYO]: *range,* northeast of Eureka Valley and southwest of the north end of Death Valley. Named on Last Chance Range (1958), Magruder Mountain (1957), and Soldier Pass (1958) 15' quadrangles. The name is from Last Chance Spring (Palmer, p. 42).

Last Chance Spring [INYO]: *spring,* 2 miles east of Last Chance Mountain (lat. 37°16'50" N, long. 117°39'45" W; sec. 2, T 8 S, R 39 E). Named on Magruder Mountain (1957) 15' quadrangle. Lieutenant D.A. Lyle and his party were near death when they reached the spring and named it in 1871 (Hanna, p. 168-169).

Latimer: see **The Racetrack** [INYO].

Latopie Lake [MONO]: *lake,* 825 feet long, 2.5 miles south of Sonora Pass (lat. 38°17'20" N, long. 119°38'10" W). Named on Sonora Pass (1979) 7.5' quadrangle.

Laurel Creek [MONO]: *stream,* flows 5.5 miles to lowlands along Hot Creek (2) 5 miles north-northwest of Mount Morrison (lat. 37° 37'25" N, long. 118°54'15" W; near S line sec. 5, T 4 S, R 28 E). Named on Mount Morrison (1953) 15' quadrangle.

Laurel Lakes [MONO]: *lakes,* two, largest 1000 feet long, 3.25 miles west-northwest of Mount Morrison (lat. 37°34'40" N, long. 118°54'45" W; sec. 29, T 4 S, R 28 E); the lakes are along Laurel Creek. Named on Mount Morrison (1953) 15' quadrangle.

Laurel Mountain [MONO]: *peak,* 2.25 miles northwest of Mount Morrison (lat. 37°34'50" N, long. 118°53'25" W; near S line sec. 21, T 4 S. R 28 E); the peak is east of Laurel Creek and Laurel Lakes. Altitude 11,812 feet. Named on Mount Morrison (1953) 15' quadrangle.

Lava Springs [MONO]: *spring,* nearly 4 miles north of Fales Hot Springs (lat. 38°24'20" N, long. 119°23'35" W; near E line sec. 36, T 7 N, R 23 E). Named on Chris Flat (1954) 7.5' quadrangle.

Laws [INYO]: *village,* nearly 4 miles northeast of Bishop (lat. 37°24'05" N, long. 118°20'45" W; sec. 27, T 6 S, R 33 E). Named on Bishop (1949) 15' quadrangle. The first depot on Carson and Colorado Railroad, called Station, was at the site in 1883; the depot later was named Laws for R.J. Laws, assistant superintendent of the railroad (Hawkins, p. 4-5). The place is called Bishop Depot on Inyo County (1883) map, and it also was called Bishop Station (Hanna, p. 169). Postal authorities established Laws post office in 1887 and discontinued it in 1963 (Salley, p. 120). A mining camp called Owensville sprang up near the future site of Laws in 1863 (Chalfant, 1933, p. 209), and had vanished by 1871 (Hoover, Rensch, and Rensch, p. 117). Goodyear (p. 238) placed the site of Owensville about 200 yards west of Bishop Station (present Laws). Postal authorities established Owensville post office in 1866, changed the name to Glen Mary in 1868, and changed it back to Owensville in 1869; they moved the post office to Bishop Creek (present Bishop) in 1870 (Frickstad, p. 50, 105).

Lead Canyon [INYO]: *canyon,* 7 miles long, opens into lowlands 5.25 miles north-northwest of the mouth of Paiute Canyon (lat. 36° 55'15" N, long. 117°56'50" W). Named on Independence (1951) and Waucoba Wash (1951) 15' quadrangles.

Leadfield [INYO]: *locality,* 6.5 miles east-northeast of the mouth of Titus Canyon in a branch of that canyon (lat. 36°50'50" N, long. 117°03'30" W). Site named on Grapevine Peak (1957) 15' quadrangle. C.C. Julian coined the name and applied it to a mining camp that was part of his promotion of a low-grade lead deposit in 1925 and 1926 (Hanna, p. 169). Postal authorities established Leadfield post office in 1926 and discontinued it the same year (Frickstad, p. 52).

Lead Gulch [INYO]: *canyon,* drained by a stream that flows 1 mile to Mazourka Canyon 7 miles east-northeast of Independence (lat. 36°50'50" N, long. 118°05' W; sec. 5, T 13 S, R 36 E). Named on Independence (1951) 15' quadrangle.

Leavitt Creek [MONO]: *stream,* flows 5.5 miles to West Walker River 5 miles east of Sonora Pass (lat. 38°19'10" N, long. 119°32'55" W; sec. 34, T 6 N, R 22 E); the stream heads at Leavitt Lake and ends in Leavitt Meadow. Named on Pickel Meadow (1954) 7.5' quadrangle. Called Leavitts Creek on Wheeler's (1876-1877) map.

Leavitt Falls [MONO]: *waterfall,* 4 miles east of Sonora Pass on Leavitt Creek (lat. 38°19'10" N, long. 119°33'40" W; sec. 33, T 6 N, R 22 E). Named on Pickel Meadow (1954) 7.5' quadrangle.

Leavitt Lake [MONO]: *lake,* 2050 feet long, 4 miles south-southeast of Sonora Pass (lat. 38°16'25" N, long. 119°37'05" W; sec. 13, 24, T 5 N, R 21 E); the lake is at the head of Leavitt Creek. Named on Pickel Meadow (1954) 7.5' quadrangle.

Leavitt Meadow [MONO]: *valley,* 5 miles east of Sonora Pass along West Walker River (lat. 38°19' N, long. 119°33' W). Named on Pickel Meadow (1954) 7.5' quadrangle. The place was called Indian Valley before Hiram L. Leavitt settled there about 1865 (Wedertz, p. 88- 89).

Leavitt Peak [MONO]: *peak,* 3 miles south-southwest of Sonora Pass on Mono-Tuolumne County line (lat. 38°17'10" N, long. 119° 39' W). Altitude 11,569 feet. Named on Sonora Pass (1979) 7.5' quadrangle. Called Leavitts Pk. on Wheeler's (1876-1877) map.

Leavitt's: see **Leavitt Station** [MONO].

Leavitt Station [MONO]: *locality,* nearly 5 miles east of Sonora Pass along West Walker River (lat. 38°19'40" N, long. 119°33'05" W; sec. 34, T 6 N, R 22 E); the place is in Leavitt Meadow. Site named on Pickel Meadow (1954) 7.5' quadrangle. Called Leavitt's on Wheeler's (1876-1877) map. Hiram L. Leavitt settled at the site about 1865 and kept a stage station there (Wedertz, p. 88- 89).

LeConte: see **Mount LeConte** [INYO]; **Mount LeConte**, under **Funeral Peak** [INYO].

Ledge Lake [INYO]: *lake,* 350 feet long, 7 miles east-southeast of Mount Darwin (lat. 37°07'45" N, long. 118°33'15" W; sec. 35, T 9 S, R 31 E). Named on Mount Goddard (1948) 15' quadrangle.

Lee: see **Lees Camp** [INYO].

Lee Flat [INYO]: *valley,* 13 miles south-southwest of Ubehebe Peak (lat. 36°30'30" N, long. 117°39' W); the valley is along upper reaches of Lee Wash. Named on Darwin (1950) and Ubehebe Peak (1950) 15' quadrangles.

Lee Pump [INYO]: *springs,* two, about 10 miles south-southeast of Ubehebe Peak in Jackass Canyon (1) (lat. 36°32'20" N, long. 117° 32'45" W). Named on Ubehebe Peak (1950) 15' quadrangle. According to Palmer (p. 11), this probably is the place that members of the Wheeler survey called Bird Spring in 1871.

Lees Camp [INYO]: *locality,* 15 miles east of Beatty Junction near California-Nevada State line (lat. 36°34'45" N, long. 116°40' W). Named on Big Dune (1952) 15' quadrangle. Called Lee's Camp on Furnace Creek (1910) 1° quadrangle. The place appears to be the mining camp that Murbarger (p. 276) called Lee, for Dick Lee, who discovered a ledge of gold there. Postal authorities established Lee post office in 1907 and discontinued it in 1912 (Frickstad, p. 52).

Lee's Well [INYO]: *well,* 15 miles north-northwest of present Death Valley Junction in Amargosa Desert (lat. 36°28'25" N, long. 116° 33'20" W).

Named on Furnace Creek (1910) 1° quadrangle.

Lee Vining [MONO]: *village,* 21 miles south-southeast of Bridgeport near Mono Lake (lat. 37°57'25" N, long. 119°07'10" W; sec. 9, T 1 N, R 26 E); the place is along Lee Vining Creek. Named on Mono Craters (1953) 15' quadrangle. The name commemorates LeRoy Vining, a miner who came to the neighborhood in 1853 (Cain, 1961, p. 2). Local farmers called the site Poverty Flat in the early days because of hard-pan and fierce winds there; Chris Mattly had the community surveyed and sold the first lots in 1926 (La Braque, p. 20, 26). The settlement at the site first was called Lakeview (Smith, Genny, p. 30). Postal authorities established Leevining post office in 1928 and changed the name to Lee Vining in 1953 (Salley, p. 120). United States Board on Geographic Names (1957, p. 2) rejected the form "Leevining" for the name.

Leevining Canyon: see **Lee Vining Creek** [MONO].

Lee Vining Creek [MONO]: *stream,* flows 17 miles to Mono Lake 1.5 miles north-northeast of Lee Vining (lat. 37°58'35" N, long. 119°06'15" W; near E line sec. 4, T 1 N, R 25 E) Named on Mono Craters (1953) and Tuolumne Meadows (1956) 15' quadrangles. Called Leevining Creek on Mount Lyell (1901) 30' quadrangle. Water now is diverted from the stream to the aqueduct that takes Mono County water to Los Angeles. The name commemorates Leroy Vining, who prospected for gold and settled along the stream in 1853 (Hanna, p. 170). United States Board on Geographic Names (1957, p. 2) rejected the names "Leevining Creek," "Levining Creek," and "Vining Creek" for the feature. A.W. von Schmidt called the stream Rescue Creek when he surveyed in the region in 1855 (Fletcher, p. 27). Warren Fork enters 9 miles upstream from the mouth of the main stream; it is 3 miles long and is named on Mono Craters (1953) 15' quadrangle. The canyon of Lee Vining Creek has been called Vining's Gulch (Bunnell, p. 173), Lee-Vining Cañon (Irelan, p. 367), Leevining Cañon (Russell, p. 275), and Levining Creek Cañon (Eakel and McLaughlin, p. 167). United States Board on Geographic Names (1957, p. 2) rejected the names "Leevining Canyon," "Levining Canyon," and "Vining Canyon" for the feature.

Lee Vining Peak [MONO]: *peak,* 4.5 miles west-northwest of Lee Vining (lat. 37°58'20" N, long. 119°11'50" W). Altitude 11,691 feet. Named on Mono Craters (1953) 15' quadrangle. Called Leevining Pk. on Mount Lyell (1901) 30' quadrangle. United States Board on Geographic Names (1957, p. 2) rejected the names "Leevining Peak," "Levining Peak," and "Vining Peak" for the feature.

Lee Wash [INYO]: *stream,* flows 18 miles to Panamint Valley 7.5 miles west of Panamint Butte (lat. 36°25'50" N, long. 117°29'20" W); the stream goes through Lee Flat. Named on Darwin (1950) and Panamint Butte (1951) 15' quadrangles.

Left Fork Wet Fork: see **Sawmill Canyon** [MONO] (2).

Left Fork Wet Fork Creek: see **Sawmill Canyon** [MONO] (2).

Leidy Creek [MONO]: *stream,* flows 5.5 miles to the State of Nevada 7.25 miles northeast of White Mountain Peak (lat. 37°43'15" N, long. 118°11' W). Named on Mount Barcroft (1962) and White Mountain Peak (1962) 15' quadrangles. The name commemorates George Leidy, who settled in Fish Lake Valley in 1882 (Gudde, 1949, p. 186).

Lemoigne Canyon [INYO]: *canyon,* 6 miles long, opens into Death Valley nearly 10 miles south of the mouth of Marble Canyon (3) (lat. 36°30'10" N, long. 117°16'15" W). Named on Marble Canyon (1951) and Panamint Butte (1951) 15' quadrangles. The name commemorates Jean Lemoigne, a prospector who owned a mine in the canyon (Palmer, p. 43). South Fork branches southwest 1.5 miles from the mouth of the main canyon; it is 3.5 miles long and is named on Panamint Butte (1951) 15' quadrangle.

Lemonade Spring [INYO]: *spring,* 3 miles southwest of Ryan in Black Mountains (lat. 36°17'40" N, long. 116°42'30" W). Named on Ryan (1952) 15' quadrangle. According to Palmer (p. 44), the name apparently is from the color of the water.

Leviathan Canyon [ALPINE]: *canyon,* about 12 miles long, along Leviathan Creek and Bryant Creek (1). Named on Heenan Lake (1979) 7.5' quadrangle, which shows Leviathan mine near the head of the canyon. The north end of the feature is in the State of Nevada

Leviathan Creek [ALPINE]: *stream,* flows 5.5 miles to join Mountaineer Creek and form Bryant Creek (1) 5 miles northeast of Mogul Peak (lat. 38°44'10" N, long. 119°38'40" W; near N line sec. 11, T 10 N, R 21 E); the stream drains the upper part of Leviathan Canyon. Named on Heenan Lake (1979) 7.5' quadrangle.

Leviathan Peak [ALPINE]: *peak,* 6 miles east of Mogul Peak (lat. 38°41' N, long. 119°36'40" W; sec. 30, T 10 N, R 22 E); the peak is 3 miles southeast of Leviathan mine. Altitude 8963 feet. Named on Topaz Lake (1956) 15' quadrangle.

Levining Canyon: see **Lee Vining Creek** [MONO].

Levining Creek: see **Lee Vining Creek** [MONO].

Levining Creek Cañon: see **Lee Vining Creek** [MONO].

Levining Peak: see **Lee Vining Peak** [MONO].

Lewis: see **Mount Lewis** [MONO].

Lexington Canyon [ALPINE]: *canyon,* 1.25 miles long, opens into the canyon of Monitor Creek 2 miles southeast of Mogul Peak (lat. 38°39'55" N, long. 119°41'25" W; sec. 32, T 10 N, R 21 E). Named on Heenan Lake (1979) 7.5' quadrangle.

Liahona Camp [ALPINE]: *locality,* 3.5 miles east of Dardanelles Cone (lat. 38°24'10" N, long. 119°48'10" W). Named on Dardanelles Cone (1956) 15' quadrangle.

Lightning Mountain [ALPINE]: *ridge,* north-northwest-trending, 1.5 miles long, 6 miles east-northeast of Dardanelles Cone (lat. 38°26'30" N, long. 119°46'30" W). Named on Dardanelles Cone (1979) 7.5' quadrangle.

Lila C: see **Ryan** [INYO] (1).

Lilly Pad Lake [ALPINE]: *lake,* 500 feet long, 6.25 miles north-northeast of Pacific Grade Summit (lat. 38°36'20" N, long. 119°53'10" W; sec. 28, T 9 N, R 19 E). Named on Pacific Valley (1979) 7.5' quadrangle.

Lime Canyon [INYO]: *canyon,* drained by a stream that flows 2 miles to lowlands 5.25 miles west-southwest of Independence (lat. 36°46'50" N, long. 118°17'15" W; sec. 28, T 13 S, R 34 E). Named on Mount Pinchot (1953) 15' quadrangle.

Lime Hill [INYO]: *peak,* 15 miles north of Waucoba Mountain (lat. 37°14'40" N, long. 117°57'45" W; sec. 19, T 8 S, R 37 E). Named on Waucoba Spring (1958) 15' quadrangle.

Limekiln Spring [INYO]: *spring,* 5.25 miles southwest of Telescope Peak in Surprise Canyon (lat. 36°06'50" N, long. 117°09' W). Named on Telescope Peak (1952) 15' quadrangle.

Lime Kiln Station: see **Kirkwood Spring** [MONO].

Linnie [INYO]: *locality,* 7.5 miles south-southeast of the village of Little Lake along Southern Pacific Railroad (lat. 35°50' N, long. 117°52' W; near W line sec. 22, T 24 S, R 38 E). Named on Little Lake (1954) 15' quadrangle. Wheeler's (1877) map shows a place called 9 Mile Station located opposite the mouth of present Ninemile Canyon near present Linnie.

Little Alkali Lake [MONO]: *lake,* 2100 feet long, 8 miles north-northeast of Mount Morrison (lat. 37°40' N, long. 118°47'30" W; on N line sec. 29, T 3 S, R 29 E); the feature is 1 mile south-southwest of Big Alkali Lake. Named on Mount Morrison (1953) 15' quadrangle.

Little Antelope Peak: see **Antelope Peak** [ALPINE].

Little Antelope Valley [MONO]:

(1) *valley,* 2.5 miles south of Coleville (lat. 38°31'45" N, long. 119° 30'30" W); the feature is southwest of Antelope Valley. Named on Desert Creek Peak (1956) and Topaz Lake (1956) 15' quadrangles. The stream in the valley is called Roderique Creek (Eakel and McLaughlin, p. 138).

(2) *valley,* 8.5 miles north of Mount Morrison (lat. 37°40'50" N, long. 118°52'30" W). Named on Mount Morrison (1953) 15' quadrangle. Mount Morrison (1914) 30' quadrangle shows Antelope Spring in the valley.

Little Blackrock Spring [INYO]: *spring,* 9.5 miles north-northwest of Independence (lat. 36°56'20" N, long. 118°14' W; near W line sec. 2, T 12 S, R 34 E); the spring is less than 1 mile north of Blackrock Springs. Named on Independence (1951) 15' quadrangle.

Little Cactus Flat: see **Cactus Flat** [INYO].

Little Cottonwood Canyon [ALPINE]: *canyon,* drained by a stream that flows nearly 3 miles to Cottonwood Canyon 4 miles north of Mogul Peak (lat. 38°44'40" N, long. 119°42'30" W; sec. 6, T 10 N, R 21 E). Named on Heenan Lake (1979) 7.5' quadrangle.

Little Cottonwood Creek [INYO]: *stream,* flows 3.5 miles to Cottonwood Creek (2) 14 miles north-northwest of Olancha (lat. 36°27'45" N, long. 118°06'45" W). Named on Olancha (1956) 15' quadrangle.

Little Cowhorn Valley [INYO]: *valley,* 15 miles east of Big Pine (lat. 37°09'40" N, long. 118°02' W); the valley is 1.5 miles northwest of Cowhorn Valley. Named on Waucoba Mountain (1951) 15' quadrangle.

Little Deep Creek [MONO]: *stream,* flows nearly 3 miles to Deep Creek 7 miles north of Fales Hot Springs (lat. 38°27'05" N, long. 119°24'55" W; sec. 14, T 7 N, R 23 E). Named on Fales Hot Springs (1956) 15' quadrangle.

Little Dodd Spring [INYO]: *spring,* 8 miles south of Ubehebe Peak (lat. 36°34'50" N, long. 117°34'10" W); the spring is less than 0.5 mile south-southeast of Big Dodd Spring. Named on Ubehebe Peak (1950) 15' quadrangle. Palmer (p. 44) called the feature Little Dodds Spring.

Little Fryingpan Canyon [MONO]: *canyon,* drained by a stream that flows 2.5 miles to Fryingpan Creek 11 miles north-northeast of Bridgeport (lat. 38°24'35" N, long. 119°10'55" W; sec. 34, T 7 N, R 25 E). Named on Bridgeport (1958) 15' quadrangle.

Little Grapevine Creek [INYO]: *stream,* flows 3 miles to Death Valley Wash 3 miles east-southeast of Ubehebe Crater (lat. 37° 00' N, long. 117°24' W; near W line sec. 15, T 11 S, R 42 E); the stream heads at Grapevine Springs. Named on Ubehebe Crater (1957) 15' quadrangle.

Little Hebe Crater [INYO]: *crater,* 0.25 mile south of Ubehebe Crater (lat. 37°00'20" N, long. 117°27' W; sec. 18, T 11 S, R 42 E). Named on Ubehebe Crater (1957) 15' quadrangle.

Little Hot Creek [MONO]: *stream,* flows 5.5 miles to Hot Creek (2) 9 miles north-northeast of Mount Morrison (lat. 37°41'15" N, long. 118°48'40" W; sec. 18, T 3 S, R 29 E). Named on Mount Morrison (1953) 15' quadrangle, which shows a hot spring along the stream.

Little Indian Valley [ALPINE]: *valley,* 5.5 miles north-northeast of Pacific

Grade Summit (lat. 38°35'45" N, long. 119°53'10" W; near SE cor. sec. 28, T 9 N, R 19 E); the valley is 1 mile west-northwest of Indian Valley. Named on Pacific Valley (1979) 7.5' quadrangle.

Little Lake [INYO]:

(1) *lake,* 1 mile long, 0.5 mile north of the village of Little Lake (lat. 35°56'50" N, long. 117°54'05" W; sec. 8, T 23 S, R 38 E). Named on Little Lake (1954) 15' quadrangle. Loew (1876b, p. 194) called the feature Little Owens Lake, and Chalfant (1933, p. 286) noted that it was called Lagunita. Postal authorities established Lagunita post office near the lake in 1873 and discontinued it in 1876 (Salley, p. 114).

(2) *village,* 38 miles south of Keeler at the south end of Rose Valley (lat. 35°56'15" N, long. 117°54'25" W); the place is 0.5 mile south of Little Lake (1). Named on Little Lake (1954) 15' quadrangle. California Mining Bureau's (1917b) map shows a place called Narka located 3 or 4 miles south of the village of Little Lake along Southern Pacific Railroad. Narka was a railroad camp before the village of Little Lake developed (Iroquois Research Institute, p. 110). Postal authorities established both Little Lake post office and Narka post office in 1909; they discontinued Little Lake post office in 1911, when they moved the service to Narka, and reestablished it in 1913, when they moved Narka post office 5 miles north and changed the name to Little Lake (Salley, p. 123, 150). California Mining Bureau's (1917b) map also shows a place called Sodan located along the railroad halfway between Narka and the village of Little Lake. California Division of Highways' (1934) map shows a place called Skyes located 6.5 miles north-northwest of the village of Little Lake along Southern Pacific Railroad.

Little Lake Canyon [INYO]: *canyon,* drained by a stream that flows 5.5 miles to Rose Valley 1.5 miles west-northwest of the village of Little Lake (lat. 35°56'50" N, long. 117°55'50" W; sec. 12, T 23 S, R 37 E). Named on Lamont Peak (1956) and Little Lake (1954) 15' quadrangles.

Little Lakes Valley [INYO]: *valley,* 3 miles northeast of Mount Abbot on upper reaches of Rock Creek (lat. 37°25' N, long. 118° 45' W). Named on Mount Abbot (1953) and Mount Tom (1949) 15' quadrangles. The name is from forty lakes located in the valley (Gudde, 1949, p. 189).

Little Long Valley [MONO]: *valley,* 2 miles southeast of Fales Hot Springs (lat. 38°19'45" N, long. 119°22'30" W; around NE cor. sec. 31, T 6 N, R 24 E); the valley is 2 miles northeast of Long Valley (1). Named on Fales Hot Springs (1956) 15' quadrangle.

Little Lost Canyon [MONO]: *canyon,* drained by a stream that flows 1.5 miles to Little Antelope Valley 4.25 miles south of Coleville (lat. 38°30'20" N, long. 119°30'10" W; sec. 25, T 8 N, R 22 E). Named on Lost Cannon Peak (1954) 7.5' quadrangle.

Little McGee Lake [MONO]: *lake,* 950 feet long, 4.5 miles south of Mount Morrison (lat. 37°29'35" N, long. 118°51' W); the lake is less than 0.5 mile west-northwest of Big McGee Lake. Named on Mount Abbot (1953) 15' quadrangle.

Little Meysan Lake [INYO]: *lake,* 350 feet long, 10 miles west-southwest of Lone Pine (lat. 36°34' N, long. 118°14' W); the lake is 1 mile northeast of Meysan Lake. Named on Lone Pine (1958) 15' quadrangle.

Little Mormon Meadow [MONO]: *area,* 9 miles south-southeast of Bridgeport (lat. 38°08' N, long. 119°09'30" W; near E line sec. 12, T 3 N, R 25 E); the place is 2.5 miles southwest of Mormon Meadow. Named on Bodie (1958) 15' quadrangle.

Little Onion Valley [INYO]: *valley,* 7 miles west of Independence along South Fork Oak Creek (lat. 36°48'45" N, long. 118°19'15" W); the feature is 3 miles north of Onion Valley. Named on Mount Pinchot (1953) 15' quadrangle.

Little Owens Lake: see **Little Lake** [INYO] (1).

Little Petroglyph Canyon: see **Renegade Canyon** [INYO].

Little Pine: see **Independence** [INYO].

Little Pine Creek [INYO]: *stream,* flows 7.5 miles to Big Pine Creek 2 miles southwest of Big Pine (lat. 37°08'30" N, long. 118°19'05" W; sec. 25, T 9 S, R 33 E). Named on Big Pine (1950) 15' quadrangle.

Little Pine Creek: see **Independence Creek** [INYO].

Little Pothole Lake [INYO]: *lake,* 350 feet long, 9 miles west-southwest of Independence (lat. 36°46'10" N, long. 118°21' W); the lake is 1.25 miles east of Big Pothole Lake. Named on Mount Pinchot (1953) 15' quadrangle.

Little Round Valley [MONO]: *valley,* 1.5 miles west of Toms Place (lat. 37°33'40" N, long. 118°42'30" W; in and near sec. 31, T 4 S, R 30 E). Named on Casa Diablo Mountain (1953) 15' quadrangle.

Little Sand Flat [MONO]: *area,* 4.5 miles south-southeast of the site of Mono Mills (lat. 37°49'30" N, long. 118°56'30" W); the place is 4.5 miles southwest of Big Sand Flat. Named on Cowtrack Mountain (1962) 15' quadrangle.

Little Sand Spring [INYO]: *spring,* 12.5 miles north-northwest of Ubehebe Crater in Death Valley (lat. 37°10'25" N, long. 117°32'20" W; sec. 17, T 9 S, R 41 E); the spring is 1.25 miles south-southeast of Sand Spring. Named on Last Chance Range (1958) 15' quadrangle.

Little Seeley Spring [INYO]: *spring,* 11 miles south-southeast of Big Pine near Owens River (lat. 37°01' N, long. 118°13'25" W; sec. 2, T 11 S, R 34 E); the spring is 0.25 mile south-southeast of Big Seeley Spring. Named on Waucoba Mountain (1951) 15' quadrangle. Waring (p. 321) called the feature Seelys Spring.

Little Slide Canyon [MONO]: *canyon,* drained by a stream that flows 2.25 miles to Robinson Creek 4 miles north-northwest of Matterhorn Peak (lat. 38°08'35" N, long. 119°25'10" W); the canyon heads across the crest of Sierra Nevada from the head of Slide Canyon in Tuolumne County. Named on Matterhorn Peak (1956) 15' quadrangle.

Little Teton Creek [ALPINE]: *stream,* flows about 2 miles to Clark Fork 3 miles southeast of Dardanelles Cone in Tuolumne County (lat. 38°22'50" N, long. 119°49'45" W). Named on Dardanelles Cone (1979) 7.5' quadrangle.

Little Walker Cow Camp [MONO]: *locality,* nearly 3 miles west-southwest of Fales Hot Springs (lat. 38°20'05" N, long. 119°26'50" W; near E line sec. 28, T 6 N, R 23 E); the place is along Little Walker River. Named on Fales Hot Springs (1954) 7.5' quadrangle.

Little Walker River [MONO]: *stream,* flows 15 miles to West Walker River 3.5 miles northwest of Fales Hot Springs (lat. 38°22'45" N, long. 119°27' W; sec. 9, T 6 N, R 23 E). Named on Fales Hot Springs (1956) and Matterhorn Peak (1956) 15' quadrangles.

Little Wolf Creek [MONO]: *stream,* flows 3.25 miles to West Walker River 5.5 miles east of Sonora Pass (lat. 38°20'25" N, long. 119°32'35" W; sec. 27, T 6 N, R 22 E); the stream joins West Walker River less than 1 mile upstream from the mouth of Wolf Creek. Named on Pickel Meadow (1954) 7.5' quadrangle.

Llewellyn Falls [ALPINE]: *waterfall,* 7 miles east of Disaster Peak along Silver King Creek (lat. 38°27'35" N, long. 119°36'15" W; near S line sec. 7, T 7 N, R 22 E). Named on Lost Cannon Peak (1954) 7.5' quadrangle.

Lobdell Lake [MONO]: *lake,* 1700 feet long, 6.5 miles north-northeast of Fales Hot Springs (lat. 38°26'36" N, long. 119°21'45" W; sec. 20, T 7 N, R 24 E). Named on Fales Hot Springs (1956) 15' quadrangle. The lake is in an area called Swamp Meadows on Bridgeport (1909) 30' quadrangle. The name "Lobdell" commemorates J.B. Lobdell, who supposedly hid out in the neighborhood of the lake to escape military service in the 1860's (Gudde, 1949, p. 190).

Loch Leven [INYO]: *lake,* 1500 feet long, 4.25 miles north-northeast of Mount Darwin along North Fork Bishop Creek (lat. 37°13'55" N, long. 118°39'15" W). Named on Mount Goddard (1948) 15' quadrangle.

Loco [INYO]; *locality,* 11.5 miles north of Coso Junction along Southern Pacific Railroad (lat. 36°12'35" N, long. 117°58'15" W; sec. 9, T 20 S, R 37 E). Named on Haiwee Reservoir (1951) 15' quadrangle. Called Loco Siding on Ballarat (1913) 1° quadrangle. The name "Loco" probably was of local Indian origin and was applied to the place when California-Nevada Railroad was built in 1910 (Gudde, 1949, p. 191).

Loco Creek [INYO]: *stream,* flows 2.25 miles to Summit Creek 5 miles south-southwest of Olancha (lat. 36°12'50" N, long. 118°01'40" W). Named on Monache Mountain (1956) 15' quadrangle.

Locomotive Point [MONO]: *relief feature,* 4.5 miles east-northeast of Bridgeport (lat. 38°17'10" N, long. 119°09'05" W; at S line sec. 18, T 5 N, R 26 E). Named on Bridgeport (1958) 15' quadrangle.

Loco Siding: see **Loco** [INYO].

Lof: see **Hans Lof's**, under **Toms Place** [MONO].

Logan Spring [MONO]: *spring,* 6.5 miles northeast of Bridgeport (lat. 38°18'50" N, long. 119°08'05" W; sec. 8, T 5 N, R 26 E). Named on Bridgeport (1958) 15' quadrangle.

Log Cabin Creek [MONO]: *stream,* flows 2.5 miles to Bridgeport Valley nearly 4 miles west of Bridgeport (lat. 38°15'30" N, long. 119°17'50" W; sec. 26, T 5 N, R 24 E). Named on Fales Hot Springs (1956) 15' quadrangle.

Logging Flat [INYO]: *area,* 8.5 miles west-southwest of Big Pine (lat. 37°08'15" N, long. 118°26'30" W; sec. 26, T 9 S, R 32 E). Named on Big Pine (1950) 15' quadrangle.

Lone Pine [INYO]: *town,* 16 miles south-southeast of Independence (lat. 36°36'20" N, long. 118°03'40" W; in and near sec. 28, T 15 S, R 36 E). Named on Lone Pine (1958) 15' quadrangle. Olmsted's (1900) map shows Lone Pine P.O. at the place, and shows Lone Pine Sta. farther northeast along Carson and Colorado Railroad at present Mount Whitney (2). Postal authorities established Lone Pine post office in 1870 (Frickstad, p. 52). The first cabin at the site was built in the winter of 1861 and 1862, and a settlement there was reported two years later; the name is from a large pine tree that stood near Lone Pine Creek and Tuttle Creek (Hoover, Rensch, and Rensch, p. 118).

Lone Pine Creek [INYO]: *stream,* flows 5.5 miles to lowlands 8 miles west of Lone Pine (lat. 36°35'45" N, long. 118°12' W; near SE cor. sec. 30, T 15 S, R 35 E). Named on Lone Pine (1958) and Mount Whitney (1956) 15' quadrangles. The stream now discharges into the aqueduct that takes Owens Valley water to Los Angeles. North Fork enters 2.5 miles upstream from the entrance of the creek into the lowlands; it is 3 miles long, and is named on Lone Pine (1958) and Mount Whitney (1956) 15' quadrangles.

Lone Pine Hills: see **Alabama Hills** [INYO].

Lone Pine Lake [INYO]: *lake,* 450 feet long, 10.5 miles west of Lone Pine (lat. 36°34'35" N, long. 118°14'45" W); the lake is at the head of a branch of Lone Pine Creek. Named on Lone Pine (1958) 15' quadrangle.

Lone Pine Peak [INYO]: *peak,* 9.5 miles west-southwest of Lone Pine (lat. 36°33'40" N, long. 118°13'30" W). Altitude 12,944 feet. Named on Lone Pine (1958) 15' quadrangle.

Lone Pine Station [INYO]: *locality,* 1.5 miles northeast of Lone Pine along Southern Pacific Railroad (lat. 36°37'10" N, long. 118°02'25" W; sec. 22, T 15 S, R 36 E). Named on Lone Pine (1958) 15' quadrangle.

Lone Pine Station: see **Mount Whitney** [INYO] (2).

Lone Star Hill: see **Snow Canyon** [INYO].

Lone Tree Creek [MONO]: *stream,* flows 7.5 miles before ending in Hamil Valley 7.5 miles west of White Mountain Peak (lat. 37° 38' N, long. 118°23'30" W; sec. 1, T 4 S, R 32 E). Named on White Mountain Peak (1962) 15' quadrangle.

Long Canyon [MONO]: *canyon,* drained by a stream that flows 4 miles to West Walker River 7 miles north of Tower Peak (lat. 38° 14'35" N, long. 119°32'40" W). Named on Tower Peak (1956) 15' quadrangle.

Long Canyon: see **Aurora Canyon** [MONO].

Long John Canyon [INYO]: *canyon,* 4.5 miles long, opens into lowlands 3.5 miles west of New York Butte (lat. 36°38'20" N, long. 117°59'30" W). Named on New York Butte (1950) 15' quadrangle.

Long Lake [INYO]:

(1) *lake,* 1900 feet long, 2 miles northeast of Mount Abbot in Little Lakes Valley (lat. 37°24'25" N, long. 118°45'30" W). Named on Mount Abbot (1953) 15' quadrangle.

(2) *lake,* 3400 feet long, 6.5 miles east-southeast of Mount Darwin (lat. 37°08'40" N, long. 118°33'20" W; on N line sec. 26, T 9 S, R 31 E). Named on Mount Goddard (1948) 15' quadrangle.

(3) *lake,* 1100 feet long, 19 miles northwest of Olancha (lat. 36°29'15" N, long. 118°13'30" W). Named on Olancha (1956) 15' quadrangle.

Long Lake: see **Lower Long Lake** [MONO]; **Upper Long Lake** [MONO].

Longley Lake: see **McGee Lake** [INYO].

Longley Meadow [INYO]: *area,* 5.5 miles east of Mount Tom (lat. 37°20'10" N, long. 118°33'15" W; sec. 15, T 7 S, R 31 E). Named on Mount Tom (1949) 15' quadrangle.

Longley Reservoir: see **McGee Lake** [INYO].

Longs Well [INYO]: *well,* 5.25 miles east-northeast of Coso Peak (lat. 36°14'40" N, long. 117°38'05" W; near NW cor. sec. 34, T 19 S, R 40 E). Named on Coso Peak (1951) 15' quadrangle.

Long Valley [ALPINE]: *valley,* 7.5 miles east-northeast of Disaster Peak along Silver King Creek (lat. 38°29' N, long. 119°36'15" W; sec. 6, T 7 N, R 22 E). Named on Lost Cannon Peak (1954) 7.5' quadrangle.

Long Valley [MONO]:

(1) *valley,* 3 miles south of Fales Hot Springs (lat. 38°18'20" N, long. 119°23'50" W). Named on Fales Hot Springs (1954) 7.5' quadrangle.

(2) *valley,* along Owens River above Owens River Gorge; center 9 miles north-northeast of Mount Morrison (lat. 37°40' N, long. 118°46' W). Named on Casa Diablo Mountain (1953) and Mount Morrison (1953) 15' quadrangles. Water of Lake Crowley covers part of the valley.

Long Valley: see **Little Long Valley** [MONO]; **Wingate Wash** [INYO].

Long Valley Creek [MONO]: *stream,* flows 7 miles to Swauger Creek 6 miles southeast of Fales Hot Springs in Huntoon Valley (lat. 38°18'15" N, long. 119°18'30" W; sec. 10, T 5 N, R 24 E); the stream heads at Long Valley Ponds and goes through Long Valley (1). Named on Fales Hot Springs (1956) 15' quadrangle.

Long Valley Ponds [MONO]: *lakes,* two, largest 750 feet long, 3.5 miles south-southwest of Fales Hot Springs (lat. 38°17'55" N, long. 119°25'05" W; sec. 11, T 5 N, R 23 E); the lakes are at the head of Long Valley Creek. Named on Fales Hot Springs (1954) 7.5' quadrangle.

Lookout Hill: see **Lookout Mountain** [INYO] (2).

Lookout Mountain [INYO]:

(1) *peak,* 10 miles east-northeast of Mount Darwin (lat. 37°14'50" N, long. 118°30'50" W; near SW cor. sec. 18, T 8 S, R 32 E). Altitude 11,261 feet. Named on Mount Goddard (1948) 15' quadrangle.

(2) *ridge,* east-trending, 2 miles long, 9 miles north-northeast of Maturango Peak in Argus Range (lat. 36°14'35" N, long. 117° 26' W). Named on Maturango Peak (1951) 15' quadrangle. Called Lookout Hill on Wheeler's (1877) map. Modock post office served Modoc mine, which was on the ridge; miners there who registered to vote in 1892 gave their address as Modock (Hubbard, Bray, and Pipkin, p. 8). Postal authorities established Modock post office in 1899 and discontinued it in 1903 (Salley, p. 143).

Lookout Mountain [MONO]: *peak,* 12.5 miles north-northwest of Mount Morrison (lat. 37°43'45" N, long. 118°56'45" W; sec. 36, T 2 S, R 27 E). Altitude 8352 feet. Named on Mount Morrison (1953) 15' quadrangle. United States Board on Geographic Names (1990, p. 7, 9) approved names for several features near Lookout Mountain: the name "Dry Creek Knoll" for a feature, altitude 8852 feet, located 4 miles southwest of Lookout Mountain (lat. 37° 40'41" N, long. 118°59'06" W; sec. 15, 16, 21, 22, T 3 S, R 27 E); the name "Earthquake Dome" for a feature, altitude 9387 feet, located 5.5 miles southwest of Lookout Mountain (lat. 37°39'59" N, long. 118°59'56" W; sec. 21, 28, T 3 S, R 27 E); the name "Gilbert Peak" for a feature, altitude 8592 feet, located 3.2 miles southeast of Lookout Mountain (lat. 37°41'56" N, long. 118°54'22" W; sec. 8, T 3 S, R 28 E)—this name commemorates Charles Merwin Gilbert, who made the first geologic map of the Long Valley neighborhood; and the name "Mammoth Knolls" for hills, altitude of highest 8777 feet, located 5.3 miles south-southwest of Lookout Mountain (lat. 37°39'35" N, long. 118°58'38" W; sec. 27, T 3 S, R 27 E).

Lookout Peak [ALPINE]: *peak,* 4 miles west-southwest of Ebbetts Pass (lat. 38°30'40" N, long. 119°52'20" W; sec. 27, T 8 N, R 19 E). Altitude 9584 feet. Named on Ebbetts Pass (1979) 7.5' quadrangle.

Lookout Peak: see **Peep Sight Peak** [ALPINE].

Lookout Point [INYO]: *peak,* 9 miles northwest of Independence (lat. 36°53'30" N, long. 118°19'15" W). Altitude 10,144 feet. Named on Mount Pinchot (1953) 15' quadrangle.

Loope [ALPINE]: *locality,* 2 miles south-southeast of Mogul Peak along Monitor Creek (lat. 38°39'55" N, long. 119°41'45" W; sec. 32, T 10 N, R 21 E). Named on Heenan Lake (1979) 7.5' quadrangle. Called Monitor on Markleeville (1889) 30' quadrangle. The mining camp of Monitor, named for the Civil War ironclad ship, began about 1862; later the place was called Loope to honor Dr. Loope, who brought money from eastern investors to reopen mines in the neighborhood (Long, p. 27) Postal authorities established Monitor post office in 1863 and discontinued it in 1888; they established Loope post office in 1898 and discontinued it in 1908 (Frickstad, p. 4). United States Board on Geographic Names (1959, p. 7) rejected the names "Loopeville" and "Monitor" for the place.

Loope Canyon [ALPINE]: *canyon,* 1 mile long, opens into the canyon of Monitor Creek 2 miles south-southeast of Mogul Peak at Loope (lat. 38°39'55" N, long. 119°41'50" W; sec. 32, T 10 N, R 21 E). Named on Heenan Lake (1979) 7.5' quadrangle.

Loopeville: see **Loope** [ALPINE].

Lorena: see **Masonic** [MONO].

Lost Burro Gap [INYO]: *narrows,* 5.25 miles northeast of Ubehebe Peak (lat. 36°44'45" N, long. 117°31'15" W); the feature is 1.5 miles north of Lost Burro mine. Named on Ubehebe Peak (1950) 15' quadrangle.

Lost Cannon Creek [MONO]: *stream,* flows 8 miles to Mill Creek (1) 11 miles north-northwest of Fales Hot Springs (lat. 38°29'35" N, long. 119°28'50" W; near W line sec. 32, T 8 N, R 23 E). Named on Chris Flat (1954) and Lost Cannon Peak (1954) 7.5' quadrangles. The name probably is from the local legend of the discovery of the cannon that Fremont left in the neighborhood in 1844 (Lewis, p. 98). United States Board on Geographic Names (1933, p. 475) rejected the name "Lost Canyon Creek" for the feature.

Lost Cannon Peak [MONO]: *peak,* 7.25 miles northeast of Sonora Pass (lat. 38°24'20" N, long. 119°32'50" W; sec. 34, T 7 N, R 22 E); the peak is near the head of Lost Cannon Creek. Altitude 11,099 feet. Named on Lost Cannon Peak (1954) 7.5' quadrangle. The origin of the name probably is the same as the origin of the name "Lost Cannon Creek" (Lewis, p. 98).

Lost Cañon: see **Mill Creek** [MONO] (1).

Lost Canyon: see **Little Lost Canyon** [MONO].

Lost Canyon Creek: see **Lost Cannon Creek** [MONO].

Lost Lake [ALPINE]: *lake,* 1300 feet long, 3.5 miles west of Dardanelles Cone (lat. 38°24'30" N, long. 119°56'10" W). Named on Spicer Meadow Reservoir (1979) 7.5' quadrangle.

Lost Lake [MONO]: *lake,* 850 feet long, 5 miles west-northwest of Mount Morrison along Sherwin Creek (lat. 37°35'35" N, long. 118° 56'20" W). Named on Mount Morrison (1953) 15' quadrangle.

Lost Lakes [ALPINE]: *lakes,* two, each 0.25 mile long, 4 miles southeast of Carson Pass (lat. 38°38'50" N, long. 119°56'45" W; sec. 1, 12, T 9 N, R 18 E). Named on Carson Pass (1979) 7.5' quadrangle.

Lost Lakes [MONO]: *lakes,* three, largest 1500 feet long, 13 miles south-southwest of Lee Vining (lat. 37°46'45" N, long. 119°12'15" W). Named on Mono Craters (1953) 15' quadrangle.

Lostman Spring [INYO]: *spring,* 8 miles east-southeast of the mouth of Titus Canyon in Titanothere Canyon (lat. 36°47'05" N, long. 117°01'50" W). Named on Grapevine Peak (1957) 15' quadrangle. Called Tule Spring on Ballarat (1913) 1° quadrangle, but United States Board on Geographic Names (1960a, p. 9) rejected this name. H.D. Curry suggested the name "Lostman Spring" in memory of Morris Titus, of Titus Canyon (Palmer, p. 45).

Lost Valley: see **Death Valley** [INYO].

Lost Wagons [INYO]: *locality,* 15 miles northwest of Stovepipe Wells (lat. 36°49'20" N, long. 117°15'45" W). Named on Ballarat (1913) 1° quadrangle. A wagon was abandoned at the place in the summer of 1889 when horses pulling it were overcome by heat (Federal Writers' Project, p. 32).

Louisiana Butte [INYO]: *peak,* 12 miles south-southeast of Coso Peak (lat. 36°02'50" N, long. 117°37'10" W; on W line sec. 1, T 22 S, R 40 E). Named on Coso Peak (1951) 15' quadrangle.

Lower Beebe Lake [ALPINE]: *lake,* 850 feet long, 6.5 miles north-northwest of Mount Reba (lat. 38°35'55" N, long. 120°03' W); the lake is 0.5 mile southeast of Beebe Lake. Named on Mokelumne Peak (1979) 7.5' quadrangle.

Lower Blue Lake [ALPINE]: *lake,* nearly 1 mile long, behind a dam on Blue Creek 6.5 miles north of Pacific Grade Summit (lat. 38°36'30" N, long. 119°55'35" W; sec. 30, T 9 N, R 19 E); the lake is less than 1 mile southeast of Upper Blue Lake. Named on Pacific Valley (1979) 7.5' quadrangle. Lower Blue Lake and Upper Blue Lake together are called Blue Lakes on Markleeville (1889) 30' quadrangle.

Lower Boy Scout Lake [INYO]: *lake,* 850 feet long, nearly 2 miles east of Mount Whitney (1) along North Fork Lone Pine Creek (lat. 36°35' N, long. 118°15'35" W); the lake is less than 1 mile downstream from Upper Boy Scout Lake. Named on Mount Whitney (1956) 15' quadrangle.

Lower Centennial Flat [INYO]: *valley,* 7.5 miles west-northwest of Darwin (lat. 36°18' N, long. 117°43'30" W); the valley is 7 miles northeast of Upper Centennial Flat. Named on Coso Peak (1951), Darwin (1950), and Keeler (1951) 15' quadrangles. Wheeler's (1877) map has the name "Orm's Sta." at a place along a toll road in the north part of present Lower Centennial Flat. Mendenhall (p. 37) noted a place called Omes situated about 6 miles north of Arab Spring (present Lower Centennial Spring).

Lower Centennial Spring [INYO]: *spring,* 16 miles south-southeast of Keeler (lat. 36°15'55" N, long. 117°45'55" W); the spring is in Centennial Canyon less than 2 miles north of Upper Centennial Spring. Named on Keeler (1951) 15' quadrangle. Called Arab Spr. on Wheeler's (1877) map.

Lower Fish Valley [ALPINE]: *valley,* 7 miles east of Disaster Peak along Silver King Creek (lat. 38°28' N, long. 119°36'40" W; on W line sec. 7, T 7 N, R 22 E); the valley is downstream from Upper Fish Valley. Named on Lost Cannon Peak (1954) 7.5' quadrangle. Lower Fish Valley and Upper Fish Valley together are called Fish Valley on Dardanelles (1898) 30' quadrangle.

Lower Gardner Meadow [ALPINE]: *area,* 8 miles northeast of Dardanelles Cone (lat. 38°29'50" N, long. 119°46'25" W; near SE cor. sec. 33, T 8 N, R 20 E); the place is 1 mile north-northeast of Upper Gardner Meadow. Named on Dardanelles Cone (1979) 7.5' quadrangle.

Lower Horse Meadow [MONO]: *area,* 2 miles south of Lee Vining (lat. 37°55'45" N, long. 119°07'30" W; sec. 20, 21, T 1 N, R 26 E); the place is 1 mile east-northeast of Upper Horse Meadow. Named on Mono Craters (1953) 15' quadrangle.

Lower Kinney Lake [ALPINE]: *lake,* 1800 feet long, 1.25 miles north-northwest of Ebbetts Pass (lat. 38°33'40" N, long. 119°49'20" W); the lake is less than 0.25 mile downstream along Silver Creek (1) from Upper Kinney Lake. Named on Ebbetts Pass (1979) 7.5' quadrangle. Lower Kinney Lake and Upper Kinney Lake together are called Kinney Lakes on Markleeville (1889) 30' quadrangle—they were known as Silver Lakes in the 1860's before they were named for David Kinney, a farmer at Silver Mountain in 1873 (Gudde, 1949, p. 175).

Lower Lamarck Lake [INYO]: *lake,* 1100 feet long, nearly 4 miles north-northeast of Mount Darwin (lat. 37°13'05" N, long. 118°38'30" W); the lake is along Lamarck Creek 0.5 mile downstream from Upper Lamarck Lake. Named on Mount Goddard (1948) 15' quadrangle.

Lower Long Lake [MONO]: *lake,* 1000 feet long, nearly 6 miles north of Tower Peak (lat. 38°13'35" N, long. 119°34'05" W); the lake is northeast of Upper Long Lake. Named on Tower Peak (1956) 15' quadrangle.

Lower Morgan Lake [INYO]: *lake,* 2000 feet long, 5.25 miles northwest of Mount Tom (lat. 37°23'10" N, long. 118°43'50" W); the lake is 0.5 mile downstream from Upper Morgan Lake. Named on Mount Tom (1949) 15' quadrangle.

Lower Rock Creek: see **Rock Creek** [INYO-MONO].

Lower Sardine Lake [MONO]: *lake,* 1200 feet long, 8 miles southwest of Lee Vining along Walker Creek (lat. 37°51'30" N, long. 119°11'55" W); the lake is 0.25 mile downstream from Upper Sardine Lake. Named on Mono Craters (1953) 15' quadrangle. Called Sardine Lake on Mount Lyell (1901) 30' quadrangle. The name supposedly is from canned sardines that a mule was carrying when it drowned in the lake (Gudde, 1949, p. 320).

Lower Summers Meadows [MONO]: *area,* 6.25 miles south of Bridgeport (lat. 38°10' N, long. 119°15' W; in and near sec. 31, 32, T 4 N, R 25 E); the place is along Summers Creek 3 miles east of Upper Summers Meadows. Named on Matterhorn Peak (1956) 15' quadrangle. Bodie (1958) 15' quadrangle has the singular form "Lower Summers Meadow" for the name.

Lower Summit City: see **Summit City Creek** [ALPINE].

Lower Sunset Lake [ALPINE]: *lake,* 1800 feet long, nearly 7 miles north-northeast of Pacific Grade Summit (lat. 38°36'45" N, long. 119°52'30" W; on S line sec. 22, T 9 N, R 19 E); the lake is northeast of Upper Sunset Lake. Named on Ebbetts Pass (1979) and Pacific Valley (1979) 7.5' quadrangles.

Lower Town: see **Masonic** [MONO].

Lower Warm Springs [INYO]: *springs,* two, 8.5 miles east-southeast of the mouth of Paiute Canyon in Saline Valley (lat. 36°48'20" N, long. 117°46'15" W; near S line sec. 18, T 13 S, R 39 E); the springs are 2.5 miles southwest of Upper Warm Spring. Named on Waucoba Wash (1951) 15' quadrangle.

Lubken Creek [INYO]: *stream,* formed by the confluence of North Fork and South Fork, flows 1.5 miles to the aqueduct that takes Owens Valley water to Los Angeles 4.25 miles south of Lone Pine (lat. 36°32'35" N, long. 118°03' W; sec. 15, T 16 S, R 36 E). Called Lubkin Creek on Lone Pine (1958) 15' quadrangle, but United States Board on Geographic Names (1983b, p. 1) rejected this form of the name, and noted that the name is for John H. Lubken, rancher and Inyo County supervisor; the Board also rejected the name "Richter Creek" for the feature. North Fork is 8 miles long and South Fork in 5.25 miles long; both forks are named on Lone Pine (1958) 15' quadrangle. North Fork is called Richter Creek on Mount Whitney (1907) 30' quadrangle. According to Gudde (1949, p. 286), the name "Richter" probably should be "Rittgers" for some early settlers in the region.

Lubkin Creek: see **Lubken Creek** [INYO].

Lucky Jim Wash [INYO]: *stream,* flows 10.5 miles to Darwin Wash 10 miles east-northeast of Coso Peak (lat. 36°14'30" N, long. 117° 32'40" W; near W line sec. 33, T 19 S, R 41 E). Named on Coso Peak (1951) and Darwin (1950) 15' quadrangles.

Lundy [MONO]: *locality,* 16 miles south of Bridgeport (lat. 38°01'40" N, long. 119°14'25" W; sec. 17, T 2 N, R 25 E); the place is in Lundy Canyon near the west end of Lundy Lake. Named on Bodie (1958) 15' quadrangle. The mining camp called Lundy began in 1879; water of Lundy Lake now covers part of the old townsite (Hoover, Rensch, and Rensch, p. 215). Postal authorities established Lundy post office in 1880 and discontinued it in 1914 (Frickstad, p. 105).

Lundy Canyon [MONO]: *canyon,* 8 miles long, along Mill Creek (2) above a point 6 miles north-northwest of Lee Vining (lat. 38°02'20" N, long. 119°09'30" W; sec. 13, T 2 N, R 25 E). Named on Bodie (1958) and Matterhorn Peak (1956) 15' quadrangles. Russell (p. 275) referred to "the gorge of Mill Creek, or Lundy Cañon, as it is frequently called, from a mining camp which has sprung up within it during the past few years." The feature also was called Mill Creek Canyon (Smith, Genny, p. 138).

Lundy Lake [MONO]: *lake,* 5800 feet long, behind a dam on Mill Creek (2) 7.5 miles northwest of Lee Vining (lat. 38°01'55" N, long. 119°13'10" W; sec. 16, 17, T 2 N, R 25 E); the lake is in Lundy Canyon. Named on Bodie (1958) 15' quadrangle. The name is for W.J. Lundy, who began operating a sawmill by the lake about 1878 (Cain, 1956, p. 89).

Lundy Pass [MONO]: *pass,* 2.5 miles northeast of Mount Conness (lat. 37°59'30" N, long. 119°17'10" W; on W line sec. 25, T 2 N, R 24 E). Named on Tuolumne Meadows (1956) 15' quadrangle.

Luther Creek [ALPINE]: *stream,* flows 4 miles to the State of Nevada 6.25 miles north of Woodfords in Carson Valley (lat. 38° 51'50" N, long. 119°48'10" W; sec. 36, T 12 N, R 19 E). Named on Woodfords (1979) 7.5' quadrangle.

Luther Pass [ALPINE]: *pass,* 5.5 miles south-southwest of Freel Peak on Alpine-El Dorado County line (lat. 38°47'15" N, long. 119°56'40" W; sec. 24, T 11 N, R 18 E). Named on Freel Peak (1955) 7.5' quadrangle. Called Luther's Pass on Wheeler's (1876-1877) map. According to Long (p. 12), one story has the pass named for Lieutenant Luther, who selected a route over the pass for an army convoy in 1857; another account has the pass named for Mr. Luther of Sacramento, who in 1854 was the first to cross it with a wagon; yet another source has the pass named for Ira M. Luther, who had a sawmill in Carson Valley in the early 1860's.

Lynford Gulch [MONO]: *canyon,* drained by a stream that flows 1 mile to Benton Valley 2.25 miles south of Benton (lat. 37°47'05" N, long. 118°28'20" W; sec. 8, T 2 S, R 32 E). Named on Benton (1962) 15' quadrangle.

—M—

Mabel: see **Mabel Siding** [INYO].

Mabel Siding [INYO]: *locality,* nearly 4 miles north-northwest of the village of Little Lake along Southern Pacific Railroad (lat. 35°59'15" N, long. 117°56'15" W). Named on Searles Lake (1915) 1° quadrangle. Called Mabel on California Mining Bureau's (1917b) map.

Mack: see **Sam Mack Lake** [INYO].

Mack Canyon [MONO]: *canyon,* drained by a stream that flows 3 miles to Swauger Creek 4 miles east of Fales Hot Springs (lat. 38°20'45" N, long. 119°19'25" W; near N line sec. 27, T 6 N, R 24 E). Named on Fales Hot Springs (1956) 15' quadrangle.

Mack Lake [INYO]: *lake,* 0.25 mile long, 3.25 miles northeast of Mount Abbot in Little Lakes Valley (lat. 37°25'40" N, long. 118°45' W). Named on Mount Abbot (1953) and Mount Tom (1949) 15' quadrangles.

Magazine Canyon [INYO]: *canyon,* drained by a stream that flows 1 mile to Surprise Canyon 3.5 miles south of Telescope Peak (lat. 37°07'05" N, long. 117°05'30" W). Named on Telescope Peak (1952) 15' quadrangle.

Mahogany Flat [INYO]:

(1) *area,* 8 miles north of Mount Whitney (1) on upper reaches of Shepherd Creek (lat. 36°41'25" N, long. 118°18'55" W). Named on Mount Whitney (1956) 15' quadrangle. The place also is called Manzanita Flat (Schumacher, p. 84).

(2) *area,* 4.25 miles north-northeast of Telescope Peak (lat. 36°13'50" N, long. 117°04' W; near N line sec. 2, T 20 S, R 45 E). Named on Telescope Peak (1952) 15' quadrangle. Colonel J.R. White, superintendent of Death

Valley National Monument, named the feature in 1935 for the growth of mountain mahogany there; the place formerly was known as White Sage Flat (Palmer, p. 46).

Mahogany Ridge [MONO]: *ridge,* south-southwest- to west-southwest-trending, 3 miles long, 3 miles south of Fales Hot Springs (lat. 38°18'30" N, long. 119°24'30" W). Named on Fales Hot Springs (1954) 7.5' quadrangle.

Malapi Spring [INYO]: *spring,* 5.5 miles north-northwest of Emigrant Pass (1) (lat. 36°24'10" N, long. 117°11'40" W). Named on Emigrant Canyon (1952) 15' quadrangle.

Mallory: see **Mount Mallory** [INYO].

Malpais Mesa [INYO]: *relief feature,* 7.5 miles east-southeast of Keeler (lat. 36°26' N, long. 117°45' W). Named on Darwin (1950) and Keeler (1951) 15' quadrangles. Called Table Hills on Wheeler's (1877) map.

Maltby Lake [MONO]: *lake,* 1200 feet long, 3 miles northwest of Matterhorn Peak (lat. 38°07'10" N, long. 119°25'25" W). Named on Matterhorn Peak (1956) 15' quadrangle.

Mamie: see **Lake Mamie** [MONO].

Mammoth: see **Old Mammoth** [MONO].

Mammoth City: see **Old Mammoth** [MONO].

Mammoth Creek [MONO]: *stream,* flows 12 miles to Hot Creek (2) 6 miles north-northwest of Mount Morrison (lat. 37°38'20" N, long. 118°54'20" W; sec. 32, T 3 S, R 28 E); the stream heads at Mammoth Crest and goes through Mammoth Lakes (1). Named on Devils Postpile (1953) and Mount Morrison (1953) 15' quadrangles. Mammoth Creek and Hot Creek (2) together are called S. Branch [Owens River] on Lee's (1906) map.

Mammoth Crest [MONO]: *ridge,* extends for 7 miles south-southeast and east from Mammoth Pass on Mono-Madera County line and on Mono-Fresno County line (lat. 37°34'15" N, long. 119° 00' W). Named on Devils Postpile (1953) and Mount Morrison (1953) 15' quadrangles.

Mammoth Knolls: see **Lookout Mountain** [MONO].

Mammoth Lakes [MONO]:

(1) *lakes,* largest 3600 feet long, southeast of Mammoth Mountain (lat. 37°36'30" N, long. 119°01' W). Named on Devils Postpile (1953) 15' quadrangle. The name is from Mammoth vein, located east of Lake Mary (DeDecker, p. 29). The group includes Crystal Lake (2), Horseshoe Lake, Lake Barrett, Lake George, Lake Mamie, Lake Mary, McCloud Lake, T.J. Lake, and Twin Lakes (2).

(2) *town,* 9 miles northwest of Mount Morrison (lat. 37°38'50" N, long. 118°58'15" W; sec. 34, 35, T 3 S, R 27 E); the town is east of Mammoth Lakes (1). Named on Mount Morrison (1953) 15' quadrangle. Postal authorities established Mammoth Lakes post office in 1923 (Frickstad, p. 105).

Mammoth Mountain [MONO]: *peak,* 23 miles south-southeast of Lee Vining (lat. 37°37'50" N, long. 119°01'55" W). Altitude 11,053 feet. Named on Devils Postpile (1953) 15' quadrangle. United States Board on Geographic Names (1990, p. 11) approved the name "White Wing Mountain" for a feature located 7 miles north of Mammoth Mountain (lat. 37°43'32" N, long. 119°02'43" W).

Mammoth Pass [MONO]: *pass,* 1.5 miles south of Mammoth Mountain on Mono-Madera County line (lat. 37°36'35" N, long. 119°01'45" W). Named on Devils Postpile (1953) 15' quadrangle. The feature also in called Pumice Gap (Smith *in* Wright, p. 92).

Mammoth Rock [MONO]: *relief feature,* 8 miles west-northwest of Mount Morrison (lat. 37°36'50" N, long. 118°59'25" W; near W line sec. 10, T 4 S, R 27 E). Altitude 9110 feet. Named on Mount Morrison (1953) 15' quadrangle. The feature was called Monumental Rock in the early days (Smith, Genny, p. 18).

Manly: see **Lake Manly**, under **Death Valley** [INYO].

Manly Beacon: see **Golden Canyon** [INYO].

Manly Fall [INYO]: *locality,* 4.25 miles west-northwest of Manly Peak at the west base of Panamint Range (lat. 35°56'15" N, long. 117°11'10" W). Named on Manly Peak (1950) 15' quadrangle, where the name applies to a group of buildings at the mouth of Redlands Canyon. Dr. John E. Wolff gave the name, which commemorates W.L. Manly, to a dry fall located within a mile of the mouth of Redlands Canyon (Palmer, p. 46).

Manly Pass [INYO]: *pass,* 10 miles east of Argus Peak in Slate Range (lat. 35°52'10" N, long. 117°16'20" W). Named on Trona (1949) 15' quadrangle. Dr. John E. Wolff gave the name in 1938 because W.L. Manly supposedly traversed the pass on his way out of Death Valley (Palmer, p. 47).

Manly Peak [INYO]: *peak,* 45 miles east of the village of Little Lake (lat. 35°54'55" N, long. 117°07' W). Altitude 7196 feet. Named on Manly Peak (1950) 15' quadrangle. Dr. John E. Wolff named the peak in 1938 to honor W.L. Manly, who supposedly ascended the peak to map out an escape route from Death Valley (Palmer, p. 47). The name "Granite Peak" was suggested for the feature when transfer of the name "Manly" to another peak was proposed (Palmer, p. 32).

Manly Peak: see **Rogers Peak** [INYO].

Manzanar [INYO]: *locality,* 9 miles north of Lone Pine along Southern Pacific Railroad (lat. 36°44'10" N, long. 118°04'35" W; sec. 8, T 14 S, R 36 E). Named on Lone Pine (1958) 15' quadrangle. Called Francis on Mount Whitney (1907) 30' quadrangle. Postal authorities established Francis post office in 1911 and discontinued it in 1914 (Frickstad, p. 51). *Manzanar* means "apple orchard" in Spanish (Gudde, 1949, p. 203)—the place was the shipping point for what was rich orchard land before Los Angeles City took water from Owens Valley (Hungerford, p. 11).

Manzanar: see **Thebe** [INYO].

Manzanita Flat: see **Mahogany Flat** [INYO] (1).

Marble Bath [INYO]: *water feature,* 4.5 miles north-northwest of Dry Mountain (lat. 36°58'10" N, long. 117°37'55" W). Named on Dry Mountain (1957) 15' quadrangle.

Marble Canyon [INYO]:

(1) *canyon,* 2 miles long, opens into Black Canyon (1) 4.5 miles west of Westgard Pass (lat. 37°17'25" N, long. 118°14' W; near S line sec. 34, T 7 S, R 34 E). Named on Blanco Mountain (1951) 15' quadrangle.

(2) *canyon,* 12 miles long, opens into an arm of Eureka Valley 11 miles northeast of Waucoba Mountain (lat. 37°07'30" N, long. 117° 52' W). Named on Waucoba Mountain (1951) and Waucoba Spring (1958) 15' quadrangles. United States Board on Geographic Names (1991, p. 4) approved the name "Eureka Peak" for a feature, altitude 6604 feet, located in Saline Range 9.9 miles southwest of Marble Canyon (lat. 37°01'34" N, long. 117°47'12" W).

(3) *canyon,* 15 miles long, opens into Death Valley 19 miles south-southeast of Tin Mountain (lat. 36°38'45" N, long. 117°16'30" W). Named on Marble Canyon (1951) 15' quadrangle. The name is for variegated limestone of the canyon walls; Lieutenant D.A. Lyle of the Wheeler survey gave the name "Marble Spring" to a feature in the canyon (Palmer, p. 47).

Marble Creek [MONO]: *stream,* flows 7.25 miles to Spring Canyon Creek 13 miles northwest of White Mountain Peak (lat. 37°44'40" N, long. 118°27'05" W; sec. 28, T 2 S, R 32 E). Named on Benton (1962) and White Mountain Peak (1962) 15' quadrangles.

Marble Spring: see **Marble Canyon** [INYO] (3).

Margaret Ann Spring [INYO]: *spring,* 8 miles north of Argus Peak in Water Canyon (5) (lat. 35°57'55" N, long. 117°27'20" W; sec. 4, T 23 S, R 42 E). Named on Trona (1949) 15' quadrangle.

Margaret Lake [INYO]: *lake,* 500 feet long, 6.5 miles east-southeast of Mount Darwin (lat. 37°08'05" N, long. 118°33'30" W; sec. 26, T 9 S, R 31 E). Named on Mount Goddard (1948) 15' quadrangle.

Marie Lakes [MONO]: *lakes,* largest 3300 feet long, 14 miles west-northwest of Mammoth Mountain (lat. 37°44'20" N, long. 119°14'45" W). Named on Devils Postpile (1953) and Merced Peak (1953) 15' quadrangles.

Mariposa Spring [INYO]: *spring,* 4 miles southeast of Coso Peak (lat. 36°09'35" N, long. 117°40'05" W; near N line sec. 32, T 20 S, R 40 E). Named on Coso Peak (1951) 15' quadrangle.

Markleeville [ALPINE]: *village,* north of the center of Alpine County along Markleeville Creek (lat. 38°41'40" N, long. 119°46'45" W; sec. 21, T 10 N, R 20 E). Named on Markleeville (1979) 7.5' quadrangle. Called Markleville on Wheeler's (1876-1877) map. Postal authorities established Markleeville post office in 1863 (Salley, p. 134). The name commemorates Jacob J. Marklee, who located a land claim on 160 acres at the site in 1861 (Long, p. 13).

Markleeville Creek [ALPINE]: *stream,* formed by the confluence of Hot Springs Creek and Pleasant Valley Creek, flows 2.25 miles to East Fork Carson River 1.25 miles northeast of Markleeville (lat. 38°42'30" N, long. 119°46'05" W; sec. 15, T 10 N, R 20 E); the stream goes past Markleeville. Named on Markleeville (1979) 7.5' quadrangle. On Markleeville (1889) 30' quadrangle, the name applies to the lower part, at least, of present Hot Springs Creek. The stream also was known as Middle Fork Carson River (Long, p. 13).

Markleeville Creek: see **Hot Springs Creek** [ALPINE].

Markleeville Peak [ALPINE]: *peak,* 5.5 miles east-southeast of Carson Pass (lat. 38°39'40" N, long. 119°53'50" W; near N line sec. 4, T 9 N, R 19 E); the peak is 6.5 miles west-southwest of Markleeville. Altitude 9415 feet. Named on Carson Pass (1979) 7.5' quadrangle. Called Markleville Pk. on Wheeler's (1876-1877) map.

Marshall Canyon [ALPINE]: *canyon,* drained by a stream that flows nearly 2 miles to Pacific Creek 6.25 miles north of Dardanelles Cone (lat. 38°29'45" N, long. 119°53'40" W; at S line sec. 33, T 8 N, R 19 E). Named on Dardanelles Cone (1979), Ebbetts Pass (1979), and Spicer Meadow Reservoir (1979) 7.5' quadrangles.

Mars Hill: see **Furnace Creek Ranch** [INYO].

Marsh Lake [INYO]: *lake,* 800 feet long, 3 miles northeast of Mount Abbot in Little Lake Valley (lat. 37°25'20" N, long. 118°45'10" W). Named on Mount Abbot (1953) 15' quadrangle.

Martell Flat [ALPINE]: *area,* 3 miles southwest of Fourth of July Peak (lat. 38°37'40" N, long. 120°03'40" W; sec. 14, T 9 N, R 17 E). Named on Caples Lake (1979) 7.5' quadrangle. Silver Lake (1956) 15' quadrangle has the plural form "Martell Flats" for the name.

Martin Pass: see **Towne Pass** [INYO].

Marvel Canyon [INYO]: *canyon,* 2.25 miles long, opens into Surprise Canyon 4 miles south-southwest of Telescope Peak (lat. 36° 06'55" N, long.

117°06'40" W). Named on Telescope Peak (1952) 15' quadrangle.

Mary: see **Lake Mary** [MONO].

Mary Austin: see **Mount Mary Austin** [INYO].

Mary Louise Lakes [INYO]: *lakes,* largest 800 feet long, 6.5 miles east of Mount Darwin (lat. 37°09'20" N, long. 118°33'15" W; sec. 23, T 9 S, R 31 E). Named on Mount Goddard (1948) 15' quadrangle.

Masonic [MONO]: *locality,* 10 miles northeast of Bridgeport (lat. 38° 21'45" N, long. 119°06'45" W; sec. 15, T 6 N, R 26 E). Site named on Bridgeport (1958) 15' quadrangle. Prospectors found promising leads in the neighborhood in 1860, and because they were Masons they called the place Masonic; development began in 1902 (Wedertz, p. 219). The first settlement, called Middle Town, had a boarding house, general store, and a post office called Masonic; two smaller settlements were called Lower Town and Upper Town (Cain, 1961, p. 82). Lower Town is named on Bridgeport (1958) 15' quadrangle. Postal authorities established Lorena post office in 1905, changed the name to Masonic in 1906, discontinued it in 1912, reestablished it in 1913, and discontinued it in 1927 (Frickstad, p. 104, 105).

Masonic Gulch [MONO]: *canyon,* drained by a stream that flows 5 miles to the State of Nevada 11 miles north-northeast of Bridgeport (lat. 38°24'15" N, long. 119°08'30" W; near N line sec. 5, T 6 N, R 26 E); the canyon heads near Masonic. Named on Bridgeport (1958) 15' quadrangle.

Masonic Mountain [MONO]: *ridge,* east-trending, 1.5 miles long, 8 miles northeast of Bridgeport (lat. 38°20'40" N, long. 119°08' W; around NE cor. sec. 29, T 6 N, R 26 E). Named on Bridgeport (1958) 15' quadrangle.

Masonic Spring [MONO]: *spring,* 9 miles northeast of Bridgeport (lat. 38°21'10" N, long. 119°07'15" W; sec. 21, T 6 N, R 26 E); the feature is less than 1 mile southwest of the site of Masonic. Named on Bridgeport (1958) 15' quadrangle.

Matlock Lake [INYO]: *lake,* 950 feet long, 9 miles west-southwest of Independence (lat. 36°45'50" N, long. 118°21'25" W). Named on Mount Pinchot (1953) 15' quadrangle. The name commemorates the man who first planted fish in the lake (Schumacher, p. 88).

Matterhorn Peak [MONO]: *peak,* 14 miles southwest of Bridgeport on Mono-Tuolumne County line (lat. 38°05'30" N, long. 119°22'50" W). Altitude 12,264 feet. Named on Matterhorn Peak (1956) 15' quadrangle.

Maturango Peak [INYO]: *peak,* 33 miles southeast of Keeler in Argus Range (lat. 36°07'10" N, long. 117°29'40" W; on W line sec. 7, T 21 S, R 42 E). Altitude 8839 feet. Named on Maturango Peak (1951) 15' quadrangle. Hanna (p. 188) believed that the name is a misspelling of *maturrango,* which means "bad horseman" or "clumsy, rough person" in Spanish, but Palmer (p. 47) stated that the name is for Indians of the region. Kroeber (p. 47) considered the name to be more probably Spanish, or corrupted Spanish, than Indian. Wheeler's (1877) map names the peak, and shows Maturango Spr. located 3 miles farther south near the west edge of Argus Range. United States Board on Geographic Names (1960b, p. 18) approved the name "Parkinson Peak" for a feature situated about 1.4 miles south of Maturango Peak—the name honors Charles Burl Parkinson, who died shortly after scouting the peak for the Sierra Club.

Maturango Spring: see **Maturango Peak** [INYO].

Maul Lake [MONO]: *lake,* 700 feet long, 2 miles east-southeast of Mount Conness (lat. 37°57'10" N, long. 119°17'10" W). Named on Tuolumne Meadows (1956) 15' quadrangle.

Maxwell Creek [ALPINE]: *stream,* flows 1.5 miles to West Fork Carson River 7 miles south-southwest of Freel Peak in Hope Valley (lat. 38°45'30" N, long. 119°56'05" W; sec. 6, T 10 N, R 19 E). Named on Freel Peak (1955) 7.5' quadrangle.

Mazourka Canyon [INYO]: *canyon,* 11 miles long, opens into lowlands 6 miles east of Independence (lat. 36°49' N, long. 118°05'30" W; near W line sec. 8, T 13 S, R 36 E). Named on Independence (1951) 15' quadrangle.

McAdie: see **Mount McAdie** [INYO].

McAfee Creek [MONO]: *stream,* formed by the confluence of North Fork and South Fork, flows 5 miles to Fish Lake Valley 9.5 miles east of White Mountain Peak (lat. 37°38'05" N, long. 118°05' W). Named on Mount Barcroft (1962) 15' quadrangle. The name commemorates A.G. McAfee, who settled in Fish Lake Valley in 1864 (Gudde, 1949, p. 198). North Fork is 4.5 miles long and South Fork is 5.5 miles long; both forks are named on Mount Barcroft (1962) 15' quadrangle.

McAfee Meadow [MONO]: *area,* 3.5 miles south-southeast of White Mountain Peak (lat. 37°35'20" N, long. 118°13'15" W); the place is along South Fork McAfee Creek. Named on Mount Barcroft (1962) 15' quadrangle.

McCloud Camp [MONO]: *locality,* 9 miles southeast of White Mountain Peak along South Fork Cottonwood Creek (2) (lat. 37° 32' N, long. 118°09'30" W). Named on Mount Barcroft (1962) 15' quadrangle.

McCloud Flat [INYO]: *area,* 8 miles northeast of Coso Junction (lat. 36°08'15" N, long. 117°51'45" W). Named on Haiwee Reservoir (1951) 15' quadrangle.

McCloud Lake [MONO]: *lake,* 1200 feet long, 1.5 miles south of Mammoth Mountain (lat. 37°36'30" N, long. 119°01'50" W). Named on Devils Postpile (1953) 15' quadrangle. United States Board on Geographic Names (1984b, p. 2) approved the name "McLeod Lake" for the feature. The name commemorates Malcolm McLeod, district ranger from 1921 until 1929 (Smith, Genny, p. 15). The lake is one of the group called Mammoth Lakes.

McCormacks Creek: see **McCormick Creek** [ALPINE].

McCormack's Well: see **Tule Spring** [INYO] (1).

McCormick Creek [ALPINE]: *stream,* flows 3.5 miles to Tuolumne County 2.5 miles southwest of Dardanelles Cone (lat. 38°22'25" N, long. 119°54'15" W; sec. 17, T 6 N, R 19 E). Named on Donnell Lake (1979) and Spicer Meadow Reservoir (1979) 7.5' quadrangles. Called McCormacks Cr. on Wheeler's (1876-1877) map.

McElvoy Canyon [INYO]: *canyon,* drained by a stream that flows nearly 6 miles to Saline Valley 6.25 miles south of the mouth of Paiute Canyon (lat. 36°45'40" N, long. 117°53'30" W). Named on New York Butte (1950) and Waucoba Wash (1951) 15' quadrangles.

McGann Springs [INYO]: *springs,* two, 6.5 miles northwest of Independence (lat. 36°51'15" N, long. 118°17'35" W; near NW cor. sec. 5, T 13 S, R 34 E). Named on Mount Pinchot (1953) 15' quadrangle.

McGee Canyon [MONO]: *canyon,* 5 miles long, along McGee Creek (1) above a point 6.25 miles north of Glass Mountain (lat. 37°52' N, long. 118°42' W; near NW cor. sec. 17, T 1 S, R 30 E). Named on Glass Mountain (1962) 15' quadrangle.

McGee Creek [INYO]: *stream,* flows 15 miles to Horton Creek nearly 6 miles west-northwest of Bishop (lat. 37°23'50" N, long. 118°29'30" W; sec. 29, T 6 S, R 32 E); the stream heads at McGee Lake. Named on Bishop (1949) and Mount Tom (1949) 15' quadrangles. The name commemorates John McGee, sheriff of Inyo County, who owned a ranch where the stream reaches lowlands (Gudde, 1949, p. 199).

McGee Creek [MONO]:

(1) *stream,* flows 11.5 miles to Adobe Creek 9 miles north of Glass Mountain (lat. 37°54'25" N, long. 118°42'10" W; sec. 31, T 1 N, R 30 E); the stream goes through McGee Meadow and McGee Canyon. Named on Glass Mountain (1962) 15' quadrangle.

(2) *stream,* flows 10.5 miles to Convict Creek 5.25 miles northeast of Mount Morrison in Long Valley (2) (lat. 37°36'25" N, long. 118°46'50" W; sec. 16, T 4 S, R 29 E); the stream heads at Big McGee Lake. Named on Mount Abbot (1953) and Mount Morrison (1953) 15' quadrangles. The name commemorates Alney McGee, John McGee, and Bart McGee, pioneer cattlemen who had their headquarters near the stream (Smith, Genny, p. 5).

McGee Lake [INYO]: *lake,* 950 feet long, nearly 4 miles south of Mount Tom (lat. 37°17'05" N, long. 118°39'40" W); the lake is at the head of McGee Creek. Named on Mount Tom (1949) 15' quadrangle. United States Board on Geographic Names (1983c, p. 5) approved the name "Longley Lake" for the feature, and rejected the names "McGee Lake" and "Longley Reservoir" for it.

McGee Lake: see **Big McGee Lake** [MONO]; **Little McGee Lake** [MONO].

McGee Meadow [INYO]: *area,* 6.5 miles east of Mount Tom (lat. 37°19'25" N, long. 118°32'15" W; sec. 23, T 7 S, R 31 E). Named on Mount Tom (1949) 15' quadrangle.

McGee Meadow [MONO]: *area,* 2.25 miles northwest of Glass Mountain (lat. 37°47'50" N, long. 118°44'10" W; sec. 1, 2, T 2 S, R 29 E); the place is near the head of McGee Canyon. Named on Glass Mountain (1962) 15' quadrangle.

McGee Mountain [INYO]: *peak,* 2.5 miles east of Mount Morrison (lat. 37°34' N, long. 118°48'35" W; near SE cor. sec. 30, T 4 S, R 29 E); the peak is northwest of McGee Creek. Altitude 10,871 feet. Named on Mount Morrison (1953) 15' quadrangle.

McGee Pass [MONO]: *pass,* 4.25 miles south of Mount Morrison on Mono-Fresno County line (lat. 37°30'05" N, long. 118°51'35" W); the pass is near the head of McGee Creek (2). Named on Mount Morrison (1953) 15' quadrangle.

McGuinnes Spring: see **China Gardens Spring** [INYO].

McKay Creek [MONO]: *stream,* flows 2.25 miles to Sardine Creek 1.5 miles southeast of Sonora Pass (lat. 38°18'45" N, long. 119°36'20" W; near E line sec. 1, T 5 N, R 21 E). Named on Pickel Meadow (1954) and Sonora Pass (1979) 7.5' quadrangles.

McLain Park [INYO]: *area,* 9 miles south-southwest of Shoshone, and south of the southeast end of Greenwater Valley (lat. 35°51' N, long. 116°19' W). Named on Shoshone (1951) 15' quadrangle. The name is for a prospector who worked in the neighborhood (Palmer, p. 48).

McLaughlin Creek [MONO]: *stream,* flows 4 miles to Owens River 11 miles south-southeast of the site of Mono Mills (lat. 37°45'10" N, long. 118°51'30" W; near S line sec. 23, T 2 S, R 28 E); the stream heads near McLaughlin Springs. Named on Cowtrack Mountain (1962) 15' quadrangle.

McLaughlin Springs [MONO]: *springs,* 9.5 miles southeast of the site of Mono Mills (lat. 37°47'35" N, long. 118°50'10" W; sec. 12, T 2 S, R 28 E); the springs are near the head of McLaughlin Creek. Named on Cowtrack Mountain (1962) 15' quadrangle.

McLean's Pass: see **Tioga Pass** [MONO].

McLean Spring [INYO]: *spring,* 5 miles southeast of Stovepipe Wells near Salt Creek (lat. 36°36'15" N, long. 117°01'10" W; sec. 31, T 15 S, R 46 E). Named on Stovepipe Wells (1952) 15' quadrangle. The name is for a member of a group that went about marking springs in the region (Palmer, p. 48). National Park Service officials proposed the name "Jayhawker Well" for the spring because the Jayhawker party of emigrants camped nearby (Palmer, p. 39-40). Mendenhall (p. 34) mentioned two small wells, which he called Salt Creek Wells, located at or near McLean Spring. Ballarat (1913) 1° quadrangle has the word "Wells" at the site.

McLeod Lake: see **McCloud Lake** [MONO].

McMillan Lake [MONO]: *lake,* 500 feet long, 11 miles north-northwest of Matterhorn Peak (lat. 38°14'25" N, long. 119°26'10" W; sec. 34, T 5 N, R 23 E). Named on Matterhorn Peak (1956) 15' quadrangle.

McMillan Spring [MONO]: *spring,* 7 miles northeast of Bridgeport (lat. 38°20'05" N, long. 119°08'40" W; sec. 29, T 6 N, R 26 E). Named on Bridgeport (1958) 15' quadrangle.

McMurry Meadows [INYO]: *area,* 7 miles south-southwest of Big Pine (lat. 37°04'35" N, long. 118°21'20" W; sec. 15, 22, T 10 S, R 33 E). Named on Big Pine (1950) 15' quadrangle.

McMurry Spring [INYO]: *spring,* 7 miles east of Big Pine (lat. 37° 10'25" N, long. 118°10'45" W; near SW cor. sec. 8, T 9 S, R 35 E). Named on Waucoba Mountain (1951) 15' quadrangle.

Meadow Creek [ALPINE]: *stream,* flows 2.25 miles from Meadow Lake to North Fork Mokelumne River 6.5 miles northwest of Pacific Grade Summit (lat. 38°34'45" N, long. 120°00' W). Named on Pacific Valley (1979) 7.5' quadrangle.

Meadow Lake [ALPINE]: *lake,* 4600 feet long, behind a dam on Meadow Creek nearly 7 miles north-northwest of Pacific Grade Summit (lat. 38°36' N, long. 119°58'30" W; near E line sec. 27, T 9 N, R 18 E). Named on Pacific Valley (1979) 7.5' quadrangle.

Meiss Lake [ALPINE]: *lake,* 1050 feet long, 5.25 miles north of Fourth of July Peak (lat. 38°44'10" N, long. 120°00'40" W; sec. 4, T 10 N, R 18 E). Named on Caples Lake (1979) 7.5' quadrangle.

Mengel Pass [INYO]: *pass,* 2.25 miles east-southeast of Manly Peak at the south end of Butte Valley (lat. 35°54' N, long. 117°04'50" W). Named on Manly Peak (1950) 15' quadrangle. The name recalls Carl Mengel, a prospector whose ashes were buried at the pass in 1946 (Belden, p. 63).

Merk Canyon [ALPINE]: *canyon,* drained by a stream that flows 1.5 miles to West Fork Carson River 1 mile west-southwest of Woodfords (lat. 38°46'05" N, long. 119°50'30" W; sec. 34, T 11 N, R 19 E). Named on Woodfords (1979) 7.5' quadrangle.

Mesa Camp [MONO]: *locality,* 7 miles east-southeast of Toms Place (lat. 37°30'25" N, long. 118°34'25" W; near S line sec. 16, T 5 S, R 31 E). Named on Casa Diablo Mountain (1953) 15' quadrangle.

Mesquite Flat [INYO]: *area,* west and northwest of Stovepipe Wells in Death Valley (lat. 36°42' N, long. 117°12' W). Named on Grapevine Peak (1957) and Stovepipe Wells (1952) 15' quadrangles. The name is for large mesquite bushes that flourish at the place (Federal Writers' Project, p. 58). United States Board on Geographic Names (1933, p. 515) rejected the names "Mesquite Valley" and "Northwest Arm of Death Valley" for the feature.

Mesquite Spring [INYO]: *spring,* 4 miles north-northeast of Sugarloaf Peak in Anvil Spring Canyon (lat. 35°56'30" N, long. 116°54'35" W). Named on Wingate Wash (1950) 15' quadrangle.

Mesquite Spring: see **Mesquite Spring Campground** [INYO].

Mesquite Spring Campground [INYO]: *locality,* 7.25 miles northeast of Tin Mountain (lat. 36°57'50" N, long. 117°22' W; at S line sec. 26, T 11 S, R 42 E). Named on Tin Mountain (1957) 15' quadrangle. Ballarat (1913) 1° quadrangle has the name "Mesquite Spr." at the place. Palmer (p. 48) noted that the spring was named for mesquite trees nearby, and mentioned that it may be the feature called Indian Spring by some writers.

Mesquite Valley [INYO]: *valley,* east and north of Kingston Range on California-Nevada State line; mainly in San Bernardino County. Named on Horse Thief Springs (1956) and Shenandoah Peak (1956) 15' quadrangles.

Mesquite Valley: see **Death Valley** [INYO]; **Mesquite Flat** [INYO].

Mesquite Well [INYO]: *well,* 7 miles south of Bennetts Well (lat. 36°03'55" N, long. 116°50'30" W). Named on Furnace Creek (1910) 1° quadrangle.

Mexican Spring [INYO]: *spring,* 7.25 miles southeast of New York Butte (lat. 36°35'20" N, long. 117°49'25" W). Named on New York Butte (1950) 15' quadrangle.

Meysan Lake [INYO]: *lake,* 1300 feet long, nearly 3 miles southeast of Mount Whitney (1) (lat. 36°33'20" N, long. 118°15' W). Named on Lone Pine (1958) and Mount Whitney (1956) 15' quadrangles.

Meysan Lake: see **Little Meysan Lake** [INYO].

Middle Canyon [MONO]: *canyon,* drained by a stream that flows 4.25 miles to Hammil Valley 8 miles northwest of White Mountain Peak (lat. 37°42'35" N, long. 118°22'10" W; near NE cor. sec. 7, T 3 S, R 33 E). Named on White Mountain Peak (1962) 15' quadrangle.

Middle Creek [ALPINE]: *stream,* flows less than 1 mile from Upper Blue Lake to Lower Blue Lake 7.25 miles north of Pacific Grade Summit (lat. 38°37'15" N, long. 119°55'55" W; sec. 19, T 9 N, R 19 E). Named on Carson Pass (1979) and Pacific Valley (1979) 7.5' quadrangles.

Middle Creek [MONO]: *stream,* flows 1.5 miles to the State of Nevada 8 miles east of Benton (lat. 37°49'25" N, long. 118°19'35" W). Named on Benton (1962) 15' quadrangle.

Middle Creek Campground [ALPINE]: *locality,* 5.5 miles south-southeast of Carson Pass (lat. 38°37'35" N, long. 119°56'10" W; near N line sec. 19, T 9 N, R 19 E); the place is along Middle Creek. Named on Carson Pass (1979) 7.5' quadrangle.

Middle Palisade [INYO]: *peak,* 12 miles southwest of Big Pine on Inyo-Fresno County line (lat. 37°04'15" N, long. 118°28'05" W). Altitude 14,040 feet. Named on Big Pine (1950) 15' quadrangle. This is one of the group that Whitney called Palisade Peaks (Hanna, p. 226). A feature situated 0.5 mile northwest of Middle Palisade (lat. 37°04'30" N, long. 118°28'19" W) is called Norman Clyde Peak, for Norman A. Clyde, who made the first ascent in 1930 (United States Board on Geographic Names, 1974b, p. 3). A glacier located less than 0.5 mile north-northwest of Norman Clyde Peak (lat. 37°04'45" N, long. 118°28'40" W) is called Norman Clyde Glacier because the mountaineer crossed it on his way to the peak that now bears his name (United States Board on Geographic Names, 1974a, p. 3).

Middle Palisade Glacier [INYO]: *glacier,* 11.5 miles southwest of Big Pine (lat. 37°04'20" N, long. 118°27'45" W); the glacier is east of Middle Palisade. Named on Big Pine (1950) 15' quadrangle.

Middle Park [INYO]: *valley,* 11.5 miles south of Telescope Peak (lat. 36°00'15" N, long. 117°05'15" W). Named on Telescope Peak (1952) 15' quadrangle. The name is for the position of the feature relative to other places called parks (Palmer, p. 49).

Middle Park Canyon [INYO]: *canyon,* drained by a stream that flows 5.5 miles to Panamint Valley 12 miles southwest of Telescope Peak (lat. 36°01'40" N, long. 117°12'55" W; near N line sec. 15, T 22 S, R 44 E); the canyon heads near Middle Park. Named on Telescope Peak (1952) 15' quadrangle.

Middle Sister [MONO]: *peak,* 12.5 miles east-southeast of Coleville (lat. 38°30'30" N, long. 119°17'40" W); the peak is between East Sister—which is in the State of Nevada—and South Sister. Altitude 10,859 feet. Named on Desert Creek Peak (1956) 15' quadrangle.

Middle Spring: see **Bruce Canyon** [INYO]; **Rock Spring** [INYO].

Middle Town: see **Masonic** [MONO].

Midnight Lake [INYO]: *lake,* 1400 feet long, 1.5 miles east of Mount Darwin (lat. 37°10' N, long. 118°38'50" W). Named on Mount Goddard (1948) 15' quadrangle. Art Schober named the feature in the 1930's for a large black horse called Midnight (Schumacher, p. 95).

Midway Well [INYO]: *well,* nearly 7 miles north-northwest of Stovepipe Wells in Death Valley (lat. 36°44'40" N, long. 117°08'05" W; sec. 18, T 14 S, R 45 E). Named on Stovepipe Wells (1952) 15' quadrangle. The name is from the position of the well about halfway between Boundary Canyon and Grapevine Canyon (1) (Palmer, p. 49).

Mildred Lake [MONO]: *lake,* 1100 feet long, 1.5 miles southwest of Mount Morrison along Convict Creek (lat. 37°32'45" N, long. 118° 52'25" W). Named on Mount Morrison (1953) 15' quadrangle.

Milk Ranch Canyon [MONO]: *canyon,* drained by a stream that flows 1.25 miles to Bodie Creek 0.25 mile north-northeast of Bodie (lat. 38°13'05" N, long. 119°00'35" W; sec. 9, T 4 N, R 27 E). Named on Bodie (1958) 15' quadrangle.

Milk Ranch Meadow [ALPINE]: *area,* 3 miles south-southwest of Ebbetts Pass (lat. 38°30'15" N, long. 119°49'30" W). Named on Ebbetts Pass (1979) 7.5' quadrangle.

Millberry Canyon [ALPINE]: *canyon,* 2.5 miles long, along Millberry Creek above a point 3.25 miles northwest of Markleeville (lat. 38°43'25" N, long. 119°49'40" W; sec. 7, T 10 N, R 20 E). Named on Markleeville (1979) 7.5' quadrangle.

Millberry Creek [ALPINE]: *stream,* flows 6.5 miles to Markleeville Creek at Markleeville (lat. 38°41'40" N, long. 119°46'40" W; sec. 21, T 10 N, R 20 E); the stream goes through Millberry Canyon. Named on Markleeville (1979) 7.5' quadrangle.

Mill Canyon [INYO]:

(1) *canyon,* 3.25 miles long, opens into the canyon of Wyman Creek 10 miles north-northeast of Westgard Pass (lat. 37°26'05" N, long. 118°05'10" W; near N line sec. 13, T 6 S, R 35 E). Named on Blanco Mountain (1951) 15' quadrangle.

(2) *canyon,* drained by a stream that flows 7.5 miles to Panamint Valley 7.25 miles west of Panamint Butte (lat. 36°26'30" N, long. 117°29' W). Named on Darwin (1950), Panamint Butte (1951), and Ubehebe Peak (1950) 15' quadrangles.

Mill Canyon [MONO]: *canyon,* extends for 4 miles along Mill Creek (1) above a point 4.5 miles south-southeast of Coleville (lat. 38°30'10" N, long. 119°28'35" W). Named on Chris Flat (1954) 7.5' quadrangle.

Mill City [MONO]: *locality,* 8.5 miles west-northwest of Mount Morrison and 0.5 mile southwest of Old Mammoth (lat. 37°37'20" N, long. 118°59'40" W; on W line sec. 9, T 4 S, R 27 E). Named on Mount Morrison (1953) 15' quadrangle. Mount Morrison (1914) 30' quadrangle has the name "Pine City" at or near the place.

Mill Creek [MONO]:
(1) *stream,* flows 9.5 miles to West Walker River 4 miles south-southeast of Coleville (lat. 38°31'05" N, long. 119°28'20" W; sec. 20, T 8 N, R 23 E). Named on Desert Creek Peak (1956) and Fales Hot Springs (1956) 15' quadrangles. Wheeler's (1876-1877) map has the name "Lost Cañon" along what appears to be the course of this stream.
(2) *stream,* flows 13 miles to Mono Lake 4 miles north of Lee Vining (lat. 38°01' N, long. 119°07'45" W; sec. 20, T 2 N, R 26 E). Named on Bodie (1958), Matterhorn Peak (1956), and Tuolumne Meadows (1956) 15' quadrangles. The name is from sawmills that operated along the stream in the early 1860's (Wedertz, p. 153). South Fork enters from the south 8 miles upstream from the mouth of the main creek; it is 3 miles long and is named on Bodie (1958) 15' quadrangle. Caesar Thiervierge had a stable and an inn in 1877 at a place called Frenchman's Station that was situated at the mouth of Mill Creek (2); Thiervierge conducted excursions to islands in Mono Lake (Fletcher, p. 57). A small mining community called Vernon, named for a placer claim, was situated along Mill Creek (2) near the mouth of Lundy Canyon (sec. 13, T 2 N, R 25 E); it was abandoned about 1889 (Wedertz, p. 203).

Mill Creek Canyon: see **Lundy Canyon** [MONO].

Miller Spring [INYO]: *spring,* 13 miles south-southwest of Eagle Mountain on a spur of Greenwater Range (lat. 36°02'10" N, long. 116°26'35" W; sec. 4, T 22 N, R 5 E). Named on Eagle Mountain (1951) 15' quadrangle. Called Millers Spr. on Furnace Creek (1910) 1° quadrangle, and called Miller's Sp. on Tucker and Sampson's (1938) map. The name may commemorate George Miller, a prospector who visited the neighborhood in 1869 (Palmer, p. 49).

Millers Spring [INYO]: *spring,* 3.5 miles east-northeast of Darwin in Darwin Canyon (lat. 36°17'35" N, long. 117°32'15" W; sec. 9, T 19 S, R 41 E). Named on Darwin (1950) 15' quadrangle.

Millersville [MONO]: *locality,* 5 miles west-northwest of Bodie (lat. 38°14'50" N, long. 119°05'55" W; sec. 34, T 5 N, R 26 E). Named on Bridgeport (1909) 30' quadrangle.

Millie Lake [MONO]: *lake,* 950 feet long, 5.5 miles east of Sonora Pass (lat. 38°20'15" N, long. 119°32'20" W; sec. 27, T 6 N, R 22 E). Named on Pickel Meadow (1954) 7.5' quadrangle.

Millner Creek: see **Milner Creek** [MONO].

Mills Lake [INYO]: *lake,* 1000 feet long, 1.25 miles north-northeast of Mount Abbot (lat. 37°24'10" N, long. 118°46'30" W); the lake is 1 mile northeast of Mount Mills. Named on Mount Abbot (1953) 15' quadrangle.

Millspaugh [INYO]: *locality,* 5.5 miles south-southeast of Maturango Peak (lat. 36°02'50" N, long. 117°27'35" W; near SE cor. sec. 5, T 22 S, R 42 E). Site named on Maturango Peak (1951) 15' quadrangle. Postal authorities established Millspaugh post office in 1902 and discontinued it in 1910; the name was for Almon N. Millspaugh, first postmaster (Salley, p. 141).

Mills Peak: see **Mount Mills** [INYO].

Milner Creek [MONO]: *stream,* flows 7.5 miles to the north end of Chalfant Valley 6 miles west-southwest of White Mountain Peak (lat. 37°35'45" N, long. 118°21' W; near W line sec. 16, T 4 S, R 33 E). Named on White Mountain Peak (1962) 15' quadrangle. United States Board on Geographic Names (1964b, p. 13) approved the form "Millner Creek" for the name.

Minaret Summit [MONO]: *pass,* 2 miles northwest of Mammoth Mountain on Mono-Madera County line (lat. 37°39'15" N, long. 119°03'25" W). Named on Devils Postpile (1953) 15' quadrangle.

Mine Creek [MONO]: *stream,* flows nearly 3 miles to Lee Vining Creek 7.25 miles west of Lee Vining (lat. 37°56'15" N, long. 119° 14'55" W; near W line sec. 20, T 1 N, R 25 E). Named on Tuolumne Meadows (1956) 15' quadrangle.

Mineral Hill: see **Old Mammoth** [MONO].

Mineral Mountain [ALPINE]: *peak,* 12.5 miles south-southeast of Mogul Peak (lat. 38°31'35" N, long. 119°37'30" W; sec. 24, T 8 N, R 21 E). Altitude 8964 feet. Named on Topaz Lake (1956) 15' quadrangle.

Mineral Park: see **Old Mammoth** [MONO].

Minnow Wash: see **Sulphur Spring** [INYO].

Minute Gun Cañon: see **Stone Canyon** [INYO].

Mirror Lake [INYO]: *lake,* 550 feet long, 1.5 miles east-southeast of Mount Whitney (1) along Lone Pine Creek (lat. 36°34'15" N, long. 118°15'45" W). Named on Mount Whitney (1956) 15' quadrangle.

Moat Lake [MONO]: *lake,* 1000 feet long, 6.25 miles east-southeast of Matterhorn Peak (lat. 38°03'20" N, long. 119°16'40" W; near N line sec. 1, T 2 N, R 24 E). Named on Matterhorn Peak (1956) 15' quadrangle. The feature is one of the group called Virginia Lakes

Mocalno: see **Hammil** [MONO].

Mock [INYO]: *locality,* 7.25 miles south of New York Butte along Southern Pacific Railroad (lat. 36°32'35" N, long. 117°56' W; sec. 15, T 16 S, R 37 E). Named on New York Butte (1950) 15' quadrangle.

Modock: see **Lookout Mountain** [INYO] (2).

Modoc Peak [MONO]: *peak,* 2.5 miles south-southwest of Benton (lat. 37°46'55" N, long. 118°29'45" W; near NW cor. sec. 18, T 2 S, R 32 E). Named on Benton (1962) 15' quadrangle.

Mogul [ALPINE]: *locality,* 4.25 miles east of Markleeville (lat. 38° 41' N, long. 119°42'10" W); less than 1 mile east-southeast of present Mogul Peak in present Mogul Canyon. Named on Markleeville (1889) 30' quadrangle. The place was a mining camp of the 1860's and 1870's (Nadeau, p. 219).

Mogul Canyon [ALPINE]: *canyon,* drained by a stream that flows 3.5 miles to East Fork Carson River 1.5 miles southwest of Mogul Peak (lat. 38°40'35" N, long. 119°44'10" W); the old mining camp called Mogul was in the canyon. Named on Heenan Lake (1979) 7.5' quadrangle.

Mogul Canyon: see **Goskey Canyon** [ALPINE].

Mogul Peak [ALPINE]: *peak,* 3.5 miles east of Markleeville (lat. 38° 41'20" N, long. 119°43' W); the peak is north of Mogul Canyon. Altitude 7583 feet. Named on Heenan Lake (1979) 7.5' quadrangle.

Moigne Mountain: see **Pinto Peak** [INYO].

Mokelumne River, North Fork [ALPINE]: *stream,* flows 21 miles to Amador County and Calaveras County nearly 2.5 miles west of Mount Reba (lat. 38°30'35" N, long. 120°04'20" W). Named on Ebbetts Pass (1979), Mokelumne Peak (1979), and Pacific Valley (1979) 7.5' quadrangles. Called Mokelumne River on Markleeville (1889) and Pyramid Peak (1896) 30' quadrangles.

Mollie Gibson Canyon [INYO]: *canyon,* 3 miles long, opens into Payson Canyon 1 mile north of Westgard Pass (lat. 37°19' N, long. 118°09'10" W; sec. 29, T 7 S, R 35 E); the canyon heads near Mollie Gibson mine. Named on Blanco Mountain (1951) 15' quadrangle.

Molybdenite Creek [MONO]: *stream,* flows 8 miles to Little Walker River 4.5 miles southwest of Fales Hot Springs (lat. 38°18'10" N, long. 119°27' W; sec. 4, T 5 N, R 23 E). Named on Fales Hot Springs (1956) and Matterhorn Peak (1956) 15' quadrangles.

Monache [INYO]: *locality,* 7.25 miles north of Olancha along Southern Pacific Railroad (lat. 36°23'10" N, long. 118°00'30" W). Named on Olancha (1907) 30' quadrangle. The name is from a division or dialect group of Indians (Gudde, 1949, p. 220-221).

Mona Lake: see **Mono Lake** [MONO].

Monarch Canyon [INYO]: *canyon,* drained by a stream that flows 3.5 miles to Death Valley 7.5 miles north of Beatty Junction (lat. 36°42'45" N, long. 116°57' W; near W line sec. 26, T 14 S, R 46 E). Named on Chloride Cliff (1952) 15' quadrangle.

Monarch Spring [INYO]: *spring,* 9.25 miles north of Beatty Junction in Funeral Mountains (lat. 36°43'20" N, long. 116°55'20" W; sec. 24, T 14 N, R 46 E); the spring is in Monarch Canyon. Named on Chloride Cliff (1952) 15' quadrangle.

Monckton: see **Dunderberg Mill** [MONO].

Monitor: see **Loope** [ALPINE].

Monitor Cañon: see **Monitor Creek** [ALPINE].

Monitor Creek [ALPINE]: *stream,* flows 4 miles to East Fork Carson River 2 miles south-southwest of Mogul Peak (lat. 38°39'40" N, long. 119°43'35" W; near N line sec. 1, T 9 N, R 20 E). Named on Heenan Lake (1979) 7.5' quadrangle. United States Board on Geographic Names (1957, p. 2) rejected the name "Heenan Creek" for the stream. Eakel (p. 8) used the name "Monitor Cañon" for the canyon of the creek

Monitor Pass [ALPINE]: *pass,* 5.25 miles east of Mogul Peak (lat. 38°40'30" N, long. 119°37'15" W; sec. 36, T 10 N, R 21 E). Named on Topaz Lake (1956) 15' quadrangle.

Mono: see **Mono Lake Post Office** [MONO]; **Mono Mills** [MONO].

Mono Basin: see **Mono Valley** [MONO].

Mono Craters [MONO]: *range,* 9 miles southeast of Lee Vining (lat. 37°52' N, long. 119°00'30" W); the feature is south of Mono Lake. Named on Cowtrack Mountain (1962) and Mono Craters (1953) 15' quadrangles.

Mono Diggings [MONO]: *locality,* 11 miles south-southeast of Bridgeport in Rattlesnake Gulch (lat. 38°05'25" N, long. 119°09'30" W; on W line sec. 30, T 3 N, R 26 E). Named on Bodie (1958) 15' quadrangle. Mining of placer gold at the place began in 1857 (Irelan, p. 366).

Mono Diggings: see **Sinnamon Cut** [MONO].

Mono Dome [MONO]: *peak,* nearly 3 miles west of Lee Vining (lat. 37°57'40" N, long. 119°10'15" W). Altitude 10,614 feet. Named on Mono Craters (1953) 15' quadrangle.

Mono Jim Peak: see **Mount Morrison** [MONO].

Monola [INYO]: *locality,* nearly 3 miles east-southeast of Big Pine along Southern Pacific Railroad (lat. 37°08'40" N, long. 118°14'35" W; on S line sec. 22, T 9 S, R 34 E). Named on Waucoba Mountain (1951) 15' quadrangle.

Mono Lake [MONO]: *lake,* 13 miles long, 21 miles southeast of Bridgeport (lat. 38°00' N, long. 119°00' W). Named on Bodie (1958), Cowtrack Mountain (1962), Mono Craters (1953), and Trench Canyon (1958) 15' quadrangles. Called Mona Lake on Mitchell's (1856) map. Russell (p. 273) called the feature Lake Mono. The name is from the designation of a division of Shoshonean Indians that lived in the region (Kroeber, p. 48).

Mono Lake: see **Mono Lake Post Office** [MONO].

Mono Lake Post Office [MONO]: *locality,* 2.5 miles north-northwest of Lee Vining near the edge of Mono Lake (lat. 37°59'30" N, long. 119°08'30" W; sec. 31, T 2 N, R 26 E). Named on Mono Craters (1953) 15' quadrangle. Bridgeport (1909) 30' quadrangle shows Mono Lake P.O. at a place called Tioga Lodge, located 1 mile farther north-northwest. The name "Mono Lake" is at the post office site on Eakel and McLaughlin's (1917) map. Postal authorities established Mono post office in 1882 and discontinued it in 1884; they moved it and changed the name to Mono Lake in 1889, and discontinued it in 1965 (Salley, p. 144).

Mono Mills [MONO]: *locality,* 9.5 miles east-southeast of Lee Vining (lat. 37°53'15" N, long. 118°57'30" W; near E line sec. 2, T 1 S, R 27 E). Site named on Cowtrack Mountain (1962) 15' quadrangle. A lumber camp at the place supplied mines at Bodie (Cain, 1956, p. 39-40). The sawmill there was completed in 1880; at first it was called Mono Saw Mill and the village by it was called Mono, but later the mill and village together were called Mono Mills (Fletcher, p. 75).

Mono Pass [INYO]: *pass,* nearly 3 miles north-northeast of Mount Abbot on Inyo-Frenso County line (lat. 37°25'30" N, long. 118°46'20" W). Named on Mount Abbot (1953) 15' quadrangle.

Mono Pass [MONO]: *pass,* 9 miles southwest of Lee Vining on Mono-Tuolumne County line at the head of Bloody Canyon (lat. 37°51'20" N, long. 119°12'45" W). Named on Mono Craters (1953) 15' quadrangle.

Mono Saw Mill: see **Mono Mills** [MONO].

Mono Valley [MONO]: *valley,* around the north side of Mono Lake. Named on Bodie (1958) and Trench Canyon (1958) 15' quadrangles. Cowtrack Mountain (1962) 15' quadrangle has the name "Mono Basin" for the valley southeast of Mono Lake.

Mono Village [MONO]: *settlement,* 11 miles southwest of Bridgeport near the west end of Twin Lakes (1) (lat. 38°09' N, long. 119°22'30" W; sec. 6, T 3 N, R 24 E). Named on Matterhorn Peak (1956) 15' quadrangle.

Monoville: see **Sinnamon Cut** [MONO].

Mono Vista Spring [MONO]: *spring,* 4.25 miles north-northwest of Lee Vining (lat. 38°01'10" N, long. 119°08'20" W; sec. 20, T 2 N, R 26 E); the spring is in Mono Valley near the edge of Mono Lake. Named on Bodie (1958) 15' quadrangle.

Monte Cristo [MONO]: *locality,* 11 miles north of Bridgeport in Sweetwater Mountains (lat. 38°24'40" N, long. 119°13'45" W; sec. 31, T 7 N, R 25 E). Site named on Bridgeport (1958) 15' quadrangle. The place was a small mining camp in the 1880's (Gudde, 1975, p. 221). A short-lived mining town called Cameron, for Robert A. Cameron, was about 1 mile from Monte Cristo; an attempt to change the name "Cameron" to "Newburg" failed (Wederz, p. 162).

Monte Diablo Creek: see **Convict Creek** [MONO].

Montenegro Spring [INYO]: *springs,* two, 2.5 miles west of Westgard Pass (lat. 37°17'45" N, long. 118°11'45" W; sec. 36, T 7 S, R 34 E). Named on Blanco Mountain (1951) 15' quadrangle.

Montgomery City [MONO]: *locality,* 2.5 miles east-northeast of Benton (lat. 37°49'45" N, long. 118°25'50" W); the place is 4.25 miles west of Montgomery Peak near the mouth of Montgomery Canyon. Site named on Benton (1962) 15' quadrangle.

Montgomery Creek [MONO]: *stream,* flows 4.5 miles to Benton Valley 3 miles east-northeast of Benton (lat. 37°50' N, long. 118° 25'30" W); the stream heads south of Montgomery Peak. Named on Benton (1962) 15' quadrangle.

Montgomery Peak [MONO]: *peak,* nearly 7 miles east of Benton (lat. 37°50'20" N, long. 118°21'20" W). Altitude 13,441 feet. Named on Benton (1962) 15' quadrangle. Called White Mountain. Peak on Wheeler's (1871) map.

Montgomery Spring [INYO]: *spring,* 10 miles west of Shoshone (lat. 35°56'50" N, long. 116°26'50" W). Named on Shoshone (1951) 15' quadrangle.

Montrose: see **Lake Jessie Montrose**, under **Tioga Lake** [MONO].

Monumental Rock: see **Mammoth Rock** [MONO].

Monument Peak [ALPINE]: *peak,* 4.5 miles north of Freel Peak on Alpine-El Dorado County line (lat. 38°55'25" N, long. 119°53'50" W; sec. 7, T 12 N, R 19 E). Altitude 10,067 feet. Named on South Lake Tahoe (1955) 7.5' quadrangle, which shows the peak on the incorrect California-Nevada State line that Von Schmidt surveyed in 1873.

Monument Ridge [MONO]: *ridge,* east-to north-northeast-trending, 2.5 miles long, 4 miles east-northeast of Matterhorn Peak (lat. 38° 06'30" N, long. 119°18'40" W). Named on Matterhorn Peak (1956) 15' quadrangle.

Moonlight Lake [INYO]: *lake,* 2100 feet long, 2 miles east of Mount Darwin (lat. 37°09'45" N, long. 118°38'05" W; near S line sec. 18, T 9 S, R 31 E). Named on Mount Goddard (1948) 15' quadrangle. United States Board on Geographic Names (1965b, p. 10) rejected the name "Hungry Packer Lake" for the feature.

Moran Spring [MONO]: *spring,* 8 miles northeast of Toms Place (lat. 37°39'15" N, long. 118°35' W; sec. 29, T 3 S, R 31 E). Named on Casa Diablo Mountain (1953) 15' quadrangle.

Morgan: see **Mount Morgan** [INYO]; **Mount Morgan** [MONO].

Morgan Creek [INYO]: *stream,* flows 2.5 miles to Pine Creek 2.5 miles west-northwest of Mount Tom (lat. 37°21'40" N, long. 118° 41'50" W; sec. 8, T 7 S, R 30 E). Named on Mount Tom (1949) 15' quadrangle.

Morgan Lake: see **Lower Morgan Lake** [INYO]; **Upper Morgan Lake** [INYO].

Morgan Pass [INYO]: *pass,* 2 miles east of Mount Abbot (lat. 37°23'30" N, long. 118°45' W); the pass is situated above Upper Morgan Lake. Named on Mount Abbot (1953) and Mount Tom (1949) 15' quadrangles.

Mormon Gulch [INYO]: *canyon,* drained by a stream that flows 1.5 miles to Pleasant Canyon 10 miles south of Telescope Peak (lat. 36°01'35" N, long. 117°04' W). Named on Telescope Peak (1952) 15' quadrangle. The name recalls the presence of Mormons in the vicinity in the early days (Palmer, p. 50).

Mormon Meadow [MONO]: *area,* 7.25 miles west-southwest of Bodie along Clear Creek (lat. 38°09'45" N, long. 119°07'45" W; sec. 32, T 4 N, R 26 E). Named on Bodie (1958) 15' quadrangle, which shows Mormon ranch nearby. The misspelled name "Mormon" is for Colonel Thomas J. Moorman, who was in the neighborhood in the early 1850's (Wedertz, p. 24-25). Fletcher (fig. 8, p. 53) showed a place called Mormon Station located about 7 miles west-southwest of Bodie along a toll road between Big Meadows (present Bridgeport) and Bodie.

Mormon Meadow: see **Little Mormon Meadow** [MONO].

Mormon Point [INYO]: *promontory,* 9.5 miles southeast of Bennetts Well on the east side of Death Valley (lat. 36°03'15" N, long. 116° 45'30" W). Named on Bennetts Well (1952) 15' quadrangle.

Mormon Station: see **Mormon Meadow** [MONO].

Morning Star Hill: see **Colorado Hill** [ALPINE].

Morris Creek [MONO]: *stream,* flows 4.5 miles, mainly in Nevada, to Benton Valley 5.5 miles northeast of Benton near California-Nevada State line (lat. 37°52'35" N, long. 118°24'20" W). Named on Benton (1962) 15' quadrangle.

Morrison: see **Mount Morrison** [MONO].

Mosaic Canyon [INYO]: *canyon,* drained by a stream that flows 2.5 miles to Death Valley 7 miles south-southwest of Stovepipe Wells (lat. 36°34'30" N, long. 117°08'45" W). Named on Stovepipe Wells (1952) 15' quadrangle. The name is from the smooth, water-worn surface of colorful conglomerate in the bottom of the canyon that gives the floor of the canyon the appearance of a mosaic (Federal Writers' Project, p. 32). Employees of Pacific Coast Borax Company named the feature (Palmer, p. 51).

Moscow Canyon [INYO]: *canyon,* drained by a stream that flows 2 miles to an unnamed valley 3 miles west of Argus Peak (lat. 35°51'05" N, long. 117°29'50" W; sec. 13, T 24 S, R 42 E). Named on Trona (1949) 15' quadrangle.

Moscow Spring [INYO]: *spring,* 2 miles northwest of Argus Peak (lat. 35°52'05" N, long. 117°28'25" W; near NW cor. sec. 8, T 24 S, R 42 E); the spring is on the north side of Moscow Canyon. Named on Trona (1949) 15' quadrangle. The spring appears to be at or near a place called Horse Camp on Wheeler's (1877) map.

Mosquito Lake [ALPINE]: *lake,* 900 feet long, less than 0.25 mile west-southwest of Pacific Grade Summit (lat. 38°30'55" N, long. 119°54'45" W; sec. 29, T 8 N, R 19 E). Named on Pacific Valley (1979) 7.5' quadrangle.

Mound Spring Valley: see **Death Valley** [INYO].

Mount Abbot [INYO]: *peak,* 22 miles west of Bishop on Inyo-Fresno County line (lat. 37°23'15" N, long. 118°47'05" W). Altitude 13,715 feet. Named on Mount Abbot (1953) 15' quadrangle. Members of the Whitney survey named the peak in 1864 for Captain Henry Larcom Abbot of the army engineers (Farquhar, 1923, p. 381). United States Board on Geographic Names (1933, p. 78) ruled against the form "Mount Abbott" for the name.

Mount Agassiz [INYO]: *peak,* 9 miles east-southeast of Mount Darwin on Inyo-Fresno County line (lat. 37°06'45" N, long. 118° 31'50" W). Altitude 13,891 feet. Named on Mount Goddard (1948) 15' quadrangle. Called Agassiz Needle on Mount Goddard (1912) 30' quadrangle, a name that Lil A. Winchell gave in 1879 to honor Professor Louis Agassiz of Harvard University (Farquhar, 1923, p. 382). This is one of the peaks that Whitney called Palisade Peaks (Hanna, p. 226). United States Board on Geographic Names (1969, p. 4) approved the name "Aperture Peak" for a feature located 0.5 mile north of Mount Agassiz (lat. 37°07'30" N, long. 118°31'47" W).

Mount Aggie [MONO]: *peak,* 1.5 miles southeast of Mount Morrison (lat. 37°32'45" N, long. 118°50'30" W). Altitude 11,561 feet. Named on Mount Morrison (1953) 15' quadrangle.

Mountaineer Creek [ALPINE]: *stream,* flows 6.5 miles to join Leviathan Creek and form Bryant Creek (1) 5 miles northeast of Mogul Peak (lat. 38°44'10" N, long. 119°38'40" W; near N line sec. 11, T 10 N, R 21 E). Named on Topaz Lake (1956) 15' quadrangle.

Mountain Lake: see **Caples Lake** [ALPINE].

Mountain Spring [INYO]: *spring,* 2 miles east-northeast of the mouth of Mountain Springs Canyon (lat. 35°56'55" N, long. 117° 33'55" W; near W line sec. 9, T 23 S, R 41 E). Named on Mountain Springs Canyon (1953) 15' quadrangle.

Mountain Springs Canyon [INYO]: *canyon,* drained by a stream that flows 5.5 miles to lowlands 17 miles east of the village of Little Lake (lat. 35°56'10" N, long. 117°35'45" W; sec. 18, T 23 S, R 41 E); Mountain Spring is in the canyon. Named on Mountain Springs Canyon (1953) 15' quadrangle.

Mount Alice [INYO]: *peak,* 10 miles west-southwest of Big Pine (lat. 37°07'25" N, long. 118°27'55" W; sec. 34, T 9 S, R 32 E). Altitude 11,630 feet. Named on Big Pine (1950) 15' quadrangle. The name commemorates Mrs. Alice Ober of Big Pine, who acted as chaperon for a group that traveled through the neighborhood; the name originally applied to present Temple Crag (Gudde, 1969, p. 7, 334).

Mount Baldwin [MONO]: *peak,* 2 miles south of Mount Morrison (lat. 37°31'55" N, long. 118°51' W). Altitude 12,614 feet. Named on Mount Morrison (1953) 15' quadrangle.

Mount Barcroft [MONO]: *peak,* 3.5 miles south of White Mountain Peak (lat. 37°34'55" N, long. 118°14'50" W). Altitude 13,040 feet. Named on Mount Barcroft (1962) and White Mountain Peak (1962) 15' quadrangles. The name commemorates Sir Joseph Barcroft, who was a British physiologist interested in high altitude effects (United States Board on Geographic Names, 1954, p. 2).

Mount Barnard [INYO]: *peak,* nearly 4 miles north-northwest of Mount Whitney (1) on Inyo-Tulare County line (lat. 36°37'40" N, long. 118°19'15" W). Altitude 13,990 feet. Named on Mount Whitney (1956) 15' quadrangle. The name honors astronomer Edward E. Barnard (United States Board on Geographic Names, 1933, p. 124).

Mount Baxter [INYO]: *peak,* 10 miles west-northwest of Independence on Inyo-Fresno County line (lat. 36°51'45" N, long. 118° 21'50" W). Altitude 13,125 feet. Named on Mount Pinchot (1953) 15' quadrangle. George R. Davis of United States Geological Survey named the peak in 1905 to commemorate John Baxter, a rancher in Owens Valley (Sowaal, p. 97).

Mount Biedeman [MONO]: *peak,* 5 miles southwest of Bodie (lat. 38°09'05" N, long. 119°04' W; on E line sec. 2, T 3 N, R 26 E). Altitude 8981 feet. Named on Bodie (1958) 15' quadrangle. The misspelled name is for Jack Biderman, a miner at Bodie (Gudde, 1975, p. 33).

Mount Bolton Brown [INYO]: *peak,* 11.5 miles southwest of Big Pine on Inyo-Fresno County line (lat. 37°02'45" N, long. 118°26'20" W). Altitude 13,538 feet. Named on Big Pine (1950) 15' quadrangle. Chester Versteeg and his party climbed the peak in 1922 and named it to honor Bolton C. Brown of the Sierra Club (Versteeg, p. 426).

Mount Bradley [INYO]: *peak,* 10.5 miles north-northwest of Mount Whitney (1) on Inyo-Tulare County line (lat. 36°43'45" N, long. 118°20'15" W). Altitude 13,289 feet. Named on Mount Whitney (1956) 15' quadrangle. Mr. and Mrs. Robert M. Price and J.C. Shinn made the first ascent of the peak in 1898 and named it for Cornelius Beach Bradley, professor at University of California (Farquhar, 1923, p. 385).

Mount Braly: see **Brawley Peaks** [MONO].

Mount Bullion [ALPINE]: *locality,* 2 miles south-southwest of Mogul Peak at the confluence of East Fork Carson River and Monitor Creek (lat. 38°39'40" N, long. 119°43'30" W; near N line sec. 1, T 9 N, R 20 E). Site named on Heenan Lake (1979) 7.5' quadrangle. Called Bullion on California Mining Bureau's (1917a) map. Postal authorities established Bullionae post office in 1869 and discontinued it in 1872 (Frickstad, p. 4). The place also was called Bullona (Hoover, Rensch, and Rensch, p. 26).

Mount Carillon [INYO]: *peak,* 1.25 miles northeast of Mount Whitney (1) on Inyo-Tulare County line (lat. 36°35'30" N, long. 118°16'40" W). Altitude 13,552 feet. Named on Mount Whitney (1956) 15' quadrangle. The named is for the fancied resemblance of the feature to a bell tower (United States Board on Geographic Names, 1938, p. 10).

Mount Conness [MONO]: *peak,* 11 miles west of Lee Vining on Mono-Tuolumne County line (lat. 37°58' N, long. 119°19'15" W). Altitude 12,590 feet. Named on Tuolumne Meadows (1956) 15' quadrangle. Members of the Whitney survey named the peak to honor John Conness, who helped pass through the legislature the bill that established the survey (Whitney, 1870, p. 100). Conness also helped establish Yosemite Valley as a park (Smith, Genny, p. 26).

Mount Corcoran [INYO]: *peak,* 11.5 miles west-southwest of Lone Pine on Inyo-Tulare County line (lat. 36°32'10" N, long. 118°14'50" W). Named on Lone Pine (1958) 15' quadrangle. United States Board on Geographic Names (1933, p. 236) rejected the names "Mount Langley," "Mount Whitney Number 1," "Old Mount Whitney," and "Sheep Rock" for the feature. The Board later (1968a, p. 6) rejected the form "Corcoran Mountain" for the name, which was given in 1868 to honor philanthropist William Wilson Corcoran.

Mount Crocker [MONO]: *peak,* nearly 6 miles south-southeast of Mount Morrison on Mono-Fresno County line (lat. 37°29' N, long. 118°49'30" W). Altitude 12,457 feet. Named on Mount Abbot (1953) 15' quadrangle. Called Crocker Pk. on Sampson's (1940) map. R.B. Marshall of United States Geological Survey named the peak to honor Charles Crocker of Central Pacific Railroad (Gudde, 1949, p. 84).

Mount Dade [INYO]: *peak,* 0.5 mile southeast of Mount Abbot on Inyo-Fresno County line (lat. 37°22'55" N, long. 118°46'45" W). Named on Mount Abbot (1953) 15' quadrangle.

Mount Dana [MONO]: *peak,* 7 miles southwest of Lee Vining on Mono-Tuolumne County line (lat. 37°54' N, long. 119°13'15" W). Altitude 13,053 feet. Named on Mono Craters (1953) 15' quadrangle. Members of the Whitney survey named the peak in 1863 to honor geologist James Dwight Dana (United States Board on Geographic Names, 1934, p. 6). Russell (p. 283) gave the name "Mount Dana Glacier" to a feature located 0.25 mile northeast of the peak at the head of Glacier Canyon. United States Board on Geographic Names (1994, p. 4) approved the name "Beartrack Canyon" for a feature, 3 miles long, that opens into Lee Vining Canyon 5 miles northeast of Mount Dana (lat. 37°58'15" N, long. 119°10'07" W).

Mount Dana Glacier: see **Mount Dana** [MONO].

Mount Darwin [INYO]: *peak,* 20 miles southwest of Bishop on Inyo-Fresno County line (lat. 37°10' N, long. 118°40'15" W). Altitude 13,830 feet. Named on Mount Goddard (1948) 15' quadrangle. Theodore S. Solomons named the peak in 1895 for Charles Darwin (Farquhar, 1923, p. 390).

Mount Davis [MONO]: *peak,* 12 miles west-northwest of Mammoth Mountain on Mono-Madera County line (lat. 37°42'55" N, long. 119°13'05" W). Altitude 12,311 feet. Named on Devils Postpile (1953) 15' quadrangle. The name commemorates Brigadier General Milton F. Davis, who climbed the peak in 1891 when he was a Lieutenant under Captain A.E. Wood, first acting superintendent of Yosemite National Park (Farquhar, 1926, p. 305).

Mount Dubois [MONO]: *peak,* 8 miles east-southeast of Benton (lat. 37°47' N, long. 118°20'30" W). Altitude 13,559 feet. Named on Benton (1962) 15' quadrangle.

Mount Emerson [INYO]: *peak,* 5.25 miles north of Mount Darwin (lat. 37°14'35" N, long. 118°39'10" W). Altitude 13,225 feet. Named on Mount Goddard (1948) 15' quadrangle. John Muir gave the name "Mount Emerson" to a peak to honor Ralph Waldo Emerson, but the feature that he named probably is the one now called Mount Humphreys (Gudde, 1949, p. 107).

Mount Emma [MONO]: *peak,* 6.5 miles southwest of Fales Hot Springs (lat. 38°16'40" N, long. 119°28'30" W; sec. 17, T 5 N, R 23 E). Altitude 10,525 feet. Named on Fales Hot Springs (1954) 7.5' quadrangle.

Mount Gayley [INYO]: *peak,* 12.5 miles west-southwest of Big Pine (lat. 37°06'10" N, long. 118°29'55" W). Altitude 13,510 feet. Named on Big Pine (1950) and Mount Goddard (1948) 15' quadrangles.

Mount Gibbs [MONO]: *peak,* 7.5 miles southwest of Lee Vining (lat. 37°52'35" N, long. 119°12'40" W). Altitude 12,764 feet. Named on Mono Craters (1953) 15' quadrangle. Frederick Law Olmsted named the peak in 1864 for Oliver Wolcott Gibbs, professor of science at Harvard University (Farquhar *in* Brewer, p. 549).

Mount Gilbert [INYO]: *peak,* 4.5 miles east-southeast of Mount Darwin on Inyo-Fresno County line (lat. 37°08'15" N, long. 118° 35'45" W; sec. 28, T 9 S, R 31 E). Altitude 13,103 feet. Named on Mount Goddard (1948) 15' quadrangle. The name honors geologist Grove Karl Gilbert (Farquhar, 1923, p. 398).

Mount Goode [INYO]: *peak,* 6.5 miles east-southeast of Mount Darwin on Inyo-Fresno County line (lat. 37°07'25" N, long. 118° 34'05" W; on W line sec. 35, T 9 S, R 31 E). Altitude 13,092 feet. Named on Mount Goddard (1948) 15' quadrangle. The name commemorates topographer Richard Urquhart Goode of United States Geological Survey (Farquhar, 1923, p. 399).

Mount Gould [INYO]: *peak,* 10 miles west of Independence on Inyo-Fresno County line (lat. 36°46'50" N, long. 118°22'35" W). Altitude 13,005 feet. Named on Mount Pinchot (1953) 15' quadrangle. The name honors Wilson S. Gould of Oakland, who climbed the peak with J.N. LeConte in 1896; LeConte had climbed it in 1890 and named it University Peak, but this name was transferred to another feature (Farquhar, 1923, p. 399).

Mount Haeckel [INYO]: *peak,* 1.25 miles south-southeast of Mount Darwin on Inyo-Fresno County line (lat. 37°09' N, long. 118°39'35" W). Altitude 13,435 feet. Named on Mount Goddard (1948) 15' quadrangle. Theodore S. Solomons named the peak in 1895 for Ernst Heinrich Haeckel, professor of zoology at University of Jena (Farquhar, 1923, p. 401).

Mount Hogue [MONO]: *peak,* 7.25 miles north-northwest of White Mountain Peak (lat. 37°44' N, long. 118°18'15" W). Altitude 12,751 feet. Named on White Mountain Peak (1962) 15' quadrangle.

Mount Humphreys [INYO]: *peak,* nearly 5 miles south-southwest of Mount Tom on Inyo-Fresno County line (lat. 37°16'15" N, long. 118°40'15" W). Altitude 13,986 feet. Named on Mount Tom (1949) 15' quadrangle. Members of the Whitney survey named the peak in 1864 for General Andrew Atkinson Humphreys (Farquhar, 1923, p. 405-406). This probably is the peak that John Muir called Mount Emerson for Ralph Waldo Emerson (Gudde, 1949, p. 107).

Mount Huntington [MONO]: *peak,* 8 miles southeast of Mount Morrison on Mono-Fresno County line (lat. 37°28'10" N, long. 118°46'35" W). Named on Mount Abbot (1953) 15' quadrangle. Called Huntington Pk. on Sampson's (1940) map. R.B. Marshall of United States Geological Survey named the feature to honor Collis P. Huntington of Central Pacific Railroad (Hanna, p. 145).

Mount Inyo [INYO]:

(1) *peak,* 9.5 miles north-northwest of the mouth of Paiute Canyon (lat. 36°58'40" N, long. 117°59'15" W). Named on Waucoba Wash (1951) 15' quadrangle.

(2) *peak,* 6.5 miles north-northwest of New York Butte (lat. 36°44'05" N,

long. 117°59'05" W). Altitude 11,107 feet. Named on New York Butte (1950) 15' quadrangle.

Mount Irvine [INYO]: *peak,* 2.25 miles southeast of Mount Whitney (1) (lat. 36°33'20" N, long. 118°15'45" W); the peak is 0.5 mile north of Mount Mallory. Altitude 13,770 feet. Named on Mount Whitney (1956) 15' quadrangle. Norman Clyde climbed the peak in 1925 and proposed the name to honor A.C. Irvine, who perished on Mount Everest in 1924 with George Leigh Mallory (Farquhar, 1926, p. 306).

Mount Jackson [MONO]: *peak,* 7.5 miles east-southeast of Fales Hot Springs in Sweetwater Mountains (lat. 38°19'30" N, long. 119° 15'55" W; near E line sec. 31, T 6 N, R 25 E). Altitude 9378 feet. Named on Fales Hot Springs (1956) 15' quadrangle.

Mount Jepson: see **Mount Sill** [INYO].

Mount Johnson [INYO]: *peak,* 5.5 miles east-southeast of Mount Darwin on Inyo-Fresno County line (lat. 37°07'45" N, long. 118° 35'05" W; on E line sec. 33, T 9 S, R 31 E). Altitude 12,868 feet. Named on Mount Goddard (1948) 15' quadrangle. The name is for Willard D. Johnson of United States Geological Survey (United States Board on Geographic Names, 1933, p. 401).

Mount Johnson: see **Mount Lewis** [MONO].

Mount Julius Caesar [INYO]: *peak,* 2 miles south of Mount Abbot on Inyo-Fresno County line (lat. 37°21'20" N, long. 118°46'50" W). Altitude 13,196 feet. Named on Mount Abbot (1953) 15' quadrangle. United States Board on Geographic Names (1978a, p. 4) rejected the form "Mount Julius Cesar" for the name.

Mount Keith [INYO]: *peak,* 9 miles north-northwest of Mount Whitney (1) on Inyo-Tulare County line (lat. 36°42' N, long. 118° 20'30" W). Altitude 13,977 feet. Named on Mount Whitney (1956) 15' quadrangle. Helen M. Gompertz named the peak in 1896 to honor California landscape painter William Keith (Hanna, p. 159).

Mount Lamarck [INYO]: *peak,* nearly 2 miles north of Mount Darwin on Inyo-Fresno County line (lat. 37°11'40" N, long. 118° 40'10" W); the peak is near the head of Lamarck Creek. Altitude 13,417 feet. Named on Mount Goddard (1948) 15' quadrangle. Called Lamarch Mtn. on Tucker and Sampson's (1938) map.

Mount Langley [INYO]: *peak,* 11.5 miles west-southwest of Lone Pine on Inyo-Tulare County line (lat. 36°31'25" N, long. 118°14'20" W). Altitude 14,042 feet. Named on Lone Pine (1958) 15' quadrangle. The name honors Samuel Pierpont Langley, secretary of Smithsonian Institution from 1877 until 1906, who led an expedition to Mount Whitney in 1881 (Farquhar, 1924, p. 52). Clarence King gave the name "Sheep Rock" (Wilkins, p. 145) or "Sheep Mountain" to the peak in 1864 (Goodyear, p. 232).

Mount Langley: see **Mount Corcoran** [INYO].

Mount LeConte [INYO]: *peak,* 3.5 miles southeast of Mount Whitney (1) on Inyo-Tulare County line (lat. 36°32'30" N, long. 118°15'05" W). Altitude 13,960 feet. Named on Mount Whitney (1956) 15' quadrangle. The name honors Joseph LeConte, professor of geology and natural history at University of California from 1869 until 1901 (Farquhar, 1924, p. 53).

Mount LeConte: see **Funeral Peak** [INYO].

Mount Lewis [MONO]: *peak,* 9 miles south-southwest of Lee Vining (lat. 37°50'30" N, long. 119°11'15" W). Altitude 12,296 feet. Named on Mono Craters (1953) 15' quadrangle. United States Board on Geographic Names (1933, p. 456) rejected the name "Mount Johnson" for the peak, and approved the name "Mount Lewis" to commemorate W.B. Lewis, who was superintendent of Yosemite National Park for eleven years.

Mount Mallory [INYO]: *peak,* 2.5 miles southeast of Mount Whitney (1) on Inyo-Tulare County line (lat. 36°33' N, long. 118°15'45" W). Altitude 13,850 feet. Named on Mount Whitney (1956) 15' quadrangle. Norman Clyde climbed the peak in 1925 and proposed the name to honor George Leigh Mallory, who perished on Mount Everest in 1924 (Farquhar, 1926, p. 306).

Mount Mary Austin [INYO]: *peak,* 9 miles west of Independence (lat. 36°48'55" N, long. 118°21'45" W). Named on Mount Pinchot (1953) 15' quadrangle. The name honors Mary Austin, prominent writer, natural historian, and resident of the region (United States Board on Geographic names, 1966b, p. 6).

Mount McAdie [INYO]: *peak,* 2.25 miles south-southeast of Mount Whitney (1) on Inyo-Tulare County line (lat. 36°33' N, long. 118° 16'30" W). Named on Mount Whitney (1956) 15' quadrangle.

Mount Mills [INYO]: *peak,* 0.5 mile north-northwest of Mount Abbot on Inyo-Fresno County line (lat. 37°23'40" N, long. 118°47'20" W). Altitude 13,468 feet. Named on Mount Abbot (1953) 15' quadrangle. Called Mills Peak on Tucker and Sampson's (1938) map. The name honors Darius Ogden Mills, pioneer California banker and mountaineer (Hanna, p. 193).

Mount Morgan [INYO]: *peak,* 6.25 miles northwest of Mount Tom (lat. 37°24'20" N, long. 118°43'55" W). Altitude 13,748 feet. Named on Mount Tom (1949) 15' quadrangle. Members of the Wheeler survey named the peak in 1878 for J.H. Morgan of the survey (Gudde, 1949, p. 224). United States Board on Geographic Names (1968b, p. 4) approved the name "Broken Finger Peak" for a feature located 0.8 mile east of Mount Morgan (lat. 37°24'20" N, long. 118°43'00" W).

Mount Morgan [MONO]: *peak,* 5.5 miles southeast of Mount Morrison (lat. 37°30'45" N, long. 118°46'45" W). Altitude 13,005 feet. Named on Mount Morrison (1953) 15' quadrangle.

Mount Morrison [MONO]: *peak,* 31 miles south-southeast of Lee Vining (lat. 37°33'45" N, long. 118°51'25" W; sec. 35, T 4 S, R 28 E); the peak is 1.5 miles south of Convict Lake. Altitude 12,268 feet. Named on Mount Morrison (1953) 15' quadrangle. The name commemorates Robert Morrison, who was killed in 1871 while serving with a posse that fought with the escaped convicts for whom nearby Convict Lake was named (Hoover, Rensch, and Rensch, p. 215). United States Board on Geographic Names (1987b, p. 1) approved the name "Mono Jim Peak" for a feature located 0.8 mile north-northeast of Mount Morrison (lat. 37°34'18" N, long. 118°51'03" W; sec. 26, T 4 S, R 28 E); the name is for a Paiute guide who was killed during the same fight with the escaped convicts.

Mount Muir [INYO]: *peak,* 1 mile south of Mount Whitney (1) on Inyo-Tulare County line (lat. 36°33'50" N, long. 118°17'25" W). Altitude 14,015 feet. Named on Mount Whitney (1956) 15' quadrangle. Professor Alexander G. McAdie named the peak for naturalist John Muir (Farquhar, 1924, p. 60).

Mount Nunn: see **Soldier Pass** [INYO].

Mount Olsen [MONO]: *peak,* 15 miles south of Bridgeport (lat. 38° 02'30" N, long. 119°14'50" W; near S line sec. 8, T 2 N, R 25 E). Altitude 11,086 feet. Named on Bodie (1958) 15' quadrangle.

Mount Palmer [INYO]: *peak,* 6 miles north-northeast of the mouth of Titus Canyon in Grapevine Mountains (lat. 36°54'20" N, long. 117°08' W). Altitude 7979 feet. Named on Grapevine Peak (1957) 15' quadrangle. The name honors T.S. Palmer, a member of the biological expedition to Death Valley in 1891 (United States Board on Geographic Names, 1957, p. 2-3).

Mount Patterson [MONO]: *peak,* 8 miles northeast of Fales Hot Springs in Sweetwater Mountains (lat. 38°26'15" N, long. 119°18'15" W; sec. 23, T 7 N, R 24 E). Altitude 11,673 feet. Named on Fales Hot Springs (1956) 15' quadrangle. Called Sweetwater Pk. on Wheeler's (1876-1877) map. United States Board on Geographic Names (1961a, p. 19) rejected the name "Sweetwater Mountain" for the feature. The name "Patterson" commemorates James H. Patterson, who discovered the first mines on the slopes of the peak (Wedertz, p. 69-70).

Mount Perkins [INYO]: *peak,* 13 miles northwest of Independence on Inyo-Fresno County line (lat. 36°55'40" N, long. 118°22'50" W). Altitude 12,591 feet. Named on Mount Pinchot (1953) 15' quadrangle. Robert D. Pike named the peak in 1906 to honor George Clement Perkins, governor of California from 1880 until 1883, and senator from California from 1893 until 1915 (Hanna, p. 233).

Mount Perry [INYO]: *peak,* 4.5 miles southwest of Ryan in Black Mountains (lat. 36°16'25" N, long. 116°43'25" W). Altitude 5739 feet. Named on Ryan (1952) 15' quadrangle. The name honors John W.S. Perry, who designed the 20-mule-team wagons used to haul borax from Death Valley in the 1880's (United States Board on Geographic Names, 1962a, p. 14).

Mount Powell [INYO]: *peak,* 3.25 miles southeast of Mount Darwin on Inyo-Fresno County line (lat. 37°08'15" N, long. 118°37'40" W; sec. 30, T 9 S, R 31 E). Named on Mount Goddard (1948) 15' quadrangle. The name presumably is for John Wesley Powell (Farquhar, 1924, p. 64).

Mount Prater [INYO]: *peak,* 12 miles southwest of Big Pine on Inyo-Fresno County line (lat. 37°02'15" N, long. 118°26' W). Altitude 13,329 feet. Named on Big Pine (1950) 15' quadrangle. The name is for Alfred Prater, who ascended the peak with his wife in 1928—they probably were the first to do so (United States Board on Geographic Names, 1933, p. 618).

Mount Reba [ALPINE]: *peak,* 13 miles south of Carson Pass (lat. 38°30'30" N, long. 120°01'40" W; near NW cor. sec. 32, T 8 N, R 18 E). Altitude 8755 feet. Named on Mokelumne Peak (1979) 7.5' quadrangle.

Mount Russell [INYO]: *peak,* less than 1 mile north-northeast of Mount Whitney (1) on Inyo-Tulare County line (lat. 36°35'25" N, long. 118°17'15" W). Altitude 14,086 feet. Named on Mount Whitney (1956) 15' quadrangle. The name honors geologist Israel Cook Russell (Hanna, p. 261).

Mount Scowden [MONO]: *peak,* 9 miles southeast of Matterhorn Peak (lat. 38°00'30" N, long. 119°15'30" W; sec. 30, T 2 N, R 25 E). Named on Matterhorn Peak (1956) 15' quadrangle.

Mount Sill [INYO]: *peak,* 10.5 miles east-southeast of Mount Darwin on Inyo-Fresno County line (lat. 37°05'45" N, long. 118°30'10" W). Altitude 14,162 feet. Named on Mount Goddard (1948) 15' quadrangle. Joseph N. LeConte named the peak in 1896 for Edward Rowland Sill, professor of literature at University of California from 1874 until 1882 (Farquhar, 1925, p. 133). This is one of the peaks that Whitney called Palisade Peaks (Hanna, p. 226). United States Board on Geographic Names (1971, p. 2) approved the name "Mount Jepson" for a peak located 0.7 mile southeast of Mount Sill (lat. 37°05'20" N, long. 118°29'40" W); the name honors Willis Linn Jepson, professor of botany at University of California from 1899 until 1937—the Board noted the variant name "Pine Martin Peak" for Mount Jepson.

Mount Smith: see **Smith Mountain** [INYO].

Mount Stanford [MONO]: *peak,* 6 miles southeast of Mount Morrison on

Mono-Fresno County line (lat. 37°29'25" N, long. 118°47'45" W). Altitude 12,851 feet. Named on Mount Abbot (1953) 15' quadrangle. Called Stanford Peak on Sampson's (1940) map, but United States Board on Geographic Names (1983a, p. 5) rejected this form of the name. R.B. Marshall of United States Geological Survey named the peak for Leland Stanford (Farquhar, 1925, p. 135).

Mount Starr [INYO]: *peak,* 3 miles north-northeast of Mount Abbot on Inyo-Fresno County line (lat. 37°25'40" N, long. 118°45'55" W). Altitude 12,870 feet. Named on Mount Abbot (1953) 15' quadrangle. The Sierra Club named the peak to honor Walter A. Starr, Jr., mountain climber and author of *Guide to the John Muir Trail and the High Sierra region* (United States Board on Geographic Names, 1939, p. 33).

Mount Thompson [INYO]: *peak,* 3.5 miles east-southeast of Mount Darwin on Inyo-Fresno County line (lat. 37°08'35" N, long. 118° 36'45" W; sec. 29, T 9 S, R 31 E). Named on Mount Goddard (1948) 15' quadrangle. R.B. Marshall of United States Geological Survey named the peak for geographer Almon Harrris Thompson (Farquhar, 1925, p. 138).

Mount Tinemaha [INYO]: *peak,* 10.5 miles south-southwest of Big Pine (lat. 37°02'10" N, long. 118°23'45" W). Altitude 12,561 feet. Named on Big Pine (1950) 15' quadrangle. Early residents of Owens Valley applied the name, which is from a Paiute Indian chief (United States Board on Geographic Names, 1938, p. 54).

Mount Tom [INYO]: *peak,* 15 miles west of Bishop (lat. 37°20'10" N, long. 118°39'20" W; sec. 14, T 7 S, R 30 E). Altitude 13,652 feet. Named on Mount Tom (1949) 15' quadrangle. Called High Pk. on Lippincott's (1902) map. The name "Tom" honors Thomas Clark, who is credited with the first ascent of the peak in the 1860's (Gudde, 1949, p. 364).

Mount Tyndall [INYO]: *peak,* 6 miles north-northwest of Mount Whitney (1) on Inyo-Tulare County line (lat. 36°39'20" N, long. 118°20'10" W). Altitude 14,018 feet. Named on Mount Whitney (1956) 15' quadrangle. Clarence King and Richard Cotter climbed the peak in 1864 and King named it for John Tyndall, professor of natural philosophy at the Royal Institution, London (Farquhar, 1925, p. 140).

Mount Versteeg [INYO]: *peak,* 5 miles north-northwest of Mount Whitney (1) on Inyo-Tulare County line (lat. 36°38'50" N, long. 118°19'25" W). Altitude 13,470 feet. Named on Mount Whitney (1956) 15' quadrangle. The name honors Chester Versteeg, who was devoted to furthering interest in the Sierra Nevada (United States Board on Geographic Names, 1965a, p. 10-11).

Mount Wallace [INYO]: *peak,* 1.5 miles south-southeast of Mount Darwin on Inyo-Fresno County line (lat. 37°08'45" N, long. 118° 39'20" W). Altitude 13,377 feet. Named on Mount Goddard (1948) 15' quadrangle. Theodore S. Solomons named the peak in 1895 to honor Alfred Russell Wallace, the contemporary of Charles Darwin (Farquhar, 1925, p. 142).

Mount Warren [MONO]: *peak,* 6 miles west-northwest of Lee Vining (lat. 37°59'25" N, long. 119°13'20" W; sec. 33, T 2 N, R 25 E). Altitude 12,327 feet. Named on Mono Craters (1953) 15' quadrangle. Members of the Whitney survey named the feature for Gouverneur Kemble Warren, who was involved in the Pacific Railroad surveys and was a Union general during the Civil War (Hanna, p. 349).

Mount Wheeler: see **Wheeler Peak** [MONO].

Mount Whitney [INYO]:

(1) *peak,* 16 miles south-southwest of Independence on Inyo-Tulare County line (lat. 36°34'45" N, long. 118°17'30" W). Altitude 14,494 feet. Named on Mount Whitney (1956) 15' quadrangle. A field party of the Whitney survey saw the peak in 1864 and named it for their chief, Josiah Dwight Whitney (Whitney, 1865, p. 382). Birnie (p. 134) called the feature both Mount Whitney and Whitney's Peak. John Lucas, Charles D. Begole, and A.H. Johnson, three Inyo County men, made the first ascent in 1873 (Gudde, 1949, p. 389). According to Goodyear (p. 231-232), Whitney came to Owens Valley in 1872 to investigate the effects of the great earthquake of that year, and became so unpopular with many residents that a movement began to change the name of Mount Whitney to Fisherman's Peak to honor the three men who first climbed the it, but the movement failed.

(2) *locality,* 3 miles east-northeast of Lone Pine along Southern Pacific Railroad (lat. 36°37'40" N, long. 118°00'50" W; sec. 13, T 15 S, R 36 E). Named on Lone Pine (1958) 15' quadrangle. Called Whitney on Lee's (1906) map, and called Lone Pine Sta. on Olmstead's (1900) map, which shows the place along Carson and Colorado Railroad.

Mount Whitney Number 1: see **Mount Corcoran** [INYO].

Mount Williamson [INYO]: *peak,* about 5.5 miles north of Mount Whitney (1) (lat. 36°39'20" N, long. 118°18'40" W). Altitude 14,375 feet. Named on Mount Whitney (1956) 15' quadrangle. Clarence King named the peak in 1864 to honor Major R.S. Williamson, well known for his topographical work in connection with the Pacific Railroad surveys (Whitney, 1865, p. 382).

Mount Winchell [INYO]: *peak,* 9 miles east-southeast of Mount Darwin on Inyo-Fresno County line (lat 37°06'15" N, long. 118°31'30" W). Altitude 13,768 feet. Named on Mount Goddard (1948) 15' quadrangle. Lil A. Winchell gave the name to a peak in 1879 to honor his father's cousin, Alexander Winchell, professor of geology at University of Michigan; United States Geological Survey transferred the name to present Mount Winchell (Farquhar, 1925, p. 144-145). This is one of the group that Whitney called Palisade Peaks (Hanna, p. 226).

Mount Wood [MONO]: *peak,* 10.5 miles south-southwest of Lee Vining (lat. 37°48'30" N, long. 119°09'40" W). Altitude 12,637 feet. Named on Mono Craters (1953) 15' quadrangle. Lieutenant N.F. McClure named the peak for Captain Abram E. Wood, acting superintendent of Yosemite National Park from 1891 until 1893 (Gudde, 1949, p. 393).

Movie Flat [INYO]: *area,* 3.5 miles west of Lone Pine (lat. 36°36'40" N, long. 118°07'30" W). Named on Lone Pine (1958) 15' quadrangle. The name is from the making of motion pictures at the place (Hoffman, p. 62).

Muah Mountain [INYO]: *peak,* 10.5 miles northwest of Olancha (lat. 36°24' N, long. 118°07'30" W). Altitude 11,016 feet. Named on Olancha (1956) 15' quadrangle. Kroeber (p. 49) suggested an Indian origin for the name.

Mud Canyon [INYO]: *canyon,* 2.5 miles long, opens into Death Valley nearly 3 miles east-southeast of Stovepipe Wells (lat. 36° 39' N, long. 117°01'50" W; near E line sec. 13, T 15 S, R 45 E). Named on Stovepipe Wells (1952) 15' quadrangle.

Mud Lake [ALPINE]:

(1) *lake,* 800 feet long, 5 miles south of Mount Reba on Alpine-Calaveras County line (lat. 38°26'10" N, long. 120°01'10" W). Named on Tamarack (1979) 7.5' quadrangle.

(2) *lake,* 1200 feet long, 5.5 miles west-northwest of Dardanelles Cone (lat. 38°25'35" N, long. 119°58' W). Named on Spicer Meadow Reservoir (1979) 7.5' quadrangle.

Mud Lake [MONO]: *lake,* 850 feet long, 6.25 miles east of Sonora Pass (lat. 38°20'15" N, long. 119°31'20" W; sec. 26, T 6 N, R 22 E). Named on Pickel Meadow (1954) 7.5' quadrangle.

Mud Spring [INYO]: *spring,* 6 miles southwest of Emigrant Pass (1) in Panamint Range (lat. 36°16'30" N, long. 117°13' W). Named on Emigrant Canyon (1952) 15' quadrangle.

Mud Spring Canyon [MONO]: *canyon,* drained by a stream that flows 2 miles to Molybdenite Creek 5.5 miles south-southwest of Fales Hot Springs (lat. 38°16'20" N, long. 119°25'35" W; near N line sec. 22, T 5 N, R 23 E). Named on Fales Hot Springs (1954) 7.5' quadrangle.

Muir: see **Mount Muir** [INYO].

Muir Lake [INYO]: *lake,* 800 feet long, 11 miles southwest of Lone Pine (lat. 36°30' N, long. 118°12'30" W). Named on Lone Pine (1958) and Olancha (1956) 15' quadrangles.

Mule Lake [INYO]: *lake,* 400 feet long, 10 miles northwest of Independence along Sawmill Creek (lat. 36°53'25" N, long. 118°20'30" W). Named on Mount Pinchot (1953) 15' quadrangle.

Mule Spring [INYO]: *spring,* 6.5 miles southeast of Big Pine near the west edge of Inyo Mountains (lat. 37°06'20" N, long. 118° 12' W; near E line sec. 1, T 10 S, R 34 E). Named on Waucoba Mountain (1951) 15' quadrangle.

Mulkey Pass [INYO]: *pass,* 13 miles northwest of Olancha on Inyo-Tulare County line (lat. 36°25'45" N, long. 118°09'55" W; near E line sec. 22, T 17 S, R 35 E). Named on Olancha (1956) 15' quadrangle. The name commemorates Cyrus Mulkey; the feature also is called "old" Mulkey Pass, in contrast to "new" Mulkey Pass, another name for nearby Trail Pass (Schumacher, p. 80).

Mumford Canyon: see **Munford Canyon** [INYO].

Munckton: see **Dunderberg Mill** [MONO].

Munford Canyon [INYO]: *canyon,* drained by a stream that flows 1.5 miles to Rattlesnake Canyon 4 miles east-northeast of Argus Peak (lat. 35°52'15" N, long. 117°22'45" W; sec. 6, T 24 S, R 43 E). Named on Trona (1949) 15' quadrangle. United States Board on Geographic Names (1983f, p. 2) approved the name "Mumford Canyon" for the feature.

Murderer's Creek: see **Deadman Creek** [MONO].

Murphy Creek [MONO]: *stream,* flows 7.25 miles to East Walker River 8 miles north-northeast of Bridgeport (lat. 38°22'15" N, long. 119°11'40" W; sec. 14, T 6 N, R 25 E). Named on Bridgeport (1958) and Fales Hot Springs (1956) 15' quadrangles.

Murphy Flat [MONO]: *area,* 7.5 miles east of Fales Hot Springs (lat. 38°21'45" N, long. 119°15'45" W; near SW cor. sec. 17, T 6 N, R 25 E); the place is south of Murphy Creek. Named on Fales Hot Springs (1956) 15' quadrangle.

Murphy Pond [MONO]: *lake,* 1600 feet long, 8 miles north-northeast of Bridgeport along East Walker River (lat. 38°22'05" N, long. 119°11'50" W; sec. 14, T 6 N, R 25 E); the lake is near the mouth of Murphy Creek. Named on Bridgeport (1958) 15' quadrangle.

Murphy Spring [MONO]: *spring,* 3 miles west-southwest of Bodie (lat. 38°11'25" N, long. 119°03'15" W; sec. 24, T 4 N, R 26 E). Named on Bodie (1958) 15' quadrangle. J.C. Murphy had a stage station at the spring in the 1880's (Gudde, 1949, p. 229).

Murray Canyon [ALPINE]: *canyon,* drained by a stream that flows 3.5 miles to East Fork Carson River 4 miles northeast of Disaster Peak (lat. 38°29'45" N, long. 119°40'55" W; near W line sec. 33, T 8 N, R 21 E). Named on Disaster Peak (1979) 7.5' quadrangle.

Mushroom Rock [INYO]: *relief feature,* 4.25 miles south of Furnace Creek Inn at the east edge of Death Valley (lat. 36°23'15" N, long. 116°51' W; at E line sec. 10, T 26 N, R 1 E). Named on Furnace Creek (1952) 15' quadrangle. The feature is a mushroom-shaped rock 6 feet high (Palmer, p. 52).

Musser and Jarvis Creek [ALPINE]: *stream,* flows 3.5 miles to Hot Springs Creek 1.5 miles west of Markleeville (lat. 38°41'25" N, long. 119°48'30" W; near N line sec. 29, T 10 N, R 20 E). Named on Markleeville (1979) 7.5' quadrangle.

Mustard Canyon [INYO]: *canyon,* 0.5 mile long, opens into Death Valley 3 miles north-northwest of Furnace Creek Inn (lat. 36°29'20" N, long. 116°52'40" W; near S line sec. 4, T 27 N, R 1 E). Named on Furnace Creek (1952) 15' quadrangle. Personnel of Pacific Coast Borax Company named the canyon for the color of the rocks there (Palmer, p. 52).

– N –

Napoleon Canyon [MONO]: *canyon,* drained by a stream that flows 1.25 miles to Slinkard Valley 2.5 miles west of Coleville (lat. 38°34'25" N, long. 119°33'15" W; sec. 3, T 8 N, R 22 E). Named on Topaz Lake (1956) 15' quadrangle.

Narboe Cañon: see **Hall Canyon** [INYO]; **Tuber Canyon** [INYO].

Narka: see **Little Lake** [INYO] (2).

Narrows: see **The Narrows** [INYO].

Natural Bridge [INYO]: *relief feature,* 12.5 miles south-southeast of Furnace Creek Inn on the west side of Black Mountains (lat. 36° 17'05" N, long. 116°45'50" W). Named on Furnace Creek (1952) 15' quadrangle. L.P. Noble discovered and named this arch of rock in 1933; the canyon where it lies is called Natural Bridge Canyon (Palmer, p. 52).

Natural Bridge Canyon: see **Natural Bridge** [INYO].

Navel Spring [INYO]: *spring,* nearly 5 miles north-northwest of Ryan (lat. 36°22'50" N, long. 116°42'55" W; sec. 13, T 26 N, R 2 E). Named on Ryan (1952) 15' quadrangle. The name refers to the position of the spring in the bank where it issues (Palmer, p. 53).

Needle Peak [INYO]: *peak,* 5.25 miles east-southeast of Manly Peak (lat. 35°53'10" N, long. 117°01'40" W). Altitude 5805 feet. Named on Manly Peak (1950) 15' quadrangle. The name is from the shape of the peak (Palmer, p. 53). On Wheeler's (1877) map, the name applies to a feature situated farther west at about the position of present Manly Peak.

Negit Island [MONO]: *island,* 4200 feet long, 5.5 miles northeast of Lee Vining in Mono Lake (lat. 38°01'15" N, long. 119°02'50" W; on E line sec. 24, T 2 N, R 26 E). Named on Bodie (1958) 15' quadrangle. Russell (p. 279) named the island and stated that the word "negit" means "blue-winged goose" in an Indian dialect.

Nelson Range [INYO]: *range,* 10 miles south-southwest of Ubehebe Peak between Inyo Mountains and Panamint Range (lat. 36°33'30" N, long. 117°39'30" W). Named on Ubehebe Peak (1950) 15' quadrangle. C. Hart Merriam named the range for Edward William Nelson, who explored the neighborhood with the Death Valley expedition of 1891 (Palmer, p. 53).

Nemo Canyon [INYO]: *canyon,* 10 miles long, opens into Wildrose Canyon 7.5 miles southwest of Emigrant Pass (1) (lat. 36°15'10" N, long. 117°13'50" W). Named on Emigrant Canyon (1952) 15' quadrangle.

Nevada Creek [MONO]: *stream,* flows 0.5 mile to the State of Nevada 9 miles north-northwest of Coleville (lat. 38°41'45" N, long. 119°33'30" W; near E line sec. 21, T 10 N, R 22 E). Named on Topaz Lake (1956) 15' quadrangle.

Nevada Lake: **Caples Lake** [ALPINE].

Nevahbe Ridge [MONO]: *ridge,* north-trending, 3 miles long, 4.5 miles east-southeast of Mount Morrison (lat. 37°31'45" N, long. 118°47' W). Named on Mount Morrison (1953) 15' quadrangle.

Nevares Peak [INYO]: *peak,* 9.5 miles southeast of Beatty Junction near the west edge of Funeral Mountains (lat. 36°30'35" N, long. 116°48'10" W). Altitude 2859 feet. Named on Chloride Cliff (1952) 15' quadrangle. The name commemorates Adolphe Joseph Nevares (Palmer, p. 53).

Nevares Springs [INYO]: *springs,* 8.5 miles southeast of Beatty Junction on the east side of Death Valley (lat. 36°30'40" N, long. 116°49'15" W; sec. 36, T 28 N, R 1 E); the springs are at the foot of Nevares Peak. Named on Chloride Cliff (1952) 15' quadrangle. Palmer (p. 71) noted that the place also may have been called Sweetwater Spring.

New Army Pass [INYO]: *pass,* 20 miles northwest of Olancha on Inyo-Tulare County line (lat. 36°29'25" N, long. 118°14'25" W); the pass is 0.5 mile south of Army Pass. Named on Olancha (1956) 15' quadrangle.

Newburg: see **Cameron**, under **Monte Cristo** [MONO].

New Owenyo: see **Owenyo** [INYO].

New Range [MONO]: *range,* 4 miles south-southeast of Fales Hot Springs (lat. 38°17'30" N, long. 119°22'30" W). Named on Fales Hot Springs (1956) 15' quadrangle.

New Ryan: see **Ryan** [INYO] (2).

New York Butte [INYO]: *peak,* 8 miles east-northeast of Lone Pine in Inyo Mountains (lat. 36°38'50" N, long. 117°55'55" W). Altitude 10,668 feet. Named on New York Butte (1950) 15' quadrangle.

New York Hill [MONO]: *peak,* 9 miles northeast of Bridgeport (lat. 38°21'30" N, long. 119°07'30" W; sec. 21, T 6 N, R 26 E). Named on Bridgeport (1958) 15' quadrangle.

Ninemile Canyon [INYO]: *canyon,* drained by a stream that flows 6 miles to Indian Wells Valley 7 miles south of the village of Little Lake (lat. 35°50'10" N, long. 117°54'15" W). Named on Little Lake (1954) 15' quadrangle. Tucker and Sampson's (1938) map has the form "Nine Mile Canyon" for the name.

9 Mile Station: see **Linnie** [INYO].

Nipple: see **The Nipple** [ALPINE].

Nobel Canyon: see **Noble Canyon** [ALPINE].

Nobel Creek: see **Noble Canyon** [ALPINE].

Nobel Lake: see **Noble Lake** [ALPINE].

Noble Canyon [ALPINE]: *canyon,* drained by a stream that flows 5.5 miles to Silver Creek (1) 4 miles north-northeast of Ebbetts Pass (lat. 38°35'50" N, long. 119°46'40" W; sec. 28, T 9 N, R 20 E). Named on Ebbetts Pass (1979) 7.5' quadrangle. Called Nobel Canyon on Markleeville (1956) 15' quadrangle, which has the name "Nobel Creek" for the stream in the canyon. Called Wobel Canyon on Markleeville (1889) 30' quadrangle. United States Board on Geographic Names (1979b, p. 7) rejected the names "Nobel Canyon," "Wobel Canyon," and "Nobel Creek," while approving the name "Noble Creek."

Noble Creek: see **Noble Canyon** [ALPINE].

Noble Lake [ALPINE]: *lake,* 600 feet long, 2.25 miles east-southeast of Ebbetts Pass (lat. 38°31'40" N, long. 119°46'35" W); the lake is near the head of Noble Canyon. Named on Ebbetts Pass (1979) 7.5' quadrangle. United States Board on Geographic Names (1979b, p. 7) rejected the names "Nobel Lake" and "Wobel Lake" for the feature.

Noname Canyon [INYO]: *canyon,* drained by a stream that flows 5 miles to Indian Wells Valley 8.5 miles south of the village of Little Lake (lat. 35°48'50" N, long. 117°54' W). Named on Little Lake (1954) 15' quadrangle.

Nopah Range [INYO]: *range,* east of Chicago Valley and west of Pahrump Valley and California Valley. Named on Stewart Valley (1958) and Tecopa (1950) 15' quadrangles. Kroeber (p. 51) suggested an Indian origin for the name. Palmer (p. 16) noted that the range also had the name "Chung Up Mountains."

Norboe Canyon: see **Tuber Canyon** [INYO].

Norfolk Cañon: see **Osborne Canyon** [INYO].

Norman Clyde Glacier: see **Middle Palisade** [INYO].

Norman Clyde Peak: see **Middle Palisade** [INYO].

North Canyon [MONO]: *canyon,* 4 miles long, opens into the canyon of Adobe Creek 8.5 miles north of Glass Mountain (lat. 37°53'40" N, long. 118°43'15" W; near NE cor. sec. 1, T 1 S, R 29 E). Named on Cowtrack Mountain (1962) and Glass Mountain (1962) 15' quadrangles.

North Crater [MONO]: *crater,* 4.5 miles east-southeast of Lee Vining (lat. 37°55'45" N, long. 119°02'40" W; sec. 19, T 1 N, R 27 E); the feature is at the north end of Mono Craters. Named on Mono Craters (1953) 15' quadrangle. Russell (p. 382) called the feature Panum Crater and stated that *panum* is an Indian word meaning "lake." United States Board on Geographic Names (1972, p. 1) approved the name "Panum Crater" for the feature.

North Lake [INYO]: *lake,* 1800 feet long, 5.5 miles northeast of Mount Darwin along North Fork Bishop Creek (lat. 37°13'55" N, long. 118°36'45" W; on S line sec. 19, T 8 S, R 31 E). Named on Mount Goddard (1948) 15' quadrangle.

North Landing [MONO]: *locality,* 6.25 miles northwest of Toms Place on the east side of Lake Crowley (lat. 37°38'10" N, long. 118°44'35" W; near N line sec. 2, T 4 S, R 29 E). Named on Casa Diablo Mountain (1953) 15' quadrangle.

North Palisade [INYO]: *peak,* 10 miles east-southeast of Mount Darwin on Inyo-Fresno County line (lat. 37°05'40" N, long. 118° 30'50" W). Altitude 14,242 feet. Named on Mount Goddard (1948) 15' quadrangle. Lil A. Winchell named the peak in 1879 for Frank Dusy, and Bolton C. Brown named it in 1895 for David Starr Jordan (Farquhar, 1924, p. 62), but neither name remains. This is one of the peaks that Whitney called Palisade Peaks (Hanna, p. 226). United States Board on Geographic Names (1985a, p. 3) approved the name "Polemonium Peak" for a feature, altitude 14,080 feet, located 0.2 mile southeast of North Palisade on Inyo-Fresno County line (lat. 37°05'37" N, long. 118°30'40" W).

North Panamints: see **Cottonwood Mountains** [INYO].

North Peak [MONO]: *peak,* 1 mile north-northeast of Mount Conness on Mono-Tuolumne County line (lat. 37°59' N, long. 119° 18'50" W; sec. 34, T 2 N, R 24 E). Altitude 12,242 feet. Named on Tuolumne Meadows (1956) 15' quadrangle.

Northwest Arm: see **Death Valley** [INYO].

Northwest Arm of Death Valley: see **Mesquite Flat** [INYO].

Norton Meadow [INYO]: *area,* 5.5 miles east of Mount Tom along McGee Creek (lat. 37°19'30" N, long. 118°33'30" W; sec. 22, T 7 S, R 31 E). Named on Mount Goddard (1912) 30' quadrangle.

Nova Canyon [INYO]: *canyon,* drained by a stream that flows 6 miles to Panamint Valley 9 miles south-southeast of Panamint Butte (lat. 36°18'25" N, long. 117°18'35" W). Named on Emigrant Canyon (1952) and Panamint Butte (1951) 15' quadrangles.

Nunn: see **Mount Nunn**, under **Soldier Pass** [INYO].

Nutter Lake [MONO]: *lake,* 550 feet long, 5 miles east-southeast of Matterhorn Peak (lat. 38°04' N, long. 119°17'45" W). Named on Matterhorn Peak (1956) 15' quadrangle. An engineer of Standard Consolidated Mining Company named the lake in 1905 for Edward H. Nutter, assistant superintendent of the company (Gudde, 1949, p. 239).

— O —

Oak Creek [INYO]: *stream,* formed by the confluence of North Fork and South Fork 3.25 miles northwest of Independence (lat. 36° 50' N, long. 118°15' W; sec. 2, T 13 S, R 34 E), and flows only 2 miles before it ends in Owens Valley. Named on Independence (1951) 15' quadrangle. North Fork is 8.5 miles long and South Fork is 8 miles long; both forks are named on Mount Pinchot (1953) 15' quadrangle. Chalfant (1933, p. 233) noted an attempt in the 1860's to start a town called Oakdale in Owens Valley about halfway between Little Pine (present Independence) and Oak Creek.

Oak Creek Camp [INYO]: *locality,* 5 miles northwest of Independence (lat. 36°50'30" N, long. 118°16'15" W; sec. 3, T 13 S, R 34 E); the place is along North Fork Oak Creek. Named on Mount Pinchot (1953) 15' quadrangle.

Oakdale: see **Oak Creek** [INYO].

Oasis [MONO]: *locality,* 20 miles east-southeast of Mount Barcroft in Fish Lake Valley (lat. 37°29'25" N, long. 117°54'45" W; near W line sec. 27, T 5 S, R 37 E). Named on Soldier Pass (1958) 15' quadrangle. Postal authorities established Oasis post office in 1873 and discontinued it in 1942; the name was for Oasis ranch, where the post office was located (Salley, p. 159).

Odell Lake [MONO]: *lake,* 1600 feet long, 2.5 miles northeast of Mount Conness (lat. 37°59'45" N, long. 119°17'10" W; on W line sec. 25, T 2 N, R 24 E). Named on Tuolumne Meadows (1956) 15' quadrangle.

O'Harrel Canyon [MONO]: *canyon,* 2.5 miles long, opens into lowlands 2.5 miles west-southwest of Glass Mountain (lat. 37°45'15" N, long. 118°44'55" W; sec. 23, T 2 S, R 29 E). Named on Glass Mountain (1962) 15' quadrangle.

O'Harrel Canyon Creek [MONO]: *stream,* flows 6.25 miles to Owens River 11 miles north-northeast of Mount Morrison (lat. 37° 42'20" N, long. 118°46'25" W; sec. 9, T 3 S, R 29 E); the stream drains O'Harrel Canyon. Named on Mount Morrison (1953) 15' quadrangle.

Oh Ridge [MONO]: *ridge,* north-northwest-trending, 0.5 mile long, 11.5 miles south-southeast of Lee Vining near June Lake (1) (lat. 37°47'50" N, long. 119°03'35" W; on S line sec. 1, T 2 S, R 26 E). Named on Mono Craters (1953) 15' quadrangle. The name is for the spontaneous exclamation "Oh!" given by travelers who have a sudden view of June Lake (1) as they cross the ridge (Bean, p. 8).

Olancha [INYO]: *village,* 37 miles south-southeast of Independence (lat. 36°17' N, long. 118°00'20" W; sec. 18, T 19 S, R 37 E). Named on Olancha (1956) 15' quadrangle. Called Olanche on Holt's (1864) map. Postal authorities established Olancha post office in 1870 (Frickstad, p. 52). Kroeber (p. 51) thought that the name "Olanche" may have an Indian origin. It first was applied to Olancha mine in the 1860's, and later to Olancha Peak and to the village (Hanna, p. 217). M.H. Farley built a small mill at the site about 1861 (Schumacher, p. 21).

Olancha Creek [INYO]: *stream,* flows 3.5 miles to lowlands 3 miles west-southwest of Olancha (lat. 36°15'45" N, long. 118°03'05" W; near SW cor. sec. 23, T 19 S, R 36 E). Named on Olancha (1956) 15' quadrangle. The stream discharges into the aqueduct that takes Owens Valley water to Los Angeles.

Olancha Pass [INYO]: *pass,* 7.25 miles southwest of Olancha on Inyo-Tulare County line (lat. 36°12'45" N, long. 118°06'15" W; sec. 5, T 20 S, R 36 E). Named on Monache Mountain (1956) 15' quadrangle.

Olancha Peak [INYO]: *peak,* 6.5 miles west of Olancha on Inyo-Tulare County line (lat. 36°15'55" N, long. 118°07' W). Altitude 12,123 feet. Named on Olancha (1956) 15' quadrangle.

Olancha Siding [INYO]: *locality,* 1 mile south-southwest of Olancha along Southern Pacific Railroad (lat. 36°16' N, long. 118°00'45" W; sec. 19, T 19 S, R 37 E). Named on Olancha (1956) 15' quadrangle.

Olancha Warm Springs: see **Dirty Socks** [INYO].

Olancha Wells: see **Dirty Socks** [INYO].

Olanche: see **Olancha** [INYO].

Old Benton: see **Benton Hot Springs** [MONO].

Old Mammoth [MONO]: *settlement,* 8.5 miles west-northwest of Mount Morrison (lat. 37°37'45" N, long. 118°59'05" W; sec. 3, 4, T 4 S, R 27 E). Named on Mount Morrison (1953) 15' quadrangle. Called Mammoth on Mount Morrison (1914) 30' quadrangle. The place had the name "Mammoth" until 1937, when businesses there moved to a better location on a newly completed highway at present Mammoth Lakes (Smith, Genny, p. 19). The name "Mammoth" originated with Mammoth vein, located east of Lake Mary (DeDecker, p. 29), and with Mammoth Mining Company, formed in 1878 (Hanna, p. 183). Mammoth City, the center for mining activity, boomed in 1878 and 1879 (Smith, Genny, p. 16). Postal authorities established Mammoth post office in 1879, discontinued it in 1881, reestablished it in 1896, and discontinued it in 1898 (Frickstad, p. 105). California Mining Bureau's (1917b) map shows a place called Mineral Park located near present Old Mammoth. Postal authorities established Mineral Park post office in 1912 and discontinued it in 1913 (Frickstad, p. 105). The ridge south of Old Mammoth, between Old Mammoth and upper reaches of Mammoth Creek, has been called Red Mountain, Gold Mountain, and Mineral Hill (Smith, Genny, p. 16).

Old Mount Whitney: see **Mount Corcoran** [INYO].

Old Ryan: see **Ryan** [INYO] (1).

Old Smelter Well [INYO]: *well,* 8 miles east-southeast of Tecopa at Tecopa Pass (lat. 35°48' N, long. 116°06' W). Named on Avawatz Mountains (1933) 1° quadrangle, which mistakenly shows the well in San Bernardino County.

Olsen: see **Mount Olsen** [MONO].

Omes: see **Lower Centennial Flat** [INYO].

Oneida Lake [MONO]: *lake,* 2200 feet long, 4.25 miles east-northeast of Mount Conness (lat. 37°59'40" N, long. 119°15' W; on E line sec. 31, T 2 N, R 25 E); the feature is in Lake Canyon. Named on Mono Craters (1953) and Tuolumne Meadows (1956) 15' quadrangles.

Onion Creek [INYO]: *stream,* flows 3 miles to Baker Creek 6 miles west of Big Pine (lat. 37°09'25" N, long. 118°23'50" W; sec. 20, T 9 S, R 33 E). Named on Big Pine (1950) 15' quadrangle.

Onion Valley [INYO]: *valley,* 7.5 miles west-southwest of Independence along Independence Creek (lat. 36°46'30" N, long. 118°19'50" W). Named on Mount Pinchot (1953) 15' quadrangle. The name is from the abundance of swamp onions in the valley (Schumacher, p. 42).

Onion Valley: see **Little Onion Valley** [INYO].

Opal Canyon [INYO]: *canyon,* 1.5 miles long, opens into Marble Canyon (2) 5.5 miles north-northeast of Waucoba Mountain (lat. 37°05'30" N, long. 117°57'50" W; near E line sec. 7, T 10 S, R 37 E). Named on Waucoba Spring (1958) 15' quadrangle.

Ophir Mountain [INYO]: *peak,* 1.5 miles north-northwest of Darwin (lat. 36°17'25" N, long. 117°35'50" W; near SW cor. sec. 12, T 19 S, R 40 E). Altitude 6010 feet. Named on Darwin (1950) 15' quadrangle. Palmer (p. 54) believed that the peak was named for Ophir Mountain at Virginia City, Nevada.

Oriental Wash [INYO]: *stream,* heads in the State of Nevada and flows 2.5 miles in Inyo County before ending 15 miles north-northwest of Ubehebe Crater in Death Valley (lat. 37°12'40" N, long. 117°33' W; near E line sec. 6, T 9 S, R 41 E). Named on Last Chance Range (1958) 15' quadrangle.

Orm's Station: see **Lower Centennial Flat** [INYO].

Orondo Canyon [INYO]: *canyon,* 2 miles long, opens into Bruce Canyon 6.5 miles northeast of Argus Peak (lat. 35°55'10" N, long. 117°21'45" W); Orondo mine is near the head of the canyon. Named on Trona (1949) 15' quadrangle.

Osborne Canyon [INYO]: *canyon,* drained by a stream that flows 6 miles to Panamint Valley 10 miles south-southwest of Panamint Butte (lat. 36°17'50" N, long. 117°24'50" W; sec. 10, T 19 S, R 42 E). Named on Panamint Butte (1951) 15' quadrangle. Called Norfolk Cañon on Wheeler's (1877) map.

Osborn Hill [ALPINE]: *peak,* 2.25 miles south-southeast of Mount Reba (lat. 38°28'30" N, long. 120°01'05" W; sec. 8, T 7 N, R 18 E). Altitude 7815 feet. Named on Tamarack (1979) 7.5' quadrangle.

Oteys Sierra Village [INYO]: *settlement,* 3.5 miles west of Bishop (lat. 37°21'30" N, long. 118°27'30" W; near NE cor. sec. 9, T 7 S, R 32 E). Named on Bishop (1949) 15' quadrangle.

Ott Well: see **The Tanks** [INYO].

Owen's Great Lake: see **Owens Lake** [INYO].

Owens Lake [INYO]: *lake,* 17 miles long, at the south end of Owens Valley, where it is the sink of Owens River. Named on Ballarat (1913) 1°quadrangle, and on Mount Whitney (1907) and Olancha (1907) 30' quadrangles—all three maps show it as a permanent lake. The more recent Keeler (1951), Lone Pine (1958), New York Butte (1950), and Olancha (1956) 15' quadrangles—made after Owens Valley water was taken to Los Angeles by aqueduct—show the feature as a dry lake. Fremont named the lake for Richard Owens, a guide for Fremont's expedition of 1845 and 1846, although Owens did not visit the lake (Chalfant, 1933, p. 98). Blake (p. 141) referred to Owens' lake, and Whitney (1865, p. 455) mentioned Owen's Lake. United States Board on Geographic Names (1933, p. 579) rejected the name "Owen Lake" for the feature, which also was known as Big Owens Lake to distinguish it from Little Owens Lake, as present Little Lake (1) sometimes was called (Hanna, p. 172). Hanks (p. 31) referred to Owen's Great Lake. Waring and Huguenin (p. 35) used the name "Owens Lake Springs" for some springs "scattered along" the southeast edge of Owens Lake. Chalfant (1933, p. 312) noted a place called Ferguson's Landing, where steamboats discharged freight at the northwest corner of the lake.

Owens Lake: see **Little Owens Lake**, under **Little Lake** [INYO] (1).

Owens Lake Springs: see **Owens Lake** [INYO].

Owens Point [INYO]: *peak,* 9 miles southwest of Lone Pine (lat. 36° 30'05" N, long. 118°09'20" W). Altitude 11,411 feet. Named on Lone Pine (1958) 15' quadrangle.

Owens River [INYO-MONO]: *stream,* heads in Mono County and flows 130 miles to Owens Lake 6 miles southeast of Lone Pine in Inyo County (lat. 36°33' N, long. 117°58'45" W; near N line sec. 17, T 16 S, R 37 E). Named on Big Pine (1950), Bishop (1949), Casa Diablo Mountain (1953), Cowtrack Mountain (1962), Independence (1951), Lone Pine (1958), Mount Morrison (1953), Mount Tom (1949), New York Butte (1950), and Waucoba Mountain (1951) 15' quadrangles. Fremont named the stream for Richard Owens, for whom he named Owens Lake (Chalfant, 1933, p. 98). United States Board on Geographic Names (1933, p. 579) rejected the form "Owen River" for the name. Present Mammoth Creek [MONO] and Hot Creek [MONO] (2) together are called South Fork [Owens River] on Lee's (1906) map.

Owens River Gorge [INYO-MONO]: *canyon,* on Inyo-Mono County line, mainly in Mono County, extends for 22 miles along Owens River above the entrance of the river into lowlands 6.5 miles west-northwest of Bishop (lat. 37°24'15" N, long. 118°30' W; sec. 30, T 6 S, R 32 E). Named on Casa Diablo Mountain (1953) and Mount Tom (1949) 15' quadrangles.

Owens River Valley: see **Chalfant Valley** [MONO]; **Hammil Valley** [MONO].

Owens Valley [INYO]: *valley,* east of Sierra Nevada and west of White Mountains and Inyo Mountains; Owens River passes through the valley on the way to Owens Lake. Named on Death Valley (1954), Fresno (1962), and Mariposa (1957) 1°x 2° quadrangles. Fremont named the valley for Richard Owens, for whom he named Owens Lake (Chalfant, 1933, p. 98). Whitney (1865, p. 455) referred to Owen's Valley. United States Board on Geographic Names (1933, p. 579) rejected the form "Owen Valley" for the name.

Owensville: see **Laws** [INYO].

Owenyo [INYO]: *locality,* 5 miles north of Lone Pine along Southern Pacific Railroad (lat. 36°40'45" N, long. 118°02'35" W; sec. 34, T 14 S, E 36 E); the place is in Owens Valley. Named on Lone Pine (1958) 15' quadrangle. On Mount Whitney (1907) 30' quadrangle, the name applies to a site located 0.5 mile farther southeast. The name, coined from the words "Owens" and "Inyo," was given to a station on Carson and Colorado Railroad in 1905; when the rail line to Mojave was built in 1910, the station was shifted to the present location and called New Owenyo, but the term "New" was dropped the next year (Gudde, 1949, p. 247). Officials of William Penn Colonial Association established a town called Owenyo as the center of a Quaker colony about 1900, but they sold the colony's land about 1905 (Schumacher, p. 34). Postal authorities established Owenyo post office in 1902, discontinued it in 1905, reestablished it in 1916, and discontinued it in 1941 (Frickstad, p. 52).

Owlshead Canyon [INYO]: *canyon,* drained by a stream that flows 3.5 miles to Death Valley 12 miles southwest of Epaulet Peak (lat. 35°51'30" N, long. 116°40'45" W); the canyon is in Owlshead Mountains. Named on Confidence Hills (1950) 15' quadrangle.

Owlshead Mountains [INYO]: *range,* southeast of Wingate Wash and southwest of the south end of Death Valley; mainly in San Bernardino County. Named on Confidence Hills (1950) and Wingate Wash (1950) 15' quadrangles. The name is from twin basins at the southwest edge of Death Valley that suggest the eyes and face of an owl (Lingenfelter, p. 83).

— P —

Pacific Creek [ALPINE]: *stream,* flows 4.5 miles to North Fork Mokelumne River 1.25 miles north of Pacific Grade Summit (lat. 38°32'05" N, long. 119°54'40" W; sec. 20, T 8 N, R 19 E); the stream goes through Pacific Valley. Named on Pacific Valley (1979) and Spicer Meadow Reservoir (1979) 7.5' quadrangles.

Pacific Grade Summit [ALPINE]: *pass,* nearly 6 miles west-southwest of Ebbetts Pass (lat. 38°31' N, long. 119°54'30" W; sec. 29, T 8 N, R 19 E); the pass is west of Pacific Valley. Named on Pacific Valley (1979) 7.5' quadrangle.

Pacific Valley [ALPINE]: *valley,* east of Pacific Grade Summit (lat. 38°31' N, long. 119°54'05" W; near E line sec. 29, T 8 N, R 19 E). Named on Pacific Valley (1979) 7.5' quadrangle. An exploring party named the valley in 1855 (Powers, p. 189).

Paert's Hot Spring: see **Benton Hot Springs** [MONO].

Page Peaks [MONO]: *peaks,* 4.25 miles east-southeast of Matterhorn Peak (lat. 38°04' N, long. 119°18'30" W). Named on Matterhorn Peak (1956) 15' quadrangle.

Pahrump Valley [INYO]: *valley,* north of Kingston Range and Northeast of Nopah Range; mainly in the State of Nevada. Named on Horse Thief Springs (1956), Pahrump (1958), and Stewart Valley (1958) 15' quadrangles. The name is of Indian origin (Palmer, p. 55).

Paiute Canyon [INYO]: *canyon,* drained by a stream that flows 8.5 miles to Saline Valley 14 miles north of New York Butte (lat. 36° 51' N, long. 117°54'50" W; near SW cor. sec. 35, T 12 S, R 37 E). Named on Independence (1951) and Waucoba Wash (1951) 15' quadrangles.

Paiute Monument [INYO]: *relief feature,* 10 miles east-northeast of Independence (lat. 36°51'50" N, long. 118°02'05" W); the feature is south of the head of Paiute Canyon. Altitude 8369 feet. Named on Independence (1951) 15' quadrangle. United States Board on Geographic Names (1984a, p. 3) approved the name "Winnedumah Paiute Monument" for the feature, and rejected the names "Paiute Monument," "Piute Monument," and "Winnedumah"—the name is for a Paiute Indian medicine man who according to legend was turned into this 60-foot high pillar of rock while he was invoking divine aid during a battle with some Digger Indians.

Palisade Crest [INYO]: *peak,* 12.5 miles west-southwest of Big Pine on Inyo-Fresno County line (lat. 37°04'40" N, long. 118°29'10" W). Named on Big Pine (1950) 15' quadrangle.

Palisade Glacier [INYO]: *glacier,* 10 miles east-southeast of Mount Darwin (lat. 37°06' N, long. 118°30'30" W); the feature is northeast of North Palisade. Named on Mount Goddard (1948) 15' quadrangle.

Palisade Peaks: see **Middle Palisade** [INYO]; **Mount Agassiz** [INYO]; **Mount Sill** [INYO]; **Mount Winchell** [INYO]; **North Palisade** [INYO].

Palmer: see **Mount Palmer** [INYO].

Palm Spring [INYO]: *spring,* 8.5 miles east-southeast of the mouth of Paiute Canyon in Saline Valley (lat. 36°48'45" N, long. 117°45'55" W; near E line sec. 18, T 13 S, R 39 E). Named on Waucoba Wash (1951) 15' quadrangle, which indicates that the spring water is hot. The name is for a single palm tree planted near the spring (Mitchell, 1971, p. 9).

Panamint [INYO]: *locality,* 3.5 miles south of Telescope Peak in Surprise Canyon (lat. 36°07'05" N, long. 117°05'40" W). Named on Telescope Peak (1952) 15' quadrangle. A copper and silver strike in 1872 started a boom town called Panamint, or Panamint City, that by 1874 had a population of 5000 and a main street 1 mile long; a cloudburst destroyed the town in 1876 (Murbarger, p. 276-277). Postal authorities established Panamint post office in 1874, discontinued it in 1877, reestablished it in 1882, discontinued it in 1883, reestablished it in 1887, and discontinued it in 1895 (Frickstad, p. 52).

Panamint Butte [INYO]: *peak,* 29 miles east of Keeler (lat. 36° 26' N, long. 117°21'15" W). Altitude 6585 feet. Named on Panamint Butte (1951) 15' quadrangle.

Panamint Canyon [INYO]: *canyon,* drained by a stream that flows 3.5 miles to Panamint Valley 2.5 miles south of Panamint Butte (lat. 36°23'45" N, long. 117°21'30" W); the canyon is in Panamint Range. Named on Panamint Butte (1951) 15' quadrangle.

Panamint City: see **Panamint** [INYO].

Panamint Pass [INYO]: *pass,* 4.5 miles south-southeast of Telescope Peak (lat. 36°06'25" N, long. 117°04'10" W); the pass is in Panamint Range. Altitude 8070 feet. Named on Telescope Peak (1952) 15' quadrangle.

Panamint Range [INYO]: *range,* west of Death Valley and north of Wingate Wash. Named on Death Valley (1954) and Trona (1957) 1°x 2° quadrangles. Members of the Darwin French party named the range in 1860 (Federal Writers' Project, p. 19) for an Indian tribe of the region (Kroeber, p. 53-54). Parts of the range were known in the early days by the names "Given's Mountain" and "Telescope Mountains"—the last name probably from Telescope Peak (Palmer, p. 30, 71-72).

Panamint Springs [INYO]: *locality,* 9 miles southwest of Panamint Butte on the west side of Panamint Valley near the mouth of Darwin Canyon (lat. 36°20'20" N, long. 117°28'05" W; sec. 30, T 18 S, R 42 E). Named on Panamint Butte (1951) 15' quadrangle. Postal authorities established Panamint Springs post office in 1940 and discontinued it in 1946 (Frickstad, p. 52).

Panamint Valley [INYO]: *valley,* west of Panamint Range, and east of Slate Range and the north part of Argus Range; extends south into San Bernardino County. Named on Death Valley (1954) and Trona (1957) 1°x 2° quadrangles. Members of the Darwin French party named the valley in 1860 (Federal Writers' Project, p. 19). Postal Route (1884) map shows a place called Reilly located on the west side of present Panamint Valley; postal authorities established Reilly post office in 1883 and discontinued it the same year (Frickstad, p. 52).

Panum Crater: see **North Crater** [MONO].

Paoha Island [MONO]: *island,* 2.25 miles long, 5.25 miles east-northeast of Lee Vining in Mono Lake (lat. 38°00' N, long. 119° 02' W). Named on Bodie (1958) and Mono Craters (1953) 15' quadrangles. Russell (p. 278-279) named the feature and stated that *paoha* is an Indian word used to designate legendary spirits supposedly seen in vapor rising from hot springs on the island—the word also is used to designate hot springs in general. Baker's (1855) map has the name "Grand Id." for what appears to be present Paoha Island. Russell (p. 288) used the name "Hot Spring Cove" for an embayment on the east side of the island, where a large thermal spring occurs at the edge of the lake.

Papoose Flat [INYO]: *area,* 5.5 miles west of Waucoba Mountain (lat. 37°01' N, long. 118°06'30" W). Named on Waucoba Mountain (1951) 15' quadrangle.

Paradise Camp [MONO]: *locality,* 7 miles southeast of Toms Place along Rock Creek (3) (lat. 37°28'45" N, long. 118°36'10" W; near SW cor. sec. 29, T 5 S, R 31 E). Named on Mount Tom (1949) 15' quadrangle. Arthur Clark of Bishop started a resort at the place in 1923 on land that he homesteaded in 1919 (Hanna, p. 229).

Paradise Valley [ALPINE]: *valley,* 1.25 miles north-northwest of Disaster Peak (lat. 38°27'55" N, long. 119°44'35" W). Named on Disaster Peak (1979) 7.5' quadrangle.

Parchers Camp [INYO]: *locality,* 6.5 miles east of Mount Darwin along South Fork Bishop Creek (lat. 37°11'10" N, long. 118°33'25" W; sec. 11, T 9 S, R 31 E). Named on Mount Goddard (1948) 15' quadrangle. William Chandler Parcher and his wife started the place in 1922 (Hanna, p. 229).

Parker Creek [MONO]: *stream,* flows 8.5 miles to Rush Creek 5.25 miles south-southeast of Lee Vining (lat. 37°53' N, long. 119°05'50" W; sec. 3, T 1 S, R 26 E). Named on Mono Craters (1953) 15' quadrangle. The name is for an early settler along the stream (United States Board on Geographic Names, 1934, p. 18). Russell (p. 325) gave the name "Parker Creek Glacier" to a feature located at the head of the canyon of Parker Creek.

Parker Creek Glacier: see **Parker Creek** [MONO].

Parker Lake [MONO]: *lake,* 1550 feet long, 9 miles south-southwest of Lee Vining (lat. 37°50' N, long. 119°09'25" W; near W line sec. 30, T 1 S, R 26 E); the lake is along Parker Creek. Named on Mono Craters (1953) 15' quadrangle.

Parker Lakes [INYO]: *lakes,* largest 650 feet long, 9 miles west of Independence near the head of South Fork Oak Creek (lat. 36°48'10" N, long. 118°21'25" W). Named on Mount Pinchot (1953) 15' quadrangle.

Parker Pass [MONO]: *pass,* 9.5 miles south-southwest of Lee Vining on Mono-Tuolumne County line (lat. 37°50'20" N, long. 119°12'25" W); the pass is near the head of Parker Creek. Named on Mono Craters (1953) 15' quadrangle. The name is from Parker Creek (United States Board on Geographic Names, 1934, p. 18).

Parker Peak [MONO]: *peak,* 10.5 miles south-southwest of Lee Vining (lat. 37°48'50" N, long. 119°11' W); the peak is near upper reaches of Parker Creek. Altitude 12,861 feet. Named on Mono Craters (1953) 15' quadrangle.

Parkinson Peak: see **Maturango Peak** [INYO].

Parson's Cañon: see **Homewood Canyon** [INYO].

Partzwick: see **Blind Spring Hill** [MONO].

Par Value Lakes [MONO]: *lakes,* three, largest 750 feet long, nearly 3 miles east of Matterhorn Peak (lat. 38°05'05" N, long. 119°19'50" W). Named on Matterhorn Peak (1956) 15' quadrangle. The name is from Par Value mining claim (Gudde, 1949, p. 254).

Pass Creek: see **Carson River, West Fork** [ALPINE].

Pass Creek Canyon: see **West Carson Canyon** [ALPINE].

Pat Keyes Canyon [INYO]: *canyon,* drained by a stream that flows 6 miles to Saline Valley 5 miles south of the mouth of Paiute Canyon (lat. 36°46'50" N, long. 117°53'45" W). Named on Waucoba Wash (1951) 15' quadrangle.

Pat Keyes Spring [INYO]: *spring,* 7.5 miles south-southwest of the mouth of Paiute Canyon (lat. 36°45'15" N, long. 117°58'40" W); the spring is in a branch of Pat Keyes Canyon. Named on Waucoba Wash (1951) 15' quadrangle.

Patterson: see **Mount Patterson** [MONO].

Patterson Canyon [MONO]: *canyon,* drained by a stream that flows 3 miles to Swauger Creek 5.25 miles west-northwest of Bridgeport (lat. 38°17'45" N, long. 119°18'30" W; sec. 15, T 5 N, R 24 E). Named on Fales Hot Springs (1956) 15' quadrangle. R.S. Patterson and J.H. Patterson acquired land in the canyon in 1870 and built a mill at its mouth (Wedertz, p. 155).

Paynesville [ALPINE]: *village,* 0.25 mile northeast of Woodfords along West Fork Carson River (lat. 38°48'35" N, long. 119°46'45" W; near S line sec. 18, T 11 N, R 20 E). Named on Woodfords (1979) 7.5' quadrangle.

Payson Canyon [INYO]: *canyon,* drained by a stream that heads at Westgard Pass and flows 5 miles to Deep Springs Valley 4 miles east-northeast of the pass (lat. 37°19' N, long. 118°05' W; near N line sec. 25, T 7 S, R 35 E). Named on Blanco Mountain (1951) 15' quadrangle. The name commemorates "Old Lew" Payson, who lived at Antelope Spring (Gudde, 1949, p. 256).

Peaceful Pines [ALPINE]: *locality,* 4.5 miles east of Dardanelles Cone in Sand Flat (lat. 38°24'20" N, long. 119°47'20" W). Named on Dardanelles Cone (1979) 7.5' quadrangle.

Peach Spring: see **Bruce Canyon** [INYO].

Pearce Peak [MONO]: *peak,* 2.5 miles south of Benton on Blind Spring Hill (lat. 37°46'50" N, long. 118°29'10" W; sec. 18, T 2 S, R 32 E). Named on Benton (1962) 15' quadrangle.

Pecks: see **Hope Valley** [ALPINE].

Peeler Lake [MONO]: *lake,* 0.5 mile long, 5 miles west-northwest of Matterhorn Peak (lat. 38°07'10" N, long. 119°28' W). Named on Matterhorn Peak (1956) 15' quadrangle. The name is for Barney Peeler (Wedertz, p. 175); the lake is 2 miles southwest of Barney Lake (1), also named for Peeler.

Peep Sight Peak [ALPINE]: *peak,* 6.5 miles north of Dardanelles Cone (lat. 38°29'50" N, long. 119°51' W). Altitude 9716 feet. Named on Dardanelles Cone (1979) 7.5' quadrangle. Called Lookout Peak on Dardanelles Cone (1956) 15' quadrangle

Pellisier Creek [MONO]: *stream,* flows 7.5 miles before ending in Hamil Valley 9 miles west-northwest of White Mountain Peak (lat. 37°41'20" N, long. 118°24'30" W); the stream heads near Pellisier Flats. Named on White Mountain Peak (1962) 15' quadrangle.

Pellisier Flats [MONO]: *area,* 9 miles east-southeast of Benton (lat. 37°46' N, long. 118°19'45" W). Named on Benton (1962) and White Mountain Peak (1962) 15' quadrangles.

Pennsylvania Creek [ALPINE]: *stream,* flows nearly 4 miles to Silver Creek (1) 4 miles north-northeast of Ebbetts Pass (lat. 38°35'50" N, long. 119°46'40" W; sec. 28, T 9 N, R 20 E); the stream goes past Pennsylvania mine. Named on Ebbetts Pass (1979) 7.5' quadrangle.

Peridido Canyon [INYO]: *canyon,* drained by a stream that flows 5 miles to Hidden Valley 13 miles west-northwest of the mouth of Marble Canyon (3) (lat. 36°44'25" N, long. 117°29'10" W). Named on Tin Mountain (1957) 15' quadrangle.

Perkins: see **Mount Perkins** [INYO].

Permanente [INYO]: *locality,* 6.25 miles north of Olancha along Southern Pacific Railroad (lat. 36°22'20" N, long. 118°00'50" W). Named on Olancha (1956) 15' quadrangle.

Perognathus Flat: see **Harrisburg Flats** [INYO].

Perry: see **Mount Perry** [INYO].

Perry Aiken Creek [MONO]: *stream,* formed by the confluence of North Fork and South Fork, flows 2 miles to the State of Nevada 9 miles east-northeast of White Mountain Peak (lat. 37°39'40" N, long. 118°06' W; sec. 27, T 3 S, R 35 E). Named on Mount Barcroft (1962) 15' quadrangle. The name commemorates Perry Aiken, who settled near the stream in 1870 (Gudde, 1949, p. 258). North Fork is 8 miles long and South Fork is 6 miles long; both forks are named on Mount Barcroft (1962) 15' quadrangle.

Perry Aiken Flat [MONO]: *area,* 3 miles north-northeast of White Mountain Peak (lat. 37°40'15" N, long. 118°13'45" W); the place is near the head of a branch of North Fork Perry Aiken Creek. Named on Mount Barcroft (1962) 15' quadrangle.

Peterson Mill [INYO]: *locality,* 9 miles south-southwest of Bishop (lat. 37°15'15" N, long. 118°28'40" W; near W line sec. 16, T 8 S, R 32 E). Named on Bishop (1949) 15' quadrangle.

Petroglyph Canyon [INYO]: *canyon,* 6.5 miles long, opens into Coso Basin 9 miles west-northwest of the mouth of Mountain Springs Canyon (lat. 35°59'20" N, long. 117°43'10" W; sec. 25, T 22 S, R 39 E). Named on Coso Peak (1951) and Mountain Springs Canyon (1953) 15' quadrangles.

Petroglyph Canyon: see **Little Petroglyph Canyon**, under **Renegade Canyon** [INYO].

Pickel Meadow [MONO]: *valley,* 7 miles east-northeast of Sonora Pass along West Walker River (lat. 38°21'10" N, long. 119°31' W). Named on Fales Hot Springs (1954) and Pickel Meadow (1954) 7.5' quadrangles. Called Pickle Meadow on Dardanelles (1898) 30' quadrangle. Wheeler's (1876-1877) map has the name "Pickle's" at the place. The name is for Frank Pickel, a stockman and prospector of the 1860's; the place first was called Duffields Valley (Gudde, 1949, p. 260).

Pickett Peak [ALPINE]: *peak,* 7 miles south of Freel Peak (lat. 38° 45'20" N, long. 119°54'10" W; sec. 4, T 10 N, R 19 E). Altitude 9118 feet. Named on Freel Peak (1956) 15' quadrangle. Edward M. Pickett ran an early stage station called Pickett Place that was near the peak (Gudde, 1949, p. 260). California Division of Highways' (1934) shows a place called Picketts situated 1.5 miles east-southeast of Luther Pass. A toll gate near the west end of present West Carson Canyon was at a place first called Green's, and later called Pickett's (Long, p. 40).

Pickett Place: see **Pickett Peak** [ALPINE].

Pickett's: see **Pickett Peak** [ALPINE].

Pickle Meadow: see **Pickel Meadow** [MONO].

Pickle's: see **Pickel Meadow** [MONO].

Pilot Spring [MONO]: *spring,* 6.5 miles southeast of the site of Mono Mills (lat. 37°49'35" N, long. 118°52'15" W; sec. 27, T 1 S, R 28 E). Named on Cowtrack Mountain (1962) 15' quadrangle.

Pimentel Meadows [MONO]: *area,* 2.5 miles east of Fales Hot Springs (lat. 38°20'55" N, long. 119°21'05" W; sec. 20, 21, T 6 N, R 24 E). Named on Fales Hot Springs (1956) 15' quadrangle. The place is in a canyon called Tamarack Can. on Wheeler's (1876-1877) map.

Pine City: see **Mill City** [MONO].

Pine Creek [INYO]: *stream,* flows 14 miles to Rock Creek 8.5 miles northeast of Mount Tom (lat. 37°26'25" N, long. 118°34'10" W; near E line sec. 9, T 6 S, R 31 E). Named on Mount Tom (1949) 15' quadrangle.

Pine Creek: see **Little Pine Creek** [INYO]; **Little Pine Creek**, under **Independence Creek** [INYO].

Pine Creek Pass [INYO]: *pass,* 4.5 miles west-southwest of Mount Tom on

Inyo-Fresno County line (lat. 37°19'05" N, long. 118°44'05" W; near N line sec. 30, T 7 S, R 30 E); the pass is near the head of Pine Creek. Named on Mount Tom (1949) 15' quadrangle.

Pine Lake [INYO]: *lake,* 1500 feet long, 4 miles west-northwest of Mount Tom (lat. 37°21'10" N, long. 118°43'40" W; sec. 7, T 7 S, R 30 E); the lake is along Pine Creek. Named on Mount Tom (1949) 15' quadrangle.

Pine Lake: see **Upper Pine Lake** [INYO].

Pine Martin Campground [ALPINE]: *locality,* 8 miles northwest of Dardanelles Cone, and northeast of Lake Alpine (1) (lat. 38°28'50" N, long. 119°59'20" W). Named on Spicer Meadow Reservoir (1979) 7.5' quadrangle.

Pine Martin Peak: see **Mount Jepson**, under **Mount Sill** [INYO].

Pinnacle Ridge [INYO]: *ridge,* east-trending, 1.5 miles long, 1 mile east-southeast of Mount Whitney (1) (lat. 36°34'25" N, long. 118° 16'35" W). Named on Mount Whitney (1956) 15' quadrangle.

Piñon Mesa [INYO]: *area,* 5 miles north-northwest of Telescope Peak (lat. 36°14'10" N, long. 117°07'05" W). Named on Telescope Peak (1952) 15' quadrangle. National Park Service officials proposed the name because of a grove of pinyons near the place (Palmer, p. 57).

Pinto Peak [INYO]: *peak,* 6 miles northwest of Emigrant Pass (1) in Panamint Range (lat. 36°23' N, long. 117°13'30" W). Altitude 7510 feet. Named on Emigrant Canyon (1952) 15' quadrangle. On Wheeler's (1877) map, the part of Panamint Range near Pinto Peak is called Pinto Range. Fairbanks (p. 473) used the names "Pinto Range" or "Calico Range" for the same part of present Panamint Range, and Gudde (1949, p. 263) noted that locally it is called Moigne Mountain for an old prospector.

Pinto Range: see **Pinto Peak** [INYO].

Pinyon Creek [INYO]: *stream,* flows 5.5 miles to Independence Creek 4.25 miles west-southwest of Independence (lat. 36°46'45" N, long. 118°16' W; sec. 27, T 13 S, R 34 E). Named on Mount Pinchot (1953) and Mount Whitney (1956) 15' quadrangles.

Pinyon Mountain [MONO]: *peak,* 6.5 miles northeast of White Mountain Peak (lat. 37°42'05" N, long. 118°10'25" W). Altitude 8773 feet. Named on Mount Barcroft (1962) 15' quadrangle.

Piper Mountain [INYO]: *peak,* 4 miles northeast of Deep Springs (lat. 37°24'35" N, long. 117°55'40" W; sec. 21, T 6 S, R 37 E). Altitude 7703 feet. Named on Soldier Pass (1958) 15' quadrangle. United States Board on Geographic Names (1975, p. 9) approved the name "Chocolate Mountain"—the name is for the fancied resemblance of dark rock on top of the peak to chocolate frosting—and listed the name "Piper Mountain" as a variant.

Piper Peak [INYO]: *peak,* 5.5 miles west of Big Pine (lat. 37°09'35" N, long. 118°23'10" W; near NE cor. sec. 20, T 9 S, R 33 E). Altitude 8199 feet. Named on Big Pine (1950) 15' quadrangle.

Piute Canyon [MONO]: *canyon,* drained by a stream that flows 1.5 miles to Little Walker River 12 miles north-northwest of Matterhorn Peak (lat. 38°14'50" N, long. 119°29'30" W; sec. 30, T 5 N, R 23 E); the canyon heads near Piute Pass. Named on Matterhorn Peak (1956) 15' quadrangle.

Piute Creek [MONO]: *stream,* flows 6 miles to Chalfant Valley 9.5 miles south-southwest of White Mountain Peak (lat. 37°30'35" N, long. 118°19'15" W; sec. 14, T 5 S, R 33 E); the stream heads near Piute Mountain. Named on Mount Barcroft (1962) and White Mountain Peak (1962) 15' quadrangles.

Piute Lake [INYO]: *lake,* 1800 feet long, 4.5 miles north of Mount Darwin along North Fork (1) Bishop Creek (lat. 37°14'10" N, long. 118°40'15" W). Named on Mount Goddard (1948) 15' quadrangle.

Piute Meadows: see **Upper Piute Meadows** [MONO].

Piute Monument: see **Paiute Monument** [INYO].

Piute Mountain [MONO]: *peak,* 7 miles south of White Mountain Peak (lat. 37°32'15" N, long. 118°13'55" W); the peak is near the head of Piute Creek. Altitude 12,564 feet. Named on Mount Barcroft (1962) 15' quadrangle.

Piute Pass [INYO]: *pass,* 5 miles north of Mount Darwin on Inyo-Fresno County line (lat. 37°14'20" N, long. 118°41' W); the pass is above Piute Lake. Altitude 11,423 feet. Named on Mount Goddard (1948) 15' quadrangle. J.N. LeConte named the pass in 1904 (Farquhar, 1924, p. 64).

Piute Pass [MONO]: *pass,* 7 miles north-northeast of Tower Peak (lat. 38°14'30" N, long. 119°30'35" W; sec. 36, T 5 N, R 22 E); the pass is near the head of Piute Canyon. Named on Tower Peak (1956) 15' quadrangle.

Pizona [MONO]: *locality,* 16 miles north-northeast of Glass Mountain (lat. 37°58'20" N, long. 118°33'30" W; sec. 4, T 1 N, R 31 E); the place is along Pizona Creek. Site named on Glass Mountain (1962) 15' quadrangle.

Pizona Creek [MONO]: *stream,* flows 5.5 miles to Adobe Valley 15 miles north-northeast of Glass Mountain (lat. 37°58'30" N, long. 118°36'10" W; sec. 6, T 1 N, R 31 E). Named on Glass Mountain (1962) 15' quadrangle.

Pizona Spring: see **Upper Pizona Spring** [MONO].

Pleasant Canyon [INYO]: *canyon,* 9 miles long, opens into Panamint Valley 11 miles southwest of Telescope Peak (lat. 36°02'40" N, long. 117°13' W). Named on Telescope Peak (1952) 15' quadrangle. Wheeler's (1877) map has the name "Pleasant Vy. Cañon." The fcature also was called Post Office Canyon (Hubbard, Bray, and Pipkin, p. 15)—Post Office Spring is near its mouth. A mining camp called Pleasant City was located in the canyon in the 1890's (Lingenfelter, p. 195). A place called Anthony's Camp also was situated in the canyon; Charles Anthony financed a mine there in 1893 (Hubbard, Bray, and Pipkin, p. 15-16).

Pleasant City: see **Pleasant Canyon** [INYO].

Pleasant Valley [ALPINE]: *valley,* 3 miles southwest of Markleeville (lat. 38°39'20" N, long. 119°48'45" W). Named on Markleeville (1979) 7.5' quadrangle.

Pleasant Valley Cañon: see **Pleasant Canyon** [INYO].

Pleasant Valley Creek [ALPINE]: *stream,* flows 9.5 miles to join Hot Springs Creek and form Markleeville Creek 0.5 mile west-southwest of Markleeville (lat. 38°41'30" N, long. 119°47'20" W; near N line sec. 28, T 10 N, R 20 E); the stream goes through Pleasant Valley. Named on Markleeville (1979) 7.5' quadrangle.

Pleasant Valley Creek: see **Jeff Davis Creek** [ALPINE].

Point Bartlett [INYO]: *promontory,* 14 miles north of Olancha on the west side of Owens Lake (lat. 36°29'15" N, long. 118°01' W); the feature is 1 mile northeast of Bartlett. Named on Olancha (1956) 15' quadrangle.

Poison Canyon [ALPINE]:

(1) *canyon,* drained by a stream that flows 1.25 miles to Bloods Creek 2 miles south of Mount Reba (lat. 38°28'35" N, long. 120° 01'40" W; near E line sec. 7, T 7 N, R 18 E). Named on Tamarack (1979) 7.5' quadrangle.

(2) *canyon,* drained by a stream that flows 1.5 miles to Highland Creek 4.25 miles north-northeast of Dardanelles Cone (lat. 38°27'45" N, long. 119°50'45" W). Named on Dardanelles Cone (1979) 7.5' quadrangle. Called Champion Canyon on Dardanelles Cone (1956) 15' quadrangle, but United States Board on Geographic Names (1979b, p. 8) rejected this name.

Poison Creek [ALPINE]:

(1) *stream,* flows 2.5 miles to Mountaineer Creek 5.25 miles east-northeast of Mogul Peak (lat. 38°43'50" N, long. 119°38' W; sec. 11, T 10 N, R 21 E). Named on Topaz Lake (1956) 15' quadrangle.

(2) *stream,* flows 3 miles to East Fork Carson River 13 miles south-southeast of Mogul Peak in Dumonts Meadow (lat. 38°30'45" N, long. 119°39'15" W; sec. 27, T 8 N, R 21 E); the stream heads at Poison Lake. Named on Disaster Peak (1979) and Wolf Creek (1979) 7.5' quadrangles.

Poison Creek [MONO]:

(1) *stream,* flows 4 miles to Little Walker River nearly 4 miles southwest of Fales Hot Springs (lat. 38°18'55" N, long. 119°27'05" W; near N line sec. 4, T 5 N, R 23 E). Named on Fales Hot Springs (1954) and Pickel Meadow (1954) 7.5' quadrangles. Called Cabin Creek on Bridgeport (1909) 30' quadrangle, but United States Board on Geographic Names (1961a, p. 19) rejected this name for the stream.

(2) *stream,* flows 3.5 miles to South Fork Cottonwood Creek (2) 9 miles southeast of White Mountain Peak (lat. 37°31'50" N, long. 118°09'50" W). Named on Mount Barcroft (1962) 15' quadrangle.

Poison Flat [ALPINE]: *area,* 13 miles south-southeast of Mogul Peak (lat. 38°30'30" N, long. 119°37'25" W; sec. 25, T 8 N, R 21 E); the place is 1.5 miles east-southeast of the mouth of Poison Creek (2). Named on Topaz Lake (1956) 15' quadrangle.

Poison Lake [ALPINE]: *lake,* 700 feet long, 5 miles east-northeast of Disaster Peak (lat. 38°28'50" N, long. 119°39'10" W); the lake is at the head of Poison Creek (2). Named on Disaster Peak (1979) 7.5' quadrangle.

Poison Meadow [INYO]: *area,* 15 miles northwest of Olancha (lat. 36°26' N, long. 118°12' W; on E line sec. 20, T 17 S, R 35 E). Named on Olancha (1956) 15' quadrangle.

Poison Spring [INYO]: *spring,* 7 miles south-southeast of Chloride Cliff in Funeral Mountains (lat. 36°36'20" N, long. 116°49'20" W). Named on Furnace Creek (1910) 1° quadrangle. National Park Service employees proposed the name "Headache Spring" for the feature because water from the spring supposedly gives headaches to those who drink it (Palmer, p. 35).

Poison Valley: see **Tamarack Creek** [ALPINE].

Polemonium Peak: see **North Palisade** [INYO].

Poleta [INYO]: *locality,* nearly 4 miles east of Bishop along Southern Pacific Railroad (lat. 37°21'40" N, long. 118°19'30" W; near S line sec. 2, T 7 S, R 33 E); the place is 2 miles west-northwest of the mouth of Poleta Canyon. Named on Bishop (1913) 30' quadrangle. Postal authorities established Poleta post office in 1895 and discontinued it in 1923 (Frickstad, p. 52).

Poleta Canyon [INYO]: *canyon,* 5.5 miles long, opens into lowlands 5.5 miles east-southeast of Bishop (lat. 37°20'10" N, long. 118°18'05" W; sec. 13, T 7 S, R 33 E). Named on Bishop (1949) and Blanco Mountain (1951) 15' quadrangles. The name is for Poleta mine, which was named for the Mexican or Spaniard who found it in the early 1880's (Gudde, 1949, p. 269).

Poor Boy Creek [ALPINE]: *stream,* flows 2 miles to East Fork Carson River nearly 2 miles east-southeast of Markleeville (lat. 38° 40'55" N, long. 119°45'05" W; sec. 26, T 10 N, R 20 E). Named on Markleeville (1979) 7.5' quadrangle.

Poore Creek [MONO]: *stream,* flows 2.5 miles to West Walker River 6 miles east of Sonora Pass in Pickel Meadow (lat. 38°20'35" N, long. 119°31'35" W; sec. 26, T 6 N, R 22 E); the stream heads at Poore Lake. Named on Pickel Meadow (1954) 7.5' quadrangle.

Poore Lake [MONO]: *lake,* 1 mile long, 6.5 miles east-southeast of Sonora Pass (lat. 38°18'30" N, long. 119°31'30" W; mainly in sec. 2, T 5 N, R 22 E); the lake is at the head of Poore Creek. Named on Pickel Meadow (1954) 7.5' quadrangle.

Pops Gulch [INYO]: *canyon,* 1 mile long, opens into Al Rose Canyon 10.5 miles northeast of Independence (lat. 36°55'35" N, long. 118°05'10" W). Named on Independence (1951) 15' quadrangle. DeDecker (p. 46-47) referred to Pop's Gulch.

Porter Peak [INYO]: *peak,* 8.5 miles south-southeast of Telescope Peak (lat. 36°03' N, long. 117°03'20" W). Altitude 9101 feet. Named on Telescope Peak (1952) 15' quadrangle.

Portuguese Bench [INYO]: *area,* 1.5 miles west of Coso Junction (lat. 36°03' N, long. 117°58'40" W; near W line sec. 3, T 22 N, R 37 E). Named on Haiwee Reservoir (1951) 15' quadrangle. Ballarat (1913) 1° quadrangle has the plural form "Portuguese Benches" for the name.

Portuguese Canyon [INYO]: *canyon,* drained by a stream that flows 3.5 miles to Rose Valley 2.5 miles southwest of Coso Junction (lat. 36°01' N, long. 117°58'25" W). Named on Haiwee Reservoir (1951) and Monache Mountain (1956) 15' quadrangles.

Post Office Canyon: see **Pleasant Canyon** [INYO].

Post Office Spring [INYO]: *spring,* 11.5 miles southwest of Telescope Peak and less than 0.5 mile south of Ballarat (lat. 36°02'30" N, long. 117°13'25" W; near NE cor. sec. 9, T 22 S, R 44 E). Named on Telescope Peak (1952) 15' quadrangle. The name reportedly is from letters and cash that outlaws left at the spring in the 1870's for certain stage drivers, who then on their return trip left provisions (Hubbard, Bray, and Pipkin, p. 4-5). According to Palmer (p. 58), the feature probably was called Soda Spring originally.

Potato Peak [MONO]: *peak,* 4.25 miles west-northwest of Bodie (lat. 38°14' N, long. 119°05'05" W; near E line sec. 3, T 4 N, R 26 E). Altitude 10,236 feet. Named on Bodie (1958) 15' quadrangle.

Pothole: see **The Pothole** [INYO].

Pothole Lake: see **Big Pothole Lake** [INYO]; **Little Pothole Lake** [INYO].

Poverty Flat: see **Lee Vining** [MONO].

Poverty Hills [INYO]: *range,* 8 miles south-southeast of Big Pine on the west side of Owens Valley (lat. 37°03' N, long. 118°15' W). Named on Big Pine (1950) and Waucoba Mountain (1951) 15' quadrangles. A storekeeper named the range because he went broke when the prospectors who were is customers could not pay their bills (Schumacher, p. 47).

Powell: see **Mount Powell** [INYO].

Prater: see **Mount Prater** [INYO].

Prospector Meadow: see **Big Prospector Meadow** [MONO].

Pumice Gap: see **Mammoth Pass** [MONO].

Pumice Valley [MONO]: *valley,* 4 miles southeast of Lee Vining (lat. 37°54'30" N, long. 119°04'30" W). Named on Mono Craters (1953) 15' quadrangle.

Punch Bowl [MONO]: *crater,* 11 miles south-southeast of Lee Vining near the south end of Mono Craters (lat. 37°48'55" N, long. 119°01'30" W). Named on Mono Craters (1953) 15' quadrangle.

Putnam's: see **Independence** [INYO].

Pyramid Pass: see **Pyramid Peak** [INYO].

Pyramid Peak [INYO]: *peak,* nearly 6 miles northeast of Ryan (2) in Funeral Mountains (lat. 36°23'30" N, long. 116°36'40" W). Altitude 6703 feet. Named on Ryan (1952) 15' quadrangle. The name is from the shape of the peak (Palmer, p. 59). M.H. Farley gave the name "Furnace Creek Pass" to a pass near Pyramid Peak in 1861; Margaret Long renamed the feature Pyramid Pass in 1941 (Palmer, p. 29, 59).

—Q—

Quail Spring [INYO]: *spring,* 4 miles north of Argus Peak (lat. 35°54'35" N, long. 117°26'55" W; sec. 28, T 23 S, R 42 E). Named on Trona (1949) 15' quadrangle.

Quaking Asp Canyon [MONO]: *canyon,* drained by a stream that flows 1.5 miles to the State of Nevada 15 miles north of Bridgeport (lat. 38°29'10" N, long. 119°14' W; sec. 18, T 7 N, R 25 E). Named on Bridgeport (1958) and Fales Hot Springs (1956) 15' quadrangles.

Quaking Aspen Campground [ALPINE]: *locality,* 3 miles west of Markleeville near Hot Springs Creek (lat. 38°41'55" N, long. 119° 50'05" W; sec. 24, T 10 N, R 19 E). Named on Markleeville (1979) 7.5' quadrangle.

Quartzite Peak: see **Shadow Mountain** [INYO].

Quartzite Spring: see **Quartz Spring** [INYO].

Quartz Spring [INYO]: *spring,* 7.5 miles south-southwest of Tin Mountain (lat. 36°46'45" N, long. 117°29'35" W). Named on Tin Mountain (1957) 15' quadrangle. The name is for quartzite that occurs near the feature, which also is called Quartzite Spring ·(Palmer, p. 59).

Queen Dicks [MONO]: *locality,* 5.5 miles southeast of Benton (lat. 37°45'50" N, long. 118°24' W; sec. 24, T 2 S, R 32 E); the place is at the mouth of Queen Dicks Canyon. Site named on Benton (1962) 15' quadrangle.

Queen Dicks Canyon [MONO]: *canyon,* drained by a stream that flows 3.5 miles to Benton Valley 5.5 miles southeast of Benton (lat. 37°45'50" N, long. 118°24'10" W; sec. 24, T 2 S, R 32 E). Named on Benton (1962) 15' quadrangle. The stream in the canyon is called Fall Cr. on Sampson's (1940) map.

Queen Valley [MONO]: *valley,* mainly in the State of Nevada, opens into Benton Valley 6 miles north-northeast of Benton (lat. 37° 54' N, long. 118°26' W). Named on Benton (1962) 15' quadrangle. This valley and Benton Valley together are called Spring Valley on Wheeler's (1871) map. Carlson (p. 196) related the name "Queen" to Indian Queen mine, located in the State of Nevada near the north end of White Mountains

—R—

Rabbit Flat: see **White Sage Flat** [INYO].

Racetrack: see **The Racetrack** [INYO].

Racetrack Valley [INYO]: *valley,* east of Ubehebe Peak in Panamint Range (lat. 36°42'30" N, long. 117°34' W); the feature called The Racetrack is in the valley. Named on Dry Mountain (1957) and Ubehebe Peak (1950) 15' quadrangles.

Railroad Canyon [ALPINE]: *canyon,* drained by a stream that flows 1.5 miles to East Fork Carson River 7 miles south-southeast of Mogul Peak (lat. 38°35'50" N, long. 119°39'50" W; sec. 27, T 9 N, R 21 E). Named on Wolf Creek (1979) 7.5' quadrangle.

Rainbow Canyon [INYO]: *canyon,* 5.5 miles long, opens into Panamint Valley 8.5 miles west-southwest of Panamint Butte (lat. 36° 22'30" N, long. 117°29'15" W; sec. 13, T 18 S, R 41 E). Named on Darwin (1950) and Panamint Butte (1951) 15' quadrangles.

Ramsey: see **Greenwater** [INYO].

Rancheria Gulch [MONO]: *canyon,* drained by a stream that flows 5 miles to Mono Valley 10.5 miles south-southwest of Bodie (lat. 38°04'10" N, long. 119°04'55" W; near S line sec. 35, T 3 N, R 26 E). Named on Bodie (1958) 15' quadrangle.

Rancheria Gulch Spring [MONO]: *spring,* 10 miles southwest of Bodie (lat. 38°06'05" N, long. 119°07'45" W; sec. 20, T 3 N, R 26 E); the spring is in the upper part of Rancheria Gulch. Named on Bodie (1958) 15' quadrangle.

Randall Creek [ALPINE]: *stream,* flows 1.25 miles to Indian Creek (1) 4.25 miles north-northwest of Markleeville (lat. 38°44'55" N, long. 119°48'50" W). Named on Markleeville (1979) 7.5' quadrangle.

Rattlesnake Cabin [INYO]: *locality,* 21 miles north of New York Butte (lat. 36°56'45" N, long. 117°52'55" W). Named on Ballarat (1913) 1° quadrangle.

Rattlesnake Canyon [INYO]: *canyon,* drained by a stream that flows 3.5 miles to Searles Valley nearly 5 miles east of Argus Peak (lat. 35°51'40" N, long. 117°21'35" W; sec. 8, T 24 S, R 43 E). Named on Trona (1949) 15' quadrangle.

Rattlesnake Gulch [INYO]: *canyon,* drained by a stream that flows 1 mile to Wildrose Canyon nearly 6 miles south-southwest of Emigrant Pass (1) (lat. 36°16' N, long. 117°11'40" W). Named on Emigrant Canyon (1952) 15' quadrangle.

Rattlesnake Gulch [MONO]: *canyon,* drained by a stream that flows 2 miles to Bacon Gulch nearly 12 miles southwest of Bodie (lat. 38°04'50" N, long. 119°08'45" W; sec. 31, T 3 N, R 26 E). Named on Bodie (1958) 15' quadrangle.

Rawson Creek [INYO]: *stream,* flows 6.5 miles to lowlands 5.25 miles south of Bishop (lat. 37°17'10" N, long. 118°24'15" W; sec. 6, T 8 S, R 33 E). Named on Big Pine (1950) and Bishop (1949) 15' quadrangles.

Raymond: see **Raymond Canyon Creek** [ALPINE].

Raymond Canyon Creek [ALPINE]: *stream,* flows 3.5 miles to Pleasant Valley nearly 4 miles south-southwest of Markleeville (lat. 38°38'50" N, long. 119°49'05" W; near S line sec. 6, T 9 N, R 20 E); the stream heads near Raymond Peak. Named on Ebbetts Pass (1979) and Markleeville (1979) 7.5' quadrangles. This appears to be the stream that on its upper reaches is called Krum's C. on Reed's (1864) map, which shows a place called Raymond situated along the stream. Long (p. 29) noted that Raymond City was located where Krumm Creek enters Pleasant Valley, and that the place was named for R.W. Raymond, who investigated and reported on mining in the neighborhood.

Raymond City: see **Raymond Canyon Creek** [ALPINE].

Raymond Lake [ALPINE]: *lake,* 750 feet long, 4.5 miles north-northwest of Ebbetts Pass (lat. 38°36'35" N, long. 119°50'05" W; near N line sec. 25, T 9 N, R 19 E); the lake is 0.25 mile north-northwest of Raymond Peak. Named on Ebbetts Pass (1979) 7.5' quadrangle.

Raymond Meadows [ALPINE]: *area,* 2.5 miles north-northwest of Ebbetts Pass (lat. 38°34'40" N, long. 119°49'40" W). Named on Ebbetts Pass (1979) 7.5' quadrangle.

Raymond Meadows Creek [ALPINE]: *stream,* flows 2.25 miles to Silver Creek (1) nearly 3 miles north-northeast of Ebbetts Pass (lat. 38°35'05" N, long. 119°47'50" W); Raymond Meadows is near the head of the creek. Named on Ebbetts Pass (1979) 7.5' quadrangle.

Raymond Peak [ALPINE]: *peak,* 4.25 miles north-northwest of Ebbetts Pass (lat. 38°36'15" N, long. 119°49'55" W; sec. 25, T 9 N, R 19 E). Altitude 10,014 feet. Named on Ebbetts Pass (1979) 7.5' quadrangle. Members of the Whitney survey named the peak in 1865 for R.W. Raymond (Gudde, 1949, p. 280), for whom Raymond City was named.

Reba: see **Mount Reba** [ALPINE].

Red Amphitheater [INYO]: *valley,* 6 miles north of Ryan in Funeral Mountains (lat. 36°24'30" N, long. 116°40' W). Named on Ryan (1952) 15' quadrangle.

Red and White Mountain [MONO]: *peak,* 5.5 miles south of Mount Morrison on Mono-Fresno County line (lat. 37°28'50" N, long. 118°51'25" W). Altitude 12,850 feet. Named on Mount Abbot (1953) 15' quadrangle. Theodore S. Solomons named the peak in 1894 for red and white rocks exposed on it (Farquhar, 1925, p. 127).

Red Cinder Hill: see **Red Hill** [INYO].

Red Cinder Mountain: see **Red Hill** [INYO].

Redding Canyon [INYO]: *canyon,* 4 miles long, enters Poleta Canyon 6 miles east-southeast of Bishop (lat. 37°20'50" N, long. 118°17'15" W; near N line sec. 18, T 7 S, R 34 E). Named on Bishop (1949) and Blanco Mountain (1951) 15' quadrangles. The name commemorates John Redding, a miner who lived in the canyon in 1879 (Gudde, 1949, p. 282).

Red Hill [INYO]: *hill,* 3.5 miles north of the village of Little Lake in Rose Valley (lat. 35°59'10" N, long. 117°55' W; sec. 30, T 22 S, R 38 E). Altitude 3952 feet. Named on Little Lake (1954) 15' quadrangle. United States Board on Geographic Names (1983f, p. 2) rejected the names "Cinder Hill," "Red Cinder Hill," and "Red Cinder Mountain" for the feature.

Red Lake [ALPINE]: *lake,* 3900 feet long, less than 1 mile east-northeast of Carson Pass (lat. 38°41'55" N, long. 119°58'25" W; mainly in sec. 23, T 10 N, R 18 E). Named on Carson Pass (1979) 7.5' quadrangle.

Red Lake [INYO]: *lake,* 900 feet long, 11.5 miles south-southwest of Big Pine (lat. 37°01'10" N, long. 118°24'10" W); the lake is at the head of Red Mountain Creek. Named on Big Pine (1950) 15' quadrangle.

Red Lake [MONO]:

(1) *lake,* 850 feet long, 7.25 miles east-southeast of Matterhorn Peak (lat. 38°02'35" N, long. 119°15'45" W; sec. 7, T 2 N, R 25 E). Named on Matterhorn Peak (1956) 15' quadrangle. The lake is one of the group called Virginia Lakes

(2) *lake,* 400 feet long, 6 miles west of Mount Morrison (lat. 37° 34' N, long. 118°58' W). Named on Mount Morrison (1953) 15' quadrangle.

Red Lake Creek [ALPINE]: *stream,* flows 4 miles to West Fork Carson River 4 miles northeast of Carson Pass (lat. 38°44' N, long. 119°55'50" W); the stream heads at Red Lake. Named on Carson Pass (1979) 7.5' quadrangle.

Red Lake Peak [ALPINE]: *peak,* 1.25 miles north of Carson Pass (lat. 38°42'50" N, long. 119°59'10" W; sec. 15, T 10 N, R 18 E); the peak is 1.25 miles north-northwest of Red Lake. Altitude 10,063 feet. Named on Carson Pass (1979) 7.5' quadrangle. The peak was called Red Mountain in the early days (Goddard, p. 105).

Redlands Canyon [INYO]: *canyon,* 4.5 miles long, opens into Panamint Valley 4.25 miles west-northwest of Manly Peak (lat. 35° 56'15" N, long. 117°11'10" W). Named on Manly Peak (1950) 15' quadrangle. The name is from Redlands Gold Mining Company, formed in the 1880's by residents of Redlands in San Bernardino County; the feature earlier was called Emigrant Canyon (Lingenfelter, p. 90, 194).

Redlands Spring [INYO]: *spring,* nearly 3.5 miles west-northwest of Manly Peak (lat. 35°56'15" N, long. 117°10'10" W); the spring is in Redlands Canyon. Named on Manly Peak (1950) 15' quadrangle.

Red Mountain [INYO]: *hill,* 9 miles south of Big Pine (lat. 37°01'45" N, long. 118°17'15" W; near SW cor. sec. 32, T 10 S, R 34 E). Altitude 5188 feet. Named on Big Pine (1950) 15' quadrangle.

Red Mountain [MONO]:

(1) *peak,* 4 miles southwest of Toms Place (lat. 37°31'25" N, long. 118°44' W). Altitude 11,472 feet. Named on Casa Diablo Mountain (1953) 15' quadrangle.

(2) *peak,* 8.5 miles east of White Mountain Peak (lat. 37°37'20" N, long. 118°06'20" W). Altitude 7754 feet. Named on Mount Barcroft (1962) 15' quadrangle.

Red Mountain: see **Old Mammoth** [MONO]; **Red Lake Peak** [ALPINE].

Red Mountain Creek [INYO]: *stream,* flows 5.5 miles to Tinemaha Creek 8 miles south of Big Pine and 2 miles northwest of Red Mountain (lat. 37°03'05" N, long. 118°18'50" W; sec. 25, T 10 S, R 33 E); the stream heads at Red Lake. Named on Big Pine (1950) 15' quadrangle.

Red Peak [MONO]: *peak,* 10.5 miles southeast of Mount Barcroft (lat. 37°28'40" N, long. 118°06'25" W). Altitude 10,094 feet. Named on Blanco Mountain (1951) 15' quadrangle.

Red Ridge [INYO]: *ridge,* north-northeast-trending, nearly 1 mile long, 14 miles south of Keeler (lat. 36°17'40" N, long. 117°54'15" W; sec. 7, T 19 S, R 38 E). Named on Keeler (1951) 15' quadrangle.

Red Rock Canyon [MONO]: *canyon,* 3 miles long, opens into Hammil Valley 11.5 miles west of White Mountain Peak (lat. 37° 39'30" N, long. 118°27'30" W; sec. 28, T 3 S, R 32 E). Named on Casa Diablo Mountain (1953) and White Mountain Peak (1962) 15' quadrangles.

Red Slate Mountain [MONO]: *peak,* 3.5 miles south of Mount Morrison on Mono-Fresno County line (lat. 37°30'30" N, long. 118°52'10" W). Altitude 13,163 feet. Named on Mount Morrison (1953) 15' quadrangle. Members of the Whitney survey gave the descriptive name to the feature (Sowaal, p. 113).

Red Top Lake [MONO]: *lake,* 350 feet long, 7 miles southeast of Sonora Pass (lat. 38°15'45" N, long. 119°32'20" W; sec. 22, T 5 N, R 22 E). Named on Pickel Meadow (1954) 7.5' quadrangle.

Red Wall Canyon [INYO]: *canyon,* drained by a stream that flows 6.5 miles to Death Valley 3.25 miles northwest of the mouth of Titus Canyon (lat. 36°51'45" N, long. 117°12'25" W). Named on Grapevine Peak (1957) 15' quadrangle.

Red Wash Creek [MONO]: *stream,* flows 2 miles to the State of Nevada 11 miles northeast of Bridgeport (lat. 38°21'40" N, long. 119°04'50" W; sec. 14, T 6 N, R 26 E). Named on Bridgeport (1958) 15' quadrangle.

Reed Flat [INYO]: *area,* 6 miles west-northwest of Westgard Pass (lat. 37°22'50" N, long. 118°11' W; near W line sec. 31, T 6 S, R 35 E). Named on Blanco Mountain (1951) 15' quadrangle.

Reilly: see **Panamint Valley** [INYO].

Renegade Canyon [INYO]: *canyon,* drained by a stream that flows 9.5 miles to Coso Basin 2.5 miles northwest of the mouth of Mountain Springs Canyon (lat. 35°57'35" N, long. 117°37'50" W; near S line sec. 2, T 23 S, R 40 E). Named on Coso Peak (1951) and Mountain Springs Canyon (1953) 15' quadrangles. The canyon, which contains a large number of petroglyphs, sometimes is called Little Petroglyph Canyon (Duffield, p. 50). Wheeler's (1877) map has the name "Kelley's Sta." for a place situated near the mouth of the canyon.

Rescue Creek: see **Lee Vining Creek** [MONO].

Resting Spring [INYO]: *spring,* 4.5 miles east-northeast of Tecopa at the south end of Resting Spring Range (lat. 35°52'35" N, long. 116°09'25" W; sec. 31, T 21 N, R 8 E). Named on Tecopa (1950) 15' quadrangle. The name dates back to about 1850, when parties of Mormons bound for San Bernardino from Salt Lake City used the place to break their long journey (Hoover, Rensch, and Rensch, p. 114). The spring was known as the Archilette to early travelers on the old Spanish trail to California; Fremont called the place Agua de Hernandez, for the lone survivor of an Indian attack there in 1844 (Fremont, p. 264-265).

Resting Spring Range [INYO]: *range,* east of Amargosa River, and west of Chicago Valley and Stewart Valley; extends south from just inside the State of Nevada to Resting Spring. Named on Ash Meadows (1952), Eagle Mountain (1951) Stewart Valley (1958), and Tecopa (1950) 15' quadrangles.

Rest Spring [INYO]: *spring,* 7.5 miles south of Tin Mountain (lat. 36°46'35" N, long. 117°27' W). Named on Tin Mountain (1957) 15' quadrangle.

Revenue Canyon [INYO]: *canyon,* 5 miles long, opens into Panamint Valley 5.5 miles east-northeast of Maturango Peak (lat. 36°09'50" N, long. 117°24'45" W). Named on Maturango Peak (1951) 15' quadrangle. The name probably is from Revenue mine (Palmer, p. 62).

Reversed Creek [MONO]: *stream,* heads at June Lake (1) and flows 3.25 miles to Rush Creek 13 miles south of Lee Vining (lat. 37° 46' N, long. 119°07'15" W; near SE cor. sec. 17, T 2 S, R 26 E). Named on Mono Craters (1953) 15' quadrangle. The name records that "the ancient drainage has been reversed by the deposition of morainal débris" (Russell, p. 343)—the stream flows toward rather than away from the Sierra Nevada.

Reversed Peak [MONO]: *peak,* 10.5 miles south of Lee Vining (lat. 37°48'20" N, long. 119°05'50" W; sec. 3, T 2 S, R 26 E); the peak is north of Reversed Creek. Altitude 9473 feet. Named on Mono Craters (1953) 15' quadrangle.

Reward [INYO]: *locality,* 9.5 miles north of Lone Pine at the west base of Inyo Mountains (lat. 36°44'45" N, long. 118°03'10" W). Named on Lone Pine (1958) 15' quadrangle. Postal authorities established Reward post office in 1900 and discontinued it in 1906; the name is from Reward Consolidated Mining Company, which had a mine at the place (Salley, p. 184).

Reynolds Peak [ALPINE]: *peak,* 3 miles north-northwest of Ebbetts Pass (lat. 38°34'50" N, long. 119°50'15" W). Altitude 9679 feet. Named on Ebbetts Pass (1979) 7.5' quadrangle. Called Reynold Peak on Markleeville (1889) 30' quadrangle, but United States Board on Geographic Names (1979b, p. 8) rejected this designation; on the recommendation of Forest Service officials, the peak was named in 1929 for G. Elmer Reynolds, editor of the *Stockton Record,* and an advocate of forest conservation.

Rhinedollar Reservoir: see **Ellery Lake** [MONO].

Rhodes Hill [INYO]: *hill,* 13 miles west-southwest of Shoshone in Black Mountains (lat. 35°55'20" N, long. 116°29'55" W); the feature is southeast of Rhodes Wash. Altitude 2872 feet. Named on Shoshone (1951) 15' quadrangle.

Rhodes Spring [INYO]: *spring,* 2.5 miles south of Epaulet Peak (lat. 35°56'

N, long. 116°31'25" W); the spring is near Rhodes Wash. Named on Confidence Hills (1950) 15' quadrangle. The name commemorates Albert Rhodes, who found silver ore in 1885, but died while bringing a prospective buyer to his discovery (Lingenfelter, p. 330).

Rhodes Wash [INYO]: *stream,* flows 9.5 mile to Death Valley 7.25 miles south-southwest of Epaulet Peak (lat. 35°52'45" N, long. 116°34'45" W). Named on Confidence Hills (1950) and Shoshone (1951) 15' quadrangles.

Rice Lake [ALPINE]: *lake,* 250 feet long, 7 miles north-northwest of Pacific Grade Summit (lat. 38°36'35" N, long. 119°57'30" W; near N line sec. 26, T 9 N, R 18 E). Named on Pacific Valley (1979) 7.5' quadrangle.

Richter Creek: see **Lubken Creek** [INYO].

Rickey Canyon [MONO]: *canyon,* 4.5 miles long, heads in the State of Nevada and opens into Antelope Valley 4 miles northeast of Coleville (lat. 38°36'30" N, long. 119°27'30" W; sec. 21, T 9 N, R 23 E). Named on Desert Creek Peak (1956) 15' quadrangle.

Rickey Peak [MONO]: *peak,* 6 miles south of Fales Hot Springs (lat. 38°15'50" N, long. 119°22'50" W; sec. 30, T 5 N, R 24 E). Altitude 10,126 feet. Named on Fales Hot Springs (1954) 7.5' quadrangle. Called Rickey's Pk. on Wheeler's (1876-1877) map.

Right Fork Wet Fork: see **Wet Fork** [MONO].

Riley: see **Barney Riley** [ALPINE]; **Barney Riley Creek** [ALPINE].

Rileys: see **Barney Riley** [ALPINE].

Ring Well: see **Ruiz Well** [INYO].

Rio Clara: see **West Walker River** [MONO].

Rio de los Payuches: see **Amargosa River** [INYO].

Rio Ida: see **East Walker River** [MONO].

Rio Salitroso: see **Salt Creek** [INYO].

River Spring [MONO]: *spring,* 12.5 mile north-northeast of Glass Mountain on the east side of Adobe Valley (lat. 37°56'20" N, long. 118°36'45" W; near NE cor. sec. 24, T 1 N, R 30 E). Named on Glass Mountain (1962) 15' quadrangle. Tucker (p. 402) used the plural form "River Springs" for the name.

River Spring Lakes [MONO]: *intermittent lakes,* 12 miles north-northeast of Glass Mountain on the east side of Adobe Valley (lat. 37°55'45" N, long. 118°36'15" W); the features are southeast of River Spring. Named on Glass Mountain (1962) 15' quadrangle. Called River Sprs. Lakes on Sampson's (1940) map, but United States Board on Geographic Names (1986, p. 2) rejected the forms "River Springs Lakes" and "River Springs Lake" for the name.

Riverview Campground [ALPINE]: *locality,* about 3.5 miles west of Dardanelles Cone along Clark Fork (lat. 38°23'55" N, long. 119° 48'10" W). Named on Dardanelles Cone (1956) 15' quadrangle.

Roachville: see **Cottonwood Creek** [INYO-MONO].

Roberts: see **Roberts Ridge** [INYO].

Roberts Ridge [INYO]: *ridge,* west-trending, 3.5 miles long, 8.5 miles north-northeast of Westgard Pass (lat. 37°25' N, long. 118° 06'30" W). Named on Blanco Mountain (1951) 15' quadrangle, which shows Roberts ranch north of the ridge. California Mining Bureau's (1917b) map has the name "Roberts" at or near the ranch site.

Robinson Creek [MONO]: *stream,* flows 20 miles, including through Twin Lakes, to Bridgeport Reservoir 1.5 miles northwest of Bridgeport (lat. 38°16'20" N, long. 119°15'05" W; near S line sec. 19, T 5 N, R 25 E). Named on Fales Hot Springs (1956) and Matterhorn Peak (1956) 15' quadrangles. The name commemorates Moses Robinson, who had a lumber mill along the stream in the 1860's (Wedertz, p. 154).

Robinson Creek Campground [MONO]: *locality,* 7 miles southwest of Bridgeport (lat. 38°11'10" N, long. 119°19'15" W; near SW cor. sec. 22, T 4 N, R 24 E); the place is along Robinson Creek. Named on Matterhorn Peak (1956) 15' quadrangle.

Robinson Lake [INYO]: *lake,* 400 feet long, 8 miles west-southwest of Independence (lat. 36°45'30" N, long. 118°20'20" W). Named on Mount Pinchot (1953) 15' quadrangle.

Robinson Peak [MONO]: *peak,* 5 miles north of Matterhorn Peak on Sawmill Ridge (lat. 38°10' N, long. 119°23'05" W; sec. 31, T 4 N, R 24 E); the peak is north of Robinson Creek. Altitude 10,806 feet. Named on Matterhorn Peak (1956) 15' quadrangle. The name is for Moses Robinson, of Robinson Creek (Wedertz, p. 154).

Rock Canyon: see **Rock Creek** [MONO] (1).

Rock Cave: see **Rock Spring** [INYO].

Rock Creek [INYO-MONO]: *stream,* flows 28 miles in Inyo County and Mono County to Owens River 9 miles northeast of Mount Tom (lat. 37°26'10" N, long. 118°33'15" W; sec. 10, T 6 S, R 31 E). Named on Casa Diablo Mountain (1953) and Mount Tom (1949) 15' quadrangles. East Fork enters from the south-southeast in Mono County 20 miles upstream from the mouth of the main creek; it is 5.5 miles long and is named on Mount Tom (1949) 15' quadrangle. United States Board on Geographic Names (1985c, p. 2) approved the name "Lower Rock Creek" for the part of former Rock Creek between Toms Place and Owens River—the name "Rock Creek" is retained for the stream above Toms Place.

Rock Creek [MONO]:

(1) *stream,* flows 7 miles to West Walker River 5 miles southeast of Coleville (lat. 38°30'45" N, long. 119°26'55" W; near E line sec. 28, T 8 N, R 23 E). Named on Desert Creek Peak (1956) and Fales Hot Springs (1956) 15' quadrangles. South Fork enters from the south 1.5 miles upstream from the mouth of the main stream; it is 4.5 miles long and is named on Desert Creek Peak (1956) and Fales Hot Springs (1956) 15' quadrangles. The canyon of the main stream is called Ross Canyon on Wellington (1893) 30' quadrangle, and is called Rock Canyon on Wellington (1893, reprinted 1942) 30' quadrangle.

(2) *stream,* flows 6 miles to Hammil Valley 11 miles northwest of White Mountain Peak (lat. 37°43'30" N, long. 118°24'50" W; sec. 35, T 2 S, R 32 E). Named on Benton (1962) and White Mountain Peak (1962) 15' quadrangles.

Rock Creek Lake [INYO]: *lake,* 2400 feet long, 9 miles north-northwest of Mount Tom (lat. 37°27'10" N, long. 118°44'10" W); the lake is along Rock Creek [INYO-MONO]. Named on Mount Tom (1949) 15' quadrangle.

Rock Island Pass [MONO]: *pass,* 4.5 miles west of Matterhorn Peak on Mono-Tuolumne County line (lat. 38°05'55" N, long. 119°27'50" W); the pass is 1.5 miles north-northeast of Rock Island Lake, which is in Tuolumne County. Named on Matterhorn Peak (1956) 15' quadrangle.

Rock Lake [ALPINE]: *lake,* 1450 feet long, 5.5 miles northwest of Dardanelles Cone (lat. 38°27'05" N, long. 119°57' W). Named on Spicer Meadow Reservoir (1979) 7.5' quadrangle.

Rock Spring [INYO]: *spring,* 6.5 miles north-northeast of Argus Peak in Bruce Canyon (lat. 37°56'05" N, long. 117°23'05" W). Named on Trona (1949) 15' quadrangle. The spring appears to be the same as the one that Thompson (1921, p. 249) called Middle Spring, and that Thompson's (1921) map shows. Federal Writers' Project (p. 49) mentioned a place near Middle Spring called Rock Cave, "a shallow cavern in a huge rock blackened with smoke," where prospectors walled up a cave and built a fireplace.

Rock Springs Canyon [MONO]: *canyon,* drained by a stream that flows 6.5 miles to Bridgeport Reservoir nearly 3 miles north-northeast of Bridgeport (lat. 38°17'45" N, long. 119°12'55" W; sec. 16, T 5 N, R 25 E). Named on Bridgeport (1958) 15' quadrangle. Called Rocky Spr. Can. on Sampson's (1940) map.

Rocky Bottom Lake [INYO]: *lake,* 900 feet long, 9 miles east-northeast of Mount Darwin (lat. 37°12' N, long. 118°31' W; sec. 6, T 9 S, R 32 E). Named on Mount Goddard (1948) 15' quadrangle.

Rocky Canyon: see **West Carson Canyon** [ALPINE].

Rocky Spring Canyon: see **Rock Springs Canyon** [MONO].

Roderique Creek: see **Little Antelope Valley** [MONO] (1).

Rodger Peak [MONO]: *peak,* 14 miles west-northwest of Mammoth Mountain on Mono-Madera County line (lat. 37°43'30" N, long. 119°15'25" W). Altitude 12,978 feet. Named on Merced Peak (1953) 15' quadrangle. Called Rodgers Peak on Mount Lyell (1901) 30' quadrangle. Lieutenant N.F. McClure named the peak in 1895 for Captain Alexander Rodgers, acting superintendent of Yosemite National Park in 1895 and 1897 (United States Board on Geographic Names, 1934, p. 21).

Rodgers Lakes [MONO]: *lakes,* largest 1100 feet long, 13 miles northwest of Mammoth Mountain (lat. 37°44'10" N, long. 119°13'35" W); the lakes are 2 miles east-northeast of Rodger Peak. Named on Devils Postpile (1953) 15' quadrangle.

Rodgers Pak: see **Rodger Peak** [MONO].

Rodriguez Flat [ALPINE-MONO]: *area,* 4 miles southwest of Coleville on Alpine-Mono County line (lat. 38°31'30" N, long. 119°33'30" W; sec. 21, 22, T 8 N, R 22 E). Named on Topaz Lake (1956) 15' quadrangle.

Rogers Peak [INYO]: *peak,* 3.25 miles north of Telescope Peak in Panamint Range (lat. 36°13'05" N, long. 117°05'05" W; near S line sec. 3, T 20 S, R 45 E). Altitude 9994 feet. Named on Telescope Peak (1952) 15' quadrangle. National Park Service personnel proposed in 1936 to rename the double peak called Baldy on Ballarat (1913) 1° quadrangle; they gave the northernmost of the two peaks the name "Manly Peak," for W.L. Manly, and gave the southern one the name "Rogers Peak," for John Rogers, Manly's companion in the rescue of emigrants stranded in Death Valley (Gudde, 1949, p. 203). However, now the northern peak is called Rogers Peak and the southern one is called Bennett Peak on Telescope Peak (1952) 15' quadrangle. United States Board on Geographic Names (1968a, p. 6) approved the name "Coville Ridge" for an east-trending ridge, 1.5 miles long, that is located 3 miles northeast of Rogers Peak (lat. 36°14'33" N, long. 117°02'30" W); the name honors Frederick Vernon Coville, a member of the expedition to Death Valley in 1890 and 1891, and author of *Botany of the Death Valley Expedition.*

Roosevelt Lake [MONO]: *lake,* 700 feet long, 5.5 miles east-southeast of Sonora Pass (lat. 38°17'45" N, long. 119°32'30" W; sec. 10, T 5 N, R 22 E). Named on Pickel Meadow (1954) 7.5' quadrangle.

Rose Canyon: see **Al Rose Canyon** [INYO]; **Wildrose Canyon** [INYO].

Rose Mountain Range: see **Carson Range** [ALPINE].

Rose Spring [INYO]: *spring,* 4.5 miles north of Coso Junction (lat. 36°06'30" N, long. 117°57'35" W); the spring is near the north end of Rose Valley. Named on Haiwee Reservoir (1951) 15' quadrangle.

Rose Spring: see **Wildrose Spring** [INYO].

Rose Spring Cañon: see **Wildrose Canyon** [INYO].

Rose Valley [INYO]: *valley,* between the Sierra Nevada and Coso Range (lat. 36°01' N, long. 117°55' W). Named on Haiwee Reservoir (1951) and Little Lake (1954) 15' quadrangles.

Ross Canyon: see **Rock Creek** [MONO] (1).

Rough Creek [MONO]: *stream,* flows 8 miles to the State of Nevada 13 miles east-northeast of Bridgeport (lat. 38°18'30" N, long. 119°00'15" W; sec. 9, T 5 N, R 27 E). Named on Bodie (1958) and Bridgeport (1958) 15' quadrangles.

Roughs: see **The Roughs** [MONO].

Round Mountain [INYO]:

(1) *peak,* 8.5 miles west-northwest of Big Pine (lat. 37°12'30" N, long. 118°25'55" W; sec. 35, T 8 S, R 32 E). Altitude 11,188 feet. Named on Big Pine (1950) 15' quadrangle.

(2) *peak,* 7.5 miles south-southwest of Olancha on Inyo-Tulare County line (lat. 36°11'25" N, long. 118°04'25" W). Altitude 9884 feet. Named on Monache Mountain (1956) 15' quadrangle.

Round Mountain [MONO]:

(1) *hill,* 4.5 miles northeast of Coleville (lat. 38°36'55" N, long. 119°27' W; sec. 21, T 9 N, R 23 E). Altitude 5806 feet. Named on Desert Creek Peak (1956) 15' quadrangle.

(2) *peak,* 4.25 miles north-northeast of Toms Place (lat. 37°36'55" N, long. 118°38'30" W; near W line sec. 11, T 4 S, R 30 E). Altitude 7625 feet. Named on Casa Diablo Mountain (1953) 15' quadrangle.

Round Top [ALPINE]: *peak,* 2.25 miles south-southwest of Carson Pass (lat. 38°39'50" N, long. 120°00' W; sec. 33, T 10 N, R 18 E). Altitude 10,381 feet. Named on Caples Lake (1979) and Carson Pass (1979) 7.5' quadrangles.

Roundtop: see **Kirkwood** [ALPINE].

Round Top Lake [ALPINE]: *lake,* 1050 feet long, nearly 1 mile northeast of Fourth of July Peak (lat. 38°40'05" N, long. 120°00'40" W; sec. 33, T 10 N, R 18 E); the lake is 0.5 mile west-northwest of Round Top. Named on Caples Lake (1979) 7.5' quadrangle.

Roundtop Lake: see **Winnemucca Lake** [ALPINE].

Round Valley [ALPINE]: *valley,* less than 1 mile southeast of Mount Reba (lat. 38°30'05" N, long. 120°01' W). Named on Mokelumne Peak (1979) 7.5' quadrangle.

Round Valley [INYO]:

(1) *valley,* 14 miles northwest of Olancha (lat. 36°26'20" N, long. 118°10'15" W; on N line sec. 22, T 17 S, R 35 E). Named on Olancha (1956) 15' quadrangle.

(2) *locality,* 7.5 miles northeast of Mount Tom (lat. 37°24'50" N, long. 118°33'10" W; sec. 22, T 6 S, R 31 E); the place is in Round Valley [INYO-MONO]. Named on Mount Goddard (1912) 30' quadrangle. Postal authorities established Round Valley post office in 1874 and discontinued it in 1919 (Frickstad, p. 52).

Round Valley [INYO-MONO]: *valley,* 6.5 miles north-northeast of Mount Tom and west of the lower end of Owens Gorge on Inyo-Mono County line (lat. 37°25' N, long. 118°35'30" W). Named on Mount Tom (1949) 15' quadrangle. Chalfant (1933, p. 198) noted that the name "Greenly's Valley" was used for the feature in the 1860's. In 1870 a detachment of soldiers from Camp Independence set up a camp on the west side of, and a little north of the center of the valley; they called the place Camp Egbert, for Major Egbert, commander at Camp Independence (Cragen, p. 89).

Round Valley: see **Little Round Valley** [MONO].

Round Valley Peak [INYO]: *peak,* 8 miles north of Mount Tom (lat. 37°26'55" N, long. 118°40'50" W); the peak is 3 miles west of the west edge of Round Valley [INYO-MONO]. Altitude 11,943 feet. Named on Mount Tom (1949) 15' quadrangle.

Rovana [INYO]: *village,* 5.5 miles north-northeast of Mount Tom (lat. 37°24'50" N, long. 118°36'40" W; sec. 19, T 6 S, R 31 E). Named on Mount Tom (1949) 15' quadrangle.

Ruby Lake [INYO]: *lake,* 1750 feet long, 2 miles north-northeast of Mount Abbot (lat. 37°24'55" N, long. 118°46'10" W). Named on Mount Abbot (1953) 15' quadrangle.

Ruby Spring [INYO]: *spring,* 4.5 miles north-northeast of Argus Peak (lat. 35°55'10" N, long. 117°25'45" W; sec. 22, T 23 S, R 42 E). Named on Trona (1949) 15' quadrangle.

Ruiz Well [INYO]: *well,* 7 miles northwest of Stovepipe Wells in Death Valley (lat. 36°43'50" N, long. 117°10'25" W). Named on Ballarat (1913) 1° quadrangle. Mendenhall (p. 33) gave the name "Ring Well" as an alternate.

Rush Creek [MONO]: *stream,* flows 22 miles to Mono Lake nearly 4 miles east of Lee Vining (lat. 37°57'10" N, long. 119°03'05" W; sec. 13, T 1 N, R 26 E). Named on Devils Postpile (1953) and Mono Craters (1953) 15' quadrangles. A.W. von Schmidt called the stream Lake Creek when he surveyed the region in 1855 (Fletcher, p. 27). Some water from the creek now is diverted to the aqueduct that takes Mono County water to Los Angeles.

Russell: see **Mount Russell** [INYO].

Russell Camp [INYO]: *locality,* 1.5 miles east of Manly Peak near the southwest end of Butte Valley (lat. 35°54'45" N, long. 117°05'15" W). Named on Manly Peak (1950) 15' quadrangle.

Russell's Valley: see **Upper Summers Meadows** [MONO].

Ruth: see **Lake Ruth** [MONO].

Ruwau Lake [INYO]: *lake,* 1400 feet long, 7.25 miles east-southeast of Mount Darwin (lat. 37°08'20" N, long. 118°32'50" W; near W line sec. 25, T 9 S, R 31 E). Named on Mount Goddard (1948) 15' quadrangle. The name was coined from the names of two power-company engineers, Rhudy and Waugh (Schumacher, p. 94).

Ryan [INYO]:

(1) *locality,* 6.25 miles southwest of Death Valley Junction at the end of a rail line to Lila C mine (lat. 36°14'30" N, long. 116°29'50" W). Named on Furnace Creek (1910) 1° quadrangle. Lila C mine produced colemanite for Pacific Coast Borax Company; W. T. Coleman named the mine for his daughter (Myrick, p. 545). The locality was known only by the name of the mine until 1907, when Tonopah and Tidewater Railroad reached the site; then it was named Ryan, for John Ryan of the borax company (Hanna, p. 262). Postal authorities established Ryan post office in 1907 (Frickstad, p. 52). The site became Old Ryan after the post office and the name "Ryan" went to present Ryan (2) (Murbarger, p. 277).

(2) *town,* 13 miles southeast of Furnace Creek Inn in Greenwater Range (lat. 36°19'20" N, long. 116°40'15" W; sec. 8, T 25 N, R 3 E). Named on Ryan (1952) 15' quadrangle. Called Devair on Furnace Creek (1910) 1° quadrangle, where it is shown at the end of Death Valley Railroad; the name "Devair" is said to come from letters in the name "Death Valley Railroad" (Palmer, p. 24). Ryan (2) was known as New Ryan for a time after the post office and the name "Ryan" were transferred to it from Ryan (1) (Murbarger, p. 277). Postal authorities established Ryan post office at Ryan (1) in 1907, moved it to Ryan (2) in 1914, and discontinued it in 1930 (Salley, p. 191).

– S –

Sabies Canyon [MONO]: *canyon,* drained by a stream that flows 4 miles to Chalfant Valley 6.25 miles southwest of White Mountain Peak (lat. 37°34'50" N, long. 118°20'40" W; sec. 21, T 4 S, R 33 E). Named on White Mountain Peak (1962) 15' quadrangle.

Sabrina: see **Camp Sabrina** [INYO]; **Lake Sabrina** [INYO].

Sacramento Canyon [MONO]: *canyon,* drained by a stream that flows 4.5 miles to Chalfant Valley 7 miles southwest of White Mountain Peak (lat. 37°32'25" N, long. 118°19'55" W; sec. 3, T 5 S, R 33 E). Named on White Mountain Peak (1962) 15' quadrangle.

Saddlebag Campground [MONO]: *locality,* 2.5 miles east of Mount Conness (lat. 37°57'55" N, long. 119°16'15" W); the place is near the outlet of Saddlebag Lake. Named on Tuolumne Meadows (1956) 15' quadrangle.

Saddlebag Lake [MONO]: *lake,* 1.5 miles long, behind a dam 2.5 miles east of Mount Conness on Lee Vining Creek (lat. 37°57'55" N, long. 119°16'20" W). Named on Tuolumne Meadows (1956) 15' quadrangle. Called Saddlebag Reservoir on Sampson's (1940) map.

Saddlebag Reservoir: see **Saddlebag Lake** [MONO].

Saddlerock Lake [INYO]: *lake,* 1900 feet long, 7 miles east-southeast of Mount Darwin (lat. 37°07'45" N, long. 118°33'10" W; sec. 35, T 9 S, R 31 E). Named on Mount Goddard (1948) 15' quadrangle. The name is from the shape of a rock on the shore of the lake (Schumacher, p. 93)

Sage Flat [INYO]:

(1) *area,* 6 miles west-southwest of Big Pine along Big Pine Creek (lat. 37°07'25" N, long. 118°23'10" W; on E line sec. 32, T 9 S, R 33 E). Named on Big Pine (1950) 15' quadrangle.

(2) *area,* 5 miles south-southwest of Olancha (lat. 36°13'25" N, long. 118°03'10" W). Named on Monache Mountain (1956) 15' quadrangle.

Sage Hen Flat [MONO]: *area,* 8 miles southeast of Mount Barcroft (lat. 37°29'10" N, long. 118°09'45" W); the place is 4 miles west of Sage Hen Peak. Named on Blanco Mountain (1951) 15' quadrangle.

Sagehen Flat [ALPINE]: *area,* 3.5 miles east-southeast of Mogul Peak (lat. 38°39'50" N, long. 119°39'50" W; on S line sec. 34, T 10 N, R 21 E). Named on Heenan Lake (1979) 7.5' quadrangle.

Sagehen Meadow [MONO]: *area,* 6 miles east-southeast of the site of Mono Mills (lat. 37°52' N, long. 118°51'25" W; near S line sec. 11, T 1 S, R 28 E); Sagehen Spring is at the place. Named on Cowtrack Mountain (1962) 15' quadrangle. Called Sagehen Meadows on Sampson's (1940) map, but United States Board on Geographic Names (1965b, p. 11) rejected this form of the name.

Sage Hen Peak [MONO]: *peak,* 11 miles southeast of Mount Barcroft in White Mountains (lat. 37°28'45" N, long. 118°05'05" W); the peak is 4 miles east of Sage Hen Flat. Named on Blanco Mountain (1951) 15' quadrangle.

Sagehen Flat [ALPINE]: *area,* 3.5 miles east-southeast of Mogul Peak (lat. 38°39'50" N, long. 119°39'50" W; on S line sec. 34, T 10 N, R 21 E). Named on Heenan Lake (1979) 7.5' quadrangle.

Sagehen Meadow [MONO]: *area,* 6 miles east-southeast of the site of Mono

Mills (lat. 37°52' N, long. 118°51'25" W; near S line sec. 11, T 1 S, R 28 E); Sagehen Spring is at the place. Named on Cowtrack Mountain (1962) 15' quadrangle. Called Sagehen Meadows on Sampson's (1940) map, but United States Board on Geographic Names (1965b, p. 11) rejected this form of the name.

Sage Hen Peak [MONO]: *peak,* 11 miles southeast of Mount Barcroft in White Mountains (lat. 37°28'45" N, long. 118°05'05" W); the peak is 4 miles east of Sage Hen Flat. Named on Blanco Mountain (1951) 15' quadrangle. Called Sage Peak on Sampson's (1940) map.

Sagehen Peak [MONO]: *peak,* 7 miles east of the site of Mono Mills (lat. 37°51'10" N, long. 118°50'30" W; near S line sec. 13, T 1 S, R 28 E); the peak is 1.25 miles southeast of Sagehen Meadow. Altitude 9193 feet. Named on Cowtrack Mountain (1962) 15' quadrangle.

Sagehen Spring [MONO]: *spring,* nearly 6 miles east-southeast of the site of Mono Mills (lat. 37°52' N, long. 118°51'30" W; near N line sec. 14, T 1 S, R 28 E); the spring is at Sagehen Meadow. Named on Cowtrack Mountain (1962) 15' quadrangle.

Sage Peak: see **Sage Hen Peak** [MONO].

Sailor Lake [INYO]: *lake,* 300 feet long, 2 miles east of Mount Darwin (lat. 37°10' N, long. 118°38'15" W; sec. 18, T 9 S, R 31 E). Named on Mount Goddard (1948) 15' quadrangle. United States Board on Geographic Names (1983d, p. 6) rejected the name "Drunken Sailor Lake" for the feature.

Saint Marys Pass [ALPINE]: *pass,* 1.5 miles north-northwest of Sonora Pass (lat. 38°20'50" N, long. 119°39'15" W). Named on Sonora Pass (1979) 7.5' quadrangle.

Salina City: see **The Racetrack** [INYO].

Salinas Valley: see **Saline Valley** [INYO].

Saline Range [INYO]: *range,* north of Saline Valley and south of Eureka Valley. Named on Dry Mountain (1957), Last Chance Range (1958), Waucoba Spring (1958), and Waucoba Wash (1951) 15' quadrangles. The name is from Saline Valley (Palmer, p. 63).

Saline Valley [INYO]: *valley,* between Inyo Mountains and Panamint Range (lat. 36°45' N, long. 117°47' W). Named on Dry Mountain (1957), New York Butte (1950), Ubehebe Peak (1950), and Waucoba Wash (1951) 15' quadrangles. The feature was called Salinas Valley in 1871 because of salt deposits found there (Palmer, p. 63). Mendenhall (p. 33) noted Saline Valley Well, dug about 1889 to furnish water for manufacture of borax on a dry lake in Saline Valley. Waring and Huguenin (p. 35) listed Saline Valley Springs, located in Saline Valley 1 mile west of Salt Lake.

Saline Valley Springs: see **Saline Valley** [INYO].

Saline Valley Well: see **Saline Valley** [INYO].

Salisbury Pass: see **Salsberry Pass** [INYO].

Salmon Flat [MONO]: *area,* 5 miles east-southeast of Coleville (lat. 38°32'35" N, long. 119°25'20" W; sec. 14, T 8 N, R 23 E). Named on Desert Creek Peak (1956) 15' quadrangle.

Salsberry Pass [INYO]: *pass,* 9.5 miles west-southwest of Shoshone near the north end of Ibex Hills (lat. 35°55'30" N, long. 116°25'40" W); the pass is about 2 miles southeast of Salsberry Peak. Named on Shoshone (1951) 15' quadrangle. Palmer (p. 63) gave the name "Salisbury Pass" as an alternate, and indicated that the name is for Jack Salsberry, or Salisbury, who promoted a mine in Death Valley and brought the first tractors to the valley.

Salsberry Peak [INYO]: *peak,* 10.5 miles west of Shoshone (lat. 35° 56'45" N, long. 116°27'15" W). Named on Shoshone (1951) 15' quadrangle.

Salsberry Spring [INYO]: *spring,* 9 miles west-southwest of Shoshone near the north end of Ibex Hills (lat. 35°55'50" N, long. 116° 25' W); the spring is less than 1 mile northeast of Salsberry Pass. Named on Shoshone (1951) 15' quadrangle.

Salt Creek [INYO]: *stream* and *dry wash,* flows 35 miles from near Stovepipe Wells to Devils Golf Course 12 miles south of Furnace Creek Inn; the stream passes through some lakes. Named on Chloride Cliff (1952), Furnace Creek (1952), and Stovepipe Wells (1952) 15' quadrangles. Spaniards called the stream Rio Salitroso in 1830 (Lingenfelter, p. 25).

Salt Creek Wells: see **McLean Spring** [INYO].

Salt Lake [INYO]: *lake,* 6000 feet long, 7.25 miles east-northeast of New York Butte in Saline Valley (lat. 36°42' N, long. 117°49' W). Named on New York Butte (1950) 15' quadrangle.

Salt Springs [INYO].

(1) *springs,* three, 5 miles southeast of Beatty Junction (lat. 36°32'05" N, long. 116°53'05" W; at E line sec. 20, T 28 N, R 1 E). Named on Chloride Cliff (1952) 15' quadrangle.

(2) *springs,* two, 6 miles south-southwest of Beatty Junction (lat. 36°30'30" N, long. 116°59'30" W). Named on Chloride Cliff (1952) 15' quadrangle. United States Board on Geographic Names (1968a, p. 10) approved the name "West Side Borax Camp" for a mining camp situated at the springs, and rejected the name "Shoveltown" for the camp.

(3) *springs,* 3 miles north of Furnace Creek Inn (lat. 36°29'35" N, long. 116°51'15" W; sec. 3, T 27 N, R 1 E). Named on Furnace Creek (1952) 15' quadrangle.

Salt Well [INYO]: *well,* nearly 5 miles southwest of Stovepipe Wells (lat. 36°37' N, long. 117°08'45" W). Named on Ballarat (1913) 1° quadrangle.

Salt Wells Valley: see **Indian Wells Valley** [INYO].

Sam Mack Lake [INYO]: *lake,* 1200 feet long, 9.5 miles east-southeast of Mount Darwin (lat. 37°06'55" N, long. 118°30'40" W). Named on Mount Goddard (1948) 15' quadrangle.

Samman Springs: see **Simons Spring** [MONO].

Sams Spring: see **Antelope Spring** [INYO].

San Carlos: see **Independence** [INYO].

Sand Canyon [INYO]:

(1) *canyon,* 2.5 miles long, opens into lowlands 8.5 miles east of Mount Tom (lat. 37°20'15" N, long. 118°30' W; sec. 18, T 7 S, R 32 E). Named on Mount Tom (1949) 15' quadrangle.

(2) *canyon,* drained by a stream that flows 6.5 miles to Indian Wells Valley in Kern County 11 miles south of the village of Little Lake (lat. 35°46'40" N, long. 117°52'45" W; sec. 9, T 25 S, R 38 E). Named on Little Lake (1954) 15' quadrangle.

Sand Canyon [MONO]: *canyon,* 1.5 miles long, along Birch Creek (1) above a point 2 miles south of Toms Place (lat. 37°31'50" N, long. 118°40'30" W). Named on Casa Diablo Mountain (1953) 15' quadrangle.

Sand Flat [ALPINE]: *area,* 4.25 miles east of Dardanelles Cone along Clark Fork on Alpine-Tuolumne County line (lat. 38°24'20" N, long. 119°47'30" W). Named on Dardanelles Cone (1979) 7.5' quadrangle.

Sand Flat [INYO]: *valley,* 8.5 miles west of the mouth of Marble Canyon (3) (lat. 36°39'15" N, long. 117°25'45" W). Named on Marble Canyon (1951) 15' quadrangle.

Sand Flat: see **Big Sand Flat** [MONO]; **Little Sand Flat** [MONO].

Sand Flat Campground [ALPINE]: *locality,* 4.5 miles east of Dardanelles Cone (lat. 38°24'15" N, long. 119°47'10" W); the place is at Sand Flat. Named on Dardanelles Cone (1979) 7.5' quadrangle.

Sand Spring [INYO]: *spring,* 14 miles north-northwest of Ubehebe Crater in Death Valley (lat. 37°11'20" N, long. 117°33'05" W; sec. 7, T 9 S, R 41 E). Named on Last Chance Range (1958) 15' quadrangle. Palmer (p. 23) mentioned that the feature was called Desert Spring in the early days.

Sand Spring: see **Little Sand Spring** [INYO].

Sand Springs Creek: see **Fish Slough** [INYO-MONO].

Sandy Meadow [ALPINE]: *area,* 2 miles west of Pacific Grade Summit (lat. 38°31'10" N, long. 119°56'45" W; sec. 25, T 8 N, R 18 E). Named on Pacific Valley (1979) 7.5' quadrangle.

Sandy Meadow Creek [ALPINE]: *stream,* flows 2.5 miles to North Fork Mokelumne River nearly 3 miles northwest of Pacific Grade Summit (lat. 38°32'40" N, long. 119°56'40" W); the stream goes through Sandy Meadow. Named on Pacific Valley (1979) 7.5' quadrangle.

Sanger Meadow [INYO]: *area,* 8.5 miles west of Big Pine (lat. 37° 10'45" N, long. 118°26'55" W). Named on Big Pine (1950) 15' quadrangle. The name commemorates the Sanger family, who ran horses at the place (Gudde, 1949, p. 304).

Sangers Slough [INYO]: *marsh,* 6.25 miles south-southeast of Big Pine along Owens River (lat. 37°05'15" N, long. 118°13'50" W; sec. 11, 14, T 10 S, R 34 E). Named on Waucoba Mountain (1951) 15' quadrangle.

San Joaquin Mountain [MONO]: *peak,* 7.5 miles northwest of Mammoth Mountain on Mono-Madera County line (lat. 37°43'10" N, long. 119°06'20" W). Altitude 11,600 feet. Named on Devils Postpile (1953) 15' quadrangle. This peak and a nearby peak formerly were called Two Teats (Gudde, 1949, p. 373-374).

San Lucas Canyon [INYO]: *canyon,* 10 miles long, opens into Saline Valley 9.5 miles west-southwest of Ubehebe Peak (lat. 36° 38'20" N, long. 117°44'30" W). Named on New York Butte (1950) and Ubehebe Peak (1950) 15' quadrangles.

Santa Anita Spring: see **Santa Rita Spring** [INYO].

Santa Rita Flat [INYO]: *area,* 10 miles north-northeast of Independence (lat. 36°55'30" N, long. 118°06'30" W). Named on Independence (1951) 15' quadrangle. The name is from an early mine (DeDecker, p. 46).

Santa Rita Spring [INYO]: *spring,* 9.5 miles north-northeast of Independence (lat. 36°55'30" N, long. 118°06'50" W); the spring is at Santa Rita Flat. Named on Independence (1951) 15' quadrangle. Called Santa Anita Spring on Mount Whitney (1907) 30' quadrangle.

Santa Rosa Flat [INYO]: *valley,* 13 miles north-northwest of Darwin (lat. 36°26'30" N, long. 117°39'45" W); the valley is west of Santa Rosa Hills. Named on Darwin (1950) 15' quadrangle.

Santa Rosa Hills [INYO]: *range,* 6.5 miles long, 13 miles north-northwest of Darwin (lat. 36°27'30" N, long. 117°38'15" W); the range is east of Santa Rosa Flat. Named on Darwin (1950) 15' quadrangle.

Santa Rosa Wash [INYO]: *stream,* flows 16 miles to Rainbow Canyon 6.5 miles north of Darwin (lat. 36°21'45" N, long. 117°34'15" W; sec. 18, T 18 S, R 41 E); the stream drains Santa Rosa Flat. Named on Darwin (1950) 15' quadrangle.

Sardine Canyon [INYO]: *canyon,* 2 miles long, opens into the canyon of South Fork Oak Creek 6 miles west of Independence (lat. 36°48'30" N, long. 118°18' W). Named on Mount Pinchot (1953) 15' quadrangle.

Sardine Creek [MONO]: *stream,* flows 4 miles to Leavitt Creek 3 miles east-southeast of Sonora Pass (lat. 38°18'25" N, long. 119° 35'20" W; sec. 6, T 5 N, R 22 E); the stream goes through Sardine Meadow. Named on

Pickel Meadow (1954) and Sonora Pass (1979) 7.5' quadrangles.

Sardine Falls [MONO]: *waterfall,* 1.5 miles south-southeast of Sonora Pass along McKay Creek (lat. 38°18'30" N, long. 119°37'15" W; sec. 1, T 5 N, R 21 E); the feature is nearly 1 mile west-southwest of Sardine Meadow. Named on Pickel Meadow (1954) 7.5' quadrangle.

Sardine Lake [INYO]: *lake,* 550 feet long, 8.5 miles west of Independence (lat. 36°47'50" N, long. 118°21'05" W); the lake is above Sardine Canyon. Named on Mount Pinchot (1953) 15' quadrangle.

Sardine Lake: see **Lower Sardine Lake** [MONO]; **Upper Sardine Lake** [MONO].

Sardine Meadow [MONO]: *area,* nearly 2 miles east-southeast of Sonora Pass (lat. 38°18'50" N, long. 119°36'30" W; near E line sec. 1, T 5 N, R 21 E); the place is along Sardine Creek. Named on Pickel Meadow (1954) 7.5' quadrangle.

Sario Canyon [MONO]: *canyon,* drained by a stream that flows 3.5 miles to Swauger Creek 5.5 miles east-southeast of Fales Hot Springs in Huntoon Valley (lat. 38°18'50" N, long. 119°18'35" W; near N line sec. 10, T 5 N, R 24 E). Named on Fales Hot Springs (1956) 15' quadrangle, which shows Sario ranch located 0.5 mile south-southwest of the mouth of the stream that drains the canyon.

Sawmill Campground [MONO]: *locality,* 3 miles east-southeast of Mount Conness along Lee Vining Creek (lat. 37°57'30" N, long. 119°16'10" W). Named on Tuolumne Meadows (1956) 15' quadrangle.

Sawmill Canyon [MONO]:

(1) *canyon,* 1.5 miles long, opens into Pumice Valley 5.25 miles south of Lee Vining (lat. 37°52'50" N, long. 119°07'10" W; near N line sec. 9, T 1 S, R 26 E). Named on Mono Craters (1953) 15' quadrangle.

(2) *canyon,* drained by a stream that flows 3 miles to Wet Fork 3.5 miles east-northeast of Glass Mountain (lat. 37°48'15" N, long. 118°39'05" W); the canyon heads at Sawmill Meadow. Named on Glass Mountain (1962) 15' quadrangle. The stream in the canyon is called Left Fork on Mount Morrison (1914) 30' quadrangle, but United States Board on Geographic Names (1964c, p. 16) approved the name "Sawmill Creek" for the stream, and rejected the names "Left Fork Wet Fork" and "Left Fork Wet Fork Creek" for it.

Sawmill Creek [ALPINE]: *stream,* flows 3.5 miles to Hot Springs Creek 4 miles west of Markleeville (lat. 38°41'45" N, long. 119°51'25" W; sec. 23, T 10 N, R 19 E). Named on Carson Pass (1979) and Markleeville (1979) 7.5' quadrangles.

Sawmill Creek [INYO]: *stream,* flows 5 miles to lowlands 9 miles north-northwest of Independence (lat. 36°54'45" N, long. 118°17'10" W); the stream heads near Sawmill Pass. Named on Independence (1951) and Mount Pinchot (1953) 15' quadrangles. The name is from Blackrock sawmill, built along the stream in the 1860's (Schumacher, p. 46). The creek now discharges into the aqueduct that takes Owens Valley water to Los Angeles.

Sawmill Creek [MONO]: *stream,* flows 1 mile to Hot Creek (1) 0.5 mile east-southeast of Fales Hot Spring (lat. 38°20'55" N, long. 119°23'25" W; sec. 19, T 6 N, R 24 E). Named on Fales Hot Springs (1956) 15' quadrangle.

Sawmill Creek: see **Sawmill Canyon** [MONO] (2).

Sawmill Lake [INYO]: *lake,* 1200 feet long, 10 miles northwest of Independence (lat. 36°53'10" N, long. 118°20'45" W); the lake is along Sawmill Creek. Named on Mount Pinchot (1953) 15' quadrangle.

Sawmill Meadow [INYO]; *area,* 10 miles northwest of Independence (lat. 36°53'50" N, long. 118°19'35" W); the place is along Sawmill Creek. Named on Mount Pinchot (1953) 15' quadrangle.

Sawmill Meadow [MONO]: *area,* nearly 2 miles east-southeast of Glass Mountain (lat. 37°46'10" N, long. 119°40'30" W; sec. 16, T 2 S, R 30 E); the place is at the head of Sawmill Canyon (2). Named on Glass Mountain (1962) 15' quadrangle.

Sawmill Pass [INYO]: *pass,* 11 miles west-northwest of Independence on Inyo-Fresno County line (lat. 36°53' N, long. 118°21'45" W); the pass is near the head of Sawmill Creek. Named on Mount Pinchot (1953) 15' quadrangle.

Sawmill Point [INYO]: *peak,* 10.5 miles northwest of Independence (lat. 36°55' N, long. 118°19'15" W). Altitude 9416 feet. Named on Mount Pinchot (1953) 15' quadrangle.

Sawmill Ridge [MONO]: *ridge,* north-northeast-trending, 3 miles long, 6 miles north of Matterhorn Peak (lat. 38°10'45" N, long. 119°21'35" W). Named on Matterhorn Peak (1956) 15' quadrangle. The name is from a sawmill operated in 1861 along Robinson Creek below the ridge (Wedertz, p. 154).

Sawtooth Peak [INYO]: *peak,* 9 miles south-southwest of the village of Little Lake on Inyo-Tulare County line (lat. 35°49'25" N, long. 117°59' W). Altitude 7970 feet. Named on Little Lake (1954) 15' quadrangle.

Sawtooth Ridge [MONO]: *ridge,* extends for 2.5 miles west-northwest from Matterhorn Peak along Mono-Tuolumne County line (lat. 38°06'15" N, long. 119°23'45" W). Named on Matterhorn Peak (1956) 15' quadrangle.

Scheelite [INYO]: *village,* 3 miles north-northwest of Mount Tom along Pine Creek (lat. 37°22'45" N, long. 118°40'25" W). Named on Mount Tom (1949) 15' quadrangle. The name is from the tungsten mineral found in mines near the place (Bateman, p. 15).

Schober Lakes [INYO]: *lakes,* three, largest 600 feet long, 1.5 miles northeast of Mount Darwin (lat. 37°11'05" N, long. 118°39'25" W). Named on Mount Goddard (1948) 15' quadrangle.

Schwaub [INYO]: *locality,* 12 miles north of present Ryan (2) in Funeral Mountains near the head of Echo Canyon (lat. 36°29'50" N, long. 116°40'45" W). Named on Furnace Creek (1910) 1° quadrangle. When gold was discovered in the neighborhood in 1905, a town was built and named for Charles M. Schwab, at one time president of United States Steel Corporation (Neal, p. 42). Postal authorities established Schwab post office in 1907 and discontinued it the same year (Frickstad, p. 52). A townsite called Echo was laid out on the crest of Funeral Mountains halfway between Schwaub and Lee—it had a couple of tents (Lingenfelter, p. 281).

Schwaub Peak [INYO]: *peak,* 10.5 miles north of Ryan (2) in Funeral Mountains (lat. 36°28'25" N, long. 116°39'10" W). Altitude 6448 feet. Named on Ryan (1952) 15' quadrangle.

Scossa Canyon [ALPINE]: *canyon,* less than 1 mile long, opens into Diamond Valley 3 miles east of Woodfords (lat. 38°46'15" N, long. 119°46'10" W; near W line sec. 32, T 11 N, R 20 E). Named on Woodfords (1979) 7.5' quadrangle.

Scott Creek [ALPINE]: *stream,* flows 3 miles to Diamond Valley 1.5 miles southeast of Woodfords (lat. 38°45'35" N, long. 119°48'30" W). Named on Markleeville (1979) and Woodfords (1979) 7.5' quadrangles.

Scotts Lake [ALPINE]: *lake,* 1750 feet long, 7.5 miles south-southwest of Freel Peak (lat. 38°45'50" N, long. 119°57'55" W; near N line sec. 2, T 10 N, R 18 E). Named on Freel Peak (1955) 7.5' quadrangle.

Scottys Canyon [INYO]: *canyon,* 4.25 miles long, opens into Death Valley 8 miles west of Epaulet Peak (lat. 35°57'35" N, long. 116° 40'10" W). Named on Confidence Hills (1950) 15' quadrangle. The name is for Walter Scott, known as Death Valley Scotty, who claimed to have a mine in the canyon; the feature originally was called Greyhound Canyon (Palmer, p. 33, 65).

Scottys Castle [INYO]: *locality,* 6.25 miles east-northeast of Ubehebe Crater in Grapevine Canyon (lat. 37°01'55" N, long. 117° 20'25" W). Named on Ubehebe Crater (1957) 15' quadrangle. Postal authorities established Scotty's Castle post office in 1947 and discontinued it in 1953 (Frickstad, p. 53). Railroad crossties used as firewood at Scotty's Castle were stored in a nearby gulch that became known as Tie Canyon (Myrick, p. 536). United States Board on Geographic Names (1983e, p. 4) approved the name "Dedeckera Canyon" for a canyon in Last Chance Range that is 2 miles long and opens into Eureka Valley 16 miles west of Scottys Castle (lat. 37°03'35" N, long. 117°38'25" W)—the name is from a rare shrub of the buckwheat family that was first discovered in the canyon.

Scotty's Grapevine Spring: see **Grapevine Springs** [INYO].

Scotty Spring [INYO]: *spring,* 12 miles northwest of Independence (lat. 36°56'20" N, long. 118°19'20" W; sec. 1, T 12 S, R 33 E). Named on Mount Pinchot (1953) 15' quadrangle.

Scout Carson Lake [ALPINE]: *lake,* 400 feet long, nearly 2 miles west-southwest of Fourth of July Peak (lat. 38°38'50" N, long. 120°03'10" W; sec. 11, T 9 N, R 17 E). Named on Caples Lake (1979) 7.5' quadrangle.

Scowden: see **Mount Scowden** [MONO].

Scranton [INYO]: *locality,* 13 miles northeast of Ryan along the abandoned route of Tonopah and Tidewater Railroad (lat. 36°27'05" N, long. 116°30'10" W; near W line sec. 25, T 27 N, R 4 E). Site named on Ryan (1952) 15' quadrangle. The name is for Scranton, Pennsylvania—a group from that city financed a company to supply water to the mining Camp of Greenwater (Palmer, p. 66).

Searles Spring: see **Indian Joe Spring** [INYO].

Searles Valley [INYO]: *valley,* east of Argus Range and west of Slate Range; mainly in San Bernardino County. Named on Trona (1949) 15' quadrangle. United States Board on Geographic Names (1961b, p. 12) rejected the name "Spangler Valley" for the feature.

Sebrina: see **Lake Sebrina**, under **Lake Sabrina** [INYO].

Second Falls [INYO]: *waterfall,* 9 miles west-southwest of Big Pine along North Fork Big Pine Creek (lat. 37°08' N, long. 118°27'10" W; sec. 26, T 9 S, R 32 E); the feature is 1 mile upstream from First Falls. Named on Big Pine (1950) 15' quadrangle.

Second Lake [INYO]: *lake,* 1750 feet long, 11 miles west-southwest of Big Pine along North Fork Big Pine Creek (lat. 37°07'25" N, long. 118°29'10" W; sec. 33, T 9 S, R 32 E); the lake is between First Lake and Third Lake. Named on Big Pine (1950) 15' quadrangle. The feature is one of the group called Big Pine Lakes.

Secret Lake [MONO]: *lake,* 800 feet long, 5.5 miles east-southeast of Sonora Pass (lat. 38°18'25" N, long. 119°32'15" W; sec. 3, T 5 N, R 22 E). Named on Pickel Meadow (1954) 7.5' quadrangle.

Seeley:Spring see **Big Seeley Spring** [INYO]; **Little Seeley Spring** [INYO].

Seelys Spring: see **Little Seeley Spring** [INYO].

Seep Hole Spring [INYO]: *spring,* 12 miles northeast of Independence (lat. 36°54'50" N, long. 118°01'35" W). Named on Independence (1951) 15' quadrangle. Called Sheep Hole Spring on Tucker and Sampson's (1938) map.

Sentinel Meadow [MONO]: *area,* 10 miles southeast of the site of Mono Mills (lat. 37°48'05" N, long. 118°49'05" W; sec. 6, T 2 S, R 29 E). Named on Cowtrack Mountain (1962) 15' quadrangle.

Sentinel Peak [INYO]: *peak,* 5 miles south of Telescope Peak in Panamint Range (lat. 36°05'45" N, long. 117°04'40" W). Altitude 9636 feet. Named on Telescope Peak (1952) 15' quadrangle. The name is from the commanding position of the feature (Palmer, p. 66).

Sentinel Rock: see **Jeff Davis Peak** [ALPINE].

Serene Lake [INYO]: *lake,* 500 feet long, 8.5 miles northwest of Mount Tom in Little Lakes Valley (lat. 37°26'20" N, long. 118°44'35" W). Named on Mount Tom (1949) 15' quadrangle.

Sevehah Cliff [MONO]: *relief feature,* 1.5 miles northwest of Mount Morrison on the west side of Convict Creek (lat. 37°34'40" N, long. 118°52'35" W; sec. 22, 27, T 4 S, R 28 E). Named on Mount Morrison (1953) 15' quadrangle.

Seven Pines [INYO]: *settlement,* 5.5 miles west of Independence along Independence Creek (lat. 36°47'10" N, long. 118°17'40" W; sec. 20, T 13 S, R 34 E). Named on Mount Pinchot (1953) 15' quadrangle.

Seventh Lake [INYO]: *lake,* 500 feet long, 9 miles east-southeast of Mount Darwin (lat. 37°08'15" N, long. 118°30'55" W; sec. 30, T 9 S, R 32 E); the lake is 700 feet west-northwest of Sixth Lake. Named on Mount Goddard (1948) 15' quadrangle.

Shadow Mountain [INYO]: *peak,* 9 miles east-southeast of Death Valley Junction in Resting Spring Range (lat. 36°15'50" N, long. 116°15'25" W; near SE cor. sec. 18, T 25 N, R 7 E). Altitude 5071 feet. Named on Ash Meadows (1952) 15' quadrangle. Called Quartzite Pk. on Furnace Creek (1910) 1° quadrangle.

Shamrock Lake [MONO]: *lake,* 1700 feet long, 2.5 miles north-northeast of Mount Conness along Mill Creek (2) (lat. 37°59'50" N, long. 119°17'45" W; sec. 26, T 2 N, R 24 E). Named on Tuolumne Meadows (1956) 15' quadrangle.

Shannon Canyon [INYO]: *canyon,* 2.5 miles long, opens into lowlands 6.25 miles northwest of Big Pine (lat. 37°13'50" N, long. 118°22' W; near NE cor. sec. 29, T 8 S, R 33 E). Named on Big Pine (1950) 15' quadrangle. North Fork branches west 1.5 miles upstream from the mouth of the main canyon; above that place, the main canyon splits to form Middle Fork and South Fork. Middle Fork is 2 miles long, North Fork is nearly 3 miles long, and South Fork is 2.25 miles long. All three forks are named on Big Pine (1950) 15' quadrangle.

Shay Creek [ALPINE]: *stream,* flows 1.5 miles to Hot Springs Creek 3 miles west of Markleeville (lat. 38°41'50" N, long. 119°50'10" W; sec. 24, T 10 N, R 19 E). Named on Markleeville (1979) 7.5' quadrangle.

Shealy [MONO]: *locality,* 15 miles west-southwest of White Mountain Peak along Southern Pacific Railroad (lat. 37°36'50" N, long. 118°23'40" W; sec. 12, T 4 S, R 32 E). Named on White Mountain (1917) 30' quadrangle.

Sheeles Camp [MONO]: *locality,* 8 miles north-northeast of Fales Hot Springs (lat. 38°27'40" N, long. 119°21'30" W; near S line sec. 8, T 7 N, R 24 E). Named on Fales Hot Springs (1956) 15' quadrangle.

Sheep Canyon [INYO]: *canyon,* 6.5 miles long, opens into Death Valley 5.5 miles west-southwest of Funeral Peak (lat. 36°05' N, long. 116°43'20" W). Named on Funeral Peak (1951) 15' quadrangle. The name is from mountain sheep that live in the vicinity; the feature also is called Sheep Creek Canyon (Palmer, p. 66).

Sheep Creek [MONO]: *stream,* flows 1 mile to the State of Nevada 13 miles east-southeast of Coleville (lat. 38°30' N, long. 119°16'45" W). Named on Desert Creek Peak (1956) 15' quadrangle.

Sheep Creek Canyon: see **Sheep Canyon** [INYO].

Sheephead Mountain [INYO]: *peak,* 9 miles west-southwest of Shoshone in Ibex Hills (lat. 35°55'15" N, long. 116°24'35" W). Altitude 4270 feet. Named on Shoshone (1951) 15' quadrangle. Palmer (p. 66) called the peak Sheepshead Mountain, and presumed that the name records the finding of one or more sheep skulls near the feature.

Sheephead Pass [INYO]: *pass,* 9.5 miles west-southwest of Shoshone in Ibex Hills (lat. 35°54'15" N, long. 116°24'45" W); the pass is 1 mile south of Sheephead Mountain. Named on Shoshone (1951) 15' quadrangle.

Sheephead Spring [INYO]: *spring,* 9 miles west-southwest of Shoshone in Ibex Hills (lat. 35°54' N, long. 116°24'20" W); the spring is 0.5 mile southeast of Sheephead Pass. Named on Shoshone (1951) 15' quadrangle.

Sheep Hole Spring: see **Seep Hole Spring** [INYO].

Sheep Meadow [ALPINE]: *area,* 3 miles west-northwest of Ebbetts Pass (lat. 38°33'50" N, long. 119°51'30" W). Named on Ebbetts Pass (1979) 7.5' quadrangle.

Sheep Mountain [MONO]: *peak,* 8 miles south-southeast of White Mountain Peak (lat. 37°31'40" N, long. 118°13' W). Altitude 12,497 feet. Named on Mount Barcroft (1962) 15' quadrangle.

Sheep Mountain: see **Mount Langley** [INYO]; **Tucki Mountain** [INYO].

Sheep Pass: see **Vacation Pass** [INYO].

Sheep Rock: see **Mount Corcoran** [INYO]; **Mount Langley** [INYO].

Sheepshead Mountain: see **Sheephead Mountain** [INYO].

Shell Lake [MONO]: *lake,* 1100 feet long, 3.5 miles east-southeast of Mount Conness along Mine Creek (lat. 37°56'25" N, long. 119°15'50" W; near NW cor. sec. 19, T 1 N, R 25 E). Named on Tuolumne Meadows (1956) 15' quadrangle.

Shepard Creek: **Shepherd Creek** [INYO].

Shepard's Cañon: see **Shepherd Canyon** [INYO].

Shepherd Canyon [INYO]: *canyon,* 8 miles long, opens into Panamint Valley 8 miles southeast of Maturango Peak (lat. 36°02'30" N, long. 117°23'30" W; sec. 12, T 22 S, R 42 E). Named on Maturango Peak (1951) 15' quadrangle. The name commemorates John Shepherd of Owens Valley, who built a toll road around the south end of Owens Lake to shorten the route to Panamint (Palmer, p. 66). Wheeler's (1877) map shows a toll house on the road in the canyon, and has the name "20 mile Spr" nearby. Birnie (p. 131) used the name "Shepperd's Cañon," and Fairbanks (p. 473) used the name "Shepard's Cañon."

Shepherd Creek [INYO]: *stream,* flows 6.5 miles to Owens Valley 9.5 miles north of Mount Whitney (1) (lat. 36°43' N, long. 118°15'30" W; sec. 15, T 14 S, R 34 E). Named on Lone Pine (1958) and Mount Whitney (1956) 15' quadrangles. United States Board on Geographic Names (1933, p. 687) rejected the form "Shepard Creek" for the name, which commemorates the Shepherd family, whose ranch was along lower reaches of the stream.

Shepherd Pass [INYO]: *pass,* 7.25 miles north-northwest of Mount Whitney (1) on Inyo-Tulare County line (lat. 36°40'20" N, long. 118°20'35" W); the pass is near the headwaters of Shepherd Creek. Named on Mount Whitney (1956) 15' quadrangle. The name commemorates the Shepherd families, pioneers of Inyo County (United States Board on Geographic Names, 1933, p. 687).

Shepperd's Cañon: see **Shepherd Canyon** [INYO].

Sheridan Creek [ALPINE]: *stream,* flows less than 0.5 mile to the State of Nevada nearly 4 miles northeast of Freel Peak (lat. 38°53'45" N, long. 119°50'55" W; near S line sec. 16, T 12 N, R 19 E). Named on Minden (1968) 7.5' quadrangle.

Sherrold Lake [ALPINE]: *lake,* 400 feet long, less than 0.5 mile north-northwest of Ebbetts Pass (lat. 38°33' N, long. 119°48'50" W; sec. 18, T 8 N, R 20 E). Named on Ebbetts Pass (1979) 7.5' quadrangle.

Sherwin Creek [MONO]: *stream,* flows 5.5 miles to Mammoth Creek 6.5 miles northwest of Mount Morrison (lat. 37°37'55" N, long. 118°56'10" W; at W line sec. 6, T 4 S, R 28 E). Named on Mount Morrison (1953) 15' quadrangle. The name commemorates James L.C. Sherwin, who settled in Round Valley in the early 1860's (Gudde, 1949, p. 329).

Sherwin Hill [MONO]: *ridge,* southeast-trending, 1 mile long, 5.5 miles southeast of Toms Place (lat. 37°30'20" N, long. 118°36'25" W). Named on Casa Diablo Mountain (1953) and Mount Tom (1949) 15' quadrangles. The name is for James L.C. Sherwin of Sherwin Creek (Gudde, 1949, p. 329).

Sherwin Lakes [MONO]: *lakes,* largest 800 feet long, 6 miles northwest of Mount Morrison (lat. 37°36'35" N, long. 118°56'35" W); the lakes are along Sherwin Creek. Named on Mount Morrison (1953) 15' quadrangle.

Sherwin Meadow [MONO]: *area,* 4 miles south-southeast of Toms Place (lat. 37°30'50" N, long. 118°38'15" W; on W line sec. 13, T 5 S, R 30 E); the place is 0.5 mile west of Sherwin Summit. Named on Casa Diablo Mountain (1953) 15' quadrangle. United States Board on Geographic Names (1985c, p. 3) approved the name "Swall Meadow" for the feature.

Sherwin Summit [MONO]: *locality,* 4.25 miles southeast of Toms Place (lat. 37°30'50" N, long. 118°37'45" W; sec. 13, T 5 S, R 30 E); the place is 1 mile west-northwest of Sherwin Hill. Named on Casa Diablo Mountain (1953) 15' quadrangle. California Division of Highways' (1934) map shows a place called Clarks located 1.25 miles south of Sherwin Summit.

Shingle Mill Bench [INYO]: *area,* 15 miles north-northwest of Independence (lat. 36°59'25" N, long. 118°21' W). Named on Mount Pinchot (1953) 15' quadrangle.

Shingle Mill Flat [ALPINE]: *area,* 2.5 miles west of Woodfords along West Fork Carson River (lat. 38°46'05" N, long. 119°52'10" W; sec. 32, T 11 N, R 19 E). Named on Woodfords (1979) 7.5' quadrangle.

Shingle Mill Flat [MONO]: *area,* 7.5 miles north-northwest of Fales Hot Springs along West Walker River (lat. 38°26'45" N, long. 119° 27'15" W: near S line sec. 16, T 7 N, R 23 E). Named on Chris Flat (1954) 7.5' quadrangle.

Shore Line Butte [INYO]: *hill,* 11 miles west-southwest of Epaulet Peak in Death Valley (lat. 35°54'30" N, long. 116°42'30" W). Altitude 648 feet. Named on Confidence Hills (1950) 15' quadrangle. H.D. Curry named the hill for several distinct shoreline terraces formed there when Death Valley held a lake (Palmer, p. 67).

Shorty Harris Canyon [INYO]: *canyon,* drained by a stream that flows 1.5 miles to Marble Canyon (3) 9 miles west-southwest of the mouth of that canyon (lat. 36°35'50" N, long. 117°26'15" W). Named on Marble Canyon (1951) 15' quadrangle.

Shortys Well [INYO]: *well,* 4.25 miles north-northwest of Bennetts Well in Death Valley (lat. 36°13'35" N, long. 116°52'45" W). Named on Bennetts Well (1952) 15' quadrangle. The name is for "Shorty" Borden, a prospector who developed water at the place (Palmer, p. 67).

Shoshone [INYO]: *village,* 14 miles east of Epaulet Peak along Amargosa River (lat. 35°58'30" N, long. 116°16'15" W; sec. 30, T 22 N, R 7 E). Named on Shoshone (1951) 15' quadrangle. A station on Tonopah and Tidewater Railroad at the place was named for Indians of the region (Palmer, p. 67). Postal authorities established Shoshone post office in 1915 and discontinued it for a time in 1920 (Frickstad, p. 53). A railroad siding built 4 miles north of Shoshone about 1921 was called Gerstley (Myrick, p. 587)—the name was for James Gerstley, an associate of F.M. Smith (Hildebrand, p. 79).

Shoshone Spring [INYO]: *spring,* at the north edge of Shoshone (lat. 35°58'45" N, long. 116°16'20" W; sec. 30, T 22 S, R 7 E). Named on Shoshone (1951) 15' quadrangle.

Shoveltown: see **West Side Borax Camp**, under **Salt Springs** [INYO] (2).

Side Hill Spring [INYO]: *spring,* 15 miles northeast of Independence (lat. 36°58'55" N, long. 118°02' W). Named on Independence (1951) 15' quadrangle.

Sierra Blanca: see **White Mountains** [INYO-MONO].

Sierra de San Marcos: see **Sierra Nevada**, under "Regional setting."

Sierra Nevada: see "Regional setting."

Sill: see **Mount Sill** [INYO].

Silverado Canyon [MONO]: *canyon,* drained by a stream that flows 3.5 miles to the State of Nevada 14 miles north of Bridgeport (lat. 38°27'15" N, long. 119°12'45" W; sec. 20, T 7 N, R 25 E). Named on Bridgeport (1958) and Fales Hot Springs (1956) 15' quadrangles.

Silver Canyon [INYO-MONO]: *canyon,* drained by a stream that heads in Mono County and flows 11.5 miles to lowlands 5.25 miles east-northeast of Bishop in Inyo County (lat. 37°24'20" N, long. 118°18'55" W; near SE cor. sec. 23, T 6 S, R 33 E). Named on Bishop (1949) and Blanco Mountain (1951) 15' quadrangles.

Silver Creek [ALPINE]:

(1) *stream,* flows 9 miles to East Fork Carson River nearly 4 miles south of Mogul Peak (lat. 38°37'55" N, long. 119°43'05" W; near NE cor. sec. 13, T 9 N, R 20 E). Named on Ebbetts Pass (1979), Heenan Lake (1979), and Wolf Creek (1979) 7.5' quadrangles.

(2) *stream,* flows 5.5 miles, including through Lake Alpine, to North Fork Stanislaus River nearly 5 miles south of Mount Reba (lat. 38°26'25" N, long. 120°00'45" W). Named on Pacific Valley (1979), Spicer Meadow Reservoir (1979), and Tamarack (1979) 7.5' quadrangles.

(3) *locality,* 5.5 miles south-southeast of Markleeville along Silver Creek (1) (lat. 38°37' N, long. 119°44'35" W). Named on Markleeville (1889) 30' quadrangle. Postal authorities established Silver Creek post office in 1879, discontinued it the same year, reestablished it in 1882, discontinued it for a time in 1888, and discontinued it finally in 1890 (Frickstad, p. 4). California Division of Highways' (1934) map shows a place called Fays Camp located 3 miles southeast of Silver Creek (3) (sec. 29, T 9 N, R 21 E).

Silver Creek [MONO]: *stream,* flows 6.25 miles to West Walker River 7.25 miles east-northeast of Sonora Pass in Pickel Meadow (lat. 38°21'20" N, long. 119°30'25" W; sec. 24, T 6 N, R 22 E). Named on Lost Cannon Peak (1954) and Pickel Meadow (1954) 7.5' quadrangles.

Silver Creek Campground [ALPINE]: *locality,* 3.25 miles north-northeast of Ebbetts Pass (lat. 38°35'20" N, long. 119°47'10" W; near N line sec. 33, T 9 N, R 20 E); the place is along Silver Creek (1). Named on Ebbetts Pass (1979) 7.5' quadrangle.

Silver Creek Meadows [MONO]: *area,* 5.25 miles northeast of Sonora Pass (lat. 38°22'35" N, long. 119°34' W; in and near sec. 9, T 6 N, R 22 E); the place is along Silver Creek. Named on Lost Cannon Peak (1954) 7.5' quadrangle.

Silver Falls [MONO]: *waterfall,* 5 miles east-northeast of Sonora Pass (lat. 38°20'40" N, long. 119°32'40" W; sec. 27, T 6 N, R 22 E). Named on Pickel Meadow (1954) 7.5' quadrangle.

Silver Hill [ALPINE]: *peak,* 3.5 miles south-southeast of Mogul Peak (lat. 38°38'15" N, long. 119°41'55" W; sec. 8, T 9 N, R 21 E). Altitude 7500 feet. Named on Heenan Lake (1979) 7.5' quadrangle.

Silver Hill [MONO]: *peak,* 0.5 mile southeast of Bodie (lat. 38°12'15" N, long. 119°00'20" W; sec. 16, T 4 N, R 27 E). Named on Bodie (1958) 15' quadrangle.

Silver King: see **Snodgrass Creek** [ALPINE].

Silver King Creek [ALPINE]: *stream,* flows 14 miles to East Fork Carson River 10 miles south-southeast of Mogul Peak in Silver King Valley (lat. 38°34'05" N, long. 119°37'35" W; sec. 1, T 8 N, R 21 E). Named on Sonora Pass (1956) and Topaz Lake (1956) 15' quadrangles. A small sawmill town called Splinterville was located near the mouth of Silver King Creek in the mid-1860's (Long, p. 29).

Silver King Valley [ALPINE]: *valley,* 10 miles south-southeast of Mogul Peak (lat. 38°34' N, long. 119°37'30" W); the valley is along Silver King Creek and East Fork Carson River. Named on Topaz Lake (1956) 15' quadrangle.

Silver Lake [MONO]: *lake,* 4200 feet long, 12.5 miles south of Lee Vining along Rush Creek (lat. 37°46'35" N, long. 119°07'25" W; mainly in sec. 17, T 2 S, R 26 E). Named on Mono Craters (1953) 15' quadrangle. It was called Goose Lake about 1880 (Bean, p. 4). The name "Silver" is from the color of the water on overcast days (Smith, Genny, p. 25). Roy Carson started a resort called Carson Camp by the lake in 1917 (Bean, p. 13). Postal authorities established Carsons Camp post office in 1924 and discontinued it in 1928 (Frickstad, p. 104).

Silver Lakes: see **Kinney Lakes**, under **Lower Kinney Lake** [ALPINE].

Silver Mountain [ALPINE]: *locality,* nearly 5 miles north-northeast of Ebbetts Pass along Silver Creek (1) (lat. 38°36'20" N, long. 119° 46'05" W); the place is 3 miles north of Silver Peak. Site named on Ebbetts Pass (1979) 7.5' quadrangle. Scandinavian miners founded the place in 1858 and called it Köngsberg, or Konigsberg (Hoover, Rensch, and Rensch, p. 26). Postal authorities established Konigsberg post office in 1863, discontinued it for a time in 1864, changed the name to Silver Mountain in 1865, and discontinued it in 1883 (Frickstad, p. 4). Wheeler (1879, p. 178) called the place Silver Mountain City. Jackson (*in* Eno, p. 151) mentioned a place called Boulder Hill, located 3 miles from Silver Mountain, where some free gold was found in large boulders. Wheeler's (1876-1877) map has the name "Anna Pk." for a feature situated about 1.25 miles north of the community of Silver Mountain.

Silver Mountain [INYO]: *ridge,* north-northwest-trending, 1 mile long, 15 miles north-northeast of Coso Junction in Coso Range (lat. 36°14'10" N, long. 117°50'10" W; sec. 34, T 19 S, R 38 E). Named on Haiwee Reservoir (1951) 15' quadrangle. M.H. Farley named the ridge for silver he found there in 1860 (Chalfant, 1933, p. 130).

Silver Mountain: see **Silver Peak** [ALPINE].

Silver Mountain City: see **Silver Mountain** [ALPINE].

Silver Mountain Peak: see **Silver Peak** [ALPINE],

Silver Peak [ALPINE]: *peak,* nearly 3 miles east-northeast of Ebbetts Pass (lat. 38°33'50" N, long. 119°45'30" W). Altitude 10,772 feet. Named on Ebbetts Pass (1979) 7.5' quadrangle. Called Silver Mt. Pk. on Wheeler's (1876-1877) map. Whitney (1865, p. 447) used the name "Silver Mountain," apparently for present Silver Peak.

Silver Peak [INYO]: *peak,* nearly 4 miles south of Coso Peak in Coso Range (lat. 36°08'50" N, long. 117°42'20" W; near W line sec. 36, T 20 S, R 39 E). Named on Coso Peak (1951) 15' quadrangle.

Silvertip Campground [ALPINE]: *locality,* 2 miles south-southeast of Mount Reba (lat. 38°28'50" N, long. 120°01' W; near S line sec. 5, T 17 N, R 18 E). Named on Tamarack (1979) 7.5' quadrangle.

Silver Valley [ALPINE]: *valley,* 3 miles south-southeast of Mount Reba (lat. 38°28'15" N, long. 120°00'30" W). Named on Big Trees (1891) 30' quadrangle. Powers (p. 188) named the valley in 1855 "on account of its proximity to the silver mine which had been visited by one of our party on a former occasion, but which proves to be nothing more valuable than plumbago."

Silver Valley Campground [ALPINE]: *locality,* 8 miles northwest of Dardanelles Cone (lat. 38°28'50" N, long. 119°59'10" W). Named on Spicer Meadow Reservoir (1979) 7.5' quadrangle.

Simons Spring [MONO]: *spring,* 5.5 miles north-northeast of the site of Mono Mills near the edge of Mono Lake (lat. 37°58' N, long. 118°55'55" W; near N line sec. 7, T 1 N, R 28 E). Named on Cowtrack Mountain (1962) 15' quadrangle. The feature first was called Samman Springs for Louis Samman, who homesteaded there (La Braque, p. 59).

Sinnamon Cut [MONO]: *locality,* 12 miles south-southeast of Bridgeport (lat. 38°05'45" N, long. 119°08'45" W; sec. 30, T 3 N, R 26 E). Named on Bodie (1958) 15' quadrangle. Calhoun (p. 130) called the place Cinnamon Cut. The feature is a large hydraulic excavation named for James Sinnamon, who mined there (Wedertz, p. 36). Wheeler's (1871) map has the name "Monoville" near the site. Gold was discovered at Monoville in 1859 and a ditch brought water from present Virginia Creek for hydraulic mining operations; the area around Monoville was known as Mono Diggings (Cain, 1961, p. 6-8). Postal authorities established Monoville post office in 1859 and discontinued it in 1862 (Salley, p. 144).

Sinnamon Meadow [MONO]: *area,* 10 miles south of Bridgeport (lat. 38°06'30" N, long. 119°13'30" W; in and near sec. 21, T 3 N, R 25 E). Named on Bodie (1958) 15' quadrangle. The name commemorates James Sinnamon of Sinnamon Cut (Wedertz, p. 36).

Sisters: see **The Sisters** [ALPINE].

Six Spring Canyon [INYO]: *canyon,* drained by a stream that flows 7 miles to Death Valley 8.5 miles south-southwest of Bennetts Well (lat. 36°03' N, long. 116°55'20" W). Named on Bennetts Well (1952) and Telescope Peak (1952) 15' quadrangles. The canyon is supposed to contain six springs (Palmer, p. 67).

Sixth Lake [INYO]: *lake,* 1200 feet long, 9 miles east-southeast of Mount Darwin (lat. 37°08'10" N, long. 118°30'40" W; sec. 29, T 9 S, R 32 E); the lake is between Fifth Lake and Seventh Lake. Named on Mount Goddard (1948) 15' quadrangle.

Skelton Lake [MONO]: *lake,* 1400 feet long, 6.5 miles west of Mount Morrison along Mammoth Creek (lat. 37°34'35" N, long. 118°58'30" W). Named on Mount Morrison (1953) 15' quadrangle. The name commemorates the Skelton brothers, early prospectors who had a stamp mill below the lake (Smith, Genny, p. 49).

Skidoo [INYO]: *locality,* 7 miles north of Emigrant Pass (1) (lat. 36° 26'10" N, long. 117°08'50" W). Named on Emigrant Canyon (1952) 15' quadrangle. Mining started at the place in 1906 (Hubbard, Bray, and Pipkin, p. 86). The slang expression "23 Skidoo" was current at the time, and according to various accounts, the name "Skidoo" was given because: (1) the mining claims were staked on the 23rd of the month; (2) 23 men established the camp; (3) the original site consisted of 23 mine claims; (4) water was brought 23 miles to the camp from Birch Spring (Gist, p. 20). Postal authorities established Hoveck post office at the place in 1906, changed the name to Skidoo in 1907, and discontinued it in 1917 (Frickstad, p. 51, 53). The name "Hoveck" was for Matt Hoveck, manager of Skiddo mines (Weight, p. 28).

Ski Lake [MONO]: *lake,* 750 feet long, 4.25 miles south-southeast of Sonora Pass (lat. 38°16'25" N, long. 119°36'05" W; near N line sec. 19, T 5 N, R 22 E). Named on Pickel Meadow (1954) 7.5' quadrangle.

Skinner: see **Diaz** [INYO].

Skyes: see **Little Lake** [INYO] (2).

Sky Meadows [MONO]: *area,* 7.5 miles west of Mount Morrison (lat. 37°34'45" N, long. 118°54'35" W). Named on Mount Morrison (1953) 15' quadrangle.

Slater: see **Hermit Valley** [ALPINE].

Slate Range [INYO]: *range,* southwest of Panamint Valley and east of Searles Valley; the south half of the feature is in San Bernardino County. Named on Manly Peak (1950) and Trona (1949) 15' quadrangles.

Slaughter Canyon [ALPINE]: *canyon,* drained by a stream that flows 1.25 miles to Highland Creek 2 miles north-northwest of Dardanelles Cone (lat. 38°25'55" N, long. 119°52'50" W). Named on Spicer Meadow Reservoir (1979) 7.5' quadrangle.

Slaughter Canyon: see **Jenkins Canyon** [ALPINE].

Slick Rock [ALPINE]: *relief feature,* 4.5 miles south of Mount Reba (lat. 38°26'45" N, long. 120°00'45" W). Named on Tamarack (1979) 7.5' quadrangle.

Slide Canyon: see **Little Slide Canyon** [MONO].

Slide Mountain [MONO]: *peak,* 3.5 miles west of Matterhorn Peak on Mono-Tuolumne County line (lat. 38°05'35" N, long. 119°26'45" W); the peak is at the head of a feature called The Slide, which is in Tuolumne County. Named on Matterhorn Peak (1956) 15' quadrangle.

Slim Lake [INYO]: *lake,* 500 feet long, 9 miles west-southwest of Independence (lat. 36°45'45" N, long. 118°21'20" W). Named on Mount Pinchot (1953) 15' quadrangle.

Slims Peak: see **Clair Camp** [INYO].

Slinkard Creek [MONO]: *stream,* flows 10.5 miles to Antelope Valley 5.25 miles north-northwest of Coleville (lat. 38°38'30" N, long. 119°31'45" W; sec. 11, T 9 N, R 22 E); the stream goes through Slinkard Valley. Named on Topaz Lake (1956) 15' quadrangle.

Slinkard Valley [MONO]: *valley,* 4 miles west-northwest of Coleville (lat. 38°35'30" N, long. 119°34'30" W). Named on Topaz Lake (1956) 15' quadrangle. Called Slinkard's Valley on Wheeler's (1876-1877) map, and called Slinkards Valley on Markleeville (1889) 30' quadrangle. The name commemorates A. James Slinkard, who build a road up Slinkard Creek into the valley (Gudde, 1949, p. 334).

Smith Mountain [INYO]: *ridge,* west-northwest-trending, 4.5 miles long, 7 miles south-southwest of Funeral Peak in Black Mountains (lat. 36°01' N, long. 116°40'30" W). Named on Confidence Hills (1950) and Funeral Peak (1951) 15' quadrangles. J.J. McGillivray named the peak in 1891 for Francis Marion Smith, president of Pacific Coast Borax Company; the ridge also is called Mount Smith (Palmer, p. 51).

Smiths Creek [ALPINE]: *stream,* flows 1.5 miles to East Fork Carson River 1.5 miles south-southwest of Mogul Peak (lat. 38°40'10" N, long. 119°43'45" W). Named on Heenan Lake (1979) 7.5' quadrangle

Snodgrass Creek [ALPINE]: *stream,* flows 2 miles to Silver King Creek 13 miles south-southeast of Mogul Peak (lat. 38°32' N, long. 119°35'35" W; near SW cor. sec. 17, T 8 N, R 22 E). Named on Topaz Lake (1956) 15' quadrangle. A place called Silver King was situated at the mouth of Snodgrass Canyon (Long, p. 29). Postal authorities established Silver King post office in 1864 and discontinued it in 1866 (Frickstad, p. 4). Wheeler's (1876-1877) map has the name "Konigs Pk." for a feature located 4.5 miles north of Silver King on present Alpine-Mono County line.

Snooky Spring [INYO]: *spring,* 7.5 miles north of Argus Peak in Water Canyon (5) (lat. 35°57'30" N, long. 117°25'30" W; near SE cor. sec. 3, T 23 S, R 42 E). Named on Trona (1949) 15' quadrangle.

Snow Canyon [ALPINE]: *canyon,* drained by a stream that flows 2 miles to Meadow Lake nearly 7 miles north-northwest of Pacific Grade Summit (lat. 38°36'05" N, long. 119°58'35" W; sec. 27, T 9 N, R 18 E). Named on Pacific Valley (1979) 7.5' quadrangle.

Snow Canyon [INYO]: *canyon,* 4.25 miles long, opens into Panamint Valley 7 miles northeast of Maturango Peak (lat. 36°11'45" N, long. 117°25' W; sec. 15, T 20 S, R 42 E). Named on Maturango Peak (1951) 15' quadrangle. Called Snow's Cañon on Wheeler's (1877) map, which has the name "Lone Star Hill" for a prominent peak north of the canyon, and has the name "Double Head" for a peak near the head of the canyon.

Snow Lake [MONO]: *lake,* 1050 feet long, 4.25 miles west of Matterhorn Peak (lat. 38°06'05" N, long. 119°27'35" W). Named on Matterhorn Peak (1956) 15' quadrangle.

Snow's Cañon: see **Snow Canyon** [INYO].

Snowshoe Springs Campground [ALPINE]: *locality,* 5.5 miles south of Freel Peak along West Fork Carson River (lat. 38°46'40" N, long. 119°53'10" W; sec. 31, T 11 N, R 19 E). Named on Freel Peak (1955) 7.5' quadrangle.

Snowslide Canyon [ALPINE]: *canyon,* 1.25 miles long, opens into the canyon of East Fork Carson River 10 miles south-southeast of Mogul Peak (lat. 38°33'35" N, long. 119°38'15" W; sec. 11, T 8 N, R 21 E). Named on Wolf Creek (1979) 7.5' quadrangle.

Snow Valley [ALPINE]: *area,* 1.25 miles southwest of Mount Reba (lat. 38°29'50" N, long. 120°02'50" W). Named on Mokelumne Peak (1979) and Tamarack (1979) 7.5' quadrangles.

Snowy Mountains: see **Sierra Nevada**, under "Regional setting."

Snowy Range: see **Sierra Nevada**, under "Regional setting."

Soda Cone [ALPINE]: *locality,* 13 miles south-southeast of Mogul Peak (lat. 38°30'35" N, long. 119°38'05" W; sec. 26, T 8 N, R 21 E). Named on Wolf Creek (1979) 7.5' quadrangle.

Sodan: see **Little Lake** [INYO] (2).

Soda Spring [ALPINE]: *spring,* 3.5 miles west of Markleeville near Grover Hot Springs (lat. 38°41'50" N, long. 119°50'45" W; sec. 24, T 10 N, R 19 E). Named on Markleeville (1979) 7.5' quadrangle.

Soda Spring: see **Post Office Spring** [INYO].

Soda Springs Station [ALPINE]: *locality,* 13 miles south-southeast of Mogul Peak in Dumonts Meadows (lat. 38°30'25" N, long. 119° 39'10" W; sec. 27, T 8 N, R 21 E). Named on Wolf Creek (1979) 7.5' quadrangle. Topaz Lake (1956) 15' quadrangle shows Soda Springs guard station at the place.

Soldier Canyon [INYO]: *canyon,* drained by a stream that flows 5.5 miles to an unnamed canyon 5.5 miles east of Big Pine (lat. 37°10'15" N, long. 118°11'30" W; sec. 18, T 9 S, R 35 E). Named on Waucoba Mountain (1951) 15' quadrangle.

Soldier Pass [INYO]: *pass,* 1.5 miles south-southeast of Deep Springs (lat. 37°20'50" N, long. 117°58'30" W; near N line sec. 13, T 7 S, R 36 E). Named on Soldier Pass (1958) 15' quadrangle. United States Board on Geographic Names (1980, p. 4) approved the name "Mount Nunn" for a peak, altitude 7830 feet, situated 4.5 miles south of Soldier Pass (lat. 37°17'02" N, long. 117°59'32" W; sec. 2, T 8 S, R 36 E)—the name honors Lucien L. Nunn, a pioneer in development of electric power and founder of Deep Springs College.

Soldier Pass Canyon [INYO]: *canyon,* 2.5 miles long, opens into Eureka Valley 3.25 miles southeast of Deep Springs (lat. 37°20'45" N, long. 117°56'15" W; sec. 17, T 7 S, R 37 E); the canyon heads near Soldier Pass. Named on Soldier Pass (1958) 15' quadrangle. According to Palmer (p. 68), the name evidently came from army use of the canyon as a route to the lands east of Owens Valley.

Sonora Bridge Campground [MONO]: *locality,* 4.25 miles west-northwest of Fales Hot Springs near West Walker River (lat. 38°21'50" N, long. 119°28'30" W; sec. 17, T 6 N, R 23 E). Named on Fales Hot Springs (1954) 7.5' quadrangle.

Sonora Junction [MONO]: *locality,* nearly 3 miles west of Fales Hot Springs (lat. 38°20'55" N, long. 119°27'05" W; sec. 21, T 6 N, R 23 E); the road from Sonora Pass joins U.S. Highway 395 at the place. Named on Fales Hot Springs (1954) 7.5' quadrangle. Mr. A. Mack built a station, often called The Junction House, at the site in the 1860's (Wedertz, p. 62).

Sonora Pass [ALPINE-MONO]: *pass,* 10 miles south-southeast of Disaster Peak, where Alpine County, Mono County, and Tuolumne County meet (lat. 38°19'40" N, long. 119°38'10" W). Named on Sonora Pass (1979) 7.5' quadrangle.

Sonora Peak [ALPINE-MONO]: *peak,* less than 2 miles north of Sonora Pass on Alpine-Mono County line (lat. 38°21'15" N, long. 119°38'05" W). Altitude 11,459 feet. Named on Sonora Pass (1979) 7.5' quadrangle.

Sorensens [ALPINE]: *locality,* 5.5 miles south of Freel Peak along West Fork Carson River (lat. 38°46'30" N, long. 119°54'05" W; near E line sec. 25, T 11 N, R 18 E). Named on Freel Peak (1955) 7.5' quadrangle.

Sourdough Canyon [INYO]: *canyon,* nearly 2 miles long, branches north from Surprise Canyon 3.5 miles south of Telescope Peak (lat. 36°07' N, long. 117°05'55" W). Named on Telescope Peak (1952) 15' quadrangle.

Sourdough Spring [INYO]: *spring,* 4 miles south-southeast of Manly Peak (lat. 35°51'35" N, long. 117°05'40" W). Named on Manly Peak (1950) 15' quadrangle.

Southeast Palisade: see **Split Mountain** [INYO].

Southern California Peak: see **Trojan Peak** [INYO].

South Fork Lakes [INYO]: *lakes,* largest 650 feet long, 18 miles northwest of Olancha (lat. 36°29' N, long. 118°13' W; near NW cor. sec. 5, T 17 S, R 35 E); the lakes are near the head of South Fork Cottonwood Creek (3). Named on Olancha (1956) 15' quadrangle.

Southfork Pass [INYO]: *pass,* 11 miles southwest of Big Pine on Inyo-Fresno

County line (lat. 37°04'05" N, long. 118°27' W); the pass is near the head of a branch of South Fork Big Pine Creek. Named on Big Pine (1950) 15' quadrangle.

South Lake [INYO]: *lake,* 1 mile long, behind a dam on South Fork (1) Bishop Creek 6 miles east of Mount Darwin (lat. 37°10'20" N, long. 118°33'55" W; near NW cor. sec. 14, T 9 S, R 31 E). Named on Mount Goddard (1948) 15' quadrangle.

South Landing [MONO]: *locality,* 3 miles west-northwest of Toms Place on the south side of Lake Crowley (lat. 37°34'50" N, long. 118°43'50" W; near SW cor. sec. 24, T 4 S, R 29 E). Named on Casa Diablo Mountain (1953) 15' quadrangle.

South Palisade: see **Split Mountain** [INYO].

South Park [INYO]: *valley,* 5.25 miles north of Manly Peak (lat. 35° 59'20" N, long. 117°05'50" W). Named on Manly Peak (1950) 15' quadrangle. The feature is named for its position relative to other valleys that are called parks (Palmer, p. 68).

South Park Canyon [INYO]: *canyon,* 5 miles long, opens into Panamint Valley 7.5 miles northwest of Manly Peak (lat. 35°59'30" N, long. 117°12'25" W; sec. 27, T 22 S, R 44 E); the canyon heads at South Park. Named on Manly Peak (1950) 15' quadrangle. Palmer (p. 73) noted that the feature also is called Thorndike Canyon, for John Thorndike, owner of a zinc mine there.

South Sister [MONO]: *peak,* 10.5 miles north-northeast of Fales Hot Springs (lat. 38°29' N, long. 119°18' W; sec. 1, 2, T 7 N, R 24 E); the peak is nearly 2 miles south of Middle Sister. Altitude 11,339 feet. Named on Fales Hot Springs (1956) 15' quadrangle.

Spangler Valley: see **Searles Valley** [INYO].

Spanish Spring [INYO]: *spring,* 8 miles south-southeast of Ubehebe Peak (lat. 36°35'15" N, long. 117°30'45" W). Named on Ubehebe Peak (1950) 15' quadrangle.

Spearhead Lake [INYO]: *lake,* 1050 feet long, 7 miles east-southeast of Mount Darwin (lat. 37°08'15" N, long. 118°33'10" W; sec. 26, T 9 S, T 31 E). Named on Mount Goddard (1948) 15' quadrangle.

Sperry Hills [INYO]: *range,* 12.5 miles south of Shoshone on Inyo-San Bernardino County line (lat. 35°47'30" N, long. 116°17' W). Named on Shoshone (1951) 15' quadrangle. United States Board on Geographic Names (1966a, p. 7) rejected the names "Alexander Hills" and "Tecopa Hills" for the range.

Spire Lake [INYO]: *lake,* 1400 feet long, 2.25 miles southeast of Mount Abbot (lat. 37°22'10" N, long. 118°45'05" W); the lake is 1 mile east of Bear Creek Spire. Named on Mount Abbot (1953) and Mount Tom (1949) 15' quadrangles.

Splinterville: see **Silver King Creek** [ALPINE].

Split Lake [INYO]: *lakes,* two, largest 700 feet long, 5 miles west-northwest of Mount Tom (lat. 37°22'05" N, long. 118°44'35" W). Named on Mount Tom (1949) 15' quadrangle.

Split Mountain [INYO]: *peak,* 12.5 miles southwest of Big Pine on Inyo-Fresno County line (lat. 37°01'15" N, long. 118°25'15" W). Altitude 14,058 feet. Named on Big Pine (1950) 15' quadrangle. Bolton C. Brown named the peak for its double summit; Wheeler called it Southeast Palisade in 1878 (Farquhar, 1925, p. 135). The feature also was called South Palisade (Hanna, p. 226).

Spook Canyon [INYO]: *canyon,* drained by a stream that flows 2 miles to Division Creek 11.5 miles northwest of Independence (lat. 36°56' N, long. 118°19'15" W; sec. 1, T 12 S, R 33 E). Named on Mount Pinchot (1953) 15' quadrangle.

Spooky Meadow [MONO]: *area,* 9.5 miles northwest of Mammoth Mountain (lat. 37°44'40" N, long. 119°07'50" W; sec. 29, T 2 S, R 26 E). Named on Devils Postpile (1953) 15' quadrangle.

Spratt Creek [ALPINE]: *stream,* flows 5 miles to Hot Springs Creek 1 mile west of Markleeville (lat. 38°41'30" N, long. 119°48'20" W; near N line sec. 29, T 10 N, R 20 E). Named on Markleeville (1979) 7.5' quadrangle.

Spring Canyon Creek [MONO]: *stream,* flows about 4 miles from the south end of Benton Valley to the north end of Hammil Valley 12 miles west-northwest of White Mountain Peak (lat. 37°34'40" N, long. 118°26'20" W; sec. 34, T 2 S, R 32 E). Named on Benton (1962) 15' quadrangle, where the name seems to apply to only a segment of a much longer stream.

Spring Creek [MONO]: *stream,* flows 2.25 miles to Antelope Valley 5 miles southeast of Coleville (lat. 38°31'15" N, long. 119°26'10" W; sec. 22, T 8 N, R 23 E). Named on Desert Creek Peak (1956) 15' quadrangle.

Spring Valley: see **Benton Valley** [MONO].

Spuller Lake [MONO]: *lake,* 600 feet long, 2.5 miles east-southeast of Mount Conness (lat. 37°56'55" N, long. 119°17'05" W). Named on Tuolumne Meadows (1956) 15' quadrangle.

Squaw Flat [INYO]: *valley,* 3 miles northwest of Waucoba Mountain (lat. 37°02'30" N, long. 118°02'45" W); the valley is 1.5 miles west of Squaw Peak. Named on Waucoba Mountain (1951) 15' quadrangle.

Squaw Peak [INYO]: *peak,* 2.25 miles north-northwest of Waucoba Mountain (lat. 37°03'15" N, long. 118°01' W). Altitude 10,358 feet. Named on Waucoba Mountain (1951) 15' quadrangle.

Squaw Ridge [ALPINE]: *ridge,* northeast-trending, 5 miles long, 3.5 miles southwest of Fourth of July Peak on Alpine-Amador County line (lat. 38°37'30" N, long. 120°04'20" W). Named on Caples Lake (1979) 7.5' quadrangle.

Squaw Spring [INYO]: *spring,* 6 miles east of Manly Peak (lat. 35°54'40" N, long. 117°00'30" W). Named on Manly Peak (1950) 15' quadrangle.

Squaw Springs [INYO]: *springs,* two, 2.25 miles southwest of Waucoba Mountain (lat. 37°00'05" N, long. 118°02'30" W); the springs are nearly 4 miles south-southwest of Squaw Peak. Named on Waucoba Mountain (1951) 15' quadrangle.

Squaw Teat: see **Thimble Peak** [INYO].

Stanford Lake [MONO]: *lake,* 1400 feet long, 6.25 miles southeast of Mount Morrison (lat. 37°29'35" N, long. 118°47'05" W); the lake is less than 1 mile east-northeast of Mount Stanford. Named on Mount Abbot (1953) 15' quadrangle.

Stanford Peak: see **Mount Stanford** [MONO].

Stanislaus Meadow [ALPINE]: *area,* 1.5 miles west-southwest of Pacific Grade Summit (lat. 38°30'10" N, long. 119°56'10" W; sec. 31, T 8 N, R 19 E); the place is along North Fork Stanislaus River. Named on Pacific Valley (1979) and Spicer Meadow Reservoir (1979) 7.5' quadrangles.

Stanislaus Peak [ALPINE]: *peak,* 5.5 miles southeast of Disaster Peak (lat. 38°23'05" N, long. 119°40' W). Altitude 11,233 feet. Named on Disaster Peak (1979) 7.5' quadrangle.

Stanislaus River, Clark's Fork: see **Clark Fork** [ALPINE].

Stanislaus River, North Fork [ALPINE]: *stream,* flows 10 miles to Calaveras County and Tuolumne County 5 miles south of Mount Reba (lat. 38°26'10" N, long. 120°01' W). Named on Pacific Valley (1979), Spicer Meadow Reservoir (1979), and Tamarack (1979) 7.5' quadrangles.

Star City [MONO]: *locality,* 11 miles north of Bridgeport in Sweetwater Mountains (lat. 38°25'05" N, long. 119°14'20" W; sec. 31, T 7 N, R 25 E). Site named on Bridgeport (1958) 15' quadrangle. The place was a mining camp in the 1880's (Wedertz, p. 163).

Starr: see **Mount Starr** [INYO].

Starvation Canyon [INYO]: *canyon,* drained by a stream that flows 10 miles to Death Valley nearly 5 miles southwest of Bennetts Well (lat. 36°07' N, long. 116°55'25" W). Named on Bennetts Well (1952) and Telescope Peak (1952) 15' quadrangles. National Park Service officials proposed the name to conform with the general nomenclature of Death Valley (Palmer, p. 69).

State Line: see **Benton** [MONO].

Station: see **Laws** [INYO]; **Zurich** [INYO].

Station Peak [MONO]: *peak,* 12 miles southeast of White Mountain Peak (lat. 37°30'45" N, long. 118°06'25" W). Altitude 10,316 feet. Named on Mount Barcroft (1962) 15' quadrangle.

Stecker Flat [INYO]: *area,* 11 miles south-southwest of Big Pine (lat. 37°00'50" N, long. 118°21'55" W). Named on Big Pine (1950) 15' quadrangle.

Steelhead Lake [MONO]:

(1) *lake,* 2000 feet long, 2 miles north-northeast of Mount Conness along Mill Creek (2) (lat. 37°59'40" N, long. 119°18'05" W; sec. 26, T 2 N, R 24 E). Named on Tuolumne Meadows (1956) 15' quadrangle.

(2) *lake,* 1500 feet long, 5 miles south-southeast of Mount Morrison at the head of a branch of McGee Creek (lat. 37°30' N, long. 118° 48'30" W). Named on Mount Abbot (1953) and Mount Morrison (1953) 15' quadrangles.

Stella Lake [MONO]: *lakes,* three connected, largest 1200 feet long, 3 miles northwest of Tower Peak (lat. 38°10'50" N, long. 119°34'40" W). Named on Tower Peak (1956) 15' quadrangle.

Steven: see **Stevens Peak** [ALPINE].

Stevenot Camp [ALPINE]: *locality,* 3.5 miles north-northwest of Pacific Grade Summit (lat. 38°33'45" N, long. 119°56'10" W; near W line sec. 7, T 8 N, R 19 E). Site named on Pacific Valley (1979) 7.5' quadrangle.

Stevens Lake [ALPINE]: *lake,* 1500 feet long, 2.5 miles southeast of Woodfords (lat. 38°45'10" N, long. 119°47'05" W; sec. 4, T 10 N, R 20 E). Named on Woodfords (1979) 7.5' quadrangle.

Stevens Peak [ALPINE]: *peak,* 2.5 miles north of Carson Pass (lat. 38°44' N, long. 119°58'55" W; near N line sec. 10, T 10 N, R 18 E). Altitude 10,059 feet. Named on Carson Pass (1979) 7.5' quadrangle. The name commemorates J.M. Stevens (Gudde, 1949, p. 343), who operated Stevens Station, a toll stop in upper Hope Valley (Long, p. 40). Wheeler's (1876-1877) map shows a place called Steven located about 1.5 miles east of Stevens Peak. Macomb (1878, p. 141) referred to Stevens' Peak and to Stevens' ranch in Hope Valley.

Stevens Station: see **Stevens Peak** [ALPINE].

Stewarts: see **Deep Springs** [INYO].

Stewart Valley [INYO]: *valley,* 15 miles east-southeast of Death Valley Junction on California-Nevada State line east of Resting Spring Range and north of Nopah Range (lat. 36°12'30" N, long. 116°10' W). Named on Stewart Valley (1958) 15' quadrangle.

Stockade Flat [MONO]: *area,* 5.5 miles southwest of Fales Hot Springs (lat. 38°17'25" N, long. 119°27'55" W; near SE cor. sec. 8, T 5 N, R 23 E). Named on Fales Hot Springs (1954) 7.5' quadrangle.

Stone Canyon [INYO]: *canyon,* 2.5 miles long, opens into lowlands 10 miles north-northeast of Maturango Peak (lat. 36°15' N, long. 117°25'25" W). Named on Maturango Peak (1951) 15' quadrangle. This appears to be the feature called Minute Gun Cañon on Wheeler's (1877) map.

Stone Corral [INYO]: *locality,* 9 miles south of Telescope Peak in Pleasant Canyon (lat. 36°02' N, long. 117°05'50" W). Named on Telescope Peak (1952) 15' quadrangle. Indians are thought to have built a stone corral found at the place (Hubbard, Bray, and Pipkin, p. 37).

Stovepipe Wells [INYO]: *well,* 11 miles east of the mouth of Marble Canyon (3) in Death Valley (lat. 36°39'30" N, long. 117°04'45" W; near N line sec. 15, T 15 S, R 45 E). Named on Stovepipe Wells (1952) 15' quadrangle. The name is from a few lengths of rusty stove pipe that were used to mark holes in the sand that furnished the only water along a road across Death Valley; the marking was needed because the holes often filled with wind-blown sand (Federal Writers' Project, p. 46). A natural amphitheater situated about 2 miles south of Stovepipe Wells is called Easter Bowl for Easter sunrise services held there (Palmer, p. 25).

Straight Canyon [MONO]: *canyon,* drained by a stream that flows 4 miles to Chalfant Valley 7 miles southwest of White Mountain Peak (lat. 37°33'30" N, long. 118°20'10" W; sec. 33, T 4 S, R 33 E). Named on White Mountain Peak (1962) 15' quadrangle.

Striped Butte [INYO]: *hill,* 3.5 miles northeast of Manly Peak in Butte Valley (lat. 35°56'55" N, long. 117°04'15" W). Altitude 4743 feet. Named on Manly Peak (1950) 15' quadrangle. Called The Butte on Searles Lake (1915) 1° quadrangle, but United States Board on Geographic Names (1985a, p. 3) rejected this designation. The name "Striped Butte" is from bands of rock; Hugh McCormack called the hill Curious Butte in 1861 (Palmer, p. 21, 69).

Striped Mountain [INYO]: *peak,* 16 miles northwest of Independence on Inyo-Fresno County line (lat. 36°57'55" N, long. 118°24'10" W). Named on Mount Pinchot (1953) 15' quadrangle. Bolton C. Brown named the peak in 1896 for its striped appearance (Farquhar, 1925, p. 136).

Stuard Canyon [ALPINE]: *canyon,* drained by a stream that flows 1.5 miles to Carson Valley 2 miles north-northeast of Woodfords (lat. 38°48'05" N, long. 119°48'35" W; sec. 23, T 11 N, R 19 E). Named on Woodfords (1979) 7.5' quadrangle.

Stutler Canyon [ALPINE]: *canyon,* drained by a stream that flows 2 miles to the State of Nevada nearly 4 miles northeast of Freel Peak (lat. 38°54'05" N, long. 119°51'20" W; sec. 16, T 12 N, R 19 E). Named on Minden (1968) and South Lake Tahoe (1955) 7.5' quadrangles.

Sugar Loaf [INYO]: *peak,* 12 miles south of Keeler in Coso Range (lat. 36°19'05" N, long. 117°52' W; near N line sec. 4, T 19 S, R 38 E). Altitude 5233 feet. Named on Keeler (1951) 15' quadrangle.

Sugarloaf [INYO]: *peak,* 8 miles west of Big Pine (lat. 37°11' N, long. 118°26' W; sec. 12, T 9 S, R 32 E). Altitude 11,026 feet. Named on Big Pine (1950) 15' quadrangle.

Sugarloaf [MONO]: *peak,* 1.5 miles south of Bodie (lat. 38°11'20" N, long. 119°00'30" W; sec. 21, T 4 N, R 27 E). Named on Bodie (1958) 15' quadrangle.

Sugarloaf: see **Sugarloaf Peak** [INYO].

Sugarloaf Mountain [INYO]: *mountain,* 7 miles east of Coso Junction in Coso Range (lat. 36°02' N, long. 117°49'15" W). Altitude 5126 feet. Named on Haiwee Reservoir (1951) 15' quadrangle.

Sugarloaf Peak [INYO]: *peak,* 10.5 miles east-southeast of Manly Peak in Panamint Range (lat. 35°53'05" N, long. 116°55'40" W). Named on Wingate Wash (1950) 15' quadrangle. Called Sugarloaf on Avawatz Mountains (1933) 1° quadrangle, and called Sugar Loaf on Wheeler's (1877) map. According to Palmer (p. 7), National Park Service officials proposed the name "Arcane Peak" in 1936, apparently for present Sugarloaf Peak, to honor J.B. Arcane, a Death Valley emigrant of 1849.

Suicide Pass: see **Jubilee Pass** [INYO].

Sullivan Lake [MONO]: *lake,* 1500 feet long, 11 miles northwest of Mammoth Mountain (lat. 37°44'30" N, long. 119°10' W). Named on Devils Postpile (1953) 15' quadrangle.

Sulphur Pond [MONO]: *lake,* 400 feet long, 9 miles south-southeast of Bodie in Mono Valley (lat. 38°05'05" N, long. 118°57'55" W; sec. 26, T 3 N, R 27 E). Named on Trench Canyon (1958) 15' quadrangle.

Sulphur Spring [INYO]: *spring,* nearly 6 miles south-southwest of Beatty Junction in Death Valley (lat. 36°30'35" N, long. 116°58'20" W). Named on Chloride Cliff (1952) 15' quadrangle. United States Board on Geographic Names (1968a, p. 6) approved the name "Cottonball Marsh" for a generally wet area located 0.5 mile northwest of Sulphur Spring (lat. 36°31'00" N, long. 116°58'35" W), and noted that the wet area is on the west side of a feature called Cottonball Basin; the Board rejected the name "Minnow Wash" for present Cottonball Marsh.

Summers Back Pasture: see **Upper Summers Meadows** [MONO].

Summers Creek [MONO]: *stream,* flows 7 miles to Green Creek (2) 4 miles south-southwest of Bridgeport (lat. 38°12' N, long. 119°15'15" W; near N line sec. 19, T 4 N, R 25 E); the stream heads in Upper Summers Meadows and goes through Lower Summers Meadows. Named on Bodie (1958) and Matterhorn Peak (1956) 15' quadrangles. The name commemorates Jesse N. Summers and G.N. Summers, who bought property along the stream in 1864 (Wedertz, p. 175).

Summers Meadows: see **Lower Summers Meadows** [MONO]: **Upper Summers Meadows** [MONO].

Summit City: see **Summit City Creek** [ALPINE].

Summit City Creek [ALPINE]: *stream,* flows 9 miles to North Fork Mokelumne River 4.25 miles north of Mount Reba (lat. 38°34'20" N, long. 120°01'40" W). Named on Caples Lake (1979), Carson Pass (1979), and Mokelumne Peak (1979) 7.5' quadrangles. Called Summit Creek on Markleeville (1889) and Pyramid Peak (1896) 30' quadrangles. Wheeler's (1876-1877) map has the designation "Lower Summit City (ab'd)" at a place situated along Summit Creek (present Summit City Creek) about 3 miles west-northwest of present Upper Blue Lake (about at S line present sec. 4, T 9 N, R 18 E), and the designation "Upper Summit City (ab'd)" at a place located along Summit Creek about 1.25 miles northwest of present Upper Blue Lake (present sec. 2, T 9 N, R 18 E). Summit City was about 2.5 miles southwest of Upper Blue Lake, and had about 600 inhabitants in 1864; a rival town called Lower Summit city was laid out about 2 miles away (Long, p. 28).

Summit Creek [INYO]: *stream,* flows 5.5 miles to lowlands 5 miles south of Olancha (lat. 36°12'30" N, long. 118°00'30" W; sec. 7, T 20 S, R 37 E). Named on Haiwee Reservoir (1951) and Monache Mountain (1956) 15' quadrangles. The stream now discharges into the aqueduct that takes Owens Valley water to Los Angeles.

Summit Creek: see **Summit City Creek** [ALPINE].

Summit Lake [ALPINE]:

(1) *lake,* 950 feet long, 3 miles north-northwest of Markleeville (lat. 38°44'10" N, long. 119°47'35" W; at NW cor. sec. 9, T 10 N, R 20 E). Named on Markleeville (1979) 7.5' quadrangle.

(2) *lake,* 1350 feet long, 5.25 miles northwest of Ebbetts Pass (lat. 38°36'15" N, long. 119°52'15" W; sec. 27, T 9 N, R 19 E). Named on Ebbetts Pass (1979) 7.5' quadrangle.

(3) *lake,* 1550 feet long, 6 miles west-northwest of Dardanelles Cone (lat. 38°25'55" N, long. 119°58'20" W). Named on Spicer Meadow Reservoir (1979) 7.5' quadrangle.

Summit Lake [MONO]: *lake,* 2800 feet long, 4.5 miles southeast of Matterhorn Peak (lat. 38°03'10" N, long. 119°19' W; sec. 3, T 2 N, R 24 E). Named on Matterhorn Peak (1956) 15' quadrangle.

Summit Lake: see **Caples Lake** [ALPINE]; **June Lake** [MONO] (1); **Lake Mary** [MONO]; **Swift Lake** [INYO].

Summit Meadow [INYO]: *area,* 9 miles west-northwest of Independence along North Fork Oak Creek (lat. 36°50' N, long. 118°21'30" W). Named on Mount Pinchot (1953) 15' quadrangle.

Summit Meadow [MONO]: *area,* 8.5 miles northeast of Sonora Pass on upper reaches of Lost Cannon Creek (lat. 38°24'40" N, long. 119°31'15" W; sec. 35, 36, T 7 N, R 22 E). Named on Lost Cannon Peak (1954) 7.5' quadrangle.

Summit Meadow Lake [ALPINE]; *lake,* 450 feet long, nearly 3 miles west-southwest of Fourth of July Peak (lat. 38°38'20" N, long. 120°04'05" W; sec. 11, T 9 N, R 17 E). Named on Caples Lake (1979) 7.5' quadrangle.

Summit Station: see **Homewood Canyon** [INYO].

Sunday Canyon [INYO]: *canyon,* nearly 1 mile long, branches northwest from Mazourka Canyon 9.5 miles northeast of Independence (lat. 36°54'25" N, long. 118°05' W). Named on Independence (1951) 15' quadrangle.

Sunset Lake [INYO]: *lake,* 1900 feet long, 3.5 miles east-southeast of Mount Darwin (lat. 37°09'15" N, long. 118°36'55" W; sec. 20, T 9 S, R 31 E). Named on Mount Goddard (1948) 15' quadrangle.

Sunset Lake: see **Lower Sunset Lake** [ALPINE]; **Upper Sunset Lake** [ALPINE].

Sunshine: see **Bodie Creek** [MONO].

Surprise Canyon [INYO]: *canyon,* 7 miles long, opens into Panamint Valley 8 miles southwest of Telescope Peak (lat. 36°06'05" N, long. 117°12' W; sec. 14, T 21 S, R 44 E). Named on Telescope Peak (1952) 15' quadrangle. According to Federal Writers' Project (p. 52-53), S.G. George gave the name to the canyon in 1860 after he became suspicious of his Indian guide and feared a surprise attack there. According to Palmer (p. 70), Charles Alvord named the canyon about 1860 because he was surprised when he found ore there.

Surprise Springs [INYO]: *springs,* two, 6 miles east of Ubehebe Crater in Grapevine Mountains (lat. 37°00'05" N, long. 117°20'35" W; sec. 18, T 11 S, R 43 E). Named on Ubehebe Crater (1957) 7.5' quadrangle.

Surveyors Well [INYO]: *well,* 7.25 miles northwest of Stovepipe Wells in Death Valley (lat. 36°44'50" N, long. 117°09'15" W). Named on Ballarat (1913) 1° quadrangle. Birnie (p. 131) called the feature Surveyors' Well; Palmer (p. 70) called it Surveyor's Well, and identified it as probably the feature that members of the Blasdel party called Wilson's Well in 1866.

Swager Canyon: see **Swauger Creek** [MONO].

Swager Creek: see **Swauger Creek** [MONO].

Swagger Creek: see **Swauger Creek** [MONO].

Swall Meadow [MONO]: *area,* 4.25 miles south-southeast of Toms Place (lat. 37°30'30" N, long. 118°38'30" W; on W line sec. 13, T 5 S, R 30 E).

Named on Casa Diablo Mountain (1953) 15' quadrangle.

Swall Meadow: see **Sherwin Meadow** [MONO].

Swamp Meadows [MONO]: *area*, 6.5 miles north-northeast of Fales Hot Springs around Lobdel Lake (lat. 38°26'45" N, long. 119°21'30" W; in and near sec. 20, T 7 N, R 24 E). Named on Bridgeport (1909) 30' quadrangle.

Swansea [INYO]: *locality*, 8.5 miles south of New York Butte near the east edge of Owens Valley (lat. 36°31'30" N, long. 117°54'10" W). Named on New York Butte (1950) 15' quadrangle. A smelter operated at the place from 1869 until 1874; the name is from the famous smelter town of Swansea in Wales (Hoover, Rensch, and Rensch, p. 119).

Swauger Creek [MONO]: *stream*, flows 14 miles to Buckeye Creek 2.5 miles west-northwest of Bridgeport (lat. 38°16'05" N, long. 119°16'15" W; sec. 25, T 5 N, R 24 E). Named on Fales Hot Springs (1956) 15' quadrangle. Called Yaney Creek on Wheeler's (1876-1877) map. The canyon of the upper part of the stream is called Swager Canyon on Bridgeport (1909) 30' quadrangle. The name "Swauger Creek" commemorates Samuel A. Swauger, who patented land along the stream in 1880 (Gudde, 1949, p. 349). United States Board on Geographic Names (1961a, p. 19) rejected the forms "Swager Creek" and "Swagger Creek" for the name. East Fork enters from the northeast 10 miles upstream from the mouth of the main stream; it is 2.5 miles long and is named on Fales Hot Springs (1956) 15' quadrangle.

Sweetwater: see **Sweetwater Mountains** [MONO].

Sweetwater Canyon [MONO]: *canyon*, drained by a stream that flows 4 miles to the State of Nevada 12 miles northeast of Fales Hot Springs (lat. 38°28'50" N, long. 119°15' W); the canyon is in Sweetwater Mountains. Named on Fales Hot Springs (1956) 15' quadrangle. Sampson's (1940) map has the name Sweetwater Cr. for the stream in the canyon.

Sweetwater Creek [INYO]: *stream*, flows 3 miles to the head of Wilson Canyon 4 miles west of Argus Peak (lat. 35°51' N, long. 117°31' W). Named on Trona (1949) 15' quadrangle. The stream is unnamed in Wilson Canyon. United States Board on Geographic Names (1983f, p. 3) approved the name "Sweetwater Wash" for the feature, and rejected the names "Sweetwater Creek" and "Wilson Creek."

Sweetwater Creek: see **Sweetwater Canyon** [MONO].

Sweetwater Mountain: see **Mount Patterson** [MONO].

Sweetwater Mountains [MONO]: *range*, between Bridgeport Valley and Antelope Valley; the northernmost part of the range is in the State of Nevada. Named on Bridgeport (1958), Desert Creek Peak (1956), and Fales Hot Springs (1956) 15' quadrangles. Called Sweetwater Range on Wheeler's (1876-1877) map and on Wellington (1893) 30' quadrangle. Postal authorities established Sweetwater post office 26 miles north of Bridgeport in 1925 and discontinued it in 1929 (Salley, p. 217)—presumably the post office was in or near Sweetwater Mountains.

Sweetwater Peak: see **Mount Patterson** [MONO].

Sweetwater Range: see **Sweetwater Mountains** [MONO].

Sweetwater Spring: see **Nevares Springs** [INYO].

Sweetwater Wash: see **Sweetwater Creek** [INYO].

Swift Lake [INYO]: *lake*, 400 feet long, 11.5 miles west of Big Pine (lat. 37°08' N, long. 118°29'55" W; sec. 29, T 9 S, R 32 E). Named on Big Pine (1950) 15' quadrangle. United States Board on Geographic Names (1985c, p. 3) approved the name "Summit Lake" for the feature.

Sword Lake [ALPINE]: *lake*, 1250 feet long, 3.25 miles west of Dardanelles Cone (lat. 38°24'25" N, long. 119°56' W). Named on Spicer Meadow Reservoir (1979) 7.5' quadrangle.

Sykes [INYO]: *locality*, 1 mile southwest of Coso Junction along Southern Pacific Railroad (lat. 36°02'10" N, long. 117°57'30" W; sec. 11, T 22 S, R 37 E). Named on Haiwee Reservoir (1951) 15' quadrangle

Sylvania Canyon [INYO]: *canyon*, 5.5 miles long, heads in the State of Nevada and opens into Fish Lake Valley 10.5 miles east-northeast of Deep Springs (lat. 37°24'45" N, long. 117°48' W; sec. 22, T 6 S, R 38 E); the canyon is in Sylvania Mountains. Named on Magruder Mountain (1957) and Soldier Pass (1958) 15' quadrangles.

Sylvania Mountains [INYO]: *range*, at the southeast end of Fish Lake Valley on California-Nevada State line. Named on Magruder Mountain (1957) and Soldier Pass (1958) 15' quadrangles. The range first was called Green Mountain and was renamed for Sylvania mining district, which is in the State of Nevada; the name "Sylvania" is from the mineral sylvanite, a telluride of silver found in the mining district (Carlson, p. 228).

Symmes Creek [INYO]: *stream*, flows 3.5 miles to Owens Valley 10.5 miles north of Mount Whitney (1) (lat. 36°43'45" N, long. 118°16'15" W; near W line sec. 10, T 14 S, R 34 E). Named on Independence (1951), Mount Pinchot (1953), and Mount Whitney (1956) 15' quadrangles. The name commemorates a pioneer family in the neighborhood (Schumacher, p. 35).

Syndicate Mill [MONO]: *locality*, 1.25 miles northeast of Bodie along Bodie Creek (lat. 38°13'25" N, long. 118°59'35" W; near E line sec. 9, T 4 N, R 27 E). Site named on Trench Canyon (1958) 15' quadrangle.

—T—

Table Hills: see **Malpais Mesa** [INYO].

Table Mountain [INYO]: *ridge*, north- to north-northeast-trending, 4.5 miles long, 5.5 miles northeast of Mount Darwin (lat. 37°12'30" N, long. 118°35'30" W). Named on Mount Goddard (1948) 15' quadrangle.

Taboose: see **Taboose Creek** [INYO].

Taboose Creek [INYO]: *stream*, flows 12 miles to Owens River 14 miles north of Independence (lat. 37°00' N, long. 118°13' W); the stream heads near Taboose Pass. Named on Big Pine (1950), Independence (1951), and Mount Pinchot (1953) 15' quadrangles. The name is from an Indian word for an edible legume that grows in the neighborhood (Hanna, p. 323). Indepedence (1951) 15' quadrangle shows Taboose ranch located near the mouth of the stream. Frickstad (p. 53) listed Taboose post office, established in 1876 and discontinued in 1878.

Taboose Pass [INYO]: *pass*, 17 miles northwest of Independence on Inyo-Fresno County line (lat. 36°59'05" N, long. 118°24'45" W); the pass is at the head of Taboose Creek. Named on Mount Pinchot (1953) 15' quadrangle.

Talc Canyon [INYO]: *canyon*, drained by a stream that flows 2 miles to Death Valley 12.5 miles southwest of Epaulet Peak (lat. 35°51'50" N, long. 116°42' W). Named on Confidence Hills (1950) 15' quadrangle.

Talc City Hills: see **Darwin** [INYO].

Talus [INYO]: *locality*, 3.25 miles north-northwest of Coso Junction along Southern Pacific Railroad (lat. 36°05'15" N, long. 117°58'20" W; near S line sec. 22, T 21 S, R 37 E); the place is near the mouth of Talus Canyon. Named on Haiwee Reservoir (1951) 15' quadrangle.

Talus Canyon [INYO]: *canyon*, drained by a stream that flows 4 miles to Rose Valley 3 miles northwest of Coso Junction (lat. 36° 04'55" N, long. 117°58'45" W; near W line sec. 27, T 21 S, R 37 E). Named on Haiwee Reservoir (1951) and Monache Mountain (1956) 15' quadrangles.

Tamarack: see **Woodfords** [ALPINE].

Tamarack Canyon [INYO]: *canyon*, 1.25 miles long, branches east from an unnamed canyon 13 miles north-northeast of Independence (lat. 36°58'20" N, long. 118°05'10" W). Named on Independence (1951) 15' quadrangle.

Tamarack Canyon: see **Pimentel Meadows** [MONO]; **Tamarack Creek** [MONO].

Tamarack Creek [ALPINE]: *stream*, flows 3.25 miles to Silver King Creek 7.5 miles east-northeast of Disaster Peak (lat. 38°29'25" N, long. 119°36'25" W; sec. 31, T 8 N, R 22 E). Named on Disaster Peak (1979) and Lost Cannon Peak (1954) 7.5' quadrangles. The canyon of present Tamarack Creek is called Poison Valley on Dardanelles (1898) 30' quadrangle. Gudde (1949, p. 268) associated the name "Poison Valley" with the death of stock that ate water hemlock and larkspur by the stream in the early days.

Tamarack Creek [MONO]: *stream*, flows 4.5 miles to Twin Lakes (1) 5.5 miles north-northeast of Matterhorn Peak (lat. 38°09'45" N, long. 119°19'40" W; sec. 33, T 4 N, R 24 E). Named on Matterhorn Peak (1956) 15' quadrangle. The canyon of the stream is called Tamarack Canyon on Bridgeport (1909) 30' quadrangle.

Tamarack Lake [ALPINE]:

(1) *lake*, 0.5 mile long, 6.5 miles north of Pacific Grade Summit (lat. 38°36'45" N, long. 119°54' W; at SW cor. sec. 21, T 9 N, R 19 E). Named on Pacific Valley (1979) 7.5' quadrangle.

(2) *lake*, 700 feet long, nearly 6 miles east of Disaster Peak (lat. 38° 27'20" N, long. 119°37'35" W). Named on Disaster Peak (1979) 7.5' quadrangle.

Tamarack Lake [MONO]: *lake*, 1300 feet long, 4.25 miles east-northeast of Matterhorn Peak (lat. 38°07'30" N, long. 119°18'55" W); the lake is along Tamarack Creek. Named on Matterhorn Peak (1956) 15' quadrangle.

Tamarack Lakes [INYO]: *lakes*, largest 1000 feet long, 6 miles north-northwest of Mount Tom (lat. 37°24'45" N, long. 118°42'30" W). Named on Mount Tom (1949) 15' quadrangle.

Tanks: see **The Tanks** [INYO].

Taylor Canyon [MONO]:

(1) *canyon*, 2 miles long, opens into Antelope Valley 4.5 miles south-southeast of Coleville (lat. 38°30'30" N, long. 119°28'15" W; sec. 29, T 8 N, R 23 E). Named on Desert Creek Peak (1956) and Fales Hot Springs (1956) 15' quadrangles.

(2) *canyon*, 5.5 miles long, drained by Adobe Creek above a point 7 miles north of Glass Mountain (lat. 37°52'15" N, long. 118°43'30" W; sec. 12, T 1 S, R 29 E). Named on Glass Mountain (1962) 15' quadrangle.

Taylor Springs: see **Benton Hot Springs** [MONO].

Taylor Valley [MONO]: *valley*, 7 miles east of Coleville on California-Nevada State line (lat. 38°34' N, long. 119°22'30" W). Named on Desert Creek Peak (1956) 15' quadrangle.

Teakettle Junction [INYO]: *locality*, 11 miles south-southeast of Dry Mountain in Racetrack Valley (lat. 36°45'40" N, long. 117°32'30" W). Named on Dry Mountain (1957) 15' quadrangle.

Tebo Creek: see **Thibaut Creek** [INYO].

Tecopa [INYO]: *village,* 9 miles south-southeast of Shoshone along Amargosa River (lat. 35°50'55" N, long. 116°13'30" W; sec. 9, T 20 N, R 7 E). Named on Tecopa (1950) 15' quadrangle, which shows a dismantled rail line at the place. The name "Tecopa" is said to be for an Indian (Lingenfelter, p. 22). Brothers William D. Brown and Robert D. Brown laid out a townsite in 1875 and called it Brownsville, but Jonas Osborne purchased the site and renamed it Tecopa (Lingenfelter, p. 137, 139). Mines were discovered in the neighborhood in the 1860's, and by 1877 most of the people in the mining district had settled at this original site of Tecopa (Paher, p. 19), which was situated 5 miles southeast of Resting Springs and just north of Tecopa Pass (Palmer, p. 71). Present Tecopa was built later along Tonopah and Tidewater Railroad, which was completed to the site in 1907 (Myrick, p. 555). Postal authorities established Tecopa post office in 1877, discontinued it in 1881, reestablished it at the new site in 1907, discontinued it in 1931, and reestablished it in 1932 (Frickstad, p. 53). Postal authorities established Kasson post office 12 miles northwest of the first site of Tecopa in 1879 and discontinued it the same year (Salley, p. 109). The name "Kasson" recalls Amasa C. Kasson, a Milwaukee investor who was swindled by the promoters of a fake mining venture at the place (Lingenfelter, p. 144).

Tecopa Hills: see **Sperry Hills** [INYO]; **Tecopa Hot Springs** [INYO].

Tecopa Hot Springs [INYO]: *spring,* 1.5 miles north of Tecopa (lat. 35°52'15" N, long. 116°13'50" W; sec. 33, T 21 S, R 7 E). Named on Tecopa (1950) 15' quadrangle. Avawatz Mountains (1933) 1° quadrangle shows some hot springs at the place. United States Board on Geographic Names (1966b, p. 7) approved the name "Tecopa Hills" for a range located just north of Tecopa and south of Tecopa Hot Springs; the Board rejected the name "Tecopa Hot Springs Hills" for the feature.

Tecopa Hot Springs Hills: see **Tecopa Hills**, under **Tecopa Hot Springs** [INYO].

Tecopa Pass [INYO]: *pass,* 8 miles east-southeast of Tecopa at the south end of Nopah Range (lat. 35°48'10" N, long. 116°06' W; sec. 27, T 20 N, R 8 E). Named on Tecopa (1950) 15' quadrangle.

Telephone Canyon [INYO]: *canyon,* 4.25 miles long, opens into lowlands 11.5 miles north-northwest of Emigrant Pass (1) (lat. 36° 29'35" N, long. 117°12'25" W). Named on Emigrant Canyon (1952) 15' quadrangle.

Telephone Gulch [ALPINE]: *canyon,* drained by a stream that flows 1.5 miles to Summit City Creek 8 miles north of Mount Reba (lat. 38°37'15" N, long. 120°02' W). Named on Caples Lake (1979) and Mokelumne Peak (1979) 7.5' quadrangles.

Telephone Spring [INYO]: *spring,* 10.5 miles north-northwest of Emigrant Pass (1) on the west side of Tucki Mountain (lat. 36°28'45" N, long. 117°11'45" W); the spring is in Telephone Canyon. Named on Emigrant Canyon (1952) 15' quadrangle, which indicates that the spring is dry. National Park Service officials proposed the name, apparently because the telephone line that ran from Rhyolite, Nevada, to Skidoo in 1906 passed through the canyon that contains the spring (Palmer, p. 71).

Telescope Mountain: see **Telescope Peak** [INYO].

Telescope Mountains: see **Panamint Range** [INYO].

Telescope Peak [INYO]: *peak,* 34 miles south of Stovepipe Wells in Panamint Range (lat. 36°10'10" N, long. 117°05'15" W; sec. 27, T 20 S, R 45 E). Altitude 11,049 feet. Named on Telescope Peak (1952) 15' quadrangle. W.T. Henderson climbed the peak in 1861 and named it for the extensive view from the top (Spears, p. 23). Hanks (p. 36) called it Telescope Mountain.

Temple Crag [INYO]: *peak,* 12 miles west-southwest of Big Pine (lat. 37°06'35" N, long. 118°29'25" W). Altitude 12,999 feet. Named on Big Pine (1950) 15' quadrangle. The peak first was called Mount Alice (Gudde, 1969, p. 7), but United States Board on Geographic Names (1933, p. 748) rejected this name for the feature.

Tennessee Spring [INYO]: *spring,* 13 miles east-southeast of Coso Peak near the west base of Argus Range (lat. 36°06'15" N, long. 117°30'45" W; near W line sec. 13, T 21 S, R 41 E). Named on Coso Peak (1951) 15' quadrangle.

Termination Valley: see **Eureka Valley** [INYO].

Terry Canyon [MONO]: *canyon,* drained by a stream that flows nearly 2 miles to Mill Creek (1) 9 miles north-northwest of Fales Hot Springs (lat. 38°27'50" N, long. 119°29'15" W; sec. 7, T 7 N, R 23 E). Named on Chris Flat (1954) 7.5' quadrangle.

Teton Creek: see **Little Teton Creek** [ALPINE].

Texas Spring [INYO]: *spring,* 1 mile east-northeast of Furnace Creek Inn (lat. 36°27'30" N, long. 116°50'15" W; near N line sec. 23, T 27 N, R 1 E). Named on Furnace Creek (1952) 15' quadrangle. The feature first was known as Tex's Spring; this name was for "Bellerin Tex" Bennett, who developed the spring (Hanna, p. 328).

Texas Spring Campground [INYO]: *locality,* 0.5 mile north of Furnace Creek Inn (lat. 36°27'30" N, long. 116°51'10" W; sec. 15, T 27 N, R 1 E); the place is 1 mile west of Texas Spring. Named on Furnace Creek (1952) 15' quadrangle.

Tex's Spring: see **Texas Spring** [INYO].

Thebe [INYO]: *locality,* 5.5 miles south-southeast of Independence (lat. 36°43'55" N, long. 118°09'30" W; sec. 10, T 14 S, R 35 E). Named on Mount Whitney (1907) 30' quadrangle. Called Manzanar on Mount Whitney (1937) 30' quadrangle. Postal authorities established Thebe post office in 1896, changed the name to Manzanar in 1911, and discontinued it in 1929 (Frickstad, p. 52, 53). Thebe developed in an area of farmland that in the early days was known as George's Creek; after the planting of large apple and pear orchards in the neighborhood, the community was named Manzanar—presumably from *manzanar,* which means "apple" in Spanish—but the orchards died after construction of the aqueduct that takes Owens Valley water to Los Angeles; during World War II, the government interned 10,000 people of Japanese ancestry at the place (Schumacher, p. 33-34).

The Butte: see **Striped Butte** [INYO].

The Cleaver [MONO]: *ridge,* north-northeast-trending, 1.25 miles long, 1.25 miles north-northwest of Matterhorn Peak (lat. 38°06'35" N, long. 119°23'20" W). Named on Matterhorn Peak (1956) 15' quadrangle.

The Dardanelles [ALPINE]: *ridge,* west- to south-southwest-trending, 5.5 miles long, 10 miles south-southwest of Ebbetts Pass (lat. 38°24'45" N, long. 119°53' W); Dardanelles Cone is the highest point on the ridge. Named on Dardanelles Cone (1979) and Spicer Meadow Reservoir (1979) 7.5' quadrangles. United States Board on Geographic Names (1978b, p. 2) rejected the name "Dardanelles Mountain" for the feature, and attributed the name "The Dardanelles" to members of the Whitney survey, who saw a fancied resemblance of rocks on the ridge to castles guarding the Dardanelles in Turkey.

The Dunes [INYO]:

(1) *area,* 6 miles southeast of the mouth of Paiute Canyon in Saline Valley (lat. 36°46' N, long. 117°51' W). Named on Waucoba Wash (1951) 15' quadrangle.

(2) *area,* 6 miles west-northwest of Panamint Butte in Panamint Valley (lat. 36°27'40" N, long. 117°27'15" W; on W line sec. 17, T 17 S, R 42 E). Named on Panamint Butte (1951) 15' quadrangle. Called White Sand Hills on Wheeler's (1877) map.

The Elbow [ALPINE]: *locality,* 2 miles west-northwest of Ebbetts Pass (lat. 38°33'10" N, long. 119°50'50" W; near N line sec. 14, T 8 N, R 19 E); the place is at a sharp bend in a road where the road crosses Elbow Creek. Named on Ebbetts Pass (1979) 7.5' quadrangle.

The Grandstand [INYO]: *hill,* 1 mile east of Ubehebe Peak (lat. 36° 41'35" N, long. 117°33'55" W); the feature is at The Racetrack. Named on Ubehebe Peak (1950) 15' quadrangle. The feature resembles a grandstand for spectators at The Racetrack (Palmer, p. 59).

The Hogsback [INYO]: *ridge,* east-northeast-trending, 1 mile long, 10 miles northwest of Independence (lat. 36°54'30" N, long. 118° 19' W). Named on Mount Pinchot (1953) 15' quadrangle.

The Hot Springs [MONO]: *springs,* 2.5 miles south-southeast of Bridgeport (lat. 38°13'25" N, long. 119°12'50" W; sec. 9, T 4 N, R 25 E); the springs are near the mouth of Hot Springs Canyon. Named on Bodie (1958) 15' quadrangle.

The Hunchback [INYO]: *peak,* 8 miles east of Mount Darwin (lat. 37°10'50" N, long. 118°31'25" W; sec. 7 T 9 S, R 32 E). Altitude 12,226 feet. Named on Mount Goddard (1948) 15' quadrangle.

The Iceberg [ALPINE]: *relief feature,* less than 2 miles south-southwest of Disaster Peak (lat. 38°25'25" N, long. 119°44'40" W). Named on Disaster Peak (1979) 7.5' quadrangle. The name is for the fancied resemblance of the feature to an iceberg (Gudde, 1949, p. 158).

The Jumpoff [MONO]: *relief feature,* 7 miles east of Benton (lat. 37° 48'45" N, long. 118°21' W); the name applies to the steep east side of a peak in White Mountains. Named on Benton (1962) 15' quadrangle.

The Junction House: see **Sonora Junction** [MONO].

The Narrows [INYO]:

(1) *narrows,* nearly 4 miles north-northwest of Waucoba Mountain at the west end of Marble Canyon (2) (lat. 37°04'30" N, long. 118° 01'30" W; sec. 15, T 10 S, R 36 E). Named on Waucoba Mountain (1951) 15' quadrangle.

(2) *narrows,* 9 miles southwest of Epaulet Peak along Amargosa River between Confidence Hills and Black Mountains (lat. 35° 52' N, long. 116°37' W). Named on Confidence Hills (1950) 15' quadrangle.

The Nipple [ALPINE]: *peak,* nearly 5 miles southeast of Carson Pass (lat. 38°38'25" N, long. 119°55'55" W; on S line sec. 7, T 9 N, R 19 E). Altitude 9342 feet. Named on Carson Pass (1979) 7.5' quadrangle.

The Pothole [INYO]: *lake,* 200 feet long, 7.5 miles north-northwest of Mount Whitney (1) on upper reaches of Shepherd Creek (lat. 36°41' N, long. 118°20'10" W). Named on Mount Whitney (1956) 15' quadrangle.

The Racetrack [INYO]: *dry lake,* nearly 3 miles long, 1.5 miles east-southeast of Ubehebe Peak (lat. 36°41' N, long. 117°33'45" W). Named on Ubehebe Peak (1950) 15' quadrangle. The name is for the resemblance of the feature to a nearly circular racetrack, complete with a rocky "grandstand" (Gudde, 1949, p. 278). Jack Salsberry laid out a townsite a couple of miles northwest of The Racetrack in the early 1900's and called it Salina City—later the place was renamed Latimer to flatter a heavy investor in mines of the neighborhood; a rival place called Ubehebe City was laid out at the south end of The Racetrack (Lingenfelter, p. 329).

The Roughs [MONO]: *area,* 7.5 miles northwest of Matterhorn Peak (lat. 38°10'40" N, long. 119°27'30" W). Named on Matterhorn Peak (1956) 15' quadrangle.

The Sisters [MONO]: *peaks,* two, less than 1 mile east-northeast of Fourth of July Peak (lat. 38°39'50" N, long. 120°00'35" W; sec. 33, T 10 N, R 18 E). Altitudes 10,045 feet and 10,153 feet. Named on Caples Lake (1979) 7.5' quadrangle.

The Tanks [INYO]: *locality,* nearly 6 miles east-southeast of Argus Peak in Searles Valley (lat. 35°50'05" N, long. 117°20'45" W; sec. 21, T 24 S, R 43 E). Named on Trona (1949) 15' quadrangle. Waring and Huguenin (p. 35) reported that good water was piped to the place from a tunnel near the mouth of what they called Argus Cañon—probably present Great Falls Basin. Wheeler's (1877) map has the name "Water Sta." along a road at about the site of The Tanks. Thompson's (1921) map shows three wells near The Tanks: Ott Well, located 1.5 miles to the northeast; Farm Well, located 1.25 miles to the southeast; and Well No. 1, located about 1.5 miles to the southeast.

The Thumb [INYO]: *peak,* 10.5 miles southwest of Big Pine (lat. 37°04'15" N, long. 118°26'45" W). Altitude 13,388 feet. Named on Big Pine (1950) 15' quadrangle. Windsor B. Putnam made the first ascent of the peak in 1921 and named it for its resemblance to the end of a thumb; the peak also is called East Palisade (Gudde, 1949, p. 361).

Thibau Creek: see **Thibaut Creek** [INYO].

Thibaut Creek [INYO]: *stream,* flows 4.5 miles to lowlands 6.5 miles northwest of Independence (lat. 36°51'50" N, long. 118° 17' W; sec, 32, T 12 S, R 34 E). Named on Independence (1951) 15' quadrangle, where it is called Thibau Creek, and on Mount Pinchot (1953) 15' quadrangle. The name commemorates a French family who lived by the creek in the 1890's; it sometimes is spelled as it is pronounced, "Tebo" (Gudde, 1949, p. 360). The stream now discharges into the aqueduct that takes Owens Valley water to Los Angeles.

Thimble Peak [ALPINE]: *peak,* 2 miles west of Fourth of July Peak (lat. 38°39'45" N, long. 120°03'35" W; sec. 2, T 9 N, R 17 E). Altitude 9805 feet. Named on Caples Lake (1979) 7.5' quadrangle.

Thimble Peak [INYO]: *peak,* 7.5 miles east of the mouth of Titus Canyon (lat. 36°48'45" N, long. 117°02'20" W). Altitude 6381 feet. Named on Grapevine Peak (1957) 15' quadrangle. The name is for the shape of the peak; the feature also is known as Squaw Teat (Palmer, p. 73).

Third Lake [INYO]: *lake,* 1300 feet long, 11.5 miles west-southwest of Big Pine along North Fork Big Pine Creek (lat. 37°07'15" N, long. 118°29'40" W; on E line sec. 32, T 9 S, R 32 E); the lake is situated between Second Lake and Fourth Lake. Named on Big Pine (1950) 15' quadrangle. The lake is one of the group called Big Pine Lakes.

Thompson: see **Mount Thompson** [INYO].

Thompson Camp [INYO]: *locality,* 3.25 miles south of Telescope Peak near the head of Surprise Canyon (lat. 36°07'20" N, long. 117°05'10" W). Named on Telescope Peak (1952) 15' quadrangle.

Thompson Canyon [INYO]: *canyon,* drained by a stream that flows 3 miles to lowlands 9 miles north-northeast of Maturango Peak (lat. 36°14' N, long. 117°25'45" W); Thompson Spring is in the canyon. Named on Maturango Peak (1951) 15' quadrangle.

Thompson Lake [INYO]: *lake,* 950 feet long, nearly 4 miles east of Mount Darwin (lat. 37°10'05" N, long. 118°36'10" W; on E line sec. 17, T 9 S, R 31 E). Named on Mount Goddard (1948) 15' quadrangle.

Thompson Peak [ALPINE]: *peak,* nearly 5 miles south-southwest of Freel Peak on Alpine-El Dorado County line (lat. 38°47'50" N, long. 119°56'35" W; sec. 13, T 11 N, R 18 E). Altitude 9340 feet. Named on Freel Peak (1955) 7.5' quadrangle. The name commemorates John A. "Snowshoe" Thompson (Gudde, 1949, p. 360).

Thompson Ridge [INYO]: *ridge,* north-trending, 3 miles long, 3.5 miles east of Mount Darwin (lat. 37°09'45" N, long. 118°36'30" W); the ridge extends north from Mount Thompson. Named on Mount Goddard (1948) 15' quadrangle.

Thompsons: see **Casa Diablo Hot Springs** [MONO].

Thompson Spring [INYO]: *spring,* 8 miles north-northeast of Maturango Peak in Argus Range (lat. 36°13'50" N, long. 117°27'40" W); the spring is in Thompson Canyon. Named on Maturango Peak (1951) 15' quadrangle.

Thornburg Canyon [ALPINE]: *canyon,* 2.5 miles long, along Spratt Creek above a point 3.25 miles southwest of Markleeville (lat. 38° 39'45" N, long. 119°49'30" W; near S line sec. 31, T 10 N, R 20 E). Named on Markleeville (1979) 7.5' quadrangle.

Thorndike Camp [INYO]: *locality,* 4.5 miles north-northeast of Telescope Peak in Wildrose Canyon (lat. 36°14'10" N, long. 117° 04'15" W; sec. 35, T 19 S, R 45 E). Named on Telescope Peak (1952) 15' quadrangle.

Thorndike Canyon: see **South Park Canyon** [INYO].

Thorndyke Canyon [INYO]: *canyon,* 2 miles long, opens into Cactus Flat 11 miles north-northeast of Coso Junction (lat. 36° 11' N, long. 117°51'20" W; sec. 21, T 20 S, R 38 E). Named on Haiwee Reservoir (1951) 15' quadrangle, which shows Thorndyke mine near the head of the canyon.

Thor Peak [INYO]: *peak,* 1.5 miles east of Mount Whitney (1) (lat. 36°34'35" N, long. 118°15'50" W). Altitude 12,300 feet. Named on Mount Whitney (1956) 15' quadrangle.

Through Canyon [INYO]: *canyon,* drained by a stream that heads in San Bernardino County and flows 4.5 miles to Death Valley 12.5 miles south-southwest of Epaulet Peak (lat. 35°48'30" N, long. 116°37' W). Named on Confidence Hills (1950) 15' quadrangle.

Thumb: see **The Thumb** [INYO].

Thunder and Lightning Lake [INYO]: *lake,* 0.5 mile long, 8.5 miles east of Mount Darwin (lat. 37°09'05" N, long. 118°31'10" W; sec. 19, T 9 S, R 32 E). Named on Mount Goddard (1948) 15' quadrangle.

Thunderbolt Peak [INYO]: *peak,* 10 miles east-southeast of Mount Darwin on Inyo-Fresno County line (lat. 37°05'50" N, long. 118° 31' W). Named on Mount Goddard (1948) 15' quadrangle.

Tibbets: see **Aberdeen** [INYO] (1).

Tibbotts: see **Aberdeen** [INYO] (2).

Tie Canyon: see **Scottys Castle** [INYO].

Timberline Tarns [INYO]: *lakes,* two, largest 700 feet long, 7.25 miles east-southeast of Mount Darwin (lat. 37°08' N, long. 118° 33' W; near SW cor. sec. 25, T 9 S, R 31 E). Named on Mount Goddard (1948) 15' quadrangle.

Timosea Peak [INYO]: *peak,* 13 miles north-northwest of Olancha (lat. 36°27'30" N, long. 118°05'10" W). Altitude 8625 feet. Named on Olancha (1956) 15' quadrangle.

Tinemaha: see **Fish Springs** [INYO] (2); **Mount Tinemaha** [INYO].

Tinemaha Creek [INYO]: *stream,* flows 13 miles to Owens River 7.5 miles south-southeast of Big Pine in Tinemaha Reservoir (lat. 37°03'55" N, long. 118°13'45" W; sec. 23, T 10 S, R 34 E). Named on Big Pine (1950) and Waucoba Mountain (1951) 15' quadrangles.

Tinemaha Lake [INYO]: *lake,* 600 feet long, 11 miles southwest of Big Pine (lat 37°02'35" N, long. 118°25'10" W); the lake is on upper reaches of Tinemaha Creek. Named on Big Pine (1950) 15' quadrangle.

Tinemaha Reservoir [INYO]: *intermittent lake,* 2 miles long, behind a dam on Owens River 8.5 miles south-southeast of Big Pine (lat. 37°03'20" N, long. 118°13'35" W; sec. 25, 26, T 10 S, R 34 E); the reservoir is at the confluence of Owens River and Tinemaha Creek. Named on Waucoba Mountain (1951) 15' quadrangle.

Tin Mountain [INYO]: *peak,* 8 miles east of Dry Mountain in Cottonwood Mountains (lat. 36°53'10" N, long. 117°27'15" W). Altitude 8953 feet. Named on Tin Mountain (1957) 15' quadrangle. According to Palmer (p. 73), the name probably is from reports of a deposit of tin ore.

Tioga: see **Bennettville** [MONO].

Tioga Crest [MONO]: *ridge,* south-trending, 2 miles long, 2.5 miles east-northeast of Mount Conness (lat. 37°59' N, long. 119°15'40" W). Named on Tuolumne Meadows (1956) 15' quadrangle.

Tioga Hill: see **Gaylor Peak** [MONO].

Tioga Lake [MONO]: *lake,* 3500 feet long, nearly 5 miles southeast of Mount Conness (lat. 37°55'30" N, long. 119°15'05" W; sec. 19, 30, T 1 N, R 25 E); the lake is less than 1 mile north-northeast of Tioga Pass. Named on Mono Craters (1953) and Tuolumne Meadows (1956) 15' quadrangles. Called Tioga Lake Reservoir on Sampson's (1940) map. The feature was known as Lake Jessie in 1860 (Hubbard), and as Lake Jessie Montrose about 1880 (DeDecker, p. 22).

Tioga Lake Reservoir: see **Tioga Lake** [MONO].

Tioga Lodge [MONO]: *locality,* 3.5 miles north-northwest of Lee Vining on the west shore of Mono Lake (lat. 38°00'05" N, long. 119°09' W; sec. 30, T 2 N, R 26 E). Named on Bridgeport (1909) 30' quadrangle, which also shows Mono Lake P.O. at the site. Mono Craters (1953) 15' quadrangle shows Mono Lake P.O. situated 1 mile farther south-southeast. The place also was known as Hammond Station, and as Hammond's (Billeb, p. 41, 155). Jack Hammond operated a stage stop and tollgate there (La Braque, p. 13).

Tioga Pass [MONO]: *pass,* 5.25 miles southeast of Mount Conness on Mono-Tuolumne County line (lat. 37°54'40" N, long. 119°15'25" W; near N line sec. 31, T 1 N, R 25 E). Named on Tuolumne Meadows (1956) 15' quadrangle. The name is from Tioga County, New York (United States Board on Geographic Names, 1934, p. 25), and was applied first to a mine near the pass, and then to the pass itself (Smith, Genny, p. 29). The feature also was known as McLean's Pass (Hubbard), and Bancroft's (1864) map shows Browns Pass at or near the site.

Tioga Peak [MONO]: *peak,* 7 miles west of Lee Vining (lat. 37° 57' N, long. 119°14'45" W; sec. 17, T 1 N, R 25 E). Altitude 11,513 feet. Named on Mono Craters (1953) and Tuolumne Meadows (1956) 15' quadrangles.

Titanothere Canyon [INYO]: *canyon,* drained by a stream that flows 8 miles to Death Valley 7.5 miles southeast of the mouth of Titus Canyon (lat. 36°45' N, long. 117°04'30" W; sec. 10, T 14 S, R 45 E). Named on Grapevine Peak (1957) 15' quadrangle. National Park Service officials proposed the name after discovery of fossil bones of a titanothere near the head of the canyon (Palmer, p. 73).

Titus Canyon [INYO]: *canyon,* heads in the State of Nevada and opens into Death Valley 16 miles east-southeast of Tin Mountain (lat. 36°49'15" N, long. 117°10'20" W; near W line sec. 14, T 13 S, R 44 E). Named on Grapevine Peak (1957) 15' quadrangle. The name recalls Morris Titus, a young mining engineer who perished in the canyon in 1906 (Cronkhite, p. 10).

T.J. Lake [MONO]: *lake,* 1400 feet long, 3 miles south-southeast of Mammoth Mountain (lat. 37°35'30" N, long. 119°00'25" W). Named on Devils Postpile (1953) 15' quadrangle. The name is from the initials of Tom Jones, one of the first supervisors of Inyo National Forest (Smith, Genny, p. 51). The lake is one of the group called Mammoth Lakes

Tobacco Flat [MONO]: *area,* 3.5 miles northeast of Mount Morrison (lat. 37°36' N, long. 118°49'05" W; sec. 18, T 4 S, R 29 E). Named on Mount Morrison (1953) 15' quadrangle.

Todd's Meadows: see **Grays Meadow** [INYO].

Toler Creek [MONO]: *stream,* flows 6 miles to Fish Lake Valley 10 miles east of White Mountain Peak (lat. 37°36'40" N, long. 118°04'45" W). Named on Mount Barcroft (1962) 15' quadrangle.

Toll House [INYO]: *locality,* 7.5 miles northeast of Big Pine on the road from Owens Valley to Westgard Pass (lat. 37°14'40" N, long. 118°11'30" W; sec. 24, T 8 S, R 34 E). Named on Waucoba Mountain (1951) 15' quadrangle, which shows a spring at the spot—the spring probably is the one that Waring and Huguenin (p. 35) called Toll House Spring.

Tollhouse Canyon [MONO]: *canyon,* drained by a stream that flows nearly 1 mile to the canyon of West Walker River 6.5 miles north-northwest of Fales Hot Springs (lat. 38°26'10" N, long. 119°27'10" W; sec. 21, T 7 N, R 23 E); the canyon is north of Tollhouse Flat. Named on Chris Flat (1954) 7.5' quadrangle.

Tollhouse Flat [MONO]: *area,* 6 miles north-northwest of Fales Hot Springs along West Walker River (lat. 38°25'50" N, long. 119° 27' W; near NW cor. sec. 27, T 7 N, R 23 E). Named on Chris Flat (1954) 7.5' quadrangle.

Toll House Spring: see **Toll House** [INYO].

Tom: see **Mount Tom** [INYO].

Toms Place [MONO]: *settlement,* 10 miles east of Mount Morrison along Rock Creek (3) (lat. 37°33'45" N, long. 118°40'45" W; sec. 32, 33, T 4 S, R 30 E). Named on Casa Diablo Mountain (1953) 15' quadrangle. A resort called Hans Lof's, for the owner, started at the place in 1919; Tom Yernby and his wife bought the resort in 1922 and changed the name (Hanna, p. 331). Postal authorities established Tom's Place post office in 1963 (Salley, p. 223).

Topaz [MONO]: *locality,* 2.5 miles north-northeast of Coleville (lat. 38°36'10" N, long. 119°29'50" W; near N line sec. 30, T 9 N, R 23 E). Named on Desert Creek Peak (1956) 15' quadrangle. According to Quimby (p. 344), T.B. Rickey had a ranch at the place, and when a village developed there, Mrs. Rickey named the community for the topaz coloring of quaking aspen trees in nearby canyons

Topaz Lake [MONO]: *lake,* 3 miles long, 8 miles north of Coleville on California-Nevada State line (lat. 38°41' N, long. 119°32' W); the lake is 4.25 miles north-northwest of Topaz. Named on Topaz Lake (1956) 15' quadrangle. Water of West Walker River inundated the site in 1920 and 1921 to form the lake; a smaller lake at the place before 1920 was called Alkali Lake (Hanna, p. 331).

Topaz Post Office [MONO]: *locality,* 3 miles north of Coleville (lat. 38°36'40" N, long. 119°31'10" W; sec. 24, T 9 N, R 22 E); the place is 1.25 miles west-northwest of Topaz. Named on Topaz Lake (1956) 15' quadrangle. Postal authorities established Topaz post office in 1885, discontinued it in 1922, and reestablished it in 1926 (Frickstad, p. 105).

Topsy Turvey Lake [INYO]: *lake,* 1300 feet long, 2 miles east-northeast of Mount Darwin (lat. 37°10'25" N, long. 118°38'05" W; near N line sec. 18, T 9 S, R 31 E). Named on Mount Goddard (1948) 15' quadrangle. Art Schober, a packer, named the lake for huge boulders scattered about every which way (Schumacher, p. 96).

Tortoise Mountains: see **Argus Range** [INYO].

Tower Canyon [MONO]: *canyon,* 2 miles long, drained by West Walker River above a point 2.5 miles north-northeast of Tower Peak (lat. 38°10'45" N, long. 119°31'50" W). Named on Tower Peak (1956) 15' quadrangle.

Tower Lake [MONO]: *lake,* 1200 feet long, 1 mile north of Tower Peak (lat. 38°09'35" N, long. 119°33' W). Named on Tower Peak (1956) 15' quadrangle.

Tower Peak [MONO]: *peak,* 19 miles west-southwest of Bridgeport on Mono-Tuolumne County line (lat. 38°08'40" N, long. 119°32'45" W). Altitude 11,755 feet. Named on Tower Peak (1956) 15' quadrangle. G.H. Goddard gave the name "Castle Peak" to the feature in 1859, but that name was transferred to another peak; members of the Whitney survey then named present Tower Peak (Hanna, p. 332).

Towne Pass [INYO]: *pass,* nearly 5 miles east-southeast of Panamint Butte in Panamint Range (lat. 36°24' N, long. 117°16'40" W). Named on Panamint Butte (1951) 15' quadrangle. Called Town's Pass on Wheeler's (1877) map. Members of the Darwin French party in 1860 called it Towne's Pass for an emigrant of 1849 (Federal Writers' Project, p. 19). The Jayhawker party of emigrants called it Martin Pass, for James Martin, another emigrant of 1849 (Palmer, p. 47). Palmer (p. 74) gave the name "Townsend Pass" as an alternate.

Towne's Pass: see **Towne Pass** [INYO].

Townsend Pass: see **Towne Pass** [INYO].

Town's Pass: see **Towne Pass** [INYO].

Toyabe Campground [ALPINE]: *locality,* 3 miles west of Markleeville near Hot Springs Creek (lat. 38°41'55" N, long. 119°49'55" W; near E line sec. 24, T 10 N, R 19 E); the place is in Toyabe National Forest. Named on Markleeville (1979) 7.5' quadrangle.

Trafton Mountain: see **Benton Hot Springs** [MONO].

Trail Canyon [INYO]: *canyon,* 8.5 miles long, opens into Death Valley 11.5 miles south-southwest of Furnace Creek Inn (lat. 36° 18'30" N, long. 116°58' W). Named on Emigrant Canyon (1952) and Furnace Creek (1952) 15' quadrangles. South Fork branches south nearly 5 miles upstream from the mouth of the main canyon; it is 3.25 miles long and is named on Emigrant Canyon (1952) 15' quadrangle.

Trail Crest [INYO]: *locality,* nearly 1.5 miles south of Mount Whitney (1) on Inyo-Tulare County line (lat. 36°33'35" N, long. 118°17'30" W). Named on Mount Whitney (1956) 15' quadrangle, which shows the trail to Mount Whitney reaching the crest of the Sierra Nevada at the spot.

Trail Pass [INYO]: *pass,* 14 miles northwest of Olancha on Inyo-Tulare County line (lat. 36°25'40" N, long. 118°10'30" W; sec. 22, T 17 S, R 35 E). Named on Olancha (1956) 15' quadrangle. Trail Pass has been called "new" Mulkey Pass, and Mulkey Pass has been called "old" Mulkey Pass (Schumacher, p. 80).

Trail Peak [INYO]: *peak,* 15 miles northwest of Olancha on Inyo-Tulare County line (lat. 36°25'40" N, long. 118°11'20" W; sec. 21, T 17 S, R 35 E); the peak is less than 1 mile west of Trail Pass. Altitude 11,623 feet. Named on Olancha (1956) 15' quadrangle.

Tramway: see **Keeler** [INYO].

Travertine Hot Springs [MONO]: *spring,* 1.5 miles east-southeast of Bridgeport (lat. 38°14'45" N, long. 119°12'15" W; sec. 34, T 5 N, R 25 E). Named on Bodie (1958) 15' quadrangle. Tucker (p. 402-403) called the feature Travertine Springs, and noted that three springs there are associated with ridges of banded onyx marble.

Travertine Point [INYO]: *relief feature,* 3.5 miles north of Ryan (lat. 36°22'10" N, long. 116°39'50" W). Named on Ryan (1952) 15' quadrangle.

Travertine Springs [INYO]: *springs,* 1.5 miles east-southeast of Furnace Creek Inn near Furnace Creek Wash (lat. 36°26'30" N, long. 116°49'40" W). Named on Furnace Creek (1952) 15' quadrangle. The name is from the abundance of travertine near the springs (Hanna, p. 333). The feature first was known as Hadley Spring, for Ebenezer Hadley, compass man of the party that surveyed the neighborhood in 1857 (Palmer, p. 34).

Travertine Springs: see **Travertine Hot Springs** [MONO].

Treasure Lakes [INYO]:

(1) *lakes,* three, largest 0.25 mile long, 1 mile east of Mount Abbot (lat. 37°23'15" N, long. 118°45'55" W). Named on Mount Abbot (1953) 15' quadrangle.

(2) *lakes,* five, largest 1000 feet long, 5.5 miles east-southeast of Mount Darwin (lat. 37°08'25" N, long. 118°34'30" W; in and near sec. 27, T 9 S, R 31 E). Named on Mount Goddard (1948) 15' quadrangle. The name is for golden trout planted in the lakes (United States Board on Geographic Names, 1938, p. 55). Mr. and Mrs. W.C. Parcher named the lakes—their son carried trout to stock them (Schumacher, p. 93).

Trench Canyon [MONO]: *canyon,* 3 miles long, opens into Mono Valley from the north-northeast 7.5 miles east-southeast of Bodie (lat. 38°10'15" N, long. 118°53'15" W). Named on Trench Canyon (1958) 15' quadrangle. Russell (p. 272) named the feature "from the peculiar form of this straight, narrow gorge."

Tres Plumas Creek [MONO]: *stream,* flows 3 miles to Cottonwood Creek (2) 9.5 miles southeast of White Mountain Peak (lat. 37°31'55" N, long. 118°08'30" W); the stream heads at Tres Plumas Meadow. Named on Mount Barcroft (1962) 15' quadrangle.

Tres Plumas Flat [MONO]: *area,* 8.5 miles southeast of White Mountain Peak (lat. 37°33'15" N, long. 118°08' W); the place is east of Tres Plumas Creek. Named on Mount Barcroft (1962) 15' quadrangle.

Tres Plumas Meadow [MONO]: *area,* 7 miles southeast of White Mountain Peak (lat. 37°33'45" N, long. 118°09'45" W). Named on Mount Barcroft (1962) 15' quadrangle.

Triangle Spring [INYO]: *spring,* 5.5 miles north-northwest of Stovepipe Wells in Death Valley (lat. 36°43'40" N, long. 117°08'05" W; sec. 19, T 14 S, R 45 E). Named on Stovepipe Wells (1952) 15' quadrangle.

Trojan Peak [INYO]: *peak,* 4.5 miles north-northwest of Mount Whitney (1) (lat. 36°38'30" N, long. 118°18'50" W). Altitude 13,950 feet. Named on Mount Whitney (1956) 15' quadrangle. United States Board on Geographic Names (1954, p. 4) approved the name, which was given to honor University of Southern California, whose students have the nickname "Trojans"—the Board rejected the name "Southern California Peak" for the feature.

Truckee River: see **Upper Truckee River** [ALPINE].

Truman Canyon [MONO]: *canyon,* on California-Nevada State line, 3 miles long, opens into Benton Valley 7 miles north of Benton (lat. 37°55' N, long. 118°28'15" W; sec. 29, T 1 N, R 32 E). Named on Benton (1962) 15' quadrangle.

Trumble Lake [MONO]: *lake,* 1000 feet long, 7.25 miles east-southeast of

Matterhorn Peak (lat. 38°03'10" N, long. 119°15'25" W; near N line sec. 7, T 2 N, R 25 E). Named on Matterhorn Peak (1956) 15' quadrangle. The name is for John S. Trumble, who patented land by the lake in 1880 (Gudde, 1949, p. 370). The feature is one of the group called Virginia Lakes.

Tryon Meadow [ALPINE]: *area,* nearly 3 miles south of Ebbetts Pass (lat. 38°30'20" N, long. 119°48'05" W; sec. 32, T 8 N, R 20 E); the place is 1.25 miles southwest of Tryon Peak. Named on Ebbetts Pass (1979) 7.5' quadrangle.

Tryon Peak [ALPINE]: *peak,* 2 miles southeast of Ebbetts Pass (lat. 38°31'20" N, long. 119°47'15" W). Altitude 9970 feet. Named on Ebbetts Pass (1979) 7.5' quadrangle.

Tuber Canyon [INYO]: *canyon,* 7.5 miles long, opens into Panamint Valley 8 miles west-northwest of Telescope Peak (lat. 36°12'40" N, long. 117°13'30" W). Named on Telescope Peak (1952) 15' quadrangle. According to Palmer (p. 52), the feature first was called Narboe Canyon, or Norboe Canyon, evidently for P.M. Narboe. Wheeler's (1877) map has the name "Narboe Cañon" for present Hall Canyon.

Tuber Spring [INYO]: *spring,* 3 miles north-northwest of Telescope Peak in Panamint Range (lat. 36°12'50" N, long. 117°06'15" W; sec. 9, T 20 S, R 45 E); the spring is in Tuber Canyon. Named on Telescope Peak (1952) 15' quadrangle.

Tub Springs [INYO]: *springs,* four, 5.5 miles west of Independence (lat. 36°48'05" N, long. 118°17'55" W; sec. 17, T 13 S, R 34 E). Named on Mount Pinchot (1953) 15' quadrangle.

Tucki Mountain [INYO]: *range,* 10 miles south of Stovepipe Wells between Emigrant Wash and Death Valley (lat. 36°31' N, long. 117°06' W). Named on Emigrant Canyon (1952), Furnace Creek (1952), and Stovepipe Wells (1952) 15' quadrangles. Mendenhall (p. 35) called the range Tucki Mountain, or Sheep Mountain. *Tucki* supposedly means "sheep" in an Indian dialect (Palmer, p. 75).

Tucki Wash [INYO]: *stream,* flows about 8 miles to Death Valley 11 miles northeast of Emigrant Pass (1) (lat. 36°27'05" N, long. 117°00' W); the stream heads on Tucki Mountain. Named on Emigrant Canyon (1952) and Furnace Creek (1952) 15' quadrangles.

Tule Holes: see **Tule Spring** [INYO] (2).

Tule Lake [MONO]: *lake,* 300 feet long, 4 miles west of Fales Hot Springs (lat. 38°21'35" N, long. 119°28'15" W; near N line sec. 20, T 6 N, R 23 E). Named on Fales Hot Springs (1954) 7.5' quadrangle.

Tule Spring [INYO]:

(1) *spring,* 5.5 miles north of Bennetts Well in Death Valley (lat. 36°14'35" N, long. 116°52'50" W). Named on Bennetts Well (1952) 15' quadrangle. The feature also was called McCormack's Well, for Hugh McCormack, who visited Death Valley in 1861 (Palmer, p. 48).

(2) *spring,* 10 miles east-southeast of Tecopa (lat. 35°49' N, long. 116°03'15" W). Named on Tecopa (1950) 15' quadrangle. Called Tule Holes on Avawatz Mountains (1933) 1° quadrangle. The name "Tule Holes" is from the presence of tules near the spring (Palmer, p. 75).

Tule Spring: see **Lostman Spring** [INYO].

Tule Station: see **Keeler** [INYO].

Tunawee Canyon [INYO]: *canyon,* drained by a stream that flows 4.5 miles to Rose Valley nearly 2.5 miles northwest of Coso Junction (lat. 36°04'20" N, long. 117°58' W; near N line sec. 34, T 21 S, R 37 E). Named on Haiwee Reservoir (1951) and Monache Mountain (1956) 15' quadrangles.

Tungsten City: see **Tungsten Hills** [INYO].

Tungsten Hills [INYO]: *range,* 7 miles east-northeast of Mount Tom and southeast of Round Valley (1) (lat. 37°21'30" N, long. 118°32'30" W). Named on Mount Tom (1949) 15' quadrangle. Knopf (1917, p. 229) suggested the name for tungsten deposits found in the range in 1913. A mining Camp called Tungsten City was laid out in Deep Canyon during World War I (Bateman, p. 14).

Tunnabora Peak [INYO]: *peak,* 2 miles north-northeast of Mount Whitney (1) on Inyo-Tulare County line (lat. 36°36'15" N, long. 118°16'50" W). Altitude 13,565 feet. Named on Mount Whitney (1956) 15' quadrangle.

Turquoise Lake [MONO]: *lake,* 700 feet long, nearly 2 miles east of Matterhorn Peak (lat. 38°05'50" N, long. 119°20'55" W). Named on Matterhorn Peak (1956) 15' quadrangle.

Tuttle Creek [INYO]: *stream,* flows 3.5 miles to lowlands 7 miles west-southwest of Lone Pine (lat. 36°33'35" N, long. 118°10'10" W). Named on Lone Pine (1958) 15' quadrangle. The name honors Lyman Tuttle, one of the organizers of Inyo County, and county surveyor from 1866 until 1872 (Gudde, 1949, p. 373). The stream now discharges into the aqueduct that takes Owens Valley water to Los Angeles.

Twelvemile Spring [INYO]: *spring,* 17 miles southeast of Eagle Mountain (lat. 36°01'20" N, long. 116°09'15" W; sec. 7 T 22 N, R 8 E). Named on Stewart Valley (1958) 15' quadrangle. The spring is 12 miles by road from Resting Spring (Palmer, p. 76).

20 Mile Spring: see **Shepherd Canyon** [INYO].

Twenty Mule Team Canyon [INYO]: *canyon,* 2 miles long, opens into the valley of Furnace Creek Wash 4.25 miles southeast of Furnace Creek Inn (lat. 36°24'30" N, long. 116°47'35" W). Named on Furnace Creek (1952) 15' quadrangle. Officials of Pacific Coast Borax Company named the canyon to advertise and commemorate their product (Palmer, p. 76), symbolized by the twenty-mule teams used in early days of the borate industry in Death Valley.

Twin Lake [ALPINE]: *lake,* 4000 feet long, 6.5 miles north-northwest of Pacific Grade Summit (lat. 38°36'25" N, long. 119°56'15" W; on E line sec. 25, T 9 N, R 18 E). Named on Pacific Valley (1979) 7.5' quadrangle. Called Twin Lakes on Markleeville (1889) 30' quadrangle, which shows the feature as two connected lakes.

Twin Lake [MONO]: *lake,* 350 feet long, 2.5 miles northeast of Mount Conness (lat. 37°59'45" N, long. 119°17'25" W; sec. 26, T 2 N, R 24 E). Named on Tuolumne Meadows (1956) 15' quadrangle.

Twin Lakes [MONO]:

(1) *lakes,* two, each 1.5 miles long, 9.5 miles southwest of Bridgeport along Robinson Creek (lat. 38°09'15" N, long. 119°20'45" W). Named on Matterhorn Peak (1956) 15' quadrangle.

(2) *lakes,* three, largest 1500 feet long, 1.5 miles east-southeast of Mammoth Mountain (lat. 37°37' N, long. 119°00'25" W; mainly in sec. 9, T 4 S, R 27 E). Named on Devils Postpile (1953) 15' quadrangle. The lakes are part of the group called Mammoth Lakes.

Twin Lakes: see **Caples Lake** [MONO]; **Twin Lake** [ALPINE].

Twin Lakes Campground [MONO]: *locality,* 8 miles southwest of Bridgeport (lat. 38°10'10" N, long. 119°19'20" W; near NE cor. sec. 33, T 4 N, R 24 E); the place is at the northeast end of Twin Lakes (1). Named on Matterhorn Peak (1956) 15' quadrangle. Sampson's (1940) map shows a place called Crags View at or near the site, and California Division of Highways' (1934) map shows Crag View Camp there.

Twin Lakes Reservoir: see **Caples Lake** [MONO].

Twin Peaks [MONO]: *peaks,* two, 1.5 miles east-southeast of Matterhorn Peak on Mono-Tuolumne County line (lat. 38°04'55" N, long. 119°21'15" W. Named on Matterhorn Peak (1956) 15' quadrangle.

Two Teats [MONO]: *peak,* nearly 7 miles northwest of Mammoth Mountain on Mono-Madera County line (lat. 37°42'45" N, long. 119°05'55" W). Altitude 11,387 feet. Named on Devils Postpile (1953) 15' quadrangle. This peak and nearby San Joaquin Mountain together formerly were called Two Teats (Gudde, 1949, p. 373-374).

Tyee Lakes [INYO]: *lakes,* largest 1300 feet long, 5.5 miles east of Mount Darwin (lat. 37°10'50" N, long. 118°34'30" W; sec. 10, T 9 N, R 31 E). Named on Mount Goddard (1948) 15' quadrangle.

Tyndall: see **Mount Tyndall** [INYO].

—U—

Uba Hebe Crater: see **Ubehebe Crater** [INYO].

Ubehebe: see **Ubehebe Crater** [INYO].

Ubehebe City: see **The Racetrack** [INYO].

Ubehebe Crater [INYO]: *crater,* 38 miles southeast of Deep Springs in the north part of Death Valley (lat. 37°00'35" N, long. 117°26'55" W; sec. 7, T 11 S, R 42 E). Named on Ubehebe Crater (1957) 15' quadrangle. According to Palmer (p. 76), the name is from an Indian word that means "big basket in the rock"—it also has the forms "Uba Hebe" and "Yuba Hebe." A gold and copper mining camp called Ubehebe was near the crater in 1906 (Hanna, p. 339).

Ubehebe Peak [INYO]: *peak,* 20 miles east of New York Butte (lat. 36°41'25" N, long. 117°35'05" W). Altitude 5678 feet. Named on Ubehebe Peak (1950) 15' quadrangle.

Uhlmeyer Spring: see **Ulymeyer Spring** [INYO].

Ulida Flat [INYO]: *valley,* 5.5 miles southeast of Ubehebe Peak (lat. 36°38'30" N, long. 117°30'30" W). Named on Marble Canyon (1951) and Ubehebe Peak (1950) 15' quadrangles.

Ulymeyer Spring [INYO]: *spring,* 3 miles east-northeast of Big Pine near the east edge of Owens Valley (lat. 37°10'55" N, long. 118°14'15" W; sec. 10, T 9 S, R 34 E). Named on Waucoba Mountain (1951) 15' quadrangle. United States Board on Geographic Names (1987a, p. 1) approved the name "Uhlmeyer Spring" for the feature.

Underwood Valley [ALPINE]: *valley,* 1.5 miles northeast of Mount Reba (lat. 38°31'20" N, long. 120°00'35" W). Named on Mokelumne Peak (1979) 7.5' quadrangle.

Union Reservoir [ALPINE]: *lake,* 1.25 miles long, behind a dam on North Fork Stanislaus River 7 miles west-northwest of Dardanelles Cone (lat. 38°25'50" N, long. 119°59'50" W). Named on Spicer Meadow Reservoir (1979) 7.5' quadrangle. Called Highland Reservoir on Dardanelles (1898) 30' quadrangle, but United States Board on Geographic Names (1960c, p. 22) rejected this name, which was from Highland City (Gudde, 1949, p. 148).

University Peak [INYO]: *peak,* 12.5 miles north-northwest of Mount Whitney (1), where Inyo County, Fresno County, and Tulare County meet (lat. 36°44'50" N, long. 118°21'40" W). Altitude 13,632 feet. Named on Mount Whitney (1956) 15' quadrangle. J.N. LeConte transferred the name—which honors University of California—from present Mount Gould to this peak in 1896 (Farquhar, 1925, p. 140).

Upper Blue Lake [ALPINE]: *lake,* 1 mile long, behind a dam on Middle Creek 5.25 miles south-southeast of Carson Pass (lat. 38° 37'40" N, long. 119°56'20" W); the lake is less than 1 mile northwest of Lower Blue Lake. Named on Carson Pass (1979) 7.5' quadrangle. Upper Blue Lake and Lower Blue Lake together are called Blue Lakes on Markleeville (1889) 30' quadrangle. Wheeler's (1876-1877) map has the name "Blue Lake Pk." for a feature situated west of present Upper Blue Lake. United States Board on Geographic Names (1980, p. 4) approved the name "Deadwood Peak" for a peak, altitude 9846 feet, located 2.2 miles west of Upper Blue Lake—this may be the feature called Blue Lake Pk. on Wheeler's map. A station or stopping place called Harmonial City was situated on the road between Upper Blue Lake and Lower Blue Lake (Long, p. 29).

Upper Boy Scout Lake [INYO]: *lake,* 800 feet long, 1 mile east-northeast of Mount Whitney (1) on upper reaches of North Fork Lone Pine Creek (lat. 36°34'55" N, long. 118°16'20" W); the lake is less than 1 mile upstream from Lower Boy Scout Lake. Named on Mount Whitney (1956) 15' quadrangle.

Upper Cactus Flat [INYO]: *area,* 9 miles northeast of Coso Junction (lat. 36°07' N, long. 117°48'45" W); the place is 6 miles southeast of Cactus Flat. Named on Haiwee Reservoir (1951) 15' quadrangle. United States Board on Geographic Names (1983e, p. 3) rejected the name "Big Cactus Flat" for the feature.

Upper Centennial Flat [INYO]: *area,* 16 miles northeast of Coso Junction (lat. 36°13'15" N, long. 117°46' W); the place is 7 miles southwest of Lower Centennial Flat. Named on Haiwee Reservoir (1951) 15' quadrangle.

Upper Centennial Spring [INYO]: *spring,* 17 miles northeast of Coso Junction (lat. 36°14'25" N, long. 117°46' W); the spring is near the head of Centennial Canyon, and less than 2 miles south of Lower Centennial Spring. Named on Haiwee Reservoir (1951) 15' quadrangle.

Upper Emigrant Spring [INYO]: *spring,* 7 miles north-northwest of Emigrant Pass (1) (lat. 36°25'30" N, long. 117°11'35" W); the spring is in Emigrant Canyon 0.5 mile south of Emigrant Spring. Named on Emigrant Canyon (1952) 15' quadrangle.

Upper Fish Valley [ALPINE]: *valley,* 7.5 miles east of Disaster Peak along Silver King Creek (lat. 38°27' N, long. 119°35'50" W); the valley is upstream from Lower Fish Valley. Named on Lost Cannon Peak (1954) 7.5' quadrangle. Upper Fish Valley and Lower Fish Valley together are called Fish Valley on Dardanelles (1898) 30' quadrangle.

Upper Gardner Meadow [ALPINE]: *area,* 7.5 miles northeast of Dardanelles Cone (lat. 38°29'10" N, long. 119°47' W); the place is 1 mile south-southwest of Lower Gardner Meadow. Named on Dardanelles Cone (1979) 7.5' quadrangle.

Upper Horse Meadow [MONO]: *area,* 2.5 miles south-southwest of Lee Vining (lat. 37°55'25" N, long. 119°08'45" W; on N line sec. 30, T 1 N, R 26 E); the place is 1 mile west-southwest of Lower Horse Meadow. Named on Mono Craters (1953) 15' quadrangle.

Upper Horton Lakes [INYO]: *lakes,* largest 0.25 mile long, 3 miles south-southwest of Mount Tom (lat. 37°18'10" N, long. 118°40'45" W); the lakes are on upper reaches of Horton Creek 1 mile upstream from Horton Lake. Named on Mount Tom (1949) 15' quadrangle.

Upper Kinney Lake [ALPINE]: *lake,* 1250 feet long, 1.25 miles northwest of Ebbetts Pass along Silver Creek (1) (lat. 38°33'30" N, long. 119°49'40" W); the lake is less than 0.25 mile upstream from Lower Kinney Lake. Named on Ebbetts Pass (1979) 7.5' quadrangle. Lower Kinney Lake and Upper Kinney Lake together are called Kinney Lakes on Markleeville (1889) 30' quadrangle. The lakes were known as Silver Lakes in the 1860's before they were named for David Kinney, a farmer at Silver Mountain in 1873 (Gudde, 1949, p. 175).

Upper Lamarck Lake [INYO]: *lake,* 0.5 mile long, 3 miles north-northeast of Mount Darwin (lat. 37°12'40" N, long. 118°39' W); the lake is along Lamarck Creek 0.5 mile upstream from Lower Lamarck Lake. Named on Mount Goddard (1948) 15' quadrangle.

Upper Long Lake [MONO]: *lake,* 1600 feet long, 5.5 miles north-northwest of Tower Peak (lat. 37°13'25" N, long. 119°33'15" W); the lake is southwest of Lower Long Lake. Named on Tower Peak (1956) 15' quadrangle.

Upper Morgan Lake [INYO]: *lake,* 1250 feet long, 6 miles northwest of Mount Tom (lat. 37°23'20" N, long. 118°44'40" W); the lake is 0.5 mile upstream from Lower Morgan Lake. Named on Mount Tom (1949) 15' quadrangle.

Upper Pine Lake [INYO]: *lake,* 1500 feet long, 4.25 miles west of Mount Tom on upper reaches of Pine Creek (lat. 37°20'40" N, long. 118°44' W; sec. 18, T 7 S, R 30 E); the lake is 0.5 mile upstream from Pine Lake. Named on Mount Tom (1949) 15' quadrangle.

Upper Piute Meadows [MONO]: *area,* 3.25 miles north of Tower Peak along West Walker River (lat. 38°11'30" N, long. 119°32'10" W). Named on Tower Peak (1956) 15' quadrangle, which shows Piute cabin at the north end of the area. Called Piute Mdw. on Sampson's (1940) map.

Upper Pizona Spring [MONO]: *spring,* 16 miles northeast of Glass Mountain (lat. 37°57'35" N, long. 118°32' W; sec. 11, T 1 N, R 31 E); the spring is near the head of Pizona Creek. Named on Glass Mountain (1962) 15' quadrangle.

Upper Sardine Lake [MONO]: *lake,* 800 feet long, 8.5 miles southwest of Lee Vining at the head of Walker Creek (lat. 37°51'15" N, long. 119°12'15" W); the lake is 0.25 mile upstream from Lower Sardine Lake. Named on Mono Craters (1953) 15' quadrangle.

Upper Summers Meadows [MONO]: *area,* 8 miles south-southwest of Bridgeport (lat. 38°09'45" N, long. 119°18'15" W; sec. 34, 35, T 4 N, R 24 E); the place is 3 miles west of Lower Summers Meadows at the head of Summers Creek. Named on Matterhorn Peak (1956) 15' quadrangle. Called Summers Back Pasture on Bridgeport (1909) 30' quadrangle. Jesse N. Summers and G.N. Summers bought property in 1864 from Charles Russell and John Russell at what was known as Russell's Valley; the place soon became known as Summers Meadows (Wedertz, p. 175).

Upper Summit City: see **Summit City Creek** [ALPINE].

Upper Sunset Lake [ALPINE]: *lake,* 1400 feet long, 6.5 miles north-northeast of Pacific Grade Summit (lat. 38°36'30" N, long. 119°52'40" W; sec. 27, T 9 N, R 19 E); the lake is southwest of Lower Sunset Lake. Named on Pacific Valley (1979) 7.5' quadrangle.

Upper Town: see **Masonic** [MONO].

Upper Truckee River [ALPINE]: *stream,* flows nearly 3 miles to El Dorado County 5.5 miles north of Fourth of July Peak (lat. 38°44'15" N, long. 120°01'15" W; sec. 5, T 10 N, R 18 E). Named on Caples Lake (1979) 7.5' quadrangle.

Upper Warm Spring [INYO]: *spring,* 9.5 miles southwest of Dry Mountain in Saline Valley (lat. 36°49'55" N, long. 117°44'15" W; near N line sec. 9, T 13 S, R 39 E); the spring is 2.5 miles northeast of Lower Warm Springs. Named on Dry Mountain (1957) 15' quadrangle.

Utica Reservoir [ALPINE]: *lake,* nearly 2 miles long, 5 miles south-southeast of Mount Reba on Alpine-Tuolumne County line, mainly in Alpine County (lat. 38°26' N, long. 120°00' W). Named on Spicer Meadow Reservoir (1979) and Tamarack (1979) 7.5' quadrangles.

—V—

Vacation Pass [INYO]: *pass,* 2.5 miles north-northwest of Mount Whitney (1) on Inyo-Tulare County line (lat. 36°36'45" N, long. 118°18' W). Named on Mount Whitney (1956) 15' quadrangle. Called Sheep Pass on Mount Whitney (1907) 30' quadrangle.

Valentine Lake [MONO]: *lake,* 2300 feet long, 4.5 miles west-northwest of Mount Morrison along Sherwin Creek (lat. 37°34'35" N, long. 118°56'10" W; on W line sec. 30, T 4 S, R 28 E). Named on Mount Morrison (1953) 15' quadrangle. The name commemorates W.L. Valentine, one of the owners of Valentine Camp, an exclusive club camp built at present Old Mammoth in 1920 (Smith, Genny, p. 44).

Valley Wells [INYO]: *locality,* 6.5 miles east-southeast of Argus Peak in Searles Valley (lat. 35°49'45" N, long. 117°19'50" W; near E line sec. 21, T 24 S, R 43 E). Named on Trona (1949) 15' quadrangle.

Vaquero Camp [ALPINE]: *locality,* 9 miles south-southeast of Mogul Peak in Silver King Valley (lat. 38°34'45" N, long. 119°37'50" W; near W line sec. 36, T 9 N, R 21 E). Named on Wolf Creek (1979) 7.5' quadrangle.

Vaughn Gulch [INYO]: *canyon,* drained by a stream that flows 3 miles to lowlands 7 miles east of Independence (lat. 36°49'10" N, long. 118°04'35" W; sec. 8, T 13 S, R 36 E). Named on Independence (1951) 15' quadrangle.

Vaughn's Creek: see **East Walker River** [MONO].

Vermillion Canyon [INYO]: *canyon,* 3 miles long, opens into lowlands 15 miles south-southwest of Keeler (lat. 36°17' N, long. 117° 55'30" W; sec. 13, T 19 S, R 37 E). Named on Keeler (1951) 15' quadrangle.

Vernon: see **Mill Creek** [MONO] (2).

Versteeg: see **Mount Versteeg** [INYO].

Victoria Peak [MONO]: *peak,* 5.5 miles north-northwest of Matterhorn Peak on Buckeye Ridge (lat. 38°10'05" N, long. 119°25'20" W). Altitude 11,732 feet. Named on Matterhorn Peak (1956) 15' quadrangle.

Vining Canyon: see **Lee Vining Creek** [MONO].

Vining Creek: see **Lee Vining Creek** [MONO].

Vining Peak: see **Lee Vining Peak** [MONO].

Vining's Gulch: see **Lee Vining Creek** [MONO].

Virgil Connell Spring [MONO]: *spring,* 9 miles north-northwest of Coleville (lat. 38°40'40" N, long. 119°35'15" W; near S line sec. 29, T 10 N, R 22 E). Named on Topaz Lake (1956) 15' quadrangle.

Virginia Creek [MONO]: *stream,* flows 16 miles to Bridgeport Valley 4 miles south of Bridgeport (lat. 38°11'45" N, long. 119° 13' W; sec. 21, T 4 N, R 25 E); the stream heads at Virginia Lakes. Named on Bodie (1958) 15' quadrangle.

Virginia Lake Camp: see **Virginia Lakes** [MONO].

Virginia Lakes [MONO]: *lakes,* 7 miles east-southeast of Matterhorn Peak (lat. 38°02'45" N, long. 119°16' W); the lakes are on upper reaches of Virginia Creek. Named on Matterhorn Peak (1956) 15' quadrangle. The group includes Blue Lake (1), Cooney Lake, Frog Lakes, Moat Lake, Red

Lake (1), and Trumbull Lake. California Division of Highways' (1934) map shows a place called Virginia Lake Camp situated at the lakes.

Virginia Pass [MONO]: *pass,* 3 miles southeast of Matterhorn Peak on Mono-Tuolumne County line (lat. 38°04' N, long. 119°20'05" W); the pass is near the head of Virginia Canyon, which is in Tuolumne County. Named on Matterhorn Peak (1956) 15' quadrangle.

Virgin Spring [INYO]: *spring,* 3.5 miles west-southwest of Epaulet Peak in Black Mountains (lat. 35°57'15" N, long. 116°35' W); the spring is on the west side of Virgin Spring Canyon. Named on Confidence Hills (1950) 15' quadrangle. National Park Service officials proposed the name, evidently for the purity of the spring water (Palmer, p. 77).

Virgin Spring Canyon [INYO]: *canyon,* 5.5 miles long, opens into lowlands 4 miles southwest of Epaulet Peak (lat. 35°55'45" N, long. 116°34'30" W); Virgin Spring is in the canyon. Named on Confidence Hills (1950) 15' quadrangle.

Voight Canyon [ALPINE]: *canyon,* drained by a stream that flows 1.5 miles to Carson Valley 1 mile north-northeast of Woodfords (lat. 38°47'15" N, long. 119°49' W; sec. 26, T 11 N, R 19 E). Named on Woodfords (1979) 7.5' quadrangle.

Volcanic Butte [MONO]: *peak,* 3.25 miles south-southeast of Fales Hot Springs (lat. 38°18'25" N, long. 119°22'55" W; sec. 7, T 5 N, R 24 E). Altitude 8607 feet. Named on Fales Hot Springs (1954) 7.5' quadrangle.

Volcanic Tableland [INYO-MONO]: *relief feature,* mainly north-northwest of Bishop on Inyo-Mono County line; Owens River Gorge is incised into the feature. Named on Bishop (1949), Casa Diablo Mountain (1953), Mount Tom (1949), and White Mountain Peak (1962) 15' quadrangles.

Volcano Butte [INYO]: *peak,* 4.25 miles northwest of the mouth of Mountain Springs Canyon (lat. 35°59'15" N, long. 117°38'30" W; near S line sec. 27, T 22 S, R 40 E). Altitude 5882 feet. Named on Mountain Springs Canyon (1953) 15' quadrangle.

Volcano Peak [INYO]: *peak,* 4.5 miles east-northeast of the village of Little Lake (lat. 35°57'20" N, long. 117°49'50" W; near N line sec. 12, T 23 S, R 38 E). Altitude 5352 feet. Named on Little Lake (1954) 15' quadrangle. Wheeler's (1877) map has the label "Crater" for the feature.

– W –

Wade Canyon [ALPINE]: *canyon,* drained by a stream that flows 1.5 miles to West Carson Canyon at Woodfords (lat. 38°46'45" N, long. 119°49'15" W; sec. 35, T 11 N, R 19 E). Named on Woodfords (1979) 7.5' quadrangle. Reed's (1864) map shows a place called Wade's situated near the mouth of present Wade Canyon.

Wade's: see **Wade Canyon** [ALPINE].

Wade Valley [ALPINE]: *valley,* 3.25 miles east-northeast of Woodfords (lat. 38°47'40" N, long. 119°46' W). Named on Woodfords (1979) 7.5' quadrangle.

Waford Spring [MONO]: *spring,* 8 miles south of Bodie in Mono Valley (lat. 38°05'45" N, long. 119°00'25" W; sec. 28, T 3 N, R 27 E). Named on Bodie (1958) 15' quadrangle.

Walker Creek [INYO]: *stream,* flows 4 miles to Olancha Creek 2.5 miles west-southwest of Olancha (lat. 36°15'55" N, long. 118°02'55" W; sec. 23, T 19 S, R 36 E). Named on Monache Mountain (1956) and Olancha (1956) 15' quadrangles. Called Walkers Cr. on Tucker and Sampson's (1938) map. The name commemorates Gus Walker, who settled in the Olancha neighborhood in 1864 (Gudde, 1949, p. 382).

Walker Creek [MONO]: *stream,* flows 8.5 miles to Rush Creek nearly 4 miles southeast of Lee Vining in Pumice Valley (lat. 37° 54'50" N, long. 119°04'45" W; sec. 26, T 1 N, R 26 E); the stream goes through Walker Lake. Named on Mono Craters (1953) 15' quadrangle.

Walker Lake [MONO]: *lake,* 3900 feet long, 6 miles south-southwest of Lee Vining in Bloody Canyon (lat. 37°52'30" N, long. 119° 09'45" W). Named on Mono Craters (1953) 15' quadrangle. The name is for William J. Walker, who settled near the lake (Smith, Genny, p. 70).

Walker Meadows [MONO]: *area,* 6.25 miles north-northwest of Tower Peak (lat. 38°14' N, long. 119°34'30" W; sec. 32, T 5 N, R 22 E); the place is along West Fork West Walker River. Named on Tower Peak (1956) 15' quadrangle.

Walker Mountain [MONO]: *peak,* 11 miles north-northwest of Matterhorn Peak (lat. 38°14'15" N, long. 119°28'20" W; sec. 32, T 5 N, R 23 E); the peak is east of Little Walker River. Altitude 11,563 feet. Named on Matterhorn Peak (1956) 15' quadrangle.

Walker River: see **East Walker River** [MONO]; **Little Walker River** [MONO]; **West Walker River** [MONO].

Wallace: see **Mount Wallace** [INYO].

Walters Canyon [MONO]: *canyon,* drained by a stream that flows 1 mile to Bridgeport Valley 3.5 miles north-northwest of Bridgeport (lat. 38°18'05" N, long. 119°15'15" W; near S line sec. 7, T 5 N, R 25 E). Named on Fales Hot Springs (1956) 15' quadrangle.

Ward: see **Dunderberg Peak** [MONO].

Warm Spring [INYO]: *spring,* 5.5 miles north of Sugarloaf Peak (lat. 35°58' N, long. 116°55'50" W). Named on Wingate Wash (1950) 15' quadrangle.

Warm Spring [MONO]: *spring,* 6 miles west of Bodie (lat. 38°12'10" N, long. 119°07'15" W; near W line sec. 16, T 4 N, R 26 E). Named on Bodie (1958) 15' quadrangle. Called Warm Sprs. on Sampson's (1940) map.

Warm Spring: see **Upper Warm Spring** [INYO].

Warm Spring Canyon [INYO]: *canyon,* 10 miles long, opens into Death Valley 6 miles north-northeast of Sugarloaf Peak (lat. 35°57'40" N, long. 116°52' W); Warm Spring is in the Canyon. Named on Manly Peak (1950) and Wingate Wash (1950) 15' quadrangles.

Warm Spring Flat: see **Big Alkali** [MONO].

Warm Springs [MONO]: *springs,* two, 14 miles south-southeast of Bodie near the edge of Mono Lake (lat. 38°02' N, long. 118°54'15" W; near E line sec. 17, T 2 N, R 28 E). Named on Trench Canyon (1958) 15' quadrangle, which shows the springs located 11 miles north of the site of Mono Mills along an old railroad grade. Billeb (p. 46) noted that a station called Warm Springs was situated along the railroad 11 miles north of Mono Mills near the east shore of Mono Lake.

Warm Springs: see **Lower Warm Springs** [INYO].

Warm Sulphur Springs [INYO]: *springs,* four, on the east side of Panamint Valley 8 miles west-southwest of Telescope Peak (lat. 36°07'15" N, long. 117°12'45" W; sec. 10, T 21 S, R 44 E). Named on Telescope Peak (1952) 15' quadrangle.

Warner Hot Springs: see **Casa Diablo Hot Springs** [MONO].

Warren: see **Mount Warren** [MONO].

Warren Bench [INYO]: *relief feature,* 2.5 miles west-northwest of Big Pine (lat. 37°10'25" N, long. 118°20'10" W; sec. 11, 14, T 9 S, R 33 E); the feature is 1.5 miles south-southwest of Warren Lake. Named on Big Pine (1950) 15' quadrangle.

Warren Fork: see **Lee Vining Creek** [MONO].

Warren Lake [INYO]: *intermittent lake,* 3900 feet long, 3 miles northwest of Big Pine (lat. 37°11'45" N, long. 118°19'45" W; sec. 2, T 9 S, R 33 E); the feature is 1.5 miles north-northeast of Warren Bench. Named on Big Pine (1950) 15' quadrangle.

Wasco Lake [MONO]: *lake,* 950 feet long, nearly 2 miles northeast of Mount Conness (lat. 37°59'10" N, long. 119°17'50" W; sec. 35, T 2 N, R 24 E). Named on Tuolumne Meadows (1956) 15' quadrangle.

Wasson: see **Lake Canyon** [MONO].

Water Canyon [INYO]:

(1) *canyon,* 2.5 miles long, opens into Mazourka Canyon from the east 9 miles northeast of Independence (lat. 36°53'25" N, long. 118°04'55" W). Named on Independence (1951) 15' quadrangle.

(2) *canyon,* drained by a stream that flows 4.5 miles to Darwin Wash 9 miles east-southeast of Coso Peak (lat. 36°10' N, long. 117°33'15" W; sec. 29, T 20 S, R 41 E). Named on Coso Peak (1951) 15' quadrangle.

(3) *canyon,* drained by a stream that flows 1.5 miles to Surprise Canyon 3 miles south of Telescope Peak (lat. 36°07'20" N, long. 117°05'05" W). Named on Telescope Peak (1952) 15' quadrangle.

(4) *canyon,* 11 miles long, opens into lowlands 10 miles north-northeast of Argus Peak (lat. 35°58'45" N, long. 117°20'50" W). Named on Trona (1949) 15' quadrangle. Called Bendere's Cañon on Wheeler's (1877) map.

Water Canyon [INYO-MONO]: *canyon,* 4.25 miles long, heads in Mono County and opens into the canyon of Wyman Creek 10 miles north-northeast of Westgard Pass in Inyo County (lat. 37°26'15" N, long. 118°06'30" W; sec. 11, T 6 S, R 35 E). Named on Blanco Mountain (1951) 15' quadrangle.

Water Canyon [MONO]: *canyon,* drained by a stream that flows 4 miles to East Walker River nearly 11 miles north-northeast of Bridgeport (lat. 38°24'10" N, long. 119°10'10" W; near NW cor. sec. 6, T 6 N, R 26 E). Named on Bridgeport (1958) 15' quadrangle.

Waterhouse Peak [ALPINE]: *peak,* 6.5 miles south-southwest of Freel Peak on Alpine-El Dorado County line (lat. 38°46'35" N, long. 119°57'50" W; sec. 26, T 11 N, R 18 E). Altitude 9497 feet. Named on Freel Peak (1955) 7.5' quadrangle. Forest Service officials named the peak in memory of Clark Waterhouse, a Forest Service employee who was killed in World War I (Gudde, 1969, p. 359).

Water Station: see **The Tanks** [INYO].

Watterson Canyon [MONO]: *canyon,* 3.5 miles long, opens into Long Valley 6 miles north-northwest of Toms Place (lat. 37°38'15" N, long. 118°43'15" W; sec. 36, T 3 S, R 29 E). Named on Casa Diablo Mountain (1953) 15' quadrangle.

Watterson Meadow [MONO]: *area,* 6.5 miles east-southeast of Glass Mountain (lat. 37°45' N, long. 118°35'30" W). Named on Casa Diablo Mountain (1953) and Glass Mountain (1962) 15' quadrangles.

Watterson Troughs [MONO]: *spring,* 8 miles north of Toms Place (lat. 37°40'45" N, long. 118°39'15" W; sec. 22, T 3 S, R 30 E). Named on Casa Diablo Mountain (1953) 15' quadrangle.

Waucoba Canyon [INYO]: *canyon,* 6 miles long, opens into the valley of Waucoba Wash 5.5 miles north of the mouth of Paiute Canyon (lat. 37°00' N, long. 117°56'10" W; near N line sec. 16, T 11 S, R 37 E). Named on Independence (1951), Waucoba Spring (1958), and Waucoba Wash (1951) 15' quadrangles.

Waucoba Mountain [INYO]: *peak,* 19 miles east-southeast of Big Pine (lat. 37°01'20" N, long. 118°00'25" W). Altitude 11,123 feet. Named on Waucoba Mountain (1951) 15' quadrangle. Palmer (p. 78) called the feature Waucoba Peak, and attributed the name to an Indian word with the meaning "round." Gudde (1949, p. 385) attributed the name to an Indian word for various kinds of pine trees.

Waucoba Peak: see **Waucoba Mountain** [INYO].

Waucoba Spring [INYO]: *spring,* 3.5 miles east-southeast of Waucoba Mountain (lat. 37°00'15" N, long. 117°56'50" W; sec. 8, T 11 S, R 37 E). Named on Waucoba Spring (1958) 15' quadrangle. According to Palmer (p. 78), the feature may also have been called Wheeler Spring, for Lieutenant George M. Wheeler, whose command explored the region in 1871.

Waucoba Wash [INYO]: *stream,* flows 18 miles from the mouth of Waucoba Canyon to a point in Saline valley 6.5 miles southeast of the mouth of Paiute Canyon (lat. 36°46'45" N, long. 117°50' W; sec. 27, T 13 S, R 38 E). Named on Waucoba Wash (1951) 15' quadrangle.

Waugh Lake [MONO]: *lake,* 1.5 miles long, behind a dam on Rush Creek 15 miles south-southwest of Lee Vining (lat. 37°45'05" N, long. 119°10'50" W). Named on Devils Postpile (1953) and Mono Craters (1953) 15' quadrangles. The name recalls E.J. Waugh, chief construction engineer for the dam that formed the lake (Smith, Genny, p. 68).

Way Lake [MONO]: *lake,* 300 feet long, 7.25 miles west of Mount Morrison (lat. 37°34'55" N, long. 118°59'10" W). Named on Mount Morrison (1953) 15' quadrangle. According to Genny Smith (p. 50), the correct name of the feature is Emerald Lake.

Weber Lake [MONO]: *lake,* 2100 feet long, 11 miles northwest of Mammoth Mountain (lat. 37°44'30" N, long. 119°10'30" W). Named on Devils Postpile (1953) 15' quadrangle.

Wedertz Flat [MONO]: *area,* 9 miles north of Bridgeport (lat. 38° 23' N, long. 119°12'30" W; sec. 10, 11, T 6 N, R 25 E). Named on Bridgeport (1958) 15' quadrangle. Called Wedertz Flats on Bridgeport (1909) 30' quadrangle. The name commemorates Louis Wedertz, a pioneer who owned land near the feature (Gudde, 1949, p. 386).

Weir Lake [INYO]: *lake,* 500 feet long, 6 miles east of Mount Darwin along South Fork (1) Bishop Creek (lat. 37°10'35" N, long. 118°33'45" W; sec. 11, T 9 S, R 31 E). Named on Mount Goddard (1948) 15' quadrangle.

Weiser Creek [ALPINE]: *stream,* flows nearly 4 miles to Highland Creek 3 miles north-northeast of Dardanelles Cone (lat. 38°26'45" N, long. 119°51'35" W). Named on Dardanelles Cone (1979) 7.5' quadrangle.

Well Number 1: see **The Tanks** [INYO].

Wells Meadow [INYO]: *area,* 7 miles north-northeast of Mount Tom near the west edge of Round Valley (1) (lat. 37°26'30" N, long. 118°37'45" W; sec. 12, T 6 S, R 30 E). Named on Mount Tom (1949) 15' quadrangle.

Wells Meadow: see **Witcher Meadow** [MONO].

Wells Peak [ALPINE-MONO]: *peak,* 5.5 miles north-northeast of Sonora Pass on Alpine-Mono County line (lat. 38°23'50" N, long. 119°34'55" W; sec. 5, T 6 N, R 22 E). Altitude 10,833 feet. Named on Lost Cannon Peak (1954) 7.5' quadrangle. The name commemorates John C. Wells, forest officer and supervisor of Mono National Forest (United States Board on Geographic Names, 1933, p. 807).

Wells Upper Meadow [INYO]: *area,* 3.5 miles east-southeast of Mount Tom (lat. 37°19'05" N, long. 118°35'45" W); the place is 9 miles south-southeast of Wells Meadow. Named on Mount Tom (1949) 15' quadrangle.

West Carson Canyon [ALPINE]: *canyon,* extends for 5 miles along West Fork Carson River from Woodfords to Hope Valley. Named on Freel Peak (1955) and Woodfords (1979) 7.5' quadrangles. Called Carson Cañon on Reed's (1864) map. According to Long (p. 9), the canyon was known in the early days as Carson Canyon, Rocky Canyon, Emigrant Canyon, and Big Canyon, and later as Woodfords Canyon. Morgan (*in* Pritchard, p. 168) noted that Mormons in 1848, and also many Forty-niners, called the feature Pass Creek Canyon—present West Fork Carson River sometimes was called Pass Creek (Decker, p. 140).

West Carson River: see **Carson River, West Fork** [ALPINE].

Wester Park [ALPINE]: *area,* 5 miles north-northwest of Mount Reba (lat. 38°34'20" N, long. 120°03'55" W). Named on Mokelumne Peak (1979) 7.5' quadrangle.

Westgard Pass [INYO]: *pass,* 14 miles east-southeast of Bishop at the south end of White Mountains (lat. 37°18' N, long. 118°09'15" W; sec. 32, T 7 S, R 35 E). Named on Blanco Mountain (1951) 15' quadrangle. The name honors A.L. Westgard, who included the pass on his recommended route for a transcontinental highway in 1913 (Schumacher, p. 51).

West Lake [MONO]: *lake,* 1900 feet long, 3.25 miles east of Matterhorn Peak (lat. 38°05'30" N, long. 119°19'15" W); the lake is 1.5 miles north-west of East Lake. Named on Matterhorn Peak (1956) 15' quadrangle.

West Side Borax Camp: see **Salt Springs** [INYO] (2).

West Walker River [MONO]: *stream,* flows 47 miles to the State of Nevada 6 miles north of Coleville (lat. 38°39' N, long. 119°29'40" W). Named on Desert Creek Peak (1956), Fales Hot Springs (1956), Sonora Pass (1956), Topaz Lake (1956), and Tower Peak (1956) 15' quadrangles. Called Rio Clara or West Fork on Bancroft's (1864) map. West Fork [of West Walker River] enters nearly 6 miles east-southeast of Sonora Pass; it is 8.5 miles long and is named on Sonora Pass (1956) and Tower Peak (1956) 15' quadrangles. On Dardanelles (1898) 30' quadrangle, present West Walker River above the junction with West Fork is called Middle Fork. West Walker River is a major tributary of Walker River, which is in the State of Nevada—Fremont named Walker River for Joseph R. Walker, one of his guides (Gudde, 1949, p. 382).

Wet Canyon [MONO]: *canyon,* drained by a stream that flows 5 miles from Wet Meadow to Dexter Creek 7 miles north-northwest of Glass Mountain (lat. 37°52'20" N, long. 118°44'40" W; sec. 11, T 1 S, R 29 E). Named on Cowtrack Mountain (1962) and Glass Mountain (1962) 15' quadrangles.

Wet Fork [MONO]: *stream,* flows 7.5 miles to join Dry Fork and form Blackwater Wash 6 miles north-northeast of Glass Mountain (lat. 37°50'45" N, long. 118°38'50" W; sec. 22, T 1 S, R 30 E). Named on Glass Mountain (1962) 15' quadrangle. On Mount Morrison (1914) 30' quadrangle, the part of the stream above the mouth of Sawmill Canyon (2) is called Right Fork, and the stream in Sawmill Canyon (2) is called Left Fork. United States Board on Geographic Names (1964c, p. 16) rejected the names "Right Fork Wet Fork" and "Wet Fork Creek" for present Wet Fork.

Wet Fork Creek: see **Wet Fork** [MONO].

Wet Meadow [MONO]: *marsh,* 11 miles east-southeast of the site of Mono Mills (lat. 37°48'40" N, long. 118°47'05" W; sec. 33, T 1 S, R 29 E); Wet Meadow is in Wet Canyon. Named on Cowtrack Mountain (1962) 15' quadrangle.

Wet Meadows: see **Wet Meadows Reservoir** [ALPINE].

Wet Meadows Reservoir [ALPINE]: *lake,* 2000 feet long, 5 miles north-northwest of Ebbetts Pass (lat. 38°36'20" N, long. 119° 52' W; sec. 27, T 9 N, R 19 E). Named on Ebbetts Pass (1979) 7.5' quadrangle. Markleeville (1956) 15' quadrangle shows Wet Meadows at the place.

Wheeler Canyon [INYO]: *canyon,* drained by a stream that flows 6.5 miles to Waucoba Wash 8 miles north of the mouth of Paiute Canyon (lat. 36°57'45" N, long. 117°53'40" W; sec. 26, T 11 S, R 37 E). Named on Waucoba Wash (1951) 15' quadrangle. The name commemorates Lieutenant George M. Wheeler, whose command explored the region in 1871 (Palmer, p. 78).

Wheeler Creek [MONO]: *stream,* flows 3.5 miles to Hot Creek (1) 1.5 miles west of Fales Hot Springs (lat. 38°20'50" N, long. 119° 25'50" W; near E line sec. 22, T 6 N, R 23 E); the stream goes through Wheeler Flat. Named on Fales Hot Springs (1956) 15' quadrangle.

Wheeler Crest [INYO-MONO]: *ridge,* north-trending, 9 miles long, south of Toms Place on Inyo-Mono County line (lat. 37°28' N, long. 118°41' W). Named on Mount Tom (1949) 15' quadrangle. United States Board on Geographic Names (1933, p. 812) called the feature Wheeler Ridge.

Wheeler Flat [MONO]: *area,* 1.5 miles west-southwest of Fales Hot Springs (lat. 38°20'20" N, long. 119°25'30" W; in and near sec. 26, 27, T 6 N, R 23 E); the place is along Wheeler Creek. Named on Fales Hot Springs (1956) 15' quadrangle.

Wheeler Lake [ALPINE]: *lake,* 1050 feet long, 4 miles west of Pacific Grade Summit (lat. 38°31'10" N, long. 119°58'50" W; sec. 27, T 8 N, R 18 E). Named on Pacific Valley (1979) 7.5' quadrangle.

Wheeler Peak [MONO]: *peak,* nearly 8 miles northeast of Fales Hot Springs in Sweetwater Mountains (lat. 36°25'05" N, long. 119°17'15" W; near S line sec. 25, T 7 N, R 24 E). Altitude 11,664 feet. Named on Fales Hot Springs (1956) 15' quadrangle. Called Mt. Wheeler on Sampson's (1940) map.

Wheeler Ridge: see **Wheeler Crest** [INYO-MONO].

Wheeler Spring: see **Waucoba Spring** [INYO].

Whippoorwill Canyon [INYO]: *canyon,* 2.5 miles long, opens into an unnamed valley 3.5 miles east-southeast of Waucoba Mountain (lat. 37°00'30" N, long. 117°56'45" W; near W line sec. 9, T 11 S, R 37 E). Named on Waucoba Spring (1958) 15' quadrangle.

Whippoorwill Flat [INYO]: *area,* 3 miles north-northeast of Waucoba Mountain (lat. 37°03'30" N, long. 117°58'45" W). Named on Waucoba Spring (1958) 15' quadrangle.

Whiskey Canyon [MONO]: *canyon,* 1.5 miles long, 1.5 miles south-southeast of Toms Place (lat. 37°32'20" N, long. 118°40'25" W). Named on Casa Diablo Mountain (1953) 15' quadrangle.

Whiskey Creek [MONO]: *stream,* flows 2.5 miles to Lake Crowley 3 miles west-northwest of Toms Place (lat. 37°34'40" N, long. 118° 44' W; near NW cor. sec. 25, T 4 S, R 29 E). Named on Casa Diablo Mountain (1953) 15' quadrangle.

Whiskey Flat: see **Adobe Valley** [MONO].

White Canyon [ALPINE]: *canyon,* 2 miles long, nearly 3.5 miles east of Disaster Peak along East Fork Carson River (lat. 38°26'40" N, long. 119°40'15" W). Named on Disaster Peak (1979) 7.5' quadrangle.

Whitecliff Lake [ALPINE]: *lake,* 750 feet long, 5.25 miles east of Disaster Peak (lat. 38°26'20" N, long. 119°38'05" W); the lake is less than 0.5 mile east-northeast of Whitecliff Peak. Named on Disaster Peak (1979) 7.5' quadrangle.

Whitecliff Peak [ALPINE]: *peak,* 5 miles east of Disaster Peak (lat. 38°26'10" N, long. 119°38'25" W). Named on Disaster Peak (1979) 7.5' quadrangle.

White Hills [INYO]: *range,* 12 miles east-southeast of the village of Little

Lake between Coso Basin and Indian Wells Valley (lat. 35° 52'15" N, long. 117°43' W). Named on Mountain Springs Canyon (1953) 15' quadrangle.

White Mountain [ALPINE-MONO]: *peak,* 4 miles north-northeast of Sonora Pass on Alpine-Mono County line (lat. 38°22'50" N, long. 119°36'50" W). Altitude 11,398 feet. Named on Lost Cannon Peak (1954) 7.5' quadrangle

White Mountain [MONO]: *peak,* 1.5 miles south-southeast of Mount Conness on Mono-Tuolumne County line (lat. 37°56'45" N, long. 119°18'30" W). Named on Tuolumne Meadows (1956) 15' quadrangle.

White Mountain City [INYO]: *locality,* 3 miles north-northwest of Deep Springs near the north end of Deep Springs Valley (lat. 37° 24'45" N, long. 117°59'50" W; sec. 23, T 6 S, R 36 E); the place is near the edge of White Mountains. Ruins named on Soldier Pass (1958) 15' quadrangle. Surveyors made a town plat at the place in the 1860's (Chalfant, 1933, p. 214).

White Mountain Peak [MONO]: *peak,* 17 miles southeast of Benton in White Mountains (lat. 37°38'05" N, long. 118°15'20" W). Altitude 14,246 feet. Named on White Mountain Peak (1962) 15' quadrangle. The name is from white rock at the summit (Gudde, 1949, p. 388).

White Mountain Peak: see **Montgomery Peak** [MONO].

White Mountain Range: see **White Mountains** [INYO].

White Mountains [INYO-MONO]: *range,* east of Owens Valley and north of Westgard Pass in Inyo County, and east of Benton Valley, Hammil Valley, and Chalfant Valley in Mono County; the range extends north into the State of Nevada. Named on Goldfield (1954) and Mariposa (1957) 1°x 2° quadrangles. The name is from white rock exposed at the crest of the range (Stewart, p. 532-533). Wheeler (1876, p. 47) referred to the feature as Sierra Blanca, and Fairbanks (p. 473) called it White Mountain Range.

White Sage Flat [INYO]: *area,* 1.5 miles west-southwest of Emigrant Pass (1) (lat. 36°19'30" N, long. 117°09'50" W). Named on Emigrant Canyon (1952) 15' quadrangle. The area also is called Rabbit Flat for the large number of jack rabbits there (Palmer, p. 59).

White Sage Flat: see **Mahogany Flat** [INYO] (2).

White Sage Wash [INYO]: *stream,* flows 2.25 miles to Nemo Canyon 4 miles southwest of Emigrant Pass (1) (lat. 36°17'35" N, long. 117°11'30" W); the stream heads near White Sage Flat. Named on Emigrant Canyon (1952) 15' quadrangle.

White Sand Hills: see **The Dunes** [INYO] (2).

White Top Mountain [INYO]: *peak,* 7.5 miles south-southeast of Tin Mountain in Cottonwood Mountains (lat. 36°46'50" N, long. 117°24'45" W). Altitude 7607 feet. Named on Tin Mountain (1957) 15' quadrangle.

White Wing Mountain: see **Mammoth Mountain** [MONO].

Whitmore Hot Springs [MONO]: *locality,* 5.5 miles north-northeast of Mount Morrison in Long Valley (2) (lat. 37°37'50" N, long. 118°48'40" W; sec. 6, T 4 S, R 29 E). Named on Mount Morrison (1953) 15' quadrangle. Mount Morrison (1914) 30' quadrangle shows marsh at the place, and has the name "Whitmore Tub" there. Mount Morrison (1953) 15' quadrangle shows a lake by the site. Eakel and McLaughlin (p. 174) referred to Whitmore Tub Spring.

Whitmore Tub: see **Whitmore Hot Springs** [MONO].

Whitmore Tub Spring: see **Whitmore Hot Springs** [MONO].

Whitney: see **Mount Whitney** [INYO].

Whitney Pass [INYO]: *pass,* less than 2 miles south-southeast of Mount Whitney (1) on Inyo-Tulare County line (lat. 36°33'15" N, long. 118°16'40" W). Named on Mount Whitney (1956) 15' quadrangle.

Whitney Portal [INYO]: *settlement,* 9 miles west of Lone Pine along Lone Pine Creek (lat. 36°35'15" N, long. 118°13'30" W). Named on Lone Pine (1958) 15' quadrangle. United States Board on Geographic Names (1938, p. 58) approved the name "Whitney Portal" for "a flat on Lone Pine Creek about 3 miles east of Mount Whitney," which is about 1 mile west of the settlement; the flat was called Whitney Portal at the official opening of a new automobile road to the place in 1936, although previously it had been called Hunter Flat for William L. Hunter, a pioneer of Owens Valley.

Whitney's Peak: see **Mount Whitney** [INYO] (1).

Wicht: see **Chris Wicht Camp** [INYO].

Wickline Canyon [INYO]: *canyon,* drained by a stream that flows 1.25 miles to lowlands 0.5 mile south-southwest of the village of Little Lake (lat. 35°55'45" N, long. 117°54'40" W; sec. 18, T 23 S, R 38 E). Named on Little Lake (1954) 15' quadrangle.

Wild Cow Canyon [MONO]: *canyon,* drained by a stream that flows 2.5 miles to Dexter Creek 10.5 miles east-southeast of the site of Mono Mills (lat. 37°49'50" N, long. 118°47' W; sec. 28, T 1 S, R 29 E). Named on Cowtrack Mountain (1962) 15' quadrangle.

Wilderness Creek [ALPINE]: *stream,* flows 5 miles to Tuolumne County 5.25 miles west of Dardanelles Cone (lat. 38°24'30" N, long. 119°58' W). Named on Spicer Meadow Reservoir (1979) 7.5' quadrangle.

Wildhorse Creek [MONO]: *stream,* flows 6 miles to Fish Lake Valley 12 miles east-southeast of White Mountain Peak (lat. 37°35'45" N, long. 118°02'40" W; near S line sec. 18, T 4 S, R 36 E). Named on Mount Barcroft (1962) 15' quadrangle.

Wild Horse Meadow [MONO]: *area,* 7.5 miles east-southeast of the site of Mono Mills (lat. 37°50'40" N, long. 118°50'10" W; sec. 24, T 1 S, R 28 E). Named on Cowtrack Mountain (1962) 15' quadrangle.

Wild Horse Mesa [INYO]: *area,* 15 miles south-southeast of Coso Peak (lat. 36°00' N, long. 117°37' W). Named on Coso Peak (1951) and Mountain Springs Canyon (1953) 15' quadrangles.

Wild Horse Mountain [MONO]: *peak,* 7 miles east-southeast of Coleville (lat. 38°31'45" N, long. 119°23'30" W; on E line sec. 24, T 8 N, R 23 E); the peak is nearly 1 mile south of Wild Horse Spring. Altitude 8685 feet. Named on Desert Creek Peak (1956) 15' quadrangle.

Wild Horse Spring [INYO]: *spring,* 4.25 miles south of Coso Peak (lat. 36°08'20" N, long. 117°42'35" W; sec. 1, T 21 S, R 39 E). Named on Coso Peak (1951) 15' quadrangle.

Wild Horse Spring [MONO]: *spring,* 6.5 miles east-southeast of Coleville (lat. 38°32'30" N, long. 119°23'40" W; sec. 13, T 8 N, R 23 E); the spring is nearly 1 mile north of Wild Horse Mountain. Named on Desert Creek Peak (1956) 15' quadrangle

Wildrose Canyon [INYO]: *canyon,* 12 miles long, opens into Panamint Valley 10 miles west-northwest of Telescope Peak (lat. 36°14'30" N, long. 117°14'30" W). Named on Emigrant Canyon (1952), Maturango Peak (1951), and Telescope Peak (1952) 15' quadrangles. Members of an exploring party led by Dr. Samuel Gregg George named the canyon in 1860, reportedly for the profusion of wild roses growing there (Hanna, p. 355). Dr. George used the name "Rose Canyon" in reminiscences written in 1875 (Weight, p. 9), and Wheeler (1876, p. 65) used the name "Rose Spring Cañon." DeGroot (p. 210) noted that Wild Rose Springs are in Windy Cañon, presumably meaning present Wildrose Canyon. A spring in Wild Rose Canyon is called Antimony Spring for a nearby antimony mine (Palmer, p. 7).

Wildrose Canyon [MONO]: *canyon,* drained by a stream that flows 2.5 miles to Watterson Meadow 13 miles north-northeast of Toms Place (lat. 37°44'20" N, long. 118°35'30" W; near S line sec. 30, T 2 S, R 31 E); Wildrose mine is in the canyon. Named on Casa Diablo Mountain (1953) 15' quadrangle.

Wildrose Peak [INYO]: *peak,* 5.5 miles southeast of Emigrant Pass (1) (lat. 36°16'30" N, long. 117°04'40" W; near SW cor. sec. 14, T 19 S, R 45 E); the peak is near the head of Wildrose Canyon. Named on Emigrant Canyon (1952) 15' quadrangle.

Wildrose Spring [INYO]: *spring,* 6.5 miles southwest of Emigrant Pass (1) (lat. 36°15'45" N, long. 117°12'40" W); the spring is in Wildrose Canyon. Named on Emigrant Canyon (1952) 15' quadrangle. Called Wild Rose Sp. on Wheeler's (1877) map. Members of an exploring party led by Dr. Samuel Gregg George named the feature Rose Spring in 1860 for the roses blooming there (Federal Writers' Project, p. 51). Dr. George used the name "Rose Springs" in reminiscences written in 1875 (Weight, p. 9).

Wildyrie: see **Lake Mary** [MONO].

Wilfred Canyon [MONO]: *canyon,* 3 miles long, opens into Long Valley (2) 10.5 miles north of Toms Place (lat. 37°42'45" N, long. 118°41'35" W; sec. 5, T 3 S, R 30 E); the canyon is drained by Wilfred Creek. Named on Casa Diablo Mountain (1953) 15' quadrangle.

Wilfred Creek [MONO]: *stream,* flows for 5.5 miles before it ends in Long Valley (2) 7 miles north-northwest of Toms Place (lat. 37° 42' N, long. 118°43'30" W; sec. 12, T 3 S, R 29 E). Named on Casa Diablo Mountain (1953) 15' quadrangle.

Wilkerson Springs [INYO]: *springs,* two, 3 miles east-northeast of Big Pine near the east edge of Owens Valley (lat. 37°11'10" N, long. 118°14'35" W; sec. 10, T 9 S, R 34 E). Named on Waucoba Mountain (1951) 15' quadrangle.

Williams [ALPINE]: *locality,* 10 miles west of Markleeville near Red Lake (lat. 38°42' N, long. 119°58'15" W). Named on Markleeville (1889) 30' quadrangle. Called William's on Wheeler's (1876-1877) map. The name is for Billy Williams, who settled at Red Lake in the early days (Gudde, 1949, p. 390).

Williams Butte [MONO]: *peak,* 2.5 miles south of Lee Vining (lat. 37°55'10" N, long. 119°06'50" W; sec. 28, T 1 N, R 26 E). Altitude 8431 feet. Named on Mono Craters (1953) 15' quadrangle. The name commemorates Thomas Williams, who owned land near the feature in 1882 (Gudde, 1949, p. 390). United States Board on Geographic Names (1994, p. 4) approved the name "Beartrack Creek" for a stream that flows 4.5 miles to Lee Vining Creek 1.6 miles north of Williams Butte (lat. 37°56'34" N, long, 119°07'07" W); the stream heads 0.5 mile south of Log Cabin mine.

Williams Canyon [INYO]: *canyon,* drained by a stream that flows 3 miles to Panamint Valley 9 miles west-northwest of Telescope Peak (lat. 36°14'05" N, long. 117°13'50" W). Named on Telescope Peak (1952) 15' quadrangle. Called William's Canyon on Murphy's (1932) map. The name is for Tom Williams, who had mining claims in the canyon (Palmer, p. 79).

Williamson: see **Mount Williamson** [INYO].

Williamson Creek [INYO]: *stream,* flows 4.25 miles to Shepherd Creek 8.5 miles north of Mount Whitney (1) (lat. 36°42'10" N, long. 118°17'20" W); the stream heads near Mount Williamson. Named on Mount Whitney

(1956) 15' quadrangle.

Willow Creek [ALPINE]: *stream,* flows 6.5 miles to West Fork Carson River 5.5 miles south of Freel Peak (lat. 38°46'40" N, long. 119°55' W). Named on Freel Peak (1955) 7.5' quadrangle.

Willow Creek [INYO]:

(1) *stream,* heads in Cucomungo Canyon and flows 5 miles to Eureka Valley 12 miles east-southeast of Deep Springs (lat. 37° 19'30" N, long. 117°46'30" W; sec. 23, T 7 N, R 38 E); Willow Spring (6) is near the head of the stream. Named on Magruder Mountain (1957) and Soldier Pass (1958) 15' quadrangles.

(2) *stream,* formed by the confluence of North Fork and South Fork, flows 1.5 miles to Saline Valley 1 mile south of the mouth of Paiute Canyon (lat. 36°50'15" N, long. 117°55' W). Named on Waucoba Wash (1951) 15' quadrangle. North Fork is 3 miles long and is named on Waucoba Wash (1951) 15' quadrangle. South Fork is nearly 6 miles long and is named on Independence (1951) and Waucoba Wash (1951) 15' quadrangles. United States Board on Geographic Names (1988, p. 4) approved the name "Willow Creek" for Willow Creek and its South Fork—as shown on the quadrangle map—together, and retained the name "North Fork Willow Creek" for the stream with that name on the map.

(3) *stream,* flows 4 miles to Death Valley 7 miles west-southwest of Funeral Peak (lat. 36°04'10" N, long. 116°44'15" W); the stream heads at Willow Spring (3). Named on Funeral Peak (1951) 15' quadrangle.

Willow Creek [MONO]: *stream,* flows 3.25 miles to an aqueduct 6 miles west-northwest of White Mountain Peak that takes water to Hammil Valley (lat. 37°40'20" N, long. 118°20'55" W). Named on White Mountain Peak (1962) 15' quadrangle.

Willow Creek Camp [INYO]: *locality,* 1 mile south of the mouth of Paiute Canyon on the west edge of Saline Valley (lat. 36°50'15" N, long. 117°55' W); the place is along Willow Creek (2). Named on Waucoba Wash (1951) 15' quadrangle.

Willow Flat [ALPINE]: *area,* nearly 4 miles southwest of Ebbetts Pass (lat. 38°30'20" N, long. 119°51'40" W; near W line sec. 35, T 8 N, R 19 E). Named on Ebbetts Pass (1979) 7.5' quadrangle.

Willow Flat [MONO]: *area,* 6.25 miles south-southwest of Fales Hot Springs along Little Walker River (lat. 38°16'20" N, long. 119°27'15" W; sec. 16, 21, T 5 N, R 23 E). Named on Fales Hot Springs (1954) 7.5' quadrangle.

Willow Lake [INYO]: *lake,* 400 feet long, 10 miles west-southwest of Big Pine along South Fork Big Pine Creek (lat. 37°06' N, long. 118°27'30" W). Named on Big Pine (1950) 15' quadrangle.

Willow Meadow [ALPINE]: *area,* nearly 3 miles west-southwest of Ebbetts Pass along Grouse Creek (2) (lat. 38°31'35" N, long. 119° 51'20" W; near S line sec. 23, T 8 N, R 19 E). Named on Ebbetts Pass (1979) 7.5' quadrangle.

Willow Spring [INYO]:

(1) *spring,* 5 miles northwest of Emigrant Pass (1) (lat. 36°23'45" N, long. 117°11'30" W). Named on Emigrant Canyon (1952) 15' quadrangle.

(2) *spring,* 2.5 miles northwest of Daylight Pass (lat. 36°48'45" N, long. 116°58' W; near W line sec. 22, T 13 S, R 46 E). Named on Bullfrog (1954) 15' quadrangle.

(3) *spring,* 5.25 miles southwest of Furnace Creek (lat. 36°03' N, long. 116°41'15" W); the spring is at the head of Willow Creek (3). Named on Funeral Peak (1951) 15' quadrangle.

(4) *spring,* 3.25 miles east of Manly Peak at the head of Anvil Spring Canyon (lat. 35°54'40" N, long. 117°03'30" W). Named on Manly Peak (1950) 15' quadrangle.

(5) *spring,* nearly 4 miles southeast of Tecopa (lat. 35°48'20" N, long. 116°11' W; near W line sec. 25, T 20 N, R 7 E). Named on Tecopa (1950) 15' quadrangle. This may be the feature that Waring (p. 343) called China Ranch Springs—China Ranch is less than 1 mile downstream from the spring along an unnamed creek.

(6) *spring,* 3.5 miles north of Last Chance Mountain in Cucomungo Canyon (lat. 37°20' N, long. 117°42'10" W); the spring is at the head of Willow Creek (1). Named on Magruder Mountain (1957) 15' quadrangle.

(7) *spring,* 8 miles east-northeast of Independence (lat. 36°49'50" N, long. 118°03'45" W); the spring is in present Willow Springs Canyon. Named on Mount Whitney (1907) 30' quadrangle.

Willow Spring: see **China Garden Spring** [INYO].

Willow Springs [MONO]: *locality,* nearly 5 miles south-southeast of Bridgeport along Virginia Creek (lat. 38°11'20" N, long. 119°12'15" W; sec. 22, T 4 N, R 25 E). Named on Bodie (1958) 15' quadrangle.

Willow Springs Canyon [INYO]: *canyon,* drained by a stream that flows 3.5 miles to lowlands 6.5 miles east-northeast of Independence (lat. 36°49'20" N, long. 118°05' W; sec. 8, T 13 S, R 36 E); Willow Spring (7) is in the canyon. Named on Independence (1951) 15' quadrangle.

Willow Wash [INYO]: *stream* and *dry wash,* extends for 4 miles to Willow Creek (1) 12.5 miles east of Deep Springs (lat. 37°20'15" N, long. 117°45'55" W; near E line sec. 14, T 7 S, R 38 E). Named on Soldier Pass (1958) 15' quadrangle.

Wilson Butte [MONO]: *crater,* 13 miles south-southeast of Lee Vining (lat. 37°47' N, long. 119°01'30" W; sec. 8, T 2 S, R 27 E). Named on Mono Craters (1953) 15' quadrangle.

Wilson Canyon [INYO]:

(1) *canyon,* 5.25 miles long, opens into Indian Wells Valley 4.25 miles south of the mouth of Mountain Springs Canyon (lat. 35°52'35" N, long. 117°35'30" W; sec. 6, T 24 S, R 41 E). Named on Mountain Springs Canyon (1953) 15' quadrangle. The stream that enters the upper end of the canyon is called Sweetwater Creek on Trona (1949) 15' quadrangle.

(2) *canyon,* drained by a stream that flows 5.25 miles to Searles Valley 4.25 miles southeast of Argus Peak (lat. 35°48'55" N, long. 117°23'15" W; sec. 25, T 25 S, R 42 E); the canyon heads near the upper end of Wilson Canyon (1) and trends in the opposite direction. Named on Trona (1949) 15' quadrangle.

Wilson Creek [MONO]: *stream,* flows 10.5 miles to a point near Mono Lake 6.5 miles north-northeast of Lee Vining (lat. 38°02'50" N, long. 119°04'45" W; sec. 11, T 2 N, R 26 E). Named on Bodie (1958) 15' quadrangle. The name commemorates James Wilson, an early settler in the neighborhood (Calhoun, p. vi).

Wilson Creek: see **Sweetwater Creek** [INYO].

Wilson's Well: see **Surveyors Well** [INYO].

Winchell: see **Mount Winchell** [INYO].

Window Rock: see **Echo Canyon** [INYO].

Windy Cañon: see **Wildrose Canyon** [INYO].

Wingate Wash [INYO]: *stream,* heads in San Bernardino County and flows 12 miles in Inyo County to Death Valley 9.5 miles east of Sugarloaf Peak (lat. 35°54'30" N, long. 116°45'50" W; sec. 21, T 21 N, R 2 E). Named on Wingate Wash (1950) 15' quadrangle, which shows the wash entering Long Valley in San Bernardino County. Wheeler's (1877) map has the name "Long Valley" along the course of the stream.

Winnedumah: see **Paiute Monument** [INYO].

Winnedumah Paiute Monument: see **Paiute Monument** [INYO].

Winnemucca Lake [ALPINE]: *lake,* 2350 feet long, 1.5 miles south of Carson Pass (lat. 38°40'10" N, long. 119°59'30" W; sec. 34, T 10 N, R 18 E); the lake is 0.5 mile northeast of Round Top. Named on Carson Pass (1979) 7.5' quadrangle. The local name of the feature, Roundtop Lake, is from the nearby peak called Roundtop (Gudde, 1949, p. 391).

Winters Peak [INYO]: *peak,* 11.5 miles east-southeast of Beatty Junction (lat. 36°31'05" N, long. 116°45'15" W). Altitude 5033 feet. Named on Chloride Cliff (1952) 15' quadrangle. United States Board on Geographic Names (1962a, p. 19) rejected the name "Echo Mountain" for the feature, and noted that the name "Winters Peak" honors Aaron Winters, who discovered borax deposits in Death Valley in 1881.

Witcher Creek [MONO]: *stream,* flows 1.5 miles to Birch Creek (1) 3.25 miles southeast of Toms Place (lat. 37°31'35" N, long. 118° 38'20" W; near W line sec. 12, T 5 S, R 30 E); the stream heads near Witcher Meadow. Named on Casa Diablo Mountain (1953) 15' quadrangle.

Witcher Meadow [MONO]: *area,* 2.5 miles south-southeast of Toms Place (lat. 37°31'45" N, long. 118°40' W); the place is near the head of Witcher Creek. Named on Casa Diablo Mountain (1953) 15' quadrangle. Called Wells Meadow on Mount Morrison (1914) 30' quadrangle.

Wit-so-nah-pah: see **Lake Wit-so-nah-pah** [MONO].

Wobel Canyon: see **Noble Canyon** [ALPINE].

Wobel Lake: see **Noble Lake** [ALPINE].

Wolf Creek [ALPINE]: *stream,* flows 11 miles to East Fork Carson River 5.5 miles south-southeast of Mogul Peak (lat. 38°36'50" N, long. 119°41'35" W; sec. 20, T 9 N, R 21 E). Named on Dardanelles Cone (1979), Disaster Peak (1979), and Wolf Creek (1979) 7.5' quadrangles. Wheeler (1879, p. 178) listed an abandoned mining camp called Centreville that was situated opposite the mouth of Wolf Creek.

Wolf Creek [MONO]: *stream,* flows 5.5 miles to West Walker River 5.5 miles east-northeast of Sonora Pass (lat. 38°20'55" N, long. 119°32'10" W; near W line sec. 23, T 6 N, R 22 E); the stream heads at Wolf Creek Lake. Named on Pickel Meadow (1954) 7.5' quadrangle.

Wolf Creek: see **Little Wolf Creek** [MONO].

Wolf Creek Camp [ALPINE]: *locality,* 6.5 miles south-southeast of Mogul Peak in Wolf Creek Meadows (lat. 38°35'45" N, long. 119° 41'25" W; sec. 29, T 9 N, R 21 E); the place is along Wolf Creek. Named on Wolf Creek (1979) 7.5' quadrangle.

Wolf Creek Lake [ALPINE]: *lake,* 600 feet long, 6.5 miles south-southeast of Mogul Peak (lat. 38°35'55" N, long. 119°40'20" W; sec. 28, T 9 N, R 21 E); the lake is less than 1 mile east of Wolf Creek. Named on Wolf Creek (1979) 7.5' quadrangle.

Wolf Creek Lake [MONO]: *lake,* 900 feet long, 2.25 miles north-northeast of Sonora Pass (lat. 38°21'25" N, long. 119°37'15" W); the lake is at the head of Wolf Creek. Named on Pickel Meadow (1954) 7.5' quadrangle.

Wolf Creek Meadows [ALPINE]: *area,* 7 miles south-southeast of Mogul Peak (lat. 38°35'20" N, long. 119°41'25" W; sec. 29, 32, T 9 N, R 21 E); the place is along Wolf Creek. Named on Wolf Creek (1979) 7.5' quadrangle.

Wolf Creek Pass [ALPINE]: *pass,* 8.5 miles northeast of Dardanelles Cone (lat. 38°29'55" N, long. 119°46'10" W); the pass is north of the head of Wolf Creek. Named on Dardanelles Cone (1979) 7.5' quadrangle.

Wonder Lakes [INYO]: *lakes,* largest 800 feet long, 3.5 miles north of Mount Darwin (lat. 37°13'10" N, long. 118°39'30" W). Named on Mount Goddard (1948) 15' quadrangle.

Wonoga Peak [INYO]: *peak,* 15 miles north-northwest of Olancha (lat. 36°29' N, long. 118°07' W). Altitude 10,371 feet. Named on Olancha (1956) 15' quadrangle.

Wood: see **Mount Wood** [MONO].

Wood Canyon [INYO]:
(1) *canyon,* drained by a stream that flows nearly 5 miles to Panamint Valley 6.25 miles northeast of Maturango Peak (lat. 36° 11' N, long. 117°25' W; sec. 22, T 20 S, R 42 E). Named on Maturango Peak (1951) 15' quadrangle.
(2) *canyon,* 1.5 miles long, opens into Redlands Canyon 2 miles north-northwest of Manly Peak (lat. 35°56'25" N, long. 117°07'40" W). Named on Manly Peak (1950) 15' quadrangle.
(3) *canyon,* 3 miles long, extends east-southeast from Emigrant Pass (1) (lat. 36°20'10" N, long. 117°08'25" W). Named on Emigrant Canyon (1952) 15' quadrangle.

Woodchuck Basin [ALPINE]: *area,* 4 miles west-southwest of Pacific Grade Summit along Silver Creek (2) (lat. 38°52'30" N, long. 119°58'50" W; mainly in sec. 34, T 8 N, R 18 E). Named on Pacific Valley (1979) and Spicer Meadow Reservoir (1979) 7.5' quadrangles.

Woodfords [ALPINE]: *village,* 6 miles north-northwest of Markleeville along West Fork Carson River (lat. 38°46'35" N, long. 119° 49'20" W; near W line sec. 35, T 11 N, R 19 E). Named on Woodfords (1979) 7.5' quadrangle. Called Woodford on Wheeler's (1876-1877) map. Sam Brannan left two men at the spot in 1847 to established an outpost, and although the site was abandoned, it still was known as Brannan Springs; later the place was known as Cary's Mills, or Carey's Mills, for a man named Cary, who built a sawmill there about 1851; still later it was known as Woodfords, for Daniel Woodford, who came to the site in 1849 and built a hotel (Hoover, Rensch, and Rensch, p. 26; Long, p. 19). Postal authorities established Carey's Mills post office in 1858, changed the name to Woodfords in 1869, discontinued it in 1914, reestablished it 1962, and discontinued it in 1974 (Salley, p. 37, 242). They established Tamarack post office 20 miles southwest of Woodfords in 1900 and discontinued it in 1905 (Salley, p. 218).

Woodfords Canyon: see **West Carson Canyon** [ALPINE].

Woodfords Peak: see **Cary Peak** [ALPINE].

Woodpecker Canyon [INYO]: *canyon,* 1.5 miles long, enters Surprise Canyon 4 miles south-southwest of Telescope Peak (lat. 36° 07' N, long. 117°07'05" W). Named on Telescope Peak (1952) 15' quadrangle.

Woods [ALPINE]: *locality,* 2.5 miles north-northeast of present Fourth of July Peak (lat. 38°41'45" N, long. 120°15' W); the place is near present Woods Lake. Named on Pyramid Peak (1896) 30' quadrangle.

Woods Creek [ALPINE]: *stream,* flows 2 miles to Caples Lake 2.5 miles north-northwest of Fourth of July Peak (lat. 38°41'50" N, long. 120°01'55" W; sec. 20, T 10 N, R 18 E); the stream heads at Woods Lake. Named on Caples Lake (1979) 7.5' quadrangle.

Woods Gulch [ALPINE]: *canyon,* drained by a stream that flows 2.5 miles to Arnot Creek 3.5 miles east-northeast of Dardanelles Cone (lat. 38°25'20" N, long. 119°48'35" W). Named on Dardanelles Cone (1979) 7.5' quadrangle.

Woods Lake [ALPINE]: *lake,* 1500 feet long, nearly 2 miles north-northeast of Fourth of July Peak (lat. 38°41' N, long. 120°00'30" W; sec. 28, T 10 N, R 18 E); the lake is at the head of Woods Creek. Named on Caples Lake (1979) 7.5' quadrangle. Called Wood's L. on Wheeler's (1876-1877) map.

Woods Lakes [MONO]: *lakes,* two, each 400 feet long, 6 miles west of Mount Morrison on upper reaches of Mammoth Creek (lat. 37° 34'15" N, long. 118°57'50" W). Named on Mount Morrison (1953) 15' quadrangle.

Wormhole Canyon [INYO]: *canyon,* drained by a stream that flows 2 miles to Cottonwood Creek (3) 11 miles north-northwest of Olancha (lat. 36°25'50" N, long. 118°03'50" W). Named on Olancha (1956) 15' quadrangle.

Wotans Throne [INYO]: *peak,* about 1 mile southeast of Mount Whitney (1) (lat. 36°34' N, long. 118°16'40" W). Named on Mount Whitney (1956) 15' quadrangle.

Wyman Creek [INYO]: *stream,* flows 14 miles to Deep Springs Valley 2.5 miles north of Deep Springs (lat. 37°24'30" N, long. 117°59'25" W; sec. 23, T 6 S, R 36 E). Named on Blanco Mountain (1951) and Soldier Pass (1958) 15' quadrangles. The name recalls Dan Wyman, who came to White Mountains in search of placer gold in 1861 (Chalfant, 1933, p. 143).

—X - Y—

Yaney Canyon [MONO]: *canyon,* drained by a stream that flows 2.25 miles to Swauger Canyon nearly 5 miles west-northwest of Bridgeport (lat. 38°17'20" N, long. 119°18'15" W; near E line sec. 15, T 5 N, R 24 E). Named on Fales Hot Springs (1956) 15' quadrangle. The name commemorates I.P. Yaney, who in the early 1860's operated a lumber mill situated about 4 miles east of Fales Hot Springs (Wedertz, p. 155).

Yaney Creek: see **Swauger Creek** [MONO].

Yellowjacket Canyon [MONO]: *canyon,* 2 miles long, opens into Hammil Valley 12.5 miles west-northwest of White Mountain Peak (lat. 37°42'25" N, long. 118°27'35" W; near E line sec 8, T 3 S, R 32 E); Yellowjacket Spring is near the head of the canyon. Named on White Mountain Peak (1962) 15' quadrangle.

Yellowjacket Spring [MONO]: *spring,* 14 miles west-northwest of White Mountain Peak (lat. 37°43' N, long. 118°29'10" W; sec. 6, T 3 S, R 32 E); the spring is in Yellowjacket Canyon. Named on White Mountain Peak (1962) 15' quadrangle, which shows three springs in the vicinity. Sampson's (1940) map has the plural form "Yellowjacket Springs" for the name.

Yost Creek [MONO]: *stream,* flows 3.25 miles to Reversed Creek 13 miles south of Lee Vining (lat. 37°45'50" N, long. 119°06'15" W; sec. 21, T 2 S, R 26 E); the stream goes through Yost Lake. Named on Devils Postpile (1953) and Mono Craters (1953) 15' quadrangles.

Yost Lake [MONO]: *lake,* 500 feet long, 8.5 miles north-northwest of Mammoth Mountain (lat. 37°44'45" N, long. 119°05'40" W; sec. 27, T 2 S, R 26 E); the lake is along Yost Creek. Named on Devils Postpile (1953) 15' quadrangle.

Yparraquirre Canyon [MONO]: *canyon,* drained by a stream that flows 2.5 miles to West Walker River 7.5 miles north of Tower Peak (lat. 38°15'05" N, long. 119°32'10" W; sec. 27, T 5 N, R 22 E). Named on Tower Peak (1956) 15' quadrangle.

Yuba Hebe Crater: see **Ubehebe Crater** [INYO].

—Z—

Zabriskie [INYO]: *locality,* 5 miles south of Shoshone along Tonopah and Tidewater Railroad (lat. 35°54' N, long. 116°15' W). Named on Avawatz Mountains (1933) 1° quadrangle. The railroad station at the place was named in 1907 for C.B. Zabriskie, an official of Pacific Coast Borax Company; the community that developed there declined when Shoshone became the trading center for the neighborhood (Paher, p. 18). Postal authorities established Zabriskie post office in 1907 and discontinued it in 1918 (Frickstad, p. 53). Waring and Huguenin (p. 34) listed a feature called Borax Well situated 1 mile southwest of Zabriskie at Amargosa borax works.

Zabriskie Point [INYO]: *peak,* 3 miles southeast of Furnace Creek Inn in Black Mountains (lat. 36°25'15" N, long. 116°48'40" W; near E line sec. 36, T 27 N, R 1 E). Altitude 710 feet. Named on Furnace Creek (1952) 1' quadrangle. The name commemorates C.B. Zabriskie of Pacific Coast Borax Company (Palmer, p. 80).

Zinc Hill [INYO]: *ridge,* north-northwest-trending, 1.5 miles long, 6 miles east-northeast of Darwin in Argus Range (lat. 36°17'45" N, long. 117°29'40" W). Named on Darwin (1950) and Panamint Butte (1951) 15' quadrangles.

"Z" Lake [MONO]: *lake,* 750 feet long, 2 miles northeast of Mount Conness (lat. 37°59'20" N, long. 119°17'30" W; sec. 26, T 2 N, R 24 E); the outline of the lake on a map resembles the letter "Z." Named on Tuolumne Meadows (1956) 15' quadrangle.

Zurich [INYO]: *locality,* 2 miles northeast of Big Pine along Southern Pacific Railroad (lat. 37°11' N, long. 118°15'35" W; sec. 9, T 9 S, R 34 E). Named on Big Pine (1950) 15' quadrangle. Called Station on Lippincott's (1902) map, and called Alvord on Lee's (1906) map.

East Sierra Region
Alpine, Inyo and Mono Counties

References Cited

BOOKS AND ARTICLES

Bateman, Paul C. 1956. *Economic geology of the Bishop tungsten district, California.* (California Division of Mines Special Report 47.) San Francisco: California Division of Mines, 87 p.

Bean, Betty. 1977. *Horseshoe Canyon, A brief history of the June Lake loop.* Bishop, California: Chalfant Press, Inc., 116 p.

Belden, L. Burr. 1966. *Mines of Death Valley.* Glendale, California: La Siesta Press, 71 p.

Belden, L. Burr, and Walker, Ardis Manly. 1962. *Searles Lake borax, 1862-1962.* (Published for the dedication of the Searles Lake Monument on November 8, 1962.) (No Place): Death Valley '49ers, Inc., 39 p.

Billeb, Emil W. 1968. *Mining camp days.* Berkeley, California: Howell-North Books, 229 p.

Birnie, R., Jr. 1876. "Executive report of Lieutenant R. Birnie, Jr., Thirteenth United States Infantry, on the operations of party no. 2, California section, field-season of 1875." *Annual report upon the geographical surveys west of the one hundredth meridian, in California, Nevada, Utah, Colorado, Wyoming, New Mexico, Arizona, and Montana.* (Appendix JJ of *The Annual Report of the Chief of Engineers for 1876.*) Washington: Government Printing Office, p. 130-135.

Blackwelder, Eliot. 1933. "Lake Manly—An extinct lake of Death Valley." *Geographical Review,* v. 23, no. 3, p. 464-471.

Blake, William P. 1857. "Geological report." *Reports of explorations and surveys, to ascertain the most practicable and economical route for a railroad from the Mississippi River to the Pacific Ocean.* Volume V, Part II. (33d Cong., 2d Sess., Sen. Ex. Doc. No. 78.) Washington: Beverley Tucker, Printer, 370 p.

Boyd, William Harland. 1972. *A California middle border; The Kern River country, 1772-1880.* Richardson, Texas: The Havilah Press, 226 p.

Brewer, William H. 1949. *Up and down California in 1860-1864.* (Edited by Francis P. Farquhar.) Berkeley and Los Angeles: University of California Press, 583 p.

Bunnell, Lafayette Houghton. 1977. *Discovery of the Yosemite.* (Reprinted from *Discovery of the Yosemite and the Indian War of 1851 which led to that event,* first published in 1880.) Olympic Valley, California: Outbooks, 184 p.

Cain, Ella M. 1956. *The story of Bodie.* San Francisco, California: Fearon Publishers, 196 p.

_____1961. *The story of early Mono County.* San Francisco, California: Fearon Publishers, Inc., 166 p.

Calhoun, Margaret. 1984. *Pioneers of Mono Basin.* Lee Vining, California: Artemisia Press, 172 p.

California Division of Highways. 1934. *California highway transportation survey, 1934.* Sacramento: Department of Public Works, Division of Highways, 130 p. + appendices.

Campbell, Marius R. 1902. *Reconnaissance of the borax deposits of Death Valley and Mohave Desert.* (United States Geological Survey Bulletin 200.) Washington: Government Printing Office, 23 p.

Carlson, Helen S. 1974. *Nevada place names.* Reno, Nevada: University of Nevada Press, 282 p.

Chalfant, W.A. 1933. *The story of Inyo.* (Revised edition.) (Author), 430 p.

_____1947. *Gold, guns, & ghost towns.* Stanford, California: Stanford University Press, 175 p.

Coy, Owen C. 1923. *California county boundaries.* Berkeley: California Historical Survey Commission, 335 p.

Cragen, Dorothy Clara. 1975. *The boys in the sky-blue pants.* Fresno, California: Pioneer Publishing Company, 211 p.

Cronkhite, Daniel. 1968. *Death Valley's victims, A descriptive chronology 1849-1966.* Verdi, Nevada: Sagebrush Press, 33 p.

Decker, Peter. 1966. *The diaries of Peter Decker; Overland to California in 1849 and life in the mines, 1850-1851.* Georgetown, California: The Talisman Press, 338 p.

DeDecker, Mary. 1966. *Mines of the eastern Sierra.* Glendale, California: La Siesta Press, 72 p.

DeGroot, Henry. 1890. "Inyo County." *Tenth annual report of the State Mineralogist, for the year ending December 1, 1890.* Sacramento: California State Mining Bureau, p. 209-218.

Duffield, Anne. 1981. "Petroglyphs of the Coso Range." *Desert,* v. 44, no. 5, p. 50-51, 53.

Eakle, Arthur S. 1919. "Alpine County." *Report XV of the State Mineralogist.* Sacramento: California State Mining Bureau, p. 5-27.

Eakle, Arthur S., and McLaughlin, R.P. 1919. "Mono County." *Report XV of the State Mineralogist.* Sacramento: California State Mining Bureau, p. 135-175.

Eno, Henry. 1965. *Twenty years on the Pacific slope, Letters of Henry Eno from California and Nevada, 1848-1871.* (Edited by W. Turrentine Jackson.) New Haven and London: Yale University Press, 224 p.

Fairbanks, Harold W. 1894. "Preliminary report on the mineral deposits of Inyo, Mono, and Alpine Counties." *Twelfth report of the State Mineralogist, (Second Biennial,) two years ending September 15, 1894.* Sacramento: California State Mining Bureau, 472-478.

Farquhar, Francis P. 1923. "Place names of the High Sierra [Part I]." *Sierra Club Bulletin,* v. 11, no. 4, p. 380-407.

_____1924. "Place names of the High Sierra, Part II." *Sierra Club Bulletin,* v. 12, no. 1, p. 47-64.

_____1925. "Place names of the High Sierra, Part III." *Sierra Club Bulletin,* v. 12, no. 2, p. 126-147.

_____1926. "Mountaineering notes." *Sierra Club Bulletin,* v. 12, no. 3, p. 304-307.

Federal Writers' Project. 1939. *Death Valley, A guide.* Boston: Houghton Mifflin Company, 75 p.

Fletcher, Thomas C. 1987. *Paiute, prospector, pioneer, The Bodie-Mono Lake area in the nineteenth century.* Lee Vining, California: Artemisia Press, 123 p.

Fremont, J.C. 1845. *Report of the exploring expedition to the Rocky Mountains in the year 1842, and to Oregon and North California in the years 1843-'44.* Washington: Blair and Rives, Printers, 583 p.

Frickstad, Walter N. 1955. *A century of California post offices, 1848 to 1954.* Oakland, California: Philatelic Research Society, 395 p.

Gist, Evalyn Slack. 1958. "Skidoo—Ghost camp in the lonely Panamints." *Desert Magazine,* v. 21, no. 4, p. 20-22.

Goddard, George H. 1856. "Report of a survey of a portion of the eastern boundary of California, and of a reconnaissance of the old Carson and Johnson immigrant roads over the Sierra Nevada." *Annual report of the Surveyor-General, of the State of California.* (Sen. Doc. No. 5, sess. of 1856.) Sacramento: State Printer, p. 89-186.

Goodyear, W.A. 1888. "Inyo County." *Eighth annual report of the State Mineralogist, for the year ending October 1, 1888.* Sacramento: California State Mining Bureau, p. 224-309.

Gudde, Erwin G. 1949. *California place names.* Berkeley and Los Angeles: University of California Press, 431 p.

_____1969. *California place names.* Berkeley and Los Angeles: University of California Press, 416 p.

_____1975. *California gold camps.* Berkeley, Los Angeles, London: University of California Press, 467 p.

Hanks, Henry G. 1883. "Report on the borax deposits of California and Nevada." *Third annual report of the State Mineralogist for the year ending June 1, 1883.* Sacramento: California State Mining Bureau, Part 2, 111 p.

Hanna, Phil Townsend. 1951. *The dictionary of California land names.* Los Angeles: The Automobile Club of Southern California, 392 p.

Hawkins, Clarabell E. 1975. *Story of Laws, California.* (Author), 29 p.

Hildebrand, George H. 1982. *Borax pioneer: Francis Marion Smith.* San Diego, California: Howell-North Books, 318 p.

Hoffman, Helen. 1984. *Owens Valley, A guide to Independence and Lone Pine.* (Author), 79 p.

Hoover, Mildred Brooke, Rensch, Hero Eugene, and Rensch, Ethel Grace. 1966. *Historic spots in California.* (Third edition, revised by William N. Abeloe.) Stanford, California: Stanford University Press, 642 p.

Hubbard, Douglass. 1958. *Ghost mines of Yosemite.* Fredericksburg, Texas:

The Awani Press, (no pagination).

Hubbard, Paul B., Bray, Doris, and Pipkin, George. 1965. *Ballarat, 1897-1917, Facts and folklore.* Lancaster, California: Paul B. and Arline B. Hubbard, 98 p.

Hungerford, John B. 1958. *The Slim Princess, The story of the Southern Pacific narrow gauge.* (Second edition.) Reseda, California: Hungerford Press, 31 p.

Irelan, William, Jr. 1888. "Report of the State Mineralogist." *Eighth annual report of the State Mineralogist. For the year ending October 1, 1888.* Sacramento: California State Mining Bureau, p. 12-695.

Iroquois Research Institute. 1979. *A land use history of Coso Hot Springs, Inyo County, California.* (Administrative publication 200.) China Lake, California: Naval Weapons Center, 228 p.

Jenkins, Marguerite. 1960. "Dirty Sock, A 'for free' spa on the Mojave Desert." *Desert Magazine,* v. 23, no. 4, p. 27-28.

Kip, Leonard. 1946. *California sketches, with recollections of the gold mines.* Los Angeles: N.A. Kovach, 58 p.

Knopf, Adolph. 1914. "The Darwin silver-lead mining district, California." *Contributions to economic geology, 1913, Part I, Metals and nonmetals except fuels.* (United States Geological Survey Bulletin 580-A.) Washington: Government Printing Office, p. 1-18.

_____1917. "Tungsten deposits of northwestern Inyo County, California." *Contributions to economic geology, 1916, Part I, Metals and nonmetals except fuels.* (United States Geological Survey Bulletin 640-L.) Washington: Government Printing Office, p. 229-249.

Koenig, George. 1984. *Beyond this place there be dragons.* Glendale, California: The Arthur H. Clark Company, 263 p.

Kroeber, A.L. 1916. "California place names of Indian origin." *University of California Publications in American Archæology and Ethnology,* v. 12, no. 2, p. 31-69.

La Braque, Lily Mathieu. 1984. *Man from Mono.* Reno, Nevada: Nevada Academic Press, 196 p.

Lee, Bourke. 1930. *Death Valley.* New York: The Macmillan Company, 210 p.

Lee, Willis T. 1906. *Geology and water resources of Owens Valley, California.* (United States Geological Survey Water-Supply and Irrigation Paper 181.) Washington: Government Printing Office, 28 p.

Lewis, Ernest Allen. 1981. *The Frémont cannon, High up and far back.* Glendale, California: The Arthur H. Clark Company, 168 p.

Lingenfelter, Richard E. 1986. *Death Valley and the Amargosa.* Berkeley, Los Angeles, London: University of California Press, 664 p.

Lippincott, Joseph Barlow. 1902. *Storage of water on Kings River, California.* (United States Geological Survey Water-Supply and Irrigation Paper No. 58.) Washington: Government Printing Office, 101 p.

Loew, Oscar. 1876a. "Report on the geological and mineralogical character of southeastern California and adjacent regions." *Annual report upon the geographical surveys west of the one hundredth meridian, in California, Nevada, Utah, Colorado, Wyoming, New Mexico, Arizona, and Montana.* (Appendix JJ of *The Annual Report of the Chief of Engineers for 1876.*) Washington: Government Printing Office, p. 173-188.

_____1876b. "Report on the alkaline lakes, thermal springs, mineral springs, and brackish waters of southern California and adjacent country." *Annual report upon the geographical surveys west of the one hundredth meridian, in California, Nevada, Utah, Colorado, Wyoming, New Mexico, Arizona, and Montana.* (Appendix JJ of *The Annual Report of the Chief of Engineers for 1876.*) Washington: Government Printing Office, p. 188-199.

Long, Ileen Price (Chairman, Centennial Book Committee). 1964. *Alpine heritage, One hundred years of history, recreation, lore, in Alpine County, California, 1864-1964.* Campbell, California: Craftsmen Typographers, Inc., 66 p.

Lyman, C.S. 1849. "Observations on California." *American Journal of Science and Arts,* (series 2), v. 7, no. 20, p. 290-292, 305-309.

Macomb, M.M. 1878. "Executive and descriptive report of Lieutenant M.M. Macomb, Fourth Artillery, on the operations of Party No. 2, California section, Field season of 1877." *Annual report upon the geographical surveys of the territory of the United States west of the 100th meridian, in the states and territories of California, Colorado, Kansas, Nebraska, Nevada, Oregon, Texas, Arizona, Idaho, Montana, New Mexico, Utah, Washington, and Wyoming.* (Appendix NN of *The Annual Report of the Chief of Engineers for 1878.*) Washington: Government Printing Office, 139-145.

_____1879. "Report of Lieutenant M.M. Macomb, Fourth Artillery, in charge of Party No. 2, California Section, field season of 1878 and 1879." *Annual report upon the geographical surveys of the territory of the United States west of the 100th Meridian, in the states and territories of California, Colorado, Kansas, Nebraska, Nevada, Oregon, Texas, Arizona, Idaho, Montana, New Mexico, Utah, Washington, and Wyoming.* (Appendix OO of *The Annual Report of the Chief of Engineers for 1879.*) Washington: Government Printing Office, p. 253-261.

Manly, William Lewis. 1929. *Death Valley in '49.* New York, Santa Barbara: Wallace Hebberd, 524 p.

Mendenhall, Walter C. 1909. *Some desert watering places in southeastern California and southwestern Nevada.* (United States Geological Survey Water-Supply Paper 224.) Washington: Government Printing Office, 98 p.

Mitchell, Roger. 1971. "Exploring Inyo's Saline Valley." *Desert Magazine,* v. 34, no. 11, p. 7-9.

_____1978. "Two of Mono's forgotten ghosts." *Desert,* v. 41, no. 7, p. 8-11.

Moorman, Madison Berryman. 1948. *The journal of Madison Berryman Moorman, 1850-1851.* (Edited by Irene D. Paden.) San Francisco: California Historical Society, 150 p.

Murbarger, Nell. 1956. *Ghosts of the glory trail.* Palm Desert, California: Desert Magazine Press, 291 p.

Murphy, F.M. 1932. "Geology of a part of the Panamint Range, California." *Mining in California,* v. 28, no. 3 and 4, p. 329-356.

Myrick, David F. 1962-1963, *Railroads of Nevada and eastern California.* Berkeley, California: Howell-North Books, (2 volumes) 933 p.

Nadeau, Remi. 1965. *Ghost towns and mining camps of California.* Los Angeles: The Ward Ritchie Press, 278 p.

Neal, Howard. 1977. "Desert ghosts, Schwab, California." *Desert,* v. 40, no. 11, p. 42-43.

Noyes, L.W. 1856. "Report of L.W. Noyes, Esq., of the Calaveras exploring expedition." *Annual report of the Surveyor-General, of the State of California.* (Sen. Doc. No. 5, Sess. of 1856.) Sacramento: State Printer, p. 325-327.

Olmsted, Frank H. 1901. "Physical characteristics of Kern River, California, with special reference to electric power development." *Reconnaissances of Kern and Yuba Rivers, California.* (United States Geological Survey Water-Supply and Irrigation Paper No. 46.) Washington: Government Printing Office, p. 11-38.

Paher, Stanley W. 1973. *Death Valley ghost towns.* Las Vegas, Nevada: Nevada Publications, 48 p.

Palmer, T.S. 1948. *Place names of the Death Valley region in California and Nevada.* (Privately printed), 80 p.

Powers, O.B. 1856. "Report on the Calaveras Route." *Annual report of the Surveyor-General, of the State of California.* (Sen. Doc. No. 5, Sess. of 1856.) Sacramento: State Printer, p. 187-191.

Pritchard, James A. 1959. *The overland diary of James A. Pritchard from Kentucky to California in 1849.* Denver, Colorado: The Old West Publishing Company, 221 p.

Quimby, Myron J. 1969. *Scratch Ankel, U.S.A., American place names and their derivation.* New York: A.S. Barnes and Company, 390 p.

Russell, Israel C. 1889. "Quaternary history of Mono Valley, California." *Eighth Annual Report of the United States Geological Survey, 1886-87.* Part I. Washington: Government Printing Office, p. 261-394.

Salley, H.E. 1977. *History of California post offices, 1849-1976.* La Mesa, California: Postal History Association, Inc., 300 p.

Sampson, R.J. 1940. "Mineral resources of Mono County." *California Journal of Mines and Geology,* v. 36, no. 2, p. 117-156.

Schumacher, Genny (editor). 1962. *Deepest Valley.* San Francisco: Sierra Club, 206 p.

Shannon, Betty. 1971. "Mono County's mines of Mount Patterson." *Desert Magazine,* v. 34, no. 7, p. 34-35, 44-45.

Sinclair, C.H. 1901. *Oblique boundary line between California and Nevada.* (United States. Coast and Geodetic Survey, Report for 1900, Appendix 3.) Washington: Government Printing Office, p. 253-484.

Smith, Jedediah S. 1977. *The southwest expedition of Jedediah S. Smith, His personal account of the journey to California, 1826-1827.* (Edited by George R. Brooks.) Glendale, California: The Arthur H. Clark Company, 259 p.

Smith, Genny (editor). 1976. *Mammoth Lakes Sierra.* (Fourth edition.) Palo Alto, California: Genny Smith Books, 147 p.

Sowaal, Marguerite. 1985. *Naming the eastern Sierra.* Bishop, California: Chalfant Press, 125 p.

Spears, John R. 1892. *Illustrated sketches of Death Valley and other borax deserts of the Pacific Coast.* Chicago and New York: Rand, McNally & Company, Publishers, 226 p.

Stewart, George R. 1970. *American place-names, A concise and selective dictionary for the continental United States of America.* New York: Oxford University Press, 550 p.

Strong, Mary Frances. 1971. "The lively marble ghost." *Desert Magazine,* v. 34, no. 7, p. 24-25.

Thompson, David G. 1921. *Routes to desert watering places in the Mohave Desert region, California.* (United States Geological Survey Water-Supply Paper 490-B.) Washington: Government Printing Office, p. 87-269.

_____1929. *The Mohave Desert region, California.* (United States Geological Survey Water-Supply Paper 578.) Washington: Government Printing Office, 759 p.

Tucker, W. Burling. 1927. "Los Angeles field division." *Mining in California,* v. 23, no. 4, p. 374-406.

Tucker, W.B., and Sampson, R. J. 1938. "Mineral resources of Inyo County." *California Journal of Mines and Geology,* v. 34, no. 4, p. 368-500.

United States Board on Geographic Names (under name "United States Geographic Board"). 1933. *Sixth report of the United States Geographic Board, 1890-1932.* Washington: Government Printing Office, 834 p.

_____(under name "United States Geographic Board"). 1934. *Decisions of the United States Geographic Board, No. 30—June 30, 1932.* (Yosemite National Park, California.) Washington: Government Printing Office, 29 p.

_____(under name "United States Board on Geographical Names"). 1938. *Decisions of the United States Board on Geographical Names, Decisions rendered between July 1, 1937, and June 30, 1938.* Washington: Government Printing Office, 62 p.

_____(under name "United States Board on Geographical Names"). 1939. *Decisions of the United States Board on Geographical Names, Decisions rendered between July 1, 1938, and June 30, 1939.* Washington: Government Printing Office, 41 p.

_____1950. *Decisions on names in the United States and Alaska rendered during April, May, and June 1950.* (Decision list no. 5006.) Washington: Department of the Interior, 47 p.

_____1954. *Decisions on names in the United States, Alaska and Puerto Rico, Decisions rendered from July 1950 to May 1954.* (Decision list no. 5401.) Washington: Department of the Interior, 115 p.

_____1957. *Decisions on names in the Unites States, Alaska and Hawaii, Decisions rendered from May 1954 through March 1957.* (Decision list no. 5701.) Washington: Department of the Interior, 23 p.

_____1959. *Decisions on names in the United States, Decisions rendered from January 1959 through April 1959.* (Decision list no. 5902.) Washington: Department of the Interior, 49 p.

_____1960a. *Decisions on names in the United States, Decisions rendered from September 1959 through December 1959.* (Decision list no. 5904.) Washington: Department of the Interior, 68 p.

_____1960b. *Decisions on names in the United States, Puerto Rico and the Virgin Islands, Decisions rendered from January through April 1960.* (Decision list no. 6001.) Washington: Department of the Interior, 79 p.

_____1960c. *Decisions on names in the United States and the Virgin Islands, Decisions rendered from May 1960 through August 1960.* (Decision list no. 6002.) Washington: Department of the Interior, 77 p.

_____1961a. *Decisions on names in the United States, Decisions rendered from September through December 1960.* (Decision list no. 6003.) Washington: Department of the Interior, 73 p.

_____1961b. *Decisions on names in the United States, Decisions rendered from January through April 1961.* (Decision list no. 6101.) Washington: Department of the Interior, 74 p.

_____1962a. *Decisions on names in the United States, Decisions rendered from September through December 1961.* (Decision list no. 6103.) Washington: Department of the Interior, 75 p.

_____1962b. *Decisions on names in the United States, Decisions rendered from May through August 1962.* (Decision list no. 6202.) Washington: Department of the Interior, 81 p.

_____1964a. *Decisions on geographic names in the United States, September through December 1963.* (Decision list no. 6303.) Washington: Department of the Interior, 66 p.

_____1964b. *Decisions on geographic names in the United States, January through April 1964.* (Decision list no. 6401.) Washington: Department of the Interior, 74 p.

_____1964c. *Decisions on geographic names in the United States, May through August 1964.* (Decision list no. 6402.) Washington: Department of the Interior, 85 p.

_____1965a. *Decisions on geographic names in the United States, September through December 1964.* (Decision list no. 6403.) Washington: Department of the Interior, 66 p.

_____1965b. *Decisions on geographic names in the United States, July through September 1965.* (Decision list no. 6503.) Washington: Department of the Interior, 74 p.

_____1966a. *Decisions on geographic names in the United States, October through December 1965.* (Decision list no. 6504.) Washington: Department of the Interior, 38 p.

_____1966b. *Decisions on geographic names in the United States, January through March 1966.* (Decision list no. 6601.) Washington: Department of the Interior, 44 p.

_____1967. *Decisions on geographic names in the United States, October through December 1966.* (Decision list no. 6604.) Washington: Department of the Interior, 36 p.

_____1968a. *Decisions on geographic names in the United States, January through March 1968.* (Decision list no. 6801.) Washington: Department of the Interior, 51 p.

_____1968b. *Decisions on geographic names in the United States, April through June 1968.* (Decision list no. 6802.) Washington: Department of the Interior, 42 p.

_____1969. *Decisions on geographic names in the United States, January through March 1969.* (Decision list no. 6901.) Washington: Department of the Interior, 31 p.

_____1970. *Decisions on geographic names in the United States, April through June 1970.* (Decision list no. 7002.) Washington: Department of the Interior, 20 p.

_____1971. *Decisions on geographic names in the United States, July through September 1971.* (Decision list no. 7103.) Washington: Department of the Interior, 18 p.

_____1972. *Decisions on geographic names in the United States, October through December 1971.* (Decision list no. 7104.) Washington: Department of the Interior, 20 p.

_____1974a. *Decisions on geographic names in the United States, October through December 1973.* (Decision list no. 7304.) Washington: Department of the Interior, 15 p.

_____1974b. *Decisions on geographic names in the United States, July through September 1974.* (Decision list no. 7403.) Washington: Department of the Interior, 34 p.

_____1975. *Decisions on geographic names in the United States, January through March 1975.* (Decision list no. 7501.) Washington: Department of the Interior, 36 p.

_____1978a. *Decisions on geographic names in the United States, April through June 1978.* (Decision list no. 7802.) Washington: Department of the Interior, 30 p.

_____1978b. *Decisions on geographic names in the United States, October through December 1978.* (Decision list no. 7804.) Washington: Department of the Interior, 48 p.

_____1979a. *Decisions on geographic names in the United States, January through March 1979.* (Decision list no. 7901.) Washington: Department of the Interior, 27 p.

_____1979b. *Decisions on geographic names in the United States, April through June 1979.* (Decision list no. 7902.) Washington: Department of the Interior, 33 p.

_____1980. *Decisions on geographic names in the United States, April through June 1980.* (Decision list no. 8002.) Washington: Department of the Interior, 33 p.

_____1983a. *Decisions on geographic names in the United States, July through September 1982.* (Decision list no. 8203.) Washington: Department of the Interior, 25 p.

_____1983b. *Decisions on geographic names in the United States, October through December 1982.* (Decision list no. 8204.) Washington: Department of the Interior, 26 p.

_____1983c. Decisions on geographic names in the United States, January through March 1983. (Decision list no. 8301.) Washington: Department of the Interior, 33 p.

_____1983d. *Decisions on geographic names in the United States, April through June 1983.* (Decision list no. 8302.) Washington: Department of the Interior, 29 p.

_____1983e. *Decisions on geographic names in the United States, July through September 1983.* (Decision list no. 8303.) Washington: Department of the Interior, 26 p.

_____1983f. *Decisions on geographic names in the United States, October through December 1983.* (Decision list no. 8304.) Washington: Department of the Interior, 20 p.

_____1984a. *Decisions on geographic names in the United States, January through March 1984.* (Decision list no. 8401.) Washington: Department of the Interior, 29 p.

_____1984b. *Decisions on geographic names in the United States, July through September 1984.* (Decision list no. 8403.) Washington: Department of the Interior, 10 p.

_____1985a. *Decisions on geographic names in the United States, January through March 1985.* (Decision list no. 8501.) Washington: Department of the Interior, 18 p.

_____1985b. *Decisions on geographic names in the United States, April through June 1985.* (Decision list no. 8502.) Washington: Department of the Interior, 12 p.

_____1985c. *Decisions on geographic names in the United States, October through December 1985.* (Decision list no. 8504.) Washington: Department of the Interior, 12 p.

_____1986. *Decisions on geographic names in the United States, July through September 1986.* (Decision list no. 8603.) Washington: Department of the Interior, 11 p.

_____1987a. *Decisions on geographic names in the United States, July through September 1987.* (Decision list no. 8703.) Washington: Department of the Interior, 18 p.

_____1987b. *Decisions on geographic names in the United States, October through December 1987.* (Decision list no. 8704.) Washington: Department of the Interior, 15 p.

_____1988. *Decisions on geographic names in the United States, October through December 1988.* (Decision list no. 8804.) Washington: Department of the Interior, 20 p.

_____1990. *Decisions on geographic names in the United States.* (Decision list 1990.) Washington: Department of the Interior, 35 p.

_____1991. *Decisions on geographic names in the United States.* (Decision list 1991.) Washington: Department of the Interior, 40 p.

_____1994. *Decisions on geographic names in the United States.* (Decision list 1994.) Washington: Department of the Interior, 17 p.

_____1995. *Decisions on geographic names in the United States.* (Decision list 1995.) Washington: Department of the Interior, 19 p.

Versteeg, Chester. 1923. "The peaks and passes of the Upper Basin, South Fork of the Kings River." *Sierra Club Bulletin,* v. 11, no. 4, p. 421-426.

Waring, Clarence A., and Huguenin, Emile. 1919. "Inyo County." *Report XV of the State Mineralogist.* Sacramento: California State Mining Bureau, p. 28-134.

Waring, Gerald A. 1915. *Springs of California.* (United States Geological Survey Water-Supply Paper 338.) Washington: Government Printing Office, 410 p.

Wedertz, Frank S. 1978. *Mono Diggings.* Bishop, California: Chalfant Press, Inc., 245 p.

Weight, Harold O. 1960. "A summer visit to the Panamints." *Desert Magazine,* v. 23, no. 7, p. 8-9, 25-28.

Wheeler, George M. 1876. *Annual report upon the geographical surveys west of the one hundredth meridian, in California, Nevada, Utah, Colorado, Wyoming, New Mexico, Arizona, and Montana.* (Appendix JJ of *The Annual Report of the Chief of Engineers for 1876.*) Washington: Government Printing Office, 355 p

_____1878. *Annual report upon the geographical surveys of the territory of the United States west of the 100th meridian, in the states and territories of California, Colorado, Kansas, Nebraska, Nevada, Oregon, Texas, Arizona, Idaho, Montana, New Mexico, Utah, Washington, and Wyoming.* (Appendix NN of *The Annual Report of the Chief of Engineers for 1878.*) Washington: Government Printing Office, 234 p.

_____1879. *Annual report upon the geographical surveys of the territory of the United States west of the 100th meridian, in the states and territories of California, Colorado, Kansas, Nebraska, Nevada, Oregon, Texas, Arizona, Idaho, Montana, New Mexico, Utah, Washington, and Wyoming.* (Appendix OO of *The Annual Report of the Chief of Engineers for 1879.*) Washington: Government Printing Office, 340 p.

Whitney, J.D. 1865. *Report of progress and synopsis of the field-work from 1860 to 1864.* (Geological Survey of California, Geology, Volume I.) Published by authority of the Legislature of California, 498 p.

_____1870. *The Yosemite guide-book.* Published by authority of the Legislature [of California], 155 p.

Wilkes, Charles. 1958. *Columbia River to the Sacramento.* Oakland, California: Biobooks, 140 p.

Wilkins, Thurman. 1958. *Clarence King, A biography.* New York: The Macmillan Company, 441 p.

Wright, James W.A. 1984. *The Lost Cement mine.* (Genny Smith, editor.) Mammoth Lakes, California: Genny Smith Books, 95 p.

Woodward, Arthur. 1961. *Camels and surveyors in Death Valley.* (Publication no. 7.) (No place): Death Valley '49ers, Inc., 73 p.

QUADRANGLE MAPS

(All maps published by United States Geological Survey. Dates identify the editions of the maps. If a reprinted or revised map was used, the year of reprinting or revision is given in parentheses, unless the reprinted or revised map is cited specifically in the text.)

Ash Meadows 15'—1952.
Aurora 15'—1956.
Avawatz Mountains 1°—1933 (reprinted 1945).
Ballarat 1°—1913 (reprinted 1947).
Bennetts Well 15'—1952.
Benton 15'—1962.
Big Dune 15'—1952 (minor corrections 1967).
Big Meadow 15'—1956.
Big Pine 15'—1950 (minor corrections 1958).
Big Trees 30'—1891.
Bishop 30'—1913 (reprinted 1941).
15'—1949.
Blanco Mountain 15'—1951.
Bodie 15'—1958.
Bridgeport 30'—1909.
15'—1958.
Bullfrog 15'—1954.
Caples Lake 7.5'—1979.
Carson Pass 7.5'—1979.
Casa Diablo Mountain 15'—1953.
Chloride Cliff 15'—1952.
Chris Flat 7.5'—1954.
Confidence Hills 15'—1950.
Coso Peak 15'—1951.
Cowtrack Mountain 15'—1962.
Dardanelle 7.5'—1979.
Dardanelles 30'—1898.
Dardanelles Cone 15'—1956.
7.5'—1979.
Darwin 15'—1950.
Davis Mountain 15'—1963.
Death Valley 1°x 2°—1954 (limited revision 1961).
Desert Creek Peak 15'—1956.
Devils Postpile 15'—1953.
Disaster Peak 7.5'—1979.
Donnell Lake 7.5'—1979.
Dry Mountain 15'—1957.
Eagle Mountain 15'—1951.
Ebbetts Pass 7.5'—1979.
Emigrant Canyon 15'—1952.
Fales Hot Springs 15'—1956.
7.5'—1954.
Freel Peak 15'—1956.
7.5'—1955 (photorevised 1969).
Fresno 1°x 2°—1962 (limited revision 1967).
Funeral Peak 15'—1951.
Furnace Creek 1°—1910 (reprinted 1941).
15'—1952.
Glass Mountain 15'—1962.
Goldfield 1°x 2°—1954.
Grapevine Peak 15'—1957.
Haiwee Reservoir 15'—1951.
Heenan Lake 7.5'—1979.
Horse Thief Springs 15'—1956.
Huntoon Valley 15'—1958.
Independence 15'—1951.
Keeler 15'—1951.
Lamont Peak 15'—1956.
Last Chance Range 15'—1958.
Lida 1°—1913.
Little Lake 15'—1954.
Lone Pine 15'—1958.
Lost Cannon Peak 7.5'—1954.
Magruder Mountain 15'—1957.
Manly Peak 15'—1950.
Marble Canyon 15'—1951.
Mariposa 1°x 2°—1957 (revised 1970).
Markleeville 30'—1889.
15'—1956.
7.5'—1979.
Matterhorn Peak 15'—1956.
Maturango Peak 15'—1951.
Merced Peak 15'—1953.
Minden 7.5'—1968 (photorevised 1974).
Mokelumne Peak 7.5'—1979.
Monache Mountain 15'—1956.
Mono Craters 15'—1953.
Mount Abbot 15'—1953.
Mountain Springs Canyon 15'—1953.
Mount Barcroft 15'—1962.
Mount Goddard 30'—1912 (reprinted 1940).
15'— 1948 (minor corrections 1957).
Mount Lyell 30'—1901 (reprinted 1948).
Mount Morrison 30'—1914 (reprinted 1950).
15'—1953.
Mount Pinchot 15'—1953.
Mount Siegel 15'—1957.
Mount Tom 15'—1949.
Mount Whitney 30'—1907 (reprinted 1910); 1937.
15'—1956 (limited revision 1967).
New York Butte 15'—1950.
Olancha 30'—1907 (reprinted 1931).
15'—1956.
Pacific Valley 7.5'—1979.
Pahrump 15'—1958.
Panamint Butte 15'—1951.
Pickel Meadow 7.5'—1954.
Piper Peak 15'—1963.
Pyramid Peak 30'—1896 (corrected 1940, reprinted 1947).
Ryan 15'—1952.
Searles Lake 1°—1915 (reprinted 1946).
Shenandoah Peak 15'—1956.
Shoshone 15'—1951.
Silver Lake 15'—1956.
Soldier Pass 15'—1958.
Sonora Pass 15'—1956.
7.5'—1979.
South Lake Tahoe 7.5'—1955 (photorevised 1969 and 1974).

Spicer Meadow Reservoir 7.5'—1979.
Stewart Valley 15'—1958.
Stovepipe Wells 15'—1952.
Tamarack 7.5'—1979.
Tecopa 15'—1950.
Telescope Peak 15'—1952.
Tin Mountain 15'—1957.
Topaz Lake 15'—1956.
Tower Peak 15'—1956.
Trench Canyon 15'—1958.
Trona 1°x 2°—1957 (limited revision 1963).
15'—1949.
Tuolumne Meadows 15'—1956.
Ubehebe Crater 15'—1957.
Ubehebe Peak 15'—1950.
Waucoba Mountain 15'—1951 (minor corrections 1958).
Waucoba Spring 15'—1958.
Waucoba Wash 15'—1951 (minor corrections 1965).
Wellington 30'—1893; 1893, reprinted 1942.
White Mountain 30'—1917 (reprinted 1951).
White Mountain Peak 15'—1962.
Wingate Wash 15'—1950 (minor corrections 1965).
Wolf Creek 7.5'—1979.
Woodfords 7.5'—1979.

MISCELLANEOUS MAPS

Baker. 1855. "Map of the mining region, of California." Drawn by Geo. A. Baker.

Bancroft. 1864. "Bancroft's map of the Pacific States." Compiled by Wm. H. Knight. Published by H.H. Bancroft & Co., Booksellers and Stationers, San Francisco, Cal.

California Division of Highways. 1934. (Appendix "A" *of* California Division of Highways, 1934.)

California Mining Bureau. 1917a. (Untitled map *in* California Mining Bureau Bulletin 74, p. 165.)

____1917b. (Untitled map in California Mining Bureau Bulletin 74, p. 170.)

Campbell. 1902. "Sketch map of Mohave Desert and Death Valley." (Plate I *in* Campbell.)

Colton. 1863. "Colton's map of California, Nevada, Utah, Colorado, Arizona, & New Mexico". Published by J.H. Colton, 172 William St., New York.

Eakel and McLaughlin. 1917. "Map of portion of Mono County, California." (Plate II *in* Eakel and McLaughlin.)

Holt. 1864. "Holt's map of the Owen's River mining county." Compiled and drawn from the most reliable information by Arthur W. Reddie; published by Warren Holt, San Francisco, Cal.

Inyo County. 1883. "Mining map of Inyo County." (Map reproduced in *Early California, Southern Edition.* Corvalis, Oregon: Western Guide Publishers, p. 26-27.)

Lee. 1906. "Map of Owens Valley, California." (Plate I *in* W.T. Lee.)

Lippincott. 1902. "Map of drainage basin of Kings River, California, showing route traversed by exploring parties." (Plate I *in* Lippincott.)

Mitchell. 1856. "Mitchell's new national map." Published by S. Augustus Mitchell, Philadelphia.

Murphy. 1932. "Reconnaissance geologic map of a part of the Panamint Range, California." (Plate IV *in* Murphy.)

Olmstead. 1900. "Map of upper Kern River." [Plate III *in* Olmstead.)

Postal Route. 1884. (Map reproduced in *Early California, Southern Edition.* Corvalis, Oregon: Western Guide Publishers, p. 34-35.)

Reed. 1864. "A map of the Silver Mountain mining districts, including the territory of the proposed new county of Alpine." Compiled by Therion Reed. San Francisco, Cal., H.H. Bancroft & Co. (Reproduced *in* Long.)

Russell. 1889. "Hydrographic basin of Lake Mono." (Plate XVII *in* Russell.)

Sampson. 1940. "Map of Mono County, showing location of principal mining properties." (Plate I *in* Sampson.)

Thompson. 1921. "Relief map of part of Mohave Desert region, California, showing desert watering places." (Plate X *in* Thompson, 1921.)

Tucker and Sampson. 1938. "Map of Inyo County, California, showing location of principal mines." (Plate III *in* Tucker and Sampson.)

Wheeler. 1871. "Parts of southern Nevada and eastern California." (Atlas Sheet No. 57.) Expedition of 1871 under the command of 1st Lieut. Geo. M. Wheeler.

____1876-1877. "Parts of eastern California and western Nevada." (Atlas Sheet No. 56B.) Expeditions of 1876 & 1877 under the command of 1st Lieut. Geo. M. Wheeler.

____1877. "Part of eastern California." (Atlas Sheet No. 65D.) Expeditions of 1871 and 1875 under command of 1st Lieut. Geo. M. Wheeler.

Part Ten
South Coast Region

Los Angeles, Orange, San Diego and Ventura Counties

Part Ten- South Coast Region

South Coast Region
Los Angeles, Orange, San Diego and Ventura Counties

Regional Setting

General.—This section concerns geographic features in four counties—Los Angeles, Orange, San Diego, and Ventura—that front on the southernmost coast of California. Townships (T) and Ranges (R) refer to San Bernardino Base and Meridian. Although the region is highly urbanized and industrialized, all four of the counties include some remote and unsettled parts. The region generally has a moderate climate near the coast and a somewhat harsher climate farther inland. Most of the inhabitants depend on water brought from outside. The map on the facing page shows the location of the South Coast Region and the counties in it.

Los Angeles County.—Los Angeles County lies along the coast between Orange County and Ventura County, and includes highlands to the north and east. The east part of Los Angeles County is at the southwest tip of Mojave Desert—the name "Mojave" for the desert is from the designation of Indians that lived farther east near Colorado River (Gudde, 1949, p. 219); United States Board on Geographic Names (1934, p. 11) rejected the form "Mohave Desert" for the name, and cited local usage for the decision. San Clemente Island and Santa Catalina Island offshore belong to Los Angeles County. The first state legislature created the county in 1850, and in 1851 the county boundaries were changed so that it included the territory of present San Bernardino County; in 1853 the east part of this huge area was lost when San Bernardino County itself was organized, and more territory was lost in 1889 with the formation of Orange County; the Los Angeles-Ventura County line was uncertain from the beginning, and it was not until 1923 that all of the Los Angeles County boundaries were finally defined (Coy, p. 140-156). Los Angeles has been the county seat from the beginning (Hoover, Rensch, and Rensch, p. 146).

Orange County.—Orange County includes lowlands adjacent to Los Angeles County and highlands farther south. The state legislature created Orange County in 1889 from part of Los Angeles County, and the county boundaries have not changed (Coy, p. 196). Santa Ana is and always has been the county seat (Hoover, Rensch, and Rensch, p. 259).

San Diego County.—San Diego County occupies the extreme southwest corner of California at the Mexican border. It extends from the low-lying coastal lands eastward across highlands to the arid depression occupied by Salton Sea in Imperial County. The state legislature created a San Diego County in 1850 that included most of present San Diego, Imperial, Riverside, and San Bernardino Counties; the legislature reduced the size of San Diego County by removing present San Bernardino County in 1851, present Riverside County in 1893, and present Imperial County in 1907 (Coy, p. 221-223). San Diego has always been the county seat; the county name is from San Diego Bay (Hoover, Rensch, and Rensch, p. 328).

Ventura County.—Ventura County extends from the coast inland to include the lower part of the valley of Santa Clara River and highlands adjacent to the river. The county includes Anacapa Island and San Nicolas Island offshore. The state legislature created Ventura County in 1872 from the east part of Santa Barbara County; some territory was added to the east by a resurvey of Los Angeles-Ventura County line in 1881, a boundary made official in 1923 (Coy, p. 291-293). Ventura has been the the seat of county government from the beginning; the county name is derived from San Buenaventura mission (Hoover, Rensch, and Rensch, p. 576).

SOUTH COAST REGION
LOS ANGELES, ORANGE, SAN DIEGO AND VENTURA COUNTIES

- A -

Abadi Creek [VENTURA]: *stream,* flows 5.25 miles to Sespe Creek 6 miles west-southwest of Reyes Peak (lat. 34°36'30" N, long. 119° 23' W; near W line sec. 13, T 6 N, R 24 W). Named on Old Man Mountain (1943) 7.5' quadrangle.

Abalone Cove [LOS ANGELES]: *embayment,* 7 miles south of Redondo Beach city hall along the coast (lat. 33°44'30" N, long. 118°22'50" W). Named on Redondo Beach (1951) 7.5' quadrangle.

Abalone Point [LOS ANGELES]: *promontory,* 0.5 mile east of Avalon on the northeast side of Santa Catalina Island (lat. 33°20'35" N, long. 118°19' W). Named on Santa Catalina East (1950) 7.5' quadrangle.

Abalone Point [ORANGE]: *promontory,* 2.25 miles west-northwest of Laguna Beach city hall along the coast (lat. 33°33'15" N, long. 117°49'10" W). Named on Laguna Beach (1965) 7.5' quadrangle. Meadows (p. 102) listed a small cove called Morro Bay that is located on the east side of Abalone Point.

Abbott's Landing: see **Balboa** [ORANGE].

Aberdeen Canyon [LOS ANGELES]: *canyon,* less than 1 mile long, 5.25 miles north-northwest of Los Angeles city hall (lat. 34°07'15" N, long. 118°17'15" W). Named on Hollywood (1953) 7.5' quadrangle.

Abrams Canyon [LOS ANGELES]: *canyon,* drained by a stream that flows 1.5 miles to Pine Canyon (3) 1 mile west of the village of Lake Hughes (lat. 34°40'40" N, long. 118°27'30" W; sec. 22, T 7 N, R 15 W). Named on Lake Hughes (1957) 7.5' quadrangle.

Absco: see **Ventura** [VENTURA].

Acelga: see **Santa Ana** [ORANGE].

Acton [LOS ANGELES]: *town,* 20 miles northeast of downtown San Fernando in Soledad Canyon (lat. 34°28'10" N, long. 118°11'45" W; mainly in sec. 36, T 5 N, R 13 W). Named on Acton (1959) 7.5' quadrangle. Postal authorities established Acton post office in 1887 (Frickstad, p. 69). According to local residents, the name is from Acton, Massachusetts (Hanna, p. 2).

Acton Camp [LOS ANGELES]: *locality,* 1.25 miles south of Acton in Soledad Canyon (lat. 34°26'55" N, long. 118°11'50" W; near NW cor. sec. 12, T 4 N, R 13 W). Named on Acton (1959) 7.5' quadrangle. Acton (1939) 6' quadrangle has the label "CCC Camp" at the place. Los Angeles County (1935) map shows a feature called Chitwood Canyon that opens into Soledad Canyon from the north opposite the site of Acton Camp.

Acton Canyon [LOS ANGELES]: *canyon,* drained by a stream that flows 2.5 miles to lowlands 1.5 miles north-northeast of Acton (lat. 34°29'15" N, long. 118°11'20" W; sec. 25, T 5 N, R 13 W). Named on Acton (1959) and Ritter Ridge (1958) 7.5' quadrangles.

Adams Barranca [VENTURA]: *gully,* extends for 2 miles from the mouth of Adams Canyon to Santa Clara River 2.5 miles south-southwest of Santa Paula (lat. 34°19'30" N, long. 119°05'10" W). Named on Santa Paula (1951) 7.5' quadrangle.

Adams Canyon [LOS ANGELES]: *canyon,* 2 miles long, opens into lowlands 17 miles east-southeast of Gorman (lat. 34°45'35" N, long. 118°33'30" W; at N line sec. 27, T 8 N, R 16 W). Named on Burnt Peak (1958) and Neenach School (1965) 7.5' quadrangles.

Adams Canyon [VENTURA]: *canyon,* drained by a stream that flows 6.25 miles to the valley of Santa Clara River 2.5 miles west of Santa Paula (lat. 34°20'45" N, long. 119°06'10" W). Named on Santa Paula (1951) and Santa Paula Peak (1951) 7.5' quadrangles. The name commemorates William G. Adams, who started digging a well for oil in a branch of the canyon in 1872 (Ricard).

Adams Hill [LOS ANGELES]: *peak,* 5.5 miles west-southwest of Pasadena city hall (lat. 34°07'45" N, long. 118°14'05" W). Named on Pasadena (1953) 7.5' quadrangle.

Adams Square [LOS ANGELES]: *locality,* 5.5 miles west of Pasadena city hall (lat. 34°08' N, long. 118°14'30" W); the place is northwest of Adams Hill. Named on Pasadena (1953) 7.5' quadrangle.

Adler Canyon: see **Alder Canyon** [SAN DIEGO].

Adobe Creek [VENTURA]: *stream,* flows 3.5 miles to Sespe Creek 8 miles north-northwest of Wheeler Springs (lat. 34°36'20" N, long. 119°21'50" W; near SW cor. sec. 18, T 6 N, R 23 W). Named on Reyes Peak (1943) and Wheeler Springs (1943) 7.5' quadrangles.

Adobe Flats [SAN DIEGO]: *area,* 6.25 miles northwest of Mesa Grande (lat. 33°14'25" N, long. 116°51'05" W). Named on Mesa Grande (1948) 7.5' quadrangle.

Adobe Mountain [LOS ANGELES]: *hill,* 11 miles north-northeast of Black Butte on Los Angeles-San Bernardino County line (lat. 34° 42'15" N, long. 117°40'15" W; around SE cor. sec. 12, T 7 N, R 8 W). Named on Adobe Mountain (1955) 7.5' quadrangle.

Adobe Springs [SAN DIEGO]: *springs,* 8.5 miles north-northwest of Warner Springs (lat. 33°23'45" N, long. 116°41'45" W; sec. 8, T 9 S, R 3 E). Named on Beauty Mountain (1960) 7.5' quadrangle.

Agoura [LOS ANGELES]: *town,* 29 miles west-northwest of Los Angeles city hall (lat. 34°08'35" N, long. 118°44'20" W). Named on Calabasas (1952) 7.5' quadrangle. Seminole (1932) 6' quadrangle has both the names "Picture City" and "Agoura P.O." at the place. Postal authorities established Agoura post office in 1927 and moved it 0.5 mile west in 1937 (Salley, p. 2). When they established the post office at the community of Picture City, they requested a one-word designation for the facility; the name "Agoura" was chosen because the site was on Agoura ranch (Gudde, 1949, p. 4). According to Hanna (p. 2), the name "Agoura" is a corruption of the surname "Lagoura" of an early settler.

Agra [SAN DIEGO]: *locality,* 2 miles south-southwest of San Onofre Mountain along Atchison, Topeka and Santa Fe Railroad (lat. 33° 20' N, long. 117°30' W). Named on Las Pulgas Canyon (1968) and San Onofre Bluff (1968) 7.5' quadrangles. The place originally was a cattle loading station (Stein, p. 1).

Agua Amarga Canyon [LOS ANGELES]: *canyon,* drained by a stream that flows 2.5 miles to the sea 5.25 miles south-southwest of Redondo Beach city hall at Lunada Bay (lat. 33°46'10" N, long. 118°25'15" W). Named on Redondo Beach (1951) 7.5' quadrangle.

Agua Blanca Creek [VENTURA]: *stream,* flows 16 miles to Piru Creek 7.5 miles southeast of Cobblestone Mountain (lat. 34°32'25" N, long. 118°45'40" W; at S line sec. 3, T 5 N, R 18 W). Named on Cobblestone Mountain (1958), Devils Heart Peak (1943), and McDonald Peak (1958) 7.5' quadrangles.

Agua Caliente: see **Los Tules** [SAN DIEGO]; **San Jose del Valle** [SAN DIEGO]; **Warner Springs** [SAN DIEGO].

Agua Caliente Creek [SAN DIEGO]: *stream* and *dry wash,* extends for 10.5 miles to San Luis Rey River 5 miles west of Warner Springs (lat. 33°16'45" N, long. 116°43'15" W). Named on Hot Springs Mountain (1960) and Warner Springs (1959) 7.5' quadrangles.

Agua Caliente de San Juan: see **San Juan Hot Springs** [ORANGE].

Agua Caliente Hot Springs: see **Agua Caliente Springs** [SAN DIEGO].

Agua Caliente Springs [SAN DIEGO]: *locality,* 52 miles east-northeast of San Diego (lat. 32°57' N, long. 116°18'10" W; sec. 18, T 14 N, R 7 E). Named on Agua Caliente Springs (1959) 7.5' quadrangle. On Cuyapaipe (1944) 15' quadrangle, the name "Agua Caliente Hot Springs" applies to springs at the place.

Agua Canyon [LOS ANGELES]: *canyon,* drained by a stream that flows less than 1 mile to Arroyo Seco 5.5 miles north-northwest of Pasadena city hall (lat. 34°13'25" N, long. 118°10'45" W). Named on Pasadena (1966) 7.5' quadrangle.

Agua Chinon Wash [ORANGE]: *stream,* flows 7.5 miles to San Diego Creek 9 miles southeast of Santa Ana city hall (lat. 33°39'05" N, long. 117°45'20" W). Named on El Toro (1968) and Tustin (1965) 7.5' quadrangles. The canyon of the upper part of the stream is called Tomato Spring Canyon on Corona (1902) 30' quadrangle. The name "Agua Chinon" is from Cañada de Agua Chinon, an early name for present Limestone Canyon (Stephenson, p. 124).

Agua del Palo Verde: see **Laguna Reservoir** [ORANGE].

Agua del Toro: see **Serrano Creek** [ORANGE].

Agua Dulce [LOS ANGELES]: *village,* 9 miles northeast of Solemint in

Sierra Pelona Valley (lat. 34°29'45" N, long. 118°19'30" W; at NW cor. sec. 26, T 5 N, R 14 W). Named on Agua Dulce (1960) 7.5' quadrangle. Postal authorities established Agua Dulce post office in 1955 (Salley, p. 2).

Agua Dulce: see **Palmdale** [LOS ANGELES].

Agua Dulce Canyon [LOS ANGELES]: *canyon,* 8 miles long, opens into Soledad Canyon 7.5 miles east-northeast of Solemint (lat. 34° 26'20" N, long. 118°19'25" W; near S line sec. 10, T 4 N, R 14 W). Named on Agua Dulce (1960) and Sleepy Valley (1958) 7.5' quadrangles. Los Angeles County (1935) map shows several canyons near Agua Dulce Canyon: Decker Canyon, which opens into Soledad Canyon from the north less than 1 mile east of the mouth of Agua Dulce Canyon (near W line sec. 11, T 4 N, R 14 W); Burke Canyon, which opens into Soledad Canyon from the north 1.25 miles east of the mouth of Agua Dulce Canyon (sec. 11, T 4 N, R 14 W); Johns Canyon, which opens into Soledad Canyon from the north 1.5 miles east of the mouth of Agua Dulce Canyon (near W line sec. 12, T 4 N, R 14 W); Alpine Canyon, which opens into Soledad Canyon from the south opposite the mouth of Agua Dulce Canyon; and Paso Canyon, which opens into Agua Dulce Canyon from the northwest about 1.5 miles north of the mouth of Agua Dulce Canyon (sec. 3, T 4 N, R 14 W).

Agua Dulce Creek [SAN DIEGO]: *stream,* flows 1.25 miles to Boiling Spring Ravine 7.5 miles north-northeast of Buckman Springs (lat. 32°52'20" N, long. 116°26'35" W; at S line sec. 11, T 15 S, R 5 E). Named on Mount Laguna (1960) 7.5' quadrangle.

Agua Dulce Well [SAN DIEGO]: *well,* 7.5 miles north-northeast of Buckman Springs (lat. 32°52'20" N, long. 116°26'35" W; at N line sec. 14, T 15 S, R 5 E); the feature is along Agua Dulce Creek. Named on Mount Laguna (1960) 7.5' quadrangle.

Agua Escondido: see **Escondido Creek** [SAN DIEGO].

Aguage del Padre Gomez: see **Tomato Spring** [ORANGE].

Aguagito: see **San Juan Capistrano** [ORANGE].

Agua Hedionda [SAN DIEGO]:

(1) *land grant,* inland from Carlsbad. Named on Encinitas (1968), Rancho Santa Fe (1968), San Luis Rey (1968), and San Marcos (1968) 7.5' quadrangles. Juan Maria Marron received 3 leagues in 1842 and claimed 13,311 acres patented in 1872 (Cowan, p. 12-13).

(2) *lake,* nearly 1.25 miles long, 4.5 miles southeast of Oceanside (lat. 33°08'30" N, long. 117°19'30" W); the feature is at the mouth of Agua Hedionda Creek on Agua Hedionda grant. Named on San Luis Rey (1968) 7.5' quadrangle.

Agua Hedionda Creek [SAN DIEGO]: *stream,* flows 9.5 miles to Agua Hedionda (2) 5.25 miles southeast of Oceanside (lat. 33°08'30" N, long. 117°18'45" W). Named on San Luis Rey (1968) and San Marcos (1968) 7.5' quadrangles.

Aguaje de la Centinela [LOS ANGELES]: *land grant,* at Inglewood. Named on Inglewood (1964) and Venice (1950) 7.5' quadrangles. Ignacio Machado received the land in 1844; Bruno Avila claimed 2219 acres patented in 1872 (Cowan, p. 13).

Aguaje del Cuate: see **Gavilan** [ORANGE].

Aguaje Lodoso: see **Mud Spring** [LOS ANGELES].

Agua Magna Canyon [LOS ANGELES]: *canyon,* 1.5 miles long, 4.5 miles south of Torrance city hall (lat. 33°46'20" N, long. 118°21'15" W). Named on Torrance (1964) 7.5' quadrangle.

Agua Negra Canyon [LOS ANGELES]: *canyon,* 1.25 miles long, 4.5 miles south-southwest of Torrance city hall (lat. 33°46'30" N, long. 118°21'30" W). Named on Torrance (1964) 7.5' quadrangle. The name is from adobe-blackened water in the canyon (Fink, p. 22).

Aguanga Creek: see **Temecula Creek** [SAN DIEGO].

Aguanga Mountain [SAN DIEGO]: *ridge,* generally west-northwest-trending, 6 miles long, 9 miles east of Boucher Hill (lat. 33°19'45" N, long. 116°45'30" W). Named on Palomar Observatory (1949) and Warner Springs (1959) 7.5' quadrangles.

Agua Tibia: see **Pala** [SAN DIEGO].

Agua Tibia Creek [SAN DIEGO]: *stream,* flows 5.25 miles to San Luis Rey River 3 miles east-southeast of Pala (lat. 33°20'40" N, long. 117°01'35" W; near S line sec. 31, T 9 S, R 1 W). Named on Boucher Hill (1948), Pala (1968), and Vail Lake (1953) 7.5' quadrangles.

Agua Tibia Mountain [SAN DIEGO]: *ridge,* generally northwest-trending, about 5 miles long, 7 miles northwest of Boucher Hill (lat. 33°25' N, long. 117°00' W). Named on Pechanga (1968) and Vail Lake (1953) 7.5' quadrangles.

Ah-DA-HI: see **Camp Ah-DA-HI** [LOS ANGELES].

Airplane Flat [LOS ANGELES]: *area,* nearly 6 miles west of Mount San Antonio (lat. 34°17'10" N, long. 117°44'50" W). Named on Mount San Antonio (1955) 7.5' quadrangle.

Airplane Ridge [SAN DIEGO]: *ridge,* southeast-trending, 1.5 miles long, 2 miles south-southeast of Cuyamaca Peak (lat. 32°55'15" N, long. 116°35'25" W). Named on Cuyamaca Peak (1960) 7.5' quadrangle.

Akens Canyon [LOS ANGELES]: *canyon,* drained by a stream that flows 1 mile to Big Tujunga Canyon 1.25 miles north of Sunland (lat. 34°16'40" N, long. 118°18'30" W). Named on Sunland (1953) 7.5' quadrangle.

Alamitos Bay [LOS ANGELES]: *bay,* opens to the sea 5 miles east-southeast of Long Beach city hall by the mouth of San Gabriel River (lat. 33°44'35" N, long. 118°07' W). Named on Long Beach (1949), Los Alamitos (1950), and Seal Beach (1950) 7.5' quadrangles. Early maps show marsh at the place fed by water of San Gabriel River; in 1934 officials of Long Beach ordered that the course of San Gabriel River be separated from the bay (Gleason p. 101-102).

Alamitos Beach [LOS ANGELES]: *locality,* less than 1 mile east-southeast of present Long Beach city hall along Los Angeles Terminal Railroad (lat. 33°46' N, long. 118°10'45" W). Named on Downey (1902) 15' quadrangle.

Alamo Camp [VENTURA]: *locality,* 1.5 miles northwest of McDonald Peak (lat. 34°39'05" N, long. 118°56'30" W; near SW cor. sec. 36, T 7 N, R 20 W); the place is along Alamo Creek (1). Named on McDonald Peak (1958) 7.5' quadrangle.

Alamo Creek [VENTURA]:

(1) *stream,* flows 5.25 miles to Mutau Creek 15 miles east-northeast of Reyes Peak (lat. 34°40'20" N, long. 119°00'55" W; near W line sec. 29, T 7 N, R 20 W); the stream heads at Alamo Mountain. Named on Lockwood Valley (1943) and McDonald Peak (1958) 7.5' quadrangles.

(2) *stream,* flows 9 miles to join Beartrap Creek and form Cuyama River 4 miles south of Reyes Peak (lat. 34°41'25" N, long. 119°17'30" W; sec. 23, T 7 N, R 23 W). Named on Reyes Peak (1943) and San Guillermo (1943) 7.5' quadrangles.

Alamo Mountain [VENTURA]: *ridge,* northwest-trending, 2 miles long, 2.25 miles north-northwest of McDonald Peak (lat. 34°39'55" N, long. 118°57'15" W). Named on McDonald Peak (1958) 7.5' quadrangle.

Alamos Canyon [VENTURA]: *canyon,* drained by a stream that flows 6 miles to Arroyo Simi 3.5 miles east of Moorpark (lat. 34° 17' N, long. 118°49' W; sec. 1, T 2 N, R 19 W). Named on Simi (1951) 7.5' quadrangle.

Alcoholic Pass [SAN DIEGO]: *pass,* 7 miles north of Borrego Springs (lat. 33°21'35" N, long. 116°22'35" W; sec. 29, T 9 S, R 6 E). Named on Borrego Palm Canyon (1959) 7.5' quadrangle.

Alder Canyon [SAN DIEGO]: *canyon,* drained by a stream that flows 0.5 mile to Riverside County 11.5 miles north-northeast of Warner Springs (lat. 33°25'35" N, long. 116°32'05" W; at N line sec. 2, T 9 S, R 4 E). Named on Bucksnort Mountain (1960) 7.5' quadrangle. Called Elder Canyon on Ramona (1903) 30' quadrangle, and called Adler Canyon on Warner Springs (1960) 15' quadrangle. The feature divides at the head to form North Fork, which is partly in Riverside County, and South Fork. Each fork is 5.25 miles long, and each is named on Bucksnort Mountain (1960) 7.5' quadrangle.

Alder Creek [LOS ANGELES]:

(1) *stream,* flows 2.25 miles to Gold Creek 4.25 miles north-northwest of Sunland (lat. 34°19'10" N, long. 118°19'50" W; sec. 27, T 3 N, R 14 W). Named on Sunland (1953) 7.5' quadrangle.

(2) *stream,* formed by the confluence of North Fork and West Fork, flows 4.25 miles to Big Tujunga Canyon 5.5 miles south-southwest of Pacifico Mountain (lat. 34°18'25" N, long. 118°04'20" W; sec. 31, T 3 N, R 11 W). Named on Chilao Flat (1959) 7.5' quadrangle. North Fork is 2 miles long and is named on Chilao Flat (1959) 7.5' quadrangle. West Fork is 2.25 miles long and is named on Chilao Flat (1959) and Pacifico Mountain (1959) 7.5' quadrangles. Present West Fork is called North Fork on Alder Creek (1941) 6' quadrangle. East Fork enters from the east 2.5 miles upstream from the mouth of the main creek and is nearly 4 miles long. Middle Fork enters 3.5 miles upstream from the mouth of the main creek and is 3 miles long. East Fork and Middle Fork are named on Chilao Flat (1959) 7.5' quadrangle.

Alder Creek [VENTURA]: *stream,* flows nearly 7 miles to Sespe Creek 2 miles northeast of Devils Heart Peak (lat. 34°33'50" N, long. 118°57'10" W; sec. 36, T 6 N, R 20 W). Named on Devils Heart Peak (1943) and McDonald Peak (1958) 7.5' quadrangles. East Fork enters from the east 1.5 miles above the mouth of the main stream; it is nearly 3 miles long and is named on Devils Heart Peak (1943) 7.5' quadrangle.

Alder Gulch [LOS ANGELES]: *canyon,* drained by a stream that flows 1.5 miles to San Gabriel River 5 miles west-northwest of Mount San Antonio (lat. 34°19'10" N, long. 117°43'40" W; at E line sec. 29, T 3 N, R 8 W). Named on Mount San Antonio (1955) 7.5' quadrangle.

Alder Saddle [LOS ANGELES]: *pass,* nearly 2 miles southeast of Pacifico Mountain (lat. 34°21'50" N, long. 118°00'45" W; near E line sec. 10, T 3 N, R 11 W); the pass is at the head of Middle Fork Alder Creek (2). Named on Chilao Flat (1959) 7.5' quadrangle.

Alder Spring [ORANGE]: *spring,* 2.5 miles south-southeast of Santiago Peak in Trabuco Canyon (lat. 33°40'45" N, long. 117°30'45" W; near NW cor. sec. 4, T 6 S, R 6 W). Named on Santiago Peak (1954) 7.5' quadrangle.

Alexander Spring [LOS ANGELES]: *spring,* 1.25 miles northeast of Crystal Lake (lat. 34°19'45" N, long. 117°49'30" W). Named on Crystal Lake (1958) 7.5' quadrangle.

Alhambra [LOS ANGELES]: *city,* 7.25 miles east-northeast of Los Angeles city hall (lat. 34°05'35" N, long. 118°07'35" W). Named on El Monte

(1953) and Los Angeles (1953) 7.5' quadrangles. Postal authorities established Alhambra post office in 1885 (Frickstad, p. 70), and the city incorporated in 1903.

Alhambra: see **North Alhambra** [LOS ANGELES]; **West Alhambra**, under **Shorb** [LOS ANGELES].

Alhambra Wash [LOS ANGELES]: *stream*, flows 6.5 miles to Rio Hondo 3 miles southwest of El Monte city hall (lat. 34°02'45" N, long. 118°04'25" W). Named on El Monte (1953) and Los Angeles (1953) 7.5' quadrangles.

Alimony Ridge [LOS ANGELES]: *ridge*, north-trending, 1 mile long, 8 miles west of Valyermo (lat. 34°27'15" N, long. 117°59'30" W). Named on Juniper Hills (1959) 7.5' quadrangle.

Aliso [ORANGE]: *locality*, about 3 miles southeast of present Santa Ana city hall along a railroad (lat. 33°43'30" N, long. 117°50" W). Named on Santa Ana (1901) 15' quadrangle.

Aliso Beach [ORANGE]: *beach*, 2 miles southeast of Laguna Beach city hall along the coast (lat. 33°30'35" N, long. 117°45'05" W; sec. 6, T 8 S, R 8 W); the feature is at the mouth of Aliso Creek. Named on Laguna Beach (1965, photorevised 1981) 7.5' quadrangle.

Aliso Canyon [LOS ANGELES]:

(1) *canyon*, drained by a stream that flows 8.5 miles to Soledad Canyon 2 miles east of Acton (lat. 34°28'15" N, long. 118°09'45" W; sec. 32, T 5 N, R 12 E). Named on Acton (1959) and Pacifico Mountain (1959) 7.5' quadrangles.

(2) *canyon*, nearly 3 miles long, opens into lowlands 4.5 miles east-northeast of Chatsworth (lat. 34°16'40" N, long. 118°31'35" W). Named on Oat Mountain (1952) 7.5' quadrangle.

Aliso Canyon [ORANGE]: *canyon*, drained by a stream that heads in Riverside County and flows 2.5 miles to Lucas Canyon 10 miles east-northeast of San Juan Capistrano (lat. 33°34'10" N, long. 117° 30'30" W; at W line sec. 10, T 7 S, R 6 W). Named on Cañada Gobernadora (1968) and Sitton Peak (1954) 7.5' quadrangles. Called Verdugo Canyon on Lake Elsinore (1942) 15' quadrangle, where present Verdugo Canyon is unnamed.

Aliso Canyon [SAN DIEGO]: *canyon*, 7.25 miles long, opens into lowlands along the coast 6.25 miles southeast of San Onofre Mountain (lat. 33°17'15" N, long. 117°25'15" W; near S line sec. 20, T 10 S, R 5 W). Named on Las Pulgas Canyon (1968) and Morro Hill (1968) 7.5' quadrangles.

Aliso Canyon [VENTURA]: *canyon*, drained by a stream that flows 8 miles to the valley of Santa Clara River 2.5 miles north of Saticoy (lat. 34°19'10" N, long. 119°08'40" W). Named on Ojai (1952) and Saticoy (1951) 7.5' quadrangles.

Aliso Canyon: see **Deer Canyon** [LOS ANGELES] (1); **Devil Canyon** [LOS ANGELES].

Aliso Canyon Wash [LOS ANGELES]: *stream*, heads at the mouth of Aliso Canyon (2) and flows 7 miles to Los Angeles River 3.5 miles east-southeast of the center of Canoga Park (lat. 34°11'25" N, long. 118°32'25" W). Named on Canoga Park (1952) and Oat Mountain (1952) 7.5' quadrangles.

Aliso City: see **El Toro** [ORANGE].

Aliso Creek [ORANGE]: *stream*, flows 18 miles to the sea 3 miles southeast of Laguna Beach city hall (lat. 33°30'40" N, long. 117° 45'10" W; sec. 6, T 8 S, R 8 W). Named on El Toro (1968), Laguna Beach (1965, photorevised 1981), and San Juan Capistrano (1968) 7.5' quadrangles. Called Alisos Creek on El Toro (1950) and Santiago Peak (1954) 7.5' quadrangles.

Aliso Point [ORANGE]: *promontory*, 3.25 miles southeast of Laguna Beach city hall along the coast (lat. 33°30'20" N, long. 117°45' W; sec. 6, T 8 S, R 8 W); the feature is southeast of Aliso Beach. Named on Laguna Beach (1965, photorevised 1981) 7.5' quadrangle.

Alisos Creek: see **Aliso Creek** [ORANGE].

Aliso Spring [LOS ANGELES]: *spring*, 2.5 miles west-northwest of Pacifico Mountain (lat. 34°23'45" N, long. 122°04'25" W); the spring is in the upper part of Aliso Canyon (1). Named on Pacifico Mountain (1959) 7.5' quadrangle.

Alla [LOS ANGELES]: *locality*, 6.5 miles north of Manhattan Beach city hall along Pacific Electric Railroad (lat. 33°58'50" N, long. 118°25'40" W). Named on Venice (1950) 7.5' quadrangle.

Alligator Rock [SAN DIEGO]: *rock*, 5.5 miles west-northwest of downtown San Diego along the coast (lat. 32°44'35" N, long 117° 15'15" W). Named on Point Loma (1967) 7.5' quadrangle.

Allison Gulch [LOS ANGELES]: *canyon*, drained by a stream that flows 2.5 miles to San Gabriel River 6 miles west-southwest of Mount San Antonio (lat. 34°15'45" N, long. 117°44'45" W). Named on Mount San Antonio (1955) 7.5' quadrangle.

Allison Springs: see **La Mesa** [SAN DIEGO].

All Nations Camp [LOS ANGELES]: *locality*, 3.5 miles west-northwest of Big Pines (lat. 34°23'50" N, long. 117°44'45" W). Named on Mescal Creek (1956) 7.5' quadrangle.

Almond [ORANGE]: *locality*, less than 1 mile east-southeast of present Buena Park civic center along Southern Pacific Railroad (lat. 33°51'35" N, long. 117°59'05" W; at S line sec. 36, T 3 S, R 11 W). Named on Anaheim (1950) 7.5' quadrangle.

Almond [SAN DIEGO]: *locality*, 5.5 miles west-southwest of Mesa Grande in Pamo Valley (lat. 33°08'35" N, long. 116°50'50" W; near S line sec. 11, T 12 S, R 1 E). Named on Ramona (1903) 30' quadrangle. Postal authorities established Almond post office in 1896, moved it 2 miles northwest in 1908, and discontinued it in 1914; the name was from an almond grove at the site (Salley, p. 5).

Almondale: see **Pearblossom** [LOS ANGELES].

Aloha [SAN DIEGO]: *locality*, 5.5 miles east of present National City civic center (lat. 32°41'10" N, long. 117°01' W). Named on San Diego (1904) 15' quadrangle.

Alolia: see **Saugus** [LOS ANGELES].

Alosta: see **Glendora** [LOS ANGELES].

Alpine [LOS ANGELES]:

(1) *locality*, nearly 3 miles south-southeast of Palmdale along Southern Pacific Railroad (lat. 34°32'20" N, long. 118°06'20" W; at S line sec. 2, T 5 N, R 12 W); the place is 0.5 mile south-southeast of Harold. Named on Palmdale (1937) 6' quadrangle. United States Board on Geographic Names (1960b, p. 8) rejected the name "Alpine" for nearby Harold. Los Angeles County (1935) map has the name "Alpine Spgs. Cany." for a feature located west of the site of Alpine (1) (sec. 10, 11, T 5 N, R 12 W).

(2) *locality*, 7 miles east of Solemint along Southern Pacific Railroad (lat. 34°26'15" N, long. 118°20'15" W; near S line sec. 10, T 4 N, R 14 W). Named on Lang (1933) 6' quadrangle. Los Angeles County (1935) map shows a feature called Alpine Canyon that opens into Soledad Canyon near Alpine (2) (at N line sec. 15, T 4 N, R 14 W).

Alpine [SAN DIEGO]: *town*, 11.5 miles east-northeast of the city of El Cajon (lat. 32°50'05" N, long. 116°46' W; in and near sec. 27, 28, T 15 S, R 2 E). Named on Alpine (1955) 7.5' quadrangle. Postal authorities established Alpine post office in 1885 (Frickstad, p. 148). B.R. Arnold founded the town in the 1880's; an elderly woman named the community because its setting reminded her of her native Switzerland (Stein, p. 4).

Alpine: see **Harold** [LOS ANGELES].

Alpine Butte [LOS ANGELES]: *mountain*, 9.5 miles north-northeast of Littlerock (lat. 34°37'50" N, long. 117°53'50" W; at SW cor. sec. 1, T 6 N, R 10 W). Altitude 3259 feet. Named on Alpine Butte (1957) and Littlerock (1957) 7.5' quadrangles.

Alpine Canyon [LOS ANGELES]: *canyon*, nearly 2 miles long, 2.25 miles southeast of Crystal Lake (lat. 34°17'40" N, long. 117°49'10" W). Named on Crystal Lake (1958) 7.5' quadrangle.

Alpine Canyon: see **Agua Dulce Canyon** [LOS ANGELES]; **Alpine** [LOS ANGELES] (2).

Alpine Creek [SAN DIEGO]: *stream*, flows nearly 4 miles to Galloway Valley 2.5 miles west of Alpine (lat. 32°50'35" N, long. 116° 48'15" W; near NW cor. sec. 29, T 15 S, R 2 E); the stream goes through Alpine. Named on Alpine (1955) 7.5' quadrangle.

Alpine Heights [SAN DIEGO]: *locality*, 1.25 miles southwest of Alpine (lat. 32°49'15" N, long. 116°46'45" W; in and near sec. 33, T 15 S, R 2 E). Named on Alpine (1955) 7.5' quadrangle.

Alpine Springs Canyon: see **Alpine** [LOS ANGELES] (1).

Alpine Springs Colony: see **Littlerock** [LOS ANGELES].

Alsace [LOS ANGELES]: *locality*, 6.25 miles north of Manhattan Beach city hall along Pacific Electric Railroad (lat. 33°58'45" N, long. 118°25' W). Named on Venice (1950) 7.5' quadrangle.

Alta: see **Grossmont** [SAN DIEGO].

Altacanyada [LOS ANGELES]: *district*, 6.5 miles north-northwest of present Pasadena city hall (lat. 34°13'20" N, long. 118°12'25" W; near N line sec. 35, T 2 N, R 13 W). Named on La Crescenta (1939) 6' quadrangle. Los Angeles County (1935) map has the form "Alta Canyada" for the name.

Altadena [LOS ANGELES]: *city*, 3 miles north-northeast of Pasadena city hall (lat. 34°11'30" N, long. 118°07'30" W). Named on Mount Wilson (1953) and Pasadena (1953) 7.5' quadrangles. Postal authorities established Altadena post office in 1894 (Frickstad, p. 70). The name, applied in 1887, is from the position of the community above Pasadena (Gudde, 1949, p. 9). California Mining Bureau's (1917a) map shows a place called La Vina located about 3 miles north of Altadena. Postal authorities established La Vina post office in 1915 (Salley, p. 119).

Altamira Canyon [LOS ANGELES]: *canyon*, drained by a stream that flows 1.25 miles to the sea 7.25 miles south of Redondo Beach city hall (lat. 33°44'25" N, long. 118°22'35" W). Named on San Pedro (1964) and Torrance (1964) 7.5' quadrangles.

Alvarado Canyon [SAN DIEGO]: *canyon*, 6 miles long, opens into Mission Valley 4.5 miles west of La Mesa (lat. 32°46'55" N, long. 117°05'45" W). Named on La Mesa (1967) 7.5' quadrangle.

Alvarado Hot Springs [LOS ANGELES]: *locality*, 4.5 miles northeast of La Habra [ORANGE] (lat. 33°58'35" N, long. 117°53'10" W). Named on La Habra (1952) 7.5' quadrangle. On La Habra (1964) 7.5' quadrangle, the name applies to a water feature. According to Berkstresser (p. A-7), water at a temperature of 112° Fahrenheit is pumped from a large-diameter oil test well drilled to about 5,000 feet in 1910—natural gas produced with the water heats a bath house

Amago: see **Palomar Mountain** [SAN DIEGO] (2).

Amargo: see **Malibu Junction** [LOS ANGELES].

Amargosa Creek [LOS ANGELES]: *stream* and *dry wash,* extends for 30 miles in an interrupted watercourse to Lancaster (lat. 34°41'20" N, long. 118°09'30" W; at N line sec. 21, T 7 N, R 12 W). Named on Del Sur (1958), Lancaster West (1958), Ritter Ridge (1958), and Sleepy Valley (1958) 7.5' quadrangles

Amargosa Creek [VENTURA]: *stream,* flows 7 miles to Lockwood Creek 13 miles northeast of Reyes Peak (lat. 34°44'05" N, long. 119°04'40" W). Named on Cuddy Valley (1943), Lockwood Valley (1943), and Sawmill Mountain (1943) 7.5' quadrangles. Called Bitter Creek on Mount Pinos (1903) 30' quadrangle, but United States Board on Geographic Names (1939, p. 4) rejected this name for the stream.

Amarillo Beach [LOS ANGELES]: *beach,* 1.25 miles west of Malibu Point along the coast (lat. 34°01'50" N, long. 118°42'20" W). Named on Malibu Beach (1951) 7.5' quadrangle. Called Amarilla Beach on Solstice Canyon (1932) 6' quadrangle.

Amarillo Canyon: see **Winter Canyon** [LOS ANGELES].

Amarus Lake: see **Santa Ana River** [ORANGE].

Ames Valley [SAN DIEGO]: *valley,* 4.5 miles northeast of Buckman Springs (lat. 32°49'20" N, long. 116°26'45" W; near W line sec. 35, T 15 S, R 5 E). Named on Mount Laguna (1960) 7.5' quadrangle.

Anacapa Island [VENTURA]: *islands,* three, 20 miles south-southwest of Ventura (lat. 34°00'55" N, long. 119°21'25" W at east end; lat. 34°00'50" N, long. 119°26'35" W at west end). Named on Anacapa Island (1973) quadrangle. Anacapa Island is one of the group called Santa Barbara Islands, which in turn is part of the larger group called Channel Islands (United States Coast and Geodetic Survey, p. 106). Early Spanish explorers gave the cluster of islands that forms present Anacapa Island the name "Tres Isleos," and in 1770 Costanso referred to one island as Falsa Vela because it looked like a ship; he called the other two islands Las Mesitas (Wagner, p. 372). Juan Perez called the cluster Islotes de Santo Tomas in 1774 (Wagner, p. 514). Yates (p. 171-173) referred to the three islands as the Anacapas, and to the individual islands as Eastern Anacapa, Middle Anacapa, and Western Anacapa. The name "Anacapa" is of Indian origin (Kroeber, p. 34).

Anacapa Passage [VENTURA]: *water feature,* between Anacapa Island and Santa Cruz Island, which is west of Anacapa Island in Santa Barbara County—the water passage is as narrow as 4.5 miles. Named on Los Angeles (1975) 1°x 2° quadrangle.

Anaheim [ORANGE]: *city,* 7 miles north-northwest of Santa Ana city hall (lat. 33°50'10" N, long. 117°54'40" W). Named on Anaheim (1965), Los Alamitos (1964), Orange (1964), and Yorba Linda (1964, photorevised 1981) 7.5' quadrangles. Postal authorities established Anaheim post office in 1861 (Frickstad, p. 115), and the city incorporated in 1878. A group of Germans, mainly from San Francisco, started a colony at the place in 1857—for years the community was known as Campo Aleman to its Spanish-speaking neighbors (Hoover, Rensch, and Rensch, p. 263). The name "Anaheim" is from Santa Ana River and *heim,* which means "home" in German (Bancroft, 1888, p. 522).

Anaheim: see **South Anaheim** [ORANGE]; **West Anaheim** [ORANGE].

Anaheim Bay [ORANGE]: *bay,* opens to the sea 7.5 miles northwest of Huntington Beach civic center (lat. 33°44'05" N, long. 118°05'40" W); the feature is along the lower part of former Anaheim Creek. Named on Seal Beach (1965) 7.5' quadrangle.

Anaheim Bay: see **Huntington Harbor** [ORANGE] (1).

Anaheim Creek [ORANGE]: *stream,* flows 8 miles to the sea 7.5 miles northwest of present Huntington Beach civic center (lat. 33° 44' N, long. 118°06' W). Named on Downey (1902) and Las Bolsas (1896) 15' quadrangles. The feature is an overflow channel of Santa Ana River (Meadows, p. 21).

Anaheim Junction: see **West Anaheim Junction** [ORANGE].

Anaheim Landing [ORANGE]: *locality,* 7.5 miles northwest of present Huntington Beach civic center along the coast (lat. 33°44' 05" N, long. 118°06' W); the site is at the mouth of Anaheim Creek. Named on Las Bolsas (1896) 15' quadrangle. The place was called El Piojo in the early days (Meadows, p. 21). Later it was a shipping point for residents of Anaheim; lighters carried produce to schooners anchored offshore and brought back supplies; the navy took over the site during World War II as part of an ammunition and net depot (Gleason, p. 101).

Anaheim Tower [ORANGE]: *locality,* 7 miles southeast of present Buena Park civic center where Atchison, Topeka and Santa Fe Railroad crossed Southern Pacific Railroad (lat. 33°48'30" N, long. 117°53'35" W; sec. 23, T 4 S, R 10 W). Named on Anaheim (1950) 7.5' quadrangle. Called Miraflores on Corona (1902) 30' quadrangle.

Anaheim Union Reservoir [ORANGE]: *lake,* 1300 feet long, 3 miles west-northwest of Yorba Linda (lat. 33°54'15" N, long. 117°51'55" W; on S line sec. 18, T 3 S, R 9 W). Named on Yorba Linda (1964) 7.5' quadrangle.

Anahuac Spring [SAN DIEGO]: *spring,* 9.5 miles north-northwest of Descanso (lat. 32°59'05" N, long. 116°39'45" W; sec. 3, T 14 S, R 3 E). Named on Tule Springs (1960) 7.5' quadrangle.

Anaverde Creek [LOS ANGELES]: *stream,* flows 7.25 miles to lowlands 1.5 miles southwest of downtown Palmdale (lat. 34°34'10" N, long. 118°08' W; sec. 34, T 6 N, R 12 W); the stream goes through Anaverde Valley. Named on Ritter Ridge (1958) 7.5' quadrangle.

Anaverde Valley [LOS ANGELES]: *valley,* 3.25 miles west-southwest of Palmdale (lat. 34°34'15" N, long. 118°10'15" W). Named on Ritter Ridge (1958) 7.5' quadrangle.

Anderson Valley [SAN DIEGO]: *area,* 4.5 miles east-southeast of El Cajon Mountain (lat. 32°52'45" N, long. 116°45'15" W; on E line sec. 10, T 15 S, R 2 E). Named on El Cajon Mountain (1955) 7.5' quadrangle.

Andrade Corner [LOS ANGELES]: *locality,* 4 miles east-southeast of the village of Lake Hughes (lat. 34°38'55" N, long. 118°22'35" W; on E line sec. 32, T 7 N, R 14 W). Named on Lake Hughes (1957) 7.5' quadrangle. Called Talamantes on Lake (1937) 6' quadrangle, but United States Board of Geographic Names (1960a, p. 11) rejected this designation for the place. The name "Andrade" recalls Andrada stage station that Pedro Andrada built in the 1880's (Hoover, Rensch, and Rensch, p. 168).

Andrews' Station: see **Lyon's Station**, under **San Fernando Pass** [LOS ANGELES].

Angelina Spring [SAN DIEGO]: *spring,* 9.5 miles southwest of Borrego Springs in Grapevine Canyon (lat. 33°09'20" N, long. 116°29'05" W). Named on Tubb Canyon (1959) 7.5' quadrangle. Brown (1920, p. 77) described the feature as "a seep of water in the canyon gravel." It was called Canebrake Spring in the 1880's (Stein, p. 5).

Angles Pass [VENTURA]: *pass,* 3.5 miles west-northwest of Piru (lat. 34°26'15" N, long. 118°50'45" W; near SW cor. sec. 11, T 4 N, R 19 W). Named on Piru (1952) 7.5' quadrangle.

Anlauf Canyon [VENTURA]: *canyon,* drained by a stream that flows 2 miles to Santa Paula Creek 4.25 miles west-southwest of Santa Paula Peak (lat. 34°25'20" N, long. 119°04'55" W; near S line sec. 16, T 4 N, R 21 W). Named on Santa Paula Peak (1951) 7.5' quadrangle. Called Onlauf Canyon on Santa Paula (1903) 15' quadrangle. The name is for the Anlauf family of Santa Paula, landowners in the neighborhood (Gudde, 1949, p. 243).

Ant Canyon [LOS ANGELES]: *canyon,* drained by a stream that flows 0.5 mile to Pacoima Canyon 6.5 miles north-northwest of Sunland (lat. 34°20'45" N, long. 118°21'55" W; sec. 17, T 3 N, R 14 W). Named on Sunland (1953) 7.5' quadrangle.

Antelope Acres [LOS ANGELES]: *settlement,* 4.5 miles north of Del Sur (lat. 34°45'15" N, long. 118°17'15" W; sec. 29, 30, 31, T 8 N, R 13 W); the place is in Antelope Valley. Named on Del Sur (1958) and Little Buttes (1965) 7.5' quadrangles.

Antelope Buttes [LOS ANGELES]: *ridge,* west-southwest-trending, 2.5 miles long, 5.5 miles north-northeast of the village of Lake Hughes (lat. 34°44'15" N, long. 118°23'15" W). Named on Del Sur (1958), Fairmont Butte (1965), Lake Hughes (1957), and Little Buttes (1965) 7.5' quadrangles.

Antelope Center [LOS ANGELES]: *locality,* 4 miles north of Littlerock (lat. 34°34'45" N, long. 117°58'05" W; on W line sec. 29, T 6 N, R 10 W). Named on Littlerock (1957) 7.5' quadrangle.

Antelope Valley [LOS ANGELES]: *valley,* part of Mojave Desert north of San Gabriel Mountains on Los Angeles-Kern County line. Named on Los Angeles (1975) and San Bernardino (1957) 1°x 2° quadrangles. Called Palma Plain on Williamson's (1853a) map. The name "Antelope" is from antelope herds in the valley in the early days (Hoover, Rensch, and Rensch, p. 148).

Antelope Valley: see **El Mirage Valley** [LOS ANGELES].

Antimony Canyon [LOS ANGELES]: *canyon,* drained by a stream that flows less than 1 mile to Kings Canyon 4 miles northeast of Burnt Peak (lat. 34°43' N, long. 118°31'05" W; near SW cor. sec. 6, T 7 N, R 15 W). Named on Burnt Peak (1958) 7.5' quadrangle.

Anton Canyon [SAN DIEGO]: *canyon,* drained by a stream that flows 3.5 miles to lowlands 4.5 miles east of Buckman Springs (lat. 32°46' N, long. 116°24'55" W; sec. 24, T 16 S, R 5 E). Named on Mount Laguna (1960) 7.5' quadrangle.

Apache Canyon [VENTURA]: *canyon,* drained by a stream that flows 16 miles to Cuyama River 11 miles northwest of Reyes Peak (lat. 34°44'45" N, long. 119°24'40" W). Named on Apache Canyon (1943), Cuyama Peak (1943), Rancho Nuevo Creek (1943), and Sawmill Mountain (1943) 7.5' quadrangles.

Apache Potrero [VENTURA]: *area,* 16 miles north of Reyes Peak (lat. 34°52' N, long. 119°19'30" W; sec. 15, T 9 N, R 23 W); the place is 5 miles north of Apache Canyon. Named on Apache Canyon (1943) 7.5' quadrangle.

Apex: see **Escondido** [SAN DIEGO].

Apple Canyon [LOS ANGELES]: *canyon,* drained by a stream that flows nearly 4 miles to Cañada de Los Alamos 8.5 miles south-southeast of Gorman (lat. 34°41'10" N, long. 118°47'10" W; near E line sec. 21, T 7 N, R 18 W). Named on Black Mountain (1958) 7.5' quadrangle.

Apple Tree Flat [LOS ANGELES]: *area,* 1.5 miles west-northwest of Big Pines (lat. 34°23'15" N, long. 117°42'40" W). Named on Mescal Creek (1956) 7.5' quadrangle.

Aqua Tibia: see **Pala** [SAN DIEGO].

Aqueduct Spring [LOS ANGELES]: *spring,* 5 miles south of the village of Lake Hughes (lat. 34°36' N, long. 118°26'45" W); the spring is less than

0.5 mile east of the aqueduct that brings Owens Valley water to Los Angeles. Named on Green Valley (1958) 7.5' quadrangle.

Ararat: see **Mount Ararat** [SAN DIEGO].

Arbolada [VENTURA]: *locality*, less than 1 mile west of downtown Ojai (lat. 34°27' N, long. 119°15'25" W). Named on Matilija (1952) 7.5' quadrangle.

Arcadia [LOS ANGELES]: *city*, 6 miles south-southeast of Mount Wilson (1) (lat. 34°08'30" N, long. 118°01'45" W). Named on Baldwin Park (1966), El Monte (1953), and Mount Wilson (1953) 7.5' quadrangles. Postal authorities established Arcadia post office in 1888 and named it for Dona Arcadia de Baker (Salley, p. 9). The city incorporated in 1903. Herman A. Unruh of San Gabriel Valley Railroad platted the place about 1888 (Gudde, 1949, p. 13).

Arcadia: see **West Arcadia** [LOS ANGELES].

Arch Beach [ORANGE]: *beach*, 2 miles south-southeast of Laguna Beach city hall along the coast (lat. 33°31'15" N, long. 117°45'50" W; sec. 36, T 7 S, R 9 W). Named on Laguna Beach (1965) 7.5' quadrangle. On Santa Ana (1901) 15' quadrangle, the name applies to an inhabited place at the site. Postal authorities established Arch Beach post office in 1889 and discontinued it in 1894 (Frickstad, p. 116). Hubbard Goff built a hotel at the site about 1886; in 1887 Goff and his brother Henry laid out a subdivision around the hotel and called it Arch Beach from an arched rock on the shore—the subdivision was unsuccessful (Meadows, p. 22). Fairview Development Company and Santa Ana Immigration Association laid out a town called Catalina-on-the-Main southeast of Arch Beach in 1888, but this venture also failed (Meadows, p. 51).

Arch Rock [ORANGE]: *relief feature*, nearly 6 miles west-northwest of Laguna Beach city hall along the coast at Corona del Mar (lat. 33°35'15" N, long. 117°52' W). Named on Laguna Beach (1965) 7.5' quadrangle. Called Hollow Rock on Corona (1902) 30' quadrangle.

Arch Rock [VENTURA]: *rock*, off the east end of Anacapa Island (lat. 34°01' N, long. 119°21'20" W). Named on Anacapa Island (1973) quadrangle. About 1936 a storm destroyed the arch that gave the rock its name; the feature also was called Grand Arch (Doran, 1980, p. 130).

Arena [LOS ANGELES]: *locality*, less than 1 mile northeast of present Manhattan Beach city hall along a railroad (lat. 33°53'45" N, long, 118°24' W). Named on Redondo (1896) 15' quadrangle.

Arkansas Canyon [SAN DIEGO]: *canyon*, drained by a stream that flows nearly 3 miles to San Felipe Valley 4.25 miles northeast of Julian (lat. 33°07' N, long. 116°32'30" W). Named on Julian (1960) and Ranchita (1960) 7.5' quadrangles. A man from Arkansas settled at the place in the 1870's and named it (Stein, p. 6).

Army Camp Beach: see **San Nicolas Island** [VENTURA].

Arnold: see **Port Hueneme** [VENTURA].

Arrastre Canyon [LOS ANGELES]: *canyon*, drained by a stream that flows 4.5 miles to Soledad Canyon 2 miles south-southwest of Acton (lat. 34°26'40" N, long. 118°12'30" W; sec. 11, T 4 N, R 13 W). Named on Acton (1959) 7.5' quadrangle.

Arrastra Flat [VENTURA]: *valley*, 2 miles east-southeast of Frazier Mountain (lat. 34°45'40" N, long. 118°56'30" W; around SE cor. sec. 24, T 8 N, R 20 W). Named on Frazier Mountain (1958) 7.5' quadrangle.

Arrowmaker Ridge [SAN DIEGO]: *ridge*, south-southwest- to west-southwest-trending, 1.25 miles long, 2.5 miles east-southeast of Cuyamaca Peak (lat. 32°55'45" N, long. 116°34'10" W). Named on Cuyamaca Peak (1960) 7.5' quadrangle.

Arrow Point [LOS ANGELES]: *promontory*, 2.25 miles northeast of Silver Peak on the north side of Santa Catalina Island (lat. 33°28'40" N, long. 118°32'15" W). Named on Santa Catalina West (1943) 7.5' quadrangle. Doran (1980, p. 66) gave the alternate names "Ram Point" and "Stony Point" for the feature.

Arroyo Calabasas [LOS ANGELES]: *stream*, flows 7 miles to join Bell Creek and form Los Angeles River 0.5 mile southwest of the center of Canoga Park (lat. 34°11'40" N, long. 118°36'05" W); the stream goes through Calabasas. United States Board on Geographic Names (1933, p. 183) rejected the forms "Arroyo Calabaces" and "Arroyo Calabazas" for the name.

Arroyo Colorado [VENTURA]: *gully*, extends for 2.25 miles to Honda Barranca 6 miles south of Santa Paula (lat. 34°16' N, long. 119°03'15" W). Named on Santa Paula (1951) 7.5' quadrangle.

Arroyo Conejo: see **Conejo Creek** [VENTURA].

Arroyo de la Quema: see **San Juan Creek** [ORANGE].

Arroyo del Mupu: see **Santa Paula Creek** [VENTURA].

Arroyo Hondo: see **San Rafael** [LOS ANGELES].

Arroyo Hueso [SAN DIEGO]: *stream*, flows 4.5 miles to Vallecito Creek 5.5 miles north-northwest of Sweeney Pass (lat. 32°54'35" N, long. 116°12'20" W; sec. 36, T 14 S, R 7 E). Named on Arroyo Tapiado (1959) 7.5' quadrangle.

Arroyo Jalisco [LOS ANGELES]: *stream*, flows 1.25 miles to Tacobi Creek 3.5 miles west-northwest of La Habra [ORANGE] (lat. 33°57'10" N, long. 117°59'55" W; sec. 35, T 2 S, R 11 W). Named on La Habra (1952) 7.5' quadrangle.

Arroyo las Posas [VENTURA]: *stream*, flows 10 miles to Calleguas Creek 2.25 miles northeast of downtown Camarillo (lat. 34°14'20" N, long. 119°00'20" W). Named on Camarillo (1950), Moorpark (1951), and Newbury Park (1951) 7.5' quadrangles.

Arroyo Pescadero [LOS ANGELES]: *stream*, flows 2.25 miles to La Canada Verde Creek 1.5 miles east-southeast of present Whittier city hall (lat. 33°57'40" N, long. 118°00'35" W; near SW cor. sec. 26, T 2 S, R 11 W). Named on La Habra (1952) and Whittier (1949) 7.5' quadrangles.

Arroyo Poco: see **Indian Rock Spring** [SAN DIEGO].

Arroyo Salada [ORANGE]: *stream*, flows 1 mile to Salt Creek 3 miles west of San Juan Capistrano (lat. 33°29'35" N, long. 117° 43' W; sec. 9, T 8 S, R 8 W). Named on Dana Point (1968) and San Juan Capistrano (1968) 7.5' quadrangles. On Dana Point (1949) 7.5' quadrangle, the name applies to the canyon of the stream.

Arroyo Salada [SAN DIEGO]: *stream*, flows nearly 6 miles to Imperial County 7.25 miles north-northeast of Ocotillo Wells (lat. 33°14'30" N, long. 116°04'55" W; at W line sec. 6, T 11 S, R 9 E). Named on Fonts Point (1959), Seventeen Palms (1956), and Shell Reef (1959) 7.5' quadrangles. Called Arroyo Salada Wash on Agua Dulce (1942) 15' quadrangle, but United States Board on Geographic Names (1961b, p. 12) rejected this name for the feature. North Fork enters the main stream in Imperial County; it is 4.5 miles long in San Diego County, and is named on Seventeen Palms (1956) 7.5' quadrangle.

Arroyo Salada: see **Salt Creek** [ORANGE]; **Sulphur Creek** [ORANGE].

Arroyo Salada Wash: see **Arroyo Salada** [SAN DIEGO].

Arroyo Salinas [LOS ANGELES]: *stream*, flows 1.25 miles to Arroyo Jalisco 3.25 miles west-northwest of La Habra [ORANGE] (lat. 33°57'20" N, long. 117°59'35" W; sec. 36, T 2 S, R 11 W). Named on La Habra (1952) 7.5' quadrangle.

Arroyo San Mateo: see **San Mateo Canyon** [SAN DIEGO].

Arroyo San Miguel [LOS ANGELES]: *stream*, flows nearly 2 miles to Tacobi Creek 3.5 miles northwest of La Habra [ORANGE] (lat. 33°57'25" N, long. 117°59'50" W; sec. 35, T 2 S, R 11 W). Named on La Habra (1952) 7.5' quadrangle.

Arroyo San Nicolas: see **Nicholas Canyon** [LOS ANGELES].

Arroyo San Onofre: see **San Onofre Canyon** [SAN DIEGO].

Arroyo Santa Rosa [VENTURA]: *stream*, flows 3 miles to Santa Rosa Valley nearly 4 miles north of Newbury Park (lat. 34°14'20" N, long. 118°54'25" W). Named on Moorpark (1951), Newbury Park (1951), and Simi (1951) 7.5' quadrangles.

Arroyo Seco [LOS ANGELES]: *stream*, flows 23 miles to Los Angeles River 2 miles north-northeast of Los Angeles city hall (lat. 34°04'45" N, long. 118°13'30" W). Named on Chilao Flat (1959), Condor Peak (1959), Los Angeles (1953), and Pasadena (1953) 7.5' quadrangles. On Tujunga (1900) 15' quadrangle, the name "Long Canyon" applies to the upper part of the canyon of present Arroyo Seco.

Arroyo Seco [SAN DIEGO]: *stream*, flows less than 1 mile to Sweetwater River 2 miles south-southeast of Cuyamaca Peak (lat. 32°54'20" N, long. 116°35' W). Named on Cuyamaca Peak (1960) 7.5' quadrangle.

Arroyo Seco Creek [SAN DIEGO]: *stream*, flows 2.5 miles to Riverside County 6.5 miles north of Boucher Hill (lat. 33°25'35" N, long. 116°56'15" W; at N line sec. 1, T 9 S, R 1 W). Named on Vail Lake (1953) 7.5' quadrangle.

Arroyo Seco del Diablo [SAN DIEGO]: *dry wash*, extends for 10 miles to Vallecito Creek 3.5 miles north-northeast of Sweeney Pass (lat. 32°53' N, long. 116°09'35" W; sec. 9, T 15 S, R 8 E). Named on Arroyo Tapiado (1959) 7.5' quadrangle.

Arroyo Sequit [LOS ANGELES-VENTURA]: *stream*, formed by the confluence of East Fork and West Fork, flows 3 miles to the sea 8 miles west-northwest of Point Dume (lat. 34°02'40" N, long. 118° 55'55" W); the mouth of the stream is just east of Sequit Point. Named on Triunfo Pass (1950) 7.5' quadrangle. United States Board on Geographic Names (1933, p. 682) rejected the forms "Arroyo Siquis" and "Arroyo Siquit" for the name. East Fork and West Fork (which heads in Ventura County) each are 2.5 miles long and are named on Triunfo Pass (1950) 7.5' quadrangle

Arroyo Simi [VENTURA]: *stream*, flows 19 miles to Arroyo Las Posas 2.25 miles west-southwest of Moorpark (lat. 34°16'10" N, long. 118°54'30" W; sec. 7, T 2 N, R 19 W); the stream goes through Simi Valley. Named on Moorpark (1951), Santa Susana (1951), and Simi (1951) 7.5' quadrangles.

Arroyo Susal: see **Los Sauces Creek** [VENTURA].

Arroyo Tapiado [SAN DIEGO]: *dry wash*, extends for 8 miles to the canyon of Vallecito Creek 4.25 miles north of Sweeney Pass (lat. 32°53'40" N, long. 116°10'45" W; sec. 5, T 15 S, R 8 E). Named on Arroyo Tapiado (1959) 7.5' quadrangle.

Arroyo Trabuco [ORANGE]: *stream*, flows 15 miles from the mouth of Trabuco Canyon to San Juan Creek less than 1 mile south of the center of San Juan Capistrano (lat. 33°29'25" N, long. 117°39'55" W; sec. 12, T 8 S, R 8 W). Named on Cañada Gobernadora (1968), San Juan Capistrano (1968), and Santiago Peak (1954) 7.5' quadrangles. Called Trabuco Creek on Dana Point (1968) 7.5' quadrangle. On Corona (1902) 30' quadrangle, the name applies to the canyon of the stream.

Arsenic Spring [SAN DIEGO]: *spring*, 2.25 miles north of Jacumba (lat. 32°39' N, long. 116°11'05" W; sec. 32, T 17 S, R 8 E). Named on Jacumba (1959) 7.5' quadrangle.

Artesia [LOS ANGELES]: *town*, 9 miles northeast of Long Beach city hall (lat. 33°51'55" N, long. 118°04'55" W). Named on Los Alamitos (1964) 7.5' quadrangle. Postal authorities established Artesia post office in 1882, discontinued it in 1902, and reestablished it in 1906 (Frickstad, p. 70). The town incorporated in 1959. Officials of Artesia Company founded and named the town in the 1870's—the company drilled artesian-water wells (Gudde, 1949, p. 16).

Artesian Spring Campgrounds [LOS ANGELES]: *locality*, 5.5 miles southwest of the village of Leona Valley (lat. 34°34'10" N, long. 118°21'51" W; sec. 33, T 6 N, R 14 W). Named on Sleepy Valley (1958) 7.5' quadrangle. Bouquet Reservoir (1937) 6' quadrangle shows an artesian spring at the site.

Arundell Barranca [VENTURA]: *gully*, extends for 4 miles from the mouth of Sexton Canyon to the sea 2.25 miles south-southeast of downtown Ventura (lat. 34°15'10" N, long. 119°16'10" W). Named on Saticoy (1951) and Ventura (1951) 7.5' quadrangles.

Arundell Peak [VENTURA]: *peak*, 3.5 miles north of Piru (lat. 34° 28' N, long. 118°47'55" W; near NE cor. sec. 6, T 4 N, R 18 W). Altitude 3216 feet. Named on Piru (1952) 7.5' quadrangle

Arundell Spring [VENTURA]: *spring*, 3.5 miles north of Piru (lat. 34°27'55" N, long. 118°47'20" W; near N line sec. 5, T 4 N, R 18 W); the spring is 0.5 mile east of Arundell Peak. Named on Piru (1952) 7.5' quadrangle.

Ascot Reservoir [LOS ANGELES]: *intermittent lake*, 1000 feet long, 3.5 miles east-northeast of Los Angeles city hall (lat. 34°04'40" N, long. 118°11'20" W; near SE cor. sec. 13, T 1 S, R 13 W). Named on Los Angeles (1953) 7.5' quadrangle.

Athens [LOS ANGELES]: *district*, 5.25 miles southeast of Inglewood city hall (lat. 33°55'20" N, long. 118°16'45" W). Named on Inglewood (1952) 7.5' quadrangle.

Atherton Canyon: see **Bouquet Canyon** [LOS ANGELES].

Atkinson: see **Ballena** [SAN DIEGO].

Atlantic Cove: see **South Cove** [SAN DIEGO].

Atmore Meadows [LOS ANGELES]: *area*, 1.5 miles west-northwest of Burnt Peak (lat. 34°41'30" N, long. 118°36'15" W). Named on Burnt Peak (1958) 7.5' quadrangle.

Atwater [LOS ANGELES]: *district*, 4.25 miles north of Los Angeles city hall (lat. 34°06'55" N, long. 118°15'25" W). Named on Hollywood (1953) 7.5' quadrangle.

Atwood [ORANGE]: *village*, 5.5 miles north-northeast of Orange city hall (lat. 33°52'05" N, long. 117°49'50" W). Named on Orange (1964) 7.5' quadrangle. Called Richfields on Corona (1902) 30' quadrangle. Postal authorities established Atwood post office in 1924 (Frickstad, p. 116). Promoters laid out a new townsite called Richfield, but when postal authorities refused to allow the name "Richfield" for a post office, the community took the name "Atwood" from W.J. Atwood, purchasing agent of Chanselor-Canfield Midway Oil Company (Meadows, p. 23). The residents of Atwood voted in 1970 to join Placenta (Carpenter, p. 242).

Atwood: see **Morena** [SAN DIEGO].

Aurant [LOS ANGELES]: *locality*, 5 miles east-northeast of Los Angeles city hall along Southern Pacific Railroad (lat. 34°04'40" N, long. 118°09'50" W). Named on Los Angeles (1966) 7.5' quadrangle.

Avalon [LOS ANGELES]: *town*, near the southeast end of Santa Catalina Island (lat. 33°20'35" N, long. 118°19'40" W). Named on Santa Catalina East (1950) 7.5' quadrangle. Postal authorities established Avalon post office in 1889 (Frickstad, p. 70), and the town incorporated in 1913. The community is at the site of Timm's Landing, where A.W. Timm raised sheep and goats in the early days (Gleason, p. 20). The town first was known as Shatto, for George R. Shatto, who bought the island in 1887 (Hanna, p. 20). Shatto's sister, Mrs. E.J. Whitney, renamed the place Avalon, a name from Tennyson's *Idylls of the King* (Gleason, p. 20).

Avalon Bay [LOS ANGELES]: *embayment*, at Avalon on Santa Catalina Island (lat. 33°20'45" N, long. 118°19'20" W). Named on Santa Catalina East (1950) 7.5' quadrangle. Preston (1890b, map following p. 278) called the feature Dakin's Cove; United States Board on Geographic Names (1936a, p. 8) rejected the name "Dakin Bay" for it. The embayment also was called "Timms Bay" and "Timms Cove" from A.W. Timm of Timm's Landing (Hanna, p. 20)

Avalon Village [LOS ANGELES]: *locality*, 4.5 miles east-southeast of Torrance city hall (lat. 33°48'50" N, long. 118°15'50" W). Named on Torrance (1964) 7.5' quadrangle.

Aventura: see **Camp Aventura** [LOS ANGELES].

Averill Canyon [LOS ANGELES]: *canyon*, less than 1 mile long, nearly 3 miles northwest of Point Fermin (lat. 33°44'10" N, long. 118°19'20" W). Named on San Pedro (1964) 7.5' quadrangle.

Avocado Creek [LOS ANGELES]: *stream*, flows nearly 2 miles to San Gabriel River 2 miles southeast of El Monte city hall (lat. 34° 02'45" N, long. 118°00'35" W). Named on Baldwin Park (1953) and El Monte (1966) 7.5' quadrangles.

Avondale [SAN DIEGO]: *locality*, 5.5 miles east of present National City civic center (lat. 32°40'50" N, long. 117°01' W). Named on San Diego (1904) 15' quadrangle.

Ayars Canyon [LOS ANGELES]: *canyon*, less than 1 mile long, 6.5 miles west-northwest of Pasadena city hall (lat. 34°11'40" N, long. 118°14'30" W). Named on Pasadena (1953) 7.5' quadrangle.

Ayers Creek [VENTURA]: *stream*, flows 1.5 miles to Lake Casitas 7.5 miles north-northwest of Ventura (lat. 34°22'25" N, long. 119° 21'20" W). Named on Ventura (1951, photorevised 1967) 7.5' quadrangle. The name is for Robert Ayers, who came to the vicinity in 1868 (Ricard).

Azalea Creek [SAN DIEGO]: *stream*, flows less than 2 miles to Boulder Creek (1) nearly 4 miles north of Cuyamaca Peak (lat. 32° 59'55" N, long. 116°36'55" W; near W line sec. 31, T 13 S, R 4 E). Named on Julian (1960) 7.5' quadrangle.

Azalea Spring [SAN DIEGO]: *spring*, 1 mile north-northeast of Cuyamaca Peak (lat. 32°57'35" N, long. 116°36' W). Named on Cuyamaca Peak (1960) 7.5' quadrangle.

Azure Vista [SAN DIEGO]: *district*, 5.25 miles west of downtown San Diego (lat. 32°43'15" N, long. 117°15'15" W). Named on Point Loma (1967) 7.5' quadrangle.

Azusa [LOS ANGELES]:

(1) *land grant*, at Duarte. Named on Azusa (1953), Baldwin Park (1953), El Monte (1953), and Mount Wilson (1953) 7.5' quadrangles. Andres Duarte received the land in 1841 and claimed 6596 acres patented in 1878 (Cowan, p. 18). The name is from an Indian village (Kroeber, p. 35).

(2) *land grant*, at Azusa. Named on Azusa (1953) and Baldwin Park (1953) 7.5' quadrangles. Luis Arenas received the land in 1841 and Harry Dalton claimed 4331 acres patented in 1876 (Cowan, p. 17-18). According to Perez (p. 54), Henry Dalton was the grantee in 1846.

(3) *city*, 20 miles east-northeast of Los Angeles city hall (lat. 34°08'05" N, long. 117°54'15" W); the place is on Azusa (2) grant. Named on Baldwin Park (1953) 7.5' quadrangle. Postal authorities established Azusa post office in 1874 and moved it 0.5 mile northeast in 1887 (Salley, p. 13). The city incorporated in 1898. Jonathan Slauson organized Azusa Land and Water Company in 1886, platted a town, and was ready to sell lots in 1887; Henry Dalton had platted a town called Benton at the same place 32 years earlier (Jackson, p. 244-245).

Azusa Avenue [LOS ANGELES]: *locality*, 3.25 miles east of Baldwin Park city hall along Pacific Electric Railroad (lat. 34°05'30" N, long. 117°54'15" W; near W line sec. 14, T 1 S, R 10 W). Named on Baldwin Park (1953) 7.5' quadrangle.

Azusa Canon: see **San Gabriel Canyon** [LOS ANGELES].

- B -

Backus Summit: see **Castro Peak** [LOS ANGELES].

Bacon Creek [LOS ANGELES]: *stream*, flows less than 1 mile to end 1 mile east-southeast of present Whittier city hall (lat. 33°58'10" N, long. 118°01' W). Named on Whittier (1949) 7.5' quadrangle.

Bad Canyon [LOS ANGELES]: *canyon*, drained by a stream that flows 2 miles to Pacoima Canyon 7.25 miles north of Sunland (lat. 34°21'50" N, long. 118°17'35" W; near NE cor. sec. 12, T 3 N, R 14 W). Named on Agua Dulce (1960) and Sunland (1953) 7.5' quadrangles.

Baden-Powell: see **Mount Baden-Powell** [LOS ANGELES].

Bahia de los Fumos: see **San Pedro Bay** [LOS ANGELES].

Bahia de San Juan Capistrano: see **Dana Cove** [ORANGE].

Bahia de San Pedro: see **San Pedro Bay** [LOS ANGELES].

Bahia Point [SAN DIEGO]: *promontory*, 5.5 miles south-southeast of Point La Jolla along the coast (lat. 32°46'30" N, long. 117°14'45" W). Named on La Jolla (1967) 7.5' quadrangle. Called Gleason Point on La Jolla (1953) 7.5' quadrangle.

Bailey Canyon [LOS ANGELES]: *canyon*, 1.25 miles long, 3 miles south of Mount Wilson (1) (lat. 34°11' N, long. 118°03'35" W; sec. 8, 17, T 1 N, R 11 W). Named on Mount Wilson (1953) 7.5' quadrangle. Called Baile Canyon on Pasadena (1900) 15' quadrangle.

Bailey Creek [SAN DIEGO]: *stream*, flows 2 miles to Jim Green Creek 2 miles southeast of Santa Ysabel (lat. 33°05'20" N, long. 116°38'40" W; sec. 35, T 12 S, R 3 E). Named on Santa Ysabel (1960) 7.5' quadrangle.

Baird Canyon [LOS ANGELES]: *canyon*, drained by a stream that flows 1 mile to San Francisquito Canyon nearly 8 miles south-southwest of the village of Lake Hughes (lat. 34°34' N, long. 118° 28'05" W). Named on Green Valley (1958) 7.5' quadrangle.

Baird Park [LOS ANGELES]: *locality*, 4 miles northeast of Los Angeles city hall (lat. 34°05'10" N, long. 118°11' W). Named on Alhambra (1926) 6' quadrangle. Postal authorities established Bairdstown post office 5 miles east of Los Angeles post office in 1904 and discontinued it in 1917; the name was for Llewelin Baird, founder of the place (Salley, p. 13).

Bairdstown: see **Baird Park** [LOS ANGELES].

Baker Cabin [VENTURA]: *locality*, 3.5 miles northeast of McDonald Peak along Snowy Creek (lat. 34°40'20" N, long. 118°53'40" W; sec. 28, T 7 N,

R 19 W). Named on McDonald Peak (1958) 7.5' quadrangle.

Baker Canyon [LOS ANGELES]: *canyon,* 2 miles long, opens into Mint Canyon (1) 3.5 miles northeast of Solemint (lat. 34°27'15" N, long. 118°25' W; near SE cor. sec. 2, T 4 N, R 15 W). Named on Mint Canyon (1960) 7.5' quadrangle.

Baker Canyon [ORANGE]: *canyon,* drained by a stream that flows 5 miles to the canyon of Santiago Creek 6.25 miles south of Sierra Peak (lat. 33°45'35" N, long. 117°40'25" W). Named on Black Star Canyon (1967) 7.5' quadrangle. The feature was called Cañada de la Vieja—*Cañada de la Vieja* means "Canyon of the Old Woman" in Spanish—before W.H. Hall took up a homestead there; for years it was called Hall's Canyon, but after Charles Baker moved there it became Baker's Canyon (Meadows, p. 49; Stephenson, p. 24-25).

Baker Wash [LOS ANGELES]: *stream,* heads in San Jose Hills and flows 2.5 miles to end in lowlands 3.25 miles southeast of Baldwin Park city hall (lat. 34°03'20" N, long. 117°54'55" W). Named on Baldwin Park (1953) 7.5' quadrangle.

Balanced Rock: see **Pyramid Head** [LOS ANGELES].

Balboa [ORANGE]: *district,* 7 miles southeast of Huntington Beach civic center in Newport Beach (lat. 33°36'10" N, long. 117°53'55" W). Named on Newport Beach (1965) 7.5' quadrangle. Postal authorities established Balboa post office in 1907 (Salley, p. 13). Officials of Newport Bay Investment Company had the community laid out in 1905; E.J. Louis, Peruvian consul in Los Angeles, suggested naming the place for the discoverer of the Pacific Ocean (Gudde, 1949, p. 20). Edward J. Abbot had bought swamp and overflow land there from the state in 1892 and built a house and a small pier known as Abbott's Landing (Gleason, p. 94-95).

Balboa Beach [ORANGE]: *beach,* 7 miles southeast of Huntington Beach civic center along the coast (lat. 33°36' N, long. 117°54' W); the beach is at Balboa. Named on Newport Beach (1965) 7.5' quadrangle.

Balboa Island [ORANGE]: *island,* 4400 feet long, 7 miles east-southeast of Huntington Beach civic center in Newport Bay (lat. 33°36'25" N, long. 117°53'30" W). Named on Newport Beach (1965) 7.5' quadrangle. Postal authorities established Balisle post office in 1927 and changed the name to Balboa Island in 1928 (Frickstad, p. 116). W.S. Collins had the island made in 1906 by dredging bay mud onto a sand flat in Newport Bay; Newport Beach annexed the island in 1916 (Meadows, p. 23). The eastern tip of the island is separated from the main part by a waterway, and this cutoff section of land is called Little Island (Gleason, p. 98).

Balboa Palisades: see **Corona del Mar** [ORANGE].

Balboa Reach: see **Newport Bay** [ORANGE].

Balcan Mountains: see **Volcan Mountains** [SAN DIEGO].

Balcom Canyon [VENTURA]: *canyon,* drained by a stream that flows 2.5 miles to the valley of Santa Clara River 5.25 miles southwest of Fillmore (lat. 34°21' N, long. 118°58'55" W; at W line sec. 9, T 3 N, R 20 W). Named on Moorpark (1951) 7.5' quadrangle. Called Sulphur Canyon on Piru (1921) 15' quadrangle.

Baldhead Spring: see **Sweetwater Spring** [SAN DIEGO].

Bald Mountain [LOS ANGELES]: *ridge,* northwest-trending, 1.25 miles long, 7.5 miles east-southeast of Gorman (lat. 34°44'45" N, long. 118°43'50" W; around NW cor. sec. 31, T 8 N, R 17 W). Named on La Liebre Ranch (1965) and Liebre Mountain (1958) 7.5' quadrangles.

Bald Peak [ORANGE]: *peak,* 5 miles southeast of Pleasants Peak on Orange-Riverside County line (lat. 33°45'20" N, long. 117°32'05" W). Altitude 3947 feet. Named on Corona South (1967) 7.5' quadrangle.

Baldwin Canyon: see **Baldwin Grade Canyon** [LOS ANGELES].

Baldwin Grade Canyon [LOS ANGELES]: *canyon,* drained by a stream that flows 1.5 miles to lowlands 5.25 miles north-northeast of Burnt Peak (lat. 34°45'10" N, long. 118°32'05" W; sec. 25, T 8 N, R 16 W). Named on Burnt Peak (1958) 7.5' quadrangle. Called Baldwin Canyon on Los Angeles County (1935) map.

Baldwin Hills [LOS ANGELES]: *range,* 3 miles north-northwest of Inglewood city hall (lat. 34°00' N, long. 118°22'30" W). Named on Beverly Hills (1950), Hollywood (1953), Inglewood (1952), and Venice (1964) 7.5' quadrangles.

Baldwin Hills Reservoir [LOS ANGELES]: *lake,* 1250 feet long, 7.5 miles west-southwest of Los Angeles city hall (lat. 34°00'30" N, long. 118°21'45" W); the feature is in Baldwin Hills. Named on Hollwood (1953) 7.5' quadrangle.

Baldwin Park [LOS ANGELES]: *city,* 4.25 miles southwest of Azusa city hall (lat. 34°05'10" N, long, 117°57'30" W); the city is on Santa Anita grant. Named on Baldwin Park (1953) 7.5' quadrangle. Pomona (1904) 15' quadrangle shows a place called Vineland at present Baldwin Park (lat. 34°05'25" N, long. 117°57'45" W). Postal authorities established Vineland post office in 1887 and changed the name to Baldwin Park in 1907 (Frickstad, p. 83). The city incorporated in 1956. The name "Baldwin" commemorates Elias Jackson "Lucky" Baldwin, who bought Santa Anita grant in 1875 (Hanna, p. 23).

Baldy [VENTURA]: *peak,* 2.5 miles north of Piru (lat. 34°27'15" N, long. 118°47'55" W; near SE cor. sec. 6, T 4 N, R 18 W). Altitude 3416 feet. Named on Piru (1952) 7.5' quadrangle.

Baldy: see **Mount Baldy** [LOS ANGELES]; **North Baldy**, under **Mount Baden-Powell** [LOS ANGELES]; **Mount San Antonio** [LOS ANGELES].

Baldy Peak: see **North Baldy Peak**, under **Throop Peak** [LOS ANGELES].

Balisle: see **Balboa Island** [ORANGE].

Ballast Point [LOS ANGELES]: *promontory,* 4 miles east-southeast of Silver Peak on Santa Catalina Island (lat. 33°25'50" N, long. 118°30'15" W). Named on Santa Catalina West (1943) 7.5' quadrangle.

Ballast Point [SAN DIEGO]: *promontory,* 4.5 miles west-southwest of downtown San Diego along Point Loma at the entrance to San Diego Bay (lat. 32°41'10" N, long. 117°13'55" W). Named on Point Loma (1967) 7.5' quadrangle. The name is from the use of stones from the place as ballast for ships returning to Boston with hides in the 1840's; Vizcaino called the feature Punta de los Guijarros in 1602—*Punta de los Guijarros* means "Point of the Pebbles" is Spanish (Hanna, p. 23).

Ballena [SAN DIEGO]: *locality,* 6.5 miles east-northeast of Ramona (lat. 33°03'40" N, long. 116°45'05" W; near N line sec. 11, T 13 S, R 2 E); the place is in Ballena Valley. Named on Ramona (1903) 30' quadrangle. Postal authorities established Ballena post office in 1870, discontinued it in 1894, reestablished it in 1896, and discontinued it in 1902 (Frickstad, p. 148). They established Atkinson post office 16 miles southwest of Ballena post office in 1878 and discontinued in 1880; the name was for Lemuel Atkinson, first postmaster (Salley, p. 11).

Ballena Valley [SAN DIEGO]: *valley,* 5 miles southwest of Santa Ysabel (lat. 33°04'15" N, long. 116°44'35" W); the valley is east of Whale Mountain. Named on Ramona (1955) and Santa Ysabel (1960) 7.5' quadrangles. The name is from nearby Whale Peak—*ballena* means "whale" in Spanish (Gudde, 1949, p. 21-22).

Ball Flat [LOS ANGELES]: *area,* 2.5 miles northwest of Big Pines (lat. 34°24'15" N, long. 117°43'30" W). Named on Mescal Creek (1956) 7.5' quadrangle.

Ballinger Canyon [VENTURA]: *canyon,* drained by a stream that heads in Kern County and flows 4.25 miles in Ventura County to enter Santa Barbara County nearly 20 miles north-northwest of Reyes Peak (lat. 34°53'10" N, long. 119°26'30" W; near N line sec. 9, T 9 N, R 24 W). Named on Ballinger Canyon (1943) and Cuyama Peak (1943) 7.5' quadrangles.

Ballona [LOS ANGELES]: *land grant,* at Venice, Playa del Rey, and Culver City. Named on Beverly Hills (1950), Hollywood (1953), Inglewood (1964), and Venice (1950) 7.5' quadrangles. Called La Ballona on Inglewood (1952) 7.5' quadrangle. Agustin Machado, Ignacio Machado, Felipe Talamantes, and Tomas Talamantes received the land in 1839 and claimed 13,920 acres patented in 1873 (Cowan, p. 18; Cowan gave the alternate name "Paso de las Carretas" for the grant). According to tradition in the Talamantes family, the name "Ballona" is from Bayona, a city in Spain that was the home of a family ancestor (Gudde, 1949, p. 22).

Ballona: see **Port Ballona**, under **Playa del Rey** [LOS ANGELES].

Ballona Creek [LOS ANGELES]: *stream,* flows 8.5 miles to the sea nearly 6 miles north-northwest of Manhattan Beach city hall (lat. 33°57'40" N, long. 118°27'20" W); the stream crosses Ballona grant. Named on Beverly Hills (1950), Hollywood (1953), and Venice (1950) 7.5' quadrangles. Called Sanjon de Agua con Alisos on a diseño of Rincon de Los Bueyes grant (Becker, 1969).

Ballona Harbor: see **Ballona Lagoon** [LOS ANGELES].

Ballona Junction: see **Redondo Junction** [LOS ANGELES].

Ballona Lagoon [LOS ANGELES] *water feature,* extends north-northwest parallel to the coast from a point on Ballona Creek 6 miles north-northwest of Manhattan Beach city hall (lat. 33°58' N, long. 118°27'15" W). Named on Venice (1950) 7.5' quadrangle. On Redondo (1896) 15' quadrangle, the name applies to a larger water feature and adjacent marsh. Venice (1964) 7.5' quadrangle has the name "Marina del Rey" at the place, and Lankershim Ranch Land and Water Company's (1888) map shows Ballona Harbor there.

Bancroft Point [SAN DIEGO]: *relief feature,* nearly 7 miles west of Jamul (lat. 32°44'15" N, long. 116°59'25" W; sec. 33, T 16 S, R 1 W). Named on Jamul Mountains (1955) 7.5' quadrangle.

Bandini [LOS ANGELES]:

(1) *district,* 5.5 miles southeast of Los Angeles city hall (lat. 34°00'25" N, long. 118°10' W). Named on Los Angeles (1953) 7.5' quadrangle.

(2) *locality,* 5 miles west of present Whittier city hall along Atchison, Topeka and Santa Fe Railroad (lat. 33°58'55" N, long. 118°07'05" W). Named on Whittier (1951) 7.5' quadrangle. On Bell (1936) 6' quadrangle, the name applies to a place located about 1 mile farther west-northwest along the railroad.

Bandy Canyon [SAN DIEGO]: *canyon,* 1.5 miles long, 1.5 miles southeast of San Pasqual along Santa Maria Creek (lat. 33°03'50" N, long. 116°57'30" W). Named on San Pasqual (1954) 7.5' quadrangle.

Bangle [LOS ANGELES]: *locality,* 4.25 miles north-northwest of Long Beach city hall along a railroad (lat. 33°49'30" N, long. 118° 13'40" W). Named on Long Beach (1949) 7.5' quadrangle.

Bankhead Spring [SAN DIEGO]: *spring,* nearly 4 miles northwest of Jacumba (lat. 32°38'50" N, long. 116°14'35" W; near E line sec. 34, T 17 S, R 7 E). Named on Jacumba (1959) 7.5' quadrangle.

Bankhead Springs [SAN DIEGO]: *locality,* nearly 4 miles northwest of Jacumba (lat. 32°39' N, long. 116°14'30" W; on E line sec. 34, T 17 S, R 7 E); the place is less than 0.25 mile north of Bankhead Spring. Named on Jacumba (1959) 7.5' quadrangle. Bert Horr, son of the first settler, gave the name "Bankhead" to the place after the road that goes through it was named Bankhead Highway in 1916 to honor Senator John Hollis Bankhead of Alabama for his promotion of a coast-to-coast highway (Stein, p. 8).

Banner [SAN DIEGO]: *locality,* 3.25 miles east of Julian (lat. 33°04'05" N, long. 116°32'45" W; at W line sec. 2, T 13 S, R 4 E). Named on Julian (1960) 7.5' quadrangle. Postal authorities established Banner post office in 1873, discontinued it for a time in 1876, discontinued it in 1877, reestablished it in 1883, moved it 0.75 mile west in 1902, and discontinued it in 1907 (Salley, p. 14). The name is from the small American flag that Louis Redman used to mark his gold claim at the site in 1870 (Ellsberg, p. 42, 45).

Banner Canyon [SAN DIEGO]: *canyon,* 3.5 miles long, along Banner Creek above a point 3.25 miles east of Julian (lat. 33°04'10" N, long. 116°32'40" W; sec. 2, T 13 S, R 4 E); the mining camp called Banner was in the canyon. Named on Julian (1960) 7.5' quadrangle. Called San Felipe Cañon on Hanks' (1886b) map.

Banner Creek [SAN DIEGO]: *stream,* flows 10 miles to San Felipe Valley 6.5 miles east-northeast of Julian (lat. 33°06'15" N, long. 116°29'40" W). Named on Earthquake Valley (1959) and Julian (1960) 7.5' quadrangles. Called San Felipe Creek on Hanks' (1886b) map.

Banner Queen Trading Post [SAN DIEGO]: *locality,* 4 miles east of Julian (lat. 33°04'30" N, long. 116°32'05" W; sec. 2, T 13 S, R 4 E). Named on Julian (1960) 7.5' quadrangle, which shows Banner Queen mine located 1 mile east-southeast of the place.

Banning: see **Mount Banning** [LOS ANGELES]; **Mount Banning**, under **Black Jack Mountain** [LOS ANGELES].

Banning Beach [LOS ANGELES]: *beach,* 2.5 miles northwest of Avalon on the northeast side of Santa Catalina Island (lat. 33°22'30" N, long. 118°21'10" W). Named on Santa Catalina East (1950) 7.5' quadrangle.

Barber City [ORANGE]: *district,* 7.5 miles south-southwest of Buena Park civic center in Westminister (lat. 33°45'25" N, long. 118°01'45" W; sec. 9, T 5 S, R 11 W). Named on Los Alamitos (1950) 7.5' quadrangle. Henry Barber laid out the place in 1924 (Meadows, p. 24).

Barber Mountain [SAN DIEGO]: *ridge,* north-northwest-trending, 1.25 miles long, 5 miles north of Barrett Junction (lat. 32°41'10" N, long. 116°42'50" W; sec. 18, 19, T 17 S, R 3 E). Named on Barrett Lake (1960) 7.5' quadrangle.

Barber Mountain: see **Elena Mountain** [SAN DIEGO].

Bardsdale [VENTURA]: *town,* 2 miles south-southwest of Fillmore (lat. 34°22'30" N, long. 118°55'50" W). Named on Fillmore (1951) and Moorpark (1951) 7.5' quadrangles. Postal authorities established Bardsdale post office in 1887 and discontinued it in 1906 (Frickstad, p. 217). R.G. Surdam founded the town in 1887 on land purchased from Thomas R. Bard, the first president of Union Oil Company, and named the town for Bard (Hanna, p. 25) An earlier community at the site commonly was called Stringtown because it was strung out along a water ditch (Ricard).

Bare Mountain [LOS ANGELES]: *peak,* 8.5 miles west-southwest of Valyermo (lat. 34°23'55" N, long. 117°59'30" W). Altitude 6388 feet. Named on Juniper Hills (1959) 7.5' quadrangle.

Bare Mountain Canyon [LOS ANGELES]: *canyon,* drained by a stream that flows 5.5 miles to Little Rock Creek 8.5 miles west of Valyermo (lat. 34°26'15" N, long. 117°59'50" W). Named on Juniper Hills (1959) and Pacifico Mountain (1959) 7.5' quadrangles. West Fork branches southwest 3.25 miles north-northeast of Pacifico Mountain; it is 2 miles long and is named on Pacifico Mountain (1959) 7.5' quadrangle.

Barham: see **Vista** [SAN DIEGO].

Barker Valley [SAN DIEGO]: *valley,* 6 miles east of Boulder Hill along West Fork San Luis Rey River (lat. 33°20' N, long. 116°49'15" W; in and near sec. 6, T 10 S, R 2 E). Named on Palomar Observatory (1949) 7.5' quadrangle. The name recalls an early homesteader at the place (Stein, p. 9).

Barley Flats [LOS ANGELES]: *area,* 7.5 miles south-southwest of Pacifico Mountain (lat. 34°16'45" N, long. 118°04'30" W; sec. 7, T 2 N, R 11 W). Named on Chilao Flat (1959) 7.5' quadrangle. Wild rye growing at the place gives it the appearance of a barley field (Robinson, J.W., 1977, p. 190).

Barlow Canyon [VENTURA]: *canyon,* drained by a stream that flows 2.25 miles to the valley of Santa Clara River 5.25 miles west of Saticoy (lat. 34°17' N, long. 119°14'25" W). Named on Saticoy (1951) 7.5' quadrangle.

Barney Knob [LOS ANGELES]: *peak,* 6.5 miles northwest of Point Dume (lat. 34°04'40" N, long. 118°52'40" W; near S line sec. 16, T 1 S, R 19 W). Altitude 1729 feet. Named on Triunfo Pass (1950) 7.5' quadrangle.

Barona [SAN DIEGO]: *locality,* 3.25 miles west-northwest of El Cajon Mountain (lat. 32°56'10" N, long. 116°52' W); the place is in Barona Valley. Named on El Cajon Mountain (1955) 7.5' quadrangle.

Barona: see **Padre Barona Creek** [SAN DIEGO].

Barona Mesa [SAN DIEGO]: *area,* 5.5 miles north-northeast of El Cajon Mountain (lat. 32°59'10" N, long. 116°46'50" W); the feature is partly on Cañada de San Vicente y Mesa del Padre Barona grant. Named on El Cajon Mountain (1955) 7.5' quadrangle. The name commemorates Padre Barona of San Diego mission (Stein, p. 9).

Barona Valley [SAN DIEGO]: *valley,* 3.5 miles northwest of El Cajon Mountain (lat. 32°56'45" N, long. 116°51'45" W); the valley is along Padre Barona Creek on Cañada de San Vicente y Mesa Del Padre Barona grant. Named on El Cajon Mountain (1955) 7.5' quadrangle. Called Padre Barona Valley on Cuyamaca (1903) 30' quadrangle.

Barrel Spring [LOS ANGELES]: *spring,* 5.5 miles north-northwest of Sunland (lat. 34°05'05" N, long. 118°20'30" W; near NW cor. sec. 22, T 3 N, R 14 W). Named on Sunland (1966) 7.5' quadrangle.

Barrel Spring [SAN DIEGO]: *spring,* 1.25 miles north-northeast of San Felipe (lat. 33°12'55" N, long. 116°35'15" W). Named on Ranchita (1960) 7.5' quadrangle. Brown (1923, p. 270) described the feature as a pool of water 5 or 6 feet in diameter with a barrel beside it that is filled with dirty water "which tastes better than it looks."

Barrel Springs [LOS ANGELES]: *springs,* 4 miles southeast of Palmdale (lat. 34°32' N, long. 118°04'05" W; sec. 7, T 5 N, R 11 E). Named on Palmdale (1958) 7.5' quadrangle.

Barrett [SAN DIEGO]: *locality,* nearly 2 miles north-northeast of Campo along San Diego and Arizona Eastern Railroad (lat. 32°37'45" N, long. 116°27'35" W; near N line sec. 10, T 18 S, R 5 E). Named on Cameron Corners (1959) 7.5' quadrangle.

Barrett: see **Barrett Junction** [SAN DIEGO]; **Sawtelle**, under **West Los Angeles** [LOS ANGELES].

Barrett Canyon [LOS ANGELES]: *canyon,* drained by a stream that heads in San Bernardino County and flows 1.25 miles to San Antonio Canyon 12.5 miles north-northeast of Pomona city hall just inside Los Angeles County (lat. 34°13'05" N, long. 117°39'50" W; sec. 36, T 2 N, R 8 W). Named on Mount Baldy (1954) 7.5' quadrangle. Called Kerkhoff Canyon on Camp Baldy (1940) 6' quadrangle, where present Cascade Canyon is called Barrett Canyon.

Barrettdam: see **Barrett Lake** [SAN DIEGO].

Barrett Junction [SAN DIEGO]: *locality,* 27 miles east-southeast of San Diego (lat. 32°36'45" N, long. 116°42'20" W; at NW cor. sec. 17, T 18 S, R 3 E). Named on Tecate (1960) 7.5' quadrangle. Called Eisenecke on Cuyamaca (1903) 30' quadrangle, and called Barrett on Tucker and Reed's (1939) map—United States Board on Geographic Names (1962a, p. 5) rejected the name "Barrett" for the place. Postal authorities established Barrett post office in 1915 and discontinued it in 1936 (Salley, p. 15). Mr. and Mrs. Billie Bloch applied the name "Eisenecke" to their ranch at the site (Gudde, 1949, p. 104). The name "Barrett" is for the Barrett family, pioneers in the neighborhood in the 1870's (Stein, p. 10).

Barrett Lake [SAN DIEGO]: *lake,* behind a dam 5 miles north-northeast of Barrett Junction along Cottonwood Creek (3) (lat. 32°40'45" N, long. 116°40'10" W; near NW cor. sec. 22, T 17 S, R 3 E). Named on Barrett Lake (1960) and Morena Reservoir (1960) 7.5' quadrangles. Called Barrett Reservoir on Tucker and Reed's (1939) map, but United States Board on Geographic Names (1962a, p. 5) rejected this name for the feature. Officials of the city of San Diego named the lake in 1919 to commemorate George W. Barrett and his sister, who homesteaded land in 1879 near the site of the dam that forms the lake (Gudde, 1949, p. 24). Postal authorities established Barrettdam post office 5 miles north of Barrett post office in 1920 and discontinued it in 1922; it was at the site of the dam that forms Barrett Lake (Salley, p. 15).

Barrett Reservoir: see **Barrett Lake** [SAN DIEGO].

Bartholomaus Canyon [LOS ANGELES]: *canyon,* drained by a stream that flows 1.5 miles to lowlands 3.5 miles east of downtown San Fernando (lat. 34°17' N, long. 118°22'35" W; at E line sec. 6, T 2 N, R 14 W). Named on San Fernando (1953) 7.5' quadrangle. Called Batholem Canyon on Los Angeles County (1935) map.

Bartlett: see **Camp Bartlett** [VENTURA].

Bartolo [LOS ANGELES]: *locality,* 3.5 miles south of El Monte city hall along Union Pacific Railroad (lat. 34°01'10" N, long. 118°02'35" W); the place is on Paso de Bartolo grant. Named on El Monte (1953) 7.5' quadrangle.

Bartolo: see **Saint Helens Spur** [LOS ANGELES].

Barton Canyon [SAN DIEGO]: *canyon,* drained by a stream that flows 2.5 miles to Riverside County 15 miles northeast of Borrego Springs (lat. 33°25'45" N, long. 116°11'30" W; at S line sec. 31, T 8 S, R 8 E). Named on Rabbit Peak (1959) 7.5' quadrangle.

Barton Mound: see **East Irvine** [ORANGE].

Bassett [LOS ANGELES]: *town,* 2.25 miles southeast of El Monte city hall (lat. 34°03' N, long. 118°00' W). Named on Baldwin Park (1953) and El Monte (1953) 7.5' quadrangles. Postal authorities established Bassett post office in 1957; after O.T. Bassett purchased the site in 1895, the place was known as Bassett ranch and was developed in the 1930's as Bassett Village (Salley, p. 15).

Bassett Village: see **Bassett** [LOS ANGELES].

Bass Rock [VENTURA]: *relief feature,* 5.5 miles southwest of Triunfo Pass along the coast (lat. 34°03'55" N, long. 118°59'40" W; sec. 20, T 1 S., R 20 W). Named on Triunfo Pass (1950) 7.5' quadrangle.

Bastanchury: see **Sunny Hills** [ORANGE].

Batholem Canyon: see **Bartholomaus Canyon** [LOS ANGELES].

Batiquitos Lagoon [SAN DIEGO]: *lake*, 2.5 miles long, 3.25 miles north of Encinitas at the mouth of San Marcos Creek (lat. 33°05'20" N, long. 117°17' W). Named on Encinitas (1968) 7.5' quadrangle.

Battle Mountain [SAN DIEGO]: *peak*, 5.25 miles south of Escondido (lat. 33°02'50" N, long. 117°04'05" W). Altitude 803 feet. Named on Escondido (1968) 7.5' quadrangle. A feature called Mule Hill is located about 1.5 miles northeast of present Battle Mountain (Harlow, 1982, p. 189)—the name, given by American troops under General Kearny, is for the mules that they ate when Mexicans besieged them at the place in 1846 (Stein, p. 85).

Baughman Spring [LOS ANGELES]: *spring*, 4.5 miles west-southwest of Pacifico Mountain along Mill Creek (lat. 34°21'20" N, long. 118°06'35" W). Named on Chilao Flat (1959) 7.5' quadrangle.

Baxos de Zuniga: see **Zuñiga Shoal** [SAN DIEGO].

Bay City: see **Seal Beach** [ORANGE].

Bay Island [ORANGE]: *island*, 450 feet long, 6.5 miles east-southeast of Huntington Beach civic center in Newport Bay (lat. 33° 36'25" N, long. 117°54'15" W). Named on Newport Beach (1965) 7.5' quadrangle. The feature was a low-lying mud flat before the level was raised by material from dredging operations; the place was called Modjeska Island after Polish actress Helene Modjeska bought a home there in 1907 (Gleason, p. 96-97).

Bay of San Pedro: see **San Pedro Bay** [LOS ANGELES-ORANGE].

Bay Park [SAN DIEGO]: *district*, 6 miles southeast of Point La Jolla (lat. 32°47' N, long. 117°12' W); the place is just east of Mission Bay. Named on La Jolla (1967) 7.5' quadrangle.

Bay Point [SAN DIEGO]: *promontory*, 5.5 miles south-southeast of present Point La Jolla in Mission Bay (lat. 32°46'45" N, long. 117° 14'20" W). Named on La Jolla (1903) 15' quadrangle.

Bayside Village [SAN DIEGO]: *locality*, 6 miles southeast of Point La Jolla (lat. 32°46'55" N, long. 117°12'15" W); the place is just east of Mission Bay. Named on La Jolla (1943) 7.5' quadrangle.

Beacon Bay [ORANGE]: *embayment*, 7 miles east-southeast of Huntington Beach civic center in Newport Bay (lat. 33°36'35" N, long. 117°53'40" W). Named on Newport Beach (1965) 7.5' quadrangle.

Beale's Cut: see **San Fernando Pass** [LOS ANGELES].

Bear Canyon [LOS ANGELES]:

(1) *canyon*, drained by a stream that flows 5 miles to Cienaga Canyon 12 miles southeast of Gorman (lat. 34°39'35" N, long. 118°40'10" W; near N line sec. 34, T 7 N, R 17 W). Named on Liebre Mountain (1958) 7.5' quadrangle.

(2) *canyon*, nearly 2 miles long, 14 miles north-northeast of Pomona city hall on Los Angeles-San Bernardino County line (lat. 34°14'45" N, long. 117°39'20" W). Named on Mount Baldy (1954) 7.5' quadrangle. West Fork branches north less than 1 mile above the mouth of the main canyon; it is 1.25 miles long and is named on Mount Baldy (1954) and Mount San Antonio (1955) 7.5' quadrangles.

(3) *canyon*, drained by a stream that flows nearly 5 miles to Santa Clara River 6.25 miles east of Solemint (lat. 34°25'35" N, long. 118°20'50" W; sec. 16, T 4 N, R 14 W). Named on Agua Dulce (1960) 7.5' quadrangle. Called Little Bear Canyon on Los Angeles County (1935) map.

(4) *canyon*, drained by a stream that flows about 2 miles to Sand Canyon (2) 4 miles southeast of Solemint (lat. 34°22'45" N, long. 118°24'10" W; sec. 1, T 3 N, R 15 W). Named on Mint Canyon (1960) and San Fernando (1953) 7.5' quadrangles.

(5) *canyon*, drained by a stream that flows 3.5 miles to Arroyo Seco 6.5 miles southeast of Condor Peak (lat. 34°15'05" N, long. 118° 08'55" W). Named on Condor Peak (1959), Mount Wilson (1953), and Pasadena (1953) 7.5' quadrangles.

(6) *canyon*, 1.5 miles long, 1.5 miles north of Gorman on Los Angeles-Kern County line (lat. 34°49'05" N, long. 118°51'10" W; at NW cor. sec. 1, T 8 N, R 19 W). Named on Lebec (1958) 7.5' quadrangle.

Bear Canyon [SAN DIEGO]: *canyon*, drained by a stream that flows 1.25 miles to Cañada Aguanga 6.5 miles northwest of Warner Springs (lat. 33°20'20" N, long. 116°43'45" W; sec. 1, T 10 S, R 2 E). Named on Warner Springs (1959) 7.5' quadrangle.

Bear Canyon [VENTURA]:

(1) *canyon*, drained by a stream that flows 3.25 miles to Cuyama River 5.5 miles northwest of Reyes Peak (lat. 34°41'05" N, long. 119°21'25" W; sec. 19, T 7 N, R 23 W). Named on Rancho Nuevo Creek (1943) and Reyes Peak (1943) 7.5' quadrangles.

(2) *canyon*, drained by a stream that flows 3.5 miles to Sespe Creek 11 miles east-northeast of Wheeler Springs (lat. 34°33'30" N, long. 119°06'10" W; near N line sec. 5, T 5 N, R 21 W). Named on Topatopa Mountains (1943) 7.5' quadrangle.

(3) *canyon*, drained by a stream that flows 3 miles to Sisar Creek 6.5 miles west of Santa Paula Peak (lat. 34°25'55" N, long. 119° 07'20" W). Named on Santa Paula Peak (1951) 7.5' quadrangle.

Bear Canyon: see **Little Bear Canyon** [LOS ANGELES]; **O'Hara Canyon** [VENTURA]; **South Portal Canyon** [LOS ANGELES].

Bear Creek [LOS ANGELES]: *stream*, flows 10.5 miles to West Fork San Gabriel River 7.5 miles north of Azusa city hall (lat. 34°14'25" N, long. 117°53' W). Named on Azusa (1953), Crystal Lake (1958), and Waterman Mountain (1959) 7.5' quadrangles. West Fork enters from the west 5.25 miles south-southeast of Waterman Mountain; it is 4.5 miles long and is named on Waterman Mountain (1959) 7.5' quadrangle.

Bear Creek [SAN DIEGO]: *stream*, flows 3.5 miles to Temescal Creek (1) 5 miles west-southwest of Mesa Grande (lat. 33°09'35" N, long. 116°51'15" W; near W line sec. 2, T 12 S, R 1 E). Named on Mesa Grande (1948) 7.5' quadrangle.

Bear Creek [VENTURA]: *stream*, flows nearly 1 mile to Maple Creek 5.5 miles north of Fillmore (lat. 34°28'55" N, long. 118°53'20" W; near N line sec. 32, T 5 N, R 19 W). Named on Fillmore (1951) 7.5' quadrangle.

Bear Creek: see **Maple Creek** [VENTURA]; **Rancho Nuevo Creek** [VENTURA].

Bear Divide [LOS ANGELES]: *pass*, 6 miles north-northeast of downtown San Fernando (lat. 34°21'35" N, long. 118°23'30" W; sec. 7, T 3 N, R 14 W); the feature is near the head of Bear Canyon (4). Named on San Fernando (1966) 7.5' quadrangle.

Beardsley Wash [VENTURA]: *stream*, flows 3.5 miles to lowlands 4 miles west-northwest of Camarillo (lat. 34°14'10" N, long. 119°06'15" W). Named on Camarillo (1950) and Santa Paula (1951) 7.5' quadrangles.

Bear Flat [ORANGE]: *area*, 3.5 miles west-northwest of Santiago Peak at the head of Halfway Canyon (lat. 33°44'10" N, long. 117° 35'15" W). Named on Santiago Peak (1954) 7.5' quadrangle. On Santiago Peak (1943) 15' quadrangle, the name applies to a place located 1.25 miles north-northwest of Santiago Peak (lat. 33°43'35" N, long. 117°32'40" W). The name is from the bear that Jonathan Watson killed at the site (Sleeper, 1976, p. 79).

Bear Gulch [LOS ANGELES]: *canyon*, drained by a stream that flows 1.25 miles to Prairie Fork 5.5 miles northwest of Mount San Antonio (lat. 34°20'55" N, long. 117°42'35" W; at W line sec. 15, T 3 N, R 8 W). Named on Mount San Antonio (1955) 7.5' quadrangle.

Bear Gulch [VENTURA]: *canyon*, nearly 2 miles long, opens into the canyon of Piru Creek 6 miles northeast of McDonald Peak (lat. 34° 42'05" N, long. 118°52'15" W; near W line sec. 14, T 7 N, R 19 W); the canyon heads northeast of Bear Mountain. Named on Black Mountain (1958) and McDonald Peak (1958) 7.5' quadrangles.

Bear Gulch: see **Halfway Canyon** [ORANGE].

Bear Gulch Camp [LOS ANGELES]: *locality*, 13 miles east-southeast of Gorman on Liebre Mountain (lat. 34°42'45" N, long. 118° 37'50" W; sec. 12, T 7 N, R 17 W); the place is near the head of Bear Canyon (1). Named on Liebre Mountain (1958) 7.5' quadrangle.

Bear Heaven [VENTURA]: *area*, 7.5 miles northwest of Fillmore (lat. 34°29' N, long. 118°59' W). Named on Fillmore (1951) and Santa Paula Peak (1951) 7.5' quadrangles.

Bear Mountain [VENTURA]: *peak*, 5.5 miles north-northeast of McDonald Peak (lat. 34°42'20" N, long. 118°53'30" W; near NE cor. sec. 16, T 7 N, R 19 W). Altitude 4777 feet. Named on McDonald Peak (1958) 7.5' quadrangle.

Bear Ridge [SAN DIEGO]: *ridge*, west-trending, 3 miles long, 6.5 miles northeast of Escondido city hall (lat. 33°11'55" N, long. 117° 00' W). Named on Rodriguez Mountain (1948) and Valley Center (1968) 7.5' quadrangles.

Bear Spring [LOS ANGELES]: *spring*, 3.5 miles south-southwest of the village of Leona Valley (lat. 34°34'10" N, long. 118°18'55" W; sec. 36, T 6 N, R 14 W). Named on Sleepy Valley (1958) 7.5' quadrangle. Los Angeles County (1935) map shows Bear Spring located a little farther north (sec. 25, T 6 N, R 14 W), and shows a feature called Pidgeon Spg. situated about 1 mile west-southwest of Bear Spring (sec. 35, T 6 N, R 14 W).

Bear Spring [SAN DIEGO]: *spring*, 2.5 miles south-southeast of Rodriguez Mountain (lat. 33°12'15" N, long. 116°52'45" W). Named on Rodriguez Mountain (1948) 7.5' quadrangle.

Bear Spring: see **Los Pinos Spring** [ORANGE].

Bear Spring Flats [SAN DIEGO]: *area*, 2.5 miles south-southeast of Rodriguez Mountain (lat. 33°12' N, long. 116°52'45" W); Bear Spring is at the place. Named on Rodriguez Mountain (1948) 7.5' quadrangle.

Bear Trap Canyon [ORANGE]: *canyon*, drained by a stream that flows 1.25 miles to Santiago Canyon 2.5 miles west-southwest of Santiago Peak (lat. 33°41'30" N, long. 117°34'20" W; at W line sec. 36, T 5 S, R 7 W). Named on Santiago Peak (1954) 7.5' quadrangle.

Beartrap Canyon [LOS ANGELES]:

(1) *canyon*, drained by a stream that flows 2.25 miles to Piru Creek 10.5 miles south-southeast of Gorman (lat. 34°39'20" N, long. 118° 46'50" W; sec. 34, T 7 N, R 18 W). Named on Black Mountain (1958) 7.5' quadrangle. Los Angeles County (1935) map shows a place called Horse Thief Flat located about 1 mile west of the mouth of Beartrap Canyon along a southern tributary of Piru Creek.

(2) *canyon,* 3.25 miles long, opens into Aliso Canyon (1) 4.25 miles east-southeast of Acton (lat. 34°26'15" N, long. 118°07'50" W; at NW cor. sec. 15, T 4 N, R 12 W). Named on Acton (1959) and Pacifico Mountain (1959) 7.5' quadrangles. A grizzly bear trapped in the canyon in 1889 was sent to the zoo in San Francisco, where it lived until 1911 (Robinson, J.W., 1977, p. 190, 195).

Beartrap Creek [VENTURA]: *stream,* flows 7.25 miles to join Alamo Creek (2) and form Cuyama River 4 miles north of Reyes Peak (lat. 34°41'25" N, long. 119°17'30" W; sec. 23, T 7 N, R 23 W). Named on Reyes Peak (1943) and San Guillermo (1943) 7.5' quadrangles.

Beartrap Spring [LOS ANGELES]: *spring,* 11 miles south-southeast of Gorman in Beartrap Canyon (1) (lat. 34°38'35" N, long. 118°47'25" W). Named on Black Mountain (1958) 7.5' quadrangle.

Bear Valley [SAN DIEGO]:

(1) *valley,* 5.25 miles southwest of Rodriguez Mountain (lat. 33° 10'50" N, long. 116°58' W). Named on Rodriguez Mountain (1948) 7.5' quadrangle. On Ramona (1903) 30' quadrangle, the name "Bear Valley" applies to both present Bear Valley and present Woods Valley.

(2) *valley,* 7.5 miles southeast of Descanso (lat. 32°47' N, long. 116°31'05" W). Named on Descanso (1960) 7.5' quadrangle.

Bear Valley: see **Valley Center** [SAN DIEGO].

Bear Valley Reservoir: see **Lake Wohlford** [SAN DIEGO].

Beatty Canyon [LOS ANGELES]: *canyon,* 1 mile long, 1.25 miles north-northeast of Azusa city hall (lat. 34°09'05" N, long. 117°53'45" W; sec. 23, 26, T 1 N, R 10 W). Named on Azusa (1953) 7.5' quadrangle.

Beaver Hollow [SAN DIEGO]: *canyon,* 3.25 miles long, opens into the canyon of Sweetwater River 6.5 miles southwest of Alpine (lat. 32°45'50" N, long. 116°50'40" W; sec. 23, T 16 S, R 1 R). Named on Alpine (1955) and Dulzura (1972) 7.5' quadrangles.

Beckley: see **Hall Beckley Canyon** [LOS ANGELES].

Bedford Peak [ORANGE]: *peak,* 2.5 miles southeast of Pleasants Peak on Orange-Riverside County line (lat. 33°46' N, long. 117°34'35" W). Named on Corona South (1967) 7.5' quadrangle. The name is from a pioneer of Riverside County (Meadows, p. 26).

Bee Canyon [LOS ANGELES]:

(1) *canyon,* drained by a stream that flows 3 miles to San Francisquito Canyon 7.5 miles south of the village of Lake Hughes (lat. 34°34'05" N, long. 118°27'45" W). Named on Green Valley (1958) 7.5' quadrangle.

(2) *canyon,* drained by a stream that flows 2.5 miles to Santa Clara River 5.25 miles east-northeast of Solemint (lat. 34°26'15" N, long. 118°21'55" W; near N line sec. 17, T 4 N, R 14 W). Named on Agua Dulce (1960) 7.5' quadrangle.

(3) *canyon,* drained by a stream that flows 0.5 mile to Pacoima Canyon 7 miles north-northwest of Sunland (lat. 34°21'05" N, long. 118°21'25" W; near SW cor. sec. 9, T 3 N, R 14 W). Named on Sunland (1953) 7.5' quadrangle.

(4) *canyon,* drained by a stream that flows 2.5 miles to lowlands 5 miles south of Newhall (lat. 34°18'25" N, long. 118°30'35" W). Named on Oat Mountain (1952) 7.5' quadrangle.

Bee Canyon [ORANGE]:

(1) *canyon,* 0.5 mile long, opens into Santa Ana Canyon 2.5 miles south-southeast of San Juan Hill (lat. 33°52'40" N, long. 117°43'15" W). Named on Prado Dam (1967) 7.5' quadrangle.

(2) *canyon,* drained by a stream that flows 2 miles to lowlands 5.5 miles north-northwest of El Toro (lat. 33°42'05" N, long. 117°42'45" W). Named on El Toro (1968) 7.5' quadrangle.

Bee Canyon [SAN DIEGO]:

(1) *canyon,* drained by a stream that flows 1.25 miles to San Luis Rey River 5 miles south of Boucher Hill (lat. 33°15'35" N, long. 116°56'15" W; sec. 36, T 10 S, R 1 W). Named on Boucher Hill (1948) and Rodriguez Mountain (1948) 7.5' quadrangles.

(2) *canyon,* drained by a stream that flows 2.25 miles to Cottonwood Creek (3) 3 miles southwest of Barrett Junction (lat. 32° 35'10" N, long. 116°44'50" W; sec. 23, T 18 S, R 2 E). Named on Otay Mountain (1972) and Tecate (1960) 7.5' quadrangles.

Bee Canyon: see **Round Canyon** [ORANGE].

Bee Canyon Wash [ORANGE]: *stream,* flows 4.5 miles from the mouth of Bee Canyon (2) to San Diego Creek 9 miles southeast of Santa Ana city hall (lat. 33°39'15" N, long. 117°45'30" W). Named on El Toro (1968) and Tustin (1965) 7.5' quadrangles.

Beeler Canyon [SAN DIEGO]: *canyon,* 6.5 miles long, opens into the upper end of Los Peñasquitos Canyon 2 miles west-southwest of Poway (lat. 32°56'55" N, long. 117°04'05" W; at NE cor. sec. 22, T 14 S, R 2 W); the lower part of the canyon is drained by present Beeler Creek, and the upper part is drained by a branch of Poway Creek. Named on Poway (1967) and San Vicente Reservoir (1955) 7.5' quadrangles. The misspelled name commemorates Julius Buehler, who homesteaded 500 acres before 1900 (Stein, p. 11).

Beeler Creek [SAN DIEGO]: *stream,* flows 4.5 miles to join Poway Creek and form Los Peñasquitos Creek 2 miles west-southwest of Poway (lat. 32°57' N, long. 117°04' W; near NE cor. sec. 22, T 14 S, R 2 W). Named on Poway (1967, photorevised 1975) 7.5' quadrangle. Called Los Peñasquitos Creek on Poway Valley (1952) 7.5' quadrangle.

Bee Rock [LOS ANGELES]: *relief feature,* 3.5 miles south-southeast of Burbank city hall (lat. 34°08'05" N, long. 118°17'35" W). Named on Burbank (1953) 7.5' quadrangle.

Bee Valley [SAN DIEGO]: *valley,* nearly 3 miles north of Barrett Junction (lat. 32°39'15" N, long. 116°42'15" W; at SW cor. sec. 29, T 17 S, R 3 E). Named on Barrett Lake (1960) 7.5' quadrangle.

Bel Air [LOS ANGELES]: *district,* 3.25 miles west-northwest of Beverly Hills city hall in Los Angeles (lat. 34°05'10" N, long. 118° 27' W). Named on Beverly Hills (1950) 7.5' quadrangle.

Bell [LOS ANGELES]: *city,* 2 miles north-northeast of South Gate city hall (lat. 33°58'45" N, long. 118°11'15" W). Named on South Gate (1952) 7.5' quadrangle. The city incorporated in 1923. Downey (1902) 15' quadrangle has the names "Obed" and "Bell Sta." for a place situated along Los Angeles Terminal Railroad about 1 mile west of present Bell city hall (lat. 33°58'40" N, long. 118°12'20" W). Postal authorities established Obed post office—named for Obed, Kentucky—in 1892 and changed the name to Bell in 1898; James G. Bell, who owned the land there, was the first postmaster of both post offices (Hanna, p. 28; Salley, p. 17, 159).

Bell Bluff [SAN DIEGO]: *relief feature,* 6 miles southwest of Descanso (lat. 32°48'30" N, long. 116°42' W; mainly in sec. 5, T 16 S, R 3 E). Named on Viejas Mountain (1960) 7.5' quadrangle.

Bell Canyon [LOS ANGELES]: *canyon,* 2 miles long, joins Volfe Canyon to form Big Dalton Canyon 5 miles northeast of Glendora city hall (lat. 34°10'55" N, long. 117°47'45" W; sec. 11, T 1 N, R 9 W). Named on Glendora (1953) 7.5' quadrangle.

Bell Canyon [LOS ANGELES-VENTURA]: *canyon,* 6 miles long, on Los Angeles-Ventura County line along Bell Creek above a point 5 miles south-southwest of Chatsworth (lat. 34°11'50" N, long. 118° 39'15" W). Named on Calabasas (1952) 7.5' quadrangle.

Bell Canyon [ORANGE]: *canyon,* drained by a stream that flows 13 miles to San Juan Creek nearly 7 miles east-northeast of San Juan Capistrano (lat. 33°32'05" N, long. 117°33'15" W; near NW cor. sec. 30, T 7 S, R 6 W). Named on Alberhill (1954), Cañada Gobernadora (1968), and Santiago Peak (1954) 7.5' quadrangles. The name is the anglicized form of the Spanish name *Cañada de la Campaña,* given to the canyon in Spanish days because of a boulder there that gave off a clear tone when struck (Meadows, p. 26).

Bell Canyon: see **Hot Spring Canyon** [ORANGE].

Bell Creek [LOS ANGELES-VENTURA]: *stream,* heads just inside Ventura County and flows 3 miles to join Arroyo Calabasas and form Los Angeles River 0.5 mile southwest of the center of Canoga Park (lat. 34°11'40" N, long. 118°36'05" W). Named on Calabasas (1952) and Canoga Park (1952) 7.5' quadrangles. South Branch enters from the southwest 1.5 miles above the mouth of the main stream; it is 0.5 mile long and is named on Calabasas (1952) 7.5' quadrangle.

Bellflower [LOS ANGELES]: *city,* 8 miles southwest of Whittier city hall (lat. 33°52'55" N, long. 118°07'15" W). Named on Long Beach (1949), Los Alamitos (1950), South Gate (1952), and Whittier (1965) 7.5' quadrangles. Postal authorities established Bellflower post office in 1910 (Frickstad, p. 70), and the city incorporated in 1957. F.E. Woodruff founded the community in 1906 and called it Somerset, but postal authorities rejected this designation; an orchard of bellflower apples suggested the present name (Gudde, 1949, p. 27).

Bell Gardens [LOS ANGELES]: *city,* 2 miles east-southeast of South Gate city hall (lat. 33°58' N, long. 118°09'30" W). Named on South Gate (1964) 7.5' quadrangle. Postal authorities established Gardens post office in 1930 and changed the name to Bell Gardens in 1943 (Salley, p. 82). The city incorporated in 1961. The community began in 1930 when promoters subdivided vegetable tracts developed there by Japanese gardeners (Gudde, 1969, p. 25).

Bell Station: see **Bell** [LOS ANGELES].

Bell Valley [SAN DIEGO]: *valley,* 3.5 miles east of Potrero (lat. 32° 35'50" N, long. 116°33'15" W; near NW cor. sec. 23, T 18 S, R 4 E). Named on Potrero (1960) 7.5' quadrangle.

Belmont Shore [LOS ANGELES]: *district,* 3.25 miles east-southeast of Long Beach city hall (lat. 33°45'30" N, long. 118°08'05" W). Named on Long Beach (1964) 7.5' quadrangle. Postal authorities established Belmont Shore post office in 1930 and discontinued it in 1962; the place, now part of Long Beach, was settled in the early 1900's as a seashore vacation spot (Salley, p. 18).

Belvedere [LOS ANGELES]:

(1) *district,* 4.5 miles east-southeast of Los Angeles city hall (lat. 34°02'10" N, long. 118°09'45" W). Named on Los Angeles (1953) 7.5' quadrangle.

(2) *locality,* 2.5 miles northeast of Redondo (present Redondo Beach) along a rail line (lat. 33°51'50" N, long. 118°21'25" W). Named on Redondo (1896) 15' quadrangle.

Belvedere Gardens [LOS ANGELES]: *district,* 5 miles east-southeast of Los Angeles city hall (lat. 34°01'40" N, long. 118°10' W). Named on Alhambra (1926) 6' quadrangle.

Benedict: see **Stanton** [ORANGE].

Benedict Canyon [LOS ANGELES]: *canyon*, 3.25 miles long, 3 miles northwest of Beverly Hills city hall (lat. 34°06'15" N, long. 118°26'10" W). Named on Beverly Hills (1950) and Van Nuys (1953) 7.5' quadrangles. The name commemorates Edson A. Benedict, a storekeeper in Los Angeles who claimed the canyon in 1868 (Gudde, 1949, p. 28).

Bennington [LOS ANGELES]: *locality*, 3 miles north of Los Angeles city hall along Los Angeles Terminal Railroad (lat. 34°05'45" N, long. 118°14' W). Named on Pasadena (1900) 15' quadrangle.

Bennis Bowl [SAN DIEGO]: *relief feature*, 9 miles northwest of Borrego Springs (lat. 33°20'45" N, long. 116°29'10" W). Named on Borrego Palm Canyon (1959) 7.5' quadrangle.

Benson Lake [SAN DIEGO]: *dry lake*, 1 mile long, just northeast of Ocotillo Wells (lat. 33°08'50" N, long. 116°07'50" W; around NW cor. sec. 10, T 12 S, R 8 E). Named on Borrego Mountain (1960) and Shell Reef (1959) 7.5' quadrangles. Called Bensons Dry Lake on Barrel Spring (1942) 15' quadrangle. The name commemorates an early homesteader and prospector (Stein, p. 11).

Bensons Dry Lake: see **Benson Lake** [SAN DIEGO].

Benton: see **Azusa** [LOS ANGELES] (3).

Bent Spring Canyon [LOS ANGELES]: *canyon*, 2.25 miles long, 4 miles south of Torrance city hall (lat. 33°46'40" N, long. 118°40'15" W). Named on Torrance (1964) 7.5' quadrangle.

Ben Weston Beach [LOS ANGELES]: *beach*, 3 miles west-southwest of Mount Banning on the west side of Santa Catalina Island (lat. 33°21'45" N, long. 118°29' W); the beach is less than 0.5 mile north-northeast of Ben Weston Point. Named on Santa Catalina South (1943) 7.5' quadrangle.

Ben Weston Point [LOS ANGELES]: *promontory*, 3.25 miles west-southwest of Mount Banning on the west side of Santa Catalina Island (lat. 33°21'25" N, long. 118°29'15" W). Named on Santa Catalina South (1943) 7.5' quadrangle. The name recalls Ben Weston, an early squatter on the island (Doran, 1980, p. 76).

Bergstrom Canyon [SAN DIEGO]: *canyon*, drained by a stream that flows nearly 2 miles to Cañada Verruga 2 miles northeast of San Felipe (lat. 33°13'10" N, long. 116°34'15" W). Named on Ranchita (1960) 7.5' quadrangle.

Bernardo [SAN DIEGO]: *locality*, 4 miles south-southeast of Escondido (lat. 33°03'35" N, long. 117°03'55" W); the place is on San Bernardo grant. Named on Escondido (1901) 15' quadrangle. Postal authorities established Bernardo post office 5 miles south of Escondido in 1872 and discontinued it in 1918 (Salley, p. 19).

Bernardo Mountain [SAN DIEGO]: *peak*, 4.25 miles south of Escondido (lat. 33°03'50" N, long. 117°05'15" W); the feature is on San Bernardo grant.. Altitude 1150 feet. Named on Escondido (1968) 7.5' quadrangle.

Bernardo River: see **San Dieguito River** [SAN DIEGO].

Berry Canyon [LOS ANGELES]: *canyon*, 1.25 miles long, 5 miles southeast of Van Nuys (lat. 34°07'55" N, long. 118°23'10" W). Named on Van Nuys (1953) 7.5' quadrangle.

Berryfield: see **Garden Grove** [ORANGE].

Berry Flat [LOS ANGELES]: *area*, 4.25 miles north of Glendora city hall (lat. 34°11'55" N, long. 117°51'10" W; near W line sec. 5, T 1 N, R 9 W). Named on Glendora (1953) 7.5' quadrangle.

Bertha Canyon [SAN DIEGO]: *canyon*, 1.5 miles long, 4.5 miles northeast of San Felipe (lat. 33°14'10" N, long. 116°32' W; around NW cor. sec. 12, T 11 S, R 4 E). Named on Ranchita (1960) 7.5' quadrangle.

Beulah Picnic Ground [SAN DIEGO]: *locality*, nearly 4 miles east of Descanso (lat. 32°51' N, long. 116°33' W; near SE cor. sec. 22, T 15 S, R 4 E). Named on Descanso (1960) 7.5' quadrangle.

Beverly: see **Beverly Hills** [LOS ANGELES].

Beverly Glen [LOS ANGELES]: *locality*, 3.5 miles northwest of Beverly Hills city hall in Brown Canyon (2) (lat. 34°06'30" N, long. 118°26'45" W). Named on Beverly Hills (1950) 7.5' quadrangle. Postal authorities established Beverly Glen post office in 1913 and discontinued it in 1916 (Frickstad, p. 71).

Beverly Hills [LOS ANGELES]: *city*, 9 miles west of Los Angeles city hall (lat. 34°04'20" N, long. 118°24' W). Named on Beverly Hills (1950) and Hollywood (1953) 7.5' quadrangles. Postal authorities established Beverly post office in 1907 and changed the name to Beverly Hills in 1911 (Salley, p. 20). The city incorporated in 1914. De Las Aguas Association of San Francisco bought Rodeo de los Aguas grant in 1869 and subdivided it to form a German colony called Santa Maria—the association reserved land for a town of Santa Maria at a site in the heart of present Beverly Hills (Robinson, W.W., p. 23-24). Another early-day community called Morocco also occupied part of present Beverly Hills (Hanna, p. 31). The name "Beverly Hills" is from Beverly Farms, Massachusetts, former home of Burton E. Green, an official of Rodeo Land and Water Company, which promoted the city (Gudde, 1949, p. 30).

Bichota Canyon [LOS ANGELES]: *canyon*, drained by a stream that flows nearly 4 miles to North Fork San Gabriel River 4 miles south of Crystal Lake (lat. 34°15'40" N, long. 117°50'35" W). Named on Crystal lake (1958) 7.5' quadrangle.

Bichota Mesa [LOS ANGELES]: *area*, 4 miles south of Crystal Lake (lat. 34°15'45" N, long. 117°50'45" W); the place is opposite the mouth of Bichota Canyon. Named on Crystal Lake (1958) 7.5' quadrangle.

Big Canyon [ORANGE]: *canyon*, drained by a stream that flows nearly 3 miles to lowlands along Upper Newport Bay 7 miles east-southeast of Huntington Beach city hall (lat. 33°37'50" N, long. 117°52'55" W). Named on Laguna Beach (1965), Newport Beach (1965), and Tustin (1965) 7.5' quadrangles.

Big Canyon [VENTURA]: *canyon*, drained by a stream that flows 1.5 miles to Upper Ojai Valley nearly 4 miles east-southeast of the town of Ojai (lat. 34°25'50" N, long. 119°09'40" W). Named on Ojai (1952) 7.5' quadrangle. The feature first was called Cataract Canyon for natural asphalt cataracts or tar seeps in it, and then it was called Pinkerton Canyon for a family of early landowners in the vicinity (Ricard).

Big Canyon Reservoir [ORANGE]: *lake*, 1350 feet long, 6.25 miles northwest of Laguna Beach city hall (lat. 33°36'40" N, long. 117° 51'20" W); the lake is at the head of a branch of Big Canyon. Named on Laguna Beach (1965) 7.5' quadrangle.

Big Cedar Creek [VENTURA]: *stream*, flows 1.5 miles to Snowy Creek 2.5 miles northeast of McDonald Peak (lat. 34°39'25" N, long. 118°54'25" W; near W line sec. 33, T 7 N, R 19 W). Named on McDonald Peak (1958) 7.5' quadrangle.

Big Cienega [LOS ANGELES]:

(1) *canyon*, drained by a stream that flows less than 1 mile to Trail Canyon nearly 1 mile northwest of Condor Peak (lat. 34°20' N, long. 118°13'45" W). Named on Condor Peak (1959) 7.5' quadrangle.

(2) *spring*, 1.5 miles north-northeast of Crystal Lake (lat. 34°20'15" N, long. 117°49'50" W). Named on Crystal Lake (1958) 7.5' quadrangle. On Crystal Lake (1941) 6' quadrangle, the name "Big Cienega" applies to a relief feature at the place.

Big Cienega Spring [LOS ANGELES]: *spring*, 3.25 miles east-northeast of Glendora city hall (lat. 34°09'30" N, long. 117°48'45" W; sec. 22, T 1 N, R 9 W). Named on Glendora (1953) 7.5' quadrangle.

Big Cone Camp [VENTURA]: *locality*, 2.5 miles west of Santa Paula Peak at the mouth of East Fork Santa Paula Canyon (lat. 34°26'55" N, long. 119°03'20" W). Named on Santa Paula Peak (1951) 7.5' quadrangle.

Big Cone Spring [ORANGE]: *spring*, 2 miles north-northwest of Santiago Peak (lat. 33°44'20" N, long. 117°32'45" W). Named on Santiago Peak (1954) 7.5' quadrangle. The name is from some bigcone-spruce trees that grow near the spring (Meadows, p. 27).

Big Dalton Canyon [LOS ANGELES]: *canyon*, 3.5 miles long, opens into lowlands 2 miles northeast of Glendora city hall (lat. 34°09'10" N, long. 117°50'10" W; at W line sec. 21, T 1 N, R 9 W). Named on Glendora (1953) 7.5' quadrangle. The canyon divides at the head to form Volfe Canyon and Bell Canyon. The name "Dalton" commemorates Henry Dalton, who claimed Azusa grant and Santa Anita grant (Gudde, 1949, p. 87). Spaniards called the feature El Cañon de la Boca Negra, supposedly for dark foliage that marked the entrance to the canyon—*El Cañon de la Boca Negra* means "the canyon with the Black Mouth" in Spanish (Robinson, J.W., 1983, p. 13).

Big Dalton Reservoir [LOS ANGELES]: *lake*, behind a dam 4 miles northeast of Glendora city hall (lat. 34°10'10" N, long. 117°48'30" W; sec. 15, T 1 N, R 9 W); the lake is in Big Dalton Canyon. Named on Glendora (1966) 7.5' quadrangle.

Big Dalton Wash [LOS ANGELES]: *stream* and *dry wash*, extends for nearly 11 miles from the mouth of Big Dalton Canyon to Walnut Creek 1.5 miles south-southwest of Baldwin Park city hall (lat. 34°04' N, long. 117°58'15" W). Named on Baldwin Park (1953), Glendora (1953), and San Dimas (1954) 7.5' quadrangles. East Branch extends for 1.25 miles from the mouth of Shuler Canyon to Big Dalton Wash 1.25 miles east-southeast of Glendora city hall. East Branch is named on Glendora (1966) 7.5' quadrangle; the upper part of present East Branch is called Shuler Creek on Glendora (1953) 7.5' quadrangle.

Bighorn: see **Valyermo** [LOS ANGELES].

Bighorn Canyon [SAN DIEGO]: *canyon*, drained by a stream that flows nearly 3 miles to lowlands 12 miles west-southwest of Ocotillo Wells (lat. 33°05'45" N, long. 116°20' W). Named on Whale Peak (1959) 7.5' quadrangle.

Big Horn Ridge [LOS ANGELES]: *ridge*, southwest-trending, 3 miles long, center 2.25 southwest of Mount San Antonio (lat. 34° 16'15" N, long. 117°40'40" W). Named on Mount San Antonio (1955) 7.5' quadrangle.

Big John Flat [LOS ANGELES]: *area*, 4 miles northwest of Big Pines (lat. 34°25'05" N, long. 117°44'30" W; sec. 19, 20, T 4 N, R 8 W). Named on Mescal Creek (1956) and Valyermo (1958) 7.5' quadrangles. Called Big John Flats on Los Angeles County (1935) map.

Big Laguna Lake [SAN DIEGO]: *lake*, 2050 feet long, 2.5 miles west-southwest of Monument Peak (lat. 32°52'50" N, long. 116°27'40" W; near W line sec. 10, T 15 S, R 5 E); the lake is in Laguna Meadow. Named on Monument Peak (1959) 7.5' quadrangle. Called Big Laguna on Tucker and Reed's (1939) map. On Cuyapaipe (1944) 15' quadrangle, present Big Laguna Lake and present Little Laguna Lake together are called Laguna Lakes, but United States Board on Geographic Names (1961b, p. 9) rejected this name for the pair.

Big Lake [SAN DIEGO]: *intermittent lake,* 1500 feet long, 3.5 miles west-southwest of Warner Springs (lat. 33°16'05" N, long. 116°41'35" W). Named on Warner Springs (1959) 7.5' quadrangle.

Big Mermaids Canyon [LOS ANGELES]: *canyon,* drained by a stream that flows 2.5 miles to West Fork San Gabriel River 7.5 miles north of Azusa city hall (lat. 34°14'45" N, long. 117°54' W); the mouth of the canyon is 1650 feet east of the mouth of Little Mermaids Canyon. Named on Azusa (1953) and Waterman Mountain (1959) 7.5' quadrangles.

Big Moore Canyon: see **Wickham Canyon** [LOS ANGELES].

Big Mountain [VENTURA]: *ridge,* west-trending, 8 miles long, center 6 miles northeast of Moorpark (lat. 34°20'15" N, long. 118° 47'45" W). Named on Santa Susana (1951) and Simi (1951) 7.5' quadrangles.

Big Narrows [VENTURA]: *narrows,* 3.25 miles south-southeast of Cobblestone Mountain along Agua Blanca Creek (lat. 34°34' N, long. 118°50'25" W; near E line sec. 36, T 6 N, R 19 W). Named on Cobblestone Mountain (1958) 7.5' quadrangle.

Big Oak Flat [LOS ANGELES]: *area,* 2.5 miles east of Whitaker Peak (lat. 34°34'35" N, long. 118°41'30" W; sec. 28, 33, T 6 N, R 17 W). Named on Whitaker Peak (1958) 7.5' quadrangle.

Big Oak Spring [LOS ANGELES]: *spring,* 4 miles southwest of the village of Leona Valley (lat. 34°34'25" N, long. 118°20'20" W; near SW cor. sec. 26, T 6 N, R 14 E). Named on Sleepy Valley (1958) 7.5' quadrangle.

Big Pines [LOS ANGELES]: *village,* nearly 7 miles north-northwest of Mount San Antonio (lat. 34°22'45" N, long. 117°41'20" W; near W line sec. 2, T 3 N, R 8 W). Named on Mescal Creek (1956) 7.5' quadrangle. Swarthout (1941) 6' quadrangle shows a place called Swarthout located 0.5 mile west-northwest of the west end of Swarthout Valley at present Big Pines. Postal authorities established Swartout post office (with the misspelled name) in 1926 and discontinued it in 1942 (Frickstad, p. 82).

Big Potrero [SAN DIEGO]: *valley,* at and north of the village of Potrero (lat. 32°37' N, long. 116°36'45" W). Named on Potrero (1960) and Tecate (1960) 7.5' quadrangles.

Big Potrero: see **Long Potrero** [SAN DIEGO].

Big Potrero Creek: see **Potrero Creek** [SAN DIEGO] (2).

Big Rock [LOS ANGELES]: *rock,* 7 miles west-northwest of present Santa Monica city hall, and 100 feet offshore (lat. 34°02'10" N, long. 118°36'30" W). Named on Las Flores (1932) 6' quadrangle.

Big Rock Beach [LOS ANGELES]: *beach,* 7.25 miles west-northwest of Santa Monica city hall (lat. 34°02'15" N, long. 118°37' W; sec. 36, T 1 S, R 17 W); Big Rock is near the east end of the beach, which is at the mouth of Piedra Gorda Canyon. Named on Topanga (1952) 7.5' quadrangle.

Big Rock Campground [LOS ANGELES]: *locality,* 5.5 miles southeast of Valyermo (lat. 34°23'15" N, long. 117°46'45" W; sec. 36, T 4 N, R 9 W). Named on Valyermo (1958) 7.5' quadrangle.

Big Rock Creek [LOS ANGELES]: *stream,* flows 11 miles to lowlands 1.5 miles north-northwest of Valyermo (lat. 34°28'30" N, long. 117°51'15" W; sec. 31, T 5 N, R 9 W). Named on Valyermo (1958) 7.5' quadrangle. Thompson (1929, p. 291) noted that the stream was called both Rock Creek and Rio del Llano, but United States Board on Geographic Names (1960d, p. 15) rejected these names for the feature. South Fork enters from the south 3 miles southeast of Valyermo; it is 5.5 miles long and is named on Crystal Lake (1958) and Valyermo (1958) 7.5' quadrangles.

Big Rock Springs [LOS ANGELES]: *locality,* 1 mile southeast of Valyermo (lat. 34°26'05" N, long. 117°50'05" W; at E line sec. 17, T 4 N, R 9 W); the place is along Big Rock Creek. Named on Valyermo (1958) 7.5' quadrangle. Rock Creek (1903) 15' quadrangle has the name "Big Rock Villa" near the site.

Big Rock Villa: see **Big Rock Springs** [LOS ANGELES].

Big Rock Wash [LOS ANGELES]: *stream* and *dry wash,* extends for 15 miles from the mouth of the canyon of Big Rock Creek to end 12 miles north-northeast of Littlerock (lat. 34°40' N, long. 117°52'15" W; sec. 30, T 7 N, R 9 W). Named on Hi Vista (1957), Littlerock (1957), Lovejoy Buttes (1957), and Valyermo (1958) 7.5' quadrangles. United States Board on Geographic Names (1961c, p. 8) rejected the names "Rio del Llano," "Rock Creek Wash," and "Rock Wash" for the feature.

Big Spring [SAN DIEGO]: *spring,* 5 miles southwest of Borrego Springs (lat. 33°12'05" N, long. 116°26' W). Named on Tubb Canyon (1959) 7.5' quadrangle.

Big Springs Canyon [LOS ANGELES]: *canyon,* drained by a stream that flows nearly 3 miles to the sea 2.5 miles west-northwest of Mount Banning on Santa Catalina Island (lat. 33°23'10" N, long. 118°28'25" W); the feature is east of Little Springs Canyon. Named on Santa Catalina North (1950) 7.5' quadrangle.

Big Springs Reservoir [LOS ANGELES]: *lake,* 200 feet long, 4.5 miles north-northwest of Mount Banning on Santa Catalina Island (lat. 33°26' N, long. 118°27'40" W). Named on Santa Catalina North (1950) 7.5' quadrangle.

Big Sycamore Canyon [VENTURA]: *canyon,* drained by a stream that flows 10 miles to the sea 5 miles east-southeast of Point Mugu (lat. 34°04'15" N, long. 119°00'50" W). Named on Newbury Park (1951), Point Mugu (1949), and Triunfo Pass (1950) 7.5' quadrangles. Called Sycamore Canyon on Camulos (1903) 30' quadrangle, but United States Board on Geographic Names (1961c, p. 8) rejected this name for the feature.

Big Tujunga Canyon [LOS ANGELES]: *canyon,* 19 miles long, opens into Tujunga Valley 1 mile north-northwest of Sunland (lat. 34°16'30" N, long. 118°18'50" W). Named on Chilao Flat (1959), Condor Peak (1959), and Sunland (1953) 7.5' quadrangles. Called Tujunga Canyon on San Fernando (1900) 15' quadrangle, which shows Tujunga River in it. Marcou (p. 160) referred to "the large cañon of the Big Tujunja or Tujunga." United States Board on Geographic Names (1968b, p. 4) rejected the names "Tahunga Canyon," "Tajunga Canyon," "Tujunga Canyon," "Tujunga Creek," and "Tuyanga Canyon." The name, which is from Tujunga grant (Robinson, J.W., 1977, p. 145), evidently is of Indian origin (Kroeber, p. 62). The canyon divides at the head to form Upper Big Tujunga Canyon and the canyon of Alder Creek (2). Present Upper Big Tujunga Canyon is called Big Tujunga Canyon on Mount Wilson (1939) 6' quadrangle, but United States Board on Geographic Names (1968b, p. 7) rejected the names "Big Tujunga Canyon," "Tahunga Canyon," "Tajunga Canyon," "Tujunga Canyon," "Tujunga Creek," and "Tuyanga Canyon" for present Upper Big Tujunga Canyon. The Board (1976a, p. 5) approved the name "Big Tujunga Creek" for the stream that flows through Upper Big Tujunga Canyon and Big Tujunga Canyon, and gave the names "Tujunga Creek" and "Tujunga River" as variants.

Big Tujunga Creek: see **Big Tujunga Canyon** [LOS ANGELES]:

Big Tujunga Station [LOS ANGELES]: *locality,* nearly 3 miles south of Condor Peak (lat. 34°17'10" N, long. 118°13'30" W; sec. 3, T 2 N, R 13 W); the place is in Big Tujunga Canyon. Named on Condor Peak (1959) 7.5' quadrangle.

Big Wash [SAN DIEGO]:

(1) *stream,* flows 4 miles to Imperial County 17 miles east-northeast of Borrego Springs (lat. 33°19'05" N, long. 116°05' W; at E line sec. 12, T 10 S, R 8 E). Named on Fonts Point (1959) and Seventeen Palms (1956) 7.5' quadrangles.

(2) *stream,* flows 3.25 miles to San Felipe Creek 6.25 miles northwest of Ocotillo Wells (lat. 33°13' N, long. 116°12' W; sec. 13, T 11 S, R 7 E). Named on Borrego Mountain (1960) 7.5' quadrangle.

Bill Lane Camp: see **Camp Bill Lane** [LOS ANGELES].

Bingham [ORANGE]: *locality,* 3.5 miles west-southwest of present Buena Park civic center along Pacific Electric Railroad at Los Angeles-Orange County line (lat. 33°50'45" N, long. 118°03'30" W). Named on Los Alamitos (1935) 7.5' quadrangle.

Binnacle Rock [LOS ANGELES]: *rock,* about 3 miles south of Avalon near the southeast end of Santa Catalina Island, and 225 feet offshore (lat. 33°18'05" N, long. 118°20' W). Named on Santa Catalina East (1950) 7.5' quadrangle.

Birch Hill [SAN DIEGO]: *ridge,* generally east-trending, about 1 mile long, 4.5 miles east-southeast of Boucher Hill (lat. 33°18'40" N, long. 116°51' W; mainly in sec. 14, T 10 S, R 1 E). Named on Palomar Observatory (1949) 7.5' quadrangle. The name commemorates Arthur Birch and Harry Birch, brothers from England who lived in the neighborhood for a time before they returned to their native land (Stein, p. 12).

Bird: see **John Bird Canyon** [LOS ANGELES].

Bird Rock [LOS ANGELES]: *rock,* 6.25 miles north-northwest of Mount Banning on the north side of Santa Catalina Island, and 1800 feet offshore (lat. 33°27'05" N, long. 118°29'10" W). Named on Santa Catalina North (1950) 7.5' quadrangle. Preston (1890b, map following p. 278) called the feature White Rock, but United States Board on Geographic Names (1936a, p. 9 rejected this name for it.

Bird Rock [SAN DIEGO]: *rock,* 2.5 miles south of Point La Jolla, and 400 feet offshore (lat. 32°48'50" N, long. 117°16'25" W). Named on La Jolla (1967) 7.5' quadrangle.

Bird Rock: see **Ship Rock** [LOS ANGELES].

Bishop Stevens Campground [SAN DIEGO]: *locality,* less than 1 mile north-northeast of Julian (lat. 33°05'15" N, long. 116°35'45" W; sec. 32, T 12 S, R 4 E). Named on Julian (1960) 7.5' quadrangle. Called Stevens Campground on Santa Ysabel (1960) 15' quadrangle.

Bisket [LOS ANGELES]: *relief feature,* 4.5 miles northeast of downtown San Fernando (lat. 34°19'50" N, long. 118°23'20" W; sec. 19, T 3 N, R 14 W). Named on San Fernando (1966) 7.5' quadrangle.

Bisnaga Alta Wash [SAN DIEGO]: *stream,* flows 4.5 miles to Vallecito Creek nearly 3 miles northwest of Agua Caliente Springs (lat. 32°58'10" N, long. 116°19'20" W; sec. 12, T 14 S, R 6 E). Named on Agua Caliente Springs (1959) and Whale Peak (1959) 7.5' quadrangles.

Bit Rock [LOS ANGELES]: *rock,* 3.25 miles south-southwest of Redondo Beach city hall, and 700 feet offshore at Flat Rock Point (lat. 33°47'45" N, long. 118°24'35" W). Named on Redondo Beach (1963) 7.5' quadrangle.

Bitter Canyon [LOS ANGELES]: *canyon,* drained by a stream that flows 3 miles to Charlie Canyon 6.5 miles south of Warm Springs Mountain (lat. 34°30'10" N, long. 118°34'45" W; sec. 20, T 5 N, R 16 W). Named on Warm Springs Mountain (1958) 7.5' quadrangle. Tejon (1903) 30' quadrangle has the name "Bitter Creek" for the stream in the canyon. Los Angeles County (1935) map shows a feature called Shaw Canyon that opens into Charlie Canyon from the north less than 1 mile east of the mouth of Bitter Canyon (near W line sec. 21, T 5 N, R 16 W), and a feature called McRay Canyon that opens into Charlie Canyon about 2 miles east-northeast of the mouth of Bitter Canyon (near W line sec. 15, T 5 N, R 16 W).

Bitter Creek: see **Amargosa Creek** [VENTURA]; **Bitter Canyon** [LOS ANGELES].

Bitter Creek Canyon [SAN DIEGO]: *canyon,* drained by a stream that flows 3 miles to Grapevine Canyon 9 miles south-southwest of Borrego Springs (lat. 33°08'45" N, long. 116°26'50" W). Named on Earthquake Valley (1959) and Tubb Canyon (1959) 7.5' quadrangles.

Bitter Creek Spring [SAN DIEGO]: *spring,* 10 miles south-southwest of Borrego Springs (lat. 33°08'05" N, long. 116°27'50" W); the spring is in Bitter Creek Canyon. Named on Tubb Canyon (1959) 7.5' quadrangle.

Bitter Point: see **Santa Ana River** [ORANGE].

Bitterwater Lake: see **Amarus Lake**, under **Santa Ana River** [ORANGE].

Bixby [LOS ANGELES]: *locality,* 4.25 miles north-northeast of present Long Beach city hall along Union Pacific Railroad (lat. 33°49'40" N, long. 118°09'50" W). Named on Clearwater (1925) 6' quadrangle.

Bixby: see **Bixby Knolls** [LOS ANGELES].

Bixby Knolls [LOS ANGELES]: *district,* 4.5 miles north of Long Beach city hall (lat. 33°50'05" N, long. 118°10'40" W). Named on Long Beach (1949) 7.5' quadrangle. Postal authorities established Bixby post office 4 miles north of Long Beach post office in 1946; the name commemorates Jotham Bixby, pioneer of Long Beach (Salley, p. 22).

Bixby Slough: see **Harbor Lake** [LOS ANGELES].

Black Butte [LOS ANGELES]: *hill,* 15 miles east-northeast of Littlerock (lat. 34°33'25" N, long. 117°43'20" W; on N line sec. 4, T 5 N, R 8 W). Altitude 3581 feet. Named on El Mirage (1956) 7.5' quadrangle.

Black Butte [SAN DIEGO]: *peak,* 4 miles west of Mesa Grande (lat. 33°11'05" N, long. 116°50'20" W; near SW cor. sec. 25, T 11 S, R 1 E). Named on Ramona (1903) 30' quadrangle.

Black Canyon [SAN DIEGO]: *canyon,* drained by a stream that flows 4.5 miles to Santa Ysabel Creek 4.25 miles south-southwest of Mesa Grande (lat. 33°07'35" N, long. 116°48'20" W; at E line sec. 18, T 12 S, R 2 E). Named on Mesa Grande (1948) 7.5' quadrangle.

Black Canyon [VENTURA]: *canyon,* drained by a stream that flows less than 1 mile to Simi Valley (1) 2.25 miles west-southwest of Santa Susana Pass (lat. 34°15'45" N, long. 118°40'15" W; near NE cor. sec. 16, T 2 N, R 17 W). Named on Santa Susana (1951) 7.5' quadrangle.

Black Jack Camp [LOS ANGELES]: *locality,* 2 miles east-northeast of Mount Banning on Santa Catalina Island (lat. 33°23'05" N, long. 118°24'20" W); the place is 0.25 mile west-southwest of Black Jack Mountain. Named on Santa Catalina North (1950) 7.5' quadrangle.

Black Jack Mountain [LOS ANGELES]: *peak,* 2.25 miles east-northeast of Mount Banning on Santa Catalina Island (lat. 33°23'15" N, long. 118°24' W). Altitude 2010 feet. Named on Santa Catalina North (1950) 7.5' quadrangle. The name is from zinc blende, also called black jack, found in some veins on spurs of the peak (Preston, 1890b, p. 278). The feature is called Mount Banning on some older maps (Doran, 1980, p. 77).

Black Mountain [SAN DIEGO]:

(1) *peak,* 2.5 miles west-southwest of Mesa Grande (lat. 33°09'35" N, long. 116°48'25" W; near E line sec. 6, T 12 S, R 2 E). Altitude 4051 feet. Named on Mesa Grande (1948) 7.5' quadrangle.

(2) *peak,* 5 miles west-northwest of Poway (lat. 32°58'55" N, long. 117°06'55" W; near SW cor. sec. 5, T 14 S, R 2 W). Altitude 1552 feet. Named on Poway (1967) 7.5' quadrangle. United States Board on Geographic Names (1963, p. 13) rejected the name "Santa Maria Mountain" for the feature.

(3) *locality,* 8 miles east of Delmar (present Del Mar) (lat. 32°58' N, long. 117°07'45" W); the place is 1.25 miles southwest of Black Mountain (2). Named on La Jolla (1903) 15' quadrangle. Postal authorities established Black Mountain post office in 1888, moved it 0.5 mile southwest in 1890, moved it 1 mile east and 0.5 mile north in 1899, and discontinued it in 1903 (Salley, p. 22).

Black Mountain [VENTURA]:

(1) *peak,* 4.5 miles east-northeast of McDonald Peak (lat. 34°39'15" N, long. 118°51'40" W; sec. 35, T 7 N, R 19 W). Altitude 6216 feet. Named on Black Mountain (1958) 7.5' quadrangle.

(2) *ridge,* west-trending, 2 miles long, 1.5 miles southeast of the town of Ojai (lat. 34°25'55" N, long. 119°13'15" W). Named on Ojai (1952) 7.5' quadrangle.

Black Mountain: see **Cowles Mountain** [SAN DIEGO].

Black Point [LOS ANGELES]: *promontory,* 1.25 miles north-northwest of Silver Peak on the north side of Santa Catalina Island (lat. 33°28'30" N, long. 118°34'40" W). Named on Santa Catalina West (1943) 7.5' quadrangle.

Blacks Beach: see **Del Mar** [SAN DIEGO].

Black Star Canyon [ORANGE]: *canyon,* drained by Black Star Creek, which flows 5 miles to Santiago Creek 5.5 miles south-southwest of Sierra Peak (lat. 33°46'20" N, long. 117°40'50" W). Named on Black Star Canyon (1967) 7.5' quadrangle, which shows Black Star coal mine near the mouth of the canyon. The feature first was called Cañada de los Indios (Meadows, p. 27). After August Witte discovered coal there in 1879, the canyon took the name of his mine (Hoover, Rensch, and Rensch, p. 264).

Black Star Creek [ORANGE]: *stream,* flows 5 miles to Santiago Creek 5.5 miles south-southwest of Sierra Peak (lat. 33°46'20" N, long. 117°40'50" W); the stream drains Black Star Canyon. Named on Black Star Canyon (1967) 7'5' quadrangle.

Blackwater Hole [SAN DIEGO]: *spring,* 5 miles east-southeast of Warner Springs (lat. 33°15'40" N, long. 116°32'55" W; near W line sec. 35, T 10 S, R 4 E). Named on Hot Springs Mountain (1960) 7.5' quadrangle.

Blair Valley [SAN DIEGO]: *valley,* 12 miles east-southeast of Julian (lat. 33°01'25" N, long. 116°24'15" W). Named on Earthquake Valley (1959) 7.5' quadrangle.

Blair Valley: see **Little Blair Valley** [SAN DIEGO].

Blanchard Canyon [LOS ANGELES]: *canyon,* 1 mile long, 3 miles east of Sunland (lat. 34°15'35" N, long. 118°15'45" W; sec. 17, T 2 N, R 13 W). Named on Sunland (1953) 7.5' quadrangle.

Blanchard Canyon [VENTURA]: *canyon,* drained by a stream that flows 2.25 miles to Piru Canyon nearly 3 miles northeast of Piru (lat. 34°26'35" N, long. 118°45'30" W). Named on Piru (1952) 7.5' quadrangle. The name commemorates Hooper Crews Blanchard (Ricard).

Blanchards: see **Santa Paula** [VENTURA].

Bleich Canyon [LOS ANGELES]: *canyon,* drained by a stream that flows 2.5 miles to lowlands 4 miles north-northeast of the village of Lake Hughes (lat. 34°43'45" N, long. 118°28'30" W; near N line sec. 4, T 7 N, R 15 W). Named on Lake Hughes (1957) 7.5' quadrangle. Called Bly Canyon on Fairmont (1937) 6' quadrangle, but United States Board on Geographic Names (1960a, p. 12) rejected this name for the feature.

Bleich Flat [LOS ANGELES]: *area,* nearly 5 miles northeast of Burnt Peak (lat. 34°43'35" N, long. 118°30'35" W; sec. 6, T 7 N, R 15 W). Named on Burnt Peak (1958) 7.5' quadrangle.

Blind Canyon [LOS ANGELES]: *canyon,* drained by a stream that flows less than 1 mile to Coldwater Canyon (2) 4.5 miles west-southwest of Mount San Antonio (lat. 34°15'15" N, long. 117°42'45" W). Named on Mount San Antonio (1955) 7.5' quadrangle.

Blind Canyon [LOS ANGELES-VENTURA]: *canyon,* drained by a stream that heads just inside Ventura County and flows 2 miles to Devil Canyon 2.5 miles north-northwest of Chatsworth in Los Angeles County (lat. 34°17'45" N, long. 118°37'05" W; sec. 36, T 3 N, R 17 W). Named on Oat Mountain (1952) and Santa Susana (1951) 7.5' quadrangles. Los Angeles County (1935) map has the name "Caradas Creek" for the stream in present Blind Canyon, and in Devil Canyon below the junction of Blind Canyon and Devil Canyon.

Blind Canyon [ORANGE]:

(1) *canyon,* drained by a stream that flows 2.5 miles to Santiago Creek 6 miles southwest of Sierra Peak (lat. 33°47'40" N, long. 117°43'50" W). Named on Black Star Canyon (1967) 7.5' quadrangle. Corona (1942) 15' quadrangle has the name "Fremont Creek" for the stream in this canyon, and has the name "Sierra Canyon" for present Fremont Canyon.

(2) *canyon,* drained by a stream that flows 2.5 miles to Christianitos Canyon about 4 miles northeast of San Clemente civic center (lat. 33°28' N, long. 117°33'45" W; near N line sec. 24, T 8 S, R 7 W). Named on San Clemente (1968) 7.5' quadrangle.

Bliss: see **Mount Bliss** [LOS ANGELES].

Bliss Canyon [LOS ANGELES]: *canyon,* 1.25 miles long, 4 miles west-northwest of Azusa city hall (lat. 34°09'50" N, long. 117° 58' W; sec. 17, 18, 19, T 1 N, R 10 W). Named on Azusa (1953) 7.5' quadrangle.

Bloomdale Creek [SAN DIEGO]: *stream,* flows 5.5 miles to Sutherland Reservoir 7.5 miles northeast of Ramona (lat. 33°07'30" N, long. 116°46'15" W; near SE cor. sec. 16, T 12 S, R 2 E). Named on Mesa Grande (1948) and Warners Ranch (1960) 7.5' quadrangles.

Blow Sand Canyon [SAN DIEGO]: *canyon,* 1.25 miles long, 4 miles northwest of Ocotillo Wells (lat. 33°10'55" N, long. 116°10'45" W). Named on Borrego Mountain (1960) 7.5' quadrangle.

Bluebird Canyon [ORANGE]: *canyon,* 1.5 miles long, opens to the sea about 1 mile south-southeast of Laguna Beach city hall (lat. 33° 31'45" N, long. 117°46'20" W; sec. 25, T 7 S, R 9 W). Named on Laguna Beach (1965) 7.5' quadrangle. The feature first was called Rim Rock Canyon, but now that name is restricted to an upper branch (Meadows, p. 119).

Blue Canyon [SAN DIEGO]: *canyon,* drained by a stream that flows 2 miles to Cañada Aguanga 5.5 miles northwest of Warner Springs (lat. 33°19'50" N, long. 116°42'30" W). Named on Warner Springs (1959) 7.5' quadrangle.

Blue Cavern Point [LOS ANGELES]: *promontory,* 5.5 miles north-northwest of Mount Banning on the north side of Santa Catalina Island (lat. 33°26'55" N, long. 118°28'35" W). Named on Santa Catalina North (1950) 7.5' quadrangle.

Bluegum Canyon [LOS ANGELES]: *canyon,* nearly 1 mile long, 2.5 miles east of Sunland (lat. 34°15'35" N, long. 118°16'10" W; sec. 17, 18, T 2 N,

R 13 W). Named on Sunland (1953) 7.5' quadrangle. Los Angeles County (1935) map has the form "Blue Gum Canyon" for the name.

Blue Mud Canyon [ORANGE]: *canyon*, drained by a stream that flows 3 miles to Santa Ana Canyon 2.25 miles east of Yorba Linda (lat. 33°52'50" N, long. 117°45'20" W). Named on Prado Dam (1967) and Yorba Linda (1964, photorevised 1981) 7.5' quadrangles.

Blue Point [VENTURA]: *promontory*, 8 miles southeast of Cobblestone Mountain on the west side of Piru Creek (lat. 34°31'35" N, long. 118°45'40" W; near SW cor. sec. 10, T 5 N, R 18 W). Named on Cobblestone Mountain (1958) 7.5' quadrangle.

Blue Point Campground [VENTURA]: *locality*, 8 miles southeast of Cobblestone Mountain along Piru Creek (lat. 34°31'50" N, long. 118°45'25" W; sec. 10, T 5 N, R 18 W); the place is just north of Blue Point. Named on Cobblestone Mountain (1958) 7.5' quadrangle.

Blue Ridge [LOS ANGELES]: *ridge*, northwest- to west-trending 9 miles long, center 6 miles north-northwest of Mount San Antonio (lat. 34°22' N, long. 117°41'30" W). Named on Mescal Creek (1956), Mount San Antonio (1955), and Valyermo (1958) 7.5' quadrangles. The southeasternmost end of the ridge is in San Bernardino County.

Blue Ridge Camp [LOS ANGELES]: *locality*, 5.5 miles north-northwest of Mount San Antonio (lat. 34°21'35" N, long. 117°41'10" W; sec. 11, T 3 N, R 8 W); the place is on Blue Ridge. Named on Mount San Antonio (1955) 7.5' quadrangle.

Blue Rock Spring [VENTURA]: *spring*, 15 miles north-northwest of Reyes Peak (lat. 34°50'40" N, long. 119°20'55" W; at SE cor. sec. 20, T 9 N, R 23 W). Named on Apache Canyon (1943) 7.5' quadrangle.

Blue Spring [SAN DIEGO]: *spring*, 13 miles west-southwest of Ocotillo Wells in Bighorn Canyon (lat. 33°04'05" N, long. 116°20'15" W; sec. 2, T 13 S, R 6 E). Named on Whale Peak (1959) 7.5' quadrangle.

Bluff Camp [VENTURA]: *locality*, 1.5 miles north of Santa Paula Peak (lat. 34°27'40" N, long. 119°00'30" W; near E line sec. 6, T 4 N, R 20 W). Named on Santa Paula Peak (1951) 7.5' quadrangle.

Bluff Cove [LOS ANGELES]: *embayment*, 3.5 miles south of Redondo Beach city hall along the coast (lat. 33°47'30" N, long. 118°24'25" W). Named on Redondo Beach (1951) 7.5' quadrangle.

Bly Canyon: see **Bleich Canyon** [LOS ANGELES].

Boal [SAN DIEGO]: *locality*, 3 miles north-northeast of Imperial Beach civic center along San Diego and Arizona Eastern Railroad (lat. 32°36'50" N, long. 117°05'20" W). Named on Imperial Beach (1967) 7.5' quadrangle.

Boat Canyon [ORANGE]: *canyon*, drained by a stream that flows nearly 2 miles to the sea less than 1 mile west of Laguna Beach city hall (lat. 33°32'40" N, long. 117°47'40" W). Named on Laguna Beach (1965) 7.5' quadrangle. Commercial fishermen landed their rowboats on the beach at the mouth of the canyon in the early days (Meadows, p. 28).

Bobcat Canyon [LOS ANGELES]:

(1) *canyon*, drained by a stream that flows 2 miles to Santa Clara River 10 miles east of Solemint (lat. 34°26'25" N, long. 118°17' W; sec. 7, T 4 N, R 13 W). Named on Agua Dulce (1960) 7.5' quadrangle.

(2) *canyon*, drained by a stream that flows 3.5 mile to West Fork San Gabriel River 3.5 miles east-northeast of Mount Wilson (1) (lat. 34°14'25" N, long. 118°00' W; sec. 23, T 2 N, R 11 W). Named on Chilao Flat (1959), Mount Wilson (1953), and Waterman Mountain (1959) 7.5' quadrangles.

Bob Owens Canyon [SAN DIEGO]: *canyon*, drained by a stream that flows 1.5 miles to Cottonwood Creek (3) 4 miles north-northeast of Barrett Junction (lat. 32°39'50" N, long. 116°40'35" W; sec. 28, T 17 S, R 3 E). Named on Barrett Lake (1960) 7.5' quadrangle.

Bobs Canyon: see **Bobs Gap** [LOS ANGELES].

Bobs Gap [LOS ANGELES]: *pass*, 2.25 miles east-northeast of Valyermo (lat. 34°27'15" N, long. 117°48'45" W; on S line sec. 3, T 4 N, R 9 W). Named on Valyermo (1958) 7.5' quadrangle. Los Angeles County (1935) map shows a feature called Bobs Canyon located about 3 miles southeast of Bobs Gap.

Boca de la Playa [ORANGE]: *land grant*, between Capistrano Beach and San Clemente. Named on Dana Point (1949) and San Clemente (1968) 7.5' quadrangles. Emigdio Vejar received 1.5 leagues in 1846 and claimed 6607 acres patented in 1879 (Cowan, p. 61).

Boca de Santa Monica [LOS ANGELES]: *land grant*, extends from Santa Monica Canyon to Topanga Canyon. Named on Beverly Hills (1950) and Topanga (1952) 7.5' quadrangles. Isidro Reyes and others received 1.5 leagues in 1839 and claimed 6657 acres patented in 1882 (Cowan, p. 94). Perez (p. 55) gave 1881 as the year of the patent.

Boden Canyon [SAN DIEGO]: *canyon*, drained by a stream that flows 5 miles to Santa Ysabel Creek 3.25 miles east of San Pasqual (lat. 33°05'30" N, long. 116°53'45" W; sec. 32, T 12 S, R 1 E). Named on Rodriguez Mountain (1948) and San Pasqual (1954) 7.5' quadrangles. Called Roden Canyon on Ramona (1903) 30' quadrangle. The name "Boden Canyon" commemorates an early homesteader in the region (Stein, p. 13).

Boden Field [SAN DIEGO]: *area*, 7.25 miles north-northwest of Warner Springs (lat. 33°23' N, long. 116°39'45" W; sec. 15, T 9 S, R 3 E). Named on Beauty Mountain (1960) 7.5' quadrangle.

Bodie Peak: see **Lobo Canyon** [LOS ANGELES] (1).

Boiler Canyon: see **Bouquet Canyon** [LOS ANGELES].

Boiling Point [LOS ANGELES]: *locality*, nearly 7 miles south-southeast of the village of Leona Valley at the head of Agua Dulce Canyon (lat. 34°31'20" N, long. 118°15'45" W; near N line sec. 17, T 5 N, R 13 W). Named on Sleepy Valley (1958) 7.5' quadrangle.

Boiling Spring Ravine [SAN DIEGO]: *canyon*, 1.25 miles long, 7.5 miles north-northeast of Buckman Springs (lat. 32°52'20" N, long. 116°26'15" W; at S line sec. 11, T 15 S, R 5 E). Named on Mount Laguna (1960) 7.5' quadrangle.

Bolcan Mountains: see **Volcan Mountains** [SAN DIEGO].

Bolsa [ORANGE]: *locality*, 6.25 miles north-northeast of present Huntington Beach civic center (lat. 33°44'40" N, long. 117°57'15" W; at NW cor. sec. 17, T 5 S, R 10 W); the place is on Las Bolsas grant. Named on Newport Beach (1951) 7.5' quadrangle. Postal authorities established Bolsa post office in 1886, discontinued it in 1891, reestablished it in 1895, discontinued it in 1904, and reestablished it 1971 (Salley, p. 24).

Bolsa Bay [ORANGE]: *water feature*, 4.25 miles northwest of Huntington Beach civic center (lat. 33°42'10" N, long. 118°03'10" W); the feature is on La Bolsa Chica grant. Named on Seal Beach (1965) 7.5' quadrangle. In the early days, a feature called Freeman River headed at some large springs located just south of Westminister and reached the sea through Bolsa Bay; the stream was named was for J.G. Freeman, who owned land along it (Meadows, p. 64).

Bolsa de Quigara: see **Newport Bay** [ORANGE].

Bolsa de San Joaquin: see **Newport Bay** [ORANGE].

Bolsas Creek [ORANGE]: *stream*, flows through marsh to the sea 4 miles northwest of present Huntington Beach civic center (lat. 33° 42'20" N, long. 118°03'35" W); Bolsa Bay now occupies part of the old stream course. Named on Las Bolsas (1896) 15' quadrangle.

Bommer Canyon [ORANGE]: *canyon*, drained by a stream that flows 2.25 miles to Bonita Creek 8 miles south of Santa Ana city hall (lat. 33°37'50" N, long. 117°50'35" W). Named on Laguna Beach (1965) and Tustin (1965) 7.5' quadrangles.

Bonebreak Canyon: see **Meier Canyon** [VENTURA].

Boneyard Canyon [LOS ANGELES]: *canyon*, on Los Angeles-San Bernardino County line, drained by a stream that flows 1.25 miles to lowlands 3.5 miles north-northeast of Big Pines (lat. 34°25'30" N, long. 117°39'25" W; near SW cor. sec. 18, T 4 N, R 7 W). Named on Mescal Creek (1956) 7.5' quadrangle.

Boneyard Canyon [SAN DIEGO]: *canyon*, drained by a stream that flows 1.25 miles to Barrett Lake 6.25 miles north-northeast of Barrett Junction (lat. 32°41'20" N, long. 116°38'50" W; sec. 14, T 17 S, R 3 E). Named on Barrett Lake (1960) 7.5' quadrangle.

Boney Mountain:[VENTURA]: *ridge*, mainly southwest-trending, 4 miles long, 2 miles west-northwest of Triunfo Pass (lat. 34°07'15" N, long. 118°57' W). Named on Newbury Park (1951) and Triunfo Pass (1950) 7.5' quadrangles. The feature has a series of sharp crags and was known in the early days as Old Boney (Ricard).

Bonita [SAN DIEGO]: *town*, 4.25 miles east-southeast of National City civic center (lat. 32°39'30" N, long. 117°02' W). Named on National City (1967) 7.5' quadrangle. Postal authorities established Bonita post office in 1898 (Frickstad, p. 148). Henry F. Cooper settled at the place in 1884 and called his property Bonita ranch; a fruit-packing center that developed at the site in 1891 retained the name "Bonita" (Stein, p. 14).

Bonita: see **Camp Bonita** [LOS ANGELES].

Bonita Creek [ORANGE]: *stream*, flows 3.5 miles to San Diego Creek 6.5 miles south of Santa Ana city hall (lat. 33°39'05" N, long. 117°51'35" W). Named on Tustin (1965) 7.5' quadrangle. Tustin (1935) 7.5' quadrangle has the name "Coyote Creek" for the lower part of the stream.

Bonita Reservoir [ORANGE]: *lake*, 1600 feet long, behind a dam 8 miles south of Santa Ana city hall (lat. 33°37'55" N, long. 117°50'50" W); the lake is along Bonita Creek. Named on Tustin (1965) 7.5' quadrangle.

Bonsall [SAN DIEGO]: *town*, 6.5 miles south-southeast of Fallbrook (lat. 33°17'20" N, long. 117°13'30" W; in and near sec. 20, T 10 S, R 3 W). Named on Bonsall (1968) 7.5' quadrangle. Postal authorities established Bonsall post office in 1890 and moved it 1.5 miles northeast in 1893 (Salley, p. 24). The place also was called Mount Fairview and Osgood—the name "Osgood" was for the chief engineer of the railroad survey in the area in the 1870's and was given in the hope that the rail line would pass through the community; the name "Bonsall" commemorates a retired Methodist minister who had a fruit-tree nursery at the site in 1889 (Stein, p. 14). Postal authorities established Mount Fairview post office in 1871 and discontinued it in 1880; they established Osgood post office in 1881, discontinued it in 1884, reestablished it in 1888, and discontinued it in 1891 (Salley, p. 148, 163).

Boomer Beach [SAN DIEGO]: *beach*, just southwest of Point La Jolla along the coast (lat. 32°51' N, long. 117°16'25" W). Named on La Jolla (1967) 7.5' quadrangle.

Boone Canyon [VENTURA]: *canyon*, drained by a stream that flows 1.5 miles to Fox Canyon 4 miles south-southeast of Santa Paula (lat. 34°18'15" N, long. 119°01'15" W). Named on Santa Paula (1951) 7.5' quadrangle.

Bootleggers Canyon [LOS ANGELES]: *canyon,* drained by a stream that flows 1.5 miles to Soledad Canyon 2.5 miles south-southwest of Acton (lat. 34°26'10" N, long. 118°13'05" W; at W line sec. 14, T 4 N, R 13 W). Named on Acton (1959) 7.5' quadrangle.

Border City: see **Valyermo** [LOS ANGELES].

Borego: see **Borrego Springs** [SAN DIEGO].

Borego Mountain: see **Borrego Mountain** [SAN DIEGO].

Borego Springs: see **Borrego Springs** [SAN DIEGO].

Borego Valley: see **Borrego Valley** [SAN DIEGO].

Boring Creek [SAN DIEGO]: *stream,* flows 1 mile to Jim Green Creek 2.25 miles east-southeast of Santa Ysabel (lat. 33°05'40" N, long. 116°38'15" W; at S line sec. 26, T 12 S, R 3 E). Named on Santa Ysabel (1960) 7.5' quadrangle.

Borrego [SAN DIEGO]: *locality,* 3.5 miles southeast of Borrego Springs (lat. 33°13'15" N, long. 116°20' W; near E line sec. 15, T 11 S, R 6 E); the place is in Borrego Valley. Named on Borrego Sink (1959) 7.5' quadrangle.

Borrego: see **Little Borrego** [SAN DIEGO].

Borrego Badlands [SAN DIEGO]: *area,* 9 miles east of Borrego Springs (lat. 33°15'30" N, long. 116°13' W). Named on Borrego Mountain (1960), Borrego Sink (1959), Clark Lake (1959), and Fonts Point (1959) 7.5' quadrangles.

Borrego Canyon [ORANGE]: *canyon,* drained by a stream that flows 4.5 miles to lowlands 3 miles north of El Toro (lat. 33°40'05" N, long. 117°42' W). Named on El Toro (1968) 7.5' quadrangle.

Borrego Canyon Wash [ORANGE]: *stream,* flows 2.5 miles to Agua Chinon Wash 3.25 miles northwest of El Toro (lat. 33°39'15" N, long. 117°44'15" W). Named on El Toro (1968) 7.5' quadrangle.

Borrego Mountain [SAN DIEGO]: *ridge,* generally northwest-trending, 4 miles long, center 4.5 miles northwest of Ocotillo Wells (lat. 33°11'15" N, long. 116°11'30" W). Named on Borrego Mountain (1960) 7.5' quadrangle. Called Borego Mt. on Tucker and Reed's (1939) map, but United States Board on Geographic Names (1950b, p. 2) rejected the names "Borego Mountain" and "Red Mountain" for the feature.

Borrego Mountain Wash [SAN DIEGO]: *stream,* flows nearly 3 miles to San Felipe Creek 6.5 miles northwest of Ocotillo Wells (lat. 33°12'45" N, long. 116°12'45" W; near S line sec. 14, T 11 S, R 7 E); the feature is at the west end of Borrego Mountain. Named on Borrego Mountain (1960) 7.5' quadrangle.

Borrego Palm Canyon [SAN DIEGO]: *canyon,* nearly 4 miles long, opens into Borrego Valley 2.5 miles west-northwest of Borrego Springs (lat. 33°16'15" N, long. 116°25' W). Named on Borrego Palm Canyon (1959) 7.5' quadrangle. Called Palm Canyon on Ramona (1903) 30' quadrangle, but United States Board on Geographic Names (1962a, p. 6) rejected this name for the feature. The canyon divides at the head to form Middle Fork and North Fork. Middle Fork is 7 miles long and is named on Borrego Palm Canyon (1959) and Hot Springs Mountain (1960) 7.5' quadrangles. United States Board on Geographic Names (1962a, p. 13) rejected the name Palm Canyon for Middle Fork. North Fork is 3.5 miles long and is named on Borrego Palm Canyon (1959) 7.5' quadrangle.

Borrego Palms Resort [SAN DIEGO]: *locality,* less than 2 miles west-northwest of Borrego Springs (lat. 33°16'10" N, long. 116° 24' W; at NW cor. sec. 31, T 10 S, R 6 E). Named on Borrego Palm Canyon (1959) 7.5' quadrangle.

Borrego Sink [SAN DIEGO]: *dry lake,* 1.5 miles long, 5 miles east-southeast of Borrego Springs (lat. 33°13'10" N, long. 116°18' W; mainly in sec. 13, T 11 S, R 6 E). Named on Borrego Sink (1959) 7.5' quadrangle.

Borrego Sink Wash [SAN DIEGO]: *stream,* flows 4 miles from Borrego Sink to San Felipe Creek 7.25 miles northwest of Ocotillo Wells (lat. 33°12'55" N, long. 116°13'30" W; near E line sec. 15, T 11 S, R 7 E). Named on Borrego Mountain (1960) and Borrego Sink (1959) 7.5' quadrangles.

Borrego Spring [SAN DIEGO]: *spring,* 6.5 miles east-southeast of Borrego Springs (lat. 33°13'35" N, long. 116°16'10" W; at S line sec. 8, T 11 S, R 7 E); the spring is along Borrego Sink Wash. Named on Borrego Sink (1959) 7.5' quadrangle. The spring is thought to have been a watering place for bighorn sheep—*borrego* means "lamb" in Spanish (Stein, p. 15).

Borrego Springs [SAN DIEGO]: *town,* 18 miles northeast of Julian (lat. 33°15'25" N, long. 116°22'25" W). Named on Borrego Palm Canyon (1959), Borrego Sink (1959), Clark Lake (1959), and Tubb Canyon (1959) 7.5' quadrangles. Called Borego Springs on Tucker and Reed's (1939) map, but United States Board on Geographic Names (1950b, p. 2) rejected the names "Borego Springs" and "Borego" for the town. Postal authorities established Borrego Springs post office in 1949 (Frickstad, p. 148). Tucker and Reed's (1939) map shows a place called Borego located about 4.5 miles west-northwest of Borrego Springs (present Borrego Springs) (NE quarter sec. 10, T 11 S, R 5 E). Postal authorities established Borego post office in 1928 and discontinued it in 1940 (Frickstad, p. 148).

Borrego Valley [SAN DIEGO]: *valley,* extends northwest from Borrego Mountain for about 15 miles. Named on Borrego Palm Canyon (1959), Borrego Sink (1959), Clark Lake (1959), and Tubb Canyon (1959) 7.5' quadrangles. Called Borego Valley on Clark Lake (1944) 15' quadrangle, but United States Board on Geographic Names (1950b, p. 2) rejected this name for the feature.

Borrego Valley: see **Lower Borrego Valley** [SAN DIEGO].

Boston Heights [LOS ANGELES]: *district,* 2.5 miles east of present Los Angeles city hall (lat. 34°03'35" N, long. 118°11'45" W). Named on Alhambra (1926) 6' quadrangle.

Bostonia [SAN DIEGO]: *district,* 2 miles northeast of El Cajon city hall (lat. 32°48'30" N, long. 116°56'15" W). Named on El Cajon (1967) 7.5' quadrangle. Postal authorities established Bostonia post office in 1894 (Frickstad, p. 148). Settlers from Boston came to the place in 1887 to raise citrus fruit and raisin grapes at what they called Boston ranch (Hanna, p. 38). The place had the early name "Meridian District" (Gudde, 1949, p. 38).

Bottle Peak [SAN DIEGO]: *peak,* 5 miles east-northeast of Escondido city hall (lat. 33°09'40" N, long. 117°00'10" W; sec. 5, T 12 S, R 1 W). Altitude 2139 feet. Named on Valley Center (1968) 7.5' quadrangle. The name is from the shape of the peak (Stein, p. 16).

Bottle Peak Spring [SAN DIEGO]: *spring,* 4.25 miles northeast of Escondido city hall (lat. 33°09'25" N, long. 117°00'40" W; near W line sec. 5, T 12 S, R 1 W); the spring is located 0.5 mile southwest of Bottle Peak. Named on Valley Center (1968) 7.5' quadrangle.

Boucher Hill [SAN DIEGO]: *peak,* 18 miles north-northeast of Escondido (lat. 33°20'05" N, long. 116°55'05" W; sec. 6, T 10 S, R 1 E). Altitude 5438 feet. Named on Boucher Hill (1948) 7.5' quadrangle. Stein (p. 16) considered the name "Boucher" a misspelling of the family name "Bougher."

Boulder Canyon [LOS ANGELES]:

(1) *canyon,* drained by a stream that flows 3 miles to lowlands 5.25 miles northwest of Big Pines (lat. 34°26'15" N, long. 117°45' W; sec. 18, T 4 N, R 8 W). Named on Mescal Creek (1956) 7.5' quadrangle.

(2) *canyon,* drained by a stream that flows 1.5 miles to Gold Creek 4 miles north of Sunland (lat. 34°19'10" N, long. 118°19'05" W; sec. 26, T 3 N, R 14 W). Named on Sunland (1953) 7.5' quadrangle. Los Angeles County (1935) map shows Boulder Creek in the canyon.

Boulder Canyon [VENTURA]: *canyon,* drained by a stream that flows 3.5 miles to the canyon of Cuyama River 5.25 miles northwest of Reyes Peak (lat. 34°41'05" N, long. 119°20'50" W; at W line sec. 20, T 7 N, R 23 W). Named on Reyes Peak (1943) 7.5' quadrangle.

Boulder Creek [SAN DIEGO]:

(1) *stream,* flows 11 miles from Cuyamaca Reservoir to San Diego River 11 miles northwest of Descanso (lat. 32°58'30" N, long. 116°44'15" W; near NE cor. sec. 11, T 14 S, R 2 E). Named on Cuyamaca Peak (1960) and Tule Springs (1960) 7.5' quadrangles.

(2) *stream,* heads in Imperial County and flows nearly 2 miles in San Diego County before reentering Imperial County 5.5 miles east-northeast of Jacumba (lat. 32°39' N, long. 116°06'20" W; at E line sec. 36, T 17 S, R 8 E). Named on In-Ko-Pah Gorge (1959) 7.5' quadrangle.

Boulder Creek [VENTURA]: *stream,* flows 5.5 miles to Santa Clara River 2.5 miles west-southwest of Fillmore (lat. 34°23' N, long. 118°57'10" W; near W line sec. 35, T 4 N, R 20 W). Named on Fillmore (1951) 7.5' quadrangle.

Boulder Creek: see **Boulder Canyon** [LOS ANGELES] (2).

Boulder Oaks [SAN DIEGO]:

(1) *locality,* 6.5 miles north of Lakeside (lat. 32°57'25" N, long. 116°55'30" W; near W line sec. 18, T 14 S, R 1 E). Named on San Vicente Reservoir (1955) 7.5' quadrangle.

(2) *locality,* 9 miles north of Campo (lat. 32°43'55" N, long. 116° 29' W; near NW cor. sec. 4, T 17 S, R 5 E). Named on Cameron Corners (1959) 7.5' quadrangle.

Boulevard [SAN DIEGO]: *locality,* 1 mile east-southeast of Manzanita (lat. 32°39'50" N, long. 116°16'25" W; sec. 28, T 17 S, R 7 E). Named on Live Oak Springs (1959) 7.5' quadrangle. Postal authorities established Boulevard post office in 1909 (Frickstad, p. 148). They established Larkinville post office near present Boulevard post office in 1876 and discontinued it the same year—the name was for Peter Larkin, first postmaster (Salley, p. 118).

Boulevard Gardens [ORANGE]: *locality,* 4.5 miles north of present Huntington Beach civic center (lat. 33°43'40" N, long. 117°59'20" W; at E line sec. 23, T 5 S, R 11 W). Named on Newport Beach (1951) 7.5' quadrangle.

Boundary Creek [SAN DIEGO]: *stream* and *dry wash,* extends for nearly 10 miles to Jacumba Valley near Jacumba (lat. 32°37'25" N, long. 116°10'50" W; near N line sec. 8, T 18 S, R 8 E); the feature is parallel to and on the Mexican boundary. Named on Jacumba (1959), Live Oak Springs (1959), and Tierra del Sol (1959) 7.5' quadrangles.

Boundary Peak [SAN DIEGO]: *peak,* 11.5 miles east of Campo (lat. 32°36'30" N, long. 116°16' W; near N line sec. 16, T 18 S, R 7 E); the peak is 0.25 mile north of the Mexican boundary. Named on Tierra del Sol (1959) 7.5' quadrangle.

Bouquet Campground Number 4 [LOS ANGELES]: *locality,* 8 miles south-southeast of the village of Lake Hughes (lat. 34°33'40" N, long. 118°24'05"

W; near S line sec. 31, T 6 N, R 14 W); the place is in Bouquet Canyon. Named on Green Valley (1958) 7.5' quadrangle.

Bouquet Campground Number 3 [LOS ANGELES]: *locality,* 8.5 miles south-southeast of the village of Lake Hughes (lat. 34°33'15" N, long. 118°24'35" W; near W line sec. 1, T 5 N, R 15 W); the place is in Bouquet Canyon. Named on Green Valley (1958) 7.5' quadrangle.

Bouquet Canyon [LOS ANGELES]: *canyon,* drained by a stream that flows 20 miles to Santa Clara River nearly 3 miles north-northwest of Newhall (lat. 34°25'30" N, long. 118°32'30" W). Named on Green Valley (1958), Mint Canyon (1960), Newhall (1952), and Sleepy Valley (1958) 7.5' quadrangles. Called Deadman Canyon on Camulos (1903) 30' quadrangle, and on Fernando (1900) 15' quadrangle. Storms (p. 248) mentioned the name "La Cañon de Los Murtes," presumably for present Bouquet Canyon. Francisco Chari, a French sailor known to the Spaniards by the nickname "El Buque"—*El Buque* means means "The Ship" in Spanish— took up land in the canyon; surveyors later misspelled his nickname when they named the canyon for him (Gudde, 1949, p. 38). Los Angeles County (1935) map names several branches of Bouquet Canyon: Boiler Canyon, which opens into Bouquet Canyon from the north about 3.5 miles north-northwest of Solemint (near W line sec. 5, T 4 N, R 15 W); Era Canyon, which opens into Bouquet Canyon from the north 0.5 mile below the mouth of Boiler Canyon (sec. 6, T 4 N, R 15 W); Kane Canyon, which opens into Bouquet Canyon from the east nearly 4 miles north of Solemint (near SE cor. sec. 32, T 5 N, R 15 W); and Atherton Canyon, which opens into Bouquet Canyon just below the mouth of Kane Canyon (at N line sec. 5, T 4 N, R 15 W).

Bouquet Canyon Reservoir: see **Bouquet Reservoir** [LOS ANGELES].

Bouquet Juntion [LOS ANGELES]: *locality,* 2.5 miles north of Newhall (lat. 34°25'20" N, long. 118°32'25" W); the road to Bouquet Canyon branches from the road to Soledad Canyon at the place. Named on Newhall (1952) 7.5' quadrangle.

Bouquet Reservoir [LOS ANGELES]: *lake,* behind a dam 7.5 miles south-southeast of the village of Lake Hughes (lat. 34°34'35" N, long. 118°23'05" W; sec. 29, T 6 N, R 14 W); the lake is in Bouquet Canyon. Named on Green Valley (1958) and Sleepy Valley (1958) 7.5' quadrangles. Called Bouquet Canyon Reservoir on Los Angeles County (1935) map.

Bouton Lake [LOS ANGELES]: *lake,* 2000 feet long, 5 miles north-northeast of Long Beach city hall (lat. 33°50'05" N, long. 118°08'50" W). Named on Long Beach (1949) 7.5' quadrangle.

Bow Willow Canyon [SAN DIEGO]: *canyon,* 3 miles long, along Bow Willow Creek above a point 3 miles west-northwest of Sweeney Pass (lat. 32°50'40" N, long. 116°13'55" W; at S line sec. 23, T 15 S, R 7 E). Named on Sombrero Peak (1959) and Sweeney Pass (1959) 7.5' quadrangles. According to Bloomquist (1979b, p. 38), the name most likely concerns the use by Indians of willow wood from the place for bows; other explanations have the name a corruption of the term "Bull Willow," used either because a bull or bulls were associated with the place, or because a stand of willows there were referred to as "bull" willows.

Bow Willow Creek [SAN DIEGO]: *stream,* flows 10.5 miles to Carrizo Creek 4.5 miles northeast of Sweeney Pass (lat. 32°52'25" N, long. 116°08'35" W; at N line sec. 15, T 15 S, R 8 E); the stream goes through Bow Willow Canyon. Named on Arroyo Tapiado (1959), Sombrero Peak (1959), and Sweeney Pass (1959) 7.5' quadrangles.

Bow Willow Palms [SAN DIEGO]: *locality,* 1 mile southeast of Sombrero Peak (lat. 32°49'15" N, long. 116°16'45" W; sec. 32, T 15 S, R 7 E); the place is along Bow Willow Creek. Named on Sombrero Peak (1959) 7.5' quadrangle.

Box Canyon [LOS ANGELES-VENTURA]: *canyon,* drained by a stream that heads in Ventura County and flows nearly 3 miles to Chatsworth Reservoir 2.5 miles southwest of Chatsworth in Los Angeles County (lat. 34°14' N, long. 118°38'25" W). Named on Calabasas (1952) and Santa Susana (1951) 7.5' quadrangles.

Box Canyon [ORANGE]: *canyon,* drained by a stream that flows 1.25 miles to Santa Ana Canyon 2 miles south of San Juan Hill (lat. 33°52'55" N, long. 117°44' W). Named on Prado Dam (1967) 7.5' quadrangle.

Box Canyon [SAN DIEGO]:

(1) *canyon,* drained by a stream that flows 5 miles to lowlands 9 miles north-northwest of Borego Springs (lat. 33°22'35" N, long. 116°25'30" W; sec. 23, T 9 S, R 5 E). Named on Collins Valley (1959) 7.5' quadrangle.

(2) *canyon,* 1.5 miles long, 10 miles east-southeast of Julian (lat. 33°00'50" N, long. 116°26'30" W; sec. 26, T 13 S, R 5 E). Named on Earthquake Valley (1959) 7.5' quadrangle. Men of Cook's Mormon Battalion hacked a wagon road through the narrow canyon in 1847 to allow the passage of wagons; later Butterfield Overland stages traversed it (Hoover, Rensch, and Rensch, p. 342). Chase (1919, p. 245) noted the early name "Puerta de San Felipe" for the feature.

Boyle: see **Boyle Heights** [LOS ANGELES].

Boyle Heights [LOS ANGELES]: *district,* 1.5 miles southeast of Los Angeles city hall (lat. 34°02' N, long. 118°12'15" W). Named on Los Angeles (1953) 7.5' quadrangle. Postal authorities established Boyle post office in the district in 1952 (Salley, p. 25). The place was known to the Spaniards as El Paredon Blanco—*El Paredon Blanco* means "The White Bluffs" in Spanish; the name "Boyle Heights" is from Boyle Workman, who subdivided the district in 1874 (Latta, p. 11).

Brace Canyon [LOS ANGELES]: *canyon,* 1 mile long, 2.25 miles north-northwest of Burbank city hall (lat. 34°12'50" N, long. 118° 19'20" W; sec. 35, T 2 N, R 14 W). Named on Burbank (1966) 7.5' quadrangle.

Bradbury [LOS ANGELES]: *town,* 3.5 miles west of Azusa city hall (lat. 34°08'40" N, long. 117°58'05" W); the place is at the mouth of Bradbury Canyon. Named on Azusa (1966) 7.5' quadrangle. Postal authorities established Bradbury post office in 1957 (Salley, p. 25), and the town incorporated the same year. The name commemorates L.L. Bradbury, who owned land at the site about 1900 (Gudde, 1969, p. 36).

Bradbury Canyon [LOS ANGELES]: *canyon,* nearly 1 mile long, 3.5 miles west-northwest of Azusa city hall (lat. 34°09'35" N, long. 117°57'40" W; mainly in sec. 19, 20, T 1 N, R 10 W). Named on Azusa (1953) 7.5' quadrangle. Los Angeles County (1935) map has the form "Bradberry Canyon" for the name.

Bradley Spring: see **Foster** [SAN DIEGO].

Brainard Canyon [LOS ANGELES]: *canyon,* 3.5 miles long, opens into lowlands 8.5 miles west-northwest of Valyermo (lat. 34°29' N, long. 117°58'15" W; near NW cor. sec. 31, T 5 N, R 10 W). Named on Juniper Hills (1959) 7.5' quadrangle.

Branagan: see **Newport Beach** [ORANGE] (2).

Brand Canyon [LOS ANGELES]: *canyon,* 1.25 miles long, 1.25 miles east-northeast of Burbank city hall (lat. 34°11'30" N, long. 118°16'10" W). Named on Burbank (1953) 7.5' quadrangle.

Branscomb Camp: see **Follows Camp** [LOS ANGELES].

Branson: see **Julian** [SAN DIEGO].

Branson City: see **Julian** [SAN DIEGO].

Bratton Valley [SAN DIEGO]: *valley,* 7.5 miles east-southeast of Jamul (lat. 32°41' N, long. 116°45'15" W; sec. 22, 23, T 17 S, R 2 E). Named on Barrett Lake (1960) and Dulzura (1972) 7.5' quadrangles. United States Board on Geographic Names (1962a, p. 6) rejected the designation "Brattan Valley" for the feature. Stein (p. 17) associated the name with Napoleon Bratton, an early setter and cattleman in the region.

Brea [ORANGE]: *city,* 12 miles north of Santa Ana (lat. 33°55' N, long. 117°54' W). Named on La Habra (1964) 7.5' quadrangle. Postal authorities established Brea post office in 1912 (Frickstad, p. 116), and the city incorporated in 1917. The school building of Randolph school district was built in Brea Canyon about 1.5 miles north of the center of present Brea in 1902; Officials of Ontario Investment Company had a townsite called Randolph laid out below the school in 1908, but the community that developed there took the name "Brea" in 1911 (Meadows, p. 118). Meadows (p. 111, 131) noted two flag stops along Pacific Electric Railroad near Brea: Pillsbury, located 0.5 mile west-northwest of the center of town, and Stewart, situated 1 mile west of the center of town—the name "Stewart" was for W.L. Stewart, vice president and general manager of Union Oil Company.

Brea Canyon [LOS ANGELES-ORANGE]: *canyon,* 12.5 miles long, along Brea Creek on Los Angeles-Orange County line above a point 4 miles south-southeast of La Habra (lat. 33°52'45" N, long. 117°55'20" W); the feature is partly on Rincon de la Brea grant. Named on La Habra (1964) and Yorba Linda (1964) 7.5' quadrangles. Called La Brea Canyon on Coyote Hills (1935) 7.5' quadrangle, called Rodeo Canyon on Anaheim (1942) 15' quadrangle—where present Tonner Canyon is called La Brea Canyon, and called Canada del Rodeo on Watts' (1898-1899) map. Watts (p. 33) noted that the feature was known locally as Rincon de la Brea.

Brea Canyon [VENTURA]: *canyon,* drained by a stream that flows 3.25 miles to Arroyo Simi 4.5 miles east of Moorpark (lat. 34° 16'45" N, long. 118°48'10" W; at S line sec. 6, T 2 N, R 18 W). Named on Simi (1951) 7.5' quadrangle.

Brea Canyon: see **Tonner Canyon** [LOS ANGELES-ORANGE].

Brea Chem [ORANGE]: *locality,* 3.5 miles west-northwest of Yorba Linda along Pacific Electric Railroad (lat. 33°55' N, long. 117°52'10" W; near NW cor. sec. 18, T 3 S, R 9 W). Named on Yorba Linda (1964) 7.5' quadrangle.

Brea Creek [ORANGE]: *stream,* flows nearly 6 miles from the mouth of Brea Canyon [LOS ANGELES-ORANGE] to Coyote Creek 1.25 miles northwest of Buena Park civic center (lat. 33°52'40" N, long. 118°00'30" W; near W line sec. 26, T 3 S, R 11 W). Named on Anaheim (1965), La Habra (1964), and Whittier (1965) 7.5' quadrangles. The stream is called Coyote Creek on Whittier (1949) 7.5' quadrangle.

Breakneck Canyon [LOS ANGELES]: *canyon,* drained by a stream that flows nearly 1 mile to Big Tujunga Canyon 3 miles south-southeast of Condor Peak (lat. 34°17' N, long. 118°11'45" W; sec. 1, T 2 N, R 13 W). Named on Condor Peak (1959) 7.5' quadrangle. On Tujunga (1900) 15' quadrangle, the stream in the canyon is called Breakneck Creek.

Breakneck Creek: see **Breakneck Canyon** [LOS ANGELES].

Breeze Hill [SAN DIEGO]: *peak,* 7 miles east of Oceanside (lat. 33° 11'30" N, long. 117°15'30" W; near W line sec. 25, T 11 S, R 4 W). Named on

San Luis Rey (1968) 7.5' quadrangle.

Brents: see **Brents Mountain** [LOS ANGELES].

Brents Junction [LOS ANGELES]: *locality,* 2.25 miles east of Agoura (lat. 34°08'50" N, long. 118°41'50" W; on N line sec. 30, T 1 N, R 17 W). Named on Calabasas (1952) 7.5' quadrangle.

Brents Mountain [LOS ANGELES]: *peak,* 4.5 miles north-northwest of Malibu Point (lat. 34°05'10" N, long. 118°43'20" W; sec. 13, T 1 S, R 18 W). Altitude 1713 feet. Named on Malibu Beach (1951) 7.5' quadrangle. Solstice Canyon (1932) 6' quadrangle shows a place called Brents Mountain Crag Camp located 0.5 mile east of Brents Mountain; Malibu Beach (1951) 7.5' quadrangle has the name "Salvation Army Camp" at the same place, and Los Angeles County (1935) map has the name "Brents" there.

Brents Mountain Crag Camp: see **Brents Mountain** [LOS ANGELES].

Brentwood [LOS ANGELES]: *district,* 4.5 miles west-southwest of Beverly Hills city hall in Los Angeles (lat. 34°03'10" N, long. 118° 28'45" W). Named on Beverly Hills (1966) 7.5' quadrangle. The place includes former Brentwood Park and Westgate.

Brentwood Heights [LOS ANGELES]: *district,* 4.5 miles west of Beverly Hills city hall in Los Angeles (lat. 34°03'40" N, long. 118° 28'35" W). Named on Beverly Hills (1950) 7.5' quadrangle. Called Westgate Heights on Sawtelle (1934) 6' quadrangle. Postal authorities established Brentwood Heights Hot Springs post office in 1926, changed the name to Brentwood Heights in 1927, and discontinued it in 1935 (Salley, p. 26).

Brentwood Heights Hot Springs: see **Brentwood Heights** [LOS ANGELES].

Brentwood Park [LOS ANGELES]: *district,* 5 miles west-southwest of Beverly Hills city hall in Los Angeles (lat. 34°03'15" N, long. 118°29' W). Named on Beverly Hills (1950) 7.5' quadrangle. On Beverly Hills (1966) 7.5' quadrangle, this district is shown as part of present Brentwood. Postal authorities established Brentwood Park post office in 1908 and discontinued it in 1909 (Salley, p. 26).

Briggs Terrace [LOS ANGELES]: *locality,* 8 miles northwest of Pasadena city hall in Pickens Canyon (lat. 34°14'25" N, long. 118° 13'30" W; near SE cor. sec. 22, T 2 N, R 13 W). Named on Pasadena (1953) 7.5' quadrangle.

Broadacres Gardens: see **Compton** [LOS ANGELES].

Broad Canyon [LOS ANGELES]:

(1) *canyon,* drained by a stream that flows 3 miles to lowlands 3.5 miles north-northwest of the village of Lake Hughes (lat. 34°43'30" N, long. 118°27'30" W; sec. 3, T 7 N, R 15 W). Named on Lake Hughes (1957) 7.5' quadrangle.

(2) *canyon,* drained by a stream that flows 3.5 miles to lowlands 7.5 miles north-northeast of the village of Lake Hughes (lat. 34°46'20" N, long. 118°22'35" W; near NW cor. sec. 21, T 8 N, R 14 W). Named on Fairmont Butte (1965) 7.5' quadrangle.

Bronco Flats [SAN DIEGO]: *area,* 4 miles west-northwest of Morena Village (lat. 32°41'40" N, long. 116°34' W; sec. 15, T 17 S, R 4 E). Named on Morena Reservoir (1960) 7.5' quadrangle. Cuyamaca (1903) 30' quadrangle has the singular form "Bronco Flat" for the name.

Brookhurst [ORANGE]: *locality,* 2.5 miles east-southeast of present Buena Park civic center along Southern Pacific Railroad (lat. 33° 50'40" N, long. 117°57'30" W). Named on Garden Grove (1935) 7.5' quadrangle. A loading platform for Brookhurst Ranch Company was at the site (Meadows, p. 30).

Brooklyn Heights [LOS ANGELES]: *district,* 1.5 miles east of present Los Angeles city hall (lat. 34°02'55" N, long. 118°13' W). Named on Pasadena (1900) 15' quadrangle.

Brooklyn Heights [SAN DIEGO]: *district,* 2 miles east-northeast of downtown San Diego (lat. 32°43'30" N, long. 117°07'45" W). Named on Point Loma (1942) 7.5' quadrangle.

Brookmann Canyon [LOS ANGELES]: *canyon,* 0.5 mile long, 3 miles east of Burbank city hall (lat. 34°10'25" N, long. 118°15'25" W). Named on Burbank (1953) 7.5' quadrangle.

Brookside Canyon [LOS ANGELES]: *canyon,* drained by a stream that flows 1.25 miles to Topanga Canyon 5.5 miles west-northwest of Santa Monica city hall (lat. 34°02'55" N, long. 118°34'50" W). Named on Topanga (1952) 7.5' quadrangle.

Brown: see **John Brown Peak**, under **Mount Lowe** [LOS ANGELES] (1).

Brown Barranca [VENTURA]: *gully,* extends from the mouth of Long Canyon (2) to Santa Clara River 0.5 mile south-southeast of Saticoy (lat. 34°16'30" N, long. 119°08'40" W). Named on Saticoy (1951) 7.5' quadrangle.

Brown Canyon [LOS ANGELES]:

(1) *canyon,* drained by a stream that flows nearly 1 mile to Arroyo Seco 7 miles north-northwest of Pasadena city hall (lat. 34°14'25" N, long. 118°11' W). Named on Pasadena (1953) 7.5' quadrangle.

(2) *canyon,* 3 miles long, 2 miles northwest of Beverly Hills city hall (lat. 34°06'15" N, long. 118°25'20" W). Named on Beverly Hills (1950) 7.5' quadrangle.

Brown Field Naval Auxilary Air Station [SAN DIEGO]: *military installation,* 8 miles west of Otay Mountain (lat. 32°34'10" N, long. 116°59'20" W). Named on Otay Mesa (1955) 7.5' quadrangle.

Browning [ORANGE]: *locality,* 4 miles east-southeast of Santa Ana city hall along Atchison, Topeka and Santa Fe Railroad (lat. 33° 44' N, long. 117°48' W). Named on Tustin (1965) 7.5' quadrangle. The name commemorates Frank Browning, who leased land near the site (Meadows, p. 30-31).

Brown Mountain [LOS ANGELES]: *peak,* 6 miles north of Pasadena city hall (lat. 34°06'40" N, long. 118°08'45" W). Altitude 4454 feet. Named on Pasadena (1953) 7.5' quadrangle. Jason Brown and Owen Brown named the feature for their father, abolitionist John Brown (Robinson, J.W., 1977, p. 103, 105).

Browns Canyon [LOS ANGELES]: *canyon,* 4 miles long, opens into lowlands 1.25 miles northeast of Chatsworth (lat. 34°16'20" N, long. 118°35'25" W). Named on Oat Mountain (1952) 7.5' quadrangle.

Browns Canyon Wash [LOS ANGELES]: *stream,* flows nearly 6 miles from the mouth of Browns Canyon to Los Angeles River 1 mile east-southeast of the center of Canoga Park (lat. 34°11'40" N, long. 116°34'50" W). Named on Canoga Park (1952) and Oat Mountain (1952) 7.5' quadrangles

Browns Flat [LOS ANGELES]: *area,* 9.5 miles north of Pomona city hall (lat. 34°11'15" N, long. 117°43'15" W; sec. 9, T 1 N, R 8 W). Named on Mount Baldy (1954) 7.5' quadrangle.

Browns Gulch [LOS ANGELES]: *canyon,* drained by a stream that flows 2.5 miles to San Gabriel Canyon 4.5 miles north of Glendora city hall (lat. 34°12'15" N, long. 117°51'45" W; sec. 6, T 1 N, R 9 W). Named on Azusa (1953) and Glendora (1966) 7.5' quadrangles.

Brownstone [VENTURA]: *locality,* 1.5 miles west-northwest of Fillmore along Southern Pacific Railroad (lat. 34°24'25" N, long. 118° 56'15" W). Named on Piru (1921) 15' quadrangle. Stone from Sespe Cañon brownstone quarry, located 5 miles to the north, was shipped from the spot (Huguenin, p. 769).

Brownstone Reservoir [VENTURA]: *lake,* 225 feet long, 2 miles west-northwest of Fillmore (lat. 34°24'55" N, long. 118°56'35" W; sec. 23, T 4 N, R 20 W). Named on Fillmore (1951) 7.5' quadrangle.

Brubaker Canyon [VENTURA]: *canyon,* drained by a stream that heads in Santa Barbara County and flows 1.5 miles in Ventura County to Cuyama River 12 miles northwest of Reyes Peak (lat. 34°45'25" N, long. 119°25'20" W; sec. 28, T 8 N, R 24 W). Named on Cuyama Peak (1943) and Rancho Nuevo Creek (1943) 7.5' quadrangles.

Brush Canyon [LOS ANGELES]: *canyon,* 2 miles long, 6.25 miles northwest of Los Angeles city hall (lat. 34°07'10" N, long. 118°18'55" W'; on S line sec. 35, T 1 N, R 14 W). Named on Burbank (1953) and Hollywood (1953) 7.5' quadrangles.

Bryant Canyon [LOS ANGELES]: *canyon,* drained by a stream that flows nearly 2 miles to Big Tujunga Canyon 3.5 miles northeast of Sunland (lat. 34°18' N, long. 118°16'25" W; near E line sec. 31, T 3 N, R 13 W). Named on Sunland (1953) 7.5' quadrangle.

Buaro: see **Santa Ana** [ORANGE].

Bubble-up Creek: see **Pala** [SAN DIEGO].

Bubbling Spring [SAN DIEGO]: *spring,* 6.5 miles southwest of Borrego Springs (lat. 33°11'40" N, long. 116°27'40" W). Named on Tubb Canyon (1959) 7.5' quadrangle.

Buck Canyon [LOS ANGELES]:

(1) *canyon,* drained by a stream that flows 2.5 miles to Little Tujunga Canyon 5 miles north-northwest of Sunland (lat. 34°19'35" N, long. 118°20'15" W; sec. 22, T 3 N, R 14 W). Named on Sunland (1953) 7.5' quadrangle.

(2) *canyon,* drained by a stream that flows less than 1 mile to Pacoima Canyon 2.5 miles north-northwest of Condor Peak (lat. 34°21'35" N, long. 118°14'15" W). Named on Condor Peak (1959) 7.5' quadrangle.

Buck Canyon [SAN DIEGO]: *canyon,* drained by a stream that flows nearly 3 miles to Cañada Verruga 2 miles northeast of San Felipe (lat. 33°13'10" N, long. 116°34'10" W). Named on Ranchita (1960) 7.5' quadrangle.

Buck Creek [VENTURA]: *stream,* flows 5.25 miles to Piru Creek 7 miles east-northeast of McDonald Peak (lat. 34°39'55" N, long. 118°49'25" W). Named on Black Mountain (1958) and McDonald Peak (1958) 7.5' quadrangles. Los Angeles County (1935) map shows a feature called Mine Canyon that opens into the canyon of Piru Creek less than 1 mile northwest of the mouth of Buck Creek.

Buck Creek Campground [VENTURA]: *locality,* 4 miles east of McDonald Peak (lat. 34°38'15" N, long. 118°52'05" W; near SW cor. sec. 2, T 6 N, R 19 W); the place is along Buck Creek. Named on Black Mountain (1958) 7.5' quadrangle.

Buck Creek Spring [VENTURA]: *spring,* 4 miles east of McDonald Peak (lat. 34°38'15" N, long. 118°52'10" W; near SW cor. sec. 2, T 6 N, R 19 W); the spring is along Buck Creek. Named on Black Mountain (1958) 7.5' quadrangle.

Buck Gully [ORANGE]: *canyon,* drained by a stream that flows 3.5 miles to the sea 6 miles west-northwest of Laguna Beach city hall (lat. 33°35'15" N, long. 117°51'55" W). Named on Laguna Beach (1965) 7.5' quadrangle.

Buckhorn [VENTURA]: *locality,* 1.5 miles southwest of Piru (lat. 34° 24'05" N, long. 118°48'55" W; sec. 25, T 4 N, R 19 W). Named on Piru (1952) 7.5' quadrangle. Postal authorities established Buckhorn post office in 1900 and discontinued it in 1906; deer antlers that decorated the post office building suggested the name (Salley, p. 28).

Buckhorn Canyon: see **Buckhorn Flat** [LOS ANGELES].

Buckhorn Flat [LOS ANGELES]: *area*, 1.5 miles east-northeast of Waterman Mountain (lat. 34°20'45" N, long. 117°54'45" W; sec. 15, T 3 N, R 10 W). Named on Waterman Mountain (1959) 7.5' quadrangle. Los Angeles County (1935) map has the form "Buckhorn Flats" for the name, and shows a feature called Buckhorn Canyon that extends for 2.5 miles from Waterman Mountain through Buckhorn Flats to Cooper Canyon.

Buckhorn Spring [LOS ANGELES]: *spring*, 1.5 miles east-northeast of Waterman Mountain (lat. 34°20'30" N, long. 117°24'30" W; sec. 15, T 3 N, R 10 W); the spring is near Buckhorn Flat. Named on Waterman Mountain (1959) 7.5' quadrangle.

Buckman Springs [SAN DIEGO]: *locality*, 9 miles south-southwest of Monument Peak along Cottonwood Creek (3) (lat. 32°46'15" N, long. 116°29'30" W; sec. 20, T 16 S, R 5 E). Named on Mount Laguna (1960) 7.5' quadrangle. The name commemorates Amos Buckman, who settled in the neighborhood in the late 1860's (Gudde, 1949, p. 42). Six small carbonated springs at the place were developed about 1876, and the water was marketed for table use under the name "California Club Water" (Waring, p. 247).

Bucksnort Mountain [SAN DIEGO]: *ridge*, north-northwest-trending, 2 miles long, 8 miles north of Warner Springs (lat. 33°23'45" N, long. 116°36'20" W). Named on Bucksnort Mountain (1960) 7.5' quadrangle.

Bucksnort Spring [VENTURA]: *spring*, 4.5 miles east of Devils Heart Peak (lat. 34°33'10" N, long. 118°53'35" W). Named on Devils Heart Peak (1943) 7.5' quadrangle.

Buena [SAN DIEGO]: *locality*, 3 miles southeast of Vista (lat. 33°10'25" N, long. 117°12'30" W); the place is along Buena Creek. Named on San Marcos (1968) 7.5' quadrangle. Postal authorities established Buena post office in 1883 and discontinued it in 1893 (Frickstad, p. 149).

Buena Creek [SAN DIEGO]: *stream*, flows 4.5 miles to Agua Hedionda Creek 3.25 miles south-southeast of Vista (lat. 33°09'25" N, long. 117°13'30" W). Named on San Marcos (1968) 7.5' quadrangle. On Escondido (1901) 15' quadrangle, present Buena Creek is shown as part of Agua Hedionda Creek.

Buena Park [ORANGE]: *city*, 11 miles northwest of Santa Ana (lat. 33°51'50" N, long 117°59'50" W). Named on Anaheim (1965), La Habra (1964), Los Alamitos (1964), and Whittier (1965) 7.5' quadrangles. Postal authorities established Buena Park post office in 1887 (Frickstad, p. 116), and the city incorporated in 1953. James A. Whitaker founded the community in 1887 on 960 acres of land that he bought the year before (Meadows, p. 31).

Buena Vista [SAN DIEGO]: *land grant*, at Vista. Named on San Marcos (1968) 7.5' quadrangle. An Indian called Felipe received 0.5 league in 1845; Jesus Machado was patentee for 1884.89 acres in 1897 (Cowan, p. 20; Perez, p. 56).

Buena Vista Creek [SAN DIEGO]:

(1) *stream*, flows 9 miles to Buena Vista Lagoon 2.5 miles east-southeast of downtown Oceanside (lat. 33°10'45" N, long. 117°20'20" W; sec. 31, T 11 S, R 4 W); the stream goes through Buena Vista grant. Named on San Luis Rey (1968) and San Marcos (1968) 7.5' quadrangles.

(2) *stream*, flows 12 miles to end near Lake Henshaw 2.5 miles north of Morettis Junction (lat. 33°14'05" N, long. 116°42' W). Named on Ranchita (1960) and Warners Ranch (1960) 7.5' quadrangles.

Buena Vista Hills [SAN DIEGO]: *ridge*, north-trending, 1.5 miles long, 1.25 miles north-northeast of Vista (lat. 33°13' N, long. 117° 14'20" W); the feature is partly on Buena Vista grant. Named on Escondido (1901) 15' quadrangle.

Buena Vista Lagoon [SAN DIEGO]: *lake*, 1.5 miles long, 2.25 miles southeast of downtown Oceanside (lat. 33°10'25" N, long. 117° 21' W); the feature is at the mouth of Buena Vista Creek (1). Named on San Luis Rey (1968) 7.5' quadrangle.

Buffalo Corral Reservoir: see **Lower Buffalo Corral Reservoir** [LOS ANGELES]; **Upper Buffalo Corral Reservoir** [LOS ANGELES].

Buffalo Springs Reservoirs [LOS ANGELES]: *lakes*, two, largest 150 feet long, 2.5 miles north-northeast of Mount Banning on Santa Catalina Island (lat. 33°24'25" N, long. 118°25' W). Named on Santa Catalina North (1950) 7.5' quadrangle.

Buford Canyon [LOS ANGELES]: *canyon*, drained by a stream that flows 1 mile to Swarthout Valley 5.5 miles north of Mount San Antonio (lat. 34°21'55" N, long. 117°39'40" W; near NE cor. sec. 12, T 3 N, R 8 W). Named on Mount San Antonio (1955) 7.5' quadrangle.

Bull Canyon [LOS ANGELES]: *canyon*, drained by a stream that flows 12 miles to Los Angeles River 2 miles southwest of Van Nuys (lat. 34°10'10" N, long. 118°28'25" W). Named on Oat Mountain (1952), San Fernando (1953), and Van Nuys (1953) 7.5' quadrangles. The stream in Bull Canyon below a point about 3 miles west of downtown San Fernando is called Bull Creek on San Fernando (1966) 7.5' quadrangle, which shows the confluence of the stream with Los Angeles River about 1.5 miles west-northwest of the location of the mouth of Bull Canyon shown on Van Nuys (1953) 7.5' quadrangle.

Bull Creek: see **Bull Canyon** [LOS ANGELES].

Bull Pasture [SAN DIEGO]: *area*, 4 miles east-southeast of Boucher Hill (lat. 33°18'55" N, long. 116°50'45" W; near S line sec. 11, T 10 S, R 1 E). Named on Palomar Observatory (1949) 7.5' quadrangle.

Bunton Flat [SAN DIEGO]: *area*, 5 miles south-southeast of Santa Ysabel (lat. 33°02'35" N, long. 116°38'15" W; sec. 14, T 13 S, R 3 E). Named on Santa Ysabel (1960) 7.5' quadrangle.

Burbank [LOS ANGELES]: *city*, 9.5 miles north-northwest of Los Angeles city hall (lat. 34°10'55" N, long. 118°18'25" W). Named on Burbank (1953) 7.5' quadrangle. Postal authorities established Burbank post office in 1887 (Frickstad, p. 71), and the city incorporated in 1911. The name is from Dr. David Burbank, a dentist in Los Angeles who was one of the subdividers of the property (Gudde, 1949, p. 45). California Mining Bureau's (1917a) map shows a place called Roberts located about 4 miles northwest of Burbank along the railroad. Postal authorities established Roberts post office 4.5 miles northwest of Burbank post office in 1912 and discontinued it in 1916; the name was from the given name of Robert B. Reed, first postmaster, who developed the site (Salley, p. 187).

Burbank Canyon [LOS ANGELES]: *canyon*, less than 1 mile long, 6.5 miles north-northeast of Pomona city hall (lat. 34°08'40" N, long. 117°43'05" W; sec. 27, 28, T 1 N, R 8 W). Named on Mount Baldy (1954) 7.5' quadrangle.

Burbank Junction [LOS ANGELES]: *locality*, less than 1 mile west-northwest of Burbank city hall along Southern Pacific Railroad (lat. 34°11'10" N, long. 118°19'15" W). Named on Burbank (1953) 7.5' quadrangle.

Burges Canyon [VENTURA]: *canyon*, drained by a stream that flows 6.5 miles to Santa Barbara County 14 miles northwest of Reyes Peak (lat. 34°47'25" N, long. 119°26'30" W; sec. 17, T 8 N, R 24 W). Named on Apache Canyon (1943) and Cuyama Peak (1943) 7.5' quadrangles. Hess (p. 28) mentioned "a hill known as French Point" situated south of the lower part of Burges Canyon (sec. 16, T 8 N, R 24 W).

Burke Canyon: see **Agua Dulce Canyon** [LOS ANGELES].

Burkhart Saddle [LOS ANGELES]: *pass*, 4.5 miles south-southwest of Valyermo (lat. 34°23'10" N, long. 117°53'35" W; sec. 35, T 4 N, R 10 W). Named on Juniper Hills (1959) 7.5' quadrangle.

Burnett: see **Long Beach** [LOS ANGELES].

Burnham: see **Mount Burnham** [LOS ANGELES].

Burns Canyon [LOS ANGELES]: *canyon*, drained by a stream that flows nearly 1.5 miles to lowlands 3.5 miles east-southeast of the village of Lake Hughes (lat. 34°39'05" N, long. 118°23'15" W; sec. 32, T 7 N, R 14 W). Named on Lake Hughes (1957) 7.5' quadrangle.

Burnside Canyon [LOS ANGELES]: *canyon*, 2 miles long, opens into lowlands 17 miles east-southeast of Gorman (lat. 34°45'30" N, long. 118°33'50" W; near N line sec. 27, T 8 N, R 16 W). Named on Burnt Peak (1958) and Neenach School (1965) 7.5' quadrangles.

Burnt Mountain [SAN DIEGO]: *peak*, 5.5 miles north of Escondido city hall (lat. 33°12'10" N, long. 117°03'55" W; near W line sec. 23, T 11 S, R 2 W). Named on Valley Center (1968) 7.5' quadrangle.

Burnt Peak [LOS ANGELES]: *peak*, 17 miles east-southeast of Gorman (lat. 34°41' N, long. 118°34'30" W). Altitude 5788 feet. Named on Burnt Peak (1958) 7.5' quadrangle.

Burnt Peak: see **Little Burnt Peak** [LOS ANGELES].

Burnt Peak Canyon [LOS ANGELES]: *canyon*, drained by a stream that flows 4.5 miles to Fish Canyon (1) 2.5 miles south-southwest of Burnt Peak (lat. 34°39' N, long. 118°35'45" W); the canyon heads east of Burnt Peak. Named on Burnt Peak (1958) 7.5' quadrangle.

Burnt Rancheria Campground [SAN DIEGO]: *locality*, 7.5 miles north-northeast of Buckman Springs (lat. 32°51'40" N, long. 116° 25' W; near SE cor. sec. 13, T 15 S, R 5 E). Named on Mount Laguna (1960) 7.5' quadrangle.

Burro Canyon [LOS ANGELES]:

(1) *canyon*, drained by a stream that flows 2.25 miles to Fish Canyon (1) 4.25 miles southwest of Burnt Peak (lat. 34°38'15" N, long. 118°37'35" W). Named on Burnt Peak (1958) 7.5' quadrangle.

(2) *canyon*, drained by a stream that flows 2 miles to San Gabriel Reservoir 7 miles north of Glendora city hall (lat. 34°14'10" N, long. 117°50'20" W). Named on Crystal Lake (1958) and Glendora (1953) 7.5' quadrangles. Called Burrow Canyon on Rock Creek (1903) 15' quadrangle.

Burro Creek [VENTURA]: *stream*, flows 3.5 miles to Sespe Creek 6 miles north-northwest of Wheeler Springs (lat. 34°35'35" N, long. 119°18'45" W). Named on Reyes Peak (1943) and Wheeler Springs (1943) 7.5' quadrangles.

Burro Flats [VENTURA]: *area*, 8 miles northeast of Thousand Oaks (lat. 34°13'45" N, long. 118°42'40" W). Named on Calabasas (1952) 7.5' quadrangle.

Burro Peak [LOS ANGELES]: *peak*, 4.25 miles south of Crystal Lake (lat. 34°15'20" N, long. 117°50'40" W). Altitude 3200 feet. Named on Crystal Lake (1958) 7.5' quadrangle.

Burro Spring [SAN DIEGO]: *spring*, less than 0.5 mile north-northwest of Agua Caliente Springs (lat. 32°57'20" N, long. 116°18'10" W; sec. 18, T

14 S, R 7 E). Named on Agua Caliente Springs (1959) 7.5' quadrangle.

Burrow Canyon: see **Burro Canyon** [LOS ANGELES] (2).

Burruel Point [ORANGE]: *promontory,* 4 miles north-northeast of Orange city hall (lat. 33°50'15" N, long. 117°49'30" W). Named on Orange (1964) 7.5' quadrangle. The name recalls Desiderio Burruel, son-in-law of Teodocio Yorba (Meadows, p. 31).

Burruel Ridge: see **Peralta Hills** [ORANGE] (1).

Bus Canyon [VENTURA]: *canyon,* 2.5 miles long, opens into Simi Valley (1) 6 miles north-northeast of Thousand Oaks (lat. 34°14'30" N, long. 118°46'40" W). Named on Thousand Oaks (1952) 7.5' quadrangle.

Buschalaugh Cove [SAN DIEGO]: *embayment,* nearly 5 miles west-northwest of Otay Mountain along Lower Otay Reservoir (lat. 32° 37'05" N, long. 116°55'10" W). Named on Otay Mesa (1955) 7.5' quadrangle.

Bushard: see **Huntington Beach** [ORANGE].

Bushnell Summit [LOS ANGELES]: *pass,* 3 miles east-northeast of Burnt Peak (lat. 34°42'10" N, long. 118°31'40" W; near S line sec. 12, T 7 N, R 16 W). Named on Burnt Peak (1958) 7.5' quadrangle.

Butler [LOS ANGELES]: *locality,* 3.5 miles west of Azusa city hall along Atchison, Topeka and Santa Fe Railroad (lat. 34°07'55" N, long. 117°57'50" W; sec. 31, T 1 N, R 10 W). Named on Azusa (1953) 7.5' quadrangle.

Butler Canyon [SAN DIEGO]: *canyon,* 4.5 miles long, opens into Clark Valley 9 miles north of Borrego Springs (lat. 33°23'10" N, long. 116°21'45" W; sec. 16, T 9 S, R 6 E). Named on Clark Lake NE (1960) and Collins Valley (1959) 7.5' quadrangles. Clark Lake (1944) 15' quadrangle shows the feature as part of Rockhouse Canyon, but United States Board on Geographic Names (1962a, p. 6) rejected the name "Rockhouse Canyon" for Butler Canyon.

Butterfield Canyon [LOS ANGELES]: *canyon,* drained by a stream that flows 2 miles to West Fork San Gabriel River nearly 8 miles north-northwest of Azusa city hall (lat. 34°14'35" N, long. 117°56'50" W). Named on Azusa (1953) 7.5' quadrangle.

Buttes Canyon [SAN DIEGO]: *canyon,* 1.5 miles long, opens into lowlands along San Felipe Creek 4.5 miles northwest of Ocotillo Wells (lat. 33°11'30" N, long. 116°11'30" W; near E line sec. 25, T 11 S, R 7 E). Named on Borrego Mountain (1960) 7.5' quadrangle.

Buttes Pass [SAN DIEGO]: *pass,* 4.5 miles west-northwest of Ocotillo Wells (lat. 33°10'25" N, long. 116°12'20" W; at W line sec. 36, T 11 S, R 7 E); the pass is at the head of Buttes Canyon. Named on Borrego Mountain (1960) 7.5' quadrangle.

Butte Street Junction [LOS ANGELES]: *locality,* 2.5 miles south-southeast of Los Angeles city hall along Union Pacific Railroad (lat. 34°01'05" N, long. 118°13'50" W). Named on Los Angeles (1966) 7.5' quadrangle.

Button Shell Beach [LOS ANGELES]: *beach,* 5 miles north-northwest of Avalon on the northeast side of Santa Catalina Island (lat. 33°24'15" N, long. 118°22'05" W). Named on Santa Catalina East (1950) 7.5' quadrangle. United States Board on Geographic Names (1976c, p. 3) gave the form "Buttonshell Beach" as a variant.

Buzzard Peak [LOS ANGELES]: *peak,* 5.5 miles west of Pomona city hall in San Jose Hills (lat. 34°03'20" N, long. 117°51' W). Altitude 1375 feet. Named on San Dimas (1954) 7.5' quadrangle.

By Jim Spring [SAN DIEGO]: *spring,* nearly 7 miles west-southwest of Borrego Springs (lat. 33°13' N, long. 116°28'50" W; near W line sec. 16, T 11 S, R 5 E); the feature is 1050 feet west of Jim Spring. Named on Tubb Canyon (1959) 7.5' quadrangle.

- C -

Caballero Creek [LOS ANGELES]: *stream,* flows nearly 4.5 miles to Los Angeles River 4 miles east-southeast of the center of Canoga Park (lat. 34°11'10" N, long. 118°31'40" W). Named on Canoga Park (1952) 7.5' quadrangle.

Cabin Canyon [LOS ANGELES]: *canyon,* drained by a stream that flows 1.25 miles to Aliso Canyon (1) 4.25 miles northwest of Pacifico Mountain (lat. 34°25'05" N, long. 118°05'35" W; sec. 24, T 4 N, R 12 W). Named on Pacifico Mountain 1959) 7.5' quadrangle.

Cabin Flat [LOS ANGELES]: *area,* 4.5 miles northwest of Mount San Antonio along Prairie Fork (lat. 34°20'35" N, long. 117°41'50" W; sec. 15, T 3 N, R 8 W). Named on Mount San Antonio (1955) 7.5' quadrangle.

Cabrillo Harbor [LOS ANGELES]: *embayment,* nearly 4 miles north-northeast of Mount Banning on the north side of Santa Catalina Island (lat. 33°25'15" N, long. 118°24'15" W). Named on Santa Catalina North (1950) 7.5' quadrangle.

Cabrini Canyon [LOS ANGELES]: *canyon,* 1 mile long, nearly 3 miles north-northwest of Burbank city hall (lat. 34°12'55" N, long. 118°20' W; in and near sec. 34, T 2 N, R 14 W). Named on Burbank (1953) 7.5' quadrangle.

Cactus Bay [LOS ANGELES]: *embayment,* 1.5 miles west-northwest of Silver Peak on the south side of Santa Catalina Island (lat. 33° 28' N, long. 118°35'35" W). Named on Santa Catalina West (1943) 7.5' quadrangle.

Cactus Garden [SAN DIEGO]: *area,* 5.25 miles west of Ocotillo Wells (lat. 33°07'50" N, long. 116°13'15" W; near E line sec. 15, T 12 S, R 7 E). Named on Borrego Mountain (1960) 7.5' quadrangle.

Cactus Peak [LOS ANGELES]: *peak,* 2.25 miles south-southwest of Mount Banning on Santa Catalina Island (lat. 33°20'15" N, long. 118°26'40" W). Altitude 1560 feet. Named on Santa Catalina South (1943) 7.5' quadrangle. The feature also was called Mount Vizcaino (Doran, 1980, p. 77).

Cactus Point [ORANGE]: *promontory,* nearly 1.5 miles south-southeast of Laguna Beach city hall along the coast (lat. 33°31'35" N, long. 117°46'15" W; at N line sec. 35, T 7 S, R 9 W). Named on Laguna Beach (1965) 7.5' quadrangle.

Cactus Valley [SAN DIEGO]: *valley,* 9 miles south-southeast of Borrego Springs (lat. 33°08'50" N, long. 116°17'45" W; on E line sec. 12, T 12 S, R 6 E). Named on Borrego Sink (1959) 7.5' quadrangle.

Cagney Island: see **Collins Island** [ORANGE].

Cahuenga [LOS ANGELES]: *land grant,* 2 miles south-southwest of Burbank city hall. Named on Burbank (1966) 7.5' quadrangle. Jose M. Triunfo was the grantee in 1843, and David W. Alexander was the patentee for 388.34 acres in 1872 (Perez, p. 57).

Cahuenga: see **Hollywood** [LOS ANGELES]; **Universal City** [LOS ANGELES].

Cahuenga Pass [LOS ANGELES]: *pass,* 7.5 miles northwest of Los Angeles city hall (lat. 34°07'30" N, long. 118°20'35" W). Named on Burbank (1953) and Hollywood (1953) 7.5' quadrangles. Marcou (p. 158) referred to Cahunga Pass, and Preston (1890a, p. 189) mentioned Cahuengo Pass. The name undoubtedly is of Indian origin (Kroeber, p. 36).

Cahuenga Peak [LOS ANGELES]: *peak,* 3.25 miles south-southwest of Burbank city hall (lat. 34°08'15" N, long. 118°19'30" W); the peak is 1.25 miles northeast of Cahuenga Pass. Altitude 1821 feet. Named on Burbank (1953) 7.5' quadrangle.

Cajon Gap: see **Mission Gorge** [SAN DIEGO].

Calabasas [LOS ANGELES]: *village,* 6 miles east of Agoura (lat. 34° 09'25" N, long. 118°38'15" W; sec. 23, T 1 N, R 17 W). Named on Calabasas (1952) 7.5' quadrangle, which shows Calabasas P.O. located 1.25 miles west-southwest of Calabasas (on W line sec. 22, T 1 N, R 17 W). Calabasas (1903) 15' quadrangle has the name "Calabasas" at both places, and Dry Canyon (1932) 6' quadrangle shows Calabasas school at the site of present Calabasas post office. Postal authorities established Calabasas post office in 1888, moved it 1 mile west in 1889, discontinued it in 1897, and reestablished it in 1898 (Salley, p. 32). The name is the Spanish version of an Indian word for "place of wild gourds," and means "pumpkin," "squash," or "wild gourd" in Spanish (Hanna, p. 49). United States Board on Geographic Names (1933, p. 183) rejected the forms "Calabaces" and "Calabazas" for the name. Postal authorities established Daices post office—named for Wencil Daic, first postmaster—6 miles west of Calabasas in 1891, changed the name to Liberty in 1899, and discontinued it in 1900 (Salley, p. 54, 122).

Calabasas Highlands [LOS ANGELES]: *locality,* 2 miles south of Calabasas (lat. 34°07'50" N, long. 118°38'40" W; near NE cor. sec. 34, T 1 N, R 17 W). Named on Calabasas (1952) 7.5' quadrangle.

Calabasas Peak [LOS ANGELES]: *peak,* 6 miles north-northeast of Malibu Point (lat. 34°06'45" N, long. 118°39' W; sec. 3, T 1 S, R 17 W); the peak is 3.25 miles south-southwest of Calabasas. Altitude 2163 feet. Named on Malibu Beach (1951) 7.5' quadrangle.

Calavera Lake [SAN DIEGO]: *lake,* 0.5 mile long, nearly 6 miles east-southeast of Oceanside (lat. 33°10'15" N, long. 117°17' W); the lake is at the north base of Cerro de la Calavera. Named on San Luis Rey (1968) 7.5' quadrangle.

Calavo Gardens [SAN DIEGO]: *locality,* 2 miles south of El Cajon city hall (lat. 32°45'45" N, long. 116°57'35" W). Named on El Cajon (1967) 7.5' quadrangle.

Cal-Baden Mineral Spring: see **Sycamore Canyon** [LOS ANGELES] (5).

Caldwell Lake [LOS ANGELES]: *lake,* 650 feet long, 4.5 miles east-southeast of Valyermo (lat. 34°24'50" N, long. 117°46'40" W; sec. 24, T 4 N, R 9 W). Named on Valyermo (1958) 7.5' quadrangle.

Calexico Lodge [SAN DIEGO]: *locality,* 0.5 mile east-southeast of Manzanita (lat. 32°40' N, long. 116°16'45" W; near NE cor. sec. 29, T 17 S, R 7 E). Named on Live Oak Springs (1959) 7.5' quadrangle.

California Heights [LOS ANGELES]: *district,* 4 miles north of Long Beach city hall (lat. 33°49'30" N, long. 118°10'45" W). Named on Long Beach (1949) 7.5' quadrangle.

California Street [LOS ANGELES]: *locality,* 1 mile south-southwest of present Pasadena city hall along Los Angeles Terminal Railroad (lat. 34°08'05" N, long. 118°09'10" W). Named on Pasadena (1900) 15' quadrangle.

Calleguas [VENTURA]: *land grant,* east of Camarillo. Named on Camarillo (1950) and Newbury Park (1951) 7.5' quadrangles. Jose Pedro Ruiz received the land in 1837; Gabriel Ruiz claimed 9998 acres patented in 1866 (Cowan, p. 22). The name is from the designation of an Indian rancheria (Kroeber, p. 37).

Calleguas Creek [VENTURA]: *stream,* flows 13 miles to Mugu Lagoon 2.25 miles northwest of Point Mugu (lat. 34°06'20" N, long. 119°05'30"

W); the stream is partly on Calleguas grant. Named on Camarillo (1950) and Point Mugu (1949) 7.5' quadrangles. Called Rio Simi on Parke's (1854-1855) map. Antisell (p. 75) used the name "Semee creek."

Calumet Canyon [VENTURA]: *canyon,* drained by a stream that flows nearly 2 miles to the valley of Santa Clara River 5 miles west-southwest of Piru (lat. 34°22'55" N, long. 118°52'10" W; sec. 33, T 4 N, R 19 W). Named on Piru (1952) and Simi (1951) 7.5' quadrangles.

Camarillo [VENTURA]: *city,* 8.5 miles east of Oxnard (lat. 34°13' N, long. 119°02'10" W). Named on Camarillo (1950) 7.5' quadrangle. Postal authorities established Camarillo post office in 1899 (Frickstad, p. 217), and the city incorporated in 1964. The name commemorates Juan Camarillo, who purchased Callequas grant (Hoover, Rensch, and Rensch, p. 581).

Camarillo Hills [VENTURA]: *ridge,* west-southwest-trending, 6 miles long, center 2.5 miles north-northwest of downtown Camarillo (lat. 34°15' N, long. 119°03'30" W). Named on Camarillo (1950) and Santa Paula (1951) 7.5' quadrangles.

Camel Rock [SAN DIEGO]: *relief feature,* 5.5 miles east of San Felipe (lat. 33°12'05" N, long. 116°30'10" W; sec. 19, T 11 S, R 4 E). Named on Ranchita (1960) 7.5' quadrangle.

Camels Head Wash [SAN DIEGO]: *stream,* flows 1.5 miles to Fish Creek Wash 10 miles north of Sweeney Pass (lat. 32°58'35" N, long. 116°09'15" W; at SE cor. sec. 4, T 14 S, R 8 E). Named on Arroyo Tapiado (1959) 7.5' quadrangle.

Cameron Corners [SAN DIEGO]: *locality,* 1.5 miles north of Campo (lat. 32°37'45" N, long. 116°28'15" W; at NW cor. sec. 10, T 18 S, R 5 E). Named on Cameron Corners (1959) 7.5' quadrangle.

Camerons Canyon: see **Cañada de Aliso** [VENTURA].

Cameron Valley [SAN DIEGO]: *valley,* 7.25 miles north of Campo (lat. 32°42'45" N, long. 116°28'15" W). Named on Cameron Corners (1959) 7.5' quadrangle. Thomas Cameron was the first settler in the valley (Stein, p. 21).

Camp Ah-DA-HI [LOS ANGELES]: *locality,* nearly 2 miles north of Mount Wilson (lat. 34°14'55" N, long. 118°03'55" W; near NE cor. sec. 19, T 2 N, R 11 W). Named on Mount Wilson (1953) 7.5' quadrangle

Camp Aventura [LOS ANGELES]: *locality,* 1 mile north-northwest of Glendora city hall (lat. 34°09'05" N, long. 117°52'15" W; at SW cor. sec. 19, T 1 N, R 9 W). Named on Glendora (1966) 7.5' quadrangle.

Camp Bartlett [VENTURA]: *locality,* 5.5 miles west of Santa Paula Peak along Sisar Creek (lat. 34°25'40" N, long. 119°06'25" W). Named on Santa Paula Peak (1951) 7.5' quadrangle.

Camp Bill Lane [LOS ANGELES]: *locality,* 1 mile north of Sunland (lat. 34°16'30" N, long. 118°18'20" W). Named on Sunland (1953) 7.5' quadrangle. Called Bill Lane Camp on Sunland (1966) 7.5' quadrangle.

Camp Bonita [LOS ANGELES]: *locality,* 8.5 miles northeast of Glendora city hall near the mouth of Cattle Canyon (lat. 34°13'45" N, long. 117°46'05" W). Named on Camp Bonita (1940) 6' quadrangle. Jay Gardner Scott founded a resort called Scott's Camp at the site in 1909 and soon changed the name to Camp Bonita; a flood destroyed the place in 1938 (Robinson, J.W., 1983, p. 96).

Camp Caula [LOS ANGELES]: *locality,* 2 miles north-northeast of Whitaker Peak (lat. 34°35'55" N, long. 118°43'20" W; sec. 19, T 6 N, R 18 W). Named on Whitaker Peak (1958) 7.5' quadrangle.

Camp Chiquita [LOS ANGELES]: *locality,* 4.25 miles north of Pasadena city hall (lat. 34°12'40" N, long. 118°08'20" W); the place is near Chiquita Canyon. Named on Pasadena (1953) 7.5' quadrangle.

Camp Christian [LOS ANGELES]: *locality,* 5.5 miles west-northwest of Waterman Mountain (lat. 34°20'55" N, long. 117°59'55" W; sec. 14, T 3 N, R 11 W). Named on Waterman Mountain (1959) 7.5' quadrangle.

Camp Comfort [VENTURA]: *locality,* 1.5 miles south-southwest of downtown Ojai along San Antonio Creek (lat. 34°25'35" N, long. 119°15'30" W). Named on Matilija (1952) 7.5' quadrangle.

Camp Cumorah Crest [LOS ANGELES]: *locality,* 3 miles west-northwest of Waterman Mountain (lat. 34°20'55" N, long. 117°59'05" W; sec. 13, T 3 N, R 11 W). Named on Waterman Mountain (1959) 7.5' quadrangle. Waterman Mountain (1941) 6' minute quadrangle has the name "Cumorah Crest" for a relief feature located near the place.

Camp Cuyamaca [SAN DIEGO]: *locality,* 3 miles east-southeast of Cuyamaca (lat. 32°55'35" N, long. 116°33'30" W). Named on Cuyamaca Peak (1960) 7.5' quadrangle.

Camp Davidson [SAN DIEGO]: *locality,* 5.5 miles south-southeast of Santa Ysabel (lat. 33°02'20" N, long. 116°37'35" W; near S line sec. 13, T 13 S, R 3 E). Named on Santa Ysabel (1960) 7.5' quadrangle.

Camp Del Mar [SAN DIEGO]: *locality,* 2.25 miles north-northwest of Oceanside on Camp Pendleton Marine Corp Base (lat. 33°13'30" N, long. 117°24' W; around NE cor. sec. 16, T 11 S, R 5 W). Named on Oceanside (1968) 7.5' quadrangle.

Camp De Luz [SAN DIEGO]: *locality,* 4.25 miles west of Fallbrook on Joseph H. Pendleton Naval Reservation (lat. 33°22'15" N, long. 117°19'15" W; near N line sec. 29, T 9 S, R 4 W). Named on Morro Hill (1949) 7.5' quadrangle.

Camp Drum: see **Wilmington** [LOS ANGELES].

Camp Elliott [SAN DIEGO]: *military installation,* 8 miles northwest of La Mesa (lat. 32°51'30" N, long. 117°06'45" W). Named on La Mesa (1953) 7.5' quadrangle, which shows the installation located on Camp Elliott Naval Reservation; Camp Elliott and part of the naval reservation later were included in Miramar Naval Air Station. Camp Elliott Naval Reservation is named on La Mesa (1953), Poway Valley (1952), and San Vicente Reservoir (1955) 7.5' quadrangles.

Camp Elliott Naval Reservation: see **Camp Elliott** [SAN DIEGO].

Camp Glenwood [LOS ANGELES]: *locality,* 1.5 miles northwest of Waterman Mountain (lat. 34°21'10" N, long. 117°57'25" W; near NW cor. sec. 17, T 3 N, R 10 W). Named on Waterman Mountain (1959) 7.5' quadrangle.

Camp Hawthorne [LOS ANGELES]: *locality,* 2 miles west-northwest of Big Pines (lat. 34°23'35" N, long. 117°43'15" W). Named on Mescal Creek (1956) 7.5' quadrangle.

Camp Hemohme [LOS ANGELES]: *locality,* 2 miles west-northwest of Big Pines (lat. 34°23'20" N, long. 117°43'15" W). Named on Mescal Creek (1956) 7.5' quadrangle.

Camp Hidden Valley [LOS ANGELES]: *locality,* 3 miles southeast of Pacifico Mountain (lat. 34°21' N, long. 118°00'10" W; sec. 14, T 3 N, R 11 W). Named on Chilao Flat (1959) 7.5' quadrangle.

Camp Hi-Hill [LOS ANGELES]: *locality,* 9.5 miles south-southwest of Pacifico Mountain near the head of West Fork San Gabriel River (lat. 34°15'15" N, long. 118°05'40" W). Named on Chilao Flat (1959) 7.5' quadrangle. Called Opids Camp on Mount Wilson (1939) 6' quadrangle. John T. Opid took out a resort lease in 1913 at what then was called Stony Gulch and began construction of a popular hostelry called Opid's Camp; the place now is known as Camp Hi-Hill (Robinson, J.W., 1977, p. 159, 161). Ernest DeVore, Chorie DeVore, and J.P. Nevins built a place called Camp West Fork in 1913 about 5 miles downstream from Opid's Camp; it lasted until the mid-1920's (Robinson, J.W., 1977, p. 162).

Camp Hual-Cu-Cuish [SAN DIEGO]: *locality,* 2.25 miles north-northeast of Cuyamaca Peak (lat. 32°58'25" N, long. 116°35' W). Named on Cuyamaca Peak (1960) 7.5' quadrangle.

Camp Huntington [LOS ANGELES]: *locality,* 4 miles west-southwest of Mount Wilson (1) in Rubio Canyon (lat. 34°12' N, long. 118°07'15" W; sec. 3, T 1 N, R 12 W). Named on Mount Wilson (1953) 7.5' quadrangle.

Camp Idle Hour: see **Idlehour Camp** [LOS ANGELES].

Camp Ivy [LOS ANGELES]: *locality,* 2 miles southeast of Mount Wilson (1) in Winter Canyon (lat. 34°12'30" N, long. 118°02' W; on S line sec. 33, T 2 N, R 11 W). Named on Mount Wilson (1953) 7.5' quadrangle. The place first was called Hoegee's Camp; Arie Hoegee and his family founded the resort in 1908 (Robinson, J.W., 1977, p. 134). It was called Camp LeRoy before LeRoy Haynes sold it to Ivy Holzer in 1947; Holzer changed the name to Camp Ivy (Owens, p. 88). A fire destroyed the place in 1953 (Robinson, J.W., 1977, p. 134).

Camp Joseph H. Pendleton Naval Reservation: see **Camp Pendleton Marine Corps Base** [SAN DIEGO].

Camp Josepho [LOS ANGELES]: *locality,* 5 miles north-northwest of Santa Monica city hall in Rustic Canyon (lat. 34°04'50" N, long. 118°31'10" W). Named on Topanga (1952) 7.5' quadrangle.

Camp Jubilee [LOS ANGELES]: *locality,* 2.5 miles north-northeast of Big Pines (lat. 34°24'40" N, long. 117°40'10" W; near N line sec. 25, T 4 N, R 8 W). Named on Mescal Creek (1956) 7.5' quadrangle.

Camp Junipero Serra [LOS ANGELES]: *locality,* 2.5 miles west-northwest of Big Pines (lat. 34°23'35" N, long. 117°43'45" W). Named on Mescal Creek (1956) 7.5' quadrangle.

Camp Kearney [SAN DIEGO]: *military installation,* 7 miles east of present Point La Jolla (lat. 32°52'15" N, long. 117°09'30" W). Named on La Jolla (1903) 15' quadrangle. The post office established at the place in 1917 had the names "Linda Vista Military Branch," "Military Branch," and "Kearney Military Branch" until 1921, when the name was changed to Camp Kearney; postal authorities discontinued Camp Kearney post office in 1926, reestablished it at a new site in 1942, discontinued it in 1943, and reestablished for a time in 1946—the army had a training camp at the place during World War I, and the navy used it during World War II (Salley, p. 34, 109). The name "Kearney" recalls an American general of Mexican War fame (Gudde, 1949, p. 171).

Camp Kole [LOS ANGELES]: *locality,* 9 miles south-southwest of Pacifico Mountain (lat. 34°15'10" N, long. 118°04'25" W; near S line sec. 18, T 2 N, R 11 W); the place is at the mouth of Valley Forge Canyon. Named on Chilao Flat (1959) 7.5' quadrangle. Mount Wilson (1939) 6' quadrangle shows Valley Forge Lodge at the site. Ernest DeVore and Cherie DeVore took a Forest Service lease in 1922 and started a resort that they called Valley Forge Lodge (Robinson, J.W., 1977, p. 162).

Camp LeRoy: see **Camp Ivy** [LOS ANGELES].

Camp Losadena: see **Switzer Camp** [LOS ANGELES].

Camp Lupin [LOS ANGELES]: *locality,* 3 miles north-northwest of Mount San Antonio (lat. 34°19'40" N, long. 117°40' W; sec. 24, T 3 N, R 8 W). Named on Mount San Antonio (1955) 7.5' quadrangle.

Camp Manzanita [LOS ANGELES]: *locality,* 2.5 miles west-northwest of

Big Pines (lat. 34°23'40" N, long. 117°43'35" W). Named on Mescal Creek (1956) 7.5' quadrangle.

Camp Marion [LOS ANGELES]: *locality,* 0.5 mile east-northeast of Mescal Creek (lat. 34°22'35" N, long. 117°40'50" W; sec. 2, T 3 N, R 8 W). Named on Mescal Creek (1956) 7.5' quadrangle.

Camp Marston [SAN DIEGO]: *locality,* 2.5 miles south-southwest of Julian (lat. 33°02'35" N, long. 116°37'15" W; near E line sec. 13, T 13 S, R 3 E). Named on Julian (1960) 7.5' quadrangle.

Camp Matthews Naval Reservation [SAN DIEGO]: *military installation,* 6 miles south-southeast of Del Mar at the site of present University of California San Diego campus (lat. 32°52'35" N, long. 117°13'35" W). Named on Del Mar (1953) 7.5' quadrangle.

Camp McClellan [LOS ANGELES]: *locality,* 0.25 mile north of Big Pines (lat. 34°23' N, long. 117°41'20" W; near NW cor. sec. 2, T 3 N, R 8 W). Named on Mescal Creek (1956) 7.5' quadrangle.

Camp McKiwanis [LOS ANGELES]: *locality,* 1.5 miles west-northwest of Big Pines (lat. 34°23'20" N, long. 117°43' W). Named on Mescal Creek (1956) 7.5' quadrangle.

Camp Merriam: see **Camp Sierra** [LOS ANGELES].

Camp Metaka [LOS ANGELES]: *locality,* 1.25 miles west-northwest of Big Pines (lat. 34°23'20" N, long. 117°42'35" W). Named on Mescal Creek (1956) 7.5' quadrangle.

Camp Minnewawa [SAN DIEGO]: *locality,* 4.5 miles south-southeast of Jamul (lat. 32°39' N, long. 116°51'15" W). Named on Jamul (1955) 15' quadrangle.

Campo [SAN DIEGO]: *town,* 40 miles east of San Diego (lat. 32°36'25" N, long. 116°28'05" W; at W line sec. 15, T 18 S, R 5 E). Named on Campo (1959) 7.5' quadrangle. Postal authorities established Campo post office in 1870, moved it 2.5 miles northwest in 1891, and moved it 3 miles east in 1892 (Salley, p. 35). They established Milguatay post office about 25 miles northeast of Campo in 1868 and discontinued it in 1875; the place also was known as New Texas (Salley, p. 140). They established Homestead post office 7 miles west of Campo in 1878, discontinued it in 1880, reestablished it in 1892, and discontinued it in 1893 (Salley, p. 99). They established Divide post office, named for Tecate Divide, 11 miles east of Campo (sec. 15, T 18 S, R 6 E) in 1889 and discontinued it in 1890 (Salley, p. 59).

Camp Oak Grove [LOS ANGELES]: *locality,* 7.5 miles north-northeast of Glendora city hall (lat. 34°14'15" N, long. 117°49'15" W). Named on Glendora (1966) 7.5' quadrangle.

Camp Oak Wilde: see **Oakwilde** [LOS ANGELES].

Campo Aleman: see **Anaheim** [ORANGE].

Campo Creek [SAN DIEGO]: *stream* and *dry wash,* extends for 19 miles to Mexico 4.5 miles east-southeast of Potrero (lat. 32°35' N, long. 116°32'25" W). Named on Cameron Corners (1959), Campo (1959), Live Oak Springs (1959), and Potrero (1960) 7.5' quadrangles.

Campo de Cahunga: see **Universal City** [LOS ANGELES].

Campo Lake [SAN DIEGO]: *lake,* 800 feet long, about 0.5 mile west of Campo (lat. 32°36'30" N, long. 116°28'55" W; sec. 16, T 18 S, R 5 E); the lake is along Campo Creek. Named on Campo (1959) 7.5' quadrangle.

Camp Ole Station [SAN DIEGO]: *locality,* 1 mile south-southwest of Monument Peak (lat. 32°52'50" N, long. 116°25'40" W; near W line sec. 12, T 15 S, R 5 E). Named on Monument Peak (1959) 7.5' quadrangle.

Campo Valley [SAN DIEGO]: *valley,* north of Campo along Campo Creek (lat. 32°37'30" N, long. 116°27'45" W). Named on Cameron Corners (1959) and Campo (1959) 7.5' quadrangles.

Camp Pajarito [LOS ANGELES]: *locality,* 1 mile north-northwest of Waterman Mountain (lat. 34°21' N, long. 117°56'30" W; near E line sec. 17, T 3 N, R 10 W). Named on Waterman Mountain (1959) 7.5' quadrangle.

Camp Pendleton Marine Corps Base [SAN DIEGO]: *military installation,* extends from Oceanside to San Onofre and Fallbrook; covers Santa Margarita y Las Flores grant. Named on Fallbrook (1968), Las Pulgas Canyon (1968), Margarita Peak (1968), Morro Hill (1968), Oceanside (1968), San Clemente (1968), San Luis Rey (1968), and San Onofre Bluff (1968) 7.5' quadrangles. Called Camp Joseph H. Pendleton Naval Reservation on Fallbrook (1949), Las Pulgas Canyon (1949), Margarita Peak (1950), Morro Hill (1949), San Clemente (1949), and San Luis Rey (1948) 7.5' quadrangles. Called Camp Pendleton Naval Reservation on Oceanside (1947) and San Onofre Bluff (1949) 7.5' quadrangles, called Camp Joseph H. Pendleton on Sitton Peak (1954) 7.5' quadrangle, and called Camp Pendleton on Santa Ana (1959) 1°x 2° quadrangle. The name "Pendleton," given in 1941, commemorates Marine Major General Joseph H. Pendleton, who was instrumental in establishment of the facility (Gudde, 1949, p. 257; Stein, p. 22).

Camp Pendleton Naval Reservation: see **Camp Pendleton Marine Corps Base** [SAN DIEGO].

Camp Pulgas [SAN DIEGO]: *locality,* 5 miles east-southeast of San Onofre Mountain on Camp Joseph H. Pendleton Naval Reservation (lat. 33°20'30" N, long. 117°24'35" W; sec. 4, T 10 S, R 5 W); the place is in Las Pulgas Canyon. Named on Las Pulgas Canyon (1949) 7.5' quadrangle.

Camp Rathke: see **Santiago Reservoir** [ORANGE].

Camp Rosenita [LOS ANGELES]: *locality,* 2.25 miles southeast of Pacifico Mountain (lat. 34°21'20" N, long. 118°00'40" W; near SE cor. sec. 10, T 3 N, R 11 W). Named on Chilao Flat (1959) 7.5' quadrangle.

Camp San Pedro: see **Drum Barracks**, under **Wilmington** [LOS ANGELES].

Camps Creek [SAN DIEGO]: *stream,* flows 3 miles to De Luz Creek 5.5 miles northwest of Fallbrook (lat. 33°26'10" N, long. 117°19'15" W; near W line sec. 32, T 8 S, R 4 W). Named on Fallbrook (1968) 7.5' quadrangle.

Camp Sierra [LOS ANGELES]: *locality,* nearly 5 miles north of Pasadena city hall (lat. 34°13' N, long. 118°07'55" W; near W line sec. 34, T 2 N, R 12 W). Named on Pasadena (1953) 7.5' quadrangle. Judge J.H. Merriam founded a place called Camp Merriam high on Sunset Ridge above Millard Canyon in 1904; C.W. Siefert took over the place and changed the name to Camp Sierra (Robinson, J.W., 1977, p. 137-138).

Camp Singing Pines [LOS ANGELES]: *locality,* 3.5 miles west-northwest of Waterman Mountain (lat. 34°21'05" N, long. 117°59'30" W; near NW cor. sec. 13, T 3 N, R 11 W). Named on Waterman Mountain (1959) 7.5' quadrangle. Called Squaw Camp on Waterman Mountain (1941) 6' quadrangle.

Camp Sizzle Spring [SAN DIEGO]: *spring,* 3.25 miles north of Jacumba (lat. 32°39'50" N, long. 116°11' W; sec. 29, T 17 S, R 8 E). Named on Jacumba (1959) 7.5' quadrangle.

Camp Slauson [LOS ANGELES]: *locality,* 5.5 miles north-northeast of Malibu Point in Red Rock Canyon (3) (lat. 34°06'15" N, long. 118°38'30" W; at SE cor. sec. 3, T 1 S, R 17 W). Named on Malibu Beach (1951) 7.5' quadrangle.

Camp Sterling [LOS ANGELES]: *locality,* 2.5 miles north-northeast of Sunland in Big Tujunga Canyon (lat. 34°17'35" N, long. 118°17'05" W; near NW cor. sec. 6, T 2 N, R 13 W). Named on La Crescenta (1939) 6' quadrangle.

Camp Sturtevant: see **Sturtevant Camp** [LOS ANGELES].

Camp Tapawingo [SAN DIEGO]: *locality,* 3.25 miles north-northeast of Cuyamaca Peak (lat. 32°59' N, long. 116°34'20" W). Named on Cuyamaca Peak (1960) 7.5' quadrangle.

Camp Teresita Pines [LOS ANGELES]: *locality,* 1.5 miles west-northwest of Big Pines (lat. 34°23'30" N, long. 117°42'55" W). Named on Mescal Creek (1956) 7.5' quadrangle.

Camp Toyon [LOS ANGELES]: *locality,* 2.5 miles northwest of Avalon on Santa Catalina Island (lat. 33°22'25" N, long. 118°21'15" W); the place is at Toyon Bay. Named on Santa Catalina East (1950) 7.5' quadrangle.

Camp 2 [LOS ANGELES]: *locality,* 8.5 miles south of the present village of Lake Hughes in Bouquet Canyon (lat. 34°33'15" N, long. 118°25'15" W; sec. 2, T 5 N, R 15 W). Named on San Francisquito (1937) 6' quadrangle.

Camp Valcrest [LOS ANGELES]: *locality,* 2.5 miles west-northwest of Waterman Mountain (lat. 34°20'40" N, long. 117°58'40" W; near E line sec. 13, T 3 N, R 11 W). Named on Waterman Mountain (1959) 7.5' quadrangle. Waterman Mountain (1941) 6' quadrangle has the name "Valcrest" at the place.

Camp Verdugo Pines [LOS ANGELES]: *locality,* 2.25 miles west-northwest of Big Pines (lat. 34°23'20" N, long. 117°43'35" W). Named on Mescal Creek (1956) 7.5' quadrangle.

Camp West Fork: see **Camp Hi-Hill** [LOS ANGELES].

Camp Wilson: see **Martins Camp** [LOS ANGELES].

Camp Wolahi [SAN DIEGO]: *locality,* 3 miles north-northeast of Cuyamaca Peak (lat. 32°59'25" N, long. 116°35'20" W). Named on Cuyamaca Peak (1960) 7.5' quadrangle.

Camp Wright: see **Oak Grove** [SAN DIEGO].

Camulas: see **Camulos** [VENTURA].

Camulos [VENTURA]: *locality,* 2.25 miles east-southeast of Piru (lat. 34°24'20" N, long. 118°45'20" W). Named on Piru (1952) 7.5' quadrangle. Postal authorities established Camulas post office in 1885, changed the name to Camulos in 1886, and discontinued it in 1914 (Frickstad, p. 218). The name is of Indian origin (Kroeber, p. 37).

Cañada Agua Caliente [SAN DIEGO]: *canyon,* 9 miles long, opens into the canyon of Agua Caliente Creek 1.25 miles west of Warners Springs (lat. 33°17'15" N, long. 116°39'15" W); Warner Hot Spring is in the canyon. Named on Hot Springs Mountain (1960) and Warner Springs (1959) 7.5' quadrangles.

Cañada Aguanga [SAN DIEGO]: *canyon,* 4.5 miles long, drained by a stream that joins San Luis Rey River 4 miles west-northwest of Warner Springs (lat. 33°18'35" N, long. 116°41'35" W); the canyon is northeast of the southeast end of Aguanga Mountain. Named on Warner Springs (1959) 7.5' quadrangle.

Cañada Buena Vista [SAN DIEGO]: *valley,* 2 miles north-northwest of San Felipe (lat. 33°13'30" N, long. 116°36'30" W); the feature is along Buena Vista Creek (2). Named on Ranchita (1960) 7.5' quadrangle.

Cañada Chiquita [ORANGE]: *canyon,* drained by a stream that flows 6.5 miles to San Juan Creek 3.5 miles east-northeast of San Juan Capistrano (lat. 33°31'35" N, long. 117°36'35" W; near NE cor. sec. 33, T 7 S, R 7

W). Named on Cañada Gobernadora (1968) 7.5' quadrangle.
Cañada de Agua Chinon: see **Limestone Canyon** [ORANGE].
Cañada de Aliso [VENTURA]: *canyon*, drained by a stream that flows 3.25 miles to Cañada Larga 5 miles north-northeast of Ventura (lat. 34°21' N, long. 119°15'30" W). Named on Ventura (1951) 7.5' quadrangle. Called Cañada del Aliso on Matilija (1952) 7.5' quadrangle. The feature also was called Camerons Canyon for Alexander M. Cameron, who owned land there (Ricard).
Cañada de la Brea: see **Rincon de la Brea** [LOS ANGELES-ORANGE].
Cañada de la Campaña: see **Bell Canyon** [ORANGE].
Cañada de la Habra: see **La Habra** [LOS ANGELES-ORANGE].
Cañada de la Madera: see **Silverado Canyon** [ORANGE]; **Walnut Canyon** [ORANGE].
Canada de la Madra: see **Shady Canyon** [ORANGE].
Cañada de la Oasis: see **Oso Canyon** [LOS ANGELES].
Cañada de las Encinas [VENTURA]: *canyon*, drained by a stream that flows 0.5 mile to the canyon of Ventura River 3.25 miles north of Ventura (lat. 34°19'35" N, long. 119°17'05" W). Named on Ventura (1951) 7.5' quadrangle.
Canada de las Lagunas: see **Laguna Canyon** [ORANGE].
Cañada de la Soledad: see **Soledad Canyon** [SAN DIEGO].
Canada de las Ranas: see **Peters Canyon** [ORANGE].
Cañada de las Yeguas: see **San Clemente Canyon** [SAN DIEGO].
Cañada de la Vieja: see **Baker Canyon** [ORANGE].
Cañada del Diablo [VENTURA]: *canyon*, drained by a stream that flows 4.5 miles to Ventura River 2 miles north-northwest of downtown Ventura (lat. 34°18'15" N, long. 119°18'10" W). Named on Ventura (1951) 7.5' quadrangle.
Cañada de Leon: see **Lion Canyon** [VENTURA] (2).
Canada del Incendio: see **San Juan Creek** [ORANGE].
Cañada de Los Alamos [LOS ANGELES]: *canyon*, nearly 7 miles long, opens into the canyon of Piru Creek 9 miles south-southeast of Gorman (lat. 34°39'15" N, long. 118°46'30" W; sec. 34, T 7 N, R 18 W). Named on Black Mountain (1958) 7.5' quadrangle, where the upper part of the feature is called Lower Hungry Valley. Beartrap Canyon (1938) and Gorman (1938) 6' quadrangles have the form "Cañada de los Alamos" (with the lower-case "l" in "los") for the name.
Cañada de los Alisos [ORANGE]: *land grant*, at and north of El Toro. Named on El Toro (1950), San Juan Capistrano (1949), and Santiago Peak (1954) 7.5' quadrangles. Jose Serrano received 2 leagues in 1842 and more land in 1846; he claimed 10,669 acres patented in 1871 (Cowan, p. 15).
Cañada de los Coches: see **El Cajon** [SAN DIEGO] (1).
Cañada de los Encinos: see **Encinitas Creek** [SAN DIEGO].
Cañada de los Indios: see **Black Star Canyon** [ORANGE].
Cañada de los Nogales [LOS ANGELES]: *land grant*, 4 miles north of Los Angeles city hall. Named on Los Angeles (1953) 7.5' quadrangle. Jose M. Aguila received 0.5 league in 1844 and claimed 1200 acres patented in 1882 (Cowan, p. 53).
Canada del Rodeo: see **Brea Canyon** [LOS ANGELES-ORANGE].
Canada del Toro: see **Serrano Creek** [ORANGE].
Cañada de Ozuna: see **Murray Canyon** [SAN DIEGO].
Cañada de Palos Verdes: see **Harbor Lake** [LOS ANGELES].
Cañada de Polomia: see **Guejito y Cañada de Polomia**, under **Guejito** [SAN DIEGO].
Cañada de Rodriguez [VENTURA]: *canyon*, drained by a stream that flows 2.25 miles to Ventura River 3.5 miles north of Ventura (lat. 34°20' N, long. 119°17'55" W); the canyon is on Cañada de San Miguelito grant, which Ramon Rodriquez received in 1846. Named on Ventura (1951) 7.5' quadrangle.
Cañada de San Alejo: see **Los Encenitos** [SAN DIEGO].
Cañada de San Buenaventura: see **Rose Canyon** [SAN DIEGO].
Cañada de San Joaquin [VENTURA]: *canyon*, drained by a stream that flows 1.5 miles to the canyon of Ventura River 2 miles north of downtown Ventura (lat. 34°18'30" N, long. 119°17'30" W). Named on Ventura (1951) 7.5' quadrangle.
Cañada de San Miguelito [VENTURA]: *land grant*, northwest of Ventura. Named on Ventura (1951) 7.5' quadrangle. Ramon Rodriguez received 2 leagues in 1846 and his heirs claimed 8877 acres patented in 1871 (Cowan, p. 86).
Cañada de Santa Ana: see **Cañon de Santa Ana** [ORANGE].
Cañada de Santa Clara: see **Santa Clara River** [VENTURA].
Cañada de San Vicente y Mesa del Padre Barona [SAN DIEGO]: *land grant*, north-northeast of Lakeside. Named on El Cajon Mountain (1955), Ramona (1955), and San Vicente Reservoir (1955) 7.5' quadrangles. Called San Vicente on El Cajon (1939) 15' quadrangle. Juan Lopez received 3 leagues in 1846; Domingo Yorba claimed 13,316 acres patented in 1873 (Cowan, p. 89).
Cañada Gobernadora [ORANGE]: *canyon*, drained by a stream that flows 8.5 miles to San Juan Creek 4 miles east-northeast of San Juan Capistrano (lat. 33°31'25" N, long. 117°35'50" W; sec. 34, T 7 S, R 7 W). Named on Cañada Gobernadora (1968) and Santiago Peak (1954) 7.5' quadrangles. Called Canada Gubernadora on Corona (1902) 30' quadrangle. *Gobernadora* means "greasewood" in Spanish (Meadows, p. 66).
Cañada Larga [VENTURA]: *canyon*, drained by a stream that flows 7.5 miles to Ventura River 4 miles north of Ventura (lat. 34°20'15" N, long. 119°17'45" W); the feature is on Cañada Larga o Verde grant. Named on Saticoy (1951) and Ventura (1951) 7.5' quadrangles. Postal authorities established Verdi post office at the mouth of the canyon in 1894 and discontinued it in 1898 (Ricard; Salley, p. 230).
Cañada Larga o Verde [VENTURA]: *land grant*, north of Ventura. Named on Matilija (1952), Ojai (1952), Saticoy (1951), and Ventura (1951) 7.5' quadrangles. Joaquina Alvarado received 0.5 league in 1841 and claimed 6659 acres patented in 1873 (Cowan, p. 44; Cowan listed the grant under the name "Cañada Larga y Verde").
Cañada Niguel: see **Salt Creek** [ORANGE].
Canada of Alamos: see **San Francisquito Canyon** [LOS ANGELES].
Canada Salada: see **Sulphur Creek** [ORANGE].
Cañada San Nicolas: see **Nicholas Canyon** [LOS ANGELES].
Cañada Seca [VENTURA]: *canyon*, drained by a stream that flows 2 miles to Cañada Larga 4.5 miles north-northeast of Ventura (lat. 34°20'40" N, long. 119°15'35" W). Named on Saticoy (1951) and Ventura (1951) 7.5' quadrangles.
Cañada Seco: see **Williams Canyon** [ORANGE].
Cañada Verde [SAN DIEGO]: *canyon*, drained by a stream that flows nearly 6 miles to lowlands 1 mile southwest of Warner Springs (lat. 33°16'20" N, long. 116°38'40" W). Named on Hot Springs Mountain (1960) and Warner Springs (1959) 7.5' quadrangles.
Cañada Verruga [SAN DIEGO]: *canyon*, 2 miles northeast of San Felipe along Buena Vista Creek (lat. 33°13'10" N, long. 116°34'20" W). Named on Ranchita (1960) 7.5' quadrangle. The name reportedly is from an Indian who had a large wart on his neck—*verruga* means "wart" in Spanish (Stein, p. 23).
Canal de Santa Barbara: see **Santa Barbara Channel** [VENTURA].
Canal Street Station [LOS ANGELES]: *locality*, 6 miles southeast of present Torrance city hall along Pacific Electric Railroad (lat. 33° 46'25" N, long. 118°15'40" W). Named on Wilmington (1925) 6' quadrangle.
Canebrake Canyon [SAN DIEGO]: *canyon*, 1.5 miles long, 4.5 miles south-southeast of Agua Caliente Springs (lat. 32°53'45" N, long. 116°15'30" W; mainly in sec. 3, 4, T 15 S, R 7 E); the canyon is along Canebrake Wash. Named on Agua Caliente Springs (1959) 7.5' quadrangle.
Canebrake Spring: see **Angelina Spring** [SAN DIEGO].
Canebreak Wash [SAN DIEGO]: *stream*, flows 11.5 miles to Vallecito Creek 6.5 miles north-northwest of Sweeney Pass (lat. 32° 55' N, long. 116°13'55" W; near N line sec. 35, T 14 S, R 7 E). Named on Agua Caliente Springs (1959), Arroyo Tapiado (1959), and Sombrero Peak (1959) 7.5' quadrangles.
Canet: see **Weldons** [VENTURA].
Canoga: see **Canoga Park** [LOS ANGELES].
Canoga Park [LOS ANGELES]: *district*, 23 miles west-northwest of Los Angeles city hall (lat. 34°12'05" N, long. 118°35'45" W). Named on Canoga Park (1952) 7.5' quadrangle. Camulos (1903) 30' quadrangle shows a place called Canoga along the railroad at the site. Called Owensmouth on Chatsworth (1927) 6' quadrangle. Postal authorities established Owensmouth post office in 1912 and changed the name to Canoga Park in 1931 (Frickstad, p. 78). Harrison Gray Otis, publisher of *Los Angeles Times*, gave the name "Owensmouth" to the place because it used water brought by aqueduct from Owens River in Inyo County (Hanna, p. 54). The west part of Canoga Park withdrew from the district to form an incorporated community called West Hills.
Cañon de la Horca: see **Fremont Canyon** [ORANGE].
Cañon de los Monos: see **Los Monos Canyon** [SAN DIEGO].
Cañon de Santa Ana [ORANGE]: *land grant*, extends from Yorba Linda to Santa Ana Canyon. Named on Black Star Canyon (1950), Orange (1950), Prado Dam (1950), and Yorba Linda (1950) 7.5' quadrangles. Bernardo Yorba received 3 leagues in 1834 and claimed 13,329 acres patented in 1866 (Cowan, p. 90; Cowan used the form "Cañada de Santa Ana" for the name).
Canterbury Lake: see **Lake Sherwood** [VENTURA].
Canton Canyon [LOS ANGELES-VENTURA]: *canyon*, drained by a stream that heads in Los Angeles County and flows 8.5 miles to Lake Piru 9 miles southeast of Cobblestone Mountain in Ventura County (lat. 34°30'45" N, long. 118°45'15" W; near S line sec. 15, T 5 N, R 18 W). Named on Cobblestone Mountain (1958) and Whitaker Peak (1958) 7.5' quadrangles. The lower part of the feature is called Stockton Canyon on Whitaker Peak (1935) 6' quadrangle, but United States Board on Geographic Names (1960b, p. 6) rejected the names "Stockton Canyon" and "Stocton Canyon" for it.
Canyon Acres [ORANGE]: *locality*, less than 1 mile northeast of Laguna Beach city hall in a branch of Laguna Canyon (lat. 33°33'10" N, long. 117°46'15" W; sec. 24, T 7 S, R 9 W). Named on Laguna Beach (1965) 7.5' quadrangle.
Canyon City [SAN DIEGO]: *locality*, 5 miles east of Potrero (lat. 32°35'40"

N, long. 116°31'35" W; sec. 24, T 18 S, R 4 E). Named on Potrero (1960) 7.5' quadrangle.

Canyon de las Encinas [SAN DIEGO]: *canyon*, drained by a stream that flows 3.5 miles to the sea 5.5 miles north-northwest of Encinitas (lat. 33°06'55" N, long. 117°19'30" W; sec. 20, T 12 S, R 4 W). Named on Encinitas (1968) 7.5' quadrangle.

Canyon sin Nombre [SAN DIEGO]: *canyon*, drained by a stream that flows 4.5 miles to Carrizo Creek (2) 3.5 miles northeast of Sweeney Pass (lat. 32°52'20" N, long. 116°08'35" W; near N line sec. 15, T 15 S, R 8 E). Named on Sweeney Pass (1959) 7.5' quadrangle.

Cape Canyon [LOS ANGELES]: *canyon*, drained by a stream that flows 3.25 miles to Middle Canyon 1.25 miles south of Mount Banning on Santa Catalina Island (lat. 33°21'15" N, long. 118° 26' W). Named on Santa Catalina North (1950) and Santa Catalina South (1943) 7.5' quadrangles.

Cape Canyon Reservoir [LOS ANGELES]: *lake*, 300 feet long, 2.5 miles east of Mount Banning on Santa Catalina Island (lat. 33°22'40" N, long. 118°23'30" W); the feature is at the head of Cape Canyon. Named on Santa Catalina North (1950) 7.5' quadrangle.

Cape Cortes [LOS ANGELES]: *promontory*, 3 miles southeast of Silver Peak on the south side of Santa Catalina Island (lat. 33°25'45" N, long. 118°31'55" W). Named on Santa Catalina West (1943) 7.5' quadrangle.

Cape Horn Canyon [LOS ANGELES]: *canyon*, drained by a stream that flows 1.5 miles to San Gabriel River 7.5 miles north-northeast of Glendora city hall (lat. 34°13'50" N, long. 117°47'55" W). Named on Glendora (1953) 7.5' quadrangle.

Capistrano: see **San Juan Capistrano** [ORANGE].

Capistrano Beach [ORANGE]: *town*, 2.5 miles south-southwest of San Juan Capistrano (lat. 33°27'55" N, long. 117°40'40" W); the place is at the mouth of San Juan Creek. Named on Dana Point (1968) 7.5' quadrangle, which shows a railroad station called Serra at the town. Capistrano (1902) 30' quadrangle has the name "San Juan" at or near the site. Postal authorities established Capistrano Beach post office in 1925, changed the name to Doheny Park in 1931, and changed it back to Capistrano Beach in 1948 (Frickstad, p. 116). United States Board Geographic Names (1963, p. 13) rejected the names "Doheny Park," "San Juan by the Sea," and "Serra" for the town. Promoters laid out a subdivision called San Juan-by-the-Sea at the site in 1887, but the development failed; it was revived in 1925 under the name "Capistrano Beach," and eventually the E.L. Doheny interests took over the enterprise (Meadows, p. 50).

Capistrano Bight [ORANGE]: *water feature*, extends southeast along the coast from Dana Point to San Mateo Point [ORANGE-SAN DIEGO]. Named on Dana Point (1968) and San Clemente (1968) 7.5' quadrangles.

Caradas Creek: see **Blind Canyon** [LOS ANGELES-VENTURA].

Carbon Beach [LOS ANGELES]: *beach*, 1.5 miles east-northeast of Malibu Point (lat. 34°02'20" N, long. 118°39'30" W); the beach is west of the mouth of Carbon Canyon. Named on Malibu Beach (1951) 7.5' quadrangle.

Carbon Canyon [LOS ANGELES]: *canyon*, drained by a stream that flows nearly 3 miles to the sea 2 miles east-northeast of Malibu Point (lat. 34°02'15" N, long. 118°38'50" W). Named on Malibu Beach (1951) 7.5' quadrangle. Called Coal Canyon on Camulos (1903) 30' quadrangle.

Carbon Canyon [ORANGE]: *canyon*, 7 miles long, heads in San Bernardino County and opens into lowlands 2.5 miles northwest of Yorba Linda (lat. 33°55' N, long. 117°50'20" W). Named on Yorba Linda (1964) 7.5' quadrangle.

Carbon Canyon Creek: see **Carbon Creek** [ORANGE].

Carbon Canyon Wash: see **Carbon Creek** [ORANGE].

Carbon Creek [ORANGE]: *stream*, flows 17 miles to Coyote Creek [LOS ANGELES-ORANGE] 5.5 miles southwest of Buena Park civic center (lat. 33°48'55" N, long. 118°04'10" W; near N line sec. 19, T 4 S, R 11 W). Named on Anaheim (1965), Los Alamitos (1964), and Orange (1964) 7.5' quadrangles. Called Carbon Canyon Creek on Anaheim (1950), Orange (1950), and Yorba Linda (1950) 7.5' quadrangles. Anaheim (1950) 7.5' quadrangle also has the name "Carbon Canyon Wash" for part of the feature (sec. 9, T 4 S, R 10 W).

Carbondale: see **Silverado Canyon** [ORANGE].

Cardiff: see **Cardiff-by-the-Sea** [SAN DIEGO].

Cardiff-by-the-Sea [SAN DIEGO]: *town*, 1.5 miles south-southeast of Encinitas (lat. 33°01'10" N, long. 117°16'45" W); the place is northwest of San Elijo Lagoon. Named on Encinitas (1968) 7.5' quadrangle. California Mining Bureau's (1917b) map shows a place called Cardiff located along the railroad at the site. J. Frank Cullen laid out the town in 1911 and named it for the seaport in Wales; the place first was called San Elijo (Gudde, 1949, p. 56).

Carey: see **Saugus** [LOS ANGELES].

Carl: see **Carlsbad** [SAN DIEGO].

Carlos Canyon [LOS ANGELES]: *canyon*, drained by a stream that flows 2 miles to Piru Creek 10 miles south-southeast of Gorman (lat. 34°39'30" N, long. 118°46'55" W; sec. 34, T 7 N, R 18 W). Named on Black Mountain (1958) 7.5' quadrangle.

Carlsbad [SAN DIEGO]: *city*, 3 miles southeast of downtown Oceanside (lat. 33°09'50" N, long. 117°20'30" W). Named on San Luis Rey (1968) and San Marcos (1968) 7.5' quadrangles. Postal authorities established Carlsbad post office in 1886, discontinued it in 1909, and reestablished it in 1910 (Salley, p. 38). The place first was called Frazier's Station for John Frazier, who homesteaded there in 1883; Frazier discovered mineral water in a well dug in 1886, and when analysis showed the water to be like that at Karlsbad in Bohemia, Frazier changed the name of the place to Carlsbad—the abbreviated name "Carl" was used at the time of anti-German feeling during World War I (Stein, p. 24). Postal authorities established Seda post office 2.5 miles south of Carlsbad in 1895 and discontinued it in 1897 (Salley, p. 200).

Carlsbad: see **North Carlsbad** [SAN DIEGO].

Carl Spring [SAN DIEGO]: *spring*, 3.5 miles south of Descanso (lat. 32°48'15" N, long. 116°37'25" W; sec. 1, T 16 S, R 3 E). Named on Descanso (1960) 7.5' quadrangle.

Carlton [ORANGE]: *locality*, 1.5 miles west-northwest of Yorba Linda along Pacific Electric Railroad (lat. 33°54'05" N, long. 117° 50'10" W; near NW cor. sec. 21, T 3 S, R 9 W). Named on Yorba Linda (1950) 7.5' quadrangle. The place preserves the name of a community called Carlton that started in 1887; by the middle of 1889 the residents were leaving, and eventually the buildings were hauled away (Carpenter, p. 94).

Carlton Hills [SAN DIEGO]: *locality*, 4.5 miles north-northwest of El Cajon city hall (lat. 32°51'10" N, long. 116°59'45" W). Named on El Cajon (1967) 7.5' quadrangle.

Carmel Cove [SAN DIEGO]: *embayment*, 5.25 south-southeast of Point La Jolla off Mission Bay (lat. 32°46'40" N, long. 117°14'55" W); the feature is just west of El Carmel Point. Named on La Jolla (1953) 7.5' quadrangle. La Jolla (1967) 7.5' quadrangle shows the embayment as part of Santa Barbara Cove.

Carmel Mountain [SAN DIEGO]: *peak*, 3.5 miles southeast of Del Mar (lat. 32°55'50" N, long. 117°13' W; sec. 29, T 14 S, R 3 W). Altitude 427 feet. Named on Del Mar (1967) 7.5' quadrangle.

Carmel Valley [SAN DIEGO]: *canyon*, 3.25 miles long, opens into Soledad Valley 2.5 miles southeast of Del Mar (lat. 32°55'45" N, long. 117°14'30" W; near NE cor. sec. 25, T 14 S, R 4 W). Named on Del Mar (1967) 7.5' quadrangle. The feature divides at the head to form McGonigle Canyon and Deer Canyon. On La Jolla (1903) 15' quadrangle, present Carmel Valley is shown as the lower part of McGonigle Canyon.

Carmenita [LOS ANGELES]: *locality*, 5.5 miles south of present Whittier city hall (lat. 33°53'25" N, long. 118°02'40" W; near SW cor. sec. 21, T 3 S, R 11 W). Named on Whittier (1949) 7.5' quadrangle. Postal authorities established Carmenita post office in 1887 and discontinued it in 1892 (Frickstad, p. 71).

Carmicle: see **Kevet** [VENTURA].

Carney Canyon [SAN DIEGO]: *canyon*, drained by a stream that flows 5 miles to Temescal Creek (1) 5 miles west-southwest of Mesa Grande (lat. 33°09'05" N, long. 116°51' W; near N line sec. 11, T 12 S, R 1 E). Named on Mesa Grande (1948) 7.5' quadrangle. The name commemorates William Carney, a stockman in the neighborhood (Stein, p. 25).

Carr Canyon [LOS ANGELES]: *canyon*, drained by a stream that flows 3 miles to Little Rock Wash 7 miles southeast of Palmdale (lat. 34°30'35" N, long. 118°01'20" W; sec. 22, T 5 N, R 11 W). Named on Juniper Hills (1959), Pacifico Mountain (1959), and Palmdale (1958) 7.5' quadrangles.

Carrista Creek [SAN DIEGO]: *stream*, flows 3 miles to Carrizo Creek (1) at Morettis Junction (lat. 33°12' N, long. 116°42'35" W). Named on Warners Ranch (1960) 7.5' quadrangle.

Carrizo Badlands [SAN DIEGO]: *area*, northeast of the lower part of Carrizo Valley; extends southeast across San Diego-Imperial County line 5 miles east-northeast of Sweeney Pass. Named on Carrizo Mountain (1957) and Sweeney Pass (1959) 7.5' quadrangles.

Carrizo Canyon [SAN DIEGO]: *canyon*, 7.5 miles long, drained by Carrizo Creek (2) above a point 1.5 miles west-northwest of Sweeney Pass (lat. 32°50'15" N, long. 116°12'10" W; sec. 25, T 15 S, R 7 E). Named on Jacumba (1959) and Sweeney Pass (1959) 7.5' quadrangles. United States Board on Geographic Names (1961b, p. 9) rejected the name "Carrizo Gorge" for the feature.

Carrizo Canyon: see **Carrizo Gorge** [SAN DIEGO] (1).

Carrizo Creek [SAN DIEGO]:

(1) *stream*, flows 6.5 miles to Lake Henshaw 0.5 mile northwest of Morettis Junction (lat. 33°12'20" N, long. 116°43' W). Named on Warners Ranch (1960) 7.5' quadrangle.

(2) *stream*, flows 11 miles to Imperial County 5.5 miles northeast of Sweeney Pass (lat. 32°52'30" N, long. 116°06'10" W; at E line sec. 12, T 15 S, R 8 E). Named on Arroyo Tapiado (1959), Carrizo Mountain (1957), Carrizo Mountain NE (1957), and Sweeney Pass (1959) 7.5' quadrangles. United States Board on Geographic Names (1961b, p. 9) rejected the name "Carrizo Wash" for the feature. Emory (p. 103) used the form "Cariso creek" for the name.

Carrizo Gorge [SAN DIEGO]:

(1) *canyon*, 6.5 miles long, along Carrizo Creek (2) above a point 9 miles north of Jacumba (lat. 32°44'45" N, long. 116°11'45" W; sec. 30, T 16 S,

R 8 E); the feature is upstream from Carrizo Canyon. Named on Jacumba (1959) 7.5' quadrangle. United States Board on Geographic Names (1961b, p. 10) rejected the name "Carrizo Canyon" for the feature.
(2) *locality,* 6.25 miles north of Jacumba along San Diego and Arizona Eastern Railroad (lat. 32°42'40" N, long. 116°11'35" W; near N line sec. 7, T 17 S, R 8 E); the place is on the east side of Carrizo Gorge (1). Named on Jacumba (1959) 7.5' quadrangle.

Carrizo Gorge: see **Carrizo Canyon** [SAN DIEGO].

Carrizo Valley [SAN DIEGO]: *valley,* 4 miles north-northwest of Sweeney Pass (lat. 32°53'15" N, long. 116°12'15" W). Named on Agua Caliente Springs (1959), Arroyo Tapiado (1959), and Sweeney Pass (1959) 7.5' quadrangles. Hanks' (1886a) map has the name "Colorado Pass" along present Carrizo Valley.

Carrizo Wash: see **Carrizo Creek** [SAN DIEGO] (2).

Carroll Canyon [SAN DIEGO]: *canyon,* drained by a stream that flows 8.5 miles to Soledad Canyon 6.25 miles southeast of Del Mar (lat. 32°53'25" N, long. 117°11'35" W; near N line sec. 9, T 15 S, R 3 W). Named on Del Mar (1967) and Poway (1967) 7.5' quadrangles. The name commemorates Thomas Carroll, an early rancher in the neighborhood (Stein, p. 26).

Carson [LOS ANGELES]: *city,* 3.5 miles east of Torrance city hall (lat. 33°49'45" N, long. 118°17' W). Named on Torrance (1964) 7.5' quadrangle. Postal authorities established North Wilmington post office in 1953 and changed the name to Carson in 1955 (Salley, p. 157). The city incorporated in 1968.

Carter's Camp: see **Little Santa Anita Canyon** [LOS ANGELES].

Casa de Oro [SAN DIEGO]: *town,* 6.5 miles west-northwest of Jamul (lat. 32°44'50" N, long. 116°58'45" W). Named on El Cajon (1967) and Jamul Mountains (1955) 7.5' quadrangles.

Casa Desierto: see **Redman** [LOS ANGELES].

Casa Loma: see **Yorba Linda** [ORANGE].

Casa Verdugo: see **Tropico** [LOS ANGELES].

Cascade Canyon [LOS ANGELES]: *canyon,* drained by a stream that heads in San Bernardino County and flows 1.25 miles to San Antonio Canyon 12 miles north-northeast of Pomona city hall in Los Angeles County (lat. 34°12'55" N, long. 117°40'05" W; sec. 36, T 2 N, R 8 W). Named on Mount Baldy (1954) 7.5' quadrangle. Called Barrett Can. on Camp Baldy (1940) 6' quadrangle, where present Barrett Canyon is called Kerkhoff Canyon.

Cascade Picnic Area: see **Cascade Public Camp** [LOS ANGELES].

Cascade Public Camp [LOS ANGELES]: *locality,* 2.25 miles east of Mount Wilson (1) in Santa Anita Canyon (lat. 34°13'05" N, long. 118°01'20" W; sec. 34, T 2 N, R 11 W). Named on Mount Wilson (1953) 7.5' quadrangle. Called Cascade Picnic Area on Mount Wilson (1966) 7.5' quadrangle.

Casells: see **Caswell** [LOS ANGELES].

Case Spring [SAN DIEGO]: *spring,* 2 miles west of Margarita Peak (lat. 33°27' N, long. 117°25'20" W; sec. 29, T 8 S, R 5 W). Named on Margarita Peak (1968) 7.5' quadrangle. The name commemorates Alden B. Case, who came to the neighborhood to farm in 1894 (Stein, p. 26).

Casino Point [LOS ANGELES]: *promontory,* 0.25 mile north of Avalon on the northeast side of Santa Catalina Island (lat. 33°20'55" N, long. 118°19'30" W). Named on Santa Catalina East (1950) 7.5' quadrangle. United States Board on Geographic Names (1936a, p. 10) rejected the name "Sugarloaf Point" for the feature.

Casitas [VENTURA]: *locality,* 5.5 miles north of Ventura along Southern Pacific Railroad (lat. 34°21'30" N, long. 119°18'35" W). Named on Ventura (1904) 15' quadrangle.

Casitas: see **Lake Casitas** [VENTURA].

Casitas Creek [VENTURA]: *stream,* flows 2.5 miles to Rincon Creek 6 miles south-southwest of White Ledge Peak (lat. 34°23'45" N, long. 119°27'10" W); the stream heads at West Casitas Pass. Named on White Ledge Peak (1952) 7.5' quadrangle.

Casitas Pass: see **East Casitas Pass** [VENTURA]; **West Casitas Pass** [VENTURA].

Casitas Reservoir: see **Lake Casitas** [VENTURA].

Casitas Springs [VENTURA]: *town,* 6 miles north of Ventura along Ventura River (lat. 34°22' N, long. 119°18'20" W). Named on Ventura (1951) 7.5' quadrangle. Postal authorities established Casitas Springs post office in 1928 and discontinued it in 1969 (Salley, p. 39).

Casitas Valley [VENTURA]: *valley,* 6 miles south of White Ledge Peak (lat. 34°22'55" N, long. 119°24' W; sec. 33, T 4 N, R 24 W); the feature is between East Casitas Pass and West Casitas Pass. Named on White Ledge Peak (1952) 7.5' quadrangle. The name is from little willow-thatched houses used by Indians in the neighborhood—*casitas* means "little houses" in Spanish (Hoover, Rensch, and Rensch, p. 578).

Cassara Canyon [LOS ANGELES]: *canyon,* drained by a stream that flows less than 1 mile to Tujunga Valley 3 miles west-northwest of Sunland (lat. 34°16'45" N, long. 118°21'20" W; at S line sec. 4, T 2 N, R 14 W). Named on Sunland (1966) 7.5' quadrangle.

Castac: see **Castaic** [LOS ANGELES].

Castac Creek: see **Castaic Creek** [LOS ANGELES].

Castac Valley [LOS ANGELES]: *valley,* mainly in Kern County, but extends southwest into Los Angeles County 2.5 miles northwest of Gorman (lat. 34°49'05" N, long. 118°53' W; at N line sec. 3, T 8 N, R 19 W). Named on Frazier Mountain (1958) 7.5' quadrangle. Called Castaic Valley on Frazier Mountain (1944) 7.5' quadrangle, but United States Board on Geographic Names (1960d, p. 16) rejected this designation for the feature. Antisell (p. 91) used the form "Cestek" for the name.

Castac Valley: see **Castaic Valley** [LOS ANGELES].

Castaic [LOS ANGELES]: *town,* 9 miles northwest of Newhall (lat. 34°29'20" N, long. 118°36'55" W; sec. 25, T 5 N, R 17 W); the place is along Castaic Creek in Castaic Valley. Named on Newhall (1952) 7.5' quadrangle. Postal authorities established Castaic post office in 1894, discontinued it in 1895, and reestablished it in 1917 (Frickstad, p. 71). The name is from Castac grant in Kern County (Hanna, p. 58), but United States Board on Geographic Names (1960d, p. 16) rejected the name "Castac" for the town. California Mining Bureau's (1917a) map shows a place called Kemp situated about 4 miles west-southwest of Castaic along the railroad. Los Angeles County (1935) map shows a feature called Nicholson Canyon located west of Castaic (sec. 25, 26, T 5 N, R 17 W).

Castaic: see **Castaic Junction** [LOS ANGELES].

Castaic Afterbay: see **Elderberry Forebay** [LOS ANGELES].

Castaic Canyon: see **Castaic Valley** [LOS ANGELES].

Castaic Creek [LOS ANGELES]: *stream,* flows 23 miles to Santa Clara River 6.5 miles west-northwest of Newhall (lat. 34°25'10" N, long. 118°37'45" W). Named on Liebre Mountain (1958), Newhall (1952), Val Verde (1952), Warm Springs Mountain (1958), and Whitaker Peak (1958) 7.5' quadrangles. Preston (1890a, p. 201) used the form "Castaca Cañon" for the name. United States Board on Geographic Names (1960d, p. 17) rejected the names "Castac Creek" and "Castiac Creek" for the feature. The name is from an Indian village located near the mouth of the stream (Kroeber, p. 37).

Castaic Forebay: see **Elderberry Forebay** [LOS ANGELES].

Castaic Junction [LOS ANGELES]: *locality,* nearly 6 miles northeast of Newhall (lat. 34°26'25" N, long. 118°36'20" W); the place is 3.5 miles south of Castaic, where the road to Castaic joins the road that lies along Santa Clara River. Named on Newhall (1952) 7.5' quadrangle. Santa Susana (1903) 15' quadrangle shows a place called Castaic located along the railroad at the site, and Castaic (1940) 6' quadrangle shows Castaic Sta. there. Newhall (1952, photorevised 1988) 7.5' quadrangle has the name "Valencia" near the place; Valencia is a new town founded after Newhall (1952) 7.5' quadrangle was made. Postal authorities established Valencia post office in 1965 (Salley, p. 229). Los Angeles County (1935) map has the name "San Jose Canyon" for a feature, about 1.5 miles long, that opens into the valley of Santa Clara River from the south near Castaic Junction, and has the name "Potrero Canyon" for a feature, about 2.5 miles long, that is parallel to San Jose Canyon and situated 0.5 mile farther east

Castaic Lagoon [LOS ANGELES]: *lake,* 6.5 miles south-southwest of Warm Springs Mountain along Castaic Creek below the dam that forms Castaic Lake (lat. 34°30'15" N, long. 118°36'30" W; on and near E line sec. 24, T 5 N, R 17 W). Named on Warm Springs Mountain (1958, photorevised 1988) 7.5' quadrangle.

Castaic Lake [LOS ANGELES]: *lake,* behind a dam on Castaic Creek 5.5 miles south-southwest of Warm Springs Mountain (lat. 34°31'10" N, long. 118°36'20" W; on W line sec. 18, T 5 N, R 16 W). Named on Warm Springs Mountain (1958, photorevised 1988) and Whitaker Peak (1958, photorevised 1974) 7.5' quadrangles.

Castaic Pumping Forebay: see **Elderberry Forebay** [LOS ANGELES].

Castaic Pumping Plant Afterbay: see **Elderberry Forebay** [LOS ANGELES].

Castaic Reservoir: see **Elderberry Forebay** [LOS ANGELES].

Castaic Station: see **Castaic Junction** [LOS ANGELES].

Castaic Valley [LOS ANGELES]: *valley,* along Castaic Creek above the entrance of the creek into the valley of Santa Clara River. Named on Newhall (1952) and Warm Springs Mountain (1958) 7.5' quadrangles. Called Castac Valley on Camulos (1903) 30' quadrangle, and Storms (p. 248) mentioned Casteca Cañon. United States Board on Geographic Names (1960d, p. 17) rejected the names "Castac Valley" and "Castaic Canyon" for the feature.

Castaic Valley: see **Castac Valley** [LOS ANGELES].

Casteca Cañon: see **Castaic Valley** [LOS ANGELES].

Castellammare: see **Castellammare Mesa** [LOS ANGELES].

Castellammare Mesa [LOS ANGELES]: *area,* 4.5 miles west-northwest of Santa Monica city hall (lat. 34°02'35" N, long. 118°33'40" W). Named on Topanga (1952) 7.5' quadrangle. Topanga Canyon (1928) 6' quadrangle has the name "Castellammare" for a locality at the place.

Castiac Creek: see **Castaic Creek** [LOS ANGELES].

Castillo Guijarros: see **Fort Rosecrans** [SAN DIEGO].

Castle Canyon [LOS ANGELES]: *canyon,* drained by a stream that flows about 0.5 mile to Rubio Canyon 3.25 miles west of Mount Wilson (1) (lat. 34°12'55" N, long. 118°07' W). Named on Mount Wilson (1966) 7.5' quadrangle.

Castle Canyon [VENTURA]: *canyon,* drained by a stream that flows nearly

4 miles to Cuyama River 7.5 miles northwest of Reyes Peak (lat. 34°42'35" N, long. 119°22'40" W). Named on Reyes Peak (1943) 7.5' quadrangle.

Castle Park [SAN DIEGO]: *district,* 4 miles northeast of Imperial Beach civic center (lat. 32°36'40" N, long. 117°03'45" W). Named on Imperial Beach (1967) 7.5' quadrangle.

Castle Rock [LOS ANGELES]:

(1) *relief feature,* 4.5 miles west-northwest of present Santa Monica city hall along the coast (lat. 34°02'30" N, long. 118°33'55" W). Named on Topanga Canyon (1928) 6' quadrangle.

(2) *rock,* 1.5 miles west of Northwest Harbor on San Clemente Island, and 2000 feet offshore (lat. 33°02'05" N, long. 118°36'50" W). Named on San Clemente Island North (1943) 7.5' quadrangle.

Castro Canyon [SAN DIEGO]: *canyon,* drained by a stream that flows 4.5 miles to Magee Creek nearly 2 miles east-northeast of Pala (lat. 32°22'45" N, long. 117°02'50" W; sec. 24, T 9 S, R 2 W). Named on Pechanga (1968) and Vail Lake (1953) 7.5' quadrangles. Jahns and Wright's (1951b) map has the name "Castro Creek" for the stream in the canyon. The name "Castro" commemorates either Ramon Castro or Zacarias Castro, residents of the canyon (Stein, p. 26).

Castro Creek: see **Castro Canyon** [SAN DIEGO].

Castro Peak [LOS ANGELES]: *peak,* 6 miles north of Point Dume (lat. 34°05'10" N, long. 118°47'05" W; sec. 17, T 1 S, R 18 W). Altitude 2824 feet. Named on Point Dume (1951) 7.5' quadrangle. Los Angeles County (1935) map shows a place called Backus Summit situated 1.25 miles west of Castro Peak.

Caswell [LOS ANGELES]: *locality,* 5.5 miles south-southeast of Gorman in Peace Valley (lat. 34°43'20" N, long. 118°47'50" W; at S line sec. 4, T 7 N, R 18 W). Named on Black Mountain (1958) 7.5' quadrangle. Called Casells on Black Mountain (1943) 7.5' quadrangle.

Catalina Channel: see **San Pedro Channel** [LOS ANGELES].

Catalina Harbor [LOS ANGELES]: *embayment,* 4 miles east-southeast of Silver Peak on the south side of Santa Catalina Island (lat. 33°25'45" N, long. 118°30'25" W). Named on Santa Catalina West (1943) 7.5' quadrangle.

Catalina Head [LOS ANGELES]: *peak,* 4 miles southeast of Silver Peak on Santa Catalina Island (lat. 33°25'25" N, long. 118°30'50" W); the feature is just west of the entrance to Catalina Harbor. Named on Santa Catalina West (1943) 7.5' quadrangle.

Catalina-on-the-Main: see **Arch Beach** [ORANGE].

Cataract Canyon: see **Big Canyon** [VENTURA].

Cat Canyon [LOS ANGELES]: *canyon,* drained by a stream that flows nearly 1 mile to San Antonio Canyon 11 miles north-northeast of Pomona city hall (lat. 34°11'50" N, long. 117°40'35" W; sec. 1, T 1 N, R 8 W). Named on Mount Baldy (1954) 7.5' quadrangle.

Catfish Spring [SAN DIEGO]: *spring,* 4 miles south of San Felipe (lat. 33°08'35" N, long. 116°35'15" W; sec. 8, T 12 S, R 4 E). Named on Ranchita (1960) 7.5' quadrangle.

Catharina Creek [VENTURA]: *stream,* flows 1.5 miles to Rincon Creek 4 miles southwest of White Ledge Peak (lat. 34°25'45" N, long. 119°26'35" W; near E line sec. 13, T 4 N, R 25 W). Named on White Ledge Peak (1952) 7.5' quadrangle. Called East Fork [of Rincon Creek] on Ventura (1904) 15' quadrangle.

Cat Rock [VENTURA]: *island,* 425 feet long, off the south side of the western Anacapa Island (lat. 34°00'15" N, long. 119°25'15" W). Named on Anacapa Island (1973) quadrangle.

Cattle Canyon [LOS ANGELES]: *canyon,* 8.5 miles long, opens into the canyon of San Gabriel River 8.5 miles northeast of Glendora city hall (lat. 34°13'45" N, long. 117°46'05" W). Named on Glendora (1953), Mount Baldy (1954), and Mount San Antonio (1955) 7.5' quadrangles.

Caula: see **Camp Caula** [LOS ANGELES].

Cavin [VENTURA]: *locality,* 3.5 miles west-southwest of Piru along Southern Pacific Railroad (lat. 34°23'40" N, long. 118°51' W; near SE cor. sec. 27, T 4 N, R 19 W). Named on Piru (1952) 7.5' quadrangle. California Division of Highways' (1934) map shows a place called Wilshire located 1.5 miles west of Cavin along the railroad.

CCC Ridge [LOS ANGELES]: *ridge,* southeast-trending, 1 mile long, 5 miles south-southeast of Condor Peak (lat. 34°15'25" N, long. 118°11'30" W; mainly in sec. 13, T 2 N, R 13 W). Named on Condor Peak (1959) 7.5' quadrangle.

Cedar Camp: see **Fish Fork** [LOS ANGELES].

Cedar Canyon [LOS ANGELES]:

(1) *canyon,* drained by a stream that flows less than 1 mile to Arroyo Seco 9 miles south-southwest of Pacifico Mountain (lat. 34°15'15" N, long. 118°05' W). Named on Chilao Flat (1959) and Mount Wilson (1953) 7.5' quadrangles.

(2) *canyon,* drained by a stream that flows 1.5 miles to Mescal Creek 2 miles northwest of Big Pines (lat. 34°23'45" N, long. 117° 43' W). Named on Mescal Creek (1956) 7.5' quadrangle.

(3) *canyon,* drained by a stream that flows 1 mile to Cogswell Reservoir 8.5 miles north-northwest of Azusa city hall (lat. 34° 14'10" N, long. 117°59'10" W; near N line sec. 25, T 2 N, R 11 W). Named on Azusa (1953) 7.5' quadrangle.

Cedar Canyon [SAN DIEGO]: *canyon,* drained by a stream that flows 5 miles to Dulzura Creek 4.5 miles south-southeast of Jamul (lat. 32°39'05" N, long. 116°51'10" W). Named on Dulzura (1972) and Otay Mountain (1972) 7.5' quadrangles.

Cedar Canyon: see **Little Cedar Canyon** [SAN DIEGO].

Cedar Creek [LOS ANGELES]: *stream,* flows 2.25 miles to Soldier Creek 1 mile east-southeast of Crystal Lake (lat. 34°18'40" N, long. 117°50' W). Named on Crystal Lake (1958) 7.5' quadrangle.

Cedar Creek [SAN DIEGO]:

(1) *stream,* flows nearly 4 miles to San Luis Rey River 5.5 miles southeast of Boucher Hill (lat. 33°16'15" N, long. 116°51'10" W; at N line sec. 35, T 10 S, R 1 E). Named on Palomar Observatory (1949) 7.5' quadrangle.

(2) *stream,* flows 10.5 miles to San Diego River 12 miles northwest of Descanso (lat. 32°59'15" N, long. 116°44'25" W; sec. 2, T 14 S, R 2 E). Named on Julian (1960), Santa Ysabel (1960), and Tule Springs (1960) 7.5' quadrangles.

Cedar Creek [VENTURA]: *stream,* flows nearly 2 miles to South Fork Piru Creek 8.5 miles east of Reyes Peak (lat. 34°38'15" N, long. 119°07'35" W; sec. 5, T 6 N, R 21 W). Named on San Guillermo (1943) 7.5' quadrangle. United States Board on Geographic Names (1990, p. 6) rejected the name "South Fork Piru Creek" for the stream.

Cedar Creek: see **Big Cedar Creek** [VENTURA].

Cedar Creek Falls [SAN DIEGO]: *waterfall,* 11.5 miles north-northwest of Descanso (lat. 32°59'25" N, long. 116°43'45" W; near N line sec. 1, T 14 S, R 2 E); the feature is along Cedar Creek (2). Named on Tule Springs (1960) 7.5' quadrangle.

Cedar Glen Camp [SAN DIEGO]: *locality,* 2.25 miles north of Julian along Dan Price Creek (lat. 33°06'35" N, long. 116°35'30" W; near S line sec. 20, T 12 S, R 4 E). Named on Julian (1960) 7.5' quadrangle.

Cedars Campground: see **Little Cedars Campground** [LOS ANGELES].

Cedar Springs [LOS ANGELES]: *locality,* 3 miles east-northeast of Waterman Mountain (lat. 34°21'05" N, long. 117°53'05" W; near NW cor. sec. 13, T 3 N, R 10 W). Named on Waterman Mountain (1959) 7.5' quadrangle. Crystal Lake (1941) 6' quadrangle shows a spring called Cedar Spring at the site.

Celery [ORANGE]: *locality,* 2.5 miles southeast of present Huntington Beach civic center along Southern Pacific Railroad (lat. 33° 38' N, long. 117°58' W). Named on Santa Ana (1901) 15' quadrangle.

Cemetery Barranca: see **Sanjon Barranca** [VENTURA].

Cemetery Ravine: see **Chavez Ravine** [LOS ANGELES].

Centennial Creek [VENTURA]: *stream,* flows 1.5 miles to Little Sespe Creek 4 miles north of Fillmore (lat. 34°27'40" N, long. 118° 54'35" W; sec. 6, T 4 N, R 19 W). Named on Fillmore (1951) 7.5' quadrangle.

Center Creek [LOS ANGELES]: *stream,* flows 1 mile to Gold Creek 4.25 miles north of Sunland (lat. 34°19'20" N, long. 118°18'40" W; at N line sec. 26, T 3 N, R 14 W). Named on Sunland (1953) 7.5' quadrangle.

Centinela [LOS ANGELES]: *locality,* less than 1 mile northeast of present Inglewood city hall along Atchison, Topeka and Santa Fe Railroad (lat. 33°58'15" N, long. 118°20'30" W); the place is on Aguaje de la Centinela grant. Named on Redondo (1896) 15' quadrangle. Postal authorities established Centinela post office in 1889 and discontinued it in 1895 (Salley, p. 41).

Centinela Creek [LOS ANGELES]: *stream,* flows 7.5 miles to Ballona Lagoon about 5.5 miles north-northwest of present Manhattan Beach city hall (lat. 33°57'45" N, long. 118°27' W); the stream heads near Centinela. Named on Redondo (1896) 15' quadrangle. Venice (1964) 7.5' quadrangle shows a feature called Centinela Creek Channel that joins Ballona Creek 2.25 miles above the mouth of that creek.

Centinela Valley Camp [LOS ANGELES]: *locality,* 0.5 mile northwest of Big Pines (lat. 34°23'05" N, long. 117°41'50" W). Named on Mescal Creek (1956) 7.5' quadrangle.

Central Avenue [LOS ANGELES]: *locality,* 5.5 miles east-northeast of present Inglewood city hall along Atchison, Topeka and Santa Fe Railroad (lat. 33°59'10" N, long. 118°15'20" W). Named on Redondo (1896) 15' quadrangle.

Centro: see **Covina** [LOS ANGELES].

Cerrito de las Ranas: see **Red Hill** [ORANGE].

Cerritos [LOS ANGELES]: *city,* 10 miles northeast of Long Beach city hall (lat. 33°51'30" N, long. 118°03'30" W). Named on Los Alamitos (1964, photorevised 1981) and Whittier, (1965, photorevised 1981) 7.5' quadrangles. Called Dairy Valley on Los Alamitos (1964) and Whittier (1965) 7.5' quadrangles. Postal authorities established Dairy Valley post office in 1962 and changed the name to Cerritos in 1967 (Salley, p. 54). The city incorporated with the name "Dairy Valley" in 1956, and changed the name to Cerritos in 1967. The place was incorporated to preserve the land for dairy farms, but by the late 1960's most of the dairy activity was gone (Van Kampen, p. 39, 41, 43).

Cerritos: see **Elftman** [LOS ANGELES].

Cerritos Channel [LOS ANGELES]: *water feature,* 3 miles west of Long Beach city hall between Terminal Island and the mainland (lat. 33°45'55"

N, long. 118°14'30" W). Named on Long Beach (1964) and Torrance (1964) 7.5' quadrangles.

Cerro Colorado: see **Red Hill** [ORANGE].

Cerro de la Calavera [SAN DIEGO]: *peak,* 6 miles east-southeast of Oceanside (lat. 33°10'05" N, long. 117°16'50" W). Altitude 513 feet. Named on San Luis Rey (1968) 7.5' quadrangle.

Cerro de la Hechicera [SAN DIEGO]: *ridge,* north-northwest-trending, 1 mile long, 1.5 miles south-southeast of San Felipe (lat. 33° 10'45" N, long. 116°35'15" W; mainly in sec. 32, T 11 S, R 4 E). Named on Ranchita (1960) 7.5' quadrangle.

Cerro de las Posas [SAN DIEGO]: *ridge,* northwest- to west-trending, 1 mile long, 6.25 miles north of Rancho Santa Fe (lat. 33°06'40" N, long. 117°11'45" W; on S line sec. 21, T 12 S, R 3 W). Named on Rancho Santa Fe (1968) 7.5' quadrangle. On San Luis Rey (1898) 30' quadrangle, the name applies to a ridge that extends west for 3 miles from Mount Whitney, and that includes present Cerro de las Posas.

Cerro Villa Heights [ORANGE]: *locality,* 4 miles northeast of Orange city hall (lat. 33°49'35" N, long. 117°48'05" W). Named on Orange (1964) 7.5' quadrangle.

Chaffee Island: see **Island Chaffee** [LOS ANGELES].

Chalk Hills [LOS ANGELES]: *ridge,* north-northwest-trending, 2 miles long, 2.5 miles south-southeast of Canoga Park (lat. 34°10'10" N, long. 118°34'40" W). Named on Canoga Park (1952) 7.5' quadrangle.

Chandler Canyon [LOS ANGELES]: *canyon,* 1 mile long, 3.5 miles northwest of Burbank city hall (lat. 34°13'30" N, long. 118°20'35" W; sec. 27, 28, T 2 N, R 14 W). Named on Burbank (1953) 7.5' quadrangle.

Chandlers [LOS ANGELES]: *locality,* 2 miles west-northwest of Gorman (lat. 34°48'40" N, long. 118°53' W). Named on Frazier Mountain (1944) 7.5' quadrangle. Called Chandler on Gorman (1938) 6' quadrangle.

Chaneys Point [ORANGE]: *promontory,* 0.5 mile south of Laguna Beach city hall along the coast (lat. 33°32'15" N, long. 117°46'45" W; at W line sec. 25, T 7 S, R 9 W). Named on Laguna Beach (1965) 7.5' quadrangle.

Channel Islands: see **Santa Barbara Channel** [VENTURA].

Channel Islands Harbor: see **Port Hueneme** [VENTURA].

Channing Meadow [SAN DIEGO]: *area,* 3.25 miles north-northeast of Buckman Springs (lat. 32°48'50" N, long. 116°28'10" W; on N line sec. 4, T 16 S, R 5 E). Named on Mount Laguna (1960) 7.5' quadrangle.

Chantry Flat [LOS ANGELES]: *area,* 3 miles southeast of Mount Wilson (1) (lat. 34°11'40" N, long. 118°01'20" W; on S line sec. 3, T 1 N, R 11 W). Named on Mount Wilson (1953) 7.5' quadrangle. Called Chantry Flats on Los Angeles County (1935) map. Charles E. Chantry received use of 20 acres at the place in 1907 (Owens, p. 17-18).

Chaparral Campground [LOS ANGELES]: *locality,* 8.5 miles south-southeast of the village of Lake Hughes (lat. 34°33'30" N, long. 118°24'20" W; near N line sec. 1, T 5 N, R 15 W). Named on Green Valley (1958) 7.5' quadrangle.

Chapman [LOS ANGELES]: *locality,* 6.5 miles south of Mount Wilson (1) along Southern Pacific Railroad (lat. 34°07'35" N, long. 118°04'30" W). Named on Pasadena (1900) 15' quadrangle.

Chapman: see **Chapman Siding** [LOS ANGELES].

Chapman Siding [LOS ANGELES]: *locality,* 5.25 miles south-southwest of Mount Wilson (1) along Atchison, Topeka and Santa Fe Railroad (lat. 34°08'55" N, long. 118°04'55" W). Named on Mount Wilson (1953) 7.5' quadrangle. Mount Wilson (1966) 7.5' quadrangle has the name "Chapman" at the place.

Chappo [SAN DIEGO]: *locality,* 9 miles southwest of Fallbrook along Atchison, Topeka and Santa Fe Railroad (lat. 33°17'35" N, long. 117°21'40" W; near W line sec. 24, T 10 S, R 5 W). Named on Morro Hill (1968) 7.5' quadrangle.

Chariot Canyon [SAN DIEGO]: *canyon,* drained by a stream that flows 5.5 miles to Banner Canyon 3 miles east-southeast of Julian (lat. 33°04'05" N, long. 116°33' W; near E line sec. 3, T 13 S, R 4 E). Named on Julian (1960) 7.5' quadrangle. The feature first was called San Felipe Canyon; the name "Chariot Canyon" is from Golden Chariot mine that George N. King discovered in 1871 (Gudde, 1975, p. 27, 68).

Chariot Mountain [SAN DIEGO]: *ridge,* west- to southwest-trending, 1.5 miles long, 6.5 miles southeast of Julian (lat. 33°01'30" N, long. 116°30'30" W). Named on Earthquake Valley (1959) and Julian (1960) 7.5' quadrangles.

Charles Cañon: see **Charlie Canyon** [LOS ANGELES].

Charlie Canyon [LOS ANGELES]: *canyon,* drained by a stream that flows 9 miles to Castaic Valley 8 miles north-northwest of Newhall (lat. 34°29' N, long. 118°36'30" W; near SE cor. sec. 25, T 5 N, R 17 W). Named on Newhall (1952) and Warm Springs Mountain (1958) 7.5' quadrangles. Preston (1890a, p. 202) called the feature Charles Cañon.

Charlton Flats [LOS ANGELES]: *area,* 5.5 miles south of Pacifico Mountain along East Fork Alder Creek (lat. 34°18'15" N, long. 118°01' W). Named on Alder Creek (1941) 6' quadrangle. The place first was called Pine Flat, but in 1925 the name was changed to honor Rush H. Charlton, who was retiring as forest supervisor (Robinson, J.W., 1977, p. 193).

Charlton Flats Picnic Ground [LOS ANGELES]: *locality,* 6 miles south of Pacifico Mountain (lat. 34°17'40" N, long. 118°01'05" W; at N line sec. 3, T 2 N, R 11 W); the place is at the south end of Charlton Flats. Named on Chilao Flat (1959) 7.5' quadrangle.

Charlton Station [LOS ANGELES]: *locality,* 6 miles south-southeast of Pacifico Mountain (lat. 34°17'55" N, long. 118°00'20" W; near S line sec. 35, T 3 N, R 11 W). Named on Chilao Flat (1959) 7.5' quadrangle.

Charter Oak [LOS ANGELES]: *district,* 6.5 miles west-northwest of Pomona city hall (lat. 34°06' N, long. 117°51' W). Named on San Dimas (1966) 7.5' quadrangle. Postal authorities established Charter Oak post office in 1899, discontinued it in 1954, and reestablished it in 1956 (Salley, p. 42).

Charter Oak Creek [LOS ANGELES]: *stream,* flows 3 miles to Walnut Creek 3.25 miles east-southeast of Baldwin Park city hall (lat. 34°04'10" N, long. 117°53'10" W); the stream heads at Charter Oak district. Named on Baldwin Park (1966) and San Dimas (1966) 7.5' quadrangles.

Chatsworth [LOS ANGELES]: *district,* 9 miles west-southwest of San Fernando in Los Angeles (lat. 34°15'25" N, long. 118°36'20" W). Named on Oat Mountain (1952) 7.5' quadrangle. Called Chatworth on California Mining Bureau's (1909b) map. Postal authorities established Chatsworth post office in 1890 and moved it 0.75 mile south in 1898 (Salley, p. 42). The name is from Chatsworth, England (Gudde, 1949, p. 64). California Mining Bureau's (1917a) map shows a place called Hasson located along the railroad northwest of Chatsworth near present Santa Susana Pass. The same map shows a place called Pisgah Grande situated about 11 miles north-northwest of Chatsworth, and north-northwest of Hasson. Postal authorities established Pisgah Grande post office 10 miles northwest of Chatsworth post office (sec. 15, T 3 N, R 17 W) in 1915 and discontinued it in 1920 (Salley, p. 173)—Finis E. Yoakum founded a religious utopian colony at the place (Hoover, Rensch, and Rensch, p. 169).

Chatsworth Creek [LOS ANGELES]: *stream,* flows 2 miles to Bell Creek 1.25 miles west of the center of Canoga Park (lat. 34°11'55" N, long. 118°37' W); the stream heads at Chatsworth Reservoir. Named on Calabasas (1952) and Canoga Park (1952) 7.5' quadrangles.

Chatsworth Lake Manor [LOS ANGELES-VENTURA]: *locality,* 2 miles south of Santa Susana Pass on Los Angeles-Ventura County line (lat. 34°14'25" N, long. 118°38'05" W); the place is at the north side of Chatsworth Reservoir. Named on Calabasas (1952) 7.5' quadrangle.

Chatsworth Peak [VENTURA]: *peak,* 1 mile south-southwest of Santa Susana Pass (lat. 34°15'25" N, long. 118°38'25" W). Altitude 2314 feet. Named on Santa Susana (1951) 7.5' quadrangle. The name is from the nearby town of Chatsworth [LOS ANGELES] (Ricard).

Chatsworth Reservoir [LOS ANGELES]: *lake,* behind a dam on Chatsworth Creek 2.5 miles south-southwest of Chatsworth (lat. 34°13'35" N, long. 118°37'45" W). Named on Calabasas (1952) and Canoga Park (1952) 7.5' quadrangles.

Chavez Ravine [LOS ANGELES]: *canyon,* 1.5 miles long, 1.25 miles north of Los Angeles city hall (lat. 34°04'30" N, long. 118°14'50" W). Named on Los Angeles (1953) 7.5' quadrangle. Stevenson's (1884) map shows four south-trending canyons east of Chavez Ravine between the ravine and Los Angeles River: Sulphur Ravine, just east of Chavez Ravine; Cemetery Ravine, the second canyon to the east; Solano Ravine, the third canyon to the east; and Reservoir Ravine, the canyon farthest to the east. Hanson's (1868) map has the name "Stone Quarry Hills" for the range that contains Chavez Ravine and the four canyons.

Cheeseboro Canyon [LOS ANGELES-VENTURA]: *canyon,* drained by a stream that heads in Ventura County and flows 5 miles to Palo Comado Canyon 0.5 miles north-northeast of Agoura in Los Angeles County (lat. 34°09'05" N, long. 118°44' W). Named on Calabasas (1952) 7.5' quadrangle.

Cherry Canyon [LOS ANGELES]:

(1) *canyon,* drained by a stream that flows 2.5 miles to Piru Creek 3.5 miles north of Whitaker Peak (lat. 34°37'20" N, long. 118°44'40" W; near W line sec. 12, T 6 N, R 18 W). Named on Liebre Mountain (1958) and Whitaker Peak (1958) 7.5' quadrangles.

(2) *canyon,* drained by a stream that flows 3.5 miles to San Francisquito Canyon nearly 6 miles south of the village of Lake Hughes (lat. 34°35'25" N, long. 118°26'50" W). Named on Green Valley (1958) 7.5' quadrangle.

Cherry Canyon [SAN DIEGO]: *canyon,* 1.5 miles long, 6 miles north-northeast of San Felipe (lat. 33°14'15" N, long. 116°30'35" W; sec. 6, 7, T 11 S, R 5 E). Named on Ranchita (1960) 7.5' quadrangle.

Cherry Cove [LOS ANGELES]: *embayment,* 4 miles east of Silver Peak on the north side of Santa Catalina Island (lat. 33°27'05" N, long. 118°30'05" W); the feature is at the mouth of Cherry Valley. Named on Santa Catalina West (1943) 7.5' quadrangle. Preston (1890b, p. 280) called the embayment Cherry Valley Harbor.

Cherry Creek [VENTURA]: *stream,* flows 2.5 miles to Sespe Creek 7.5 miles north-northwest of Wheeler Springs (lat. 34°36'15" N, long. 119°21'20" W; near S line sec. 18, T 6 N, R 23 W). Named on Wheeler Springs (1943) 7.5' quadrangle.

Cherry Creek Campground [VENTURA]: *locality,* 7 miles north-northwest of Wheeler Springs (lat. 34°35'50" N, long. 119°21'10" W; sec. 19, T 6 N, R 23 W); the place is along Cherry Creek. Named on Wheeler Springs

(1943) 7.5' quadrangle.

Cherry Flat [SAN DIEGO]: *area,* 0.25 mile north of Cuyamaca Peak (lat. 32°57'05" N, long. 116°36'25" W). Named on Cuyamaca Peak (1960) 7.5' quadrangle.

Cherry Valley [LOS ANGELES]: *canyon,* drained by a stream that flows 1 mile to the sea nearly 4 miles east of Silver Peak on the north side of Santa Catalina Island (lat. 33°27' N, long. 118°30'05" W). Named on Santa Catalina West (1943) 7.5' quadrangle.

Cherry Valley Harbor: see **Cherry Cove** [LOS ANGELES].

Chicarita Creek [SAN DIEGO]: *stream,* flows 3 miles to Los Peñasquitos Canyon 3.5 miles west-southwest of Poway (lat. 32°56'50" N, long. 117°05'50" W; near NE cor. sec. 21, T 14 S, R 2 W). Named on Poway (1967) 7.5' quadrangle.

Chicken Canyon [LOS ANGELES]: *canyon,* 0.5 mile long, 8 miles north-northeast of Pomona city hall (lat. 34°09'30" N, long. 117° 41'35" W; sec. 23, T 1 N, R 8 W). Named on Mount Baldy (1954) 7.5' quadrangle.

Chico Ravine [SAN DIEGO]: *canyon,* drained by a stream that flows less than 1 mile to Los Rasalies Ravine nearly 7 miles north-northeast of Buckman Springs (lat. 32°52' N, long. 116°27'10" W; sec. 15, T 15 S, R 5 E). Named on Mount Laguna (1960) 7.5' quadrangle.

Chief Mountain [SAN DIEGO]: *peak,* 2 miles northeast of Pala (lat. 33°23'15" N, long. 117°02'55" W; at SW cor. sec. 13, T 9 S, R 2 W). Altitude 502 feet. Named on Pechanga (1968) 7.5' quadrangle, which shows Pala Chief mine situated 500 feet west of the peak.

Chief Mountain: see **Little Chief Mountain** [SAN DIEGO].

Chihuahua Creek [SAN DIEGO]: *stream,* flows 13 miles to Temecula Creek nearly 8 miles northeast of Boucher Hill (lat. 33°23'50" N, long. 116°48'30" W; near NE cor. sec. 18, T 9 S, R 2 E); the stream drains Chihuahua Valley. Named on Aguanga (1954) and Beauty Mountain (1960) 7.5' quadrangles. On Ramona (1903) 30' quadrangle, the name applies to the stream in present Cooper Canyon.

Chihuahua Valley [SAN DIEGO]: *valley,* 7.5 miles north-northwest of Warner Springs (lat. 33°23'15" N, long. 116°40' W). Named on Beauty Mountain (1960), Hot Springs Mountain (1960), and Warner Springs (1959) 7.5' quadrangles. Jose Melandras, a goatherd, named the feature for his native state in Mexico (Stein, p. 27-28).

Chilao Campground [LOS ANGELES]: *locality,* 4 miles south of Pacifico Mountain (lat. 34°19'25" N, long. 118°01'05" W; near N line sec. 27, T 3 N, R 11 W); the place is at Chilao Flat. Named on Chilao Flat (1959) 7.5' quadrangle.

Chilao Creek [LOS ANGELES]: *stream,* flows 3.5 miles to East Fork Alder Creek (2) 4 miles south of Pacifico Mountain (lat. 34°19'20" N, long. 118°01'35" W; near NW cor. sec. 27, T 3 N, R 11 W). Named on Chilao Flat (1959) and Waterman Mountain (1959) 7.5' quadrangles.

Chilao Flat [LOS ANGELES]: *area,* 3.5 miles south of Pacifico Mountain (lat. 34°19'50" N, long. 118°01'20" W; mainly in sec. 21, 22, T 3 N, R 11 W). Named on Chilao Flat (1959) 7.5' quadrangle. Called Pine Flats on Tujunga (1900) 15' quadrangle. The name is for Chileo Silvas, who reportedly herded cattle and lassoed bears at the place for 40 years (Robinson, J.W., 1983, p. 217).

Chilao Station [LOS ANGELES]: *locality,* nearly 4 miles south-southeast of Pacifico Mountain (lat. 34°19'40" N, long. 118°00'30" W; sec. 22, T 3 N, R 11 W); the place is at Chilao Flat. Named on Chilao Flat (1959) 7.5' quadrangle.

Childs Canyon [LOS ANGELES]: *canyon,* 1 mile long, 1.5 miles northeast of Burbank city hall (lat. 34°11'30" N, long. 118°16'35" W). Named on Burbank (1953) 7.5' quadrangle.

Chileno Canyon [LOS ANGELES]: *canyon,* drained by a stream that flows 2.25 miles to West Fork San Gabriel River 8 miles north-northwest of Azusa city hall (lat. 34°14'30" N, long. 117°56'55" W). Named on Azusa (1953) and Waterman Mountain (1959) 7.5' quadrangles.

Chimney Canyon [LOS ANGELES]: *canyon,* drained by a stream that flows nearly 1.5 miles to Pacoima Canyon 2.5 miles north of Condor Peak (lat. 34°21'40" N, long. 118°12'35" W). Named on Acton (1959) and Condor Peak (1959) 7.5' quadrangles.

Chimney Creek [SAN DIEGO]: *stream,* flows 1 mile to Doane Creek 1.5 miles east of Boucher Hill (lat. 33°19'55" N, long. 116°53'30" W; near SW cor. sec. 4, T 10 S, R 1 E). Named on Boucher Hill (1948) 7.5' quadrangle.

Chimney Flats [SAN DIEGO]: *area,* 1.25 miles east of Rodriguez Mountain (lat. 33°14' N, long. 116°52'50" W). Named on Rodriguez Mountain (1948) 7.5' quadrangle.

Chimney Lake [SAN DIEGO]: *intermittent lake,* 1050 feet long, nearly 2 miles west of Warner Springs (lat. 33°16'45" N, long. 116°39'50" W). Named on Warner Springs (1959) 7.5' quadrangle.

Chimney Rock [SAN DIEGO]: *relief feature,* 7 miles west-southwest of Tubb Canyon (lat. 33°13'30" N, long. 116°29'25" W; at S line sec. 8, T 11 S, R 5 E). Named on Tubb Canyon (1959) 7.5' quadrangle.

Chimney Spring [SAN DIEGO]: *spring,* nearly 6 miles west-southwest of Borrego Springs (lat. 33°12'50" N, long. 116°27'40" W; near W line sec. 15, T 11 S, R 5 E). Named on Tubb Canyon (1959) 7.5' quadrangle.

China Flat [VENTURA]: *area,* 4.25 miles northeast of Thousand Oaks (lat. 34°12'30" N, long. 118°46'05" W; near S line sec. 33, T 2 N, R 18 W). Named on Thousand Oaks (1952) 7.5' quadrangle.

China Point [LOS ANGELES]:

(1) *promontory,* 3.5 miles south-southwest of Mount Banning on the south side of Santa Catalina Island (lat. 33°19'45" N, long. 118° 28' W). Named on Santa Catalina South (1943) 7.5' quadrangle.

(2) *promontory,* 4.5 miles west-northwest of Pyramid Point at the south end of San Clemente Island (lat. 32°48'05" N, long. 118°25'30" W). Named on San Clemente Island South (1943) 7.5' quadrangle.

Chino Creek [LOS ANGELES]: *stream,* flows 2 miles to San Bernardino County 2.5 miles south-southeast of Pomona city hall (lat. 34° 01'05" N, long. 117°44'05" W). Named on Ontario (1954) and San Dimas (1954) 7.5' quadrangles.

Chino Flat [VENTURA]: *area,* 2.5 miles north of Piru (lat. 34°27'05" N, long. 118°47'05" W; near N line sec. 8, T 4 N, R 18 W). Named on Piru (1952) 7.5' quadrangle.

Chino Hills [LOS ANGELES-ORANGE]: *range,* extends east in Los Angeles, Orange, and San Bernardino Counties from Brea Canyon to Santa Ana River; the range is south of Chino, which is in San Bernardino County. Named on Prado Dam (1967) and Yorba Linda (1950) 7.5' quadrangles.

Chiquita: see **Camp Chiquita** [LOS ANGELES].

Chiquita Canyon [LOS ANGELES]: *canyon,* 1.5 miles long, 4.25 miles north of Pasadena city hall (lat. 34°12'30" N, long. 118°08'30" W). Named on Pasadena (1953) 7.5' quadrangle. Called Chiquita Ravine on Los Angeles County (1935) map.

Chiquita Ravine: see **Chiquita Canyon** [LOS ANGELES].

Chiquito Peak [SAN DIEGO]: *ridge,* east-trending, 1 mile long, 2 miles west of Descanso (lat. 32°50'55" N, long. 116°39' W). Named on Viejas Mountain (1960) 7.5' quadrangle. Called Descanso Peak on Everhart's (1951) map.

Chiquito Spring [ORANGE]: *spring,* 4.5 miles south of Trabuco Peak (lat. 33°38'20" N, long. 117°28'10" W). Named on Alberhill (1954) 7.5' quadrangle. Kenneth Munhall, a forest ranger, named the spring in 1927 for his horse (Meadows, p. 52).

Chismahoo Creek [VENTURA]: *stream,* flows less than 1 mile to Lake Casitas 8 miles southwest of the town of Ojai (lat. 34°23' N, long. 119°22'10" W). Named on Matilija (1952, photorevised 1967) and White Ledge Peak (1952) 7.5' quadrangles.

Chismahoo Mountain [VENTURA]: *peak,* 2.25 miles southwest of White Ledge Peak (lat. 34°26'40" N, long. 119°25'10" W; sec. 8, T 4 N, R 24 W). Altitude 2923 feet. Named on White Ledge Peak (1952) 7.5' quadrangle.

Chitwood Canyon: see **Acton Camp** [LOS ANGELES].

Chivo Canyon [LOS ANGELES-VENTURA]: *canyon,* drained by a stream that heads in Los Angeles County and flows 5 miles to Simi Valley (1) 4 miles west-northwest of Santa Susana Pass in Ventura County (lat. 34°18' N, long. 118°41'30" W; near E line sec. 31, T 3 N, R 17 W). Named on Santa Susana (1951) 7.5' quadrangle.

Chocolate Canyon [SAN DIEGO]: *canyon,* 2 miles long, 2.5 miles northwest of Alpine (lat. 32°51'30" N, long. 116°48' W; sec. 17, 20, T 15 S, R 2 E). Named on Alpine (1955) 7.5' quadrangle. Cuyamaca (1903) 30' quadrangle has the name "Chocolate Cr." for the stream in the canyon.

Chocolate Creek: see **Chocolate Canyon** [SAN DIEGO].

Chollas Creek [SAN DIEGO]: *stream,* flows nearly 6 miles to San Diego Bay 2.5 miles southeast of downtown San Diego (lat. 32°41'15" N, long. 117°08' W). Named on National City (1967) and Point Loma (1967) 7.5' quadrangles. United States Board on Geographic Names (1968b, p. 5) rejected the name "Las Chollas Creek" for the stream. On Point Loma (1967) 7.5' quadrangle, the name "Chollas Creek Channel" applies to a water feature at the mouth of Chollas Creek.

Chollas Creek Channel: see **Chollas Creek** [SAN DIEGO].

Chollas Reservoir [SAN DIEGO]: *lake,* 1500 feet long, 5 miles north-northeast of National City civic center (lat. 32°44'15" N, long. 117°03'45" W). Named on National City (1967) 7.5' quadrangle.

Chollas Valley [SAN DIEGO]: *canyon,* drained by Chollas Creek, which flows nearly 6 miles to San Diego Bay 2.5 miles southeast of downtown San Diego (lat. 32°41'15" N, long. 117°08' W). Named on La Mesa (1967) and National City (1967) 7.5' quadrangles. Called Las Choyas Valley on La Jolla (1903) 15' quadrangle.

Chollas Valley: see **South Chollas Valley** [SAN DIEGO].

Chorro Grande Canyon [VENTURA]: *canyon,* drained by a stream that flows 3.5 miles to Sespe Creek 6.25 miles north-northwest of Wheeler Springs (lat. 34°35'35" N, long. 119°19'35" W; sec. 21, T 6 N, R 23 W). Named on Reyes Peak (1943) and Wheeler Springs (1943) 7.5' quadrangles.

Chrisman [VENTURA]: *locality,* 1.5 miles north-northwest of downtown Ventura along Southern Pacific Railroad (lat. 34°17'50" N, long. 119°18'05" W). Named on Ventura (1951) 7.5' quadrangle.

Christian: see **Camp Christian** [LOS ANGELES].

Chuchupate Campground [VENTURA]: *locality,* 2 miles west-northwest of Frazier Mountain (lat. 34°47'15" N, long. 118°59'55" W; sec. 16, T 8 N, R 20 W). Named on Frazier Mountain (1958) 7.5' quadrangle. The name is of Indian origin (Ricard).

Chuckwalla Canyon [SAN DIEGO]: *canyon*, about 1 mile long, along Chuckwalla Wash 12 miles east of Julian (lat. 33°06' N, long. 116°24' W). Named on Earthquake Valley (1959) 7.5' quadrangle.

Chuckwalla Wash [SAN DIEGO]: *stream* and *dry wash*, extends for 3.5 miles to San Felipe Creek nearly 8.5 miles south of Borrego Springs (lat. 33°08'10" N, long. 116°21'20" W; sec. 16, T 12 S, R 6 E). Named on Borrego Sink (1959) and Earthquake Valley (1959) 7.5' quadrangles.

Chula Vista [SAN DIEGO]: *city*, 2.5 miles south-southeast of National City civic center (lat. 32°38'25" N, long. 117°05'05" W). Named on Imperial Beach (1967) and National City (1967) 7.5' quadrangles. Postal authorities established Chulavista post office in 1890, and changed the name to Chula Vista in 1906 (Salley, p. 43). The city incorporated in 1911. Officials of San Diego Land and Town Company had the community laid out and named it in 1888 (Gudde, 1949, p. 68). United States Board on Geographic Names (1981, p. 2) approved the name "Chula Vista Small Boat Basin" for a harbor on the east side of San Diego Bay at Chula Vista (lat. 32°37'23" N, long. 117°06'05" W).

Chula Vista Junction [SAN DIEGO]: *locality*, 2.5 miles south of present National City civic center along San Diego and Arizona Eastern Railroad (lat. 32°38'15" N, long. 117°05'50" W); the place is 1 mile west-southwest of downtown Chula Vista. Named on National City (1944) 7.5' quadrangle.

Chula Vista Small Boat Basin: see **Chula Vista** [SAN DIEGO].

Church Rock [LOS ANGELES]: *rock*, 3 miles south of Avalon at the southeast end of Santa Catalina Island, and 750 feet offshore (lat. 33°17'50" N, long. 118°19'35" W). Named on Santa Catalina East (1950) 7.5' quadrangle.

Cibbets Flat [SAN DIEGO]: *area*, 2.5 miles east of Buckman Springs at the mouth of Long Canyon (2) (lat. 32°46'40" N, long. 116°26'45" W; at SW cor. sec. 14, T 16 S, R 5 E). Named on Mount Laguna (1960) 7.5' quadrangle.

Cienaga Campground [LOS ANGELES]: *locality*, 6.25 miles east-northeast of Whitaker Peak in Fish Canyon (1) (lat. 34°37'10" N, long. 118°38'10" W; near SW cor. sec. 12, T 6 N, R 17 W); the place is near Cienaga Spring. Named on Whitaker Peak (1958) 7.5' quadrangle. Called Cienaga Camp on Redrock Mountain (1936) 6' quadrangle.

Cienaga Canyon [LOS ANGELES]: *canyon*, 5 miles long, along Castaic Creek above a point 15 miles southeast of Gorman (lat. 34° 38'15" N, long. 118°40'10" W; sec. 3, T 6 N, R 17 W). Named on Liebre Mountain (1958) 7.5' quadrangle.

Cienaga Flats [SAN DIEGO]: *area*, less than 1 mile east of Rodriguez Mountain (lat. 33°14'10" N, long. 116°53'20" W). Named on Rodriguez Mountain (1948) 7.5' quadrangle.

Cienaga Spring [LOS ANGELES]: *spring*, 6.25 miles east-northeast of Whitaker Peak (lat. 34°37'05" N, long. 118°38'15" W; sec. 12, T 6 N, R 17 W). Named on Whitaker Peak (1958) 7.5' quadrangle.

Cienega [LOS ANGELES]: *locality*, 5.25 miles west-southwest of Los Angeles city hall along Southern Pacific Railroad (lat. 34°01'15" N, long. 118°19'35" W); the place is at the boundary of Las Cienegas grant. Named on Hollywood (1966) 7.5' quadrangle.

Cienega Camp [VENTURA]: *locality*, 0.5 mile northwest of Santa Paula Peak (lat. 34°26'55" N, long. 119°00'55" W; sec. 7, T 4 N, R 20 W). Named on Santa Paula Peak (1951) 7.5' quadrangle.

Cienega de la San Joaquin: see **Newport Bay** [ORANGE].

Cienega de las Ranas: see **Upper Newport Bay** [ORANGE].

Cienega de San Joaquin: see **Cienega de las Ranas**, under **Upper Newport Bay** [ORANGE].

Cienega o Paso de la Tijera [LOS ANGELES]: *land grant*, at Baldwin Hills. Named on Hollywood (1953) and Inglewood (1952) 7.5' quadrangles. Vicente Sanchez received the land in 1843; Tomas Sanchez and others claimed 4481 acres patented in 1873 (Cowan, p. 28). The term "Cienega" in the name is from natural springs and marsh; the term "Paso de la Tijera" in the name is from the fancied resemblance of two narrow valleys to an open pair of scissors (Hoover, Rensch, and Rensch, p. 162)—*tijera* means "scissors" in Spanish. Postal authorities established La Tijera post office, named for the grant, in 1938 (Salley, p. 119).

Cigarette Hills [SAN DIEGO]: *peaks*, two, 5.5 miles east and east-northeast of Julian (lat. 33°05'55" N, long. 116°30'15" W; lat. 33° 04'50" N, long. 116°30'15" W). Named on Julian (1960) 7.5' quadrangle.

Cima Mesa [LOS ANGELES]: *area*, 6 miles west-northwest of Valyermo (lat. 34°27'45" N, long. 117°57'15" W; at W line sec. 5, T 4 N, R 10 W). Named on Juniper Hills (1959) 7.5' quadrangle.

Circle Camp: see **Coldwater Canyon** [LOS ANGELES] (1).

Citrus: see **Covina** [LOS ANGELES].

City Heights: see **East San Diego** [SAN DIEGO].

City Lands of Los Angeles [LOS ANGELES]: *land grant*, at downtown Los Angeles. Named on Hollywood (1953) and Los Angeles (1953) 7.5' quadrangles.

City of Commerce: see **Commerce** [LOS ANGELES].

City of Industry: see **Industry** [LOS ANGELES].

City of Orangethorpe: see **Placentia** [ORANGE].

City Terrace [LOS ANGELES]:
(1) *district*, 3.5 miles east of Los Angeles city hall (lat. 34°03'05" N, long. 118°10'55" W). Named on Los Angeles (1953) 7.5' quadrangle.
(2) *locality*, nearly 4 miles east of Los Angeles city hall along Pacific Electric Railroad (lat. 34°03'35" N, long. 118°10'40" W); the place is northeast of City Terrace (1). Named on Alhambra (1926) 6' quadrangle.

Clair [ORANGE]: *locality*, 4.25 miles south of Buena Park along Southern Pacific Railroad (lat. 33°48'20" N, long. 117°59'05" W). Named on Corona (1902) 30' quadrangle. Postal authorities established Clair post office in 1895 and discontinued it in 1900 (Frickstad, p. 116).

Clairemont [SAN DIEGO]: *district*, 5.5 miles southeast of Point La Jolla in San Diego (lat. 32°48' N, long. 117°12'15" W). Named on La Jolla (1967) 7.5' quadrangle.

Clairemont: see **North Clairemont** [SAN DIEGO].

Clamshell Canyon [LOS ANGELES]: *canyon*, drained by a stream that flows 1.5 miles to Santa Anita Wash 4 miles southeast of Mount Wilson (1) (lat. 34°10'30" N, long. 118°01'05" W; sec. 15, T 1 N, R 11 W). Named on Mount Wilson (1953) 7.5' quadrangle.

Clamshell Peak [LOS ANGELES]: *peak*, 7 miles northwest of Azusa city hall (lat. 34°12'05" N, long. 117°59'50" W; near E line sec. 2, T 1 N, R 11 W). Named on Azusa (1953) 7.5' quadrangle.

Clapp Canon: see **Soquel Canyon** [ORANGE].

Claremont [LOS ANGELES]: *city*, 3.5 miles northeast of Pomona city hall (lat. 34°05'45" N, long. 117°43' W). Named on Mount Baldy (1967) and Ontario (1967) 7.5' quadrangles. Postal authorities established Claremont post office in 1887 (Frickstad, p. 72), and the city incorporated in 1907. Officials of Pacific Land and Improvement Company had the town platted in 1887 and named it for Claremont, New Hampshire, former home of a director of the company (Gudde, 1949, p. 69). Lankershim Ranch Land and Water Company's (1888) map shows a place called Palomares located along the railroad west of Claremont, between Claremont and Lordsburg.

Clark Canyon [SAN DIEGO]: *canyon*, 2.25 miles long, opens into Sycamore Canyon (3) 4.5 miles northwest of Lakeside (lat. 32°53'55" N, long. 116°59'15" W). Named on San Vicnete Reservoir (1955) 7.5' quadrangle.

Clarke Dry Lake: see **Clark Lake** [SAN DIEGO].

Clark Gulch [LOS ANGELES]: *canyon*, drained by a stream that flows 1.5 miles to San Gabriel River 5.25 miles west of Mount San Antonio (lat. 34°18' N, long. 117°44'10" W). Named on Mount San Antonio (1955) 7.5' quadrangle. Called Clarks Gulch on Los Angeles County (1935) map.

Clark Lake [SAN DIEGO]: *dry lake*, 2.5 miles long, 7.5 miles northeast of Borrego Springs (lat. 33°20'10" N, long. 116°16'45" W). Named on Clark Lake (1959) 7.5' quadrangle. Tucker and Reed's (1939) map has the form "Clarke Dry Lake" for the name, which was given in the 1890's to commemorates the Clark brothers, who developed the feature as a watering place for their stock (Gudde, 1949, p. 69).

Clark Lake: see **Little Clark Lake** [SAN DIEGO].

Clarks Peak [VENTURA]: *peak*, 3.25 miles southwest of Triunfo Pass (lat. 34°05' N, long. 118°57'45" W; sec. 15, T 1 N, R 20 W). Altitude 1965 feet. Named on Triunfo Pass (1950) 7.5' quadrangle. The name commemorates a pioneer family in the neighborhood (Ricard).

Clark Valley [SAN DIEGO]: *valley*, center 9 miles northeast of Borrego Springs (lat. 33°20'45" N, long. 116°15'30" W). Named on Clark Lake (1959), Clark Lake NE (1960), and Fonts Point (1959) 7.5' quadrangles. Stein (p. 29) associated the name with Fred Clark and Frank Clark, cattlemen in the neighborhood.

Clark Well [SAN DIEGO]: *well*, 9.5 miles northeast of Borrego Springs (lat. 33°21'20" N, long. 116°15'45" W; near SE cor. sec. 29, T 9 S, R 7 E); the well is in Clark Valley. Named on Clark Lake (1959) 7.5' quadrangle.

Clayton [LOS ANGELES]: *locality*, 2.5 miles south of El Monte city hall along Union Pacific Railroad (lat. 34°01'35" N, long. 118°01'55" W). Named on El Monte (1953) 7.5' quadrangle.

Clear Creek [LOS ANGELES]: *stream*, flows 3.5 miles to Big Tujunga Canyon 3.25 miles south-southeast of Condor Peak (lat. 34°16'55" N, long. 118°11'50" W; near S line sec. 1, T 2 N, R 13 W). Named on Condor Peak (1959) 7.5' quadrangle.

Clear Creek Station [LOS ANGELES]: *locality*, 5.25 miles southeast of Condor Peak (lat. 34°16'15" N, long. 118°09'10" W); the place is near the head of Clear Creek. Named on Condor Peak (1959) 7.5' quadrangle.

Clear Spring [LOS ANGELES]: *spring*, 2 miles southeast of the village of Lake Hughes (lat. 34°39'10" N, long. 118°25'20" W; sec. 36, T 7 N, R 15 W). Named on Lake Hughes (1957) 7.5' quadrangle.

Clearwater: see **Clearwater Canyon** [LOS ANGELES]; **Clearwater Station** [LOS ANGELES]; **South Clearwater**, under **Paramount** [LOS ANGELES].

Clearwater Canyon [LOS ANGELES]: *canyon*, drained by a stream that flows 2.25 miles to San Francisquito Canyon 6 miles south of the village of Lake Hughes (lat. 34°35' N, long. 118°27'10" W). Named on Green

Valley (1958) 7.5' quadrangle. Thompson's (1921) map shows a place called Clearwater situated near the mouth of Clearwarer Canyon.

Clearwater Station [LOS ANGELES]: *locality*, 4.5 miles southeast of South Gate city hall along Pacific Electric Railroad (lat. 33°54'10" N, long. 118°09'30" W). Named on South Gate (1952) 7.5' quadrangle. Downey (1902) 15' quadrangle shows a community called Clearwater located less than 1 mile southwest of present Clearwater Station (lat. 33°53'35" N, long. 118°09'45" W). Postal authorities established Clearwater post office in 1888 and discontinued it in 1953; the name was from a small lake created by water from artesian wells (Salley, p. 45).

Clef: see **Mount Clef** [VENTURA].

Clemente Canyon: see **San Clemente Canyon** [SAN DIEGO].

Clement Junction [LOS ANGELES]: *locality*, nearly 3 miles south of Los Angeles city hall along Southern Pacific Railroad (lat. 34°00'50" N, long. 118°14'20" W). Named on Los Angeles (1966) 7.5' quadrangle.

Clevenger Canyon [SAN DIEGO]: *canyon*, 2.5 miles long, opens into the canyon of Santa Ysabel Creek 3 miles east of San Pasqual (lat. 33°05'20" N, long. 116°54'05" W; sec. 32, T 12 S, R 1 E). Named on San Pasqual (1954) 7.5' quadrangle. The name commemorates Archibald Clevenger, an early settler in the neighborhood (Stein, p. 30).

Clifton [LOS ANGELES]: *district*, 1.25 miles south-southeast of Redondo Beach city hall (lat. 33°40'35" N, long. 118°22'45" W). Named on Redondo Beach (1951) and Torrance (1964) 7.5' quadrangles. Called Clifton Heights on Los Angeles County (1935) map.

Clifton Heights: see **Clifton** [LOS ANGELES].

Cloudburst Canyon [LOS ANGELES]:

(1) *canyon*, drained by a stream that flows less than 1 mile to Arroyo Seco 9.5 miles south-southwest of Pacifico Mountain (lat. 34°15'40" N, long. 118°07' W). Named on Chilao Flat (1959) 7.5' quadrangle.

(2) *canyon*, drained by a stream that flows 1.5 miles to Squaw Canyon 2 miles north-northwest of Waterman Mountain (lat. 34° 21'45" N, long. 117°57'15" W; sec. 8, T 3 N, R 10 W). Named on Waterman Mountain (1959) 7.5' quadrangle.

(3) *canyon*, 1.5 miles long, nearly 2 miles southeast of Crystal Lake (lat. 34°18'05" N, long. 117°49'25" W). Named on Crystal Lake (1958) 7.5' quadrangle.

Cloudburst Summit [LOS ANGELES]: *pass*, 1 mile north of Waterman Mountain (lat. 34°21'05" N, long. 117°56' W; near N line sec. 16, T 3 N, R 10 W); the pass is at the head of Cloudburst Canyon (2). Named on Waterman Mountain (1959) 7.5' quadrangle.

Cloud Peak: see **Cuyamaca Peak** [SAN DIEGO].

Clover Flat [SAN DIEGO]:

(1) *area*, 5.5 miles north-northeast of Campo along Miller Creek (lat. 32°40'10" N, long. 116°24'45" W; sec. 30, T 17 S, R 6 E). Named on Cameron Corners (1959) 7.5' quadrangle.

(2) *locality*, 5 miles northeast of Campo along San Diego and Arizona Eastern Railroad (lat. 32°39'45" N, long. 116°24'50" W; near SW cor. sec. 30, T 17 S, R 6 E); the place is at Clover Flat (1). Named on Cameron Corners (1959) 7.5' quadrangle.

Coachwhip Canyon [SAN DIEGO]: *canyon*, 0.5 mile long, 13 miles east of Borrego Springs (lat. 33°17'35" N, long. 116°09'05" W). Named on Fonts Point (1959) 7.5' quadrangle.

Coal Canyon [ORANGE]: *canyon*, drained by a stream that flows 2.25 miles to Santa Ana Canyon 2.5 miles northwest of Sierra Peak (lat. 33°52'20" N, long. 117°41'15" W). Named on Black Star Canyon (1967) 7.5' quadrangle. Corona (1942) 15' quadrangle has the name "Coal Cr." for the stream in the canyon.

Coal Canyon: see **Carbon Canyon** [LOS ANGELES].

Coal Creek: see **Coal Canyon** [ORANGE].

Coarse Gold Canyon [LOS ANGELES]: *canyon*, drained by a stream that flows nearly 1.5 miles to Bouquet Canyon 4.5 miles north of Solemint (lat. 34°25' N, long. 118°27'15" W; sec. 21, T 4 N, R 15 W). Named on Mint Canyon (1960) 7.5' quadrangle.

Coast Guard Beach: see **San Nicolas Island** [VENTURA].

Cobal Canyon [LOS ANGELES]: *canyon*, drained by a stream that flows 1.25 miles to lowlands 6.5 miles north-northeast of Pomona city hall (lat. 34°08'35" N, long. 117°42'30" W; sec. 27, T 1 N, R 8 W). Named on Mount Baldy (1954) 7.5' quadrangle.

Cobblestone Mountain [VENTURA]: *peak*, 14 miles north of Fillmore (lat. 34°36'30" N, long. 118°52' W; sec. 14, T 6 N, R 19 W). Altitude 6730 feet. Named on Cobblestone Mountain (1958) 7.5' quadrangle.

Cobblestone Spring [VENTURA]: *spring*, 0.5 mile east of Cobblestone Mountain (lat. 34°36'25" N, long. 118°51'20" W; at E line sec. 14, T 6 N, R 19 E). Named on Cobblestone Mountain (1958) 7.5' quadrangle.

Coche Canyon [VENTURA]: *canyon*, drained by a stream that flows 3.5 miles to Cañada Larga nearly 8 miles northwest of Saticoy (lat. 34°21'45" N, long. 119°14'50" W). Named on Matilija (1952), Ojai (1952), and Saticoy (1951) 7.5' quadrangles.

Cockatoo Grove [SAN DIEGO]: *locality*, 8 miles southwest of Jamul (lat. 32°38'30" N, long. 116°58'55" W; on S line sec. 33, T 17 S, R 1 W). Named on Jamul Mountains (1955) 7.5' quadrangle. A former Austrian sailor, who had a vineyard and winepress at the place, named it (Gudde, 1949, p. 72).

Cockleburr Canyon [SAN DIEGO]: *canyon*, drained by a stream that flows 2 miles to the sea 8.5 miles south-southeast of San Onofre Mountain (lat. 33°15'05" N, long. 117°25'50" W; sec. 5, T 11 S, R 5 W). Named on Las Pulgas Canyon (1968) 7.5' quadrangle

Cogswell Reservoir [LOS ANGELES]: *lake*, behind a dam on West Fork San Gabriel River 8 miles north-northwest of Azusa city hall (lat. 34°14'40" N, long. 117°57'50" W). Named on Azusa (1953) 7.5' quadrangle.

Colb Valley [SAN DIEGO]: *canyon*, drained by a stream that flows 2.5 miles to West Fork San Luis Rey River 5 miles east of Boucher Hill (lat. 33°20'10" N, long. 117°49'55" W; sec. 1, T 10 S, R 1 E). Named on Palomar Observatory (1949) 7.5' quadrangle. The misspelled name recalls William Kolb, a homesteader in the neighborhood (Stein, p. 30).

Colby Canyon [LOS ANGELES]: *canyon*, drained by a stream that flows nearly 2 miles to Arroyo Seco 6 miles southeast of Condor Peak (lat. 34°15'55" N, long. 118°08'35" W). Named on Chilao Flat (1959) and Condor Peak (1959) 7.5' quadrangles.

Cold Brook: see **Coldbrook Camp** [LOS ANGELES].

Coldbrook Camp [LOS ANGELES]: *locality*, 2 miles south of Crystal Lake (lat. 34°17'40" N, long. 117°50'20" W); the place is at the mouth of Coldbrook Creek. Named on Camp Rincon (1940) 6' quadrangle. Postal authorities established Cold Brook post office in 1911 and discontinued it in 1916; the name was from Cold Brook Camp (Salley, p. 47). R.W. Dawson took over management of a resort at the place in 1904 and named it Coldbrook Camp; the site had the early name "Sycamore Flats" (Robinson, J.W., 1983, p. 57, 92).

Coldbrook Creek [LOS ANGELES]: *stream*, flows less than 2 miles to join Soldier Creek and form North Fork San Gabriel River 2 miles south of Crystal Lake (lat. 34°17'25" N, long. 117°50'20" W). Named on Crystal Lake (1958) 7.5' quadrangle.

Cold Canyon [LOS ANGELES]: *canyon*, drained by a stream that flows 2.5 miles to Salt Creek 9 miles southeast of Gorman (lat. 34° 41'55" N, long. 118°42'20" W; sec. 17, T 7 S, R 17 W). Named on Liebre Mountain (1958) 7.5' quadrangle.

Cold Creek [LOS ANGELES]: *stream*, flows 4.5 miles to Malibu Creek 3.5 miles north-northwest of Malibu Point (lat. 34°04'40" N, long. 118°42'05" W; sec. 18, T 1 S, R 17 W). Named on Malibu Beach (1951) 7.5' quadrangle.

Cold Spring [SAN DIEGO]:

(1) *spring*, 4 miles north northwest of Margarita Peak (lat. 33°29'25" N, long. 117°25'05" W; sec. 8, T 8 S, R 5 W). Named on Margarita Peak (1968) 7.5' quadrangle.

(2) *spring*, 2.5 miles east of Cuyamaca Peak (lat. 32°56'35" N, long. 116°33'55" W); the spring is along Cold Stream. Named on Cuyamaca Peak (1960) 7.5' quadrangle.

Cold Spring Canyon [ORANGE]: *canyon*, drained by a stream that flows 4.5 miles to San Juan Creek 10 miles northeast of San Juan Capistrano (lat. 33°35'10" N, long. 117°31'10" W; near W line sec. 4, T 7 S, R 6 W). Named on Cañada Gobernadora (1968) and Santiago Peak (1954) 7.5' quadrangles.

Cold Spring Canyon [SAN DIEGO]: *canyon*, drained by a stream that flows 2 miles to Devil Canyon 4 miles northwest of Margarita Peak (lat. 33°28'45" N, long. 117°26'30" W; sec. 18, T 8 S, R 5 W); Cold Spring (1) is at the head of the canyon. Named on Margarita Peak (1968) 7.5' quadrangle.

Cold Springs Canyon [LOS ANGELES]: *canyon*, drained by a stream that flows 1.5 miles to Fish Canyon (2) 5 miles north-northwest of Azusa city hall (lat. 34°12' N, long. 117°56'30" W; near W line sec. 4, T 1 N, R 10 W). Named on Azusa (1953) 7.5' quadrangle.

Cold Stream [SAN DIEGO]: *stream*, flows 2.5 miles to Sweetwater River 3 miles east-southeast of Cuyamaca Peak in Green Valley (3) (lat. 32°55'25" N, long. 116°33'30" W). Named on Cuyamaca Peak (1960) 7.5' quadrangle.

Coldwater Canyon [LOS ANGELES]:

(1) *canyon*, drained by a stream that flows 1.25 miles to Big Tujunga Canyon 7 miles southwest of Pacifico Mountain (lat. 34° 18'35" N, long. 118°06'55" W). Named on Chilao Flat (1959) 7.5' quadrangle. Los Angeles County (1935) map shows a place called Circle Camp located about 0.25 mile north of the mouth of Coldwater Canyon (1) in Big Tujunga Canyon.

(2) *canyon*, drained by a stream that flows nearly 7 miles to Cattle Canyon 12.5 miles north of Pomona city hall (lat. 34°14'05" N, long. 117°43'40" W). Named on Mount Baldy (1954) and Mount San Antonio (1955) 7.5' quadrangles.

(3) *canyon*, 2 miles long, 2.5 miles north of Beverly Hills city hall (lat. 34°06'30" N, long. 118°24'15" W). Named on Beverly Hills (1950) 7.5' quadrangle.

Coldwater Canyon [VENTURA]: *canyon*, drained by a stream that flows 2 miles to Sespe Creek 5 miles north-northwest of Filllmore (lat. 34°27'55" N, long. 118°56'35" W; near N line sec. 2, T 4 N, R 20 W). Named on Fillmore (1951) 7.5' quadrangle.

Coldwater Fork [VENTURA]: *stream,* flows 3.5 miles to Hot Springs Canyon 2.5 miles north-northwest of Devils Heart Peak (lat. 34°34'55" N, long. 118°59'25" W; sec. 27, T 6 N, R 20 W). Named on Devils Heart Peak (1943) 7.5' quadrangle.

Colegrove [LOS ANGELES]: *district,* 5.5 miles west-northwest of present Los Angeles city hall (lat. 34°05'30" N, long. 118°19'45" W). Named on Santa Monica (1902) 15' quadrangle. Postal authorities established Colegrove post office in 1888 and discontinued it in 1917; the name was for Seward Cole, first postmaster and promoter of the community (Salley, p. 47). A spa called Radium Sulphur Spring was situated near Colegrove (Merrill, 1919, p. 508); the place, which also was called Hollywood Spa, obtained water from an old oil test well, probably drilled in 1905 (Berkstresser, p. A-7).

Coleman City: see **Wynola** [SAN DIEGO].

Coleman Creek [SAN DIEGO]: *stream,* flows 6.25 miles to San Diego River 1 mile southeast of Santa Ysabel (lat. 33°05'50" N, long. 116°39'40" W; sec. 27, T 12 S, R 3 E). Named on Julian (1960) and Santa Ysabel (1960) 7.5' quadrangles. The name commemorates Fred Coleman, who along with Elza Wood, discovered gold in the stream (Stein, p. 30).

Coleman Flat [SAN DIEGO]: *area,* 4.5 miles south-southeast of Santa Ysabel (lat. 33°03'05" N, long. 116°38'15" W; near SE cor. sec. 11, T 13 S, R 3 E). Named on Santa Ysabel (1960) 7.5' quadrangle. The name is for Fred Coleman of Coleman Creek (Stein, p. 30).

Colima [LOS ANGELES]: *locality,* 2.25 miles south-southeast of Whittier city hall along Southern Pacific Railroad (lat. 33°56'40" N, long. 118°00'55" W). Named on Whittier (1965) 7.5' quadrangle.

College Settlement: see **Downey** [LOS ANGELES].

Collier Flat [SAN DIEGO]: *area,* 4.5 miles south-southwest of Santa Ysabel (lat. 33°03'25" N, long. 116°43' W; sec. 7, T 13 S, R 3 E). Named on Santa Ysabel (1960) 7.5' quadrangle.

Collins Island [ORANGE]: *island,* 325 feet long, nearly 7 miles east-southeast of Huntington Beach civic center in Newport Bay at the northwest tip of Balboa Island (lat. 33°36'30" N, long. 117°53'55" W). Named on Newport Beach (1965) 7.5' quadrangle. The name commemorates W.S. Collins, who created this feature and nearby Balboa Island; Collins Island also was called Cagney Island for the movie star who later owned it (Gleason, p. 97).

Collins Valley [SAN DIEGO]: *valley,* 10 miles north-northwest of Borrego Springs along Coyote Creek (lat. 33°22'55" N, long. 116° 27'30" W). Named on Borrego Palm Canyon (1959) 7.5' quadrangle. The name commemorates John Collins, who homesteaded at the place in the 1890's (Gudde, 1969, p. 70).

Colonia Independencia [ORANGE]: *locality,* 4.25 miles south-southeast of present Buena Park civic center (lat. 33°48'20" N, long. 117°58'05" W; near S line sec. 19, T 4 S, R 10 W). Named on Anaheim (1950) 7.5' quadrangle.

Colonia Juarez [ORANGE]: *locality,* 4.5 miles northeast of present Huntington Beach civic center (lat. 33°42'50" N, long. 117°56'45" W; sec. 29, T 5 S, R 10 W). Named on Newport Beach (1951) 7.5' quadrangle.

Colonia Manzanillo [ORANGE]: *locality,* 8 miles south-southeast of present Buena Park civic center (lat. 33°45'30" N, long. 117°56'05" W; near NW cor. sec. 9, T 5 S, R 10 W). Named on Anaheim (1950) 7.5' quadrangle.

Colorado Lagoon [LOS ANGELES]: *lake,* 1750 feet long, 3.25 miles east of Long Beach city hall (lat. 33°46'15" N, long. 118°08' W). Named on Long Beach (1964) 7.5' quadrangle.

Colorado Pass: see **Carrizo Valley** [SAN DIEGO].

Coltrell Flat [VENTURA]: *area,* 2.5 miles north-northwest of Devils Heart Peak along Sespe Creek (lat. 34°34'40" N, long. 118°59'45" W; at SW cor. sec. 27, T 6 N, R 20 W). Named on Devils Heart Peak (1943) 7.5' quadrangle. United States Board on Geographic Names (1990, p. 7) approved the name "Cottriel Flat" for the feature, and pointed out that the name is for George W. Cottriel, who patented land at the place in 1891.

Columbine Spring [LOS ANGELES]: *spring,* 2.5 miles north-northwest of Mount San Antonio (lat. 34°19'20" N, long. 117°40' W; near N line sec. 25, T 3 N, R 8 W). Named on Mount San Antonio (1955) 7.5' quadrangle.

Combs Camp [SAN DIEGO]: *locality,* 6.25 miles north of Warner Springs (lat. 33°22'25" N, long. 116°36'45" W; sec. 19, T 9 S, R 4 E). Named on Hot Springs Mountain (1960) 7.5' quadrangle.

Combs Peak [SAN DIEGO]: *peak,* 8 miles north of Warner Springs on Bucksnort Mountain (lat. 33°23'40" N, long. 116°36'15" W; sec. 7, T 9 S, R 4 E). Altitude 6193 feet. Named on Bucksnort Mountain (1960) 7.5' quadrangle.

Comfort: see **Camp Comfort** [VENTURA]; **Old Point Comfort** [LOS ANGELES].

Commerce [LOS ANGELES]: *town,* 6 miles southeast of Los Angeles city hall (lat. 34°00'05" N, long. 118°09'15" W). Named on Los Angeles (1966) and South Gate (1964) 7.5' quadrangles. Postal authorities established City of Commerce post office there in 1963 (Salley, p. 44). The place is an industrial enclave that incorporated in 1960.

Commercial Basin [SAN DIEGO]: *embayment,* 3.5 miles west of downtown San Diego off San Diego Bay (lat. 32°43'20" N, long. 117°13'20" W). Named on Point Loma (1967) 7.5' quadrangle.

Community Center: see **Simi Valley** [VENTURA] (2).

Como [ORANGE]: *locality,* 5.25 miles southeast of Santa Ana city hall along Atchison Topeka and Santa Fe Railroad (lat. 33°41'55" N, long. 117°47'30" W). Named on Tustin (1965) 7.5' quadrangle.

Compton [LOS ANGELES]: *city,* 4.25 miles south-southwest of South Gate (lat. 33°53'40" N, long. 118°13'25" W). Named on Inglewood (1952) and South Gate (1952) 7.5' quadrangles. Postal authorities established Compton post office in 1869 (Frickstad, p. 72), and the city incorporated in 1888. The Reverend G.D. Compton started the community, first called Comptonville, in 1869 under the sponsorship of the Methodist Church (Hanna, p. 70). Lankershim Ranch Land and Water Company's (1888) map shows a place called Broadacres Gardens located just southeast of Compton.

Compton Creek [LOS ANGELES]: *stream,* flows 8.5 miles to Los Angeles River 5 miles north of Long Beach city hall (lat. 33°50'30" N, long. 118°12'10" W). Named on Inglewood (1952) and South Gate (1952) 7.5' quadrangles. Before 1938, when part of the watercourse was paved and joined to Los Angeles River, the creek flowed to San Pedro Bay through Wilmington Lagoon (Poland, Garrett, and Sinnott, p. 21).

Comptonville: see **Compton** [LOS ANGELES].

Condor Canyon [LOS ANGELES]: *canyon,* drained by a stream that flows 1.25 miles to Trail Canyon 5.5 miles northeast of Sunland (lat. 34°19'30" N, long. 118°15'15" W); the canyon heads near Condor Peak. Named on Condor Peak (1959) and Sunland (1953) 7.5' quadrangles.

Condor Peak [LOS ANGELES]: *peak,* 19 miles north of Los Angeles city hall (lat. 34°19'30" N, long. 118°13'10" W). Named on Condor Peak (1959) 7.5' quadrangle.

Conejo Creek [VENTURA]: *stream,* flows 19 miles to Calleguas Creek 2 miles south-southeast of Camarillo (lat. 34°11'20" N, long. 119°01'20" W). Named on Camarillo (1950) and Newbury Park (1951) 7.5' quadrangles. The feature is called Arroyo Conejo above Santa Rosa Valley on Newbury Park (1951) and Thousand Oaks (1952) 7.5' quadrangles. North Fork Arroyo Conejo enters 2 miles north-northwest of Newbury Park; it is 6.25 miles long and is named on Newbury Park (1951) 7.5' quadrangle. South Branch Arroyo Conejo enters from the south 0.5 mile north-northeast of Newbury Park; it is 6.25 miles long—including an interruption of the stream course through Conejo Valley—and is named on Newbury Park (1951) 7.5' quadrangle.

Conejo Mountain [VENTURA]: *peak,* 4.25 miles west of Newbury Park (lat. 34°11'15" N, long. 118°59' W); the peak is 1.5 miles west of Conejo Valley. Altitude 1814 feet. Named on Newbury Park (1951) 7.5' quadrangle.

Conejos Creek [SAN DIEGO]: *stream,* flows 10.5 miles to El Capitan Reservoir 2.5 miles east-southeast of El Cajon Mountain (lat. 32°53'35" N, long. 116°45'50" W; sec. 3, T 15 S, R 2 E). Named on El Cajon Mountain (1955) and Tule Springs (1960) 7.5' quadrangles. On Cuyamaca (1903) 30' quadrangle, present Conejos Creek below its junction with King Creek is called South Fork [San Diego River]—this map shows South Fork formed by the confluence of Conejos Creek and King Creek.

Conejos Valley [SAN DIEGO]: *valley,* 6 miles northwest of Descanso (lat. 32°54'25" N, long. 116°42'10" W); the valley is along Conejos Creek. Named on Tule Springs (1960) 7.5' quadrangle.

Conejo Valley [VENTURA]: *valley,* west of Newbury Park (lat. 34° 11' N, long. 118°56' W); the feature is on El Conejo grant. Named on Newbury Park (1951) 7.5' quadrangle.

Coney Island [ORANGE]: *hill,* nearly 7 miles east-southeast of Huntington Beach civic center along Newport Bay (lat. 33°37'10" N, long. 117°53'30" W). Named on Newport Beach (1965) 7.5' quadrangle. Newport Beach (1951) 7.5' quadrangle shows the feature surrounded by marsh and water.

Conservation Camp 37 [LOS ANGELES]: *locality,* 6.25 miles south-southwest of Valyermo (lat. 34°21'15" N, long. 117°52'40" W; near S line sec. 12, T 3 N, R 10 W). Named on Waterman Mountain (1959) 7.5' quadrangle.

Contract Point [LOS ANGELES]: *relief feature,* 4.5 miles north-northeast of downtown San Fernando (lat. 34°20'30" N, long. 118° 24'25" W; sec. 13, T 3 N, R 15 W). Named on San Fernando (1966, photorevised 1972) 7.5' quadrangle.

Cooks Canyon [LOS ANGELES]: *canyon,* 1 mile long, 3.5 miles east of Sunland (lat. 34°15'25" N, long. 118°15'05" W; mainly in sec. 16, T 2 N, R 13 W). Named on Condor Peak (1959) and Sunland (1953) 7.5' quadrangles. Called Cook Cany. on Los Angeles County (1935) map.

Coon Canyon: see **Fern Canyon** [LOS ANGELES] (1).

Cooper Canyon [LOS ANGELES]: *canyon,* drained by a stream that flows 2.5 miles to Little Rock Creek 2.5 miles northeast of Waterman Mountain (lat. 34°21'45" N, long. 117°54' W; sec. 11, T 3 N, R 10 W). Named on Waterman Mountain (1959) 7.5' quadrangle. The name commemorates brothers Ike Cooper and Tom Cooper, hunters who favored the canyon (Robinson, J.W., 1977, p. 189).

Cooper Canyon [SAN DIEGO]: *canyon,* drained by a stream that heads in Riverside County and flows 6.5 miles to Chihuahua Creek 10.5 miles north-northwest of Warner Springs in San Diego County (lat. 33°24'55" N, long. 116°42'50" W; sec. 6, T 9 S, R 3 E). Named on Beauty Mountain (1960) 7.5' quadrangle.

Cooper Canyon [VENTURA]: *canyon,* 1 mile long, opens into Santa Ana Valley 5 miles west of the town of Ojai (lat. 34°26'15" N, long. 119°19'50" W). Named on Matilija (1952) 7.5' quadrangle. Joseph Harrison Cooper once owned the canyon (Ricard).

Cooper Cienega [SAN DIEGO]: *area,* 9.5 miles north-northwest of Warner Springs (lat. 33°24'55" N, long. 116°40'50" W; sec. 4, T 9 S, R 3 E). Named on Beauty Mountain (1960) 7.5' quadrangle. Ramona (1903) 30' quadrangle has the form "Cooper Cienaga" for the name.

Copter Ridge [LOS ANGELES]: *ridge,* south-southeast-trending, 3 miles long, 3.25 miles east of Crystal Lake (lat. 34°19'30" N, long. 117°47'30" W) Named on Crystal Lake (1958) 7.5' quadrangle.

Cordero: see **Huntington Beach** [ORANGE].

Cordero Canyon: see **McGonigle Canyon** [SAN DIEGO].

Cordorniz: see **Garden Grove** [ORANGE].

Cordova Canyon: see **Elderberry Canyon** [LOS ANGELES].

Cornell [LOS ANGELES]: *village,* 8 miles north of Point Dume in Triunfo Canyon (lat. 34°06'50" N, long. 118°46'35" W; sec. 4, T 1 S, R 18 W). Named on Point Dume (1951) 7.5' quadrangle.

Cornell: see **Seminole Hot Springs** [LOS ANGELES].

Corona del Mar [ORANGE]: *district,* 6.25 miles west-northwest of Laguna Beach city hall in Newport Beach (lat. 33°35'30" N, long. 117°52'15" W). Named on Laguna Beach (1965) and Newport Beach (1965) 7.5' quadrangles. Postal authorities established Corona Del Mar (with a capital "D") post office in 1926, moved it about 0.25 mile northwest in 1940, moved it 0.5 mile southeast in 1941, and changed the name to Corona del Mar (with a lower-case "d") in 1950 (Salley, p. 50). George E. Hart developed and named the place in 1904; F.D. Cornell Company acquired it in 1915 and named it Balboa Palisades, but the old name was restored (Gudde, 1949, p. 79). The place was called Pacific Palisades for a short time after a hotel called Palisades Inn was built there (Meadows, p. 109).

Coronado [SAN DIEGO]: *town,* 2 miles south-southwest of, and across San Diego Bay from downtown San Diego (lat. 32°41'30" N, long. 117°10'45" W). Named on Imperial Beach (1967) and Point Loma (1967) 7.5' quadrangles. Postal authorities established Coronado post office in 1887 (Frickstad, p. 149), and the town incorporated in 1890. Elisha Babcock and H.L. Story organized Coronado Beach Company in 1886 and built a resort hotel and town; according to tradition, the name "Coronado" is from Coronado Islands off Mexico that Vizcaino discovered and named in 1602 (Stein, p. 31).

Coronado Heights [SAN DIEGO]: *locality,* 1.5 miles north-northwest of present Imperial Beach civic center (lat. 32°36' N, long. 117°07'30" W). Named on San Ysidro (1943) 7.5' quadrangle.

Corral Beach [LOS ANGELES]: *beach,* 3 miles west of Malibu Point along the coast (lat. 34°02' N, long. 118°44' W); the beach is at the mouth of Corral Canyon. Named on Malibu Beach (1951) 7.5' quadrangle.

Corral Canyon [LOS ANGELES]: *canyon,* drained by a stream that flows 4 miles to the sea 3 miles west of Malibu Point (lat. 34°02' N, long. 118°44' W). Named on Malibu Beach (1951) 7.5' quadrangle.

Corral Canyon [SAN DIEGO]: *canyon,* drained by a stream that flows 5.5 miles to Skye Valley 7.5 miles west-northwest of Morena Village (lat. 32°43'10" N, long. 116°37'25" W; near E line sec. 1, T 17 S, R 3 E). Named on Morena Reservoir (1960) 7.5' quadrangle.

Corral Canyon [VENTURA]: *canyon,* drained by a stream that flows 5.5 miles to Cuyama River 9 miles northwest of Reyes Peak (lat. 34°43'30" N, long. 119°23'15" W). Named on Apache Canyon (1943), Rancho Nuevo Creek (1943), and Reyes Peak (1943) 7.5' quadrangles.

Corral de Luz Warm Springs: see **De Luz** [SAN DIEGO] (1).

Corral Harbor: see **San Nicolas Island** [VENTURA].

Corral Mountain [SAN DIEGO]: *peak,* 3.5 miles south of Mesa Grande (lat. 33°07'55" N, long. 116°46'45" W; sec. 16, T 12 S, R 2 E). Altitude 3249 feet. Named on Mesa Grande (1948) 7.5' quadrangle.

Corriganville [VENTURA]: *locality,* 1.25 miles west-southwest of Santa Susana Pass (lat. 34°15'50" N, long. 118°39'10" W). Named on Santa Susana (1951) 7.5' quadrangle. Ray "Crash" Corrigan made western movies at the place (Ricard).

Cortelyou Spring [LOS ANGELES]: *spring,* 2.5 miles north of Crystal Lake (lat. 34°21'20" N; long. 117°50'35" W; sec. 8, T 3 N, R 9 W). Named on Crystal Lake (1958) 7.5' quadrangle.

Corte Madera Mountain [SAN DIEGO]: *peak,* 7 miles south of Descanso (lat. 32°45'25" N, long. 116°35'20" W; at N line sec. 29, T 16 S, R 4 E). Altitude 4657 feet. Named on Descanso (1960) 7.5' quadrangle.

Corte Madera Valley [SAN DIEGO]: *valley,* 6.5 miles south-southeast of Descanso (lat. 32°46' N, long. 116°34'15" W; in and near sec. 21, T 16 S, R 4 E); the valley is 1.25 miles northeast of Corte Madera Mountain. Named on Descanso (1960) 7.5' quadrangle.

Cortes: see **Cape Cortes** [LOS ANGELES].

Corvallis: see **Norwalk** [LOS ANGELES].

Cosmit Peak [SAN DIEGO]: *peak,* 5 miles south of Julian (lat. 33°00'25" N, long. 116°36'55" W; near SW cor. sec. 30, T 13 S, R 4 E). Altitude 4575 feet. Named on Julian (1960) 7.5' quadrangle. The name is of Indian origin (Kroeber, p. 40).

Costa: see **Ponto** [SAN DIEGO].

Costa Brava: see **Silver Strand** [SAN DIEGO].

Costa Mesa [ORANGE]: *city,* 4.5 miles east-southeast of Huntington Beach civic center (lat. 33°38'35" N, long. 117°55'35" W). Named on Newport Beach (1965) and Tustin (1965) 7.5' quadrangles. Postal authorities established Harper post office 3 miles northeast of Newport Beach post office in 1909 and changed the name to Costa Mesa in 1920 (Salley, p. 93). The name "Harper" was for a local rancher; Alice Plummer's entry "Costa Mesa" won a contest held in 1915 to choose a new name for the community (Hanna, p. 75).

Cota [LOS ANGELES]: *locality,* 5 miles north of Long Beach city hall along a railroad (lat. 33°50'20" N, long. 118°12'20" W). Named on Long Beach (1949) 7.5' quadrangle.

Cota: see **Pala** [SAN DIEGO].

Cottonwood Campground [LOS ANGELES]: *locality,* 5 miles southeast of Burnt Peak in Elizabeth Lake Canyon (lat. 34°38'25" N, long. 118°30'15" W). Named on Burnt Peak (1958) 7.5' quadrangle.

Cottonwood Canyon [LOS ANGELES]:

(1) *canyon,* drained by a stream that flows 1 mile to Little Tujunga Canyon 3.5 miles north-northwest of Sunland (lat. 34°18'10" N, long. 118°20'45" W; sec. 33, T 3 N, R 14 W). Named on Sunland (1966) 7.5' quadrangle.

(2) *canyon,* drained by a stream that flows 5.25 miles to the sea 2.5 miles west of Mount Banning on Santa Catalina Island (lat. 33°22'35" N, long. 118°28'40" W). Named on Santa Catalina North (1950) 7.5' quadrangle.

Cottonwood Canyon [SAN DIEGO]: *canyon,* drained by a stream that flows 3 miles to Mason Valley 5 miles north-northwest of Monument Peak (lat. 32°57'45" N, long. 116°27'15" W; near S line sec. 10, T 14 S, R 5 E). Named on Monument Peak (1959) 7.5' quadrangle.

Cottonwood Creek [SAN DIEGO]:

(1) *stream,* flows 2.5 miles to De Luz Creek 6.5 miles northwest of Fallbrook (lat. 33°27'15" N, long. 117°19'25" W; sec. 29, T 8 S, R 4 W). Named on Fallbrook (1968) 7.5' quadrangle.

(2) *stream,* flows 6.25 miles to Riverside County 7 miles north-northeast of Boucher Hill (lat. 33°25'35" N, long. 116°52' W). Named on Aguanga (1954) and Palomar Observatory (1949) 7.5' quadrangles.

(3) *stream,* flows 36 miles to join Tecate Creek and form Tijuana River 5 miles east-southeast of Otay Mountain (lat. 32°34' N, long. 116°45'55" W; sec. 34, T 18 S, R 2 E). Named on Barrett Lake (1960), Cameron Corners (1959), Morena Reservoir (1960), Mount Laguna (1960), Otay Mountain (1972), and Tecate (1960) 7.5' quadrangles. United States Board on Geographic Names (1968a, p. 6) rejected the name "Tia Juana River" for the stream.

Cottonwood Creek: see **Little Cottonwood Creek**, under **Oso Canyon** [LOS ANGELES].

Cottonwood Glen [LOS ANGELES]: *locality,* 3.5 miles north-northwest of Sunland in Little Tujunga Canyon (lat. 34°18'05" N, long. 118°20'50" W; sec. 33, T 3 N, R 14 W); the place is at the mouth of Cottonwood Canyon (1). Named on Sunland (1953) 7.5' quadrangle.

Cottonwood Spring [SAN DIEGO]: *spring,* 6.5 miles southwest of Borrego Springs (lat. 33°12'15" N, long. 116°28' W; near E line sec. 21, T 11 S, R 5 E). Named on Tubb Canyon (1959) 7.5' quadrangle.

Cottonwood Valley [SAN DIEGO]: *valley,* 9.5 miles north of Campo (lat. 32°44'20" N, long. 116°29'15" W); the valley is along Cottonwood Creek (3). Named on Cameron Corners (1959) and Mount Laguna (1960) 7.5' quadrangles.

Cottriel Flat: see **Coltrell Flat** [VENTURA].

Couger Canyon [LOS ANGELES]: *canyon,* nearly 1 mile long, opens into Pacoima Canyon 5 miles north-northeast of downtown San Fernando (lat. 34°20'35" N, long. 118°23'35" W; sec. 18, T 3 N, R 14 W). Named on San Fernando (1953) 7.5' quadrangle.

Cougar Canyon [SAN DIEGO]: *canyon,* drained by a stream that flows 6 miles to Indian Canyon 9 miles northwest of Borrego Springs (lat. 33°21'20" N, long. 116°28'45" W). Named on Borrego Palm Canyon (1959) and Hot Springs Mountain (1960) 7.5' quadrangles. Called Indian Canyon on Clark Lake (1944) and Warner Springs (1942) 15' quadrangles, but United States Board on Geographic Names (1962a, p. 9) rejected this name for the canyon. The feature first was called Krueger Canyon to honor George Krueger of Brawley Chamber of Commerce in Imperial County, but this name was transformed by local usage (Stein, p. 33-34).

County Farm: see **Poor Farm Station** [LOS ANGELES].

Couser Canyon [SAN DIEGO]: *canyon,* drained by a stream that flows 3 miles to the valley of San Luis Rey River 3.5 miles southwest of Pala (lat. 33°20' N, long. 117°07'30" W; sec. 6, T 10 S, R 2 W). Named on Pala (1968) 7.5' quadrangle. The name is for R.V. Couser, who settled in the canyon about 1900 (Stein, p. 34).

Cove: see **The Cove** [SAN DIEGO].

Cove Campground [VENTURA]: *locality,* 4.5 miles south-southeast of Cobblestone Mountain along Agua Blanca Creek (lat. 34°33'10" N, long.

118°49'35" W). Named on Cobblestone Mountain (1958) 7.5' quadrangle.

Covina [LOS ANGELES]: *city,* 4 miles east of Baldwin Park city hall (lat. 34°05'15" N, long. 117°53'20" W). Named on Baldwin Park (1966) and San Dimas (1966) 7.5' quadrangles. Postal authorities established Covina post office in 1887 (Frickstad, p. 72), and the city incorporated in 1901. J.S. Phillips, landowner in the neighborhood, and Fred Eaton, engineer and surveyor, named the community in 1882 for its covelike setting and the large number of abandoned grape vines there (Hanna, p. 75-76). Postal authorities established Citrus post office at the site of present Covina in 1878 and discontinued in 1887 (Salley, p. 44). They established Centro post office 1.25 miles north of Citrus post office in 1885, changed the name to Gladstone in 1888, and discontinued it in 1892—an admirer of the British Prime Minister was responsible for the name "Gladstone" (Salley, p. 41, 85).

Covina: see **West Covina** [LOS ANGELES].

Cowan Heights [ORANGE]: *locality,* 4.5 miles east-southeast of Orange city hall (lat. 33°46'30" N, long. 117°46'15" W). Named on Orange (1964) 7.5' quadrangle.

Cow Canyon [LOS ANGELES]: *canyon,* drained by a stream that flows 4.25 miles to Cattle Canyon 12.5 miles north of Pomona city hall (lat. 34°13'45" N, long. 117°43'15" W). Named on Mount Baldy (1954) 7.5' quadrangle.

Cow Canyon [SAN DIEGO]: *canyon,* drained by a stream that flows 2.5 miles to Cañada Aguanga nearly 6 miles northwest of Warner Springs (lat. 33°20'10" N, long. 116°42'45" W). Named on Warner Springs (1959) 7.5' quadrangle.

Cow Canyon Saddle [LOS ANGELES]: *pass,* 12 miles north-northeast of Pomona city hall (lat. 34°13'40" N, long. 117°40'10" W; sec. 25, T 2 N, R 8 W); the pass is at the head of Cow Canyon. Named on Mount Baldy (1954) 7.5' quadrangle.

Cowhead Potrero [VENTURA]: *area,* 16 miles north of Reyes Peak (lat. 34°52'15" N, long. 119°17'10" W; at N line sec. 12, T 9 N, R 23 W). Named on Apache Canyon (1943) 7.5' quadrangle.

Cowles: see **Santee** [SAN DIEGO].

Cowles Mountain [SAN DIEGO]: *peak,* 3.25 miles north of La Mesa (lat. 32°48'45" N, long. 117°01'50" W). Altitude 1591 feet. Named on La Mesa (1967) 7.5' quadrangle. The feature also was called Mission Peak and Black Mountain (Stein, p. 13, 34).

Cowles Spring: see **Dog Spring** [SAN DIEGO].

Cow Spring [VENTURA]: *spring,* 4 miles east-northeast of Devils Heart Peak (lat. 34°33'35" N, long. 119°54'25" W). Named on Devils Heart Peak (1943) 7.5' quadrangle.

Cow Spring Canyon [LOS ANGELES]: *canyon,* drained by a stream that flows 5 miles to lowlands 12 miles east of Gorman (lat. 34°46'45" N, long. 118°38'10" W; sec. 13, T 8 N, R 17 W). Named on La Liebre Ranch (1965) and Liebre Mountain (1958) 7.5' quadrangles. Called Cow Springs Canyon on Liebre (1938) 6' quadrangle, but United States Board on Geographic Names (1959, p. 6) rejected this form of the name.

Coxey Hill [SAN DIEGO]: *peak,* 7.5 miles east-southeast of Oceanside (lat. 33°09'35" N, long. 117°15'15" W). Altitude 570 feet. Named on San Luis Rey (1968) 7.5' quadrangle.

Coyote Bluff [ORANGE]: *relief feature,* nearly 3 miles south-southeast of San Juan Capistrano along Prima Deshecha Canyon (lat. 33°27'50" N, long. 117°38'30" W; on E line sec. 19, T 8 S, R 7 W). Named on Dana Point (1968) 7.5' quadrangle.

Coyote Canyon [LOS ANGELES]:

(1) *canyon,* drained by a stream that flows 2.25 miles to Cañada de Los Alamos 7.25 miles south-southeast of Gorman (lat. 34°41'40" N, long. 118°47'30" W); near S line sec. 16, T 7 N, R 18 W). Named on Black Mountain (1958) 7.5' quadrangle.

(2) *canyon,* drained by a stream that flows nearly 2 miles to Sand Canyon (2) 3.5 miles southeast of Solemint (lat. 34°22'45" N, long. 118°24'30" W; near NW cor. sec. 1, T 3 N, R 15 W). Named on Mint Canyon (1960) and San Fernando (1953) 7.5' quadrangles.

Coyote Canyon [ORANGE]: *canyon,* 2.5 miles long, opens into the canyon of Bonita Creek 8 miles south of Santa Ana city hall (lat. 33°37'50" N, long. 117°50'30" W). Named on Laguna Beach (1965) and Tustin (1965) 7.5' quadrangles. On Tustin (1935) 7.5' quadrangle, the name "Coyote Creek" applies to present Bonita Creek below the mouth of present Coyote Canyon.

Coyote Canyon [SAN DIEGO]:

(1) *canyon,* on San Diego-Riverside County line along Coyote Creek above a point 13 miles north-northwest of Borrego Springs (lat. 33°25'25" N, long. 116°28'35" W). Named on Collins Valley (1959) 7.5' quadrangle.

(2) *canyon,* about 2 miles long, 8 miles north-northwest of Borrego Springs (lat. 33°21'55" N, long. 116°24'45" W); the canyon is along Coyote Creek. Named on Borrego Palm Canyon (1959) 7.5' quadrangle.

Coyote Canyon [VENTURA]: *canyon,* drained by a stream that flows 6.25 miles to Arroyo Las Posas 6.5 miles west-southwest of Moorpark (lat. 34°15'30" N, long. 118°59'15" W). Named on Moorpark (1951) and Santa Paula (1951) 7.5' quadrangles.

Coyote Creek [LOS ANGELES-ORANGE]: *stream,* heads in Orange County and flows 13 miles in and out of Orange County across Los Angeles-Orange County line to San Gabriel River 6.5 miles east-northeast of Long Beach city hall in Los Angeles County (lat. 33° 47'40" N, long. 118°05'20" W; sec. 25, T 4 S, R 12 W). Named on La Habra (1952), Los Alamitos (1964), and Whittier (1965) 7.5' quadrangles. Los Alamitos (1950) 7.5' quadrangle shows the creek formed by the confluence of East Fork and Middle Fork 7 miles above the mouth of the stream—on this map the present main stream is called East Fork, and present La Cañada Verde Creek is called West Fork. On Whittier (1949) 7.5' quadrangle, the name "Coyote Creek" applies to present Brea Creek.

Coyote Creek [SAN DIEGO]: *stream* and *dry wash,* heads in Riverside County and extends for 20 miles in San Diego County to Borrego Sink 5 miles east-southeast of Borrego Springs (lat. 33°13'20" N, long. 116°17'50" W; sec. 13, T 11 S, R 6 E). Named on Borrego Palm Canyon (1959), Borrego Sink (1959), Clark Lake (1959), and Collins Valley (1959) 7.5' quadrangles.

Coyote Creek [VENTURA]: *stream,* flows nearly 15 miles to Ventura River 5.25 miles north-northwest of Ventura (lat. 34°21'15" N, long. 119°18'35" W). Named on Matilija (1952), Ventura (1951), and White Ledge Peak (1952) 7.5' quadrangles. East Fork enters 3.5 miles south-southeast of White Ledge Peak; it is 2.5 miles long and is named on Matilija (1952) and White Ledge Peak (1952) 7.5' quadrangles. West Fork enters from the southwest 3.25 miles south of White Ledge Peak; it is nearly 3 miles long and is named on White Ledge Peak (1952) 7.5' quadrangle.

Coyote Creek: see **Bonita Creek** [ORANGE].

Coyote Flat [LOS ANGELES]: *area,* nearly 9 miles northeast of Glendora city hall along San Gabriel River (lat. 34°14'05" N, long. 117°46' W). Named on Glendora (1966) 7.5' quadrangle.

Coyote Hills: see **East Coyote Hills** [ORANGE]; **West Coyote Hills** [ORANGE].

Coyote Mountain [SAN DIEGO]: *ridge,* southeast-trending, 6 miles long, 6.5 miles north-northeast of Borrego Springs (lat. 33°20'45" N, long. 116°19'45" W); the ridge is northeast of Coyote Creek. Named on Clark Lake (1959) 7.5' quadrangle.

Coyote Mountains [SAN DIEGO]: *range,* 15 miles southeast of Agua Caliente Springs on San Diego-Imperial County line (lat. 32° 49'30" N, long. 116°06' W). Named on Carrizo Mountain (1957) and Sweeney Pass (1959) 7.5' quadrangles.

Coyote Pass [LOS ANGELES]: *canyons,* two, that provide a passage through highlands in Monterey Park 5.25 miles east of Los Angeles city hall (lat. 34°03'15" N, long. 118°08'50" W). Named on Los Angeles (1953) 7.5' quadrangle. The feature also is called Monterey Pass (Gudde, 1949, p. 223).

Cozy Dell Canyon [VENTURA]: *canyon,* drained by a stream that flows 3.25 miles to Ojai Valley nearly 3 miles west-northwest of the town of Ojai (lat. 34°28'05" N, long. 119°17'05" W; near SE cor. sec. 33, T 5 N, R 23 W). Named on Matilija (1952) 7.5' quadrangle.

Crab Hollow Diggings: see **San Gabriel River** [LOS ANGELES].

Craig Beach: see **Mills Landing** [LOS ANGELES].

Craig Canyon [LOS ANGELES]: *canyon,* 0.5 mile long, nearly 2 miles north-northwest of Burbank city hall (lat. 34°12'25" N, long. 118°19' W). Named on Burbank (1953) 7.5' quadrangle.

Craig Spring [LOS ANGELES]: *spring,* 4 miles southeast of the village of Lake Hughes in San Francisquito Canyon (lat. 34°37'40" N, long. 118°23'50" W; near NE cor. sec. 7, T 6 N, R 14 W). Named on Lake Hughes (1957) 7.5' quadrangle.

Crane Canyon [LOS ANGELES]: *canyon,* 2 miles long, 2 miles north-northeast of Gorman on Los Angeles-Kern County line (lat. 34°49'05" N, long. 118°50'10" W; near NW cor. sec. 6, T 8 N, R 18 W). Named on Lebec (1958) 7.5' quadrangle.

Crane Lake: see **Quail Lake** [LOS ANGELES].

Cranes Peak [SAN DIEGO]: *peak,* less than 1 mile east-southeast of San Pasqual (lat. 33°05'20" N, long. 116°56'20" W; sec. 36, T 12 S, R 1 W). Altitude 1054 feet. Named on San Pasqual (1954) 7.5' quadrangle.

Crater Camp [LOS ANGELES]: *locality,* 3.5 miles north-northwest of Malibu Point (lat. 34°04'45" N, long. 118°41'55" W; sec. 18, T 1 S, R 17 W). Named on Malibu Beach (1951) 7.5' quadrangle.

Crater Lake: see **Echo Lake** [LOS ANGELES].

Crawfish George's: see **San Pedro** [LOS ANGELES] (2).

Crawfish Rock [ORANGE]: *rock,* 3.5 miles south-southwest of San Juan Capistrano, and 0.5 mile offshore (lat. 33°27'15" N, long. 117°41'15" W). Named on Dana Point (1968) 7.5' quadrangle.

Crawford Canyon [ORANGE]: *canyon,* less than 1 mile long, 3.25 miles east of Orange city hall (lat. 33°47' N, long. 117°47'40" W). Named on Orange (1964) 7.5' quadrangle.

Crescent [LOS ANGELES]: *district,* 8 miles west-northwest of present Los Angeles city hall (lat. 34°05'25" N, long. 118°22'25" W). Named on Hollywood (1926) 6' quadrangle.

Crescent Bay [ORANGE]: *embayment,* 1.25 miles west of Laguna Beach city hall along the coast (lat. 33°32'45" N, long. 117°48'05" W). Named

on Laguna Beach (1965) 7.5' quadrangle.
Crescent Bay: see **Sail Bay** [SAN DIEGO].
Crestline Camp [SAN DIEGO]: *locality,* 3.5 miles east-southeast of Boucher Hill (lat. 33°18'50" N, long. 116°51'45" W; at N line sec. 15, T 10 S, R 1 E). Named on Palomar Observatory (1949) 7.5' quadrangle.
Cristianitos Canyon [ORANGE]: *canyon,* 4.25 miles long, along Cristianitos Creek above a point 3 miles northeast of San Clemente civic center (lat. 33°27'15" N, long. 117°34'05" W). Named on Cañada Gobernadora (1968) and San Clemente (1968) 7.5' quadrangles.
Cristianitos Creek [ORANGE-SAN DIEGO]: *stream,* heads in Orange County and flows 6.5 miles to San Mateo Creek 2.25 miles east-southeast of San Clemente [ORANGE] civic center in San Diego County (lat. 33°25'10" N, long. 117°34'10" W; sec. 1, T 9 S, R 7 W). Named on San Clemente (1968) 7.5' quadrangle. The name recalls two little Indian girls who were ill and who became Christians when the padres with Portola baptized them at the place in 1769—*Cristianitos* means "little Christians" in Spanish (Hoover, Rensch, and Rensch, p. 259).
Crosley Saddle [SAN DIEGO]: *pass,* 5.5 miles north-northwest of Boucher Hill (lat. 33°24' N, long. 116°58'15" W; near S line sec. 10, T 9 S, R 1 W). Named on Vail Lake (1953) 7.5' quadrangle, which shows Crosley homestead situated 2.25 miles northeast of the pass.
Croswell Springs: see **Lovejoy Springs** [LOS ANGELES].
Crouch Valley [SAN DIEGO]: *valley,* 5.5 miles north of Buckman Springs (lat. 32°51'10" N, long. 116°28'20" W). Named on Mount Laguna (1960) 7.5' quadrangle.
Crow Canyon [ORANGE]: *canyon,* drained by a stream that flows 4.25 miles to Bell Canyon 8 miles northeast of San Juan Capistrano (lat. 33°35' N, long. 117°34'05" W; near N line sec. 12, T 7 S, R 7 W). Named on Cañada Gobernadora (1968) and Santiago Peak (1954) 7.5' quadrangles.
Crown Cove [SAN DIEGO]: *embayment,* 5.5 miles south-southeast of downtown San Diego along San Diego Bay (lat. 32°38'10" N, long. 117°08'20" W). Named on Point Loma (1967) 7.5' quadrangle.
Crown Point [SAN DIEGO]: *district,* 5 miles south-southeast of Point La Jolla on a peninsula in Mission Bay (lat. 32°47'10" N, long. 117°14'10" W). Named on La Jolla (1967) 7.5' quadrangle.
Crow Spring [ORANGE]: *spring,* 11 miles northeast of San Juan Capistrano (lat. 33°37'05" N, long. 117°32' W; sec. 29, T 6 S, R 6 W); the spring is in Crow Canyon. Named on Cañada Gobernadora (1968) 7.5' quadrangle.
Crushton [LOS ANGELES]: *locality,* less than 1 mile northeast of Baldwin Park city hall along Pacific Electric Railroad (lat. 34°05'30" N, long. 117°57' W; on N line sec. 17, T 1 S, R 10 W). Named on Baldwin Park (1953) 7.5' quadrangle.
Cruthers Creek [LOS ANGELES]: *stream,* flows 4.5 miles to Holmes Creek 2.25 west of Valyermo (lat. 34°26'40" W; long. 117°53'20" W; near SE cor. sec. 11, T 4 N, R 10 W). Named on Juniper Hills (1959) 7.5' quadrangle. On Los Angeles County (1935) map, present Holmes Creek is called East Fork Cruthers Creek. The same map shows a feature called Moss Spring located hear the head of Cruthers Creek (sec. 35, T 4 N, R 10 W).
Cruzan Canyon: see **Cruzan Mesa** [LOS ANGELES].
Cruzan Mesa [LOS ANGELES]: *area,* 3.25 miles north-northeast of Solemint (lat. 34°27'45" N, long. 118°26'25" W; mainly in sec. 3, T 4 N, R 15 W). Named on Mint Canyon (1960) 7.5' quadrangle. Los Angeles County (1935) map has the name "Cruzan Canyon" for a feature, 1.25 miles long, that opens into Mint Canyon (1) 1 mile east-southeast of present Cruzan Mesa.
Crystal Cove [ORANGE]: *locality,* 4 miles west-northwest of Laguna Beach city hall along the coast (lat. 33°34'30" N, long. 117°50'25" W). Named on Laguna Beach (1965) 7.5' quadrangle.
Crystal Lake [LOS ANGELES]: *lake,* 650 feet long, 5 miles east-southeast of Waterman Mountain (lat. 34°19'10" W; long. 117°50'45" W). Named on Crystal Lake (1958) 7.5' quadrangle. R.W. Dawson visited the lake in 1876 and laid claim to it; Dawson was a pioneer settler at Sycamore Flat (2), and apparently he gave the name "Sycamore Lake" to the feature (Robinson, J.W., 1983, p. 105).
Crystal Spring [LOS ANGELES]: *spring,* nearly 3 miles west of Mount Wilson (1) (lat. 34°13'30" N, long. 118°06'35" W). Named on Pasadena (1900) 15' quadrangle. Water from the spring was bottled for table use (Waring, p. 367).
Cuati: see **Prospero Tract** [LOS ANGELES].
Cuca [SAN DIEGO]: *land grant,* 4 miles south-southeast of Boucher Hill. Named on Boucher Hill (1948) and Palomar Observatory (1949) 7.5' quadrangles. Maria Juan de los Angeles received 0.5 league in 1845 and claimed 2174 acres patented in 1878 (Cowan, p. 31; Cowan gave the name "El Potrero" as an alternate).
Cudahy [LOS ANGELES]: *town,* 1.25 miles east-northeast of South Gate city hall (lat. 33°57'45" N, long. 118°10'45" W). Named on South Gate (1964) 7.5' quadrangle. Postal authorities established Cudahy post office in 1930; the name was for Peter Cudahy, who settled at the place and founded Cudahy Meat Packing Company (Salley, p. 53). The town incorporated in 1960. Bell (1936) 6' quadrangle shows Cudahy Sta. located along the railroad in the town (lat. 33°57'20" N, long. 118°11' W).
Cudahy Slough [SAN DIEGO]: *lake,* 500 feet long, 7 miles south-southeast of Point La Jolla (lat. 32°46' N, long. 117°12'15" W). Named on La Jolla (1953) 7.5' quadrangle.
Cudahy Station: see **Cudahy** [LOS ANGELES].
Cuddy Peak: see **Frazier Mountain** [VENTURA].
Culp Canyon [SAN DIEGO]: *canyon,* 1.5 miles long, 4.25 miles southwest of Borrego Springs (lat. 33°12'35" N, long. 116°25'30" W). Named on Tubb Canyon (1959) 7.5' quadrangle. Stein (p. 35) associated the name with John Kolp, an early cattleman in the neighborhood.
Culp Valley [SAN DIEGO]: *valley,* 5.5 miles southwest of Borrego Springs (lat. 33°12'30" N, long. 116°27'15" W; mainly in sec. 15, 22, T 11 S, R 5 E). Named on Tubb Canyon (1959) 7.5' quadrangle.
Culver: see **Culver City** [LOS ANGELES].
Culver City [LOS ANGELES]: *city,* 3.5 miles south of Beverly Hills city hall (lat. 34°01'15" N, long. 118°23'45" W). Named on Beverly Hills (1950), Hollywood (1953), and Venice (1950) 7.5' quadrangles. Called Culver on Sawtelle (1925) 6' quadrangle. Postal authorities established Culver City post office in 1915 (Frickstad, p. 72), and the city incorporated in 1917. T. McCarey named the place for Harry H. Culver when Culver Investment Company announced plans for the community in 1913 (Hanna, p. 79).
Culver Garden [LOS ANGELES]: *district,* 7.5 miles north of present Manhattan Beach city hall (lat. 33°59'45" N, long. 118°25'20" W). Named on Venice (1924) 6' quadrangle.
Culver Junction [LOS ANGELES]: *locality,* 3 miles south of Beverly Hills city hall along Southern Pacific Railroad (lat. 34°01'40" N, long. 118°23'20" W); a branch rail line to Culver City joins the main rail line at the place. Named on Beverly Hills (1966) 7.5' quadrangle.
Cumorah Crest: see **Camp Cumorah Crest** [LOS ANGELES].
Cunnane Barranca: see **Prince Barranca** [VENTURA].
Cunningham Canyon [LOS ANGELES]. *canyon,* drained by a stream that flows less than 1 mile to Verdugo Wash 4 miles northeast of Burbank city hall (lat. 34°13'25" N, long. 118°15'25" W). Named on Burbank (1966) 7.5' quadrangle.
Cutca Valley [SAN DIEGO]: *valley,* 4 miles north of Boucher Hill (lat. 33°23'40" N, long. 116°55'05" W; sec. 18, T 9 S, R 1 E). Named on Vail Lake (1953) 7.5' quadrangle. Called Hut Cut Valley on Ramona (1903) 30' quadrangle, and Hutcut Valley on Ellis and Lee's (1919) map.
Cuyamaca [SAN DIEGO]:
(1) *land grant,* between Descanso and Cuyamaca Reservoir. Named on Descanso (1960) and Julian (1960) 7.5' quadrangles—Cuyamaca Peak (1960) 7.5' quadrangle has the name "Cuyamaca Rancho" for the grant. Agustin Olvera received 11 leagues in 1845 and claimed 35,501 acres patented in 1874 (Cowan, p. 32; Cowan gave the alternate names "Cayamaca" and "Cujamaca" for the grant).
(2) *locality,* 3.5 miles northeast of Cuyamaca Peak (lat. 32°59' N, long. 116°34'15" W). Named on Cuyamaca (1903) 30' quadrangle. Postal authorities established Stratton post office at a supply center for mines in 1887, changed the name to Cuyamaca in 1888, and discontinued it in 1907; the name "Stratton" was for James Stratton, a mine owner (Salley, p. 54, 214).
Cuyamaca: see **Camp Cuyamaca** [SAN DIEGO].
Cuyamaca Lodge [SAN DIEGO]: *locality,* 3 miles north-northeast of Cuyamaca Peak (lat. 32°59'15" N, long. 116°35'05" W). Named on Cuyamaca Peak (1960) 7.5' quadrangle.
Cuyamaca Mountains [SAN DIEGO]: *range,* extends for 10 miles south from a spot west of Cuyamaca Reservoir to Sweetwater River. Named on Descanso (1960), Julian (1960), Tule Springs (1960), and Viejas Mountain (1960) 7.5' quadrangles.
Cuyamaca Peak [SAN DIEGO]: *peak,* 6.25 miles north of Descanso (lat. 32°56'50" N, long. 116°36'20" W); the peak is in Cuyamaca Mountains. Altitude 6512 feet. Named on Cuyamaca Peak (1960) 7.5' quadrangle. United States Board on Geographic Names (1933, p. 250) rejected the name "Cloud Peak" for the feature.
Cuyamaca Reservoir: see **Lake Cuyamaca** [SAN DIEGO].
Cuyama River [VENTURA]: *stream,* formed by the confluence of Beartrap Creek and Alamo Creek (2), flows 12.5 miles to Santa Barbara County 14 miles northwest of Reyes Peak (lat. 34°47' N, long. 119°26'30" W; sec. 17, T 8 N, R 24 W). Named on Cuyama Peak (1943), Rancho Nuevo Creek (1943), and Reyes Peak (1943) 7.5' quadrangles. Called Guyamas River on Goddard's (1857) map, Rio S. Maria on Parke's (1854-1855) map, and Santa Maria River on California Mining Bureau's (1909a) map.
Cycuan Creek: see **Sycuan Creek** [SAN DIEGO].
Cycuan Peak: see **Sycuan Peak** [SAN DIEGO].
Cypave [LOS ANGELES]. *locality,* 3.5 miles south-southeast of present Inglewood city hall along Pacific Electric Railroad (lat. 33° 55'10" N, long. 118°19'35" W). Named on Inglewood (1924) 6' quadrangle.
Cypress [ORANGE]: *city,* 3.5 miles southwest of Buena Park civic center (lat. 33°49'15" N, long. 118°02'10" W). Named on Los Alamitos (1964) 7.5' quadrangle. Postal authorities established Cypress post office in 1927

(Frickstad, p. 116), and the city incorporated in 1956. The name recalls Cypress school district, organized in 1895 (Meadows, p. 56). The community began in 1899 and first was called Waterville because it was practically surrounded by the uncontrolled flow of water from artesian wells; the residents disliked the name "Waterville" and chose the new name "Cypress" about 1905 (Hanna, p. 80).

Cypress Canyon [SAN DIEGO]: *canyon,* drained by a stream that flows nearly 3 miles to Los Peñasquitos Canyon 4.25 miles west-southwest of Poway (lat. 32°56'40" N, long. 117°06'25" W; sec. 20, T 14 S, R 2 W). Named on Poway (1967) 7.5' quadrangle.

Cypress Grove [LOS ANGELES]. *locality,* 7.25 miles north of present Manhattan Beach city hall along Pacific Electric Railroad (lat. 34°59'30" N, long, 118°25'15" W). Named on Venice (1924) 6' quadrangle.

- D -

Dagger Flat [LOS ANGELES]. *area,* 7 miles north-northwest of Sunland in Pacoima Canyon (lat. 34°21'35" N, long. 118°20'30" W; at W line sec. 10, T 3 N, R 14 W). Named on Sunland (1953) 7.5' quadrangle.

Dagger Flat Canyon [LOS ANGELES]: *canyon,* drained by a stream that flows 2 miles to Pacoima Canyon 7 miles north-northwest of Sunland (lat. 34°21'35" N, long. 118°20'30" W; at W line sec. 10, T 3 N, R 14 W); the mouth of the canyon is at Dagger Flat. Named on Agua Dulce (1960) and Sunland (1953) 7.5' quadrangles.

Daices: see **Calabasas** [LOS ANGELES].

Dairyland: see **La Palma** [ORANGE].

Dairy Valley: see **Cerritos** [LOS ANGELES].

Daisy Canyon [LOS ANGELES]: *canyon,* drained by a stream that flows 1.25 miles to Colby Canyon 6 miles southeast of Condor Peak (lat. 34°16'15" N, long. 118°08'05" W). Named on Chilao Flat (1959) and Condor Peak (1959) 7.5' quadrangles.

Dakin Bay: see **Avalon Bay** [LOS ANGELES].

Dakin's Cove: see **Avalon Bay** [LOS ANGELES].

Dalewood [ORANGE]: *locality,* 6 miles south of present Buena Park civic center (lat. 33°46'40" N, long. 117°58'50" W; sec. 36, T 4 S, R 11 W). Named on Anaheim (1950) 7.5' quadrangle.

Daley Flat [SAN DIEGO]: *area,* 3.25 miles south of Santa Ysabel (lat. 33°03'45" N, long. 116°40' W; at NW cor. sec. 10, T 13 S, R 3 E). Named on Santa Ysabel (1960) 7.5' quadrangle.

Dalton Campground: see **Little Dalton Campground** [LOS ANGELES].

Dalton Canyon: see **Big Dalton Canyon** [LOS ANGELES]; **Little Dalton Canyon** [LOS ANGELES].

Dalton Reservoir: see **Big Dalton Reservoir** [LOS ANGELES].

Dalton Wash: see **Big Dalton Wash** [LOS ANGELES]; **Little Dalton Wash** [LOS ANGELES].

Daly Creek [SAN DIEGO]: *stream,* flows less than 1 mile to Longs Gulch 4 miles north-northwest of El Cajon Mountain (lat. 32°57'45" N, long. 116°51'30" W). Named on El Cajon Mountain (1955) 7.5' quadrangle.

Dameron Valley [SAN DIEGO]: *valley,* 8 miles northeast of Boucher Hill (lat. 33°25'10" N, long. 116°49'25" W). Named on Aguanga (1954) 7.5' quadrangle. The misspelled name commemorates Mit Damron, who settled in the neighborhood in the 1860's (Stein, p. 37).

Dana Basin [SAN DIEGO]: *embayment,* 6.25 miles south-southeast of Point La Jolla along Mission Bay (lat. 32°46' N, long. 117°14'05" W). Named on La Jolla (1953) 7.5' quadrangle.

Dana Cove [ORANGE]: *embayment,* 3.5 miles southwest of San Juan Capistrano (lat. 33°27'45" N, long. 117°42'15" W). Named on Dana Point (1968) 7.5' quadrangle. The feature was called Bahia de San Juan Capistrano when it was used as an anchorage for San Juan Capistrano mission (Gudde, 1949, p. 88). The name "Dana" recalls Richard Henry Dana, who described the embayment in his book *Two Years before the Mast* (Hoover, Rensch, and Rensch, p. 261).

Dana Point [ORANGE]:

(1) *promontory,* 4 miles southwest of San Juan Capistrano along the coast (lat. 33°27'40" N, long. 117°42'55" W); the feature is west of Dana Cove. Named on Dana Point (1968) 7.5' quadrangle. Called San Juan Capistrano Point on San Juan Capistrano (1941) 15' quadrangle, but United States Board on Geographic Names (1938, p. 17) rejected the names "San Juan Capistrano Point" and "San Juan Point" for the feature. Wagner (p. 410) noted that the promontory was called Punta de Arbolada on a Spanish chart. Richard Egan is credited with applying the name "Dana" to the promontory in the 1870's after he visited the spot with Richard Henry Dana's son (Hanna, p. 82).

(2) *town,* 3 miles southwest of San Juan Capistrano (lat. 33°28'05" N, long. 117°41'50" W); the center of the town is 1 mile northeast of Dana Point (1). Named on Dana Point (1968) 7.5' quadrangle. Postal authorities established Dana Point post office in 1929 (Frickstad, p. 116). S.H. Woodruff laid out the town in 1924 (Meadows, p. 57).

Dana Point Harbor [ORANGE]: *water feature,* 3.5 miles southwest of San Juan Capistrano along the coast at Dana Cove (lat. 33°27'35" N, long. 117°41'50" W). Named on Dana Point (1968) 7.5' quadrangle.

Daney Canyon [SAN DIEGO]: *canyon,* drained by a stream that flows 2 miles to San Vicente Creek 8 miles north-northeast of Lakeside (lat. 32°58'25" N, long. 116°53'05" W). Named on San Pasqual (1954) and San Vicente Reservoir (1955) 7.5' quadrangles.

Dan Price Creek [SAN DIEGO]: *stream,* flows 1.5 miles to Santa Ysabel Creek 2.5 miles north of Julian (lat. 33°07' N, long. 116°36'30" W). Named on Julian (1960) 7.5' quadrangle.

Dark Canyon [LOS ANGELES]:

(1) *canyon,* drained by a stream that flows 1.5 miles to Arroyo Seco 7 miles north-northwest of Pasadena city hall (lat. 34°14'45" N; long. 118°11' W). Named on Condor Peak (1959) and Pasadena (1953) 7.5' quadrangles.

(2) *canyon,* drained by a stream that flows 2 miles to Cold Canyon 4.5 miles north of Malibu Point (lat. 34°04'55" N, long. 118°41'25" W; near W line sec. 17, T 1 S, R 17 W). Named on Malibu Beach (1951) 7.5' quadrangle.

(3) *canyon,* 0.5 mile long, 3.5 miles south-southwest of Burbank city hall (lat. 34°08'20" N, long. 118°20'25" W). Named on Burbank (1953) 7.5' quadrangle.

Dark Canyon [SAN DIEGO]: *canyon,* drained by a stream that flows 1.5 miles to Cañada Aguanga 7.5 miles northwest of Warner Springs (lat. 33°20'45" N, long. 117°44'15" W; near SE cor. sec. 35, T 9 S, R 2 E). Named on Warner Springs (1959) 7.5' quadrangle.

Dark Canyon: see **Sycamore Canyon** [LOS ANGELES] (5).

Daum [ORANGE]: *locality,* 1.5 miles west-northwest of Yorba Linda along Atchison, Topeka and Santa Fe Railroad (lat. 33°53'50" N, long. 117°50'15" W). Named on Olinda (1935) 7.5' quadrangle.

Dave McCain Spring [SAN DIEGO]: *spring,* 9 miles southwest of Ocotillo Wells (lat. 33°03' N, long. 116°14'15" W). Named on Harper Canyon (1959) 7.5' quadrangle.

Davidson: see **Camp Davidson** [SAN DIEGO].

Davidson City: see **Dominguez** [LOS ANGELES] (2).

Daviston: see **Jamacha** [SAN DIEGO].

Dawson Saddle [LOS ANGELES]: *pass,* 4 miles north-northeast of Crystal Lake (lat. 34°22'05" N, long. 117°48'10" W; near SE cor. sec. 3, T 3 N, R 9 W). Named on Crystal Lake (1958) 7.5' quadrangle.

Dayton Avenue [LOS ANGELES]: *locality,* 2.25 miles north-northeast of Los Angeles city hall along Southern Pacific Railroad (lat. 34°05' N, long. 118°13'30" W). Named on Los Angeles (1966) 7.5' quadrangle.

Dayton Canyon [LOS ANGELES]: *canyon,* 1.25 miles long, drained by Dayton Creek above a point 3.5 miles southwest of Chatsworth (lat. 34°13'10" N, long. 118°38'45" W). Named on Calabasas (1952) 7.5' quadrangle.

Dayton Creek [LOS ANGELES]: *stream,* flows 2.25 miles to Chatsworth Creek 3 miles south-southwest of Chatsworth (lat. 34°12'55" N, long. 118°37'30" W); the stream drains Dayton Canyon. Named on Calabasas (1952) 7.5' quadrangle.

Dead Horse Canyon [LOS ANGELES]: *canyon,* 2 miles long, 6 miles west-northwest of Pasadena city hall (lat. 34°10'20" N, long. 118° 14'45" W). Named on Burbank (1953) and Pasadena (1953) 7.5' quadrangles.

Deadhorse Canyon [LOS ANGELES]: *canyon,* drained by a stream that flows less than 1 mile to South Long Canyon 4.5 miles northeast of Burnt Peak (lat. 34°43'30" N, long. 118°31'05" W; near W line sec. 6, T 7 N, R 15 W). Named on Burnt Peak (1958) 7.5' quadrangle.

Deadhorse Canyon: see **Dead Horse Creek** [VENTURA].

Dead Horse Creek [VENTURA]: *stream,* flows 2 miles to Snowy Creek 4.5 miles northeast of McDonald Peak (lat. 34°40'30" N, long. 118°52'30" W; sec. 27, T 7 N, R 19 W). Named on Black Mountain (1958) and McDonald Peak (1958) 7.5' quadrangles. Called Deadhorse Cr. on Tejon (1903) 30' quadrangle. The canyon of the stream is called Deadhorse Canyon on Los Angeles County (1935) map.

Deadman Canyon: see **Bouquet Canyon** [LOS ANGELES].

Deadman Flat [SAN DIEGO]: *area,* 5.25 miles south of Santa Ysabel (lat. 33°01'50" N, long. 116°40'10" W; near E line sec. 21, T 13 S, R 3 E). Named on Santa Ysabel (1960) 7.5' quadrangle.

Deadman Hole [SAN DIEGO]: *relief feature,* 6.5 miles northwest of Warner Springs in Cañada Aguanga (lat. 33°20'30" N, long. 116° 43'15" W; near NE cor. sec. 1, T 10 S, R 2 E). Named on Warner Springs (1959) 7.5' quadrangle. Called Deadman's Hole on Tucker and Reed's (1939) map. The name came after a Butterfield Overland stage driver found a corpse at the place in 1858 (Gudde, 1949, p. 90).

Deadman Island: see **Reservation Point** [LOS ANGELES].

Deal Canyon [VENTURA]: *canyon,* drained by a stream that flows 4.5 miles to Rancho Nuevo Creek 8.5 miles west-northwest of Reyes Peak (lat. 34°41'20" N, long. 119°24'50" W). Named on Rancho Nuevo Creek (1943) 7.5' quadrangle.

Deals Flat [VENTURA]: *area,* 3.5 miles west-southwest of Triunfo Pass (lat. 34°05'15" N, long. 118°58'15" W; at NE cor. sec. 16, T 1 S, R 20 W). Named on Triunfo Pass (1950) 7.5' quadrangle.

De Anza Cove [SAN DIEGO]: *embayment,* 5.25 miles southeast of Point La Jolla off Fiesta Bay (lat. 32°47'45" N, long. 117°12'45" W); the feature is north of De Anza Point. Named on La Jolla (1967) 7.5' quadrangle.

De Anza Point [SAN DIEGO]: *promontory,* 5.25 miles southeast of Point La Jolla along Fiesta Bay (lat. 32°47'40" N, long. 117°12'40" W). Named on La Jolla (1967) 7.5' quadrangle.

Decker Canyon: see **Agua Dulce Canyon** [LOS ANGELES].

Deep Canyon [ORANGE]: *canyon,* 1 mile long, 2.25 miles south-southeast of San Juan Capistrano (lat. 33°28'15" N, long. 117°38'55" W). Named on Dana Point (1968) 7.5' quadrangle.

Deep Tank Reservoir [LOS ANGELES]: *lake,* 300 feet long, nearly 4 miles north of Mount Banning on Santa Catalina Island (lat. 33°25'30" N, long. 118°27' W). Named on Santa Catalina North (1950) 7.5' quadrangle.

Deer Canyon [LOS ANGELES]:

(1) *canyon,* drained by a stream that flows nearly 2 miles to Elizabeth Lake Canyon 3.25 miles southwest of the village of Lake Hughes (lat. 34°38'50" N, long. 118°29'10" W; near SE cor. sec. 32, T 7 N, R 15 W). Named on Lake Hughes (1957) 7.5' quadrangle. On Los Angeles County (1935) map, the name "Aliso Canyon" applies to the lower part of present Deer Canyon (1) and to a western branch of that canyon.

(2) *canyon,* drained by a stream that flows nearly 1 mile to Sunset Canyon 2 miles northeast of Burbank (lat. 34°12'05" W; long. 118°17'10" W). Named on Burbank (1953) 7.5' quadrangle.

Deer Canyon [SAN DIEGO]: *canyon,* drained by a stream that flows 3.5 miles to Carmel Valley 4.5 miles east of Del Mar (lat. 32° 57' N, long. 117°11'15" W; near SE cor. sec. 16, T 14 S, R 3 W). Named on Del Mar (1967) 7.5' quadrangle.

Deer Canyon [VENTURA]: *canyon,* drained by a stream that flows 2.25 miles to the sea 5.25 miles southwest of Triunfo Pass (lat. 34°03'40" N, long. 118°59'05" W; sec. 21, T 1 S, R 20 W). Named on Triunfo Pass (1950) 7.5' quadrangle.

Deer Creek [LOS ANGELES]: *stream,* flows 1.5 miles to Verdugo Canyon 6 miles west-northwest of Pasadena city hall (lat. 34°11'35" N, long. 118°14'05" W). Named on Burbank (1953) and Pasadena (1953) 7.5' quadrangles.

Deer Flat Campground [LOS ANGELES]: *locality,* 1 mile north-northeast of Crystal Lake (lat. 34°20' N, long. 117°50'15" W). Named on Crystal Lake (1958) 7.5' quadrangle.

Deerhorn Flat: see **Deerhorn Valley** [SAN DIEGO].

Deerhorn Spring [SAN DIEGO]: *spring,* 5 miles north of Barrett Junction (lat. 32°40'45" N, long. 116°43'30" W; sec. 24, T 17 S, R 2 E); the spring is in Deerhorn Valley. Named on Barrett Lake (1960) 7.5' quadrangle.

Deerhorn Valley [SAN DIEGO]: *valley,* 4.5 miles north-northwest of Barrett Junction (lat. 32°40'30" N, long. 116°43'30" W; mainly in sec. 24, T 17 S, R 2 E). Named on Barrett Lake (1960) 7.5' quadrangle. Called Deerhorn Flat on Cuyamaca (1903) 30' quadrangle, but United States Board on Geographic Names (1962a, p. 10) rejected this name for the place.

Deering Canyon [SAN DIEGO]: *canyon,* drained by a stream that flows nearly 1 mile to Indian Canyon 8.5 miles northwest of Borrego Springs (lat. 33°20'30" N, long. 116°29'05" W). Named on Borrego Palm Canyon (1959) 7.5' quadrangle.

Deer Lake [SAN DIEGO]: *intermittent lake,* 225 feet long, 1.5 miles south of Julian (lat. 33°03'15" N, long. 116°36'10" W; sec. 7, T 13 S, R 4 E). Named on Julian (1960) 7.5' quadrangle.

Deer Lake Highlands [LOS ANGELES]: *locality,* 2 miles north-northeast of Chatsworth (lat. 34°17' N, long. 118°35'45" W; sec. 6, T 2 N, R 16 W). Named on Oat Mountain (1952) 7.5' quadrangle. Called Twin Lakes on Chatsworth (1940) and Zelzah (1941) 6' quadrangles, and called Twin Lakes Park on Santa Susana (1943) 15' quadrangle.

Deer Lodge [LOS ANGELES]: *locality,* 3 miles north of Burnt Peak (lat. 34°43'35" N, long. 118°34'25" W; near E line sec. 4, T 7 N, R 16 W). Named on Burnt Peak (1958) 7.5' quadrangle.

Deer Park [LOS ANGELES]: *locality,* 5.5 miles northwest of Azusa city hall (lat. 34°11'40" N, long. 117°57'50" W; on S line sec. 6, T 1 N, R 10 W). Named on Azusa (1953) 7.5' quadrangle. The name is from the abundance of deer at the place in the 1880's (Robinson, J.W., 1983, p. 74).

Deer Park [SAN DIEGO]: *area,* nearly 7 miles east-southeast of Cuyamaca Peak (lat. 32°54'05" N, long. 116°30'05" W; on N line sec. 6, T 15 S, R 5 E). Named on Cuyamaca Peak (1960) 7.5' quadrangle.

Deer Park Branch [LOS ANGELES]: *stream,* flows 1 mile to Eaton Canyon 1.5 miles west-southwest of Mount Wilson (1) (lat. 34°13'05" N, long. 118°05'05" W). Named on Mount Wilson (1953) 7.5' quadrangle.

Deer Park Canyon [VENTURA]: *canyon,* drained by a stream that flows 2.25 miles to Santa Barbara County 18 miles north-northwest of Reyes Peak (lat. 34°51'10" N, long. 119°26'30" W; sec. 21, T 9 N, R 24 W). Named on Cuyama Peak (1943) 7.5' quadrangle.

Deer Ridge Camp [LOS ANGELES]: *locality,* 0.5 mile east-southeast of Big Pines (lat. 34°22'35" N, long. 117°40'55" W; sec. 2, T 3 N, R 8 W). Named on Mescal Creek (1956) 7.5' quadrangle.

Deer Spring [LOS ANGELES]: *spring,* 6.5 miles south of Acton (lat. 34°22'35" N, long. 118°10'50" W). Named on Acton (1959) 7.5' quadrangle. Los Angeles County (1935) map has the plural form "Deer Springs" for the name.

Deer Spring [SAN DIEGO]: *spring,* less than 1 mile north-northeast of Cuyamaca Peak (lat. 32°57'20" N, long. 116°36' W). Named on Cuyamaca Peak (1960) 7.5' quadrangle.

Deer Spring Campground [LOS ANGELES]: *locality,* 4 miles north-northeast of Condor Peak (lat. 34°22'30" N, long. 118°10'55" W); the campground is near Deer Spring. Named on Condor Peak (1959) 7.5' quadrangle.

Deguynos Canyon [SAN DIEGO]: *canyon,* drained by a stream that flows nearly 7 miles to Imperial County 8 miles north-northeast of Sweeney Pass (lat. 32°55'20" N, long. 116°06'10" W; at E line sec. 25, T 14 S, R 8 E). Named on Arroyo Tapiado (1959) and Carrizo Mountain NE (1957) 7.5' quadrangles.

Dehesa [SAN DIEGO]: *locality,* 6 miles southwest of Alpine (lat. 32° 46'55" N, long. 116°50'55" W; sec. 14, T 16 S, R 1 E); the place is near the south end of present Dehesa Valley. Named on Cuyamaca (1903) 30' quadrangle. Postal authorities established Dehesa post office at the former site of Sweetwater post office in 1888 and discontinued it in 1917 (Salley, p. 56, 217).

Dehesa Valley [SAN DIEGO]: *valley,* 5.5 miles southwest of Alpine (lat. 32°47'10" N, long. 116°50'30" W; sec. 11, 12, 14, T 16 S, R 1 E). Named on Alpine (1955) 7.5' quadrangle.

Dehr Creek [SAN DIEGO]: *stream,* flows nearly 5 miles to Cedar Creek (2) 6.25 miles south-southeast of Santa Ysabel (lat. 33°01'10" N, long. 116°38'25" W; near N line sec. 26, T 13 S, R 3 E). Named on Julian (1960) and Santa Ysabel (1960) 7.5' quadrangles.

Del Amo [LOS ANGELES]: *locality,* 5.5 miles north of Long Beach city hall along Pacific Electric Railroad (lat. 33°50'50" N, long. 118°12'35" W). Named on Long Beach (1949) 7.5' quadrangle.

Del Dios [SAN DIEGO]: *district,* 4.25 miles south-southwest of Escondido city hall along Lake Hodges (lat. 33°04'25" N, long. 117°07'05" W; mainly at E line sec. 6, T 13 S, R 2 W). Named on Escondido (1968) 7.5' quadrangle.

Delhi [ORANGE]: *locality,* 2.5 miles south-southeast of Santa Ana along Southern Pacific Railroad (lat. 33°42'50" N, long. 117°51'15" W). Named on Tustin (1935) 7.5' quadrangle, which shows Gloryetta post office at the place. Postal authorities established Harbor post office in 1914, changed the name to Gloryetta in 1915, and discontinued it in 1936 (Frickstad, p. 117). The name "Delhi" is from Delhi, New York, former home of the McFaldden brothers, who developed several hundred acres of land in Orange County (Meadows, p. 57).

Del Mar [SAN DIEGO]: *town,* 18 miles north-northwest of downtown San Diego along the coast (lat. 32°57'35" N, long. 117°15'50" W; sec. 11, 14, T 14 S, R 4 W). Named on Del Mar (1967) 7.5' quadrangle. Postal authorities established Del Mar post office in 1885 (Frickstad, p. 149), and the town incorporated in 1959. Colonel J.S. Taylor arrived at the place in 1882 and began a real-estate promotion; Mrs. Loop, wife of one of Taylor's partners, suggested the name "Del Mar" from Bayard Taylor's poem *Paseo del Mar* (Stein, p. 38). Hanks' (1886a) map shows a place called Weed P.O. located about 3 miles south-southeast of present Del Mar near the mouth of Soledad Valley. Postal authorities established Weed post office in 1880 and discontinued it in 1886; the name was for William S. Weed, first postmaster (Salley, p. 236). United States Board on Geographic Names (1992, p. 4) approved the name "Blacks Beach" for a beach situated 4.5 miles south of Del Mar along the coast—the name is for the Black family.

Del Mar: see **Camp Del Mar** [SAN DIEGO].

Del Mar Mesa [SAN DIEGO]: *ridge,* north-trending, 1.25 miles long, 5 miles east-southeast of Del Mar (lat. 32°56'30" N, long. 117°10'50" W; sec. 22, T 14 S, R 3 W). Named on Del Mar (1967) 7.5' quadrangle.

Del Rey [LOS ANGELES]: *locality,* 7 miles north of present Manhattan Beach city hall along Pacific Electric Railroad (lat. 33°59'10" N, long. 118°25'30" W). Named on Venice (1924) 6' quadrangle.

Del Sur [LOS ANGELES]: *locality,* 8.5 miles east of the village of Lake Hughes (lat. 34°41'20" N, long. 118°17'20" W; at NE cor. sec. 19, T 7 N, R 13 W). Named on Del Sur (1958) 7.5' quadrangle. Postal authorities established Maynard post office in 1884, moved it 0.5 mile east in 1890, changed the name to Del Sur the same year, moved it 0.5 mile west in 1891, and discontinued it in 1925; the name "Maynard" was for Levi C. Maynard, first postmaster (Salley, p. 57, 135).

Del Sur Ridge [LOS ANGELES]: *ridge,* 7.5 miles long, center about 11 miles south of the village of Lake Hughes (lat. 34°31' N, long. 118°28'15" W). Named on Green Valley (1958) and Mint Canyon (1960) 7.5' quadrangles.

Delta [LOS ANGELES]: *locality,* 3.5 miles south-southeast of Inglewood city hall (lat. 33°55'10" N, long. 118°19'15" W; sec. 11, T 3 S, R 14 W). Named on Inglewood (1964) 7.5' quadrangle.

Delta Canyon [LOS ANGELES]: *canyon,* 1.5 miles long, opens into Big Tujunga Canyon 4 miles northeast of Sunland (lat. 34°18'05" N, long. 118°15'35" W). Named on Condor Peak (1959) and Sunland (1953) 7.5' quadrangles.

De Luz [SAN DIEGO]:

(1) *locality,* 5.5 miles northwest of Fallbrook (lat. 33°26'15" N, long.

117°19'25" W; sec. 32, T 8 S, R 4 W). Named on Fallbrook (1968) 7.5' quadrangle. The name supposedly is from the Spanish term "Corral de Luz" given by Mexicans to a corral built by Mr. Luce (Stein, p. 38). Postal authorities established Deluz post office in 1882, changed the name De Luz in 1891, moved it 1.5 miles northeast in 1895, moved it 1.5 miles west in 1902, moved it 1 mile west in 1906, moved it 1 mile southeast in 1909, moved it 0.25 mile north in 1937, moved it 0.5 mile south in 1938, and discontinued it in 1955—the moves of the post office generally were for the convenience of various postmasters (Salley, p. 57). Berkstresser (p. A-12) listed De Luz Warm Springs, located near present De Luz (lat. 33°26'09" N, long. 117°19'30" W). Waring (p. 48) noted that the springs supported a small resort in 1888 and 1889. Anderson (p. 122) used the name "Corral de Luz Warm Springs" for the resort. Postal authorities established Recluse post office 4 miles northwest of De Luz post office in 1893 and discontinued it in 1898 (Salley, p. 182).

(2) *locality,* 2 miles south-southwest of Fallbrook along Atchison, Topeka and Santa Fe Railroad (lat. 33°21'35" N, long. 117°16'10" W; at S line sec. 26, T 9 S, R 4 W). Named on Morro Hill (1968) 7.5' quadrangle.

De Luz: see **Camp De Luz** [SAN DIEGO].

De Luz Creek [SAN DIEGO]: *stream,* heads in Riverside County and flows 8.5 miles in San Diego County to Santa Margarita River 4.25 miles west-southwest of Fallbrook (lat. 33°21'40" N, long. 117°19'20" W; sec. 29, T 9 S, R 4 W); De Luz (1) is along the stream. Named on Fallbrook (1968) and Morro Hill (1968) 7.5' quadrangles. Called Deluz Creek on San Luis Rey (1898) 30' quadrangle.

Deluz Station [SAN DIEGO]: *locality,* 4.25 miles west-southwest of Fallbrook along Southern California Railroad (lat. 33°21'45" N, long. 117°19'30" W). Named on San Luis Rey (1898) 30' quadrangle. Margarita Peak (1944) 15' quadrangle has the name for a place located 2.5 miles farther south-southeast along a realignment of the railroad.

Deluz Warm Springs: see **De Luz** [SAN DIEGO] (1).

Del Valle [LOS ANGELES]: *locality,* 8 miles west-northwest of Newhall along Southern Pacific Railroad (lat. 34°25'05" N, long. 118°39'25" W); the place is on San Francisco grant, which Antonio del Valle received. Named on Val Verde (1952) 7.5' quadrangle. Camulos (1903) 30' quadrangle had the form "Delvalle" for the name.

Denis [LOS ANGELES]: *locality,* 6 miles south of Lancaster along Southern Pacific Railroad (lat. 34°38' N, long. 118°07'30" W; sec. 2, 11, T 6 N, R 12 W). Named on Lancaster East (1958), Lancaster West (1958), and Palmdale (1958) 7.5' quadrangles.

Dennery Canyon [SAN DIEGO]: *canyon,* drained by a stream that flows 1.5 miles to Otay Valley 5.5 miles east of Imperial Beach civic center (lat. 32°35'20" N, long. 117°01'10" W). Named on Imperial Beach (1967) 7.5' quadrangle.

Dennis Park: see **Mission Hills** [LOS ANGELES].

Derrydale Creek [VENTURA]: *stream,* flows 3.5 miles to Sespe Creek 5.5 miles north-northeast of Wheeler Springs (lat. 34°35' N, long. 119°15'40" W; near E line sec. 25, T 6 N, R 23 E). Named on Lion Canyon (1943) and Wheeler Springs (1943) 7.5' quadrangles.

Descanso [SAN DIEGO]: *town,* 33 miles east-northeast of San Diego (lat. 32°51'25" N, long. 116°36'55" W). Named on Descanso (1960) 7.5' quadrangle. Postal authorities established Descanso post office in 1877 and moved it 2 miles southeast in 1884 (Salley, p. 58).

Descanso Bay [LOS ANGELES]: *embayment,* 0.5 mile north of Avalon on the northeast side of Santa Catalina Island (lat. 33°21'05" N, long. 118°19'35" W). Named on Santa Catalina East (1950) 7.5' quadrangle.

Descanso Campground [SAN DIEGO]: *locality,* 0.5 mile west of Descanso (lat. 32°51'20" N, long. 116°37'35" W; near N line sec. 24, T 15 S, R 3 E). Named on Viejas Mountain (1960) 7.5' quadrangle.

Descanso Creek [SAN DIEGO]: *stream,* flows 6 miles to Sweetwater River at Descanso (lat. 32°51'30" N, long. 116°36'45" W). Named on Cuyamaca Peak (1960) and Descanso (1960) 7.5' quadrangles.

Descanso Junction [SAN DIEGO]: *locality,* 1 mile south of Descanso (lat. 32°50'30" N, long. 116°36'45" W; near NW cor. sec. 30, T 15 S, R 4 E). Named on Descanso (1960) 7.5' quadrangle.

Descanso Peak: see **Chiquito Peak** [SAN DIEGO].

Descanso Valley [SAN DIEGO]: *valley,* at and east of Descanso (lat. 32°51'15" N, long. 116°36'25" W). Named on Descanso (1960) 7.5' quadrangle.

Desert Lodge [SAN DIEGO]: *locality,* 4.25 miles southeast of Borrego Springs (lat. 33°12'35" N, long. 116°19'40" W; sec. 22, 23, T 11 S, R 6 E). Named on Borrego Sink (1959) 7.5' quadrangle.

Des Moines [ORANGE]: *locality,* 1.5 miles west of downtown La Habra along Pacific Electric Railroad (lat. 33°55'40" N, long. 117° 58' W). Named on La Habra (1964) 7.5' quadrangle. The site also had the name "Laon Junction" (Meadows, p. 77).

De Soto Heights: see **Soto Street Junction** [LOS ANGELES].

Devil Canyon [LOS ANGELES]: *canyon,* drained by a stream that flows 4.5 miles to Browns Canyon 1.5 miles north-northwest of Chatsworth (lat. 34°16'40" N, long. 118°35'30" W). Named on Oat Mountain (1952) and Santa Susana (1951) 7.5' quadrangles. Camulos (1903) 30' quadrangle has the name "Aliso Canyon" for the upper part of present Devil Canyon, and shows Devil Creek in the lower part. Santa Susana (1903) 15' quadrangle has the name "Ybarra Canyon" for the upper part of present Devil Canyon, and leaves present Ybarra Canyon unnamed. Los Angeles County (1935) map shows Devils Canyon Creek in present Devil Canyon.

Devil Canyon [LOS ANGELES-VENTURA]: *canyon,* drained by a stream that heads in Los Angels County and flows 6 miles to Lake Piru 6 miles north-northeast of Piru in Ventura County (lat. 34°29'15" N, long. 118°44'25" W). Named on Val Verde (1952, photorevised 1969) and Whitaker Peak (1958) 7.5' quadrangles. Los Angeles County (1935) map has the form "Devils Canyon" for the name.

Devil Canyon [SAN DIEGO]: *canyon,* drained by a stream that flows 7.5 miles to San Mateo Canyon 5 miles west-northwest of Margarita Peak (lat. 33°28'25" N, long. 117°27'55" W). Named on Margarita Peak (1968) 7.5' quadrangle. Called Devils Canyon on Tucker and Reed's (1939) map.

Devil Creek: see **Devil Canyon** [LOS ANGELES].

Devil Gulch [LOS ANGELES]: *canyon,* drained by a stream that flows 2.5 miles to San Gabriel River 6 miles east-southeast of Crystal Lake (lat. 34°16'50" N, long. 117°45'10" W). Named on Crystal Lake (1958) 7.5' quadrangle. Called Devils Canyon on Rock Creek (1903) 15' quadrangle, but United States Board on Geographic Names (1939, p. 13) rejected this form for the name.

Devil Gulch: see **Devils Gulch** [VENTURA].

Devils Canyon [LOS ANGELES]: *canyon,* nearly 10 miles long, opens into the canyon of West Fork San Gabriel River 8.5 miles north-northwest of Azusa city hall (lat. 34°14'30" N, long. 117°58'15" W). Named on Azusa (1953) and Waterman Mountain (1959) 7.5' quadrangles.

Devils Canyon [SAN DIEGO]: *canyon,* drained by a stream that flows 1.5 miles to Imperial County 6.5 miles northeast of Jacumba (lat. 32°41'05" N, long. 116°06'20" W; at E line sec. 13, T 17 S, R 8 E). Named on In-Ko-Pah Gorge (1959) 7.5' quadrangle.

Devils Canyon: see **Devil Canyon** [LOS ANGELES-VENTURA]; **Devil Canyon** [SAN DIEGO]; **Devil Gulch** [LOS ANGELES].

Devils Canyon Creek: see **Devil Canyon** [LOS ANGELES].

Devils Chair [LOS ANGELES]: *relief feature,* 3 miles south of Valyermo (lat. 34°24'05" N, long. 117°50'50" W; sec. 29, T 4 N, R 9 W). Named on Valyermo (1958) 7.5' quadrangle.

Devils Gate [LOS ANGELES]:

(1) *narrows,* 3 miles north-northwest of present Pasadena city hall along Arroyo Seco (lat. 34°11'05" N, long. 118°10'30" W). Named on Pasadena (1900) 15' quadrangle.

(2) *locality,* 2.5 miles north-northwest of present Pasadena city hall along Los Angeles Terminal Railroad (lat. 34°10'50" N, long. 118° 10'05" W); the place is 0.5 mile east-southeast of Devils Gate (1). Named on Pasadena (1900) 15' quadrangle.

Devils Gate [VENTURA]: *narrows,* 4.5 miles north-northwest of Fillmore along Sespe Creek (lat. 34°27'50" N, long. 118°56'35" W; sec. 2, T 4 N, R 20 W). Named on Fillmore (1951) 7.5' quadrangle.

Devils Gate Reservoir [LOS ANGELES]: *intermittent lake,* behind a dam three miles north-northwest of Pasadena along Arroyo Seco (lat. 34°11'05" N, long. 118°10'30" W); the dam is at Devils Gate (1). Named on Pasadena (1966) 7.5' quadrangle.

Devils Gateway [VENTURA]: *narrows,* 5.5 miles southeast of Cobblestone Mountain along Agua Blanca Creek (lat. 34°33' N, long. 118°48'05" W; sec. 6, T 5 N, R 18 W). Named on Cobblestone Mountain (1958) 7.5' quadrangle.

Devils Gulch [LOS ANGELES]: *canyon,* 1 mile long, 2 miles north-northeast of Burnt Peak (lat. 34°42'20" N, long. 118°33'25" W; on S line sec. 10, T 7 N, R 16 W). Named on Burnt Peak (1958) 7.5' quadrangle.

Devils Gulch [VENTURA]: *relief feature,* 5 miles southwest of the town of Ojai near Ventura River (lat. 34°24'25" N, long. 119°17'50" W). Named on Matilija (1952) 7.5' quadrangle. Called Devil Gulch on Ventura (1904) 15' quadrangle.

Devils Heart Peak [VENTURA]: *peak,* 10.5 miles north-northwest of Fillmore (lat. 34°32'45" N, long. 118°58'30" W). Altitude 5203 feet. Named on Devils Heart Peak (1943) 7.5' quadrangle.

Devils Jumpoff [SAN DIEGO]: *relief feature,* 7 miles south-southwest of San Ysabel (lat. 33°01'20" N, long. 116°43'55" W; near S line sec. 24, T 13 S, R 2 E). Named on Santa Ysabel (1960) 7.5' quadrangle.

Devils Potrero [VENTURA]: *area,* 6 miles southeast of Cobblestone Mountain (lat. 34°32'10" N, long. 118°48'25" W; sec. 7, T 5 N, R 18 W). Named on Cobblestone Mountain (1958) 7.5' quadrangle.

Devils Punchbowl [LOS ANGELES]: *relief feature,* 1.5 miles south of Valyermo (lat. 34°25'15" N, long. 117°51'10" W; sec. 18, 19, 20, T 4 N, R 9 W). Named on Valyermo (1958) 7.5' quadrangle.

Devils Punchbowl [SAN DIEGO]: *relief feature,* 9 miles north-northwest of Descanso (lat. 32°58'10" N, long. 116°41' W; near W line sec. 9, T 14 S, R 3 E). Named on Tule Springs (1960) 7.5' quadrangle.

Devil Wash: see **Little Devil Wash** [SAN DIEGO].

Devore Campground [LOS ANGELES]: *locality,* 2 miles northeast of Mount Wilson (1) along West Fork San Gabriel River (lat. 34°14'35" N, long.

118°02'05" W; sec. 21, T 2 N, R 11 W). Named on Mount Wilson (1966) 7.5' quadrangle.

Dewitt Canyon [LOS ANGELES]: *canyon*, drained by a stream that flows nearly 2 miles to Pico Canyon 3.25 miles west of Newhall (lat. 34°22'35" N, long. 118°35'15" W; near NW cor. sec. 5, T 3 N, R 16 W). Named on Oat Mountain (1952) 7.5' quadrangle.

Dexter Peak [SAN DIEGO]: *peak*, 0.5 mile southwest of Descanso (lat. 32°50'55" N, long. 116°37'20" W; sec. 24, T 15 S, R 3 E). Named on Descanso (1960) 7.5' quadrangle. The name commemorates John Porter Dexter, an early resident of the neighborhood (United States Board on Geographic Names, 1961a, p. 18).

Diabold Canyon [SAN DIEGO]: *canyon*, 2.5 miles long, 4 miles west of Manzanita (lat. 32°40'45" N, long. 116°21'25" W). Named on Live Oak Springs (1959) 7.5' quadrangle.

Diamond Bar [LOS ANGELES]: *town*, 4 miles west-southwest of Pomona city hall (lat. 34°01'30" N, long. 117°48'45" W). Named on San Dimas (1966, photorevised 1981) and Yorba Linda (1964, photorevised 1981) 7.5' quadrangles.

Diamond Bar Creek [LOS ANGELES]: *stream*, flows nearly 3 miles to San Jose Creek 7.25 miles west-southwest of Pomona city hall (lat. 34°00'15" N, long. 117°51'45" W). Named on San Dimas (1966) 7.5' quadrangle.

Diamond Campground [LOS ANGELES]: *locality*, about 8 miles north-northeast of Sunland in Pacoima Canyon (lat. 34°22'10" N, long. 118°15'55" W). Named on Sunland (1966) 7.5' quadrangle.

Dick Spring [SAN DIEGO]: *spring*, 10.5 miles northwest of Warner Springs (lat. 33°24'20" N, long. 116°44'20" W; near SE cor. sec. 11, T 9 S, R 2 E). Named on Beauty Mountain (1960) 7.5' quadrangle. The name reportedly is from a dog that slipped into the spring (Stein, p. 39).

Dictionary Hill [SAN DIEGO]: *ridge*, west-trending, 1 mile long, 7 miles west of Jamul (lat. 32°43'30" N, long. 116°59'45" W). Named on Jamul Mountains (1955) and National City (1967) 7.5' quadrangles. Purchasers of encyclopedias received as a bonus lots in a subdivision laid out on the ridge in 1911; the term "encyclopedia" somehow was transformed into "dictionary" and applied to the place (Stein, p. 39).

Dillon Canyon [SAN DIEGO]: *canyon*, drained by a stream that flows nearly 1 mile to Spring Canyon (2) 6.5 miles east-southeast of Imperial Beach (lat. 32°03'15" N, long. 117°00'20" W; at N line sec. 5, T 19 S, R 1 W). Named on Imperial Beach (1967) 7.5' quadrangle.

Dillon Divide [LOS ANGELES]: *pass*, 6.25 miles north-northwest of Sunland (lat. 34°20'40" N, long. 118°20'55" W; sec. 16, T 3 N, R 14 W). Named on Sunland (1966) 7.5' quadrangle, which shows Dillon ranch located 0.5 mile west-northwest of the pass.

Dime Canyon [LOS ANGELES]: *canyon*, drained by a stream that flows less than 1 mile to Cattle Canyon 8.5 miles northeast of Glendora city hall (lat. 34°13'40" N, long. 117°45'50" W). Named on Glendora (1966) 7.5' quadrangle.

Disappointment: see **Mount Disappointment** [LOS ANGELES].

Divide: see **Campo** [SAN DIEGO].

Divide Forest Camp [VENTURA]: *locality*, 2.5 miles east-northeast of McDonald Peak at the head of Big Cedar Creek (lat. 34°38'35" N, long. 118°53'40" W; sec. 4, T 6 N, R 19 W). Named on McDonald Peak (1958) 7.5' quadrangle.

Division [SAN DIEGO]: *locality*, 4.5 miles east-southeast of Potrero along San Diego and Arizona Eastern Railroad (lat. 32°35'10" N, long. 116°32'05" W). Named on Potrero (1960) 7.5' quadrangle.

Dix Canyon [LOS ANGELES]: *canyon*, drained by a stream that flows 1.5 miles to Topanga Canyon 7.5 miles northwest of Santa Monica city hall (lat. 34°04'55" N, long. 118°35'45" W; sec. 18, T 1 S, R 16 W). Named on Topanga (1952) 7.5' quadrangle.

Doane Canyon [LOS ANGELES]: *canyon*, drained by a stream that flows 2 miles to Big Tujunga Canyon 1 mile north of Sunland (lat. 34°16'35" N, long. 118°18'40" W). Named on Sunland (1953) 7.5' quadrangle.

Doane Creek [SAN DIEGO]: *stream*, flows 2.25 miles to join French Creek and form Pauma Creek 1 mile north-northeast of Boucher Hill (lat. 33°20'55" N, long. 116°54'45" W; near E line sec. 31, T 9 S, R 1 E). Named on Boucher Hill (1948) 7.5' quadrangle. The name is from the Doane brothers, homesteaders in the valley in the late 1860's (Gudde, 1949, p. 96).

Doane Valley: see **Lower Doane Valley** [SAN DIEGO]; **Lower French Valley** [SAN DIEGO]; **Upper Doane Valley** [SAN DIEGO].

Dodge Valley [SAN DIEGO]: *valley*, 9 miles east-northeast of Boucher Hill along Temecula Creek (lat. 33°22'15" N, long. 116° 46'15" W). Named on Aguanga (1954), Beauty Mountain (1960), Palomar Observatory (1949), and Warner Springs (1959) 7.5' quadrangles. The name commemorates F.E. Dodge, a stockman who settled in the neighborhood in 1887 (Stein, p. 40).

Doe Flat [LOS ANGELES]: *area*, 8.5 miles north-northeast of Glendora city hall (lat. 34°14'50" N, long. 117°48' W). Named on Crystal Lake (1958) and Glendora (1966) 7.5' quadrangles.

Doe Spring [LOS ANGELES]: *spring*, 4.5 miles southwest of Waterman Mountain (lat. 34°18' N, long. 118°00' W). Named on Waterman Mountain (1959) 7.5' quadrangle.

Doghouse Junction [SAN DIEGO]: *locality*, 0.5 mile north-northeast of Otay Mountain (lat. 32°35'40" N, long. 116°50'35" W). Altitude 3566 feet. Named on Otay Mountain (1972) 7.5' quadrangle.

Dog Spring [SAN DIEGO]: *spring*, 4 miles north-northwest of La Mesa (lat. 32°49'10" N, long. 117°03' W). Named on La Mesa (1953) 7.5' quadrangle. The feature first was called Cowles Spring (Stein, p. 34).

Doheny Cattle Camp Number 2 [LOS ANGELES]: *locality*, 13 miles west-northwest of Newhall at the mouth of Oak Canyon (1) (lat. 34°28'35" N, long. 118°43'05" W). Named on Santa Felicia Canyon (1935) 6' quadrangle.

Doheny Park: see **Capistrano Beach** [ORANGE].

Delanco Junction [LOS ANGELES]: *locality*, 2.25 miles east of Torrance city hall (lat. 33°50'45" N, long. 118°17'55" W). Named on Torrance (1964) 7.5' quadrangle. Called Dolanco on Compton (1930) 6' quadrangle.

Dolgeville: see **Shorb** [LOS ANGELES].

Dolley [LOS ANGELES]: *locality*, 9 miles northeast of present Long Beach city hall along Pacific Electric Railroad (lat. 33°51'55" N, long. 118°05'25" W). Named on Artesia (1925) 6' quadrangle.

Dolores [LOS ANGELES]: *locality*, nearly 5 miles north-northwest of Long Beach city hall along Southern Pacific Railroad (lat. 33° 50' N, long. 118°13'30" W). Named on Long Beach (1964) 7.5' quadrangle.

Dome Mountain [LOS ANGELES-VENTURA]: *peak*, 4 miles east-northeast of Cobblestone Mountain on Los Angeles-Ventura County line (lat. 34°37'45" N, long. 118°48'05" W). Named on Black Mountain (1958) 7.5' quadrangle.

Domingo: see **Lake Domingo** [SAN DIEGO].

Dominguez [LOS ANGELES]:

(1) *district*, nearly 5 miles north-northwest of Long Beach city hall (lat. 33°50'10" N, long. 118°13'10" W). Named on Long Beach (1949) 7.5' quadrangle.

(2) *locality*, 7 miles north of present Long Beach city hall along Southern Pacific Railroad (lat. 33°52' N, long. 118°13' W). Named on Downey (1902) 15' quadrangle. Compton (1930) 6' quadrangle shows a place called Davidson City at the site. Davidson City was named for Davidson Investment Company (Gudde, 1949, p. 97).

Dominguez Campground [VENTURA]: *locality*, 4.5 miles north of Piru (lat. 34°28'50" N, long. 118°47'50" W; near NW cor. sec. 32, T 5 N, R 18 W); the place is in Dominguez Canyon. Named on Piru (1952) 7.5' quadrangle.

Dominguez Canyon [VENTURA]: *canyon*, drained by a stream that flows 3 miles to Reasoner Canyon 4.5 miles north-northeast of Piru (lat. 34°28'45" N, long. 118°46'15" W; sec. 33, T 5 N, R 18 W). Named on Piru (1952) 7.5' quadrangle. Called Reasoner Canyon on Camulos (1903) 30' quadrangle.

Dominguez Channel [LOS ANGELES]: *water feature*, extends for 16 miles to Los Angeles Harbor 3.25 miles west of Long Beach city hall (lat. 33°46'05" N, long. 118°15' W). Named on Inglewood (1964), Long Beach (1964), and Torrance (1964) 7.5' quadrangles. Inglewood (1952) 7.5' quadrangle has the name "Laguna Dominguez" for marsh situated mainly at the upper part of present Dominguez Channel; Los Angeles Board of Supervisors adopted the name "Laguna Dominguez" in 1938 for the swampy lake formerly called Nigger Slough (Gudde, 1949, p. 97).

Dominguez Hills [LOS ANGELES]: *ridge*, east-northeast-trending, about 3 miles long, 2 miles north-northeast of Dominguez (lat. 33° 51'45" N, long. 118°14'15" W). Named on Inglewood (1964), Long Beach (1964), South Gate (1964), and Torrance (1964) 7.5' quadrangles. On Downey (1902) 15' quadrangle, the name "Dominguez Hill" applies to the high point on present Domingues Hills.

Dominguez Junction [LOS ANGELES]: *locality*, 6.5 miles north of Long Beach city hall along the railroad (lat. 33°51'45" N, long. 118°12'55" W); the place is near the east end of Dominguez Hills. Named on Long Beach (1949) 7.5' quadrangle.

Dominguez Reservoir [LOS ANGELES]: *lake*, 450 feet long, 0.5 mile north-northwest of present Torrance city hall (lat. 33°50'45" N, long. 118°20'30" W). Named on Torrance (1924) 6' quadrangle.

Don [SAN DIEGO]: *locality*, nearly 4 miles south-southeast of San Onofre Mountain along Atchison, Topeka and Santa Fe Railroad (lat. 33°18'45" N, long. 117°28'35" W; sec. 14, T 10 S, R 6 W). Named on Las Pulgas Canyon (1949) 7.5' quadrangle. Railroad officials named the place in 1907 (Hanna, p. 88).

Donohoe Mountain [SAN DIEGO]: *peak*, 4 miles east-northeast of Otay Mountain (lat. 32°37'20" N, long. 116°46'50" W; sec. 9, T 18 S, R 2 E). Named on Otay Mountain (1972) 7.5' quadrangle. The name commemorates Stuart Donohue, an early settler and mine operator in the region (Stein, p. 40).

Donohoe Spring [SAN DIEGO]: *spring*, 4.5 miles east of Otay Mountain (lat. 32°35'30" N, long. 116°46'05" W; near W line sec. 22, T 18 S, R 2 E); the spring is 2 miles south-southeast of Donohue Mountain. Named on Otay Mountain (1972) 7.5' quadrangle.

Don Spring [SAN DIEGO]: *spring*, nearly 6 miles west-southwest of Borrego

Springs (lat. 33°13' N, long. 116°27'50" W; near W line sec. 15, T 11 S, R 5 E). Named on Tubb Canyon (1959) 7.5' quadrangle.

Dorothy Canyon [LOS ANGELES]: *canyon,* drained by a stream that flows 1.5 miles to Pacoima Canyon 7 miles north of Sunland (lat. 34°21'45" N, long. 118°19'35" W; near NE cor. sec. 10, T 3 N, R 14 W). Named on Sunland (1953) 7.5' quadrangle.

Dorr Canyon [LOS ANGELES]: *canyon,* drained by a stream that flows 3 miles to Big Rock Creek nearly 5 miles southeast of Valyermo (lat. 34°23'35" N, long. 117°47'45" W; near NW cor. sec. 35, T 4 N, R 9 W). Named on Crystal Lake (1958) and Valyermo (1958) 7.5' quadrangles.

Dos Cabezas [SAN DIEGO]: *locality,* nearly 9.5 miles north-northeast of Jacumba along San Diego and Arizona Eastern Railroad (lat. 32°44'45" N, long. 116°08'15" W; near E line sec. 27, T 16 S, R 8 E). Named on Jacumba (1959) 7.5' quadrangle. Called Dos Cabezas Siding on Jacumba (1939) 15' quadrangle.

Dos Cabezas Spring [SAN DIEGO]: *spring,* 7 miles north-northeast of Jacumba (lat. 32°42'50" N, long. 116°08'35" W; near S line sec. 3, T 17 S, R 8 E). Named on Jacumba (1959) 7.5' quadrangle. The name is from two heaps of boulders that resemble two heads—*dos cabezas* means "two heads" in Spanish (Stein, p. 40).

Double Canyon [SAN DIEGO]: *canyon,* drained by a stream that flows 2 miles to Couger Canyon 3.5 mile southwest of Pala (lat. 33°19'45" N, long. 117°07'20" W; at SE cor. sec. 6, T 10 S, R 2 W). Named on Pala (1968) 7.5' quadrangle.

Double Peak [SAN DIEGO]: *peak,* 6.25 miles north-northeast of Rancho Santa Fe (lat. 33°06'35" N, long. 117°10'35" W; at N line sec. 27, T 12 S, R 3 W). Altitude 1644 feet. Named on Rancho Santa Fe (1968) 7.5' quadrangle.

Dougherty Peak: see **Throop Peak** [LOS ANGELES].

Dough Flat [VENTURA]: *area,* 5 miles east-southeast of Devils Heart Peak (lat. 34°31'20" N, long. 118°53'35" W; sec. 17, T 5 N, R 19 W). Named on Devils Heart Peak (1943) 7.5' quadrangle.

Douglas Junction [LOS ANGELES]: *locality,* 6 miles north-northeast of Long Beach city hall along Union Pacific Railroad (lat. 33°51'20" N, long. 118°09'50" W). Named on Long Beach (1949) 7.5' quadrangle.

Dove Canyon [ORANGE]: *canyon,* drained by a stream that flows 3 miles to Bell Canyon 10 miles northeast of San Juan Capistrano (lat. 33°37'10" N, long. 117°33'45" W; sec. 25, T 6 S, R 7 W). Named on Cañada Gobernadora (1968) and Santiago Peak (1954) 7.5' quadrangles. The name is from the abundance of mourning doves in the canyon (Meadows, p. 58).

Dove Canyon: see **Peters Canyon** [ORANGE].

Dowd Canyon [LOS ANGELES]: *canyon,* drained by a stream that flows 3 miles to San Francisquito Canyon 4.25 miles south-southeast of the village of Lake Hughes (lat. 34°37' N, long. 118°25' W; at S line sec. 12, T 6 N, R 15 W). Named on Green Valley (1958) and Sleepy Valley (1958) 7.5' quadrangles.

Downey [LOS ANGELES]: *city,* 4.5 miles east-southeast of South Gate city hall (lat. 33°56'25" N, long. 118°07'45" W). Named on South Gate (1964) and Whittier (1949) 7.5' quadrangles. Called Downey City on Stevenson's (1884) map. Postal authorities established Downey post office in 1876 (Salley, p. 61), and the city incorporated in 1956. The name commemorates John G. Downey, governor California from 1860 until 1862, who subdivided Santa Gertrudis grant where the city lies (Gudde, 1949, p. 98). Bancroft (1888, p. 522) referred to Downey City, "which absorbed Gallatin and College Settlement." The community called Gallatin was started in 1868, and a church and a college opened in 1869 at a place called College Settlement—both Gallatin and College Settlement were moved to Downey when Downey was founded (Thompson and West, p. 150). Postal authorities established Vultee Field post office 1.75 miles south of Downey post office in 1940 and discontinued it in 1947; the name was for Vultee Aircraft, Incorporated, military aircraft manufacturers in World War II (Salley, p. 233).

Downey: see **Mount Downey**, under **Santiago Peak** [ORANGE].

Downey Road [LOS ANGELES]: *locality,* 3.5 miles southeast of Los Angeles city hall (lat. 34°00'50" N, long. 118°12'15" W). Named on Los Angeles (1966) 7.5' quadrangle.

Drinkwater Canyon [LOS ANGELES]: *canyon,* drained by a stream that flows 1.5 miles to San Francisquito Canyon 5.5 miles south-southeast of Warm Springs Mountain (lat. 34°31'40" N, long. 118°31'40" W; near S line sec. 11, T 5 N, R 16 W). Named on Warm Springs Mountain (1958) 7.5' quadrangle. Los Angeles County (1935) map shows several canyons related to San Francisquito Canyon: LeBrun Canyon, which opens into San Francisquito Canyon from the north about 2 miles north-northeast of the mouth of Drinkwater Canyon; Peters Canyon, which opens into LeBrun Canyon from the north near the mouth of LeBrun Canyon; and Hunter Canyon, which opens into San Francisquito Canyon about 1.5 miles northeast of the mouth of LeBrun Canyon. According to Outland (1963, p. 27), Raggio ranch and stage station was located about 0.5 mile below the mouth Drinkwater Canyon.

Drinkwater Flat [LOS ANGELES]: *area,* 9.5 miles south-southwest of the village of Lake Hughes in Dry Canyon (1) (lat. 34°32'30" N, long. 118°30' W). Named on Green Valley (1958) and Warm Springs Mountain (1958) 7.5' quadrangles. Red Mountain (1936) 6' quadrangle has the name "Drinkwater Flat" for a place located about 0.5 mile farther west at the head of Drinkwater Canyon.

Drinkwater Reservoir [LOS ANGELES]: *lake,* 600 feet long, 4.5 miles southeast of Warm Springs Mountain (lat. 34°31'50" N, long. 118°31'15" W; near E line sec. 11, T 5 N, R 16 W); the feature is near Drinkwater Canyon. Named on Warm Springs Mountain (1958) 7.5' quadrangle.

Dripping Springs [VENTURA]: *spring,* 3.5 miles northeast of Devils Heart Peak (lat. 34°34'30" N, long. 118°55'20" W; near N line sec. 32, T 6 N, R 19 W). Named on Devils Heart Peak (1943) 7.5' quadrangle.

Drum Barracks: see **Wilmington** [LOS ANGELES].

Dry Canyon [LOS ANGELES]:

(1) *canyon,* drained by a stream that flows 18 miles to Bouquet Canyon 3 miles north of Newhall (lat. 34°25'50" N, long. 118° 32' W). Named on Green Valley (1958), Newhall (1952), and Warm Springs Mountain (1958) 7.5' quadrangles.

(2) *canyon,* drained by a stream that flows 2.5 miles to lowlands less than 1 mile southeast of Calabasas (lat. 34°08'50" N, long. 118°37'45" W; at N line sec. 26, T 1 N, R 17 W). Named on Calabasas (1952) 7.5' quadrangle.

(3) *canyon,* 2.5 miles long, 4 miles west-northwest of Beverly Hills city hall (lat. 34°05'45" N, long. 118°27'45" W). Named on Beverly Hills (1950) 7.5' quadrangle.

(4) *canyon,* drained by a stream that flows nearly 2 miles to Solstice Canyon 3.5 miles west of Malibu Point (lat. 34°02'15" N, long. 118°44'45" W). Named on Malibu Beach (1951) 7.5' quadrangle.

Dry Canyon [SAN DIEGO]: *canyon,* drained by a stream that flows 2.5 miles to lowlands 3 miles southwest of Borrego Springs (lat. 33°13'25" N, long. 116°24'25" W). Named on Tubb Canyon (1959) 75' quadrangle.

Dry Canyon [VENTURA]:

(1) *canyon,* drained by a stream that flows about 2 miles to Simi Valley (1) 6.5 miles west-northwest of Santa Susana Pass (lat. 34° 17'25" N, long. 118°44'45" W; sec. 3, T 2 N, R 18 W). Named on Santa Susana (1951) 7.5' quadrangle. Called Oak Canyon on Santa Susana (1943) 15' quadrangle.

(2) *canyon,* drained by a stream that flows 10 miles to Cuyama River 4 miles north of Reyes Peak (lat. 34°41'25" N, long. 119°17'30" W; sec. 23, T 7 N, R 23 W). Named on Reyes Peak (1943), San Guillermo (1943), and Sawmill Mountain (1943) 7.5' quadrangles. West Fork branches north-northwest nearly 4 miles above the mouth of the main canyon; it is 3 miles long and is named on Apache Canyon (1943) and Reyes Peak (1943) 7.5' quadrangles.

Dry Canyon: see **Gillibrand Canyon** [VENTURA].

Dry Canyon Reservoir [LOS ANGELES]: *lake,* 3700 feet long, behind a dam 6.5 miles north of Newhall (lat. 34°28'55" N, long. 118°31'30" W; on S line sec. 26, T 5 N, R 16 W); the lake is in Dry Canyon (1). Named on Newhall (1952) 7.5' quadrangle.

Dry Creek [VENTURA]: *stream,* flows about 5.5 miles to end 6.5 miles north-northeast of McDonald Peak (lat. 34°43'40" N, long. 118°54'35" W; sec. 5, T 7 N, R 19 W). Named on McDonald Peak (1958) 7.5' quadrangle.

Dry Gulch [LOS ANGELES]:

(1) *canyon,* drained by a stream that flows 2.5 miles to Elizabeth Lake Canyon 3 miles south of Warm Springs Mountain (lat. 34°33'10" N, long. 118°34'35" W; sec. 5, T 5 N, R 16 W). Named on Warm Springs Mountain (1958) 7.5' quadrangle.

(2) *canyon,* drained by a stream that flows 1.5 miles to Coldwater Canyon (2) nearly 4 miles west-southwest of Mount San Antonio (lat. 34°15'55" N, long. 117°42'20" W). Named on Mount San Antonio (1955) 7.5' quadrangle.

Dry Lake Canyon [LOS ANGELES]: *canyon,* drained by a stream that flows 1 mile to San Antonio Canyon 11 miles north-northeast of Pomona city hall (lat. 34°12'10" N, long. 117°40'30" W; sec. 1, T 1 N, R 8 W). Named on Mount Baldy (1954) 7.5' quadrangle.

Dry Valley [SAN DIEGO]: *canyon,* drained by a stream that flows nearly 1 mile to Bob Owens Canyon 4 miles north-northeast of Barrett Junction (lat. 32°40'05" N, long. 116°41'05" W; at S line sec. 21, T 17 S, R 3 E). Named on Barrett Lake (1960) 7.5' quadrangle.

Duarte [LOS ANGELES]: *town,* 3.5 miles west of Azusa city hall (lat. 34°08'25" N, long. 117°58'10" W); the place is on Andres Duarte's Azusa (1) grant. Named on Azusa (1966) and Baldwin Park (1966) 7.5' quadrangles. Postal authorities established Duarte post office in 1882 (Frickstad, p. 72), and the town incorporated in 1957. The community began with subdivision of Azusa (1) grant in 1864 and 1865 (Gudde, 1949, p. 100).

Dubber Spur [SAN DIEGO]: *locality,* 2.5 miles north of Jacumba along San Diego and Arizona Eastern Railroad (lat. 32°39'25" N, long. 116°11'20" W; near W line sec. 29, T 17 S, R 8 E). Named on Jacumba (1959) 7.5' quadrangle.

Duckville [SAN DIEGO]: *locality,* 6.5 miles south-southeast of present Point La Jolla in marsh along Mission Bay (lat. 32°46' N, long. 117°13'10" W).

Named on La Jolla (1903) 15' quadrangle.

Dudmore [LOS ANGELES]: *locality*, 1.5 miles north-northwest of Torrance city hall along Atchison, Topeka and Santa Fe Railroad (lat. 33°51'25" N, long. 118°21' W). Named on Torrance (1964) 7.5' quadrangle.

Duena: see **Santa Ana** [ORANGE].

Dulah [VENTURA]: *settlement*, 4.5 miles west-northwest of Ventura along the coast (lat. 34°18'45" N, long. 119°21'30" W). Named on Ventura (1951) 7.5' quadrangle.

Dulzura [SAN DIEGO]: *village*, 7.5 miles southeast of Jamul (lat. 32°38'40" N, long. 116°46'50" W; near S line sec. 33, T 17 S, R 2 E). Named on Dulzura (1972) 7.5' quadrangle. Postal authorities established Dulzura post office in 1886, discontinued it in 1933, and reestablished it in 1936 (Frickstad, p. 150). The name reportedly is from the honey industry at the place—*dulzura* means "sweetness" in Spanish (Gudde, 1949, p. 100).

Dulzura Creek [SAN DIEGO]: *stream*, flows 9 miles to Jamul Creek 4.5 miles south of Jamul (lat. 32°38'55" N, long. 116°52'10" W). Named on Dulzura (1972) and Otay Mountain (1972) 7.5' quadrangles.

Dulzura Summit [SAN DIEGO]: *pass*, nearly 2 miles west of Barrett Junction (lat. 32°37' N, long. 116°44'15" W; at E line sec. 11, T 18 S, R 2 E). Named on Tecate (1960) 7.5' quadrangle.

Dume: see **Point Dume** [LOS ANGELES].

Dume Canyon: see **Zuma Canyon** [LOS ANGELES].

Dume Cove [LOS ANGELES]: *embayment*, just northeast of Point Dume along the coast (lat. 34°00'15" N, long. 118°48' W). Named on Point Dume (1951) 7.5' quadrangle. United States Board on Geographic Names (1961c, p. 13) rejected the name "Dume Cove" for present Paradise Cove.

Dume Point: see **Point Dume** [LOS ANGELES].

Dumetz: see **Point Dumetz**, under **Point Dume** [LOS ANGELES].

Dundee [LOS ANGELES]: *locality*, 3.5 miles northwest of present Burbank city hall along Southern Pacific Railroad (lat. 34°12'30" N, long. 118°21'20" W). Named on Santa Monica (1902) 15' quadrangle. Postal authorities established Dundee post office in 1887 and discontinued it in 1909; the name was from Dundee, Scotland (Salley, p. 62).

Dunsmore Canyon [LOS ANGELES]: *canyon*, 1.5 miles long, 5 miles south-southwest of Condor Peak (lat. 34°15'30" N, long. 118°14'20" W; mainly in sec. 15, 16, T 2 N, R 13 W). Named on Condor Peak (1959) 7.5' quadrangle.

DuPont: see **Fort DuPont**, under **Old Town** [SAN DIEGO].

Durasnitos Spring [SAN DIEGO]: *spring*, 6.5 miles south-southeast of San Pasqual (lat. 33°00'20" N, long. 116°54'10" W; at N line sec. 32, T 13 S, R 1 E). Named on San Pasqual (1954) 7.5' quadrangle.

Dutch Flat [SAN DIEGO]: *marsh*, 2.25 miles west-northwest of downtown San Diego in San Diego Bay (lat. 32°44' N, long. 117° 11'45" W). Named on Point Loma (1942) 7.5' quadrangle.

Dutch Harbor [VENTURA]: *embayment*, on the south side of San Nicolas Island (lat. 33°13'05" N, long. 119°29'10" W). Named on San Nicolas Island (1943) quadrangle.

Dutch Louie Camp [LOS ANGELES]: *locality*, 7 miles north-northwest of Sunland in Pacoima Canyon (lat. 34°21'30" N, long. 118° 21'10" W; sec. 9, T 3 N, R 14 W). Named on Sunland (1953) 7.5' quadrangle. Called Dutch Louie Campground on Sunland (1966) 7.5' quadrangle.

Dutchman Canyon [SAN DIEGO]: *canyon*, drained by a stream that flows 2 miles to Dulzura Creek 8 miles southeast of Jamul (lat. 32° 38'20" N, long. 116°46'05" W; near NW cor. sec. 3, T 18 S, R 2 E). Named on Dulzura (1972) 7.5' quadrangle. The name is from a shepherd who lived in the canyon before 1880; Dorothy Clark Schmid, a resident of the region, won approval of the name (United States Board on Geographic Names, 1974, p. 2; Stein, p. 41).

Dutchmans Camp [VENTURA]: *locality*, 2.5 miles northwest of McDonald Peak (lat. 34°39'50" N, long. 119°58'05" W; near S line sec. 26, T 7 N, R 20 W). Named on McDonald Peak (1958) 7.5' quadrangle.

Dyar Spring [SAN DIEGO]: *spring*, 4 miles east-southeast of Cuyamaca Peak (lat. 32°54'55" N, long. 116°32'45" W). Named on Cuyamaca Peak (1960) 7.5' quadrangle.

Dyche Valley [SAN DIEGO]: *valley*, 6.5 miles east-southeast of Boucher Hill (lat. 33°17'35" N, long. 116°48'50" W; mainly in sec. 19, T 10 S, R 2 E). Named on Palomar Observatory (1949) 7.5' quadrangle. The name commemorates George Dyche, who settled in the neighborhood in 1868 (Stein, p. 41).

Dye Canyon [SAN DIEGO]: *canyon*, 1.5 miles long, 6 miles south-southwest of Santa Ysabel (lat. 33°02' N, long. 116°43'45" W; sec. 13, 24, T 13 S, R 2 E). Named on Santa Ysabel (1960) 7.5' quadrangle. The name commemorates John Dye, a pioneer settler (Stein, p. 41).

Dye Mountain [SAN DIEGO]: *ridge*, north-northeast-trending, 5.5 miles long, center about 4 miles south-southwest of Santa Ysabel (lat. 33°03'15" N, long. 116°42'20" W). Named on Santa Ysabel (1960) 7.5' quadrangle.

Dyer [ORANGE]: *locality*, 2.5 miles south-southeast of Santa Ana city hall along Southern Pacific Railroad (lat. 33°42'35" N, long. 117°51'15" W). Named on Tustin (1965) 7.5' quadrangle.

- E -

Eagle Canyon [LOS ANGELES]: *canyon*, 1.5 miles long, 8.5 miles north-west of Pasadena city hall (lat. 34°14'40" N, long. 118°14'10" W; sec. 22, T 2 N, R 13 W). Named on Condor Peak (1959) and Pasadena (1953) 7.5' quadrangles.

Eagle Canyon Channel [LOS ANGELES]: *stream*, extends for 1.5 miles to Verdugo Wash nearly 8 miles northwest of Pasadena city hall (lat. 34°13'05" N, long. 118°14'55" W); the feature heads at the mouth of Eagle Canyon. Named on Pasadena (1966) 7.5' quadrangle.

Eagle Crag [SAN DIEGO]: *peak*, 4 miles north-northwest of Boucher Hill (lat. 33°23'15" N, long. 116°57'20" W; near S line sec. 14, T 9 S, R 1 W). Altitude 5077 feet. Named on Vail Lake (1953) 7.5' quadrangle.

Eagle Peak [SAN DIEGO]: *peak*, 10.5 miles north-northwest of Descanso (lat. 32°59'05" N, long. 116°42'30" W; sec. 6, T 14 S, R 3 E). Altitude 3226 feet. Named on Tule Springs (1960) 7.5' quadrangle.

Eagle Reef: see **Isthmus Cove** [LOS ANGELES].

Eagle Rock [LOS ANGELES]:

(1) *relief feature*, 2.25 miles west of Pasadena city hall (lat. 34°08'35" N, long. 118°10'55" W). Named on Pasadena (1953) 7.5' quadrangle. The name is from the figure of an eagle in flight caused by shadows cast on the face of the feature by an overhanging rock outcrop (Diller and others, p. 98).

(2) *rock*, 2.25 miles west-northwest of Silver Peak near the west end of Santa Catalina Island, and 750 feet offshore (lat. 33°28'20" N, long. 118°36'15" W). Named on Santa Catalina West (1943) 7.5' quadrangle.

(3) *district*, 3.5 miles west-southwest of Pasadena city hall in Los Angeles (lat. 34°08' N, long. 118°12' W); the place is southwest of Eagle Rock (1). Named on Pasadena (1953) 7.5' quadrangle.

Eagle Rock Reservoir [LOS ANGELES]: *lake*, 1100 feet long, 2.5 miles west of Pasadena city hall (lat. 34°08'50" N, long. 118°11'20" W); the feature is northeast of Eagle Rock district. Named on Pasadena (1953) 7.5' quadrangle.

Eagle Rock Valley [LOS ANGELES]: *valley*, 3.5 miles west-southwest of present Pasadena city hall (lat. 34°08'20" N, long. 118°12'30" W); the place is at and around present Eagle Rock district. Named on Pasadena (1900) 15' quadrangle.

Eagles Nest [LOS ANGELES]: *ridge*, generally west-trending, about 1 mile long, 1 mile southwest of Mount Banning on Santa Catalina Island (lat. 33°21'45" N, long. 118°26'45" W). Named on Santa Catalina South (1943) 7.5' quadrangle.

Eagles Nest [SAN DIEGO]: *locality*, 2.25 miles east of Warner Springs in Cañada Verde (lat. 33°17'15" N, long. 116°35'40" W; near SW cor. sec. 20, T 10 S, R 4 E). Named on Hot Springs Mountain (1960) 7.5' quadrangle. Hiram Keyes homesteaded at the site in the 1880's, and he and his wife operated a commercial summer camp there—Keyes translated the Indian name for the spot, which meant "place of the eagle" (Stein, p. 42).

Eagle Spring [LOS ANGELES]: *spring*, 8 miles northwest of Santa Monica city hall (lat. 34°06'25" N, long. 118°34' W). Named on Topanga (1952) 7.5' quadrangle.

Earlham: see **El Modeno** [ORANGE].

Earthquake Bay: see **Gulf of Santa Catalina** [ORANGE-SAN DIEGO].

Earthquake Valley [SAN DIEGO]: *valley*, 9.5 miles east of Julian (lat. 33°04'30" N, long. 116°26' W). Named on Earthquake Valley (1959) 7.5' quadrangle.

East Basin [SAN DIEGO]: *embayment*, 1.5 miles west-northwest of downtown San Diego off San Diego Bay (lat. 32°43'35" N, long. 117°11'30" W). Named on Point Loma (1967) 7.5' quadrangle. United States Board on Geographic Names (1981, p. 2) rejected the name "Harbor Island East Basin" for the feature.

East Butte [SAN DIEGO]: *ridge*, northwest-trending, 2 miles long, 2.5 miles northwest of Ocotillo Wells (lat. 33°10'10" N, long. 116° 10' W); the feature is at the southeast end of Borrego Mountain. Named on Borrego Mountain (1960) 7.5' quadrangle.

East Canyon [LOS ANGELES]: *canyon*, drained by a stream that flows 1.25 miles to Gavin Canyon 2 miles south-southwest of Newhall (lat. 34°20'45" N, long. 118°32'30" W; sec. 15, T 3 N, R 16 W). Named on Oat Mountain (1952) 7.5' quadrangle.

East Canyon Channel [LOS ANGELES]: *water feature*, extends for 2.5 miles to Pacoima Wash 1.25 miles south of downtown San Fernando (lat. 34°15'45" N, long. 118°26'30" W). Named on San Fernando (1966) 7.5' quadrangle.

East Casitas Pass [VENTURA]: *pass*, nearly 6 miles south of White Ledge Peak (lat. 34°23'10" N, long. 119°22'50" W; sec. 34, T 4 N, R 24 W); the feature is 2 miles east of West Casitas Pass. Named on White Ledge Peak (1952) 7.5' quadrangle.

East Coyote Hills [ORANGE]: *range*, 4 miles southeast of downtown La Habra (lat. 33°53'30" N, long. 117°54' W); the feature is east of West Coyote Hills. Named on La Habra (1964) 7.5' quadrangle.

Eastern Anacapa: see **Anacapa Island** [VENTURA].

East Fish Camp [VENTURA]: *locality,* on the south side of the middle Anacapa Island (lat. 34°00'25" N, long. 119°23'05" W). Named on Anacapa Island (1973) quadrangle.

East Irvine [ORANGE]: *village,* 8 miles southeast of Santa Ana city hall (lat. 33°40'35" N, long. 117°45'35" W); the place is about 3.5 miles east of the center of present Irvine. Named on Tustin (1965, photorevised 1981) 7.5' quadrangle. Tustin (1965) 7.5' quadrangle has the designation "Irvine (Valencia Siding)" at the site, but United States Board on Geographic Names (1965c, p. 8) rejected the name "Irvine" for the village. Corona (1902) 30' quadrangle has both the names "Irvine" and "Myford" along Atchison, Topeka and Santa Fe Railroad at the place. Postal authorities established Myford post office in 1899, changed the name to Irvine in 1914, and to East Irvine in 1965; the name "Myford" was for Myford Irvine, first postmaster (Salley, p. 64, 149). Atchison, Topeka and Santa Fe Railroad established a shipping center at the site in 1888 and named it Irvine for Irvine ranch, owned by James Irvine; because a post office named Irvine already existed in California, the post office at the site was called Myford for Irvine's son; the village and post office became East Irvine when the new city of Irvine was started nearby (Meadows, p. 73). A feature called Barton Mound lies 1.5 miles south of East Irvine; the name recalls Sheriff James Barton, whom outlaws killed there in 1857 (Hoover, Rensch, and Rensch, p. 265; Meadows, p. 24).

East Las Virgenes Canyon [VENTURA]: *canyon,* drained by a stream that flows 2 miles to Las Virgenes Canyon 7.5 miles east of Thousand Oaks (lat. 34°10'15" N, long. 118°42'05" W). Named on Calabasas (1952) 7.5' quadrangle. Called East Fork on Camulos (1903) 30' quadrangle.

East Los Angeles [LOS ANGELES]:
(1) *district,* 2 miles northeast of present Los Angeles city hall (lat. 34°04'35" N, long. 118°12'45" W). Named on Pasadena (1900) 15' quadrangle.
(2) *district,* 4.5 miles southeast of Los Angeles city hall (lat. 34°00'55" N, long. 118°10'45" W). Named on Los Angeles (1953) 7.5' quadrangle.

East Mesa [SAN DIEGO]:
(1) *area,* 4.5 miles southeast of Cuyamaca Peak (lat. 32°54'25" N, long. 116°32'30" W). Named on Cuyamaca Peak (1960) 7.5' quadrangle.
(2) *area,* 8.5 miles north-northeast of Sweeney Pass (lat. 32°57'10" N, long. 116°08'15" W). Named on Arroyo Tapiado (1959) and Carrizo Mountain NE (1957) 7.5' quadrangles.

Eastmont [LOS ANGELES]: *district,* 5.5 miles east-southeast of Los Angeles city hall (lat. 34°01'25" N, long. 118°09' W). Named on Alhambra (1926) 6' quadrangle.

East Pasadena [LOS ANGELES]: *district,* east of the main part of Pasadena (lat. 34°09' N, long. 118°05'30" W). Named on Mount Wilson (1953) 7.5' quadrangle. Pasadena (1900) 15' quadrangle has the name "Lamanda" along the railroad at the place, and Mount Wilson (1966) 7.5' quadrangle has the name "Lamanda Park" for the railroad station at East Pasadena. Postal authorities established Lamanda Park post office in 1886, changed the name to Lamanda in 1894, to La Manda in 1905, to Lamanda Park in 1920, and to East Pasadena in 1930 (Salley, p. 116). They first established East Pasadena post office in 1887, discontinued it in 1896, reestablished it in 1904, discontinued it in 1907, and reestablished it in 1930 (Salley, p. 64). The name "Lamanda" is from Amanda Rose—her husband, Lenard J. Rose, owned the land at the place (Gudde, 1949, p. 102).

East San Diego [SAN DIEGO]: *district,* 5 miles north of National City civic center in San Diego (lat. 32°44'45" N, long. 117°06'15" W). Named on La Mesa (1967) and National City (1967) 7.5' quadrangles. Postal authorities established Teralta post office in 1911 and changed the name to East San Diego in 1912—the district also was called City Heights (Salley, p. 220).

East San Gabriel [LOS ANGELES]: *locality,* 3.25 miles west-northwest of El Monte city hall along Southern Pacific Railroad (lat. 34° 05'35" N, long. 118°04'50" W); the place is 1.5 miles east of downtown San Gabriel. Named on El Monte (1953) 7.5' quadrangle.

East San Pedro [LOS ANGELES]: *locality,* 3 miles northeast of Point Fermin on Terminal Island (lat. 33°44'15' N, long. 118°15'45" W). Named on San Pedro (1964) 7.5' quadrangle. Postal authorities established East San Pedro post office 1 mile east of San Pedro post office in 1906 and discontinued in 1924 (Salley, p. 64).

East Whittier [LOS ANGELES]: *district,* 1.25 miles southeast of present Whittier city hall (lat. 33°57'50" N, long. 118°01' W). Named on Whittier (1949) 7.5' quadrangle.

East Whittier Siding [LOS ANGELES]: *locality,* nearly 3 miles south-southeast of present Whittier city hall along Atchison, Topeka and Santa Fe Railroad (lat. 33°56'10" N, long. 118°00'50" W). Named on Whittier (1949) 7.5' quadrangle.

East Wilmington: see **Wilmington** [LOS ANGELES].

Eastwood: see **Julian** [SAN DIEGO].

Eastwood Creek [SAN DIEGO]: *stream,* flows 1.5 miles to Coleman Creek 1.25 miles west of Julian (lat. 33°04'50" N, long. 116°37'20" W; near S line sec. 36, T 12 S, R 3 E). Named on Julian (1960) 7.5' quadrangle.

Eastwood Hill [SAN DIEGO]: *peak,* 1 mile north-northwest of Julian (lat. 33°05'30" N, long. 116°36'30" W; near N line sec. 31, T 12 S, R 4 E); the peak is north of Eastwood Creek. Named on Julian (1960) 7.5' quadrangle.

Eaton Canyon [LOS ANGELES]: *canyon,* drained by a stream that flows 5 miles to leave San Gabriel Mountains 3.25 miles southwest of Mount Wilson (lat. 34°11'30" N, long. 118°06'10" W; at S line sec. 2, T 1 N, R 12 W). Named on Mount Wilson (1953) 7.5' quadrangle. The name commemorates Judge Benjamin S. Eaton, who had property 3 miles below the mouth of the canyon; the feature had the early name "Precipicio Canyon" (Robinson, J.W., 1977, p. 102).

Eaton Canyon Wash: see **Eaton Wash** [LOS ANGELES].

Eaton Wash [LOS ANGELES]: *stream,* extends for 9.5 miles from the mouth of Eaton Canyon to Rio Hondo 1.5 miles west of El Monte city hall (lat. 34°04'10" N, long. 118°03'20" W). Named on El Monte (1966) and Mount Wilson (1953) 7.5' quadrangles. El Monte (1926) 6' quadrangle has the name "Eaton Canyon Wash" for the stream.

Ebey Canyon [LOS ANGELES]: *canyon,* drained by a stream that flows nearly 1.5 miles to Tujunga Valley 1 mile north-northwest of Sunland (lat. 34°16'25" N, long. 118°19'05" W). Named on Sunland (1953) 7.5' quadrangle. Called Ebe Cany. on Los Angeles County (1935) map.

Echo Dell: see **Echo Valley** [SAN DIEGO].

Echoes: see **Fall Brook** [SAN DIEGO].

Echo Falls Canyon [VENTURA]: *canyon,* drained by a stream that flows 2.5 miles to Santa Paula Canyon 4 miles west of Santa Paula Peak (lat. 34°26'30" N, long. 119°04'45" W). Named on Santa Paula Peak (1951) 7.5' quadrangle.

Echo Lake [LOS ANGELES]: *lake,* 400 feet long, 3.25 miles northeast of Mount Banning on Santa Catalina Island (lat. 33°24' N, long. 118°23'25" W). Named on Santa Catalina North (1950) 7.5' quadrangle. Doran (1980, p. 77) gave the alternate name "Crater Lake" for the feature.

Echo Mountain [LOS ANGELES]: *locality,* 3.5 miles west-southwest of Mount Wilson (lat. 34°12'45" N, long. 118°07'15" W; sec. 34, T 2 N, R 12 W). Site named on Mount Wilson (1953) 7.5' quadrangle. Pasadena (1900) 15' quadrangle has both the names "Echo Mountain" and "Mount Lowe Hotel" at the spot. Mount Lowe (1939) 6' quadrangle has the name "Echo Mountain" for a place along the Pacific Electric incline cable, and Mount Wilson (1966) 7.5' quadrangle has the name "Echo Mountain" for a peak at the place. Postal authorities established Echo Mountain post office in 1893, moved it 3.5 miles northeast in 1904, and changed the name to Mount Lowe in 1910 (Salley, p. 65).

Echo Mountain [SAN DIEGO]: *ridge,* south-southwest-trending, 1.5 miles long, 4.25 miles north-northeast of Barrett Junction (lat. 32° 39'55" N, long. 116°40'15" W). Named on Barrett Lake (1960) 7.5' quadrangle.

Echo Rock [LOS ANGELES]: *peak,* 0.25 mile northeast of Mount Wilson (1) (lat. 34°13'30" N, long. 118°03'20" W). Named on Pasadena (1900) 15' quadrangle.

Echo Spring [SAN DIEGO]: *spring,* 4.25 miles east of Otay Mountain (lat. 32°36'25" N, long. 116°46'15" W). Named on Otay Mountain (1972) 7.5' quadrangle.

Echo Valley [SAN DIEGO]: *valley,* 4.25 miles north-northwest of Descanso (lat. 32°54'30" N, long. 116°39'15" W; mainly in sec. 34, T 14 S, R 3 E). Named on Tule Springs (1960) 7.5' quadrangle. Everhart's (1951) map shows a place called Echo Dell located nearly 1 mile up King Creek from the mouth of present Echo Valley.

Echo Well: see **Echoes**, under **Fallbrook** [SAN DIEGO].

Edendale [LOS ANGELES]: *locality,* 2.5 miles north-northwest of Los Angeles city hall (lat. 34°05'25" N, long. 118°15'25" W). Named on Hollywood (1953) 7.5' quadrangle. Postal authorities established Edendale post office in 1952 (Salley, p. 65).

Eden Gardens [SAN DIEGO]: *locality,* 2 miles north-northeast of Del Mar (lat. 32°59'15" N, long. 117°15'15" W; sec. 1, 2, T 14 S, R 4 W). Named on Del Mar (1967) 7.5' quadrangle.

Edfu: see **Lemon** [VENTURA].

Edgemont [LOS ANGELES]: *locality,* 4.5 miles northwest of present Los Angeles city hall (lat. 34°06'35" N, long. 118°17"35" W). Named on Santa Monica (1902) 15' quadrangle.

Edwards Air Force Base: see **Rosamond Lake** [LOS ANGELES].

Edwards Canyon [VENTURA]: *canyon,* drained by a stream that flows 1 mile to the valley of Santa Clara River 1 mile west of Piru (lat. 34°24'45" N, long. 118°48'35" W; sec. 19, T 4 N, R 18 W). Named on Piru (1952) 7.5' quadrangle.

Eel Point [LOS ANGELES]: *promontory,* 8 miles south-southeast of Northwest Harbor on the west side of San Clemente Island (lat. 32° 55'05" N, long. 118°32'45" W). Named on San Clemente Island Central (1943) 7.5' quadrangle.

Egg Mountain [SAN DIEGO]: *hill,* 2 miles northwest of Sweeney Pass (lat. 32°50'55" N, long. 116°12'25" W; sec. 24, T 15 S, R 7 E). Named on Sweeney Pass (1959) 7.5' quadrangle.

Eisenecke: see **Barrett Junction** [SAN DIEGO].

Elanus Canyon [SAN DIEGO]: *canyon,* drained by a stream that flows 4 miles to Murphy Canyon 7 miles northwest of La Mesa (lat. 32°49'45" N, long. 117°07' W). Named on La Mesa (1967, photorevised 1975) 7.5' quadrangle. The name is from *Elanus leucurus,* the scientific name of the white-tailed kites that live in the canyon (United States Board on Geographic Names, 1977, p. 4).

Elayon [LOS ANGELES]: *locality,* less than 1 mile south-southeast of Newhall along Southern Pacific Railroad (lat. 34°22'15" N, long. 118°31'20" W). Named on Santa Susana (1903) 15' quadrangle.

El Cajon [SAN DIEGO]:

(1) *land grant,* at and around the city of El Cajon. Named on Alpine (1955), El Cajon (1967), El Cajon Mountain (1955), La Mesa (1967), Poway (1967), and San Vicente Reservoir (1955) 7.5' quadrangles. Maria Antonio Estudillo de Pedrorena received 11 leagues in 1845; Thomas W. Sutherland, guardian for heirs of Miguel Pedrorena, claimed 48,800 acres patented in 1876 (Cowan, p. 21). A grant of 400 varas called Cañada de los Coches that lay within El Cajon grant was given to Apolinaria Lorenzana in 1843; A. Lestrada claimed 28 acres patented in 1873 (Cowan, p. 28).

(2) *city,* 13 miles east-northeast of downtown San Diego (lat. 32°47'35" N, long. 116°57'40" W); the place is on El Cajon grant. Named on El Cajon (1967) and La Mesa (1967) 7.5' quadrangles. Postal authorities established Elcajon post office in 1878 and changed the name to El Cajon in 1905 (Salley, p. 66). The city incorporated in 1912. Postal authorities established Sweetwater post office 8 miles southeast of El Cajon (2) along Agua Dulce Creek in 1885 and discontinued it in 1888; they established Dehesa post office at the same site in 1888 (Salley, p. 217). Tucker (1925b, p. 381) described El Granito Mineral Springs, located about 1 mile southeast of El Cajon (2); the spring water was bottled as early as 1913.

El Cajon Mountain [SAN DIEGO]: *peak,* 11.5 miles northeast of El Cajon city hall (lat. 32°54'55" N, long. 116°49'10" W; near W line sec. 31, T 14 S, R 2 E). Altitude 3675 feet. Named on El Cajon Mountain (1955) 7.5' quadrangle. United States Board on Geographic Names (1990, p. 10) approved the name "Silverdome" for a peak, altitude 2388 feet, located 2.6 miles west of El Cajon Mountain (lat. 32°54'54" N, long. 116°51'50" W).

El Cajon Valley [SAN DIEGO]: *valley,* at and near the city of El Cajon (lat. 32°48'30" N, long. 116°57'15" W); the valley is on El Cajon grant. Named on El Cajon (1967) 7.5' quadrangle.

El Cañon de la Boca Negra: see **Big Dalton Canyon** [LOS ANGELES].

El Capitan [SAN DIEGO]: *locality,* 3 miles east-northeast of El Cajon Mountain along San Diego River (lat. 32°56' N, long. 116° 46'30" W; at NE cor. sec. 28, T 14 S, R 2 E). Named on Cuyamaca (1903) 30' quadrangle. Postal authorities established El Capitan post office in 1886, discontinued it in 1887, reestablished it in 1891, and discontinued it in 1895 (Salley, p. 66).

El Capitan Lake: see **El Capitan Reservoir** [SAN DIEGO].

El Capitan Reservoir [SAN DIEGO]: *lake,* behind a dam on San Diego River 2.25 miles south-southeast of El Cajon Mountain (lat. 32°53'05" N, long. 116°48'30" W; sec. 7, T 15 S, R 2 E); water of the lake covers the site of El Capitan. Named on Alpine (1955) and El Cajon Mountain (1955) 7.5' quadrangles. United States Board on Geographic Names (1979b, p. 6) approved the name "El Capitan Lake" for the feature.

El Carmel Point [SAN DIEGO]: *promontory,* 5.25 miles south-southeast of Point La Jolla in Mission Bay (lat. 32°46'45" N, long. 117°14'50" W). Named on La Jolla (1967) 7.5' quadrangle.

El Conejo [LOS ANGELES-VENTURA]: *land grant,* around Newbury Park and Thousands Oaks; mainly in Ventura County, but extends south into Los Angeles County. Named on Newbury Park (1951), Point Dume (1951), Thousand Oaks (1952), and Triunfo Pass (1950) 7.5' quadrangles. Jose Polanco and Ignacio Rodriguez received 11 leagues in 1803; Jose de la Guerra y Noriega received the grant in 1822 and claimed 48,672 acres patented in 1873 (Cowan, p. 29; Cowan gave the name "Señora de Altagracia" as an alternate). Font first used the name "Conejo" in the neighborhood in 1776—*conejo* means "rabbit" in Spanish (Ricard).

Elderberry Canyon [LOS ANGELES]: *canyon,* drained by a stream that flows 3.5 miles to Castaic Creek nearly 6 miles east of Whitaker Peak (lat. 34°34'05" N, long. 118°37'50" W; sec. 36, T 6 N, R 17 W). Named on Warm Springs Mountain (1958) and Whitaker Peak (1958) 7.5' quadrangles. Los Angeles County (1935) map names several other branches of the canyon of Castaic Creek: Simon Canyon, which opens into the canyon of Castaic Creek from the east about 0.5 mile downstream from the mouth of Elderberry Canyon; Cordova Canyon, which opens into the canyon of Castaic Creek from the northeast about 0.25 mile upstream from the mouth of Elderberry Canyon; Funks Canyon, which opens into the canyon of Castaic Creek from the north about 1 mile upstream from the mouth of Elderberry Canyon; Haynes Canyon, which opens into the canyon of Castaic Creek from the northeast about 1 mile upstream from the mouth of Funks Canyon; Sycamore Canyon, which opens into the canyon of Castaic Creek from the southwest about 0.25 mile upstream from the mouth of Haynes Canyon; and Randolph Canyon, which opens into the canyon of Castaic Creek from the southwest about 0.5 mile upstream from the mouth of Sycamore Canyon.

Elderberry Forebay [LOS ANGELES]: *water feature,* behind a dam on Castaic Creek 6 miles east of Whitaker Peak (lat. 34°33'40" N, long. 118°37'45" W; near S line sec. 36, T 6 N, R 17 W); the feature is at and above the mouth of Elderberry Canyon. Named on Whitaker Peak (1958, photorevised 1974) 7.5' quadrangle. United States Board on Geographic Names (1973, p. 3) gave the variant names "Castaic Afterbay," "Castaic Forebay," "Castaic Pumping Forebay," "Castaic Pumping Plant Afterbay," and "Castaic Reservoir" for the feature.

Elder Canyon: see **Alder Canyon** [SAN DIEGO].

Eldon: see **Lancaster** [LOS ANGELES].

Eldoradoville: see **Eldoradoville Campground** [LOS ANGELES].

Eldoradoville Campground [LOS ANGELES]: *locality,* 8.5 miles northeast of Glendora city hall along San Gabriel River (lat. 34° 13'45" N, long. 117°46'10" W). Named on Glendora (1966) 7.5' quadrangle. The name recalls the mining camp of Eldoradoville, which was situated near the intersection of East Fork San Gabriel River and Cattle Canyon; the first settlement at the site, called Prospect Bar, was destroyed by a flood in 1859, and Eldoradoville was wiped out by a flood in 1862—a shanty settlement of unemployed men and their families at the site in the depression years of the early 1930's had the informal name "Hooverville" (Robinson, J.W., 1983, p. 18-20, 40).

Eleanor: see **Lake Eleanor** [VENTURA].

Electric: see **Pico Heights** [LOS ANGELES].

Elena Mountain [SAN DIEGO]: *peak,* 5.5 miles north-northwest of Barrett Junction (lat. 32°41'25" N, long. 116°43'40" W; sec. 13, T 17 S, R 2 E). Altitude 3339 feet. Named on Barrett Lake (1960) 7.5' quadrangle. Called Barber Mt. on Cuyamaca (1903) 30' quadrangle.

El Encanto [LOS ANGELES]: *locality,* 2 miles north-northeast of Azusa city hall (lat. 34°09'40" N, long. 117°53'30" W; near E line sec. 23, T 1 N, R 10 W). Named on Azusa (1953) 7.5' quadrangle.

El Encino[LOS ANGELES]: *land grant,* at and north of Encino. Named on Canoga Park (1952) and Van Nuys (1966) 7.5' quadrangles. Ramon, Francisco, and Roque (presumably Indians) received 1 league in 1845; Vicente de la Ossa claimed 4461 acres patented in 1873 (Cowan, p. 34).

Elephant Hill [LOS ANGELES]: *peak,* 2.5 miles west of Pomona city hall (lat. 34°03'05" N, long. 117°47'45" W). Altitude 1160 feet. Named on San Dimas (1954) 7.5' quadrangle.

El Escorpion [LOS ANGELES]: *land grant,* north of Calabasas. Named on Calabasas (1952) 7.5' quadrangle. Odon, Urbano, and Manuel (who were Indians) received the land in 1845 and claimed 1110 acres patented in 1876 (Cowan, p. 34).

Elftman [LOS ANGELES]: *locality,* 5 miles north-northwest of Long Beach city hall along Southern Pacific Railroad (lat. 33°50'25" N, long. 118°13'20" W). Named on Long Beach (1964) 7.5' quadrangle. Downey (1902) 15' quadrangle has the name "Cerritos" at the site. Postal authorities established Cerritos post office in 1888, discontinued it in 1890, reestablished it in 1902, and discontinued it in 1903 (Salley, p. 41).

El Granito Mineral Springs: see **El Cajon** [SAN DIEGO] (2).

Elisio: see **Santa Paula** [VENTURA].

Elizabeth Lake [LOS ANGELES]:

(1) *intermittent lake,* 1.25 miles long, 2.25 miles east-southeast of the village of Lake Hughes (lat. 34°40' N, long. 118°24'10" W; mainly in sec. 30, T 7 N, R 14 W). Named on Lake Hughes (1957) 7.5' quadrangle. Baker's (1911) map shows two lakes at the place, and has the name "Elizabeth Lakes" for them. Elizabeth Lake (1917) 30' quadrangle shows one permanent lake there. Hughes Lake (1937) 6' quadrangles shows two lakes at the place, and has the name "Elizabeth Lake" for the pair. The feature long was known as La Laguna de Chico Lopez for its owner; the present name came after Elizabeth Wingfield fell into the lake (Latta, p. 29, 81). It also was called Laguna del Diablo (Bell, p. 202) and Rabbit Lake (Barras, p. 17). Blake (p. 57) used the form "Lake Elizabeth" for the name.

(2) *locality,* 3.25 miles east-southeast of the present village of Lake Hughes (lat. 34°39'45" N, long. 118°22'50" W; near S line sec. 29, T 7 N, R 14 W); the place is less than 0.5 mile east-southeast of the east end of Elizabeth Lake (1). Named on Elizabeth Lake (1917) 30' quadrangle. Postal authorities established Elizabeth Lake post office in 1878, discontinued it in 1892, reestablished it in 1893, discontinued it in 1918, reestablished it in 1923, and discontinued it finally in 1925 (Frickstad, p. 73). California Mining Bureau's (1917a) map shows a place called Pinchot located 6 miles southwest of Elizabeth Lake (2). Postal authorities established Pinchot post office in 1908 and discontinued it in 1911; the name was for Gifford Pinchot, head of the Forest Service (Salley, p. 171).

Elizabeth Lake Campground [LOS ANGELES]: *locality,* 2.25 miles northeast of Warm Springs Mountain (lat. 34°37'15" N, long. 118° 33'25" W); the place is in Elizabeth Lake Canyon. Named on Warm Springs Mountain (1958) 7.5' quadrangle.

Elizabeth Lake Canyon [LOS ANGELES]: *canyon,* drained by a stream that flows 16 miles to Castaic Creek 5.5 miles south-southwest of Warm Springs Mountain (lat. 34°31' N, long. 118°36'15" W; near W line sec. 18, T 5 N, R 16 W); the feature heads 3 miles west of Elizabeth Lake (1). Named on Burnt Peak (1958), Lake Hughes (1957), and Warm Springs Mountain (1958) 7.5' quadrangles.

Elkhorn Camp [LOS ANGELES]: *locality,* 6.25 miles northwest of present Santa Monica city hall in Topanga Canyon (lat. 34°03'35" N, long. 118°35' W). Named on Topanga Canyon (1928) 6' quadrangle.

Elkhorn Lodge [LOS ANGELES]: *locality,* 10 miles northeast of Solemint (lat. 34°29'40" N, long. 118°18'30" W; near NE cor. sec. 26, T 5 N, R 14 W). Named on Lang (1933) 6' quadrangle.

Ella Wash [SAN DIEGO]: *dry wash,* extends for 2 miles from the mouth of Coachwhip Canyon to Palo Verde Wash 13 miles east of Borrego Springs (lat. 33°15'55" N, long. 116°09'40" W). Named on Fonts Point (1959) 7.5' quadrangle.

Eller Slough [LOS ANGELES]: *stream,* flows 4 miles to end 5.25 miles north-northwest of Black Butte (lat. 34°37'40" N, long. 117° 44'40" W; sec. 8, T 6 N, R 8 W)). Named on Adobe Mountain (1955) and El Mirage (1956) 7.5' quadrangles.

Elliott: see **Camp Elliott** [SAN DIEGO].

Ellis Apiary Campground [VENTURA]: *locality,* 6 miles east-southeast of Cobblestone Mountain (lat. 34°34' N, long. 118°46'40" W). Named on Cobblestone Mountain (1958) 7.5' quadrangle. A small commercial beehive operation was at the site (Gagnon, p. 79).

Ellis Spring [SAN DIEGO]: *spring,* 2.25 miles west-southwest of Descanso (lat. 32°50'35" N, long. 116°38'50" W; near NW cor. sec. 26, T 15 S, R 3 E). Named on Viejas Mountain (1960) 7.5' quadrangle.

Ellsworth Barranca [VENTURA]: *gully,* extends for 2 miles from the mouth of Aliso Canyon to Santa Clara River 1 mile east-northeast of Saticoy (lat. 34°17'30" N, long. 119°07'50" W). Named on Saticoy (1951) 7.5' quadrangle. The name commemorates Daniel Ellsworth and Charles Ellsworth, farmers near Saticoy in the 1870's (Ricard).

Elm Creek [VENTURA]: *stream,* flows 1.5 miles to Tar Creek 6.5 miles north of Fillmore (lat. 34°29'35" N, long. 118°53'05" W; near E line sec. 29, T 5 N, R 19 W). Named on Cobblestone Mountain (1958) and Fillmore (1951) 7.5' quadrangles.

El Merrie Dell [LOS ANGELES]: *locality,* 4.5 miles northwest of Sunland in Kagel Canyon (lat. 34°17'45" N, long. 118°22'35" W; on E line sec. 31, T 3 N, R 14 W). Named on Sunland (1942) 6' quadrangle.

El Mirage Valley [LOS ANGELES]: *valley,* mainly in San Bernardino County, but extends northwest into Los Angeles County 12 miles north-northeast of Black Butte (lat. 34°44' N, long. 117°40' W). Named on Adobe Mountain (1955) and Jackrabbit Hill (1973) 7.5' quadrangles. Called Mirage Valley on Kramer (1942) 15' quadrangle, and called Antelope Valley on Adobe (1934) 6' quadrangle.

El Modena: see **El Modeno** [ORANGE].

El Modena Station [ORANGE]: *locality,* 2.25 miles east-southeast of present Orange city hall (lat. 33°46'50" N, long. 117°48'40" W). Named on Orange (1950) 7.5' quadrangle.

El Modeno [ORANGE]: *district,* 2 miles east of Orange city hall (lat. 33°47'15" N, long. 117°48'45" W). Named on Orange (1964) 7.5' quadrangle. Called El Modena on Corona (1902) 30' quadrangle. Lankershim Ranch Land and Water Company's (1888) map has the form "Elmodena" for the name. Postal authorities established Earlham post office in 1887 and changed the name to El Modena in 1888, to El Modino in 1910, and back to El Modena in 1970; a group from Earlham, Indiana, planned to found a university at the spot and gave the site the name "Earlham" (Salley, p. 63, 68). United States Board on Geographic Names (1965b, p. 11) rejected the names "El Modena" and "Modena" for the place, but later (1970a, p. 2) approved the name "El Modena" and listed the names "El Modeno" and "Modena" as variants. Earlham began in 1886 as a Quaker settlement; the name was changed to Modena for the city in Italy, but postal authorities added the Spanish article "El" to the name to distinguish the post office from another one in California—later the terminal letter "a" was changed to "o" apparently in the mistaken belief that the gender of the word should agree with the Spanish article "El" (Hanna, p. 196).

El Molino [LOS ANGELES]: *district,* 6 miles west-northwest of El Monte city hall in San Marino (lat. 34°06'40" N, long. 118°07'15" W). Named on El Monte (1953) 7.5' quadrangle.

El Monte [LOS ANGELES]: *city,* 12 miles east of Los Angeles city hall (lat. 34°04'15" N, long. 118°01'45" W). Named on El Monte (1953) 7.5' quadrangle. A.W. Whipple (p. 135) referred to "the town of Monte," and Trask (p. 19) used the name "the Monte" for the place. Postal authorities established Monte post office in 1853, changed the name to Elmonte in 1875, and changed it to El Monte in 1905 (Salley, p. 68, 145). The city incorporated in 1912. Squatters came to the site in 1852, and a dense stand of willows there gave the name "El Monte" to the place—*el monte* means "the thicket" in Spanish (Gudde, 1949, p. 106). Henry Dalton laid out the town, which by 1852 had a dozen frame buildings and was called Lexington, Lickskillit, and El Monte; it was the first town of English-speaking people in Southern California (Jackson, p. 150). Postal authorities established Four Corners post office 6 miles northeast of El Monte post office (NE quarter sec. 17, T 1 S, R 10 W) in 1876 and discontinued it in 1878 (Salley, p. 79).

El Monte: see **South El Monte** [LOS ANGELES].

El Monte Park [SAN DIEGO]: *locality,* 2.25 miles southwest of El Cajon Mountain along San Diego River (lat. 32°53'30" N, long. 116°50'45" W). Named on El Cajon Mountain (1955) 7.5' quadrangle.

El Moro: see **Morro Hill** [SAN DIEGO].

Elmwood Canyon [LOS ANGELES]: *canyon,* 1 mile long, 1.5 miles east-northeast of Burbank city hall (lat. 34°11'40" N, long. 118°16'55" W). Named on Burbank (1953) 7.5' quadrangle.

El Nido [LOS ANGELES]:

(1) *locality,* 3.5 miles west-northwest of Malibu Point (lat. 34°02'35" N, long. 118°44'20" W; sec. 35, T 1 S, R 18 W). Named on Malibu Beach (1951) 7.5' quadrangle.

(2) *district,* 2.25 miles north-northwest of Torrance city hall (lat. 33°51'55" N, long. 118°21'25" W). Named on Torrance (1964) 7.5' quadrangle.

El Nido: see **Jamul** [SAN DIEGO] (2).

El Paredon Blanco: see **Boyle Heights** [LOS ANGELES].

El Piojo: see **Anaheim Landing** [ORANGE].

El Potrero: see **Cuca** [SAN DIEGO].

El Potrero del Tenaja [SAN DIEGO]: *valley,* 10 miles northwest of Fallbrook on San Diego-Riverside County line (lat. 33°29'15" N, long. 117°21'45" W). Named on San Luis Rey (1898) 30' quadrangle.

El Prado Meadow [SAN DIEGO]: *area,* 2 miles west of Monument Peak (lat. 32°53'20" N, long. 116°27'05" W; near S line sec. 3, T 15 S, R 5 E). Named on Monument Peak (1959) 7.5' quadrangle.

El Prieto [LOS ANGELES]: *canyon,* drained by a stream that flows 1.5 miles to Arroyo Seco 4.5 miles north-northwest of Pasadena city hall (lat. 34°12'30" N, long. 118°10'10" W; at SE cor. sec. 31, T 2 N, R 12 W). Named on Pasadena (1953) 7.5' quadrangle. Called El Prieto Cany. on Los Angeles County (1935) map. For many years the feature was called Negro Canyon, for Robert Owen, a freed slave who lived there in the 1850's (Robinson, J.W., 1977, p. 103).

El Prieto Canyon: see **El Prieto** [LOS ANGELES].

El Pueblo de Nuestra Señora la Reina de los Angeles de la Porciuncula: see **Los Angeles** [LOS ANGELES].

El Rincon [VENTURA]: *land grant,* at Rincon Point on Ventura-Santa Barbara County line. Named on White Ledge Peak (1952) 7.5' quadrangle. Teodoro Arellanes received 1 league in 1835 and claimed 4460 acres patented in 1872 (Cowan, p. 68).

El Rio [VENTURA]: *town,* 2.5 miles north of Oxnard (lat. 34°14'05" N, long. 119°10'15" W); the place is near Santa Clara River. Named on Oxnard (1949) 7.5' quadrangle. Called Elrio on Hueneme (1904) 15' quadrangle. Postal authorities established New Jerusalem post office in 1882, changed the name to Jerusalem in 1895, changed it to El Rio the same year, discontinued it in 1911, reestablished it in 1953, and discontinued it in 1966 (Salley, p. 68, 107). The name "Jerusalem" was from Jewish merchants at the place (Ricard).

El Rio de los Temblores: see **San Gabriel River** [LOS ANGELES-ORANGE].

El Salto [SAN DIEGO]: *water feature,* nearly 5 miles east-southeast of Oceanside along Buena Vista Creek (lat. 33°10'45" N, long. 117°17'55" W). Named on San Luis Rey (1948) 7.5' quadrangle.

El Segundo [LOS ANGELES]: *town,* 2.25 miles north of Manhattan Beach city hall (lat. 33°55'05" N, long. 118°25' W). Named on Venice (1950) 7.5' quadrangle. Postal authorities established El Segundo post office in 1911 (Frickstad, p. 73), and the town incorporated in 1917. Colonel Rheem of Standard Oil Company applied the name "El Segundo" to the refinery that the company had at the place, the second refinery of the company in California—*el segundo* means "the second" in Spanish (Gudde, 1949, p. 107).

El Segundo Station [LOS ANGELES]:

(1) *locality,* 2 miles northeast of Manhattan Beach city hall along Atchison, Topeka and Santa Fe Railroad (lat. 33°54'30" N, long. 118°23' W). Named on Venice (1950) 7.5' quadrangle.

(2) *locality,* 1.25 miles north-northwest of present Manhattan Beach city hall along Pacific Electric Railroad (lat. 33°55' N, long. 118° 25'40" W). Named on Venice (1924) 6' quadrangle.

El Sereno [LOS ANGELES]: *district,* 4.25 miles east-northeast of Los Angeles city hall (lat. 34°04'55" N, long. 118°10'30" W; sec. 18, T 1 S, R 12 W). Named on Los Angeles (1953) 7.5' quadrangle. Postal authorities established El Sereno post office in 1949 (Salley, p. 68).

Elsmere Canyon [LOS ANGELES]: *canyon,* nearly 3 miles long, opens into the canyon of Newhall Creek 2 miles southeast of Newhall (lat. 34°21'40" N, long. 118°30'15" W). Named on San Fernando (1953) 7.5' quadrangle. On San Fernando (1945) 15' quadrangle, the name follows a southeasterly branch of the canyon rather than the present main canyon above the mouth of the branch.

El Toro [ORANGE]: *city,* 18 miles southeast of Santa Ana (lat. 33° 37'35" N, long. 117°41'35" W); the city is on Cañada de los Alisos grant. Named on El Toro (1968) and San Juan Capistrano (1968) 7.5' quadrangles. Postal authorities established Eltoro post office in 1888 and changed the name to El Toro in 1905 (Salley, p. 69). A townsite called Aliso City laid out at the place in 1887 failed to develop as planned (Meadows, p. 19). When railroad officials asked Mrs. Dwight Whiting to name their station at the site, she selected the designation "El Toro" from a bull that had fallen into a well there and drowned—*el toro* means "the bull" in Spanish (Hanna, p.

332).

El Toro Air Station: see **El Toro Marine Corps Air Station** [ORANGE].

El Toro Canyon [LOS ANGELES]: *canyon*, drained by a stream that flows nearly 2 miles to Las Llajas Canyon [LOS ANGELES-VENTURA] 7.5 miles west-southwest of Newhall (lat. 34°19'35" N, long. 118°38'45" W). Named on Santa Susana (1951) 7.5' quadrangle.

El Toro Marine Corps Air Station [ORANGE]: *military installation*, 4 miles north-northwest of El Toro (lat. 33°40'45" N, long. 117°43'30" W). Named on El Toro (1968) 7.5' quadrangle. Called El Toro Air Station on El Toro (1950) 7.5' quadrangle.

El Toro Reservoir [ORANGE]: *lake*, 0.25 mile long, 1.5 miles east of El Toro (lat. 33°37'25" N, long. 118°39'55" W; at N line sec. 25, T 6 S, R 8 W). Named on El Toro (1968) and San Juan Capistrano (1968) 7.5' quadrangles.

El Valle de Santa Catalina de Bononia de los Encinos: see **San Fernando Valley** [LOS ANGELES].

El Venado: see **Point Dume** [LOS ANGELES].

Elvira [SAN DIEGO]: *locality*, 2.5 miles east-southeast of Point La Jolla along Atchison, Topeka and Santa Fe Railroad (lat. 32°50'15" N, long. 117°13'55" W). Named on La Jolla (1967) 7.5' quadrangle. La Jolla (1953) 7.5' quadrangle has the name for a place located about 1 mile farther north along the railroad (lat. 32°51'05" N, long. 117°13'55" W).

Elysian Garden [LOS ANGELES]: *locality*, 3.5 miles north-northwest of Los Angeles city hall (lat. 34°06'20" N, long. 118°15'30" W); the place is north of present Elysian Heights. Named on Glendale (1928) 6' quadrangle.

Elysian Heights [LOS ANGELES]: *district*, 2.5 miles north of Los Angeles city hall (lat. 34°05'15" N, long. 118°15' W). Named on Hollywood (1953) and Los Angeles (1953) 7.5' quadrangles.

Emerald Bay [LOS ANGELES]: *embayment*, 2.5 miles east of Silver Peak on the north side of Santa Catalina Island (lat. 33°27'55" N, long. 118°31'25" W). Named on Santa Catalina West (1943) 7.5' quadrangle. The feature also was called Wilson's Cove, for Spencer H. Wilson (Doran, 1980, p. 68). During the mining boom of the 1860's, streets were laid out on the shore of Emerald Bay for a town to be called Queen City (Doran, 1963, p. 100; Gleason, p. 15-16).

Emerald Bay [ORANGE]: *village*, 1.5 miles west of Laguna Beach city hall along the coast (lat. 33°33'05" N, long. 117°48'20" W). Named on Laguna Beach (1965) 7.5' quadrangle. Los Angeles Title Insurance Company developed the exclusive residential community in 1929 (Meadows, p. 60).

Emerald Canyon [ORANGE]: *canyon*, drained by a stream that flows 3.25 miles to the sea 1.5 miles west-northwest of Laguna Beach city hall (lat. 33°33'05" N, long. 117°48'25" W); the mouth of the canyon is at Emerald Bay. Named on Laguna Beach (1965, photorevised 1981) 7.5' quadrangle. Called Niger Canyon on Santa Ana (1942) 15' quadrangle, and called Nigger Canyon on Laguna Beach (1949) 7.5' quadrangle. United States Board on Geographic Names (1969a, p. 3) rejected the names "Niger Canyon" and "Mayate Canyon" for the feature. The word "Nigger" was a corruption of the name "Niguel" (Meadows, p. 105).

Emerson Flats [LOS ANGELES]: *area*, 5.5 miles west-northwest of Azusa city hall (lat. 34°10'35" N, long. 117°59'15" W; sec. 13, T 1 N, R 11 W). Named on Azusa (1953) 7.5' quadrangle. The name commemorates L.H. Emerson, who filed for land just below the junction of Monrovia Canyon and Sawpit Canyon, and built a log cabin there in the 1880's (Robinson, J.W., 1983, p. 73-74).

Emery: see **Un Gallo Flat** [SAN DIEGO].

Emily City: see **Coleman City**, under **Wynola** [SAN DIEGO].

Emma: see **Mount Emma** [LOS ANGELES].

Emory: see **Fort Emory**, under **Silver Strand** [SAN DIEGO].

Empire Landing [LOS ANGELES]: *locality*, 4 miles north of Mount Banning on the north side of Santa Catalina Island (lat. 33°25'35" N, long. 118°26' W). Named on Santa Catalina North (1950) 7.5' quadrangle. The place also was known as Pot Hole Harbor (Doran, 1980, p. 72).

Encanto [SAN DIEGO]: *district*, 4 miles northeast of National City civic center (lat. 32°42'45" N, long. 117°03'30" W). Named on National City (1967) 7.5' quadrangle. Postal authorities established Encanto post office in 1909 (Frickstad, p. 150). Alice Klauber, whose family first developed the place, gave the name to the district in 1889—previously it was called Klauber Park (Stein, p. 44).

Enchanted Cove [SAN DIEGO]: *embayment*, 6 miles south-southeast of Point La Jolla along Fiesta Island (lat. 32°46'35" N, long. 117° 12'55" W). Named on La Jolla (1967) 7.5' quadrangle.

Enchanto: see **Lake Enchanto** [LOS ANGELES].

Encinal Canyon [LOS ANGELES]: *canyon*, drained by a stream that flows 2.5 miles to the sea 4.5 miles northwest of Point Dume (lat. 34°02'10" N, long. 118°52'10" W). Named on Point Dume (1951) 7.5' quadrangle.

Encinitas [SAN DIEGO]: *town*, 12 miles south-southeast of Oceanside (lat. 33°02'30" N, long. 117°17'30" W); the town is west of Los Encinitos grant. Named on Encinitas (1968) 7.5' quadrangle. Postal authorities established Encinitos post office in 1882 and changed the name to Encinitas in 1887 (Frickstad, p. 150). They established Vaileta post office 4.5 miles northwest of Encinitas in 1887 and discontinued it in 1888; the name was for Albert H. Vail, first postmaster (Salley, p. 228-229).

Encinitas: see **Los Encenitos** [SAN DIEGO].

Encinitas Creek [SAN DIEGO]: *stream*, flows 4.5 miles to Batiquitos Lagoon 3.5 miles north-northeast of Encinitas (lat. 33°05'15" N, long. 117°16'05" W; sec. 35, T 12 S, R 4 W); the stream is mainly on Los Encinitos grant. Named on Encinitas (1968) and Rancho Santa Fe (1968) 7.5' quadrangles. Crespi gave the name "Cañada de los Encinos" to the valley of the stream at the time of the Portola expedition (Stein, p. 45).

Encinitos: see **Encinitas** [SAN DIEGO].

Encino [LOS ANGELES]: *district*, 6.25 miles east-southeast of the center of Canoga Park in Los Angeles (lat. 34°09'35" N, long. 118° 30' W); the place is on El Encino grant. Named on Canoga Park (1952) and Van Nuys (1953) 7.5' quadrangles. Called Encino Park on Reseda (1928) 6' quadrangle. Postal authorities established En Cino post office in 1873, discontinued in it 1877, and reestablished it 1 mile farther north with the name "Encino" in 1938 (Salley, p. 70).

Encino Creek [LOS ANGELES]: *stream*, flows 2 miles to Los Angeles River 2 miles south-southwest of Van Nuys (lat. 34°10'05" N, long. 118°28'25" W); the stream is in Encino. Named on Van Nuys (1966) 7.5' quadrangle.

Encino Park: see **Encino** [LOS ANGELES].

Encino Reservoir [LOS ANGELES]: *lake*, 0.5 mile long, 6 miles southeast of the center of Canoga Park (lat. 34°08'45" N, long. 118°30'45" W); the feature is 1.25 miles southwest of Encino. Named on Canoga Park (1952) 7.5' quadrangle.

Encino Siding [LOS ANGELES]: *locality*, 5.5 miles east of the center of Canoga Park along Southern Pacific Railroad (lat. 34°11'10" N, long. 118°30'15" W); the place is 2 miles north of Encino. Named on Canoga Park (1952) 7.5' quadrangle. Reseda (1928) 6' quadrangle shows a place called "Encino" located along the railroad 0.25 mile farther south before the rails were realigned.

Engineer Springs [SAN DIEGO]: *locality*, nearly 9 miles southeast of Jamul (lat. 32°37'45" N, long. 116°45'50" W; near S line sec. 3, T 18 S, R 2 E). Named on Dulzura (1972) 7.5' quadrangle.

Engleheard Canyon [LOS ANGELES]: *canyon*, drained by a stream that flows 1.5 miles to Verdugo Wash 7 miles northwest of Pasadena city hall (lat. 34°12'25" N, long. 118°14'25" W). Named on Burbank (1953) and Pasadena (1966) 7.5' quadrangles.

Englewild Canyon [LOS ANGELES]: *canyon*, 1 mile long, 2 miles north-northeast of Glendora city hall (lat. 34°09'40" N, long. 117° 51'05" W; mainly in sec. 20, T 1 N, R 9 W). Named on Glendora (1953) 7.5' quadrangle.

English Canyon [ORANGE]: *canyon*, drained by a stream that flows 3.5 miles to Aliso Creek less than 1 mile east of El Toro (lat. 33° 37'45" N, long. 117°40'50" W). Named on El Toro (1968) 7.5' quadrangle. The name is from settlers who came to the place from England in 1890 (Meadows, p. 61).

Ensenada de Baxa Entrada: see **Mission Bay** [SAN DIEGO].

Ensenada de San Andres: see **San Pedro Bay** [LOS ANGELES-ORANGE].

Entrance Channel [SAN DIEGO]: *channel*, 6.5 miles south of Point La Jolla (lat. 32°45'30" N, long. 117°14'50" W); the feature is at the entrance to Mission Bay. Named on La Jolla (1967) 7.5' quadrangle.

Epworth [VENTURA]: *locality*, 2 miles north-northwest of Moorpark (lat. 34°18'55" N, long. 118°53'25" W; sec. 29, T 3 N, R 19 W). Named on Moorpark (1951) 7.5' quadrangle.

Era Canyon: see **Bouquet Canyon** [LOS ANGELES].

Escondido [SAN DIEGO]: *city*, 28 miles north of San Diego (lat. 33° 07'30" N, long. 117°04'30" W). Named on Escondido (1968), San Marcos (1968), and Valley Center (1968) 7.5' quadrangles. Postal authorities established Apex post office in 1881, moved it 5 miles south in 1883, and moved it 8 miles south and changed the name to Escondido in 1884; they moved Escondido post office 0.5 mile east in 1886 (Salley, p. 8, 70). The city incorporated in 1888. A syndicate of businessmen bought Rincon del Diablo grant in 1885 and laid out the community, which they named for Escondido Creek (Gudde, 1949, p. 109).

Escondido Beach [LOS ANGELES]: *beach*, 2.5 miles northeast of Point Dume along the coast (lat. 34°01'30" N, long. 118°46' W); the beach is at the mouth of Escondido Canyon (2). Named on Point Dume (1951) 7.5' quadrangle.

Escondido Canyon [LOS ANGELES]:

(1) *canyon*, drained by a stream that flows 6 miles to Agua Dulce Canyon 8 miles east-northeast of Solemint (lat. 34°27'50" N, long. 118°19'45" W; near NE cor. sec. 3, T 4 N, R 14 W). Named on Agua Dulce (1960) 7.5' quadrangle. Los Angeles County (1935) map shows North Fork opening into the main canyon from the northeast about 1.5 miles above the mouth of the main canyon.

(2) *canyon*, drained by a stream that flows 4.5 miles to the sea 3 miles northeast of Point Dume (lat. 34°01'30" N, long. 118°45'50" W). Named on Point Dume (1951) 7.5' quadrangle.

Escondido Creek [SAN DIEGO]: *stream*, flows 24 miles to San Elijo Lagoon 2.5 miles west of Rancho Santa Fe (lat. 33°01'10" N, long. 117°14'40" W; sec. 25, T 13 S, R 4 W). Named on Escondido (1968), Rancho Santa Fe (1968), Rodriguez Mountain (1948), and Valley Center (1968) 7.5' quadrangles. Members of the Anza expedition camped by the stream and called it Agua Escondido (Stein, p. 46).

Escondido Junction [SAN DIEGO]: *locality,* 1.25 miles south-southeast of downtown Oceanside along Atchison, Topeka and Santa Fe Railroad (lat. 33°10'50" N, long. 117°22'10" W; near NE cor. sec. 35, T 11 S, R 5 W). Named on San Luis Rey (1968) 7.5' quadrangle.

Escondido Lake: see **Lake Wohlford** [SAN DIEGO].

Escondido Ravine [SAN DIEGO]: *canyon,* drained by a stream that flows 1 mile to Boiling Spring Ravine 7.5 miles north-northeast of Buckman Springs (lat. 32°52'20" N, long. 116°26'05" W; at S line sec. 11, T 15 S, R 5 E). Named on Mount Laguna (1960) 7.5' quadrangle.

Esperanza [ORANGE]: *locality,* 3.5 miles east-southeast of Yorba Linda along Atchison, Topeka and Santa Fe Railroad (lat. 33°52'35" N, long. 117°45'15" W). Named on Orange (1964), Prado Dam (1967), and Yorba Linda (1950) 7.5' quadrangles. The name is for Esperanza Yorba, daughter of Prudencio Yorba (Meadows, p. 61).

Esperanza: see **Lancaster** [LOS ANGELES].

Espinosa Creek [SAN DIEGO]: *stream,* flows 4.5 miles to Pine Valley Creek 9.5 miles north-northeast of Barrett Junction (lat. 32° 44'40" N, long. 116°39' W; near SW cor. sec. 26, T 16 S, R 3 E). Named on Barrett Lake (1960), Descanso (1960), Morena Reservoir (1960), and Viejas Mountain (1960) 7.5' quadrangles.

Eucalyptus Hills [SAN DIEGO]: *settlement,* 5.5 miles north of El Cajon city hall (lat. 32°52'25" N, long. 116°56'30" W). Named on El Cajon (1967) and San Vicente Reservoir (1955) 7.5' quadrangles.

Eucalyptus Pass [SAN DIEGO]: *pass,* less than 2 miles southwest of present El Cajon city hall (lat. 32°46'45" N, long. 116°59'15" W). Named on Cuyamaca (1903) 30' quadrangle.

Eucalyptus Reservoir [SAN DIEGO]: *lake,* 750 feet long, 1.5 miles northeast of La Mesa (lat. 32°46'55" N, long. 117°00'10" W; sec. 17, T 16 S, R 1 W). Named on La Mesa (1953) 7.5' quadrangle.

Eureka Canyon [VENTURA]: *canyon,* drained by a stream that flows 4 miles to the valley of Santa Clara River 1.5 miles south-southeast of Piru (lat. 34°23'35" N, long. 118°46'55" W). Named on Piru (1952), Santa Susana (1951), and Val Verde (1952) 7.5' quadrangles.

Evans Point [SAN DIEGO]: *peak,* 6 miles southeast of Oceanside (lat. 33°08'25" N, long. 117°17'50" W). Altitude 357 feet. Named on San Luis Rey (1968) 7.5' quadrangle.

Evergreen [LOS ANGELES]: *locality,* nearly 1 mile west-southwest of present Whittier city hall along Southern Pacific Railroad (lat. 33°58' N, long. 118°02'55" W). Named on Downey (1902) 15' quadrangle.

Evey Canyon [LOS ANGELES]: *canyon,* drained by a stream that flows 2 miles to San Antonio Canyon 8.5 miles north-northeast of Pomona city hall (lat. 34°09'45" N, long. 117°40'50" W; near NE cor. sec. 23, T 1 N, R 8 W). Named on Mount Baldy (1954) 7.5' quadrangle. The name commemorates Judge Evey, who settled in San Antonio Canyon in the late 1870's (Robinson, J.W., 1983, p. 136).

Ex Mission de San Fernando [LOS ANGELES]: *land grant,* in San Fernando Valley at and around San Fernando mission. Named on Calabasas (1952), Canoga Park (1952), Oat Mountain (1952), San Fernando (1953), Sunland (1953), and Van Nuys (1953) 7.5' quadrangles. Eulogio de Célis bought 13 leagues in 1846 and claimed 116,858 acres patented in 1873 (Cowan, p. 76).

Ex Mission San Diego: see **Mission San Diego** [SAN DIEGO].

Eyrie: see **The Eyrie**, under **Mount Harvard** [LOS ANGELES].

- F -

Fagan Canyon [VENTURA]: *canyon,* drained by a stream that flows 3 miles to the valley of Santa Clara River 1 mile west of downtown Santa Paula (lat. 34°21'20" N, long. 119°04'40" W). Named on Santa Paula (1951) and Santa Paula Peak (1951) 7.5' quadrangles. The name commemorates Michael Fagan, who settled in Ventura County in 1869 and raised sheep in the canyon (Ricard).

Fairmont [LOS ANGELES]: *locality,* 4 miles north-northeast of the village of Lake Hughes (lat. 34°44'05" N, long. 118°25'25" W; sec. 36, T 8 N, R 15 W). Named on Lake Hughes (1957) 7.5' quadrangle. Postal authorities established Fairmont post office in 1888 and discontinued it in 1939; the name was transferred from a place in Illinois (Salley, p. 72).

Fairmont Butte [LOS ANGELES]: *ridge,* generally north-northeast-trending, nearly 2 miles long, 6 miles north-northeast of the village of Lake Hughes (lat. 34°45'30" N, long. 118°24' W). Named on Fairmont Butte (1965) and Lake Hughes (1957) 7.5' quadrangles.

Fairmont Reservoir [LOS ANGELES]: *lake,* 4300 feet long, 2 miles north of the village of Lake Hughes (lat. 34°42'25" N, long. 118° 25'55" W; sec. 11, 12, T 7 N, R 15 W); the feature is 2 miles south-southwest of Fairmont. Named on Lake Hughes (1957) 7.5' quadrangle. Johnson's (1911) map shows an inhabited place called North Portal located at present Fairmont Reservoir at the north end of a tunnel for the aqueduct that brings Owens Valley water from Inyo County to Los Angeles—the place was a temporary headquarters for operations at the north end of the tunnel (Johnson, p. 9).

Fair Oaks [LOS ANGELES]: *locality,* 6.5 miles northeast of present Los Angeles city hall along a rail line (lat. 34°07'05" N, long. 118° 09'15" W). Named on Pasadena (1900) 15' quadrangle.

Fairview [ORANGE]: *locality,* 6 miles south-southwest of Santa Ana (lat. 33°40'15" N, long. 117°55' W). Named on Corona (1902) 30' quadrangle. Postal authorities established Fairview post office in 1888 and discontinued it in 1903 (Frickstad, p. 116). Promoters bought land in 1887 and laid out a town of Fairview, but the enterprise failed and the land reverted to farming; Santa Ana Army Air Base was established at the site in 1943 (Meadows, p. 62, 123-124). Waring (p. 37) described a place called Fairview Hot Spring that was located south of Santa Ana; water for the establishment originally came from a spring, but later from an artesian well 700 feet deep—in 1908 a hotel and cottages accommodated about 50 people.

Fairview [VENTURA]: *locality,* 3 miles northwest of Moorpark (lat. 34°18'55" N, long. 118°54'50" W; sec. 30, T 3 N, R 19 W). Named on Moorpark (1951) 7.5' quadrangle.

Fairview: see **Mount Fairview**, under **Bonsall** [SAN DIEGO].

Fairview Canyon [VENTURA]: *canyon,* drained by a stream that flows 1.25 miles to the valley of Santa Clara River 4 miles west-southwest of Piru (lat. 34°23'55" N, long. 118°51'40" W; sec. 27, T 4 N, R 19 W). Named on Piru (1952) 7.5' quadrangle.

Fairview Hot Spring: see **Fairview** [ORANGE].

Falda: see **Loma Alta Mountain** [SAN DIEGO].

Fallbrook [SAN DIEGO]: *town,* 21 miles north-northwest of Escondido (lat. 33°22'55" N, long. 117°15' W). Named on Bonsall (1968), Fallbrook (1968), Morro Hill (1968), and Temecula (1968) 7.5' quadrangles. Called Fall Brook on Tucker and Reed's (1939) map. Postal authorities established Fall Brook post office in 1878, moved it 5 miles northwest and changed the name to West Fall Brook in 1888, moved it 5 miles southeast and changed the name back to Fall Brook in 1888, and changed the name to Fallbrook in 1950 (Salley, p. 72, 237). Charles Reche came to the place from Fallbrook, Pennsylvania, in 1858 and produced honey that he sold under the brand-name "Fallbrook," which eventually became the name of the town (Stein, p. 47). Hanks' (1886a) map shows a place called Howe P.O. located about 4 miles northwest of Fallbrook post office, and just west of Fallbrook Station. Postal authorities established Howe post office in 1882 and discontinued it in 1891 (Frickstad, p. 151). They established Echoes post office 4 miles northeast of Howe post office in 1886 and discontinued it in 1887; the name was from Echo Well, which was dry and produced only echoes (Salley, p. 65).

Fallbrook Junction [SAN DIEGO]: *locality,* 2 miles north-northwest of Oceanside along Atchison, Topeka and Santa Fe Railroad (lat. 33°13'25" N, long. 117°23'35" W; sec. 15, T 11 S, R 5 W). Named on Oceanside (1968) 7.5' quadrangle.

Fallbrook Naval Reservation [SAN DIEGO]: *military installation,* 2.5 miles southwest of Fallbrook (lat. 33°21'30" N, long. 117°16'30" W). Named on Bonsal (1948), Fallbrook (1949), and Morro Hill (1949) 7.5' quadrangles. Fallbrook (1968) 7.5' quadrangle has the designation "Naval Weapons Station (Fallbrook Annex)" for the place.

Fallbrook Station [SAN DIEGO]: *locality,* 1.25 miles north of Fallbrook along Southern California Railroad (lat. 33°24' N, long. 117° 15' W). Named on San Luis Rey (1898) 30' quadrangle.

Fall Canyon [LOS ANGELES]: *canyon,* drained by a stream that flows nearly 3 miles to Texas Canyon 11 miles south of the village of Lake Hughes (lat. 34°30'55" N, long. 118°24'20" W; sec. 13, T 5 N, R 15 W). Named on Green Valley (1958) 7.5' quadrangle. On Los Angeles County (1935) map, the stream in the canyon is called Fall Creek.

Fall Creek [LOS ANGELES]: *stream,* flows 1.5 miles to Big Tujunga Canyon 3.5 miles east-southeast of Condor Peak (lat. 34°18'20" N, long. 118°09'45" W). Named on Condor Peak (1959) 7.5' quadrangle, which shows waterfalls near the mouth of the creek.

Fall Creek: see **Fall Canyon** [LOS ANGELES].

Fallen Leaf Spring [LOS ANGELES]: *spring,* 11.5 miles north-northeast of Pomona city hall (lat. 34°13'05" N, long. 117°41'50" W). Named on Mount Baldy (1954) 7.5' quadrangle.

Falling Springs [LOS ANGELES]: *locality,* 1.25 miles south-southeast of Crystal Lake (lat. 34°18'10" N, long. 117°50'15" W). Named on Crystal Lake (1958) 7.5' quadrangle. Called La Cienega on Crystal Lake (1941) 6' quadrangle, but United States Board on Geographic Names (1962a, p. 11) rejected this name. The site first was known as Little Cienega; Frank Headlee built a small resort there in 1931 that he called La Cienega, then Headlee's, and finally Falling Springs Resort (Robinson, J.W., 1983, p. 94).

Fallon: see **Rowland** [LOS ANGELES].

Falls: see **The Falls** [SAN DIEGO].

Falls Canyon [LOS ANGELES]:
(1) *canyon,* drained by a stream that flows nearly 1.5 miles to West Fork San Gabriel River 9 miles south-southwest of Pacifico Mountain (lat. 34°15'10" N, long. 118°04'20" W; near S line sec. 18, T 2 N, R 11 W). Named on Chilao Flat (1959) and Mount Wilson (1953) 7.5' quadrangles.
(2) *canyon,* drained by a stream that flows nearly 1 mile to Arroyo Seco 6.25 miles north-northwest of Pasadena city hall (lat. 34° 14' N, long. 118°10'40" W). Named on Pasadena (1953) 7.5' quadrangle.

Falls Canyon [ORANGE]: *canyon,* drained by a stream that flows 1.5 miles to Trabuco Canyon 2.5 miles south of Santiago Peak (lat. 33° 40'25" N, long. 117°32'10" W; near W line sec. 5, T 6 S, R 6 W). Named on Santiago Peak (1954) 7.5' quadrangle. A place called Surprise City was situated at the mouth of Falls Canyon; it provided housing for workers involved with the tin mine in Trabuco Canyon from about 1902 until 1908 (Meadows, p. 132). A flood in 1916 swept away the abandoned houses there (Sleeper, 1968, p. 166).

Falls Creek [LOS ANGELES]: *stream,* flows 2.5 miles to Devil Canyon 1.5 miles north of Chatsworth (lat. 34°16'55" N, long. 118° 36'20" W; at E line sec. 1, T 2 N, R 17 W). Named on Oat Mountain (1952) 7.5' quadrangle. The canyon of the stream has the name "Twin Lakes Canyon" on Los Angeles County (1935) map.

Falls Gulch [LOS ANGELES]: *canyon,* drained by a stream that flows 1.25 miles to San Gabriel River 5 miles west of Mount San Antonio (lat. 34°18'10" N, long. 117°44' W; sec. 32, T 3 N, R 8 W). Named on Mount San Antonio (1955) 7.5' quadrangle.

Falsa Vela: see **Anacapa Island** [VENTURA].

False Bay: see **Mission Bay** [SAN DIEGO].

False Point [SAN DIEGO]: *promontory,* 3 miles south of Point La Jolla along the coast (lat. 32°48'25" N, long. 117°16' W). Named on La Jolla (1967) 7.5' quadrangle.

Fanita: see **Santee** [SAN DIEGO].

Farley Flat [SAN DIEGO]: *area,* 3 miles east of Descanso (lat. 32° 51'10" N, long. 116°33'50" W; on W line sec. 22, T 15 S, R 4 E). Named on Descanso (1960) 7.5' quadrangle.

Farnsworth Bank: see **Lands End** [LOS ANGELES].

Farr [SAN DIEGO]: *locality,* 5.25 miles south-southeast of Oceanside along Atchison, Topka and Santa Fe Railroad (lat. 33° 07'50" N, long. 117°19'45" W). Named on San Luis Rey (1968) 7.5' quadrangle.

Fascination Spring [LOS ANGELES]: *spring,* 2.25 miles north-northwest of Sunland (lat. 34°17'30" N, long. 118°19'20" W; near NW cor. sec. 2, T 2 N, R 14 W). Named on Sunland (1953) 7.5' quadrangle.

Fault Wash [SAN DIEGO]: *stream* and *dry wash,* extends for 7.5 miles to San Felipe Creek 2.5 miles north-northwest of Ocotillo Wells (lat. 33°10'35" N, long. 116°09' W). Named on Borrego Mountain (1960) 7.5' quadrangle.

Featherstone Canyon [SAN DIEGO]: *canyon,* 2.5 miles long, opens into Barrona Valley 2.25 miles northwest of El Cajon Mountain (lat. 32°56'15" N, long. 116°51' W). Named on El Cajon Mountain (1955) 7.5' quadrangle. The name reportedly is from some boulders in the canyon that are marked with crude feather patterns (Stein, p. 47).

Fellowship Farm [LOS ANGELES]: *locality,* 3 miles south-southeast of Baldwin Park (lat. 34°02'45" N, long. 117°56'15" W). Named on Puente (1927) 6' quadrangle.

Fenner Canyon [LOS ANGELES]: *canyon,* drained by a stream that flows 1.5 miles to Big Rock Creek 5.5 miles southeast of Valyermo (lat. 34°23'25" N, long. 117°46'40" W). Named on Valyermo (1958) 7.5' quadrangle.

Ferguson Flat [SAN DIEGO]: *area,* 3.25 miles north-northeast of Julian (lat. 33°07'20" N, long. 116°34'55" W; near SE cor. sec. 17, T 12 S, R 4 E). Named on Julian (1960) 7.5' quadrangle.

Fermin: see **Point Fermin** [LOS ANGELES].

Fernandez: see **Juan Fernandez Spring** [VENTURA].

Fernando: see **San Fernando** [LOS ANGELES].

Fernando Pass: see **San Fernando Pass** [LOS ANGELES].

Fern Ann Falls [LOS ANGELES]: *locality,* 2 miles north-northwest of Chatsworth (lat. 34°17'05" N, long. 118°36'55" W; sec. 1, T 2 N, R 17 W); the place is along Falls Creek. Named on Oat Mountain (1952) 7.5' quadrangle.

Fernbrook [SAN DIEGO]: *locality,* 7.5 miles north of Lakeside (lat. 32°58'05" N, long. 116°54'40" W; near E line sec. 7, T 14 S, R 1 E). Named on San Vicente Reservoir (1955) 7.5' quadrangle.

Fern Canyon [LOS ANGELES]:
(1) *canyon,* drained by a stream that flows 2 miles to Arroyo Seco (lat. 34°12'50" N, long. 118°10'20" W; sec. 31, T 2 N, R 12 W). Named on Pasadena (1953) 7.5' quadrangle. Los Angeles County (1935) map shows a feature called Coon Canyon situated between Fern Canyon (1) and El Prieto.
(2) *canyon,* drained by a stream that flows less than 1 mile to Fish Canyon (2) 2.5 miles north-northwest of Azusa city hall (lat. 34° 10'10" N, long. 117°55'30" W; near E line sec. 16, T 1 N, R 10 W). Named on Azusa (1953) 7.5' quadrangle.
(3) *canyon,* drained by a stream that flows 3.5 miles to East Fork San Dimas Canyon nearly 10 miles north of Pomona city hall (lat. 34°11'45" N, long. 117°44'20" W; near S line sec. 5, T 1 N, R 8 W). Named on Mount Baldy (1954) 7.5' quadrangle.
(4) *canyon,* 0.5 mile long, nearly 4 miles south-southeast of Burbank city hall (lat. 34°07'45" N, long. 118°17'05" W). Named on Burbank (1953) 7.5' quadrangle.

Fern Creek [SAN DIEGO]: *stream,* flows 2 miles to Camps Creek 6 miles northwest of Fallbrook (lat. 33°26'15" N, long. 117°19'40" W; at E line sec. 31, T 8 S, R 4 W). Named on Fallbrook (1968) 7.5' quadrangle.

Fern Flat [SAN DIEGO]: *area,* 1 mile east-northeast of Cuyamaca Peak (lat. 32°57'10" N, long. 116°35'20" W). Named on Cuyamaca Peak (1960) 7.5' quadrangle.

Fern Lodge [LOS ANGELES]: *locality,* 2.5 miles east-southeast of Mount Wilson (1) in Santa Anita Canyon (lat. 34°12'30" N, long. 118°01' W; on N line sec. 3, T 1 N, R 11 W). Named on Mount Wilson (1953) 7.5' quadrangle. Earl Topping built Fern Lodge in 1916 (Robinson, J.W., 1977, p. 134).

Fern Springs [LOS ANGELES]: *spring,* 6.25 miles north of Glendora city hall (lat. 34°13'40" W, long. 117°52'10" W; sec. 30, T 2 N, R 9 W). Named on Glendora (1953) 7.5' quadrangle.

Fernwood [LOS ANGELES]: *settlement,* 8 miles northwest of Santa Monica city hall (lat. 34°04'45" N, long. 118°36' W; sec. 18, T 1 S, R 16 W). Named on Topanga (1952) 7.5' quadrangle. Called Wildwood on Topanga Canyon (1928) 6' quadrangle.

Fiesta Bay [SAN DIEGO]: *embayment,* 5 miles south-southeast of Point La Jolla off Mission Bay (lat. 32°47'20" N, long. 117°13'30" W). Named on La Jolla (1967) 7.5' quadrangle.

Fiesta Island [SAN DIEGO]: *island,* 1.5 miles long, 6 miles south-southeast of Point La Jolla (lat. 32°47'20" N, long. 117°13'20" W); the feature is southeast of Fiesta Bay. Named on La Jolla (1967) 7.5' quadrangle.

Filaree Flat [SAN DIEGO]: *area,* 3.25 miles west-northwest of Monument Peak (lat. 32°54'40" N, long. 116°28'15" W; sec. 33, T 14 S, R 5 E). Named on Monument Peak (1959) 7.5' quadrangle.

Fillmore [VENTURA]: *town,* 9 miles east-northeast of Santa Paula (lat. 34°24'05" N, long. 118°54'40" W; sec. 30, T 4 N, R 19 W). Named on Fillmore (1951) 7.5' quadrangle. Postal authorities established Fillmore post office in 1887 (Frickstad, p. 218), and the town incorporated in 1914. The name is for J.A. Fillmore of Southern Pacific Railroad (Hanna, p. 105). Postal authorities established Scenega post office 12 miles east of Santa Paula in 1875, discontinued it for a time in 1876, and discontinued it finally in 1888—the name was a corruption of the Spanish word *cienega* (Salley, p. 199).

Fillmore: see **North Fillmore** [VENTURA].

Fine Gold Canyon: see **Santa Felicia Canyon** [LOS ANGELES-VENTURA].

Finger Canyon [SAN DIEGO]: *canyon,* drained by a stream that flows less than 0.5 mile to Dillon Canyon 6.25 miles east-southeast of Imperial Beach (lat. 32°33'20" N, long. 117°00'35" W; near S line sec. 32, T 18 S, R 1 W). Named on Imperial Beach (1967) 7.5' quadrangle.

Fire Mountain [SAN DIEGO]: *peak,* 2.5 miles east of downtown Oceanside (lat. 33°11'40" N, long. 117°19'50" W; at E line sec. 30, T 11 S, R 4 W). Named on San Luis Rey (1968) 7.5' quadrangle.

Firestone Park [LOS ANGELES]: *locality,* 1.5 miles west-northwest of South Gate city hall along Southern Pacific Railroad (lat. 33°57'50" N, long. 118°13'55" W). Named on South Gate (1964) 7.5' quadrangle. Called Firestone Park Sta. on South Gate (1952) 7.5' quadrangle.

Firestone Park Station: see **Firestone Park** [LOS ANGELES].

Firmin: see **Point Fermin** [LOS ANGELES].

Firth: see **Paramount** [LOS ANGELES].

Fish Camp: see **East Fish Camp** [VENTURA].

Fish Canyon [LOS ANGELES].
(1) *canyon,* drained by a stream that flows 12 miles to Castaic Creek 4.5 miles east-northeast of Whitaker Peak (lat. 34°36'05" N, long. 118°39'50" W; near N line sec. 22, T 6 N, R 17 W). Named on Burnt Peak (1958), Liebre Mountain (1958), and Whitaker Peak (1958) 7.5' quadrangles. East Fork branches east 6.5 miles east-northeast of Whitaker Peak; it is 3.5 miles long and is named on Burnt Peak (1958), Warm Springs Mountain (1958), and Whitaker Peak (1958) 7.5' quadrangles. North Fork branches north 1 mile west-northwest of Burnt Peak; it is 1.5 miles long and is named on Burnt Peak (1958) 7.5' quadrangle.
(2) *canyon,* drained by a stream that flows 6.25 miles to lowlands 2 miles north-northwest of Azusa city hall (lat. 34°09'30" N, long. 117°55'25" W; at W line sec. 22, T 1 N, R 10 W). Named on Azusa (1953) 7.5' quadrangle.

Fish Creek [LOS ANGELES]: *stream,* flows 4 miles to Elizabeth Lake Canyon 4.25 miles southeast of Burnt Peak (lat. 34°38'30" N, long. 118°31'15" W). Named on Burnt Peak (1958) 7.5' quadrangle.

Fish Creek [VENTURA]: *stream,* flows 5 miles to Piru Creek 4 miles east of Cobblestone Mountain (lat. 34°36'30" N, long. 118°47'45" W). Named on Cobblestone Mountain (1958) 7.5' quadrangle. North Fork enters from the north 1.25 miles above the mouth of the main stream; it is 3 miles long and is named on Black Mountain (1958) and Cobblestone Mountain (1958) 7.5' quadrangles.

Fish Creek Wash [SAN DIEGO]: *stream* and *dry wash*, extends for 17 miles to Imperial County 7.5 miles south-southeast of Ocotillo Wells (lat. 33°02'15" N, long. 117°06'10" W; at E line sec. 13, T 13 S, R 8 E). Named on Arroyo Tapiado (1959), Borrego Mountain SE (1958), Carrizo Mountain NE (1957), and Harper Canyon (1959) 7.5' quadrangles. North Fork enters 11.5 miles north-northeast of Sweeney Pass; it is 5 miles long and is named on Arroyo Tapiado (1959) and Harper Canyon (1959) 7.5' quadrangles.

Fisher Canyon [LOS ANGELES]: *canyon*, 1 mile long, 3.25 miles north-west of Burbank city hall (lat. 34°12'50" N, long. 118°20'15" W; in and near sec. 34, T 2 N, R 14 W). Named on Burbank (1953) 7.5' quadrangle.

Fisherman Point [SAN DIEGO]: *promontory*, 4 miles west of downtown San Diego along San Diego Bay (lat. 32°43'05" N, long. 117° 13'45" W). Named on Point Loma (1967) 7.5' quadrangle.

Fishermans Cove [LOS ANGELES]: *embayment*, nearly 6 miles north-north-west of Mount Banning on the north side of Santa Catalina Island (lat. 33°26'40" N, long. 118°29'05" W). Named on Santa Catalina North (1950) 7.5' quadrangle. United States Coast and Geodetic Survey (p. 108) used the form "Fisherman Cove" for the name.

Fisher Spring [LOS ANGELES]: *spring*, 1.5 miles northeast of Whitaker Peak (lat. 34°35'25" N, long. 118°42'55" W; near SE cor. sec. 19, T 6 N, R 17 W). Named on Whitaker Peak (1958) 7.5' quadrangle.

Fish Fork [LOS ANGELES]: *stream*, flows 4 miles to San Gabriel River 5 miles west of Mount San Antonio (lat. 34°18'20" N, long. 117°43'55" W; sec. 32, T 3 N, R 8 W). Named on Mount San Antonio (1955) 7.5' quadrangle. Los Angeles County (1935) map shows a place called Cedar Camp located 2 miles northwest of San Antonio Peak (present Mount San Antonio) along a tributary to Fish Fork (sec. 36, T 3 N, R 8 W).

Fish Fork Camp [LOS ANGELES]: *locality*, 5 miles west of Mount San Antonio along San Gabriel River (lat. 34°18'20" N, long. 117° 43'55" W; sec. 32, T 3 N, R 8 W); the place is opposite the mouth of Fish Fork. Named on Mount San Antonio (1955) 7.5' quadrangle.

Fish Harbor [LOS ANGELES]: *water feature*, 2.5 miles northeast of Point Fermin at the southwest end of Terminal Island (lat. 33°44'10" N, long. 118°16' W). Named on San Pedro (1964) 7.5' quadrangle.

Five Palms Spring [SAN DIEGO]: *spring*, 7.5 miles north of Ocotillo Wells (lat. 33°14'55" N, long. 116°06'15" W). Named on Shell Reef (1959) 7.5' quadrangle.

Five Points [LOS ANGELES]: *locality*, less than 1 mile southeast of El Monte city hall (lat. 34°03'45" N, long. 118°01'05" W). Named on El Monte (1953) 7.5' quadrangle.

Five Points [SAN DIEGO]: *locality*, 2 miles north-northwest of downtown San Diego (lat. 32°44'30" N, long. 117°10'55" W). Named on Point Loma (1953) 7.5' quadrangle.

Flathead Flats [SAN DIEGO]: *area*, 1 mile west of Monument Peak (lat. 32°53'30" N, long. 116°26'10" W; sec. 2, T 15 S, R 5 E). Named on Monument Peak (1959) 7.5' quadrangle.

Flat Rock [LOS ANGELES]: *rock*, 3.25 miles south-southwest of Redondo Beach city hall, and 500 feet offshore (lat. 33°47'45" N, long. 118°24'35" W). Named on Redondo Beach (1963) 7.5' quadrangle.

Flat Rock Point [LOS ANGELES]: *promontory*, 3.25 miles south-south-west of Redondo Beach city hall along the coast (lat. 33°47'50" N, long. 118°24'30" W); Flat Rock is off the promontory. Named on Redondo Beach (1963) 7.5' quadrangle. Redondo Beach (1951) 7.5' quadrangle has the form "Flatrock Point" for the name.

Fleetridge [SAN DIEGO]: *district*, 4.5 miles west of downtown San Diego (lat. 32°43'45" N, long. 117°14'15" W). Named on Point Loma (1967) 7.5' quadrangle.

Fletcher Hills [SAN DIEGO]: *ridge*, north-northwest-trending, 2.5 miles long, nearly 2 miles north-northwest of El Cajon city hall (lat. 32°48'15" N, long. 116°59'15" W). Named on El Cajon (1967) 7.5' quadrangle.

Flint Peak [LOS ANGELES]: *peak*, 3.25 miles west-northwest of Pasadena city hall (lat. 34°09'50" N, long. 118°11'45" W). Altitude 1888 feet. Named on Pasadena (1953) 7.5' quadrangle.

Flintridge [LOS ANGELES]: *district*, 4 miles northwest of Pasadena city hall (lat. 34°11' N, long. 118°11'45" W). Named on Pasadena (1953) 7.5' quadrangle. The place was subdivided in 1920 and Frank P. Flint, senator from California from 1905 until 1911, named it (Gudde, 1949, p. 116). Flintridge and La Cañada (2) incorporated in 1976 with the name "La Cañada Flintridge."

Florence [LOS ANGELES]: *district*, 3 miles west-northwest of South Gate city hall (lat. 33°58'30" N, long. 118°14'55" W). Named on Inglewood (1964) and South Gate (1964) 7.5' quadrangles. Postal authorities established Florence post office in 1878, discontinued it in 1918, and reestablished it in 1926 (Salley, p. 76). Downey (1902) 15' quadrangle has the name "Florence" for a place located along Southern Pacific Railroad in present Florence (lat. 33°58'25" N, long. 118°14'05" W), and has the name "Florence Sta." for a place situated along the railroad less than 1 mile farther south (lat. 33°57'45" N, long. 118°14' W).

Florence Station: see **Florence** [LOS ANGELES].

Florentine: see **Oneonta** [SAN DIEGO].

Flume Canyon [LOS ANGELES]: *canyon*, drained by a stream that heads in Los Angeles County and flows 1.5 miles to Swarthout Valley 5.25 miles north of Mount San Antonio in San Bernardino County (lat. 34°21'50" N, long. 117°39'05" W; sec. 7, T 3 N, R 7 W). Named on Mount San Antonio (1955) 7.5' quadrangle. On Los Angeles County (1935) map, the stream in the canyon is called Flume Creek.

Flume Creek: see **Flume Canyon** [LOS ANGELES].

Flynn Springs [SAN DIEGO]: *locality*, 5.5 miles west of Alpine along Los Coches Creek (lat. 32°50'50" N, long. 116°51'45" W). Named on El Cajon (1939) 15' quadrangle. James E. Flinn and his family settled at the place in the 1870's (Stein, p. 49).

Foley Canyon [SAN DIEGO]: *canyon*, drained by a stream that flows 2 miles to the sea 2 miles southwest of San Onofre Mountain (lat. 33°20'50" N, long. 117°31'20" W; near E line sec. 32, T 9 S, R 6 W). Named on San Onofre Bluff (1968) 7.5' quadrangle.

Follows Camp [LOS ANGELES]: *locality*, 7.5 miles north-northeast of Glendora city hall along San Gabriel River (lat. 34°14' N, long. 117°48'10" W; near NE cor. sec. 27, T 2 N, R 9 W). Named on Glendora (1966) 7.5' quadrangle. Ralph Follows came to live along San Gabriel River to restore his health in 1891 and soon started the camp that bears his name (Robinson, J.W., 1983, p. 86-87). A place called Branscomb Camp started just east of Follows Camp in 1913 and washed away the next year (Robinson, J.W., 1983, p. 97).

Follows Camp West: see **Shady Oaks Camp** [LOS ANGELES].

Folsom Ridge [ORANGE]: *ridge*, generally west-trending, less than 1 mile long, 2.25 miles south-southeast of San Juan Capistrano (lat. 33°28'05" N, long. 117°39'15" W). Named on Dana Point (1968) 7.5' quadrangle.

Fonts Point [SAN DIEGO]: *peak*, 8.5 miles east of Borrego Springs (lat. 33°15'25" N, long. 116°13'55" W; near S line sec. 34, T 10 S, R 7 E). Altitude 1294 feet. Named on Fonts Point (1959) 7.5' quadrangle. Padre Font described the view of Borrego Badlands from the place in the diary that he kept during the Anza expedition of 1775 and 1776 (Stein, p. 49).

Fonts Point Wash [SAN DIEGO]: *stream* and *dry wash*, extends for 5 miles to end in Clark Valley 8 miles east-northeast of Borrego Springs (lat. 33°19'20" N, long. 116°15'10" W; sec. 9, T 10 S, R 7 E); the feature heads near Fonts Point. Named on Clark Lake (1959) and Fonts Point (1959) 7.5' quadrangles.

Foot and Walker Pass [SAN DIEGO]: *pass*, 11.5 miles east of Julian (lat. 33°02'15" N, long. 116°24'05" W; near SE cor. sec. 18, T 13 S, R 6 E). Named on Earthquake Valley (1959) 7.5' quadrangle.

Foothill Station: see **Sulphur Springs** [LOS ANGELES].

Forbes Siding [LOS ANGELES]: *locality*, 5.5 miles northwest of present Pomona city hall along Atchison, Topeka and Santa Fe Railroad (lat. 34°07'05" N, long. 117°49'45" W). Named on Glendora (1927) 6' quadrangle.

Forester Creek [SAN DIEGO]: *stream*, flows 9 miles to the valley of San Diego River 3.5 miles north-northwest of El Cajon city hall (lat. 32°50'20" N, long. 116°59'45" W). Named on Alpine (1955) and El Cajon (1967) 7.5' quadrangles.

Forest Park [LOS ANGELES]: *settlement*, 2.5 miles north-northeast of Solemint (lat. 34°26'45" N, long. 118°25'40" W; sec. 11, T 4 N, R 15 W). Named on Mint Canyon (1960) 7.5' quadrangle.

Forster: see **San Onofre Creek** [SAN DIEGO].

Forster Lake [ORANGE]: *lake*, behind a dam 3.5 miles south-southeast of San Juan Capistrano in Prima Deshecha Canyon (lat. 33°26'55" N, long. 117°38'45" W). Named on Dana Point (1949) 7.5' quadrangle.

Forsythe Canyon [LOS ANGELES]: *canyon*, drained by a stream that flows 1 mile to Pine Canyon (3) 2 miles west-northwest of the village of Lake Hughes (lat. 34°41'20" N, long. 118°28'45" W; sec. 21, T 7 N, R 15 W). Named on Lake Hughes (1957) 7.5' quadrangle.

Fort DuPont: see **Old Town** [SAN DIEGO].

Fort Emory: see **Silver Strand** [SAN DIEGO].

Fort Hill: see **Los Angeles** [LOS ANGELES].

Fort Latham: see **Playa del Rey** [LOS ANGELES].

Fort MacArthur [LOS ANGELES]: *military installation*, near Point Fermin. Fort MacArthur Upper Reservation is 0.5 mile north of Point Fermin (lat. 33°42'45" N, long. 118°17'40" W), and Fort MacArthur Lower Reservation is 1 mile north-northeast of Point Fermin (lat. 33°43' N, long. 118°17'10" W). Named on San Pedro (1964) 7.5' quadrangle, which also shows Fort MacArthur Military Reservation situated 1.5 miles northwest of Point Fermin (lat. 33° 43'05" N, long. 118°18'50" W). Land for the lower reservation was reserved in 1888, and land for the upper reservation was purchased in 1910; when construction of the facility began in 1914, the army named the installation to honor Lieutenant General Arthur MacArthur (Gudde, 1949, p. 198; Whiting and Whiting, p. 43).

Fort Moore: see **Los Angeles** [LOS ANGELES].

Fort Pio Pico: see **Zuñiga Point** [SAN DIEGO].

Fort Rosecrans [SAN DIEGO]: *military installation*, 5 miles west-south-west of downtown San Diego on Point Loma (1) at the entrance to San

Diego Bay (lat. 32°41' N, long. 117°14'15" W). Named on Point Loma (1967) 7.5' quadrangle, which shows the place on a naval reservation—the reservation is called Fort Rosecrans Military Reservation on Point Loma (1953) 7.5' quadrangle. Postal authorities established Fort Rosecrans post office in 1906, discontinued it in 1922, reestablished it in 1941, and discontinued it in 1946 (Salley, p. 78). A military reservation was established at the place in 1852, and the first fortifications were at Ballast Point, about at the site of the Spanish fortification called Castillo Guijarros; the army began an earthwork to protect the entrance to San Diego Bay in 1873, and the name "Fort Rosecrans" was given to the place in 1899 to honor General William S. Rosecrans—the facility was transferred to the navy in 1959 (Frazer, p. 29-30).

Fort San Diego: see **Old Town** [SAN DIEGO].

Fort Stockton: see **Old Town** [SAN DIEGO].

Fort Tejon Pass: see **Tejon Pass** [LOS ANGELES].

Fortuna Mountain [SAN DIEGO]: *peak*, 6 miles north-northwest of La Mesa (lat. 32°50'55" N, long. 117°03'40" W). Named on La Mesa (1967) 7.5' quadrangle.

Fossil Canyon [LOS ANGELES]: *canyon*, drained by a stream that flows 1 mile to Coldwater Canyon (2) 4.5 miles southwest of Mount San Antonio (lat. 34°15'20" N, long. 117°42'40" W). Named on Mount San Antonio (1955) 7.5' quadrangle.

Foss Lake [SAN DIEGO]: *lake*, 6300 feet long, 9.5 miles south-southwest of Fallbrook (lat. 33°15'30" N, long. 117°19' W). Named on Margarita Peak (1944) 15' quadrangle. The name commemorates David Foss, a merchant, farmer, and justice of the peace, who came to the neighborhood in 1872 (Stein, p. 50).

Foster [SAN DIEGO]: *locality*, 3.25 miles north of Lakeside along San Vicente Creek (lat. 32°54'30" N, long. 116°55'30" W; near SW cor. sec. 31, T 14 S, R 1 E). Named on San Vicente Reservoir (1955) 7.5' quadrangle. Postal authorities established Foster post office in 1893 and discontinued it in 1916; the name was for Joseph Foster, rancher, stagecoach operator, and county supervisor (Salley, p. 79). Waring (p. 350-351) listed Bradley Spring, located 6 miles by road north from Foster; the water was taken to San Diego and bottled for table use.

Foster Canyon [SAN DIEGO]: *canyon*, drained by a stream that flows nearly 2 miles to San Vicente Reservoir 5 miles north of Lakeside (lat. 32°55'55" N, long. 116°56'10" W). Named on San Vicente Reservoir (1955) 7.5' quadrangle.

Foster Park [VENTURA]: *town*, 5 miles north of Ventura along Ventura River (lat. 34°21'10" N, long. 119°18'15" W). Named on Los Angeles (1975) 1°x 2° quadrangle. Postal authorities established Foster Park post office in 1952 and discontinued it in 1966 (Salley, p. 79). The name is from Foster Memorial Park, located nearby and given to the county by Mr. and Mrs. Eugene P. Foster in memory of their son; freeway construction destroyed the community in 1969 (Ricard).

Fountainhead Spring [LOS ANGELES]: *spring*, 0.5 mile east-southeast of Pacifico Mountain (lat. 34°22'45" N, long. 118°01'40" W; near NW cor. sec. 3, T 3 N, R 11 W). Named on Pacifico Mountain (1959) 7.5' quadrangle.

Fountain Valley [ORANGE]: *city*, 4.25 miles northeast of Huntington Beach civic center (lat. 33°42'30" N, long. 117°57' W). Named on Newport Beach (1965) 7.5' quadrangle. Postal authorities established Fountain Valley post office in 1958 (Salley, p. 79); the city had incorporated in 1957. Santa Ana River changed its course in 1828 and left about 30,000 acres of marsh land between the old and new courses; this area was called Squatters Country because of illegal residents there, it was called Fountain Valley for the abundance of artesian water in the neighborhood, and it was called Gospel Swamp for the devout residents who held camp meetings there; the city of Fountain Valley now covers most of the area (Meadows, p. 63, 67).

Four Corners [SAN DIEGO]:

(1) *locality*, 5 miles north-northeast of El Cajon Mountain (lat. 32° 58'40" N, long. 116°46'35' W; at N line sec. 9, T 14 S, R 2 E). Named on El Cajon Mountain (1955) 7.5' quadrangle.

(2) *locality*, 4.5 miles northwest of Morena Village (lat. 32°43'30" N, long. 116°33'30" W; near E line sec. 3, T 17 S, R 4 E). Named on Morena Reservoir (1960) 7.5' quadrangle.

Four Corners: see **El Monte** [LOS ANGELES].

Fourfork Creek [VENTURA]: *stream*, flows 1.5 miles to Little Sespe Creek 4 miles north of Fillmore (lat. 34°27'40" N, long. 118°54'35" W; sec. 6, T 4 N, R 19 W); Fourfork Creek and Centennial Creek join Little Sespe Creek at the same point, so that stream courses radiate in four directions from the place. Named on Fillmore (1951) 7.5' quadrangle.

Four Points [LOS ANGELES]: *locality*, 5.5 miles east-southeast of Palmdale (lat. 34°32'35" N, long. 118°01'45" W; near NE cor. sec. 9, T 5 N, R 11 W). Named on Palmdale (1958) 7.5' quadrangle.

Fourth of July Cove [LOS ANGELES]: *embayment*, 4 miles east-southeast of Silver Peak on the north side of Santa Catalina Island (lat. 33°26'50" N, long. 118°30' W). Named on Santa Catalina North (1950) and Santa Catalina West (1943) 7.5' quadrangles. Preston (1890b, p. 280) referred to July Harbor.

Fox Barranca [VENTURA]: *gully*, extends for 3.25 miles from the mouth of Fox Canyon to Arroyo Las Posas 6.5 miles west-southwest of Moorpark (lat. 34°15'30" N, long. 118°59'15" W). Named on Santa Paula (1951) 7.5' quadrangle.

Fox Canyon [ORANGE]: *canyon*, drained by a stream that flows 1.25 miles to Bell Canyon 10.5 miles northeast of San Juan Capistrano (lat. 33°37'25" N, long. 117°33'25" W). Named on Cañada Gobernadora (1968) 7.5' quadrangle. The name commemorates Samuel Fox, who homesteaded on the ridge between Fox Canyon and Crow Canyon in 1879 (Meadows, p. 64).

Fox Canyon [VENTURA]: *canyon*, drained by a stream that flows 3.25 miles to lowlands 5 miles south-southeast of Santa Paula (lat. 34°17'10" N, long. 119°01'25" W). Named on Santa Paula (1951) 7.5' quadrangle.

Fox Creek [LOS ANGELES]: *stream*, flows 7 miles to Big Tujunga Canyon 3 miles east-southeast of Condor Peak (lat. 34°18'10" N, long. 118°10'35" W). Named on Condor Peak (1959) 7.5' quadrangle. West Fork enters from the northwest 2.5 miles upstream from the mouth of the main creek; it is 3 miles long and is named on Condor Peak (1959) 7.5' quadrangle. A place called Wagon Wheels Camp was situated near the mouth of Fox Creek; the name was from a pair of wagon wheels abandoned at the site (Robinson, J.W., 1977, p. 145).

Frances [ORANGE]: *locality*, 6.25 miles east-southeast of Santa Ana city hall along Atchison, Topeka and Santa Fe Railroad (lat. 33°42'40" N, long. 117°45'45" W). Named on Tustin (1965) 7.5' quadrangle. The name commemorates Frances Anita Plum, first wife of James Irvine, Jr. (Meadows, p. 64).

Franklin Canyon [LOS ANGELES]: *canyon*, 2.5 miles long, 2.5 miles north-northwest of Beverly Hills city hall (lat. 34°06'30" N, long. 118°24'50" W). Named on Beverly Hills (1950) 7.5' quadrangle.

Franklin Canyon Reservoir [LOS ANGELES]: *lake*, 3300 feet long, behind a dam 1.5 miles north-northwest of Beverly Hills city hall (lat. 34°05'40" N, long. 118°24'35" W); the lake is in Franklin Canyon. Named on Beverly Hills (1950) 7.5' quadrangle.

Franklin Canyon Reservoir: see **Upper Franklin Canyon Reservoir** [LOS ANGELES].

Franks Peak [SAN DIEGO]: *peak*, 6.5 miles north-northeast of Rancho Santa Fe (lat. 33°06'20" N, long. 117°09'25" W; at E line sec. 26, T 12 S, R 3 W). Altitude 1688 feet. Named on Rancho Santa Fe (1968) 7.5' quadrangle.

Frazier Creek [VENTURA]: *stream*, flows 3.5 miles to Piru Creek 4 miles north-northeast of McDonald Peak (lat. 34°41'20" N, long. 118°54'40" W; sec. 20, T 7 N, R 19 W). Named on McDonald Peak (1958) 7.5' quadrangle.

Frazier Mountain [VENTURA]: *peak*, 26 miles north of Fillmore (lat. 34°46'30" N, long. 118°58'05" W; at S line sec. 14, T 8 N, R 20 W). Named on Frazier Mountain (1958) 7.5' quadrangle. United States Board on Geographic Names (1933, p. 311) rejected the name "Cuddy Peak" for the feature. The name "Frazier" is for a pioneer family of the neighborhood (Ricard).

Frazier Point [SAN DIEGO]: *relief feature*, 3.25 miles east-southeast of Boucher Hill (lat. 33°18'30" N, long. 116°52'15" W; sec. 15, T 10 S, R 1 E). Named on Palomar Observatory (1949) 7.5' quadrangle.

Frazier's Station: see **Carlsbad**.

Fred Canyon [SAN DIEGO]: *canyon*, drained by a stream that flows 3.25 miles to Kitchen Creek 2.5 miles east-southeast of Buckman Springs (lat. 32°45'35" N, long. 116°27' W; near N line sec. 5, T 16 S, R 5 E). Named on Mount Laguna (1960) 7.5' quadrangle.

Freeman Canyon [LOS ANGELES]: *canyon*, drained by a stream that flows 6 miles to Cañada de Los Alamos 6.5 miles south-southeast of Gorman (lat. 34°42'30" N, long. 118°49' W; near SW cor. sec. 8, T 7 N, R 18 W). Named on Black Mountain (1958) and Lebec (1958) 7.5' quadrangles.

Freeman Island: see **Island Freeman** [LOS ANGELES].

Freeman River: see **Bolsa Bay** [ORANGE].

Freeway Park [ORANGE]: *locality*, 2.25 miles southeast of present Buena Park civic center (lat. 33°50'40" N, long. 117°57'45" W; near NE cor. sec. 7, T 4 S, R 10 W). Named on Anaheim (1950) 7.5' quadrangle.

Fremont Canyon [ORANGE]: *canyon*, drained by a stream that flows nearly 7 miles to Santiago Creek 7 miles southwest of Sierra Peak (lat. 33°47'30" N, long. 117°43'35" W). Named on Black Star Canyon (1967) 7.5' quadrangle. Called Sierra Canyon on Corona (1902) 30' quadrangle. In the early days the feature was called Cañon de la Horca because it narrows down to a gorge—*Cañon de la Horca* means "Canyon that was Choked" in Spanish, later it was called Sierra Canyon because it heads at Sierra Peak, and finally it took the nickname of a shepherd called "Fremont" Smith because he had campaigned with John C. Fremont (Meadows, p. 64-65). A large depression in the cliff on the east side of Fremont Canyon 1.4 miles above its mouth is called Robbers Cave (Meadows, p. 120).

Fremont Creek: see **Blind Canyon** [ORANGE] (1).

Fremont Pass: see **San Fernando Pass** [LOS ANGELES].

Fremontville [VENTURA]: *locality*, 2 miles west of Moorpark (lat. 34°16'40" N, long. 118°54'30" W). Named on Camulos (1903) 30' quadrangle. Postal authorities established Fremontville post office in 1894 and discontinued it in 1905 (Frickstad, p. 218).

French Canyon [SAN DIEGO]: *canyon,* drained by a stream that flows nearly 4 miles to the sea 7.5 miles south-southeast of San Onofre Mountain (lat. 33°15'40" N, long. 117°26'25" W). Named on Las Pulgas Canyon (1968) 7.5' quadrangle.

French Creek [SAN DIEGO]: *stream,* flows nearly 3 miles to join Doane Creek and form Pauma Creek 1 mile north-northeast of Boucher Hill (lat. 33°20'55" N, long. 116°54'45" W; near E line sec. 31, T 9 S, R 1 E). Named on Boucher Hill (1948) 7.5' quadrangle.

French Flat: see **Frenchmans Flat** [LOS ANGELES].

French Hill [ORANGE]: *peak,* 7.5 miles south-southeast of Santa Ana city hall (lat. 33°39' N, long. 117°48'30" W). Altitude 426 feet. Named on Tustin (1965) 7.5' quadrangle. The name commemorates C.E. French, first superintendent of Irvine ranch (Meadows, p. 65).

Frenchmans Flat [LOS ANGELES]: *area,* 3 miles north-northwest of Whitaker Peak along Piru Creek (lat. 34°36'55" N, long. 118°44'45" W; near NW cor. sec. 13, T 6 N, R 18 W). Named on Whitaker Peak (1958) 7.5' quadrangle. Called French Flat on Beartrap Canyon (1938) 6' quadrangle, but United States Board on Geographic Names (1960b, p. 8) rejected this name for the place. The name "Frenchmans Flat" recalls Harry Latour and Pete Augustura, who had a cabin at the site (Suter, p. 20).

Frenchmans Flat Campground [LOS ANGELES]: *locality,* 3 miles north of Whitaker Peak (lat. 34°37' N, long. 118°44'35" W; near NW cor. sec. 13, T 6 N, R 18 W); the place is at Frenchman Flat. Named on Whitaker Peak (1958) 7.5' quadrangle.

French Mountain [SAN DIEGO]: *peak,* 6 miles southwest of Rodriguez Mountain (lat. 33°10'05" N, long. 116°58'20" W; at S line sec. 34, T 11 S, R 1 W). Altitude 2008 feet. Named on Rodruguez Mountain (1948) 7.5' quadrangle.

French Point: see **Burges Canyon** [VENTURA].

French Valley: see **Lower French Valley** [SAN DIEGO]; **Upper French Valley** [SAN DIEGO].

Frenchys Cove [VENTURA]: *embayment,* on the north side of the gap between middle Anacapa Island and western Anacapa Island (lat. 34°00'25" N, long. 119°24'25" W). Named on Anacapa Island (1973) quadrangle.

Fresno Canyon [VENTURA]: *canyon,* drained by a stream that flows 2.5 miles to Ventura River 6 miles north of Ventura (lat. 34°21'50" N, long. 119°18'30" W). Named on Matilija (1952) and Ventura (1951) 7.5' quadrangles.

Frey Canyon [VENTURA]: *canyon,* drained by a stream that flows 2 miles to the valley of Santa Clara River 4.25 miles southwest of Piru (lat. 34°22'50" N, long. 118°51'20" W; sec. 34, T 4 N, R 19 W). Named on Piru (1952) and Simi (1951) 7.5' quadrangles. Called Guiberson Canyon on Piru (1921) 15' quadrangle, and called Garberson Canyon on Eldridge and Arnold's (1907) map.

Frey Creek [SAN DIEGO]: *stream,* flows 5 miles to San Luis Rey River 3.5 miles east-southeast of Pala (lat. 33°20'35" N, long. 117° 01'15" W; at S line sec. 31, T 9 S, R 1 W). Named on Boucher Hill (1948) and Pala (1968) 7.5' quadrangles. Stein (p. 50) associated the name with George Frey and John Frey, homesteaders in the neighborhood before 1900.

Friendly Hills [LOS ANGELES]: *district,* 2.25 miles east-southeast of Whittier city hall (lat. 33°59' N, long. 118°00' W). Named on La Habra (1964) and Whittier (1965) 7.5' quadrangles.

Frog Rock [LOS ANGELES]: *rock,* 1.25 miles north-northwest of Avalon, and 75 feet offshore on the northeast side of Santa Catalina Island (lat. 33°21'40" N, long. 118°20'05" W). Named on Santa Catalina East (1950) 7.5' quadrangle.

Fruitdale [SAN DIEGO]: *locality,* 2.25 miles north-northeast of present Imperial Beach civic center (lat. 32°36' N, long. 117°05'30" W; near S line sec. 16, T 18 S, R 2 W). Named on San Diego (1904) 15' quadrangle.

Fruitland [LOS ANGELES]: *locality,* 10 miles west of Whittier along Los Angeles Terminal Railroad (lat. 33°59'50" N, long. 118°12'25" W). Named on Downey (1902) 15' quadrangle.

Fry Creek [SAN DIEGO]: *stream,* flows nearly 2 miles to join Iron Springs Creek and form West Fork San Luis Rey River 3.25 miles east of Boucher Hill (lat. 33°20'10" N, long. 116°51'45" W; sec. 3, T 10 S, R 1 E). Named on Boucher Hill (1948) and Palomar Observatory (1949) 7.5' quadrangles.

Fryer Canyon [LOS ANGELES]: *canyon,* drained by a stream that flows 1 mile to Soledad Canyon (lat. 34°26'15" N, long. 118° 16' W; at N line sec. 17, T 4 N, R 13 W). Named on Agua Dulce (1960) 7.5' quadrangle.

Fryingpan Springs [LOS ANGELES]: *springs,* 4 miles south of the village of Leona Valley (lat. 34°33'35" N, long. 118°17'25" W; near SE cor. sec. 31, T 6 N, R 13 W). Named on Sleepy Valley (1958) 7.5' quadrangle.

Fryman Canyon [LOS ANGELES]: *canyon,* drained by a stream that flows 1 mile to Berry Canyon 5 miles southeast of Van Nuys (lat. 34°08' N, long. 118°23'25" W). Named on Beverly Hills (1950) and Van Nuys (1953) 7.5' quadrangles.

Fuller Park [ORANGE]: *locality,* 1 mile east-northeast of present Buena Park civic center (lat. 33°52'05" N, long. 117°58'35" W; near E line sec. 36, T 3 S, R 11 W). Named on Anaheim (1950) 7.5' quadrangle.

Fullerton [ORANGE]: *city,* 4 miles east of Buena Park civic center (lat. 33°52'15" N, long. 117°55'45" W). Named on Anaheim (1965), La Habra (1964), and Yorba Linda (1964) 7.5' quadrangles. Postal authorities established Fullerton post office in 1888 (Frickstad, p. 116), and the city incorporated in 1904. George H. Amerige and Edward R. Amerige purchased land at the place and laid out a townsite; Fullerton Land and Trust Company, a subsidiary of Atchison, Topeka and Santa Fe Railroad, acquired an interest in the project and the community was named to honor George H. Fullerton, president of the company; after Fullerton lost his position with the company, officials of the railroad called their station at the site La Habra, but the residents of the community insisted on retaining the old name (Meadows, p. 65).

Fullerton Creek [ORANGE]: *stream,* flows 12.5 miles to Coyote Creek 2.25 miles west of Buena Park civic center (lat. 33°51'50" N, long. 118°02'05" W; sec. 33, T 3 S, R 11 W). Named on Anaheim (1965), La Habra (1964), and Los Alamitos (1964) 7.5' quadrangles.

Fulton Wells: see **Santa Fe Springs** [LOS ANGELES].

Funks Canyon: see **Elderberry Canyon** [LOS ANGELES].

Fusier Canyon [LOS ANGELES]: *canyon,* drained by a stream that flows 2.5 miles to Big Tujunga Canyon 3.25 miles south of Condor Peak (lat. 34°16'45" N, long. 118°12'30" W). Named on Condor Peak (1959) 7.5' quadrangle.

Fustero Point [VENTURA]: *promontory,* 9 miles southeast of Cobblestone Mountain on the east side of Lake Piru (lat. 34°30'40" N, long. 118°45'10" W; near N line sec. 22, T 5 N, R 18 W). Named on Cobblestone Mountain (1958) 7.5' quadrangle. The name commemorates Juan Fustero, an Indian who lived at the place (Ricard).

- G -

Gabino Canyon [ORANGE]: *canyon,* drained by a stream that flows nearly 7 miles to Christianitos Canyon about 4 miles northeast of San Clemente civic center (lat. 33°28' N, long. 117°33'45" W; near N line sec. 24, T 8 S, R 7 W). Named on Cañada Gobernadora (1968) and San Clemente (1968) 7.5' quadrangles.

Gable Promontory: see **South Gable Promontory**, under **Mount Harvard** [LOS ANGELES].

Gage [LOS ANGELES]: *locality,* 4.5 miles east-northeast of present South Gate city hall along Pacific Electric Railroad (lat. 33°58'30" N, long. 118°07'30" W). Named on Bell (1936) 6' quadrangle.

Gail Canyon [LOS ANGELES]: *canyon,* 0.5 mile long, 6 miles north-northeast of Pomona city hall (lat. 34°08'20" N, long. 117°43'15" W; sec. 28, T 1 N, R 8 W). Named on Mount Baldy (1954) 7.5' quadrangle.

Gallagher Beach [LOS ANGELES]: *beach,* 2.25 miles north-northwest of Avalon on the northeast side of Santa Catalina Island (lat. 33°22'15" N, long. 118°20'55" W); the beach is at the mouth of Gallagher Canyon. Named on Santa Catalina East (1950) 7.5' quadrangle. The name commemorates Tom Gallagher, who lived at the place as a squatter for many years (Gudde, 1949, p. 123-124).

Gallagher Canyon [LOS ANGELES]: *canyon,* drained by a stream that flows 1.25 miles to the sea 2.25 miles north-northwest of Avalon on the northeast side of Santa Catalina Island (lat. 33°22'10" N, long. 118°20"50" W). Named on Santa Catalina East (1950) 7.5' quadrangle.

Gallatin: see **Downey** [LOS ANGELES].

Galleta Meadows [SAN DIEGO]: *area,* nearly 4 miles north-northwest of Borrego Springs (lat. 33°18'20" N, long. 116°24'20" W). Named on Borrego Palm Canyon (1959) 7.5' quadrangle. Called Gueyetta Meadows on Clark Lake (1944) 15' quadrangle, but United States Board on Geographic Names (1962a, p. 11) rejected the names "Gueyetta Meadows" and "Galletta Meadows" for the place.

Galloway Valley [SAN DIEGO]: *valley,* 2.5 miles west of Alpine (lat. 32°50'15" N, long. 116°48'40" W; mainly in sec. 30, T 15 S, R 2 E). Named on Alpine (1955) 7.5' quadrangle.

Gamewell: see **Huntington Beach** [ORANGE].

Ganesha Junction [LOS ANGELES]: *locality,* nearly 2 miles north-northwest of present Pomona city hall (lat. 34°04'50" N, long. 117° 45'35" W). Named on Claremont (1928) 6' quadrangle.

Ganesha Park [LOS ANGELES]: *district,* 1.5 miles north-northwest of present Pomona city hall (lat. 34°04'30" N, long. 117°45'40" W). Named on Claremont (1928) 6' quadrangle.

Garapito Creek [LOS ANGELES]: *stream,* flows 2.5 miles to Topanga Canyon 9 miles northwest of Santa Monica city hall (lat. 34°06'45" N, long. 118°35'25" W; sec. 6, T 1 S, R 16 W). Named on Topanga (1952) 7.5' quadrangle. Calabasas (1903) 15' quadrangle shows Garapito Creek in present Topanga Canyon above the mouth of present Old Topanga Canyon.

Garberson Canyon: see **Frey Canyon** [VENTURA].

Garcia Canyon [LOS ANGELES]: *canyon,* drained by a stream that flows 1 mile to Morris Reservoir nearly 4 miles north of San Dimas city hall (lat. 34°11'25" N, long. 117°51'30" W; near NE cor. sec. 7, T 1 N, R 9 W). Named on Glendora (1953) 7.5' quadrangle.

Gardena [LOS ANGELES]: *city,* 6 miles south-southeast of Inglewood city hall (lat. 33°52'55" N, long. 118°18'20" W). Named on Inglewood (1964) and Torrance (1964) 7.5' quadrangles. Postal authorities established Gardena post office in 1890 and moved it 1.5 miles southeast in 1892; the name recalls truck gardens at the site (Salley, p. 82). The city incorporated in 1930.

Garden Acres [ORANGE]: *locality,* 6 miles south of present Buena Park civic center (lat. 33°46'35" N, long. 117°58'25" W; near SW cor. sec. 31, T 4 S, R 10 W). Named on Anaheim (1950) 7.5' quadrangle.

Garden Grove [ORANGE]: *city,* 7 miles south-southeast of Buena Park civic center (lat. 33°46'35" N, long. 117°56' W). Named on Anaheim (1965) and Los Alamitos (1964, photorevised 1981) 7.5' quadrangles. California Mining Bureau's (1909b) map has the form "Gardengrove" for the name. Postal authorities established Garden Grove post office in 1877 (Frickstad, p. 117), and the city incorporated in 1956. Dr. A.G. Cook and Converse Howe founded the community in 1877 (Guinn, p. 195). A loading platform situated along Pacific Electric Railroad about 2 miles west-northwest of present Garden Grove city hall was called Berryfield, and later it was known as Harperville (Meadows, p. 26-27). A flag stop located along Pacific Electric Railroad 2.5 miles northwest of present Garden Grove city hall was called Cordorniz, and a flag stop located along the same railroad 1.25 miles northwest of present Garden Grove city hall was called Mesto (Meadows, p. 54, 99).

Garden Gulch [LOS ANGELES]: *canyon,* drained by a stream that flows 1.25 miles to an unnamed canyon 4 miles north-northwest of Burnt Peak (lat. 34°43'40" N, long. 118°36'50" W; sec. 6, T 7 N, R 16 W). Named on Burnt Peak (1958) 7.5' quadrangle.

Garden of the Gods [LOS ANGELES]: *area,* 1 mile north-northwest of Chatsworth (lat. 34°16'25" N, long. 118°36'35" W; sec. 12, T 2 N, R 17 W). Named on Oat Mountain (1952) 7.5' quadrangle.

Gardens: see **Bell Gardens** [LOS ANGELES].

Garlic Flats [SAN DIEGO]: *area,* nearly 3 miles south-southeast of Rodriguez Mountain (lat. 33°11'50" N, long. 116°53'05" W). Named on Rodriguez Mountain (1948) 7.5' quadrangle.

Garnet Mountain [SAN DIEGO]: *ridge,* north-northwest-trending, 1 mile long, 5 miles northwest of Monument Peak (lat. 32°56'30" N, long. 116°29'10" W; sec. 20, T 14 S, R 5 E). Named on Monument Peak (1959) 7.5' quadrangle.

Garnet Peak [SAN DIEGO]: *peak,* 3.25 miles northwest of Monument Peak (lat. 32°55'30" N, long. 116°27'30" W; near W line sec. 27, T 14 S, R 5 E). Named on Monument Peak (1959) 7.5' quadrangle.

Garnsey [LOS ANGELES]: *locality,* 3 miles east-southeast of Van Nuys along Southern Pacific Railroad (lat. 34°10'10" N, long. 118° 24'15" W). Named on Van Nuys (1926) 6' quadrangle.

Garvalia: see **San Gabriel** [LOS ANGELES].

Garvanza [LOS ANGELES]: *district,* 3.5 miles northeast of Los Angeles city hall in Los Angeles (lat. 34°07' N, long. 118°10'30" W). Named on Los Angeles (1953) 7.5' quadrangle. Postal authorities established Garvanza post office in 1887 and discontinued it in 1921; the name is from chickpeas planted at the place—*garbanzo* means "chickpeas" in Spanish (Salley, p. 83). United States Board on Geographic Names (1933, p. 319) rejected the form "Garvanzo" for the name.

Garvanza Station [LOS ANGELES]: *locality,* nearly 5 miles northeast of present Los Angeles city hall along Atchison, Topeka and Santa Fe Railroad (lat. 34°06'35" N, long. 118°11'35" W); the place is 0.5 mile west-southwest of Garvanza. Named on Pasadena (1900) 15' quadrangle.

Garvey: see **South San Gabriel** [LOS ANGELES].

Garvey Avenue: see **South San Gabriel** [LOS ANGELES].

Garvey Reservoir [LOS ANGELES]: *lake,* 5 miles west-southwest of El Monte city hall (lat. 34°03' N, long. 118°07' W); the feature is southwest of South San Gabriel, which also was called Garvey. Named on El Monte (1966) 7.5' quadrangle.

Gaskill Peak [SAN DIEGO]: *peak,* 8.5 miles north of Barrett Junction (lat. 32°44'20" N, long. 116°42'55" W). Altitude 3836 feet. Named on Barrett Lake (1960) 7.5' quadrangle.

Gaspur [LOS ANGELES]: *locality,* 1.5 miles west-northwest of Long Beach city hall along Pacific Electric Railroad (lat. 33°46'55" N, long. 118°13'05" W). Named on Long Beach (1949) 7.5' quadrangle.

Gaston [LOS ANGELES]: *locality,* 4 miles north of present Los Angeles city hall along Los Angeles Terminal Railroad (lat. 34°06'30" N, long. 118°14'40" W). Named on Pasadena (1900) 15' quadrangle.

Gates Canyon [LOS ANGELES-VENTURA]: *canyon,* drained by a stream that heads just inside Ventura County and flows 1.5 miles to Las Virgenes Creek 2.5 miles east-northeast of Agoura (lat. 34°09'10" N, long. 118°41'45" W; sec. 19, T 1 N, R 17 W). Named on Calabasas (1952) 7.5' quadrangle.

Gavilan [ORANGE]: *locality,* 4.5 miles north of San Juan Capistrano along Atchison, Topeka and Santa Fe Railroad (lat. 33°34'10" N, long. 117°40'25" W). Named on San Juan Capistrano (1968) 7.5' quadrangle. Construction of the railroad in 1887 destroyed springs called Aguaje del Cuate that were situated 0.6 mile north of Gavilan; travelers had always found fresh water at the springs (Meadows, p. 18).

Gavin Canyon [LOS ANGELES]: *canyon,* drained by a stream that flows 3 miles to lowlands nearly 2 miles west-southwest of downtown Newhall (lat. 34°22'30" N, long. 118°33' W). Named on Oat Mountain (1952) 7.5' quadrangle.

Gemco [LOS ANGELES]: *locality,* 2 miles north-northeast of Van Nuys along Southern Pacific Railroad (lat. 34°12'35" N, long. 118° 26'05" W). Named on Van Nuys (1966) 7.5' quadrangle.

Gem Hill [SAN DIEGO]: *peak,* 2.5 miles northwest of Mesa Grande (lat. 33°12'35" N, long. 116°48' W; near N line sec. 20, T 11 S, R 2 E). Altitude 4058 feet. Named on Mesa Grande (1948) 7.5' quadrangle.

George Canyon [LOS ANGELES]: *canyon,* 2 miles long, 5 miles south of Torrance city hall (lat. 33°45'45" N, long. 118°20'10" W). Named on Torrance (1964) 7.5' quadrangle.

George Mountain: see **Old George Mountain** [SAN DIEGO].

Georges Gap [LOS ANGELES]: *pass,* 5 miles southeast of Condor Peak (lat. 34°16'10" N, long. 118°10' W). Named on Condor Peak (1959) 7.5' quadrangle.

German [LOS ANGELES]: *locality,* 2.25 miles east-southeast of Gorman (lat. 34°47' N, long. 118°49' W; near NW cor. sec. 17, T 8 N, R 18 W). Named on Tejon (1903) 30' quadrangle.

German Canyon: see **Gorman Canyon** [LOS ANGELES].

Gert Wash [SAN DIEGO]: *stream,* flows 4 miles to Imperial County 6.5 miles northeast of Sweeney Pass (lat. 32°53'50" N, long. 116° 06'10" W; at E line sec. 1, T 15 S, R 8 E). Named on Arroyo Tapiado (1959) and Carrizo Mountain NE (1957) 7.5' quadrangles.

Ghost Mountain [SAN DIEGO]: *ridge,* west-southwest-trending, less than 1 mile long, 14 miles east-southeast of Julian (lat. 33°00'15" N, long. 116°22'45" W; at NE cor. sec. 32, T 13 S, R 6 E). Named on Earthquake Valley (1959) 7.5' quadrangle.

Gibraltar: see **Little Gibraltar** [LOS ANGELES].

Gibson: see **Point Fermin** [LOS ANGELES].

Gillibrand Canyon [VENTURA]: *canyon,* drained by a stream that flows 4 miles to Tapo Canyon (1) 6 miles west-northwest of Santa Susana Pass (lat. 34°19' N, long. 118°43' W; sec. 25, T 3 N, R 18 E). Named on Santa Susana (1951) 7.5' quadrangle. Called Dry Canyon on Santa Susana (1903) 15' quadrangle. The name "Gillibrand Canyon" is for Edward Clayton Gillibrand, who settled in the neighborhood about 1889 (Ricard).

Gilman Peak [ORANGE]: *peak,* 3 miles northeast of Yorba Linda (lat. 33°55'25" N, long. 117°46'30" W; sec. 12, T 3 S, R 9 W). Altitude 1678 feet. Named on Yorba Linda (1950) 7.5' quadrangle. The name commemorates Richard Hall Gilman, an early settler (Meadows, p. 66).

Girard: see **Woodland Hills** [LOS ANGELES].

Girard Reservoir [LOS ANGELES]: *lake,* 400 feet long, 3.5 miles south of Canoga Park (lat. 34°09'05" N, long. 118°36'35" W); the feature is just south of Woodland Hills, which once was called Girard. Named on Canoga Park (1952) 7.5' quadrangle.

Gladstone: see **Covina** [LOS ANGELES].

Glassell Park [LOS ANGELES]: *district,* 4 miles north of Los Angeles city hall (lat. 34°06'40" N, long. 118°14'20" W). Named on Los Angeles (1953) 7.5' quadrangle.

Gleason Canyon [LOS ANGELES]: *canyon,* drained by a stream that flows 5.5 miles to Aliso Canyon (1) 3 miles east-southeast of Acton (lat. 34°26'40" N, long. 118°08'55" W; at E line sec. 8, T 4 N, R 12 W); the canyon heads near Mount Gleason. Named on Acton (1959) 7.5' quadrangle.

Gleason Mountain: see **Mount Gleason** [LOS ANGELES].

Gleason Point: see **Bahia Point** [SAN DIEGO].

Glen Campground [LOS ANGELES]: *locality,* nearly 8 miles west-northwest of Azusa city hall along West Fork San Gabriel River (lat. 34°14'25" N, long. 117°57'05" W). Named on Azusa (1966) 7.5' quadrangle.

Glen Canyon [LOS ANGELES]: *canyon,* drained by a stream that flows 2 miles to West Fork San Gabriel River nearly 8 miles north-northwest of Azusa city hall (lat. 34°14'25" N, long. 117°57'05" W). Named on Azusa (1953) 7.5' quadrangle.

Glen Cliff: see **Emery**, under **Un Gallo Flat** [SAN DIEGO].

Glencliff Campground [SAN DIEGO]: *locality,* 2 miles north of Buckman Springs (lat. 32°48'05" N, long. 116°29'55" W; at E line sec. 7, T 16 S, R 5 E). Named on Mount Laguna (1960) 15' quadrangle.

Glendale [LOS ANGELES]: *city,* 6 miles west of Pasadena city hall (lat. 34°08'50" N, long. 118°14'50" W). Named on Burbank (1953), Hollywood (1953), Pasadena (1966), and Sunland (1953) 7.5' quadrangles. Called Riverdale on Stevenson's (1884) map. Postal authorities established Mason post office in 1886 and changed the name Glendale in 1891 (Salley, p. 134). The city incorporated in 1906. The community began soon after the railroad was built from Los Angeles to San Fernando in 1873 and 1874; it first was called Riverdale, but postal authorities rejected this name and called the post office there Mason (Gudde, 1949, p. 128). The place also was called Verdugo before 1883, when an artist from Chicago proposed the name "Glendale," which was adopted by popular acclaim (Hanna, p. 121).

Glendale: see **North Glendale** [LOS ANGELES]; **West Glendale** [LOS AN-

GELES].

Glendale Junction [LOS ANGELES]: *locality,* 2 miles north-northeast of Los Angeles city hall along a rail line (lat. 34°04'30" N, long. 118°13'25" W). Named on Los Angeles (1966) 7.5' quadrangle.

Glendora [LOS ANGELES]: *city,* 2.5 miles east of Azusa city hall (lat. 34°08'10" N, long. 117°51'50" W). Named on Azusa (1953), Glendora (1953), and San Dimas (1966) 7.5' quadrangles. Postal authorities established Alosta post office in 1883 and moved it 0.5 mile west in 1887, when they changed the name to Glendora; they reestablished Alosta post office in 1888 and discontinued it in 1899—when it was discontinued finally, Alosta post office was situated 1 mile south of Glendora post office (Salley, p. 5, 86). Glendora incorporated in 1911. George Whitcomb coined the name "Glendora" in 1887 from the word "glen" and his wife's name "Ledora" (Gudde, 1949, p. 128).

Glendora Mountain [LOS ANGELES]: *peak,* 4 miles north-northeast of Glendora city hall (lat. 34°11'30" N, long. 117°50'15" W; near NE cor. sec. 8, T 1 N, R 9 W). Altitude 3322 feet. Named on Glendora (1966) 7.5' quadrangle.

Glen Lonely [SAN DIEGO]: *valley,* 8 miles southwest of Descanso (lat. 32°46'20" N, long. 116°42'40" W; on N line sec. 19, T 16 S, R 3 E). Named on Viejas Mountain (1960) 7.5' quadrangle. On Cuyamaca (1903) 30' quadrangle, the name applies to a settlement at the place.

Glen Oaks [SAN DIEGO]: *locality,* 2 miles west of Alpine (lat. 32° 50'15" N, long. 116°48' W; sec. 29, T 15 S, R 2 E). Named on Alpine (1955) 7.5' quadrangle.

Glenview [LOS ANGELES]: *locality,* 10 miles northwest of Santa Monica city hall near the head of Topanga Canyon (lat. 34°07'30" N, long. 118°36' W). Named on Canoga Park (1952) and Topanga (1952) 7.5' quadrangles. Called Mohn Springs on Dry Canyon (1932) 6' quadrangle. Los Angeles County (1935) map shows a place called Veteran Springs located in Topanga Canyon at or near present Glenview. Sampson (p. 206) mentioned Mohn Mineral Springs and noted that the water was bottled for sale.

Glenview [SAN DIEGO]: *locality,* 2.25 miles south-southeast of Lakeside (lat. 32°49'55" N, long. 116°54'20" W). Named on El Cajon (1967) 7.5' quadrangle.

Glenwood: see **Camp Glenwood** [LOS ANGELES].

Glorietta Bay [SAN DIEGO]: *embayment,* nearly 3 miles south of downtown San Diego along San Diego Bay (lat. 32°40'40" N, long. 117°10'10" W). Named on Point Loma (1967) 7.5' quadrangle.

Gloryetta: see **Delhi** [ORANGE].

Goat Buttes [LOS ANGELES]: *relief feature,* 5.5 miles northwest of Malibu Point (lat. 34°05'50" N, long. 118°44'25" W; mainly in sec. 11, T 1 S, R 18 W). Named on Malibu Beach (1951) 7.5' quadrangle.

Goat Canyon [SAN DIEGO]:

(1) *canyon,* drained by a stream that flows 1.5 miles to Carrizo Gorge 8 miles north of Jacumba (lat. 32°44" N, long. 116°11'20" W; sec. 31, T 16 S, R 8 E). Named on Jacumba (1959) 7.5' quadrangle.

(2) *canyon,* heads in Mexico, 0.5 mile long in San Diego County, opens into lowlands 2.5 miles south-southeast of Imperial Beach civic center (lat. 32°32'25" N, long. 117°06'20" W). Named on Imperial Beach (1967) 7.5' quadrangle.

Goat Canyon: see **Tick Canyon** [LOS ANGELES].

Goat Harbor [LOS ANGELES]: *embayment,* 4 miles northeast of Mount Banning on the north side of Santa Catalina Island (lat. 33° 25' N, long. 118°23'40" W). Named on Santa Catalina North (1950) 7.5' quadrangle.

Goat Island [SAN DIEGO]: *island,* 2.25 miles northwest of Morena Village in Morena Reservoir (lat. 32°42'25" N, long. 116°31'35" W; sec. 12, T 17 S, R 4 E). Named on Morena Reservoir (1960) 7.5' quadrangle.

Goat Mountain [SAN DIEGO]: *peak,* 2.5 miles south-southeast of Manzanita (lat. 32°38'10" N, long. 116°15'50" W; sec. 4, T 18 S, R 7 E). Named on Live Oak Springs (1959) 7.5' quadrangle.

Goat Peak [SAN DIEGO]: *peak,* 7.5 miles north-northwest of Lakeside (lat. 32°57'30" N, long. 116°58'35" W; near NW cor. sec. 15, T 14 S, R 1 W). Altitude 1728 feet. Named on San Vicente Reservoir (1955) 7.5' quadrangle.

Gobblers Knob [SAN DIEGO]: *relief feature,* 7.5 miles west-southwest of Jamul (lat. 32°40'05" N, long. 116°59'30" W; near N line sec. 28, T 17 S, R 1 W). Named on Jamul Mountains (1955) 7.5' quadrangle.

Godde Pass [LOS ANGELES]: *pass,* 8.5 miles southwest of Lancaster (lat. 34°36'30" N, long. 118°14'35" W; sec. 15, T 6 N, R 13 W). Named on Ritter Ridge (1958) 7.5' quadrangle.

Godwin Canyon [VENTURA]: *canyon,* drained by a stream that flows nearly 4 miles to Sespe Creek 7 miles north-northwest of Wheeler Springs (lat. 34°36' N, long. 119°20'50" W; near W line sec. 20, T 6 N, R 23 W). Named on Reyes Peak (1943) and Wheeler Springs (1943) 7.5' quadrangles.

Goff Island [ORANGE]: *peninsula,* 2.5 miles southeast of Laguna Beach city hall along the coast (lat. 33°30'50" N, long, 117°45'35" W; near S line sec. 31, T 7 S, R 8 W). Named on Laguna Beach (1965) 7.5' quadrangle. On Santa Ana (1901) 15' quadrangle, the name applies to a small island at the site. The name commemorates four Goff brothers who settled along the coast near the feature in the early 1870's (Meadows, p. 66-67).

Gold Canyon [LOS ANGELES]: *canyon,* drained by a stream that flows 2.25 miles to Big Tujunga Canyon 3.5 miles northeast of Sunland (lat. 34°18'05" N, long. 118°16'15" W; near W line sec. 32, T 3 N, R 13 W). Named on Sunland (1953) 7.5' quadrangle.

Gold Canyon Saddle [LOS ANGELES]: *pass,* 4 miles north of Sunland (lat. 34°19' N, long. 118°17'35" W; sec. 25, T 3 N, R 14 W); the feature is at the head of Gold Canyon. Named on Sunland (1966) 7.5' quadrangle.

Gold Creek [LOS ANGELES]: *stream,* flows nearly 6 miles to Little Tujunga Canyon 4 miles north-northwest of Sunland (lat. 34°18'35" N, long. 118°20'40" W; near SE cor. sec. 28, T 3 N, R 14 W). Named on Sunland (1953) 7.5' quadrangle. Gold-mining operations along Gold Creek around the turn of the century constituted what was called Little Nugget Placers (Robinson, J.W., 1973, p. 36).

Gold Creek Saddle [LOS ANGELES]: *pass,* 5.25 miles north-northeast of Sunland (lat. 34°19'50" N, long. 118°16'35" W). Named on Sunland (1966) 7.5' quadrangle.

Goldenrod Spring [LOS ANGELES]: *spring,* 2 miles north-northwest of Sunland (lat. 34°17'25" N, long. 118°19'10" W; sec. 2, T 2 N, R 14 W). Named on Sunland (1966) 7.5' quadrangle.

Goldfish Point [SAN DIEGO]: *promontory,* 0.25 mile east of Point La Jolla along the coast (lat. 32°51' N, long. 117°16'10" W). Named on La Jolla (1967) 7.5' quadrangle.

Gold Hill [VENTURA]: *peak,* 5 miles north-northeast of McDonald Peak (lat. 34°42'15" N, long 118°55' W; sec. 17, T 7 N, R 19 W). Altitude 4838 feet. Named on McDonald Peak (1958) 7.5' quadrangle.

Gold Hill Campground [VENTURA]: *locality,* 5 miles north of McDonald Peak (lat. 34°42'15" N, long. 118°56'05" W; sec. 18, T 7 N, R 19 W); the place is 1 mile west of Gold Hill. Named on McDonald Peak (1958) 7.5' quadrangle.

Gomez Creek [SAN DIEGO]: *stream,* flows 4 miles to the valley of San Luis Rey River 1.25 miles west of Pala (lat. 33°21'55" N, long. 117°05'55" W; sec. 28, T 9 S, R 2 W). Named on Pala (1968) and Pechanga (1968) 7.5' quadrangles.

Gonzales Canyon [SAN DIEGO]: *canyon,* drained by a stream that flows 3.5 miles to San Dieguito Valley nearly 2 miles east-northeast of Delmar (lat. 32°58'10" N, long. 117°13'45" W; sec. 7, T 14 S, R 3 W). Named on Del Mar (1967) 7.5' quadrangle.

Gookin Gulch: see **Pine Canyon** [LOS ANGELES] (1).

Gookins Dry Lake [LOS ANGELES]: *dry lake,* 500 feet long, 11 miles east-southeast of Gorman (lat. 34°44'35" N, long. 118°37'45" W; on N line sec. 36, T 8 N, R 17 W). Named on Liebre Mountain (1958) 7.5' quadrangle.

Gooseberry Canyon [LOS ANGELES]: *canyon,* drained by a stream that flows 1 mile to Pacoima Canyon 7 miles north of Sunland (lat. 34°21'45" N, long. 118°18'45" W; sec. 11, T 3 N, R 14 W). Named on Sunland (1953) 7.5' quadrangle.

Gooseberry Spring: see **Little Jimmy Spring** [LOS ANGELES].

Goose Valley [SAN DIEGO]: *valley,* 1.5 miles northeast of Ramona along Santa Maria Creek (lat. 33°03'40" N, long. 116°50'40" W). Named on Ramona (1955) 7.5' quadrangle.

Gopher Canyon [SAN DIEGO]: *canyon,* drained by a stream that flows 4.25 miles to San Luis Rey River 8 miles south of Fallbrook (lat. 33°15'55" N, long. 117°14'05" W; sec. 31, T 10 S, R 3 W). Named on Bonsall (1968) 7.5' quadrangle. South Fork branches south 2 miles above the mouth of the main canyon; it is 3.25 miles long and is named on Bonsall (1968) and San Marcos (1968) 7.5' quadrangles. On Tucker and Reed's (1939) map, the name "Gopher Canyon" applies to present South Fork.

Gordon Canyon [LOS ANGELES]:

(1) *canyon,* drained by a stream that flows less than 1 mile to Pacoima Canyon 7 miles north of Sunland (lat. 34°21'45" N, long. 118°19'15" W; sec. 11, T 3 N, R 14 W). Named on Sunland (1966) 7.5' quadrangle.

(2) *canyon,* 1 mile long, 2.25 miles east-northeast of Glendora city hall (lat. 34°08'45" N, long. 117°49'30" W; sec. 21, 28, T 1 N, R 9 W). Named on Glendora (1953) 7.5' quadrangle.

Gordon Point [SAN DIEGO]: *peak,* 2.25 miles north of Boucher Hill (lat. 33°22' N, long. 116°55'05" W; sec. 30, T 9 S, R 1 E). Named on Boucher Hill (1948) 7.5' quadrangle. The name commemorates Donald H. Gordon, a pioneer aviator who spent the last 25 years of his life at the place; the feature, which is 0.3 mile south of Morgan Hill, has the alternate name "Morgan Hill" (United States Board on Geographic Names, 1971, p. 2).

Gorman [LOS ANGELES]: *village,* 42 miles northwest of San Fernando (lat. 34°47'45" N, long. 118°51'10" W; at W line sec. 12, T 8 N, R 19 W). Named on Lebec (1958) 7.5' quadrangle. Postal authorities established Gorman's Station post office in 1877, discontinued in it 1878, reestablished it the same year, changed the name to Gorman Station in 1894, discontinued it in 1896, reestablished it with name "Gorman" in 1896, discontinued it in 1898, reestablished it in 1904, discontinued it in 1908, and reestablished it in 1915; the name was for Henry Gorman, first postmaster (Salley, p. 87). Gorman was a soldier at Fort Tejon in Kern County who settled in the neighborhood after his discharge in 1864 (Hanna, p. 124).

Gorman Canyon [LOS ANGELES]: *canyon*, drained by a stream that flows 1.5 miles to Sand Canyon (2) 3.5 miles southeast of Solemint (lat. 34°22'45" N, long. 118°24'40" W; near NW cor. sec. 1, T 3 N, R 15 W). Named on Mint Canyon (1960) and San Fernando (1953) 7.5' quadrangles. Called German Canyon on San Fernando (1900) 15' quadrangle.

Gorman Creek [LOS ANGELES]: *stream*, flows 10.5 miles to Cañada de Los Alamos 7 miles south-southeast of Gorman (lat. 34° 42'10" N, long. 118°47'40" W; sec. 16, T 7 N, R 18 W); Gorman is along upper reaches of the creek. Named on Black Mountain (1958) and Lebec (1958) 7.5' quadrangles.

Gorman's Station: see **Gorman** [LOS ANGELES].

Gosnell Hill [VENTURA]: *relief feature*, 2 miles north of downtown Ventura (lat. 34°18'40" N, long. 119°17'25" W). Named on Ventura (1951) 7.5' quadrangle. The name commemorates Truman Barrick Gosnell, who farmed at the place in the 1890's (Ricard).

Gospel Swamp: see **Fountain Valley** [ORANGE].

Goss Canyon [LOS ANGELES]: *canyon*, nearly 1 mile long, 8 miles northwest of Pasadena city hall (lat. 34°14'20" N, long. 118°13'55" W; heads in sec. 22, T 2 N, R 13 W). Named on Pasadena (1953) 7.5' quadrangle.

Gould Canyon [LOS ANGELES]: *canyon*, 1.5 miles long, 6 miles northnorthwest of Pasadena city hall (lat. 34°13'15" N, long. 118° 11'40" W; sec. 25, 36, T 2 N, R 13 W). Named on Pasadena (1953) 7.5' quadrangle.

Government Canyon [LOS ANGELES]: *canyon*, drained by a stream that flows 1 mile to Swarthout Valley 5.5 miles north-northwest of Mount San Antonio (lat. 34°22'05" N, long. 117°40'05" W; at N line sec. 12, T 3 N, R 8 W). Named on Mount San Antonio (1955) 7.5' quadrangle.

Government Well [SAN DIEGO]: *springs*, 4.5 miles east-northeast of San Felipe (lat. 33°13'40" N, long. 116°31'40" W; sec. 12, T 11 S, R 4 E). Named on Ranchita (1960) 7.5' quadrangle.

Gower: see **Mount Gower** [SAN DIEGO].

Grabino Canyon [ORANGE]: *canyon*, drained by a stream that flows 7 miles to Cristianitos Canyon about 4 miles northeast of San Clemente civic center (lat. 33°28' N, long. 117°33'45" W; near N line sec. 24, T 8 S, R 7 W). Named on Cañada Gobernadora (1968) and San Clemente (1968) 7.5' quadrangles.

Grace Hill [LOS ANGELES]: *hill*, 1.5 miles south-southwest of Pasadena city hall (lat. 34°07'35" N, long. 118°09'05" W). Named on Pasadena (1953) 7.5' quadrangle.

Graham [LOS ANGELES]: *district*, 2.25 miles west-southwest of present South Gate city hall (lat. 33°56'40" N, long. 118°14'35" W). Named on Watts (1937) 6' quadrangle. Postal authorities established Seal Garden post office 1 mile north of Watts post office in 1908, changed the name to Graham Station in 1911, and discontinued it in 1918; the name "Seal Garden" was for a farm project that failed, and the name "Graham Station" was for a place along Pacific Electric Railroad (Salley, p. 87, 200).

Graham Canyon [LOS ANGELES]: *canyon*, drained by a stream that flows 2.25 miles to lowlands 5.5 miles north-northwest of Big Pines (lat. 34°27'15" N, long. 117°43'50" W; near NE cor. sec. 8, T 4 N, R 8 W). Named on Mescal Creek (1956) 7.5' quadrangle.

Graham Station: see **Graham** [LOS ANGELES].

Granada: see **Granada Hills** [LOS ANGELES].

Granada Hills [LOS ANGELES]: *district*, 5 miles east of Chatsworth in Los Angeles (lat. 34°16' N, long. 118°31' W). Named on Oat Mountain (1952) and San Fernando (1966) 7.5' quadrangles. Called Granada on Zelzah (1941) 6' quadrangle. Postal authorities established Granada Hills post office in 1942 (Salley, p. 88).

Grand Arch: see **Arch Rock** [VENTURA].

Grand Canyon [LOS ANGELES]:

(1) *canyon*, drained by a stream that flows 1 mile to Millard Canyon 5.5 miles north of Pasadena city hall (lat. 34°13'45" N, long. 118° 07'40" W). Named on Mount Wilson (1953) and Pasadena (1953) 7.5' quadrangles.

(2) *canyon*, drained by a stream that flows 2.25 miles to Silver Canyon 3 miles west of Avalon on Santa Catalina Island (lat. 33° 20'05" N, long. 118°22'30" W). Named on Santa Catalina East (1950) 7.5' quadrangle.

Grandview Canyon [LOS ANGELES]: *canyon*, drained by a stream that flows 4.5 miles to lowlands nearly 5 miles east of Valyermo (lat. 34°26'15" N, long. 117°46' W; near NE cor. sec. 13, T 4 N, R 9 W). Named on Mescal Creek (1956) and Valyermo (1958) 7.5' quadrangles.

Granite Mountain [LOS ANGELES]: *peak*, 2.25 miles west-southwest of Pacifico Mountain (lat. 34°22'15" N, long. 118°04'10" W; sec. 6, T 3 N, R 11 W). Named on Chilao Flat (1959) 7.5' quadrangle.

Granite Mountain [SAN DIEGO]: *ridge*, southeast- to northeast-trending, 2 miles long, 7 miles east-southeast of Julian (lat. 33°02'45" N, long. 116°29'15" W). Named on Earthquake Valley (1959) and Julian (1960) 7.5' quadrangles. On Borrego (1939) 15' quadrangle, the name "Oriflamme Mountain" applies to present Granite Mountain, and the name "Granite Mountain" identifies the high point on Oriflamme Mountain.

Granite Spring [SAN DIEGO]: *spring*, 5.25 miles southeast of Cuyamaca Peak (lat. 32°54'05" N, long. 116°32' W). Named on Cuyamaca Peak (1960) 7.5' quadrangle.

Grantville [SAN DIEGO]: *district*, 4.5 miles west-northwest of La Mesa in San Diego (lat. 32°47'20" N, long. 117°05'25" W). Named on La Mesa (1967) 7.5' quadrangle. La Jolla (1903) 15' quadrangle has both the names "Grantville" and "Gravilla" at the place. Postal authorities established Grantville post office in 1960; the name honors General U.S. Grant, and was given in 1887 to promote a soldiers home—the place was renamed Orcutt in 1890 (Salley, p. 88). Postal authorities established Orcutt post office in 1890 and discontinued it in 1896; the name was for Herman C. Orcutt, first postmaster (Salley, p. 162). They established Gravilla post office in 1897 and discontinued it in 1905; the name, coined from the words "gravel" and "villa," was for the location of the post office in a villa by gravel pits (Salley, p. 88-89).

Grape Arbor [LOS ANGELES]: *locality*, 1 mile east-southeast of present Agoura in Liberty Canyon (lat. 34°08'15" N, long. 118°43'30" W). Named on Camulos (1903) 30' quadrangle.

Grapevine Canyon [LOS ANGELES]: *canyon*, 1.5 miles long, opens into lowlands 3.5 miles northwest of downtown San Fernando (lat. 34°18'55" N, long. 118°29'10" W). Named on San Fernando (1953) 7.5' quadrangle.

Grapevine Canyon [SAN DIEGO]: *canyon*, 7.5 miles long, opens into Yaqui Flat along San Felipe Creek 9 miles south-southwest of Borrego Springs (lat. 33°08'15" N, long. 116°26' W). Named on Ranchita (1960) and Tubb Canyon (1959) 7.5' quadrangles.

Grapevine Creek [SAN DIEGO]: *stream*, flows 3.25 miles to Potrero Creek (2) 3 miles east-southeast of Barrett Junction (lat. 32°35'50" N, long. 116°39'20" W; near SW cor. sec. 14, T 18 S, R 3 E). Named on Barrett Lake (1960) and Tecate (1960) 7.5' quadrangles.

Grapevine Hills [SAN DIEGO]: *area*, 8 miles southwest of Borrego Springs (lat. 33°10' N, long. 116°28' W); the feature is on the north side of Grapevine Canyon. Named on Tubb Canyon (1959) 7.5' quadrangle.

Grapevine Mountain [SAN DIEGO]: *peak*, 8.5 miles east-northeast of Julian (lat. 33°07'15" N, long. 116°28' W). Altitude 3955 feet. Named on Earthquake Valley (1959) 7.5' quadrangle.

Grapevine Spring [SAN DIEGO]: *spring*, 4.5 miles east-southeast of San Felipe (lat. 33°10'35" N, long. 116°31'25" W; sec. 36, T 11 S, R 4 E); the spring is in Grapevine Canyon. Named on Ranchita (1960) 7.5' quadrangle. The name is from grapevines that cover the canyon walls below the spring (Brown, 1923, p. 222).

Grasshopper Canyon [LOS ANGELES]: *canyon*, drained by a stream that flows 5.25 miles to Castaic Creek 6.25 miles south-southwest of Warm Springs Mountain (lat. 34°30'30" N, long. 118°36'45" W; near N line sec. 24, T 5 N, R 17 W). Named on Warm Springs Mountain (1958) 7.5' quadrangle.

Grass Mountain [LOS ANGELES]: *peak*, nearly 3 miles south-southwest of the village of Lake Hughes (lat. 34°38'30" N, long. 118°24'45" W). Altitude 4605 feet. Named on Lake Hughes (1957) 7.5' quadrangle.

Grassy Hollow [LOS ANGELES]: *area*, 2 miles west of Big Pines (lat. 34°22'35" N, long. 117°43'25" W; sec. 4, T 3 N, R 8 W). Named on Mescal Creek (1956) 7.5' quadrangle.

Grave Wash [SAN DIEGO]: *stream*, flows 1.5 miles to Imperial County 17 miles east-northeast of Borrego Springs (lat. 33°18'15" N, long. 116°05' W; at E line sec. 13, T 10 S, R 8 E). Named on Seventeen Palms (1956) 7.5' quadrangle.

Graveyard Barranca: see **Sanjon Barranca** [VENTURA].

Graveyard Canyon [LOS ANGELES]: *canyon*, drained by a stream that flows nearly 4 miles to San Gabriel River 7.5 miles north-northeast of Glendora city hall (lat. 34°14'10" N, long. 117°48'35" W). Named on Crystal Lake (1958) and Glendora (1953) 7.5' quadrangles. The name is from Indian burial grounds (Gudde, 1969, p. 127).

Gravilla: see **Grantville** [SAN DIEGO].

Gray Mountain [SAN DIEGO]: *ridge*, northwest-trending, 1 mile long, 2.5 miles north-northeast of Jacumba (lat. 32°38'45" N, long. 116°10' W; sec. 33, T 17 S, R 8 E). Named on Jacumba (1959) 7.5' quadrangle.

Green: see **Jim Green Creek** [SAN DIEGO].

Greenleaf Canyon [LOS ANGELES]: *canyon*, drained by a stream that flows 2.5 miles to Topanga Canyon 8.5 miles northwest of Santa Monica city hall (lat. 34°05'25" N, long. 118°36'15" W). Named on Topanga (1952) 7.5' quadrangle.

Green Meadows [LOS ANGELES]: *locality*, 5 miles east of Inglewood (lat. 33°57'30" N, long. 118°16' W). Named on Redondo (1896) 15' quadrangle. Postal authorities established Green Meadows post office at a farming community in 1894 and discontinued it in 1902 (Salley, p. 89).

Green Valley [LOS ANGELES]: *settlement*, 4.25 miles south-southeast of the village of Lake Hughes (lat. 34°37'15" N, long. 118°24'45" W). Named on Lake Hughes (1957) 7.5' quadrangle. Hughes Lake (1937) 6' quadrangle has the name "La Joya" at the site.

Green Valley [SAN DIEGO]:

(1) *valley*, 7.5 miles south-southeast of Escondido (lat. 33°01' N, long. 117°02'15" W; in and near sec. 25, T 13 S, R 2 W). Named on Escondido (1968) 7.5' quadrangle.

(2) *canyon*, 1.5 miles long, nearly 3 miles north-northeast of Encinitas along

Encinitas Creek (lat. 33°04'30" N, long. 117°15'55" W; mainly in sec. 2, T 13 S, R 4 W). Named on Encinitas (1968) 7.5' quadrangle.
(3) *valley,* 3 miles east-southeast of Cuyamaca Peak along Sweetwater River (lat. 32°55'35" N, long. 116°33'30" W). Named on Cuyamaca Peak (1960) 7.5' quadrangle.

Green Valley: see **Upper Green Valley** [SAN DIEGO].

Green Valley Area Campground [SAN DIEGO]: *locality,* 3 miles south-southeast of Cuyamaca Peak along Sweetwater River (lat. 32°54'15" N, long. 116°35' W); the place is near the southwest end of Green Valley (3). Named on Cuyamaca Peak (1960) 7.5' quadrangle.

Green Valley Falls [SAN DIEGO]: *waterfall,* 3.5 miles south-southeast of Cuyamaca Peak along Sweetwater River (lat. 32°54' N, long. 116°35' W); the feature is downstream from the southwest end of Green Valley (3). Named on Cuyamaca Peak (1960) 7.5' quadrangle.

Green Verdugo Reservoir [LOS ANGELES]: *intermittent lake,* 500 feet long, 1.25 miles west of downtown Sunland (lat. 34°15'25" N, long. 118°20'05" W). Named on Sunland (1966) 7.5' quadrangle.

Greenville [ORANGE]: *locality,* 6 miles east-northeast of Huntington Beach civic center (lat. 33°42'10" N, long. 117°54'25" W). Named on Newport Beach (1965) 7.5' quadrangle. Newport school was built at the site in 1874, and after the community of Newport Beach was started, the village around the school was referred to as Old Newport (Meadows, p. 106-107). A flag stop located along Pacific Electric Railroad 0.5 mile west of Greenville was called Von Schritz (Meadows, p. 137).

Greenwich Village [VENTURA]: *locality,* about 1.5 miles west-northwest of downtown Thousand Oaks (lat. 34°10"50" N, long. 118°51'45" W; sec. 10, T 1 N, R 19 W). Named on Thousand Oaks (1952) 7.5' quadrangle.

Gridley Canyon [VENTURA]: *canyon,* drained by a stream that flows 3.5 miles to Ojai Valley 2.5 miles east-northeast of the town of Ojai (lat. 34°28' N, long. 119°12'10" W; sec. 32, T 5 N, R 22 E). Named on Ojai (1952) 7.5' quadrangle.

Griffin [VENTURA]: *locality,* 15 miles east-northeast of Reyes Peak at the east end of Lockwood Valley (lat. 34°44' N, long. 119°02'45" W; near SW cor. sec. 31, T 8 N, R 20 W). Named on Mount Pinos (1903) 30' quadrangle. Postal authorities established Griffin post office in 1896 and discontinued it in 1905 (Frickstad, p. 218).

Grimes Canyon [VENTURA]: *canyon,* drained by a stream that flows 3.25 miles to the valley of Santa Clara River 2.25 miles south of Fillmore (lat. 34°22' N, long. 118°55'10" W; near SE cor. sec. 1, T 3 N, R 20 W). Named on Moorpark (1951) 7.5' quadrangle. The name commemorates Brice Grimes of Bardsdale (Ricard).

Grissom Island: see **Island Grissom** [LOS ANGELES].

Grizzly Flat [LOS ANGELES]: *area,* 4 miles south of Condor Peak (lat. 34°16'10" N, long. 118°12'25" W; sec. 11, T 2 N, R 13 W). Named on Condor Peak (1959) 7.5' quadrangle. Called Grizzly Flats on Los Angeles County (1935) map.

Grossmont [SAN DIEGO]: *town,* 2 miles southwest of El Cajon city hall (lat. 32°46'35" N, long. 116°59'30" W). Named on El Cajon (1967) 7.5' quadrangle. Cuyamaca (1903) 30' quadrangle shows a place called Alta situated along San Diego Cuyamaca and Eastern Railroad at the site. Postal authorities established Grossmont post office in 1910 and discontinued it in 1971 (Salley, p. 90). The name "Grossmont" is from William B. Gross, who with Colonel Ed Fletcher promoted the place as an artist's colony about 1900 (Gudde, 1949, p. 136).

Grossmont Reservoir [SAN DIEGO]: *lake,* 1200 feet long, 1.5 miles west-southwest of El Capitan city hall (lat. 32°47'05" N, long. 116° 59'15" W); the feature is north of Grossmont. Named on El Cajon (1967) 7.5' quadrangle.

Grotto Creek [LOS ANGELES]: *stream,* flows 1.5 miles to Big Tujunga Canyon 7 miles southwest of Pacifico Mountain (lat. 34° 18'35" N, long. 118°07'05" W). Named on Chilao Flat (1959) 7.5' quadrangle.

Grotto Spring [ORANGE]: *spring,* 1.25 miles west-northwest of Santiago Peak (lat. 33°43'15" N, long. 117°33'05" W; sec. 19, T 5 S, R 6 W). Named on Santiago Peak (1954) 7.5' quadrangle.

Grundy: see **Mother Grundy Peak** [SAN DIEGO].

Guadalasca [VENTURA]: *land grant,* at Point Mugu and inland to Conejo Mountain. Named on Camarillo (1950), Newbury Park (1951), Point Mugu (1949), and Triunfo Pass (1950) 7.5' quadrangles. Isabel Yorba received 6 leagues in 1836 and claimed 30,594 acres patented in 1873 (Cowan, p. 37-38; Cowan gave the alternate name "La Laguna" for the grant).

Guajome [SAN DIEGO]: *land grant,* north-northwest of Vista. Named on Morro Hill (1968), San Luis Rey (1968), and San Marcos (1968) 7.5' quadrangles. Andres, Manual, and Jose (Indians) received 1 league in 1845; Andres and others claimed 2219 acres patented in 1871 (Cowan, p. 38; Perez, p. 68). The name is of Indian origin (Kroeber, p. 41).

Guajome Lake [SAN DIEGO]: *lake,* 0.5 mile long, nearly 7 miles east-northeast of Oceanside (lat. 33°14'50" N, long. 117°16'35" W); the lake is on Guajome grant. Named on San Luis Rey (1968) 7.5' quadrangle.

Guard Canyon: see **Morgan Canyon** [LOS ANGELES].

Guatay [SAN DIEGO]: *village,* 3.5 miles east of Descanso (lat. 32° 51' N, long. 116°33'20" W; sec. 22, T 15 S, R 4 E); the place is 1 mile east-northeast of Guatay Mountain. Named on Descanso (1960) 7.5' quadrangle. Postal authorities established Guatay post office in 1917, discontinued it in 1936, and reestablished it in 1947 (Frickstad, p. 151). The name is of Indian origin (Kroeber, p. 41).

Guatay Campground [SAN DIEGO]: *locality,* 2.5 miles east of Descanso (lat. 32°51'10" N, long. 116°34'20" W; sec. 21, T 15 S, R 4 E); the place is less than 1 mile north of Guatay Mountain. Named on Descanso (1960) 7.5' quadrangle.

Guatay Mountain [SAN DIEGO]: *peak,* 2.5 miles east-southeast of Descanso (lat. 32°50'35" N, long. 116°34'25" W; near N line sec. 28, T 15 S, R 4 E). Altitude 4885 feet. Named on Descanso (1960) 7.5' quadrangle.

Guejito [SAN DIEGO]: *land grant,* about halfway between Escondido and Lake Henshaw. Named on Mesa Grande (1948) and Rodriguez Mountain (1948) 7.5' quadrangles. Jose Maria Orozco received 3 leagues in 1845; George W. Hamley claimed 13,299 acres patented in 1866 (Cowan, p. 38-39; Cowan listed the grant under the designation "Guejito (or Quejito) y Cañada de Palomia").

Guejito Creek [SAN DIEGO]: *stream,* flows 10.5 miles to Rockwood Canyon 1.5 miles north of San Pasqual (lat. 33°06'50" N, long. 116°57'20" W; sec. 23, T 12 S, R 1 W); the stream is largely on Guejito grant. Named on Rodriguez Mountain (1948) and San Pasqual (1954) 7.5' quadrangles.

Guejito y Cañada de Palomia: see **Guejito** [SAN DIEGO].

Gueyetta Meadows: see **Galleta Meadows** [SAN DIEGO].

Guffy Camp [LOS ANGELES]: *locality,* 3.5 miles north of Mount San Antonio (lat. 34°20'30" N, long. 117°39'15" W; at S line sec. 18, T 3 N, R 7 W). Named on Mount San Antonio (1955) 7.5' quadrangle. Called Guffys Camp on Swarthout (1941) 6' quadrangle.

Guiberson Canyon: see **Frey Canyon** [VENTURA].

Gulf of Santa Catalina [LOS ANGELES-ORANGE]: *water feature,* separates the mainland from Santa Catalina and San Clemente Islands. Named on Long Beach (1957) and Santa Ana (1959) 1°x 2° quadrangles. On Blake's (1857) map, the name "Earthquake Bay" applies to the sea along the coast from San Pedro to San Diego.

Gum Tree Cove [SAN DIEGO]: *embayment,* 7 miles west of Jamul along Sweetwater Reservoir (lat. 32°42' N, long. 116°59'40" W). Named on Jamul Mountains (1955) 7.5' quadrangle.

Gunn Canyon [SAN DIEGO]: *canyon,* less than 0.5 mile long, 3 miles northwest of Warner Springs (lat. 33°19'05" N, long. 116°39'50" W; at W line sec. 10, T 10 S, R 3 E). Named on Warner Springs (1959) 7.5' quadrangle.

Guyamas River: see **Cuyama River** [VENTURA].

Gypsum [ORANGE]: *locality,* 3.25 miles southeast of San Juan Hill along Atchison, Topeka and Santa Fe Railroad (lat. 33°52'40" N, long. 117°42' W); the place is north of the mouth of Gypsum Canyon. Named on Prado Dam (1950) 7.5' quadrangle.

Gypsum Canyon [ORANGE]: *canyon,* drained by a stream that flows 3.5 miles to Santa Ana Canyon 3.5 miles west-northwest of Sierra Peak (lat. 33°52' N, long. 117°42'35" W). Named on Black Star Canyon (1967) 7.5' quadrangle. Corona (1942) 15' quadrangle has the name "Gypsum Creek" for the stream in the canyon. A deposit of gypsum occurs in the canyon (Tucker, 1925a, p. 67).

Gypsum Creek: see **Gypsum Canyon** [ORANGE].

- H -

Hacienda Heights [LOS ANGELES]: *city,* 5.5 miles south of Baldwin Park city hall (lat. 34°00'20" N, long. 117°57'50" W). Named on Baldwin Park (1966) and La Habra (1964) 7.5' quadrangles.

Hahaonuput: see **San Rafael** [LOS ANGELES].

Haines [VENTURA]: *locality,* 3 miles southwest of Santa Paula along Southern Pacific Railroad (lat. 34°19'30" N, long. 119°06'05" W); the place is near Haines Barranca. Named on Santa Paula (1951) 7.5' quadrangle. The name commemorates Abner Haines, who came to the neighborhood in 1867 (Ricard).

Haines Barranca [VENTURA]: *gully,* extends for 2 miles from the mouth of O'Hara Canyon to Santa Clara River nearly 3 miles southwest of Santa Paula (lat. 34°19'15" N, long. 119°05'20" W). Named on Santa Paula (1951) 7.5' quadrangle.

Haines Canyon [LOS ANGELES]: *canyon,* drained by a stream that flows 2.5 miles to lowlands 2 miles east of Sunland, where it enters Haines Canyon Channel (lat. 34°15'30" N, long. 118°16'35" W; sec. 18, T 2 N, R 13 W). Named on Condor Peak (1959) and Sunland (1953) 7.5' quadrangles.

Haines Canyon [VENTURA]: *canyon,* 1 mile long, opens into the valley of Santa Clara River 2.25 miles east of Fillmore (lat. 34'23'50" N, long. 118°52'20" W; near S line sec. 28, T 4 N, R 19 W). Named on Camulos (1903) 30' quadrangle. The name commemorates Herman Haines, who was killed by gunfire on the main street of Santa Paula in 1886 (Ricard).

Haines Canyon Channel [LOS ANGELES]: *stream,* flows 3.5 miles from the mouth of Haines Canyon to Tujunga Valley 0.5 mile northwest of the center of Sunland (lat. 34°16' N, long. 118°19'05" W). Named on Burbank (1953) and Sunland (1953) 7.5' quadrangles.

Halcon [ORANGE]: *locality*, 3 miles southwest of present Buena Park civic center along Pacific Electric Railroad (lat. 33°49'40" N, long. 118°01'40" W). Named on Los Alamitos (1935) 7.5' quadrangle.

Halfhill Dry Lake: see **Halfhill Lake** [SAN DIEGO].

Halfhill Lake [SAN DIEGO]: *dry lake*, 4 miles south-southeast of Ocotillo Wells (lat. 33°05'30" N, long. 116°06'15" W; mainly in sec. 26, T 12 S, R 8 E). Named on Borrego Mountain SE (1958) 7.5' quadrangle. Called Halfhill Dry Lake on Barrel Spring (1942) 15' quadrangle.

Halfway Canyon [ORANGE]: *canyon*, drained by a stream that flows 1 mile to Silverado Canyon nearly 4 miles northwest of Santiago Peak (lat. 33°44'45" N, long. 117°35'05" W; near S line sec. 11, T 5 S, R 7 W); Bear Flat (1) is at the head of the canyon. Named on Santiago Peak (1954) 7.5' quadrangle. The feature also was called Bear Gulch (Sleeper, 1976, p. 79).

Halfway House: see **Martins Camp** [LOS ANGELES].

Halfway Inn [LOS ANGELES]: *locality*, 10 miles southeast of Gorman (lat. 34°41'05" N, long. 118°43'45" W; at W line sec. 19, T 7 N, R 17 W). Named on Liebre Mountain (1958) 7.5' quadrangle.

Halfway Rock [ORANGE]: *rock*, 1 mile south of Laguna Beach city hall, and 400 feet offshore (lat. 33°31'50" N, long. 117°46'30" W). Named on Laguna Beach (1965) 7.5' quadrangle. The feature is half way between Laguna Beach and Arch Beach (Meadows, p. 68).

Halfway Spring Campground [VENTURA]: *locality*, 3.5 miles east-southeast of Cobblestone Mountain (lat. 34°35' N, long. 118°48'55" W; sec. 29, T 6 N, R 18 W). Named on Cobblestone Mountain (1958) 7.5' quadrangle.

Hall Beckley Canyon [LOS ANGELES]: *canyon*, 1.5 miles long, 7 miles north-northwest of Pasadena city hall (lat. 34°14' N, long. 118°12'30" W; sec. 23, 26, T 2 N, R 13 W). Named on Pasadena (1953) 7.5' quadrangle. Called Hall Canyon on Los Angeles County (1935) map.

Hall Canyon [VENTURA]: *canyon*, drained by a stream that flows 4 miles to lowlands 2 miles east of downtown Ventura (lat. 34°16'55" N, long. 119°15'25" W). Named on Ventura (1951) 7.5' quadrangle. The name commemorates brothers Dick Hall and Bill Hall, who raised sheep in the canyon in the 1870's (Ricard). East Fork branches northeast nearly 2 miles above the mouth of the main canyon; it is 3.5 miles long and is named on Saticoy (1951) and Ventura (1951) 7.5' quadrangles.

Hall Canyon [ORANGE]: *canyon*, drained by a stream that flows nearly 2 miles to Baker Canyon 6.25 miles south of Sierra Peak (lat. 33°45'35" N, long. 117°39'40" W; sec. 1, T 5 S, R 8 W). Named on Black Star Canyon (1967) 7.5' quadrangle. Meadows (p. 68) associated the name with W.H. Hall, who kept bees in present Baker Canyon.

Hall Canyon: see **Hall Beckley Canyon** [LOS ANGELES].

Hall's Canyon: see **Baker Canyon** [ORANGE].

Halls Canyon Channel [LOS ANGELES]: *stream*, extends for 2 miles from the mouth of Hall Beckley Canyon to Verdugo Wash 6.5 miles northwest of Pasadena city hall (lat. 34°12'15" N, long. 118°14'15" W). Named on Pasadena (1966) 7.5' quadrangle.

Halsey Canyon [LOS ANGELES]: *canyon*, drained by a stream that flows 5 miles to Castaic Creek 6.25 miles northwest of Newhall (lat. 34°26'25" N, long. 118°37'10" W). Named on Newhall (1952) and Val Verde (1952) 7.5' quadrangles. Called Hasley Canyon on Santa Susana (1903) 15' quadrangle. Los Angeles County (1935) map shows a feature called Stevens Canyon that opens into Halsey Canyon from the west near the mouth of Halsey Canyon.

Ham Canyon [LOS ANGELES]: *canyon*, 1.5 miles long, 4.5 miles east of Glendora city hall (lat. 34°08'45" N, long. 117°47'15" W; mainly in sec. 26, T 1 N, R 9 W). Named on Glendora (1953) 7.5' quadrangle.

Hamilton Beach [LOS ANGELES]: *beach*, less than 1 mile north of Avalon on the northeast side of Santa Catalina Island (lat. 33°21'15" N, long. 118°19'45" W). Named on Santa Catalina East (1950) 7.5' quadrangle.

Hammell: see **Ventura** [VENTURA].

Hammond Canyon [VENTURA]: *canyon*, drained by a stream that flows 4.5 miles to Sulphur Canyon 8 miles northwest of Saticoy (lat. 34°22'20" N, long. 119°14'05" W). Named on Ojai (1952) and Saticoy (1951) 7.5' quadrangles. The name is for Elisha George Hammond and his wife, who owned land in the canyon in 1875 (Ricard).

Hampton Canyon [VENTURA]: *canyon*, drained by a stream that flows 2.5 miles to Wheeler Canyon 4.25 miles north of Saticoy (lat. 34°20'50" N, long. 119°08'45" W). Named on Saticoy (1951) 7.5' quadrangle. The name commemorates Wade Hampton, who reportedly was in the region as early as 1867 (Ricard).

Handy Creek [ORANGE]: *stream*, flows 2.5 miles to the canyon of Santiago Creek 4 miles east-northeast of Orange city hall (lat. 33° 48'45" N, long. 117°47'15" W). Named on Orange (1964) 7.5' quadrangle.

Hansen [ORANGE]: *locality*, 3.25 miles south-southwest of Buena Park civic center along Southern Pacific Railroad (lat. 33°49' N, long. 118°00'35" W). Named on Los Alamitos (1964) 7.5' quadrangle. The name recalls Charles Hansen and Peter Hansen, who raised wheat in the neighborhood in the 1880's (Meadows, p. 69). A flag stop called Lobo was situated along Pacific Electric Railroad less than 1 mile southeast of Hansen (Meadows, p. 79).

Hansen Canyon [LOS ANGELES]: *canyon*, drained by a stream that flows nearly 1 mile to Big Tujunga Canyon 3 miles south-southeast of Condor Peak (lat. 34°17'20" N, long. 118°11'40" W; sec. 1, T 2 N, R 13 W). Named on Condor Peak (1959) 7.5' quadrangle.

Hansen Flood Control Basin: see **Hansen Lake** [LOS ANGELES].

Hansen Lake [LOS ANGELES]: *lake*, 3 miles east-southeast of downtown San Fernando along Tujunga Wash (lat. 34°16' N, long. 118°23'15" W). Named on San Fernando (1966) 7.5' quadrangle. San Fernando (1953) 7.5' quadrangle shows Hansen Flood Control Basin at the place.

Hapaha Flat [SAN DIEGO]: *area*, 10 miles southwest of Ocotillo Wells (lat. 33°02' N, long. 116°15' W). Named on Harper Canyon (1959) and Whale Peak (1959) 7.5' quadrangles.

Happy Camp [VENTURA]: *locality*, 35 miles north of Moorpark (lat. 34°20'15" N, long. 118°51'55" W; near SE cor. sec. 16, T 3 N, R 19 W). Named on Simi (1951) 7.5' quadrangle.

Happy Camp Canyon [VENTURA]: *canyon*, drained by a stream that flows 10 miles to Arroyo Simi 1 mile east of Moorpark (lat. 34°17'10" N, long. 118°51'40" W; sec. 3, T 2 N, R 19 W); Happy Camp is in the canyon. Named on Simi (1951) 7.5' quadrangle.

Happy Valley [LOS ANGELES]:

(1) *canyon*, 1 mile long, opens into Pine Canyon (1) 14 miles east of Gorman (lat. 34°45'20" N, long. 118°36' W). Named on Burnt Peak (1958) and Neenach School (1965) 7.5' quadrangles.

(2) *district*, 3.5 miles northeast of Los Angels city hall (lat. 34°05'10" N, long. 118°11'50" W). Named on Los Angeles (1953) 7.5' quadrangle.

Harbison Canyon [SAN DIEGO]:

(1) *canyon*, drained by a stream that flows 3 miles to Dehesa Valley 5.5 miles southwest of Alpine (lat. 32°47'45" N, long. 116°50'40" W; sec. 11, T 16 S, R 1 E). Named on Alpine (1955) 7.5' quadrangle. The name commemorates John Harbison, an apiarist who homesteaded in the canyon in 1869 (Stein, p. 57).

(2) *village*, 4 miles west-southwest of Alpine (lat. 32°49' N, long. 116°50' W; mainly in sec. 36, T 15 S, R 1 E); the place is in Harbison Canyon (1). Named on Alpine (1955) 7.5' quadrangle. Postal authorities established Harbison Canyon post office in 1927 and discontinued it in 1936 (Salley, p. 93).

Harbor: see **Delhi** [ORANGE].

Harbor City [LOS ANGELES]: *district*, 4 miles southeast of Torrance city hall in Los Angeles (lat. 33°47'30" N, long. 118°17'45" W). Named on Torrance (1964) 7.5' quadrangle. Postal authorities established Harbor City post office in 1916; the full name of the place is Harbor Industrial City (Salley, p. 93).

Harbor Hills [LOS ANGELES]: *district*, 4.25 miles south-southeast of Torrance city hall (lat. 33°46'50" N, long. 118°18'40" W). Named on Torrance (1964) 7.5' quadrangle.

Harbor Industrial City: see **Harbor City** [LOS ANGELES].

Harbor Island [ORANGE]: *island*, 1200 feet long, 6.5 miles east-southeast of Huntington Beach civic center in Newport Bay (lat. 33°36'40" N, long. 117°54'10" W). Named on Newport Beach (1965) 7.5' quadrangle. Joseph A. Beck created the island in 1926 by adding fill to a sandbar (Meadows, p. 69).

Harbor Island [SAN DIEGO]: *island*, 1.5 miles long, 2.25 miles west-northwest of downtown San Diego in San Diego Bay (lat. 32°43'30' N, long. 117°12' W). Named on Point Loma (1967) 7.5' quadrangle.

Harbor Island East Basin: see **East Basin** [SAN DIEGO].

Harbor Island Reach: see **Newport Bay** [ORANGE].

Harbor Island West Basin: see **West Basin** [SAN DIEGO].

Harbor Lake [LOS ANGELES]: *lake*, crescent shaped, 1.5 miles long, 4.5 miles southeast of Torrance city hall (lat. 33°47'05" N, long. 118°37'35" W). Named on Torrance (1964) 7.5' quadrangle. Called Bixby Slough on Redondo (1896) 15' quadrangle. The old name "Bixby Slough" was for Jotham Bixby, a pioneer landowner; the feature was called Cañada de Palos Verdes in Spanish days (Gudde, 1949, p. 32). It also was called Machado Lake or Lake Machado (Fink, p. 22).

Harbor Side [SAN DIEGO]: *district*, 3 miles northeast of Imperial Beach (lat. 32°36'40" N, long. 117°04'55" W). Named on Imperial Beach (1967) 7.5' quadrangle.

Harding Canyon [ORANGE]: *canyon*, drained by a stream that flows 5.5 miles to Santiago Creek nearly 7 miles northeast of El Toro (lat. 33°42'30" N, long. 117°37'40" W; sec. 29, T 5 S, R 7 W). Named on El Toro (1950) and Santiago Peak (1954) 7.5' quadrangles. The name commemorates Isaac Harding, who homesteaded at the place; Harding sold out to Madame Modjeska in 1898 (Meadows, p. 69). The feature first was called Shrewsbury Canyon for Lewis Shrewsbury, who had an apiary there (Sleeper, 1976. p. 87, 89).

Hardluck Campground [VENTURA]: *locality*, 6.5 miles northeast of McDonald Peak along Piru Creek (lat. 34°41'30" N, long. 118° 51' W; at N line sec. 24, T 7 N, R 19 W). Named on Black Mountain (1958) 7.5' quadrangle.

Hargraves: see **Orange** [ORANGE].

Harmon Barranca [VENTURA]: *gully,* extends for 3 miles from the mouth of Harmon Canyon to Santa Clara River 3.5 miles north of Oxnard (lat. 34°14'45" N, long. 119°11'30" W). Named on Saticoy (1951) 7.5' quadrangle.

Harmon Canyon [VENTURA]: *canyon,* drained by a stream that flows 4.25 miles to the valley of Santa Clara River 2.5 miles west of Saticoy (lat. 34°17'20" N, long. 119°11'50" W). Named on Saticoy (1951) 7.5' quadrangle. The name commemorates Silas Solon Harmon, a Presbyterian minister who farmed at the place in the late 1860's (Ricard).

Harmony Grove [SAN DIEGO]: *locality,* 6.5 miles northeast of Rancho Santa Fe (lat. 33°05'45" N, long. 117°08'05" W; near SW cor. sec. 30, T 12 S, R 2 W). Named on Rancho Santa Fe (1968) 7.5' quadrangle.

Harold [LOS ANGELES]: *locality,* 2.5 miles south of Palmdale along Southern Pacific Railroad (lat. 34°32'40" N, long. 118°06'30" W; sec. 2, T 5 N, R 12 W). Named on Palmdale (1958) 7.5' quadrangle. Postal authorities established Trego post office in 1884, changed the name to Harold in 1890, discontinued it in 1894, reestablished it in 1895, and discontinued it finally in 1901 (Salley, p. 93, 224). United States Board on Geographic Names (1960b, p. 8) rejected the name "Alpine" for the place. Los Angeles County (1935) map shows a feature called Harold Canyon located southwest of Harold (mainly in sec. 10, T 5 N, R 12 W). Postal authorities established Myrtle post office 10 miles east of Harold in 1891, moved it 4 miles east in 1894, discontinued it for a time in 1895, moved it 1.5 miles west in 1899, and discontinued it in 1902 (Salley, p. 149).

Harold Canyon: see **Harold** [LOS ANGELES].

Harold Lake: see **Lake Palmdale** [LOS ANGELES].

Harold Reservoir: see **Lake Palmdale** [LOS ANGELES].

Harper: see **Costa Mesa** [ORANGE].

Harper Canyon [SAN DIEGO]: *canyon,* nearly 3 miles long, opens into lowlands 6.5 miles west-southwest of Ocotillo Wells (lat. 33° 07'20" N, long. 116°14'15" W). Named on Harper Canyon (1959) 7.5' quadrangle. The name commemorates Julius Harper and Amby Harper, brothers who raised cattle in the neighborhood (Stein, p. 57).

Harper Creek [SAN DIEGO]: *stream,* flows 4.5 miles to Green Valley (3) 3.5 miles east-southeast of Cuyamaca Peak (lat. 32° 56' N, long. 116°32'55" W). Named on Cuyamaca Peak (1960) 7.5' quadrangle.

Harper Flat [SAN DIEGO]: *area,* 9 miles southwest of Ocotillo Wells (lat. 32°04'15" N, long. 116°15'30" W). Named on Harper Canyon (1959) and Whale Peak (1959) 7.5' quadrangles.

Harperville: see **Garden Grove** [ORANGE].

Harrisburg: see **Carbondale**, under **Silverado Canyon** [ORANGE].

Harrison Canyon [SAN DIEGO]: *canyon,* drained by a stream that flows 3 miles to Pauma Valley 2.5 miles west-southwest of Boucher Hill (lat. 33°19'15" N, long. 116°58'15" W). Named on Boucher Hill (1948) 7.5' quadrangle. Called Nigger Canyon on Boucher Hill (1950) 7.5' quadrangle. United States Board on Geographic Names (1970c, p. 1-2) gave the alternate names "Negro Canyon" and "Nigger Canyon" for the feature; the name "Harrison Canyon" is for Nathan Harrison, a freed Negro who lived in the neighborhood after the Civil War.

Harrison Park [SAN DIEGO]: *settlement,* 4 miles south-southeast of Julian (lat. 33°01'30" N, long. 116°34'15" W; sec. 21, T 13 S, R 4 E). Named on Julian (1960) 7.5' quadrangle.

Harrow Canyon [LOS ANGELES]: *canyon,* 1 mile long, 1.5 miles north of Glendora city hall (lat. 34°09'25" N, long. 117°51'40" W; sec. 19, T 1 N, R 9 W). Named on Glendora (1953) 7.5' quadrangle.

Hartford [LOS ANGELES]: *locality,* 7 miles west-southwest of present Pomona city hall (lat. 34°00'20" N, long. 117°51'20" W). Named on Pomona (1904) 15' quadrangle. Postal authorities established Hartford post office in 1893 and discontinued it in 1895 (Frickstad, p. 74).

Hartley Hill [SAN DIEGO]: *ridge,* west-trending, 0.5 mile long, 7.5 miles west-southwest of Morena Village (lat. 32°38'30" N, long. 116°37'20" W; at SW cor. sec. 31, T 17 S, R 4 E). Named on Barrett Lake (1960) and Morena Reservoir (1960) 7.5' quadrangles.

Hart's Ranch: see **San Fernando Pass** [LOS ANGELES].

Harvard: see **Mount Harvard** [LOS ANGELES].

Harvard Branch [LOS ANGELES]: *stream,* flows nearly 1 mile to Eaton Canyon 1.5 miles southwest of Mount Wilson (1) (lat. 34° 12'25" N, long. 118°05' W). Named on Mount Wilson (1953) 7.5' quadrangle.

Harvard Observatory Point: see **Mount Wilson** [LOS ANGELES] (1).

Haskell Canyon [LOS ANGELES]: *canyon,* drained by a stream that flows 8.5 miles to Bouquet Canyon 4.25 miles north of Newhall (lat. 34°26'45" N, long. 118°30'40" W; sec. 12, T 4 N, R 16 E). Named on Green Valley (1958), Mint Canyon (1960), and Newhall (1952) 7.5' quadrangles. The name commemorates John Haskell, who bought a ranch in the canyon in 1890 and mined gold there (Robinson, J.W., 1973, p. 19).

Hasley Canyon: see **Halsey Canyon** [LOS ANGELES].

Hasson: see **Chatsworth** [LOS ANGELES].

Hastings Canyon [LOS ANGELES]: *canyon,* 1 mile long, 3 miles south of Mount Wilson (1) (lat. 34°10'50" N, long. 118°04'05" W; sec. 7, 18, T 1 N, R 11 W). Named on Mount Wilson (1953) 7.5' quadrangle.

Hatfield Creek [SAN DIEGO]: *stream,* flows 9 miles to Santa Maria Creek 1 mile north-north east of downtown Ramona (lat. 33°03'30" N, long. 116°51'10" W). Named on Ramona (1955) and Santa Ysabel (1960) 7.5' quadrangles. The name is for a homesteader (Stein, p. 57).

Hauser Canyon [LOS ANGELES]: *canyon,* drained by a stream that flows 2.25 miles to Sierra Pelona Valley 6 miles south of the village of Leona Valley (lat. 34°31'45" N, long. 118°16'35" W; sec. 7, T 5 N, R 13 W). Named on Sleepy Valley (1958) 7.5' quadrangle. Red Rover (1937) 6' quadrangle shows Hauser ranch in the canyon.

Hauser Canyon [SAN DIEGO]: *canyon,* about 5.5 miles long, 4 miles west of Morena Village (lat. 32°40'20" N, long. 116°34'30" W); the feature is along Hauser Creek and Cottonwood Creek (3). Named on Morena Reservoir (1960) 7.5' quadrangle. The name is for a settler who came to the neighborhood soon after the Civil War (Stein, p. 57).

Hauser Creek [SAN DIEGO]: *stream,* flows 4 miles to Cottonwood Creek (3) nearly 4 miles west of Morena Village (lat. 32°40'20" N, long. 116°34' W; at N line sec. 27, T 17 S, R 4 E). Named on Morena Reservoir (1960) 7.5' quadrangle.

Hauser Mountain [SAN DIEGO]: *ridge,* generally northwest-trending, about 4.5 miles long, 2.25 miles south-southwest of Morena Village (lat. 32°38'30" N, long. 116°32' W); the ridge is southwest of Hauser Creek. Named on Morena Reservoir (1960) and Potrero (1960) 7.5' quadrangles.

Hawaiian Gardens [LOS ANGELES]: *town,* 8.5 miles east-northeast of Long Beach city hall (lat. 33°49'45" N, long. 118°04'15" W). Named on Los Alamitos (1964) 7.5' quadrangle. Postal authorities established Hawaiian Gardens post office in 1951 (Salley, p. 94), and the town incorporated in 1964.

Hawk Canyon [SAN DIEGO]: *canyon,* 0.5 mile long, 5 miles west-northwest of Ocotillo Wells (lat. 33°11' N, long. 116°12'15" W; at NW cor. sec. 36, T 11 S, R 7 E). Named on Borrego Mountain (1960) 7.5' quadrangle.

Hawkins: see **Mount Hawkins** [LOS ANGELES]; **South Mount Hawkins** [LOS ANGELES].

Hawthorne [LOS ANGELES]: *city,* 3 miles south of Inglewood city hall (lat. 33°55'05" N, long. 118°21'15" W). Named on Inglewood (1952) and Venice (1964) 7.5' quadrangles. Postal authorities established Hawthorne post office in 1908 (Frickstad, p. 74), and the city incorporated in 1922. Mrs. Laurine H. Woolwine, whose father was a founder of the city, named the place about 1906 for Nathaniel Hawthorne (Gudde, 1949, p. 144).

Hawthorne: see **Camp Hawthorne** [LOS ANGELES].

Hay Canyon [LOS ANGELES]: *canyon,* less than 1 mile long, 6.5 miles north-northwest of Pasadena city hall (lat. 34°13'35" N, long. 118°12'05" W; mainly in sec. 25, T 2 N, R 13 W). Named on Pasadena (1953) 7.5' quadrangle. Los Angeles County (1935) map shows a feature called Sargent Canyon located east of Hay Canyon, between Hay Canyon and Gould Canyon.

Hayden Valley: see **Jewell Valley** [SAN DIEGO].

Hayes [LOS ANGELES]: *locality,* less than 1 mile east of El Monte along Pacific Electric Railroad (lat. 34°04'30" N, long. 118°01'05" W). Named on El Monte (1926) 6' quadrangle.

Haynes Canyon: see **Elderberry Canyon** [LOS ANGELES].

Haypress Reservoir [LOS ANGELES]: *lake,* 950 feet long, 2 miles west-northwest of Avalon on Santa Catalina Island (lat. 33°21'10" N, long. 118°21'40" W). Named on Santa Catalina East (1950) 7.5' quadrangle.

Headlee's: see **Falling Springs** [LOS ANGELES].

Heaton Flat [LOS ANGELES]: *area,* 9 miles northeast of Glendora city hall along San Gabriel River (lat. 34°14'25" N, long. 117°45'35" W). Named on Glendora (1953) 7.5' quadrangle. William Tecumseh Heaton came to the neighborhood in 1891 and settled at Peachtree Flat, which now is called Heaton Flat (Robinson, J.W., 1983, p. 35).

Helix [SAN DIEGO]: *locality,* 8 miles northeast of present National City civic center (lat. 32°44'50" N, long. 117°00'10" W). Named on San Diego (1904) 15' quadrangle. Postal authorities established Helix post office 1885 and changed the name to Spring Valley in 1909 (Salley, p. 95).

Helix: see **Mount Helix** [SAN DIEGO].

Hell Creek [SAN DIEGO]: *stream,* flows 4.5 miles to Paradise Creek (1) 3.25 miles west of Rodriguez Mountain (lat. 33°14'10" N, long. 116°57'35" W; near W line sec. 11, T 11 S, R 1 W). Named on Rodriguez Mountain (1948) 7.5' quadrangle.

Hellers Bend [SAN DIEGO]: *locality,* 4.5 miles south of Fallbrook (lat. 33°19' N, long. 117°14'05" W; sec. 7, T 10 S, R 3 W). Named on Bonsall (1968) 7.5' quadrangle.

Hellhole: see **Lower Hellhole** [SAN DIEGO]; **Upper Hellhole** [SAN DIEGO].

Hellhole Canyon [SAN DIEGO]: *canyon,* drained by a stream that flows 4 miles to lowlands 3.5 miles west-southwest of Borrego Springs (lat. 33°14'35" N, long. 116°25'35" W). Named on Tubb Canyon (1959) 7.5' quadrangle. South Fork branches southwest 1.5 miles above the mouth of the main canyon; it is 2 miles long and is named on Tubb Canyon (1959) 7.5' quadrangle.

Hellhole Flat [SAN DIEGO]: *area,* 5 miles west of Borrego Springs (lat. 33°15'20" N, long. 116°27'40" W). Named on Borrego Palm Canyon (1959) and Tubb Canyon (1959) 7.5' quadrangles.

Hellhole Palms [SAN DIEGO]: *locality*, 4 miles west-southwest of Borrego Springs (lat. 33°14'15" N, long. 116°26'25" W); the place is in Hellhole Canyon. Named on Tubb Canyon (1959) 7.5' quadrangle.

Hemohme: see **Camp Hemohme** [LOS ANGELES].

Henderson Canyon [LOS ANGELES]: *canyon*, drained by a stream that flows 1.5 miles to Verdugo Wash 7.5 miles northwest of Pasadena city hall (lat. 34°12'55" N, long. 118°14'50" W). Named on Burbank (1966) 7.5' quadrangle.

Henderson Canyon [SAN DIEGO]: *canyon*, drained by a stream that flows 3.25 miles to Borrego Valley 4 miles north-northwest of Borrego Springs (lat. 33°18'20" N, long. 116°24'35" W). Named on Borrego Palm Canyon (1959) 7.5' quadrangle. The name commemorates Dave Henderson, a mining engineer in Julian mining district (Stein, p. 58).

Henninger Flats [LOS ANGELES]: *area*, 2.5 miles south-southwest of Mount Wilson (1) (lat. 34°11'35" N, long. 118°05'10" W; at N line sec. 12, T 1 N, R 12 W). Named on Mount Wilson (1953) 7.5' quadrangle. The name recalls William K. Henninger, who built a house at the place in 1884 (Robinson, J.W., 1977, p. 67).

Hen Rock [LOS ANGELES]: *rock*, 4.5 miles north-northwest of Avalon off Santa Catalina Island (lat. 33°24' N, long. 118°22' W). Named on Santa Catalina East (1950) 7.5' quadrangle.

Henry Ridge [LOS ANGELES]: *ridge*, south-trending, 2.25 miles long, 9.5 miles northwest of Santa Monica city hall (lat. 34°06'30" N, long. 118°36'40" W). Named on Topanga (1952) 7.5' quadrangle.

Henshaw: see **Lake Henshaw** [SAN DIEGO].

Heriot Mountain [SAN DIEGO]: *peak*, 2.5 miles east-northeast of Pala (lat. 33°22'40" N, long. 117°02'10" W; near E line sec. 24, T 9 S, R 2 W). Altitude 1766 feet. Named on Pala (1950) and Pechanga (1968) 7.5' quadrangles. Called Hiriart Mtn. on Jahns and Wright's (1951a) map.

Hermon: see **Highland Park** [LOS ANGELES].

Hermosa: see **Hermosa Beach** [LOS ANGELES]; **South Pasadena** [LOS ANGELES].

Hermosa Beach [LOS ANGELES]: *town*, 1.5 miles north-northwest of Redondo Beach city hall (lat. 33°51'45" N, long. 118°23'55" W). Named on Redondo Beach (1951) and Venice (1950) 7.5' quadrangles. Postal authorities established Hermosa Beach post office in 1903 (Frickstad, p. 75), and the town incorporated in 1907. Called Hermosa on California Mining Bureau's (1917a) map.

Hermosillo: see **Hermosillo Station** [LOS ANGELES].

Hermosillo Station [LOS ANGELES]: *locality*, 6.5 miles south-southeast of Inglewood city hall (lat. 33°52'45" N, long. 118°17'50" W). Named on Inglewood (1952) 7.5' quadrangle. Called Hermosillo on Compton (1930) 6' quadrangle.

Herrick Canyon: see **Marek Canyon** [LOS ANGELES].

Heryford Canyon [LOS ANGELES]: *canyon*, 1.25 miles long, 2 miles northeast of Burnt Peak (lat. 34°42' N, long. 118°33' W; sec. 11, 14, T 7 N, R 16 W). Named on Burnt Peak (1958) 7.5' quadrangle.

Hewes Park [ORANGE]: *locality*, 2.25 miles east of present Orange city hall (lat. 33°46'50" N, long. 117°48'35" W). Named on Orange (1964) 7.5' quadrangle. David Hewes planned to build a home at the site as early as 1886, but when the house was not built, the property was open to the public as a park—the place was subdivided in 1928 (Meadows, p. 70).

Hewitt [LOS ANGELES]: *locality*, 3.5 miles east-northeast of Van Nuys along Southern Pacific Railroad (lat. 34°12' N, long. 118°23'25" W). Named on Van Nuys (1953) 7.5' quadrangle.

Hialeah Springs [LOS ANGELES]: *spring*, 9 miles southwest of Newhall (lat. 34°16'40" N, long. 118°37'45" W). Named on Santa Susana (1951) 7.5' quadrangle. Los Angeles County (1935) map has the name "Hi-Lea Canyon" for the canyon that contains Hialeah Springs.

Hiatt Canyon [LOS ANGELES]: *canyon*, drained by a stream that flows 2 miles to Elizabeth Lake Canyon 1.25 miles southwest of the village of Lake Hughes (lat. 34°39'45" N, long. 118°27'20" W; sec. 27, T 7 N, R 15 W). Named on Lake Hughes (1957) 7.5' quadrangle.

Hickey Canyon [ORANGE]: *canyon*, drained by a stream that flows 2.5 miles to Arroyo Trabuco 5 miles southwest of Santiago Peak (lat. 33°39'20" N, long. 117°40' W; near NE cor. sec. 15, T 6 S, R 7 W). Named on Santiago Peak (1954) 7.5' quadrangle. The name commemorates Jim Hickey, who came to the canyon in 1877 and kept bees there (Meadows, p. 70). The feature first was called Weakly Canyon for Labon Weakly, who was a pioneer beekeeper in the mid-1870's; later it was called Rowell Canyon for Edward Rowell, a resident of the place (Sleeper, 1976, p. 165-166).

Hicks Canyon [ORANGE]: *canyon*, drained by a stream that flows 2 miles to lowlands about 7 miles north-northwest of El Toro (lat. 33°43'10" N, long. 117°44' W). Named on El Toro (1968) 7.5' quadrangle. The name is from Jim Hickey, who moved his bees to the canyon in the 1880's (Meadows, p. 70).

Hick's Canyon: see **Rose Canyon** [ORANGE].

Hicks Canyon Wash [ORANGE]: *stream*, flows 2.5 miles from the mouth of Hicks Canyon to Rattlesnake Canyon Wash 5.5 miles east-southeast of Santa Ana city hall (lat. 33°43'35" N, long. 117° 46'15" W). Named on El Toro (1968) and Tustin (1965) 7.5' quadrangles.

Hickson [LOS ANGELES]: *locality*, 2.5 miles southwest of downtown San Fernando along Pacific Electric Railroad (lat. 34°15'25" N, long. 118°28' W). Named on Pacoima (1927) 6' quadrangle.

Hidden Anchorage [SAN DIEGO]: *embayment*, 6.25 miles south-southeast of Point La Jolla along Fiesta Island (lat. 32°46'15" N, long. 117°13'10" W). Named on La Jolla (1967) 7.5' quadrangle.

Hidden Glen [SAN DIEGO]: *valley*, 9 miles southwest of Descanso (lat. 32°46'25" N, long. 116°43'40" W; sec. 13, 24, T 16 S, R 2 E). Named on Viejas Mountain (1960) 7.5' quadrangle.

Hidden Hills [LOS ANGELES]: *town*, northwest of Calabasas (lat. 34°09'45" N, long. 118°39' W). Named on Calabasas (1952, photorevised 1967) 7.5' quadrangle. The town incorporated in 1961.

Hidden Lake [LOS ANGELES]: *lake*, 300 feet long, 2.5 miles northeast of Burnt Peak (lat. 34°42'30" N, long. 118°32'45" W; sec. 11, T 7 N, R 16 W). Named on Burnt Peak (1958) 7.5' quadrangle. Manzana (1938) 6' quadrangle shows an intermittent lake.

Hidden Spring [SAN DIEGO]: *spring*, 11.5 miles north of Borrego Springs (lat. 33°25'20" N, long. 116°23'15" W; near E line sec. 6, T 9 S, R 6 E). Named on Collins Valley (1959) 7.5' quadrangle.

Hidden Springs [LOS ANGELES]: *locality*, 5 miles east of Condor Peak along Mill Creek (lat. 34°19'05" N, long. 118°07'50" W). Named on Condor Peak (1959) 7.5' quadrangle. Los Angeles County (1935) map has the singular form "Hidden Spring" for the name.

Hidden Valley [VENTURA]: *valley*, 2.5 miles south of Newbury Park (lat. 34°08'50" N, long. 118°54'20" W). Named on Newbury Park (1951) 7.5' quadrangle. Called Potrero on Camulos (1903) 30' quadrangle.

Hidden Valley: see **Camp Hidden Valley** [LOS ANGELES].

Hideaway Canyon [LOS ANGELES]: *canyon*, about 1 mile long, 2.5 miles northeast of Burnt Peak (lat. 34°42'15" N, long. 118°32'30" W; sec. 11, 14, T 7 N, R 16 W). Named on Burnt Peak (1958) 7.5' quadrangle.

Hideaway Lake [SAN DIEGO]: *lake*, 700 feet long, 7.5 miles north of Escondido city hall (lat. 33°14' N, long. 117°03'20" W; sec. 11, T 11 S, R 2 W). Named on Valley Center (1968) 7.5' quadrangle.

Hide Park: see **La Playa** [SAN DIEGO].

Higgins Canyon [LOS ANGELES]: *canyon*, 2.5 miles long, 2.5 miles north-northwest of Beverly Hills city hall (lat. 34°06'20" N, long. 118°25' W). Named on Beverly Hills (1950) 7.5' quadrangle.

High Knob Mountain: see **San Marcos Mountains** [SAN DIEGO].

Highland Park [LOS ANGELES]: *district*, 5 miles north-northeast of Los Angeles city hall (lat. 34°06'45" N, long. 118°12' W). Named on Los Angeles (1953) 7.5' quadrangle. Postal authorities established Highland Park post office in 1892 (Salley, p. 97). They established Hermon post office in 1904 and discontinued it in 1916; the name was for the developer of a community that now is in Highland Park (Salley, p. 96).

Highland Park: see **North Highland Park** [LOS ANGELES].

Highland Valley [SAN DIEGO]: *valley*, 5.5 miles southeast of Escondido (lat. 33°04'05" N, long. 117°00'30" W; near S line sec. 5, T 13 S, R 1 W). Named on Escondido (1968) and San Pasqual (1954) 7.5' quadrangles.

Highline Saddle [LOS ANGELES]: *pass*, 6.25 miles north of downtown Sunland on Mendenhall Ridge (lat. 34°21'05" N, long. 118° 19'30" W; at NE cor. sec. 15, T 3 N, R 14 W). Named on Sunland (1966) 7.5' quadrangle.

High Point [SAN DIEGO]: *peak*, 5 miles east-northeast of Boucher Hill (lat. 33°21'50" N, long. 116°50'10" W; sec. 25, T 9 S, R 1 E); the feature is the highest point on Palomar Mountain. Altitude 6140 feet. Named on Palomar Observatory (1949) 7.5' quadrangle. Called Palomar Mountain on Ramona (1903) 30' quadrangle.

Highway Highlands [LOS ANGELES]: *locality*, 4.5 miles northeast of Burbank city hall (lat. 34°14'15" N, long. 118°15'55" W). Named on Burbank (1953) 7.5' quadrangle. Postal authorities established Highway Highlands post office in 1925 and discontinued it in 1954 (Salley, p. 97). Mark S. Collins, one of the promoters of the place, named it in 1923 for its position along a state highway (Gudde, 1949, p. 148).

Hi-Hill: see **Camp Hi-Hill** [LOS ANGELES].

Hi-Lea Canyon: see **Hialeah Springs** [LOS ANGELES].

Hill: see **Sorrento** [SAN DIEGO].

Hillcrest [SAN DIEGO]: *district*, 2 miles north-northeast of downtown San Diego (lat. 32°44'50" N, long. 117°09' W). Named on Point Loma (1967) 7.5' quadrangle.

Hillcrest Canyon [LOS ANGELES]: *canyon*, less than 1 mile long, 2.5 miles east of Burbank city hall (lat. 34°10'40" N, long. 118°15'40" W). Named on Burbank (1953) 7.5' quadrangle.

Hillgrove [LOS ANGELES]: *district*, nearly 5 miles south-southwest of Baldwin Park city hall (lat. 34°01'05" N, long. 117°58'45" W). Named on Baldwin Park (1966) 7.5' quadrangle. On Puente (1927) 6' quadrangle, the name "Hill Grove" applies to a place along a rail line.

Hillsdale [SAN DIEGO]: *locality*, 2.25 miles east-southeast of El Cajon city hall (lat. 32°46'35" N, long. 116°55'35" W). Named on El Cajon (1967) 7.5' quadrangle.

Hills of the Moon Wash [SAN DIEGO]: *stream*, flows 3.25 miles to lowlands along San Felipe Creek 7 miles northwest of Ocotillo Wells (lat. 33°13'15" N, long. 116°12'40" W; sec. 14, T 11 S, R 7 E). Named on Borrego Mountain (1960) 7.5' quadrangle.

Hill Valley [SAN DIEGO]: *valley*, 4 miles west of Manzanita along Campo Creek (lat. 32°40'10" N, long. 116°20'30" W; sec. 26, T 17 S, R 6 E). Named on Live Oak Springs (1959) 7.5' quadrangle.

Hillyer: see **Mount Hillyer** [LOS ANGELES].

Himmel Canyon [SAN DIEGO]: *canyon*, 3.5 miles long, along San Vicente Creek above a point 7 miles east-southeast of Ramona (lat. 33°00'05" N, long. 116°45'25" W). Named on Ramona (1955) and Santa Ysabel (1960) 7.5' quadrangles.

Hines Peak [VENTURA]: *peak*, 12 miles east of Wheeler Springs at the west end of Topatopa Mountains (lat. 34°30'40" N, long. 119° 04'30" W; near SW cor. sec. 15, T 5 N, R 21 W). Altitude 6704 feet. Named on Topatopa Mountains (1943) 7.5' quadrangle. The name is for Colonel J.D. Hines, first superior court judge in Ventura County (Outland, 1969, p. 7).

Hinton: see **Mount Hinton** [SAN DIEGO].

Hipass: see **Tierra del Sol** [SAN DIEGO].

Hipass Station: see **Tierra del Sol** [SAN DIEGO].

Hiriart Mountain: see **Heriot Mountain** [SAN DIEGO].

Hi Vista [LOS ANGELES]: *locality*, 19 miles northeast of Littlerock (lat. 34°44'05" N, long. 117°46'35" W; on S line sec. 36, T 8 N, R 9 W). Named on Hi Vista (1957) 7.5' quadrangle. Mrs. M.R. Card, wife of the developer of the site, named the place in 1930 for the view from there (Gudde, 1949, p. 148).

Hoagland Canyon: see **Stokes Canyon** [LOS ANGELES].

Hoar: see **Mount Hoar**, under **Rincon Mountain** [VENTURA].

Hobart [LOS ANGELES]: *locality*, 3.5 miles southeast of Los Angeles city hall along Atchison, Topeka and Santa Fe Railroad (lat. 34°00'40" N, long. 118°12'10" W). Named on Los Angeles (1953) 7.5' quadrangle. Called Manhattan on Pasadena (1900) 15' quadrangle.

Hobo Canyon [ORANGE]: *canyon*, 1 mile long, opens to the sea 2.25 miles south-southeast of Laguna Beach city hall (lat. 33°31' N, long. 117°45'35" W; sec. 31, T 7 S, R 8 W). Named on Laguna Beach (1965) 7.5' quadrangle.

Hodges: see **Lake Hodges** [SAN DIEGO].

Hoegee Campground [LOS ANGELES]: *locality*, 2 miles southeast of Mount Wilson (1) along Winter Creek (lat. 34°12'25" N, long. 118°01'55" W; near NE cor. sec. 4, T 1 N, R 11 W). Named on Mount Wilson (1966) 7.5' quadrangle. The name recalls Arie Hoegee and his family, founders of Hoegee's Camp, later called Camp Ivy (Robinson, J.W., 1977, p. 134).

Hoegee's Camp: see **Camp Ivy** [LOS ANGELES].

Hog Back [LOS ANGELES]: *relief feature*, 12.5 miles north-northeast of Pomona city hall (lat. 34°13'10" N, long. 117°40' W; sec. 36, T 2 N, R 8 W). Named on Mount Baldy (1954) 7.5' quadrangle. Camp Baldy (1940) 6' quadrangle has the form "Hogback" for the name.

Hogback: see **The Hogback**, under **Mount Harvard** [LOS ANGELES].

Hog Canyon [LOS ANGELES]: *canyon*, 1.25 miles long, opens into lowlands 3.5 miles north-northwest of downtown San Fernando (lat. 34°19'45" N, long. 118°27'50" W; near W line sec. 21, T 3 N, R 15 W). Named on San Fernando (1953) 7.5' quadrangle.

Hog Canyon: see **Tapo Canyon** [VENTURA] (1).

Hog Island [ORANGE]: *island*, 6.5 miles northwest of Huntington Beach civic center in marsh along Anaheim Bay (lat. 33°43'55" N, long. 118°04'20" W). Named on Seal Beach (1965) 7.5' quadrangle.

Holabird: see **San Diego** [SAN DIEGO].

Holcomb Canyon [LOS ANGELES]: *canyon*, drained by a stream that flows 3.5 miles to Big Rock Creek 2 miles south-southeast of Valyermo (lat. 34°25' N, long. 117°50'15" W; sec. 20, T 4 N, R 9 W). Named on Valyermo (1958) 7.5' quadrangle. Los Angeles County (1935) map has the name "Holcomb Creek" for the stream in the canyon.

Holcomb Creek: see **Holcomb Canyon** [LOS ANGELES].

Holcomb Ridge [LOS ANGELES]: *ridge*, west- to west-northwest-trending, 3 miles long, center 1 mile northeast of Valyermo (lat. 34°27'30" N, long. 117°50'30" W). Named on Valyermo (1958) 7.5' quadrangle.

Holcomb Village [SAN DIEGO]: *locality*, 7.5 miles northwest of Warner Springs (lat. 33°21'05" N, long. 116°44'15" W; at E line sec. 35, T 9 S, R 2 E). Named on Warner Springs (1959) 7.5' quadrangle.

Holdansville: see **San Francisquito Canyon** [LOS ANGELES].

Hole-in-the-Wall [VENTURA]: *relief feature*, 7 miles south-southeast of Cobblestone Mountain along Hopper Canyon (lat. 34°30'40" N, long. 118°50'10" W). Named on Cobblestone Mountain (1958) 7.5' quadrangle.

Holiday Lake [LOS ANGELES]: *lake*, 15 miles east of Gorman (lat. 34°47'55" N, long. 118°34'25" W; sec. 9, T 8 N, R 16 W). Named on Neenach School (1965) 7.5' quadrangle.

Holland Summit: see **Tejon Pass** [LOS ANGELES].

Hollenbeck Canyon [SAN DIEGO]: *canyon*, drained by a stream that flows 5 miles to Dulzura Creek 4.25 miles south-southeast of Jamul (lat. 32°39'55" N, long. 116°50'05" W). Named on Dulzura (1972) 7.5' quadrangle.

Hollister Campground [VENTURA]: *locality*, 5 miles southeast of Cobblestone Mountain along Agua Blanca Creek (lat. 34°32'55" N, long. 118°49' W). Named on Cobblestone Mountain (1958) 7.5' quadrangle.

Hollister Valley: see **Thing Valley** [SAN DIEGO].

Hollow Rock: see **Arch Rock** [ORANGE].

Hollydale [LOS ANGELES]: *district*, 4 miles southeast of South Gate city hall (lat. 33°54'55" N, long. 118°09'35" W). Named on South Gate (1952) 7.5' quadrangle. Postal authorities established Hollydale post office in 1926 (Salley, p. 99).

Hollywood [LOS ANGELES]: *district*, 5 miles west-northwest of Los Angeles city hall in Los Angeles (lat. 34°05'30" N, long. 118° 19' W). Named on Hollywood (1953) 7.5' quadrangle. Postal authorities established Hollywood post office in 1897 (Salley, p. 99). Horace H. Wilcox laid out the community in 1886; his wife suggested the name (Gudde, 1969, p. 143). Promoters projected an elaborate townsite called Cahuenga at present Hollywood in 1888, but the older community of Hollywood soon eclipsed it (Hanna, p. 48).

Hollywood: see **Mount Hollywood** [LOS ANGELES]; **North Hollywood** [LOS ANGELES]; **West Hollywood** [LOS ANGELES].

Hollywood Beach [VENTURA]: *settlement*, 3.5 miles southwest of Oxnard along the coast (lat. 34°10'05" N, long. 119°13'50" W). Named on Oxnard (1949) 7.5' quadrangle. The name, given after a movie called *The Sheik* was filmed at the place, was supposed to attract residents (Ricard).

Hollywood by the Sea [VENTURA]: *town*, 3.5 miles southwest of Oxnard along the coast (lat. 34°09'35" N, long. 119°13'25" W). Named on Oxnard (1949) 7.5' quadrangle. The name has the same origin as the name of neighboring Hollywood Beach (Ricard).

Hollywood Lake: see **Hollywood Reservoir** [LOS ANGELES].

Hollywood Reservoir [LOS ANGELES]: *lake*, 0.5 mile long, 7 miles northwest of Los Angeles city hall (lat. 34°07'15" N, long. 118°19'55" W; on S line sec. 34, T 1 N, R 14 W). Named on Burbank (1953) and Hollywood (1953) 7.5' quadrangles. Called Hollywood Lake on Burbank (1926) 6' quadrangle.

Hollywood Riviera [LOS ANGELES]: *district*, 2 miles south-southeast of Redondo Beach city hall (lat. 33°48'45" N, long. 118°22'50" W). Named on Redondo Beach (1951) 7.5' quadrangle.

Hollywood Spa: see **Colegrove** [LOS ANGELES].

Holmes Creek [LOS ANGELES]: *stream*, flows 4 miles to Pallett Creek 2 miles west-northwest of Valyermo (lat. 34°27'10" N, long. 117°53'45" W; sec. 11, T 4 N, R 10 W). Named on Juniper Hills (1959) 7.5' quadrangle. On Los Angeles County (1935) map, present Holmes Creek above its confluence with Cruthers Creek is called East Fork Cruthers Creek.

Holser Canyon [LOS ANGELES-VENTURA]: *canyon*, drained by a stream that heads in Los Angeles County and flows 3.5 miles to Piru Canyon 3 miles northeast of Piru in Ventura County (lat. 34° 26'25" N, long. 118°45'10" W). Named on Piru (1952) and Val Verde (1952) 7.5' quadrangles. The name commemorates a family of landowners in the canyon (Ricard).

Holt Canyon: see **Humphreys** [LOS ANGELES].

Holton [LOS ANGELES]: *locality*, 3.5 miles north-northwest of present Manhattan Beach city hall along Pacific Electric Railroad (lat. 33°56'50" N, long. 118°26'35" W). Named on Venice (1924) 6' quadrangle.

Holton: see **Karl Holton Camp** [LOS ANGELES].

Holy Jim Canyon [ORANGE]: *canyon*, drained by a stream that flows nearly 3 miles to Trabuco Canyon 2.5 miles south-southeast of Santiago Peak (lat. 33°40'35" N, long. 117°31' W; at W line sec. 4, T 6 S, R 6 W). On Santiago Peak (1943) 15' quadrangle, the name applies to the lower part of the canyon and to a northeast branch. The feature was named in jest for James "Cussin' Jim" Smith, who had an apiary in the canyon (Gudde, 1949, p. 151).

Home Junction [LOS ANGELES]: *locality*, 3.25 miles southwest of Beverly Hills city hall along Southern Pacific Railroad (lat. 34°02'05" N, long. 118°26' W). Named on Beverly Hills (1966) 7.5' quadrangle. Beverly Hills (1950) 7.5' quadrangle shows the place along Pacific Electric Railroad. On Santa Monica (1902) 15' quadrangle, a branch rail line to Soldiers Home joins the main line at the site.

Homelands [SAN DIEGO]: *locality*, 5.5 miles west-northwest of Jamul (lat. 32°44'35" N, long. 116°58' W). Named on Jamul Mountains (1955) 7.5' quadrangle.

Home Ranch: see **Ranch House** [SAN DIEGO].

Homestead: see **Campo** [SAN DIEGO].

Honby [LOS ANGELES]: *locality*, 2.25 miles west of Solemint along Southern Pacific Railroad (lat. 34°25'15" N, long. 118°29'40" W; near N line sec. 19, T 4 N, R 15 W). Named on Mint Canyon (1960) 7.5' quadrangle. Los Angeles County (1935) map shows a feature called McCoy Canyon that opens into Solemint Canyon from the northeast 0.5 mile northwest of Honby.

Honda Barranca [VENTURA]: *gully*, extends for 3.5 miles to Beardsley Wash 7 miles south of Santa Paula (lat. 34°15'15" N, long. 119°04'05" W). Named on Santa Paula (1951) 7.5' quadrangle.

Hondo: see **Poor Farm Station** [LOS ANGELES].

Hondo Canyon [LOS ANGELES]: *canyon*, drained by a stream that flows

1.5 miles to Old Topanga Canyon 9 miles northwest of Santa Monica city hall (lat. 34°05'50" N, long. 118°36'55" W; sec. 12, T 1 S, R 17 W). Named on Topanga (1952) 7.5' quadrangle.

Honeybee Campground [LOS ANGELES]: *locality*, 7 miles north-northwest of Sunland in Pacoima Canyon (lat. 34°21'15" N, long. 118°21'10" W; near S line sec. 9, T 3 N, R 14 W). Named on Sunland (1966) 7.5' quadrangle. The place is at the mouth of a feature called Honey Bee Canyon on Los Angels County (1935) map.

Honey Bee Canyon: see **Honeybee Campground** [LOS ANGELES].

Hoover Canyon [SAN DIEGO]: *canyon*, drained by a stream that flows 2.25 miles to Buena Vista Creek 2.25 miles east-northeast of San Felipe (lat. 33°12'50" N, long. 116°33'50" W). Named on Ranchita (1960) 7.5' quadrangle.

Hooverville: see **Eldoradoville Campground** [LOS ANGELES].

Hopper Canyon [VENTURA]: *canyon*, drained by a stream that flows 11 miles to the valley of Santa Clara River 2 miles west of Piru (lat. 34°24'30" N, long. 118°49'40" W; near SW cor. sec. 24, T 4 N, R 19 W); the canyon is east of Hopper Mountain. Named on Cobblestone Mountain (1958) and Piru (1952) 7.5' quadrangles. The name commemorates Ari Hopper, a mountaineer who homesteaded above the canyon (Outland, 1969, p. 27).

Hopper Mountain [VENTURA]: *peak*, 6 miles northwest of Piru (lat. 34°28'40" N, long. 118°51'50" W; near W line sec. 34, T 5 N, R 19 W). Altitude 4524 feet. Named on Piru (1952) 7.5' quadrangle.

Hormiguero [SAN DIEGO]: *locality*, 3.5 miles east-northeast of Pala (lat. 33°23'15" N, long. 117°01'15" W; near S line sec. 18, T 9 S, R 1 W). Named on Pechanga (1949) 7.5' quadrangle.

Horn Canyon [VENTURA]: *canyon*, 2.5 miles long, along Thatcher Creek above a point 4 miles east-northeast of the town of Ojai (lat. 34°27'50" N, long. 119°10'40" W; near SW cor. sec. 34, T 5 N, R 22 W). Named on Ojai (1952) 7.5' quadrangle.

Horno Canyon [SAN DIEGO]: *canyon*, nearly 3 miles long, opens into lowlands along the coast 2 miles south of San Onofre Mountain (lat. 33°20'05" N, long. 117°29'35" W; sec. 3, T 10 S, R 6 W); the canyon is southeast of Horno Hill. Named on Las Pulgas Canyon (1968) 7.5' quadrangle.

Horno Creek [ORANGE]: *stream*, flows 5.5 miles to San Juan Creek 0.5 mile east-southeast of San Juan Capistrano (lat. 33°29'55" N, long. 117°39'15" W; at S line sec. 6, T 8 S, R 7 W). Named on San Juan Capistrano (1968) 7.5' quadrangle. The name is from kilns situated along the stream that were used to make roof tiles and floor tiles for San Juan Capistrano mission—*horno* means "kiln" in Spanish (Meadows, p. 71).

Horno Hill [SAN DIEGO]: *peak*, 3500 feet south of San Onofre Mountain (lat. 33°21'15" N, long. 117°29'30" W; sec. 34, T 9 S, R 6 W). Altitude 1481 feet. Named on Las Pulgas Canyon (1968) 7.5' quadrangle. Berkstresser (p. A-12) listed a feature called Horno Ridge Springs, located 0.5 mile northeast of Horno Hill (lat. 33°21'30" N, long. 117°29' W).

Horno Ridge Springs: see **Horno Hill** [SAN DIEGO].

Horno Summit [SAN DIEGO]: *pass*, 3.5 miles east-northeast of San Onofre Mountain (lat. 33°22'30" N, long. 117°26' W). Named on Las Pulgas Canyon (1968) and Margarita Peak (1968) 7.5' quadrangles.

Horse Camp [LOS ANGELES]: *locality*, 9.5 miles east-southeast of Gorman (lat. 34°43'40" N, long. 118°39'40" W). Named on Liebre (1938) 6' quadrangle.

Horse Camp Canyon [LOS ANGELES]: *canyon*, 4 miles long (the course of the canyon is interrupted by San Andreas rift zone), opens into lowlands 11 miles east of Gorman (lat. 34°46'50" N, long. 118°39'20" W; sec. 14, T 8 N, R 17 W); Horse Camp is in the canyon. Named on La Liebre Ranch (1965) and Liebre Mountain (1958) 7.5' quadrangles.

Horse Canyon [LOS ANGELES]: *canyon*, drained by a stream that flows 2.25 miles to San Gabriel River nearly 8 miles north-northeast of Glendora city hall (lat. 34°13'55" N, long. 117°47'30" W). Named on Glendora (1953) 7.5' quadrangle. East Fork branches southeast 0.5 mile above the mouth of the main canyon; it is nearly 1.5 miles long and is named on Glendora (1953) 7.5' quadrangle.

Horse Canyon [SAN DIEGO]: *canyon*, drained by a stream that flows 4.5 miles to Kitchen Creek 2.25 miles southeast of Buckman Springs (lat. 32°44'55" N, long. 116°27'45" W; near SW cor. sec. 27, T 16 S, R 5 E). Named on Mount Laguna (1960) 7.5' quadrangle.

Horse Canyon Saddle [LOS ANGELES]: *pass*, 5.5 miles north-northeast of Glendora city hall (lat. 34°12'15" N, long. 117°48'30" W; sec. 3, T 1 N, R 9 W). Named on Glendora (1953) 7.5' quadrangle.

Horse Flats [LOS ANGELES]:

(1) *area*, 4 miles northeast of Chatsworth (lat. 34°17'45" N, long. 118°33' W; around SW cor. sec. 34, T 3 N, R 16 W). Named on Oat Mountain (1952) 7.5' quadrangle.

(2) *area*, 3 miles south-southeast of Pacifico Mountain (lat. 34°20'45" N, long. 118°00'30" W). Named on Alder Creek (1941) 6' quadrangle.

Horse Flats Campground [LOS ANGELES]: *locality*, 3 miles south-southeast of Pacifico Mountain (lat. 34°20'35" N, long. 118°00'30" W; near W line sec. 14, T 3 N, R 11 W); the place is at Horse Flats (2). Named on Chilao Flat (1959) 7.5' quadrangle.

Horse Heaven Group Camp [SAN DIEGO]: *locality*, 1.25 miles west-southwest of Monument Peak (lat. 32°53'10" N, long. 116°26'30" W; near N line sec. 11, T 15 S, R 5 E). Named on Monument Peak (1959) 7.5' quadrangle.

Horse Meadow [SAN DIEGO]: *area*, 6 miles northeast of Buckman Springs (lat. 32°50'20" N, long. 116°25'20" W; sec. 25, T 15 S, R 5 E). Named on Mount Laguna (1960) 7.5' quadrangle.

Horseshoe Bend [ORANGE]:

(1) *bend*, 2 miles south of San Juan Hill along Santa Ana River (lat. 33°52'50" N, long. 117°44'15" W). Named on Prado Dam (1967) 7.5' quadrangle.

(2) *locality*, 2.5 miles south-southwest of San Juan Hill along Atchison, Topeka and Santa Fe Railroad (lat. 33°52'50" N, long. 117°44'40" W); the place is near Horseshoe Bend (1). Named on Prado (1941) 7.5' quadrangle.

Horseshoe Bend [SAN DIEGO]: *ridge*, south- to northwest-trending, about 1 mile long, 7 miles west-southwest of Jamul (lat. 32°40'10" N, long. 116°59' W; on N line sec. 28, T 17 S, R 1 W); the ridge has a horseshoe shape. Named on Jamul Mountains (1955) 7.5' quadrangle.

Horsethief Canyon [SAN DIEGO]:

(1) *canyon*, drained by a stream that flows 1.25 miles to Paradise Creek (1) 3.25 miles west-northwest of Rodriguez Mountain (lat. 33°15' N, long. 116°57'20" W; sec. 2, T 11 S, R 1 W). Named on Rodriguez Mountain (1948) 7.5' quadrangle.

(2) *canyon*, drained by a stream that flows 5.5 miles to Pine Valley Creek 7.5 miles south-southwest of Descanso (lat. 32°45'10" N, long. 116°38'55" W; near W line sec. 26, T 16 S, R 3 E). Named on Viejas Mountain (1960) 7.5' quadrangle. Horse thieves hid stolen horses in the canyon in the 1870's and 1880's before taking them to Mexico for sale (Stein, p. 59).

Horse Thief Flat: see **Beartrap Canyon** [LOS ANGELES] (1).

Horsethief Ridge [SAN DIEGO]: *ridge*, generally south-southwest-trending, 4 miles long, 5.5 miles south-southwest of Descanso (lat. 32°46'45" N, long. 116°38'30" W); the ridge is east of Horsethief Canyon (2). Named on Viejas Mountain (1960) 7.5' quadrangle.

Horse Trail Campground [LOS ANGELES]: *locality*, 11.5 miles east-southeast of Gorman (lat. 34°34'15" N, long. 118°39'15" W; sec. 35, T 8 N, R 17 W). Named on Liebre Mountain (1958) 7.5' quadrangle.

Horsetrough Spring [ORANGE]: *spring*, 2.25 miles south of Sierra Peak (lat. 33°49'05" N, long. 117°38'55" W; sec. 18, T 4 S, R 7 W). Named on Black Star Canyon (1967) 7.5' quadrangle.

Hot Spring Canyon [ORANGE]: *canyon*, drained by a stream that flows 7.25 miles to San Juan Creek 10 miles northeast of San Juan Capistrano (lat. 33°35'15" N, long. 117°30'55" W; sec. 4, T 7 S, R 6 W). Named on Alberhill (1954), Cañada Gobernadora (1968), and Santiago Peak (1954) 7.5' quadrangles. Cañada Gobernadora (1968) 7.5' quadrangle shows a hot spring near the mouth of the canyon. Called Bell Canyon on Lake Elsinore (1942) 15' quadrangle, where present Bell Canyon is unnamed.

Hot Springs Canyon [VENTURA]: *canyon*, drained by a stream that flows 5.25 miles to Sespe Creek 2.25 miles north-northwest of Devils Heart Peak (lat. 34°34'35" N, long. 118°59'05" W; at S line sec. 27, T 6 N, R 20 W); the feature called Sespe Hot Springs is in the canyon. Named on Devils Heart Peak (1943) and Topatopa Mountains (1943) 7.5' quadrangles. Called Hot Spring Canyon on Mount Pinos (1903) 30' quadrangle. Tejon (1903) 30' quadrangle has the name "Hot Springs Cr." for the stream in the canyon.

Hot Springs Creek: see **Hot Springs Canyon** [VENTURA].

Hot Springs Mountain [SAN DIEGO]: *ridge*, generally west-northwest-trending, nearly 3 miles long, 4.5 miles east-northeast of Warner Springs (lat. 33°18'30" N, long. 116°34' W). Named on Hot Springs Mountain (1960) 7.5' quadrangle.

Howard Creek [VENTURA]: *stream*, flows 3.5 miles to Sespe Creek 6 miles northeast of Wheeler Springs (lat. 34°33'20" N, long. 119° 12'20" W; near N line sec. 5, T 5 N, R 22 W). Named on Lion Canyon (1943) 7.5' quadrangle. The name commemorates Jeff Howard, a homesteader in the neighborhood in the 1870's (Ricard).

Howard Summit [LOS ANGELES]: *locality*, 4.5 miles southeast of Inglewood along a rail line (lat. 33°55'15" N, long. 118°17'35" W). Named on Redondo (1896) 15' quadrangle. Postal authorities established Howard Summit post office on a small hill (NE quarter sec. 12, T 3 S, R 13 W) in 1892, changed the name to Loma Vista in 1902, and discontinued it in 1904; the name "Howard Summit" was for William W. Howard, first postmaster (Salley, p. 101, 125).

Howe: see **Fallbrook** [SAN DIEGO].

Hual-Cu-Cuish: see **Camp Hual-Cu-Cuish** [SAN DIEGO].

Hubbard Spring [SAN DIEGO]: *spring*, 7 miles south-southeast of Dulzura (lat. 32°37'45" N, long. 116°49' W; near S line sec. 6, T 18 S, R 2 E). Named on Dulzura (1972) 7.5' quadrangle.

Hubbert Lake [SAN DIEGO]: *intermittent lake*, 1850 feet long, 2.5 miles north-northeast of Oceanside (lat. 33°13'35" N, long. 117°21'15" W; on S line sec. 12, T 11 S, R 5 W). Named on San Luis Rey (1968) 7.5' quadrangle. San Luis Rey (1948) 7.5' quadrangle shows a permanent lake.

Hudsons Bay Camp [LOS ANGELES]: *locality,* 8 miles north-northeast of Glendora city hall along San Gabriel River (lat. 34°13'55" N, long. 117°47'30" W). Named on Glendora (1966) 7.5' quadrangle.

Hueneme: see **Port Hueneme** [VENTURA].

Hueneme Point: see **Point Hueneme** [VENTURA].

Huerta de Cuati [LOS ANGELES]: *land grant,* at San Marino. Named on El Monte (1953) and Mount Wilson (1953) 7.5' quadrangles. Victoria Reid received the land in 1830 or 1838, and claimed 128 acres patented in 1859 (Cowan, p. 31; Cowan used the form "Huerta de Coati" for the name).

Hughes: see **Lake Hughes** [LOS ANGELES].

Hughes Canyon [LOS ANGELES]: *canyon,* drained by a stream that flows nearly 3 miles to Santa Clara River 12 miles east of Solemint (lat. 34°26'25" N, long. 118°15'15" W; near SE cor. sec. 8, T 4 N, R 13 W). Named on Acton (1959) and Agua Dulce (1960) 7.5' quadrangles.

Hughes Canyon: see **Price Canyon** [LOS ANGELES].

Hughes Lake [LOS ANGELES]: *lake,* 2000 feet long, at the village of Lake Hughes (lat. 34°40'35" N, long. 118°26'40" W; near SW cor. sec. 23, T 7 N, R 15 W). Named on Lake Hughes (1957) 7.5' quadrangle. G.O. Hughes owned land along the lake (Gudde, 1949, p. 156). The lake is in what was known as Tweedy Canyon as late as 1875; Bill Tweedy and his family lived there for years (Latta, p. 211). Los Angeles County (1935) map shows a place called Judahy Flats located 1.5 miles northwest of Hughes Lake (SW cor. sec. 15, T 7 N, R 15 W).

Hughes Lake: see **Lake Hughes** [LOS ANGELES].

Hulburd Grove [SAN DIEGO]: *locality,* 0.5 mile northwest of Descanso (lat. 32°51'45" N, long. 116°37'15" W). Named on Descanso (1960) and Viejas Mountain (1960) 7.5' quadrangles. The name commemorates Ebenezer Wallace Hulburd, who settled at the place in 1884 (Hanna, p. 143).

Humingbird Creek [LOS ANGELES]: *stream,* flows less than 1 mile to San Dimas Canyon nearly 8 miles northeast of Glendora city hall (lat. 34°12'20" N, long. 117°45'15" W; sec. 6, T 1 N, R 8 W). Named on Glendora (1966) 7.5' quadrangle.

Humphreys [LOS ANGELES]: *locality,* 1 mile east-southeast of Solemint along Southern Pacific Railroad (lat. 34°24'35" N, long. 118°26'25" W; near S line sec. 22, T 4 N, R 15 W). Named on Mint Canyon (1960) 7.5' quadrangle. Los Angeles County (1935) map shows a feature called Holt Canyon that opens into Solemint Canyon from the south at present Humphreys. Lankershim Ranch Land and Water Company's (1888) map shows a place called Kent Sta. located along the railroad between Saugus and Lang, at or near the site of present Humphreys.

Hungry Valley [VENTURA]: *valley,* 8.5 miles north-northeast of McDonald Peak (lat. 34°44'40" N, long. 118°52'30" W). Named on Black Mountain (1958), Frazier Mountain (1958), Lebec (1958), and McDonald Peak (1958) 7.5' quadrangles.

Hungry Valley: see **Lower Hungry Valley**, under **Cañada de Los Alamos** [LOS ANGELES].

Hunt Canyon [LOS ANGELES]: *canyon,* 3.25 miles long, 7.5 miles north-northwest of Pacifico Mountain (lat. 34°29'20" N, long. 118° 03'50" W). Named on Pacifico Mountain (1959) 7.5' quadrangle. Los Angeles County (1935) map has the form "Hunts Cany." for the name.

Hunter Canyon: see **Drinkwater Canyon** [LOS ANGELES].

Huntington: see **Camp Huntington** [LOS ANGELES].

Huntington Beach [ORANGE]: *city,* 10 miles southwest of Santa Ana (lat. 33°39'40" N, long. 117°59'55" W). Named on Los Alamitos (1964), Newport Beach (1965), and Seal Beach (1965) 7.5' quadrangles. Postal authorities established Huntington Beach post office in 1903 (Frickstad, p. 117), and the city incorporated in 1909. Philip Stanton and others laid out a community called Pacific City in 1901 at what was known as Shell Beach; after Henry E. Huntington bought controlling interest in the project in 1902, the town was renamed Huntington Beach (Meadows, p. 72). Meadows listed several stops situated along Pacific Electric Railroad in and near Huntington Beach: Bushard, named for John B. Bushard, a farmer, located 2.25 miles east-northeast of Huntington Beach civic center (p. 31); Cordero, located 3 miles northeast of the civic center (p. 54); Gamewell, located 1.5 miles southeast of the civic center (p. 65); Lambs, located 2.5 miles northeast of the civic center (p. 77); Nimock, located 3.25 miles north-northeast of the civic center (p. 106); Thompsonville, located a little more than 0.5 mile north-northeast of the civic center (p. 134); and Xalisco, located 1.5 miles east of the civic center (p. 140).

Huntington Harbour [ORANGE]:

(1) *water feature,* 5.5 miles northwest of Huntington Beach civic center (lat. 33°43'15" N, long. 118°03'45" W); the feature is inland from Sunset Beach. Named on Seal Beach (1965) 7.5' quadrangle. Seal Beach (1950) 7.5' quadrangle has the name "Sunset Bay" at the place. United States Board on Geographic Names (1978b, p. 4) rejected the names "Anaheim Bay" and "Huntington Harbor" for the feature.

(2) *district,* 5 miles northwest of Huntington Beach civic center (lat. 33°43' N, long. 118°03'15" W); the place is at Huntington Harbour (1). Named on Seal Beach (1965, photorevised 1981) 7.5' quadrangle.

Huntington Park [LOS ANGELES]: *city,* less than 2 miles north-northwest of South Gate city hall (lat. 33°58'45" N, long. 118°13'05" W). Named on South Gate (1952) 7.5' quadrangle. Postal authorities established La Park post office in 1904 and changed the name to Huntington Park in 1906 (Salley, p. 117). The city incorporated in 1906. E.V. Baker laid out the community in 1903 and named it for Henry E. Huntington (Gudde, 1949, p. 157).

Hunts Canyon: see **Hunt Canyon** [LOS ANGELES].

Hutak Canyon [LOS ANGELES]: *canyon,* 1 mile long, 6 miles west of Valyermo (lat. 34°26'15" N, long. 117°57' W; sec. 8, 17, T 4 N, R 10 W). Named on Juniper Hills (1959) 7.5' quadrangle.

Hut Cut Valley: see **Cutca Valley** [SAN DIEGO].

Hutton Peak [VENTURA]: *peak,* 3.25 miles west-northwest of Piru (lat. 34°26' N, long. 118°50'40" W; sec. 14, T 4 N, R 19 W). Altitude 2239 feet. Named on Piru (1952) 7.5' quadrangle.

Hyde Park [LOS ANGELES]: *district,* 2 miles east of Inglewood city hall (lat. 33°57'55" N, long. 118°19'15" W). Named on Inglewood (1952) 7.5' quadrangle. On Inglewood (1964) 7.5' quadrangle, the name applies to a place located 1 mile farther north-northwest. Postal authorities established Hyde Park post office in 1888, changed the name to Hydepark in 1895, changed it back to Hyde Park in 1924, and discontinued the post office in 1969 (Salley, p. 102). Moses L. Wicks laid out a community at the place in 1887 and named it for the owner of a lumber yard there (Gudde, 1949, p. 158).

Hynes: see **Paramount** [LOS ANGELES].

Hyperion [LOS ANGELES]: *locality,* 3 miles north-northwest of present Manhattan Beach city hall along Pacific Electric Railroad (lat. 33°55'35" N, long. 118°25'55" W). Named on Venice (1924) 6' quadrangle.

– I –

Icy Springs [LOS ANGELES]: *spring,* 6.25 miles southeast of Valyermo along Big Rock Creek (lat. 34°22'55" N, long. 117°46'15" W; near N line sec. 1, T 3 N, R 9 W). Named on Valyermo (1958) 7.5' quadrangle.

Idlehour Camp [LOS ANGELES]: *locality,* 1.5 miles southwest of Mount Wilson (1) (lat. 34°12'35" N, long. 118°05' W). Named on Mount Wilson (1953) 7.5' quadrangle. The name recalls Camp Idle Hour, which Emile Gunther started in 1915 in Eaton Canyon (Robinson, J.W., 1977, p. 134). Mount Wilson (1966) 7.5' quadrangle shows a place called Idlehour Campground located about 400 feet farther south.

Idlewood Canyon [LOS ANGELES]: *canyon,* less than 0.5 mile long, 2 miles east of Burbank city hall (lat. 34°10'50" N, long. 118°16'10" W). Named on Burbank (1953) 7.5' quadrangle.

Ikanhoffer Canyon: see **Maple Canyon** [LOS ANGELES] (1).

Imperial Beach [SAN DIEGO]: *town,* 6.5 miles south of National City civic center (lat. 32°34'35" N, long. 117°06'55" W). Named on Imperial Beach (1967) 7.5' quadrangle. Postal authorities established South San Diego post office at the site in 1888 and discontinued it in 1902 (Salley, p. 209). They established Imperial Beach post office in 1909 (Frickstad, p. 151), and the town incorporated in 1956. E.W. Peterson named the town in 1906 to appeal to residents of Imperial Valley, in Imperial County, as a place for their summer homes (Hanna, p. 147).

Imperial Crest [LOS ANGELES]: *locality,* 4 miles southwest of present Whittier city hall (lat. 33°55'35" N, long. 118°04'25" W). Named on Whittier (1949) 7.5' quadrangle. The place includes a crescent-shaped street, and is located off of Imperial Highway.

Inceville [LOS ANGELES]: *locality,* 4 miles west-northwest of present Santa Monica city hall along the coast (lat. 34°02'20" N, long. 118°33'20" W). Named on Topanga Canyon (1928) 6' quadrangle.

Indiana Colony: see **Pasadena** [LOS ANGELES].

Indian Ben Saddle [LOS ANGELES]: *pass,* 2 miles north of Condor Peak (lat. 34°21'10" N, long. 118°12'50" W). Named on Condor Peak (1959) 7.5' quadrangle.

Indian Bill Canyon [LOS ANGELES]: *canyon,* nearly 2 miles long, 6 miles west of Valyermo (lat. 34°26'20" N, long. 117°57'25" W). Named on Juniper Hills (1959) 7.5' quadrangle.

Indian Canyon [LOS ANGELES]:

(1) *canyon,* drained by a stream that flows 3.25 miles to Santa Clara River 10 miles east of Solemint (lat. 34°26'20" N, long. 118°16'40" W; near S line sec. 7, T 4 N, R 13 W). Named on Agua Dulce (1960) 7.5' quadrangle. On Ravenna (1934) 6' quadrangle, the stream in the canyon is called Indian Creek.

(2) *canyon,* drained by a stream that flows 1.25 miles to Lopez Canyon 2.5 miles east-northeast of downtown San Fernando (lat. 34°17'45" N, long. 118°23'55" W; near SE cor. sec. 36, T 3 N, R 15 W). Named on San Fernando (1953) 7.5' quadrangle.

Indian Canyon [SAN DIEGO]: *canyon,* 3.5 miles long, along Indian Creek (1) above a point 9.5 miles northwest of Borrego Springs (lat. 33°22' N, long. 116°28'10" W; near NW cor. sec. 28, T 9 S, R 5 E). Named on Borrego Palm Canyon (1959) 7.5' quadrangle.

Indian Canyon: see **Cougar Canyon** [SAN DIEGO].

Indian Canyon Campground [LOS ANGELES]: *locality,* 11 miles east of Solemint (lat. 34°25'10" N, long. 118°16' W); the place is in present Indian Canyon (1). Named on Ravena (1934, reprinted 1949) 6' quadrangle.

Indian Creek [SAN DIEGO]:

(1) *stream,* flows nearly 6 miles to Coyote Creek 9 miles north-northwest of Borego Springs (lat. 33°22'25" N, long. 116°26'15" W; near E line sec. 22, T 9 S, R 5 E). Named on Borrego Palm Canyon (1959) 7.5' quadrangle.

(2) *stream,* flows nearly 4 miles to Pine Valley Creek 6.25 miles east-southeast of Cuyamaca Peak (lat. 32°53'55" N, long. 116°30'45" W; sec. 6, T 15 S, R 5 E). Named on Cuyamaca Peak (1960) and Monument Peak (1959) 7.5' quadrangles.

Indian Creek: see **Indian Canyon** [LOS ANGELES] (1).

Indian Flats [SAN DIEGO]: *area,* nearly 5 miles north-northwest of Warner Springs (lat. 33°21' N, long. 116°39'40" W; on S line sec. 27, T 9 S, R 3 E). Named on Warner Springs (1959) 7.5' quadrangle.

Indian Gorge [SAN DIEGO]: *canyon,* 1 mile long, nearly 4 miles northwest of Sweeney Pass (lat. 32°52'20" N, long. 116°13'35" W; sec. 12, 14, T 15 S, R 7 E). Named on Sweeney Pass (1959) 7.5' quadrangle.

Indian Head [SAN DIEGO]: *peak,* nearly 5 miles north of El Cajon Mountain (lat. 32°59'05" N, long. 116°48'35" W; sec. 6, T 14 S, R 2 E). Altitude 2355 feet. Named on El Cajon Mountain (1955) 7.5' quadrangle.

Indianhead [SAN DIEGO]: *peak,* 4 miles northwest of Borrego Springs (lat. 33°17'35" N, long. 116°25'45" W). Named on Borrego Palm Canyon (1959) 7.5' quadrangle.

Indian Head Spring [SAN DIEGO]: *spring,* 4.5 miles north of El Cajon Mountain (lat. 32°58'55" N, long. 116°49' W); the spring is nearly 0.5 mile southwest of Indian Head. Named on El Cajon (1939) 15' quadrangle.

Indian Hill [LOS ANGELES]: *relief feature,* 4.5 miles north-northeast of Pomona city hall (lat. 34°06'55" N, long. 117°42'50" W; on W line sec. 3, T 1 S, R 8 W). Named on Ontario (1954) 7.5' quadrangle. The name recalls an Indian rancheria that was the last of its kind in the vicinity; smallpox decimated the Indians in 1892 and 1893 (Anonymous, 1976, p. 2).

Indian Hill [SAN DIEGO]: *hill,* 5 miles south of Sweeney Pass (lat. 32°45'30" N, long. 116°10'20" W; near SE cor. sec. 20, T 16 S, R 8 E). Named on Sweeney Pass (1959) 7.5' quadrangle.

Indian Point [SAN DIEGO]: *promontory,* 2.25 miles south-southeast of downtown San Diego along San Diego Bay (lat. 32°41'25" N, long. 117°08'30" W). Named on Point Loma (1967) 7.5' quadrangle.

Indian Potrero [SAN DIEGO]:

(1) *area,* 5.5 miles northwest of Margarita Peak (lat. 33°30' N, long. 117°27'45" W). Named on Margarita Peak (1968) and Sitton Peak (1954) 7.5' quadrangles.

(2) *area,* nearly 5 miles west-northwest of Monument Peak (lat. 32°55'10" N, long. 116°29'45" W; mainly in sec. 29, T 14 S, R 5 E). Named on Monument Peak (1959) 7.5' quadrangle.

Indian Rock [LOS ANGELES]: *rock,* 2.5 miles east-northeast of Silver Peak, and 600 feet offshore on the north side of Catalina Island (lat. 33°28'05" N, long. 118°31'35" W). Named on Santa Catalina West (1943) 7.5' quadrangle.

Indian Rock Spring [SAN DIEGO]: *spring,* 1.5 miles west-northwest of Escondido city hall (lat. 33°07'55" N, long. 117°06'05" W). Named on Valley Center (1968) 7.5' quadrangle. United States Board on Geographic Names (1990, p. 10) approved the name "Arroyo Poco" for a stream that flows southeast for 1.2 miles to an unnamed stream 0.8 miles north-northeast of Indian Rock Spring in Escondido (lat. 33°08'28" N, long. 117°05'45" W).

Indian Spring [LOS ANGELES]: *spring,* nearly 3 miles east-northeast of the village of Lake Hughes (lat. 34°41'40" N, long. 118°23'40" W; near E line sec. 18, T 7 N, R 14 W). Named on Lake Hughes (1957) 7.5' quadrangle.

Indian Spring: see **Allison Spring**, under **La Mesa** [SAN DIEGO].

Indian Springs [LOS ANGELES]:

(1) *spring,* 5.5 miles north-northwest of Sunland (lat. 34°20'10" N, long. 118°20'05" W; near N line sec. 22, T 3 N, R 14 W). Named on Sunland (1966) 7.5' quadrangle.

(2) *locality,* 5 miles north-northwest of Sunland (lat. 34°19'55" N, long. 118°20' W; sec. 22, T 3 N, R 14 W); the place is 0.5 mile south of Indian Springs (1). Named on Sunland (1953) 7.5' quadrangle. Los Angeles County (1935) map has the form "Indian Spring" for the name.

Indian Springs [SAN DIEGO]: *locality,* 1 mile northwest of Jamul (lat. 32°43'10" N, long. 116°52'50" W; sec. 4, T 17 S, R 1 E). Named on Jamul Mountains (1955) 7.5' quadrangle.

Indian Valley [SAN DIEGO]: *valley,* 3 miles northeast of Sombrero Peak (lat. 32°51'45" N, long. 116°14'45" W). Named on Sombrero Peak (1959) and Sweeney Pass (1959) 7.5' quadrangles. The canyon divides at the head to form North Fork and South Fork; both forks are named on Sombrero Peak (1959) 7.5' quadrangle.

Indian Well: see **Yaqui Well** [SAN DIEGO].

Industry [LOS ANGELES]: *town,* the city hall is 4.5 miles south of Baldwin Park city hall (lat. 34°01'15" N, long. 117°57'20" W). Named on Baldwin Park (1966), El Monte (1966), La Habra (1964), San Dimas (1966), and Yorba Linda (1964) 7.5' quadrangles. Postal authorities established City of Industry post office at the place in 1957 (Salley, p. 44). The town incorporated in 1957 to promote and protect industrial development.

Inglewood [LOS ANGELES]: *city,* 16 miles northwest of Long Beach city hall (lat. 33°57'50" N, long. 118°21'10" W). Named on Inglewood (1952) 7.5' quadrangle. Postal authorities established Inglewood post office in 1895 (Salley, p. 104), and the city incorporated in 1908.

Inglewood Rancho: see **Lennox** [LOS ANGELES].

In-Ko-Pah Mountains [SAN DIEGO]: *range,* extends for about 10 miles southeast from Canebrake Wash to Carrizo Creek; center 9 miles south of Agua Caliente (lat. 32°49' N, long. 116°17' W). Named on Jacumba (1959), Live Oak Springs (1959), Mount Laguna (1960), Sombrero Peak (1959), and Sweeney Pass (1959) 7.5' quadrangles. On Cuyapaipe (1944) 15' quadrangle, the hyphens are omitted from the name.

Inner Pasture [SAN DIEGO]: *valley,* 2.25 miles south-southwest of Agua Caliente Springs (lat. 32°55'20" N, long. 116°19'20" W). Named on Agua Caliente Springs (1959) 7.5' quadrangle.

Inspiration Point [LOS ANGELES]:

(1) *peak,* nearly 3 miles west of Mount Wilson (1) (lat. 34°13'20" N, long. 118°06'35" W; at S line sec. 26, T 2 N, R 12 W). Altitude 4715 feet. Named on Mount Wilson (1953) 7.5' quadrangle.

(2) *promontory,* nearly 5 miles west-northwest of Point Fermin along the coast (lat. 33°44'10" N, long. 118°22'05" W). Named on San Pedro (1964) 7.5' quadrangle.

Inspiration Point [SAN DIEGO]:

(1) *peak,* 8 miles east of Borrego Springs (lat. 33°16'05" N, long. 116°14'15" W; at S line sec. 27, T 10 S, R 7 E). Named on Fonts Point (1959) 7.5' quadrangle.

(2) *relief feature,* 0.5 mile south-southeast of Warner Springs (lat. 33°16'35" N, long. 116°37'35" W). Named on Warner Springs (1959) 7.5' quadrangle.

(3) *relief feature,* 2.5 miles southeast of Julian (lat. 33°03' N, long. 116°34'05" W; near SE cor. sec. 9, T 13 S, R 4 E). Named on Julian (1960) 7.5' quadrangle.

Iredell Canyon [LOS ANGELES]: *canyon,* drained by a stream that flows less than 1 mile to Fryman Canyon 5 miles southeast of Van Nuys (lat. 34°07'55" N, long. 118°23'25" W). Named on Van Nuys (1953) 7.5' quadrangle.

Iron Bound Bay [LOS ANGELES]: *embayment,* 1 mile south-southwest of Silver Peak on the south side of Santa Catalina Island (lat. 33°26'50" N, long. 118°34'25" W). Named on Santa Catalina West (1943) 7.5' quadrangle.

Iron Canyon [LOS ANGELES]:

(1) *canyon,* drained by a stream that flows 4.5 miles to Sand Canyon (2) 2.5 miles east-southeast of Solemint (lat. 34°23'50" N, long. 118°25' W; near SE cor. sec. 26, T 4 N, R 15 W). Name on Agua Dulce (1960) and Mint Canyon (1960) 7.5' quadrangles.

(2) *canyon,* drained by a stream that flows 2 miles to Pacoima Canyon 3 miles north-northwest of Condor Peak (lat. 34°21'45" N, long. 118°14'40" W). Named on Acton (1959) and Condor Peak (1959) 7.5' quadrangles.

Iron Fork [LOS ANGELES]: *stream,* flows 6 miles to San Gabriel River 5.5 miles west of Mount San Antonio (lat. 34°17'45" N, long. 117°44'25" W). Named on Crystal Lake (1958) and Mount San Antonio (1955) 7.5' quadrangles. South Fork enters 5 miles east of Crystal Lake; it is 4.25 miles long and is named on Crystal Lake (1958) 7.5' quadrangle.

Iron Mountain [SAN DIEGO]: *peak,* 8 miles north-northwest of Lakeside (lat. 32°58'15" N, long. 116°57'15" W; sec. 11, T 14 S, R 1 W). Altitude 2696 feet. Named on San Vicente Reservoir (1955) 7.5' quadrangle.

Iron Mountain: see **Magic Mountain** [LOS ANGELES].

Iron Mountain Saddle [LOS ANGELES]: *pass,* 7 miles north-northeast of Sunland (lat. 34°21' N, long. 118°15'30" W). Named on Sunland (1966) 7.5' quadrangle.

Iron Peak [LOS ANGELES]:

(1) *peak,* 1.5 miles north-northwest of Condor Peak (lat. 34°20'55" N, long. 118°13'40" W). Altitude 5635 feet. Named on Condor Peak (1959) 7.5' quadrangle.

(2) *peak,* 4.5 miles southwest of Pacifico Mountain (lat. 34°20'20" N, long. 118°05'25" W). Named on Chalao Flat (1959) 7.5' quadrangle.

(3) *peak,* nearly 4 miles west of Mount San Antonio (lat. 34°17'20" N, long. 117°42'45" W). Altitude 8002 feet. Named on Mount San Antonio (1955) 7.5' quadrangle.

Ironsides [LOS ANGELES]: *locality,* nearly 3 miles southeast of Torrance city hall along Atchison, Topeka and Santa Fe Railroad (lat. 33°48'35" N, long. 118°18'10" W). Named on Torrance (1964) 7.5' quadrangle.

Ironside Spring [SAN DIEGO]: *spring,* 4.5 miles south of San Felipe (lat. 33°08' N, long. 116°35'45" W; sec. 17, T 12 S, R 4 E). Named on Ranchita (1960) 7.5' quadrangle.

Iron Spring [SAN DIEGO]:

(1) *spring,* 10 miles north of Descanso (lat. 32°59'50" N, long. 116° 37'50"

W; sec. 36, T 13 S, R 3 E). Named on Tule Springs (1960) 7.5' quadrangle.

(2) *spring*, 3.5 miles north-northwest of Jacumba (lat. 32°39'50" N, long. 116°13'05" W; sec. 25, T 17 S, R 7 E). Named on Jacumba (1959) 7.5' quadrangle.

Iron Springs Canyon [SAN DIEGO]: *canyon*, drained by a stream that flows nearly 2 miles to San Diego River 4.25 miles south-southwest of Santa Ynez (lat. 32°03' N, long. 116°41'45" W; at S line sec. 8, T 13 S, R 3 E). Named on Santa Ynez (1960) 7.5' quadrangle.

Iron Springs Creek [SAN DIEGO]: *stream*, flows nearly 2 miles to join Fry Creek and form West Fork San Luis Rey River 3.25 miles east of Boucher Hill (lat. 33°20'10" N, long. 116°51'45" W; sec. 3, T 10 S, R 1 E). Named on Boucher Hill (1948) and Palomar Observatory (1949) 7.5' quadrangles.

Iron Trough Canyon [VENTURA]: *canyon*, drained by a stream that flows 1.25 miles to Tripas Canyon nearly 7 miles northwest of Santa Susana Pass (lat. 34°19'55" N, long. 118°43'20" W; sec. 24, T 3 N, R 18 W). Named on Santa Susana (1951) 7.5' quadrangle.

Irvine: [ORANGE]: *city*, 5 miles southeast of Santa Ana city hall (lat. 33°41' N, long. 117°49' W). Named on Tustin (1965, photorevised 1981) 7.5' quadrangle. Postal authorities transferred Irvine post office to the place from present East Irvine in 1965 (Salley, p. 105), and the city incorporated in 1971.

Irvine: see **East Irvine** [ORANGE].

Irvine Lake: see **Santiago Reservoir** [ORANGE].

Irvine Mesa [ORANGE]: *area*, 8 miles north-northeast of El Toro on the ridge between Silverado Canyon and Santiago Creek (lat. 33° 44'30" N, long. 117°39'30" W). Named on El Toro (1968) 7.5' quadrangle.

Irvine Siding [ORANGE]: *locality*, 3.5 miles southeast of Santa Ana city hall along Atchison, Topeka and Santa Fe Railroad (lat. 33° 43' N, long. 117°49' W). Named on Tustin (1965) 7.5' quadrangle. Called Venta on Tustin (1950) 7.5' quadrangle.

Irvings Crest [SAN DIEGO]: *locality*, 8 miles north of Lakeside (lat. 32°58'50" N, long. 116°54'40" W; near SE cor. sec. 6, T 14 S, R 1 E). Named on San Vicente Reservoir (1955) 7.5' quadrangle.

Irwin Canyon: see **Solemint** [LOS ANGELES].

Irwindale [LOS ANGELES]:

(1) *town*, 2 miles northeast of Baldwin Park city hall (lat. 34°06'15" N, long. 117°56' W). Named on Azusa (1966), Baldwin Park (1966), and El Monte (1966) 7.5' quadrangles. Postal authorities established Irwindale post office in 1899 (Frickstad, p. 75), and the town incorporated in 1957. The name commemorates a citrus grower (Gudde, 1969, p. 153).

(2) *locality*, 1.5 miles east-northeast of Baldwin Park city hall along Pacific Electric Railroad (lat. 34°05'30" N, long. 117°56' W; sec. 16, T 1 S, R 10 W). Named on Baldwin Park (1953) 7.5' quadrangle.

Irwindale Siding [LOS ANGELES]: *locality*, 1.5 miles northeast of Baldwin Park city hall along Southern Pacific Railroad (lat. 34°05'50" N, long. 117°56'20" W; sec. 9, T 1 S, R 10 W). Named on Baldwin Park (1966) 7.5' quadrangle.

Isham Creek [SAN DIEGO]: *stream*, flows 3 miles to El Capitan Reservoir 4.5 miles northeast of El Cajon Mountain (lat. 32°57'30" N, long. 116°45'25" W; near E line sec. 15, T 14 S, R 2 E). Named on El Cajon Mountain (1955) and Tule Springs (1960) 7.5' quadrangles.

Isham Spring: see **Sweetwater Spring** [SAN DIEGO].

Isla Hermosa Camp Ground [LOS ANGELES]: *locality*, 2.5 miles south-southeast of Valyermo along Big Rock Creek (lat. 34°24'50" N, long. 117°49'45" W; sec. 21, T 4 N, R 9 W). Named on Valyermo (1940) 6' quadrangle.

Island Chaffee [LOS ANGELES]: *island*, 850 feet long, 3.5 miles southeast of Long Beach city hall, and 4600 feet offshore (lat. 33°44'25" N, long. 118°08'20" W). Named on Long Beach (1964) 7.5' quadrangle. Called Chaffee Island on Long Beach (1964, photorevised 1972) 7.5' quadrangle, but United States Board on Geographic Names (1979b, p. 5) rejected this form of the name; the Board noted that officials of Long Beach named the feature to honor American astronaut Roger B. Chaffee. The island is artificial and is used for oil wells.

Island Freeman [LOS ANGELES]: *island*, 1100 feet long, 2.5 miles southeast of Long Beach city hall, and 1.25 miles offshore (lat. 33° 44'30" N, long. 118°09'40" W). Named on Long Beach (1964) 7.5' quadrangle. Called Freeman Island on Long Beach (1964, photorevised 1972) 7.5' quadrangle, but United States Board on Geographic Names (1979b, p. 6) rejected this form of the name; the Board noted that officials of Long Beach named the feature to honor American astronaut Theodore C. Freeman. The island is artificial and is used for oil wells.

Island Grissom [LOS ANGELES]: *island*, 950 feet long, 1 mile southeast of Long Beach city hall, and 1100 feet offshore (lat. 33° 45'35" N, long. 118°10'50" W). Named on Long Beach (1964) 7.5' quadrangle. Called Grissom Island on Long Beach (1964, photorevised 1972) 7.5' quadrangle, but United States Board on Geographic Names (1979b, p. 6) rejected this form of the name; the Board noted that officials of Long Beach named the feature to honor American Astronaut Virgil I. Grissom. The island is artificial and is used for oil wells.

Island or Peninsula of San Diego [SAN DIEGO]: *land grant*, at Coronado along the west side of San Diego Bay. Named on Imperial Beach (1967) and Point Loma (1967) 7.5' quadrangles. Pedro C. Carrillo, Arch.C. Peachy, and W.H. Aspinwall received the land in 1846 and claimed 4185 acres patented in 1869 (Cowan, p. 74-75).

Island White [LOS ANGELES]: *island*, 950 feet long, 2.25 miles east-southeast of Long Beach city hall, and 0.5 mile offshore (lat. 33°45'10" N, long. 118°09'30" W). Named on Long Beach (1964) 7.5' quadrangle. Called White Island on Long Beach (1964, photorevised 1972) 7.5' quadrangle, but United States Board on Geographic Names (1979b, p. 9) rejected this form of the name; the Board noted that officials of the city of Long Beach named the feature to honor American astronaut Edward H. White. The island is artificial and is used for oil wells.

Islip: see **Mount Islip** [LOS ANGELES].

Islip Canyon [LOS ANGELES]: *canyon*, drained by a stream that flows 1.5 miles to Morris Reservoir 4 miles north of Glendora city hall (lat. 34°11'35" N, long. 117°51'50" W; near N line sec. 7, T 1 N, R 9 W). Named on Azusa (1953) and Glendora (1953) 7.5' quadrangles.

Islip Saddle [LOS ANGELES]: *pass*, 2.5 miles north of Crystal Lake (lat. 34°21'25" N, long. 117°51' W; sec. 8, T 3 N, R 9 W); the pass is 1 mile northwest of Mount Islip. Named on Crystal Lake (1958) 7.5' quadrangle.

Islotes de Santo Tomas: see **Anacapa Island** [VENTURA].

Isthmus: see **The Isthmus** [LOS ANGELES].

Isthmus Cove [LOS ANGELES]: *embayment*, 6 miles northwest of Mount Banning on the north side of Santa Catalina Island (lat. 33°26'35" N, long. 118°29'40" W). Named on Santa Catalina North (1950) 7.5' quadrangle. Isthmus Cove, Fourth of July Cove, and Fishermans Cove together were called Union Bay in Civil War times; Union Bay was used by the vessel that transported troops and supplies to the island (Gleason, p. 17). A feature called Eagle Reef is west of the entrance to Isthmus Cove (United States Coast and Geodetic Survey, p. 108).

Italian Gardens [LOS ANGELES]: *locality*, 4 miles northeast of Mount Banning on the north side of Santa Catalina Island (lat. 33° 24'40" N, long. 118°22'55" W). Named on Santa Catalina North (1950) 7.5' quadrangle.

Iva [LOS ANGELES]: *locality*, 18 miles east of Gorman (lat. 34°46' N, long. 118°31'40" W). Named on Tejon (1903) 30' quadrangle.

Ivanhoe [LOS ANGELES]:

(1) *locality*, 4 miles north-northwest of present Los Angeles city hall (lat. 34°0630" N, long. 118°16'30" W). Named on Santa Monica (1902) 15' quadrangle. Postal authorities established Ivanhoe post office in 1904, changed the name to Sunset Hills in 1908, and discontinued it in 1911 (Salley, p. 105, 216).

(2) *locality*, 4.5 miles north-northwest of present Los Angeles city hall along Pacific Electric Railroad (lat. 34°06'35" N, long. 118°15'45" W). Named on Glendale (1928) 6' quadrangle.

Ivy:[LOS ANGELES]: *locality*, 3 miles south of present Beverly Hills city hall (lat. 34°01'35" N, long. 118°23'15" W). Named on Santa Monica (1902) 15' quadrangle.

Ivy: see **Camp Ivy** [LOS ANGELES].

- J -

Jackass Flat [SAN DIEGO]: *valley*, 12 miles north of Borrego Springs on San Diego-Riverside County line (lat. 33°25'30" N, long. 116°24' W; around NE cor. sec. 1, T 9 S, R 5 E). Named on Collins Valley (1959) 7.5' quadrangle.

Jackson Camp [VENTURA]: *locality*, 3 miles west-northwest of Santa Paula Peak in Santa Paula Canyon (lat. 34°27'45" N, long. 119°03'20" W). Named on Santa Paula Peak (1951) 7.5' quadrangle

Jackson Flat [LOS ANGELES]: *area*, 2.5 miles west of Big Pines (lat. 34°22'50" N, long. 117°44' W; at N line sec. 5, T 3 N, R 8 W). Named on Mescal Creek (1956) 7.5' quadrangle.

Jackson Hill: see **San Nicolas Island** [VENTURA].

Jackson Lake [LOS ANGELES]: *lake*, 0.25 mile long, 2.25 miles west-northwest of Big Pines (lat. 34°23'30" N, long. 117°43'30" W). Named on Mescal Creek (1956) 7.5' quadrangle.

Jacumba [SAN DIEGO]: *village*, 17 miles east of Campo (lat. 32°37'05" N, long. 116°11'20" W; mainly in sec. 8, T 18 S, R 8 E). Named on Jacumba (1959) 7.5' quadrangle. Postal authorities established Jacumba post office in 1915 (Frickstad, p. 151). California Mining Bureau's (1917b) map shows Jacumba Hot Springs near the place. According to Mendenhall (1909, p. 87), the owners of Jacumba Spring provided a bathhouse for users of the water, which was considered medicinal.

Jacumba Hot Springs: see **Jacumba** [SAN DIEGO].

Jacumba Mountains [SAN DIEGO]: *range*, extends for about 10 miles south and southeast from Carrizo Creek to Imperial County; center 18 miles south-southeast of Agua Caliente Springs (lat. 32° 43' N, long. 116°11' W). Named on In-Ko-Pah Gorge (1959), Jacumba (1959), and Sweeney Pass (1959) 7.5' quadrangles.

Jacumba Peak [SAN DIEGO]: *peak,* less than 1 mile north-northwest of Jacumba (lat. 32°37'30" N, long. 116°12' W; on N line sec. 7, T 18 S, R 8 E). Altitude 3363 feet. Named on Jacumba (1959) 7.5' quadrangle.

Jacumba Spring: see **Jacumba** [SAN DIEGO].

Jacumba Valley [SAN DIEGO]: *valley,* at Jacumba (lat. 32°37'30" N, long. 116°10'30" W). Named on Jacumba (1959) 7.5' quadrangle.

Jamacao: see **Jamacha** [SAN DIEGO].

Jamacha [SAN DIEGO]: *locality,* 2.5 miles northwest of Jamul (lat. 32°44'30" N, long. 116°54'35" W). Named on Jamul Mountains (1955) 7.5' quadrangle. Called Jamacho on Cuyamaca (1903) 30' quadrangle. United States Board on Geographic Names (1970c, p. 2) gave the variant names "Jamacho" and "Jamacao" for the place. Postal authorities established Daviston post office 5 miles northwest of Jamul in 1895, changed the name to Jamacha the same year, and discontinued it in 1922 (Salley, p. 56, 106)

Jamacha: see **Jamacho** [SAN DIEGO].

Jamacha Junction [SAN DIEGO]: *locality,* 4 miles west-northwest of Jamul (lat. 32°44'20" N, long. 116°56'30" W); the place is at the west end of Jamacha Valley. Named on Jamul Mountains (1955) 7.5' quadrangle.

Jamacha Valley [SAN DIEGO]: *valley,* 3 miles west-northwest of Jamul along Sweetwater River (lat. 32°44'25" N, long. 116°55'15" W). Named on El Cajon (1967) and Jamul Mountains (1955) 7.5' quadrangles.

Jamacho [SAN DIEGO]: *land grant,* at Sweetwater Reservoir. Named on El Cajon (1967), Jamul Mountains (1955), and National City (1967) 7.5' quadrangles. Apolinaria Lorenzana received the land in 1840 and claimed 8881 acres patented in 1871 (Cowan, p. 41; Cowan used the form "Jamacha" for the name). The name is of Indian origin (Kroeber, p. 44).

Jamacho: see **Jamacha** [SAN DIEGO].

James Canyon: see **Mint Canyon** [LOS ANGELES] (1).

Jamison Spring [ORANGE]: *spring,* 0.5 mile west of Santiago Peak (lat. 33°42'35" N, long. 117°32'45" W; near N line sec. 30, T 5 S, R 6 W). Named on Santiago Peak (1954) 7.5' quadrangle. The name commemorates a miner and hunter who settled near the spring in the 1880's (Meadows, p. 74).

Jamul [SAN DIEGO]:

(1) *land grant,* southeast of Jamul. Named on Dulzura (1972) and Jamul Mountains (1955) 7.5' quadrangles. Pio Pico received the land in 1831 and 1845; heirs of H.S. Burton claimed 8926 acres patented in 1876 (Cowan, p. 41). The name is of Indian origin (Kroeber, p. 44).

(2) *town,* 7 miles southeast of El Cajon (lat. 32°43' N, long. 116°52'30" W). Named on Dulzura (1972) and Jamul Mountains (1955) 7.5' quadrangles. Postal authorities established Janal post office in 1876, moved it 6 miles east in 1880 when they changed the name to Jamul, discontinued it in 1882, reestablished it in 1883, discontinued it in 1884, reestablished it in 1885, and moved it 0.5 mile west in 1937 (Salley, p. 106). They established El Nido post office 8 miles south of Jamul (SW quarter sec. 5, T 18 S, R 1 E) in 1888, moved it 1 mile southeast in 1899, and discontinued it in 1900 (Salley, p. 68).

Jamul: see **North Jamul** [SAN DIEGO].

Jamul Butte [SAN DIEGO]: *peak,* 2.25 miles southeast of Jamul (lat. 32°41'40" N, long. 116°50'40" W). Altitude 1448 feet. Named on Dulzura (1972) 7.5' quadrangle.

Jamul Creek [SAN DIEGO]: *stream,* flows 10 miles to Lower Otay Reservoir 6 miles south of Jamul (lat. 32°37'55" N, long. 116°53'15" W; sec. 4, T 18 S, R 1 E). Named on Dulzura (1972) and Jamul Mountains (1955) 7.5' quadrangles.

Jamul Mountains [SAN DIEGO]: *range,* 3.5 miles south-southwest of Jamul (lat. 32°40' N, long. 116°53'30" W). Named on Dulzura (1972) and Jamul Mountains (1955) 7.5' quadrangles.

Jamul Valley [SAN DIEGO]: *valley,* 6 miles south of Jamul (lat. 32° 37'55" N, long. 116°53' W; sec. 4, T 18 S, R 1 E); the feature is along Jamul Creek. Named on Jamul Mountains (1955) 7.5' quadrangle.

Janal: see **Jamul** [SAN DIEGO] (2); **Otay** [SAN DIEGO] (1).

Japacha Creek [SAN DIEGO]: *stream,* flows nearly 2 miles to Sweetwater River 3 miles southeast of Cuyamaca Peak (lat. 32°54'55" N, long. 116°34'10" W). Named on Cuyamaca Peak (1960) 7.5' quadrangle.

Japacha Peak [SAN DIEGO]: *peak,* 1 mile south-southeast of Cuyamaca Peak (lat. 32°56'05" N, long. 116°36' W). Altitude 5825 feet. Named on Cuyamaca Peak (1960) 7.5' quadrangle.

Japacha Spring [SAN DIEGO]: *spring,* 2 miles southeast of Cuyamaca Peak (lat. 32°55'35" N, long. 116°34'45" W); the spring is 1.25 miles east-southeast of Japacha Peak along a tributary of Japacha Creek. Named on Cuyamaca Peak (1960) 7.5' quadrangle.

Japatul Valley [SAN DIEGO]: *valley,* 6 miles southwest of Descanso (lat. 32°47'30" N, long. 116°40'40" W; mainly in sec. 9, T 16 S, R 3 E). Named on Viejas Mountain (1960) 7.5' quadrangle.

Jardine Canyon [SAN DIEGO]: *canyon,* drained by a stream that flows nearly 4 miles to North Fork San Onofre Canyon 6 miles west-southwest of Margarita Peak (lat. 33°24'20" N, long. 117°29'25" W). Named on Margarita Peak (1968) 7.5' quadrangle.

Jaunita Cove: see **San Juan Cove** [SAN DIEGO].

Javon Canyon [VENTURA]: *canyon,* drained by a stream that flows nearly 3 miles to the sea 1.25 miles northwest of Pitas Point (lat. 34°19'55" N, long. 119°24'05" W; sec. 21, T 3 N, R 24 W). Named on Pitas Point (1950) 7.5' quadrangle. The name is from *jabón,* which means "soap" in Spanish—an abrasive material called rock-soap was produced in the canyon in the 1870's (Gudde, 1949, p. 165).

Jaybird Creek [SAN DIEGO]: *stream,* flows 2 miles to Pauma Valley 3.5 miles west of Boucher Hill (lat. 33°19'35" N, long. 116° 58'40" W). Named on Boucher Hill (1948) 7.5' quadrangle.

Jean: see **Lake Jean** [SAN DIEGO].

Jefferson [LOS ANGELES]: *locality,* 2.25 miles southwest of Los Angeles city hall along Southern Pacific Railroad (lat. 34°01'05" N, long. 118°16'25" W). Named on Hollywood (1966) 7.5' quadrangle.

Jefferson: see **Lennox** [LOS ANGELES].

Jeffrey [LOS ANGELES]: *locality,* 2.5 miles north-northeast of present Los Angeles city hall along Los Angeles Terminal Railroad (lat. 34°05'20" N, long. 118°13'30" W). Named on Pasadena (1900) 15' quadrangle.

Jeffries Canyon [LOS ANGELES]: *canyon,* less than 1 mile long, 3.25 miles northwest of Burbank city hall (lat. 34°13'05" N, long. 118°20'35" W; sec. 27, 33, 34, T 2 N, R 14 W). Named on Burbank (1953) 7.5' quadrangle.

Jeff Valley [SAN DIEGO]: *canyon,* 1 mile long, 5.25 miles east-southeast of Boucher Hill along upper reaches of Cedar Creek (1) (lat. 33°18'20" N, long. 116°50'10" W; sec. 13, T 10 S, R 1 E). Named on Palomar Observatory (1949) 7.5' quadrangle.

Jehemy Beach: see **San Nicolas Island** [VENTURA].

Jennings: see **Lake Jennings** [SAN DIEGO].

Jerusalem: see **El Rio** [VENTURA].

Jesmond Dene [SAN DIEGO]: *locality,* 4 miles north-northwest of Escondido city hall (lat. 33°10'45" N, long. 117°06'30" W; near N line sec. 32, T 11 S, R 2 W). Named on Valley Center (1968) 7.5' quadrangle. Postal authorities established Jesmond Dene post office in 1933 and discontinued it in 1935 (Frickstad, p. 152). Subdividers named the place for part of the city of Newcastle-on-Tyne in England (Stein, p. 63).

Jessee: see **Palomar Mountain** [SAN DIEGO] (2).

Jesus Canyon [LOS ANGELES]: *canyon,* drained by a stream that flows 4 miles to lowlands 4.5 miles north of Big Pines (lat. 34°26'45" N, long. 117°41'35" W; at E line sec. 10, T 4 N, R 8 W). Named on Mescal Creek (1956) 7.5' quadrangle.

Jewell Valley [SAN DIEGO]: *valley,* 2.25 miles south-southeast of Manzanita along Boundary Creek (lat. 32°38'20" N, long. 116°16'30" W). Named on Live Oak Springs (1959) and Tierra del Sol (1959) 7.5' quadrangles. United States Board on Geographic Names (1961b, p. 10) rejected the names "Hayden Valley" and "Jewel Valley" for the place.

Jewfish Point [LOS ANGELES]: *promontory,* 2 miles southeast of Avalon near the southeast end of Santa Catalina Island (lat. 33°19'10" N, long. 118°18'10" W). Named on Santa Catalina East (1950) 7.5' quadrangle.

Jim Green Creek [SAN DIEGO]: *stream,* flows 3 miles to Coleman Creek 2 miles southeast of Santa Ysabel (lat. 33°05'18" N, long. 116°38'40" W; sec. 35, T 12 S, R 3 E). Named on Julian (1960) and Santa Ysabel (1960) 7.5' quadrangles.

Jimmy Campground: see **Little Jimmy Campground** [LOS ANGELES].

Jimmy Spring: see **Little Jimmy Spring** [LOS ANGELES].

Jim Spring [SAN DIEGO]: *spring,* 6.5 miles west-southwest of Borrego Springs (lat. 33°13' N, long. 116°28'40" W; sec. 16, T 11 S, R 5 E). Named on Tubb Canyon (1959) 7.5' quadrangle.

Joaquin Valley: see **Little Joaquin Valley** [ORANGE].

Jofegan [SAN DIEGO]: *locality,* 6.5 miles southwest of Fallbrook along Atchison, Topeka and Santa Fe Railroad on Camp Pendleton Marine Corps Base (lat. 33°18'55" N, long. 117°19'50" W; at SW cor. sec. 8, T 10 S, R 4 W). Named on Morro Hill (1968) 7.5' quadrangle. The place first was a cattle shipping station called Stock Pen; it was enlarged in 1942 to accommodate the needs of the Marine Corps and named for General Joseph Fegan, first commander of the base (Stein, p. 63-64).

John Bird Canyon [LOS ANGELES]: *canyon,* 1 mile long, 4.25 miles west-southwest of Valyermo (lat. 34°25'20" N, long. 117°55'20" W; sec. 21, 22, T 4 N, R 10 W). Named on Juniper Hills (1959) 7.5' quadrangle.

John Brown Peak: see **Mount Lowe** [LOS ANGELES] (1).

John Muirs Peak: see **Muir Peak**, under **Mount Wilson** [LOS ANGELES] (1)

Johnnie Spring [SAN DIEGO]: *spring,* nearly 6 miles west-southwest of Borrego Springs (lat. 33°12'55" N, long. 116°27'45" W; near W line sec. 15, T 11 S, R 5 E). Named on Tubb Canyon (1959) 7.5' quadrangle.

Johns Canyon: see **Agua Dulce Canyon** [LOS ANGELES].

Johnson Canyon [SAN DIEGO]:

(1) *canyon,* drained by a stream that flows 3 miles to San Luis Rey River 5.5 miles north of Warner Springs (lat. 33°21'50" N, long. 116°38'25" W; at S line sec. 23, T 9 S, R 3 E). Named on Beauty Mountain (1960), Bucksnort Mountain (1960), and Warner Springs (1959) 7.5' quadrangles.

(2) *canyon,* drained by a stream that flows 3.5 miles to Otay Valley nearly 7 miles west of Otay Mountain (lat. 32°35'30" N, long. 116° 57'30" W). Named on Otay Mesa (1955) 7.5' quadrangle. The name is for the Johnson

brothers, early ranchers in the region (Stein, p. 64).

Johnson Creek [SAN DIEGO]: *stream,* flows 2.5 miles to Boulder Creek (1) 8.5 miles north-northwest of Descanso (lat. 32°58'10" N, long. 116°40'20" W; sec. 9, T 14 S, R 3 E). Named on Tule Springs (1960) 7.5' quadrangle.

Johnson Ridge: see **Johnston Ridge**, under **Mutau Flat** [VENTURA].

Johnsons Landing [LOS ANGELES]: *locality,* 2.25 miles east-northeast of Silver Peak on the north side of Santa Catalina Island (lat. 33°28'05" N, long. 118°31'50" W). Named on Santa Catalina West (1943) 7.5' quadrangle.

Johnson Summit [LOS ANGELES]: *pass,* 4.25 miles west-southwest of Del Sur on Portal Ridge (lat. 34°39'30" N, long. 118°21'15" W; near NW cor. sec. 34, T 7 N, R 14 W). Named on Del Sur (1958) 7.5' quadrangle.

Johnstone Peak [LOS ANGELES]: *peak,* 4.25 miles east-northeast of Glendora city hall (lat. 34°09'40" N, long. 117°47'45" W; sec. 23, T 1 N, R 9 W). Altitude 3201 feet. Named on Glendora (1953) 7.5' quadrangle. The name commemorates W.A. Johnstone, a conservation leader in California (United States Board on Geographic Names, 1940, p. 23). The feature first was called San Dimas Peak (Robinson, J.W., 1983, p. 125).

Johnston Ridge: see **Mutau Flat** [VENTURA].

Johnstown [SAN DIEGO]: *locality,* 2 miles southeast of Lakeside (lat. 32°50'15" N, long. 116°53'50" W). Named on El Cajon (1967) 7.5' quadrangle.

Jojoba Wash [SAN DIEGO]: *stream,* flows 3.25 miles to end 3.5 miles east-southeast of Sweeney Pass (lat. 32°48'35" N, long. 116° 07'30" W; sec. 2, T 16 S, R 8 E). Named on Sweeney Pass (1959) 7.5' quadrangle.

Jones Canyon [LOS ANGELES]: *canyon,* drained by a stream that flows nearly 2 miles to lowlands 1.25 miles northwest of Acton (lat. 34°28'55" N, long. 118°12'40" W; near S line sec. 26, T 5 N, R 13 W). Named on Acton (1959) 7.5' quadrangle.

Joseph H. Pendleton: see **Camp Joseph H. Pendleton**, under **Camp Pendleton Marine Corps Base** [SAN DIEGO].

Josephine Creek [LOS ANGELES]: *stream,* flows 1.5 miles to Big Tujunga Canyon 3 miles east-southeast of Condor Peak (lat. 34°18'05" N, long. 118°10'20" W); the stream heads near Josephine Peak. Named on Condor Peak (1959) 7.5' quadrangle.

Josephine Mountain: see **Josephine Peak** [LOS ANGELES].

Josephine Peak [LOS ANGELES]: *peak,* 4.5 miles southeast of Condor Peak (lat. 34°17'10" N, long. 118°09'10" W). Altitude 5558 feet. Named on Condor Peak (1959) 7.5' quadrangle. Called Josephine Mt. on Tujunga (1900) 15' quadrangle. Joseph Barlow Lippencott used the peak as a triangulation point and named it for his wife when he was mapping Tujunga quadrangle for United States Geological Survey in 1894 (Robinson, J.W., 1977, p. 154).

Josephine Saddle [LOS ANGELES]: *pass,* nearly 6 miles east-southeast of Condor Peak (lat. 34°16'55" N, long. 118°08' W); the pass is 1 mile east of Josephine Peak. Named on Condor Peak (1959) 7.5' quadrangle.

Josepho: see **Camp Josepho** [LOS ANGELES].

Joy Meadow [SAN DIEGO]: *area,* 5.5 miles north-northeast of Buckman Springs (lat. 32°50'55" N, long. 116°27'30" W; sec. 22, T 15 S, R 5 E). Named on Mount Laguna (1960) 7.5' quadrangle.

Juan Fernandez Spring [VENTURA]: *spring,* nearly 6 miles north-northeast of Piru (lat. 34°29'40" N, long. 118°45'35" W; sec. 27, T 5 N, R 18 W). Named on Piru (1952) 7.5' quadrangle. The name is for Juan Bautista Fernandez and his son (Ricard).

Juan Flat [SAN DIEGO]: *area,* 5.25 miles southeast of Morettis Junction (lat. 33°09'30" N, long. 116°38' W; at W line sec. 1, T 12 S, R 3 E). Named on Warners Ranch (1960) 7.5' quadrangle.

Juaquapin Creek [SAN DIEGO]: *stream,* flows 2.25 miles to Sweetwater River 3 miles southeast of Cuyamaca Peak (lat. 32°54'50" N, long. 116°34'05" W). Named on Cuyamaca Peak (1960) 7.5' quadrangle.

Jubilee: see **Camp Jubilee** [LOS ANGELES].

Juch Canyon [SAN DIEGO]: *canyon,* 1.5 miles long, along Jim Green Creek above a point 2.5 miles east-southeast of Santa Ysabel (lat. 33°05'45" N, long. 116°38' W; near SE cor. sec. 26, T 12 S, R 3 E). Named on Julian (1960) and Santa Ysabel (1960) 7.5' quadrangles.

Judahy Flats: see **Hughes Lake** [LOS ANGELES].

Judson Reservoir [SAN DIEGO]: *lake,* 2150 feet long, 4.5 miles northeast of present Imperial Beach civic center (lat. 32°36'50" N, long. 117°02'55" W). Named on San Ysidro (1953) 7.5' quadrangle.

Julian [SAN DIEGO]: *town,* 28 miles east of Escondido (lat. 33°04'40" N, long. 116°36'05" W; near NE cor. sec. 6, T 13 S, R 4 E). Named on Julian (1960) 7.5' quadrangle. Called Julian City on Hanks' (1886b) map. Postal authorities established Julian post office in 1870 (Frickstad, p. 152). Drury D. Bailey laid out the townsite after discovery of gold nearby and named it for his cousin, M.S. Julian, who was mining recorder at the place; the town was an active mining center from 1870 until 1880 (Stein, p. 64; Tucker and Reed, p. 15). Lewis C. Branson laid out a town about 1 mile east of present Julian in 1870 and called it Branson City (Ellsberg, p. 18). Postal authorities established Branson post office in 1870 and discontinued it the same year (Frickstad, p. 149). Joseph Stancliff started a town 1 mile west of Julian in 1870 and called it Eastwood (Ellsberg, p. 18). Postal authorities established Stonewall post office 7.5 miles south of Julian (sec. 9, T 14 S, R 4 E) in 1873 and discontinued it in 1876; the name was for Stonewall Jackson mine (Salley, p. 213). They established Powells Store post office in 1878 and discontinued it in 1879, when they moved the service to Julian; Joseph L. Powell was the first postmaster (Salley, p. 177). They established McGee's post office 10 miles west of Julian in 1891 and discontinued it in 1893; the name was for Richard W. McGee, first postmaster (Salley, p. 136).

July Harbor: see **Fourth of July Harbor** [LOS ANGELES].

June Wash [SAN DIEGO]: *stream,* flows nearly 7 miles to Vallecito Creek 2.5 miles east-southeast of Agua Caliente Springs (lat. 32° 56'10" N, long. 116°15'30" W; near W line sec. 22, T 14 S, R 7 E). Named on Agua Caliente Springs (1959) and Whale Peak (1959) 7.5' quadrangles.

Juniper Hills [LOS ANGELES]: *locality,* 4.5 miles west of Valyermo (lat. 34°26'40" N, long. 117°56' W; sec. 9, T 4 N, R 10 W). Named on Juniper Hills (1959) 7.5' quadrangle.

Junipero Serra: see **Camp Junipero Serra** [LOS ANGELES].

Jupiter Mountain [LOS ANGELES]: *ridge,* generally west-trending, 3 miles long, 5.25 miles south-southeast of the village of Lake Hughes (lat. 34°36'20" N, long. 118°24'40" W). Named on Green Valley (1958) 7.5' quadrangle.

- K -

Kagel Canyon [LOS ANGELES]: *canyon,* nearly 4 miles long, opens into Little Tujunga Canyon 4 miles west-northwest of Sunland (lat. 34°16'55" N, long. 118°22'20" W). Named on San Fernando (1953) and Sunland (1953) 7.5' quadrangles. The name commemorates Henry Kagel, who claimed land at the mouth of the canyon (Gudde, 1949, p. 170).

Kagel Divide [LOS ANGELES]: *pass,* 5.25 miles northwest of Sunland (lat. 34°19'20" N, long. 118°21'50" W; on N line sec. 29, T 3 N, R 14 W); the pass is at the head of a branch of Kagel Canyon. Named on Sunland (1966) 7.5' quadrangle.

Kagel Mountain [LOS ANGELES]: *peak,* nearly 5 miles northeast of downtown San Fernando (lat. 34°20' N, long. 118°23' W; sec. 19, T 3 N, R 14 W). Named on San Fernando (1966) 7.5' quadrangle.

Kanaka Flat [SAN DIEGO]: *area,* 2 miles north-northwest of Julian (lat. 33°06'25" N, long. 116°37' W; at NE cor. sec. 25, T 12 S, R 3 E). Named on Julian (1960) 7.5' quadrangle.

Kane Canyon: see **Bouquet Canyon** [LOS ANGELES].

Kanoshaz Spur [LOS ANGELES]: *locality,* 6 miles southwest of El Monte city hall along Union Pacific Railroad (lat. 34°00'20" N, long. 118°05'50" W). Named on El Monte (1966) 7.5' quadrangle.

Kanter Canyon [LOS ANGELES]: *canyon,* 2 miles long, 5.25 miles west of Beverly Hills city hall (lat. 34°05' N, long. 118°29'30" W). Named on Beverly Hills (1950) 7.5' quadrangle.

Karl Holton Camp [LOS ANGELES]: *locality,* 4 miles northwest of Sunland in Marek Canyon (lat. 34°18'05" N, long. 118°21'35" W; on W line sec. 33, T 3 N, R 14 W). Named on Sunland (1966) 7.5' quadrangle.

Kashmere Canyon [LOS ANGELES]: *canyon,* drained by a stream that flows nearly 2 miles to lowlands at Acton (lat. 34°28'25" N, long. 118°04'35" W; at E line sec. 35, T 5 N, R 13 W). Named on Acton (1959) 7.5' quadrangle.

Kathryn [ORANGE]: *locality,* 7.25 miles east-southeast of Santa Ana city hall along Atchison, Topeka and Santa Fe Railroad (lat. 33°42'15" N, long., 117°45'10" W). Named on Tustin (1965) 7.5' quadrangle. The name is for Kathryn Helene Irvine, daughter of James Irvine, Jr. (Meadows, p. 75).

Katrina: see **Lake Katrina**, under **Tweedy Lake** [LOS ANGELES].

Kearchoffer Flat [SAN DIEGO]: *area,* 9 miles southwest of Descanso (lat. 32°45'50" N, long. 116°43'25" W; near E line sec. 24, T 16 S, R 2 E). Named on Viejas Mountain (1960) 7.5' quadrangle. United States Board on Geographic Names (1981, p. 2) rejected the name "Sunrise Valley" for the place.

Kearney: see **Camp Kearney** [SAN DIEGO].

Kearney Military Branch: see **Camp Kearney** [SAN DIEGO].

Kearny Mesa [SAN DIEGO]: *area,* 10 miles southeast of Del Mar (lat. 32°52'30" N, long. 117°07'30" W). Named on Del Mar (1967), La Jolla (1967), La Mesa (1967), and Poway (1967) 7.5' quadrangles.

Keeler Flats [LOS ANGELES]: *area,* 4.5 miles east-northeast of Burnt Peak (lat. 34°42'50" N, long. 118°30' W; sec. 7, 8, T 7 N, R 15 W). Named on Burnt Peak (1958) and Lake Hughes (1957) 7.5' quadrangles.

Keith [VENTURA]: *locality,* 3 miles west of Fillmore along Southern Pacific Railroad (lat. 34°23'40" N, long. 118°57'30" W; at S line sec. 27, T 4 N, R 20 W). Named on Fillmore (1951) 7.5' quadrangle. The name is from Keith Spalding, owner of Sespe grant (Ricard).

Kellers Shelter [LOS ANGELES]: *embayment,* just east of Malibu Point along the coast (lat. 34°02'10" N, long. 118°40'30" W). Named on Malibu Beach (1951) 7.5' quadrangle. The name commemorates Mathew Keller, first American owner of the feature (Femling, p. 65).

Kelly: see **Mount Kelly** [SAN DIEGO].

Kelly Creek [SAN DIEGO]: *stream,* flows nearly 3 miles to Cedar Creek (2) 7 miles west-northwest of Cuyamaca Peak (lat. 32°59'45" N, long. 116°42'35" W; sec. 31, T 13 S, R 3 E). Named on Tule Springs (1960) 7.5' quadrangle.

Kelp Point [LOS ANGELES]: *promontory,* 2.25 miles southeast of Silver Peak on the south side of Santa Catalina Island (lat. 33° 26' N, long. 118°32'30" W). Named on Santa Catalina West (1943) 7.5' quadrangle.

Kemp: see **Castaic** [LOS ANGELES].

Kennedy Canyon [VENTURA]: *canyon,* drained by a stream that flows 2 miles to Ventura River 3.25 miles west-northwest of Ojai (lat. 34°28'25" N, long. 119°17'25" W; sec. 33, T 5 N, R 23 W). Named on Matilija (1952) 7.5' quadrangle. The name commemorates John Logan Kennedy, who came to Ventura in 1872 (Ricard).

Kent Station: see **Humphreys** [LOS ANGELES].

Kentucky Springs [LOS ANGELES]: *springs,* 6 miles northwest of Pacifico Mountain (lat. 34°26'45" N, long. 118°06'30" W; sec. 11, T 4 N, R 12 W). Named on Pacifico Mountain (1959) 7.5' quadrangle. On Tujunga (1900) 15' quadrangle, the name applies to a locality near the site of the springs.

Kentucky Springs Canyon [LOS ANGELES]: *canyon,* drained by a stream that flows 7 miles to Soledad Canyon 3.25 miles east-northeast of Acton (lat. 34°28'50" N, long. 118°08'30" W; near S line sec. 28, T 5 N, R 12 W); Kentucky Springs are in the canyon. Named on Acton (1959) and Pacifico Mountain (1959) 7.5' quadrangles.

Kentwood-In-The-Pines [SAN DIEGO]: *settlement,* 1.5 miles east-southeast of Julian (lat. 33°04'20" N, long. 116°34'30" W; sec. 4, T 13 S, R 4 E). Named on Julian (1960) 7.5' quadrangle. Santa Ysabel (1943) 15' quadrangle omits hyphens from the name.

Kenyon Cove [SAN DIEGO]: *relief feature,* nearly 9 miles south of Borrego Springs (lat. 33°07'50" N, long. 116°24'15" W). Named on Tubb Canyon (1959) 7.5' quadrangle.

Keril Canyon [LOS ANGELES]: *canyon,* drained by a stream that flows less than 1 mile to Big Dalton Canyon 4 miles northeast of Glendora city hall (lat. 34°10'10" N, long. 117°48'30" W; sec. 15, T 1 N, R 9 W). Named on Glendora (1953) 7.5' quadrangle.

Kerkhoff Canyon [LOS ANGELES]: *canyon,* drained by a stream that heads in San Bernardino County and flows 2 miles to San Antonio Canyon 13 miles north-northeast of Pomona city hall in Los Angeles County (lat. 34°13'35" N, long. 117°39'55" W; sec. 25, T 2 N, R 8 W). Named on Mount Baldy (1954) 7.5' quadrangle. Present Barrett Canyon is called Kerkhoff Canyon on Camp Baldy (1940) 6' quadrangle.

Kessler Flat [SAN DIEGO]: *area,* 6 miles south of Santa Ysabel (lat. 33°01'15" N, long. 116°41'15" W; at SE cor. sec. 20, T 13 S, R 3 E). Named on Santa Ysabel (1960) 7.5' quadrangle.

Kester [LOS ANGELES]: *locality,* 1.5 miles east-southeast of Van Nuys along Southern Pacific Railroad (lat. 34°10'25" N, long. 118° 25'20" W). Named on Van Nuys (1926) 6' quadrangle.

Kester Canyon: see **Sharps Canyon** [LOS ANGELES-VENTURA].

Kesters Camp [VENTURA]: *locality,* 7.5 miles southeast of Cobblestone Mountain near the mouth of Agua Blanca Creek (lat. 34°32'30" N, long. 118°45'50" W; near SE cor. sec. 4, T 5 N, R 18 W). Named on Cobblestone Mountain (1958) 7.5' quadrangle.

Kevet [VENTURA]: *locality,* 1.25 miles east-northeast of downtown Santa Paula along Southern Pacific Railroad (lat. 34°21'45" N, long. 119°02'15" W; at N line sec. 12, T 3 N, R 21 W). Named on Santa Paula (1951) 7.5' quadrangle. California Mining Bureau's (1917a) map shows a place called Carmicle located about 1.5 miles north-northeast of Kevet along the railroad.

Kewen Lake [LOS ANGELES]: *lake,* 1100 feet long, 6.25 miles west-northwest of present El Monte city hall (lat. 34°07' N, long. 118°07'30" W). Named on Pasadena (1900) 15' quadrangle.

Keys Canyon [SAN DIEGO]: *canyon,* 3.25 miles long, along Keys Creek below a point 5.25 miles south-southwest of Pala (lat. 33°17'30" N, long. 117°06'10" W). Named on Bonsall (1968) and Pala (1968) 7.5' quadrangles.

Keys Creek [SAN DIEGO]: *stream,* flows 12 miles to San Luis Rey River 6.5 miles southeast of Fallbrook (lat. 33°19'05" N, long. 117° 09'50" W). Named on Pala (1968) 7.5' quadrangle.

Keystone [LOS ANGELES]: *district,* 3.5 miles east of Torrance city hall (lat. 33°49'40" N, long. 118°16'35" W). Named on Torrance (1964) 7.5' quadrangle.

Kimball [VENTURA]: *locality,* 3 miles southwest of Saticoy along Southern Pacific Railroad (lat. 34°15'20" N, long. 119°11'15" W). Named on Saticoy (1951) 7.5' quadrangle.

Kimball Valley [SAN DIEGO]: *valley,* 7.25 miles north of Lakeside along San Vicente Creek (lat. 32°57'50" N, long. 116°53'45" W; sec. 8, T 14 S, R 1 E). Named on San Vicente Reservoir (1955) 7.5' quadrangle.

Kimbrough Canyon [LOS ANGELES]: *canyon,* drained by a stream that flows 1 mile to Oakdale Canyon (1) 4.25 miles north-northwest of Burnt Peak (lat. 34°44'10" N, long. 118°37' W; sec. 31, T 8 N, R 16 W). Named on Burnt Peak (1958) and Liebre Mountain (1958) 7.5' quadrangles.

Kincaid [LOS ANGELES]: *locality,* 1.5 miles west-southwest of Azusa city hall along Atchison, Topeka and Santa Fe Railroad (lat. 34°07'45" N, long. 117°55'45" W; at E line sec. 33, T 1 N, R 10 W). Named on Azusa (1953) 7.5' quadrangle.

Kincaid Cabin [VENTURA]: *locality,* 14 miles east-northeast of Reyes Peak along Piru Creek (lat. 34°40'25" N, long. 119°02'10" W; sec. 30, T 7 N, R 20 W). Named on Lockwood Valley (1943) 7.5' quadrangle.

Kineloa Canyon: see **Pasadena Glen** [LOS ANGELES].

King Creek [SAN DIEGO]: *stream,* flows 10 miles to Conejos Creek nearly 7 miles west-northwest of Descanso (lat. 32°53'55" N, long. 116°43'05" W; at W line sec. 6, T 15 S, R 3 E). Named on Cuyamaca Peak (1960) and Tule Springs (1960) 7.5' quadrangles. West Fork enters 3.25 miles north-northwest of Descanso; it is nearly 3 miles long and is named on Cuyamaca Peak (1960) and Tule Springs (1960) 7.5' quadrangles. Everhart's (1951) map shows present West Fork as the main stream.

King Harbor [LOS ANGELES]: *water feature,* 0.5 mile west of Redondo Beach city hall along the coast (lat. 33°50'45" N, long. 118°23'45" W). Named on Redondo Beach (1963) 7.5' quadrangle.

Kings Campground [VENTURA]: *locality,* 5.5 miles north of McDonald Peak (lat. 34°43' N, long. 118°55'40" W; sec. 7, T 7 N, R 19 W). Named on McDonald Peak (1958) 7.5' quadrangle.

Kings Canyon [LOS ANGELES]: *canyon,* drained by a stream that flows 4.25 miles to lowlands 4.5 miles northwest of the village of Lake Hughes (lat. 34°43'50" N, long. 118°29'15" W; near N line sec. 5, T 7 N, R 15 W). Named on Burnt Peak (1958) and Lake Hughes (1957) 7.5' quadrangles.

Kingsley Canyon: see **Necktie Canyon** [LOS ANGELES].

Kinneyloa: see **Mount Kinneyloa**, under **Mount Wilson** [LOS ANGELES] (1).

Kirby Canyon [LOS ANGELES]: *canyon,* 0.5 miles long, 4.5 miles west-northwest of Pasadena city hall (lat. 34°10'20" N, long. 118° 13'10" W). Named on Pasadena (1953) 7.5' quadrangle.

Kitchen Creek [SAN DIEGO]: *stream,* flows nearly 8 miles to Cottonwood Creek (3) 9 miles north of Campo (lat. 32°44' N, long. 116°29'15" W; at NE cor. sec. 5, T 17 S, R 5 E); the stream goes through Kitchen Valley. Named on Cameron Corners (1959) and Mount Laguna (1960) 7.5' quadrangles.

Kitchen Valley [SAN DIEGO]: *valley,* 3.5 miles northeast of Buckman Springs (lat. 32°48'45" N, long. 116°27'15" W; mainly in sec. 3, T 16 S, R 5 E). Named on Mount Laguna (1960) 7.5' quadrangle. The misspelled name is for Augustus Caesar Kitching, an early rancher in the neighborhood (Stein, p. 65).

Kitter Canyon [LOS ANGELES]: *canyon,* drained by a stream that flows 2.5 miles to Little Rock Creek 4.5 miles north-northeast of Pacifico Mountain (lat. 34°26'40" N, long. 118°00'35" W). Named on Pacifico Mountain (1959) 7.5' quadrangle.

Klauber Park: see **Encanto** [SAN DIEGO].

Kleine Canyon [LOS ANGELES]: *canyon,* drained by a stream that flows nearly 2 miles to Elizabeth Lake Canyon 2 miles north-northeast of Warm Springs Mountain (lat. 34°37'20" N, long. 118° 33'20" W). Named on Burnt Peak (1958) and Warm Springs Mountain (1958) 7.5' quadrangles.

Klondike Canyon [LOS ANGELES]: *canyon,* 1 mile long, 4.5 miles northwest of Point Fermin (lat. 33°44'40" N, long. 118°21'10" W). Named on San Pedro (1964) 7.5' quadrangle.

Klondike Creek [SAN DIEGO]: *stream,* flows 2.5 miles to San Vicente Creek 5.5 miles north-northwest of El Cajon Mountain (lat. 33°59'35" N, long. 116°50'45" W). Named on El Cajon Mountain (1955) 7.5' quadrangle.

Kohler Canyon [SAN DIEGO]: *canyon,* drained by a stream that flows nearly 3 miles to Temecula Creek 8.5 miles east-northeast of Boucher Hill (lat. 33°22'30" N, long. 116°46'30" W; sec. 21, T 9 S, R 2 E). Named on Palomar Observatory (1949) 7.5' quadrangle.

Kole: see **Camp Kole** [LOS ANGELES].

Kratka Ridge [LOS ANGELES]: *ridge,* generally southwest- to west-trending, 2.5 miles long, 3 miles east-northeast of Waterman Mountain (lat. 34°21' N, long. 117°53' W). Named on Waterman Mountain (1959) 7.5' quadrangle.

Krotona Hill [VENTURA]: *ridge,* west-northwest-trending, 1.25 miles long, 2 miles west-southwest of downtown Ojai (lat. 34°26'15" N, long. 119°16'25" W). Named on Matilija (1952) 7.5' quadrangle. The name is from a Theosophical colony called Krotona that Albert P. Warrington founded in 1911 and moved to the place in 1924 (Hine, p. 57).

Krueger Canyon: see **Cougar Canyon** [SAN DIEGO].

Krum Reservoir [ORANGE]: *water feature,* 1.5 miles southeast of San Juan Capistrano (lat. 33°29'05" N, long. 117°38'40" W; near SE cor. sec. 7, T 8 S, R 7 W). Named on Dana Point (1968) 7.5' quadrangle.

Kumpahui Creek [SAN DIEGO]: *stream,* flows 1.5 miles to Lake Henshaw 1.5 miles west-northwest of Morettis Junction (lat. 33°12'35" N, long. 116°43'50" W). Named on Warners Ranch (1960) 7.5' quadrangle.

- L -

La Ballona: see **Ballona** [LOS ANGELES].

La Bolsa [ORANGE]: *locality,* less than 2 miles north of present Huntington Beach civic center along Southern Pacific Railroad (lat. 33°41'10" N, long. 117°59'50" W; at N line sec. 2, T 6 S, R 11 W); the place is on Las Bolsas grant. Named on Newport Beach (1951) 7.5' quadrangle.

La Bolsa Chica [ORANGE]: *land grant,* inland from Sunset Beach. Named on Los Alamitos (1950), Newport Beach (1951), and Seal Beach (1950) 7.5' quadrangles. Joaquin Ruiz received 2 leagues in 1841 and claimed 8107 acres patented in 1874 (Cowan, p. 19).

La Brea [LOS ANGELES]: *land grant,* southwest of Hollywood. Named on Beverly Hills (1950) and Hollywood (1953) 7.5' quadrangles. Jose Antonio Bocha received 1 league in 1828 and claimed 4439 acres patented in 1873 (Cowan, p. 20).

La Brea Canyon: see **Brea Canyon** [LOS ANGELES-ORANGE]; **Tonner Canyon** [LOS ANGELES-ORANGE].

La Broche Canyon [VENTURA]: *canyon,* drained by a stream that flows 1.5 miles to Santa Paula Canyon 4.25 miles west of Santa Paula Peak (lat. 34°26'40" N, long. 119°05' W). Named on Santa Paula Peak (1951) 7.5' quadrangle.

La Brun [LOS ANGELES]: *locality,* 8.5 miles south-southwest of the present village of Lake Hughes in San Francisquito Canyon (lat. 34°33'30" N, long. 118°29'15" W; near N line sec. 6, T 5 N, R 15 W). Named on Elizabeth Lake (1917) 30' quadrangle.

La Cañada [LOS ANGELES]:

(1) *land grant,* north of Verdugo Mountains and San Rafael Hills at La Cañada and La Crescenta. Named on Burbank (1953), Pasadena (1953), and Sunland (1953) 7.5' quadrangles. Ignacio Coronel received 2 leagues in 1843; J.R. Scott and others claimed 5832 acres patented in 1866 (Cowan, p. 23).

(2) *town,* 5 miles northwest of Pasadena city hall (lat. 34°12'15" N, long. 118°12' W); the town is on La Cañada grant. Named on Pasadena (1953) 7.5' quadrangle. Postal authorities established La Canada post office in 1884 and discontinued it for a time in 1888 (Frickstad, p. 75). La Cañada and nearby Flintridge incorporated in 1976 with the name "La Cañada Flintridge." United States Board on Geographic Names (1979b, p. 7) rejected both the names "La Canada" and "Flintridge" for the newly incorporated community.

La Cañada del Violin: see **Violin Canyon** [LOS ANGELES].

La Cañada Flintridge: see **La Cañada** [LOS ANGELES] (2).

La Cañada Verde Creek [LOS ANGELES-ORANGE]: *stream,* heads in Los Angeles County and flows 9.5 miles to Coyote Creek 12 miles northeast of Long Beach city hall just inside Orange County.(lat. 33°52'05" N, long. 118°01'55" W; sec. 33, T 3 S, R 11 W). Named on La Habra (1952) and Los Alamitos (1964) 7.5' quadrangles. The stream is called West Fork [of Coyote Creek] on Los Alamitos (1950) 7.5' quadrangle.

La Cañon de Los Murtes: see **Bouquet Canyon** [LOS ANGELES].

Lachusa Canyon [LOS ANGELES]: *canyon,* drained by a stream that flows nearly 3 miles to the sea 5.5 miles west-northwest of Point Dume (lat. 34°02'20" N, long. 118°53'40" W). Named on Triunfo Pass (1950) 7.5' quadrangle. Called Lechuza Canyon on Camulos (1903) 30' quadrangle

Lachusa Point: see **Lechuza Point** [LOS ANGELES].

La Cienaga [SAN DIEGO]: *spring,* 6 miles west-northwest of Borrego Springs (lat. 33°12'35" N, long. 116°27'55" W; at NE cor. sec. 21, T 11 S, R 5 E). Named on Tubb Canyon (1959) 7.5' quadrangle.

La Cienega: see **Falling Springs** [LOS ANGELES].

Lacosca Creek [VENTURA]: *stream,* flows nearly 3 miles to Agua Blanca Creek 5 miles southeast of Cobblestone Mountain (lat. 34° 32'50" N, long. 118°48'55" W). Named on Cobblestone Mountain (1958) 7.5' quadrangle.

Lacosta: see **Ponto** [SAN DIEGO].

La Costa Beach [LOS ANGELES]: *beach,* 2.25 miles east-northeast of Malibu Point (lat. 34°02'15" N, long. 118°38'30" W). Named on Malibu Beach (1951) 7.5' quadrangle.

La Crescenta [LOS ANGELES]: *town,* 7.5 miles northwest of Pasadena city hall (lat. 34°05'55" N, long. 118°14'20" W). Named on Pasadena (1953) 7.5' quadrangle. Postal authorities established La Crescenta post office in 1888 (Frickstad, p. 75). Dr. Benjamin Briggs is said to have named the community for the crescent shape of the alluvial fans that he could see from his home at the place (Hanna, p. 76).

La Cresta [SAN DIEGO]: *locality,* 6 miles west-southwest of Alpine (lat. 32°48'45" N, long. 116°51'45" W; mainly in sec. 3, T 16 S, R 1 E). Named on Alpine (1955) 7.5' quadrangle.

La Cross: see **Lacrosse** [VENTURA].

Lacrosse [VENTURA]: *locality,* 7 miles north of Ventura along Southern Pacific Railroad (lat. 34°22'35" N, long. 119°18'25" W). Named on Ventura (1904) 15' quadrangle. California Division of Highways' (1934) map has the form "La Cross" for the name.

Ladd Canyon [ORANGE]: *canyon,* drained by a stream that flows 5 miles to Silverado Canyon 9 miles north-northeast of El Toro (lat. 33°44'55" N, long. 117°38'20" W); Mustang Spring in on the side of the canyon. Named on Black Star Canyon (1967), Corona South (1967), and El Toro (1968) 7.5' quadrangles. Present Ladd Canyon was called Mustang Spring Canyon before H.C. Ladd settled there in 1872 (Meadows, p. 76, 103). East Fork branches northeast 2 miles south of Pleasants Peak; it heads in Riverside County, is 2 miles long, and is named on Corona South (1967) 7.5' quadrangle. West Fork branches north 2.5 miles south-southwest of Pleasants Peak; it is 2.5 miles long and is named on Corona South (1967) 7.5' quadrangle. On Corona (1942) 15' quadrangle, Ladd Canyon divides at the head to form East Fork and West Fork.

Ladrillo [SAN DIEGO]: *locality,* 3.5 miles southeast of present Point La Jolla along Atchison, Topeka and Santa Fe Railroad (lat. 32°49'10" N, long. 117°13'40" W). Named on La Jolla (1903) 15' quadrangle.

Ladybug Canyon [LOS ANGELES]: *canyon,* drained by a stream that flows 1.25 miles to Arroyo Seco 9.5 miles south-southwest of Pacifico Mountain (lat. 34°15'40" N, long. 118°07' W). Named on Chilao Flat (1959) 7.5' quadrangle.

Ladybug Creek [VENTURA]: *stream,* flows 2.25 miles to Sespe Creek 6.25 miles north-northwest of Wheeler Springs (lat. 34°35'45" N, long. 119°19'45" W; sec. 21, T 6 N, R 23 W). Named on Wheeler Springs (1943) 7.5' quadrangle.

Ladyface [LOS ANGELES]: *peak,* 2 miles west-southwest of Agoura (lat. 34°08'05" N, long. 118°46'20" W). Altitude 2036 feet. Named on Thousand Oaks (1952) 7.5' quadrangle.

Lady Waterman Mountain: see **Waterman Mountain** [LOS ANGELES].

La Fetra [LOS ANGELES]: *locality,* 1.25 miles east-northeast of Azusa city hall along Pacific Electric Railroad (lat. 34°08'20" N, long. 117°52'50" W). Named on Azusa (1953) 7.5' quadrangle.

La Fresa [LOS ANGELES]: *district,* 2.5 miles north of Torrance city hall (lat. 33°52'25" N, long. 118°20' W). Named on Torrance (1964) 7.5' quadrangle.

Lagol [VENTURA]: *locality,* 4.25 miles west-southwest of Moorpark along Southern Pacific Railroad (lat. 34°16'10" N, long. 118° 57' W). Named on Moorpark (1951) 7.5' quadrangle. Called Lagol Siding on Camulos (1903) 30' quadrangle.

Lagona: see **Laguna Beach** [ORANGE].

Lagona Beach: see **Laguna Beach** [ORANGE].

La Granada Mountain [VENTURA]: *peak,* 4 miles south-southwest of White Ledge Peak (lat. 34°25'05' N, long. 119°25'20" W; at W line sec. 20, T 4 N, R 24 W). Altitude 2291 feet. Named on White Ledge Peak (1952) 7.5' quadrangle.

Laguna [LOS ANGELES]:

(1) *lake,* 6.5 miles west of Whittier (lat. 33°59'15" N, long. 118° 09' W). Named on Downey (1902) 15' quadrangle.

(2) *locality,* 6 miles west of Whittier along Atchison, Topeka and Santa Fe Railroad (lat. 33°59'15" N, long. 118°08'10" W); the place is just east of Laguna (1). Named on Downey (1902) 15' quadrangle.

(3) *locality,* 4 miles east-northeast of South Gate city hall along Southern Pacific Railroad (lat. 33°58'40" N, long. 118°08'25" W). Named on South Gate (1964, photorevised 1981) 7.5' quadrangle.

Laguna: see **Laguna Beach** [ORANGE]; **Lagunas** [ORANGE]; **Mount Laguna** [SAN DIEGO]; **South Laguna** [ORANGE]; **The Laguna**, under **Laguna Meadow** [SAN DIEGO].

Laguna Beach [ORANGE]: *town,* 17 miles south-southeast of Santa Ana along the coast (lat. 33°32'45" N, long. 117°46'50" W); the town is at the mouth of Laguna Canyon. Named on Laguna Beach (1965) and San Juan Capistrano (1968) 7.5' quadrangles. Called Laguna on Santa Ana (1896) 15' quadrangle. Postal authorities established Lagona Beach post office in 1891 and discontinued it in 1893; they established Lagona post office in 1894 and changed the name to Laguna Beach in 1904 (Salley, p. 114). The town incorporated in 1927. George Rogers purchased land at the mouth of Laguna Canyon in 1887 and laid out the town (Meadows, p. 76).

Laguna Campground [SAN DIEGO]: *locality,* 1.5 miles west of Monument Peak (lat. 32°53'20" N, long. 116°26'50" W; at SE cor. sec. 3, T 15 S, R 5 E). Named on Monument Peak (1959) 7.5' quadrangle.

Laguna Canyon [ORANGE]: *canyon,* 6.25 miles long, opens to the sea 0.25 mile southwest of Laguna Beach city hall (lat. 33°32'35" N, long. 117°47'05" W). Named on Laguna Beach (1965) 7.5' quadrangle. The feature was called Canada de las Lagunas in the early days for fresh-water lagoons situated near its head (Meadows, p. 32).

Laguna Creek [VENTURA]: *stream,* flows 1.25 miles to Rincon Creek 5.25 miles south-southwest of White Ledge Peak (lat. 34°24'25" N, long. 119°26'40" W; near NE cor. sec. 25, T 4 N, R 25 W). Named on White Ledge Peak (1952) 7.5' quadrangle.

Laguna del Diablo: see **Elizabeth Lake** [LOS ANGELES] (1).

Laguna Dominguez: see **Dominguez Channel** [LOS ANGELES].

Laguna Hills [ORANGE]: *city,* 1.5 miles southwest of El Toro (lat. 33°36'45" N, long. 117°43' W). Named on San Juan Capistrano (1968) 7.5' quadrangle. Postal authorities established Laguna Hills post office in 1964; the post office name is from a retirement community called Leisure World Laguna Beach Hills (Salley, p. 114).

Laguna Junction [SAN DIEGO]: *locality,* nearly 7 miles east-southeast of Descanso (lat. 32°48'35" N, long. 116°30'40" W; near W line sec. 6, T 16 S, R 5 E). Named on Descanso (1960) 7.5' quadrangle.

Laguna Lake [ORANGE]: *lake,* 1500 feet long, nearly 2 miles south-southeast of downtown La Habra (lat. 33°54'30" N, long. 117°56'10" W). Named on La Habra (1964) 7.5' quadrangle.

Laguna Lake: see **Big Laguna Lake** [SAN DIEGO]; **Little Laguna Lake** [SAN DIEGO].

Laguna Lakes: see **Big Laguna Lake** [SAN DIEGO].

Laguna Meadow [SAN DIEGO]: *valley*, 2.5 miles west-southwest of Monument Peak (lat. 32°53' N, long. 116°27'45" W); Big Laguna Lake is in the valley. Named on Monument Peak (1959) and Mount Laguna (1960) 7.5' quadrangles. Brown's (1920) map shows a lake called The Laguna at the place.

Laguna Mountains [SAN DIEGO]: *range*, extends for about 15 miles southeast from Cuyamaca Reservoir to La Posta Creek. Named on Cameron Corners (1959), Cuyamaca Peak (1960), Descanso (1960), Monument Peak (1959), and Mount Laguna (1960) 7.5' quadrangles. The name is from two lakes, called Laguna Lakes, located in the range (Gudde, 1949, p. 179-180).

Laguna Niguel [ORANGE]: *town*, 3.5 miles west-northwest of San Juan Capistrano (lat. 33°31'15" N, long. 117°42'45" W); the town is on Niguel grant. Named on San Juan Capistrano (1968) 7.5' quadrangle. Postal authorities established Laguna Niguel post office in 1968 (Salley, p. 114).

Laguna Peak [VENTURA]: *peak*, 1.5 miles north of Point Mugu (lat. 34°06'30" N, long. 119°03'50" W). Named on Point Mugu (1949) 7.5' quadrangle.

Laguna Point [VENTURA]: *promontory*, 3 miles west-northwest of Point Mugu along the coast (lat. 34°05'40" N, long. 119°06'30" W). Named on Point Mugu (1949) 7.5' quadrangle. Point Mugu (1950) 7.5' quadrangle gives the alternate name "Sandy Point" for the feature.

Laguna Reservoir [ORANGE]: *lake*, 1600 feet long, 9.5 miles southeast of Santa Ana city hall (lat. 33°38'30" N, long. 117°45'30" W). Named on Tustin (1965) 7.5' quadrangle. The feature is at the head of a stream called Agua del Palo Verde in the early days (Meadows, p. 17).

Laguna Ridge [VENTURA]: *ridge*, west-trending, 3.5 miles long, 4.5 miles south of White Ledge Peak (lat. 34°24'10" N, long. 119°23'10" W). Named on Matilija (1952) and White Ledge Peak (1952) 7.5' quadrangles.

Lagunas [ORANGE]: *intermittent lakes*, largest 1000 feet long, 4.5 miles north-northeast of Laguna Beach city hall (lat. 33°36'35" N, long. 117°45'25" W); the features are in Laguna Canyon. Named on Laguna Beach (1965) 7.5' quadrangle. Santa Ana (1901) 15' quadrangle shows a single lake called Laguna at the place.

Laguna Seca: see **Nigger Slough** [LOS ANGELES].

La Habra [LOS ANGELES-ORANGE]: *land grant*, at and near the city of La Habra [ORANGE]. Named on La Habra (1964) 7.5' quadrangle. Maríano Roldan received 1.5 leagues in 1839; Andres Pico and others claimed 6699 acres patented in 1872 (Cowan, p. 39; Cowan used the name "Cañada de la Habra" for the grant).

La Habra [ORANGE]: *city*, 13 miles north-northwest of Santa Ana (lat. 33°55'55" N, long. 117°56'45" W); the city is on La Habra [LOS ANGELES-ORANGE] grant. Named on La Habra (1964) 7.5' quadrangle. Postal authorities established La Habra post office in 1895, discontinued it in 1903, and reestablished it in 1912 (Frickstad, p. 117). The city incorporated in 1925.

La Habra: see **Fullerton** [ORANGE].

La Habra Heights [LOS ANGELES]: *town*, 2 miles north of La Habra [ORANGE] (lat. 33°57'30" N, long. 117°57' W). Named on La Habra (1952) 7.5' quadrangle. The town incorporated in 1978.

La Honda Spring [SAN DIEGO]: *spring*, 0.5 mile west-northwest of Jamul (lat. 32°43'20" N, long. 116°53'05" W; sec. 33, T 16 S, R 1 E). Named on Jamul Mountains (1955) 7.5' quadrangle.

Lairport [LOS ANGELES]: *locality*, 3 miles north-northeast of Manhattan Beach city hall along Atchison, Topeka and Santa Fe Railroad (lat. 33°55'25" N, long. 118°22'40" W). Named on Venice (1964) 7.5' quadrangle. Called Wiseburn on Redondo (1896) 15' quadrangle. Postal authorities established Wiseburn post office in 1891, discontinued it the same year, reestablished it in 1896, moved it 2 miles southeast in 1898, and discontinued it in 1906 (Salley, p. 242).

La Isla de la Culebra de Cascabel: see **Terminal Island** [LOS ANGELES] (1).

La Isla del Muerto: see **Reservation Point** [LOS ANGELES].

La Jolla [ORANGE]: *locality*, 5 miles north-northwest of Orange city hall (lat. 33°51'30" N, long. 117°52'25" W). Named on Anaheim (1950) and Orange (1964) 7.5' quadrangles.

La Jolla [SAN DIEGO]: *district*, south of Point La Jolla in San Diego (lat. 32°50'15" N, long. 117°16'30" W). Named on La Jolla (1967) 7.5' quadrangle. Postal authorities established La Jolla Park post office in 1888, discontinued it in 1893, reestablished it with the name "Lajolla" in 1894, and changed the name to La Jolla in 1905 (Salley, p. 115). F.T. Botsford laid out the townsite in 1887 (Hanna, p. 156). Goodyear (1888b, p. 522) claimed that the name "La Jolla" is a misspelling of the earlier name "La Joya."

La Jolla: see **Point La Jolla** [SAN DIEGO].

La Jolla Amago [SAN DIEGO]: *locality*, 5 miles southeast of Boucher Hill (lat. 33°17' N, long. 116°51'45" W; sec. 27, T 10 S, R 1 E). Named on Palomar Observatory (1949) 7.5' quadrangle.

La Jolla Bay [SAN DIEGO]: *embayment*, northeast of Point La Jolla along the coast (lat. 32°51'15" N, long. 117°15'40" W). Named on La Jolla (1967) 7.5' quadrangle.

La Jolla Canyon [VENTURA]: *canyon*, 1.5 miles long, opens to the sea 1.5 miles east of Point Mugu (lat. 34°05' N, long. 119°02'05" W); the feature heads at La Jolla Valley. Named on Point Mugu (1949) 7.5' quadrangle.

La Jolla Caves [SAN DIEGO]: *caves*, 0.5 mile east of Point La Jolla along the coast (lat. 32°50'55" N, long. 117°15'55" W). Named on La Jolla (1967) 7.5' quadrangle.

La Jolla Hermosa [SAN DIEGO]: *locality*, 2.25 miles south of Point La Jolla (lat. 32°49'05" N, long. 117°16'10" W). Named on La Jolla (1943) 7.5' quadrangle.

La Jolla Mesa [SAN DIEGO]: *area*, 2 miles south-southeast of Point La Jolla (lat. 32°49'35" N, long. 117°15'40" W). Named on La Jolla (1967) 7.5' quadrangle.

La Jolla Park: see **La Jolla** [SAN DIEGO].

La Jolla Peak [VENTURA]: *peak*, 2 miles north-northeast of Point Mugu (lat. 34°06'55" N, long. 119°02'55" W). Altitude 1567 feet. Named on Point Mugu (1949) 7.5' quadrangle. Called La Joya Pk. on Hueneme (1904) 15' quadrangle, but United States Board on Geographic Names (1961c, p. 10) rejected this name for the feature.

La Jolla Shores Beach [SAN DIEGO]: *beach*, 1.25 miles east-northeast of Point La Jolla along the coast (lat. 32°51'35" N, long. 117°15'20" W). Named on La Jolla (1967) 7.5' quadrangle.

La Jolla Valley [SAN DIEGO]: *valley*, along Lusardi Creek above a point 3.5 miles east-southeast of Rancho Santa Fe (lat. 33°00'20" N, long. 117°08'40" W; sec. 36, T 13 S, R 3 W). Named on Escondido (1968) and Rancho Santa Fe (1968) 7.5' quadrangles.

La Jolla Valley [VENTURA]: *valley*, 1.25 miles north-northeast of Point Mugu (lat. 34°06'15" N, long. 119°03'05" W); the feature is less than 1 mile south of La Jolla Peak. Named on Point Mugu (1949) 7.5' quadrangle.

La Joya: see **Green Valley** [LOS ANGELES]; **La Jolla** [SAN DIEGO].

La Joya Peak: see **La Jolla Peak** [VENTURA].

Lake Campground [LOS ANGELES]: *locality*, 2 miles west-northwest of Big Pines (lat. 34°23'25" N, long. 117°43'20" W); the place is near Jackson Lake. Named on Mescal Creek (1956) 7.5' quadrangle.

Lake Canyon [VENTURA]: *canyon*, drained by a stream that flows 2.5 miles to Sexton Canyon 4 miles west-northwest of Saticoy (lat. 34°18' N, long. 119°13'05" W). Named on Saticoy (1951) 7.5' quadrangle.

Lake Casitas [VENTURA]: *lake*, behind a dam on Coyote Creek 7 miles north-northwest of Ventura (lat. 34°22'15" N, long. 119° 20' W). Named on Matilija (1952, photorevised (1967) and Ventura (1951, photorevised 1967) 7.5' quadrangles. United States Board on Geographic Names (1960a, p. 13) first approved and then (1962a, p. 9) rejected the name "Casitas Reservoir" for the lake.

Lake Cuyamaca [SAN DIEGO]: *lake*, behind a dam on Boulder Creek 3.25 miles north-northeast of Cuyamaca Peak (lat. 32°59'25" N, long. 116°35'10" W). Named on Cuyamaca Peak (1960, photorevised 1988) 7.5' quadrangle. Called Cuyamaca Reservoir on Cuyamaca Peak (1960) and Julian (1960) 7.5' quadrangles.

Lake Domingo [SAN DIEGO]: *lake*, 900 feet long, 11.5 miles east of Campo (lat. 32°36'55" N, long. 116°16'15" W; sec. 9, T 18 S, R 7 E). Named on Tierra del Sol (1959) 7.5' quadrangle.

Lake Eleanor [VENTURA]: *intermittent lake*, behind a dam on Lake Eleanor Creek 2.5 miles south-southwest of Thousand Oaks (lat. 34°08'05" N, long. 119°51' W; at E line sec. 27, T 1 N, R 19 W). Named on Thousand Oaks (1952) 7.5' quadrangle.

Lake Eleanor Creek [LOS ANGELES-VENTURA]: *stream*, heads in Los Angeles County and flows nearly 3 miles to Potrero Valley about 2 miles south-southwest of Thousand Oaks in Ventura County (lat. 34°08'45" N, long. 118°50'55" W; near NW cor. sec. 26, T 1 N, R 19 W). Named on Thousand Oaks (1952) 7.5' quadrangle.

Lake Elizabeth: see **Elizabeth Lake** [LOS ANGELES]; **West Lake Elizabeth**, under **Lake Hughes** [LOS ANGELES].

Lake Enchanto [LOS ANGELES]: *lake*, 1450 feet long, 8 miles north of Point Dume in Triunfo Canyon (lat. 34°06'50" N, long. 118°46'40" W; near W line sec. 4, T 1 S, R 18 W). Named on Point Dume (1951) 7.5' quadrangle.

Lake Henshaw [SAN DIEGO]:

(1) *lake*, behind a dam on San Luis Rey River 4 miles north of Mesa Grande (lat. 33°14'25" N, long. 116°45'45" W). Named on Mesa Grande (1948), Palomar Observatory (1949), Warner Springs (1959), and Warners Ranch (1960) 7.5' quadrangles. The reservoir was completed in 1924 and named for William G. Henshaw, who owned land flooded by water of the lake (Gudde, 1949, p. 147).

(2) *locality*, 2.5 miles north of Mesa Grande (lat. 33°13'55" N, long. 116°45'35" W); the place is along Lake Henshaw (1). Named on Mesa Grande (1948) 7.5' quadrangle.

Lake Hodges [SAN DIEGO]: *lake*, behind a dam on San Dieguito River 4.5

miles east-northeast of Rancho Santa Fe (lat. 33°02'40" N, long. 117°07'40" W; sec. 18, T 13 S, R 2 W). Named on Escondido (1968) and Rancho Santa Fe (1968) 7.5' quadrangles. Postal authorities established Lake Hodges post office in 1924 and discontinued it in 1926 (Frickstad, p. 152). Officials of Atchison, Topeka and Santa Fe Railroad had the dam built in 1922 and named the lake for W.E. Hodges, vice president of the railroad (Gudde, 1949, p. 150).

Lake Hughes [LOS ANGELES]: *village*, 26 miles north of San Fernando (lat. 34°40'35" N, long. 118°26'25" W; in and near sec. 23, T 7 N, R 15 W); the village is near Hughes Lake. Named on Lake Hughes (1957) 7.5' quadrangle. Hughes Lake (1937) 6' quadrangle has the name "Hughes Lake" for the village, and shows Lake Hughes P.O. at the place. Postal authorities established Lake Hughes post office in 1925; the name was for G.O. Hughes, owner of the land—the community first was known as West Lake Elizabeth (Salley, p. 115).

Lake Jean [SAN DIEGO]: *lake*, 450 feet long, 7.25 miles northwest of Warner Springs (lat. 33°20'55" N, long. 116°43'55" W; near W line sec. 36, T 9 S, R 2 E). Named on Warner Springs (1959) 7.5' quadrangle. Mr. Donato, who owned the property, named the lake for his wife (Stein, p. 69).

Lake Jennings [SAN DIEGO]: *lake*, 1 mile long, 2 miles east of Lakeside (lat. 32°51'30" N, long. 116°53'15" W). Named on El Cajon (1967) 7.5' quadrangle.

Lake Katarina: see **Tweedy Lake** [LOS ANGELES].

Lake Machado: see **Harbor Lake** [LOS ANGELES].

Lake Mathiessen: see **Lake Sherwood** [VENTURA].

Lake Miramar: see **Miramar Reservoir** [SAN DIEGO].

Lake Palmdale [LOS ANGELES]: *lake*, 1 mile long, 2 miles south of Palmdale (lat. 34°33'05" N, long. 118°07'15" W; mainly in sec. 3, T 5 N, R 12 W). Named on Palmdale (1958) and Ritter Ridge (1958) 7.5' quadrangles. Called Harold Reservoir on Elizabeth Lake (1917) 30' quadrangle, and called Palmdale Reservoir on Palmdale (1937) 6' quadrangle, but United States Board on Geographic Names (1960a, p. 16) rejected the names "Harold Lake," "Harold Reservoir," "Palmdale Lake," "Palmdale Reservoir," and "Shoulder Lake" for the feature.

Lake Piru [VENTURA]: *lake*, behind a dam 4 miles northeast of Piru (lat. 34°27'40" N, long. 118°45'05" W); the lake is along Piru Creek. Named on Cobblestone Mountain (1958), Piru (1952, photorevised 1969), and Val Verde (1952, photorevised 1969) 7.5' quadrangles. United Water Conservation District built the dam that formed the lake in 1956 (Ricard).

Lake Salinas: see **Salt Pond** [LOS ANGELES].

Lake San Marcos [SAN DIEGO]:

(1) *lake*, 1.25 miles long, behind a dam 6 miles north of Rancho Santa Fe (lat. 33°06'35" N, long. 117°12'30" W; at NE cor. sec. 29, T 12 S, R 3 W); the lake is along San Marcos Creek. Named on Rancho Santa Fe (1968) and San Marcos (1968) 7.5' quadrangles.

(2) *locality*, 7 miles north of Rancho Santa Fe (lat. 33°07'25" N, long. 117°12' W); the place is at Lake San Marcos (1). Named on Rancho Santa Fe (1968) and San Marcos (1968) 7.5' quadrangles.

Lake Shangri La [LOS ANGELES]: *dry lake*, nearly 2 miles west of Baldwin Park city hall in a gravel pit (lat. 34°05'25" N, long. 117° 59'30" W; sec. 13, T 1 S, R 11 W). Named on Baldwin Park (1953) 7.5' quadrangle.

Lake Sherwood [VENTURA]: *lake*, behind a dam on Potrero Valley Creek 2.25 miles south-southwest of Thousand Oaks (lat. 34°08'20" N, long. 118°51'25" W). Named on Newbury Park (1951) and Thousand Oaks (1952) 7.5' quadrangles. Called Sherwood Lake on Los Angeles County (1935) map. The name is from the filming of the movie *Robin Hood* at the place in 1922; a reservoir built at the site in 1889 was called Canterbury Lake until about 1898, when F.W. Mathiessen, Jr., purchased the land—the early lake then was known as Lake Mathiessen (Ricard).

Lakeside [SAN DIEGO]: *town*, 5.25 miles north-northeast of El Cajon city hall (lat. 32°51'40" N, long. 116°55'15" W). Named on El Cajon (1967) 7.5' quadrangle. Postal authorities established Lakeside post office in 1887 (Frickstad, p. 152). El Cajon Valley Company had the townsite laid out in 1887 beside Lindo Lake (Stein, p. 69). Waring (p. 305) listed Lakeside Mineral Wells, dug about 1906 on property of the inn at Lakeside to provide mineralized drinking water.

Lakeside Farms [SAN DIEGO]: *settlement*, 1.25 miles west-northwest of Lakeside (lat. 32°52'05" N, long. 116°56'15" W). Named on El Cajon (1967) 7.5' quadrangle.

Lakeside Mineral Wells: see **Lakeside** [SAN DIEGO].

Lakeside Park [LOS ANGELES]: *locality*, 3.25 miles southwest of Chatsworth (lat. 34°13'40" N, long. 118°38'50" W); the place is west of Chatsworth Reservoir. Named on Calabasas (1952) 7.5' quadrangle.

Lake Sutherland: see **Sutherland Lake** [SAN DIEGO].

Lakeview [SAN DIEGO]: *locality*, 1.5 miles southeast of Lakeside (lat. 32°50'35" N, long. 116°54'10" W). Named on El Cajon (1967) 7.5' quadrangle.

Lake Wohlford [SAN DIEGO]: *lake*, behind a dam on Escondido Creek 5 miles northeast of Escondido city hall (lat. 33°10' N, long. 117°00'15" W; near N line sec. 5, T 12 S, R 1 W). Named on Rodriguez Mountain (1948) and Valley Center (1968) 7.5' quadrangles. Called Wohlford Res. on Tucker and Reed's (1939) map, but United States Board on Geographic Names (1965a, p. 16) rejected the names "Wohlford Reservoir" and "Lake Wolford" for the feature. The first small dam at the site was built in 1890 and formed a lake called Bear Valley Reservoir; later the feature was called Escondido Lake, and in 1924 the present lake was named for Alvin W. Wohlford, who was prominent in development of a water supply for the neighborhood (Stein, p. 69).

Lakewood [LOS ANGELES]: *city*, 6.5 miles north-northeast of Long Beach city hall (lat. 33°51' N, long. 118°07'55" W). Named on Los Alamitos (1964) 7.5' quadrangle. Postal authorities established Lakewood post office in 1949 (Salley, p. 116), and the city incorporated in 1954.

Lakewood Village [LOS ANGELES]: *district*, 6 miles northeast of Long Beach city hall (lat. 33°50' N, long. 118°07'30" W). Named on Long Beach (1949) and Los Alamitos (1950) 7.5' quadrangles. Clark J. Bonner and Charles B. Hopper had the community laid out in 1934; the name is from nearby Bouton Lake (Gudde, 1949, p. 180-181).

La Laguna [SAN DIEGO]: *lake*, 1200 feet long, 2.5 miles east-northeast of present Point La Jolla (lat. 32°52'10" N, long. 117°14'10" W). Named on La Jolla (1903) 15' quadrangle.

La Laguna: see **Guadalasca** [VENTURA].

La Laguna de Chico Lopez: see **Elizabeth Lake** [LOS ANGELES] (1).

La Laguna Seca: see **Quail Lake** [LOS ANGELES].

La Liebra [LOS ANGELES]: *land grant*, west of Antelope Valley on Los Angeles-Kern County line. Named on La Liebre Ranch (1965), Lebec (1958), Liebre Mountain (1958), and Neenach School (1965) 7.5' quadrangles. Jose M. Flores received 11 leagues in 1846 and claimed 48,800 acres patented in 1875 (Cowan, p. 45). Johnson's (1911) map shows a feature called Liebre Creek on La Liebra grant; the stream heads east of Quail Lake and flows about 3.5 miles easterly to a spot in the lowlands (sec. 15, T 8 N, R 17 W).

Lamanda: see **East Pasadena** [LOS ANGELES].

Lamanda Park: see **East Pasadena** [LOS ANGELES].

Lambert Reservoir [ORANGE]: *lake*, 1000 feet long, 4.5 miles north-northwest of El Toro (lat. 33°41'35" N, long. 117°42'35" W). Named on El Toro (1968) 7.5' quadrangle. The name is for Ray Lambert, who had a citrus grove at the mouth of Bee Canyon (Meadows, p. 77).

Lambs: see **Huntington Beach** [ORANGE].

Lamel Spring [LOS ANGELES]: *spring*, 6 miles northeast of Crystal Lake (lat. 34°22'05" N, long. 117°45'20" W). Named on Crystal Lake (1958) 7.5' quadrangle.

La Merced [LOS ANGELES]: *land grant*, north of Montebello. Named on El Monte (1953) and Los Angeles (1953) 7.5' quadrangles. Casilda Soto received 1 league in 1844; Francis Pliny F. Temple and others claimed 2364 acres patented in 1872 (Cowan, p. 47).

La Mesa [SAN DIEGO]: *city*, 8.5 miles east-northeast of downtown San Diego (lat. 32°46' N, long. 117°01'15" W). Named on El Cajon (1967), La Mesa (1967), and National City (1967) 7.5' quadrangles. Postal authorities established Lamesa post office in 1891 and changed the name to La Mesa in 1905; the place was called La Mesa Heights in 1886 (Salley, p. 116). The city incorporated in 1912. The site was called Allison Springs for an artesian spring on Robert Allison's ranch; the townsite laid out at the place in 1894 was called La Mesa Springs, but in 1904 the name was shortened to La Mesa (Stein, p. 69-70). Berkstresser (p. A-13) listed the names "La Mesa Spring," "Lamesa Spring," "Indian Spring" and "Allison Springs" for the artesian spring.

La Mesa Heights: see **La Mesa** [SAN DIEGO].

La Mesa Springs: see **La Mesa** [SAN DIEGO].

La Mirada [LOS ANGELES]: *city*, 4 miles south-southeast of Whittier city hall (lat. 33°55'35" N, long. 118°00'40" W); La Mirada Creek goes through the city. Named on La Habra (1964) and Whittier (1965) 7.5' quadrangles. Postal authorities established La Mirada post office in 1895 (Frickstad, p. 76), and the city incorporated in 1960. Whittier (1949) 7.5' quadrangle has the name for a place along Atchison, Topeka and Santa Fe Railroad in the present city of La Mirada (lat. 33°53'40" N, long. 118°01'25" W; sec. 22, T 3 S, R 11 W).

La Mirada Creek [LOS ANGELES-ORANGE]: *stream*, heads in Los Angeles County and flows 8.5 miles, partly in Orange County, to La Cañada Verde Creek nearly 6 miles south of Whittier city hall (lat. 33°53'25" N, long. 118°01'55" W; sec. 21, T 3 S, R 11 W). Named on La Habra (1952) and Whittier (1965) 7.5' quadrangles.

La Nacion [SAN DIEGO]: *land grant*, at National City and Chula Vista. Named on Imperial Beach (1967), Jamul Mountains (1955), National City (1967), and Otay Mesa (1955) 7.5' quadrangles. John Forster received 6 leagues in 1845 and claimed 26,632 acres patented in 1866 (Cowan, p. 50).

Lancaster [LOS ANGELES]: *city*, 32 miles north-northeast of San Fernando (lat. 34°41'50" N, long. 118°08'15" W). Named on Lancaster East (1958) and Lancaster West (1958) 7.5' quadrangles. Postal authorities established Lancaster post office in 1884 (Frickstad, p. 76), and the city incorporated in 1977. M.L. Wicks laid out the townsite in 1884 and named it for his home town of Lancaster, Pennsylvania (Settle, p. 29). Postal authorities established Eldon post office 13 miles east of Lancaster in 1892 and discontinued it the same year (Salley, p. 66). Johnson's (1911) map shows a place called Esperanza located 5.5 miles west-northwest of Lancaster.

Lancaster Mountain [SAN DIEGO]: *peak*, 8 miles east-southeast of Fallbrook (lat. 33°19'20" N, long. 117°08' W; sec. 7, T 10 S, R 2 W). Altitude 1485 feet. Named on Bonsall (1968) 7.5' quadrangle. The name commemorates A.W. Lancaster, who bought a farm near the peak in 1872 (Gudde, 1949, p. 181).

Landing Hill [ORANGE]: *relief feature*, 8 miles northwest of Huntington Beach civic center (lat. 33°44'55" N, long. 118°05'35" W; sec. 11, 12, T 5 S, R 12 W). Named on Los Alamitos (1964) and Seal Beach (1965) 7.5' quadrangles. The name is from Anaheim Landing, which was located about 1 mile south of Landing Hill (Meadows, p. 77).

Lands End [LOS ANGELES]: *promontory*, 2.5 miles west-northwest of Silver Peak at the extreme west end of Santa Catalina Island (lat. 33°28'45" N, long. 118°36'20" W). Named on Santa Catalina West (1943) 7.5' quadrangle, which shows Catalina Island West End light near the place. United States Board on Geographic Names (1978c, p. 5) approved the name "West End" for the promontory. The Board (1936b, p. 22) approved the name "Farnsworth Bank" for a feature situated about 1 mile southwest of Santa Catalina Island (lat. 33°20'36" N, long. 118°31' W)—they noted that name commemorates Samuel Stephen Farnsworth, who built a road on the Island and died there. According to United States Coast and Geodetic Survey (p. 107), Farnsworth Bank is located 9.2 miles southeast of West End.

Lane: see **Camp Bill Lane** [LOS ANGELES].

Lang [LOS ANGELES]: *locality*, 5 miles east of Solemint along Southern Pacific Railroad (lat. 34°26'05" N, long. 118°22'10" W; sec. 17, T 4 N, R 14 W). Named on Agua Dulce (1960) and Mint Canyon (1960) 7.5' quadrangles. Postal authorities established Lang post office in 1881, discontinued it in 1882, reestablished it in 1883, and discontinued it in 1933; the name was for John Lang, first postmaster (Salley, p. 117). The golden spike that marked completion of Southern Pacific Railroad's line connecting Los Angeles and San Francisco was driven at Lang in 1876 (Hanna, p. 167). Los Angeles County (1935) map shows a feature called Lang Canyon that opens into Soledad Canyon from the north about 0.5 mile west of Lang.

Lang Canyon: see **Lang** [LOS ANGELES].

Lankershim: see **North Hollywood** [LOS ANGELES].

Lanoitan: see **Lincoln Acres** [SAN DIEGO].

Laon Junction: see **Des Moins** [ORANGE].

La Paco [LOS ANGELES]: *locality*, 3 miles west-southwest of present Burbank city hall along Southern Pacific Railroad (lat. 34° 10'05" N, long. 118°21'25" W). Named on Burbank (1926) 6' quadrangle.

La Paleta Valley [SAN DIEGO]: *valley*, 4 miles southeast of downtown San Diego between Paradise Valley and South Las Choyas Valley (lat. 32°41' N, long. 117°06'30" W). Named on San Diego (1904) 15' quadrangle.

La Palma [ORANGE]: *town*, 3 miles west-southwest of Buena Park civic center (lat. 33°50'45" N, long. 118°02'35" W; on S line sec. 4, T 4 S, R 11 W). Named on Los Alamitos (1964) 7.5' quadrangle. Postal authorities established La Palma post office in 1966; the name was from La Palma Avenue (Salley, p. 117). The town incorporated with the name "Dairyland" in 1955; residents changed the name to La Palma in 1957.

La Paloma [ORANGE]: *locality*, 2.25 miles east-southeast of Orange city hall (lat. 33°46'50" N, long. 117°48'10" W). Named on Orange (1964) 7.5' quadrangle. Lawrence Phillips laid out a Latin-American colony at the place in 1923 (Meadows, p. 75).

La Palonia Flat [LOS ANGELES]: *area*, 3 miles south of Condor Peak in Big Tujunga Canyon (lat. 34°17' N, long. 118°13'20" W; sec. 3, T 2 N, R 13 W). Named on Condor Peak (1959) 7.5' quadrangle.

La Park: see **Huntington Park** [LOS ANGELES].

La Paz: see **Mission Viejo or La Paz** [ORANGE].

La Paz Canyon [ORANGE]: *canyon*, drained by a stream that heads in Riverside County and flows 3 miles in Orange County to Gabino Canyon 5.5 miles northeast of San Clemente (lat. 33°28'55" N, long. 117°32'10" W; near W line sec. 8, T 8 S, R 6 W); the feature is on Mission Viejo or La Paz grant. Named on Cañada Gobernadora (1968) and San Clemente (1968) 7.5' quadrangles.

La Placerita Canyon: see **Placerita Canyon** [LOS ANGELES].

La Playa [SAN DIEGO]: *district*, 4.5 miles west of downtown San Diego on Point Loma (lat. 32°42'35" N, long. 117°14'15" W). Named on Point Loma (1967) 7.5' quadrangle. The place was the site of a flourishing trade in cattle hides from 1824 until 1846—Yankees called the spot Hide Park (Hoover, Rensch, and Rensch, p. 339-340).

La Posta Creek [SAN DIEGO]: *stream*, flows 20 miles to Cottonwood Creek (3) 8 miles north of Campo (lat. 32°42'55" N, long. 116°29'50" W; sec. 8, T 17 S, R 5 E). Named on Cameron Corners (1959), Mount Laguna (1960), and Sombrero Peak (1959) 7.5' quadrangles.

La Posta Service [SAN DIEGO]: *locality*, 8 miles north of Campo (lat. 32°43'05" N, long. 116°27' W; near SW cor. sec. 2, T 17 S, R 5 E); the place is along La Posta Creek. Named on Cameron Corners (1959) 7.5' quadrangle.

La Posta Valley [SAN DIEGO]: *valley*, 8.5 miles north-northeast of Campo (lat. 32°43'30" N, long. 116°25'45" W; sec. 1, T 17 S, R 5 E); the valley is partly along La Posta Creek. Named on Cameron Corners (1959) 7.5' quadrangle.

La Presa [SAN DIEGO]: *locality*, 7 miles west of Jamul (lat. 32°42'30" N, long. 116°59'45" W). Named on Jamul Mountains (1955) 7.5' quadrangle. Postal authorities established La Presa post office in 1888, discontinued it the same year, reestablished it in 1889, and discontinued it in 1895; the name is from a nearby dam along Sweetwater River—*la presa* means "the dam" in Spanish (Salley, p. 118).

La Puente [LOS ANGELES]:

(1) *land grant*, north of Puente Hills between San Gabriel River and San Jose Creek. Named on Baldwin Park (1953), El Monte (1953), La Habra (1952), San Dimas (1954), Whittier (1951), and Yorba Linda (1950) 7.5' quadrangles. John Rowland and William Workman received the land in 1845; they claimed 48,791 acres patented in 1867 (Cowan, p. 64; Cowan listed the grant under the wrong name).

(2) *city*, 4.5 miles south of Baldwin Park city hall (lat. 34°02'10" N, long. 117°57' W); the city is on La Puente (1) grant. Named on Baldwin Park (1966) 7.5' quadrangle. Called Puente on Baldwin Park (1953) 7.5' quadrangle. Postal authorities established Puente post office in 1884 and changed the name to La Puente in 1956 (Salley, p. 118).

La Puerta Springs [SAN DIEGO]: *springs*, 1.5 miles north of Cuyamaca Peak (lat. 32°58'05" N, long. 116°36'15" W). Named on Cuyamaca Peak (1960) 7.5' quadrangle.

La Punta [SAN DIEGO]: *locality*, 1.5 miles northeast of present Imperial Beach civic center along San Diego and Arizona Eastern Railroad (lat. 32°35'35" N, long. 117°05'45" W; sec. 21, T 18 S, R 2 W). Named on San Diego (1904) 15' quadrangle.

La Quinta [LOS ANGELES]: *locality*, 7.5 miles west-southwest of Newhall in Las Llajas Canyon [LOS ANGELES-VENTURA] (lat. 34°19'40" N, long. 118°38'25" W). Named on Pico (1940) 6' quadrangle.

Largo Vista [LOS ANGELES]: *locality*, 5 miles east-southeast of Valyermo in Grandview Canyon (lat. 34°25'40" N, long. 117°45'55" W; near SE cor. sec. 13, T 4 N, R 9 W). Named on Valyermo (1958) 7.5' quadrangle.

Lark Canyon [SAN DIEGO]: *canyon*, drained by a stream that flows 2.5 miles to McCain Valley 3 miles north-northeast of Manzanita (lat. 32°42'10" N, long. 116°15'35" W; near E line sec. 9, T 17 S, R 7 E). Named on Live Oak Springs (1959) 7.5' quadrangle.

Larkinville: see **Boulevard** [SAN DIEGO].

Larres Canyon: see **Potrero Canyon** [LOS ANGELES].

Las Bancas [SAN DIEGO]: *relief feature*, nearly 3 miles southeast of Descanso (lat. 32°49'35" N, long. 116°34'50" W; near W line sec. 33, T 15 S, R 4 E). Named on Descanso (1960) 7.5' quadrangle.

Las Barras Canyon [LOS ANGELES]: *canyon*, less than 1 mile long, 4 miles north-northeast of Burbank city hall (lat. 34°14' N, long. 118°16'35" W). Named on Burbank (1953) 7.5' quadrangle.

Las Bolsas [ORANGE]: *land grant*, at and west of present Fountain Valley. Named on Anaheim (1950), Los Alamitos (1950), Newport Beach (1951), and Seal Beach (1950) 7.5' quadrangles. Catarina Ruis, widow of Manuel Nieto, received confirmation of 7 leagues of this part of the original Los Nietos grant in 1834; Maria C. Nieto claimed half of 33,460 acres patented in 1877, and Ramon Yorba and others claimed the other half, patented in 1874 (Cowan, p. 19).

Las Casetas [LOS ANGELES]: *locality*, 4.5 miles north-northwest of present Pasadena city hall (lat. 34°12'30" N, long. 118°10' W). Named on Pasadena (1900) 15' quadrangle. United States Board on Geographic Names (1933, p. 449) rejected the forms "Las Casitas" and "Los Casitos" for the name. Jason Brown and Owen Brown, sons of John Brown of Civil War fame, laid out a farm at the place in the 1880's and called it Las Casitas—*las casitas* means "the little houses" in Spanish (Robinson, J.W., 1977, p. 103).

Las Casetas Station [LOS ANGELES]: *locality*, 3.25 miles north-northwest of present Pasadena city hall along Los Angeles Terminal Railroad (lat. 34°11'30" N, long. 118°09'30" W); the place is 1.25 miles south-southeast of Las Casetas. Named on Pasadena (1900) 15' quadrangle.

Las Casitas: see **Las Casetas** [LOS ANGELES].

Las Chollas Creek: see **Chollas Creek** [SAN DIEGO].

Las Choyas Valley: see **Chollas Valley** [SAN DIEGO]; **South Las Choyas Valley**, under **South Chollas Valley** [SAN DIEGO].

Las Cienegas [LOS ANGELES]: *land grant*, 5.5 miles west of Los Angeles city hall. Named on Hollywood (1953) 7.5' quadrangle. Januario Avila received 1 league in 1823 and claimed 4439 acres patented in 1871 (Cowan, p. 28). According to Perez (p. 62), Francisco Abila was grantee in 1843, and Januario Abila was patentee in 1871.

Las Flores [LOS ANGELES]: *locality*, nearly 3 miles east of Malibu Point along the coast (lat. 34°02'15" N, long, 118°38' W); the place is on Topanga Malibu Sequit grant at the mouth of Las Flores Canyon. Named on Malibu Beach (1951) 7.5' quadrangle, which shows Malibu post office at the place. Postal authorities established Malibu post office 1947; the name is from the grant (Salley, p. 131).

Las Flores [SAN DIEGO]: *locality,* 6 miles south-southeast of San Onofre along Atchison, Topeka and Santa Fe Railroad (lat. 33°17'10" N, long. 117°27'05" W; at SE cor. sec. 24, T 10 S, R 6 W); the place is 0.5 mile southeast of the railroad crossing of Las Flores Creek. Named on Las Pulgas Canyon (1968) 7.5' quadrangle.

Las Flores: see **Santa Margarita y las Flores** [SAN DIEGO].

Las Flores Canyon [LOS ANGELES]:

(1) *canyon,* 1 mile long, 3.5 miles west of Mount Wilson (1) (lat. 34°12'55" N, long. 118°07'25" W; sec. 34, T 2 N, R 12 W). Named on Mount Wilson (1953) and Pasadena (1953) 7.5' quadrangles.

(2) *canyon,* drained by a stream that flows 3.5 miles to the sea 2.5 miles east of Malibu Point (lat. 34°02'10" N, long. 118°38'05" W). Named on Malibu Beach (1951) 7.5' quadrangle.

Las Flores Canyon: see **Little Las Flores Canyon** [LOS ANGELES].

Las Flores Creek [SAN DIEGO]: *stream,* flows nearly 2 miles from the mouth of Las Pulgas Canyon to the sea 5.5 miles south-southeast of San Onofre Mountain (lat. 33°17'25" N, long. 117°27'50" W; sec. 24, T 10 S, R 6 W); the stream is on Santa Margarita y Las Flores grant. Named on Las Pulgas Canyon (1968) 7.5' quadrangle.

La Sierra Canyon [LOS ANGELES]: *canyon,* drained by a stream that flows 2.5 miles to Triunfo Canyon 8 miles north of Point Dume (lat. 34°07'05" N, long. 118°47' W). Named on Point Dume (1951) 7.5' quadrangle.

La Sierra de San Gabriel: see **San Gabriel Mountains** [LOS ANGELES].

Laskey Mesa [VENTURA]: *area,* 8.5 miles east of Thousand Oaks (lat. 34°10'30" N, long. 118°40'50" W). Named on Calabasas (1952) 7.5' quadrangle.

Las Llajas Canyon [LOS ANGELES-VENTURA]: *canyon,* drained by a stream that heads in Los Angeles County and flows 5.5 miles to Simi Valley (1) 4 miles west-northwest of Santa Susana Pass in Ventura County (lat. 34°18' N, long. 118°41'30" W; near E line sec. 31, T 3 N, R 17 W). Named on Santa Susana (1951) 7.5' quadrangle.

Las Lomas [LOS ANGELES]: *locality,* 2.5 miles west-northwest of Azusa city hall along Pacific Electric Railroad (lat. 34°08'35" N, long. 117°56'45" W). Named on Azusa (1953) 7.5' quadrangle.

Las Lomas Muertas [SAN DIEGO]: *ridge,* south-trending, 2.25 miles long, 4.5 miles east-southeast of Escondido city hall (lat. 33° 09' N, long. 117°00'05" W). Named on Valley Center (1949) 7.5' quadrangle.

Las Mesitas: see **Anacapa Island** [VENTURA].

La Soledad Pass: see **Soledad Pass** [LOS ANGELES].

Las Penasquitas: see **Los Peñasquitos** [SAN DIEGO].

Las Penasquitas Canyon: see **Los Peñasquitos Canyon** [SAN DIEGO].

Las Pitas: see **Point Las Pitas**, under **Pitas Point** [VENTURA].

Las Posas [VENTURA]: *land grant,* at and around Somis. Named on Camarillo (1950), Moorpark (1951), Newbury Park (1951), and Santa Paula (1951) 7.5' quadrangles. Jose Carrillo received 6 leagues in 1834; Jose de la Guerra y Noriega claimed 26,623 acres patented in 1881 (Cowan, p. 63; Cowan used the form "Las Pozas" for the name). Perez (p. 82) gave the date 1871 for the patent.

Las Posas: see **Saticoy** [VENTURA].

Las Posas Hills [VENTURA]: *ridge,* west-trending, 7 miles long, center 4 miles southwest of Moorpark (lat. 34°15'10" N, long. 118° 56' W). Named on Moorpark (1951) and Newbury Park (1951) 7.5' quadrangles.

Las Pozas: see **Las Posas** [VENTURA].

Las Pulgas Canyon [SAN DIEGO]: *canyon,* 8 miles long, opens into flatlands along the coast 5 miles southeast of San Onofre Mountain (lat. 33°18'30" N, long. 117°26'30" W; sec. 18, T 10 S, R 5 W). Named on Fallbrook (1968), Las Pulgas Canyon (1968), and Margarita Peak (1968) 7.5' quadrangles.

Las Pulgas Canyon: see **Pulga Canyon** [LOS ANGELES].

Las Salinas: see **Salt Pond** [LOS ANGELES].

Last Chance Camp [VENTURA]: *locality,* 4.5 miles north-northwest of Santa Paula Peak (lat. 34°29'50" N, long. 119°03'15" W). Named on Santa Paula Peak (1951) 7.5' quadrangle.

Las Tunas Beach [LOS ANGELES]: *beach,* 6.25 miles west-northwest of Santa Monica city hall along the coast (lat. 34°02'20" N, long. 118°35'45" W; sec. 31, 32, T 1 S, R 16 W); the beach is at the mouth of Tuna Canyon. Named on Topanga (1952) 7.5' quadrangle.

Las Virgenes [LOS ANGELES]: *land grant,* at and near Agoura. Named on Calabasas (1952), Malibu Beach (1951), Point Dume (1951), and Thousand Oaks (1952) 7.5' quadrangles. Jose Maria Dominguez received the land in 1837; M. Antonio Machado claimed 8885 acres patented in 1883 (Cowan, p. 58; Cowan listed the grant under the name "Paraje de las Virgenes"). Perez (p. 104) gave 8878.76 acres as the size of the grant.

Las Virgenes Canyon [LOS ANGELES-VENTURA]: *canyon,* 6.5 miles long, on Los Angeles-Ventura County line along Las Virgenes Creek above a point 2.25 miles east of Agoura (lat. 34°09' N, long. 118°41'45" W; sec. 19, T 1 N, R 17 E). Named on Calabasas (1952) 7.5' quadrangle.

Las Virgenes Canyon: see **East Las Virgenes Canyon** [VENTURA].

Las Virgenes Creek [LOS ANGELES-VENTURA]: *stream,* heads in Ventura County and flows 10.5 miles in Los Angeles and Ventura Counties to Malibu Creek 5 miles north-northwest of Malibu Point in Los Angeles County (lat. 34°05'50" N, long. 118°43'15" W; sec. 12, T 1 S, R 18 W). Named on Calabasas (1952) and Malibu Beach (1951) 7.5' quadrangles. Whitney (p. 122) called the stream Virgenes Creek.

Lateen [LOS ANGELES]: *locality,* 2 miles east-northeast of Baldwin Park city hall along Pacific Electric Railroad (lat. 34°05'30" N, long. 117°55'25" W; near W line sec. 15, T 1 S, R 10 W). Named on Baldwin Park (1953) 7.5' quadrangle.

Latham: see **Fort Latham**, under **Playa del Rey** [LOS ANGELES].

Latigo Canyon [LOS ANGELES]: *canyon,* 3 miles long, opens to the sea 3.5 miles northeast of Point Dume (lat. 34°01'50" N, long. 118° 45'10" W). Named on Point Dume (1951) 7.5' quadrangle.

La Tijera: see **Cienega o Paso de La Tijera** [LOS ANGELES].

Latrango Canon: see **Telegraph Canyon** [ORANGE].

La Tuna Canyon [LOS ANGELES]: *canyon,* 5.5 miles long, opens into lowlands 4.5 miles northwest of Burbank city hall (lat. 34° 14' N, long. 118°21'30" W; near NW cor. sec. 28, T 2 N, R 14 W). Named on Burbank (1953) 7.5' quadrangle.

Laurel Canyon [LOS ANGELES]:

(1) *canyon,* drained by a stream that flows 1.25 miles to Pacoima Canyon 7 miles north of Sunland (lat. 34°21'35" N, long. 118° 20' W; sec. 10, T 3 N, R 14 W). Named on Sunland (1953) 7.5' quadrangle.

(2) *canyon,* 1.5 miles long, 8.5 miles west-northwest of Los Angeles city hall (lat. 34°06'50" N, long. 118°22'20" W). Named on Hollywood (1966) 7.5' quadrangle.

Laurel Gulch [LOS ANGELES]: *canyon,* drained by a stream that flows 2.5 miles to San Gabriel River 6 miles west-southwest of Mount San Antonio (lat. 34°15'30" N, long. 117°44'45" W). Named on Mount San Antonio (1955) 7.5' quadrangle.

Laurel Spring [ORANGE]: *spring,* nearly 3 miles west of Santiago Peak (lat. 33°42'50" N, long. 117°34'50" W). Named on Santiago Peak (1954) 7.5' quadrangle.

Lava Flow Wash [SAN DIEGO]: *stream,* flows 2.5 miles to Imperial County 5.25 miles east-southeast of Sweeney Pass (lat. 32°47'25" N, long. 116°06'10" W; at E line sec. 12, T 16 S, R 8 E). Named on Sweeney Pass (1959) 7.5' quadrangle.

La Verne [LOS ANGELES]: *town,* 3.25 miles north-northwest of Pomona city hall (lat. 34°06' N, long. 117°46'10" W). Named on Glendora (1966) and San Dimas (1954) 7.5' quadrangles. Pomona (1904) 15' quadrangle has the name "Lordsburg" at present La Verne, and has the name "La Verne" for a place located about 1.25 miles farther northwest. Postal authorities established Lordsburg post office in 1887; they established La Vern post office 2 miles northwest of Lordsburg post office in 1888 and moved it to Lordsburg in 1889; they changed the name of Lordsburg post office to La Verne in 1918 (Salley, p. 119, 126). La Verne incorporated in 1906. Lordsburg, named for its founder, I.W. Lord, originally was a Dunkard colony (Garner, p. 209). The name "La Verne" is from La Verne Heights, a subdivision that had the given name of its promoter (Gudde, 1949, p. 184).

Lavida Hot Springs: see **La Vida Mineral Springs** [ORANGE].

La Vida Mineral Springs [ORANGE]: *locality,* 3 miles north-northeast of Yorba Linda in Carbon Canyon (lat. 33°56' N, long. 117°47'35" W; near S line sec. 2, T 3 S, R 9 W). Named on Yorba Linda (1950) 7.5' quadrangle. Anaheim (1942) 15' quadrangle shows a water feature called Lavida Hot Springs at the site. A resort at the place uses water from an artesian well drilled at or near a former natural spring (Berkstresser, p. A-9).

La Vina: see **Altadena** [LOS ANGELES].

Lawlor: see **Mount Lawlor** [LOS ANGELES].

Lawndale [LOS ANGELES]: *town,* 4.5 miles south of Inglewood city hall (lat. 33°53'10" N, long. 118°21' W). Named on Inglewood (1964) 7.5' quadrangle. Postal authorities established Lawndale post office in 1906 (Frickstad, p. 76), and the town incorporated in 1959. Charles Hopper founded and named the community in 1905 (Gudde, 1949, p. 184).

Lawrence Canyon [SAN DIEGO]: *canyon,* drained by a stream that flows less than 1 mile to San Luis Rey River nearly 1 mile north of downtown Oceanside (lat. 33°12'30" N, long. 117°22'55" W; at W line sec. 23, T 11 S, R 5 W). Named on Oceanside (1968) and San Luis Rey (1948) 7.5' quadrangles.

Lawson Creek [SAN DIEGO]: *stream,* flows 6 miles to Sweetwater River nearly 5 miles south-southwest of Alpine (lat. 32°46'20" N, long. 116°47'50" W; near N line sec. 20, T 16 S, R 2 E). Named on Alpine (1955), Barrett Lake (1960), and Dulzura (1972) 7.5' quadrangles. The name commemorates I.J. Lawson, a pioneer of the neighborhood in the 1870's (Stein, p. 72).

Lawson Peak [SAN DIEGO]: *peak,* nearly 8 miles north of Barrett Junction (lat. 32°43'35" N, long. 116°43'30" W; sec. 1, T 17 S, R 2 E). Altitude 3660 feet. Named on Barrett Lake (1960) 7.5' quadrangle.

Lawson Valley [SAN DIEGO]: *valley,* 7 miles north of Dulzura (lat. 32°44'45" N, long. 116°45'15" W); the valley is along upper reaches of Lawson Creek. Named on Alpine (1955), Barrett Lake (1960), Dulzura (1972), and Viejas Mountain (1960) 7.5' quadrangles. Postal authorities established Lawson Valley post office 8 miles northeast of Jamul in 1890 and discontinued it in 1891 (Salley, p. 120).

La Zanja: see **San Rafael** [LOS ANGELES].

La Zanja Canyon [SAN DIEGO]: *canyon*, drained by a stream that flows 4.5 miles to San Dieguito Valley 4 miles east-northeast of Del Mar (lat. 32°58'45" N, long. 117°12'10" W; sec. 4, T 14 S, R 3 W). Named on Del Mar (1967) 7.5' quadrangle.

Leach Canyon [ORANGE]: *canyon*, drained by a stream that flows 0.5 mile to Riverside County 3.5 miles southeast of Trabuco Peak (lat. 33°40'15" N, long. 117°25'40" W; near N line sec. 8, T 6 S, R 5 W). Named on Alberhill (1954) 7.5' quadrangle.

Leaming Canyon [LOS ANGELES]: *canyon*, drained by a stream that flows 1 mile to Gavin Canyon 2.25 miles south-southwest of Newhall (lat. 34°21'05" N, long. 118°32'50" W; near N line sec. 15, T 3 N, R 16 W). Named on Oat Mountain (1952) 7.5' quadrangle. The name commemorates Christopher Leaming, a pioneer of the 1860's (Reynolds, p. 13).

Le Brun Canyon: see **Drinkwater Canyon** [LOS ANGELES].

Lechler Canyon [LOS ANGELES-VENTURA]: *canyon*, drained by a stream that heads in Los Angeles County and flows nearly 3 miles to Lake Piru 5.5 miles northeast of Piru in Ventura County (lat. 34°28'10" N, long. 118°44' W). Named on Val Verde (1952, photorevised 1969) 7.5' quadrangle, which shows Lechler ranch in nearby in Oak Canyon [LOS ANGELES] (1). Called Leckler Canyon on Santa Susana (1903) 15' quadrangle.

Lechusa Canyon: see **Lachusa Canyon** [LOS ANGELES].

Lechuza Point [LOS ANGELES]: *promontory*, 4 miles northwest of Point Dume (lat. 34°02'05" N, long. 118°51'40" W). Named on Point Dume (1951) 7.5' quadrangle. Called Lachusa Point on Dume Point (1932) 6' quadrangle.

Leckler Canyon: see **Lechler Canyon** [LOS ANGELES-VENTURA].

Lee: see **Mount Lee** [LOS ANGELES].

Leesdale [VENTURA]: *locality*, 4 miles west-southwest of Camarillo along Southern Pacific Railroad (lat. 34°11'50" N, long. 119°05'50" W). Named on Camarillo (1950) 7.5' quadrangle.

Lees Lake [LOS ANGELES]: *lake*, 650 feet long, nearly 3 miles south-southwest of Chatsworth along Chatsworth Creek (lat. 34° 13'20" N, long. 118°37'45" W). Named on Calabasas (1952) 7.5' quadrangle.

Lee Valley [SAN DIEGO]: *valley*, nearly 4 miles east of Jamul at the head of Jamul Creek (lat. 32°43'20" N, long. 116°48'30" W; sec. 6, T 17 S, R 2 E). Named on Dulzura (1972) 7.5' quadrangle. The name is for an early settler (Stein, p. 72).

Leffingwell [LOS ANGELES]: *locality*, 2.5 miles west of La Habra [ORANGE] along Union Pacific Railroad (lat. 33°56' N, long. 117° 59'30" W). Named on La Habra (1952) 7.5' quadrangle.

Leffingwell Creek [LOS ANGELES-ORANGE]: *stream*, heads in Los Angeles County and flows 3.5 miles, partly in Orange County, to La Cañada Verde Creek 2.5 miles south of present Whittier city hall (lat. 33°56'20" N, long. 118°01'25" W). Named on La Habra (1952) and Whittier (1949) 7.5' quadrangles.

Legg Lake [LOS ANGELES]: *lakes*, two, largest 2000 feet long, 3 miles south-southwest of El Monte city hall in a flood control basin of San Gabriel River and Rio Hondo (lat. 34°02' N, long. 118°03'30" W). Named on El Monte (1966) 7.5' quadrangle.

Lemon [VENTURA]: *locality*, 2.25 miles east-southeast of downtown Ventura along Southern Pacific Railroad (lat. 34°15'45" N, long. 119°15'20" W). Named on Ventura (1951) 7.5' quadrangle. The name is from a packing house for lemons (Ricard). California Division of Highways' (1934) map shows a place called Edfu located along the railroad 1 mile east-southeast of Lemon.

Lemon: see **Siempreviva**, under **Otay** [SAN DIEGO] (3); **Walnut** [LOS ANGELES].

Lemon Creek [LOS ANGELES]: *stream*, flows 3 miles to San Jose Creek 7.25 miles south-southwest of Pomona city hall (lat. 34°00'20" N, long. 117°51'40" W); the stream goes through Walnut, which formerly was called Lemon. Named on San Dimas (1966) 7.5' quadrangle.

Lemon Grove [SAN DIEGO]: *town*, 6.5 miles northeast of National City civic center (lat. 32°44'35" N, long. 117°01'45" W). Named on National City (1967) 7.5' quadrangle. Called Lemongrove on San Diego (1904) 15' quadrangle, but United States Board on Geographic Names (1961c, p. 11) rejected this one-word form of the name. Postal authorities established Lemon Grove post office in 1893, changed the name to Lemongrove in 1895, and changed it back to Lemon Grove in 1950 (Salley, p. 121). The Allison brothers laid out the townsite in 10-acre and 20-acre plots (Stein, p. 72).

Lemon Heights [ORANGE]: *locality*, 4.5 miles east-southeast of Orange city hall (lat. 33°45'30" N, long. 117°46'45" W). Named on Orange (1964) 7.5' quadrangle.

Le Montaine Creek [LOS ANGELES]: *stream*, flows 3.5 miles to lowlands 3.5 miles north-northeast of Big Pines (lat. 34°25'30" N, long. 117°40' W; near N line sec. 24, T 4 N, R 8 W). Named on Mescal Creek (1956) 7.5' quadrangle.

Lennox [LOS ANGELES]: *town*, 1.5 miles south of Inglewood city hall (lat. 33°56'25" N, long. 118°21' W). Named on Inglewood (1952) 7.5' quadrangle. Postal authorities established Lennox post office in 1930, discontinued it in 1936, and reestablished it in 1940 (Salley, p. 121). The name is from Lennox, Massachusetts, former home of a resident of the place; it also was known as Inglewood Rancho and as Jefferson (Gudde, 1949, p. 186).

Leona Valley [LOS ANGELES]:

(1) *valley*, 11 miles long, center 10 miles west-southwest of Lancaster (lat. 34°37'15" N, long. 118°17'30" W). Named on Del Sur (1958), Ritter Ridge (1958), and Sleepy Valley (1958) 7.5' quadrangles. Called Leonis Valley on Elizabeth Lake (1917) 30' quadrangle, but United States Board on Geographic Names (1959, p. 6-7) rejected this name, which is from Miguel Leonis, a Basque shepherd (Gudde, 1949, p. 186).

(2) *village*, 9.5 miles east-southeast of the village of Lake Hughes (lat. 34°37'05" N, long. 118°17'15" W; near SW cor. sec. 8, T 6 N, R 13 W); the village is in Leona Valley (1). Named on Sleepy Valley (1958) 7.5' quadrangle.

Leon Canyon [VENTURA]: *canyon*, drained by a stream that flows 2.5 miles to Cañada Larga 5.5 miles north-northeast of Ventura (lat. 34°21'25" N, long. 119°15'05" W). Named on Saticoy (1951) 7.5' quadrangle.

Leonis Valley: see **Leona Valley** [LOS ANGELES].

LeRoy: see **Camp LeRoy**, under **Camp Ivy** [LOS ANGELES]

Latteau Canyon [LOS ANGELES]: *canyon*, drained by a stream that flows 2 miles to Sierra Pelona Valley 6 miles south of the village of Lenna Valley (lat. 34°31'45" N, long. 118°16'40" W; sec. 7, T 5 N, R 13 W). Named on Sleepy Valley (1958) 7.5' quadrangle.

Letterbox Canyon [SAN DIEGO]: *canyon*, less than 1 mile long, 7 miles southeast of Oceanside (lat. 33°08'20" N, long. 117°16'45" W). Named on San Luis Rey (1968) 7.5' quadrangle.

Leucadia [SAN DIEGO]: *town*, 2 miles north-northwest of Encinitas (lat. 33°04'10" N, long. 117°18'10" W). Named on Encinitas (1968) 7.5' quadrangle. Postal authorities established Leucadia post office in 1888, discontinued it the same year, reestablished it in 1889, discontinued it in 1890, reestablished it in 1891, discontinued it in 1894, and reestablished it in 1926 (Frickstad, p. 152). A group of British spiritualists started the community in 1885 and named it for a Greek island (Gudde, 1949, p. 186; Stein, p. 72).

Lewis: see **Mount Lewis** [LOS ANGELES].

Lewis Paul Canyon [LOS ANGELES]: *canyon*, drained by a stream that flows 1.25 miles to Big Dalton Canyon nearly 4 miles northeast of Glendora city hall (lat. 34°10'10" N, long. 117°48'35" W; sec. 15, T 1 N, R 9 W). Named on Glendora (1953) 7.5' quadrangle.

Lews Spring [SAN DIEGO]: *spring*, 5.5 miles west-southwest of Borrego Springs (lat. 33°12'55" N, long. 116°27'35" W; sec. 15, T 11 S, R 5 E). Named on Tubb Canyon (1959) 7.5' quadrangle.

Lexington: see **El Monte** [LOS ANGELES]; **Lockwood Flat** [VENTURA].

Lexington Wash: see **Rio Hondo** [LOS ANGELES] (1).

Libby Lake: see **Little Libby Lake** [SAN DIEGO].

Liberty: see **Calabasas** [LOS ANGELES].

Liberty Canyon [LOS ANGELES]: *canyon*, drained by a stream that flows nearly 4 miles to Las Virgenes Creek 5.5 miles north-northwest of Malibu Point (lat. 34°06'20" N, long. 118°42'40" W; near SE cor. sec. 1, T 1 S, R 18 W). Named on Calabasas (1952) and Malibu Beach (1951) 7.5' quadrangles.

Liberty Park [ORANGE]: *locality*, 3.25 miles north of present Huntington Beach civic center (lat. 33°42'25" N, long. 117°59'20" W; at E line sec. 26, T 5 S, R 11 W). Named on Newport Beach (1951) 7.5' quadrangle.

Lickskillit: see **El Monte** [LOS ANGELES].

Lido Isle [ORANGE]: *island*, 1 mile long, 6 miles southeast of Huntington Beach civic center in Newport Bay (lat. 33°36'45" N, long. 117°55' W). Named on Newport Beach (1965) 7.5' quadrangle. W.K. Parkinson purchased the property from Pacific Electric Land Company in 1923, had the island built up with dredged material, and opened a subdivision there in 1928—the name is from an island southeast of Venice, Italy (Meadows, p. 78). When Henry E. Huntington owned the place, it was known as Pacific Electric Island (Gleason, p. 98).

Lido Isle Reach: see **Newport Bay** [ORANGE].

Liebre Creek: see **La Liebra** [LOS ANGELES].

Liebre Gulch [LOS ANGELES]: *canyon*, drained by a stream that flows 8 miles to Piru Creek 11 miles south-southeast of Gorman (lat. 34°38'50" N, long. 118°45'45" W; near N line sec. 2, T 6 N, R 18 W); the canyon heads near the west end of Liebre Mountain. Named on Black Mountain (1958) and Liebre Mountain (1958) 7.5' quadrangles. West Fork branches off about 0.5 mile above the mouth of the main canyon; it is 7 miles long and is named on Black Mountain (1958) 7.5' quadrangle. United States Board on Geographic Names (1960c, p. 19) rejected the name "West Liebre Gulch" for West Fork.

Liebre Mountain [LOS ANGELES]: *ridge*, west-northwest-trending, 6 miles long, 12.5 miles east-southeast of Gorman (lat. 34°43' N, long. 118°40" W). Named on Burnt Peak (1958) and Liebre Mountain (1958) 7.5' quadrangles. Called Liebre Mountains on Neenach (1943) 15' quadrangle. Fairbanks (p. 493) referred to a range called Sierra Libre, and Marcou (p. 166) mentioned a range that he called both Sierra Liebra and Sierra de Liebre.

Lilac [SAN DIEGO]: *locality,* 5.25 miles south of Pala (lat. 33°17'15" N, long. 117°05' W; near SW cor. sec. 22, T 10 S, R 2 W). Named on Pala (1968) 7.5' quadrangle. Postal authorities established Lilac post office in 1898 and discontinued it in 1912 (Frickstad, p. 152).

Lillian Hill [SAN DIEGO]: *peak,* 9 miles north-northwest of Descanso (lat. 32°58'35" N, long. 116°40'50" W; near NW cor. sec. 9, T 14 S, R 3 E). Named on Tule Springs (1960) 7.5' quadrangle.

Lilly Meadows [VENTURA]: *area,* 12.5 miles northeast of Reyes Peak (lat. 34°46' N, long. 119°08' W; at W line sec. 20, T 8 N, R 21 W). Named on Sawmill Mountain (1943) 7.5' quadrangle.

Lily Spring [LOS ANGELES]: *spring,* nearly 3 miles northeast of Crystal Lake (lat. 34°20'40" N, long. 117°48'30" W). Named on Crystal Lake (1958) 7.5' quadrangle.

Limco: see **Limon** [VENTURA].

Lime Canyon [VENTURA]:

(1) *canyon,* drained by a stream that flows 3 miles to Piru Canyon 3.25 miles north-northeast of Piru (lat. 34°27'15" N, long. 118°45'40" W). Named on Piru (1952) 7.5' quadrangle.

(2) *canyon,* drained by a stream that flows nearly 2 miles to Matilija Creek 4.5 miles west of Wheeler Springs (lat. 34°30'10" N, long. 119°22'10" W; near W line sec. 23, T 5 N, R 24 W). Named on Matilija (1952) and White Ledge Peak (1952) 7.5' quadrangles.

Limekiln Canyon [LOS ANGELES]:

(1) *canyon,* 4 miles long, opens into lowlands 3 miles east-northeast of Chatsworth (lat. 34°16'20" N, long. 118°33'25" W; sec. 9, T 2 N, R 16 W). Named on Oat Mountain (1952) 7.5' quadrangle.

(2) *canyon,* 1.5 miles long, opens into lowlands 3.5 miles northeast of San Fernando (lat. 34°19'10" N, long. 118°23'50" W; sec. 25, T 3 N, R 15 W). Named on San Fernando (1953) 7.5' quadrangle.

Limekiln Canyon Wash [LOS ANGELES]: *stream,* flows nearly 4 miles to Aliso Canyon Wash 3.5 miles northeast of the center of Canoga Park (lat. 34°13'50" N, long. 118°32'40" W); the stream heads at the mouth of Limekiln Canyon (1). Named on Canoga Park (1952) and Oat Mountain (1952) 7.5' quadrangles.

Limerock Canyon [LOS ANGELES]: *canyon,* drained by a stream that flows 1.5 miles to Little Tujunga Canyon 4 miles north-northwest of Sunland (lat. 34°18'45" N, long. 118°20'35" W; near E line sec. 28, T 3 N, R 14 W); the canyon is northeast of Limerock Peak. Named on Sunland (1953) 7.5' quadrangle.

Limerock Peak [LOS ANGELES]: *peak,* nearly 5 miles northwest of Sunland (lat. 34°19'05" N, long. 118°21'25" W; sec. 28, T 3 N, R 14 W). Altitude 2986 feet. Named on Sunland (1966) 7.5' quadrangle.

Limestone Canyon [ORANGE]: *canyon,* drained by a stream that flows 5.5 miles to Santiago Reservoir 6.5 miles south-southwest of Sierra Peak (lat. 33°45'50" N, long. 117°42'35" W). Named on Black Star Canyon (1967) and El Toro (1968) 7.5' quadrangles. Called Rabbit Canyon on Corona (1902) 30' quadrangle. The feature also was called Cañada de Agua Chinon for a spring that was named for a curly-headed man who lived by it—*chinon* means "curly" in Spanish (Meadows, p. 32; Stephenson, p. 99). The name "Limestone Canyon" was given in 1862 when Sam Shrewsbury built a limekiln in the canyon (Meadows, p. 78).

Limon [VENTURA]: *locality,* 3.5 miles southwest of Santa Paula along Southern Pacific Railroad (lat. 34°19'15" N, long. 119°06'25" W); a spur rail line to Limoneira leaves the main line at the place. Named on Santa Paula (1951) 7.5' quadrangle. Called Limco on California Mining Bureau's (1917a) map.

Limoneira [VENTURA]: *locality,* 4 miles west-southwest of Santa Paula (lat. 34°19'50" N, long. 119°07'25" W). Named on Santa Paula (1951) and Saticoy (1951) 7.5' quadrangles. The name is from a packing house for lemons (Ricard).

Lincoln Acres [SAN DIEGO]: *district,* 2 miles east-southeast of National City civic center (lat. 32°39'55" N, long. 117°04'20" W). Named on National City (1967) 7.5' quadrangle. Postal authorities established Lincoln Acres post office in 1927 (Salley, p. 122). They established Lanoitan post office 3 miles southeast of National City in 1925 and moved it to Lincoln Acres in 1928—Lanoitan is the word "national" spelled backwards (Salley, p. 117).

Lincoln Crest [LOS ANGELES]: *pass,* 2.25 miles south-southwest of the village of Leona Valley at the head of Bouquet Canyon (lat. 34°35'10" N, long. 118°18'15" W; at NW cor. sec. 30, T 6 N, R 13 W). Named on Sleepy Valley (1958) 7.5' quadrangle.

Lincoln Heights [LOS ANGELES]: *district,* 2.5 miles east-northeast of Los Angeles city hall (lat. 34°04'15" N, long. 118°12'15" W). Named on Los Angeles (1953) 7.5' quadrangle. Alhambra (1926) 6' quadrangle has the name "Lincoln Park" at the place. Postal authorities established Lincoln Heights post office in 1949 (Salley, p. 122).

Lincoln Park [LOS ANGELES]: *locality,* 6 miles northeast of present Los Angeles city hall (lat. 34°06'35" N, long. 118°10'30" W). Named on Pasadena (1900) 15' quadrangle.

Lincoln Park: see **Lincoln Heights** [LOS ANGELES].

Lincoln Village [LOS ANGELES]: *district,* 4.5 miles north-northwest of Long Beach city hall (lat. 33°49'45" N, long. 118°13'15" W). Named on Long Beach (1949) 7.5' quadrangle.

Linda Isle [ORANGE]: *island,* 1500 feet long, 6.5 miles east-southeast of Huntington Beach civic center in Newport Bay (lat. 33°36'50" N, long. 117°54'05" W). Named on Newport Beach (1965) 7.5' quadrangle. Called Shark Island on Newport Beach 7.5' (1951) quadrangle, but United States Board on Geographic Names (1967a, p. 3) rejected this designation. Teenagers found the place a romantic playground and named it Shark Island in the 1930's; the name "Linda Isle" is for a granddaughter of James Irvine, Jr. (Meadows, p. 78, 127).

Linda Vista [LOS ANGELES]: *locality,* 3.5 miles northwest of Pasadena city hall (lat. 34°10'15" N, long. 118°10'40" W). Named on Pasadena (1953) 7.5' quadrangle.

Linda Vista [SAN DIEGO]: *district,* 7.5 miles southeast of Point La Jolla in San Diego (lat. 32°47'05" N, long. 117°10' W). Named on La Jolla (1967) 7.5' quadrangle. Postal authorities reestablished Linda Vista post office in 1943 at the place, which is 5 miles east of the former site of Linda Vista post office at present Miramar (2)—the community provided housing for aircraft workers during World War II (Salley, p. 122). Ellis and Lee's (1919) map shows a place called Rosedale situated less than 2 miles north of present Linda Vista, where La Jolla (1943) 7.5' quadrangle shows Rosedale landing field.

Linda Vista: see **Miramar** [SAN DIEGO] (1) and (2).

Linda Vista Military Branch: see **Camp Kearny** [SAN DIEGO].

Lindero Canyon [LOS ANGELES-VENTURA]: *canyon,* drained by a stream that heads in Ventura County and flows 6.5 miles to Medea Creek 1 mile west of Agoura in Los Angeles County (lat. 34°08'20" N, long. 118°45'30" W). Named on Thousand Oaks (1952) 7.5' quadrangle. The feature is on the boundary between two land grants—*lindero* means "boundary" in Spanish (Ricard).

Lindo Lake [SAN DIEGO]: *lake,* 2500 feet long, at Lakeside (lat. 32° 51'30" N, long. 116°54'55" W). Named on El Cajon (1939) 15' quadrangle.

Lindys: see **Nintynine Oaks** [LOS ANGELES].

Lion Canyon [LOS ANGELES]: *canyon,* drained by a stream that flows 1.25 miles to Burnt Peak Canyon 2.25 miles south of Burnt Peak (lat. 34°38'50" N, long. 118°34'40" W). Named on Burnt Peak (1958) 7.5' quadrangle.

Lion Canyon [ORANGE]: *canyon,* drained by a stream that flows nearly 4 miles to San Juan Canyon 7 miles south of Trabuco Peak (lat. 33°36'05" N, long. 117°27'35" W; sec. 36, T 6 S, R 6 W). Named on Alberhill (1954) and Sitton Peak (1954) 7.5' quadrangles.

Lion Canyon [VENTURA]:

(1) *canyon,* drained by a stream that flows 6.5 miles to Sespe Creek 8 miles east-northeast of Wheeler Springs (lat. 34°33'35" N, long. 119°09'35" W; near NW cor. sec. 2, T 5 N, R 22 W). Named on Lion Canyon (1943) and Topatopa Mountains (1943) 7.5' quadrangles.

(2) *canyon,* 4.5 miles long, along Lion Creek above a point 2 miles south-southwest of the town of Ojai (lat. 34°25'20" N, long. 119° 15'50" W). Named on Matilija (1952) and Ojai (1952) 7.5' quadrangles. Called Cañada de Leon on Peckham's (1866) map.

Lion Creek [SAN DIEGO]: *stream,* flows 2.25 miles to Pauma Creek 1.5 miles west-northwest of Boucher Hill (lat. 33°20'45" N, long. 116°56'30" W; near SW cor. sec. 36, T 9 S, R 1 W). Named on Boucher Hill (1948) 7.5' quadrangle.

Lion Creek [VENTURA]: *stream,* flows 8 miles to San Antonio Creek 2 miles south-southwest of the town of Ojai (lat. 34°25'20" N, long. 119°15'50" W); the stream passes through Lion Canyon (2). Named on Ojai (1952) 7.5' quadrangle.

Lion Head: see **Lions Head** [LOS ANGELES].

Lions Canyon [LOS ANGELES-ORANGE]: *canyon,* drained by a stream that heads in Los Angeles County and flows 1.5 miles, partly in San Bernardino County, to Carbon Canyon 4.25 miles north-northeast of Yorba Linda just inside Orange County (lat. 33°56'40" N, long. 117°46'50" W; near NW cor. sec. 1, T 3 S, R 9 W). Named on Yorba Linda (1950) 7.5' quadrangle.

Lions Head [LOS ANGELES]: *promontory,* 4 miles east of Silver Peak on the north side of Santa Catalina Island (lat. 33°27'10" N, long. 118°30' W). Named on Santa Catalina West (1943) 7.5' quadrangle. United States Board on Geographic Names (1976c, p. 4) approved the singular form "Lion Head" for the name, and gave the names "Lions Head" and "Lions Head Point" as variants.

Lions Head Point: see **Lions Head** [LOS ANGELES].

Lithia Spring [SAN DIEGO]: *spring,* nearly 3 miles east of San Felipe in Hoover Canyon (lat. 33°12'15" N, long. 116°33'05" W; at E line sec. 22, T 11 S, R 4 E). Named on Ranchita (1960) 7.5' quadrangle.

Little Bear Canyon [LOS ANGELES]: *canyon,* drained by a stream that flows 2 miles to Arroyo Seco 6.5 miles southeast of Condor Peak (lat. 34°15'10" N, long. 118°08'55" W); the mouth of the canyon is 500 feet north of the mouth of Bear Canyon (5). Named on Condor Peak (1959)

7.5' quadrangle. Tujunga (1900) 15' quadrangle has the name "Little Bear Creek" for the stream in the canyon.

Little Bear Canyon: see **Bear Canyon** [LOS ANGELES] (3).

Little Bear Creek: see **Little Bear Canyon** [LOS ANGELES].

Little Blair Valley [SAN DIEGO]: *valley*, 14 miles east-southeast of Julian (lat. 33°01'15" N, long. 116°22'45" W); the feature is east of Blair Valley. Named on Earthquake Valley (1959) and Whale Peak (1959) 7.5' quadrangles.

Little Borrego [SAN DIEGO]: *locality*, 3 miles south of Ocotillo Wells (lat. 33°06' N, long. 116°07'30" W; sec. 27, T 12 S, R 8 E). Site named on Borrego Mountain SE (1958) 7.5' quadrangle.

Little Burnt Peak [LOS ANGELES]: *peak*, 0.5 mile north of Burnt Peak (lat. 34°41'20" N, long. 118°34'35" W). Named on Burnt Peak (1958) 7.5' quadrangle.

Little Buttes [LOS ANGELES]: *hill*, 11.5 miles northeast of the village of Lake Hughes (lat. 34°47'55" N, long. 118°18'10" W; sec. 7, T 8 N, R 13 W). Named on Little Buttes (1965) 7.5' quadrangle.

Little Cedar Canyon [SAN DIEGO]: *canyon*, drained by a stream that flows 3.25 miles to Jamul Creek 5 miles south of Jamul (lat. 32°38'35" N, long. 116°52'15" W); the mouth of the canyon is 1 mile west-southwest of the mouth of Cedar Canyon. Named on Dulzura (1972) and Otay Mountain (1972) 7.5' quadrangles.

Little Cedars Campground [LOS ANGELES]: *locality*, 7.5 miles west-southwest of Valyermo along South Fork Little Rock Creek (lat. 34°23'50" N, long. 117°58'10" W; near S line sec. 30, T 4 N, R 10 W). Named on Juniper Hills (1959) 7.5' quadrangle.

Little Chief Mountain [SAN DIEGO]: *peak*, nearly 2 miles northeast of Pala (lat. 32°22'45" N, long. 117°02'55" W; near W line sec. 24, T 9 S, R 2 W); the peak is 0.5 mile south of Chief Mountain. Altitude 1154 feet. Named on Pechanga (1968) 7.5' quadrangle.

Little Cienega: see **Falling Spring** [LOS ANGELES].

Little Clark Lake [SAN DIEGO]: *dry lake*, 1500 feet long, 9.5 miles northeast of Borrego Springs (lat. 33°20'10" N, long. 116°14'15" W; sec. 3, T 10 S, R 7 E); the feature is in Clark Valley. Named on Fonts Point (1959) 7.5' quadrangle.

Little Cottonwood Creek: see **Oso Canyon** [LOS ANGELES].

Little Dalton Campground [LOS ANGELES]: *locality*, 2.5 miles north-northeast of Glendora city hall (lat. 34°10'05" N, long. 117° 50'15" W; near SE cor. sec. 17, T 1 N, R 9 W); the place is in Little Dalton Canyon. Named on Glendora (1953) 7.5' quadrangle. Glendora (1966) 7.5' quadrangle shows Little Dalton Picnic Area at the site

Little Dalton Canyon [LOS ANGELES]: *canyon*, 4 miles long, opens into lowlands 2 miles northeast of Glendora city hall (lat. 34°09'15" N, long. 117°50'15" W; at E line sec. 20, T 1 N, R 9 W); the mouth of the canyon is just west of the mouth of Big Dalton Canyon. Named on Glendora (1953) 7.5' quadrangle.

Little Dalton Wash [LOS ANGELES]: *stream*, flows nearly 7 miles from the mouth of Little Dalton Canyon to Big Dalton Wash 2.5 miles east-northeast of Baldwin Park city hall (lat. 34°06' N, long. 117°55'25" W; near W line sec. 10, T 1 S, R 10 W). Named on Baldwin Park (1953) 7.5' quadrangle.

Little Devil Wash [SAN DIEGO]: *stream*, flows 1.25 miles to Vallecito Creek 4.25 miles north of Sweeney Pass (lat. 32°53'30" N, long. 116°10'20" W; at W line sec. 4, T 15 S, R 8 E). Named on Arroyo Tapiado (1959) 7.5' quadrangle.

Little Gibraltar [LOS ANGELES]: *promontory*, nearly 4 miles north-northeast of Mount Banning on the north side of Santa Catalina Island (lat. 33°25'20" N, long. 118°24'15" W). Named on Santa Catalina North (1950) 7.5' quadrangle.

Little Harbor [LOS ANGELES]: *embayment*, 2.5 miles west-northwest of Mount Banning on the west side of Santa Catalina Island (lat. 33°23' N, long. 118°28'30" W). Named on Santa Catalina North (1950) 7.5' quadrangle.

Little Island: see **Balboa Island** [ORANGE].

Little Jimmy Campground [LOS ANGELES]: *locality*, 2 miles north-northeast of Crystal Lake (lat. 34°20'50" N, long. 117°49'45" W); the place is 750 feet north of Little Jimmy Spring. Named on Crystal Lake (1958) 7.5' quadrangle.

Little Jimmy Spring [LOS ANGELES]: *spring*, 2 miles north-northeast of Crystal Lake (lat. 34°20'45" N, long. 117°49'40" W). Named on Crystal Lake (1958) 7.5' quadrangle. The feature first was called Gooseberry Spring for the gooseberry bushes around it; Jimmy Swinnerton, a well-known newspaper cartoonist, camped at the place in 1909 and painted a likeness of his cartoon character "Little Jimmy" on a tree stump—the spring took the name of the character, and the place was called Swinnerton Camp (Robinson, J.W., 1983, p. 109).

Little Joaquin Valley [ORANGE]: *valley*, 6.5 miles east of Santa Ana city hall (lat. 33°44'50" N, long. 117°44'15" W). Named on Orange (1964) and Tustin (1965) 7'5 quadrangles. The name is from the fancied resemblance of the feature to a miniature version of San Joaquin Valley of central California (Meadows, p. 78).

Little Laguna Lake [SAN DIEGO]: *intermittent lake*, 1000 feet long, 2 miles west-southwest of Monument Peak (lat. 32°53'10" N, long. 116°27'10" W; near N line sec. 10, T 15 S, R 5 E); the feature is 0.5 mile northeast of Big Laguna Lake. Named on Monument Peak (1959) 7.5' quadrangle. This lake and nearby Big Laguna Lake together are called Laguna Lakes on Cuyapaipe (1944) 15' quadrangle, but United States Board on Geographic Names (1961b, p. 11) rejected this name.

Little Lake [LOS ANGELES]: *intermittent lake*, 800 feet long, 4 miles south-west of present Whittier city hall (lat. 33°55'50" N, long. 118°04'55" W). Named on Whittier (1925) 6' quadrangle.

Littlelands: see **Tujunga** [LOS ANGELES] (2).

Little Las Flores Canyon [LOS ANGELES]: *canyon*, drained by a stream that flows 1.5 miles to Las Flores Canyon (2) 3 miles northeast of Malibu Point (lat. 34°03'25" N, long. 118°38'10" W; near NW cor. sec. 26, T 1 S, R 17 W). Named on Malibu Beach (1951) and Topanga (1952) 7.5' quadrangles.

Little Libby Lake [SAN DIEGO]: *intermittent lake*, 0.25 mile long, 4 miles south-southwest of Morro Hill (lat. 33°15'05" N, long. 117° 18'25" W; sec. 4, T 11 S, R 4 W). Named on Morro Hill (1968) 7.5' quadrangle. The name commemorates William Libby and Catherine Libby, who homesteaded by the lake in 1868 (Stein, p. 73).

Little Mermaids Canyon [LOS ANGELES]: *canyon*, drained by a stream that flows 2.25 miles to West Fork San Gabriel River 7.5 miles north of Azusa city hall (lat. 34°14'45" N, long. 117°54'20" W); the mouth of the canyon is 1650 feet west of the mouth of Big Mermaid Canyon. Named on Azusa (1953) and Waterman Mountain (1959) 7.5' quadrangles.

Little Mutau Creek [VENTURA]: *stream*, flows 5 miles to Mutau Creek 15 miles east of Reyes Peak (lat. 34°39'20" N, long. 119°01'30" W; sec. 32, T 7 N, R 20 W). Named on Lockwood Valley (1943) and McDonald Peak (1958) 7.5' quadrangles.

Little Nicholas Canyon: see **Willow Creek** [LOS ANGELES].

Little Nugget Placers: see **Gold Creek** [LOS ANGELES].

Little Potrero Creek [SAN DIEGO]: *stream*, flows 2 miles to Potrero Creek (2) 7 miles west-southwest of Morena Village (lat. 32°37'45" N, long. 116°36'25" W; near NW cor. sec. 8, T 18 S, R 4 E). Named on Morena Reservoir (1960) 7.5' quadrangle.

Little Rattlesnake Canyon: see **Shoemaker Canyon** [LOS ANGELES] (2).

Littlerock [LOS ANGELES]: *locality*, 27 miles north of Azusa (lat. 34°31'15" N, long. 117°58'50" W; sec. 13, T 5 N, R 11 W). Named on Littlerock (1957) 7.5' quadrangle. Called Little Rock on Little Rock (1934) 6' quadrangle, but United States Board on Geographic Names (1983b, p. 5) rejected this form of the name. Postal authorities established Little Rock post office in 1893 and changed the name to Littlerock in 1894; the place also was known as Alpine Springs Colony and as Tierra Bonita (Salley, p. 123).

Little Rock Creek [LOS ANGELES]: *stream*, flows 14 miles to Little Rock Reservoir 6 miles north of Pacifico Mountain (lat. 34°28'10" N, long. 118°01'10" W; near S line sec. 34, T 5 N, R 11 W). Named on Crystal Lake (1958), Juniper Hills (1959), Pacifico Mountain (1959), and Waterman Mountain (1959) 7.5' quadrangles. On Mount Emma (1940) 6' quadrangle, the name "Little Rock Creek" applies both to present Little Rock Creek and to present Little Rock Wash, which is below Little Rock Reservoir. South Fork enters from the south 7.25 miles west-southwest of Valyermo; it is 5.5 miles long and is named on Chilao Flat (1959), Juniper Hills (1959), and Waterman Mountain (1959) 7.5' quadrangles.

Little Rock Reservoir [LOS ANGELES]: *lake*, 1.25 miles long, behind a dam 7 miles north of Pacifico Mountain (lat. 34°29'10" N, long. 118°01'20" W; near S line sec. 27, T 5 N, R 11 W); the dam is on Little Rock Creek. Named on Pacifico Mountain (1959) 7.5' quadrangle.

Little Rock Station [LOS ANGELES]: *locality*, nearly 8 miles north of Pacifico Mountain (lat. 34°29'45" N, long. 118°01'35" W; at W line sec. 27, T 5 N, R 11 W); the place is along Little Rock Wash. Named on Pacifico Mountain (1959) 7.5' quadrangle.

Little Rock Wash [LOS ANGELES]: *stream* and *dry wash*, extends for 19 miles to end 6.5 miles east of Lancaster (lat. 34°42'15" N, long. 118°01'30" W; at N line sec. 15, T 7 N, R 11 W); the feature heads at Little Rock Reservoir. Named on Lancaster East (1958), Littlerock (1957), Pacifico Mountain (1959), and Palmdale (1958) 7.5' quadrangles. Called Little Rock Cr. on Elizabeth Lake (1917) 30' quadrangle.

Little Santa Anita Canyon [LOS ANGELES]: *canyon*, 3.25 miles long, the mouth is 3.5 miles south-southeast of Mount Wilson (1) (lat. 34° 10'30" N, long. 118°02'30" W; sec. 18, T 1 N, R 11 W); the mouth of the canyon is about 1.5 miles west of the mouth of Santa Anita Canyon. Named on Mount Wilson (1953) 7.5' quadrangle. The Carter brothers started a resort in 1906 called Carter's Camp that was located just below the mouth of Little Santa Anita Canyon; the place was sold in 1913, subdivided, and renamed Sierra Madre Canyon Park (Robinson, J.W., 1977, p. 128). A place called both Quarterway House and The Old Trading Post was situated 2 miles up the canyon from Carter's Camp (Robinson, J.W., 1977, p. 130).

Little Sespe Creek [VENTURA]: *stream*, flows 2 miles to Sespe Creek 3.5

miles north-northwest of Fillmore (lat. 34°27'05" N, long. 118°55'25" W; at S line sec. 1, T 4 N, R 20 W). Named on Fillmore (1951) 7.5' quadrangle.

Little Simi Valley [VENTURA]: *valley,* at and near Moorpark (lat. 34°16'30" N, long. 118°53'45" W); the feature is along Arroyo Simi. Named on Moorpark (1951) and Simi (1951) 7.5' quadrangles.

Little Springs Canyon [LOS ANGELES]: *canyon,* drained by a stream that flows nearly 4 miles to the sea 2.5 miles west-northwest of Mount Banning on Santa Catalina Island (lat. 33°23'10" N, long. 118°28'25" W); the feature is west of Big Springs Canyon. Named on Santa Catalina North (1950) 7.5' quadrangle.

Little Stonewall Creek [SAN DIEGO]: *stream,* flows 2.25 miles to Cuyamaca Reservoir 3 miles northeast of Cuyamaca Peak (lat. 32° 58'50" N, long. 116°34'15" W). Named on Cuyamaca Peak (1960) 7.5' quadrangle.

Little Stonewall Peak [SAN DIEGO]: *peak,* nearly 3 miles east-northeast of Cuyamaca Peak (lat. 32°57'55" N, long. 116°33'50" W); the feature is 0.5 mile northeast of Stonewall Peak. Altitude 5250 feet. Named on Cuyamaca Peak (1960) 7.5' quadrangle.

Little Sycamore Canyon [SAN DIEGO]: *canyon,* drained by a stream that flows 2.25 miles to San Diego River 5.5 miles north of La Mesa (lat. 32°50'40" N, long. 117°01'50" W). Named on La Mesa (1967) 7.5' quadrangle.

Little Sycamore Canyon [VENTURA]: *canyon,* drained by a stream that flows nearly 5 miles to the sea 5 miles south-southwest of the mouth of Big Sycamore Canyon (lat. 34°03'10" N, long. 118°57'45" W; sec. 27, T 1 S, R 20 W). Named on Triumfo Pass (1950) 7.5' quadrangle.

Little Tahunga Canyon: see **Little Tujunga Canyon** [LOS ANGELES].

Little Tecate Mountain: see **Little Tecate Peak** [SAN DIEGO].

Little Tecate Peak [SAN DIEGO]: *peak,* nearly 2 miles west-southwest of Barrett Junction (lat. 32°35'55" N, long. 116°43'50" W; at N line sec. 24, T 18 S, R 2 E); the feature is nearly 3 miles west-northwest of Tecate Peak. Altitude 2366 feet. Named on Tecate (1960) 7.5' quadrangle. Called Little Tecate Mt. on Cuyamaca (1903) 30' quadrangle, and called Little Tecate on Tucker and Reed's (1939) map.

Little Trough Canyon [LOS ANGELES]: *canyon,* 0.5 mile long, opens into Lobo Canyon (1) 8 miles north of Point Dume (lat. 34° 07'05" N, long. 118°48'55" W; near SE cor. sec. 36, T 1 N, R 19 W); the mouth of the canyon is 1700 feet west of the mouth of Trough Canyon (2). Named on Point Dume (1951) 7.5' quadrangle.

Little Tujunga Canyon [LOS ANGELES]: *canyon,* drained by a stream that flows 5.5 miles to lowlands 4 miles west-northwest of downtown Sunland (lat. 34°17' N, long. 118°22'10" W; sec. 5, T 2 N, R 14 W). Named on Sunland (1953) 7.5' quadrangle. United States Board on Geographic Names (1933, p. 467) rejected the form "Little Tahunga Canyon" for the name, and (1975a, p. 5) approved the name "Little Tujunga Creek" for the stream in the canyon.

Little Tujunga Creek: see **Little Tujunga Canyon** [LOS ANGELES].

Little Valley [SAN DIEGO]: *valley,* 3.5 miles south of Manzanita (lat. 32°37'45" N, long. 116°17'25" W; sec. 5, T 18 S, R 7 E). Named on Live Oak Springs (1959) 7.5' quadrangle.

Live Oak Acres [VENTURA]: *settlement,* 4.5 miles southwest of the town of Ojai along Ventura River (lat. 34°24'30" N, long. 119°18'25" W). Named on Matilija (1952) 7.5' quadrangle.

Live Oak Campground [LOS ANGELES]: *locality,* 4 miles southeast of Solemint in Sand Canyon (2) (lat. 34°22'45" N, long. 118°24'10" W; sec. 1, T 3 N, R 15 W). Named on Mint Canyon (1960) 7.5' quadrangle.

Live Oak Canyon [LOS ANGELES]: *canyon,* 3 miles long, opens into lowlands 4.5 miles north of Pomona city hall (lat. 34°07'30" N, long. 117°44'35" W; sec. 32, T 1 N, R 8 W). Named on Mount Baldy (1954) 7.5' quadrangle. Cucamonga (1903) 15' quadrangle has the name "Liveoak Creek" for the stream in the canyon.

Live Oak Canyon [ORANGE]: *canyon,* drained by a stream that flows nearly 3 miles to lowlands along Arroyo Trabuco 5.5 miles southwest of Santiago Peak (lat. 33°39'10" N, long. 117°35'55" W; sec. 15, T 6 S, R 7 W). Named on Santiago Peak (1954) 7.5' quadrangle.

Liveoak Creek: see **Live Oak Canyon** [LOS ANGELES]; **Live Oak Wash** [LOS ANGELES].

Live Oak Spring Canyon: see **Sand Canyon** [LOS ANGELES] (2).

Live Oak Springs [SAN DIEGO]: *locality,* 3 miles west-northwest of Manzanita (lat. 32°41'25" N, long. 116°20' W; around SE cor. sec. 14, T 17 S, R 6 E). Named on Live Oak Springs (1959) 7.5' quadrangle. Charles Hill settled at the small resort in 1886 (Stein, p. 73).

Live Oak Wash [LOS ANGELES]: *stream,* flows 3.5 miles to Puddingstone Reservoir 3.5 miles northwest of Pomona city hall (lat. 34°05'40" N, long. 117°47'15" W). Named on Ontario (1954) and San Dimas (1954) 7.5' quadrangles. Called Liveoak Creek on Cucamonga (1903) 15' quadrangle.

Lizard Canyon [SAN DIEGO]: *canyon,* less than 1 mile long, opens into the canyon of San Felipe Creek 8.5 miles south of Borrego Springs (lat. 33°07'55" N, long. 116°23'35" W). Named on Tubb Canyon (1959) 7.5' quadrangle. The canyon divides at the head into East Fork and West Fork. East Fork is nearly 1 mile long and West Fork is 1.25 miles long; both forks are named on Earthquake Valley (1959) 7.5' quadrangle.

Llano [LOS ANGELES]: *locality,* 10 miles east of Littlerock (lat. 34° 30'20" N, long. 117°49' W; on E line sec. 21, T 5 N, R 9 W). Named on Lovejoy Buttes (1957) 7.5' quadrangle. Llano (1934) 6' quadrangle shows Llano post office located 1 mile farther west (sec. 21, T 5 N, R 9 W). Postal authorities established Llano post office in 1890, discontinued it in 1900, and reestablished it in 1915 (Frickstad, p. 76). The name recalls a socialistic colony called Llano del Rio that operated at the place from 1914 until 1918 (Hoover, Rensch, and Rensch, p. 168).

Llano del Rio: see **Llano** [LOS ANGELES].

Loara: see **West Anaheim** [ORANGE].

Lobe Canyon: see **Lobo Canyon** [LOS ANGELES] (1).

Lobo: see **Hansen** [ORANGE].

Lobo Canyon [LOS ANGELES]:

(1) *canyon,* drained by a stream that flows 3.25 miles to Triunfo Canyon 8.5 miles north of Point Dume (lat. 34°07'25" N, long. 118°47'35" W; sec. 32, T 1 N, R 18 W). Named on Point Dume (1951) 7.5' quadrangle Called Lobe Canyon on Camulos (1903) 30' quadrangle. Los Angeles County (1935) map shows a feature called Bodie Peak located near the head of the canyon (sec. 2, T 1 S, R 19 W).

(2) *canyon,* drained by a stream that flows 1.5 miles to Cogswell Reservoir 9 miles north-northwest of Azusa city hall (lat. 34°14'30" N, long. 117°59'15" W; sec. 24, T 2 N, R 11 W). Named on Azusa (1953) and Waterman Mountain (1959) 7.5' quadrangles.

Lobster Bay [LOS ANGELES]: *embayment,* 3.25 miles southeast of Silver Peak on the south side of Santa Catalina Island (lat. 33°25'45" N, long. 118°31'30" W). Named on Santa Catalina West (1943) 7.5' quadrangle.

Lobster Point [LOS ANGELES]: *promontory,* 4 miles southeast of Silver Peak on the south side of Santa Catalina Island (lat. 33°25'20" N, long. 118°30'45" W); the feature is east of Lobster Bay. Named on Santa Catalina West (1943) 7.5' quadrangle.

Lockwood Creek [VENTURA]: *stream,* flows 11 miles to Piru Creek 5.5 miles northwest of McDonald Peak (lat. 34°41'55" N, long. 118°59'50" W; near E line sec. 16, T 7 N, R 20 W); the stream goes through Lockwood Valley. Named on Lockwood Valley (1943), McDonald Peak (1958), and San Guillermo (1943) 7.5' quadrangles. North Fork enters in Lockwood; it is 8.5 miles long and is named on Lockwood Valley (1943) and Sawmill Mountain (1943) 7.5' quadrangles. Middle Fork enters North Fork in Lockwood Valley; it is 7 miles long and is named on Cuddy Valley (1943), Lockwood Valley (1943), and Sawmill Mountain (1943) 7.5' quadrangles.

Lockwood Flat [VENTURA]: *valley,* 5.5 miles northwest of McDonald Peak along Piru Creek (lat. 34°42' N, long. 118°59'45" W; on E line sec. 16, T 7 N, R 20 W); the feature is at the mouth of Lockwood Creek. Named on McDonald Peak (1958) 7.5' quadrangle. A town called Lexington was laid out at the place in 1887 during mining excitement (Outland, 1969, p. 54).

Lockwood Mesa: see **Solana Beach** [SAN DIEGO].

Lockwood Valley [VENTURA]: *valley,* 13 miles northeast of Reyes Peak (lat. 34°44'15" N, long. 119°05'30" W); the feature is along Lockwood Creek. Named on Cuddy Valley (1943), Lockwood Valley (1943), San Guillermo (1943), and Sawmill Mountain (1943) 7.5' quadrangles.

Lodgepole Picnic Area [LOS ANGELES]: *locality,* 4.25 miles northeast of Crystal Lake (lat. 34°21'40" N, long. 117°47'30" W; sec. 11, T 3 N, R 9 W). Named on Crystal Lake (1958) 7.5' quadrangle.

Lodi Canyon [LOS ANGELES]: *canyon,* drained by a stream that flows 2 miles to San Dimas Canyon 5.25 miles east of Glendora city hall (lat. 34°09'05" N, long. 117°46'20" W; near S line sec. 24, T 1 N, R 9 W). Named on Glendora (1953) 7.5' quadrangle.

Loftus [ORANGE]: *locality,* 3.25 miles west-northwest of Yorba Linda along Pacific Electric Railroad (lat. 33°54'50" N, long. 117° 51'45" W). Named on Olinda (1935) 7.5' quadrangle. The name commemorates William Loftus, an oil man (Meadows, p. 79).

Loftus Canyon [VENTURA]: *canyon,* drained by a stream that flows 0.5 mile to the valley of Santa Clara River 3.25 miles east of Santa Paula (lat. 34°21'05" N, long. 119°00' W; near S line sec. 8, T 3 N, R 20 W). Named on Santa Paula (1951) 7.5' quadrangle.

Logan Heights [SAN DIEGO]: *district,* 2.5 miles east-southeast of downtown San Diego (lat. 32°42' N, long. 117°07'45" W). Named on Point Loma (1942) 7.5' quadrangle.

Log Cabin Campground [VENTURA]: *locality,* 5.5 miles southeast of Cobblestone Mountain along Agua Blanca Creek (lat. 34°32'55" N, long. 118°48'15" W; sec. 6, T 5 N, R 18 W). Named on Cobblestone Mountain (1958) 7.5' quadrangle.

Loki Canyon [SAN DIEGO]: *canyon,* drained by a stream that flows 1.5 miles to Tubb Canyon nearly 4 miles southwest of Borrego Springs (lat. 33°12'45" N, long. 116°24'45" W). Named on Tubb Canyon (1959) 7.5' quadrangle.

Loma: see **Point Loma** [SAN DIEGO].

Loma Alta [SAN DIEGO]: *locality,* 5.5 miles east of Oceanside along Southern California Railroad (lat. 33°12'15" N, long. 117°17'10" W); the place is 0.5 mile northeast of Loma Alta Mountain. Named on Oceanside (1898) 15' quadrangle.

Loma Alta Creek [SAN DIEGO]: *stream,* flows nearly 7.5 miles to the sea 1.5 miles south-southeast of downtown Oceanside (lat. 33° 10'35" N, long. 117°22'05" W; sec. 35, T 11 S, R 5 W); the stream is north of Loma Alta Mountain. Named on San Luis Rey (1968) 7.5' quadrangle.

Loma Alta Mountain [SAN DIEGO]: *ridge,* about 1 mile long, 5 miles east of Oceanside (lat. 33°11'55" N, long. 117°17'25" W; on S line sec. 22, T 11 S, R 4 W). Named on San Luis Rey (1968) 7.5' quadrangle. California Mining Bureau's (1917b) map shows a place called Falda situated along the railroad 5 miles east of Oceanside. Gudde (1949, p. 112) thought that the name "Falda" was chosen because the place is near the steep slope of Loma Alta—*falda,* which means "skirt" in Spanish, also is used for the lower part of a slope.

Loma Portal [SAN DIEGO]: *district,* 2.5 miles west-northwest of downtown San Diego (lat. 32°44'50" N, long. 117°12'50" W). Named on Point Loma (1967) 7.5' quadrangle. Postal authorities established Loma Portal post office in 1915, discontinued it for a time in 1918, and discontinued it finally in 1928 (Frickstad, p. 153).

Lomarias de la Costa: see **San Joaquin Hills** [ORANGE].

Loma Ridge [ORANGE]: *ridge,* generally northwest-trending, 6.5 miles long, center about 8 miles north of El Toro (lat. 33°44'45" N, long. 117°42'30" W); the place is on Lomas de Santiago grant. Named on Black Star Canyon (1967), El Toro (1968), and Orange (1964) 7.5' quadrangles.

Lomas de Santiago [ORANGE]: *land grant,* east of Tustin and north of El Toro. Named on Black Star Canyon (1950), El Toro (1950), Orange (1950), Prado Dam (1950), and Tustin (1950) 7.5' quadrangles. Teodosio Yorba received the land in 1846 and claimed 47,227 acres patented in 1868 (Cowan, p. 96).

Loma Verde [LOS ANGELES]: *peak,* 11.5 miles northwest of Newhall (lat. 34°29'45" N, long. 118°40'05" W; on S line sec. 21, T 5 N, R 17 W). Named on Val Verde (1952) 7.5' quadrangle. Called Loma Verde Pk. on Los Angeles County (1935) map.

Loma Verde Peak: see **Loma Verde** [LOS ANGELES].

Loma Vista: see **Howard Summit** [LOS ANGELES].

Lomita [LOS ANGELES]: *town,* 3.5 miles south-southeast of Torrance city hall (lat. 33°47'30" N, long. 118°19' W). Named on Torrance (1964) 7.5' quadrangle. Postal authorities established Lomita post office in 1910 (Frickstad, p. 76), and the town incorporated in 1964. W.I. Hollingsworth Company of Los Angeles founded and named the community in 1907: the place first was planned as a Dunker colony (Hanna, p. 175).

Lone Hill [LOS ANGELES]: *locality,* 5.5 miles northwest of Pomona city hall along Southern Pacific Railroad (lat. 34°06'10" N, long. 117°49'30" W). Named on San Dimas (1966) 7.5' quadrangle. On Glendora (1939) 6' quadrangle, the name "San Dimas Junction" applies to a place situated along the railroad at or near present Lone Hill.

Lone Oak Canyon [VENTURA]: *canyon,* drained by a stream that flows 1 mile to Bus Canyon 5.25 miles northeast of Thousand Oaks (lat. 34°13'10" N, long. 118°45'50" W; sec. 33, T 2 N, R 18 W). Named on Calabasas (1952) and Thousand Oaks (1952) 7.5' quadrangles.

Lone Point: see **Long Point** [LOS ANGELES] (2).

Lone Tiger Spring [SAN DIEGO]: *spring,* 3 miles north of Jacumba (lat. 32°39'40" N, long. 116°10'50" W; sec. 29, T 17 S, R 8 E). Named on Jacumba (1939) 15' quadrangle.

Lonetree Canyon [LOS ANGELES]: *canyon,* drained by a stream that flows 1.5 miles to Pacoima Canyon 8 miles north-northeast of Sunland (lat. 34°22'20" N, long. 118°16'40" W). Named on Agua Dulce (1960) and Sunland (1953) 7.5' quadrangles. Called Long Tree Canyon on Los Angeles County (1935) map.

Long Beach [LOS ANGELES]: *city,* 19 miles south of Los Angeles city hall (lat. 33°46'10" N, long. 118°11'35" W). Named on Long Beach (1949), Los Alamitos (1950), Seal Beach (1950), and South Gate (1952) 7.5' quadrangles. Postal authorities established Long Beach post office in 1885, changed the name to Longbeach in 1895, and changed it back to Long Beach in 1914 (Salley, p. 125). The city incorporated in 1897. William E. Willmore founded the community in 1882 and called it Willmore City (Gudde, 1949, p. 193). Postal authorities established Burnett post office 3 miles north of Long Beach post office in 1897 and discontinued it in 1929; the name was for the developer of a farming community at the site (Salley, p. 30). They established Roosevelt post office in 1937 and discontinued it in 1942; it was named for Franklin D. Roosevelt and was in Long Beach at Pier G, Navy Landing Building (Salley, p. 188).

Long Beach: see **North Long Beach** [LOS ANGELES].

Long Beach Channel [LOS ANGELES]: *channel,* leads to Long Beach Middle Harbor 2 miles southwest of Long Beach city hall (lat. 33°44'45" N, long. 118°12'55" W). Named on Long Beach (1964) 7.5' quadrangle.

Long Beach Harbor [LOS ANGELES]: *water feature,* 2 miles southwest of Long Beach city hall (lat. 33°45' N, long. 118°13'15" W). Named on Long Beach (1949) 7.5' quadrangle. Called Long Beach Middle Harbor on Long Beach (1964) 7.5' quadrangle, which shows Long Beach Outer Harbor seaward of this feature, and Long Beach Inner Harbor farther inland.

Long Buttes [LOS ANGELES]: *ridge,* north-northeast-trending, 3 miles long, center 17 miles north-northeast of Little Rock near Hi Vista (lat. 34°43' N, long. 117°48'45" W). Named on Alpine Butte (1945) 15' quadrangle.

Long Canyon [LOS ANGELES]:

(1) *canyon,* drained by a stream that flows 2 miles to Santa Clara River 9 miles east of Solemint (lat. 34°26'25" N, long. 118°17'50" W; sec. 12, T 4 N, R 14 W). Named on Agua Dulce (1960) 7.5' quadrangle.

(2) *canyon,* drained by a stream that flows 1 mile to Arroyo Seco 5.5 miles south-southeast of Condor Peak (lat. 34°15'10" N, long. 118°10'20" W). Named on Condor Peak (1959) 7.5' quadrangle. On Tujunga (1900) 15' quadrangle, the name "Long Canyon" applies to the upper part of the canyon of present Arroyo Seco.

Long Canyon [ORANGE]: *canyon,* drained by a stream that flows nearly 3 miles to Riverside County 5.25 miles south-southeast of Trabuco Peak (lat. 33°38'10" N, long. 117°25'50" W). Named on Alberhill (1954) 7.5' quadrangle.

Long Canyon [SAN DIEGO]:

(1) *canyon,* drained by a stream that flows 4.25 miles to Riverside County 6.5 miles north of Boucher Hill (lat. 33°25'35" N, long. 116°53'40" W). Named on Aguanga (1954), Palomar Observatory (1949), and Vail Lake (1953) 7.5' quadrangles.

(2) *canyon,* drained by a stream that flows 5.5 miles to Kitchen Creek 2.5 miles east of Buckman Springs (lat. 32°46'40" N, long. 116°26'55" W; at SE cor. sec. 15, T 16 S, R 5 E). Named on Mount Laguna (1960) 7.5' quadrangle.

(3) *canyon,* drained by a stream that flows nearly 3 miles to Sweetwater Valley 4.5 miles east of National City civic center (lat. 32°39'50" N, long. 117°01'20" W). Named Jamul Mountains (1955) and National City (1967) 7.5' quadrangles.

Long Canyon [VENTURA]:

(1) *canyon,* drained by a stream that flows 4 miles to lowlands 4 miles west of Moorpark (lat. 34°17'40" N, long. 118°57' W). Named on Moorpark (1951) 7.5' quadrangle.

(2) *canyon,* drained by a stream that flows 2.25 miles to the valley of Santa Clara River nearly 2 miles west-northwest of Saticoy (lat. 34°17'50" N, long. 119°10'30" W). Named on Saticoy (1951) 7.5' quadrangle.

(3) *canyon,* drained by a stream that flows 5 miles to Apache Canyon 11 miles north-northwest of Reyes Peak (lat. 34°47' N, long. 119°19'45" W; at W line sec. 16, T 8 N, R 23 W). Named on Apache Canyon (1943) 7.5' quadrangle.

(4) *canyon,* drained by a stream that flows 1.5 miles to Oak Canyon (2) 5.5 miles north-northeast of Thousand Oaks (lat. 34° 14'10" N, long. 118°47' W; at S line sec. 20, T 2 N, R 18 W). Named on Thousand Oaks (1952) 7.5' quadrangle.

Long Canyon: see **Arroyo Seco** [LOS ANGELES]; **North Long Canyon** [LOS ANGELES]; **South Long Canyon** [LOS ANGELES].

Long Dave Canyon [VENTURA]: *canyon,* drained by a stream that flows 2.5 miles to Lockwood Creek 6 miles east-northeast of Reyes Peak (lat. 34°42'50" N, long. 119°00'45" W; near W line sec. 9, T 7 N, R 20 W). Named on Lockwood Valley (1943) and McDonald Peak (1958) 7.5' quadrangles.

Long Dave Valley [VENTURA]: *valley,* 8 miles north-northwest of McDonald Peak (lat. 34°44'30" N, long. 118°59'15" W); the valley extends north-northeast from the upper end of Long Dave Canyon. Named on McDonald Peak (1958) 7.5' quadrangle.

Long Grade Canyon [VENTURA]: *canyon,* drained by a stream that flows 3.25 miles to lowlands 3.5 miles south of Camarillo (lat. 34° 09'55" N, long. 119°02'30" W). Named on Camarillo (1950) and Newbury Park (1951) 7.5' quadrangles.

Long Point [LOS ANGELES]:

(1) *promontory,* 7.25 miles south of Redondo Beach city hall along the coast (lat. 33°44'10" N, long. 118°23'50" W). Named on Redondo Beach (1951) 7.5' quadrangle.

(2) *promontory,* 5 miles north-northwest of Avalon on the northeast side of Santa Catalina Island (lat. 33°24'20" N, long. 118°21'55" W). Named on Santa Catalina East (1950) 7.5' quadrangle. Preston (1890b, map following p. 278) called the feature Lone Pt., but United States Board on Geographic Names (1936b, p. 28) rejected this name for the feature.

Long Potrero [SAN DIEGO]: *valley,* 5.25 miles west-southwest of Morena Village (lat. 32°38'30" N, long. 116°35' W); the place is along Potrero Creek (2). Named on Morena Reservoir (1960) 7.5' quadrangle. On Potrero (1944) 15' quadrangle, present Long Potrero is shown as part of Big Potrero, but United States Board on Geographic Names (1962a, p. 12) rejected the name "Big Potrero" for present Long Potrero.

Longs Gulch [SAN DIEGO]: *canyon,* drained by a stream that flows nearly 4 miles to San Vicente Creek 7.5 miles north-northeast of Lakeside (lat. 32°58' N, long. 116°53'35" W). Named on El Cajon Mountain (1955) and San Vicente Reservoir (1955) 7.5' quadrangles.

Long Tree Canyon: see **Lonetree Canyon** [LOS ANGELES].

Long Valley [SAN DIEGO]:

(1) *valley,* 7.5 miles southeast of Descanso (lat. 32°46'15" N, long.

116°32'30" W; sec. 14, 23, T 16 S, R 4 E). Named on Descanso (1960) 7.5' quadrangle.

(2) *valley*, nearly 6 miles northwest of Mesa Grande (lat. 33°13'55" N, long. 116°50'50" W). Named on Mesa Grande (1948) 7.5' quadrangle.

Long Valley [VENTURA]: *valley*, 2.5 miles west-southwest of downtown Ojai at present Mira Monte (lat. 34°25'45" N, long. 119°16'55" W). Named on Ventura (1904) 15' quadrangle.

Long Valley Peak [SAN DIEGO]: *peak*, 6.25 miles southeast of Descanso (lat. 32°47'50" N, long. 116°31'55" W; near W line sec. 12, T 16 S, R 4 E); the feature is near the head of Long Valley (1). Altitude 4906 feet. Named on Descanso (1960) 7.5' quadrangle.

Longview [LOS ANGELES]: *locality*, 4 miles northwest of Valyermo (lat. 34°29'40" N long. 117°53'30" W; sec. 26, T 5 N, R 10 W). Named on Valyermo (1940) 6' quadrangle.

Lookout Gates [LOS ANGELES]: *locality*, 1.5 miles northeast of Chatsworth (lat. 34°16'20" N, long. 118°35'10" W; sec. 8, T 2 N, R 16 W). Named on Oat Mountain (1952) 7.5' quadrangle.

Lookout Mountain [LOS ANGELES]: *peak*, 14 miles north-northeast of Pomona city hall (lat. 34°14'55" N, long. 117°40'25" W). Altitude 6812 feet. Named on Mount Baldy (1954) 7.5' quadrangle. A fire lookout functioned on the peak from 1915 until 1927 (Robinson, J.W., 1983, p. 172).

Lookout Point [LOS ANGELES]: *relief feature*, 2 miles south-southeast of Mount Wilson (1) (lat. 34°11'50" N, long. 118°02'50" W; near E line sec. 5, T 1 N, R 11 W). Named on Mount Wilson (1953) 7.5' quadrangle.

Loop Canyon [LOS ANGELES]: *canyon*, nearly 2 miles long, opens into lowlands 3.5 miles north-northeast of downtown San Fernando (lat. 34°19'35" N, long. 118°24'40" W; near W line sec. 24, T 3 N, R 15 W). Named on San Fernando (1953) 7.5' quadrangle.

Loop Wash [SAN DIEGO]: *dry wash*, 1.5 miles long, opens into the canyon of Fish Creek Wash 10.5 miles north of Sweeney Pass (lat. 32°58'50" N, long. 116°08'55" W; sec. 3, T 14 S, R 8 E). Named on Arroyo Tapiado (1959) 7.5' quadrangle.

Lopez: see **Palmdale** [LOS ANGELES].

Lopez Canyon [LOS ANGELES]: *canyon*, 3.5 miles long, opens into lowlands 2 miles east of downtown San Fernando (lat. 34°17'10" N, long. 118°24'15" W). Named on San Fernando (1953) 7.5' quadrangle.

Lopez Station: see **San Fernando** [LOS ANGELES].

Lordsburg: see **La Verne** [LOS ANGELES].

Lorenzo Beach [LOS ANGELES]: *beach*, 1 mile north of Silver Peak (lat. 33°28'25" N, long. 118°33'50" W). Named on Santa Catalina West (1943) 7.5' quadrangle.

Losadena: see **Camp Losadena**, under **Switzer Camp** [LOS ANGELES].

Los Alamitos [LOS ANGELES-ORANGE]: *land grant*, extends from Long Beach [LOS ANGELES] to the town of Los Alamitos [ORANGE]. Named on Anaheim (1950), Long Beach (1949), Los Alamitos (1950), and Seal Beach (1950) 7.5' quadrangles. Juan Jose Nieto received 6 leagues in 1834 and Abel Stearns claimed 28,027 acres patented in 1874 (Cowan, p. 14).

Los Alamitos [ORANGE]: *town*, 6 miles southwest of Buena Park civic center (lat. 33°48'15" N, long. 118°04'15" W); the town is on Los Alamitos grant. Postal authorities established Los Alamitos post office in 1897 (Frickstad, p. 117), and the town incorporated in 1960. The Clark brothers purchased 8000 acres of Los Alamitos grant in 1896 and built a sugar factory there; the town began as a village that grew around the factory (Meadows, p. 79).

Los Alamitos Armed Forces Reserve Center: see **Los Alamitos Naval Air Station** [ORANGE].

Los Alamitos Junction [ORANGE]: *locality*, 4 miles south of Buena Park along Southern Pacific Railroad (lat. 33°48'25" N, long. 117° 59'45" W; near E line sec. 23, T 4 S, R 11 W). Named on Anaheim (1965) 7.5' quadrangle.

Los Alamitos Naval Air Station [ORANGE]: *military installation*, 6 miles south-southwest of Buena Park civic center (lat. 33°47'40" N, long. 118°03'15" W); the place is south of the town of Los Alamitos on Los Alamitos grant. Named on Los Alamitos (1964) 7.5' quadrangle. Called Los Alamitos Armed Forces Reserve Center on Los Alamitos (1964, photorevised 1981) 7.5' quadrangle.

Los Alisos Canyon [LOS ANGELES]: *canyon*, drained by a stream that flows nearly 3 miles to the sea 6 miles west-northwest of Point Dume (lat. 34°02'25" N, long. 118°53'50" W). Named on Triunfo Pass (1950) 7.5' quadrangle. Called Nicolas Canyon on Triunfo Pass (1921) 15' quadrangle, and called Nicholas Canyon on Camulos (1903) 30' quadrangle. United States Board on Geographic Names (1943, p. 9) rejected the name "Nicholas Canyon" for the feature.

Los Altos [LOS ANGELES]: *district*, 2.25 miles east-northeast of Long Beach city hall (lat. 33°47'35" N, long. 118°07'35" W). Named on Long Beach (1964) and Los Alamitos (1964) 7.5' quadrangles. Called Los Altos Terrace on Long Beach (1949) and Los Alamitos (1950) 7.5' quadrangles.

Los Altos Terrace: see **Los Altos** [LOS ANGELES].

Los Amigos: see **Poor Farm Station** [LOS ANGELES].

Los Angeles [LOS ANGELES]: *city*, occupies much of the ground from the west end of San Gabriel Mountains to the sea at San Pedro (city hall near lat. 34°03'15" N, long. 118°14'30" W). Named on Long Beach (1957) and Los Angeles (1975) 1°x 2° quadrangles. Called Pueblo de Los Angeles on Parke's (1854-1855) map. Postal authorities established Los Angeles post office in 1850 (Frickstad, p. 76), and the city incorporated the same year. The pueblo that became the city was established in 1781 with the name "El Pueblo de Nuestra Señora la Reina de los Angeles de la Porciuncula" (Hoover, Rensch, and Rensch, p. 149). An elevation called Fort Hill, located less than 1000 feet north of present Los Angeles city hall (Dumke *in* Evans, p. 190) was used as a base during the first American occupation of Los Angeles in 1846; Lieutenant Davidson built Fort Moore there in 1847 and named it to honor Captain Benjamin D. Moore, who was killed in battle at San Pasqual in 1846 (Frazer, p. 28).

Los Angeles: see **East Los Angeles** [LOS ANGELES]; **North Los Angeles**, under **Northridge** [LOS ANGELES]; **Port Los Angeles** [LOS ANGELES]; **South Los Angeles** [LOS ANGELES]; **West Los Angeles** [LOS ANGELES].

Los Angeles Harbor [LOS ANGELES]: *water feature*, 6 miles southwest of Long Beach city hall at the west end of San Pedro Bay. Named on Long Beach (1957) 1°x 2° quadrangle. San Pedro (1964) 7.5' quadrangle shows Los Angeles Outer Harbor east of Point Fermin. United States Coast and Geodetic Survey (p. 97) described Los Angeles Harbor as including the districts of San Pedro and Wilmington, and a major part of Terminal Island.

Los Angeles Junction [SAN DIEGO]: *locality*, 2 miles north-northwest of downtown Oceanside along Southern California Railroad (lat. 33°13'15" N, long. 117°23'45" W). Named on Oceanside (1898) 15' quadrangle.

Los Angeles Lake [LOS ANGELES]: *lake*, 1350 feet long, 7 miles north-northwest of Manhattan Beach city hall (lat. 33°58'50" N, long. 118°27'20" W). Named on Venice (1950) 7.5' quadrangle.

Los Angeles River [LOS ANGELES]: *stream*, flows 50 miles to the sea less than 1 mile west-southwest of Long Beach city hall (lat. 33°45'50" N, long. 118°12'15" W). Named on Burbank (1953), Canoga Park (1952), Hollywood (1953), Long Beach (1949), Los Angeles (1953), South Gate (1952), and Van Nuys (1953) 7.5' quadrangles. Called R. de los Angeles on Eddy's (1854) map. Marcou (p. 158) called it Rio de los Angeles, or Rio de Porciuncula. Members of the Portola expedition camped along the stream in 1769 and gave it the name "Nuestra Señora de los Angeles de Porciuncula" on the day after the feast day of that saint—the cradle of the Franciscan order is the Porciuncula chapel in the basilica of Our Lady of the Angels near Assisi, Italy (Gudde, 1949, p. 194). Los Angeles River reached the sea just north of present Playa del Rey before the flood of 1825 diverted the water to San Gabriel River, which emptied into San Pedro Bay (Poland and others, p. 35). But before 1825, water of Los Angeles River seldom reached the sea at all, for it spread over lowlands where it formed lakes, ponds, and marshes in part of now highly urbanized Los Angels (Warner, Hayes, and Widney, p. 17-18). United States Board on Geographic Names (1978a, p. 7) approved the name "Queensway Bay" for the place at the present mouth of Los Angeles River in Long Beach (lat. 33°45'30" N, long. 118°11'45" W) where the former British liner *Queen Mary* is permanently anchored.

Los Bueyos Canyon: see **Weir Canyon** [ORANGE].

Los Caballos Campground [SAN DIEGO]: *locality*, 2.5 miles northeast of Cuyamaca Peak (lat. 32°58'20" N, long. 116°34'15" W). Named on Cuyamaca Peak (1960) 7.5' quadrangle.

Los Casitos: see **Las Casetas** [LOS ANGELES].

Los Cerritos [LOS ANGELES]:

(1) *land grant*, north of Long Beach between Los Angeles River and San Gabriel River. Named on Long Beach (1949), Los Alamitos (1950), South Gate (1952) and Whittier (1951) 7.5' quadrangles. Manuela Nieto received 5 leagues in 1834; John Temple claimed 27,054 acres patented in 1867 (Cowan, p. 26).

(2) *locality*, 4 miles north of present Long Beach city hall along Pacific Electric Railroad (lat. 33°49'40" N, long. 118°12' W); the place is on Los Cerritos grant. Named on Clearwater (1925) 6' quadrangle.

Los Cerritos: see **San Miguel** [VENTURA]; **Signal Hill** [LOS ANGELES] (1).

Los Cochas: see **Los Cochas Creek** [SAN DIEGO].

Los Coches Creek [SAN DIEGO]: *stream*, flows 8 miles to the valley of San Diego River at Lakeside (lat. 32°51'25" N, long. 116° 55'35" W). Named on Alpine (1955) and El Cajon (1967) 7.5' quadrangles. Hanks' (1886a) map shows a place called Los Cochas situated about 4 miles northeast of El Cajon (2) near present Los Coches Creek.

Los Coyotes [LOS ANGELES-ORANGE]: *land grant*, at and around Buena Park [ORANGE]. Named on Anaheim (1950), La Habra (1952), Los Alamitos (1950), and Whittier (1949) 7.5' quadrangles. Juan Jose Nieto received 10 leagues in 1834; Andres Pico and others claimed 48,806 acres patented in 1875 (Cowan, p. 30-31).

Los Encenitos [SAN DIEGO]: *land grant*, east of Encinitas. Named on Encinitas (1968) and Rancho Santa Fe (1968) 7.5' quadrangles. Called Encinitas on Oceanside (1898) 15' quadrangle. Andres Ibarra received 1 league in 1842 and claimed 4431 acres patented in 1871 (Cowan, p. 33-

34; Cowan gave the alternate name "Cañada de San Alejo" for the grant). Perez (p. 65) gave 1846 as the year of the grant.

Los Felis [LOS ANGELES]: *land grant*, northeast of Hollywood at the east end of Santa Monica Mountains. Named on Burbank (1953), Hollywood (1953), and Los Angeles (1953) 7.5' quadrangles. Vincente Felix received 1.5 leagues in 1802 and Juan Diego claimed 6647 acres patented in 1871 (Cowan, p. 36). According to Perez (p. 67), Maria Berdugo was the grantee in 1843 and the patentee in 1871.

Los Gatos Ravine [SAN DIEGO]: *canyon*, about 0.5 mile long, 7.25 miles north-northeast of Buckman Springs (lat. 32°52'10" N, long. 116°26'45" W; at NW cor. sec. 14, T 15 S, R 5 E). Named on Mount Laguna (1960) 7.5' quadrangle.

Los Monos Canyon [SAN DIEGO]: *canyon*, about 1 mile long, nearly 8 miles east-southeast of Oceanside along Agua Hedionda Creek (lat. 33°08'45" N, long. 117°15'30" W). Named on San Luis Rey (1968) 7.5' quadrangle. Chase (1913, p. 41) used the designation "Cañon de los Monos or Monkey Cañon" for the feature.

Los Nietos [LOS ANGELES]: *town*, 2.25 miles west-southwest of present Whittier city hall (lat. 33°57'40" N, long. 118°04'10" W). Named on Whittier (1949) 7.5' quadrangle. Postal authorities established Los Nietos post office in 1867, discontinued it in 1876, reestablished it in 1891, discontinued it in 1904, and reestablished it in 1924 (Salley, p. 128). The name recalls the five heirs of Manuel Nieto (*los Nietos* in Spanish), who were granted again the lands that the elder Nieto got in 1784 (Gudde, 1949, p. 195).

Los Nietos Junction [LOS ANGELES]: *locality*, 2.25 miles west-southwest of Whittier city hall along Southern Pacific Railroad (lat. 33°57'35" N, long. 118°04'10" W); the place is at the south edge of Los Nietos. Named on Whittier (1965) 7.5' quadrangle.

Los Nietos Station [LOS ANGELES]: *locality*, 2.5 miles west-southwest of Whittier city hall along Southern Pacific Railroad (lat. 33° 57'35" N, long. 118°04'30" W). Named on Whittier (1965) 7.5' quadrangle.

Los Nogales [LOS ANGELES]: *land grant*, west-southwest of downtown Pomona. Named on San Dimas (1954) 7.5' quadrangle. Jose de la Cruz Linares received 1 league in 1840; M. de Jesus Garcia and others claimed 1004 acres patented in 1882 (Cowan, p. 52-53).

Los Osos Valley: see **Oso Creek** [ORANGE].

Los Palos Colorados: see **Los Palos Verdes** [LOS ANGELES].

Los Palos Verdes [LOS ANGELES]: *land grant*, at Palos Verdes Hills. Named on Redondo Beach (1951), San Pedro (1964), and Torrance (1964) 7.5' quadrangles. Jose L. Sepulveda and others received the land in 1827 and 1846; they claimed 31,629 acres patented in 1880 (Cowan, p. 57; Cowan gave the alternate name "Los Palos Colorados" for the grant). The name is from Cañada de los Palos Verdes, the early name for the place later called Bixby Slough—*Cañada de los Palos Verdes* means "Valley of Green Trees" in Spanish (Gudde, 1949, p. 251). Postal authorities established Palos Verdes post office on the grant 3.5 miles northwest of Wilmington post office in 1880 and discontinued it the same year (Salley, p. 166).

Los Patos [ORANGE]: *locality*, 5 miles northwest of Huntington Beach civic center along Pacific Electric Railroad (lat. 33°42'40" N, long. 118°03'50" W). Named on Seal Beach (1950) 7.5' quadrangle.

Los Peñasquitos [SAN DIEGO]: *land grant*, between Poway and Del Mar. Named on Del Mar (1967) and Poway (1967) 7.5' quadrangles. Francisco Maria Ruiz and Francisco Maria Alvarado received the land in 1823 and 1834; Ruiz claimed 8486 acres patented in 1876 (Cowan, p. 94; Cowan used the name "Santa Maria de Peñasquitos" for the grant). According to Perez (p. 81), Francisco M. Alvarado was the patentee in 1876. United States Board on Geographic Names (1933, p. 475) rejected the forms "Las Penasquitas," "Paguay," "Penasquitos," and "Pinasquitos" for the name.

Los Peñasquitos Canyon [SAN DIEGO]: *canyon*, drained by Los Peñasquitos Creek, which flows 11 miles to Soledad Valley 4.25 miles south-southeast of Del Mar (lat. 32°54'15" N, long. 117° 13'30" W). Named on Del Mar (1967) and Poway (1967) 7.5' quadrangles. Chase (1913, p. 45) referred to Las Peñasquitas Cañon. United States Board on Geographic Names (1933, p. 475) rejected the names "Las Penasquitas Canyon," "Paguay Canyon," "Penasquitos Canyon," and "Pinasquitos Canyon" for the feature.

Los Peñasquitos Creek [SAN DIEGO]: *stream*, formed by the confluence of Beeler Creek and Poway Creek, flows 11 miles to Soledad Valley 4.25 miles south-southeast of Del Mar (lat. 32° 54'15" N, long. 117°13'30" W). Named on Poway (1967, photorevised 1975) 7.5' quadrangle. On Poway Valley (1952) 7.5' quadrangle, present Beeler Creek is called Los Peñasquitos Creek.

Los Pinetos Canyon [LOS ANGELES]: *canyon*, drained by a stream that flows 1.5 miles to Placerita Canyon nearly 3 miles south-southeast of Solemint (lat. 34°22'35" N, long. 118°26'35" W; sec. 3, T 3 N, R 15 W). Named on San Fernando (1953) 7.5' quadrangle.

Los Pinetos Spring [LOS ANGELES]: *spring*, 5.25 miles north of downtown San Fernando (lat. 34°21'30" N, long. 118°26'50" W; near W line sec. 10, T 3 N, R 15 W); the spring is near the head of Los Pinetos Canyon. Named on San Fernando (1966) 7.5' quadrangle.

Los Pinos Mountain [SAN DIEGO]: *peak*, 5.5 miles northwest of Morena Village (lat. 32°44'05" N, long. 116°34'35" W; sec. 33, T 16 S, R 4 E). Altitude 4805 feet. Named on Morena Reservoir (1960) 7.5' quadrangle.

Los Pinos Peak [ORANGE]: *peak*, 2.5 miles south of Trabuco Peak (lat. 33°39'35" N, long. 117°28'15" W; at N line sec. 11, T 6 S, R 6 W). Altitude 4510 feet. Named on Alberhill (1954) 7.5' quadrangle.

Los Pinos Potrero: see **Los Pinos Spring** [ORANGE].

Los Pinos Spring [ORANGE]: *spring*, 3.25 miles south-southeast of Trabuco Peak (lat. 33°39'35" N, long. 117°27'05" W; near E line sec. 12, T 6 S, R 6 W); the place is 1 mile east-southeast of Los Pinos Peak near the head of Hot Spring Canyon. Named on Alberhill (1954) 7.5' quadrangle. Meadows (p. 25) called the feature Bear Spring, but (p. 80) noted that an open grassy area at the head of Hot Spring Canyon is called Los Pinos Potrero.

Los Pitas: see **Point Los Pitas**, under **Pitas Point** [VENTURA].

Los Rasaltes Ravine [SAN DIEGO]: *canyon*, drained by a stream that flows 1.25 miles to Laguna Meadow 7 miles north-northeast of Buckman Springs (lat. 32°52'05" N, long. 116°27'25" W; sec. 15, T 15 S, R 5 E). Named on Mount Laguna (1960) 7.5' quadrangle.

Los Sauces Creek [VENTURA]: *stream*, flows 4.5 miles to the sea 3 miles northwest of Pitas Point (lat. 34°20'55" N, long. 119°25'20" W; at S line sec. 8, T 3 N, R 24 W). Named on Pitas Point (1950) and White Ledge Peak (1952) 7.5' quadrangles. Called Arroyo Susal on Peckham's (1866) map.

Lost Canyon [LOS ANGELES]: *canyon*, drained by a stream that flows nearly 2 miles to North Fork San Gabriel River 3 miles south of Crystal Lake (lat. 34°16'20" N, long. 117°50'40" W). Named on Crystal Lake (1958) 7.5' quadrangle.

Lost Canyon: see **Oak Spring Canyon** [LOS ANGELES] (1).

Los Terrenitos [SAN DIEGO]: *locality*, 1.5 miles south-southwest of Descanso (lat. 32°50'05" N, long. 116°37'20" W; sec. 25, T 15 S, R 3 E). Named on Descanso (1960) 7.5' quadrangle.

Lost Lake [SAN DIEGO]: *intermittent lake*, 0.25 mile long, 4 miles west-southwest of Warner Springs (lat. 33°16'15" N, long. 116°42'05" W). Named on Warner Springs (1959) 7.5' quadrangle.

Lost Point [LOS ANGELES]: *promontory*, 13 miles south-southeast of Northwest Harbor on the west side of San Clemente Island (lat. 32°51'10" N, long. 118°30' W). Named on San Clemente Island Central (1943) 7.5' quadrangle.

Los Trancos Canyon [ORANGE]: *canyon*, drained by a stream that flows nearly 3 miles to the sea 4 miles west-northwest of Laguna Beach city hall (lat. 33°34'25" N, long. 117°50'05" W). Named on Laguna Beach (1965) 7.5' quadrangle. On Santa Ana (1942) 15' quadrangle, present Muddy Canyon is called Los Trancos Canyon. The name is from bars that kept trespassers out of the canyon—*los trancos* means "the bars" in Spanish (Meadows, p. 97).

Lost Spring [SAN DIEGO]: *spring*, 5.25 miles east of San Felipe (lat. 33°11'20" N, long. 116°31'35" W; sec. 25, T 11 S, R 4 E). Named on Ranchita (1960) 7.5' quadrangle.

Lost Trough Canyon [ORANGE]: *canyon*, drained by a stream that flows nearly 1.5 miles to Bee Canyon (1) 2.25 miles south-southeast of San Juan Hill (lat. 33°53' N, long. 117°43'20" W). Named on Prado Dam (1967) 7.5' quadrangle.

Los Tules [SAN DIEGO]: *settlement*, 0.5 mile east of Warner Springs (lat. 33°17' N, long. 116°37'05" W). Named on Hot Springs Mountain (1960) 7.5' quadrangle. Warner Springs (1942) 15' quadrangle shows a place called Agua Caliente at the site.

Lost Valley [LOS ANGELES]: *valley*, 2.25 miles west-southwest of the village of Leona Valley (lat. 34°36'20" N, long. 118°19'20" W; at E line sec. 14, T 6 N, R 14 W). Named on Sleepy Valley (1958) 7.5' quadrangle.

Lost Valley [SAN DIEGO]:

(1) *valley*, 6 miles north-northeast of Warner Springs along Agua Caliente Creek (lat. 33°21'15" N, long. 116°34'15" W). Named on Hot Springs Mountain (1960) 7.5' quadrangle.

(2) *area*, 5 miles south of Sombrero Peak (lat. 32°45'35" N, long. 116°16'30" W; on E line sec. 20, T 16 S, R 7 E). Named on Sombrero Peak (1959) 7.5' quadrangle.

Lost Woman Canyon [ORANGE]: *canyon*, drained by a stream that flows 1.5 miles to Silverado Canyon 4 miles southeast of Pleasants Peak (lat. 33°45'10" N, long. 117°33'30" W; sec. 12, T 5 S, R 7 W). Named on Corona South (1967) and Santiago Peak (1954) 7.5' quadrangles.

Los Vallecitos [SAN DIEGO]: *valley*, 7 miles north of Rancho Santa Fe along San Marcos Creek (lat. 33°07'15" N, long. 117°12'15" W). Named on Rancho Santa Fe (1968) 7.5' quadrangle.

Los Vallecitos de San Marcos [SAN DIEGO]: *land grant*, at San Marcos. Named on Rancho Santa Fe (1968), San Marcos (1968), and Valley Center (1968) 7.5' quadrangles. Jose M. Alvarado received the land in 1840 and Lorenzo Soto claimed 8975 acres patented in 1883 (Cowan, p. 84).

Louies Cabin [LOS ANGELES]: *locality*, 3.5 miles west of Waterman Mountain (lat. 34°19'50" N, long. 117°59'40" W; near E line sec. 23, T 3 N, R 11 W). Named on Waterman Mountain (1959) 7.5' quadrangle.

Lovejoy Buttes [LOS ANGELES]: *range*, 10 miles northeast of Littlerock (lat. 34°36'15" N, long. 117°50'30" W). Named on Lovejoy Buttes (1957) 7.5' quadrangle. On Los Angeles County (1935) map, the name "Lovejoy Butte" applies to a high point in the range (sec. 20, T 6 N, R 10 W).

Lovejoy Lake [LOS ANGELES]: *lake*, 100 feet long, 10 miles northeast of Littlerock (lat. 34°36'20" N, long. 117°49'45" W); the lake is at Lovejoy Springs. Named on Alpine Butte (1945) 15' quadrangle.

Lovejoy Springs [LOS ANGELES]: *spring*, 10 miles northeast of Littlerock (lat. 34°40'20" N, long. 117°49'40" W; sec. 16, T 6 N, R 9 W); the feature is at Lovejoy Buttes. Named on Lovejoy Buttes (1957) 7.5' quadrangle. Los Angeles County (1935) map has the singular form "Lovejoy Spring" for the name. Johnson (p. 52) gave the alternate name "Croswell Springs" for the feature.

Loveland Reservoir [SAN DIEGO]: *lake*, behind a dam on Sweetwater River 4 miles south-southwest of Alpine (lat. 32°46'55" N, long. 116°47'35" W; sec. 17, T 16 S, R 2 E). Named on Alpine (1955) and Viejas Mountain (1960) 7.5' quadrangles. United States Board on Geographic Names (1962a, p. 12) rejected the name "Sweetwater Falls Reservoir" for the feature. The name "Loveland" is for Fremont Loveland, a prominent citizen (Stein, p. 76).

Lovell Canyon [LOS ANGELES]: *canyon*, drained by a stream that flows 1 mile to Little Tujunga Canyon nearly 4 miles north-northwest of Sunland (lat. 34°18'25" N, long. 118°20'45" W; near NE cor. sec. 33, T 3 N, R 14 W). Named on Sunland (1966) 7.5' quadrangle.

Love Valley [SAN DIEGO]: *valley*, 10 miles southeast of Boucher Hill (lat. 33°15'20" N, long. 116°46'30" W; on S line sec. 33, T 10 S, R 2 E). Named on Palomar Observatory (1949) 7.5' quadrangle.

Lowe: see **Mount Lowe** [LOS ANGELES].

Lower Borrego Valley [SAN DIEGO]: *valley*, extends from a point 7 miles west of Ocotillo Wells southeast into Imperial County. Named on Borrego Mountain (1960), Borrego Mountain SE (1958), and Harper Canyon (1959) 7.5' quadrangles.

Lower Buffalo Corral Reservoir [LOS ANGELES]: *lake*, 650 feet long, 3.5 miles northwest of Mount Banning on Santa Catalina Island in Little Springs Canyon (lat. 33°24'45" N, long. 118°28'15" W); the feature is 1 mile south of Upper Buffalo Corral Reservoir. Named on Santa Catalina North (1950) 7.5' quadrangle.

Lower Doane Valley [SAN DIEGO]: *valley*, 1 mile northeast of Boucher Hill (lat. 33°20'45" N, long. 116°54'25" W; near SW cor. sec. 32, T 9 S, R 1 E); the valley is about 1 mile northwest of Upper Doane Valley along Doane Creek. Named on Boucher Hill (1948) 7.5' quadrangle.

Lower French Valley [SAN DIEGO]: *valley*, 1.25 miles north-northeast of Boucher Hill (lat. 33°21'15" N, long. 116°54'45" W; near NE cor. sec. 31, T 9 S, R 1 E); the feature is 1.5 miles west-southwest of Upper French Valley along French Creek. Named on Boucher Hill (1948) 7.5' quadrangle. On Ramona (1903) 30' quadrangle, the name "Doane Valley" applies to present Lower French Valley and to Lower Doane Valley together.

Lower Hellhole [SAN DIEGO]: *canyon*, 2.25 miles west-southwest of Rodriguez Mountain (lat. 33°13'40" N, long. 116°56'40" W); the canyon is along Hell Creek downstream from Upper Hellhole. Named on Rodriguez Mountain (1948) 7.5' quadrangle. Ramona (1903) 30' quadrangle has the name "Hellhole" at the place.

Lower Hungry Valley: see **Cañada de Los Alamos** [LOS ANGELES].

Lowerotay: see **Lower Otay Reservoir** [SAN DIEGO].

Lower Otay Camp: see **Lower Otay Camping Area** [SAN DIEGO].

Lower Otay Camping Area [SAN DIEGO]: *locality*, 5 miles west of Otay Mountain (lat. 32°36'25" N, long. 116°55'45" W); the place is just below the dam that forms Lower Otay Reservoir. Named on Otay Mesa (1955) 7.5' quadrangle. Called Lower Otay Camp on Jamul (1955) 15' quadrangle.

Lower Otay Lake: see **Lower Otay Reservoir** [SAN DIEGO].

Lower Otay Reservoir [SAN DIEGO]: *lake*, behind a dam 5 miles west of Otay Mountain (lat. 32°36'35" N, long. 116°55'30" W; near NW cor. sec. 18, T 18 S, R 1 E); the lake is along Otay River. Named on Jamul Mountains (1955) and Otay Mesa (1955) 7.5' quadrangles. Unites States Board on Geographic Names (1979b, p. 7) approved the name "Lower Otay Lake" for the feature, and rejected the names "Lower Otay Reservoir" and "Otay Reservoir" for it. Postal authorities established Lowerotay post office 3 miles northeast of Bonita post office at Lower Otay Reservoir in 1917 and discontinued it in 1920 (Salley, p. 128).

Lower Pacifico Campground [LOS ANGELES]: *locality*, 0.25 mile west-southwest of Pacifico Mountain (lat. 34°22'50" N, long. 118° 02'20" W; near N line sec. 4, T 3 N, R 11 W). Named on Pacifico Mountain (1959) 7.5' quadrangle.

Lower Peters Canyon Reservoir [ORANGE]: *lake*, 750 feet long, 5 miles east-southeast of Orange city hall (lat. 33°45'35" N, long. 117°46'10" W); the feature is in Peters Canyon. Named on Orange (1964) 7.5' quadrangle.

Lower San Juan Campground [ORANGE]: *locality*, 7 miles south of Trabuco Peak (lat. 33°35'55" N, long. 117°27'35" W; near S line sec. 36, T 6 S, R 6 W); the place is in San Juan Canyon near Orange-Riverside County line. Named on Sitton Peak (1954) 7.5' quadrangle, which shows Upper San Juan Campground farther up the canyon in Riverside County.

Lower Shake Campground [LOS ANGELES]: *locality*, 3 miles east-northeast of Burnt Peak (lat. 34°41'55" N, long. 118°31'30" W; sec. 13, T 7 N, R 16 W); the place is 0.5 mile north-northeast of Upper Shake Campground. Named on Burnt Peak (1958) 7.5' quadrangle.

Lower Switzer Campground [LOS ANGELES]: *locality*, nearly 6 miles southeast of Condor Peak along Arroyo Seco (lat. 34°16' N, long. 118°08'45" W); the place is 0.25 mile west of Upper Switzer Campground. Named on Condor Peak (1959) 7.5' quadrangle.

Lower Willows [SAN DIEGO]: *locality*, 9 miles north-northwest of Borrego Springs along Coyote Creek (lat. 33°22'35" N, long. 116° 26'30" W; sec. 22, T 9 S, R 5 E). Named on Collins Valley (1959) 7.5' quadrangle.

Lowler: see **Mount Lowler,** under **Mount Lawlor** [LOS ANGELES].

Lucas: see **Tom Lucas Campground** [LOS ANGELES].

Lucas Canyon [ORANGE]: *canyon*, drained by a stream that heads in Riverside County and flows 5.5 miles to San Juan Creek 7.5 miles east-northeast of San Juan Capistrano (lat. 33°33'20" N, long. 117° 33' W; sec. 18, T 7 S, R 6 W). Named on Cañada Gobernadora (1968) and Sitton Peak (1954) 7.5' quadrangles. The name is for a Christianized Indian who lived in the canyon (Meadows, p. 97).

Lucas Creek [LOS ANGELES]: *stream*, flows 2.25 miles to Big Tujunga Canyon 4 miles east-southeast of Condor Peak (lat. 34°18'20" N, long. 118°09'20" W). Named on Condor Peak (1959) 7.5' quadrangle.

Lucas Creek [SAN DIEGO]: *stream*, flows nearly 2 miles to Indian Creek (2) 4 miles west-northwest of Monument Peak (lat. 32°54'35" N, long. 116°29'10" W; sec. 32, T 14 S, R 5 E). Named on Monument Peak (1959) 7.5' quadrangle.

Lucky Canyon [LOS ANGELES]: *canyon*, less than 1 mile long, 1 mile southeast of the village of Lake Hughes (lat. 34°39'50" N, long. 118°25'40" W; mainly in sec. 25, T 7 N, R 15 W). Named on Lake Hughes (1957) 7.5' quadrangle.]

Lukens: see **Mount Lukens** [LOS ANGELES].

Lunada Bay [LOS ANGELES]: *embayment*, 5.25 miles south-southwest of Redondo Beach city hall along the coast (lat. 33°46'10" N, long. 118°25'20" W). Named on Redondo Beach (1951) 7.5' quadrangle.

Lupe Spring [SAN DIEGO]: *spring*, 4.5 miles east of Otay Mountain (lat. 32°35'20" N, long. 116°46'05" W; near W line sec. 22, T 18 S, R 2 E). Named on Otay Mountain (1972) 7.5' quadrangle.

Lupin: see **Camp Lupin** [LOS ANGELES].

Lusardi [SAN DIEGO]: *locality*, 8.5 miles south-southwest of Escondido at the west end of La Jolla Valley (lat. 33°00'20" N, long. 117°08'30" W); the place is along present Lusardi Creek. Named on Escondido (1901) 15' quadrangle. Postal authorities established Lusardi post office in 1889, moved it 0.5 mile northwest in 1892, discontinued it for a time in 1903, and discontinued it finally in 1911 (Salley, p. 129). The name is from Pete Lusardi (Hanna, p. 178).

Lusardi Canyon [SAN DIEGO]: *canyon*, drained by a stream that flows 4 miles to San Luis Rey River 7.5 miles southeast of Boucher Hill (lat. 33°16' N, long. 116°49'15" W; near W line sec. 31, T 10 S, R 2 E). Named on Mesa Grande (1948) and Palomar Observatory (1949) 7.5' quadrangles.

Lusardi Creek [SAN DIEGO]: *stream*, flows 5 miles to San Dieguito River 2 miles east-southeast of Rancho Santa Fe (lat. 33°00'45" N, long. 117°10'20" W; sec. 27, T 13 S, R 3 W). Named on Rancho Santa Fe (1968) 7.5' quadrangle.

Lux Canyon [SAN DIEGO]: *canyon*, about 1 mile long, 2.25 miles east-southeast of Encinitas (lat. 33°01'50" N, long. 117°15'20" W; at E line sec. 23, T 13 S, R 4 E). Named on Encinitas (1968) 7.5' quadrangle.

Lycium Wash [SAN DIEGO]: *stream* and *dry wash*, extends for 2.25 miles to North Fork Fish Creek Wash 11.5 miles north-northeast of Sweeney Pass (lat. 32°59'30" N, long. 116°07'55" W). Named on Arroyo Tapiado (1959) and Harper Canyon (1959) 7.5' quadrangles.

Lynwood [LOS ANGELES]: *city*, 2 miles south of South Gate city hall (lat. 33°55'40" N, long. 118°12'40" W). Named on South Gate (1952) 7.5' quadrangle. Postal authorities established Lynwood post office in 1922 (Frickstad, p. 77). The city incorporated in 1921. The name is from Lynwood dairy, which the owner of the dairy named for his wife, Lynn Wood Sessions (Gudde, 1949, p. 198).

Lynwood Gardens [LOS ANGELES]: *district*, 3 miles south-southeast of South Gate city hall in Lynwood (lat. 33°54'45" N, long. 118°11'30" W). Named on South Gate (1952) 7.5' quadrangle.

Lynwood Hills [SAN DIEGO]: *locality*, 3.5 miles east-southeast of National City civic center (lat. 32°38'45" N, long. 117°03' W). Named on National City (1967) 7.5' quadrangle.

Lynwood Station [LOS ANGELES]: *locality*, 2.5 miles south-southwest of South Gate city hall along Southern Pacific Railroad (lat. 33°55'30" N, long. 118°13'25" W); the place is at the west side of Lynwood. Named on South Gate (1964) 7.5' quadrangle.

Lynx Gulch [LOS ANGELES]: *canyon*, drained by a stream that flows 3.25 miles to Big Tujunga Canyon 6 miles south-southwest of Pacifico Mountain (lat. 34°18'35" N, long. 118°05'20" W; near N line sec. 36, T 3 N, R 12 W). Named on Chilao Flat (1959) 7.5' quadrangle.

Lyon Canyon [LOS ANGELES]: *canyon*, drained by a stream that flows 3 miles to Gavin Canyon nearly 2 miles west-southwest of downtown

Newhall (lat. 34°22'15" N, long. 118°33'40" W; sec. 4, T 3 N, R 16 W). Named on Oat Mountain (1952) 7.5' quadrangle. Sanford Lyon of Lyon's Station owned the feature (Reynolds, p. 13).

Lyons Hot Springs: see **Matilija Hot Springs** [VENTURA].

Lyons Peak [SAN DIEGO]: *peak,* 4 miles north of Dulzura (lat. 32° 42'10" N, long. 116°45'45" W; at S line sec. 10, T 17 S, R 2 E). Named on Dulzura (1972) 7.5' quadrangle.

Lyon Springs: see **Matilija Hot Springs** [VENTURA].

Lyon's Station: see **San Fernando Pass** [LOS ANGELES].

Lyons Valley [SAN DIEGO]: *valley,* 6.5 miles east of Jamul (lat. 32° 42'55" N, long. 116°45'40" W). Named on Barrett Lake (1960) and Dulzura (1972) 7.5' quadrangles. The name is for General Nathaniel Lyons, who owned land in the valley (Gudde, 1949, p. 198).

- M -

MacArthur: see **Fort MacArthur** [LOS ANGELES].

Machado [LOS ANGELES]: *locality,* 7.25 miles north-northwest of Manhattan Beach city hall along Pacific Electric Railroad (lat. 33° 59'10" N, long. 118°27'05" W); the place is on Ballona grant, received by Agustin Machado and Ignacio Machado. Named on Venice (1950) 7.5' quadrangle. Called Machada on Redondo (1896) 15' quadrangle. On Venice (1924) 6' quadrangle, the name "Machado" applies to a place located nearly 0.5 mile farther east-southeast along the rail line. Postal authorities established Machado post office in 1874, discontinued it in 1875, reestablished it in 1878, and discontinued it in 1887 (Salley, p. 130).

Machado Lake: see **Harbor Lake** [LOS ANGELES].

Maddock Canyon [LOS ANGELES]: *canyon,* less than 1 mile long, 3 miles west-northwest of Azusa city hall (lat. 34°09'30" N, long. 117°57' W; sec. 20, T 1 N, R 10 W). Named on Azusa (1953) 7.5' quadrangle.

Madero Ravine [SAN DIEGO]: *canyon,* 0.5 mile long, nearly 7 miles north-northeast of Buckman Springs (lat. 32°51'40" N, long. 116° 26'30" W; near S line sec. 14, T 15 S, R 5 E). Named on Mount Laguna (1960) 7.5' quadrangle.

Madranio Canyon [VENTURA]: *canyon,* drained by a stream that flows 3.5 miles to the sea 2.5 miles northwest of Pitas Point at Sea Cliff (lat. 34°20'40" N, long. 119°25'05" W; sec. 17, T 3 N, R 24 W). Named on Pitas Point (1950) 7.5' quadrangle.

Madre Grande: see **Mother Grundy Peak** [SAN DIEGO].

Magee Creek [SAN DIEGO]: *stream,* flows 3.25 miles to the valley of San Luis Rey River 2.25 miles east-northeast of Pala (lat. 33°22'10" N, long. 117°03'15" W; sec. 26, T 9 S, R 2 W). Named on Pala (1968) and Pechanga (1968) 7.5' quadrangles. Jahns and Wright's (1951a) map has the name "McGee Can." for the canyon of the stream.

Magic Mountain [LOS ANGELES]: *peak,* 8 miles east-southeast of Solemint (lat. 34°23'10" N, long. 118°19'40" W; sec. 34, T 4 N, R 14 W). Named on Agua Dulce (1960) 7.5' quadrangle. Called Iron Mountain on San Fernando (1900) 15' quadrangle.

Magnolia Park [LOS ANGELES]: *locality,* 2.5 miles west-southwest of Burbank city hall (lat. 34°10'10" N, long. 118°21'10" W). Named on Burbank (1953) 7.5' quadrangle.

Maher Canyon [LOS ANGELES]: *canyon,* drained by a stream that flows 3 miles to Santa Clara River 10 miles east of Solemint (lat. 34°26'25" N, long. 118°17'15" W; near SW cor. sec. 7, T 4 N, R 13 W). Named on Agua Dulce (1960) 7.5' quadrangle.

Maidenhair Falls [SAN DIEGO]: *waterfall,* 4 miles west-southwest of Borrego Springs in Hellhole Canyon (lat. 33°14'15" N, long. 116°26'20" W). Named on Tubb Canyon (1959) 7.5' quadrangle.

Maizeland: see **Rivera**, under **Pico Rivera** [LOS ANGELES].

Malaga Canyon [LOS ANGELES]: *canyon,* drained by a stream that flows less than 3 miles to the sea nearly 3 miles south of Redondo Beach city hall (lat. 33°48'10" N, long. 118°23'45" W). Named on Redondo Beach (1951) 7.5' quadrangle

Malaga Cove [LOS ANGELES]: *embayment,* 2.5 miles south of Redondo Beach city hall along the coast (lat. 33°48'15" N, long. 118°23'45" W); the feature is at the mouth of Malaga Canyon. Named on Redondo Beach (1951) 7.5' quadrangle.

Malaga Creek: see **Malibu Creek** [LOS ANGELES].

Malaga Point: see **Malibu Point** [LOS ANGELES].

Maliba Sequit Creek: see **Malibu Creek** [LOS ANGELES].

Maliba Sequit Point: see **Malibu Point** [LOS ANGELES].

Malibo Creek: see **Malibu Creek** [LOS ANGELES].

Malibo Point: see **Malibu Point** [LOS ANGELES].

Malibu: see **Las Flores** [LOS ANGELES].

Malibu Bowl [LOS ANGELES]: *locality,* 4 miles west-northwest of Malibu Point (lat. 34°03'40" N, long. 118°44'30" W; near SW cor. sec. 23, T 1 S, R 18 W). Named on Malibu Beach (1951) 7.5' quadrangle.

Malibu Beach [LOS ANGELES]: *locality,* at and west of Malibu Point (lat. 34°01'55" N, long. 118°41'15" W). Named on Malibu Beach (1951) 7.5' quadrangle.

Malibu Creek [LOS ANGELES]: *stream,* flows 9.5 miles to the sea at Malibu Point (lat. 34°01'55" N, long. 118°40'45" W). Named on Malibu Beach (1951) 7.5' quadrangle. United States Board on Geographic Names (1933, p. 494) rejected the names "Malaga Creek," "Malibo Creek," "Maliba Sequit Creek," and "Topanga Malibu Sequit Creek" for the stream.

Malibu Hills [LOS ANGELES]: *locality,* 3.5 miles west-northwest of Malibu Point (lat. 34°02'50" N, long. 118°44'35" W; near SW cor. sec. 26, T 1 S, R 18 W). Named on Malibu Beach (1951) 7.5' quadrangle.

Malibu Junction [LOS ANGELES]: *locality,* 1 mile west of Agoura (lat. 34°08'35" N, long. 118°45'20" W). Named on Thousand Oaks (1952) 7.5' quadrangle. Camulos (1903) 30' quadrangle shows a place called Vejor located at or near present Malibu Junction. Postal authorities established Amargo post office in 1880 at a place known as Vejar that was situated 7 miles east of Newbury Park [VENTURA] and discontinued it in 1885; Delores M. Vejar was the first postmaster (Salley, p. 6).

Malibu Lake [LOS ANGELES]: *lake,* less than 1 mile long, behind a dam on Malibu Creek nearly 8 miles north-northeast of Point Dume (lat. 34°06'15" N, long. 118°45' W; near S line sec. 3, T 1 S, R 18 W). Named on Malibu Beach (1951) and Point Dume (1951) 7.5' quadrangles. The feature had the early name "Russell's Lake" (Anonymous, 1950, p. 33).

Malibu Mar Vista [LOS ANGELES]: *locality,* nearly 5 miles north-northeast of Point Dume (lat. 34°03'40" N, long. 118°45'50" W). Named on Solstice Canyon (1932) 6' quadrangle.

Malibu Point [LOS ANGELES]: *promontory,* 25 miles west of Los Angeles city hall along the coast (lat. 34°01'50" N, long. 118°40'55" W); the feature is on Topanga Malibu Sequit grant. Named on Malibu Beach (1951) 7.5' quadrangle. United States Board on Geographic Names (1933, p. 494) rejected the names "Malaga Point," "Malibo Point," "Maliba Sequit Point," and "Topanga Malibu Sequit Point" for the promontory

Malibu Riviera [LOS ANGELES]: *locality,* at and north of Point Dume (lat. 34°00'55" N, long. 118°48'10" W). Named on Point Dume (1951) 7.5' quadrangle.

Malibu Trading Station: see **Trancas** [LOS ANGELES].

Malibu Vista [LOS ANGELES]: *locality,* nearly 4 miles north-northeast of Point Dume (lat. 34°02'55" N, long. 118°46'20" W; sec. 28, T 1 S, R 18 W). Named on Point Dume (1951) 7.5' quadrangle.

Mandalay Beach [VENTURA]: *beach,* nearly 4 miles west of Oxnard along the coast (lat. 34°11'50" N, long. 119°14'50" W). Named on Oxnard (1949) 7.5' quadrangle.

Mand Canyon [LOS ANGELES]: *canyon,* 0.5 mile long, 3 miles east of Burbank city hall (lat. 34°10'20" N, long. 118°15'15" W). Named on Burbank (1953) 7.5' quadrangle.

Mandeville Canyon [LOS ANGELES]: *canyon,* drained by a stream that flows 5 miles to Santa Monica Canyon 5.5 miles west of Beverly Hills city hall (lat. 34°03'40" N, long. 118°29'35" W). Named on Beverly Hills (1950), Canoga Park (1952), and Topanga (1952) 7.5' quadrangles.

Mangalar Spring [SAN DIEGO]: *spring,* 12 miles north-northeast of Warner Springs (lat. 33°25'20" N, long. 116°31'10" W; sec. 1, T 9 S, R 4 E). Named on Bucksnort Mountain (1960) 7.5' quadrangle.

Manhattan: see **Hobart** [LOS ANGELES]; **Manhattan Beach** [LOS ANGELES].

Manhattan Beach [LOS ANGELES]: *city,* 15 miles west-northwest of Long Beach city hall (lat. 33°53'15" N, long. 118°24'35" W). Named on Redondo Beach (1951) and Venice (1950) 7.5' quadrangles. Postal authorities established Manhattan post office in 1903 and changed the name to Manhattan Beach in 1927 (Frickstad, p. 77). The city incorporated in 1912. The place first was called Shore Acres; Stewart Merrill, founder of the community, suggested the name Manhattan Beach from Manhattan Island in New York (Gudde, 1949, p. 203).

Manhattan Beach Station [LOS ANGELES]: *locality,* 1.25 miles north-northwest of Manhattan Beach city hall along Pacific Electric Railroad (lat. 33°54'15" N, long. 118°25'15" W). Named on Venice (1924) 6' quadrangle.

Manuel Canyon [VENTURA]: *canyon,* drained by a stream that flows nearly 2 miles to the canyon of Ventura River 3.5 miles north of Ventura (lat. 34°20' N, long. 119°17'05" W). Named on Ventura (1951) 7.5' quadrangle. The name commemorates John Manuel, a native of Portugal who had a farm at the place (Ricard).

Manzana [LOS ANGELES]: *locality,* 18 miles east of Gorman (lat. 34°46' N, long. 118°31'40" W). Named on Tejon (1903) 30' quadrangle. Postal authorities established Manzana post office in 1892, moved it 1.5 miles northeast in 1899, moved it 4 miles south in 1902, and discontinued it in 1908; the place was in an apple-growing region—*manzana* means "apple" in Spanish (Salley, p. 132).

Manzanita [SAN DIEGO]: *village,* 11 miles east-northeast of Campo (lat. 32°40'10" N, long. 116°17'20" W; at N lines sec. 29, 30, T 17 S, R 7 E). Named on Live Oak Springs (1959) 7.5' quadrangle.

Manzanita: see **Camp Manzanita** [LOS ANGELES].

Manzanita Canyon: see **Oak Spring Canyon** [LOS ANGELES] (1).

Maple Canyon [LOS ANGELES]:

(1) *canyon,* 1.25 miles long, opens into an unnamed canyon 2 miles south

of the village of Leona Valley (lat. 34°35'15" N, long. 118° 17'15" W; near NE cor. sec. 30, T 6 N, R 13 W). Named on Sleepy Valley (1958) 7.5' quadrangle. Los Angeles County (1935) map has the name "Ikanhoffer Canyon" for a presently unnamed canyon at the mouth of Maple Canyon. (2) *canyon*, drained by a stream that flows 1.25 miles to North Fork San Gabriel River 2.5 miles south of Crystal Lake (lat. 34°16'50" N, long. 117°50'25" W). Named on Crystal Lake (1958) 7.5' quadrangle. (3) *canyon*, drained by a stream that flows nearly 1 mile to Pacoima Canyon 5.25 miles north east of downtown San Fernando (lat. 34° 20'40" N, long. 118°23' W; sec. 18, T 3 N, R 14 W). Named on San Fernando (1953) 7.5' quadrangle. (4) *canyon*, drained by a stream that flows less than 1 mile to Big Tujunga Canyon 3 miles south-southeast of Condor Peak (lat. 34° 17'10" N, long. 118°11'35" W; sec. 1, T 2 N, R 13 W). Named on Condor Peak (1959) 7.5' quadrangle. (5) *canyon*, drained by a stream that flows 1 mile to Sawtooth Canyon 5.25 miles northwest of Azusa city hall (lat. 34°10'40" N, long. 117°58'50" W; near NE cor. sec. 13, T 1 N, R 11 W). Named on Azusa (1953) 7.5' quadrangle.

Maple Canyon [VENTURA]: *canyon*, drained by a stream that flows nearly 1 mile to Dominguez Canyon 4.5 miles north of Piru (lat. 34°28'50" N, long. 118°47'50" W; near NW cor. sec. 32, T 5 N, R 18 W). Named on Piru (1952) 7.5' quadrangle.

Maple Creek [VENTURA]: *stream*, flows nearly 3 miles to Tar Creek 6.25 miles north of Fillmore (lat. 34°29'30" N, long. 118° 55' W). Named on Fillmore (1951) 7.5' quadrangle. Called Bear Cr. on Camulos (1903) 30' quadrangle—Fillmore (1951) 7.5' quadrangle has the name "Bear Creek" for a tributary of Maple Creek.

Maple Spring [ORANGE]: *spring*, 1.5 miles north-northwest of Santiago Peak (lat. 33°43'55" N, long. 117°32'50" W). Named on Santiago Peak (1954) 7.5' quadrangle. The name is for a cluster of maple trees at the spring (Meadows, p. 99).

Marek Canyon [LOS ANGELES]: *canyon*, drained by a stream that flows nearly 2 miles to Little Tujunga Canyon 4 miles northwest of Sunland (lat. 34°17'35" N, long. 118°21'40" W; at NE cor. sec. 5, T 2 N, R 14 W). Named on Sunland (1953) 7.5' quadrangle. Called Herrick Canyon on San Fernando (1900) 15' quadrangle, and called Merrick Canyon on Los Angeles County (1935) map.

Marengo [LOS ANGELES]: *locality*, 3.5 miles north-northwest of present Pasadena city hall along Los Angeles Terminal Railroad (lat. 34°11'15" N, long. 118°09' W). Named on Pasadena (1900) 15' quadrangle.

Margarita: see **Ranch House** [SAN DIEGO].

Margarita Peak [SAN DIEGO]: *peak*, 9.5 miles west-northwest of Fallbrook (lat. 33°26'40" N, long. 117°23'20" W; near N line sec. 34, T 8 S, R 5 W); the peak is at the edge of Santa Margarita y las Flores grant. Altitude 3189 feet. Named on Margarita Peak (1968) 7.5' quadrangle.

Marie Canyon [LOS ANGELES]: *canyon*, drained by a stream that flows 1.5 miles to the sea 1.5 miles west of Malibu Point (lat. 34° 01'50" N, long. 118°42'35" W). Named on Malibu Beach (1951) 7.5' quadrangle.

Mariette Creek [SAN DIEGO]: *stream*, flows 1.25 miles to Jim Green Creek 1.5 miles northwest of Julian (lat. 33°05'50" N, long. 116°37'10" W; sec. 25, T 12 S, R 3 E). Named on Julian (1960) 7.5' quadrangle.

Marina Del Rey [LOS ANGELES]: *water feature*, boat harbor 6.5 miles north-northwest of Manhattan Beach city hall near the mouth of Ballona Creek (lat. 33°58'30" N, long. 118°27' W). Named on Venice (1964) 7.5' quadrangle. Redondo (1896) 15' quadrangle shows Ballona Lagoon at the site, and Venice (1950) 7.5' quadrangle shows marsh there.

Marina Passage: see **Pacific Passage** [SAN DIEGO].

Mariners Basin [SAN DIEGO]: *embayment*, 6 miles south of Point La Jolla off Mission Bay (lat. 32°45'55" N, long. 117°14'50" W). Named on La Jolla (1967) 7.5' quadrangle.

Mariners Point [SAN DIEGO]: *promontory*, 6.25 miles south-southeast of Point La Jolla (lat. 32°45'50" N, long. 117°14'45" W); the feature is on the north side of the entrance to Mariners Basin. Named on La Jolla (1967) 7.5' quadrangle.

Marion: see **Camp Marion** [LOS ANGELES]; **Reseda** [LOS ANGELES].

Marion Canyon [SAN DIEGO]: *canyon*, drained by a stream that flows 5.25 miles to San Luis Rey River 2 miles east-southeast of Pala (lat. 33°21'30" N, long. 117°02'30" W; at S line sec. 25, T 9 S, R 2 W). Named on Pala (1968), Pechanga (1968), and Vail Lake (1953) 7.5' quadrangles.

Markham: see **Mount Markham** [LOS ANGELES].

Marlboro [ORANGE]: *locality*, nearly 2 miles north-northwest of Orange city hall along Southern Pacific Railroad (lat. 33°48'45" N, long. 117°51'30" W). Named on Orange (1964) 7.5' quadrangle.

Marle Canyon [LOS ANGELES]: *canyon*, drained by a stream that flows 1.5 miles to the sea 1.5 miles west of Malibu Point (lat. 34°01'50" N, long. 118°42'35" W). Named on Malibu Beach (1951) 7.5' quadrangle.

Marmon Canyon: see **Mormon Canyon** [LOS ANGELES].

Marne [LOS ANGELES]: *locality*, 6.25 miles south-southeast of Baldwin Park city hall along Southern Pacific Railroad (lat. 34°00'20" N, long. 117°54'20" W). Named on Baldwin Park (1953) 7.5' quadrangle.

Marple Canyon [LOS ANGELES]: *canyon*, drained by a stream that flows 6.5 miles to Castaic Valley 9 miles north-northwest of downtown Newhall at Castaic (lat. 34°29'25" N, long. 118° 36'45" W; sec. 25, T 5 N, R 17 W). Named on Whitaker Peak (1958) 7.5' quadrangle.

Marron: see **Mount Marron** [SAN DIEGO].

Marron Canyon [SAN DIEGO]: *canyon*, about 1.25 miles long, 5.25 miles east of Oceanside along Buena Vista Creek (lat. 33°10'50" N, long. 117°17"20" W); the feature is on Agua Hedionda grant, owned by Juan Maria Marron. Named on San Luis Rey (1968) 7.5' quadrangle.

Marron Valley [SAN DIEGO]: *valley*, 4.5 miles east-southeast of Otay Mountain on upper reaches of Tijuana River on the Mexican border (lat. 32°34' N, long. 116°46'20" W). Named on Otay Mountain (1972) 7.5' quadrangle.

Marshall Canyon [LOS ANGELES]: *canyon*, nearly 1 mile long, along Marshall Creek above a point 7 miles north of Pomona city hall (lat. 34°09'10" N, long. 117°44'50" W; near SW cor. sec. 20, T 1 N, R 8 W). Named on Mount Baldy (1954) 7.5' quadrangle.

Marshall Creek [LOS ANGELES]: *stream*, flows 4.5 miles to end in lowlands 4.5 miles north-northwest of Pomona city hall (lat. 34° 07' N, long. 117°46'25" W). Named on Glendora (1953), Mount Baldy (1954), and San Dimas (1954) 7.5' quadrangles.

Marston: see **Camp Marston** [SAN DIEGO].

Marston Meadow [SAN DIEGO]: *area*, 9.5 miles north of Descanso (lat. 32°59'35" N, long. 116°38'40" W; on S line sec. 35, T 13 S, R 3 E). Named on Tule Springs (1960) 7.5' quadrangle.

Martindale Canyon [LOS ANGELES]: *canyon*, drained by a stream that flows 3.5 miles to Bouquet Reservoir 5.5 miles west-southwest of the village of Leona Valley (lat. 34°34'40" N, long. 118°22'10" W; sec. 28, T 6 N, R 14 W). Named on Sleepy Valley (1958) 7.5' quadrangle.

Martins [LOS ANGELES]: *locality*, 4.25 miles east of Whitaker Peak (lat. 34°33'55" N, long. 118°39'35" W; near W line sec. 35, T 6 N, R 17 W). Named on Whitaker Peak (1958) 7.5' quadrangle.

Martins Camp [LOS ANGELES]: *locality*, 0.5 mile south of Mount Wilson (1) (lat. 34°13' N, long. 118°04' W; on W line sec. 32, T 2 N, R 11 W). Named on Pasadena (1900) 15' quadrangle. Clarence S. Martin bought a place called Steils Camp in 1891 and renamed it Camp Wilson, but to most visitors it was known as Martin's Camp; George Schneider built his Halfway House in 1894 about 4 miles below Martin's Camp (Robinson, J.W., 1977, p. 30, 38).

Martin's Peak: see **Mount Harvard** [LOS ANGELES].

Mar Vista [LOS ANGELES]: *district*, 5 miles south-southwest of Beverly Hills city hall in Los Angeles (lat. 34°00'10" N, long. 118°25'30" W). Named on Beverly Hills (1950) 7.5' quadrangle. Postal authorities established Mar Vista post office in 1925 (Frickstad, p. 77). The place was called Ocean Park Heights before 1904 (Gudde, 1949, p. 206).

Mason: see **Glendale** [LOS ANGELES].

Mason Valley [SAN DIEGO]: *valley*, 7 miles north-northwest of Monument Peak (lat. 32°59'30" N, long. 116°27' W). Named on Earthquake Valley (1959) and Monument Peak (1959) 7.5' quadrangles. The name commemorates James E. Mason, who homesteaded in the neighborhood in 1884 (Stein, p. 78).

Matagua Creek: see **Matagual Creek** [SAN DIEGO].

Matagual Creek [SAN DIEGO]: *stream*, flows 7.25 miles to Lake Henshaw 2.25 miles north of Morettis Junction (lat. 33°13'50" N, long. 116°42'50" W). Named on Warners Ranch (1960) 7.5' quadrangle. United States Board on Geographic Names (1962b, p. 19) rejected the names "Matagua Creek," "Mataguay Creek," and "Matajuai Creek" for the stream. According to Kroeber (p. 47), the name "Matagual" is a misprint of the word "Matajuai," which is of Indian origin.

Matagual Valley [SAN DIEGO]: *valley*, 2.5 miles east-northeast of Morettis Junction (lat. 33°12'45" N, long. 116°40' W); the valley is along Matagual Creek. Named on Warners Ranch (1960) 7.5' quadrangle. United States Board on Geographic Names (1962b, p. 19) rejected the names "Matagua Valley," "Mataguay Valley," and "Matajuai Valley" for the place.

Matagua Valley: see **Matagual Valley** [SAN DIEGO].

Mataguay Creek: see **Matagual Creek** [SAN DIEGO].

Mataguay Valley: see **Matagual Valley** [SAN DIEGO].

Matajuai Creek: see **Matagual Creek** [SAN DIEGO].

Matajuai Valley: see **Matagual Valley** [SAN DIEGO].

Matay Canyon [LOS ANGELES]: *canyon*, 1.5 miles long, 5.25 miles west of Valyermo (lat. 34°26'15" N, long. 118°56'40" W; sec. 8, 17, T 4 N, R 10 W). Named on Juniper Hills (1959) 7.5' quadrangle.

Mateo: see **Serra** [ORANGE].

Mathiessen: see **Lake Mathiessen**, under **Lake Sherwood** [VENTURA].

Matiliha Cañon: see **Matilija Creek** [VENTURA].

Matilija [VENTURA]: *locality*, 1.25 miles west-southwest of downtown Ojai along Southern Pacific Railroad (lat. 34°26'20" N, long. 119°15'40" W). Named on Ventura (1904) 15' quadrangle. California Division of Highways' (1934) map shows a place called Tico located 1.5 miles west-southwest of Matilija along the railroad.

Matilija: see **Matilija Hot Springs** [VENTURA].

Matilija Creek [VENTURA]: *stream*, flows 15 miles to join its North Fork and form Ventura River 4 miles northwest of the town of Ojai (lat. 34°29'05" N, long. 119°18' W; near W line sec. 28, T 5 N, R 23 W). Named on Matilija (1952), Old Man Mountain (1943), and Wheeler Springs (1943) 7.5' quadrangles. The canyon of the stream is called Matiliha Cañon on Parke's (1854-1855) map. Antisell (p. 67) used the form "Matilihah" for the name, which is of Indian origin (Kroeber, p. 47). North Fork is 7.5 miles long and is named on Matilija (1952) and Wheeler Springs (1943) 7.5' quadrangles; it is called North Fork Ventura River on Wheeler Springs (1944) 7.5' quadrangle. Upper North Fork enters the main stream 5.5 miles west of Wheeler Springs; it is 6.5 miles long and is named on Old Man Mountain (1943) and Wheeler Springs (1943) 7.5' quadrangles. On Ventura (1904) 15' quadrangle, the stream in present Murietta Canyon is called West Fork Matilija Cr.

Matilija Hot Springs [VENTURA]: *locality*, 4.25 miles northwest of the town of Ojai (lat. 34°29' N, long. 119°18'15" W; sec. 29, T 5 N, R 23 W); the place is along Matilija Creek. Named on Matilija (1952) 7.5' quadrangle. Called Matilija on Ventura (1904) 15' quadrangle. Postal authorities established Matilija post office in 1889 and discontinued it in 1916 (Frickstad, p. 218). The place was a resort as early as about 1890; in 1908 it had accommodations for 200 guests (Waring, p. 63). Berkstresser (p. A-19) gave the alternate name "Ojai Hot Sulphur Springs" for the place. Ventura (1941) 15' quadrangle shows Lyons Hot Springs along Matilija Creek above Matilija Hot Springs. Waring (p. 278) noted that Lyons Spring is in Matilija Canyon about 1 mile northwest of Matilija Hot Springs. Postal authorities established Nogales post office in 1906, moved it and changed the name to Lyon Springs in 1907, and discontinued it in 1914; the name "Lyon" was for Gertrude A. Lyon, owner of the place, and the name "Nogales" was for native walnut trees at the site—*nogales* means "walnut trees" in Spanish (Salley, p 129-130, 155).

Matthews: see **Camp Matthews Naval Reservation** [SAN DIEGO].

Mattox Canyon [LOS ANGELES]: *canyon*, drained by a stream that flows 2.5 miles to Soledad Canyon 3.5 miles southwest of Acton (lat. 34°26'10" N, long. 118°14'40" W; near N line sec. 16, T 4 N, R 13 W). Named on Acton (1959) and Agua Dulce (1960) 7.5' quadrangles.

Maxson [LOS ANGELES]: *locality*, nearly 2 miles east of El Monte along Pacific Electric Railroad (lat. 34°04'35" N, long. 118°00'25" W). Named on El Monte (1926) 6' quadrangle.

Maxy Canyon [VENTURA]: *canyon*, drained by a stream that flows 6.5 miles to Hungry Valley 7.5 miles north-northeast of McDonald Peak (lat. 34°44'15" N, long. 118°53'20" W; near E line sec. 34, T 8 N, R 19 W). Named on Frazier Mountain (1958) and McDonald Peak (1958) 7.5' quadrangles.

Mayate Canyon: see **Emerald Canyon** [ORANGE].

May Canyon [LOS ANGELES]: *canyon*, nearly 1.5 miles long, opens into lowlands 3.25 miles north of downtown San Fernando (lat. 34° 19'45" N, long. 118°25'40" W; sec. 23, T 3 N, R 15 W). Named on San Fernando (1953) 7.5 quadrangle.

May Canyon Saddle [LOS ANGELES]: *pass*, 5 miles north of downtown San Fernando (lat. 34°21'20" N, long. 118°25'50" W; at W line sec. 11, T 3 N, R 15 W). Named on San Fernando (1966) 7.5' quadrangle.

Mayfair [LOS ANGELES]: *district*, 7.25 miles north-northeast of Long Beach city hall (lat. 33°51'55" N, long. 118°08'15" W). Named on Long Beach (1949) and Los Alamitos (1950) 7.5' quadrangles. Postal authorities established Mayfair post office in 1958 and discontinued it in 1963 (Salley, p. 135).

Maynard: see **Del Sur** [LOS ANGELES].

Mayo Spur [LOS ANGELES]: *locality*, 9 miles west-northwest of Newhall along Southern Pacific Railroad (lat. 34°24'35" N, long. 118°40'25" W). Named on Val Verde (1952) 7.5' quadrangle.

Maywood [LOS ANGELES]: *town*, 2.5 miles north-northeast of South Gate city hall (lat. 33°59'25" N, long. 118°11'15" W). Named on South Gate (1964) 7.5' quadrangle. Postal authorities established Maywood post office in 1925; the name is from May Wood, who was an employee of Laguna Land and Water Company—the company founded the community (Salley, p. 136). The city incorporated in 1924.

McAlmond Canyon [SAN DIEGO]: *canyon*, drained by a stream that flows 4 miles to Cottonwood Creek (3) 2.5 miles north-northeast of Barrett Junction (lat. 32°38'40" N, long. 116°40'45" W; sec. 33, T 17 S, R 3 E). Named on Barrett Lake (1960) and Morena Reservoir (1960) 7.5' quadrangles. The name is for Captain C.G. McAlmond, who became pilot commissioner for the port of San Diego in 1873 (Stein, p. 77).

McCain: see **Dave McCain Spring** [SAN DIEGO].

McCain Valley [SAN DIEGO]: *valley*, 2.5 miles north of Manzanita along Tule Creek (lat. 32°42'15" N, long. 116°17'20" W). Named on Jacumba (1959) and Live Oak Springs (1959) 7.5' quadrangles. The name is for John McCain, a homesteader who settled at the place in 1869 (Stein, p. 77).

McCampbell [LOS ANGELES]: *locality*, 4.5 miles west of present Whittier city hall along Pacific Electric Railroad (lat. 33°58'20" N, long. 118°06'50" W). Named on Bell (1936) 6' quadrangle.

McClellan: see **Camp McClellan** [LOS ANGELES].

McClure Canyon [LOS ANGELES]:

(1) *canyon*, 1.25 miles long, 4.5 miles west-southwest of Valyermo (lat. 34°25'25" N, long. 117°55'30" W; sec. 16, 21, T 14 N, R 10 W). Named on Juniper Hills (1959) 7.5' quadrangle.

(2) *canyon*, 1.5 miles long, 2 miles north-northwest of Burbank city hall (lat. 34°12'40" N, long. 118°19'05" W). Named on Burbank (1953) 7.5' quadrangle.

McCorkle Canyon [LOS ANGELES]: *canyon*, drained by a stream that flows 1 mile to Kings Canyon 4.5 miles northeast of Burnt Peak (lat. 34°43'05" N, long. 118°30'40" W; near S line sec. 6, T 7 N, R 15 W). Named on Burnt Peak (1958) 7.5' quadrangle.

McCoy Canyon [LOS ANGELES]: *canyon*, 4 miles long, along Arroyo Calabasas above a point 0.25 mile south-southwest of Calabasas (lat. 34°09' N, long. 118°38'30" W; at E line sec. 22, T 1 N, R 17 W). Named on Calabasas (1952) 7.5' quadrangle.

McCoy Canyon: see **Honby** [LOS ANGELES].

McCraken Reservoir [ORANGE]: *water feature*, 1.5 miles south of San Juan Capistrano (lat. 33°28'45" N, long. 117°39'50" W). Named on Dana Point (1968) 7.5' quadrangle.

McDill: see **Mount McDill** [LOS ANGELES].

McDonald Cabin [VENTURA]: *locality*, 5.25 miles north of Devils Heart Peak (lat. 34°37'10" N, long. 118°57'20" W; at S line sec. 12, T 6 N, R 20 W); the place is 1.25 miles southwest of McDonald Peak. Named on Devils Heart Peak (1943) 7.5' quadrangle.

McDonald Canyon [VENTURA]: *canyon*, drained by a stream that flows 1.5 miles to Ojai Valley 2 miles west-northwest of the town of Ojai (lat. 34°27'25" N, long. 119°16'30" W; sec. 3, T 4 N, R 23 W). Named on Matilija (1952) 7.5' quadrangle.

McDonald Creek [LOS ANGELES]: *stream*, flows 1.5 miles to La Tuna Canyon 4.5 miles north-northwest of Burbank city hall (lat. 34°14'05" N, long. 118°20'55" W; near S line sec. 21, T 2 N, R 14 W). Named on Burbank (1953) 7.5' quadrangle.

McDonald Peak [VENTURA]: *peak*, 16 miles north of Fillmore (lat. 34°38' N, long. 118°56'20" W; near NW cor. sec. 7, T 6 N, R 19 W). Altitude 6870 feet. Named on McDonald Peak (1958) 7.5' quadrangle.

McFadden's Landing: see **Newport Beach** [ORANGE] (2).

McGee Canyon: see **Magee Creek** [SAN DIEGO].

McGee Flat [SAN DIEGO]: *area*, 5.5 miles south-southeast of Santa Ysabel (lat. 33°01'50" N, long. 116°38'50" W; near W line sec. 23, T 13 S, R 3 E). Named on Santa Ysabel (1960) 7.5' quadrangle.

McGee's: see **Julian** [SAN DIEGO].

McGill: see **Mount McGill**, under **Mount Pinos** [VENTURA].

McGinty Mountain [SAN DIEGO]: *ridge*, generally west-northwest-trending, 2.5 miles long, 2.5 miles northeast of Jamul (lat. 32°44'40" N, long. 116°50'55" W). Named on Alpine (1955) and Dulzura (1972) 7.5' quadrangles.

McGonigle Canyon [SAN DIEGO]: *canyon*, drained by a stream that flows 5 miles to Carmel Valley 4 miles east of Del Mar (lat. 32° 57' N, long 117°11'30" W; sec. 16, T 14 S, R 3 W). Named on Del Mar (1967) 7.5' quadrangle. On La Jolla 1903) 15' quadrangle, the name extends southwest along present Carmel Valley. The feature first was known as Cordero Canyon for the Cordero brothers, who were soldiers with the Portola expedition; the name McGonigle, given in the 1870's, is for Felix McGonigle, an early settler in the neighborhood (Gudde, 1949, p. 199).

McGrath: see **Oxnard** [VENTURA].

McGrath Lake [VENTURA]: *lake*, 3000 feet long, 4.25 miles west-northwest of Oxnard near the coast (lat. 34°12'50" N, long. 119°15'10" W). Named on Oxnard (1949) 7.5' quadrangle. The lake is named for a family that had land in the neighborhood (Ricard).

McKinley [LOS ANGELES]: *district*, 3 miles northeast of present Torrance city hall (lat. 33°51'50" N, long. 118°18'05" W). Named on Torrance (1924) 6' quadrangle.

McKinley: see **Mount McKinley** [LOS ANGELES].

McKinley Canyon [LOS ANGELES]: *canyon*, drained by a stream that flows 1.25 miles to Trail Canyon 5.5 miles northeast of Sunland (lat. 34°19'20" N, long. 118°15'20" W); the canyon heads near Mount McKinley. Named on Sunland (1953) 7.5' quadrangle.

McKiwanis: see **Camp McKiwanis** [LOS ANGELES].

McNeil [LOS ANGELES]: *locality*, 2.5 miles west-southwest of present Burbank city hall along Southern Pacific Railroad (lat. 34° 10'15" N, long. 118°21' W). Named on Burbank (1926) 6' quadrangle.

McPherson [ORANGE]: *locality*, 1.5 miles east of Orange city hall along Southern Pacific Railroad (lat. 33°47'20" N, long. 117°49'20" W). Named on Orange (1964) 7.5' quadrangle. Postal authorities established McPherson post office in 1886 and discontinued it in 1900; the name was for Robert McPherson, first postmaster (Salley, p. 136-137).

McRay Canyon: see **Bitter Canyon** [LOS ANGELES].

McVicker Canyon [ORANGE]: *canyon*, drained by a stream that flows 1 mile to Riverside County 2.5 miles southeast of Trabuco Peak (lat. 33°40'40" N, long. 117°26'15" W; sec. 6, T 6 S, R 5 W). Named on Alberhill (1954) 7.5' quadrangle.

Medanos Point: see **Point Medanos** [SAN DIEGO].

Medea Creek [LOS ANGELES-VENTURA]: *stream,* heads in Ventura County and flows 7.25 miles to Malibu Lake 8.5 miles north-northeast of Point Dume in Los Angeles County (lat. 34°06'45" N, long. 118°45'20" W; sec. 3, T 1 S, R 18 W). Named on Malibu Beach (1951), Point Dume (1951), and Thousand Oaks (1952) 7.5' quadrangles.

Meier Canyon [VENTURA]: *canyon,* 3 miles long, opens into Simi Valley (1) 5 miles west of Santa Susana Pass (lat. 34°15'55" N, long. 118°43'15" W; at S line sec. 12, T 2 N, R 18 W). Named on Calabasas (1952) 7.5' quadrangle. The feature first was called Bonebreak Canyon, probably for George H. Bonebreak, then it was called Sycamore Canyon, and finally it was called Meier Canyon for Eddie Meier, who owned land in the neighborhood (Ricard).

Meiners Oaks [VENTURA]: *town,* 2 miles west of downtown Ojai (lat. 34°27' N, long. 119°16'45" W). Named on Matilija (1952) 7.5' quadrangle.

Mendenhall: see **Mendenhall Valley** [SAN DIEGO].

Mendenhall Peak [LOS ANGELES]: *peak,* 6 miles north of Sunland (lat. 34°20'55" N, long. 118°18'45" W; near N line sec. 14, T 3 N, R 14 W); the peak is on Mendenhall Ridge. Named on Sunland (1953) 7.5' quadrangle. Forest Service officials named the feature for Frank Mendenhall, a hunter (Gudde, 1949, p. 210).

Mendenhall Ridge [LOS ANGELES]: *ridge,* generally west-trending, 6 miles long, 6 miles north of Sunland (lat. 34°20'55" N, long. 118° 18'15" W). Named on Sunland (1966) 7.5' quadrangle.

Mendenhall Saddle [LOS ANGELES]: *pass,* 6 miles north of Sunland (lat. 34°20'55" N, long. 118°18'15" W; near NW cor. sec. 13, T 3 N, R 14 W); the pass is near the center of Mendenhall Ridge. Named on Sunland (1966) 7.5' quadrangle.

Mendenhall Valley [SAN DIEGO]: *valley,* 4.5 miles east of Boucher Hill (lat. 33°19'45" N, long. 116°50'15" W). Named on Palomar Observatory (1949) 7.5' quadrangle. Tucker and Reed's (1939) map shows a place called Mendenhall in the valley. The name commemorates Enos Mendenhall, who settled at the valley in 1870 (Gudde, 1949, p. 210).

Mentryville: see **Pico Canyon** [LOS ANGELES].

Meridian District: see **Bostonia** [SAN DIEGO].

Merigan: see **San Marcos** [SAN DIEGO].

Merle [SAN DIEGO]: *locality,* 2.5 miles north-northwest of Encinitas along Southern California Railroad (lat. 33°04'30" N, long. 117°18'30" W). Named on Oceanside (1898) 15' quadrangle. Postal authorities established Merle post office in 1888, discontinued it for a time in 1892, and discontinued it in 1909; the name was for the son of the first settler at the place (Salley, p. 138).

Mermaids Canyon: see **Big Mermaids Canyon** [LOS ANGELES]; **Little Mermaids Canyon** [LOS ANGELES].

Merriam: see **Camp Merriam**, under **Camp Sierra** [LOS ANGELES].

Merriam Mountains [SAN DIEGO]: *ridge,* south-southeast-trending, 7 miles long, center 6 miles east of Vista (lat. 33°12'15" N, long. 117°08'15" W). Named on San Marcos (1968) and Valley Center (1968) 7.5' quadrangles. The name commemorates Major Gustavus F. Merriam, who settled in the neighborhood in 1875 to raise bees and operate a winery (Stein, p. 79).

Merrick Canyon: see **Marek Canyon** [LOS ANGELES].

Merton [SAN DIEGO]: *locality,* 1 mile southwest of present Poway (lat. 32°56'55" N, long. 117°03'20" W). Named on La Jolla (1903) 15' quadrangle. Postal authorities established Merton post office in 1890, moved it 0.5 mile east in 1900, and discontinued it in 1902 (Salley, p. 138).

Mesa: see **Mount Mesa** [LOS ANGELES]; **The Mesa** [SAN DIEGO].

Mesa del Padre Barona: see **Cañada de San Vicente y Mesa del Padre Barona** [SAN DIEGO].

Mesa Grande [SAN DIEGO]: *locality,* 11 miles north-northeast of Ramona (lat. 33°10'50" N, long. 116°46'05" W; near NW cor. sec. 34, T 11 S, R 2 E). Named on Mesa Grande (1948) 7.5' quadrangle. Postal authorities established Mesa Grande post office in 1879, discontinued it the same year, reestablished it in 1883 with the name Mesaville, changed the name to Mesa Grande the same year; moved it 1.5 miles north in 1892, moved it 1 mile northwest in 1899, and discontinued it in 1953 (Salley, p. 138).

Mesa Peak [LOS ANGELES]: *peak,* 3 miles northwest of Malibu Point (lat. 34°03'45" N, long. 118°43'05" W; near S line sec. 24, T 1 S, R 18 W). Altitude 1844 feet. Named on Malibu Beach (1951) 7.5' quadrangle.

Mesaville: see **Mesa Grande** [SAN DIEGO].

Mescal Bajada [SAN DIEGO]: *area,* 12 miles west of Ocotillo Wells (lat. 33°07' N, long. 116°20'30" W). Named on Whale Peak (1959) 7.5' quadrangle.

Mescal Campground [LOS ANGELES]: *locality,* 2 miles west-northwest of Big Pines (lat. 34°23'30" N, long. 117°43'15" W); the place is less than 0.5 mile west of Mescal Creek. Named on Mescal Creek (1956) 7.5' quadrangle.

Mescal Creek [LOS ANGELES]: *stream,* flows 5.5 miles to lowlands 5 miles north of Big Pines (lat. 34°27' N, long. 117°42'15" W; sec. 10, T 4 N, R 8 W). Named on Mescal Creek (1956) 7.5' quadrangle.

Mesmer [LOS ANGELES]: *locality,* 6.5 miles north of present Manhattan Beach city hall along Atchison, Topeka and Santa Fe Railroad (lat. 33°59' N, long. 118°24' W). Named on Redondo (1896) 15' quadrangle.

Mesquite Oasis [SAN DIEGO]: *locality,* 6.5 miles north-northwest of Sweeney Pass (lat. 32°55'15" N, long. 116°13' W; near S line sec. 25, T 14 S, R 7 E). Named on Arroyo Tapiado (1959) 7.5' quadrangle.

Messenger Flats [LOS ANGELES]: *area,* 6 miles south of Acton (lat. 34°22'55" N, long. 118°11'35" W; at S line sec. 36, T 4 N, R 13 W). Named on Acton (1959) 7.5' quadrangle.

Mesto: see **Garden Grove** [ORANGE].

Metaka: see **Camp Metaka** [LOS ANGELES].

Metate Hill [SAN DIEGO]: *hill,* 5.5 miles east-southeast of Borrego Springs (lat. 33°13'10" N, long. 116°17'10" W; sec. 18, T 11 S, R 7 E). Named on Borrego Sink (1959) 7.5' quadrangle.

Mexican Canyon [SAN DIEGO]: *canyon,* drained by a stream that flows 3 miles to lowlands 1.5 miles northwest of Jamul (lat. 32°44'15" N, long. 116°53'30" W; at W line sec. 33, T 16 S, R 1 E). Named on Dulzura (1972) and Jamul Mountains (1955) 7.5' quadrangles.

Michael Canyon: se **Michael Creek** [LOS ANGELES-VENTURA].

Michael Creek [LOS ANGELES-VENTURA]: *stream,* heads in Los Angeles County and flows 2.25 miles to Piru Creek 7 miles southeast of Cobblestone Mountain in Ventura County (lat. 34°32'50" N, long. 118°46'15" W; sec. 4, T 5 N, R 18 W). Named on Cobblestone Mountain (1958) and Whitaker Peak (1958) 7.5' quadrangles. Los Angeles County (1935) map has the name "Michael Cany." for the canyon of the stream.

Middle Anacapa: see **Anacapa Island** [VENTURA].

Middle Canyon [LOS ANGELES]: *canyon,* drained by a stream that flows 7.25 miles to the sea nearly 3 miles west of Mount Banning on Santa Catalina Island (lat. 33°22'05" N, long. 118°28'50" W). Named on Santa Catalina South (1943) 7.5' quadrangle.

Middle Lake [LOS ANGELES]: *lake,* 3.5 miles east-southeast of downtown San Fernando (lat. 34°15'45" N, long. 118°22'45" W). Named on San Fernando (1966) 7.5' quadrangle.

Middle Mesa [SAN DIEGO]: *area,* 7.5 miles north of Sweeney Pass (lat. 32°56'35" N, long. 116°11' W); the feature is situated between West Mesa (2) and East Mesa (2). Named on Arroyo Tapiado (1959) 7.5' quadrangle.

Middle Mesa Peak: see **Middle Peak** [SAN DIEGO].

Middle Mountain [SAN DIEGO]: *ridge,* west-trending, 1.25 miles long, nearly 7 miles southwest of Descanso (lat. 32°47'35" N, long. 116°42' W; sec. 7, 8, T 16 S, R 3 E). Named on Viejas Mountain (1960) 7.5' quadrangle.

Middle Peak [SAN DIEGO]: *peak,* 2.25 miles north of Cuyamaca Peak (lat. 32°58'50" N, long. 116°36' W). Altitude 5883 feet. Named on Cuyamaca Peak (1960) 7.5' quadrangle. Stein (p. 80) called the feature Middle Mesa Peak, and noted that it lies between Cuyamaca Peak and North Peak.

Middle Point [VENTURA]: *promontory,* 4 miles west-northwest of Point Mugu along the coast (lat. 34°05'55" N, long. 119°07'45" W); the feature is situated between Hueneme Point (present Point Hueneme) and Mugu Point (present Point Mugu). Named on Hueneme (1904) 15' quadrangle.

Middle Ranch Cove: see **Mills Landing** [LOS ANGELES].

Middle Ridge [SAN DIEGO]: *ridge,* south-trending, 3 miles long, 4 miles west of Mesa Grande (lat. 33°10'50" N, long. 116°50'25" W). Named on Mesa Grande (1948) 7.5' quadrangle.

Middle Spring [SAN DIEGO]: *spring,* 4.5 miles southwest of Borrego Springs in Tubb Canyon (lat. 33°12'25" N, long. 116°25'30" W). Named on Tubb Canyon (1959) 7.5' quadrangle.

Middle Willows [SAN DIEGO]: *locality,* 13 miles north-northwest of Borrego Springs in Coyote Canyon (1) (lat. 33°25'30" N, long. 116°29'15" W). Named on Collins Valley (1959) 7.5' quadrangle.

Midway City [ORANGE]: *town,* 6 miles north of Huntington Beach civic center (lat. 33°45' N, long. 117°59' W). Named on Anaheim (1965) and Newport Beach (1965) 7.5' quadrangles. Postal authorities established Midway City post office in 1929 (Frickstad, p. 117).

Miguel: see **Mother Miguel Mountain** [SAN DIEGO].

Mildred Falls [SAN DIEGO]: *waterfall,* 7 miles south-southwest of Santa Ysabel along Ritchie Creek (lat. 33°00'50" N, long. 116°42'50" W; sec. 30, T 13 S, R 3 E). Named on Santa Ysabel (1960) 7.5' quadrangle.

Mile High [LOS ANGELES]: *locality,* 5.5 miles east-southeast of Valyermo (lat. 34°24'45" N, long. 117°46'20" W; sec. 24, T 4 N, R 9 W). Named on Valyermo (1958) 7.5' quadrangle.

Milguatay: see **Campo** [SAN DIEGO].

Millard Canyon [LOS ANGELES]: *canyon,* drained by a stream that flows 3.5 miles to Arroyo Seco 4 miles north-northwest of Pasadena city hall (lat. 34°12'15" N, long. 118°09'50" W; sec. 5, T 1 N, R 12 W). Named on Pasadena (1953) 7.5' quadrangle. The name recalls Henry W. Millard and his family, who took up a homestead in the canyon in 1862 (Robinson, J.W., 1977, p. 101).

Mill Canyon [LOS ANGELES]: *canyon,* drained by a stream that flows 5.5 miles to Soledad Canyon 3.5 miles southwest of Acton (lat. 34°26'10" N, long. 118°14'35" W; near N line sec. 16, T 4 N, R 13 W). Named on Acton (1959) 7.5' quadrangle.

Mill Creek [LOS ANGELES]: *stream,* flows 8 miles to Big Tujunga Canyon 4.5 miles east-southeast of Condor Peak (lat. 34°18'35" N, long. 118°08'30"

W). Named on Chilao Flat (1959), Condor Peak (1959), and Pacifico Mountain (1959) 7.5' quadrangles. Middle Fork enters 2.5 miles upstream from the mouth of the main creek; it is nearly 4 miles long and is named on Chilao Flat (1959) and Condor Peak (1959) 7.5' quadrangles. North Fork enters from the north nearly 1 mile upstream from the mouth of the main stream; it is 5.5 miles long and is named on Condor Peak (1959) 7.5' quadrangle.

Mill Creek Picnic Grounds [LOS ANGELES]: *locality,* 5 miles southwest of Pacifico Mountain along Mill Creek (lat. 34°20'35" N, long. 118°06'30" W). Named on Chilao Flat (1959) 7.5' quadrangle.

Mill Creek Summit [LOS ANGELES]: *pass,* nearly 3 miles west-northwest of Pacifico Mountain (lat. 34°23'30" N, long. 118°04'50" W). Named on Pacifico Mountain (1959) 7.5' quadrangle.

Miller Canyon [LOS ANGELES]: *canyon,* 1.25 miles long, 5 miles west of Valyermo (lat. 34°25'45" N, long. 117°56' W; sec. 16, 21, T 4 N, R 10 W). Named on Juniper Hills (1959) 7.5' quadrangle.

Miller Creek [SAN DIEGO]: *stream,* flows 5.25 miles to the canyon of Campo Creek 4.5 miles northeast of Campo (lat. 32°38'50" N, long. 116°24'30" W; at S line sec. 31, T 17 S, R 6 E). Named on Cameron Corners (1959) and Live Oak Springs (1959) 7.5' quadrangles.

Miller Mountain [SAN DIEGO]: *ridge,* west-trending, 1 mile long, 4 miles north of Margarita Peak (lat. 33°30'05" N, long. 117°23'15" W). Named on Margarita Peak (1968) and Sitton Peak (1954) 7.5' quadrangles.

Miller Valley [SAN DIEGO]: *valley,* 8 miles north-northeast of Campo (lat. 32°41'50" N, long. 116°23'45" W; mainly in sec. 17, T 17 S, R 6 E); the valley is along Miller Creek. Named on Cameron Corners (1959) 7.5' quadrangle.

Millhouse Canyon: see **Wheeler Canyon** [VENTURA].

Milligan Barranca [VENTURA]: *gully,* extends for 2.5 miles to Honda Barranca nearly 7 miles south of Santa Paula (lat. 34°15'20" N, long. 119°04' W). Named on Santa Paula (1951) 7.5' quadrangle.

Mills Crossing Station: see **Tierra del Sol** [SAN DIEGO].

Mills Landing [LOS ANGELES]: *locality,* nearly 3 miles west of Mount Banning on the west side of Santa Catalina Island (lat. 33° 22'05" N, long. 118°28'50" W). Named on Santa Catalina South (1943) 7.5' quadrangle. Smith's (1897) map shows Middle Ranch C. [Cove] at the site. The place was called Craig Beach in 1893 (Doran, 1980, p. 76).

Mine Canyon [SAN DIEGO]:

(1) *canyon,* 2.5 miles long, opens into Mescal Bajada 14 miles west-southwest of Ocotillo Wells (lat. 33°05'45" N, long. 116°21'45" W). Named on Whale Peak (1959) 7.5' quadrangle.

(2) *canyon,* drained by a stream that flows 4.25 miles to Tijuana River 4 miles east-southeast of Otay Mountain (lat. 32°34'10" N, long. 116°46'50" W). Named on Otay Mountain (1972) 7.5' quadrangle.

Mine Canyon: see **Buck Creek** [VENTURA].

Mine Gulch [LOS ANGELES]: *canyon,* drained by a stream that flows 2.25 miles to San Gabriel River 6 miles northwest of Mount San Antonio (lat. 34°20'35" N, long. 117°43'35" W; at W line sec. 16, T 3 N, R 8 W). Named on Crystal Lake (1958) and Mount San Antonio (1955) 7.5' quadrangles.

Mine Gulch Camp [LOS ANGELES]: *locality,* 6 miles northwest of Mount San Antonio (lat. 34°20'40" N, long. 117°43'30" W; near W line sec. 16, T 3 N, R 8 W); the place is at the mouth of Mine Gulch. Named on Mount San Antonio (1955) 7.5' quadrangle.

Mineral Hill [SAN DIEGO]: *peak,* 8 miles north-northwest of Descanso (lat. 32°58'10" N, long. 116°39'20" W; sec. 10, T 14 S, R 3 E). Altitude 3495 feet. Named on Tule Springs (1960) 7.5' quadrangle.

Minero Canyon [LOS ANGELES]: *canyon,* drained by a stream that flows 1 mile to San Gabriel Reservoir 7.25 miles north-northeast of Glendora city hall (lat. 34°14'10" N, long. 117°49'45" W; at N line sec. 28, T 2 N, R 9 W). Named on Glendora (1953) 7.5' quadrangle.

Mine Wash [SAN DIEGO]: *stream* and *dry wash,* extends for nearly 4 miles to San Felipe Creek 8.5 miles south-southeast of Borrego Springs (lat. 33°08'10" N, long. 116°19'45" W; sec. 14, T 12 S, R 6 E); the feature heads at the mouth of Mine Canyon (1). Named on Borrego Sink (1959) and Whale Peak (1959) 7.5' quadrangles.

Minnewawa: see **Camp Minnewawa** [SAN DIEGO].

Mint Canyon [LOS ANGELES]:

(1) *canyon,* drained by a stream that flows 15 miles to Santa Clara River at Solemint (lat. 34°24'50" N, long, 118°27'15" W; sec. 21, T 4 N, R 15 W). Named on Green Valley (1958), Mint Canyon (1960), and Sleepy Valley (1958) 7.5' quadrangles. Los Angeles County (1935) map shows a feature called James Canyon that opens into Mint Canyon about 5.5 miles northeast of Solemint (sec. 31, T 5 N, R 14 W), and a feature called Wright Canyon that opens into Mint Canyon about 6 miles northeast of Solemint (at S line sec. 30, T 5 N, R 14 W).

(2) *settlement,* less than 1 mile north-northeast of Solemint (lat. 34°25'45" N, long. 118°26'30" W; sec. 15, T 4 N, R 15 W); the place is in Mint Canyon (1). Named on Mint Canyon (1960) 7.5' quadrangle. Called St. Johns on Humphreys (1932) 6' quadrangle, and called Thompson on San Fernando (1945) 15' quadrangle, although San Fernando (1900) 15' quadrangle has the name "Thompson" at present Solemint. Postal authorities established Thompson post office in 1888 and discontinued it in 1903 (Frickstad, p. 82).

Mint Canyon Campground [LOS ANGELES]: *locality,* 12.5 miles south-southwest of the village of Lake Hughes (lat. 34°30'05" N, long. 118°22'50" W; near E line sec. 19, T 5 N, R 14 W); the place is in Mint Canyon (1). Named on Green Valley (1958) 7.5' quadrangle.

Mint Canyon Spring [LOS ANGELES]: *locality,* 6.5 miles northeast of Solemint (lat. 34°29'35" N, long. 118°23'05" W; sec. 30, T 5 N, R 14 W); the place is in Mint Canyon (1). Named on Mint Canyon (1960) 7.5' quadrangle.

Miraflores: see **Anaheim Tower** [ORANGE].

Mirage Valley: see **El Mirage Valley** [LOS ANGELES].

Miraleste [LOS ANGELES]: *district,* 6 miles south of Torrance city hall (lat. 33°45'05" N, long. 118°19'25" W). Named on Torrance (1964) 7.5' quadrangle. Officials of a land-development company named the place in 1924 (Gudde, 1949, p. 217).

Miraleste Canyon [LOS ANGELES]: *canyon,* 2.5 miles long, nearly 6 miles south-southeast of Torrance city hall (lat. 33°45'20" N, long. 118°18'45" W); Miraleste is in the canyon. Named on Torrance (1964) 7.5' quadrangle.

Miramar [SAN DIEGO]:

(1) *locality,* 6.5 miles southwest of Poway (lat. 32°53'35" N, long. 117°07' W; at SE cor. sec. 6, T 15 S, R 2 W). Named on Poway (1967) 7.5' quadrangle. Postal authorities established Miramar post office 4.5 miles east of present Linda Vista in 1892, moved it 1.25 miles northeast in 1904, and moved it 0.5 mile south in 1910 (Salley, p. 142). The name is from E.W. Scripps' Linda Vista ranch (Gudde, 1949, p. 217). Both the names "Linda Vista" and "Miramar" applied to the place; the railroad used the name "Linda Vista" for its station, and the post office had the name "Miramar" (Hanna, p. 194).

(2) *locality,* nearly 8 miles southeast of Del Mar along Atchison, Topeka and Santa Fe Railroad (lat. 32°52'35" N, long. 117°10'25" W; near S line sec. 10, T 15 S, R 3 W). Named on Del Mar (1967) 7.5' quadrangle. The place is called Linda Vista on Del Mar (1953) 7.5' quadrangle, and is called Lindavista on La Jolla (1903) 15' quadrangle.

Miramar Air Station Naval Reservation: see **Miramar Naval Air Station** [SAN DIEGO].

Miramar Lake: see **Miramar Reservoir** [SAN DIEGO].

Miramar Naval Air Station [SAN DIEGO]: *military installation,* 10 miles north of downtown San Diego (lat. 32°52' N, long. 117° 08' W); the place is south of Miramar (1). Named on Del Mar (1967), La Jolla (1967), La Mesa (1967), and Poway (1967) 7.5' quadrangles. Called Miramar Air Station Naval Reservation on Del Mar (1953) and Poway Valley (1952) 7.5' quadrangles.

Miramar Reservoir [SAN DIEGO]: *lake,* 1.25 miles long, 4.5 miles southwest of Poway (lat. 32°55' N, long. 117°05'45" W; mainly in sec. 32, 33, T 14 S, R 2 W); the feature is less than 2 miles northeast of Miramar (1). Named on Poway (1967) 7.5' quadrangle. Called Miramar Lake on Poway (1967, photorevised 1975) 7.5' quadrangle. United States Board on Geographic Names (1979b, p. 7) approved the name "Lake Miramar" for the feature.

Mira Monte [VENTURA]: *settlement,* 2.5 miles west-southwest of the town of Ojai (lat. 34°26' N, long. 119°17' W). Named on Matilija (1952) 7.5' quadrangle. Development of the place began in 1928 (Ricard).

Mirror Lake [VENTURA]: *intermittent lake,* 1900 feet long, 3 miles southwest of the town of Ojai (lat. 34°25'20" N, long. 119°17'25" W). Named on Matilija (1952) 7.5' quadrangle.

Mission Acres: see **Sepulveda** [LOS ANGELES] (1).

Mission Bay [SAN DIEGO]: *bay,* opens to the sea 6.5 miles south of Point La Jolla (lat. 32°45'30" N, long. 117°15'10" W). Named on La Jolla (1967) 7.5' quadrangle. Called Ensenada de Baxa Entrada on a Spanish map of 1602 (Harlow, 1987, p. 52), and called Puerto Falso on Dalrymple's (1789) map. Emory (p. 113) called the feature False Bay, but United States Board on Geographic Names (1933, p. 523) rejected this name

Mission Bay Channel [SAN DIEGO]: *channel,* 6 miles south-southeast of Point La Jolla in Mission Bay (lat. 32°46'05" N, long. 117° 14'20" W). Named on La Jolla (1967) 7.5' quadrangle.

Mission Beach [SAN DIEGO]: *district,* 5 miles south of Point La Jolla (lat. 32°46'05" N, long. 117°15'05" W); the place is between Mission Bay and the sea. Named on La Jolla (1967) 7.5' quadrangle. Postal authorities established Mission Beach post office in 1922 and discontinued it in 1951 (Salley, p. 142).

Mission Creek [LOS ANGELES]: *stream,* flows 1.25 miles from Legg Lake to Rio Hondo 4 miles southwest of El Monte city hall (lat. 34°01'35" N, long. 118°04'20" W). Named on El Monte (1966) 7.5' quadrangle.

Mission Gorge [SAN DIEGO]: *canyon,* nearly 3 miles long, along San Diego River above a point 4.25 miles northwest of La Mesa (lat. 32°48'45" N, long. 117°04'15" W). Named on La Mesa (1967) 7.5' quadrangle. Poole (p. 18) called the feature Cajon Gap.

Mission Hills [LOS ANGELES]: *district,* 2.25 miles southwest of downtown San Fernando in Los Angeles (lat. 34°15'30" N, long. 118°27'45"

W). Named on San Fernando (1966) 7.5' quadrangle. Postal authorities established Dennis Park post office in 1957 and changed the name was to Mission Hills in 1959 (Salley, p. 58).

Mission Hills [SAN DIEGO]: *district,* 2.5 miles north-northwest of downtown San Diego (lat. 32°45'15" N, long. 117°11'10" W). Named on La Jolla (1967) 7.5' quadrangle.

Mission Junction [LOS ANGELES]: *locality,* 1 mile east-northeast of Los Angeles city hall along a rail line (lat. 34°03'45" N, long. 118° 13'35" W). Named on Los Angeles (1966) 7.5' quadrangle.

Mission Knoll: see **San Luis Rey** [SAN DIEGO].

Mission Mountain [SAN DIEGO]: *ridge,* south-southwest- to northwest-trending, 2 miles long, 1.5 miles east-northeast of downtown Oceanside (lat. 33°12'15" N, long. 117°21' W); the feature is 1.5 miles southwest of San Luis Rey de Trancia mission. Named on San Luis Rey (1968) 7.5' quadrangle.

Mission Peak: see **Mission Point** [LOS ANGELES]; **Cowles Mountain** [SAN DIEGO].

Mission Point [LOS ANGELES]: *peak,* 4.5 miles south of Newhall (lat. 34°18'40" N, long. 118°32' W). Altitude 2771 feet. Named on Oat Mountain (1952) 7.5' quadrangle. Called Mission Pk. on Los Angeles County (1935) map.

Mission Point [SAN DIEGO]: *promontory,* 6.25 miles south-southeast of Point La Jolla (lat. 32°45'40" N, long. 117°14'40" W); the feature is near the entrance to Mission Bay. Named on La Jolla (1967) 7.5' quadrangle.

Mission San Diego [SAN DIEGO]: *land grant,* at San Diego. Named on Del Mar (1967), La Jolla (1967), La Mesa (1967), and National City (1967) 7.5' quadrangles. Called Ex Mission San Diego on La Jolla (1903) 15' quadrangle. Santiago Arguello received the land in 1846 and claimed 58,875 acres patented in 1876; the Catholic Church claimed 22 acres patented in 1862 (Cowan, p. 75).

Mission Valley [SAN DIEGO]: *valley,* along San Diego River above a point 7.5 miles south-southeast of Point La Jolla (lat. 32°45'45" N, long. 117°11'30" W); San Diego de Alcala mission is in the valley. Named on La Jolla (1967) and La Mesa (1967) 7.5' quadrangles.

Mission Vieja Valley: see **San Juan Canyon**, under **San Juan Creek** [ORANGE].

Mission Viejo [ORANGE]: *city,* 2 miles southeast of El Toro (lat. 33° 36' N, long. 117°40'15" W); the city is north of the northwest end of Mission Viejo or La Paz grant. Named on San Juan Capistrano (1968) 7.5' quadrangle. Postal authorities established Mission Viejo post office in 1966 (Salley, p. 143).

Mission Viejo or La Paz [ORANGE]: *land grant,* east of San Juan Capistrano. Named on Cañada Gobernadora (1968), San Clemente (1968), San Juan Capistrano (1968), and Santiago Peak (1954) 7.5' quadrangles. Called simply Mission Viejo on Cañada Gobernadora (1949), San Clemente (1949), and San Juan Capistrano (1949) 7.5' quadrangles. Agustin Olvera received the land in 1845, and John Forster claimed 46,433 acres patented in 1866 (Cowan, p. 48).

Mitchell Camp [SAN DIEGO]: *locality,* 8 miles north-northwest of Warner Springs (lat. 33°23'45" N, long. 116°41' W; near W line sec. 9, T 9 S, R 3 E). Named on Beauty Mountain (1960) 7.5' quadrangle.

Mixville [LOS ANGELES]: *locality,* 3.25 miles north-northwest of Los Angeles city hall (lat. 34°05'55" N, long. 118°15'30" W). Named on Hollywood (1953) 7.5' quadrangle.

Modelo Canyon [VENTURA]: *canyon,* drained by a stream that flows 2.5 miles to Piru Canyon 1.5 miles east-northeast of Piru (lat. 34°25'30" N, long. 118°46'10" W). Named on Piru (1952) 7.5' quadrangle.

Modelo Peak [VENTURA]: *peak,* 2.5 miles north of Piru (lat. 34° 27' N, long. 118°48' W; near N line sec. 7, T 4 N, R 18 W); the peak is at the head of Modelo Canyon. Altitude 3298 feet. Named on Piru (1952) 7.5' quadrangle.

Modena: see **El Modino** [ORANGE].

Modie Canyon: see **Moody Canyon** [LOS ANGELES].

Modjeska [ORANGE]: *village,* 6.5 miles northeast of El Toro along Santiago Creek (lat. 33°42'30" N, long. 117°37'45" W; sec. 28, 29, T 5 S, R 7 W). Named on El Toro (1968) and Santiago Peak (1954) 7.5' quadrangles.

Modjeska Canyon [ORANGE]: *canyon,* less than 1 mile long, 6.5 miles northeast of El Toro along Santiago Creek (lat. 33°42'30" N, long. 117°37'45" W). Named on El Toro (1968) 7.5' quadrangle. The name commemorates actress Helena Modjeska, who with her husband financed a Polish farming project in the canyon (Gudde, 1949, p. 218).

Modjeska Island: see **Bay Island** [ORANGE].

Modjeska Peak [ORANGE]: *peak,* nearly 1 mile northwest of Santiago Peak (lat. 33°43'10" N, long. 117°32'35" W; sec. 19, T 5 S, R 6 W). Altitude 5496 feet. Named on Santiago Peak (1954) 7.5' quadrangle. J.B. Stephenson, a forest ranger, named the peak in memory of actress Helena Modjeska after her death in 1909 (Gudde, 1949, p. 218). Previously the feature was known locally as North Peak (Stephenson, p. 7). United States Board on Geographic Names (1961c, p. 12) rejected the name "Santiago Northwest Peak" for the feature.

Modjeska Reservoir [ORANGE]: *lake,* 400 feet long, 5 miles west of Santiago Peak (lat. 33°42'55" N, long. 117°37'20" W; near NW cor. sec. 28, T 5 S, R 7 W); the feature is less than 0.5 mile north-northeast of Modjeska. Named on Santiago Peak (1954) 7.5' quadrangle. Promoters laid out a place called Santiago City in Harding Canyon during the mining excitement of 1878, but it never materialized; water of Modjeska Reservoir now covers the site (Meadows, p. 125).

Mohave Desert: see "Regional setting."

Mohn Springs: see **Glenview** [LOS ANGELES].

Mojave Desert: see "Regional setting."

Mollusk Wash [SAN DIEGO]: *dry wash,* extends for 1.5 miles to North Fork Fish Creek Wash 11.5 miles north of Sweeney Pass (lat. 32°59'40" N, long. 116°09'40" W). Named on Arroyo Tapiado (1959) 7.5' quadrangle. The name is from fossil marine mollusks found in the dry wash (Stein, p. 81).

Monaco [LOS ANGELES]: *locality,* nearly 3 miles north-northwest of Torrance city hall along Atchison Topeka and Santa Fe Railroad (lat. 33°52'30" N, long. 118°21'30" W). Named on Inglewood (1964) and Torrance (1964) 7.5' quadrangles.

Moneta [LOS ANGELES]: *locality,* 6.25 miles south-southeast of Inglewood city hall along Pacific Electric Railroad (lat. 33°52'45" N, long. 118°18'35" W). Named on Inglewood (1952) 7.5' quadrangle. Postal authorities established Moneta post office in 1890 and discontinued it in 1947 (Salley, p. 144).

Monkey Cañon: see **Los Monos Canyon** [SAN DIEGO].

Monkey Hill [SAN DIEGO]:

(1) *hill,* 2.5 miles north-northwest of Morettis Junction (lat. 33° 14' N, long. 116°43'45" W). Named on Warners Ranch (1960) 7.5' quadrangle. The feature forms an island in Lake Henshaw when the lake is full.

(2) *hill,* 11.5 miles north-northwest of Borrego Springs (lat. 33°24'15" N, long. 116°27'55" W; sec. 9, T 9 S, R 5 E). Named on Collins Valley (1959) 7.5' quadrangle.

Monroe Canyon [LOS ANGELES]: *canyon,* drained by a stream that flows 2.25 miles to Big Dalton Reservoir 4 miles northeast of Glendora city hall (lat. 34°10'25" N, long. 117°48'30" W; sec. 15, T 1 N, R 9 W). Named on Glendora (1966) 7.5' quadrangle.

Monrovia [LOS ANGELES]: *city,* 5.5 miles west of Azusa city hall (lat. 34°08'50" N, long. 117°55'50" W). Named on Azusa (1953), El Monte (1966), and Mount Wilson (1953) 7.5' quadrangles. Postal authorities established Monrovia post office in 1886 (Frickstad, p. 77), and the city incorporated in 1887. The name recalls William N. Monroe, one of the founders of the community in 1886 (Gudde, 1949, p. 221).

Monrovia Canyon [LOS ANGELES]: *canyon,* drained by a stream that flows 2.5 miles to Sawpit canyon 5.5 miles west-northwest of Azusa city hall (lat. 34°10'25" N, long. 117°59'20" W; sec. 13, T 1 N, R 11 W). Named on Azusa (1953) 7.5' quadrangle.

Monrovia Hill: see **Monrovia Peak** [LOS ANGELES].

Monrovia Peak [LOS ANGELES]: *peak,* 6.5 miles northwest of Azusa city hall (lat. 34°12'45" N, long. 117°58'05" W); the peak is 4.5 miles north-northeast of downtown Monrovia. Altitude 5412 feet. Named on Azusa (1953) 7.5' quadrangle. Called Monrovia Hill on Pomona (1904) 15' quadrangle.

Monserate [SAN DIEGO]: *land grant,* southeast of Fallbrook. Named on Bonsall (1968) 7.5' quadrangle. Isidro M. Alvarado received 3 leagues in 1846 and claimed 13,323 acres patented in 1872 (Cowan, p. 49; Cowan gave the alternate form "Monserrate" for the name). Postal authorities established Montserrat post office in 1874, discontinued it in 1876, reestablished it with the name "Monserrate" in 1889. and discontinued it in 1891; the name was from the grant (Salley, p. 144).

Monserate Mountain [SAN DIEGO]: *ridge,* generally south-trending, 4 miles long, 6.25 miles east of Fallbrook (lat. 33°22' N, long. 117°08'35" W); the feature is at the northeast corner of Monserate grant. Named on Bonsal (1968) and Temecula (1968) 7.5' quadrangles.

Monserrate: see **Monserate** [SAN DIEGO].

Montalvo [VENTURA]: *town,* 4 miles southwest of Saticoy (lat. 34° 15' N, long. 119°12'15" W). Named on Oxnard (1949) and Saticoy (1951) 7.5' quadrangles. Postal authorities established Montalvo post office in 1888 (Frickstad, p. 218). The name commemorates the early Spanish writer who first used the name "California" (Hoover, Rensch, and Rensch, p. 582).

Monte: see **El Monte** [LOS ANGELES].

Montebello [LOS ANGELES]: *city,* 6 miles southwest of El Monte city hall (lat. 34°00'40" N, long. 118°06'15" W). Named on El Monte (1953), Los Angeles (1953), South Gate (1952), and Whittier (1949) 7.5' quadrangles. Postal authorities established Montebello post office in 1902, discontinued it in 1907, and reestablished it in 1913 (Frickstad, p. 77). The city incorporated in 1920. California Mining Bureau's (1917a) map shows a place called Newmark located 2.5 miles east of Montebello along a railroad. Harris Newmark bought land at the place in 1887, and in 1889 he and Kaspare Cohn applied the name "Montebello" to their development there, which included a town called Newmark—residents dropped the name "Newmark" in 1920 (Gudde, 1949, p. 222; Hanna, p. 199).

Montebello Gardens [LOS ANGELES]: *district,* 3.5 miles southwest of El Monte city hall in present Pico Rivera (lat. 34°00'30" N, long. 118°05'30" W); the place is east of Montebello. Named on El Monte (1953) 7.5' quadrangle.

Montebello Hills [LOS ANGELES]: *range,* 4.25 miles southwest of El Monte city hall (lat. 34°01'55" N, long. 118°05'15" W); the range is northeast of downtown Montebello. Named on El Monte (1966) 7.5' quadrangle.

Monte Cristo Creek [LOS ANGELES]: *stream,* flows nearly 3 miles to Mill Creek 5 miles west-southwest of Pacifico Mountain (lat. 34°20'40" N, long. 118°06'30" W). Named on Chilao Flat (1959) 7.5' quadrangle, which shows Monte Cristo mine along the stream.

Monte Nido [LOS ANGELES]: *village,* 3.5 miles north of Malibu Point (lat. 34°04'50" N, long. 118°41'10" W; sec. 17, T 1 S, R 17 W). Named on Malibu Beach (1951) 7.5' quadrangle.

Monterey Acres [LOS ANGELES]: *district,* 8.5 miles northeast of Long Beach city hall (lat. 33°50'25" N, long. 118°04'40" W). Named on Los Alamitos (1950) 7.5' quadrangle.

Monterey Park [LOS ANGELES]: *city,* 6.5 miles east of Los Angeles city hall (lat. 34°03'35" N, long. 118°07'30" W). Named on El Monte (1953) and Los Angeles (1953) 7.5' quadrangles. Postal authorities established Monterey Park post office in 1922 (Salley, p. 145). The city incorporated in 1916. A subdivision developed at the site in 1906 was called Ramona Acres; when Monterey Park incorporated it took its name from nearby Monterey Pass (present Coyote Pass) (Gudde, 1949, p. 223).

Monterey Pass: see **Coyote Pass** [LOS ANGELES].

Monteria Lake [LOS ANGELES]: *lake,* 900 feet long, 2 miles east-northeast of Chatsworth (lat. 34°16'05" N, long. 118°34'10" W; on E line sec. 8, T 2 N, R 16 W). Named on Oat Mountain (1952) 7.5' quadrangle.

Monte Vista: see **Sun Valley** [LOS ANGELES] (2).

Montezuma Valley [SAN DIEGO]: *valley,* 4.5 miles east of San Felipe (lat. 33°12'40" N, long. 116°31'15" W). Named on Ranchita (1960) 7.5' quadrangle.

Montgomery Canyon [VENTURA]: *canyon,* drained by a stream that flows 1 mile to Oak Canyon (2) 5.5 miles north-northeast of Thousand Oaks (lat. 34°14'05" N, long. 118°47' W; at N line sec. 29, T 2 N, R 18 W). Named on Thousand Oaks (1952) 7.5' quadrangle.

Montrose [LOS ANGELES]: *town,* 6.5 miles northwest of Pasadena city hall (lat. 34°12'35" N, long. 118°13'40" W). Named on Pasadena (1953) 7.5' quadrangle. Postal authorities established Montrose post office in 1923 (Frickstad, p. 77). The name of the town was chosen by means of a contest in 1913 (Gudde, 1949, p. 223).

Montserrat: see **Monserate** [SAN DIEGO].

Monument Peak [SAN DIEGO]: *peak,* 8 miles southwest of Agua Caliente Springs (lat. 32°53'35" N, long. 116°25'10" W; sec. 1, T 15 S, R 5 E). Altitude 6271 feet. Named on Monument Peak (1959) 7.5' quadrangle. The name is from a pile of boulders five feet high that was used by surveyors (Stein, p. 82).

Moody [ORANGE]: *settlement,* 3.5 miles southwest of Buena Park civic center (lat. 33°50'10" N, long. 118°02'50" W; mainly in sec. 8, T 4 S, R 11 W). Named on Los Alamitos (1950) 7.5' quadrangle.

Moody Canyon [LOS ANGELES]: *canyon,* drained by a stream that flows nearly 4 miles to Arrastre Canyon 2.5 miles south of Acton (lat. 34°25'50" N, long. 118°11'20" W; sec. 13, T 4 N, R 13 W). Named on Acton (1959) 7.5' quadrangle. Called Modie Canyon on Acton (1939) 6' quadrangle.

Moody Canyon [SAN DIEGO]: *canyon,* drained by a stream that flows 1.5 miles to lowlands 4.5 miles east-southeast of Imperial Beach civic center at San Ysidro (lat. 32°33'15" N, long. 117°02'30" W). Named on Imperial Beach (1967) 7.5' quadrangle.

Moody Creek [LOS ANGELES-ORANGE]: *stream,* heads in Orange County and flows 2 miles to Coyote Creek [LOS ANGELES-ORANGE] 4 miles west-southwest of Buena Park civic center just inside Los Angeles County (lat. 33°50'05" N, long. 118°03'35" W; near SW cor. sec. 8, T 4 S, R 11 W). Named on Los Alamitos (1964) 7.5' quadrangle.

Moody Springs [LOS ANGELES]: *springs,* 4 miles north-northeast of Black Butte along Eller Slough (lat. 34°36'45" N, long. 117°42'30" W; sec. 15, T 6 N, R 8 W). Named on El Mirage (1956) 7.5' quadrangle. Shadow Mountains (1942) 15' quadrangle has the singular form "Moody Spr." for the name

Mooney: see **Mount Mooney** [LOS ANGELES].

Moonlight Canyon [SAN DIEGO]: *canyon,* drained by a stream that flows 1.5 miles to Carrizo Valley less than 0.5 mile east-southeast of Agua Caliente Springs (lat. 32°56'50" N, long. 116°17'45" W; near SE cor. sec. 18, T 14 S, R 7 E). Named on Agua Caliente Springs (1959) 7.5' quadrangle.

Moonstone Beach [LOS ANGELES]: *beach,* 4 miles northwest of Avalon on the northeast side of Santa Catalina Island (lat. 33°23'20" N, long. 118°22' W). Named on Santa Catalina East (1950) 7.5' quadrangle. United States Board on Geographic Names (1975a, p. 10) approved the name "Moonstone Cove" for the embayment at the place.

Moonstone Cove: see **Moonstone Beach** [LOS ANGELES].

Moore: see **Fort Moore,** under **Los Angeles** [LOS ANGELES].

Moore Canyon: see **Big Moore Canyon**, under **Wickham Canyon** [LOS ANGELES].

Moorpark [VENTURA]: *town,* 8 miles south-southeast of Fillmore in Little Simi Valley (lat. 34°17'10" N, long. 118°52'45" W; near W line sec. 4, T 2 N, R 19 W). Named on Moorpark (1951) and Simi (1951) 7.5' quadrangles. Postal authorities established Moorpark post office in 1900 (Frickstad, p. 218). The name is from a variety of apricot (Gudde, 1949, p. 224).

Moorpark Home Acres [VENTURA]: *settlement,* 2.25 miles southwest of Moorpark (lat. 34°16' N, long. 118°54'50" W; near SW cor. sec. 7, T 2 N, R 19 W). Named on Moorpark (1951) 7.5' quadrangle.

Moor's: see **San Francisquito Canyon** [LOS ANGELES].

Moosa [SAN DIEGO]: *locality,* 9.5 miles north-northwest of Escondido (lat. 33°14'50" N, long. 117°08'30" W; on W line sec. 6, T 11 S, R 2 W). Named on Escondido (1901) 15' quadrangle. Postal authorities established Moosa post office in 1881 and discontinued it in 1912 (Frickstad, p. 153). The place first was called Pomoosa, but when the post office was established the name was changed to avoid confusion with the name "Pomona" (Hanna, p. 200).

Moosa Canyon [SAN DIEGO]: *canyon,* 14 miles long, opens into the canyon of San Luis Rey River 7.25 miles south of Fallbrook (lat. 33°16'35" N, long. 117°13'30" W; near W line sec. 29, T 10 S, R 3 W); Moosa was in the canyon. Named on Bonsall (1968), Pala (1968), and Valley Center (1968) 7.5' quadrangles. South Fork branches south 6.5 miles northeast of Vista; it is 4.5 miles long and is named on San Marcos (1968) 7.5' quadrangle.

Morena [SAN DIEGO]: *locality,* 6 miles southeast of Point La Jolla (lat. 32°46'55" N, long. 117°12'25" W). Named on La Jolla (1967) 7.5' quadrangle. Called Morena Siding on La Jolla (1953) 7.5' quadrangle. On La Jolla (1903) 15' quadrangle, the name applies to an inhabited place at the site. Ellis and Lee's (1919) map shows a locality called Atwood situated along the railroad about 1.5 miles north-northwest of Morena.

Morena Butte [SAN DIEGO]: *ridge,* north-northwest-trending, 1 mile long, 2.25 miles west of Morena Village (lat. 32°40'35" N, long. 116°32'35" W; mainly in sec. 23, T 17 S, R 4 E). Named on Morena Reservoir (1960) 7.5' quadrangle.

Morena Creek [SAN DIEGO]: *stream,* flows 3.5 miles to Morena Reservoir 3 miles north-northwest of Morena Village (lat. 32°43'05" N, long. 116°31'45" W; near S line sec. 1, T 17 S, R 4 E). Named on Morena Reservoir (1960) 7.5' quadrangle.

Morena Lake: see **Morena Reservoir** [SAN DIEGO].

Morena Reservoir [SAN DIEGO]: *lake,* behind a dam on Cottonwood Creek (3) 2.5 miles west of Morena Village (lat. 32°41'10" N, long. 116°32'45" W; near N line sec. 23, T 17 S, R 4 E). Named on Morena Reservoir (1960) 7.5' quadrangle. Called Morena Lake on Potrero (1944) 15' quadrangle, but United States Board on Geographic Names (1962a, p. 13) rejected this name for the feature.

Morena Siding: see **Morena** [SAN DIEGO].

Morena Valley [SAN DIEGO]: *valley,* at and northwest of Morena Village (lat. 32°42'15" N, long. 116°31' W); the valley is along Morena Creek and Cottonwood Creek (3) at their confluence. Named on Morena Reservoir (1960) 7.5' quadrangle. The name is from Felipe Morena, a secondary character in Helen Hunt Jackson's novel *Ramona* (Stein, p. 83).

Morena Village [SAN DIEGO]: *locality,* 38 miles east of San Diego (lat. 32°40'50" N, long. 116°30'10" W); the place is southeast of Morena Reservoir at the south end of Morena Valley. Named on Cameron Corners (1959) and Morena Reservoir (1960) 7.5' quadrangles.

Moreno [SAN DIEGO]: *locality,* 1 mile north of Lakeview (lat. 32° 52'30" N, long. 116°55'25" W); the place is at the south end of Moreno Valley. Named on El Cajon (1967) and San Vicente Reservoir (1955) 7.5' quadrangles.

Moreno Valley [SAN DIEGO]: *valley,* 2 miles north of Lakeside along San Vicente Creek (lat. 32°53'15" N, long. 116°55'15" W). Named on San Vicente Reservoir (1955) 7.5' quadrangle.

Morettis: see **Morettis Junction** [SAN DIEGO].

Morettis Junction [SAN DIEGO]: *locality,* 10.5 miles northwest of Julian (lat. 33°12' N, long. 116°42'35" W). Named on Warners Ranch (1960) 7.5' quadrangle. Called Morettis on Santa Ysabel (1943) 15' quadrangle, but United States Board on Geographic Names (1962b, p. 19) rejected this designation for the place. The name recalls a Swiss-Italian resident of the neighborhood about 1900 (Hanna, p. 201).

Morgan [LOS ANGELES]: *locality,* 3 miles north-northeast of present Los Angeles city hall along Los Angeles Terminal Railroad (lat. 34°05'15" N, long. 118°12'45" W). Named on Pasadena (1900) 15' quadrangle

Morgan Canyon [LOS ANGELES]: *canyon,* 1.25 miles long, 3 miles east-northeast of Glendora city hall (lat. 34°08'40" N, long. 117°48'55" W; mainly in sec. 27, T 1 N, R 9 W). Named on Glendora (1953) 7.5' quadrangle. Called Guard Canyon on Los Angeles County (1935) map.

Morgan Canyon [VENTURA]: *canyon,* drained by a stream that flows 1.25 miles to the valley of Santa Clara River 1.25 miles east-southeast of downtown Santa Paula (lat. 34°20'55" N, long. 119° 02'10" W; at N line sec. 13, T 3 N, R 21 W). Named on Santa Paula (1951) 7.5' quadrangle.

Morgan Hill [SAN DIEGO]: *peak*, 2.5 miles north of Boucher Hill (lat. 33°27'10" N, long. 116°55'15" W; near N line sec. 30, T 9 S, R 1 E). Altitude 5596 feet. Named on Boucher Hill (1948) 7.5' quadrangle.

Morgan Hill: see **Gordon Point** [SAN DIEGO].

Mormon Canyon [LOS ANGELES]: *canyon*, drained by a stream that flows 2.25 miles to Browns Canyon 2.5 miles north-northeast of Chatsworth (lat. 34°17'45" N, long. 118°35'30" W; sec. 31, T 3 N, R 16 W). Named on Oat Mountain (1952) 7.5' quadrangle. Called Marmon Canyon on Los Angeles County (1935) map.

Mormon Island [LOS ANGELES]: *area*, nearly 6 miles southeast of Torrance city hall at Los Angeles Harbor (lat. 33°45'35" N, long. 118°15'45" W). Named on Torrance (1964) 7.5' quadrangle. On Redondo (1896) 15' quadrangle, the feature is shown as marsh in Wilmington Lagoon. Some soldiers from the Mormon Battalion settled at the place after they were mustered out in 1848 (Gleason, p. 116).

Morningside Park [LOS ANGELES]: *district*, 1.5 miles east-southeast of Inglewood city hall (lat. 33°57'25" N, long. 118°19'30" W). Named on Inglewood (1964) 7.5' quadrangle.

Moro Canyon [ORANGE]: *canyon*, drained by a stream that flows 3.25 miles to the sea 2.5 miles west-northwest of Laguna Beach city hall (lat. 33°33'40" N, long. 117°49'15" W). Named on Laguna Beach (1965) 7.5' quadrangle. The name is a misspelling of *morro*, which means "round" in Spanish—the name refers to the dome-shaped feature now called Abalone Point (Meadows, p. 102).

Morocco: see **Beverly Hills** [LOS ANGELES].

Morris Reservoir [LOS ANGELES]: *lake*, behind a dam on San Gabriel River 3 miles north-northeast of Azusa city hall (lat. 34°10'25" N, long. 117°52'45" W; sec. 13, T 1 N, R 10 W). Named on Azusa (1953) and Glendora (1953) 7.5' quadrangles.

Morro Bay: see **Abalone Point** [ORANGE].

Morro Hill [SAN DIEGO]: *peak*, 5.5 miles south of Fallbrook (lat. 33°18' N, long. 117°16'10" W; on S line sec. 14, T 10 S, R 4 W). Named on Morro Hill (1968) 7.5' quadrangle. Called El Moro on Hanks' (1886a) map.

Morro Hill [VENTURA]: *peak*, 11 miles northwest of Reyes Peak (lat. 34°44'20" N, long. 119°25'40" W). Altitude 4584 feet. Named on Rancho Nuevo Creek (1943) 7.5' quadrangle.

Mortero Canyon [SAN DIEGO]: *canyon*, 1.5 miles long, 5.5 miles southeast of Sweeney Pass (lat. 32°46'15" N, long. 116°07'25" W). Named on Sweeney Pass (1959) 7.5' quadrangle.

Mortero Palms [SAN DIEGO]: *locality*, 7.5 miles north-northeast of Jacumba along Palm Canyon Wash (lat. 32°43'15" N, long. 116° 08'50" W; sec. 3, T 17 S, R 8 E). Named on Jacumba (1959) 7.5' quadrangle.

Mortimer Park: see **Santa Susana Knolls** [VENTURA].

Morton [LOS ANGELES]: *locality*, 3.25 miles south-southeast of South Gate city hall along Pacific Electric Railroad (lat. 33°54'50" N, long. 118°10'50" W). Named on South Gate (1952) 7.5' quadrangle.

Mosquito Cove [LOS ANGELES]: *embayment*, 4 miles northwest of Pyramid Head on the northeast side of San Clemente Island (lat. 32°51'35" N, long. 118°23'55" W). Named on San Clemente Island South (1943) 7.5' quadrangle. Doran (1980, p. 52) called the place Mosquito Harbor, and attributed the name to mosquitos that breed in rock basins at the place.

Mosquito Harbor: see **Mosquito Cove** [LOS ANGELES].

Moss Spring: see **Cruthers Creek** [LOS ANGELES].

Mother Grundy Peak [SAN DIEGO]: *peak*, 3.25 miles northwest of Barrett Junction (lat. 32°39' N, long. 116°44'25" W; sec. 35, T 17 S, R 2 E). Altitude 3076 feet. Named on Barrett Lake (1960) 7.5' quadrangle. According to Stein (p. 84), the name is derived from the original name "Madre Grande."

Mother Miguel Mountain [SAN DIEGO]: *peak*, 5.5 miles west-southwest of Jamul (lat. 32°41'05" N, long. 116°57'45" W; at NE cor. sec. 22, T 17 S, R 1 W). Named on Jamul Mountains (1955) 7.5' quadrangle.

Motordrome [LOS ANGELES]: *locality*, nearly 6 miles north-northwest of present Manhattan Beach city hall along Pacific Electric Railroad (lat. 33°55'10" N, long. 118°26'15" W). Named on Venice (1924) 6' quadrangle.

Mountain Meadows [SAN DIEGO]: *area*, 4.5 miles south-southwest of Julian (lat. 33°00'50" N, long. 116°37'15" W; at E line sec. 25, T 13 S, R 3 E). Named on Julian (1960) 7.5' quadrangle.

Mountain Palm Springs [SAN DIEGO]: *springs*, 3.5 miles northwest of present Sweeney Pass (lat. 32°51'55" N, long. 116°13'25" W). Named on Carrizo Mountain (1944) 15' quadrangle.

Mountain Spring [SAN DIEGO]: *spring*, 6 miles northeast of Jacumba (lat. 32°40'25" N, long. 116°06'25" W; near E line sec. 24, T 17 S, R 8 E). Named on In-Ko-Pah Gorge (1959) 7.5' quadrangle, which shows a locality called Mountain Spring situated a short distance to the east in Imperial County. Brown's (1920) map shows a feature called Smuggler Spring located about 1.5 miles south of Mountain Springs (present Mountain Spring).

Mountain View: see **Villa Park** [ORANGE].

Mount Ararat [SAN DIEGO]: *peak*, 8 miles southeast of Fallbrook (lat. 33°17'10" N, long. 117°10'25" W; at SW cor. sec. 23, T 10 S, R 3 W). Altitude 891 feet. Named on Bonsall (1968) 7.5' quadrangle.

Mount Baden-Powell [LOS ANGELES]: *peak*, 5.5 miles northeast of Crystal Lake (lat. 34°21'30" N, long. 117°45'50" W). Altitude 9399 feet. Named on Crystal Lake (1958) 7.5' quadrangle. Called North Baldy on Rock Creek (1903) 15' quadrangle, but United States Board on Geographic Names (1933, p. 112) rejected this designation for the feature; the present name honors the founder of the Boy Scout movement.

Mount Baldy [LOS ANGELES]: *village*, 14 miles north-northeast of Pomona city hall in San Antonio Canyon on Los Angeles-San Bernardino County line (lat. 34°14'10" N, long. 117°39'25" W; sec. 19, 30, T 2 N, R 7 W). Named on Mount Baldy (1954) 7.5' quadrangle. Postal authorities established Camp Baldy post office in San Bernardino County in 1913, changed the name to Mt. Baldy in 1951, changed it to Mount Baldy in 1966, and changed it back to Mt. Baldy in 1975; the name is from Mount San Antonio, also known as Old Baldy from the lack of vegetation at the top (Salley, p. 33, 148).

Mount Banning [LOS ANGELES]: *peak*, 6.5 miles west-northwest of Avalon on Santa Catalina Island (lat. 33°22'20" N, long. 118°26'05" W). Altitude 1734 feet. Named on Santa Catalina South (1943) 7.5' quadrangle.

Mount Banning: see **Black Jack Mountain** [LOS ANGELES].

Mount Bliss [LOS ANGELES]: *peak*, 4.25 miles northwest of Azusa city hall (lat. 34°11'05" N, long. 117°57' W; sec. 8, T 1 N, R 10 W). Altitude 3725 feet. Named on Azusa (1953) 7.5' quadrangle.

Mount Burnham [LOS ANGELES]: *peak*, 4.5 miles northeast of Crystal Lake (lat. 34°21'35" N, long. 117°46'50" W; near W line sec. 12, T 3 N, R 9 W). Altitude 8997 feet. Named on Crystal Lake (1958) 7.5' quadrangle. The name honors Major Frederick Russell Burnham, explorer and scout leader (United States Board on Geographic Names, 1954, p. 2).

Mount Clef [VENTURA]: *peak*, 3.5 miles north-northeast of Newbury Park (lat. 34°14' N, long. 118°53'10" W). Altitude 994 feet. Named on Newbury Park (1950, photorevised 1967) 7.5' quadrangle.

Mountclef Ridge [VENTURA]: *ridge*, west-southwest-trending, 3 miles long, 3 miles north-northeast of Newbury Park (lat. 34°13'35" N, long. 118°53'50" W); Mount Clef is on the ridge. Named on Newbury Park (1950, photorevised 1967) and Thousand Oaks (1950, photorevised 1981) 7.5' quadrangles.

Mountclef Village [VENTURA]: *locality*, 3.25 miles northeast of Newbury Park (lat. 34°13'20" N, long. 118°52'35" W); the place is 1 mile south-southeast of Mount Clef. Named on Newbury Park (1950, photorevised 1967) 7.5' quadrangle.

Mount Disappointment [LOS ANGELES]: *peak*, 3 miles west-northwest of Mount Wilson (1) (lat. 34°14'45" N, long. 118°06'15" W). Altitude 5994 feet. Named on Mount Wilson (1953) 7.5' quadrangle. Three members of the Wheeler Survey climbed the peak in 1875 to use it as a triangulation point, but were disappointed to find that it was lower than nearby San Gabriel Peak (Robinson, J.W., 1977, p. 154).

Mount Downey: see **Santiago Peak** [ORANGE].

Mount Emma [LOS ANGELES]: *peak*, 6 miles north-northwest of Pacifico Mountain (lat. 34°27'35" N, long. 118°04'05" W). Altitude 5273 feet. Named on Pacifico Mountain (1959) 7.5' quadrangle.

Mount Emma Ridge [LOS ANGELES]: *ridge*, generally northeast-trending, 2.25 miles long, 6 miles north-northwest of Pacifico Mountain (lat. 34°27'55" N, long. 118°03'45" W); Mount Emma is on the ridge. Named on Pacifico Mountain (1959) 7.5' quadrangle.

Mount Fairview: see **Bonsall** [SAN DIEGO].

Mount Gleason [LOS ANGELES]: *peak*, 6.5 miles south of Acton (lat. 34°22'35" N, long. 118°10'35" W). Named on Acton (1959) 7.5' quadrangle. Called Gleason Mt. on Tujunga (1900) 15' quadrangle. The name commemorates George Gleason, who with his companions discovered gold ore on the slopes of the feature in 1869 (Robinson, J.W., 1973, p. 26).

Mount Gleason Campground [LOS ANGELES]: *locality*, nearly 4 miles north-northeast of Condor Peak (lat. 34°22'20" N, long. 118° 10'55" W); the place is 0.5 mile west-southwest of Mount Gleason. Named on Condor Peak (1959) 7.5' quadrangle.

Mount Gower [SAN DIEGO]: *peak*, 6.25 miles east-southeast of Ramona (lat. 33°01' N, long. 116°45'45" W; sec. 27, T 13 S, R 2 E). Altitude 3103 feet. Named on Ramona (1955) 7.5' quadrangle. The name recalls an early surveyor who worked in the vicinity (Stein, p. 85).

Mount Harvard [LOS ANGELES]: *peak*, less than 1 mile south of Mount Wilson (1) (lat. 34°12'45" N, long. 118°03'40" W; sec. 32, T 2 N, R 11 W). Altitude 5440 feet. Named on Mount Wilson (1953) 7.5' quadrangle. The feature had the names "The Hogback," "South Gable Promontory," and "Martin's Peak" before Charles W. Eliot, president of Harvard University, visited the place in 1892; the peak was renamed Mount Harvard in the hope that Harvard University would build an observatory there—the university did put up a small observatory building in 1889 at what became known as Harvard Observatory Point (Robinson, J.W., 1977, p. 24, 34, 155). Peter Steil started a tent camp in the saddle between Mount Harvard and Mount Wilson and called the place The Eyrie, but soon it became known as Steil's Camp (Robinson, J.W., 1977, p. 25).

Mount Hawkins [LOS ANGELES]: *peak,* nearly 3 miles northeast of Crystal Lake (lat. 34°20'30" N, long. 117°48'15" W). Altitude 8850 feet. Named on Crystal Lake (1958) 7.5' quadrangle. The name commemorates Nellie Hawkins, who was a popular waitress at a resort along North Fork San Gabriel River from 1901 until about 1906 (Robinson, J.W., 1983, p. 92).

Mount Hawkins: see **South Mount Hawkins** [LOS ANGELES].

Mount Helix [SAN DIEGO]: *peak,* 2 miles south-southwest of El Cajon city hall (lat. 32°46' N, long. 116°58'55" W). Altitude 1373 feet. Named on El Cajon (1967) 7.5' quadrangle. Captain Rufus K. Porter named the feature in the early 1870's for the configuration of the trail that winds around to the top of the peak (Gudde, 1949, p. 145)..

Mount Helix Reservoir [SAN DIEGO]: *lake,* 1000 feet long, 2 miles southwest of El Cajon city hall (lat. 32°46'20" N, long. 116° 59' W); the lake is less than 0.5 mile north of Mount Helix. Named on El Cajon (1967) 7.5' quadrangle.

Mount Hillyer [LOS ANGELES]: *peak,* 2.5 miles south-southeast of Pacifico Mountain (lat. 34°21' N, long. 118°00'50" W; sec. 15, T 3 N, R 11 W). Altitude 6162 feet. Named on Chilao Flat (1959) 7.5' quadrangle. Forest Service officials named the peak for Margaret Hillyer, a Forest Service employee (Gudde, 1949, p. 149).

Mount Hinton [SAN DIEGO]: *peak,* nearly 8 miles east-southeast of Oceanside (lat. 33°09' N, long. 117°15'20" W). Altitude 587 feet. Named on San Luis Rey (1968) 7.5' quadrangle.

Mount Hoar: see **Rincon Mountain** [VENTURA].

Mount Hollywood [LOS ANGELES]: *peak,* nearly 4 miles south of Burbank city hall (lat. 34°07'40" N, long. 118°18' W); the feature is north of Hollywood. Altitude 1652 feet. Named on Burbank (1953) 7.5' quadrangle.

Mount Islip [LOS ANGELES]: *peak,* nearly 2 miles north of Crystal Lake (lat. 34°20'40" N, long. 117°50'20" W). Altitude 8250 feet. Named on Crystal Lake (1958) 7.5' quadrangle. The name commemorates George Islip, who homesteaded in San Gabriel Canyon in the 1880's (Robinson, J.W., 1983, p. 111).

Mount Kelly [SAN DIEGO]: *peak,* 4 miles southeast of downtown Oceanside (lat. 33°09'50" N, long. 117°19'20" W). Named on San Luis Rey (1968) 7.5' quadrangle.

Mount Kinneyloa: see **Mount Wilson** [LOS ANGELES] (1).

Mount Laguna [SAN DIEGO]: *settlement,* 8 miles north-northeast of Buckman Springs (lat. 32°52'15" N, long. 116°25' W). Named on Monument Peak (1959) and Mount Laguna (1960) 7.5' quadrangles. Postal authorities established Resort post office in 1920 and moved it in 1930 when they changed the name to Mount Laguna; the settlement is a vacation and recreation community (Salley, p. 148, 184).

Mount Lawlor [LOS ANGELES]: *peak,* 8.5 miles south-southwest of Pacifico Mountain (lat. 34°16'15" N, long. 118°06'10" W). Altitude 5957 feet. Named on Chilao Flat (1959) 7.5' quadrangle. Called Mt. Lowler on Los Angeles County (1935) map. Forest Service officials named the peak about 1890 for Oscar Lawlor, a Los Angeles attorney.(Gudde, 1969, p. 174).

Mount Lee [LOS ANGELES]: *peak,* 3.25 miles south of Burbank city hall (lat. 34°08'05" N, long. 118°19'10" W). Named on Burbank (1966) 7.5' quadrangle. The peak is unnamed on Burbank (1953) 7.5' quadrangle, which shows Don Lee television tower on it.

Mount Lewis [LOS ANGELES]: *peak,* 4.25 miles north-northeast of Crystal Lake (lat. 34°22'20" N, long. 117°48'15" W; sec. 3, T 3 N, R 9 W). Named on Crystal Lake (1958) 7.5' quadrangle.

Mount Lowe [LOS ANGELES]:

(1) *peak,* 2.5 miles west of Mount Wilson (1) (lat. 34°13'55" N, long. 118°06'20" W; sec. 26, T 2 N, R 12 W). Altitude 5593 feet. Named on Mount Wilson (1953) 7.5' quadrangle. Owen Brown and Jason Brown, sons of abolitionist John Brown, named the feature John Brown Peak in 1887, but later they transferred the name to another peak; present Mount Lowe then was known as Oak Mountain until it was renamed to honor Professor Thaddeus Sobieski Coulincourt Lowe, who built the incline and electric railroad to Echo Mountain (Hanna, p. 177).

(2) *locality,* 2.5 miles west of Mount Wilson (1) (lat. 34°13'35" N, long. 118°06'30" W; sec. 26, T 2 N, R 12 W); the place is nearly 0.5 mile south-southwest of Mount Lowe (1). Site named on Mount Wilson (1953) 7.5' quadrangle, which shows it at the end of an abandoned Pacific Electric Railroad line. Mount Lowe (1939) 6' quadrangle shows Mt. Lowe Tavern at the site, and Mount Wilson (1966) 7.5' quadrangle shows Mt. Lowe Campground there. Postal authorities established Mount Lowe post office in 1910 and discontinued it in 1937 (Salley, p. 148).

Mount Lowe Campground: see **Mount Lowe** [LOS ANGELES] (2).

Mount Lowe Hotel: see **Echo Mountain** [LOS ANGELES].

Mount Lowe Tavern: see **Mount Lowe** [LOS ANGELES] (2).

Mount Lowler: see **Mount Lawlor** [LOS ANGELES].

Mount Lukens [LOS ANGELES]: *peak,* 4 miles south-southwest of Condor Peak (lat. 34°16'05" N, long. 118°14'15" W; near SE cor. sec. 9, T 2 N, R 13 W). Altitude 5074 feet. Named on Condor Peak (1959) 7.5' quadrangle. Called Sister Elsie Pk. on Tujunga (1900) 15' quadrangle. Members of the Wheeler Survey called the feature Sister Elsie Peak in 1875 to honor the good deeds of a Roman Catholic nun; the name "Mount Lukens" was given in the 1920's to commemorate Theodore P. Lukens, a Pasadena civic and business leader who was appointed acting supervisor of San Gabriel Forest Reserve in 1906 (Robinson, J.W., 1977, p. 69, 154).

Mount Markham [LOS ANGELES]: *peak,* 2.25 miles west-northwest of Mount Wilson (1) (lat. 34°14'10" N, long. 118°05'55" W; near NE cor. sec. 26, T 2 N, R 12 W). Altitude 5752 feet. Named on Mount Wilson (1953) 7.5' quadrangle. The feature first was called Square Top or Table Mountain for its appearance from Mount Wilson; Forest Service officials renamed it in the 1890's to honor Henry H. Markham, a prominent citizen of Pasadena and governor of California from 1891 until 1895 (Robinson, J.W., 1977, p. 155).

Mount Marron [SAN DIEGO]: *peak,* 8 miles east-southeast of Oceanside (lat. 33°08'45" N, long. 117°15'10" W). Named on San Luis Rey (1968) and San Marcos (1968) 7.5' quadrangles.

Mount McDill [LOS ANGELES]: *peak,* 3.5 miles south-southeast of the village of Leona Valley (lat. 34°34' N, long. 118°16'30" W; sec. 32, T 6 N, R 13 W). Altitude 5187 feet. Named on Sleepy Valley (1958) 7.5' quadrangle.

Mount McGill: see **Mount Pinos** [VENTURA].

Mount McKinley [LOS ANGELES]: *peak,* 6 miles north-northeast of Sunland (lat. 34°20'20" N, long. 118°15'50" W). Altitude 4926 feet. Named on Sunland (1966) 7.5' quadrangle.

Mount Mesa [LOS ANGELES]: *peak,* 10.5 miles east of Redman (lat. 34°46'25" N, long. 117°47'05" W; sec. 24, T 8 N, R 9 W). Altitude 3175 feet. Named on Rogers Lake South (1973) 7.5' quadrangle.

Mount Mooney [LOS ANGELES]: *peak,* 5.5 miles south-southeast of Pacifico Mountain (lat. 34°18'20" N, long. 118°00'25" W; sec. 35, T 3 N, R 11 W). Named on Chilao Flat (1959) 7.5' quadrangle. The name commemorates John L. Mooney, a Forest Service employee who died in France during World War I (United States Board on Geographic Names, 1933, p. 529).

Mount Oak Campground [LOS ANGELES]: *locality,* 2.25 miles west-northwest of Big Pines (lat. 34°23'40" N, long. 117°43'45" W). Named on Mescal Creek (1956) 7.5' quadrangle.

Mount Olympus [SAN DIEGO]: *peak,* 3.5 miles north-northwest of Pala (lat. 33°24'40" N, long. 117°06'05" W; near W line sec. 9, T 9 S, R 2 W). Altitude 2224 feet. Named on Pechanga (1968) 7.5' quadrangle.

Mount Orizaba [LOS ANGELES]: *peak,* 1 mile east-northeast of Mount Banning on Santa Catalina Island (lat. 33°22'30" N, long. 118°25'05" W). Altitude 2125 feet. Named on Santa Catalina North (1950) 7.5' quadrangle.

Mount Parkinson: see **Parker Mountain** [LOS ANGELES].

Mount Pinos [VENTURA]: *peak,* 15 miles north-northeast of Reyes Peak at Ventura-Kern County line (lat. 34°48'45" N, long. 119°08'40" W; at N line sec. 6, T 8 N, R 21 W). Altitude 8831 feet. Named on Sawmill Mountain (1943) 7.5' quadrangle. United States Board on Geographic Names (1933, p. 606) rejected the name "Mount McGill" for the peak.

Mount Pinos Camp [VENTURA]: *locality,* 15 miles northeast of Reyes Peak (lat. 34°47'10" N, long. 119°04'50" W; near W line sec. 14, T 8 N, R 21 W); the place is 4 miles east-southeast of Mount Pinos. Named on Cuddy Valley (1943) 7.5' quadrangle. Called Mt. Pinos CCC Camp on Cuddy Valley (1944) 7.5' quadrangle.

Mount Sally [LOS ANGELES]: *peak,* 7.5 miles south of Pacifico Peak (lat. 34°16'20" N, long. 118°00'45" W; near E line sec. 10, T 2 N, R 11 W). Altitude 5408 feet. Named on Chilao Flat (1959) 7.5' quadrangle.

Mount San Antonio [LOS ANGELES]: *peak,* 18 miles northeast of Azusa city hall on Los Angeles-San Bernardino County line (lat. 34°17'20" N, long. 117°38'45" W; sec. 6, T 2 N, R 17 W). Named on Mount San Antonio (1955) 7.5' quadrangle. Called San Antonio Peak on Camp Baldy (1940) 6' quadrangle. United States Board on Geographic Names (1961c, p. 14) rejected the names "Baldy," "North Bald," "Old Baldy," "Old Baldy Peak," "San Antonia Peak," and "San Antonio Peak" for the feature.

Mount Smith: see **Smith Mountain** [LOS ANGELES].

Mount Tecate: see **Tecate Peak** [SAN DIEGO].

Mount Torquemada [LOS ANGELES]: *peak,* 3.25 miles east-southeast of Silver Peak on Santa Catalina Island (lat. 33°26'05" N, long. 118°31'15" W). Altitude 1336 feet. Named on Santa Catalina West (1943) 7.5' quadrangle.

Mount Tule [SAN DIEGO]: *peak,* 6 miles north-northwest of Jacumba (lat. 32°42'05" N, long. 116°13'35" W; near E line sec. 11, T 17 S, R 7 E). Altitude 4647 feet. Named on Jacumba (1959) 7.5' quadrangle.

Mount Van Dam: see **Van Dam Peak** [SAN DIEGO].

Mount Vizcaino: see **Cactus Peak** [LOS ANGELES].

Mount Washington [LOS ANGELES]: *district,* 3.5 miles north-northeast of Los Angeles city hall (lat. 34°06' N, long. 118°13' W). Named on Los Angeles (1953) 7.5' quadrangle.

Mount Waterman: see **Waterman Mountain** [LOS ANGELES].

Mount Whitney [SAN DIEGO]: *peak,* 6.5 miles north-northeast of Rancho Santa Fe (lat. 33°06'30" N, long. 117°09'15" W; at NW cor. sec. 25, T 12 S, R 3 W). Named on Rancho Santa Fe (1968) 7.5' quadrangle. The name commemorates William J. Whitney, who homesteaded near the peak in

1869 (Stein, p. 85).

Mount Williamson [LOS ANGELES]: *peak,* 3.5 miles north of Crystal Lake (lat. 34°22'15" N, long. 117°51'25" W; sec. 6, T 3 N, R 9 W). Altitude 8214 feet. Named on Crystal Lake (1958) 7.5' quadrangle. The name commemorates Lieutenant Robert Stockton Williamson, who made a reconnaissance along the north side of San Gabriel Mountains in 1855 for the Pacific Railroad Survey (Robinson, J.W., 1983, p. 111).

Mount Wilson [LOS ANGELES]:

(1) *peak,* 15 miles northeast of Los Angeles city hall (lat. 34°13'25" N, long. 118°03'40" W; near S line sec. 29, T 2 N, R 11 W). Altitude 5710 feet. Named on Mount Wilson (1953) 7.5' quadrangle. The feature was known as Wilson's Peak after Benjamin D. Wilson built a trail to the top; government surveyors attempted unsuccessfully in 1887 to change the name to Mount Kinneyloa, from Abbot Kinney's ranch called Kinneyloa that was located in present Altadena—Kinney was head of the Board of Forestry of California (Robinson, J.W., 1977, p. 20, 22). Visitors to Mount Wilson in the early days commonly built a huge bonfire on a south-facing promontory—called Signal Point—at the top to let friends below know that they had arrived safely (Robinson, J.W., 1977, p. 21). A feature called Harvard Observatory Point was located near Signal Point: a small observatory building built there in 1889 gave it the name (Robinson, J.W., 1977, p. 24). United States Board on Geographic Names (1992, p. 4) approved the name "Muir Peak" for a feature situated 2.5 miles southwest of Mount Wilson (lat. 34°12'56" N, long. 118°06'05" W; sec. 35, T 2 N, R 12 W), and rejected the names "John Muirs Peak" and "Muirs Peak" for it; the name commemorates naturalist John Muir.

(2) *locality,* less than 0.5 mile northwest of Mount Wilson (1) (lat. 34°13'35" N, long. 118°03'55" W; on W line sec. 29, T 2 N, R 11 W). Named on Mount Wilson (1966) 7.5' quadrangle. Mount Wilson (1953) 7.5' quadrangle shows Mount Wilson P.O. at the place. Postal authorities established Mount Wilson post office in 1904 (Frickstad, p. 77).

Mount Zion [LOS ANGELES]: *peak,* 2 miles east-southeast of Mount Wilson (1) (lat. 34°12'50" N, long. 118°01'35" W; sec. 34, T 2 N, R 11 W). Altitude 3578 feet. Named on Mount Wilson (1953) 7.5' quadrangle.

Moyle: see **Norwalk** [LOS ANGELES].

Mud Creek Canyon [VENTURA]: *canyon,* drained by a stream that flows 3.5 miles to Santa Paula Creek 5 miles southwest of Santa Paula Peak (lat. 34°23'45" N, long. 119°04'30" W; near SW cor. sec. 27, T 4 N, R 21 W). Named on Santa Paula Peak (1951) 7.5' quadrangle.

Muddy Canyon [ORANGE]: *canyon,* drained by a stream that flows nearly 3.5 miles to the sea 3 miles west-northwest of Laguna Beach city hall (lat. 33°33'40" N, long. 117°49'40" W). Named on Laguna Beach (1965) 7.5' quadrangle. Called Los Trancos Canyon on Santa Ana (1942) 15' quadrangle, where present Los Trancos Canyon is unnamed.

Muddy Springs: see **Mud Spring** [LOS ANGELES].

Mud Palisades [SAN DIEGO]: *relief feature,* 12 miles south-southwest of Ocotillo Wells (lat. 33°00'15" N, long. 116°14'35" W). Named on Harper Canyon (1959) 7.5' quadrangle.

Mud Spring [LOS ANGELES]: *spring,* 2.5 miles north-northeast of the village of Lake Hughes (lat. 34°42'35" N, long. 118°25' W; sec. 12, T 7 N, R 15 W). Named on Lake Hughes (1957) 7.5' quadrangle. Latta (p. 59) called the feature Aguaje Lodoso, or Muddy Springs.

Mud Springs [SAN DIEGO]: *spring,* 1.25 miles north-northeast of Margarita Peak (lat. 33°27'40" N, long. 117°23'10" W; near S line sec. 22, T 8 S, R 5 W). Named on Margarita Peak (1968) 7.5' quadrangle.

Mud Springs: see **San Dimas** [LOS ANGELES].

Mud Town: see **Watts** [LOS ANGELES].

Mugu Lagoon [VENTURA]: *water feature,* 2.5 miles west-northwest of Point Mugu along the coast (lat. 34°06'05" N, long. 119°06' W). Named on Point Mugu (1949) 7.5' quadrangle. Called Mugu Laguna on Hueneme (1904) 15' quadrangle.

Mugu Laguna: see **Mugu Lagoon** [VENTURA].

Mugu Peak [VENTURA]: *peak,* 0.5 mile north-northeast of Point Mugu (lat. 34°05'35" N, long. 119°03'15" W). Altitude 1266 feet. Named on Point Mugu (1949) 7.5' quadrangle.

Mugu Point: see **Point Mugu** [VENTURA].

Muir Peak: see **Mount Wilson** [LOS ANGELES] (1).

Mule Fork [LOS ANGELES]: *stream,* flows 2 miles to Alder Creek (2) 4.5 miles south-southwest of Pacifico Mountain (lat. 34°19'10" N, long. 118°03' W; sec. 29, T 3 N, R 11 W). Named on Chilao Flat (1959) 7.5' quadrangle.

Mule Hill: see **Battle Mountain** [SAN DIEGO].

Mullally Canyon [LOS ANGELES]: *canyon,* drained by a steam that flows 1.25 miles to Pickens Canyon 7.5 miles northwest of Pasadena city hall (lat. 34°14'10" N, long. 118°13'30" W; near N line sec. 27, T 2 N, R 13 W). Named on Pasadena (1953) 7.5' quadrangle.

Mull Canyon [LOS ANGELES]: *canyon,* 1 mile long, 2.5 miles east-northeast of Glendora city hall (lat. 34°08'45" N, long. 117°49'20" W; sec. 22, 27, 28, T 1 N, R 9 W). Named on Glendora (1953) 7.5' quadrangle.

Munger Creek [ORANGE]: *stream,* flows 2.5 miles to Aliso Creek at El Toro (lat. 33°37'25" N, long. 117°41'20" W). Named on El Toro (1950) 7.5' quadrangle. The name commemorates Sam Munger and his family, who settled along the creek in the late 1880's (Meadows, p. 103).

Municipal Yacht Harbor: see **Shelter Island Yacht Basin**, under **Shelter Island** [SAN DIEGO].

Munson Creek [VENTURA]: *stream,* flows 3.5 miles to Sespe Creek 5.5 miles north of Wheeler Springs (lat. 34°35'20" N, long. 119°17'25" W; near S line sec. 23, T 6 N, R 23 W). Named on Reyes Peak (1943) and Wheeler Springs (1943) 7.5' quadrangles.

Munz Canyon [LOS ANGELES]: *canyon,* drained by a stream that flows 1.5 miles to lowlands about 1.5 miles southeast of the village of Lake Hughes (lat. 34°39'50" N, long. 118°25'15" W; sec. 25, T 7 N, R 15 W). Named on Lake Hughes (1957) 7.5' quadrangle, which shows Munz ranch near the mouth of the canyon. Elizabeth Lake (1917) 30' quadrangle has the name "Roosevelt" for a place located near the mouth of present Munz Canyon. Postal authorities established Roosevelt post office in 1902, moved it 1.5 miles southeast in 1906, and discontinued it in 1925; the name was for Theodore Roosevelt (Salley, p. 188).

Munz Lakes [LOS ANGELES]: *lakes,* 0.5 mile east-southeast of the village of Lake Hughes (lat. 34°40'20" N, long. 118°25'50" W; near NE cor. sec. 26, T 7 N, R 15 W). Named on Lake Hughes (1957) 7.5' quadrangle.

Mupu Cañon: see **Santa Paula Canyon** [VENTURA].

Murietta Canyon [VENTURA]: *canyon,* drained by a stream that flows 3.25 miles to the canyon of Matilija Creek 5 miles west of Wheeler Springs (lat. 34°30'20" N, long. 119°22'40" W; sec. 22, T 5 N, R 24 W). Named on Old Man Mountain (1943) and White Ledge Peak (1952) 7.5' quadrangles. The stream in the canyon is called West Fork Matilija Cr. on Ventura (1904) 15' quadrangle.

Murietta Divide [VENTURA]: *pass,* 3 miles west-northwest of White Ledge Peak (lat. 34°29'25" N, long. 119°26'05" W); the pass is at the head of Murietta Canyon. Named on White Ledge Peak (1952) 7.5' quadrangle.

Muroc Dry Lake Center: see **Edwards Air Force Base**, under **Rosamond Lake** [LOS ANGELES].

Murphy Canyon [SAN DIEGO]: *canyon,* drained by a stream that flows 8 miles to San Diego River 5.5 miles west of La Mesa (lat. 32°46'50" N, long. 117°06'50" W). Named on La Mesa (1967) 7.5' quadrangle. The name is for John Murphy, who settled at the place in 1860 (Stein, p. 86).

Murray Canyon [SAN DIEGO]: *canyon,* drained by a stream that flows 3.5 miles to San Diego River 8.5 miles southeast of Point La Jolla (lat. 32°46'10" N, long. 117°09'30" W). Named on La Jolla (1967) 7.5' quadrangle. The name is for John Murray, who homesteaded in the neighborhood in the 1880's (Stein, p. 86). Harlow (1987, p. 79) identified present Murray Canyon as the feature called Cañada de Ozuna on Harry D. Fitch's map of Pueblo lands of San Diego made in 1845.

Murray Reservoir [SAN DIEGO]: *lake,* 1 mile long, nearly 2 miles northwest of La Mesa (lat. 32°47'15" N, long. 117°02'30" W). Named on La Mesa (1967) 7.5' quadrangle. The name recalls James A. Murray, who was largely responsible for the dam that formed the lake in 1916 (Stein, p. 86).

Music Mountain [SAN DIEGO]: *hill,* 3 miles south-southeast of Manzanita (lat. 32°37'50" N, long. 116°15'55" W; sec. 4, T 18 S, R 7 E). Named on Live Oak Springs (1959) 7.5' quadrangle.

Mussel Cove [ORANGE]: *embayment,* 4.25 miles west-southwest of San Juan Capistrano along the coast (lat. 33°29'15" N, long. 117° 44'05" W). Named on Dana Point (1968) 7.5' quadrangle.

Mussey Grove [SAN DIEGO]: *locality,* 4.5 miles north of Lakeside (lat. 32°55'45" N, long. 116°54'20" W). Named on El Cajon (1939) 15' quadrangle. Water of San Vicente Reservoir now covers the site.

Mustang Spring [ORANGE]: *spring,* 6.5 miles south of Sierra Peak (lat. 33°45'20" N, long. 117°38'10" W; sec. 8, T 5 S, R 7 W). Named on Black Star Canyon (1967) 7.5' quadrangle.

Mustang Spring Canyon: see **Ladd Canyon** [ORANGE].

Mutau Creek [VENTURA]: *stream,* flows 10 miles to Piru Creek 15 miles east-northeast of Reyes Peak (lat. 34°40'55" N, long. 119°01'10" W; sec. 20, T 7 N, R 20 W); the stream goes through Mutau Flat. Named on Lockwood Valley (1943) and Topatopa Mountains (1943) 7.5' quadrangles.

Mutau Creek: see **Little Mutau Creek** [VENTURA].

Mutau Flat [VENTURA]: *valley,* 13 miles east of Reyes Peak (lat. 34°37'30" N, long. 119°02'45" W). Named on Lockwood Valley (1943) and Topatopa Mountains (1943) 7.5' quadrangles. The name commemorates William Mutau, who came to the region in the 1850's—the name "Mutah" in its various spellings may be an Indian alias given to a wanted man by his native wife (Outland, 1969, p. 100). United States Board on Geographic Names (1990, p. 8) approved the name "Johnston Ridge" for a feature that extends for 3.3 miles southeast from Mutau Flat to Hot Springs Canyon, and rejected name "Johnson Ridge" for it.

Muth Valley [SAN DIEGO]: *valley,* 3 miles north-northeast of Lakeside (lat. 32°54'05" N, long. 116°54' W; on S line sec. 32, T 14 S, R 1 E). Named on San Vicente Reservoir (1955) 7.5' quadrangle. The name is for A.M. Muth, a beekeeper in the neighborhood (Stein, p. 86).

Myford: see **East Irvine** [ORANGE].

Myrick Canyon [LOS ANGELES]: *canyon,* drained by a stream that flows

5.25 miles to lowlands 5 miles west-northwest of Del Sur (lat. 34°42'55" N, long. 118°22' W; near N line sec. 9, T 7 N, R 14 W). Named on Del Sur (1958) and Lake Hughes (1957) 7.5' quadrangles. Called Myric Canyon on Los Angeles County (1935) map, which also names a North Fork.

Myrtle: see **Harold** [LOS ANGELES].

Mystery Spring [VENTURA]: *spring*, 10.5 miles north of Reyes Peak (lat. 34°47'05" N, long. 119°16'55" W; sec. 14, T 8 N, R 23 W). Named on Apache Canyon (1943) 7.5' quadrangle.

Mystic Canyon [LOS ANGELES]:

(1) *canyon*, drained by a stream that flows 2.25 miles to Texas Canyon 11.5 miles south of the village of Lake Hughes (lat. 34°30'40" N, long. 118°25' W; at S line sec. 14, T 5 N, R 15 W). Named on Green Valley (1958) 7.5' quadrangle.

(2) *canyon*, drained by a stream that flows 1.5 miles to Big Dalton Canyon 2.5 miles northeast of Glendora city hall (lat. 34°09'30" N, long. 117°49'40" W; sec. 21, T 1 N, R 9 W). Named on Glendora (1953) 7.5' quadrangle.

- N -

Nadeau [LOS ANGELES]: *locality*, 2.25 miles west-northwest of South Gate city hall along Southern Pacific Railroad (lat. 33°58' N, long. 118°14'35" W). Named on South Gate (1964) 7.5' quadrangle.

Nadeau Canyon: see **Solemint** [LOS ANGELES].

Nadeau Park [LOS ANGELES]: *locality*, 2 miles northwest of present South Gate city hall along Atchison, Topeka and Santa Fe Railroad (lat. 33°59'15" N, long. 118°14'15" W). Named on Downey (1902) 15' quadrangle. The name is from Gernert and Nadeau Beet Sugarie established at the place in 1881 (Gudde, 1949, p. 230).

Nago [ORANGE]: *locality*, 2.5 miles southeast of present Huntington Beach civic center along Pacific Electric Railroad (lat. 33°38'05" N, long. 117°57'45" W). Named on Newport Beach (1951) 7.5' quadrangle.

Naples [LOS ANGELES]: *district*, 4.25 miles east-southeast of Long Beach city hall (lat. 33°45'20" N, long. 118°07'15" W). Named on Long Beach (1949) and Los Alamitos (1950) 7.5' quadrangles.

Narrows: see **The Narrows** [LOS ANGELES]; **The Narrows** [ORANGE]; **The Narrows** [SAN DIEGO].

National City [SAN DIEGO]: *city*, 4.5 miles southeast of downtown San Diego (lat. 32°40'20" N, long. 117°06'15" W); the city is on La Nacion grant. Named on National City (1967) 7.5' quadrangle. Postal authorities established National City post office in 1869 and moved it 1 mile northeast in 1898 (Salley, p. 150). The city incorporated in 1887. The Kimball brothers bought La Nacion grant in 1869, subdivided part of it into farm lots, built a wharf, and laid out a community by San Diego Bay (Guinn, p. 129).

Natural Arch [LOS ANGELES]: *relief feature*, 5.25 miles west-northwest of present Santa Monica city hall along the coast (lat. 34°02'25" N, long. 118°34'30" W). Named on Topanga Canyon (1928) 6' quadrangle.

Natural Rock Tanks [SAN DIEGO]: *water feature*, 13 miles east-northeast of Borrego Springs in Smoke Tree Canyon (lat. 33°19'10" N, long. 116°09'35" W). Named on Fonts Point (1959) 7.5' quadrangle.

Naud Junction [LOS ANGELES]: *locality*, 0.5 mile northeast of Los Angeles city hall along a railroad (lat. 34°03'35" N, long. 118°14'05" W). Named on Los Angeles (1966) 7.5' quadrangle.

Naumann: see **Oxnard** [VENTURA].

Neal Cove [SAN DIEGO]: *embayment*, 6.5 miles west of Jamul along Sweetwater Reservoir (lat. 32°42'20" N, long. 116°59' W). Named on Jamul Mountains (1955) 7.5' quadrangle.

Necktie Basin [LOS ANGELES]: *area*, 0.5 mile west of Warm Springs Mountain (lat. 34°35'45" N, long. 118°35'15" W); the place is near the head of Necktie Canyon. Named on Warm Springs Mountain (1958) 7.5' quadrangle.

Necktie Canyon [LOS ANGELES]: *canyon*, drained by a stream that flows 4 miles to Castaic Creek 4.25 miles south-southwest of Warm Springs Mountain (lat. 34°32'45" N, long. 118°37'20" W; near W line sec. 1, T 5 N, R 17 W). Named on Warm Springs Mountain (1958) 7.5' quadrangle. Los Angeles County (1935) map names three branches of the canyon of Castaic Creek near Necktie Canyon: Owl Canyon, which opens into the canyon of Castaic Creek from the northeast about 0.5 mile below the mouth of Necktie Canyon; Oak Canyon, which opens into the canyon of Castaic Creek from the northeast less than 1 mile downstream from the mouth of Owl Canyon; and Kingsley Canyon, which opens into the canyon of Castaic Creek from the northeast less than 0.25 mile below the mouth of Oak Canyon.

Nedo: see **Ozena** [VENTURA].

Neenach [LOS ANGELES]: *locality*, 13 miles east of Gorman (lat. 34°47' N, long. 118°36'55" W; sec. 18, T 8 N, R 16 W). Named on Tejon (1903) 30' quadrangle. Neenach School (1965) 7.5' quadrangle shows Neenach school situated about 0.5 mile farther east. Postal authorities established Neenach post office in 1888, moved it 2 miles southeast in 1904, moved it 3.5 miles southwest in 1910, and discontinued it in 1929; the place was a gold-mining camp (Salley, p. 152). Kroeber (p. 50) suggested an Indian origin for the name.

Neff [ORANGE]: *locality*, 5 miles southeast of present Buena Park civic center along Southern Pacific Railroad (lat. 33°48'35" N, long. 117°55'55" W). Named on Garden Grove (1935) 7.5' quadrangle.

Negro Canyon: see **El Prieto** [LOS ANGELES]; **Harrison Canyon** [SAN DIEGO].

Nehr Canyon [LOS ANGELES]: *canyon*, drained by a stream that flows 1.25 miles to Little Tujunga Canyon 4.5 miles north-northwest of Sunland (lat. 34°19'20" N, long. 118°20'15" W; near N line sec. 27, T 3 N, R 14 W). Named on Sunland (1953) 7.5' quadrangle.

Nellie: see **Palomar Mountain** [SAN DIEGO] (2).

Nellus Canyon [LOS ANGELES]: *canyon*, drained by a stream that flows 1.5 miles to Santa Clara River 9 miles east of Solemint (lat. 34°26'25" N, long. 118°17'45" W; sec. 12, T 4 N, R 14 W). Named on Agua Dulce (1960) 7.5' quadrangle.

Nelson Canyon [LOS ANGELES]: *canyon*, drained by a stream that flows 2 miles to Santa Clara River 9.5 miles east of Solemint (lat. 34°26'25" N, long. 118°17'30" W; near SE cor. sec. 12, T 4 N, R 14 W). Named on Agua Dulce (1960) 7.5' quadrangle. Los Angeles County (1935) map shows a feature called Portland Canyon that opens into Soledad Canyon from the south about 1 mile west of the mouth of Nelson Canyon, and shows a feature called Redman Canyon that opens into Soledad Canyon from the south less than 1 mile west of the mouth of Nelson Canyon.

Nelson Canyon [SAN DIEGO]: *canyon*, drained by a stream that flows 2.5 miles to Pine Valley Creek 4 miles south of Descanso (lat. 32°47'55" N, long. 116°36'25" W; sec. 7, T 16 S, R 4 E). Named on Descanso (1960) 7.5' quadrangle. The name is for an early resident of the neighborhood (Stein, p. 88).

Nestor [SAN DIEGO]: *district*, nearly 2 miles east of Imperial Beach civic center in San Diego (lat. 32°34'30" N, long. 117°05' W; on E line sec. 28, T 18 S, R 2 W). Named on Imperial Beach (1967) 7.5' quadrangle. Postal authorities established Nestor post office in 1890 (Frickstad, p. 154). The name commemorates Nestor A. Young, a state assemblyman in the 1880's who was appointed harbormaster for San Diego in 1889 (Stein, p 88-89).

Nettle Spring [VENTURA]: *spring*, 11 miles north of Reyes Peak (lat. 34°48'10" N, long. 119°17'30" W; sec. 11, T 8 N, R 23 W). Named on Apache Canyon (1943) 7.5' quadrangle.

Nevin [LOS ANGELES]: *locality*, nearly 3 miles south of Los Angeles city hall along Southern Pacific Railroad (lat. 34°00'50" N, long. 118°14'45" W). Named on Los Angeles (1966) 7.5' quadrangle.

Newbury Park [VENTURA]: *town*, 16 miles east of Oxnard (lat. 34° 11' N, long. 118°54'30" W). Named on Newbury Park (1951) 7.5' quadrangle. Postal authorities established Newbury Park post office in Ventura County in 1875, moved it into Los Angeles County in 1882, moved it 1.25 miles north and back into Ventura County in 1883, moved it 5 miles west in 1891, and moved it 1 mile west in 1908; the name is for Egbert S. Newbury, first postmaster (Salley, p. 153). They established Timberville post office 7 miles west of Newbury Park post office in 1888 and discontinued it in 1893 (Salley, p. 222).

Newcomb Pass [LOS ANGELES]: *pass*, 2 miles east-northeast of Mount Wilson (1) (lat. 34°13'55" N, long. 118°01'05" W; sec. 27, T 2 N, R 11 W). Named on Mount Wilson (1953) 7.5' quadrangle. The name commemorates Louie Newcomb, who laid out a trail over the pass (Robinson, J.W., 1977, p. 125).

Newhall [LOS ANGELES]: *town*, 7.5 miles north-northwest of San Fernando (lat. 34°23'05" N, long. 118°31'50" W). Named on Newhall (1952) and Oat Mountain (1952) 7.5' quadrangles. Postal authorities established Newhall post office in 1877 (Frickstad, p. 78). Officials of Southern Pacific Railroad built a station at present Saugus in 1876 and named it "Newhall" for Henry M. Newhall, owner of the land; in 1878 they moved the station and name to present Newhall (Gudde, 1949, p. 235). Los Angeles County (1935) map shows a feature called Railroad Canyon that extends for 2 miles south from Newhall along the rail line; the same map has the name "Wildwood Cany." for the next north-trending canyon west of and parallel to Railroad Canyon.

Newhall Creek [LOS ANGELES]: *stream*, flows 4.25 miles to South Fork Santa Clara River 0.5 miles north-northeast of downtown Newhall (lat. 34°23'40" N, long. 118°32'15" W); the stream goes through Newhall. Named on Newhall (1952) and Oat Mountain (1952) 7.5' quadrangles.

New Jerusalem: see **El Rio** [VENTURA].

Newman Point [LOS ANGELES]: *relief feature*, 4.5 miles north-northeast of Glendora city hall (lat. 34°11'55" N, long. 117°50'25" W; sec. 5, T 1 N, R 9 W). Named on Glendora (1953) 7.5' quadrangle.

Newmark: see **Montebello** [LOS ANGELES].

New Pass: see **Soledad Pass** [LOS ANGELES].

Newport [ORANGE]: *locality*, 6 miles north-northwest of Newport Beach (lat. 33°41'45" N, long. 117°54'15" W). Named on Corona (1902) 30' quadrangle.

Newport: see **Newport Beach** [ORANGE] (2); **Old Newport**, under **Greenville** [ORANGE].

Newport Bay [ORANGE]: *bay*, the entrance channel is 3.25 miles east-southeast of Newport Beach city hall (lat. 33°35'35" N, long. 117°52'45" W); the bay is at the city of Newport Beach. Named on Newport Beach (1965) 7.5' quadrangle. Newport Bay and Upper Newport Bay together are called San Joaquin Bay on Lankershim Ranch Land and Water Company's (1888) map. The combined bays also were called Cienega de la San Joaquin, Cienega de las Ranas (Hanna, p. 211), Bolsa de San Joaquin, and Bolsa de Quigara (Gleason, p. 88-90). Newport Beach (1965) 7.5' quadrangle names three channels in the bay: Balboa Reach south of Balboa Island, Harbor Island Reach south of Harbor Island, and Lido Isle Reach between Lido Isle and the mainland. Rocky Point was a conspicuous feature on the east side of the entrance to Newport Bay before jetties were built there (Meadows, p. 120).

Newport Bay: see **Upper Newport Bay** [ORANGE].

Newport Beach [ORANGE]:

(1) *beach*, 6 miles southeast of Huntington Beach civic center along the coast (lat. 33°36'20" N, long. 117°55'05" W). Named on Newport Beach (1965) 7.5' quadrangle. The feature first was known as Sand Beach (Meadows, p. 123).

(2) *city*, 5 miles southeast of Huntington Beach civic center along the coast (lat. 33°37' N, long. 117°55'45" W). Named on Laguna Beach (1965), Newport Beach (1965), and Tustin (1965) 7.5' quadrangles. Postal authorities established Newport Beach post office in 1891 (Frickstad, p. 117), and the city incorporated in 1906. In 1872 Captain S.S. Dunnells and Mr. D.M. Dorman set up a small dock and warehouse called Newport Landing just below the bluff that divides Newport Bay from Upper Newport Bay 1.25 miles east of present Newport Beach city hall; the McFadden brothers purchased the facility in 1873, and it became known as McFadden's Landing and as Port Orange—after the McFaddens built a wharf along the ocean, it was called Old Landing (Hoover, Rensch, and Rensch, p. 264). Postal authorities established Newport post office at Newport Landing in 1875, discontinued it in 1876, reestablished it in 1882, and discontinued it in 1901 (Salley, p. 154). The present city developed around the long wharf that the McFadden brothers built in 1888 along the ocean (Meadows, p. 104-105). Branagan Glass Company built a factory next to the bluff in the city of Newport Beach in 1913, and Southern Pacific Railroad built a spur line called Branagan to the factory; the spur line was abandoned in 1927 (Meadows, p. 30).

Newport Heights [ORANGE]: *district*, 5 miles east-southeast of Huntington Beach civic center (lat. 33°37'25" N, long. 117°55'15" W). Named on Newport Beach (1965) 7.5' quadrangle.

Newport Island [ORANGE]: *island*, 1400 feet long, 4.5 miles southeast of Huntington Beach civic center in Newport Harbor (lat. 33° 37'10" N, long. 117°56' W). Named on Newport Beach (1965) 7.5' quadrangle.

Newport Landing: see **Newport Beach** [ORANGE] (2).

New River: see **San Gabriel River** [LOS ANGELES].

New San Diego: see **San Diego** [SAN DIEGO].

New San Gabriel River: see **San Gabriel River** [LOS ANGELES-ORANGE].

New San Pedro: see **Wilmington** [LOS ANGELES].

New Texas: see **Milguatay**, under **Campo** [SAN DIEGO].

Newton Canyon [LOS ANGELES]: *canyon*, drained by a stream that flows 2 miles to Zuma Canyon 5.25 miles north of Point Dume (lat. 34°04'35" N, long. 118°49'05" W; near SE cor. sec. 13, T 1 S, R 19 W). Named on Point Dume (1951) 7.5' quadrangle.

Newton Canyon [SAN DIEGO]: *canyon*, drained by a stream that flows 2.5 miles to Santa Margarita River 3 miles north-northwest of Oceanside (lat. 33°14'15" N, long. 117°23'40" W; sec. 10, T 11 S, R 5 W). Named on Las Pulgas Canyon (1968) and Oceanside (1968) 7.5' quadrangles.

Newton Park [LOS ANGELES]: *district*, 4.5 miles northeast of present Los Angeles city hall (lat. 34°05'25" N, long. 118°10'35" W). Named on Alhambra (1926) 6' quadrangle.

New Town: see **San Diego** [SAN DIEGO].

Newtown: see **Wilmington** [LOS ANGELES].

Nicholas Canyon [LOS ANGELES]: *canyon*, drained by a stream that flows 2.5 miles to the sea 6.5 miles west-northwest of Point Dume (lat. 34°02'30" N, long. 118°54'50" W). Named on Triunfo Pass (1950) 7.5' quadrangle. On Camulos (1903) 30' quadrangle, the name applies to present Los Alisos Canyon. United States Board on Geographic Names (1943, p. 13) approved the name "San Nicolas Canyon" for the feature, and rejected the names "Arroyo San Nicolas," "Cañada San Nicolas," and "Nicholas Canyon."

Nicholas Canyon: see **Little Nicholas Canyon**, under **Willow Creek** [LOS ANGELES]; **Los Alisos Canyon** [LOS ANGELES].

Nicholas Flat [LOS ANGELES]: *area*, 7.25 miles northwest of Point Dume (lat. 34°04' N, long. 118°54'30" W; sec. 19, T 1 S, R 19 W). Named on Triunfo Pass (1950) 7.5' quadrangle, which shows the place near the head of Nicholas Canyon.

Nichols Canyon [LOS ANGELES]: *canyon*, 1.25 miles long, 8 miles west-northwest of Los Angeles city hall (lat. 34°06'45" N, long. 118°21'35" W; at W line sec. 4, T 1 S, R 14 W). Named on Hollywood (1966) 7.5' quadrangle.

Nicholson Canyon: see **Castaic** [LOS ANGELES].

Nicolas Canyon: see **Los Alsiso Canyon** [LOS ANGELES].

Niger Canyon: see **Emerald Canyon** [ORANGE].

Nigger Canyon: see **Emerald Canyon** [ORANGE]; **Harrison Canyon** [SAN DIEGO]; **Warring Canyon** [VENTURA].

Nigger Creek [VENTURA]: *stream*, flows 3.5 miles to Piru Creek 14 miles east-northeast of Reyes Peak (lat. 34°40' N, long. 119°02'35" W; near S line sec. 30, T 7 N, R 20 W). Named on Lockwood Valley (1943) 7.5' quadrangle.

Niggerhead Mountain [LOS ANGELES]: *peak*, 7.5 miles north of Point Dume (lat. 34°06'35" N, long. 118°48'30" W; sec. 6, T 1 S, R 18 W). Altitude 2039 feet. Named on Point Dume (1951) 7.5' quadrangle. Called Niggerhead on Los Angeles County (1935) map. The name is from the outline of the feature (Gudde, 1949, p. 233).

Nigger Slough [LOS ANGELES]: *lake*, 4 miles long, 7 miles east of Redondo (present Redondo Beach) (lat. 33°50'45" N, long. 118° 16' W). Named on Redondo (1896) 15' quadrangle. It is called Laguna Seca on a diseño of Sausal Redondo grant (Becker, 1969). Los Angeles Board of Supervisors adopted the name "Laguna Dominguez" for the swamps and lake formerly known as Nigger Slough (Gudde, 1949, p. 97)—present Dominguez Channel extends through the feature.

Nigger Wash [VENTURA]: *stream*, flows 1.5 miles to Santa Clara River 1.25 miles south of Piru (lat. 34°23'50" N, long. 118°47'50" W; sec. 30, T 4 N, R 18 W); the stream heads at the mouth of Nigger Canyon (present Warring Canyon). Named on Piru (1952) 7.5' quadrangle.

Niguel [ORANGE]: *land grant*, extends southwest from El Toro to Laguna Beach (2). Named on Dana Point (1949), Laguna Beach (1949), and San Juan Capistrano (1949) 7.5' quadrangles. Juan Avila and others received 3 leagues in 1842, and Avila claimed 13,316 acres patented in 1873 (Cowan, p. 52). Perez (p. 78) gave 1875 as the date of the patent. The name is the Spanish rendition of the designation of an Indian village (Meadows, p. 105).

Niguel Hill [ORANGE]: *peak*, 4 miles west-northwest of San Juan Capistrano (lat. 33°30'45" N, long. 117°44' W); the feature is on Niguel grant. Altitude 926 feet. Named on San Juan Capistrano (1968) 7.5' quadrangle.

Nimock: see **Huntington Beach** [ORANGE].

Nino Canyon [LOS ANGELES]: *canyon*, drained by a stream that flows less than 0.5 mile to Arroyo Seco nearly 6 miles north-northwest of Pasadena city hall (lat. 34°13'35" N, long. 118°10'45" W). Named on Pasadena (1953) 7.5' quadrangle.

9th Street Junction [LOS ANGELES]: *locality*, nearly 3 miles south-southeast of Los Angeles city hall along Union Pacific Railroad (lat. 34°01'10" N, long. 118°13'10" W). Named on Los Angeles (1953) 7.5' quadrangle.

Nintynine Oaks [LOS ANGELES]: *locality*, 8 miles northwest of Newhall (lat. 34°31' N, long. 118°36'55" W; sec. 36, T 5 N, R 17 W). Named on Newhall (1952) 7.5' quadrangle. Castaic (1940) 6' quadrangle shows a place called Lindys at the site.

Noble Canyon [SAN DIEGO]: *canyon*, drained by a stream that flows 5 miles to Pine Valley Creek 5.5 miles east of Descanso (lat. 32°51'50" N, long. 116°31'05" W; near SE cor. sec. 13, T 15 S, R 4 E). Named on Descanso (1960), Monument Peak (1959), and Mount Laguna (1960) 7.5' quadrangles. The name commemorates Jack Noble and Tom Noble, brothers who had a successful gold mine in the neighborhood (Stein, p. 89).

Noel Canyon [LOS ANGELES]: *canyon*, drained by a stream that flows 0.5 mile to Pacoima Canyon 7 miles north of Sunland (lat. 34°21'40" N, long. 118°18'10" W; sec. 12, T 3 N, R 14 W). Named on Sunland (1953) 7.5' quadrangle. Called Pinery Canyon on Los Angeles County (1935) map.

Nogales: see **Matilija Hot Springs** [VENTURA].

Nolina Wash [SAN DIEGO]: *stream*, flows 4.25 miles to Pinyon Wash 10.5 miles west of Ocotillo Wells (lat. 33°06'40" N, long. 116°18'50" W). Named on Whale Peak (1959) 7.5' quadrangle.

Nordhoff: see **Ojai** [VENTURA] (2).

Nordhoff Peak [VENTURA]: *peak*, 3.5 miles north of the town of Ojai, which originally was called Nordhoff (lat. 34°29'50" N, long. 119°14'30" W; sec. 24, T 5 N, R 23 W). Altitude 4485 feet. Named on Ojai (1952) 7.5' quadrangle.

Nordhoff Ridge [VENTURA]: *ridge*, west-trending, 3 miles long, 3.5 miles north-northwest of the town of Ojai (lat. 34°29'45" N, long. 119°15'35" W); Nordhoff Peak is at the east end of the ridge. Named on Matilija (1952) and Ojai (1952) 7.5' quadrangles.

Normal Heights [SAN DIEGO]: *district*, 5.5 miles west of La Mesa (lat. 32°45'50" N, long. 117°07'15" W). Named on La Jolla (1967) and La Mesa (1967) 7.5' quadrangles.

North Alhambra [LOS ANGELES]: *locality*, 5.25 miles west-northwest of El Monte along Southern Pacific Railroad (lat. 34°05'55" N, long. 118°07'30" W); the place is north of Alhambra. Named on Pasadena (1900) 15' quadrangle.

Northam [ORANGE]: *locality*, 1.25 miles north of Buena Park along Southern California Railroad (lat. 33°52'50" N, long. 118°00' W). Named on Corona (1902) 30' quadrangle. The name commemorates Robert Northam, a landowner and ranch manager (Meadows, p. 106).

North Bald: see **Mount San Antonio** [LOS ANGELES].

North Baldy: see **Mount Baden-Powell** [LOS ANGELES].

North Baldy Peak: see **Throop Peak** [LOS ANGELES].

North Carlsbad [SAN DIEGO]: *district,* 2.25 miles east-southeast of downtown Oceanside (lat. 33°11'15" N, long. 117°20'25" W); the place is 1.5 miles north of Carlsbad. Named on San Luis Rey (1948) 7.5' quadrangle.

North Clairemont [SAN DIEGO]: *district,* 4.25 miles east-southeast of Point La Jolla in San Diego (lat. 32°49'45" N, long. 117°12' W); the place is north of Clairemont district. Named on La Jolla (1967) 7.5' quadrangle.

North Cove [SAN DIEGO]: *embayment,* 5.5 miles south-southeast of Point La Jolla on the north side of Vacation Isle in Mission Bay (lat. 32°46'35" N, long. 117°14'15" W). Named on La Jolla (1967) 7.5' quadrangle. Called Pacific Cove on La Jolla (1953) 7.5' quadrangle.

North Fillmore [VENTURA]: *town,* less than 1 mile west-northwest of downtown Fillmore (lat. 34°24'25" N, long. 118°55'20" W; at NE cor. sec. 25, T 4 N, R 20 W). Named on Fillmore (1951) 7.5' quadrangle.

North Glendale [LOS ANGELES]: *district,* 2.5 miles southeast of Burbank city hall (lat. 34°09'40" N, long. 118°16' W); the district is 1.5 miles northwest of Glendale civic center. Named on Burbank (1953) 7.5' quadrangle.

North Highland Park [LOS ANGELES]: *district,* 5.25 miles north-northeast of present Los Angeles city hall (lat. 34°07'25" N, long. 118°12'20" W); the district is north of Highland Park. Named on Glendale (1928) 6' quadrangle.

North Hollywood [LOS ANGELES]: *district,* 4.25 miles east-southeast of Van Nuys in Los Angeles (lat. 34°10' N, long. 118°22'30" W). Named on Burbank (1953) and Van Nuys (1953) 7.5' quadrangles. Called Toluca on Santa Monica (1902) 15' quadrangle, and called Lankershim on Burbank (1926) 6' quadrangle. Postal authorities established Toluca post office in 1893, changed the name to Lankershim in 1906, and changed it to North Hollywood in 1926 (Salley, p. 117, 223). The name "Lankershim" recalls Isaac Lankershim, a developer of the place (Hanna, p. 140).

North Island [SAN DIEGO]: *area,* 3 miles west-southwest across San Diego Bay from downtown San Diego at the northwest end of the peninsula occupied by Coronado (lat. 32°42' N, long. 117°12'15" W). Named on Point Loma (1967) 7.5' quadrangle. A spring on North Island provided fresh water for ships in the early days—the spring was called Russian Wells from a legend about a little Russian girl who was the sole survivor of a shipwreck (Gleason, p. 77).

North Jamul [SAN DIEGO]: *locality,* 0.5 mile north-northeast of Jamul (lat. 32°43'30" N, long. 116°52'15" W; mainly in sec. 3, T 17 S, R 1 E). Named on Dulzura (1972) 7.5' quadrangle.

North Long Beach [LOS ANGELES]: *district,* 6 miles north of Long Beach city hall (lat. 33°51'20" N, long. 118°11' W). Named on Long Beach (1949) 7.5' quadrangle. Postal authorities established Virginia City post office in 1923 and changed the name to North Long Beach in 1928 (Salley, p. 232).

North Long Canyon [LOS ANGELES]: *canyon,* drained by a stream that flows 1.5 miles to lowlands 5.25 miles northeast of Burnt Peak (lat. 34°44'30" N, long. 118°30'55" W; sec. 31, T 8 N, R 15 W); the feature is less than 1 mile north of South Long Canyon. Named on Burnt Peak (1958) 7.5' quadrangle.

North Los Angeles: see **Northridge** [LOS ANGELES].

North Park [SAN DIEGO]: *district,* 2.5 miles northeast of downtown San Diego (lat. 32°44'30" N, long. 117°07'45" W). Named on Point Loma (1967) 7.5' quadrangle.

North Peak [SAN DIEGO]: *peak,* 5 miles south of Julian (lat. 33°00'25" N, long. 116°35'05" W). Altitude 5993 feet. Named on Julian (1960) 7.5' quadrangle.

North Peak: see **Modjeska Peak** [ORANGE].

North Pinon Mountains [SAN DIEGO]: *ridge,* generally northwest-trending, 1.5 miles long, 15 miles west of Ocotillo Wells (lat. 33° 06' N, long. 116°24'30" W); the feature is 4.5 miles northwest of Pinyon Mountains. Named on Borrego Sink (1959), Earthquake Valley (1959), and Tubb Canyon (1959) 7.5' quadrangles. United States Board on Geographic Names (1961b, p. 11) rejected the names "Pinyon Mountains" and "Vallecito Mountains" for the feature.

North Pinyon Mountains: see **Pinyon Mountains** [SAN DIEGO]; **Vallecito Mountains** [SAN DIEGO].

North Pomona [LOS ANGELES]: *district,* 2.25 miles north of Pomona city hall (lat. 34°05'20" N, long. 117°44'45" W). Named on Ontario (1954) 7.5' quadrangle. Postal authorities established North Pomona post office in 1891 and discontinued it in 1949 (Salley, p. 156).

North Portal: see **Fairmont Reservoir** [LOS ANGELES].

Northridge [LOS ANGELES]: *district,* 4 miles east-northeast of the center of Canoga Park in Los Angeles (lat. 34°13'45" N, long. 118° 32'35" W). Named on Canoga Park (1952) 7.5' quadrangle. Called Zelzah on Zelzah (1941) 6' quadrangle, which shows Northridge P.O. and Sta. at the place. Postal authorities established Zelzah post office in 1911, changed the name to North Los Angeles in 1929, and changed it to Northridge in 1938 (Frickstad, p. 78, 84). The name "Zelzah" was given to the place because it, like the biblical Zelzah, was a watering spot in the desert; Carl S. Dentzel proposed the name "Northridge" from Northridge Stampede, which was at the base of the ridge north of San Fernando Valley (Gudde, 1969, p. 224).

North San Diego [SAN DIEGO]: *district,* 8 miles south-southeast of present Point La Jolla (lat. 32°45' N, long. 117°12' W); the place is situated just south of Old Town. Named on La Jolla (1903) 15' quadrangle. Postal authorities established North San Diego post office at Old Town in 1870, discontinued it for a time in 1889, changed the name to Old San Diego in 1943, and moved it 1 mile northwest in 1972 (Salley, p. 160).

North San Gabriel [LOS ANGELES]: *locality,* 4.5 miles northwest of El Monte along Southern Pacific Railroad (lat. 34°07' N, long. 118°06' W); the place is north of San Gabriel. Named on Pasadena (1900) 15' quadrangle.

North Sherman Way [LOS ANGELES]: *locality,* 1 mile north of Van Nuys along Pacific Electric Railroad (lat. 34°12' N, long. 118°26'55" W). Named on Pacoima (1927) and Van Nuys (1926) 6' quadrangles.

North Wash [SAN DIEGO]: *stream,* flows 4.5 miles to Canebrake Wash 4.25 miles south-southeast of Agua Caliente Springs (lat. 32° 53'35" N, long. 116°16'20" W; near W line sec. 4, T 15 S, R 7 E). Named on Agua Caliente Springs (1959) 7.5' quadrangle.

Northwest Harbor [LOS ANGELES]: *embayment,* at the north end of San Clemente Island (lat. 33°01'55" N, long. 118°35' W). Named on San Clemente Island North (1943) 7.5' quadrangle.

North Whittier Heights [LOS ANGELES]: *district,* 5.25 miles south-southwest of Baldwin Park city hall (lat. 34°00'50" N, long. 117° 59'10" W). Named on Baldwin Park (1953) 7.5' quadrangle.

North Wilmington: see **Carson** [LOS ANGELES].

Norwalk [LOS ANGELES]: *city,* 4.5 miles south-southwest of Whittier city hall (lat. 33°54'55" N, long. 118°04'15" W). Named on Whittier (1965) 7.5' quadrangle. Postal authorities established Corvallis post office in 1875, and changed the name to Norwalk in 1877 (Frickstad, p. 72). The city incorporated in 1957. Postal authorities established Moyle post office 4.5 miles south of Norwalk post office in 1900 and discontinued it in 1903; the name was for Thomas Moyle, first postmaster (Salley, p. 148). They established Sunshine post office in present Norwalk 4.5 miles southwest of Whittier post office in 1944 and discontinued it in 1962; the name was for the location of the facility along Sunshine Avenue (Salley, p. 216).

Nude Wash [SAN DIEGO]: *stream,* flows 1.25 miles to San Felipe Creek 9.5 miles south-southeast of Borrego Springs (lat. 33°08'25" N, long. 116°17'15" W; at N line sec. 18, T 12 S, R 7 E). Named on Borrego Sink (1959) and Whale Peak (1959) 7.5' quadrangles.

Nuevo: see **Ramona** [SAN DIEGO].

Nuevo Canyon [VENTURA]: *canyon,* drained by a stream that flows 1.25 miles to Holser Canyon 3.25 miles east-northeast of Piru (lat. 34°26'15" N, long. 118°44'25" W; at N line sec. 14, T 4 N, R 18 W). Named on Val Verde (1952) 7.5' quadrangle.

Nutwood [ORANGE]: *locality,* 4.5 miles south-southeast of Buena Park along Southern Pacific Railroad (lat. 33°48'20" N, long. 117° 57'30" W). Named on Corona (1902) 30' quadrangle.

Nuvida Spring: see **Sweetwater Spring** [SAN DIEGO].

Nyland [VENTURA]: *town,* 3 miles northeast of Oxnard (lat. 34°13'30" N, long. 119°08'05" W). Named on Oxnard (1949) 7.5' quadrangle.

-O-

Oak Canyon [LOS ANGELES]:

(1) *canyon,* drained by a stream that flows 2.25 miles to Santa Felicia Canyon 13 miles west-northwest of Newhall (lat. 34°28'35" N, long. 118°43'05" W). Named on Val Verde (1952) 7.5' quadrangle.

(2) *canyon,* drained by a stream that flows 1.5 miles to San Gabriel River 8 miles northeast of Glendora city hall (lat. 34°13'45" N, long. 117°46'40" W). Named on Glendora (1953) 7.5' quadrangle.

Oak Canyon [SAN DIEGO]: *canyon,* drained by a stream that flows 4 miles to San Diego River 5.25 miles north-northwest of La Mesa (lat. 32°50'25" N, long. 117°02'35" W). Named on La Mesa (1967) and Poway (1967) 7.5' quadrangles.

Oak Canyon [VENTURA]:

(1) *canyon,* drained by a stream that flows less than 1 mile to Dry Canyon (1) 7 miles west-northwest of Santa Susana Pass (lat. 34° 18'25" N, long. 118°44'40" W; near NE cor. sec. 34, T 3 N, R 18 W). Named on Santa Susana (1951) 7.5' quadrangle.

(2) *canyon,* drained by a stream that flows 2.5 miles to Simi Valley (1) nearly 6 miles north-northeast of Thousand Oaks (lat. 34°14'30" N, long. 118°47' W; sec. 20, T 2 N, R 18 W). Named on Thousand Oaks (1952) 7.5' quadrangle.

Oak Canyon: see **Dry Canyon** [VENTURA] (1); **Necktie Canyon** [LOS ANGELES].

Oakdale Canyon [LOS ANGELES]:

(1) *canyon,* nearly 2 miles long, opens into Pine Canyon (1) 4 miles north-northwest of Burnt Peak (lat. 34°44'05" N, long. 118°36'10" W; sec. 32, T

8 N, R 16 W). Named on Burnt Peak (1958) and Liebre Mountain (1958) 7.5' quadrangles.

(2) *canyon,* 1.5 miles long, opens into the valley of South Fork Santa Clara River 1 mile north of downtown Newhall (lat. 34°24'05" N, long. 118°32'05" W). Named on Newhall (1952) 7.5' quadrangle.

Oak Creek [VENTURA]: *stream,* flows 1 mile to Cuyama River 9 miles northwest of Reyes Peak (lat. 34°43'40" N, long. 119°23'35" W). Named on Rancho Nuevo Creek (1943) 7.5' quadrangle.

Oak Flat [LOS ANGELES]: *area,* 3 miles north-northeast of Burnt Peak (lat. 34°43'15" N, long. 118°36'10" W; near SW cor. sec. 5, T 7 N, R 16 W). Named on Burnt Peak (1958) 7.5' quadrangle.

Oak Flat [ORANGE]: *area,* 1.5 miles south-southeast of Sierra Peak (lat. 33°49'40" N, long. 117°38'15" W; at NW cor. sec. 17, T 4 S, R 7 W). Named on Black Star Canyon (1967) 7.5' quadrangle.

Oak Flat [VENTURA]:

(1) *area,* 13 miles east-northeast of Wheeler Springs along Sespe Creek (lat. 34°33'35" N, long. 119°03'55" W; near N line sec. 3, T 5 N, R 21 W). Named on Topatopa Mountains (1943) 7.5' quadrangle.

(2) *area,* 5 miles north of Fillmore (lat. 34°28'20" N, long. 118°54'25" W). Named on Fillmore (1951) 7.5' quadrangle.

Oak Flat: see **Big Oak Flat** [LOS ANGELES]; **Oak Flats** [LOS ANGELES].

Oak Flats [LOS ANGELES]: *area,* 2.25 miles north of Whitaker Peak (lat. 34°36'15" N, long. 118°43'45" W; at and near SW cor. sec. 18, T 6 N, R 17 W). Named on Whitaker Peak (1958) 7.5' quadrangle. Los Angeles County (1935) map has the singular form "Oak Flat" for the name.

Oak Flats [SAN DIEGO]: *area,* 6 miles west-northwest of Mesa Grande (lat. 33°12'50" N, long. 116°52' W). Named on Mesa Grande (1948) 7.5' quadrangle.

Oak Flat Spring [LOS ANGELES]: *spring,* 2 miles north-northeast of Whitaker Peak at Camp Caula (lat. 34°35'55" N, long. 118°43'20" W; sec. 19, T 6 N, R 17 W); the spring is near the southeast end of Oak Flats. Named on Whitaker Peak (1958) 7.5' quadrangle.

Oak Grove [SAN DIEGO]: *locality,* 8.5 miles east-northeast of Boulder Hill (lat. 33°23'05" N, long. 117°47'20" W). Named on Aguanga (1954) 7.5' quadrangle, which shows Camp Wright historical marker located just northwest of Oak Grove, and Oak Grove stage station historical marker nearby. Postal authorities established Oak Grove post office in 1870, discontinued it for a time in 1887, changed the name to Oakgrove in 1894, moved it 1.25 miles southeast in 1895, and discontinued it in 1900 (Salley, p. 158). Oak Grove was a station on Butterfield Overland stage line, and was near the site of Camp Wright, which was built to guard the route between California and Arizona from 1861 until 1866 (Hoover, Rensch, and Rensch, p. 342).

Oak Grove: see **Camp Oak Grove** [LOS ANGELES].

Oakgrove Canyon [LOS ANGELES]: *canyon,* drained by a stream that flows 2 miles to Pine Canyon (1) nearly 4 miles north-northwest of Burnt Peak (lat. 34°44'05" N, long. 118°35'55" W; sec. 32, T 8 N, R 16 W). Named on Burnt Peak (1958) 7.5' quadrangle.

Oak Grove Valley [SAN DIEGO]: *valley,* 9 miles east-northeast of Boucher Hill (lat. 33°23'45" N, long. 116°46'45" W); Oak Grove is at the southwest corner of the valley. Named on Aguanga (1954) and Beauty Mountain (1960) 7.5' quadrangles.

Oak Hill [LOS ANGELES]: *locality,* 4.5 miles north-northeast of Point Dume (lat. 34°03'45" N, long. 118°47' W; sec. 20, T 1 S, R 18 W). Named on Solstice Canyon (1932) 6' quadrangle.

Oak Knoll [LOS ANGELES]: *district,* 8 miles northeast of Los Angeles city hall in Pasadena (lat. 34°07'25" N, long. 118°08'15" W). Named on Los Angeles (1953) 7.5' quadrangle.

Oak Lake [SAN DIEGO]: *lake,* 600 feet long, 7.25 miles southeast of Oceanside along Agua Hedionda Creek (lat. 33°08'35" N, long. 117°16'20" W). Named on San Luis Rey (1968) 7.5' quadrangle.

Oak Mountain: see **Mount Lowe** [LOS ANGELES] (1).

Oak Ridge [SAN DIEGO]: *ridge,* north-trending, 0.5 mile long, 3.5 miles south-southwest of San Felipe (lat. 33°08'45" N, long. 116° 36'45" W; near W line sec. 7, T 12 S, R 4 E). Named on Ranchita (1960) 7.5' quadrangle.

Oak Ridge [VENTURA]: *ridge,* generally west-trending, 16 miles long, center 5 miles southeast of Fillmore (lat. 34°21'20" N, long. 118°51' W). Named on Moorpark (1951), Piru (1952), Santa Susana (1951), Simi (1951), and Val Verde (1952) 7.5' quadrangles.

Oaks: see **The Oaks** [LOS ANGELES].

Oak Spring [LOS ANGELES]: *spring,* 3.5 miles north of Sunland (lat. 34°18'30" N, long. 118°19'30" W; at NE cor. sec. 34, T 3 N, R 14 W). Named on Sunland (1953) 7.5' quadrangle. Los Angeles County (1935) map has the plural form "Oak Springs" for the name.

Oak Spring [SAN DIEGO]: *spring,* 3.5 miles northeast of San Felipe (lat. 33°13'35" N, long. 116°32'35" W; near S line sec. 11, T 11 S, R 4 E). Named on Ranchita (1960) 7.5' quadrangle.

Oak Spring: see **Big Oak Spring** [LOS ANGELES]; **Oak Spring Canyon** [LOS ANGELES] (2).

Oak Spring Canyon [LOS ANGELES]:

(1) *canyon,* drained by a stream that flows nearly 5 miles to Santa Clara River 1.25 miles east-northeast of Solemint (lat. 34°25'30" N, long. 118°25' W; near SE cor. sec. 14, T 4 N, R 15 W). Named on Agua Dulce (1960) and Mint Canyon (1960) 7.5' quadrangles. Called Oak Springs Can. on Los Angeles County (1935) map, where the name follows a branch of present Oak Spring Canyon to the east (sec. 24, T 4 N, R 15 W, and sec. 19, T 4 N, R 14 W); the upper part of present Oak Spring Canyon has the name "Lost Canyon" on this map. Los Angeles County (1935) map also shows a feature called Rabbitt Canyon that opens into present Oak Spring Canyon from the south about 1.25 miles above the mouth of present Oak Spring Canyon (near SE cor. sec. 24, T 4 N, R 15 W), and a feature called Manzanita Canyon that opens into Solemint Canyon from the north opposite the mouth of present Oak Spring Canyon.

(2) *canyon,* drained by a stream that flows 2.25 miles to Little Tujunga Canyon 3.5 miles north-northwest of Sunland (lat. 34°18'20" N, long. 118°20'40" W; near NE cor. sec. 33, T 3 N, R 14 W). Named on Sunland (1953) 7.5' quadrangle. Los Angeles County (1935) map shows Oak Spring in the canyon.

Oak Springs: see **Oak Spring** [LOS ANGELES].

Oak Valley [SAN DIEGO]: *valley,* 5 miles southeast of Descanso (lat. 32°48'45" N, long. 116°32'35" W; sec. 2, T 16 S, R 4 E). Named on Descanso (1960) 7.5' quadrangle.

Oak Valley Creek [SAN DIEGO]: *stream,* flows 2.5 miles to Pine Valley Creek 4.5 miles southeast of Descanso (lat. 32°48'20" N, long. 116°34'15" W; sec. 4, T 16 S, R 4 E); a branch of the stream drains Oak Valley. Named on Descanso (1960) 7.5' quadrangle.

Oak View [VENTURA]: *town,* 4.5 miles southwest of the town of Ojai along Ventura River (lat. 34°23'50" N, long. 119°17'55" W). Named on Matilija (1952) 7.5' quadrangle. On Ventura (1904) 15' quadrangle, the name applies to a place along Southern Pacific Railroad. Postal authorities established Oak View post office in 1947; the name is from a real-estate promotion that was called Oak View Home Gardens (Salley, p. 158).

Oak Village [VENTURA]: *locality,* 3 miles west of Fillmore (lat. 34° 23'30" N, long. 118°57'40" W; near N line sec. 34, T 4 N, R 20 W). Named on Fillmore (1951) 7.5' quadrangle.

Oakwilde [LOS ANGELES]: *locality,* 7 miles north-northwest of Pasadena city hall along Arroyo Seco (lat. 34°14'40" N, long. 118° 10'55" W). Named on Pasadena (1953) 7.5' quadrangle. J.R. Phillips obtained a permit in 1911 to build a resort along Arroyo Seco at the mouth of Dark Canyon, and his resort became known as Camp Oak Wilde; a small tourist camp called Teddy's Outpost was situated 2 miles down Arroyo Seco below Camp Oak Wilde (Robinson, J.W., 1977, p. 113, 116).

Oakzanita Peak [SAN DIEGO]: *peak,* 4.5 miles south-southeast of Cuyamaca Peak (lat. 32°53'25" N, long. 116°13'40" W). Altitude 5054 feet. Named on Cuyamaca Peak (1960) 7.5' quadrangle. The coined name is from <u>oak</u> and man<u>zanita</u> vegetation at the place (Stein, p. 91).

Oakzanita Springs Campground [SAN DIEGO]: *locality,* 4.5 miles south-southeast of Cuyamaca Peak (lat. 32°53'05" N, long. 116°34'25" W); the place is less than 1 mile southwest of Oakzanita Peak. Named on Cuyamaca Peak (1960) 7.5' quadrangle.

Oasis Spring [SAN DIEGO]: *spring,* 2 miles west-northwest of Monument Peak (lat. 32°54'15" W, long. 116°27'15" W; sec. 34, T 14 S, R 5 E). Named on Monument Peak (1959) 7.5' quadrangle.

Oat Hills [SAN DIEGO]: *ridge,* generally northwest-trending, 3 miles long, 6.5 miles north of Escondido city hall (lat. 33°13'15" N, long. 117°06' W). Named on Valley Center (1968) 7.5' quadrangle.

Oat Mountain [LOS ANGELES]: *ridge,* west-northwest-trending, 5 miles long, 5 miles southwest of Newhall (lat. 34°19'40" N, long. 118°35'15" W). Named on Oat Mountain (1952) 7.5' quadrangle.

Oat Mountain [VENTURA]: *peak,* 3.25 miles north of Fillmore (lat. 34°26'55" N, long. 118°54'10" W; at NE cor. sec. 7, T 4 N, R 19 W). Altitude 3124 feet. Named on Fillmore (1951) 7.5' quadrangle.

Oban [LOS ANGELES]: *locality,* 5.5 miles north of Lancaster along Southern Pacific Railroad (lat. 34°46'25" N, long. 118°08'50" W; near W line sec. 22, T 8 N, R 12 W). Named on Rosamond (1973) 7.5' quadrangle. On Oban (1933) 6' quadrangle, the name applies to a place located nearly 0.5 mile farther north along the railroad—this place is called Oban Siding on Los Angeles County (1935) map, which shows a place called Waterdale situated about 2 miles east of Oban Siding (sec. 14, T 8 N, R 12 W).

Obed: see **Bell** [LOS ANGELES].

Oberg [LOS ANGELES]: *locality,* 5 miles northwest of Newhall along Southern Pacific Railroad (lat. 34°26' N, long. 118°35'30" W). Named on Saugus (1933) 6' quadrangle.

Observatory Peak: see **San Gabriel Peak** [LOS ANGELES].

Occidental Peak [LOS ANGELES]: *peak,* 1.5 miles west-northwest of Mount Wilson (lat. 34°14'05" N, long. 118°05' W). Altitude 5730 feet. Named on Mount Wilson (1953) 7.5' quadrangle. The feature first was called Precipicio Peak for its location above Precipicio Canyon (present Eaton Canyon); students from Occidental College built a trail to the top about 1915, and Forest Service officials named the peak for their school (Robinson, J.W., 1977, p. 155).

Ocean Beach [SAN DIEGO]: *district,* 5.25 miles west-northwest of downtown San Diego (lat. 32°44'35" N, long. 117°14'45" W). Named on La Jolla (1967) and Point Loma (1967) 7.5' quadrangles. Postal authorities established Ocean Beach post office in 1909 (Frickstad, p. 154).

Ocean Park [LOS ANGELES]: *district,* 0.5 mile southeast of Santa Monica city hall (lat. 34°00'10" N, long. 118°28'55" W). Named on Beverly Hills (1966) 7.5' quadrangle. Postal authorities established Ocean Park post office in 1899 (Salley, p. 159). Abbot Kinney and F.G. Ryan founded and named the place in 1892 (Gudde, 1949, p. 240).

Ocean Park Heights: see **Mar Vista** [LOS ANGELES].

Oceanside [SAN DIEGO]: *city,* 35 miles north-northwest of San Diego (lat. 33°11'45" N, long. 117°22'45" W); the city is situated beside the ocean. Named on Bonsall (1968), Morro Hill (1968), Oceanside (1968), San Luis Rey (1968), and San Marcos (1968) 7.5' quadrangles. Postal authorities established Oceanside post office in 1883 (Frickstad, p. 154), and the city incorporated in 1888.

Oceanside: see **South Oceanside** [SAN DIEGO].

Oceanside Harbor [SAN DIEGO]: *water feature,* 1 mile northwest of downtown Oceanside along the coast (lat. 33°12'25" N, long. 117° 23'35" W; mainly in sec. 22, T 11 S, R 5 W). Named on Oceanside (1968) 7.5' quadrangle.

Ocean View [ORANGE]: *locality,* 4 miles north of Huntington Beach civic center (lat. 33°42'55" N, long. 117°59'15" W; at NW cor. sec. 25, T 5 S, R 11 W). Named on Newport Beach (1965) 7.5' quadrangle.

Ocotillo: see **Ocotillo Wells** [SAN DIEGO].

Ocotillo Badlands [SAN DIEGO]: *area,* center 2.5 miles southeast of Ocotillo Wells (lat. 33°07'30" N, long. 116°06' W). Named on Borrego Mountain SE (1958) and Shell Reef (1959) 7.5' quadrangles.

Ocotillo Flat [SAN DIEGO]: *area,* 8 miles north-northwest of Borrego Springs in Coyote Canyon (2) (lat. 33°27' N, long. 116°24'30" W; mainly in sec. 25, T 9 S, R 5 E). Named on Borrego Palm Canyon (1959) 7.5' quadrangle.

Ocotillo Wells [SAN DIEGO]: *village,* 16 miles east-southeast of Borrego Springs (lat. 33°08'40" N, long. 116°07'55" W; on E line sec. 9, T 12 S, R 8 E). Named on Borrego Mountain (1960) 7.5' quadrangle. Called Ocotillo on Barrel Spring (1942) 15' quadrangle, but United States Board on Geographic Names (1962b, p. 20) rejected this name for the place.

O'Hara Canyon [VENTURA]: *canyon,* drained by a stream that flows nearly 4 miles to the valley of Santa Clara River 3 miles west of Santa Paula (lat. 34°20'40" N, long. 119°06'25" W). Named on Ojai (1952), Santa Paula (1951), and Saticoy (1951) 15' quadrangles. Members of the O'Hara family settled in the canyon in the 1860's; the feature first was called Bear Canyon (Ricard).

Ohjai Valley: see **Otay Valley** [SAN DIEGO].

Ojai [VENTURA]:

(1) *land grant,* in Ojai Valley and Upper Ojai Valley. Named on Matilija (1952), Ojai (1952), and Santa Paula Peak (1951) 7.5' quadrangles. Fernando Tico received 6 leagues in 1837 and claimed 17,717 acres patented in 1870 (Cowan, p. 54). The name is of Indian origin (Kroeber, p. 51).

(2) *town,* 12 miles north of Ventura (lat. 34°26'55" N, long. 119°14'35" W); the place is in Ojai Valley. Named on Matilija (1952) and Ojai (1952) 7.5' quadrangles. Postal authorities established Nordhoff post office in 1874 and changed the name to Ojai in 1917 (Frickstad, p. 218). The town incorporated in 1921. R.G. Surdam laid out the community in 1874 and named it for Charles Nordhoff, who wrote enthusiastically of Ojai Valley; the town was renamed for the valley in 1916 (Gudde, 1949, p. 241).

(3) *locality,* 3 miles west-southwest of downtown Ojai along Southern Pacific Railroad (lat. 34°25'35" N, long. 119°17'20" W). Named on Ventura (1904) 15' quadrangle.

Ojai Hot Sulphur Springs: see **Matilija Hot Springs** [VENTURA].

Ojai Valley [VENTURA]: *valley,* at and near the town of Ojai. Named on Matilija (1952) and Ojai (1952) 7.5' quadrangles.

Ojai Valley: see **Upper Ojai Valley** [VENTURA].

Ojala [VENTURA]: *locality,* 4 miles northwest of the town of Ojai at the head of Ventura River (lat. 34°29'05" N, long. 119°17'50" W; sec. 28, T 5 N, R 23 W). Named on Matilija (1952) 7.5' quadrangle.

Old Baldy: see **Mount San Antonio** [LOS ANGELES].

Old Baldy Peak: see **Mount San Antonio** [LOS ANGELES].

Old Boney: see **Boney Mountain** [VENTURA].

Old Camp [LOS ANGELES]: *locality,* 4 miles south-southeast of Pacifico Mountain along Chilao Creek (lat. 34°19'35" N, long. 118°00'15" W; near S line sec. 23, T 3 N, R 11 W). Named on Chilao Flat (1959) 7.5' quadrangle.

Old Camp [ORANGE]: *locality,* nearly 1.5 miles southeast of Santiago Peak (lat. 33°41'50" N, long. 117°33' W; near NW cor. sec. 31, T 5 S, R 6 W). Named on Santiago Peak (1954) 7.5' quadrangle.

Old George Mountain [SAN DIEGO]: *peak,* 3 miles south-southeast of Manzanita (lat. 32°37'55" N, long. 116°15'40" W; near E line sec. 4, T 18 S, R 7 E). Named on Live Oak Springs (1959) 7.5' quadrangle.

Old Landing: see **Newport Beach** [ORANGE] (2).

Old Man Canyon [VENTURA]: *canyon,* drained by a stream that flows 3.25 miles to Matilija Creek 6.5 miles west of Wheeler Springs (lat. 34°31'05" N, long. 119°24'15" W; sec. 16, T 5 N, R 24 W); the canyon heads at Old Man Mountain, which is in Santa Barbara County. Named on Old Man Mountain (1943) 7.5' quadrangle.

Old Newport: see **Greenville** [ORANGE].

Old Palmdale: see **Palmdale** [LOS ANGELES].

Old Point Comfort [LOS ANGELES]: *locality,* 2.25 miles south-southeast of Valyermo along Big Rock Creek (lat. 34°24'55" N, long. 117°50' W; at W line sec. 21, T 4 N, R 9 W). Named on Valyermo (1958) 7.5' quadrangle.

Old Saddleback: see **Santiago Peak** [ORANGE].

Old San Diego: see **North San Diego** [SAN DIEGO].

Old San Gabriel River: see **Rio Hondo**, under **San Gabriel River** [LOS ANGELES-ORANGE].

Old Santa Ana: see **Olive** [ORANGE].

Old Topanga Canyon [LOS ANGELES]: *canyon,* drained by a stream that flows 3.5 miles to Topanga Canyon 8.5 miles northwest of Santa Monica city hall (lat. 34°05'25" N, long. 118°36'15" W; at SW cor. sec. 7, T 1 S, R 16 W). Named on Malibu Beach (1950, photorevised 1981) 7.5' quadrangle. Called Topanga Canyon on Malibu Beach (1951) 7.5' quadrangle, but United States Board on Geographic Names (1960c, p. 18) rejected this name for the feature.

Old Town [SAN DIEGO]: *district,* 3.5 miles north-northwest of downtown San Diego (lat. 32°45'15" N, long. 117°11'45" W). Named on La Jolla (1967) 7.5' quadrangle. San Diego began as a village at present Old Town; the village was situated at the foot of a feature called Presidio Hill, named for the presidio that Portola established on the elevation to protect the mission that Junipero Serra founded there in 1769 (Frazer, p. 30; Hoover, Rensch, and Rensch, p. 330, 335). Earthworks thrown up by the Mexicans in 1838 on Presidio Hill were improved by Commodore Stockton in 1846, and unofficially were called Fort Stockton, Fort San Diego, and Fort DuPont—the name DuPont was for Captain Samuel F. DuPont of the sloop-of-war *Cyane* (Hoover, Rensch, and Rensch, p. 332; Whiting and Whiting, p. 71, 80). After the Americans realized that present Old Town was unsuitable for a seaport, it was superceded by New San Diego, located at present downtown San Diego along San Diego Bay (Hoover, Rensch, and Rensch, p. 336).

Old Trading Post: see **The Old Trading Post**, under **Little Santa Anita Canyon** [LOS ANGELES].

Ole: see **Camp Ole Station** [SAN DIEGO].

Oleo [ORANGE]: *locality,* 1 mile east of downtown Brea along Pacific Electric Railroad (lat. 33°55'15" N, long. 117°52'40" W). Named on Coyote Hills (1935) 7.5' quadrangle.

Olga [LOS ANGELES]: *locality,* 6 miles northeast of Los Angeles city hall along Atchison, Topeka and Santa Fe Railroad (lat. 34°06'45" N, long. 118°09'55" W). Named on Los Angeles (1953) 7.5' quadrangle.

Olinda [ORANGE]: *locality,* 2.5 miles northwest of Yorba Linda near the mouth of Carbon Canyon (lat. 33°55'20" N, long. 117°50'10" W; on E line sec. 8, T 3 S, R 9 W). Named on Yorba Linda (1950) 7.5' quadrangle. Goodyear (1888a, p. 70) called the place Petrolia. It was built for oil workers and was a busy community in the 1920's, but it was gone by the 1960's (Carpenter, p. 94).

Olive [ORANGE]: *village,* 3.5 miles north of Orange city hall (lat. 33°50'15" N, long. 117°50'40" W). Named on Orange (1964) 7.5' quadrangle. Postal authorities established Olive post office in 1887 and discontinued it for a time in 1900 (Frickstad, p. 117). The Yorba and Peralta families built adobe homes on Santiago de Santa Ana grant at the place, and this cluster of buildings was called Santa Ana, or Santa Ana Abajo—*abajo* means "lower" in Spanish—to distinguish it from Santa Ana Arriba—*arriba* means "upper" in Spanish—which was located on Bernardo Yorba's Cañon de Santa Ana grant farther up Santa Ana River; after the present city of Santa Ana was laid out in 1868, present Olive became known as Old Santa Ana (Hoover, Rensch, and Rensch, p. 261-262; Meadows, p. 107). The name "Olive" came from olive trees on Burruel Point, and was applied to a school district before it was applied to the village (Meadows, p. 107-108). The community was called Olive Heights when it was laid out in 1880, but the name "Olive" was used for the post office (Gudde, 1949, p. 242).

Olivehain [SAN DIEGO]: *locality,* 2.5 miles northwest of Rancho Santa Fe (lat. 33°02'45" N, long. 117°14' W). Named on Rancho Santa Fe (1968) 7.5' quadrangle. Postal authorities established Olivehain post office in 1887, discontinued it in 1909, and reestablished it in 1969 (Salley, p. 160). The place was founded in 1884 as a German colony (Hoover, Rensch, and Rensch, p. 344).

Olive Heights: see **Olive** [ORANGE].

Olive Hill [LOS ANGELES]: *hill,* 4.25 miles northwest of Los Angeles city hall (lat. 34°06' N, long. 118°17'35" W; sec. 12, T 1 S, R 14 W). Named on Hollywood (1953) 7.5' quadrangle.

Olive Hills: see **Peralta Hills** [ORANGE] (1).

Olive Hills Reservoir [ORANGE]: *lake,* 650 feet long, 3.5 miles north-northeast of Orange city hall (lat. 33°50'05" N, long. 117°49'20" W). Named on Orange (1964) 7.5' quadrangle.

Oliver Canyon [LOS ANGELES]: *canyon*, drained by a stream that flows less than 1 mile to Tujunga Valley 2.5 miles west-northwest of Sunland (lat. 34°16'30" N, long. 118°20'55" W; sec. 9, T 2 N, R 14 W). Named on Sunland (1953) 7.5' quadrangle.

Olive View [LOS ANGELES]: *locality*, 3 miles north of downtown San Fernando (lat. 34°19'30" N, long. 118°26'40" W). Named on San Fernando (1966) 7.5' quadrangle. Postal authorities established Olive View post office in 1923 and discontinued it in 1973; the name was from olive orchards present below the place.(Salley, p. 161).

Olive Wood [LOS ANGELES]: *locality*, less than 0.5 mile east-northeast of present Pasadena city hall along Atchison, Topeka and Santa Fe Railroad (lat. 34°09' N, long. 118°08'10" W). Named on Pasadena (1900) 15' quadrangle.

Olivewood [SAN DIEGO]: *locality*, 1.25 miles southeast of present National City civic center (lat. 32°39'40" N, long. 117°05'30" W). Named on San Diego (1904) 15' quadrangle.

Olla Wash [SAN DIEGO]: *dry wash*, extends for nearly 2 miles to Fish Creek Wash 11 miles north of Sweeney Pass (lat. 32°59'15" N, long. 116°13'10" W; sec. 1, T 14 S, R 7 E). Named on Arroyo Tapiado (1959) and Harper Canyon (1959) 7.5' quadrangles.

Olympus: see **Mount Olympus** [SAN DIEGO].

Omaha Heights [LOS ANGELES]: *district*, 3.5 miles northeast of present Los Angeles city hall (lat. 34°04'50" N, long. 118°11'25" W). Named on Alhambra (1926) 6' quadrangle.

O'Neal Canyon [SAN DIEGO]: *canyon*, drained by a stream that flows 6 miles to Otay River 5.5 miles west of Otay Mesa (lat. 32° 36' N, long. 116°56'30" W). Named on Otay Mesa (1955) and Otay Mountain (1972) 7.5' quadrangles. The name recalls an early homesteader in the neighborhood (Stein, p. 93).

O'Neill Lake [SAN DIEGO]: *lake*, 4400 feet long, 5.5 miles southwest of Fallbrook (lat. 33°19'50" N, long. 117°19'15" W). Named on Morro Hill (1968) 7.5' quadrangle. Called O'Neil Lake on Margarita Peak (1944) 15' quadrangle.

Oneonta [SAN DIEGO]: *locality*, 1 mile southeast of present Imperial Beach civic center (lat. 32°34' N, long. 117°06'15" W; near NE cor. sec. 32, T 18 S, R 2 W). Named on San Diego (1904) 15' quadrangle. Postal authorities established Oneonta post office in 1888 and discontinued it in 1900; the name is from a place in New York State (Salley, p. 161). They established Florentine post office 4.5 miles northwest of Oneonta in 1890 and discontinued it in 1892 (Salley, p. 76).

Oneonta Park [LOS ANGELES]: *district*, 6 miles east-northeast of present Los Angeles city hall (lat. 34°06'15" N, long. 118°09'20" W). Named on Altadena (1928) 6' quadrangle. The name is for Oneonta, New York, birthplace of Henry E. Huntington (Gudde, 1949, p. 243).

Oneonta Slough [SAN DIEGO]: *water feature*, 1 mile southwest of Imperial Beach civic center near the coast (lat. 32°33'55" N, long. 117°07'45" W). Named on Imperial Beach (1967) 7.5' quadrangle.

One Thousand Palms Canyon: see **Salvador Canyon** [SAN DIEGO].

Onlauf Canyon: see **Anlauf Canyon** [VENTURA].

Opids Camp: see **Camp Hi-Hill** [LOS ANGELES].

Orange [ORANGE]: *city*, 6 miles north-northwest of Santa Ana (lat. 33°47'15" N, long. 117°51' W). Named on Anaheim (1965) and Orange (1964) 7.5' quadrangles. Postal authorities established Orange post office in 1873 (Frickstad, p. 117), and the city incorporated in 1888. Chapman and Glassell laid out the community in 1872 and called it Richland; postal authorities refused this name for a post office, and Glassell substituted the name "Orange" from his native county in Virginia (Gudde, 1949, p. 244; Hanna, p. 219). Anaheim (1898) 15' quadrangle shows a place called Orange Station located along Southern Pacific Railroad 1.5 miles west-southwest of downtown Orange; Corona (1902) 30' quadrangle has the name "Orange" at the site. A Pacific Electric Railroad station called Hargraves was situated less than 1 mile southwest of present Orange city hall (Meadows, p. 69).

Orange: see **Port Orange**, under **Newport Beach** [ORANGE] (2); **West Orange,** under **Santa Ana** [ORANGE].

Orange Avenue Junction [LOS ANGELES]: *locality*, 1 mile east- northeast of Baldwin Park city hall along Southern Pacific Railroad (lat. 34°05'30" N, long. 117°56'30" W). Named on Baldwin Park (1966) 7.5' quadrangle.

Orange Park Acres [ORANGE]: *settlement*, 4 miles east-northeast of Orange city hall (lat. 33°48'05" N, long. 117°46'50" W). Named on Orange (1964) 7.5' quadrangle. E.F. Mead developed the place in 1928 (Meadows, p. 108).

Orange Station: see **Orange** [ORANGE].

Orangethorpe: see **City of Orangethorpe**, under **Placentia** [ORANGE].

Orasco Ridge [SAN DIEGO]: *ridge*, generally south-trending, 4 miles long, 4.5 miles east-northeast of San Pasqual (lat. 33°07' N, long. 116°52'45" W). Named on Rodriguez Mountain (1948) and San Pasqual (1954) 7.5' quadrangles.

Orchard Camp [LOS ANGELES]: *locality*, nearly 2 miles south-southeast of Mount Wilson (1) in Little Santa Anita Canyon (lat. 34°11'55" N, long. 118°03'05" W; sec. 5, T 1 N, R 11 W). Named on Mount Wilson (1953) 7.5' quadrangle. George Islip planted cherry, apple, pear, and plum trees at the place, which came to be called Orchard Camp (Robinson, J.W., 1977, p. 21).

Orcutt: see **Grantville** [SAN DIEGO].

Orcutt Canyon [VENTURA]: *canyon*, drained by a stream that flows 4.25 miles to the valley of Santa Clara River 2 miles northeast of Santa Paula (lat. 34°22'35" N, long. 119°02'15" W; sec. 1, T 3 N, R 21 W). Named on Santa Paula Peak (1951) 7.5' quadrangle. The name commemorates John Hall Orcutt, a pioneer of Santa Paula (Ricard).

Oriflamme Canyon [SAN DIEGO]: *canyon*, drained by a stream that flows 7.25 miles to the canyon of Vallecito Wash 8 miles east-southeast of Julian (lat. 33°01' N, long. 116°29' W; near W line sec. 28, T 13 S, R 5 E). Named on Cuyamaca Peak (1960), Earthquake Valley (1959), Julian (1960), and Monument Peak (1959) 7.5' quadrangles. United States Board on Geographic Names (1961b, p. 11) rejected the name "Oroflamme Canyon" for the feature. Ramona (1903) 30' quadrangle has the name "Oriflamme Creek" for the stream in the canyon; United States Board on Geographic Names (1961b, p. 11) approved this name for the stream, and rejected the name "Oroflamme Creek" for it. The name is from Oriflamme gold mine (Gudde, 1975, p. 255).

Oriflamme Creek: see **Oriflamme Canyon** [SAN DIEGO].

Oriflamme Mountain [SAN DIEGO]: *ridge*, southwest- to south-southeast-trending, 3.5 miles long, 8 miles north-northwest of Monument Peak (lat. 32°59'30" N, long. 116°29'50" W). Named on Earthquake Valley (1959), Julian (1960), and Monument Peak (1959) 7.5' quadrangles. Present Granite Mountain is called Oriflamme Mountain on Borrego (1939) 15' quadrangle. United States Board on Geographic Names (1961b, p. 11) rejected the names "Oriflamme Mountains" and "Oroflamme Mountains" for the ridge.

Orinoco Creek [SAN DIEGO]: *stream*, flows 3.5 miles to Temescal Creek (2) 3.5 miles south of Santa Ysabel (lat. 33°03'20" N, long. 116°39'40" W; sec. 10, T 13 S, R 3 E). Named on Julian (1960) and Santa Ysabel (1960) 7.5' quadrangles.

Orizaba: see **Mount Orizaba** [LOS ANGELES].

Ormond Beach [VENTURA]: *beach*, 4 miles south of Oxnard along the coast (lat. 34°08'15" N, long. 119°11' W). Named on Oxnard (1949) 7.5' quadrangle.

Oro Fino Canyon [LOS ANGELES]: *canyon*, 1.5 miles long, 2 miles east-northeast of Newhall (lat. 34°23'55" N, long. 118°30' W). Named on Mint Canyon (1960) and Newhall (1952) 7.5' quadrangles.

Oroflamme Canyon: see **Oriflamme Canyon** [SAN DIEGO].

Oroflamme Creek: see **Oriflamme Creek**, under **Oriflamme Canyon** [SAN DIEGO].

Oroflamme Mountains: see **Oriflamme Mountain** [SAN DIEGO].

Orr Spring Canyon [LOS ANGELES]: *canyon*, drained by a stream that flows 0.5 mile to Pine Canyon (3) 2 miles west-northwest of the village of Lake Hughes (lat. 34°41'05" N, long. 118°28'20" W; sec. 21, T 7 N, R 15 W). Named on Lake Hughes (1957) 7.5' quadrangle.

Ortega Hill [VENTURA]: *peak*, nearly 6 miles northwest of Wheeler Springs (lat. 34°34'25" N, long. 119°21'15" W; at N line sec. 31, T 6 N, R 23 W). Named on Wheeler Springs (1943) 7.5' quadrangle.

Ortonville [VENTURA]: *village*, 3 miles north of Ventura along Ventura River (lat. 34°19'15" N, long. 119°17'25" W). Named on Ventura (1951) 7.5' quadrangle. The name recalls Robert Orton, a miller at Ventura flour mill; a railroad siding at the place served the mill (Ricard).

Osgood: see **Bonsall** [SAN DIEGO].

Osito Canyon [LOS ANGELES]: *canyon*, drained by a stream that flows 3.5 miles to Piru Creek 3 miles north-northwest of Whitaker Peak at Frenchman Flat (lat. 34°36'55" N, long. 118°44'40" W; near NW cor. sec. 13, T 6 N, R 18 W). Named on Liebre Mountain (1958) and Whitaker Peak (1958) 7.5' quadrangles.

Oso Canyon [LOS ANGELES]: *canyon*, drained by a stream that heads just inside Kern County and flows 8 miles, mainly in Los Angeles County, to Los Angeles-Kern County line 8 miles east of Gorman (lat. 34°49'05" N, long. 118°42'40" W; near NE cor. sec. 6, T 8 N, R 17 W). Named on La Liebra Ranch (1965) and Lebec (1958) 7.5' quadrangles. The stream in the canyon is called Little Cottonwood Creek on Johnson's (1911) map. United States Board on Geographic Names (1967a, p. 4) rejected the name "Canada de la Oasis" for the canyon.

Oso Creek [ORANGE]: *stream*, flows 12.5 miles to Arroyo Trabuco 1.5 miles north-northwest of San Juan Capistrano (lat. 33°31'10" N, long. 117°40'15" W; sec. 36, T 7 S, R 8 W). Named on El Toro (1968), San Juan Capistrano (1968), and Santiago Peak (1954) 7.5' quadrangles. The name "Los Osos Valley" applies to the valley of the upper part of Oso Creek on some early maps (Meadows, p. 80).

Osuna Valley [SAN DIEGO]: *valley*, 1 mile south-southeast of the center of Rancho Santa Fe along San Dieguito River (lat. 33°00'30" N, long. 117°11'50" W). Named on Rancho Santa Fe (1968) 7.5' quadrangle.

Otay [SAN DIEGO]:

(1) *land grant*, around Lower Otay Reservoir. Named on Jamul Mountains (1955) and Otay Mesa (1955) 7.5' quadrangles. Jose Antonio Estudillo received 1 league in 1829 and 1846; his widow, Victoria Dominguez, and others claimed 4437 acres patented in 1872 (Cowan, p. 41-42; Cowan gave the alternate name "Janal" for the grant).

(2) *land grant*, east of Otay (3). Named on Imperial Beach (1967), Jamul Mountains (1955), and Otay Mesa (1955) 7.5' quadrangles. Jose Antonio Estudillo received 2 leagues in 1829 and 1846; Magdalena Estudillo claimed 6658 acres patented in 1872 (Cowan, p. 55).

(3) *locality*, 3.25 miles east-northeast of Imperial Beach civic center (lat. 32°35'45" N, long. 117°03'50" W); the place is in Otay Valley. Named on Imperial Beach (1967) 7.5' quadrangle. Postal authorities established Otay post office in 1870, discontinued it in 1872, reestablished it in 1887, discontinued it in 1925, and reestablished it in 1968 (Salley, p. 163). They established Siempreviva post office 10 miles southeast of Otay post office in 1889 and moved it 3.25 miles west in 1892, when they changed the name to Lemon (Salley, p. 204).

Otay Lake: see **Upper Otay Lake**, under **Upper Otay Reservoir** [SAN DIEGO].

Otay Mesa [SAN DIEGO]: *area*, east of San Ysidro (2) (lat. 32° 34' N, long. 116°59' W); the feature is south of Otay Valley. Named on Imperial Beach (1967) and Otay Mesa (1955) 7.5' quadrangles.

Otay Mountain [SAN DIEGO]: *peak*, 8.5 miles south of Jamul (lat. 32°35'40" N, long. 116°50'40" W). Altitude 3566 feet. Named on Otay Mountain (1972) 7.5' quadrangle.

Otay Reservoir: see **Lower Otay Reservoir** [SAN DIEGO]; **Upper Otay Reservoir** [SAN DIEGO].

Otay River [SAN DIEGO]: *stream* and *dry wash*, extends for 13 miles from Lower Otay Reservoir to the south end of San Diego Bay 1.5 miles north of Imperial Beach civic center (lat. 32°36' N, long. 117°06'55" W). Named on Imperial Beach (1967) and Otay Mesa (1955) 7.5' quadrangles.

Otay Valley [SAN DIEGO]: *valley*, along Otay River, which extends for 13 miles to the south end of San Diego Bay 1.5 miles north of Imperial Beach civic center (lat. 32°36' N, long. 117°06'55" W). Named on Imperial Beach (1967) and Otay Mesa (1955) 7.5' quadrangles. United States Board on Geographic Names (1933, p. 576) rejected the name "Ohjai Valley" for the feature.

Otterbein [LOS ANGELES]: *locality*, 5.5 miles northeast of La Habra [ORANGE] (lat. 33°59'45" N, long. 117°53' W). Named on La Habra (1952) 7.5' quadrangle. Bishop William M. Bell gave the name in 1911 to a settlement for retired ministers of the Church of the United Brethern in Christ; Philip W. Otterbein founded the church (Gudde, 1949, p. 247).

Overlook [SAN DIEGO]: *locality*, 7 miles southeast of Point La Jolla (lat. 32°46'10" N, long. 117°11'55" W). Named on La Jolla (1943) 7.5' quadrangle.

Owens: see **Bob Owens Canyon** [SAN DIEGO].

Owensmouth: see **Canoga Park** [LOS ANGELES].

Owl Canyon: see **Necktie Canyon** [LOS ANGELES].

Oxnard [VENTURA]: *city*, 8 miles southeast of Ventura (lat. 34°11'50" N, long. 119°10'45" W). Named on Oxnard (1949) 7.5' quadrangle. Postal authorities established Oxnard post office in 1898 (Frickstad, p. 218), and the city incorporated in 1903. The name is for Henry T. Oxnard, who started a sugar-beet refinery at the place in 1897 (Gudde, 1949, p. 247). California Division of Highways' (1934) map shows a place called McGrath located 4 miles west-northwest of Oxnard at the end of a railroad spur, a place called Todd located 3 miles east of Oxnard along the railroad, and a place called Naumann located 4.5 miles east-southeast of Oxnard along the railroad.

Oyster Shell Wash [SAN DIEGO]: *stream* and *dry wash*, extends for nearly 2 miles to North Fork Fish Creek Wash 11.5 miles north-northeast of Sweeney Pass (lat. 32°59'35" N, long. 116°07'35" W). Named on Arroyo Tapiado (1959) and Harper Canyon (1959) 7.5' quadrangles.

Ozena [VENTURA]: *locality*, 5.5 miles northwest of Reyes Peak along Cuyama River at the mouth of Boulder Canyon (lat. 34°41'55" N, long. 119°21' W; at E line sec. 19, T 7 N, R 23 W). Named on Mount Pinos (1903) 30' quadrangle. Postal authorities established Ozena post office in 1890, moved it 3 miles south in 1901, moved it 1 mile east in 1904, moved it 3 miles east in 1909, and discontinued it in 1921 (Salley, p. 164). California Mining Bureau's (1917a) map shows a place called Nedo located about 7 miles northwest of Ozena on the southwest side of Cuyama River near Ventura-Santa Barbara County line. Postal authorities established Nedo post office in 1915 and discontinued it in 1918 (Frickstad, p. 218).

- P -

Pacific Beach [SAN DIEGO]:

(1) *district*, 3.5 miles south-southeast of Point La Jolla in San Diego (lat. 32°48'20" N, long. 117°15' W). Named on La Jolla (1967) 7.5' quadrangle. Postal authorities established Pacific Beach post office in 1888 (Salley, p. 164).

(2) *locality*, 4.5 miles southeast of Point La Jolla along Atchison, Topeka and Santa Fe Railroad (lat. 32°48'30" N, long. 117°12'55" W); the place is east of Pacific Beach district. Named on La Jolla (1967) 7.5' quadrangle. Called Pacific Beach Siding on La Jolla (1953) 7.5' quadrangle.

Pacific City: see **Huntington Beach** [ORANGE].

Pacifico Campground: see **Lower Pacifico Campground** [LOS ANGELES]; **Upper Pacifico Campground** [LOS ANGELES].

Pacific Cove: see **North Cove** [SAN DIEGO].

Pacific Electric Island: see **Lido Isle** [ORANGE].

Pacific Palisades: see **Corona del Mar** [ORANGE].

Pacific Passage [SAN DIEGO]: *channel*, 6.5 miles south-southeast of Point La Jolla in Mission Bay between Fiesta Island and the mainland (lat. 32°46'30" N, long. 117°12'40" W). Named on La Jolla (1967) 7.5' quadrangle. United States Board on Geographic Names (1969b, p. 5) rejected the name "Marina Passage" for the feature.

Pacoima Canyon [LOS ANGELES]: *canyon*, drained by a stream that flows 20 miles to lowlands 3.5 miles north-northeast of downtown San Fernando (lat. 34°19'40" N, long. 118°24'10" W; near S line sec. 24, T 3 N, R 15 W). Named on Acton (1959), Agua Dulce (1960), Condor Peak (1959), San Fernando (1953), and Sunland (1953) 7.5' quadrangles. San Fernando (1900) 15' quadrangle shows Pacoima Creek in the canyon. Marcou (p. 160) gave the name "Pacoña Cañon" as an alternate. North Fork branches northeast 8 miles north-northeast of Sunland; it is 2 miles long and is named on Acton (1959) and Agua Dulce (1960) 7.5' quadrangles. South Fork branches southeast 7.25 miles north of Sunland; it is 2.5 miles long and in named on Sunland (1953) 7.5' quadrangle.

Pacoima Creek: see **Pacoima Canyon** [LOS ANGELES].

Pacoima Reservoir [LOS ANGELES]: *lake*, behind a dam 4.25 miles north-northeast of downtown San Fernando (lat. 34°20'05" N, long. 118°23'45" W; near NW cor. sec. 19, T 3 N, R 14 W); the lake is in Pacoima Canyon. Named on San Fernando (1966) 7.5' quadrangle.

Pacoima Wash [LOS ANGELES]: *stream* and *dry wash*, extends for 9.5 miles from the mouth of Pacoima Canyon to end in central Van Nuys (lat. 34°11'50" N, long. 118°26'45" W). Named on San Fernando (1953) and Van Nuys (1966) 7.5' quadrangles.

Pacoña Cañon: see **Pacoima Canyon** [LOS ANGELES].

Padre Barona Creek [SAN DIEGO]: *stream*, flows 6.25 miles to San Vicente Reservoir 5.25 miles north-northeast of Lakeside (lat. 32° 55'55" N, long. 116°53'40" W; near S line sec. 20, T 14 S, R 1 E); the stream is on Cañada de San Vicente y Mesa del Padre Barona grant. Named on El Cajon Mountain (1955) and San Vicente Reservoir (1955) 7.5' quadrangles.

Padre Barona Valley: see **Barona Valley** [SAN DIEGO].

Padre Juan Canyon [VENTURA]: *canyon*, drained by a stream that flows 3.5 miles to the sea at Pitas Point (lat. 34°19'10" N, long. 119°23'25" W; near SW cor. sec. 22, T 3 N, R 24 W). Named on Pitas Point (1950) and Ventura (1951) 7.5' quadrangles. The name commemorates Juan Comapla, priest at San Buenavenura mission from 1861 until 1877, who had a small ranch in the canyon (Ricard).

Paguay Canyon: see **Los Peñasquitos Canyon** [SAN DIEGO].

Paine Bottom [SAN DIEGO]: *canyon*, about 1 mile long, 4.5 miles south-southeast of Santa Ysabel (lat. 33°02'40" N, long. 116°39'10" W; near E line sec. 15, T 13 S, R 3 E). Named on Santa Ysabel (1960) 7.5' quadrangle.

Painter Lagoon [LOS ANGELES]: *lake*, nearly 1 mile long, 2 miles south-southwest of present Whittier city hall (lat. 33°56'40" N, long. 118°02'30" W). Named on Whittier (1949) 7.5' quadrangle. Whittier (1965) 7.5' quadrangle shows a drain through the place.

Painters [LOS ANGELES]: *locality*, 2 miles north-northwest of present Pasadena city hall along Los Angeles Terminal Railroad (lat. 34°10'25" N, long. 118°09'40" W). Named on Pasadena (1900) 15' quadrangle.

Pajarito: see **Camp Pajarito** [LOS ANGELES].

Pala [SAN DIEGO]: *town*, 10 miles east of Fallbrook (lat. 33°21'55" N, long. 117°04'30" W; sec. 27, T 9 S, R 2 W). Named on Pala (1968) 7.5' quadrangle. Postal authorities established Pala post office in 1875 (Frickstad, p. 154). The name is of Indian origin (Kroeber, p. 53). Postal authorities established Aqua Tibia post office 4 miles south of Pala at some warm sulphur springs in 1884, changed the name to Agua Tibia in 1886, and discontinued it in 1888 (Salley, p. 2). They established Cota post office 8 miles southeast of Agua Tibia post office in 1886 and discontinued it in 1890 (Salley, p. 51). United States Board on Geographic Names (1991, p. 3) approved the name "Bubble-up Creek" for a stream that flows 3 miles to disappear 1 mile south of Pala in the valley of San Luis Rey River (lat. 33°21'07" N, long. 117°04'25" W; sec. 34, T 9 S, R 2 W).

Pala Canyon: see **Pala Creek** [SAN DIEGO].

Pala Creek [SAN DIEGO]: *stream*, flows 7.25 miles to the valley of San Luis Rey River at Pala (lat. 33°21'55" N, long. 117°04'45" W; sec. 27, T 9 S, R 2 W). Named on Pala (1968) and Pechanga (1968) 7.5' quadrangles. Jahns and Wright's (1951a) map has the name "Pala Can." for the canyon of present Pala Creek.

Pala Mesa [SAN DIEGO]: *village*, 6 miles east-southeast of Fallbrook (lat. 33°19'55" N, long. 117°09'45" W). Named on Bonsall (1968) 7.5'

quadrangle.

Pala Mountain [SAN DIEGO]: *ridge,* northwest-trending, 3.5 miles long, 2.5 miles southeast of Pala (lat. 33°20'25" N, long. 117°02'40" W). Named on Pala (1968) 7.5' quadrangle. On Temecula (1945) 15' quadrangle, the name applies to the high point on the ridge.

Palisades [LOS ANGELES]: *escarpment,* west-northwest-trending, 3.25 miles long, center 2.5 miles south-southwest of Avalon on the south side of Santa Catalina Island (lat. 33°18'55" N, long. 118°21'15" W). Named on Santa Catalina East (1950) 7.5' quadrangle.

Palisades Beach [LOS ANGELES]: *beach,* 1.25 miles west-northwest of present Santa Monica city hall along the coast (lat. 34°01'20" N, long. 118°30'35" W). Named on Topanga Canyon (1928) 6' quadrangle.

Palisades del Rey: see **Playa del Rey** [LOS ANGELES].

Palisades Reservoir [ORANGE]: *lake,* 650 feet long, 2.5 miles south-southeast of San Juan Capistrano (lat. 33°27'55" N, long. 117°39' W; sec. 19, T 8 S, R 7 W). Named on Dana Point (1968) 7.5' quadrangle.

Pallett [LOS ANGELES]: *locality,* 2.5 miles west-northwest of present Valyermo (lat. 34°27'05" N, long. 117°53'50" W; near N line sec. 11, T 4 N, R 10 W); the place is along Pallett Creek. Named on Rock Creek (1903) 15' quadrangle.

Pallett Creek [LOS ANGELES]: *stream,* flows nearly 7 miles to Big Rock Creek 1.25 miles north-northwest of Valyermo (lat. 34°27'40" N, long. 117°51'50" W; sec. 6, T 4 N, R 9 W). Named on Juniper Hills (1959) and Valyermo (1958) 7.5' quadrangles.

Pallett Mountain [LOS ANGELES]: *peak,* 4.5 miles south-southwest of Valyermo (lat. 34°23'10" N, long. 117°53'05" W; near SW cor. sec. 36, T 4 N, R 10 W); the peak is near the head of Pallett Creek. Named on Juniper Hills (1959) 7.5' quadrangle.

Palma: see **Palms** [LOS ANGELES].

Palma Plain: see **Antelope Valley** [LOS ANGELES].

Palmas: see **Palms** [LOS ANGELES].

Palm Avenue: see **Palm City** [SAN DIEGO].

Palm Canyon: see **Borrego Palm Canyon** [SAN DIEGO].

Palm Canyon Camp Grounds [SAN DIEGO]: *locality,* 2.5 miles west-northwest of present Borrego Springs (lat. 33°16'15" N, long. 116°25' W); the place is at the mouth of Palm Canyon (present Borrego Palm Canyon). Named on Clark Lake (1944) 15' quadrangle.

Palm Canyon Wash [SAN DIEGO]: *stream,* flows 5 miles to Imperial County 9 miles north-northeast of Jacumba (lat. 32°43'55" N, long. 116°06'10" W; at E line sec. 36, T 16 S, R 8 E). Named on In-Ko-Pah Gorge (1959) and Jacumba (1959) 7.5' quadrangles.

Palm City [SAN DIEGO]: *district,* 2 miles east-northeast of Imperial Beach civic center in San Diego (lat. 32°35' N, long. 117°05' W). Named on Imperial Beach (1967) 7.5' quadrangle. On San Ysidro (1953) 7.5' quadrangle, the name "Palm City" applies to present South San Diego. Postal authorities established Palm City post office in 1914 and discontinued it in 1956 (Salley, p. 165). The place first was called Palm Avenue for the palm trees planted along its main street, but because post office authorities objected to this name the place was renamed Palm City (Stein, p. 96).

Palmdale [LOS ANGELES]: *town,* 8 miles south of Lancaster (lat. 34°34'45" N, long. 118°07' W; in and near sec. 25, 26, T 6 N, R 12 W). Named on Palmdale (1958) and Ritter Ridge (1958) 7.5' quadrangles. Baker's (1911) map shows a place called West Palmdale located about 2 miles west-northwest of Palmdale near the railroad; the place called Palmdale on Baker's (1911) map is called Old Palmdale on Johnson's (1911) map. Postal authorities established Palmenthal post office in 1888, changed the name to Palmdale in 1890, and discontinued it in 1899 when service moved to West Palmdale post office; they changed the name of West Palmdale post office to Palmdale the same year (Frickstad, p. 78, 79). German Lutherans founded the community in 1886 and named it for Joshua trees found there—Joshua trees sometimes were called yucca palms (Gudde, 1949, p. 250). The community began about 2 miles farther east, but eventually it was moved to the railroad (Hanna, p. 227). The site originally was known as Agua Dulce for a spring of sweet water there (Latta, p. 170). Postal authorities established Lopez post office in 1894 and discontinued it in 1896, when service moved to West Palmdale post office (Salley, p. 126).

Palmdale Lake: see **Lake Palmdale** [LOS ANGELES].

Palmdale Reservoir: see **Lake Palmdale** [LOS ANGELES].

Palmenthal: see **Palmdale** [LOS ANGELES].

Palmer Canyon [LOS ANGELES]: *canyon,* drained by a stream that flows 2.5 miles to lowlands 6.5 miles north-northeast of Pomona city hall (lat. 34°08'35" N, long. 117°42'25" W; sec. 27, T 1 N, R 8 W) Named on Mount Baldy (1954) 7.5' quadrangle. West Fork branches northwest 1.25 miles above the mouth of the main canyon; it is less than 1 mile long and is named on Mount Baldy (1954) 7.5' quadrangle.

Palm Grove [SAN DIEGO]: *locality,* 8 miles north of Jacumba (lat. 32°44'10" N, long. 116°12'25" W; near E line sec. 36, T 16 S, R 7 E). Named on Jacumba (1959) 7.5' quadrangle.

Palm Mesa [SAN DIEGO]: *area,* 7 miles northwest of Borrego Springs (lat. 33°19'10" N, long. 116°28'25" W). Named on Borrego Palm Canyon (1959) 7.5' quadrangle. The name is from native palm trees at the place (United States Board on Geographic Names, 1962a, p. 14).

Palms [LOS ANGELES]: *district,* 3.5 miles south of Beverly Hills city hall in Los Angeles (lat. 34°01'20" N, long. 118°24'15" W). Named on Beverly Hills (1950) 7.5' quadrangle. Called Palmas on California Mining Bureau's (1909b) map, and called Palma on Diller and others' (1915) map. Postal authorities established Palms post office in 1887 (Frickstad, p. 79).

Palm Spring [SAN DIEGO]: *spring,* 6.5 miles north-northwest of Sweeney Pass (lat. 32°55'15" N, long. 116°13' W; near S line sec. 25, T 14 S, R 7 E). Named on Arroyo Tapiado (1959) 7.5' quadrangle. Travelers in the 1850's destroyed the native palm trees that gave the spring its name (Bloomquist, 1979a, p. 14).

Palm Wash [SAN DIEGO]: *stream,* flows 3.25 miles to Imperial County 17 miles east of Borrego Springs (lat. 33°17'20" N, long. 116°05' W; at E line sec. 24, T 10 S, R 8 E). Named on Seventeen Palms (1956) 7.5' quadrangle. North Fork enters from the north at San Diego-Imperial County line; it is 2.5 miles long and is named on Seventeen Palms (1956) 7.5' quadrangle. South Fork enters from the southwest in Imperial County less than 1 mile below the mouth of North Fork; it is 3.25 miles long and is named on Seventeen Palms (1956) 7.5' quadrangle.

Palo Comado Canyon [LOS ANGELES-VENTURA]: *canyon,* drained by a stream that heads in Ventura County and flows nearly 5 miles to lowlands at Agura in Los Angeles County (lat. 34°09'05" N, long. 118°44' W). Named on Calabasas (1952) 7.5' quadrangle. Called Posita Canyon on Camulos (1903) 30' quadrangle.

Palomar: see **Palomar Mountain** [SAN DIEGO] (2).

Paloma Ravine [SAN DIEGO]: *canyon,* drained by a stream that flows nearly 0.5 mile to Los Rasaltes Ravine 6.25 miles north-northeast of Buckman Springs (lat. 32°51'20" N, long. 116°27' W; near NE cor. sec. 22, T 15 S, R 5 E). Named on Mount Laguna (1960) 7.5' quadrangle.

Palomares: see **Claremont** [LOS ANGELES].

Palomar Mountain [SAN DIEGO]:

(1) *ridge,* west-northwest- to west-trending, 4 miles long, 5 miles east-northeast of Boucher Hill (lat. 33°21'50" N, long. 116°50'15" W). Named on Palomar Observatory (1949) 7.5' quadrangle. Called Smith's Mountain on Hanks' (1886a) map, but United States Board on Geographic Names (1933, p. 583) rejected the name "Smith Mountain" for the feature. On Ramona (1903) 30' quadrangle, the name "Palomar Mt." applies to present High Point, which is on the ridge. The name "Smith" was for Joseph Smith, a homesteader of 1868 who was murdered (Stine, p. 96).

(2) *village,* 2.5 miles east-southeast of Boucher Hill (lat. 33°19'20" N, long. 116°52'40" W; near E line sec. 9, T 10 S, R 1 E). Named on Boucher Hill (1948) 7.5' quadrangle. Called Palomar on Palomar Mountain (1942) 15' quadrangle. Ramona (1903) 30' quadrangle shows a place called Nellie located about 0.5 mile southwest of the present village of Palomar Mountain. Postal authorities established Nellie post office in 1883, moved it 2 miles northwest in 1891, and moved it and changed the name to Palomar Mountain in 1920; the name "Nellie" was for Nellie McQueen, first postmaster (Salley, p. 153). They established Amago post office 5.5 miles southeast of Nellie post office in 1900 and discontinued it in 1902; the name was for Pio B. Amago, first postmaster (Salley, p. 6). They established Jessee post office 7 miles southeast of Nellie post office in 1896, moved it 1.5 miles northwest in 1898, and discontinued it in 1904; the name was for Harriet L. Jessee, first postmaster (Salley, p. 107). They established Soboyame post office 3.5 miles southeast of Nellie post office in 1910 and discontinued it in 1911 (Salley, p. 207).

Palomas Canyon [LOS ANGELES]: *canyon,* drained by a stream that flows 2.25 miles to Violin Canyon nearly 6 miles southeast of Whitaker Peak (lat. 34°31'10" N, long. 118°39'15" W; sec. 15, T 5 N, R 17 W). Named on Whitaker Peak (1958) 7.5' quadrangle.

Palo Verde [LOS ANGELES]: *locality,* 8 miles south-southwest of present Whittier city hall (lat. 33°52'35" N, long. 118°06'30" W). Named on Whittier (1949) 7.5' quadrangle.

Palo Verde Canyon [SAN DIEGO]: *canyon,* drained by a stream that flows 4.5 miles to lowlands 12 miles east-northeast of Borrego Springs (lat. 33°18'40" N, long. 116°11' W). Named on Fonts Point (1959) 7.5' quadrangle.

Palos Verdes: see **Los Palos Verdes** [LOS ANGELES].

Palos Verdes Estates [LOS ANGELES]: *town,* 3 miles south of Redondo Beach city hall (lat. 33°48' N, long. 118°23'25" W); the town is in Palos Verdes Hills. Named on Redondo Beach (1963) and Torrance (1964) 7.5' quadrangles. Postal authorities established Palos Verdes Estates post office in 1925 (Frickstad, p. 79).

Palos Verdes Hills [LOS ANGELES]: *range,* 10 miles west of Long Beach city hall (lat. 33°46' N, long. 118°22' W). Named on Redondo Beach (1951), San Pedro (1964), and Torrance (1964) 7.5' quadrangles. Called San Pedro Hills on Redondo (1896) 15' quadrangle.

Palos Verdes Point [LOS ANGELES]: *promontory,* 5.25 miles south-southwest of Redondo Beach city hall along the coast (lat. 33°46'25" N, long. 118°25'40" W); the promontory is at Palos Verdes Hills. Named on Redondo Beach (1951) 7.5' quadrangle. Called Rocky Point on Redondo (1896) 15' quadrangle, but United States Board on Geographic Names

(1940, p. 32-33) rejected this name for the feature.

Palo Verde Spring [SAN DIEGO]: *spring,* 13 miles east-northeast of Borrego Springs (lat. 33°20'05" N, long. 116°10'30" W); the spring is in Palo Verde Canyon. Named on Fonts Point (1959) 7.5' quadrangle.

Palos Verdes Reservoir [LOS ANGELES]: *intermittent lake,* 1450 feet long, 4.5 miles south of Torrance city hall (lat. 33°46'20" N, long. 118°19'20" W). Named on Torrance (1964) 7.5' quadrangle.

Palo Verde Wash [SAN DIEGO]: *dry wash,* heads at the mouth of Palo Verde Canyon and extends for 11 miles to San Felipe Creek 2 miles north of Ocotillo Wells (lat. 33°10'30" N, long. 116°08'30" W). Named on Borrego Mountain (1960) and Fonts Point (1959) 7.5' quadrangles.

Pamitas Spring [SAN DIEGO]: *spring,* 3.25 miles north-northeast of Sweeney Pass (lat. 33°52'30" N, long. 116°10' W). Named on Carrizo Mountain (1944) 15' quadrangle.

Pamo Canyon: see **Quail Canyon** [SAN DIEGO] (1).

Pamo Valley [SAN DIEGO]: *valley,* 5.25 miles long, along Santa Ysabel Creek and Temescal Creek (1) above a point on Santa Ysabel Creek 4 miles north of Ramona (lat. 33°06'20" N, long. 116°51'25" W; near NW cor. sec. 26, T 12 S, R 1 E). Named on Mesa Grande (1948) and Ramona (1955) 7.5' quadrangles.

Panawatt Springs [SAN DIEGO]: *springs,* 5.25 miles east of Warner Springs (lat. 33°16'25" N, long. 116°32'25" W; sec. 26, T 10 S, R 4 E). Named on Hot Springs Mountain (1960) 7.5' quadrangle.

Pancho Canyon [ORANGE]: *canyon,* drained by a stream that flows less than 1 mile to Santiago Creek 7 miles north-northeast of El Toro (lat. 33°43'30" N, long. 117°38'50" W). Named on El Toro (1968) 7.5' quadrangle.

Panorama City [LOS ANGELES]: *district,* 3 miles north of Van Nuys (lat. 34°13'40" N, long. 118°26'30" W). Named on Van Nuys (1953) 7.5' quadrangle. Postal authorities established Panorama City post office in 1953; the name is from Panorama moving picture studio (Salley, p. 166).

Panorama Heights [ORANGE]: *locality,* 3 miles east-southeast of Orange city hall (lat. 33°46'35" N, long. 117°47'50" W). Named on Orange (1964) 7.5' quadrangle. L.S. Leeson and G.E. Lindley developed the subdivision in 1928 (Meadows, p. 110).

Panorama Outlook [SAN DIEGO]: *promontory,* 2.25 miles west-northwest of Borrego Springs (lat. 33°15'55" N, long. 116°24'45" W; sec. 36, T 10 S, R 5 E). Named on Borrego Palm Canyon (1959) 7.5' quadrangle.

Paradise Canyon [LOS ANGELES]: *canyon,* nearly 1 mile long, 5 miles north-northwest of Pasadena city hall (lat. 34°12'40" N, long. 118°10'50" W; sec. 31, T 2 N, R 12 W). Named on Pasadena (1953) 7.5' quadrangle.

Paradise Cove [LOS ANGELES]: *embayment,* 1.5 miles northeast of Point Dume (lat. 34°01'10" N, long. 118°47'05" W). Named on Point Dume (1951) 7.5' quadrangle. Gleason (p. 121) called the feature Dume Cove, and noted that it has the popular name "Paradise Cove." United States Board on Geographic Names (1961c, p. 13) rejected the name "Dume Cove" for the place.

Paradise Creek [SAN DIEGO]:

(1) *stream,* flows nearly 6 miles to San Luis Rey River 5.25 miles south-southwest of Boucher Hill (lat. 33°15'50" N, long. 116°57'15" W; sec. 35, T 10 S, R 1 W). Named on Boucher Hill (1948) and Rodriguez Mountain (1948) 7.5' quadrangles.

(2) *stream,* flows 5 miles to San Diego Bay 1.5 miles south-southwest of National City civic center (lat. 32°39'05" N, long. 117° 07' W). Named on National City (1953) 7.5' quadrangle.

Paradise Mountain [SAN DIEGO]: *relief feature,* 3.5 miles southwest of Rodriguez Mountain (lat. 33°12'10" N, long. 116°56'15" W). Named on Rodriguez Mountain (1948) 7.5' quadrangle.

Paradise Springs [LOS ANGELES]: *locality,* 4.25 miles southeast of Valyermo along Big Rock Creek (lat. 34°23'45" N, long. 117°48'15" W; on S line sec. 27, T 4 N, R 9 W). Named on Valyermo (1958) 7.5' quadrangle.

Paradise Valley [SAN DIEGO]: *valley,* in National City (lat. 32°40'30" N, long. 117°05'20" W); the valley is along Paradise Creek (2). Named on National City (1967) 7.5' quadrangle.

Paradise Valley [VENTURA]: *locality,* 4.25 miles south of Chatsworth [LOS ANGELES] in Dayton Canyon just inside Ventura County (lat. 34°13'20" N, long. 118°40'05" W). Named on Chatsworth (1940) 6' quadrangle.

Paraje de las Virgenes: see **Las Virgenes** [LOS ANGELES].

Paramount [LOS ANGELES]: *city,* 5.5 miles south-southeast of South Gate city hall (lat. 33°53'05" N, long. 118°09'35" W). Named on South Gate (1964) 7.5' quadrangle. Called South Clearwater on Downey (1902) 15' quadrangle, and called Hynes on Clearwater (1925) 6' quadrangle. Postal authorities established Hynes post office in 1898 and changed the name to Paramount in 1948 (Frickstad, p. 75). The name "Hynes" was for C.B. Hynes, superintendent of Salt Lake Railroad (Gudde, 1949, p. 158). Paramount incorporated in 1957. When the communities of Hynes and Clearwater merged to form a new city, Frank Zamboni proposed the name "Paramount" for the place because Paramount Boulevard was its main street—the boulevard was named for Paramount motion picture company (Gudde, 1969, p. 238). Postal authorities established Firth post office 3 miles east of Hynes post office in 1908 and discontinued it in 1909 (Salley, p. 75).

Parayne Hill [SAN DIEGO]: *peak,* 9 miles east-southeast of Boucher Hill (lat. 33°17' N, long. 116°46'50" W; near N line sec. 28, T 10 S, R 2 E). Altitude 4407 feet. Named on Palomar Observatory (1949) 7.5' quadrangle.

Pardee [LOS ANGELES]: *locality,* 2 miles north-northwest of Newhall along Southern Pacific Railroad near Saugus (lat. 34°24'55" N, long. 118°32'25" W). Named on Newhall (1952) 7.5' quadrangle.

Paris [LOS ANGELES]: *locality,* 1 mile east of Acton along Southern Pacific Railroad (lat. 34°28'20" N, long. 118°10'50" W; near W line sec. 31, T 5 N, R 12 W). Named on Acton (1959) 7.5' quadrangle.

Park Canyon [VENTURA]: *canyon,* drained by a stream that flows 4 miles to Wagon Road Canyon 7 miles northeast of Reyes Peak (lat. 34°42'35" N, long. 119°12'25" W; at SW cor. sec. 10, T 7 N, R 22 W). Named on San Guillermo (1943) 7.5' quadrangle.

Park Creek [VENTURA]: *stream,* flows 3 miles to Sespe Creek 15 miles east-northeast of Wheeler Springs (lat. 34°34'10" N, long. 119°01'25" W; sec. 32, T 6 N, R 20 W). Named on Devils Heart Peak (1943) and Topatopa Mountains (1943) 7.5' quadrangles.

Parker Canyon [LOS ANGELES]: *canyon,* drained by a stream that flows 1 mile to the sea nearly 5 miles west-northwest of Santa Monica city hall (lat. 34°02'30" N, long. 118°34' W). Named on Topanga (1952) 7.5' quadrangle.

Parker Mesa [LOS ANGELES]: *area,* 5.25 miles west-northwest of Santa Monica city hall (lat. 34°02'40" N, long. 118°34'20" W); the place is west of the lower part of Parker Canyon. Named on Topanga (1952) 7.5' quadrangle.

Parker Mountain [LOS ANGELES]: *peak,* 1.5 miles west-southwest of Acton (lat. 34°27'35" N, long. 118°13'05" W; at W line sec. 2, T 4 N, R 13 W). Altitude 4131 feet. Named on Acton (1959) 7.5' quadrangle. The feature also was called Mount Parkinson (Gudde, 1949, p. 254).

Parkinson: see **Mount Parkinson**, under **Parker Mountain** [LOS ANGELES].

Paroli Spring [SAN DIEGO]: *spring,* 3.5 miles southeast of San Felipe (lat. 33°09'50" N, long. 116°33'20" W; sec. 3, T 12 S, R 4 E). Named on Ranchita (1960) 7.5' quadrangle.

Parsons Landing [LOS ANGELES]: *locality,* 1.5 miles north of Silver Peak on the north side of Santa Catalina Island (lat. 33°28'25" N, long. 118°33' W). Named on Santa Catalina West (1943) 7.5' quadrangle.

Pasadena [LOS ANGELES]: *city,* 8 miles northeast of Los Angeles city hall (lat. 34°08'50" N, long. 118°08'35" W). Named on Los Angeles (1953), Mount Wilson (1953), and Pasadena (1953) 7.5' quadrangles. Postal authorities established Pasadena post office in 1875, discontinued it the same year, and reestablished it in 1876 (Frickstad, p. 79). The city incorporated in 1886. The community first was called Indiana Colony because the original promoters of the place came from Indiana; Dr. T.B. Elliott, president of Indiana Colony, proposed the name "Pasadena," which supposedly is a Chippewa Indian word (Gudde, 1949, p. 254), but Kroeber (p. 54) expressed doubt about an Indian origin for the name.

Pasadena: see **East Pasadena** [LOS ANGELES]; **South Pasadena** [LOS ANGELES].

Pasadena Camp [LOS ANGELES]: *locality,* 3.25 miles west-northwest of Waterman Mountain (lat. 34°21'10" N, long. 117°59'30" W; near NW cor. sec. 13, T 3 N, R 11 W). Named on Waterman Mountain (1959) 7.5' quadrangle.

Pasadena Glen [LOS ANGELES]: *canyon,* 1.5 miles long, 2.5 miles south-southwest of Mount Wilson (1) (lat. 34°11'15" N, long. 118° 04'30" W; mainly in sec. 7, T 1 N, R 11 W). Named on Mount Wilson (1953) 7.5' quadrangle. Los Angeles County (1935) map has the name "Kineloa Canyon" for the canyon just west of Pasadena Glen, where Mount Wilson (1953) 7.5' quadrangle shows Kineloa ranch.

Paso Canyon: see **Agua Dulce Canyon** [LOS ANGELES].

Paso de Bartolo [LOS ANGELES]: *land grant,* at Pico Rivera and Whittier. Named on El Monte (1953) and Whittier (1949) 7.5' quadrangles. Juan Crispin Perez received 2 leagues in 1835; Pio Pico and others claimed 8991 acres patented in 1881; Rafael Guirado claimed 876 acres granted in 1836 and patented in 1867; Joaquin Sepulveda claimed 208 acres patented in 1881 (Cowan, p. 18; Cowan listed the grant under the designation "Paso de Bartolo Viejo, (or) San Rafael").

Paso de Bartolo Viejo: see **Paso de Bartolo** [LOS ANGELES].

Paso de las Carretas: see **Ballona** [LOS ANGELES].

Paso Picacho Campground [SAN DIEGO]: *locality,* 1.5 miles east-northeast of Cuyamaca Peak (lat. 32°57'30" N, long. 116°34'50" W). Named on Cuyamaca Peak (1960) 7.5' quadrangle.

Patrick Reservoir [LOS ANGELES]: *lake,* 650 feet long, 2.25 miles west of Avalon on Santa Caltalina Island (lat. 33°21' N, long. 118° 21'50" W). Named on Santa Catalina East (1950) 7.5' quadrangle.

Patricks Shelter [LOS ANGELES]: *locality,* 2.25 miles north-northwest of Avalon on the northeast side of Santa Catalina Island (lat. 33°22'10" N, long. 118°20'45" W). Named on Santa Catalina East (1950) 7.5' quadrangle.

Pats Canyon [SAN DIEGO]: *canyon,* drained by a stream that flows nearly 2 miles to Barrett Lake 3 miles north-northeast of Barrett Junction (lat. 33°41' N, long. 116°40'30" W; near SE cor. sec. 16, T 17 S, R 3 E). Named on Barrett Lake (1960) 7.5' quadrangle.

Paul: see **Lewis Paul Canyon** [LOS ANGELES].

Paulerino [ORANGE]: *locality,* 7 miles east of present Huntington Beach civic center along Southern Pacific Railroad (lat. 33°40'55" N, long. 117°52'40" W). Named on Newport Beach (1935) 7.5' quadrangle.

Pauma [SAN DIEGO]: *land grant,* north of Rincon. Named on Boucher Hill (1948) and Pala (1968) 7.5' quadrangles. Jose Antonio Serrano and others received 3 leagues in 1844; they claimed 13,310 acres patented in 1871 (Cowan, p. 59; Cowan gave the alternate name "Potrero de Pauma" for the grant). The name is of Indian origin (Kroeber, p. 54).

Pauma Creek [SAN DIEGO]: *stream,* formed by the confluence of Doane Creek and French Creek, flows 6.5 miles to San Luis Rey River 5 miles southeast of Pala (lat. 33°19'05" N, long. 117°00'30" W). Named on Boucher Hill (1950) and Pala (1968) 7.5' quadrangles.

Pauma Valley [SAN DIEGO]:
(1) *valley,* 4.5 miles west-southwest of Boucher Hill along San Luis Rey River (lat. 33°18'30" N, long. 116°59'30" W); the feature is on Pauma grant. Named on Boucher Hill (1948) and Pala (1968) 7.5' quadrangles.
(2) *village,* 4.25 miles west-southwest of Boucher Hill (lat. 33°18'15" N, long. 116°59' W); the place is in Pauma Valley (1). Named on Boucher Hill (1948) 7.5' quadrangle. Postal authorities established Pauma Valley post office in 1951 (Salley, p. 168).

Peace Valley [LOS ANGELES]: *valley,* 9 miles long, along Gorman Creek above the entrance of that creek into Cañada de Los Alamos 7 miles south-southeast of Gorman (lat. 34°42'10" N, long. 118°47'40" W; sec. 16, T 7 N, R 18 W). Named on Black Mountain (1958) and Lebec (1958) 7.5' quadrangles.

Peachtree Flat: see **Heaton Flat** [LOS ANGELES].

Peacock Canyon [LOS ANGELES]: *canyon,* drained by a stream that flows nearly 1 mile to Cattle Canyon 12 miles north of Pomona city hall (lat. 34°13'45" N, long. 117°45' W). Named on Mount Baldy (1954) 7.5' quadrangle.

Peacock Saddle [LOS ANGELES]: *pass,* 8.5 miles northeast of Glendora city hall (lat. 34°13' N, long. 117°45' W); the pass is near the head of Peacock Canyon. Named on Glendora (1953) and Mount Baldy (1954) 7.5' quadrangles.

Pearblossom [LOS ANGELES]: *locality,* 4.25 miles east-southeast of Littlerock (lat. 34°30'20" N, long. 117°54'30" W). Named on Littlerock (1957) 7.5' quadrangle. Called Pearblossom Heights on Alpine Butte (1945) 15' quadrangle. Postal authorities established Pearblossom post office in 1933 (Salley, p. 169). Guy C. Chase named the place in 1924 for the pear orchards that surrounded it (Gudde, 1949, p. 256). Johnson's (1911) map has the name "Almondale" at a spot situated about 0.5 mile west of present Pearblossom.

Pearblossom Heights: see **Pearblossom** [LOS ANGELES].

Pearland [LOS ANGELES]: *village,* 4.25 miles east-southeast of Palmdale (lat. 34°33'40" N, long. 118°02'40" W; near S line sec. 33, T 6 N, R 11 W). Named on Palmdale (1958) 7.5' quadrangle. The name was given to the place in 1919 (Gudde, 1949, p. 256).

Peavine Campground [LOS ANGELES]: *locality,* 1.5 miles west-northwest of Big Pines (lat. 34°23'20" N, long. 117°43' W). Named on Mescal Creek (1956) 7.5' quadrangle.

Peavine Canyon [LOS ANGELES]: *canyon,* nearly 2 miles long, 2.5 miles north-northwest of Beverly Hills city hall (lat. 34°06'15" N, long. 118°25'20" W). Named on Beverly Hills (1950) 7.5' quadrangle.

Pebbly Beach [LOS ANGELES]: *locality,* 1 mile east-southeast of Avalon on the northeast side of Santa Catalina Island (lat. 33°20'05" N, long. 118°18'40" W). Named on Santa Catalina East (1950) 7.5' quadrangle.

Pechner Canyon [LOS ANGELES]: *canyon,* drained by a stream that flows 2 miles to Pallet Creek 3 miles west-southwest of Valyermo (lat. 34°25'30" N, long. 117°53'45" W; near N line sec. 23, T 4 N, R 10 W). Named on Juniper Hills (1959) 7.5' quadrangle.

Pechstein Reservoir [SAN DIEGO]: *lake,* 1150 feet long, 4 miles east-southeast of Vista (lat. 33°11'05" N, long. 117°10'40" W; near S line sec. 27, T 11 S, R 3 W). Named on San Marcos (1968) 7.5' quadrangle. Stein (p. 98) associated the name with William Pechstein, an early developer of land and promoter of irrigation in the neighborhood.

Pedley Valley [SAN DIEGO]: *area,* 4 miles east-southeast of Boucher Hill (lat. 33°19'10" N, long. 116°51'05" W; sec. 11, T 10 S, R 1 E). Named on Palomar Observatory (1949) 7.5' quadrangle.

Pelican Hill [ORANGE]: *peak,* 4.5 miles northwest of Laguna Beach city hall (lat. 33°35'35" N, long. 117°50'15" W); the peak is 1.25 miles northeast of Pelican Point. Named on Laguna Beach (1965) 7.5' quadrangle.

Pelican Point [ORANGE]: *promontory,* nearly 5 miles west-northwest of Laguna Beach city hall along the coast (lat. 33°34'45" N, long. 117°51'10" W). Named on Laguna Beach (1965) 7.5' quadrangle.

Pellissier Spur [LOS ANGELES]: *locality,* 3 miles south of El Monte city hall along Union Pacific Railroad (lat. 34°01'50" N, long. 118° 01'30" W). Named on El Monte (1966) 7.5' quadrangle.

Peña Canyon [LOS ANGELES]: *canyon,* drained by a stream that flows nearly 2 miles to the sea 6.25 miles west-northwest of Santa Monica city hall (lat. 34°02'20" N, long. 118°35'45" W). Named on Topanga (1952) 7.5' quadrangle.

Pena Spring [SAN DIEGO]: *spring,* 5.5 miles west-southwest of Borrego Springs in South Fork Hellhole Canyon (lat. 33°13'35" N, long. 116°27'50" W). Named on Tubb Canyon (1959) 7.5' quadrangle.

Penasquitos Canyon: see **Los Peñasquitos Canyon**[SAN DIEGO].

Pendleton: see **Camp Pendleton Marine Corps Base** [SAN DIEGO].

Penin Canyon [SAN DIEGO]: *canyon,* 2 miles long, 3.5 miles south of Santa Ysabel along Temescal Creek (2) (lat. 33°03'30" N, long. 116°40'30" W; in and near sec. 9, T 13 S, R 3 E). Named on Santa Ysabel (1960) 7.5' quadrangle.

Peninsula of San Diego: see **Island or Peninsula of San Diego** [SAN DIEGO].

Peninsula Point [SAN DIEGO]: *promontory,* 3 miles west-northwest of downtown San Diego along San Diego Bay (lat. 32°44'10" N, long. 117°12'15" W). Named on Point Loma (1942) 7.5' quadrangle.

Penrose [VENTURA]: *locality,* 3 miles northwest of Moorpark (lat. 34°18'50" N, long. 118°54'35" W). Named on Camulos (1903) 30' quadrangle. Postal authorities established Penrose post office in 1893 and discontinued it in 1905 (Frickstad, p. 219).

Pensinger Canyon: see **Persinger Canyon** [LOS ANGELES].

Peppertree Canyon [VENTURA]: *canyon,* drained by a stream that flows 3.5 miles to the valley of Santa Clara River 1.5 miles north of Saticoy (lat. 34°18'30" N, long. 119°09' W). Named on Saticoy (1951) 7.5' quadrangle.

Pepper Tree Spring [SAN DIEGO]: *spring,* 8 miles north-northwest of Monument Peak (lat. 32°59'40" N, long. 116°29'10" W; near SE cor. sec. 32, T 13 S, R 5 E). Named on Monument Peak (1959) 7.5' quadrangle.

Peralta: see **Walnut Canyon** [ORANGE].

Peralta Hills [ORANGE]:
(1) *ridge,* west-trending, 3.5 miles long, 4.5 miles northeast of Orange city hall (lat. 33°50'05" N, long. 117°47'45" W). Named on Orange (1964) 7.5' quadrangle. United States Board on Geographic Names (1965c, p. 10) rejected the names "Burruel Ridge" and "Olive Hills" for the feature.
(2) *settlement,* 4.25 miles north-northeast of Orange city hall (lat. 33°50'40" N, long. 117°48'45" W). Named on Orange (1964, photorevised 1981) 7.5' quadrangle.

Perdition Caves [LOS ANGELES]: *caves,* 5.5 miles north-northwest of Mount Banning along the north side of Santa Catalina Island (lat. 33°26'50" N, long. 118°28'35" W). Named on Santa Catalina North (1950) 7.5' quadrangle.

Perez Cove [SAN DIEGO]: *embayment,* 6.25 miles south-southeast of Point La Jolla off Mission Bay (lat. 32°46'05" N, long. 117°13'50" W). Named on La Jolla (1967) 7.5' quadrangle.

Perry [LOS ANGELES]: *district,* 2 miles north of Torrance city hall (lat. 33°51'55" N, long. 118°20'30" W). Named on Torrance (1964) 7.5' quadrangle. Postal authorities established Perry post office in 1905 and discontinued it in 1916; the name was for the president of Pacific Electric Railroad (Salley, p. 170).

Persinger Canyon [LOS ANGELES]: *canyon,* drained by a stream that flows 2.5 miles to San Gabriel Reservoir 5.5 miles north of Glendora city hall (lat. 34°12'50" N, long. 117°51'05" W; sec. 32, T 2 N, R 9 W). Named on Glendora (1966) 7.5' quadrangle. Called Pensinger Canyon on Glendora (1953) 7.5' quadrangle. The name recalls Bate Persinger and Mary Persinger, who owned a resort at a site now under water of San Gabriel Reservoir (Robinson, J.W., 1983, p. 83-85).

Perspiration Point [LOS ANGELES]: *locality,* 5 miles south of Acton (lat. 34°23'50" N, long. 118°12'05" W; at E line sec. 26, T 4 N, R 13 W). Named on Acton (1959) 7.5' quadrangle.

Peters Canyon [ORANGE]: *canyon,* drained by a stream that flows nearly 2 miles to lowlands 5 miles east-southeast of Orange city hall (lat. 33°45'20" N, long. 117°46'05" W). Named on Orange (1964) 7.5' quadrangle. The name is for James Peters, who farmed land that he leased in the canyon; the feature was known in the early days as Canada de las Ranas from nearby Cienega de las Ranas—hunters called it Rabbit Canyon, Quail Canyon, and Dove Canyon for game there (Stephenson, p. 72, 73, 74).

Peters Canyon: see **Drinkwater Canyon** [LOS ANGELES].

Peters Canyon Reservoir [ORANGE]: *lake,* 2200 feet long, 5 miles east of Orange city hall (lat. 33°46'55" N, long. 117°45'40" W); the feature is at the head of Peters Canyon. Named on Orange (1964) 7.5' quadrangle.

Peters Canyon Reservoir: see **Lower Peters Canyon Reservoir** [ORANGE].

Peters Canyon Wash [ORANGE]: *stream,* flows 8 miles from the mouth of Peters Canyon to San Diego Creek 5.5 miles south-southeast of Santa Ana city hall (lat. 33°40'05" N, long. 117° 50'05" W). Named on Orange (1964) and Tustin (1965) 7.5' quadrangles.

Peterson Canyon [SAN DIEGO]: *canyon,* drained by a stream that flows 5 miles to Loveland Reservoir 8.5 miles west-southwest of Descanso (lat. 32°47'40" N, long. 116°44'30" W; sec. 11, T 16 S, R 2 E). Named on

Viejas Mountain (1960) 7.5' quadrangle.

Petrolia: see **Olinda** [ORANGE].

Petroliopolis: see **Lyon's Station**, under **San Fernando Pass** [LOS ANGELES].

Pettinger Canyon [LOS ANGELES]: *canyon*, drained by a stream that flows 2.5 miles to Haskell Canyon 7 miles north of Newhall (lat. 34°28'55" N, long. 118°30'30" W; near S line sec. 25, T 5 N, R 16 W). Named on Newhall (1952) and Warm Springs Mountain (1958) 7.5' quadrangles.

Peutz Valley [SAN DIEGO]: *canyon*, drained by a stream that flows 3.5 miles to El Capitan Reservoir 2.5 miles northwest of Alpine (lat. 32°51'55" N, long. 116°47'35" W; sec. 17, T 15 S, R 2 E). Named on Alpine (1955) 7.5' quadrangle. Stein (p. 98) associated the name with Nicholas Peutz, who settled in the neighborhood in the 1870's.

Phelps Corner [SAN DIEGO]: *locality*, nearly 4 miles east of Dulzura in Lee Valley (lat. 32°43'20" N, long. 116°48'40" W; sec. 6, T 17 S, R 2 E). Named on Dulzura (1972) 7.5' quadrangle.

Phipps Canyon [LOS ANGELES]: *canyon*, drained by a stream that flows 1 mile to West Fork San Gabriel River 7.25 miles north of Azusa city hall (lat. 34°14'25" N, long. 117°53'35" W). Named on Azusa (1953) 7.5' quadrangle.

Pickens Canyon [LOS ANGELES]: *canyon*, 2.5 miles long, 8 miles northwest of Pasadena city hall (lat. 34°14'30" N, long. 118°13'20" W). Named on Condor Peak (1959) and Pasadena (1953) 7.5' quadrangles. On Los Angeles County (1935) map, present Sutton Canyon is called East Fork [Pickens Canyon].

Pickens Canyon Channel [LOS ANGELES]: *stream*, flows 1.25 miles from the mouth of Pickens Canyon to Verdugo Wash 7 miles northwest of Pasadena city Hall (lat. 34°12'25" N, long. 118°14'20" W). Named on Pasadena (1953) 7.5' quadrangle.

Pico [LOS ANGELES]: *locality*, 4.5 miles west of Newhall (lat. 34° 22'40" N, long. 118°36'40" W; at N line sec. 1, T 3 N, R 17 W); the place is in Pico Canyon. Site named on Newhall (1952) 7.5' quadrangle.

Pico: see **Fort Pio Pico**, under **Zuñiga Point** [SAN DIEGO]; **Pico Rivera** [LOS ANGELES].

Pico Camp: see **Mentryville**, under **Pico Canyon** [LOS ANGELES].

Pico Canyon [LOS ANGELES]: *canyon*, 4.25 miles long, opens into lowlands 2 miles west of downtown Newhall (lat. 34°23'10" N, long. 118°34' W). Named on Newhall (1952), Oat Mountain (1952), and Santa Susana (1951) 7.5' quadrangles. The name is for Andreas Pico, who in 1855 dipped crude oil from hand-dug pits in the canyon (Franks and Lambert, p. 41). C.A. Mentry, a veteran of Titusville oil fields in Pennsylvania, completed the first commercially productive oil well in California in Pico Canyon in the 1870's; the town that sprang up there was called Mentryville (Harrington, p. 39). The place earlier was called Pico Springs, or Pico Camp (Reynolds, p. 25).

Pico Heights [LOS ANGELES]: *district*, 3.5 miles west of Los Angeles city hall (lat. 34°02'50" N, long. 118°18' W). Named on Santa Monica (1902) 15' quadrangle. Postal authorities established Electric post office in 1887, changed the name to Pico Heights in 1891, discontinued it in 1897, and reestablished it in 1898; the name "Electric" was for Pacific Electric Railroad (Salley, p. 67, 171).

Pico Rivera [LOS ANGELES]: *city*, 3 miles west of Whittier city hall (lat. 33°58'55" N, long. 118°05'15" W). Named on El Monte (1966) and Whittier (1965) 7.5' quadrangles. The communities of Pico and Rivera incorporated under the name "Pico Rivera" in 1958 (Gudde, 1969, p. 245). Pico was 3 miles northwest of present Whittier city hall (lat. 33°59'50" N, long. 118°04'40" W) and is named on El Monte (1953) and Whittier (1949) 7.5' quadrangles. Postal authorities established Pico post office in 1925 and combined it with Rivera post office in 1958 under the name "Pico Rivera" (Salley, p. 171). The place is on the part of Paso de Bartolo grant owned by Pio Pico. Rivera was 4.25 miles west of present Whittier city hall (lat. 33°57'45" N, long. 118°06'30" W) and is named on Whittier (1949) 7.5' quadrangle. Postal authorities established Rivera post office in 1888 and discontinued it in 1958 (Salley, p. 186). The place was called Maizeland in 1866 for corn grown there (Gudde, 1949, p. 288); Senator R.F. del Valle gave the name "Rivera" to the community in 1886 for its position between San Gabriel River and Rio Hondo (Hanna, p. 256).

Pico's Lake: see **Whalen Lake** [SAN DIEGO].

Pico Springs: see **Mentryville**, under **Pico Canyon** [LOS ANGELES].

Picture City: see **Agoura** [LOS ANGELES].

Pidgeon Spring: see **Bear Spring** [LOS ANGELES].

Piedra Blanca Camp [VENTURA]: *locality*, 8 miles east-northeast of Wheeler Springs along Sespe Creek (lat. 34°33'40" N, long. 119° 09'50" W; at S line sec. 36, T 6 N, R 22 W); the place is less than 1 mile upstream from the mouth of Piedra Blanca Creek. Named on Lion Canyon (1943) 7.5' quadrangle. Called Piedra Blanca CCC Camp on Lion Canyon (1944) 7.5' quadrangle.

Piedra Blanca Creek [VENTURA]: *stream*, flows nearly 9 miles to Sespe Creek 8.5 miles east-northeast of Wheeler Springs (lat. 34° 33'30" N, long. 119°09'05" W; near N line sec. 2, T 5 N, R 22 W). Named on Lion Canyon (1943) and San Guillermo (1943) 7.5' quadrangles. North Fork enters from the northeast 2.5 miles above the mouth of the main stream; it is 3 miles long and is named on Lion Canyon (1943) 7.5' quadrangle.

Piedra de Lumbre Canyon [SAN DIEGO]: *canyon*, 5 miles long, opens into lowlands along the coast 4.5 miles south-southeast of San Onofre Mountain (lat. 33°18'45" N, long. 117°27' W; near NW cor. sec. 18, T 10 S, R 5 W). Named on Las Pulgas Canyon (1968) 7.5' quadrangle.

Piedra Gorda Canyon [LOS ANGELES]: *canyon*, drained by a stream that flows 1.5 miles to the sea 7 miles west-northwest of Santa Monica city hall (lat. 34°02'10" N, long. 118°36'30" W; sec. 36, T 1 S, R 17 W); the mouth of the canyon is at Big Rock Beach. Named on Topanga (1952) 7.5' quadrangle.

Piedras Grandes [SAN DIEGO]: *ridge*, west-northwest-trending, about 1 mile long, 8.5 miles north-northeast of Jacumba (lat. 32°44'15" N, long. 116°08'50" W; sec. 34, T 16 S, R 8 E). Named on Jacumba (1959) 7.5' quadrangle.

Pierpont Bay [VENTURA]:

(1) *embayment*, along the coast at Ventura (lat. 34°16'15" N, long. 119°17'15" W). Named on Ventura (1951) 7.5' quadrangle. The name commemorates Ernest Pierpont, a resident of Ojai Valley in the 1890's (Gudde, 1949, p. 261).

(2) *district*, 1.5 miles southeast of downtown Ventura near the coast (lat. 34°15'45" N, long. 119°16'15" W); the district is east of Pierpont Bay (1). Named on Ventura (1951) 7.5' quadrangle. The place was laid out in 1925, and Ventura annexed it in 1968 (Ricard).

Pigeon Flat [VENTURA]: *area*, 3 miles east of Devils Heart Peak (lat. 34°32'40" N, long. 118°55'25" W). Named on Devils Heart Peak (1943) 7.5' quadrangle.

Pigeon Ridge [LOS ANGELES]: *ridge*, southwest-trending, 3 miles long, 2.5 miles southeast of Crystal Lake (lat. 34°17'15" N, long. 117°49'05" W). Named on Crystal Lake (1958) 7.5' quadrangle.

Pilgrim Creek [SAN DIEGO]: *stream*, flows 9.5 miles to San Luis Rey River 5.25 miles north of Oceanside city hall (lat. 33°14'25" N, long. 117°20'05" W; near N line sec. 7, T 11 S, R 4 W). Named on Morro Hill (1968) 7.5' quadrangle. Stein (p. 98) associated the name with Charles Pilgrim, who farmed in the region in the 1880's.

Pillsbury: see **Brea** [ORANGE].

Pinasquitos Canyon: see **Los Peñasquitos Canyon** [SAN DIEGO].

Pinchot: see **Elizabeth Lake** [LOS ANGELES] (2).

Pine Canyon [LOS ANGELES]:

(1) *canyon*, 2.25 miles long, opens into lowlands 14 miles east of Gorman (lat. 34°46' N, long. 118°35'45" W; sec. 20, T 8 N, R 16 W). Named on Burnt Peak (1958) and Neenach School (1965) 7.5' quadrangles. Called Gookin Gulch on Johnson's (1911) map. The feature divides at the head to form Oakdale Canyon (1) and Oakgrove Canyon.

(2) *canyon*, drained by a stream that flows 2 miles to Bear Canyon (1) 12 miles southeast of Gorman (lat. 34°40'25" N, long. 118°39'10" W; sec. 26, T 7 N, R 17 W). Named on Burnt Peak (1958) and Liebre Mountain (1958) 7.5' quadrangles.

(3) *canyon*, drained by a stream that flows 4.25 miles to Hughes Lake at the village of Lake Hughes (lat. 34°40'35" N, long. 118° 26'50" W; at E line sec. 22, T 7 N, R 15 W). Named on Burnt Peak (1958) and Lake Hughes (1957) 7.5' quadrangles.

(4) *canyon*, 0.5 mile long, opens into the canyon of Gold Creek 4.5 miles north of Sunland (lat. 34°19'40" N, long. 118°17'55" W; sec. 24, T 3 N, R 14 W). Named on Sunland (1953) 7.5' quadrangle.

(5) *canyon*, drained by a stream that flows 1.25 miles to Arroyo Seco 6.25 miles north-northwest of Pasadena city hall (lat. 34°14'10" N, long. 118°10'35" W). Named on Pasadena (1953) 7.5' quadrangle.

(6) *canyon*, drained by a stream that flows less than 1 mile to Morris Reservoir 3 miles north of Glendora city hall (lat. 34°10'40" N, long. 117°52'05" W; near N line sec. 18, T 1 N, R 9 W). Named on Glendora (1953) 7.5' quadrangle.

(7) *canyon*, drained by a stream that flows less than 1 mile to Big Dalton Canyon nearly 4 miles northeast of Glendora city hall (lat. 34°10'05" N, long. 117°48'35" W; near S line sec. 15, T 1 N, R 9 W). Named on Glendora (1953) 7.5' quadrangle.

Pine Canyon [ORANGE]: *canyon*, drained by a stream that flows 1.5 miles to Silverado Canyon nearly 4 miles northwest of Santiago Peak (lat. 33°44'45" N, long. 117°35' W; sec. 11, T 5 S, R 7 W). Named on Santiago Peak (1954) 7.5' quadrangle.

Pine Canyon [VENTURA]: *canyon*, drained by a stream that flows 3.25 miles to Sespe Creek 4.5 miles north-northwest of Fillmore (lat. 34°27'40" N, long. 118°56'30" W; sec. 2, T 4 N, R 20 W). Named on Fillmore (1951) 7.5' quadrangle.

Pine Creek [LOS ANGELES]: *stream*, flows 2.25 miles to Amargosa Creek 9 miles southwest of Lancaster (lat. 34°36'05" N, long. 118° 14'35" W; at S line sec. 15, T 6 N, R 13 W). Named on Ritter Ridge (1958) and Sleepy Valley (1958) 7.5' quadrangles.

Pine Creek Campground [SAN DIEGO]: *locality*, nearly 5 miles east of Descanso (lat. 32°50'35" N, long. 116°32' W; near E line sec. 26, T 15 S, R 4 E); the place is in Pine Valley (2). Named on Descanso (1960) 7.5'

quadrangle.

Pine Flat: see **Charlton Flats** [LOS ANGELES]; **Pine Flats** [LOS ANGELES]; **West Pine Flat** [LOS ANGELES].

Pine Flats [LOS ANGELES]: *area,* northeast of Crystal Lake (lat. 34° 19'25" N, long. 117°50'10" W). Named on Crystal Lake (1958) 7.5' quadrangle. Called Pine Flat on Rock Creek (1903) 15' quadrangle, but United States Board on Geographic Names (1962a, p. 14) rejected this form of the name.

Pine Flats: see **Chilao Flat** [LOS ANGELES].

Pine Grove [SAN DIEGO]: *locality,* 9.5 miles northwest of Descanso (lat. 32°56'45" N, long. 116°42'45" W; sec. 19, T 14 S, R 3 E). Named on Tule Springs (1960) 7.5' quadrangle.

Pine Hills [SAN DIEGO]:

(1) *ridge,* east-trending, 1.5 miles long, 7.5 miles east-southeast of Boucher Hill (lat. 33°16'55" N, long. 116°48'10" W). Named on Palomar Observatory (1949) 7.5' quadrangle.

(2) *settlement,* about 2.5 miles southwest of Julian (lat. 33°02'45" N, long. 116°37'40" W; sec. 12, 13, T 13 S, R 3 E). Named on Julian (1960) and Santa Ysabel (1960) 7.5' quadrangles. Postal authorities established Pine Hills post office in 1913 and discontinued it in 1931; the name was from Pine Hills Lodge, a vacation resort (Salley, p. 172).

Pine Hollow Picnic Area [LOS ANGELES]: *locality,* 2.5 miles north-northeast of Crystal Lake (lat. 34°21'15" N, long. 117°50'05" W; near SW cor. sec. 9, T 3 N, R 9 W). Named on Crystal Lake (1958) 7.5' quadrangle.

Pine Mountain [LOS ANGELES]: *peak,* 6 miles north of Azusa city hall (lat. 34°13'25" N, long. 117°54' W). Altitude 4540 feet. Named on Azusa (1953) 7.5' quadrangle.

Pine Mountain [SAN DIEGO]:

(1) *peak,* 4.5 miles north-northwest of Warner Springs (lat. 33°20'40" N, long. 116°39'25" W; sec. 34, T 9 S, R 3 E). Altitude 3913 feet. Named on Warner Springs (1959) 7.5' quadrangle.

(2) *peak,* 4.5 miles west-northwest of Monument Peak (lat. 32°55'05" N, long. 116°29'35" W; near S line sec. 29, T 14 S, R 5 E). Named on Monument Peak (1959) 7.5' quadrangle.

(3) *peak,* 6.5 miles northwest of Mesa Grande (lat. 33°14'05" N, long. 116°51'30" W). Altitude 4221 feet. Named on Mesa Grande (1948) 7.5' quadrangle.

Pine Mountain [VENTURA]: *ridge,* generally west-northwest-trending, 10 miles long, center 1 mile east of Reyes Peak (lat. 34°37'55" N, long. 119°15'55" W). Named on Lion Canyon (1943), Reyes Peak (1943), and San Guillermo (1943) 7.5' quadrangles.

Pine Mountain: see **Vetter Mountain** [LOS ANGELES].

Pine Mountain Lodge [VENTURA]: *locality,* 6 miles east of Reyes Peak (lat. 34°37' N, long. 119°10'35" W; near N line sec. 14, T 6 N, R 22 W). Named on Lion Canyon (1943) 7.5' quadrangle.

Pine Mountain Ridge [LOS ANGELES]: *ridge,* west-northwest-trending, 5 miles long, center 3.5 miles northwest of Mount San Antonio on Los Angeles-San Bernardino County line (lat. 34°19'30" N, long. 117°41'05" W); Pine Mountain of San Bernardino County is at the east end of the ridge. Named on Mount San Antonio (1955) 7.5' quadrangle.

Pine Ridge [SAN DIEGO]: *ridge,* generally southeast-trending, 1 mile long, 3 miles south-southeast of Cuyamaca Peak (lat. 32°54'20" N, long. 116°35'30" W). Named on Cuyamaca Peak (1960) 7.5' quadrangle.

Pinery Canyon: see **Noel Canyon** [LOS ANGELES].

Pines Camp Ground: see **The Pines Camp Ground** [VENTURA].

Pine Springs [VENTURA]: *spring,* 9.5 miles east-northeast of Reyes Peak (lat. 34°41'25" N, long. 119°07'55" W; near W line sec. 20, T 7 N, R 21 W). Named on San Guillermo (1943) 7.5' quadrangle.

Pine Valley [SAN DIEGO]:

(1) *canyon,* 0.5 mile long, 6.5 miles east-southeast of Boucher Hill (lat. 33°18'35" N, long. 116°48'35" W; sec. 18, T 10 S, R 2 E). Named on Palomar Observatory (1949) 7.5' quadrangle.

(2) *valley,* 5.25 miles east-southeast of Descanso (lat. 32°50'20" N, long. 116°31'45" W). Named on Descanso (1960) 7.5' quadrangle.

(3) *town,* 5.5 miles east-southeast of Descanso (lat. 32°49'15" N, long. 116°31'45" W; mainly in sec. 36, T 15 S, R 4 E); the place is at the south end of Pine Valley (2). Named on Descanso (1960) 7.5' quadrangle. Postal authorities established Pine Valley post office in 1924 (Frickstad, p. 155).

Pine Valley Creek [SAN DIEGO]: *stream,* flows 23 miles to Barrett Lake 7.5 miles north-northeast of Barrett Junction (lat. 32°43'05" N, long. 116°39'50" W; sec. 3, T 17 S, R 3 E); the stream goes through Pine Valley (2). Named on Barrett Lake (1960), Cuyamaca Peak (1960), Descanso (1960), and Viejas Mountain (1960) 7.5' quadrangles.

Pine Valley Station [SAN DIEGO]: *locality,* 8 miles northeast of Dulzura (lat. 32°42'30" N, long. 116°40' W; near N line sec. 10, T 17 S, R 3 E). Named on Cuyamaca (1903) 30' quadrangle.

Pinkerton Canyon: see **Big Canyon** [VENTURA].

Pinnacle: see **The Pinnacle** [LOS ANGELES].

Pinnacle Rocks: see **Twin Rocks** [LOS ANGELES].

Piñon Point [SAN DIEGO]: *relief feature,* 8 miles north-northeast of Buckman Springs at Mount Laguna (lat. 32°52'15" N, long. 116° 25' W; near N line sec. 13, T 15 S, R 5 E). Named on Mount Laguna (1960) 7.5' quadrangle.

Pinos: see **Mount Pinos** [VENTURA].

Pin Rock [LOS ANGELES]: *rock,* near the mouth of Catalina Harbor on the south side of Santa Catalina Island, and 300 feet offshore (lat. 33°25'30" N, long. 118°30'20" W). Named on Santa Catalina West (1943) 7.5' quadrangle.

Pinyon Canyon [SAN DIEGO]: *canyon,* 4.5 miles long, along Pinyon Wash above a point 10 miles west-southwest of Ocotillo Wells (lat. 33°05'25" N, long. 116°17'45" W). Named on Whale Peak (1959) 7.5' quadrangle.

Pinyon Flats [LOS ANGELES]: *area,* 9 miles west-southwest of Valyermo (lat. 34°22'35" N, long. 117°59'15" W; near NW cor. sec. 1, T 3 N, R 11 W). Named on Juniper Hills (1959) and Waterman Mountain (1959) 7.5' quadrangles.

Pinyon Mountains [SAN DIEGO]: *range,* 12 miles west-southwest of Ocotillo Wells (lat. 33°04' N, long. 116°19'45" W). Named on Whale Peak (1959) 7.5' quadrangle. United States Board on Geographic Names (1961b, p. 12) rejected the names "North Pinyon Mountains" and "Vallecito Mountains" for the range.

Pinyon Mountains: see **North Pinyon Mountains** [SAN DIEGO]; **Vallecito Mountains** [SAN DIEGO].

Pinyon Mountain Valley [SAN DIEGO]: *valley,* 13 miles west-southwest of Ocotillo Wells (lat. 33°03' N, long. 116°19'45" W); the valley is south of Pinyon Mountains. Named on Whale Peak (1959) 7.5' quadrangle.

Pinyon Ridge [LOS ANGELES]: *ridge,* west-northwest-trending, 5.5 miles long, center 4 miles southeast of Valyermo (lat. 34°24'30" N, long., 117°48' W). Named on Valyermo (1958) 7.5' quadrangle.

Pinyon Ridge [SAN DIEGO]: *ridge,* east- to east-southeast-trending, 7 miles long, center 6 miles south-southwest of Borrego Springs (lat. 33°10'15" N, long. 116°24'45" W). Named on Tubb Canyon (1959) 7.5' quadrangle.

Pinyon Spring [SAN DIEGO]: *spring,* 8.5 miles southwest of Borrego Springs (lat. 33°10'20" N, long. 116°28'50" W). Named on Tubb Canyon (1959) 7.5' quadrangle.

Pinyon Wash [SAN DIEGO]: *stream,* flows 4 miles to San Felipe Creek 9 miles south-southeast of Borrego Springs (lat. 33°08' N, long. 116°18'30" W; sec. 13, T 12 S, R 6 E); the stream heads at the mouth of Pinyon Canyon. Named on Borrego Sink (1959) and Whale Peak (1959) 7.5' quadrangles.

Pioneer Pass [VENTURA]: *pass,* 1.25 miles southwest of Santa Susana Pass (lat. 34°15'25" N, long. 118°38'55" W). Named on Santa Susana (1951) 7.5' quadrangle.

Pio Pico: see **Fort Pio Pico**, under **Zuñiga Point** [SAN DIEGO].

Pipe Canyon [LOS ANGELES]: *canyon,* drained by a stream that flows 1.5 miles to Big Tujunga Canyon 2.5 miles north-northeast of Sunland (lat. 34°17'35" N, long. 118°17'05" W; sec. 6, T 2 N, R 13 W). Named on Sunland (1953) 7.5' quadrangle.

Piru [VENTURA]: *town,* 7 miles east of Fillmore (lat. 34°24'50" N, long. 118°47'35" W; sec. 20, T 4 N, R 18 W); the place is near the mouth of Piru Creek. Named on Piru (1952) 7.5' quadrangle. Postal authorities established Piru Rancho post office in 1888, changed the name to Piru City the same year, and changed it to Piru in 1903 (Salley, p. 173). David Cook founded the town in 1887 (Hoover, Rensch, and Rensch, p. 580). California Division of Highways' (1934) map shows a place called Rockbank located 0.5 mile east-northeast of Piru along a rail line.

Piru: see **Lake Piru** [VENTURA].

Piru Canyon [VENTURA]: *canyon,* 6.5 miles long, along Piru Creek above Piru (mouth at lat. 34°25'10" N, long. 118°47'15" W). Named on Piru (1952) 7.5' quadrangle.

Piru City: see **Piru** [VENTURA].

Piru Creek [LOS ANGELES-VENTURA]: *stream,* flows 68 miles, partly in Los Angeles County, to Santa Clara River 1 mile south-southeast of Piru in Ventura County (lat. 34°24' N, long. 118° 47' W). Named on Black Mountain (1958), Cobblestone Mountain (1958), Liebre Mountain (1958), Lockwood Valley (1943), McDonald Peak (1958), Piru (1952), San Guillermo (1943), Val Verde (1952), and Whitaker Peak (1958) 7.5' quadrangles. Called Rio Piru on Parke's (1854-1855) map. Antisell (p. 67) referred to Peyrou river, and Marcou (p. 166) used the designation "Rio de Peru." The name is of Indian origin (Kroeber, p. 54). South Fork enters 10 miles east of Reyes Peak; it is 4.25 miles long and is named on Lockwood Valley (1943) and San Guillermo (1943) 7.5' quadrangles. United States Board on Geographic Names (1990, p. 6) rejected the name "South Fork Piru Creek" for present Cedar Creek [VENTURA].

Piru Gorge [LOS ANGELES]: *narrows,* 11 miles south-southeast of Gorman (lat. 34°38'30" N, long. 118°45'50" W; mainly in sec. 2, T 6 N, R 18 W); the feature is along Piru Creek. Named on Black Mountain (1958) 7.5' quadrangle.

Piru Rancho: see **Piru** [VENTURA].

Pisgah Grande: see **Chatsworth** [LOS ANGELES].

Pitas Point [VENTURA]: *promontory,* 6 miles west-northwest of Ventura along the coast (lat. 34°19'05" N, long. 119°23'15" W; sec. 27, T 3 N, R 24 W). Named on Pitas Point (1950) 7.5' quadrangle. United States Board on Geographic Names (1961c, p. 14) rejected the names "Point las Petes,"

"Point Las Pitas," and "Point Los Pitas" for the feature, and pointed out that the name is from *los pitos,* which means "the whistles" in Spanish—Portola gave this designation to an Indian village at the place in 1769 after members of his party were kept awake at night by noise that Indians made with pipes or whistles (Hoover, Rensch, and Rensch, p. 577).

Piute Butte [LOS ANGELES]: *hill,* 12.5 miles northeast of Littlerock (lat. 34°39'30" N, long. 117°51' W; mainly in sec. 32, T 7 N, R 9 W). Named on Hi Vista (1957) 7.5' quadrangle.

Piute Ponds [LOS ANGELES]: *lake,* about 1.25 miles long, 6.25 miles north-northeast of Lancaster (lat. 34°47'20" N, long. 118°06'50" W; sec. 13, 14, T 8 N, R 12 W). Named on Rosamond (1973) and Rosamond Lake (1973) 7.5' quadrangles.

Placentia [ORANGE]: *city,* 6 miles north of Orange city hall (lat. 33° 52'15" N, long. 117°52'10" W). Named on Anaheim (1965), La Habra (1964), Orange (1964), and Yorba Linda (1964) 7.5' quadrangles. Postal authorities established Placentia post office in 1893, discontinued it in 1903, and reestablished it in 1911 (Frickstad, p. 117). The city incorporated in 1926. The name is from Placentia school district, which was organized at the place in 1879 (Meadows, p. 111). Residents of an area along Orangethorpe Avenue near Placentia incorporated in 1920 as the City of Orangethorpe to keep neighboring Fullerton from putting a sewer farm in their midst; after the threat from Fullerton passed, the City of Orangethorpe disincorporated (Carpenter, p. 194).

Placerita Canyon [LOS ANGELES]: *canyon,* drained by Placerita Creek, which flows 7 miles to South Fork Santa Clara River at Newhall (lat. 34°23'30" N, long., 118°32'10" W). Named on Mint Canyon (1960) and Newhall (1952) 7.5' quadrangles. Called La Placerita Canyon on Newhall (1933) 6' quadrangle. Preston (1890a, p. 200) referred to Placerito Cañon. The name recalls placer gold that Francisco Lopez found at the place in 1842 (Bunje and Kean, p. 9).

Placerita Creek [LOS ANGELES]: *stream,* flows 7 miles to South Fork Santa Clara River at Newhall (lat. 34°23'30" N, long. 118°32'10" W). Named on Newhall (1952) 7.5' quadrangle.

Plaisted Creek [SAN DIEGO]: *stream,* flows 2.5 miles to Potrero Creek (1) 2.25 miles south-southwest of Boucher Hill (lat. 33°18'05" N, long. 116°55'50" W). Named on Boucher Hill (1948) 7.5' quadrangle.

Plano Trabuco [ORANGE]: *area,* extends southwest from the mouth of Trabuco Canyon between Arroyo Trabuco and Tiejeras Canyon; center about 6 miles southwest of Santiago Peak (lat. 33°38'15" N, long. 117°36' W). Named on Cañada Gobernadora (1949) and Santiago Peak (1954) 7.5' quadrangles. The feature now is called Trabuco Mesa (Meadows, p. 111).

Playa del Rey [LOS ANGELES]: *district,* 5 miles north-northwest of Manhattan Beach city hall in Los Angeles (lat. 33°57'05" N, long. 118°26'40" W). Named on Venice (1964) 7.5' quadrangle. Postal authorities established Playa del Rey post office in 1904, discontinued it in 1914, reestablished it in 1939, and changed the name to Playa Del Rey (with a capital "D") in 1960 (Salley, p. 174). Redondo (1896) 15' quadrangle shows a place called Port Ballona located at present Playa del Rey near the present mouth of Ballona Creek. Postal authorities established Port Ballona post office in 1887 and discontinued it in 1889 (Salley, p. 176). Moye L. Wicks attempted to develop a port and town called Port Ballona at the mouth of Ballona Creek in 1886, but the promotion failed; the venture was revived in 1902 and renamed Playa del Rey (Gleason, p. 120). A place called Tell's Landing, operated by Captain William Tell, also was situated at present Playa del Rey (Burnham, p. 339). During the Civil War a garrison of California volunteers occupied Fort Latham, which was located just back of present Playa Del Rey; the estuary at the mouth of Ballona Creek was considered a possible shipping and landing place for Southern sympathizers (Bell, p. 75). Venice (1924) 6' quadrangle has the name "Palisades del Rey" at present Playa del Rey.

Playa del Rey Beach [LOS ANGELES]: *beach,* 4 miles north-northwest of Manhattan Beach city hall along the coast (lat. 33°56'30" N, long. 118°26'30" W); the beach is at Playa del Rey. Named on Venice (1950) 7.5' quadrangle.

Pleasant Ranchos [ORANGE]: *locality,* nearly 6 miles south-southeast of present Buena Park civic center (lat. 33°47' N, long. 117°58'05" W; sec. 31, T 4 S, R 10 W). Named on Anaheim (1950) 7.5' quadrangle.

Pleasants Peak [ORANGE]: *peak,* 15 miles east of Santa Ana on Orange-Riverside County line (lat. 33°47'45" N, long. 117°36'20" W; at E line sec. 28, T 4 S, R 7 W). Altitude 4007 feet. Named on Corona South (1967) 7.5' quadrangle. Called Sugarloaf Peak on Corona (1942) 15' quadrangle, but United States Board on Geographic Names (1934, p. 14) rejected this name for the feature, and noted that Orange County Historical Society suggested the name "Pleasants Peak" to honor J.E. Pleasants, who was associated with the peak since 1860.

Pleasant Valley [VENTURA]: *valley,* at and near Camarillo (lat. 34° 13' N, long. 119°02'15" W). Named on Camarillo (1950) and Newbury Park (1951) 7.5' quadrangles.

Pleasant View Ridge [LOS ANGELES]: *ridge,* generally northwest-trending, 5 miles long, 5 miles southwest of Valyermo (lat. 34°24'45" N, long. 117°55'45" W). Named on Crystal Lake (1958), Juniper Hills (1959), and Valyermo (1958) 7.5' quadrangles.

Plum Canyon [LOS ANGELES]: *canyon,* drained by a stream that flows 4 miles to Bouquet Canyon 3.5 miles northwest of Solemint (lat. 34°27'05" N, long. 118°29'55" W; near NW cor. sec. 7, T 4 N, R 15 W). Named on Mint Canyon (1960) 7.5' quadrangle.

Plum Canyon [SAN DIEGO]: *canyon,* drained by a stream that flows 2.5 miles to San Felipe Creek 9 miles south-southwest of Borrego Springs (lat. 33°07'50" N, long. 116°25'30" W). Named on Earthquake Valley (1959) and Tubb Canyon (1959) 7.5' quadrangles.

Plum Spring [LOS ANGELES]: *spring,* 6 miles south-southwest of the village of Lake Hughes in Clearwater Canyon (lat. 34°35'35" N, long. 118°28'45" W). Named on Green Valley (1958) 7.5' quadrangle.

Poche [ORANGE]: *locality,* 4.25 miles south-southeast of San Juan Capistrano along Atchison, Topeka and Santa Fe Railroad (lat. 33° 26'30" N, long. 117°38'35" W). Named on Dana Point (1968) 7.5' quadrangle.

Poggi Canyon [SAN DIEGO]: *canyon,* drained by a stream that flows 6.25 miles to Otay River 4.5 miles east-northeast of Imperial Beach (lat. 32°35'25" N, long. 117°02'25" W; sec. 24, T 18 S, R 2 W). Named on Imperial Beach (1967), Jamul Mountains (1955), and Otay Mesa (1955) 7.5' quadrangles. The name commemorates Joseph Poggi, who was a cattleman in the neighborhood (Stein, p. 99).

Point Comfort: see **Old Point Comfort** [LOS ANGELES].

Point Dume [LOS ANGELES]: *promontory,* 33 miles east of Los Angeles city hall along the coast (lat. 34°00' N, long. 118°48'20" W). Named on Point Dume (1951) 7.5' quadrangle. Called Dume Pt. on Camulos (1903) 30' quadrangle, and called Pt. Duma on Park's (1854-1855) map. Preston (1890a, p. 208) referred to Point Dumas. United States Board on Geographic Names (1933, p. 275) rejected the forms "Point Duma" and "Point Dumetz" for the name. Vancouver (p. 174) named the feature in 1793 to honor Father Francisco Dumetz, but used the misspelled name "Point Dume." California Mining Bureau's (1917a) map shows a place called El Venado located about 2.5 miles north of Point Dume. Postal authorities established El Venado post office 27 miles northwest of Santa Monica (SE quarter of SE quarter sec. 20, T 1 S, R 18 W) in 1914 and discontinued it in 1917 (Salley, p. 69).

Point Dumetz: see **Point Dume** [LOS ANGELES].

Point Fermin [LOS ANGELES]: *promontory,* 7.5 miles southwest of Long Beach city hall along the coast (lat. 33°42'15" N, long. 118° 17'35" W). Named on San Pedro (1964) 7.5' quadrangle. Vancouver (p. 63. 176) named the feature in 1793 to honor Fermin Francisco de Lasuen, father president of the Franciscan order. Postal authorities established Firmin post office near Point Fermin in 1911 and moved it in 1912 when they changed the name to Point Fermin; they moved it again in 1918 when they changed the name to Gibson, and discontinued it in 1948 (Salley, p. 75, 84, 174).

Point Gorda: see **Punta Gorda** [VENTURA].

Point Hueneme [VENTURA]: *promontory,* 4 miles south-southwest of Oxnard (lat. 34°08'45" N, long. 119°12'55" W). Named on Oxnard (1949) 7.5' quadrangle. Called Hueneme Point on Hueneme (1904) 15' quadrangle. The name is of Indian origin (Kroeber, p. 43).

Point La Jolla [SAN DIEGO]: *promontory,* 11.5 miles northwest of downtown San Diego along the coast (lat. 32°51'05" N, long. 117° 16'20" W). Named on La Jolla (1967) 7.5' quadrangle. The name also had the form "Point Lajolla" (Gudde, 1949, p. 168).

Point Las Petes: see **Pitas Point** [VENTURA].

Point Las Pitas: see **Pitas Point** [VENTURA].

Point Loma [SAN DIEGO]:

(1) *peninsula,* 13 miles long, west of San Diego Bay, center 5 miles west-southwest of downtown San Diego (lat. 32°41'45" N, long. 117°14'40" W). Named on Point Loma (1967) 7.5' quadrangle. A Spanish map of 1769 has the name "La Loma que cubre puerto" for the feature (Harlow, 1987, p. 56), and Dalrymple's (1789) map has the name "Pta. de la Loma" for it.

(2) *locality,* 4 miles west of downtown San Diego (lat. 32°43'30" N, long. 117°13'50" W); the place is at the north end of present Point Loma (1). Named on San Diego (1904) 15' quadrangle. Point Loma (1942) 7.5' quadrangle has both the names "Point Loma P.O." and "Roseville" at the site. Postal authorities established Point Loma post office in 1893 (Frickstad, p. 155).

Point Loma Junction [SAN DIEGO]: *locality,* 7.25 miles south-southeast of Point La Jolla along San Diego Electric Railroad (lat. 32°45'15" N, long. 117°13'05" W). Named on La Jolla (1943) 7.5' quadrangle.

Point Los Pitas: see **Pitas Point** [VENTURA].

Point Medanos [SAN DIEGO]: *promontory,* 6.5 miles south of Point La Jolla on the north side of the entrance to Mission Bay (lat. 32° 45'35" N, long. 117°15' W). Named on La Jolla (1967) 7.5' quadrangle. Called Medanos Pt. on La Jolla (1903) 15' quadrangle.

Point Mugu [VENTURA]: *promontory,* 10 miles southeast of Oxnard along the coast (lat. 34°05'10" N, long. 119°03'35" W). Named on Point Mugu (1949) 7.5' quadrangle. Called Mugu Point on Hueneme (1904) 15' quadrangle. Vizcaino called the feature Punta de Rio Dulce in 1602 because of a stream of fresh water near it; then on the return voyage of the expedition early in 1603 it was called Punta de la Conversion for the conversion of San Pablo, celebrated January 25 (Wagner, p. 399). The name "Mugu" is of Indian origin (Kroeber, p. 49).

Point Mugu Navel Reservation [VENTURA]: *military installation,* at Mugu Lagoon. Named on Point Mugu (1949) 7.5' quadrangle.

Point Vicente [LOS ANGELES]: *promontory,* 7 miles south of Redondo Beach city hall along the coast (lat. 33°44'30" N, long. 118°24'40" W). Named on Redondo Beach (1951) 7.5' quadrangle. Called Point Vincente on San Pedro (1944) 15' quadrangle. United States Board on Geographic Names (1933, p. 789) rejected the forms "Point Vincent" and "Point Vincente" for the feature, although they admitted that Vancouver named it Point Vincente in 1793 for Friar Vincente Santa Maria of Buenaventura mission. It is called Relis del Codo on a diseño of Palos Verdes grant—*Relis del Codo* means "Landslide Corner" in Spanish (Becker, 1964).

Point Vincente: see **Point Vicente** [LOS ANGELES].

Poison Oak Canyon [LOS ANGELES]: *canyon,* 1.25 miles long, 10 miles east-southeast of Gorman (lat. 34°44'15" N, long. 118°41'05" W; mainly in sec. 33, T 8 N, R 17 W). Named on Liebre Mountain (1958) 7.5' quadrangle.

Pole Canyon [LOS ANGELES]: *canyon,* drained by a stream that flows nearly 4 miles to Soledad Canyon 5 miles east-northeast of Solemint (lat. 34°25'50" N, long. 118°22'20" W; sec. 17, T 4 N, R 14 W). Named on Agua Duce (1960) 7.5' quadrangle.

Pole Canyon: see **Pole Creek** [VENTURA].

Polecat Gulch [LOS ANGELES]: *canyon,* drained by a stream that flows 1.25 miles to San Gabriel Reservoir 5.25 miles north of Glendora city hall (lat. 34°12'40" N, long. 117°51'35" W; sec. 31, T 2 N, R 9 W). Named on Glendora (1953) 7.5' quadrangle.

Pole Creek [VENTURA]: *stream,* flows 6.5 miles to the valley of Santa Clara River at Fillmore (lat. 34°24'35" N, long. 118°54'20" W; near S line sec. 19, T 4 N, R 19 W). Named on Fillmore (1951) 7.5' quadrangle. On Camulos (1903) 30' quadrangle, the canyon of the stream is called Pole Canyon. The name is from some poles found near the stream—poles that were used in the early days for fence posts; the stream also was called Yellow Creek (Ricard).

Pomeroy Canyon [LOS ANGELES]: *canyon,* drained by a stream that flows 1 mile to Brand Canyon 2 miles east of Burbank city hall (lat. 34°11'10" N, long. 118°16'25" W). Named on Burbank (1953) 7.5' quadrangle.

Pomona [LOS ANGELES]: *city,* 28 miles east of Los Angeles city hall (lat. 34°03'20" N, long. 117°45' W). Named on Ontario (1954) and San Dimas (1954) 7.5' quadrangles, which show a siding called Pomona situated 2.5 miles north of Pomona city hall along Atchison, Topeka and Santa Fe Railroad (lat. 34°05'40" N, long. 117°00' W). Postal authorities established Pomona post office in 1875 (Frickstad, p. 79), and the city incorporated in 1888. Solomon Gates submitted the name "Pomona" in a contest to name the new community in 1875; Gates, a nurseryman, was familiar with the Pomona of the Grangers, and with Pomona, goddess of fruit and trees in Roman mythology (Anonymous, 1976, p. 14).

Pomona: see **North Pomona** [LOS ANGELES].

Pomona Junction [LOS ANGELES]: *locality,* nearly 1.5 miles north of present Pomona city hall along Pacific Electric Railroad (lat. 34° 04'30" N, long. 117°45'10" W). Named on Claremont (1928) 6' quadrangle.

Pomoosa: see **Moosa** [SAN DIEGO].

Ponto [SAN DIEGO]: *locality,* 4 miles north-northwest of Encinitas along Atchison, Topeka and Santa Fe Railroad (lat. 33°05'45" N, long. 117°18'45" W; at SW cor. sec. 28, T 12 S, R 4 W). Named on Encinitas (1968) 7.5' quadrangle. Called Lacosta on San Luis Rey (1898) 30' quadrangle, and called Costa on California Mining Bureau's (1917b) map. Postal authorities established La Costa post office in 1896 and discontinued it in 1905 (Salley, p. 114).

Poor Farm Station [LOS ANGELES]: *locality,* 3.25 miles southeast of present South Gate city hall along Los Angeles Terminal Railroad (lat. 33°55'15" N, long. 118°10' W). Named on Downey (1902) 15' quadrangle. Postal authorities established County Farm post office 2.5 miles northeast of Clearwater at the county home for the indigent in 1908, changed the name to Hondo in 1918, and changed it to Los Amigos in 1957 (Salley, p. 51, 99). South Gate (1952) 7.5' quadrangle shows Hondo post office at Rancho Los Amigos, which is by the site of Poor Farm Station.

Poplar Creek [VENTURA]: *stream,* flows 2.25 miles to Hot Springs Canyon 3.5 miles north-northwest of Devils Heart Peak (lat. 34°35'40" N, long. 119°00' W; sec. 21, T 6 N, R 20 W). Named on Devils Heart Peak (1943) 7.5' quadrangle.

Poplin Creek [VENTURA]: *stream,* flows 2.5 miles to Coyote Creek 7 miles west-southwest of the town of Ojai (lat. 34°24'45" N, long. 119°21'35" W). Named on Matilija (1952) 7.5' quadrangle.

Poppy Peak [LOS ANGELES]: *peak,* 2.5 miles west-southwest of Pasadena city hall (lat. 34°07'50" N, long. 118°10'50" W). Altitude 1038 feet. Named on Pasadena (1953) 7.5' quadrangle.

Portal Ridge [LOS ANGELES]: *ridge,* west-northwest-trending, 18 miles long, northeast of Pine Canyon (1) and Leona Valley (1); center near Elizabeth Lake. Named on Burnt Peak (1958), Del Sur (1958), Lake Hughes (1957), Lancaster West (1958), Ritter Ridge (1958), and Sleepy Valley (1958) 7.5' quadrangles.

Port Ballona: see **Playa del Rey** [LOS ANGELES].

Port Hueneme [VENTURA]: *town,* 3.25 miles south-southwest of Oxnard near the coast (lat. 34°09' N, long. 119°11'45" W). Named on Oxnard (1949) 7.5' quadrangle. Called Hueneme on Hueneme (1904) 15' quadrangle, but United States Board on Geographic Names (1950c, p. 6) rejected this name for the place. Postal authorities established Wynema post office in 1870, changed the name to Hueneme in 1874, and to Port Hueneme in 1940 (Frickstad, p. 219, 220). The town incorporated in 1948. W.E. Barnard and a group of squatters started the community of Wynema in 1870; Thomas R. Bard, owner of the land, laid out the town of Hueneme in 1872—the name of the place became Port Hueneme after construction of a harbor there in 1939 (Ricard). United States Board on Geographic Names (1965a, p. 13) approved the name "Channel Islands Harbor" for a place situated about 1.5 miles northwest of Port Hueneme (lat. 34°09'45" N, long. 119°13'23" W), and rejected the name "Ventura County Small Craft Harbor" for the feature; the name "Channel Islands Harbor" is from the position of the feature at the gateway to the northernmost of the Channel Islands. Ricard listed a place called Arnold located 3 miles southeast of Port Hueneme—the name recalls a family of early residents at the spot.

Portland Canyon: see **Nelson Canyon** [LOS ANGELES].

Port Los Angeles [LOS ANGELES]: *locality,* 2.5 miles west-northwest of present Santa Monica city hall (lat. 34°31'20" N, long. 118° 32'15" W). Named on Calabasas (1903) 15' quadrangle, which shows a pier about 1 mile long there. Officials of Southern Pacific Railroad built a rail line to the place to attract coastal trade away from San Pedro, but eventually railroad officials abandoned the enterprise (Gleason, p. 113-114). Postal authorities established Port Los Angeles post office in 1897 and discontinued it in 1908 (Frickstad, p. 79).

Port Orange: see **McFadden's Landing**, under **Newport Beach** [ORANGE] (2).

Portuguese Bend [LOS ANGELES]:

(1) *embayment,* 4.5 miles west-northwest of Point Fermin (lat. 33° 44'10" N, long. 118°21'45" W). Named on San Pedro (1964) 7.5' quadrangle. The name is from two Portuguese whaling companies that operated at the place in the mid-nineteenth century (Fink, p. 19).

(2) *district,* 5 miles west-northwest of Point Fermin (lat. 33°44'30" N, long. 118°22' W); the place is above Portuguese Bend (1). Named on San Pedro (1964) 7.5' quadrangle.

Portuguese Canyon [LOS ANGELES]: *canyon,* 1.5 miles long, opens to the sea 4.5 miles west-northwest of Point Fermin at Portuguese Bend (1) (lat. 33°44'15" N, long. 118°21'40" W). Named on San Pedro (1964) and Torrance (1964) 7.5' quadrangles.

Portuguese Point [LOS ANGELES]: *promontory,* 5 miles west-northwest of Point Fermin along the coast (lat. 33°44'15" N, long. 118° 22'25" W); the place is 0.5 mile west of Portuguese Bend (1). Named on San Pedro (1964) 7.5' quadrangle.

Poser Mountain [SAN DIEGO]: *ridge,* west-southwest-trending, 1 mile long, 3.5 miles west-northwest of Descanso (lat. 32°52'15" N, long. 116°40'15" W; mainly in sec. 16, T 15 S, R 3 E). Named on Viejas Mountain (1960) 7.5' quadrangle. The name is for Heinrich von Poser, an early settler in the neighborhood (Stein, p. 99).

Posey Canyon [LOS ANGELES]: *canyon,* drained by a stream that flows 2.25 miles to Piru Creek 11.5 miles south-southeast of Gorman (lat. 34°38'45" N, long. 118°45'45" W; near W cor. sec. 2, T 6 N, R 18 W). Named on Black Mountain (1958) and Liebre Mountain (1958) 7.5' quadrangles.

Posita Canyon: see **Palo Comado Canyon** [LOS ANGELES-VENTURA].

Post New San Diego: see **San Diego** [SAN DIEGO].

Potato Mountain [LOS ANGELES]: *peak,* 8.5 miles north-northeast of Pomona city hall (lat. 34°09'55" N, long. 117°41'30" W; near S line sec. 14, T 1 N, R 8 W). Altitude 3422 feet. Named on Mount Baldy (1954) 7.5' quadrangle.

Pothole: see **The Pothole** [VENTURA].

Pothole Canyon [SAN DIEGO]: *canyon,* about 2 miles long, opens into the canyon of Pine Valley Creek 4.25 miles south-southeast of Descanso (lat. 32°47'55" N, long. 116°35'25" W; sec. 8, T 16 S, R 4 E). Named on Descanso (1960) 7.5' quadrangle.

Pot Hole Harbor: see **Empire Landing** [LOS ANGELES].

Potholes: see **The Potholes** [LOS ANGELES].

Pothole Spring [VENTURA]: *spring,* nearly 6 miles southeast of Cobblestone Mountain (lat. 34°32'30" N, long. 118°48'20" W; near S line sec. 6, T 5 N, R 18 W); the spring is 0.5 mile north-northwest of The Pothole. Named on Cobblestone Mountain (1958) 7.5' quadrangle.

Potrero [SAN DIEGO]: *village,* 5.5 miles east of Barrett Junction (lat. 32°36'20" N, long. 116°36'35" W; sec. 18, T 18 S, R 4 E). Named on Potrero (1960) 7.5' quadrangle. Postal authorities established Potrero post office in 1876 and moved it 1 mile southwest in 1900 (Salley, p. 177).

Potrero: see **Hidden Valley** [VENTURA]; **The Potrero** [SAN DIEGO].

Potrero Canyon [LOS ANGELES]: *canyon,* 7.25 miles long, opens into the valley of Santa Clara River 8.5 miles west of Newhall (lat. 34°24'10" N, long. 118°40'25" W). Named on Newhall (1952) and Val Verde (1952) 7.5' quadrangles. Called Larres Canyon on Los Angeles County (1935) map.

Potrero Canyon: see **Castaic Junction** [LOS ANGELES].

Potrero Chico [LOS ANGELES]: *land grant,* 3.5 miles southwest of El Monte city hall along Rio Hondo south of Potrero Grande grant. Named on El Monte (1953) 7.5' quadrangle. According to Cowan (p. 62-63), Antonio Valenzuela received the land in 1843, and Ramon Valenzuela and others claimed it. According to Perez (p. 82), who listed the grant under the name "Potrero de la Mission Vieja de San Gabriel," Juan Alvitre and Antonio Valenzuela were the grantees in 1844, and they were the patentees for 83.46 acres in 1923.

Potrero Creek [SAN DIEGO]:

(1) *stream,* flows 5.5 miles to San Luis Rey River 4.5 miles southwest of Boucher Hill (lat. 33°16'50" N, long. 116°58'05" W; sec. 27, T 10 S, R 1 W). Named on Boucher Hill (1948) 7.5' quadrangle.

(2) *stream,* flows 10.5 miles to Cottonwood Creek (3) 0.5 mile east-southeast of Barett Junction (lat. 32°36'35" N, long. 116°41'50" W; near N line sec. 17, T 18 S, R 3 E); the stream goes through Long Potrero and Big Potrero. Named on Morena Reservoir (1960), Potrero (1960), and Tecate (1960) 7.5' quadrangles. United States Board on Geographic Names (1962a, p. 15) rejected the name "Big Potrero Creek" for the stream.

Potrero Creek: see **Little Potrero Creek** [SAN DIEGO].

Potrero de Felipe Lugo [LOS ANGELES]: *land grant,* 2 miles south of El Monte city hall along San Gabriel River. Named on El Monte (1953) 7.5' quadrangle. Teodoro Romero and others received the land in 1845; Jorge Morillo claimed 2042 acres patented in 1871 (Cowan, p. 63).

Potrero de la Mission Vieja de San Gabriel: see **Potrero Chico** [LOS ANGELES].

Potrero de Pauma: see **Pauma** [SAN DIEGO].

Potrero Grande [LOS ANGELES]: *land grant,* southwest of downtown El Monte. Named on El Monte (1953) 7.5' quadrangle. Manuel Antonio received 1 league in 1845; J. Matias Sanchez claimed 4432 acres patented in 1859 (Cowan, p. 63).

Potrero John Creek [VENTURA]: *stream,* flows nearly 4 miles to Sespe Creek 5.25 miles north-northeast of Wheeler Springs (lat. 34°35'05" N, long. 119°16' W; sec. 25, T 6 N, R 23 W). Named on Wheeler Springs (1943) 7.5' quadrangle.

Potrero los Pinos [ORANGE]: *land grant,* 4 miles south of Trabuco Peak. Named on Alberhill (1954) 7.5' quadrangle.

Potrero Peak [SAN DIEGO]: *peak,* 1.5 miles northwest of Potrero (lat. 32°37'10" N, long. 116°38' W; sec. 12, 18 S, R 3 E). Altitude 3344 feet. Named on Tecate (1960) 7.5' quadrangle.

Potrero Seco [VENTURA]: *valley,* 8 miles west of Reyes Peak (lat. 34°38'10" N, long. 119°25'20" W). Named on Rancho Nuevo Creek (1943) 7.5' quadrangle.

Potrero Valley [VENTURA]: *valley,* 3.5 miles southwest of Newbury Park (lat. 34°09'25" N, long. 118°57'45" W). Named on Newbury Park (1951) 7.5' quadrangle.

Potrero Valley Creek [LOS ANGELES-VENTURA]: *stream,* heads in Ventura County and flows 12 miles to Malibu Lake 7.5 miles north-northeast of Point Dume in Los Angeles County (lat. 34°06'20" N, long. 118°45'50" W; near SE cor. sec. 4, T 1 S, R 18 W). Named on Thousand Oaks (1952) 7.5' quadrangle.

Pots Valley: see **Valley of Ollas** [LOS ANGELES].

Pound Cake Hill: see **Signal Hill** [LOS ANGELES] (1).

Poverty Canyon [VENTURA]: *canyon,* drained by a stream that flows 1.25 miles to Casitas Valley 6 miles south of White Ledge Peak (lat. 34°23'05" N, long. 119°23'50" W; sec. 33, T 4 N, R 24 W). Named on White Ledge Peak (1952) 7.5' quadrangle.

Poverty Gulch [SAN DIEGO]: *canyon,* about 1 mile long, 3.5 miles northwest of Descanso (lat. 32°53'05" N, long. 116°40'05" W; sec. 9, 10, T 15 S, R 3 E). Named on Tule Springs (1960) 7.5' quadrangle.

Poway [SAN DIEGO]: *city,* 18 miles north-northeast of San Diego (lat. 32°57'35" N, long. 117°02'10" W). Named on Poway (1967) 7.5' quadrangle. Postal authorities established Poway post office in 1870 (Frickstad, p. 155), and the city incorporated in 1980. Postal authorities established Virginia post office 8 miles southwest of Poway in 1890 and discontinued it in 1900; the name was for Virginia A. Tower, first postmaster (Salley, p. 232). According to an item in *The Weekly Philatelic Era* for September 27, 1902:

> The post office building in Virginia, Cal., has the distinction of being the smallest in the world. It is located on the stage road which runs north from San Diego, and it is far from any other building or habitation. Upon the days which bring the stage past the tiny edifice the postmaster comes to the roadside office and awaits the coming of the stage which brings the mail. When it arrives the mail which has been deposited in the letter drop by the five or six patrons of the office is exchanged for that which the stage has brought for the Virginia office, and it is distributed in the rude lock boxes—the locks being padlocks—which have been attached to the office building. These being accessible from the outside, the presence of the postmaster at times other than the coming of the stage is not essential.

Poway Creek [SAN DIEGO]: *stream,* flows 7.25 miles to join Beeler Creek and form Los Peñasquitos Creek 2 miles west-southwest of Poway (lat. 32°57' N, long. 117°04' W; near NE cor. sec. 22, T 14 S, R 2 W). Named on Poway (1967, photorevised 1975) and San Vicente Reservoir (1955) 7.5' quadrangles.

Poway Grove [SAN DIEGO]: *locality,* 2 miles southwest of Poway near the mouth of Beeler Canyon (lat. 32°56'30" N, long. 117°03'55" W; near W line sec. 23, T 14 S, R 2 W). Named on Poway Valley (1952) 7.5' quadrangle.

Poway Valley [SAN DIEGO]: *valley,* at Poway (lat. 32°58' N, long. 117°02'15" W). Named on Poway (1967) 7.5' quadrangle.

Powder Canyon [LOS ANGELES]: *canyon,* 1.5 miles long, 2.5 miles north-northeast of La Habra [ORANGE] (lat. 33°57'50" N, long. 117°50'30" W). Named on La Habra (1964) 7.5' quadrangle.

Powder Dump Wash [SAN DIEGO]: *stream,* flows less than 0.5 mile to the canyon of San Felipe Creek 9.5 miles south-southeast of Borrego Springs (lat. 33°07'50" N, long. 116°18'05" W; sec. 13, T 12 S, R 6 E). Named on Borrego Sink (1959) 7.5' quadrangle.

Powells Store: see **Julian** [SAN DIEGO].

Powerhouse Canyon [SAN DIEGO]: *canyon,* about 2 miles long, 1.5 miles northeast of downtown San Diego (lat. 32°43'55" N, long. 117°08'35" W). Named on Point Loma (1967) 7.5' quadrangle.

Prairie Fork [LOS ANGELES]: *stream,* heads just inside San Bernardino County and flows 4.5 miles to San Gabriel River nearly 6 miles northwest of Mount San Antonio (lat. 34°20'35" N, long. 117°43'25" W; sec. 16, T 3 N, R 8 W). Named on Mount San Antonio (1955) 7.5' quadrangle.

Pratt Canyon [LOS ANGELES]: *canyon,* drained by a stream that flows 1.5 miles to an unnamed canyon 3.5 miles north-northwest of Burnt Peak (lat. 34°43'35" N, long. 118°36'25" W; at E line sec. 6, T 7 N, R 16 W). Named on Burnt Peak (1958) 7.5' quadrangle.

Precipicio Canyon: see **Eaton Canyon** [LOS ANGELES].

Precipicio Peak: see **Occidental Peak** [LOS ANGELES].

Presidio Hill: see **Old Town** [SAN DIEGO].

Previtt Canyon [SAN DIEGO]: *canyon,* drained by a stream that flows 2.5 miles to Dodge Valley 9 miles northwest of Warner Springs (lat. 33°22'35" N, long. 116°44'16" W; at E line sec. 23, T 9 S, R 2 E). Named on Beauty Mountain (1960) and Warner Springs (1959) 7.5' quadrangles.

Price: see **Dan Price Creek** [SAN DIEGO].

Price Canyon [LOS ANGELES]: *canyon,* drained by a stream that flows 2 miles to Fairmont Reservoir 2 miles north of the village of Lake Hughes (lat. 34°42'15" N, long. 118°26'15" W; near S line sec. 11, T 7 N, R 15 W). Named on Lake Hughes (1957) 7.5' quadrangle. Los Angeles County (1935) map has the name "Hughes Canyon" for a feature that branches east from Price Canyon just above Fairmont Reservoir.

Prima Deshecha Cañada [ORANGE]: *canyon,* drained by a stream that flows 5 miles to the sea 4.25 miles south-southeast of San Juan Capistrano (lat. 33°26'25" N, long. 117°38'40" W). Named on Dana Point (1949) and San Clemente (1968) 7.5' quadrangles. On Capistrano (1902) 30' quadrangle, the name applies to the stream in the canyon. The feature is the first difficult canyon to cross on the road south from San Juan Capistrano mission—*Prima Deshecha Cañada* means "First Rough Canyon" in Spanish (Meadows, p. 112-113).

Primitive Camp [SAN DIEGO]: *locality,* 2 miles south-southeast of Cuyamaca Peak (lat. 32°55'10" N, long. 116°35'55" W). Named on Cuyamaca Peak (1960) 7.5' quadrangle.

Prince Barranca [VENTURA]: *gully,* extends for 0.5 mile from the mouth of Hall Canyon 1.5 miles east of downtown Ventura (lat. 34°16'45" N, long. 119°15'45" W). Named on Ventura (1951) 7.5' quadrangle. The name commemorates Francis Munroe Prince, an early settler; the feature also had the name "Cunnane Barranca" for Dr. Cunnane, who owned property there (Ricard).

Pringle Canyon [SAN DIEGO]: *canyon,* 3 miles long, opens into the canyon of Dulzura Creek 7 miles southeast of Jamul (lat. 32°39' N, long. 116°47'05" W; near W line sec. 33, T 17 S, R 2 E). Named on Dulzura (1972) 7.5' quadrangle.

Prisoner Creek [SAN DIEGO]: *stream,* flows 3 miles to San Luis Rey River 8 miles southeast of Boucher Hill (lat. 33°15'45" N, long. 116°48'15" W; sec. 31, T 10 S, R 2 E). Named on Mesa Grande (1948) and Palomar Observatory (1949) 7.5' quadrangles.

Proctor Valley [SAN DIEGO]: *valley,* 4 miles southwest of Jamul (lat. 32°40'15" N, long. 116°55'20" W). Named on Jamul (1955) 7.5' quadrangle. The name recalls Professor Richard Proctor, an English astronomer whose wife wanted to build an observatory on San Miguel Mountain as a memorial to her husband (Stein, p. 101).

Prospect Bar: see **Eldoradoville Campground** [LOS ANGELES].

Prospect Canyon [LOS ANGELES]: *canyon,* drained by a stream that flows

1.5 miles to Elizabeth Lake Canyon 2.25 miles north-northeast of Warm Springs Mountain (lat. 34°37'20" N, long. 118°33'20" W). Named on Burnt Peak (1958) and Warm Springs Mountain (1958) 7.5' quadrangles.

Prospect Park [LOS ANGELES]: *locality*, 4.5 miles northwest of present Los Angeles city hall (lat. 34°05'45" N, long. 118°17'55" W). Named on Santa Monica (1902) 15' quadrangle. Postal authorities established Prospect Park post office in 1888 and discontinued it in 1912 (Salley, p. 178).

Prospero Tract [LOS ANGELES]: *land grant*, at San Marino. Named on El Monte (1953) and Mount Wilson (1953) 7.5' quadrangles. Antonio Valenzuela and Prospero Valenzuela received the land in 1843; Ramon Valenzuela and others claimed 24 acres patented in 1875 (Cowan, p. 31; Cowan listed the grant under the designation "Cuati, (or) Prospero").

Providencia [LOS ANGELES]: *land grant*, extends from southwest of downtown Burbank to Cahuenga Peak. Named on Burbank (1953) 7.5' quadrangle. Vicente de la Osa was the grantee in 1843; David W. Alexander and Francis Mellus were the petentees for 4064 acres in 1872 (Perez, p. 83).

Puckett Canyon: see **Vasquez Canyon** [LOS ANGELES].

Puddingstone Reservoir [LOS ANGELES]: *lake*, nearly 4 miles northwest of Pomona city hall in San Jose Hills (lat. 34°05'15" N, long. 117°48'20" W). Named on San Dimas (1954) 7.5' quadrangle.

Pueblitos Canyon [SAN DIEGO]: *canyon*, 2 miles long, opens into the valley of Santa Margarita River 10 miles southwest of Fallbrook (lat. 33°16'20" N, long. 117°22'15" W; near S line sec. 26, T 10 S, R 5 W). Named on Morro Hill (1968) 7.5' quadrangle.

Pueblo de Los Angeles: see **Los Angeles** [LOS ANGELES].

Pueblo Lands of San Diego [SAN DIEGO]: *land grant*, at San Diego. Named on Del Mar (1967), La Jolla (1967), National City (1967), and Point Loma (1967) 7.5' quadrangles.

Pueblo Siding [SAN DIEGO]: *locality*, 6 miles east-northeast of Campo along San Diego and Arizona Eastern Railroad (lat. 32° 38' N, long. 116°27'15" W). Named on Campo (1939) 15' quadrangle.

Puente: see **La Puente** [LOS ANGELES] (2).

Puente Creek [LOS ANGELES]: *stream*, flows 5.5 miles to San Jose Creek 4.5 miles south-southwest of Baldwin Park city hall (lat. 34° 01'30" N, long. 117°58'45" W); the stream is on La Puente grant. Named on Baldwin Park (1966) 7.5' quadrangle.

Puente Hills [LOS ANGELES-ORANGE]: *range*, north of Whittier and La Habra between San Gabriel River and Brea Canyon in Los Angeles, Orange, and San Bernardino Counties. Named on Los Angeles (1975), San Bernardino (1957), and Santa Ana (1959) 1°x 2° quadrangles. Baldwin Park (1953) 7.5' quadrangle also has the name "Puente Hills" for a small range located just east of downtown La Puente and separated from the main Puente Hills by San Jose Creek. Parke's (1854-1855) map has the name "Sierra de Santa Ana" for present Puente Hills and present Santa Ana Mountains combined. English (p. 5) applied the name "Puente Hills" to "The whole group of hills lying between the towns of Pomona, Whittier, and Corona and a small area directly south of the town of Puente," and noted that "the name should preferably be used for the group of hills lying between Santa Ana and San Gabriel rivers." English (p. 5) noted also that "The part of the Puente Hills directly north of the city of Whittier and east to La Habra Canyon" is called Whittier Hills. Poland and others' (1956) map has the name "Whittier Narrows" for the place that both San Gabriel River and Rio Hondo pass the west end of Puente Hills.

Puente Junction [LOS ANGELES]: *locality*, 5 miles south of Baldwin Park city hall along Union Pacific Railroad (lat. 34°00'50" N, long. 117°57'35" W). Named on Baldwin Park (1966) 7.5' quadrangle. Called Puente Sta. on Puente (1927) 6' quadrangle.

Puente Largo [LOS ANGELES]: *locality*, 1 mile west-northwest of Azusa city hall along Pacific Electric Railroad (lat. 34°08'20" N, long. 117°55'30" W). Named on Azusa (1953) 7.5' quadrangle.

Puente Station: see **Puente Junction** [LOS ANGELES].

Puerco Beach [LOS ANGELES]: *beach*, 2 miles west of Malibu Point along the coast (lat. 34°01'50" N, long. 118°43'05" W); the beach is mainly east of the mouth of Puerco Canyon. Named on Malibu Beach (1951) 7.5' quadrangle.

Puerco Canyon [LOS ANGELES]: *canyon*, drained by a stream that flows 2.25 miles to the sea 2.5 miles west of Malibu Point (lat. 34° 01'55" N, long. 118°43'25" W). Named on Malibu Beach (1951) 7.5' quadrangle.

Puerta de San Felipe: see **Box Canyon** [SAN DIEGO] (2).

Puerta la Cruz [SAN DIEGO]: *locality*, 4 miles west-northwest of Warner Springs (lat. 33°18'35" N, long. 116°41'30" W). Named on Warner Springs (1959) 7.5' quadrangle. The name evidently is from a cross that Spaniards erected at the site in 1821 (Hill, p. 42).

Puerto Falsa: see **Mission Bay** [SAN DIEGO].

Pulga Canyon [LOS ANGELES]: *canyon*, drained by a stream that flows nearly 3 miles to the sea 3.5 miles west-northwest of Santa Monica city hall (lat. 34°02'20" N, long. 118°32'35" W). Named on Topanga (1952) 7.5' quadrangle. Called Las Pulgas Canyon on Los Angeles County (1935) map.

Pulgas: see **Camp Pulgas** [SAN DIEGO].

Pulgas Lake [SAN DIEGO]: *lake*, 1700 feet long, 3.5 miles east-southeast of San Onofre Mountain in Piedra de Lumbre Canyon (lat. 33°20'45" N, long. 117°26'10" W; near SE cor. sec. 31, T 9 S, R 5 W). Named on Las Pulgas Canyon (1968) 7.5' quadrangle.

Punchbowl Canyon [LOS ANGELES]: *canyon*, drained by a stream that flows 3.5 miles to Big Rock Creek 2 miles south-southeast of Valyermo (lat. 34°25'20" N, long. 117°50'15" W; sec. 20, T 4 N, R 9 W); part of the canyon is in Devils Punchbowl. Named on Valyermo (1958) 7.5' quadrangle. On Los Angeles County (1935) map, the stream in the canyon is called Punchbowl Creek.

Punchbowl Creek: see **Punchbowl Canyon** [LOS ANGELES].

Punta [VENTURA]: *settlement*, 4.5 miles northwest of Pitas Point (lat. 34°21'50" N, long. 119°26'50" W; on S line sec. 1, T 3 N, R 25 W); the place is 0.5 mile north-northwest of Punta Gorda. Named on Pitas Point (1950) 7.5' quadrangle. Called Punta Gorda on Ventura (1904) 15' quadrangle. Postal authorities established Punta Gorda post office in 1888 and discontinued it in 1916 (Frickstad, p. 219).

Punta de Arbolada: see **Dana Point** [ORANGE].

Punta de la Conversion: see **Point Mugu** [VENTURA].

Punta de los Guijarros: see **Ballast Point** [SAN DIEGO].

Punta de los Muertos: see **San Diego** [SAN DIEGO].

Punta de Rio Dulce: see **Point Mugu** [VENTURA].

Punta Gorda [VENTURA]: *promontory*, 4 miles northwest of Pitas Point (lat. 34°21'20" N, long. 119°26'30" W; near W line sec. 7, T 3 N, R 24 W). Named on Pitas Point (1950) 7.5' quadrangle. United States Board on Geographic Names (1961c, p. 10) rejected the form "Point Gorda" for the name.

Punta Gorda: see **Punta** [VENTURA].

Puzzle Canyon [LOS ANGELES]: *canyon*, drained by a stream that flows nearly 3 miles to lowlands 4.25 miles north of Big Pines (lat. 34°26'30" N, long. 117°40'35" W; near SE cor. sec. 11, T 4 N, R 8 W). Named on Mescal Creek (1956) 7.5' quadrangle.

Pyramid Cove [LOS ANGELES]: *embayment*, 2 miles west of Pyramid Head at the southeast end of San Clemente Island (lat. 32° 49'20" N, long. 118°23' W). Named on San Clemente Island South (1943) 7.5' quadrangle. Called Smugglers Cove on Smith's (1898) map.

Pyramid Head [LOS ANGELES]: *promontory*, at the southeast end of San Clement Island (lat. 32°49'15" N, long. 118°20'55" W). Named on San Clemente Island South (1943) 7.5' quadrangle. The name is from the resemblance of the promontory to a pyramid (Doran, 1980, p. 52). United States Board on Geographic Names (1978c, p. 3) approved the name "Balanced Rock" for a feature situated 0.5 mile southwest of Pyramid Head (lat. 32°48'58" N, long. 118°21'15" W), and rejected the names "Whitewashed Rock" and "White Washed Rock" for it.

Pyramid Lake [LOS ANGELES]: *lake*, behind a dam on Piru Creek 11 miles south-southeast of Gorman in Piru Gorge (lat. 34°38'35" N, long. 118°45'45" W; sec. 2, T 6 N, R 18 W); Pyramid Rock is just south of the dam. Named on Black Mountain (1958, photorevised 1974) 7.5' quadrangle.

Pyramid Rock [LOS ANGELES]: *relief feature*, 11.5 miles south-southeast of Gorman in Piru Gorge (lag. 34°38'30" N, long. 118°45'50" W; sec. 2, T 6 N, R 18 W). Named on Black Mountain (1958) 7.5' quadrangle.

- Q -

Quail [LOS ANGELES]: *locality*, nearly 6 miles east-southeast of Gorman at the northwest edge of present Quail Lake (lat. 34°46'20" N, long. 118°45'05" W; near SE cor. sec. 14, T 8 N, R 18 W). Named on Tejon (1903) 30' quadrangle. Postal authorities established Quail post office in 1898 and discontinued it in 1902; the name was from large coveys of quail at the place (Salley, p. 179).

Quail Canyon [SAN DIEGO]:

(1) *canyon*, drained by a stream that flows 2.5 miles to Bear Creek nearly 6 miles west of Mesa Grande (lat. 33°10'40" N, long. 116° 52'05" W; sec. 34, T 11 S, R 1 E). Named on Mesa Grande (1948) and Rodriguez Mountain (1948) 7.5' quadrangles. Called Pamo Canyon on Ramona (1903) 30' quadrangle—the name "Pamo" is of Indian origin (Kroeber, p. 53).

(2) *canyon*, 1.25 miles long, 5 miles west-northwest of Alpine (lat. 32°51'50" N, long. 116°52' W; sec. 15, T 15 S, R 1 E). Named on Alpine (1955) 7.5' quadrangle.

(3) *canyon*, drained by a stream that flows nearly 2 miles to Sycamore Canyon (3) 6.5 miles north of La Mesa (lat. 32°51'45" N, long. 117°00'35" W). Named on La Mesa (1967) and Poway (1967) 7.5' quadrangles.

Quail Canyon: see **Peters Canyon** [ORANGE].

Quail Lake [LOS ANGELES]: *lake*, 1600 feet long, 6 miles east-southeast of Gorman (lat. 34°46'20" N, long. 118°45'05" W). Named on La Liebra Ranch (1965) and Lebec (1958) 7.5' quadrangles. Quail (1938) 6' quadrangle shows the feature as an intermittent lake. The Spaniards called it La Laguna Seca (Latta, p. 31), and later it had the name "Crane Lake" (Suter, p. 20).

Quail Lake Inn [LOS ANGELES]: *locality,* 4.5 miles east-southeast of Gorman (lat. 34°46'35" N, long. 118°46'25" W); the place is 1.25 miles northwest of Quail Lake. Named on Lebec (1945) 7.5' quadrangle.

Quail Spring [LOS ANGELES]: *spring,* 10.5 miles east of Soledad (lat. 34°24' N, long. 118°16'45" W; sec. 30, T 4 N, R 13 W). Named on Agua Dulce (1960) 7.5' quadrangle.

Quanai Canyon [SAN DIEGO]: *canyon,* 1 mile long, 1.5 miles southeast of Santa Ysabel (lat. 33°05'30" N, long. 116°39'30" W; mainly in sec. 34, T 12 S, R 3 E). Named on Santa Ysabel (1960) 7.5' quadrangle.

Quarry Canyon [LOS ANGELES]: *canyon,* drained by a stream that flows 1 mile to Santa Ynez Canyon 6.5 miles northwest of Santa Monica city hall (lat. 34°05'05" N, long. 118°34' W). Named on Topanga (1952) 7.5' quadrangle.

Quarry Spring [LOS ANGELES]: *spring,* about 13 miles south-southeast of Gorman in Cherry Canyon (1) (lat. 34°37'35" N, long. 118°44'15" W; sec. 12, T 6 N, R 18 W). Named on Liebre Mountain (1958) 7.5' quadrangle.

Quarterway House: see **Little Santa Anita Canyon** [LOS ANGELES].

Quartz Hill [LOS ANGELES]:

(1) *ridge,* west-trending, 1.5 miles long, 5 miles southwest of downtown Lancaster (lat. 34°38'45" N, long. 118°12'15" W; at and near SE cor. sec. 36, T 7 N, R 13 W). Named on Lancaster West (1958) 7.5' quadrangle.

(2) *town,* 6 miles southwest of Lancaster (lat. 34°38'45" N, long. 118°13'05" W); the town is at and near Quartz Hill (1). Named on Lancaster West (1958) 7.5' quadrangle. Postal authorities established Quartz Hill post office in 1948 (Salley, p. 179).

Quartz Vein Wash [SAN DIEGO]: *stream,* flows nearly 2 miles to San Felipe Creek 9.5 miles south-southeast of Borrego Springs (lat. 33°08' N, long. 116°18' W; sec. 13, T 12 S, R 6 E). Named on Borrego Sink (1959) and Whale Peak (1959) 7.5' quadrangles.

Quatal Canyon [VENTURA]: *canyon,* drained by a stream that heads in Kern County and flows 14 miles through Ventura County to Santa Barbara County 16 miles northwest of Reyes Peak (lat. 34° 49' N, long. 119°26'30" W; near S line sec. 33, T 9 N, R 24 W). Named on Apache Canyon (1943) and Cuyama Peak (1943) 7.5' quadrangles.

Queen City: see **Emerald Bay** [LOS ANGELES].

Queen Mountain: see **Tourmaline Queen Mountain** [SAN DIEGO].

Queensway Bay: see **Los Angeles River** [LOS ANGELES].

Quejito y Cañada de Polomia: see **Guejito** [SAN DIEGO].

Quigley Canyon [LOS ANGELES]: *canyon,* 1.25 miles long, 1.5 miles east of Newhall (lat. 34°23'20" N, long. 118°30' W). Named on Mint Canyon (1960) and Newhall (1952) 7.5' quadrangles.

Quivira Basin [SAN DIEGO]: *embayment,* 6.5 miles south-southeast of Point La Jolla off the entrance to Mission Bay (lat. 32°45'45" N, long. 117°14'15" W). Named on La Jolla (1967) 7.5' quadrangle.

- R -

Rabbit Lake: see **Elizabeth Lake** [LOS ANGELES] (1).

Rabbit Canyon: see **Limestone Canyon** [ORANGE]; **Peters Canyon** [ORANGE].

Rabbit Peak [LOS ANGELES]: *peak,* nearly 4 miles west-southwest of Pacifico Mountain (lat. 34°21'25" N, long. 118°05'40" W). Altitude 5307 feet. Named on Chilao Flat (1959) 7.5' quadrangle.

Rabbitt Canyon: see **Oak Spring Canyon** [LOS ANGELES] (1).

Radford Canyon [LOS ANGELES]: *canyon,* drained by a stream that flows 1 mile to Berry Canyon 5 miles southeast of Van Nuys (lat. 34°07'55" N, long. 118°22'50" W). Named on Burbank (1953) and Van Nuys (1953) 7.5' quadrangles.

Radium Sulphur Spring: see **Colegrove** [LOS ANGELES].

Raggio: see **Drinkwater Canyon** [LOS ANGELES].

Railroad Canyon [LOS ANGELES]: *canyon,* less than 1 mile long 4.25 miles south-southeast of Del Sur (lat. 34°37'50" N, long. 118° 15'45" W; on S line sec. 4, T 6 N, R 13 W). Named on Del Sur (1958) 7.5' quadrangle.

Railroad Canyon: see **Newhall** [LOS ANGELES].

Rainbow [SAN DIEGO]: *town,* 6.25 miles east-northeast of Fallbrook (lat. 33°24'40" N, long. 117°08'50" W; sec. 12, T 9 S, R 3 W). Named on Temecula (1968) 7.5' quadrangle. Postal authorities established Rainbow post office in 1889, discontinued it in 1914, and reestablished it with the name "Rainbow Valley" in 1967 (Salley, p. 180). The name commemorates J.P.M. Rainbow, who with his partner purchased land for a town at the site in 1888 (Stein, p. 103).

Rainbow Creek [SAN DIEGO]: *stream,* flows nearly 6 miles to Santa Margarita River 2.5 miles northeast of Fallbrook (lat. 33°24'40" N, long. 117°12'55" W; sec. 8, T 9 S, R 3 W; the stream heads in Rainbow Valley. Named on Temecula (1968) 7.5' quadrangle.

Rainbow Spring [SAN DIEGO]: *spring,* 4 miles east of Warner Springs (lat. 33°17'15" N, long. 116°33'50" W; sec. 22, T 10 S, R 4 E). Named on Hot Springs Mountain (1960) 7.5' quadrangle.

Rainbow Valley [SAN DIEGO]: *valley,* 6.5 miles east-northeast of Fallbrook (lat. 33°25' N, long. 117°08'45" W); Rainbow is in the valley. Named on Temecula (1968) 7.5' quadrangle.

Rainbow Valley: see **Rainbow** [SAN DIEGO].

Rainbow Wash [SAN DIEGO]: *stream,* flows 2.5 miles to lowlands 8 miles northwest of Ocotillo Wells (lat. 33°13'45" N, long. 116°13'45" W). Named on Borrego Mountain (1960) 7.5' quadrangle.

Ramera Canyon [LOS ANGELES]: *canyon,* drained by a stream that flows 4.25 miles to the sea nearly 2 miles northeast of Point Dume (lat. 34°01'10" N, long. 118°47'10" W). Named on Point Dume (1951) 7.5' quadrangle.

Ramona [LOS ANGELES]: *locality,* 6 miles east of present Los Angeles city hall (lat. 34°04'30" N, long. 118°08'30" W). Named on Pasadena (1900) 15' quadrangle. Postal authorities established Ramona post office in 1887 and discontinued it in 1895 (Frickstad, p. 80).

Ramona [SAN DIEGO]: *town,* 13 miles east-southeast of Escondido (lat. 33°02'35" N, long. 116°51'50" W). Named on Ramona (1955) and San Pasqual (1954) 7.5' quadrangles. Postal authorities established Nuevo post office in 1883, changed the name to Ramona in 1886, changed it back to Nuevo in 1887, and changed it finally to Ramona in 1895 (Frickstad, p. 154). The community at the place was named Nuevo in 1883 soon after it began, but officials of Santa Maria Water and Land Company had a town laid out in 1886 that included the site of Nuevo and gave the name "Ramona" to the new development in 1895 (Stein, p. 104). The name is from the heroine of Helen Hunt Jackson's novel *Ramona* (Gudde, 1949, p. 279).

Ramona Acres: see **Monterey Park** [LOS ANGELES].

Ramona Canyon [VENTURA]: *canyon,* drained by a stream that flows less than 1 mile to Holser Canyon 4 miles east-northeast of Piru (lat. 34°26'20" N, long. 118°43'50" W; near SE cor. sec. 11, T 4 N, R 18 W). Named on Val Verde (1952) 7.5' quadrangle.

Ramona Park [LOS ANGELES]: *district,* 7.25 miles east of Los Angeles city hall (lat. 34°04'15" N, long. 118°07'20" W). Named on Alhambra (1926) 6' quadrangle.

Ram Point: see **Arrow Point** [LOS ANGELES].

Ranch House [SAN DIEGO]: *locality,* 7.5 miles southwest of Fallbrook along Atchison, Topeka and Santa Fe Railroad (lat. 33°18'10" N, long. 117°20'35" W; near SW cor. sec. 18, T 10 S, R 4 W). Named on Morro Hill (1968) 7.5' quadrangle. Called Ranch House Siding on Morro Hill (1949) 7.5' quadrangle. San Luis Rey (1898) 30' quadrangle has the name "Home Ranch" near the site. The place first was called Margarita because it is on Santa Margarita y las Flores grant, but before 1900 the name was changed to Ranch House for the nearby adobe house of the Picos, early owners of the grant (Gudde, 1949, p. 279).

Ranchita [SAN DIEGO]: *locality,* 4.5 miles east of San Felipe (lat. 33°12'40" N, long. 116°31'15" W; at S line sec. 13, T 11 S, R 4 E). Named on Ranchita (1960) 7.5' quadrangle. Postal authorities established Ranchita post office in 1935 (Frickstad, p. 155). They established Verruga post office 3 miles northwest of Ranchita in 1917 and discontinued it in 1926; the name was from Verruga Marble Company, producers of stone at the site (Salley, p. 231). Tucker and Reed's (1939) map shows Verruga marble deposit situated about 1 mile north of the east end of Cañada Verruga (sec. 10, T 11 S, R 4 E).

Ranchito [LOS ANGELES]: *locality,* 3 miles west-northwest of present Whittier city hall (lat. 33°59'15" N, long. 118°05'05" W). Named on Downey (1902) 15' quadrangle. Postal authorities established Ranchito post office in 1877 and discontinued it in 1886 (Frickstad, p. 80).

Rancho Bernardo [SAN DIEGO]: *district,* 7.25 miles south of Escondido in San Diego (lat. 33°01'05" N, long. 117°03'35" W); the place is on San Bernardo grant. Named on Escondido (1968) 7.5' quadrangle. Postal authorities established Rancho Bernardo post office in 1976 (Salley, p. 181).

Rancho del Otay [SAN DIEGO]: *locality,* 6 miles southwest of Jamul (lat. 32°38'50" N, long. 116°56'05" W); the place is by Upper Otay Reservoir. Named on Jamul Mountains (1955) 7.5' quadrangle.

Rancho Los Amigos: see **County Farm Station** [LOS ANGELES].

Rancho Nuevo Creek [VENTURA]: *stream,* heads in Santa Barbara County and flows 5 miles in Ventura County to Cuyama River 7.5 miles northwest of Reyes Peak (lat. 34°42'15" N, long. 119°22'55" W). Named on Rancho Nuevo Creek (1943) 7.5' quadrangle. United States Board on Geographic Names (1950a, p. 1) rejected the name "Bear Creek" for the stream, or for its upper part.

Rancho Santa Clarita [LOS ANGELES]: *town,* 4 miles north of Newhall (lat. 34°26'30" N, long. 118°32' W). Named on Newhall (1952) 7.5' quadrangle. A small placer-mining camp of the 1890's known as Ratsburg was situated at the junction of San Francisquito Canyon and Bouquet Canyon in present Rancho Santa Clarita (Robinson, J.W., 1973, p. 19).

Rancho Santa Fe [SAN DIEGO]: *town,* 10 miles southwest of Escondido (lat. 33°01'10" N, long. 117°12'10" W). Named on Rancho Santa Fe (1968) 7.5' quadrangle. Postal authorities established Rancho Santa Fe post office in 1924 (Frickstad, p. 155). The name recalls the experimental planting of eucalyptus trees for use as railroad ties that officials of Atchison, Topeka and Santa Fe Railroad tried on land purchased in 1906; the ex-

periment failed, but the failure turned into a successful land-development promotion (Stein, p. 105-106).
Rancho Viejo [SAN DIEGO]: *locality,* 7 miles east-southeast of Fallbrook (lat. 33°19'15" N, long. 117°08'55" W). Name on Bonsall (1968) 7.5' quadrangle.
Randolph: see **Brea** [ORANGE].
Randolph Canyon: see **Elderberry Canyon** [LOS ANGELES].
Rankin Peak [LOS ANGELES]: *peak,* 6.5 miles northwest of Azusa city hall (lat. 34°12'30" N, long. 117°58'25" W; on N line sec. 6, T 1 N, R 10 W). Named on Azusa (1966) 7.5' quadrangle. The name commemorates the Reverend Edward Payson Rankin of Monrovia (United States Board on Geographic Names, 1949, p. 4).
Rathke: see **Camp Rathke**, under **Santiago Reservoir** [ORANGE].
Ratsburg: see **Rancho Santa Clarita** [LOS ANGELES].
Rattlesnake Canyon [LOS ANGELES]:
(1) *canyon,* drained by a stream that flows 3.25 miles to East Fork Fish Canyon (1) 3.5 miles west-northwest of Warm Springs Mountain (lat. 34°36'55" N, long. 118°37'10" W). Named on Burnt Peak (1958) and Warm Springs Mountain (1958) 7.5' quadrangles.
(2) *canyon,* drained by a stream that flows 1 mile to San Gabriel River 6 miles east-southeast of Crystal Lake (lat. 34°16'40" N, long. 117°45'10" W); the canyon heads at Rattlesnake Peak. Named on Crystal Lake (1958) 7.5' quadrangle.
(3) *canyon,* drained by a stream that flows 2 miles to Pacoima Canyon 7.25 miles north of Sunland (lat. 34°21'55" N, long. 118° 18'45" W; near N line sec. 11, T 3 N, R 14 E). Named on Agua Dulce (1960) and Sunland (1953) 7.5' quadrangles.
Rattlesnake Canyon [ORANGE]: *canyon,* drained by a stream that flows 2.5 miles to lowlands 7.5 miles north-northwest of El Toro (lat. 33°43'40" N, long. 117°44'40" W). Named on El Toro (1950) 7.5' quadrangle.
Rattlesnake Canyon [SAN DIEGO]:
(1) *canyon,* drained by a stream that flows 4 miles to lowlands 11 miles east-northeast of Borrego Springs (lat. 33°19'10" N, long. 116°11'45" W; near E line sec. 12, T 10 S, R 7 E). Named on Fonts Point (1959) 7.5' quadrangle.
(2) *canyon,* along Rattlesnake Creek (2) above a point 1.5 miles northeast of Poway (lat. 32°58'30" N, long. 117°00'45" W; at W line sec. 8, T 14 S, R 1 W). Named on Poway (1967) 7.5' quadrangle.
(3) *canyon,* less than 1 mile long, 6 miles southwest of Fallbrook (lat. 33°18'55" N, long. 117°19'20" W; on S line sec. 8, T 10 S, R 4 W). Named on Morro Hill (1968) 7.5' quadrangle.
(4) *canyon,* drained by a stream that flows 3 miles to Cottonwood Creek (3) 2.5 miles north-northeast of Barrett Junction (lat. 32°38'45" N, long. 116°40'45" W; sec. 33, T 17 S, R 3 E). Named on Barrett Lake (1960) 7.5' quadrangle.
Rattlesnake Canyon: see **Shoemaker Canyon** [LOS ANGELES] (2).
Rattlesnake Canyon Wash [ORANGE]: *stream,* flows 3.25 miles from the mouth of Rattlesnake Canyon to Peters Canyon Wash 5 miles east-southeast of Santa Ana city hall (lat. 33°43'05" N, long. 117°47'20" W). Named on El Toro (1968) and Tustin (1965) 7.5' quadrangles.
Rattlesnake Creek [SAN DIEGO]:
(1) *stream,* flows 3 miles to Temecula Creek 8.5 miles east-northeast of Boucher Hill (lat. 33°22'35" N, long. 116°46'50" W; sec. 21, T 9 S, R 2 E). Named on Aguanga (1954) and Palomar Observatory (1949) 7.5' quadrangles.
(2) *stream,* flows nearly 5 miles to Poway Creek in Poway (lat. 32° 57'05" N, long. 117°02'55" W; near SW cor. sec. 13, T 14 S, R 2 W); the stream drains Rattlesnake Canyon (2). Named on Poway (1967) 7.5' quadrangle.
Rattlesnake Island: see **Terminal Island** [LOS ANGELES] (1).
Rattlesnake Mountain [SAN DIEGO]: *ridge,* north-northwest-trending, nearly 2 miles long, 10 miles east of Campo (lat. 32°37' N, long. 116°17'30" W). Named on Live Oak Springs (1959) and Tierra del Sol (1959) 7.5' quadrangles.
Rattlesnake Peak [LOS ANGELES]: *peak,* 5 miles southeast of Crystal Lake (lat. 34°16'20" N, long. 117°46'35" W). Altitude 5826 feet. Named on Crystal Lake (1958) 7.5' quadrangle.
Rattlesnake Peak [ORANGE]: *peak,* 5 miles east-northeast of Orange city hall (lat. 33°49' N, long. 117°46'15" W). Altitude 772 feet. Named on Orange (1964) 7.5' quadrangle.
Rattlesnake Reservoir [ORANGE]: *lake,* nearly 0.5 mile long, behind a dam at the mouth of Rattlesnake Canyon 7.5 miles north-northwest of El Toro (lat. 33°43'45" N, long. 117°44'15" W). Named on El Toro (1968) 7.5' quadrangle.
Rattlesnake Spring [LOS ANGELES]: *spring,* 3.25 miles east-northeast of Waterman Mountain (lat. 34°21'35" N, long. 117°53'10" W; near W line sec. 12, T 3 N, R 10 W). Named on Waterman Mountain (1959) 7.5' quadrangle.
Rattlesnake Spring [SAN DIEGO]: *spring,* 13 miles northeast of Borrego Springs (lat. 33°21'10" N, long. 116°11'25" W); the spring is in a branch of Rattlesnake Canyon (1). Named on Fonts Point (1959) 7.5' quadrangle.
Rattlesnake Terminal Island: see **Terminal Island** [LOS ANGELES] (1).
Rattlesnake Valley [SAN DIEGO]: *valley,* 5.25 miles east of Cuyamaca Peak along upper reaches of Harper Creek (lat. 32°56'40" N, long. 116°30'50" W). Named on Cuyamaca Peak (1960) 7.5' quadrangle.
Ravena City: see **Ravenna** [LOS ANGELES].
Ravenna [LOS ANGELES]: *locality,* 2.5 miles south-southwest of Acton along Southern Pacific Railroad in Soledad Canyon (lat. 34° 26'20" N, long. 118°13'25" W; near S line sec. 10, T 4 N, R 13 W). Named on Acton (1959) 7.5' quadrangle. Postal authorities established Ravena City post office in 1868, discontinued it in 1871, reestablished it with the name "Ravena" in 1875, changed the name to Ravenna in 1876, discontinued it in 1877, reestablished it in 1878, and discontinued it in 1895 (Salley, p. 181). A mining town called Soledad sprang up at the place in 1862, but because of confusion with the town of Soledad in Monterey County, the community was renamed Ravenna for Don Manuel Ravenna, president of Soldedad Gold, Silver and Copper Mining Company; the railroad listed both the names "Ravenna" and "Soledad City" at the place (Robinson, J.W., 1973, p. 21).
Raymer [LOS ANGELES]: *locality,* 2.25 miles north-northwest of Van Nuys along Southern Pacific Railroad (lat. 34°12'50" N, long. 118°27'45" W). Named on Van Nuys (1953) 7.5' quadrangle.
Raymond [LOS ANGELES]: *locality,* 1.5 miles south of present Pasadena city hall along Los Angeles Terminal Railroad (lat. 34° 07'30" N, long. 118°09' W). Named on Pasadena (1900) 15' quadrangle.
Raymond Hill [LOS ANGELES]: *district,* 7 miles northeast of Los Angeles city hall in South Pasadena (lat. 34°07'20" N, long. 118° 08'50" W). Named on Los Angeles (1953) 7.5' quadrangle.
Real Canyon [VENTURA]: *canyon,* drained by a stream that flows 1 mile to the valley of Santa Clara River 0.5 mile west-northwest of Piru (lat. 34°25' N, long. 118°48'05" W; sec. 19, T 4 N, R 18 W). Named on Piru (1952) 7.5' quadrangle. The Real family lived in the canyon in 1874 (Ricard).
Real Wash [VENTURA]: *stream,* flows 1.5 miles from the mouth of Real Canyon to Santa Clara River 1.25 miles south-southwest of Piru (lat. 34°23'50" N, long. 118°48'05" W; sec. 30, T 4 N, R 18 W). Named on Piru (1952) 7.5' quadrangle.
Reasoner Canyon [VENTURA]: *canyon,* drained by a stream that flows 4 miles to Lake Piru 4.5 miles north-northeast of Piru (lat. 34°28'45" N, long. 118°46' W; sec. 33, T 5 N, R 18 W). Named on Cobblestone Mountain (1958) and Piru (1952, photorevised 1969) 7.5' quadrangles. On Camulos (1903) 30' quadrangle, the name applies to present Domingez Canyon. The Reasoner family lived in the canyon (Ricard).
Reba: see **Sorrento** [SAN DIEGO].
Recluse: see **De Luz** [SAN DIEGO] (1).
Recreation Point [ORANGE]: *promontory,* 0.5 mile west-southwest of Laguna Beach city hall along the coast (lat. 33°32'35" N, long. 117°47'30" W). Named on Laguna Beach (1965) 7.5' quadrangle.
Red Box Gap [LOS ANGELES]: *pass,* 9.5 miles south-southwest of Pacifico Mountain (lat. 34°15'30" N, long. 118°06'15" W). Named on Chilao Flat (1959) 7.5' quadrangle. The name is from a fire box painted red that forest rangers placed at the site about 1908 (Robinson, J.W., 1977, p. 158-159).
Red Box Station [LOS ANGELES]: *locality,* 9.5 miles south-southwest of Pacifico Mountain (lat. 34°15'30" N, long. 118°06'15" W); the place is at Red Box Gap. Named on Chilao Flat (1959) 7.5' quadrangle.
Redcastle: see **Sepulveda** [LOS ANGELES] (2).
Red Fox Canyon [LOS ANGELES]: *canyon,* drained by a stream that flows 1.5 miles to Elizabeth Lake Canyon 4.25 miles southeast of Burnt Peak (lat. 34°37'50" N, long. 118°32' W). Named on Burnt Peak (1958) and Warm Springs Mountain (1958) 7.5' quadrangles.
Red Hill [ORANGE]: *hill,* 4.25 miles east of Santa Ana city hall (lat. 33°45' N, long. 117°47'30" W). Altitude 345 feet. Named on Orange (1964) and Tustin (1965) 7.5' quadrangles. In the early days the feature was a landmark called Cerro Colorado for its red color given by cinnabar, the quicksilver ore; it also was called Cerrito de las Ranas for its proximity to Cienega de las Ranas (Meadows, p. 51, 118).
Red Hill [SAN DIEGO]: *peak,* nearly 4 miles southeast of Sweeney Pass (lat. 32°47'35" N, long. 116°08'15" W; at W line sec. 11, T 16 S, R 8 E). Named on Sweeney Pass (1959) 7.5' quadrangle.
Redman [LOS ANGELES]: *locality,* 17 miles north of Littlerock (lat. 34°45'50" N, long. 117°58'05" W; at SW cor. sec. 20, T 8 N, R 10 W). Named on Redman (1973) 7.5' quadrangle. Thompson's (1921) map shows Casa Desierto P.O. situated 3 miles east of Redman school at present Redman. Postal authorities established Redman post office in 1908, moved it 3 miles east in 1914 when they changed the name to Casa Desierto, and discontinued it in 1922; the name "Redman" was for the developer of the site (Salley, p. 39, 182).
Redman Canyon: see **Nelson Canyon** [LOS ANGELES].
Red Mountain [LOS ANGELES]: *peak,* 3.25 miles east of Warm Springs Mountain (lat. 34°35'10" N, long. 118°31'25" W). Named on Warm Springs Mountain (1958) 7.5' quadrangle.
Red Mountain [SAN DIEGO]:
(1) *peak,* 3.5 miles east-northeast of Fallbrook (lat. 33°24' N, long.

117°11'25" W; near NW cor. sec. 15, T 9 S, R 3 W). Altitude 1617 feet. Named on Temecula (1968) 7.5' quadrangle.

(2) *peak,* 8 miles north of Escondido city hall (lat. 33°14'50" N, long. 117°04'45" W; sec. 3, T 11 S, R 2 W). Altitude 1812 feet. Named on Valley Center (1968) 7.5' quadrangle.

Red Mountain [VENTURA]: *ridge,* generally east-trending, 3.5 miles long, 5.5 miles north-northwest of Ventura (lat. 34°21' N, long. 119°20'30" W). Named on Ventura (1951) 7.5' quadrangle.

Red Mountain: see **Borrego Mountain** [SAN DIEGO].

Redondo: see **Redondo Beach** [LOS ANGELES].

Redondo Beach [LOS ANGELES]: *city,* 12 miles west-northwest of Long Beach city hall (lat. 33°50'35" N, long. 118°23'20" W). Named on Inglewood (1952), Torrance (1964), and Venice (1950) 7.5' quadrangles. Called Redondo on Redondo (1896) 15' quadrangle. Postal authorities established Redondo Beach post office in 1889, changed the name to Redondo in 1895, and changed it back to Redondo Beach in 1909 (Salley, p. 183). The city incorporated in 1892.

Redondo Flat [SAN DIEGO]: *area,* 8 miles north-northwest of Jacumba (lat. 32°43'35" N, long. 116°14'20" W; around SE cor. sec. 34, T 16 S, R 7 E). Named on Jacumba (1959) 7.5' quadrangle.

Redondo Junction [LOS ANGELES]: *locality,* 2.5 miles south-southeast of Los Angeles city hall along Atchison, Topeka and Santa Fe Railroad (lat. 34°01' N, long. 118°13'30" W). Named on Los Angeles (1953) 7.5' quadrangle. Called Ballona Junction on Pasadena (1900) 15' quadrangle.

Redondo Spring [SAN DIEGO]: *spring,* nearly 8 miles north-northwest of Jacumba (lat. 32°43'30" N, long. 116°14'10" W; near N line sec. 2, T 17 S, R 7 E); the spring is at Redondo Flat. Named on Jacumba (1959) 7.5' quadrangle.

Red Reef Canyon [VENTURA]: *canyon,* drained by a stream that flows 2.5 miles to Sespe Creek 14 miles east-northeast of Wheeler Springs (lat. 34°33'50" N, long. 119°03'10" W; near SE cor. sec. 36, T 6 N, R 21 W). Named on Topatopa Mountains (1943) 7.5' quadrangle.

Redrock Canyon [LOS ANGELES]:

(1) *canyon,* drained by a stream that flows 3.5 miles to Castaic Creek 16 miles southeast of Gorman (lat. 34°37'30" N, long. 118° 39'30" W; at W line sec. 11, T 6 N, R 17 W); the canyon heads at Redrock Mountain. Named on Liebre Mountain (1958) 7.5' quadrangle.

(2) *canyon,* drained by a stream that flows less than 1 mile to Spencer Canyon 5 miles north of Burnt Peak (lat. 34°44'15" N, long. 118°34'55" W; sec. 33, T 8 N, R 16 W). Named on Burnt Peak (1958) 7.5' quadrangle.

(3) *canyon,* drained by a stream that flows 1.5 miles to Topanga Canyon 6 miles north-northeast of Malibu Point (lat. 34°06'20" N, long. 118°37'40" W; sec. 2, T 1 S, R 17 W). Named on Malibu Beach (1951) 7.5' quadrangle.

Redrock Creek [VENTURA]: *stream,* flows 4.25 miles to Tar Creek 5.25 miles southeast of Devils Heart Peak (lat. 34°30' N, long. 118° 54' W; near W line sec. 20, T 5 N, R 19 W). Named on Devils Heart Peak (1943) 7.5' quadrangle.

Redrock Mountain [LOS ANGELES]: *ridge,* north- to west-trending, 2.5 miles long, 13 miles southeast of Gorman (lat. 34°39'30" N, long. 118°38'20" W). Named on Liebre Mountain (1958) 7.5' quadrangle. On Tejon (1903) 30' quadrangle, the name "Redrock Mt." applies to a peak located at the south end of the ridge, and on Red Mountain (1936) 6' quadrangle, the name applies to a peak situated about 1 mile farther west.

Red Rover Canyon [LOS ANGELES]: *canyon,* 3 miles northwest of Acton (lat. 34°29'50" N, long. 118°13'25" W; sec. 22, 27, T 5 N, R 13 W). Named on Ravena (1934, reprinted 1949) 6' quadrangle.

Red Top [SAN DIEGO]:

(1) *peak,* 5 miles south-southwest of Agua Caliente Springs (lat. 32° 53'05" N, long. 116°20'30" W; near NW cor. sec. 11, T 15 S, R 6 E). Altitude 4467 feet. Named on Agua Caliente Springs (1959) 7.5' quadrangle.

(2) *peak,* 9 miles north-northeast of Barrett Junction (lat. 32°43'45" N, long. 116°38' W; at SW cor. sec. 36, T 16 S, R 3 E). Named on Barrett Lake (1960) 7.5' quadrangle.

Redwing Lake [LOS ANGELES]: *lake,* 800 feet long, 3.5 miles north of downtown Sunland in a flood control basin (lat. 34°15'50" N, long. 118°22'25" W). Named on Sunland (1966) 7.5' quadrangle.

Reed Reservoir [ORANGE]: *water feature,* 1.5 miles east-southeast of San Juan Capistrano (lat. 33°29'35" N, long. 117°38'15" W; sec. 8, T 8 S, R 7 W). Named on Dana Point (1968) 7.5' quadrangle.

Reed Spring [LOS ANGELES]: *spring,* 3.25 miles north of Crystal Lake (lat. 34°22' N, long. 117°50'50" W; at N line sec. 8, T 3 N, R 9 W). Named on Crystal Lake (1958) 7.5' quadrangle.

Reef Point [ORANGE]: *promontory,* 2.25 miles west-northwest of Laguna Beach city hall along the coast (lat. 33°33'25" N, long. 117°49'10" W). Named on Laguna Beach (1965) 7.5' quadrangle.

Reeves Creek [VENTURA]: *stream,* flows 5.25 miles to Thatcher Creek 3 miles east of the town of Ojai (lat. 34°26'55" N, long. 119° 11'25" W). Named on Ojai (1952) 7.5' quadrangle.

Reidy Canyon [SAN DIEGO]: *canyon,* nearly 3 miles long, 5 miles north of Escondido city hall (lat. 33°11'45" N, long. 117°05'25" W). Named on Valley Center (1968) 7.5' quadrangle. The name commemorates Maurice Reidy, an early homesteader in the vicinity (Stein, p. 106-107).

Relis del Codo: see **Point Vicente** [LOS ANGELES].

Remolacha: see **Talbert** [ORANGE].

Rendalia [LOS ANGELES]: *locality,* 6 miles southeast of South Gate city hall along Pacific Electric Railroad (lat. 33°53'25" N, long. 118°08' W). Named on South Gate (1952) 7.5' quadrangle.

Repollo: see **Talbert** [ORANGE].

Reseda [LOS ANGELES]: *district,* 3.5 miles east of the center of Canoga Park in Los Angeles (lat. 34°12'05" N, long. 118°32'05" W). Named on Canoga Park (1952) 7.5' quadrangle. On Calabasas (1903) 15' quadrangle, the name "Reseda" applies to a place along Southern Pacific Railroad where Reseda (1928) 6' quadrangle has the name "Reseda Siding" and Canoga Park (1952) 7.5' quadrangle has the name "Tarzana Siding." Calabasas (1903) 15' quadrangle also shows a place called Marion located 1.5 miles north of Reseda. Postal authorities established Reseda post office in 1922 (Frickstad, p. 80). The name "Reseda" originally was applied to a station on a Southern Pacific Railroad line built from Burbank to Chatsworth about 1895; after 1920 the name was transferred to a station of Pacific Electric Railroad known previously as Marion (Gudde, 1949, p. 284).

Reseda Siding: see **Tarzana Siding** [LOS ANGELES].

Reservation Point [LOS ANGELES]: *promontory,* 2 miles northeast of Point Fermin (lat. 33°43'20" N, long. 118°16' W). Named on San Pedro (1964) 7.5' quadrangle. Reservation Point received its name in 1915 when the Treasury Department established a quarantine station there (Gudde, 1949, p. 284). Stevenson's (1884) map shows Dead Man Is. connected to the southwest end of Rattlesnake Is. (present Terminal Island) by a breakwater. The entrance to Los Angeles harbor originally lay between present Terminal Island and Dead Man's Island, but in 1872 a breakwater was built to connect the two islands with the hope that this structure would cause a new channel to be scoured out elsewhere; with the aid of dredging a new channel was made, and in 1928 this channel was widened by removal of the island and by deposit of its material along the breakwater, an operation that formed present Reservation Point (Gleason, p. 113-116). United States Board on Geographic Names (1933, p. 639) rejected the names "Deaman Island" and "Deadmans Island" for Reservation Point. The name "Deadman's Island" is from burials made at the site, including burial of six United States Marines killed in battle with the Mexicans in 1846—the place also was known as La Isla del Muerto (Gleason, p. 114-116).

Reservoir Canyon [ORANGE]: *canyon,* 1 mile long, 1.5 miles south-southeast of San Juan Capistrano (lat. 33°28'40" N, long. 117°39'20" W). Named on Dana Point (1968) 7.5' quadrangle.

Reservoir Hill [LOS ANGELES]: *peak,* 10 miles south-southeast of Gorman (lat. 34°39'40" N, long. 118°43'30" W). Named on Liebre Mountain (1958) 7.5' quadrangle, which shows a small reservoir on the feature.

Reservoir Ravine: see **Chavez Ravine** [LOS ANGELES].

Reservoir Summit [LOS ANGELES]: *pass,* 10 miles south-southeast of Gorman (lat. 34°39'45" N, long. 118°43'40" W); the pass is 1000 feet northwest of Reservoir Hill. Named on Liebre Mountain (1958) 7.5' quadrangle.

Resort: see **Mount Laguna** [SAN DIEGO].

Resort Point [LOS ANGELES]: *promontory,* 5.5 miles south-southwest of Redondo Beach city hall along the coast (lat. 33°46' N, long. 118°25'25" W). Named on Redondo Beach (1951) 7.5' quadrangle.

Revolon Slough [VENTURA]: *stream,* flows 7 miles to Calleguas Creek 6.5 miles south-southwest of Camarillo (lat. 34°07'40" N, long. 119°04'35" W). Named on Camarillo (1950) 7.5' quadrangle. The Revolon family farmed near the stream in the 1870's (Ricard).

Reyes Creek [VENTURA]: *stream,* flows 6 miles to Cuyama River 5 miles north-northwest of Reyes Peak (lat. 34°41'40" N, long. 119° 19' W; near N line sec. 21, T 7 N, R 23 W); the stream heads near Reyes Peak. Named on Reyes Peak (1943) 7.5' quadrangle. C.W. Whipple (p. 148) referred to Ray's Creek.

Reyes Peak [VENTURA]: *peak,* 24 miles north of Ventura on Pine Mountain (lat. 34°37'50" N, long. 119°16'50" W; near NE cor. sec. 11, T 6 N, R 23 W). Altitude 7510 feet. Named on Reyes Peak (1943) 7.5' quadrangle. The name commemorates Jacinto Damien Reyes, who was a forest ranger in the neighborhood for more than 30 years (Hanna, p. 253).

Reynier Canyon [LOS ANGELES]: *canyon,* less than 1 mile long, opens into Sand Canyon (2) 3 miles southeast of Solemint (lat. 34° 23'10" N, long. 118°25'05" W; sec. 35, T 4 N, R 15 W). Named on Mint Canyon (1960) 7.5' quadrangle.

Rheba [SAN DIEGO]: *locality,* 3.5 miles south-southeast of Del Mar along Atchison, Topeka and Santa Fe Railroad (lat. 32°55' N, long. 117°14'15" W). Named on Del Mar (1953) 7.5' quadrangle.

Ribbon Beach [LOS ANGELES]: *beach,* nearly 1 mile southwest of Silver Peak on the south side of Santa Catalina Island (lat. 33° 27' N, long. 118°34'40" W); the beach is less than 1 mile north-northwest of Ribbon Rock. Named on Santa Catalina West (1943) 7.5' quadrangle.

Ribbon Rock [LOS ANGELES]: *ridge*, west-southwest-trending, 0.5 miles long, 1.25 miles south of Silver Peak on the south side of Santa Catalina Island (lat. 33°26'30" N, long. 118°34'15" W). Named on Santa Catalina West (1943) 7.5' quadrangle. The feature is a wall of dark rock with a vein of quartz that is visible from a distance of many miles at sea (United States Coast and Geodetic Survey, p. 107).

Rice Canyon [LOS ANGELES]: *canyon*, drained by a stream that flows 2.25 miles to Gavin Canyon 2.25 miles south-southwest of Newhall (lat. 34°20'45" N, long. 118°32'30" W; near N line sec. 15, T 3 N, R 16 W). Named on Oat Mountain (1952) 7.5' quadrangle.

Rice Canyon [SAN DIEGO]:
(1) *canyon*, drained by a stream that flows 3.5 miles to San Luis Rey River 7.5 miles east-southeast of Fallbrook (lat. 33°20'20" N, long. 117°07'55" W; sec. 6, T 10 S, R 2 W). Named on Bonsall (1968) and Temecula (1968) 7.5' quadrangles.
(2) *canyon*, drained by a stream that flows nearly 4 miles to Sweetwater Valley 3 miles southeast of National City civic center (lat. 32°38'50" N, long. 117°03'30" W). Named on National City (1967) 7.5' quadrangle.

Rice Canyon [VENTURA]: *canyon*, 1 mile long, opens into Ojai Valley 3 miles west-northwest of the town of Ojai (lat. 34°27'30" N, long. 119°17'40" W). Named on Matilija (1952) 7.5' quadrangle.

Richardson Canyon [LOS ANGELES]: *canyon*, drained by a stream that flows 1.5 miles to Oakdale Canyon (1) 11 miles east-southeast of Gorman (lat. 34°44' N, long. 118°37'35" W; sec. 36, T 8 N, R 17 W). Named on Liebre Mountain (1958) 7.5' quadrangle.

Richardson Canyon [VENTURA]: *canyon*, drained by a stream that flows 1.5 miles to the valley of Santa Clara River 1 mile southeast of downtown Santa Paula (lat. 34°20'40" N, long. 119°02'45" W). Named on Santa Paula (1951) 7.5' quadrangle. The name is for a pioneer family that owned the place (Ricard).

Richfields: see **Atwood** [ORANGE].

Richland [SAN DIEGO]: *locality*, 4 miles west-northwest of Escondido along Southern California Railroad (lat. 33°08'20" N, long. 117°08'30" W). Named on Escondido (1901) 15' quadrangle. Postal authorities established Richland post office in 1894 and discontinued it in 1905; the promotional name was from a farm development (Salley, p. 185).

Richland: see **Orange** [ORANGE].

Ridge Crest Picnic Ground [LOS ANGELES]: *locality*, 3 miles east-northeast of Waterman Mountain (lat. 34°21'10" N, long. 117°53'15" W; at NW cor. sec. 13, T 3 N, R 10 W). Named on Waterman Mountain (1959) 7.5' quadrangle.

Ridge View: see **Saugus** [LOS ANGELES].

Rim Rock Canyon [ORANGE]: *canyon*, drained by a stream that flows 1.25 miles to Bluebird Canyon 1 mile southeast of Laguna Beach city hall (lat. 33°32'05" N, long. 117°46'05" W; sec, 25, T 7 S, R 9 W). Named on Laguna Beach (1965) 7.5' quadrangle. The name once applied also to present Bluebird Canyon, but now it is restricted (Meadows, p. 119).

Rincon [SAN DIEGO]: *locality*, 4 miles southwest of Boucher Hill (lat. 33°17'15" N, long. 116°57'25" W; sec. 23, T 10 S, R 1 W). Named on Boucher Hill (1948) 7.5' quadrangle.

Rincon Beach [VENTURA]: *beach*, center 2 miles northwest of Pitas Point along the coast (near lat. 34°20'15" N, long. 119°24'30" W). Named on Pitas Point (1950) 7.5' quadrangle.

Rincon Canyon [LOS ANGELES]: *canyon*, drained by a stream that flows 1 mile to the canyon of West Fork San Gabriel River 7 miles north of Glendora city hall (lat. 34°14'10" N, long. 117°51'35" W; near N line sec. 30, T 2 N, R 9 W). Named on Glendora (1953) 7.5' quadrangle.

Rincon Creek [VENTURA]: *stream*, flows 9.5 miles, mainly along Ventura-Santa Barbara County line, to the sea 12.5 miles west-northwest of Ventura (lat. 34°22'25" N, long. 119°28'35" W); the mouth of the stream is at Rincon Point. Named on Pitas Point (1950) and White Ledge Peak (1952) 7.5' quadrangles. On Ventura (1904) 15' quadrangle, present Catharina Creek is called East Fork Rincon Creek.

Rincon de la Brea [LOS ANGELES-ORANGE]: *land grant*, at and near Brea Canyon. Named on La Habra (1952), San Dimas (1954), and Yorba Linda (1950) 7.5' quadrangles. Gil Ibarra received 1 league in 1841 and claimed 4453 acres patented in 1864; the grant first was called Cañada de la Brea (Cowan, p. 20).

Rincon de la Brea: see **Brea Canyon** [LOS ANGELES-ORANGE].

Rincon del Diablo [SAN DIEGO]: *land grant*, at Escondido. Named on Escondido (1968) and Valley Center (1968) 7.5' quadrangles. Juan B. Alvarado received 3 leagues in 1843, and his heirs claimed 12,654 acres patented in 1872 (Cowan, p. 32-33).

Rincon de Los Bueys [LOS ANGELES]: *land grant*, south of Beverly Hills. Named on Beverly Hills (1950) and Hollywood (1953) 7.5' quadrangles. Bernardo Higuera received three-fifths of a league in 1821 and 1843; Francisco Higuera and others claimed 3128 acres patented in 1872 (Cowan, p. 21).

Rincon de San Pasqual: see **San Pasqual** [LOS ANGELES].

Rincon Mountain [VENTURA]: *peak*, 4.25 miles north-northwest of Pitas Point (lat. 34°22'20" N, long. 119°25'15" W); the peak is 3.25 miles east of Rincon Point. Altitude 2161 feet. Named on Pitas Point (1950) 7.5' quadrangle. Called Mt. Hoar on Peckham's (1866) map.

Rincon Point [VENTURA]: *promontory*, 6.25 miles northwest of Pitas Point along the coast (lat. 34°22'20" N, long. 119°28'35" W); the feature is on El Rincon grant at the mouth of Rincon Creek. Named on Pitas Point (1950) and White Ledge Peak (1952) 7.5' quadrangles.

Rincon Refugio: see **Valle de los Amigos** [SAN DIEGO].

Rio de la Santa Clara: see **Santa Clara River** [VENTURA].

Rio del Dulcissimo Nombre de Jesus del Temblores: see **Santa Ana River** [ORANGE].

Rio del Llano: see **Big Rock Creek** [LOS ANGELES]; **Big Rock Wash** [LOS ANGELES].

Rio de los Angeles: see **Los Angeles River** [LOS ANGELES].

Rio del Tecate: see **Tecate Creek** [SAN DIEGO].

Rio Del Tia Juana: see **Tijuana River** [SAN DIEGO].

Rio de Porciuncula: see **Los Angeles River** [LOS ANGELES].

Rio de San Gabriel: see **San Gabriel River** [LOS ANGELES-ORANGE].

Rio de Santa Ana: see **Santa Ana River** [ORANGE].

Rio de Santa Clara [VENTURA]: *land grant*, at and near Oxnard and Port Hueneme. Named on Camarillo (1950), Oxnard (1949), and Point Mugu (1949) 7.5' quadrangles. Valentin Cota received the land in 1837 and claimed 44,883 acres patented in 1872 (Cowan, p. 92).

Rio Hondo [LOS ANGELES]:
(1) *stream*, flows 17 miles to Los Angeles River 2.25 miles southeast of South Gate city hall (lat. 33°56'05" N, long. 118°10'25" W). Named on El Monte (1953), South Gate (1952), and Whittier (1949) 7.5' quadrangles. Called Lexington Wash near El Monte on Pasadena (1900) 15' quadrangle—El Monte had the early name "Lexington." San Gabriel River followed the course of present Rio Hondo until the flood of 1867, when it took a new course and the former course took the name "Rio Hondo" (Gudde, 1949, p. 152).
(2) *locality*, 5.25 miles west of present Whittier city hall along Pacific Electric Railroad (lat. 33°58'40" N, long. 118°07'20" W). Named on Bell (1936) 6' quadrangle.

Rio Piru: see **Piru Creek** [VENTURA].

Rio San Bernadino: see **Santa Ana River** [ORANGE].

Rio San Bernardo: see **San Dieguito River** [SAN DIEGO].

Rio San Buenaventura: see **Ventura River** [VENTURA].

Rio San Gabriel: see **San Gabriel River** [LOS ANGELES].

Rio Santa Ana: see **Santa Ana River** [ORANGE].

Rio Santa Anna: see **Santa Ana River** [ORANGE].

Rio Santa Margarita: see **Santa Margarita River** [SAN DIEGO].

Rio Santa Maria: see **Cuyama River** [VENTURA].

Rios Canyon [SAN DIEGO]: *canyon*, drained by a stream that flows 2.25 miles to Los Coches Creek 3 miles east-southeast of Lakeside (lat. 32°50'30" N, long. 116°52'40" W). Named on Alpine (1955) and El Cajon (1967) 7.5' quadrangles.

Rio Simi: see **Calleguas Creek** [VENTURA].

Rio Tecate: see **Tijuana River** [SAN DIEGO].

Rio Tia Juana: see **Tijuana River** [SAN DIEGO].

Rio Tijuana: see **Tijuana River** [SAN DIEGO].

Ritchie Creek [SAN DIEGO]: *stream*, flows 5.25 miles to San Diego River nearly 8 miles south-southwest of Santa Ysabel (lat. 33°00'20" N, long. 116°43'35" W; near N line sec. 36, T 13 S, R 2 E). Named on Santa Ysabel (1960) 7.5' quadrangle.

Ritter Canyon [LOS ANGELES]: *canyon*, drained by a stream that flows 2.25 miles to Leona Valley (1) 7 miles west of Palmdale (lat. 34°36' N, long. 118°14'30" W; near N line sec. 22, T 6 N, R 13 W). Named on Ritter Ridge (1958) 7.5' quadrangle.

Ritter Ridge [LOS ANGELES]: *ridge*, east-southeast-trending, 3.25 miles long, 5.5 miles west-northwest of Palmdale (lat. 34°36'15" N, long. 118°12'30" W). Named on Ritter Ridge (1958) 7.5' quadrangle.

Rivera: see **Pico Rivera** [LOS ANGELES]; **Riviera** [LOS ANGELES].

Rivera Canyon [LOS ANGELES]: *canyon*, drained by a stream that flows 1.25 miles to lowlands 17 miles east of Gorman (lat. 34°45'25" N, long. 118°32'55" W; sec. 26, T 8 N, R 16 W). Named on Burnt Peak (1958) and Neenach School (1965) 7.5' quadrangles.

River Bottom Reservoir [SAN DIEGO]: *intermittent lake*, 8 miles west of Otay Mountain along Otay River (lat. 32°35'10" N, long. 116°58'45" W). Named on Otay Mesa (1955) 7.5' quadrangle.

Riverdale: see **Glendale** [LOS ANGELES].

Riverview [SAN DIEGO]: *locality*, 4.5 miles north-northeast of El Cajon (lat. 32°51'25" N, long. 116°56" W); the place is along San Diego River. Named on El Cajon (1967) 7.5' quadrangle.

Riverview Farms [SAN DIEGO]: *locality*, 1 mile southwest of Lakeside (lat. 32°50'55" N, long. 116°55'50" W). Named on El Cajon (1967) 7.5' quadrangle.

Riviera [LOS ANGELES]: *district*, 6 miles west of Beverly Hills city hall in Los Angels (lat. 34°03'30" N, long. 118°30' W). Named on Beverly Hills (1950) and Topanga (1952) 7.5' quadrangles. Called Rivera on Sawtell (1934) 6' quadrangle.

Riviera Villas [SAN DIEGO]: *district,* 5 miles west of downtown San Diego (lat. 32°43'40" N, long. 117°05' W). Named on Point Loma (1942) 7.5' quadrangle.

Robbers Cave: see **Fremont Canyon** [ORANGE].

Robbers Peak [ORANGE]: *peak,* 6 miles east-northeast of Orange city hall (lat. 33°49'40" N, long. 117°45'25" W). Altitude 1152 feet. Named on Orange (1964) 7.5' quadrangle. Bulldozers destroyed the feature in 1973 (Sleeper, 1976, p. 165).

Robbers' Roost: see **Vasquez Rocks** [LOS ANGELES].

Robbs Gulch [LOS ANGELES]: *canyon,* drained by a stream that flows less than 1 mile to San Gabriel Reservoir 6 miles north of Glendora city hall (lat. 34°13'15" N, long. 117°51'10" W). Named on Glendora (1966) 7.5' quadrangle.

Roberts: see **Burbank** [LOS ANGELES].

Roberts Camp [LOS ANGELES]: *locality,* 3 miles east-southeast of Mount Wilson in Santa Anita Canyon (lat. 34°12' N, long. 118°01'05" W; sec. 3, T 1 N, R 11 W). Named on Mount Wilson (1953) 7.5' quadrangle. Postal authorities established Roberts Camp post office in 1922 and discontinued it in 1933 (Frickstad, p. 80). Otto L. Roberts settled at the place in 1911 and started a resort there in 1912 (Robinson, J.W., 1977, p. 133).

Roberts Canyon [LOS ANGELES]: *canyon,* drained by a stream that flows 5.5 miles to lowlands 2 miles north of Azusa city hall (lat. 34°09'45" N, long. 117°54'20" W; near NW cor. sec. 23, T 1 N, R 10 W). Named on Azusa (1953) 7.5' quadrangle. Called Rogers Canyon on Los Angeles County (1935) map. The name "Roberts Canyon" commemorates H.C. Roberts, a settler of 1856 (Gudde, 1949, p. 288).

Roberts Canyon: see **Williams Canyon** [LOS ANGELES] (1).

Robinson Canyon [LOS ANGELES]: *canyon,* 1.5 miles long, 9 miles east-southeast of Gorman (lat. 34°44' N, long. 118°40' W; mainly in sec. 34, T 8 N, R 17 W). Named on Liebre Mountain (1958) 7.5' quadrangle.

Roblar: see **Simi Valley** [VENTURA] (2).

Roblar Creek [SAN DIEGO]: *stream,* flows 6.5 miles to De Luz Creek 4 miles west of Fallbrook (lat. 33°23'15" N, long. 117°19'15" W). Named on Fallbrook (1968) and Margarita Peak (1968) 7.5' quadrangles.

Rocamp [ORANGE]: *locality,* 1.25 miles west-northwest of Huntington Beach civic center along Pacific Electric Railroad (lat. 33°40'10" N, long. 118°01'05" W). Named on Seal Beach (1950) 7.5' quadrangle.

Rock [VENTURA]: *locality,* 4.5 miles north of Ventura along Southern Pacific Railroad (lat. 34°20'45" N, long. 119°17'50" W). Named on Ventura (1904) 15' quadrangle.

Rockbank: see **Piru** [VENTURA].

Rockbound Canyon [LOS ANGELES]: *canyon,* drained by a stream that flows less than 2 miles to Soldier Creek 1.5 miles south-southeast of Crystal Lake (lat. 34°17'50" N, long. 117°50'05" W). Named on Crystal Lake (1958) 7.5' quadrangle.

Rock Canyon [SAN DIEGO]: *canyon,* drained by a stream that flows nearly 2 miles to Cañada Aguanga 5.5 miles northwest of Warner Springs (lat. 33°20' N, long. 116°42'30" W). Named on Warner Springs (1959) 7.5' quadrangle.

Rock Creek [LOS ANGELES]: *stream,* diverges from Big Rock Wash and flows 9 miles to end 8.5 miles north-northeast of Littlerock (lat. 34°38'15" N, long. 117°56' W; at W line sec. 3, T 6 N, R 10 W). Named on Alpine Butte (1957), Littlerock (1957), and Lovejoy Buttes (1957) 7.5' quadrangles.

Rock Creek [VENTURA]: *stream,* flows 2.5 miles to Sheep Creek 14 miles east-northeast of Reyes Peak (lat. 34°40'25" N, long. 119°02'35" W; sec. 30, T 7 N, R 20 W). Named on Lockwood Valley (1943) 7.5' quadrangle.

Rock Creek: see **Big Rock Creek** [LOS ANGELES]; **Little Rock Creek** [LOS ANGELES].

Rock Creek Wash: see **Big Rock Wash** [LOS ANGELES].

Rock Haven: see **Rock Haven Spring** [SAN DIEGO].

Rock Haven Spring [SAN DIEGO]: *spring,* 9.5 miles north-northwest of Lakeside (lat. 32°59'45" N, long. 116°58'05" W; sec. 34, T 13 S, R 1 W). Named on San Vicente Reservoir (1955) 7.5' quadrangle. El Cajon (1939) 15' quadrangle has a locality called Rock Haven at the site.

Rockhouse Canyon [SAN DIEGO]:

(1) *canyon,* heads in Riverside County, 3.5 miles long in San Diego County, opens into Clark Valley 9.5 miles north of Borrego Springs (lat. 33°23'30" N, long. 116°21'30" W; sec. 16, T 9 S, R 6 E). Named on Clark Lake NE (1960) and Collins Valley (1959) 7.5' quadrangles.

(2) *canyon,* drained by a stream that flows 4.5 miles to Carrizo Canyon 2.25 miles southwest of Sweeney Pass (lat. 32°48'40" N, long. 116°12'40" W; near N line sec. 1, T 16 S, R 7 E). Named on Sombrero Peak (1959) and Sweeney Pass (1959) 7.5' quadrangles.

Rockhouse Canyon: see **Butler Canyon** [SAN DIEGO].

Rock Mountain [SAN DIEGO]:

(1) *peak,* 1.25 miles north-northeast of El Cajon Mountain (lat. 32°55'55" N, long. 116°48'35" W; sec. 30, T 14 S, R 2 E). Altitude 3299 feet. Named on El Cajon Mountain (1955) 7.5' quadrangle.

(2) *ridge,* north-northeast-trending, 1 mile long, 8 miles west of Otay Mountain (lat. 32°35'50" N, long. 116°58'50" W). Named on Otay Mesa (1955) 7.5' quadrangle.

Rock Spring [SAN DIEGO]: *spring,* nearly 5 miles south of San Felipe (lat. 33°07'50" N, long. 116°35'10" W; sec. 17, T 12 S, R 4 E). Named on Ranchita (1960) 7.5' quadrangle.

Rock Springs: see **Big Rock Springs** [LOS ANGELES].

Rock Wash: see **Big Rock Wash** [LOS ANGELES].

Rockwood Canyon [SAN DIEGO]: *canyon,* drained by a stream that flows 4.5 miles to Santa Ysabel Creek 0.5 mile west of San Pasqual (lat. 33°05'25" N, long. 116°57'50" W; near E line sec. 34, T 12 S, R 1 W). Named on Rodriguez Mountain (1948) and San Pasqual (1954) 7.5' quadrangles. The name is for B.B. Rockwood, an early settler in the region (Stein, p. 109).

Rocky Buttes [LOS ANGELES]: *peaks,* 11 miles northeast of Littlerock (lat. 34°38'45" N, long. 117°52'15" W; on and near S line sec. 31, T 7 N, R 9 W). Named on Alpine Butte (1957) and Hi Vista (1957) 7.5' quadrangles.

Rocky Flat [VENTURA]: *area,* 6.5 miles north of Ventura along Ventura River at the site of present Casitas Springs (lat. 34°22'05" N, long. 119°18'30" W). Named on Ventura (1904) 15' quadrangle.

Rocky Mountain [SAN DIEGO]: *ridge,* south- to south-southwest-trending, 1.5 miles long, 5.5 miles north-northwest of Warner Springs (lat. 33°20'55" N, long. 116°41'15" W; on S line sec. 29, T 9 S, R 3 E). Named on Warner Springs (1959) 7.5' quadrangle.

Rocky Peak [LOS ANGELES-VENTURA]: *peak,* 1.5 miles north of Santa Susana pass on Los Angeles-Ventura County line (lat. 34°17'30" N, long. 118°38'10" W). Altitude 2714 feet. Named on Santa Susana (1951) 7.5' quadrangle.

Rocky Peak [SAN DIEGO]: *peak,* nearly 8 miles northwest of Fallbrook (lat. 33°27'20" N, long. 117°21'15" W; sec. 25, T 8 S, R 5 W). Altitude 2365 feet. Named on Fallbrook (1968) 7.5' quadrangle.

Rocky Point [SAN DIEGO]: *promontory,* 1100 feet southwest of Point La Jolla along the coast (lat. 32°50'55" N, long. 117°16'40" W). Named on La Jolla (1967) 7.5' quadrangle.

Rocky Point: see **Newport Bay** [ORANGE]; **Palos Verdes Point** [LOS ANGELES].

Roden Canyon: see **Boden Canyon** [SAN DIEGO].

Rodeo Canyon: see **Brea Canyon** [LOS ANGELES-ORANGE].

Rodeo de las Aguas: see **San Antonio or Rodeo de Las Agues** [LOS ANGELES].

Rodeo Flat [VENTURA]: *area,* 4.5 miles north of Piru (lat. 34°28'45" N, long. 118°48'30" W; sec. 31, T 5 N, R 18 W). Named on Piru (1952) 7.5' quadrangle.

Rodeo Grounds [SAN DIEGO]: *area,* nearly 5 miles northeast of Buckman Springs (lat. 32°49'15" N, long. 116°25'55" W; at E line sec. 35, T 15 S, R 5 E). Named on Mount Laguna (1960) 7.5' quadrangle.

Rodeo Spring [VENTURA]: *spring,* 4.25 miles north of Piru (lat. 34° 28'30" N, long. 118°48'30" W; sec. 31, T 5 N, R 18 W); the feature is near Rodeo Flat. Named on Piru (1952) 7.5' quadrangle.

Roderick Mountain: see **Rodriguez Mountain** [SAN DIEGO].

Rodriguez Canyon [SAN DIEGO]: *canyon,* drained by a stream that flows 3.5 miles to the canyon of Vallecito Wash 8 miles east-southeast of Julian (lat. 33°01'10" N, long. 116°29'05" W; near NW cor. sec. 28, T 13 S, R 5 E). Named on Earthquake Valley (1959) and Julian (1960) 7.5' quadrangles.

Rodriguez Mountain [SAN DIEGO]: *peak,* 13 miles north of Ramona (lat. 33°14' N, long. 116°54'10" W; sec. 8, T 11 S, R 1 E). Altitude 3886 feet. Named on Rodrigues Mountain (1948) 7.5' quadrangle. Called Roderick Mountain on Ramona (1903) 30' quadrangle.

Rogers Camp [LOS ANGELES]: *locality,* 17 miles southeast of Gorman in Fish Canyon (1) (lat. 34°38'05" N, long. 118°37'35" W). Named on Liebre Mountain (1958) 7.5' quadrangle.

Rogers Canyon: see **Roberts Canyon** [LOS ANGELES].

Rogers Creek [LOS ANGELES]: *stream,* flows 2.5 miles to Amargosa Creek nearly 2 miles east-southeast of the village of Leona Valley (lat. 34°36'20" N, long. 118°15'30" W; sec. 16, T 6 N, R 13 W). Named on Sleepy Valley (1958) 7.5' quadrangle.

Roger Young Village [LOS ANGELES]: *locality,* 2.5 miles south-southeast of Burbank city hall (lat. 34°09'05" N, long. 118°16'50" W). Named on Burbank (1953) 7.5' quadrangle.

Rolling Hills [LOS ANGELES]: *town,* 5.5 miles south of Torrance city hall in Palos Verdes Hills (lat. 33°45'45" N, long. 118°21' W). Named on San Pedro (1964) and Torrance (1964) 7.5' quadrangles. Postal authorities established Rolling Hills post office in 1937, discontinued it in 1942, and reestablished it in 1949 (Salley, p. 188). The town incorporated in 1957.

Rolling Hills Estates [LOS ANGELES]: *town,* 3.5 miles south-southwest of Torrance city hall in Palos Verdes Hills (lat. 33°47'15" N, long. 118°21'45" W). Named on Redondo Beach (1963) and Torrance (1964) 7.5' quadrangles. Postal authorities established Rolling Hills Estates post office in 1964 as a branch of Palos Verdes Peninsula post office, which they had established in 1962 in Palos Verdes Hills (Salley, p. 166, 188). Rolling Hills Estates incorporated in 1957.

Romero Canyon [LOS ANGELES]: *canyon,* drained by a stream that flows

3.5 miles to Halsey Canyon 9.5 miles northwest of Newhall (lat. 34°27'50" N, long. 118°39'30" W). Named on Val Verde (1952) and Whitaker Peak (1958) 7.5' quadrangles.

Roosevelt [LOS ANGELES]:
(1) *locality*, 7.5 miles east-northeast of Lancaster (lat. 34°43'10" N, long. 118°00'20" W; around NE cor. sec. 11, T 7 N, R 11 W). Named on Lancaster East (1958) 7.5' quadrangle. Postal authorities established Roosevelt Corner post office 9 miles east of Lancaster post office in 1966; the name was from Roosevelt school at the place (Salley, p. 188).
(2) *district*, 2.5 miles northeast of Torrance city hall (lat. 33°51'50" N, long. 118°18'15" W). Named on Torrance (1964) 7.5' quadrangle.

Roosevelt: see **Long Beach** [LOS ANGELES]; **Munz Canyon** [LOS ANGELES].

Roosevelt Corner: see **Roosevelt** [LOS ANGELES] (1).

Rosamond Dry Lake: see **Rosamond Lake** [LOS ANGELES].

Rosamond Lake [LOS ANGELES]: *dry lake*, about 5 miles long, 10 miles north-northeast of Lancaster on Los Angeles-Kern County line (lat. 34°50' N, long. 118°04' W). Named on Rosamond Lake (1973) 7.5' quadrangle. Called Rosamond Dry Lake on Rosamond (1943) 15' quadrangle. Rosamond Lake (1973) 7.5' quadrangle has the designation "Air Force Flight Test Center, Edwards Air Force Base" at the dry lake. Defense Department officials named the air force base in 1949 to honor Captain Glenn W. Edwards, a pilot killed in 1948 while testing a jet plane—previously the place was called Muroc Dry Lake Center (Hanna, p. 95).

Roscoe: see **Sun Valley** [LOS ANGELES] (1).

Rose Canyon [ORANGE]: *canyon*, drained by a stream that flows 2 miles to Arroyo Trabuco 4.5 miles southwest of Santiago Peak (lat. 33°39'35" N, long. 117°35'05" W; near S line sec. 11, T 6 S, R 7 W). Named on Santiago Peak (1954) 7.5' quadrangle. The feature was called Hick's Canyon on some early maps for Jim Hickey, who kept bees there beginning in 1875; later it was called Wild Rose Canyon, and then Rose Canyon after 1886 (Sleeper, 1976, p. 166).

Rose Canyon [SAN DIEGO]: *canyon*, drained by a stream that flows 14 miles to Mission Bay 5 miles southeast of Point La Jolla (lat. 32°47'45" N, long. 117°13'10" W). Named on Del Mar (1967), La Jolla (1967), and Poway (1967) 7.5' quadrangles. Harlow (1987, p. 79) identified present Rose Canyon as the feature called Cañada de San Buenaventura on a map of the Pueblo lands of San Diego that Henry D. Fitch made in 1845. The name "Rose" commemorates Louis Rose, a prominent citizen of San Diego who had a tannery in the canyon (Stein, p. 110).

Rosecrans [LOS ANGELES]: *locality*, 5.5 miles southeast of present Inglewood city hall along a railroad (lat. 33°53'55" N, long. 118° 17'30" W). Named on Redondo (1896) 15' quadrangle. Postal authorities established Rosecrans post office in 1888, discontinued it in 1890, reestablished in 1951, and discontinued it in 1962; the name commemorates Union General William S. Rosecrans of Civil War fame (Salley, p. 189).

Rosecrans: see **Fort Rosecrans** [SAN DIEGO].

Rosecrans Hills [LOS ANGELES]: *ridge*, north-northwest-trending, about 8 miles long, center 3.5 miles southeast of Inglewood city hall (lat. 33°56' N, long. 118°18'15" W). Named on Inglewood (1964) 7.5' quadrangle.

Rose Creek [VENTURA]: *stream*, flows 1.5 miles to Snowy Creek 4.25 miles northeast of McDonald Peak (lat. 34°40'25" N, long. 118°52'50" W; sec. 27, T 7 N, R 19 W). Named on McDonald Peak (1958) 7.5' quadrangle.

Rosedale: see **Linda Vista** [SAN DIEGO].

Rose Gulch [LOS ANGELES]: *canyon*, drained by a stream that flows 1 mile to Iron Fork nearly 6 miles west of Mount San Antonio (lat. 34°18'05" N, long. 117°44'50" W). Named on Mount San Antonio (1955) 7.5' quadrangle.

Rose Hill [LOS ANGELES]: *district*, 3.5 miles east-northeast of Los Angeles city hall (lat. 34°04'50" N, long. 118°11'35" W). Named on Alhambra (1926) 6' quadrangle.

Rosemead [LOS ANGELES]: *city*, 2.5 miles west-northwest of El Monte city hall (lat. 34°04'50" N, long. 118°04'20" W). Named on El Monte (1953) 7.5' quadrangle. Postal authorities established Rosemead post office in 1924 (Salley, p. 189), and the city incorporated in 1959. The name first applied in the 1870's to Leonard J. Rose's horse farm (Gudde, 1949, p. 290).

Rosemont [SAN DIEGO]: *locality*, 6.5 miles south-southeast of San Pasqual (lat. 33°00' N, long. 116°55'30" W; near W line sec. 31, T 13 S, R 1 E). Named on San Pasqual (1954) and San Vicente Reservoir (1955) 7.5' quadrangles.

Rosenita: see **Camp Rosenita** [LOS ANGELES].

Rose Valley Creek [VENTURA]: *stream*, flows 3.5 miles to Howard Creek 5.5 miles northeast of Wheeler Springs (lat. 34°33'05" N, long. 119°12'30" W; sec. 5, T 5 N, R 22 W). Named on Lion Canyon (1943) 7.5' quadrangle.

Rose Valley Falls [VENTURA]: *waterfall*, 6.5 miles east-northeast of Wheeler Springs along Rose Valley Creek (lat. 34°31'35" N, long. 119°10'40" W; at E line sec. 9, T 5 N, R 22 W). Named on Lion Canyon (1943) 7.5' quadrangle.

Roseville [SAN DIEGO]: *district*, 4 miles west-northwest of downtown San Diego (lat. 32°43'55" N, long. 117°13'30" W). Named on Point Loma (1967) 7.5' quadrangle. Point Loma (1942) 7.5' quadrangle has both the names "Roseville" and "Point Loma P.O." at a site situated about 0.5 mile farther south near present Commercial Basin (lat. 32°43'30" N, long. 117°13'40" W). San Diego (1904) 15' quadrangle has the name "Roseville" for a community located 1 mile farther southwest (lat. 32°42'50" N, long. 117°14'40" W). The name "Roseville" is for Louis Rose of Rose Canyon, who built a wharf at the place in 1870 (Gudde, 1949, p. 290).

Ross Lake [SAN DIEGO]: *lake*, 1600 feet long, 4.5 miles north-northwest of Fallbrook (lat. 33°26'25" N, long. 117°12'05" W; sec. 34, T 8 S, R 4 W). Named on Fallbrook (1968) 7.5' quadrangle.

Rossmoor [ORANGE]: *town*, 7 miles southwest of Buena Park civic center (lat. 33°47'10" N, long. 118°04'45" W). Named on Los Alamitos (1964) 7.5' quadrangle. Postal authorities established Rossmoor post office in 1962; the name is from Ross W. Cortese, who built the community (Salley, p. 189).

Ross Mountain [LOS ANGELES]: *peak*, 5.25 miles east of Crystal Lake (lat. 34°19'30" N, long. 117°45'20" W). Altitude 7402 feet. Named on Crystal Lake (1958) 7.5' quadrangle.

Round Canyon [ORANGE]: *canyon*, 3 miles long, opens into lowlands 4.5 miles north-northwest of El Toro (lat. 33°41'25" N, long. 117°42'30" W). Named on El Toro (1968) 7.5' quadrangle. Called Bee Canyon on Corona (1902) 30' quadrangle, where present nearby Bee Canyon is unnamed.

Round Granite Hill [SAN DIEGO]: *hill*, 9 miles south-southeast of Borrego Springs (lat. 33°07'45" N, long. 116°19'45" W; on E line sec. 15, T 12 S, R 6 E). Altitude 1502 feet. Named on Borrego Sink (1959) 7.5' quadrangle.

Round Mountain [SAN DIEGO]: *peak*, 1.5 miles north-northeast of Jacumba (lat. 32°38'20" N, long. 116°10'55" W; at N line sec. 5, T 18 S, R 8 E). Altitude 3367 feet. Named on Jacumba (1959) 7.5' quadrangle.

Round Mountain [VENTURA]: *hill*, 4 miles south-southwest of Camarillo (lat. 34°09'45" N, long. 119°03'20" W). Altitude 554 feet. Named on Camarillo (1950) 7.5' quadrangle.

Round Potrero [SAN DIEGO]: *valley*, 7 miles west-southwest of Morena Village (lat. 32°39'30" N, long. 116°37' W; mainly in sec. 30, 31, T 17 S, R 4 E). Named on Barrett Lake (1960) and Morena Reservoir (1960) 7.5' quadrangles.

Round Spring Canyon [VENTURA]: *canyon*, drained by a stream that flows 8 miles to Cuyama River 8 miles northwest of Reyes Peak (lat. 34°42'50" N, long. 119°22'55" W). Named on Apache Canyon (1943) and Reyes Peak (1943) 7.5' quadrangles.

Roundtop [LOS ANGELES]: *peak*, nearly 3 miles southwest of Pacifico Mountain (lat. 34°21'10" N, long. 118°04' W; near N line sec. 18, T 3 N, R 11 W). Altitude 6316 feet. Named on Chilao Flat (1959) 7.5' quadrangle.

Rowell Canyon: see **Hickey Canyon** [ORANGE].

Rowher Canyon [LOS ANGELES]: *canyon*, drained by a stream that flows 4 miles to Mint Canyon (1) 12.5 miles south-southeast of the village of Lake Hughes (lat. 34°30'10" N, long. 118°22'45" W; near E line sec. 19, T 5 N, R 14 W). Named on Green Valley (1958) and Sleepy Valley (1958) 7.5' quadrangles.

Rowland [LOS ANGELES]: *locality*, 6 miles south-southeast of Baldwin Park city hall along Union Pacific Railroad (lat. 34°00'05" N, long. 117°55'45" W). Named on Baldwin Park (1953) 7.5' quadrangle. Postal authorities established Rowland post office in 1903 and discontinued it in 1904; the name was for Bernard F. Rowland, first postmaster (Salley, p. 190). California Mining Bureau's (1917a) map shows a place called Fallon located 2 miles east of Rowland along the railroad.

Rowland Heights [LOS ANGELES]: *city*, 4 miles northeast of La Habra [ORANGE] (lat. 33°58'30" N, long. 117°54'15" W). Named on La Habra (1964) 7.5' quadrangle. Postal authorities established Rowland Heights post office in 1963 (Salley, p. 190).

Rowland Siding [LOS ANGELES]: *locality*, 5.5 miles south-southeast of present Baldwin Park city hall along Southern Pacific Railroad (lat. 34°00'30" N, long. 117°55'45" W). Named on Pomona (1904) 15' quadrangle.

Rowley Canyon [LOS ANGELES]: *canyon*, 1.25 miles long, 2 miles east-northeast of Sunland (lat. 34°16' N, long. 118°16'45" W; mainly at S line sec. 7, T 2 N, R 13 W). Named on Sunland (1953) 7.5' quadrangle.

Royball Spring [LOS ANGELES]: *spring*, 12.5 miles south-southeast of Gorman (lat. 34°37'45" N, long. 118°45'25" W). Named on Black Mountain (1958) 7.5' quadrangle.

Rubio Canyon [LOS ANGELES]:
(1) *canyon*, 2.25 miles long, opens into lowlands 3 miles west-southwest of Mount Wilson (1) (lat. 34°11'50" N, long. 118°07'20" W; sec. 3, T 1 N, R 12 W). Named on Mount Wilson (1953) 7.5' quadrangle. The name commemorates Jesus Rubio Maron, who came to the place in 1867 and built a cabin near the mouth of the canyon (Robinson, J.W., 1977, p. 101).
(2) *locality*, 3.5 miles west-southwest of Mount Wilson (1) along Pacific Electric Railroad (lat. 34°12'20" N, long. 118°07' W); the place is in Rubio

Canyon (1). Named on Mount Lowe (1939) 6' quadrangle.

Rubio Wash [LOS ANGELES]: *stream,* flows 5 miles to Rio Hondo 2.25 miles west of El Monte city hall (lat. 34°03'20" N, long. 118° 04' W). Named on El Monte (1953) 7.5' quadrangle.

Ruby Canyon [LOS ANGELES]:

(1) *canyon,* drained by a stream that flows 3 miles to Piru Creek 15 miles south-southeast of Gorman (lat. 34°34'35" N, long. 118°46'30" W). Named on Cobblestone Mountain (1958) and Whitaker Peak (1958) 7.5' quadrangles. Called Whitaker Canyon on Los Angeles County (1935) map.

(2) *canyon,* drained by a stream that flows 4 miles to Elizabeth Lake Canyon 1.5 miles east-northeast of Warm Springs Mountain (lat. 34°36'10" N, long. 118°33'15" W). Named on Green Valley (1958) and Warm Springs Mountain (1958) 7.5' quadrangles.

(3) *canyon,* 1 mile long, 6 miles west-northwest of Azusa city hall (lat. 34°10'20" N, long. 118°00' W; sec. 14, T 1 N, R 11 W). Named on Azusa (1953) 7.5' quadrangle.

Ruby Spring [LOS ANGELES]: *spring,* 4.25 miles east of Warm Springs Mountain (lat. 34°35'40" N, long. 118°30'10" W); the spring is in Ruby Canyon (2). Named on Warm Springs Mountain (1958) 7.5' quadrangle.

Runkle Canyon [VENTURA]: *canyon,* 3.25 miles long, opens into Simi Valley (1) 6 miles west of Santa Susana Pass (lat. 34°15'40" N, long. 118°44'15" W; sec. 14, T 2 N, R 18 W). Named on Calabasas (1952) and Santa Susana (1951) 7.5' quadrangles.

Runkle Reservoir [VENTURA]: *lake,* 750 feet long, 5 miles west-southwest of Santa Susana Pass (lat. 34°14'35" N, long. 118°43'50" W); the lake is in Runkle Canyon. Named on Calabasas (1952) 7.5' quadrangle.

Runnymead: see **Tarzana** [LOS ANGELES].

Rush Canyon [LOS ANGELES]: *canyon,* drained by a stream that flows 1.25 miles to Mint Canyon 12.5 miles south-southeast of the village of Lake Hughes (lat. 34°30' N, long. 118°22'50" W; near E line sec. 19, T 5 N, R 14 W). Named on Green Valley (1958) 7.5' quadrangle.

Rush Creek [LOS ANGELES]: *stream,* flows about 1.25 miles to West Fork San Gabriel River 1.5 miles north-northeast of Mount Wilson (1) (lat. 34°14'45" N, long. 118°02'50" W; near E line sec. 20, T 2 N, R 11 W). Named on Mount Wilson (1953) 7.5' quadrangle.

Russ [LOS ANGELES]: *locality,* 8 miles east of Solemint along Southern Pacific Railroad (lat. 34°26'25" N, long. 118°18'50" W; near S line sec. 11, T 4 N, R 14 W). Named on Agua Dulce (1960) 7.5' quadrangle. Called Russ Siding on San Fernando (1900) 15' quadrangle.

Russell's Lake: see **Malibu Lake** [LOS ANGELES].

Russell Valley [LOS ANGELES-VENTURA]: *valley,* 5.5 miles west of Agoura on Los Angeles-Ventura County line (lat. 34°08'55" N, long. 118°49' W). Named on Thousand Oaks (1952) 7.5' quadrangle. The name commemorates A.D. Russell and H.M. Russell, who bought land in the neighborhood in 1881 (Ricard). The town of Westlake Village now occupies much of the valley. Postal authorities established Westlake Village post office 4 miles south of Thousand Oaks post office in 1966 and discontinued it in 1972 (Salley, p. 237). Westlake Village incorporated in 1981.

Russian Wells: see **North Island** [SAN DIEGO].

Russ Siding: see **Russ** [LOS ANGELES].

Rustic Canyon [LOS ANGELES]: *canyon,* drained by a stream that flows 8 miles to the sea 2 miles west-northwest of Santa Monica city hall (lat. 34°01'40" N, long. 118°31'05" W). Named on Topanga (1952) 7.5' quadrangle.

Rusty Spring [SAN DIEGO]: *spring,* nearly 6 miles west-southwest of Borrego Springs (lat. 33°12'55" N, long. 116°27'55" W; near W line sec. 15, T 11 S, R 5 E). Named on Tubb Canyon (1959) 7.5' quadrangle.

- S -

Sacotone Spring [SAN DIEGO]: *spring,* 7 miles north-northwest of Jacumba (lat. 32°42'45" N, long. 116°13'50" W; at S line sec. 2, T 17 S, R 7 E). Named on Jacumba (1959) 7.5' quadrangle.

Saddleback [SAN DIEGO]: *pass,* 7.5 miles south-southwest of Santa Ysabel (lat. 33°00'10" N, long. 116°42'50" W; sec. 31, T 13 S, R 3 E). Named on Santa Ysabel (1960) 7.5' quadrangle.

Saddleback: see **Old Saddleback**, under **Santiago Peak** [ORANGE].

Saddleback Buttes [LOS ANGELES]: *ridge,* north-northeast-trending, 2 miles long, 15 miles northeast of Littlerock (lat. 34°40'30" N, long. 117°48' W; in and near sec. 23, 26, T 7 N, R 9 W). Named on Hi Vista (1957) 7.5' quadrangle.

Saddle Peak [LOS ANGELES]: *ridge,* generally northeast-trending, 0.5 mile long, 3.5 miles north-northeast of Malibu Point (lat. 34° 04'35" N, long. 118°39'15" W; near SW cor. sec. 15, T 1 S, R 17 W). Named on Malibu Beach (1951) 7.5' quadrangle.

Saddle Rock [LOS ANGELES]: *peak,* 6.5 miles north-northwest of Point Dume (lat. 34°05'40" N, long. 118°49'45" W; near W line sec. 12, T 1 S, R 19 W). Named on Point Dume (1951) 7.5' quadrangle.

Saddle Rock Lodge [LOS ANGELES]: *locality,* nearly 7 miles north of Dume Point (present Point Dume) (lat. 34°05'55" N, long. 118° 49' W); the place is less than 1 mile east-northeast of present Saddle Rock. Named on Dume Point (1932) 6' quadrangle.

Sail Bay [SAN DIEGO]: *embayment,* 4.5 miles south-southeast of Point La Jolla off Mission Bay (lat. 32°47'15" N, long. 117°14'45" W). Named on La Jolla (1967) 7.5' quadrangle. Called Crescent Bay on La Jolla (1953) 7.5' quadrangle, and shown as part of Mission Bay on La Jolla (1943) 7.5' quadrangle.

Saint Helens Spur [LOS ANGELES]: *locality,* 5 miles south-southwest of El Monte city hall along Union Pacific Railroad (lat. 34°00'20" N, long. 118°03'45" W); the place is on Paso de Bartolo grant. Named on El Monte (1953) 7.5' quadrangle. Called Bartolo on El Monte (1966) 7.5' quadrangle.

Saint Johns: see **Mint Canyon** [LOS ANGELES] (2).

Salazar Canyon [SAN DIEGO]: *canyon,* drained by a stream that flows 2.5 miles to Cottonwood Creek (3) 6.25 miles west of Morena Village (lat. 32°40'45" N, long. 116°36'40" W; sec. 19, T 17 S, R 4 E). Named on Morena Reservoir (1960) 7.5' quadrangle.

Salazar Spring [SAN DIEGO]: *spring,* 7.5 miles west-northwest of Morena Village (lat. 32°44'10" N, long. 116°37'05" W; near E line sec. 36, T 16 S, R 3 E). Named on Morena Reservoir (1960) 7.5' quadrangle.

Salinas: see **Lake Salinas**, under **Salt Pond** [LOS ANGELES].

Sally: see **Mount Sally** [LOS ANGELES].

Salmons City: see **Trujillo Creek** [SAN DIEGO].

Salmons Creek: see **Trujillo Creek** [SAN DIEGO].

Salta Verde Point [LOS ANGELES]: *promontory,* nearly 4 miles south of Mount Banning on the south side of Santa Catalina Island (lat. 33°19' N, long. 118°25'15" W). Named on Santa Catalina South (1943) 7.5' quadrangle.

Salt Canyon [LOS ANGELES-VENTURA]: *canyon,* drained by a stream that heads in Los Angeles County and flows 6 miles to Santa Clara River 9.5 miles west of Newhall just inside Ventura County (lat. 34°23'55" N, long. 118°42'15" W). Named on Santa Susana (1951) and Val Verde (1952) 7.5' quadrangles. Called Salt Creek Canyon on Santa Susana (1943) 15' quadrangle. East Fork branches east 3 miles above the mouth of the main canyon; it is 2 miles long and is named on Santa Susana (1951) and Val Verde (1952) 7.5' quadrangles. Present East Fork is called No. Fork on Los Angeles County (1935) map,which shows a So. Fork farther upstream.

Salt Creek [LOS ANGELES]: *stream,* flows 7 miles to Castaic Creek 13 miles southeast of Gorman (lat. 34°38'15" N, long. 118°40'10" W; sec. 3, T 6 N, R 17 W). Named on Liebre Mountain (1958) 7.5' quadrangle. The name is from salt pools situated near the head of the stream (Preston, 1890a, p. 204).

Salt Creek [ORANGE]: *stream,* flows 4 miles to the sea nearly 4 miles west-southwest of San J2uan Capistrano (lat. 33°28'55" N, long. 117°43'25" W). Named on Dana Point (1968) and San Juan Capistrano (1968) 7.5' quadrangles. Old maps have the names "Arroyo Salada" and "Cañada Niguel" for the feature (Meadows, p. 121). According to Preston (1890a, p. 210), Mexican shepherds obtained rock salt near the head of the stream.

Salt Creek [SAN DIEGO]:

(1) *stream,* flows 1.5 miles to Mason Valley 5.5 miles north-northwest of Monument Peak (lat. 32°57'50" N, long. 116°27'35" W; sec. 10, T 14 S, R 5 E). Named on Monument Peak (1959) 7.5' quadrangle.

(2) *stream,* flows 6 miles to Otay River 6 miles west of Otay Mountain (lat. 32°35'55" N, long. 116°56'55" W). Named on Jamul (1955) and Otay Mesa (1955) 7.5' quadrangles.

Salt Creek Canyon: see **Salt Canyon** [LOS ANGELES].

Salt Marsh Canyon [VENTURA]: *canyon,* drained by a stream that flows 3.5 miles to Adams Canyon 6.25 miles west-southwest of Santa Paula Peak (lat. 34°23'35" N, long. 119°06'10" W). Named on Ojai (1952) and Santa Paula Peak (1951) 7.5' quadrangles. United States Board on Geographic Names (1969b, p. 5) approved the form "Saltmarsh Canyon" for the name, which commemorates John Saltmarsh (Goodyear, 1888a, p. 108).

Salt Pond [LOS ANGELES]: *lake,* 1500 feet long, less than 0.5 mile north-northwest of present Redondo Beach city hall (lat. 33°51' N, long. 118°23'45" W). Named on Redondo (1896) 15' quadrangle. Called Las Salinas on Hall's (1887) map. Preston (1890b, p. 281) called the feature Lake Salinas. Indians obtained salt from the lake; in the 1850's Johnson and Allanson built a works that produced 450 tons of salt by evaporation in 1879 (Grenier, p. 175).

Salvador Canyon [SAN DIEGO]: *canyon,* drained by a stream that flows 3 miles to Collins Valley 11 miles north-northwest of Borrego Springs (lat. 33°23'45" N, long. 116°28'30" W). Named on Bucksnort Mountain (1960) and Collins Valley (1959) 7.5' quadrangles. Called Thousand Palms Canyon on Ramona (1903) 30' quadrangle, and called One Thousand Palms Canyon on Clark Lake (1944) 15' quadrangle, but United States Board on Geographic Names (1962a, p. 15) rejected both names for the feature. The name "Salvador Canyon" honors Salvador Ygnacio Linares, who was born at nearby Upper Willows in Coyote Canyon on Christmas Eve, 1775, at the time of the second Anza expedition (Bloomquist, 1978b, p. 35).

South Fork branches south 1 mile above the mouth of the main canyon; it is 1.25 miles long and is named on Collins Valley (1959) 7.5' quadrangle.

Samagatuma Creek [SAN DIEGO]: *stream,* flows 4.5 miles to Sweetwater River at Descanso (lat. 32°51'20" N, long. 116°36'40" W); the stream drains Samagatuma Valley. Named on Descanso (1960) 7.5' quadrangle.

Samagatuma Valley [SAN DIEGO]: *valley,* 3 miles east of Descanso (lat. 32°51'55" N, long. 116°33'55" W). Named on Descanso (1960) 7.5' quadrangle. The name is from an Indian rancheria (Gudde, 1949, p. 297).

San Alejo: see **San Elijo Canyon** [SAN DIEGO].

San Antonio [LOS ANGELES]: *land grant,* extends from Lynwood to Montebello. Named on El Monte (1953), Los Angeles (1953), South Gate (1952), and Whittier (1951) 7.5' quadrangles. Antonio Maria Lugo received the land in 1810, 1823, 1827, and 1838; Lugo claimed 29,513 acres patented in 1866 (Cowan, p. 71-72).

San Antonio: see **Mount San Antonio** [LOS ANGELES]; **Yorba** [ORANGE].

San Antonio Canyon [LOS ANGELES]: *canyon,* heads in San Bernardino County and extends for about 6 miles in Los Angeles County and along Los Angeles-San Bernardino County line to open into lowlands 8.5 miles north-northeast of Pomona city hall (lat. 34°09'30" N, long. 117°40'45" W; sec. 23, 24, T 1 N, R 8 W). Named on Mount Baldy (1954) 7.5' quadrangle.

San Antonio Creek [VENTURA]: *stream,* flows 14 miles to Ventura River 6 miles southwest of the town of Ojai (lat. 34°22'50" N, long. 119°18'25" W). Named on Matilija (1952) and Ojai (1952) 7.5' quadrangles.

San Antonio or Rodeo de las Aguas [LOS ANGELES]: *land grant,* at Beverly Hills. Named on Beverly Hills (1950) and Hollywood (1953) 7.5' quadrangles. Maria Rita Valdes received the land in 1841 and claimed 4449 acres patented in 1871 (Cowan, p. 69).

San Antonio Peak: see **Mount San Antonio** [LOS ANGELES].

San Antonio Ridge [LOS ANGELES]: *ridge,* generally west-trending, 5 miles long, center 2.5 miles west of Mount San Antonio (lat. 34° 17'30" N, long. 117°41'20" W); Mount San Antonio is at the east end. Named on Mount San Antonio (1955) 7.5' quadrangle.

San Antonio Wash [LOS ANGELES]: *stream* and *dry wash,* extends for 9 miles from the mouth of San Antonio Canyon along and near Los Angeles-San Bernardino County line to enter San Bernardino County finally 2.25 miles southeast of Pomona city hall (lat. 34°02'25" N, long. 117°43'30" W). Named on Mount Baldy (1954) and Ontario (1954) 7.5' quadrangles.

San Bernardino Mountains: see **San Gabriel Mountains** [LOS ANGELES].

San Bernardino Range: see **San Gabriel Mountains** [LOS ANGELES].

San Bernardo [SAN DIEGO]: *land grant,* south of Escondido. Named on Escondido (1968) and Poway (1967) 7.5' quadrangles. Joseph F. Snook received 4 leagues in 1842 and 1845; his widow claimed 17,763 acres patented in 1874 (Cowan, p. 73). Emory's (1848) map shows Snook's Rancho. United States Board on Geographic Names (1976b, p. 3) approved the name "San Bernardo Valley" for the valley of San Dieguito River on the grant, and gave the variant name "Valle de San Bernardo" for the feature. Emory's (1848) map has the name "Rio San Bernardo" for present San Dieguito River at the place.

San Bernardo River: see **San Dieguito River** [SAN DIEGO].

San Bernardo Valley: see **San Bernardo** [SAN DIEGO].

San Buenaventura: see **Ventura** [VENTURA].

San Buenaventura Plain: see **Santa Clara River** [VENTURA].

San Buenaventura River: see **Ventura River** [VENTURA].

San Cayetano: see **Sespe** [VENTURA] (1).

San Cayetano Mountain [VENTURA]: *peak,* 5 miles northwest of Fillmore (lat. 34°26'20" N, long. 118°58'50" W; near S line sec. 9, T 4 N, R 20 W). Named on Fillmore (1951) 7.5' quadrangle. Called San Cayetano Pk. on Los Angeles County (1935) map. Goodyear (1888a, p. 112) referred to Mount San Cayatana. The name is from the alternate name "San Cayetano" for Sespe grant (Gudde, 1949, p. 300).

San Clemente [ORANGE]: *city,* 30 miles southeast of Santa Ana along the coast (lat. 33°25'40" N, long. 117°36'30" W). Named on Dana Point (1968) and San Clemente (1968) 7.5' quadrangles. Postal authorities established San Clemente post office in 1926 (Frickstad, p. 117), and the city incorporated in 1928. Ole Hanson founded the community in 1925 (Meadows, p. 121).

San Clemente Canyon [SAN DIEGO]: *canyon,* drained by a stream that flows 13 miles to Rose Canyon 2.5 miles east-southeast of Point La Jolla (lat. 32°50'15" N, long. 117°13'50" W). Named on La Jolla (1967), La Mesa (1967), and Poway (1967) 7.5' quadrangles. United States Board on Geographic Names (1933, p. 664) rejected the names "Clemente Canyon" and "San Clemento Canyon" for the feature. Harlow (1987, p. 79) identified present San Clemente Canyon as the feature called Cañada de las Yeguas on the map of Pueblo lands of San Diego that Henry D. Fitch made in 1845.

San Clemente Island [LOS ANGELES]: *island,* 21 miles long, 55 miles south of Point Fermin (lat. 32°54' N, long. 118°29' W). Named on Long Beach (1957) 1°x 2° quadrangles. Vizcaino named the island in 1602 for Saint Clement, third Pope and Bishop of Rome (Gudde, 1949, p. 300). United States Board on Geographic Names (1933, p. 664) rejected the form "San Clements Island" for the name.

Sand Beach: see **Newport Beach** [ORANGE].

Sandberg [LOS ANGELES]: *locality,* 8.5 miles east-southeast of Gorman (lat. 34°44'25" N, long. 118°42'30" W; near NW cor. sec. 32, T 8 N, R 17 W). Named on Liebre Mountain (1958) 7.5' quadrangle. Postal authorities established Sandberg post office in 1918 and discontinued it in 1944 (Salley, p. 193). The name is for Herman Sandberg, who operated a tavern at the place (Hanna, p. 270).

Sand Canyon [LOS ANGELES]:

(1) *canyon,* drained by a stream that flows 0.5 mile to Kings Canyon 3 miles northeast of Burnt Peak (lat. 34°42'45" N, long. 118°32'05" W; near W line sec. 12, T 7 N, R 16 W). Named on Burnt Peak (1958) 7.5' quadrangle.

(2) *canyon,* drained by a stream that flows 8 miles to Santa Clara River nearly 2 miles east of Solemint (lat. 34°25'15" N, long. 118° 25'25" W; sec. 23, T 4 N, R 15 W). Named on Agua Dulce (1960), Mint Canyon (1960), San Fernando (1953), and Sunland (1953) 7.5' quadrangles. Los Angeles County (1935) map shows a feature called Live Oak Spring Canyon that opens into Sand Canyon from the southeast about 2 miles east-southeast of Solemint (at S line sec. 23, T 4 N, R 15 W).

Sand Canyon Reservoir [ORANGE]: *lake,* 0.5 mile long, behind a dam at the head of Sand Canyon Wash 8 miles south-southeast of Santa Ana city hall (lat. 33°38'50" N, long. 117°47'45" W). Named on Tustin (1965) 7.5' quadrangle.

Sand Canyon Wash [ORANGE]: *stream,* flows 3 miles to San Diego Creek 6.25 miles south-southeast of Santa Ana city hall (lat. 33°39'30" N, long. 117°50'30" W); the feature heads at Sand Canyon Reservoir. Named on Tustin (1965) 7.5' quadrangle.

Sand Creek [SAN DIEGO]: *stream,* flows 6.25 miles to El Capitan Reservoir 4 miles northeast of El Cajon Mountain (lat. 32°56'45" N, long. 116°45'40" W; sec. 22, T 14 S, R 2 E). Named on El Cajon Mountain (1955) and Tule Springs (1960) 7.5' quadrangles.

Sandia Canyon [SAN DIEGO]: *canyon,* drained by a stream that heads in Riverside County and flows 3 miles in San Diego County to Santa Margarita River 2.25 miles north of Fallbrook (lat. 33°24'50" N, long. 117°14'40" W; near NE cor. sec. 12, T 9 S, R 4 W). Named on Fallbrook (1968) and Temecula (1968) 7.5' quadrangles.

San Diegito: see **San Dieguito** [SAN DIEGO].

San Diegito Valley: see **San Dieguito Valley** [SAN DIEGO].

San Diego [SAN DIEGO]: *city,* at the southwest corner of San Diego County (downtown near lat. 32°43' N, long. 117°09'45" W). Named on Del Mar (1967), Imperial Beach (1967), La Jolla (1967), La Mesa (1967), National City (1967), Otay Mesa (1955), Point Loma (1967), and Poway (1967) 7.5' quadrangles. Postal authorities established San Diego post office at present Old Town in 1849, moved it 4 miles south and changed the name to South San Diego in 1869, and changed the name to San Diego in 1876 (Salley, p. 193). The community incorporated in 1850. Dalrymple's (1789) map shows a feature called Pta. de los Muertos located along San Diego Bay near present downtown San Diego—the name is from the burial at the spot of scurvy victims at the time of the first survey of San Diego Bay by the Spaniards in 1782 (Hoover, Rensch, and Rensch, p. 340). Gray's (1856) map has the name "New San Diego" for a place located 3.25 miles south-southeast of San Diego (present Old Town) on the east side of San Diego Bay. William Heath Davis founded the American city at present Old town in 1850 (Hanna, p. 271). At about the same time promoters hired Gray, who was United States Surveyor to the Boundary Commission, to lay out a community called New Town or New San Diego along San Diego Bay 3 miles south of present Old Town, and contracted with Davis to build the place (Bartlett, v. 2, p. 97; Gleason, p. 75). The venture at New San Diego was a failure until Alonzo E. Horton came in 1867 and laid out the nucleus of present San Diego (Hoover, Rensch, and Rensch, p. 336). An American military installation, first called Post New San Diego and then called San Diego Barracks, was built in 1851 about 0.5 mile southwest of present downtown San Diego, and was abandoned in 1921 (Hoover, Rensch, and Rensch, p. 340). Postal authorities established Holabird post office 7 miles northeast of San Diego post office in 1888 and discontinued it the same year (Salley, p. 99).

San Diego: see **East San Diego** [SAN DIEGO]; **Fort San Diego**, under **Old Town** [SAN DIEGO]; **North San Diego** [SAN DIEGO]; **South San Diego** [SAN DIEGO]; **South San Diego**, under **Imperial Beach** [SAN DIEGO].

San Diego Barracks: see **San Diego** [SAN DIEGO].

San Diego Bay [SAN DIEGO]: *bay,* opens to the sea 4.5 miles west-southwest of downtown San Diego (lat. 32°41' N, long. 117°13'45" W). Named on Imperial Beach (1967) and Point Loma (1967) 7.5' quadrangles. Called Puerto bueno de S. Diego on a Spanish map of 1602 (Harlow, 1987, p. 52). Cabrillo discovered the bay in 1542 and called it San Miguel for the saint on whose day he was there; Vizcaino gave the present name to the feature in 1602 on the day of San Diego de Alcala (Wagner, p. 408).

San Diego Creek [ORANGE]: *stream,* flows 13 miles to Upper Newport

Bay nearly 7 miles south of Santa Ana city hall (lat. 33°38'55" N, long. 117°52'25" W). Named on El Toro (1968) and Tustin (1965) 7.5' quadrangles. The old road to San Diego followed the stream for several miles (Meadows, p. 121).

San Diego River [SAN DIEGO]: *stream* and *dry wash*, extends for 50 miles to the sea 6.5 miles south of Point La Jolla (lat. 32°45'20" N, long. 117°15'10" W). Named on El Cajon (1967), El Cajon Mountain (1955), La Jolla (1967), La Mesa (1967), San Vicente Reservoir (1955), Santa Ysabel (1960), and Tule Springs (1960) 7.5' quadrangles. The river emptied into San Diego Bay before 1853, when the flow of water was diverted into Mission Bay to prevent the silting up of San Diego Bay (Ellis and Lee, p. 25). On Cuyamaca (1903) 30' quadrangle, the name South Fork [San Diego River] applies to present Conejos Creek; the map shows South Fork formed by the confluence of Conejos Creek and King Creek.

San Dieguito [SAN DIEGO]: *land grant*, at and near Rancho Santa Fe. Named on Del Mar (1967) and Rancho Santa Fe (1968) 7.5' quadrangles. Juan Maria Osuna received 2 leagues in 1840 or 1841, and in 1845; his heirs claimed 8825 acres patented in 1871 (Cowan, p. 75). United States Board on Geographic Names (1933, p. 665) rejected the forms "San Diegito" and "San Digitas" for the name. Postal authorities established San Dieguito post office 20 miles north of San Diego in 1874, discontinued it in 1876, reestablished it in 1877, and discontinued it in 1886 (Salley, p. 193).

San Dieguito Reservoir [SAN DIEGO]: *lake*, 3000 feet long, 1.5 miles north-northeast of Rancho Santa Fe (lat. 33°02'20" N, long. 117°11'35" W). Named on Rancho Santa Fe (1968) 7.5' quadrangle.

San Dieguito River [SAN DIEGO]: *stream*, formed by the confluence of Santa Maria Creek and Santa Ysabel Creek, flows 23 miles to the sea 1 mile north of Del Mar (lat. 32°58'30" N, long. 117°16'10" W). Named on Del Mar (1967), Escondido (1968), and Rancho Santa Fe (1968) 7.5' quadrangles. Called Rio San Bernardo on Emory's (1848) map. United States Board on Geographic Names (1933, p. 665) rejected the names "Bernardo River," "San Bernardo River," and "San Pasqual River" for the stream.

San Dieguito Valley [SAN DIEGO]: *valley*, 2.5 miles east-northeast of Del Mar (lat. 32°58'45" N, long. 117°13'30" W); the feature is along lower reaches of San Dieguito River. Named on Del Mar (1967) 7.5' quadrangle. United States Board on Geographic Names (1933, p. 665) rejected the forms "San Diegito Valley" and "San Digitas Valley" for the name.

San Digitas: see **San Dieguito** [SAN DIEGO].

San Digitas Valley: see **San Dieguito Valley** [SAN DIEGO].

San Dimas [LOS ANGELES]: *town*, 5 miles northwest of Pomona city hall (lat. 34°06'30" N, long. 117°48'30" W). Named on Glendora (1966) and San Dimas (1966) 7.5' quadrangles. Postal authorities established San Dimas post office in 1888 (Frickstad, p. 80), and the town incorporated in 1960. The site first was called Mud Springs (Robinson, J.W., 1983, p. 49).

San Dimas Canyon [LOS ANGELES]: *canyon*, drained by a stream that flows 6.5 miles to lowlands 5 miles east of Glendora city hall (lat. 34°08'40" N, long. 117°46'30" W; sec. 25, T 1 N, R 9 W). Named on Glendora (1953) and Mount Baldy (1954) 7.5' quadrangles. East Fork branches east 3.5 miles above the mouth of the main canyon; it is 5 miles long and is named on Glendora (1966) and Mount Baldy (1954) 7.5' quadrangles. West Fork branches northwest less than 2 miles above the mouth of the main canyon; it is nearly 3 miles long and is named on Glendora (1966) 7.5' quadrangle.

San Dimas Junction: see **Lone Hill** [LOS ANGELES].

San Dimas Peak: see **Johnstone Peak** [LOS ANGELES].

San Dimas Reservoir [LOS ANGELES]: *lake*, behind a dam 5.25 miles east-northeast of Glendora city hall (lat. 34°09'15" N, long. 117°46'15" W; sec. 24, T 1 N, R 9 W); the lake is in San Dimas Canyon. Named on Glendora (1966) 7.5' quadrangle.

San Dimas Wash [LOS ANGELES]: *stream* and *dry wash*, extends for 9 miles from the mouth of San Dimas Canyon to Big Daulton Wash 2.5 miles east-northeast of Baldwin Park city hall (lat. 34° 06' N, long. 117°55'05" W; sec. 10, T 1 S, R 10 W). Named on Baldwin Park (1966), Glendora (1953), and San Dimas (1954) 7.5' quadrangles.

Sandrock Creek [LOS ANGELES]: *stream*, flows 2.5 miles to Big Rock Creek 0.5 miles north-northwest of Valyermo (lat. 34°27'15" N, long. 117°51'20" W); the stream goes past Sandrock. Named on Valyermo (1958) 7.5' quadrangle.

Sand Rock Peak [LOS ANGELES]: *peak*, 4.5 miles west-southwest of Newhall (lat. 34°22'05" N, long. 118°36'20" W; near SW cor. sec. 6, T 3 N, R 16 W). Altitude 2511 feet. Named on Oat Mountain (1952) 7.5' quadrangle. Pico (1940) 6' quadrangle has the form "Sandrock Pk" for the name.

Sandrocks [LOS ANGELES]: *relief feature*, about 1 mile south-southwest of Valyermo (lat. 34°25'50" N, long. 117°51'50" W; sec. 18, T 4 N, R 9 W). Named on Valyermo (1958) 7.5' quadrangle.

Sandstone Camp [VENTURA]: *locality*, 8 miles north-northwest of Wheeler Springs along Adobe Creek (lat. 34°36'35" N, long. 119° 21'55" W; near W line sec. 18, T 6 N, R 23 W). Named on Wheeler Springs (1943) 7.5' quadrangle.

Sandstone Canyon [SAN DIEGO]: *canyon*, 3 miles long, opens into the canyon of Fish Creek Wash 10.5 miles north of Sweeney Pass (lat. 32°58'45" N, long. 116°12'50" W; sec. 1, T 14 S, R 7 E). Named on Agua Caliente Springs (1959) and Arroyo Tapiado (1959) 7.5' quadrangles.

Sandstone Peak [VENTURA]: *peak*, 1 mile west-northwest of Triunfo Pass (lat. 34°07'15" N, long. 118°55'50" W; near S line sec. 36, T 1 N, R 20 W). Altitude 3111 feet. Named on Triunfo Pass (1950) 7.5' quadrangle.

Sandy Creek [SAN DIEGO]: *stream*, flows 2.25 miles to Cedar Creek (2) 6.5 miles south-southeast of Santa Ysabel (lat. 33°01'10" N, long. 116°38'25" W; near N line sec. 26, T 13 S, R 3 E). Named on Julian (1960) and Santa Ysabel (1960) 7.5' quadrangles.

Sandy Point: see **Laguna Point** [VENTURA].

San Elijo: see **Cardiff-by-the-Sea** [SAN DIEGO].

San Elijo Canyon [SAN DIEGO]: *canyon*, 2.5 miles long, along Escondido Creek above a point 5 miles north-northeast of Rancho Santa Fe (lat. 33°04'35" N, long. 117°09'25" W; near N line sec. 2, T 13 S, R 3 W). Named on Rancho Santa Fe (1968) 7.5' quadrangle. The name is from a place that members of the Portola expedition called San Alejo in 1769 (Gudde, 1949, p. 301).

San Elijo Lagoon [SAN DIEGO]: *marsh*, 3 miles southeast of Encinitas at the mouth of Escondido Creek (lat. 33°00'35" N, long. 117° 15'30" W). Named on Encinitas (1968) and Rancho Santa Fe (1968) 7.5' quadrangles.

San Emigdio Mesa [VENTURA]: *area*, 12 miles north of Reyes Peak (lat. 34°48'15" N, long. 119°14'30" W). Named on Apache Canyon (1943) and Sawmill Mountain (1943) 7.5' quadrangles.

San Felipe [SAN DIEGO]: *locality*, 8.5 miles north of Julian (lat. 33° 11'55" N, long. 116°35'50" W; near SW cor. sec. 20, T 11 S, R 4 E). Named on Ranchita (1960) 7.5' quadrangle. United States Board on Geographic Names (1975b, p. 5) approved the name "Teofulio Summit" for a place located 0.5 mile north of San Felipe; the name is for Teofulio Helm, a mission Indian who homesteaded in the neighborhood—this appears to be the feature called Warner Pass on Hanks' (1886a) map.

San Felipe Canyon: see **Banner Canyon** [SAN DIEGO]; **Chariot Canyon** [SAN DIEGO].

San Felipe Creek [SAN DIEGO]: *stream* and *dry wash*, extends for 36 miles to Imperial County 3.25 miles east-northeast of Ocotillo Wells (lat. 33°09'40" N, long. 116°04'50" W; at NE cor. sec. 1, T 12 S, R 8 E). Named on Borrego Mountain (1960), Borrego Sink (1959), Julian (1960), Ranchita (1960), Shell Reef (1959), and Tubb Canyon (1959) 7.5' quadrangles.

San Felipe Creek: see **Banner Creek** [SAN DIEGO].

San Felipe Hills [SAN DIEGO]: *ridge*, northwest-trending, 6 miles long, center 3 miles east-southeast of San Felipe (lat. 33°11' N, long. 116°33'15" W); the ridge is northeast of the upper part of San Felipe Creek. Named on Ranchita (1960) 7.5' quadrangle.

San Felipe Valley [SAN DIEGO]: *valley*, about 9 miles long, along San Felipe Creek above a point 7.5 miles east of Julian (lat. 33° 06' N, long. 116°28'30" W). Named on Earthquake Valley (1959), Julian (1960), and Ranchita (1960) 7.5' quadrangles. The name is from the camping place that Pedro Fages called San Phelipe in 1782 (Gudde, 1949, p. 302).

San Fernando [LOS ANGELES]: *town*, 22 miles northwest of Los Angeles city hall (lat. 34°16'55" N, long. 118°16'25" W). Named on San Fernando (1953) 7.5' quadrangle; which shows San Fernando mission near the edge of the town. Called Fernando on Fernando (1900) 15' quadrangle. Postal authorities established San Fernando post office in 1873, discontinued it for a time in 1876, moved it and changed the name to Fernando in 1892, and changed the name back to San Fernando in 1905 (Salley, p. 74, 194). Jeronimo Lopez started a stage station, called Lopez Station, 1.5 miles west of present San Fernando; the place reportedly had a post office in 1869 (Salley, p. 126). Water of a reservoir now covers the site (Latta, p. 57).

San Fernando Bay: see **Santa Monica Bay** [LOS ANGELES].

San Fernando Mountains: see **San Gabriel Mountains** [LOS ANGELES].

San Fernando Pass [LOS ANGELES]: *pass*, 2.5 miles south-southeast of Newhall (lat. 34°20'45" N, long. 118°30'35" W; sec. 13, T 3 N, R 16 W). Named on Oat Mountain (1952) 7.5' quadrangle. Called Fernando Pass on Camulos (1903) 30' quadrangle. Oat Mountain (1952) 7.5' quadrangle has the name "Fremont Pass" for a pass situated just east of San Fernando Pass (lat. 34°20'40" N, long. 118°30'25" W). Fremont traversed the highlands between Santa Clara River and San Fernando Valley in 1847, and his route there became known as Fremont Pass; General E.F. Beale had his men cut a trench 50 feet deep in the pass to ease the way for vehicles crossing it—this feature became known as Beale's Cut (Hoover, Rensch, and Rensch, p. 167). The cut, which also was called San Fernando Pass, was the main route north from Los Angeles until the early 1900's; a tunnel replaced the road through the pass in 1910, and a new road in present San Fernando Pass replaced the tunnel in 1939 (Barras, p. 22). A place called Hart's Ranch, later Lyon's Station, was situated 8 miles from San Fernando and north of Beale's Cut; it was an important stop on the stage line before the railroad came (Ormsby, p. 117; Barras, p. 22)—the place also was called Petroliopolis (Marcou, p. 161). Postal authorities established Petroliopolis post office in 1867 and discontinued it in 1871 (Salley, p. 170). They established Lyon's Station post office in 1874, changed the name to Andrews' Station in 1875, and discontinued it in 1879 (Frickstad, p. 77; Salley, p. 7). Lyon's Station was named for Sanford Lyons and Cyrus Lyons, who ran the stopping place in the 1850's and 1860's (Grenier, p. 311). Andrews Station post office was named for Andrew J. Krasyynski, first postmaster (Salley, p. 7).

San Fernando Plain: see **San Fernando Valley** [LOS ANGELES].

San Fernando Reservoir [LOS ANGELES]: *lake*, 1.5 miles long, 2.25 miles west-northwest of downtown San Fernando (lat. 34°17'30" N, long. 118°28'35" W). Named on San Fernando (1953) 7.5' quadrangle. San Fernando (1966) 7.5' quadrangle shows an unnamed debris basin at the place. Los Angeles County (1935) map shows two lakes, called San Fernando Reservoirs, there.

San Fernando Reservoir: see **Upper San Fernando Reservoir** [LOS ANGELES].

San Fernando Valley [LOS ANGELES]: *valley*, between San Gabriel Mountains and Santa Monica Mountains. Named on Los Angeles (1975) 1°x 2° quadrangle. Called San Fernando Plain on Parke's (1854-1855) map. Crespi called the feature El Valle de Santa Catalina de Bononia de los Encinos when he was there with Portola in 1769 (Hanna, p. 272).

San Francisco [LOS ANGELES-VENTURA]: *land grant*, along Santa Clara River between Newhall and Piru on Los Angeles-Ventura County line, mainly in Los Angeles County. Named on Newhall (1952), Oat Mountain (1952), Piru (1952), and Val Verde (1952) 7.5' quadrangles. Antonio del Valle received 8 leagues in 1839; Jacoba Felix and others claimed 48,612 acres patented in 1875 (Cowan, p. 76).

San Francisco Peak [SAN DIEGO]: *peak*, 7 miles east-southeast of Oceanside (lat. 33°10'10" N, long. 117°15'50" W). Named on San Luis Rey (1968) 7.5' quadrangle.

San Francisquito [LOS ANGELES]: *land grant*, at El Monte. Named on Baldwin Park (1953) and El Monte (1953) 7.5' quadrangles. Henry Dalton received 2 leagues in 1845 and claimed 8894 acres patented in 1867 (Cowan, p. 77).

San Francisquito Canyon [LOS ANGELES]: *canyon*, drained by a stream that flows 21 miles to Santa Clara River 4 miles northwest of Newhall (lat. 34°25'35" N, long. 118°34'30" W). Named on Green Valley (1958), Lake Hughes (1957), Newhall (1952), and Warm Springs Mountain (1958) 7.5' quadrangles. Barras (p. 17) noted the alternate name "Canada of Alamos" used for the canyon in 1851, and mentioned (p. 22) that a way station called Moor's or Holdansville was situated at the mouth of the canyon in 1860. Goddard's (1857) map has the name "S. Francisquito Pass" along present San Francisquito Canyon, and Whitney (p. 195-196) noted that San Francisquito Pass follows the canyon to Lake Elizabeth. Blake (p. 57) noted that "The ascent from the valley of Lake Elizabeth to the summit-level of the pass is short." Baker's (1911) map shows Turner Pass near Elizabeth Lake, and Antisell (p. 87) noted the alternate name "Turner's Pass" for San Francisquito Pass.

San Francisquito Pass: see **San Francisquito Canyon** [LOS ANGELES].

San Gabriel [LOS ANGELES]: *city*, 5 miles west-northwest of El Monte city hall (lat. 34°05'45" N, long. 118°06'25" W). Named on El Monte (1953) 7.5' quadrangle, which shows San Gabriel mission in the city. Postal authorities established San Gabriel post office in 1854 (Frickstad, p. 81), and the city incorporated in 1913. They established Garvalia post office 2.5 miles south of San Gabriel post office in 1898 and discontinued it in 1902; the name was for Richard Garvey, who started a community of small farms and homes at the place(Salley, p. 83).

San Gabriel: see East San Gabriel [LOS ANGELES]; **North San Gabriel** [LOS ANGELES]; **South San Gabriel** [LOS ANGELES].

San Gabriel Canyon [LOS ANGELES]: *canyon*, 9 miles long, along San Gabriel River above a point nearly 2 miles north of Azusa city hall (lat. 34°09'35" N, long. 117°54'20" W; at W line sec. 23, T 1 N, R 10 W). Named on Azusa (1953) and Glendora (1953) 7.5' quadrangles. The feature was called Azusa Canon in the 1840's (Robinson, J.W., 1983, p. 15).

San Gabriel Mountains [LOS ANGELES]: *range*, south of Mojave Desert and east of Soledad Canyon; extends east into San Bernardino County. Named on Los Angeles (1975) and San Bernardino (1966) 1°x 2° quadrangles. Goddard's (1857) map shows present San Gabriel Mountains as part of a much lager feature called San Bernardino Range. On Stevenson's (1884) map, the westernmost end of present San Gabriel Mountains and the east end of present Santa Susana Mountains together are called San Fernando Mountains; on the same map, present San Gabriel Mountains farther east near Little Tujunga Cañon is called Tujunga Mts., and the range still farther the east is called San Bernardino Range. Garces used the name "La Sierra de San Gabriel" in 1776 for the range north of San Gabriel mission (Robinson, J.W., 1983, p. 14). Azusa (1928) 6' quadrangle has the name "Sierra Madre" for present San Gabriel Mountains north of Monrovia and Azusa (3), but Azusa (1939) 6' quadrangle has the name "San Gabriel Mountains" there. United States Board on Geographic Names (1933, p. 666) rejected the names "San Bernardino Mountains," "Sierra Madre," and "Sierra San Gabriel" for present San Gabriel Mountains.

San Gabriel Peak [LOS ANGELES]: *peak*, 2.5 miles west-northwest of Mount Wilson (1) (lat. 34°14'35" N, long. 118°05'50" W). Altitude 6161 feet. Named on Mount Wilson (1953) 7.5' quadrangle. Members of the Wheeler Survey named the peak in 1875 for its apparent domination of the watershed of West Fork San Gabriel River; previously the feature was known as Observatory Peak because Professor T.S.C. Lowe had planned to built an astronomical observatory on it (Robinson, J.W., 1977, p. 154-155).

San Gabriel Reservoir [LOS ANGELES]: *lake*, behind a dam nearly 5 miles north of Glendora city hall (lat. 34°12'15" N, long. 117°51'25" W; sec. 6, T 1 N, R 9 W); the lake is along San Gabriel River. Named on Glendora (1953) 7.5' quadrangle.

San Gabriel River [LOS ANGELES-ORANGE]: *stream*, heads in Los Angeles County and flows 60 miles, partly at Los Angeles-Orange County line, to the sea 5 miles east-southeast of Long Beach city hall (lat. 33°44'35" N, long. 118°06'50" W). Named on Azusa (1953), Baldwin Park (1966), Crystal Lake (1958), El Monte (1953), Glendora (1953), Los Alamitos (1950), Mount San Antonio (1955), Seal Beach (1950), and Whittier (1949) 7.5' quadrangles. Called Rio de S. Gabriel on Parke's (1854-1855) map, and R. San Gabriel on Eddy's (1854) map, which shows the stream as a tributary of R. de los Angeles. Stevenson's (1884) map shows San Gabriel Riv. dividing below about the mouth of San Jose Creek; the eastern stream below the split is called New San Gabriel Riv. (present San Gabriel River), and the westernmost stream below the split is called Old San Gabriel Riv. (present Rio Hondo)—on the map this stream joins Los Angeles Riv, and below this junction Los Angeles River also is called Old San Gabriel Riv. Present San Gabriel River first was called El Rio de los Temblores (Thompson and West, p. 20). Before the flood of 1867 and 1868, water of San Gabriel River reached San Pedro Bay, but during that flood it cut a new course from the west end of Puente Hills to the sea at Alamitos Bay; this new course was known as New River (Poland and others, p. 35). Present San Gabriel River is called East Fork San Gabriel River on Camp Bonita (1940) and Camp Rincon (1940) 6' quadrangles, and on Glendora (1953) 7.5' quadrangle, but United States Board on Geographic Names (1962a, p. 16) rejected this name for the stream. A mining place called Crab Hollow Diggings was situated at the headwaters of East Fork in the 1850's (Gudde, 1975, p. 87). West Fork enters the main stream from the west 6.5 miles north of Glendora city hall; it is 19 miles long and is named on Azusa (1953), Chilao Flat (1959), Glendora (1953), and Mount Wilson (1953) 7.5' quadrangles. North Fork, which is formed by the confluence of Coldbrook Creek and Soldier Creek, enters West Fork 2 miles upstream from the mouth of West Fork; it is 4.5 miles long and is named on Crystal Lake (1958) and Glendora (1953) 7.5' quadrangles. United States Board on Geographic Names (1962a, p. 16) rejected the name "North Fork San Gabriel River" for present Soldier Creek. The stream in present Shortcut Canyon is called Trail Fork San Gabriel R. on Tujunga (1900) 15' quadrangle. The watercourse below the mouth of San Gabriel Canyon is called San Gabriel Wash on Pomona (1904) 15' quadrangle.

San Gabriel Wash: see **San Gabriel River** [LOS ANGELES-ORANGE].

San Guillermo Creek [VENTURA]: *stream*, flows 6.25 miles to Lockwood Creek 13 miles northeast of Reyes Peak (lat. 34°43'55" N, long. 119°05'15" W; near S line sec. 34, T 8 N, R 21 W); the stream heads at San Guillermo Mountain. Named on Lockwood Valley (1943) 7.5' quadrangle.

San Guillermo Mountain [VENTURA]: *peak*, 9 miles east-northeast of Reyes Peak (lat. 34°41'45" N, long. 119°08'50" W; sec. 18, T 7 N, R 21 W). Altitude 6602 feet. Named on San Guillermo (1943) 7.5' quadrangle.

San Ignacio [SAN DIEGO]: *locality*, nearly 7 miles east-northeast of Warner Springs in Middle Fork Borrego Palm Canyon (lat. 33°18'20" N, long. 116°31'05" W; at E line sec. 13, T 10 S, R 4 E). Named on Hot Springs Mountain (1960) 7.5' quadrangle.

San Joaquin [ORANGE]: *land grant*, mainly between Upper Newport Bay and Laguna Canyon in and near San Joaquin Hills. Named on El Toro (1950), Laguna Beach (1949), Newport Beach (1951), San Juan Capistrano (1949), and Tustin (1950) 7.5' quadrangles. Jose Sepulveda received 11 leagues in 1842 and claimed 48,803 acres patented in 1867 (Cowan, p. 79).

San Joaquin Bay: see **Newport Bay** [ORANGE].

San Joaquin Hills [ORANGE]: *range*, between Upper Newport Bay and Laguna Canyon (center near lat. 33°37'30" N, long. 117° 48' W); the range is on San Joaquin grant. Named on Laguna Beach (1965) and Tustin (1965) 7.5' quadrangles. Called Lomarias de la Costa on a diseño of San Joaquin grant made in the 1840's (Becker, 1969), and called Sierra San Juan on Goddard's (1857) map.

San Joaquin Reservoir [ORANGE]: *lake*, 0.5 mile long, 6 miles northwest of Laguna Beach city hall (lat. 33°37' N, long. 117°50'30" W); the feature is in San Joaquin Hills on San Joaquin grant. Named on Laguna Beach (1965) 7.5' quadrangle.

San Joaquin Swamp: see **Cienega de las Ranas**, under **Upper Newport Bay** [ORANGE].

Sanjon Barranca [VENTURA]: *canyon*, 1.5 miles long, opens into lowlands in downtown Ventura (lat. 34°16'50" N, long. 119°16'40" W). Named on Ventura (1951) 7.5' quadrangle. The feature also had the names "Cemetery Barranca" and "Graveyard Barranca" because it is next to a cemetery (Ricard).

Sanjon de Agua con Alisos: see **Ballona Creek** [LOS ANGELES].

San Jose Canyon: see **Castaic Junction** [LOS ANGELES].

San Jose Creek: see **South San Jose Creek** [LOS ANGELES].

San Jose de Gracia de Simi: see **Simi** [LOS ANGELES-VENTURA].

San Jose del Valle [SAN DIEGO]: *land grant,* at and west of Warner Springs. Named on Hot Springs Mountain (1960), Palomar Observatory (1949), Ranchita (1960), Warner Springs (1959), and Warners Ranch (1960) 7.5' quadrangles. Jose Antonio Bernardino Pico received 11 leagues in 1840; Juan Jose Warner received the land in 1844 and claimed 20,689 acres patented in 1880; the land originally was part of neighboring Valle de San Jose grant (Cowan, p. 81; Cowan gave the alternate name "Agua Caliente" for the grant). According to Perez (p. 92), Juan J. Warner was the grantee in 1834.

San Juan: see **Capistrano Beach** [ORANGE].

San Juan Anchorage [ORANGE]: *anchorage,* 3.5 miles southwest of San Juan Capistrano off Dana Cove (lat. 33°27'25" N, long. 117° 42' W). Named on Dana Point (1949) 7.5' quadrangle. United States Coast and Geodetic Survey (p. 96) called the feature San Juan Capistrano Anchorage.

San-Juan-by-the-Sea: see **Capistrano Beach** [ORANGE]; **Serra** [ORANGE].

San Juan Cajon de Santa Ana [ORANGE]: *land grant,* around Fullerton, Anaheim, and Placentia. Named on Anaheim (1950), La Habra (1952), Orange (1950), and Yorba Linda (1950) 7.5' quadrangles. Juan P. Ontiveros received the land in 1837 and claimed 35,971 acres patented in 1877 (Cowan, p. 82).

San Juan Campground: see **Lower San Juan Campground** [ORANGE].

San Juan Canyon [ORANGE]: *canyon,* drained by a stream that flows 2 miles to Salt Creek 2.5 miles west of San Juan Capistrano (lat. 33°30'30" N, long. 117°42'20" W; sec. 3, T 8 S, R 8 W). Named on San Juan Capistrano (1968) 7.5' quadrangle.

San Juan Canyon: see **San Juan Creek** [ORANGE].

San Juan Capistrano [ORANGE]: *town,* 23 miles southeast of Santa Ana (lat. 33°30'05" N, long. 117°39'45" W). Named on Cañada Gobernadora (1968), Dana Point (1968), San Clemente (1968), and San Juan Capistrano (1968) 7.5' quadrangles. Called Capistrano on Corona (1902) 30' quadrangle. Postal authorities established Capistrano post office in 1867 and changed the name to San Juan Capistrano in 1905 (Salley, p. 195). The community incorporated in 1961. The town name is from San Juan Capistrano mission, founded at the place in 1776; before that the site was called Santa Maria Magdalena, a name given by members of the Portola expedition in 1769 (Hanna, p. 278). A spring called Aguagito was situated 0.8 mile north of the mission and provided good drinking water (Meadows, p. 19).

San Juan Capistrano Anchorage: see **San Juan Anchorage** [ORANGE].

San Juan Capistrano Hot Springs: see **San Juan Hot Springs** [ORANGE].

San Juan Capistrano Point: see **Dana Point** [ORANGE] (1).

San Juan Cove [SAN DIEGO]: *embayment,* 5 miles south-southeast of Point La Jolla (lat. 32°46'50" N, long. 117°14'55" W). Named on La Jolla (1967) 7.5' quadrangle. Called Juanita Cove on La Jolla (1953) 7.5' quadrangle.

San Juan Creek [ORANGE]: *stream,* heads in Riverside County and flows 20 miles in Orange County to the sea 3 miles south-southwest of San Juan Capistrano (lat. 33°27'45" N, long. 117°41' W). Named on Cañada Gobernadora (1968), Dana Point (1968), San Juan Capistrano (1968), and Sitton Peak (1954) 7.5' quadrangles. The upper part of the canyon of the stream is called San Juan Canyon on Cañada Gobernadora (1968) and Sitton Peak (1954) 7.5' quadrangles; the whole canyon is called San Juan Canyon on Corona (1902) 30' quadrangle. Before construction of San Juan Capistrano mission, the canyon was known as Arroyo de la Quema because members of the Portola expedition observed Indians burning vegetation there to scare out small game—*Arroyo de la Quema* means "Creek of the Burned" in Spanish; Costanso in his account of the Portola expedition called it Canada del Incendio (Meadows, p. 22, 49). Cañada Gobernadora (1968) 7.5' quadrangle shows the site of Mission Vieja along San Juan Creek at the mouth of Cañada Gobernadora, and Cañada Gobernadora (1949) quadrangle has the term "Old Mission Site" at the place. San Juan Canyon had the name "Mission Vieja Valley" on the first official map of Orange County made in 1889 (Meadows, p. 101).

San Juan Hill [ORANGE]: *peak,* 12 miles northeast of Santa Ana on Orange-San Bernardino County line (lat. 33°54'50" N, long. 117° 44'15" W; sec. 17, T 3 S, R 8 W). Altitude 1781 feet. Named on Prado Dam (1967) 7.5' quadrangle.

San Juan Hot Springs [ORANGE]: *village,* 15 miles northeast of San Juan Capistrano (lat. 33°35'30" N, long. 117°30'30" W); the place is in San Juan Canyon less than 0.5 mile northeast of the mouth of Hot Spring Canyon. Named on Cañada Gobernadora (1968) 7.5' quadrangle. Corona (1902) 30' quadrangle shows a water feature called San Juan Hot Spring at the mouth of Hot Spring Canyon. The spring was called Agua Caliente de San Juan in the early days (Meadows, p. 17). Waring (p. 48-49) called the feature San Juan Capistrano Hot Springs, and noted that it consists of two main springs, four minor ones, and several marshy patches; the water was as hot as 124° Fahrenheit and was used first by Indians, and then about 1885 buildings were constructed and the place became a resort for campers and for the ailing. Postal authorities established Talega post office at the site in 1895 and discontinued it in 1896 (Frickstad, p. 118; Meadows, p. 133).

San Juan Point: see **Dana Point** [ORANGE] (1).

San Juan Rocks [ORANGE]: *rocks,* about 4.25 miles southwest of San Juan Capistrano, and 300 feet to 1200 feet offshore at Dana Point (1) (lat. 33°27'30" N, long. 117°42'55" W). Named on Dana Point (1968) 7.5' quadrangle. Capistrano (1902) 30' quadrangle shows San Juan Rock. United States Coast and Geodetic Survey (p. 96) described San Juan Rock as 10 feet high, about 50 feet in extent, and 340 yards south of the highest point on the cliff at Dana Point (1).

San Luis Rey [SAN DIEGO]: *district,* 4 miles northeast of downtown Oceanside (lat. 33°13'50" N, long. 117°19'30" W); the place is along San Luis Rey River at the site of San Luis Rey de Francia mission. Postal authorities established San Luis Rey post office in 1861 and discontinued it for a time in 1865 (Frickstad, p. 156). Hanks' (1886a) map shows San Luis Rey railroad station south of the mouth of San Luis Rey River, and shows San Luis Rey post office located farther inland south of San Luis Rey River. Tucker and Reed's (1939) map has the name "Mission Knoll" for a peak situated about 1 mile south-southwest of San Luis Rey.

San Luis Rey Camp [SAN DIEGO]: *locality,* 9 miles southeast of Boucher Hill (lat. 33°15'10" N, long. 116°47'30" W; near NE cor. sec. 5, T 11 S, R 2 E); the place is along San Luis Rey River. Named on Palomar Observatory (1949) 7.5' quadrangle.

San Luis Rey Heights [SAN DIEGO]: *locality,* 5 miles south-southeast of Fallbrook (lat. 33°19' N, long. 117°12'25" W); the place is north of San Luis Rey River. Named on Bonsall (1968) 7.5' quadrangle.

San Luis Rey River [SAN DIEGO]: *stream* and *dry wash,* extends for 64 miles to the sea less than 1 mile west-northwest of downtown Oceanside (lat. 33°12'10" N, long. 117°23'25" W; sec. 22, T 11 S, R 5 W); San Luis Rey de Francis mission is along the stream. Named on Bonsall (1968), Boucher Hill (1948), Mesa Grande (1948), Morro Hill (1968), Oceanside (1968), Pala (1968), Palomar Observatory (1949), San Luis Rey (1968), and Warner Springs (1959) 7.5' quadrangles. West Fork joins the main stream in Lake Henshaw; it is formed by the confluence of Fry Creek and Iron Springs Creek, is 10.5 miles long, and is named on Palomar Observatory (1949) and Warner Springs (1959) 7.5' quadrangles.

San Marcos [SAN DIEGO]: *town,* 6 miles southeast of Vista (lat. 33° 08'35" N, long. 117°10' W); the town is along San Marcos Creek. Named on San Marcos (1968) and Valley Center (1968) 7.5' quadrangles. On Escondido (1901) 15' quadrangle, the name applies to a place located 1.5 miles farther west. Postal authorities established San Marcos post office in 1888 and moved it 1.25 miles northeast in 1901 (Salley, p. 196). The town incorporated in 1963. Officials of San Marcos Land Company purchased property in the 1880's and started a town about 2.5 miles west of present San Marcos; they moved the community to the present site along the railroad in 1901 (Stein, p. 117-118). Postal authorities established Merigan post office in 1889, moved it 1.5 miles southeast to a spot 2.5 miles southwest of San Marcos and changed the name to Sumac in 1890, and discontinued it in 1891; the name "Merigan" was for Michael Merigan, first postmaster (Salley, p. 138, 215).,

San Marcos: see **Lake San Marcos** [SAN DIEGO].

San Marcos Creek [SAN DIEGO]: *stream,* flows 15 miles to Batiquitos Lagoon 3.5 miles north-northeast of Encinitas (lat. 33° 05'15" N, long. 117°16'05" W; sec. 35, T 12 S, R 4 W). Named on Encinitas (1968), Rancho Santa Fe (1968), and San Marcos (1949) 7.5' quadrangles.

San Marcos Mountains [SAN DIEGO]: *ridge,* north-northwest-trending, 4 miles long, center 3 miles east-northeast of Vista (lat. 33°13'30" N, long. 117°11'30" W). Named on San Marcos (1968) 7.5' quadrangle. Tucker and Reed's (1939) map has the name "High Knob Mt." for a high point on the ridge (on S line sec. 15, T 11 S, R 3 W).

San Marcos Valley [SAN DIEGO]: *valley,* 5 miles southeast of Vista (lat. 33°08'15" N, long. 117°11' W); the valley is along San Marcos Creek at San Marcos. Named on San Luis Rey (1898) 30' quadrangle.

San Mateo: see **San Onofre** [SAN DIEGO].

San Mateo Canyon [SAN DIEGO]: *canyon,* heads in Riverside County and is 8.5 miles long in San Diego County; extends along San Mateo Creek (2) above a point 4.5 miles east of San Clemente [ORANGE] civic center (lat. 33°25'25" N, long. 117°31'45" W; sec. 5, T 9 S, R 6 W). Named on Margarita Peak (1968), San Clemente (1968), and Sitton Peak (1954) 7.5' quadrangles. Called Arroyo San Mateo on Capistrano (1902) 30' quadrangle.

San Mateo Creek [SAN DIEGO]:

(1) *stream,* flows 1 mile to Devil Canyon 2.5 miles north of Margarita Peak (lat. 33°28'50" N, long. 117°22'50" W; at E line sec. 15, T 8 S, R 5 W). Named on Fallbrook (1968) and Margarita Peak (1968) 7.5' quadrangles.

(2) *stream,* heads in Riverside County and flows 14 miles in San Diego County to the sea 3 miles south-southeast of San Clemente [ORANGE] civic center (lat. 33°23'05" N, long. 117°35'30" W; near E line sec. 15, T

9 S, R 7 W). Named on San Clemente (1968) 7.5' quadrangle.

San Mateo Point [ORANGE-SAN DIEGO]: *promontory,* 3 miles south-southeast of San Clemente civic center along the coast on Orange-San Diego County line (lat. 33°23'15" N, long. 117°35'45" W; sec. 15, T 9 S, T 7 W); the feature is just west of the mouth of San Mateo Creek [SAN DIEGO] (2). Named on San Clemente (1968) 7.5' quadrangle.

San Mateo Rocks [ORANGE]: *rocks,* 1.5 miles south-southwest of San Clemente civic center, and 0.5 mile offshore (lat. 33°24'15" N, long. 117°37' W); the rocks are 1.5 miles northwest of San Mateo Point. Named on San Clemente (1968) 7.5' quadrangle.

San Miguel [VENTURA]: *land grant,* between the mouth of Santa Clara River and downtown Ventura. Named on Oxnard (1949), Saticoy (1951), and Ventura (1951) 7.5' quadrangles. Raimundo Olivas and Felipe Lorenzana received the land in 1841 and claimed 4694 acres patented in 1873 (Cowan, p. 85—Cowan gave the alternate name "Los Cerritos" for the grant; Perez, p. 94).

San Miguel Mountain [SAN DIEGO]: *peak,* nearly 4 miles west-southwest of Jamul (lat. 32°41'45" N, long. 116°56'05" W; near N line sec. 13, T 17 S, R 1 W). Altitude 2565 feet. Named on Jamul Mountains (1955, photorevised 1971 and 1975) 7.5' quadrangle. Jamul Mountains (1955) 7.5' quadrangle has the plural form "San Miguel Mountains" for the name, but United States Board on Geographic Names (1965c, p. 11) rejected this.

San Nicolas Canyon: see **Nicholas Canyon** [LOS ANGELES].

San Nicolas Island [VENTURA]: *island,* 9.5 miles long, 36 miles south of Ventura (lat. 33°14'45" N, long. 119°30'30" W). Named on San Nicolas Island (1943) quadrangle. The crew of Vizcaino's launch *Tres Reyes* named the island on December 6, 1602, the day of the saint (Wagner, p. 412). Vedder's (1963) map names several features on the island: Vizcaino Point, located at the extreme west end (lat. 33°16'40" N, long. 119°34'40" W); Thousand Springs, located along the north coast nearly 3 miles east-northeast of Vizcaino Point (lat. 33°17' N, long. 119°31'45" W); Corral Harbor, located on the north coast 3.5 miles east of Vizcaino Point (lat. 33°16'40" N, long. 119°30'55" W); Army Camp Beach, located on the north coast 5 miles east of Vizcaino Point (lat. 33°15'55" N, long. 119°29'40" W); Seal Beach, located on the south coast 4 miles southeast of Vizcaino Point (lat. 33°13'55" N, long. 119°32'15" W); Jackson Hill, located 5 miles east-southeast of Vizcaino Point (lat. 33°14'25" N, long. 119°30'15" W); Coast Guard Beach, located 1.5 miles west-northwest of the east tip of the island (lat. 33°14'25" N, long. 119°26'35" W); and Jehemy Beach, located on the side of the east tip (lat. 33°13'35" N, long. 119°25' W). These names, for the most part, are from local usage of military personnel on the island (J.G. Vedder, personal communication, 1986).

San Olene Canyon [LOS ANGELES]: *canyon,* drained by a stream that flows 1 mile to Santa Anita Canyon 3 miles southeast of Mount Wilson (1) (lat. 34°11'50" N, long. 118°01'10" W; sec. 3, T 1 N, R 11 W). Named on Mount Wilson (1953) 7.5' quadrangle. J.W. Robinson (1977, p. 123) referred to Santa Oline Creek, named for Miss Oline Newall, one of a group of hikers who had lunch at the place in 1896.

San Onofre [SAN DIEGO]: *locality,* 4 miles south-southeast of San Clemente [ORANGE] civic center along Atchison, Topeka and Santa Fe Railroad (lat. 33°22'45" N, long. 117°34'10" W; sec. 24, T 9 S, R 7 W). Named on San Clemente (1968, photorevised 1975) 7.5' quadrangle. Called San Mateo on San Juan Capistrano (1941) 15' quadrangle. Postal authorities established San Onofre post office in 1917, discontinued it in 1919, reestablished it in 1920, discontinued it in 1936, reestablished it in 1938, and discontinued it in 1943 (Frickstad, p. 156). The name "San Onofre" is from an Egyptian saint (Gudde, 1949, p. 311).

San Onofre: see **Santa Margarita y San Onofre**, under **Santa Margarita y las Flores** [SAN DIEGO].

San Onofre Beach [SAN DIEGO]: *beach,* 4.5 miles southeast of San Clemente [ORANGE] along the coast (lat. 33°22'20" N, long. 117° 33'50" W; sec. 24, T 9 S, R 7 W); the beach is southeast of San Onofre. Named on San Onofre Bluff (1968) 7.5' quadrangle.

San Onofre Bluff [SAN DIEGO]: *escarpment,* 5.5 miles southeast of San Clemente [ORANGE] civic center along the coast (lat. 33°21'40" N, long. 117°32'20" W); the feature is southeast of San Onofre. Named on San Onofre Bluff (1968) 7.5' quadrangle.

San Onofre Canyon [SAN DIEGO]: *canyon,* 11 miles long, along San Onofre Creek above a point 4.5 miles southeast of San Clemente [ORANGE] civic center (lat. 33°23'15" N, long. 117°32'55" W; at S line sec. 18, T 9 S, R 6 W). Named on Margarita Peak (1968) and San Clemente (1968) 7.5' quadrangles. Called Arroyo San Onofre on Capistrano (1902) 30' quadrangle. North Fork branches northeast 3.5 miles above the mouth of the main canyon; it is 7.25 miles long and is named on Margarita Peak (1968) 7.5' quadrangle. South Fork branches southeast 2.5 miles above the mouth of the main canyon; it is 6.5 miles long and is named on Margarita Peak (1968) and San Clemente (1968) 7.5' quadrangles.

San Onofre Creek [SAN DIEGO]: *stream,* flows 16 miles to the sea 3.5 miles south-southeast of San Clemente [ORANGE] civic center (lat. 33°22'50" N, long. 117°34'40" W; sec. 23, T 9 S, R 7 W). Named on San Clemente (1968) 7.5' quadrangle. Hanks' (1886a) map shows a place called Forster P.O. located at the mouth of San Onofre Creek. Postal authorities established Forster post office in 1879 and discontinued it in 1883—they later reestablished the post office 6 miles to the northwest in Orange County; the name was for John O. Forster, owner of Santa Margarita y Flores grant (Salley, p. 77).

San Onofre Hills: see **San Onofre Mountain** [SAN DIEGO].

San Onofre Mountain [SAN DIEGO]: *peak,* 14 miles west of Fallbrook (lat. 33°21'50" N, long. 117°29'35" W; sec. 27, T 9 S, R 6 W). Altitude 1725 feet. Named on Las Pulgas Canyon (1968) 7.5' quadrangle. Ellis and Lee (p. 31) used the name "San Onofre Hills" for the range that includes San Onofre Mountain.

San Padro: see **San Pedro** [LOS ANGELES] (2).

San Pasqual [LOS ANGELES]: *land grant,* at and near Pasadena. Named on El Monte (1953), Los Angeles (1953), Mount Wilson (1953), and Pasadena (1953) 7.5' quadrangles. Manuel Garfias received 3.5 leagues in 1843 and claimed 13,694 acres patented in 1863; Benjamin D. Wilson claimed 709 acres patented in 1881 (Cowan, p. 86; Cowan listed the grant under the designation "Rincon de San Pasqual (or) Pascual").

San Pasqual [SAN DIEGO]: *town,* 6 miles west-northwest of Ramona (lat. 33°05'30" N, long. 116°57'15" W; in and near sec. 35, T 12 S, R 1 W). Named on San Pasqual (1954) 7.5' quadrangle. Postal authorities established San Pasqual post office in 1874, discontinued it in 1880, reestablished it in 1887, moved it 3 miles east in 1891, and discontinued it in 1901 (Salley, p. 196).

San Pasqual Creek: see **Santa Ysabel Creek** [SAN DIEGO].

San Pasqual River: see **San Dieguito River** [SAN DIEGO].

San Pasqual Valley [SAN DIEGO]: *valley,* extends west from San Pasqual along Santa Ysabel Creek. Named on Escondido (1968) and San Pasqual (1954) 7.5' quadrangles.

San Pedro [LOS ANGELES]:

(1) *land grant,* mainly between Wilmington, Compton, and Redondo Beach. Named on Inglewood (1952), Long Beach (1949), Redondo Beach (1963), San Pedro (1964), South Gate (1952), and Torrance (1964) 7.5' quadrangles. Juan Jose Dominguez received the land before 1784; Manuel Dominguez received it in 1839 and claimed 43,119 acres patented in 1858 (Cowan, p. 86; Perez, p. 95).

(2) *district,* 2 miles north of Point Fermin in Los Angeles (lat. 33° 44'10" N, long. 118°17'45" W). Named on San Pedro (1964) 7.5' quadrangle. Postal authorities established San Padro post office in 1854, discontinued it in 1864, and reestablished it with the name "San Pedro" in 1882 (Salley, p. 196). The place developed at what was called Sepulveda's Landing, and later called Timm's Point (Hoover, Rensch, and Rensch, p. 154). The Sepulveda brothers built a crude dock and landing there in 1835, and sold it to August Timms in 1852; Timms' name was applied to the landing as well as to a nearby promontory, Timms' Point, which previously was known as San Pedro Point (Grenier, p. 183-184). Arnold and Arnold's (1902) map has the name "Crawfish George's" for a locality situated along the coast just southwest of Timms Point.

San Pedro: see **Camp San Pedro**, under **Wilmington** [LOS ANGELES]; **East San Pedro** [LOS ANGELES]; **New San Pedro**, under **Wilmington** [LOS ANGELES].

San Pedro Bay [LOS ANGELES-ORANGE]: *embayment,* extends from San Pedro [LOS ANGELES] to Seal Beach [ORANGE]. Named on Long Beach (1949), Los Alamitos (1950), San Pedro (1964), and Seal Beach (1950) 7.5' quadrangles. Called Bay of S. Pedro on Parke's (1854-1855) map. Cabrillo named the feature Bahia de los Fumos in 1542 for the smoke from fires that the Indians set to drive out small game; Vizcaino renamed it Ensenada de San Andres to record the saint on whose day he was there, but he was mistaken on the days of the Catholic calendar; Cabrera Buena named it Bahia de San Pedro in 1784 for Saint Peter, Bishop of Alexandria (Gleason, p. 103-104). Davidson (p. 194) believed that the name "Bahia de los Fumos" of Cabrillo referred to present Santa Monica Bay.

San Pedro Canyon [LOS ANGELES]: *canyon,* drained by a stream that flows 2 miles to end 2.5 miles north of Point Fermin in San Pedro (lat. 33°44'20" N, long. 118°18'10" W); the canyon heads at San Pedro Hill. Named on San Pedro (1964) 7.5' quadrangle.

San Pedro Channel [LOS ANGELES]: *water feature,* between Santa Catalina Island and the mainland at Palos Verdes Hills. Named on Long Beach (1957) 1°x 2° quadrangle. United States Board on Geographic Names (1961a, p. 19) rejected the name "Catalina Channel" for the feature.

San Pedro Hill [LOS ANGELES]: *peak,* 3.5 miles northwest of Point Fermin (lat. 33°44'45" N, long. 118°20'05" W). Named on San Pedro (1964) 7.5' quadrangle.

San Pedro Hills: see **Palos Verdes Hills** [LOS ANGELES].

San Pedro Point: see **Timms Point**, under **San Pedro** [LOS ANGELES] (2).

San Rafael [LOS ANGELES]: *land grant,* between Arroyo Seco and Los Angeles River around Glendale. Named on Burbank (1953), Hollywood (1953), Los Angeles (1953), and Pasadena (1953) 7.5' quadrangles. Jose Maria Verdugo received the land in 1784; Julio Verdugo and others claimed 36,403 acres patented in 1882 (Cowan, p. 87; Cowan gave the alternate name "La Zanja" for the grant). Perez (p. 95) gave the date 1798 for the grant to Jose M. Verdugo. Gudde (1949, p. 312) noted that the grant also was called Hahaonuput and Arroyo Hondo.

San Rafael: see **Paso de Bartolo** [LOS ANGELES].

San Rafael Hills [LOS ANGELES]: *range,* 3.5 miles northwest of Pasadena city hall between Arroyo Seco and Verdugo Wash (lat. 34°10'30" N, long. 118°12' W); the range is on San Rafael grant. Named on Pasadena (1953) 7.5' quadrangle.

San Rafael Peak [VENTURA]: *peak,* 16 miles east of Reyes Peak (lat. 34°37'25" N, long. 119°00'05" W; sec. 9, T 6 N, R 20 W). Altitude 6666 feet. Named on Devils Heart Peak (1943), Lockwood Valley (1943), and Topatopa Mountains (1943) 7.5' quadrangles.

Santa Ana [ORANGE]: *city,* near the center of the north part of Orange County (lat. 33°44'50" N, long. 117°52' W). Named on Anaheim (1965), Newport Beach (1965), Orange (1964), and Tustin (1965) 7.5' quadrangles. Postal authorities established Santa Ana post office in 1870 (Frickstad, p. 117), and the city incorporated in 1886. William H. Spurgeon founded the place in 1869 (Guinn, p. 192). Meadows listed places along Pacific Electric Railroad at Santa Ana: Acelga, a flag stop located 4.25 miles southwest of Santa Ana city hall (p, 17); Buaro, a flag stop located 3 miles west-northwest of the city hall (p. 31); Duena, a flag stop located 3.25 miles west-northwest of the city hall (p. 58); and West Orange, a station located 2.25 miles northwest of the city hall (p. 139).

Santa Ana [VENTURA]: *land grant,* around Lake Casitas. Named on Matilija (1952), Pitas Point (1950), Ventura (1951), and White Ledge Peak (1952) 7.5' quadrangles. Crisogono Ayala and others received the land in 1837; they claimed 21,522 acres patented in 1870 (Cowan, p. 89-90).

Santa Ana: see **Olive** [ORANGE]; **South Santa Ana** [ORANGE].

Santa Ana Abajo: see **Olive** [ORANGE].

Santa Ana Army Air Base: see **Fairview** [ORANGE].

Santa Ana Arriba: see **Olive** [ORANGE].

Santa Ana Canyon [ORANGE]: *canyon,* 7.5 miles long, mainly in Orange County, but extends east into Riverside County and San Bernardino County; along Santa Ana River above a point 6 miles northeast of Orange city hall (lat. 33°51'30" N, long. 117°47' W). Named on Black Star Canyon (1967), Orange (1964), and Prado Dam (1967) 7.5' quadrangles.

Santa Ana Creek [VENTURA]: *stream,* formed by the confluence of North Fork and West Fork, flows 3.5 miles to Lake Casitas 6 miles west-southwest of the town of Ojai (lat. 34°24'35" N, long. 119°20'15" W); the stream is partly on Santa Ana grant. Named on Matilija (1952, photorevised 1967) 7.5' quadrangle. North Fork is 2.25 miles long and is named on Matilija (1952) 7.5' quadrangle West Fork is 4.5 miles long and is named on Matilija (1952) and White Ledge Peak (1952) 7.5' quadrangles.

Santa Ana Gardens [ORANGE]: *locality,* 7 miles northeast of present Huntington Beach civic center (lat. 33°43'35" N, long. 117° 54' W). Named on Newport Beach (1951) 7.5' quadrangle.

Santa Ana Heights [ORANGE]: *district,* 6 miles east of Huntington Beach civic center (lat. 33°39'15" N, long. 117°53'45" W). Named on Newport Beach (1965) 7.5' quadrangle.

Santa Ana Mountains [ORANGE]: *range,* extends southeast for about 20 miles along Orange-Riverside County line from Santa Ana River to a point southeast of the head of Trabuco Canyon. Named on Santa Ana (1959) 1°x 2° quadrangle. Called Sierra Santiago on Goddard's (1857) map. On Parke's (1854-1855) map, the name "Sierra de Santa Ana" applies to present Santa Ana Mountains and to present Puente Hills together. Whitney (p. 175) used the form "Santa Anna Range" for the name. Hanna (p. 287) noted use of the name "Sierra del Trabuco" for the south part of the range. Meadows (p. 133) pointed out that some people who live east of the feature call it Temescal Range.

Santa Ana Peak: see **Santiago Peak** [ORANGE].

Santa Ana River [ORANGE]: *stream,* enters Orange County from Riverside County and flows 28 miles in Orange County to the sea 3.25 miles southeast of Huntington Beach civic center (lat. 33°37'45" N, long. 117°57'25" W). Named on Anaheim (1965), Black Star Canyon (1967), Newport Beach (1965), Orange (1964), and Prado Dam (1967) 7.5' quadrangles. Called Rio S. Bernadino on Gibbes' (1852) map, called Rio Santa Anna on Williamson's (1853b) map, called R. Sta. Anna on Eddy's (1854) map, called Rio de Sta. Ana on Parke's (1854-1855) map, called Santa Anna R. on Goddard's (1857) map, and called Rio Santa Anna on Rogers and Johnsron's (1857) map. Crespi named the stream Rio del Dulcissimo Nombre de Jesus del Temblores when members of the Portola expedition felt a severe earthquake while they were camped along the stream in 1769—*Rio del Dulcissimo Nombre de Jesus del Temblores* means "River of the Sweetest Name of Jesus of the Earthquakes" in Spanish; the soldiers of the expedition called the feature Rio Santa Ana because it seemed to come from Santa Ana Mountains (Meadows, p. 119, 124). Before a flood in 1825, Santa Ana River reached the sea several miles northwest of its present mouth (Poland and others, p. 35). Before the river was confined to its modern course, it entered the west end of Newport Bay; backwater from the stream formed a shallow lake of bitter water west of the river that was 2 miles long and 0.5 mile wide—this feature was called Amarus Lake or Bitterwater Lake (Meadows, p. 20). The lake extended west from a headland called Bitter Point that is 0.5 mile east-northeast of the present mouth of Santa Ana River—a dike built in 1920 from Bitter Point to the sea prevents the river from discharging into Newport Bay (Meadows, p. 27).

Santa Ana Valley [VENTURA]: *valley,* 5.25 miles west-southwest of Ojai (lat. 34°25'15" N, long. 119°20'25" W); the valley is along Santa Ana Creek. Named on Matilija (1952) 7.5' quadrangle. Water of Lake Casitas now covers part of the feature.

Santa Anita [LOS ANGELES]:

(1) *land grant,* at and near Arcadia and Sierra Madre. Named on Azusa (1953), El Monte (1953), and Mount Wilson (1953) 7.5' quadrangles. Hugo Perfecto Reid received 3 leagues in 1841 and 1846; Henry Dalton claimed 13,319 acres patented in 1866 (Cowan, p. 90). Perez (p. 97) gave 1845 as the date of the grant to Reid.

(2) *locality,* 5.25 miles south of Mount Wilson (1) along Atchison, Topeka and Santa Fe Railroad (lat. 34°08'50" N, long. 118°03'20" W); the place is on Santa Anita grant. Named on Pasadena (1900) 15' quadrangle. Postal authorities established Santa Anita post office in 1886, discontinued it in 1910, reestablished it in 1914, and discontinued it in 1940 (Frickstad, p. 81).

Santa Anita Canyon [LOS ANGELES]: *canyon,* 5.25 miles long, opens into lowlands 4.25 miles south-southeast of Mount Wilson (1) (lat. 34°10'15" N, long. 118°01'15" W; sec. 15, T 1 N, R 11 W). Named on Mount Wilson (1953) 7.5' quadrangle. East Fork branches east 3 miles above the mouth of the main canyon; it is 2.5 miles long and is named on Azusa (1953) and Mount Wilson (1953) 7.5' quadrangles. North Fork branches north 3.25 miles above the mouth of the main canyon; it is nearly 1.5 miles long and is named on Mount Wilson (1953) 7.5' quadrangle. On Pasadena (1900) 15' quadrangle, the name "Santa Antia Canyon" applies to present North Fork, and present Santa Anita Canyon above the junction is called West Fork.

Santa Antia Canyon: see **Little Santa Anita Canyon** [LOS ANGELES].

Santa Anita Falls: see **Sturtevant Falls** [LOS ANGELES].

Santa Anita Wash [LOS ANGELES]: *stream,* extends for 5.25 miles to Rio Hondo 2.25 miles north-northwest of El Monte city hall (lat. 34°06'10" N, long. 118°00'50" W); the feature heads at the mouth of Santa Anita Canyon. Named on El Monte (1953) and Mount Wilson (1953) 7.5' quadrangles.

Santa Anna Range: see **Santa Ana Mountains** [ORANGE].

Santa Anna River: see **Santa Ana River** [ORANGE].

Santa Barbara Channel [VENTURA]: *water feature,* between the coast and Anacapa Island, and between the coast and islands of Santa Barbara County. Named on Los Angeles (1975) 1°x 2° quadrangle. Vizcaino gave the name "Canal de Santa Barbara" to the feature when he sailed through it on December 4, 1602, the day of the saint (Wagner, p. 118, 413). The islands on the south side of Santa Barbara Channel—Anacapa in Ventura County, and Santa Cruz, Santa Rosa, and San Miguel in Santa Barbara County—are called Santa Barbara Islands; they are part of the larger group—including San Clemente and Santa Catalina in Los Angeles County, San Nicholas in Ventura County, and Santa Barbara in Santa Barbara County—that is called the Channel Islands (United States Coast and Geodetic Survey, p. 106).

Santa Barbara Cove [SAN DIEGO]: *embayment,* 5.5 miles south-southeast of Point La Jolla off Mission Bay (lat. 32°46'30" N, long. 117°14'55" W). Named on La Jolla (1967) 7.5' quadrangle. On La Jolla (1953) 7.5' quadrangle, the name "Santa Barbara Cove" applies to present Santa Barbara Cove and to present Carmel Cove together.

Santa Barbara Islands: see **Santa Barbara Channel** [VENTURA].

Santa Barbara Mountains: see **Santa Ynez Mountains** [VENTURA].

Santa Catalina Island [LOS ANGELES]: *island,* 21 miles long, 21 miles south-southwest of Point Fermin across San Pedro Channel (lat. 33°24' N, long. 118°25' W). Named on Long Beach (1957) 1°x 2° quadrangle. Cabrillo discovered the island in 1542, and believed that he had found two islands that he named La Vitoria and San Salvador for his two ships; Vizcaino sighted the island on the eve of Saint Catherine's Day in 1603 and named it Santa Catalina (Hanna, p. 288; Hoover, Rensch, and Rensch, p. 146).

Santa Catarina Spring [SAN DIEGO]: *spring,* 9 miles north-northwest of Borrego Springs (lat. 33°22'20" N, long. 116°26'30" W; sec. 22, T 9 S, R 5 E). Named on Borrego Palm Canyon (1959) 7.5' quadrangle. Called Santa Caterina Springs on Clark Lake (1944) 15' quadrangle.

Santa Clara Cove [SAN DIEGO]: *embayment,* nearly 5 miles south-southeast of Point La Jolla off Sail Bay (lat. 32°47'05" N, long. 117°15' W); the feature is just west of Santa Clara Point. Named on La Jolla (1967) 7.5' quadrangle.

Santa Clara del Norte [VENTURA]: *land grant,* south of Saticoy. Named on Camarillo (1950), Oxnard (1949), Santa Paula (1951), and Saticoy (1951) 7.5' quadrangles. Juan Sanchez received the land in 1837 and claimed 13,989 acres patented in 1869 (Cowan, p. 91).

Santa Clara Plain: see **Santa Clara River** [VENTURA].

Santa Clara Point [SAN DIEGO]: *promontory,* nearly 5 miles south-southeast of Point La Jolla along Mission Bay (lat. 32°47' N, long. 117°14'55" W). Named on La Jolla (1967) 7.5' quadrangle.

Santa Clara River [LOS ANGELES-VENTURA]: *stream,* heads in Los Angeles County and flows 68 miles to the sea 5.25 miles west-northwest of Oxnard in Ventura County (lat. 34°14' N, long. 119° 15'55" W). Named on Agua Dulce (1960), Fillmore (1951), Mint Canyon (1960), Moorpark (1951), Newhall (1952), Oxnard (1949), Piru (1952), Santa Paula (1951), Saticoy (1951), and Val Verde (1952) 7.5' quadrangles. Called Rio de la Sta. Clara on Parke's (1854-1855) map, which has the name "Sta. Clara Plain" for lowlands near the mouth of the river. Whitney (p, 124-125) called the same lowlands San Buenaventura or Santa Clara Plain, and (p. 121) used the name "Santa Clara Valley" for the valley of the stream. Members of the Portola expedition gave the name "Cañada de Santa Clara" to the valley of the river when they reached the place on August 12, 1769, the day of the saint (Wagner, p. 414). South Fork, formed by the confluence of the streams in Lyon Canyon and Gavin Canyon, enters from the southeast 3 miles north-northwest of Newhall (lat. 34°25'30" N, long. 118°33'30" W); it is 4.5 miles long and is named on Newhall (1952) 7.5' quadrangle.

Santa Clara Valley: see **Santa Clara River** [LOS ANGELES-VENTURA].

Santa Felicia Canyon [LOS ANGELES-VENTURA]: *canyon,* drained by a stream that heads in Los Angeles County and flows 5 miles to Lake Piru 5.5 miles northeast of Piru in Ventura County (lat. 34° 28'30" N, long. 118°43'55" W). Named on Val Verde (1952, photorevised 1969) and Whitaker Peak (1958) 7.5' quadrangles. Called Santa Feliciana Canyon on Los Angeles County (1935) map, which also names three tributaries: Fine Gold Canyon, which branches from main canyon about 5.5 miles south-southeast of Whitaker Peak; Well Canyon, which branches from the main canyon less than 1 mile downstream from the mouth of Fine Gold Canyon; and Temescal Canyon, which branches from the main canyon less than 1 mile downstream from the mouth of Well Canyon on Temescal grant.

Santa Feliciana Canyon: see **Santa Felicia Canyon** [LOS ANGELES-VENTURA].

Santa Fe Springs [LOS ANGELES]: *town,* 3.5 miles southwest of Whittier city hall (lat. 33°56'50" N, long. 118°05'05" W). Named on Whittier (1965) 7.5' quadrangle. Downey (1902) 15' quadrangle shows a place called Fulton Wells located along Southern Pacific Railroad in present Santa Fe Springs (lat. 33°56'30" N, long. 118° 04'50" W), a community called Santa Fe Springs situated 0.5 mile to the east (lat. 33°56'25" N, long. 118°04'20" W), and a place called Santa Fe Springs Sta. located along Atchison, Topeka and Santa Fe Railroad 0.5 mile east-northwest of the community of Santa Fe Springs (lat. 33°56'35" N, long. 118°03'45" W). Postal authorities established Sulphur Wells post office—with James E. Fulton as the first postmaster—in 1878, changed the name to Fulton Wells in 1879, and changed the name to Santa Fe Springs in 1888; the name "Santa Fe Springs" was from Atchison, Topeka and Santa Fe Railroad (Salley, p. 82, 197, 215). The town incorporated in 1957. Dr. J.E. Fulton put down three wells at the place in the 1870's and obtained sulphur water which he used at a resort called Santa Fe Springs or Fulton Wells (Waring, p. 282).

Santa Gertrudes [LOS ANGELES]: *land grant,* at and near Downey and Santa Fe Springs. Named on La Habra (1952), South Gate (1952), and Whittier (1951) 7.5' quadrangles. Josefa Cota de Nieto received 5 leagues in 1833 and 1834; Antonio Maria Nieto received the land in 1845; James P. McFarland and John G. Downey claimed 17,602 acres patented in 1870; Tomás Sanches Colima claimed 3696 acres patented in 1877 (Cowan, p. 92).

Santa Inez Range: see **Santa Ynez Mountains** [VENTURA].

Santa Isabel: see **Santa Ysabel** [SAN DIEGO] (1).

Santa Margarita Canyon [LOS ANGELES]: *canyon,* drained by a stream that flows 2 miles to Escondido Canyon 12 miles east-northeast of Solemint (lat. 34°28'40" N, long. 118°15'45" W; sec. 32, T 5 N, R 13 W). Named on Agua Dulce (1960) 7.5' quadrangle.

Santa Margarita Creek: see **Santa Margarita River** [SAN DIEGO].

Santa Margarita Mountains [SAN DIEGO]: *ridge,* generally south-southeast-trending, 6 miles long, center about 1 mile north-northwest of Margarita Peak (lat. 33°27'25" N, long. 117°23'45" W). Named on Margarita Peak (1968) and Sitton Peak (1954) 7.5' quadrangles.

Santa Margarita River [SAN DIEGO]: *stream* and *dry wash,* heads in Riverside County and extends for 25 miles in San Diego County to the sea 3.25 miles northwest of Oceanside (lat. 33°13'50" N, long. 117°24'55" W; near W line sec. 9, T 11 S, R 5 W). Named on Fallbrook (1968), Las Pulgas Canyon (1968), Morro Hill (1968), Oceanside (1968), and Temecula (1968) 7.5' quadrangles. United States Board on Geographic Names (1943, p. 13) rejected the names "Rio Santa Margarita," "Santa Margarita Creek," "Temecula Creek," and "Temecula River" for the stream or part of it. Members of the Portola expedition named the river in 1769 (Gudde, 1949, p. 316).

Santa Margarita y las Flores [SAN DIEGO]: *land grant,* along the coast between Oceanside and San Mateo Point, and inland to Fallbrook. Named on Fallbrook (1968), Las Pulgas Canyon (1968), Margarita Peak (1968), Morro Hill (1968), Oceanside (1968), San Clemente (1968), San Luis Rey (1968), and San Onofre Bluff (1968) 7.5' quadrangles. Pio Pico and Andres Pico received the land in 1841 and claimed 133,441 acres patented in 1879; Las Flores grant was added to the original Santa Margarita grant by purchase in 1844—the grant was called Santa Margarita y San Onofre before that time (Cowan, p. 93). The federal government purchased most of the land in 1942 for Camp Pendleton Marine Corps Base (Stein, p. 120).

Santa Margarita y San Onofre: see **Santa Margarita y las Flores** [SAN DIEGO].

Santa Maria: see **Beverly Hills** [LOS ANGELES]; **Valle de Pomo or Santa Maria** [SAN DIEGO].

Santa Maria Creek [LOS ANGELES]: *stream,* flows 1.5 miles to Garapita Creek 9 miles northwest of Santa Monica city hall (lat. 34°07'05" N, long. 118°35'05" W; at N line sec. 5, T 1 S, R 16 W). Named on Canoga Park (1952) and Topanga (1952) 7.5' quadrangles.

Santa Maria Creek [SAN DIEGO]: *stream,* flows 16 miles to join Santa Ysabel Creek and form San Dieguito River 3 miles west of San Pasqual (lat. 33°05' N, long. 117°00' W; near SE cor. sec. 34, T 12 S, R 1 W). Named on Ramona (1955) and San Pasqual (1954) 7.5' quadrangles.

Santa Maria de Peñasquitos: see **Los Peñasquitos** [SAN DIEGO].

Santa Maria Magdalena: see **San Juan Capistrano** [ORANGE].

Santa Maria Mountain: see **Black Mountain** [SAN DIEGO] (2).

Santa Maria River: see **Cuyama River** [VENTURA].

Santa Maria Valley [SAN DIEGO]: *valley,* around and west of Ramona (center near lat. 33°02' N, long. 116°55' W); Santa Maria Creek drains the valley. Named on Ramona (1955) and San Pasqual (1954) 7.5' quadrangles.

Santa Monica [LOS ANGELES]: *city,* 14 miles west of Los Angeles city hall (lat. 34°00'40" N, long. 18°29'25" W); the city is partly on San Vicente y Santa Monica grant. Named on Beverly Hills (1950), Topanga (1952), and Venice (1950) 7.5' quadrangles. Postal authorities established Santa Monica post office in 1875 (Frickstad, p. 81), and the city incorporated in 1886.

Santa Monica see **San Vicente y Santa Monica** [LOS ANGELES]; **South Santa Monica** [LOS ANGELES].

Santa Monica Bay [LOS ANGELES]: *embayment,* extends east from Point Dume past Santa Monica to Redondo Beach. Named on Beverly Hills (1950), Malibu Beach (1951), Point Dume (1951), Topanga (1952), and Venice (1950) 7.5' quadrangles. Called S. Fernando B. on Sage's (1846) map.

Santa Monica Canyon [LOS ANGELES]: *canyon,* drained by a stream that flows nearly 3 miles to Rustic Canyon 2 miles west-northwest of Santa Monica city hall (lat. 34°01'45" N, long. 118° 30'55" W). Named on Beverly Hills (1950) and Topanga (1952) 7.5' quadrangles. The canyon divides at the head to form Mandeville Canyon and Sullivan Canyon.

Santa Monica Mountains [LOS ANGELES-VENTURA]: *range,* on Los Angeles-Ventura County line; extends east for about 42 miles from Point Mugu to Los Angeles River. Named on Los Angeles (1975) 1°x 2° quadrangle. Called Sierra de la Monica on Parke's (1854-1855) map. Antisell (p. 76) referred to the Sierra Monica, Whitney (p. 168) mentioned Sierra Santa Monica, and Marcou (p. 159) described Sierra de Santa Monica. Preston (1890a, p. 189, 207) called the feature both Santa Monica Range and Sierra Santa Monica.

Santa Monica Range: see **Santa Monica Mountains** [LOS ANGELES-VENTURA].

Santa Monica Ridge [SAN DIEGO]: *ridge,* west-southwest-trending, 1.5 miles long, 5 miles east of Del Mar between McGonigle Canyon and Deer Canyon (lat. 32°57'20" N, long. 117°10'40" W; mainly in sec. 15, T 14 S, R 3 W). Named on Del Mar (1967) 7.5' quadrangle.

Santa Paula [VENTURA]: *town,* 14 miles east-northeast of Ventura (lat. 34°21'15" N, long. 119°03'30" W); the town is on Santa Paula y Saticoy grant near the mouth of Santa Paula Creek. Named on Santa Paula (1951) and Santa Paula Peak (1951) 7.5' quadrangles. Postal authorities established Santa Paula post office in 1874 (Frickstad, p. 219), and the town incorporated in 1902. They established Elisio post office 6 miles west of Santa Paula in Wheeler Canyon in 1893 and discontinued it in 1900 (Salley, p. 67). Ricard listed a place called Blanchards located 1 mile west of Santa Paula along Southern Pacific Railroad; the name recalls Nathan Weston Blanchard, who founded Santa Paula.

Santa Paula Canyon [VENTURA]: *canyon,* 9 miles long, along Santa Paula Creek above a point 4.5 miles west-southwest of Santa Paula Peak (lat. 34°25'25" N, long. 119°05'05" W). Named on Santa Paula Peak (1951) and Topatopa Mountains (1943) 7.5' quadrangles. The feature first was called Mupu Cañon (Goodyear, 1888a, p. 105). East Fork branches east nearly 3 miles west of Santa Paula Peak; it is 3.25 miles long and is named on Santa Paula Peak (1951) 7.5' quadrangle.

Santa Paula Creek [VENTURA]: *stream,* flows 15 miles to Santa Clara River 0.5 mile east-southeast of downtown Santa Paula (lat. 34°20'55" N, long. 119°02'55" W); the stream drains Santa Paula Canyon. Named on Santa Paula (1951) and Santa Paula Peak (1951) 7.5' quadrangles. Called Arroyo del Mupu on the diseño of Sespe grant in 1833 (Becker, 1964).

Santa Paula Peak [VENTURA]: *peak,* 7 miles north-northeast of Santa Paula (lat. 34°26'25" N, long. 119°00'30" W; near SE cor. sec. 7, T 4 N, R 20 W). Altitude 4957 feet. Named on Santa Paula Peak (1951) 7.5' quadrangle.

Santa Paula Ridge [VENTURA]: *ridge*, west-trending, 4.5 miles long, center 2.25 miles west of Santa Paula Peak (lat. 34°26'10" N, long. 119°02'45" W); Santa Paula Peak is at the east end of the ridge. Named on Santa Paula Peak (1951) 7.5' quadrangle.

Santa Paula Sulphur Springs: see **Sulphur Springs** [VENTURA].

Santa Paula y Saticoy [VENTURA]: *land grant*, along the valley of Santa Clara River from near Ventura to Santa Paula. Named on Oxnard (1949), Santa Paula (1951), Santa Paula Peak (1951), Saticoy (1951), and Ventura (1951) 7.5' quadrangles. Manuel Jimeno Casarin received 4 leagues in 1843; J.P. Davidson claimed 17,773 acres patented in 1872 (Cowan, p. 94).

Santa Rosa Mountains [SAN DIEGO]: *range*, mainly in Riverside County, but extends southeast into San Diego County 14 miles north-northeast of Borrego Springs (lat. 33°25'40" N, long. 116°14'20" W). Named on Fonts Point (1959), Oasis (1956), Rabbit Peak (1959), and Seventeen Palms (1956) 7.5' quadrangles.

Santa Rosa Valley [VENTURA]: *valley*, 4 miles north-northwest of Newbury Park (lat. 34°14'15" N, long. 118°55'45" W). Named on Newbury Park (1951) 7.5' quadrangle.

Santa Sinforosa Ridge [SAN DIEGO]: *ridge*, generally east-trending, about 1 mile long, 7.25 miles east-southeast of Oceanside (lat. 33°10' N, long. 117°15'30" W). Named on San Luis Rey (1968) 7.5' quadrangle.

Santa Susana: see **Simi Valley** [VENTURA] (2).

Santa Susana Canyon: see **Santa Susana Pass** [VENTURA].

Santa Susana Knolls [VENTURA]: *settlement*, 2 miles west-southwest of Santa Susana Pass (lat. 34°15'40" N, long. 118°40' W; mainly in sec. 16, T 2 N, R 17 W). Named on Santa Susana (1951) 7.5' quadrangle. Called Mortimer Park on Santa Susana (1943) 15' quadrangle.

Santa Susana Mountains [LOS ANGELES-VENTURA]: *range*, west of Newhall between Santa Clara River and San Fernando Valley; mainly in Los Angeles County, but extends west into Ventura County. Named on Los Angeles (1975) 1°x 2° quadrangle. Called Sierra De La St. Susana on Parke's (1854-1855) map. Antisell (p. 75) mentioned both Sierra Santa Susana and Sierra Susanna. Williamson (p. 29) referred to Susannah range. Whitney (p. 120) called the feature Sierra Santa Susanna, and noted that it also is known as Scorpion Hills.

Santa Susana Pass [LOS ANGELES-VENTURA]: *pass*, nearly 10 miles southwest of Newhall on Los Angeles-Ventura County line (lat. 34°16'05" N, long. 118°37'55" W; at W line sec 11, T 2 N, R 17 W); the feature is east of Simi Valley [VENTURA] (1). Named on Santa Susana (1951) 7.5' quadrangle. Called Simi Pass on Parke's (1854-1855) map. Los Angeles County (1935) map has the name "Santa Susana Cany." for the canyon west of the pass.

Santa Susana Pass Wash [LOS ANGELES]: *stream*, flows 7.5 miles to Browns Canyon Wash less than 2 miles north of the center of Canoga Park (lat. 34°13'40" N, long. 118°35'30" W); the stream heads at Santa Susana Pass. Named on Canoga Park (1952) and Oat Mountain (1952) 7.5' quadrangles.

Santa Teresa Valley [SAN DIEGO]: *valley*, 5.25 miles east-northeast of Ramona (lat. 33°04'35" N, long. 116°46'55" W; mainly in sec. 4, T 13 S, R 2 E). Named on Ramona (1955) 7.5' quadrangle.

Santa Ynez Canyon [LOS ANGELES]: *canyon*, 5.5 miles long, opens to the sea 4 miles west-northwest of Santa Monica city hall (lat. 34°02'15" N, long. 118°33'15" W). Named on Topanga (1952) 7.5' quadrangle.

Santa Ynez Lake [LOS ANGELES]: *lake*, 275 feet long, 4 miles west-northwest of Santa Monica city hall (lat. 34°02'35" N, long. 118°33'05" W). Named on Topanga (1952) 7.5' quadrangle.

Santa Ynez Mountains [VENTURA]: *range*, mainly in Santa Barbara County, but extends east into Ventura County as far as Ventura River 4 miles northwest of the town of Ojai. Named on Matilija (1952) and White Ledge Peak (1952) 7.5' quadrangles. Called Sierra de la Santa Inez on Parke's (1854-1855) map. Blake (p. 137) called the feature Santa Inez range, Antisell (p. 65) called it Santa Barbara Mountains, and Whitney (p. 111) called it Sierra Santa Iñez.

Santa Ysabel [ORANGE]: *locality*, 6.5 miles east of present Buena Park civic center along Atchison, Topeka and Santa Fe Railroad (lat. 33°52' N, long. 117°53'05" W; sec. 36, T 3 S, R 10 W). Named on Anaheim (1950) 7.5' quadrangle.

Santa Ysabel [SAN DIEGO]:

(1) *land grant*, at and north of the village of Santa Ysabel. Named on Julian (1960), Ranchita (1960), Santa Ysabel (1960), and Warners Ranch (1960) 7.5' quadrangles. Jose Joaquin Ortega and Edward Stokes received 4 leagues in 1844; Ortega and others claimed 17,719 acres patented in 1872 (Cowan, p. 93—Cowan used the form "Santa Isabel" for the name; Perez, p. 98).

(2) *village*, 4.5 miles west-northwest of Julian (lat. 33°06'35" N, long. 116°40'20" W); the place is at the south end of Santa Ysabel Valley on Santa Ysabel grant. Named on Santa Ysabel (1960) 7.5' quadrangle. Postal authorities established Santa Ysabel post office in 1889 (Frickstad, p. 156).

Santa Ysabel Creek [SAN DIEGO]: *stream*, flows 31 miles to join Santa Maria Creek and form Santa Dieguito River 3 miles west of San Pasqual (lat. 33°05' N, long. 117°00' W; near SE cor. sec. 34, T 12 S, R 1 W). Named on Julian (1960), Mesa Grande (1948), Ramona (1955), Ranchita (1960), San Pasqual (1954), Santa Ysabel (1960) and Warners Ranch (1960) 7.5' quadrangles. United States Board on Geographic Names (1933, p. 670) rejected the names "San Pasqual Creek" and "San Ysabell Creek" for the stream.

Santa Ysabel Peak [SAN DIEGO]: *peak*, nearly 6 miles south-southwest of Morettis Junction (lat. 33°09'45" N, long. 116°39'35" W; sec. 3, T 12 S, R 3 E). Altitude 4767 feet. Named on Warners Ranch (1960) 7.5' quadrangle.

Santa Ysabel Valley [SAN DIEGO]: *valley*, center about 1.25 miles north-northwest of the village of Santa Ysabel (lat. 33°07'30" N, long. 116°40'50" W); the valley is along Santa Ysabel Creek. Named on Santa Ysabel (1960) and Warners Ranch (1960) 7.5' quadrangles.

Santee [SAN DIEGO]: *city*, 2.25 miles west-southwest of Lakeside (lat. 32°50'20" N, long. 116°58'20" W). Named on El Cajon (1967) 7.5' quadrangle. Postal authorities established Santee post office in 1891, and named it for Milton Santee, first postmaster (Salley, p. 198). The city incorporated in 1980. The place also was known as Fanita, for Mrs. Fanita McCoon, and as Cowles, for George Cowles, who settled there in 1877 (Gudde, 1949, p. 319; Hanna, p. 294).

Santee Recreational Lakes [SAN DIEGO]: *lakes*, 6 miles north of La Mesa in Sycamore Canyon (3) near the mouth of the canyon (lat. 32°06'10" N, long. 117°00'20" W). Named on La Mesa (1967) 7.5' quadrangle.

Santiago Canyon [LOS ANGELES]: *canyon*, drained by a stream that flows 7.5 miles to Little Rock Creek 6 miles north of Pacifico Mountain (lat. 34°28'05" N, long. 118°01'10" W). Named on Pacifico Mountain (1959) 7.5' quadrangle.

Santiago Canyon: see **Santiago Creek** [ORANGE].

Santiago City: see **Modjeska Reservoir** [ORANGE].

Santiago Creek [ORANGE]: *stream* and *dry wash*, extends for 27 miles to Santa Ana River 9 miles southeast of Buena Park civic center (lat. 33°46'10" N, long. 117°53'20" W; sec. 2, T 5 S, R 10 W). Named on Anaheim (1965), Black Star Canyon (1967), El Toro (1968), and Orange (1964) 7.5' quadrangles. Corona (1942) 15' quadrangle has the name "Santiago Canyon" for the canyon of the stream, and Santiago Peak (1954) 7.5' quadrangle has this name for the canyon, but leaves the stream unnamed. On Corona (1902) 30' quadrangle, the name "Santiago Canyon" applies to the upper part of the canyon of Santiago Creek. Members of the Portola expedition named the stream for Saint James in 1769 (Meadows, p. 22).

Santiago de Santa Ana [ORANGE]: *land grant*, at Orange, Santa Ana, and Newport Beach. Named on Anaheim (1950), Black Star Canyon (1950), Newport Beach (1951), Orange (1950), Prado Dam (1950), and Tustin (1950) 7.5' quadrangles. Antonio Yorba received 11 leagues in 1810 and his heirs claimed 78,941 acres patented in 1883 (Cowan, p. 90).

Santiago Northwest Peak: see **Modjeska Peak** [ORANGE].

Santiago Peak [ORANGE]: *peak*, 20 miles east of Santa Ana on Orange-Riverside County line (lat. 33°42'40" N, long. 117°32' W). Named on Santiago Peak (1954) 7.5' quadrangle, which shows the alternate name "Old Saddleback" for the feature. United States Board on Geographic Names (1961c, p. 15) rejected the names "Old Saddleback," "Temescal Peak," and "Trabuco Peak" for it. The name "Old Saddleback" properly applies to two peaks together, Santiago Peak and Mojeska Peak, and to the ridge between them (Stephenson, p. 3-4). Whitney (p. 177) climbed Santiago peak in 1861 and named it Mount Downey to honor J.G. Downey, then governor of California. Bowers (p. 399) called the feature Saddleback or Santa Ana Peak.

Santiago Reservoir [ORANGE]: *lake*, behind a dam 6 miles southwest of Sierra Peak (lat. 33°47'10" N, long. 117°43'30" W); the lake is along on Santiago Creek . Named on Black Star Canyon (1967) 7.5' quadrangle. Called Irvine Lake on Black Star Canyon (1950) 7.5' quadrangle. The dam that forms the lake is at a place called Sycamore Flat for the sycamore trees there (Meadows, p. 133). During World War II, the army had a post called Camp Rathke situated in Santiago Canyon below the lake at a county park (Sleeper, 1976, p. 194).

San Vicente: see **Cañada de San Vicente y Mesa del Padre Barona** [SAN DIEGO].

San Vicente Creek [SAN DIEGO]: *stream*, flows 19 miles to the valley of San Diego River 1 mile north of Lakeside (lat. 32°52'30" N, long. 116°55'15" W). Named on El Cajon Mountain (1955), Ramona (1955), Santa Ysabel (1960), and San Vicente Reservoir (1955) 7.5' quadrangles. West Branch, which is named on San Vicente Reservoir (1955) 7.5' quadrangle, flows 4.25 miles to San Vicente Reservoir, where it joins the main stream.

San Vicente Mountain [LOS ANGELES]: *peak*, 7 miles southwest of the center of Canoga Park (lat. 34°07'45" N, long. 118°30'45" W); the peak is on San Vicente y Santa Monica grant. Altitude 1961 feet. Named on Canoga Park (1952) 7.5' quadrangle.

San Vicente Mountain [SAN DIEGO]: *peak*, 3.5 miles north of El Cajon

Mountain (lat. 32°58'05" N, long. 116°48'40" W; sec. 7, T 14 S, R 2 E). Altitude 2855 feet. Named on El Cajon Mountain (1955) 7.5' quadrangle.

San Vicente Reservoir [SAN DIEGO]: *lake,* behind a dam on San Vicente Creek 3.5 miles north of Lakeside (lat. 32°54'45" N, long. 116°55'25" W; near W line sec. 31, T 14 S, R 1 E). Named on San Vicente Reservoir (1955) 7.5' quadrangle.

San Vicente Valley [SAN DIEGO]: *valley,* 4.5 miles southeast of Ramona (lat. 33°00'05" N, long. 116°48'15" W); the valley is along and near San Vicente Creek. Named on El Cajon Mountain (1955) and Ramona (1955) 7.5' quadrangles.

San Vicente y Santa Monica [LOS ANGELES]: *land grant,* extends from Santa Monica to Topanga Canyon. Named on Beverly Hills (1950), Canoga Park (1952), Topanga (1952), and Van Nuys (1953) 7.5' quadrangles. Francisco Sepulveda received the land in 1828, 1839, and 1846; Ramona Sepulveda claimed 30,260 acres patented in 1881; Boca de Santa Monica grant was made from the original San Vicente grant in 1839 (Cowan, p. 89).

San Ysabell Creek: see **Santa Ysabel Creek** [SAN DIEGO].

San Ysidro [SAN DIEGO]:

(1) *locality,* 4.5 miles east-southeast of Warner Springs (lat. 33°15'20" N, long. 116°33'45" W; near SW cor. sec. 34, T 10 S, R 4 E); the place is along San Ysidro Creek. Named on Hot Springs Mountain (1960) 7.5' quadrangle.

(2) *district,* 4.5 miles east-southeast of Imperial Beach civic center in San Diego (lat. 32°33'20" N, long. 117°02'35" W); the place is along Tijuana River. Named on Imperial Beach (1967) 7.5' quadrangle. The community and its post office first had the name "Tia Juana" from the town just across the border in Mexico; William E. Smythe changed the name to San Ysidro when he founded a farming colony at the place in 1909 (Gudde, 1949, p. 320). Postal authorities established Tia Juana post office in 1876, discontinued it in 1881, reestablished it in 1887, moved it 1 mile southeast in 1901, and discontinued it in 1904; they established San Ysidro post office in 1910 (Salley, p. 198, 221).

San Ysidro Creek [SAN DIEGO]: *stream,* flows 11 miles to Buena Vista Creek (2) 4 miles northeast of Morettis Junction (lat. 33°14'35" N, long. 116°39'50" W). Named on Hot Springs Mountain (1960), Ranchita (1960), and Warners Ranch (1960) 7.5' quadrangles.

San Ysidro Mountain [SAN DIEGO]: *ridge,* northeast- to east-trending, 4 miles long, 6.5 miles west of Borrego Springs (lat. 33°15'45" N, long. 116°29'15" W). Named on Borrego Palm Canyon (1959), Hot Springs Mountain (1960), and Ranchita (1960) 7.5' quadrangles.

San Ysidro Mountains [SAN DIEGO]: *range,* 20 miles east-southeast of San Diego (lat. 32°35'30" N, long. 116°51' W). Named on Dulzura (1972), Jamul Mountains (1955), Otay Mesa (1955), and Otay Mountain (1972) 7.5' quadrangles.

San Ysidro Station [SAN DIEGO]: *locality,* 5.5 miles east-southeast of Imperial Beach civic center along San Diego and Arizona Eastern Railroad at the Mexican border (lat. 32°32'35" N, long. 117°01'35" W; sec. 6, T 19 S, R 1 W). Named on Imperial Beach (1967) 7.5' quadrangle. Called Tia Juana on San Diego (1904) 15' quadrangle.

Sargent Canyon: see **Hay Canyon** [LOS ANGELES].

Saticoy [VENTURA]: *town,* 7.5 miles east of Ventura (lat. 34°17' N, long. 119°08'50" W); the town is on Santa Paula y Saticoy grant. Named on Saticoy (1951) 7.5' quadrangle. Postal authorities established Saticoy post office in 1873 and discontinued it for a time in 1892 (Salley, p. 198). The name is of Indian origin (Kroeber, p. 56). The name "Saticoy" first applied to present West Saticoy, but in 1887 the name was transferred to the present community, which is along the railroad (Ricard). Postal authorities established Las Posas post office 6 miles southeast of Saticoy in 1892 and discontinued it in 1897—the name was from Las Posas grant (Salley, p. 118).

Saticoy: see **Santa Paula y Saticoy** [VENTURA]; **West Saticoy** [VENTURA].

Saucer Branch [LOS ANGELES]: *canyon,* drained by a stream that flows 1.25 miles to Millard Canyon 5 miles north of Pasadena city hall (lat. 34°13'10" N, long. 118°08'10" W). Named on Pasadena (1953) 7.5' quadrangle.

Saugus [LOS ANGELES]: *town,* 2 miles north-northwest of downtown Newhall (lat. 34°24'40" N, long. 118°32'20" W). Named on Newhall (1952) 7.5' quadrangle. Camulos (1903) 30' quadrangle has both the names "Saugus" and "Surrey" at the site. Postal authorities established Surrey post office in 1891 and changed the name to Saugus in 1915; the town was called Saugus after 1877, but the post office retained the old name for years (Salley, p. 216). The railroad station at the site first was called Newhall, for Henry M. Newhall, but when this name was transferred to present Newhall in 1878, the place was renamed Saugus for Newhall's birthplace in Massachusetts (Gudde, 1949, p. 321). Postal authorities established Alolia post office 18 miles northwest of Saugus on the old ridge route from Los Angeles to Bakersfield in 1916, changed the name to Ridge View the same year, and discontinued it in 1918 (Salley, p. 5, 185). Postal authorities established Carey post office 5 miles north of Saugus (sec. 34, T 5 N, R 16 W) in 1927 and discontinued in 1928; the name was for Western movie star Harry Carey, on whose ranch the post office was situated (Salley, p. 37).

Sausal Redondo [LOS ANGELES]: *land grant,* mainly between Redondo Beach and Inglewood. Named on Inglewood (1952), Redondo Beach (1951), Torrance (1964), and Venice (1950) 7.5' quadrangles. Antonio Ignacio Avila received 5 leagues in 1822, 1837, and 1846; he claimed 22,459 acres patented in 1875 (Cowan, p. 96; Cowan used the form "Sauzal Redondo" for the name).

Savage Creek [LOS ANGELES]: *stream,* flows 1 mile to end 0.5 mile east of Whittier city hall (lat. 33°58'20" N, long. 118°01'30" W). Named on Whittier (1965) 7.5' quadrangle.

Savannah [LOS ANGELES]: *locality,* 1.5 miles west-northwest of El Monte along Southern Pacific Railroad (lat. 34°05' N, long. 118°03'30" W). Named on Pasadena (1900) 15' quadrangle. Postal authorities established Savannah post office in 1876 and discontinued it in 1900 (Frickstad, p. 81). United States Board on Geographic Names (1933, p. 674) rejected the form "Savanna" for the name.

Sawmill Campground [LOS ANGELES]: *locality,* 1.25 miles north of Burnt Peak (lat. 34°42'05" N, long. 118°34'15" W); the place is on Sawmill Mountain. Named on Burnt Peak (1958) 7.5' quadrangle.

Sawmill Canyon [LOS ANGELES]:

(1) *canyon,* less than 1 mile long, nearly 2 miles north of Burnt Peak (lat. 34°42'30" N, long. 118°34'20" W; near E line sec. 9, T 7 N, R 16 W); the canyon is on the north side of Sawmill Mountain. Named on Burnt Peak (1958) 7.5' quadrangle.

(2) *canyon,* drained by a stream that flows nearly 1 mile to Swarthout Valley 6 miles north-northwest of Mount San Antonio (lat. 34°22'20" N, long. 117°40'45" W; sec. 2, T 3 N, R 8 W). Named on Mount San Antonio (1955) 7.5' quadrangle.

Sawmill Mountain [LOS ANGELES]: *ridge,* generally west-trending, 8 miles long, center 3 miles east of Burnt Peak (lat. 34°41'10" N, long. 118°31'15" W). Named on Burnt Peak (1958) and Lake Hughes (1957) 7.5' quadrangles.

Sawmill Mountain [VENTURA]: *peak,* 14 miles north-northeast of Reyes Peak on Ventura-Kern County line (lat. 34°48'50" N, long. 119°10' W; on N line sec. 1, T 8 N, R 22 W). Named on Sawmill Mountain (1943) 7.5' quadrangle.

Sawpit Canyon [LOS ANGELES]: *canyon,* drained by a stream that flows 5 miles to lowlands 5.5 miles west-northwest of Azusa city hall (lat. 34°09'45" N, long. 117°59'30" W). Named on Azusa (1953) 7.5' quadrangle. The name is from a sawpit located near the mouth of the canyon; the sawpit appeared old when the first settlers discovered it in the 1870's (Robinson, J.W., 1983, p. 15, 73).

Sawpit Wash [LOS ANGELES]: *stream* and *dry wash,* extends for 5 miles from the mouth of Sawpit Canyon to Rio Hondo 2.5 miles north-northeast of present El Monte city hall (lat. 34°06'40" N, long. 118°00'15" W). Named on Azusa (1953), Baldwin Park (1953), and El Monte (1953) 7.5' quadrangles.

Sawtelle: see **West Los Angeles** [LOS ANGELES].

Sawtooth Mountain [LOS ANGELES]: *ridge,* east-trending, 3 miles long, 2 miles southeast of Burnt Peak (lat. 34°39'40" N, long. 118° 33'05" W). Named on Burnt Peak (1958) 7.5' quadrangle.

Sawtooth Mountains [SAN DIEGO]: *ridge,* southwest- to south-trending, 6 miles long, 3.5 miles west-southwest of Agua Caliente Springs (lat. 32°55'30" N, long. 116°21' W). Named on Agua Caliente Springs (1959) 7.5' quadrangle.

Sawtooth Range [SAN DIEGO]: *ridge,* northeast- to east-trending, nearly 3 miles long, 4 miles north-northwest of Monument Peak (lat. 32°57' N, long. 116°26' W). Named on Monument Peak (1959) 7.5' quadrangle.

Saxonia Park [LOS ANGELES]: *locality,* 1 mile east-northeast of downtown Newhall (lat. 34°23'20" N, long. 118°30'45" W). Named on Newhall (1952) 7.5' quadrangle.

Scenega: see **Fillmore** [VENTURA].

Scheideck: see **Scheideck Camp** [VENTURA].

Scheideck Camp [VENTURA]: *locality,* 4 miles north-northwest of Reyes Peak along Reyes Creek (lat. 34°40'55" N, long. 119°18'30" W; at E line sec. 22, T 7 N, R 23 W). Named on Reyes Peak (1943) 7.5' quadrangle. California Division of Highways' (1934) map shows a place called Scheideck located 4 miles north of Reyes Peak and 1.25 miles east-northeast of the site of Scheideck Camp. Postal authorities established Scheideck post office in 1921 and discontinued it in 1935; the name was for Martin Scheideck, first postmaster and operator of a vacation camp (Salley, p. 199).

Scholder Creek [SAN DIEGO]: *stream,* flows 2.5 miles to an unnamed stream 1.25 miles northwest of Mesa Grande (lat. 33°11'35" N, long. 116°47' W; sec. 28, T 11 S, R 2 E). Named on Mesa Grande (1948) 7.5' quadrangle.

Scholl Canyon [LOS ANGELES]: *canyon,* nearly 3 miles long, opens into Sycamore Canyon (2) 5 miles west of Pasadena city hall (lat. 34°09'05" N, long. 118°13'40" W). Named on Pasadena (1953) 7.5' quadrangle.

Schoolhouse Canyon [LOS ANGELES]: *canyon*, 1.5 miles long, opens into lowlands 3 miles north-northwest of downtown San Fernando (lat. 34°19'30" N, long. 118°27'30" W; near S line sec. 21, T 3 N, R 15 W). Named on San Fernando (1953) 7.5' quadrangle. Sylmar (1935) 6' quadrangle has the form "School House Canyon" for the name. San Fernando (1966) 7.5' quadrangle shows Schoolhouse Debris Basin at the mouth of the canyon.

Schoolhouse Canyon [SAN DIEGO]: *canyon*, drained by a stream that flows nearly 2 miles to San Pasqual Valley at San Pasqual (lat. 33°05'10" N, long. 116°56'45" W; at W line sec. 36, T 12 S, R 1 W). Named on San Pasqual (1954) 7.5' quadrangle.

Schoolhouse Canyon [VENTURA]: *canyon*, drained by a stream that flows 2.25 miles to Russell Valley 1.25 miles southeast of Thousand Oaks (lat. 34°09'35" N, long. 118°49'05" W). Named on Thousand Oaks (1952) 7.5' quadrangle.

Schoolhouse Debris Basin: see **Schoolhouse Canyon** [LOS ANGELES].

Schumacher Point [LOS ANGELES]: *relief feature*, 3.5 miles north of Burnt Peak (lat. 34°44' N, long. 118°34'10" W; near SW cor. sec. 34, T 8 N, R 16 W). Named on Burnt Peak (1958) 7.5' quadrangle.

Schwartz Canyon [LOS ANGELES]: *canyon*, drained by a stream that flows less than 1 mile to Tujunga Valley 2 miles west-northwest of Sunland (lat. 34°16'30" N, long. 118°20'35" W; at W line sec. 10, T 2 N, R 14 W). Named on Sunland (1953) 7.5' quadrangle.

Scissors Crossing [SAN DIEGO]: *locality*, 7.5 miles east of Julian (lat. 33°05'50" N, long. 116°28'30" W). Named on Earthquake Valley (1959) 7.5' quadrangle.

Scorpion Hills: see **Santa Susana Mountains** [LOS ANGELES-VENTURA].

Scott Canyon [LOS ANGELES]: *canyon*, 0.5 mile long, 3.5 miles west-northwest of Azusa city hall (lat. 34°08'55" N, long. 117°57'45" W). Named on Azusa (1953) 7.5' quadrangle.

Scott's Camp: see **Camp Bonita** [LOS ANGELES].

Scove Canyon [SAN DIEGO]: *canyon*, drained by a stream that flows nearly 4 miles to Pine Valley 6 miles east-southeast of Descanso (lat. 32°49'30" N, long. 116°31'15" W; sec. 36, T 15 S, R 4 E). Named on Descanso (1960) and Mount Laguna (1960) 7.5' quadrangles.

Scully Hill [ORANGE]: *peak*, 4.25 miles southeast of San Juan Hill on Orange-San Bernardino County line (lat. 33°52'40" N, long. 117°40'40" W). Named on Prado Dam (1967) 7.5' quadrangle. The name commemorates Thomas J. Scully, a pioneer school teacher who lived near the feature; a promontory along Santa Ana River south of the peak is called Scully Point (Meadows, p. 126).

Scully Point: see **Scully Hill** [ORANGE].

Seabright [LOS ANGELES]: *locality*, 1.5 miles northwest of present Long Beach city hall (lat. 33°47' N, long. 118°12'40" W). Named on Downey (1902) 15' quadrangle.

Sea Cliff [VENTURA]: *locality*, 2.5 miles northwest of Pitas Point along Southern Pacific Railroad (lat. 34°20'40" N, long. 119° 25' W; sec. 17, T 3 N, R 24 W). Named on Pitas Point (1950) 7.5' quadrangle. Diller and others' (1915) map has the form "Seacliff" for the name.

Seal Beach [ORANGE]: *city*, 8 miles northwest of Huntington Beach civic center (lat. 33°44'30" N, long. 118°06'15" W). Named on Los Alamitos (1964) and Seal Beach (1965) 7.5' quadrangles. Postal authorities established Bay City post office in 1904 and changed the name to Seal Beach in 1914 (Frickstad, p. 116). The city incorporated in 1915. Philip A. Stanton and I.A. Lothian purchased land and laid out a townsite called Bay City at the place in 1903; the name was changed to Seal Beach because of the abundance of harbor seals at the spot (Meadows, p. 126).

Seal Beach: see **San Nicolas Island** [VENTURA].

Seal Cove [LOS ANGELES]: *embayment*, 10 miles south-southeast of Northwest Harbor on the west side of San Clemente Island (lat. 32° 54'15" N, long. 118°31'50" W). Named on San Clemente Island Central (1943) 7.5' quadrangle. Called Seal Hbr. on Smith's (1898) map.

Seal Garden: see **Graham** [LOS ANGELES].

Seal Harbor: see **Seal Cove** [LOS ANGELES].

Seal Rock [SAN DIEGO]: *promontory*, 2100 feet southwest of Point La Jolla along the coast (lat. 32°50'50" N, long. 117°16'40" W). Named on La Jolla (1967) 7.5' quadrangle.

Seal Rocks [LOS ANGELES]: *rocks*, 2.5 miles south-southeast of Avalon near the southeast end of Santa Catalina Island (lat. 33°18'25" N, long. 118°18'20" W). Named on Santa Catalina East (1950) 7.5' quadrangle.

Seco Canyon: see **Williams Canyon** [ORANGE].

Secret Canyon [SAN DIEGO]: *canyon*, drained by a stream that flows 3 miles to Pine Valley Creek nearly 7 miles south of Descanso (lat. 32°45'45" N, long. 116°38'25" W; sec. 23, T 16 S, R 3 E). Named on Descanso (1960) and Viejas Mountain (1960) 7.5' quadrangles.

Seda: see **Carlsbad** [SAN DIEGO].

Segunda Deshecha Cañada [ORANGE]: *canyon*, drained by a stream that flows 5.25 miles to the sea 1.5 miles west of San Clemente civic center (lat. 33°25'55" N, long. 117°38'05" W; sec. 32, T 8 S, R 7 W); the canyon is less than 1 mile southeast of Prima Deshecha Cañada. Named on San Clemente (1968) 7.5' quadrangle. The feature is the second difficult canyon to cross on the road south from the San Juan Capistrano mission—*Segunda Deshecha Cañada* means "Second Rough Canyon" in Spanish (Meadows, p. 126).

Sekwan Creek: see **Sycuan Creek** [SAN DIEGO].

Sekwan Peak: see **Sycuan Peak** [SAN DIEGO].

Selwyn [SAN DIEGO]: *locality*, 4.5 miles east of present Point La Jolla along Atchison, Topeka and Santa Fe Railroad in Rose Canyon (lat. 32°51'40" N, long. 117°11'45" W). Named on La Jolla (1903) 15' quadrangle.

Seminole: see **Seminole Hot Springs** [LOS ANGELES].

Seminole Hot Springs [LOS ANGELES]: *locality*, 7.5 miles north of Point Dume in La Sierra Canyon (lat. 34°06'30" N, long. 118°47'25" W; sec. 5, T 1 S, R 18 W). Named on Point Dume (1951) quadrangle, which shows Cornell school near the place. Called Cornell on Triunfo Pass (1921) 15' quadrangle. Seminole (1932) 6' quadrangle shows both Seminole and Cornell P.O. at the site. Postal authorities established Cornell post office in 1912 (Salley, p. 50). Water from an oil test well, reportedly about 3000 feet deep, is used for health-bathing and swimming at the place (Berkstresser, p.A-7).

Senior Canyon: see **Señor Canyon** [VENTURA].

Sennet Canyon [LOS ANGELES]: *canyon*, drained by a stream that flows 1.5 miles to Los Angeles River 2.25 miles south-southwest of Burbank city hall (lat. 34°09'10" N, long. 118°19'30" W). Named on Burbank (1953) 7.5' quadrangle.

Señora de Altagracia: see **El Conejo** [LOS ANGELES-VENTURA].

Señor Canyon [VENTURA]: *canyon*, 3.5 miles long, along San Antonio Creek above a point 4 miles northeast of the town of Ojai (lat. 34°28'15" N, long. 119°11'55" W; sec. 32, T 5 N, R 22 W). Named on Ojai (1952) 7.5' quadrangle. United States Board on Geographic Names (1968a, p. 9) approved the name "Senior Canyon" for the feature.

Sentenac Canyon [SAN DIEGO]: *canyon*, nearly 3 miles long, along San Felipe Creek above a point 9 miles south-southwest of Borrego Springs (lat. 33°07'45" N, long. 116°25'50" W). Named on Earthquake Valley (1959) and Tubb Canyon (1959) 7.5' quadrangles. The name is for Pete Sentenac and Paul Sentenac, brothers who homesteaded at the place in the 1880's (Stein, p. 125).

Sentenac Cienaga [SAN DIEGO]: *marsh*, 8 miles east of Julian along San Felipe Creek (lat. 33°06'05" N, long. 116°27'15" W); the place is at the head of Sentenac Canyon. Named on Earthquake Valley (1959) 7.5' quadrangle.

Sentenac Creek [SAN DIEGO]: *stream*, flows 2.25 miles to San Diego River 2 miles south of Santa Ysabel (lat. 33°04'45" N, long. 116°40'15" W; at N line sec. 4, T 13 S, R 3 E). Named on Santa Ysabel (1960) 7.5' quadrangle.

Sentenac Mountain [SAN DIEGO]: *peak*, 9 miles east of Julian (lat. 33°06'25" N, long. 116°26'35" W; near NE cor. sec. 27, T 12 S, R 5 E); the feature is east of the head of Sentenac Canyon. Altitude 3068 feet. Named on Earthquake Valley (1959) 7.5' quadrangle.

Sentinel Rock [LOS ANGELES]: *rock*, 3 miles west of Mount Banning, and 550 feet off the west side of Santa Catalina Island (lat. 33°22'20" N, long. 118°29'10" W). Named on Santa Catalina South (1943) 7.5' quadrangle.

Sentous [LOS ANGELES]: *locality*, 7.5 miles west-southwest of Los Angeles city hall along Southern Pacific Railroad (lat. 34°01'35" N, long. 118°22'10" W). Named on Hollywood (1966) 7.5' quadrangle.

Sepulveda [LOS ANGELES]:

(1) *district*, 3.25 miles north-northwest of Van Nuys in Los Angeles (lat. 34°13'40" N, long. 118°28' W). Named on Van Nuys (1953) 7.5' quadrangle. Called Mission Acres on Pacoima (1927) 6' quadrangle. Postal authorities established Mission Acres post office in 1926 and changed the name to Sepulveda in 1927 (Salley, p. 142).

(2) *locality*, 2 miles southeast of Burbank city hall along Southern Pacific Railroad (lat. 34°09'45" N, long. 118°17' W). Named on Burbank (1953) 7.5' quadrangle. Called Redcastle on Santa Monica (1902) 15' quadrangle. Postal authorities established Redcastle post office in 1895 and discontinued it the same year (Frickstad, p. 80).

Sepulveda Canyon [LOS ANGELES]:

(1) *canyon*, 4 miles long, 5 miles west-northwest of Beverly Hills city hall (lat. 34°06' N, long. 118°28'40" W). Named on Beverly Hills (1950) 7.5' quadrangle. The name is for Francisco Sepulveda, who received San Vicente y Santa Monica grant (Gudde, 1949, p. 325).

(2) *canyon*, nearly 2 miles long, 4.5 miles south of Torrance city hall (lat. 33°46'25" N, long. 118°21'05" W). Named on Torrance (1964) 7.5' quadrangle.

Sepulveda Channel [LOS ANGELES]: *water feature*, joins Ballona Creek 7 miles north of Manhattan Beach city hall (lat. 33°59'35" N, long. 118°24'25" W). Named on Venice (1964) 7.5' quadrangle.

Sepulveda's Landing: see **San Pedro** [LOS ANGELES] (2).

Sequan Creek: see **Sycuan Creek** [SAN DIEGO].

Sequan Peak: see **Sycuan Peak** [SAN DIEGO].

Sequit Point [LOS ANGELES]: *promontory*, 8 miles west-northwest of Point Dume along the coast (lat. 34°02'35" N, long. 118°56'10" W); the feature is on Topanga Malibu Sequit grant. Named on Triunfo Pass (1950) 7.5' quadrangle.

Serra [ORANGE]: *locality,* 2.5 miles south-southwest of San Juan Capistrano along Atchison, Topeka and Santa Fe Railroad at Capistrano Beach (lat. 33°28' N, long. 117°40'45" W). Named on Dana Point (1968) 7.5' quadrangle. The place first was called San Juan-by-the-Sea (Meadows, p. 126-127). California Mining Bureau's (1917a) map shows a place called Mateo located along the railroad about 3 miles southeast of Serra.

Serra: see **Capistrano Beach** [ORANGE].

Serra Mesa [SAN DIEGO]: *district,* 8.5 miles east-southeast of Point La Jolla (lat. 32°48' N, long. 117°08'15" W). Named on La Jolla (1967) 7.5' quadrangle.

Serrano Canyon [VENTURA]: *canyon,* drained by a stream that flows 3.5 miles to Big Sycamore Canyon nearly 3 miles east of Point Mugu (lat. 34°05'25" N, long. 119°00'40" W). Named on Point Mugu (1949) and Triunfo Pass (1950) 7.5' quadrangles.

Serrano Creek [ORANGE]: *stream,* flows nearly 5 miles to San Diego Creek 2.5 miles west-northwest of El Toro (lat. 33°38'10" N, long. 117°44' W). Named on El Toro (1968) 7.5' quadrangle. The stream was called Agua del Toro in the early days (Meadows, p. 18). Stevenson's (1884) map shows Canada del Toro.

Sespe [VENTURA]:

(1) *land grant,* along the valley of Santa Clara River near Fillmore. The river divides the grant into two parts: Sespe No. 1, south of the river, is named on Fillmore (1951), Moorpark (1951), and Santa Paula (1951) 7.5' quadrangles; Sespe No. 2, north of the river, is named on Fillmore (1951), Moorpark (1951), Piru (1952), Santa Paula (1951), and Santa Paula Peak (1951) 7.5' quadrangles. Carlos Antonio Carrillo received 2 leagues in 1833; T.W. Moore and others claimed 6 leagues and received 8881 acres patented in 1872 (Cowan, p. 97; Cowan gave the alternate name "San Cayetano" for the grant). The name "Sespe " is of Indian origin (Kroeber, p. 57).

(2) *locality,* 1.5 miles west-northwest of Fillmore (lat. 34°24'40" N, long. 118°56' W); the place is along Sespe Creek. Named on Piru (1921) 15' quadrangle.

(3) *locality,* 2.25 miles west of Fillmore along Southern Pacific Railroad (lat. 34°24' N, long. 118°57' W; sec. 26, T 4 N, R 20 W). Named on Fillmore (1951) 7.5' quadrangle. Called Sespe Sta. on Piru (1921) 15' quadrangle. Postal authorities established Sespe post office in 1894 and discontinued it in 1932 (Frickstad, p. 219).

Sespe Creek [VENTURA]: *stream,* flows 58 miles to Santa Clara River 2.5 miles west-southwest of Fillmore (lat. 34°22'55" N, long. 118°57'05" W; near SW cor. sec. 35, T 4 N, R 20 W). Named on Devils Heart Peak (1943), Fillmore (1951), Lion Canyon (1943), Old Man Mountain (1943), Topatopa Mountains (1943), and Wheeler Springs (1943) 7.5' quadrangles. Called Sespe R. on Goddard's (1857) map. Rothrock (p. 209) called the stream Sespo Creek, and C.W. Whipple (p. 148) called it Cespe Creek. West Fork enters from the west 2.5 miles south-southeast of Devils Heart Peak; it is 6.25 miles long and is named on Devils Heart Peak (1943) and Topatopa Mountains (1943) 7.5' quadrangles.

Sespe Creek: see **Little Sespe Creek** [VENTURA].

Sespe Gorge [VENTURA]: *narrows,* 5.25 miles north-northeast of Wheeler Springs (lat. 34°34'45" N, long. 119°15'25" W; near W line sec. 30, T 6 N, R 22 W); the feature is along Sespe Creek. Named on Wheeler Springs (1943) 7.5' quadrangle.

Sespe Hot Springs [VENTURA]: *spring,* 3.5 miles north-northwest of Devils Heart Peak in Hot Springs Canyon (lat. 34°35'40" N, long. 118°59'50" W). Named on Devils Heart Peak (1943) 7.5' quadrangle.

Sespe Station: see **Sespe** [VENTURA] (3).

Sespe Village [VENTURA]: *locality,* nearly 3 miles west-southwest of Fillmore (lat. 34°23'10" N, long. 118°57'20" W; at E line sec. 34, T 4 N, R 20 W); the place is near the mouth of Sespe Creek. Named on Fillmore (1951) 7.5' quadrangle.

Seven Pines Forest Camp [VENTURA]: *locality,* 2.5 miles northeast of McDonald Peak along Snowy Creek (lat. 34°39'25" N, long. 118°54'25" W; near W line sec. 33, T 7 N, R 19 W). Named on McDonald Peak (1958) 7.5' quadrangle.

Seventeen Palms [SAN DIEGO]: *locality,* 15 miles east of Borrego Springs (lat. 33°15'20" N, long. 116°06'35" W; sec. 35, T 10 S, R 8 E). Named on Seventeen Palms (1956) 7.5' quadrangle. According to Mendenhall (1909, p. 82-83), the name is from the number of native palm trees that once grew at the place.

Sewart Mountain [VENTURA]: *peak,* 2 miles east-northeast of McDonald Peak (lat. 34°38'25" N, long. 118°54'20" W; near W line sec. 4, T 6 N, R 19 W). Altitude 6825 feet. Named on McDonald Peak (1958) 7.5' quadrangle. Called Stewart Pk. on California Mining Bureau's (1917a) map.

Sexton Canyon [VENTURA]: *canyon,* drained by a stream that flows 4.25 miles to the valley of Santa Clara River 4 miles west of Saticoy (lat. 34°17'05" N, long. 119°13' W). Named on Saticoy (1951) 7.5' quadrangle.

Seymour Creek [VENTURA]: *stream,* flows 8 miles to Lockwood Creek 15 miles east-northeast of Reyes Peak (lat. 34°44' N, long. 119°02'25" W; near S line sec. 31, T 8 N, R 20 W). Named on Cuddy Valley (1943) and Lockwood Valley (1943) 7.5' quadrangles. Dr. Stephen Bowers named the stream in the late 1880's for Louisa Seymour, a friend of his (Ricard).

Shady Canyon [ORANGE]: *canyon,* 2.25 miles long, opens into an unnamed canyon nearly 9 miles south-southeast of Santa Ana city hall (lat. 33°38' N, long. 117°47'45" W). Named on Laguna Beach (1965) and Tustin (1965) 7.5' quadrangles. The upper part of the feature is called Cañada de la Madra on a map of 1841 (Meadows, p. 127).

Shady Dell [SAN DIEGO]: *locality,* nearly 8 miles north of Lakeside along West Fork San Vicente Creek (lat. 32°58'20" N, long. 116° 55' W; sec. 7, T 14 S, R 11 E). Named on San Vicente Reservoir (1955) 7.5' quadrangle.

Shady Oaks Camp [LOS ANGELES]: *locality,* 7.5 miles north-northeast of Glendora city hall along San Gabriel River (lat. 34°14'05" N, long. 117°48'20" W; near NE cor. sec. 27, T 2 N, R 9 W). Named on Glendora (1966) 7.5 quadrangle. Tony Galleta bought the place in the early 1950's and named it Shady Oaks; it also was called Follows Camp West (Robinson, J.W, 1983, p. 96-97).

Shake Campground: see **Lower Shake Campground** [LOS ANGELES]; **Upper Shake Campground** [LOS ANGELES].

Shake Canyon [LOS ANGELES]: *canyon,* drained by a stream that flows 2 miles to Pine Canyon (3) 3.25 miles east-northeast of Burnt Peak (lat. 34°42'05" N, long. 118°31'25" W; near N line sec. 13, T 7 N, R 16 W). Named on Burnt Peak (1958) 7.5' quadrangle.

Shan Canyon: see **Tick Canyon** [LOS ANGELES].

Shangri La: see **Lake Shangri La** [LOS ANGELES].

Shark Island: see **Linda Isle** [ORANGE].

Sharps Canyon [LOS ANGELES]: *canyon,* drained by a stream that flows 1 mile to Morris Reservoir 3.25 miles north of Glendora city hall (lat. 34°11' N, long. 117°51'55" W; sec. 7, T 1 N, R 9 W). Named on Glendora (1966) 7.5' quadrangle.

Sharps Canyon [LOS ANGELES-VENTURA]: *canyon,* drained by a stream that heads in Los Angeles County and flows nearly 3 miles to Piru Creek 17 miles south-southeast of Gorman just inside Ventura County (lat. 34°32'15" N, long. 118°45'30" W; sec. 10, T 5 N, R 18 E). Named on Cobblestone Mountain (1958) and Whitaker Peak (1958) 7.5' quadrangles. Los Angeles County (1935) map shows a feature called Kester Canyon that opens into the canyon of Piru Creek just above the mouth of Sharps Canyon.

Shatto: see **Avalon** [LOS ANGELES].

Shaw Canyon: see **Bitter Canyon** [LOS ANGELES].

Shaw Valley [SAN DIEGO]: *canyon,* drained by a stream that flows 2 miles to Carmel Valley 3.25 miles east-southeast of Del Mar (lat. 32°56'25" N, long. 117°12'45" W; sec. 20, T 14 S, R 3 W). Named on Del Mar (1967) 7.5' quadrangle.

Shay Canyon [LOS ANGELES]: *canyon,* 0.5 mile long, 3.25 miles east of Glendora city hall (lat. 34°07'50" N, long. 117°48'20" W; sec. 34, T 1 N, R 9 W). Named on Glendora (1953) 7.5' quadrangle.

Sheas Lodge [LOS ANGELES]: *locality,* 6 miles west of Del Sur (lat. 34°41'50" N, long. 118°23'40" W; on W line sec. 17, T 5 N, R 14 W). Named on Lake (1937) 6' quadrangle. Lake Hughes (1957) 7.5' quadrangle shows Sheas Castle at the site.

Sheep Camp Creek [SAN DIEGO]: *stream,* flows 1.5 miles to Boulder Creek 9.5 miles north-northwest of Descanso (lat. 32°58'30" N, long. 116°41'20" W; near NE cor. sec. 8, T 14 S, R 3 E). Named on Tule Springs (1960) 7.5' quadrangle.

Sheep Camp Spring [LOS ANGELES]: *spring,* 0.25 mile north-northwest of Pacifico Mountain (lat. 34°23'10" N, long. 118°02'10" W). Named on Pacifico Mountain (1959) 7.5' quadrangle. Alder Creek (1941) 6' quadrangle has the form "Sheepcamp Spring" for the name.

Sheep Canyon [SAN DIEGO]: *canyon,* drained by a stream that flows 5 miles to Collins Valley 9.5 miles northwest of Borrego Springs (lat. 33°22'05" N, long. 116°28'25" W). Named on Bucksnort Mountain (1960) and Hot Springs Mountain (1960) 7.5' quadrangles. The name is from desert bighorn sheep in the neighborhood (Bloomquist, 1978c, p. 36). South Fork branches southwest less than 1 mile above the mouth of the main canyon; it is 5.25 miles long and is named on Borrego Palm Canyon (1959) and Hot Springs Mountain (1960) 7.5' quadrangles.

Sheep Corral Canyon [LOS ANGELES]: *canyon,* drained by a stream that flows 1.25 miles to Verdugo Wash 4 miles northeast of Burbank city hall (lat. 34°13'40" N, long. 118°15'40" W). Named on Burbank (1966) 7.5' quadrangle.

Sheep Creek [VENTURA]: *stream,* flows 3.5 miles to Piru Creek 14 miles east-northeast of Reyes Peak (lat. 34°40'20" N, long. 119°02'10" W; sec. 30, T 7 N, R 20 W). Named on Lockwood Valley (1943) 7.5' quadrangle.

Sheephead Mountain [SAN DIEGO]: *ridge,* south-trending, 1.5 miles long, nearly 4 miles north-northeast of Buckman Springs (lat. 32°49'10" N, long. 116°27'45" W). Named on Mount Laguna (1960) 7.5' quadrangle.

Sheep Hills [ORANGE]: *range,* 5.5 miles northwest of San Juan Capistrano (lat. 33°33'15" N, long. 117°43'50" W). Named on San Juan Capistrano (1968) 7.5' quadrangle.

Shell Beach: see **Huntington Beach** [ORANGE].

Shelter Island [SAN DIEGO]: *island,* nearly 1.25 miles long, about 4 miles west of downtown San Diego in San Diego Bay (lat. 32° 42'50" N, long. 117°13'30" W). Named on Point Loma (1967) 7.5' quadrangle. Artificial fill connects the feature to land. The island was a sandbar before the surface was raised by dredged material in 1951 (Gleason, p. 85). United States Board on Geographic Names (1979a, p. 6) approved the name "Shelter Island Yacht Basin" for the harbor formed by the island, and rejected the names "Municipal Yacht Harbor" and "Yacht Harbor" for the place.

Shelter Island Yacht Basin: see **Shelter Island** [SAN DIEGO].

Shepherd Canyon [SAN DIEGO]: *canyon,* drained by a stream that flows nearly 4 miles to Murphy Canyon 6.5 miles northwest of La Mesa (lat. 32°49'20" N, long. 117°07' W). Named on La Mesa (1967) 7.5' quadrangle.

Sherer Canyon [LOS ANGELES]: *canyon,* drained by a stream that flows less than 1 mile to Hillcrest Canyon 2.5 miles east of Burbank city hall (lat. 34°10'40" N, long. 118°15'50" W). Named on Burbank (1953) 7.5' quadrangle.

Sherman [LOS ANGELES]: *locality,* 1.25 miles northeast of present Beverly Hills city hall (lat. 34°05'05" N, long. 118°22'55" W). Named on Hollywood (1926) 6' quadrangle. Postal authorities established Shermanton post office in 1896, changed the name to Sherman in 1899; and changed it to West in 1928; the name "Shermanton" was for General M.H. Sherman, railroad builder and land developer (Salley, p. 203).

Sherman Junction [LOS ANGELES]: *locality,* 1.5 miles east of Beverly Hills city hall along Pacific Electric Railroad (lat. 34°04'15" N, long. 118°22'30" W). Named on Beverly Hills (1950) 7.5' quadrangle.

Sherman Oaks [LOS ANGELES]: *district,* 2.25 miles south of the center of Van Nuys in Los Angeles (lat. 34°09' N, long. 118°26'50" W). Named on Van Nuys (1953) 7.5' quadrangle. Postal authorities established Sherman Oaks post office in 1931 (Salley, p. 203).

Shermanton: see **Sherman** [LOS ANGELES].

Sherman Way: see **North Sherman Way** [LOS ANGELES].

Sherwood Lake: see **Lake Sherwood** [VENTURA].

Shields Canyon [LOS ANGELES]: *canyon,* less than 1 mile long, nearly 9 miles northwest of Pasadena city hall (lat. 34°14'50" N, long. 118°14'15" W; on E line sec. 21, T 2 N, R 13 W). Named on Condor Peak (1959) and Pasadena (1953) 7.5' quadrangles.

Shields Canyon: see **Shiells Canyon** [VENTURA].

Shiells Canyon [VENTURA]: *canyon,* drained by a stream that flows 1.5 miles to the valley of Santa Clara River 2.25 miles southeast of Fillmore (lat. 34°22'50" N, long. 118°52'45" W). Named on Fillmore (1951), Moorpark (1951), and Simi (1951) 7.5' quadrangles. Called Shields Canyon on Camulos (1903) 30' quadrangle. The name "Shiells" commemorates brothers William Shiells and James Shiells (Ricard).

Shifting Sands [LOS ANGELES]: *area,* 1 mile south-southwest of Northwest Harbor on San Clemente Island (lat. 33°01' N, long. 118°35'30" W). Named on San Clemente Island North (1943) 7.5' quadrangle.

Shingle Spring [SAN DIEGO]: *spring,* 6.5 miles northwest of Warner Springs (lat. 33°21'30" N, long. 116°33'45" W; sec. 27, T 9 S, R 4 E). Named on Hot Springs Mountain (1960) 7.5' quadrangle. Stein (p. 127) associated the name with shingles that homesteaders got from cedar trees at the place.

Ship Rock [LOS ANGELES]: *rock,* 7 miles north-northwest of Mount Banning, and 1.25 miles off the north side of Santa Catalina Island (lat. 33°27'50" N, long. 118°29'30" W). Named on Santa Catalina North (1950) 7.5' quadrangle. United States Board on Geographic Names (1936a, p. 23) rejected the name "Bird Rock" for the feature. According to Gleason (p. 34), early navigators often mistook the rock for a vessel.

Shirley [ORANGE]: *locality,* 3 miles south-southwest of present Buena Park civic center along Pacific Electric Railroad (lat. 33°49'30" N, long. 118°01'25" W; sec. 15, T 4 S, R 11 W). Named on Los Alamitos (1950) 7.5' quadrangle.

Shoemaker [LOS ANGELES]: *locality,* 1.25 miles east-southeast of present Valyermo (lat. 34°25'50" N, long. 117°50'10" W). Named on Rock Creek (1903) 15' quadrangle. Postal authorities established Shoemaker post office in 1901, moved it 1.5 miles west in 1909, and moved it 1 mile northwest when they changed the name to Valyermo in 1910; the name "Shoemaker" was for Abram H. Shoemaker, first postmaster (Salley, p. 203). Johnson's (1911) map shows a place called Tilghman located 3.5 miles north of Shoemaker.

Shoemaker Canyon [LOS ANGELES]:

(1) *canyon,* drained by a stream that flows 2.5 miles to the canyon of Big Rock Creek 1.25 miles southeast of Valyermo (lat. 34°25'55" N, long. 117°50'05" W; at E line sec. 17, T 4 N, R 9 W); the mouth of the canyon is near the site of Shoemaker. Named on Valyermo (1958) 7.5' quadrangle.

(2) *canyon,* drained by a stream that flows nearly 1 mile to San Gabriel River 6.5 miles southeast of Crystal Lake (lat. 34°15'20" N, long. 117°45'30" W). Named on Crystal Lake (1958) 7.5' quadrangle. Called Rattlesnake Canyon on Rock Creek (1903) 15' quadrangle, but United States Board on Geographic Names (1962a, p. 16) rejected the names "Rattlesnake Canyon" and "Little Rattlesnake Canyon" for the feature. The name "Shoemaker" commemorates Alonzo Schoemaker, who owned land above the canyon (Robinson, J.W., 1983, p. 35).

Shorb [LOS ANGELES]: *locality,* 6 miles east-northeast of present Los Angeles city hall along Southern Pacific Railroad (lat. 34°04'45" N, long. 118°08'50" W). Named on Pasadena (1900) 15' quadrangle. Postal authorities established Shorb post office in 1895 and discontinued it in 1909; the name was for J. De Barth Shorb, a businessman (Salley, p. 203). California Mining Bureau's (1917a) map shows a place called Dolgeville located about 1 mile north of Shorb along the railroad. Postal authorities established Dolgeville post office in 1904, changed the name to West Alhambra in 1911, and discontinued it in 1920; the name was for Alfred Dolge, who built a factory for the manufacture of felt at the site (Salley, p. 60, 237).

Shore Acres: see **Manhattan Beach** [LOS ANGELES].

Shortcut Canyon [LOS ANGELES]: *canyon,* drained by a stream that flows 2.25 miles to West Fork San Gabriel River nearly 3 miles north-northeast of Mount Wilson (1) (lat. 34°14'50" N, long. 118° 02'55" W; near E line sec. 20, T 2 N, R 11 W). Named on Chilao Flat (1959) and Mount Wilson (1953) 7.5' quadrangles. The stream in the canyon has the name "Trail Fork San Gabriel R." on Tujunga (1900) 15' quadrangle.

Shortcut Picnic Grounds [LOS ANGELES]: *locality,* 7.5 miles south of Pacifico Mountain (lat. 34°16'25" N, long. 118°02'20" W; sec. 9, T 2 N, R 11 W); the place is near the head of Shortcut Canyon. Named on Chilao Flat (1959) 7.5' quadrangle.

Short Wash [SAN DIEGO]: *stream* and *dry wash,* extends for 2.25 miles to Palo Verde Wash 13 miles east of Borrego Springs (lat. 33°16'05" N, long. 116°09'55" W). Named on Fonts Point (1959) 7.5' quadrangle.

Shoulder Lake: see **Lake Palmdale** [LOS ANGELES].

Shrewsbury Canyon: see **Harding Canyon** [ORANGE].

Shrewsbury Spring [ORANGE]: *spring,* 4 miles west-northwest of Santiago Peak (lat. 33°44' N, long. 117°35'45" W; sec. 15, T 5 S, R 7 W). Named on Santiago Peak (1954) 7.5' quadrangle. The name is for Sam Shrewsbury, an early resident of Santiago Canyon (Meadows, p. 128).

Shuler Canyon [LOS ANGELES]: *canyon,* less than 1 mile long, 3.25 miles east of Glendora (lat. 34°08' N, long. 117°48'25" W; sec. 34, T 1 N, R 9 W). Named on Glendora (1953) 7.5' quadrangle.

Shuler Creek: see **East Branch**, under **Big Dalton Wash** [LOS ANGELES].

Siempreviva: see **Otay** [SAN DIEGO] (3).

Sierra: see **Camp Sierra** [LOS ANGELES].

Sierra Canyon: see **Fremont Canyon** [ORANGE].

Sierra de la Monica: see **Santa Monica Mountains** [LOS ANGELES-VENTURA].

Sierra de la Santa Inez: see **Santa Ynez Mountains** [VENTURA].

Sierra de Liebre: see **Liebre Mountain** [LOS ANGELES].

Sierra de los Berdugos: see **Verdugo Mountains** [LOS ANGELES].

Sierra del Trabuco: see **Santa Ana Mountains** [ORANGE].

Sierra de Santa Ana: see **Santa Ana Mountains** [ORANGE].

Sierra de Santa Monica: see **Santa Monica Mountains** [LOS ANGELES-VENTURA].

Sierra Liebra: see **Liebre Mountain** [LOS ANGELES].

Sierra Madre [LOS ANGELES]: *town,* 4 miles south of Mount Wilson (1) (lat. 34°09'45" N, long. 118°03'10" W). Named on Mount Wilson (1953) 7.5' quadrangle. Postal authorities established Sierra Madre post office in 1882 (Frickstad, p. 81), and the town incorporated in 1907. The name recalls Sierra Madre Villa, one of the earliest resorts in Los Angeles County and nucleus of the present town (Hanna, p. 305).

Sierra Madre: see **San Gabriel Mountains** [LOS ANGELES].

Sierra Madre Canyon Park: see **Carter's Camp**, under **Little Santa Anita Canyon** [LOS ANGELES].

Sierra Monica: see **Santa Monica Mountains** [LOS ANGELES-VENTURA].

Sierra Peak [ORANGE]: *peak,* 14 miles east-northeast of Santa Ana on Orange-Riverside County line (lat. 33°51' N, long. 117°39'10" W; sec. 6, T 4 S, R 7 W). Altitude 3045 feet. Named on Black Star Canyon (1967) 7.5' quadrangle.

Sierra Pelona [LOS ANGELES]: *range,* west- to southwest-trending, 18 miles long, east of Bouquet Canyon and north of Mint Canyon. Named on Green Valley (1958), Ritter Ridge (1958), and Sleepy Valley (1958) 7.5' quadrangles. Called Sierra Pelona Ridge on Los Angeles County (1935) map.

Sierra Pelona Ridge: see **Sierra Pelona** [LOS ANGELES].

Sierra Pelona Valley [LOS ANGELES]: *valley,* 7 miles south of the village of Leona Valley (lat. 34°30'45" N, long. 118°18'30" W); the valley is south of Sierra Pelona. Named on Agua Dulce (1960) and Sleepy Valley (1958) 7.5' quadrangles.

Sierra San Gabriel: see **San Gabriel Mountains** [LOS ANGELES].

Sierra San Juan: see **San Joaquin Hills** [ORANGE].

Sierra Santa Iñez: see **Santa Ynez Mountains** [VENTURA].

Sierra Santa Monica: see **Santa Monica Mountains** [LOS ANGELES-VENTURA].

Sierra Santa Susana: see **Santa Susana Mountains** [LOS ANGELES-

VENTURA].

Sierra Santiago: see **Santa Ana Mountains** [ORANGE].

Sierra Susana: see **Santa Susana Mountains** [VENTURA].

Sierra Vista [LOS ANGELES]: *district,* 5.5 miles east-northeast of present Los Angeles city hall (lat. 34°05'40" N, long. 118°09'25" W). Named on Alhambra (1926) 6' quadrangle.

Signal Hill [LOS ANGELES]:

(1) *peak,* 2.5 miles northeast of Long Beach city hall (lat. 33°48' N, long. 118°09'45" W). Named on Long Beach (1949) 7.5' quadrangle. Called Los Cerritos on Downey (1902) 15' quadrangle—the peak is on the boundary of Los Cerritos grant. The feature was known as Los Cerritos in Spanish times, but it was called Signal Hill after members of the Coast Survey put a signal there (Gudde, 1949, p. 332). It also was called Pound Cake Hill (Hanna, p. 306).

(2) *town,* 3 miles north-northeast of Long Beach city hall (lat. 33° 48'20" N, long. 118°10' W); Signal Hill (1) is at the town. Named on Long Beach (1949) 7.5' quadrangle. Postal authorities established Signal Hill post office in 1926, discontinued it in 1950, and reestablished it in 1956 (Salley, p. 204). The town incorporated in 1924.

(3) *locality,* 2.25 miles north-northeast of present Long Beach city hall along Los Angeles Terminal Railroad (lat. 33°48' N, long. 118°10'50" W). Named on Downey (1902) 15' quadrangle.

Signal Peak [ORANGE]: *peak,* 4.5 miles north-northwest of Laguna Beach city hall (lat. 33°36'20" N, long. 117°48'40" W). Named on Laguna Beach (1965) 7.5' quadrangle. The feature was used as a signal point for early surveys in Orange County (Meadows, p. 129).

Signal Point: see **Mount Wilson** [LOS ANGELES] (1).

Sill Hill [SAN DIEGO]: *peak,* 7.5 miles north of Descanso (lat. 32°57'50" N, long. 116°38'15" W; near SE cor. sec. 11, T 14 S, R 3 E). Named on Tule Springs (1960) 7.5' quadrangle.

Silvano [SAN DIEGO]: *locality,* 11.5 miles north-northwest of Ramona (lat. 33°11' N, long. 116°58'15" W; near S line sec. 27, T 11 S, R 1 W). Named on Ramona (1903) 30' quadrangle. Postal authorities established Silvano post office in 1893, discontinued it in 1894, reestablished in it 1900, and discontinued it in 1901 (Salley, p. 204).

Silver Acres [ORANGE]: *locality,* 7 miles north-northeast of present Huntington Beach civic center (lat. 33°45' N, long. 117°56'15" W). Named on Anaheim (1950) and Newport Beach (1951) 7.5' quadrangles.

Silverado [ORANGE]: *locality,* 9 miles north-northeast of El Toro (lat. 33°44'45" N, long. 117°38' W); the place is in Silverado Canyon. Named on El Toro (1968) 7.5' quadrangle. Postal authorities established Silverado post office in 1878, discontinued it in 1883, reestablished it in 1906, discontinued it in 1907, and reestablished it in 1931 (Salley, p. 204). J.W. Clark laid out a townsite called Silverado after a reported silver strike in Santa Ana Mountains in 1877 (Meadows, p, 129).

Silverado Canyon [ORANGE]: *canyon,* drained by a stream that flows 9 miles to Santiago Creek 6.5 miles south of Sierra Peak (lat. 33°45'30" N, long. 117°40'45" W). Named on Corona South (1967), El Toro (1968), and Santiago Peak (1954) 7.5' quadrangles. The feature first was called Cañada de la Madera for the trees there that provided lumber in the early days (Meadows, p. 49). The name "Silverado Canyon" came after Hank Smith and William Curry discovered silver in the canyon in 1877 (Hoover, Rensch, and Rensch, p. 264). Black Star Canyon (1950) 7.5' quadrangle has the name "Silverado Creek" for the stream in the canyon. After Ramon Mesquida discovered coal in the canyon in 1878, a mining town called Carbondale sprang up 1.5 miles above the mouth of the canyon; Tom Harris supervised the mine, and the community was known as Harrisburg before Carbondale post office opened (Hoover, Rensch, and Rensch, p. 264; Meadows, p. 50). Postal authorities established Carbondale post office in 1881 and discontinued it in 1884 (Salley, p. 37).

Silverado Creek: see **Silverado Canyon** [ORANGE].

Silver Canyon [LOS ANGELES]: *canyon,* drained by a stream that flows nearly 3 miles to the sea 4.25 miles southeast of Mount Banning on Santa Catalina Island (lat. 33°19'15" N, long. 118°23'20" W). Named on Santa Catalina East (1950) and Santa Catalina South (1943) 7.5' quadrangles.

Silver Canyon Landing [LOS ANGELES]: *locality,* 4.25 miles southeast of Mount Banning on the south side of Santa Catalina Island (lat. 33°19'15" N, long. 118°23'20" W); the place is at the mouth of Silver Canyon. Named on Santa Catalina South (1943) 7.5' quadrangle. Smith's (1897) map has the name "Silver C." (the "C" presumably for "Cove") at the site.

Silver Cove: see **Silver Canyon Landing** [LOS ANGELES].

Silver Creek [LOS ANGELES]: *stream,* flows 1 mile to Big Tujunga Canyon 3.5 miles south of Condor Peak (lat. 34°16'35" N, long. 118°12'50" W; sec. 11, T 2 N, R 13 W). Named on Condor Peak (1959) 7.5' quadrangle.

Silverdome: see **El Cajon Mountain** [SAN DIEGO].

Silver Hill: see **Silver Peak** [LOS ANGELES].

Silver Lake: see **Silver Lake Reservoir** [LOS ANGELES].

Silver Lake Heights [LOS ANGELES]: *district,* 3.5 miles north-northwest of Los Angeles city hall (lat. 34°06'10" N, long. 118°15'20" W); the place is east of Silver Lake Reservoir. Named on Glendale (1928) 6' quadrangle.

Silver Lake Reservoir [LOS ANGELES]: *lake,* 4400 feet long, 3.25 miles north-northwest of Los Angeles city hall (lat. 34°05'50" N, long. 118°15'45" W). Named on Hollywood (1953) 7.5' quadrangle. Called Silver Lake on Los Angeles (1928) 6' quadrangle.

Silver Mountain [LOS ANGELES]: *peak,* 4.5 miles north of Azusa city hall (lat. 34°11'50" N, long. 117°53'20" W; on E line sec. 2, T 1 N, R 10 W). Altitude 3391 feet. Named on Azusa (1953) 7.5' quadrangle. Mines near the peak produced silver in the 1880's (Robinson, J.W., 1983, p. 30).

Silver Peak [LOS ANGELES]: *peak,* 16 miles northwest of Avalon on Santa Catalina Island (lat. 33°27'35" N, long. 118°34'05" W). Named on Santa Catalina West (1943) 7.5' quadrangle. Doran (1980, p. 66) associated the name with the discovery of silver-bearing galena; the feature also was called Silver Hill.

Silver Strand [SAN DIEGO]: *beach,* 3.5 miles south of downtown San Diego along the seaward side of the peninsula that forms San Diego Bay. Named on Point Loma (1967) 7.5' quadrangle. Dalrymple's (1789) map has the name "Costa Brava" at the place. The army built an installation called Fort Emory, for army officer W.H. Emory, at the south end of Silver Strand in 1942; the navy took over the facility in 1948 (Whiting and Whiting, p. 26).

Silver Strand [VENTURA]: *town,* nearly 4 miles south-southwest of Oxnard near the coast (lat. 34°09'05" N, long. 119°13' W). Named on Oxnard (1949) 7.5' quadrangle.

Simi [LOS ANGELES-VENTURA]: *land grant,* at and around Simi Valley (1) on Los Angeles-Ventura County line. Named on Calabasas (1952), Moorpark (1951), Newbury Park (1951), Santa Susana (1951), Simi (1951), Thousand Oaks (1952), and Val Verde (1952) 7.5' quadrangles. Francisco Javier Pico, Miguel Pico, and Patricio Pico received 14 leagues in 1795 and 1821; Manuel Pico and Patricio Pico received the grant in 1842; Jose de la Guerra y Noriega claimed 113,009 acres patented in 1865 (Cowan, p. 98; Cowan listed the grant under the name "San Jose de Gracia de Simi"). The name "Simi" is of Indian origin (Kroeber, p. 58).

Simi: see **Simi Valley** [VENTURA] (2).

Simi Hills [VENTURA]: *range,* 7 miles northeast of Thousand Oaks (lat. 34°13'30" N, long. 118°44'50" W); the range is south of Simi Valley (1). Named on Calabasas (1952), Santa Susana (1951), and Thousand Oaks (1952) 7.5' quadrangles.

Simiopolis: see **Simi Valley** [VENTURA] (2).

Simi Pass: see **Santa Susana Pass** [LOS ANGELES-VENTURA].

Simi Peak [VENTURA]: *peak,* 4 miles northeast of Thousand Oaks (lat. 34°12'15" N, long. 118°46'50" W; near NE cor. sec. 5, T 1 N, R 18 W); the feature is in Simi Hills. Altitude 2403 feet. Named on Thousand Oaks (1952) 7.5' quadrangle.

Simi Station [VENTURA]: *locality,* 6 miles east of Moorpark along Southern Pacific Railroad in the present city of Simi Valley (lat. 34°16'30" N, long. 118°46'35" W; at W line sec. 9, T 2 N, R 18 W). Named on Simi (1951) 7.5' quadrangle.

Simi Valley [VENTURA]:

(1) *valley,* west of Santa Susana Pass (center near lat. 34°16'30" N, long. 118°44'30" W). Named on Santa Susana (1951), Simi (1951), and Thousand Oaks (1952) 7.5' quadrangles.

(2) *city,* 32 miles east of Ventura in Simi Valley (1) (lat. 34°16'15" N, long. 118°43'15" W). Named on Los Angeles (1975) 1°x 2° quadrangle. The communities of Simi, Santa Susana, and Community Center combined in 1969 as the incorporated city of Simi Valley. The former community of Simi was in the east part of Simi Valley (1) (lat. 34°16'10" N, long. 118°46'50" W; at E line sec. 8, T 2 N, R 18 W) and is named on Simi (1951) 7.5' quadrangle. The former community of Santa Susana was in the west part of Simi Valley (1) (lat. 34°16'20" N, long. 118°42'30" W; on E line sec. 12, T 2 N, R 18 W) and is named on Santa Susana (1951) 7.5' quadrangle. The town of Community Center began about 1924 when schools and a church were established midway between the communities of Santa Susana and Simi (Ricard). Community Center was situated near the center of Simi Valley (1) (lat. 34°16'15" N, long. 118°44'10" W; sec. 11, T 2 N, R 18 W) and is named on Santa Susana (1951) 7.5' quadrangle—it is called Simi Valley Community on Santa Susana (1943) 15' quadrangle. Postal authorities established Simiopolis post office in 1889, changed the name to Simi the same year, and changed it to Simi Valley in 1971 (Salley, p. 205). They established Santa Susana post office in 1904 and it became a station of Simi Valley post office in 1971 (Salley, p. 198). They established Roblar post office 5 miles east of Simi post office in 1894 and discontinued it the same year (Salley, p. 187).

Simi Valley: see **Little Simi Valley** [VENTURA].

Simi Valley Community: see **Community Center**, under **Simi Valley** [VENTURA] (2).

Simmons Canyon [SAN DIEGO]: *canyon,* drained by a stream that flows 4 miles to La Posta Creek 5.25 miles east-southeast of Buckman Springs (lat. 32°45'05" N, long. 116°24'20" W; sec. 30, T 16 S, R 6 E). Named on Mount Laguna (1960) and Sombrero Peak (1959) 7.5' quadrangles.

Simmons Flat [SAN DIEGO]: *area,* 2.5 miles north-northeast of Julian (lat. 33°06'30" N, long. 116°34'50" W; near SE cor. sec. 20, T 12 S, R 4 E).

Named on Julian (1960) 7.5' quadrangle.

Simon Canyon: see **Elderberry Canyon** [LOS ANGELES].

Simons [LOS ANGELES]: *locality*, 4.5 miles east-northeast of South Gate city hall along Atchison, Topeka and Santa Fe Railroad (lat. 33°59'15" N, long. 118°07'55" W). Named on South Gate (1952) 7.5' quadrangle. The name is from Walter Simons, who started a brickyard at the place in 1905 (Gudde, 1949, p. 333). Postal authorities established Simons post office in 1908 and discontinued it in 1934 (Salley, p. 205).

Singing Pines: see **Camp Singing Pines** [LOS ANGELES].

Singing Springs [LOS ANGELES]: *locality*, 5.25 miles east of Condor Peak along Mill Creek (lat. 34°19'15" N, long. 118°07'40" W). Named on Condor Peak (1959) 7.5' quadrangle.

Sinks: see **The Sinks** [ORANGE].

Siphon Reservoir [ORANGE]: *lake*, 1800 feet long, 6 miles northwest of El Toro (lat. 33°42'40" N, long. 117°43'45" W). Named on El Toro (1968) 7.5' quadrangle.

Sisar Canyon [VENTURA]: *canyon*, 4.25 miles long, along Sisar Creek above a point 6.25 miles east of the town of Ojai (lat. 34°26'40" N, long. 119°08' W; sec. 12, T 4 N, R 22 W). Named on Ojai (1952) and Santa Paula Peak (1951) 7.5' quadrangles. The name is of Indian origin (Kroeber, p. 58).

Sisar Creek [VENTURA]: *stream*, flows 7.5 miles to Santa Paula Creek 4.25 miles west of Santa Paula Peak (lat. 34°25'35" N, long. 119°05'25" W). Named on Ojai (1952) and Santa Paula Peak (1951) 7.5' quadrangles.

Sister Elsie Peak: see **Mount Lukens** [LOS ANGELES].

Sizzle Spring: see **Camp Sizzle Spring** [SAN DIEGO].

Skeleton Canyon [VENTURA]: *canyon*, 2.5 miles long, opens into Russell Valley at Thousand Oaks (lat. 34°10'05" N, long. 118°49'30" W). Named on Thousand Oaks (1952) 7.5' quadrangle.

Ski Beach [SAN DIEGO]: *beach*, 5.5 miles south-southeast of Point La Jolla on the east side of Vacation Isle (lat. 32°46'35" N, long. 117°13'55" W). Named on La Jolla (1967) 7.5' quadrangle.

Ski Islands [SAN DIEGO]: *islands*, two, largest 550 feet long, 5.25 miles south-southeast of Point La Jolla in Fiesta Bay (lat. 32°47'10" N, long. 117°13'35" W). Named on La Jolla (1967) 7.5' quadrangle.

Skunk Hollow [SAN DIEGO]: *canyon*, 0.5 mile long, 1.5 miles north-northwest of Barrett Junction (lat. 32°38' N, long. 116°42'55" W; sec. 6, T 18 S, R 3 E). Named on Barrett Lake (1960) 7.5' quadrangle.

Skunk Spring [SAN DIEGO]: *spring*, 4 miles north-northwest of El Cajon Mountain (lat. 32°58'15" N, long. 116°50'20" W). Named on El Cajon Mountain (1955) 7.5' quadrangle.

Skye Valley [SAN DIEGO]: *valley*, 8.5 miles north-northeast of Barrett Junction (lat. 32°43'10" N, long. 116°37'55" W; sec. 1, T 17 S, R 3 E). Named on Barrett Lake (1960) and Morena Reservoir (1960) 7.5' quadrangles. The McLean brothers, who came from Scotland to homestead in the valley, gave the place a name from their native land (Stein, p. 127).

Slaughter Canyon [LOS ANGELES]: *canyon*, drained by a stream that flows 1 mile to Gold Canyon 5.5 miles north-northeast of Sunland (lat. 34°20'15" N, long. 118°17'10" W). Named on Sunland (1953) 7.5' quadrangle.

Slaughterhouse Canyon [SAN DIEGO]: *canyon*, drained by a stream that flows 3.5 miles to San Vicente Creek 2.5 miles north of Lakeside (lat. 32°53'50" N, long. 116°55'50" W). Named on San Vicente Reservoir (1955) 7.5' quadrangle.

Slauson [LOS ANGELES]: *locality*, 4.25 miles east-northeast of present Inglewood city hall along Atchison, Topeka and Santa Fe Railroad (lat. 33°59'15" N, long. 118°17' W). Named on Redondo (1896) 15' quadrangle.

Slauson: see **Camp Slauson** [LOS ANGELES].

Sleeper Canyon [LOS ANGELES]: *canyon*, drained by a stream that flows 1 mile to Malibu Creek nearly 4 miles north-northwest of Malibu Point (lat. 34°04'55" N, long. 118°42'20" W; sec. 18, T 1 S, R 17 W). Named on Malibu Beach (1951) 7.5' quadrangle.

Sleepy Hollow [SAN DIEGO]: *relief feature*, 7.5 miles east-southeast of Borrego Springs (lat. 33°11'55" N, long. 116°16' W; sec. 20, 29, T 11 S, R 7 E). Named on Borrego Sink (1959) 7.5' quadrangle.

Sleepy Valley [LOS ANGELES]: *settlement*, 8.5 miles south-southwest of the village of Leona Valley in Mint Canyon (1) (lat. 34°30'35" N, long. 118°21'50" W; at NE cor. sec. 20, T 5 N, R 14 W). Named on Sleepy Valley (1958) 7.5' quadrangle.

Sloan Canyon [LOS ANGELES]: *canyon*, drained by a stream that flows 2.5 miles to Halsey Canyon 9 miles northwest of Newhall (lat. 34°27'45" N, long. 118°39'10" W; sec. 3, T 4 N, R 17 W). Named on Val Verde (1952) 7.5' quadrangle.

Slot: see **The Slot** [SAN DIEGO].

Smeltzer [ORANGE]: *locality*, 4.5 miles north of Huntington Beach civic center along Southern Pacific Railroad (lat. 33°43'45" N, long. 117°59'50" W; at N line sec. 23, T 5 S, R 11 W). Named on Newport Beach (1965) 7.5' quadrangle. Postal authorities established Smeltzer post office 2 miles south of Westminister post office in 1900 and discontinued it the same year; the name was for Daniel E. Smeltzer, first postmaster (Salley, p. 206)—Mr. Smeltzer introduced the raising of celery to the region in 1894, and the railroad siding at a packing house was named for him (Meadows, p. 130). Santa Ana (1942) 15' quadrangle shows a place called Sugar located along the railroad 0.5 mile north of Smeltzer.

Smith Canyon [LOS ANGELES]: *canyon*, drained by a stream that flows 2.25 miles to Romero Canyon 9.5 miles northwest of Newhall (lat. 34°28'20" N, long. 118°39'30" W). Named on Santa Susana (1943) 15' quadrangle.

Smith Canyon [SAN DIEGO]: *canyon*, drained by a stream that flows 2.25 miles to Campo Valley 2.5 miles east-northeast of Campo (lat. 32°37'30" N, long. 116°26' W; sec. 12, T 18 S, R 5 E). Named on Campo (1959) 7.5' quadrangle.

Smith Canyon [VENTURA]: *canyon*, drained by a stream that flows 2 miles to the valley of Santa Clara River 1.5 miles south of Piru (lat. 34°23'30" N, long. 118°47'30" W; sec. 32, T 4 N, R 18 W). Named on Piru (1952) 7.5' quadrangle.

Smith Fork [VENTURA]: *stream*, flows 2.5 miles to Piru Creek 6.25 miles northeast of McDonald Peak (lat. 34°42'10" N, long. 118° 52' W; sec. 14, T 7 N, R 19 W). Named on Black Mountain (1958) and McDonald Peak (1958) 7.5' quadrangles.

Smith Mountain [LOS ANGELES]: *peak*, nearly 3 miles south-southwest of Crystal Lake (lat. 34°16'55" N, long. 117°51'45" W). Altitude 5111 feet. Named on Crystal Lake (1958) 7.5' quadrangle. Gudde (1949, p. 335) used the form "Mount Smith" for the name.

Smith Mountain: see **Palomar Mountain** [SAN DIEGO] (1).

Smoke Tree Canyon [SAN DIEGO]: *canyon*, drained by a stream that flows 3.5 miles to lowlands 13 miles east of Borrego Springs (lat. 33°17'25" N, long. 116°09'25" W). Named on Fonts Point (1959) 7.5' quadrangle.

Smoke Tree Forest [SAN DIEGO]: *locality*, 1.5 miles west of Sweeney Pass along Carrizo Creek (2) (lat. 32°50' N, long. 116°12'30" W; sec. 25, T 15 S, R 7 E). Named on Sweeney Pass (1959) 7.5' quadrangle.

Smoke Tree Wash [SAN DIEGO]: *dry wash*, extends for nearly 1 mile from the mouth of Smoke Tree Canyon to Palo Verde Wash 12.5 miles east of Borrego Springs (lat. 33°16'45" N, long. 116°09'45" W). Named on Fonts Point (1959) 7.5' quadrangle.

Smuggler Canyon [SAN DIEGO]: *canyon*, drained by a stream that flows 6 miles to Vallecito Creek 2 miles northwest of Agua Caliente Springs (lat. 32°58'10" N, long. 116°19'50" W; near E line sec. 11, R 14 S, R 6 E). Named on Agua Caliente Springs (1959) and Whale Peak (1959) 7.5' quadrangles.

Smuggler Gulch [SAN DIEGO]: *canyon*, extends north for 0.5 mile from the Mexican border 3 miles south-southeast of Imperial Beach civic center (lat. 32°32'30" N, long. 117°05'10" W; on S line sec. 4, T 19 S, R 2 W). Named on Imperial Beach (1967) 7.5' quadrangle.

Smugglers Cove: see **Pyramid Cove** [LOS ANGELES].

Smuggler Spring: see **Mountain Spring** [SAN DIEGO].

Snail Canyon [VENTURA]: *canyon*, drained by a stream that flows 4.5 miles to the canyon of Cuyama River 5 miles northwest of Reyes Peak (lat. 34°41'15" N, long. 119°20'15" W; sec. 20, T 7 N, R 23 W). Named on Reyes Peak (1943) 7.5' quadrangle.

Snobel Valley [SAN DIEGO]: *valley*, 5.25 miles northwest of Mesa Grande (lat. 33°13'20" N, long. 116°50'30" W). Named on Mesa Grande (1948) 7.5' quadrangle.

Snover Canyon [LOS ANGELES]: *canyon*, 0.5 mile long, 7.25 miles northwest of Pasadena city hall (lat. 34°14' N, long. 118°13' W; sec. 26, 27, T 2 N, R 13 W). Named on Pasadena (1953) 7.5' quadrangle.

Snow Canyon [VENTURA]: *canyon*, drained by a stream that flows 2.25 miles to the valley of Santa Clara River 2.25 miles west-northwest of Fillmore (lat. 34°25'10" N, long. 118°56'45" W; sec. 23, T 4 N, R 20 W). Named on Fillmore (1951) 7.5' quadrangle.

Snowslide Canyon [LOS ANGELES]: *canyon*, drained by a stream that flows 1 mile to Pine Flats 1 mile northeast of Crystal Lake (lat. 34°19'45" N, long. 117°49'50" W). Named on Crystal Lake (1958) 7.5' quadrangle.

Snow Spring [LOS ANGELES]: *spring*, 1.25 miles north of Crystal Lake (lat. 34°20'20" N, long. 117°51'05" W). Named on Crystal Lake (1958) 7.5' quadrangle.

Snowy Creek [VENTURA]: *stream*, flows 7.5 miles to Piru Creek 6.25 miles northeast of McDonald Peak (lat. 34°41'35" N, long. 118°51'40" W; near S line sec. 14, T 7 N, R 19 W). Named on Black Mountain (1958) and McDonald Peak (1958) 7.5' quadrangles.

Snowy Forest Camp [VENTURA]: *locality*, 3 miles northeast of McDonald Peak (lat. 34°39'45" N, long. 118°54'15" W; near N line sec. 33, T 7 N, R 19 W); the place is along Snowy Creek. Named on McDonald Peak (1958) 7.5' quadrangle.

Snowy Peak [VENTURA]: *peak*, 3 miles east-northeast of McDonald Peak (lat. 34°39' N, long. 118°53'15" W; near SW cor. sec. 34, T 7 N, R 19 W). Altitude 6559 feet. Named on McDonald Peak (1958) 7.5' quadrangle.

Soboyame: see **Palomar Mountain** [SAN DIEGO] (2).

Solamint: see **Solemint** [LOS ANGELES].

Solana Beach [SAN DIEGO]: *town*, 2.25 miles north of Del Mar along the coast (lat. 32°59'30" N, long. 117°16'15" W). Named on Del Mar (1967) and Encinitas (1968) 7.5' quadrangles. Postal authorities established Solana

Beach post office in 1924 (Frickstad, p. 156). Colonel Ed Fletcher laid out and named the town in 1923 at a place previously called Lockwood Mesa (Stein, p. 128).

Solano Ravine: see **Chavez Ravine** [LOS ANGELES].

Sold Canyon [LOS ANGELES]: *canyon,* drained by a stream that flows 1 mile to Pacoima Canyon 8 miles north-northeast of Sunland (lat. 34°22' N, long. 118°15'15" W). Named on Condor Peak (1959) and Sunland (1953) 7.5' quadrangles.

Soldier Creek [LOS ANGELES]: *stream,* flows 3 miles to join Coldbrook Creek and form North Fork San Gabriel River 2 miles south of Crystal Lake (lat. 34°17'25" N, long. 117°50'20" W). Named on Crystal Lake (1958) 7.5' quadrangle. United States Board on Geographic Names (1962a, p. 16) rejected the name "North Fork San Gabriel River" for the stream.

Soldiers Home: see **West Los Angeles** [LOS ANGELES].

Soledad: see **Ravenna** [LOS ANGELES].

Soledad Campground [LOS ANGELES]: *locality,* 8.5 miles east of Solemint (lat. 34°26'25" N, long. 118°18'25" W; near E line sec. 11, T 4 N, R 14 W); the place is in Soledad Canyon. Named on Agua Dulce (1960) 7.5' quadrangle.

Soledad Canyon [LOS ANGELES]: *canyon,* 32 miles long, along Santa Clara River above a point 2.5 miles north of Newhall (lat. 34°25'30" N, long. 118°32'15" W). Named on Acton (1959), Agua Dulce (1960), Mint Canyon (1960), Newhall (1952), and Pacifico Mountain (1959) 7.5' quadrangles.

Soledad Canyon [SAN DIEGO]: *canyon,* drained by a stream that flows 4.5 miles to marsh in Soledad Valley 4.5 miles south-southeast of Del Mar (lat. 32°54'05" N, long. 117°13'20" W). Named on Del Mar (1967) 7.5' quadrangle. Members of the Portola expedition called the feature Valle Santa Isabel in 1769 (Wagner, p. 511-512). The feature had the alternate name "Sorrento Canyon," and has the name "Cañada de la Soledad" on the map of Pueblo lands of San Diego that Henry D. Fitch made in 1845 (Harlow, 1987, p. 79).

Soledad City: see **Ravenna** [LOS ANGELES].

Soledad Mountain [SAN DIEGO]: *ridge,* west-northwest-trending, 1 mile long, 1.5 miles east-southeast of Point La Jolla (lat. 32°50'30" N, long. 117°15'15" W). Named on La Jolla (1967) 7.5' quadrangle.

Soledad Pass [LOS ANGELES]: *pass,* 5.5 miles south of Palmdale at Vincent (lat. 34°30' N, long. 118°06'55" W; sec. 22, 23, T 5 N, R 12 W); the pass is approached from the southwest by way of Soledad Canyon, but it is not at the head of that canyon. Named on Pacifico Mountain (1959) and Palmdale (1958) 7.5' quadrangles. Called Williamson's Pass on Blake's (1857) map, and called La Soledad Pass on Gray's (1873) map. Williamson (p. 30) called the feature New Pass.

Soledad Sulphur Springs [LOS ANGELES]: *locality,* 6 miles east of Solemint (lat. 34°26' N, long. 118°21'35" W; at W line sec. 16, T 4 N, R 14 W). Named on Lang (1933) 6' quadrangle.

Soledad Valley [SAN DIEGO]: *valley,* extends for nearly 3 miles from the mouth of Soledad Canyon to the sea 1.5 miles south of Del Mar (lat. 32°56' N, long. 117°15'35" W). Named on Del Mar (1967) 7.5' quadrangle, where the feature is largely covered by marsh. Hanks' (1886a) map shows a place called Solidad (with an "i") near the mouth of present Soledad Canyon.

Solemint [LOS ANGELES]: *town,* 9 miles north of San Fernando (lat. 34°25' N, long. 118°27'15" W; sec. 21, T 4 N, R 15 W); the place is at the junction of Soledad Canyon and Mint Canyon. Named on Mint Canyon (1960) 7.5' quadrangle. Called Solamint on Humphreys (1932) 6' quadrangle. San Fernando (1900) 15' quadrangle has the name "Thompson" at the site. Los Angeles County (1935) map names four branches of Soledad Canyon near Solemint: Whites Canyon, which opens into Soledad Canyon from the northeast about 1 mile northwest of Solemint (sec. 17, T 4 N, R 15 W); Irwin Canyon, which opens into Soledad Canyon from the south about 1.5 miles west of Solemint (sec. 20, T 4 N, R 15 W); Suracco Canyon, which opens into Soledad Canyon from the south about 1 mile southwest of Solemint (near SE cor. sec. 20, T 4 N, R 15 W); and Nadeau Canyon, which opens into Soledad Canyon from the south 0.5 mile south-southwest of Solemint (at N line sec. 28, T 4 N, R 15 W).

Solidad: see **Soledad Valley** [SAN DIEGO].

Solromar [VENTURA]: *locality,* 5 miles south-southwest of Triunfo Pass along the coast (lat. 34°03' N, long. 118°57'15" W; on W line sec. 26, T 1 S, R 20 W). Named on Triunfo Pass (1950) 7.5' quadrangle. Postal authorities established Solromar post office in 1944 and discontinued it in 1956 (Salley, p. 207). The name was coined from sol, oro, and mar—the Spanish words for "sun," "gold," and "sea"—to suggest a golden sunset on the sea (Gudde, 1949, p. 338).

Solstice Canyon [LOS ANGELES]: *canyon,* drained by a stream that flows 4.5 miles to the sea 3.5 miles west of Malibu Point (lat. 34° 01'55" N, long. 118°44'30" W). Named on Malibu Beach (1951) and Point Dume (1951) 7.5' quadrangles.

Sombrero Canyon [LOS ANGELES]: *canyon,* 2 miles long, opens into lowlands 3.5 miles north-northwest of downtown San Fernando (lat. 34°19'45" N, long. 118°28'05" W near E line sec. 20, T 3 N, R 15 W). Named on San Fernando (1953) 7.5' quadrangle. West Fork branches northwest near the mouth of the main canyon; it is 1.25 miles long and is named on San Fernando (1966) 7.5' quadrangle.

Sombrero Peak [SAN DIEGO]: *peak,* 8 miles south of Agua Caliente Springs (lat. 32°49'55" N, long. 116°17'30" W; at W line sec. 29, T 15 S, R 7 E). Named on Sombrero Peak (1959) 7.5' quadrangle. The feature is shaped like the crown of a Mexican hat (Bloomquist, 1970, p. 34).

Sombrero Peak Palm Grove [SAN DIEGO]: *locality,* 0.5 mile east of Sombrero Peak (lat. 32°49'50" N, long. 116°17' W; near S line sec. 29, T 15 S, R 7 E). Named on Sombrero Peak (1959) 7.5' quadrangle.

Somerset: see **Bellflower** [LOS ANGELES].

Somis [VENTURA]: *town,* 7 miles west-southwest of Moorpark (lat. 34°15'25" N, long. 118°59'45" W). Named on Moorpark (1951) 7.5' quadrangle. Postal authorities established Somis post office in 1893 (Frickstad, p. 219). The name is of Indian origin (Kroeber, p. 59).

Sonome Canyon [LOS ANGELES-ORANGE]: *canyon,* drained by a stream that heads in Los Angeles County and flows 2.25 miles to Carbon Canyon 2.5 miles north-northeast of Yorba Linda in Orange County (lat. 33°55'40" N, long. 117°48' W; near W line sec. 11, T 3 S, R 9 W). Named on Yorba Linda (1950) 7.5' quadrangle.

Sopers Hot Springs [VENTURA]: *locality,* 4 miles northwest of Ojai (lat. 34°28'55" N, long. 119°17'25" W). Named on Ventura (1941) 15' quadrangle. Matilija (1952) 7.5' quadrangle shows Sopers ranch at or near the site.

Soquel Canyon [ORANGE]: *canyon,* drained by a stream that heads in San Bernardino County and flows 2.5 miles in Orange County to Carbon Canyon 2.5 miles north-northeast of Yorba Linda (lat. 33° 55'25" N, long. 117°48' W; at W line sec. 11, T 3 S, R 9 W). Named on Yorba Linda (1950) 7.5' quadrangle. Called Clapp Canon on Watts' (1898-1899) map.

Sorrento [SAN DIEGO]: *locality,* 4.5 miles south-southeast of Del Mar along Atchison, Topeka and Santa Fe Railroad (lat. 32°54'05" N, long. 117°13'20" W). Named on Del Mar (1967) 7.5' quadrangle. Officials of San Diego Town and Land Company named the place in 1887 for the Italian city (Stein, p. 129). Del Mar (1953) 7.5' quadrangle shows Sorrento P.O. situated in Soledad Canyon 1.25 miles southeast of present Sorrento, and California Mining Bureau's (1917b) map has the designation "Hill (Sorrento)" for the same place. Postal authorities established Sorrento post office in 1888, discontinued it in 1904, reestablished it in 1927, and discontinued it in 1959 (Salley, p. 208). They established Hill post office 5 miles southeast of Del Mar in 1909, and moved it and changed the name to Sorrento in 1927 (Salley, p. 97). California Mining Bureau's (1917b) map shows a place called Reba located along the railroad 4 miles south-southeast of Del Mar and 1.5 miles north-northeast of Hill.

Sorrento Canyon: see **Soledad Canyon** [SAN DIEGO].

Soto Street Junction [LOS ANGELES]: *locality,* nearly 3 miles south-southeast of Los Angeles city hall along Union Pacific Railroad (lat. 34°01'05" N, long. 118°13'05" W). Named on Los Angeles (1966) 7.5' quadrangle. Lankershim Ranch Land and Water Company's (1888) map shows a place called De Soto Heights located just east of downtown Los Angeles near present Soto Street Junction.

Sourdough Spring [SAN DIEGO]: *spring,* 5.25 miles east-northeast of Boucher Hill (lat. 33°21'55" N, long. 116°49'50" W; sec. 25, T 9 S, R 1 E). Named on Palomar Observatory (1949) 7.5' quadrangle.

South Anaheim [ORANGE]: *locality,* 7 miles southeast of Buena Park civic center along Southern Pacific Railroad (lat. 33°48'30" N, long. 117°54' W; sec. 23, T 4 S, R 10 W). Named on Anaheim (1965) 7.5' quadrangle. Called Tustin Junction on Anaheim (1950) 7.5' quadrangle

South Chollas Valley [SAN DIEGO]: *canyon,* drained by a stream that flows 6 miles to Chollas Creek 1.5 miles northwest of National City civic center (lat. 32°41'30" N, long. 117°07'20" W). Named on National City (1967) 7.5' quadrangle. Called South Las Choyas Valley on San Diego (1904) 15' quadrangle.

South Clearwatrer: see **Paramount** [LOS ANGELES].

South Cove [SAN DIEGO]: *embayment,* nearly 6 miles south-southeast of Point La Jolla off Mission Bay on the south side of Vacation Isle (lat. 32°46'20" N, long. 117°14'10" W). Named on La Jolla (1967) 7.5' quadrangle. Called Atlantic Cove on La Jolla (1953) 7.5' quadrangle.

South El Monte [LOS ANGELES]: *town,* 2 miles southwest of El Monte city hall (lat. 34°03'10" N, long. 118°03'15" W). Named on El Monte (1966) 7.5' quadrangle. Postal authorities established South El Monte post office in 1958 (Salley, p. 208), and the town incorporated the same year.

South Fork Campground [LOS ANGELES]: *locality,* 4 miles south-southeast of Valyermo (lat. 34°23'40" N, long. 117°49'10" W; near NE cor. sec. 33, T 4 N, R 9 W); the place is along South Fork Big Rock Creek. Named on Valyermo (1958) 7.5' quadrangle.

South Gable Promontory: see **Mount Harvard** [LOS ANGELES].

South Gate [LOS ANGELES]: *city,* 12 miles north of Long Beach city hall (lat. 33°57'20" N, long. 118°12'15" W). Named on South Gate (1952) 7.5' quadrangle. Postal authorities established South Gate post office in 1923 (Salley, p. 209), and the city incorporated the same year. The place was named in 1918 from South Gate Gardens of Cudahy ranch, opened to the public in 1917 (Gudde, 1949, p. 340).

South Hills [LOS ANGELES]: *range*, 7 miles northwest of Pomona city hall (lat. 34°07'15" N, long. 117°50'45" W). Named on Glendora (1953) and San Dimas (1954) 7.5' quadrangles.

South Laguna [ORANGE]: *town*, 4.5 miles west of San Juan Capistrano (lat. 33°30' N, long. 117°44'30" W); the place is southeast of Laguna Beach along the coast. Named on Dana Point (1968) and San Juan Capistrano (1968) 7.5' quadrangles. Postal authorities established Three Arches post office in 1933 and changed the name to South Laguna in 1934 (Frickstad, p. 118). The Whiting Company and Blanch L. Dolph started a subdivision at the place in 1927 (Meadows, p. 134).

South Las Choyas Valley: see **South Chollas Valley** [SAN DIEGO].

South Long Canyon [LOS ANGELES]: *canyon*, drained by a stream that flows 2 miles to lowlands 5.5 miles northeast of Burnt Peak (lat. 34°44' N, long. 118°30'15" W; sec. 31, T 8 N, R 15 W); the canyon is less than 1 mile south of North Long Canyon. Named on Burnt Peak (1958) 7.5' quadrangle.

South Los Angeles [LOS ANGELES]:

(1) *district*, 3.5 miles south-southwest of present Los Angeles city hall (lat. 34°00'10" N, long. 118°15'20" W). Named on Santa Monica (1902) 15' quadrangle. Postal authorities established South Los Angeles post office in 1891 and discontinued it in 1897 (Frickstad, p. 81).

(2) *locality*, 5 miles east-southeast of Inglewood city hall along Southern Pacific Railroad (lat. 33°55'40" N, long. 118°16'35" W). Named on Inglewood (1964, photorevised 1981) 7.5' quadrangle.

South Mesa [SAN DIEGO]: *area*, 6 miles north-northeast of Sweeney Pass (lat. 32°54'45" N, long. 116°08'15" W); the feature is south of East Mesa (2). Named on Arroyo Tapiado (1959) and Carrizo Mountain NE (1957) 7.5' quadrangles.

South Mountain [VENTURA]: *ridge*, generally southwest-trending, 9.5 miles long, center 2.25 miles south of Santa Paula (lat. 34°19'15" N, long. 119°03'30" W). Named on Moorpark (1951) and Santa Paula (1951) 7.5' quadrangles.

South Mount Hawkins [LOS ANGELES]: *peak*, 2 miles east-southeast of Crystal Lake (lat. 34°18'40" N, long. 117°48'35" W); the peak is 2 miles south of Mount Hawkins. Altitude 7783 feet. Named on Crystal Lake (1958) 7.5' quadrangle.

South Oceanside [SAN DIEGO]: *district*, 1.5 miles southeast of downtown Oceanside (lat. 33°10'45" N, long. 117°21'30" W). Named on San Luis Rey (1968) 7.5' quadrangle. Postal authorities established South Oceanside post office in 1888 and discontinued it in 1889 (Frickstad, p. 157).

South Park [SAN DIEGO]: *district*, 2 miles east of downtown San Diego (lat. 33°43'20" N, long. 117°07'45" W). Named on Point Loma (1967) 7.5' quadrangle.

South Pasadena [LOS ANGELES]: *city*, 7 miles northeast of Los Angeles city hall (lat. 34°06'55" N, long. 118°09'05" W); the city is south of Pasadena. Named on Los Angeles (1953) 7.5' quadrangle. Postal authorities established Hermosa post office in 1882 and changed the name to South Pasadena in 1884 (Salley, p. 96). The city incorporated in 1888. The name "Hermosa" was from Hermosa Vista Hotel, where Hermosa post office was located (Hanna, p. 312).

South Portal: see **South Portal Canyon** [LOS ANGELES].

South Portal Campground [LOS ANGELES]: *locality*, 3.5 miles south of the village of Lake Hughes (lat. 34°37'20" N, long. 118° 26'30" W); the place is in South Portal Canyon. Named on Green Valley (1958) 7.5' quadrangle.

South Portal Canyon [LOS ANGELES]: *canyon*, drained by a stream that flows 3.5 miles to San Francisquito Canyon 4.5 miles south of the village of Lake Hughes (lat. 34°36'35" N, long. 118°26'15" W). Named on Green Valley (1958) and Lake Hughes (1957) 7.5' quadrangles. Called Bear Canyon on Elizabeth Lake (1917) 30' quadrangle. Johnson'a (1911) map shows an inhabited place called South Portal situated in the canyon near the south end of a tunnel along the aqueduct that brings Owens Valley water from Inyo County to Los Angeles.

South Rim [SAN DIEGO]: *relief feature*, 6.25 miles east-southeast of Imperial Beach civic center at the southwest end of Otay Mesa (lat. 32°32'55" N, long. 117°00'50" W; sec. 5, 6, T 19 S, R 1 W). Named on Imperial Beach (1967) 7.5' quadrangle.

South San Diego [SAN DIEGO]: *district*, 1.25 miles east-northeast of Imperial Beach civic center in San Diego (lat. 32°34'50" N, long. 117°05'45" W). Named on Imperial Beach (1967) 7.5' quadrangle. Called Palm City on San Ysidro (1953) 7.5' quadrangle.

South San Diego: see **Imperial Beach** [SAN DIEGO]; **San Diego** [SAN DIEGO].

South San Gabriel [LOS ANGELES]: *town*, 4 miles west of El Monte city hall (lat. 34°03'45" N, long. 118°05'55" W); the town is south of San Gabriel. Named on El Monte (1953) 7.5' quadrangle, which gives the alternate name "Garvey" for the place. Postal authorities established Garvey Avenue post office in 1925, changed the name to Gavey in 1930, and discontinued it in 1952 (Salley, p. 83). They established South San Gabriel post office in 1938, discontinued it in 1948, and reestablished it in 1949 (Salley, p. 209). The name "Garvey" commemorates Richard Garvey, who started a subdivision of small farms and homesites at present South San Gabriel (Hanna, p. 118).

South San Jose Creek [LOS ANGELES]: *stream*, flows 2.5 miles to San Jose Creek nearly 5 miles west-southwest of Pomona city hall (lat. 34°01'40" N, long. 117°49'45" W). Named on San Dimas (1966) 7.5' quadrangle. Called San Jose Creek on San Dimas (1954) 7.5' quadrangle, but United States Board on Geographic Names (1967b, p. 5) rejected this name.

South Santa Ana [ORANGE]: *locality*, 2.5 miles south of Santa Ana city hall along Southern Pacific Railroad (lat. 33°42'40" N, long. 117°52'05" W). Named on Tustin (1965) 7.5' quadrangle.

South Santa Monica [LOS ANGELES]: *locality*, 8.5 miles north-northwest of present Manhattan Beach city hall along Atchison, Topeka and Santa Fe Railroad (lat. 34°00' N, long. 118°29' W). Named on Redondo (1896) 15' quadrangle.

South Tapo Canyon: see **Tapo Canyon** [VENTURA] (1).

South Tule Canyon [LOS ANGELES]: *canyon*, drained by a stream that flows 2.5 miles to Tule Canyon 4.5 miles east-northeast of Warm Springs Mountain (lat. 34°36'40" N, long. 118°30'05" W). Named on Green Valley (1958) and Warm Springs Mountain (1958) 7.5' quadrangles.

South Vista [SAN DIEGO]: *district*, 0.5 mile southeast of downtown Vista (lat. 33°11'45" N, long. 117°14'15" W). Named on San Marcos (1949) 7.5' quadrangle.

Southwest Village [LOS ANGELES]: *locality*, nearly 2 miles east-northeast of Torrance city hall (lat. 33°50'45" N, long. 118°18'35" W). Named on Torrance (1964) 7.5' quadrangle.

South Whittier [LOS ANGELES]: *district*, 1 mile south-southwest of present Whittier city hall (lat. 33°57'35" N, long. 118°02'30" W). Named on Whittier (1949) 7.5' quadrangle. Postal authorities established South Whittier post office in 1964 (Salley, p. 209).

South Whittier Heights [LOS ANGELES]: *district*, 3.5 miles south of present Whittier city hall (lat. 33°55'15" N, long. 118°01'30" W). Named on Whittier (1949) 7.5' quadrangle.

Spade Canyon [LOS ANGELES]: *canyon*, drained by a stream that flows 2.5 miles to Rowher Canyon 8 miles south-southwest of the village of Leona Valley (lat. 34°31' N, long. 118°21'45" W; near E line sec. 17, T 5 N, R 14 W). Named on Sleepy Valley (1958) 7.5' quadrangle. On Los Angeles County (1935) map, the name "Spade Canyon" applies to present Spade Spring Canyon.

Spade Spring Canyon [LOS ANGELES]: *canyon*, drained by a stream that flows 4.5 miles to Mint Canyon 8 miles south-southwest of the village of Leona Valley (lat. 34°30'40" N, long. 118°21'25" W; at S line sec. 16, T 5 N, R 14 W). Named on Sleepy Valley (1958) 7.5' quadrangle. Called Spring Canyon on Bouquet Reservoir (1937) 6' quadrangle, but United States Board on Geographic Names (1959, p. 7) rejected this name for the feature. Called Spade Canyon on Los Angeles County (1935) map.

Spadra [LOS ANGELES]:

(1) *locality*, 3.25 miles west of Pomona city hall along Southern Pacific Railroad (lat. 34°03'05" N, long. 117°48'30" W). Named on San Dimas (1954) 7.5' quadrangle. Postal authorities established Spadra post office in 1868, discontinued it for a time in 1875, and discontinued it finally in 1955 (Salley, p. 210). Billy Rubotton built a tavern at the place in 1866 and applied for a post office named from his former home at Spadra Bluff, Arkansas (Anonymous, 1976, p. 13-14). The railroad station at the place took the name in 1874 (Gudde, 1949, p. 340).

(2) *locality*, nearly 3 miles west of Pomona city hall along Union Pacific Railroad (lat. 34°03'10" N, long. 117°48' W). Named on San Dimas (1966) 7.5' quadrangle.

Spangler Peak [SAN DIEGO]: *peak*, 3.25 miles south-southeast of Ramona (lat. 33°00'20" N, long. 116°50' W; sec. 36, T 13 S, R 1 E). Altitude 1984 feet. Named on Ramona (1955) 7.5' quadrangle.

Spanish Bight [SAN DIEGO]: *embayment*, 2 miles southwest of downtown San Diego off San Diego Bay between North Island and Coronado (lat. 32°42' N, long. 117°11'30" W). Named on Point Loma (1942) 7.5' quadrangle.

Spanish Canyon [LOS ANGELES]: *canyon*, drained by a stream that flows 2 miles to Sawpit Canyon 5.5 miles west-northwest of Azusa city hall (lat. 34°10'05" N, long. 117°59'25" W; sec. 13, T 1 N, R 11 W). Named on Azusa (1953) 7.5' quadrangle.

Spanishtown [LOS ANGELES]: *locality*, 2.25 miles north-northwest of present South Gate city hall (lat. 33°59'30" N, long. 118°14'20" W). Named on Downey (1902) 15' quadrangle.

Sparr Heights [LOS ANGELES]: *locality*, 5.5 miles northwest of Pasadena city hall (lat. 34°11'45" N, long. 118°13'30" W). Named on Glendale (1928) 6' quadrangle.

Spencer Canyon [LOS ANGELES]: *canyon*, 2.5 miles long, opens into lowlands 15 miles east of Gorman (lat. 34°45'35" N, long. 118°34'30" W; at N line sec. 28, T 8 N, R 16 W). Named on Burnt Peak (1958) and Neenach School (1965) 7.5' quadrangles. Manzana (1938) 6' quadrangle shows Spencer ranch in the canyon.

Spencer Valley [SAN DIEGO]: *valley*, 2 miles east-southeast of Santa Ysabel (lat. 33°05'45" N, long. 116°38'30" W; sec. 26, 35, T 12 S, R 3 E). Named on Santa Ysabel (1960) 7.5' quadrangle.

Spinks Canyon [LOS ANGELES]: *canyon*, drained by a stream that flows 1.25 miles to Scott Canyon 3.5 miles west-northwest of Azusa city hall (lat. 34°08'55" N, long. 117°57'45" W). Named on Azusa (1953) 7.5' quadrangle.

Split Mountain [SAN DIEGO]: *ridge*, generally west-trending, 1.5 miles long, 12 miles north-northeast of Sweeney Pass (lat. 32°59'55" N, long. 116°07' W); the canyon of Fish Creek Wash divides the ridge. Named on Borrego Mountain SE (1958) and Carrizo Mountain NE (1957) 7.5' quadrangles.

Split Rock [SAN DIEGO]: *relief feature*, 11 miles southwest of Ocotillo Wells (lat. 33°02'40" N, long. 116°16'20" W). Named on Whale Peak (1959) 7.5' quadrangle.

Spooners Mesa [SAN DIEGO]: *relief feature*, 2.5 miles south-southeast of Imperial Beach civic center at the Mexican boundary (lat. 32°32'25" N, long. 117°05'35" W; sec. 4, 9, T 19 S, R 2 W). Named on Imperial Beach (1967) 7.5' quadrangle.

Spouting Caves [LOS ANGELES]: *caves*, 5.5 miles north-northwest of Mount Banning along the north side of Santa Catalina Island (lat. 33°26'40" N, long. 118°28'30" W). Named on Santa Catalina North (1950) 7.5' quadrangle.

Spring: see **Spring Valley** [SAN DIEGO] (2).

Spring Camp [LOS ANGELES]: *locality*, 7 miles northwest of Azusa city hall (lat. 34°12'50" N, long. 117°58'40" W; at E line sec. 36, T 2 N, R 11 W). Named on Azusa (1953) 7.5' quadrangle. The camp, which appears to date from the early 1900's, is named from an ever-flowing spring there (Owens, p. 53).

Spring Canyon [LOS ANGELES]:
(1) *canyon*, drained by a stream that flows 1 mile to Kings Canyon 3.5 miles northeast of Burnt Peak (lat. 34°43'05" N, long. 118°31'55" W; sec. 12, T 7 N, R 16 W). Named on Burnt Peak (1958) 7.5' quadrangle.
(2) *canyon*, drained by a stream that flows 2.5 miles to Tapie Canyon 4.5 miles east-northeast of Solemint (lat. 34°26'10" N, long. 118°22'35" W; near NW cor. sec. 17, T 4 N, R 14 W). Named on Agua Dulce (1960) 7.5' quadrangle.
(3) *canyon*, less than 0.5 mile long, about 3 miles east of Glendora city hall (lat. 34°07'50" N, long. 117°48'45" W; sec. 34, T 1 N, R 9 W). Named on Glendora (1953) 7.5' quadrangle.
(4) *canyon*, 0.5 mile long, 3.5 miles south-southeast of Burbank city hall (lat. 34°07'55" N, long. 118°17'35" W). Named on Burbank (1953) 7.5' quadrangle.

Spring Canyon [ORANGE]: *canyon*, drained by a stream that flows 0.5 mile to Williams Canyon 7.5 miles north-northeast of El Toro (lat. 33°43'45" N, long. 117°38'40" W; at S line sec. 18, T 5 S, R 7 W). Named on El Toro (1968) 7.5' quadrangle.

Spring Canyon [SAN DIEGO]:
(1) *canyon*, 1.25 miles long, opens into Skye Valley 7.5 miles west-northwest of Morena Village (lat. 32°43'35" N, long. 116°37'15" W; near NW cor. sec. 6, T 17 S, R 4 E). Named on Morena Reservoir (1960) 7.5' quadrangle.
(2) *canyon*, drained by a stream that flows 2.5 miles to Mexico 6.25 miles east-southeast of Imperial Beach civic center (lat. 32°32'35" N, long. 117°00'50" W; at E line sec. 6, T 19 S, R 1 W). Named on Imperial Beach (1967) and Otay Mesa (1955) 7.5' quadrangles.
(3) *canyon*, drained by a stream that flows 3.5 miles to the canyon of San Diego River 5.5 miles north of La Mesa (lat. 32°50'45" N, long. 117°02'10" W). Named on La Mesa (1967) and Poway (1967) 7.5' quadrangles.

Spring Canyon: see **Spade Spring Canyon** [LOS ANGELES]; **Spring Creek** [LOS ANGELES].

Spring Canyon Creek [VENTURA]: *stream*, flows 2.5 miles to Tar Creek 6.5 miles north of Fillmore (lat. 34°29'40" N, long. 118°53'40" W; near N line sec. 29, T 5 N, R 19 W). Named on Devils Heart Peak (1943) and Fillmore (1951) 7.5' quadrangles. Called North Fork Tar Cr. on Tejon (1903) 30' quadrangle, but United States Board on Geographic Names (1990, p. 11) rejected this name for the feature.

Spring Creek [LOS ANGELES]: *stream*, flows nearly 2 miles to Pacoima Canyon 7.25 miles north of Sunland (lat. 34°21'55" N, long. 118°18'30" W; at NE cor. sec. 11, T 3 N, R 14 W). Named on Agua Dulce (1960) and Sunland (1953) 7.5' quadrangles. The canyon of the stream is called Spring Canyon on Los Angeles County (1935) map.

Spring Hill [LOS ANGELES]: *relief feature*, nearly 12 miles north-northeast of Pomona city hall (lat. 34°12'35" N, long. 117°40'05" W; sec. 36, T 2 N, R 8 W). Named on Mount Baldy (1954) 7.5' quadrangle.

Spring Landing [LOS ANGELES]: *locality*, nearly 1 mile southwest of Silver Peak on the south side of Santa Catalina Island (lat. 33° 27'05" N, long. 118°34'50" W). Named on Santa Catalina West (1943) 7.5' quadrangle.

Springs: see **Sulphur Springs** [VENTURA].

Springs Canyon: see **Little Springs Canyon** [LOS ANGELES].

Spring Valley [SAN DIEGO]:
(1) *valley*, 6.5 miles northeast of National City civic center (lat. 32° 43'30" N, long. 117°00'45" W). Named on National City (1967) 7.5' quadrangle.
(2) *city*, 1.25 miles southeast of downtown La Mesa (lat. 32°45'10" N, long. 117°00'40" W); the city is at the north end of Spring Valley (1). Named on El Cajon (1967), Jamul Mountains (1955), La Mesa (1967), and National City (1967) 7.5' quadrangles. Postal authorities established Spring Valley post office in 1909 (Frickstad, p. 157). California Mining Bureau's (1917b) map shows a place called Spring located along the railroad in the present city of Spring Valley.

Springville [VENTURA]: *locality*, 3.25 miles west of downtown Camarillo (lat. 34°13'15" N, long. 119°05'25" W). Named on Camarillo (1950) 7.5' quadrangle. Postal authorities established Springville post office in 1875 and discontinued it in 1903 (Frickstad, p. 219).

Spruce Canyon [LOS ANGELES]: *canyon*, drained by a stream that flows 1.25 miles to San Antonio Canyon 10 miles north-northeast of Pomona city hall (lat. 34°11'15" N, long. 117°40'30" W; sec. 12, T 1 N, R 8 W). Named on Mount Baldy (1954) 7.5' quadrangle.

Spruce Canyon [ORANGE]: *canyon*, drained by a stream that flows less than 1 mile to Silverado Canyon 4.25 miles southeast of Pleasants Peak (lat. 33°45'05" N, long. 117°33'05" W. Named on Corona South (1967) and Santiago Peak (1954) 7.5' quadrangles.

Spruce Draw [LOS ANGELES]: *canyon*, drained by a stream that flows 0.5 mile to South Portal Canyon 2.5 miles southeast of the village of Lake Hughes (lat. 34°38'50" N, long. 118°25'05" W; near S line sec. 36, T 7 N, R 15 W). Named on Lake Hughes (1957) 7.5' quadrangle.

Spruce Grove Campground [LOS ANGELES]: *locality*, nearly 2 miles east of Mount Wilson (1) in Santa Anita Canyon (lat. 34°13'15" N, long. 118°01'45" W; near NW cor. sec. 34, T 2 N, R 11 W). Named on Mount Wilson (1966) 7.5' quadrangle.

Spunky Canyon [LOS ANGELES]: *canyon*, drained by a stream that flows nearly 3 miles to Bouquet Reservoir 6.5 miles south-southeast of the village of Lake Hughes (lat. 34°35'35" N, long. 118°22'55" W; sec. 20, T 6 N, R 14 W). Named on Green Valley (1958) and Sleepy Valley (1958) 7.5' quadrangles.

Spunky Canyon Campground [LOS ANGELES]: *locality*, 5.25 miles south-southeast of the village of Lake Hughes (lat. 34°36'35" N, long. 118°23'25" W; near W line sec. 17, T 6 N, R 14 W); the place is nearly 1 mile northwest of Spunky Canyon. Named on Green Valley (1958) 7.5' quadrangle.

Spur Meadow [SAN DIEGO]: *area*, 6 miles northwest of Morena Village (lat. 32°43'45" N, long. 116°35'15" W; near NW cor. sec. 4, T 17 S, R 4 E). Named on Morena Reservoir (1960) 7.5' quadrangle.

Square Top: see **Mount Markham** [LOS ANGELES].

Squatters Country: see **Fountain Valley** [ORANGE].

Squaw Camp: see **Camp Singing Pines** [LOS ANGELES].

Squaw Canyon [LOS ANGELES]: *canyon*, drained by a stream that flows 3.5 miles to South Fork Little Rock Creek 8.5 miles southwest of Valyermo (lat. 34°22'35" N, long. 117°58'25" W; near W line sec. 6, T 3 N, R 10 W). Named on Juniper Hills (1959) and Waterman Mountain (1959) 7.5' quadrangles.

Squaw Canyon [SAN DIEGO]: *canyon*, 1.5 miles long, 1 mile west of Agua Caliente Springs (lat. 32°56'55" N, long. 116°19'05" W). Named on Agua Caliente Springs (1959) 7.5' quadrangle.

Squaw Flat [VENTURA]: *area*, 4.5 miles east of Devils Heart Peak (lat. 34°32'20" N, long. 118°53'45" W). Named on Devils Heart Peak (1943) 7.5' quadrangle.

Squaw Peak [SAN DIEGO]: *peak*, 1.5 miles north-northeast of Ocotillo Wells (lat. 33°10'40" N, long. 116°06'55" W). Named on Shell Reef (1959) 7.5' quadrangle.

Squaw Spring [VENTURA]: *spring*, 4.5 miles east of Devils Heart Peak (lat. 34°32'10" N, long. 118°53'50" W); the spring is at Squaw Flat. Named on Devils Heart Peak (1943) 7.5' quadrangle.

Squaw Tit [SAN DIEGO]: *peak*, nearly 4 miles northeast of Jacumba on Table Mountain (lat. 32°39' N, long. 116°08'15" W; near W line sec. 35, T 17 S, R 8 E). Named on Jacumba (1959) 7.5' quadrangle.

Squirrel Inn [LOS ANGELES]: *locality*, 2 miles south-southeast of Crystal Lake along North Fork San Gabriel River (lat. 34°17'30" N, long. 117°50'30" W; near N line sec. 5, T 2 N, R 9 W). Named on Rock Creek (1903) 15' quadrangle.

Stag Cove [SAN DIEGO]: *relief feature*, 8.5 miles south of Borrego Springs (lat. 33°07'55" N, long. 116°22' W). Named on Borrego (1959) 15' quadrangle.

Stanton [ORANGE]: *town*, 4 miles south of Buena Park civic center (lat. 33°48'10" N, long. 117°59'45" W). Named on Anaheim (1965) and Los Alamitos (1964) 7.5' quadrangles. Postal authorities established Stanton post office in 1912 and discontinued it for a time in 1921 (Frickstad, p. 118). The town incorporated in 1956. California Mining Bureau's (1909b) map shows a place called Benedict at the site. The crossing of Pacific Electric Railroad and Southern Pacific Railroad at the place was called Benedict; Philip A Stanon laid out a subdivision called Benedict there in 1905, and later the community of Stanton was named for him (Meadows,

p. 26, 131). A flag stop along Pacific Electric Railroad called Vignola was situated less than 1 mile east-southeast of present Stanton city hall (Meadows, p. 137).

Star Bay [LOS ANGELES]: *embayment*, 1.25 miles west of Silver Peak on the south side of Santa Catalina Island (lat. 33°27'40" N, long. 118°35'20" W). Named on Santa Catalina West (1943) 7.5' quadrangle.

Starvation Mountain [SAN DIEGO]: *peak*, 3.25 miles southwest of San Pasqual (lat. 33°03'10" N, long. 116°59'15" W; near S line sec. 9, T 13 S, R 1 W). Altitude 2140 feet. Named on San Pasqual (1954) 7.5' quadrangle.

Stauffer [VENTURA]: *locality*, 15 miles northeast of Reyes Peak in Lockwood Valley (lat. 34°45'15" N, long. 119°03'55" W; on E line sec. 26, T 8 N, R 21 W). Named on Cuddy Valley (1943) 7.5' quadrangle. Postal authorities established Stauffer post office in 1905, discontinued it in 1933, reestablished it in 1937, and discontinued it in 1942 (Frickstad, p. 219). The name was for John Stauffer, who with Thomas Thorkildsen formed Frazier Borate Company and had the company camp and store at the place (Bailey, p. 63).

Stearn: see **Yorba Linda** [ORANGE].

Steele Canyon [SAN DIEGO]: *canyon*, drained by a stream that flows 5.25 miles to Sweetwater River 4 miles west-northwest of Jamul (lat. 32°43'55" N, long. 116°56'30" W). Named on Jamul Mountains (1955) 7.5' quadrangle.

Steep Hill Canyon [LOS ANGELES]: *canyon*, drained by a stream that flows 1.25 miles to the sea 4 miles northwest of Point Dume (lat. 34°02'10" N, long. 118°51'30" W). Named on Point Dume (1951) 7.5' quadrangle.

Steil's Camp: see **Martins Camp** [LOS ANGELES]; **Mount Harvard** [LOS ANGELES].

Steiner Canyon [LOS ANGELES]: *canyon*, drained by a stream that flows less than 1 mile to Pine Canyon (3) 3 miles west-northwest of the village of Lake Hughes (lat. 34°41'35" N, long. 118°29'30" W; sec. 17, T 7 N, R 15 W). Named on Lake Hughes (1957) 7.5' quadrangle.

Stephenson Peak [SAN DIEGO]: *peak*, 1.25 miles south-southeast of Monument Peak (lat. 32°52'35" N, long. 116°24'50" W; near E line sec. 12, T 15 S, R 5 E). Named on Monument Peak (1959) and Mount Laguna (1960) 7.5' quadrangles.

Sterling: see **Camp Sterling** [LOS ANGELES].

Stevens Campground: see **Bishop Stevens Campground** [SAN DIEGO].

Stevens Canyon: see **Halsey Canyon** [LOS ANGELES].

Stewart: see **Brea** [ORANGE].

Stewart Canyon [VENTURA]: *canyon*, drained by a stream that flows nearly 3 miles to Ojai Valley 1.25 miles north-northwest of downtown Ojai (lat. 34°27'40" N, long. 119°15'10" W; near N line sec. 2, T 4 N, R 23 W). Named on Matilija (1952) 7.5' quadrangle.

Stewart Peak: see **Sewart Mountain** [VENTURA].

Stingleys Hot Springs: see **Vickers Hot Springs** [VENTURA].

Stock Pen: see **Jofegan** [SAN DIEGO].

Stockton: see **Fort Stockton**, under **Old Town** [SAN DIEGO].

Stockton Canyon: see **Canton Canyon** [LOS ANGELES-VENTURA].

Stokes Canyon [LOS ANGELES]: *canyon*, drained by a stream that flows 4.25 miles to Las Virgenes Creek 5 miles north-northwest of Malibu Point (lat. 34°05'45" N, long. 118°43' W; sec. 12, T 1 S, R 18 W). Named on Malibu Beach (1951) 7.5' quadrangle. Los Angeles County (1935) map shows a feature called Hoagland Cany. that opens into Stokes Canyon from the north 1.5 miles northeast of the mouth of Stokes Canyon (at W line sec. 5, T 1 S, R 17 W).

Stokes Valley [SAN DIEGO]: *area*, 6.25 miles west-northwest of Morena Village (lat. 32°42'15" N, long. 116°36'25" W; sec. 7, 8, T 17 S, R 4 E). Named on Morena Reservoir (1960) 7.5' quadrangle.

Stone Cabin Flat [LOS ANGELES]: *area*, 5.5 miles north-northwest of Azusa city hall (lat. 34°12'20" N, long. 117°56'45" W; near NE cor. sec. 5, T 21 N, R 10 W). Named on Azusa (1966) 7.5' quadrangle. Azusa (1953) 7.5' quadrangle shows a feature called Stone Cabin at the site. The name is from the cabin that Hardy Harris and several school boys built in 1911 using boulders from the bed of the nearby stream (Robinson, J.W., 1983, p. 78).

Stone Canyon [LOS ANGELES]:

(1) *canyon*, drained by a stream that flows 1.25 miles to Big Tujunga Canyon 2.5 miles south-southwest of Condor Peak (lat. 34°17'35" N, long. 118°14'10" W; at W line sec. 3, T 2 N, R 13 W). Named on Condor Peak (1959) 7.5' quadrangle.

(2) *canyon*, 3 miles long, 3.5 miles west-northwest of Beverly Hills city hall (lat. 34°06' N, long. 118°27'15" W). Named on Beverly Hills (1950) 7.5' quadrangle.

Stone Canyon Reservoir [LOS ANGELES]: *lake*, nearly 1 mile long, behind a dam 4 miles northwest of Beverly Hills city hall (lat. 34° 06'15" N, long. 118°27'05" W); the lake is in Stone Canyon (2). Named on Beverly Hills (1950) 7.5' quadrangle.

Stone Canyon Reservoir: see **Upper Stone Canyon Reservoir** [LOS ANGELES].

Stone Corral Creek [VENTURA]: *stream*, flows nearly 4 miles to Sespe Creek 2 miles east-northeast of Devils Heart Peak (lat. 34° 33'25" N, long. 118°56'35" W). Named on Devils Heart Peak (1943) 7.5' quadrangle. Tejon (1903) 30' quadrangle shows a feature called Stone Corral located along upper reaches of the stream.

Stonehurst [LOS ANGELES]: *district*, 3.5 miles west-southwest of Sunland (lat. 34°15' N, long. 118°22'15" W). Named on Burbank (1953) and Sunland (1953) 7.5' quadrangles.

Stoneman [LOS ANGELES]: *locality*, 5.5 miles west-northwest of El Monte city hall along Southern Pacific Railroad (lat. 34°05'20" N, long. 118°07'15" W). Named on El Monte (1953) 7.5' quadrangle.

Stone Quarry Hills: see **Chavez Ravine** [LOS ANGELES].

Stonewall: see **Julian** [SAN DIEGO].

Stonewall Creek [SAN DIEGO]: *stream*, flows 2 miles to Green Valley (3) 3 miles east of Cuyamaca Peak (lat. 32°56'25" N, long. 116°33'05" W). Named on Cuyamaca Peak (1960) 7.5' quadrangle.

Stonewall Creek: see **Little Stonewall Creek** [SAN DIEGO].

Stonewall Peak [SAN DIEGO]: *peak*, 2.25 miles east-northeast of Cuyamaca Peak (lat. 32°57'40" N, long. 116°34'15" W). Altitude 5730 feet. Named on Cuyamaca Peak (1960) 7.5' quadrangle.

Stonewall Peak: see **Little Stonewall Peak** [SAN DIEGO].

Stone Wash [SAN DIEGO]: *stream* and *dry wash*, extends for 2.25 miles to Lycium Wash nearly 10 miles south of Ocotillo Wells (lat. 33°00'05" N, long. 116°08'45" W). Named on Harper Canyon (1959) 7.5' quadrangle.

Stony Gulch: see **Camp Hi-Hill** [LOS ANGELES].

Stony Point [LOS ANGELES]:

(1) *hill*, 1 mile north of Chatsworth (lat. 34°16'15" N, long. 118°36'10" W; near W line sec. 7, T 2 N, R 16 W). Named on Oat Mountain (1952) 7.5' quadrangle.

(2) *promontory*, 1.25 miles northeast of Silver Peak on the north side of Santa Catalina Island (lat. 33°28'30" N, long. 118°33'20" W). Named on Santa Catalina West (1943) 7.5' quadrangle.

Stony Point [SAN DIEGO]: *promontory*, 6 miles south-southeast of Point La Jolla at the southwest end of Fiesta Island (lat. 32°46'15" N, long. 117°13'45" W). Named on La Jolla (1967) 7.5' quadrangle.

Stony Point: see **Arrow Point** [LOS ANGELES].

Storm Canyon [SAN DIEGO]: *canyon*, 2.25 miles long, nearly 2 miles northwest of Monument Peak (lat. 32°54'50" N, long. 116° 26'15" W). Named on Monument Peak (1959) 7.5' quadrangle.

Story Canyon [LOS ANGELES]: *canyon*, 0.5 mile long, 1.5 miles northeast of Burbank city hall (lat. 34°11'45" N, long. 118°17'20" W). Named on Burbank (1953) 7.5' quadrangle.

Stough Canyon [LOS ANGELES]: *canyon*, 1.5 miles long, 2 miles north of Burbank city hall (lat. 34°12'30" N, long. 118°18'10" W). Named on Burbank (1953) 7.5' quadrangle.

Stowe [SAN DIEGO]: *locality*, 6 miles northwest of Lakeside in Sycamore Canyon (3) (lat. 32°55'35" N, long. 116°59'10" W; near E line sec. 28, T 14 S, R 1 W). Named on Cuyamaca (1903) 30' quadrangle. Postal authorities established Stowe post office in 1889 and discontinued it in 1905 (Frickstad, p. 157).

Strathearn [VENTURA]: *locality*, 4.5 miles east of Moorpark along Southern Pacific Railroad (lat. 34°16'50" N, long. 118°47'45" W; near SE cor. sec. 6, T 2 N, R 18 W). Named on Simi (1951) 7.5' quadrangle. The name is for the Strathearn family, owners of part of Simi grant (Ricard).

Stratton: see **Cuyamaca** [SAN DIEGO].

Strawberry Park [LOS ANGELES]: *district*, 5.25 miles southeast of Inglewood city hall (lat. 33°54' N, long. 118°18' W). Named on Inglewood (1952) 7.5' quadrangle. Redondo (1896) 15' quadrangle has the name for a place located along a railroad in or near the district.

Strawberry Peak [LOS ANGELES]: *peak*, 8.5 miles south-southwest of Pacifico Mountain (lat. 34°17' N, long. 118°07'10" W). Altitude 6164 feet. Named on Chilao Flat (1959) 7.5' quadrangle. The name, given in the 1880's, is from the shape of the peak (Robinson, J.W., 1977, p. 155).

Strayns Canyon [LOS ANGELES]: *canyon*, drained by a stream that flows 2.25 miles to West Fork San Gabriel River 1.5 miles north of Mount Wilson (lat. 34°14'55" N, long. 118°03'30" W; sec. 20, T 2 N, R 11 W). Named on Mount Wilson (1953) 7.5' quadrangle.

Stringtown: see **Bardsdale** [VENTURA].

Stuart [SAN DIEGO]: *locality*, 9 miles south-southeast of San Onofre Mountain along Atchison, Topeka and Santa Fe Railroad (lat. 33° 15'05" N, long. 117°25'10" W; near E line sec. 5, T 11 S, R 5 W). Named on Las Pulgas Canyon (1968) 7.5' quadrangle. The name, given in 1908, commemorates E.B. Stuart, an agent for the railroad (Hanna, p. 319).

Stuart Mesa [SAN DIEGO]: *area*, 4 miles north-northwest of Oceanside (lat. 33°14'55" N, long. 117°24'45" W; sec. 4, 5, T 11 S, R 5 W); the north end of the feature is near Stuart. Named on Las Pulgas Canyon (1968) and Oceanside (1968) 7.5' quadrangles.

Stuart Spring [SAN DIEGO]: *spring*, 6 miles east-southeast of San Felipe (lat. 33°09'45" N, long. 116°30'20" W). Named on Ranchita (1960) 7.5' quadrangle. The feature also was called Sumac Spring (Brown, 1923, p. 223).

Studebaker [LOS ANGELES]: *locality*, 5.5 miles southwest of present

Whittier city hall (lat. 33°55'25" N, long. 118°06'20" W). Named on Whittier (1949) 7.5' quadrangle. On Downey (1902) 15' quadrangle, the name refers to a place along Southern Pacific Railroad.

Studio City [LOS ANGELES]: *district*, 4 miles southeast of the center of Van Nuys in Los Angeles (lat. 34°08'50" N, long. 118°23'45" W). Named on Van Nuys (1953) 7.5' quadrangle. Postal authorities established Studio City post office in 1928; the name is from Republic movie studio (Salley, p. 214).

Sturtevant Camp [LOS ANGELES]: *locality*, 1.5 miles east of Mount Wilson (1) in Santa Anita Canyon (lat. 34°13'20" N, long. 118°02'05" W; near N line sec. 33, T 2 N, R 11 W). Named on Mount Wilson (1953) 7.5' quadrangle. The name commemorates William M. Sturtevant, who opened the resort in 1893; the Methodist Church bought the place in 1945 and operated it as a religious retreat called Camp Sturtevant (Robinson, J.W., 1977, p. 119, 125).

Sturtevant Falls [LOS ANGELES]: *waterfall*, 2.5 miles east-southeast of Mount Wilson (1) in Santa Anita Canyon (lat. 34°12'40" N, long. 118°01'05" W; sec. 34, T 2 N, R 11 W). Named on Mount Wilson (1953) 7.5' quadrangle. The feature first was called Santa Anita Falls (Owens, p. 1).

Sucrosa [VENTURA]: *locality*, 2.5 miles west-southwest of Camarillo along Southern Pacific Railroad (lat. 34°11'40" N, long. 119° 04'20" W). Named on Hueneme (1904) 15' quadrangle.

Sugar: see **Smeltzer** [ORANGE].

Sugarloaf [LOS ANGELES]: *peak*, nearly 4 miles east-northeast of downtown San Fernando (lat. 34°18'40" N, long. 118°23' W; sec. 30, T 3 N, R 14 W). Named on San Fernando (1966) 7.5' quadrangle.

Sugarloaf [ORANGE]: *peak*, 5.25 miles south of Trabuco Peak (lat. 33°37'35" N, long. 117°28'50" W; near W line sec. 23, T 6 S, R 6 W). Altitude 3227 feet. Named on Alberhill (1954) 7.5' quadrangle.

Sugarloaf Peak: see **Pleasants Peak** [ORANGE].

Sugarloaf Point [ORANGE]: *promontory*, 2 miles south-southeast of Laguna Beach city hall along the coast (lat. 33°31'10" N, long. 117°45'45" W; on E line sec. 36, T 7 S, R 9 W). Named on Laguna Beach (1965) 7.5' quadrangle.

Sugarloaf Point: see **Casino Point** [LOS ANGELES].

Sullivan Canyon [LOS ANGELES]: *canyon*, drained by a stream that flows 5.25 miles to Santa Monica Canyon 5.5 miles west of Beverly Hills city hall (lat. 34°03'40" N, long. 118°29'40" W). Named on Beverly Hills (1950), Canoga Park (1952), and Topanga (1952) 7.5' quadrangles.

Sullivans Beach [LOS ANGELES]: *beach*, 2.5 miles east of Silver Peak on the north side of Santa Catalina Island (lat. 33°27'40" N, long. 118°31'15" W). Named on Santa Catalina West (1943) 7.5' quadrangle.

Sulphur Canyon [LOS ANGELES]: *canyon*, drained by a stream that flows 2 miles to Las Llajas Canyon [LOS ANGELES-VENTURA] 7.5 miles west-southwest of Newhall (lat. 34°19'40" N, long. 118°38'20" W). Named on Oat Mountain (1952) and Santa Susana (1951) 7.5' quadrangles

Sulphur Canyon [VENTURA]: *canyon*, drained by a stream that flows 3 miles to Cañada Larga 8 miles northwest of Saticoy (lat. 34°22'05" N, long. 119°14'15" W); the canyon heads on Sulphur Mountain (1). Named on Ojai (1952) and Saticoy (1951) 7.5' quadrangles.

Sulphur Canyon: see **Balcom Canyon** [VENTURA].

Sulphur Creek [ORANGE]: *stream*, flows 4.5 miles to Aliso Creek 4.5 miles northwest of San Juan Capistrano (lat. 33°33' N, long. 117°43'05" W). Named on San Juan Capistrano (1968) 7.5' quadrangle. Santiago Peak (1943) 15' quadrangle has the name "Arroyo Salada" for the canyon of the upper part of the stream, and Corona (1902) 30' quadrangle has the name "Canada Salada" for it.

Sulphur Creek [VENTURA]:
(1) *stream*, flows 3 miles to Agua Blanca Creek 4.5 miles southeast of Cobblestone Mountain (lat. 34°33'05" N, long. 118°49'25" W). Named on Cobblestone Mountain (1958) 7.5' quadrangle.
(2) *stream*, flows 1 mile to Rincon Creek 5 miles south-southwest of White Ledge Peak (lat. 34°24'35" N, long. 119°26'40" W; sec. 24, T 4 N, R 25 W). Named on White Ledge Peak (1952) 7.5' quadrangle.

Sulphur Creek Reservoir [ORANGE]: *lake*, 0.5 mile long, behind a dam 4.25 miles northwest of San Juan Capistrano (lat. 33°33' N, long. 117°42'25" W); the lake is along Sulphur Creek. Named on San Juan Capistrano (1968) 7.5' quadrangle.

Sulphur Mountain [VENTURA]:
(1) *ridge*, generally west-trending, 13 miles long, extends from Santa Paula Creek to Ventura River, mainly south of Ojai Valley and Upper Ojai Valley (center near lat. 34°24'45" N, long. 119°11'30" W). Named on Matilija (1952), Ojai (1952), and Santa Paula Peak (1951) 7.5' quadrangles. Goodyear (1888a, p. 109) noted that the feature "is well named on account of the numerous sulphur springs on all sides of it."
(2) *peak*, 3.5 miles west of Piru (lat. 34°25' N, long. 118°51'15" W; sec. 22, T 4 N, R 19 W). Altitude 2130 feet. Named on Piru (1952) 7.5' quadrangle.

Sulphur Mountain Spring: see **Sulphur Springs** [VENTURA].

Sulphur Peak [VENTURA]: *peak*, 3.5 miles east-southeast of Devils Heart Peak (lat. 34°31'05" N, long. 118°55'30" W). Altitude 4528 feet. Named on Devils Heart Peak (1943) 7.5' quadrangle.

Sulphur Ravine: see **Chavez Ravine** [LOS ANGELES].

Sulphur Spring [LOS ANGELES]: *spring*, 3.5 miles northwest of Waterman Mountain (lat. 34°22' N, long. 117°59'10" W; near N line sec. 12, T 3 N, R 11 W). Named on Waterman Mountain (1959) 7.5' quadrangle. Los Angeles County (1935) map has the plural form "Sulphur Springs" for the name.

Sulphur Spring [VENTURA]: *spring*, 2 miles northeast of Ojai (lat. 34°28'10" N, long. 119°13'15" W; sec. 31, T 5 N, R 22 W). Named on Santa Paula (1903) 15' quadrangle.

Sulphur Spring Canyon [VENTURA]: *canyon*, drained by a stream that flows 5 miles to Dry Canyon (2) 4.5 miles north of Reyes Peak (lat. 34°41'45" N, long. 119°17'10" W). Named on Apache Canyon (1943) and Reyes Peak (1943) 7.5' quadrangles.

Sulphur Springs [LOS ANGELES]: *locality*, 8 miles northwest of Newhall (lat. 34°28'40" N, long. 118°36'50" W; sec. 36, T 5 N, R 17 W). Named on Newhall (1952) 7.5' quadrangle. Castaic (1940) 6' quadrangle shows a place called Foothill Sta. near the site.

Sulphur Springs [VENTURA]: *locality*, 5 miles west of Santa Paula Peak along Sisar Creek (lat. 34°25'40" N, long. 119°05'40" W). Named on Santa Paula Peak (1951) 7.5' quadrangle. Santa Paula (1903) 15' quadrangle has the name "Sulphur Mt. Spring" for a spring at or near the place. Postal authorities established Springs post office at the site in 1909 and discontinued it in 1912 (Salley, p. 210). Crawford (p. 524) called the place Santa Paula Sulphur Springs, and Waring (p. 279) called it Sulphur Mountain Springs.

Sulphur Wells: see **Santa Fe Springs** [LOS ANGELES].

Sumac: see **San Marcos** [SAN DIEGO].

Sumac Spring: see **Stuart Spring** [SAN DIEGO].

Summit [LOS ANGELES]: *locality*, 8.5 miles west-southwest of Palmdale (lat. 34°31'20" N, long. 118°14'45" W; sec. 16, T 5 N, R 13 W). Named on Ritter Ridge (1958) 7.5' quadrangle.

Summit Reservoir [LOS ANGELES]: *lake*, 350 feet long, 5.25 miles north-northwest of Mount Banning on Santa Catalina Island (lat. 33°26'15" N, long. 118°28'50" W). Named on Santa Catalina North (1950) 7.5' quadrangle.

Suncrest [SAN DIEGO]: *locality*, 6 miles west-southwest of Alpine (lat. 32°48'20" N, long. 116°51'50" W; mainly in sec. 3, T 16 S, R 1 E). Named on Alpine (1955) 7.5' quadrangle. Allen Houser and Ray Coast bought the place in 1924 to develop a resort community (Stein, p. 134).

Sunday School Flats [SAN DIEGO]: *area*, 2.5 miles east of Boucher Hill (lat. 33°19'50" N, long. 116°52'40" W; sec. 4, T 10 S, R 1 E). Named on Boucher Hill (1948) 7.5' quadrangle. Theodore O. Bailey established an open-air sunday school at the site (Stein, p. 134).

Sun Garden Village [ORANGE]: *locality*, 6.5 miles south of present Buena Park civic center (lat. 33°46'20" N, long. 117°58'45" W; near N line sec. 1, T 5 S, R 11 W). Named on Anaheim (1950) 7.5' quadrangle.

Sunland [LOS ANGELES]: *district*, 7 miles east of San Fernando in Los Angeles (lat. 34°15'35" N, long. 118°18'40" W). Named on Sunland (1953) 7.5' quadrangle. Postal authorities established Sunland post office in 1887 (Frickstad, p. 82).

Sunny Hills [ORANGE]: *district*, 2.25 miles south-southeast of downtown La Habra in Fullerton (lat. 33°54'05" N, long. 117° 56' W). Named on La Habra (1964) 7.5' quadrangle. Postal authorities established Sunny Hills post office in 1969 (Salley, p. 215). La Habra (1952) 7.5' quadrangle shows Sunny Hills ranch at the place, and Coyote Hills (1935) 7.5' quadrangle shows Bastanchury ranch there. Sunny Hills Ranch Company bought Bastanchury ranch and subdivided it in 1940 (Gudde, 1949, p. 347). Pacific Electric Railroad had a station called Bastanchury that was named for Domingo Bastanchury, who owned 6000 acres of land north of Fullerton (Meadows, p. 24).

Sunnyside [LOS ANGELES]: *locality*, 4 miles east-southeast of present Inglewood city hall along a railroad (lat. 33°56'35" N, long. 118°17'30" W). Named on Redondo (1896) 15' quadrangle.

Sunnyside [SAN DIEGO]: *town*, 5 miles east of National City civic center (lat. 32°40'20" N, long. 117°01' W). Named on National City (1967) 7.5' quadrangle. Postal authorities established Sunnyside post office in 1892 and discontinued it in 1974 (Salley, p. 215). J.C. Frisbie founded and named the town in 1876 (Gudde, 1949, p. 347).

Sunny Slope [LOS ANGELES]: *locality*, 6.5 miles south of Mount Wilson (1) along Southern Pacific Railroad (lat. 34°07'30" N, long. 118°05'05" W). Named on Pasadena (1900) 15' quadrangle. The name is from Leonard J. Rose's Sunny Slope farm (Gudde, 1949, p. 347).

Sunny Vista [SAN DIEGO]: *locality*, 3 miles southeast of National City civic center (lat. 32°38'45" N, long. 117°03'45" W). Named on National City (1967) 7.5' quadrangle.

Sunrise [LOS ANGELES]: *locality*, 1.5 miles south of Lancaster along Southern Pacific Railroad (lat. 34°40'25" N, long. 118°07'55" W). Named on Lancaster West (1958) 7.5' quadrangle.

Sunrise Valley: see **Kearchoffer Flat** [SAN DIEGO].

Sunset: see **Westwood** [LOS ANGELES].

Sunset Bay: see **Huntington Harbor** [ORANGE] (1).
Sunset Beach [ORANGE]: *town*, 5.5 miles northwest of Huntington Beach civic center along the coast (lat. 33°43' N, long. 118°04'05" W). Named on Seal Beach (1965) 7.5' quadrangle. Postal authorities established Sunset Beach post office in 1905, discontinued it in 1924, and reestablished it in 1925 (Frickstad, p. 118).
Sunset Canyon [LOS ANGELES]: *canyon*, 2 miles long, 2 miles northeast of Burbank city hall (lat. 34°12'15" N, long. 118°17'05" W). Named on Burbank (1953) 7.5' quadrangle.
Sunset Cliffs [SAN DIEGO]:
(1) *relief feature*, 5.5 miles west of downtown San Diego along the coast (lat. 32°44' N, long. 117°15'20" W). Named on Point Loma (1967) 7.5' quadrangle.
(2) *district*, 5.25 miles west of downtown San Diego (lat. 32°43'50" N, long. 117°15'10" W); the district is at Sunset Cliffs (1). Named on Point Loma (1967) 7.5' quadrangle.
Sunset Hills: see **Ivanhoe** [LOS ANGELES] (1).
Sunset Mountain [SAN DIEGO]: *ridge*, north-northwest-trending, 1 mile long, 9 miles west-southwest of Ocotillo Wells (lat. 33°06'15" N, long. 116°16'45" W). Named on Whale Peak (1959) 7.5' quadrangle.
Sunset Peak [LOS ANGELES]: *peak*, 12 miles north-northeast of Pomona city hall (lat. 34°13' N, long. 117°41'20" W). Altitude 5796 feet. Named on Mount Baldy (1954) 7.5' quadrangle.
Sunset Point [SAN DIEGO]: *promontory*, 6 miles south-southeast of Point La Jolla along Mission Bay (lat. 32°46' N, long. 117°14'20" W). Named on La Jolla (1967) 7.5' quadrangle.
Sunset Wash [SAN DIEGO]: *stream*, flows 2 miles to San Felipe Creek 9.5 miles south-southeast of Borrego Springs (lat. 33°08'25" N, long. 116°17'15" W; at N line sec. 18, T 12 S, R 7 E); the feature heads near Sunset Mountain. Named on Borrego Sink (1959) and Whale Peak (1959) 7.5' quadrangles.
Sunshine: see **Norwalk** [LOS ANGELES].
Sunshine Acres [LOS ANGELES]: *district*, nearly 3 miles south of present Whittier city hall (lat. 33°55'25" N, long. 118°02'45" W). Named on Whittier (1949) 7.5' quadrangle.
Sunshine Canyon: see **Tunnel** [LOS ANGELES].
Sunshine Mountain [SAN DIEGO]: *ridge*, west-northwest-trending, 1 mile long, 10.5 miles north-northwest of Descanso (lat. 32°59'50" N, long. 116°40'35" W; mainly in sec. 33, T 13 S, R 3 E). Named on Tule Springs (1960) 7.5' quadrangle.
Sunshine Summit [SAN DIEGO]: *pass*, 7.5 miles northwest of Warner Springs (lat. 33°21'05" N, long. 116°44'20" W; near E line sec. 35, T 9 S, R 2 E). Named on Warner Springs (1959) 7.5' quadrangle.
Sun Valley [LOS ANGELES]:
(1) *district*, 4.25 miles northwest of Burbank city hall in Los Angeles (lat. 34°13'05" N, long. 118°22'05" W). Named on Burbank (1953) and Van Nuys (1953) 7.5' quadrangles. Called Roscoe on Santa Monica (1902) 15' quadrangle. Postal authorities established Roscoe post office in 1924 and changed the name to Sun Valley in 1948; the name "Roscoe" was for a brakeman for Southern Pacific Railroad (Salley, p. 188). Residents of the place chose the name "Sun Valley" by popular vote in 1948 to replace the name "Roscoe" (Hanna, p. 320).
(2) *locality*, 5 miles northeast of Van Nuys along Southern Pacific Railroad (lat. 34°13'35" N, long. 118°22'40" W); the place is north of Sun Valley (1). Named on Van Nuys (1953) 7.5' quadrangle. Called Monte Vista on Santa Monica (1902) 15' quadrangle.
Suracco Canyon: see **Solemint** [LOS ANGELES].
Surfside [ORANGE]: *district*, 6.5 miles northwest of Huntington Beach city hall along the coast in Seal Beach (lat. 33°43'40" N, long. 118°04'55" W). Named on Seal Beach (1965) 7.5' quadrangle. Postal authorities established Surfside post office in 1943 (Frickstad, p. 118).
Surprise City: see **Falls Canyon** [ORANGE].
Surrey: see **Saugus** [LOS ANGELES].
Susanna Canyon [LOS ANGELES]: *canyon*, drained by a stream that flows nearly 3 miles to San Gabriel River 7.5 miles north-northeast of Glendora city hall (lat. 34°14'15" N, long. 117°49'05" W). Named on Crystal Lake (1958) and Glendora (1953) 7.5' quadrangles. East Fork branches northeast 0.5 mile upstream from the mouth of the main canyon; it is 1.25 miles long and is named on Glendora (1953) 7.5' quadrangle.
Susannah Range: see **Santa Susana Range** [LOS ANGELES-VENTURA].
Sutherland [SAN DIEGO]: *locality*, 6.5 miles northeast of Ramona (lat. 33°06'15" N, long. 116°47'10" W; sec. 28, T 12 S, R 2 E). Named on Ramona (1903) 30' quadrangle. Postal authorities established Sutherland post office in 1895 and discontinued it in 1903; the name was for John P. Sutherland, a pioneer real-estate dealer (Salley, p. 216).
Sutherland Lake [SAN DIEGO]: *lake*, behind a dam on Santa Ysabel Creek 7 miles northeast of Ramona (lat. 33°07'05" N, long. 116°47'10" W; near W line sec. 21, T 12 S, R 2 E); the site of Sutherland is along the lake. Named on Ramona (1955) 7.5' quadrangle. Called Sutherland Reservoir on Ramona (1955, photorevised 1971) 7.5' quadrangle. United States Board on Geographic Names (1979b, p. 8) approved the name "Lake Sutherland" for the feature.
Sutherland Reservoir: see **Sutherland Lake** [SAN DIEGO].
Sutton Canyon [LOS ANGELES]: *canyon*, drained by a stream that flows 1.25 miles to Pickens Canyon 8 miles northwest of Pasadena city hall (lat. 34°14'35" N, long. 118°13'20" W; near E line sec. 22, T 2 N, R 13 W). Named on Condor Peak (1959) and Pasadena (1953) 7.5' quadrangles. Called East Fork [Pickens Canyon] on Los Angeles County (1935) map.
Swain Canyon [LOS ANGELES]: *canyon*, drained by a stream that flows 1.25 miles to the sea 2.5 miles north-northwest of Avalon on Santa Catalina Island (lat. 33°22'30" N, long. 118°21'10" W). Named on Santa Catalina East (1950) 7.5' quadrangle.
Swain's Landing: see **Whites Landing** [LOS ANGELES].
Swan Lake [SAN DIEGO]: *intermittent lake*, 0.25 mile long, 3.25 miles west of Warner Springs (lat. 33°16'30" N, long. 116°41'25" W). Named on Warner Springs (1959) 7.5' quadrangle.
Swarthout: see **Big Pines** [LOS ANGELES].
Swarthout Valley [LOS ANGELES]: *valley*, 5.25 miles north of Mount San Antonio on Los Angeles-San Bernardino County line (lat. 34°22' N, long. 117°39' W). Named on Mount San Antonio (1955) 7.5' quadrangle. C.W. Whipple (p. 148) referred to Swarthows Cañon. The name commemorates Nathan Swarthout and Truman Swarthout, brothers who settled in the valley about 1851 (Robinson, J.W., 1983, p. 196).
Swartout: see **Big Pines** [LOS ANGELES].
Swartz Canyon [SAN DIEGO]: *canyon*, drained by a stream that flows 4.5 miles to San Vicente Creek 4.5 miles southeast of Ramona (lat. 33°00'05" N, long. 116°48'10" W). Named on Ramona (1955) 7.5' quadrangle.
Sweeney Canyon [SAN DIEGO]: *canyon*, drained by a stream that flows 4.5 miles to Carrizo Creek (2) 1.5 miles northwest of Sweeney Pass (lat. 32°50'45" N, long. 116°12' W; near SW cor. sec. 19, T 15 S, R 8 E). Named on Sweeney Pass (1959) 7.5' quadrangle. The misspelled name is for Lieutenant Thomas William Sweeny, an army officer who was stationed at Fort Yuma in present Imperial County in the 1850's (Stein, p. 135).
Sweeney Pass [SAN DIEGO]: *pass*, 11 miles southeast of Agua Caliente Springs (lat. 32°49'55" N, long. 116°10'50" W; near S line sec. 29, T 15 S, R 8 E). Named on Sweeney Pass (1959) 7.5' quadrangle.
Sweetwater: see **El Cajon** [SAN DIEGO] (2).
Sweetwater Falls Reservoir: see **Loveland Reservoir** [SAN DIEGO].
Sweetwater Junction [SAN DIEGO]: *locality*, 2 miles southeast of present National City civic center (lat. 32°39'20" N, long. 117° 05' W); the place is in Sweetwater Valley. Named on San Diego (1904) 15' quadrangle.
Sweetwater Pass [SAN DIEGO]: *pass*, 2.5 miles southeast of present El Cajon city hall (lat. 32°46'30" N, long. 116°55'40" W). Named on Cuyamaca (1903) 30' quadrangle.
Sweetwater Reservoir [SAN DIEGO]: *lake*, behind a dam nearly 6 miles east-northeast of National City civic center (lat. 32°41'30" N, long. 117°00'25" W); the lake is along Sweetwater River. Named on Jamul Mountains (1955) and National City (1967) 7.5' quadrangles. The dam that forms the lake was completed in 1886 (Stein, p. 136).
Sweetwater River [SAN DIEGO]: *stream* and *dry wash*, extends for 50 miles to San Diego Bay 1.5 miles south-southwest of National City civic center (lat. 32°38'35" N, long. 117°06'55" W). Named on Alpine (1955), Cuyamaca Peak (1960), El Cajon (1967), Jamul Mountains (1955), National City (1953), and Viejas Mountain (1960) 7.5' quadrangles. North Fork enters from the northeast 6.25 miles southwest of Alpine; it is 6.25 miles long and is named on Alpine (1955) 7.5' quadrangle.
Sweetwater Spring [SAN DIEGO]: *spring*, 5.5 miles west of Jamul (lat. 32°43'35" N, long. 116°58'10" W). Named on Jamul Mountains (1955) 7.5' quadrangle. Called Isham Spr. on Jamul (1943) 15' quadrangle. The feature was known locally as Baldhead Spring because use of the mineralized water was supposed to prevent baldness (Waring, p. 311). According to Merrill (1916, p. 718), the feature also was called Nuvida Spring.
Sweetwater Valley [SAN DIEGO]: *valley*, 3.5 miles east-southeast of National City civic center (lat. 32°39'30" N, long. 117°02'45" W); the valley is along lower reaches of Sweetwater River. Named on National City (1967) 7.5' quadrangle.
Swinnerton Camp: see **Little Jimmy Spring** [LOS ANGELES].
Switzer Camp [LOS ANGELES]: *locality*, 6 miles southeast of Condor Peak along Arroyo Seco (lat. 34°15'30" N, long. 118°09'15" W). Named on Condor Peak (1959) 7.5' quadrangle. Called Switzers Camp on Mount Lowe (1939) 6' quadrangle. Perry Switzer built a trail to the place in 1884 and opened Switzer's Camp, the first tourist resort in San Gabriel Mountains; after a forest fire destroyed the camp in 1896, Lloyd B. Austin took over the site in 1912 and built a mountain hostelry first called Camp Losadena, but renamed Switzer-land (Robinson, J.W., 1977, p. 108, 110-111).
Switzer Campground: see **Lower Switzer Campground** [LOS ANGELES]; **Upper Switzer Campground** [LOS ANGELES].
Switzer-land: see **Switzer Camp** [LOS ANGELES].
Switzer Station [LOS ANGELES]: *locality*, 6 miles southeast of Condor Peak along Arroyo Seco (lat. 34°16' N, long. 118°08'35" W). Named on Condor Peak (1959) 7.5' quadrangle.
Sycamore Campground [LOS ANGELES]: *locality*, 7 miles west-south-

west of Valyermo along Little Rock Creek (lat. 34°25'05" N, long. 117°58'20" W; sec. 19, T 4 N, R 10 W). Named on Juniper Hills (1959) 7.5' quadrangle.

Sycamore Canyon [LOS ANGELES]:

(1) *canyon,* drained by a stream that flows nearly 2 miles to San Dimas Wash 4 miles east of Glendora city hall (lat. 34°07'35" N, long. 117°47'35" W; sec. 35, T 1 N, R 9 W). Named on Glendora (1953) 7.5' quadrangle.

(2) *canyon,* 3.5 miles long, 4 miles west-northwest of Pasadena city hall (lat. 34°10' N, long. 118°12'20" W). Named on Pasadena (1953) 7.5' quadrangle.

(3) *canyon,* drained by a stream that flows 1.5 miles to Sawpit Canyon 5 miles northwest of Azusa city hall (lat. 34°10'45" N, long. 117°58'20" W; near N line sec. 18, T 1 N, R 10 W). Named on Azusa (1953) 7.5' quadrangle.

(4) *canyon,* less than 1 mile long, 4.25 miles southwest of El Monte city hall (lat. 34°02'10" N, long. 118°05'20" W). Named on El Monte (1966) 7.5' quadrangle.

(5) *canyon,* drained by a stream that flows 3.5 miles to lowlands along San Gabriel River 4.5 miles south-southwest of El Monte city hall (lat. 34°00'40" N, long. 118°03'15" W). Named on El Monte (1953) 7.5' quadrangle. Watts' (1898-1899) map shows a feature called Dark Canyon that opens into Sycamore Canyon from the east near the west end of Puente Hills. Berkstresser (p. A-7) listed a place called Cal-Baden Mineral Spring located in Sycamore Canyon (5) near the canyon mouth (lat. 34°00'12" N, long. 118°02'55"W).

Sycamore Canyon [SAN DIEGO]:

(1) *canyon,* drained by a stream that flows 4 miles to Dulzura Creek nearly 6 miles southeast of Jamul (lat. 32°39'20" N, long. 116°48'20" W; near NE cor. sec. 31, T 17 S, R 2 E). Named on Dulzura (1972) and Otay Mountain (1972) 7.5' quadrangles.

(2) *canyon,* drained by a stream that flows 1.5 miles to Pauma Valley 3.5 miles west-southwest of Boucher Hill (lat. 33°18'45" N, long. 116°58'20" W). Named on Boucher Hill (1948) 7.5' quadrangle.

(3) *canyon,* drained by a stream that flows 8 miles to the canyon of San Diego River 5.5 miles north of La Mesa (lat. 32°50'40" N, long. 117°00'20" W). Named on La Mesa (1967), Poway (1967), and San Vicente Reservoir (1955) 7.5' quadrangles.

Sycamore Canyon [VENTURA]:

(1) *canyon,* drained by a stream that flows 1.5 miles to Alder Creek 4.25 miles north-northeast of Devils Heart Peak (lat. 34°36'05" N, long. 118°56'30" W; near W line sec. 19, T 6 N, R 19 W). Named on Devils Heart Peak (1943) 7.5' quadrangle.

(2) *canyon,* drained by a stream that flows 2 miles to an unnamed canyon 6 miles north-northeast of Thousand Oaks (lat. 34°15'05" N, long. 118°48'10" W). Named on Thousand Oaks (1952) 7.5' quadrangle.

Sycamore Canyon: see **Big Sycamore Canyon** [VENTURA]; **Elderberry Canyon** [LOS ANGELES]; **Little Sycamore Canyon** [SAN DIEGO]; **Little Sycamore Canyon** [VENTURA]; **Meier Canyon** [VENTURA]; **West Sycamore Canyon** [SAN DIEGO].

Sycamore Creek [VENTURA]:

(1) *stream,* flows 3 miles to Sespe Creek 14 miles east-northeast of Wheeler Springs (lat. 34°34' N, long. 119°03' W; at E line sec. 36, T 6 N, R 21 W). Named on Topatopa Mountains (1943) 7.5' quadrangle.

(2) *stream,* flows 2.5 miles to Lion Creek 4.5 miles east of the town of Ojai in Upper Ojai Valley (lat. 34°26'10" N, long. 119°09'45" W). Named on Ojai (1952) 7.5' quadrangle.

Sycamore Flat [LOS ANGELES]:

(1) *area,* 2 miles south-southeast of Crystal Lake along North Fork San Gabriel River (lat. 34°17'20" N, long. 117°50'25" W; sec. 5, T 2 N, R 9 W). Named on Rock Creek (1903) 15' quadrangle.

(2) *area,* 4 miles east-northeast of Glendora city hall (lat. 34°09'05" N, long. 117°47'35" W; at S line sec. 23, T 1 N, R 9 W). Named on Glendora (1953) 7.5' quadrangle. The name is from Sycamore Canyon (1), which is located below the area (Robinson, J.W., 1983, p. 118).

Sycamore Flat: see **Santiago Reservoir** [ORANGE].

Sycamore Flat Campground [LOS ANGELES]: *locality,* 2.5 miles southeast of Valyermo along Big Rock Creek (lat. 34°24'45" N, long. 117°49'25" W; sec. 21, T 4 N, R 9 W). Named on Valyermo (1958) 7.5' quadrangle.

Sycamore Flats [SAN DIEGO]: *area,* 5.5 miles south-southwest of Rodriguez Mountain (lat. 33°09'20" N, long. 116°56' W). Named on Rodriguez Mountain (1948) 7.5' quadrangle.

Sycamore Flats: see **Coldbrook Camp** [LOS ANGELES].

Sycamore Lake: see **Crystal Lake** [LOS ANGELES].

Sycamore Park [LOS ANGELES]: *locality,* 4 miles north-northeast of present Los Angeles city hall along Los Angeles Terminal Railroad (lat. 34°05'50" N, long. 118°12'15" W). Named on Pasadena (1900) 15' quadrangle.

Sycuan Creek [SAN DIEGO]: *stream,* flows 2 miles to North Fork Sweetwater River 5 miles southwest of Alpine (lat. 32°47'15" N, long. 116°49'50" W; near S line sec. 12, T 16 S, R 1 E). Named on Alpine (1955, photorevised 1988) 7.5' quadrangle. Called Sequan Creek on Alpine (1955) 7.5' quadrangle. United States Board on Geographic Names (1977, p. 6) listed the variant names "Cycuan Creek," "Sekwan Creek," "Sequan Creek," and "Syenan Creek" for the feature.

Sycuan Peak [SAN DIEGO]: *peak,* 6 miles south-southwest of Alpine (lat. 32°45'15" N, long. 116°48'20" W; at E line sec. 30, T 16 S, R 2 E). Altitude 2801 feet. Named on Alpine (1955, photorevised 1988) 7.5' quadrangle. Called Sequan Peak on Alpine (1955) 7.5' quadrangle. The name is of Indian origin (Kroeber, p. 57). United States Board on Geographic Names (1977, p. 6) listed the variant names "Cycuan Peak," "Sekwan Peak," "Sequan Peak," and "Syenan Peak" for the feature.

Syenan Creek: see **Sycuan Creek** [SAN DIEGO].

Syenan Peak: see **Sycuan Peak** [SAN DIEGO].

Sylmar [LOS ANGELES]: *district,* 2.5 miles northwest of downtown San Fernando in Los Angeles (lat. 34°18'35" N, long. 118°28'20" W). Named on San Fernando (1953) 7.5' quadrangle.

Sylvana: see **Valley Center** [SAN DIEGO].

Sylvano [SAN DIEGO]: *locality,* 5.25 miles southwest of Roderick (present Rodriguez) Mountain in Bear Valley (1) (lat. 33°11' N, long. 116°58'30" W). Named on Ramona (1903) 30' quadrangle.

Sylvia Park [LOS ANGELES]: *locality,* 9 miles northwest of Santa Monica city hall (lat. 34°06'50" N, long. 118°34'55" W; sec. 5, T 1 S, R 16 W). Named on Topanga (1952) 7.5' quadrangle.

- T -

Table Mountain [LOS ANGELES]: *ridge,* west-northwest-trending, 2.5 miles long, center less than 1 mile east-northeast of Big Pine (lat. 34°22'55" N, long. 117°40'40" W). Named on Mescal Creek (1956) 7.5' quadrangle.

Table Mountain [SAN DIEGO]: *relief feature,* nearly 4 miles northeast of Jacumba (lat. 32°39'10" N, long. 116°08'20" W; around NE cor. sec. 34, T 17 S, R 8 E). Named on Jacumba (1959) 7.5' quadrangle.

Table Mountain: see **Mount Markham** [LOS ANGELES].

Table Mountain Campground [LOS ANGELES]: *locality,* 0.5 mile north of Big Pines (lat. 34°23'15" N, long. 117°41'20" W); the place is on Table Mountain. Named on Mescal Creek (1956) 7.5' quadrangle.

Table Rock [LOS ANGELES]: *relief feature,* 11 miles south-southeast of the village of Lake Hughes in Texas Canyon (lat. 34°31'25" N, long. 118°23'15" W; near N line sec. 18, T 5 N, R 14 W). Named on Green Valley (1958) 7.5' quadrangle.

Tacobi Creek [LOS ANGELES]: *stream,* flows 3 miles to Leffingwell Creek nearly 3 miles south-southeast of present Whittier city hall (lat. 33°56'10" N, long. 118°00'35" W). Named on La Habra (1952) and Whittier (1949) 7.5' quadrangles.

Tahunga Canyon: see **Big Tujunga Canyon** [LOS ANGELES].

Tajauta [LOS ANGELES]: *land grant,* near Watts. Named on Inglewood (1964) and South Gate (1952) 7.5' quadrangles. Called Tajuata on Inglewood (1952) 7.5' quadrangle. Anastasio Avila received 1 league in 1843; Enrique Avila claimed 3560 acres patented in 1873 (Cowan, p. 101).

Tajunga Canyon: see **Big Tujunga Canyon** [LOS ANGELES].

Talamantes: see **Andrade Corner** [LOS ANGELES].

Talbert [ORANGE]: *locality,* 3.5 miles northeast of present Huntington Beach civic center (lat. 33°42'05" N, long. 117°57'45" W; on N line sec. 31, T 5 S, R 10 W). Named on Newport Beach (1951) 7.5' quadrangle. Postal authorities established Talbert post office in 1899 and discontinued it in 1907 (Frickstad, p. 118). The Talbert family bought land at the place in 1896 and established a small trading center (Meadows, p. 133). Pacific Electric Railroad had a flag stop called Remolacha located 1.5 miles south of Talbert, and a flag stop called Repollo located about 2 miles east of Talbot (Meadows, p. 118, 119).

Talega: see **San Juan Hot Springs** [ORANGE].

Talega Canyon [ORANGE-SAN DIEGO]: *canyon,* drained by a stream that heads in Riverside County and flows 6 miles back and forth across Orange-San Diego County line to Christianitos Creek nearly 3 miles northeast of San Clemente civic center (lat. 33° 27'05" N, long. 117°34'10" W; sec. 25, T 8 S, R 7 W). Named on Margarita Peak (1968), San Clemente (1968), and Sitton Peak (1954) 7.5' quadrangles.

Talich [SAN DIEGO]: *locality,* 3.5 miles east of downtown Oceanside along Atchison, Topeka and Santa Fe Railroad (lat. 33°12' N, long. 117°19' W; near SE cor. sec. 20, T 11 S, R 4 W). Named on San Luis Rey (1968) 7.5' quadrangle.

Talone Lake [SAN DIEGO]: *marsh,* nearly 6 miles east-northeast of Oceanside (lat. 33°14'20" N, long. 117°17'35" W; near NW cor. sec. 10, T 11 S, R 4 W). Named on San Luis Rey (1948) 7.5' quadrangle.

Tamarisk Grove Campground [SAN DIEGO]: *locality,* 8 miles south of Borrego Springs along San Felipe Creek (lat. 33°08'20" N, long. 113°22'30" W). Named on Borrego Sink (1959) and Tubb Canyon (1959) 7.5' quadrangles.

Tanbark Creek: see **Tanbark Flats** [LOS ANGELES].

Tanbark Flats [LOS ANGELES]: *locality,* 7.5 miles northeast of Glendora city hall near the head of San Dimas Canyon (lat. 34°12'15" N, long. 117°45'35" W; sec. 6, T 1 N, R 8 W). Named on Glendora (1953) 7.5' quadrangle. On Glendora (1966) 7.5' quadrangle, the name "Tanbark Creek" applies to the stream in San Dimas Canyon at and near Tanbark Flats.

Tapawingo: see **Camp Tapawingo** [SAN DIEGO].

Tapia Canyon [LOS ANGELES]: *canyon,* drained by a stream that flows 4 miles to Castaic Canyon nearly 8 miles northwest of Newhall (lat. 34°28'40" N, long. 118°36'25" W; at E line sec. 36, T 5 N, R 17 W). Named on Newhall (1952) 7.5' quadrangle.

Tapie Canyon [LOS ANGELES]: *canyon,* drained by a stream that flows nearly 3 miles to Santa Clara River 4.25 miles east-northeast of Solemint (lat. 34°25'55" N, long. 118°23' W; sec. 18, T 4 N, R 14 W). Named on Agua Dulce (1960) 7.5' quadrangle. Called Vorhees Canyon on Los Angeles County (1935) map.

Tapo Canyon [VENTURA]:

(1) *canyon,* drained by a stream that flows nearly 4 miles to Simi Valley (1) 5.5 miles west-northwest of Santa Susana Pass (lat. 34° 18' N, long. 118°43'05" W; sec. 36, T 3 N, R 18 W). Named on Santa Susana (1951) 7.5' quadrangle. Tapo Canyon (1) and Tapo Canyon (2) head on opposite sides of the pass located between Santa Susana Mountains and Oak Ridge. The upper part of Tapo Canyon (1) is called Hog Canyon on Santa Susana (1943) 15' quadrangle, and the lower part is called South Tapo Canyon on that map. The name "Tapo" is of Indian origin (Kroeber, p. 61).

(2) *canyon,* drained by a stream that flows 3 miles to the valley of Santa Clara River 4.5 miles east-southeast of Piru (lat. 34°23'35" N, long. 118°53'15" W). Named on Santa Susana (1951) and Val Verde (1952) 7.5' quadrangles.

Tar Creek [VENTURA]: *stream,* flows 5.5 miles to Sespe Creek 6.5 miles north-northwest of Fillmore (lat. 34°29'25" N, long. 118°56'30" W). Named on Fillmore (1951) and Piru (1952) 7.5' quadrangles. Present Spring Canyon Creek is called North Fork Tar Cr. on Tejon (1903) 30' quadrangle, but United States Board on Geographic Names (1990, p. 11) rejected this designation for the stream.

Tarzana [LOS ANGELES]: *district,* 3.25 miles southeast of the center of Canoga Park in Los Angeles (lat. 34°10'20" N, long. 118° 33' W). Named on Canoga Park (1952) 7.5' quadrangle. Postal authorities established Tarzana post office in 1930 at a place first called Runnymead (Salley, p. 218). The name "Tarzana" is from Edgar Rice Burroughs' estate at the place; Burroughs named the estate for his fictional character "Tarzan" (Gudde, 1949, p. 354).

Tarzana Siding [LOS ANGELES]: *locality,* 4 miles east-southeast of Canoga Park along Southern Pacific Railroad (lat. 34°10'50" N, long, 118°32' W); the place is 1 mile northeast of Tarzana. Named on Canoga Park (1952) 7.5' quadrangle. Called Reseda on Camulos (1903) 30' quadrangle, and called Reseda Siding on Reseda (1928) 6' quadrangle.

Taylor Campground [LOS ANGELES]: *locality,* 3 miles south of Warm Springs Mountain in Elizabeth Lake Canyon (lat. 34°33' N, long. 118°34'35" W; sec. 5, T 5 N, R 16 W). Named on Warm Springs Mountain (1958) 7.5' quadrangle.

Taylor Creek [SAN DIEGO]: *stream,* flows 5.25 miles to Peterson Canyon 7.5 miles southwest of Descanso (lat. 32°47'35" N, long. 116°43'15" W; near E line sec. 12, T 16 S, R 2 E). Named on Viejas Mountain (1960) 7.5' quadrangle.

Taylor Junction [LOS ANGELES]: *locality,* 1.5 miles east-northeast of Los Angeles city hall along Southern Pacific Railroad (lat. 34° 03'45" N, long. 118°13'15" W). Named on Los Angeles (1966) 7.5' quadrangle.

Taylor Spring [SAN DIEGO]: *spring,* 7.25 miles north-northwest of Monument Peak (lat. 32°59'15" N, long. 116°28'35" W; sec. 4, T 14 S, R 5 E). Named on Monument Peak (1959) 7.5' quadrangle.

Tecate [SAN DIEGO]: *village,* 1.5 miles south-southwest of Potrero (lat. 32°35' N, long. 116°37'10" W; near NW cor. sec. 30, T 18 S, R 4 E). Named on Potrero (1960) and Tecate (1960) 7.5' quadrangles. Postal authorities established Tecate post office in 1912 (Frickstad, p. 157).

Tecate Creek [SAN DIEGO]: *stream,* heads in Mexico and flows 1.25 miles in San Diego County to join Cottonwood Creek (3) and form Tijuana River 5 miles east-southeast of Otay Mountain (lat. 32°34' N, long. 116°45'55" W; sec. 34, T 18 S, R 2 E). Named on Otay Mountain (1972) and Tecate (1960) 7.5' quadrangles. Called Rio del Tecate on Cuyamaca (1903) 30' quadrangle.

Tecate Divide [SAN DIEGO]: *ridge,* generally south-trending, 10 miles long, center near Live Oak Springs (lat. 32°41'30" N, long. 116°19'15" W). Named on Live Oak Springs (1959), Sombrero Peak (1959), and Tierra del Sol (1959) 7.5' quadrangles.

Tecate Mountain: see **Tecate Peak** [SAN DIEGO].

Tecate Peak [SAN DIEGO]: *peak,* 2.5 miles south-southeast of Barrett Junction (lat. 32°34'45" N, long. 116°41'15" W; near NW cor. sec. 28, T 18 S, R 3 E). Altitude 3885 feet. Named on Tecate (1960) 7.5' quadrangle. Called Tecate Mt. on Cuyamaca (1903) 30' quadrangle, but United States Board on Geographic Names (1961c, p. 17) rejected the names "Mount Tecate" and "Tecate Mountain" for the feature.

Tecate Peak: seed **Little Tecate Peak** [SAN DIEGO].

Tecolote Creek [SAN DIEGO]: *stream,* flows 6.25 miles to Mission Bay 6.5 miles southeast of Point La Jolla (lat. 32°46'15" N, long. 117°12'30" W). Named on La Jolla (1967) 7.5' quadrangle. La Jolla (1903) 15' quadrangle has the name "Tecolote Valley" for the valley along the lower part of the stream.

Tecolote Valley: see **Tecolote Creek** [SAN DIEGO].

Teddy's Outpost: see **Oakwilde** [LOS ANGELES].

Tehachapi Mountains [LOS ANGELES]: *range,* mainly in Kern County, but extends southwest into Los Angeles County northeast of Gorman (lat. 34°49' N, long. 118°48'30" W). Named on Los Angeles (1975) 1°x 2° quadrangle.

Tejon Pass [LOS ANGELES]: *pass,* 1.5 miles west-northwest of Gorman (lat. 34°48'05" N, long. 118°52'30" W; at N line sec. 10, T 8 N, R 19 W). Named on Frazier Mountain (1958) and Lebec (1958) 7.5' quadrangles. Called Holland Summit on Lebec (1945) 7.5' quadrangle. The feature first was known as Fort Tejon Pass, for the fort in Kern County, and later as Tejon Pass; the name "Tejon Pass" earlier applied to a feature in Kern County (Gudde, 1949, p. 356).

Telegraph Canyon [ORANGE]: *canyon,* drained by a stream that heads in San Bernardino County and flows nearly 5 miles in Orange County to Carbon Canyon 2.25 miles north-northwest of Yorba Linda (lat. 33°55'10" N, long. 117°49'35" W; near S line sec. 9, T 3 S, R 9 W). Named on Prado Dam (1950) and Yorba Linda (1950) 7.5' quadrangles. Watts' (1898-1899) map has the designation "Latrango or Telegraph Canon" for the feature. The name "Telegraph Canyon" is from a telegraph line in the canyon (Meadows, p. 133).

Telegraph Canyon [SAN DIEGO]: *canyon,* drained by a stream that flows 10 miles to San Diego Bay 3 miles north-northeast of Imperial Beach civic center (lat. 32°37'05" N, long. 117°05'35" W). Named on Imperial Beach (1967), Jamul Mountains (1955), and National City (1967) 7.5' quadrangles. The name is from a telegraph line in the canyon in 1870 (Stein, p. 138).

Tell's Landing: see **Playa del Rey** [LOS ANGELES].

Temecula Creek [SAN DIEGO]: *stream,* flows 8.5 miles to Riverside County 7.5 miles north-northeast of Boucher Hill (lat. 33°25'35" N, long. 116°50'50" W; at N line sec. 2, T 9 S, R 1 E). Named on Aguanga (1954), Palomar Observatory (1949), and Warner Springs (1959) 7.5' quadrangles. United States Board on Geographic Names (1943, p. 14) rejected the names "Aguanga Creek" and "Temecula River" for any part of the stream.

Temecula Creek: see **Santa Margarita River** [SAN DIEGO].

Temecula River: see **Santa Margarita River** [SAN DIEGO]; **Temecula Creek** [SAN DIEGO].

Temescal [LOS ANGELES-VENTURA]: *land grant,* northeast of Piru on Los Angeles-Ventura County line. Named on Piru (1952), Val Verde (1952), and Whitaker Peak (1958) 7.5' quadrangles. Francisco Lopez R. de la Custa received 3 leagues in 1843 and claimed 13,339 acres patented in 1871 (Cowan, p. 101-102).

Temescal Canyon [LOS ANGELES]: *canyon,* drained by a stream that flows nearly 5.5 miles to the sea 3 miles west-northwest of Santa Monica city hall (lat. 34°02'05" N, long. 118°32'05" W). Named on Topanga (1952) 7.5' quadrangle.

Temescal Canyon: see **Santa Felicia Canyon** [LOS ANGELES-VENTURA].

Temescal Creek [SAN DIEGO]:

(1) *stream,* flows 8.5 miles to Santa Ysabel Creek 5.25 miles north of Ramona (lat. 33°07'15" N, long. 116°51'05" W; sec. 23, T 12 S, R 1 E). Named on Mesa Grande (1948) and Ramona (1955) 7.5' quadrangles.

(2) *stream,* flows 3.5 miles to San Diego River nearly 4 miles south-southwest of Santa Ynez (lat. 33°03'20" N, long. 116°41'25" W; sec. 8, T 13 S, R 3 E). Named on Santa Ysabel (1960) 7.5' quadrangle.

Temescal Peak: see **Santiago Peak** [ORANGE].

Temescal Range: see **Santa Ana Mountains** [ORANGE].

Temescal Valley [SAN DIEGO]: *canyon,* 4 miles west-northwest of Mesa Grande (lat. 33°12'15" N, long. 116°50' W; sec. 24, T 11 S, R 1 E); the feature is along Temescal Creek (1). Named on Mesa Grande (1948) 7.5' quadrangle.

Temple: see **Temple City** [LOS ANGELES].

Temple City [LOS ANGELES]: *city,* 3 miles north-northwest of El Monte city hall (lat. 34°06'30" N, long. 118°03'25" W). Named on El Monte (1953) 7.5' quadrangle. Called Temple on Sierra Madre (1928) 6' quadrangle. Postal authorities established Temple post office in 1924 and changed the name to Temple City in 1928 (Frickstad, p. 82). The city incorporated in 1960. Walter Paul Temple founded the community in 1922 (Hanna, p. 327).

Temple Hill [ORANGE]: *ridge,* south-trending, 1.25 miles long, 1.5 miles east-northeast of Laguna Beach city hall (lat. 33°33' N, long. 117°45'15" W; sec. 19, T 7 S, R 8 W). Named on Laguna Beach (1965) 7.5' quadrangle.

Ten Sycamore Flat [VENTURA]: *area,* 15 miles east-northeast of Wheeler Springs (lat. 34°34'15" N, long. 119°02'40" W; sec. 31, T 6 N, R 20 W). Named on Topatopa Mountains (1943) 7.5' quadrangle.

Tent City [SAN DIEGO]: *locality,* nearly 3 miles south of downtown San

Diego across San Diego Bay (lat. 32°40'35" N, long. 117°10'15" W). Named on Point Loma (1942) 7.5' quadrangle.

Tentrock Canyon [LOS ANGELES]: *canyon,* drained by a stream that flows 4.5 miles to lowlands 10 miles east of Gorman (lat. 34° 46'30" N, long. 118°40'30" W; near SW cor sec. 15, T 8 N, R 17 W). Named on La Liebre Ranch (1965) and Liebre Mountain (1958) 7.5' quadrangles.

Teofulio Summit: see **San Felipe** [SAN DIEGO].

Teralta: see **East San Diego** [SAN DIEGO].

Teresita Pines: see **Camp Teresita Pines** [LOS ANGELES].

Terminal: see **Terminal Island** [LOS ANGELES] (2).

Terminal Island [LOS ANGELES]:

(1) *island,* 2 miles long, 3 miles west-southwest of Long Beach city hall (lat. 33°45'30" N, long. 118°14'30" W). Named on Long Beach (1949), San Pedro (1964), and Torrance (1964) 7.5' quadrangles. Called Rattle Snake Is. on Lankershim Ranch Land and Water Company's (1888) map, and called Rattlesnake I. on Mendenhall's (1908) map, but United States Board on Geographic Names (1933, p. 750) rejected the names "Rattlesnake Island" and "Rattlesnake Terminal Island" for the feature. The Spaniards called the it La Isla de la Culebra de Cascabel because it was infested with rattlesnakes—*La Isla de la Culebra de Cascabel* means "The Island of the Snake of the Rattle" in Spanish; after Terminal Railroad Company bought the place in 1891, the name was changed to Terminal Island and it became a popular summer resort (Gleason, p. 116, 118).

(2) *locality,* nearly 4 miles west-southwest of Long Beach city hall along Union Pacific Railroad (lat. 33°45'10" N, long. 118°15'20" W); the place is on Terminal Island (1). Named on Wilmington (1925) 6' quadrangle. Called Terminal on California Mining Bureau's (1917a) map. Postal authorities established Terminal post office in 1898, changed the name to Terminal Island in 1924, and discontinued it in 1943 (Frickstad, p. 82).

Ternez [VENTURA]: *locality,* 3 miles west-southwest of Moorpark along Southern Pacific Railroad (lat. 34°16'15" N, long. 118°56'15" W). Named on Piru (1921) 15' quadrangle. Called Ternez Siding on Camulos (1903) 30' quadrangle, and called Tarnez on Los Angeles County (1955) map.

Texas: see **New Texas**, under **Campo** [SAN DIEGO].

Texas Canyon [LOS ANGELES]: *canyon,* drained by a stream that flows 8 miles to Bouquet Canyon 5.25 miles north of Solemint (lat. 34°29'30" N, long. 118°27'35" W; sec. 28, T 5 N, R 15 W). Named on Green Valley (1958), Mint Canyon (1960), and Sleepy Valley (1958) 7.5' quadrangles.

Thatcher Creek [VENTURA]: *stream,* flows 6.5 miles to San Antonio Creek less than 1 mile east-southeast of downtown Ojai (lat. 34°26'35" N, long. 119°13'50" W). Named on Ojai (1952) 7.5' quadrangle.

The Cove [SAN DIEGO]: *embayment,* just east of Point La Jolla along the coast (lat. 32°51' N, long. 117°16'20" W). Named on La Jolla (1967) 7.5' quadrangle.

The Eyrie: see **Steil's Camp**, under **Mount Harvard** [LOS ANGELES].

The Falls [SAN DIEGO]: *waterfall,* 4.5 miles north-northwest of Morena Village along a branch of Morena Creek (lat. 32°44'15" N, long. 116°32'30" W). Named on Morena Reservoir (1960) 7.5' quadrangle.

The Hogback: see **Mount Harvard** [LOS ANGELES].

The Isthmus [LOS ANGELES]: *relief feature,* 0.5 miles southwest of Northwest Harbor on San Clemente Island (lat. 33°01'30" N, long. 118°35'25" W). Named on San Clemente Island North (1943) 7.5' quadrangle.

The Laguna: see **Laguna Meadow** [SAN DIEGO].

The Mesa [SAN DIEGO]: *ridge,* west-northwest-trending, less than 1 mile long, 7.25 miles southwest of Alpine (lat. 32°46'10" N, long. 116°51'50" W; sec. 22, T 16 S, R 1 E). Named on Alpine (1955) 7.5' quadrangle.

Thenard [LOS ANGELES]: *locality,* 3 miles west-northwest of Long Beach city hall along Southern Pacific Railroad (lat. 33°47'15" N, long. 118°14'30" W). Named on Long Beach (1949) 7.5' quadrangle. Called Thenard Junc. on Downey (1902) 15' quadrangle.

Thenard Junction: see **Thenard** [LOS ANGELES].

The Narrows [LOS ANGELES]:

(1) *narrows,* 4.5 miles east-northeast of Condor Peak in Big Tujunga Canyon (lat. 34°18'35" N, long. 118°08'30" W). Named on Chilao Flat (1959) and Condor Peak (1959) 7.5' quadrangles.

(2) *narrows,* 5.5 miles west of Mount San Antonio along San Gabriel River (lat. 34°17'35" N, long. 117°44'30" W). Named on Mount San Antonio (1955) 7.5' quadrangle.

The Narrows [ORANGE]: *relief feature,* constricted part of Upper Newport Bay 6.5 miles east-southeast of Huntington Beach city hall (lat. 33°38'15" N, long. 117°53'15" W). Named on Newport Beach (1965) 7.5' quadrangle.

The Narrows [SAN DIEGO]:

(1) *narrows,* 9.5 miles south-southeast of Borrego Springs along San Felipe Creek (lat. 33°08'05" N, long. 116°18' W; sec. 13, T 12 S, R 6 E). Named on Borrego Sink (1959) 7.5' quadrangle.

(2) *narrows,* 6.5 miles north of Campo along La Posta Creek (lat. 32°42' N, long. 116°28'45" W; sec. 16, T 17 S, R 5 E). Named on Cameron Corners (1959) 7.5' quadrangle.

The Oaks [LOS ANGELES]: *locality,* 8 miles south-southwest of the village of Leona Valley in Mint Canyon (lat. 34°30'40" N, long. 118°21'15" W; at N line sec. 21, T 5 N, R 14 W). Named on Sleepy Valley (1958) 7.5' quadrangle.

The Old Trading Post: see **Little Santa Anita Canyon** [LOS ANGELES].

The Pines Camp Ground [VENTURA]: *locality,* 5.5 miles east-northeast of the town of Ojai (lat. 34°29'05" N, long. 119°09'30" W; sec. 26, T 5 N, R 22 W). Named on Ojai (1952) 7.5' quadrangle.

The Pinnacle [LOS ANGELES]: *peak,* 6.5 miles north-northwest of Sunland (lat. 34°20'55" N, long. 118°20'35" W; near NE cor. sec. 16, T 3 N, R 14 W). Altitude 3836 feet. Named on Sunland (1966) 7.5' quadrangle.

The Pothole [VENTURA]: *relief feature,* closed depression 6.25 miles southeast of Cobblestone Mountain (lat. 34°32' N, long. 118° 48'10" W; sec. 7, T 5 N, R 18 W). Named on Cobblestone Mountain (1958) 7.5' quadrangle. Called The Potholes on California Mining Bureau's (1917a) map.

The Potholes [LOS ANGELES]: *water feature,* 4 miles east of Burnt Peak along upper reaches of Fish Creek (lat. 34°40'25" N, long. 118°30'15" W; on S line sec. 19, T 7 N, R 15 W). Named on Burnt Peak (1958) 7.5' quadrangle.

The Potrero [SAN DIEGO]: *valley,* center 3 miles northeast of Monument Peak (lat. 32°55' N, long. 116°22'30" W). Named on Agua Caliente Springs (1959) and Monument Peak (1959) 7.5' quadrangles.

The Sinks [ORANGE]: *relief feature,* 6.25 miles north-northeast of El Toro near the head of Agua Chinon Wash (lat. 33°42'55" N, long. 117°39'55" W). Named on El Toro (1968) 7.5' quadrangle.

The Slot [SAN DIEGO]: *canyon,* 1250 feet long, 5.5 miles west-northwest of Ocotillo Wells at the head of Borrego Mountain Wash (lat. 33°10'55" N, long. 116°12'55" W; near N line sec. 35, T 11 S, R 7 E). Named on Borrego Mountain (1960) 7.5' quadrangle.

The Thimble [SAN DIEGO]: *peak,* 7 miles west of Borrego Springs (lat. 33°14'50" N, long. 116°29'50" W; sec. 5, T 11 S, R 5 E). Altitude 5779 feet. Named on Tubb Canyon (1959) 7.5' quadrangle.

The Willows [SAN DIEGO]: *locality,* 6.5 miles west-southwest of Descanso (lat. 32°50'10" N, long. 116°43'15" W; sec. 25, T 15 S, R 2 E). Named on Viejas Mountain (1960) 7.5' quadrangle. A popular cabin resort was at the place, where by 1896 Frederick B. Walker established an inn called The Willows (Stein, p. 139).

Thimble: see **The Thimble** [SAN DIEGO].

Thing Valley [SAN DIEGO]: *valley,* 7 miles east-northeast of Buckman Springs along La Posta Creek (lat. 32°48'25" N, long. 116°22'50" W). Named on Mount Laguna (1960) and Sombrero Peak (1959) 7.5' quadrangles. The name commemorates Damon Thing, who purchased the valley about 1870 and had a cattle ranch there; the feature first was called Hollister Valley for a man who raised sheep at the place (Gudde, 1949, p. 360).

Third Wash [SAN DIEGO]: *stream,* flows 3 miles to San Felipe Creek 5.5 miles northwest of Ocotillo Wells (lat. 33°12'40" N, long. 116°11'25" W; at SE cor. sec. 13, T 11 S, R 7 E). Named on Borrego Mountain (1960) 7.5' quadrangle.

Thompson: see **Mint Canyon** [LOS ANGELES] (2); **Solemint** [LOS ANGELES].

Thompson Creek: see **Thompson Wash** [LOS ANGELES].

Thompson Flat [LOS ANGELES]: *area,* 12.5 miles north of Pomona city hall (lat. 34°14'05" N, long. 117°43'35" W). Named on Mount Baldy (1954) 7.5' quadrangle, which shows Thompson ranch by the place.

Thompsonville: see **Huntington Beach** [ORANGE].

Thompson Wash [LOS ANGELES]: *stream,* flows 4 miles to end in lowlands 2.5 miles north of Pomona city hall (lat. 34°05'45" N, long. 117°45'20" W). Named on Ontario (1954) and San Dimas (1954) 7.5' quadrangles. On Mount Baldy (1954) 7.5' quadrangle, the name "Thompson Creek" applies to the upper part of present Thompson Wash.

Thorn Meadows [VENTURA]: *area,* 9.5 miles east of Reyes Peak (lat. 34°37'55" N, long. 119°06'40" W; at N line sec. 9, T 6 N, R 21 W). Named on Lockwood Valley (1943) 7.5' quadrangle. Mount Pinos (1903) 30' quadrangle shows marsh in the area.

Thorn Point [VENTURA]: *peak,* 9 miles east of Reyes Peak (lat. 34° 36'20" N, long. 119°07'35" W; near S line sec. 17, T 6 N, R 21 W). Altitude 6935 feet. Named on Lion Canyon (1943) 7.5' quadrangle.

Thousand Oaks [VENTURA]: *city,* 20 miles east of Oxnard (lat. 34° 10'15" N, long. 118°50'15" W). Named on Thousand Oaks (1952) 7.5' quadrangle. Called Thousand Oaks Community on Triunfo Pass (1940) 15' quadrangle. Postal authorities established Thousand Oaks post office in 1938 (Frickstad, p. 219), and the city incorporated in 1964.

Thousand Palms Canyon: see **Salvador Canyon** [SAN DIEGO].

Thousand Springs: see **San Nicolas Island** [VENTURA].

Thrall: see **Will Thrall Peak** [LOS ANGELES].

Three Arch Bay [ORANGE]: *locality,* 4 miles west of San Juan Capistrano along the coast (lat. 33°29'30" N, long. 117°43'30" W). Named on Dana Point (1968) 7.5' quadrangle. The name is from three natural arches at the place (Gudde, 1949, p. 361).

Three Arches: see **South Laguna** [ORANGE].

Threemile House [LOS ANGELES]: *locality,* 3.25 miles north of present Los Angeles city hall along Los Angeles Terminal Railroad (lat. 34°06'05"

N, long. 118°14'20" W). Named on Pasadena (1900) 15' quadrangle.

Threepoint: see **Three Points** [LOS ANGELES] (1).

Three Points [LOS ANGELES]:

(1) *locality,* 4 miles north-northwest of Burnt Peak at the mouth of Oakgrove Canyon (lat. 34°44'05" N, long. 118°35'50" W; sec. 32, T 8 N, R 16 W). Named on Burnt Peak (1958) 7.5' quadrangle. Called Threepoint on Manzana (1938) 6' quadrangle, but United States Board on Geographic Names (1960a, p. 18) rejected the forms "Threepoint" and "Three Point" for the name. Los Angeles County (1935) map shows a place called Voltaire located about 1 mile southeast of Three Points. Postal authorities established Voltair post office in 1912 and discontinued it in 1922 (Frickstad, p. 83).

(2) *locality,* 2.5 miles west of Waterman Mountain (lat. 34°20'35" N, long. 117°58'55"W; sec. 13, T 3 N, R 11 W). Named on Waterman Mountain (1959) 7.5' quadrangle.

3 Sister Buttes: see **Three Sisters** [LOS ANGELES].

Three Sisters [LOS ANGELES]: *peaks,* three, 1.5 miles southeast of Black Butte (lat. 34°32'15" N, long. 117°42'15" W; sec. 10, T 5 N, R 8 W). Named on El Mirage (1956) 7.5' quadrangle. Called 3 Sister Buttes on Los Angeles County (1935) map.

Throop Mountain: see **Throop Peak** [LOS ANGELES].

Throop Peak [LOS ANGELES]: *peak,* 3.5 miles northeast of Crystal Lake (lat. 34°21' N, long. 117°47'55" W). Altitude 9138 feet. Named on Crystal Lake (1958) 7.5' quadrangle. United States Board on Geographic Names (1962a, p. 17) rejected the names "North Baldy Peak" and "Throop Mountain" for the feature, and noted that the name "Throop" commemorates Amos G. Throop, who in 1891 founded Throop University, a forerunner of California Institute of Technolgy. Students from the school climbed the peak and named it in 1916; previously the feature was called Dougherty Peak for A.A. Dougherty of Coldbrook Camp (Robinson, J.W., 1983, p. 112).

Thunder Valley [SAN DIEGO]: *valley,* 6.5 miles northeast of Buckman Springs (lat. 32°50'05" N, long. 116°24'15" W; sec. 30, T 15 S, R 6 E). Named on Mount Laguna (1960) 7.5' quadrangle.

Thurin [ORANGE]: *locality,* 5.5 miles east of present Huntington Beach civic center along Southern Pacific Railroad (lat. 33°39'15" N, long. 117°54'15" W). Named on Newport Beach (1935) 7.5' quadrangle.

Tia Juana: see **San Ysidro** [SAN DIEGO] (2); **San Ysidro Station** [SAN DIEGO].

Tia Juana River: see **Cottonwood Creek** [SAN DIEGO] (3); **Tijuana River** [SAN DIEGO].

Tick Canyon [LOS ANGELES]: *canyon,* drained by a stream that flows 5.5 miles to Santa Clara River nearly 4 miles east-northeast of Solemint (lat. 34°25'55" N, long. 118°23'30" W; sec. 18, T 4 N, R 14 W). Named on Agua Dulce (1960) and Mint Canyon (1960) 7.5' quadrangles. Los Angeles County (1935) map shows a feature called Goat Canyon that opens into Tick Canyon from the north about 2 miles above the mouth of Tick Canyon (at E line sec. 6, T 4 N, R 14 W), and a feature called Shan Canyon that opens into Tick Canyon from the north about 1 mile above the mouth of Tick Canyon (sec. 7, T 4 N, R 14 W).

Tico: see **Matilija** [VENTURA].

Tie Canyon [LOS ANGELES]: *canyon,* drained by a stream that flows 1.25 miles to Aliso Canyon (1) 2.5 miles west-northwest of Pacifico Mountain (lat. 34°23'55" N, long. 118°04'25" W). Named on Pacifico Mountain (1959) 7.5' quadrangle.

Tierra Blanca Mountains [SAN DIEGO]: *range,* extends for 8 miles southeast and south from a point west of Agua Caliente Springs (center near lat. 32°53'30" N, long. 116°16' W). Named on Agua Caliente Springs (1959), Arroyo Tapiado (1959), Sombrero Peak (1959), and Sweeney Pass (1959) 7.5' quadrangles.

Tierra Bonita: see **Littlerock** [LOS ANGELES].

Tierra del Fuego: see **Vacation Isle** [SAN DIEGO].

Tierra del Sol [SAN DIEGO]: *locality,* 8.5 miles east of Campo (lat. 32°37'20" N, long. 116°19'20" W; sec. 12, T 18 S, R 6 E). Named on Tierra del Sol (1959) 7.5' quadrangle. Called Hipass on Campo (1939) 15' quadrangle, but United States Board on Geographic Names (1961b, p. 13) rejected this name for the place. Postal authorities established Hipass post office in 1917, changed the name to Tierra del Sol in 1956, and discontinued it in 1964; railroad officials gave the name "Hipass" to the place because it is at the highest point on the rail line (Salley, p. 98, 222). Campo (1939) 15' quadrangle has the name Hipass Sta. for a place located 1 mile east-southeast of Hypass (present Tierra del Sol) along San Diego and Arizona Eastern Railroad (lat. 32°37' N, long. 116°18'25" W). Campo (1944) 15' quadrangle shows a place called Mills Crossing Station situated along the railroad just south of Hipass (present Tierra del Sol) (lat. 32°37'10" N, long. 116°19'15" W).

Tierra Rejada Valley [VENTURA]: *valley,* 2.5 miles southeast of Moorpark (lat. 34°15'25" N, long. 118°51'15" W). Named on Simi (1951) 7.5' quadrangle. Called Tierra Rejada on Piru (1921) 15' quadrangle.

Tie Summit Station [LOS ANGELES]: *locality,* 2.5 miles west-northwest of Pacifico Mountain (lat. 34°23'25" N, long. 118°04'45" W); the place is less than 1 mile south-southwest of the mouth of Tie Canyon by Mill Creek Summit. Named on Pacifico Mountain (1959) 7.5' quadrangle.

Tijeras Canyon [ORANGE]: *canyon,* drained by a stream that flows 5.25 miles to Arroyo Trabuco 4 miles southeast of El Toro (lat. 33° 35'35" N, long. 117°37'55" W). Named on Cañada Gobernadora (1968), San Juan Capistrano (1968), and Santiago Peak (1954) 7.5' quadrangles.

Tijuana River [SAN DIEGO]: *stream,* formed by the confluence of Cottonwood Creek (3) and Tecate Creek, and flows 2.25 miles before entering Mexico; the stream continues mainly in Mexico before reentering San Diego County to flow 6.25 miles to the sea 1.5 miles south-southwest of Imperial Beach civic center (lat. 32° 33'25" N, long. 117°07'50" W; sec. 31, T 18 S, R 2 W). Named on Imperial Beach (1967) and Otay Mountain (1972) 7.5' quadrangles. Called Rio Tia Juana on Goddard's (1857) map, called Ti Juana River on Hanks' (1886a) map, called Rio Del Tia Juana on Cuyamaca (1903) 30' quadrangle, and called Tia Juana River on San Ysidro (1953) 7.5' quadrangle. United States Board on Geographic Names (1968a, p. 10) rejected the names "Rio Tecate," "Rio Tiajuana," "Rio Tijuana," "Tia Juana," "Tia Juana River," and "Tiajuana River" for the stream.

Tilghman: see **Shoemaker** [LOS ANGELES].

Timber Canyon [VENTURA]: *canyon,* 2.25 miles long, opens into the valley of Santa Clara River 4 miles northeast of Santa Paula (lat. 34°23'30" N, long. 119°00'45" W). Named on Santa Paula Peak (1951) 7.5' quadrangle.

Timber Creek [VENTURA]: *stream,* flows 4.5 miles to Sespe Creek 13 miles east-northeast of Wheeler Springs (lat. 34°33'25" N, long. 119°04'10" W; sec. 3, T 5 N, R 21 W). Named on Topatopa Mountains (1943) 7.5' quadrangle.

Timberville: see **Newbury Park** [VENTURA].

Timms Bay: see **Avalon Bay** [LOS ANGELES].

Timms Cove: see **Avalon Bay** [LOS ANGELES].

Timm's Landing: see **Avalon** [LOS ANGELES].

Timms' Point: see **San Pedro** [LOS ANGELES] (2).

Tims Canyon [SAN DIEGO]: *canyon,* drained by a stream that flows 2 miles to Santa Ysabel Creek 1.5 miles east of San Pasqual (lat. 33°05'20" N, long. 116°55'30" W; near W line sec. 31, T 12 S, R 1 E). Named on San Pasqual (1954) 7.5' quadrangle. The name recalls Mr. Tim, who homesteaded in the neighborhood about 1900 (Stein, p. 140).

Tin Can Cabin Campground [VENTURA]: *locality,* 2.5 miles south of Cobblestone Mountain along Agua Blanca Creek (lat. 34°34'10" N, long. 118°51'40" W; sec. 35, T 6 N, R 19 W). Named on Cobblestone Mountain (1958) 7.5' quadrangle.

Tin Can Flat [SAN DIEGO]: *area,* 2 miles west of Boucher Hill (lat. 33°19'50" N, long. 116°57'05" W). Named on Boucher Hill (1948) 7.5' quadrangle. The place was a popular picnic spot (Stein, p. 140).

Tin Mine Canyon [ORANGE]: *canyon,* drained by a stream that flows nearly 0.5 mile to Riverside County 2.25 miles southeast of Serra Peak (lat. 33°49'20" N, long. 117°37'45" W; sec. 17, T 4 S, R 7 W). Named on Black Star Canyon (1967) 7.5' quadrangle.

Tinta Creek [VENTURA]: *stream,* heads in Santa Barbara County and flows 4.5 miles in Ventura County to Rancho Nuevo Creek 8 miles northwest of Reyes Peak (lat. 34°42'15" N, long. 119°23'20" W). Named on Rancho Nuevo Creek (1943) 7.5' quadrangle.

Titus [SAN DIEGO]: *locality,* 1 mile north-northeast of Jacumba along San Diego and Arizona Eastern Railroad (lat. 32°37'50" N, long. 116°10'45" W; sec. 5, T 18 S, R 8 E). Named on Jacumba (1959) 7.5' quadrangle.

Tobanao Canyon: see **Topanga Canyon** [LOS ANGELES].

Tobanca Canyon: see **Topanga Canyon** [LOS ANGELES].

Todd: see **Oxnard** [VENTURA].

Todd Barranca [VENTURA]: *gully,* extends for 3 miles from the mouth of Wheeler Canyon to Santa Clara River 4.5 miles southwest of Santa Paula (lat. 34°18'10" N, long. 119°06'40" W). Named on Santa Paula (1951) and Saticoy (1951) 7.5' quadrangles. The name commemorates Marquis de LaFayette Todd, who came to Ventura in 1869 (Ricard).

Toll Canyon [LOS ANGELES]: *canyon,* less than 0.5 mile long, nearly 3 miles east of Burbank city hall (lat. 34°10'30" N, long. 118°15'40" W). Named on Burbank (1953) 7.5' quadrangle.

Toluca: see **North Hollywood** [LOS ANGELES].

Toluca Lake [LOS ANGELES]: *lake,* less than 0.5 mile long, 3.5 miles southwest of Burbank city hall (lat. 34°08'45" N, long. 118° 20'45" W). Named on Burbank (1953) 7.5' quadrangle.

Tomato Spring [ORANGE]: *spring,* 5 miles north of El Toro (lat. 33° 41'45" N, long. 117°42'30" W). Named on El Toro (1968) 7.5' quadrangle. The feature first was called Aguage del Padre Gomez because Padre Gomez of the Portola expedition discovered it in 1769; the present name is from tomato plants found growing wild at the spot early in American times (Meadows, p. 18, 135).

Tomato Spring Canyon: see **Agua Chinon Wash** [ORANGE].

Tom Lucas Campground [LOS ANGELES]: *locality,* nearly 1.5 miles west-northwest of Condor Peak in Trail Canyon (lat. 34°19'50" N, long. 118°14'30" W). Named on Condor Peak (1959) 7.5' quadrangle. The name commemorates "Barefoot Tom" Lucas, a forest ranger who lived in Big

Tujunga Canyon for more than 30 years (Robinson, J.W., 1977, p. 148-149).

Toms Canyon [VENTURA]: *canyon*, drained by a stream that flows 3.5 miles to Hopper Canyon 2.5 miles west-northwest of Piru (lat. 34°25'25" N, long. 118°50'05" W; at S line sec. 14, T 4 N, R 19 W). Named on Piru (1952) 7.5' quadrangle.

Tonner Canyon [LOS ANGELES-ORANGE]: *canyon*, drained by a stream that heads in Los Angeles County and flows 9 miles, partly in San Bernardino County but mainly in Los Angeles County, to Brea Canyon 4 miles west of La Habra in Orange County (lat. 33° 56'20" N, long. 117°52'35" W). Named on San Dimas (1954) and Yorba Linda (1950) 7.5' quadrangles. Called La Brea Canyon on La Brea (1928) 6' quadrangle, and called Brea Canyon on Watts' (1898-1899) map, where present Brea Canyon is called Canada del Rodeo.

Topanga [LOS ANGELES]: *town*, 8.5 miles north-northwest of Santa Monica city hall (lat. 34°05'45" N, long. 118°36' W; sec. 7, T 1 S, R 16 W); the place is in Topanga Canyon. Named on Topanga (1952) 7.5' quadrangle. Postal authorities established Topanga post office in 1908 (Frickstad, p. 82).

Topanga Beach [LOS ANGELES]: *town*, 5.5 miles west-northwest of Santa Monica city hall along the coast (lat. 34°02'20" N, long. 118° 34'50" W); the place is at the mouth of Topanga Canyon. Named on Topanga (1952) 7.5' quadrangle.

Topanga Canyon [LOS ANGELES]: *canyon*, drained by a stream that flows 8 miles to the sea 5.5 miles west-northwest of Santa Monica city hall (lat. 34°02'15" N, long. 118°34'55" W). Named on Canoga Park (1952) and Topanga (1952) 7.5' quadrangles. United States Board on Geographic Names (1960c, p. 19) rejected the names "Tobanao Canyon," "Tobanca Canyon," and "Topango Canyon" for the feature. Calabasas (1903) 15' quadrangle shows Garapito Creek in present Topanga Canyon above the mouth of present Old Topanga Canyon. On Malibu Beach (1951) 7.5' quadrangle, present Old Topanga Canyon is called Topanga Canyon, but on Malibu Beach (1950, photorevised 1981) 7.5' quadrangle, present Old Topanga Canyon is named properly.

Topanga Canyon: see **Old Topanga Canyon** [LOS ANGELES].

Topanga Malibu Sequit [LOS ANGELES]: *land grant*, extends along the coast from Sequit Point to Las Flores Canyon (2). Named on Malibu Beach (1951), Point Dume (1951), and Triunfo Pass (1950) 7.5' quadrangles. Jose Bartolome Tapia received the land in 1804; Matthew Keller claimed 13,316 acres patented in 1872 (Cowan, p. 104). The words "Topanga" and "Malibu" have an Indian origin, and the word "Sequit" evidently has also (Kroeber, p. 46, 57, 63). According to Perez (p. 102), Jose J. Tapia was the grantee in 1805.

Topanga Malibu Sequit Creek: see **Malibu Creek** [LOS ANGELES].

Topanga Malibu Sequit Point: see **Malibu Point** [LOS ANGELES].

Topanga Park [LOS ANGELES]: *locality*, 6 miles north-northeast of Malibu Point (lat. 34°06'20" N, long. 118°37'40" W; sec. 2, T 1 S, R 17 W); the place is in Topanga Canyon. Named on Malibu Beach (1951) 7.5' quadrangle.

Topango Canyon: see **Topanga Canyon** [LOS ANGELES].

Topatopa Bluff [VENTURA]: *escarpment*, north-northwest-trending, 1.5 miles long, 6.25 miles west-northwest of Santa Paula Peak (lat. 34°29'15" N, long. 119°06'15" W; mainly in sec. 29, T 5 N, R 21 W). Named on Santa Paula Peak (1951) 7.5' quadrangle.

Topatopa Mountains [VENTURA]: *ridge*, northeast- to east-trending, 6 miles long, center 15 miles east of Wheeler Springs (near lat. 34°32' N, long. 119°02' W); Topatopa Peak is at the east end of the ridge. Named on Devils Heart Peak (1943) and Topatopa Mountains (1943) 7.5' quadrangles. Called Topatopa Ridge on Los Angeles County (1935) map. C.W. Whipple (p. 148) used the form "Topa Topa Mountains" for the name, which is of Indian origin (Kroeber, p. 63).

Topatopa Peak [VENTURA]: *peak*, less than 1 mile west-southwest of Devils Heart Peak (lat. 34°32'20" N, long. 118°59'15" W). Altitude 6210 feet. Named on Devils Heart Peak (1943) 7.5' quadrangle.

Topatopa Ridge: see **Topatopa Mountains** [VENTURA].

Top of the World [ORANGE]: *locality*, 1.5 miles east of Laguna Beach city hall at the south end of Temple Hill (lat. 33°32'35" N, long. 117°45'10" W; near S line sec. 19, T 7 S, R 8 W). Named on Laguna Beach (1965) 7.5' quadrangle.

Torote Canyon [SAN DIEGO]: *canyon*, drained by a stream that flows 2.5 miles to Indian Gorge 4 miles northwest of Sweeney Pass (lat. 32°52'15" N, long. 116°14'05" W; sec. 14, T 15 S, R 7 E). Named on Agua Caliente Springs (1959), Sombrero Peak (1959), and Sweeney Pass (1959) 7.5' quadrangles. Elephant trees grow along the canyon—*torote* means "elephant tree" in Spanish (Bloomquist, 1970, p. 34).

Torqua Spring [LOS ANGELES]: *spring*, 3.5 miles northwest of Avalon on Santa Catalina Island (lat. 33°23'05" N, long. 118° 22' W). Named on Santa Catalina East (1950) 7.5' quadrangle.

Torquemada: see **Mount Torquemada** [LOS ANGELES].

Torrance [LOS ANGELES]: *city*, 10 miles west-northwest of Long Beach city hall (lat. 33°50'15" N, long. 118°20'25" W). Named on Inglewood (1952), Redondo Beach (1951), and Torrance (1964) 7.5' quadrangles. Postal authorities established Torrance post office in 1912 (Frickstad, p. 82), and the city incorporated in 1921. The name is for Jared S. Torrance, who founded the community and named it in 1911 (Gudde, 1949, p. 366).

Torrey Canyon [VENTURA]: *canyon*, drained by a stream that flows 1.5 miles to the valley of Santa Clara River nearly 1.5 miles south of Piru (lat. 34°23'20" N, long. 118°47'45" W; at E line sec. 31, T 4 N, R 18 W). Named on Piru (1952) and Simi (1951) 7.5' quadrangles. The name commemorates Dr. John Torrey, who visited the place in 1865 while inspecting petroleum deposits (White, p. 96).

Tourmaline Queen Mountain [SAN DIEGO]: *peak*, 1.5 miles north of Pala (lat. 33°23'25" N, long. 117°04'15" W; near SE cor. sec. 15, T 9 S, R 2 W). Altitude 1922 feet. Named on Pechanga (1968) 7.5' quadrangle, which shows Tourmaline Queen mine situated 850 feet east of the peak. Called Queen Mountain on Jahns and Wright's (1951a) map.

Townsend Peak [LOS ANGELES]: *peak*, 2.5 miles east-southeast of Whitaker Peak (lat. 34°33'35" N, long. 118°41'20" W; near S line sec. 33, T 6 N, R 17 W). Altitude 3184 feet. Named on Whitaker Peak (1958) 7.5' quadrangle.

Towsley Canyon [LOS ANGELES]: *canyon*, drained by a stream that flows 4 miles to Gavin Canyon 2.25 miles southwest of Newhall (lat. 34°21'30" N, long. 118°33'20" W; sec. 9, T 3 N, R 16 W). Named on Oat Mountain (1952) 7.5' quadrangle. The name commemorates Darius Towsley, a pioneer in the canyon (Reynolds, p. 13).

Toyon: see **Camp Toyon** [LOS ANGELES].

Toyon Bay: see **Willow Cove** [LOS ANGELES].

Trabuco [ORANGE]: *land grant*, along and near the upper part of Arroyo Trabuco. Named on Cañada Gobernadora (1949), El Toro (1950), San Juan Capistrano (1949), and Santiago Peak (1954) 7.5' quadrangles. Santiago Arguello and others received 5 leagues in 1841 and 1846; John Forster claimed 22,184 acres patented in 1866 (Cowan, p. 104). According to Perez (p. 102), Juan Forster was the grantee in 1846.

Trabuco: see **Trabuco Oaks** [ORANGE].

Trabuco Campground [ORANGE]: *locality*, 2.5 miles south of Santiago Peak (lat. 33°40'30" N, long. 117°31'15" W; near E line sec. 5, T 6 S, R 6 W); the place is in Trabuco Canyon. Named on Santiago Peak (1954) 7.5' quadrangle.

Trabuco Canyon [ORANGE]: *canyon*, drained by a stream that flows nearly 7 miles to lowlands 3.5 miles south-southwest of Santiago Peak (lat. 33°40'05" N, long. 117°33'45" W; sec. 12, T 6 S, R 7 W). Named on Alberhill (1954) and Santiago Peak (1954) 7.5' quadrangles. The name recalls a blunderbuss that one of Portola's soldiers lost at the place in 1769—*trabuco* means "blunderbuss" in Spanish (Gudde, 1949, p. 367).

Trabuco Canyon: see **Trabuco Oaks** [ORANGE].

Trabuco Creek: see **Arroyo Trabuco** [ORANGE].

Trabuco Mesa: see **Plano Trabuco** [ORANGE].

Trabuco Oaks [ORANGE]: *village*, 4.5 miles southwest of Santiago Peak in Hickey Canyon (lat. 33°39'50" N, long. 117°35'20" W; at W line sec. 11, T 6 S, R 7 W). Named on Santiago Peak (1954) 7.5' quadrangle, which shows Trabuco Canyon post office at the site. Postal authorities established Trabuco Canyon post office in 1938 (Frickstad, p. 118). United States Board on Geographic Names (1970a, p. 2) approved the name "Trabuco Canyon" for the place, and gave the names "Trabuco Oaks" and "Trabuco" as variants.

Trabuco Peak [ORANGE]: *peak*, 26 miles east of Santa Ana on Orange-Riverside County line (lat. 33°42'10" N, long. 117°28'30" W; sec. 26, T 5 S, R 6 W). Named on Alberhill (1954) 7.5' quadrangle.

Trabuco Peak: see **Santiago Peak** [ORANGE].

Trail Canyon [LOS ANGELES]: *canyon*, drained by a stream that flows 5 miles to Big Tujunga Canyon 4.25 miles northeast of Sunland (lat. 34°18'10" N, long. 118°15'20" W; near E line sec. 32, T 3 N, R 13 W). Named on Condor Peak (1959) and Sunland (1953) 7.5' quadrangles. North Fork branches from the main canyon 1.5 miles west of Condor Peak; it is 9 miles long and is named on Condor Peak (1959) 7.5' quadrangle.

Trail Canyon [VENTURA]: *canyon*, drained by a stream that flows 1.5 miles to Piru Creek nearly 5 miles north-northeast of McDonald Peak (lat. 34°41'25" N, long. 118°53'30" W; near NE cor. sec. 21, T 7 N, R 19 W). Named on McDonald Peak (1958) 7.5' quadrangle.

Trailer Canyon [LOS ANGELES]: *canyon*, drained by a stream that flows 1.25 miles to Santa Ynez Canyon 6 miles northwest of Santa Monica city hall (lat. 34°04'25" N, long. 118°33'50" W). Named on Topanga (1952) 7.5' quadrangle.

Trail Fork [LOS ANGELES]: *canyon*, 2 miles long, opens into Shortcut Canyon 8 miles south of Pacifico Mountain (lat. 34°15'40" N, long. 118°02'45" W; near W line sec. 16, T 2 N, R 11 W). Named on Chilao Flat (1959) 7.5' quadrangle.

Trail Fork: see **San Gabriel River** [LOS ANGELES].

Trampas Canyon [ORANGE]: *canyon*, drained by a stream that flows 2 miles to San Juan Creek nearly 5 miles east of San Juan Capistrano (lat. 33°30'50" N, long. 117°34'55" W; near S line sec. 35, T 7 S, R 7 W). Named on Cañada Gobernadora (1968) and San Clemente (1968) 7.5'

quadrangles.

Trancas [LOS ANGELES]: *locality,* 3 miles northwest of Point Dume (lat. 34°01'50" N, long. 118°50'35" W); the place is at the mouth of Trancas Canyon. Dume Point (1932) 6' quadrangle shows a place called Malibu Trading Sta. at the site.

Trancas Beach [LOS ANGELES]: *beach,* 3 miles northwest of Point Dume along the coast (lat. 34°02' N, long. 118°51' W); the beach is at and west of the mouth of Trancas Canyon. Named on Point Dume (1951) 7.5' quadrangle. On Dume Point (1932) 6' quadrangle, the name "Trancas Beach" applies also to the beach southeast of the mouth of Trancas Canyon, where Point Dume (1951) 7.5' quadrangle has the name "Zuma Beach County Park."

Trancas Canyon [LOS ANGELES]: *canyon,* drained by a stream that flows 6 miles to the sea 3 miles northwest of Point Dume (lat. 34° 01'45" N, long. 118°50'30" W). Named on Point Dume (1951) 7.5' quadrangle.

Travertine Palms [SAN DIEGO]: *locality,* 19 miles northeast of Borrego Springs (lat. 32°24'05" N, long. 116°05'50" W; near W line sec. 12, T 9 S, R 8 E). Named on Rabbit Peak (1959) 7.5' quadrangle.

Travertine Palms Wash [SAN DIEGO]: *stream,* flows 5 miles to Imperial County 20 miles northeast of Borrego Springs (lat. 33° 25' N, long. 116°05'05" W; at E line sec. 1, T 9 S, R 8 E); Travertine Palms is along a branch of the stream. Named on Oasis (1956) 7.5' quadrangle.

Trego: see **Harold** [LOS ANGELES].

Tres Isleos: see **Anacapa Island** [VENTURA].

Tripas Canyon [VENTURA]: *canyon,* drained by a stream that flows 5.25 miles to Tapo Canyon (1) 6.25 miles northwest of Santa Susana Pass (lat. 34°19'30" N, long. 118°43'10" W; near S line sec. 24, T 3 N, R 18 W). Named on Santa Susana (1951) and Simi (1951) 7.5' quadrangles.

Triunfo: see **Triunfo Corner** [VENTURA].

Triunfo Canyon [LOS ANGELES]: *canyon,* extends for 10 miles along Potrero Valley Creek [LOS ANGELES-VENTURA] below Russell Valley [LOS ANGELES-VENTURA], and along Malibu Creek above a point 4 miles north-northwest of Malibu Point (lat. 34°05' N, long. 118°42'30" W; sec. 18, T 1 S, R 17 W). Named on Malibu Beach (1951), Point Dume (1951), and Thousand Oaks (1952) 7.5' quadrangles. The name recalls the designations "El triunfo del Dulcisimo Nombre de Jeses" and "El triunfo de Jesus" that Crespi gave to places in the vicinity of the canyon in 1770—*El triunmfo del Dulcisimo Nombre de Jeses* means "The triumph of the Sweet Name of Jesus" in Spanish. (Gudde, 1949, p. 369). Parke (p. 3) used the form "Triompho" for the name.

Triunfo Corner [VENTURA]: *locality,* 1.25 miles southeast of downtown Thousand Oaks (lat. 34°09'20" N, long. 118°49'20" W; sec. 24, T 1 N, R 19 W). Named on Thousand Oaks (1952) 7.5' quadrangle. Called Triunfo on Triunfo Pass (1921) 15' quadrangle. Postal authorities established Triumfo (with an "m") post office in 1915, changed the name to Triunfo in 1917, and discontinued it in 1936 (Frickstad, p. 219). They established Yerba Buena post office 3 miles west of Triumfo post office (NW quarter sec. 11, T 1 S, R 20 W) in 1916 and discontinued it in 1917 (Salley, p. 244).

Triunfo Pass [VENTURA]: *pass,* 5 miles south-southwest of Newbury Park (lat. 34°06'45" N, long. 118°55' W; near W line sec. 6, T 1 S, R 19 W). Named on Triunfo Pass (1950) 7.5' quadrangle.

Troedel Spring [LOS ANGELES]: *spring,* 2 miles north-northwest of the village of Lake Hughes (lat. 34°42' N, long. 118°27'40" W; sec. 15, T 7 N, R 15 W). Named on Lake Hughes (1957) 7.5' quadrangle.

Tropico [LOS ANGELES]: *locality,* 5 miles south-southeast of Burbank along Southern Pacific Railroad (lat. 34°07'25" N, long. 118° 15'45" W). Named on Santa Monica (1902) 15' quadrangle. Postal authorities established Tropico post office in 1888, discontinued it in 1918, and reestablished it in 1964; developers of the community coined the name (Salley, p. 225). Postal authorities established Casa Verdugo post office 3 miles north of Tropico in 1906 and discontinued it in 1918 (Salley, p. 39).

Trough Canyon [LOS ANGELES]:

(1) *canyon,* drained by a stream that flows 3.5 miles to Salt Creek 11.5 miles southeast of Gorman (lat. 34°39'05" N, long. 118°41'20" W; sec. 33, T 7 N, R 17 W). Named on Liebre Mountain (1958) 7.5' quadrangle.

(2) *canyon,* drained by a stream that flows less than 1 mile to Lobo Canyon (1) 8 miles north of Point Dume (lat. 34°07'05" N, long. 118°31' W; near S line sec. 31, T 1 N, R 18 W). Named on Point Dume (1951) 7.5' quadrangle.

Trough Canyon [VENTURA]: *canyon,* drained by a stream that flows 1 mile to Bus Canyon 6 miles northeast of Thousand Oaks (lat. 34°14'15" N, long. 118°45'55" W; near SE cor. sec. 21, T 2 N, R 18 W). Named on Thousand Oaks (1952) 7.5' quadrangle.

Trough Canyon: see **Little Trough Canyon** [LOS ANGELES].

Trout Creek [VENTURA]: *stream,* flows 4 miles to Sespe Creek 9 miles east-northeast of Wheeler Springs (lat. 34°33'35" N, long. 119°08'35" W; near NW cor. sec. 1, T 5 N, R 22 W). Named on Lion Canyon (1943) 7.5' quadrangle.

Troutman Mountain [SAN DIEGO]: *hill,* nearly 5 miles north of Monument Peak in Vallecito Valley (lat. 32°57'40" N, long. 116° 24'20" W; on S line sec. 7, T 14 S, R 6 E). Altitude 2086 feet. Named on Monument Peak (1959) 7.5' quadrangle.

Troy Canyon [SAN DIEGO]: *canyon,* drained by a stream that flows 4 miles to Long Canyon (2) 3.25 miles east-northeast of Buckman Springs (lat. 32°47'20" N, long. 116°26'20" W; near N line sec. 14, T 16 S, R 5 E). Named on Mount Laguna (1960) 7.5' quadrangle.

Troy Flat [SAN DIEGO]: *area,* 4 miles northeast of Buckman Springs (lat. 32°48'25" N, long. 116°26'25" W; at S line sec. 2, T 16 S, R 5 E); the feature is in Troy Canyon. Named on Mount Laguna (1960) 7.5' quadrangle.

Trujillo Creek [SAN DIEGO]: *stream,* flows 5 miles to San Luis Rey River at Pala (lat. 33°21'50" N, long. 117°04'15" W; sec. 27, T 9 S, R 2 W). Named on Pala (1968) and Pechanga (1968) 7.5' quadrangles. Called Salmons Creek on Jahns and Wright's (1951b) map, which shows the abandoned site of Salmons City along the stream northwest of Chief Mountain. The name "Salmons" recalls F.A. Salmons, who with his associates located Tourmaline Queen mine in 1903 (Jahns and Wright, p. 56).

Tubb Canyon [SAN DIEGO]: *canyon,* 2 miles long, 4.5 miles southwest of Borrego Springs (lat. 33°12'25" N, long. 116°25'30" W). Named on Tubb Canyon (1959) 7.5' quadrangle. The name reportedly is from a sunken wooden tub that held water for cattle (Stein, p. 142).

Tubb Canyon Spring [SAN DIEGO]: *spring,* nearly 4 miles south-southwest of Borrego Springs (lat. 33°12'45" N, long. 116°24'45" W); the spring is near the mouth of Tubb Canyon. Named on Tubb Canyon (1959) 7.5' quadrangle.

Tuhunga: see **Tujunga** [LOS ANGELES] (2).

Tujunga [LOS ANGELES]:

(1) *land grant,* at Sunland and Tujunga (2). Named on Burbank (1953) and Sunland (1953) 7.5' quadrangles. Pedro Lopez and others received 1.5 leagues in 1840; D.W. Alexander and others claimed 6661 acres patented in 1874 (Cowan, p. 105).

(2) *district,* 1.25 miles east-southeast of Sunland in Los Angeles (lat. 34°15' N, long. 118°17' W); the place is on Tujunga grant. Named on Burbank (1953) and Sunland (1953) 7.5' quadrangles. Postal authorities established Tuhunga post office in 1855, discontinued it in 1894, and reestablished it with the name Tujunga in 1916 (Salley, p. 225). California Mining Bureau's (1917a) map shows a place called Littlelands located about halfway between Sunland and La Crescenta. Postal authorities established Littlelands post office 9 miles southeast of San Fernando in 1914; they moved it and changed the name to Tujunga in 1916 (Salley, p. 123).

Tujunga Canyon: see **Big Tujunga Canyon** [LOS ANGELES]; **Little Tujunga Canyon** [LOS ANGELES].

Tujunga Creek: see **Big Tujunga Canyon** [LOS ANGELES]; **Little Tujunga Creek**, under **Little Tujunga Canyon** [LOS ANGELES].

Tujunga Mountains: see **San Gabriel Mountains** [LOS ANGELES].

Tujunga River: see **Big Tujunga Canyon** [LOS ANGELES].

Tujunga Valley [LOS ANGELES]: *valley,* 3.5 miles long, center 1.5 miles west-northwest of Sunland (lat. 34°16'05" N, long. 118° 20' W); the valley is below the mouth of Big Tujunga Canyon. Named on Sunland (1953) 7.5' quadrangle.

Tujunga Wash [LOS ANGELES]: *dry wash,* extends for 9 miles from Hansen Flood Control Basin to Los Angeles River 4.25 miles southeast of Van Nuys (lat. 34°08'45" N, long. 118°23'15" W). Named on San Fernando (1966) and Van Nuys (1953) 7.5' quadrangles. Van Nuys (1953) 7.5' quadrangle also shows a feature called Tujunga Wash Flood Control Channel, which occupies an artificial watercourse that diverges from Tujunga Wash 4.5 miles northeast of Van Nuys and extends for 7.5 miles to Los Angeles River 4.25 miles southeast of Van Nuys (lat. 34°08'45" N, long. 118°23'15" W). The Tujunga Wash Flood Control Channel of Van Nuys (1953) 7.5' quadrangle is called Tujunga Wash on Van Nuys (1966) 7.5' quadrangle, which shows Hollywood freeway following the original Tujunga Wash, which it calls Central Branch Tujunga Wash.

Tule: see **Mount Tule** [SAN DIEGO].

Tule Canyon [LOS ANGELES]: *canyon,* drained by a stream that flows 5 miles to Ruby Canyon (2) nearly 4 miles east of Warm Springs Mountain (lat. 34°35'50" N, long. 118°30'40" W. Named on Green Valley (1958), Lake Hughes (1957), and Warm Springs Mountain (1958) 7.5' quadrangles.

Tule Canyon [SAN DIEGO]: *canyon,* 2.5 miles long, opens into Carrizo Gorge 4 miles north of Jacumba (lat. 32°40'30" N, long. 116°12' W; sec. 19, T 17 S, R 8 E). Named on Jacumba (1959) 7.5' quadrangle.

Tule Canyon: see **South Tule Canyon** [LOS ANGELES].

Tule Creek [SAN DIEGO]: *stream,* flows 9 miles to end in McCain Valley 1.5 north of Manzanita (lat. 32°41'35" N, long. 116°17'05" W; sec. 17, T 17 S, R 7 E). Named on Live Oak Springs (1959) and Sombrero Peak (1959) 7.5' quadrangles.

Tule Creek [VENTURA]: *stream,* flows 5.25 miles to Sespe Creek 3.5 miles north-northeast of Wheeler Spring (lat. 34°33'30" N, long. 119°16' W; at S line sec. 36, T 6 N, R 23 W). Named on Wheeler Springs (1943) 7.5' quadrangle.

Tule Lake [SAN DIEGO]: *lake,* 0.5 mile long, 5 miles northwest of Jacumba (lat. 32°40'30" N, long. 116°14'45" W; sec. 22, T 17 S, R 7 E). Named on

Jacumba (1959) 7.5' quadrangle.

Tule Ridge [LOS ANGELES]: *ridge*, southeast-trending, 4.25 miles long, 4 miles south-southwest of the village of Lake Hughes (lat. 34°37'15" N, long. 118°27'50" W); the ridge is southeast of Tule Canyon and South Tule Canyon. Named on Green Valley (1958) and Lake Hughes (1957) 7.5' quadrangles.

Tule Springs [SAN DIEGO]: *spring*, 8 miles northwest of Descanso (lat. 32°56'20" N, long. 116°42'45" W; sec. 19, T 14 S, R 3 E). Named on Tule Springs (1960) 7.5' quadrangle. Tucker and Reed's (1939) map has the singular form "Tule Spr." for the name.

Tule Wash [SAN DIEGO]: *stream*, flows nearly 3 miles to Imperial County 6.5 miles north-northeast of Ocotillo Wells (lat. 33°13'45" N, long. 116°04'55" W; at W line sec. 7, T 11 S, R 9 E). Named on Shell Reef (1959) 7.5' quadrangle.

Tuley Canyon [SAN DIEGO]: *canyon*, about 1 mile long, opens into the canyon of San Luis Rey River 2.25 miles north-northeast of downtown Oceanside (lat. 33°13'15" N, long. 117°21'35" W; sec. 13, T 11 S, R 5 W). Named on San Luis Rey (1968) 7.5' quadrangle.

Tumble Inn [LOS ANGELES]: *locality*, 7 miles southeast of Gorman (lat. 34°42'30" N, long. 118°43'15" W; sec. 7, T 7 N, R 17 W). Named on Liebre Mountain (1958) 7.5' quadrangle.

Tumble Inn Campground [LOS ANGELES]: *locality*, 7 miles southeast of Gorman (lat. 34°42'55" N, long. 118°43' W; sec. 7, T 7 N, R 17 W); the place is 0.5 mile north-northeast of the site of Tumble Inn. Named on Liebre Mountain (1958) 7.5' quadrangle.

Tumbler Canyon [LOS ANGELES]: *canyon*, drained by a stream that flows 1.5 miles to Cogswell Reservoir 8.5 miles north-northwest of Azusa city hall (lat. 34°14'20" N, long. 117°58'45" W; near SE cor. sec. 24, T 2 N, R 11 W). Named on Azusa (1953) 7.5' quadrangle.

Tuna Canyon [LOS ANGELES]: *canyon*, drained by a stream that flows 3 miles to the sea 6 miles west-northwest of Santa Monica city hall (lat. 34°02'20" N, long. 118°35'20" W; at E line sec. 31, T 1 S, R 16 W); the mouth of the canyon is at Las Tunas Beach. Named on Topanga (1952) 7.5' quadrangle.

Tunnel [LOS ANGELES]: *locality*, 3.5 miles south-southeast of Newhall along Southern Pacific Railroad (lat. 34°19'45" N, long. 118° 30'10" W); the place is at the south end of a railroad tunnel. Named on Oat Mountain (1952) 7.5' quadrangle. Postal authorities established Tunnel post office in 1876 and discontinued it the same year (Frickstad, p. 82). Los Angeles County (1935) map shows a feature called Sunshine Canyon that is about 2 miles long and opens into Weldon Canyon from the west less than 0.5 mile south-southeast of Tunnel.

Turkey Canyon [LOS ANGELES]: *canyon*, drained by a stream that flows nearly 3 miles to Elizabeth Lake Canyon 4.25 miles southeast of Burnt Peak (lat. 34°38'05" N, long. 118°31'45" W). Named on Burnt Peak (1958) 7.5' quadrangle.

Turnbull Canyon [LOS ANGELES]: *canyon*, drained by a stream that flows nearly 2 miles to end less than 1 mile north of present Whittier city hall (lat. 33°59'05" N, long. 118°01'55" W). Named on Whittier (1949) 7.5' quadrangle.

Turnbull Creek [LOS ANGELES]: *stream*, flows less than 1 mile from Painter Lagoon to La Canada Verde Creek 2.5 miles south of present Whittier city hall (lat. 33°56'05" N, long. 118°02'15" W). Named on Whittier (1949) 7.5' quadrangle. Whittier (1965) 7.5' quadrangle shows a drain along the course of the stream

Turner's Pass: see **San Francisquito Pass**, under **San Francisquito Canyon** [LOS ANGELES].

Turtle Canyon [VENTURA]: *canyon*, drained by a stream that flows 2.5 miles to Piru Creek 5.5 miles east-southeast of Cobblestone Mountain (lat. 34°34'05" N, long. 118°46'40" W). Named on Cobblestone Mountain (1958) 7.5' quadrangle.

Tustin [ORANGE]: *city*, 2.5 miles east of Santa Ana city hall (lat. 33° 44'35" N, long. 117°49'25" W). Named on Orange (1964) and Tustin (1965) 7.5' quadrangles. Postal authorities established Tustin City post office in 1872 and changed the name to Tustin in 1894 (Frickstad, p. 118). The city incorporated in 1927. Columbus Tustin bought land at the place in 1868 and laid out Tustin City in 1870 (Meadows, p. 136).

Tustin City: see **Tustin** [ORANGE].

Tustin Junction: see **South Anaheim** [ORANGE].

Tuyanga Canyon: see **Big Tujunga Canyon** [LOS ANGELES].

Tweedy Canyon: see **Hughes Lake** [LOS ANGELES].

Tweedy Lake [LOS ANGELES]: *lake*, 650 feet long, 3.25 miles north of Burnt Peak (lat. 34°43'50" N, long. 118°34' W; on N line sec. 3, T 7 N, R 16 W). Named on Burnt Peak (1958) 7.5' quadrangle. The name is for Robert Tweedy, a homesteader who was the first owner of the lake (Gudde, 1969, p. 348). The feature now is called Lake Katrina (Settle, p. 36).

Twin Canyon [LOS ANGELES]: *canyon*, drained by a stream that flows less than 0.5 mile to Arroyo Seco 7 miles north-northwest of Pasadena city hall (lat. 34°14'30" N, long. 118°11' W). Named on Pasadena (1953) 7.5' quadrangle.

Twin Flats [SAN DIEGO]: *area*, 2.5 miles south-southeast of Rodriguez Mountain (lat. 33°11'10" N, long. 116°52'55" W). Named on Rodriguez Mountain (1948) 7.5' quadrangle.

Twin Lakes [LOS ANGELES]: *locality*, 1.5 miles north of Chatsworth (lat. 34°16'40" N, long. 118°35'50" W; on N line sec. 7, T 2 N, R 16 W). Named on Oat Mountain (1952) 7.5' quadrangle. On Chatsworth (1940) and Zelzah (1941) 6' quadrangles, present Deer Lake Highlands is called Twin Lakes.

Twin Lakes [SAN DIEGO]: *lakes*, two, largest 600 feet long, about 9.5 miles north-northwest of Warner Springs in Cooper Canyon (lat. 33°25'05" N, long. 116°40'55" W; near NW cor. sec. 4, T 9 S, R 3 E). Named on Beauty Mountain (1960) 7.5' quadrangle.

Twin Lakes Canyon: see **Falls Creek** [LOS ANGELES].

Twin Lakes Park: see **Deer Lake Highlands** [LOS ANGELES].

Twin Oaks [SAN DIEGO]: *locality*, 5.25 miles east-southeast of Vista (lat. 33°11'05" N, long. 117°09'15" W). Named on San Marcos (1968) 7.5' quadrangle. Postal authorities established Twin Oaks post office in 1889 and discontinued it in 1901 (Frickstad, p. 157). Tucker and Reed's (1939) map has the singular form "Twin Oak" for the name.

Twin Oaks Valley [SAN DIEGO]: *valley*, 5.5 miles east-southeast of Vista (lat. 33°10'40" N, long. 117°09'05" W); Twin Oaks is in the valley. Named on San Marcos (1968) 7.5' quadrangle.

Twin Peaks [LOS ANGELES]: *peaks*, two, 1.5 miles south of Waterman Mountain (lat. 34°19' N, long. 117°55'50" W). Named on Waterman Mountain (1959) 7.5' quadrangle. Called Waterman Mountain on Rock Creek (1903) 15' quadrangle, but United States Board on Geographic Names (1939, p. 35) rejected this name for the feature.

Twin Peaks [SAN DIEGO]: *peak*, 2 miles north of Poway (lat. 32°59'15" N, long. 117°02'30" W; sec. 1, T 14 S, R 2 W). Altitude 1306 feet. Named on Poway (1967) 7.5' quadrangle. Called Twin Peak on La Jolla (1903) 15' quadrangle.

Twin Pines Camp [VENTURA]: *locality*, 2.5 miles north-northwest of McDonald Peak (lat. 34°40'10" N, long. 118°57'05" W; sec. 25, T 7 N, R 20 W). Named on McDonald Peak (1958) 7.5' quadrangle.

Twin Points [ORANGE]: *promontory*, 1 mile west of Laguna Beach city hall along the coast (lat. 33°32'40" N, long. 117°47'55" W). Named on Laguna Beach (1965) 7.5' quadrangle.

Twin Rocks [LOS ANGELES]: *relief feature*, 4 miles northeast of Mount Banning on the north side of Santa Catalina Island (lat. 33° 25'05" N, long. 118°23'20" W). Named on Santa Catalina North (1950) 7.5' quadrangle. The feature first was called Pinnacle Rocks (Doran, 1980, p. 66).

Twin Springs Canyon [LOS ANGELES]: *canyon*, drained by a stream that flows 1 mile to Sawpit Canyon 5 miles northwest of Azusa city hall (lat. 34°11' N, long. 117°57'55" W; sec. 7, T 1 N, R 10 W). Named on Azusa (1953) 7.5' quadrangle.

Twin Valley Camp [LOS ANGELES]: *locality*, 3 miles west-northwest of Big Pines (lat. 34°23'55" N, long. 117°44'15" W). Named on Mescal Creek (1956) 7.5' quadrangle.

Twomile Point [LOS ANGELES]: *relief feature*, 8 miles north-northwest of Azusa city hall along Cogswell Reservoir (lat. 34°14'20" N, long. 117°58'25" W). Named on Azusa (1953) 7.5' quadrangle.

Two Rock Point [ORANGE]: *promontory*, 1.25 miles west of Laguna Beach city hall along the coast (lat. 33°32'45" N, long. 117°48'10" W). Named on Laguna Beach (1965) 7.5' quadrangle.

- U -

Una Lake [LOS ANGELES]: *lake*, 1100 feet long, 2 miles south of Palmdale (lat. 34°33' N, long. 118°06'40" W; near W line sec. 2, T 5 N, R 12 W); a road and railroad separate the feature from Lake Palmdale. Named on Palmdale (1958) 7.5' quadrangle.

Un Gallo Flat [SAN DIEGO]: *area*, 2.5 miles north of Buckman Springs along Cottonwood Creek (3) (lat. 32°48'30" N, long. 116° 29'45" W; mainly in sec. 5, T 16 S, R 5 E). Named on Mount Laguna (1960) 7.5' quadrangle. The name recalls an old rooster that was the lone survivor of a flock of chickens at the site; after Captain William Emery bought the place, Mrs. Emery chose the name "Glen Cliff" for a post office, but when postal authorities established a post office there in 1882, they named it instead "Emery" for William S. Emery, first postmaster—they discontinued it in 1887 (Salley, p. 69; Stein, p. 143-144).

Union Bay: see **Isthmus Cove** [LOS ANGELES].

Universal City [LOS ANGELES]: *locality*, 4 miles southwest of Burbank city hall (lat. 34°08'15" N, long. 118°21'15" W). Named on Burbank (1966) 7.5' quadrangle. Postal authorities established Universal City post office in 1915 (Frickstad, p. 83). The name is from Universal Pictures Company (Gudde, 1969, p. 350). Burbank (1966) 7.5' quadrangle shows a place called Campo de Cahunga located 1.25 miles northwest of Cahuenga Pass at Universal City. It was here that Fremont accepted the surrender of Andreas Pico in 1847; postal authorities established Cahuenga post office at or near the place in 1881, discontinued it in 1886, reestablished it in 1904, and discontinued it in 1907 (Salley, p. 31). Lankershim Ranch Land

and Water Company's (1888) map shows a place called Wyneka situated just west of Cahuenga.

University [LOS ANGELES]: *district,* 3.5 miles southwest of Los Angeles city hall (lat. 34°01'05" N, long. 118°17' W); present University of Southern California campus is at the place. Named on Santa Monica (1902) 15' quadrangle.

University City [SAN DIEGO]: *district,* 4 miles east of Point La Jolla in San Diego (lat. 32°51'15" N, long. 117°12'15" W); the place is 1.5 miles southeast of University of California San Diego campus. Named on La Jolla (1967) 7.5' quadrangle.

University Heights [SAN DIEGO]: *district,* 10 miles southeast of Point La Jolla in San Diego (lat. 32°45'20" N, long. 117°08'15" W). Named on La Jolla (1967) 7.5' quadrangle.

Upper Big Tujunga Canyon: see **Big Tujunga Canyon** [LOS ANGELES].

Upper Buffalo Corral Reservoir [LOS ANGELES]: *lake,* 650 feet long, 4.25 miles north-northwest of Mount Banning in Little Springs Canyon on Santa Catalina Island (lat. 33°25'35" N, long. 118°28'05" W); the lake is 1 mile north of Lower Buffalo Corral Reservoir. Named on Santa Catalina North (1950) 7.5' quadrangle.

Upper Doane Valley [SAN DIEGO]: *valley,* 1.25 miles east of Boucher Hill (lat. 33°20'15" N, long. 116°53'45" W); the valley is along Doane Creek about 1 mile southeast of Lower Doane Valley. Named on Boucher Hill (1948) 7.5' quadrangle.

Upper Falls Public Camp [LOS ANGELES]: *locality,* about 2.5 miles east-northeast of Mount Wilson (1) in Santa Anita Canyon (lat. 34°12'55" N, long. 118°01'10" W; sec. 34, T 2 N, R 11 W); the place is 0.25 mile north of Sturtevant Falls. Named on Mount Wilson (1953) 7.5' quadrangle.

Upper Franklin Canyon Reservoir [LOS ANGELES]: *lake,* 1200 feet long, behind a dam 3.25 miles north of Beverly Hills city hall (lat. 34°07'10" N, long. 118°24'35" W; at S line sec. 36, T 1 N, R 15 W); the dam is in Franklin Canyon about 2 miles upstream from the dam that forms Franklin Canyon Reservoir. Named on Beverly Hills (1966) 7.5' quadrangle. Called Upper Res. on Beverly Hills (1950) 7.5' quadrangle.

Upper French Valley [SAN DIEGO]: *valley,* 2.5 miles northeast of Boucher Hill (lat. 33°21'35" N, long. 116°52'55" W); the valley is along French Creek 1.5 miles east-northeast of Lower French Valley. Named on Boucher Hill (1948) and Palomar Observatory (1949) 7.5' quadrangles. Called French Valley on Ramona (1903) 30' quadrangle.

Upper Green Valley [SAN DIEGO]: *canyon,* 2 miles long, 4 miles east of Cuyamaca Peak on upper reaches of Sweetwater River (lat. 32°57'10" N, long. 116°32'30" W); the canyon is upstream from Green Valley (3). Named on Cuyamaca Peak (1960) 7.5' quadrangle.

Upper Hellhole [SAN DIEGO]: *canyon,* 1.5 miles southwest of Rodriguez Mountain (lat. 33°13'20" N, long. 116°55'15" W); the feature is along Hell Creek upstream from Lower Hellhole. Named on Rodriguez Mountain (1948) 7.5' quadrangle.

Upper Newport Bay [ORANGE]: *bay,* 6.5 miles east of Huntington Beach civic center (lat. 33°38'30" N, long. 117°53'15" W); the feature extends inland from Newport Bay. Named on Newport Beach (1965) 7.5' quadrangle. Called Newport Bay on Newport Beach (1935) 7.5' quadrangle. In the early days, millions of tree frogs lived in a swamp in lowlands between Upper Newport Bay and Red Hill; the place was known as Cienega de las Ranas—*Cienega de las Ranas* means "Swamp of the Frogs" in Spanish—and later it was called San Joaquin Swamp or Cienega de San Joaquin for San Joaquin grant (Meadows, p. 52).

Upper Ojai Valley [VENTURA]: *valley,* 4 miles east of the town of Ojai (lat. 34°26'15" N, long. 119°10'15" W); the feature is southeast of the east end of Ojai Valley, and at a higher elevation. Named on Ojai (1952) 7.5' quadrangle.

Upper Otay Lake: see **Upper Otay Reservoir** [SAN DIEGO].

Upper Otay Reservoir [SAN DIEGO]: *lake,* behind a dam 5.5 miles south-southwest of Jamul (lat. 32°38'55" N, long. 116°55'50" W); the lake is just above Lower Otay Reservoir. Named on Jamul Mountains (1955) 7.5' quadrangle. United States Board on Geographic Names (1979b, p. 8-9) approved the name "Upper Otay Lake" for the feature, and rejected the names "Otay Reservoir" and "Upper Otay Reservoir" for it.

Upper Pacifico Campground [LOS ANGELES]: *locality,* at Pacifico Mountain (lat. 34°22'55" N, long. 118°02' W). Named on Pacifico Mountain (1959) 7.5' quadrangle.

Upper San Fernando Reservoir [LOS ANGELES]: *lake,* 0.5 mile long, 3.5 miles west-northwest of downtown San Fernando (lat. 34°18'25" N, long. 118°29'30" W). Named on San Fernando (1953) 7.5' quadrangle. Called Upper Van Norman Lake on San Fernando (1966) 7.5' quadrangle.

Upper Shake Campground [LOS ANGELES]: *locality,* 2.5 miles east-northeast of Burnt Peak (lat. 34°41'25" N, long. 118°31'45" W; near S line sec. 13, T 7 N, R 16 W); the place is in Shake Canyon 0.5 mile south-southwest of Lower Shake Campground. Named on Burnt Peak (1958) 7.5' quadrangle.

Upper Stone Canyon Reservoir [LOS ANGELES]: *lake,* 0.25 miles long, behind a dam 4.5 miles northwest of Beverly Hills city hall (lat. 34°07'05" N, long. 118°27'15" W); the lake is in Stone Canyon (2) just above Stone Canyon Reservoir. Named on Beverly Hills (1966) 7.5' quadrangle.

Upper Switzer Campground [LOS ANGELES]: *locality,* 6 miles southeast of Condor Peak along Arroyo Seco (lat. 34°16' N, long. 118°08'30" W); the place is 0.25 mile east of Lower Switzer Campground. Named on Condor Peak (1959) 7.5' quadrangle.

Upper Van Norman Lake: see **Upper San Fernando Reservoir** [LOS ANGELES].

- V -

Vacation Isle [SAN DIEGO]: *island,* 5.5 miles south-southeast of Point La Jolla in Mission Bay (lat. 32°46'30" N, long. 117°14'10" W). Named on La Jolla (1967) 7.5' quadrangle. Called Tierra del Fuego on La Jolla (1953) 7.5' quadrangle.

Vaileta: see **Encinitas** [SAN DIEGO].

Valcrest: see **Camp Valcrest** [LOS ANGELES].

Valencia: see **Castaic Junction** [LOS ANGELES].

Valencia Siding: see **East Irvine** [ORANGE].

Valinda [LOS ANGELES]: *district,* 3 miles south-southeast of Baldwin Park city hall (lat. 34°02'40" N, long. 117°56'30" W). Named on Baldwin Park (1966) 7.5' quadrangle.

Valla [LOS ANGELES]: *locality,* nearly 2 miles southwest of Whittier city hall along Southern Pacific Railroad (lat. 33°57'30" N, long. 118°03'35" W). Named on Whittier (1965) 7.5' quadrangle. Called Valla Siding on Whittier (1949) 7.5' quadrangle, which shows the place along Pacific Electric Railroad.

Vallecito: see **Vallecito Valley** [SAN DIEGO].

Vallecito Creek [SAN DIEGO]: *stream* and *dry wash,* extends for 19 miles to Carrizo Creek (2) 3.5 miles northeast of Sweeney Pass (lat. 32°52'25" N, long. 116°08'35" W; near N line sec. 15, T 15 S, R 8 E). Named on Agua Caliente Springs (1959), Arroyo Tapiado (1959), and Monument Peak (1959) 7.5' quadrangles. United States Board on Geographic Names (1961b, p. 13) rejected the names "Vallecitos Wash" and "Vallecito Wash" for the feature.

Vallecito Creek: see **Vallecito Wash** [SAN DIEGO].

Vallecito Mountains [SAN DIEGO]: *range,* southwest of Ocotillo Wells. Named on Borrego Mountain SE (1958), Borrego Sink (1959), Harper Canyon (1959), and Whale Peak (1959) 7.5' quadrangles. United States Board on Geographic Names (1961b, p. 13) rejected the names "North Pinyon Mountains" and "Pinyon Mountains" for the range.

Vallecito Mountains: see **North Pinyon Mountains** [SAN DIEGO]; **Pinyon Mountains** [SAN DIEGO].

Vallecitos [SAN DIEGO]:

(1) *valley,* 1.5 miles west of Margarita Peak near the head of North Fork San Onofre Canyon (lat. 33°27' N, long. 117°25' W). Named on Margarita Peak (1968) 7.5' quadrangle.

(2) *area,* 9 miles north-northwest of Lakeside (lat. 32°59' N, long. 116°58'45" W; in and near sec. 3, 4, T 14 S, R 1 W). Named on San Vicente Reservoir (1955) 7.5' quadrangle.

Vallecitos Wash: see **Vallecito Wash** [SAN DIEGO].

Vallecito Valley [SAN DIEGO]: *valley,* 5.25 miles north-northeast of Monument Peak (lat. 32°57'45" N, long. 116°23' W). Named on Agua Caliente Springs (1959) and Monument Peak (1959) 7.5' quadrangles. Brown's (1920) map shows a place called Vallecito located at the east end of Vallecito Valley; Vallecito was a noted watering place in the early days (Brown, 1923, p. 231). Agua Caliente Springs (1959) 7.5' quadrangle shows Vallecito Stage Station county park at the place.

Vallecito Wash [SAN DIEGO]: *stream,* flows 4.5 miles to the southeast end of Mason Valley, where the name changes to Vallecito Creek 6.25 miles north of Monument Peak (lat. 32°59'05" N, long. 116°25'15" W; sec. 1, T 14 S, R 5 E). Named on Earthquake Valley (1959) and Monument Peak (1959) 7.5' quadrangles. United States Board on Geographic Names (1961b, p. 13) rejected the names "Vallecito Creek" and "Vallecitos Wash" for the feature.

Vallecito Wash: see **Vallecito Creek** [SAN DIEGO].

Valle de los Amigos [SAN DIEGO]: *valley,* 3 miles north-northeast of Ramona along Santa Maria Creek (lat. 33°04'50" N, long. 116° 50'10" W). Named on Ramona (1955) 7.5' quadrangle. Called Rincon Refugio on Ramona (1903) 30' quadrangle.

Valle de los Viejas: see **Viejas Valley** [SAN DIEGO].

Valle de Pamo or Santa Maria [SAN DIEGO]: *land grant,* covers much of Santa Maria Valley around Ramona. Named on Ramona (1955) and San Pasqual (1954) 7.5' quadrangles. Jose Joaquin Ortega and Edward Stokes received 4 leagues in 1843; they claimed 17,709 acres patented in 1872 (Cowan, p. 57).

Valle de San Bernardo: see **San Bernardo** [SAN DIEGO].

Valle de San Felipe [SAN DIEGO]: *land grant,* east-northeast of Julian along San Felipe Creek. Named on Earthquake Valley (1959), Julian (1960), and Ranchita (1960) 7.5' quadrangles. Felipe Costillo received 3 leagues in 1846; John Forster claimed 9972 acres patented in 1866 (Cowan, p. 75).

Valle de San Jose [SAN DIEGO]: *land grant*, at and east of Lake Henshaw. Named on Mesa Grande (1948), Palomar Observatory (1949), Ranchita (1960), Warner Springs (1959), and Warners Ranch (1960) 7.5' quadrangles. Silvestre de la Portilla received the land in 1834 and claimed 17,634 acres patented in 1880; Warner claimed San Jose del Valle grant from the center of this land, leaving the original grant in one large and two small sections (Cowan, p. 81). Perez (p. 103) gave 1836 as the date of the grant.

Valle Las Viejas: see **Viejas Valley** [SAN DIEGO].

Valle Santa Isabel: see **Soledad Canyon** [SAN DIEGO].

Valley: see **Valley Center** [SAN DIEGO].

Valley Center [SAN DIEGO]: *town*, 7 miles north-northeast of Escondido city hall (lat. 33°13'05" N, long. 117°02' W). Named on Valley Center (1968) 7.5' quadrangle. Escondido (1901) 15' quadrangle shows the place situated in Bear Valley. Postal authorities established Valley post office in 1874, changed the name to Valley Centre in 1878, discontinued it for a time in 1879, moved it 1.5 miles north in 1885, and changed the name to Valley Center in 1887 (Salley, p. 220). Postal authorities established Sylvana post office 5 miles east of Valley Center in 1907 and discontinued it in 1912 (Salley, p. 217).

Valley Forge Canyon [LOS ANGELES]: *canyon*, drained by a stream that flows 1.5 miles to West Fork San Gabriel River 9 miles south-southwest of Pacifico Mountain (lat. 34°15'10" N, long. 118°04'20" W; near S line sec. 18, T 2 N, R 11 W). Named on Chilao Flat (1959) 7.5' quadrangle.

Valley Forge Lodge: see **Camp Kole** [LOS ANGELES].

Valley of Ollas [LOS ANGELES]: *canyon*, drained by a stream that flows less than 1 mile to the sea nearly 4 miles north of Mount Banning at Empire Landing on Santa Catalina Island (lat. 33°25'35" N, long. 118°26' W). Named on Santa Catalina North (1950) 7.5' quadrangle. Doran (1980, p. 72) gave the alternate name "Pots Valley" for the feature.

Valley of the Springs [SAN DIEGO]: *valley*, 6.25 miles south-southeast of Boucher Hill (lat. 33°15' N, long. 116°52'45" W; sec. 4, T 11 S, R 1 E). Named on Boucher Hill (1948) and Rodriguez Mountain (1948) 7.5' quadrangles.

Valley of the Thousand Springs [SAN DIEGO]: *canyon*, about 0.5 mile long, 9 miles northwest of Borrego Springs (lat. 33°20'40" N, long. 116°29'10" W). Named on Borrego Palm Canyon (1959) 7.5' quadrangle.

Val Verde [LOS ANGELES]: *settlement*, 9 miles west-northwest of Newhall in San Martinez Chiquito Canyon (lat. 34°26'50" N, long. 118°39'45" W; sec. 9, 10, T 4 N, R 17 W). Named on Val Verde (1952) 7.5' quadrangle, which shows Val Verde county park at the place. Castaic (1940) 6' quadrangle shows Valverde Lodge there, and has the name "Valverde Park" for the county park. Postal authorities established Val Verde Park post office in 1954, discontinued it in 1965, and reestablished it in 1966 (Salley, p. 229).

Valverde Lodge: see **Val Verde** [LOS ANGELES].

Val Verde Park: see **Val Verde** [LOS ANGELES].

Valyermo [LOS ANGELES]: *village*, 9 miles southeast of Littlerock along Big Rock Creek (lat. 34°26'40" N, long. 117°51'05" W; at W line sec. 8, T 4 N, R 9 W). Named on Valyermo (1958) 7.5' quadrangle. On Valyermo (1940) 6' quadrangle, the name "Valyermo" applies to a place located about 1 mile farther southeast (near E line sec. 17, T 4 N, R 9 W). Postal authorities established Valyermo post office in 1910, discontinued it in 1920, and reestablished in it 1930 (Frickstad, p. 83). W.C. Petchner, who owned Valyermo ranch, named the village in 1909 (Gudde, 1949, p. 376). California Mining Bureau's (1917a) map shows a place called Bighorn situated about 8 miles southeast of Valyermo. Postal authorities established Bighorn post office in 1904 and discontinued it in 1908 (Frickstad, p. 71). California Division of Highways' (1934) map shows a place called Border City located 10 miles east of Valyermo at the east border of Los Angeles County (sec. 1, T 4 N, R 8 W).

Van Dam Peak [SAN DIEGO]: *peak*, 2.5 miles west of Poway (lat. 32°37'15" N, long. 117°04'45" W; sec. 15, T 14 S, R 2 W). Altitude 1038 feet. Named on Poway (1967, photorevised 1975) 7.5' quadrangle. United States Board on Geographic Names (1984, p. 5) rejected the name "Mount Van Dam" for the peak, and noted that the feature is named for Edward Van Dam, county superintendent of roads from 1933 until 1961.

Van Norman Lake: see **Upper Van Norman Lake**, under **Upper San Fernando Reservoir** [LOS ANGELES].

Van Nuys [LOS ANGELES]: *district*, 15 miles northwest of Los Angeles city hall (lat. 34°11' N, long. 118°26'45" W). Named on Van Nuys (1953) 7.5' quadrangle. Postal authorities established Van Nuys post office in 1911 (Frickstad, p. 83). The name is for I.N. Van Nuys, who came to Los Angeles County in 1870 and later helped organize San Fernando Farm and Homestead Association (Bancroft, 1890, p. 759).

Van Tassel Canyon [LOS ANGELES]: *canyon*, drained by a stream that flows 2.5 miles to lowlands 2 miles northwest of Azusa city hall (lat. 34°09'15" N, long. 117°55'55" W; sec. 21, T 1 N, R 10 W). Named on Azusa (1953) 7.5' quadrangle.

Van Tassel Ridge [LOS ANGELES]: *ridge*, generally south-southeast-trending, 2.25 miles long, center 3 miles northwest of Azusa city hall (lat. 34°10'15" N, long. 117°56'15" W); the feature is east of Van Tassel Canyon. Named on Azusa (1953) 7.5' quadrangle.

Vasquez Canyon [LOS ANGELES]: *canyon*, drained by a stream that flows 4.5 miles to the stream in Bouquet Canyon 4 miles north of Solemint (lat. 34°28'25" N, long. 118°27'55" W; near W line sec. 33, T 5 N, R 15 W). Named on Green Valley (1958) and Mint Canyon (1960) 7.5' quadrangles. Los Angeles County (1935) map shows a feature called Puckett Canyon that opens into Vasquez Canyon from the east near the mouth of Vasquez Canyon.

Vasquez Creek [LOS ANGELES]: *stream*, flows 1.25 miles to Big Tujunga Canyon 3.5 miles south of Condor Peak (lat. 34°16'35" N, long. 118°12'35" W; sec. 11, T 2 N, R 13 W). Named on Condor Peak (1959) 7.5' quadrangle. Called Vasques Cr. on Los Angeles County (1935) map.

Vasquez Rocks [LOS ANGELES]: *relief feature*, 9 miles east-northeast of Solemint (lat. 34°29'05" N, long. 118°19' W; sec. 26, T 5 N, R 14 W). Named on Agua Dulce (1960) 7.5' quadrangle. Lang (1933) 6' quadrangle has the singular form "Vasquez Rock" for the name. The feature also is called Robbers' Roost—the outlaw Tiburcio Vasquez is said to have hid there (Hoover, Rensch, and Rensch, p. 168).

Vassar Canyon [LOS ANGELES]: *canyon*, drained by a stream that flows 1 mile to Sawpit Canyon 5 miles northwest of Azusa city hall (lat. 34°10'45" N, long. 117°58'20" W; at N line sec. 18, T 1 N, R 10 W). Azusa (1953) 7.5' quadrangle.

Veeh Reservoir [ORANGE]: *lake*, 2000 feet long, 2.25 miles west of El Toro (lat. 33°37'20" N, long. 117°43'50" W; near NE cor. sec. 29, T 6 S, R 8 W). Named on El Toro (1968) and San Juan Capistrano (1968) 7.5' quadrangles.

Vegala [LOS ANGELES]: *locality*, 5 miles southeast of Los Angeles city hall along Atchison, Topeka and Santa Fe Railroad (lat. 34°00'05" N, long. 118°10'30" W). Named on Alhambra (1926) 6' quadrangle.

Vejor: see **Malibu Junction** [LOS ANGELES].

Venedo Canyon [LOS ANGELES]: *canyon*, drained by a stream that flows 1.5 miles to San Gabriel Reservoir 6.5 miles north of Glendora city hall (lat. 34°13'40" N, long. 117°50'30" W; sec. 29, T 2 N, R 9 W). Named on Glendora (1953) 7.5' quadrangle.

Venice [LOS ANGELES]: *district*, 8 miles north-northwest of Manhattan Beach city hall in Los Angeles (lat. 33°59'30" N, long. 118° 27'30" W). Named on Beverly Hills (1950) and Venice (1950) 7.5' quadrangles. Postal authorities established Venice post office in 1905 (Frickstad, p. 83). Abbot Kinney designed and built the community in 1904 with a system of canals in the style of Venice, Italy (Gudde, 1949, p. 377). It became part of Los Angeles in 1925 (Hanna, p. 343).

Venice Beach [LOS ANGELES]: *beach*, along the coast north of the mouth of Ballona Creek at Venice (lat. 33°58'45" N, long. 118° 28' W). Named on Venice (1950) 7.5' quadrangle.

Venta: see **Irvine Siding** [ORANGE].

Ven-Tu Park [VENTURA]: *settlement*, 0.5 mile south of Newbury Park (lat. 34°10'30" N, long. 118°54'30" W; sec. 18, T 1 N, R 19 W). Named on Newbury Park (1951) 7.5' quadrangle.

Ventura [VENTURA]: *city*, along the coast between the mouth of Ventura River and the mouth of Santa Clara River (lat. 34°16'45" N, long. 119°17'25" W). Named on Saticoy (1951) and Ventura (1951) 7.5' quadrangles. Ventura (1951) 7.5' quadrangle has the alternate name "San Buenaventura" for the place. Postal authorities established San Buenaventura post office in 1862 and changed the name to Ventura in 1889 (Frickstad, p. 219). The community incorporated under the name "San Buenaventura" in 1866, but United States Board on Geographic Names (1933, p. 788) rejected this designation for the city. The name is from San Buenaventura mission, founded at the site in 1782 (Hoover, Rensch, and Rensch, p. 576, 577). Postal authorities established Hammell post office 21 miles east of San Buenaventura post office in 1882 and discontinued it in 1883; the name was for James Hammell, first postmaster (Salley, p. 92). Ricard listed a place called Absco located 2 miles southeast of Ventura along Southern Pacific Railroad and named from initial letters of the term "American Beet Sugar Company"—the company built a refinery at the site in 1897.

Ventura County Small Craft Harbor: see **Channel Islands Harbor**, under **Port Hueneme** [VENTURA].

Ventura Cove [SAN DIEGO]: *embayment*, 5.5 miles south-southeast of Point La Jolla off Mission Bay (lat. 32°46'20" N, long. 117°14'40" W); the feature is just northwest of Ventura Point. Named on La Jolla (1967) 7.5' quadrangle.

Ventura Harbor: see **Ventura Keys** [VENTURA].

Ventura Keys [VENTURA]: *water feature*, small-boat harbor 2 miles southeast of downtown Ventura along the coast (lat. 34°15'25" N, long. 119°15'50" W). Named on Ventura (1951, photorevised 1967) 7.5' quadrangle. United States Board on Geographic Names (1986, p. 2) approved the name "Ventura Harbor" for the place, and rejected the name "Ventura Marina."

Ventura Marina: see **Ventura Keys** [VENTURA].

Ventura Point [SAN DIEGO]: *promontory*, 6 miles south-southeast of Point

La Jolla along Mission Bay (lat. 32°46'10" N, long. 117° 14'30" W). Named on La Jolla (1967) 7.5' quadrangle.

Ventura River [VENTURA]: *stream,* formed by the confluence of Matilija Creek and North Fork Matilija Creek, flows 16 miles to the sea 1 mile west-southwest of downtown Ventura (lat. 34°16'25" N, long. 119°18'25" W). Named on Matilija (1952) and Ventura (1951) 7.5' quadrangles. Called Rio San Buenaventura on Peckham's (1866) map. Whitney (p. 125) called it San Buenaventura River. On Wheeler Springs (1944) 7.5' quadrangle, present North Fork Matilija Creek is called North Fork Ventura River.

Verde Ravine [SAN DIEGO]: *canyon,* 0.5 mile long, 6 miles north-northeast of Buckman Springs (lat. 32°50'45" N, long. 116°26'10" W; on S line sec. 23, T 15 S, R 5 E). Named on Mount Laguna (1960) 7.5' quadrangle.

Verdi: see **Cañada Larga** [VENTURA].

Verdugo [LOS ANGELES]: *locality,* 5.5 miles west of present Pasadena city hall (lat. 34°08'25" N, long. 118°14'35" W). Named on Pasadena (1900) 15' quadrangle. Postal authorities established Verdugo post office in 1884 and discontinued it in 1902 (Frickstad, p. 83).

Verdugo: see **Glendale** [LOS ANGELES].

Verdugo Canyon [LOS ANGELES]: *canyon,* 5.5 miles west-northwest of Pasadena city hall (lat. 34°11'15" N, long. 118°13'35" W); the canyon is at the east end of Verdugo Hills along Verdugo Wash. Named on Pasadena (1966) 7.5' quadrangle. On Pasadena (1953) 7.5' quadrangle, the name applies to the canyon a little father upstream along Verdugo Wash

Verdugo Canyon [ORANGE]: *canyon,* drained by a stream that heads in Riverside County and flows 5.5 miles to San Juan Creek 6.5 miles east-northeast of San Juan Capistrano (lat. 33°31'25" N, long. 117°33'30" W). Named on Cañada Gobernadora (1968) and Sitton Peak (1954) 7.5' quadrangles. Members of the Verdugo family lived in the canyon (Meadows, p. 137).

Verdugo Canyon: see **Aliso Canyon** [ORANGE].

Verdugo City [LOS ANGELES]: *district,* 7 miles northwest of Pasadena city hall in Glendale (lat. 34°12'45" N, long. 118°14'30" W); the district is north of Verdugo Mountains on San Rafael grant. Named on Pasadena (1953) 7.5' quadrangle. Postal authorities established Verdugo City post office in 1924 (Frickstad, p. 83). Harry Fowler laid out the community in 1925 (Gudde, 1949, p. 378). The name recalls Jose Maria Verdugo, who received San Rafael grant.

Verdugo Creek: see **Verdugo Wash** [LOS ANGELES].

Verdugo Mountains [LOS ANGELES]: *range,* 11 miles north-northwest of Los Angeles city hall between La Canada (2) and Burbank (lat. 34°13' N, long. 118°17'30" W). Named on Burbank (1953) and Pasadena (1953) 7.5' quadrangles. The feature was called Sierra de los Berdugos on a diseño in 1843 (Gudde, 1949, p. 378).

Verdugo Park [LOS ANGELES]: *locality,* 5 miles west-northwest of present Pasadena city hall (lat. 34°10'05" N, long. 118°13'45" W); the place is in Verdugo Canyon. Named on Pasadena (1900) 15' quadrangle.

Verdugo Pines: see **Camp Verdugo Pines** [LOS ANGELES].

Verdugo Wash [LOS ANGELES]: *stream,* flows 9 miles to Los Angeles River 2.5 miles southeast of Burbank city hall (lat. 34°09'15" N, long. 118°16'40" W). Named on Burbank (1966) and Pasadena (1966) 7.5' quadrangles. The upper part of the stream is called Verdugo Creek on Burbank (1953) 7.5' quadrangle.

Vermont Canyon [LOS ANGELES]: *canyon,* 1 mile long, 5.5 miles northwest of Los Angeles city hall (lat. 34°07'10" N, long. 118°17'40" W). Named on Burbank (1953) and Hollywood (1953) 7.5' quadrangles.

Vernon [LOS ANGELES]: *locality,* industrial area 3.5 miles south of Los Angeles city hall (lat. 34°00'20" N, long. 118°13'45" W). Named on Los Angeles (1953) and South Gate (1952) 7.5' quadrangles. Pasadena (1900) 15' quadrangle shows a place called Vernondale located along the railroad at present Vernon. Postal authorities established Vernondale post office in 1888 and discontinued it in 1897; they established Vernon post office in 1926 (Salley, p. 231). Vernon incorporated in 1905. The name commemorates George R. Vernon, who settled at the place after 1871 (Gudde, 1949, p. 379).

Vernondale: see **Vernon** [LOS ANGELES].

Verruga: see **Ranchita** [SAN DIEGO].

Veteran Springs: see **Glenview** [LOS ANGELES].

Vetter Mountain [LOS ANGELES]: *peak,* nearly 6 miles south of Pacifico Mountain (lat. 34°17'50" N, long. 118°01'40" W; at SW cor. sec. 34, T 3 N, R 11 W). Altitude 5908 feet. Named on Chilao Flat (1959) 7.5' quadrangle. Called Pine Mt. on Tujunga (1900) 15' quadrangle. The name "Vetter Mountain" commemorates Victor P. Vetter, Forest Service district ranger (Gudde, 1949, p. 379).

Vicente: see **Point Vicente** [LOS ANGELES].

Vickers Hot Springs [VENTURA]: *locality,* 6 miles west-northwest of the town of Ojai along Matilija Creek (lat. 34°29'35" N, long. 119°20'10" W). Named on Ventura (1904) 15' quadrangle. Waring (p. 63) mentioned a feature called Stingleys Hot Springs located about 0.5 mile below Vickers Hot Springs on the property of S.G.Stingley.

Victoria Beach [ORANGE]: *beach,* 2.25 miles south-southeast of Laguna Beach city hall along the coast (lat. 33°31' N, long. 117°45'35" W; near W line sec. 31, T 7 S, R 8 W). Named on Laguna Beach (1965) 7.5' quadrangle. The name is from Victoria Drive, a street that leads to the beach (Meadows, p. 137).

Viejas: see **Viejas Valley** [SAN DIEGO].

Viejas Creek [SAN DIEGO]: *stream,* flows 8.5 miles to Sweetwater River 8 miles west-southwest of Descanso (lat. 32°48'45" N, long. 116°44'40" W; near N line sec. 2, T 16 S, R 2 E); the stream drains Viejas Valley. Named on Alpine (1955) and Viejas Mountain (1960) 7.5' quadrangles.

Viejas Mountain [SAN DIEGO]: *peak,* 6.5 miles west of Descanso (lat. 32°51'40" N, long. 116°43'30" W; near S line sec. 13, T 15 S, R 2 E). Altitude 4187 feet. Named on Viejas Mountain (1960) 7.5' quadrangle.

Viejas Valley [SAN DIEGO]: *valley,* 4.5 miles west of Descanso (lat. 32°50'45" N, long. 116°41'30" W). Named on Viejas Mountain (1960) 7.5' quadrangle. James Graham Cooper mentioned a place called Valle de los Viejas, named for some old Indians that the first Spanish visitors found there (Coan, p. 132). Hanks' (1886a) map shows a place called Viejas located in Valle Las Viejas. Postal authorities established Viejas post office in 1873 and discontinued it in 1893 (Frickstad, p. 158).

Viejo Siding [ORANGE]: *locality,* 2 miles south-southeast of La Habra along Union Pacific Railroad (lat. 33°54'15" N, long. 117° 55'35" W). Named on Coyote Hills (1935) 7.5' quadrangle.

View Park [LOS ANGELES]: *district,* 2.5 miles north-northeast of Inglewood city hall (lat. 34°00' N, long. 118°20'30" W). Named on Hollywood (1966) and Inglewood (1964) 7.5' quadrangles.

Vignola: see **Stanton** [ORANGE].

Villa Canyon [LOS ANGELES]: *canyon,* drained by a stream that flows nearly 2 miles to Castaic Valley 7.5 miles northwest of Newhall (lat. 34°28'05" N, long. 118°37' W; at S line sec. 36, T 5 N, R 17 W). Named on Newhall (1952) and Val Verde (1952) 7.5' quadrangles.

Villager Peak [SAN DIEGO]: *peak,* 13 miles northeast of Borrego Springs (lat. 33°23'20" N, long. 116°13'05" W). Altitude 5756 feet. Named on Rabbit Peak (1959) 7.5' quadrangle. The name reportedly is from two Indian villages that once were situated on the side of the peak (Stein, p. 146).

Villa Park [ORANGE]: *town,* 3 miles northeast of Orange city hall (lat. 33°48'50" N, long. 117°48'45" W). Named on Orange (1964) 7.5' quadrangle. Postal authorities established Villa Park post office in 1888, discontinued it for a time in 1900, discontinued it again in 1906, and reestablished it 1964 (Salley, p. 232). Villa Park incorporated in 1962. The original name of the community was Mountain View for the school at the place, but when postal authorities rejected this name for a post office, the name of the town was changed to Villa Park—the post office opened in a country store at Wanda (Meadows, p. 137). The Southern Pacific Railroad station that opened 0.5 mile west of Villa Park in 1888 was called Wanda (Meadows, p. 138). Corona (1902) 30' quadrangle shows Wanda located along the railroad at the site of present Villa Park, and the name "Villa Park" applies to a place situated a little farther east.

Vicente: see **Point Vicente** [LOS ANGELES].

Vincent [LOS ANGELES]: *locality,* 5.5 miles south of Palmdale along Southern Pacific Railroad at Soledad Pass (lat. 34°30' N, long. 118°06'55" W; near E line sec. 22, T 5 N, R 12 W). Named on Pacifico Mountain (1959) and Palmdale (1958) 7.5' quadrangles. Postal authorities established Vincent post office in 1892 and discontinued it in 1896 (Salley, p. 232).

Vincente: see **Point Vincente**, under **Point Vicente** [LOS ANGELES].

Vincent Gap [LOS ANGELES]: *pass,* 6.5 miles northeast of Crystal Lake (lat. 34°22'25" N, long. 117°45'10" W; sec. 6, T 3 N, R 8 W); the pass is at the head of Vincent Gulch. Named on Crystal Lake (1958) 7.5' quadrangle.

Vincent Gulch [LOS ANGELES]: *canyon,* 3 miles long, along San Gabriel River above a point 6 miles northwest of Mount San Antonio (lat. 34°20'35" N, long. 117°43'25" W; sec. 16, T 3 N, R 8 W). Named on Mount San Antonio (1955) 7.5' quadrangle. The name commemorates Charles Vincent Dougherty, alias Charles Tom Vincent, who lived a solitary life in San Gabriel Mountains from 1870 until 1926 (Robinson, J.W., 1983, p. 164).

Vine Creek [LOS ANGELES]: *stream,* flows 2.5 miles to Walnut Creek Wash (present Walnut Creek) 3.25 miles east-southeast of Baldwin Park city hall (lat. 34°03'50" N, long. 117°54'35" W). Named on Baldwin Park (1953) 7.5' quadrangle.

Vineland: see **Baldwin Park** [LOS ANGELES].

Vineyard [LOS ANGELES]: *locality,* 5.5 miles west of Los Angeles city hall (lat. 34°02'50" N, long. 118°20'05" W). Named on Hollywood (1926) 6' quadrangle.

Vineyard [SAN DIEGO]: *locality,* 5 miles south of Rodriguez Mountain (lat. 33°09'50" N, long. 116°54' W). Named on Ramona (1903) 30' quadrangle. Postal authorities established Vineyard post office in vinyards on Guejito grant in 1884, moved it 2 miles south in 1904, and discontinued it in 1922 (Salley, p. 232).

Vinvale [LOS ANGELES]: *locality,* 2.5 miles east of South Gate city hall along Southern Pacific Railroad (lat. 33°57'10" N, long. 118° 09'45" W). Named on South Gate (1952) 7.5' quadrangle.

Violin Canyon [LOS ANGELES]: *canyon,* drained by a stream that flows

6.5 miles to Marple Canyon 7.25 miles southeast of Whitaker Peak (lat. 34°30'30" N, long. 118°37'45" W; sec. 23, T 5 N, R 17 W). Named on Whitaker Peak (1958) 7.5' quadrangle. After Juan Yuca and Estanislao Olaje played the violin for grizzly bears there, the canyon was known as La Cañada del Violin—early American settlers preserved the name as Violin Canyon (Latta, p. 173).

Violin Summit [LOS ANGELES]: *pass,* 3 miles east of Whitaker Peak (lat. 34°33'55" N, long. 118°41'05" W; sec. 33, T 6 N, R 17 W); the pass is near the head of Violin Canyon. Named on Whitaker Peak (1958) 7.5' quadrangle.

Virgenes Creek: see **Las Virgenes Creek** [LOS ANGELES-VENTURA].

Virginia: see **Poway** [SAN DIEGO].

Virginia City: see **North Long Beach** [LOS ANGELES].

Virginia Colony [VENTURA]: *locality,* 1 mile east of Moorpark (lat. 34°17'15" N, long. 118°51'35" W; sec. 3, T 2 N, R 19 W). Named on Simi (1951) 7.5' quadrangle. The name is from the given name of a woman who did missionary and social work with Mexicans who lived at the place in the early 1920's (Ricard).

Vista [SAN DIEGO]: *city,* 7 miles east of Oceanside (lat. 33°12'15" N, long. 117°14'40" W); the city is on Buena Vista grant. Named on San Luis Rey (1968) and San Marcos (1968) 7.5' quadrangles. Postal authorities established Vista post office in 1882, discontinued in it 1886, and reestablished it in 1888; the named is from Buena Vista grant (Salley, p. 233). The city incorporated in 1963. Postal authorities established Barham post office 5 miles east of Vista in 1883, moved it 1 mile west in 1886, and discontinued it in 1888; the name was for J.H. Barham, first postmaster (Salley, p. 15).

Vista: see **South Vista** [SAN DIEGO].

Vista del Malpais [SAN DIEGO]: *locality,* 10.5 miles east of Borrego Springs (lat. 33°15'40" N, long. 116°11'40" W; sec. 36, T 10 S, R 7 E); the place is in Borrego Badlands —*vista del malpais* means "view of the badlands" in Spanish. Named on Fonts Point (1959) 7.5' quadrangle.

Vista del Malpais Wash [SAN DIEGO]: *dry wash,* less than 1 mile long, joins Short Wash 11 miles east of Borrego Springs (lat. 33° 16'10" N, long. 116°11'10" W); the feature heads at Vista del Malpais. Named on Fonts Point (1959) 7.5' quadrangle.

Vista del Mar [LOS ANGELES]: *district,* 3.25 miles north of Long Beach city hall (lat. 33°49'05" N, long. 118°11'55" W). Named on Long Beach (1949) 7.5' quadrangle.

Vista Picnic Ground [LOS ANGELES]: *locality,* 2.5 miles east-northeast of Waterman Mountain (lat. 34°20'55" N, long. 117°53'30" W; sec. 14, T 3 N, R 10 W). Named on Waterman Mountain (1959) 7.5' quadrangle.

Vizcaino: see **Mount Vizcaino**, under **Cactus Peak** [LOS ANGELES].

Vizcaino Point: see **San Nicolas Island** [VENTURA].

Vogel Canyon [LOS ANGELES]: *canyon,* drained by a stream that flows nearly 3 miles to Big Tujunga Canyon 2.5 miles south of Condor Peak (lat. 34°17'20" N, long. 118°13'35" W; sec. 3, T 2 N, R 13 W). Named on Condor Peak (1959) 7.5' quadrangle.

Vogel Flat [LOS ANGELES]: *area,* 2.5 miles south of Condor Peak in Big Tujunga Canyon (lat. 34°17'20" N, long. 118°13'35" W; sec. 3, T 2 N, R 13 W); the place is at the mouth of Vogel Canyon.. Named on Condor Peak (1959) 7.5' quadrangle.

Volcanic Hills [SAN DIEGO]: *range,* about 4 miles south-southeast of Sweeney Pass (lat. 32°47'10" N, long. 116°08'45" W). Named on Sweeney Pass (1959) 7.5' quadrangle.

Volcan Mountains [SAN DIEGO]: *range,* extends for about 14 miles between San Felipe Creek and Santa Ysabel Creek (center near lat. 33°09' N, long. 116°36'30" W). Named on Ranchita (1960) and Warners Ranch (1960) 7.5' quadrangles. Called Volcan Mountain on Julian (1960) 7.5' quadrangle. United States Board on Geographic Names (1962b, p. 21) rejected the names "Balcan Mountains," "Bolcan Mountains," "Volcan Mountain," and "Volcano Mountain" for the feature.

Volcano Mountain: see **Volcan Mountains** [SAN DIEGO].

Volfe Canyon [LOS ANGELES]: *canyon,* less than 2 miles long, joins Bell Canyon to form Big Dalton Canyon 5 miles northeast of Glendora city hall (lat. 34°10'55" N, long. 117°47'45" W; sec. 11, T 1 N, R 9 W). Named on Glendora (1953) 7.5' quadrangle.

Voltaire: see **Three Points** [LOS ANGELES] (1).

Von Schritz: see **Greenville** [ORANGE].

Vorhees Canyon: see **Tapie Canyon** [LOS ANGELES].

Vultee Field: see **Downey** [LOS ANGELES].

Vulture Crags [ORANGE]: *relief feature,* 4 miles west-southwest of Santiago Peak (lat. 33°41'35" N, long. 117°36'10" W; sec. 34, T 5 S, T 7 W). Named on Santiago Peak (1954) 7.5' quadrangle. J.E. Pleasants and Samuel Shrewsbury named the feature for California condors that frequented the place (Stephenson, p. 129).

-W-

Wadstrom [VENTURA]: *locality,* 2.5 miles north of Ventura along Southern Pacific Railroad (lat. 34°18'55" N, long. 119°17'25" W). Named on Ventura (1951) 7.5' quadrangle.

Wagon Road Canyon [VENTURA]: *canyon,* drained by a stream that flows 9 miles to Alamo Creek (2) 4.5 miles north-northeast of Reyes Peak (lat. 34°41'35" N, long. 119°15'20" W; near N line sec. 19, T 7 N, R 22 W). Named on San Guillermo (1943) 7.5' quadrangle.

Wagon Wheel Canyon [ORANGE]: *canyon,* drained by a stream that flows 2.5 miles to Cañada Gobernadora 6 miles northeast of San Juan Capistrano (lat. 33°33'35" N, long. 117°35'10" W; near W line sec. 14, T 7 S, R 7 W). Named on Cañada Gobernadora (1968) 7.5' quadrangle.

Wagon Wheels Camp: see **Fox Creek** [LOS ANGELES].

Wahoo [LOS ANGELES]: *locality,* 5 miles west-southwest of Sunland along Southern Pacific Railroad (lat. 34°14'35" N, long. 118° 23'50" W). Named on Sunland (1942) 6' quadrangle.

Walker: see **Foot and Walker Pass** [SAN DIEGO].

Walker Canyon [SAN DIEGO]: *canyon,* drained by a stream that flows 5.25 miles to Carrizo Gorge 3 miles north of Jacumba (lat. 32°39'50" N, long. 116°11'35" W; near E line sec. 30, T 17 S, R 8 E). Named on Jacumba (1959) and Live Oak Springs (1959) 7.5' quadrangles. The name commemorates George P. Walker, a homesteader of the 1860's (Stein, p. 148).

Walker Creek [SAN DIEGO]: *stream,* flows 2.5 miles to the west end of Walker Canyon 0.5 mile east-southeast of Manzanita (lat. 32°40' N, long. 116°16'55" W; sec. 29, T 17 S, R 7 E). Named on Live Oak Springs (1959) 7.5' quadrangle.

Walnut [LOS ANGELES]: *town,* 6.5 miles west-southwest of Pomona city hall (lat. 34°00'55" N, long. 117°51'15" W). Named on Baldwin Park (1966) and San Dimas (1966) 7.5' quadrangles. Called Lemon on Pomona (1904) 15' quadrangle. Postal authorities established Lemon post office in 1895 and changed the name to Walnut in 1908 (Frickstad, p. 76). The town incorporated in 1959.

Walnut Canyon [LOS ANGELES]: *canyon,* drained by a stream that flows 1.5 miles to the sea 1.25 miles northeast of Point Dume (lat. 34°00'50" N, long. 118°47'30" W). Named on Point Dume (1951) 7.5' quadrangle.

Walnut Canyon [ORANGE]: *canyon,* drained by a stream that flows 2.5 miles to Santa Ana Canyon 6 miles northeast of Orange city hall (lat. 33°50'50" N, long. 117°46'40" W). Named on Black Star Canyon (1950) and Orange (1964) 7.5' quadrangles. The feature also was called Cañada de la Madera (Meadows, p. 138). An inhabited place in Santa Ana Canyon near the mouth of Walnut Canyon was called Peralta—the headquarters of the Peralta family was there (Meadows, p. 110).

Walnut Canyon Reservoir [ORANGE]: *lake,* 2000 feet long, behind a dam 6.5 miles east-northeast of Orange city hall (lat. 33°50'25" N, long. 117°45'05" W); the lake is in Walnut Canyon. Named on Black Star Canyon (1967, photorevised 1988) and Orange (1964, photorevised 1981) 7.5' quadrangles.

Walnut Creek [LOS ANGELES]: *stream,* flows 14 miles to San Gabriel River 1.5 miles southeast of El Monte city hall (lat. 34°03'35" N, long. 118°00'15" W). Named on Baldwin Park (1966), El Monte (1966), and San Dimas (1954) 7.5' quadrangles. Called Walnut Creek Wash on Baldwin Park (1953) 7.5' quadrangle, but United States Board on Geographic Names (1967b, p. 5) rejected this name for the feature

Walnut Creek Wash: see **Walnut Creek** [LOS ANGELES].

Walnut Park [LOS ANGELES]: *district,* 1.5 miles northwest of South Gate city hall (lat. 33°58'10" N, long. 118°13'15" W). Named on South Gate (1964) 7.5' quadrangle.

Walnut Siding [LOS ANGELES]: *locality,* 7 miles west-southwest of Pomona city hall along Union Pacific Railroad (lat. 34°00'15" N, long. 117°51'10" W). Named on San Dimas (1966) 7.5' quadrangle.

Walnut Station [LOS ANGELES]: *locality,* nearly 7 miles west-southwest of present Pomona city hall along Union Pacific Railroad (lat. 34°00'15" N, long. 117°51'15" W); the place is 0.5 mile south-southeast of Walnut. Named on Covina (1927) 6' quadrangle.

Walteria [LOS ANGELES]: *district,* 2.5 miles south of Torrance city hall (lat. 33°48'05" N, long. 118°21' W). Named on Torrance (1964) 7.5' quadrangle. Postal authorities established Walteria post office in 1926 and discontinued it in 1954 (Frickstad, p. 83). The name is from Captain Walters, who built Walters hotel in the early part of the twentieth century (Gudde, 1969, p. 358).

Waltz [LOS ANGELES]: *locality,* 1.5 miles south-southeast of Newhall along Southern Pacific Railroad (lat. 34°21'35" N, long. 118° 31'10" W). Named on Newhall (1933) 6' quadrangle. Called Waltz Jct. on California Division of Highways' (1934) map.

Wanda: see **Villa Park** [ORANGE].

Ward Canyon [LOS ANGELES]: *canyon,* 0.5 mile long, 9 miles northwest of Pasadena city hall (lat. 34°14'55" N, long. 118°14'50" W; sec. 21, T 2 N, R 13 W). Named on Condor Peak (1959) and Pasadena (1953) 7.5' quadrangles.

Ward Canyon [SAN DIEGO]: *canyon,* drained by a stream that flows 3.5 miles to lowlands 2.5 miles west of Warner Springs (lat. 33°17'25" N, long. 116°40'35" W). Named on Warner Springs (1959) 7.5' quadrangle.

Warm Spring: see **Warm Springs Camp** [LOS ANGELES].

Warm Springs Camp [LOS ANGELES]: *locality,* 1.25 miles northeast of Warm Springs Mountain in Elizabeth Lake Canyon (lat. 34° 36'30" N, long. 118°33'35" W). Named on Warm Springs Mountain (1958) 7.5' quadrangle. Tejon (1903) 30' quadrangle shows a spring called Warm Spring at the site, and Los Angeles County (1935) map has the name "Warm Springs" there.

Warm Springs Canyon [LOS ANGELES]: *canyon,* drained by a stream that flows nearly 3 miles to Elizabeth Lake Canyon 1.5 miles northeast of Warm Springs Mountain (lat. 34°36'25" N, long. 118°33'35" W). Named on Warm Springs Mountain (1958) 7.5' quadrangle.

Warm Springs Mountain [LOS ANGELES]: *peak,* 14 miles north of Newhall (lat. 34°35'45" N, long. 118°34'45" W). Altitude 4020 feet. Named on Warm Springs Mountain (1958) 7.5' quadrangle.

Warner [SAN DIEGO]: *locality,* 18 miles northeast of Ramona (lat. 33°14' N, long. 116°38'35" W). Named on Ramona (1903) 30' quadrangle. Warners Ranch (1960) 7.5' quadrangle shows a Butterfield Overland stage station historical marker at the site, and shows Warners ranch situated 1.5 miles farther west-northwest (lat. 33°14'30" N, long. 116°39'55" W). Postal authorities established Warner's Ranch post office in 1859, discontinued it in 1860, reestablished it in 1861, discontinued it in 1862, reestablished it for a time in 1867, reestablished it in 1870, discontinued it in 1875, reestablished it with the name "Warner" in 1881, discontinued it in 1884, reestablished it in 1890, and discontinued it in 1907 (Salley, p. 234). The name commemorates Jonathan Trumbull Warner, who came to California in 1831 and owned the land at the place; his ranch was a Butterfield Overland stage stop in 1858 (Hoover, Rensch, and Rensch, p. 341).

Warner Hot Spring [SAN DIEGO]: *spring,* at Warner Springs (lat. 33°17'05" N, long. 116°37'50" W). Named on Warner Springs (1959) 7.5' quadrangle. Waring (p. 45-46) noted that springs at the place discharge about 150 gallons a minute of water as hot as 139° Fahrenheit, and that a resort uses the water.

Warner Pass: see **Teofulio Summit**, under **San Felipe** [SAN DIEGO].

Warner Springs [SAN DIEGO]: *village,* 28 miles east-northeast of Escondido (lat. 33°17' N, long. 116°37'55" W); Warner Hot Spring is at the place. Named on Warner Springs (1959) 7.5' quadrangle. Called Agua Caliente on Ramona (1903) 30' quadrangle. Postal authorities established Warner Springs post office in 1905 (Frickstad, p. 158).

Warner's Ranch: see **Warner** [SAN DIEGO].

Warren Canyon [SAN DIEGO]: *canyon,* drained by a stream that flows nearly 4 miles to an unnamed canyon 8 miles south-southeast of Escondido (lat. 33°01' N, long. 117°00'30" W). Named on San Vicente Reservoir (1955) 7.5' quadrangle.

Warring Canyon [VENTURA]: *canyon,* drained by a stream that flows 2 miles to the valley of Santa Clara River at Piru (lat. 34°25'05" N, long. 118°47'50" W; sec. 19, T 4 N, R 18 W). Named on Piru (1952, photorevised 1969) 7.5' quadrangle. Called Nigger Canyon on Piru (1952) 7.5' quadrangle; United States Board on Geographic Names (1970b, p. 3) gave this name as a variant.

Wash Hollow Creek [SAN DIEGO]: *stream,* flows 4 miles to Hatfield Creek 3.25 miles east of Ramona (lat. 33°03'05" N, long. 116°48'35" W; near NE cor. sec. 8, T 13 S, R 2 E). Named on Ramona (1955) 7.5' quadrangle.

Washington: see **Mount Washington** [LOS ANGELES].

Washtub Falls [SAN DIEGO]: *waterfall,* 1.25 miles west-southwest of Mesa Grande (lat. 33°10'20" N, long. 116°47'10" W; near W line sec. 33, T 11 S, R 2 E). Named on Mesa Grande (1948) 7.5' quadrangle.

Wason Barranca [VENTURA]: *gully,* extends for 2.25 miles from the mouth of Peppertree Canyon to Santa Clara River 0.5 mile east-southeast of Saticoy (lat. 34°16'55" N, long. 119°08'20" W). Named on Saticoy (1951) 7.5' quadrangle. The name commemorates Milton Wason, who was the first county judge of Ventura County (Ricard).

Water Canyon [LOS ANGELES]: *canyon,* drained by a stream that flows 1 mile to Morris Reservoir 3.5 miles north-northeast of Azusa city hall (lat. 34°11' N, long. 117°52'40" W; sec. 12, T 1 N, R 10 W). Named on Azusa (1953) 7.5' quadrangle.

Waterdale: see **Oban** [LOS ANGELES].

Waterman Mountain [LOS ANGELES]: *peak,* 12 miles north-northwest of Azusa (lat. 34°20'10" N, long. 117°56'10" W). Altitude 8038 feet. Named on Waterman Mountain (1959) 7.5' quadrangle. Called Mt. Waterman on Los Angeles County (1935) map. Rock Creek (1903) 15' quadrangle has the name "Waterman Mt." for present Twin Peaks, located 1.5 miles farther south. Bob Waterman, his wife Liz, and Perry Switzer climbed the peak in 1889; the men named it Lady Waterman Mountain for Liz, whom they believed was the first white woman to cross San Gabriel Mountains, but the name became simply Mount Waterman (Robinson, J.W., 1977, p. 191).

Water Street [LOS ANGELES]: *locality,* 2.5 miles northeast of Los Angeles city hall along Atchison, Topeka and Santa Fe Railroad (lat. 34°05' N, long. 118°13' W). Named on Los Angeles (1953) 7.5' quadrangle.

Waterville: see **Cypress** [ORANGE].

Watkins Creek [LOS ANGELES]: *stream,* flows 2 miles to Holmes Creek nearly 2 miles west-southwest of Valyermo (lat. 34°26'10" N, long. 117°52'40" W; sec. 13, T 4 N, R 10 W). Name on Valyermo (1958) 7.5' quadrangle.

Watson [LOS ANGELES]: *locality,* 3.5 miles northwest of Long Beach city hall along Southern Pacific Railroad (lat. 33°48'30" N, long. 118°14'05" W). Named on Long Beach (1964) 7.5' quadrangle. Called Watson Crossing on Downey (1902) 15' quadrangle. The name is from Maria Dominguez de Watson, who was allocated the part of San Pedro grant where the place is situated (Gudde, 1949, p. 384).

Watson Crossing: see **Watson** [LOS ANGELES].

Watson Junction [LOS ANGELES]: *locality,* 5.5 miles east-southeast of Torrance city hall along Atchison Topeka and Santa Fe Railroad (lat. 33°48' N, long. 118°15'10" W). Named on Torrance (1964) 7.5' quadrangle.

Watts [LOS ANGELES]: *district,* 2.25 miles west-southwest of South Gate city hall in Los Angeles (lat. 33°56'30" N, long. 118°14'30" W). Named on South Gate (1952) 7.5' quadrangle. Postal authorities established Watts post office in 1904 (Frickstad, p. 83). The name commemorates C.H. Watts, who had a ranch at the place; the community originally was called Mud Town—Los Angeles annexed the district in 1926 (Gudde, 1969, p. 359).

Way Hill [LOS ANGELES]: *ridge,* east-trending, 0.5 mile long, 4.25 miles northeast of Pomona city hall (lat. 34°06'45" N, long. 117° 48'50" W). Named on San Dimas (1954) 7.5' quadrangle.

Wayside Canyon [LOS ANGELES]: *canyon,* drained by a stream that flows 3 miles to Castaic Valley 7 miles northwest of Newhall (lat. 34°27'55" N, long. 118°36'15" W). Named on Newhall (1952) 7.5' quadrangle, which shows Wayside Honor Ranch at the mouth of the canyon.

Weakly Canyon: see **Hickey Canyon** [ORANGE].

Weaver Mountain [SAN DIEGO]: *peak,* 4.5 miles south of Pala (lat. 33°18' N, long. 117°04'20" W; near N line sec. 22, T 10 S, R 2 W). Altitude 1593 feet. Named on Pala (1968) 7.5' quadrangle.

Webb Canyon [LOS ANGELES]: *canyon,* drained by a stream that flows 1.5 miles to Thompson Wash 4.5 miles north of Pomona city hall (lat. 34°07'15" N, long. 117°44'15" W; at N line sec. 5, T 1 S, R 8 W). Named on Mount Baldy (1954) and Ontario (1954) 7.5' quadrangles.

Webber Canyon [LOS ANGELES]: *canyon,* 0.5 mile long, 7 miles northwest of Pasadena city hall (lat. 34°13'45" N, long. 118°12'55" W; sec. 26, T 2 N, R 13 W). Named on Pasadena (1953) 7.5' quadrangle.

Webbers Camp: see **Weber Camp** [LOS ANGELES].

Weber Camp [LOS ANGELES]: *locality,* 4.5 miles west-southwest of Mount San Antonio in Coldwater Canyon (2) (lat. 34°15'25" N, long. 117°42'50" W). Named on Mount San Antonio (1955) 7.5' quadrangle. Called Webbers Camp on Los Angeles County (1935) map. John P. Weber founded Weber's Camp in 1906—it lasted until 1924 (Robinson, J.W., 1983, p. 97-98).

Weed: see **Del Mar** [SAN DIEGO].

Weeks Poultry Community: see **Winnetka** [LOS ANGELES].

Weir Canyon [ORANGE]: *canyon,* drained by a stream that flows 3.25 miles to Santiago Creek 5.25 miles east-northeast of present Orange city hall (lat. 33°48'35" N, long. 117°45'35" W). Named on Black Star Canyon (1967) and Orange (1950) 7.5' quadrangles. The feature first was called Los Bueyos Canyon for the oxen that drew carretas over the road there; the name "Weir Canyon" is from a weir built in the canyon (Meadows, p. 80, 138).

Weldon Canyon [LOS ANGELES]: *canyon,* 1.25 miles long, 3 miles south-southeast of Newhall (lat. 34°20'20" N, long. 118°30'50" W; on S line sec. 13, T 3 N, R 16 W). Named on Oat Mountain (1952) 7.5' quadrangle.

Weldon Canyon [VENTURA]: *canyon,* drained by a stream that flows 3 miles to Ventura River 4.5 miles north of Ventura (lat. 34° 20'40" N, long. 119°17'50" W); the mouth of the stream is at Weldons. Named on Ventura (1951) 7.5' quadrangle.

Weldons [VENTURA]: *locality,* 4.5 miles north of Ventura along Southern Pacific Railroad (lat. 34°20'40" N, long. 119°17'45" W); the place is on Cañada Larga o Verde grant. Named on Ventura (1951) 7.5' quadrangle. The name commemorates W.R.H. Weldon, who owned and operated Canet ranch in the 1890's (Ricard). California Division of Highways' (1934) map shows a place called Canet located 1 mile northwest of Weldons along the railroad. The name "Canet" recalls Anselme Canet, a Frenchman who settled in Ventura in 1873 and purchased part of Cañada Larga o Verde grant (Hanna, p. 54).

Well Canyon: see **Santa Felicia Canyon** [LOS ANGELES-VENTURA].

Wellington Heights [LOS ANGELES]: *district,* 3.25 miles east-southeast of Los Angeles city hall (lat. 34°02'20" N, long. 118°11'10" W). Named on Los Angeles (1953) 7.5' quadrangle.

Well of the Eight Echoes [SAN DIEGO]: *well,* 4.25 miles north-northwest of Sweeney Pass (lat. 32°53'05" N, long. 116°13' W; sec. 12, T 15 S, R 7 E). Named on Arroyo Tapiado (1959) 7.5' quadrangle.

Weowlet Spring [SAN DIEGO]: *spring,* 5 miles east-southeast of Warner Springs (lat. 33°15'35" N, long. 116°33' W; at E line sec. 34, T 10 S, R 4 E). Named on Hot Springs Mountain (1960) 7.5' quadrangle.

Werner Camp [LOS ANGELES]: *locality,* 3.25 miles south-southeast of Acton in Arrastre Canyon (lat. 34°25'20" N, long. 118°10'55" W; at NW cor. sec. 19, T 4 N, R 12 W). Named on Acton (1959) 7.5' quadrangle.

West: see **Sherman** [LOS ANGELES].

West Alhambra: see **Dolgeville**, under **Shorb** [LOS ANGELES].

West Anaheim [ORANGE]: *locality,* 4.25 miles east-southeast of Buena Park civic center along Southern Pacific Railroad (lat. 33° 49'50" N, long. 117°55'55" W; sec. 16, T 4 S, R 10 W). Named on Anaheim (1965) 7.5' quadrangle. Called Loara on California Mining Bureau's (1909b) map. Postal authorities established Loara post office in 1900 and discontinued it in 1907; the name was for the wife of the first postmaster (Salley, p. 124).

West Anaheim Junction [ORANGE]: *locality,* 7.25 miles southeast of Buena Park civic center along Southern Pacific Railroad (lat. 33°47'50" N, long. 117°53'45" W; sec. 26, T 4 S, R 10 W). Named on Anaheim (1950) 7.5' quadrangle.

West Arcadia [LOS ANGELES]: *district,* in the southwest part of Arcadia (lat. 34°07'30" N, long. 118°03'15" W). Named on El Monte (1953) and Mount Wilson (1953) 7.5' quadrangles.

West Basin [SAN DIEGO]: *embayment,* 2.5 miles west-northwest of downtown San Diego off San Diego Bay (lat. 32°43'40" N, long. 117°12'15" W). Named on Point Loma (1967) 7.5' quadrangle. United States Board on Geographic Names (1981, p. 3) rejected the name "Harbor Island West Basin" for the feature.

West Butte [SAN DIEGO]: *relief feature,* 5.5 miles northwest of Ocotillo Wells (lat. 33°11'30" N, long. 116°12'30" W); the feature is at the northwest end of Borrego Mountain. Named on Borrego Mountain (1960) 7.5' quadrangle.

West Casitas Pass [VENTURA]: *pass,* 5.5 miles south of White Ledge Peak (lat. 34°23'20" N, long. 119°24'50" W; sec. 32, T 4 N, R 24 W); the feature is 2 miles west of East Casitas pass at the head of Casitas Creek. Named on White Ledge Peak (1952) 7.5' quadrangle.

Westchester [LOS ANGELES]: *district,* 5 miles north of Manhattan Beach city hall in Los Angeles (lat. 33°57'35" N, long. 118°24' W). Named on Venice (1950) 7.5' quadrangle.

West Cove [LOS ANGELES]: *embayment,* 1.5 miles south-southwest of Northwest Harbor on San Clemente Island (lat. 33°00'50" N, long. 118°35'50" W); the feature is on the west side of the island. Named on San Clemente Island North (1943) 7.5' quadrangle.

West Covina [LOS ANGELES]: *city,* 1.5 miles southeast of Baldwin Park city hall (lat. 34°04'15" N, long. 117°56'10" W). Named on Baldwin Park (1966) and San Dimas (1966) 7.5' quadrangles. Postal authorities established West Covina post office in 1954 (Salley, p. 237). The city incorporated in 1923.

West Coyote Hills [ORANGE]: *range,* extends for 3 miles east from Los Angeles-Orange County line to Brea Canyon; center 2.5 miles south of downtown La Habra (lat. 33°54' N, long. 117°57'45" W); the range is on Los Coyotes grant. Named on La Habra (1964) 7.5' quadrangle. Called Coyote Hills on La Habra (1952) 7.5' quadrangle.

West End: see **Lands End** [LOS ANGELES].

Western Anacapa: see **Anacapa Island** [VENTURA].

West Fall Brook: see **Fallbrook** [SAN DIEGO].

West Fork: see **Camp West Fork**, under **Camp Hi-Hill** [LOS ANGELES].

Westgate [LOS ANGELES]: *district,* 4.25 miles west-southwest of Beverly Hills city hall in Los Angeles (lat. 34°03'20" N, long. 118° 28'15" W). Named on Beverly Hills (1950) 7.5' quadrangle. Postal authorities established Westgate post office in 1909 and discontinued it in 1915 (Frickstad, p. 83).

Westgate Heights: see **Brentwood Heights** [LOS ANGELES].

West Glendale [LOS ANGELES]: *locality,* 1.5 miles west of Glendale city hall along Southern Pacific Railroad (lat. 34°08'55" N, long. 118°16'20" W). Named on Burbank (1953) 7.5' quadrangle. Postal authorities established West Glendale post office in 1888 and discontinued it in 1893 (Frickstad, p. 83).

West Hills: see **Canoga Park** [LOS ANGELES].

West Hollywood [LOS ANGELES]: *city,* 8 miles west-northwest of Los Angeles city hall (lat. 34°05'30" N, long. 118°22'30" W). Named on Beverly Hills (1950) and Hollywood (1953) 7.5' quadrangles.

West Lake [LOS ANGELES]: *lake,* 1200 feet long, 2.25 miles west of present Los Angeles city hall (lat. 34°03'25" N, long. 118°16'45" W). Named on Santa Monica (1902) 15' quadrangle.

West Lake Elizabeth: see **Lake Hughes** [LOS ANGELES].

Westlake Village: see **Russell Valley** [LOS ANGELES-VENTURA].

West Liebre Gulch: see **West Fork**, under **Liebre Gulch** [LOS ANGELES].

West Los Angeles [LOS ANGELES]: *district,* 3.5 miles southwest of Beverly Hills city hall in Los Angeles (lat. 34°02'30" N, long. 118° 27'15" W). Named on Beverly Hills (1966) 7.5' quadrangle. Beverly Hills (1950) 7.5' quadrangle has the designation "Sawtelle (West Los Angeles P.O.)" at the place. Postal authorities established Sawtelle post office in 1899 and discontinued it in 1929; the named "Sawtell" was for W.E Sawtelle, owner of the site and manager of Pacific Land Company—the place also was known as Barrett (Salley, p. 199). Postal authorities established West Los Angeles post office in 1922, discontinued it in 1926 when they moved the post office to Sawtelle, and reestablished it in 1929 (Salley, p. 238). California Mining Bureau's (1909b) map shows a place called Soldiers Home located just northwest of Sawtelle. Postal authorities established Soldiers Home post office in 1889 and discontinued it in 1915 (Frickstad, p. 81).

West Mesa [SAN DIEGO]:

(1) *area,* 2 miles southeast of Cuyamaca Peak (lat. 32°55'25" N, long. 116°34'40" W). Named on Cuyamaca Peak (1960) 7.5' quadrangle.

(2) *area,* 8.5 miles north of Sweeney Pass (lat. 32°57' N, long. 116° 12'15" W). Named on Arroyo Tapiado (1959) 7.5' quadrangle.

Westminister [ORANGE]: *city,* 5.5 miles north-northeast of Huntington Beach city hall (lat. 33°44'15" N, long. 117°58'15" W). Named on Anaheim (1965), Los Alamitos (1964), Newport Beach (1965), and Seal Beach (1965) 7.5' quadrangles. Postal authorities established Westminister post office in 1874 (Frickstad, p. 118), and the city incorporated in 1957. The Reverend L.P. Weber started a colony at the place in the 1870's for people sympathetic with the principles of the Presbyterian Church as formulated in the seventeenth century by the Westminister Assembly (Gudde, 1949, p. 387).

Weston: see **Ben Weston Beach** [LOS ANGELES]; **Ben Weston Point** [LOS ANGELES].

West Orange: see **Santa Ana** [ORANGE].

West Palmdale: see **Palmdale** [LOS ANGELES].

West Pine Flat [LOS ANGELES]: *area,* less than 0.5 mile east of Crystal Lake (lat. 34°19'05" N, long. 117°50'20" W); the place is at the southwest end of Pine Flats. Named on Crystal Lake (1958) 7.5' quadrangle.

West Ravine [LOS ANGELES]: *canyon,* less than 1 mile long, 4 miles north of Pasadena city hall (lat. 34°12'20" N, long. 118° 09' W; on W line sec. 4, T 1 N, R 12 W). Named on Pasadena(1953) 7.5' quadrangle.

West Saticoy [VENTURA]: *settlement,* less than 1 mile west of Saticoy (lat. 34°17'05" N, long. 119°09'35" W). Named on Saticoy (1951) 7.5' quadrangle. Postal authorities established West Saticoy post office in 1892 and discontinued it in 1913 (Salley, p. 238). The place first was called Saticoy, but when in 1887 the railroad was built nearly a mile to the east, a new community (present Saticoy) at the railroad took the name (Ricard).

West Sycamore Canyon [SAN DIEGO]: *canyon,* drained by a stream that flows 3.5 miles to Sycamore Canyon (3) 6 miles south-southeast of Poway (lat. 32°52'30" N, long. 117°00'15" W). Named on Poway (1967) 7.5' quadrangle. La Jolla (1903) 15' quadrangle shows the feature as part of present Sycamore Canyon (3).

Westward Beach [LOS ANGELES]: *beach,* extends for 1 mile along the coast northwest from Point Dume (lat. 34°00'30" N, long. 118° 48'50" W). Named on Point Dume (1951) 7.5' quadrangle. Called Zuma Beach on Dume Point (1932) 6' quadrangle.

West Whittier [LOS ANGELES]: *district,* 2 miles northwest of present Whittier city hall (lat. 33°59'25" N, long. 118°03'45" W). Named on Whittier (1949) 7.5' quadrangle. Postal authorities established West Whittier post office in 1926 and discontinued it that year (Salley, p. 238).

Westwood [LOS ANGELES]: *district,* 2 miles west-southwest of Beverly Hills city hall (lat. 34°03'25" N, long. 118°25'45" W). Named on Beverly Hills (1966) 7.5' quadrangle. Called Sunset on Lankershim Ranch Land and Water Company's (1888) map, and called Westwood Hills on Sawtelle (1934) 6' quadrangle.

Westwood Hills: see **Westwood** [LOS ANGELES].

Westwood Village [LOS ANGELES]: *locality,* nearly 2 miles west-southwest of Beverly Hills city hall (lat. 34°03'35" N, long. 118° 26'40" W). Named on Beverly Hills (1950) 7.5' quadrangle.

Whale Mountain [SAN DIEGO]: *peak,* 6.25 miles east-northeast of Ramona (lat. 33°04'30" N, long. 116°45'35" W; sec. 3, T 13 S, R 2 E). Altitude 3043 feet. Named on Ramona (1955) 7.5' quadrangle.

Whalen Lake [SAN DIEGO]: *lake,* 0.5 mile long, 4 miles northeast of Oceanside (lat. 33°14'35" N, long. 117°20'10" W; mainly in sec. 6, T 11 S, R 4 W). Named on San Luis Rey (1968) 7.5' quadrangle. Unites States Board on Geographic Names (1969c, p. 4) approved the name "Whelan Lake" for the feature. It was known as Pico's Lake after the Pico family won it on a horse race; John Whelan later leased the property from the Pico family (Stein, p. 151).

Whalen Lake: see **Windmill Lake** [SAN DIEGO].

Whale Peak [SAN DIEGO]: *peak,* 12.5 miles southwest of Ocotillo Wells (lat. 33°01'45" N, long. 116°18'55" W; near E line sec. 24, T 13 S, R 6 E). Altitude 5349 feet. Named on Whale Peak (1959) 7.5' quadrangle.

Whale Rock [LOS ANGELES]: *rock,* 2 miles south-southeast of Silver Peak, and 200 feet off the south side of Santa Catalina Island (lat. 33°25'55" N, long. 118°33'35" W). Named on Santa Catalina West (1943) 7.5' quadrangle.

Whale View Point [SAN DIEGO]: *promontory,* 3600 feet southwest of Point La Jolla along the coast (lat. 32°50'35" N, long. 117°16'50" W). Named on La Jolla (1967) 7.5' quadrangle.

Wheeler Canyon [VENTURA]: *canyon,* drained by a stream that flows 7 miles to the valley of Santa Clara River 3.5 miles north of Saticoy (lat. 34°20'05" N, long. 119°08'20" W). Named on Ojai (1952) and Saticoy (1951) 7.5' quadrangles. The feature was called Millhouse Canyon in the 1860's for Dr. Millhouse, who kept a boarding house for oil-field workers there (Ricard).

Wheeler Gorge [VENTURA]: *narrows,* 1 mile east of Wheeler Springs along North Fork Matilija Creek (lat. 34°30'30" N, long. 119°16'30" W; at S line sec. 15, T 5 N, R 23 W). Named on Wheeler Springs (1943) 7.5' quadrangle.

Wheeler's Cold Spring: see **Wheeler Springs** [VENTURA].

Wheeler's Hot Springs: see **Wheeler Springs** [VENTURA].

Wheeler Springs [VENTURA]: *locality,* 16 miles north of Ventura (lat. 34°30'30" N, long. 119°17'25" W; at S line sec. 16, T 5 N, R 23 W). Named on Wheeler Springs (1943) 7.5' quadrangle. Postal authorities established Wheeler Springs post office in 1913 and discontinued it in 1962 (Salley, p. 239). Huguenin (p. 766-767) called the place Wheeler's Hot Springs, mentioned that it had been a resort since 1890, and noted that the resort owner conducted a summer camp at Wheeler's Cold Spring, located 9 miles by trail north of Wheeler's Hot Springs in the canyon of Sespe Creek.

Whelan Lake: see **Whalen Lake** [SAN DIEGO].

Whisky Spring [LOS ANGELES]: *spring,* 11 miles south-southeast of the village of Lake Hughes (lat. 34°31'25" N, long. 118°22'35" W; near NW cor. sec. 17, T 5 N, R 14 W). Named on Green Valley (1958) 7.5' quadrangle.

Whispering Pines [SAN DIEGO]: *settlement,* 1 mile east-northeast of Julian (lat. 33°05'10" N, long. 116°35'05" W; sec. 32, T 12 S, R 4 E). Named on Julian (1960) 7.5' quadrangle.

Whitaker Canyon: see **Ruby Canyon** [LOS ANGELES] (1).

Whitaker Peak [LOS ANGELES]: *peak,* nearly 17 miles south-southeast of Gorman (lat. 34°34'20" N, long. 118°44' W; near N line sec. 36, T 6 N, R 18 W). Altitude 4148 feet. Named on Whitaker Peak (1958) 7.5' quadrangle.

Whitaker Summit [LOS ANGELES]: *pass,* 1.5 miles northeast of Whitaker Peak (lat. 34°35'15" N, long. 118°42'50" W; near NE cor. sec. 30, T 6 N, R 17 W). Named on Whitaker Peak (1958) 7.5' quadrangle.

Whiteacre Peak [VENTURA]: *peak,* 4.5 miles south of Cobblestone Mountain (lat. 34°32'30" N, long. 118°52'20" W). Altitude 5079 feet. Named on Cobblestone Mountain (1958) 7.5' quadrangle.

White Canyon [ORANGE]: *canyon,* about 0.5 mile long, opens into Silverado Canyon 9 miles north-northeast of El Toro at Silverado (lat. 33°44'45" N, long. 117°38'05" W). Named on El Toro (1968) 7.5' quadrangle.

White Cove [LOS ANGELES]: *embayment,* 4.25 miles north-northwest of Avalon on the northeast side of Santa Catalina Island (lat. 33°23'35" N, long. 118°22'05" W). Named on Santa Catalina East (1950) 7.5' quadrangle. Smith's (1897) map has the name "Whitley's Cove" for an embayment that includes present White Cove.

White Heather [LOS ANGELES]: *locality,* 7 miles south of the village of Leona Valley in Sierra Pelona Valley (lat. 34°31'10" N, long. 118°18'15" W; near W line sec. 13, T 5 N, R 14 W). Named on Sleepy Valley (1958) 7.5' quadrangle.

White Island: see **Island White** [LOS ANGELES].

White Ledge Peak [VENTURA]: *peak,* 15 miles north-northwest of Ventura (lat. 34°28'10" N, long. 119°23'30" W). Altitude 4640 feet. Named on White Ledge Peak (1952) 7.5' quadrangle.

White Mountain [SAN DIEGO]: *peak,* 2.25 miles north-northwest of Barrett Junction (lat. 32°38'40" N, long. 116°43' W; sec. 31, T 17 S, R 3 E). Altitude 3297 feet. Named on Barrett Lake (1960) 7.5' quadrangle.

White Mountain [VENTURA]: *ridge,* west- to southwest-trending, 3 miles long, 2 miles north-northeast of Cobblestone Mountain (lat. 34°37'55" N, long. 118°50'50" W). Named on Black Mountain (1958) and Cobblestone Mountain (1958) 7.5' quadrangles.

White Oak Canyon [LOS ANGELES]: *canyon,* drained by a stream that flows 1 mile to Big Tujunga Canyon 2.5 miles southeast of Condor Peak (lat. 34°18' N, long. 118°11'05" W). Named on Condor Peak (1959) 7.5' quadrangle.

White Oak Springs [SAN DIEGO]: *springs,* two, 6 miles west-northwest of Margarita Peak (lat. 33°29'25" N, long. 117°28'40" W). Named on Margarita Peak (1968) 7.5' quadrangle. Margarita Peak (1944) 15' quadrangle has the singular form "White Oak Spring" for the name.

White Point: see **Whites Point** [LOS ANGELES].

White Rock [LOS ANGELES]: *relief feature,* 7.25 miles northwest of Pyramid Head on the northeast side of San Clemente Island (lat. 32°53'30" N, long. 118°26'25" W). Named on San Clemente Island Central (1943) 7.5' quadrangle.

White Rock [SAN DIEGO]: *relief feature,* 2.5 miles north of Encinitas (lat. 33°04'40" N, long. 117°17'30" W; near NE cor. sec. 4, T 13 S, R 4 W). Named on San Luis Rey (1898) 30' quadrangle.

White Rock: see **Bird Rock** [LOS ANGELES].

White Saddle [LOS ANGELES]: *pass,* 5.25 miles northwest of Azusa city hall (lat. 34°11'50" N, long. 117°57'25" W; near SW cor. sec. 5, T 1 N, R 10 W). Named on Azusa (1953) 7.5' quadrangle.

Whites Canyon: see **Solemint** [LOS ANGELES].

Whites Landing [LOS ANGELES]: *locality,* 4.25 miles north-northwest of Avalon on the northeast side of Santa Catalina Island (lat. 33°23'40" N, long. 118°22'10" W); the place is at White Cove. Named on Santa Catalina East (1950) 7.5' quadrangle. Called Swain's Ldg. on Smith's (1897) map.

Whites Point [LOS ANGELES]: *promontory,* 1.5 miles west-northwest of Point Fermin (lat 33°42'50" N, long. 118°19' W). Named on San Pedro (1964) 7.5' quadrangle. United States Board on Geographic Names (1983a, p. 5) approved the form "White Point" for the name.

Whites Point Hot Springs [LOS ANGELES]: *locality,* 1.5 miles west-northwest of Point Fermin (lat. 33°43' N, long. 118°19'10" W); the place is near Whites Point (present White Point). Named on San Pedro Hills (1928) 6' quadrangle.

Whitewashed Rock: see **Balanced Rock**, under **Pyramid Head** [LOS ANGELES].

Whitewater Canyon [LOS ANGELES]: *canyon,* drained by a stream that flows 0.5 mile to Pacoima Canyon 7 miles north-northwest of Sunland (lat. 34°21'20" N, long. 118°21'10" W; sec. 9, T 3 N, R 14 W). Named on Sunland (1953) 7.5' quadrangle.

Whitley's Cove: see **White Cove** [LOS ANGELES].

Whitleys Peak [LOS ANGELES]: *peak,* 3.5 miles northwest of Avalon on Santa Catalina Island (lat. 33°22'55" N, long. 118°22'05" W). Altitude 1302 feet. Named on Santa Catalina East (1950) 7.5' quadrangle.

Whitney: see **Mount Whitney** [SAN DIEGO].

Whitney Canyon [LOS ANGELES]: *canyon,* 3.5 miles long, opens into the canyon of Newhall Creek 2 miles southeast of Newhall (lat. 34°21'55" N, long. 118°30'15" W). Named on San Fernando (1953) 7.5' quadrangle.

Whittier [LOS ANGELES]: *city,* 17 miles north-northeast of Long Beach city hall (lat. 33°58'25" N, long. 118°02' W). Named on El Monte (1966) and Whittier (1965) 7.5' quadrangles. Postal authorities established Whittier post office in 1887 (Frickstad, p. 83), and the city incorporated in 1898. An organization of Quakers founded the place in 1887, and at the suggestion of Micajah D. Johnson named it for John Greenleaf Whitter, the Quaker poet (Gudde, 1949, p. 389).

Whittier: see **East Whittier** [LOS ANGELES]; **North Whittier Heights** [LOS ANGELES]; **South Whittier** [LOS ANGELES]; **South Whittier Heights** [LOS ANGELES]; **West Whittier** [LOS ANGELES].

Whittier Creek [LOS ANGELES]: *stream,* flows 1.5 miles to Painter Lagoon 2 miles south-southwest of present Whittier city hall (lat. 33°56'45" N, long. 118°02'45" W). Named on Whittier (1949) 7.5' quadrangle.

Whittier Hills: see **Puente Hills** [LOS ANGELES].

Whittier Junction [LOS ANGELES]: *locality,* 5 miles south-southwest of El Monte city hall along Union Pacific Railroad (lat. 34°00'15" N, long. 118°04' W). Named on El Monte (1953) 7.5' quadrangle.

Whittier Narrows: see **Puente Hills** [LOS ANGELES].

Wicham Canyon [LOS ANGELES]: *canyon,* drained by a stream that flows 1.5 miles to Pico Canyon 3.5 miles west of Newhall (lat. 34° 22'40" N, long. 118°35'40" W; near N line sec. 6, T 3 N, R 16 W). Named on Newhall (1952) and Oat Mountain (1952) 7.5' quadrangles. Called Big Moore Canyon on Pico (1940) 6' quadrangle.

Wickiup Campground [LOS ANGELES]: *locality,* 6.5 miles southwest of Pacifico Mountain in Big Tujunga Canyon (lat. 34°18'20" N, long. 118°06'30" W; sec. 35, T 3 N, R 12 W); the place is nearly 0.5 mile southwest of the mouth of Wickiup Canyon. Named on Chilao Flat (1959) 7.5' quadrangle

Wigham Creek [SAN DIEGO]: *stream,* flows 1.5 miles to San Luis Rey River 8.5 miles southeast of Boucher Hill (lat. 33°15'30" N, long. 116°47'55" W; near S line sec. 32, T 10 S, R 2 E). Named on Palomar Observatory (1949) 7.5' quadrangle.

Wilbur Wash [LOS ANGELES]: *stream,* flows 2.25 miles to Aliso Canyon Wash 4.25 miles northeast of the center of Canoga Park (lat. 34°14'40" N, long. 118°32'35" W). Named on Canoga Park (1952) and Oat Mountain (1952) 7.5' quadrangles.

Wildasin [LOS ANGELES]: *locality,* 3.5 miles east-northeast of Inglewood city hall along Atchison, Topeka and Santa Fe Railroad (lat. 33°59'20" N, long. 118°17'50" W). Named on Inglewood (1964) 7.5' quadrangle. Called Wildeson on Redondo (1896) 15' quadrangle.

Wildcat Canyon [SAN DIEGO]: *canyon,* drained by a stream that flows 3.25 miles to the valley of San Diego River 1.5 miles north-northeast of Lakeside (lat. 32°52'35" N, long. 116°54'25" W). Named on San Vicente Reservoir (1955) 7.5' quadrangle.

Wildcat Gulch [LOS ANGELES]: *canyon,* drained by a stream that flows 2 miles to Upper Big Tujunga Canyon nearly 6 miles south-southwest of Pacifico Mountain (lat. 34°18'30" N, long. 118°04'45" W; near NW cor. sec. 31, T 3 N, R 11 W). Named on Chilao Flat (1959) 7.5' quadrangle.

Wildcat Spring [SAN DIEGO]: *spring,* 6.25 miles north of Descanso (lat. 32°56'35" N, long. 116°38'10" W; near E line sec. 23, T 14 S, R 3 E). Named on Tule Springs (1960) 7.5' quadrangle.

Wildeson: see **Wildasin** [LOS ANGELES].

Wild Mans Canyon [SAN DIEGO]: *canyon,* 1 mile long, 6.5 miles west-southwest of Jamul (lat. 32°40'30" N, long. 116°58'30" W; mainly in sec. 22, T 17 S, R 1 W). Named on Jamul Mountains (1955) 7.5' quadrangle.

Wild Pigeon Flat [SAN DIEGO]: *area,* 4 miles east of Descanso (lat. 32°51'30" N, long. 116°32'45" W; near NW cor. sec. 23, T 15 S, R 4 E).

Named on Descanso (1960) 7.5' quadrangle.

Wild Rose Canyon: see **Rose Canyon** [ORANGE].

Wildwood [LOS ANGELES]: *locality*, 2.5 miles south-southwest of Condor Peak in Big Tujunga Canyon (lat. 34°17'40" N, long. 118° 14'25" W; near NE cor. sec. 4, T 2 N, R 13 W). Named on Condor Peak (1959) 7.5' quadrangle.

Wildwood: see **Fernwood** [LOS ANGELES].

Wildwood Canyon [LOS ANGELES]:

(1) *canyon*, 1.5 miles long, 2 miles north-northeast of Burbank city hall (lat. 34°12'30" N, long. 118°17'30" W). Named on Burbank (1966) 7.5' quadrangle.

(2) *canyon*, 1.5 miles long, 3 miles east of Glendora city hall (lat. 34°08'20" N, long. 117°48'40" W; sec. 27, 34, T 1 N, R 9 W). Named on Glendora (1953) 7.5' quadrangle.

Wildwood Canyon: see **Newhall** [LOS ANGELES].

Wiley Canyon [LOS ANGELES]: *canyon*, drained by a stream that flows 1.25 miles to Towsley Canyon 2.25 miles southwest of Newhall (lat. 34°21'25" N, long. 118°33'25" W; sec. 9, T 3 N, R 16 W). Named on Oat Mountain (1952) 7.5' quadrangle. Henry Clay Wiley, a merchant and expressman, was a pioneer in the canyon (Reynolds, p. 13).

Wiley Canyon [VENTURA]: *canyon*, drained by a stream that flows 2 miles to the valley of Santa Clara River 3 miles southwest of Piru (lat. 34°22'55" N, long. 119°49'50" W). Named on Piru (1952) and Simi (1951) 7.5' quadrangles.

Willard Canyon [VENTURA]: *canyon*, drained by a stream that flows 1.25 miles to the valley of Santa Clara River 2 miles east of Santa Paula (lat. 34°21'10" N, long. 119°01'20" W; sec. 7, T 3 N, R 20 W). Named on Santa Paula (1951) 7.5' quadrangle.

Williams Camp: see **Williams Flat** [LOS ANGELES].

Williams Canyon [LOS ANGELES]:

(1) *canyon*, drained by a stream that flows 1.5 miles to San Gabriel River 8 miles northeast of Glendora city hall (lat. 34°14' N, long. 117°47'20" W). Named on Glendora (1953) 7.5' quadrangle. Called Roberts Canyon on Pomona (1904) 15' quadrangle.

(2) *canyon*, 0.5 mile long, 7 miles north-northeast of Pomona city hall (lat. 34°09'05" N, long. 117°42'15" W; on S line sec. 22, T 1 N, R 8 W). Named on Mount Baldy (1954) 7.5' quadrangle.

Williams Canyon [ORANGE]: *canyon*, drained by a stream that flows 3.25 miles to Santiago Creek 7.5 miles north-northeast of El Toro (lat. 33°43'40" N, long. 117°39' W). Named on El Toro (1968) and Santiago Peak (1954) 7.5' quadrangles. The name commemorates Marshall Williams, who lived in the canyon; the feature also was known as Cañada Seco and as Seco Canyon in the early days (Meadows, p. 50, 126, 139).

Williams Flat [LOS ANGELES]: *area*, 8 miles north-northeast of Glendora city hall along San Gabriel River (lat. 34°13'55" N, long. 117°47'25" W); the place is opposite the mouth of Williams Canyon (1). Named on Glendora (1953) 7.5' quadrangle. Camp Bonita (1940) 6' quadrangle shows Williams Camp near the site. Jim Williams founded Williams Camp 1.25 miles downstream from Camp Bonita in 1913 (Robinson, J.W., 1983, p. 96).

Williamson: see **Mount Williamson** [LOS ANGELES].

Williamson's Pass: see **Soledad Pass** [LOS ANGELES].

Willmore City: see **Long Beach** [LOS ANGELES].

Willowbrook [LOS ANGELES]: *district*, 3 miles south-southwest of South Gate city hall (lat. 33°55' N, long. 118°13'45" W). Named on South Gate (1952) 7.5' quadrangle. South Gate (1964) 7.5' quadrangle has the designation "Willowbrook (Willow Brook P.O.)" at the place. Postal authorities established Willowbrook post office in 1906 and changed the name to Willow Brook in 1952: the name is from willow trees that grew along a stream at the site when Pacific Electric Railroad built a station there (Salley, p. 241).

Willow Cove [LOS ANGELES]: *embayment*, 2.5 miles north-northwest of Avalon on the northeast side of Santa Catalina Island (lat. 33°22'30" N, long. 118°21'10" W). Named on Santa Catalina East (1950) 7.5' quadrangle, which shows Camp Toyon at the place. United States Board on Geographic Names (1975a, p. 12) approved the name "Toyon Bay" for the feature, and approved the name "Willow Cove" for an embayment situated 0.25 mile north-northwest of present Toyon Bay (lat. 33°22'39" N, long. 118°21'18" W).

Willow Creek [LOS ANGELES]: *stream*, flows 1 mile to the sea 7.5 miles west-northwest of Point Dume (lat. 34°02'45" N, long. 118° 55'40" W). Named on Triunfo Pass (1950) 7.5' quadrangle. Los Angeles County (1935) map has the name "Little Nicholas Canyon" for the canyon of present Willow Creek—the feature is less than 1 mile west of Nicholas Canyon.

Willow Creek [VENTURA]: *stream*, flows nearly 2 miles to Lake Casitas 8 miles southwest of the town of Ojai (lat. 34°23'25" N, long. 119°21'40" W). Named on Matilija (1952, photorevised 1967) and White Ledge Peak (1952) 7.5' quadrangles.

Willows: see **Lower Willows** [SAN DIEGO]; **The Willows** [SAN DIEGO].

Willow Spring [LOS ANGELES]: *spring*, 5 miles southwest of the village of Leona Valley (lat. 34°34' N, long. 118°21'10" W; sec. 34, T 6 N, R 14 W). Named on Sleepy Valley (1958) 7.5' quadrangle.

Willow Spring [SAN DIEGO]:

(1) *spring*, 10.5 miles northwest of Fallbrook (lat. 33°29'25" N, long. 117°22'15" W; sec. 11, T 8 S, R 5 W). Named on Fallbrook (1968) 7.5' quadrangle.

(2) *spring*, 5 miles east-southeast of San Felipe (lat. 33°10'40" N, long. 116°31' W; on E line sec. 36, T 11 S, R 4 E). Named on Ranchita (1960) 7.5' quadrangle.

Willow Springs Canyon [LOS ANGELES]:

(1) *canyon*, drained by a stream that flows 3.5 miles to lowlands 4 miles west-northwest of Del Sur (lat. 34°42'30" N, long. 118°21'20" W; sec. 10, T 7 N, R 14 W). Named on Del Sur (1958) and Lake Hughes (1957) 7.5' quadrangles.

(2) *canyon*, drained by a stream that flows 1.5 miles to Hauser Canyon 5.25 miles south of the village of Leona Valley (lat. 34°32'30" N, long. 118°16'10" W; near SW cor. sec. 5, T 5 N, R 13 W). Named on Sleepy Valley (1958) 7.5' quadrangle. Called Willow Springs Gulch on Red Rover (1937) 6' quadrangle, but United States Board on Geographic Names (1959, p. 8) rejected this name for the feature.

Willow Springs Gulch: see **Willow Springs Canyon** [LOS ANGELES] (2).

Willowville [LOS ANGELES]: *locality*, 2.5 miles north of Long Beach city hall along Pacific Electric Railroad (lat. 33°48'20" N, long. 118°11'15" W). Named on Long Beach (1949) 7.5' quadrangle.

Wills Canyon [VENTURA]: *canyon*, 2 miles long, opens into Ojai Valley 3 miles west of the town of Ojai (lat. 34°27' N, long. 119° 17'45" W). Named on Matilija (1952) 7.5' quadrangle.

Will Thrall Peak [LOS ANGELES]: *peak*, 5 miles south-southwest of Valyermo (lat. 34°23'05" N, long. 117°54'05" W; near SW cor. sec. 35, T 4 N, R 10 W). Named on Juniper Hills (1959) 7.5' quadrangle. The name commemorates William H. Thrall, an early conservationist (United States Board on Geographic Names, 1963, p. 15).

Will Valley [SAN DIEGO]: *valley*, 8 miles east-southeast of Boucher Hill (lat. 33°17'20" N, long. 116°47'25" W; in and near sec. 20, T 10 S, R 2 E). Named on Palomar Observatory (1949) 7.5' quadrangle. The name is for Will Cook, a homesteader in the valley (Stein, p. 152).

Wilmar [LOS ANGELES]: *district*, 2 miles south of present San Gabriel city hall (lat. 34°04'15" N, long. 118°05'10" W). Named on Alhambra (1926) and El Monte (1926) 6' quadrangles.

Wilmington [LOS ANGELES]: *district*, 6 miles southeast of Torrance city hall in Los Angeles (lat. 33°47' N, long. 118°15'40" W). Named on Long Beach (1964) and Torrance (1964) 7.5' quadrangles. Postal authorities established Wilmington post office in 1864 (Frickstad, p. 84). Los Angeles annexed the place in 1909 (Hanna, p. 356). Phineas Banning named the community after his birthplace in Delaware; until 1863 the place was known as New San Pedro or Newtown (Gudde, 1949, p. 391). Postal authorities established East Wilmington post office in 1912, discontinued it in 1918, reestablished it in 1919, and discontinued it in 1921 (Frickstad, p. 73). Redondo (1896) 15' quadrangle shows a place called Drum Barracks located less than 1 mile northeast of the center of Wilmington (lat. 33°47' N, long. 118°15'30" W). The place first was called Camp San Pedro, then Camp Drum to honor Adjutant-General Richard C. Drum, and after December 1, 1863, it was designated Drum Barracks (Hart, p. 54).

Wilmington: see **North Wilmington**, under **Carson** [LOS ANGELES].

Wilmington Lagoon [LOS ANGELES]: *water feature*, south of Wilmington between Wilmington and present Terminal Island (lat. 33° 45'30" N, long. 118°16" W). Named on Redondo (1896) 15' quadrangle. The feature now is modified to form part of Los Angeles Harbor.

Wilshire: see **Cavin** [VENTURA].

Wilsie Canyon [VENTURA]: *canyon*, 4 miles long, drained by Reeves Creek above a point 4 miles east of the town of Ojai (lat. 34°27'15" N, long. 119°10'25" W; sec. 3, T 4 N, R 22 W). Named on Ojai (1952) 7.5' quadrangle.

Wilson: see **Camp Wilson**, under **Martins Camp** [LOS ANGELES]; **Mount Wilson** [LOS ANGELES].

Wilsona [LOS ANGELES]: *locality*, 14 miles east-northeast of Littlerock (lat. 34°36'50" N, long. 117°46'05" W; near N line sec. 18, T 6 N, R 8 W). Named on Wilsona (1935) 6' quadrangle. Postal authorities established Wilsona post office in 1917 and discontinued it in 1933; the name was for President Woodrow Wilson (Salley, p. 241).

Wilsona Gardens [LOS ANGELES]: *locality*, 14 miles northeast of Littlerock (lat. 34°40' N, long. 117°49'30" W; sec. 27, T 7 N, R 9 W). Named on Hi Vista (1957) 7.5' quadrangle.

Wilson Canyon [LOS ANGELES]: *canyon*, 2 miles long, opens into lowlands 3.25 miles north of downtown San Fernando (lat. 34°19'45" N, long. 118°26'40" W; sec. 22, T 3 N, R 15 W). Named on San Fernando (1953) 7.5' quadrangle.

Wilson Canyon Saddle [LOS ANGELES]: *pass*, 5 miles north of downtown San Fernando (lat. 34°21'25" N, long. 118°27'05" W; near E line sec. 9, T 3 N, R 15 W); the pass is near the head of Wilson Canyon. Named on San Fernando (1966) 7.5' quadrangle.

Wilson Cove [LOS ANGELES]: *embayment*, 2.5 miles southeast of Northwest Harbor on the east side of San Clemente Island (lat. 33° 30' N, long. 118°33'25" W). Named on San Clemente Island North (1943) 7.5' quadrangle.

Wilson Creek [SAN DIEGO]: *stream*, flows 5.25 miles to Barrett Lake 5.5 miles north-northeast of Barrett Junction (lat. 32°41'15" N, long. 116°40'20" W; at E line sec. 16, T 17 S, R 3 E). Named on Barrett Lake (1960) 7.5' quadrangle.

Wilson Lake [LOS ANGELES]: *intermittent lake*, 2.25 miles south-southeast of present Pasadena city hall (lat. 34°07'10" N, long. 118°07'20" W). Named on Altadena (1928) 6' quadrangle.

Wilson's Cove: see **Emerald Bay** [LOS ANGELES].

Wilson's Peak: see **Mount Wilson** [LOS ANGELES] (1).

Windmill Canyon [LOS ANGELES-VENTURA]: *canyon*, 0.5 mile long, 2 miles east-southeast of Thousand Oaks on Los Angeles-Ventura County line (lat. 34°09'45" N, long. 118°48' W). Named on Thousand Oaks (1952) 7.5' quadrangle.

Windmill Canyon [SAN DIEGO]: *canyon*, drained by a stream that flows 4 miles to the valley of San Luis Rey River 6 miles north of Oceanside city hall (lat. 33°14'55" N, long. 117°19'55" W; near E line sec. 6, T 11 S, R 4 W). Named on Morro Hill (1968) 7.5' quadrangle.

Windmill Canyon [VENTURA]: *canyon*, drained by a stream that flows nearly 3 miles to Gillibrand Canyon 5.5 miles northwest of Santa Susana Pass (lat. 34°19'40" N, long. 118°41'50" W; sec. 19, T 3 N, R 17 W). Named on Santa Susana (1951) 7.5' quadrangle.

Windmill Flat [SAN DIEGO]: *area*, 5 miles north of El Cajon Mountain (lat. 33°59'50" N, long. 116°49'30" W). Named on El Cajon Mountain (1955) 7.5' quadrangle.

Windmill Lake [SAN DIEGO]: *intermittent lake*, 1800 feet long, 5 miles southwest of Morro Hill (lat. 33°15'10" N, long. 117°19'55" W; near E line sec. 6, T 11 S, R 4 W); the feature is at the mouth of Windmill Canyon. Named on Morro Hill (1968) and San Luis Rey (1968) 7.5' quadrangles. Called Whalen Lake on Margarita Peak (1944) 15' quadrangle. Morro Hill (1949) 7.5' quadrangle shows a permanent lake.

Windsor Hills [LOS ANGELES]: *district*, 2 miles north of Inglewood city hall (lat. 33°59'25" N, long. 118°21'10" W). Named on Inglewood (1964) 7.5' quadrangle.

Windy Gap [LOS ANGELES]: *pass*, 2 miles north-northeast of Crystal Lake (lat. 34°20'35" N, long. 117°49'40" W). Named on Crystal Lake (1958) 7.5' quadrangle.

Windy Spring [LOS ANGELES]: *spring*, 2 miles north-northeast of Crystal Lake (lat. 34°20'50" N, long. 117°50'05" W). Named on Crystal Lake (1958) 7.5' quadrangle.

Winery Canyon [LOS ANGELES]: *canyon*, about 1 mile long, 6.5 miles north-northwest of Pasadena city hall (lat. 34°13'45" N, long. 118°12'20" W; mainly in sec. 26, T 2 N, R 13 W). Named on Pasadena (1953) 7.5' quadrangle.

Wingfoot [LOS ANGELES]: *locality*, 6 miles east-northeast of Inglewood city hall along Atchison, Topeka and Santa Fe Railroad (lat. 33°59'20" N, long. 118°15'15" W). Named on Inglewood (1964) 7.5' quadrangle.

Winnetka [LOS ANGELES]: *district*, less than 2 miles east-northeast of the center of Canoga Park in Los Angeles (lat. 34°12'50" N, long. 118°34'10" W). Named on Canoga Park (1952) 7.5' quadrangle. Postal authorities established Winnetka post office in 1935 (Salley, p. 242). The place first was called Weeks Poultry Community (Gudde, 1969, p. 366).

Winston Peak [LOS ANGELES]: *peak*, 1.5 miles north of Waterman Mountain (lat. 34°21'30" N, long. 117°56'05" W; sec. 9, T 3 N, R 10 W); the peak is at the southeast end of Winston Ridge. Altitude 7502 feet. Named on Waterman Mountain (1959) 7.5' quadrangle.

Winston Ridge [LOS ANGELES]: *ridge*, generally west-northwest-trending, 3.5 miles long, 7.25 miles southwest of Valyermo (lat. 34°22'25" N, long. 117°56'30" W). Named on Juniper Hills (1959) and Waterman Mountain (1959) 7.5' quadrangles. The name commemorates L.C. Winston, a Pasadena businessman who froze to death on the ridge during a blizzard in 1893 (Robinson, J.W., 1977, p. 191-192).

Winston Spring [LOS ANGELES]: *spring*, 1 mile northwest of Waterman Mountain (lat. 34°20'50" N, long. 117°57' W; sec. 17, T 3 N, R 10 W); the spring is about 1 mile southwest of Winston Peak. Named on Waterman Mountain (1959) 7.5' quadrangle.

Winter Camp Creek: see **Winter Creek** [LOS ANGELES].

Winter Canyon [LOS ANGELES]: *canyon*, 1 mile long, 1.5 miles northwest of Malibu Point (lat. 34°02'35" N, long. 118°42'10" W; on S line sec. 30, T 1 S, R 17 W). Named on Malibu Beach (1951) 7.5' quadrangle. Called Amarillo Canyon on Los Angeles County (1935) map.

Winter Creek [LOS ANGELES]: *stream*, flows 3 miles to Santa Anita Canyon 3 miles southeast of Mount Wilson (1) (lat. 34° 12' N, long. 118°01'10" W; sec. 3, T 1 N, R 11 W). Named on Mount Wilson (1953) 7.5' quadrangle. Called Winter Camp Creek on Los Angeles County (1935) map. Wilbur M. Sturtevant began work on a trail in 1895 and set up a camp, called Sturtevant's Winter Camp, which gave its name to Winter Camp Creek (Owens, p. 4-5).

Winter Gardens [LOS ANGELES]: *district*, 5 miles east-southeast of Los Angeles city hall (lat. 34°01' N, long. 118°10' W). Named on Alhambra (1926) 6' quadrangle.

Winter Gardens [SAN DIEGO]: *locality*, 2 miles south-southwest of Lakeside (lat. 32°50'05" N, long. 116°55'55" W). Named on El Cajon (1967) 7.5' quadrangle.

Wintersburg [ORANGE]: *locality*, nearly 4 miles north of Huntington Beach civic center along Southern Pacific Railroad (lat. 33°43'05" N, long. 117°59'50" W; near S line sec. 23, T 5 S, R 11 W). Named on Newport Beach (1965) 7.5' quadrangle. The name commemorates Henry Winters, an early-day celery farmer (Meadows, p. 139).

Winterwarm [SAN DIEGO]: *settlement*, 3.25 miles south-southeast of Fallbrook (lat. 33°20'30" N, long. 117°13'15" W). Named on Bonsall (1968) 7.5' quadrangle.

Wire Mountain [SAN DIEGO]: *ridge*, south-southeast-trending, nearly 2 miles long, 2.5 miles north-northeast of Oceanside (lat. 33°13'50" N, long. 117°22'05" W). Named on San Luis Rey (1968) 7.5' quadrangle. On Oceanside (1898) 15' quadrangle, the name applies to a peak on the ridge.

Wire Springs Canyon [ORANGE]: *canyon*, drained by a stream that flows nearly 1 mile to Blue Mud Canyon 1.25 miles south-southeast of San Juan Hill (lat. 33°53'50" N, long. 117°44' W). Named on Prado Dam (1967) 7.5' quadrangle.

Wiseburn: see **Lairport** [LOS ANGELES].

Witch Creek [SAN DIEGO]:

(1) *stream*, flows 4 miles to Santa Ysabel Creek 4 miles west of Santa Ysabel (lat. 33°06'30" N, long. 116°44'20" W; near NE cor. sec. 26, T 12 S, R 2 E). Named on Santa Ysabel (1960) 7.5' quadrangle.

(2) *locality*, 3 miles southwest of Santa Ysabel (lat. 33°04'50" N, long. 116°42'50" W; at S line sec. 31, T 12 S, R 3 E); the place is along Witch Creek (1). Named on Santa Ysabel (1960) 7.5' quadrangle. Postal authorities established Witch Creek post office in 1893 and discontinued it in 1938 (Frickstad, p. 158).

Witch Creek Mountain [SAN DIEGO]: *peak*, 3.5 miles southwest of Santa Ysabel (lat. 33°04'40" N, long. 116°43'30" W; near N line sec. 1, T 13 S, R 2 E); the peak is south of Witch Creek (1). Altitude 3279 feet. Named on Santa Ysabel (1960) 7.5' quadrangle.

Woersham Cañon: see **Worsham Creek** [LOS ANGELES].

Wohlford Reservoir: see **Lake Wohlford** [SAN DIEGO].

Wolahi: see **Camp Wolahi** [SAN DIEGO].

Wolf Canyon [SAN DIEGO]: *canyon*, drained by a stream that flows nearly 3 miles to Otay Valley 9 miles west of Otay Mountain (lat. 32°35'30" N, long. 116°59'35" W). Named on Otay Mesa (1955) 7.5' quadrangle.

Wolfe Well [SAN DIEGO]: *well*, 4 miles northeast of Ocotillo Wells (lat. 33°10'55" N, long. 116°05' W). Named on Shell Reef (1959) 7.5' quadrangle, which indicates that the well is dry.

Wolfskill Camp [LOS ANGELES]: *locality*, 8.5 miles north of Pomona city hall (lat. 34°10'30" N, long. 117°45'05" W); the place is in Wolfskill Canyon. Named on La Verne (1940) 6' quadrangle.

Wolfskill Canyon [LOS ANGELES]: *canyon*, drained by a stream that flows nearly 4 miles to San Dimas Canyon 7 miles east-northeast of Glendora city hall (lat. 34°10'35" N, long. 117°45'20" W; sec. 18, T 1 N, R 8 W). Named on Glendora (1953) and Mount Baldy (1954) 7.5' quadrangles. The name commemorates William Wolfskill, who settled at Los Angeles in 1836 and was a pioneer of the fruit-growing industry (Gudde, 1949, p. 392).

Wolfskill Falls [LOS ANGELES]: *waterfall*, 8.5 miles north of Pomona city hall (lat. 34°10'35" N, long. 117°44'55" W; near W line sec. 17, T 1 N, R 8 W); the feature is in Wolfskill Canyon. Named on Mount Baldy (1954) 7.5' quadrangle. J.W. Robinson (1983, p. 118) described Wolfskill Falls Camp, a resort that Albert Coulatti and his wife Marion built 100 yards downstream from Wolfskill Falls in 1923—the resort operated until 1934.

Wolfskill Falls Camp: see **Wolfskill Falls** [LOS ANGELES].

Wonderstone Wash [SAN DIEGO]: *stream*, flows 4 miles to Imperial County 18 miles east-northeast of Borrego Springs (lat. 33°20'50" N, long. 116°05'05" W; at E line sec. 36, T 9 S, R 8 E). Named on Fonts Point (1959) and Seventeen Palms (1956) 7.5' quadrangles.

Wood Canyon [ORANGE]: *canyon*, drained by a stream that flows nearly 4 miles to Aliso Creek 5 miles west-northwest of San Juan Capistrano (lat. 33°32'30" N, long. 117°44'10" W). Named on San Juan Capistrano (1968) 7.5' quadrangle. The name is from oak trees in the canyon (Meadows, p. 140).

Wood Canyon [SAN DIEGO]: *canyon*, drained by a stream that flows 2 miles to Santa Margarita River 5.5 miles southwest of Fallbrook (lat. 33°20'25" N, long. 117°19'55" W; at E line sec. 6, T 10 S, R 4 W). Named on Morro Hill (1968) 7.5' quadrangle.

Wood Canyon [VENTURA]: *canyon*, drained by a stream that flows 3.5 miles to Big Sycamore Canyon 3.5 miles northeast of Point Mugu (lat. 34°06'40" N, long. 119°00'35" W). Named on Camarillo (1950) and Point Mugu (1949) 7.5' quadrangles.

Wooded Hill [SAN DIEGO]: *peak*, 6.25 miles north-northeast of Buckman Springs (lat. 32°51'05" N, long. 116°26'20" W). Altitude 6223 feet. Named on Mount Laguna (1960) 7.5' quadrangle.

Woodland Hills [LOS ANGELES]: *district*, 2.5 miles south of the center of Canoga Park in Los Angeles (lat. 34°09'45" N, long. 118° 36'15" W). Named on Calabasas (1952) and Canoga Park (1952) 7.5' quadrangles. Called Girard on Dry Canyon (1932) 6' quadrangle, but United States Board on Geographic Names (1950c, p. 7) rejected this name for the place. Postal authorities established Girard post office in 1923 and changed the name to Woodland Hills in 1941; the name "Girard" was for Victor Girard, who subdivided the place (Salley, p. 85).

Woodland Park [LOS ANGELES]: *district*, 8 miles northeast of Long Beach city hall (lat. 33°50'30" N, long. 118°05' W; sec. 12, T 4 S, R 12 W). Named on Los Alamitos (1950) 7.5' quadrangle.

Wood Ranch Reservoir [VENTURA]: *lake*, 1 mile long, 4.5 miles north of Thousand Oaks (lat. 34°14'15" N, long. 118°49'30" W). Named on Thousand Oaks (1950, photorevised 1981) 7.5' quadrangle.

Woods Cove [ORANGE]: *embayment*, 1.5 miles south-southeast of Laguna Beach city hall along the coast (lat. 33°31'30" N, long. 117°46'05" W). Named on Laguna Beach (1965) 7.5' quadrangle.

Woodson Mountain [SAN DIEGO]: *peak*, 5.5 miles south of San Pasqual (lat. 33°00'30" N, long. 116°58'10" W; at S line sec. 27, T 13 S, R 1 W). Altitude 2894 feet. Named on San Pasqual (1954) 7.5' quadrangle. The name commemorates Dr. Marshall Clay Woodson, who homesteaded at the base of the feature in 1873 (Stein, p. 153).

Woods Valley [SAN DIEGO]: *valley*, 4.25 miles west-southwest of Rodriguez Mountain (lat. 33°12'20" N, long. 116°58'15" W; mainly in sec. 22, T 11 S, R 1 W). Named on Rodriguez Mountain (1948) 7.5' quadrangle. On Ramona (1903) 30' quadrangle, present Woods Valley is shown as part of Bear Valley (1).

Wood Valley [SAN DIEGO]: *valley*, 4.5 miles east-northeast of Jamul (lat. 32°44'30" N, long. 116°48' W; sec. 31, 32, T 16 S, R 2 E). Named on Dulzura (1972) 7.5' quadrangle.

Woodwardia Canyon [LOS ANGELES]: *canyon*, drained by a stream that flows less than 1 mile to Dark Canyon (1) 5.25 miles south-southeast of Condor Peak (lat. 34°15'10" N, long. 118°11'30" W; near S line sec. 13, T 2 N, R 13 W). Named on Condor Peak (1959) 7.5' quadrangle.

Woolsey Canyon [LOS ANGELES-VENTURA]: *canyon*, drained by a stream that heads just inside Ventura County and flows 1.5 miles to lowlands at Chatsworth Reservoir nearly 3 miles southwest of Chatsworth in Los Angeles County (lat. 34°13'55" N, long. 118° 38'40" W). Named on Calabasas (1952) 7.5' quadrangle.

Workman [LOS ANGELES]: *locality*, nearly 3 miles southeast of South Gate city hall along Union Pacific Railroad (lat. 33°55'40" N, long. 118°10'05" W). Named on South Gate (1952) 7.5' quadrangle. Postal authorities established Workman post office in 1878, discontinued it the same year, reestablished it in 1892, discontinued it in 1893, reestablished it in 1898, discontinued it in 1904, reestablished it in 1911, and discontinued it in 1913; the name was for William Workman, a pioneer of 1841 (Salley, p. 243).

Workman Hill [LOS ANGELES]: *peak*, 2.25 miles east-northeast of present Whittier city hall (lat. 33°59'30" N, long. 118°00'05" W); the feature is near La Puente grant. Altitude 1387 feet. Named on La Habra (1952) and Whittier (1949) 7.5' quadrangles. The name is for William Workman, who was one of the recipients of La Puente grant (Gudde, 1949, p. 393).

Worsham Creek [LOS ANGELES]: *stream*, flows less than 2 miles to end 0.5 mile east of present Whittier city hall (lat. 33°58'20" N, long. 118°01'30" W). Named on Whittier (1949) 7.5' quadrangle. Watts' (1898-1899) map has the name "Woersham Cañon" for the canyon of the stream.

Woyden [LOS ANGELES]: *locality*, 2.5 miles southeast of El Monte along Southern Pacific Railroad (lat. 34°03'05" N, long. 118°00'10" W). Named on Pasadena (1900) 15' quadrangle.

Wright: see **Camp Wright**, under **Oak Grove** [SAN DIEGO].

Wright Canyon [SAN DIEGO]: *canyon*, drained by a stream that flows 3.25 miles to Padre Barona Creek 2.5 miles north-northwest of El Cajon Mountain (lat. 32°57' N, long. 116°50'25" W). Named on El Cajon Mountain (1955) 7.5' quadrangle.

Wright Canyon: see **Mint Canyon** [LOS ANGELES] (1).

Wrigley Reservoir [LOS ANGELES]: *lake*, 500 feet long, 1.5 miles west-northwest of Avalon on Santa Catalina Island (lat. 33°21'10" N, long. 118°21'05" W). Named on Santa Catalina East (1950) 7.5' quadrangle.

Wruck Canyon [SAN DIEGO]: *canyon*, drained by a stream that flows 1.25 miles to Spring Canyon (2) 6.5 miles east-southeast of Imperial Beach civic center (lat. 32°32'55" N, long. 117°00'20" W; at N line sec. 5, T 19 S, R 1 W). Named on Imperial Beach (1967) and Otay Mesa (1955) 7.5' quadrangles.

Wyatt [LOS ANGELES]: *locality*, 6 miles northeast of present Los Angeles city hall along Los Angeles Terminal Railroad (lat. 34° 07' N, long. 118°10' W). Named on Pasadena (1900) 15' quadrangle.

Wyneka: see **Cahuenga**, under **Universal City** [LOS ANGELES].

Wynema: see **Port Hueneme** [VENTURA].

Wynola [SAN DIEGO]: *village*, nearly 2 miles east-southeast of Santa Ysabel in Spencer Valley near Coleman Creek (lat. 33°05'50" N, long. 116°38'40" W; near SW cor. sec. 26, T 12 S, R 3 E). Named on Santa Ysabel (1960) 7.5' quadrangle. Postal authorities established Wynola post office in 1889 and discontinued it in 1913; the name was from Lake Wynola, Pennsylvania—the place also was known as Coleman City (Salley, p. 243-244). Posal authorities rejected the name "Spencer Valley" for the post office (Hanna, p. 359). A.E. Coleman found gold at the place in 1869, and the mining camp that developed at the site first was called Emily City, then Coleman City—the place consisted almost entirely of tents (Ellsberg, p. 14-15, 18).

- X - Y -

Xalisco: see **Huntington Beach** [ORANGE].

Yacht Harbor: see **Shelter Island Yacht Basin**, under **Shelter Island** [SAN DIEGO].

Yaeger Mesa [ORANGE]: *relief feature*, 1.5 miles south-southwest of Trabuco Peak (lat. 33°40'50" N, long. 117°29'15" W; near NE cor. sec. 3, T 6 S, R 6 W). Named on Alberhill (1954) 7.5' quadrangle. The name commemorates Jacob Yaeger, who came to the neighborhood in 1899 and settled at the upper end of Trabuco Canyon (Meadows, p. 140).

Yaqui Flat [SAN DIEGO]: *area*, nearly 9 miles south-southwest of Borrego Springs (lat. 33°08'15" N, long. 116°25'40" W). Named on Tubb Canyon (1959) 7.5' quadrangle.

Yaqui Meadows [SAN DIEGO]: *area*, 4.5 miles south of Borrego Springs (lat. 33°11'15" N, long. 116°21'45" W). Named on Borrego Sink (1959) and Tubb Canyon (1959) 7.5' quadrangles.

Yaqui Pass [SAN DIEGO]: *pass*, 7.5 miles south of Borrego Springs (lat. 33°08'45" N, long. 116°21'05" W; sec. 9, T 12 S, R 6 E); the pass is at the west end of Yaqui Ridge. Named on Borrego Sink (1959) 7.5' quadrangle.

Yaqui Ridge [SAN DIEGO]: *ridge*, east-southeast-trending, nearly 3 miles long, 8 miles south-southeast of Borrego Springs (lat. 33°08'45" N, long. 116°19'30" W). Named on Borrego Sink (1959) 7.5' quadrangle.

Yaqui Well [SAN DIEGO]: *spring*, 8 miles south of Borrego Springs near San Felipe Creek (lat. 33°08'20" N, long. 116°23'15" W). Named on Tubb Canyon (1959) 7.5' quadrangle. The name is for a Yaqui Indian (Bloomquist, 1978a, p. 16). The feature also was called Indian Well (Brown, 1923, p. 223).

Ybarra Canyon [LOS ANGELES]:

(1) *canyon*, drained by a stream that flows 2.5 miles to Devil Canyon 2.5 miles north-northwest of Chatsworth (lat. 34°17'35" N, long. 118°36'50" W; at S line sec. 36, T 3 N, R 17 W). Named on Oat Mountain (1952) 7.5' quadrangle. On Santa Susana (1903) 15' quadrangle, the upper part of present Devil Canyon is called Ybarra Canyon, and part of present Ybarra Canyon is unnamed.

(2) *canyon*, drained by a stream that flows nearly 3 miles to Big Tujunga Canyon 2.5 miles southwest of Condor Peak (lat. 34°17'50" N, long. 118°14'45" W; sec. 33, T 3 N, R 13 W). Named on Condor Peak (1959) 7.5' quadrangle, which shows Ybarra ranch located near the mouth of the canyon.

Yellow Creek: see **Pole Creek** [VENTURA].

Yellow Rose Spring [SAN DIEGO]: *spring*, 2.5 miles east-southeast of Buckman Springs along Kitchen Creek (lat. 32°45'10" N, long 116°27' W; sec. 27, T 16 S, R 5 E). Named on Mount Laguna (1960) 7.5' quadrangle.

Yerba Buena: see **Triunfo Corner** [VENTURA].

Yerba Buena Ridge [LOS ANGELES]: *ridge*, southwest-trending, 2.25 miles long, 5.5 miles north-northeast of Sunland (lat. 34° 20' N, long. 118°16'45" W). Named on Sunland (1966) 7.5' quadrangle.

Yerba Buena Spring [LOS ANGELES]: *spring*, 6 miles north-northeast of Sunland (lat. 34°20'25" N, long. 118°16'15" W); the spring is near the northeast end of Yerba Buena Ridge. Named on Sunland (1953) 7.5' quadrangle.

Yorba [ORANGE]: *locality*, 6 miles north-northeast of Orange city hall along Atchison, Topeka and Santa Fe Railroad (lat. 33°51'55" N, long. 117°48'30" W). Named on Orange (1950) 7.5' quadrangle. Postal authorities established Yorba post office in 1880, discontinued it in 1881, reestablished it in 1888, discontinued it in 1900, reestablished it in 1902, and discontinued it in 1905—the place also was known as San Antonio (Salley, p. 245).

Yorba Linda [ORANGE]: *city*, 10 miles north-northeast of Santa Ana (lat. 33°53'20" N, long. 117°48'45" W). Named on Orange (1964, photorevised 1981) and Yorba Linda (1964) 7.5' quadrangles. Postal authorities established Yorba Linda post office in 1912 (Frickstad, p. 118), and the city incorporated in 1967. The place began in 1909 as a station along Pacific Electric Railroad (Meadows, p. 141). A flag stop called Casa Loma was located along the same railroad 1 mile northwest of Yorba Linda; a station called Stearn, named for Jacob Stearn, a landowner there, was situated along the railroad 1.4 miles southeast of Yorba Linda (Meadows, p. 51, 131).

Yorba Linda Reservoir [ORANGE]: *lake*, 0.5 mile long, 1 mile south of Yorba Linda (lat. 33°52'30" N, long. 117°48'40" W). Named on Orange (1950) and Yorba Linda (1950) 7.5' quadrangles.

Young: see **Roger Young Village** [LOS ANGELES].

Young Canyon [LOS ANGELES]: *canyon,* drained by a stream that flows 2.5 miles to Santa Clara River 11.5 miles east of Solemint (lat. 34°26'25" N, long. 118°15'45" W; near S line sec. 8, T 4 N, R 13 W). Named on Agua Dulce (1960) 7.5' quadrangle.

Ysidora [SAN DIEGO]: *locality,* 6.5 miles west-southwest of Morro Hill along Atchison, Topeka and Santa Fe Railroad (lat. 33°15'40" N, long. 117°22'10" W; sec. 35, T 10 S, R 5 W). Named on Morro Hill (1949) 7.5' quadrangle.

Ysidora Basin [SAN DIEGO]: *valley,* 6.5 miles west-southwest of Morro Hill (lat. 33°15'20" N, long. 117°22' W). Named on Morro Hill (1968) and San Luis Rey (1968) 7.5' quadrangles.

Yucca Valley [SAN DIEGO]: *valley,* 13 miles north-northwest of Borrego Springs (lat. 33°25'15" N, long. 116°29'15" W). Named on Collins Valley (1959) 7.5' quadrangle.

Yuima Creek [SAN DIEGO]: *stream,* flows 5 miles to San Luis Rey River 4.5 miles southwest of Boucher Hill (lat. 33°16'55" N, long. 116°58'10" W; sec. 27, T 10 S, R 1 W). Named on Boucher Hill (1948) 7.5' quadrangle.

- Z -

Zachau Canyon [LOS ANGELES]: *canyon,* 1.25 miles long, 2 miles east-northeast of Sunland (lat. 34°16'20" N, long. 118°16'45" W; sec. 7, T 2 N, R 13 W). Named on Sunland (1953) 7.5' quadrangle.

Zelzah: see **Northridge** [LOS ANGELES].

Zion: see **Mount Zion** [LOS ANGELES].

Zuma Beach: see **Westward Beach** [LOS ANGELES].

Zuma Canyon [LOS ANGELES]: *canyon,* drained by a stream that flows 7 miles to the sea 1.25 miles northwest of Point Dume (lat. 34°00'50" N, long. 118°49'15" W). Named on Point Dume (1951) 7.5' quadrangle. Called Dume Canyon on Camulos (1903) 30' quadrangle, but United States Board on Geographic Names (1961c, p. 18) rejected the names "Dume Canyon" and "Zuma Valley" for the feature.

Zuma Valley: see **Zuma Canyon** [LOS ANGELES].

Zuñiga Point [SAN DIEGO]: *promontory,* 4.25 miles southwest of downtown San Diego at the southwest corner of North Island, and at the entrance to San Diego Bay (lat. 33°41' N, long. 117°13'20" W). Named on Point Loma (1967) 7.5' quadrangle. United States Board on Geographic Names (1936b, p. 44) rejected the name "Zuninga Point" for the feature. A military installation called Fort Pio Pico, named in honor of the governor of California under Mexican rule, was established at the place in 1906 and abandoned in 1919 (Whiting and Whiting, p. 60).

Zuñiga Shoal [SAN DIEGO]: *shoal,* 4.25 miles southwest of downtown San Diego (lat. 32°40'40" N, long. 117°13'10" W); the feature is 0.5 mile south-southeast of Zuñiga Point. Named on Point Loma (1967) 7.5' quadrangle. Called Baxos de Zuniga on Dalrymple's (1789) map. United States Board on Geographic Names (1936b, p. 44) rejected the name "Zuninga Shoal" for the feature.

Zuninga Point: see **Zuñiga Point** [SAN DIEGO].

Zuninga Shoal: see **Zuñiga Shoal** [SAN DIEGO].

South Coast Region Los Angeles, Orange, San Diego and Ventura Counties

References Cited

BOOKS AND ARTICLES

Anderson, Winslow. 1892. *Mineral springs and health resorts of California*. San Francisco: The Bancroft Company, 347 p.

Anonymous. 1950. "A run into the country." *Westways,* v. 42, no. 12, p. 32-33.

_____1976. *Pomona centennial history*. Pomona, California: Pomona Centennial-Bicentennial Committee, 198 p.

Antisell, Thomas. 1856. "Geological report." *Reports of explorations and surveys, to ascertain the most practicable and economical route for a railroad from the Mississippi River to the Pacific Ocean*. Volume VII, Part II. (33d Cong., 2d Sess., Sen. Ex. Doc. No. 78.) Washington: Beverley Tucker, Printer, 204 p.

Arnold, Delos, and Arnold, Ralph. 1902. "The marine Pliocene and Pleistocene stratigraphy of the coast of southern California." *The Journal of Geology,* v. 10, no. 2, p. 117-138.

Bailey, Richard C. 1962. *Explorations in Kern*. Bakersfield, California: Kern County Historical Society, 81 p.

Baker, Charles Laurence. 1911. "Notes on the later Cenozoic history of the Mohave Desert region in southeastern California." *University of California Publications, Bulletin of the Department of Geology,* v. 6, no. 15, p. 333-383.

Bancroft, Hubert Howe. 1888. *History of California, Volume VI, 1848-1859*. San Francisco: The History Company, Publishers, 787 p.

_____1890. *History of California, Volume VII, 1860-1890*. San Francisco: The History Company, Publishers, 826 p.

Barras, Judy. 1976. *The long road to Tehachapi*. Tehachapi, California: (Author), 231 p.

Bartlett, John Russell. 1854. *Personal narrative of explorations and incidents in Texas, New Mexico, California, Sonora, and Chihuahua, connected with the United States and Mexican Boundary Commission, during the years 1850, '51, '52, and '53*. New York: D. Appleton & Company, (2 volumes) 506 p. + 624 p.

Becker, Robert H. 1964. *Diseños of California ranchos*. San Francisco: The Book Club of California, (no pagination).

_____1969. *Designs on the land*. San Francisco: The Book Club of California, (no pagination).

Bell, Horace. 1930. *On the old West Coast*. New York: William Morrow & Co., 336 p.

Berkstresser, C.F., Jr. 1968. *Data for springs in the Southern Coast, Transverse, and Peninsular Ranges of California*. (United States Geological Survey, Water Resources Division, Open-file report.) Menlo Park, California, 21 p. + appendices.

Blake, William P. 1857. "Geological report." *Reports of explorations and surveys, to ascertain the most practicable and economical route for a railroad from the Mississippi River to the Pacific Ocean,* Volume V, Part II. (33d Cong., 2d Sess., Sen. Ex. Doc. No. 78.) Washington: Beverly Tucker, Printer, 370 p.

Bloomquist, Richard A. 1970. "Beyond Indian Gorge." *Desert,* v. 33, no. 12, p. 34-36.

_____1978a. "Seventeen Palms Oasis." *Desert,* v. 41, no. 7. p. 16-17.

_____1978b. "Salvador Canyon." *Desert,* v. 41, no. 10, p. 34-35.

_____1978c. "South Fork of Sheep Canyon." *Desert,* v. 41, no. 11, p. 36-37.

_____1979a. "Palm Spring." *Desert,* v. 42, no. 1, p. 14-15.

_____1979b. "South Fork of Bow Willow Canyon." *Desert,* v. 42, no. 9, p. 38.

Bowers, Stephen. 1890. "Orange County." *Tenth annual report of the State Mineralogist, for the year ending December 1, 1890*. Sacramento: California State Mining Bureau, p. 399-409.

Brown, John S. 1920. *Routes to desert watering places in the Salton Sea region, California*. (United States Geological Survey Water-Supply Paper 490-A.) Washington: Government Printing Office, 86 p.

_____1923. *The Salton Sea region, California*. (United States Geological Survey Water-Supply Paper 497.) Washington: Government Printing Office, 292 p.

Bunje, Emil T.H., and Kean, James C. 1983. *Pre-Marshall gold in California. Volume II*. Sacramento, California: Historic California Press, 70 p.

Burnham, Frederick R. 1927. "The remarks of Major Frederick R. Burnham." *Annual Publications*. Los Angeles, California: Historical Society of Southern California, p. 334-352.

California Division of Highways. 1934. *California highway transportation survey, 1934*. Sacramento: Department of Public Works, Division of Highways, 130 p. + appendices.

Carpenter, Virginia L. 1977. *Placentia, A pleasant place*. Santa Ana, California: Friis-Pioneer Press, 285 p.

Chase, J. Smeaton. 1913. *California coast trails*. Boston and New York: Houghton Mifflin Company, 326 p.

_____1919. *California desert trails*. Boston and New York: Houghton Mifflin Company, 387 p.

Coan, Eugene. 1981. *James Graham Cooper, pioneer Western naturalist*. Moscow, Idaho: The University Press of Idaho, 255 p.

Cowan, Robert G. 1956. *Ranchos of California*. Fresno, California: Academy Library Guild, 151 p.

Coy, Owen C. 1923. *California county boundaries*. Berkeley: California Historical Survey Commission, 335 p.

Crawford, J.J. 1896. "Report of the State Mineralogist." *Thirteenth report (Third Biennial) of the State Mineralogist for the two years ending September 15, 1896*. Sacramento: California State Mining Bureau, p. 10-646.

Davidson, George. 1887. "An examination of some of the early voyages of discovery and exploration on the northwest coast of America, from 1539 to 1603." *Report of the Superintendent of the U.S. Coast and Geodetic Survey, showing progress of the work during the fiscal year ending with June, 1886*. Appendix No. 7. Washington: Government Printing Office, p. 155-247.

Diller, J.S., and others. 1915. *Guidebook of the Western United States, Part D. The Shasta Route and Coast Line*. (United States Geological Survey Bulletin 614.) Washington: Government Printing Office, 142 p.

Doran, Adelaide LeMert. 1963. *The ranch that was Robbins'*. Los Angeles: (Author), 211 p.

_____1980. *Pieces of eight Channel Islands, A bibliographical guide and source book*. Glendale, California: The Arthur H. Clark Company, 340 p.

Eldridge, George Homans, and Arnold, Ralph. 1907. *The Santa Clara Valley, Puente Hills, and Los Angeles oil districts, southern California*. (Unites States Geological Survey Bulletin 309.) Washington: Government Printing Office, 266 p.

Ellis, Arthur J., and Lee, Charles H. 1919. *Geology and ground waters of the western part of San Diego County, California*. (United States Geological Survey Water-Supply Paper 446.) Washington: Government Printing Office, 321 p.

Ellsberg, Helen. 1972. *Mines of Julian*. Glendale, California: La Siesta Press, 71 p.

Emory, W.H. 1848. *Notes of a military reconnoissance, from Fort Leavenworth, in Missouri, to San Diego, in California, including parts of the Arkansas, Del Norte, and Gila Rivers*. (30th Cong., 1st Sess., Sen. Ex. Doc. No. 7.) Washington: Wendell and Van Benthuysen, Printers, 416 p.

English, Walter A. 1926. *Geology and oil resources of the Puente Hills region, southern California*. (United States Geological Survey Bulletin 768.) Washington: Government Printing Office, 110 p.

Evans, George W.B. 1945. *Mexican gold trail, The journal of a forty-niner*. (Edited by Glenn S. Dumke.) San Marino, California: The Huntington Library, 340 p.

Everhart, Donald L. 1951. "Geology of the Cuyamaca Peak quadrangle, San Diego County, California." *Crystalline rocks of southwestern California*. (California Division of Mines Bulletin 159.) San Francisco: Division of Mines, p. 51-115.

Fairbanks, Harold W. 1894. "Geology of northern Ventura, Santa Barbara, San Luis Obispo, Monterey, and San Benito Counties." *Twelfth report of the State Mineralogist, (Second Biennial,) two years ending September 15, 1894*. Sacramento: California State Mining Bureau, p. 493-526.

Femling, Jean. 1984. *Great piers of California*. Santa Barbara, California:

Capra Press, 137 p.

Fink, Augusta. 1966. *Time and the terraced land*. Berkeley, California: Howell-North Books, 136 p.

Franks, Kenny A., and Lambert, Paul F. 1985. *Early California oil*. College Station: Texas A & M University Press, 243 p.

Frazer, Robert W. 1965. *Forts of the West*. Norman: University of Oklahoma Press, 246 p.

Frickstad, Walter N. 1955. *A century of California post offices, 1848 to 1954*. Oakland, California: Philatelic Research Society, 395 p.

Gagnon, Dennis R. 1981. *Exploring the Santa Barbara backcountry*. Santa Cruz: Western Tanager Press, 151 p.

Garner, Bess Adams. 1939. *Windows in an old adobe*. Claremont, California: Sauders Press, 246 p.

Gay, Thomas E., Jr., and Hoffman, Samuel R. 1954. "Mines and mineral deposits of Los Angeles County, California." *California Journal of Mines and Geology,* v. 50, nos. 3 and 4, p. 467-709.

Gleason, Duncan. 1958. *The islands and ports of California*. New York: The Devin-Adair Company, 201 p.

Goodyear, W.A. 1888a. "Petroleum, asphaltum, and natural gas." *Seventh annual report of the State Mineralogist, for the year ending October 1, 1887*. Sacramento: California State Mining Bureau, p. 63-114.

_____1888b "San Diego County." *Eighth annual report of the State Mineralogist, for the year ending October 1, 1888*. Sacramento: California State Mining Bureau, p. 516-528.

Grenier, Judson A. 1978. *A guide to historic places in Los Angeles County*. Dubuque, Iowa: Kedall/Hunt Publishing Company, 324 p.

Gudde, Erwin G. 1949. *California place names*. Berkeley and Los Angeles: University of California Press, 431 p.

_____1969. *California place names*. Berkeley and Los Angeles: University of California Press, 416 p.

_____1975. *California gold camps*. Berkeley, Los Angeles, London: University of California Press, 467 p.

Guinn, J.M. 1902. *Historical and biographical record of Southern California*. Chicago: Chapman Publishing Company, 1019 p,

Hanks, Henry G. 1886. *Sixth annual report of the State Mineralogist. Part I. For the year ending June 1, 1886*. Sacramento: California State Mining Bureau, 145 p.

Hanna, Phil Townsend. 1951. *The dictionary of California land names*. Los Angeles: The Automobile Club of Southern California, 392 p.

Harlow, Neal. 1976. *Maps and surveys of the pueblo lands of Los Angeles*. Los Angeles: Dawson's Book Shop, 169 p.

_____1982. *California conquered*. Berkeley, Los Angeles, London: University of California Press, 499 p.

_____1987. *Maps of the Pueblo lands of San Diego, 1602-1874*. Los Angeles: Dawson's Book Shop, 244 p.

Harrington, Marie. 1978. "California's pioneer oil town." *Desert,* v. 41, no. 10, p. 38-40.

Hart, Herbert M. 1965. *Old forts of the Far West*. New York: Bonanza Books, 192 p.

Hess, Frank L. 1910. *A reconnaissance of the gypsum deposits of California*. (United States Geological Survey Bulletin 413.) Washington: Government Printing Office, 36 p.

Hill, Joseph J. 1927. *The history of Warner's ranch and its environs*. Los Angeles, California: (Privately printed), 221 p.

Hine, Robert V. 1983. *California's utopian colonies*. Berkeley, Los Angeles, London: University of California Press, 209 p.

Hoover, Mildred Brooke, Rensch, Hero Eugene, and Rensch, Ethel Grace. 1966. *Historic spots in California*. (Third edition, revised by William N. Abeloe.) Stanford, California: Stanford University Press, 642 p.

Huguenin, Emile. 1919. "Ventura County." *Report XV of the State Mineralogist*. Sacramento: California State Mining Bureau, p. 751-769.

Jackson, Sheldon G. 1977. *A British ranchero in old California*. Glendale and Azusa, California: Arthur H. Clark Company and Azusa Pacific College, 265 p.

Jahns, Richard H., and Wright, Lauren A. 1951 *Gem- and lithium-bearing pegmatites of the Pala district, San Diego County, California*. (California Division of Mines Special Report 7-A.) San Francisco: Division of Mines, 72 p.

Johnson, Harry R. 1911. *Water resources of Antelope Valley, California*. (United States Geological Survey Water-Supply Paper 278.) Washington: Government Printing Office, 92 p.

Kroeber, A.L. 1916. "California place names of Indian origin." *University of California Publications in American Archæology and Ethnology,* v. 12, no. 2, p. 31-69.

Latta, Frank F. 1976. *Saga of Rancho El Tejón*. Santa Cruz, California: Bear State Books, 293 p.

Marcou, Jules. 1876. "Report on the geology of a portion of southern California." *Annual report upon the geographical surveys west of the one hudredth meridian, in California, Nevada, Utah, Colorado, Wyoming, New Mexico, Arizona, and Montana*. (Appendix JJ of *The Annual Report of the Chief of Engineers for 1876*.) Washington: Government Printing Office, p. 158-172.

Meadows, Don. 1966. *Historic place names in Orange County*. Balboa Island, California: Paisano Press, Inc., 141 p.

Mendenhall, Walter C. 1908. *Ground waters and irrigation enterprises in the Foothill belt, southern California*. (United States Geological Survey Water-Supply Paper 219.) Washington: Government Printing Office, 180 p.

_____1909. *Some desert watering places in southeastern California and southwestern Nevada.,* (United States Geological Survey Water-Supply Paper 224.) Washington: Government Printing Office, 98 p.

Merrill, Frederick J.H. 1916. "The counties of San Diego, Imperial." *Report XIV of the State Mineralogist*. Sacramento: California State Mining Bureau, p. 635-743.

_____1919. "Los Angeles County, Orange County, Riverside County." *Report XV of the State Mineralogist*. Sacramento: California State Mining Bureau, p. 461-589.

Ormsby, Waterman L. 1968. *The Butterfield Overland mail*. San Marino, California: The Huntington Library, 179 p.

Outland, Charles F. 1963. *Man-made disaster, The story of St. Francis Dam*. Glendale, California: The Arthur H. Clark Company, 249 p.

_____1969. *Mines, murders, and grizzlies, Tales of California's Ventura back country*. (No place): Ventura County Historical Society and The Ward Ritchie Press, 134 p.

Owens, Glen. 1981. *The heritage of the Big Santa Anita*. (No place): Big Santa Anita Historical Society, 105 p.

Parke, John G. 1857. "General report." *Reports of explorations and surveys, to ascertain the most practicable and economical route for a railroad from the Mississippi River to the Pacific Ocean*. Volume VII, part I. (33d. Cong., 2d Sess., Sen. Ex. Doc. No. 78.) Washington: Beverley Tucker, Printer, 42 p.

Peckham, S.F. 1882. (Prepared in 1866.) "Examination of the bituminous substances occurring in southern California." *The Coast Ranges*. (Geological Survey of California, Geology, Volume II, Appendix F; the complete Volume II was not published.) Cambridge, Massachusetts: John Wilson & Son, University Press, p. 49-90.

Perez, Crisostomo N. 1996. *Land grants in Alta California*. Rancho Cordova, California: Landmark Enterprises, 264 p.

Poland, J.F., and others. 1956. *Ground-water geology of the coastal zone, Long Beach-Santa Ana area, California*. (United States Geological Survey Water-Supply Paper 1109.) Washington: Government Printing Office, 162 p.

Poland, J.F., Garrett, A.A., and Sinnott, Allen. 1959. *Geology, hydrology, and chemical character of ground waters in the Torrance-Santa Monica area, California*. (United States Geological Survey Water-Supply Paper 1461.) Washington: Government Printing Office, 425 p.

Poole, Charles H. 1857. "Report upon the route from San Diego to Fort Yuma, via San Diego River, Warner's Pass, and San Felipe Canon." *Reports of explorations and surveys, to ascertain the most practicable and economical route for a railroad from the Mississippi River to the Pacific Ocean*. Volume VII, Appendix B. (33d Cong., 2d Sess., Sen. Ex. Doc. No. 78.) Washington: Beverley Tucker, Printer, 28 p.

Preston, E.B. 1890a. "Los Angeles County." *Ninth annual report of the State Mineralogist, for the year ending December 1, 1889*. Sacramento: California State Mining Bureau, p. 189-210.

_____1890b. "Los Angeles County." *Tenth annual report of the State Mineralogist, for the year ending December 1, 1890*. Sacramento: California State Mining Bureau, p. 277-298.

Reynolds, Gerald G. 1985. *Pico Canyon chronicles, The story of California's pioneer oil field*. Newhall, California: Santa Clara Valley Historical Society, 46 p.

Ricard, Herbert F. 1972. "Place names of Ventura County." *Ventura County Historical Society Quarterly,* v. 17, no. 2, (no pagination).

Robinson, John W. 1973. *Mines of the San Gabriels*. Glendale, California: La Siesta Press, 71 p.

_____1977. *The San Gabriels, Southern California mountain country*. San Marino, California: Golden West Books, 214 p.

_____1983. *The San Gabriels II, The mountains from Monrovia Canyon to Lytle Creek*. Arcadia, California: Big Santa Anita Historical Society, 224 p.

Robinson, W.W. 1966. *Maps of Los Angeles from Ord's Survey of 1849 to the end of the Boom of the Eighties*. Los Angeles: Dawson's Bookshop, 87 p.

Rothrock, J.T. 1876. "Report upon the operations of a special natural-history party and main field-party No. 1, California section, field-season of 1875." *Annual report upon the geographical surveys west of the one hudredth meridian, in California, Nevada, Utah, Colorado, Wyoming, New Mexico Arizona, and Montana*. (Appendix JJ of *The Annual Report of the Chief of Engineers for 1876*.) Washington: Government Printing Office, p. 202-213.

Salley, H.E. 1977. *History of California post offices, 1849-1976*. La Mesa, California: Postal History Associates, Inc., 300 p.

Sampson, R.J. 1937. "Mineral resources of Los Angeles County." *California Journal of Mines and Geology*, v. 33, no. 3, p. 173-213.

Settle, Glen A. 1963. *Here roamed the antelope*. Rosamond, California: The Kern-Antelope Historical Society, Inc., 64 p.

Sleeper, Jim. 1968. "Trabuco tin faces axe." *Mineral Information Service*, v. 21, no. 11, p. 164-167.

_____1976. *A Boys' book of bear stories (Not for boys). A grizzly introduction to the Santa Ana Mountains*. Trabuco Canyon, California: California Classics, 212 p.

Smith, William Sidney Tangier. 1897. "The geology of Santa Catalina Island." *Proceedings of the California Academy of Sciences* (third series), v. 1, no. 1, p. 1-71.

_____1898. "A geological sketch of San Clemente Island." *Eighteenth annual report of the United States Geological Survey, 1896-97*. Part II. Washington: Government Printing Office, p. 450-496.

Stein, Lou. 1975. *San Diego County place-names*. San Diego, California: Tofua Press, 163 p.

Stephenson, Terry E. 1948. *The shadows of Old Saddleback*. (No place): The Fine Arts Press, 207 p.

Storms, W.H. 1893. "Los Angeles County." *Eleventh report of the State Mineralogist, (First Biennial,) Two years ending September 15, 1892*. Sacramento: California State Mining Bureau, p. 243-248.

Suter, Coral. 1993. "Riding high on the old Ridge Route." *The Californians*, v. 10, no. 5, p. 18-31.

Thompson, David G. 1921. *Routes to desert watering places in the Mohave Desert region, California*. (United States Geological Survey Water-Supply Paper 490-B.) Washington: Government Printing Office, p. 87-269.

_____1929. *The Mohave Desert region, California*. (United States Geological Survey Water-Supply Paper 578.) Washington: Government Printing Office, 759 p.

Thompson and West. 1880. *History of Los Angeles County, California*. Oakland, California: Thompson & West, 192 p.

Trask, John B. 1856 *Report on the geology of northern and southern California*. (Sen. Sess. of 1856, Doc. No. 14.) Sacramento: State Printer, 66 p.

Tucker, W. Burling. 1925a. "Los Angeles field division (Orange County)." *Mining in California*, v. 21, no. 1, p. 58-71.

_____1925b "Los Angeles field division (San Diego County)." *Mining in California*, v. 21, no. 3, p. 325-382.

Tucker, W.B., and Reed, Charles H. 1939. "Mineral resources of San Diego County." *California Journal of Mines and Geology*, v. 35, no. 1, p. 8-78.

United States Board on Geographic Names (under name "United States Geographic Board"). 1933. *Sixth report of the United States Geographic Board, 1890-1932*. Washington: Government Printing Office, 834 p.

_____(under name "United States Geographic Board"). 1934. *Decisions of the United States Geographic Board, No. 34—Decisions June 1933-March 1934*. Washington: Government Printing Office, 20 p.

_____(under name "United States Board on Geographical Names"). 1936a. *Decisions of the United States Board on Geographical Names, Decisions rendered between July 1, 1934, and June 30, 1935*. Washington: Government Printing Office, 26 p.

_____(under name "United States Board on Geographical Names"). 1936b. *Decisions of the United States Board on Geographical Names, Decisions rendered between July 1, 1935, and June 30, 1936*. Washington: Government Printing Office, 44 p.

_____(under name "United States Board on Geographical Names"). 1938. *Decisions of the United States Board on Geographical Names, Decisions rendered between July 1, 1937, and June 30, 1938*. Washington: Government Printing Office, 62 p.

_____(under name "United States Board on Geographical Names"). 1939. *Decisions of the United States Board on Geographical Names, Decisions rendered between July 1, 1938, and June 30, 1939*. Washington: Government Printing Office, 41 p.

_____(under name "United States Board on Geographical Names"). 1940. *Decisions of the United States Board on Geographical Names, Decisions rendered between July 1, 1939, and June 30, 1940*. Washington: Government Printing Office, 46 p.

_____(under name "United States Board on Geographical Names"). 1943. *Decisions rendered between July 1, 1941, and June 30, 1943*. Washington: Department of the Interior, 104 p.

_____1949. *Decision lists nos. 4907, 4908, 4909, July, August, September, 1949*. Washington: Department of the Interior, 24 p.

_____1950a. *Decision lists nos. 4910, 4911, 4912, October, November, December, 1949*. Washington: Department of the Interior, 10 p.

_____1950b. *Decision list no. 5003, January, February, March, 1950*. Washington: Department of the Interior, 24 p.

_____1950c. *Decisions on names in the United States and Alaska rendered during April, May, and June 1950*. (Decision list no. 5006.) Washington: Department of the Interior, 47 p.

_____1954. *Decisions on names in the United States, Alaska and Puerto Rico, Decisions rendered from July 1950 to May 1954*. (Decision list no. 5401.) Washington: Department of the Interior, 115 p.

_____1959. *Decisions on names in the United States, Decisions rendered from January, 1959 through April, 1959*. (Decision list no. 5902.) Washington: Department of the Interior, 49 p.

_____1960a. *Decisions on names in the United States and Puerto Rico, Decisions rendered in May, June, July, and August, 1959*. (Decision list no. 5903.) Washington: Department of the Interior, 79 p.

_____1960b. *Decisions on names in the United States, Decisions rendered from September 1959 through December 1959*. (Decision list no. 5904.) Washington: Department of the Interior, 68 p.

_____1960c. *Decisions on names in the United States, Puerto Rico and the Virgin Islands, Decisions rendered from January through April 1960*. (Decision list no. 6001.) Washington: Department of the Interior, 79 p.

_____1960d. *Decisions on names in the United States and the Virgin Islands, Decisions rendered from May 1960 through August 1960*. (Decision list no. 6002.) Washington: Department of the Interior, 77 p.

_____1961a. *Decisions on names in the United States, Decisions rendered from September through December 1960*. (Decision list no. 6003.) Washington: Department of the Interior, 73 p.

_____1961b. *Decisions on names in the United States, Decisions rendered from January through April 1961*. (Decision list no. 6101.) Washington: Department of the Interior, 74 p.

_____1961c. *Decisions on names in the United States, Decisions rendered from May through August 1961*. (Decision list no. 6102.) Washington: Department of the Interior, 81 p.

_____1962a. *Decisions on names in the United States, Decisions rendered from September through December 1961*. (Decision list no. 6103.) Washington: Department of the Interior, 75 p.

_____1962b. *Decisions on names in the United States, Decisions rendered from January through April 1962*. (Decision list no. 6201.) Washington: Department of the Interior, 72 p.

_____1963. *Decisions on geographic names in the United States, May through August 1963*. (Decision list no. 6302.) Washington: Department of the Interior, 81 p.

_____1965a. *Decisions on geographic names in the United States, January through March 1965*. (Decision list no. 6501.) Washington: Department of the Interior, 85 p.

_____1965b. *Decisions on geographic names in the United States, April through June 1965*. (Decision list no. 6502.) Washington: Department of the Interior, 39 p.

_____1965c. *Decisions on geographic names in the United States, July through September 1965*. (Decision list no. 6503.) Washington: Department of the Interior, 74 p.

_____1967a. *Decisions on geographic names in the United States, April through June 1967*. (Decision list no. 6702.) Washington: Department of the Interior, 26 p.

_____1967b. *Decisions on geographic names in the United States, July through September 1967*. (Decision list no. 6703.) Washington: Department of the Interior, 29 p.

_____1968a. *Decisions on geographic names in the United States, January through March 1968*. (Decision list no. 6801). Washington: Department of the Interior, 51 p.

_____1968b. *Decisions on geographic names in the United States, April through June 1968*. (Decision list no. 6802.) Washington: Department of the Interior, 42 p.

_____1969a. *Decisions on geographic names in the United States, October through December 1968*. (Decision list no. 6804.) Washington: Department of the Interior, 33 p.

_____1969b. *Decisions on geographic names in the United States, January through March 1969*. (Decision list no. 6901.) Washington: Department of the Interior, 31 p.

_____1969c. *Decisions on geographic names in the United States, April through June 1969*. (Decision list no. 6902.) Washington: Department of the Interior, 28 p.

_____1970a. *Decisions on geographic names in the United States, January through March 1970*. (Decision list no. 7001.) Washington: Department of the Interior, 31 p.

_____1970b. *Decisions on geographic names in the United States, April through June 1970*. (Decision list. no. 7002.) Washington: Department of the Interior, 20 p.

_____1970c. *Decisions on geographic names in the United States, July through September 1970*. (Decision list no. 7003.) Washington: Department of the Interior, 15 p.

_____1971. *Decisions on geographic names in the United States, October through December 1970*. (Decision list no. 7004.) Washington: Department of the Interior, 28 p.

_____1973. *Decisions on geographic names in the United States, July through September 1973*. (Decision list no. 7303.) Washington: Department of the Interior, 14 p.

_____1974. *Decisions on geographic names in the United States, July through September 1974* (Decision list no. 7403.) Washington: Department of the Interior, 34 p.

_____1975a. *Decisions on geographic names in the United States, January through March 1975*. (Decision list no. 7501.) Washington: Department of the Interior, 36 p.

_____1975b. *Decisions on geographic names in the United States, April through June 1975*. (Decision list no. 7502.) Washington: Department of the Interior, 32 p.

_____1976a. *Decisions on geographic names in the United States, October through December 1975*. (Decision list no. 7504.) Washington: Department of the Interior, 45 p.

_____1976b. *Decisions on geographic names in the United States, January through March 1976*. (Decision list no. 7601.) Washington: Department of the Interior, 30 p.

_____1976c. *Decisions on geographic names in the United States, July through September 1976*. (Decision list no. 7603.) Washington: Department of the Interior, 25 p.

_____1977. *Decisions on geographic names in the United States, April through June 1977*. (Decision list no. 7702.) Washington: Department of the Interior, 40 p.

_____1978a. *Decisions on geographic names in the United States, October through December 1977*. (Decision list no. 7704.) Washington: Department of the Interior, 29 p.

_____1978b. *Decisions on geographic names in the United States, January through March 1978*. (Decision list no. 7801.) Washington: Department of the Interior, 18 p.

_____1978c. *Decisions on geographic names in the United States, April through June 1978*. (Decision list no. 7802.) Washington: Department of the Interior, 30 p.

_____1979a. *Decisions on geographic names in the United States, January through March 1979*. (Decision list no. 7901.) Washington: Department of the Interior, 27 p.

_____1979b. *Decisions on geographic names in the United States, April through June 1979*. (Decision list no. 7902.) Washington: Department of the Interior, 33 p.

_____1981. *Decisions on geographic names in the United States, October through December 1980*. (Decision list no. 8004.) Washington: Department of the Interior, 21 p.

_____1983a. *Decisions on geographic names in the United States, July through September 1982*. (Decision list no. 8203.) Washington: Department of the Interior, 25 p.

_____1983b. *Decisions on geographic names in the United States, January through March 1983*. (Decision list no. 8301.) Washington: Department of the Interior, 33 p.

_____1984. *Decisions on geographic names in the United States, April through June 1984*. (Decision list no. 8402.) Washington: Department of the Interior, 22 p.

_____1986. *Decisions on geographic names in the United States, January through March 1986*. (Decision list no. 8601.) Washington: Department of the Interior, 13 p.

_____1990. *Decisions on geographic names in the United States*. (Decision list 1990.) Washington: Department of the Interior, 35 p.

_____1991. *Decisions on geographic names in the United States*. (Decision list 1991.) Washington: Department of the Interior, 40 p.

_____1992. *Decisions on geographic names in the United States*. (Decision list 1992.) Washington: Department of the Interior, 21 p.

United States Coast and Geodetic Survey. 1963. *United States Coast Pilot 7, Pacific Coast, California, Oregon, Washington, and Hawaii*. (Ninth edition.) Washington: United States Government Printing Office, 336 p.

Vancouver, George. 1953. *Vancouver in California, 1792-1794*. (The original account edited and annotated by Marguerite Eyer Wilbur.) Los Angeles: Glen Dawson, 274 p.

Van Kampen, Carol. 1977. "From Dairy Valley to Chino: An example of urbanization in southern California's dairy land." *The California Geographer*, v. 17, p. 39-48.

Vedder, J.G., and Norris, Robert M. 1963. *Geology of San Nicolas Island*. (United States Geological Survey Professional Paper 369.) Washington: Government Printing Office, 65 p.

Wagner, Henry R. 1968. *The cartography of the Northwest Coast of America to the year 1800*. (One-volume reprint of 1937 edition.) Amsterdam: N. Israel, 543 p.

Warner, J.J., Hayes, Benjamin, and Widney, J.P. 1876. *An historical sketch of Los Angeles County, California*. Los Angeles: Louis Lewis & Co., 159 p.

Waring, Gerald A. 1915. *Springs of California*. (United States Geological Survey Water-Supply Paper 338.) Washington: Government Printing Office, 410 p.

Watts, W.L. 1901. *Oil and gas yielding formations of California*. (California State Mining Bureau Bulletin No. 19.) Sacramento: California State Mining Bureau, 236 p.

Whipple, A.W. 1856. "Itinerary." *Reports of explorations and surveys, to ascertain the most practicable and economical route for a railroad from the Mississippi River to the Pacific Ocean*. Volume III, Part I. (33d Cong., 2d Sess, Sen. Ex. Doc. No. 78.) Washington: Beverley Tucker Printer, 136 p.

Whipple, C.W. 1876. "Executive report of Lieutenant C.W. Whipple, Ordnance Corps, on the operations of special party, California section, field-season of 1875." *Annual report upon the geographical surveys west of the one hundredth meridian, in California, Nevada, Utah, Colorado, Wyoming, New Mexico, Arizona, and Montana*. (Appendix JJ of *The Annual Report of the Chief of Engineers for 1876*.) Washington: Government Printing Office, p. 147-150.

White, Gerald T. 1968. *Scientists in conflict, The beginnings of the oil industry in California*. San Marino, California: The Huntington Library, 272 p.

Whiting, J.S., and Whiting, Richard J. 1960. *Forts of the State of California*. (Authors), 90 p.

Whitney, J.D. 1865. *Report of progress and synopsis of the field-work from 1860 to 1864*. (Geological Survey of California, Geology, Volume I.) Published by authority of the Legislature of California, 498 p.

Williamson, R.S. 1855. "Report." *Reports of explorations and surveys, to ascertain the most practicable and economical route for a railroad from the Mississippi River to the Pacific Ocean*. Volume V, part I. (33d Cong., 2d Sess., Sen. Ex. Doc. No. 78.) Washington: Beverley Tucker, Printer, 43 p.

Yates, Lorenzo Z. 1890. "Stray notes on the geology of the Channel Islands." *Ninth annual report of the State Mineralogist, for the year ending December 1, 1889*. Sacramento: California State Mining Bureau, p. 171-174.

QUADRANGLE MAPS

(All maps published by United States Geological Survey, except as noted. Dates identify the editions of the maps. If a reprinted or revised map was used, the year or reprinting or revision is given in parentheses, unless the reprinted or revised map is cited specifically in the text.)

Acton 7.5'—1959.
6'—1939
Adobe 6'—1934.
Adobe Mountain 7.5'—1955 (photorevised 1968).
Agua Caliente Springs 7.5'—1959.
Agua Dulce 15' (same area as Rabbit Peak 15')—1942 (Army).
7.5'—1960.
Aguanga 7.5'—1954 (photorevised 1971).
Alberhill 7.5'—1954.
Alder Creek 6'—1941 (reprinted 1948).
Alhambra 6'—1926 (reprinted 1939).
Alpine 7.5'—1955 (photorevised 1977); 1955, photorevised 1988.
Alpine Butte 15'—1945 (Army).
7.5'—1957.
Altadena 6'—1928.
Anacapa Island—1973 (part of Channel Island National Monument map).
Anaheim 15'—1898; 1942 (Army).
7.5' (same area as Garden Grove 7.5')—1950; 1965.
Apache Canyon 7.5'—1943.
Arroyo Tapiado 7.5'—1959.
Artesia 6'—1925.
Azusa 7.5'—1953; 1966.
6'—1928; 1939.
Baldwin Park 7.5'—1953; 1966.
Ballinger Canyon 7.5'—1943.
Barrel Spring 15' (same area as Borrego Mountain 15')—1942 (Army).
Barrett Lake 7.5'—1960.
Beartrap Canyon 6'—1938 (reprinted 1948).
Beauty Mountain 7.5'—1960.
Bell 6'—1936.
Beverly Hills 7.5'—1950; 1966 (photorevised 1972).
Black Mountain 7.5'—1943 (Army); 1958; 1958, photorevised 1974.
Black Star Canyon 7.5'—1950; 1967; 1967, photorevised 1988.
Bonsall 7.5'—1948; 1968.
Borrego 15'—1939; 1959.
Borrego Mountain 7.5'—1960.
Borrego Mountain SE 7.5'—1958.
Borrego Palm Canyon 7.5'—1959 (photorevised 1974).
Borrego Sink 7.5'—1959.
Boucher Hill 7.5'—1948 (photorevised 1988); 1950.
Bouquet Reservoir 6'—1937.
Bucksnort Mountain 7.5'—1960.
Burbank 7.5'—1953; 1966.
6'—1926 (reprinted 1932).
Burnt Peak 7.5'—1958.
Calabasas 15'—1903 (reprinted 1924).
7.5'—1952; 1952, photorevised 1967.
Camarillo 7.5'—1950.
Cameron Corners 7.5'—1959 (photorevised 1977).
Camp Baldy 6'—1940.
Camp Bonita 6'—1940.

Campo 15'—1939; 1944 (Army).
7.5'—1959.
Camp Rincon 6'—1940.
Camulos 30'—1903 (reprinted 1938).
Cañada Gobernadora 7.5'—1949; 1968.
Canoga Park 7.5'—1952.
Capistrano 30'—1902 (reprinted 1941).
Carrizo Mountain 15'—1944 (Army).
7.5'—1957.
Carrizo Mountain NE 7.5'—1957.
Castaic 6'—1940.
Chatsworth 6'—1927; 1940.
Chilao Flat 7.5'—1959.
Claremont 6'—1928 (reprinted 1932).
Clark Lake 15'—1944 (Army).
7.5'—1959 (photorevised 1974).
Clark Lake NE 7.5'—1960.
Clearwater 6'—1925 (reprinted 1932).
Cobblestone Mountain 7.5'—1958.
Collins Valley 7.5'—1959.
Compton 6'—1930.
Condor Peak 7.5'—1959.
Corona 30'—1902 (reprinted 1946).
15'—1942 (Army).
Corona South 7.5'—1967.
Covina 6'—1927.
Coyote Hills 7.5' (same area as La Habra 7.5')—1935.
Crystal Lake 7.5'—1958 (photorevised 1972).
6'—1941.
Cucamonga 15' (same area as Ontario 15')—1903 (reprinted 1932).
Cuddy Valley 7.5'—1943; 1944 (Army).
Cuyamaca 30'—1903 (reprinted 1942).
Cuyamaca Peak 7.5'—1960; 1960, photorevised 1988.
Cuyama Peak 7.5'—1943.
Cuyapaipe 15' (same area as Mount Laguna 15')—1944 (Army).
Dana Point 7.5'—1949; 1968.
Del Mar 7.5'—1953; 1967.
Del Sur 7.5'—1958.
Descanso 7.5'—1960.
Devils Heart Peak 7.5'—1943.
Downey 15'—1902 (reprinted 1929).
Dry Canyon 6'—1932.
Dulzura 7.5'—1972.
Dume Point 6'—1932.
Earthquake Valley 7.5'—1959.
El Cajon 15'—1939.
7.5'—1967.
El Cajon Mountain 7.5'—1955 (photorevised 1971).
Elizabeth Lake 30'—1917 (reprinted 1941).
El Mirage 7.5'—1956 (photorevised 1968).
El Monte 7.5'—1953; 1966 (photorevised 1981).
6'—1926 (reprinted 1932).
El Toro 7.5'—1950; 1968.
Encinitas 7.5'—1968.
Escondido 15'—1901.
7.5'—1968.
Fairmont 6'—(1937 (reprinted 1951).
Fairmont Butte 7.5'—1965.
Fallbrook 7.5'—1949; 1968.
Fernando 15' (same area as San Fernando 15')—1900 (reprinted 1910).
Fillmore 7.5'—1951.
Fonts Point 7.5'—1959.
Frazier Mountain 7.5'—1944 (Army); 1958.
Garden Grove 7.5' (same area as Anaheim 7.5')—1935.
Glendale 6'—1928 (reprinted 1948).
Glendora 7.5'—1953; 1966 (photorevised 1972).
6'—1927; 1939
Gorman 6'—1938.
Green Valley 7.5'—1958.
Harper Canyon 7.5'—1959.
Hi Vista 7.5'—1957.
Hollywood 7.5'—1953; 1966 (photorevised 1972).
6'—1926.
Hot Springs Mountain 7.5'—1960.
Hueneme 15'—1904 (reprinted 1940).
Hughes Lake 6'—1937.
Humphreys 6'—1932 (reprinted 1946).
Imperial Beach 7.5' (same area as San Ysidro 7.5')—1967.
Inglewood 7.5'—1952; 1964; 1964, photorevised 1981.
6'—1924.
In-Ko-Pah Gorge 7.5'—1959 (photorevised 1975).
Jackrabbit Hill 7.5'—1973.
Jacumba 15'—1939.
7.5'—1959 (photorevised 1975).
Jamul 15'—1943; 1955.
Jamul Mountains 7.5'—1955; 1955, photorevised 1971 and 1975.
Julian 7.5'—1960.
Juniper Hills 7.5'—1959 (photorevised 1974).
Kramer 15'—1942 (reprinted 1947).
La Brea 6'—1928 (reprinted 1932).
La Crescenta 6'—1939.
Laguna Beach 7.5'—1949; 1965; 1965, photorevised 1981.
La Habra 7.5' (same area as Coyote Hills 7.5')—1952; 1964.
La Jolla 15'—1903 (reprinted 1942).
7.5'—1943; 1953; 1967.
Lake 6'—1937.
Lake Elsinore 15'—1942 (Army).
Lake Hughes 7.5'—1957.
La Liebre Ranch 7.5'—1965.
La Mesa 7.5'—1953; 1967, 1967, photorevised 1975.
Lancaster East 7.5'—1958.
Lancaster West 7.5'—1958.
Lang 6'—1933.
Las Bolsas 15'—1896 (reprinted 1926).
Las Flores 6'—1932.
Las Pulgas Canyon 7.5'—1949; 1968.
La Verne 6'—1940.
Lebec 7.5'—1945 (Army); 1958.
Liebre 6'—1938.
Liebre Mountain 7.5'—1958.
Lion Canyon 7.5'—1943; 1944 (Army).
Little Buttes 7.5'—1965.
Little Rock 6'—1934 (reprinted 1949).
Littlerock 7.5'—1957.
Live Oak Springs 7.5'—1959.
Llano 6'—1934 (reprinted 1949).
Lockwood Valley 7.5'—1943.
Long Beach 1°x 2°—1957 (revised 1970).
7.5'—1949; 1964; 1964, photorevised 1972.
Los Alamitos 7.5'—1935; 1950; 1964; 1964, photorevised 1981.
Los Angeles 1°x 2°—1975.
7.5'—1953; 1966 (photorevised 1981).
6'—1928 (reprinted 1931).
Lovejoy Buttes 7.5'—1957.
Malibu Beach 7.5'—1951; 1950, photorevised 1981.
Manzana 6'—1938 (reprinted 1943).
Margarita Peak 15'—1944 (Army).
7.5'—1950; 1968.
Matilija 7.5'—1952; 1952, photorevised 1967.
McDonald Peak 7.5' (same area as Alamo Mountain 7.5')—1958.
Mesa Grande 7.5'—1948 (photorevised 1971).
Mescal Creek 7.5—1956 (photorevised 1968).
Mint Canyon 7.5'—1960.
Monument Peak 7.5'—1959.
Moorpark 7.5'—1951.
Morena Reservoir 7.5'—1960.
Morro Hill 7.5'—1949; 1968.
Mount Baldy 7.5'—1954; 1967.
Mount Emma 6'—1940 (reprinted 1948).
Mount Laguna 15' (same area as Cuyapaipe 15')—1960.
7.5'—1960 (photorevised 1975).
Mount Lowe 6'—1939.
Mount Pinos 30'—1903 (reprinted 1918).
Mount San Antonio 7.5'—1955 (photorevised 1968).
Mount Wilson 7.5'—1953; 1966 (photorevised 1988).
6'—1939.
National City 7.5'—1944; 1953; 1967.
Neenach 15'—1943.
Neenach School 7.5'—1965.
Newbury Park 7.5'—1951; 1950, photorevised 1967.
Newhall 7.5'—1952; 1952, photorevised 1988.
6'—1933.
Newport Beach 7.5'—1935; 1951; 1965.
Oasis 7.5'—1956 (photorevised 1974).
Oat Mountain 7.5'—1952.
Oban 6'—1933 (reprinted 1949).
Oceanside 15'—1898.
7.5'—1947; 1968.
Ojai 7.5'—1952.
Old Man Mountain 7.5'—1943.
Olinda 7.5' (same area as Yorba Linda 7.5')—1935 (Army).
Ontario 7.5'—1954; 1967 (photorevised 1981).

Orange 7.5'—1950; 1964; 1964, photorevised 1981.
Otay Mesa 7.5'—1955 (photorevised 1971).
Otay Mountain 7.5'—1972.
Oxnard 7.5'—1949.
Pacifico Mountain 7.5'—1959.
Pacoima 6'—1927.
Pala 7.5'—1950; 1968.
Palmdale 7.5'—1958.
6'—1937.
Palomar Mountain 15'—1942 (Army).
Palomar Observatory 7.5'—1949 (revised 1971).
Pasadena 15'—1900 (reprinted 1931).
7.5'—1953; 1966 (photorevised 1988).
Pechanga 7.5'—1949; 1968.
Pico 6'—1940.
Piru 15'—1921 (reprinted 1927).
7.5'—1952, 1952, photorevised 1969.
Pitas Point 7.5'—1950.
Point Dume 7.5'—1951.
Point Loma 7.5'—1942; 1953; 1967 (photorevised 1975).
Point Mugu 7.5'—1949; 1950.
Pomona 15'—1904.
Potrero 15'—1944 (reprinted 1948).
7.5'—1960.
Poway 7.5' (same area as Poway Valley 7.5')—1967; 1967, photorevised 1975.
Poway Valley 7.5' (same area as Poway 7.5')—1952.
Prado 7.5' (same area as Prado Dam 7.5')—1941.
Prado Dam 7.5' (same area as Prado 7.5')—1950; 1967.
Puente 6'—1927 (reprinted 1937).
Quail 6'—1938.
Rabbit Peak 7.5'—1959.
Ramona 30'—1903 (reprinted 1948).
7.5'—1955 (photorevised 1988); 1955, photorevised 1971.
Ranchita 7.5'—1960.
Rancho Nuevo Creek 7.5'—1943.
Rancho Santa Fe 7.5'—1968.
Ravenna 6'—1934; 1934, reprinted 1949.
Redman 7.5'—1973.
Red Mountain 6'—1936 (reprinted 1943).
Redondo 15'—1896 (reprinted 1927).
Redondo Beach 7.5'—1951; 1963.
Redrock Mountain 6'—1936.
Red Rover 6'—1937.
Reseda 6'—1928 (reprinted 1932).
Reyes Peak 7.5'—1943.
Ritter Ridge 7.5'—1958.
Rock Creek 15' (same area as Valyermo 15')—1903.
Rodriguez Mountain 7.5'—1948 (photorevised 1971).
Rogers Lake South 7.5'—1973.
Rosamond 15'—1943 (Army)
7.5'—1973.
Rosamond Lake 7.5'—1973.
San Bernardino 1°x 2°—1957 1966.
San Clemente 7.5'—1949; 1968; 1968, photorevised 1975.
San Clemente Island Central 7.5'—1943.
San Clemente Island North 7.5'—1943.
San Clemente Island South 7.5'—1943.
San Diego 15'—1904 (reprinted 1941).
San Dimas 7.5'—1954; 1966; 1966, photorevised 1981.
San Fernando 15' (same area as Fernando 15')—1900 (reprinted 1930); 1945 (Army).
7.5'—1953; 1966 (photorevised 1972).
San Francisquito 6'—1937.
San Guillermo 7.5'—1943.
San Juan Capistrano 15'—1941.
7.5'—1949; 1968.
San Luis Rey 30'—1898 (reprinted 1942).
7.5'—1948; 1968.
San Marcos 7.5'—1949; 1968.
San Nicolas Island—1943.
San Onofre Bluff 7.5'—1949; 1968.
San Pasqual 7.5'—1954 (photorevised 1971).
San Pedro 15'—1944 (Army).
7.5'—1964.
San Pedro Hills 6'—1928 (reprinted 1932).
Santa Ana 1°x 2°—1959 (revised 1969).
15'—1896 (reprinted 1899); 1901 (reprinted 1945); 1942 (Army).
Santa Catalina East 7.5'—1950.
Santa Catalina North 7.5'—1950.
Santa Catalina South 7.5'—1943.
Santa Catalina West 7.5'—1943.
Santa Felicia Canyon 6'—1935.
Santa Monica 15'—1902.
Santa Paula 15'—1903 (reprinted 1942).
7.5'—1951.
Santa Paula Peak 7.5'—1951.
Santa Susana 15'—1903 (reprinted 1939); 1943 (Army).
7.5'—1951.
Santa Ysabel 15'—1943 (Army); 1960.
7.5'—1960.
Santiago Peak 15'—1943 (Army).
7.5'—1954.
San Vicente Reservoir 7.5'—1955 (photorevised 1971).
San Ysidro 7.5' (same area as Imperial Beach 7.5')—1943; 1953.
Saticoy 7.5'—1951.
Saugus 6'—1933 (reprinted 1939).
Sawmill Mountain 7.5'—1943.
Sawtelle 6'—1925 (reprinted 1931); 1934.
Seal Beach 7.5'—1950; 1965; 1965, photorevised 1981.
Seminole 6'—1932.
Seventeen Palms 7.5'—1956 (photorevised 1974).
Shadow Mountains 15'—(1942 (reprinted 1948).
Shell Reef 7.5'—1959.
Sierra Madre 6'—1928.
Simi 7.5'—1951.
Sitton Peak 7.5'—1954.
Sleepy Valley 7.5'—1958.
Solstice Canyon 6'—1932.
Sombrero Peak 7.5'—1959 (photorevised 1975).
South Gate 7.5'—1952; 1964; 1964, photorevised 1981.
Sunland 7.5'—1953; 1966 (photorevised 1972).
6'—1942 (reprinted 1949).
Swarthout 6'—1941.
Sweeney Pass 7.5'—1959.
Sylmar 6'—1935 (reprinted 1944).
Tecate 7.5'—1960.
Tejon 30'—1903 (reprinted 1948).
Temecula 15'—1945 (Army).
7.5'—1968.
Thousand Oaks 7.5'—1950, photorevised 1981; 1952.
Tierra del Sol 7.5'—1959.
Topanga 7.5'—1952.
Topanga Canyon 6'—1928.
Topatopa Mountains 7.5'—1943.
Torrance 7.5'—1964.
6'—1924.
Triunfo Pass 15'—1921 (reprinted 1942); 1940 (Army).
7.5'—1950.
Tubb Canyon 7.5'—1959 (minor corrections 1965).
Tujunga 15' (same area as Acton 15')—1900 (reprinted 1929).
Tule Springs 7.5'—1960.
Tustin 7.5'—1935; 1950; 1965; 1965, photorevised 1981.
Vail Lake 7.5'—1953 (photorevised 1971).
Valley Center 7.5'—1949; 1968.
Val Verde 7.5'—1952; 1952, photorevised 1969.
Valyermo 7.5'—1958 (photorevised 1974).
6'—1940 (reprinted 1949).
Van Nuys 7.5'—1953; 1966.
6'—1926.
Venice 7.5'—1950; 1964.
6'—1924 (reprinted 1942).
Ventura 15'—1904 (reprinted 1946); 1941 (Army).
7.5'—1951; 1951, photorevised 1967.
Viejas Mountain 7.5'—1960.
Warm Springs Mountain 7.5'—1958; 1958, photorevised 1988).
Warner Springs 15'—1942 (Army); 1960.
7.5'—1959.
Warners Ranch 7.5'—1960.
Waterman Mountain 7.5'—1959.
6'—1941 (reprinted 1948).
Watts 6'—1937.
Whale Peak 7.5'—1959.
Wheeler Springs 7.5'—1943; 1944 (Army).
Whitaker Peak 7.5'—1958; 1958, photorevised 1974.
6'—1935 (reprinted 1951).
White Ledge Peak 7.5'—1952.
Whittier 7.5'—1949; 1951; 1965; 1965, photorevised 1981.
6'—1925 (reprinted 1932).
Wilmington 6'—1925.
Wilsona 6'—1935.
Yorba Linda 7.5' (same area as Olinda 7.5')—1950; 1964; 1964, photorevised 1981.

Zelzah 6'—1941.

MISCELLANEOUS MAPS

Arnold and Arnold. 1902. "Sketch map of San Pedro and vicinity." (*In* Arnold and Arnold, p. 119.)

Baker. 1911. (Untitled map. Plate 34 *in* Baker.)

Blake. 1857. "Geological map of a part of the State of California explored in 1855 by Lieut. R.S. Williamson, U.S. Top. Engr." (*Accompanies* Blake.)

Brown. 1920. "Relief map of the western part of the Salton Sea region, Calif., showing desert watering places." (Plate VI *in* Brown, 1920.)

California Division of Highways. 1934. (Appendix "A" *of* California Division of Highways.)

California Mining Bureau. 1909a. "Santa Barbara and Ventura Counties." (*In* California Mining Bureau Bulletin 56.)

_____1909b. "Los Angeles and Orange Counties." (*In* California Mining Bureau Bulletin 56.)

_____1917a. (Untitled map *in* California Mining Bureau Bulletin 74, p. 174.)

_____1917b. (Untitled map *in* California Mining Bureau Bulletin 74, p. 176.)

Dalrymple. 1789. "Plan of port Sn. Diego on the west coast of California."

Diller and others. 1915. "Geologic and topographic map of the Coast Route from Los Angeles, California, to San Francisco, California." (*In* Diller and others.)

Eddy. 1854. "Approved and declared to be the official map of the State of California by an act of the Legislature passed March 25th 1853." Compiled by W.M. Eddy, State Surveyor General. Published for R.A. Eddy, Marysville, California, by J.H. Colton, New York.

Eldridge and Arnold, 1907. "Geologic map of the Santa Clara Valley and adjacent oil fields, Ventura and Los Angels Counties, California." (Plate I *in* Eldridge and Arnold).

Ellis and Lee. 1919. "Map of the San Diego area, California, showing topography and location of wells." (Plate II *in* Ellis and Lee.)

Emory. 1848. "Sketch of the actions fought at San Pasqual in Upper California between the Americans and Mexicans Dec. 6th & 7th, 1846." (*In* Emory.)

Everhart. 1951. "Economic map of the Cuyamaca Peak quadrangle, California." (Plate 3 *in* Everhart.)

Gibbes. 1852. "A new map of California." By Charles Drayton Gibbes, from his own and other recent surveys and explorations. Published by C.D. Gibbes, Stockton, Cal.

Goddard. 1857. "Britton & Rey's map of the State of California." By George H. Goddard.

Gray. 1856. "Sketch of the Port of San Diego." Surveyed by the U.S. Boundary Commission in 1849 and 1850. Hon. John B. Weller, U.S. Commissioner. A.B. Gray; U.S. Surveyor. Chs. J. Whiting, principal assistant.

Gray. 1873. "Gray's Atlas, New rail road and county map of the States of Oregon, California and Nevada." Compiled and drawn by Frank A. Gray. Published by O.W. Gray. Philadelphia.

Hall. 1887. "Plan of Redondo Beach, Los Angeles County, California." Designed and drawn under the direction of Wm. Ham Hall, consulting civil engineer. (Reproduced *in* Robinson, W.W., map 76.)

Hanks. 1886a. "Sketch map of San Diego County showing the position of mines and minerals referred to in the 6th Annual Report of the State Mineralogist of California for the year ending June 1st, 1886." (*Accompanies* Hanks.)

_____1886b. "Map of Julian district, San Diego Co., Cal." (*Accompanies* Hanks.)

Hanson. 1868. "Map of the 35 acre tracts of the Los Angeles City lands, Hancocks survey, situate on the southern slope of the Stone Quarry Hills." Surveyed in August 1868 by Geo. Hansen, County Surv., assisted by Captain Wm. Moore and August Ashbrand. (Reproduced *in* Harlow, 1976).

Jahns and Wright. 1951a. "Geologic map and section of the central and northern parts of the Pala pegmatite district, San Diego, County, California." (Plate 1 *in* Jahns and Wright.)

_____1951b. "Map showing distribution of pegmatite dikes and principal mines and prospects, northern part of the Pala district, San Diego County, California." (Plate 2 *in* Jahns and Wright.)

Johnson. 1911. "Reconnaissance hydrographic map of Antelope Valley region, California." (Plate VI *in* Johnson.)

Lankershim Ranch Land and Water Company. 1888. (Untitled map reproduced *in* Robinson, W.W., map 91.)

Los Angeles County. 1935. "Map of Los Angeles County, California." Prepared by The Department of Forester and Firewarden, County of Los Angeles. (Printed 1935; 1947 edition.) (Used as base map for Plates 5 and 6 *in* Gay and Hoffman.)

Mendenhall. 1908. "Map showing the artesian areas and hydrographic contours in the valley of southern California." (Plate III *in* Mendenhall, 1908.)

Parke. 1854-1855. "Map No. 1, San Francisco Bay to the plains of Los Angeles." From explorations and surveys made by Lieut. John C. Parke. Constructed and drawn by H. Custer. (In *Reports of explorations and surveys, to ascertain the most practicable and economical route for a railroad from the Mississippi River to the Pacific Ocean*. Volume XI. 1861).

Peckham. 1866. "Topographical sketch of a portion of the oil region of southern California." (Plate B *in* Peckham,)

Poland and others. 1956. "Map of the Long Beach-Santa Ana area, California, showing landform elements and generalized contours on base of principal fresh-water body." (Plate 1 *in* Poland and others.)

Rogers and Johnston. 1857. "State of California." By Prof. H.D. Rogers & A. Keith Johnston.

Sage. 1846. "Map of Oregon, California, New Mexico, N.W. Texas, & the proposed Territory of Ne-Bras-ka." By Rufus B. Sage.

Smith. 1897. "Geological map of Santa Catalina Island." (Plate I *in* Smith , 1897.)

_____1898. "Geological map of San Clemente Island." (Plate LXXXIV *in* Smith, 1898.)

Stevenson. 1884. "Map of the county of Los Angeles, California." By H.J. Stevenson, U.S. Dept. Surveyor. (Reproduced *in* Robinson, W.W.)

Thompson. 1921. "Relief map of part of Mohave Desert region, California, showing desert watering places." (Plates IX, X *in* Thompson, 1921.)

Tucker and Reed. 1939. "Map of San Diego County, showing locations of principal mineral deposits." (Plate I *in* Tucker and Reed.)

Vedder. 1963. "Geologic map and sections of San Nicolas Island, California." (Plate 3 *in* Vedder and Norris.)

Watts. 1898-1899. "Geological relief map of the Puente Hills, California." (Fig. 1 *in* Watts.)

Williamson. 1853a. "Map of passes in the Sierra Nevada from Walker's Pass to the Coast Range." By Lieut. R.S. Williamson, Topl. Engr., assisted by Lieut. J.G. Parke, Topl. Engr., and Mr. Isaac Williams Smith, Civ. Engr. (In *Reports of explorations and surveys, to ascertain the most practicable and economical route for a railroad from the Mississippi River to the Pacific Ocean*. Volume XI. 1861).

_____1853b. "General map of explorations and surveys in California." By Lieut. R.S. Williamson, Topl. Engr., assisted by Lieut. J.G. Parke, Topl. Engr., and Mr. Isaac William Smith, Civ. Engr. (In *Reports of explorations and surveys, to ascertain the most practicable and economical route for a railroad from the Mississippi River to the Pacific Ocean*. Volume XI. 1861).

Part Eleven
Southeast Region

Imperial, Riverside and San Bernardino Counties

Part Eleven-Southeast Region

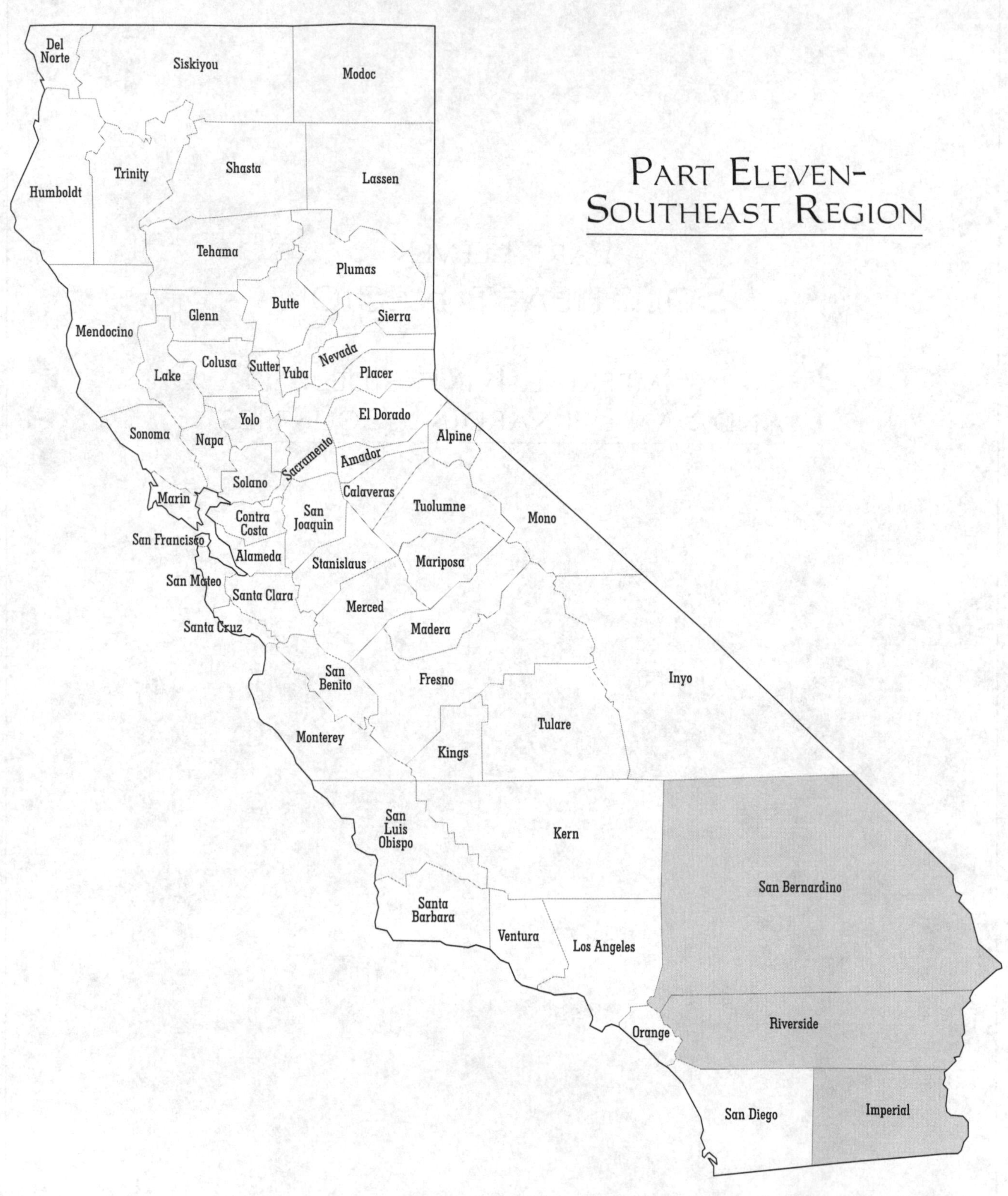

Southeast Region Imperial, Riverside and San Bernardino Counties

Regional Setting

General.—This section concerns geographic features in three counties—Imperial, Riverside, and San Bernardino—that occupy in the southeast part of California. Townships (T) 25 South to 32 South, and Ranges (R) 41 East to 47 East refer to Mount Diablo Base and Meridian; others Townships and Ranges refer to Mount Diablo Base and Meridian. Except for the high San Bernardino Mountains and San Jacinto Mountains, the Southeast Region is arid—most of it is in Mojave Desert. The name "Mojave" is from the designation of Indians that lived along Colorado River (Gudde, 1949, p. 219); United States Board on Geographic Names (1934, p. 11) rejected the form "Mohave Desert" for the name, and cited local usage for the decision. The region also includes arid lowlands, partly below sea level, that extend northwest from the head of Gulf of California in Mexico to San Gorgonio Pass. Salton Sea occupies the lowest part of this trough in the United States. Blake (p. 228) used the name "Colorado Desert" for this troughlike area because of its proximity to Colorado River. He named it on his (1857) map, which has the notation "Valley of the Ancient Lake" there. But the name "Colorado Desert" has fallen into disfavor. In modern usage, the name "Coachella Valley" refers to the northwest part, the name "Salton Basin" refers to the central part around Salton Sea, and the name "Imperial Valley" refers to the southeast part—the Spaniards called the whole Colorado Desert *La Palma de la Mano de Dios,* which means "The Hollow of God's Hand" in Spanish (Darton, p. 251). Irrigation has made rich agriculture land of parts of this depression. The map on the facing page shows the location of the Southeast Region and the counties in it.

Imperial County.—Imperial County occupies the extreme southeast corner of California. The state legislature created the county in 1907 from the east part of San Diego County; the boundaries have remained unchanged, except for a slight modification of California-Arizona State line at Colorado River (Coy, p. 113). El Centro is and always has been the county seat (Hoover, Rensch, and Rensch, p. 105).

Riverside County.—Riverside County extends westward from Colorado River nearly to the sea. Most of the residents are in the west part of the county, where water is more plentiful than in most of the east part. The state legislature created Riverside County in 1893 from sections of San Diego and San Bernardino Counties; the Riverside County boundaries remain about as first defined (Coy, p. 207-209). Riverside has been the county seat from the beginning (Hoover, Rensch, and Rensch, p. 286).

San Bernardino County.—San Bernardino County extends west from the States of Nevada and Arizona nearly to the sea. It consists mainly of desert ranges and valleys, but at the southwest corner it includes less arid places. The state legislature created San Bernardino County in 1853 from the east part of the original Los Angeles County; San Bernardino County lost territory to Inyo County in 1872 and to newly created Riverside County in 1893, but otherwise its boundaries have changed only slightly (Coy, p. 216-220). San Bernardino is and always has been the county seat (Hoover, Rensch, and Rensch, p. 316).

Southeast Region
Imperial, Riverside and San Bernardino Counties

- A -

Abacherli Canyon [SAN BERNARDINO]: *canyon,* drained by a stream that flows 1.5 miles to lowlands along Chino Creek 5 miles east of San Juan Hill (lat. 33°55'30" N, long. 117°39'15" W; sec. 7, T 3 S, R 7 W). Named on Prado Dam (1967) 7.5' quadrangle.

Abe Lincoln [RIVERSIDE]: *relief feature,* 2.5 miles southwest of present downtown Palm Springs (lat. 33°48'40" N, long. 116°34'50" W). Named on San Jacinto (1901) 30' quadrangle.

Acme [SAN BERNARDINO]: *locality,* 34 miles north of Baker along Tonopah and Tidewater Railroad (lat. 35°47'15" N, long. 116° 12' W). Named on Avawatz Mountains (1933) 1° quadrangle. According to Myrick (p. 569), Acme had the early name "Morrison," but California Mining Bureau's (1917a) map shows Morrison located just north of Acme in Inyo County. Palmer (p. 14) noted that a feature called Bully Hill is situated 0.25 mile northwest of Acme on San Bernardino-Inyo County line; the name is from Bully Hill in South Africa.

Acolita [IMPERIAL]: *locality,* 8 miles northwest of Glamis along Southern Pacific Railroad (lat. 33°04'15" N, long. 115°10'50" W; sec. 2, T 13 S, R 17 E). Named on Acolita (1953) 15' quadrangle.

Acorn Canyon [SAN BERNARDINO]: *canyon,* drained by a stream that flows 1 mile to Swarthout Valley 4.5 miles north of Mount San Antonio (lat. 34°21'15" N, long. 117°38'15" W; near SW cor. sec. 8, T 3 N, R 7 W). Named on Mount San Antonio (1955) 7.5' quadrangle. Called Oak Canyon on San Antonio (1942) 15' quadrangle.

Adahi: see **Rim Forest** [SAN BERNARDINO].

Adelanto [SAN BERNARDINO]: *town,* 7.25 miles west-northwest of Victorville (lat. 34°35' N, long. 117°24'15" W; mainly in sec. 28, T 6 N, R 5 W). Named on Adelanto (1956) 7.5' quadrangle. Postal authorities established Adelanto post office in 1916 (Frickstad, p. 137), and the town incorporated in 1970.

Adobe Corners [SAN BERNARDINO]: *locality,* 6.5 miles west-southwest of Victorville (lat. 34°30'25" N, long. 117°23'55" W; on W line sec. 22, T 5 N, R 5 W). Named on Adelanto (1956) 7.5' quadrangle.

Adobe Mountain [SAN BERNARDINO]: *hill,* 24 miles west-northwest of Victorville on San Bernardino-Los Angeles County line (lat. 34°42'15" N, long. 117°40'15" W; around SE cor. sec. 12, T 7 N, R 8 W). Named on Adobe Mountain (1955) 7.5' quadrangle.

Adobe Spring [RIVERSIDE]:

(1) *spring,* 14 miles south of Hemet (lat. 33°32'55" N, long. 116°59'55" W). Named on Sage (1954) 7.5' quadrangle.

(2) *spring,* 5.5 miles east-northeast of Murrieta (lat. 33°35'30" N, long. 117°07'45" W; sec. 6, T 7 S, R 2 W). Named on Murrieta (1953) 7.5' quadrangle.

Afton [SAN BERNARDINO]: *locality,* 23 miles southwest of Baker along Union Pacific Railroad (lat. 35°02'10" N, long. 116°22'40" W; near SE cor. sec. 18, T 11 N, R 6 E). Named on Cave Mountain (1948) 15' quadrangle.

Afton Canyon [SAN BERNARDINO]: *canyon,* 7 miles long, along Mojave River above a point 20 miles southwest of Baker (lat. 35° 02'30" N, long. 116°18'30" W; at W line sec. 13, T 11 N, R 7 E); Afton is in the canyon. Named on Cave Mountain (1948) 15' quadrangle. The feature had the early name "Cave Canyon"—caves there were a favorite camping place for travelers on the old Mojave trail (Casebier, p. 111).

Agua Alta Canyon [RIVERSIDE]: *canyon,* 8 miles long, opens into Martinez Canyon 14 miles south of Indio (lat. 33°30'50" N, long. 116°13'50" W; near SW cor. sec. 35, T 7 S, R 7 E). Named on Palm Desert (1959) 15' quadrangle, and on Valerie (1956) 7.5' quadrangle.

Agua Alta Spring [RIVERSIDE]: *spring,* 13 miles south of Palm Desert (lat. 33°31'55" N, long. 116°20'05" W; on W line sec. 26, T 7 S, R 6 E); the spring is near the head of a branch of Agua Alta Canyon. Named on Palm Desert (1959) 15' quadrangle.

Agua Bonito Mineral Spring: see **Aqua Bonita Spring** [RIVERSIDE].

Agua Caliente: see **Palm Springs** [RIVERSIDE].

Agua Caliente Spring [RIVERSIDE]: *spring,* in downtown Palm Springs (lat. 33°49'25" N, long. 116°32'40" W; at W line sec. 14, T 4 S, R 4 E). Named on Palm Springs (1957) 7.5' quadrangle.

Agua de Tomaso: see **Bitter Spring** [SAN BERNARDINO].

Agua Dulce: see **Oasis** [RIVERSIDE].

Agua Fuerte Spring [RIVERSIDE]: *spring,* 8 miles east-southeast of Idyllwild (lat. 33°42'45" N, long. 116°35'20" W; sec. 29, T 5 S, R 4 E). Named on Idyllwild (1959) 15' quadrangle.

Agua Mansa: see **Colton** [SAN BERNARDINO]

Aguanga [RIVERSIDE]: *village,* 22 miles south-southeast of Hemet (lat. 32°26'35" N, long 116°51'50" W; near S line sec. 27, T 8 S, R 1 E). Named on Aguanga (1954) 7.5' quadrangle. Postal authorities established Bergman post office in 1894, moved it 3 miles west in 1896, moved it 2.5 miles east in 1899, and moved it 0.5 mile southwest in 1901, when they changed the name to Aguanga; the name "Bergman" was for Jacob Bergman, driver of the first Butterfield Overland stage that passed by the site of the post office (Salley, p. 19). The name "Aguanga" is of Indian origin (Kroeber, p. 33-34).

Aguanga Creek: see **Temecula Creek** [RIVERSIDE].

Aguanga Valley [RIVERSIDE]: *valley,* 22 miles south-southeast of Hemet (lat. 33°26'20" N, long. 116°52'30" W); Aguanga is near the east end of the valley. Named on Aguanga (1954) and Vail Lake (1953) 7.5' quadrangles.

Ailsa [SAN BERNARDINO]: *locality,* 2.25 miles south of present Fontana city hall along Southern Pacific Railroad (lat. 34°04' N, long. 117°26' W). Named on Fontana (1943) 7.5' quadrangle. Called Aliso on California Mining Bureau's (1917a) map.

Air Corps Advanced Flying School: see **George Air Force Base** [SAN BERNARDINO].

Akela: see **Camp Akela** [SAN BERNARDINO].

Akers Camp [SAN BERNARDINO]: *locality,* 6 miles west of San Gorgonio Mountain (lat. 34°05'20" N, long. 116°56' W). Named on San Gorgonio (1902) 30' quadrangle.

Alamo Bonito: see **Mecca** [RIVERSIDE].

Alamorio [IMPERIAL]: *village,* 12.5 miles north-northwest of Holtville (lat. 32°58'45" N, long. 115°27'40" W; sec. 31, T 13 S, R 15 E); the place is near Alamo River. Named on Alamorio (1956) 7.5' quadrangle. Postal authorities established Alamorio post office in 1909 and discontinued it in 1917 (Frickstad, p. 48).

Alamo River [IMPERIAL]: *stream,* heads in Mexico and flows 55 miles in Imperial County to Salton Sea 8.5 miles northwest of Calipatria (lat. 33°12'45" N, long. 115°37'15" W; sec. 16, T 11 S, R 13 E). Named on Alamorio (1956), Bonds Corner (1957), Calexico (1957), Holtville East (1957), Holtville West (1956), Niland (1956), Westmorland (1956), and Wiest (1956) 7.5' quadrangles.

Alamos: see **Murrieta** [RIVERSIDE].

Alberhill [RIVERSIDE]: *village,* 5.5 miles northwest of the town of Lake Elsinore (lat. 33°43'35" N, long. 117°24' W; near NE cor. sec. 21, T 5 S, T 5 W). Named on Alberhill (1954) 7.5' quadrangle. Postal authorities established Alberhill post office in 1915 and discontinued it in 1969 (Salley, p. 3). United States Board on Geographic Names (1933, p. 86) rejected the form "Alberhil" for the name. Officials of California Southern Railroad named their station at the place in 1896 for C.H. Albers, James Hill, and George Hill, owners of coal and clay deposits there (Gunther, p. 9). United States Board on Geographic Names (1990, p. 5) approved the name "Bishop Canyon" for a feature, 1.9 miles long, that opens into lowlands 1.7 miles south of Alberhill (lat. 33°42'04" N, long. 117°24'09" W; sec. 28, T 5 S, R 5 W); the name commemorates William M. Bishop, Sr., who owned land in the canyon.

Alberta: see **Rockwood** [IMPERIAL].

Alder Canyon [RIVERSIDE]:

(1) *canyon,* heads in San Diego County and extends for 1.25 miles to Fig Tree Valley 21 miles south-southwest of Palm Desert in Riverside County (lat. 33°25'50" N, long. 116°31'40" W; near S line sec. 36, T 8 S, R 4 E). Named on Bucksnort Mountain (1960) 7.5' quadrangle. Called Elder Can-

yon on Ramona (1903) 30' quadrangle.

(2) *canyon*, drained by a stream that flows 7 miles to the head of Rockhouse Canyon (2) 18 miles south of Palm Desert (lat. 33° 27' N, long. 116°21'55" W; sec. 28, T 8 S, R 6 E). Named on Collins Valley (1959) 7.5' quadrangle. United States Board on Geographic Names (1962a, p. 4) rejected the name "Rockhouse Canyon" for the feature.

Alder Creek [SAN BERNARDINO]: *stream*, flows 3.5 miles to Hemlock Creek 3.5 miles south-southwest of Keller Peak (lat. 34°08'50" N, long. 117°04'05" W; near W line sec. 26, T 1 N, R 2 W). Named on Keller Peak (1967) 7.5' quadrangle. Middle Fork enters 1 mile above the mouth of the main stream; it is 2 miles long and is named on Keller Peak (1967) 7.5' quadrangle.

Alessandro [RIVERSIDE]: *locality*, 9 miles southeast of Riverside city hall along Atchison, Topeka and Santa Fe Railroad (lat. 33°53'10" N, long. 117°16'10" W; at N line sec. 26, T 3 S, R 4 W). Named on Riverside East (1967) 7.5' quadrangle. Postal authorities established Alessandro post office in 1888 and discontinued it in 1902 (Frickstad, p. 126). Messers. French, Packard and Rockwell laid out a town at the place in 1887 and named it for the husband of the heroine of Helen Hunt Jackson's novel *Romona* (Gunther, p. 11).

Alessandro Aviation Field: see **March Air Force Base** [RIVERSIDE].

Alessandro Valley: see **Moreno Valley** [RIVERSIDE].

Alexander Hills [SAN BERNARDINO]: *range*, 33 miles north of Baker at the east end of Sperry Hills (lat. 35°45' N, long. 116° 06' W). Named on Trona (1957) 1°x 2° quadrangle.

Alexander Hills: see **Sperry Hills** [SAN BERNARDINO].

Alexis: see **Hinda** [RIVERSIDE].

Alger Creek [SAN BERNARDINO]: *stream*, flows 2.25 miles to Mill Creek Canyon 5 miles west of San Gorgonio Mountain (lat. 34°05'25" N, long. 116°54'40" W; near NE cor. sec. 18, T 1 S, R 1 E). Named on Forest Falls (1970) 7.5' quadrangle.

Algodones Dunes: see **Sand Hills** [IMPERIAL].

Aliso: see **Ailsa** [SAN BERNARDINO].

Aliso Canyon [RIVERSIDE]: *canyon*, drained by a stream that flows 1 mile to Orange County 3 miles southwest of Sitton Peak (lat. 33° 33'45" N, long. 117°29'15" W; near NE cor. sec. 15, T 7 S, R 6 W). Named on Sitton Peak (1954) 7.5' quadrangle. Called Verdugo Canon on Lake Elsinore (1941) 15' quadrangle, where present Verdugo Canyon is unnamed.

Aliso Canyon [RIVERSIDE-SAN BERNARDINO]: *canyon*, drained by a stream that heads in San Bernardino County and flows 6 miles to Santa Ana River 4.5 miles east-southeast of San Juan Hill just inside Riverside County (lat. 33°53' N, long. 117°39'55" W; sec. 25, T 3 S, R 8 W). Named on Prado Dam (1967) 7.5' quadrangle.

Alkali Creek: see **Amargosa River** [SAN BERNARDINO].

Alkali Wash: see **Horse Canyon** [RIVERSIDE].

Allen Peak [SAN BERNARDINO]: *peak*, 9 miles west of San Gorgonio Mountain (lat. 34°04'50" N, long. 116°59'10" W; near SE cor. sec. 16, T 1 S, R 1 W). Altitude 5795 feet. Named on Forest Falls (1970) 7.5' quadrangle. United States Board on Geographic Names (1964b, p. 13) rejected the name "Old Allen Peak" for the feature.

Allen Peak: see **Birch Mountain** [SAN BERNARDINO].

Alligator [RIVERSIDE]: *ridge*, northeast-trending, 1 mile long, 1 mile south-southwest of Desert Center (lat. 33°42'05" N, long. 115°24'40" W; on SW cor. sec. 27, T 5 S, R 15 E). Named on Chuckwalla Mountains (1963) 15' quadrangle.

Alligator Slough [RIVERSIDE]: *water feature*, 7 miles south-southeast of Vidal [SAN BERNARDINO] in a cut off meander of Colorado River (lat. 34°01'30" N, long. 114°29' W). Named on Parker (1949) 15' quadrangle.

Almond Cove [SAN BERNARDINO]: *relief feature*, 7.5 miles east of the village of Red Mountain (lat. 35°19'45" N, long. 117°28'30" W); the place is south of Almond Mountain. Named on Cuddeback Lake (1954) 15' quadrangle.

Almond Mountain [SAN BERNARDINO]: *peak*, 9 miles east of the village of Red Mountain (lat. 35°22'10" N, long. 117°27'30" W; sec. 34, T 29 S, R 42 E). Named on Cuddeback Lake (1954) 15' quadrangle.

Alray [SAN BERNARDINO]: *locality*, 2.5 miles northwest of Cajon along Atchison, Topeka and Santa Fe Railroad (lat. 34°19'40" N, long. 117°28'55" W; near SW cor. sec. 23, T 3 N, R 6 W). Named on Cajon (1956) 7.5' quadrangle.

Alta Loma [SAN BERNARDINO]: *town*, 5.25 miles north-northeast of Ontario city hall (lat. 34°07'30" N, long. 117°35'45" W). Named on Cucamonga Peak (1966) and Guasti (1966) 7.5' quadrangles. Called Ioamosa on Cucamonga (1903) 15' quadrangle. Postal authorities established Ioamosa post office in 1895 and changed the name to Alta Loma in 1913; the name "Ioamosa" was from tracts of land called Iowa and Hermosa (Salley, p. 105). Residents of the place chose the name "Alta Loma" for a station along Pacific Electric Railroad by popular vote in 1912 (Gudde, 1949, p. 9).

Alta Vista [RIVERSIDE]: *locality*, 6 miles west of Corona at Riverside-Orange County line (lat. 33°52'10" N, long. 117°40'15" W). Named on Prado (1941) 7.5' quadrangle. Promoters laid out an unsuccessful resort townsite at the place in 1910 (Meadows, p. 20).

Altura: see **Cadiz** [SAN BERNARDINO].

Alvin Meadows [RIVERSIDE]: *area*, 12.5 miles east of Hemet (lat. 33°44'30" N, long. 116°45'15" W; on E line sec. 15, T 5 S, R 2 E). Named on Hemet (1957) 15' quadrangle.

Alvord: see **May** [RIVERSIDE].

Alvord Mountain [SAN BERNARDINO]: *range*, 33 miles west-southwest of Baker (lat. 35°05'15" N, long. 116°37' W). Named on Alvord Mountain (1948) 15' quadrangle. United States Board on Geographic Names (1962a, p. 4) rejected the plural form "Alvord Mountains" for the name. At the same time (p. 9), the Board approved the name "Clews Ridge" for a northeast-trending feature, about 1.5 miles long, located in the east part of Alvord Mountain—the name is for Joe Clews, a prospector of the 1860's. Gudde (1969, p. 9) associated the name "Alvord" with Charles Alvord, another prospector of the 1860's.

Alvord Mountain: see **Alvord Peak** [SAN BERNARDINO].

Alvord Peak [SAN BERNARDINO]: *peak*, 32 miles west-southwest of Baker (lat. 35°05'50" N, long. 116°37'10" W); the feature is the high point of Alvord Mountain. Named on Trona (1957) 1°x 2° quadrangle. United States Board on Geographic Names (1962a, p. 4) rejected the name "Alvord Mountain" for the peak.

Alvord Well [SAN BERNARDINO]: *well*, 34 miles west-southwest of Baker (lat. 35°03'20" N, long. 116°37'30" W; near E line sec. 11, T 11 N, R 3 E); the well is at the south edge of Alvord Mountain. Named on Alvord Mountain (1948) 15' quadrangle. United States Board on Geographic Names (1962a, p. 17) approved the name "Spanish Canyon" for a feature, 4.5 miles long, that opens into lowlands about 1.6 miles east-northeast of Alvord Well on the south side of Alvord Mountain (sec. 7, T 11 N, R 4 E); an old Spanish trail passed through the canyon.

Amaral Spring [SAN BERNARDINO]: *spring*, 13 miles east of Victorville (lat. 34°31'05" N, long. 117°03'50" W; sec. 14, T 5 N, R 2 W). Named on Fairview Valley (1970) 7.5' quadrangle.

Amargosa: see **South Amargosa**, under **Salt Creek** [SAN BERNARDINO].

Amargosa Desert: see **Death Valley** [SAN BERNARDINO].

Amargosa River [SAN BERNARDINO]: *stream*, heads in Inyo County and flows 32 miles in San Bernardino County to reenter Inyo County 45 miles northwest of Baker (lat. 35°47'40" N, long. 116°33'30" W). Named on Avawatz Pass (1948), Confidence Hills (1950), Leach Lake (1948), Silurian Hills (1956), and Tecopa (1950) 15' quadrangles. Antonio Armijo called the stream Rio de los Payuches in 1830 (Lingenfelter, 1986, p. 25). Fremont (p. 264) noted that it "is called by the Spaniards *Amargosa*—the bitter water of the desert." Hafen and Hafen (p. 67, 92) gave the early names "Alkali Creek" and "Bitter Water Creek" for the stream. Mendenhall (1909a, p. 48) referred to present Salt Creek as "south branch Amargosa River."

Amboy [SAN BERNARDINO]: *village*, 68 miles west-southwest of Needles (lat. 34°33'30" N, long. 115°44'30" W; at N line sec. 5, T 5 N, R 12 E). Named on Cadiz (1956) 15' quadrangle. Postal authorities established Amboy post office in 1904 (Salley, p. 6). Lewis Kingman reportedly named the place; Kingman's Atlantic and Pacific Railroad became Atchison, Topeka and Santa Fe Railroad, and after this company took over the rail line from Needles to Mojave from Southern Pacific Railroad in 1884, Kingman built a series of sidings from Amboy to Colorado River and named them in alphabetical order: Amboy, Bristol, Cadiz, Danby, Edson, Fenner, Goffs, Homer, Ibex, and Java (Hanna, p. 10; Myrick, p. 766). The company built a half-mile spur in 1916 to a new gypsum mill near Amboy; the junction with the main line was named Funston in 1917 following the death of General Funston (Myrick, p. 837).

Amboy Crater [SAN BERNARDINO]: *crater*, 3 miles west-southwest of Amboy (lat. 34°32'40" N, long. 115°47'20" W; at SW cor. sec. 1, T 5 N, R 11 E). Named on Bagdad (1956) 15' quadrangle.

American Girl Wash [IMPERIAL]: *stream*, flows 10.5 miles to end 3.25 miles southwest of Ogilby (lat. 32°46'40" N, long. 114°52'15" W; at S line sec. 9, T 16 S, R 20 E). Named on Ogilby (1963) 15' quadrangle, which shows American Girl mine located near the stream.

Amerosa Wash [IMPERIAL]: *stream*, flows 3.5 miles to end near Truckhaven (lat. 33°17'45" N, long. 115°58'05" W; near S line sec. 18, T 10 S, R 10 E). Named on Seventeen Palms (1956) and Truckhaven (1956) 7.5' quadrangles.

Ames: see **Dawes** [SAN BERNARDINO].

Ames Canyon [SAN BERNARDINO]: *canyon*, drained by a stream that flows 1.25 miles to lowlands 1.25 miles north-northeast of Devore (lat. 34°13'55" N, long. 117°23'25" W; sec. 27, T 2 N, R 5 W). Named on Devore (1966) 7.5' quadrangle.

Ames Well [SAN BERNARDINO]: *well*, 10 miles north-northeast of Landers (lat. 34°24'30" N, long. 116°20'35" W; sec. 27, T 4 N, R 6 E). Named on Hidalgo Mountain (1954) 7.5' quadrangle.

Amity Spring [SAN BERNARDINO]: *spring*, 10 miles east-southeast of Trona (lat. 35°39'20" N, long. 117°08'40" W). Named on Wingate Pass (1950) 15' quadrangle.

Amos [IMPERIAL]: *locality*, 15 miles east of Calipatria along Southern Pacific Railroad (lat. 33°07'05" N, long. 115°15'15" W; at N line sec. 24, T 12 S, R 16 E). Named on Amos (1956) 7.5' quadrangle. Called Mammoth on Mendenhall's (1908b) map. Hanks' (1886) map has the name "Mammoth Tank" at or near the site. The early name "Mammoth" for present Amos suggests the proximity of Mammoth Wash (Brown, 1923, p. 208). Postal authorities established Amos post office in 1920 and discontinued it in 1931 (Frickstad, p. 48).

Anderson Canyon [RIVERSIDE]: *canyon,* 2.5 miles long, opens into Temescal Valley 8.5 miles south-southeast of Corona (lat. 33°45'45" N, long. 117°30'10" W; near E line sec. 4, T 5 S, R 6 W). Named on Corona South (1967) and Santiago Peak (1954) 7.5' quadrangles.

Anderson Canyon: see **Indian Canyon** [RIVERSIDE].

Anderson Flat [SAN BERNARDINO]: *area,* 8 miles south of downtown Big Bear Lake (lat. 34°07'45" N, long. 116°53'20" W; near W line sec. 33, T 1 N, R 1 E); the place is less than 0.5 mile northeast of Anderson Peak. Named on Big Bear Lake (1970) 7.5' quadrangle.

Anderson Peak [SAN BERNARDINO]: *peak,* 4.25 miles west-northwest of San Gorgonio Mountain (lat. 34°07'30" N, long. 116°53'35" W; near E line sec. 32, T 1 N, R 1 E). Named on Big Bear Lake (1970) and Forest Falls (1970) 7.5' quadrangles.

Andrade [IMPERIAL]: *locality,* 1.5 miles east-southeast of Pilot Knob (lat. 32°43'35" N, long. 114°43'30" W; sec. 35, T 16 S, R 21 E). Site named on Yuma West (1965) 7.5' quadrangle, which shows an old railroad grade at the place. California Division of Highways' (1934) map has both the names "Cantu" and "Andrade P.O." at the site. Postal authorities established Andrade post office in 1909, discontinued it in 1910, reestablished it in 1912, and discontinued it in 1942 (Frickstad, p. 48). The name "Andrade" was for Don Guillermo Andrade, who bought land for a colony along Colorado River (Hanna, p. 12). The name "Cantu" for the railroad station at the site honored Colonel Esteban Cantu, governor of the northern district of Baja California from 1915 until 1920 (Gudde, 1949, p. 55; Hanna, p. 54).

Andreas Canyon [RIVERSIDE]: *canyon,* drained by a stream that flows 6.5 miles to Palm Canyon 5 miles south of Palm Springs (lat. 33°45'35" N, long. 116°32'45" W; near SE cor. sec. 3, T 5 S, R 4 E). Named on Idyllwild (1959) 15' quadrangle, and on Palm Springs (1957) and San Jacinto Peak (1981) 7.5' quadrangles. The name recalls Captain Andreas, an Indian resident of the canyon (Chase, p. 20).

Andreas Falls [RIVERSIDE]: *waterfall,* 6.5 miles southwest of Palm Springs (lat. 33°45'30" N, long. 116°37' W; near NE cor. sec. 12, T 5 S, R 3 E); the feature is in Andreas Canyon. Named on Palm Springs (1957) 7.5' quadrangle.

Angalls Canyon [SAN BERNARDINO]: *canyon,* 0.5 mile long, 8 miles north-northeast of Ontario city hall (lat. 34°10'05" N, long. 117°36'15" W; sec. 15, T 1 N, R 7 W). Named on Cucamonga Peak (1966) 7.5' quadrangle.

Angel Camp: see **Mount San Antonio** [SAN BERNARDINO].

Angelus: see **Camp Angelus** [SAN BERNARDINO].

Angelus Hill [RIVERSIDE]: *peak,* 6.25 miles east of San Jacinto (lat. 33°47'20" N, long. 116°51'10" W; sec. 23, T 4 S, R 1 E). Altitude 4111 feet. Named on Lake Fulmor (1956) 7.5' quadrangle.

Angelus Oaks: see **Camp Angelus** [SAN BERNARDINO].

Annie Orton Canyon: see **Railroad Canyon** [RIVERSIDE] (1).

Anon: see **Murrieta** [RIVERSIDE].

Antelope Creek [SAN BERNARDINO]: *stream,* flows 8.5 miles to Antelope Wash 12 miles north of downtown Morongo Valley (lat. 34°13' N, long. 116°32'30" W; near NW cor. sec. 35, T 2 N, R 4 E). Named on Onyx Peak (1972) and Rimrock (1972) 7.5' quadrangles. Called Sleepy Creek on Morongo Valley (1955) 15' quadrangle, but United States Board on Geographic Names (1975a, p. 8) gave this name as a variant.

Antelope Valley [SAN BERNARDINO]: *area,* 11 miles south of Victorville (lat. 34°23' N, long. 117°17' W). Named on Cedar Springs (1956) and Hesperia (1956) 7.5' quadrangles.

Antelope Wash [SAN BERNARDINO]: *stream,* flows 5.5 miles to Pipes Canyon Wash 10.5 miles north-northeast of downtown Morongo Valley (lat. 34°11'20" N, long. 116°30'30" W; near W line sec. 7, T 1 N, R 5 E). Named on Rimrock (1972) 7.5' quadrangle.

Anthony: see **Upland** [SAN BERNARDINO].

Anti-Fat Hot Springs: see **Glen Ivy Hot Springs** [RIVERSIDE].

Antimony Gulch [SAN BERNARDINO]: *canyon,* drained by a stream that flows 6 miles to end 15 miles northwest of Ivanpah (lat. 35°31'20" N, long. 115°28' W; near SE cor. sec. 9, T 16 N, R 14 E). Named on Clark Mountain (1956) and Roach Lake (1955) 15' quadrangles.

Antsell Rock [RIVERSIDE]: *relief feature,* 4.25 miles east of Idyllwild (lat. 33°43'50" N, long. 116°38'30" W; at N line sec. 23, T 5 S, R 3 E). Named on Idyllwild (1959) 15' quadrangle. Edmond Perkins, a topographer with United States Geological Survey, reportedly named the feature in 1897 or 1898 for an artist he saw making a painting of it (Gunther, p. 25).

Anza [IMPERIAL]: *locality,* 3.5 miles east of El Centro along Holtville Inter-urban Railroad (lat. 32°48' N, long. 115°30' W; near W line sec. 35, T 15 S, R 14 E). Named on El Centro (1957) and Holtville West (1956) 7.5' quadrangles. Called Brice Siding on Holtville (1907) 30' quadrangle.

Anza [RIVERSIDE]: *village,* 13 miles south of Idyllwild (lat. 33°33'20" N, long. 116°40'30" W; mainly in sec. 16, 21, T 7 S, R 3 E); the place is in Anza Valley. Named on Idyllwild (1959) 15' quadrangle. Postal authorities established Anza post office in 1926 (Salley, p. 8).

Anza: see **Camp Anza**, under **Arlanza** [RIVERSIDE].

Anza Ditch [IMPERIAL]: *stream,* flows 7 miles to Salton Sea 3 miles northeast of Truckhaven (lat. 33°19'15" N, long. 115°56'05" W; sec. 9, T 10 S, R 10 E). Named on Seventeen Palms (1956) and Truckhaven (1956) 7.5' quadrangles.

Anza Valley [RIVERSIDE]: *valley,* 13 miles south of Idyllwild (lat. 33°33' N, long. 116°40' W). Named on Idyllwild (1959) 15' quadrangle. San Jacinto (1901) 30' quadrangle shows the feature as part of Terwilliger Valley, but United States Board on Geographic Names (1982a, p. 2) rejected this designation. The Board (1963b, p. 14) earlier rejected the names "Cahuilla Valley" and "Coahuila Valley" for present Anza Valley. The name "Anza" is for Juan Bautista de Anza, whose expedition of 1774 and expedition of 1775 to 1776 traversed the place; in the 1880's the valley was known as Hamilton Plains for James Hamilton (Gunther, p. 26).

Apache Peak [RIVERSIDE]: *peak,* 5.5 miles east-southeast of Idyllwild (lat. 33°43'10" N, long. 116°37'30" W; sec. 24, T 5 S, R 3 E). Named on Idyllwild (1959) 15' quadrangle.

Apache Spring [RIVERSIDE]: *spring,* 6 miles east-southeast of Idyllwild (lat. 33°43'15" N, long. 116°37'10" W; sec. 24, T 5 S, R 3 E); the spring is nearly 0.5 mile east of Apache Peak. Named on Idyllwild (1959) 15' quadrangle.

Aplin [SAN BERNARDINO]: *locality,* 3 miles east-northeast of Redlands along Southern California Railroad (lat. 34°05'45" N, long. 117°08'40" W). Named on Redlands (1901) 15' quadrangle. United States Geological Survey's (1943) map shows a place called Browns located along Atchison, Topeka and Santa Fe Railroad 0.5 mile southeast of the site of Aplin.

Apolitana: see **Colton** [SAN BERNARDINO].

Apple Canyon [RIVERSIDE]: *canyon,* 1.5 miles long, 5 miles east-southeast of Idyllwild (lat. 33°42'50" N, long. 116°38'30" W; sec. 23, 26, T 5 S, R 3 E). Named on Idyllwild (1959) 15' quadrangle.

Apple Valley [SAN BERNARDINO]:

(1) *valley,* 6 miles east of Victorville (lat. 34°30' N, long. 117° 11' W). Named on Apple Valley North (1970), Apple Valley South (1971), Fairview Valley (1970), Fifteenmile Valley (1971), and Victorville (1956) 7.5' quadrangles. Mrs. Ursula M. Poates named the place at the turn of the century; she planted three apple trees there to convince buyers of real estate that fruit could be grown in the desert (Gudde, 1969, p. 12). Peirson (p. 115) noted the alternate name "East Mesa" for the place.

(2) *town,* 7 miles east-southeast of Victorville (lat. 34°29'45" N, long 117°11'20" W); the town is in Apple Valley (1). Named on Apple Valley North (1970) and Apple Valley South (1971) 7.5' quadrangles. Postal authorities established Apple Valley post office in 1949 (Salley, p. 8).

Apple White Camp: see **Lytle Creek** [SAN BERNARDINO] (2).

Applewhite Campground [SAN BERNARDINO]: *locality,* 3.25 miles southwest of Cajon along North Fork Lytle Creek (lat. 34°15'40" N, long. 117°29'35" W; sec. 15, T 2 N, R 6 W). Named on Cajon (1956) 7.5' quadrangle.

Aqua Bonita Spring [RIVERSIDE]: *spring,* 13 miles east-southeast of Idyllwild in Palm Canyon (lat. 33°40' N, long. 116°31' W; sec. 12, T 6 S, R 4 E). Named on Idyllwild (1959) 15' quadrangle. Called Agua Bonito Mineral Spring on Hemet Reservoir (1942) 15' quadrangle.

Arabia: see **Thermal** [RIVERSIDE].

Araz [IMPERIAL]: *locality,* 8.5 miles west-southwest of Bard along Southern Pacific Railroad (lat. 32°45'15" N, long. 114°41'30" W; sec. 19, T 16 S, R 22 E). Site named on Araz (1964) 7.5' quadrangle. Pilot Knob station of Butterfield Overland stage line was at the place (Hoover, Rensch, and Rensch, p. 108).

Araz Junction [IMPERIAL]: *locality,* 2.5 miles east-northeast of Pilot Knob along Southern Pacific Railroad (lat. 32°44'55" N, long. 114°42'45" W; sec. 24, T 16 S, R 21 E). Named on Yuma West (1965) 7.5' quadrangle.

Araz Wash [IMPERIAL]: *stream* and *dry wash,* extends for 8.5 miles to Colorado River 2.5 miles east-northeast of Pilot Knob (lat. 32°44'30" N, long. 114°42'20" W; sec. 25, T 16 S, R 21 E). Named on Ogilby (1963) 15' quadrangle, and on Araz (1964) and Yuma West (1965) 7.5' quadrangles.

Arbolado: see **Camp Arbolado** [SAN BERNARDINO].

Arch Creek [SAN BERNARDINO]: *stream,* flows nearly 6 miles to lowlands 9 miles east of Vidal along Colorado River (lat. 34°08'20" N, long. 114°20'35" W; near S line sec. 27, T 1 N, R 20 W). Named on Parker (1970) and Parker NW (1970) 7.5' quadrangles.

Archer [SAN BERNARDINO]: *locality,* 15 miles south of Essex along Atchison, Topeka and Santa Fe Railroad (lat. 34°25'15" N, long. 115°22' W; at W line sec. 24, T 4 N, R 15 E). Named on Cadiz Lake (1956) 15' quadrangle.

Arcilla [RIVERSIDE]: *locality,* 3.5 miles west-northwest of Estelle Mountain along Atchison, Topeka and Santa Fe Railroad (lat. 33° 47' N, long.

117°28'45" W; near N line sec. 35, T 4 S, R 6 W). Named on Lake Mathews (1967) 7.5' quadrangle. The place is a shipping point for clay—*arcilla* means "clay" in Spanish (Gunther, p. 28).

Arctic Canyon [SAN BERNARDINO]: *canyon,* drained by a stream that flows 3 miles to lowlands 7.5 miles north-northeast of Fawnskin (lat. 34°21'55" N, long. 116°52'30" W; near NE cor. sec. 9, T 3 N, R 1 E). Named on Fawnskin (1971) 7.5' quadrangle.

Argos [SAN BERNARDINO]: *locality,* 5 miles west of Ludlow along Atchison Topeka and Santa Fe Railroad (lat. 34°43'30" N, long. 116°15' W; sec. 4, T 7 N, R 7 E). Named on Lavic (1955) and Ludlow (1955) 15' quadrangles.

Argos Mountain [SAN BERNARDINO]: *peak,* 18 miles west-southwest of Ludlow (lat. 34°35'40" N, long. 116°25'40" W; sec. 23, T 6 N, R 5 E); the peak is 14 miles southwest of Argos. Named on Lavic (1955) 15' quadrangle.

Argus [SAN BERNARDINO]: *locality,* 1.5 miles southwest of Trona (lat. 35°44'50" N, long. 117°23'40" W; mainly in sec. 19, T 25 S, R 43 E). Named on Trona (1949) 15' quadrangle, and on Westend (1973) 7.5' quadrangle.

Argus Range [SAN BERNARDINO]: *range,* mainly in Inyo County, but extends south into San Bernardino County west of Trona. Named on Mountain Springs Canyon (1953) and Trona (1949) 15' quadrangles, and on Lone Butte (1973) and Westend (1973) 7.5' quadrangles. Lieutenant Lyle called the feature Tortoise Mountains in 1871; others called it Darwin Range in the early days (Palmer, p. 8, 22).

Arica: see **Freda** [SAN BERNARDINO].

Arica Mountains [RIVERSIDE]: *range,* 25 miles west-southwest of Vidal [SAN BERNARDINO] (lat. 34°01'15" N, long. 114°55'45" W). Named on Rice (1954) 15' quadrangle.

Arimo: see **Danby** [SAN BERNARDINO].

Arlanza [RIVERSIDE]: *locality,* 6 miles west-southwest of Riverside city hall (lat. 33°56'30" N, long. 117°28' W). Named on Riverside West (1967) 7.5' quadrangle. Called Arlanza Village on Riverside West (1953) 7.5' quadrangle. The name is from the words "Arlington" and "Anza"—Camp Anza, a World War II army installation named for Juan Bautista de Anza, was at the site (Gunther, p. 30, 95).

Arlanza Village: see **Arlanza** [RIVERSIDE].

Arlington [RIVERSIDE]: *district,* 6 miles southwest of Riverside city hall (lat. 33°55'15" N, long. 117°26'45" W). Named on Riverside West (1967) 7.5' quadrangle. Called Arlington Place on Riverside (1901) 15' quadrangle, where present Arlington Station is called Arlington. Postal authorities established Arlington post office in 1881, discontinued it in 1892, reestablished it with the name "Arlington Place" in 1891, and changed the post office name back to Arlington in 1900 (Salley, p. 10). Riverside Land and Irrigation Company developed the place in 1875; residents chose the name "Arlington" by popular vote (Gudde, 1949, p. 14). United States Geological Survey's (1942b) map has the name "Institute" for a place along Pacific Electric Railroad about 0.5 mile northeast of Arlington at present Sherman Indian Institute.

Arlington Heights [RIVERSIDE]: *area,* 6.5 miles south-southwest of Riverside city hall (lat. 33°54'05" N, long. 117°25'40" W); the area is in highlands southeast of Arlington. Named on Riverside West (1967) 7.5' quadrangle. Matthew Gage named the place when he began to develop it for citrus groves (Gunther, p. 31-32).

Arlington Mountain [RIVERSIDE]: *peak,* 7.5 miles north-northwest of Estelle Mountain (lat. 33°52'15" N, long. 117°28'15" W); the feature is 3.5 miles south-southwest of Arlington. Altitude 1853 feet. Named on Lake Mathews (1967) 7.5' quadrangle.

Arlington Place: see **Arlington** [RIVERSIDE].

Arlington Station [RIVERSIDE]: *locality,* 6 miles southwest of Riverside city hall along Atchison, Topeka and Santa Fe Railroad (lat. 33°54'50" N, long. 117°26'25" W; near NE cor. sec. 18, T 3 S, R 5 W). Named on Riverside West (1967) 7.5' quadrangle. Called Arlington on Riverside (1901) 15' quadrangle.

Armada [RIVERSIDE]: *locality,* 9.5 miles north of Perris (lat. 33° 55' N, long. 117°13'30" W). Named on Elsinore (1901) 30' quadrangle. Postal authorities established Armada post office in 1895 and discontinued it in 1920 (Frickstad, p. 127). The place first was called Midland for its position halfway between Alessandro and Moreno, but postal authorities refused the name "Midland" and substituted the name "Armada" (Gunther, p. 323). Perris (1943) 15' quadrangle shows Midland school near the site.

Arnold Heights [RIVERSIDE]: *locality,* 8 miles southeast of Riverside city hall (lat. 33°53'35" N, long. 117°16'40" W; sec. 22, 23, T 3 S, R 4 W). Named on Riverside East (1967) 7.5' quadrangle. The place began in 1945 as a residential community for personnel of March Air Force Base; it is on land used during World War II for Camp Haan—the name "Arnold" is for General H.H. Arnold (Gunther, p. 32-33).

Arnold Reservoir [SAN BERNARDINO]: *lake,* 1000 feet long, 6 miles north-northwest of San Juan Hill in Tonner Canyon (lat. 33° 59'25" N, long. 117°47'10" W). Named on Yorba Linda (1964) 7.5' quadrangle.

Arrastra Wash [IMPERIAL]: *stream,* flows nearly 4 miles to Little Picacho Wash 2.5 miles northeast of Picacho Peak (lat. 32°59'50" N, long. 114°37'45" W). Named on Picacho Peak (1965) 7.5' quadrangle.

Arrastre Canyon [SAN BERNARDINO]: *canyon,* drained by a stream that flows 8.5 miles to Apple Valley (1) 13 miles southeast of Victorville (lat. 34°26'15" N, long. 117°06'40" W; sec, 17, T 4 N, R 2 W). Named on Apple Valley South (1971), Butler Peak (1971), and Fifteenmile Valley (1971) 7.5' quadrangles.

Arrastre Creek [SAN BERNARDINO]: *stream,* flows 16 miles to lowlands less than 0.5 mile southeast of Old Woman Springs (lat. 34°23'15" N, long. 116°42'10" W; near SE cor. sec. 31, T 4 N, R 3 E). Named on Big Bear City (1971), Old Woman Springs (1972), Onyx Peak (1972), and Rattlesnake Canyon (1972) 7.5' quadrangles.

Arrastre Flat [SAN BERNARDINO]: *area,* 3 miles north-northwest of Big Bear City (lat. 34°18'10" N, long. 116°51'50" W; sec. 34, T 3 N, R 1 E). Named on Big Bear City (1971) 7.5' quadrangle.

Arrastre Spring [SAN BERNARDINO]: *spring,* 27 miles northwest of Baker (lat. 35°33'40" N, long. 116°24' W). Named on Avawatz Pass (1948) 15' quadrangle. The name is from an arrastre that prospectors found in 1907 at the site of an old Mexican mining camp in Avawatz Mountains (Gudde, 1969, p. 14).

Arrow Bear: see **Arrowbear Lake** [SAN BERNARDINO] (2).

Arrowbear Lake [SAN BERNARDINO]:

(1) *lake,* 450 feet long, 2 miles northwest of Keller Peak along South Fork Deep Creek (1) (lat. 34°12'45" N, long. 117°04'35" W; sec. 34, T 2 N, R 2 W). Named on Keller Peak (1967) 7.5' quadrangle.

(2) *village,* 2 miles west-northwest of Keller Peak (lat. 34°12'40" N, long. 117°04'50" W); Arrowbear Lake (1) is at the place. Named on Keller Peak (1967) 7.5' quadrangle. Postal authorities established Arrow Bear post office in 1927, changed the name to Arrowbear Lake in 1928, discontinued the post office in 1929, reestablished it in 1931, discontinued in it 1968, and reestablished in it 1971 (Salley, p. 10).

Arrowhead: see **Arrowhead Station** [SAN BERNARDINO]; **Lake Arrowhead** [SAN BERNARDINO].

Arrowhead Highlands [SAN BERNARDINO]: *district,* 9 miles north of San Bernardino city hall (lat. 34°13'45" N, long. 117°15'30" W; sec. 26, T 2 N, R 4 W). Named on San Bernardino North (1967) 7.5' quadrangle.

Arrowhead Junction [SAN BERNARDINO]: *locality,* 14 miles west-northwest of Needles (lat. 34°56'30" N, long. 114°49'25" W; sec. 19, T 10 N, R 21 E). Named on Bannock (1956) 15' quadrangle.

Arrowhead Peak [SAN BERNARDINO]: *peak,* 7 miles north of San Bernardino city hall (lat. 34°12'20" N, long. 117°15'45" W; near NE cor. sec. 2, T 1 N, R 4 W); the peak is 1.5 miles north of Arrowhead Springs. Altitude 4237 feet. Named on San Bernardino North (1967) 7.5' quadrangle.

Arrowhead Springs [SAN BERNARDINO]: *locality,* 6 miles north-northeast of San Bernardino city hall (lat. 34°11'10" N, long. 117° 15'40" W; at E line sec. 11, T 1 N, R 4 W). Named on San Bernardino North (1967) 7.5' quadrangle. Postal authorities established Arrowhead Springs post office in 1887, discontinued it in 1895, reestablished it in 1906, changed the name to Arrow Head Springs in 1907, discontinued it in 1924, reestablished it in 1925, and discontinued it in 1942 (Salley, p. 10). The twenty or more hot springs at the site came to general notice in 1858 (Anderson, p. 89-90). Dr. D.N. Smith built a resort to utilize the water in 1863 and named the facility for an arrowhead-shaped scar on the slope above the place (Hanna, p. 17). Waring (p. 33) reported that bathers used water at Waterman Hot Springs, located less than 1 mile west of Arrowhead Springs.

Arrowhead Station [SAN BERNARDINO]: *locality,* 2.5 miles north of present San Bernardino city hall along Southern California Railroad (lat. 34°08'40" N, long. 117°17'15" W); the place is 3 miles south-southwest of Arrowhead Springs. Named on San Bernardino (1901) 15' quadrangle. Called Arrowhead on Arrowhead (1941) 7.5' quadrangle. Postal authorities established Arrowhead post office in 1895 and discontinued it in 1906 (Frickstad, p. 137).

Arrowweed Spring [SAN BERNARDINO]: *spring,* 22 miles north-northeast of Amboy (lat. 34°51' N, long. 115°36' W; at S line sec. 22, T 9 N, R 13 E). Named on Flynn (1956) 15' quadrangle.

Arrowweed Springs [IMPERIAL]: *spring,* 17 miles south of Palo Verde along Vinagre Wash (lat. 33°11'30" N, long. 114°45'30" W; near NE cor. sec. 28, T 11 S, R 21 E). Named on Quartz Peak (1953) 15' quadrangle. On Picacho (1951) 15' quadrangle, the name applies to a spring located less than 1 mile farther east along Vinagre Wash.

Arrowweed Well [IMPERIAL]: *well,* 17 miles south of Palo Verde (lat. 33°11'30" N, long. 114°45'30" W; near NE cor. sec. 28, T 11 S, R 21 E); the well is by Arrowweed Springs. Named on Quartz Peak (1953) 15' quadrangle.

Arroyo de los Martires: see **Mojave River** [SAN BERNARDINO].

Arroyo de los Negros: see **Lytle Creek** [SAN BERNARDINO] (1).

Arroyo del Toro [RIVERSIDE]: *stream,* flows 3.5 miles to Warm Springs Valley 3 miles north of Lake Elsinore city hall (lat. 33°42'40" N, long. 117°19'55" W; near N line sec. 30, T 5 S, R 4 W). Named on Lake Elsinore (1953, photorevised 1988) and Steele Peak (1967) 7.5' quadrangles. On

Elsinore (1901) 30' quadrangle, the name applies to the canyon of the stream.

Arroyo Salada [IMPERIAL]: *stream,* heads in San Diego County and flows 13 miles in Imperial County to Salton Sea 4 miles east of Truckhaven (lat. 33°17'50" N, long. 115°54'20" W; sec. 14, T 10 S, R 10 E). Named on Kane Spring NW (1956), Shell Reef (1959), and Truckhaven (1956) 7.5' quadrangles. Called Arroyo Salada Wash on Barrel Spring (1942) 15' quadrangle, but United States Board on Geographic Names (1961b, p. 12) rejected this form of the name. North Fork enters 8 miles above the mouth of the main stream; it heads in San Diego County, is nearly 5 miles long in Imperial County, and is named on Seventeen Palms (1956) and Shell Reef (1959) 7.5' quadrangles.

Arroyo Salada Wash: see **Arroyo Salada** [IMPERIAL].

Arroyo Seco [IMPERIAL-RIVERSIDE]: *stream,* heads in Riverside County and flows 16 miles to Milpitas Wash 24 miles north of Glamis in Imperial County (lat. 33°20'10" N, long. 115°06'15" W; sec. 5, T 10 S, R 18 E). Named on Chuckwalla Spring (1953) and Iris Pass (1963) 15' quadrangles.

Arroyo Seco: see **Arroyo Seco Creek** [RIVERSIDE]; **Milpitas Wash** [IMPERIAL].

Arroyo Seco Creek [RIVERSIDE]: *stream,* heads in San Diego County and flows 6.25 miles in Riverside County to Vail Lake 7 miles west-northwest of Aguanga (lat. 33°29'05" N, long. 116°58'35" W). Named on Vail Lake (1953) 7.5' quadrangle. Called Arroyo Seco on Ramona (1903) 30' quadrangle.

Asbestos Mountain [RIVERSIDE]: *peak,* 8 miles southwest of Palm Desert (lat. 33°37'40" N, long. 116°27'30" W; near SW cor. sec. 22, T 6 S, R 5 E). Altitude 5265 feet. Named on Rancho Mirage (1957) 7.5' quadrangle. Palm Desert (1959) 15' quadrangle shows an asbestos mine located less than 2 miles southwest of the peak.

Asbestos Spring [RIVERSIDE]: *spring,* 9 miles southwest of Palm Desert (lat. 33°37'30" N, long. 116°28'15" W; sec. 28, T 6 S, R 5 E); the spring is less than 1 mile west-southwest of Asbestos Mountain. Named on Palm Desert (1959) 15' quadrangle.

Ash Hill [SAN BERNARDINO]: *locality,* 6.25 miles east of Ludlow along Atchison, Topeka and Santa Fe Railroad (lat. 34°42'25" N, long. 116°03'15" W; near SW cor. sec. 9, T 7 N, R 9 E). Named on Ash Hill (1955) 7.5' quadrangle. The name commemorates Ben Ash, a railroad surveyor who died of thirst at the place (Gudde, 1949, p. 16).

Ash Meadows [SAN BERNARDINO]: *area,* 5 miles south-southwest of Luna Mountain (lat. 34°16'45" N, long 117°10'05" W; near NW cor. sec. 11, T 2 N, R 3 W). Named on Lake Arrowhead (1971) 7.5' quadrangle.

Ash Meadows: see **Stove Flats** [SAN BERNARDINO].

Astley Rancho [SAN BERNARDINO]: *locality,* 27 miles west-southwest of Barstow (lat. 34°46'40" N, long. 117°28'45" W; near S line sec. 14, T 8 N, R 6 W). Named on Astley Rancho (1973) 7.5' quadrangle.

Asylum: see **Patton** [SAN BERNARDINO].

Atolia [SAN BERNARDINO]: *locality,* 3 miles south of the village of Red Mountain (lat. 35°18'55" N, long. 117°36'30" W; sec. 20, T 30 S, R 41 E). Named on Red Mountain (1967) 7.5' quadrangle. Postal authorities established Atolia post office in 1906, discontinued it in 1922, reestablished it in 1927, and discontinued it in 1944 (Frickstad, p. 138). The place was a tungsten mining camp that began in 1905 and boomed during World War I (Wynn, p. 5). Officials of Tungsten Mining Company named the camp for two company officers, Messers. Atkins and DeGolia (Gudde, 1949, p. 17).

Auburndale [RIVERSIDE]: *locality,* 3 miles north-northwest of Corona (lat. 33°55' N, long. 117°35'30" W). Named on Corona (1902) 30' quadrangle. Promoters laid out a community at the place in 1887, but the enterprise failed after plans for a railroad to the site were abandoned (Gunther, p. 34-35).

Augustine Pass [RIVERSIDE]: *pass,* 18 miles south-southeast of Desert Center (lat. 33°28'55" N, long. 115°15'25" W). Named on Iris Pass (1963) 15' quadrangle. The name commemorates Martin Augustine, who discovered gold in the neighborhood in 1917 (Gunther, p. 35).

Auld [RIVERSIDE]: *locality,* 12.5 miles east of Murrieta in Los Alamos Valley (present Auld Valley) (lat. 33°35'05" N, long. 117° 03'30" W). Named on Elsinore (1901) 30' quadrangle. Postal authorities established Auld post office in 1899 and discontinued it in 1921; the name was for George Auld, first postmaster (Salley, p. 12).

Auld Valley [RIVERSIDE]: *valley,* 11 miles east of Murrieta (lat. 33° 35'15" N, long. 117°04'15" W). Named on Bachelor Mountain (1953) 7.5' quadrangle. Called Los Alamos Valley on Elsinore (1901) 30' quadrangle, which shows the place called Auld located in the valley. George Auld came to the valley to farm in the early 1880's (Gunther, p. 35).

Ausland Well: see **East Well** [SAN BERNARDINO].

Avawatz: see **Cave Spring** [SAN BERNARDINO].

Avawatz Mountains [SAN BERNARDINO]: *range,* 22 miles northwest of Baker (lat. 35°31' N, long. 116°20' W). Named on Avawatz Pass (1948), Baker (1956), and Red Pass Lake (1948) 15' quadrangles. The name, which also had the forms "Ivawatz," "Ivanwatz," "Ivowatz," and "Ivawatch," is from Ava Watts mining district of the early 1870's (Lingenfelter, 1986, p. 136; Palmer, p. 9).

Avawatz Pass [SAN BERNARDINO]: *pass,* 27 miles northwest of Baker (lat. 35°31'25" N, long. 116°26'30" W); the feature is in Avawatz Mountains. Named on Avawatz Pass (1948) 15' quadrangle.

Avenaloca Mesa [RIVERSIDE]: *relief feature,* 10 miles west of Temecula (lat. 33°29'40" N, long. 117°19'35" W). Named on Fallbrook (1968) 7.5' quadrangle.

Avery Canyon [RIVERSIDE]: *canyon,* nearly 3 miles long, opens into Diamond Valley 3.5 miles south-southeast of downtown Hemet (lat. 33°42'05" N, long. 116°57'10" W; near S line sec. 26, T 5 S, R 1 W). Named on Hemet (1953) 7.5' quadrangle, which shows Mission ranch in the canyon. The feature also was called Mission Canyon (Gunther, p. 36).

Awahanes: see **Camp Awahanes** [SAN BERNARDINO].

Azalea Creek [RIVERSIDE]: *stream,* flows 4 miles to Twin Pines Creek 3.5 miles south of Cabazon (lat. 33°52' N, long. 116°47'30" W; near E line sec. 32, T 3 S, R 2 E). Named on Lake Fulmor (1956) 7.5' quadrangle.

Azalea Trails Camp [RIVERSIDE]: *locality,* 3 miles west of San Jacinto Peak (lat. 33°48'30" N, long. 116°43'40" W; sec. 24, T 4 S, R 2 E). Named on San Jacinto Peak (1981) 7.5' quadrangle.

Azalea Wash [SAN BERNARDINO]: *stream,* 2 miles long, 15 miles south-southeast of Essex (lat. 34°32'10" N, long. 115°08'45" W; in and near sec. 12, T 5 N, R 17 E). Named on Essex (1956) 15' quadrangle.

Aztec Spring [SAN BERNARDINO]: *spring,* 2.25 miles north of Ord Mountain (lat. 34°42'20" N, long. 116°49'15" W; at SE cor. sec. 12, T 7 N, R 1 E). Named on Ord Mountains (1955) 15' quadrangle.

Aztec Well [RIVERSIDE]: *well,* nearly 6 miles south-southeast of Desert Center (lat. 33°38' N, long. 115°22'30" W). Named on Chuckwalla Mountains (1963) 15' quadrangle. The name is from Aztec mining claim, located in 1896 (Gunther, p. 36).

- B -

Babtiste: see **Kenworthy** [RIVERSIDE].

Babtiste Canyon: see **Bautista Creek** [RIVERSIDE].

Bachelor Mountain [RIVERSIDE]: *mountain,* 9.5 miles east-northeast of Murrieta (lat. 33°36'20" N, long. 117°03'40" W; in and near sec. 35, T 6 S, R 2 W). Altitude 2555 feet. Named on Bachelor Mountain (1953) 7.5' quadrangle.

Bacon Flats [SAN BERNARDINO]: *area,* 3.5 miles south of Luna Mountain (lat. 34°17'35" N, long. 117°08' W; near NW cor. sec. 6, T 2 N, R 2 W). Named on Lake Arrowhead (1971) 7.5' quadrangle.

Badger Canyon [SAN BERNARDINO]: *canyon,* drained by a stream that flows 1.25 miles to lowlands 6 miles north of San Bernardino city hall (lat. 34°11'30" N, long. 117°18'40" W). Named on San Bernardino North (1967) 7.5' quadrangle.

Badger Lake: see **El Centro** [IMPERIAL].

Badlands: see **The Badlands** [RIVERSIDE].

Bagdad [SAN BERNARDINO]: *locality,* 8 miles west-northwest of Amboy along Atchison, Topeka and Santa Fe Railroad (lat. 34° 35' N, long. 115°52'30" W; sec. 30, T 6 N, R 11 E). Named on Bagdad (1956) 15' quadrangle. Postal authorities established Bagdad post office in 1889, discontinued it in 1921, reestablished it in 1922, and discontinued it in 1923 (Frickstad, p. 138). Thompson's (1921) map shows a place called Haynes located 3.5 miles west of Bagdad along the railroad.

Bailey Canyon [SAN BERNARDINO]: *canyon,* drained by a stream that flows 1.5 miles to lowlands 8 miles north-northwest of San Bernardino city hall (lat. 34°12'30" N, long. 117°20'55" W; at SE cor. sec. 36, T 2 N, R 5 W). Named on San Bernardino North (1967) 7.5' quadrangle.

Baileys Well [IMPERIAL]: *well,* 21 miles south of Desert Shores (lat. 33°06'10" N, long. 116°02'50" W; near NE cor. sec. 29, T 12 S, R 9 E). Named on Borrego Mountain SE (1958) 7.5' quadrangle, which indicates that the well is dry.

Bairdstown: see **Doble** [SAN BERNARDINO].

Baisley Creek [RIVERSIDE]: *stream,* flows 2.5 miles to Bautista Creek 11 miles southeast of Hemet (lat. 33°39'10" N, long. 116° 49' W; sec. 18, T 6 S, R 2 E). Named on Hemet (1957) 15' quadrangle. The name commemorates William D. Baisley, who built a house by the stream in 1894 (Gunther, p. 38).

Baker [SAN BERNARDINO]: *town,* 60 miles east-northeast of Barstow (lat. 35°16' N, long. 116°04'30" W; around SE cor. sec. 25, T 14 N, R 8 E). Named on Baker (1956) 15' quadrangle. Called Berry on California Mining Bureau's (1909a) map. Postal authorities established Baker post office in 1933 (Salley, p. 13). The name commemorates Richard Charles Baker, founder of Pacific Borax and Redwoods Chemical Works, Ltd., in 1896, and Borax Consolidated Ltd., in 1899 (Palmer, p. 10).

Balch [SAN BERNARDINO]: *locality,* 15 miles south of Baker along Union Pacific Railroad (lat. 35°02'35" N, long. 116°01'15" W; near N line sec. 16, T 11 N, R 9 E). Named on Soda Lake (1956) 15' quadrangle.

Bald Mountain [RIVERSIDE]: *peak,* 11 miles east-southeast of Idyllwild (lat. 33°40'30" N, long. 116°32'30" W; near W line sec. 2, T 6 S, R 4 E).

Altitude 4454 feet. Named on Idyllwild (1959) 15' quadrangle.

Bald Peak [RIVERSIDE]: *peak,* 8.5 miles south of Corona on Riverside-Orange County line (lat. 33°45'20" N, long. 117°32'05" W). Altitude 3947 feet. Named on Corona South (1967) 7.5' quadrangle.

Baldwin Lake [SAN BERNARDINO]: *intermittent lake,* 2.5 miles long, just east of Big Bear City (lat. 34°16'30" N, long. 116°48'30" W). Named on Big Bear City (1971) 7.5' quadrangle. The name commemorates C.G. Baldwin, first president of Pomona College, who investigated the neighborhood before 1891 to find a site for a dam to store water for power and irrigation; Baldwin reported this then unnamed lake, which the college faculty named for him (Hanna, p. 23). Postal authorities established Baldwin Lake post office in 1916, discontinued it in 1917, reestablished it in 1924, and discontinued it in 1931, when they moved the service to Big Bear City (Frickstad, p. 138)—presumably the post office was near the intermittent lake.

Baldy: see **Mount Baldy** [SAN BERNARDINO]; **Mount San Antonio** [SAN BERNARDINO].

Baldy Mesa [SAN BERNARDINO]: *area,* 13 miles southwest of Victorville (lat. 34°23'30" N, long. 117°27' W). Named on Baldy Mesa (1956) and Cajon (1956) 7.5' quadrangles. Baldy Mesa is the elevated part of an area now called West Mesa, but that earlier was called Sunrise Valley (Peirson, p. 115).

Baldy Mountain [RIVERSIDE]: *peak,* 4 miles south of the center of Idyllwild (lat. 33°41'10" N, long. 116°42'50" W; near NW cor. sec. 6, T 6 S, R 3 E). Named on Idyllwild (1959) 15' quadrangle.

Baldy Notch [SAN BERNARDINO]: *relief feature,* 2.5 miles east-southeast of Mount San Antonio (lat. 34°16'25" N, long. 117°36'30" W; on W line sec. 10, T 2 N, R 7 W). Named on Telegraph Peak (1956) 7.5' quadrangle.

Baldy Summit Inn: see **Mount San Antonio** [SAN BERNARDINO].

Baldy Village: see **Camp Baldy**, under **Mount Baldy** [SAN BERNARDINO].

Balky Horse Canyon [SAN BERNARDINO]: *canyon,* drained by a stream that flows 1.5 miles to Arrastre Creek 4.25 miles east-northeast of Sugarloaf Mountain (lat. 34°13'40" N, long. 116°44'55" W; sec. 26, T 2 N, R 2 E). Named on Moonridge (1970) 7.5' quadrangle.

Ballou [SAN BERNARDINO]: *locality,* 2.5 miles east-southeast of Ontario city hall along Union Pacific Railroad (lat. 34°03' N, long. 117°36'30" W; near SW cor. sec. 27, T 1 S, R 7 W). Named on Guasti (1966) 7.5' quadrangle. United States Geological Survey's (1941) map shows a place called Collins located 1.5 miles east-southeast of present Ballou along Union Pacific Railroad.

Bandit Pass [SAN BERNARDINO]: *narrows,* 20 miles northeast of Vidal (lat. 34°17'45" N, long. 114°13'45" W; near NE cor. sec. 3, T 2 N, R 26 E). Named on Gene Wash (1959) 7.5' quadrangle.

Bane Canyon [SAN BERNARDINO]: *canyon,* drained by a stream that flows 2.25 miles to Aliso Canyon 2 miles east of San Juan Hill (lat. 33°55' N, long. 117°42'05" W). Named on Prado Dam (1967) 7.5' quadrangle.

Banning [RIVERSIDE]: *town,* 28 miles east of Riverside (lat. 33°55'35" N, long. 116°52'35" W). Named on Beaumont (1953) and Cabazon (1956) 7.5' quadrangles. Postal authorities established Banning post office in 1877 and discontinued it for a time in 1880 (Salley, p. 14). The town incorporated in 1913. The name commemorates Phineas Banning; Ransom B. Moore, owner of land at the site, first called the place Moore City (Gunther, p. 40).

Banning: see **Camp Banning**, under **Sycamore Flat** [SAN BERNARDINO].

Banning Bench [RIVERSIDE]: *relief feature,* north-northwest of Banning along the west side of San Gorgonio River (lat. 33°58'30" N, long. 116°54'30" W). Named on Beaumont (1953) and Forest Falls (1970) 7.5' quadrangles.

Banning Canyon [RIVERSIDE-SAN BERNARDINO]: *canyon,* 4 miles long, on Riverside-San Bernardino County line, along San Gorgonio River above a point 5.25 miles north-northwest of Banning (lat. 34°00' N, long. 116°54'25" W). Named on Forest Falls (1970) and San Gorgonio Mountain (1970) 7.5' quadrangles. The canyon forks at the head to form Burnt Canyon and Sawmill Canyon, both in San Bernardino County.

Banning's Well: see **Government Holes** [SAN BERNARDINO].

Bannock [SAN BERNARDINO]: *locality,* 16 miles west-northwest of Needles along Atchison, Topeka and Santa Fe Railroad (lat. 34°56'10" N, long. 114°52' W; near N line sec. 26, T 10 N, R 20 E). Named on Bannock (1956) 15' quadrangle.

Barber Canyon [SAN BERNARDINO]: *canyon,* drained by a stream that flows 3 miles to lowlands 22 miles northwest of Essex (lat. 34° 59'28" N, long. 115°28'20" W; sec. 34, T 11 N, R 14 E). Named on Colton Well (1956) and Mid Hills (1955) 15' quadrangles.

Barber Well [SAN BERNARDINO]: *well,* 25 miles south-southwest of Ivanpah (lat. 35°00'15" N, long. 115°28'45" W; near W line sec. 27, T 11 N, R 14 E); the well is in Barber Canyon. Named on Mid Hills (1955) 15' quadrangle. Called Barber's Well on Thompson's (1921) map.

Bard [IMPERIAL]: *locality,* 14 miles south-southeast of Picacho Peak (lat. 32°47'20" N, long. 114°33'20" W; at S line sec. 4, T 16 S, R 23 E). Named on Bard (1965) 7.5' quadrangle. Postal authorities established Bard post office in 1910, discontinued it in 1933, and reestablished it in 1937 (Salley, p. 14). The name commemorates Thomas R. Bard, who promoted a 13,000-acre irrigation district in the neighborhood (Gudde, 1949, p. 23). California Mining Bureau's (1917b) map shows a place called Sellew located about 2 miles northeast of Bard along the rail line from Bard to Potholes.

Bard Lake [IMPERIAL]: *lake,* 1.25 miles south of Bard along a former course of Colorado River (lat. 32°46'20" N, long. 114°33'20" W). Named on Bard (1965) 7.5' quadrangle.

Bare Tree Spring [RIVERSIDE]: *spring,* 9 miles northeast of Garnet in Long Canyon [RIVERSIDE-SAN BERNARDINO] (lat. 34°00'25" N, long. 116°26'55" W; sec. 10, T 2 S, R 5 E). Named on Yucca Valley South (1972) 7.5' quadrangle, which indicates that the spring is dry.

Barker Peak [RIVERSIDE]: *peak,* 5.5 miles southeast of Banning (lat. 33°53' N, long. 116°50'05" W; near N line sec. 25, T 3 S, R 1 E). Altitude 4357 feet. Named on Cabazon (1956) 7.5' quadrangle. Called Barton Peak on Banning (1956) 15' quadrangle, but United States Board on Geographic Names (1968, p. 4) rejected the names "Barton Peak" and "Braton Peak" for the feature. The name "Barker" commemorates C.O. Barker, who came to Banning in 1884 (Gunther, p. 43).

Barns: see **Imperial** [IMPERIAL].

Barnwell [SAN BERNARDINO]: *locality,* 5 miles southeast of Ivanpah (lat. 35°17'35" N, long. 115°14'10" W; near W line sec. 14, T 14 N, R 16 E). Site named on Crescent Peak (1956) 15' quadrangle. Postal authorities established Manvel post office in 1893, discontinued it for a time that same year, changed the name to Barnwell in 1907, and discontinued it in 1915; the name "Manvel" was for Allen A. Manvel, president of Atlantic and Pacific Railroad (Salley, p. 15, 132).

Barnwell Sink: see **Lanfair Valley** [SAN BERNARDINO].

Barrel Spring [SAN BERNARDINO]:

(1) *spring,* 4 miles southeast of Luna Mountain (lat. 34°17'50" N, long. 117°05' W; near SW cor. sec. 34, T 3 N, R 2 W). Named on Butler Peak (1971) 7.5' quadrangle.

(2) *spring,* 5.25 miles east-southeast of Essex (lat. 34°42' N, long. 115°09'40" W; at NW cor. sec. 13, T 7 N, R 17 E). Named on Essex (1956) 15' quadrangle.

Barrett Canyon [IMPERIAL]: *canyon,* 6.5 miles long, opens into lowlands 6 miles south of Carrizo Mountain (lat. 32°54'20" N, long. 116°01'45" W; near SW cor. sec. 35, T 14 S, R 9 E). Named on Carrizo Mountain NE (1957) and Plaster City NW (1956) 7.5' quadrangles.

Barrett Canyon [SAN BERNARDINO]: *canyon,* drained by a stream that flows 1.25 miles to San Antonio Canyon 11 miles north of Ontario city hall just inside Los Angeles County (lat. 34°13'05" N, long. 117°39'50" W; sec. 36, T 2 N, R 8 W). Named on Mount Baldy (1967) 7.5' quadrangle. North Fork branches northeast 0.5 mile above the mouth of the main canyon; it is 1 mile long and is named on Mount Baldy (1967) 7.5' quadrangle.

Barrow: see **Mount Barrow** [IMPERIAL].

Barstow [SAN BERNARDINO]: *city,* 56 miles north-northeast of San Bernardino (lat. 34°53'30" N, long. 117°01'30" W). Named on Barstow (1971) and Nebo (1953) 7.5' quadrangles. Postal authorities established Barstow post office in 1886 (Frickstad, p. 138), and the city incorporated in 1947. The railroad stop at present Barstow was called Grapevine until about 1880, when it was renamed Waterman Junction (Peirson, p. 156, 158). The company town for the mill that processed ore from Waterman silver mine, which Robert W. Waterman and John L. Porter had filed on in 1880, was called Waterman's; it was situated on the north bank of Mojave River about 1 mile west of present Barstow (Miller and Miller, p. 31, 33; Myrick, p. 765). When tracks of Atchison, Topeka and Santa Fe Railroad reached the south bank of Mojave River just east of Waterman's, the junction point to Waterman's was named Barstow in honor of William Barstow Strong, president of the railroad (Myrick, p. 765-766). Postal authorities established Waterman post office in 1881 and discontinued it in 1887; they established another Waterman post office on Waterman Avenue in San Bernardino in 1961, discontinued it in 1962, reestablished it in 1966, and discontinued in 1974 (Salley, p. 235). They established Ulmer post office 15 miles southwest of Barstow in 1888 and discontinued it in 1890 (Salley, p. 227). Thompson's (1921) map shows a place called Todd located 5 miles west-southwest of Barstow along the railroad.

Barth Well [IMPERIAL]: *well,* 14 miles northeast of Calipatria (lat. 33°14'40" N, long. 115°19'20" W; sec. 5, T 11 S, R 16 E). Named on Tortuga (1955) 7.5' quadrangle, which indicates that the well is dry.

Bartlett Mountains [SAN BERNARDINO]: *range,* 2 miles north-northwest of Joshua Tree (lat. 34°09'45" N, long. 116°19'50" W). Named on Joshua Tree North (1972) 7.5' quadrangle.

Barton Canyon [RIVERSIDE]: *canyon,* 5 miles long, 21 miles south of Indio on Riverside-San Diego County line (lat. 33°25'45" N, long. 116°11'30" W). Named on Rabbit Peak (1959) 7.5' quadrangle.

Barton Creek [SAN BERNARDINO]: *stream,* formed by the confluence of East Fork and West Fork, flows 1.5 miles to Santa Ana River 4 miles south of downtown Big Bear Lake (lat. 34° 11'05" N, long. 116°55'15" W; sec.

7, T 1 N, R 1 E); the stream heads at Hathaway Flat. Named on Big Bear Lake (1970) 7.5' quadrangle. East Fork is 3 miles long and West Fork is 2.5 miles long; both forks are named on Big Bear Lake (1970) 7.5' quadrangle. Present East Fork is called Hathaway Creek on San Gorgonio (1902) 30' quadrangle.

Barton Flats [SAN BERNARDINO]: *area*, 3 miles southwest of Sugarloaf Mountain (lat. 34°10'25" N, long. 116°51'15" W; mainly in sec. 14, 15, T 1 N, R 1 E). Named on Big Bear Lake (1970) and Moonridge (1970) 7.5' quadrangles.

Barton Flats Campground [SAN BERNARDINO]: *locality*, 4 miles west-southwest of Sugarloaf Mountain (lat. 34°10'20" N, long. 116°52'25" W; at W line sec. 15, T 1 N, R 1 E); the place is at Barton Flats. Named on Moonridge (1970) 7.5' quadrangle.

Barton Peak: see **Barker Peak** [RIVERSIDE].

Base Line: see **East Highlands** [SAN BERNARDINO].

Basin: see **Baxter** [SAN BERNARDINO].

Bass [SAN BERNARDINO]: *locality*, 15 miles east-southeast of Victorville along Atchison, Topeka and Santa Fe Railroad (lat. 34° 25'30" N, long. 117°03'55" W; near W line sec. 23, T 4 N, R 2 W). Named on Fifteenmile Valley (1971) 7.5' quadrangle.

Bat Cave [SAN BERNARDINO]: *cave*, 11 miles southeast of Needles (lat. 34°42'45" N, long. 114°29'40" W; sec. 8, T 7 N, R 24 E). Named on Topoc (1970) 7.5' quadrangle.

Bat Caves Buttes [IMPERIAL-RIVERSIDE]: *hills*, 5 miles southeast of Salton on Imperial-Riverside County line (lat. 33°25'45" N, long. 115°48'45" W; in and near sec. 35, T 8 S, R 11 E). Named on Durmid (1956) 7.5' quadrangle.

Bat Cave Wash [SAN BERNARDINO]: *stream*, flows 7 miles to Colorado River 10 miles southeast of Needles (lat. 34°43'30" N, long. 114°29'30" W; sec. 5, T 7 N, R 24 E); Bat Cave is situated nearly 1 mile above the mouth of the stream. Named on Topock (1970) and Whale Mountain (1971) 7.5' quadrangles.

Bathtub Spring [SAN BERNARDINO]: *spring*, 9.5 miles south-southwest of Ivanpah (lat. 35°12'55" N, long. 115°22'55" W; near SW cor. sec. 9, T 13 N, R 15 E). Named on Mid Hills (1955) 15' quadrangle.

Bautista: see **Kenworthy** [RIVERSIDE].

Bautista Creek [RIVERSIDE]: *stream* and *dry wash*, extends for 17 miles to San Jacinto River 3.25 miles east-southeast of San Jacinto (lat. 33°45'55" N, long. 116°54'30" W). Named on Hemet (1957) and Idyllwild (1959) 15' quadrangles, and on San Jacinto (1953) 7.5' quadrangle. Juan Bautista de Anza traveled along the course of the stream on his expedition of 1774 and on his expedition of 1775 to 1776; on some early maps the feature is called Babtiste Canyon (Hanna, p. 27).

Bautista Wash [RIVERSIDE]: *stream*, diverges from Bautista Creek and flows 5.25 miles to end 1.5 miles southeast of San Jacinto (lat. 33°46'05" N, long. 116°56'25" W). Named on Hemet (1957) 15' quadrangle, and on San Jacinto (1953) 7.5' quadrangle.

Baxter [SAN BERNARDINO]: *locality*, 20 miles southwest of Baker along Union Pacific Railroad (lat. 35°02'30" N, long. 116°17'30" W). Named on Avawatz Mountains (1933) 1° quadrangle. Postal authorities established Baxter post office in 1914, discontinued it in 1919, reestablished it in 1923, and discontinued it in 1926 (Frickstad, p. 138). The name is from Baxter and Ballardie quarry; the place now is called Basin (Myrick, p. 760).

Baynham: see **Camp Baynham**, under **Mount Baldy** [SAN BERNARDINO].

Bay Tree Spring [RIVERSIDE]: *spring*, 10 miles east-northeast of San Jacinto (lat. 33°49'10" N, long. 116°47'20" W; at E line sec. 17, T 4 S, R 2 E). Named on Lake Fulmor (1956) 7.5' quadrangle.

Beal [SAN BERNARDINO]: *locality*, 6.5 miles south-southeast of Needles along Atchison, Topeka and Santa Fe Railroad (lat. 34° 45'30" N, long. 114°32'55" W; sec. 26, T 8 N, R 23 E). Named on Needles (1904) 30' quadrangle. The name commemorates A.M. Beal, superintendent of Atlantic and Pacific Railroad when that rail line reached Needles about 1884 (Hanna, p. 27). California Mining Bureau's (1917a) map shows a place called Mellen located 4 miles southeast of Beal at the west end of the railroad bridge over Colorado River.

Beale: see **Fort Beale**, under **Fort Piute** [SAN BERNARDINO].

Beal Well [IMPERIAL]: *well*, 18 miles northeast of Calipatria (lat. 33°20'15" N, long. 115°19'45" W; near NE cor. sec. 6, T 10 S, R 16 E). Named on Iris Pass (1963) 15' quadrangle.

Bear Canyon [IMPERIAL]: *canyon*, drained by a stream that flows 6.5 miles to lowlands along Colorado River 28 miles south of Palo Verde (lat. 33°01'45" N, long. 114°39'50" W; sec. 21, T 13 S, R 22 E). Named on Picacho Peak (1965) and Picacho SW (1965) 7.5' quadrangles. Called Bear Gulch on Picacho Peak (1945) 15' quadrangle.

Bear Canyon [RIVERSIDE]: *canyon*, drained by a stream that flows 1.25 miles to San Juan Canyon 1.5 miles north-northeast of Sitton Peak (lat. 33°36'20" N, long. 117°25'55" W; at W line sec. 32, T 6 S, R 5 W). Named on Sitton Peak (1954) 7.5' quadrangle.

Bear Canyon [SAN BERNARDINO]: *canyon*, nearly 2 miles long, 12.5 miles north of Ontario city hall on San Bernardino-Los Angeles County line (lat. 34°14'45" N, long. 117°39'20" W; mainly in sec. 19, T 2 N, R 7 W). Named on Mount Baldy (1967) 7.5' quadrangle.

Bear Canyon: see **Sandia Canyon** [RIVERSIDE].

Bear Canyon Bluff [IMPERIAL]: *relief feature*, 28 miles south of Palo Verde (lat. 33°01'55" N, long. 114°39'25" W; sec. 22, T 13 S, R 22 E); the feature is along Colorado River just below the mouth of Bear Canyon. Named on Picacho SW (1965) 7.5' quadrangle.

Bear Canyon Falls [IMPERIAL]: *waterfall*, 29 miles south of Palo Verde (lat. 33°00'55" N, long. 114°40'10" W); the feature is in Bear Canyon. Named on Picacho SW (1965) 7.5' quadrangle.

Bear Canyon Resort: see **Mount Baldy** [SAN BERNARDINO].

Bear Canyon Tank [IMPERIAL]: *water feature*, 29 miles south of Palo Verde (lat. 33°00'55" N, long. 114°40'10" W); the feature is in Bear Canyon. Named on Picacho SW (1965) 7.5' quadrangle.

Bearclaw Well [SAN BERNARDINO]: *well*, 20 miles northwest of Essex (lat. 34°58'40" N, long. 115°26'45" W; near N line sec. 7, T 10 N, R 15 E). Named on Colton Well (1956) 15' quadrangle.

Bear Creek [RIVERSIDE]: *stream*, flows 4.5 miles to lowlands 6 miles south-southeast of Palm Desert (lat. 33°38'45" N, long. 116° 19'05" W; sec. 13, T 6 S, R 6 E). Named on Palm Desert (1959) 15' quadrangle.

Bear Creek [SAN BERNARDINO]: *stream*, flows 8.5 miles to Santa Ana River 3 miles southeast of Keller Peak (lat. 34°09'35" N, long. 117°00'50" W; near E line sec. 19, T 1 N, R 1 W); the stream heads at Big Bear Lake (1). Named on Big Bear Lake (1970) and Keller Peak (1967) 7.5' quadrangles. North Fork enters from the north 3 miles northeast of Keller Peak; it is 2.25 miles long and is named on Keller Peak (1967) 7.5' quadrangle.

Bear Creek: see **Little Bear Creek** [SAN BERNARDINO].

Bear Creek Campground [SAN BERNARDINO]: *locality*, 3 miles southeast of Keller Peak (lat. 34°09'55" N, long. 117°00'45" W; at SE cor. sec. 18, T 1 N, R 1 W); the place is along Bear Creek. Named on Keller Peak (1967) 7.5' quadrangle.

Bear Flat [SAN BERNARDINO]: *area*, 2.5 miles south of Mount San Antonio (lat. 34°15' N, long. 117°39' W; near N line sec. 19, T 2 N, R 7 W). Named on Mount Baldy (1967) and Mount San Antonio (1955) 7.5' quadrangles. The place also was called Fern Flats (Robinson, J.W., 1983, p. 167).

Bear Gulch: see **Bear Canyon** [IMPERIAL].

Bear Lake: see **Big Bear Lake** [SAN BERNARDINO]; **Little Bear Lake**, under **Lake Arrowhead** [SAN BERNARDINO].

Bear Peak: see **Little Bear Peak** [SAN BERNARDINO].

Bear Spring [RIVERSIDE]: *spring*, 12 miles south of Corona (lat. 33°42'40" N, long. 117°31'05" W). Named on Santiago Peak (1954) 7.5' quadrangle.

Bear Spring: see **Little Bear Spring** [SAN BERNARDINO].

Bear Trap Canyon [RIVERSIDE]: *canyon*, drained by a stream that flows 2.5 miles to Strawberry Valley 1 mile west-southwest of the center of Idyllwild (lat. 33°44'10" N, long. 16°44'15" W; at W line sec. 13, T 5 S, R 2 E). Named on Idyllwild (1959) and Palm Springs (1957) 15' quadrangles.

Bear Valley [SAN BERNARDINO]: *valley*, at Big Bear Lake (1) (lat. 34°15' N, long. 116°54' W). Named on San Gorgonio Mountain (1954) 15' quadrangle, and on Big Bear City (1971) and Moonridge (1970) 7.5' quadrangles. The feature also is named on San Gorgonio (1902) 30' quadrangle, where present Big Bear Lake (1) is called Bear Lake. Don Benito Wilson claimed to have named the valley in 1845 when he and his companions found many bears there (Beattie and Beattie, p. 62-63).

Bear Valley: see **Little Bear Valley**, under **Lake Arrowhead** [SAN BERNARDINO] (1).

Bear Wallow Spring [RIVERSIDE]: *spring*, 8.5 miles northeast of Banning (lat. 34°00'45" N, long. 116°45'45" W; sec. 10, T 2 S, R 2 E). Named on San Gorgonio Mountain (1970) 7.5' quadrangle.

Beatty Well: see **Rock Spring** [SAN BERNARDINO].

Beaumont [RIVERSIDE]: *town*, 6 miles west of Banning (lat. 33°55'45" N, long. 116°58'50" W). Named on Beaumont (1953) 7.5' quadrangle. Postal authorities established San Gargonia post office in 1879, discontinued it in 1881, reestablished it with the name "San Gorgonia" in 1884, and changed the name to Beaumont in 1886 (Salley, p. 194). The town incorporated in 1912. The site was known as San Gorgonio in 1875 before officials of Southern Pacific Railroad changed the name of their station there to Summit; George C. Egan purchased 800 acres of land from the railroad in 1884 and restored the old name, which was used until 1887, when an investment company headed by H.C. Sigler of Beaumont, Texas, bought Egan's holdings and renamed the place for the Texas community (Hanna, p. 28).

Beauty Mountain [RIVERSIDE]: *ridge*, north-northeast-trending, 1 mile long, 21 miles south of Idyllwild (lat. 33°26'35" N, long. 116° 43'15" W). Named on Beauty Mountain (1960) 7.5' quadrangle.

Beauty Peak [RIVERSIDE]: *peak*, 21 miles south of Idyllwild (lat. 33°26'20" N, long. 116°43'25" W; near NE cor. sec. 36, T 8 S, R 2 E); the peak is the high point on Beauty Mountain. Altitude 5548 feet. Named on Beauty Mountain (1960) 7.5' quadrangle. Ramona (1903) 30' quadrangle has the name "Beauty Mt." for the peak.

Beck Spring [SAN BERNARDINO]: *spring*, 46 miles northwest of Ivanpah (lat. 35°47' N, long. 115°55'55" W; near E line sec. 31, T 20 N, R 10 E). Named on Horse Thief Springs (1956) 15' quadrangle. The name is for William Beck, a prospector (Palmer, p. 11).

Bedford Canyon [RIVERSIDE]: *canyon*, nearly 5 miles long, opens into lowlands 5 miles southeast of Corona (lat. 33°49' N, long. 117°31' W; near NE cor. sec. 20, T 4 S, R 6 W). Named on Corona South (1967) 7.5' quadrangle, which shows a Butterfield Overland stage station historical marker near the mouth of the canyon. The name "Bedford" commemorates Thomas Jefferson Bedford, who ran the stage station from 1869 until 1872 (Gunther, p. 46-47).

Bedford Peak [RIVERSIDE]: *peak*, 7.5 miles south of Corona on Riverside-Orange County line (lat. 33°46' N, long. 117°34'40" W); the peak is at the head of Bedford Canyon. Named on Corona South (1967) 7.5' quadrangle.

Bedford Wash [RIVERSIDE]: *stream*, flows 5.5 miles to Temescal Canyon 5 miles southeast of Corona (lat. 33°49'20" N, long. 117° 30'35" W; sec. 16, T 4 S, R 6 W); the stream drains Bedford Canyon. Named on Corona South (1967) 7.5' quadrangle.

Bedrock Spring [SAN BERNARDINO]: *spring*, 9.5 miles northeast of the village of Red Mountain (lat. 35°27'25" N, long. 117°30'10" W; near W line sec. 31, T 28 S, R 42 E). Named on Klinker Mountain (1967) 7.5' quadrangle.

Bee Canyon [RIVERSIDE]: *canyon*, drained by a stream that flows 1.25 miles to San Jacinto River 7.5 miles east of Hemet (lat. 33°44'30" N, long. 116°50'15" W; near NW cor. sec. 13, T 5 S, R 1 E). Named on Banning (1956) and Hemet (1957) 15' quadrangles.

Beecher Canyon [SAN BERNARDINO]: *canyon*, drained by a stream that flows 4 miles to lowlands 22 miles northwest of Essex (lat. 34° 59'30" N, long. 115°27'45" W; near W line sec. 35, T 11 N, R 14 E). Named on Colton Well (1956) and Mid Hills (1955) 15' quadrangles.

Beechers Corners: see **Kramer Junction** [SAN BERNARDINO].

Beecher Spring: see **Cooks Well** [SAN BERNARDINO].

Bee Wash [IMPERIAL]: *stream*, flows 5.5 miles to lowlands along Colorado River 4.25 miles west of Bard (lat. 32°47'10" N, long. 114°37'40" W; sec. 11, T 16 S, R 22 E). Named on Araz (1964) 7.5' quadrangle.

Belardes Potrero [RIVERSIDE]: *area*, 4 miles south-southwest of Sitton Peak (lat. 33°31'35" N, long. 117°28'45" W; sec. 26, T 7 S, R 6 W). Named on Sitton Peak (1954) 7.5' quadrangle.

Belfast: see **Crucero** [SAN BERNARDINO].

Belle Campground [RIVERSIDE]: *locality*, 31 miles east-northeast of Garnet (lat. 34°00'10" N, long. 116°01'05" W). Named on Queen Mountain (1972) 7.5' quadrangle.

Belleville [SAN BERNARDINO]: *locality*, 4 miles northeast of Fawnskin (lat. 34°18' N, long. 116°53' W; sec. 33, T 3 N, R 1 E). Site named on Fawnskin (1971) 7.5' quadrangle. According to tradition, Betsy Van Dusen made a flag for the first Fourth-of-July celebration at the mining camp and the residents then called the place Belleville for Betsy's little daughter Belle (La Fuze, p. 56).

Bell Mountain [RIVERSIDE]: *peak*, 9.5 miles south-southeast of Perris (lat. 33°39'35" N, long. 117°09'05" W; near SW cor. sec. 12, T 6 S, R 3 W). Named on Romoland (1953) 7.5' quadrangle.

Bell Mountain [SAN BERNARDINO]:

(1) *hill*, 5 miles northeast of Victorville (lat. 34°35' N, long. 117° 13' W; sec. 29, T 6 N, R 3 W). Altitude 3896 feet. Named on Apple Valley North (1970) 7.5' quadrangle

(2) *locality*, 8 miles northeast of Victorville (lat. 34°37'20" N, long. 117°12'20" W); the place is 3 miles north of Bell Mountain (1). Named on Apple Valley North (1970) and Turtle Valley (1970) 7.5' quadrangles. Postal authorities established Bell Mountain post office in 1953 and discontinued it in 1956 (Salley, p. 18).

Bell Mountain Wash [SAN BERNARDINO]: *stream*, flows 11 miles to Mojave River nearly 2 miles north of Victorville (lat. 34°33'45" N, long. 117°17'55" W; sec. 33, T 6 N, R 4 W); the stream passes just north of Bell Mountain (1). Named on Apple Valley North (1970), Turtle Valley (1970), and Victorville (1956) 7.5' quadrangles.

Belltown [RIVERSIDE]: *locality*, 2 miles north of Riverside (lat. 34° 00'40" N, long. 117°23'10" W). Named on Fontana (1967) 7.5' quadrangle. N.R. Bell filed a subdivision map in 1907 for a community that he named for himself (Gunther, p. 48).

Bellyache Springs [SAN BERNARDINO]: *spring*, 3.5 miles southwest of downtown Big Bear Lake (lat. 34°12'20" N, long. 116°57'15" W; near N line sec. 2, T 1 N, R 1 W). Named on Big Bear Lake (1970) 7.5' quadrangle.

Belvedere Heights [RIVERSIDE]: *locality*, 3.5 miles east of Riverside (lat. 33°59' N, long. 117°18'40" W; sec. 21, T 2 S, R 4 W). Named on Riverside East (1967) 7.5' quadrangle.

Bendel's Corner: see **Valerie** [RIVERSIDE].

Bengal: see **Bolo**, under **Cadiz** [SAN BERNARDINO].

Bennett Wash [SAN BERNARDINO]: *stream* and *dry wash*, extends for 8.5 miles to Colorado River 17 miles east-northeast of Vidal (lat. 34°12'05" N, long. 114°13'35" W; near W line sec. 2, T 1 N, R 26 E). Named on Cross Roads (1959), Parker (1970), and Whipple Wash (1970) 7.5' quadrangles.

Berdoo Camp: see **Berdoo Canyon** [RIVERSIDE].

Berdoo Canyon [RIVERSIDE]: *canyon*, 6 miles long, opens into lowlands 7.25 miles north-northeast of Indio (lat. 33°48'50" N, long. 116°10'15" W; sec. 20, T 4 S, R 8 E). Named on Lost Horse Mountain (1958) 15' quadrangle. Postal authorities established Berdoo Camp post office in Berdoo Canyon in 1934 and discontinued it in 1937; the post office was at a construction camp for the aqueduct that takes Colorado River water to Los Angeles (Salley, p. 19; Wight, p. 12).

Berdoo Canyon: see **West Berdoo Canyon** [RIVERSIDE].

Bergman: see **Aguanga** [RIVERSIDE].

Bernasconi Hills [RIVERSIDE]: *ridge*, northeast-trending, 3.25 miles long, 6 miles northeast of Perris (lat. 33°50'45" N, long. 117°09'15" W). Named on Perris (1967) 7.5' quadrangle. The name is for Bernardo Bernasconi, a landowner in the neighborhood (Gunther, p. 50).

Bernasconi Hot Springs: see **Lakeview Hot Springs** [RIVERSIDE].

Bernasconi Pass [RIVERSIDE]: *pass*, 5.5 miles northeast of Perris (lat. 33°50'25" N, long. 117°09'35" W; sec. 11, T 4 S, R 3 W); the feature is in Bernasconi Hills. Named on Perris (1967) 7.5' quadrangle.

Bernice [IMPERIAL]: *locality*, 1.25 miles south-southeast of Calipatria along Southern Pacific Railroad (lat. 33°06'30" N, long. 115° 30'30" W). Named on Calipatria (1943) 15' quadrangle. Postal authorities established Bernice post office in 1913 and discontinued it in 1914 (Salley, p. 19).

Berry: see **Baker** [SAN BERNARDINO].

Bertha Peak [SAN BERNARDINO]: *peak*, 2.5 miles east-northeast of Fawnskin (lat. 34°17' N, long. 116°53'55" W; sec. 5, T 2 N, R 1 E); the feature is near the west end of Bertha Ridge. Altitude 8201 feet.. Named on Fawnskin (1971) 7.5' quadrangle.

Bertha Ridge [SAN BERNARDINO]: *ridge*, east-trending, 2.5 miles long, 3.5 miles east-northeast of Fawnskin (lat. 34°16'55" N, long. 116°53' W). Named on Big Bear City (1971) and Fawnskin (1971) 7.5' quadrangles.

Bertram [IMPERIAL]: *locality*, 24 miles northwest of Calipatria along Southern Pacific Railroad (lat. 33°22'40" N, long. 115°46'55" W; sec. 24, T 9 S, R 11 E). Named on Durmid (1956) and Durmid SE (1956) 7.5' quadrangles.

Bethune [SAN BERNARDINO]: *locality*, 2 miles south-southwest of present San Bernardino city hall along Pacific Electric Railroad (lat. 34°04'40" N, long. 117°18'20" W). Named on Colton (1943) 7.5' quadrangle.

Betz Beach [RIVERSIDE]: *beach*, less than 2 miles northwest of Salton along Salton Sea (lat. 33°29'35" N, long. 115°54'25" W; sec. 11, T 8 S, R 10 E). Named on Salton (1956) 7.5' quadrangle.

B Hill [SAN BERNARDINO]: *hill*, less than 0.5 mile west-northwest of downtown Barstow (lat. 34°54'05" N, long. 117°02' W; sec. 1, T 9 N, R 2 W). Named on Barstow (1971) 7.5' quadrangle.

Bicycle Lake [SAN BERNARDINO]: *dry lake*, 2.5 miles long, 31 miles west of Baker (lat. 35°16'45" N, long. 116°37'30" W). Named on Tiefort Mountain (1948) 15' quadrangle. The feature also had the name "Garlic Lake" (Thompson, 1929, p. 257).

Big Bear City [SAN BERNARDINO]: *locality*, 28 miles east-northeast of San Bernardino (lat. 34°15'40" N, long. 116°50'55" W); the place is at the east end of Big Bear Lake (1). Named on Big Bear City (1971) 7.5' quadrangle. Postal authorities established Van Dusen post office in 1927, changed the name to Big Bear City in 1928, and moved the post office 0.5 mile south in 1939; the name "Van Dusen" was for Jed Van Dusen, a settler of the 1860's (Salley, p. 21, 230). United States Board on Geographic Names (1989b, p. 1) approved the name "Lone Valley" for a feature, 5.5 miles long, situated 4.5 miles northeast of Big Bear City.

Big Bear Lake [SAN BERNARDINO]:

(1) *lake*, 5 miles long, 23 miles east-northeast of San Bernardino (lat. 34°15'15" N, long. 116°55' W). Named on Big Bear City (1971), Big Bear Lake (1970), and Fawnskin (1971) 7.5' quadrangles. Called Bear Lake on San Gorgonio (1902) 30' quadrangle. Bear Valley Reservoir and Bear Valley Irrigation Company placed a temporary dam in 1883 in Bear Valley and the next year completed a permanent dam there that formed the lake; the word "Big" became attached to the name to distinguish the lake from Little Bear Lake, an early designation of present Lake Arrowhead (Richards).

(2) *town*, 11 miles north-northwest of San Gorgonio Mountain (lat. 34°14'35" N, long. 116°54'35" W); the place is along Big Bear Lake (1). Named on Big Bear Lake (1970), Fawnskin (1971), and Moonridge (1970, photorevised 1988) 7.5' quadrangles. Postal authorities established Big Bear Lake post office in 1938 (Frickstad, p. 138), and the town incorporated in 1980. San Gorgonio (1902) 30' quadrangle shows a community called Pine Lake at the site of present downtown Big Bear Lake (lat. 34°14'15" N, long. 116°54'45" W; on W line sec. 20, T 2 N, R 1 E). Postal authorities established Pinelake post office at a lumber camp in 1891 and discontinued it in 1905 (Salley, p. 172). California Mining Bureau's (1917a) map shows a place called Pine Knot located southeast of Bear Lake (present Big Bear Lake). Postal authorities established Pine Knot post office in 1912, discontinued in it 1913, reestablished it in 1916, and changed the

name to Big Bear Lake in 1938 (Frickstad, p. 144). They established Reservoir post office 38 miles northeast of San Bernardino at a reservoir construction camp in 1892 and discontinued it the same year (Salley, p. 184), and they established Bear Lake post office 5 miles west of Pine Knot at a vacation resort along Big Bear Lake in 1924 and discontinued it in 1931 (Salley, p. 17).

Big Bear Park: see **Sugarloaf** [SAN BERNARDINO] (2).

Big Butch Wash [SAN BERNARDINO]: *stream*, drained by a stream that flows nearly 1.5 miles to Manker Flat 2 miles southeast of Mount San Antonio (lat. 34°15'55" N, long. 117°37'20" W; at N line sec. 16, T 2 N, R 7 W). Named on Telegraph Peak (1956) 7.5' quadrangle.

Big Falls [SAN BERNARDINO]: *waterfall*, 4 miles west-southwest of San Gorgonio Mountain along Falls Creek (lat. 34°05'10" N, long. 116°53'40" W; near E line sec. 17, T 1 S, R 1 E). Named on Forest Falls (1970) 7.5' quadrangle.

Big Falls Campground [SAN BERNARDINO]: *locality*, 4 miles west-southwest of San Gorgonio Mountain in Mill Creek Canyon (lat. 34°04'55" N, long. 116°53'30" W; near W line sec. 16, T 1 S, R 1 E); the place is 1700 feet south-southeast of Big Falls. Named on Forest Falls (1970) 7.5' quadrangle.

Bighorn Basin [SAN BERNARDINO]: *relief feature*, 19 miles north of Amboy (lat. 34°49'40" N, long. 115°41'45" W; sec. 35, T 9 N, R 12 E). Named on Flynn (1956) 15' quadrangle.

Bighorn Canyon [SAN BERNARDINO]: *canyon*, drained by a stream that flows 4.5 miles to lowlands 8 miles southeast of Old Woman Springs (lat. 34°19'25" N, long. 116°35'50" W; near NE cor. sec. 30, T 3 N, R 4 E); the canyon heads at Bighorn Mountains. Named on Bighorn Canyon (1972) 7.5' quadrangle.

Bighorn Mountains [SAN BERNARDINO]: *ridge*, south-southeast-to east-trending, 3 miles long, 7.5 miles southeast of Old Woman Springs (lat. 34°18'20" N, long. 116°37'30" W). Named on Bighorn Canyon (1972) and Rattlesnake Canyon (1972) 7.5' quadrangles.

Bighorn Peak [SAN BERNARDINO]: *peak*, 12 miles north-northeast of Ontario city hall (lat. 34°14' N, long. 117°35'45" W; sec. 27, T 2 N, R 7 W). Altitude 8441 feet. Named on Cucamonga Peak (1966) 7.5' quadrangle.

Big Laguna: see **Temescal** [RIVERSIDE].

Big Maria Mountains [RIVERSIDE]: *range*, 16 miles north of Blythe (lat. 33°50' N, long. 114°38' W). Named on Big Maria Mountains (1951) and Midland (1952) 15' quadrangles, and on Blythe NE (1951) 7.5' quadrangle.

Big Meadows [SAN BERNARDINO]: *area*, 3 miles south-southeast of Sugarloaf Mountain along Santa Ana River (lat. 34°09'25" N, long. 116°47'35" W; sec. 20, T 1 N, R 2 E). Named on Moonridge (1970) 7.5' quadrangle.

Big Morongo Canyon [RIVERSIDE-SAN BERNARDINO]: *canyon*, 4 miles long, on Riverside-San Bernardino County line, opens into Coachella Valley 11 miles north of Palm Springs (lat. 34°00'05" N, long. 116°33'30" W; sec. 15, T 2 S, R 4 E). Named on Morongo Valley (1972) 7.5' quadrangle.

Big Morongo Canyon [SAN BERNARDINO]: *canyon*, 9 miles long, opens into Morongo Valley (1) 2.25 miles north-northeast of downtown Morongo Valley (lat. 34°04'40" N, long. 116°33'55" W; near SE cor. sec. 16, T 1 S, R 4 E). Named on Catclaw Flat (1972), Morongo Valley (1972), and Onyx Peak (1972) 7.5' quadrangles.

Big Morongo Creek [RIVERSIDE-SAN BERNARDINO]: *stream*, heads in San Bernardino County and flows 16 miles through Big Morongo Canyon [SAN BERNARDINO], across Morongo Valley [SAN BERNARDINO] (1), and through Big Morongo Canyon [RIVERSIDE-SAN BERNARDINO] to Big Morongo Wash 11 miles north of Palm Springs in Riverside County (lat. 34°00'05" N, long. 116°33'30" W; sec. 15, T 2 S, R 4 E). Named on Morongo Valley (1972) 7.5' quadrangle.

Big Morongo Wash [RIVERSIDE]: *dry wash*, extends for 3.5 miles from the mouth of Big Morongo Canyon [RIVERSIDE-SAN BERNARDINO] to join Little Morongo Wash and form Morongo Wash 9 miles north of Palm Springs (lat. 33°57'45" N, long. 116°31'35" W; near SW cor. sec. 25, T 2 S, R 4 E). Named on Desert Hot Springs (1955) 7.5' quadrangle.

Big Oaks Canyon [RIVERSIDE-SAN BERNARDINO]: *canyon*, 1.5 miles long, 4.5 miles south-southwest of San Gorgonio Mountain on Riverside-San Bernardino County line (lat. 34°02' N, long. 116° 50'30" W). Named on San Gorgonio Mountain (1970) 7.5' quadrangle.

Big Palm Spring: see **Palm Springs** [RIVERSIDE].

Big Pine Flat [SAN BERNARDINO]: *area*, 7 miles east-southeast of Luna Mountain (lat. 34°19'15" N, long. 117°00'30" W; sec. 20, 29, T 3 N, R 1 W). Named on Butler Peak (1971) and Fawnskin (1971) 7.5' quadrangles. On Deep Creek (1902) 15' quadrangle, the name "Big Pine Flat" applies to a place situated 2.5 miles south-southwest of present Big Pine Flat.

Big Wash [IMPERIAL]: *stream*, heads in San Diego County and flows 8 miles to Salton Sea 4.5 miles north of Truckhaven (lat. 33° 21'40" N, long. 115°58'55" W; near E line sec. 25, T 9 S, R 9 E). Named on Seventeen Palms (1956) 7.5' quadrangle.

Big Wash [RIVERSIDE]:

(1) *stream*, flows 14 miles to Chuckwalla Valley 6.5 miles northwest of Desert Center (lat. 33°47'10" N, long. 115°28' W; sec. 36, T 4 S, R 14 E). Named on Coxcomb Mountains (1963) and Pinto Basin (1963) 15' quadrangles.

(2) *stream*, flows 9.5 miles to Colorado River 23 miles north of Blythe (lat. 33°56'10" N, long. 114°32'05" W; sec. 11, T 3 S, R 23 E). Named on Big Maria Mountains NE (1954) and Vidal (1971) 7.5' quadrangles.

Big Wash [SAN BERNARDINO]: *stream*, flows 10 miles to end 19 miles east-southeast of Essex in Ward Valley (lat. 34°35'30" N, long. 114°58'30" W; sec. 22, T 6 N, R 19 E). Named on Essex (1956) 15' quadrangle.

Billie Mountain [SAN BERNARDINO]: *hill*, 25 miles southeast of Ivanpah (lat. 35°02'50" N, long. 115°03' W; at E line sec. 8, T 11 N, R 18 E). Named on Lanfair Valley (1956) 15' quadrangle.

Billy Goat Mountain [RIVERSIDE]: *peak*, 2.5 miles north of Aguanga (lat. 33°28'45" N, long. 116°51'40" W; sec. 15, T 8 S, R 1 E). Altitude 2921 feet. Named on Aguanga (1954) 7.5' quadrangle.

Biloxi Wash [IMPERIAL]: *stream*, flows nearly 1 mile to Iberia Wash 1.5 miles east-southeast of Truckhaven (lat. 33°17'25" N, long. 115°57'10" W; sec. 20, T 10 S, R 10 E). Named on Truckhaven (1956) 7.5' quadrangle.

Binkley Canyon: see **Mayhew Canyon** [RIVERSIDE].

Binkley's Diggings: see **Cottonwood Canyon** [RIVERSIDE] (3).

Birch Creek [SAN BERNARDINO]: *stream*, flows nearly 3 miles to Oak Glen Creek 9 miles west-southwest of San Gorgonio Mountain (lat. 34°03'15" N, long. 116°58'50" W; at W line sec. 27, T 1 S, R 1 W). Named on Forest Falls (1970) 7.5' quadrangle.

Birch Mountain [SAN BERNARDINO]: *peak*, 7 miles west-southwest of San Gorgonio Mountain (lat. 34°04'35" N, long. 116°56'50" W; near NE cor. sec. 23, T 1 S, R 1 W). Altitude 7826 feet. Named on Forest Falls (1970) 7.5' quadrangle. United States Board on Geographic Names (1964b, p. 13) rejected the name "Allen Peak" for the feature.

Bird Spring [SAN BERNARDINO]: *spring*, 20 miles east-southeast of the village of Red Mountain (lat. 35°11'50" N, long. 117°18'45" W; near NW cor. sec. 31, T 31 S, R 44 E). Named on Fremont Peak (1956) 15' quadrangle.

Bishop Canyon: see **Alberhill** [RIVERSIDE].

Biskra Palms [RIVERSIDE]: *locality*, 12.5 miles east of Cathedral City (lat. 33°47'25" N, long. 116°15'05" W; sec. 28, T 4 S, R 7 E). Named on Myoma (1958) 7.5' quadrangle. The name is from the ancient Algerian town of Biskra, which was the source of some date palms planted in Coachella Valley (Gunther, p. 53).

Bismark [SAN BERNARDINO]: *locality*, 7.25 miles north of Daggett (lat. 34°57'55" N, long. 116°51'35" W; near NE cor. sec. 15, T 10 N, R 1 E). Site named on Yermo (1953) 7.5' quadrangle.

Bitter Spring [SAN BERNARDINO]: *spring*, 20 miles west of Baker (lat. 35°13'40" N, long. 116°25'45" W; at SE cor. sec. 10, T 13 N, R 5 E). Named on Cave Mountain (1948) 15' quadrangle. Thompson (1929, p. 546) identified this spring as almost certainly the feature that Fremont and other early explorers called Agua de Tomaso.

Bitter Water Creek: see **Amargosa River** [SAN BERNARDINO].

Bixby Canyon [RIVERSIDE]: *canyon*, nearly 2 miles long, opens into Temescal Valley 8 miles south-southeast of Corona (lat. 33° 45'55" N, long. 117°30'30" W; sec. 4, T 5 S, R 6 W). Named on Corona South (1967) 7.5' quadrangle. The name recalls Jotham Bixby, who owned the canyon (Gunther, p. 54).

Blackburn [SAN BERNARDINO]: *locality*, 20 miles south-southeast of Ivanpah (lat. 35°04'30" N, long. 115°10' W). Named on Ivanpah (1912) 1° quadrangle.

Blackburn Canyon [RIVERSIDE]: *canyon*, drained by a stream that flows 4 miles to Bautista Creek 8 miles east-southeast of Hemet (lat. 33°41'45" N, long. 116°51' W; sec. 35, T 5 S, R 1 E). Named on Hemet (1957) 15' quadrangle. The name is for Fred Abner Blackburn, whose homestead was at and near the mouth of the canyon (Gunther, p. 56).

Black Butte [RIVERSIDE]: *peak*, 11 miles south-southeast of Desert Center (lat. 33°33'45" N, long. 115°20'40" W). Altitude 4504 feet. Named on Chuckwalla Mountains (1963) 15' quadrangle.

Black Butte [SAN BERNARDINO]: *hill*, nearly 2 miles north of Newberry (lat. 34°51'15" N, long. 116°41'30" W; sec. 20, T 9 N, R 3 E). Altitude 1978 feet. Named on Newberry (1955) 15' quadrangle.

Black Canyon [SAN BERNARDINO]:

(1) *canyon*, 2 miles long, 16 miles south-southwest of Ivanpah (lat. 35°07'15" N, long. 115°24'10" W; sec. 18, T 12 N, R 15 E). Named on Mid Hills (1955) 15' quadrangle.

(2) *canyon*, 4.5 miles long, opens into lowlands 25 miles southeast of the village of Red Mountain (lat. 35°08' N, long. 117°15'40" W; near E line sec. 21, T 32 S, R 44 E); the canyon is northwest of Black Mountain (4). Named on Fremont Peak (1956) and Opal Mountain (1955) 15' quadrangles.

Black Canyon: see **Dark Canyon** [RIVERSIDE].

Black Canyon Wash [SAN BERNARDINO]: *stream*, flows 22 miles from the mouth of Black Canyon (1) to end 7.5 miles north-northwest of Essex (lat. 34°50'30" N, long. 115°16'45" W; sec. 26, T 9 N, R 16 E). Named on Colton Well (1956) and Mid Hills (1955) 15' quadrangles.

Black Eagle Well [RIVERSIDE]: *well,* 18 miles north-northwest of Desert Center (lat. 33°56'35" N, long. 115°33'40" W; near NE cor. sec. 1, T 3 S, R 13 E). Named on Pinto Basin (1963) 15' quadrangle.

Blackhawk Canyon [SAN BERNARDINO]: *canyon,* drained by a stream that heads at Blackhawk Mountain and flows 1.5 miles to lowlands 7.25 miles north-northeast of Big Bear City (lat. 34°21'35" N, long. 116°47'45" W; sec. 8, T 3 N, R 2 E). Named on Big Bear City (1971) 7.5' quadrangle.

Blackhawk Mountain [SAN BERNARDINO]: *ridge,* west- to northwest-trending, 2.25 miles long, 5.5 miles north-northeast of Big Bear City (lat. 34°20'15" N, long. 116°48'45" W). Named on Big Bear City (1971) 7.5' quadrangle.

Blackhawk Well [SAN BERNARDINO]: *well,* 5.5 miles east-southeast of the village of Red Mountain (lat. 35°19'40" N, long. 117° 31'30" W; near E line sec. 13, T 30 N, R 41 E). Named on Red Mountain (1967) 7.5' quadrangle.

Black Hill [RIVERSIDE]:

(1) *peak,* 6.5 miles south-southwest of Palm Desert (lat. 33°37'40" N, long. 116°24'40" W; near SE cor. sec. 24, T 6 S, R 5 E). Altitude 3689 feet. Named on Rancho Mirage (1957) 7.5' quadrangle.

(2) *hill,* 15 miles north-northwest of Blythe (lat. 33°48'40" N, long. 114°42'05" W). Altitude 1225 feet. Named on Big Maria Mountains SW (1971) 7.5' quadrangle.

Black Hill [SAN BERNARDINO]: *ridge,* west- to southwest-trending, 2.5 miles long, 10 miles north-northeast of downtown Morongo Valley (lat. 34°10'40" N, long. 116°30' W). Named on Rimrock (1972) and Yucca Valley North (1972) 7.5' quadrangles.

Black Hills [IMPERIAL]: *range,* 28 miles north of Glamis (lat. 33° 23'15" N, long. 115°02'40" W). Named on Chuckwalla Spring (1953) 15' quadrangle.

Black Hills [RIVERSIDE]: *ridge,* northeast-trending, 1.5 miles long, 15 miles south of Hemet (lat. 33°31'40" N, long. 116°58'20" W; on N line sec. 34, T 7 S, R 1 W). Named on Sage (1954) 7.5' quadrangle.

Black Hills [SAN BERNARDINO]: *ridge,* north-trending, 7.5 miles long, 17 miles east of the village of Red Mountain (lat. 35°23'30" N, long. 117°18'30" W). Named on Cuddeback Lake (1954) 15' quadrangle.

Black Lava Butte [SAN BERNARDINO]: *ridge,* south-southwest-trending, 2.5 miles long, 8 miles north-northwest of Yucca Valley (lat. 34°13'45" N, long. 116°30' W). Named on Rimrock (1972) and Yucca Valley North (1972) 7.5' quadrangles.

Black Meadow Landing [SAN BERNARDINO]: *locality,* 24 miles northeast of Vidal along Lake Havasu (lat. 34°21'05" N, long. 114° 11'55" W; sec. 13, T 3 N, R 26 E). Named on Gene Wash (1959) 7.5' quadrangle.

Black Metal Wash [SAN BERNARDINO]: *stream* and *dry wash,* extends for 4.5 miles to Lake Havasu 24 miles northeast of Vidal (lat. 34°21'05" N, long. 114°11'45" W; sec. 13, T 3 N, R 26 E). Named on Gene Wash (1959) 7.5' quadrangle.

Black Mountain [IMPERIAL]: *ridge,* northwest-trending, 4 miles long, 14 miles east-northeast of Glamis (lat. 33°04' N, long. 114° 50'45" W). Named on Quartz Peak (1953) 15' quadrangle.

Black Mountain [RIVERSIDE]:

(1) *ridge,* generally northeast-trending, 2.25 miles long, 4 miles west-northwest of San Jacinto Peak (lat. 33°50'15" N, long. 116° 44'30" W). Named on Lake Fulmor (1956) and San Jacinto Peak (1981) 7.5' quadrangles.

(2) *peak,* 13 miles east-northeast of Murrieta (lat. 33°37'10" N, long. 117°00'05" W). Altitude 3040 feet. Named on Bachelor Mountain (1953) and Sage (1954) 7.5' quadrangles.

Black Mountain [SAN BERNARDINO]:

(1) *hill,* 20 miles west of Victorville (lat. 34°35'30" N, long. 117° 38'35" W; mainly in sec. 20, T 6 N, R 7 W). Altitude 3425 feet. Named on El Mirage (1956) 7.5' quadrangle.

(2) *range,* 19 miles south-southwest of Barstow (lat. 34°38'10" N, long. 117°07'15" W). Named on Apple Valley North (1970), Fairview Valley (1970), Stoddard Well (1970), and Turtle Valley (1970) 7.5' quadrangles.

(3) *peak,* 13 miles north of downtown Morongo Valley (lat. 34°13'55" N, long. 116°35'15" W; on N line sec. 29, T 2 N, R 4 E). Altitude 6149 feet. Named on Rimrock (1972) 7.5' quadrangle.

(4) *mountain,* 26 miles east-southeast of the village of Red Mountain (lat. 35°08'30" N, long. 117°14' W). Named on Fremont Peak (1956) and Opal Mountain (1955) 15' quadrangles.

Black Mountain: see **Ibex Hills** [SAN BERNARDINO].

Black Mountain Camp [RIVERSIDE]: *locality,* nearly 4 miles west-northwest of San Jacinto Peak (lat. 33°50' N, long. 116°44'25" W; near E line sec. 11, T 4 S, R 2 E); the place is by present Black Mountain (1). Named on Palm Springs (1957) 15' quadrangle.

Black Mountain Creek [RIVERSIDE]: *stream,* flows nearly 1 mile to North Fork San Jacinto River 11 miles east of San Jacinto (lat. 33°47'30" N, long. 116°45'55" W; sec. 27, T 4 S, R 2 E); the stream heads at Black Mountain (1). Named on Lake Fulmor (1956) 7.5' quadrangle.

Black Mountains: see **Dead Mountains** [SAN BERNARDINO]; **Ibex Hills** [SAN BERNARDINO].

Black Point [RIVERSIDE]: *promontory,* 11 miles north-northeast of Blythe along Colorado River (lat. 33°45'15" N, long. 114°31' W; at W line sec. 7, T 5 S, R 24 E). Named on Big Maria Mountains SE (1955) 7.5' quadrangle.

Black Rabbit Canyon [RIVERSIDE]: *canyon,* drained by a stream that flows 4.5 miles to Martinez Canyon 14 miles south of Palm Desert (lat. 33°31' N, long. 116°21' W; near W line sec. 34, T 7 S, R 6 E). Named on Palm Desert (1959) 15' quadrangle.

Black Rabbit Canyon: see **Martinez Canyon** [RIVERSIDE].

Black Ridge [SAN BERNARDINO]: *ridge,* northwest-trending, 2.5 miles long, 8.5 miles north-northwest of Bagdad (lat. 34°41'30" N, long. 115°57' W). Named on Bagdad (1956) 15' quadrangle.

Black Rock Canyon [SAN BERNARDINO]: *canyon,* drained by a stream that flows 2.25 miles to lowlands 4.5 miles southeast of Yucca Valley (lat. 34°04'30" N, long. 116°23'10" W; near NW cor. sec. 20, T 1 S, R 6 E). Named on Yucca Valley South (1972) 7.5' quadrangle.

Black Rocks [RIVERSIDE]: *relief feature,* 3.25 miles north-northwest of Estelle Mountain (lat. 33°48'35" N, long. 117°26'35" W; sec. 19, T 4 S, R 5 W). Named on Lake Mathews (1967) 7.5' quadrangle.

Black Rock Spring [SAN BERNARDINO]: *spring,* 5.25 miles south-southeast of Yucca Valley (lat. 34°03'25" N, long. 116°23'45" W; sec. 30, T 1 S, R 6 E); the spring is in Black Rock Canyon. Named on Yucca Valley South (1972) 7.5' quadrangle.

Black's Well: see **Harper Lake** [SAN BERNARDINO].

Black Tank [SAN BERNARDINO]: *water feature,* 24 miles west of Ivanpah (lat. 35°17'15" N, long. 115°43'40" W; sec. 20, T 14 N, R 12 E). Named on Mescal Range (1955) 15' quadrangle.

Blackwater Well [SAN BERNARDINO]: *well,* 15 miles east of the village of Red Mountain (lat. 35°21'30" N, long. 117°20'45" W; near NW cor. sec. 2, T 30 S, R 43 E). Named on Cuddeback Lake (1954) 15' quadrangle. Soldiers dug the well (Mendenhall, 1908a, p. 52).

Blaisdell Canyon [RIVERSIDE]: *canyon,* drained by a stream that flows 2.5 miles to lowlands 5.25 miles northwest of Palm Springs (lat. 33°53' N, long. 116°37' W; near E line sec. 25, T 3 S, R 3 E). Named on Desert Hot Springs (1955), Palm Springs (1957), and San Jacinto Peak (1981) 7.5' quadrangles. The misspelled name is for E.S. Blasdell, who was in the vicinity as early as 1894 (Gunther, p. 57).

Blake: see **Goffs** [SAN BERNARDINO].

Blake Hill: see **Mecca** [RIVERSIDE].

Blanca: see **Casa Blanca** [RIVERSIDE].

Blankenship Bend [SAN BERNARDINO]: *bend,* 20 miles south-southeast of Needles along Colorado River on California-Arizona State line (lat. 34°35'45" N, long. 114°26'05" W; sec. 23, 26, T 6 N, R 24 E). Named on Castle Rock (1970) 7.5' quadrangle.

Bledsoe Gulch [SAN BERNARDINO]: *gully,* 1.5 miles long, 4.5 miles north of Redlands city hall (lat. 34°07'15" N, long. 117°10'20" W). Named on Redlands (1967) 7.5' quadrangle.

Blind Canyon [RIVERSIDE]: *canyon,* 1 mile long, 15 miles north of Cathedral City (lat. 33°59'30" N, long. 116°29'50" W; sec. 18, 19, T 2 S, R 5 E). Named on Desert Hot Springs (1955) and Seven Palms Valley (1958) 7.5' quadrangles.

Blind Hills [SAN BERNARDINO]: *ridge,* north-trending, 2.25 miles long, 9 miles northwest of Essex (lat. 34°50'30" N, long. 115°20'45" W; sec. 19, 30, 31, T 9 N, R 16 E). Named on Colton Well (1956) 15' quadrangle.

Blind Spring [SAN BERNARDINO]: *spring,* 28 miles north-northeast of Amboy (lat. 34°55'20" N, long. 115°31'15" W; near S line sec. 28, T 10 N, R 14 E). Named on Flynn (1956) 15' quadrangle.

Blodgett Flat [RIVERSIDE]: *area,* 1.5 miles south-southwest of the center of Idyllwild (lat. 33°43'05" N, long. 116°43'45" W). Named on Idyllwild (1959) 15' quadrangle.

Bloomington [SAN BERNARDINO]: *town,* 3.25 miles southeast of Fontana city hall (lat. 34°04'15" N, long. 117°23'30" W). Named on Fontana (1967) 7.5' quadrangle. Postal authorities established Bloomington post office in 1892 (Frickstad, p. 138). Semi-Tropic Land and Water Company subdivided the place in 1888; Eugene Weston, an official of the company, named the community for the profusion of wildflowers there (Hanna, p. 35).

Blue Angels Peak: see **Smugglers Cave** [IMPERIAL].

Blue Chalcedony Spring [SAN BERNARDINO]: *spring,* 26 miles southeast of Trona (lat. 35°28'20" N, long. 117°04'55" W). Named on Pilot Knob (1954) 15' quadrangle.

Blue Cut [SAN BERNARDINO]:

(1) *relief feature,* 2.5 miles south of Cajon in Cajon Canyon (lat. 34°15'50" N, long. 117°28' W; near NW cor. sec. 13, T 2 N, R 6 W). Named on Cajon (1956) 7.5' quadrangle.

(2) *relief feature,* 15 miles north-northwest of downtown Morongo Valley (lat. 34°14'45" N, long. 116°40'30" W; sec. 21, T 2 N, R 3 E). Named on Onyx Peak (1972) 7.5' quadrangle.

Blue Cut: see **The Blue Cut** [RIVERSIDE].

Bluegill Island [SAN BERNARDINO]: *island,* 300 feet long, 24 miles northeast of Vidal in Lake Havasu (lat. 34°20'40" N, long. 114°10'55" W; sec.

18, T 3 N, R 27 E). Named on Gene Wash (1959) 7.5' quadrangle.

Blue Jay [SAN BERNARDINO]: *village,* 6.25 miles north-northwest of Harrison Mountain (lat. 34°14'45" N, long. 117°12'30" W; near E line sec. 20, T 2 N, R 3 W). Named on Harrison Mountain (1967) 7.5' quadrangle. Postal authorities established Blue Jay post office in 1924 (Frickstad, p. 138).

Blue Jay Bay [SAN BERNARDINO]: *embayment,* 7.25 miles south-southwest of Luna Mountain along Lake Arrowhead (1) (lat. 34° 15'10" N, long. 117°11'45" W; near S line sec. 16, T 2 N, R 3 W). Named on Lake Arrowhead (1971) 7.5' quadrangle.

Blue Jay Canyon [SAN BERNARDINO]: *canyon,* drained by a stream that flows less than 1 mile to Little Bear Creek 6.25 miles north-northwest of Harrison Mountain (lat. 34°14'50" N, long. 117°12'25" W); the mouth of the canyon is at Blue Jay. Named on Harrison Mountain (1967) 7.5' quadrangle.

Blue Lake: see **El Centro** [IMPERIAL].

Blue Mountain [IMPERIAL]: *ridge,* northwest-trending, 2.5 miles long, 25 miles east-northeast of Calipatria (lat. 33°14'30" N, long. 115°06'15" W). Named on Acolita (1953) and Chuckwalla Spring (1953) 15' quadrangles.

Blue Mountain [SAN BERNARDINO]: *peak,* 5.5 miles south of San Bernardino city hall (lat. 34°01'20" N, long. 117°17'45" W; on E line sec. 4, T 2 S, R 4 W). Named on San Bernardino South (1967) 7.5' quadrangle.

Blue Ridge [SAN BERNARDINO]: *ridge,* generally east-trending, 1.5 miles long, 3 miles north-northeast of Mount San Antonio (lat. 34° 19'40" N, long. 117°37' W). Named on Telegraph Peak (1956) 7.5' quadrangle.

Bluewater Canyon [RIVERSIDE]: *canyon,* drained by a stream that flows 4 miles to San Mateo Canyon 4.25 miles south-southeast of Sitton Peak (lat. 33°31'35" N, long. 117°25'30" W). Named on Sitton Peak (1954) 7.5' quadrangle.

Bluff Lake [SAN BERNARDINO]: *lake,* 1150 feet long, 3.5 miles west-southwest of downtown Big Bear Lake along Siberia Creek (lat. 34°13'10" N, long. 116°58'05" W; sec. 34, T 2 N, R 1 W). Named on Big Bear Lake (1970) 7.5' quadrangle.

Bly [RIVERSIDE]: *locality,* inhabited place 6.5 miles west of present Riverside city hall (lat. 34°59'30" N, long. 117°29'30" W). Named on Riverside (1943) 15' quadrangle. United States Geological Survey's (1942b) map shows a railroad junction called Bly located just northeast of the inhabited place of the same name. San Pedro, Los Angeles and Salt Lake Railroad ran a spur line in 1903 or 1904 to Bly Brothers and McGilliard Stone Company quarries in Jurupa Mountains, and railroad officials gave the name "Bly" to the junction of the spur with the main line (Gunther, p. 58). California Mining Bureau's (1917b) map has the name "Bly Jc." for the rail connection.

Blythe [RIVERSIDE]: *town,* 160 miles east of Riverside (lat. 33°36'35" N, long. 114°35'45" W; in and near sec. 32, T 6 S, R 23 E). Named on Blythe (1951) 7.5' quadrangle. Postal authorities established Blythe post office in 1882, discontinued it the same year, reestablished it in 1883, discontinued it in 1884, and reestablished it in 1908 (Salley, p. 23). The town incorporated in 1916. The name commemorates Thomas H. Blythe, who was involved in development of irrigation of Palo Verde Valley in the 1870's and 1880's (Gunther, p. 59).

Blythe: see **East Blythe** [RIVERSIDE]; **Harvard** [SAN BERNARDINO].

Blythe Junction: see **Rice** [SAN BERNARDINO].

B Mountain: see **Lone Butte** [SAN BERNARDINO].

Bobcat Canyon [SAN BERNARDINO]: *canyon,* 1 mile long, 10 miles northeast of Victorville (lat. 34°38'35" N, long. 117°10'20" W; sec. 2, 3, T 6 N, R 3 W). Named on Turtle Valley (1970) 7.5' quadrangle.

Bobcat Hills [SAN BERNARDINO]: *hills,* 19 miles south-southeast of Ivanpah (lat. 35°05'20" N, long. 115°09'15" W; mainly in sec. 28, T 12 N, R 17 E). Named on Lanfair Valley (1956) 15' quadrangle.

Bobo Springs Reservoir [SAN BERNARDINO]: *water feature,* 14 miles north-northeast of downtown Morongo Valley (lat. 34°14'20" N, long. 116°30'05" W). Named on Morongo Valley (1955) 15' quadrangle.

Bolo: see **Cadiz** [SAN BERNARDINO].

Bombay: see **Cadiz** [SAN BERNARDINO].

Bombay Beach [IMPERIAL]: *beach,* 4 miles west-southwest of Frink along Salton Sea (lat. 33°20'55" N, long. 115°43' W; sec. 33, 34, T 9 S, R 12 E). Named on Frink (1956) 7.5' quadrangle.

Bonanza King Well [SAN BERNARDINO]: *well,* 22 miles northwest of Essex (lat. 34°59' N, long. 115°29'50" W; near SW cor. sec. 33, T 11 N, R 14 E). Named on Colton Well (1956) 15' quadrangle. Workers of Bonanza King mining company dug the well, which also was known as Providence Well (Mendenhall, 1909a, p. 66). A community called Providence was located just east of Bonanza King mine in the 1880's (Lorey, p. 29). Postal authorities established Providence post office in 1882 and discontinued it in 1892 (Salley, p. 178).

Bonanza Spring [SAN BERNARDINO]: *spring,* 9.5 miles west-southwest of Essex (lat. 34°41' N, long. 115°24' W; sec. 22, T 7 N, R 15 E); the spring is 5 miles northwest of Danby. Named on Danby (1956) 15' quadrangle. The feature also was known as Danby Spring; locomotives used water carried by pipeline from the spring to Danby (Thompson, 1929, p. 688).

Bonds Corner [IMPERIAL]: *locality,* 9 miles east of Calexico (lat. 32°41'35" N, long. 115°20'10" W; at N line sec. 9, T 17 S, R 16 E). Named on Bonds Corner (1957) 7.5' quadrangle. Postal authorities established Bonds Corner post office in 1929 and discontinued it in 1930; the name was for Dr. J.L. Bond, a homesteader (Salley, p. 24).

Boneyard Canyon [SAN BERNARDINO]: *canyon,* on San Bernardino-Los Angeles County line, drained by a stream that flows 1.25 miles to lowlands 9.5 miles north of Mount San Antonio (lat. 34° 25'30" N, long. 117°39'25" W; near SW cor. sec. 18, T 4 N, R 7 W). Named on Mescal Creek (1956) 7.5' quadrangle.

Bonita Falls [SAN BERNARDINO]: *waterfall,* 14 miles north-northeast of Ontario city hall along a tributary to South Fork Lytle Creek (lat. 34°13'45" N, long. 117°30'15" W; near W line sec. 27, T 2 N, R 6 W). Named on Cucamonga Peak (1966) 7.5' quadrangle.

Bonnie Bell [RIVERSIDE]: *locality,* 9.5 miles northwest of Palm Springs along Whitewater River (lat. 33°56'55" N, long. 116°38'30" W; at S line sec. 35, T 2 S, R 3 E). Named on Whitewater (1955) 7.5' quadrangle.

Borate: see **Yermo** [SAN BERNARDINO].

Borax Flat [SAN BERNARDINO]: *area,* 3 miles east-northeast of Trona at the north end of Searles Lake (lat. 35°46'30" N, long. 117°19'30" W; in and near sec. 10, 11, T 25 S, R 43 E). Named on Trona (1949) 15' quadrangle.

Borax Flat: see **Searles Lake** [SAN BERNARDINO].

Borax Lake: see **Searles Lake** [SAN BERNARDINO].

Borea Canyon [SAN BERNARDINO]: *canyon,* drained by a stream that flows 1.5 miles to lowlands 5 miles west of Harrison Mountain (lat. 34°10' N, long. 117°14'35" W; near SE cor. sec. 13, T 1 N, R 4 W). Named on Harrison Mountain (1967) 7.5' quadrangle.

Borosolvay [SAN BERNARDINO]: *locality,* 2.5 miles southwest of Trona (lat. 35°44'05" N, long. 117°24' W; near NW cor. sec. 30, T 25 N, R 43 E). Site named on Westend (1973) 7.5' quadrangle. Postal authorities established Borosolvay post office in 1917 and discontinued it in 1921 (Frickstad, p. 139). Pacific Coast Borax Company and Solvay Process Company started the community in 1916 and named it for the two firms (Gudde, 1949, p. 38).

Borrego Valley: see **Lower Borrego Valley** [IMPERIAL].

Boulder Bay [SAN BERNARDINO]:

(1) *embayment,* 2.5 miles west of downtown Big Bear Lake along Big Bear Lake (1) (lat. 34°14'25" N, long. 116°57'15" W; sec. 23, T 2 N, R 1 W). Named on Big Bear Lake (1970) 7.5' quadrangle.

(2) *district,* 2 miles west of downtown Big Bear Lake (lat. 34°14'20" N, long. 116°56'45" W; sec. 23, 24, T 2 N, R 1 W); the place is at Boulder Bay (1). Named on Big Bear Lake (1970) 7.5' quadrangle.

Boulder Canyon [RIVERSIDE]: *canyon,* 0.5 mile long, 13 miles east-northeast of Chiriaco Summit (lat. 33°43'40" N, long. 115°30'40" W; at N line sec. 22, T 5 S, R 14 E). Named on Hayfield (1963) 15' quadrangle.

Boulder Creek [IMPERIAL]: *stream,* flows nearly 5 miles, partly in San Diego County, to Myer Creek 11 miles south-southwest of Carrizo Mountain (lat. 32°40'20" N, long. 116°04'30" W; sec. 21, T 17 S, R 9 E). Named on In-Ko-Pah Gorge (1959) 7.5' quadrangle.

Boulder Park [IMPERIAL]: *locality,* 12.5 miles south-southwest of Carrizo Mountain (lat. 32°39'30" N, long. 116°06' W; sec. 30, T 17 S, R 9 E); the place is near Boulder Creek. Named on In-Ko-Pah Gorge (1959) 7.5' quadrangle.

Boundary Canyon [RIVERSIDE]: *canyon,* drained by a stream that flows nearly 2 miles to Grape Canyon 11 miles northeast of Banning (lat. 34°01'35" N, long. 116°43'05" W; at W line sec. 6, T 2 S, R 3 E); a national forest boundary line follows the canyon. Named on Catclaw Flat (1972) 7.5' quadrangle.

Bousic Canyon [SAN BERNARDINO]: *canyon,* drained by a stream that flows 1.5 miles to lowlands 7 miles north-northeast of Fawnskin (lat. 34°22' N, long. 116°54'45" W; at S line sec. 6, T 3 N, R 1 E). Named on Fawnskin (1971) 7.5' quadrangle.

Bow Canyon [SAN BERNARDINO]: *canyon,* 2 miles long, 2.5 miles northwest of Sugarloaf Mountain (lat. 34°13'25" N, long. 116°50'50" W). Named on Moonridge (1970) 7.5' quadrangle.

Bowden Flat [SAN BERNARDINO]: *area,* 11 miles north-northeast of downtown Morongo Valley (lat. 34°11'55" N, long. 116°31'15" W). Named on Rimrock (1972) 7.5' quadrangle.

Bowers: see **San Jacinto** [RIVERSIDE].

Bowmans Wash [SAN BERNARDINO]: *stream* and *dry wash,* extends for 9 miles to Colorado River 18 miles east-northeast of Vidal (lat. 34°12'45" N, long. 114°12'40" W; sec. 35, T 2 N, R 26 E). Named on Cross Roads (1959), Parker (1970), and Whipple Wash (1970) 7.5' quadrangles.

Box Canyon [RIVERSIDE]: *canyon,* 7 miles long, opens into lowlands 5 miles northwest of Mortmar (lat. 33°34'50" N, long. 115° 59' W; sec. 7, T 7 S, R 10 E). Named on Mortmar (1958) 7.5' quadrangle.

Box Canyon [SAN BERNARDINO]: *canyon,* 4 miles long, opens into lowlands 10 miles east-southeast of Newberry (lat. 34°44'45" N, long. 116°32'30" W; near NE cor. sec. 34, T 8 N, R 4 E). Named on Rodman

Mountains (1955) 15' quadrangle.

Box Canyon Wash [RIVERSIDE]: *stream,* flows 5.25 miles from the mouth of Box Canyon to Salton Sea 19 miles southeast of Indio (lat. 33°31'05" N, long. 116°00'30" W; on W line sec. 36, T 7 S, R 9 E). Named on Cottonwood Spring (1943) 15' quadrangle, and on Mecca (1955) 7.5' quadrangle. Mortmar (1958) 7.5' quadrangle shows the stream diverted into a canal before it reaches Salton Sea.

Box Springs [RIVERSIDE]:

(1) *locality,* 5 miles east-southeast of Riverside city hall (lat. 33° 56'45" N, long. 117°17'45" W; at SE cor. sec. 33, T 2 S, R 4 W). Named on Riverside East (1967) 7.5' quadrangle. United States Board on Geographic Names (1975a, p. 9) approved the name "Cassina Springs" for a feature situated about 2.5 miles north of Box Springs (1) (sec. 22, T 2 S, R 4 W).

(2) *locality,* 6 miles southeast of Riverside city hall along Atchison, Topeka and Santa Fe Railroad (lat. 33°55'55" N, long. 117°17'20" W; at S line sec. 3, T 3 S, R 4 W); the place is 1 mile south-southeast of Box Springs (1). Named on Riverside East (1967) 7.5' quadrangle. Called Box Springs Siding on Riverside East (1953) 7.5' quadrangle.

Box Springs: see **Edgemont** [RIVERSIDE].

Box Springs Canyon [RIVERSIDE]: *canyon,* 2.25 miles long, 4 miles east-southeast of Riverside city hall (lat. 33°57'25" N, long. 117°18'30" W); Box Springs (1) is at the upper end of the canyon. Named on Riverside West (1967) 7.5' quadrangle.

Box Springs Mountains [RIVERSIDE]: *range,* 4.5 miles east of Riverside city hall (lat. 33°59' N, long. 117°17'15" W); the range is north of Box Springs (1). Named on Riverside East (1967) and San Bernardino South (1967) 7.5' quadrangles.

Box Springs Siding: see **Box Springs** [RIVERSIDE] (2).

Box S Springs [SAN BERNARDINO]: *springs,* 5.5 miles southeast of the town of Lucerne Valley (lat. 34°23'10" N, long. 116°52'40" W; at S line sec. 33, T 4 N, R 1 E). Named on Lucerne Valley (1971) 7.5' quadrangle. San Gorgonio (1902) 30' quadrangle shows Box S ranch at the site of the present town of Lucerne Valley.

Bradley Canyon [RIVERSIDE]: *canyon,* nearly 1 mile long, opens into lowlands 2.25 miles southeast of Cathedral City (lat. 33°45'15" N, long. 116°26'15" W; sec. 11, T 5 S, R 5 E). Named on Cathedral City (1958) and Rancho Mirage (1957) 7.5' quadrangles.

Bradtmoore: see **Heber** [IMPERIAL].

Brant [SAN BERNARDINO]: *locality,* 6 miles southwest of Ivanpah along Union Pacific Railroad (lat. 35°17'30" N, long. 115°22'15" W; near SW cor. sec. 15, T 14 N, R 15 E). Named on Ivanpah (1956) 15' quadrangle.

Braton Peak: see **Barker Peak** [RIVERSIDE].

Brawley [IMPERIAL]: *town,* 13 miles north of El Centro (lat. 32°58'45" N, long. 115°32' W). Named on Brawley (1957) 7.5' quadrangle. Postal authorities established Brawley post office in 1903 (Frickstad, p. 48), and the the town incorporated in 1908. Officers of Imperial Land Company had the town laid out in 1902 and called it Braly, for J.H. Braly, who had owned the property; after Braly refused permission to use his name, A.H. Heber, general manager of the company, suggested the name "Brawley" to honor one of Heber's friends (Gudde, 1949, p. 39).

Brea Canyon: see **Tonner Canyon** [SAN BERNARDINO].

Breakneck Creek [SAN BERNARDINO]: *stream,* flows 2.25 miles to Santa Ana River 3.25 miles south-southeast of Keller Peak (lat. 34° 09'15" N, long. 117°01'10" W; sec. 19, T 1 N, R 1 W). Named on Keller Peak (1967) 7.5' quadrangle.

Breezy Point [SAN BERNARDINO]: *relief feature,* 19 miles south of Victorville (lat. 34°15'45" N, long. 117°18'50" W; near E line sec. 17, T 2 N, R 4 W). Named on Cedar Springs (1956) 7.5' quadrangle.

Brice Siding: see **Anza** [IMPERIAL].

Bridal Veil Creek [SAN BERNARDINO]: *stream,* flows 1 mile to Mill Creek Canyon 6 miles west of San Gorgonio Mountain (lat. 34°05'20" N, long. 116°56' W; near N line sec. 13, T 1 S, R 1 W). Named on Forest Falls (1970) 7.5' quadrangle.

Brisbane Valley [SAN BERNARDINO]: *valley,* 16 miles southwest of Barstow (lat. 34°45' N, long. 117°15' W). Named on Hodge (1971), Turtle Valley (1970), and Wild Crossing (1973) 7.5' quadrangles.

Bristol: see **Bolo**, under **Cadiz** [SAN BERNARDINO].

Bristol Lake [SAN BERNARDINO]: *dry lake,* 13 miles long, center 7 miles south-southeast of Amboy (lat. 34°28' N, long. 115°41' W). Named on Bagdad (1956), Bristol Lake (1956), Cadiz (1956), and Lead Mountain (1955) 15' quadrangles.

Bristol Mountains [SAN BERNARDINO]: *range,* extends northwest for 40 miles from the neighborhood of Amboy and Bristol Lake. Named on Bagdad (1956), Broadwell Lake (1955), Cadiz (1956), Kerens (1957), Ludlow (1955), Old Dad Mountain (1956), and Soda Lake (1956) 15' quadrangles.

Bristol Spring [SAN BERNARDINO]: *spring,* 23 miles east-northeast of Vidal (lat. 34°15'50" N, long. 114°08'40" W; sec. 16, T 2 N, R 27 E). Named on Gene Wash (1959) 7.5' quadrangle.

Broadwell [SAN BERNARDINO]: *locality,* 10.5 miles north of Ludlow (lat. 34°52'25" N, long. 116°11'30" W; sec. 13, T 9 N, R 7 E). Site named on Broadwell Lake (1955) 15' quadrangle. The place was a siding along Tonopah and Tidewater Railroad named about 1905 for a prospector and owner of a nearby mine (Hanna, p. 41).

Broadwell Lake [SAN BERNARDINO]: *dry lake,* 4.25 miles long, 8 miles north of Ludlow (lat. 34°50'30" N, long. 116°11' W); the site of Broadwell is at the north end of the feature. Named on Broadwell Lake (1955) 15' quadrangle. Thompson (1929, p. 656) used the names "Broadwell Valley" and "Ludlow Valley" for the valley at and around the dry lake.

Broadwell Mesa [SAN BERNARDINO]: *area,* 13 miles north-northeast of Ludlow (lat. 34°53'30" N, long. 116°04' W); the place is 7.5 miles east-northeast of Broadwell Lake. Named on Broadwell Lake (1955) 15' quadrangle.

Broadwell Valley: see **Broadwell Lake** [SAN BERNARDINO].

Brooks Canyon [RIVERSIDE]: *canyon,* nearly 1 mile long, 5.5 miles south of Alberhill (lat. 33°38'45" N, long. 117°22'50" W; sec. 15, T 6 S, R 5 W). Named on Alberhill (1954, photorevised 1988) 7.5' quadrangle. The name honors Andrew C. Brooks, a Forest Service employee killed in a fire in 1959 (United States Board on Geographic Names, 1960c, p. 16).

Brooks Cienaga: see **Two Springs** [SAN BERNARDINO].

Brookside: see **Redlands** [SAN BERNARDINO] (2).

Brooks Springs: see **Two Springs** [SAN BERNARDINO].

Brooks Switch: see **Rico** [IMPERIAL].

Broom Flat [SAN BERNARDINO]: *area,* 15 miles northwest of downtown Morongo Valley (lat. 34°13'30" N, long. 116°43'30" W; sec. 25, T 2 N, R 2 E). Named on Onyx Peak (1972) 7.5' quadrangle.

Broom Spring [SAN BERNARDINO]: *spring,* 14 miles north-northwest of downtown Morongo Valley (lat. 34°13'30" N, long. 116° 42'25" W; near S line sec. 30, T 2 N, R 3 E); the spring is 1 mile east of Broom Flat. Named on Onyx Peak (1972) 7.5' quadrangle.

Brown Buttes [SAN BERNARDINO]: *relief feature,* 11 miles north-northeast of Amboy (lat. 34°42'45" N, long. 115°41'15" W; sec. 11, T 7 N, R 12 E). Named on Cadiz (1956) 15' quadrangle.

Brown Canyon [RIVERSIDE]:

(1) *canyon,* drained by a stream that flows 2.25 miles to Temescal Valley 7.25 miles south-southeast of Corona (lat. 33°46'40" N, long. 117°30'35" W; sec. 33, T 4 S, R 6 W). Named on Corona South (1967) 7.5' quadrangle. The name is for A.H. Brown, who lived in the canyon at least as early as 1886 (Gunther, p. 71).

(2) *canyon,* drained by a stream that flows 2 miles to Cactus Valley 6.5 miles south-southeast of Hemet (lat. 33°40' N, long. 116°54'05" W; sec. 8, T 6 S, R 1 E). Named on Hemet (1953) 7.5' quadrangle.

Brown Creek [RIVERSIDE]: *stream,* flows 4.25 miles to Twin Pines Creek 5.5 miles southeast of Banning (lat. 33°52'50" N, long. 116° 47'55" W; sec. 29, T 3 S, R 2 E). Named on Cabazon (1956), Lake Fulmor (1956), and San Jacinto Peak (1981) 7.5' quadrangles.

Brownlands: see **Mystic Lake** [RIVERSIDE].

Brown Mountain [SAN BERNARDINO]: *peak,* 5.25 miles east-southeast of Trona (lat. 35°41'15" N, long. 117°01' W). Altitude 5125 feet. Named on Wingate Pass (1950) 15' quadrangle.

Browns: see **Aplin** [SAN BERNARDINO].

Brown's Lake: see **Mystic Lake** [RIVERSIDE].

Browns Wash [SAN BERNARDINO]: *stream,* flows 6 miles before ending 16 miles south-southeast of Essex (lat. 34°25' N, long. 115° 15'15" W; sec. 24, T 4 N, R 16 E). Named on Cadiz Lake (1956) and Milligan (1956) 15' quadrangles.

Browns Well [RIVERSIDE]: *well,* 31 miles north-northwest of Blythe (lat. 33°59'45" N, long. 114°53'10" W; sec. 16, T 2 S, R 20 E). Site named on Midland (1952) 15' quadrangle. Floyd Brown lived at the well, which was 300 feet deep (Mendenhall, 1909a, p. 79).

Brown Valley: see **Indian Wells Valley** [SAN BERNARDINO].

Brush Canyon [SAN BERNARDINO]: *canyon,* drained by a stream that flows 2 miles to Orange County 3 miles east-southeast of San Juan Hill (lat. 33°53'15" N, long. 117°41'45" W). Named on Prado Dam (1967) 7.5' quadrangle.

Bryman [SAN BERNARDINO]: *locality,* 10 miles north-northwest of Victorville (lat. 34°40'30" N, long. 117°20'40" W; near SW cor. sec. 19, T 7 N, R 4 W). Named on Helendale (1956) 7.5' quadrangle.

Bryn Mawr [SAN BERNARDINO]: *locality,* nearly 3 miles west of Redlands city hall (lat. 34°02'50" N, long. 117°13'50" W; near N line sec. 31, T 1 S, R 3 W). Named on Redlands (1967) 7.5' quadrangle. Called Brynmawr on California Mining Bureau's (1909a) map, but United States Board on Geographic Names (1933, p. 168) rejected this form of the name. Redlands (1901) 15' quadrangle has both the names "Bryn Mawr" and "Redlands Junction" at the place. Postal authorities established Brynmawr post office in 1895 and changed the name to Bryn Mawr in 1924 (Salley, p. 28).

Buck Mesa [RIVERSIDE]: *relief feature,* 9.5 miles east of Murrieta (lat. 33°32'15" N, long. 117°02'50" W). Named on Bachelor Mountain (1953) 7.5' quadrangle.

Buck Point [SAN BERNARDINO]: *relief feature,* 12.5 miles north-northeast of Ontario city hall (lat. 34°13'10" N, long. 117°32'40" W; sec. 31, T 2 N, R 6 W). Named on Cucamonga Peak (1966) 7.5' quadrangle.

Buck Ridge [RIVERSIDE]: *ridge,* east-southeast-trending, 5 miles long, 18 miles south of Palm Desert (lat. 33°27'30" N, long. 116° 24'40" W). Named on Collins Valley (1959) 7.5' quadrangle.

Buck Spring [RIVERSIDE]: *spring,* 8.5 miles east-northeast of San Jacinto (lat. 33°50'20" N, long. 116°49'40" W; sec. 12, T 4 S, R 1 E). Named on Lake Fulmor (1956) 7.5' quadrangle.

Buckthorn Canyon: see **Buckthorn Wash** [SAN BERNARDINO].

Buckthorn Wash [SAN BERNARDINO]: *dry wash,* extends for 11 miles to Mojave River 20 miles west-southwest of Barstow (lat. 34°45'20" N, long. 117°19'30" W; sec. 29, T 8 N, R 4 W). Named on Astley Rancho (1973) and Wild Crossing (1973) 7.5' quadrangles. Hawes (1956) 15' quadrangle has the name "Buckthorn Canyon" for the canyon of the dry wash.

Buckwheat Wash [SAN BERNARDINO]: *dry wash,* 42 miles north-northwest of Baker on San Bernardino-Inyo County line (lat. 35° 47'40" N, long. 116°26'30" W). Named on Shoshone (1951) 15' quadrangle.

Budweiser Spring [SAN BERNARDINO]: *spring,* 17 miles north-northeast of Amboy (lat. 34°46'20" N, long. 115°44'30" W; sec. 20, T 8 N, R 12 E); the spring is near Budweiser Wash. Named on Flynn (1956) 15' quadrangle.

Budweiser Wash [SAN BERNARDINO]: *stream,* flows 18 miles to Devils Playground Wash 26 miles north-northwest of Amboy (lat. 34°55'25" N, long. 115°52'15" W; near SW cor. sec. 30, T 10 N, R 11 E). Named on Flynn (1956) and Kerens (1957) 15' quadrangles.

Bull Canyon [RIVERSIDE]: *canyon,* drained by a stream that flows 4.5 miles to the head of Palm Canyon 16 miles southeast of Idyllwild (lat. 33°34'10" N, long. 116°31'40" W; sec. 13, T 7 S, R 4 E). Named on Idyllwild (1959) 15' quadrangle.

Bull Canyon [SAN BERNARDINO]:

(1) *canyon,* drained by a stream that flows 7.5 miles to Devils Playground Wash 22 miles north of Amboy (lat. 34°52'30" N, long. 115°46'35" W; sec. 13, T 9 N, R 11 E). Named on Flynn (1956) 15' quadrangle.

(2) *canyon,* drained by a stream that flows 1.25 miles to Deer Canyon (2) 9.5 miles north-northeast of Ontario city hall (lat. 34° 10'55" N, long. 117°34'10" W; sec. 12, T 1 N, R 7 W). Named on Cucamonga Peak (1966) 7.5' quadrangle.

Bull Canyon: see **Penrod Canyon** [RIVERSIDE].

Bullhead Slough [IMPERIAL]: *stream,* flows 2 miles to New River 8.5 miles west of El Centro (lat. 32°48'15" N, long. 115°42'30" W; at E line sec. 3, T 16 S, R 12 E). Named on Seeley (1957) 7.5' quadrangle.

Bullion Mountains [SAN BERNARDINO]: *range,* extends southeast from a point south of Lavic Lake to a spot north of Dale Lake. Named on Needles (1956) and San Bernardino (1966) 1°x 2° quadrangles. The name is from Bullion mine of the 1880's and later (Hanna, p. 45).

Bullion Wash [SAN BERNARDINO]: *stream* and *dry wash,* extends for about 6 miles to the valley that contains Deadman Lake 16 miles east-northeast of Landers (lat. 34°22'30" N, long. 118°09'15" W; sec. 4, T 3 N, R 8 E); the feature is along the southwest side of Bullion Mountains. Named on Deadman Lake (1955) 15' quadrangle.

Bullock Spring [SAN BERNARDINO]: *spring,* 20 miles south-southwest of Ivanpah (lat. 35°05'40" N, long. 115°29' W; near E line sec. 28, T 12 N, R 14 E). Named on Mid Hills (1955) 15' quadrangle.

Bullocks Well [SAN BERNARDINO]: *well,* 27 miles north-northwest of Ivanpah near the southeast end of Mesquite Valley (lat. 35°40'50" N, long. 115°31'45" W). Named on Ivanpah (1912) 1° quadrangle. Sinclair (p. 326) called the feature Bullock's well.

Bullseye Rock [RIVERSIDE]: *relief feature,* 11 miles east-southeast of Idyllwild (lat. 33°41'50" N, long. 116°32'15" W; sec. 35, T 5 S, R 4 E). Named on Idyllwild (1959) 15' quadrangle.

Bull Spring [SAN BERNARDINO]: *spring,* 32 miles west-northwest of Ivanpah (lat. 35°26'30" N, long. 115°51'50" W). Named on Halloran Spring (1956) 15' quadrangle.

Bull Spring Wash [SAN BERNARDINO]: *stream,* flows 7.5 miles before disappearing 34 miles west of Ivanpah (lat. 35°23'15" N, long. 115°54'30" W; sec. 15, T 15 N, R 10 E); the stream passes 0.5 mile southeast of Bull Spring. Named on Halloran Spring (1956) 15' quadrangle. Called Halloran Wash on Ivanpah (1912) 1° quadrangle.

Bully Hill: see **Acme** [SAN BERNARDINO].

Bundy Canyon [RIVERSIDE]: *canyon,* 2.25 miles long, opens into lowlands nearly 5 miles southeast of Lake Elsinore city hall (lat. 33°37'35" N, long. 117°15'35" W; near NE cor. sec. 26, T 6 S, R 4 W). Named on Lake Elsinore (1953) and Romoland (1953) 7.5' quadrangles. The name recalls Mr. and Mrs. Joseph W. Bundy and their two sons, who camped in the canyon in the 1880's; the sons filed for homesteads there in the 1890's (Gunther, p. 77).

Bundys Elsinore Hot Spring: see **Lake Elsinore** [RIVERSIDE] (2).

Bunker Hill [SAN BERNARDINO]: *locality,* nearly 2 miles south-southwest of present San Bernardino city hall along the railroad (lat. 34°04'45" N, long. 117°18'20" W). Named on San Bernardino (1901) 15' quadrangle.

Bunker Mountain [SAN BERNARDINO]: *ridge,* west- to southwest-trending, 1.25 miles long, 4 miles north-northeast of Joshua Tree (lat. 34°10'55" N, long. 116°16'25" W; mainly in sec. 8, 17, T 1 N, R 7 E). Named on Joshua Tree North (1972) 7.5' quadrangle.

Burcham: see **Summit** [SAN BERNARDINO].

Buried Mountain [RIVERSIDE]: *hill,* 10 miles north-northeast of Mortmar in Shavers Valley (lat. 33°39' N, long. 115°51'30" W; sec. 17, T 6 S, R 11 E). Altitude 1472 feet. Named on Cottonwood Spring (1958) 15' quadrangle.

Burkhardt Lake [SAN BERNARDINO]: *intermittent lake,* 0.25 mile long, 2 miles north-northwest of Victorville near Mojave River (lat. 34°33'50" N, long. 117°18'35" W; near W line sec. 33, T 6 N, R 4 W). Named on Victorville (1956) 7.5' quadrangle.

Burns Canyon [SAN BERNARDINO]: *canyon,* drained by a stream that flows 3.5 miles to lowlands 10.5 miles north of downtown Morongo Valley (lat. 34°11'45" N, long. 116°33'30" W; sec. 3, T 1 N, R 4 E). Name on Rimrock (1972) 7.5' quadrangle.

Burns Flat [SAN BERNARDINO]: *area,* nearly 5 miles north of Big Bear City (lat. 34°19'45" N, long. 116°51'10" W; sec. 23, T 3 N, R 1 E). Named on Big Bear City (1971) 7.5' quadrangle.

Burns Spring [SAN BERNARDINO]:

(1) *spring,* 5.5 miles east-southeast of Luna Mountain (lat. 34°18'50" N, long. 117°02'20" W; sec. 25, T 3 N, R 2 W). Named on Butler Peak (1971) 7.5' quadrangle.

(2) *spring,* 11 miles north of downtown Morongo Valley (lat. 34°12'15" N, long. 116°34'55" W; near SE cor. sec. 32, T 2 N, R 4 E); the spring is in Burns Canyon. Named on Rimrock (1972) 7.5' quadrangle.

Burnt Canyon [SAN BERNARDINO]: *canyon,* drained by a stream that flows 2 miles to Banning Canyon 4.25 miles south-southwest of San Gorgonio Mountain (lat. 34°02'30" N, long. 116°51'05" W; sec. 35, T 1 S, R 1 E). Named on San Gorgonio Mountain (1970) 7.5' quadrangle.

Burnt Flats [SAN BERNARDINO]: *area,* 4 miles west-southwest of Luna Mountain (lat. 34°19'50" N, long. 117°11'45" W; sec. 21, T 3 N, R 3 W). Named on Lake Arrowhead (1971) 7.5' quadrangle.

Burnt Mill Canyon [SAN BERNARDINO]: *canyon,* drained by a stream that flows 1.5 miles to Miller Canyon 18 miles south of Victorville (lat. 34°16'30" N, long. 117°18'40" W; at E line sec. 8, T 2 N, R 4 W). Named on Cedar Springs (1956) 7.5' quadrangle.

Burnt Mill Creek [SAN BERNARDINO]: *stream,* flows less than 1 mile to Lake Arrowhead 6.25 miles north-northwest of Harrison Mountain (lat. 34°15'05" N, long. 117°11'35" W; near N line sec. 21, T 2 N, R 3 W). Named on Harrison Mountain (1967) 7.5' quadrangle.

Burnt Mountain [SAN BERNARDINO]: *hill,* 2.5 miles east-southeast of Yucca Valley (lat. 34°06'15" N, long. 116°24'15" W; around NE cor. sec. 12, T 1 S, R 5 E). Named on Yucca Valley South (1972) 7.5' quadrangle.

Burnt Palms Spring: see **Sheep Hole Oasis** [RIVERSIDE].

Burnt Valley [RIVERSIDE]: *valley,* 15 miles south-southeast of Idyllwild (lat. 33°33'15" N, long. 116°35'40" W; near N line sec. 20, T 7 S, R 4 E). Named on Idyllwild (1959) 15' quadrangle.

Burris: see **Crafton** [SAN BERNARDINO].

Burro Canyon [SAN BERNARDINO]:

(1) *canyon,* drained by a stream that heads in San Bernardino County and flows 2 miles, partly in Inyo County, to enter Inyo County finally 6.5 miles west-northwest of Trona (lat. 35°47'45" N, long. 117°29'15" W; at S line sec. 31, T 24 N, R 42 E). Named on Trona (1949) 15' quadrangle.

(2) *canyon,* drained by a stream that flows nearly 3 miles to Black Canyon Wash 22 miles south of Ivanpah (lat. 35°01'15" N, long. 115°20'40" W; sec. 23, T 11 N, R 15 E). Named on Mid Hills (1955) 15' quadrangle.

Burro Flats [RIVERSIDE]: *area,* 5 miles north-northeast of Banning (lat. 33°59'50" N, long. 116°51' W; sec. 14, T 2 S, R 1 E). Named on Cabazon (1956) and San Gorgonio Mountain (1970) 7.5' quadrangles.

Burro Flats [SAN BERNARDINO]: *area,* 3.25 miles west-southwest of Sugarloaf Mountain along Santa Ana River (lat. 34°11'05" N, long. 116°52' W; sec. 10, T 1 N, R 1 E). Named on Moonridge (1970) 7.5' quadrangle.

Burro Spring [SAN BERNARDINO]:

(1) *spring,* 16 miles northwest of Ivanpah (lat. 35°30'10" N, long. 115°30'45" W; sec. 1, T 16 N, R 13 E). Named on Clark Mountain (1956) 15' quadrangle.

(2) *spring,* 12 miles southwest of Ivanpah (lat. 35°12'20" N, long. 115°27'20" W; sec. 14, T 13 N, R 14 E). Named on Mid Hills (1955) 15' quadrangle. Called The Trough Spring on Ivanpah (1912) 1° quadrangle, and The Troughs Spring on Thompson's (1921) map. United States Board on Geographic Names (1960a, p. 12) rejected the name "The Troughs" for it.

Burro Wash [IMPERIAL]: *stream,* flows nearly 4 miles to Little Picacho Wash 1.5 miles east-northeast of Picacho Peak (lat. 32°58'45" N, long. 114°38'10" W). Named on Picacho Peak (1965) 7.5' quadrangle.

Burt's Dry Lake: see **Dale Lake** [SAN BERNARDINO].

Bush [SAN BERNARDINO]: *locality,* 28 miles south of Amboy at Dale Lake (lat. 34°09' N, long. 115°42'05" W; at SE cor. sec. 22, T 1 N, R 12 E). Named on Dale Lake (1956) 15' quadrangle.

Butcher Knife Canyon [SAN BERNARDINO]: *canyon,* 2 miles long, 7 miles south of Ivanpah (lat. 35°14'10" N, long. 115°22'45" W). Named on Mid Hills (1955) 15' quadrangle.

Butch Wash: see **Big Butch Wash** [SAN BERNARDINO].

Butler Fork [SAN BERNARDINO]: *stream,* flows less than 0.5 mile to North Fork Bear Creek nearly 4 miles north-northeast of Keller Peak (lat. 34°14'35" N, long. 117°00'45" W; at W line sec. 20, T 2 N, R 1 W). Named on Keller Peak (1967) 7.5' quadrangle.

Butler Peak [SAN BERNARDINO]: *peak,* 9 miles southeast of Luna Mountain (lat. 34°15'25" N, long. 117°00'25" W; sec. 17, T 2 N, R 1 W). Altitude 8535 feet. Named on Butler Peak (1971) 7.5' quadrangle.

Butterfield Valley [RIVERSIDE]: *valley,* 6 miles west-northwest of Aguanga along Temescal Creek (lat. 33°28'45" N, long. 116°57'30" W). Named on Vail Lake (1953) 7.5' quadrangle. Called Nigger Valley on Ramona (1903) 30' quadrangle, but United States Board on Geographic Names (1970, p. 1) rejected the names "Nigger Valley" and "Negro Valley" for the place, and noted that the name "Butterfield" commemorates Butterfield Overland stage line, which passed through the valley. The name "Nigger Valley" was for James Hamilton, who settled at the place in the 1860's (Gunther, p. 352).

Butterfly Mountain [RIVERSIDE]: *peak,* 11.5 miles southeast of Idyllwild (lat. 33°37'25" N, long. 116°34'50" W; on W line sec. 28, T 6 S, R 4 E). Named on Idyllwild (1959) 15' quadrangle. United States Board on Geographic Names (1978, p. 3) approved the name "Butterfly Peak" for the feature.

Butterfly Peak: see **Butterfly Mountain** [RIVERSIDE].

Butters [IMPERIAL]: *locality,* 10.5 miles southeast of Calipatria along Southern Pacific Railroad (lat. 33°00'10" N, long. 115°24'30" W). Named on Iris (1945) 15' quadrangle.

Buttes: see **The Buttes** [SAN BERNARDINO].

Buzzards Peak [IMPERIAL]: *peak,* 21 miles south-southwest of Palo Verde (lat. 32°08'35" N, long. 114°51'45" W; on W line sec. 10, T 12 S, R 20 E). Named on Quartz Peak (1953) 15' quadrangle.

Buzzard Spring [RIVERSIDE]: *spring,* 11 miles northwest of Desert Center (lat. 33°49'35" N, long. 115°31'45" W). Named on the Pinto Basin (1963) 15' quadrangle.

- C -

Cabarker: see **El Centro** [IMPERIAL].

Cabazon [RIVERSIDE]: *town,* 5.25 miles east of Banning (lat. 33° 55' N, long. 116°47' W; sec. 16, 17, T 3 S, R 2 E). Named on Cabazon (1956) 7.5' quadrangle. Postal authorities established Cabazon post office in 1886 (Frickstad, p. 127). The railroad stop at the site first was called Hall's Siding, for Colonel M.S. Hall, who had a contract for grading the rail bed; by 1876 the name was changed to Jacinto, and finally it was changed to Cabazon to honor an old chief, Cabezón, of the Cahilla Indians (Gunther, p. 81).

Cabazon Peak [RIVERSIDE]: *peak,* 6.5 miles east-southeast of Banning (lat. 33°52'55" N, long. 116°46'25" W; near NE cor. sec. 28, T 3 S, R 2 E); the peak is 2.5 miles south-southeast of Cabazon. Named on Cabazon (1956) 7.5' quadrangle.

Cabin Spring [SAN BERNARDINO]: *spring,* 10 miles south-southwest of Ivanpah (lat. 35°12'45" N, long. 115°24'30" W; near NE cor. sec. 18, T 13 N, R 15 E). Named on Mid Hills (1955) 15' quadrangle.

Cable Canyon [SAN BERNARDINO]: *canyon,* 1.25 miles long, opens into lowlands 1 mile east-northeast of Devore (lat. 34°13'20" N, long. 117°23'05" W). Named on Devore (1966) and San Bernardino North (1967) 7.5' quadrangles. The canyon divides at the head to form East Fork and West Fork. East Fork is 1.5 miles long and is named on San Bernardino North (1967) 7.5' quadrangle. West Fork is 2 miles long and is named on Cedar Springs (1956) and San Bernardino North (1967) 7.5' quadrangles.

Cable Creek [SAN BERNARDINO]: *stream,* flows 6 miles from the mouth of Cable Canyon to Cajon Wash 6 miles northwest of San Bernardino city hall (lat. 34°09'45" N, long. 117°21'50" W). Named on Devore (1966) and San Bernardino North (1967) 7.5' quadrangles.

Cactus [IMPERIAL]: *locality,* 4.5 miles northwest of Ogilby along Southern Pacific Railroad (lat. 32°51'45" N, long. 114°53'45" W; at W line sec. 17, T 15 S, R 20 E). Named on Ogilby (1963) 15' quadrangle. Postal authorities established Cactus post office at a railroad construction camp in 1883, discontinued it the same year, reestablished in in 1885, and discontinued it again in 1886 (Salley, p. 31).

Cactus City [RIVERSIDE]: *locality,* 11 miles north of Mortmar (lat. 33°40'45" N, long. 115°57'45" W; sec. 5, T 6 S, R 10 E). Named on Cottonwood Spring (1958) 15' quadrangle. Steve Ragsdale, who built a store, cafe, and garage at the site in 1935, named the place for cholla cactus growing nearby (Hanna, p. 47-48).

Cactus Flat [SAN BERNARDINO]: *area,* 4.5 miles north-northeast of Big Bear City (lat. 34°19'25" N, long. 116°48'55" W). Named on Big Bear City (1971) 7.5' quadrangle.

Cactus Flat Spring: see **Cactus Spring** [SAN BERNARDINO].

Cactus Spring [RIVERSIDE]: *spring,* about 11 miles south of Palm Desert (lat. 33°34' N, long. 116°23' W; near NW cor. sec. 17, T 7 S, R 6 E). Named on Palm Desert (1959) 15' quadrangle.

Cactus Spring [SAN BERNARDINO]: *spring,* 4.25 miles north-northeast of Big Bear City (lat. 34°18'50" N, long. 116°48'30" W; sec. 30, T 3 N, R 2 E); the spring is nearly 1 mile south-southeast of Cactus Flat. Named on Big Bear City (1971) 7.5' quadrangle. Waring (p. 347) called the feature Cactus Flat Spring, and noted that it also was known as Hidden Spring.

Cactus Valley [RIVERSIDE]: *valley,* 6 miles south-southeast of Hemet (lat. 33°40'15" N, long. 116°55'30" W). Named on Hemet (1953) 7.5' quadrangle. The first American settlers at the place in the 1860's and early 1870's called it Cholla Valley (Gunther, p. 84).

Cadiz [SAN BERNARDINO]: *locality,* 14 miles east of Amboy along Atchison, Topeka and Santa Fe Railroad (lat. 34°31'15" N, long. 115°30'40" W; sec. 16, T 5 N, R 14 W). Named on Cadiz (1956) and Danby (1956) 15' quadrangles. Postal authorities established Cadiz post office in 1939 (Frickstad, p. 139). Amboy (1942) 1° quadrangle shows a place called Bolo located 7.5 miles west of Cadiz along Atchison, Topeka and Santa Fe Railroad. Bolo first was called Bristol; the name was changed to Bombay in 1898, then to Bengal, and finally to Bolo in 1915 (Gudde, 1949, p. 36). Thompson's (1921) map shows a place called McCoy located 5.5 miles southeast of Cadiz along Atchison, Topeka and Santa Fe Railroad, and a place called Altura situated 4 miles west of Cadiz along the railroad.

Cadiz Lake [SAN BERNARDINO]: *dry lake,* 11 miles long, 27 miles southeast of Amboy (lat. 34°18' N, long. 115°24' W); the feature is 17 miles south-southeast of Cadiz in Cadiz Valley. Named on Cadiz Lake (1956) and Cadiz Valley (1956) 15' quadrangles.

Cadiz Summit [SAN BERNARDINO]: *pass,* 18 miles southwest of Essex (lat. 34°34'05" N, long. 115°29'15" W; sec. 35, T 6 N, R 14 E). Named on Danby (1956) 15' quadrangle.

Cadiz Valley [RIVERSIDE-SAN BERNARDINO]: *valley,* at and south-southeast of Cadiz, mainly in San Bernardino County, but extends south into Riverside County. Named on Bristol Lake (1956), Cadiz Lake (1956), Cadiz Valley (1956), and Iron Mountains (1956) 15' quadrangles.

Cady: see **Camp Cady** [SAN BERNARDINO].

Cady Mountains [SAN BERNARDINO]: *range,* center about 12 miles northwest of Ludlow (lat. 34°50' N, long. 116°20' W). Named on Broadwell Lake (1955), Cady Mountains (1955), Cave Mountain (1948), Ludlow (1955), and Newberry (1955) 15' quadrangles.

Cady Spring [SAN BERNARDINO]: *spring,* 9.5 miles northeast of Newberry (lat. 34°56'10" N, long. 116°35'20" W; near NW cor. sec. 29, T 10 N, R 4 E); the spring is less than 1 mile south of the site of Camp Cady. Named on Newberry (1955) 15' quadrangle.

Cahillas Creek: see **Cahuilla Creek** [RIVERSIDE].

Cahillas Valley: see **Cahuilla Valley** [RIVERSIDE].

Cahuilla [RIVERSIDE]: *village,* 14 miles south of Idyllwild (lat. 33° 32'30" N, long. 116°44'35" W; on N line sec. 26, T 7 S, R 2 E); the place is in Cahuilla Valley. Named on Idyllwild (1959) 15' quadrangle. Called Coahuila on San Jacinto (1901) 30' quadrangle, but United States Board on Geographic Names (1963b, p. 15) rejected the names "Coahuila," "Coahuilla," "Cohuilla," and "Kawia" for the place. Postal authorities established Cahuilla post office 1888, moved it 2 miles northeast in 1889, moved it 6 miles west in 1895, discontinued it in 1903, reestablished it in 1909, discontinued it for a time in 1919, discontinued it in 1921, reestablished it in 1924, and discontinued it finally in 1926 (Salley, p. 31). The name is from the designation of an Indian dialect group (Kroeber, p. 36).

Cahuilla Creek [RIVERSIDE]: *stream,* flows 18 miles to Wilson Creek 4 miles north of Aguanga (lat. 33°30' N, long. 116°51'30" W; at SE cor. sec. 3, T 8 S, R 1 E). Named on Hemet (1957) and Idyllwild (1959) 15' quadrangles, and on Aguanga (1954) 7.5' quadrangle. Called Coahuila Cr. on San Jacinto (1901) 30' quadrangle, but United States Board on Geographic Names (1963b, p. 15) rejected the names "Coahuila Creek," "Cahillas Creek," "Coahuilla Creek," and "Cohuilla Creek" for the stream.

Cahuilla Hills [RIVERSIDE]: *locality,* 3 miles southwest of Palm Desert (lat. 33°41'20" N, long. 116°24'45" W; sec. 36, T 5 S, R 5 E). Named on Rancho Mirage (1957) 7.5' quadrangle.

Cahuilla Mountain [RIVERSIDE]: *peak,* 16 miles southeast of Hemet (lat. 33°35' N, long. 116°47' W; near N line sec. 9, T 7 S, R 2 E). Altitude 5604 feet. Named on Hemet (1957) 15' quadrangle. Called Coahuila Mt. on San Jacinto (1901) 30' quadrangle, and called Cahuilla Pk. on California Mining Bureau's (1917b) map. United States Board on Geographic Names (1963b, p. 15) rejected the names "Coahuilla Mountain," "Cahuilla Peak," "Coahilla Peak," "Coahuila Mountain," "Cohuila Mountain," and "Cohuilla Mountain" for the feature.

Cahuilla Mountain: see **Little Cahuilla Mountain** [RIVERSIDE].

Cahuilla Peak: see **Cahuilla Mountain** [RIVERSIDE].

Cahuilla Valley [RIVERSIDE]: *valley,* 19 miles southeast of Hemet (lat. 33°31'45" N, long. 116°46'30" W); the valley is along Cahuilla Creek. Named on Hemet (1957) 15' quadrangle. Called Coahuila Valley on San Jacinto (1901) 30' quadrangle, but United States Board on Geographic Names (1963b, p. 15) rejected the names "Coahuila Valley," "Cahillas Valley," "Coahilla Valley," and "Cohuilla Valley" for the place.

Cahuilla Valley: see **Anza Valley** [RIVERSIDE].

Cajalco Canyon [RIVERSIDE]: *canyon,* 3 miles long, opens into the canyon of Temescal Wash 6 miles northwest of Estelle Mountain (lat. 33°49'25" N, long. 117°30' W). Named on Lake Mathews (1967) 7.5' quadrangle.

Cajalco Reservoir: see **Lake Mathews** [RIVERSIDE].

Cajon [SAN BERNARDINO]: *locality,* 19 miles south-southwest of Victorville along the railroad (lat. 34°18' N, long. 117°27'35" W; sec. 36, T 3 N, R 6 W). Named on Cajon (1956) 7.5' quadrangle. Thompson's (1929) map shows a place called Camp Cajon located less than 1 mile north-northwest of Cajon.

Cajon: see **Cajon Junction** [SAN BERNARDINO].

Cajon Campground [SAN BERNARDINO]: *locality,* nearly 2 miles south-southeast of Cajon (lat. 34°16'30" N, long. 117°27' W; near W line sec. 7, T 2 N, R 5 W); the place is in Cajon Canyon. Named on Cajon (1956) 7.5' quadrangle.

Cajon Canyon [SAN BERNARDINO]: *canyon,* 15 miles long, opens into lowlands at Devore (lat. 34°13' N, long. 117°24' W). Named on Cajon (1956), Devore (1966), Phelan (1956), and Telegraph Peak (1956) 7.5' quadrangles.

Cajon Junction [SAN BERNARDINO]: *locality,* 1.25 miles northwest of Cajon (lat. 34°18'45" N, long. 117°28'30" W; near S line sec. 26, T 3 N, R 6 W). Named on Cajon (1956) 7.5' quadrangle. Hesperia (1942) 15' quadrangle shows Cajon post office at the site. Postal authorities established Cajon post office in 1889, discontinued it in 1918, reestablished it in 1919, and discontinued it in 1944 (Frickstad, p. 139).

Cajon Mountain [SAN BERNARDINO]: *peak,* 2.5 miles southeast of Cajon (lat. 34°16'20" N, long. 117°25'10" W; near E line sec. 8, T 2 N, R 5 W); the feature is east of Cajon Canyon. Named on Cajon (1956) 7.5' quadrangle.

Cajon Pass [SAN BERNARDINO]: *pass,* 2.5 miles northeast of Cajon (lat. 34°19'30" N, long. 117°25'40" W; at S line sec. 20, T 3 N, R 5 W). Named on Cajon (1956) 7.5' quadrangle. Don Pedro Fages traversed the pass in 1772, and later travelers on the Old Spanish trail from New Mexico to Los Angeles followed it; the Spaniards used the names "El Cajon de los Mexicanos" and "El Cajon de Muscupiabe" for the feature—the term "Muscupiabe" was from an Indian village located at present Camp Cajon (Hanna, p. 49). Several places have been considered the summit of Cajon Pass at one time or another: the most easterly place is at present Summit Station; a second place is on the route of the Old Spanish trail 1.5 miles north of Summit Station; a third place is on the route of the state highway 1 mile west of the Old Spanish trail crossing; a fourth place is on what is shown on early government maps as the old road about 5 miles west of the state highway route; and another place is on Sanford's road 1.5 miles still farther west (Beattie and Beattie, p. 328). This last spot was on the road that Captain William B.T. Sandford laid out over what was known as Sanford's Pass (La Fuze, p. 42).

Cajon Summit [SAN BERNARDINO]: *locality,* 3.5 miles north of Cajon (lat. 34°21' N, long. 117°26'45" W; near W line sec. 18, T 3 N, R 5 W). Named on Cajon (1956) 7.5' quadrangle.

Cajon Wash [SAN BERNARDINO]: *dry wash,* extends for 5.25 miles from the mouth of Cajon Canyon to Lytle Creek Wash 5 miles northwest of San Bernardino city hall (lat. 34°08'50" N, long. 117° 21'35" W). Named on Devore (1966) and San Bernardino North (1967) 7.5' quadrangles.

Calada [SAN BERNARDINO]: *locality,* 17 miles north-northwest of Ivanpah along Union Pacific Railroad (lat. 35°34'50" N, long. 115° 22'10" W; sec. 21, T 17 N, R 15 E); the place is near California-Nevada State line. Named on Roach Lake (1955) 15' quadrangle.

Calamity Canyon [SAN BERNARDINO]: *canyon,* drained by a stream that flows 0.5 mile to Deer Canyon (2) 10 miles north-northeast of Ontario city hall (lat. 34°11'50" N, long. 117°34'55" W; sec. 2, T 1 N, R 7 W). Named on Cucamonga Peak (1966) 7.5' quadrangle.

Caleb [RIVERSIDE]: *locality,* 17 miles southeast of Indio along Southern Pacific Railroad (lat. 33°32'15" N, long. 116°00'45" W). Named on Coachella (1943) 15' quadrangle.

Calexico [IMPERIAL]: *town,* 9.5 miles south-southeast of El Centro at the Mexican border (lat. 32°40'15" N, long. 115°29'30" W; sec. 13, 14, T 17 S, R 14 E). Named on Calexico (1957) and Heber (1957) 7.5' quadrangles. Postal authorities established Calexico post office in 1902 (Frickstad, p. 48), and the town incorporated in 1908. L.M. Holt, publicity director for Imperial Land Company, coined the name from the words "California" and "Mexico"; he also coined the name "Mexicali" for the Mexican town situated just across the border.from Calexico (Hanna, p. 50). Lieutenant Cave J. Couts, commander of the escort for the International Boundary Commission, set up an installation in 1849 at the site of present Calexico and called it Camp Salvation; the place provided aid for distressed overland emigrants (Hoover, Rensch, and Rensch, p. 111).

Calhoun: see **Camp Calhoun**, under **Pilot Knob** [IMPERIAL].

Calico [SAN BERNARDINO]: *locality,* 6 miles north-northeast of Daggett (lat. 34°56'55" N, long. 116°51'50" W; sec. 22, T 10 N, R 1 E). Named on Yermo (1953) 7.5' quadrangle. Postal authorities established Calico post office in 1882 and discontinued it in 1898 (Salley, p. 32).

Calico: see **Daggett** [SAN BERNARDINO].

Calico Mountains [SAN BERNARDINO]: *range,* 9.5 miles north of Daggett (lat. 35°00' N, long. 116°51' W). Named on Daggett (1956) and Lane Mountain (1948) 15' quadrangles. The name is from the multicolored rocks that make up the feature (Thompson, 1929, p. 442).

Calico Peak [SAN BERNARDINO]: *peak,* 9.5 miles north-northeast of Daggett (lat. 34°59'45" N, long. 116°50'15" W; at NE cor. sec. 2, T 10 N, R 1 E); the peak is in Calico Mountains. Altitude 4542 feet. Named on Yermo (1953) 7.5' quadrangle.

Calimesa [RIVERSIDE-SAN BERNARDINO]: *district,* 2.25 miles south-southwest of Yucaipa on Riverside-San Bernardino County line (lat. 34°00'25" N, long. 117°03'30" W; sec. 11, T 2 S, R 2 W). Named on El Casco (1967) and Yucaipa (1967) 7.5' quadrangles.

Calipatria [IMPERIAL]: *town,* 23 miles north of El Centro (lat. 33° 07'30" N, long. 115°30'50" W; sec. 15, 16, T 12 S, R 14 E). Named on Niland (1956) and Westmorland (1956) 7.5' quadrangles. Postal authorities established Calipatria post office in 1914 (Salley, p. 32), and the town incorporated in 1919. Imperial Valley Farm Lands Association purchased land and laid out the town in 1914; the community first was known as Date City (Hanna, p. 51).

Calumet Mountains [SAN BERNARDINO]: *range,* 17 miles southeast of Amboy (lat. 34°20'30" N, long. 115°34'30" W). Named on Bristol Lake (1956) 15' quadrangle.

Calzona [SAN BERNARDINO]: *locality,* 6 miles east of Vidal along Atchison, Topeka and Santa Fe Railroad (lat. 34°07'45" N, long. 114°24'35" W; sec. 36, T 1 N, R 24 E); the place is 1.25 miles north of California-Arizona State line. Named on Parker NW (1970) 7.5' quadrangle. Postal authorities established Calzona post office in 1909 and discontinued it in 1914 (Frickstad, p. 139).

Cameron Lake: see **New River** [IMPERIAL].

Camino [SAN BERNARDINO]: *locality,* 20 miles west of Needles (lat. 34°50'45" N, long. 114°57'50" W; near NW cor. sec. 26, T 9 N, R 19 E). Named on Bannock (1956) 15' quadrangle.

Camp Akela [SAN BERNARDINO]: *locality,* 4.5 miles northwest of Sugarloaf Mountain (lat. 34°14'50" N, long. 116°51'45" W; sec. 22, T 2 N, R 1 E). Named on Moonridge (1970) 7.5' quadrangle.

Camp Angelus [SAN BERNARDINO]: *locality,* 8 miles south-southwest of downtown Big Bear Lake (lat. 34°08'40" N, long. 116°58'50" W; at and near E line sec. 28, T 1 N, R 1 W). Named on Big Bear Lake (1970) 7.5' quadrangle, which shows Angelus Oaks post office at the spot. United States Board on Geographic Names (1976a, p. 4) approved the name "Angelus Oaks" for the place. Postal authorities established Camp Angelus post office in 1924 and discontinued it in 1943; they established Angelus Oaks post office in 1962 (Salley, p. 7, 33).

Camp Anza: see **Arlanza** [RIVERSIDE].

Camp Arbolado [SAN BERNARDINO]: *locality,* 5 miles south-southeast of downtown Big Bear Lake (lat. 34°10'25" N, long. 116°53'20" W; near W line sec. 16, T 1 N, R 1 E). Named on Big Bear Lake (1970) 7.5' quadrangle.

Camp Awahanes [SAN BERNARDINO]: *locality,* 3.25 miles northwest of Keller Peak (lat. 34°13'30" N, long. 117°05'35" W; near S line sec. 28, T 2 N, R 2 W). Named on Keller Peak (1967) 7.5' quadrangle. Called Larrys Boys Camp on Redlands (1954) 15' quadrangle.

Camp Baldy: see **Mount Baldy** [SAN BERNARDINO].

Camp Banning: see **Sycamore Flat** [SAN BERNARDINO].

Camp Baynham: see **Mount Baldy** [SAN BERNARDINO].

Campbell Hill [SAN BERNARDINO]: *hill,* 2.5 miles northeast of Twentynine Palms (lat. 34°09'20" N, long. 116°01'10" W; on E line sec. 22, T 1 N, R 9 E). Altitude 2162 feet. Named on Twentynine Palms (1973) 7.5' quadrangle.

Campbell Wash [IMPERIAL]: *stream,* flows 8 miles to Tule Wash 4.25 miles southeast of Truckhaven (lat. 33°15'40" N, long. 115° 55' W; sec. 34, T 10 S, R 10 E). Named on Kane Spring NW (1956) and Truckhaven (1956) 7.5' quadrangles.

Camp Cady [SAN BERNARDINO]: *locality,* 9.5 miles northeast of Newberry (lat. 34°56'45" N, long. 116°35'15" W; at W line sec. 20, T 10 N, R 4 E). Site named on Newberry (1955) 15' quadrangle. Major Carleton established the military post in 1860; the post was reactivated in 1862 to warn of Confederate attack, and was reactivated again in 1864 to control depredations by Indians; it was reopened in 1865 and moved 0.5 mile west in 1868—stockmen bought the buildings in 1871 (Hart, p. 124-126). Carleton named the post to honor Major Albemarle Cady of the 6th Infantry (Casebier, p. 127).

Camp Cajon: see **Cajon** [SAN BERNARDINO].

Camp Calhoun: see **Pilot Knob** [IMPERIAL].

Camp Carleton: see **Norton Air Force Base** [SAN BERNARDINO].

Camp Cedar Crest [SAN BERNARDINO]: *locality,* 2.5 miles northwest of Keller Peak (lat. 34°13'30" N, long. 117°04'30" W; near S line sec. 27, T 2 N, R 2 W). Named on Keller Peak (1967) 7.5' quadrangle.

Camp Cedar Falls [SAN BERNARDINO]: *locality,* 5.5 miles south-southwest of downtown Big Bear Lake (lat. 34°09'50" N, long. 116°56'10" W; on N line sec. 24, T 1 N, R 1 W). Named on Big Bear Lake (1970) 7.5'

quadrangle.

Camp Cohila [SAN BERNARDINO]: *locality*, 1 mile southwest of Big Bear City (lat. 34°15'05" N, long. 116°51'40" W; sec. 15, T 2 N, R 1 E). Named on Big Bear City (1971) 7.5' quadrangle.

Camp Conifer [SAN BERNARDINO]: *locality*, 2 miles west-northwest of Keller Peak (lat. 34°12'25" N, long. 117°05' W; near NW cor. sec. 3, T 1 N, R 2 W). Named on Keller Peak (1967) 7.5' quadrangle.

Camp Conrad [SAN BERNARDINO]: *locality*, 3.5 miles southeast of Sugarloaf Mountain (lat. 34°09'45" N, long. 116°51'50" W; near S line sec. 15, T 1 N, R 1 E). Named on Moonridge (1970) 7.5' quadrangle.

Camp Creek [SAN BERNARDINO]:

(1) *stream*, flows less than 0.5 mile to Bear Creek 2.5 miles east-northeast of Keller Peak (lat. 34°12'50" N, long. 117°00'35" W; near W line sec. 32, T 2 N, R 1 W). Named on Keller Peak (1967) 7.5' quadrangle.

(2) *stream*, flows 1 mile to Mill Creek Canyon nearly 4 miles west-southwest of San Gorgonio Mountain (lat. 34°04'50" N, long. 116° 53'10" W; sec. 16, T 1 S, R 1 E). Named on Forest Falls (1970) 7.5' quadrangle.

Camp De Benneville Pines [SAN BERNARDINO]: *locality*, 6 miles south-southeast of downtown Big Bear Lake (lat. 34°09'35" N, long. 116°53'35" W; on E line sec. 20, T 1 N, R 1 E). Named on Big Bear Lake (1970) 7.5' quadrangle.

Camp Dolores: see **Colton** [SAN BERNARDINO].

Camp Dunlap [IMPERIAL]: *locality*, 10 miles north-northeast of Calipatria (lat. 33°15'30" N, long. 115°27'45" W; in and near sec. 36, T 10 S, R 14 E). Site named on Iris Pass (1963) 15' quadrangle.

Camp Edwards [SAN BERNARDINO]: *locality*, nearly 4 miles southwest of Sugarloaf Mountain (lat. 34°09'45" N, long. 116°51'50" W; near N line sec. 22, T 1 N, R 1 E). Named on Moonridge (1970) 7.5' quadrangle.

Camp Emerson [RIVERSIDE]: *locality*, 1 mile west-southwest of the center of Idyllwild (lat. 33°44'05" N, long. 116°44' W; near W line sec. 13, T 5 S, R 2 E). Named on Idyllwild (1959) 15' quadrangle. The name honors C.L. Emerson, who donated the site for a Boy Scout camp (Gunther, p. 95).

Camp Evans [RIVERSIDE]: *locality*, 1 mile west-northwest of Riverside city hall (lat. 33°59'25" N, long. 117°23'15" W); the place is 0.5 mile southwest of Lake Evans. Named on Riverside West (1967) 7.5' quadrangle.

Camp Good News [SAN BERNARDINO]: *locality*, 3 miles southwest of Sugarloaf Mountain (lat. 34°10'20" N, long. 116°51'15" W; sec. 14, T 1 N, R 1 E). Named on Moonridge (1970) 7.5' quadrangle.

Camp Haan [RIVERSIDE]: *military installation*, 9 miles southeast of Riverside city hall (lat. 33°52'30" N, long. 117°16' W). Named on Riverside (1943) 15' quadrangle. Postal authorities established Camp Haan post office in 1941 and discontinued it in 1947 (Salley, p. 34). The name honored Major General William G. Haan, a field artillery officer in the Philippines in 1898 and in France during World War I; anti-aircraft artillery personnel trained at the camp—in 1945 the installation was made part of adjacent March Air Force Base, and for a time was known as West March (Gunther, p. 95-96).

Camp Independence: see **Pilot Knob** [IMPERIAL].

Camp Irwin [SAN BERNARDINO]: *military installation*, 34 miles west of Baker on part of a huge area that has the name "Camp Irwin Military Reservation" or "Marine Corps Training Center" on most maps (lat. 35°15'45" N, long. 116°41' W; in and near sec. 32, T 14 N, R 3 E). Named on Tiefort Mountains (1948) 15' quadrangle. Trona (1957) 1°x 2° quadrangle has the designation "Camp Irwin (Fort Irwin P.O.)" at the site. Postal authorities established Camp Irwin post office, named for Major General George L. Irwin, in 1943, discontinued it in 1945, reestablished it in 1961, and changed the name to Fort Irwin the same year (Salley, p. 34).

Camp JCA [SAN BERNARDINO]: *locality*, 3.5 miles southwest of Sugarloaf Mountain (lat. 34°10'15" N, long. 116°52' W; sec. 15, T 1 N, R 1 E). Named on Moonridge (1970) 7.5' quadrangle.

Camp Juniper: see **Minnelusa** [SAN BERNARDINO].

Camp Lackey [RIVERSIDE]: *locality*, 3.5 miles northwest of San Jacinto Peak (lat. 33°50'55" N, long. 116°43'20" W; near E line sec. 1, T 4 S, R 2 E). Named on San Jacinto Peak (1981) 7.5' quadrangle.

Camp La Verne [SAN BERNARDINO]: *locality*, 6 miles south-southeast of downtown Big Bear Lake (lat. 34°09'40" N, long. 116°53'05" W; near N line sec. 21, T 1 N, R 1 E). Named on Big Bear Lake (1970) 7.5' quadrangle.

Camp Maria Stella [SAN BERNARDINO]: *locality*, 4.25 miles north of Mount San Antonio (lat. 34°21'05" N, long. 117°38'30" W; near NE cor. sec. 18, T 3 N, R 7 W). Named on Mount San Antonio (1955) 7.5' quadrangle.

Camp Marl Springs: see **Marl Spring** [SAN BERNARDINO].

Camp Nawakwa [SAN BERNARDINO]: *locality*, 3.5 miles southwest of Sugarloaf (lat. 34°10' N, long. 116°51'50" W; sec. 15, T 1 N, R 1 E). Named on Moonridge (1970) 7.5' quadrangle.

Camp Norris [SAN BERNARDINO]: *locality*, 3.25 miles southwest of Sugarloaf Mountain (lat. 34°10'15" N, long. 116°51'30" W; near E line sec. 15, T 1 N, R 1 E). Named on Moonridge (1970) 7.5' quadrangle.

Camp Oakes [SAN BERNARDINO]: *locality*, 4 miles northeast of Sugarloaf Mountain (lat. 34°13'50" N, long. 116°45'10" W; near E line sec. 27, T 2 N, R 2 E). Named on Moonridge (1970) 7.5' quadrangle.

Camp Osceola [SAN BERNARDINO]: *locality*, 3.25 miles southwest of Sugarloaf Mountain (lat. 34°09'40" N, long. 116°51' W; near N line sec. 23, T 1 N, R 1 E). Named on Moonridge (1970) 7.5' quadrangle.

Camp Osito Rancho [SAN BERNARDINO]: *locality*, 2 miles south-southwest of downtown Big Bear Lake (lat. 34°13'10" N, long. 116°55'50" W; sec. 36, T 2 N, R 1 W). Named on Big Bear Lake (1970) 7.5' quadrangle.

Camp Paivika [SAN BERNARDINO]: *locality*, 9 miles north of San Bernardino city hall (lat. 34°14'10" N, long. 117°19'10" W; at N line sec. 29, T 2 N, R 4 W). Named on San Bernardino North (1967) 7.5' quadrangle.

Camp Prentiss: see **Norton Air Force Base** [SAN BERNARDINO].

Camp Radford [SAN BERNARDINO]: *locality*, 3 miles south of downtown Big Bear Lake (lat. 34°11'55" N, long. 116°54'10" W; sec. 5, T 1 N, R 1 E). Named on Big Bear Lake (1970) 7.5' quadrangle.

Camp River Glen [SAN BERNARDINO]: *locality*, 3 miles west-southwest of Sugarloaf Mountain along Santa Ana River (lat. 34° 10'55" N, long. 116°51'40" W; sec. 10, T 1 N, R 1 E). Named on Moonridge (1970) 7.5' quadrangle.

Camp Rock [SAN BERNARDINO]: *relief feature*, 6 miles north-northeast of Daggett (lat. 34°56'20" N, long. 116°50'15" W; near SE cor. sec. 23, T 10 N, R 1 E). Named on Yermo (1953) 7.5' quadrangle.

Camp Rock Springs: see **Rock Spring** [SAN BERNARDINO].

Camp Roosevelt [RIVERSIDE]: *locality*, 5 miles south-southeast of Idyllwild (lat. 33°40'50" N, long. 116°40'30" W; sec. 4, T 6 S, R 3 E). Named on Idyllwild (1959) 15' quadrangle.

Camp Round Meadow [SAN BERNARDINO]: *locality*, 5.5 miles south of downtown Big Bear Lake (lat. 34°09'40" N, long. 116°54'20" W; near NW cor. sec. 20, T 1 N, R 1 E). Named on Big Bear Lake (1970) 7.5' quadrangle.

Camp Salvation: see **Calexico** [IMPERIAL].

Camp San Antonio [SAN BERNARDINO]: *locality*, 2 miles south-southeast of Mount San Antonio (lat. 34°15'40" N, long. 117° 38' W; sec. 17, T 2 N, R 7 W); the place is in San Antonio Canyon. Named on Mount San Antonio (1955) 7.5' quadrangle.

Camp Seeley [SAN BERNARDINO]: *locality*, 19 miles south of Victorville (lat. 34°15'20" N, long. 117°18'10" W; sec. 16, T 2 N, R 4 W); the place is at Seeley Flat. Named on Cedar Springs (1956) 7.5' quadrangle.

Camp Sky Meadow [SAN BERNARDINO]: *locality*, 3.5 miles south of downtown Big Bear Lake (lat. 34°11'35" N, long. 116°54'30" W; at SW cor. sec. 5, T 1 N, R 1 E). Named on Big Bear Lake (1970) 7.5' quadrangle.

Camp Soda Springs: see **Soda Springs** [SAN BERNARDINO].

Camp Spring: see **Little Camp Spring** [RIVERSIDE].

Camp Tahquitz [RIVERSIDE]: *locality*, 0.5 mile north of the center of Idyllwild (lat. 33°44'55" N, long. 116°43'10" W; at W line sec. 7, T 5 S, R 3 E). Named on Idyllwild (1959) 15' quadrangle.

Camp Tahquitz [SAN BERNARDINO]: *locality*, 5.5 miles south of downtown Big Bear Lake (lat. 34°09'55" N, long. 116°53'45" W; near SE cor. sec. 17, T 1 N, R 1 E). Named on Big Bear Lake (1970) 7.5' quadrangle.

Camp Ta Ta Pochon [SAN BERNARDINO]: *locality*, 6 miles south-southeast of downtown Big Bear Lake (lat. 34°09'25" N, long. 116°53'10" W; sec. 21, T 1 N, R 1 E). Named on Big Bear Lake (1970) 7.5' quadrangle.

Camp Tautona [SAN BERNARDINO]: *locality*, 3 miles southwest of Sugarloaf Mountain (lat. 34°10'10" N, long. 116°51'15" W; near W line sec. 14, T 1 N, R 1 E). Named on Moonridge (1970) 7.5' quadrangle.

Camp Tree Mont [RIVERSIDE]: *locality*, 4.5 miles northeast of Sunnymead (lat. 33°59'30" N, long. 117°11'50" W; near S line sec. 16, T 2 S, R 3 W). Named on Sunnymead (1967) 7.5' quadrangle.

Camp Tulake [SAN BERNARDINO]: *locality*, 4 miles southwest of Sugarloaf Mountain (lat. 34°09'40" N, long. 116°52'10" W; near N line sec. 22, T 1 N, R 1 E). Named on Moonridge (1970) 7.5' quadrangle.

Camp Wintaka [SAN BERNARDINO]: *locality*, 2.5 miles northwest of Keller Peak (lat. 34°13'20" N, long. 117°04'45" W; at N line sec. 34, T 2 N, R 2 W). Named on Keller Peak (1967) 7.5' quadrangle.

Camp Young: see **Chiriaco Summit** [RIVERSIDE].

Camp Yuma: see **Pilot Knob** [IMPERIAL].

Cañada de Santa Ana: see **Cañon de Santa Ana** [SAN BERNARDINO].

Canadian Hot Springs: see **Eden Hot Springs** [RIVERSIDE].

Cane Spring: see **Kane Spring** [IMPERIAL].

Cañon de Santa Ana [SAN BERNARDINO]: *land grant*, mainly in Orange County, but extends northeast into San Bernardino County in Chino Hills. Named on Black Star Canyon (1967) and Prado Dam (1967) 7.5' quadrangles. Bernardo Yorba received 3 leagues in 1834 and claimed 13,329 acres patented in 1866 (Cowan, p. 90; Cowan used the form "Cañada de Santa Ana" for the name).

Cantu: see **Andrade** [IMPERIAL].

Canyon Crest: see **Canyon Crest Heights** [RIVERSIDE].

Canyon Crest Heights [RIVERSIDE]: *district*, 2.5 miles east of Riverside city hall (lat. 33°58'50" N, long. 117°19'40" W; at W line sec. 20, T 2 S, R

4 W). Named on Riverside East (1967) 7.5' quadrangle. Postal authorities established Canyon Crest post office in 1963 (Salley, p. 36). The place began about 1941 as a housing annex for personnel from March Field; it was built on the east side of Canyon Crest Drive and was named for that street—by the time postal authorities established the post office there, the place was part of University of California Riverside (Gunther, p. 98).

Canyon Siding [RIVERSIDE]: *locality,* 5.5 miles northeast of present Lake Elsinore city hall (lat. 33°43' N, long. 117°15'30" W); the place is in Railroad Canyon. Named on Elsinore (1901) 30' quadrangle.

Canyon Spring [RIVERSIDE]: *spring,* 9 miles south-southeast of Chiriaco Summit (lat. 33°32'45" N, long. 115°39'10" W; sec. 20, T 7 S, R 13 E). Named on Hayfield (1963) 15' quadrangle. The old Canyon Spring stage station is just south of the spring (Brown, 1923, p. 248).

Canyon Spring [SAN BERNARDINO]: *spring,* 3.5 miles east-northeast of Big Bear City (lat. 34°17'20" N, long. 116°47'30" W; sec. 5, T 2 N, R 2 E). Named on Big Bear City (1971) 7.5' quadrangle.

Caramba Camp [RIVERSIDE]: *locality,* 5.5 miles southwest of Palm Springs (lat. 33°47' N, long. 116°37'25" W; sec. 36, T 4 S, R 3 E). Named on Palm Springs (1957) 7.5' quadrangle. The name, which is from a Spanish exclamation, was given to the feature after some cowboys were terrified by sounds that they heard there during the night (Gunther, p. 98-99).

Carbonate Gulch [SAN BERNARDINO]: *canyon,* drained by a stream that flows 4 miles to lowlands 13 miles south of Essex (lat. 34°32'25" N, long. 115°15'30" W; sec. 12, T 5 N, R 16 E); the feature heads near Carbonate Peak. Named on Danby (1956) and Essex (1956) 15' quadrangles.

Carbonate Peak [SAN BERNARDINO]: *peak,* 12.5 miles south-southeast of Essex (lat. 34°33'30" N, long. 115°11'25" W; near S line sec. 34, T 6 N, R 17 E). Named on Essex (1956) 15' quadrangle.

Carbon Canyon [SAN BERNARDINO]: *canyon,* drained by a stream that flows nearly 3 miles to Orange County 3 miles northwest of San Juan Hill (lat. 33°56'40" N, long. 117°46'50" W). Named on Yorba Linda (1964) 7.5' quadrangle.

Carbon Canyon Mineral Springs [SAN BERNARDINO]: *locality,* 3.5 miles northwest of San Juan Hill (lat. 33°56'45" N, long. 117° 46'50" W; at N line sec. 1, T 3 S, R 9 W); the place is in Carbon Canyon. Named on Yorba Linda (1950) 7.5' quadrangle. Water used at the facility is from a well drilled for oil (Berkstresser, 1968, p. A-12).

Cargo Muchacho Mountains [IMPERIAL]: *range,* 5 miles northeast of Ogilby (lat. 32°52' N, long. 114°46'30" W). Named on Ogilby (1963) 15' quadrangle, and on Araz (1964) 7.5' quadrangle. Called Cargo Mechaco Mts. on Hanks' (1886) map.

Caribou Creek [SAN BERNARDINO]: *stream,* flows 7.25 miles to Baldwin Lake at Big Bear City (lat. 34°16'10" N, long. 116°49'50" W; sec. 12, T 2 N, R 1 E). Named on Big Bear City (1971) and Fawnskin (1971) 7.5' quadrangles.

Carleton: see **Camp Carleton**, under **Norton Air Force Base** [SAN BERNARDINO].

Carrillo Spring [RIVERSIDE]: *spring,* 3.25 miles southwest of Sitton Peak (lat. 33°33'20" N, long. 117°29'10" W; near E line sec. 15, T 7 S, R 6 W). Named on Sitton Peak (1954) 7.5' quadrangle.

Carrizo Badlands [IMPERIAL]: *relief feature,* mainly in San Diego County, but extends east-southeast into Imperial County 5 miles west-northwest of Carrizo Mountain (lat. 32°50'45" N, long. 116° 06' W). Named on Carrizo Mountain (1957) 7.5' quadrangle.

Carrizo Creek [IMPERIAL]: *stream,* heads in San Diego County and flows 3.5 miles in Imperial County to become Carrizo Wash (2) 4 miles north-northwest of Carrizo Mountain (lat. 32°52'35" N, long. 116°02'45" W; sec. 9, T 15 S, R 9 E). Named on Carrizo Mountain (1957) and Carrizo Mountain NE (1957) 7.5' quadrangles. United States Board on Geographic Names (1961b, p. 9) rejected the name "Carrizo Wash" for Carrizo Creek.

Carrizo Creek [RIVERSIDE]: *stream,* flows 5.25 miles to Dead Indian Creek 4 miles south-southwest of Palm Desert (lat. 33°40'15" N, long. 116°24'20" W; near SW cor. sec. 6, T 6 S, R 6 E). Named on Palm Desert (1959) 15' quadrangle.

Carrizo Creek: see **Carrizo Wash** [IMPERIAL] (1).

Carrizo Falls [IMPERIAL]: *waterfall,* 28 miles south of Palo Verde (lat. 33°01'10" N, long. 114°41'20" W); the feature is along Carrizo Wash (2). Named on Picacho SW (1965) 7.5' quadrangle.

Carrizo Mountain [IMPERIAL]: *peak,* 26 miles west of El Centro (lat. 32°49'30" N, long. 116°00'50" W; near NW cor. sec. 35, T 15 S, R 9 E); the peak is in Coyote Mountains. Altitude 2408 feet. Named on Carrizo Mountain (1957) 7.5' quadrangle. The peak also is called Coyote Mountain (Brown, 1923, p. 215).

Carrizo Spring [IMPERIAL]: *spring,* 28 miles south of Palo Verde (lat. 33°01'15" N, long. 114°41'20" W); the spring is along Carrizo Wash (2). Named on Picacho SW (1965) 7.5' quadrangle.

Carrizo Springs: see **Old Carrizo Stage Station** [IMPERIAL].

Carrizo Stage Station: see **Old Carrizo Stage Station** [IMPERIAL].

Carrizo Wash [IMPERIAL]:

(1) *stream* and *dry wash,* extends for 21 miles from where Carrizo Creek becomes Carrizo Wash to San Felipe Creek 5.25 miles west of Kane Spring (lat. 33°05'55" N, long. 115°55'35" W; near E line sec. 28, T 12 S, R 10 E). Named on Carrizo Mountain (1957), Carrizo Mountain NE (1957), Harpers Well (1956), and Plaster City NW (1956) 7.5' quadrangles. Called Carrizo Creek on Carrizo Mountain (1944) 15' quadrangle, but United States Board on Geographic Names (1961b, p. 10) rejected this name for the feature.

(2) *stream,* flows 7.25 miles to Colorado River 27 miles south of Palo Verde (lat. 33°02'15" N, long. 114°40'15" W; at S line sec. 16, T 13 S, R 22 E). Named on Picacho Peak (1965) and Picacho SW (1965) 7.5' quadrangles.

Carrizo Wash: see **Carrizo Creek** [IMPERIAL].

Carrizo Wells: see **Old Carrizo Stage Station** [IMPERIAL].

Carsons Wells [SAN BERNARDINO]: *wells,* 28 miles northwest of Vidal (lat. 34°25'35" N, long. 114°49'15" W). Named on Turtle Mountains (1954) 15' quadrangle.

Carson Wash [SAN BERNARDINO]: *stream,* flows 2.5 miles to end 6.5 miles southeast of Essex (lat. 34°39'25" N, long. 115°10'35" W; near NW cor. sec. 35, T 7 N, R 17 E). Named on Essex (1956) 15' quadrangle.

Cartridge Spring [RIVERSIDE]: *spring,* 5.5 miles east-southeast of Idyllwild (lat. 33°42'25" N, long. 116°38' W; near E line sec. 26, T 5 S, R 3 E). Named on Idyllwild (1959) 15' quadrangle.

Caruthers Canyon [SAN BERNARDINO]: *canyon,* 2 miles long, 7 miles south of Ivanpah (lat. 35°14' N, long. 115°18' W). Named on Mid Hills (1955) 15' quadrangle.

Casa Blanca [RIVERSIDE]: *district,* 4 miles south-southwest of Riverside city hall (lat. 33°55'55" N, long. 117°24' W; around SE cor. sec. 4, T 3 S, R 5 W). Named on Riverside West (1967) 7.5' quadrangle. Called Blanca on California Mining Bureau's (1917b) map. The neighborhood became known as Casa Blanca soon after Henry Benedict Lockwood moved into a white adobe house there in 1878; Lockwood subdivided some of his land when a rail line reached the site in 1886 (Gunther, p. 100).

Casa de Cuerva [RIVERSIDE]: *area,* 15 miles south-southeast of Palm Desert (lat. 33°32' N, long. 116°15' W). Named on Coachella (1956) and Palm Desert (1959) 15' quadrangles.

Casa Loma [RIVERSIDE]: *locality,* 5 miles east of Lakeview (lat. 33°49'40" N, long. 117°02' W). Named on Elsinore (1901) 30' quadrangle.

Cascade Canyon [SAN BERNARDINO]: *canyon,* drained by a stream that flows nearly 1 mile to Los Angeles County 10.5 miles north of Ontario city hall (lat. 34°12'45" N, long. 117°39'50" W; sec. 36, T 2 N, R 8 W). Named on Mount Baldy (1967) 7.5' quadrangle.

Cassina Springs: see **Box Springs** [RIVERSIDE] (1).

Castile Canyon [RIVERSIDE]: *canyon,* drained by a stream that flows 3 miles to Poppet Creek 4 miles east of San Jacinto (lat. 33° 47'20" N, long. 116°53'10" W; at S line sec. 28, T 4 S, R 1 E). Named on San Jacinto (1953) 7.5' quadrangle. The misspelled name commemorates Jose Jesus Castillo, who received land near San Jacinto patented in 1890 (Gunther, p. 104).

Castle Dome [SAN BERNARDINO]: *peak,* 7.5 miles west of Essex (lat. 34°43'45" N, long. 115°22'40" W; near N line sec. 2, T 7 N, R 15 E). Altitude 3299 feet. Named on Danby (1956) 15' quadrangle.

Castle Mountains [SAN BERNARDINO]: *range,* 14 miles east of Ivanpah on California-Nevada State line (lat. 35°19' N, long. 115° 05' W). Named on Crescent Peak (1956) 15' quadrangle.

Castle Peaks [SAN BERNARDINO]: *peaks,* 9 miles east-northeast of Ivanpah (lat. 35°22'15" N, long. 115°09'30" W). Named on Crescent Peak (1956) 15' quadrangle.

Castle Rock [SAN BERNARDINO]:

(1) *hill,* 18 miles west-northwest of Vidal (lat. 34°16' N, long. 114° 46'40" W). Altitude 2979 feet. Named on Turtle Mountains (1954) 15' quadrangle.

(2) *relief feature,* 3 miles west-southwest of downtown Big Bear Lake (lat. 34°13'50" N, long. 116°57'40" W; near W line sec. 26, T 2 N, R 1 W). Named on Big Bear Lake (1970) 7.5' quadrangle.

Castle Rocks [RIVERSIDE]: *relief feature,* 2.25 miles west-northwest of San Jacinto Peak on Fuller Ridge (lat. 33°49'55" N, long. 116°42'50" W; on S line sec. 7, T 4 S, R 3 E). Named on San Jacinto Peak (1981) 7.5' quadrangle.

Catclaw Flat [RIVERSIDE-SAN BERNARDINO]: *area,* 6 miles west of downtown Morongo Valley on Riverside-San Bernardino County line (lat. 34°02'15" N, long. 116°41'05" W; on E line sec. 32, T 1 S, R 3 E). Named on Catclaw Flat (1972) 7.5' quadrangle. United States Board on Geographic Names (1975a, p. 9) noted that the designation is from catclaw acacia, a common desert plant; the Board gave the form "Cat Claw Flat" as a variant.

Cat Creek [RIVERSIDE]: *stream,* flows 3.5 miles to lowlands 3.25 miles southwest of Palm Desert (lat. 33°41'30" N, long. 116°25'15" W; sec. 36, T 5 S, R 5 E). Named on Rancho Mirage (1957) 7.5' quadrangle.

Catfish Bay [SAN BERNARDINO]: *embayment,* 25 miles south-southeast of Needles along Lake Havasu (lat. 34°31'30" N, long. 114°23'20" W; on E line sec. 18, T 5 N, R 25 E). Named on Castle Rock (1970) 7.5' quadrangle.

Cathedral Canyon [RIVERSIDE]: *canyon,* 4 miles long, opens into lowlands at Cathedral City (lat. 33°46'40" N, long. 116°27'50" W). Named on Cathedral City (1958) and Rancho Mirage (1957) 7.5' quadrangles.

Cathedral City [RIVERSIDE]: *town,* 5.5 miles southeast of downtown Palm Springs (lat. 33°46'50" N, long. 116°27'50" W; sec. 33, T 4 S, R 5 E); the place is at the mouth of Cathedral Canyon. Named on Cathedral City (1958) 7.5' quadrangle. Postal authorities established Cathedral City post office in 1928 (Frickstad, p. 127), and the town incorporated in 1981. Development of the community began in 1925 (Gunther, p. 105).

Cathedral City: see **The Pinnacles** [SAN BERNARDINO] (1).

Catholic Hill [SAN BERNARDINO]: *peak,* 4 miles east of Victorville (lat. 34°32'30" N, long. 117°13'30" W; on E line sec. 6, T 5 N, R 3 W). Named on Apple Valley North (1970) 7.5' quadrangle.

Cave Canyon: see **Afton Canyon** [SAN BERNARDINO].

Cave Mountain [SAN BERNARDINO]: *ridge,* northeast-trending, 4 miles long, 20 miles southwest of Baker (lat. 35°04'30" N, long. 116°18'30" W). Named on Cave Mountain (1948) 15' quadrangle.

Cave Mountains: see **Cronese Mountains** [SAN BERNARDINO].

Cave of the Winding Stairs: see **Winding Stair Cave** [SAN BERNARDINO].

Cave Rocks [RIVERSIDE]: *relief feature,* 12.5 miles south of Idyllwild (lat. 33°33'30" N, long. 116°42'15" W; near SE cor. sec. 18, T 7 S, R 3 E). Named on Idyllwild (1959) 15' quadrangle.

Cave Spring [RIVERSIDE]: *spring,* 8 miles east of San Jacinto (lat. 33°46'20" N, long. 116°49'20" W; near NW cor. sec. 6, T 5 S, R 2 E). Named on Lake Fulmor (1956) 7.5' quadrangle. Called Sycamore Spring on Banning (1942) 15' quadrangle.

Cave Spring [SAN BERNARDINO]: *spring,* 27 miles northwest of Baker (lat. 35°32'25" N, long. 116°25'50" W). Named on Avawatz Pass (1948) 15' quadrangle. Two springs at the place occur in large grottoes or caves (Mendenhall, 1909a, p. 47). The old mining camp known as Crackerjack was situated about 2 miles southwest of Cave Springs (Thompson, 1929, p. 199). The name "Crackerjack" is from Crackerjack mining district, organized in 1906 and named by the miners for their "crackerjack" find (Lingenfelter, 1986, p. 331). Postal authorities established Crackerjack post office in 1907, moved it 3 miles northeast and changed the name to Avawatz in 1908, and discontinued it in 1910 (Salley, p. 12, 52).

Cedar Canyon [SAN BERNARDINO]:

(1) *canyon,* 4 miles long, opens into lowlands 14 miles south-southwest of Ivanpah (lat. 35°09'40" N, long. 115°27' W; sec. 35, T 13 N, R 14 E). Named on Mid Hills (1955) 15' quadrangle.

(2) *canyon,* 1.5 miles long, 2.5 miles southeast of Mount San Antonio (lat. 34°15'25" N, long. 117°37'05" W; mainly in sec. 16, T 2 N, R 7 W). Named on Telegraph Peak (1956) 7.5' quadrangle.

Cedar Creek [SAN BERNARDINO]: *stream,* flows nearly 2 miles to Shake Creek 6 miles south of Luna Mountain (lat. 34°15'40" N, long. 117°07'40" W; sec. 18, T 2 N, R 2 W). Named on Harrison Mountain (1967) and Lake Arrowhead (1971) 7.5' quadrangles.

Cedar Crest: see **Camp Cedar Crest** [SAN BERNARDINO].

Cedar Falls: see **Camp Cedar Falls** [SAN BERNARDINO].

Cedar Glen [SAN BERNARDINO]: *village,* 6.5 miles south-southwest of Luna Mountain (lat. 34°15'15" N, long. 117°09'45" W; sec. 14, T 2 N, R 3 W). Named on Lake Arrowhead (1971) 7.5' quadrangle. Postal authorities established Cedar Glen post office in 1939 (Frickstad, p. 139).

Cedar Lake [SAN BERNARDINO]: *lake,* 750 feet long, 2 miles west-southwest of downtown Big Bear Lake (lat. 34°13'50" N, long. 116°56'25" W; sec. 25, T 2 N, R 1 W). Named on Big Bear Lake (1970) 7.5' quadrangle.

Cedar Mountain [SAN BERNARDINO]: *peak,* 6 miles west-southwest of San Gorgonio Mountain (lat. 34°04'05" N, long. 116°55'40" W; at W line sec. 19, T 1 S, R 1 E). Altitude 8324 feet. Named on Forest Falls (1970) 7.5' quadrangle.

Cedar Pines: see **Cedarpines Park** [SAN BERNARDINO].

Cedarpines Park [SAN BERNARDINO]: *village,* 20 miles south of Victorville (lat. 34°15'05" N, long. 117°19'40" W). Named on Cedar Springs (1956) and San Bernardino North (1967) 7.5' quadrangles. Called Cedar Pines on Hesperia (1942) 15' quadrangle. Postal authorities established Cedarpines Park post office in 1927, discontinued it in 1943, and reestablished it in 1946 (Frickstad, p. 139).

Cedar Spring [RIVERSIDE]:

(1) *spring,* 9.5 miles east-southeast of Idyllwild (lat. 33°40'40" N, long. 116°34'40" W; sec. 4, T 6 S, R 4 W). Named on Idyllwild (1959) 15' quadrangle.

(2) *spring,* 13 miles south-southwest of Palm Desert (lat. 33°32'10" N, long. 116°26'30" W; sec. 26, T 7 S, R 5 E). Named on Palm Desert (1959) 15' quadrangle. Called Virgin Spring on United States Geological Survey's (1904) map.

Cedar Springs [SAN BERNARDINO]: *locality,* 18 miles south of Victorville (lat. 34°02'05" N, long. 117°19'50" W; near E line sec. 6, T 2 N, R 4 W). Named on Cedar Springs (1956) 7.5' quadrangle. Water of Silverwood Lake now covers the site.

Cedar Wash [SAN BERNARDINO]: *stream,* flows 14 miles from the mouth of Cedar Canyon to Kelso Wash 26 miles southwest of Ivanpah (lat. 35°03'20" N, long. 115°37'55" W; sec. 7, T 11 N, R 13 E). Named on Kelso (1955) and Mid Hills (1955) 15' quadrangles.

Cerrito Solo [SAN BERNARDINO]: *relief feature,* 1 mile southwest of present Colton civic center (lat. 34°03'35" N, long. 117°20'10" W). Named on Colton (1943) 7.5' quadrangle.

Cerro de San Pablo: see **Pilot Knob** [IMPERIAL].

Chalk Hill [RIVERSIDE]: *ridge,* southwest-trending, 1 mile long, 1 mile south of the center of Idyllwild (lat. 33°43'35" N, long. 116° 43'15" W; on E line sec. 24, T 5 S, R 2 E). Named on Idyllwild (1959) 15' quadrangle.

Chambers Well [SAN BERNARDINO]: *well,* 10.5 miles north of Vidal (lat. 34°16'35" N, long. 114°29'10" W; near W line sec. 8, T 2 N, R 24 E). Named on Whipple Mountains SW (1970) 7.5' quadrangle, which indicates that the well is dry. Thompson (1929, p. 747) noted that the 48-foot well held only 6 inches of water in 1917.

Chambless [SAN BERNARDINO]: *locality,* 11.5 miles east of Amboy (lat. 34°33'40" N, long. 115°32'35" W; near SW cor. sec. 32, T 6 N, R 14 E). Named on Cadiz (1956) 15' quadrangle.

Champagne [SAN BERNARDINO]: *locality,* 5.5 miles east-southeast of Ontario city hall along Union Pacific Railroad (lat. 34°02' N, long. 117°33'30" W; near SE cor. sec. 36, T 1 S, R 7 W). Named on Guasti (1966) 7.5' quadrangle.

Chaney Hill [RIVERSIDE]: *hill,* 2.25 miles northwest of Murrieta (lat. 33°34'45" N, long. 117°14'25" W). Named on Murrieta (1953) 7.5' quadrangle. The misspelled name is for Madison Cheney and his wife, who discovered coal in the neighborhood in 1883 (Gunther, p. 108).

Chaparrosa Peak [SAN BERNARDINO]: *peak,* 7.25 miles north of downtown Morongo Valley (lat. 34°09' N, long. 116°33'45" W; near SE cor. sec. 21, T 1 N, R 4 E). Altitude 5541 feet. Named on Rimrock (1972) 7.5' quadrangle.

Chaparrosa Spring [SAN BERNARDINO]: *spring,* 8 miles north-northeast of downtown Morongo Valley (lat. 34°08'40" N, long. 116°30'50" W; near NE cor. sec. 25, T 1 N, R 4 E); the spring is along Chaparrosa Wash. Named on Rimrock (1972) 7.5' quadrangle.

Chaparrosa Wash [SAN BERNARDINO]: *stream,* flows 5.25 miles to Pipes Wash 4.5 miles north of Yucca Valley (lat. 34°11'10" N, long. 116°27'25" W; at E line sec. 9, T 1 N, R 5 E). Named on Rimrock (1972) and Yucca Valley North (1972) 7.5' quadrangles.

Charlton Peak [SAN BERNARDINO]: *peak,* nearly 2 miles west-northwest of San Gorgonio Mountain (lat. 34°06'50" N, long. 116° 51'10" W; sec. 2, T 1 S, R 1 E). Altitude 10,806 feet. Named on San Gorgonio Mountain (1970) 7.5' quadrangle.

Charlton Peak: see **Little Charlton Peak** [SAN BERNARDINO].

Chase [SAN BERNARDINO]: *locality,* 15 miles southwest of Ivanpah (lat. 35°11' N, long. 115°30'15" W; sec. 29, T 13 N, R 14 E). Named on Kelso (1955) 15' quadrangle.

Chemehuevi Mountains [SAN BERNARDINO]: *range,* center 15 miles south-southeast of Needles (lat. 34°37' N, long. 114°33' W). Named on Sawtooth Range (1950) and Topock (1950) 15' quadrangles. The name is from an Indian tribe of the neighborhood (Kroeber, p. 38). United States Board on Geographic Names (1965a, p. 9) rejected the names "Mohave Mountains," "Chemehuevis Mountains," and "Chemehuevitz Mountains" for the range.

Chemehuevi Peak [SAN BERNARDINO]: *peak,* 20 miles south of Needles (lat. 34°33'10" N, long. 114°33'45" W); the peak is in Chemehuevi Mountains. Altitude 3694 feet. Named on Chemehuevi Peak (1971) 7.5' quadrangle.

Chemehuevi Valley [SAN BERNARDINO]: *valley,* west and south of Chemehuevi Mountains; extends across Colorado River into Arizona. Named on Savahia Peak (1950), Sawtooth Range (1950), Stepladder Mountains (1956), Topock (1950), Turtle Mountains (1954), and Whipple Mountains (1950) 15' quadrangles.

Chemehuevi Valley: see **Little Chemehuevi Valley** [SAN BERNARDINO].

Chemehuevi Wash [SAN BERNARDINO]: *stream* and *dry wash,* extends for 33 miles to Lake Havasu 25 miles north-northeast of Vidal (lat. 34°28'25" N, long. 114°24'15" W); the feature goes through Chemehuevi Valley. Named on Savahia Peak (1950), Sawtooth Range (1950), and Stepladder Mountains (1956) 15' quadrangles.

Cherry Canyon [RIVERSIDE-SAN BERNARDINO]: *canyon,* on Riverside-San Bernardino County line, 3 miles long, along Noble Creek above a point 6 miles northwest of Banning (lat. 33°58'55" N, long. 116°57'30" W). Named on Beaumont (1953) and Forest Falls (1970) 7.5' quadrangles. The name is from Cherry Valley Land and Water Company; the feature first was known as Noble Canyon (Gunther, p. 109).

Cherry Canyon [SAN BERNARDINO]: *canyon,* 1 mile long, 12 miles north of Ontario city hall (lat. 34°14'10" N, long. 117°37'45" W). Named on Cucamonga Peak (1966) and Mount Baldy (1967) 7.5' quadrangles.

Cherry Valley [RIVERSIDE]: *town,* 6.5 miles west-northwest of Banning (lat. 33°58'20" N, long. 116°58'35" W). Named on Beaumont (1953) 7.5' quadrangle. Postal authorities established Cherry Valley post office in 1958 (Salley, p. 42). Cherry Valley Land and Water Company began developing land at place in 1885 (Gunther, p. 109).

Chicken Water Spring [SAN BERNARDINO]: *spring,* 16 miles south-southwest of Ivanpah (lat. 35°06'30" N, long. 115°28' W; sec. 22, T 12 N, R 14 E). Named on Mid Hills (1955) 15' quadrangle.

Chicopee Canyon: see **Jacoby Canyon** [SAN BERNARDINO].

Chimney Flats [RIVERSIDE]: *area*, 11.5 miles east of Hemet (lat. 33°44'10" N, long. 116°46'30" W; sec. 16, T 5 S, R 2 E). Named on Hemet (1957) 15' quadrangle. A chimney standing at the place is left from the CCC program of the 1930's (Jennings, p. 14).

Chimney Peak: see **Picacho Peak** [IMPERIAL].

Chimney Rock [SAN BERNARDINO]:

(1) *relief feature*, 6 miles northeast of Daggett (lat. 34°55'50" N, long. 117°49'20" W; near E line sec. 25, T 10 N, R 1 E). Named on Yermo (1953) 7.5' quadrangle.

(2) *relief feature*, 17 miles east-southeast of Victorville (lat. 34°28'05" N, long. 117°00'55" W; near E line sec. 6, T 4 N, R 1 W). Named on Fifteenmile Valley (1971) 7.5' quadrangle.

Chimney Rock: see **Picacho Peak** [IMPERIAL].

China Borax Lake: see **China Lake** [SAN BERNARDINO].

China Lake [SAN BERNARDINO]: *dry lake*, 14 miles west-southwest of Trona on San Bernardino-Kern County line (lat. 35°43' N, long. 117°37'30" W). Named on Mountain Springs Canyon (1953) 15' quadrangle, and on Lone Butte (1973) and Ridgecrest North (1973) 7.5' quadrangles. The name presumably is from Chinese borax workers at the place; the feature also was called China Borax Lake (Gale, p. 269).

China Lake Naval Weapons Center [SAN BERNARDINO]: *military installation*, at and near China Lake on San Bernardino-Kern County line. Named on Christmas Canyon (1973), Lone Butte (1973), Ridgecrest North (1973), Searles Lake (1973), Spangler Hills East (1973), Spangler Hills West (1973), and Westend (1973) 7.5' quadrangles. Construction of the facility began in 1943 (Wines, p. 81).

China Spring [SAN BERNARDINO]: *spring*, 14 miles west-northwest of Ivanpah (lat. 35°27'15" N, long. 115°30'30" W). Named on Mescal Range (1955) 15' quadrangle.

Chino [SAN BERNARDINO]: *city*, 4 miles south-southwest of Ontario city hall (lat. 34°00'45" N, long. 117°41'15" W); the place is on Santa Ana del Chino grant. Named on Ontario (1967) and Prado Dam (1967) 7.5' quadrangles. Postal authorities established Chino post office in 1873 and discontinued it for a time in 1887 (Salley, p. 43). The city incorporated in 1910.

Chino Canyon [RIVERSIDE]: *canyon*, 4.5 miles long, opens into lowlands 2 miles northwest of Palm Springs (lat. 33°51' N, long. 116°34'30" W). Named on Palm Springs (1957) and San Jacinto Peak (1981) 7.5' quadrangles. The name commemorates an Indian called Chino, who lived in the neighborhood of Palm Springs (Chase, p. 17).

Chino Creek [RIVERSIDE-SAN BERNARDINO]: *stream*, heads in Los Angeles County and flows 11.5 miles in San Bernardino and Riverside Counties to Santa Ana River 4.5 miles west of Corona (lat. 33°53'30" N, long, 117°38'35" W; sec. 20, T 3 S, R 7 W). Named on Ontario (1967) and Prado Dam (1967) 7.5' quadrangles.

Chino Creek: see **Little Chino Creek** [SAN BERNARDINO].

Chino Hills [SAN BERNARDINO]: *range*, north of Santa Ana River and south of Chino in San Bernardino, Los Angeles, and Orange Counties. Named on Prado Dam (1967) and Yorba Linda (1964) 7.5' quadrangles.

Chipmunk Spring [SAN BERNARDINO]: *spring*, nearly 5 miles southeast of Luna Mountain (lat. 34°17'30" N, long. 117°04'15" W; near NE cor. sec. 3, T 2 N, R 2 W). Named on Butler Peak (1971) 7.5' quadrangle.

Chiriaco Summit [RIVERSIDE]: *village*, 19 miles west-southwest of Desert Center (lat. 33°39'40" N, long. 115°43'10" W; sec. 10, T 6 S, R 12 E); the place is at the east end of Shavers Valley. Named on Hayfield (1963) 15' quadrangle. Called Shaver Summit on Canyon Spring (1943) 15' quadrangle. Postal authorities established Chiriaco Summit post office in 1959 (Salley, p. 43). The name "Chiriaco" commemorates Joseph L. Chiriaco, who started a gas station and store at Shaver's Summit in 1933 (Gunther, p. 112). Camp Young, a World War II army desert training center named for Lieutenant General Samuel B.M. Young, functioned near Chiriaco Summit from 1942 until 1944 (Gunther, p. 96).

Chocolate Drop [SAN BERNARDINO]: *relief feature*, 2 miles west-northwest of the center of Twentynine Palms (lat. 34°08'55" N, long. 116°05'10" W; near NW cor. sec. 30, T 1 N, R 9 E). Named on Twentynine Palms (1973) 7.5' quadrangle.

Chocolate Mountains [IMPERIAL-RIVERSIDE]: *range*, northeast of Salton Sea and Imperial Valley; mainly in Imperial County, but the northwest end is in Riverside County. Named on El Centro (1958) and Salton Sea (1959) 1°x 2° quadrangles. According to Orcutt (p. 899), the name is from the color of the range.

Cholla Canyon [RIVERSIDE]: *canyon*, drained by a stream that flows 3 miles to Cactus Valley 7 miles south-southeast of Hemet (lat. 33°39'35" N, long. 116°54'05" W; at N line sec. 17, T 6 S, R 1 E). Named on Hemet (1957) 15' quadrangle.

Cholla Valley: see **Cactus Valley** [RIVERSIDE].

Cholla Wash [RIVERSIDE]: *stream*, 1.5 miles long, 5 miles northeast of Chiriaco Summit (lat. 33°42'30" N, long. 115°39'30" W). Named on Hayfield (1963) 15' quadrangle.

Christmas Canyon [SAN BERNARDINO]: *canyon*, 2 miles long, opens into Searles Valley 17 miles south of Trona (lat. 35°31'35" N, long. 117°21'55" W). Named on Christmas Canyon (1973) 7.5' quadrangle.

Chubbuck [SAN BERNARDINO]: *locality*, 30 miles east-southeast of Amboy along Atchison, Topeka and Santa Fe Railroad (lat. 34° 22' N, long. 115°17'15" W; sec. 10, T 3 N, R 16 E). Named on Cadiz Lake (1956) 15' quadrangle. Called Kilbeck on Thompson's (1921) map. Postal authorities established Chubbuck post office in 1938 and discontinued it in 1950 (Frickstad, p. 139). The name "Kilbeck" was for a railroad employee; the name "Chubbuck" is for the developer of local lime deposits (Gudde, 1949, p. 68).

Chuckawalla Bill Spring [RIVERSIDE]: *spring*, 10 miles north-northeast of Garnet (lat. 34°01'40" N, long. 116°27'20" W; near W line sec. 3, T 2 S, R 5 E). Named on Yucca Valley South (1972) 7.5' quadrangle.

Chuckwalla Mountains [RIVERSIDE]: *range*, center 12 miles south-southeast of Desert Center (lat. 33°34' N, long. 115°20' W). Named on Chuckwalla Mountains (1963), Chuckwalla Spring (1953), Hayfield (1963), Iris Pass (1963), and Sidewinder Well (1952) 15' quadrangles. According to Jaeger (p. 23), the local Indians used the name "chuckawalla" for a tall slender variety of cactus; later the name was applied to a kind of lizard—the Indians always pronounced the "a" in the middle of the word.

Chuckwalla Mountains: see **Little Chuckwalla Mountains** [RIVERSIDE].

Chuckwalla Spring [RIVERSIDE]: *spring*, 20 miles south-southeast of Desert Center (lat. 33°28'35" N, long. 115°12'40" W); the spring is in Chuckwalla Mountains. Named on Chuckwalla Spring (1953) 15' quadrangle.

Chuckwalla Spring [SAN BERNARDINO]: *spring*, 8 miles west-northwest of Essex (lat. 34°46'10" N, long. 115°22'40" W; sec. 23, T 8 N, R 15 E). Named on Colton Well (1956) 15' quadrangle.

Chuckwalla Valley [RIVERSIDE]: *valley*, north and northeast of Chuckwalla Mountains. Named on Chuckwalla Mountains (1963), Coxcomb Mountains (1963), Hayfield (1963), McCoy Spring (1952), Palen Mountains (1952), and Sidewinder Well (1952) 15' quadrangles.

Chuckwalla Well [RIVERSIDE]: *well*, 21 miles south-southeast of Desert Center (lat. 33°26'35" N, long. 115°13' W; at N line sec. 33, T 8 S, R 17 E); the well is near the southeast end of Chuckwalla Mountains. Named on Chuckwalla Spring (1953) 15' quadrangle.

Chukar Spring [SAN BERNARDINO]: *spring*, 3 miles east of Luna Mountain (lat. 34°20'50" N, long. 117°04'30" W; sec. 15, T 3 N, R 2 W). Named on Butler Peak (1971) 7.5' quadrangle.

Chung Up Mountains: see **Kingston Range** [SAN BERNARDINO].

Cibola Valley [IMPERIAL]: *valley*, along Colorado River on California-Arizona State line; extends south of Palo Verde Valley for about 12 miles. Named on Cibola (1951) 15' quadrangle, and on Cibola (1965), Palo Verde (1965), and Picacho NW (1965) 7.5' quadrangles.

Cienaga Grande [SAN BERNARDINO]: *water feature*, 5.25 miles south of downtown Big Bear Lake (lat. 34°10'05" N, long. 116°54'20" W; near W line sec. 17, T 1 N, R 1 E). Named on Big Bear Lake (1970) 7.5' quadrangle.

Cienaga Larga: see **Cienega Larga** [SAN BERNARDINO].

Cienaga Redonda: see **Cienega Redonda** [SAN BERNARDINO].

Cienaga Rincon: see **Dry Ranch** [RIVERSIDE].

Cienaga Seca [SAN BERNARDINO]: *area*, 12.5 miles northwest of downtown Morongo Valley (lat. 34°11'05" N, long. 116°43'15" W; sec. 12, T 1 N, R 2 E). Named on Onyx Peak (1972) 7.5' quadrangle.

Cienaga Seca: see **Little Cienaga Seca** [SAN BERNARDINO].

Cienaga Seca Creek [SAN BERNARDINO]: *stream*, flows 7 miles to Santa Ana River 2.5 miles south of Sugarloaf Mountain (lat. 34° 09'40" N, long. 116°48'20" W; near NE cor. sec. 19, T 1 N, R 2 E); Cienaga Seca is north of the stream. Named on Moonridge (1970) and Onyx Peak (1972) 7.5' quadrangles.

Cienega Larga [SAN BERNARDINO]: *area*, 7 miles east-southeast of Luna Mountain (lat. 34°18'05" N, long. 117°00'50" W; near E line sec. 31, T 3 N, R 1 W). Named on Butler Peak (1971) 7.5' quadrangle. United States Board on Geographic Names (1960b, p. 7) rejected the form "Cienaga Larga" for the name.

Cienega Redonda [SAN BERNARDINO]: *area*, 6.5 miles east-southeast of Luna Mountain (lat. 34°18'05" N, long. 117°01'20" W; sec. 31, T 3 N, R 1 W). Named on Butler Peak (1971) 7.5' quadrangle. United States Board on Geographic Names (1960b, p. 7) rejected the form "Cienaga Redonda" for the name. On Deep Creek (1902) 15' quadrangle, the name applies to a canyon that extends for 1.5 miles from present Cienega Redonda to present Big Pine Flat.

Cienega Spring [SAN BERNARDINO]: *spring*, 5.5 miles southeast of Luna Mountain (lat. 34°17'45" N, long. 117°02'45" W; at S line sec. 36, T 3 N, R 2 W). Named on Butler Peak (1971) 7.5' quadrangle.

Cima [SAN BERNARDINO]: *locality*, 13 miles southwest of Ivanpah along Union Pacific Railroad (lat. 35°14'10" N, long. 115°30' W; near SE cor sec. 5, T 13 N, R 14 E). Named on Kelso (1955) and Mid Hills (1955) 15' quadrangles. Postal authorities established Cima post office in 1905

(Frickstad, p. 139). *Cima* means "summit" in Spanish; the place is at the top of the pass between Kelso and Ivanpah (Gudde, 1949, p. 69).

Cinco Poses Spring [RIVERSIDE]: *spring,* 6.5 miles south-southeast of Cabazon (lat. 33°49'30" N, long. 116°45' W; sec. 14, T 4 S, R 2 E). Named on Lake Fulmor (1956) 7.5' quadrangle.

Circle Mountain [SAN BERNARDINO]: *peak,* 5 miles northeast of Mount San Antonio (lat. 34°20'35" N, long. 117°35'05" W; near SW cor. sec. 14, T 3 N, R 7 W). Named on Telegraph Peak (1956) 7.5' quadrangle.

Citrus: see **Highgrove** [RIVERSIDE].

City Creek [SAN BERNARDINO]: *stream,* formed by the confluence of East Fork and West Fork, flows 7.25 miles to an artificial watercourse 1 mile east of San Bernardino city hall (lat. 34°06'15" N, long. 117°16'25" W). Named on Harrison Mountain (1967), Redlands (1967), and San Bernardino South (1967) 7.5' quadrangles. East Fork is 5 miles long and West Fork is 5.25 miles long; both forks are named on Harrison Mountain (1967) 7.5' quadrangle.

City Well: see **Mountain Well** [SAN BERNARDINO].

Clapboard Town: see **Holcomb Valley** [SAN BERNARDINO].

Clapp Spring [IMPERIAL]: *spring,* 7.5 miles west-southwest of Palo Verde near the north end of Palo Verde Mountains (lat. 33°24'40" N, long. 114°51'20" W). Named on Palo Verde Mountains (1953) 15' quadrangle. Brown (1920, p. 83) gave the alternate name "Red Butte Spring" for present Clapp Spring, and noted that the name "Red Butte" is from "a sharp-pointed round peak" located 0.25 mile southwest of the spring.

Claremont [RIVERSIDE]: *peak,* 3 miles north-northeast of San Jacinto (lat. 33°49'25" N, long. 116°56'20" W; sec. 13, T 4 S, R 1 W). Named on San Jacinto (1953) 7.5' quadrangle. Called Claremont Pk. on California Mining Bureau's (1917b) map.

Claremont Peak: see **Claremont** [RIVERSIDE].

Clark Mountain [SAN BERNARDINO]: *peak,* 20 miles northwest of Ivanpah (lat. 35°31'30" N, long. 115°35'15" W; near SW cor. sec. 28, T 17 N, R 13 E). Altitude 7929 feet. Named on Clark Mountain (1956) 15' quadrangle. The name is from Clarke mining district, named for William H. Clarke, one of the group that found rich copper and silver deposits at the place (Lingenfelter, 1986, p. 135). Thompson's (1921) map shows Pachalka Spring located 2.5 miles west of Clark Mountain. The name "Pachalka" is for an Indian who lived at the place (Gudde, 1949, p. 247).

Clark Mountain Range [SAN BERNARDINO]: *range,* 21 miles northwest of Ivanpah (lat. 35°34' N, long. 115°34' W); Clark Mountain is near the southwest end of the range. Named on Clark Mountain (1956), Ivanpah (1956), Mescal Range (1955), and Roach Lake (1955) 15' quadrangles.

Clark Mountain Station [SAN BERNARDINO]: *locality,* 18 miles west-northwest of Ivanpah (lat. 35°28'20" N, long. 115°35'30" W; at E line sec. 17, T 16 N, R 13 E); the place is 4 miles south of Clark Mountain. Named on Mescal Range (1955) 15' quadrangle.

Clarks Pass [SAN BERNARDINO]: *pass,* 35 miles south-southeast of Amboy (lat. 34°04'20" N, long. 115°33'15" W; sec. 19, T 1 S, R 14 E). Named on Dale Lake (1956) 15' quadrangle.

Clarks Summit [SAN BERNARDINO]: *locality,* 3 miles southwest of downtown Big Bear Lake (lat. 34°12'30" N, long. 116°56'40" W; at SE cor. sec. 35, T 2 N, R 1 W). Named on Big Bear Lake (1970) 7.5' quadrangle.

Clay Point [IMPERIAL]: *promontory,* 1.5 miles south-southwest of Truckhaven (lat. 33°16'35" N, long. 115°59'15" W; sec. 25, T 10 S, R 9 E). Named on Truckhaven (1956) 7.5' quadrangle.

Clear Bay [SAN BERNARDINO]: *embayment,* 23 miles south-southeast of Needles along Lake Havasu (lat. 34°33'05" N, long. 114° 24' W; on S line sec. 6, T 5 N, R 25 E). Named on Castle Rock (1970) 7.5' quadrangle.

Cleghorn Canyon [SAN BERNARDINO]: *canyon,* drained by a stream that flows nearly 3 miles to Cajon Canyon 1.5 miles south-southeast of Cajon (lat. 34°16'40" N, long. 117°27'05" W; near NW cor. sec. 7, T 2 N, R 5 W). Named on Cajon (1956) 7.5' quadrangle.

Cleghorn Lakes [SAN BERNARDINO]: *dry lakes,* two, largest 1 mile long, 20 miles south of Amboy (lat. 34°16'30" N, long. 115°47'45" W; sec. 2, 11, 13, T 2 N, R 11 E). Named on Lead Mountain (1955) 15' quadrangle.

Cleghorn Mountain [SAN BERNARDINO]: *peak,* nearly 3 miles east of Cajon (lat. 34°17'40" N, long. 117°24'40" W; near N line sec. 4, T 2 N, R 5 W); the peak is on Cleghorn Ridge. Altitude 5333 feet. Named on Cajon (1956) 7.5' quadrangle. The name is for Mathew Cleghorn and his son John, who leased timber land near the peak in the 1870's (Gudde, 1949, p. 70).

Cleghorn Pass [SAN BERNARDINO]:

(1) *pass,* 17 miles southwest of Amboy (lat. 34°21' N, long. 115°56'45" W; near NW cor. sec. 16, T 3 N, R 10 E). Named on Lead Mountain (1955) 15' quadrangle.

(2) *pass,* 3.25 miles east-southeast of Cajon (lat. 34°17'10" N, long. 117°24'25" W; sec. 4, T 2 N, R 5 W); the pass is at the head of Cleghorn Canyon. Named on Cajon (1956) 7.5' quadrangle.

Cleghorn Ridge [SAN BERNARDINO]: *ridge,* generally east-trending, 5.5 miles long, center 4.5 miles east of Cajon (lat. 34°17'30" N, long. 117°23' W). Named on Cajon (1956) and Cedar Springs (1956) 7.5' quadrangles.

Clemens Well [RIVERSIDE]: *well,* 10 miles south-southeast of Chiriaco Summit along Salt Creek (lat. 33°31'15" N, long. 115° 40' W). Named on Hayfield (1963) 15' quadrangle, which indicates that the well is dry.

Clews Ridge: see **Alvord Mountain** [SAN BERNARDINO].

Cliff Canyon [SAN BERNARDINO]: *canyon,* drained by a stream that flows 2.5 miles to Ivanpah Valley 5 miles southwest of Ivanpah (lat. 35°17' N, long. 115°22'10" W; sec. 22, T 14 N, R 15 E). Named on Ivanpah (1956) 15' quadrangle.

Cliff Canyon Spring [SAN BERNARDINO]: *spring,* nearly 5 miles south-southwest of Ivanpah (lat. 35°16'15" N, long. 115°22'05" W; sec. 27, T 14 N, R 15 E); the spring is in Cliff Canyon. Named on Ivanpah (1956) 15' quadrangle.

Clipper Mountains [SAN BERNARDINO]: *range,* 10 miles west of Essex (lat. 34°44'30" N, long. 115°25' W). Named on Cadiz (1956), Colton Well (1956), and Danby (1956) 15' quadrangles.

Clipper Valley [SAN BERNARDINO]: *valley,* northwest of Clipper Mountains (lat. 34°51'30" N, long. 115°28' W). Named on Colton Well (1956) and Flynn (1956) 15' quadrangles.

Clipper Wash [SAN BERNARDINO]: *stream* and *dry wash,* extends for 5 miles to loose its identity 16 miles northeast of Amboy (lat. 34°41' N, long. 115°30'30" W; near E line sec. 21, T 7 N, R 14 E); the feature is at the southwest end of Clipper Mountains. Named on Cadiz (1956) 15' quadrangle.

Clyde [IMPERIAL]: *locality,* 7 miles northwest of Ogilby along Southern Pacific Railroad (lat. 32°51'45" N, long. 114°53'45" W; at W line sec. 17, T 15 S, R 20 E). Named on Ogilby (1963) 15' quadrangle. Called Drylyn on Yuma (1905) 30' quadrangle.

Coachella [RIVERSIDE]: *town,* nearly 4 miles southeast of Indio (lat. 33°40'45" N, long. 116°10'30" W; mainly in sec. 5, T 6 S, R 8 E); the town is in Coachella Valley. Named on Indio (1956) 7.5' quadrangle. Postal authorities established Coachella post office in 1901 (Frickstad, p. 127). James L. Rector founded the place in 1898 as a loading site for mesquite firewood sent to Los Angeles by rail—it first was called Woodspur (Rollins, p. 14). United States Geological Survey's (1904) map shows a place called La Mesa situated 2.25 miles south-southwest of Coachella (sec. 18, T 6 S, R 8 E). La Mesa was an Indian village (Gunther, p. 284).

Coachella Valley [RIVERSIDE]: *valley,* northeast of San Jacinto Mountains and Santa Rosa Mountains between San Gorgonio Pass and Salton Sea. Named on Santa Ana (1959) 1°x 2° quadrangle. Called Cohuilla Valley on Goddard's (1857) map, and shown as the north part of Colorado Desert on Mendenhall's (1908a) map. United States Board on Geographic Names (1933, p. 225) rejected the name "Conchilla Valley" for the feature.

Coahilla Peak: see **Cahuilla Mountain** [RIVERSIDE].

Coahilla Valley: see **Cahuilla Valley** [RIVERSIDE].

Coahuila: see **Cahuilla** [RIVERSIDE].

Coahuila Creek: see **Cahuilla Creek** [RIVERSIDE].

Coahuila Mountain: see **Cahuilla Mountain** [RIVERSIDE].

Coahuila Valley: see **Anza Valley** [RIVERSIDE]; **Cahuilla Valley** [RIVERSIDE].

Coahuilla: see **Cahuilla** [RIVERSIDE].

Coahuilla Creek: see **Cahuilla Creek** [RIVERSIDE].

Coahuilla Mountain: see **Cahuilla Mountain** [RIVERSIDE].

Coal Mine Canyon: see **Tin Mine Canyon** [RIVERSIDE].

Coats Spring [SAN BERNARDINO]: *spring,* 10 miles east of Ivanpah (lat. 35°21'15" N, long. 115°07'50" W; sec. 27, T 15 N, R 17 E). Named on Crescent Peak (1956) 15' quadrangle.

Cobarts Valley: see **Fifteenmile Valley** [SAN BERNARDINO].

Coffee's Bath House: see **Desert Hot Springs** [RIVERSIDE].

Coffin Spring [SAN BERNARDINO]: *spring,* 26 miles northwest of Vidal (lat. 34°23'45" N, long. 114°48'40" W). Named on Turtle Mountains (1954) 15' quadrangle. According to Thompson (1929, p. 741), the name is from the configuration of the rocks around the spring.

Cohila: see **Camp Cohila** [SAN BERNARDINO].

Cohuila Mountain: see **Cahilla Mountain** [RIVERSIDE].

Cohuilla: see **Cahuilla** [RIVERSIDE].

Cohuilla Creek: see **Cahuilla Creek** [RIVERSIDE].

Cohuilla Mountain: see **Cahuilla Mountain** [RIVERSIDE].

Cohuilla Valley: see **Cahuilla Valley** [RIVERSIDE]; **Coachella Valley** [RIVERSIDE].

Coldbrook Campground [SAN BERNARDINO]: *locality,* 1.25 miles west-southwest of downtown Big Bear Lake (lat. 34°14'05" N, long. 116°55'50" W; near NE cor. sec. 25, T 2 N, R 1 W). Named on Big Bear Lake (1970) 7.5' quadrangle.

Cold Creek [SAN BERNARDINO]: *stream,* flows 2 miles to Santa Ana River 6.5 miles south-southwest of downtown Big Bear Lake (lat. 34°09'50" N, long. 116°58'35" W; at S line sec. 15, T 1 N, R 1 W). Named on Big Bear Lake (1970) 7.5' quadrangle.

Coldwater Canyon [RIVERSIDE]: *canyon,* heads just inside Orange County and extends for 3.5 miles to Temescal Valley 4.25 miles west of Estelle Mountain (lat. 33°45'15" N, long. 117°29'40" W; near N line sec. 10, T 5 S, R 6 W). Named on Corona South (1967), Lake Mathews (1967), and Santiago Peak (1954) 7.5' quadrangles.

Coldwater Canyon [SAN BERNARDINO]:
(1) *canyon*, drained by a stream that flows nearly 3 miles to North Fork Lytle Creek 4.25 miles east of Mount San Antonio (lat. 34° 17'45" N, long. 117°34'10" W; near NW cor. sec. 1, T 2 N, R 7 W). Named on Telegraph Peak (1956) 7.5' quadrangle.
(2) *canyon*, 3 miles long, along East Twin Creek above a point 6 miles north-northeast of San Bernardino city hall (lat. 34°11'10" N, long. 117°15'15" W; sec. 12, T 1 N, R 4 W). Named on Harrison Mountain (1967) and San Bernardino North (1967) 7.5' quadrangles.

Cold Water Canyon House in Temescal Canyon: see **Glen Ivy Hot Springs** [RIVERSIDE].

Coldwater Creek [RIVERSIDE]: *stream*, flows 3.25 miles to Dry Creek 3 miles south-southwest of the center of Idyllwild (lat. 33° 42'20" N, long. 116°44'45" W; sec. 26, T 5 S, R 2 E). Named on Idyllwild (1959) 15' quadrangle.

Cole Canyon [RIVERSIDE]: *canyon*, 2 miles long, opens into lowlands along Murrieta Creek 1.5 miles west-northwest of Murrieta (lat. 33°33'45" N, long. 117°14'30" W). Named on Murrieta (1953) and Wildomar (1953) 7.5' quadrangles.

College Camp [SAN BERNARDINO]: *locality*, 2.25 miles south of Sugarloaf Mountain (lat. 34°10' N, long. 116°49' W; near S line sec. 18, T 1 N, R 2 E). Named on Moonridge (1970) 7.5' quadrangle.

College Heights [SAN BERNARDINO]: *district*, 3.5 miles northwest of Ontario city hall (lat. 34°06'05" N, long. 117°41'05" W). Named on Ontario (1967) 7.5' quadrangle. Called College Hill on United States Geological Survey's (1942a) map. L.W. Campbell named the place in 1909 or 1910 for its proximity to Pomona College (Gudde, 1949, p. 74).

College Hill: see **College Heights** [SAN BERNARDINO].

Collins: see **Ballou** [SAN BERNARDINO].

Colony Heights [RIVERSIDE]: *locality*, 2.25 miles north-northeast of Lakeview (lat. 33°52' N, long. 117°07'45" W). Named on Elsinore (1901) 30' quadrangle. Faulty land titles and lack of water forced a religious colony that started at the place in 1894 to move to Riverside about 1901 (Gunther, p. 125-126).

Colorado: see **Winterhaven** [IMPERIAL].

Colorado Desert: see "Regional setting."

Colorado River: *stream*, extends for 235 miles along California-Arizona State line (including 7 miles in Arizona by a change of the river course) to enter Mexico 2 miles east-southeast of Pilot Knob [IMPERIAL] (lat. 32°43'05" N, long. 114°43'10" W; sec. 35, T 16 S, R 21 E). Named on El Centro (1958), Needles (1956), and Salton Sea (1959) 1°x 2° quadrangles. Called R°G° [Rio Grande] de los Martyres on a Spanish map of 1710 (Wheat, p. 76) and called Rio Colorado on Farnham's (1845) map. Melchior Diaz, one of Coronado's lieutenants, gave the name "Rio del Tizon" (or "Tison") to the stream when he crossed it in 1540—*Rio del Tizon* means "River of the Torch," or "River of the Firebrand" in Spanish, and refers to the burning sticks that the naked Yuma Indians carried for warmth in the winter; Hernando Alarcon discovered the mouth of the river at about the same time and gave it the name "Buena Gula" (Wheat, p. 36).

Colosseum Gorge [SAN BERNARDINO]: *canyon*, 3 miles long, 19 miles northwest of Ivanpah (lat. 35°33' N, long. 115°32'50" W). Named on Clark Mountain (1956) 15' quadrangle, which shows Colosseum mine near the head of the canyon.

Colton [SAN BERNARDINO]: *city*, 3 miles southwest of San Bernardino city hall (lat. 34°04'15" N, long. 117°19'15" W). Named on San Bernardino South (1967) 7.5' quadrangle. Postal authorities established Colton post office in 1876 (Frickstad, p. 139), and the city incorporated in 1887. Members of Slover Mountain Colony came to the site in 1873, and when Southern Pacific Railroad reached the place in 1875, railroad officials named their station there for David D. Colton, financial director of Central Pacific Railroad (Gudde, 1949, p. 75). The first colonists at the site came from New Mexico and settled there in 1843; their community was known as Politana, Politan, Apolitana, Epolitan, Napolitan, and Hypolitan—the name no doubt was from Hipolito Espinosa, an earlier settler; these colonists left the place in 1845 and moved 3 or 4 miles farther down Santa Ana River, where a community on the north side of the river was called Agua Mansa, and a community on the south side was called San Salvadore—the name "San Salvadore" was applied to more than one place in the neighborhood (Beattie and Beattie, p. 60-61, 101; Hanna, p. 69). A flood destroyed Agua Mansa in 1862, but San Bernardino South (1967) 7.5' quadrangle shows Agua Mansa cemetery situated 3.25 miles southwest of Colton civic center. Postal authorities established San Salvadore post office 3 miles north of Riverside in 1873, discontinued it in 1876, reestablished it in 1878, discontinued it in 1879, reestablished it in 1883, and discontinued it in 1886 (Salley, p. 197). General J.H. Bean, commander of militia in southern California, organized a company of volunteers that were stationed in Cajon Pass in the winter of 1850 and 1851; later he moved the company to a facility called Camp Dolores that was situated near Apolitana (Beattie and Beattie, p. 84). Postal authorities established Reche post office 13 miles southeast of Colton in 1883 and discontinued it in 1888; the name was for Antonie C. Reche, first postmaster (Salley, p. 182).

Colton: see **West Colton** [SAN BERNARDINO].

Colton Heights: see **East Colton Heights** [SAN BERNARDINO].

Colton Hills [SAN BERNARDINO]: *range*, 19 miles northwest of Essex (lat. 34°57'30" N, long. 115°26' W). Named on Colton Well (1956) 15' quadrangle.

Colton Wash [SAN BERNARDINO]: *stream*, flows 15 miles to Homer Wash 23 miles southeast of Essex (lat. 34°31' N, long. 114° 56'45" W; near SE cor. sec. 14, T 5 N, R 19 E). Named on Essex (1956) 15' quadrangle.

Colton Well [SAN BERNARDINO]: *well*, 17 miles northwest of Essex (lat. 34°56' N, long. 115°25'25" W; at NE cor. sec. 29, T 10 N, R 15 E); the well is at the south end of Colton Hills. Named on Colton Well (1956) 15' quadrangle.

Columbia Mountain [SAN BERNARDINO]: *peak*, 20 miles south-southwest of Ivanpah (lat. 35°05' N, long. 115°28'15" W; sec. 34, T 12 N, R 14 E). Named on Mid Hills (1955) 15' quadrangle.

Columbine Spring [SAN BERNARDINO]:
(1) *spring*, 13 miles north of Ontario city hall in Icehouse Canyon (lat. 34°14'30" N, long. 117°36'10" W; sec. 22, T 2 N, R 7 W). Named on Cucamonga Peak (1966) 7.5' quadrangle.
(2) *spring*, 7.5 miles south of downtown Big Bear Lake (lat. 34° 08'10" N, long. 116°56'25" W; near S line sec. 25, T 1 N, R 1 W). Named on Big Bear Lake (1970) 7.5' quadrangle.

Compton Canyon: see **Mayhew Canyon** [RIVERSIDE].

Compton Siding [RIVERSIDE]: *locality*, 2.5 miles southeast of Corona along Atchison, Topeka and Santa Fe Railroad (lat. 33°50'45" N, long. 117°32'05" W; on W line sec. 5, T 4 S, R 6 W). Named on Corona South (1954) 7.5' quadrangle, which shows the place situated along Compton Avenue.

Conchilla Valley: see **Coachella Valley** [RIVERSIDE].

Concrete: see **Pedley** [RIVERSIDE].

Conejo Well [RIVERSIDE]: *well*, 7 miles north of Chiriaco Summit (lat. 33°45'40" N, long. 115°44' W). Named on Pinto Basin (1963) 15' quadrangle.

Cone Peak [RIVERSIDE]: *peak*, 8.5 miles southeast of Idyllwild (lat. 33°40' N, long. 116°35'50" W; on E line sec. 7, T 6 S, R 4 E). Named on Idyllwild (1959) 15' quadrangle.

Conifer: see **Camp Conifer** [SAN BERNARDINO].

Conrad: see **Camp Conrad** [SAN BERNARDINO].

Console Springs [RIVERSIDE]: *locality*, 3.5 miles north-northeast of Sunnymead in Reche Canyon (lat. 33°59'10" N, long. 117°13'10" W; sec. 20, T 2 S, R 3 W). Named on Sunnymead (1967) 7.5' quadrangle. Giovanni Consoli laid claim to three springs at the place in 1906 and sold bottled water under the name "Prof. John Console" (Gunther, p. 131).

Constance Peak [SAN BERNARDINO]: *peak*, 8.5 miles south-southwest of downtown Big Bear Lake (lat. 34°08'20" N, long. 116°59'45" W; near SW cor. sec. 28, T 1 N, R 1 W). Altitude 6645 feet. Named on Big Bear Lake (1970) 7.5' quadrangle.

Converse Creek [SAN BERNARDINO]: *stream*, flows 2.25 miles to Santa Ana River 4 miles south of downtown Big Bear Lake (lat. 34°11'10" N, long. 116°54'30" W; near W line sec. 8, T 1 N, R 1 E). Named on Big Bear Lake (1970) 7.5' quadrangle.

Converse Flat [SAN BERNARDINO]: *area*, 3.5 miles south of downtown Big Bear Lake (lat. 34°11'25" N, long. 116°54'45" W; near NE cor. sec. 7, T 1 N, R 1 E); the place is west of Converse Creek. Named on Big Bear Lake (1970) 7.5' quadrangle. Called Covers Flat on San Gorgonio (1902) 30' quadrangle.

Convict Spring [SAN BERNARDINO]: *spring*, 3.5 miles west-southwest of Devore (lat. 34°12'10" N, long. 117°27'40" W; sec. 1, T 1 N, R 6 W). Named on Devore (1966) 7.5' quadrangle.

Cook Canyon [SAN BERNARDINO]: *canyon*, drained by a stream that flows 1.5 miles to lowlands 2.25 miles south-southwest of Harrison Mountain (lat. 34°08'10" N, long. 117°10'30" W; near SE cor. sec. 27, T 1 N, R 3 W). Named on Harrison Mountain (1967) 7.5' quadrangle.

Cooks Well [SAN BERNARDINO]: *spring*, 30 miles north-northeast of Amboy (lat. 34°56'30" N, long. 115°30'05" W; sec. 22, T 10 N, R 14 E). Named on Flynn (1956) 15' quadrangle, which shows the feature located 0.5 mile east of Mitchell Caverns state park. The name "Mitchell Caverns" commemorates Jack Mitchell and his wife, who from 1932 until 1954 provided guided tours of caves that first were called Providence Caves or Crystal Caves (Anonymous, 1985, p. 34). Thompson's (1921) map shows a feature called Beecher Spring located 5 miles northeast of Cook's Well.

Coolgardie Camp [SAN BERNARDINO]: *locality*, 36 miles east-southeast of the village of Red Mountain (lat. 35°06' N, long. 117° 03' W; sec. 33, T 32 S, R 46 E). Named on Opal Mountain (1955) 15' quadrangle. The name is from a mining place in Western Australia (Hanna, p. 72).

Coolidge Springs [IMPERIAL]: *village*, 1 mile southwest of Desert Shores (lat. 33°23'40" N, long. 116°03' W; on W line sec. 16, T 9 S, R 9 E). Named on Oasis (1956) 7.5' quadrangle.

Coon Canyon [SAN BERNARDINO]: *canyon*, drained by a stream that flows 1.5 miles to lowlands 38 miles southeast of the village of Red Mountain (lat. 35°01'30" N, long. 117°04'30" W; sec. 22, T 11 N, R 2 W). Named on Opal Mountain (1955) 15' quadrangle.

Coon Creek [SAN BERNARDINO]: *stream,* flows 4 miles to join Heart Bar Creek and form Santa Ana River 4.25 miles southeast of Sugarloaf Mountain (lat. 34°09' N, long. 116°46'15" W; near SE cor. sec. 21, T 1 N, R 2 E). Named on Moonridge (1970) and Onyx Peak (1972) 7.5' quadrangles.

Coon Creek Jumpoff [SAN BERNARDINO]: *relief feature,* 10 miles northwest of downtown Morongo Valley (lat. 34°08'50" N, long. 116°42'40" W; near N line sec. 30, T 1 N, R 3 E); the feature is near the head of Coon Creek. Named on Onyx Peak (1972) 7.5' quadrangle.

Coon Hollow [RIVERSIDE]: *relief feature,* 19 miles southwest of Blythe in Mule Mountains (lat. 33°27'10" N, long. 114°52' W). Named on Palo Verde Mountains (1953) 15' quadrangle.

Cooper Canyon [RIVERSIDE]: *canyon,* drained by a stream that flows 1.25 miles to San Diego County 22 miles south of Idyllwild (lat. 33°25'40" N, long. 116°38'25" W; at S line sec. 35, T 8 S, R 3 E). Named on Beauty Mountain (1960) 7.5' quadrangle.

Copper Basin [IMPERIAL]: *valley,* 2.5 miles east of Picacho Peak (lat. 32°58'45" N, long. 114°37' W). Named on Little Picacho Peak (1965) 7.5' quadrangle.

Copper Basin [SAN BERNARDINO]: *valley,* 19 miles northeast of Vidal (lat. 34°18' N, long. 114°14'30" W). Named on Gene Wash (1959) and Whipple Wash (1970) 7.5' quadrangles.

Copper Basin Reservoir [SAN BERNARDINO]: *lake,* 1.5 miles long, behind a dam on Copper Basin Wash 20 miles northeast of Vidal (lat. 34°16'45" N, long. 114°13'20" W; sec. 11, T 2 N, R 26 E). Named on Gene Wash (1959) 7.5' quadrangle.

Copper Basin Wash [SAN BERNARDINO]: *stream,* flows 8.5 miles to Colorado River 21 miles east-northeast of Vidal (lat. 34°14'50" N, long. 114°10'30" W; near E line sec. 19, T 2 N, R 27 E). Named on Gene Wash (1959) 7.5' quadrangle.

Copper Canyon [SAN BERNARDINO]: *canyon,* 5 miles long, opens into Lake Havasu 23 miles north-northeast of Vidal (lat. 34°25'35" N, long. 114°19'20" W). Named on Lake Havasu City South (1970) 7.5' quadrangle.

Copper City [SAN BERNARDINO]: *locality,* 31 miles south-southeast of Trona (lat. 35°21' N, long. 117°11' W; sec. 5, T 30 S, R 45 E). Site named on Pilot Knob (1954) 15' quadrangle. The place was a mining camp begun in the 1880's (Paher, p. 43).

Copper Mountain [SAN BERNARDINO]: *ridge,* generally north-northwest-trending, 6 miles long, 9 miles west-northwest of Twentynine Palms (lat. 34°10'45" N, long. 116°12' W). Named on Sunfair (1972) 7.5' quadrangle. The name is from a copper prospect opened on the ridge (Thompson, 1929, p. 645).

Copper Queen Canyon [SAN BERNARDINO]: *canyon,* drained by a stream that heads in Inyo County and flows 3.5 miles in San Bernardino County to Searles Lake 4 miles east-northeast of Trona (lat. 35°46'30" N, long. 117°18'20" W; sec. 12, T 25 S, R 44 E). Named on Trona (1949) 15' quadrangle.

Coral Wash [IMPERIAL]: *stream,* flows 6.5 miles to Salton Sea 3.25 miles north-northeast of Truckhaven (lat. 33°20'20" N, long. 115° 57'05" W; at N line sec. 5, T 10 S, R 10 E). Named on Seventeen Palms (1956) and Truckhaven (1956) 7.5' quadrangles.

Cornell Peak [RIVERSIDE]: *peak,* 1 mile east of San Jacinto Peak (lat. 33°48'50" N, long. 116°39'45" W; near N line sec. 22, T 4 S, R 3 E). Altitude 9750 feet. Named on San Jacinto Peak (1981) 7.5' quadrangle. Edmund Taylor Perkins, Jr., topographer with United States Geological Survey, named the peak for Cornell University, the alma mater of geologist Robert T. Hill, who was camping with Perdins within sight of the peak (Robinson and Risher, p. 45).

Cornfield Spring [SAN BERNARDINO]: *spring,* 30 miles north-northeast of Amboy (lat. 34°58'15" N, long. 115°34'15" W; near W line sec. 12, T 10 N, R 13 E). Named on Flynn (1956) 15' quadrangle.

Corn Spring [RIVERSIDE]: *spring,* 7.5 miles southeast of Desert Center (lat. 33°37'30" N, long. 115°19'30" W). Named on Chuckwalla Mountains (1963) 15' quadrangle. The name is from corn that kept coming up at the place long after the Indians that had planted corn there were gone (Gunther, p. 132).

Corn Springs Wash [RIVERSIDE]: *stream* and *dry wash,* extends for 9 miles to lowlands 9 miles southeast of Desert Center (lat. 33° 37'15" N, long. 115°18' W); Corn Spring is along the feature. Named on Chuckwalla Mountains (1963) 15' quadrangle.

Corona [RIVERSIDE]: *city,* 13 miles southwest of Riverside (lat. 32° 52'30" N, long. 117°33'55" W). Named on Corona North (1967) and Corona South (1967) 7.5' quadrangles. After officials of South Riverside Land Company had the community laid out, postal authorities established South Riverside post office there in 1887 and changed the name to Corona in 1897 (Salley, p. 209). The city incorporated in 1896.

Corral Canyon [RIVERSIDE]: *canyon,* 1.25 miles long, 5 miles northeast of Banning (lat. 33°59'05" N, long. 116°49'10" W; sec. 18, 19, T 2 S, R 2 E). Named on Cabazon (1956) 7.5' quadrangle.

Cosy Dell [SAN BERNARDINO]: *locality,* 1.5 miles south-southeast of Cajon in Cajon Canyon (lat. 34°16'45" N, long. 117°27'10" W; near NE cor. sec. 12, T 2 N, R 6 W). Named on Cajon (1956) 7.5' quadrangle. The name is from Cozy Dell ranch that Jesse Tay and C.M. Lawrence started about 1878 (Hanna, p. 76).

Cotners Corner [SAN BERNARDINO]: *locality,* 8 miles east-southeast of Victorville (lat. 34°28'20" N, long. 117°10'15" W; at SW cor. sec. 35, T 5 N, R 3 W). Named on Apple Valley South (1971) 7.5' quadrangle.

Cottage Gardens [SAN BERNARDINO]: *district,* 1.25 miles east of present San Bernardino city hall (lat. 34°06'15" N, long. 117° 16' W). Named on Colton (1943) 7.5' quadrangle.

Cotton Spring [RIVERSIDE]: *spring,* 17 miles north-northeast of Mortmar (lat. 33°44'30" N, long. 115°48'30" W; near N line sec. 14, T 5 S, R 11 E). Named on Cottonwood Spring (1958) 15' quadrangle.

Cottonwood: see **Hodge** [SAN BERNARDINO]; **Wild**, under **Helendale** [SAN BERNARDINO].

Cottonwood Basin [RIVERSIDE]: *valley,* 15 miles north of Mortmar (lat. 33°44'30" N, long. 115°54'30" W); the place is in Cottonwood Mountains. Named on Cottonwood Spring (1958) and Hexie Mountains (1963) 15' quadrangles.

Cottonwood Canyon [RIVERSIDE]:

(1) *canyon,* drained by a stream that flows 4.25 miles to San Gorgonio Pass 11.5 miles northwest of Palm Springs (lat. 33°56'45" N, long. 116°41'25" W; near N line sec. 5, T 3 S, R 3 E). Named on Whitewater (1955) 7.5' quadrangle.

(2) *canyon,* 3.5 miles long, opens into Shavers Valley 14 miles north-northeast of Mortmar (lat. 33°42' N, long. 115°48' W; near NE cor. sec. 35, T 5 S, R 11 E). Named on Cottonwood Spring (1958) 15' quadrangle.

(3) *canyon,* drained by a stream that flows 4.25 miles to San Jacinto River 3.25 miles east of Lake Elsinore city hall (lat. 33°40'25" N, long. 117°16'15" W; sec. 2, T 6 S, R 4 W). Named on Lake Elsinore (1953) and Romoland (1953) 7.5' quadrangles. A gold-mining place called Binkley's Diggings, for Frank Binkely, was near the mouth of the canyon (Gunther, p. 53).

(4) *canyon,* drained by a stream that flows 1.5 miles to Bautista Creek 9.5 miles south of Idyllwild (lat. 33°36'30" N, long. 116°44'30" W; sec. 35, T 6 S, R 2 E). Named on Idyllwild (1959) 15' quadrangle.

Cottonwood Canyon [SAN BERNARDINO]: *canyon,* 2 miles long, 9 miles south-southwest of Ivanpah (lat. 35°13'45" N, long. 115° 24' W). Named on Mid Hills (1955) 15' quadrangle.

Cottonwood Canyon: see **Railroad Canyon** [RIVERSIDE] (1).

Cottonwood Creek [RIVERSIDE]: *stream,* heads in San Diego County and flows 1.5 miles in Riverside County to Temecula Creek 1 mile west of Aguanga (lat. 33°26'30" N, long. 116°53' W; at S line sec. 28, T 8 S, R 1 E). Named on Aguanga (1954) and Vail Lake (1953) 7.5' quadrangles.

Cottonwood Lake [RIVERSIDE]: *lake,* 1300 feet long, 11 miles east of Perris (lat. 33°47'05" N, long. 117°01'55" W; near NW cor. sec. 31, T 4 S, R 1 W). Named on Lakeview (1967) 7.5' quadrangle.

Cottonwood Mountains [RIVERSIDE]: *range,* 14 miles north of Mortmar (lat. 33°43' N, long. 115°55' W). Named on Cottonwood Spring (1958) and Hexie Mountains (1963) 15' quadrangles.

Cottonwood Pass [RIVERSIDE]: *narrows,* 16 miles north-northeast of Mortmar (lat. 33°43'30" N, long. 115°48'45" W; sec. 23, T 5 S, R 11 E); the feature is in Cottonwood Canyon (2). Named on Cottonwood Spring (1958) 15' quadrangle.

Cottonwood Spring [RIVERSIDE]:

(1) *spring,* 17 miles north-northeast of Mortmar (lat. 33°44'10" N, long. 115°48'30" W; sec. 14, T 5 S, R 11 E). Named on Cottonwood Spring (1958) 15' quadrangle. A large clump of tall cottonwood trees marks the site (Brown, 1923, p. 265).

(2) *spring,* 18 miles south of Palm Desert (lat. 33°27'40" N, long. 116°22'40" W; sec. 20, T 8 S, R 6 E). Named on Collins Valley (1959) 7.5' quadrangle. United States Geological Survey's (1904) map shows a place called Old Santa Rosa situated 1.5 miles north-northwest of present Cottonwood Spring (2) (near NE cor. sec. 18, T 8 S, R 6 E).

Cottonwood Spring [SAN BERNARDINO]:

(1) *spring,* 9 miles south-southwest of Ivanpah (lat. 35°13'35" N, long. 115°24' W; near NW cor. sec. 8, T 13 N, R 15 E); the spring is in Cottonwood Canyon. Named on Mid Hills (1955) 15' quadrangle.

(2) *spring,* 17 miles north-northeast of Amboy (lat. 34°33'15" N, long. 115°39'45" W; near NW cor. sec. 7, T 8 N, R 13 E); the spring is near Cottonwood Wash. Named on Flynn (1956) 15' quadrangle. United States Board on Geographic Names (1986a, p. 2) approved the name "Cottonwood Spring" for a feature about 0.5 mile west of Cottonwood Spring (2) in the upper course of Cottonwood Wash (lat. 34°48'20" N, long. 115°40'20" W; sec. 12, T 8 N, R 12 E).

(3) *spring,* about 1 mile northwest of Old Woman Springs (lat. 34°24'20" N, long. 116°43'10" W; near E line sec. 25, T 4 N, R 2 E). Named on Old Woman Springs (1972) 7.5' quadrangle. The water comes from a tunnel in a hillside (Thompson, 1929, p. 629).

Cottonwood Spring: see **Sacaton Spring** [SAN BERNARDINO].

Cottonwood Wash [SAN BERNARDINO]: *stream*, flows 16 miles to Kelso Wash 29 miles north of Amboy (lat. 34°58'30" N, long. 115° 44'30" W; sec. 8, T 10 N, R 12 E). Named on Flynn (1956) 15' quadrangle.

Cougar Buttes [SAN BERNARDINO]: *ridge*, west-northwest-trending, 2.5 miles long, 8 miles east-northeast of the town of Lucerne Valley (lat. 34°28'30" N, long. 116°48'45" W). Named on Couger Buttes (1971) 7.5' quadrangle.

County Well [IMPERIAL]: *well*, 22 miles south of Desert Shores (lat. 33°05'10" N, long. 116°01'15" W; sec. 34, T 12 S, R 9 E). Named on Borrego Mountain SE (1958) 7.5' quadrangle, which indicates that the well is dry.

Covers Flat: see **Converse Flat** [SAN BERNARDINO].

Cove Spring [SAN BERNARDINO]: *spring*, 17 miles north-northeast of Amboy (lat. 34°47'40" N, long. 115°38'10" W; near S line sec. 8, T 8 N, R 13 E). Named on Flynn (1956) 15' quadrangle.

Covington Flat: see **Lower Covington Flat** [RIVERSIDE-SAN BERNARDINO]; **Upper Covington Flat** [RIVERSIDE].

Covington Spring [RIVERSIDE]: *spring*, 16 miles east-northeast of Garnet (lat. 34°01' N, long. 116°17'25" W; sec. 7, T 2 S, R 7 E). Named on Joshua Tree South (1972) 7.5' quadrangle, which indicates that the spring is dry.

Covington Well [RIVERSIDE]: *well*, 17 miles east-northeast of Garnet (lat. 34°01'20" N, long. 116°16'55" W; on W line sec. 5, T 2 S, R 7 E). Named on Joshua Tree South (1972) 7.5' quadrangle, which indicates that the well is dry.

Cow Canyon [RIVERSIDE]: *canyon*, drained by a stream that flows 2.5 miles to Horsethief Canyon 2.25 miles west of Alberhill (lat. 33°43'20" N, long. 117°26'10" W; sec. 19, T 5 S, R 5 W). Named on Alberhill (1954) 7.5' quadrangle.

Cow Cove [SAN BERNARDINO]: *relief feature*, 24 miles west of Ivanpah (lat. 35°20'30" N, long. 115°43'50" W; sec. 31, 32, T 15 N, R 12 E). Named on Mescal Range (1955) 15' quadrangle.

Cowhole Mountain [SAN BERNARDINO]: *range*, 41 miles west-southwest of Ivanpah (lat. 35°08' N, long. 115°59'30" W). Named on Old Dad Mountain (1956) and Soda Lake (1956) 15' quadrangles

Cowhole Mountain: see **Little Cowhole Mountain** [SAN BERNARDINO].

Cox [RIVERSIDE]: *locality*, 16 miles northwest of Bly along Atchison, Topeka and Santa Fe Railroad (lat. 33°50'15" N, long. 114°46'15" W; at E line sec. 9, T 4 S, R 21 E). Named on Midland (1952) 15' quadrangle. The name commemorates H.J. Cox, construction superintendent of California Southern Railroad; the place first was called English Siding for P.A. English, who owned gypsum mines nearby—the place also was called Midland, and was called Mineral, or Mineral Switch, because manganese and gypsum were shipped from there (Gunther, p. 141, 181, 324, 326).

Coxcomb Mountains [RIVERSIDE-SAN BERNARDINO]: *range*, on Riverside-San Bernardino County line, mainly in Riverside County, about 14 miles north-northeast of Desert Center (lat. 33°55' N, long. 115°21' W). Named on Cadiz Valley (1956) and Coxcomb Mountains (1963) 15' quadrangles.

Cox Creek [SAN BERNARDINO]: *stream*, flows 4 miles to Holcomb Creek 5.5 miles south-southeast of Luna Mountain (lat. 34°16'35" N, long. 117°04'35" W; sec. 10, T 2 N, R 2 W). Named on Butler Peak (1971) 7.5' quadrangle.

Coxey Creek [SAN BERNARDINO]: *stream*, flows 7 miles to Deep Creek (1) 2 miles south-southwest of Luna Mountain (lat. 34° 19' N, long. 117°08'15" W; at E line sec. 25, T 3 N, R 3 W). Named on Butler Peak (1971) and Lake Arrowhead (1971) 7.5' quadrangles. Called Mill Creek on Lake Arrowhead (1956) 15' quadrangle, and United States Board on Geographic Names (1974a, p. 4) gave this name as a variant.

Coxey Meadow [SAN BERNARDINO]: *area*, 3.5 miles east of Luna Mountain (lat. 34°20' N, long. 117°04'10" W; at E line sec. 22, T 3 N, R 2 W); the place is along Coxey Creek. Named on Butler Peak (1971) 7.5' quadrangle.

Cox Spring [SAN BERNARDINO]: *spring*, 5.25 miles east-southeast of Luna Mountain (lat. 34°18'35" N, long. 117°02'30" W; at S line sec. 25, T 3 N, R 2 W); the spring is along Cox Creek. Named on Butler Peak (1971) 7.5' quadrangle.

Coyote Canyon [RIVERSIDE]: *canyon*, 4.5 miles long, along Coyote Creek (2) above a point 21 miles south-southwest of Palm Desert just inside San Diego County (lat. 33°25'20" N, long. 116°28'35" W); the feature divides at the head to form Horse Canyon, Nance Canyon, and Tule Canyon. Named on Bucksnort Mountain (1960) and Collins Valley (1959) 7.5' quadrangles. On Ramona (1903) 30' quadrangle, the name "Coyote Canyon" applies both to present Coyote Canyon and to present Nance Canyon.

Coyote Creek [RIVERSIDE]:

(1) *stream*, flows 2 miles to Deep Canyon (2) 5 miles south of Palm Desert (lat. 33°39' N, long. 116°22'10" W; sec. 16, T 6 S, R 6 E). Named on La Quinta (1959) 7.5' quadrangle.

(2) *stream* and *dry wash*, extends for 13 miles through Horse Canyon and Coyote Canyon to San Diego County 21 miles south-southwest of Palm Desert (lat. 33°25'40" N, long. 116°29'45" W; at S line sec. 32, T 8 S, R 5 E). Named on Idyllwild (1959) and Palm Desert (1959) 15' quadrangles, and on Bucksnort Mountain (1960) and Collins Valley (1959) 7.5' quadrangles.

Coyote Flat [SAN BERNARDINO]: *area*, 3.25 miles east-northeast of Luna Mountain (lat. 34°21'30" N, long. 117°03'30" W; in and near sec. 11, T 3 N, R 2 W). Named on Butler Peak (1971) 7.5' quadrangle.

Coyote Hole Canyon [SAN BERNARDINO]: *canyon*, about 1 mile long, 1 mile south-southeast of Joshua Tree (lat. 34°07'15" N, long. 116°18'30" W; on S line sec. 36, T 1 N, R 6 E). Named on Joshua Tree South (1972) 7.5' quadrangle.

Coyote Holes [SAN BERNARDINO]: *spring*, 42 miles west-northwest of Ivanpah along Kingston Wash (lat. 35°38'30" N, long. 115°57'30" W). Named on Kingston Peak (1955) 15' quadrangle. Mendenhall (1909a, p. 50) listed Cunningham Spring, a feature located about 6 miles southeast of Coyote Holes.

Coyote Hole Spring [SAN BERNARDINO]: *spring*, 1.5 miles south of Joshua Tree (lat. 34°07' N, long. 116°18'25" W; sec. 1, T 1 S, R 6 E); the spring is in Coyote Hole Canyon. Named on Joshua Tree South (1972) 7.5' quadrangle.

Coyote Lake [SAN BERNARDINO]:

(1) *dry lake*, 4.5 miles long, 40 miles west-southwest of Baker (lat. 35°04' N, long. 116°45'30" W). Named on Alvord Mountain (1948) and Lane Mountain (1948) 15' quadrangles.

(2) *dry lake*, 2.5 miles long, 10 miles west-northwest of Twentynine Palms (lat. 34°10' N, long. 116°13'20" W). Named on Sunfair (1972) 7.5' quadrangle.

Coyote Mountain: see **Carrizo Mountain** [IMPERIAL].

Coyote Mountains [IMPERIAL]: *range*, 5 miles west of Carrizo Mountain on Imperial-San Diego County line (lat. 32°49'20" N, long. 116°06'10" W). Named on Carrizo Mountain (1957) and Painted Gorge (1957) 7.5' quadrangles.

Coyote Springs [SAN BERNARDINO]: *spring*, 20 miles north of Amboy (lat. 34°50'50" N, long. 115°40'15" W; near N line sec. 25, T 9 N, R 12 E). Named on Flynn (1956) 15' quadrangle.

Coyote Valley [SAN BERNARDINO]: *valley*, 10 miles west of Twentynine Palms (lat. 34°10' N, long. 116°13'45" W); Coyote Lake (2) is in the valley. Named on Joshua Tree North (1972) and Sunfair (1972) 7.5' quadrangles.

Coyote Wash [IMPERIAL]: *stream* and *dry wash*, extends for 15 miles to end 3.5 miles east-northeast of Plaster City (lat. 32°48'35" N, long. 115°48' W; sec. 2, T 16 S, R 11 E). Named on Coyote Wells (1957), Painted Gorge (1957), and Plaster City (1957) 7.5' quadrangles. South Fork enters 1.25 miles northeast of Coyote Wells, it is nearly 4 miles long and is named on Coyote Wells (1957) 7.5' quadrangle.

Coyote Well [SAN BERNARDINO]: *well*, 42 miles west-southwest of Baker (lat. 35°01'30" N, long. 116°45'50" W; at SW cor. sec. 22, T 11 N, R 2 E); the well is about 1 mile south of Coyote Lake (1). Named on Lane Mountain (1948) 15' quadrangle.

Coyote Wells [IMPERIAL]: *locality*, 24 miles west of El Centro along San Diego and Eastern Arizona Railroad (lat. 32°44'20" N, long. 115°50'58" W; near NW cor. sec. 32, T 16 S, R 10 E). Named on Coyote Wells (1957) 7.5' quadrangle. The name is from a well located 1.5 miles farther east—coyotes dug holes in sand there to obtain water (Brown, 1923, p. 214).

Crab Creek [SAN BERNARDINO]: *stream*, flows 5 miles to Deep Creek (1) 6 miles south of Luna Mountain (lat. 34°15'15" N, long. 117°07' W; near SW cor. sec. 17, T 2 N, R 2 W). Named on Butler Peak (1971) and Keller Peak (1967) 7.5' quadrangles.

Crab Flats [SAN BERNARDINO]: *area*, 6 miles south-southeast of Luna Mountain (lat. 34°15'45" N, long. 117°05'30" W; sec. 16, T 2 N, R 2 W); the place is along Crab Creek. Named on Butler Peak (1971) 7.5' quadrangle.

Crackerjack: see **Cave Spring** [SAN BERNARDINO].

Crafton [SAN BERNARDINO]: *locality*, 5 miles west-northwest of Yucaipa along Southern Pacific Railroad (lat. 34°03'45" N, long. 117°07'15" W; at SW cor. sec. 20, T 1 S, R 2 W). Named on Redlands (1967) and Yucaipa (1967, photorevised 1973) 7.5' quadrangles. On Redlands (1901) 15' quadrangle, the name "Crafton" applies to a place located about 1 mile farther west along the railroad (lat. 34°03'45" N, long. 117°08'20" W), and the name "Craftonville" appears at present Crafton. Myron H. Crafts developed a resort at the site of present Crafton in the 1870's and called it Crafton Retreat; officials of Crafton Land and Water Company had present Crafton laid out about 1885 (Gudde, 1949, p. 83). Postal authorities established Crafton Retreat post office in 1886 and discontinued it in 1887; they reestablished the post office with the name "Craftonville" in 1892, and discontinued it in 1920 (Salley, p. 52). The site of Crafton was called Eastberne Valley before Mr. Crafts arrived (Hanna, p. 76). Postal authorities established Burris post office 17.5 miles east of Craftonville post office in 1908 and discontinued it in 1910; the name was for Oscar V. Burris, mine owner and first postmaster (Salley, p. 30).

Crafton Hills [SAN BERNARDINO]: *ridge*, east-northeast-trending, 4 miles long, 3 miles northwest of Yucaipa (lat. 34°03'30" N, long. 117°04'30"

W); the ridge is east of Crafton. Named on Yucaipa (1967) 7.5' quadrangle.

Crafton Peak: see **Heaps Peak** [SAN BERNARDINO].

Crafton Reservoir [SAN BERNARDINO]: *lake,* 650 feet long, 4.25 miles west-northwest of Yucaipa (lat. 34°03'35" N, long. 117°06'25" W; near NE cor. sec. 29, T 1 S, R 2 W); the lake is less than 1 mile east-southeast of Crafton. Named on Yucaipa (1967) 7.5' quadrangle.

Crafton Retreat: see **Crafton** [SAN BERNARDINO].

Craftonville: see **Crafton** [SAN BERNARDINO].

Crafts Fork [SAN BERNARDINO]: *stream,* flows 0.5 mile to Snow Fork 3.5 miles north-northeast of Keller Peak (lat. 34°14'30" N, long. 117°01' W; near E line sec. 19, T 2 N, R 1 W). Named on Keller Peak (1967) 7.5' quadrangle. Redlands (1901) 15' quadrangle shows the stream as the uppermost part of North Fork Bear Creek.

Crafts Peak [SAN BERNARDINO]: *peak,* 8.5 miles southeast of Luna Mountain (lat. 35°15'05" N, long. 117°01'45" W; at N line sec. 19, T 2 N, R 1 W). Altitude 8364 feet. Named on Butler Peak (1971) 7.5' quadrangle.

Cram Peak [SAN BERNARDINO]: *peak,* 5.5 miles north-northwest of Yucaipa (lat. 34°06'30" N, long. 117°04' W; on E line sec. 3, T 1 S, R 2 W). Altitude 4162 feet. Named on Yucaipa (1967) 7.5' quadrangle.

Cramville: see **East Highlands** [SAN BERNARDINO].

Cree Camp [SAN BERNARDINO]: *locality,* 36 miles west of Ivanpah (lat. 35°22'30" N, long. 115°57'30" W; sec. 19, T 15 N, R 10 E). Named on Halloran Spring (1956) 15' quadrangle.

Crestline [SAN BERNARDINO]: *town,* 9.5 miles north of San Bernardino city hall (lat. 34°14'25" N, long. 117°17'15" W; in and near sec. 22, T 2 N, R 4 W). Named on San Bernardino North (1967) 7.5' quadrangle. Postal authorities established Incline post office in 1907, changed the name to Skyland Heights in 1910, and changed it to Crestline in 1919 (Frickstad, p. 142, 146).

Crestmore [RIVERSIDE]: *locality,* 3 miles north of Riverside along Union Pacific Railroad (lat. 34°01'25" N, long. 117°23'15" W); the place is 1.5 miles south-southwest of Crestmore [SAN BERNARDINO]. Named on Fontana (1967) 7.5' quadrangle.

Crestmore [SAN BERNARDINO]: *locality,* 4.5 miles south-southeast of Fontana city hall (lat. 34°02'40" N, long. 117°23'45" W; sec. 33, 34, T 1 S, R 5 W). Named on Fontana (1967) 7.5' quadrangle.

Crest Park [SAN BERNARDINO]: *village,* 5.25 miles north-northwest of Harrison Mountain (lat. 34°14' N, long. 117°12' W; near N line sec. 28, T 2 N, R 3 W). Named on Harrison Mountain (1967) 7.5' quadrangle. Postal authorities established Crest Park post office in 1949 (Frickstad, p. 140). The name is from Crest Park campgrounds (Gudde, 1969, p. 80).

Crest Summit [SAN BERNARDINO]: *locality,* 5.25 miles north-northwest of Harrison Mountain (lat. 34°13'50" N, long. 117°12'30" W; at E line sec. 29, T 2 N, R 3 W). Named on Harrison Mountain (1967) 7.5' quadrangle.

Cronese Lake: see **East Cronese Lake** [SAN BERNARDINO]; **West Cronese Lake** [SAN BERNARDINO].

Cronese Mountains [SAN BERNARDINO]: *ridge,* generally northeast-trending, 4 miles long, 17 miles southwest of Baker (lat. 35° 07' N, long. 116°18'30" W); the ridge is north of Cave Mountain. Named on Cave Mountain (1948) 15' quadrangle. United States Board on Geographic Names (1987, p. 1) approved the form "Cronise Mountains" for the name, and rejected the names "Cronese Mountains" and "Cave Mountains" for the feature.

Cronese Valley [SAN BERNARDINO]:

(1) *valley,* 15 miles southwest of Baker (lat. 34°06' N, long. 116° 17'30" W); the valley is southeast of Cronese Mountains. Named on Cave Mountain (1948) 15' quadrangle. United States Board on Geographic Names (1987, p. 1) approved the form "Cronise Valley" for the name.

(2) *locality,* 16 miles southwest of Baker (lat. 35°06' N, long. 116° 16'30" W; sec. 30, T 12 N, R 7 E); the place is in Cronese Valley (1). Named on Cave Mountain (1948) 15' quadrangle. Called Cronise on Avawatz Mountains (1933) 1° quadrangle.

Cronise: see **Cronese Valley** [SAN BERNARDINO] (2).

Cronise Lake: see **East Cronise Lake**, under **East Cronese Lake** [SAN BERNARDINO]; **West Cronise Lake**, under **West Cronese Lake** [SAN BERNARDINO].

Cronise Mountains: see **Cronese Mountains** [SAN BERNARDINO].

Cronise Valley: see **Cronese Valley** [SAN BERNARDINO] (1).

Cross Roads [SAN BERNARDINO]: *locality,* 18 miles east-northeast of Vidal (lat. 34°12'50" N, long. 114°12'55" W; sec. 35, T 2 N, R 26 E). Named on Cross Roads (1959) 7.5' quadrangle. Postal authorities established Cross Roads post office in 1935 and discontinued it in 1968 (Salley, p. 53).

Crowder Canyon [SAN BERNARDINO]: *canyon,* drained by a stream that flows 3.5 miles to Cajon Canyon 0.5 mile northwest of Cajon (lat. 34°18'20" N, long. 117°27'55" W; near W line sec. 36, T 3 N, R 6 W). Named on Cajon (1956) 7.5' quadrangle.

Crown Jewel [SAN BERNARDINO]: *locality,* 2.25 miles northwest of Redlands city hall along Atchison, Topeka and Santa Fe Railroad (lat. 34°04'35" N, long. 117°12'30" W). Named on Redlands (1967) 7.5' quadrangle.

Crown Valley [RIVERSIDE]: *valley,* 6.5 miles south-southwest of Hemet (lat. 33°39'15" N, long. 116°59'50" W). Named on Hemet (1953) and Winchester (1953) 7.5' quadrangles. T.S. Brown gave the name to the valley because the peaks that surround it suggest the points of a crown (Gunther, p. 144).

Crucero [SAN BERNARDINO]: *locality,* 15 miles south-southwest of Baker along Union Pacific Railroad (lat. 35°02'50" N, long. 116° 09'50" W; at SW cor. sec. 8, T 11 N, R 8 E). Named on Soda Lake (1956) 15' quadrangle. Called Belfast on Avawatz Mountains (1933) 1° quadrangle, and called Epson on California Mining Bureau's (1917a) map. Postal authorities established Crucero post office in 1911, discontinued it in 1917, reestablished it in 1922, and discontinued it in 1943; Tonopah and Tidewater Railroad and Los Angeles Salt Lake Railroad crossed at the site—*crucero* means "crossing" in Spanish (Salley, p. 53). California Mining Bureau's (1909a) map shows a place called Mesquite located 4 miles south of Crucero along the railroad at present Mesquite Hills. Thompson (1929, p. 528) listed Mesquite Spring, a feature situated about 3.25 miles southwest of Crucero (SW quarter sec. 25, T 11 N, R 7 E).

Crucero Hill [SAN BERNARDINO]: *ridge,* north-northeast-trending, 1.25 miles long, 15 miles south-southwest of Baker (lat. 35°02' N, long. 116°09'30" W; sec. 17, 20, T 11 N, R 8 E); the ridge is 1 mile south-southeast of Crucero. Named on Soda Lake (1956) 15' quadrangle. Thompson (1929, p. 513) noted that a low pass located south of Crucero Hills (sec. 20, T 11 N, R 8 E) is known locally as Mormon Pass.

Crutts: see **Crutts Well** [SAN BERNARDINO].

Crutts Well [SAN BERNARDINO]: *well,* 32 miles east-southeast of the village of Red Mountain (lat. 35°13'05" N, long. 117°03'40" W; near SW cor. sec. 21, T 31 S, R 46 E). Named on Opal Mountain (1955) 15' quadrangle. Postal authorities established Crutts post office at the site in 1916 and discontinued it in 1922, when the well went dry (Salley, p. 53).

Crystal Caves: see **Mitchell Caverns**, under **Cooks Well** [SAN BERNARDINO].

Crystal Creek [SAN BERNARDINO]:

(1) *stream,* flows 2.5 miles to lowlands 6.5 miles north of Fawnskin (lat. 34°22' N, long. 116°56'25" W; at N line sec. 12, T 3 N, R 1 W). Named on Fawnskin (1971) 7.5' quadrangle.

(2) *stream,* flows 2.5 miles to Santa Ana River 3.5 miles south of Keller Peak (lat. 34°08'30" N, long. 117°02'35" W; sec. 25, T 1 N, R 2 W). Named on Keller Peak (1967) and Yucaipa (1967) 7.5' quadrangles.

Crystal Springs Canyon [RIVERSIDE]: *canyon,* drained by a stream that flows 2.5 miles to Red Cloud Canyon 9 miles south of Desert Center (lat. 33°35'30" N, long. 115°26' W). Named on Chuckwalla Mountains (1963) 15' quadrangle.

Cub Lee Spring: see **Cub Lee Well** [SAN BERNARDINO].

Cub Lee Well [SAN BERNARDINO]: *well,* 33 miles north-northwest of Ivanpah (lat. 35°45'05" N, long. 115°37'20" W; at S line sec. 19, T 19 N, R 13 E). Named on Shenandoah Peak (1956) 15' quadrangle. Called Cub Lee Spring on Ivanpah (1912) 1° quadrangle.

Cucamonga [SAN BERNARDINO]: *land grant,* at Cucamonga (present Rancho Cucamonga), Alta Loma, and Upland. Named on Cucamonga Peak (1966), Guasti (1966), Mount Baldy (1967), and Ontario (1967) 7.5' quadrangles. Tiburcio Tapia received 3 leagues in 1839; L.V. Prudhomme claimed 13,045 acres patented in 1872 (Cowan, p. 31). The name is of Indian origin (Kroeber, p. 41). Father Nuez, diarist of the Moraga expedition of 1819, used the name "Nuestra Señora del Pilar de Cucamonga" (Hanna, p. 78). Early American visitors had many bizarre forms for the name of the grant, including Coco Mongo Ranch, Cocomouga's Ranch, and Qui-qual-mun-go Ranch (Marcy, p. 278, 315, 316), rancho of Quiquai-mungo (Blake, p. 80), Kikal Mungo ranch (Antisell p. 79), and Rancho Cocoa-Mungo (Hafen and Hafen, p. 94).

Cucamonga: see **North Cucamonga**, under **Rancho Cucamonga** [SAN BERNARDINO]; **South Cucamonga**, under **Guasti** [SAN BERNARDINO].

Cucamonga Canyon [SAN BERNARDINO]: *canyon,* 5.5 miles long, opens into lowlands 7 miles north of Ontario city hall (lat. 34°09'45" N, long. 117°38'10" W; near N line sec. 20, T 1 N, R 7 W). Named on Cucamonga Peak (1966) and Mount Baldy (1967) 7.5' quadrangles.

Cucamonga Canyon Wash: see **Cucamonga Creek** [SAN BERNARDINO].

Cucamonga Creek [RIVERSIDE-SAN BERNARDINO]: *stream* and *dry wash,* extends for 6.25 miles, almost entirely in San Bernardino County, from the mouth of Cucamonga Canyon to Mill Creek [RIVERSIDE-SAN BERNARDINO] 7.5 miles east-northeast of San Juan Hill (lat. 33°56'45" N, long. 117°36'50" W; at S line sec. 33, T 2 S, R 7 W). Named on Corona North (1967), Cucamonga Peak (1966), Guasti (1966), and Mount Baldy (1967) 7.5' quadrangles. Called Cucamonga Canyon Wash on United States Geological Survey's (1941) map.

Cucamonga Peak [SAN BERNARDINO]: *peak,* 12 miles north-northeast of Ontario city hall (lat. 34°13'20" N, long. 117°35'05" W; at N line sec. 35, T 2 N, R 7 W). Altitude 8859 feet. Named on Cucamonga Peak (1966)

7.5' quadrangle.

Cuddeback Lake [SAN BERNARDINO]: *dry lake,* 6 miles long, 9 miles east-southeast of the village of Red Mountain (lat. 35°17' N, long. 117°28'30" W). Named on Cuddeback Lake (1954) and Fremont Peak (1956) 15' quadrangles. Thompson (1929, p. 223) noted that the feature also had the names "Golden Lake" and "Willard Lake."

Culp Valley [RIVERSIDE]: *valley,* 4.5 miles east of Aguanga (lat. 33°26'35" N, long. 116°47'15" W). Named on Aguanga (1954) 7.5' quadrangle.

Cunningham Spring: see **Coyote Holes** [SAN BERNARDINO].

Cup Spring [SAN BERNARDINO]: *spring,* 4.25 miles southeast of Luna Mountain (lat. 34°18'10" N, long. 117°04'15" W; near E line sec. 34, T 3 N, R 2 W). Named on Butler Peak (1971) 7.5' quadrangle.

Curlew [IMPERIAL]: *locality,* 8.5 miles north of Holtville along Southern Pacific Railroad (lat. 32°56' N, long. 115°24'20" W; sec. 15, T 14 S, R 15 E). Named on Alamorio (1956) 7.5' quadrangle.

Cushenbury [SAN BERNARDINO]: *locality,* 6.5 miles north of Big Bear City along Atchison, Topeka and Santa Fe Railroad (lat. 34° 21'15" N, long. 116°51'30" W; near SE cor. sec. 10, T 3 N, R 1 E). Named on Big Bear City (1971) 7.5' quadrangle. John Cushenbury had a community laid out in the early 1860's and called it Cushenbury City; the place probably was near present Cushenbury (La Fuze, v. I, p. 59, xxiii).

Cushenbury Canyon [SAN BERNARDINO]: *canyon,* 2.5 miles long, opens into lowlands 6.25 miles north of Big Bear City (lat. 34°21'05" N, long. 116°50'45" W; at N line sec. 14, T 3 N, R 1 E). Named on Big Bear City (1971) 7.5' quadrangle.

Cushenbury Springs [SAN BERNARDINO]: *springs,* 7 miles north or Big Bear City (lat. 34°21'45" N, long. 116°51'30" W; near NE cor. sec. 10, T 3 N, R 1 E); the springs are about 1 mile northwest of the mouth of Cushenbury Canyon. Named on Big Bear City (1971) 7.5' quadrangle.

Cut Spring [SAN BERNARDINO]: *spring,* 14 miles west-southwest of Ivanpah (lat. 35°16'45" N, long. 115°33'15" W; sec. 23, T 14 N, R 13 E). Named on Mescal Range (1955) 15' quadrangle.

- D -

Daggett [SAN BERNARDINO]: *town,* 9 miles east-southeast of Barstow (lat. 34°51'45" N, long. 116°53' W; in and near sec. 21, T 9 N, R 1 E). Named on Daggett (1971) 7.5' quadrangle. Postal authorities established Daggett post office in 1883 (Frickstad, p. 140). The railroad station at the site first was called Calico, but to avoid confusion with the mining camp of Calico, the station name was changed in 1883 to Daggett (Myrick, p. 766, 816). The name "Daggett" is for John R. Daggett, owner of a mine in Calico Mountains and lieutenant governor of California (Peirson, p. 190). Postal authorities established Hawley post office 8 miles northeast of Daggett in 1883, discontinued it the same year, reestablished it in 1884, and discontinued it in 1888; the name was for Isaac Hawley, who built accommodations for travelers at the place—the site also was called Forks of Road and Punta de Agua (Salley, p. 94). A place called Fish Ponds was about 3 miles above Daggett along Mojave River (Crossman, p. 219).

Daggett Ridge [SAN BERNARDINO]: *ridge,* west-northwest-trending, about 4 miles long, 6.25 miles south-southwest of Daggett (lat. 34°46'50" N, long. 116°55'40" W). Named on Daggett (1971) 7.5' quadrangle.

Daggett Wash [SAN BERNARDINO]: *stream,* flows 12 miles to Mojave River less than 1 mile west of Daggett (lat. 34°52' N, long. 116°54' W; near W line sec. 17, T 9 N, R 1 E). Named on Daggett (1971) and Minneola (1971) 7.5' quadrangles.

Dale: see **New Dale** [SAN BERNARDINO]; **Old Dale** [SAN BERNARDINO].

Dale Lake [SAN BERNARDINO]: *dry lake,* 3 miles long, 29 miles south of Amboy (lat. 34°08'30" N, long. 115°42'30" W); the dry lake is 5 miles east-northeast of Old Dale and 6 miles north of New Dale. Named on Dale Lake (1956) 15' quadrangle. The feature first was called Burt's Dry Lake; John Burt found mines in the neighborhood in 1892 or 1893 (O'Neal, p. 64).

Daley Canyon [SAN BERNARDINO]: *canyon,* less than 0.5 mile long, nearly 6 miles northwest of Harrison Mountain (lat. 34°14'05" N, long. 117°13' W; on N line sec. 29, T 2 N, R 3 W). Named on Harrison Mountain (1967) 7.5' quadrangle.

Danaher: see **San Bernardino** [SAN BERNARDINO] (2).

Danby [SAN BERNARDINO]: *locality,* 9 miles southwest of Essex along Atchison, Topeka and Santa Fe Railroad (lat. 34°38' N, long. 115°20'45" W; sec. 6, T 6 N, R 16 E). Named on Danby (1956) 15' quadrangle. Postal authorities established Danby post office in 1898, discontinued it in 1900, reestablished it in 1901, and discontinued it in 1913 (Frickstad, p. 140). Thompson's (1921) map shows a place called Arimo located along the railroad 5 miles north-northeast of Danby.

Danby Lake [SAN BERNARDINO]: *dry lake,* 14 miles long, 36 miles south-southeast of Essex (lat. 34°13' N, long. 115°05'30" W). Named on Iron Mountains (1956) and Milligan (1958) 15' quadrangles.

Danby Spring: see **Bonanza Spring** [SAN BERNARDINO].

Dark Canyon [RIVERSIDE]: *canyon,* about 2.5 miles long, along North Fork San Jacinto River 3.25 miles west-southwest of San Jacinto Peak (lat. 33°38'10" N, long. 116°43'55" W). Named on San Jacinto Peak (1981) 7.5' quadrangle. Called Black Canyon on Palm Springs (1957) 15' quadrangle, but United States Board on Geographic Names (1983c, p. 4) rejected this name for the feature.

Dark Canyon Camp [RIVERSIDE]: *locality,* 3.25 miles west-southwest of San Jacinto Peak (lat. 33°48'05" N, long. 116°44' W; near SW cor. sec. 24, T 4 S, R 2 E). Named on Palm Springs (1957) 15' quadrangle.

Dart Creek [SAN BERNARDINO]: *stream,* flows 1.5 miles to Houston Creek 19 miles south of Victorville (lat. 34°15'20" N, long. 117°16' W; sec. 14, T 2 N, R 4 W). Named on Cedar Springs (1956) and Harrison Mountain (1967) 7.5' quadrangles.

Darwin Range: see **Argus Range** [SAN BERNARDINO].

Date City [IMPERIAL]: *village,* 4.25 miles east-southeast of Holtville (lat. 32°47'30" N, long. 115°18'30" W; sec. 3, T 16 S, R 16 E). Named on Holtville East (1957) 7.5' quadrangle.

Date City: see **Calipatria** [IMPERIAL].

Date Palm Beach: see **Desert Beach** [RIVERSIDE].

Davies Canyon [IMPERIAL]: *canyon,* 1.5 miles long, opens into lowlands 25 miles west-southwest of El Centro (lat. 32°42'05" N, long. 115°59'05" W; near W line sec. 5, T 17 S, R 10 E). Named on Coyote Wells (1957) 7.5' quadrangle.

Davies Valley [IMPERIAL]: *valley,* 27 miles west-southwest of El Centro (lat. 32°39'15" N, long. 116°00' W). Named on Coyote Wells (1957) and In-Ko-Pah Gorge (1959) 7.5' quadrangles. The feature extends south-southeast into Mexico.

Davis: see **Mount Davis** [RIVERSIDE].

Davis Lake [IMPERIAL]: *lake,* 1600 feet long, 8.5 miles south of Palo Verde near Colorado River (lat. 33°18'45" N, long. 114°43'50" W; sec. 14, T 10 S, R 21 E). Named on Cibola (1965) 7.5' quadrangle.

Dawes [SAN BERNARDINO]: *locality,* 22 miles southwest of Ivanpah along Union Pacific Railroad (lat. 35°05'30" N, long. 115°33'40" W; sec. 26, T 12 N, R 13 E). Named on Kelso (1955) 15' quadrangle. Ivanpah (1912) 1° quadrangle shows a place called Ames situated along San Pedro, Los Angeles and Salt Lake Railroad at the site.

Dawn O'Day Canyon [SAN BERNARDINO]: *canyon,* drained by a stream that flows 4.25 miles to Coxey Creek 2.5 miles east-southeast of Luna Mountain (lat. 34°20'10" N, long. 117°05' W; near NW cor. sec. 22, T 3 N, R 2 W). Named on Butler Peak (1971) 7.5' quadrangle.

Dawson Canyon [RIVERSIDE]: *canyon,* 5.25 miles long, opens into the canyon of Temescal Wash 3 miles west-northwest of Estelle Mountain (lat. 33°46'50" N, long. 117°28'15" W; sec. 35, T 4 S, R 6 W). Named on Lake Mathews (1967) 7.5' quadrangle. The name commemorates Daniel Spangler Dawson, a farmer in the neighborhood (Gunther, p. 146-147).

Dawson Peak [SAN BERNARDINO]: *peak,* 1.25 miles north-northeast of Mount San Antonio (lat. 34°18'15" N, long. 117°38'05" W; sec. 32, T 3 N, R 7 W). Altitude 9575 feet. Named on Mount San Antonio (1955) 7.5' quadrangle.

Day Canyon [SAN BERNARDINO]: *canyon,* 4 miles long, opens into lowlands 10.5 miles northeast of Ontario city hall (lat. 34°11' N, long. 117°32'20" W; near W line sec. 8, T 1 N, R 6 W). Named on Cucamonga Peak (1966) 7.5' quadrangle. The name commemorates George Day, who filed a claim to water rights in the canyon in 1867 (Hanna, p. 83).

Day Canyon Wash [SAN BERNARDINO]: *stream* and *dry wash,* extends for 2 miles from the mouth of Day Canyon to Day Creek 8.5 miles northeast of Ontario city hall (lat. 34°09'20" N, long. 117°33'10" W; sec. 19, T 1 N, R 6 W). Named on Cucamonga Peak (1966) 7.5' quadrangle.

Day Creek [SAN BERNARDINO]: *stream* and *dry wash,* extends for 9 miles from Day Canyon Wash to end at Riverside County line (lat. 34°02' N, long. 117°32'40" W; at S line sec. 31, T 1 S, R 6 W). Named on Cucamonga Peak (1966) and Guasti (1966) 7.5' quadrangles.

Dead Indian Creek [RIVERSIDE]: *stream,* flows 5.5 miles to lowlands 2.5 miles south-southwest of Palm Desert (lat. 33°41'15" N, long. 116°23'30" W; near SE cor. sec. 31, T 5 S, R 6 E). Named on Rancho Mirage (1957) 7.5' quadrangle.

Deadman Lake [SAN BERNARDINO]: *dry lake,* 3.5 miles long, 15 miles east-northeast of Landers (lat. 34°18'50" N, long. 116°08'15" W). Named on Deadman Lake SE (1955) and Deadman Lake SW (1955) 7.5' quadrangles.

Deadman Point [SAN BERNARDINO]: *hill,* 11 miles east-southeast of Victorville (lat. 34°28'20" N, long. 117°07'25" W; near SE cor. sec. 31, T 5 N, R 2 W). Named on Fifteenmile Valley (1971) 7.5' quadrangle. Peirson (p. 127) called the feature Deadman's Point.

Deadmans Canyon [SAN BERNARDINO]: *canyon,* 1 mile long, 3 miles east-northeast of Sugarloaf Mountain (lat. 34°13'15" N, long. 116°46' W). Named on Moonridge (1970) 7.5' quadrangle.

Deadmans Holes: see **Mesquite Lake** [SAN BERNARDINO] (1).

Deadmans Lake [SAN BERNARDINO]: *lake,* 1900 feet long, 3 miles northeast of Sugarloaf Mountain (lat. 34°13'55" N, long. 116°46'30" W; sec. 28, T 2 N, R 2 E); the lake is south of Deadmans Ridge. Named on

Moonridge (1970) 7.5' quadrangle. On San Gorgonio Mountain (1954) 15' quadrangle, the name applies to a dry lake.

Deadmans Ridge [SAN BERNARDINO]: *ridge,* west- to west-southwest-trending, 2.5 miles long, 3.25 miles east of Sugarloaf Mountain (lat. 34°14'05" N, long. 116°46'30" W). Named on Moonridge (1970) 7.5' quadrangle.

Dead Mountains [SAN BERNARDINO]: *range,* center 11.5 miles northwest of Needles (lat. 34°57'30" N, long. 114°45" W). Named on Bannock (1956), Davis Dam (1950), Homer Mountain (1956), and Needles (1950) 15' quadrangles. United States Board on Geographic Names (1933, p. 257) rejected the name "Black Mountains" for the range.

Death Valley [SAN BERNARDINO]: *valley,* mainly in Inyo County, but extends south into San Bernardino County 45 miles northwest of Baker (lat. 35°47'40" N, long. 116°32'30" W). Named on Avawatz Pass (1948) and Confidence Hills (1950) 15' quadrangles. United States Board on Geographic Names (1933, p. 258) rejected the names "Amargosa Desert" and "Lost Valley" for present Death Valley.

De Benneville Pines: see **Camp De Benneville Pines** [SAN BERNARDINO].

Deception Canyon: see **East Deception Canyon** [RIVERSIDE]; **West Deception Canyon** [RIVERSIDE].

Decker Canyon [RIVERSIDE]: *canyon,* drained by a stream that flows 2.5 miles to Morrell Canyon 2.25 miles north-northeast of Sitton Peak (lat. 33°37' N, long. 117°25'30" W; sec. 29, T 6 S, R 5 W). Named on Alberhill (1954) and Sitton Peak (1954) 7.5' quadrangles. The name commemorates an early settler in the neighborhood (Gunther, p. 148).

Declez [SAN BERNARDINO]: *locality,* 3.5 miles southwest of present Fontana city hall along Southern Pacific Railroad (lat. 34°03'50" N, long. 117°28'50" W). Named on San Bernardino (1901) 15' quadrangle. Fontana (1943) 7.5' quadrangle has both the names "Declez" and "South Fontana Sta." at the place. Postal authorities established Declez post office in 1900 and discontinued it in 1913 (Frickstad, p. 140).

Declezville [SAN BERNARDINO]: *locality,* nearly 5 miles south-southwest of Fontana city hall (lat. 34°02'40" N, long. 117°28'50" W; sec. 35, T 1 S, R 6 W). Named on Fontana (1967) 7.5' quadrangle. Postal authorities established Declezville post office in 1888 and discontinued it in 1898 (Frickstad, p. 140). Officials of Southern Pacific Railroad gave the name "Declezville" to the terminus of a rail spur to granite quarries owned by William Declez; the junction of the spur with the main rail line was at Declez (Gudde, 1949, p. 90).

Deep Canyon [RIVERSIDE]:

(1) *canyon,* nearly 2 miles long, opens into San Gorgonio Pass 5.5 miles east-northeast of Banning (lat. 33°56'40" N, long. 116°46'55" W; near N line sec. 4, T 3 S, R 2 E). Named on Cabazon (1956) 7.5' quadrangle.

(2) *canyon,* 8.5 miles long, opens into lowlands 4 miles south of Palm Desert (lat. 33°39'45" N, long. 116°22'15" W; near W line sec. 9, T 6 S, R 6 E). Named on Palm Desert (1959) 15' quadrangle.

Deep Canyon [SAN BERNARDINO]: *canyon,* drained by a stream that flows 2.5 miles to Silver Creek 7.5 miles north-northwest of Fawnskin (lat. 34°22'35" N, long. 116°59' W; sec. 4, T 3 N, R 1 W). Named on Fawnskin (1971) 7.5' quadrangle.

Deep Creek [SAN BERNARDINO]:

(1) *stream,* flows 22 miles to join West Fork Mojave River and form Mojave River 14 miles south-southeast of Victorville (lat. 34° 20'30" N, long. 117°14'10" W; sec. 18, T 3 N, R 3 W). Named on Butler Peak (1971), Keller Peak (1967), and Lake Arrowhead (1971) 7.5' quadrangles. North Fork enters 2 miles north-northwest of Keller Peak and is 2 miles long. South Fork enters from the south 2 miles northwest of Keller Peak and is 2.5 miles long. Both forks are named on Keller Peak (1967) 7.5' quadrangle. Deep Creek (1) often is called East Fork Mojave River (Peirson, p. 32).

(2) *stream,* flows 1.25 miles to Santa Ana River 6 miles northwest of Yucaipa (lat. 34°06'15" N, long. 117°05'55" W; near N line sec. 9, T 1 S, R 2 W). Named on Yucaipa (1967) 7.5' quadrangle.

Deep Creek Lake [SAN BERNARDINO]: *lake,* 450 feet long, 2.5 miles west-northwest of Keller Peak (lat. 34°12'50" N, long. 117° 05'10" W; on W line sec. 34, T 2 N, R 2 W); the lake is along Deep Creek (1). Named on Keller Peak (1967) 7.5' quadrangle.

Deer Canyon [SAN BERNARDINO]:

(1) *canyon,* 1 mile long, nearly 4 miles west-northwest of Sugarloaf Mountain (lat. 34°13' N, long. 116°51'25" W). Named on Moonridge (1970) 7.5' quadrangle.

(2) *canyon,* 3.5 miles long, opens into lowlands 9.5 miles north-northeast of Ontario city hall (lat. 34°10'40" N, long. 117°34'15" W; near N line sec. 13, T 1 N, R 7 W). Named on Cucamonga Peak (1966) 7.5' quadrangle.

Deer Canyon Wash [SAN BERNARDINO]: *stream* and *dry wash,* extends for about 2 miles from the mouth of Deer Canyon (2) to Deer Creek (1) 8 miles northeast of Ontario city hall (lat. 34°09' N, long. 117°33'25" W; near SW cor. sec, 19, T 1 N, R 6 W). Named on Cucamonga Peak (1966) 7.5' quadrangle.

Deer Creek [SAN BERNARDINO]:

(1) *stream* and *dry wash,* extends for 11 miles from the mouth of Deer Canyon Wash to Cucamonga Creek 5 miles southeast of Ontario city hall (lat. 34°00'15" N, long. 117°35'55" W; at S line sec. 10, T 2 S, R 7 W). Named on Cucamonga Peak (1966) and Guasti (1966) 7.5' quadrangles.

(2) *stream,* flows 4.25 miles to Santa Ana River 7.5 miles southwest of downtown Big Bear Lake (lat. 34°09'45" W, long. 117°00'05" W; sec. 20, T 1 N, R 1 W). Named on Big Bear Lake (1970) 7.5' quadrangle.

Deer Creek: see **Holcomb Creek** [SAN BERNARDINO].

Deer Creek Public Camp: see **Fishermans Campground** [SAN BERNARDINO].

Deer Island [SAN BERNARDINO]: *island,* 2 miles long, 7.5 miles east of Vidal along Colorado River on California-Arizona State line (lat. 34°07'05" N, long. 114°22'15" W). Named on Parker SE (1970) and Parker SW (1970) 7.5' quadrangles.

Deer Lodge Park [SAN BERNARDINO]: *district,* 6.5 miles southwest of Luna Mountain (lat. 34°16'40" N, long. 117°12'35" W; near NE cor. sec. 8, T 2 N, R 3 W). Named on Lake Arrowhead (1971) 7.5' quadrangle.

Deer Mountain [SAN BERNARDINO]: *peak,* 3.5 miles south-southeast of Butler Peak (lat. 34°17'40" N, long. 117°06'40" W; near N line sec. 5, T 2 N, R 2 W). Altitude 5536 feet. Named on Butler Peak (1971) 7.5' quadrangle.

Deer Peak [IMPERIAL]: *relief feature,* 10 miles northeast of Holtville (lat. 32°53'55" N, long. 115°14'20" W; near S line sec. 29, T 14 S, R 17 E). Altitude 125 feet. Named on Glamis NW (1954) 7.5' quadrangle.

Deer Spring [RIVERSIDE]: *spring,* 10 miles northeast of Banning (lat. 34°01'40" N, long. 116°47'25" W; near E line sec. 5, T 2 S, R 2 E). Named on San Gorgonio Mountain (1970) 7.5' quadrangle.

Deer Spring [SAN BERNARDINO]:

(1) *spring,* 18 miles south-southwest of Ivanpah (lat. 35°17'10" N, long. 115°36'35" W; sec. 20, T 14 N, R 13 E). Named on Mescal Range (1955) 15' quadrangle.

(2) *spring,* 15 miles northwest of downtown Morongo Valley (lat. 34°12'50" N, long. 116°44'25" W; sec. 35, T 2 N, R 2 E). Named on Onyx Peak (1972) 7.5' quadrangle.

Deer Springs [RIVERSIDE]: *spring,* 1.25 miles south-southwest of San Jacinto Peak (lat. 33°47'55" N, long. 116°41'20" W; sec. 29, T 4 S, R 3 E). Named on San Jacinto Peak (1981) 7.5' quadrangle. On Palm Springs (1957) 15' quadrangle, the name applies to a feature located nearly 1 mile farther west-northwest near present Deer Springs Camp.

Deer Springs Camp [RIVERSIDE]: *locality,* 1.5 miles southwest of San Jacinto Peak (lat. 33°48'05" N, long. 116°41'55" W; near NW cor. sec. 29, T 4 S, R 3 E); the place is 0.5 mile west-northwest of Deer Springs. Named on San Jacinto Peak (1981) 7.5' quadrangle.

Deguynos Canyon [IMPERIAL]: *canyon,* drained by a stream that heads in San Diego County and flows 4 miles to Gert Wash 5 miles north-northwest of Carrizo Mountain (lat. 32°53'10" N, long. 116° 03'35" W; near S line sec. 5, T 15 S, R 9 E). Named on Carrizo Mountain NE (1957) 7.5' quadrangle.

Delamar Mountain [SAN BERNARDINO]: *peak,* 1.5 miles north of Fawnskin (lat. 34°17'30" N, long. 116°56'40" W; at E line sec. 2, T 2 N, R 1 W). Altitude 8398 feet. Named on Fawnskin (1971) 7.5' quadrangle.

Delamar Spring [SAN BERNARDINO]: *spring,* 1.5 miles north-northwest of Fawnskin (lat. 34°17'35" N, long. 116°57'20" W; near N line sec. 2, T 2 N, R 1 W); the spring is 0.5 mile west-northwest of Delamar Mountain. Named on Fawnskin (1971) 7.5' quadrangle.

Delker Canyon [SAN BERNARDINO]: *canyon,* drained by a stream that flows less than 1 mile to Ice house Canyon 13 miles north of Ontario city hall (lat. 34°14'35" N, long. 117°36'20" W; sec. 22, T 2 N, R 7 W). Named on Cucamonga Peak (1966) 7.5' quadrangle.

Dell: see **Summit** [SAN BERNARDINO].

Dellamont [RIVERSIDE]: *peak,* 3.25 miles north-northeast of San Jacinto (lat. 33°49'25" N, long. 116°55'30" W; near W line sec. 18, T 4 S, R 1 E). Named on San Jacinto (1953) 7.5' quadrangle.

Dells [SAN BERNARDINO]: *locality,* 12.5 miles north of Ontario city hall in San Antonio Canyon (lat. 34°14'15" N, long. 117°39'15" W; near S line sec. 19, T 2 N, R 7 W). Named on Cucamonga (1903) 15' quadrangle. The name recalls Fred Dell, who filed on land at the place in 1886, and leased the land in 1894 to Frank Keyes, who turned Dell's Camp into the most popular resort in San Antonio Canyon (Robinson, J.W., 1983, p. 138).

Dell's Camp: see **Dells** [SAN BERNARDINO].

Del Rosa [SAN BERNARDINO]: *district,* 5 miles west-southwest of Harrison Mountain (lat. 34°13'45" N, long. 117°14'30" W). Named on Harrison Mountain (1967) and San Bernardino North (1967) 7.5' quadrangles. Postal authorities established Del Rosa post office in 1898, changed the name to Delrosa in 1895, discontinued it in 1901, reestablished it in 1903, and changed the name back to Del Rosa in 1905 (Salley, p. 57). Following a severe drought in the early 1950's, residents of Del Rosa elected to become part of San Bernardino (Richards).

De Luz Creek [RIVERSIDE]: *stream,* flows 4 miles to San Diego County 10 miles west of the town of Temecula (lat. 33°28'20" N, long. 117°18'50" W). Named on Fallbrook (1968) and Wildomar (1953) 7.5' quadrangles.

Demens Canyon [SAN BERNARDINO]: *canyon,* 1.25 miles long, 8.5 miles north-northeast of Ontario city hall (lat. 34°10'35" N, long. 117°35'45" W; sec. 10, 15, T 1 N, R 7 W). Named on Cucamonga Peak (1966) 7.5' quadrangle.

Denning Spring [SAN BERNARDINO]: *spring,* 31 miles northwest of Baker (lat. 35°35'15" N, long. 116°28' W). Named on Avawatz Pass (1948) 15' quadrangle. The misspelled name commemorates Andrew Demming, a member of California-Nevada boundary commission in 1861 (Hanna, p. 85).

Desert [SAN BERNARDINO]: *locality,* 12.5 miles north of Ivanpah along Union Pacific Railroad (lat. 35°36'25" N, long. 115°18'55" W; sec. 12, T 16 N, R 15 E). Named on Roach Lake (1955) 15' quadrangle. Ivanpah (1912) 1° quadrangle has both the names "Desert" and "Lyons Sta." at the place. Postal authorities established Desert post office in 1908 and discontinued it in 1927 (Salley, p. 58).

Desert: see **Oro Grande** [SAN BERNARDINO].

Desert Angel [RIVERSIDE]: *peak,* 4.5 miles northwest of Palm Springs (lat. 33°52'30" N, long. 116°36'15" W; at S line sec. 30, T 3 S, R 4 E). Altitude 2356 feet. Named on Desert Hot Springs (1955) and Palm Springs (1957) 7.5' quadrangles.

Desert Beach [RIVERSIDE]: *locality,* less than 1 mile southeast of Mortmar along Salton Sea (lat. 33°30'45" N, long. 115°55'35" W; at S line sec. 34, T 7 S, R 10 E). Named on Mortmar (1958) 7.5' quadrangle. Called Date Palm Beach on Cottonwood Spring (1943) 15' quadrangle.

Desert Camp [RIVERSIDE]: *locality,* 3 miles west-northwest of Mortmar (lat. 33°32' N, long. 115°59' W; sec. 30, T 7 S, R 10 E). Named on Mortmar (1958) 7.5' quadrangle.

Desert Center [RIVERSIDE]: *village,* 47 miles west of Blythe (lat. 33°42'50" N, long. 115°24'10" W; sec. 22, T 5 S, R 15 E). Named on Chuckwalla Mountains (1963) 15' quadrangle. Postal authorities established Desert Center post office in 1934 (Frickstad, p. 127). Steve Ragsdale and his wife founded and named the place in 1925 (Gunther, p. 150).

Desert Heights [SAN BERNARDINO]: *locality,* 7 miles northwest of Twentynine Palms (lat. 34°13' N, long. 116°08' W). Named on Sunfair (1972) and Twentynine Palms (1973) 7.5' quadrangles.

Desert Hot Springs [RIVERSIDE]: *town,* 9 miles north-northeast of Palm Springs (lat. 33°57'40" N, long. 116°30' W). Named on Desert Hot Springs (1955) and Seven Palms Valley (1958) 7.5' quadrangles. The place began in 1933 as Coffee's Bath House, a winter vacation resort and year-around residential community; postal authorities established Desert Hot Springs post office in 1944 (Salley, p. 58). The town incorporated in 1963.

Desert King Spring [SAN BERNARDINO]: *spring,* 40 miles west-northwest of Baker (lat. 35°31'35" N, long. 116°42'45" W). Named on Leach Lake (1948) 15' quadrangle.

Desert Queen Well [RIVERSIDE]: *well,* 27 miles east-northeast of Garnet (lat. 34°01'50" N, long. 116°08' W; sec. 3, T 2 S, R 8 E). Named on Indian Cove (1972) 7.5' quadrangle.

Desert Shores [IMPERIAL]: *village,* 36 miles west-northwest of Calipatria along Salton Sea (lat. 33°24'15" N, long. 116°02'15" W; sec. 9, T 9 S, R 9 E). Named on Oasis (1956) 7.5' quadrangle. Called Fish Springs on Agua Dulce (1944) 15' quadrangle. Rabbit Peak (1959) 15' quadrangle shows a water feature called Fish Springs at the site. The name "Fish Springs" is from small fish in water of the spring (Burns, p. 26). A beach called Sundial opened in 1955 along Salton Sea between Desert Shores and Salton Sea Beach (Burns, p. 28).

Desert Spring [SAN BERNARDINO]: *spring,* 16 miles north-northwest of Essex (lat. 34°57'25" N, long. 115°20'30" W; sec. 18, T 10 N, R 16 E). Named on Colton Well (1956) 15' quadrangle.

Desert Springs: see **Pinon Hills** [SAN BERNARDINO].

Desert View [RIVERSIDE]: *locality,* 2.5 miles east-southeast of San Jacinto Peak (lat. 33°48'05" N, long. 116°38'20" W; sec. 26, T 4 S, R 3 E). Named on San Jacinto Peak (1981) 7.5' quadrangle.

Desert Well: see **Saltmarsh** [SAN BERNARDINO].

Desilt Wash [SAN BERNARDINO]: *stream,* flows nearly 2 miles to Colorado River 24 miles east-northeast of Vidal (lat. 34°17'15" N, long. 114°08'15" W; sec. 3, T 2 N, R 27 E). Named on Gene Wash (1959) 7.5' quadrangle.

Desmont: see **Pinon Hills** [SAN BERNARDINO].

Devers Hill [RIVERSIDE]: *hill,* 7.25 miles north of Palm Springs (lat. 33°56'15" N, long. 116°33'45" W; at E line sec. 4, T 3 S, R 4 E). Altitude 1170 feet. Named on Desert Hot Springs (1955) 7.5' quadrangle.

Devil Canyon [RIVERSIDE]: *canyon,* drained by a stream that flows 5.25 miles to lowlands 10 miles south-southeast of Palm Desert (lat. 33°35'50" N, long. 116°17'15" W; near N line sec. 6, T 7 S, R 7 E). Named on Palm Desert (1959) 15' quadrangle.

Devil Canyon [SAN BERNARDINO]: *canyon,* 1.5 miles long, opens into lowlands 6 miles north-northwest of San Bernardino city hall (lat. 34°12' N, long. 117°20'10" W). Named on San Bernardino North (1967) 7.5' quadrangle. The name is from an incident in 1842 that involved an Indian workman who was bit by a rattlesnake and screamed "El Diablo" as he died (La Fuze, v. I, p. 15). The canyon divides at the head into East Fork and West Fork. East Fork is nearly 2 miles long and is named on San Bernardino North (1967) 7.5' quadrangle. West Fork is 3 miles long and is named on Cedar Springs (1956) and San Bernardino North (1967) 7.5' quadrangles. On San Bernardino (1901) 15' quadrangle, the name "Devil Canyon" applies to present Devil Canyon and present West Fork together.

Devils Backbone [SAN BERNARDINO]: *ridge,* east-trending, 0.5 mile long, 1.5 miles east-southeast of Mount San Antonio (lat. 34° 17' N, long. 117°37'15" W; near S line sec. 4, T 2 N, R 7 W). Named on Telegraph Peak (1956) 7.5' quadrangle.

Devils Canyon [IMPERIAL]:

(1) *canyon,* drained by a stream that flows 2.25 miles to Colorado River 30 miles south-southeast of Palo Verde (lat. 33°01'45" N, long. 114°32' W; sec. 23, T 13 S, R 23 E). Named on Picacho (1964) 7.5' quadrangle.

(2) *canyon,* heads in San Diego County and is nearly 4 miles long in Imperial County; opens into lowlands 8 miles south-southwest of Carrizo Mountain (lat. 32°43'30" N, long. 116°04'15" W; at N line sec. 4, T 17 S, R 9 E). Named on In-Ko-Pah Gorge (1959) 7.5' quadrangle.

Devils Elbow [SAN BERNARDINO]: *promontory,* 15 miles south-southeast of Needles (lat. 34°39'30" N, long. 114°27'30" W; sec. 34, T 7 N, R 24 W). Named on Topock (1970) 7.5' quadrangle.

Devils Garden [RIVERSIDE]: *area,* 10.5 miles north-northwest of Palm Springs (lat. 33°58'10" N, long. 116°37'05" W; sec. 25, T 2 S, R 3 E). Named on Desert Hot Springs (1955) 7.5' quadrangle.

Devils Gate Pass [SAN BERNARDINO]: *pass,* 11.5 miles north of downtown Morongo Valley (lat. 34°12'55" N, long. 116°35'15" W; near N line sec. 32, T 2 N, R 4 E). Named on Rimrock (1972) 7.5' quadrangle.

Devils Hole [RIVERSIDE]: *valley,* 4 miles west of Aguanga (lat. 33° 26'15" N, long. 116°56' W; sec. 25, 36, T 8 S, R 1 W). Named on Vail Lake (1953) 7.5' quadrangle.

Devils Hole [SAN BERNARDINO]: *relief feature,* 3.25 miles south of Luna Mountain (lat. 34°17'50" N, long. 117°07' W; near SW cor. sec. 32, T 3 N, R 2 W). Named on Butler Peak (1971) 7.5' quadrangle.

Devils Playground [SAN BERNARDINO]: *area,* southwest of Old Dad Mountain and north of Granite Mountains. Named on Flynn (1956), Kerens (1957), Old Dad Mountain (1956) and Soda Lake (1956) 15' quadrangles.

Devils Playground Wash [SAN BERNARDINO]: *stream,* flows 20 miles to Kelso Wash 29 miles north-northwest of Amboy (lat. 34° 58'30" N, long. 115°51'10" W; near W line sec. 8, T 10 N, R 11 E). Named on Flynn (1956) and Kerens (1957) 15' quadrangles.

Devils Rockpile [RIVERSIDE]: *area,* 11.5 miles southeast of Idyllwild (lat. 33°38'45" N, long. 116°33'35" W; near SW cor. sec. 15, T 6 S, R 4 E). Named on Idyllwild (1959) 15' quadrangle.

Devore [SAN BERNARDINO]: *town,* 10 miles northwest of San Bernardino city hall at the mouth of Cajon Canyon (lat. 34°13' N, long. 117°24' W). Named on Devore (1966) 7.5' quadrangle. Postal authorities established Devore post office in 1908 and discontinued it in 1930 (Frickstad, p. 140). The place first was called Kenwood for a landowner at the site; the name "Devore" commemorates John Devore, another landowner there (Gudde, 1949, p. 94).

Devore Heights [SAN BERNARDINO]: *district,* 1.5 miles north-northwest of Devore (lat. 34°14'15" N, long. 117°24'50" W). Named on Devore (1966) 7.5' quadrangle.

Devouge Spring [SAN BERNARDINO]: *spring,* 32 miles west-northwest of Baker (lat. 35°28'30" N, long. 116°34'45" W; sec. 17, T 16 N, R 4 E). Named on Tiefort Mountains (1948) 15' quadrangle.

Diamente: see **Diamond Valley** [RIVERSIDE].

Diamond Lake: see **El Centro** [IMPERIAL].

Diamond Valley [RIVERSIDE]: *valley,* 4 miles south of downtown Hemet (lat. 33°41'20" N, long. 116°58'45" W). Named on Hemet (1953) and Winchester (1953) 7.5' quadrangles. Postal authorities established Diamente post office 5 miles southwest of San Jacinto in Diamond Valley in 1891 and discontinued it in 1896 (Salley, p. 59). The name "Diamente" is a misspelling of *diamante,* which means "diamond" in Spanish (Gunther, p. 156).

Diaz: see **El Casco** [RIVERSIDE].

Dickey Canyon [RIVERSIDE]: *canyon,* 1 mile long, 4 miles south of Alberhill (lat. 33°40' N, long. 117°24'20" W; mainly in sec. 9, T 6 S, R 5 W). Named on Alberhill (1954) 7.5' quadrangle. The name is for James E. Dickey, a homesteader who settled at the place in 1883 (Gunther, p. 157).

Diego: see **Juan Diego Flat** [RIVERSIDE].

Difficult Canyon [RIVERSIDE]: *canyon,* 1.5 miles long, 12.5 miles east-northeast of Chiriaco Summit (lat. 33°43'30" N, long. 115°31'15" W; in and near sec. 21, T 5 S, R 14 E). Named on Hayfield (1963) 15' quadrangle.

Dishpan Spring [SAN BERNARDINO]: *spring,* 5.5 miles south of Luna Mountain (lat. 34°15'50" N, long. 117°07' W; near NW cor. sec. 17, T 2 N, R 2 W). Named on Butler Peak (1971) 7.5' quadrangle.

Ditch Creek: see **Dutch Creek** [RIVERSIDE].

Dixieland [IMPERIAL]: *village,* 5 miles east of Plaster City (lat. 32° 47'30" N, long. 115°46'15" W; sec. 7, T 16 S, R 12 E). Named on Plaster City

(1957) 7.5' quadrangle. Postal authorities established Dixieland post office in 1912 and discontinued it in 1935 (Frickstad, p. 48).

Dixon [SAN BERNARDINO]: *locality,* 7.25 miles east of Ontario city hall along Union Pacific Railroad (lat. 34°02'35" N, long. 117°31'25" W; at W line sec. 33, T 1 S, R 6 W). Named on Guasti (1966) 7.5' quadrangle.

Dobbs Camp [SAN BERNARDINO]: *locality,* 3.5 miles west of San Gorgonio Mountain along Falls Creek (lat. 34°05'15" N, long. 116° 53'40" W). Named on San Gorgonio (1902) 30' quadrangle.

Dobbs Peak [SAN BERNARDINO]: *peak,* nearly 2 miles west of San Gorgonio Mountain (lat. 34°05'55" N, long. 116°51'30" W; at W line sec. 11, T 1 S, R 1 E). Altitude 10,459 feet. Named on San Gorgonio Mountain (1970) 7.5' quadrangle.

Dobe Spring [RIVERSIDE]: *spring,* 5 miles south-southwest of Sitton Peak in Talega Canyon (lat. 33°31'05" N, long. 117°28'20" W; near N line sec. 35, T 7 S, R 6 W). Named on Sitton Peak (1954) 7.5' quadrangle.

Doble [SAN BERNARDINO]: *locality,* 3 miles north-northeast of Big Bear City (lat. 34°17'55" N, long. 116°49'15" W; near W line sec. 31, T 3 N, R 2 E). Named on Big Bear City (1971) 7.5' quadrangle. Postal authorities established Doble post office in 1900, moved it 2 miles north in 1905, and discontinued it in 1906; the name was for Budd Doble, who found gold near the place about 1860 (Salley, p. 60). The site had an earlier mining camp called Bairdstown for Samuel H. Baird, who built the first structure there in 1874 (Robinson, J.W., 1975, p. 34-35). Postal authorities established and discontinued Bairdstown post office in 1875 (Salley, p. 13).

Dog Wash [SAN BERNARDINO]: *stream* and *dry wash,* extends for 21 miles to Dale Lake 29 miles south of Amboy (lat. 34°08' N, long. 115°43'30" W; at N line sec. 33, T 1 N, R 12 E). Named on Valley Mountain (1956) 15' quadrangle.

Dogwood Campground [SAN BERNARDINO]: *locality,* 5.5 miles north-northwest of Harrison Mountain (lat. 34°14'05" N, long. 117°12'40" W; near NE cor. sec. 29, T 2 N, R 3 W); the place is above the head of Dogwood Canyon. Named on Harrison Mountain (1967) 7.5' quadrangle.

Dogwood Canyon [SAN BERNARDINO]: *canyon,* drained by a stream that flows less than 0.5 mile to Little Bear Creek 6.25 miles north-northwest of Harrison Mountain (lat. 34°14'45" N, long. 117°12'30" W; near E line sec. 20, T 2 N, R 3 W). Named on Harrison Mountain (1967) 7.5' quadrangle.

Dollar Lake [SAN BERNARDINO]: *lake,* 400 feet long, 2 miles northwest of San Gorgonio Mountain (lat. 34°07'20" N, long. 116° 51'05" W; sec. 35, T 1 N, R 1 E). Named on San Gorgonio Mountain (1970) 7.5' quadrangle. According to Gudde (1949, p. 97), the lake has the shape and color of a silver dollar.

Dollar Lake Saddle [SAN BERNARDINO]: *pass,* 2 miles northwest of San Gorgonio Mountain (lat. 34°07'05" N, long. 116°51'35" W; at NE cor. sec. 3, T 1 S, R 1 E); the pass is 0.5 mile southwest of Dollar Lake. Named on San Gorgonio Mountain (1970) 7.5' quadrangle.

Dolores: see **Camp Dolores**, under **Colton** [SAN BERNARDINO].

Dome Mountain [SAN BERNARDINO]: *peak,* 7.5 miles northeast of the village of Red Mountain (lat. 35°25'40" N, long. 117°30'50" W; sec. 7, T 29 S, R 42 E). Altitude 4974 feet. Named on Klinker Mountain (1967) 7.5' quadrangle. Called Dome Pk. on California Mining Bureau's (1917a) map.

Domenigoni Valley [RIVERSIDE]: *valley,* 12 miles southeast of Perris (lat. 33°40'15" N, long. 117°03'45" W). Named on Winchester (1953) 7.5' quadrangle. The name is for Angelo Domenigoni, the first settler in the valley (Gunther, p. 158).

Dome Peak: see **Dome Mountain** [SAN BERNARDINO].

Domingo Spring [SAN BERNARDINO]: *spring,* 22 miles northwest of Essex (lat. 34°59'40" N, long. 115°27'30" W; near N line sec. 35, T 11 N, R 14 E). Named on Colton Well (1956) 15' quadrangle.

Donnell Hill [SAN BERNARDINO]: *hill,* less than 1 mile west-southwest of the center of Twentynine Palms (lat. 34°08' N, long. 116° 03'55" W; near N line sec. 32, T 1 N, R 9 E). Named on Twentynine Palms (1973) 7.5' quadrangle.

Dorners Camp [SAN BERNARDINO]: *locality,* 18 miles north-northeast of Amboy (lat. 34°48'30" N, long. 115°37'35" W; near SW cor. sec. 4, T 8 N, R 13 E). Named on Flynn (1956) 15' quadrangle.

Dos Palmas Corners [RIVERSIDE]: *locality,* 7 miles north-northeast of Palm Springs (lat. 33°55'30" N, long. 116°30'05" W; sec. 7, T 3 S, R 5 E). Named on Desert Hot Springs (1955) 7.5' quadrangle.

Dos Palmas Spring [RIVERSIDE]:

(1) *spring,* 7.5 miles south-southwest of Palm Desert (lat. 33°37'10" N, long. 116°25'30" W; at W line sec. 25, T 6 S, R 5 E). Named on Palm Desert (1959) 15' quadrangle. Called Dos Palmos Spring on Toro Peak (1943) 15' quadrangle, but United States Board on Geographic Names (1978, p. 4) rejected this form of the name.

(2) *spring,* 6.5 miles east of Mortmar (lat. 33°30'30" N, long. 115° 49'35" W; near N line sec. 3, T 8 S, R 11 E). Named on Orocopia Canyon (1958) 7.5' quadrangle. The spring was a well-known stopping place marked by two large palm trees, which gave the site its name (Mendenhall, 1909a, p. 80-81).

Double Butte [RIVERSIDE]: *range,* 8 miles east-southeast of Perris (lat. 33°43'45" N, long. 117°06'30" W). Named on Romoland (1953) and Winchester (1953) 7.5' quadrangles.

Double Canyon: see **East Double Canyon** [RIVERSIDE]; **West Double Canyon** [RIVERSIDE].

Dove Spring [SAN BERNARDINO]: *spring,* 6 miles east-northeast of Ivanpah (lat. 35°21'45" N, long. 115°12' W; near S line sec. 19, T 15 N, R 17 E). Named on Crescent Peak (1956) 15' quadrangle.

Dragon Wash [RIVERSIDE]: *stream,* 2 miles long, 13 miles east-northeast of Hayfield (lat. 33°44' N, long. 115°30'30" W). Named on Hayfield (1963) 15' quadrangle.

Draper Lake [IMPERIAL]: *lake,* 0.5 mile long, 19 miles south of Palo Verde along Colorado River (lat. 33°09'35" N, long. 114° 41' W; sec. 5, T 12 S, R 22 E). Named on Picacho NW (1965) 7.5' quadrangle, which shows Draper ranch near the lake.

Draper Wash [IMPERIAL]: *stream,* flows 4.5 miles to Draper Lake 19 miles south of Palo Verde (lat. 33°09'20" N, long. 114°41'05" W; near SW cor. sec. 5, T 12 S, R 22 E). Named on Picacho (1951) 15' quadrangle.

Drennan: see **Earp** [SAN BERNARDINO].

Drew [SAN BERNARDINO]: *locality,* 3 miles west-northwest of Redlands along Southern California Railroad (lat. 34°03'50" N, long. 117°14' W). Named on Redlands (1901) 15' quadrangle.

Drinkwater Lake [SAN BERNARDINO]: *dry lake,* less than 2 miles long, 30 miles west-northwest of Baker (lat. 35°29'50" N, long. 116°31'50" W); the feature is 4 miles east-northeast of Drinkwater Spring. Named on Tiefort Mountains (1948) 15' quadrangle.

Drinkwater Spring [SAN BERNARDINO]: *spring,* 32 miles west-northwest of Baker (lat. 35°28' N, long. 116°35'45" W; at S line sec. 18, T 16 N, R 4 E). Named on Tiefort Mountains (1948) 15' quadrangle.

Dripping Spring [SAN BERNARDINO]:

(1) *spring,* 16 miles north-northeast of Amboy (lat. 34°47' N, long. 115°38'15" W). Named on Needles (1956) 1°x 2° quadrangle.

(2) *spring,* 12.5 miles south of Essex (lat. 34°33'30" N, long. 115° 12'30" W; near S line sec. 33, T 6 N, R 17 E). Named on Essex (1956) 15' quadrangle.

Dripping Springs [RIVERSIDE]: *spring,* 7.5 miles west-northwest of Aguanga (lat. 33°28'20" N, long. 116°59'15" W). Named on Vail Lake (1953) 7.5' quadrangle. Called Dripping Spring on Ramona (1903) 30' quadrangle.

Drury: see **Newton Drury Peak**, under **San Jacinto Peak** [RIVERSIDE].

Dry Camp [RIVERSIDE]: *locality,* 6.25 miles east of Cathedral City along Southern Pacific Railroad (lat. 33°47' N, long. 116°21' W). Named on Edom (1943) 15' quadrangle. In 1876 the place was a railroad construction camp that had no local water (Gunther, p. 164).

Dry Canyon [SAN BERNARDINO]: *canyon,* less than 1 mile long, opens into lowlands 6.5 miles north of Fawnskin (lat. 34°21'45" N, long. 116°57'50" W; sec. 10, T 3 N, R 1 W). Named on Fawnskin (1971) 7.5' quadrangle. The canyon divides at the head to form East Fork and West Fork; each fork is about 1.5 miles long and is named on Fawnskin (1971) 7.5' quadrangle.

Dry Creek [RIVERSIDE]: *stream,* flows 4.5 miles to Strawberry Creek 12 miles east-southeast of Hemet (lat. 33°42'30" N, long. 116°46'10" W; near W line sec. 27, T 5 S, R 2 E). Named on Hemet (1957) and Idyllwild (1959) 15' quadrangles.

Dry Creek [SAN BERNARDINO]: *stream,* flows 2.5 miles to Deep Creek (1) 3 miles west-northwest of Keller Peak (lat. 34°12'40" N, long. 117°05'35" W; sec. 33, T 2 N, R 2 W). Named on Keller Peak (1967) 7.5' quadrangle.

Dry Lake [RIVERSIDE]: *lake,* 1000 feet long, 7.5 miles west of Riverside (lat. 33°59'45" N, long. 117°29'40" W). Named on Riverside (1901) 15' quadrangle. Bolton (p. 100) identified this as the feature that Anza called Laguna del Principe in 1774.

Dry Lake [SAN BERNARDINO]: *lake,* 1150 feet long, 1.5 miles north of San Gorgonio Mountain (lat. 34°07'10" N, long. 116°49'35" W; on S line sec. 36, T 1 N, R 1 E). Named on San Gorgonio Mountain (1970) 7.5' quadrangle.

Drylyn: see **Clyde** [IMPERIAL].

Dry Morongo Creek [RIVERSIDE-SAN BERNARDINO]: *stream* and *dry wash,* heads in San Bernardino County and extends for 4.5 miles to Coachella Valley 7.5 miles north of Garnet in Riverside County (lat. 34°00'30" N, long. 116°34'25" W; sec. 9, T 2 S, R 4 E). Named on Catclaw Flat (1972) and Morongo Valley (1972) 7.5' quadrangles.

Dry Morongo Wash [RIVERSIDE]: *dry wash,* extends for 2 miles from the mouth of the canyon of Dry Morongo Creek to Big Morongo Wash 10.5 miles north of Palm Springs (lat. 33°59'15" N, long. 116°33'15" W; sec. 22, T 2 S, R 4 E). Named on Desert Hot Springs (1955) and Morongo Valley (1972) 7.5' quadrangles.

Dry Ranch [RIVERSIDE]: *valley,* 2 miles northeast of Aguanga along Tule Creek (lat. 33°27'55" N, long. 116°50'20" W; sec. 23, 24, T 8 S, R 1 E). Named on Aguanga (1954) 7.5' quadrangle. Called Cienaga Rincon on Ramona (1903) 30' quadrangle.

Dry Wash [RIVERSIDE]:
(1) *stream* and *dry wash,* extends for 3 miles to Palm Canyon 11 miles east of Idyllwild (lat. 33°42'55" N, long. 116°31'45" W; at SE cor. sec. 23, T 5 S, R 4 E). Named on Idyllwild (1959) 15' quadrangle, and on Rancho Mirage (1957) 7.5' quadrangle. On Hemet Reservoir (1942) 15' quadrangle, the name "Rock Canyon" applies to the canyon of the feature, but United States Board on Geographic Names (1983a, p. 3) rejected this name.
(2) *stream,* flows 6 miles to San Diego County 20 miles south of Palm Desert at Jackass Flat (lat. 33°25'40" N, long. 116°24'30" W; at S line sec. 31, T 8 S, R 6 E). Named on Collins Valley (1959) 7.5' quadrangle.

Dumont [SAN BERNARDINO]: *locality,* 30 miles north of Baker (lat. 35°41'35" N, long. 116°10'20" W; near W line sec. 31, T 19 N, R 8 E). Site named on Silurian Hills (1956) 15' quadrangle. The place was along Tonopah and Tidewater Railroad and was named for Harry Dumont, an official of Pacific Coast Borax Company (Palmer, p. 25).

Dumont Dunes [SAN BERNARDINO]: *relief feature,* 30 miles north-northwest of Baker (lat. 35°39'30" N, long. 116°17'15" W; sec. 12, 13, T 18 N, R 6 E). Named on Avawatz Pass (1948) 15' quadrangle. United States Board on Geographic Names (1965b, p. 14) approved the name "Little Dumont Dunes" for the feature.

Dumont Dunes: see **Dumont Sand Dunes** [SAN BERNARDINO].

Dumont Hills [SAN BERNARDINO]: *relief feature,* 30 miles north of Baker (lat. 35°42'45" N, long. 116°07'15" W). Named on Silurian Hills (1956) 15' quadrangle.

Dumont Sand Dunes [SAN BERNARDINO]: *relief feature,* 30 miles north-northwest of Baker (lat. 35°41'15" N, long. 116°13' W); the feature is west of the site of Dumont. Named on Silurian Hills (1956) 15' quadrangle. United States Board on Geographic Names (1984, p. 4) approved the name "Dumont Dunes" for the feature.

Dunbar: see **Vontrigger** [SAN BERNARDINO].

Duncan Canyon [SAN BERNARDINO]: *canyon,* drained by a stream that flows 1.25 miles to lowlands 4 miles southwest of Devore (lat. 34°10'35" N, long. 117°27'05" W; near NW cor. sec. 18, T 1 N, R 5 W). Named on Devore (1966) 7.5' quadrangle.

Dunes [IMPERIAL]: *locality,* 3.5 miles southeast of Ogilby along Southern Pacific Railroad (lat. 32°47' N, long. 114°47'45" W; sec. 7, T 16 S, R 21 E). Named on Ogilby (1963) 15' quadrangle.

Dunkel Spring [RIVERSIDE]: *spring,* 12 miles west-northwest of Palm Springs (lat. 33°53'50" N, long. 116°44'40" W; sec. 23, T 3 S, R 2 E). Named on Whitewater (1955) 7.5' quadrangle.

Dunlap: see **Camp Dunlap** [IMPERIAL]:

Dunlap Acres [SAN BERNARDINO]: *district,* 3.5 miles west of Yucaipa (lat. 34°01'40" N, long. 117°06' W). Named on Yucaipa (1967) 7.5' quadrangle.

Dunn [SAN BERNARDINO]: *locality,* 26 miles southwest of Baker along Union Pacific Railroad (lat. 35°02'45" N, long. 116°26'10" W; sec. 15, T 11 N, R 5 E). Named on Cave Mountain (1948) 15' quadrangle.

Dunn: see **New Dunn** [SAN BERNARDINO].

Durant Siding [RIVERSIDE]: *locality,* 3.5 miles northwest of Elsinore (present Lake Elsinore) city hall along Atchison, Topeka and Santa Fe Railroad (lat. 33°42'20" N, long. 117°21'50" W; sec. 26, T 5 S, R 5 W). Named on Elsinore (1953) 7.5' quadrangle.

Durasno Valley [RIVERSIDE]: *valley,* 16 miles south of Idyllwild (lat. 33°30'30" N, long. 116°41'45" W). Named on Idyllwild (1959) 15' quadrangle, and on Beauty Mountain (1960) 7.5' quadrangle. Called Durasna Valley on Warner Springs (1950) 15' quadrangle.

Durmid [RIVERSIDE]: *locality,* 4.25 miles southeast of Salton along Southern Pacific Railroad (lat. 33°25'50" N, long. 115°49'55" W; near SW cor. sec. 34, T 8 S, R 11 E). Named on Durmid (1956) 7.5' quadrangle.

Dustin Spring [SAN BERNARDINO]: *spring,* 13 miles northeast of Ontario city hall (lat. 34°12'30" N, long. 117°30'30" W; near SE cor. sec. 33, T 2 N, R 6 W). Named on Cucamonga Peak (1966) 7.5' quadrangle.

Dutch Charlie Canyon [RIVERSIDE]: *canyon,* drained by a stream that flows nearly 1 mile to Palm Canyon 14 miles east-southeast of Idyllwild (lat. 33°38'45" N, long. 116°30'35" W; near W line sec. 18, T 6 S, R 5 E). Named on Idyllwild (1959) 15' quadrangle, and on Rancho Mirage (1957) 7.5' quadrangle. The name recalls a man who came to San Jacinto Mountains suffering from tuberculosis, and left cured (Gunther, p. 165).

Dutch Creek [RIVERSIDE]: *stream,* flows 4.5 miles to Twin Pines Creek 3.25 miles south of Cabazon (lat. 33°52'15" N, long. 116°47'35" W; at N line sec. 32, T 3 S, R 2 E). Named on Lake Fulmor (1956) and San Jacinto Peak (1981) 7.5' quadrangles. Called Ditch Creek on Banning (1956) and Palm Springs (1957) 15' quadrangles.

Dutchess Canyon [RIVERSIDE]: *canyon,* 1.5 miles long, 8 miles southeast of Idyllwild (lat. 33°40'10" N, long. 116°36'35" W). Named on Idyllwild (1959) 15' quadrangle.

Dutch Flat [RIVERSIDE]: *area,* 5 miles southwest of San Jacinto Peak (lat. 33°45'25" N, long. 116°43'30" W; near N line sec. 12, T 5 S, R 2 E). Named on San Jacinto Peak (1981) 7.5' quadrangle.

Duval Spring [RIVERSIDE]: *spring,* 14 miles southeast of Hemet (lat. 33°35'10" N, long. 116°48'45" W; near S line sec. 6, T 7 S, R 2 E). Named on Hemet (1957) 15' quadrangle.

- E -

Eads [SAN BERNARDINO]: *locality,* 14 miles west of Barstow along Atchison, Topeka and Santa Fe Railroad (lat. 34°56'45" N, long. 117°17' W; sec. 22, T 10 N, R 4 W). Named on Hawes (1956) 15' quadrangle.

Eagle Canyon [RIVERSIDE]: *canyon,* 2 miles long, opens into lowlands 4 miles south of Corona (lat. 33°49' N, long. 117°33'55" W; sec. 13, T 4 S, R 7 W). Named on Corona South (1967) 7.5' quadrangle. The feature also was known as Manning Canyon, for W.S. Manning, who filed for water there in 1886 (Gunther, p. 166).

Eagle Crags [SAN BERNARDINO]: *relief feature,* 31 miles southeast of Trona (lat. 35°23'45" N, long. 117°03'40" W). Named on Pilot Knob (1954) 15' quadrangle.

Eagle Creek [RIVERSIDE]: *stream,* flows 3.25 miles to lowlands 11 miles north-northwest of Desert Center (lat. 33°51'40" N, long. 115°29'20" W); the stream is in Eagle Mountains. Named on Coxcomb Mountains (1963) and Pinto Basin (1963) 15' quadrangles.

Eagle Hill: see **Lanfair Buttes**, under **Grotto Hills** [SAN BERNARDINO].

Eagle Mountain [RIVERSIDE]: *town,* 11 miles north-northwest of Desert Center (lat. 33°51'20" N, long. 115°29' W; sec. 2, T 4 S, R 14 E); the place is at Eagle Mountains. Named on Coxcomb Mountains (1963) 15' quadrangle. Postal authorities established Eagle Mountain post office in 1951 (Frickstad, p. 128). Management of Kaiser Steel Corporation founded the community in 1948 for employees of their Eagle Mountain iron mine; the mine and post office closed in 1983 (Gunther, p. 167-168).

Eagle Mountain: see **Lanfair Buttes, under Grotto Hills** [SAN BERNARDINO].

Eagle Mountains [RIVERSIDE]: *range,* about 11 miles northeast of Desert Center. Named on Cottonwood Spring (1958), Coxcomb Mountains (1963), Hayfield (1963), Hexie Mountains (1963), and Pinto Basin (1963) 15' quadrangles.

Eagle Pass [SAN BERNARDINO]: *pass,* 9.5 miles southwest of Needles (lat. 34°46'15" N, long. 114°45' W; near E line sec. 23, T 8 N, R 21 E); the feature is just south of Eagle Peak. Named on Bannock (1956) 15' quadrangle, and on Needles SW (1970) 7.5' quadrangle.

Eagle Peak [SAN BERNARDINO]: *peak,* 9.5 miles west-southwest of Needles (lat. 34°46'45" N, long. 114°45'15" W; at S line sec. 14, T 8 N, R 21 E). Altitude 3308 feet. Named on Bannock (1956) 15' quadrangle.

Eagle Point [SAN BERNARDINO]:
(1) *promontory,* 6.25 miles south-southwest of Luna Mountain along Lake Arrowhead (1) (lat. 34°15'45" N, long. 117°10'45" W; sec. 15, T 2 N, R 3 W). Named on Lake Arrowhead (1971) 7.5' quadrangle.
(2) *promontory,* 2.5 miles east-southeast of Fawnskin along Big Bear Lake (1) (lat. 34°15'15" N, long. 116°54'10" W; sec. 17, T 2 N, R 1 E). Named on Fawnskin (1971) 7.5' quadrangle.

Eagle Spring [RIVERSIDE]: *spring,* 9.5 miles east-southeast of Idyllwild (lat. 33°40'10" N, long. 116°34'50" W; at NE cor. sec. 8, T 6 S, R 4 E). Named on the Idyllwild (1959) 15' quadrangle.

Eagle Tank [RIVERSIDE]: *water feature,* 16 miles northwest of Desert Center (lat. 33°53'30" N, long. 115°35'10" W). Named on Pinto Basin (1963) 15' quadrangle. Eagle Tank (1943) 15' quadrangle shows the feature situated about 1.5 miles farther north-northeast (lat. 33°54'50" N, long. 115°34'20" W). Eagle Tank is a natural rock basin about 20 feet in diameter (Brown, 1920, p. 79).

Eagle Valley [RIVERSIDE]: *valley,* 7.25 miles north-northwest of Estelle Mountain (lat. 33°51'30" N, long. 117°29' W). Named on Lake Mathews (1967) 7.5' quadrangle. K.C. O'Bryan, Sterling Ferguson, and Bud Eisenlohr bought the place in 1954 and developed it for citrus; they named the valley in 1960 for a pair of eagles that they saw there (Gunther, p. 169-170).

Early Spring [SAN BERNARDINO]: *spring,* 16 miles east-southeast of Trona (lat. 35°39'10" N, long. 117°08' W). Named on Wingate Pass (1950) 15' quadrangle. Called Earlys Spr. on Thompson's (1921) map.

Earp [SAN BERNARDINO]: *village,* 12 miles east-northeast of Vidal (lat. 34°09'50" N, long. 114°18'10" W; near N line sec. 24, T 1 N, R 25 E). Named on Parker (1970) 7.5' quadrangle. Called Drennan on California Mining Bureau's (1917a) map. Postal authorities established Earp post office in 1930 (Frickstad, p. 140). Residents chose the name for the post office to honor Wyatt Earp, who had a gold claim near the place; Mr. Earp died the year before the post office opened (Gudde, 1949, p. 102; Hanna, p. 94).

Eastberne Valley: see **Crafton** [SAN BERNARDINO].

East Blythe [RIVERSIDE]: *town,* about 1 mile east of downtown Blythe (lat. 33°36'40" N, long. 114°34'35" W; mainly in sec. 33, T 6 S, R 23 E). Named on Blythe (1951) 7.5' quadrangle.

East Colton Heights [SAN BERNARDINO]: *locality,* nearly 4 miles south of present San Bernardino city hall (lat. 34°02'55" N, long. 117°17'50" W). Named on Colton (1943) 7.5' quadrangle.

East Cronese Lake [SAN BERNARDINO]: *dry lake,* 2.5 miles long, 15 miles southwest of Baker (lat. 35°07'45" N, long. 116°16'30" W); the feature is east of the north end of Cronese Mountains, and is 3 miles east-southeast of West Cronese Lake. Named on Cave Mountain (1948) 15' quadrangle. On Avawatz Mountains (1933) 1° quadrangle, the name "Cronese Lake" applies to present East Cronese Lake and present West Cronese Lake together. United States Board on Geographic Names (1987, p. 1) approved the form "East Cronise Lake" for the name, and rejected the names "Cronese Lake" and "East Cronise Dry Lake" for the feature.

East Cronise Dry Lake: see **East Cronese Lake** [SAN BERNARDINO].

East Cronise Lake: see **East Cronese Lake** [SAN BERNARDINO].

East Deception Canyon [RIVERSIDE]: *canyon,* 6 miles long, opens into lowlands 12 miles northeast of Cathedral City (lat. 33°54'30" N, long. 116°19'30" W; sec. 14, T 3 S, R 6 E); the mouth of the feature is 1 mile east of the mouth of West Deception Canyon. Named on Thousand Palms (1958) 15' quadrangle.

East Double Canyon [RIVERSIDE]: *canyon,* drained by a stream that flows nearly 2 miles to lowlands 10 miles east of Indio (lat. 33°43'40" N, long. 116°02'55" W); the feature is 0.5 mile east of West Double Canyon. Named on Thermal Canyon (1956) 7.5' quadrangle.

East Etiwanda Canyon [SAN BERNARDINO]: *canyon,* 3.25 miles long, opens into lowlands 10.5 miles northeast of Ontario city hall (lat. 34°10'25" N, long. 117°31'15" W; near W line sec. 16, T 1 N, R 6 W). Named on Cucamonga Peak (1966) 7.5' quadrangle.

East Etiwanda Creek [SAN BERNARDINO]: *stream,* flows nearly 7 miles from the mouth of East Etiwanda Canyon to end 7.25 miles east of Ontario city hall (lat. 34°05' N, long. 117°31'15" W; near W line sec. 16, T 1 S, R 6 W). Named on Cucamonga Peak (1966) and Guasti (1966) 7.5' quadrangles.

East Highland Reservoir [SAN BERNARDINO]: *lake,* 1600 feet long, 2.5 miles south of Harrison Mountain (lat. 34°07'40" N, long. 117°10'05" W; sec. 35, T 1 N, R 3 W); the feature is east of Highland. Named on Harrison Mountain (1967) 7.5' quadrangle.

East Highlands [SAN BERNARDINO]: *village,* 4 miles north of Redlands city hall (lat. 34°06'30" N, long. 117°10'15" W; near SW cor. sec. 2, T 1 S, R 3 W); the place is 2.5 miles east-southeast of Highland. Named on Redlands (1967) 7.5' quadrangle. Called East Highland on California Mining Bureau's (1917a) map, but United States Board on Geographic Names (1933, p. 281) rejected this form of the name. Postal authorities established East Highlands post office in 1892, discontinued it in 1901, and reestablished it in 1902 (Frickstad, p. 140). The place originally was called Cramville, for Louis Cram, the first settler there (Gudde, 1969, p. 140). California Mining Bureau's (1917a) map shows a place called Base Line situated along the railroad just northwest of East Highland.

East Kimbark Canyon [SAN BERNARDINO]: *canyon,* drained by a stream that flows nearly 2 miles to lowlands 1.5 miles north of Devore (lat. 34°14'15" N, long. 117°24'05" W); the mouth of the canyon is 1800 feet east-southeast of the mouth of Kimbark Canyon. Named on Cajon (1956) and Devore (1966) 7.5' quadrangles.

East Mesa [IMPERIAL]: *relief feature,* extends along the east side of Imperial Valley for about 50 miles from a point east of Wister all the way to Mexico. Named on El Centro (1958) and Salton Sea (1959) 1°x 2° quadrangles.

East Mesa: see **Apple Valley** [SAN BERNARDINO] (1).

East Ord Mountain [SAN BERNARDINO]: *range,* 4 miles southeast of Ord Mountain (lat. 34°38' N, long. 116°46' W); the range is the east part of Ord Mountains (1). Named on Ord Mountains (1955) and Rodman Mountains (1955) 15' quadrangles

East Riverside: see **Highgrove** [RIVERSIDE].

Eastside: see **Holtville** [IMPERIAL].

East Twin Creek [SAN BERNARDINO]: *stream,* flows 7.5 miles to Warm Creek 5 miles north-northeast of San Bernardino city hall (lat. 34°10'20" N, long. 117°16' W; sec. 14, T 1 N, R 4 W). Named on Harrison Mountain (1967), San Bernardino North (1967), and San Bernardino South (1967) 7.5' quadrangles.

East Well [SAN BERNARDINO]: *well,* 35 miles east of the village of Red Mountain at the east end of Superior Lake (lat. 35°14'40" N, long. 117°00'15" W; near S line sec. 12, T 31 S, R 46 E). Named on Opal Mountain (1955) 15' quadrangle. Called Ausland Well on Searles Lake (1915) 1°quadrangle.

East Wide Canyon [RIVERSIDE]: *valley,* 12 miles north-northeast of Cathedral City (lat. 33°56'30" N, long. 116°23' W; on N line sec. 5, T 3 S, R 6 E); the feature is 0.5 mile east of West Wide Canyon. Named on Seven Palms Valley (1958) 7.5' quadrangle.

Ebbens Creek [RIVERSIDE]: *stream,* flows 3 miles to Dead Indian Creek 4.5 miles southwest of Palm Desert (lat. 33°40'10" N, long. 116°25'25" W; near NW cor. sec. 12, T 6 S, R 5 E). Named on the Rancho Mirage (1957) 7.5' quadrangle. The name commemorates Theodore Ebbens, who was a prospector around the turn of the century (Bloomquist, 1977b, p. 7).

Ebbens Valley [RIVERSIDE]: *valley,* 15 miles south of Palm Desert (lat. 33°30'40" N, long. 116°22'40" W; on S line sec. 32, T 7 S, R 6 E). Named on Palm Desert (1959) 15' quadrangle.

Eden [RIVERSIDE]: *locality,* 12 miles northeast of Perris (lat. 33°52'40" N, long. 117°03'10" W); the place is 1.5 miles south of Eden Hot Springs. Named on Perris (1943) 15' quadrangle. Postal authorities established Eden post office in 1924 and discontinued it in 1934 (Frickstad, p. 128).

Eden: see **Mount Eden** [RIVERSIDE].

Eden Hot Springs [RIVERSIDE]: *locality,* 13 miles northeast of Perris (lat. 33°53'45" N, long. 117°03'15" W; sec. 23, T 3 S, R 2 W). Named on El Casco (1967) 7.5' quadrangle. Eight small hot springs were the basis of a resort at the place; the owners changed the name from Eden Hot Springs to Riverside Hot Sulphur Springs in 1893, but the old name prevailed (Gunther, p. 170). Berkstresser (1968, p. A-10) gave the alternate name "Canadian Hot Springs" for the place.

Edgar [IMPERIAL]: *locality,* 10 miles west of El Centro along San Diego and Arizona Eastern Railroad (lat. 32°47'20" N, long. 115° 44' W; sec. 9, T 16 S, R 12 E). Named on Seeley (1957) 7.5' quadrangle.

Edgemont [RIVERSIDE]: *town,* 6.5 miles southeast of Riverside city hall (lat. 33°55'15" N, long. 117°16'30" W; sec. 10, 11, T 3 S, R 4 W). Named on Riverside East (1967) 7.5' quadrangle. Called Box Springs on Riverside (1943) 15' quadrangle. Postal authorities established Edgemont post office in 1947 (Salley, p. 65). The place first was known as Rose Arbor because a Mr. Rose had a restaurant there; it was subdivided for poultry ranches in 1923 (Gunther, p. 172).

Edna: see **Mount Edna** [RIVERSIDE].

Edom [RIVERSIDE]: *locality,* 4.5 miles east-northeast of Cathedral City along Southern Pacific Railroad (lat. 33°48'25" N, long. 116° 23'25" W; at E line sec. 19, T 4 S, R 6 E). Named on Cathedral City (1958) 7.5' quadrangle. Postal authorities established Edom post office in 1913, moved it 0.75 mile northwest in 1938, and changed the name to Thousand Palms in 1939 (Salley, p. 65).

Edom Hill [RIVERSIDE]: *peak,* 6.5 miles north-northeast of Cathedral City (lat. 33°52'15" N, long. 116°25'45" W; sec. 35, T 3 S, R 5 E); the feature is 5 miles north-northwest of Edom. Altitude 1614 feet. Named on Cathedral City (1958) 7.5' quadrangle.

Edson: see **Essex** [SAN BERNARDINO].

Edwards: see **Camp Edwards** [SAN BERNARDINO].

Edwards Canyon [RIVERSIDE]: *canyon,* 0.5 mile long, 6 miles south of Alberhill (lat. 33°38'25" N, long. 117°22'40" W; sec. 14, 23, T 6 S, R 5 W). Named on Alberhill (1954, photorevised 1988) 7.5' quadrangle. The name honors Boyd M. Edwards, a Forest Service employee who lost is life in a fire in 1959 (United States Board on Geographic Names, 1960c, p. 18).

Egan [RIVERSIDE]: *locality,* 11.5 miles east-southeast of Perris along Atchison, Topeka and Santa Fe Railroad (lat. 33°44' N, long. 117°00'35" W; near W line sec. 17, T 5 S, R 1 W). Named on Winchester (1953) 7.5' quadrangle. The name, given in 1888, is for Judge Richard Egan, who was right-of-way agent for Southern California Railroad (Gunther, p. 172).

Eightmile Tank [SAN BERNARDINO]: *water feature,* 17 miles southwest of Ivanpah (lat. 35°09'55" N, long. 115°31'45" W; near W line sec. 31, T 13 N, R 14 E). Named on Kelso (1955) 15' quadrangle.

Eisenhower Mountain [RIVERSIDE]: *peak,* 3 miles southeast of Palm Desert (lat. 33°41'30" N, long. 116°20'10" W; near W line sec. 35, T 5 S, R 6 E). Altitude 1952 feet. Named on La Quinta (1959) 7.5' quadrangle. United States Board on Geographic Names (1973, p. 2) gave the variant names "Ike's Peak" and "Mount Eisenhower" for the feature; the name commemorates Dwight David Eisenhower, who spent several winters near the base of the peak.

El Cajon de los Mejicanos: see **Muscupiabe** [SAN BERNARDINO].

El Cajon de los Mexicanos: see **Cajon Pass** [SAN BERNARDINO].

El Cajon de Muscupiabe: see **Cajon Pass** [SAN BERNARDINO]; **Muscupiabe** [SAN BERNARDINO].

El Casco [RIVERSIDE]: *locality,* 15 miles north-northeast of Perris along Southern Pacific Railroad in San Timoteo Canyon (lat. 33° 58'50" N, long. 117°07' W; near W line sec. 20, T 2 S, R 2 W). Named on El Casco (1967) 7.5' quadrangle. Postal authorities established El Casco post office in 1888, moved it 0.5 mile west in 1904, and discontinued it in 1914 (Salley, p. 66). They established Diaz post office 4.5 miles west of El Casco in 1906 and discontinued it in 1907; the name was for Manuel Diaz, who opened a store at the place in 1854 (Salley, p. 59).

El Casco Lake [RIVERSIDE]: *lake,* 1150 feet long, 15 miles north-northeast of Perris (lat. 33°58'35" N, long. 117°06'30" W; at S line sec. 20, T 2 S, R 2 W). Named on El Casco (1967) 7.5' quadrangle.

El Centro [IMPERIAL]: *town,* in the south-central part of Imperial County in the heart of Imperial Valley (lat. 32°47'30" N, long. 115° 33'35" W). Named on El Centro (1957) 7.5' quadrangle. Postal authorities established El Centro post office in 1905 (Frickstad, p. 48), and the town incorporated in 1918. Before the town began, the railroad station at the site was called Cabarker, for C.A. Barker, a friend of the owner of land at the place (Gudde, 1949, p. 104). California Mining Bureau's (1917b) map shows a place called Mobile located 5 miles west of El Centro along the railroad. Postal authorities established Mobile post office in 1910 and discontinued it in 1912 (Frickstad, p. 49). United States Geological Survey's (1908) map shows a place called Silsbee located about 6 miles west-southwest of El Centro; Seeley (1957) 7.5' quadrangle shows the abandoned Silsbee school situated 5 miles west-southwest of El Centro (lat. 32°45'35" N, long. 115°38'15" W). Postal authorities established Silsbee post office in 1902 and discontinued it in 1909; the name was for Thomas Silsbee, who ran stock in the neighborhood—overflow from Colorado River destroyed the place (Salley, p. 204). United States Geological Survey's (1908) map shows several other features in the neighborhood: Gleason, a place located 6.5 miles east of El Centro along Holton Inter-urban Railroad; Pelican Lake, located 10.5 miles west-northwest of El Centro; Badger Lake, located 11 miles west of El Centro; Diamond Lake, located 10 miles west-southwest of El Centro; and Blue Lake, located 6 miles west-southwest of El Centro near Silsbee.

El Cerrito [RIVERSIDE]: *town,* 3.5 miles southeast of Corona (lat. 33°50'25" N, long. 117°31'20" W). Named on Corona South (1967) 7.5' quadrangle. Called El Cerrito Village on Corona South (1954) 7.5' quadrangle.

El Cerrito Village: see **El Cerrito** [RIVERSIDE].

Elder Canyon: see **Alder Canyon** [RIVERSIDE] (1).

Elder Creek [RIVERSIDE]: *stream,* flows 5.25 miles to Cahuilla Valley 20 miles southeast of Hemet (lat. 33°31'15" N, long. 116° 46'30" W; sec. 33, T 7 S, R 2 E). Named on Aguanga (1954) and Beauty Mountain (1960) 7.5' quadrangles.

Elder Gulch [SAN BERNARDINO]: *canyon,* drained by a stream that flows 2 miles to lowlands 2.5 miles south of Harrison Mountain (lat. 34°07'45" N, long. 117°09'45" W; sec. 35, T 1 N, R 3 W). Named on Harrison Mountain (1967) and Redlands (1967) 7.5' quadrangles.

Elephant Mountain [SAN BERNARDINO]: *ridge,* north-northeast- to north-trending, 1 mile long, 1.5 miles north-northwest of Daggett (lat. 34°53'10" N, long. 116°53'45" W; mainly in sec. 8, T 9 N, R 1 E). Named on Nebo (1953) 7.5' quadrangle.

Eleven Oaks: see **Mount Baldy** [SAN BERNARDINO].

Elizabeth Spring: see **Halloran Spring** [SAN BERNARDINO].

Ellis [RIVERSIDE]: *locality,* 1 mile southeast of the center of Perris along Atchison, Topeka and Santa Fe Railroad (lat. 33°46'15" N, long. 117°13' W; at N line sec. 5, T 5 S, R 3 W). Named on Perris (1967) 7.5' quadrangle. The name commemorates W.H. Ellis, who owned land at the place (Gunther, p. 177-178).

El Mirage [SAN BERNARDINO]: *locality,* 19 miles west-northwest of Victorville (lat. 34°36'10" N, long. 117°37'50" W; at SE cor. sec. 17, T 6 N, R 7 W); the place is in El Mirage Valley near the south end of Gray Mountain. Named on El Mirage (1956) 7.5' quadrangle. Postal authorities established Gray Mountain post office in 1913, moved it in 1917 when they changed the name to El Mirage, discontinued it in 1923, reestablished it in 1927, and discontinued it in 1934 (Salley, p. 68, 89).

El Mirage Lake [SAN BERNARDINO]: *dry lake,* 5.5 miles long, 19 miles west-northwest of Victorville (lat. 34°38'45" N, long. 117° 36'30" W); the feature is in El Mirage Valley. Named on Adobe Mountain (1955) and Shadow Mountains (1955) 7.5' quadrangles. Called Mirage Lake on Shadow Mountains (1942) 15' quadrangle.

El Mirage Valley [SAN BERNARDINO]: *valley,* 20 miles west-northwest of Victorville, partly in Los Angeles County (lat. 34°40' N, long. 117°36'30" W). Named on Adobe Mountain (1955), El Mirage (1956), Shadow Mountains (1955), and Shadow Mountains SE (1955) 7.5' quadrangles. Called Mirage Valley on Shadow Mountains (1942) 15' quadrangle.

Elmo: see **Mount Elmo** [SAN BERNARDINO].

Elora [SAN BERNARDINO]: *locality,* 19 miles southwest of Ivanpah along Union Pacific Railroad (lat. 35°08'20" N, long. 115°31'40" W; sec. 7, T 12 N, R 14 E). Named on Kelso (1955) 15' quadrangle.

El Potrero del Tenaja [RIVERSIDE]: *area,* 12 miles west of the town of Temecula on Riverside-San Diego County line (lat. 33°29'20" N, long. 117°21'45" W). Named on San Luis Rey (1898) 30' quadrangle.

El Rincon [RIVERSIDE-SAN BERNARDINO]: *land grant,* west of Chino on Riverside-San Bernardino County line. Named on Corona North (1967) and Prado Dam (1967) 7.5' quadrangles. Juan Bandini received 1 league in 1839; Bernardo Yorba claimed 4431 acres patented in 1879 (Cowan, p. 68).

El Rio [IMPERIAL]: *locality,* 3.25 miles east-northeast of Pilot Knob along Colorado River (lat. 32°45' N, long. 114°41'40" W; sec. 19, T 16 S, R 22 E). Named on Yuma (1905) 30' quadrangle. Postal authorities established El Rio post office in 1880 and discontinued it in 1881 (Frickstad, p. 150). A custom mill built at the place in 1878 and 1879 treated gold ore (Merrill, p. 725).

Elsie Caves [SAN BERNARDINO]: *caves,* nearly 2 miles southwest of downtown Big Bear Lake (lat. 34°13'25" N, long. 116°55'50" W; near SE cor. sec. 25, T 2 N, R 1 W). Named on Big Bear Lake (1970) 7.5' quadrangle.

Elsinore: see **Lake Elsinore** [RIVERSIDE]; **North Elsinore** [RIVERSIDE].

Elsinore Junction [RIVERSIDE]: *locality,* 1.5 miles east-southeast of the present town of Lake Elsinore (lat. 33°39'35" N, long. 117°18'10" W); the place is at Laguna grant. Named on Elsinore (1901) 30' quadrangle. Postal authorities established Laguna post office at the site in 1889 and discontinued it in 1891—the place also was called Laguna Station (Salley, p. 114).

Elsinore Lake: see **Lake Elsinore** [RIVERSIDE] (1).

Elsinore Mountains [RIVERSIDE]: *range,* southwest of Lake Elsinore (1) (lat. 33°37'30" N, long. 117°22' W). Named on Alberhill (1954), Lake Elsinore (1953), and Wildomar (1953) 7.5' quadrangles.

Elsinore Peak [RIVERSIDE]: *peak,* 3.5 miles west of Wildomar (lat. 33°36'10" N, long. 117°20'30" W; near W line sec. 31, T 6 S, R 4 W); the peak is in Elsinore Mountains. Altitude 3575 feet. Named on Wildomar (1953) 7.5' quadrangle.

El Sobrante de San Jacinto [RIVERSIDE]: *land grant,* at Corona and Lake Mathews. Named on Corona North (1967), Corona South (1967), Lake Mathews (1967), Riverside West (1967), and Steele Peak (1967) 7.5' quadrangles. Maria del Rosario Estudillo de Aguirre received 5 leagues in 1846; Jose Antonio Aguirre claimed 48,847 acres patented in 1867 (Cowan, p. 79).

Emerson: see **Camp Emerson** [RIVERSIDE].

Emerson Lake [SAN BERNARDINO]: *dry lake,* 3 miles long, 13 miles north of Landers (lat. 34°27' N, long. 116°24' W). Named on Emerson Lake (1954) and Hidalgo Mountain (1954) 7.5' quadrangles.

English Siding: see **Cox** [RIVERSIDE].

Ennis [RIVERSIDE]: *locality,* 3.5 miles northwest of Riverside along Union Pacific Railroad (lat. 34°00'35" N, long. 117°25'45" W). Named on Fontana (1967) 7.5' quadrangle.

Epolitan: see **Colton** [SAN BERNARDINO].

Epsom: see **Crucero** [SAN BERNARDINO].

Erwin Lake [SAN BERNARDINO]: *dry lake,* 4300 feet long, 3.5 miles north-northeast of Sugarloaf Mountain (lat. 34°14'40" N, long. 116°47'10" W; sec. 20, 21, T 2 N, R 2 E). Named on Big Bear City (1971) and Moonridge (1970) 7.5' quadrangles.

Essex [SAN BERNARDINO]: *village,* 36 miles west-southwest of Needles (lat. 34°44' N, long. 115°14'30" W; sec. 31, T 8 N, R 17 E). Named on Essex (1956) 15' quadrangle. Postal authorities established Essex post office in 1932 and moved it 0.5 mile northeast in 1937 (Salley, p. 70). The place first was called Edson (Myrick, p. 766).

Estelle [IMPERIAL]: *locality,* 3.5 miles north of Calipatria along Southern Pacific Railroad (lat. 33°10'30" N, long. 115°30'30" W; at NE cor. sec. 33, T 11 S, R 14 E). Named on Niland (1956) 7.5' quadrangle.

Estelle Mountain [RIVERSIDE]: *peak,* 15 miles south of Riverside (lat. 33°46' N, long. 117°25'15" W; sec. 5, T 5 S, R 5 W). Altitude 2767 feet. Named on Lake Mathews (1967) 7.5' quadrangle.

Eswena: see **Rancho Cucamonga** [SAN BERNARDINO].

Etengvo Wumoma: see **Lake Elsinore** [RIVERSIDE] (2).

Ethanac: see **Ethanac Siding** [RIVERSIDE].

Ethanac Siding [RIVERSIDE]: *locality,* 4 miles southeast of Perris along Atchison, Topeka and Santa Fe Railroad at Romoland (lat. 33°44'50" N, long. 117°10'40" W; sec. 10, T 5 S, R 3 W). Named on Romoland (1953) 7.5' quadrangle. Postal authorities established Ethanac post office in 1900 and discontinued it in 1925 (Salley, p. 71). The place is named for Ethan Allen Chase, who owned land there (Gunther, p. 181).

Etiwa: see **Kaiser** [SAN BERNARDINO] (1).

Etiwanda [SAN BERNARDINO]:

(1) *district,* in Rancho Cucamonga (lat. 34°07'15" N, long. 117°31'20" W). Named on Cucamonga Peak (1966) and Guasti (1966) 7.5' quadrangles. Postal authorities established Etiwanda post office in 1883 (Frickstad, p. 141). George Chaffey and W.B. Chaffey founded an agricultural colony at the place in 1881 and named it for an Indian chief who had been a friend of the Chaffey family in Canada (Hanna, p. 100).

(2) *locality,* 7.5 miles east-northeast of Ontario city hall along Atchison, Topeka and Santa Fe Railroad (lat. 34°05'35" N, long. 117°31'30" W; near SE cor. sec. 8, T 1 S, R 6 W). Named on Guasti (1966) 7.5' quadrangle. Called West Etiwanda on Cucamonga (1903) 15' quadrangle, which shows a place called Etiwanda Station located along the railroad about 1.25 miles east of West Etiwanda.

Etiwanda Canyon: see **East Etiwanda Canyon** [SAN BERNARDINO].

Etiwanda Creek: see **East Etiwanda Creek** [SAN BERNARDINO].

Etiwanda Station: see **Etiwanda** [SAN BERNARDINO] (2).

Eureka Wash [SAN BERNARDINO]: *stream,* flows 2.5 miles to Colorado River 23 miles east-northeast of Vidal (lat. 34°16'40" N, long. 114°08'10" W; sec. 10, T 2 N, R 27 E). Named on Gene Wash (1959) 7.5' quadrangle.

Evans: see **Camp Evans** [RIVERSIDE]; **Fishel** [SAN BERNARDINO].

Evans Lake: see **Lake Evans** [RIVERSIDE].

- F -

Fairmont Hill: see **North Hill** [RIVERSIDE].

Fairview Mountain [SAN BERNARDINO]: *range,* 9 miles east-northeast of Victorville (lat. 34°34'15" N, long. 117°08'15" W). Named on Apple Valley North (1970) and Fairview Valley (1970) 7.5' quadrangles.

Fairview Valley [SAN BERNARDINO]: *valley,* 12 miles east of Victorville (lat. 34°33'45" N, long. 117°05' W); the valley is mainly east of Fairview Mountain. Named on Fairview Valley (1970) 7.5' quadrangle.

Falling Rock Canyon [SAN BERNARDINO]: *canyon,* drained by a stream that flows 1.5 miles to Icehouse Canyon 13 miles north of Ontario city hall (lat. 34°14'55" N, long. 117°37'40" W). Named on Cucamonga Peak (1966) and Mount Baldy (1967) 7.5' quadrangles.

Falls Creek [RIVERSIDE]: *stream,* flows 5 miles to Snow Creek (1) 4.5 miles north of San Jacinto Peak (lat. 33°52'40" N, long. 116°40'25" W; sec. 28, T 3 S, R 3 E). Named on San Jacinto Peak (1981) 7.5' quadrangle.

Falls Creek [SAN BERNARDINO]: *stream,* flows 3.5 miles to Mill Creek Canyon 4 miles west-southwest of San Gorgonio Mountain (lat. 34°05'05" N, long. 116°53'45" W; near E line sec. 17, T 1 S, R 1 E). Named on Forest Falls (1970) and San Gorgonio Mountain (1970) 7.5' quadrangles.

Fallsvale: see **Forest Falls** [SAN BERNARDINO].

Fallsville: see **Forest Falls** [SAN BERNARDINO].

Fan Canyon [SAN BERNARDINO]: *canyon,* drained by a stream that flows 0.5 mile to Deer Canyon (2) 9.5 miles north-northeast of Ontario city hall (lat. 34°11'05" N, long. 117°34'25" W; near W line sec. 12, T 1 N, R 7 W). Named on Cucamonga Peak (1966) 7.5' quadrangle.

Fan Hill [RIVERSIDE]: *hill,* 14 miles northeast of Cathedral City (lat. 33°53'15" N, long. 116°15'35" W; near N line sec. 28, T 3 S, R 7 E). Named on Thousand Palms (1958) 15' quadrangle.

Fan Hill Canyon [RIVERSIDE]: *canyon,* 1 mile long, opens into lowlands 14 miles northeast of Cathedral City (lat. 33°53'40" N, long. 116°15'40" W; sec. 21, T 3 S, R 7 E); the feature is 0.5 mile north of Fan Hill. Named on Thousand Palms (1958) 15' quadrangle.

Fargo Canyon [RIVERSIDE]: *canyon,* 5 miles long, opens into lowlands 7.5 miles east-northeast of Indio (lat. 33°45'30" N, long. 116° 05'40" W; near NE cor. sec. 12, T 5 S, R 8 E). Named on Lost Horse Mountain (1958) 15' quadrangle. The name is from Fargo Camp, a facility set up in 1933 to house workmen on the aqueduct that takes Colorado River water to Los Angeles (Gunther, p. 184).

Fargo Canyon: see **Little Fargo Canyon** [RIVERSIDE].

Fawnskin [SAN BERNARDINO]: *town,* 5.5 miles west of Big Bear City along Big Bear Lake (1) (lat. 34°16'10" N, long. 116°56'35" W; mainly in sec. 11, 12, T 2 N, R 1 W); the town is at the mouth of Grout Creek. Named on Fawnskin (1971) 7.5' quadrangle. Postal authorities established Oso Grande post office in 1918 and changed the name to Fawnskin the same year—*Oso Grande* means "Big Bear" in Spanish; the name "Fawnskin" is from Fawnskin Valley (Salley, p. 73, 163). The place first was called Grout, for Grout Creek (Quinby, p. 130).

Fawnskin Valley [SAN BERNARDINO]: *valley,* 1.5 miles northwest of Fawnskin (lat. 34°17'05" N, long. 116°57'55" W; mainly in sec. 3, T 2 N, R 1 W). Named on Fawnskin (1971) 7.5' quadrangle. The name is from the skins that hunters stretched on trees at the place in 1891, and left there for years (Gudde, 1949, p. 114).

Fawn Spring [RIVERSIDE]: *spring,* 9 miles east of San Jacinto (lat. 33°45'50" N, long. 116°48' W; sec. 5, T 5 S, R 2 E). Named on Lake Fulmor (1956) 7.5' quadrangle.

Fenner [SAN BERNARDINO]: *village,* 7 miles north-northeast of Essex (lat. 34°49' N, long. 115°10'30" W; at NW cor. sec. 2, T 8 N, R 17 E). Named on Fenner (1956) 15' quadrangle. Postal authorities established Fenner post office in 1892, discontinued it in 1893, reestablished it for a time in 1902, reestablished it again in 1905, discontinued it in 1912, reestablished it in 1928, and discontinued it in 1974 (Salley, p. 74).

Fenner Hills [SAN BERNARDINO]: *range,* 13 miles north-northeast of Essex (lat. 34°54'30" N, long. 115°10'30" W); the range is north of Fenner in Fenner Valley. Named on Fenner (1956) 15' quadrangle.

Fenner Spring [SAN BERNARDINO]: *spring,* 8 miles east of Essex (lat. 34°45'15" N, long. 115°06'10" W; sec. 28, T 8 N, R 18 E); the spring is 6 miles southeast of Fenner. Named on Fenner (1956) 15' quadrangle.

Fenner Valley [SAN BERNARDINO]: *valley,* north and southwest of Essex; Fenner is in the valley. Named on Colton Well (1956), Danby (1956), Essex (1956), Fenner (1956), and Lanfair Valley (1956) 15' quadrangles.

Ferguson Lake [IMPERIAL]: *lake,* 9.5 miles east of Picacho Peak near Colorado River (lat. 32°58'45" N, long. 114°30' W). Named on Imperial Reservoir (1955), Little Picacho Peak (1965), and Picacho (1964) 7.5' quadrangles.

Ferguson Wash [IMPERIAL]: *stream,* flows 5.25 miles to Ferguson Lake 9 miles east of Picacho Peak (lat. 32°58'05" N, long. 114°29'45" W; sec. 7, T 14 S, R 24 E). Named on Imperial Reservoir (1955) and Little Picacho Peak (1965) 7.5' quadrangles.

Fern Basin Campground [RIVERSIDE]: *locality,* 4 miles west-southwest of San Jacinto Peak (lat. 33°47'20" N, long. 116°44'10" W; at E line sec. 26, T 4 S, R 2 E). Named on San Jacinto Peak (1981) 7.5' quadrangle. Called Fern Basin Camp on Palm Springs (1957) 15' quadrangle.

Fern Canyon: see **Wentworth Canyon** [RIVERSIDE].

Fern Creek [SAN BERNARDINO]: *stream,* flows 1.25 miles to Hooks Creek 6 miles south of Luna Mountain (lat. 34°15'45" N, long. 117°08'45" W; sec. 13, T 2 N, R 3 W). Named on Harrison Mountain (1967) and Lake Arrowhead (1971) 7.5' quadrangles.

Fern Flats: see **Bear Flat** [SAN BERNARDINO].

Fern Valley [RIVERSIDE]: *locality,* 4.25 miles south-southwest of San Jacinto Peak in Strawberry Valley (lat. 33°45'15" N, long. 116°42' W; sec. 7, 8, T 5 S, R 3 E). Named on San Jacinto Peak (1981) 7.5' quadrangle.

Ferrum [RIVERSIDE]: *locality,* less than 2 miles southeast of Salton along Southern Pacific Railroad (lat. 33°27'30" N, long. 115°51'35" W; at S line sec. 20, T 8 S, R 11 E). Named on Durmid (1956) 7.5' quadrangle. Iron ore shipped by rail from Eagle Mountain to the steel plant at Fontana passed through the place—*ferrum* is the Latin word for "iron ore."

Fertilla [RIVERSIDE]: *locality,* 4 miles north of Blythe (lat. 33°40'10" N, long. 114°35'50" W; sec. 8, T 6 S, R 23 E). Site named on Blythe NE (1951) 7.5' quadrangle. Postal authorities established Fertilla post office in 1914 and discontinued it in 1930 (Salley, p. 74). James Walsh coined the name to suggest the fertility of the region (Gunther, p. 185).

Field [SAN BERNARDINO]: *locality,* 15 miles northeast of Newberry along Union Pacific Railroad (lat. 34°59'55" N, long. 116°31'15" W). Named on Newberry (1955) 15' quadrangle.

Fifteenmile Point [SAN BERNARDINO]: *promontory,* 15 miles east-southeast of Victorville (lat. 34°27'15" N, long. 117°03'30" W; sec. 11, T 4 N, R 2 W); the feature is at the east side of Fifteenmile Valley. Named on Fifteenmile Valley (1971) 7.5' quadrangle.

Fifteenmile Valley [SAN BERNARDINO]: *valley,* 16 miles east-southeast of Victorville (lat. 34°27' N, long. 117°01'45" W). Named on Fifteenmile Valley (1971) 7.5' quadrangle. San Bernardino (1966) 1°x 2° quadrangle shows the feature as part of Lucerne Valley. Thompson (1929, p. 411) noted that Fifteenmile Valley is known locally as Cobarts Valley.

Figtree John: see **Mecca** [RIVERSIDE].

Fig Tree Valley [RIVERSIDE]: *valley,* 21 miles south-southwest of Palm Desert (lat. 33°26'30" N, long. 116°31' W; around SE cor. sec. 25, T 8 S, R 4 E). Named on Bucksnort Mountain (1960) 7.5' quadrangle.

Filaree Flat [SAN BERNARDINO]: *area,* 6.25 miles south-southwest of downtown Big Bear Lake along Santa Ana River (lat. 34°10'05" N, long. 116°58'20" W; sec. 15, T 1 N, R 1 W). Named on Big Bear Lake (1970) 7.5' quadrangle. Called Filirea Flat on San Gorgonio (1902) 30' quadrangle.

Filirea Flat: see **Filaree Flat** [SAN BERNARDINO].

Fingal [RIVERSIDE]: *locality,* 11 miles west-northwest of Palm Springs along Southern Pacific Railroad (lat. 33°55'15" N, long. 116°42'15" W; near SE cor. sec. 7, T 3 S, R 3 E). Named on Whitewater (1955) 7.5' quadrangle.

Finney Lake [IMPERIAL]: *intermittent lake,* 1150 feet long, 4.5 miles south of Calipatria near Alamo River (lat. 33°03'40" N, long. 115°30'10" W; on W line sec. 2, T 13 S, R 14 E). Named on Westmorland (1956) 7.5' quadrangle.

Fir Draw [SAN BERNARDINO]: *canyon,* drained by a stream that flows less than 0.5 mile to Icehouse Canyon 13 miles north of Ontario city hall (lat. 34°14'50" N, long. 117°37'30" W; sec. 21, T 2 N, R 7 W). Named on Cucamonga Peak (1966) 7.5' quadrangle.

Fish Camp [SAN BERNARDINO]: *locality,* 14 miles northeast of Redlands along North Fork Deep Creek (lat. 34°13'10" N, long. 117°02'40" W; at N line sec. 36, T 2 N, R 2 W). Named on Redlands (1901) 15' quadrangle.

Fish Creek [SAN BERNARDINO]: *stream,* flows 5 miles to Santa Ana River 2 miles south of Sugarloaf Mountain (lat. 34°10'10" N, long. 116°48'55" W; sec. 18, T 1 N, R 2 E). Named on Moonridge (1970) 7.5' quadrangle.

Fish Creek Meadows [SAN BERNARDINO]: *area,* 5.25 miles south-southeast of Sugarloaf Mountain (lat. 34°07'30" N, long. 116°46'45" W; sec. 33, T 1 N, R 2 E). Named on Moonridge (1970) and San Gorgonio Mountain (1970) 7.5' quadrangles.

Fish Creek Mountain: see **Fish Creek Mountains** [IMPERIAL]; **Grinnell Mountain** [SAN BERNARDINO].

Fish Creek Mountains [IMPERIAL]: *range,* 29 miles west of Brawley (lat. 33°00' N, long. 116°02' W); the range is south of Fish Creek Wash. Named on Borrego Mountain SE (1958), Carrizo Mountain NE (1957), Harpers Well (1956), and Plaster City NW (1956) 7.5' quadrangles. United States Board on Geographic Names (1961b, p. 10) rejected the singular form "Fish Creek Mountain" for the name.

Fish Creek Wash [IMPERIAL]: *stream* and *dry wash,* heads in San Diego County and extends for 11.5 miles in Imperial County to San Felipe Creek 6.5 miles west-southwest of Kane Spring (lat. 33° 05'25" N, long. 115°56'45" W; at N line sec. 32, T 12 S, R 10 E). Named on Borrego Mountain SE (1958) and Harpers Well (1956) 7.5' quadrangles.

Fishel [SAN BERNARDINO]: *locality,* 29 miles south of Essex along Atchison, Topeka and Santa Fe Railroad (lat. 34°18'50" N, long. 115°14'30" W; at S line sec. 30, T 3 N, R 17 E). Named on Milligan (1956) 15' quadrangle. Called Fishnel on California Mining Bureau's (1917a) map, which shows a place called Evans located 2.5 miles southeast of Fishnel along the railroad.

Fisher Cove [SAN BERNARDINO]: *embayment,* 3 miles west of downtown Big Bear Lake along Big Bear Lake (1) (lat. 34°14'25" N, long. 116°57'40" W; on E line sec. 22, T 2 N, R 1 W). Named on Big Bear Lake

(1970) 7.5' quadrangle.

Fishermans Camp [RIVERSIDE]: *locality,* 4.25 miles south-southeast of Sitton Peak near the mouth of Tenaja Canyon (lat. 33°31'40" N, long. 117°24'25" W). Named on Sitton Peak (1954) 7.5' quadrangle.

Fishermans Campground [SAN BERNARDINO]: *locality,* 5 miles northwest of Keller Peak (lat. 34°14'45" N, long. 117°06'35" W; sec. 20, T 2 N, R 2 W). Named on Keller Peak (1967) 7.5' quadrangle. Called Deer Creek Public Camp on Redlands (1954) 15' quadrangle.

Fish Head Rocks [SAN BERNARDINO]: *relief feature,* 7.5 miles south-southwest of Trona (lat. 35°40' N, long. 117°25'50" W; sec. 23, T 26 S, R 42 E). Named on Westend (1973) 7.5' quadrangle.

Fishnel: see **Fishel** [SAN BERNARDINO].

Fish Ponds: see **Daggett** [SAN BERNARDINO].

Fish Springs [IMPERIAL]: *spring,* at Desert Shores (lat. 33°24'25" N, long. 116°02'05" W; near E line sec. 9, T 9 S, R 9 E). Named on Rabbit Peak (1959) 15' quadrangle. The name is from tiny fish that live in the tepid water of the spring (Brown, 1923, p. 203; Chase, p. 189).

Fish Springs: see **Desert Shores** [IMPERIAL].

Flamingo Heights [SAN BERNARDINO]: *locality,* 8 miles north of Yucca Valley (lat. 34°14'30" N, long. 116°26'20" W). Named on Landers (1972) and Yucca Valley North (1972) 7.5' quadrangles.

Flat Top [SAN BERNARDINO]: *relief feature,* 6 miles north-northwest of Yucca Valley (lat. 34°12'15" N, long. 116°28'30" W; around NE cor. sec. 5, T 1 N, R 5 E). Named on Yucca Valley North (1972) 7.5' quadrangle.

Flat Top Mountain [RIVERSIDE]: *ridge,* east-southeast-trending, 1.25 miles long, 6 miles north of Cathedral City (lat. 33°51'55" N, long. 116°28'05" W). Named on Cathedral City (1958) 7.5' quadrangle.

Flattop Mountain [SAN BERNARDINO]: *peak,* 13 miles west of Needles (lat. 34°49'50" N, long. 114°49'30" W). Altitude 3029 feet. Named on Bannock (1956) 15' quadrangle.

Flat Tops [IMPERIAL]: *peaks,* two, 8.5 miles southwest of Palo Verde (lat. 33°22' N, long. 114°51'30" W). Named on Palo Verde Mountains (1953) 15' quadrangle.

Fleming Creek [SAN BERNARDINO]: *stream,* flows less than 1 mile to Lake Arrowhead (1) 6 miles north-northwest of Harrison Mountain (lat. 34°14'55" N, long. 117°11' W; near N line sec. 22, T 2 N, R 3 W). Named on Harrison Mountain (1967) 7.5' quadrangle.

Florida: see **Valle Vista** [RIVERSIDE].

Flowingwell: see **Flowing Wells** [IMPERIAL].

Flowing Wells [IMPERIAL]: *locality,* 7 miles north-northeast of Calipatria along Southern Pacific Railroad (lat. 33°13' N, long. 115°27'10" W; sec. 18, T 11 S, R 15 E). Named on Iris (1956) 7.5' quadrangle. Called Flowing Well Siding on Iris (1940) 15' quadrangle, and called Flowing Well on Iris (1945) 15' quadrangle. Postal authorities established Flowingwell post office in 1900, moved it 4 miles west in 1902, and discontinued it in 1904 (Salley, p. 76). The name is from an old watering spot that consisted of a marsh with brackish water (Brown, 1923, p. 207).

Flume Canyon [SAN BERNARDINO]: *canyon,* drained by a stream that heads in Los Angeles County and flows 1.5 miles to Swarthout Valley 5.25 miles north of Mount San Antonio (lat. 34°21'50" N, long. 117°39'05" W; sec. 7, T 3 N, R 7 W). Named on Mount San Antonio (1955) 7.5' quadrangle.

Flynn [SAN BERNARDINO]: *locality,* 29 miles north of Amboy along Union Pacific Railroad (lat. 34°58'40" N, long. 115°43'50" W; near NW cor. sec. 9, T 10 N, R 12 E). Named on Flynn (1956) 15' quadrangle.

Folly Peak [RIVERSIDE]: *peak,* 0.5 mile northwest of San Jacinto Peak (lat. 33°49'05" N, long. 116°41'05" W; at SE cor. sec. 17, T 4 S, R 3 E). Named on San Jacinto Peak (1981) 7.5' quadrangle. The name reportedly came after a climber ascended this peak thinking that it was nearby San Jacinto Peak, and then fell and injured himself when he tried to get to the desired summit (Robinson and Risher, p. 45).

Fondo [IMPERIAL]: *locality,* 6.5 miles west of Calipatria along Southern Pacific Railroad (lat. 33°06'45" N, long. 115°37'25" W; sec. 21, T 12 S, R 13 E). Named on Westmorland (1956) 7.5' quadrangle.

Fontana [SAN BERNARDINO]: *city,* 8.5 miles west of San Bernardino city hall (lat. 34°06'05" N, long. 117°26' W). Named on Fontana (1967) and Guasti (1966) 7.5' quadrangles. Postal authorities established Fontana post office in 1914 (Frickstad, p. 141), and the city incorporated in 1952. Mike Fontana subdivided his property and started the modern community in 1913 (Hanna, p. 108). San Bernardino (1901) 15' quadrangle shows a place called Rosena at the site. Postal authorities established Rosena post office in 1893 and discontinued it in 1901; the named was for Mike Fontana's daughter (Salley, p. 189). Darton and others' (1915) map shows a place called Wade located 3.25 miles west of Fontana along the railroad.

Fontana: see **South Fontana** [SAN BERNARDINO].

Fontana Station: see **South Fontana Station**, under **Declez** [SAN BERNARDINO].

Ford Canyon [SAN BERNARDINO]: *canyon,* about 1 mile long, 7 miles west-southwest of San Gorgonio Mountain (lat. 34°03'15" N, long. 116°56'15" W; sec. 25, T 1 S, R 1 W). Named on Forest Falls (1970) 7.5' quadrangle.

Ford Dry Lake [RIVERSIDE]: *dry lakes,* two, 7.5 miles long together, 23 miles east-southeast of Desert Center (lat. 33°38'15" N, long. 115°00'30" W). Named on McCoy Spring (1952) and Sidewinder Well (1952) 15' quadrangles.

Fords Dry Lake [SAN BERNARDINO]: *dry lake,* nearly 0.5 mile long, 19 miles south of Ivanpah (lat. 35°04' N, long. 115°15'45" W; sec. 4, T 11 N, R 16 E). Named on Mid Hills (1955) 15' quadrangle.

Ford Well [RIVERSIDE]: *well,* 28 miles east-southeast of Desert Center (lat. 33°37' N, long. 114°56'10" W; sec. 30, T 6 S, R 20 E); the well is about 0.5 mile east of the east end of Ford Dry Lake. Named on McCoy Spring (1952) 15' quadrangle. Called Ford's Well on California Mining Bureau's (1917b) map.

Forest Falls [SAN BERNARDINO]: *locality,* 5 miles west-southwest of San Gorgonio Mountain in Mill Creek Canyon (lat. 34°05'05" N, long. 116°54'30" W). Named on Forest Falls (1970) 7.5' quadrangle. United States Board on Geographic Names (1975b, p. 5) gave the variant names "Fallsvale," "Fallsville," and "Forest Home" for the place. Postal authorities established Fallsvale post office in 1929 and moved it 1.5 miles northeast in 1960, when they changed the name to Forest Falls (Salley, p. 73). They established Forest Home post office at a vacation resort located 11 miles east of Crafton in 1906 and discontinued it in 1960, when they moved the service to Forest Falls (Salley, p. 77).

Forest Home: see **Forest Falls** [SAN BERNARDINO].

Forest of the Sky: see **Skyforest** [SAN BERNARDINO].

Forks of Road: see **Hawley**, under **Daggett** [SAN BERNARDINO].

Forks Springs [SAN BERNARDINO]: *springs,* 6.5 miles west-northwest of downtown Morongo Valley (lat. 34°06' N, long. 116°40'50" W; sec. 9, T 1 S, R 3 E); the springs are near the confluence of North Fork Mission Creek and South Fork Mission Creek. Named on Catclaw Flat (1972) 7.5' quadrangle. Morongo Valley (1955) 15' quadrangle shows a single spring, called Forks Spring, at the site.

Forsee Creek [SAN BERNARDINO]: *stream,* flows 5 miles to Santa Ana River 5 miles south-southwest of downtown Big Bear Lake (lat. 34°10'25" N, long. 116°56'45" W; near E line sec. 14, T 1 N, R 1 W). Named on Big Bear Lake (1970) 7.5' quadrangle. Called Foxesee Creek on San Gorgonio (1902) 30' quadrangle.

Fort Beale: see **Fort Piute** [SAN BERNARDINO].

Fort Irwin: see **Camp Irwin** [SAN BERNARDINO].

Fort Piute [SAN BERNARDINO]: *locality,* 25 miles southeast of Ivanpah (lat. 35°06'50" N, long. 114°59' W; near S line sec. 13, T 12 N, R 18 E); the place is 3700 feet east-northeast of Piute Spring. Ruins named on Homer Mountain (1956) 15' quadrangle. Captain James H. Carleton set up a military post at the site in 1859 and called it Fort Beale for Edward F. Beale, who surveyed a wagon road in the region; the troops left it at the end of the Civil War, reoccupied it in 1866 when they gave it the name "Fort Piute," and abandoned it about 1868 (Frazer, p. 28-29).

Fort Soda: see **Soda Springs** [SAN BERNARDINO].

Fortynine Palms Canyon [SAN BERNARDINO]: *canyon,* drained by a stream that flows 5 miles to lowlands 2.5 miles west-southwest of Twentynine Palms (lat. 34°07'25" N, long. 116°05'30" W; sec. 36, T 1 N, R 8 E). Named on Queen Mountain (1972) 7.5' quadrangle.

Fortynine Palms Oasis [SAN BERNARDINO]: *spring,* 3.5 miles southwest of Twentynine Palms (lat. 34°06'20" N, long. 116°06'15" W); the spring is in Fortynine Palms Canyon. Named on Queen Mountain (1972) 7.5' quadrangle.

Fort Yuma: see **Pilot Knob** [IMPERIAL].

Foshay Pass [SAN BERNARDINO]: *pass,* 27 miles north-northeast of Amboy (lat. 34°54'50" N, long. 115°32'45" W; at W line sec. 32, T 10 N, R 14 E). Named on Flynn (1956) 15' quadrangle.

Foshay Spring [SAN BERNARDINO]: *spring,* 27 miles north-northeast of Amboy (lat. 34°55' N, long. 115°32' W; sec. 32, T 10 N, R 14 E); the spring is less than 1 mile east of Foshay Pass. Named on Flynn (1956) 15' quadrangle.

Fossil Canyon [IMPERIAL]: *canyon,* 2 miles long, opens into lowlands 3 miles south of Carrizo Mountain (lat. 32°47' N, long. 116° 01'10" W; near SE cor. sec. 10, T 16 S, R 9 E). Named on Carrizo Mountain (1957) 7.5' quadrangle.

Fossil Canyon [SAN BERNARDINO]: *canyon,* drained by a stream that flows 4.5 miles to lowlands 36 miles east-southeast of the village of Red Mountain (lat. 35°02'40" N, long. 117°06' W; near W line sec. 16, T 11 N, R 2 W). Named on Opal Mountain (1955) 15' quadrangle.

Foster Lake [RIVERSIDE]: *lake,* 1150 feet long, nearly 5 miles southwest of San Jacinto Peak (lat. 33°45'25" N, long. 116°43'30" W; near N line sec. 12, T 5 S, R 2 E). Named on San Jacinto Peak (1981) 7.5' quadrangle.

Fountain Peak [SAN BERNARDINO]: *peak,* 29 miles north-northeast of Amboy (lat. 34°56'45" N, long. 115°32'10" W; sec. 20, T 10 N, R 14 E). Altitude 6996 feet. Named on Flynn (1956) 15' quadrangle.

Four Corners [SAN BERNARDINO]: *locality,* at the center of Twentynine Palms (lat. 34°08'10" N, long. 116°03'15" W; at NW cor. sec. 33, T 1 N, R 9 E). Named on Twentynine Palms (1973) 7.5' quadrangle.

Four Corners: see **Kramer Junction** [SAN BERNARDINO].

Four Palms Spring [IMPERIAL]: *spring,* 9 miles south of Desert Shores (lat. 33°16'50" N, long. 116°01'35" W; at S line sec. 22, T 10 S, R 9 E). Named on Seventeen Palms (1956) 7.5' quadrangle. Agua Dulce (1944) 15' quadrangle has the plural name "Four Palms Springs."

Fourth of July Canyon [SAN BERNARDINO]: *canyon,* 1.5 miles long, 6.5 miles south of Ivanpah (lat. 35°14'30" N, long. 115°20' W). Named on Mid Hills (1955) 15' quadrangle.

Foxesee Creek: see **Forsee Creek** [SAN BERNARDINO].

Fox Spring [RIVERSIDE]: *spring,* 2 miles southwest of Sitton Peak (lat. 33°34' N, long. 117°28'10" W; near SE cor. sec. 11, T 7 S, R 6 W). Named on Sitton Peak (1954) 7.5' quadrangle.

Francis Spring [SAN BERNARDINO]: *spring,* 31 miles west-northwest of Ivanpah (lat. 35°29' N, long. 115°50'10" W; near SE cor. sec. 7, T 16 N, R 11 E). Named on Halloran Spring (1956) 15' quadrangle. Thompson (1929, p. 604) reported that the feature "is really a well dug in gravel to a depth of 10 feet and partly walled."

Frankish Peak [SAN BERNARDINO]: *peak,* 8 miles north of Ontario city hall (lat. 34°10'30" N, long. 117°39'20" W; sec. 18, T 1 N, R 7 W). Altitude 4198 feet. Named on Mount Baldy (1967) 7.5' quadrangle.

Freda [SAN BERNARDINO]: *locality,* 23 miles west of Vidal along Atchison, Topeka and Santa Fe Railroad (lat. 34°06'05" N, long. 114°54'30" W; on W line sec. 8, T 1 S, R 20 E). Named on Rice (1954) 15' quadrangle. California Mining Bureau's (1917a) map shows a place called Arica located along the railroad at or near present Freda.

Fredalba [SAN BERNARDINO]: *village,* 3 miles north-northeast of Harrison Mountain (lat. 34°12' N, long. 117°08' W; near W line sec. 6, T 1 N, R 2 W). Named on Harrison Mountain (1967) 7.5' quadrangle. Postal authorities established Fredalba post office in 1896, discontinued it in 1915, reestablished it in 1920, and discontinued it in 1924; the name was for Fred Smiley and Albert Smiley, pioneer residents—the place first was a lumber camp and then a vacation resort (Salley, p. 80).

Fredalba Creek [SAN BERNARDINO]: *stream,* flows 4.5 miles to Little Mill Creek 1.5 miles east-southeast of Harrison Mountain (lat. 34°09'20" N, long. 117°08'05" W; sec. 19, T 1 N, R 2 W). Named on Harrison Mountain (1967) and Keller Peak (1967) 7.5' quadrangles.

Fremont [SAN BERNARDINO]: *locality,* 11 miles south of the village of Red Mountain (lat. 35°11'30" N, long. 117°34'30" W; at W line sec. 34, T 31 S, R 41 E); the place is 7 miles west of Fremont Peak. Site named on Boron NE (1973) 7.5' quadrangle. Searles Lake (1915) 1° quadrangle shows the place along Atchison, Topeka and Santa Fe Railroad.

Fremont Peak [SAN BERNARDINO]: *peak,* 14 miles southeast of the village of Red Mountain (lat. 35°11'40" N, long. 117°27'10" W; on W line sec. 35, T 31 S, R 42 E). Altitude 4584 feet. Named on Fremont Peak (1956) 15' quadrangle. Mendenhall (1909a, p. 57) listed a feature called Goleta Spring located at the southeast base of Fremont Peak—the name goes back to the time of Fremont's last homeward trip across Mohave Desert. Mendenhall (1909a, p. 58) also listed Star Springs, located about 3 miles east of Fremont Peak.

Fremont Wash [SAN BERNARDINO]: *stream,* flows more than 17 miles to Mojave River 20 miles southwest of Barstow (lat. 34°44'20" N, long. 117°20'15" W; sec. 31, T 8 N, R 4 W). Named on Helendale (1956) and Victorville NW (1956) 7.5' quadrangles.

French Lake [IMPERIAL]: *intermittent lake,* 2.25 miles long, 11 miles north-northwest of Holtville (lat. 32°57' N, long. 115°28'45" W). Named on Holtville (1907) 30' quadrangle.

French Valley [RIVERSIDE]: *valley,* 9 miles northeast of Murrieta (lat. 33°37'15" N, long. 117°05'30" W). Named on Bachelor Mountain (1953) and Winchester (1953) 7.5' quadrangles. The name is from the many settlers from France and French-speaking Switzerland that came to the place in the 1860's to 1880's (Gunther, p. 191).

Fresno Canyon [RIVERSIDE]: *canyon,* drained by a stream that flows nearly 3 miles to Santa Ana River 5 miles west of Corona (lat. 33°52'55" N, long. 117°39' W). Named on Black Star Canyon (1967) and Prado Dam (1967) 7.5' quadrangles.

Fried Liver Wash [RIVERSIDE]: *stream,* flows 11.5 miles from Pleasant Valley to Pinto Wash 20 miles north-northwest of Chiriaco Summit (lat. 33°55'45" N, long. 115°50'30" W; near NE cor. sec. 8, T 3 S, R 11 E). Named on Hexie Mountains (1963) 15' quadrangle. The name is from the liver-colored flat rocks in the wash (Gunther, p. 191-192).

Frink [IMPERIAL]: *locality,* 18 miles north-northwest of Calipatria along Southern Pacific Railroad (lat. 33°21'45" N, long. 115°38'55" W; near E line sec. 30, T 9 S, R 13 E). Named on Frink (1956) 7.5' quadrangle.

Frink Spring [IMPERIAL]: *spring,* 1 mile northeast of Frink (lat. 33° 22'25" N, long. 115°38'15" W; sec. 20, T 9 S, R 13 E). Named on Frink (1956) 7.5' quadrangle. The name is for Horace Monroe Frink, who discovered the spring in 1862 while he was guiding a group of soldiers from San Bernardino to Fort Yuma (Hanna, p. 114).

Frog Creek [SAN BERNARDINO]: *stream,* flows 2.25 miles to East Fork Barton Creek 5 miles south-southeast of downtown Big Bear Lake (lat. 34°10'20" N, long. 116°53'20" W; near W line sec. 16, T 1 N, R 1 E). Named on Big Bear Lake (1970) and Moonridge (1970) 7.5' quadrangles.

Front Hill Canyon [RIVERSIDE]: *canyon,* about 0.5 mile long, 11.5 miles east of Indio (lat. 33°42'45" N, long. 116°00'55" W; sec. 26, T 5 S, R 9 E). Named on Thermal Canyon (1956) 7.5' quadrangle.

Frost [SAN BERNARDINO]: *locality,* 2 miles south-southeast of Victorville along the railroad (lat. 34°30'40" N, long. 117°16'45" W; near NE cor. sec. 22, T 5 N, R 4 W). Named on Victorville (1956) 7.5' quadrangle.

Frustration Creek [SAN BERNARDINO]: *stream,* flows nearly 1 mile to Mill Creek Canyon 8 miles west of San Gorgonio Mountain (lat. 34°05'50" N, long. 116°58' W; near E line sec. 10, T 1 S, R 1 W). Named on Forest Falls (1970) 7.5' quadrangle. Called Monkeyface Creek on San Gorgonio Mountain (1954) 15' quadrangle.

Fry Mountains [SAN BERNARDINO]: *range,* 2.5 miles southeast of Ord Mountain (lat. 34°34' N, long. 116°42'30" W). Named on Old Woman Springs (1955) and Rodman Mountains (1955) 15' quadrangles.

Fry Valley [SAN BERNARDINO]: *valley,* 3.5 miles north of Old Woman Springs (lat. 34°27'30" N, long. 116°43' W); the valley is southwest of the southeast end of Fry Mountains. Named on Old Woman Springs (1972) 7.5' quadrangle.

Fuller [IMPERIAL]: *locality,* 3.5 miles north-northwest of Holtville along Southern Pacific Railroad (lat. 32°51'35" N, long. 115°24'20" W; sec. 10, T 15 S, R 15 E). Named on Holtville West (1956) 7.5' quadrangle.

Fuller Mill Creek [RIVERSIDE]: *stream,* flows 3.25 miles to North Fork San Jacinto River 4.25 miles west-southwest of San Jacinto Peak (lat. 33°47'40" N, long. 116°44'55" W; sec. 26, T 4 S, R 2 E). Named on San Jacinto Peak (1981) 7.5' quadrangle. The name is from a sawmill that Mr. Fuller operated before 1900 (Gunther, p. 192).

Fuller Mill Creek Camp [RIVERSIDE]: *locality,* 12 miles west-southwest of Palm Springs (lat. 33°47'55" N, long. 116°44'45" W; near N line sec. 26, T 4 S, R 2 E). Named on Palm Springs (1957) 15' quadrangle.

Fuller Ridge [RIVERSIDE]: *ridge,* northwest- to west-trending, 2.5 miles long, 2.5 miles west-northwest of San Jacinto Peak (lat. 33° 50' N, long. 116°43' W); the ridge is at the head of Fuller Mill Creek. Named on San Jacinto Peak (1981) 7.5' quadrangle.

Fulmor: see **Lake Fulmor** [RIVERSIDE].

Funston: see **Amboy** [SAN BERNARDINO].

Fun Valley [RIVERSIDE]: *valley,* 9.5 miles north-northeast of Cathedral City (lat. 33°54'30" N, long. 116°23'45" W). Named on Seven Palms Valley (1958) 7.5' quadrangle.

Furnace Canyon [SAN BERNARDINO]: *canyon,* drained by a stream that flows 2.5 miles to lowlands 6.25 miles north of Fawnskin (lat. 34°21'45" N, long. 116°55'20" W; sec. 7, T 3 N, R 1 E). Named on Fawnskin (1971) 7.5' quadrangle.

Furnace Spring [SAN BERNARDINO]: *spring,* 6 miles north of Fawnskin (lat. 34°21'30" N, long. 116°55'40" W; near E line sec. 12, T 3 N, R 1 W). Named on Fawnskin (1971) 7.5' quadrangle.

- G -

Gables Wash [IMPERIAL]: *stream,* flows 5 miles to lowlands 9 miles northeast of Glamis (lat. 33°04'45" N, long. 114°56'30" W; sec. 35, T 12 S, R 19 E); the stream heads west of Imperial Gables. Named on Quartz Peak (1953) 15' quadrangle.

Gale [SAN BERNARDINO]: *locality,* 2.5 miles east of Daggett along Atchison, Topeka and Santa Fe Railroad (lat. 34°51'20" N, long. 116°50'30" W; at E line sec. 23, T 9 N, R 1 E). Named on Minneola (1971) 7.5' quadrangle.

Galena Peak [SAN BERNARDINO]: *peak,* 2.25 miles south-southwest of San Gorgonio Mountain (lat. 34°04'15" N, long. 116°50'45" W; near E line sec. 23, T 1 S, R 1 E). Altitude 9324 feet. Named on San Gorgonio Mountain (1970) 7.5' quadrangle. United States Board on Geographic Names (1988c, p. 4) approved the name "Snow Peak" for a feature, altitude 7920 feet, located 3 miles southeast of Galena Peak (lat. 34°02'16" N, long. 116°48'48" W; sec. 31, T 1 S, R 2 E); the name commemorates Charles Alden Snow, founder of Snow Peak Communications.

Galivan: see **Queen Valley** [RIVERSIDE-SAN BERNARDINO].

Galway Lake [SAN BERNARDINO]: *dry lake,* 3 miles long, 5.5 miles southwest of Ludlow (lat. 34°32'45" N, long. 116°28'30" W). Named on Lavic (1955) and Rodman Mountains (1955) 15' quadrangles.

Gamma Gulch [SAN BERNARDINO]: *canyon,* 0.5 mile long, 12 miles north of downtown Morongo Valley (lat. 34°13'20" N, long. 116°33'05" W; sec. 27, T 2 N, R 4 E). Named on Rimrock (1972) 7.5' quadrangle.

Garden of Eden: see **Palm Canyon** [RIVERSIDE].

Garden Park [SAN BERNARDINO]: *district,* 1.5 miles southeast of present San Bernardino city hall (lat. 34°05'25" N, long. 117° 16' W). Named on Colton (1943) 7.5' quadrangle.

Garlic Lake: see **Bicycle Lake** [SAN BERNARDINO].

Garlic Spring [SAN BERNARDINO]: *spring,* 32 miles west of Baker (lat. 36°13'45" N, long. 116°38'30" W; near SW cor. sec. 11, T 13 N, R 3 E). Named on Alvord Mountain (1948) 15' quadrangle.

Garner Valley [RIVERSIDE]: *valley,* 7.5 miles south-southeast of Idyllwild (lat. 33°38'45" N, long. 116°39' W). Named on Idyllwild (1959) 15' quadrangle. The name is for Robert F. Garner, who bought land in the valley in 1905; before that time, the place was called Thomas Valley for Charles Thomas, who moved there in 1872 or 1873 (Gunther, p. 194, 542-543).

Garner Wash [IMPERIAL-RIVERSIDE]: *stream,* heads in Imperial County and flows 8 miles to Salton Sea 1.5 miles north of Desert Shores in Riverside County (lat. 33°25'50" N, long. 116°02'25" W; sec. 34, T 8 S, R 9 E). Named on Oasis (1956) 7.5' quadrangle.

Garnet [RIVERSIDE]: *locality,* 4.5 miles north of Palm Springs (lat. 33°54'05" N, long. 116°32'40" W; at E line sec. 22, T 3 S, R 4 E); the place is just west of Garnet Hill. Named on Desert Hot Springs (1955) 7.5' quadrangle. Postal authorities established Garnett post office in 1927, discontinued it the same year, reestablished it with the name "Garnet" in 1930, and discontinued it in 1943 (Salley, p. 82). The Southern Pacific Railroad station at the place was named Palms in 1875; by 1889 it was called Seven Palms, in 1900 it was called Palm Springs, and in 1923 the name was changed to Garnet when the name "Palm Springs" was transferred to what had been called Whitewater station (Gudde, 1949, p. 250). California Mining Bureau's (1909b) map has the name "Pierce" at present Garnet. Postal authorities established Pierce post office in 1898 and discontinued it in 1902 (Frickstad, p. 130). California Mining Bureau's (1917b) map has the name "Gray" at present Garnet. Postal authorities established Gray post office in 1913, changed the name to Noria in 1918, and discontinued it in 1920; the name "Gray" was for Hilda M. Gray, the proposed postmaster (Salley, p. 89, 155). California Mining Bureau's (1917b) map shows a place called Monad situated about 3 miles southeast of Gray.

Garnet Gardens: see **North Palm Springs** [RIVERSIDE].

Garnet Hill [RIVERSIDE]: *ridge,* west-northwest-trending, 1.5 miles long, 4.5 miles north of Palm Springs (lat. 33°53'45" N, long. 116° 32' W; sec. 23, 24, T 3 S, R 4 E). Named on Desert Hot Springs (1955) 7.5' quadrangle.

Garnet Queen Canyon: see **Horse Canyon** [RIVERSIDE].

Garnet Queen Creek [RIVERSIDE]: *stream,* flows 3.25 miles to Vanderventer Flat 18 miles southeast of Idyllwild (lat. 33°31'55" N, 116°30'55" W; near SW cor. sec. 30, T 7 S, R 5 E). Named on Idyllwild (1959) 15' quadrangle—which shows the stream continuing on westward beyond Vanderventer Flat—and on Palm Desert (1959) 15' quadrangle, which shows Garnet Queen mine by the stream. United States Board on Geographic Names (1982a, p. 3) corrected the mistaken extent of the feature shown on Idyllwild (1959) 15' quadrangle.

Garnet Ridge [RIVERSIDE]: *ridge,* north-northeast-trending, 1 mile long, 8.5 miles east-southeast of Idyllwild (lat. 33°41'35" N, long. 116°34'30" W; mainly in sec. 33, T 5 S, T 4 E). Named on Idyllwild (1959) 15' quadrangle.

Garnett: see **Garnet** [RIVERSIDE].

Garnet Wash [RIVERSIDE]: *stream* and *dry wash,* extends for 4 miles to Whitewater River 4.5 miles north of Palm Springs (lat. 33°53'55" N, long. 116°33'05" W; sec. 22, T 3 S, R 4 E); the feature joins Whitewater River near Garnet. Named on Desert Hot Springs (1955) 7.5' quadrangle.

Gary Wash [SAN BERNARDINO]: *stream,* flows 12.5 miles to Chemehuevi Wash 22 miles north-northwest of Vidal (lat. 34°25'40" N, long. 114°35'50" W; near SE cor. sec. 18, T 4 N, R 23 E). Named on Savahia Peak NE (1971), Savahia Peak NW (1971), and Savahia Peak SW (1971) 7.5' quadrangles.

Gatuna Wash [IMPERIAL]: *stream,* flows 3.25 miles to Carrizo Wash (2) 30 miles south of Palo Verde (lat. 33°00'15" N, long. 114°41'55" W). Named on Picacho Peak (1965) and Picacho SW (1965) 7.5' quadrangles.

Gavilan Mountain [RIVERSIDE]: *peak,* 5 miles southwest of Temecula (lat. 33°26'35" N, long. 117°12'45" W; sec. 32, T 8 S, R 3 W). Altitude 1831 feet. Named on Temecula (1968) 7.5' quadrangle.

Gavilan Peak [RIVERSIDE]: *hill,* 3.5 miles northeast of Estelle Mountain (lat. 33°48'15" N, long. 117°22'30" W). Altitude 2442 feet. Named on Lake Mathews (1967) and Steele Peak (1967) 7.5' quadrangles.

Gavilan Plateau [RIVERSIDE]: *area,* 3.25 miles northeast of Estelle Mountain (lat. 33°47'45" N, long. 117°22'30" W). Named on Lake Mathews (1967) and Steele Peak (1967) 7.5' quadrangles. Called The Gavilan on Elsinore (1901) 30' quadrangle.

Gavilan Wash [IMPERIAL]: *stream* and *dry wash,* extends for 8 miles to lowlands along Colorado River 26 miles south of Palo Verde (lat. 33°03'05" N, long. 114°40'45" W; near NE cor. sec. 17, T 13 S, R 22 E). Named on Quartz Peak (1953) 15' quadrangle, and on Picacho SW (1965) 7.5' quadrangle.

Gays Pass [SAN BERNARDINO]: *pass,* 17 miles southwest of Ludlow (lat. 34°33'05" N, long. 116°22'30" W; sec. 5, T 5 N, R 6 E). Named on Lavic (1955) 15' quadrangle.

General: see **Mount General** [SAN BERNARDINO].

Gene Wash [SAN BERNARDINO]: *stream,* flows 4.25 miles to Lake Havasu 24 miles northeast of Vidal (lat. 34°18'20" N, long. 114° 09'15" W; near W line sec. 33, T 3 N, R 27 E). Named on Gene Wash (1959) 7.5' quadrangle.

Gene Wash Reservoir [SAN BERNARDINO]: *lake,* nearly 1.25 miles long, behind a dam on Gene Wash 23 miles northeast of Vidal (lat. 34°18' N, long. 114°10' W; sec. 32, T 3 N, R 27 E). Named on Gene Wash (1959) 7.5' quadrangle.

George Air Force Base [SAN BERNARDINO]: *military installation,* 5.5 miles northwest of Victorville (lat. 34°35' N, long. 117°22' W). Named on Adlelanto (1956) and Victorville (1956) 7.5' quadrangles. Postal authorities established Air Corps Advanced Flying School post office in 1941 and changed the name to George Air Force Base in 1950; the place also was called Victorville Air Force Base—the name "George" commemorates Brigadier General Harold H. George (Salley, p. 3, 84).

German Diggins Wash [IMPERIAL]: *stream,* flows 3.25 miles to lowlands 21 miles north-northwest of Glamis (lat. 33°16'10" N, long. 115°15' W; sec. 25, T 10 S, R 16 E). Named on Acolita (1953) and Chuckwalla Spring (1953) 15' quadrangles.

Gert Wash [IMPERIAL]: *stream,* heads in San Diego County and flows 5 miles to Carrizo Creek 4 miles north-northwest of Carrizo Mountain (lat. 32°52'35" N, long. 116°02'45" W; sec. 9, T 15 S, R 9 E). Named on Carrizo Mountain NE (1957) 7.5' quadrangle.

Giant Rock [SAN BERNARDINO]: *relief feature,* 4.5 miles north of Landers (lat. 34°20' N, long. 116°23'25" W; sec. 19, T 3 N, R 6 E). Named on Landers (1972) 7.5' quadrangle. On Emerson Lake (1955) 15' quadrangle, the name applies to a locality near the feature.

Gibbel Flat [RIVERSIDE]: *area,* 3.5 miles southeast of downtown Hemet (lat. 33°42'35" N, long. 116°56' W; sec. 25, T 5 S, R 1 W). Named on Hemet (1953) 7.5' quadrangle.

Gieselmann Lake [IMPERIAL]: *lake,* 1750 feet long, 7.5 miles south-southeast of Calipatria near Alamo River (lat. 33°01'25" N, long. 115°28'35" W; sec. 13, T 13 S, R 14 E). Named on Wiest (1956) 7.5' quadrangle.

Gillman Canyon [RIVERSIDE-SAN BERNARDINO]: *canyon,* drained by a stream that heads in San Bernardino County and flows 2.5 miles to San Gorgonio River 6.5 miles south-southwest of San Gorgonio Mountain in Riverside County (lat. 34°01'20" N, long. 116°53'30" W; near SW cor. sec. 4, T 2 S, R 1 E). Named on Forest Falls (1970) 7.5' quadrangle.

Gillner Point: see **Gilner Point** [SAN BERNARDINO].

Gilman Hot Springs [RIVERSIDE]: *locality,* 4 miles north-northwest of San Jacinto (lat. 33°50'05" N, long. 116°59'15" W). Named on San Jacinto (1953) 7.5' quadrangle. Called Relief Hot Springs on San Jacinto (1901) 30' quadrangle. Postal authorities established Gilman Hot Springs post office in 1938 (Frickstad, p. 128). Sidney James Branch homesteaded at the place in 1881, and by 1888 he had built Relief Springs hotel there—the hotel name was from the relief that Mrs. Branch received from arthritis, rheumatism, and chronic stomach trouble by use of water at the place (Gunther, p. 198). Waring (p. 38) noted that the name was changed to San Jacinto Hot Springs before 1915. The name "Gilman Hot Springs" is for William E. Gilman and his wife Josephine, who bought the place in 1913 (Gudde, 1949, p. 127).

Gilner Point [SAN BERNARDINO]: *promontory,* 1.25 miles south-southeast of Fawnskin along Big Bear Lake (1) (lat. 34°15'10" N, long. 116°56'20" W; at S line sec. 13, T 2 N, R 1 W). Named on Fawnskin (1971) 7.5' quadrangle. Called Gillner Point on Lucerne Valley (1947) 15' quadrangle.

Gilroy Canyon [SAN BERNARDINO]: *canyon,* 1.5 miles long, 30 miles north-northeast of Amboy (lat. 34°58' N, long. 115°31'40" W). Named on Flynn (1956) 15' quadrangle.

Ginsberg Hot Springs: see **Lakeview Hot Springs** [RIVERSIDE].

Gish: see **Summit** [SAN BERNARDINO].

Glacier Camp [SAN BERNARDINO]: *locality,* 2.25 miles south-southeast of Mount San Antonio (lat. 34°15'25" N, long. 117°38'10" W; sec. 17, T 2 N, R 7 W). Named on Mount San Antonio (1955) 7.5' quadrangle. Called Snow Crest Camp on San Antonio (1942) 15' quadrangle. Mr. and Mrs. A.R. Collins founded the place in 1925 (Robinson, J.W., 1983, p. 147).

Gladysta [SAN BERNARDINO]: *locality,* 2.25 miles west-northwest of Redlands along Southern California Railroad (lat. 34°03'50" N, long. 117°13'10" W). Named on Redlands (1901) 15' quadrangle.

Gladysta: see **Nevada** [SAN BERNARDINO].

Glamis [IMPERIAL]: *village,* 22 miles northeast of Holtville (lat. 32° 59'50" N, long. 115°04'15" W). Named on Glamis (1955) 7.5' quadrangle. Postal authorities established Glamis post office in 1886, discontinued it in 1888, reestablished it in 1899, discontinued it in 1901, reestablished it in 1917, discontinued it in 1920, reestablished it in 1921, discontinued it in 1923, and reestablished it in 1940 (Salley, p. 85).

Glamis Dunes: see **Sand Hills** [IMPERIAL].

Glasgow [SAN BERNARDINO]: *locality,* 30 miles north-northwest of Amboy along Union Pacific Railroad (lat. 34°59' N, long. 115° 52' W; sec. 6, T 10 N, R 11 E). Named on Kerens (1957) 15' quadrangle.

Gleason: see **El Centro** [IMPERIAL].

Gleason Switch: see **Meloland** [IMPERIAL].

Glen Avon [RIVERSIDE]: *town,* 6 miles west-northwest of Riverside (lat. 34°00'40" N, long. 117°28'45" W). Named on Fontana (1967) and Guasti (1966) 7.5' quadrangles. Called Glen Avon Heights on Ontario (1954) and San Bernardino (1954) 15' quadrangles. Officials of Riverside Development Company gave the name "Glen Avon Heights" to their subdivision in 1909 at what had been called West Riverside since 1887 (Gunther, p. 200). On United States Geological Survey's (1941) map, the name "Glenavon" applies to a place along Union Pacific Railroad at the west edge of the town (lat. 34°00'20" N, long. 117°30'05" W; near S line sec. 10, T 1 S, R 6 W).

Glen Avon Heights: see **Glen Avon** [RIVERSIDE].

Glen Ivy: see **Glen Ivy Hot Springs** [RIVERSIDE].

Glen Ivy Hot Springs [RIVERSIDE]: *locality*, 4.25 miles west of Estelle Mountain (lat. 33°45'20" N, long. 117°29'35" W; at N line sec. 10, T 5 S, R 6 W). Named on Lake Mathews (1967) 7.5' quadrangle. Called Glen Ivy on Elsinore (1901) 30' quadrangle, and called Temescal Hot Springs on California Mining Bureau's (1917b) map. Riverside (1901) 15' quadrangle shows a water feature called Sulphur Spring at the site. W.G. Steer and his wife took over Temescal Hot Springs in 1890, rebuilt the resort, and gave it the name "Cold Water Canyon House in Temescal Canyon"—the owners changed the name by 1893 to Hotel Glen Ivy, and changed it again in 1896 to Glen Ivy Hot Sulphur Springs (Gunther, p. 200-201). The place also was called Anti-Fat Hot Springs (Berkestresser, 1968, p. A-11).

Glen Martin [SAN BERNARDINO]: *locality*, 8 miles south-southwest of downtown Big Bear Lake (lat. 34°08'45" N, long. 116°59'05" W; sec. 28, T 1 N, R 1 W). Named on Big Bear Lake (1970) 7.5' quadrangle. Called Martin Glen on San Gorgonio (1902) 30' quadrangle.

Glen Martin Creek [SAN BERNARDINO]: *stream*, flows nearly 2 miles to Mountain Home Creek 9 miles west of San Gorgonio Mountain (lat. 34°07'10" N, long. 116°59'20" W; at S line sec. 33, T 1 N, R 1 W). Named on Big Bear Lake (1970) and Forest Falls (1970) 7.5' quadrangles.

Glenn Ranch [SAN BERNARDINO]: *locality*, 3.5 miles south-southwest of Cajon along North Fork Lytle Creek (lat. 34°15'25" N, long. 117°29'20" W; near E line sec. 15, T 2 N, R 6 W). Named on Cajon (1956) 7.5' quadrangle. After Silas Glenn died in 1878, his widow gave management of the place to her daughter and son-in-law, Mr. and Mrs. James Applewhite, who in the 1880's turned the ranch into a resort (Robinson, J.W., 1983, p. 187). Hesperia (1902) 15' quadrangle has the name "Glenn Ranch" at present Lytle Creek (2). Postal authorities established Glenn Ranch post office in 1921 and changed the name to Lytle Creek in 1953 (Salley, p. 86).

Glenoak Valley [RIVERSIDE]: *canyon*, 3 miles long, 13 miles south of Hemet (lat. 33°33'40" N, long. 116°58'45" W). Named on Sage (1954) 7.5' quadrangle.

Glen Valley [RIVERSIDE]: *locality*, 8.5 miles northeast of Estella Mountain (lat. 33°51'40" N, long. 117°19'35" W; sec. 32, T 3 S, R 4 W). Named on Steele Peak (1967) 7.5' quadrangle. Development of the site began in 1927 (Gunther, p. 201).

Globe Canyon [SAN BERNARDINO]: *canyon*, 3 miles long, opens into lowlands 24 miles south-southwest of Ivanpah (lat. 35°03'15" N, long. 115°32'45" W). Named on Kelso (1955) 15' quadrangle.

Goat Mountain [SAN BERNARDINO]:

(1) *mountain*, 2.5 miles north-northeast of Landers (lat. 34°17'50" N, long. 116°22'05" W). Altitude 3660 feet. Named on Goat Mountain (1955) 7.5' quadrangle.

(2) *peak*, 6.25 miles west of Ord Mountain (lat. 34°40' N, long. 116°55'20" W; near W line sec. 30, T 7 N, R 1 E). Altitude 5162 feet. Named on Ord Mountains (1955) 15' quadrangle.

Goat Spring [SAN BERNARDINO]: *spring*, 6.5 miles west of Ord Mountain (lat. 34°40'20" N, long. 116°55'30" W; near NW cor. sec. 30, T 7 N, R 1 E); the spring is 0.5 mile north of Goat Mountain (2). Named on Ord Mountains (1955) 7.5' quadrangle.

Gocke Valley [SAN BERNARDINO]: *valley*, 3.5 miles northeast of Sugarloaf Mountain (lat. 34°13'50" N, long. 116°45'45" W; sec. 27, T 2 N, R 2 E). Named on Moonridge (1970) 7.5' quadrangle.

Goff Flat [RIVERSIDE]: *area*, 10 miles southeast of Idyllwild (lat. 33°38'20" N, long. 116°35'40" W; near NW cor. sec. 20, T 6 S, R 4 E). Named on Idyllwild (1959) 15' quadrangle.

Goffs [SAN BERNARDINO]: *village*, 16 miles northeast of Essex along Atchison, Topeka and Santa Fe Railroad (lat. 34°55'10" N, long. 115°03'45" W; at SE cor. sec. 26, T 10 N, R 18 E). Named on Fenner (1956) 15' quadrangle. Postal authorities established Goffs post office in 1893 and discontinued it in 1894; they established Blake post office in 1896, changed the name to Goffs in 1911, and discontinued it in 1932 (Frickstad, p. 138, 141). The name "Blake" was for Isaac E. Blake, who in 1892 had Nevada Southern Railroad built north from Goffs to serve his mines (Gudde, 1975, p. 39-40). Amboy (1942) 1° quadrangle shows a place called Piute located 4.5 miles south-southwest of Goffs along the railroad

Goffs Butte [SAN BERNARDINO]: *mountain*, 14 miles northeast of Essex (lat. 34°52'50" N, long. 115°04' W; sec. 10, 11, T 9 N, R 18 E); the feature is 2.5 miles south of Goffs. Altitude 3612 feet. Named on Fenner (1956) 15' quadrangle.

Gold Basin [IMPERIAL]: *area*, 20 miles south-southwest of Palo Verde (lat. 33°09'30" N, long. 114°50'40" W; sec. 2, 3, T 12 S, R 20 E). Named on Quartz Peak (1953) 15' quadrangle.

Goldbridge: see **Lucerne Valley** [SAN BERNARDINO] (2).

Golden Lake: see **Cuddeback Lake** [SAN BERNARDINO].

Gold Mountain [SAN BERNARDINO]: *peak*, 2 miles north-northeast of Big Bear City (lat. 34°17'20" N, long. 116°50'20" W; at W line sec. 1, T 2 N, R 1 E). Altitude 8235 feet. Named on Big Bear City (1971) 7.5' quadrangle. California Mining Bureau's (1917a) map shows a place called Gold Mountain City located about 2 miles east of Gold Mountain.

Gold Mountain City: see **Gold Mountain** [SAN BERNARDINO].

Gold Park [RIVERSIDE]: *area*, 29 miles north-northeast of Chiriaco Summit (lat. 34°01'15" N, long. 115°59'15" W). Named on Valley Mountain (1956) 15' quadrangle.

Gold Ridge [SAN BERNARDINO]: *ridge*, northwest-trending, 0.5 mile long, 2.5 miles east-southeast of Mount San Antonio (lat. 34° 16'15" N, long. 117°36'15" W; sec. 10, T 2 N, R 7 W). Named on Telegraph Peak (1956) 7.5' quadrangle.

Gold Rose Well [RIVERSIDE]: *well*, 24 miles northwest of Desert Center along Pinto Wash (lat. 33°57'30" N, long. 115°41'10" W; near N line sec. 35, T 2 S, R 12 E). Named on Pinto Basin (1963) 15' quadrangle.

Goldstone [SAN BERNARDINO]: *locality*, 47 miles west of Baker (lat. 35°17'50" N, long. 116°54'45" W; sec. 19, T 14 N, R 1 E); the place is 3.25 miles south-southwest of the south end of Goldstone Lake. Named on Goldstone Lake (1948) 15' quadrangle.

Goldstone Lake [SAN BERNARDINO]: *dry lake*, 3 miles long, 46 miles west of Baker (lat. 35°22' N, long. 116°53'30" W; in and around sec. 29, T 15 N, R 1 E). Named on Goldstone Lake (1948) 15' quadrangle.

Goldstone Spring [SAN BERNARDINO]: *spring*, 27 miles north-northeast of Amboy (lat. 34°54'25" N, long. 115°33'05" W; near SW cor. sec. 31, T 10 N, R 14 E). Named on Flynn (1956) 15' quadrangle.

Gold Valley [SAN BERNARDINO]: *valley*, 17 miles south-southwest of Ivanpah (lat. 35°05'30" N, long. 115°23'30" W). Named on Mid Hills (1955) 15' quadrangle. United States Board on Geographic Names (1986b, p. 3) approved the name "Little Thorne Mountains" for a feature situated southeast of Gold Valley (lat. 35°05'06" N, long. 115°26'05" W).

Gold Valley Spring [SAN BERNARDINO]: *spring*, 19 miles south-southwest of Ivanpah (lat. 35°04'40" N, long. 115°24'45" W; sec. 31, T 12 N, R 15 E); the spring is at the southwest edge of Gold Valley. Named on Mid Hills (1955) 15' quadrangle.

Goleta Spring: see **Fremont Peak** [SAN BERNARDINO].

Goodhart Canyon [RIVERSIDE]: *canyon*, 2.5 miles long, opens into Diamond Valley 5.5 miles south of Hemet (lat. 33°40'15" N, long. 116°58'30" W; near NW cor. sec. 10, T 6 S, R 1 W). Named on Hemet (1953) 7.5' quadrangle. The name commemorates Henry Goodhart, who had land south of Diamond Valley patented in 1895 (Gunther, p. 201).

Goodman Slough [RIVERSIDE]: *marsh*, 1.25 miles southeast of downtown Blythe in a former meander of Colorado River (lat. 33° 35'55" N, long. 114°34'45" W; sec. 3, 4, 9, T 7 S, R 23 E). Named on Blythe (1951) 7.5' quadrangle.

Good News: see **Camp Good News** [SAN BERNARDINO].

Gooseberry Spring [RIVERSIDE]: *spring*, 7 miles east-southeast of Idyllwild (lat. 33°42' N, long. 116°36'30" W; near S line sec. 30, T 5 S, R 4 E). Named on Idyllwild (1959) 15' quadrangle.

Gordons Well [IMPERIAL]: *locality*, 10.5 miles southwest of Ogilby (lat. 32°42'30" N, long. 114°57'50" W; on S line sec. 36, T 16 S, R 19 E). Named on Grays Well (1964) 7.5' quadrangle.

Government Canyon [SAN BERNARDINO]: *canyon*, drained by a stream that flows 3.5 miles to Santa Ana River 6.5 miles north-northwest of Yucaipa (lat. 34°07'05" N, long. 117°05'50" W; near N line sec. 4, T 1 S, R 2 W); the canyon heads near Government Peak. Named on Keller Peak (1967) and Yucaipa (1967) 7.5' quadrangles.

Government Holes [SAN BERNARDINO]: *locality*, 12 miles south of Ivanpah (lat. 35°08'55" N, long. 119°21'30" W; sec. 3, T 12 N, R 15 E). Named on Mid Hills (1955) 15' quadrangle. After Phineas Banning received a contract in 1859 to transport goods by wagon over the Mojave road, his men dug a well along the route and called it Banning's Well, but by 1860 it was called Government Wells or Government Holes (Casebier, p. 96, 119).

Government Peak [SAN BERNARDINO]: *peak*, 3.5 miles south-southwest of Keller Peak (lat. 34°09'10" N, long. 117°05'05" W; at W line sec. 22, T 1 N, R 12 W). Named on Keller Peak (1967) 7.5' quadrangle.

Government Wells: see **Government Holes** [SAN BERNARDINO].

Graham Pass [RIVERSIDE]: *pass*, 24 miles southeast of Desert Center between Chuckwalla Mountains and Little Chuckwalla Mountains (lat. 33°27'15" N, long. 115°08' W). Named on Chuckwalla Spring (1953) 15' quadrangle.

Grand Terrace [SAN BERNARDINO]: *town*, 5 miles south-southwest of San Bernardino city hall (lat. 34°02' N, long. 117°18'45" W). Named on San Bernardino South (1967) 7.5' quadrangle. Postal authorities established Grand Terrace post office in 1959 (Salley, p. 88), and the town incorporated in 1978.

Grandview [SAN BERNARDINO]: *district*, 4.5 miles west of Barstow (lat.

34°53'15" N, long. 117°06'15" W; mainly in sec. 8, T 9 N, R 2 W). Named on Barstow (1971) 7.5' quadrangle.

Grand View Point [SAN BERNARDINO]: *peak,* 2.25 miles south-southwest of downtown Big Bear Lake (lat. 34°12'50" N, long. 116°55'20" W; sec. 31, T 2 N, R 1 E). Altitude 7784 feet. Named on Big Bear Lake (1970) 7.5' quadrangle.

Granite Cove [SAN BERNARDINO]: *canyon,* nearly 1 mile long, 16 miles north-northeast of Amboy (lat. 34°47' N, long. 115°39'15" W; sec. 18, T 8 N, R 13 E). Named on Flynn (1956) 15' quadrangle.

Granite Mountain [SAN BERNARDINO]: *peak,* 28 miles south-southeast of Trona (lat. 35°21'55" N, long. 117°14'10" W; sec. 35, T 29 S, R 44 E). Altitude 4781 feet. Named on Pilot Knob (1954) 15' quadrangle.

Granite Mountain: see **Granite Mountains** [SAN BERNARDINO] (3); **Pilot Knob** [SAN BERNARDINO].

Granite Mountains [RIVERSIDE]: *range,* 25 miles northeast of Desert Center (lat. 33°59' N, long. 115°05' W). Named on Iron Mountains (1956) and Palen Mountains (1952) 15' quadrangles.

Granite Mountains [SAN BERNARDINO]:

(1) *range,* 39 miles east-southeast of Trona (lat. 35°31' N, long. 116°45' W). Named on Leach Lake (1948), Quail Mountains (1948), and Tiefort Mountains (1948) 15' quadrangles. Called Leach Point Mountains on Campbell's (1902) map.

(2) *range,* 17 miles north of Amboy (lat. 34°48' N, long. 115° 43' W). Named on Flynn (1956) and Kerens (1957) 15' quadrangles. United States Board on Geographic Names (1988a, p. 2-3) approved names for several features in Granite Mountains: the name "Granite Peak" for a peak, altitude 6762 feet (lat. 34°47'37" N, long. 115°41'40" W; sec. 11, T 8 N, R 12 E); the name "Granite Peak Plateau" for a mesa, 1 mile long (lat. 34°47'03" N, long. 115° 41'03" W; sec. 11, 12, 13, 14, T 8 N, R 12 E); the name "Silver Peak" for a peak, altitude 6365 feet (lat. 34°48'38" N, long. 115° 41'49" W; sec. 2, T 8 N, R 12 E); and the name "White Fang" for a peak, altitude 4659 feet (lat. 34°46'57" N, long. 115°38'20" W; sec. 17, T 8 N, R 13 E).

(3) *range,* 14 miles east of Victorville (lat. 34°31' N, long. 117° 03' W). Named on Ord Mountains (1955) 15' quadrangle, and on Fairview Valley (1970), Fifteenmile Valley (1971), and Lucerne Valley (1971) 7.5' quadrangles. Barstow (1934) 30' quadrangle has the singular form "Granite Mountain" for the name.

Granite Pass [RIVERSIDE]: *pass,* 27 miles north-northeast of Desert Center (lat. 34°03'50" N, long. 115°11'30" W; at SW cor. sec. 22, T 1 S, R 17 E); the pass is north of the northwest end of Granite Mountains. Named on Iron Mountains (1956) 15' quadrangle.

Granite Pass [SAN BERNARDINO]:

(1) *pass,* 29 miles north-northwest of Baker (lat. 35°25'30" N, long. 116°33' W); the pass is at the southeast end of Granite Mountains (1). Named on Avawatz Mountains (1933) 1° quadrangle.

(2) *pass,* 19 miles north-northeast of Amboy (lat. 34°48'45" N, long. 115°36'30" W; sec. 3, T 8 N, R 13 E). Named on Flynn (1956) 15' quadrangle.

Granite Peak: see **Granite Mountains** [SAN BERNARDINO] (2); **Granite Peaks** [SAN BERNARDINO].

Granite Peak Plateau: see **Granite Mountains** [SAN BERNARDINO] (2).

Granite Peaks [SAN BERNARDINO]: *peaks,* 6.5 miles south-southwest of Old Woman Springs (lat. 34°17'55" N, long. 116°44' W). Named on Rattlesnake Canyon (1972) 7.5' quadrangle. On Old Woman Springs (1955) 15' quadrangle, the name "Granite Peak" applies to one of present Granite Peaks. United States Board on Geographic Names (1975a, p. 10) gave the variant name "Granite Peak" for present Granite Peaks.

Granite Spring [SAN BERNARDINO]:

(1) *spring,* 5.5 miles east of Big Bear City (lat. 34°16'20" N, long. 116°45'05" W; at W line sec. 11, T 2 N, R 2 E). Named on Big Bear City (1971) 7.5' quadrangle.

(2) *spring,* 28 miles west of Ivanpah (lat. 36°19'05" N, long. 115° 48'55" W). Named on Halloran Spring (1956) 15' quadrangle.

Granite Spring: see **Pilot Knob** [SAN BERNARDINO].

Granite Spur [RIVERSIDE]: *locality,* 3.5 miles north-northwest of Perris along Atchison, Topeka and Santa Fe Railroad (lat. 33°50'05" N, long. 117°14'50" W; sec. 12, T 4 S, R 4 W). Named on Steel Peak (1967) 7.5' quadrangle.

Granite Tank [SAN BERNARDINO]: *spring,* 13 miles southeast of Essex (lat. 34°37'15" N, long. 115°03'25" W; on E line sec. 11, T 6 N, R 18 E). Named on Essex (1956) 15' quadrangle. Thompson (1929, p. 711) described the feature as "a depression about 10 feet long and 7 feet wide, hollowed in the granite bed of a stream channel."

Granite Well [RIVERSIDE]: *well,* 3 miles southwest of Desert Center (lat. 33°41' N, long. 115°26'15" W). Named on Chuckwalla Mountains (1963) 15' quadrangle, which indicates that the well is dry.

Granite Well [SAN BERNARDINO]: *well,* 19 miles south-southwest of Ivanpah (lat. 35°04'35" N, long. 115°25'50" W; near SE cor. sec. 36, T 12 N, R 14 E). Named on Mid Hills (1955) 15' quadrangle. Called Granite Wells on Kingman (1954) 1°x 2° quadrangle.

Granite Wells [SAN BERNARDINO]: *locality,* 26 miles south-southeast of Trona (lat. 35°23'50" N, long. 117°14'50" W; sec. 22, T 29 S, R 44 E); the place is 2.25 miles north-northwest of Granite Mountain. Named on Pilot Knob (1954) 15' quadrangle. Mendenhall (1909a, p. 53) listed a feature called Pilot Spring located between 3 and 4 miles southeast of Granite Wells.

Grant Springs: see **Harper Lake** [SAN BERNARDINO].

Grape [SAN BERNARDINO]: *locality,* 1.5 miles west of Fontana city hall along Atchison, Topeka and Santa Fe Railroad (lat. 34°05'50" N, long. 117°27'50" W; sec. 12, T 1 S, R 6 W). Named on Fontana (1967) 7.5' quadrangle. Called Grape Spur on Fontana (1943) 7.5' quadrangle, and called Grape Siding on San Bernardino (1954) 15' quadrangle.

Grape Canyon [RIVERSIDE]: *canyon,* drained by a stream that flows 2.5 miles to Whitewater River 11 miles northeast of Banning (lat. 34°01'45" N, long. 116°43' W; sec. 6, T 2 S, R 3 E). Named on Catclaw Flat (1972) 7.5' quadrangle.

Grapeland [SAN BERNARDINO]:

(1) *locality,* 7 miles northeast of Ontario city hall along Southern Pacific Railroad (lat. 34°07'30" N, long. 117°33'30" W; at E line sec. 36, T 1 N, R 7 W). Named on Cucamonga Peak (1966) 7.5' quadrangle. United States Geological Survey's (1941) map shows a place called Las Uvas situated less than 1 mile west of Grapeland along Pacific Electric Railroad.

(2) *locality,* 5.25 miles southwest of present Devore (lat. 34°09'20" N, long. 117°27'30" W). Named on San Bernardino (1901) 15' quadrangle. Postal authorities established Hesperides post office in 1888, changed the name to Grapeland in 1889; moved it 1 mile southwest in 1891, moved it 1.5 miles southwest in 1904, and discontinued it in 1905 (Salley, p. 88, 96).

Grape Siding [IMPERIAL]: *locality,* 4.25 miles south-southwest of Brawley along Southern Pacific Railroad (lat. 32°55'10" N, long. 115°32'50" W). Named on Brawley (1945) 15' quadrangle.

Grape Siding: see **Grape** [SAN BERNARDINO].

Grape Spur: see **Grape** [SAN BERNARDINO].

Grapevine: see **Barstow** [SAN BERNARDINO].

Grapevine Canyon [SAN BERNARDINO]:

(1) *canyon,* drained by a stream that flows 4.5 miles to lowlands 17 miles east-southeast of Victorville (lat. 34°24'35" N, long. 117° 02'45" W; sec. 25, T 4 N, R 2 W). Named on Butler Peak (1971) and Fifteenmile Valley (1971) 7.5' quadrangles.

(2) *canyon,* drained by a stream that flows nearly 2 miles to the canyon of Lytle Creek 3 miles west-southwest of Devore (lat. 34° 11'55" N, long. 117°26'45" W; sec. 6, T 1 N, R 5 W). Named on Devore (1966) 7.5' quadrangle.

Grapevine Creek [RIVERSIDE]: *stream,* flows 4.25 miles to Dead Indian Creek 4 miles south-southeast of Palm Desert (lat. 33°40'10" N, long. 116°25'15" W; near N line sec. 12, T 6 S, R 5 E). Named on Rancho Mirage (1957) 7.5' quadrangle.

Grapevine Creek [SAN BERNARDINO]: *stream,* flows 3.5 miles to a spot 7 miles northeast of Big Bear City (lat. 34°20'35" N, long. 116°46'20" W; near SW cor. sec. 16, T 3 N, R 2 E). Named on Big Bear City (1971) 7.5' quadrangle.

Grapevine Spring [SAN BERNARDINO]: *spring,* 4.5 miles west-southwest of Devore (lat. 34°12'05" N, long. 117°28'45" W; sec. 2, T 1 N, R 6 W); the spring is at the head of Grapevine Canyon (2). Named on Devore (1966) 7.5' quadrangle.

Grass Canyon [SAN BERNARDINO]: *canyon,* drained by a stream that flows 1.5 miles to Black Canyon Wash 21 miles south of Ivanpah (lat. 35°01'50" N, long. 115°21'15" W; sec. 15, T 11 N, R 15 E). Named on Mid Hills (1955) 15' quadrangle.

Grass Island [SAN BERNARDINO]: *island,* 1000 feet long, 24 miles north-northeast of Vidal in Lake Havasu (lat. 34°26'50" N, long. 114°20'15" W). Named on Lake Havasu City South (1970) 7.5' quadrangle.

Grass Valley [SAN BERNARDINO]:

(1) *valley,* 8 miles southwest of Luna Mountain (lat. 34°15'25" N, long. 117°13'05" W; sec. 17, T 2 N, R 3 W). Named on Lake Arrowhead (1971) 7.5' quadrangle.

(2) *valley,* 21 miles east-southeast of the village of Red Mountain (lat. 35°17' N, long. 117°15' W). Named on Cuddeback Lake (1954) and Pilot Knob (1954) 15' quadrangles.

Grass Valley Creek [SAN BERNARDINO]: *stream,* flows 9 miles to West Fork Mojave River 14 miles south of Victorville (lat. 34°20'20" N, long. 117°16'10" W; near N line sec. 23, T 3 N, R 4 W); the stream goes through Grass Valley (1). Named on Cedar Springs (1956), Harrison Mountain (1967), and Lake Arrowhead (1971) 7.5' quadrangles.

Grass Valley Lake [SAN BERNARDINO]: *lake,* 1550 feet long, 7.5 miles southwest of Luna Mountain (lat. 34°15'40" N, long. 117°13'05" W; sec. 17, T 2 N, R 3 W); the lake is in Grass Valley (1). Named on Lake Arrowhead (1971) 7.5' quadrangle.

Gravel Hills [SAN BERNARDINO]: *ridge,* west-northwest-trending, 12 miles long, 20 miles east-southeast of the village of Red Mountain (lat. 35°11'30" N, long. 117°21' W). Named on Fremont Peak (1956) 15' quadrangle.

Gravel Wash [IMPERIAL]: *stream,* flows 5.5 miles to Salton Sea 4.5 miles north of Truckhaven (lat. 33°21'45" N, long. 115°59' W; sec. 25, T 9 S, R 9 E). Named on Seventeen Palms (1956) and Truckhaven (1956) 7.5' quadrangles.

Grave Summit [SAN BERNARDINO]: *pass,* 26 miles northwest of Baker (lat. 35°29'30" N, long. 116°27' W). Named on Avawatz Mountains (1933) 1° quadrangle.

Grave Wash [IMPERIAL]: *stream,* heads in San Diego County and flows 9 miles in Imperial County to Salton Sea 3.5 miles north of Truckhaven (lat. 33°21' N, long. 115°57'40" W). Named on Seventeen Palms (1956) and Truckhaven (1956) 7.5' quadrangles.

Graveyard Hills: see **Lanfair Buttes**, under **Grotto Hills** [SAN BERNARDINO].

Gray: see **Garnet** [RIVERSIDE].

Grayback Peak: see **San Gorgonio Mountain** [SAN BERNARDINO].

Gray Mountain [SAN BERNARDINO]: *ridge,* north-northwest-trending, 1.5 miles long, 19 miles west-northwest of Victorville (lat. 34°37' N, long. 117°37'40" W). Named on Adobe Mountain (1955), El Mirage (1956), and Shadow Mountains SE (1955) 7.5' quadrangles.

Gray Mountain: see **El Mirage** [SAN BERNARDINO].

Grays Campsite [SAN BERNARDINO]: *locality,* 1.5 miles west of Fawnskin (lat. 34°16'25" N, long. 116°58'10" W; sec. 10, T 2 N, R 1 W); the place is less than 1 mile north of Grays Peak. Named on Fawnskin (1971) 7.5' quadrangle.

Grays Peak [SAN BERNARDINO]: *peak,* 1.5 miles west-southwest of Fawnskin (lat. 34°15'40" N, long. 116°58'10" W; sec. 15, T 2 N, R 1 W). Named on Fawnskin (1971) 7.5' quadrangle.

Grays Well [IMPERIAL]: *locality,* 9 miles south-southwest of Ogilby (lat. 32°42'35" N, long. 114°55'25" W; near SE cor. sec. 32, T 16 S, R 20 E). Site named on Grays Well (1964) 7.5' quadrangle. The name was for Newt Gray of Holtville, a pioneer road builder; a camp for workers on a plank road was at the place in 1915 (Gudde, 1949, p. 134).

Great Piute Wash: see **Piute Wash** [SAN BERNARDINO].

Greda [RIVERSIDE]: *locality,* 4.5 miles west of Corona along Atchison, Topeka and Santa Fe Railroad when the rail line was on the north side of Santa Ana River (lat. 33°53'05" N, long. 117°38'50" W). Named on Prado (1941) 7.5' quadrangle.

Green Canyon [RIVERSIDE]: *canyon,* drained by a stream that flows 2 miles to lowlands nearly 6 miles south of Hemet (lat. 33° 40' N, long. 116°56'45" W; near E line sec. 11, T 6 S, R 1 W). Named on Hemet (1953) 7.5' quadrangle.

Green Canyon [SAN BERNARDINO]:

(1) *canyon,* 2.25 miles long, 1.5 miles northeast of Sugarloaf Mountain (lat. 34°12'55" N, long. 116°47'45" W). Named on Moonridge (1970) 7.5' quadrangle.

(2) *canyon,* drained by a stream that flows 2.25 miles to Mill Creek Canyon 5 miles north-northeast of Yucaipa (lat. 34°06'10" N, long. 117°01'05" W; sec. 7, T 1 S, R 1 W). Named on Yucaipa (1967) 7.5' quadrangle.

Green Canyon Group Camp [SAN BERNARDINO]: *locality,* less than 2 miles north-northeast of Sugarloaf Mountain (lat. 34°13'25" N, long. 116°48'20" W; near SE cor. sec. 30, T 2 N, R 2 E). Named on Moonridge (1970) 7.5' quadrangle.

Greenlead Camp [SAN BERNARDINO]: *locality,* 3.5 miles north-northwest of Fawnskin (lat. 34°19'10" N, long. 116°58'45" W; at E line sec. 28, T 3 N, R 1 W). Named on Lucerne Valley (1947) 15' quadrangle.

Greenlead Creek [SAN BERNARDINO]: *stream,* flows 2.25 miles to Holcomb Creek nearly 3 miles northwest of Fawnskin (lat. 34°18'10" N, long. 116°58'35" W; near W line sec. 34, T 3 N, R 1 W). Named on Fawnskin (1971) 7.5' quadrangle.

Green Spot [SAN BERNARDINO]: *locality,* 1.5 miles north of Sugarloaf Peak (lat. 34°13'15" N, long. 116°48'45" W; at S line sec. 30, T 2 N, R 2 E); the place is west of Green Canyon (1). Named on San Gorgonio Mountain (1954) 15' quadrangle. Moonridge (1970) 7.5' quadrangle shows Green Spot picnic area near the site.

Greenspot: see **Redlands** [SAN BERNARDINO] (1).

Green Spring [SAN BERNARDINO]: *spring,* 1.5 miles east-northeast of Sugarloaf Mountain (lat. 34°12'40" N, long. 116°47'15" W; at E line sec. 32, T 2 N, R 2 E); the spring is in Green Canyon. Named on Moonridge (1970) 7.5' quadrangle.

Greens Well [SAN BERNARDINO]: *well,* 20 miles northwest of Ivanpah (lat. 35°33'25" N, long. 115°34' W; sec. 15, T 17 N, R 13 E). Named on Clark Mountain (1956) 15' quadrangle, which shows Greens mine near the well.

Green Valley [SAN BERNARDINO]: *valley,* 3.25 miles north-northwest of Keller Peak (lat. 34°14'35" N, long. 117°04' W; sec. 22, 23, T 2 N, R 2 W). Named on Redlands (1954) 15' quadrangle.

Green Valley: see **Little Green Valley** [SAN BERNARDINO].

Green Valley Campground [SAN BERNARDINO]: *locality,* 3.5 miles north-northwest of Keller Peak (lat. 34°14'40" N, long. 117° 03'45" W; sec. 23, T 2 N, R 2 W); the place is in Green Valley. Named on Keller Peak (1967) 7.5' quadrangle.

Green Valley Creek [SAN BERNARDINO]: *stream,* flows 3.5 miles to Deep Creek (1) 4.25 miles northwest of Keller Peak (lat. 34°13'55" N, long. 117°06'30" W; sec. 29, T 2 N, R 2 W); the stream heads at Green Valley. Named on Keller Peak (1967) 7.5' quadrangle.

Green Valley Lake [SAN BERNARDINO]:

(1) *lake,* 0.25 mile long, nearly 3.5 miles north-northwest of Keller Peak (lat. 34°14'15" N, long. 117°04'45" W; at S line sec. 22, T 2 N, R 2 W); the feature is along Green Valley Creek. Named on Keller Peak (1967) 7.5' quadrangle.

(2) *village,* 3.5 miles north-northwest of Keller Peak (lat. 34°14'25" N, long. 117°04'30" W; sec. 22, T 2 N, R 2 W); the place is at Green Valley Lake (1). Named on Keller Peak (1967) 7.5' quadrangle. Postal authorities established Green Valley Lake post office at a vacation resort in 1939 (Salley, p. 89).

Greenwade's: see **Weisel** [RIVERSIDE].

Greeson Wash [IMPERIAL]: *stream,* flows 7.25 miles to New River 10.5 miles west-northwest of Calexico (lat. 32°44'40" N, long. 115°39' W; sec. 20, T 16 S, R 13 E). Named on Heber (1957) and Mount Signal (1957) 7.5' quadrangles.

Gregory: see **Lake Gregory** [SAN BERNARDINO].

Grinnell Mountain [SAN BERNARDINO]: *peak,* 5 miles south of Sugarloaf Mountain (lat. 34°07'35" N, long. 116°48'30" W; near E line sec. 31, T 1 N, R 2 E). Altitude 10,284 feet. Named on Moonridge (1970) and San Gorgonio Mountain (1970) 7.5' quadrangles. United States Board on Geographic Names (1964b, p. 14) rejected the names "Fish Creek Mountain" and "Grinell Mountain" for the feature, and noted that the name "Grinnell" commemorates Joseph Grinnell, professor, author, and early conservationist.

Groaner Spring [SAN BERNARDINO]: *spring,* 14 miles west-northwest of Ivanpah (lat. 35°27'15" N, long. 115°31'20" W; near SE cor. sec. 24, T 16 N, R 13 E). Named on Mescal Range (1955) 15' quadrangle.

Grommet [SAN BERNARDINO]: *locality,* 11 miles west of Vidal along Atchison, Topeka and Santa Fe Railroad (lat. 34°06'10" N, long. 114°42' W; at E line sec. 7, T 1 S, R 22 E). Named on Vidal (1949) 15' quadrangle. The name commemorates a sub-contractor for construction of the railroad.(Hanna, p. 128).

Grotto: see **The Grotto** [RIVERSIDE].

Grotto Hills [SAN BERNARDINO]: *hills,* 13 miles south-southeast of Ivanpah (lat. 35°09'30" N, long. 115°12'30" W). Named on Lanfair Valley (1956) 15' quadrangle. United States Board on Geographic Names (1985, p. 3) approved the name "Lanfair Buttes" for a hill, altitude of 4360 feet, situated 3 miles east-southeast of Grotto Hills (lat. 35°09'08" N, long. 115°09'07" W; sec. 4, 9, T 12 N, R 17 E), and rejected the names "Eagle Hill," "Eagle Mountain," "Graveyard Hills," and "Indian Hill" for the feature.

Grout: see **Fawnskin** [SAN BERNARDINO].

Grout Bay [SAN BERNARDINO]: *embayment,* at Fawnskin along Big Bear Lake (1) (lat. 34°15'50" N, long. 116°56'30" W); the feature is at the mouth of Grout Creek. Named on Fawnskin (1971) 7.5' quadrangle.

Grout Creek [SAN BERNARDINO]: *stream,* flows 3.5 miles to Big Bear Lake (1) at Fawnskin (lat. 34°16' N, long. 116°56'45" W; near SE cor. sec. 11, T 2 N, R 1 W). Named on Fawnskin (1971) 7.5' quadrangle.

Gruendike Well [RIVERSIDE]: *well,* 6 miles east-northeast of Desert Center (lat. 33°44'40" N, long. 115°18'20" W). Named on Chuckwalla Mountains (1943) 15' quadrangle. Peter S. Gruendike had a homestead patented at the site in 1916 (Gunther, p. 212).

Guadalupe Creek [RIVERSIDE]: *stream,* flows 4 miles to Devil Canyon 9.5 miles south-southeast of Palm Desert (lat. 33°36' N, long. 116°18' W; near S line sec. 31, T 6 S, R 7 E). Named on Palm Desert (1959) 15' quadrangle.

Guasti [SAN BERNARDINO]: *locality,* 3.5 miles east of Ontario city hall along Southern Pacific Railroad (lat. 34°03'50" N, long. 117° 35'15" W; at S line sec. 23, T 1 S, R 7 W). Named on Guasti (1966) 7.5' quadrangle. Cucamonga (1903) 15' quadrangle has the designation "South Cucamonga Sta. (Zucker)" at the site. Postal authorities established Zucker post office 5 miles east of Ontario in 1887 and discontinued it in 1900; the name was for Fred Zucker, first postmaster (Salley, p. 246). The name of the railroad station called South Cucamonga was changed to Guasti when Italian Vineyard Company began operations at the place soon after 1900; the name "Guasti" was for Secondo Guasti, founder of the company (Gudde, 1949, p. 138). Postal authorities established Guasti post office in 1910 (Frickstad, p. 141). United States Geological Survey's (1941) map shows a place called Racimo located 1.25 miles west of Guasti along the railroad, and a place called Viento located 2.5 miles east of Guasti along the railroad. Postal authorities established Viento post office in 1903 and discontinued it in 1910 (Frickstad, p. 147).

Guenther's Murrieta Hot Springs: see **Murrieta Hot Springs** [RIVERSIDE].

Guerneys Mill [SAN BERNARDINO]: *locality,* 6.25 miles northwest of Harrison Mountain (lat. 34°14'15" N, long. 117°13'30" W; near SW cor. sec. 20, T 2 N, R 3 W). Named on Redlands (1901) 15' quadrangle.

Gulliday Well [RIVERSIDE]: *well,* 12.5 miles south-southeast of Desert Center (lat. 33°32'25" N, long. 115°21'05" W). Named on Chuckwalla Mountains (1963) 15' quadrangle.

Gunsight Pass [SAN BERNARDINO]: *pass,* 4.25 miles south of San Gorgonio Mountain (lat. 34°02'20" N, long. 116°49'45" W; sec. 36, T 1 S, R 1 E). Named on San Gorgonio Mountain (1970) 7.5' quadrangle.

Guthrie Canyon [RIVERSIDE]: *canyon,* 0.5 mile long, 6 miles south of Alberhill (lat. 33°38'30" N, long. 117°22'35" W; sec. 14, 23, T 6 S, R 5 W). Named on Alberhill (1954, photorevised 1988) 7.5' quadrangle. The name honors John D. Guthrie, a Forest Service employee who lost his life in a fire in 1959 (United States Board on Geographic Names, 1960c, p. 19).

Gypsum Canyon: see **Main Street Canyon** [RIVERSIDE]; **Tin Mine Canyon** [RIVERSIDE].

Gypsum Canyon Creek: see **Main Street Wash** [RIVERSIDE].

Gypsum Ridge [SAN BERNARDINO]: *ridge,* southeast-trending, 1 mile long, 14 miles northeast of Landers (lat. 34°23' N, long. 116° 10'45" W). Named on Deadman Lake NW (1955) 7.5' quadrangle.

Gypsum Well [RIVERSIDE]: *well,* 24 miles north-northwest of Blythe (lat. 33°54'40" N, long. 114°49'40" W; sec. 13, T 3 S, R 20 E). Site named on Midland (1952) 15' quadrangle. Called Gyp Well on Brown's (1920) map. Officials of United Gypsum Company had the well drilled in 1914 to get water for the company's camp situated 3 miles to the south (Brown, 1923, p. 260).

Gyp Well: see **Gypsum Well** [RIVERSIDE].

- H -

Haakers [RIVERSIDE]: *locality,* 18 miles north-northeast of Blythe along Colorado River (lat. 33°51'15" N, long. 114°31'55" W; sec. 2, T 4 S, R 23 E). Named on Big Maria Mountains SE (1955) 7.5' quadrangle.

Haan: see **Camp Haan** [RIVERSIDE].

Hackberry Mountain [SAN BERNARDINO]: *range,* 20 miles south-southeast of Ivanpah (lat. 35°02'45" N, long. 115°13' W). Named on Fenner (1956), Lanfair Valley (1956), and Mid Hills (1955) 15' quadrangles.

Hackberry Spring [SAN BERNARDINO]: *spring,* 20 miles south-southeast of Ivanpah (lat. 35°03'30" N, long. 115°12'50" W; sec. 1, T 11 N, R 16 E); the spring is at Hackberry Mountain. Named on Lanfair Valley (1956) 15' quadrangle.

Haerle City: see **Riverside Mountain** [RIVERSIDE].

Hagador Canyon [RIVERSIDE]: *canyon,* 3 miles long, opens into lowlands 3 miles southwest of Corona (lat. 33°50'30" N, long. 117° 35'50" W; sec. 10, T 4 S, R 7 W). Named on Corona South (1967) 7.5' quadrangle. Gunther (p. 217) associated the name with J.T. Hagadorn, who filed a water claim in the canyon in 1886.

Halfway Hill [SAN BERNARDINO]: *hill,* 11 miles north-northwest of Essex (lat. 34°52'20" N, long. 115°19'40" W; sec. 17, T 9 N, R 16 E). Altitude 2696 feet. Named on Colton Well (1956) 15' quadrangle.

Halfway Spring [RIVERSIDE]: *spring,* 10.5 miles east of Hemet (lat. 33°44'30" N, long. 116°47' W; near NW cor. sec. 16, T 5 S, R 2 E). Named on Hemet (1957) 15' quadrangle.

Hall Canyon [RIVERSIDE]: *canyon,* 1.5 miles long, 11 miles east of San Jacinto (lat. 33°48'50" N, long. 116°46'10" W). Named on Lake Fulmor (1956) 7.5' quadrangle. The name commemorates Colonel Milton Sanders Hall, who had a contract with Southern Pacific Railroad for grading, for railroad ties, and for wood to fuel locomotives (Gunther, p. 219-220).

Hall Canyon Public Camp: see **Trailfinders Camp** [RIVERSIDE].

Halleck: see **Oro Grande** [SAN BERNARDINO].

Hall Island [RIVERSIDE]: *island,* 1.5 miles long, 19 miles north-northeast of Blythe along Colorado River (lat. 33°52'15" N, long. 114°31' W). Named on Big Maria Mountains NE (1954) and Big Maria Mountains SE (1955) 7.5' quadrangles.

Halloran Spring [SAN BERNARDINO]: *spring,* 33 miles west of Ivanpah (lat. 35°23' N, long. 115°53'30" W; sec. 14, T 15 N, R 10 E). Named on Halloran Spring (1956) 15' quadrangle. On Kingman (1954) 1°x 2° quadrangle, the name "Halloran Springs" applies to a locality near the spring. The name commemorates F.J. Halloran, who owned *The Mining and Scientific Press* (Hanna, p. 132). Mendenhall (1909a, p. 56) listed a camp used by turquoise miners that was called Toltec and that was situated about 6 miles northeast of Halloran Springs at the south end of Shadow Mountains. California Mining Bureau's (1917a) map shows a feature called Elizabeth Spring located just east of Toltec.

Halloran Wash [SAN BERNARDINO]: *stream,* flows 7 miles to end 34 miles west of Ivanpah (lat. 35°22'35" N, long. 115°55' W; sec. 22, T 15 N, R 10 E); the stream goes past Halloran Spring. Named on Halloran Spring (1956) 15' quadrangle. On Ivanpah (1912) 1° quadrangle, present Bull Spring Wash is called Halloran Wash.

Hall's Siding: see **Cabazon** [RIVERSIDE].

Hamburger Mill [SAN BERNARDINO]: *locality,* 15 miles southeast of the village of Red Mountain (lat. 35°12'30" N, long. 117°24'55" W; near W line sec. 30, T 31 S, R 43 E). Site named on Fremont Peak (1956) 15' quadrangle.

Hamilton Creek [RIVERSIDE]: *stream,* flows 3.25 miles to Anza Valley 13 miles south-southeast of Idyllwild (lat. 33°33'50" N, long. 116°37'40" W; near W line sec. 13, T 7 S, R 3 E). Named on Idyllwild (1959) 15' quadrangle. The name commemorates James Hamilton, who settled at Anza Valley in the 1870's (Gunther, p. 222-223).

Hamilton Creek [SAN BERNARDINO]: *stream,* flows nearly 2 miles to Santa Ana River 4 miles south of downtown Big Bear Lake (lat. 34°11'10" N, long. 116°55'10" W; sec. 7, T 1 N, R 1 E). Named on Big Bear Lake (1970) 7.5' quadrangle.

Hamilton Plains: see **Anza Valley** [RIVERSIDE].

Hancock Redoubt: see **Soda Springs** [SAN BERNARDINO].

Hanksite: see **Westend** [SAN BERNARDINO].

Hanlon's Ferry: see **Pilot Knob** [IMPERIAL].

Hanna Flat [SAN BERNARDINO]: *area,* 2.25 miles west-northwest of Fawnskin (lat. 34°17'25" N, long. 116°58'45" W; on E line sec. 4, T 2 N, R 1 W). Named on Fawnskin (1971) 7.5' quadrangle.

Hanna Rocks [SAN BERNARDINO]: *relief feature,* 2.5 miles west of Fawnskin (lat. 34°16'20" N, long. 116°59'25" W; sec. 9, T 2 N, R 1 W); the feature is 1.25 miles south-southwest of Hanna Flat. Named on Fawnskin (1971) 7.5' quadrangle.

Hansen Well [RIVERSIDE]: *well,* 13 miles north-northeast of Indio (lat. 33°53' N, long. 116°06'50" W). Named on Pinyon Well (1943) 15' quadrangle.

Happy: see **Point Happy** [RIVERSIDE].

Hardrock Queen Spring [SAN BERNARDINO]: *spring,* 15 miles northwest of Ivanpah (lat. 35°27'20" N, long. 115°31'40" W; sec. 24, T 16 N, R 13 E). Named on Mescal Range (1955) 15' quadrangle. Ivanpah (1912) 1° quadrangle has the name "Mescal Spr." at or near the place. Gudde (1975, p. 213) noted that a mining camp called Nantan or Mescal was situated near Mescal Spring. Postal authorities established Nantan post office in 1887 and discontinued it in 1891—the name was from a silver mine (Salley, p. 149).

Harford Spring [RIVERSIDE]: *spring,* 4.5 miles northeast of Estelle Mountain (lat. 33°48'45" N, long. 117°21'30" W). Named on Steele Peak (1967, photorevised 1973) 7.5' quadrangle. Called Hartford Springs on Steele Peak (1953) 7.5' quadrangle, and called Hartford Spring on Steele Peak (1967) 7.5' quadrangle, but United States Board on Geographic Names (1978, p. 4) rejected the name "Hartford Spring" for the feature. Henry M. Harford, who came to Perris in 1900, was owner of the spring (Gunther, p. 224-225).

Harlan Canyon [RIVERSIDE]: *canyon,* 0.5 mile long, nearly 6 miles south of Alberhill (lat. 33°38'35" N, long. 117°22'55" W; mainly in sec. 15, T 6 S, R 5 W). Named on Alberhill (1954, photorevised 1988) 7.5' quadrangle. The name honors Nelson D. Harlan, a Forest Service employee who lost his life in a fire in 1959 (United States Board on Geographic Names, 1960c, p. 19).

Harlem Springs [SAN BERNARDINO]: *locality,* 5.5 miles north-northwest of Redlands city hall (lat. 34°07'15" N, long. 117°13'45" W). Named on Redlands (1967) 7.5' quadrangle. Postal authorities established Harlem Springs post office in 1949 and discontinued it in 1957 (Salley, p. 93). The promoters of a resort at the place named it for the Harlem School for Young Ladies in New York; the school was the alma mater of a neighboring property owner (Gudde, 1949, p. 142). United States Geological Survey's (1943) map shows a place called Warm Springs situated about 1 mile west of Harlem Springs.

Harmony Acres [SAN BERNARDINO]: *locality,* 3.25 miles west-northwest of Twentynine Palms (lat. 34°08'40" N, long. 116°06'30" W; sec. 26, T 1 N, R 8 E). Named on Twentynine Palms (1973) 7.5' quadrangle.

Harold F. Whittle Camp [SAN BERNARDINO]: *locality,* 1.5 miles northwest of Fawnskin (lat. 34°16'55" N, long. 116°57'50" W; near SE cor. sec. 3, T 2 N, R 1 W). Named on Fawnskin (1971) 7.5' quadrangle.

Harper Lake [SAN BERNARDINO]: *dry lake,* 6.5 miles long, 29 miles southeast of the village of Red Mountain (lat. 35°01'30" N, long. 117°17' W). Named on Fremont Peak (1956) and Opal Mountain (1955) 15' quadrangles. The name commemorates J.D. Harper, who lived at the edge of the dry lake (Gudde, 1949, p. 142-143). Mendenhall (1909a, p. 58) noted that a feature called Black's Well was located at the east end of Harper Lake. Opal Mountain (1955) 15' quadrangle shows Blacks ranch near the east end of the lake (lat. 35°01' N, long. 117°13'45" W; sec. 30, T 11 N, R 3 W). Mendenhall (1909a, p. 58) also listed Grant Springs, located 1.5 miles northwest of Black ranch.

Harpers Well [IMPERIAL]: *well,* 4 miles west-southwest of Kane Spring (lat. 33°05'45" N, long. 115°54'20" W; near W line sec. 26, T 12 S, R 10 E). Named on Harpers Well (1956) 7.5' quadrangle. Mendenhall (1909a, p. 85) gave the alternate name "Mesquite Well" for the feature, which was drilled in search of oil. The name "Harper" is for the man who drilled the unsuccessful oil well (Brown, 1923, p. 227). Anza and his party camped at the spot in 1774; Anza's Indian guide, Sebasitan Tarabal, is commemorated by the name "San Sebastian Marsh" for a nearby place at the junction of San Felipe Wash and Carrizo Creek (Leetch, p. 14).

Harrison Mountain [SAN BERNARDINO]: *peak*, 7.5 miles north of Redlands city hall (lat. 34°09'50" N, long. 117°09'30" W; at S line sec. 14, T 1 N, R 3 W). Altitude 4743 feet. Named on Harrison Mountain (1967) 7.5' quadrangle. Myron H. Crafts named the feature in the 1880's for President Benjamin Harrison (Hanna, p. 134).

Harry Spring [SAN BERNARDINO]: *spring*, 2.5 miles northwest of Fawnskin (lat. 34°17'35" N, long. 116°59' W; near N line sec. 4, T 2 N, R 1 W). Named on Fawnskin (1971) 7.5' quadrangle.

Hart [SAN BERNARDINO]: *locality*, 12 miles east-southeast of Ivanpah (lat. 35°17'15" N, long. 115°06'15" W; at N line sec. 24, T 14 N, R 17 E); the place is 4 miles south-southwest of Hart Peak. Site named on Crescent Peak (1956) 15' quadrangle. Postal authorities established Hart post office in 1908 and discontinued it in 1915 (Frickstad, p. 141).

Hartford Spring: see **Harford Spring** [RIVERSIDE].

Hart Peak [SAN BERNARDINO]: *peak*, 13 miles east of Ivanpah (lat. 35°20'30" N, long. 115°04'45" W; sec. 31, T 15 N, R 18 E). Altitude 5543 feet. Named on Crescent Peak (1956) 15' quadrangle. The name recalls James H. Hart, who was one of the discoverers of gold in Castle Mountains in 1907 (Linder, p. 134).

Harvard [SAN BERNARDINO]: *locality*, 9 miles north of Newberry along Union Pacific Railroad (lat. 34°57'10" N, long. 116°39'40" W; at SE cor. sec. 16, T 10 N, R 3 E). Named on Newberry (1955) 15' quadrangle. The place was known as Blythe as late as 1909 (Hanna, p. 134).

Harvard Hill [SAN BERNARDINO]: *hill*, 8 miles north of Newberry (lat. 34°56'15" N, long. 116°40'10" W; sec. 21, 28, T 10 N, R 3 E); the feature is 1 mile south-southwest of Harvard. Named on Newberry (1955) 15' quadrangle.

Harwood: see **Mount Harwood** [SAN BERNARDINO]; **Mount Harwood**, under **Thunder Mountain** [SAN BERNARDINO].

Hatchery Creek [SAN BERNARDINO]: *stream*, flows 0.5 mile to Mill Creek Canyon 6 miles west of San Gorgonio Mountain (lat. 34°05'30" N, long. 116°55'55" W; near SE cor. sec. 12, T 1 S, R 1 W). Named on Forest Falls (1970) 7.5' quadrangle. The name is from a fish hatchery that was located at the mouth of the stream (United States Board on Geographic Names, 1975b, p. 5). On San Gorgonio Mountain (1954) 15' quadrangle, present Oak Cove Creek is called Hatchery Creek

Hathaway Creek [RIVERSIDE]: *stream*, flows nearly 5 miles to San Gorgonio Pass 2 miles north-northeast of Banning (lat. 33°57'10" N, long. 116°51'35" W; near E line sec. 34, T 2 S, R 1 E). Named on Cabazon (1956) and San Gorgonio Mountain (1970) 7.5' quadrangles. The feature first mistakenly was called Hearst Creek for Andy Hurst, who had a bee ranch at the mouth of the canyon of the stream; Walter Scott Hathaway and his partners bought Hurst's property in the 1880's, and the canyon of the stream sometimes was called Scott Canyon (Gunther, p. 227). West Branch enters from the northwest 5 miles north of Banning; it is 1.5 miles long and is named on Forest Falls (1970) and San Gorgonio Mountain (1970) 7.5' quadrangles.

Hathaway Creek: see **Barton Creek** [SAN BERNARDINO].

Hathaway Flat [SAN BERNARDINO]: *area*, nearly 5 miles south of downtown Big Bear Lake (lat. 34°10'25" N, long. 116°53'45" W; mainly in sec. 17, T 1 N, R 1 E). Named on Big Bear Lake (1970) 7.5' quadrangle.

Haughtelin Lake [IMPERIAL]: *lake*, 2 miles southwest of Bard along a former course of Colorado River (lat. 32°46'20" N, long. 114° 35' W). Named on Bard (1965) 7.5' quadrangle.

Havasu: see **Havasu Lake** [SAN BERNARDINO]; **Lake Havasu** [SAN BERNARDINO].

Havasu Lake [SAN BERNARDINO]: *locality*, 25 miles north of Vidal (lat. 34°28'50" N, long. 114°24'45" W; sec. 36, T 5 N, R 24 E); the place is along Lake Havasu. Named on Havasu Lake (1970) 7.5' quadrangle. Postal authorities established Havasu post office in 1961 and changed the name to Havasu Lake in 1962 (Salley, p. 94).

Havasu Lake: see **Lake Havasu** [SAN BERNARDINO].

Havasu Palms [SAN BERNARDINO]: *locality*, 23 miles north-northeast of Vidal (lat. 34°23'55" N, long. 114°16'45" W); the place is along Lake Havasu. Named on Lake Havasu City South (1970) 7.5' quadrangle. Whipple Mountains (1950) 15' quadrangle has the name "Roads End Camp" at the site.

Havens Canyon: see **Mabey Canyon** [RIVERSIDE].

Haverstick Wells [SAN BERNARDINO]: *wells*, 36 miles north-northwest of Ivanpah in Mesquite Valley (lat. 35°47' N, long. 115° 40'45" W). Named on Ivanpah (1912) 1° quadrangle.

Hawes [SAN BERNARDINO]: *locality*, 19 miles west of Barstow along Atchison, Topeka and Santa Fe Railroad (lat. 34°56'20" N, long. 117°21'45" W; near SW cor. sec. 24, T 10 N, R 5 W). Named on Hawes (1956) 15' quadrangle. The name commemorates Dave Hawes, a popular railroad conductor (Hanna, p. 134).

Hawes Peak [SAN BERNARDINO]: *peak*, 5.25 miles southeast of Luna Mountain (lat. 34°17'55" N, long. 117°03'05" W; at E line sec. 35, T 3 N, R 2 W). Altitude 6751 feet. Named on Butler Peak (1971) 7.5' quadrangle. United States Board on Geographic Names (1966c, p. 4) rejected the name "Shay Mountains" for the feature.

Hawes Peak: see **Little Shay Mountain** [SAN BERNARDINO].

Hawley: see **Daggett** [SAN BERNARDINO].

Hayden [SAN BERNARDINO]: *locality*, 26 miles southwest of Ivanpah along Union Pacific Railroad (lat. 35°02'45" N, long. 115°36'30" W; near SE cor. sec. 8, T 11 N, R 13 E). Named on Kelso (1955) 15' quadrangle.

Hayden Well [IMPERIAL]: *well*, 16 miles east-northeast of Calipatria along Mammoth Wash (lat. 33°12'20" N, long. 115°15' W; on S line sec. 13, T 11 S, R 16 E). Named on Tortuga (1955) 7.5' quadrangle, which indicates that the well is dry.

Hayfield [RIVERSIDE]: *locality*, 6 miles northeast of Chiriaco Summit (lat. 33°42'20" N, long. 115°38'05" W); the place is just north of the west part of Hayfield Lake. Named on Hayfield (1963) 15' quadrangle.

Hayfield Lake [RIVERSIDE]: *dry lake*, 4.5 miles long, 7 miles east-northeast of Chiriaco Summit (lat. 33°41'15" N, long. 115°36'15" W). Named on Hayfield (1963) 15' quadrangle. Canyon Spring (1943) 15' quadrangle shows an intermittent lake called Hayfield Reservoir at the place. The name "Hayfield" is from grass that grows on the usually barren lake bed after water from heavy rains floods the place (Brown, 1923, p. 238-239).

Hayfield Reservoir: see **Hayfield Lake** [RIVERSIDE].

Hayfield Spring [RIVERSIDE]: *spring*, 8.5 miles northeast of Chiriaco Summit (lat. 33°43'45" N, long. 115°35'50" W); the spring is 3 miles northeast of Hayfield. Named on Hayfield (1963) 15' quadrangle.

Hayfield Summit Spring [RIVERSIDE]: *spring*, 10.5 miles east-northeast of Chiriaco Summit (lat. 33°43'05" N, long. 115°33'15" W); the spring is 5 miles east-northeast of Hayfield. Named on Hayfield (1963) 15' quadrangle.

Haynes: see **Bagdad** [SAN BERNARDINO].

Haystack Butte [SAN BERNARDINO]: *ridge*, east-trending, less than 1 mile long, 33 miles west of Barstow (lat. 34°51'55" N, long. 117°37'05" W; on N line sec. 21, T 9 N, R 7 W). Named on Red Buttes (1973) 7.5' quadrangle. San Bernardino (1958) 1°x 2° quadrangle has the form "Hay Stack Butte" for the name.

Haystack Mountain [RIVERSIDE]: *peak*, 5.5 miles west-southwest of Palm Desert (lat. 33°40'55" N, long. 116°27'35" W; near NE cor. sec. 4, T 6 S, R 5 E). Altitude 3808 feet. Named on Rancho Mirage (1957) 7.5' quadrangle.

Hazard Canyon: see **Indian Canyon** [RIVERSIDE].

Hazelwood: see **Holtville** [IMPERIAL].

Heaps Peak [SAN BERNARDINO]: *peak*, 5 miles north-northeast of Harrison Mountain (lat. 34°14'35" N, long. 117°08'25" W; near NE cor. sec. 25, T 2 N, R 3 W). Altitude 6421 feet. Named on Harrison Mountain (1967) 7.5' quadrangle. California Mining Bureau's (1917a) map shows a feature called Crafton Peak situated about 6 miles east of Heaps Peak.

Hearst Creek: see **Hathaway Creek** [RIVERSIDE].

Heart Bar Campground [SAN BERNARDINO]: *locality*, 3.25 miles south-southeast of Sugarloaf Mountain (lat. 34°09'30" N, long. 116°47'10" W; near W line sec. 21, T 1 N, R 2 E). Named on Moonridge (1970) 7.5' quadrangle.

Heart Bar Creek [SAN BERNARDINO]: *stream*, flows 2 miles to join Coon Creek and form Santa Ana River 4.25 miles southeast of Sugarloaf Mountain (lat. 34°09' N, long. 116°46'15" W; near SE cor. sec. 21, T 1 N, R 2 E). Named on Moonridge (1970) and Onyx Peak (1972) 7.5' quadrangles.

Heart Bar Peak [SAN BERNARDINO]: *peak*, nearly 4 miles southeast of Sugarloaf Mountain (lat. 34°09'50" N, long. 116°45'45" W; at S line sec. 15, T 1 N, R 2 E). Altitude 8332 feet. Named on Moonridge (1970) 7.5' quadrangle.

Heartbreak Ridge [SAN BERNARDINO]: *ridge*, east-trending, 3 miles long, 11.5 miles north-northwest of downtown Morongo Valley (lat. 34°12'55" N, long. 116°40'45" W). Named on Onyx Peak (1972) 7.5' quadrangle.

Heath Canyon [SAN BERNARDINO]: *canyon*, drained by a stream that flows 1 mile to Swarthout Valley 4.5 miles north-northeast of Mount San Antonio (lat. 34°21'05" N, long. 117°37'40" W; sec. 17, T 3 N, R 7 W). Named on Mount San Antonio (1955) and Telegraph Peak (1956) 7.5' quadrangles. The name recalls Harry Heath, who homesteaded at the place in 1886 (Robinson, J.W., 1983, p. 196).

Heber [IMPERIAL]: *town*, 4.5 miles north-northwest of Calexico (lat. 32°43'50" N, long. 115°31'40" W; sec. 28, T 16 S, R 14 E). Named on Heber (1957) 7.5' quadrangle. Postal authorities established Bradtmoore post office in 1903 and moved it 0.5 mile south in 1904, when they changed the name to Heber; the name "Bradtmoore" was coined from letters in the name Bradley T. Moore, founder of the community (Salley, p. 26). Officials of California Development Company founded Heber in 1903 and named it for A.H. Heber, president of the company (Gudde, 1949, p. 145). A townsite called Paringa, laid out east of present Heber in 1901 and 1902, was abandoned in 1903; George Chaffey named the place for Paringa, Australia, where he was involved in a reclamation project (Hanna, p. 136).

Hector [SAN BERNARDINO]: *locality*, 13 miles east of Newberry along Atchison, Topeka and Santa Fe Railroad (lat. 34°48'15" N, long. 116°27'15" W; near NE cor. sec. 9, T 8 N, R 5 E). Named on Cady Mountains (1955) 15' quadrangle.

Hedges [IMPERIAL]: *locality,* 4.25 miles north of Ogilby (lat. 32°52'45" N, long. 114°50' W; near NE cor. sec. 11, T 15 S, R 20 E). Site named on Ogilby (1963) 15' quadrangle, which shows Tumco mine near the place. Postal authorities established Hedges post office in 1894 and discontinued it in 1905 (Salley, p. 95). The name was for a track walker of Southern Pacific Railroad who discovered gold in the neighborhood; later the place had the name "Tumco" from letters in the name of The United Mines Company, which took over the property (West, p. 11).

Helen: see **Helendale** [SAN BERNARDINO].

Helendale [SAN BERNARDINO]: *village,* 20 miles southwest of Barstow (lat. 34°44'35" N, long. 117°19'20" W; sec. 32, T 8 N, R 4 W). Named on Helendale (1956) 7.5' quadrangle. Called Helen on Baker's (1911) map, and called Judson on California Mining Bureau's (1917a) map. Postal authorities established Judson post office in 1909 and changed the name to Helendale in 1918 (Salley, p. 108). The Atchison, Topeka and Santa Fe Railroad station at the site first was called Point of Rocks; the station name was changed in 1897 to Helen, for the daughter of A.G. Wells, vice-president of the railroad, and changed again in 1918 to Helendale (Gudde, 1949, p. 145). Thompson's (1921) map shows a place called Wild situated along the railroad 4.5 miles northeast of Helendale; Wild first was known as Cottonwood (Thompson, 1921, p. 268). Postal authorities established Wild post office in 1928 and discontinued it in 1931; the name was for A.G. Wild, who was trainmaster for Atchison, Topeka and Santa Fe Railroad (Salley, p. 240). Thompson's (1921) map also shows a feature called McNeal Spring located 7 miles east of Helendale.

Heliograph Hill: see **Telegraph Peak** [SAN BERNARDINO].

Hell [RIVERSIDE]: *locality,* 8 miles east of Desert Center (lat. 33°41'30" N, long. 115°16'20" W; at W line sec. 36, T 5 S, R 16 E). Named on Chuckwalla Mountains (1963) 15' quadrangle.

Heller Spring [RIVERSIDE]: *spring,* 16 miles south-southeast of Idyllwild (lat. 33°31'30" N, long. 116°36'30" W; sec. 31, T 7 S, R 4 E). Named on Idyllwild (1959) 15' quadrangle. The name recalls Albert E. Heller, who built a cabin at the place and killed himself when a posse cornered him there (Gunther, p. 228).

Hell For Sure Canyon [SAN BERNARDINO]: *canyon,* drained by a stream that flows 4.25 miles to Whitewater River 8.5 miles west of downtown Morongo Valley (lat. 34°03'25" N, long. 116°43'25" W; sec. 25, T 1 S, R 2 E). Named on Catclaw Flat (1972) and San Gorgonio Mountain (1970) 7.5' quadrangles.

Hells Kitchen [RIVERSIDE]: *area,* 11 miles east-southeast of Idyllwild (lat. 33°39'30" N, long. 116°33'40" W; at SW cor. sec. 10, T 6 S, R 4 E). Named on Idyllwild (1959) 15' quadrangle.

Hemet [RIVERSIDE]: *town,* 28 miles southeast of Riverside (lat. 33° 44'55" N, long. 116°58'05" W). Named on Hemet (1953) and San Jacinto (1953) 7.5' quadrangles. Postal authorities established Hemet post office in 1892 (Frickstad, p. 128), and the town incorporated in 1910.

Hemet Butte [RIVERSIDE]: *peak,* nearly 3 miles south of downtown Hemet (lat. 33°42'35" N, long. 116°57'30" W; sec. 26, T 5 S, R 1 W). Altitude 2311 feet. Named on Hemet (1953) 7.5' quadrangle. Called Hemet Peak on California Mining Bureau's (1917b) map.

Hemet Lake: see **Lake Hemet** [RIVERSIDE].

Hemet Peak: see **Hemet Butte** [RIVERSIDE].

Hemet Reservoir: see **Lake Hemet** [RIVERSIDE].

Hemlock Creek [SAN BERNARDINO]: *stream,* flows 4 miles to Santa Ana River nearly 4 miles south-southwest of Keller Peak (lat. 34°08'35" N, long. 117°04'05" W; at W line sec. 26, T 1 N, R 2 W). Named on Keller Peak (1967) 7.5' quadrangle. East Fork enters from the northeast 1.5 miles upstream from the mouth of the main stream; it is 2.25 miles long and is named on Keller Peak (1967) 7.5' quadrangle.

Hencks Meadow [SAN BERNARDINO]: *area,* 5 miles north of Harrison Mountain (lat. 34°14' N, long. 117°10' W; near NW cor. sec. 26, T 2 N, R 3 W). Named on Harrison Mountain (1967) 7.5' quadrangle.

Henderson Canyon [SAN BERNARDINO]: *canyon,* nearly 2 miles long, opens into lowlands 11 miles northeast of Ontario city hall (lat. 34°10'20" N, long. 117°30'35" W; sec. 16, T 1 N, R 6 W). Named on Cucamonga Peak (1966) 7.5' quadrangle.

Henry Spring [SAN BERNARDINO]: *spring,* 31 miles west of Ivanpah (lat. 35°18'55" N, long. 115°51'40" W). Named on Halloran Spring (1956) 15' quadrangle.

Henshaw [RIVERSIDE]: *locality,* 5 miles west-northwest of Riverside (lat. 34°00'05" N, long. 117°27'50" W; near N line sec. 13, T 2 S, R 6 W). Named on Fontana (1953) 7.5' quadrangle.

Herkey Creek [RIVERSIDE]: *stream,* flows 7 miles to Lake Hemet 5.5 miles south-southeast of Idyllwild (lat. 33°40'15" N, long. 116° 40'35" W). Named on Idyllwild (1959) 15' quadrangle, and on San Jacinto Peak (1981) 7.5' quadrangle. United States Board on Geographic Names (1983d, p. 5) rejected the form "Hurkey Creek" for the name, which commemorates a lumberman who died from injuries inflicted by a bear (Gunther, p. 245).

Herkey Creek Camp [RIVERSIDE]: *locality,* 5 miles south-southeast of Idyllwild (lat. 33°40'35" N, long. 116°40'45" W; sec. 4, T 6 S, R 3 E); the place is near the mouth of Herkey Creek. Named on Idyllwild (1959) 15' quadrangle.

Hermits Bench [RIVERSIDE]: *relief feature,* 10.5 miles east of Idyllwild in Palm Canyon (lat. 33°44'20" N, long. 116°32'10" W; sec. 14, T 5 S, R 4 E). Named on Idyllwild (1959) 15' quadrangle. Billy Pester lived as a hermit there in a shack of palm fronds (Gunther, p. 232).

Hesperia [SAN BERNARDINO]: *town,* 8 miles south of Victorville (lat. 34°25'30" N, long. 117°18' W). Named on Hesperia (1956) 7.5' quadrangle. Postal authorities established Hesperia post office in 1888 (Frickstad, p. 142).

Hesperides: see **Grapeland** [SAN BERNARDINO] (2).

Hewitt Town: see **San Jacinto** [RIVERSIDE].

Hexie Mountains [RIVERSIDE]: *range,* 20 miles northwest of Chiriaco Summit (lat. 33°52' N, long. 115°57' W). Named on Hexie Mountains (1963) and Lost Horse Mountain (1958) 15' quadrangles. The name is from Hexahedron mine, also called Hexie mine (Gunther, p. 232).

Hidalgo Mountain [SAN BERNARDINO]: *ridge,* north-northwest-trending, 5 miles long, 12 miles north-northeast of Landers (lat. 34°26' N, long. 116°18'30" W). Named on Hidalgo Mountain (1954) 7.5' quadrangle.

Hidden Falls [RIVERSIDE]: *waterfall,* 14 miles east-southeast of Idyllwild near the mouth of Oak Canyon (lat. 33°38'10" N, long. 116°30'30" W; near W line sec. 19, T 6 S, R 5 E). Named on Idyllwild (1959) 15' quadrangle.

Hidden Fork [RIVERSIDE]: *stream,* flows 2.25 miles to Tahquitz Creek 4.25 miles southwest of Palm Springs (lat. 33°47'40" N, long. 116°36'15" W; sec. 30, T 4 S, R 4 E); the stream heads near Hidden Lake. Named on Palm Springs (1957) and San Jacinto Peak (1981) 7.5' quadrangles.

Hidden Hill [SAN BERNARDINO]: *relief feature,* 20 miles north-northeast of Amboy (lat. 34°48'45" N, long. 115°33' W; at and near sec. 6, T 8 N, R 14 E). Named on Flynn (1956) 15' quadrangle.

Hidden Lake [RIVERSIDE]: *intermittent lake,* 350 feet long, nearly 2.5 miles east-southeast of San Jacinto Peak (lat. 33°48' N, long. 116°38'25" W; near N line sec. 26, T 4 S, R 3 E). Named on San Jacinto Peak (1981) 7.5' quadrangle.

Hidden Lake Divide [RIVERSIDE]: *pass,* 2.25 miles east-southeast of San Jacinto Peak (lat. 33°48' N, long. 116°38'30" W; near N line sec. 26, T 4 S, R 3 E); the place is 700 feet west of Hidden Lake. Named on San Jacinto Peak (1981) 7.5' quadrangle.

Hidden Pair Canyon [RIVERSIDE]: *canyon,* less than 1 mile long, opens into Deep Canyon (2) 7 miles south of Palm Desert (lat. 33° 37'15" N, long. 116°23'45" W; sec. 30, T 6 S, R 6 E). Named on Palm Desert (1959) 15' quadrangle.

Hidden Palms [RIVERSIDE]: *locality,* 8.5 miles east-northeast of Cathedral City (lat. 33°49'15" N, long. 116°18'05" W; at E line sec. 13, T 4 S, R 6 E). Named on Myoma (1958) 7.5' quadrangle.

Hidden River [SAN BERNARDINO]: *locality,* 3 miles north of Joshua Tree (lat. 34°10'45" N, long. 116°18'15" W). Named on Joshua Tree North (1972) 7.5' quadrangle.

Hidden Spring [RIVERSIDE]: *spring,* 4.5 miles north-northeast of Mortmar (lat. 33°35' N, long. 115°54'20" W; near NE cor. sec. 11, T 7 S, R 10 E). Named on Mortmar (1958) 7.5' quadrangle. The spring and a cluster of palm trees are hidden behind a barricade of rocks in a maze of ravines (Burns, p. 28).

Hidden Spring [SAN BERNARDINO]: *spring,* 25 miles east-southeast of Trona (lat. 35°39'20" N, long. 116°56'25" W). Named on Quail Mountains (1948) 15' quadrangle.

Hidden Spring: see **Cactus Spring** [SAN BERNARDINO].

Hidden Spring Canyon [RIVERSIDE]: *canyon,* drained by a stream that flows nearly 4 miles to lowlands 2.5 miles north of Mortmar (lat. 33°33'30" N, long. 115°56'25" W; sec. 16, T 7 S, R 10 E); Hidden Spring is in the canyon. Named on Mortmar (1958) 7.5' quadrangle.

Hidden Tank [RIVERSIDE]: *water feature,* 20 miles north-northeast of Indio (lat. 33°57'30" N, long. 116°01' W; near NW cor. sec. 35, T 2 S, R 9 E). Named on Lost Horse Mountain (1958) 15' quadrangle.

Hidden Valley [RIVERSIDE]:

(1) *valley,* 23 miles east-northeast of Garnet (lat. 34°01' N, long. 116°10'15" W; near NW cor. sec. 8, T 2 S, R 8 E). Named on Indian Cove (1972) 7.5' quadrangle. A wall of rocks screens the valley, which made the place an ideal hideout for rustlers (O'Neal, p. 132).

(2) *valley,* 2.25 miles south-southeast of Palm Desert (lat. 33°41'35" N, long. 116°21'30" W; near E line sec. 33, T 5 S, R 6 E). Named on La Quinta (1959) 7.5' quadrangle.

Hidden Valley Campground [RIVERSIDE]: *locality,* 23 miles east-northeast of Garnet (lat. 34°01' N, long. 116°09'45" W; near N line sec. 8, T 2 S, R 8 E); the place is 0.5 mile east of Hidden Valley (1). Named on Indian Cove (1972) 7.5' quadrangle.

High Creek [SAN BERNARDINO]: *stream,* flows 1.5 miles to Mill Creek Canyon 2 miles southwest of San Gorgonio Mountain (lat. 34°04'35" N, long. 116°51'20" W; at N line sec. 23, T 1 S, R 1 E). Named on San Gorgonio Mountain (1970) 7.5' quadrangle.

Highgrove [RIVERSIDE]: *town,* 3.5 miles northeast of Riverside (lat. 34°00'50" N, long. 117°19'50" W; sec. 7, 8, T 2 S, R 4 W). Named on San

Bernardino South (1967) 7.5' quadrangle. Called High Grove on San Bernardino (1901) 15' quadrangle. Postal authorities established East Riverside post office in 1888 and changed the name to Highgrove in 1897 (Frickstad, p. 128). A syndicate of investors from Iowa, including Samuel Merrill, an ex-governor of Iowa, bought a tract of land at the place and called it Riverside Heights; they laid out a town in 1886 and called it Merrill for the ex-governor, but railroad officials called their station there Citrus—eventually the community became East Riverside (Gunther, p. 235-236), and later Highgrove.

Highland [SAN BERNARDINO]: *town,* 3.5 miles southwest of Harrison Mountain (lat. 34°07'45" N, long. 117°12'30" W). Named on Harrison Mountain (1967) 7.5' quadrangle. United States Board on Geographic Names (1933, p. 365) rejected the form "Highlands" for the name. Postal authorities established Messina post office in 1887, changed the name to Highland in 1898, and moved it 0.5 mile north in 1899 (Salley, p. 97, 139). W.H. Randall, W.T. Noyes, and others applied the name "Highland" to the place in 1883 for its elevation (Hanna, p. 138).

Highland Home: see **Highland Springs** [RIVERSIDE].

Highland Junction [SAN BERNARDINO]: *locality,* nearly 2 miles north-northwest of present San Bernardino city hall along the railroad (lat. 34°07'40" N, long. 117°18'10" W). Named on Arrowhead (1941) 7.5' quadrangle.

Highland Reservoir: see **East Highland Reservoir** [SAN BERNARDINO].

Highlands: see **East Highlands** [SAN BERNARDINO]; **West Highlands** [SAN BERNARDINO].

Highland Springs [RIVERSIDE]: *locality,* 5 miles northwest of Banning near Smith Creek (lat. 33°58'10" N, long. 116°56'30" W; sec. 25, T 2 S, R 1 W). Named on Beaumont (1953) 7.5' quadrangle. Called Highland Springs Resort on Banning (1942) 15' quadrangle. Smith's Station, a stage stop named for Dr. Isaac William Smith, was at the site in the 1860's; a company bought the place in 1884 and built a hotel there called Highland Home—Fred Hirsch and William Hirsch bought the site in 1927 and renamed it Highland Springs Village (Gunther, p. 238, 497).

Highland Springs Village: see **Highland Springs** [RIVERSIDE].

Highline: see **Holtville** [IMPERIAL].

High Meadow Springs [SAN BERNARDINO]: *springs,* 2.5 miles northwest of San Gorgonio Mountain (lat. 34°07'25" N, long. 116° 52' W; sec. 34, T 1 N, R 1 E). Named on San Gorgonio Mountain (1970) 7.5' quadrangle.

Hinda [RIVERSIDE]: *locality,* 15 miles northeast of Perris along Southern Pacific Railroad (lat. 33°57'10" N, long. 117°03'30" W). Named on El Casco (1967) 7.5' quadrangle. Called Alexis on Elsinore (1901) 30' quadrangle.

Hinkley [SAN BERNARDINO]: *town,* 10 miles west-northwest of Barstow (lat. 34°56' N, long. 117°11'50" W; sec. 28, T 10 N, R 3 W). Named on Hinkley (1971) 7.5' quadrangle. Postal authorities established Hinkley post office in 1908; the name commemorates Hinkley Henderson (Salley, p. 98).

Hinkley Valley [SAN BERNARDINO]: *valley,* 7 miles west-northwest of Barstow (lat. 34°55'30" N, long. 117°09' W); Hinkley is at the west edge of the valley. Named on Barstow (1971) and Hinkley (1971) 7.5' quadrangles.

Hitchcock Spring [SAN BERNARDINO]: *spring,* 3 miles north of Fawnskin (lat. 34°18'45" N, long. 116°57'15" W; sec. 26, T 3 N, R 1 W). Named on Fawnskin (1971) 7.5' quadrangle.

Hitt [SAN BERNARDINO]: *locality,* 9 miles east-southeast of Ivanpah along Atchison, Tonopah and Santa Fe Railroad (lat. 35°18'30" N, long. 115°09'20" W). Named on Crescent Peak (1956) 15' quadrangle.

Hixon Flat [RIVERSIDE]: *area,* 9 miles southeast of Hemet (lat. 33° 39'40" N, long. 116°51'15" W; near W line sec. 11, T 6 S, R 1 E). Named on Hemet (1957) 15' quadrangle. The name recalls a homesteader of the early 1900's (Gunther, p. 238-239).

Hobgood: see **Niland** [IMPERIAL].

Hodge [SAN BERNARDINO]: *locality,* 11.5 miles west-southwest of Barstow along Atchison, Topeka and Santa Fe Railroad (lat. 34°48'55" N, long. 117°11'30" W; sec. 4, T 8 N, R 3 W). Named on Hodge (1971) 7.5' quadrangle. Called Paliser on California Mining Bureau's (1917a) map. The place was known as Cottonwood in the early days (Hanna, p. 139), and also as Point of Timbers (Gudde, 1975, p. 84). Postal authorities established Paliser post office in 1914, changed the name to Hodge in 1925, and discontinued it in 1941—the name "Paliser" was for a railroad official; the name "Hodge" is for Gilbert Hodge and Robert Hodge, who homesteaded at the place in 1913 (Salley, p. 98, 165).

Hogbacks [RIVERSIDE]: *ridge,* northeast-trending, 2 miles long, 4 miles northeast of Murrieta (lat. 33°35'15" N, long. 117°09'05" W). Named on Murrieta (1953) 7.5' quadrangle.

Hog Canyon: see **Wildwood Canyon** [SAN BERNARDINO].

Hog Lake [RIVERSIDE]: *lake,* 550 feet long, 8.5 miles south of Idyllwild (lat. 33°37' N, long. 116°42'30" W; near S line sec. 30, T 6 S, R 3 E). Named on Idyllwild (1959) 15' quadrangle.

Holcomb Creek [SAN BERNARDINO]: *stream,* flows 17 miles to Deep Creek (1) 4 miles south of Luna Mountain (lat. 34°17'15" N, long. 117°07'35" W; sec. 6, T 2 N, R 2 W); the stream goes through Holcomb Valley and Upper Holcomb Valley. Named on Butler Peak (1971) and Fawnskin (1971) 7.5' quadrangles. United States Board on Geographic Names (1949, p. 4) rejected the name "Deer Creek" for the stream.

Holcomb Creek: see **Wildhorse Creek** [SAN BERNARDINO].

Holcomb Valley [SAN BERNARDINO]: *valley,* 2.5 miles northeast of Fawnskin (lat. 34°18'05" N, long. 116°55'05" W; sec. 31, T 3 N, R 1 E). Named on Fawnskin (1971) 7.5' quadrangle, which shows Hitchcock ranch in the valley. The name "Holcomb" commemorates William Francis Holcomb, who made the first discovery of gold in the valley in 1860 (Hoover, Rensch, and Rensch, p. 326). The area around Hitchcock ranch was known as Lower Holcomb, and a mining camp called Clapboard Town was situated about 0.5 mile south of there (Gudde, 1975, p. 74, 200).

Holcomb Valley: see **Upper Holcomb Valley** [SAN BERNARDINO].

Hole-in-the-Wall [SAN BERNARDINO]: *relief feature,* 21 miles south-southwest of Ivanpah (lat. 35°02'40" N, long. 115°23'50" W; near SW cor. sec. 8, T 11 N, R 15 E). Named on Mid Hills (1955) 15' quadrangle.

Hole-in-the-Wall Spring: see **Morongo Valley** [SAN BERNARDINO] (2).

Hole Lake [RIVERSIDE]: *lake,* 3500 feet long, 5.5 miles west-southwest of Riverside city hall (lat. 33°57'15" N, long. 117°27'40" W). Named on Riverside West (1967) 7.5' quadrangle. The name is for W.J. Hole, who had the dam built that forms the reservoir (Gunther, p. 239).

Holton: see **Holtville** [IMPERIAL].

Holtville [IMPERIAL]: *town,* 10.5 miles east of El Centro (lat. 32°48'45" N, long. 115°22'45" W). Named on Holtville East (1957) and Holtville West (1956) 7.5' quadrangles. Postal authorities established Eastside post office in 1903; they moved it 3.5 miles south and changed the name to Holtville in 1904 (Salley, p. 64). The town incorporated in 1908. W.F. Holt, an organizer of irrigation in Imperial Valley, started the community in 1903 and first called it Holton (Gudde, 1949, p. 151). California Mining Bureau's (1917b) map shows a place called Highline located about 12 miles northeast of Holtville. Postal authorities established Highline post office in 1914, discontinued it in 1918, reestablished it in 1919, and discontinued it in 1920; the name was from Highline canal (Salley, p. 97). They established Hazelwood post office 10 miles southeast of Holtville in 1910 and discontinued it in 1912; the name was from Hazelwood drop, a gate in Highline canal (Salley, p. 95).

Home Gardens [RIVERSIDE]: *town,* 2.5 miles east of Corona (lat. 33°52'40" N, long. 117°31'05" W). Named on Corona North (1967) and Corona South (1967) 7.5' quadrangles. The promoter who subdivided the place in 1924 called it Riverside Valley Home Gardens; residents changed the name to Home Gardens in the early 1940's (Gunther, p. 240).

Homeland [RIVERSIDE]: *town,* 7 miles east-southeast of Perris (lat. 33°44'35" N, long. 117°06'30" W). Named on Winchester (1953) 7.5' quadrangle. Postal authorities established Homeland post office in 1949 (Frickstad, p. 128). The community began in 1925 (Gunther, p. 240).

Homer [SAN BERNARDINO]: *locality,* 10 miles west-northwest of Needles along Atchison, Topeka and Santa Fe Railroad (lat. 34°55'10" N, long. 114°56' W; at NE cor. sec. 36, T 10 N, R 19 E). Named on Bannock (1956) 15' quadrangle.

Homer Mountain [SAN BERNARDINO]: *range,* 30 miles southeast of Ivanpah (lat. 35°01'30" N, long. 114°55'30" W). Named on Homer Mountain (1956) 15' quadrangle.

Homer Wash [SAN BERNARDINO]: *stream* and *dry wash,* extends for 46 miles to Danby Lake 35 miles south-southeast of Essex (lat. 34°14'30" N, long. 115°06' W); the feature heads south of Homer. Named on Needles (1956) 1°x 2° quadrangle.

Homestead Valley [SAN BERNARDINO]: *valley,* at and near Landers. Named on Landers (1972) and Yucca Valley North (1972) 7.5' quadrangles.

Honeymoon Spring [SAN BERNARDINO]: *spring,* 9.5 miles south-southeast of Essex (lat. 34°36'45" N, long. 115°09'45" W; near NW cor. sec. 13, T 6 N, R 17 E). Named on Essex (1956) 15' quadrangle.

Honeymoon Wash [SAN BERNARDINO]: *stream,* flows 3.5 miles to end 6.5 miles south-southeast of Essex (lat. 34°39'15" N, long. 115°11' W; sec. 34, T 7 N, R 17 E); the stream heads near Honeymoon Spring. Named on Essex (1956) 15' quadrangle.

Hons Tanks [SAN BERNARDINO]: *water feature,* 20 miles northeast of present Vidal (lat. 34°17'20" N, long. 114°13' W). Named on Parker (1911) 30' quadrangle.

Hooks Creek [SAN BERNARDINO]: *stream,* flows 3 miles to Little Bear Creek 5 miles south of Luna Mountain (lat. 34°16'10" N, long. 117°08'15" W; at E line sec. 12, T 2 N, R 3 W). Named on Harrison Mountain (1967) and Lake Arrowhead (1971) 7.5' quadrangles.

Hoover Well [IMPERIAL]: *well,* 7.5 miles west of Plaster City in Painted Gorge (lat. 32°48'40" N, long. 115°59' W). Named on Plaster City (1944) 15' quadrangle.

Hopi Spring [SAN BERNARDINO]: *spring,* 4 miles east-southeast of Luna Mountain (lat. 34°19'45" N, long. 117°03'35" W; sec. 23, T 3 N, R 2 W). Named on Butler Peak (1971) 7.5' quadrangle.

Hopkins Well [RIVERSIDE]: *well,* 25 miles east-southeast of Desert Center (lat. 33°36'45" N, long. 114°59'45" W; at NE cor. sec. 33, T 6 S, R 19 E). Named on McCoy Spring (1952) 15' quadrangle. J.W. Hopkins drilled the well in 1911; the feature also was called Teague Well and San Dimas Well (Brown, 1923, p. 241).

Hop Patch Spring [RIVERSIDE]: *spring,* 9.5 miles southeast of Idyllwild (lat. 33°39'40" N, long. 116°35' W; near E line sec. 8, T 6 S, R 4 E). Named on Idyllwild (1959) 15' quadrangle.

Hopper Canyon [SAN BERNARDINO]: *canyon,* drained by a stream that flows nearly 1 mile to lowlands 1 mile north of Devore (lat. 34°13'40" N, long. 117°23'50" W). Named on Devore (1966) 7.5' quadrangle.

Horn Peak [SAN BERNARDINO]: *peak,* 18 miles west-northwest of Vidal (lat. 34°13'45" N, long. 114°48'20" W). Altitude 3866 feet. Named on Rice (1954) 15' quadrangle.

Horn Spring [SAN BERNARDINO]: *spring,* 17 miles west-northwest of Vidal (lat. 34°12'30" N, long. 114°47'15" W); the spring is nearly 2 miles southeast of Horn Peak. Named on Rice (1954) 15' quadrangle.

Horse Canyon [RIVERSIDE]: *canyon,* 6.5 miles long, opens into Coyote Canyon 20 miles south-southwest of Palm Desert (lat. 33° 28'15" N, long. 116°32'30" W; at S line sec. 14, T 8 S, R 4 E). Named on Bucksnort Mountain (1960) 7.5' quadrangle. On Idyllwild (1959) 15' quadrangle, the upper extension of the feature is called Garnet Queen Canyon, but United States Board on Geographic Names (1982b, p. 2) approved the name "Alkali Wash" for this upper extension, which joins Horse Canyon 7 miles east-southeast of Anza (lat. 33°31'21" N, long. 116°33'30" W; sec. 34, T 7 S, R 4 E).

Horse Canyon [SAN BERNARDINO]: *canyon,* drained by a stream that flows 4.5 miles to lowlands 9 miles north-northeast of Mount San Antonio (lat. 34°24'20" N, long. 117°34'40" W; sec. 26, T 4 N, R 7 W). Named on Phelan (1956) and Telegraph Peak (1956) 7.5' quadrangles.

Horse Creek [RIVERSIDE]: *stream,* flows 4.25 miles to Bautista Creek 12 miles southeast of Hemet (lat. 33°38'40" N, long. 116°48'35" W; near SE cor. sec. 18, T 6 S, R 2 E). Named on Hemet (1957) and Idyllwild (1959) 15' quadrangles.

Horse Creek Ridge [RIVERSIDE]: *ridge,* generally northwest-trending, 6.25 miles long, 6 miles south-southwest of Idyllwild (lat. 33°39'25" N, long. 116°45' W); Horse Creek heads at the ridge. Named on Hemet (1957) and Idyllwild (1959) 15' quadrangles. United States Board on Geographic Names (1983b, p. 2) approved the name "Rouse Ridge" for the feature, and rejected the names "Horse Creek Ridge" and "Spotted Ridge" for it.

Horse Hills [SAN BERNARDINO]: *range,* 20 miles north-northeast of Amboy (lat. 34°49'10" N, long. 115°35'30" W; around SW cor. sec. 35, T 9 N, R 13 E). Named on Flynn (1956) 15' quadrangle.

Horse Island [RIVERSIDE]: *island,* less than 1 mile long, 18 miles north-northeast of Blythe in Colorado River (lat. 33°51'40" N, long. 114°30'50" W). Named on Big Maria Mountains SE (1955) 7.5' quadrangle.

Horse Meadows [SAN BERNARDINO]: *area,* 4.25 miles southwest of Sugarloaf Mountain (lat. 34°09'10" N, long. 116°51'45" W; near SE cor. sec. 22, T 1 N, R 1 E). Named on Moonridge (1970) 7.5' quadrangle.

Horse Potrero Canyon [RIVERSIDE]: *canyon,* drained by a stream that flows 2 miles to Palm Canyon 13 miles east-southeast of Idyllwild (lat. 33°40'10" N, long. 116°30'50" W; near NE cor. sec. 12, T 6 S, R 4 E). Named on Idyllwild (1959) 15' quadrangle, and on Rancho Mirage (1957) 7.5' quadrangle. United States Board on Geographic Names (1983c, p. 6) approved the name "Potrero Canyon" for the feature, which heads at Potrero Spring.

Horseshoe Lake [RIVERSIDE]: *lake,* 850 feet long, 6 miles west of Riverside city hall (lat. 33°58'10" N, long. 117°28'35" W; sec. 26, T 2 S, R 6 W). Named on Riverside West (1967) 7.5' quadrangle.

Horse Spring [SAN BERNARDINO]:

(1) *spring,* 12.5 miles east of Victorville (lat. 34°31'15" N, long. 117°04'45" W; sec. 15, T 5 N, R 2 W). Named on Fairview Valley (1970) 7.5' quadrangle.

(2) *spring,* 3.25 miles east of Luna Mountain (lat. 34°21'10" N, long. 117°04'20" W; at N line sec. 15, T 3 N, R 2 W). Named on Lake Arrowhead (1956) 15' quadrangle.

Horse Spring: see **Horsethief Springs** [SAN BERNARDINO].

Horse Spring Campground [SAN BERNARDINO]: *locality,* 3.5 miles east of Luna Mountain (lat. 34°21'05" N, long. 117°04'10" W; near NE cor. sec. 15, T 3 N, R 2 W); Horse Spring (2) is near the place. Named on Butler Peak (1971) 7.5' quadrangle. Lake Arrowhead (1956) 15' quadrangle has the form "Horse Spring Camp" for the name.

Horsethief Canyon [RIVERSIDE]: *canyon,* 3 miles long, opens into lowlands 2 miles west of Alberhill (lat. 33°43'20" N, long. 117°26'15" W; sec. 19, T 5 S, R 5 W). Named on Alberhill (1954) 7.5' quadrangle. The feature also was called Pine Creek Canyon, Indian Canyon, and Peter Wall Canyon—the last name for Peter Wall, a prominent Elsinore druggist who moved to the place in 1884 and took up farming there (Gunther, p. 244, 387).

Horsethief Canyon [SAN BERNARDINO]: *canyon,* 5.5 miles long, forms part of Summit Valley, and opens into the wide part of Summit Valley 16 miles south of Victorville (lat. 34°18'35" N, long. 117°20' W; near NE cor. sec. 31, T 3 N, R 4 W). Named on Cajon (1956) and Cedar Springs (1956) 7.5' quadrangles. The name recalls horsethieves who in the early days pastured their stolen animals in the neighborhood before taking them across the desert (Hoover, Rensch, and Rensch, p. 319).

Horsethief Canyon: see **Indian Canyon** [RIVERSIDE]; **Little Horsethief Canyon** [SAN BERNARDINO].

Horsethief Creek [RIVERSIDE]: *stream,* flows 4.5 miles to Deep Canyon (2) 10 miles south-southwest of Palm Desert (lat. 33° 35' N, long. 116°25'15" W; sec. 12, T 7 S, R 5 E). Named on Palm Desert (1959) 15' quadrangle.

Horsethief Flat [SAN BERNARDINO]: *area,* 6 miles northeast of Big Bear City (lat. 34°19'05" N, long. 116°46'05" W). Named on Big Bear City (1971) 7.5' quadrangle.

Horse Thief Springs [SAN BERNARDINO]: *springs,* 44 miles northwest of Ivanpah at Tecopa Pass (lat. 35°46'20" N, long. 115°53'15" W). Named on the Horse Thief Springs (1956) 15' quadrangle. Called Horse Spring on Ivanpah (1912) 1° quadrangle.

Hotel Glen Ivy: see **Glen Ivy Hot Springs** [RIVERSIDE].

Hot Mineral Spa [IMPERIAL]: *water feature,* 5 miles north-northwest of Frink (lat. 33°25'35" N, long. 115°41'10" W; near N line sec. 2, T 9 S, R 12 E). Named on Frink NW (1956) 7.5' quadrangle. Berkstresser (1969, p. 9) gave the alternate names "Hot Mineral Spring" and "Hot Mineral Well" for the feature.

Hot Mineral Spring: see **Hot Mineral Spa** [IMPERIAL].

Hot Mineral Well: see **Hot Mineral Spa** [IMPERIAL].

Hot Springs Canyon: see **Waterman Canyon** [SAN BERNARDINO].

Hot Sulphur Springs: see **Murrieta Hot Springs** [RIVERSIDE].

Houston Creek [SAN BERNARDINO]: *stream,* flows 2.25 miles to East Fork of North Fork Mojave River 18 miles south of Victorville (lat. 34°16'15" N, long. 117°16'45" W; near E line sec. 10, T 2 N, R 4 W). Named on Cedar Springs (1956) and San Bernardino North (1967) 7.5' quadrangles.

Hovley [IMPERIAL]: *locality,* 8.5 miles south of Calipatria along Southern Pacific Railroad (lat. 33°00'10" N, long. 115°31'15" W; on W line sec. 22, T 13 S, R 14 E). Named on Westmorland (1956) 7.5' quadrangle.

Howe Spring [SAN BERNARDINO]: *spring,* 8.5 miles south-southwest of Ivanpah (lat. 35°13'20" N, long. 115°22'20" W; sec. 9, T 13 N, R 15 E). Named on Mid Hills (1955) 15' quadrangle.

Hugo [RIVERSIDE]: *locality,* 5 miles north-northwest of Palm Springs along Southern Pacific Railroad (lat. 33°54'05" N, long. 116°35'30" W; near N line sec. 20, T 3 S, R 4 E). Named on Palm Springs (1957) 15' quadrangle.

Humabba Canyon: see **Reche Canyon** [RIVERSIDE-SAN BERNARDINO].

Humbug Mountain [SAN BERNARDINO]: *hill,* 33 miles south of Amboy (lat. 34°04'15" N, long. 115°47'30" W). Named on Valley Mountain (1956) 15' quadrangle.

Hummingbird Spring [SAN BERNARDINO]: *spring,* 5.5 miles west-northwest of Essex (lat. 34°45'15" N, long. 115°20'35" W; sec. 30, T 8 N, R 16 E). Named on Colton Well (1956) 15' quadrangle.

Hundred Palms: see **Thousand Palms Oasis** [RIVERSIDE].

Hungry Hollow [RIVERSIDE]: *relief feature,* 8.5 miles northeast of San Jacinto (lat. 33°50'50" N, long. 116°50'15" W; near W line sec. 1, T 4 S, R 1 E). Named on Lake Fulmor (1956) 7.5' quadrangle.

Hunsaker Flat [SAN BERNARDINO]: *area,* 3.5 miles west-northwest of Keller Peak at present Running Springs (lat. 34°12'20" N, long. 117°06'45" W; on S line sec. 32, T 2 N, R 2 W). Named on Redlands (1901) 15' quadrangle.

Hunters Spring [RIVERSIDE]: *spring,* 5.5 miles east-northeast of Salton (lat. 33°29'20" N, long. 115°47'30" W; sec. 12, T 8 S, R 11 E). Named on Durmid (1956) 7.5' quadrangle.

Huntington: see **Victorville** [SAN BERNARDINO].

Hurkey Creek: see **Herkey Creek** [RIVERSIDE].

Hurley Flat [RIVERSIDE]: *area,* 6.5 miles east-southeast of Banning (lat. 33°52'30" N, long. 116°46'35" W; sec. 28, T 3 S, R 2 E). Named on Cabazon (1956) and Lake Fulmor (1956) 7.5' quadrangles.

Huston Flat [SAN BERNARDINO]: *area,* 9.5 miles north of present San Bernardino city hall (lat. 34°14'20" N, long. 117°16'40" W). Named on San Bernardino (1942) 15' quadrangle. The place was known as James' Flat or Knapp's Flat in the 1850's (Beattie and Beattie, p. 220). The name "James' Flat" was for Jonathan M. James, lumber mill manager at the place (La Fuze, v. I, p. 50).

Hutt [SAN BERNARDINO]: *locality,* 3 miles west-northwest of Barstow along Atchison, Topeka and Santa Fe Railroad (lat. 34°54'25" N, long. 117°04'25" W; near S line sec. 34, T 10 N, R 2 W). Named on Barstow (1971) 7.5' quadrangle.

Hypolitan: see **Colton** [SAN BERNARDINO].

Hyten Spring [SAN BERNARDINO]: *spring,* 14 miles north-northeast of Ludlow (lat. 34°55'10" N, long. 116°03'20" W; sec. 32, T 10 N, R 9 E). Named on Broadwell Lake (1955) 15' quadrangle. Called Hytens Spring on Thompson's (1921) map.

Hytens Well [SAN BERNARDINO]: *well,* 37 miles west of Ivanpah (lat. 35°24' N, long. 115°56'40" W; sec. 8, T 15 N, R 10 E). Named on Halloran Spring (1956) 15' quadrangle.

- I -

Iberia Wash [IMPERIAL]: *stream,* flows nearly 4 miles to Salton Sea 3.5 miles east of Truckhaven (lat. 33°18' N, long. 115°55' W; sec. 15, T 10 S, R 10 E). Named on Truckhaven (1956) 7.5' quadrangle.

Ibex: see **Ibis** [SAN BERNARDINO].

Ibex Dunes [SAN BERNARDINO]: *relief feature,* 34 miles north-northwest of Baker (lat. 35°41'45" N, long. 116°22' W). Named on Avawatz Pass (1948) 15' quadrangle.

Ibex Hills [SAN BERNARDINO]: *range,* 43 miles north-northwest of Baker on San Bernardino-Inyo County line (lat. 35°49'30" N, long. 116°24'15" W). Named on Avawatz Pass (1948) and Shoshone (1951) 15' quadrangles. Irelan (p. 502) used the name "Tom Walters Mountains" for the range. Mendenhall (1909a, p. 47) used the name "Black Mountains" for present Ibex Hills near Saratoga Spring. Thompson (1929, p. 587) called the range Black Mountain. According to Palmer (p. 37), the name "Ibex" is from mountain sheep locally known as ibex, but according to Lingenfelter (1986, p. 144), the name is from Ibex Mining Company of Chicago, which operated in the neighborhood in the 1880's.

Ibex Pass [SAN BERNARDINO]: *pass,* 39 miles north-northwest of Baker on San Bernardino-Inyo County line (lat. 35°47'40" N, long. 116°20'10" W). Named on Shoshone (1951) 15' quadrangle.

Ibex Pass: see **Old Ibex Pass** [SAN BERNARDINO].

Ibex Spring [SAN BERNARDINO]: *spring,* 40 miles north-northwest of Baker (lat. 35°46'20" N, long. 116°24'35" W). Named on Shoshone (1951) 15' quadrangle.

Ibis [SAN BERNARDINO]: *locality,* 12.5 miles west-northwest of Needles (lat. 34°56'30" N, long. 114°47'30" W; sec. 21, T 10 N, R 21 E). Named on Bannock (1956) 15' quadrangle. Postal authorities established Ibis post office in 1904 and discontinued it in 1908 (Frickstad, p. 142). Officials of Atchison, Topeka and Santa Fe Railroad named the place Ibex in 1896, but changed the name to Ibis in 1904—Ibis mine was in the neighborhood (Gudde, 1949, p. 158). California Mining Bureau's (1917a) map has the name "King Sp." for a feature located about halfway between Ibis and Klinefelter.

Icehouse Canyon [SAN BERNARDINO]: *canyon,* drained by a stream that flows nearly 2 miles to San Antonio Canyon 13 miles north of Ontario city hall (lat. 34°14'55" N, long. 117°38'20" W; near N line sec. 20, T 2 N, R 7 W). Named on Cucamonga Peak (1966) and Mount Baldy (1967) 7.5' quadrangles. An enterprise in the canyon supplied ice to Los Angeles as early as the late 1850's (Robinson, J.W., 1983, p. 132-133).

Icehouse Saddle [SAN BERNARDINO]: *pass,* 12.5 miles north-northeast of Ontario city hall (lat. 34°14'20" N, long. 117°35'35" W; near SE cor. sec. 22, T 2 N, R 7 W); the pass is at the head of Icehouse Canyon. Named on Cucamonga Peak (1966) 7.5' quadrangle.

Idlewild [SAN BERNARDINO]: *locality,* 3.5 miles west of Redlands along Southern Pacific Railroad (lat. 34°03'35" N, long. 117°14'40" W). Named on Redlands (1901) 15' quadrangle.

Idlewild: see **Idyllwild** [RIVERSIDE].

Idyllwild [RIVERSIDE]: *town,* 14 miles east of Hemet (lat. 33°44'30" N, long. 116°43' W). Named on Idyllwild (1959) 15' quadrangle, and on San Jacinto Peak (1981) 7.5' quadrangle. Postal authorities established Idlewild post office at a lumber camp in 1900 and discontinued it in 1901; they established Idyllwild post office at a vacation resort in 1901, discontinued it in 1912, and reestablished it in 1913 (Salley, p. 102, 103). The place was known as Strawberry Valley soon after he first settlers arrived in 1865 (Hanna, p. 147).

Ike's Peak: see **Eisenhower Mountain** [RIVERSIDE].

Imperial [IMPERIAL]: *town,* nearly 4 miles north of El Centro (lat. 32°50'50" N, long. 115°34'10" W; on E line sec. 13, T 15 S, R 13 E). Named on El Centro (1957) 7.5' quadrangle. Postal authorities established Imperial post office in 1901 (Frickstad, p. 48), and the town incorporated in 1904. George Chaffey named the community (Hanna, p. 148). United States Geological Survey's (1908) map shows a place called Keystone situated 5 miles north-northeast of Imperial along Southern Pacific Railroad. The same map shows a feature called Mesquite Lake located 5 miles north-northeast of Imperial; the lake is nearly 3 miles long. Postal authorities established Barnes post office, named for Peter Barnes, first postmaster, 15 miles southeast of Imperial in 1901 and discontinued it in 1903; they established Laparra post office 8 miles northwest of Imperial in 1908 and discontinued it in 1911 (Salley, p. 15, 117).

Imperial Dunes: see **Sand Hills** [IMPERIAL].

Imperial Gables [IMPERIAL]: *locality,* 12.5 miles northeast of Glamis (lat. 33°07'35" N, long. 114°55'35" W; sec. 13, T 12 S, R 19 E). Named on Quartz Peak (1953) 15' quadrangle.

Imperial Junction: see **Niland** [IMPERIAL].

Imperial Reservoir [IMPERIAL]: *lake,* behind a dam 13 miles east-southeast of Picacho Peak on Colorado River (lat. 33°53' N, long. 114°27'45" W). Named on Imperial Reservoir (1955) 7.5' quadrangle

Imperial Sand Dunes: see **Sand Hills** [IMPERIAL].

Imperial Valley [IMPERIAL]: *valley,* extends from the south end of Salton Sea to Mexico. Named on El Centro (1958) 1°x 2° quadrangle. George Chaffey, who was chiefly responsible for construction of canals and ditches for irrigation of the valley, named the place (Hoover, Rensch, and Rensch, p. 110).

Inca [RIVERSIDE]: *locality,* 16 miles northwest of Blythe along Atchison, Topeka and Santa Fe Railroad (lat. 33°48' N, long. 114° 46' W; sec. 27, T 4 S, R 21 E). Named on Midland (1952) 15' quadrangle.

Incline: see **Crestline** [SAN BERNARDINO].

Inconsistent River: see **Mojave River** [SAN BERNARDINO].

Independence: see **Camp Independence**, under **Pilot Knob** [IMPERIAL].

Indian Canyon [RIVERSIDE]: *canyon,* 4.5 miles long, opens into Temescal Valley 3 miles west-northwest of Alberhill (lat. 33°44'30" N, long. 117°26'45" W; at N line sec. 18, T 5 S, R 5 W). Named on Alberhill (1954) 7.5' quadrangle. The feature was known by several names: Anderson Canyon, for Isaiah Anderson and George Anderson, who kept bees there; McCarthy Canyon, for Edward McCarthy, who filed a water claim there in 1885; Hazard Canyon, for F.M. Hazard, who filed a water claim there in 1889; Horsethief Canyon; and Peter Wall Canyon (Gunther, p. 247-248).

Indian Canyon: see **Horsethief Canyon** [RIVERSIDE].

Indian Cove [SAN BERNARDINO]: *valley,* 6 miles west-southwest of Twentynine Palms (lat. 34°06'30" N, long. 116°09' W). Named on Indian Cove (1972) 7.5' quadrangle.

Indian Cove Campground [SAN BERNARDINO]: *locality,* 6.5 miles west-southwest of Twentynine Palms (lat. 34°05'35" N, long. 116° 09'30" W); the place is at the edge of Indian Cove. Named on Indian Cove (1972) 7.5' quadrangle.

Indian Creek [RIVERSIDE]: *stream,* flows 9 miles to San Jacinto River 4.5 miles east-southeast of San Jacinto (lat. 32°45'45" N, long. 116°53' W); the stream passes 1 mile northeast of Indian Mountain. Named on Lake Fulmor (1956) and San Jacinto (1953) 7.5' quadrangles.

Indian Creek [SAN BERNARDINO]: *stream,* flows 8 miles to Willow Wash 34 miles west-southwest of Ivanpah (lat. 35°13'55" N, long. 115°54'20" W; sec. 10, T 13 N, R 10 E). Named on Old Dad Mountain (1956) 15' quadrangle.

Indian Hill: see **Lanfair Buttes**, under **Grotto Hills** [SAN BERNARDINO].

Indian Mountain [RIVERSIDE]: *ridge,* west-southwest-trending, 1.5 miles long, 10 miles east of San Jacinto (lat. 33°46'45" N, long. 116°47'25" W; sec. 32, 33, T 4 S, R 2 E). Named on Lake Fulmor (1956) 7.5' quadrangle.

Indian Pass [IMPERIAL]: *pass,* 17 miles east of Glamis (lat. 33°01'10" N, long. 114°46'25" W). Named on Quartz Peak (1953) 15' quadrangle.

Indian Potrero [RIVERSIDE]: *area,* 11.5 miles east-southeast of Idyllwild in Palm Canyon (lat. 33°41'55" N, long. 116°31'35" W; mainly in sec. 25, 36, T 5 S, R 4 E). Named on Idyllwild (1959) 15' quadrangle.

Indian Spring [RIVERSIDE]: *spring,* 9.5 miles east of Idyllwild (lat. 33°43'15" N, long. 116°33'30" W; sec. 22, T 5 S, R 4 E). Named on Idyllwild (1959) 7.5' quadrangle.

Indian Spring [SAN BERNARDINO]:

(1) *spring,* 34 miles south-southeast of Trona (lat. 35°21'25" N, long. 117°02'45" W). Named on Pilot Knob (1954) 15' quadrangle.

(2) *spring,* 10 miles east-northeast of Ivanpah (lat. 35°22'30" N, long. 115°08'45" W; at SE cor. sec. 16, T 15 N, R 17 E). Named on the Crescent Peak (1956) 15' quadrangle.

(3) *spring,* 30 miles west-southwest of Ivanpah (lat. 35°13'55" N, long. 115°49'10" W; near N line sec. 9, T 13 N, R 11 E); the spring is along Indian Creek. Named on Old Dad Mountain (1956) 15' quadrangle.

Indian Well [IMPERIAL]: *well,* 28 miles northeast of Calipatria (lat. 33°25'25" N, long. 115°11' W; sec. 3, T 9 S, R 17 E). Named on Chuckwalla Spring (1953) 15' quadrangle.

Indian Well: see **Indian Wells** [RIVERSIDE].

Indian Wells [RIVERSIDE]: *town,* 4 miles east of Palm Desert (lat. 33°43'05" N, long. 116°18'30" W). Named on La Quinta (1959) 7.5' quadrangle. United States Geological Survey's (1904) map shows a water feature called Indian Well at the site. Postal authorities established Indian Wells post office in 1915, discontinued it in 1933, reestablished it in 1968, and discontinued it in 1972 (Salley, p. 104). The town incorporated in 1967.

Indian Wells: see **Indio** [RIVERSIDE]; **Seeley** [IMPERIAL].

Indian Wells Valley [SAN BERNARDINO]: *valley,* mainly in Kern County and Los Angeles County, but extends east into San Bernardino County 15 miles east of Trona. Named on Trona (1957) 1°x 2° quadrangle. United States Board on Geographic Names (1933, p. 388) rejected the names "Salt Wells Valley," "Brown Valley," "Inyo-Kern Valley," and "Inyokern Valley" for the feature.

Indio [RIVERSIDE]: *town,* 68 miles east-southeast of Riverside (lat. 33°43'10" N, long. 116°13'05" W). Named on Indio (1956) 7.5' quadrangle. Postal authorities established Indio post office in 1888 (Frickstad, p. 128), and the town incorporated in 1930. The Southern Pacific Railroad station at the site was called Indian Wells until 1877, when the name was changed to Indio; developers filed the townsite plat for the community in 1888 (Gunther, p. 251).

Indio Canyon [RIVERSIDE]: *canyon,* 4 miles long, opens into lowlands 6 miles north-northeast of Indio (lat. 33°47'30" N, long. 116° 09'40" W; at W line sec. 28, T 4 S, R 8 E). Named on Lost Horse Mountain (1958) 15' quadrangle.

Indio Hills [RIVERSIDE]: *range,* center 10 miles northwest of Indio (lat. 33°50' N, long. 116°19' W). Named on Lost Horse Mountain (1958) 15' quadrangle, and on Cathedral City (1958), Indio (1956), Myoma (1958), and Seven Palms Valley (1958) 7.5' quadrangles.

Indio Mountain [RIVERSIDE]: *peak,* 4 miles south-southeast of Palm Desert (lat. 33°40'15" N, long. 116°20'30" W; at S line sec. 3, T 6 S, R 6 E). Altitude 2226 feet. Named on La Quinta (1959) 7.5' quadrangle.

Ingham Peak [SAN BERNARDINO]: *peak,* 4.5 miles southeast of Luna Mountain (lat. 34°17'25" N, long. 117°04'35" W; sec. 3, T 2 N, R 2 W). Altitude 6355 feet. Named on Butler Peak (1971) 7.5' quadrangle.

In-Ko-Pah Gorge [IMPERIAL]: *canyon,* 4.5 miles long, along Myer Creek above a point 8 miles south-southwest of Carrizo Mountain (lat. 32°43'15" N, long. 116°02'45" W; sec. 3, T 17 S, R 9 E). Named on In-Ko-Pah Gorge (1959) 7.5' quadrangle.

Inscription Canyon [SAN BERNARDINO]: *canyon,* nearly 1 mile long, 26 miles east-southeast of the village of Red Mountain (lat. 35°11'45" N, long. 117°11'40" W; sec. 31, T 31 S, R 45 E). Named on Opal Mountain (1955) 15' quadrangle, which indicates petroglyphs near the feature.

Inspiration Point [SAN BERNARDINO]:
(1) *promontory,* 2.5 miles west of downtown Big Bear Lake along Big Bear Lake (1) (lat. 34°14'40" N, long. 116°57'20" W; sec. 23, T 2 N, R 1 W). Named on Big Bear Lake (1970) 7.5' quadrangle.
(2) *locality,* 6 miles north of San Bernardino city hall (lat. 34°11'20" N, long. 117°16'30" W; at W line sec. 11, T 1 N, R 4 W). Named on San Bernardino North (1967) 7.5' quadrangle.
(3) *locality,* nearly 4 miles north-northwest of Keller Peak (lat. 34° 14'35" N, long. 117°05' W; at W line sec. 22, T 2 N, R 2 W). Named on Keller Peak (1967) 7.5' quadrangle.

Inspiration Point: see **Salton View** [RIVERSIDE].

Institute: see **Arlington** [RIVERSIDE].

Inyo-Kern Valley: see **Indian Wells Valley** [SAN BERNARDINO].

Ioamosa: see **Alta Loma** [SAN BERNARDINO].

Iodine Spring [RIVERSIDE]: *spring,* 4.25 miles north-northwest of Murrieta (lat. 33°36'50" N, long. 117°14'10" W; near SW cor. sec. 30, T 6 S, R 3 W). Named on Murrieta (1953) 7.5' quadrangle.

Iris [IMPERIAL]: *locality,* 8 miles northeast of Calipatria along Southern Pacific Railroad (lat. 33°11'50" N, long. 115°24'20" W; at E line sec. 21, T 11 S, R 15 E). Named on Iris (1956) 7.5' quadrangle.

Irish Wash [RIVERSIDE]: *stream* and *dry wash,* extends for 4 miles to Corn Springs Wash 5.5 miles south of Desert Center (lat. 33°38'10" N, long. 115°23'15" W). Named on Chuckwalla Mountains (1963) 15' quadrangle.

Iris Pass [RIVERSIDE]: *pass,* 17 miles south of Desert Center (lat. 33°28'45" N, long. 115°24'45" W; near W line sec. 15, T 8 S, R 15 E). Named on Iris Pass (1963) 15' quadrangle.

Iris Wash [IMPERIAL-RIVERSIDE]: *stream* and *dry wash,* heads in Riverside County and extends for 19 miles before ending 9 miles southeast of Frink in Imperial County (lat. 33°17' N, long. 115°31'30" W; sec. 21, T 10 S, R 14 E). Named on Frink (1956) and Iris Pass (1963) 15' quadrangles.

Iron Mountain [SAN BERNARDINO]: *range,* 12.5 miles west of Barstow (lat. 34°52' N, long. 117°14'30" W). Named on Hinkley (1971), Hodge (1971), Twelve Gauge Lake (1973), and Wild Crossing (1973) 7.5' quadrangles.

Iron Mountains [SAN BERNARDINO]: *range,* 20 miles south of Essex (lat. 34°10' N, long. 115°13' W). Named on Cadiz Valley (1956) and Iron Mountains (1956) 15' quadrangles.

Iron Ridge [SAN BERNARDINO]: *range,* 17 miles south-southeast of Newberry (lat. 34°37' N, long. 116°32' W). Named on Rodman Mountains (1955) 15' quadrangle.

Iron Spring [RIVERSIDE]: *spring,* 22 miles south of Idyllwild (lat. 33°25'45" N, long. 116°41'40" W; near S line sec. 32, T 8 S, R 3 E). Named on Beauty Mountain (1960) 7.5' quadrangle.

Iron Spring Canyon [RIVERSIDE]: *canyon,* drained by a stream that flows nearly 4 miles to Cooper Canyon 22 miles south of Idyllwild in San Diego County (lat. 33°25'20" N, long. 116°41'15" W). Named on Beauty Mountain (1960) 7.5' quadrangle.

Iron Spring Mountain [RIVERSIDE]: *ridge,* north-trending, 2 miles long, 20 miles south of Idyllwild (lat. 33°26'45" N, long. 116°41'50" W); Iron Spring is near the south end of the feature. Named on Beauty Mountain (1960) 7.5' quadrangle.

Ironwood Campsite [SAN BERNARDINO]: *locality,* 7.25 miles east-southeast of Luna Mountain (lat. 34°18'15" N, long. 117°00'40" W; near W line sec. 32, T 3 N, R 1 W). Named on Butler Peak (1971) 7.5' quadrangle.

Ironwood Mountains: see **McCoy Mountains** [RIVERSIDE].

Ironwood Wash [SAN BERNARDINO]: *stream,* 3.5 miles long, 27 miles south of Essex (lat. 34°21' N, long. 115°13'15" W). Named on Milligan (1956) 15' quadrangle.

Irvington Station: see **Verdemont** [SAN BERNARDINO].

Irwin: see **Camp Irwin** [SAN BERNARDINO].

Isabelle Spring [SAN BERNARDINO]: *spring,* 12 miles east of Victorville (lat. 34°32'05" N, long. 117°05'30" W; sec. 9, T 5 N, R 2 W). Named on Fairview Valley (1970) 7.5' quadrangle.

Island: see **The Island** [IMPERIAL]; **The Island** [SAN BERNARDINO].

Ivanpah [SAN BERNARDINO]: *village,* 142 miles northeast of San Bernardino (lat. 35°20'25" N, long. 115°18'30" W; sec. 31, T 15 N, R 16 E). Named on Ivanpah (1956) 15' quadrangle. Postal authorities established Ivanpah post office in 1878, discontinued it in 1899, reestablished it in 1903, and moved it 6 miles southeast in 1906, when they changed the name to Leastalk; they reestablished Ivanpah post office in 1914 and discontinued it in 1966 (Salley, p. 106). California Mining Bureau's (1917a) map has the designation "Ivanpah (old)" for a place located about 6 miles northwest of present Ivanpah at the end of a rail line. The name "Ivanpah" first applied to a mining camp of the 1870's located at the foot of Clark Mountains; California Eastern Railroad built a branch line into Ivanpah Valley in 1901, and took the name "Ivanpah" for the terminus of the line although the terminus was not at the mining camp (Gudde, 1975, p. 171). The junction of California Eastern Railroad with Union Pacific Railroad first was called Leastalk, then South Ivanpah, and finally it became present Ivanpah after abandonment of the California Eastern railhead—the original mining camp of Ivanpah was located 15 miles north of the California Eastern Railroad station of that name (Myrick, p. 845, 848). The name "Leastalk" is from letters in the term "Salt Lake" (Gudde, 1949, p. 163). Postal authorities established Leastalk post office in 1906, discontinued it in 1911, reestablished it in 1912, and changed the name to Ivanpah in 1914 (Frickstad, p. 143).

Ivanpah Lake [SAN BERNARDINO]: *dry lake,* 8 miles long, 15 miles north-northwest of Ivanpah (lat. 35°33' N, long. 115°23'45" W); the lake is in Ivanpah Valley. Named on Ivanpah (1956) and Roach Lake (1955) 15' quadrangles. Mendenhall (1909a, p. 57) noted a feature called Ivanpah Well located about 1 mile east of Ivanpah at the south end of Ivanpah Lake.

Ivanpah Mountains [SAN BERNARDINO]: *range,* 11 miles west-northwest of Ivanpah (lat. 35°23' N, long. 115°30' W); the range is west of Ivanpah Valley. Named on Ivanpah (1956) and Mescal Range (1955) 15' quadrangles.

Ivanpah Springs [SAN BERNARDINO]: *springs,* 19 miles northwest of Ivanpah (lat. 35°32'30" N, long. 115°31'40" W; sec. 24, T 17 N, R 13 E); the springs are on the west side of Ivanpah Valley. Named on Clark Mountain (1956) 15' quadrangle.

Ivanpah Tank [RIVERSIDE]: *water feature,* 22 miles north-northeast of Indio (lat. 33°59'55" N, long. 116°02'50" W; sec. 16, T 2 S, R 9 E). Named on Lost Horse Mountain (1958) 15' quadrangle.

Ivanpah Valley [SAN BERNARDINO]: *valley,* between Ivanpah Mountains and New York Mountains on California-Nevada State line; Ivanpah is near the south end of the valley. Named on Clark Mountain (1956), Crescent Peak (1956), Ivanpah (1956), and Roach Lake (1955) 15' quadrangles.

Ivanpah Well: see **Ivanpah Lake** [SAN BERNARDINO].

Ivawatz Mountains: see **Avawatz Mountains** [SAN BERNARDINO].

- J -

Jacinto: see **Cabazon** [RIVERSIDE].

Jackass Flat [RIVERSIDE]: *valley,* 20 miles south of Palm Desert on Riverside-San Diego County line (lat. 33°25'30" N, long. 116° 24' W; on S line sec. 31, T 8 S, R 6 E). Named on Collins Valley (1959) 7.5' quadrangle.

Jackhammer Gap [SAN BERNARDINO]: *relief feature,* 48 miles west-southwest of Baker (lat. 35°02'05" N, long. 116°53'30" W; near E line sec. 20, T 11 N, R 1 E). Named on Lane Mountain (1948) 15' quadrangle

Jack Rabbit Spring [SAN BERNARDINO]: *spring,* 40 miles west-southwest of Baker (lat. 35°06'05" N, long. 116°44'55" W; at E line sec. 27, T 12 N, R 2 E). Named on Alvord Mountain (1948) 15' quadrangle.

Jackrabbit Spring [SAN BERNARDINO]: *spring,* 5 miles east-southeast of Luna Mountain (lat. 34°19'20" N, long. 117°02'45" W; near N line sec. 25, T 3 N, R 2 W). Named on Butler Peak (1971) 7.5' quadrangle.

Jackson Gulch [IMPERIAL]: *canyon,* drained by a stream that flows 3 miles to lowlands 3.5 miles east of Ogilby (lat. 32°49' N, long. 114°46'35" W; near N line sec. 32, T 15 S, R 21 E). Named on Ogilby (1963) 15' quadrangle.

Jack Spring [SAN BERNARDINO]: *spring,* 39 miles west-southwest of Baker (lat. 35°09'10" N, long. 116°45'25" W; at N line sec. 10, T 12 N, R 2 E). Named on Lane Mountain (1948) 15' quadrangle.

Jacoby Canyon [SAN BERNARDINO]: *canyon,* drained by a stream that flows 1.5 miles to Cushenbury Canyon 5 miles north-northeast of Big

Bear City (lat. 34°19'45" N, long. 116°49'40" W; sec. 24, T 3 N, R 1 E). Named on Big Bear City (1971) 7.5' quadrangle. Called Chicopee Canyon on Lucerne Valley (1947) 15' quadrangle. United States Board on Geographic Names (1975a, p. 10) noted that the name "Jacoby Canyon" is for Frank Jacoby, a miner who lived in the canyon; the Board gave the name "Chicopee Canyon" as a variant.

Jacoby Spring [SAN BERNARDINO]: *spring,* 4 miles north-northeast of Big Bear City (lat. 34°19'05" N, long. 116°49'50" W; sec. 25, T 3 N, R 1 E); the spring is in Jacoby Canyon. Named on Big Bear City (1971) 7.5' quadrangle.

Jacumba Mountains [IMPERIAL]: *range,* mainly in San Diego County, but extends southeast into Imperial County 11 miles south-southwest of Carrizo Mountain (lat. 32°41'30" N, long. 116° 06'20" W). Named on In-Ko-Pah Gorge (1959) 7.5' quadrangle.

Jaeger City: see **Pilot Knob** [IMPERIAL].

Jaeger's Ferry: see **Pilot Knob** [IMPERIAL].

James' Flat: see **Huston Flat** [SAN BERNARDINO].

Java [SAN BERNARDINO]: *locality,* 7.5 miles west-northwest of Needles along Atchison, Topeka and Santa Fe Railroad (lat. 34°53'15" N, long. 114°43'30" W; sec. 7, T 9 N, R 22 E). Named on Needles NW (1970) 7.5' quadrangle.

JCA: see **Camp JCA** [SAN BERNARDINO].

Jean Peak [RIVERSIDE]: *peak,* 0.5 mile south of San Jacinto Peak (lat. 33°48'20" N, long. 116°40'40" W; sec. 21, T 4 S, R 3 E). Altitude 10,670 feet. Named on San Jacinto Peak (1981) 7.5' quadrangle. Edmond Taylor Perkins, Jr., topographer with United States Geological Survey, named the peak in 1897 for Jean Waters, whom he later married (Gunther, p. 256).

Jenks Lake [SAN BERNARDINO]: *lake,* 0.25 mile long, 5.5 miles south-southeast of downtown Big Bear Lake (lat. 34°09'50" N, long. 116°52'50" W; on S line sec. 16, T 1 N, R 1 E). Named on Big Bear Lake (1970) 7.5' quadrangle.

Jenks Meadows [SAN BERNARDINO]: *area,* 4.5 miles south of downtown Big Bear Lake (lat. 34°10'35" N, long. 116°54'20" W; near NW cor. sec. 17, T 1 N, R 1 E). Named on Big Bear Lake (1970) 7.5' quadrangle.

Jennings Spring [SAN BERNARDINO]: *spring,* 21 miles northeast of present Vidal (lat. 34°21'35" N, long. 114°16'45" W). Named on Parker (1911) 30' quadrangle.

Jenson Creek [RIVERSIDE]: *stream,* flows 3 miles to San Gorgonio Pass 12.5 miles west-northwest of Palm Springs (lat. 33°53'55" N, long. 116°44'50" W; sec. 23, T 3 S, R 2 E). Named on San Jacinto Peak (1981) and Whitewater (1955) 7.5' quadrangles. The misspelled name recalls Hans P. Jensen, who settled in the canyon after 1900 (Gunther, p. 256).

Jepson Peak [SAN BERNARDINO]: *peak,* 1.25 miles west of San Gorgonio Mountain (lat. 34°06'10" N, long. 116°50'35" W; near E line sec. 11, T 1 S, R 1 E). Altitude 11,205 feet. Named on San Gorgonio Mountain (1970) 7.5' quadrangle.

Jessie Saddle [SAN BERNARDINO]: *pass,* 6 miles north of Victorville (lat. 34°37'25" N, long. 117°18'30" W; sec. 9, T 6 N, R 4 W). Named on Victorville (1956) 7.5' quadrangle.

Jimgrey [SAN BERNARDINO]: *locality,* 25 miles west of Barstow along Atchison, Topeka and Santa Fe Railroad (lat. 34°58'40" N, long. 117°28'10" W; sec. 12, T 10 N, R 6 W). Named on Kramer Hills (1973) 7.5' quadrangle. The name is for Jim Grey, a locomotive engineer for Atchison, Topeka and Santa Fe Railroad (Hanna, p. 154).

Jobs Peak [SAN BERNARDINO]: *peak,* 19 miles south of Victorville (lat. 34°15'25" N, long. 117°19'40" W; at W line sec. 17, T 2 N, R 4 W). Named on Cedar Springs (1956) 7.5' quadrangle.

John Bull Flat [SAN BERNARDINO]: *area,* 4.5 miles northeast of Fawnskin (lat. 34°19'30" N, long. 116°53'35" W; at SE cor. sec. 20, T 3 N, R 1 E). Named on Fawnskin (1971) 7.5' quadrangle.

Johnny Lang Canyon [RIVERSIDE-SAN BERNARDINO]: *canyon,* drained by a stream that heads in Riverside County and flows 3.5 miles to lowlands 12 miles southwest of Twentynine Palms in San Bernardino County (lat. 34°02'30" N, long. 116°13'45" W; at W line sec. 35, T 1 S, R 7 E). Named on Indian Cove (1972) 7.5' quadrangle. The name commemorates Johnny Lang, who for many years lived in a cabin in the canyon (Weight, p. 30).

Johns Camp [RIVERSIDE]: *locality,* 28 miles east-northeast of Garnet (lat. 34°01'10" N, long. 116°02'30" W). Site named on Queen Mountain (1972) 7.5' quadrangle.

Johns Meadow [SAN BERNARDINO]: *area,* 7 miles south of downtown Big Bear Lake along Forsee Creek (lat. 34°08'35" N, long. 116°55'15" W; sec. 30, T 1 N, R 1 E). Named on Big Bear Lake (1970) 7.5' quadrangle. The name commemorates John B. Surr, a local civic leader and supporter of San Gorgonio wilderness area (United States Board on Geographic Names, 1972b, p. 3).

Johnson Canyon [RIVERSIDE]:

(1) *canyon,* about 0.5 mile long, 6.5 miles west-northwest of Riverside (lat. 34°01'25" N, long. 117°28'25" W; sec. 2, T 2 S, R 6 W). Named on Fontana (1967) 7.5' quadrangle.

(2) *canyon,* less than 0.5 mile long, 5.5 miles south of Alberhill (lat. 33°38'40" N, long. 117°22'50" W; mainly in sec. 15, T 6 S, R 5 W). Named on Alberhill (1954, photorevised 1988) 7.5' quadrangle. The name is for Steven W. Johnson, a Forest Service employee who lost his life in a fire in 1959 (United States Board on Geographic Names, 1960c, p. 19).

Johnson Creek [SAN BERNARDINO]: *stream,* flows 0.5 mile to Bear Creek 2 miles east of Keller Peak (lat. 34°11'50" N, long. 117°00'45" W; near W line sec. 5, T 1 N, R 1 W). Named on Keller Peak (1967) 7.5' quadrangle.

Johnson Flat: see **Johnson Meadow** [RIVERSIDE].

Johnson Meadow [RIVERSIDE]: *area,* 3 miles south-southeast of Idyllwild (lat. 33°42' N, long. 116°42'20" W; at N line sec. 31, T 5 S, R 3 E). Named on Idyllwild (1959) 15' quadrangle. United States Board on Geographic Names (1983c, p. 5) approved the name "Johnston Meadow" for the feature, and rejected the names "Johnson Flat," "Johnson Meadow," and "Johnston Flat" for it; the name reportedly is for Hancock Johnston, who owned land and built a cabin at the place.

Johnson Spring [SAN BERNARDINO]: *spring,* 7 miles west-southwest of Twentynine Palms (lat. 34°05'05" N, long. 116°09'30" W). Named on Indian Cove (1972) 7.5' quadrangle.

Johnsons Well [SAN BERNARDINO]: *well,* 25 miles west-northwest of Vidal (lat. 34°15'55" N, long. 114°54'15" W). Named on Turtle Mountains (1954) 15' quadrangle.

Johnson Valley [SAN BERNARDINO]: *valley,* center 5 miles east of Old Woman Springs (lat. 34°24' N, long. 116°37'30" W). Named on Old Woman Springs (1955) 15' quadrangle. The place sometimes is called Old Woman Springs Valley (Thompson, 1929, p. 625).

Johnson Valley: see **Upper Johnson Valley** [SAN BERNARDINO].

Johnston Flat: see **Johnson Meadow** [RIVERSIDE].

Johnston Meadow: see **Johnson Meadow** [RIVERSIDE].

Johnstons Corner [SAN BERNARDINO]: *locality,* 10 miles west-southwest of Barstow (lat. 34°49'50" N, long. 117°10'45" W; sec. 34, T 9 N, R 3 W). Named on Hodge (1971) 7.5' quadrangle.

Jolley Spring [RIVERSIDE]: *spring,* 3 miles south of San Jacinto Peak (lat. 33°46'20" N, long. 116°40'50" W; near NW cor. sec. 4, T 5 S, R 3 E). Named on San Jacinto Peak (1981) 7.5' quadrangle.

Joseph Canyon [RIVERSIDE]: *canyon,* 1.5 miles long, opens into lowlands 4.25 miles south-southeast of Corona (lat. 33°49' N, long. 117°32'40" W; sec. 18, T 4 S, R 6 W). Named on Corona South (1967) 7.5' quadrangle. The name is for N.S. Joseph and Noah G. Joseph, early settlers at the place (Gunther, p. 257).

Joshua [SAN BERNARDINO]: *locality,* 9.5 miles west-southwest of Ivanpah along Union Pacific Railroad (lat. 35°16'10" N, long. 115°27'15" W; sec. 26, T 14 N, R 14 E). Named on Ivanpah (1956) 15' quadrangle.

Joshua Cove [SAN BERNARDINO]: *relief feature,* 2.5 miles north-northwest of Joshua Tree (lat. 34°10'05" N, long. 116°19'45" W; near SW cor. sec. 14, T 1 N, R 6 E). Named on Joshua Tree North (1972) 7.5' quadrangle.

Joshua Mountain [SAN BERNARDINO]: *peak,* 3 miles south of Twentynine Palms (lat. 34°05'35" N, long. 116°03'15" W; near SE cor. sec. 8, T 1 S, R 9 E). Named on Queen Mountain (1972) 7.5' quadrangle.

Joshua Tree [SAN BERNARDINO]: *town,* 57 miles east of San Bernardino (lat. 34°08'05" N, long. 116°18'50" W). Named on Joshua Tree North (1972) and Joshua Tree South (1972) 7.5' quadrangles. Postal authorities established Joshua Tree post office in 1946 (Frickstad, p. 142).

Jost Canyon: see **Potrero Creek** [RIVERSIDE] (1).

Jozee Spring [RIVERSIDE]: *spring,* 6.5 miles south of Idyllwild (lat. 33°39' N, long. 116°42' W; at W line sec. 17, T 6 S, R 3 E). Named on Idyllwild (1959) 15' quadrangle.

Juan [SAN BERNARDINO]: *locality,* 13 miles east of Ivanpah on California-Nevada State line (lat. 35°22' N, long. 115°05'15" W; sec. 19, T 15 N, R 18 E). Site named on Crescent Peak (1956) 15' quadrangle.

Juan Diego Flat [RIVERSIDE]: *area,* 15 miles southeast of Hemet (lat. 33°35'50" N, long. 116°47'55" W; near N line sec. 5, T 7 S, R 2 E). Named on Hemet (1957) 15' quadrangle. The name is from Juan Diego, the Cahuilla Indian that Helen Hunt Jackson immortalized with the name "Alessandro" in her novel *Ramona* (Gunther, p. 258).

Juaro Canyon [RIVERSIDE]: *canyon,* drained by a stream that flows 3.25 miles to San Jacinto Valley 2 miles east of San Jacinto (lat. 33°47'05" N, long. 116°55'10" W; sec. 31, T 4 S, R 1 E). Named on San Jacinto (1953) 7.5' quadrangle.

Judson: see **Helendale** [SAN BERNARDINO].

Julian Wash [IMPERIAL]: *stream,* flows 9 miles to Colorado River 24 miles south of Palo Verde (lat. 33°05'25" N, long. 114°42'30" W; at S line sec. 25, T 12 S, R 21 E). Named on Quartz Peak (1953) 15' quadrangle, and on Picacho SW (1965) 7.5' quadrangle.

Jumbo Rocks Campground [RIVERSIDE]: *locality,* 21 miles north-northeast of Indio (lat. 33°59'30" N, long. 116°04' W; near S line sec. 17, T 2 S, R 9 E). Named on Lost Horse Mountain (1958) 15' quadrangle.

Juniper: see **Camp Juniper**, under **Minnelusa** [SAN BERNARDINO].

Juniper Flat [RIVERSIDE]: *valley,* 5 miles south-southeast of Lakeview (lat. 33°46'20" N, long. 117°05' W; around SW cor sec. 34, T 4 S, R 2 W).

Named on Lakeview (1967) 7.5' quadrangle.

Juniper Flats [RIVERSIDE]: *area,* 19 miles north of Indio (lat. 33° 59'30" N, long. 116°14' W). Named on Lost Horse Mountain (1958) 15' quadrangle.

Juniper Flats [SAN BERNARDINO]: *area,* 12 miles southeast of Victorville (lat. 34°23'25" N, long. 117°10'15" W). Named on Apple Valley South (1971) 7.5' quadrangle.

Juniper Spring [SAN BERNARDINO]: *spring,* 9 miles east-northeast of Ivanpah (lat. 35°24' N, long. 115°09'50" W; at E line sec. 8, T 15 N, R 17 E). Named on Crescent Peak (1956) 15' quadrangle.

Juniper Springs [RIVERSIDE]: *locality,* 5.25 miles south-southeast of Lakeview (lat. 33°46' N, long. 117°05' W; at W line sec. 3, T 5 S, R 2 W); the place is at Juniper Flat. Named on Lakeview (1967) 7.5' quadrangle.

Jurupa [RIVERSIDE]: *land grant,* at and near Riverside. Named on Fontana (1967), Riverside East (1967), Riverside West (1967), and San Bernardino South (1967) 7.5' quadrangles. Juan Bandini received the land in 1838; Louis Robidoux claimed 6750 acres patented in 1876 (Cowan, p. 88; Cowan listed the grant under the name "San Timoteo"). The name "Jurupa" is of Indian origin (Kroeber, p. 44).

Jurupa [RIVERSIDE-SAN BERNARDINO]: *land grant,* at and near Riverside—the grant extends north into San Bernardino County south-southwest of Colton. Named on Corona North (1967), Fontana (1967), Guasti (1966), Riverside West (1967), and San Bernardino South (1967) 7.5' quadrangles. Juan Bandini received the land in 1838; Abel Stearns claimed 13,819 acres patented in 1879 (Cowan, p. 43). Perez (p. 70) gave 32,259.16 acres as the size of the grant. The name is of Indian origin (Kroeber, p. 44).

Jurupa: see **Mount Jurupa** [RIVERSIDE]; **Riverside** [RIVERSIDE].

Jurupa Mountains [RIVERSIDE-SAN BERNARDINO]: *range,* 5 miles south of Fontana city hall on Riverside-San Bernardino County line (lat. 34°01'45" N, long. 117°26'45" W); the range is partly on Jurupa [RIVERSIDE-SAN BERNARDINO] grant. Named on Fontana (1967) and Guasti (1966) 7.5' quadrangles.

- K -

Kaiser [SAN BERNARDINO]:

(1) *locality,* 7.5 miles east of Ontario city hall along Southern Pacific Railroad (lat. 34°03'50" N, long. 117°31'15" W; near SW cor. sec. 21, T 1 S, R 6 W). Named on Guasti (1966) 7.5' quadrangle. Called Etiwa on United States Geological Survey' (1941) map. The name "Kaiser" is for Henry Kaiser, who had a steel plant near the place (Gudde, 1949, p. 170).

(2) *locality,* 3 miles west of Fontana city hall along Atchison, Topeka and Santa Fe Railroad (lat. 34°05'35" N, long. 117°29'20" W; near SE cor. sec. 10, T 1 S, R 6 W). Named on Fontana (1967) 7.5' quadrangle. Called Kaiser Siding on Fontana (1953) 7.5' quadrangle.

Kane: see **Peter Kane Mountain** [IMPERIAL]; **Peter Kane Water Hole** [IMPERIAL].

Kane Spring [IMPERIAL]: *locality,* 18 miles west of Calipatria (lat. 33°06'35" N, long. 115°50'15" W; near W line sec. 21, T 12 S, R 11 E). Named on Kane Spring (1956) 7.5' quadrangle. United States Board on Geographic Names (1961b, p. 10) rejected the names "Cane Spring" and "Kane Springs" for the place. Garces called it San Anselmo when the Anza expedition stopped there in 1774 (Hanna, p. 158).

Kane Springs [SAN BERNARDINO]: *springs,* 6 miles south of Newberry (lat. 34°44'25" N, long. 116°41'45" W; at W line sec. 32, T 8 N, R 3 E); the springs are along Kane Wash. Named on Rodman Mountains (1955) 15' quadrangle.

Kane Wash [SAN BERNARDINO]: *stream,* flows 10 miles to lowlands 4.5 miles south-southeast of Newberry (lat. 34°45'50" N, long. 116°39'45" W; near NW cor. sec. 27, T 8 N, R 3 E). Named on Ord Mountains (1955) and Rodman Mountains (1955) 15' quadrangles.

Karmack: see **Winterhaven** [IMPERIAL].

Kawia: see **Cahuilla** [RIVERSIDE].

Keany Pass [SAN BERNARDINO]: *pass,* 22 miles northwest of Ivanpah (lat. 35°35'45" N, long. 115°34' W; sec. 3, T 17 N, R 13 E). Named on Clark Mountain (1956) 15' quadrangle.

Keenbrook [SAN BERNARDINO]: *locality,* 3.25 miles south of Cajon along the railroad (lat. 34°15' N, long. 117°27'30" W; near N line sec. 24, T 2 N, R 6 W). Named on Cajon (1956) and Devore (1966) 7.5' quadrangles. Postal authorities established Keenbrook post office in 1894, discontinued it the same year, reestablished it in 1910, and discontinued it in 1921 (Frickstad, p. 142). The name is from Keenbrook ranch, owned by Messers. Keene and Bailey of San Bernardino (Robinson, J.W., 1983, p. 187).

Keen Camp: see **Mountain Center** [RIVERSIDE].

Keen Camp Summit [RIVERSIDE]: *pass,* nearly 4 miles south of Idyllwild (lat. 33°40'10" N, long. 116°42' W; at NW cor. sec. 5, T 6 S, R 3 E). Named on Idyllwild (1959) 15' quadrangle.

Keen Ridge [RIVERSIDE]: *ridge,* generally west-trending, 1 mile long, 3.25 miles south-southeast of Idyllwild (lat. 33°41'50" N, long. 116°41'45" W; sec. 31, 32, T 5 S, R 3 E). Named on Idyllwild (1959) 15' quadrangle.

Keller Cliffs [SAN BERNARDINO]: *relief feature,* nearly 2 miles south of Keller Peak (lat. 34°10'10" N, long. 117°02'45" W; sec. 13, T 1 N, R 2 W); the feature is along Keller Creek. Named on Keller Peak (1967) 7.5' quadrangle.

Keller Creek [SAN BERNARDINO]: *stream,* flows 4.25 miles to Santa Ana River 3.5 miles south of Keller Peak (lat. 34°08'45" N, long. 117°03'35" W; sec. 26, T 1 N, R 2 W); the stream heads near Keller Peak. Named on Keller Peak (1967) 7.5' quadrangle.

Keller Meadows [SAN BERNARDINO]: *marsh,* 1.5 miles south of Keller Peak (lat. 34°10'30" N, long. 117°02'55" W; near W line sec. 13, T 1 N, R 2 W). Named on Keller Peak (1967) 7.5' quadrangle.

Keller Peak [SAN BERNARDINO]: *peak,* 12.5 miles northeast of Redlands city hall (lat. 34°11'45" N, long. 117°02'55" W; near SW cor. sec. 1, T 1 N, R 2 W). Altitude 7882 feet. Named on Keller Peak (1967) 7.5' quadrangle. Gudde (1949, p. 172) associated the name with Francis D. Keller, a pioneer farmer in the neighborhood after 1854.

Kelley Camp [SAN BERNARDINO]: *locality,* 12 miles north-northeast of Ontario city hall (lat. 34°14' N, long. 117°36'15" W; sec. 27, T 2 N, R 7 W). Named on Cucamonga Peak (1953) 7.5' quadrangle. The name recalls John Kelly, who discovered a gold prospect at the place in 1905 and worked his claim there for several years; Henry Delker took a resort lease at the spot in 1922, built cabins, and opened Kelly's Camp to the public (Robinson, J.W., 1983, p. 28, 147).

Kelso [SAN BERNARDINO]: *village,* 30 miles southwest of Ivanpah (lat. 35°00'45" N, long. 115°39' W; at N line sec. 25, T 11 N, R 12 E). Named on Kelso (1955) 15' quadrangle. Postal authorities established Kelso post office in 1905 (Frickstad, p. 142). The name commemorates an official of San Pedro, Los Angeles and Salt Lake Railroad (Gudde, 1949, p. 172).

Kelso Dunes [SAN BERNARDINO]: *relief feature,* 24 miles north of Amboy (lat. 34°54'30" N, long. 115°45' W). Named on Flynn (1956) and Kerens (1957) 15' quadrangles.

Kelso Mountains [SAN BERNARDINO]: *range,* 30 miles southwest of Ivanpah (lat. 35°04' N, long. 115°44' W). Named on Kelso (1955) and Old Dad Mountain (1956) 15' quadrangles.

Kelso Peak [SAN BERNARDINO]: *peak,* 28 miles southwest of Ivanpah (lat. 35°06'15" N, long. 115°43'25" W; near S line sec. 20, T 12 N, R 12 E); the peak is in Kelso Mountains. Altitude 4764 feet. Named on Kelso (1955) 15' quadrangle.

Kelso Wash [SAN BERNARDINO]: *stream,* flows 37 miles before losing its identity 32 miles north-northwest of Amboy (lat. 35° 00' N, long. 115°55" W). Named on Flynn (1956), Kelso (1955), Kerens (1957), and Mid Hills (1955) 15' quadrangles.

Kenton Mill [SAN BERNARDINO]: *locality,* 12 miles west-southwest of Ludlow (lat. 34°38'20" N, long. 116°21'15" W; sec. 4, T 6 N, R 6 E). Named on Lavic (1955) 15' quadrangle.

Kenwood: see **Devore** [SAN BERNARDINO].

Kenworthy [RIVERSIDE]: *locality,* 10 miles south-southeast of present Idyllwild (lat. 33°36'30" N, long. 116°36' W). Named on San Jacinto (1901) 30' quadrangle. Idyllwild (1959) 15' quadrangle has the name "Kenworthy Station" at or near the site. Postal authorities established Kenworthy post office in 1897 and discontinued it in 1900 (Frickstad, p. 128). The place was a gold-mining camp started in 1897 and named for Eugene Kenworthy, an English mining man (Gudde, 1975, p. 185). California Mining Bureau's (1917b) map shows a place called Babtiste located 4 miles southwest of Kenworthy. Postal authorities established Babtiste post office in Bautista Canyon in 1913, changed the post office name to Bautista in 1924, and discontinued it in 1928 (Salley, p. 16).

Kerens [SAN BERNARDINO]: *locality,* 28 miles north of Amboy along Union Pacific Railroad (lat. 34°58' N, long. 115°48'30" W; near S line sec. 10, T 10 N, R 11 E). Named on Kerens (1957) 15' quadrangle. The name commemorates Richard C. Kerens, who promoted construction of Los Angeles, San Pedro and Salt Lake Railroad (Hanna, p. 160).

Kerkhoff Canyon [SAN BERNARDINO]: *canyon,* drained by a stream that flows nearly 2 miles to Los Angeles County 11.5 miles north of Ontario city hall (lat. 34°13'35" N, long. 117°39'55" W; near W line sec. 30, T 2 N, R 7 W). Named on Mount Baldy (1967) 7.5' quadrangle.

Kessler Peak [SAN BERNARDINO]: *peak,* 12 miles west of Ivanpah (lat. 35°18'55" N, long. 115°31'45" W; sec. 7, T 14 N, R 14 E); the peak is 1.25 miles north-northeast of Kessler Spring. Named on Mescal Range (1955) 15' quadrangle.

Kessler Spring [SAN BERNARDINO]: *spring,* 13 miles west-southwest of Ivanpah (lat. 35°17'55" N, long. 115°32' W; at W line sec. 18, T 14 N, R 14 E). Named on Mescal Range (1955) 15' quadrangle. The name commemorates a settler who was killed about 1890; one of the suspected killers, an Indian, was hanged from a tree at the spring (Gudde, 1949, p. 173).

Keystone: see **Imperial** [IMPERIAL].

Keystone Canyon [SAN BERNARDINO]: *canyon,* 2 miles long, 5 miles south of Ivanpah (lat. 35°16'15" N, long. 115°17'30" W). Named on Ivanpah (1956) 15' quadrangle.

Keystone Spring [SAN BERNARDINO]: *spring,* 5.25 miles south-southeast of Ivanpah (lat. 35°16' N, long. 115°17'20" W; near W line sec. 29, T 14 N, R 16 E); the spring is in Keystone Canyon. Named on Ivanpah (1956) 15' quadrangle.

Keys View: see **Salton View** [RIVERSIDE].

Khartoum [SAN BERNARDINO]: *locality,* 3.5 miles west-northwest of Needles along Atchison, Topeka and Santa Fe Railroad (lat. 34° 51'45" N, long. 114°39'30" W). Named on Needles (1904) 30' quadrangle.

Kidd Cove [SAN BERNARDINO]: *embayment,* 3.5 miles west of downtown Big Bear Lake along Big Bear Lake (1) (lat. 34°14'30" N, long. 116°58'10" W; sec. 22, T 2 N, R 1 W); the feature is at the mouth of Kidd Creek. Named on Big Bear Lake (1970) 7.5' quadrangle.

Kidd Creek [SAN BERNARDINO]: *stream,* flows nearly 1 mile to Big Bear Lake (1) 3.5 miles west of downtown Big Bear Lake (lat. 34°14'25" N, long. 116°58'10" W; sec. 22, T 2 N, R 1 W). Named on Big Bear Lake (1970) 7.5' quadrangle.

Kilbeck: see **Chubbuck** [SAN BERNARDINO].

Kilbeck Hills [SAN BERNARDINO]: *range,* 30 miles southeast of Amboy (lat. 34°18' N, long. 115°18'30" W). Named on Cadiz Lake (1956) and Cadiz Valley (1956) 15' quadrangles.

Kilpecker Creek [SAN BERNARDINO]: *stream,* flows 1.5 miles to Santa Ana River 6 miles south-southwest of downtown Big Bear Lake (lat. 34°10'10" N, long. 116°58'05" W; sec. 15, T 1 N, R 1 W). Named on Big Bear Lake (1970) 7.5' quadrangle.

Kimbark Canyon [SAN BERNARDINO]: *canyon,* drained by a stream that flows 2 miles to lowlands 1.5 miles north of Devore (lat. 34°14'25" N, long. 117°24'25" W). Named on Cajon (1956) and Devore (1966) 7.5' quadrangles.

Kimbark Canyon: see **East Kimbark Canyon** [SAN BERNARDINO].

Kimmel Canyon [RIVERSIDE]: *canyon,* drained by a stream that flows 2.25 miles to Saint Johns Canyon 8 miles south-southeast of Hemet (lat. 33°37'50" N, long. 116°56' W; sec. 24, T 6 S, R 1 W). Named on Hemet (1953) 7.5' quadrangle. The misspelled name is for Samuel B. Kimmell, who had land in the canyon patented in 1898 (Gunther, p. 270).

King [SAN BERNARDINO]: *locality,* 17 miles south-southwest of Baker along Union Pacific Railroad (lat. 35°02'45" N, long. 116° 12'30" W). Named on Avawatz Mountains (1933) 1° quadrangle.

King Spring: see **Ibis** [SAN BERNARDINO].

Kingston Peak [SAN BERNARDINO]: *peak,* 43 miles northwest of Ivanpah (lat. 35°48'35" N, long. 115°54'50" W); the feature is in Kingston Range. Altitude 7323 feet. Named on Kingston Peak (1955) 15' quadrangle.

Kingston Range [SAN BERNARDINO]: *range,* 44 miles northwest of Ivanpah on San Bernardino-Inyo County line (lat. 35°45' N, long. 115°55' W). Named on Horse Thief Springs (1956), Kingston Peak (1955), and Tecopa (1950) 15' quadrangles. United States Board on Geographic Names (1933, p. 428) rejected the names "Chung Up Mountains" and "Resting Spring Mountains" for the range. The name "Kingston" is for a mail carrier on the route between Salt Lake City and San Bernardino (Crossman, p. 217).

Kingston Spring [SAN BERNARDINO]: *spring,* 41 miles west-northwest of Ivanpah (lat. 35°37'15" N, long. 115°57'45" W). Named on Kingston Peak (1955) 15' quadrangle. Ivanpah (1912) 1° quadrangle has the plural form "Kingston Sprs." for the name.

Kingston Wash [SAN BERNARDINO]: *stream* and *dry wash,* extends for 50 miles to Salt Creek 25 miles north-northwest of Baker (lat. 35°36' N, long. 116°13'40" W; near SW cor. sec. 34, T 18 N, R 7 E). Named on Clark Mountain (1956), Kingston Peak (1955), and Silurian Hills (1956) 15' quadrangles.

Kinley Creek [SAN BERNARDINO]: *stream,* flows 4 miles to Deep Creek (1) 3.5 miles west of Luna Mountain (lat. 34°20'30" N, long. 117°11'25" W; near E line sec. 16, T 3 N, R 3 W). Named on Lake Arrowhead (1971) 7.5' quadrangle.

Kitching Peak [RIVERSIDE]: *peak,* 16 miles northwest of Palm Springs (lat. 33°59'55" N, long. 116°44'25" W; sec. 14, T 2 S, R 2 E). Altitude 6598 feet. Named on Whitewater (1955) 7.5' quadrangle.

Klinefelter [SAN BERNARDINO]: *locality,* 10 miles west-northwest of Needles along Atchison, Topeka and Santa Fe Railroad (lat. 34° 54' N, long. 114°46' W; at W line sec. 2, T 9 N, R 21 E). Named on Bannock (1956) 15' quadrangle. Postal authorities established Klinefelter post office in 1894 and discontinued it in 1895; the name is said to be for an employee of Atlantic and Pacific Railroad (Salley, p. 113).

Klinefelter Wash: see **Piute Wash** [SAN BERNARDINO].

Klinker Mountain [SAN BERNARDINO]: *peak,* 6 miles northeast of the village of Red Mountain (lat. 35°24'55" N, long. 117°33'15" W; sec. 14, T 29 S, R 41 E). Altitude 4562 feet. Named on Klinker Mountain (1967) 7.5' quadrangle. Called Mt. Klinker on California Mining Bureau's (1917a) map.

Klondike [SAN BERNARDINO]: *locality,* 9.5 miles east-southeast of Ludlow (lat. 34°40'05" N, long. 116°00'10" W; near W line sec. 25, T 7 N, R 9 E). Named on Ash Hill (1955) 7.5' quadrangle.

Knapp's Flat: see **Huston Flat** [SAN BERNARDINO].

Knob [IMPERIAL]: *locality,* 6 miles southeast of Ogilby along Southern Pacific Railroad (lat. 32°45'30" N, long. 114°46' W; near N line sec. 21, T 16 S, R 21 E); the place is 2 miles north-northwest of Pilot Knob. Named on Yuma (1905) 30' quadrangle.

Kokell: see **Thermal** [RIVERSIDE].

Kokoweef Peak [SAN BERNARDINO]: *peak,* 11.5 miles west-northwest of Ivanpah (lat. 35°25'15" N, long. 115°29'35" W; sec. 4, T 15 N, R 14 E). Altitude 6038 feet. Named on Ivanpah (1956) 15' quadrangle.

Kolb Creek [RIVERSIDE]: *stream,* flows 2 miles to the canyon of Arroyo Seco Creek 7.25 miles west-northwest of Aguanga (lat. 33°28'25" N, long. 116°59'10" W). Named on Pechanga (1968) and Vail Lake (1953) 7.5' quadrangles.

Kouns: see **Yermo** [SAN BERNARDINO].

Kramer [SAN BERNARDINO]: *locality,* 32 miles west of Barstow (lat. 34°59'40" N, long. 117°35'05" W; sec. 2, T 10 N, R 7 W). Named on Kramer (1956) 15' quadrangle. Postal authorities established Kramer post office in 1896, discontinued it in 1911, reestablished it in 1912, and discontinued it in 1918; the name is for Moritz Kramer, owner of the site (Salley, p. 113).

Kramer Arch [SAN BERNARDINO]: *relief feature,* 6.5 miles north-northeast of Daggett (lat. 34°57'05" N, long. 116°50'30" W; near N line sec. 23, T 10 N, R 1 E). Named on Yermo (1953) 7.5' quadrangle.

Kramer Hills [SAN BERNARDINO]:

(1) *range,* 28 miles west of Barstow (lat. 34°54'45" N, long. 117° 18' W); the range is 5.5 miles south-southeast of Kramer Junction. Named on Kramer Hills (1973) and Kramer Junction (1973) 7.5' quadrangles.

(2) *locality,* 25 miles west of Barstow (lat. 34°55'15" N, long. 117°24' W; near NW cor. sec. 36, T 10 N, R 6 W); the place is at the northeast edge of Kramer Hills (1). Named on Kramer Hills (1973) 7.5' quadrangle.

Kramer Junction [SAN BERNARDINO]: *village,* 30 miles west of Barstow (lat. 34°59' N, long. 117°32'25" W; near W line sec. 5, T 10 N, R 6 W). Named on Kramer Junction (1973) 7.5' quadrangle. Called Four Corners on San Bernardino (1966) 1° x 2° quadrangle, but United States Board on Geographic Names (1960a, p. 15) rejected the names "Four Corners" and "Beechers Corners" for the place.

Kuffel Canyon [SAN BERNARDINO]: *canyon,* drained by a stream that flows less than 1 mile to Fleming Creek 6 miles north-northwest of Harrison Mountain (lat. 34°14'45" N, long. 117°11' W; sec. 22, T 2 N, R 3 W). Named on Harrison Mountain (1967) 7.5' quadrangle.

- L -

Laborde Canyon [RIVERSIDE]: *canyon,* 4.5 miles long, opens into San Jacinto Valley 5.5 miles east-northeast of Lakeview (lat. 33° 51'45" N, long. 117°01'30" W; sec. 31, T 3 S, R 1 W). Named on El Casco (1967) and Lakeview (1967) 7.5' quadrangles. Called Laborda Canyon on Elsinore (1901) 30' quadrangle, and called La Borda Canyon on Riverside (1943) 15' quadrangle. The name commemorates Jacques La Borde, a farmer in San Jacinto Valley; the feature first was called Necochea Canyon for Jose Maria de Necochea, who homesteaded at the place in 1890 (Gunther, p. 272, 348).

Lackey: see **Camp Lackey** [RIVERSIDE].

Ladd Canyon Spring [RIVERSIDE]: *spring,* 6.5 miles south of Corona (lat. 33°46'45" N, long. 117°35'10" W; near W line sec. 35, T 4 S, R 7 W); the spring is in East Fork Ladd Canyon (Ladd Canyon is in Orange County). Named on Corona South (1967) 7.5' quadrangle.

La Delta [SAN BERNARDINO]: *locality,* 7.5 miles north-northwest of Victorville (lat. 34°38'30" N, long. 117°20'35" W; sec. 6, T 6 N, R 4 W). Named on Helendale (1956) 7.5' quadrangle.

Laguna: see **Elsinore Junction** [RIVERSIDE]; **Lake Elsinore** [RIVERSIDE] (2); **Potholes** [IMPERIAL].

Laguna del Principe: see **Dry Lake** [RIVERSIDE].

Laguna de temecula: see **Lake Elsinore** [RIVERSIDE] (1).

Laguna Grande: see **Lake Elsinore** [RIVERSIDE] (1); **Lake Elsinore** [RIVERSIDE] (2).

Laguna Palo Verde: see **Palo Verde Lagoon** [IMPERIAL-RIVERSIDE].

Laguna Sal: see **Lake Elsinore** [RIVERSIDE] (1).

Laguna Station: see **Elsinore Junction** [RIVERSIDE].

Lake Arrowhead [SAN BERNARDINO]:

(1) *lake,* 2 miles long, 7 miles south-southwest of Luna Mountain (lat. 34°15'30" N, long. 117°11' W). Named on Lake Arrowhead (1971) 7.5' quadrangle. Deep Creek (1902) 15' quadrangle shows Little Bear Valley along Little Bear Creek at the site of the present lake. United States Board on Geographic Names (1933, p. 103) rejected the name "Little Bear Lake" for the feature. Officials of Arrowhead Reservoir Company had work started in 1892 on the dam that forms the lake (Hanna, p. 17).

(2) *town,* 6.5 miles south-southwest of Luna Mountain (lat. 34°15'20" N, long. 117°10'10" W); the town is at Lake Arrowhead (1). Named on Harrison Mountain (1967) and Lake Arrowhead (1971) 7.5' quadrangles. Postal authorities established Little Bear Lake post office in 1917, changed the name to Sagital in 1922, and changed it to Lake Arrowhead the same

year—the name "Sagital" was for an Indian who greeted visitors at the place (Salley, p. 123, 191).

Lake Creek: see **Siberia Creek** [SAN BERNARDINO].

Lake Elsinore [RIVERSIDE]:

(1) *lake*, about 3.5 miles long, 22 miles south of Riverside (lat 33° 39'25" N, long. 117°20'45" W); the lake is on La Laguna grant. Named on Alberhill (1954, photorevised 1988) and Lake Elsinore (1953) 7.5' quadrangles. Called Elsinore Lake on Elsinore (1901) 30' quadrangle. The lake has the name "Laguna de temecula" on a diseño of 1844 (Becker), and the name "Laguna Sal" on Goddard's (1857) map. Spaniards called the feature Laguna Grande, but Franklin H. Heald renamed it for the community of Elsinore (present Lake Elsinore) (Gunther, p. 179, 275, 277).

(2) *town*, 21 miles south of Riverside (lat. 33°40' N, long. 117°19'10" W). Named on Lake Elsinore (1953) 7.5' quadrangle. Called Elsinore on Elsinore (1953) 7.5' quadrangle, but residents gave the name "Lake Elsinore" to the town in 1972 (Gunther, p. 277). Postal authorities established Elsinore post office in 1883 and changed the name to Lake Elsinore in 1972 (Salley, p. 115). The town incorporated in 1888. United States Board on Geographic Names (1976b, p. 3) gave the variant names "Elsinore," "Etengvo Wumoma," "Laguna," and "Machado" for the place. The Butterfield Overland stage stop at the site was called Laguna or Laguna Grande (Ormsby, p. 111). Margaret Collier Graham, whose husband Donald Graham was a partner in the purchase and subdivision of La Laguna grant, chose the name "Elsinore" for the town (Hanna, p. 97). Waring (p. 43) listed a resort called Bundys Elsinore Hot Spring that was situated about 250 yards north of Elsinore train station—a well there provided guests at a hotel and cottages with sulphureted water for drinking and bathing.

Lake Evans [RIVERSIDE]: *lake*, 1850 feet long, 1 mile north-northwest of Riverside city hall (lat. 33°59'45" N, long. 117°22'40" W). Named on Riverside West (1967) 7.5' quadrangle. Called Evans Lake on Riverside West (1953) 7.5' quadrangle. Riverside city officials dedicated the lake in 1924 and named it for Samuel Cary Evans, Jr., mayor of Riverside, who donated the site to the city (Gunther, p. 277).

Lake Fulmor [RIVERSIDE]: *lake*, 1100 feet long, 10.5 miles east of San Jacinto (lat. 33°48'20" N, long. 116°46'45" W; sec. 21, T 4 S, R 2 E). Named on Lake Fulmor (1956) 7.5' quadrangle. The name commemorates A.C. Fulmor, Riverside County road commissioner who promoted formation of the lake (Hanna, p. 114).

Lake Gregory [SAN BERNARDINO]: *lake*, less than 1 mile long, 9.5 miles north of San Bernardino city hall (lat. 34°14'35" N, long. 117°16'05" W; sec. 23, T 2 N, R 4 W). Named on San Bernardino North (1967) 7.5' quadrangle.

Lake Havasu [SAN BERNARDINO]: *lake*, behind a dam on Colorado River 24 miles east-northeast of Vidal on California-Arizona State line (lat. 34°17'45" N, long. 114°08'20" W). Named on Castle Rock (1970), Havasu Lake (1970), Lake Havasu City South (1970), and Standard Wash (1959) 7.5' quadrangles. Called Havasu Lake on Topock (1950) 15' quadrangle, but United States Board on Geographic Names (1964a, p. 10) rejected the designations "Havasu Lake" and "Parker Dam Reservoir" for the feature. The name "Lake Havasu" was given after a Mohave Indian chief viewed the lake and used the term "havasu" to describe it—*havasu* means "the water is blue" in the Mohave language (Hanna, p. 134).

Lake Hemet [RIVERSIDE]: *lake*, about 2.25 miles long, behind a dam on South Fork San Jacinto River 5.25 miles south of Idyllwild (lat. 33°39'55" N, long. 116°42'20" W; sec. 7, T 6 S, R 3 E). Named on Idyllwild (1959) 15' quadrangle. Called Hemet Reservoir on San Jacinto (1901) 30' quadrangle, but United States Board on Geographic Names (1962b, p. 17) rejected the names "Hemet Reservoir" and "Hemet Lake" for the feature. W.F. Whittier, a San Francisco capitalist, had construction of the dam begun in 1890 (Hanna, p. 136).

Lakeland Village [RIVERSIDE]: *town*, 2.25 miles south-southwest of Lake Elsinore city hall (lat. 33°38'15" N, long. 117°20'30" W); the place is on the southwest side of Lake Elsinore (1). Named on Lake Elsinore (1953) 7.5' quadrangle.

Lake Mathews [RIVERSIDE]: *lake*, behind a dam 5.25 miles north-northwest of Estelle Mountain (lat. 33°50'15" N, long. 117°27'40" W; sec. 12, T 4 S, R 6 W); the feature is at the head of Cajalco Canyon. Named on Lake Mathews (1967) 7.5' quadrangle. The lake, a storage facility for the aqueduct that brings Colorado River water to Los Angeles, first was called Cajalco Reservoir; the name "Lake Mathews" is for William Burgess Mathews, general counsel for Metropolitan Water District from 1929 until 1931 (Gunther, p. 278).

Lake Moreno: see **Mystic Lake** [RIVERSIDE].

Lake Norconian [RIVERSIDE]: *lake*, 2000 feet long, 3.25 miles north of Corona (lat. 33°55'25" N, long. 117°34'10" W; sec. 12, T 3 S, R 7 W); the lake is at Norco. Named on Corona North (1967) 7.5' quadrangle. United States Geological Survey's (1942c) map shows Norconian club by the lake. Rex B. Clark of Norco gave the name "Norconian" to the country club and to the lake (Gunther, p. 354).

Lake Peak [SAN BERNARDINO]: *ridge*, southwest-trending, 0.5 mile long, 1.25 miles northeast of San Gorgonio Mountain (lat. 34° 06'45" N, long. 116°48'45" W; sec. 6, T 1 S, R 2 E). Named on San Gorgonio Mountain (1970) 7.5' quadrangle.

Lake San Antonio Bucareli: see **Mystic Lake** [RIVERSIDE].

Lakeview [RIVERSIDE]: *town*, 7.5 miles east-northeast of Perris (lat. 33°50'15" N, long. 117°07'05" W; sec. 7, 8, T 4 S, R 2 W). Named on Lakeview (1967) 7.5' quadrangle. Postal authorities established Lake View post office in 1894, discontinued it in 1911, and reestablished it in 1920; the named is from Lake Moreno (present Mystic Lake) (Salley, p. 116).

Lakeview Hot Springs [RIVERSIDE]: *locality*, 6 miles northeast of Perris (lat. 33°50'15" N, long. 117°08'40" W; sec. 12, T 4 S, R 3 W); the place is 1.5 miles west of Lakeview and southeast of Bernasconi Hills. Named on Perris (1967) 7.5' quadrangle. Called Bernasconi Hot Springs on Perris (1943) 15' quadrangle; this name is for Marcellini Orsi Bernasconi, wife of Bernardo Bernasconi of Bernasconi Hills—the place also was called Ramona Hot Springs, Ginsberg Hot Springs, Stewart Hot Springs (Gunther, p. 50-51), and Pilares Hot Spring (Berkstresser, 1968, p. A-10).

Lakeview Mountains [RIVERSIDE]: *range*, 4.5 miles south-southeast of Lakeview (lat. 33°47' N, long. 117°05' W). Named on Lakeview (1967), Perris (1967), and Winchester (1953) 7.5' quadrangles.

Lakeview Point [SAN BERNARDINO]: *locality*, nearly 3 miles north-northeast of Keller Peak (lat. 34°14' N, long. 117°01'35" W; sec. 30, T 2 N, R 1 W). Named on Keller Peak (1967) 7.5' quadrangle.

Laguna de Temecula: see **La Laguna** [RIVERSIDE].

La Laguna [RIVERSIDE]: *land grant*, around Lake Elsinore (1). Named on Alberhill (1954), Lake Elsinore (1953), Murrieta (1953), and Wildomar (1953) 7.5' quadrangles. Julian Manrique received 3 leagues in 1844; Abel Stearns claimed 13,339 acres patented in 1872 (Cowan, p. 43). Perez (p. 71) used the name "Laguna de Temecula" for the grant.

La Loma Hills [SAN BERNARDINO]: *ridge*, north-trending, 2 miles long, 6 miles south-southwest of San Bernardino city hall (lat. 34° 02' N, long. 117°20'45" W). Named on San Bernardino South (1967) 7.5' quadrangle.

Lamb Canyon [RIVERSIDE]: *canyon*, 8 miles long, opens into San Jacinto Valley 6 miles east of Lakeview (lat. 33°51'20" N, long. 117°01' W; near E line sec. 6, T 4 S, R 1 W). Named on Beaumont (1953), Lakeview (1967), and San Jacinto (1953) 7.5' quadrangles. The name is for members of the Lamb family who lived in the canyon (Gunther, p. 282).

La Mesa: see **Coachella** [RIVERSIDE].

Lancaster Valley [RIVERSIDE]: *valley*, 3.5 miles northwest of Aguanga along Wilson Creek (lat. 33°28'55" N, long. 116°54' W). Named on Vail Lake (1953) 7.5' quadrangle. The name recalls Alfred Harris Lancaster and Albert Lancaster, both of whom had homesteads patented in the 1880's in the neighborhood (Gunther, p. 284-285).

Landers [SAN BERNARDINO]: *locality*, 10.5 miles north-northeast of Yucca Valley (lat. 34°15'55" N, long. 116°23'30" W). Named on Landers (1972) 7.5' quadrangle. Postal authorities established Landers post office in 1962; the name is for Newlin Landers, who first envisioned the desert retreat (Salley, p. 117).

Landslide Spring [RIVERSIDE]: *spring*, 8 miles east-southeast of Idyllwild (lat. 33°41'30" N, long. 116°35'55" W; near W line sec. 32, T 5 S, R 4 E). Named on Idyllwild (1959) 15' quadrangle.

Lane Mountain [SAN BERNARDINO]: *peak*, 25 miles west-southwest of Baker (lat. 35°05'25" N, long. 116°56'15" W; sec. 36, T 12 N, R 1 W). Altitude 4522 feet. Named on Lane Mountain (1948) 15' quadrangle.

Lane's Crossing: see **Oro Grande** [SAN BERNARDINO].

Lane Well [SAN BERNARDINO]: *well*, 50 miles west-southwest of Baker (lat. 35°06'30" N, long. 116°56'15" W; near NW cor. sec. 34, T 32 S, R 47 E); the well is 1.25 miles north of Lane Mountain. Named on Lane Mountain (1948) 15' quadrangle. Thompson (1929, p. 288) used the form "Lane's well" for the name.

Lanfair [SAN BERNARDINO]: *locality*, 16 miles south-southeast of Ivanpah (lat. 35°07'40" N, long. 115°11' W). Named on Kingman (1954) 1°x 2° quadrangle. Postal authorities established Lanfair post office in 1912 and discontinued it in 1927 (Frickstad, p. 142). United States Board on Geographic Names (1969, p. 5) rejected the names "Lanfair Corner," "Lanfair Junction," and "Lanfair Site" for the place.

Lanfair Buttes: see **Grotto Hills** [SAN BERNARDINO].

Lanfair Corner: see **Lanfair** [SAN BERNARDINO].

Lanfair Junction: see **Lanfair** [SAN BERNARDINO].

Lanfair Site: see **Lanfair** [SAN BERNARDINO].

Lanfair Valley [SAN BERNARDINO]: *valley*, 16 miles southeast of Ivanpah (lat. 35°10' N, long. 115°07' W). Named on Crescent Peak (1956), Lanfair Valley (1956), and Mid Hills (1955) 15' quadrangles. The name commemorates E.L. Lanfair, a pioneer settler (Hanna, p. 167). Thompson (1929, p. 29) rejected the earlier name "Barnwell Sink" for the place, and suggested that it be called Lanfair Valley because "most of the settlements in it are near Lanfair and that town is not far from its center."

Lang: see **Johnny Lang Canyon** [RIVERSIDE-SAN BERNARDINO].

Langford Dry Lake: see **Langford Well Lake** [SAN BERNARDINO].

Langford Valley: see **Langford Well Lake** [SAN BERNARDINO].

Langford Well [SAN BERNARDINO]: *well*, 31 miles west of Baker (lat.

35°12'05" N, long. 116°37'50" W; sec. 23, T 13 N, R 3 E). Named on Alvord Mountain (1948) 15' quadrangle.

Langford Well Lake [SAN BERNARDINO]: *dry lake,* nearly 1.5 miles long, 31 miles west of Baker (lat. 35°11'45" N, long. 116°37'15" W; around NW cor. sec. 25, T 13 N, R 3 E); Langford Well is at the northwest edge of the dry lake. Named on Alvord Mountain (1948) 15' quadrangle. Thompson (1929, p. 259) called the feature Langford Dry Lake, and noted that it occupies the lowest part of Langford Valley.

Langville: see **Lost Horse Well** [RIVERSIDE].

Lano: see **Wister** [IMPERIAL].

La Palma de la Mano de Dios: see "Regional setting."

Laparra: see **Imperial** [IMPERIAL].

La Paz Canyon [RIVERSIDE]: *canyon,* drained by a stream that flows 2.5 miles to Orange County 15 miles southwest of the present town of Lake Elsinore (lat. 33°30'45" N, long. 117°30'30" W; sec. 33, T 7 S, R 6 W). Named on Cañada Gobernadora (1968) and Sitton Peak (1954) 7.5' quadrangles.

La Purisima Concepcion: see **Pilot Knob** [IMPERIAL].

La Quinta [RIVERSIDE]: *town,* 5.25 miles southeast of Palm Desert (lat. 33°40' N, long. 116°18'30" W). Named on La Qunta (1959) 7.5' quadrangle. Postal authorities established La Quinta post office in 1930, discontinued it in 1943, and reestablished it in 1948 (Frickstad, p. 129). The place began in 1927 with plans for a winter resort featuring a hotel and golf course (Gunther, p. 286).

Larga Flat: see **Lower Larga Flat** [SAN BERNARDINO].

Larrys Boys Camp: see **Camp Awahanes** [SAN BERNARDINO].

La Sierra [RIVERSIDE]:

(1) *land grant,* west of Riverside. Named on Corona North (1967) and Riverside West (1967) 7.5' quadrangles. Vicente Sepulveda received 4 leagues in 1846 and claimed 17,774 acres patented in 1877 (Cowan, p. 98).

(2) *land grant,* at Corona. Named on Black Star Canyon (1967), Corona North (1967), Corona South (1967), and Prado Dam (1967) 7.5' quadrangles. Bernardo Yorba received 4 leagues in 1846 and claimed 17,787 acres patented in 1875 (Cowan, p. 98).

(3) *district,* 8.5 miles west-southwest of Riverside city hall (lat. 33°55'10" N, long. 117°29'45" W); the place is on La Sierra (1) grant. Named on Corona North (1967) and Riverside West (1967) 7.5' quadrangles.

La Sierra Heights [RIVERSIDE]: *locality,* 7 miles west-southwest of Riverside city hall (lat. 33°56'30" N, long. 117°29'15" W); the place is 1.5 miles north-northeast of La Sierra (3) on La Sierra (1) grant. Named on Corona North (1967) and Riverside West (1967) 7.5' quadrangles.

Las Uvas: see **Grapeland** [SAN BERNARDINO] (1).

Lava Bed Mountains [SAN BERNARDINO]: *range,* 16 miles west-southwest of Ludlow (lat. 34°38'30" N, long. 116°26' W). Named on Lavic (1955) 15' quadrangle.

Lava Flow Wash [IMPERIAL]: *stream,* heads in San Diego County and flows 3.5 miles to an unnamed stream 4.5 miles west-southwest of Carrizo Mountain in Imperial County (lat. 32°47'30" N, long. 116°05' W). Named on Carrizo Mountain (1959) 15' quadrangle.

Lava Hills [SAN BERNARDINO]: *range,* 4 miles north of Bagdad (lat. 34°38'30" N, long. 115°53' W). Named on Bagdad (1956) 15' quadrangle.

Lava Mountains [SAN BERNARDINO]: *range,* 6 miles northeast of the village of Red Mountain (lat. 35°26' N, long. 117°32' W). Named on Cuddeback Lake (1954) and Randsburg (1911) 15' quadrangles.

La Verne: see **Camp La Verne** [SAN BERNARDINO].

Lavic [SAN BERNARDINO]: *locality,* 8.5 miles west of Ludlow along Atchison, Topeka and Santa Fe Railroad (lat. 34°43'45" N, long. 116°18'45" W; on E line sec. 2, T 7 N, R 6 E). Named on Lavic (1955) 15' quadrangle. Postal authorities established Lavic post office in 1902, discontinued it in 1903, reestablished it in 1904, and discontinued it in 1909 (Salley, p. 119).

Lavic Lake [SAN BERNARDINO]: *dry lake,* nearly 3 miles long, 11 miles west-southwest of Ludlow (lat. 34°40'15" N, long. 116°20'30" W); the feature is 4.25 miles south-southwest of Lavic. Named on Lavic (1955) 15' quadrangle.

Laws Camp [RIVERSIDE]: *locality,* 3 miles southeast of San Jacinto Peak (lat. 33°46'45" N, long. 116°38'45" W; sec. 35, T 4 S, R 3 E). Named on San Jacinto Peak (1981) 7.5' quadrangle. The name commemorates George Law, a writer who built a stone cabin near the site in 1916 and came there every summer for years (Gunther, p. 287).

Layton Canyon [SAN BERNARDINO]: *canyon,* 3.5 miles long, opens into Searles Valley 10 miles southeast of Trona (lat. 35°40'35" N, long. 117°13'30" W; near NE cor. sec. 15, T 26 S, R 44 E). Named on Wingate Pass (1950) 15' quadrangle. United States Board on Geographic Names (1966c, p. 5) approved the designation "Layton Pass" for a feature located at the head of Layton Canyon (lat. 35°40'55" N, long. 117°09'20" W).

Layton Pass: see **Layton Canyon** [SAN BERNARDINO].

Layton Spring [SAN BERNARDINO]: *spring,* 12 miles east-southeast of Trona (lat. 35°40'45" N, long. 117°11' W); the spring is in Layton Canyon. Named on Wingate Pass (1950) 15' quadrangle

Layton Well [SAN BERNARDINO]: *well,* 14 miles southeast of Trona (lat. 35°39'30" N, long. 117°10' W). Named on Wingate Pass (1950) 15' quadrangle.

Leach Canyon [RIVERSIDE]: *canyon,* 2.5 miles long, heads in Orange County and opens into lowlands 2.25 miles south of Alberhill in Riverside County (lat. 33°40'35" N, long. 117°24'05" W; sec. 4, T 6 S, R 5 W). Named on Alberhill (1954) 7.5' quadrangle. The misspelled name is for Charles Leech, who came to the place in 1884 and filed on a homestead there (Gunther, p. 287).

Leach Lake [SAN BERNARDINO]: *dry lake,* 2.5 miles long, 40 miles northwest of Baker (lat. 35°35'30" N, long. 116°40'30" W). Named on Leach Lake (1948) 15' quadrangle.

Leach Point Mountains: see **Granite Mountains** [SAN BERNARDINO] (1).

Leach Spring [SAN BERNARDINO]: *spring,* 34 miles east-southeast of Trona (lat. 35°33'10" N, long. 116°49'50" W). Named on Quail Mountains (1948) 15' quadrangle.

Lead Mountain [SAN BERNARDINO]:

(1) *peak,* 4.5 miles northwest of Daggett (lat. 34°55'15" N, long. 116°56'05" W; on S line sec. 25, T 10 N, R 1 W). Altitude 2783 feet. Named on Nebo (1953) 7.5' quadrangle.

(2) *peak,* 13 miles west-southwest of Amboy (lat. 34°28' N, long. 115°56'15" W; near N line sec. 4, T 4 N, R 10 E). Altitude 2891 feet. Named on Lead Mountain (1955) 15' quadrangle.

Lead Pipe Spring [SAN BERNARDINO]: *spring,* 24 miles south-southeast of Trona (lat. 35°27'15" N, long. 117°10'45" W). Named on Pilot Knob (1954) 15' quadrangle.

Leastalk: see **Ivanpah** [SAN BERNARDINO].

Lechuga Store [IMPERIAL]: *locality,* about 4.5 miles south-southeast of Holtville (lat. 32°45'20" N, long. 115°20'15" W; sec. 17, T 16 S, R 16 E). Named on Holtville East (1957) 7.5' quadrangle.

Lecyr Well [SAN BERNARDINO]: *well,* 6 miles south-southeast of Ivanpah (lat. 35°16'45" N, long. 115°15' W; sec. 22, T 14 N, R 16 E). Named on Ivanpah (1956) 15' quadrangle.

Lee: see **Ruby Lee Well** [RIVERSIDE].

Lee Lake [RIVERSIDE]: *lake,* 1350 feet long, 3 miles west-northwest of Alberhill along Temescal Wash (lat. 33°44'55" N, long. 117°26'35" W; sec. 7, T 5 S, R 5 W). Named on Alberhill (1954) 7.5' quadrangle.

Ledge [SAN BERNARDINO]: *locality,* 1 mile southeast of Ivanpah along Atchison, Topeka and Santa Fe Railroad (lat. 35°12' N, long. 115°12' W). Named on Ivanpah (1912) 1° quadrangle. Thompson's (1921) map has the names "Ledge" and "Maruba P.O." at the site. Postal authorities established Maruba post office in 1915 and discontinued it in 1926 (Frickstad, p. 143).

Lemona [RIVERSIDE]: *locality,* 3 miles east of Riverside city hall along Atchison, Topeka and Santa Fe Railroad (lat. 33°58'50" N, long. 117°19'20" W; sec. 20, T 2 S, R 4 W). Named on Riverside East (1967) 7.5' quadrangle. The name is from Lemona Heights Company, which owned a tract of orange groves and lemon groves (Gunther, p. 289).

Lenwood [SAN BERNARDINO]: *town,* 4.5 miles west-southwest of Barstow (lat. 34°52'40" N, long. 117°06'15" W; mainly in sec. 17, T 9 N, R 2 W). Named on Barstow (1971) and Barstow SE (1971) 7.5' quadrangles. Frank Woods subdivided the place in the early 1920's and named it for his wife, Ellen Woods (Gudde, 1949, p. 186).

Leon [RIVERSIDE]: *locality,* 8.5 miles northeast of Murrieta (lat. 33° 38'30" N, long. 117°07' W; at S line sec. 17, T 6 S, R 2 W). Named on Elsinore (1901) 30' quadrangle, which shows Leon mine situated 1.25 miles west-northwest of the place. Postal authorities established Leon post office in 1888, moved it 1 mile northeast in 1892, moved it 1.25 miles east in 1894, moved it 1.5 miles west in 1907, and discontinued it in 1911; the name was the middle name of the postmaster, Emil L. Plath (Salley, p. 121).

Leon [SAN BERNARDINO]: *locality,* 1.5 miles north-northwest of Victorville along the railroad (lat. 34°33'25" N, long. 117°18'25" W; at S line sec. 33, T 6 N, R 4 W). Named on Victorville (1956) 7.5' quadrangle. Southwestern Portland Cement Company broke ground for a cement plant at Leon in 1915, and Mojave Northern Railroad brought limestone to the plant—the loading place at the limestone quarries was called Powell to honor F.H. Powell, who later became president of the cement company (Myrick, p. 860).

Leopard Spring [SAN BERNARDINO]: *spring,* 2.5 miles north-northeast of downtown Morongo Valley (lat. 34°05'35" N, long. 116°32'55" W; near SE cor. sec. 10, T 1 S, R 4 E). Named on Morongo Valley (1972) 7.5' quadrangle.

Lewis Canyon: see **Main Street Canyon** [RIVERSIDE].

Lewis Valley [RIVERSIDE]: *valley,* 15 miles south-southeast of Hemet (lat. 33°32'35" N, long. 116°54'10" W; mainly in sec. 20, 29, T 7 S, R 1 E). Named on Sage (1954) 7.5' quadrangle. The name is for Charles Lewis and his wife Katy, who settled in the neighborhood before 1900 (Gunther, p. 290).

Lightning Gulch [SAN BERNARDINO]: *canyon,* drained by a stream that flows 2.25 miles to Cienega Seca Creek nearly 4 miles east-southeast of Sugarloaf Mountain (lat. 34°10'25" N, long. 116°45'10" W; near NE cor. sec. 15, T 1 N, R 2 E). Named on Moonridge (1970) and Onyx Peak

(1972) 7.5' quadrangles.

Lightning Spring [SAN BERNARDINO]: *spring,* 7 miles southeast of Luna Mountain (lat. 34°16'10" N, long. 117°02'45" W; sec. 12, T 2 N, R 2 W). Named on Butler Peak (1971) 7.5' quadrangle.

Lilly Creek [RIVERSIDE]: *stream,* flows less than 1 mile to Strawberry Valley 0.25 mile west-northwest of the center of Idyllwild (lat. 33°44'30" N, long. 116°43'20" W; near NE cor. sec. 13, T 5 S, R 2 E). Named on Idyllwild (1959) 15' quadrangle, and on San Jacinto Peak (1981) 7.5' quadrangle.

Lilly Rock: see **Lily Rock** [RIVERSIDE].

Lily Cup [RIVERSIDE]: *locality,* 3 miles east-northeast of Riverside along Atchison, Topeka and Santa Fe Railroad (lat. 34°00'25" N, long. 117°20' W; sec. 7, T 2 S, R 4 W). Named on San Bernardino South (1967) 7.5' quadrangle.

Lily Rock [RIVERSIDE]: *relief feature,* nearly 4 miles south of San Jacinto Peak (lat. 33°45'35" N, long. 116°40'55" W; near SW cor. sec. 4, T 5 S, R 3 E); the feature is 0.5 mile northwest of Tahquitz Peak. Named on San Jacinto Peak (1981) 7.5' quadrangle. United States Board on Geographic Names (1983c, p. 5) rejected the designations "Tahquitz Rock" and "Lilly Rock" for the feature.

Limber Pine Bench [SAN BERNARDINO]: *area,* 8 miles south of downtown Big Bear Lake (lat. 34°07'40" N, long. 116°56'05" W; sec. 36, T 1 N, R 1 W); the place is 0.5 mile west of Limber Pine Springs. Named on Big Bear Lake (1970) 7.5' quadrangle.

Limber Pine Springs [SAN BERNARDINO]: *spring,* 8 miles south of downtown Big Bear Lake (lat. 34°07'40" N, long. 116°55'40" W; near E line sec. 36, T 1 N, R 1 W). Named on Big Bear Lake (1970) 7.5' quadrangle.

Lindarosa [RIVERSIDE]: *locality,* 2.5 miles southeast of Murrieta along Southern California Railroad (lat. 33°31'25" N, long. 117°11'15" W); the place is near Santa Rosa grant. Named on Elsinore (1901) 30' quadrangle. Called Linda Rose on Murrieta (1943) 15' quadrangle. Postal authorities established Linda Rosa post office in 1888 and discontinued it in 1890 (Frickstad, p. 153). Santa Rosa Land and Improvement Company plated a townsite at the site in 1888 (Gunther, p. 291).

Line Spring [SAN BERNARDINO]: *spring,* 4.25 miles southeast of Luna Mountain (lat. 34°18'20" N, long. 117°04'05" W; at E line sec. 34, T 3 N, R 2 W). Named on Butler Peak (1971) 7.5' quadrangle.

Lion Canyon [RIVERSIDE]: *canyon,* 3 miles long, opens into San Gorgonio Pass 6.5 miles east of Banning (lat. 33°56'05" N, long. 116°45'30" W; sec. 3, T 3 S, R 2 E). Named on Cabazon (1956) 7.5' quadrangle.

Lion Canyon [SAN BERNARDINO]: *canyon,* drained by a stream that flows 3 miles to Deep Creek (1) 1.5 miles south-southwest of Luna Mountain (lat. 34°19'30" N, long. 117°08'35" W; near S line sec. 24, T 3 N, R 3 W). Named on Butler Peak (1971) and Lake Arrowhead (1971) 7.5' quadrangles.

Lion Head Mountain [IMPERIAL]: *hill,* 15 miles northeast of Calipatria (lat. 33°18'25" N, long. 115°21' W; on N line sec. 18, T 10 S, R 16 E). Named on Iris Pass (1963) 15' quadrangle.

Lion Peak [RIVERSIDE]: *peak,* 11 miles southeast of Idyllwild (lat. 33°38'30" N, long. 116°34'15" W; on S line sec. 16, T 6 S, R 4 E). Altitude 6868 feet. Named on Idyllwild (1959) 15' quadrangle.

Lions Canyon [SAN BERNARDINO]: *canyon,* 1.5 miles long, 4 miles northwest of San Juan Hill in San Bernardino, Los Angeles, and Orange Counties (lat. 33°57'10" N, long. 117°47'20" W; mainly in sec. 35, T 2 S, R 9 W). Named on Yorba Linda (1964) 7.5' quadrangle.

Lion Spring [RIVERSIDE]:

(1) *spring,* 6.5 miles south of Alberhill (lat. 33°37'55" N, long. 117° 22'50" W; at E line sec. 22, T 6 S, R 5 W). Named on Alberhill (1954) 7.5' quadrangle.

(2) *spring,* 9 miles east-southeast of Idyllwild (lat. 33°40'30" N, long. 116°34'50" W; on W line sec. 4, T 6 S, R 4 E). Named on Idyllwild (1959) 15' quadrangle.

Little Baldy: see **Mount Harwood** [SAN BERNARDINO].

Little Bear Creek [SAN BERNARDINO]: *stream,* flows 6.5 miles to Deep Creek (1) 5 miles south of Luna Mountain (lat. 34°16'25" N, long. 117°07'35" W; sec. 7, T 2 N, R 2 W). Named on Harrison Mountain (1967) and Lake Arrowhead (1971) 7.5' quadrangles.

Little Bear Lake: see **Lake Arrowhead** [SAN BERNARDINO].

Little Bear Peak [SAN BERNARDINO]: *peak,* 2 miles northwest of Fawnskin (lat. 34°17'30" N, long. 116°58'10" W; near N line sec. 3, T 2 N, R 1 W). Altitude 7621 feet. Named on Fawnskin (1971) 7.5' quadrangle.

Little Bear Spring [SAN BERNARDINO]: *spring,* 2.5 miles northwest of Fawnskin (lat. 34°17'50" N, long. 116°58'25" W; near SW cor. sec. 34, T 3 N, R 1 W); the spring is 0.5 mile northwest of Little Bear Peak. Named on Fawnskin (1971) 7.5' quadrangle.

Little Bear Valley: see **Lake Arrowhead** [SAN BERNARDINO] (1).

Little Cahuilla Mountain [RIVERSIDE]: *peak,* 13 miles southeast of Hemet (lat. 33°36'30" N, long. 116°48'35" W; sec. 31, T 6 S, R 2 E); the peak is 2.5 miles northwest of Cahuilla Mountain. Named on Hemet (1957) 15' quadrangle. United States Board on Geographic Names (1963b, p. 16) rejected the name "Little Coahuila Mountain" for the feature.

Little Camp Spring [RIVERSIDE]: *spring,* 9 miles east-southeast of Idyllwild (lat. 33°41'10" N, long. 116°34'50" W; near SW cor. sec. 33, T 5 S, R 4 E). Named on Idyllwild (1959) 15' quadrangle.

Little Charlton Peak [SAN BERNARDINO]: peak, 1.5 miles west-northwest of San Gorgonio Mountain (lat. 34°06'35" N, long. 116° 50'55" W; sec. 2, T 1 S, R 1 E); the feature is less than 0.5 mile south-southeast of Charlton Peak. Altitude 10,696 feet. Named on San Gorgonio Mountain (1970) 7.5' quadrangle.

Little Chemehuevi Valley [SAN BERNARDINO]: *canyon,* 23 miles north-northeast of Vidal (lat. 34°24'10" N, long. 114°16'30" W). Named on Parker (1911) 30' quadrangle. Water of Lake Havasu now floods the feature.

Little Chino Creek [SAN BERNARDINO]: *stream,* flows 3.5 miles to Chino Creek 5.25 miles north-northeast of San Juan Hill (lat. 33° 59'10" N, long. 117°42'20" W). Named on Prado Dam (1967) 7.5' quadrangle.

Little Chuckwalla Mountains [RIVERSIDE]: *range,* 25 miles west-southwest of Blythe (lat. 33°29'15" N, long. 115°00'30" W); the range is east of the southeast end of Chuckwalla Mountains. Named on Chuckwalla Spring (1953), McCoy Spring (1952), Palo Verde Mountains (1953), and Sidewinder Well (1952) 15' quadrangles.

Little Cienaga Seca [SAN BERNARDINO]: *area,* 12.5 miles northwest of downtown Morongo Valley (lat. 34°10'30" N, long. 116° 44' W; near NW cor. sec. 13, T 1 N, R 2 E); the place is 1 mile southwest of Cienaga Seca. Named on Onyx Peak (1972) 7.5' quadrangle.

Little Coahuila Mountain: see **Little Cahuilla Mountain** [RIVERSIDE].

Little Cowhole Mountain [SAN BERNARDINO]: *ridge,* west-trending, 2 miles long, 42 miles west-southwest of Ivanpah (lat. 35°10'30" N, long. 116°30' W). Named on Old Dad Mountain (1956) and Soda Lake (1956) 15' quadrangles.

Little Desert [RIVERSIDE]: *area,* 10 miles east-southeast of Idyllwild (lat. 33°39'50" N, long. 116°34'05" W; sec. 9, T 6 S, R 4 E). Named on Idyllwild (1959) 15' quadrangle.

Little Dry Lake [SAN BERNARDINO]: *dry lake,* 1700 feet long, 5 miles north of the village of Red Mountain (lat. 35°25'50" N, long. 117°35'45" W; sec. 8, 9, T 29 S, R 41 E). Named on Klinker Mountain (1967) 7.5' quadrangle.

Little Dumont Dunes: see **Dumont Dunes** [SAN BERNARDINO].

Little Fargo Canyon [RIVERSIDE]: *canyon,* 4.5 miles long, opens into Fargo Canyon 7.5 miles east-northeast of Indio (lat. 33°45'40" N, long. 116°05'45" W; sec. 1, T 5 S, R 8 E). Named on Lost Horse Mountain (1958) 15' quadrangle.

Little Green Valley [SAN BERNARDINO]: *valley,* 2.5 miles north of Keller Peak (lat. 34°14' N, long. 117°03' W; near NE cor. sec. 26, T 2 N, R 2 W); the place is 1 mile southeast of Green Valley. Named on Keller Peak (1967) 7.5' quadrangle.

Little Horsethief Canyon [SAN BERNARDINO]: *canyon,* drained by a stream that flows 5 miles to Horsethief Canyon 16 miles south of Victorville (lat. 34°18'45" N, long. 117°21'20" W). Named on Cajon (1956) and Cedar Springs (1956) 7.5' quadrangles.

Little Lake [RIVERSIDE]: *intermittent lake,* 1250 feet long, 3.25 miles east-southeast of downtown Hemet (lat. 33°43'40" N, long. 116°55' W; near N line sec. 19, T 5 S, R 1 E). Named on Hemet (1953) 7.5' quadrangle.

Little Maria Mountains [RIVERSIDE]: *range,* 25 miles northwest of Blythe (lat. 33°53' N, long. 114°53'30" W). Named on Midland (1952) 15' quadrangle.

Little Mill Creek [SAN BERNARDINO]: *stream,* flows 4.25 miles to Plunge Creek 1.5 miles east-southeast of Harrison Mountain (lat. 34°09'05" N, long. 117°08' W; sec. 19, T 1 N, R 2 W). Named on Harrison Mountain (1967) 7.5' quadrangle. Redlands (1901) 15' quadrangle shows the stream as part of Plunge Creek.

Little Morongo Canyon [RIVERSIDE-SAN BERNARDINO]: *canyon,* 7.5 miles long, on Riverside-San Bernardino County line along Little Morongo Creek above a point 11 miles north of Palm Springs (lat. 33°59'20" N, long. 116°31'30" W; near NW cor. sec. 24, T 2 S, R 4 E). Named on Desert Hot Springs (1955) and Morongo Valley (1972) 7.5' quadrangles.

Little Morongo Canyon [SAN BERNARDINO]: *canyon,* 12.5 miles long, opens into Morongo Valley (1) 4.5 miles northeast of downtown Morongo Valley (lat. 34°05'45" N, long. 116°31'30" W; near W line sec. 12, T 1 S, R 4 E). Named on Morongo Valley (1972), Onyx Peak (1972), and Rimrock (1972) 7.5' quadrangles.

Little Morongo Creek [RIVERSIDE-SAN BERNARDINO]: *stream* and *dry wash,* heads in San Bernardino County and extends for 21 miles to Little Morongo Wash 11 miles north of Palm Springs in Riverside County (lat. 33°59'20" N, long. 116°31'30" W; near NW cor. sec. 24, T 2 S, R 4 E); the stream goes through Little Morongo Canyon [SAN BERNARDINO], across Morongo Valley [SAN BERNARDINO] (1), and through Little Morongo Canyon [RIVERSIDE-SAN BERNARDINO]. Named on Morongo Valley (1972) 7.5' quadrangle.

Little Morongo Heights [SAN BERNARDINO]: *district,* 5 miles northeast of downtown Morongo Valley (lat. 34°05'45" N, long. 116°31' W; sec. 12, T 1 S, R 4 E); the place is at the northeast end of Morongo Valley (1).

Named on Morongo Valley (1972) 7.5' quadrangle.

Little Morongo Wash [RIVERSIDE]: *dry wash,* extends for 1.5 miles to join Big Morongo Wash and form Morongo Wash 9 miles north of Palm Springs (lat. 33°57'45" N, long. 116°31'35" W; near SW cor. sec. 25, T 2 S, R 4 E). Named on Desert Hot Springs (1955) 7.5' quadrangle.

Little Mountain: see **Shandin Hills** [SAN BERNARDINO].

Little Mule Mountains [IMPERIAL]: *range,* 22 miles north of Glamis (lat. 33°19'45" N, long. 115°05'45" W). Named on Chuckwalla Spring (1953) 15' quadrangle.

Little Paradise [RIVERSIDE]: *locality,* 13 miles east-southeast of Idyllwild in Palm Canyon (lat. 33°40' N, long. 116°31' W; sec. 12, T 6 S, R 4 E). Named on Idyllwild (1959) 15' quadrangle.

Little Picacho Peak [IMPERIAL]: *peak,* 6.5 miles east-northeast of Picacho Peak (lat. 32°59'50" N, long. 114°33'05" W; sec. 34, T 13 S, R 23 E). Named on Little Picacho Peak (1965) 7.5' quadrangle. On Picacho Peak (1945) 15' quadrangle, the name "Little Picacho Peak" applies to a feature located 1 mile north of Picacho Peak.

Little Picacho Wash [IMPERIAL]: *stream* and *dry wash,* extends for 4 miles to Colorado River 29 miles south-southeast of Palo Verde at Picacho (lat. 33°01'30" N, long. 114°36'45" W; sec. 24, T 13 S, R 22 E). Named on Picacho (1964), Picacho Peak (1965), and Picacho SW (1965) 7.5' quadrangles. Called Picacho Wash on Picacho (1945) 15' quadrangle.

Little Pigeon Pass [SAN BERNARDINO]: *pass,* 4.5 miles south of San Bernardino city hall (lat. 34°02'20" N, long. 117°18' W; sec. 33, T 1 S, R 4 W). Named on San Bernardino South (1967) 7.5' quadrangle.

Little Pine Flat [SAN BERNARDINO]: *area,* 4.5 miles east-southeast of Luna Mountain (lat. 34°19' N, long. 117°03'20" W; sec. 26, T 3 N, R 2 W). Named on Butler Peak (1971) 7.5' quadrangle.

Little Pinyon Flat [RIVERSIDE]: *area,* 10.5 miles south of Palm Desert (lat. 33°34'05" N, long. 116°23' W); the place is 5 miles east-southeast of Pinyon Flat. Named on Palm Desert (1959) 15' quadrangle.

Little Piute Mountains [SAN BERNARDINO]: *range,* 12.5 miles east-southeast of Essex (lat. 34°38'30" N, long. 115°03'30" W); the range is 7.5 miles southeast of the south end of Piute Mountains. Named on Essex (1956) 15' quadrangle.

Little Round Valley [RIVERSIDE]: *relief feature,* 0.5 mile west-southwest of San Jacinto Peak (lat. 33°48'45" N, long. 118°41'20" W; sec. 20, T 4 S, R 3 E). Named on San Jacinto Peak (1981) 7.5' quadrangle.

Little San Bernardino Mountains [RIVERSIDE-SAN BERNARDINO]: *range,* east and southeast of Morongo Valley [SAN BERNARDINO] (1) along the northeast side of Coachella Valley on Riverside-San Bernardino County line Named on San Bernardino (1966) and Santa Ana (1959) 1°x 2° quadrangles. The range also is called Morongo Mountains (O'Neal, p. 14).

Little Sand Canyon [SAN BERNARDINO]: *canyon,* drained by a stream that flows 2.25 miles to lowlands 4.5 miles west of Harrison Mountain (lat. 34°09'25" N, long. 117°14'10" W; sec. 19, T 1 N, R 3 W); the mouth of the canyon is less than 1 mile west-northwest of the mouth of Sand Canyon (2). Named on Harrison Mountain (1967) 7.5' quadrangle. Redlands (1954) 15' quadrangle has the name "Little Sand Creek" for the stream in the canyon.

Little Sand Creek: see **Little Sand Canyon** [SAN BERNARDINO].

Little San Gorgonio Creek [RIVERSIDE SAN BERNARDINO]: *stream,* heads in San Bernardino County and flows 10.5 miles to San Timoteo Canyon 17 miles northeast of Perris in Riverside County (lat. 33°56'30" N, long. 117°00'15" W; sec. 5, T 3 S, R 1 W). Named on Beaumont (1953), El Casco (1967), and Forest Falls (1970) 7.5' quadrangles.

Little San Gorgonio Peak [SAN BERNARDINO]: *peak,* 4.25 miles southwest of San Gorgonio Mountain (lat. 34°03'35" N, long. 116° 53' W; sec. 28, T 1 S, R 1 E). Altitude 9133 feet. Named on Forest Falls (1970) 7.5' quadrangle.

Little Shay Mountain [SAN BERNARDINO]: *peak,* 4.5 miles southeast of Luna Mountain (lat. 34°17'50" N, long. 117°04'20" W; near SE cor. sec. 34, T 3 N, R 2 W); the peak is 1 mile southeast of Shay Mountain. Altitude 6635 feet. Named on Butler Peak (1971) 7.5' quadrangle. United States Board on Geographic Names (1966c, p. 5) rejected the names "Hawes Peak" and "Shay Mountains" for the feature.

Little Tahquitz Valley [RIVERSIDE]: *area,* 3.5 miles south-southeast of San Jacinto Peak (lat. 33°45'50" N, long. 113°39'45" W; near W line sec. 3, T 5 S, R 3 E); the place is less than 0.5 mile south of Tahquitz Meadow, which is called Tahquitz Valley on Palm Springs (1957) 15' quadrangle. Named on San Jacinto Peak (1981) 7.5' quadrangle.

Little Temecula [RIVERSIDE]: *land grant,* 3 miles southeast of the town of Temecula. Named on Pechanga (1968) 7.5' quadrangle. Pablo Apis, an Indian, received 0.5 league in 1845 and claimed 2233 acres patented in 1873 (Cowan, p. 101). Perez (p. 101), who used the name "Lands in Valley of Temecula" for the grant, gave Maria A. Apis as the patentee.

Little Thomas Mountain [RIVERSIDE]: *peak,* 7.5 miles south of Idyllwild (lat. 33°37'50" N, long. 116°41'50" W; near SW cor. sec. 20, T 6 S, R 3 E); the peak is on the ridge called Thomas Mountain. Altitude 6559 feet. Named on Idyllwild (1959) 15' quadrangle.

Little Thorne Mountains: see **Gold Valley** [SAN BERNARDINO].

Live Oak Canyon [RIVERSIDE]: *canyon,* drained by a stream that flows 3.25 miles to Palm Canyon 15 miles east-southeast of Idyllwild (lat. 33°37'30" N, long. 116°30'30" W; near NW cor. sec. 30, T 6 S, R 5 E). Named on Idyllwild (1959) 15' quadrangle.

Live Oak Canyon [RIVERSIDE-SAN BERNARDINO]: *canyon,* heads in San Bernardino County and extends for nearly 4 miles along Yucaipa Creek to open into San Timoteo Canyon 12.5 miles east of Riverside in Riverside County (lat. 34°00'10" N, long. 117°09'50" W; sec. 14, T 2 S, R 3 W). Named on Redlands (1967) and Yucaipa (1967) 7.5' quadrangles.

Live Oak Canyon [SAN BERNARDINO]: *canyon,* 0.5 mile long, 5 miles south of Ivanpah (lat. 35°16'15" N, long. 115°17'45" W; near NE cor. sec. 30, T 14 N, R 16 E). Named on Ivanpah (1956) 15' quadrangle.

Live Oak Spring [RIVERSIDE]: *spring,* 12.5 miles southeast of Idyllwild (lat. 33°37'20" N, long. 116°33'20" W; sec. 27, T 6 S, R 4 E); the spring is in Live Oak Canyon. Named on Idyllwild (1959) 15' quadrangle.

Live Oak Spring [SAN BERNARDINO]: *spring,* 12 miles south-southwest of Ivanpah (lat. 35°11'45" N, long. 115°25'35" W; near W line sec. 19, T 13 N, R 15 E). Named on Mid Hills (1955) 15' quadrangle.

Live Oak Tank [RIVERSIDE]: *water feature,* 22 miles north-northeast of Indio (lat. 34°00' N, long. 116°03'15" W; at W line sec. 16, T 2 S, R 9 E). Named on Lost Horse Mountain (1958) 15' quadrangle.

Liverpool Landing [SAN BERNARDINO]: *locality,* 26 miles north-northeast of Vidal along Colorado River (lat. 34°28'25" N, long. 114°22'30" W). Named on Parker (1911) 30' quadrangle. Water of Lake Havasu now covers the site.

Lizard Spring [SAN BERNARDINO]: *spring,* 4.25 miles east of Luna Mountain (lat. 34°20'15" N, long. 117°03'15" W; near NE cor. sec. 23, T 3 N, R 2 W). Named on Butler Peak (1971) 7.5' quadrangle.

Lobecks Pass [SAN BERNARDINO]: *canyon,* 11.5 miles south of Needles (lat. 34°40'35" N, long. 114°37'15" W). Named on Monumental Pass (1971) and Whale Mountain (1971) 7.5' quadrangles.

Lockhart [SAN BERNARDINO]:

(1) *locality,* 28 miles southeast of the village of Red Mountain (lat. 35°00'50" N, long. 117°19'45" W; at E line sec. 30, T 11 N, R 4 W). Named on Fremont Peak (1956) 15' quadrangle. Postal authorities established Lockart post office in 1953 and discontinued it in 1958; the name commemorates L.M. Lockhart and his family, early settlers at the place (Salley, p. 124).

(2) *locality,* 17 miles west of Barstow along Atchison, Topeka and Santa Fe Railroad (lat. 34°56'30" N, long. 117°20' W; sec. 19, T 10 N, R 4 W). Named on Hawes (1956) 15' quadrangle.

Lodge Canyon [SAN BERNARDINO]: *canyon,* drained by a stream that flows 1 mile to Slide Creek (2) 5.5 miles west-southwest of San Gorgonio Mountain (lat. 34°04'40" N, long. 116°55'15" W; near S line sec. 18, T 1 S, R 1 E). Named on Forest Falls (1970) 7.5' quadrangle.

Lodgepole Spring [SAN BERNARDINO]: *spring,* nearly 1.5 miles north of San Gorgonio Mountain (lat. 34°07'05" N, long. 116°49'20" W; near NW cor. sec. 6, T 1 S, R 2 E). Named on San Gorgonio Mountain (1970) 7.5' quadrangle.

Logan Creek [RIVERSIDE]: *stream,* flows 3.5 miles to North Fork San Jacinto River 10.5 miles east of San Jacinto (lat. 33°45'35" N, long. 116°46'55" W; near S line sec. 4, T 5 S, R 2 E). Named on Lake Fulmor (1956) and San Jacinto Peak (1981) 7.5' quadrangles.

Loma Linda [SAN BERNARDINO]: *town,* 4.25 miles south-southeast of San Bernardino city hall (lat. 34°02'55" N, long. 117°15'35" W). Named on San Bernardino South (1967) 7.5' quadrangle. San Bernardino (1901) 15' quadrangle has the name "Mound City" at the site. Postal authorities established Mound Station post office at the place in 1876 and discontinued it in 1877 (Salley, p. 147). They established Lomalinda post office in 1901, discontinued it in 1905, and established Loma Linda post office in 1908 (Frickstad, p. 143). The town incorporated in 1970. The railroad stop at the site in the 1870's was called Mound Station, and a tourist development started there in the early 1880's was called Mound City, but the project was abandoned; in the late 1890's the place was revived as a health resort called Loma Linda, but this closed in 1904—eventually the Seventh Day Adventists bought the property (Gudde, 1949, p. 192; Richards).

Lone Butte [SAN BERNARDINO]: *ridge,* north-northeast-trending, 2.25 miles long, 14 miles west-southwest of Trona (lat. 35°39'45" N, long. 117°36'15" W). Named on Lone Butte (1973) 7.5' quadrangle. United States Board on Geographic Names (1975b, p. 5) gave the variant name "B Mountain" for the feature.

Lone Pine Canyon [SAN BERNARDINO]: *canyon,* 9 miles long, center 5.5 miles west-northwest of Cajon (lat. 34°19' N, long. 117° 32'45" W). Named on Cajon (1956) and Telegraph Peak (1956) 7.5' quadrangles.

Lone Pine Island [SAN BERNARDINO]: *island,* 300 feet long, 7.5 miles south-southwest of Luna Mountain in Lake Arrowhead (1) (lat. 34°15'10" N, long. 117°11'45" W). Named on Lake Arrowhead (1971) 7.5' quadrangle.

Lone Pine Reservoir [RIVERSIDE]: *water feature,* 22 miles south of Idyllwild (lat. 33°25'40" N, long. 116°38'25" W; near S line sec. 35, T 8 S,

R 3 E). Named on Beauty Mountain (1960) 7.5' quadrangle.

Lone Valley: see **Big Bear City** [SAN BERNARDINO].

Lone Willow Spring [SAN BERNARDINO]: *spring,* 15 miles east-southeast of Trona (lat. 35°39'30" N, long. 117°08' W). Named on Wingate Pass (1950) 15' quadrangle. A stage station and a rest stop on the twenty-mule-team route from Death Valley were at the spring; the single willow tree that gave the spring its name came from a willow branch that some driver had used as a horse whip and then stuck in the moist ground (Federal Writers Project, p. 69).

Lone Wolf Colony [SAN BERNARDINO]: *locality,* 9.5 miles east-southeast of Victorville (lat. 34°28'15" N, long. 117°09'20" W; at NE cor. sec. 2, T 4 N, R 3 W). Named on Apple Valley South (1971) 7.5' quadrangle.

Long Canyon [RIVERSIDE]:

(1) *canyon,* heads in Orange County and extends for 1.5 miles in Riverside County to Morrell Canyon 2.25 miles north-northeast of Sitton Peak (lat. 33°37'05" N, long. 117°25'45" W; sec. 29, T 6 S, R 5 W). Named on Alberhill (1954) and Sitton Peak (1954) 7.5' quadrangles.

(2) *canyon,* 5.5 miles long, opens into lowlands along Murrieta Creek 5 miles southeast of Murrieta (lat. 33°30'20" N, long. 117° 08'55" W). Named on Bachelor Mountain (1953) and Murrieta (1953) 7.5' quadrangles.

(3) *canyon,* on Riverside-San Diego County line, 2.25 miles long in Riverside County, opens into the canyon of Temecula Creek 2.5 miles west of Aguanga (lat. 33°26'45" N, long. 116°54'25" W; near W line sec. 29, T 8 S, R 1 E). Named on Vail Lake (1953) 7.5' quadrangle.

Long Canyon [RIVERSIDE-SAN BERNARDINO]: *canyon,* drained by a stream that heads in San Bernardino County and flows 9.5 miles to lowlands 11.5 miles north of Cathedral City in Riverside County (lat. 33°56'50" N, long. 116°27'15" W; near SW cor. sec. 34, T 2 S, R 5 E). Named on Seven Palms Valley (1958) and Yucca Valley South (1972) 7.5' quadrangles.

Long Canyon [SAN BERNARDINO]: *canyon,* drained by a stream that flows less than 1 mile to Slide Creek (2) 5.5 miles west-southwest of San Gorgonio Mountain (lat. 34°04'45" N, long. 116°55'15" W; near S line sec. 18, T 1 S, R 1 E). Named on Forest Falls (1970) 7.5' quadrangle.

Long Point [SAN BERNARDINO]:

(1) *peninsula,* 7 miles south-southwest of Luna Mountain along Lake Arrowhead (1) (lat. 34°15'30" N, long. 117°11'40" W; mainly in sec. 16, T 2 N, R 3 W). Named on Lake Arrowhead (1971) 7.5' quadrangle.

(2) *ridge,* south-southwest-trending, 1 mile long, 2.5 miles north of Harrison Mountain (lat. 34°12' N, long. 117°09' W; sec. 1, T 1 N, R 3 W). Named on Harrison Mountain (1967) 7.5' quadrangle.

Long Valley [RIVERSIDE]:

(1) *valley,* 2.25 miles east of San Jacinto Peak (lat. 33°48'40" N, long. 116°38'20" W; sec. 23, T 4 S, R 3 E). Named on San Jacinto Peak (1981) 7.5' quadrangle.

(2) *canyon,* drained by a stream that flows 7.5 miles to Santa Gertrudis Creek 6.5 miles east of Murrieta (lat. 33°32'35" N, long. 117°06'30" W; sec. 20, T 7 S, R 2 W). Named on Bachelor Mountain (1953) 7.5' quadrangle.

Long Valley [SAN BERNARDINO]: *valley,* 25 miles east of Trona (lat. 35°46' N, long. 116°55' W). Named on Wingate Wash (1950) 15' quadrangle. The name is from the length of the feature (Palmer, p. 45).

Long Valley Creek [RIVERSIDE]: *stream,* flows 4.25 miles to Hidden Fork 4.5 miles west-southwest of Palm Springs (lat. 33°47'50" N, long. 116°37'05" W; near E line sec. 25, T 4 S, R 3 E); the stream goes through Long Valley (1). Named on Palm Springs (1957) and San Jacinto Peak (1981) 7.5' quadrangles.

Lookout Mountain [RIVERSIDE]: *ridge,* southeast-trending, 1.5 miles long, 15 miles south-southeast of Idyllwild (lat. 33°33'15" N, long. 116°34'15" W). Named on Idyllwild (1959) 15' quadrangle.

Lookout Point [SAN BERNARDINO]: *locality,* 4.5 miles southwest of downtown Big Bear Lake (lat. 34°12'15" N, long. 116°58'45" W; near NW cor. sec. 3, T 1 N, R 1 W). Named on Big Bear Lake (1970) 7.5' quadrangle.

Lord's Canyon: see **Main Street Canyon** [RIVERSIDE].

Lorenz Canyon [RIVERSIDE]: *canyon,* drained by a stream that flows nearly 1 mile to Diamond Valley 4 miles south-southeast of downtown Hemet (lat. 33°41'35" N, long. 116°57'10" W; sec. 35, T 5 S, R 1 W). Named on Hemet (1953) 7.5' quadrangle.

Los Alamos Canyon [RIVERSIDE]: *canyon,* drained by a stream that flows 6.5 miles to San Mateo Canyon 4 miles southeast of Sitton Peak (lat. 33°33'05" N, long. 117°23'35" W). Named on Sitton Peak (1954) and Wildomar (1953) 7.5' quadrangles.

Los Alamos Valley: see **Auld Valley** [RIVERSIDE].

Los Chinos Spring [RIVERSIDE]: *spring,* 3.5 miles southwest of Sitton Peak (lat. 33°32'45" N, long. 117°29' W; near W line sec. 23, T 7 S, R 6 W). Named on Sitton Peak (1954) 7.5' quadrangle.

Los Serranos [SAN BERNARDINO]: *locality,* 4.5 miles north-northeast of San Juan Hill (lat. 33°58'15" N, long. 117°42'30" W). Named on Prado Dam (1967) 7.5' quadrangle. Postal authorities established Los Serranos post office in 1954 (Salley, p. 128).

Lost Creek [SAN BERNARDINO]:

(1) *stream,* flows nearly 1 mile to Icehouse Canyon 13 miles north of Ontario city hall (lat. 34°14'45" N, long. 117°36'35" W; at E line sec. 21, T 2 N, R 7 W). Named on Cucamonga Peak (1966) 7.5' quadrangle.

(2) *stream,* flows 3 miles to Santa Ana River 2 miles south-southwest of Sugarloaf Mountain (lat. 34°10'10" N, long. 116°49'25" W; near E line sec. 13, T 1 N, R 1 E). Named on Moonridge (1970) 7.5' quadrangle.

Lost Creek: see **Momyer Creek** [SAN BERNARDINO]; **Stubbe Canyon** [RIVERSIDE].

Lost Horse Mountain [RIVERSIDE]: *ridge,* northwest-trending, 1.5 miles long, 16 miles north-northeast of Indio (lat. 33°56' N, long. 116°07'45" W). Named on Lost Horse Mountain (1958) 15' quadrangle, which shows Lost Horse mine by the feature.

Lost Horse Mountain: see **Ryan Mountain** [RIVERSIDE].

Lost Horse Spring: see **Lost Horse Well** [RIVERSIDE].

Lost Horse Valley [RIVERSIDE]: *valley,* 19 miles north of Indio (lat. 33°59'30" N, long. 116°09'45" W). Named on Lost Horse Mountain (1958) 15' quadrangle, and on Indian Cove (1972) 7.5' quadrangle.

Lost Horse Well [RIVERSIDE]: *well,* 19 miles north-northeast of Indio (lat. 33°59' N, long. 116°08'45" W); the feature is 2.5 miles north-northwest of Lost Horse Mountain. Named on Lost Horse Mountain (1958) 15' quadrangle. The feature also was known as Lost Horse Spring (Brown, 1920, p. 81) and as Witch Springs (Weight, p. 9). The mining camp at the spot in 1894 was called Langville for Johnny Lang, who filed on Lost Horse mine in 1893 (Weight, p. 10).

Lost Lake [RIVERSIDE]: *lake,* 2050 feet long, 7 miles south-southeast of Vidal in a cutoff meander of Colorado River (lat. 34°01'20" N, long. 114°28'15" W). Named on Parker SW (1970) 7.5' quadrangle.

Lost Lake [SAN BERNARDINO]:

(1) *dry lake,* 2.25 miles long, 30 miles east of Trona (lat. 35°45'10" N, long. 116°49'30" W; sec. 12, 13, T 19 N, R 1 E). Named on Quail Mountains (1948) and Wingate Wash (1950) 15' quadrangles.

(2) *lake,* 500 feet long, nearly 2 miles south of Cajon (lat. 34°16'20" N, long. 117°27'50" W; sec. 12, T 2 N, R 6 W). Named on Cajon (1956) 7.5' quadrangle.

Lost Lake Landing: see **Lost Lake Resort** [RIVERSIDE].

Lost Lake Resort [RIVERSIDE]: *locality,* 7.5 miles south-southeast of Vidal [SAN BERNARDINO] (lat. 34°00'40" N, long. 114°28'25" W; near E line sec 8, T 2 S, R 24 E). Named on Parker SW (1970) 7.5' quadrangle. Parker (1949) 15' quadrangle shows Lost Lake Landing at the site.

Lost Palms Canyon [RIVERSIDE]: *canyon,* 5 miles long, opens into lowlands 1.5 miles north of Chiriaco Summit (lat. 33°41' N, long. 115°43' W; at N line sec. 3, T 6 S, R 12 E); Lost Palms Oasis is in the canyon.. Named on Cottonwood Spring (1958) and Hayfield (1963) 15' quadrangles.

Lost Palms Oasis [RIVERSIDE]: *spring,* 4.5 miles north-northwest of Chiriaco Summit (lat. 33°43'20" N, long. 115°44'50" W; at E line sec. 20, T 5 S, R 12 E). Named on Hayfield (1963) 15' quadrangle. Philip Johnston, a writer for *Touring Topics,* visited the canyon in 1930 and named it (Gunther, p. 299).

Lost Valley: see **Death Valley** [SAN BERNARDINO].

Lovelace Canyon [SAN BERNARDINO]: *canyon,* drained by a stream that flows 2.5 miles to lowlands 15 miles southeast of Victorville (lat. 34°24'45" N, long. 117°04'20" W; at N line sec. 27, T 4 N, R 2 W). Named on Fifteenmile Valley (1971) 7.5' quadrangle.

Lower Borrego Valley [IMPERIAL]: *valley,* 21 miles south of Desert Shores on Imperial-San Diego County line (lat. 33°05'30" N, long. 116°04'50" W); the feature is southeast of of Borrego Valley, which is in San Diego County. Named on Borrego Mountain SE (1958) and Harpers Well (1956) 7.5' quadrangles.

Lower Covington Flat [RIVERSIDE-SAN BERNARDINO]: *valley,* 6.5 miles south of Joshua Tree on Riverside-San Bernardino County line (lat. 34°02'45" N, long. 116°19' W); the place is 1.5 miles northeast of Upper Covington Flat [RIVERSIDE]. Named on Joshua Tree South (1972) 7.5' quadrangle.

Lower Holcomb: see **Holcomb Valley** [SAN BERNARDINO].

Lower Larga Flat [SAN BERNARDINO]: *area,* 7.5 miles southeast of Luna Mountain (lat. 34°17'05" N, long. 117°01'05" W; sec. 6, T 2 N, R 1 W). Named on Butler Peak (1971) 7.5' quadrangle.

Lower Lytle Creek Ridge [SAN BERNARDINO]: *ridge,* southeast-trending, 7 miles long, center 3.25 miles west-northwest of Devore (lat. 34°14' N, long. 117°27'15" W); the feature is the southeast extension of Upper Lytle Creek Ridge. Named on Cajon (1956) and Devore (1966) 7.5' quadrangles.

Lower Narrows [SAN BERNARDINO]: *narrows,* 3 miles north-northwest of Victorville along Mojave River (lat. 34°34'25" N, long. 117°19'10" W; near S line sec. 29, T 6 N, R 4 W); the feature is nearly 4 miles downstream from Upper Narrows. Named on Victorville (1956) 7.5' quadrangle.

Lower Slough [SAN BERNARDINO]: *marsh,* 1.25 miles southeast of downtown Victorville near Mojave River (lat. 34°31'15" N, long. 117°16'45" W; near E line sec. 15, T 5 N, R 4 W). Named on Victorville (1956) 7.5' quadrangle.

Lucas Canyon [RIVERSIDE]: *canyon,* drained by a stream that flows nearly 2 miles to Orange County 2.25 miles west-southwest of Sitton Peak (lat.

33°34'20" N, long. 117°28'50" W; sec. 11, T 7 S, R 6 W). Named on Sitton Peak (1954) 7.5' quadrangle.

Lucerne [RIVERSIDE]: *locality*, 3.5 miles west-northwest of the present town of Lake Elsinore (lat. 33°41'30" N, long. 117°23'10" W). Named on Elsinore (1901) 30' quadrangle. Promoters laid out a townsite at the place in 1887 (Gunther, p. 301).

Lucerne Dry Lake: see **Lucerne Lake** [SAN BERNARDINO].

Lucerne Lake [SAN BERNARDINO]: *dry lake*, 5 miles long, 15 miles south-southwest of Ord Mountain (lat. 34°30' N, long. 116° 57'30" W); the feature is in Lucerne Valley (1). Named on Ord Mountains (1955) 15' quadrangle, and on Lucerne Valley (1971) 7.5' quadrangle. Called Lucerne Dry Lake on Lucerne Valley (1947) 15' quadrangle.

Lucerne Valley [SAN BERNARDINO]:

(1) *valley*, 21 miles east-southeast of Victorville (lat. 34°26' N, long. 116°57' W). Named on Ord Mountains (1955) 15' quadrangle, and on Couger Buttes (1971), Fifteenmile Valley (1971), and Lucerne Valley (1971) 7.5' quadrangles. James E. Goulding settled at the place in 1897, and later suggested the name "Lucerne Valley" because the place appeared to be a good one for growing alfalfa, which also is called lucerne (Gudde, 1969, p. 185-186).

(2) *town*, 21 miles east-southeast of Victorville (lat. 34°26'35" N, long. 116°57' W); the place is in Lucerne Valley (1). Named on Lucerne Valley (1971) 7.5' quadrangle. Postal authorities established Lucerne Valley post office in 1912; they established Goldbridge post office 19 miles north of Lucerne Valley post office (NW quarter sec. 31, T 6 N, R 1 E) in 1917 and discontinued it in 1918—the name "Goldbridge" was from Goldbridge mine (Salley, p. 86. 129).

Lucerne Valley: see **North Lucerne Valley** [SAN BERNARDINO].

Ludlow [SAN BERNARDINO]: *village*, 52 miles east-southeast of Barstow (lat. 34°43'15" N, long. 116°09'40" W; at S line sec. 5, T 7 N, R 8 E). Named on Ludlow (1955) 7.5' quadrangle. Thompson's (1921) map has the designation "Ludlow (Stagg P.O.)" at the site. Postal authorities established Stagg post office in 1902, changed the name to Ludlow in 1926, and discontinued it in 1974 (Salley, p. 129, 211). The name "Stagg" was for E.H. Stagg, general manager of Bagdad Mining and Milling Company (Myrick, p. 828). The name "Ludlow" commemorates William B. Ludlow, master car-repairer of Western Division of Central Pacific Railroad (Palmer, p. 45). United States Board on Geographic Names (1961b, p. 11) approved the name "Pacific Mesa" for a feature situated about 9 miles south of Ludlow on the east side of Bullion Mountains (sec. 20, 21, 28, T 6 N, R 8 E).

Ludlow Valley: see **Broadwell Valley** [SAN BERNARDINO].

Lugo [SAN BERNARDINO]: *locality*, 12 miles south-southwest of Victorville along the railroad (lat. 34°22'05" N, long. 117°20'30" W; near NW cor. sec. 7, T 3 N, R 4 W). Named on Cedar Springs (1956) 7.5' quadrangle. Postal authorities established Lugo post office in 1917 and discontinued it in 1924 (Frickstad, p. 143).

Lugonia: see **Redlands** [SAN BERNARDINO] (1).

Luna Canyon [SAN BERNARDINO]: *canyon*, drained by a stream that flows 2 miles to Deep Creek (1) 2 miles west-southwest of Luna Mountain (lat. 34°20'10" N, long. 117°09'40" W; near N line sec. 23, T 3 N, R 3 W). Named on Lake Arrowhead (1971) 7.5' quadrangle.

Luna Mountain [SAN BERNARDINO]: *peak*, 19 miles north-northeast of San Bernardino (lat. 34°20'40" N, long. 117°07'35" W; sec. 18, T 3 N, R 2 W). Altitude 5967 feet. Named on Lake Arrowhead (1971) 7.5' quadrangle.

Luna Spring [SAN BERNARDINO]: *spring*, less than 1 mile east-southeast of Luna Mountain (lat. 34°20'25" N, long. 117°06'55" W; near S line sec. 17, T 3 N, R 2 W). Named on Butler Peak (1971) 7.5' quadrangle.

Lynx Cat Mountain [SAN BERNARDINO]: *hill*, 13 miles west-northwest of Barstow (lat. 34°59' N, long. 117°14'15" W; in and near sec. 8, T 10 N, R 3 W). Altitude 2563 feet. Named on Hinkley (1971) 7.5' quadrangle.

Lyons Crossing [IMPERIAL]: *locality*, 7.25 miles west-northwest of Calexico (lat. 32°43' N, long. 115°36'10" W; sec. 35, T 16 S, R 13 E); a road crosses New River at the place. Named on Heber (1957) 7.5' quadrangle.

Lyons Station: see **Desert** [SAN BERNARDINO].

Lytle Canyon: see **Lytle Creek** [SAN BERNARDINO] (1).

Lytle Creek [SAN BERNARDINO]:

(1) *stream* and *dry wash*, formed by the confluence of Middle Fork and North Fork, extends for 5.25 miles to lowlands 2.5 miles southwest of Devore (lat. 34°11'30" N, long. 117°26' W). Named on Devore (1966) 7.5' quadrangle. On San Bernardino (1901) 15' quadrangle, the name "Lytle Canyon" applies to the canyon of Lytle Creek. The name commemorates Andrew Lytle, a Mormon Battalion member who settled at San Bernardino in 1851 (Hanna, p. 179). Spaniards called the stream Arroyo de los Negros (Beattie and Beattie, p. 91). Middle Fork is 6 miles long and is named on Cucamonga Peak (1966) and Telegraph Peak (1956) 7.5' quadrangles. North Fork is 11 miles long and is named on Cajon (1956), Devore (1966), Mount San Antonio (1955), and Telegraph Peak (1956) 7.5' quadrangles. South Fork, which enters just below the confluence of Middle Fork and North Fork, is nearly 4 miles long and is named on Cucamonga Peak (1966) and Devore (1966) 7.5' quadrangles.

(2) *village*, 3.5 miles southwest of Cajon (lat. 34°15'35" N, long. 117°29'55" W; sec. 15, T 2 N, R 6 W); the place is along West Fork Lytle Creek. Named on Cajon (1956) and Telegraph Peak (1956) 7.5' quadrangles. Called Glenn Ranch on Hesperia (1902) 15' quadrangle, called Applewhite Camp on Hesperia (1942) 15' quadrangle, and called Apple White Camp on San Antonio (1942) 15' quadrangle. Postal authorities established Glenn Ranch post office in 1921 and changed the name to Lytle Creek in 1953 (Frickstad, p. 143).

Lytle Creek Ridge: see **Lower Lytle Creek Ridge** [SAN BERNARDINO]; **Upper Lytle Creek Ridge** [SAN BERNARDINO].

Lytle Creek Wash [SAN BERNARDINO]: *stream* and *dry wash*, extends for 12 miles from the mouth of Lytle Creek to Warm Creek 2 miles south-southwest of San Bernardino city hall (lat. 34°04'30" N, long. 117°18'05" W). Named on Devore (1966), San Bernardino North (1967), and San Bernardino South (1967) 7.5' quadrangles. On San Bernardino South (1967) 7.5' quadrangle, the lowermost part of the feature is called Lytle Creek.

- M -

Mabey Canyon [RIVERSIDE]: *canyon*, drained by a stream that heads just inside Orange County and flows nearly 3 miles to lowlands 3 miles southwest of Corona (lat. 33°51' N, long. 117°36'40" W; sec. 4, T 4 S, R 7 W). Named on Black Star Canyon (1967) and Corona South (1967) 7.5' quadrangles. Corona (1942) 15' quadrangle shows Mabey Creek in the canyon. The name commemorates George Mabey, who had an orange grove and a nursery at the mouth of the canyon; earlier the feature had the name "Havens Canyon" for John Havens, who lived there (Gunther, p. 305).

Mabey Creek: see **Mabey Canyon** [RIVERSIDE].

Mace [SAN BERNARDINO]: *locality*, 5 miles west-northwest of Barstow (lat. 34°54'55" N, long. 117°06'30" W; sec. 32, T 10 N, R 2 W). Named on Barstow (1956) 15' quadrangle.

Macedonia Canyon [SAN BERNARDINO]: *canyon*, 5.5 miles long, opens into lowlands 21 miles south-southwest of Ivanpah (lat. 35° 04'45" N, long. 115°31'15" W; sec. 31, T 12 N, R 14 E). Named on Kelso (1955) and Mid Hills (1955) 15' quadrangles.

Macedonia Spring [SAN BERNARDINO]: *spring*, 20 miles south-southwest of Ivanpah (lat. 35°04' N, long. 115°30'10" W; sec. 5, T 11 N, R 14 E); the spring is in Macedonia Canyon. Named on Kelso (1955) 15' quadrangle.

Machado: see **Lake Elsinore** [RIVERSIDE] (2).

Macks Peak [SAN BERNARDINO]: *peak*, 6 miles north of Victorville (lat. 34°37'15" N, long. 117°18'05" W; sec. 9, T 6 N, R 4 W). Altitude 3587 feet. Named on Victorville (1956) 7.5' quadrangle.

Macomber Palms [RIVERSIDE]: *locality*, 12 miles east of Cathedral City (lat. 33°47'55" N, long. 116°15'10" W; sec. 28, T 4 S, R 7 E). Named on Myoma (1958) 7.5' quadrangle.

Mad Women Spring [RIVERSIDE]: *spring*, 10 miles east-southeast of Idyllwild (lat. 33°41'30" N, long. 116°33'20" W; sec. 34, T 5 S, R 4 E). Named on Idyllwild (1959) 15' quadrangle.

Magee Hills [RIVERSIDE]: *ridge*, northwest-trending, 2.5 miles long, 11 miles south of Hemet (lat. 33°35'30" N, long. 116°56'45" W). Named on Sage (1954) 7.5' quadrangle.

Magee Spring [RIVERSIDE]: *spring*, 9 miles south-southeast of Idyllwild (lat. 33°37'20" N, long. 116°40' W; at W line sec. 27, T 6 S, R 3 E). Named on Idyllwild (1959) 15' quadrangle.

Maggies Well [IMPERIAL]: *well*, 8.5 miles east-northeast of Pilot Knob (lat. 32°47'20" N, long. 114°36'55" W; at SW cor. sec. 1, T 16 S, R 22 E). Named on Yuma (1905) 30' quadrangle.

Magnesia Spring [RIVERSIDE]: *spring*, 3.5 miles west of Palm Desert (lat. 33°43'30" N, long. 116°26'10" W; sec. 23, T 5 S, R 5 E). Named on Rancho Mirage (1957) 7.5' quadrangle.

Magnesia Spring Canyon [RIVERSIDE]: *canyon*, 3.25 miles long, opens into lowlands 3 miles west-northwest of Palm Desert (lat. 33°44' N, long. 116°25'30" W; at E line sec. 14, T 5 S, R 5 E); Magnesia Spring is in the canyon. Named on Rancho Mirage (1957) 7.5' quadrangle.

Magnolia Avenue [RIVERSIDE]: *locality*, 3.25 miles west-southwest of Riverside city hall along Union Pacific Railroad (lat. 33°57'30" N, long. 117°25'25" W). Named on Riverside West (1967) 7.5' quadrangle. Called Streeter on Riverside West (1953) 7.5' quadrangle. On United States Geological Survey's (1942b) map, the name "Magnolia Ave." applies to a place located 0.5 mile farther east at the railroad crossing of the street called Magnolia Avenue (lat. 33°57'25" N, long. 117°23'35" W), and the name "Streeter" applies to the present locality called Magnolia Avenue. Officials of San Pedro, Los Angeles and Salt Lake Railroad gave the name "Streeter" to their station where the tracks crossed Streeter Avenue—the street name commemorates H.M. Streeter, a prominent citizen of Riverside in the early days (Gunther, p. 513).

Mail Spring [SAN BERNARDINO]: *spring,* 6 miles south-southeast of Ivanpah (lat. 35°15'45" N, long. 115°15'30" W; near E line sec. 28, T 14 N, R 16 E). Named on Ivanpah (1956) 15' quadrangle.

Main Street Canyon [RIVERSIDE]: *canyon,* 2.25 miles long, opens into lowlands 3.5 miles south of Corona (lat. 33°49'25" N, long. 117°34'35" W; sec. 14, T 4 S, R 7 W). Named on Corona South (1967) 7.5' quadrangle, which shows a thoroughfare called Main Street extending north from the mouth of the canyon to the center of Corona. Called Gypsum Canyon on Corona (1902) 30' quadrangle. The feature also was known as Lewis Canyon, and as Lord's Canyon for George William Lord (Gunther, p. 308).

Main Street Wash [RIVERSIDE]: *stream,* flows 4 miles from the mouth of Main Street Canyon to Temescal Wash 1 mile east of the center of Corona (lat. 33°52'25" N, long. 117°32'50" W). Named on Corona South (1967) 7.5' quadrangle. The feature also had the name "Gypsum Canyon Creek" (Gunther, p. 308).

Mais Canyon: see **Mias Canyon** [RIVERSIDE].

Malapai Hill [RIVERSIDE]: *hill,* 17 miles north-northeast of Indio (lat. 33°56'15" N, long. 116°05'15" W; on E line sec. 1, T 3 S, R 8 E). Altitude 4223 feet. Named on Lost Horse Mountain (1958) 15' quadrangle.

Mallard Lagoon [SAN BERNARDINO]: *embayment,* 1 mile west-northwest of downtown Big Bear Lake along Big Bear Lake (1) (lat. 34°14'55" N, long. 116°55'45" W; sec. 24, T 2 N, R 1 W). Named on Big Bear Lake (1970) 7.5' quadrangle.

Maloney Canyon [SAN BERNARDINO]: *canyon,* drained by a stream that flows 3.25 miles to Willow Creek 3.25 miles southwest of Luna Mountain (lat. 34°18'50" N, long. 117°10'15" W; at W line sec. 26, T 3 N, R 3 W). Named on Lake Arrowhead (1971) 7.5' quadrangle.

Malpais Springs [SAN BERNARDINO]: *springs,* 11 miles east-northeast of Ivanpah (lat. 35°22'20" N, long. 115°07'35" W; near NW cor. sec. 23, T 15 N, R 17 E). Named on Crescent Peak (1956) 15' quadrangle.

Mammoth: see **Amos** [IMPERIAL].

Mammoth Tank: see **Amos** [IMPERIAL].

Mammoth Wash [IMPERIAL]: *stream* and *dry wash,* extends for 15 miles to end 8 miles east of Calipatria (lat. 33°07'30" N, long. 115°22'20" W; at W line sec. 13, T 12 S, R 15 E). Named on Acolita (1953) 15' quadrangle, and on Tortuga (1955) 7.5' quadrangle.

Manchester: see **Mount Manchester** [SAN BERNARDINO].

Maniobra Valley [RIVERSIDE]: *valley,* center 2.5 miles south of Chiriaco Summit (lat. 33°37'15" N, long. 115°42'45" W). Named on Hayfield (1963) 15' quadrangle.

Manix [SAN BERNARDINO]: *locality,* 12 miles north-northeast of Newberry along Union Pacific Railroad (lat. 34°58'55" N, long. 116°35'40" W; near SE cor. sec. 6, T 10 N, R 4 E). Named on Newberry (1955) 15' quadrangle.

Manix Wash [SAN BERNARDINO]: *stream* and *dry wash,* extends for 2.5 miles to Mojave River 13 miles northeast of Newberry (lat. 34°58'30" N, long. 116°32'05" W; sec. 10, T 10 N, R 4 E). Named on Newberry (1955) 15' quadrangle.

Manker Canyon [SAN BERNARDINO]: *canyon,* nearly 1 mile long, 1.5 miles southeast of Mount San Antonio (lat. 34°16'25" N, long. 117°37'20" W; near W line sec. 9, T 2 N, R 7 W). Named on Telegraph Peak (1956) 7.5' quadrangle.

Manker Flat [SAN BERNARDINO]: *area,* nearly 2 miles south-southeast of Mount San Antonio (lat. 34°15'55" N, long. 117°37'40" W; around NE cor. sec. 17, T 2 N, R 17 W); the place is at the mouth of Manker Canyon. Named on Mount San Antonio (1955) and Telegraph Peak (1956) 7.5' quadrangles. The name commemorates Fletcher Manker, who lived at the place in the 1890's (Hanna, p. 184).

Manning Canyon: see **Eagle Canyon** [RIVERSIDE].

Manvel: see **Barnwell** [SAN BERNARDINO].

Manzanita Flat [SAN BERNARDINO]: *area,* 2.5 miles south of Keller Peak (lat. 34°09'35" N, long. 117°02'35" W; sec. 24, T 1 N, R 2 W). Named on Keller Peak (1967) 7.5' quadrangle.

Manzanita Springs [SAN BERNARDINO]: *spring,* 7.25 miles south of downtown Big Bear Lake (lat. 34°08'10" N, long. 116°56'25" W; sec. 25, T 1 N, R 1 W). Named on Big Bear Lake (1970) 7.5' quadrangle.

Manzanita Wash [SAN BERNARDINO]: *stream,* flows 5.5 miles before ending 12 miles southwest of Victorville (lat. 34°25'30" N, long. 117°26'55" W; near NW cor. sec. 19, T 4 N, R 5 W). Named on Baldy Mesa (1956) and Cajon (1956) 7.5' quadrangles.

Marble Canyon [SAN BERNARDINO]:

(1) *canyon,* drained by a stream that flows 2.5 miles to lowlands 6.5 miles north of Big Bear City (lat. 34°21'10" N, long. 116°52'20" W; near SW cor. sec. 10, T 3 N, R 1 E). Named on Big Bear City (1971) 7.5' quadrangle.

(2) *canyon,* drained by a stream that flows nearly 1 mile to lowlands 9 miles north-northeast of Ontario city hall (lat. 34°10'15" N, long. 117°33'20" W; near W line sec. 18, T 1 N, R 6 W). Named on Cucamonga Peak (1953) 7.5' quadrangle.

Marble Mountains [SAN BERNARDINO]: *range,* 11 miles east-northeast of Amboy (lat. 34°38' N, long. 115°34'30" W). Named on Cadiz (1956) and Danby (1956) 15' quadrangles.

March: see **March Air Force Base** [RIVERSIDE]; **West March** [RIVERSIDE]; **West March**, under **Camp Haan** [RIVERSIDE].

March Air Force Base [RIVERSIDE]: *military installation,* north-northwest of Perris. Named on Perris (1967), Riverside East (1967), Steele Peak (1967), and Sunnymead (1967) 7.5' quadrangles. Riverside East (1967) 7.5' quadrangle has the name "March Field" for part of the base. Postal authorities established March post office in 1918, changed the name to March Field in 1921, and changed it to March Air Force Base in 1949 (Salley, 132). The installation opened in 1918 with the name "Alessandro Aviation Field" for its location on the former Alessandro tract, but army officials soon changed the name to March Field to honor Lieutenant Peyton C. March, Jr., who was killed in a training-plane accident in 1918—the lieutenant's father was Chief of Staff of the United States Army during World War I (Gunther, p. 13, 309-310).

March Field: see **March Air Force Base** [RIVERSIDE].

Marcus Wash [IMPERIAL]: *stream* and *dry wash,* extends for 6.25 miles to Colorado River 29 miles south-southeast of Palo Verde (lat. 33°01'20" N, long. 114°35'40" W; near N line sec. 30, T 13 S, R 23 E). Named on Little Picacho Peak (1965) and Picacho (1964) 7.5' quadrangles.

Maria Mountains: see **Big Maria Mountains** [RIVERSIDE]; **Little Maria Mountains** [RIVERSIDE].

Marian [SAN BERNARDINO]: *locality,* 1.5 miles northwest of Yermo (lat. 34°55' N, long. 116°51' W; sec. 35, T 10 N, R 1 E). Site named on Daggett (1956) 15' quadrangle.

Maria Stella: see **Camp Maria Sella** [SAN BERNARDINO].

Marida: see **Verdemont** [SAN BERNARDINO].

Marie Louise: see **Mount Marie Louise** [SAN BERNARDINO].

Marigold [SAN BERNARDINO]: *locality,* 3.5 miles west-northwest of Redlands city hall along Southern Pacific Railroad (lat. 34°04'35" N, long. 117°14'25" W). Named on Redlands (1967) 7.5' quadrangle.

Marion Creek [RIVERSIDE]: *stream,* flows 2.5 miles to Strawberry Creek 4.5 miles southwest of San Jacinto Peak (lat. 33°45'15" N, long. 116°42'20" W; sec. 7, T 5 S, R 3 E); the stream heads near Marion Mountain. Named on San Jacinto Peak (1981) 7.5' quadrangle.

Marion Mountain [RIVERSIDE]: *peak,* 1.25 miles south-southwest of San Jacinto Peak (lat. 33°47'45" N, long. 116°41'15" W; near E line sec. 29, T 4 S, R 3 E). Altitude 10,362 feet. Named on San Jacinto Peak (1981) 7.5' quadrangle. Edmund Taylor Perkins, Jr., a topographer with United States Geological Survey, named the peak in 1897 for Marion Kelly, an Indian Bureau employee at the reservation in Morongo Valley, whom he met while she was camping near the peak (Gunther, p. 311).

Marion Mountain Campground [RIVERSIDE]: *locality,* 3.25 miles west-southwest of San Jacinto Peak (lat. 33°47'30" N, long. 116° 43'50" W; sec. 25, T 4 S, R 2 E); the place is 2.5 miles west of Marion Mountain. Named on San Jacinto Peak (1981) 7.5' quadrangle. Called Marion Mountain Camp on Palm Springs (1957) 15' quadrangle.

Marion Ridge [RIVERSIDE]: *ridge,* west-southwest-trending, 2.5 miles long, 3.5 miles south-southwest of San Jacinto Peak (lat. 33° 46'30" N, long. 116°43' W). Named on San Jacinto Peak (1981) 7.5' quadrangle.

Marl Mountains [SAN BERNARDINO]: *range,* 24 miles southwest of Ivanpah (lat. 35°09'30" N, long. 115°40'30" W). Named on Kelso (1955) 15' quadrangle.

Marl Spring [SAN BERNARDINO]: *spring,* 22 miles southwest of Ivanpah (lat. 35°10'15" N, long. 115°38'50" W; near E line sec. 36, T 13 N, R 12 E); the spring is at the northwest edge of Marl Mountains. Named on Kelso (1955) 15' quadrangle. The army provided token protection at the place in the 1860's with a small post called Camp Marl Springs (Hart, p. 120-121).

Marshall Peak [SAN BERNARDINO]: *peak,* 7.25 miles north of San Bernardino city hall (lat. 34°12'40" N, long. 117°18'05" W; near SE cor. sec. 33, T 2 N, R 4 W). Altitude 4003 feet. Named on San Bernardino North (1967) 7.5' quadrangle.

Martinez [RIVERSIDE]: *locality,* 11.5 miles south-southeast of Indio (lat. 33°33'45" N, long. 116°09'10" W; sec. 16, T 7 S, R 8 E); the place is on Torres Martinez Indian Reservation. Named on Valerie (1956) 7.5' quadrangle. Coachella (1943) 15' quadrangle shows the headquarters of the reservation at the place.

Martinez Canyon [RIVERSIDE]: *canyon,* 12 miles long, opens into lowlands 14 miles south of Indio (lat. 33°32'15" N, long. 116° 12' W; sec. 36, T 7 S, R 7 E). Named on Palm Desert (1959) 15' quadrangle, and on Clark Lake NE (1960) and Valerie (1956) 7.5' quadrangles. United States Board on Geographic Names (1962a, p. 13) rejected the name "Black Rabbit Canyon" for the feature.

Martinez Gulch [IMPERIAL]: *canyon,* drained by a stream that flows 0.5 mile to German Diggins Wash 21 miles north-northwest of Glamis (lat. 33°16' N, long. 115°14'40" W; near E line sec. 25, T 10 S, R 16 E). Named on Chuckwalla Spring (1953) 15' quadrangle.

Martinez Mountain [RIVERSIDE]: *peak,* 11.5 miles south of Palm Desert (lat. 33°33'30" N, long. 116°20'40" W; sec. 15, T 7 S, R 6 E). Altitude

6548 feet. Named on Palm Desert (1959) 15' quadrangle.

Martin Glen: see **Glen Martin** [SAN BERNARDINO].

Martins Well [SAN BERNARDINO]: *well,* 27 miles west-northwest of Vidal (lat. 34°18'40" N, long. 114°55' W). Named on Turtle Mountains (1954) 15' quadrangle.

Maruba: see **Ledge** [SAN BERNARDINO].

Massacre Canyon [RIVERSIDE]: *canyon,* 1.5 miles long, along Potrero Creek above a point 4.5 miles north-northwest of San Jacinto (lat. 33°50'35" N, long. 116°59'45" W). Named on San Jacinto (1953) 7.5' quadrangle. The name is from the tradition that some Indians killed their Indian enemies at the place (Hoover, Rensch, and Rensch, p. 289).

Mathews: see **Lake Mathews** [RIVERSIDE].

Matterdome: see **The Matterdome**, under **White Water Post Office** [RIVERSIDE].

May [RIVERSIDE]: *locality,* 9 miles southwest of Riverside city hall along Atchison, Topeka and Santa Fe Railroad (lat. 33°53'35" N, long. 117°29'25" W). Named on Riverside West (1967) 7.5' quadrangle. Called Alvord on California Mining Bureau's (1917b) map—the name was changed to May in 1910 (Gunther, p. 314).

Maybe Canyon [RIVERSIDE]: *canyon,* drained by a stream that flows nearly 2 miles to lowlands 3 miles southwest of Corona (lat. 33°51' N, long. 117°36'40" W; sec. 4, T 4 S, R 7 W). Named on Black Star Canyon (1967) and Corona South (1967) 7.5' quadrangles.

Mayer Farms [RIVERSIDE]: *locality,* 2.5 miles north-northwest of Perris along Atchison, Topeka and Santa Fe Railroad (lat. 33° 49' N, long. 117°14'20" W; near SW cor. sec. 18, T 4 S, R 3 W). Named on Perris (1967) 7.5' quadrangle

Mayhew Canyon [RIVERSIDE]: *canyon,* drained by a stream that flows 3.25 miles to Temescal Valley 4.5 miles west-northwest of Alberhill (lat. 33°44'30" N, long. 117°28'30" W). Named on Alberhill (1954) and Santiago Peak (1954) 7.5' quadrangles. The name commemorates James Thomas Mayhew, who filed on water in the canyon in 1883 and 1884; previously the feature was called Binkley Canyon for Frank Binkley, who homesteaded there in 1876, and Compton Canyon for Ambrose Compton and his brother Charles, who lived near the mouth of the canyon in 1874 (Gunther, p. 53, 315).

May Spring [SAN BERNARDINO]: *spring,* 2.5 miles northeast of Sugarloaf Mountain (lat. 34°13'25" N, long. 116°46'55" W; sec. 28, T 2 N, R 2 E). Named on Moonridge (1970) 7.5' quadrangle.

May Van Canyon [SAN BERNARDINO]: *canyon,* 1.5 miles long, 2.5 miles northeast of Sugarloaf Mountain (lat. 34°13'20" N, long. 116°46'50" W). Named on Moonridge (1970) 7.5' quadrangle.

McBride Canyon [RIVERSIDE]: *canyon,* drained by a stream that flows 2.5 miles to Temescal Valley 7 miles south-southeast of Corona (lat. 33°47'20" N, long. 117°30'30" W; sec. 28, T 4 S, R 6 W). Named on Corona South (1967) 7.5' quadrangle.

McCain Spring [IMPERIAL]: *spring,* 9.5 miles northwest of Kane Spring (lat. 33°11'20" N, long. 115°58'30" W; near N line sec. 30, T 11 S, R 10 E). Named on Kane Spring (1940) 15' quadrangle.

McCarthy Canyon: see **Indian Canyon** [RIVERSIDE].

McCoy: see **Cadiz** [SAN BERNARDINO].

McCoy Mountains [RIVERSIDE]: *range,* 17 miles west-northwest of Blythe (lat. 33°43'30" N, long. 114°52' W). Named on McCoy Spring (1952) and Midland (1952) 15' quadrangles. United States Board on Geographic Names (1933, p. 484) rejected the name "Ironwood Mountains" for the range.

McCoy Peak [RIVERSIDE]: *peak,* 15 miles west of Blythe (lat. 33° 39' N, long. 119°51'10" W); the peak is in McCoy Mountains. Altitude 2054 feet. Named on McCoy Spring (1952) 15' quadrangle.

McCoy Spring [RIVERSIDE]: *spring,* 20 miles west-northwest of Blythe (lat. 33°44' N, long. 114°54'25" W); the spring is at the west end of McCoy Mountains. Named on McCoy Spring (1952) 15' quadrangle. The name is for W.W. McCoy, who took pack trains into the neighborhood as early as 1857 (Gunther, p. 303).

McCoy Wash [RIVERSIDE]: *stream,* flows 18 miles to Palo Verde Valley 3.5 miles northwest of Blythe (lat. 33°38'40" N, long. 114° 38'30" W; near NE cor. sec. 23, T 6 S, R 22 E); the stream heads in McCoy Mountains. Named on McCoy Spring (1952) and Midland (1952) 15' quadrangles, and on McCoy Wash (1951) 7.5' quadrangle.

McDermont Spring [SAN BERNARDINO]: *spring,* 0.5 mile north of San Juan Hill (lat. 33°55'20" N, long. 117°44'20" W; sec. 8, T 3 S, R 8 W). Named on Prado Dam (1967) 7.5' quadrangle.

McDonald Well [SAN BERNARDINO]: *well,* 21 miles southeast of the village of Red Mountain (lat. 35°06'55" N, long. 117°22'25" W; sec. 28, T 32 S, R 43 E). Named on Fremont Peak (1956) 15' quadrangle. Searles Lake (1915) 1° quadrangle shows McDonalds ranch at the site.

McGregor Flat [RIVERSIDE]: *area,* 10.5 miles southeast of Idyllwild (lat. 33°38'05" N, long. 116°35'30" W; sec. 20, T 6 S, R 4 E). Named on Idyllwild (1959) 15' quadrangle.

McInnis Spring [SAN BERNARDINO]: *spring,* 11 miles east of Victorville (lat. 34°31'55" N, long. 117°06'05" W; near SW cor. sec. 9, T 5 N, R 2 W). Named on Fairview Valley (1970) 7.5' quadrangle.

McKinley Mountain [SAN BERNARDINO]: *peak,* 2.25 miles west of Harrison Mountain (lat. 34°10'05" N, long. 117°11'55" W; sec. 16, T 1 N, R 3 W). Altitude 3795 feet. Named on Harrison Mountain (1967) 7.5' quadrangle.

McLean Lake [SAN BERNARDINO]: *dry lake,* 1.5 miles long, 42 miles west-northwest of Baker (lat. 35°29'30" N, long. 116°45'50" W; at NE cor. sec. 9, T 16 N, R 2 E). Named on Goldstone Lake (1948) 15' quadrangle.

McMullen Flat [RIVERSIDE]: *area,* 4.25 miles south-southeast of Banning (lat. 33°52'20" N, long. 116°50'05" W; sec. 25, 36, T 3 S, R 1 E). Named on Lake Fulmor (1956) 7.5' quadrangle. The name is for Silas J. McMullen, a settler of the 1880's (Gunther, p. 305).

McNeal Spring: see **Helendale** [SAN BERNARDINO].

McVicker Canyon [RIVERSIDE]: *canyon,* nearly 4 miles long, heads in Orange County and opens into lowlands 2.5 miles south of Alberhill (lat. 33°41'10" N, long. 117°23'50" W; near SW cor. sec. 34, T 5 S, R 5 W). Named on Alberhill (1954) 7.5' quadrangle. The misspelled name is for William G. McVickar, who came to the neighborhood in 1884 and claimed land that includes the canyon (Gunther, p. 305).

Meadow Bay [SAN BERNARDINO]: *embayment,* 7.25 miles south-southwest of Luna Mountain along Lake Arrowhead (1) (lat. 34° 15'25" N, long. 117°11'50" W; sec. 16, T 2 N, R 3 W). Named on Lake Arrowhead (1971) 7.5' quadrangle.

Meadowbrook Woods [SAN BERNARDINO]: *locality,* 5.5 miles north-northwest of Harrison Mountain (lat. 34°14' N, long. 117°12'10" W; near NW cor. sec. 28, T 2 N, R 3 W). Named on Harrison Mountain (1967) 7.5' quadrangle.

Mead Valley [RIVERSIDE]: *valley,* 9 miles northeast of Estelle Mountain (lat. 33°51' N, long. 117°18' W; in and near sec. 4, T 4 S, R 4 W). Named on Steele Peak (1967) 7.5' quadrangle.

Means Lake [SAN BERNARDINO]: *dry lake,* 1.25 miles long, 8.5 miles east-northeast of Old Woman Springs (lat. 34°24'35" N, long. 116°30'20" W). Named on Emerson Lake (1954) and Melville Lake (1972) 7.5' quadrangles.

Means Wells [SAN BERNARDINO]: *wells,* 11 miles east of Old Woman Springs (lat. 34°24'45" N, long. 116°31' W); the wells are at the northwest end of present Means Lake. Named on San Gorgonio (1902) 30' quadrangle.

Mecca [RIVERSIDE]: *town,* 13 miles southeast of Indio (lat. 33°34'20" N, long. 116°04'20" W; sec. 8, T 7 S, R 9 E). Named on Mecca (1955) 7.5' quadrangle. Postal authorities established Walters post office 13 miles southeast of Indio in 1896, and changed the name to Mecca in 1903 (Salley, p. 234). Robert Holtby Myers planted the first commercial date trees at the place and named it "Mecca" (Hanna, p. 188). United States Board on Geographic Names (1960c, p. 16) approved the name "Blake Hill" for an elevation about 9 miles northeast of Mecca (SE quarter sec. 27, T 6 S, R 10 E). United States Geological Survey's (1904) map shows a place called Alamo Bonito situated 4.5 miles south-southwest of Mecca (near SE cor. sec. 35, T 7 S, R 8 E), and a place called Figtree John located 9 miles south of Mecca (sec. 33, T 8 S, R 9 E). The name "Figtree John" recalls Figtree John's Springs, named for an Indian, Juanita Razon—better known as Figtree John for the fig trees that he cared for—who lived with his family at the springs and cultivated a garden and orchard there before rising water of Salton Sea flooded the spot in 1907 (Gunther, p. 186; Mendenhall, 1909a, p. 83-84; Waring, p. 314-315).

Mecca Hills [RIVERSIDE]: *range,* 15 miles east-southeast of Indio (lat. 33°37' N, long. 116°00' W); the range is northeast of Mecca. Named on Mecca (1955), Mortmar (1958), and Thermal Canyon (1956) 7.5' quadrangles.

Meechem Canyon [SAN BERNARDINO]: *canyon,* nearly 2 miles long, 8.5 miles north-northwest of San Bernardino city hall (lat. 34°13' N, long. 117°21'15" W; sec. 25, 36, T 2 N, R 5 W). Named on San Bernardino (1954) 15' quadrangle.

Mellen: see **Beal** [SAN BERNARDINO].

Mellor Creek [RIVERSIDE]: *stream,* flows 4.5 miles to Indian Creek 7 miles east of San Jacinto (lat. 33°47'05" N, long. 116°50'15" W; sec. 36, T 4 S, R 1 E). Named on Lake Fulmer (1956) 7.5' quadrangle.

Meloland [IMPERIAL]: *locality,* nearly 4 miles west of Holtville along Holton Inter-urban Railroad (lat. 32°48'10" N, long. 115°26'40" W; sec. 32, T 15 S, R 15 E). Named on Holtville West (1956) 7.5' quadrangle. Called Gleason Switch on Holtville (1907) 30' quadrangle. Postal authorities established Meloland post office in 1908 and discontinued it in 1911 (Frickstad, p. 49).

Melson Well [IMPERIAL]: *well,* 12 miles northeast of Calipatria (lat. 33°13'55" N, long. 115°20'50" W; sec. 7, T 11 S, R 16 E). Named on Tortuga (1955) 7.5' quadrangle, which indicates that the well is dry.

Melville Lake [SAN BERNARDINO]: *dry lake,* nearly 3 miles long, 8.5 miles east-southeast of Old Woman Springs (lat. 34°26'45" N, long. 116°34' W). Named on Melville Lake (1972) 7.5' quadrangle.

Menifee [RIVERSIDE]: *locality,* 6 miles southeast of Perris along Atchison,

Topeka and Santa Fe Railroad (lat. 33°43'40" N, long. 117°08'40" W; at N line sec. 24, T 5 S, R 3 W). Named on Romoland (1953) 7.5' quadrangle. Postal authorities established Menifee post office in 1887 and discontinued it in 1896 (Frickstad, p. 129).

Menifee Valley [RIVERSIDE]: *valley,* 7.5 miles south-southeast of Perris (lat. 33°41'15" N, long. 117°10'45" W). Named on Romoland (1953) 7.5' quadrangle. The name is for S. Menifee Wilson, who found a gold mine in the neighborhood about 1880 (Gunther, p. 319).

Mentone [SAN BERNARDINO]: *town,* 3 miles east-northeast of Redlands city hall (lat. 34°04'15" N, long. 117°07'50" W; sec. 18, 19, T 1 S, R 2 W). Named on Redlands (1967) and Yucaipa (1967) 7.5' quadrangles. Postal authorities established Mentone post office in 1891 (Frickstad, p. 143). Officials of Mentone Company had the town laid out in 1887 (Gudde, 1949, p. 210-211).

Mercury Mountain [SAN BERNARDINO]: *peak,* 8 miles south-southeast of Essex (lat. 34°37'25" N, long. 115°11'35" W; near W line sec. 10, T 6 N, R 17 E). Altitude 3720 feet. Named on Essex (1956) 15' quadrangle.

Merrill: see **Highgrove** [RIVERSIDE].

Merriman Meadows [SAN BERNARDINO]: *area,* 2 miles south-southwest of downtown Big Bear Lake (lat. 34°13' N, long. 116° 55'45" W; near E line sec. 36, T 2 N, R 1 W). Named on Big Bear Lake (1970) 7.5' quadrangle.

Mesa de Burro [RIVERSIDE]: *relief feature,* 2.25 miles south-southwest of Murrieta (lat. 33°31'30" N, long. 117°14' W). Named on Murrieta (1953) 7.5' quadrangle.

Mesa De Colorado [RIVERSIDE]: *relief feature,* 6.5 miles south of Wildomar (lat. 33°30'20" N, long. 117°17'15" W). Named on Wildomar (1953) 7.5' quadrangle.

Mesa De La Punta [RIVERSIDE]: *relief feature,* 6.5 miles south-southeast of Wildomar (lat. 33°30'15" N, long. 117°15'15" W). Named on Murrieta (1953) and Wildomar (1953) 7.5' quadrangles.

Mesa Verde: see **Nicholls Warm Springs** [RIVERSIDE].

Mesaville [RIVERSIDE]: *locality,* 7 miles north-northwest of Blythe along Atchison, Topeka and Santa Fe Railroad (lat. 33°41'40" N, long. 114°39' W; sec. 35, T 5 S, R 22 E); the place is on Palo Verde Mesa. Named on McCoy Wash (1951) 7.5' quadrangle. Postal authorities established Mesaville post office in 1911 and discontinued it in 1914 (Salley, p. 139).

Mescal: see **Nantan**, under **Hardrock Queen Spring** [SAN BERNARDINO].

Mescal Range [SAN BERNARDINO]: *range,* 15 miles west-northwest of Ivanpah (lat. 35°21'30" N, long. 115°33'30" W). Named on Mescal Range (1955) 15' quadrangle.

Mescal Spring: see **Hardrock Queen Spring** [SAN BERNARDINO].

Mesquite [IMPERIAL]: *locality,* 3 miles northwest of Glamis along Southern Pacific Railroad (lat. 33°01'30" N, long. 115°06'45" W). Named on Acolita (1953) 15' quadrangle.

Mesquite: see **Crucero** [SAN BERNARDINO].

Mesquite Flat [RIVERSIDE]: *area,* 12 miles east-southeast of Idyllwild (lat. 33°41' N, long. 116°31'10" W; at N line sec. 1, T 6 S, R 4 E). Named on Idyllwild (1959) 15' quadrangle.

Mesquite Hills [SAN BERNARDINO]: *range,* 18 miles south-southwest of Baker (lat. 35°00'15' N, long. 116°10' W). Named on Soda Lake (1956) 15' quadrangle.

Mesquite Lake [SAN BERNARDINO]:

(1) *dry lake,* 4.5 miles long, 30 miles north-northwest of Ivanpah (lat. 35°43' N, long. 115°35' W); the feature is near the southeast end of Mesquite Valley. Named on Clark Mountain (1956) 15' quadrangle. Waring (p. 303) listed a water feature called Deadmans Holes that is made up of small pools at the northwest side of the dry lake.

(2) *dry lake,* 2 miles long, 5.5 miles north of Twentynine Palms (lat. 34°13'15" N, long. 116°03'55" W). Named on Twentynine Palms (1973) 7.5' quadrangle.

Mesquite Lake: see **Imperial** [IMPERIAL].

Mesquite Mountains [SAN BERNARDINO]: *range,* 31 miles northwest of Ivanpah (lat. 35°42' N, long. 115°40'30" W); the range is southwest of Mesquite Lake (1). Named on Clark Mountain (1956) and Kingston Peak (1955) 15' quadrangles.

Mesquite Pass [SAN BERNARDINO]: *pass,* 26 miles northwest of Ivanpah (lat. 35°37'30" N, long. 115°37'30" W); the pass is at the southeast end of Mesquite Mountains. Named on Clark Mountain (1956) 15' quadrangle.

Mesquite Spring [SAN BERNARDINO]:

(1) *spring,* 32 miles southeast of Trona (lat. 35°24'05" N, long. 117°01' W). Named on Pilot Knob (1954) 15' quadrangle.

(2) *spring,* 5.5 miles north-northwest of Twentynine Palms (lat. 34° 12'50" N, long. 116°04'30" W; sec. 31, T 2 N, R 9 E). Named on Twentynine Palms (1973) 7.5' quadrangle. A mesquite grove marks the site (Mendenhall, 1909a, p. 75).

Mesquite Spring: see **Crucero** [SAN BERNARDINO].

Mesquite Valley [SAN BERNARDINO]: *valley,* 36 miles north-northwest of Ivanpah on San Bernardino-Inyo County line, and on California-Nevada State line (lat. 35°48' N, long. 115°38' W). Named on Clark Mountain (1956), Roach Lake (1955), and Shenandoah Peak (1956) 15' quadrangles.

Mesquite Well: see **Harpers Well** [IMPERIAL].

Messina: see **Highland** [SAN BERNARDINO].

Metate Flat [RIVERSIDE]: *area,* 12 miles east of San Jacinto (lat. 33°48'10" N, long. 116°45'20" W; near SE cor. sec. 22, T 4 S, R 2 E). Named on Lake Fulmor (1956) 7.5' quadrangle.

Metcalf Bay [SAN BERNARDINO]: *embayment,* 1.5 miles west of downtown Big Bear Lake along Big Bear Lake (1) (lat. 34°14'40" N, long. 116°56'15" W; sec. 24, T 2 N, R 1 W); the feature is at the mouth of Metcalf Creek. Named on Big Bear Lake (1970) 7.5' quadrangle.

Metcalf Creek [SAN BERNARDINO]: *stream,* flows 2 miles to Big Bear Lake (1) 1.5 miles west of downtown Big Bear Lake (lat. 34°14'25" N, long. 116°56'10" W; sec. 24, T 2 N, R 1 W). Named on Big Bear Lake (1970) 7.5' quadrangle. Called Mill Creek on San Gorgonio Mountain (1954) 15' quadrangle.

Mexican Spring [SAN BERNARDINO]: *spring,* 3.5 miles southeast of Ivanpah (lat. 35°18' N, long. 115°17' W). Named on Ivanpah (1912) 1° quadrangle.

Mexican Water Spring [SAN BERNARDINO]: *spring,* 20 miles south-southwest of Ivanpah (lat. 35°05'40" N, long. 115°28'30" W; sec. 27, T 12 N, R 14 E). Named on Mid Hills (1955) 15' quadrangle.

Mexican Well [SAN BERNARDINO]: *well,* 14 miles northwest of Ivanpah (lat. 35°28'10" N, long. 115°31'10" W; near W line sec. 31, T 16 N, R 14 E). Named on Mescal Range (1955) 15' quadrangle.

Meyer Canyon [SAN BERNARDINO]: *canyon,* drained by a stream that flows 2.5 miles to Lytle Creek 2.5 miles west-southwest of Devore (lat. 34°12'10" N, long. 117°26'40" W; sec. 6, T 1 N, R 5 W). Named on Devore (1966) 7.5' quadrangle.

Meyers Canyon [SAN BERNARDINO]: *canyon,* drained by a stream that flows 1.5 miles to lowlands 8.5 miles north-northwest of San Bernardino city hall (lat. 34°12'40" N, long. 117°22'10" W). Named on San Bernardino North (1967) 7.5' quadrangle.

Mias Canyon [RIVERSIDE]: *canyon,* 4.5 miles long, opens into the canyon of San Gorgonio River 2 miles north of Banning (lat. 33° 57'20" N, long. 116°52'45" W; sec. 33, T 2 S, R 1 E). Named on Beaumont (1953) and Forest Falls (1970) 7.5' quadrangles. Called Mais Canyon on Banning (1956) 15' quadrangle.

Mica Butte [RIVERSIDE]: *ridge,* north-northwest-trending, 1 mile long, 5 miles south of Hemet (lat. 33°39'45" N, long. 116°58' W; sec. 10, T 6 S, R 1 W). Named on Hemet (1953) 7.5' quadrangle.

Middle Fork Jumpoff [SAN BERNARDINO]: *relief feature,* 2.5 miles southeast of San Gorgonio Mountain (lat. 34°04'05" N, long. 116°47'50" W; sec. 20, T 1 S, R 2 E). Named on San Gorgonio Mountain (1970) 7.5' quadrangle.

Middle Hills [SAN BERNARDINO]: *range,* 15 miles northeast of Amboy (lat. 34°43' N, long. 115°34'30" W; mainly in sec. 1, 12, T 7 N, R 13 E). Named on Cadiz (1956) 15' quadrangle.

Middle Lake [SAN BERNARDINO]: *lake,* 2300 feet long, 1.5 miles south-southeast of downtown Victorville (lat. 34°30'50" N, long. 117°16'35" W; at NW cor. sec. 23, T 5 N, R 4 W). Named on Victorville (1956) 7.5' quadrangle. Victorville (1956) 15' quadrangle shows a smaller Middle Lake located between features called Lower Slough and Upper Slough; present Middle Lake includes part of former Upper Slough.

Middleman Falls [SAN BERNARDINO]: *waterfall,* 2.5 miles north-northwest of Devore (lat. 34°14'55" N, long. 117°25'10" W; near E line sec. 20, T 2 N, R 5 W). Named on Devore (1966) 7.5' quadrangle.

Middle Spring [RIVERSIDE]: *spring,* 2.5 miles south of San Jacinto Peak (lat. 33°46'35" N, long. 116°40'40" W; near S line sec. 33, T 4 S, R 3 E). Named on San Jacinto Peak (1981) 7.5' quadrangle.

Mid Hills [SAN BERNARDINO]: *range,* 14 miles south-southwest of Ivanpah (lat. 35°09' N, long. 115°26' W). Named on Mid Hills (1955) 15' quadrangle.

Midland [RIVERSIDE]: *locality,* 21 miles north-northwest of Blythe (lat. 33°51'30" N, long. 114°48' W; sec. 5, T 4 S, R 21 E). Named on Midland (1952) 15' quadrangle. Postal authorities established Midland post office in 1927 and discontinued it in 1967 (Salley, p. 140). The place housed workers at a gypsum plant that closed in 1966 (Gunther, p. 323-324).

Midland: see **Armada** [RIVERSIDE]; **Cox** [RIVERSIDE].

Midway [SAN BERNARDINO]: *locality,* 27 miles southwest of Baker (lat. 35°01'55" N, long. 116°28'20" W; sec. 20, T 11 N, R 5 E). Named on Cave Mountain (1948) 15' quadrangle.

Midway Canyon [RIVERSIDE]: *canyon,* 2 miles long, opens into lowlands 11 miles north of Palm Springs (lat. 33°59'40" N, long. 116°32'55" W; near SE cor. sec. 15, T 2 S, R 4 E). Named on Desert Hot Springs (1955) and Morongo Valley (1972) 7.5' quadrangles.

Midway Mountains [IMPERIAL]: *range,* 18 miles south-southwest of Palo Verde (lat. 33°11' N, long. 114°50' W); the range is southeast of Midway Well (1). Named on Salton Sea (1959) 1°x 2° quadrangle.

Midway Well [IMPERIAL]:

(1) *well,* 17 miles south-southwest of Palo Verde (lat. 33°13' N, long. 114°51'45" W; near W line sec. 15, T 11 S, R 20 E). Named on Quartz

Peak (1953) 15' quadrangle.
(2) *locality,* 24 miles east of Calexico (lat. 32°42'30" N, long. 115° 04'25" W; on S line sec. 35, T 16 S, R 18 E). Named on Midway Well (1954) 7.5' quadrangle.

Mile Creek [SAN BERNARDINO]: *stream,* flows 2.25 miles to Santa Ana River 4 miles south-southwest of downtown Big Bear Lake (lat. 34°10'35" N, long. 116°56'30" W; near NW cor. sec. 13, T 1 N, R 1 W). Named on Big Bear Lake (1970) 7.5' quadrangle.

Mile High Pines Camp [SAN BERNARDINO]: *locality,* 3.5 miles southwest of Sugarloaf Mountain (lat. 34°10'10" N, long. 116°51'45" W; sec. 15, T 1 N, R 1 E). Named on Moonridge (1970) 7.5' quadrangle.

Milky Spring [RIVERSIDE]: *spring,* 14 miles east-southeast of Hemet (lat. 33°39'40" N, long. 116°45'40" W; at S line sec. 10, T 6 S, R 2 E). Named on Hemet (1957) 15' quadrangle. The name is from the milky appearance of the water (Gunther, p. 325).

Millard Canyon [RIVERSIDE]: *canyon,* 7 miles long, opens into San Gorgonio Pass 4.5 miles east-northeast of Banning (lat. 33°56'30" N, long. 116°47'45" W; sec. 5, T 3 S, R 2 E). Named on Cabazon (1956) and San Gorgonio Mountain (1970) 7.5' quadrangles. The name commemorates Solomon Z. Millard, who settled at the mouth of the canyon in 1877; the feature first was called Weaver Canyon for Powell Weaver, who appropriated the former San Gabriel mission lands there for his own use (Gunther, p. 325). East Branch enters from the east 3.5 miles above the mouth of the main canyon; it is nearly 3 miles long and is named on Cabazon (1956) and San Gorgonio Mountain (1970) 7.5' quadrangles. Middle Branch enters 5 miles above the mouth of the main stream; it is nearly 2 miles long and is named on San Gorgonio Mountain (1970) 7.5' quadrangle. On San Jacinto (1901) 30' quadrangle, the name "Middle Br." applies to present Millard Canyon above the mouth of present East Branch. West Branch enters from the northwest 2 miles above the mouth of the main canyon; it is 1 mile long and is named on Cabazon (1956) 7.5' quadrangle.

Mill Creek [RIVERSIDE-SAN BERNARDINO]: *stream,* heads in San Bernardino County and flows 3.25 miles to Chino Creek 5 miles east of San Juan Hill in Riverside County (lat. 33°54'50" N, long. 117°38'40" W). Named on Corona North (1967) and Prado Dam (1967) 7.5' quadrangles.

Mill Creek [SAN BERNARDINO]: *dry wash,* extends for 5.25 miles from the mouth of Mill Creek Canyon to Santa Ana Wash 6 miles northwest of Yucaipa (lat. 34°05'30" N, long. 117°07'05" W; at NW cor. sec. 17, T 1 S, R 2 W). Named on Yucaipa (1967) 7.5' quadrangle.

Mill Creek: see **Coxey Creek** [SAN BERNARDINO]; **Little Mill Creek** [SAN BERNARDINO]; **Metcalf Creek** [SAN BERNARDINO]; **Mill Creek Canyon** [SAN BERNARDINO].

Mill Creek Campgrounds [SAN BERNARDINO]: *locality,* 5 miles north-northeast of Yucaipa (lat. 34°06' N, long. 117°00'10" W; sec. 8, T 1 S, R 1 W); the place is in Mill Creek Canyon. Named on Yucaipa (1967) 7.5' quadrangle. Redlands (1954) 15' quadrangle has the singular form "Mill Creek Campground" for the name.

Mill Creek Canyon [SAN BERNARDINO]: *canyon,* 12 miles long, opens into the valley of Mill Creek nearly 4 miles north of Yucaipa (lat. 34°05'20" N, long. 117°02'15" W; sec. 13, T 1 S, R 2 W). Named on Forest Falls (1970), San Gorgonio Mountain (1970), and Yucaipa (1967) 7.5' quadrangles. The name is from a sawmill that Daniel Sexton built in 1852 (Beattie and Beattie, p. 193). San Gorgonio (1902) 30' quadrangle has the name "Mill Creek" for the stream in the canyon.

Mill Creek Jumpoff [SAN BERNARDINO]: *relief feature,* nearly 2 miles south-southwest of San Gorgonio Mountain (lat. 34°04'35" N, long. 116°50'30" W; at NW cor. sec. 24, T 1 S, R 1 E). Named on San Gorgonio Mountain (1970) 7.5' quadrangle

Miller Canyon [RIVERSIDE]: *canyon,* drained by a stream that flows 1.5 miles to Murrieta Creek less than 0.5 mile south-southwest of Murrieta (lat. 33°32'50" N, long. 117°13' W). Named on Murrieta (1953) 7.5' quadrangle.

Miller Canyon [SAN BERNARDINO]: *canyon,* along East Fork of West Fork Mojave River, which flows 6.5 miles to join West Fork Mojave River 18 miles south of Victorville at Cedar Springs (lat. 34°02'25" N, long. 117°19'45" W; near E line sec. 6, T 2 N, R 4 W). Named on Cedar Springs (1956) and Lake Arrowhead (1971) 7.5' quadrangles.

Miller Narrows [SAN BERNARDINO]: *narrows,* 5 miles west of Devore along Lytle Creek (lat. 34°13'50" N, long. 117°29'05" W; near W line sec. 26, T 2 N, R 6 W). Named on Devore (1966) 7.5' quadrangle.

Miller Peak [RIVERSIDE]: *peak,* less than 0.5 mile east of San Jacinto Peak (lat. 33°48'55" N, long. 116°40'20" W; near N line sec. 21, T 4 S, R 3 E). Named on San Jacinto Peak (1981) 7.5' quadrangle. Members of the State Park Commission of California named the peak in 1935 to honor Frank A. Miller, civic leader and proprietor of Mission Inn at Riverside (United States Board on Geographic Names, 1938, p. 36).

Millers [IMPERIAL]: *locality,* 7.25 miles south of Carrizo Mountain (lat. 32°43'30" N, long. 116°02'15" W; near N line sec. 2, T 17 S, R 9 E). Named on In-Ko-Pah Gorge (1959) 7.5' quadrangle.

Milligan [SAN BERNARDINO]: *locality,* 32 miles south of Essex along Atchison, Topeka and Santa Fe Railroad (lat. 34°16'40" N, long. 115°10' W; sec. 11, T 2 N, R 17 E). Named on Milligan (1956) 15' quadrangle. Officials of Atchison, Topeka and Santa Fe Railroad named the place for one of the partners in the mercantile firm of Drennan and Milligan in Parker, Arizona (Hanna, p. 192).

Million Dollar Canyon [RIVERSIDE]: *canyon,* drained by a stream that flows 2 miles to Rogers Canyon (lat. 33°28' N, long. 116°44'25" W; sec. 23, T 8 S, R 2 E). Named on Beauty Mountain (1960) 7.5' quadrangle.

Million Dollar Spring [RIVERSIDE]: *spring,* 20 miles south of Idyllwild (lat. 33°27'15" N, long. 116°44'20" W; near NE cor. sec. 26, T 8 S, R 2 E); the spring is in Million Dollar Canyon. Named on Beauty Mountain (1960) 7.5' quadrangle.

Mill Peak [SAN BERNARDINO]: *peak,* nearly 2 miles west of Keller Peak (lat. 34°11'30" N, long. 117°04'45" W; near N line sec. 10, T 1 N, R 2 W). Altitude 6670 feet. Named on Keller Peak (1967) 7.5' quadrangle.

Milpitas Wash [IMPERIAL]: *stream* and *dry wash,* extends for 35 miles to lowlands along Colorado River 11 miles south of Palo Verde (lat. 33°16'15" N, long. 114°43' W; sec. 36, T 10 S, R 21 E). Named on Chuckwalla Spring (1953), Cibola (1951), and Palo Verde Mountains (1953) 15' quadrangles. Called Arroyo Seco on Cibola (1945) 15' quadrangle.

Mineral: see **Cox** [RIVERSIDE].

Mineral Hill [SAN BERNARDINO]: *ridge,* southeast-trending, 3 miles long, 11.5 miles northwest of Ivanpah (lat. 35°26' N, long. 115°28'30" W). Named on Ivanpah (1956) 15' quadrangle.

Mineral Mountain [SAN BERNARDINO]: *ridge,* east-southeast-trending, 14 miles north-northeast of downtown Morongo Valley (lat. 34°14'10" N, long. 116°40'40" W; near SW cor. sec. 21, T 2 N, R 3 E). Named on Onyx Peak (1972) 7.5' quadrangle.

Mineral Spring [SAN BERNARDINO]: *spring,* 10 miles west-northwest of Ivanpah (lat. 35°24'40" N, long. 115°27'40" W; near W line sec. 2, T 15 N, R 14 E); the spring is near the south tip of Mineral Hill. Named on Ivanpah (1956) 15' quadrangle.

Mineral Switch: see **Cox** [RIVERSIDE].

Miners Bowl [SAN BERNARDINO]: *relief feature,* 2.25 miles east-southeast of Mount San Antonio (lat. 34°16'15" N, long. 117°36'40" W; near E line sec. 9, T 2 N, R 7 W). Named on Telegraph Peak (1956) 7.5' quadrangle.

Mine Shaft Saddle [SAN BERNARDINO]: *pass,* less than 1 mile north of San Gorgonio Mountain (lat. 34°06'35" N, long. 116°49'25" W; near W line sec. 6, T 1 S, R 2 E). Named on San Gorgonio Mountain (1970) 7.5' quadrangle.

Minnelusa [SAN BERNARDINO]: *locality,* 3 miles east of Fawnskin (lat. 34°15'55" N, long. 116°53'30" W; around SE cor. sec. 8, T 2 N, R 1 E); the place is near the mouth of Minnelusa Canyon. Named on Lucerne Valley (1947) 15' quadrangle. Postal authorities established Minnelusa post office in 1928 and discontinued it in 1940; the place first was called Camp Juniper (Salley, p. 142).

Minnelusa Canyon [SAN BERNARDINO]: *canyon,* drained by a stream that flows 1.25 miles to Big Bear Lake (1) 3 miles east of Fawnskin (lat. 34°15'45" N, long. 116°53'30" W; near NW cor. sec. 16, T 2 N, R 1 E). Named on Fawnskin (1971) 7.5' quadrangle.

Minneola [SAN BERNARDINO]: *locality,* 6 miles east of Daggett along Atchison Topeka and Santa Fe Railroad (lat. 34°50'45" N, long. 116°46'30" W; sec. 28, T 9 N, R 2 E). Named on Minneola (1971) 7.5' quadrangle. Postal authorities established Minneola post office in 1896 and discontinued it in 1897 (Frickstad, p. 143). Southern California Improvement Company built an irrigation canal about 1895 and projected a town called Minneola at the terminus of the canal, but the project failed—the name was for Minnie Dieterle, wife of a company official; the railroad adopted the name of the town for a station at the site in 1902 (Gudde, 1949, p. 217).

Minneola Ridge [SAN BERNARDINO]: *ridge,* generally northwest-trending, 2.5 miles long, 9 miles southeast of Daggett (lat. 34°46'15" N, long. 116°46'10" W); the feature is 5.25 miles south of Minneola. Named on Minneola (1971) 7.5' quadrangle.

Miracle Hill [RIVERSIDE]: *hill,* 11.5 miles north of Cathedral City (lat. 33°56'55" N, long. 116°28'55" W; at S line sec. 32, T 2 S, R 5 E). Altitude 1144 feet. Named on Seven Palms Valley (1958) 7.5' quadrangle.

Mirage Lake: see **El Mirage Lake** [SAN BERNARDINO].

Mirage Valley: see **El Mirage Valley** [SAN BERNARDINO].

Mira Loma [RIVERSIDE]: *town,* 8.5 miles north-northeast of Corona (lat. 33°59'20" N, long. 117°30'50" W). Named on Corona North (1967) and Guasti (1966) 7.5' quadrangles. Postal authorities established Mira Loma post office in 1930 (Frickstad, p. 129).

Mira Loma Station [RIVERSIDE]: *locality,* 8.5 miles east-northeast of Riverside along Union Pacific Railroad (lat. 34°01' N, long. 117°31'25" W; near NW cor. sec. 9, T 2 S, R 6 W). Named on Guasti (1966) 7.5' quadrangle. United States Geological Survey's (1941) map has the name "Mira Loma" at present Mira Loma Station. Cucamonga (1903) 15' quadrangle has the name "Stalder" at or near present Mira Loma Station before the railroad reached the place. Postal authorities established Stalder post office in 1896, changed the name to Wineville in 1908, moved it 1.25 miles south in 1909, and changed the name to Mira Loma in 1930; the name "Stalder" was for Arnold J. Stalder, first postmaster and a pioneer settler; the name "Wineville" was for Charles Stern winery at the site (Salley, p. 211, 241).

Mirror Lake [SAN BERNARDINO]: *dry lake,* 800 feet long, 16 miles west-southwest of Trona on San Bernardino-Kern County line (lat. 35°38'45" N, long. 117°38'15" W; on E line sec. 26, T 26 S, R 40 E). Named on Ridgecrest North (1973) 7.5' quadrangle.

Missed Spring [SAN BERNARDINO]: *spring,* 14 miles northwest of downtown Morongo Valley (lat. 34°12'20" N, long. 116°43'45" W; near N line sec. 1, T 1 N, R 2 E). Named on Onyx Peak (1972) 7.5' quadrangle.

Mission Canyon: see **Avery Canyon** [RIVERSIDE].

Mission Creek [RIVERSIDE-SAN BERNARDINO]: *stream* and *dry wash,* formed by the confluence of North Fork and South Fork in San Bernardino County, extends for 20 miles to Whitewater River 3.5 miles north-northeast of Palm Springs in Riverside Canyon (lat. 33°52'55" N, long. 116°31'40" W; at W line sec. 25, T 3 S, R 4 E). Named on Catclaw Flat (1972), Desert Hot Springs (1955), and Morongo Valley (1972) 7.5' quadrangles. North Fork is 5 miles long and is named on Catclaw Flat (1972) and Onyx Peak (1972) 7.5' quadrangles. South Fork is 5 miles long and is named on Catclaw Flat (1972) and San Gorgonio Mountain (1970) 7.5' quadrangles. West Fork enters from the west 11.5 miles above the mouth of the main stream; it is 3.5 miles long and is named on Catclaw Flat (1972) 7.5' quadrangle.

Mission Wash [IMPERIAL]: *stream,* flows 4 miles to lowlands along Colorado River 3.25 miles north of Bard (lat. 32°50' N, long. 114° 32'40" W). Named on Bard (1965) and Little Picacho Peak (1965) 7.5' quadrangles. The name recalls San Pedro y San Pablo mission that four Franciscan padres founded in 1780 about 12 miles from La Purisima Concepcion mission; the place was abandoned after an Indian uprising in 1781 (Hoover, Rensch, and Rensch, p. 108).

Mission Well [RIVERSIDE]: *well,* 24 miles northwest of Desert Center along Pinto Wash (lat. 33°57'30" N, long. 115°41'10" W; near N line sec. 35, T 2 S, R 12 E). Named on Pinto Basin (1963) 15' quadrangle.

Mitchell Caverns: see **Cooks Well** [SAN BERNARDINO].

Mitchel Range [SAN BERNARDINO]: *range,* 3.5 miles north-northeast of Barstow (lat. 34°56'40" N, long. 117°00'30" W). Named on Barstow (1971) 7.5' quadrangle.

Mobile: see **El Centro** [IMPERIAL].

Mockingbird Canyon [RIVERSIDE]: *canyon,* 5.5 miles long, opens into lowlands 6.5 miles south-southwest of Riverside city hall (lat. 33°53'40" N, long. 117°25'05" W; at E line sec. 20, T 3 S, R 5 W). Named on Lake Mathews (1967), Riverside West (1967), and Steele Peak (1967) 7.5' quadrangles.

Mockingbird Canyon Lake: see **Mockingbird Reservoir** [RIVERSIDE].

Mockingbird Reservoir [RIVERSIDE]: *lake,* behind a dam at the mouth of Mockingbird Canyon (lat. 33°53'40" N, long. 117°25'05" W; at E line sec. 20, T 3 S, R 5 W). Named on Riverside West (1967) 7.5' quadrangle. Called Mockingbird Canyon Lake on Riverside (1943) 15' quadrangle. The dam was built in 1913 to provide water storage (Gunther, p. 329).

Mohave Canyon [SAN BERNARDINO]: *canyon,* 5.5 miles long, along Colorado River 16 miles southeast of Needles on California-Arizona State line (lat. 34°38'30" N, long. 114°26'30" W). Named on Castle Rock (1970) and Topock (1970) 7.5' quadrangles.

Mohave Desert: see **Mojave Desert**, under "Regional setting."

Mohave Mountains: see **Chemehuevi Mountains** [SAN BERNARDINO].

Mohave River: see **Mojave River** [SAN BERNARDINO]; **Piute Wash** [SAN BERNARDINO].

Mohave Wash [SAN BERNARDINO]: *stream,* flows 5.25 miles to Colorado River 12 miles southeast of Needles (lat. 34°41'55" N, long. 114°28'05" W). Named on Topock (1970) and Whale Mountain (1971) 7.5' quadrangles.

Mohawk Hill [SAN BERNARDINO]: *ridge,* west-southwest- to west-trending, 4 miles long, 18 miles west-southwest of Ivanpah (lat. 35°29' N, long. 115°35' W). Named on Mescal Range (1955) 15' quadrangle, which shows Mohawk mine near the west end of the ridge.

Mohawk Spring [SAN BERNARDINO]: *spring,* 29 miles northwest of Vidal (lat. 34°25'55" N, long. 114°50'40" W). Named on Turtle Mountains (1954) 15' quadrangle.

Mojave Desert: see "Regional setting."

Mojave Heights [SAN BERNARDINO]: *locality,* 3 miles northwest of Victorville (lat. 34°04'10" N, long. 117°19'30" W; sec. 32, T 6 N, R 4 W). Named on Victorville (1956) 7.5' quadrangle.

Mojave River [SAN BERNARDINO]: *stream* and *dry wash,* formed by the confluence of Deep Creek (1) and West Fork Mojave River, extends for about 100 miles to the mouth of Afton Canyon 20 miles southwest of Baker (lat. 35°02'30" N, long. 116°18'30" W; at W line sec. 13, T 11 N, R 7 E)—the extension of the stream course on from the mouth of Afton Canyon to Soda Lake is called Mojave River Wash. Named on San Bernardino (1966) and Trona (1957) 1°x 2° quadrangles. Called Inconsistent R. on Burr's (1839) map, a name that Jedediah Smith gave to the stream (Morgan, p. 200). Called Mohahve R. on Fremont's (1848) map. Garces named the feature Arroyo de los Martires in 1776 (Thompson, 1929, p. 10). The name "Mojave River" is from Mohave Indians, who lived along Colorado River—Mojave River once mistakenly was thought to reach Colorado River (Kroeber, p. 48). United States Board on Geographic Names (1933, p. 526) rejected the form "Mohave River" for the name. West Fork is 12 miles long and is named on Cajon (1956), Cedar Springs (1956), and Lake Arrowhead (1971) 7.5' quadrangles. East Fork of West Fork enters West Fork from the southeast 18 miles south of Victorville; it is 6.5 miles long and is named on Cedar Springs (1956) and Lake Arrowhead (1971) 7.5' quadrangles. Deep Creek (1), which joins North Fork to form Mojave River, often is called East Fork Mojave River (Peirson, p. 32).

Mojave River Camp [SAN BERNARDINO]: *locality,* 6 miles west of Luna Mountain (lat. 34°20'30" N, long. 117°13'45" W; sec. 18, T 3 N, R 3 W); the place is near the head of Mojave River. Named on Lake Arrowhead (1956) 15' quadrangle.

Mojave River Forks Reservoir [SAN BERNARDINO]: *lake,* behind a dam 14 miles southeast of Victorville along Mojave River (lat. 34°20'35" N, long. 117°14'10" W; sec. 18, T 3 N, R 3 W); water of the lake covers the site of the confluence of West Fork Mojave River and Deep Creek (1). Named on Lake Arrowhead (1971) 7.5' quadrangle.

Mojave River Wash [SAN BERNARDINO]: *dry wash,* extends from the mouth of Afton Canyon, which is 20 miles southwest of Baker (lat. 35°02'30" N, long. 116°18'30" W), for about 15 miles to Soda Lake. Named on Cave Mountain (1948) and Soda Lake (1956) 15' quadrangles. The end of the dry wash is called Sink of Mohave on Goddard's (1857) map. It also was known as Soda Sink (Gudde, 1949, p. 219).

Mojave Tank [RIVERSIDE]: *water feature,* 24 miles northwest of Blythe (lat. 33°53'50" N, long. 114°50'10" W). Named on Midland (1952) 15' quadrangle. Flood waters pouring over a cliff 15 feet high formed a basin that never is entirely dry (Brown, 1920, p. 82).

Mojave Valley [SAN BERNARDINO]: *valley,* extends eastward from Daggett along Mojave River (center near lat. 34°53' N, long. 116°40' W). Named on San Bernardino (1966) 1°x 2° quadrangle. According to Thompson (1929, p. 437), the lower part of Mojave Valley, especially the part near Yermo, has been called Yermo Valley or Otis Valley.

Molino [SAN BERNARDINO]: *locality,* 5 miles north of Redlands along Atchison, Topeka and Santa Fe Railroad (lat. 34°07'30" N, long. 117°11'45" W; sec. 33, T 1 N, R 3 W). Named on Redlands (1954) 15' quadrangle.

Momyer Creek [SAN BERNARDINO]: *stream,* flows nearly 2 miles to Mill Creek Canyon 5.5 miles west of San Gorgonio Mountain (lat. 34°05'25" N, long. 116°55'30" W; near NW cor. sec. 18, T 1 S, R 1 E). Named on Forest Falls (1970) 7.5' quadrangle. Called Lost Creek on San Gorgonio Mountain (1954) 15' quadrangle. United States Board on Geographic Names (1975c, p. 4) gave the name "Lost Creek" as a variant, and noted that the name "Momyer Creek" honors Joe R. Momyer, who was a conservationist and president of the organization called Defenders of the San Gorgonio Wilderness.

Monad: see **Garnet** [RIVERSIDE].

Monarch Flat [SAN BERNARDINO]: *area,* 6 miles north of Big Bear City (lat. 34°20'50" N, long. 116°50' W; near NW cor. sec. 13, T 3 N, R 1 E). Named on Big Bear City (1971) 7.5. quadrangle.

Monkeyface Creek [SAN BERNARDINO]: *stream,* flows 1.5 miles to Mill Creek Canyon 7.25 miles west of San Gorgonio Mountain (lat. 34°05'45" N, long. 116°57'20" W; sec. 11, T 1 S, R 1 W). Named on Forest Falls (1970) 7.5' quadrangle. Called Oak Cove Creek on San Gorgonio Mountain (1954) 15' quadrangle, where present Frustration Creek is called Monkeyface Creek. United States Board on Geographic Names (1975b, p. 5) gave the names "Oak Cove Creek" and "Monkey Face Creek" as variants.

Monkeyface Falls [SAN BERNARDINO]: *waterfall,* 7.25 miles west of San Gorgonio Mountain (lat. 34°05'55" N, long. 116°57'15" W; sec. 11, T 1 S, R 1 W). Named on Forest Falls (1970) 7.5' quadrangle.

Monroe Canyon [SAN BERNARDINO]: *canyon,* drained by a stream that flows 2 miles to Keller Creek 3 miles south of Keller Peak (lat. 34°09'05" N, long. 117°03'30" W; near S line sec. 23, T 1 N, R 2 W). Named on Keller Peak (1967) 7.5' quadrangle.

Mons [RIVERSIDE]: *locality,* 7 miles east of Banning along Southern Pacific Railroad (lat. 33°55'10" N, long. 116°45'10" W; near SW cor. sec. 11, T 3 S, R 2 E). Named on Cabazon (1956) 7.5' quadrangle.

Monta Vista Resort: see **San Antonio Heights** [SAN BERNARDINO].

Montclair [SAN BERNARDINO]: *town,* 2.5 miles west-northwest of Ontario city hall (lat. 34°04'25" N, long. 117°41'30" W). Named on Ontario (1967) 7.5' quadrangle, which shows Monte Vista school at the place. Postal authorities established Montclair post office in 1958 (Salley, p. 144). The town incorporated with the name "Monte Vista" in 1956, but the residents changed the name to Montclair in 1958.

Monte Vista: see **Montclair** [SAN BERNARDINO].

Montgomery Creek [RIVERSIDE]: *stream,* flows 5.25 miles to Smith Creek 1.25 miles south of Banning (lat. 33°54'35" N, long. 116°52'55" W; sec.

16, T 3 S, R 1 E). Named on Beaumont (1953) 7.5' quadrangle.

Monumental Pass [SAN BERNARDINO]: *canyon,* 10 miles south-southwest of Needles (lat. 34°43'25" N, long. 114°42' W; sec. 5, T 7 N, R 22 E). Named on Monumental Pass (1971) 7.5' quadrangle.

Monument Mountain [RIVERSIDE]: *peak,* 15 miles northwest of Chiriaco Summit (lat. 33°48'50" N, long. 115°53'45" W; near NW cor. sec. 24, T 4 S, R 10 E). Altitude 4834 feet. Named on Hexie Mountains (1963) 15' quadrangle.

Monument Peak [RIVERSIDE]: *peak,* 2.5 miles north of Estelle Mountain (lat. 33°48'10" N, long. 117°25'20" W). Altitude 2333 feet. Named on Lake Mathews (1967) 7.5' quadrangle. The feature was known as Sentinel Peak in 1892 (Gunther, p. 332).

Monument Peak [SAN BERNARDINO]:
(1) *peak,* 10.5 miles north-northwest of San Bernardino city hall (lat. 34°14'45" N, long. 117°21'10" W; sec. 24, T 2 N, R 5 W. Altitude 5290 feet. Named on San Bernardino North (1967) 7.5' quadrangle.
(2) *peak,* 18 miles northeast of Vidal (lat. 34°16'50" N, long. 114° 15'15" W; near N line sec. 9, T 2 N, R 26 E). Altitude 2453 feet. Named on Whipple Wash (1970) 7.5' quadrangle.

Moon Lake [SAN BERNARDINO]: *intermittent lake,* 500 feet long, 10 miles north of San Bernardino city hall (lat. 34°14'40" N, long. 117°15'25" W; near W line sec. 24, T 2 N, R 4 W). Named on San Bernardino North (1967) 7.5' quadrangle.

Moonlake: see **Valley of the Moon** [SAN BERNARDINO].

Moonlight Mesa [SAN BERNARDINO]: *area,* 5.5 miles north-northeast of Joshua Tree (lat. 34°12'45" N, long. 116°17'15" W). Named on Joshua Tree North (1972) 7.5' quadrangle.

Moon Ridge [SAN BERNARDINO]: *ridge,* northwest-trending, 1.5 miles long, 2.5 miles northwest of Sugarloaf Mountain (lat. 34°13'25" N, long. 116°50'40" W). Named on Moonridge (1970) 7.5' quadrangle.

Moonridge [SAN BERNARDINO]: *district,* 3.5 miles northwest of Sugarloaf Mountain in the town of Big Bear Lake (lat. 34°14' N, long. 116°51'15" W); the place is northwest of Moon Ridge. Named on Moonridge (1970) 7.5' quadrangle.

Moonshine Spring [SAN BERNARDINO]: *spring,* 26 miles southeast of Trona (lat. 35°28'05" N, long. 117°06'05" W). Named on Pilot Knob (1954) 15' quadrangle.

Moore [SAN BERNARDINO]: *locality,* 4.25 miles northeast of Ivanpah along Union Pacific Railroad (lat. 35°23'20" N, long. 115°15'45" W; at N line sec. 15, T 15 N, R 16 E). Named on Ivanpah (1956) 15' quadrangle.

Moore City: see **Banning** [RIVERSIDE].

Moovalya Lake [SAN BERNARDINO]: *lake,* behind a dam 14 miles east-northeast of Vidal along Colorado River on California-Arizona State line (lat. 34°10'05" N, long. 114°16'35" W). Named on Parker (1970) 7.5' quadrangle.

Mopah Peaks [SAN BERNARDINO]: *peaks,* 19 miles northwest of Vidal (lat. 34°03'15" N, long. 114°45'45" W); the peaks are near the northwest end of Mopah Range. Named on Turtle Mountains (1954) 15' quadrangle.

Mopah Range [SAN BERNARDINO]: *range,* 16 miles northwest of Vidal (lat. 34°16' N, long. 114°44' W). Named on Savahia Peak (1950) and Turtle Mountains (1954) 15' quadrangles.

Mopah Spring [SAN BERNARDINO]: *spring,* 20 miles northwest of Vidal (lat. 34°18'50" N, long. 114°46'30" W); the spring is in Mopah Range. Named on Turtle Mountains (1954) 15' quadrangle.

Moreno [RIVERSIDE]: *town,* 5.25 miles east-southeast of Sunnymead (lat. 33°55'05" N, long. 117°09'20" W; at SE cor. sec. 11, T 3 S, R 3 W). Named on Sunnymead (1967) 7.5' quadrangle. Postal authorities established Moreno post office in 1891 (Frickstad, p. 129). Officials of Bear Valley and Alessandro Development Company named the place to honor Frank E. Brown of the company—*moreno* means "brown" in Spanish (Gunther, p. 333).

Moreno: see **Lake Moreno**, under **Mystic Lake** [RIVERSIDE].

Moreno Valley [RIVERSIDE]: *valley,* 4 miles southeast of Sunnymead (lat. 33°53'45" N, long. 117°12' W); Moreno is at the east end of the valley. Named on Sunnymead (1967) 7.5' quadrangle. Called Alessandro Valley on Elsinore (1901) 30' quadrangle—Alessandro is near the west end of the valley.

Morgans Well [SAN BERNARDINO]: *well,* 15 miles south of Ludlow (lat. 34°30'45" N, long. 116°11'30" W; near SW cor. sec. 18, T 5 N, R 8 E). Named on Morgans Well (1955) 7.5' quadrangle.

Mormon Crossing: see **Victorville** [SAN BERNARDINO].

Mormon Pass: see **Crucero Hill** [SAN BERNARDINO].

Mormon Spring: see **Old Mormon Spring** [SAN BERNARDINO].

Morongo Canyon: see **Big Morongo Canyon** [RIVERSIDE-SAN BERNARDINO]; **Big Morongo Canyon** [SAN BERNARDINO]; **Little Morongo Canyon** [RIVERSIDE-SAN BERNARDINO]; **Little Morongo Canyon** [SAN BERNARDINO].

Morongo Creek: see **Big Morongo Creek** [RIVERSIDE-SAN BERNARDINO]: **Little Morongo Creek** [RIVERSIDE-SAN BERNARDINO].

Morongo Heights: see **Little Morongo Heights** [SAN BERNARDINO].

Morongo Lakes [SAN BERNARDINO]: *lakes,* largest 350 feet long, 4 miles east-northeast of downtown Morongo Valley (lat. 34°04'20" N, long. 116°31'10" W; sec. 24, T 1 S, R 4 E). Named on Morongo Valley (1972) 7.5' quadrangle.

Morongo Mountains: see **Little San Bernardino Mountains** [RIVERSIDE-SAN BERNARDINO].

Morongo Valley [SAN BERNARDINO]:
(1) *valley,* at and northeast of the town of Morongo Valley (lat. 34°04'30" N, long. 116°32'30" W). Named on Morongo Valley (1972) and Yucca Valley South (1972) 7.5' quadrangles. The name is from the designation of an Indian village in the valley or along Mission Creek (Kroeber, p. 49).
(2) *town,* 41 miles east of San Bernardino (lat. 34°02'50" N, long. 116°34'45" W). Named on Morongo Valley (1972) 7.5' quadrangle. Postal authorities established Morongo Valley post office in 1947 (Frickstad, p. 143). Thompson's (1921) map shows a feature called Hole-in-the-Wall Spring situated about 1.5 miles southwest of present downtown Morongo Valley.

Morongo Valley Canyon [RIVERSIDE]: *canyon,* 2 miles long, along Dry Morongo Creek 12 miles north of Palm Springs (lat. 34°00'30" N, long. 116°34'30" W). Named on Morongo Valley (1955) 15' quadrangle.

Morongo Wash [RIVERSIDE]: *dry wash,* formed by the confluence of Big Morongo Wash and Little Morongo Wash, extends for 6.5 miles to end 6.5 miles north-northwest of Cathedral City (lat. 33° 52'15" N, long. 116°29'30" W; near NW cor. sec. 32, T 3 S, R 5 E). Named on Cathedral City (1958), Desert Hot Springs (1955), and Seven Palms Valley (1958) 7.5' quadrangles.

Morongo Wash: see **Big Morongo Wash** [RIVERSIDE]; **Little Morongo Wash** [RIVERSIDE].

Morrell Canyon [RIVERSIDE]: *canyon,* drained by a stream that flows 6 miles to San Juan Canyon 2 miles north-northeast of Sitton Peak (lat. 33°36'50" N, long. 117°26'05" W; at S line sec. 30, T 6 S, R 5 W); the canyon heads near Morrell Potrero. Named on Alberhill (1954) and Sitton Peak (1954) 7.5' quadrangles. Called Morrill Canyon on Elsinore (1901) 30' quadrangle.

Morrell Potrero [RIVERSIDE]: *area,* 4.5 miles west-northwest of Wildomar (lat. 33°36'50" N, long. 117°21'20" W; sec. 25, 36, T 6 S, R 5 W). Named on Wildomar (1953) 7.5' quadrangle. Called Morvell Potrero on Lake Elsinore (1941) 15' quadrangle. The name "Morrell Potrero" is for Marquis Lafayette Morrell, who homesteaded in the vicinity and worked in 1884 for Oliver Sandford, United States deputy surveyor (Gunther, p. 335).

Morrill Canyon: see **Morrell Canyon** [RIVERSIDE].

Morrison: see **Acme** [SAN BERNARDINO].

Morse Canyon [SAN BERNARDINO]: *canyon,* drained by a stream that flows 2 miles to lowlands 6.5 miles southwest of Devore (lat. 34°10'10" N, long. 117°29'50" W; sec. 15, T 1 N, R 6 W). Named on Cucamonga Peak (1966) and Devore (1966) 7.5' quadrangles.

Mortmar [RIVERSIDE]: *locality,* 22 miles southeast of Indio along Southern Pacific Railroad (lat. 33°31'20" N, long. 115°56'05" W; sec. 34, T 7 S, R 10 E); the place is near Salton Sea. Named on Mortmar (1958) 7.5' quadrangle. Called Mortmere on California Mining Bureau's (1917b) map. On United States Geological Survey's (1904) map, the name applies to a place located 18 miles southeast of Indio along Southern Pacific Railroad (lat. 33°30'30" N, long. 116°01' W; sec. 2, T 8 S, R 9 E)—water of Salton Sea now covers this earlier site.

Mortmere: see **Mortmar** [RIVERSIDE].

Morton Canyon [SAN BERNARDINO]: *canyon,* drained by a stream that flows nearly 4 miles to Santa Ana Wash 6 miles northwest of Yucaipa (lat. 34°06'05" N, long. 117°06'05" W; at W line sec. 9, T 1 S, R 2 W); the canyon heads near Morton Peak. Named on Yucaipa (1967) 7.5' quadrangle.

Morton Peak [SAN BERNARDINO]: *peak,* 4.5 miles north of Yucaipa (lat. 34°06'10" N, long. 117°02'25" W; sec. 12, T 1 S, R 2 W). Altitude 4624 feet. Named on Yucaipa (1967) 7.5' quadrangle.

Morvell Potrero: see **Morrell Potrero** [RIVERSIDE].

Moss [IMPERIAL]: *locality,* 13 miles north of Holtville along Southern Pacific Railroad (lat. 32°59'50" N, long. 115°24'25" W; near N line sec. 27, T 13 S, R 15 E). Named on Alamorio (1956) 7.5' quadrangle.

Mound City: see **Loma Linda** [SAN BERNARDINO].

Mound Spring [SAN BERNARDINO]: *spring,* 10 miles south-southeast of Old Woman Springs (lat. 34°15'20" N, long. 116°39'20" W; sec. 15, T 2 N, R 3 E). Named on Rattlesnake Canyon (1972) 7.5' quadrangle.

Mound Station: see **Loma Linda** [SAN BERNARDINO].

Mountain Center [RIVERSIDE]: *village,* 2.5 miles south of the center of Idyllwild (lat. 33°42'20" N, long. 116°43'30" W; sec. 25, T 5 S, R 2 E). Named on Idyllwild (1959) 15' quadrangle. Postal authorities established Keen Camp post office in 1909 and moved it 2 miles northwest in 1945, when they changed the name to Mountain Center (Salley, p. 110). The name "Keen Camp" was for Mary E. Keen, who began catering to vacationers in 1892 (Gunther, p. 261).

Mountain Home Creek [SAN BERNARDINO]: *stream,* flows 3.25 miles to Mill Creek Canyon 9.5 miles west of San Gorgonio Mountain (lat. 34°06'10" N, long. 116°59'45" W); the mouth of the stream is at Mountain Home Village. Named on Big Bear Lake (1970) and Forest Falls (1970) 7.5' quadrangles. East Fork enters from the northeast 1 mile upstream from the mouth of the main stream; it is 1.25 miles long and is named on Big Bear Lake (1970) and Forest Falls (1970) 7.5' quadrangles.

Mountain Home Peak [SAN BERNARDINO]: *peak*, 10 miles west of San Gorgonio Mountain (lat. 34°07'15" N, long. 116°59'45" W; at SW cor. sec. 33, T 1 N, R 1 W); the peak is 1.5 miles north of Mountain Home Village. Named on Forest Falls (1970) 7.5' quadrangle.

Mountain Home Spring [RIVERSIDE]: *spring*, 14 miles south-southwest of Palm Desert (lat. 33°32'20" N, long. 116°29' W; on E line sec. 29, T 7 S, R 5 E). Named on Palm Desert (1959) 15' quadrangle.

Mountain Home Village [SAN BERNARDINO]: *locality*, 5 miles north-northeast of Yucaipa in Mill Creek Canyon (lat. 34°06'05" N, long. 117°00' W; on E line sec. 8, T 1 S, R 1 W). Named on Forest Falls (1970) and Yucaipa (1967) 7.5' quadrangles.

Mountain Pass [SAN BERNARDINO]: *locality*, 16 miles west-northwest of Ivanpah (lat. 35°28'15" N, long. 115°32'35" W; sec. 14, T 16 N, R 13 E). Named on Mescal Range (1955) 15' quadrangle. Postal authorities established Mountain Pass post office in 1929, discontinued it in 1932, and reestablished it in 1966 (Salley, p. 147).

Mountain Ranch Springs: see **Pan Hot Springs** [SAN BERNARDINO].

Mountain Spring [IMPERIAL]: *locality*, 11.5 miles south-southwest of Carrizo Mountain (lat. 32°40'25" N, long. 116°06'15" W; at W line sec. 19, T 17 S, R 9 E). Named on In-Ko-Pah Gorge (1959) 7.5' quadrangle, which shows a water feature called Mountain Spring located 900 feet to the west in San Diego County.

Mountain Spring Camp [SAN BERNARDINO]: *locality*, 13 miles north-east of Essex (lat. 34°04'45" N, long. 115°03'10" W; near N line sec. 36, T 9 N, R 18 E). Named on Fenner (1956) 15' quadrangle.

Mountain Top Junction [SAN BERNARDINO]: *locality*, 8 miles north-northeast of Mount San Antonio (lat. 34°23'25" N, long. 117°34'30" W; sec. 35, T 4 N, R 7 W). Named on Phelan (1956) 7.5' quadrangle.

Mountain View [SAN BERNARDINO]: *settlement*, 4.25 miles southwest of Victorville (lat. 34°30' N, long. 117°21'15" W). Named on Adelanto (1956), Hesperia (1956), and Victorville (1956) 7.5' quadrangles.

Mountain Well [SAN BERNARDINO]: *well*, nearly 4 miles northeast of the village of Red Mountain (lat. 35°23'30" N, long. 117°33'45" W; near SE cor. sec. 22, T 29 S, R 41 E). Named on Klinker Mountain (1967) 7.5' quadrangle. Called City Well on Randsburg (1911) 15' quadrangle

Mount Baldy [SAN BERNARDINO]: *village*, 12 miles north of Ontario city hall in San Antonio Canyon on San Bernardino-Los Angeles County line (lat. 34°14'10" N, long. 117°39'25" W; sec. 19, 30, T 2 N, R 7 W). Named on Mount Baldy (1967) 7.5' quadrangle. Postal authorities established Camp Baldy post office in 1913, changed the name to Mt. Baldy in 1951, changed it to Mount Baldy in 1966, and changed it back to Mt. Baldy in 1975—the name is from Mount San Antonio, known as Old Baldy (Salley, p. 33, 148). Charles R. Baynham bought the property in 1906 and called it Camp Baynham; F.W. Palmer purchased the place in 1910 and changed the name to Camp Baldy (Hanna, p. 23). Ann Courtney and Fred Courtney opened Bear Canyon Resort just below Camp Baldy in 1921, and R.D.Shiffer started a resort called Eleven Oaks next to Bear Canyon Resort the same year; the community of Mount Baldy is known locally as Baldy Village (Robinson, J.W., 1983, p. 142, 157).

Mount Barrow [IMPERIAL]: *peak*, 23 miles south-southwest of Palo Verde (lat. 33°09' N, long. 114°56'35" W; near S line sec. 2, T 12 S, R 19 E). Altitude 2475 feet. Named on Quartz Peak (1953) 15' quadrangle.

Mount Davis [RIVERSIDE]: *peak*, 7 miles west of Banning (lat. 33° 54'30" N, long. 116°59'45" W; near W line sec. 16, T 3 S, R 1 W). Altitude 2861 feet. Named on Beaumont (1953) 7.5' quadrangle.

Mount Eden [RIVERSIDE]: *peak*, 13 miles northeast of Perris (lat. 33°53'30" N, long. 117°02'45" W; near SW cor. sec. 24, T 3 S, R 2 W); the feature is 0.5 mile southeast of Eden Hot Springs. Altitude 2353 feet. Named on El Casco (1967) 7.5' quadrangle.

Mount Edna [RIVERSIDE]: *peak*, 3.25 miles south of Banning (lat. 33°52'45" N, long. 116°52'50" W). Altitude 4357 feet. Named on Beaumont (1953) 7.5' quadrangle.

Mount Eisenhower: see **Eisenhower Mountain** [RIVERSIDE].

Mount Elmo [SAN BERNARDINO]: *hill*, 21 miles west-northwest of Victorville (lat. 34°36'45" N, long. 117°39'25" W; mainly in sec. 18, T 6 N, R 7 W). Altitude 3254 feet. Named on El Mirage (1956) 7.5' quadrangle.

Mount General [SAN BERNARDINO]: *hill*, 9 miles west-northwest of Barstow (lat. 34°57'15" N, long. 117°07'45" W; mainly in sec. 18, 19, T 10 N, R 2 W). Altitude 2925 feet. Named on Barstow (1971) and Hinkley (1971) 7.5' quadrangles.

Mount Harwood [SAN BERNARDINO]: *peak*, less than 1 mile east-southeast of Mount San Antonio (lat. 34°17'10" N, long. 117°37'55" W; sec. 5, T 2 N, R 7 W). Altitude 9552 feet. Named on Mount San Antonio (1955) 7.5' quadrangle. The name commemorates Aurelia Squire Harwood, California educator and conservationist (United States Board on Geographic Names, 1965c, p. 9). The feature also was called Little Baldy (Robinson, J.W., 1983, p. 179).

Mount Harwood: see **Thunder Mountain** [SAN BERNARDINO].

Mount Jurupa [RIVERSIDE]: *peak*, 5 miles northwest of Riverside (lat. 34°01'55" N, long. 117°26'30" W); the peak is the high point of Jurupa Mountains. Altitude 2217 feet. Named on Fontana (1967) 7.5' quadrangle.

Mount Klinker: see **Klinker Mountain** [SAN BERNARDINO].

Mount Manchester [SAN BERNARDINO]: *peak*, 38 miles southeast of Ivanpah (lat. 35°01'40" N, long. 114°44'50" W; near S line sec. 18, T 11 N, R 21 E). Altitude 3600 feet. Named on Mount Manchester (1970) 7.5' quadrangle.

Mount Marie Louise [SAN BERNARDINO]: *peak*, 7.5 miles southwest of Luna Mountain (lat. 34°17'05" N, long. 117°14'20" W; sec. 6, T 2 N, R 3 W). Altitude 5507 feet. Named on Lake Arrowhead (1971) 7.5' quadrangle.

Mount Pisgah: see **Pisgah Crater** [SAN BERNARDINO].

Mount R [SAN BERNARDINO]: *peak*, 3 miles west of Keller Peak (lat. 34°11'25" N, long. 117°06' W; sec. 9, T 1 N, R 2 W). Altitude 6355 feet. Named on Keller Peak (1967) 7.5' quadrangle.

Mount Robidoux: see **Mount Rubidoux** [RIVERSIDE].

Mount Roubedeau: see **Mount Rubidoux** [RIVERSIDE].

Mount Rubidoux [RIVERSIDE]: *hill*, 1.25 miles west of Riverside city hall (lat. 33°59' N, long. 117°23'30" W); the feature is mainly on Jurupa grant. Altitude 1399 feet. Named on Riverside West (1967) 7.5' quadrangle. Called Rubidoux Mt. on Riverside (1901) 15' quadrangle. The feature had the name "Pachappa Hill" in the early days (Gunther, p. 365). United States Board on Geographic Names (1933, p. 652) rejected the forms "Mount Robidoux," "Mount Roubedeau," and "Mount Rubideau" for the name, which recalls Louis Rubidoux, owner of Jurupa grant (Hoover, Rensch, and Rensch, p. 293).

Mount Rudolph [RIVERSIDE]: *peak*, 3 miles east-southeast of Lakeview (lat. 33°49'20" N, long. 117°04'10" W). Altitude 2649 feet. Named on Lakeview (1967) 7.5' quadrangle. The misspelled name is for Rudolf Wosslick, who bought land in the neighborhood in 1898 (Gunther, p. 339).

Mount Russell [RIVERSIDE]: *peak*, 6 miles east-southeast of Sunnymead (lat. 33°53'50" N, long. 117°09'20" W). Altitude 2664 feet. Named on Sunnymead (1967) 7.5' quadrangle.

Mount San Antonio [SAN BERNARDINO]: *peak*, 23 miles northwest of San Bernardino on San Bernardino-Los Angeles County line (lat. 34°17'20" N, long. 117°38'45" W; sec. 6, T 2 N, R 17 W). Named on Mount San Antonio (1955) 7.5' quadrangle. Called Old Baldy Peak on San Bernardino (1958) 1°x 2° quadrangle. United States Board on Geographic Names (1961c, p. 14) rejected the names "Baldy," "North Bald," "Old Baldy," "Old Baldy Peak," "San Antonia Peak," and "San Antonio Peak" for the feature. William B. Dewey established a trail camp in 1910 only 80 yards from the summit of the peak; he called it Angel Camp, and later he called it Baldy Summit Inn—fire destroyed the place in 1913 (Robinson, J.W., 1983, p. 169).

Mount Signal [IMPERIAL]: *locality*, 8.5 miles west of Calexico (lat. 32°40'45" N, long. 115°38'15" W; at NE cor. sec. 16, T 17 S, R 13 E). Named on Mount Signal (1957) 7.5' quadrangle. Postal authorities established Mount Signal post office in 1916 and discontinued it in 1934; the name is from nearby Signal Mountain in Mexico, which Lieutenant Amiel Whipple christened in 1849 when he surveyed the Mexican boundary line (Salley, p. 148).

Mount Sorenson [SAN BERNARDINO]: *peak*, 5 miles north of Harrison Mountain (lat. 34°14'15" N, long. 117°09'20" W; near SE cor. sec. 23, T 2 N, R 3 W). Altitude 6273 feet. Named on Harrison Mountain (1967) 7.5' quadrangle, which shows Lake Arrowhead boy scout camps located 1.25 miles east-northeast of the peak. The name commemorates Arnold C. Sorenson, scout executive of Los Angeles area boy scout council (United States Board on Geographic Names, 1979, p. 6).

Muddy Spring [SAN BERNARDINO]: *spring*, 3.25 miles south-southeast of Luna Mountain (lat. 34°18'10" N, long. 117°06' W; near W line sec. 33, T 3 N, R 2 W). Named on Butler Peak (1971) 7.5' quadrangle.

Mud Flat [SAN BERNARDINO]: *area*, 4 miles northwest of Harrison Mountain (lat. 34°12'30" N, long. 117°12'15" W; on N line sec. 4, T 1 N, R 3 W). Named on Harrison Mountain (1967) 7.5' quadrangle.

Mud Hills [SAN BERNARDINO]: *range*, 40 miles east-southeast of the village of Red Mountain (lat. 35°03' N, long. 117°02'30" W). Named on Opal Mountain (1955) 15' quadrangle.

Mud Spring [SAN BERNARDINO]: *spring*, 5 miles east-southeast of Luna Mountain (lat. 34°19'30" N, long. 117°02'30" W; near S line sec. 24, T 3 N, R 2 W). Named on Butler Peak (1971) 7.5' quadrangle.

Mule Canyon [SAN BERNARDINO]: *canyon*, 2.25 miles long, opens into lowlands 5.5 miles north-northeast of Daggett (lat. 34°55'45" N, long. 116°50'25" W; near E line sec. 26, T 10 N, R 1 E). Named on Yermo (1953) 7.5' quadrangle.

Mule Mountains [RIVERSIDE]: *range*, 16 miles west-southwest of Blythe (lat. 33°30' N, long. 114°50' W). Named on McCoy Spring (1952) and Palo Verde Mountains (1953) 15' quadrangles.

Mule Mountains: see **Little Mule Mountains** [IMPERIAL].

Mullet Island [IMPERIAL]: *island*, 1050 feet long, 8.5 miles northwest of

Calipatria in Salton Sea (lat. 33°13'30" N, long. 115°36'30" W; sec. 10, T 11 S, R 13 E). Named on Niland (1956) 7.5' quadrangle.

Mundo [IMPERIAL]: *locality,* 7.5 miles southeast of Frink along Southern Pacific Railroad (lat. 33°16'25" N, long. 115°34'05" W; sec. 25, T 10 S, R 13 E). Named on Wister (1956) 7.5' quadrangle. Called Volcano on United States Geological Survey's (1908) map. Postal authorities established Volcano Springs post office at the place in 1901 and discontinued it in 1902 (Salley, p. 233).

Munsen Canyon [RIVERSIDE]: *canyon,* 3.5 miles long, opens into lowlands nearly 2 miles north-northeast of Chiriaco Summit (lat. 33°41'05" N, long. 115°42'35" W; at SE cor. sec. 34, T 5 S, R 12 E). Named on Hayfield (1963) 15' quadrangle.

Munyon [IMPERIAL]: *locality,* 8 miles southeast of Calipatria along Southern Pacific Railroad (lat. 33°02'25" N, long. 115°24'50" W; near NW cor. sec. 10, T 13 S, R 15 E). Named on Wiest (1956) 7.5' quadrangle.

Murphy Dry-Placer Camp: see **Murphys Well** [SAN BERNARDINO].

Murphys Well [SAN BERNARDINO]: *well,* 33 miles east-southeast of the village of Red Mountain (lat. 35°07'40" N, long. 117°06' W; near SE cor. sec. 24, T 32 S, R 45 E). Named on Opal Mountain (1955) 15' quadrangle. Called Murphy Well on Searles Lake (1915) 1° quadrangle. Murphy Dry-Placer Camp was at the well site (Mendenhall, 1909a, p. 58).

Murphy Well [SAN BERNARDINO]: *well,* 5 miles north-northwest of Ivanpah (lat. 35°27'15" N, long. 115°20'45" W). Named on Ivanpah (1956) 15' quadrangle.

Murray Canyon [RIVERSIDE]: *canyon,* drained by a stream that flows 7.5 miles to Palm Canyon nearly 6 miles south of Palm Springs (lat. 33°45'10" N, long. 116°32'45" W). Named on Idyllwild (1959) 15' quadrangle, and on Palm Springs (1957) and San Jacinto Peak (1981) 7.5' quadrangles. The name commemorates Welwood Murray, who filed a water claim in the canyon in 1887 (Gunther, p. 343).

Murray Hill [RIVERSIDE]: *peak,* 2.25 miles west-southwest of Cathedral City (lat. 33°45'55" N, long. 116°29'55" W; sec. 6, T 5 S, R 5 E). Named on Cathedral City (1958) and Palm Springs (1957) 7.5' quadrangles.

Murrieta [RIVERSIDE]: *village,* 10 miles southeast of the town of Lake Elsinore (lat. 33°33'15" N, long. 117°12'50" W); the place is along Murrieta Creek. Named on Murrieta (1953) 7.5' quadrangle. Postal authorities established Murrietta (with the second "t") post office in 1885 and changed the name to Murrieta in 1924 (Salley, p. 149). United States Board on Geographic Names (1933, p. 538) rejected the form "Murrietta" for the name. Officials of Temecula Land and Water Company founded the community in 1884 and named it for Juan Murrieta; the old Willow Springs or Alamos stage station was at the site (Gunther, p. 343-344). Postal authorities established Anon post office 8 miles northeast of Murrietta post office (SE quarter sec. 14, T 6 S, R 3 W) in 1886 and discontinued it in 1887; the name was from letters of Andrew Kittilson's name—Kittilson homesteaded at the site (Salley, p. 8).

Murrieta Creek [RIVERSIDE]: *stream* and *dry wash,* extends for 13 miles to join Temecula Creek and form Santa Margarita River 1.5 miles south-southwest of the town of Temecula (lat. 33°28'30" N, long. 117°08'25" W). Named on Murrieta (1953), Temecula (1968), and Wildomar (1953) 7.5' quadrangles.

Murrieta Hot Springs [RIVERSIDE]: *town,* 3.25 miles east of Murrieta (lat. 33°33'45" N, long. 117°09'20" W). Named on Murrieta (1953, photorevised 1979) 7.5' quadrangle. Called Hot Sulphur Springs on Elsinore (1901) 30' quadrangle. The springs at the place first were called Temecula Hot Springs for Temecula grant where they occur, and were renamed in 1884 for the nearby new town of Murrieta; Fritz Guenther visited the place in 1902 and bought it to develop a spa known as Guenther's Murrieta Hot Springs (Gunther, p. 345).

Muscoy [SAN BERNARDINO]: *town,* 5 miles northwest of San Bernardino city hall (lat. 34°09'15" N, long. 117°20'45" W). Named on San Bernardino North (1967) 7.5' quadrangle.

Muscupiabe [SAN BERNARDINO]: *land grant,* extends from northwest of San Bernardino to the mouth of Cajon Canyon. Named on Devore (1966), Harrison Mountain (1967), San Bernardino North (1967), and San Bernardino South (1967) 7.5' quadrangles. Michael White received 1 league in 1843 and claimed 30,145 acres patented in 1872 (Cowan, p. 50; Cowan listed the alternate names "El Cajon de Muscupiabe" and "El Cajon de los Mejicanos" for the grant). The name is of Indian origin (Kroeber, p. 50).

Music Valley [RIVERSIDE-SAN BERNARDINO]: *valley,* 29 miles north-northwest of Chiriaco Summit on Riverside-San Bernardino County line (lat. 34°02' N, long. 115°57'15" W). Named on Hexie Mountains (1963) and Valley Mountain (1956) 15' quadrangles. The name is from the sound that wind makes blowing through the valley (Gunther, p. 346).

Myer Creek [IMPERIAL]: *stream,* flows for 8.5 miles before ending 6 miles south of Carrizo Mountain near Ocotillo (lat. 32°44'20" N, long. 116°00'05" W; near NE cor. sec. 35, T 16 S, R 9 E). Named on In-Ko-Pah Gorge (1959) 7.5' quadrangle.

Myer Valley [IMPERIAL]: *valley,* 11.5 miles south of Carrizo Mountain (lat. 32°40'30" N, long. 116°03' W; sec. 22, T 17 S, R 9 E); the place is near the head of a tributary to Myer Creek. Named on In-Ko-Pah Gorge (1959) 7.5' quadrangle.

Myoma [RIVERSIDE]: *locality,* 11 miles east of Cathedral City along Southern Pacific Railroad (lat. 33°45'10" N, long. 116°16'50" W; sec. 8, T 5 S, R 7 E). Named on La Quinta (1959) and Myoma (1958) 7.5' quadrangles.

Myrick Spring [SAN BERNARDINO]: *spring,* 29 miles southeast of Trona (lat. 35°30'25" N, long. 116°58'10" W). Named on Quail Mountains (1948) 15' quadrangle.

Mystic Lake [RIVERSIDE]: *lake,* 1500 feet long, 3 miles east-northeast of Lakeview (lat. 33°51'10" N, long. 117°04'25" W). Named on Elsinore (1901) 30' quadrangle. Lakeview (1967) 7.5' quadrangle shows duck ponds at the site. The lake, which had water only in wet years, also was called San Jacinto Lake, Lake Moreno, Brown's Lake, and Lake San Antonio Bucareli; the south part of the feature was subdivided during some dry years as a development called Brownlands, for Frank E. Brown, the developer (Bolton, p. 101; Gunther, p. 346-348). Postal authorities established Brownlands post office 2 miles southeast of Moreno post office in 1914 and discontinued in 1915 (Salley, p. 28).

- N -

Nance Canyon [RIVERSIDE]: *canyon,* 2.5 miles long, opens into Coyote Canyon 20 miles south-southwest of Palm Desert (lat. 33° 28'15" N, long. 116°32'45" W; at S line sec. 14, T 8 S, R 4 E). Named on Bucksnort Mountain (1960) 7.5' quadrangle. Ramona (1903) 30' quadrangle shows present Nance Canyon as part of Coyote Canyon.

Nantan: see **Hardrock Queen Spring** [SAN BERNARDINO].

Napolitan: see **Colton** [SAN BERNARDINO].

Narod [SAN BERNARDINO]:

(1) *district,* 2 miles west of Ontario city hall (lat. 34°03'30" N, long. 117°41' W; at E line sec. 26, T 1 S, R 8 W); the place is just southeast of Narod (2). Named on Ontario (1967) 7.5' quadrangle.

(2) *locality,* 2.25 miles west of Ontario city hall along Southern Pacific Railroad (lat. 34°03'40" N, long. 117°41'15" W; near N line sec. 26, T 1 S, R 8 W). Named on Ontario (1954) 7.5' quadrangle. The word "narod" is the name, spelled backward, of a railroad section foreman (Gudde, 1969, p. 217).

Nash Hill [SAN BERNARDINO]: *hill,* 21 miles west-northwest of Victorville (lat. 34°40'25" N, long. 117°38'15" W; on N line sec. 29, T 7 N, R 7 W). Altitude 3273 feet. Named on Adobe Mountain (1955) 7.5' quadrangle.

Nawakwa: see **Camp Nawakwa** [SAN BERNARDINO].

Nealeys Corner [SAN BERNARDINO]: *locality,* 3 miles southwest of Devore (lat. 34°11'15" N, long. 117°26'20" W). Named on Devore (1966) 7.5' quadrangle.

Nebo [SAN BERNARDINO]: *locality,* 5 miles east-southeast of Barstow along Atchison, Topeka and Santa Fe Railroad (lat. 34°52'45" N, long. 116°57'15" W; sec. 11, T 9 N, R 1 W). Named on Nebo (1953) 7.5' quadrangle.

Necochea Canyon: see **Laborde Canyon** [RIVERSIDE].

Needles [SAN BERNARDINO]: *town,* 160 miles east-northeast of San Bernardino (lat. 34°50'20" N, long. 114°36'15" W). Named on Needles (1970) and Needles SW (1970) 7.5' quadrangles. Postal authorities established Needles post office in 1883 (Frickstad, p. 144), and the town incorporated in 1913. Railroad construction crews working from east and west met at the place in 1883; the name "Needles" is from a group of pinnacles called The Needles located 15 miles southeast of the town in Arizona (Lingenfelter, 1978, p. 82).

Needles Boat Landing [SAN BERNARDINO]: *locality,* 25 miles north-northeast of Vidal along Lake Havasu (lat. 34°28'55" N, long. 114°24'15" W; sec. 31, T 5 N, R 25 E). Named on Whipple Mountains (1950) 15' quadrangle.

Needles Eye [RIVERSIDE]: *relief feature,* 8.5 miles east of Idyllwild along West Fork Palm Canyon (lat. 33°43'10" N, long. 116°34'15" W; sec. 21, T 5 S, R 4 E). Named on Idyllwild (1959) 15' quadrangle.

Negro Butte [SAN BERNARDINO]: *hill,* 10 miles east of the town of Lucerne Valley (lat. 34°27'55" N, long. 116°46'25" W; sec. 4, T 4 N, R 2 E). Altitude 3555 feet. Named on Cougar Buttes (1971) 7.5' quadrangle.

Negro Hill [RIVERSIDE]: *hill,* 28 miles east-northeast of Garnet (lat. 34°01'35" N, long. 116°05'05" W). Altitude 4875 feet. Named on Queen Mountain (1972) 7.5' quadrangle.

Negro Peak [SAN BERNARDINO]: *peak,* 14 miles northwest of Vidal (lat. 34°14'45" N, long. 114°42'15" W). Altitude 2524 feet. Named on Vidal (1949) 15' quadrangle.

Negro Valley: see **Butterfield Valley** [RIVERSIDE].

Neighbors [RIVERSIDE]: *locality,* 4.25 miles southwest of Blythe (lat. 33°34'25" N, long. 114°39'20" W; at NW cor. sec. 14, T 7 S, R 22 E). Named on Ripley (1952) 7.5' quadrangle. Postal authorities established Neighbours (with the "u") post office in 1905 and discontinued it in 1920; the name was for James E. Neighbours, first postmaster (Salley, p. 152).

Nelson Lake [SAN BERNARDINO]: *dry lake,* 1.5 miles long, 40 miles west-northwest of Baker (lat. 35°25'50" N, long. 116°46'30" W; sec. 32, 33, T

16 N, R 2 E). Named on Goldstone Lake (1948) 15' quadrangle.

Nelson Ridge [SAN BERNARDINO]: *ridge*, northwest-trending, 3.5 miles long, 3.5 miles northeast of Big Bear City (lat. 34°17'45" N, long. 116°48'20" W). Named on Big Bear City (1971) 7.5' quadrangle.

Nettle Spring [RIVERSIDE]: *spring*, 3.5 miles south of Idyllwild (lat. 33°41'15" N, long. 116°42'40" W; at S line sec. 31, T 5 S, R 3 E). Named on Idyllwild (1959) 15' quadrangle.

Nevada [SAN BERNARDINO]: *locality*, 2.25 miles west-northwest of Redlands city hall along Atchison Topeka and Santa Fe Railroad (lat. 34°03'55" N, long. 117°13' W). Named on Redlands (1967) 7.5' quadrangle. Called Gladysta on Redlands (1901) 15' quadrangle.

Newberry [SAN BERNARDINO]: *town*, 20 miles east-southeast of Barstow (lat. 34°49'40" N, long. 116°41'15" W; sec. 32, T 9 N, R 3 E). Named on Newberry (1955) 15' quadrangle. Thompson's (1921) map has the designation "Newberry (Water P.O.)" at the site. United States Board on Geographic Names (1967, p. 7) approved the name "Newberry Springs" for the town. Postal authorities established Watson post office at a railroad construction site at present Newberry Springs in 1883 and discontinued it the same year; the name was for Josiah Watson, first postmaster (Salley, p. 235). They established Newberry post office in 1899, discontinued it the same year, reestablished it with the name "Wagner" in 1911, changed the name to Water in 1919, changed it to Newberry in 1924, and change it to Newberry Springs in 1967 (Salley, p. 153). The springs called Newberry Springs are situated about 600 yards south of Newberry (Mendenhall, 1909a, p. 65); an estimated 300,000 to 500,000 gallons of water a day were pumped from the springs for use by the railroad (Thompson, 1929, p. 498). Thompson's (1921) map shows a place called Troy located about 6.5 miles east-southeast of Newberry along the railroad near present Troy Lake. Schuiling Cave is a small feature situated about 2 miles southeast of Newberry (SW quarter, NE quarter, sec. 9, T 8 N, R 3 E); the cave, named for Walter Schuiling who discovered it in 1953, contained the remains of prehistoric life (Downs, Howard, Clements, and Smith, p. 3).

Newberry Mountains [SAN BERNARDINO]: *range*, 10 miles southeast of Daggett (lat. 34°46' N, long. 116°45' W). Named on Daggett (1956) and Newberry (1955) 15' quadrangles

Newberry Springs: see **Newberry** [SAN BERNARDINO].

New Dale [SAN BERNARDINO]: *locality*, 35 miles south of Amboy (lat. 34°03' N, long. 115°43'10" W); the place is 7 miles south-southeast of Old Dale. Site named on Dale Lake (1956) 15' quadrangle. Postal authorities moved Dale post office from present Old Dale to New Dale in 1902 and discontinued it in 1915 (Salley, p 55). When deposits of placer gold at Dale (present Old Dale) were exhausted, the community moved to New Dale (Hanna, p. 217).

New Dunn [SAN BERNARDINO]: *locality*, 24 miles southwest of Baker along Union Pacific Railroad (lat. 35°03' N, long. 116°25'30" W; near N line sec. 14, T 11 N, R 5 E); the place is less than 1 mile east-northeast of Dunn. Named on Cave Mountain (1948) 15' quadrangle.

New River [IMPERIAL]: *stream*, heads in Mexico and flows 63 miles in Imperial County to Salton Sea 10.5 miles west of Calipatria (lat. 33°08'20" N, long. 115°41'40" W; sec. 11, T 12 S, R 12 E). Named on Brawley (1957), Brawley NW (1957), Calexico (1957), Calipatria SW (1956), Heber (1957), Mount Signal (1957), Obsidian Butte (1956), Seeley (1957), and Westmorland (1956) 7.5' quadrangles. Overflow from Colorado River formed the stream course in 1849; emigrants of that year named the feature (Edwards, p. 21). California Mining Bureau's (1917b) map shows a feature called Cameron Lake located northwest of Calexico along New River.

Newton Drury Peak: see **San Jacinto Peak** [RIVERSIDE].

New Trail Canyon [SAN BERNARDINO]: *canyon*, 1.5 miles long, 10 miles west-northwest of Ivanpah (lat. 35°23'15" N, long. 115°28'30" W; sec. 9, 10, 15, T 15 N, R 14 E). Named on Ivanpah (1956) 15' quadrangle.

New York Canyon [SAN BERNARDINO]: *canyon*, 3.5 miles long, opens into Searles Valley 10 miles east-southeast of Trona (lat. 35°41'45" N, long. 117°13'30" W; near SE cor. sec. 3, T 26 S, R 44 E); the canyon is in Slate Range. Named on Wingate Pass (1950) 15' quadrangle. Hubbard, Bray, and Pipkin (p. 7) noted that a place called Slate Range City was situated in New York Canyon. Postal authorities established Slaterange post office in 1900 and discontinued it in 1901 (Frickstad, p. 146).

New York Mountains [SAN BERNARDINO]: *range*, 6 miles east of Ivanpah on California-Nevada State line (lat. 35°20' N, long. 115° 13' W). Named on Mid Hills (1955) 15' quadrangle.

Nicholas Canyon: see **Nicholias Canyon** [RIVERSIDE].

Nicholias Canyon [RIVERSIDE]: *canyon*, drained by a stream that flows 3.5 miles to Alder Canyon (2) 17 miles south of Palm Desert (lat. 33°28'10" N, long. 116°24'30" W; near N line sec. 19, T 8 S, R 6 E). Named on Palm Desert (1959) 15' quadrangle, and on Collins Valley (1959) 7.5' quadrangle. Called Old Nicholas Canyon on Clark Lake (1942) 15' quadrangle, but United States Board on Geographic Names (1962a, p. 14) rejected the names "Old Nicholas Canyon," "Old Nichols Canyon," and "Nicholas Canyon" for the feature. The name commemorates Nicolas Guanche, who lived in the canyon for many years and died around 1918 (Robinson and Risher, p. 164, 165).

Nicholls Warm Springs [RIVERSIDE]: *locality*, 8 miles west of Blythe (lat. 33°36'20" N, long. 114°43'45" W; near SE cor. sec. 36, T 6 S, R 21 E). Named on Ripley (1952) 7.5' quadrangle. California Mining Bureau's (1917b) map shows a place called Palowalla at the site. Promoters laid out a townsite called Palowalla in 1911; after a resubdivision of the site in 1949, the place had the name "Nicholls Warm Springs" to honor A.E. Nicholls, a booster of Palo Verde Valley; after another subdivision of the property in 1964, Edward Soehnel gave the place the name "Mesa Verde" (Gunther, p. 322, 352, 377-378).

Nichols Canyon: see **Old Nichols Canyon**, under **Nicholias Canyon** [RIVERSIDE].

Nickel Canyon [RIVERSIDE]: *canyon*, drained by a stream that flows 4 miles to San Mateo Canyon 5.5 miles south of Sitton Peak (lat. 33°30'25" N, long. 117°26'50" W). Named on Sitton Peak (1954) 7.5' quadrangle.

Nicklin [RIVERSIDE]: *locality*, 16 miles northeast of Perris along Southern Pacific Railroad (lat. 33°56'35" N, long. 117°00'45" W; near W line sec. 5, T 3 S, R 1 W). Named on El Casco (1967) 7.5' quadrangle.

Nigger Canyon [RIVERSIDE]: *canyon*, along present Temecula Creek west of Nigger Valley (present Butterfield Valley) below present Vail Lake (lat. 33°29'40" N, long. 116°59' W). Named on Ramona (1903) 30' quadrangle.

Nigger Head [SAN BERNARDINO]: *relief feature*, 30 miles west of Ivanpah (lat. 35°23'50" N, long. 115°49'50" W; sec. 8, T 15 N, R 11 E). Named on Halloran Spring (1956) 15' quadrangle.

Nigger Valley: see **Butterfield Valley** [RIVERSIDE].

Nightingale [RIVERSIDE]: *village*, 10 miles south-southwest of Palm Desert (lat. 33°35'20" N, long. 116°27'10" W; sec. 3, T 7 S, R 5 E). Named on Palm Desert (1959) 15' quadrangle. United States Board on Geographic Names (1983e, p. 4) approved the name "Pinyon Pines" for the place, and rejected the names "Nightingale" and "Pinon Pines."

Niland [IMPERIAL]: *town*, 8 miles north of Calipatria (lat. 33°14'15" N, long. 115°30'45" W; mainly in sec. 4, T 11 S, R 14 E). Named on Niland (1956) 7.5' quadrangle. Called Imperial Junction on United States Geological Survey's (1908) map, and called Old Beach on Mendenhall's (1908b) map. Postal authorities established Old Beach post office in 1905 and discontinued it in 1907 (Salley, p. 160). They established Imperial Junction post office in 1910, changed the name to Hobgood in 1913, and changed it to Niland in 1914; the name Hobgood was for Richard H. Hobgood, a pioneer of the neighborhood (Salley, p. 98, 103). Officials of Imperial Farm Lands Association named the community from a contraction of the term "Nile land" to suggest the fertility of the region (Gudde, 1949, p. 236).

Nippeno: see **Nipton** [SAN BERNARDINO].

Nipton [SAN BERNARDINO]: *locality*, 9 miles north-northeast of Ivanpah along Union Pacific Railroad (lat. 35°28' N, long. 115°16'15" W; at W line sec. 33, T 16 N, R 16 E). Named on Ivanpah (1956) 15' quadrangle. Postal authorities established Nipton post office in 1905, discontinued it in 1909, reestablished it in 1911, discontinued it in 1919, and reestablished it in 1923; the name is from nearby Nipano mine (Salley, p. 154). The place first was called Nippeno (Myrick, p. 850).

Noble Canyon: see **Cherry Canyon** [RIVERSIDE-SAN BERNARDINO].

Noble Creek [RIVERSIDE-SAN BERNARDINO]: *stream*, heads in Riverside County and flows 8 miles, partly in San Bernardino County, to Little San Gorgonio Creek 7.25 miles west of Banning (lat. 33°56'30" N, long. 117°00'05" W). Named on Forest Falls (1970) 7.5' quadrangle. The name commemorates Newton Noble, who was a rancher, horseman, and stagecoach driver (Gunther, p. 352).

Noble Pass [SAN BERNARDINO]: *pass*, 20 miles northeast of Landers (lat. 34°29'30" N, long. 116°10'20" W; near W line sec. 29, T 5 N, R 8 E). Named on Deadman Lake NW (1955) 7.5' quadrangle.

Noble Well [SAN BERNARDINO]: *well*, 50 miles west-southwest of Baker (lat. 35°06'20" N, long. 116°56'15" W; at W line sec. 34, T 32 S, R 47 E). Named on Lane Mountain (1948) 15' quadrangle.

Noels Knoll [SAN BERNARDINO]: *relief feature*, 3.5 miles west of Twentynine Palms (lat. 34°08'35" N, long. 116°06'50" W; sec. 26, T 1 N, R 8 E). Named on Twentynine Palms (1973) 7.5' quadrangle.

Nolina Cove [SAN BERNARDINO]: *relief feature*, 5 miles south of Joshua Tree (lat. 34°03'55" N, long. 116°19'40" W; sec. 23, T 1 S, R 6 E). Named on Joshua Tree South (1972) 7.5' quadrangle.

Norco [RIVERSIDE]: *town*, 3.5 miles north of Corona (lat. 33°55'40" N, long. 117°33'10" W). Named on Corona North (1967) 7.5' quadrangle. Postal authorities established Norco post office in 1923 (Frickstad, p. 129), and the town incorporated in 1964. Rex B. Clark, president of North Corona Land Company, coined the name from the term "North Corona" (Gunther, p. 354).

Norconian: see **Lake Norconian** [RIVERSIDE].

Noria: see **Garnet** [RIVERSIDE].

Norris: see **Camp Norris** [SAN BERNARDINO].

North Bald: see **Mount San Antonio** [SAN BERNARDINO].

North Bay [SAN BERNARDINO]: *embayment*, nearly 7 miles south-southwest of Luna Mountain on the north side of Lake Arrowhead (1) (lat.

34°15'50" N, long. 117°11'40" W). Named on Lake Arrowhead (1971) 7.5' quadrangle.

North Creek [SAN BERNARDINO]: *stream,* flows 1.5 miles to Big Bear Lake (1) 2.5 miles west-southwest of downtown Big Bear Lake (lat. 34°14'25" N, long. 116°56'05" W; sec. 24, T 2 N, R 1 W). Named on Big Bear Lake (1970) 7.5' quadrangle.

North Cucamonga: see **Rancho Cucamonga** [SAN BERNARDINO].

North Elsinore [RIVERSIDE]: *locality,* 1.5 miles north-northwest of Lake Elsinore city hall (lat. 33°41'25" N, long. 117°20'20" W; sec. 31, T 5 S, R 4 W). Named on Lake Elsinore (1953) 7.5' quadrangle. Promoters laid out a townsite at the place in 1887 (Gunther, p. 354).

North Fork Meadows [SAN BERNARDINO]: *area,* 1.5 miles east of San Gorgonio Mountain (lat. 34°06'10" N, long. 116°47'50" W; sec. 8, T 1 S, R 2 E); the place is at the head of North Fork Whitewater River. Named on San Gorgonio Mountain (1970) 7.5' quadrangle.

North Hill [RIVERSIDE]: *hill,* less than 1 mile north of Riverside city hall (lat. 33°29'35" N, long. 117°22'20" W). Altitude 915 feet. Named on Riverside East (1967) 7.5' quadrangle. The feature first was called Fairmont Hill for the Fairmont Heights tract of 1895 (Gunther, p. 355).

North Lucerne Valley [SAN BERNARDINO]: *valley,* 18 miles south of Barstow (lat. 34°38' N, long. 117°00' W). Named on Ord Mountains (1955) 15' quadrangle, and on Fairview Valley (1970) 7.5' quadrangle. Called Lucerne Valley on Barstow (1934) 30' quadrangle, and called Upper Lucerne Valley on San Bernardino (1966) 1°x 2° quadrangle.

North Ontario: see **Upland** [SAN BERNARDINO].

North Palm Springs [RIVERSIDE]: *locality,* 6 miles north of Palm Springs (lat. 33°55'20" N, long. 116°32'30" W; sec. 11, T 3 S, R 4 E). Named on Desert Hot Springs (1955) 7.5' quadrangle. Postal authorities established North Palm Springs post office in 1950 at a place first called Garnet Gardens (Salley, p. 156).

North Park Peak [SAN BERNARDINO]: *peak,* 2 miles west of Yucca Valley (lat. 34°07'30" N, long. 116°28'45" W; sec. 32, T 1 N, R 5 E); the feature is 5.5 miles northwest of South Park Peak. Named on Yucca Valley South (1972) 7.5' quadrangle.

North Peak [SAN BERNARDINO]: *peak,* nearly 6 miles east-northeast of Luna Mountain (lat. 34°21'50" N, long. 117°01'45" W; near NW cor. sec. 7, T 3 N, R 1 W). Altitude 7094 feet. Named on Butler Peak (1971) 7.5' quadrangle.

North Shore [SAN BERNARDINO]: *district,* 6 miles south-southwest of Luna Mountain along the north side of Lake Arrowhead (1) (lat. 34°16'05" N, long. 117°11'10" W). Named on Lake Arrowhead (1971) 7.5' quadrangle.

North Shore Campground [SAN BERNARDINO]: *locality,* 5.5 miles south-southwest of Luna Mountain (lat. 34°16' N, long. 117°09'50" W; near S line sec. 11, T 2 N, R 3 W). Named on Lake Arrowhead (1971) 7.5' quadrangle.

Norton Air Force Base [SAN BERNARDINO]: *military installation,* 2.5 miles east-southeast of San Bernardino city hall (lat. 34°05'45" N, long. 117°15' W). Named on Redlands (1967) and San Bernardino South (1967) 7.5' quadrangles. The name, given in 1950, commemorates Leland F. Norton, who died in action over France in 1944 (Richards). The army set up a post in 1859 called Camp Prentiss along Santa Ana River at the site of present Norton Air Force Base—the name honored a medical officer; the site was reoccupied during the Civil War, when Major E.E. Eyre named it Camp Carleton for Colonel Carleton (Beattie and Beattie, p. 323, 384-385).

Nuevo [RIVERSIDE]: *town,* 5 miles east-northeast of Perris (lat. 33° 48'10" N, long. 117°08'40" W; on S line sec. 24, T 4 S, R 3 W); the town is at San Jacinto Nuevo y Potrero grant. Named on Perris (1967) 7.5' quadrangle. Postal authorities established Nuevo post office in 1915 (Frickstad, p. 129). Officials of Lakeview Land Company started the community of small fruit farms about 1890 (Hanna, p. 215).

- O -

Oakadena: see **Weisel** [RIVERSIDE].

Oak Canyon [RIVERSIDE]: *canyon,* drained by a stream that flows 4.25 miles to Palm Canyon 14 miles east-southeast of Idyllwild (lat. 33°38'05" N, long. 116°30'20" W; sec. 19, T 6 S, R 5 E). Named on Idyllwild (1959) 15' quadrangle.

Oak Canyon: see **Acorn Canyon** [SAN BERNARDINO]:

Oak Cove Creek [SAN BERNARDINO]: *stream,* flows 1.5 miles to Mill Creek Canyon 6.5 miles west of San Gorgonio Mountain (lat. 34°05'40" N, long. 116°56'20" W; sec. 12, T 1 S, R 1 W). Named on Forest Falls (1970) 7.5' quadrangle. Called Hatchery Creek on San Gorgonio Mountain (1954) 15' quadrangle, where present Hatchery Creek is unnamed. United States Board on Geographic Names (1975b, p. 5) noted that the name is for the abundance of oak trees at the mouth of the stream, and gave the name "Hatchery Creek" as a variant.

Oak Cove Creek: see **Monkeyface Creek** [SAN BERNARDINO].

Oak Creek [SAN BERNARDINO]:
(1) *stream,* flows nearly 1 mile to Mill Creek Canyon 6.5 miles west of San Gorgonio Mountain (lat. 34°05'35" N, long. 116°56'45" W; near SE cor. sec. 11, T 1 S, R 1 W). Named on Forest Falls (1970) 7.5' quadrangle.
(2) *stream,* flows 3.5 miles to Plunge Creek 4.5 miles north-northeast of Redlands city hall (lat. 34°06'45" N, long. 117°08'20" W; near E line sec. 1, T 1 S, R 3 W). Named on Harrison Mountain (1967), Keller Peak (1967), and Redlands (1967) 7.5' quadrangles.

Oakes: see **Camp Oakes** [SAN BERNARDINO].

Oak Flat [RIVERSIDE]: *area,* 7.25 miles east-northeast of San Jacinto (lat. 33°49'10" N, long. 116°50'25" W; near SW cor. sec. 13, T 4 S, R 1 E). Named on Lake Fulmor (1956) 7.5' quadrangle.

Oak Flats [RIVERSIDE]: *area,* 2.25 miles south of Sitton Peak (lat. 33°33'15" N, long. 117°27'05" W; at E line sec. 13, T 7 S, R 6 W). Named on Sitton Peak (1954) 7.5' quadrangle.

Oak Glen [SAN BERNARDINO]: *locality,* 7.5 miles west-southwest of San Gorgonio Mountain (lat. 34°03' N, long. 116°56'30" W; near NW cor. sec. 36, T 1 S, R 1 W). Named on Forest Falls (1970) 7.5' quadrangle.

Oak Glen Creek [SAN BERNARDINO]: *stream,* flows 11 miles to Yucaipa Creek 4.25 miles west-southwest of Yucaipa (lat. 34°00'35" N, long. 117°06'25" W); the stream heads at Oak Glen. Named on Forest Falls (1970) and Yucaipa (1967) 7.5' quadrangles.

Oak Glen Peak [SAN BERNARDINO]: *peak,* nearly 6 miles west-southwest of San Gorgonio Mountain (lat. 34°04' N, long. 116°55'15" W; sec. 19, T 1 S, R 1 E). Altitude 8404 feet. Named on Forest Falls (1970) 7.5' quadrangle.

Oak Glen Peak: see **Wilshire Peak** [SAN BERNARDINO].

Oak Mountain [RIVERSIDE]:
(1) *ridge,* west-trending, 2 miles long, 16 miles south of Hemet (lat. 33°31' N, long. 116°58'45" W). Named on Sage (1954) 7.5' quadrangle.
(2) *peak,* 8 miles east of the town of Temecula (lat. 33°29'10" N, long. 117°00'35" W). Altitude 2130 feet. Named on Pechanga (1968) 7.5' quadrangle.

Oaks Canyon: see **Big Oaks Canyon** [RIVERSIDE-SAN BERNARDINO].

Oak Slope [RIVERSIDE]: *relief feature,* 10 miles west of the town of Temecula (lat. 33°29'15" N, long. 117°19' W). Named on Fallbrook (1968) 7.5' quadrangle.

Oak Spring [RIVERSIDE]: *spring,* 8 miles east-southeast of San Jacinto (lat. 33°45'05" N, long. 116°49'15" W; near W line sec. 7, T 5 S, R 2 E). Named on Lake Fulmor (1956) 7.5' quadrangle.

Oak Spring [SAN BERNARDINO]:
(1) *spring,* 7 miles north of Mount San Antonio (lat. 34°23'10" N, long. 117°38'10" W; sec. 32, T 4 N, R 7 W). Named on San Antonio (1942) 15' quadrangle.
(2) *spring,* nearly 2 miles northeast of Luna Mountain (lat. 34°21'45" N, long. 117°06'15" W; near E line sec. 8, T 3 N, R 2 W). Named on Butler Peak (1971) 7.5' quadrangle.

Oasis [RIVERSIDE]: *village,* 20 miles south-southeast of Indio (lat. 33°27'55" N, long. 116°05'55" W; sec. 24, T 8 S, R 8 E). Named on Oasis (1956) 7.5' quadrangle. United States Geological Survey's (1904) map has the name "Agua Dulce" at or near present Oasis.

Oasis of Mora [SAN BERNARDINO]: *locality,* less than 1 mile southeast of the center of Twentynine Palms (lat. 34°07'45" N, long. 116°02'30" W; sec. 33, T 1 N, R 9 E). Named on Twentynine Palms (1973) 7.5' quadrangle.

Obregon [IMPERIAL]: *locality,* 4 miles northeast of Ogilby (lat. 32° 51'30" N, long. 114°47'15" W). Named on Ogilby (1963) 15' quadrangle.

Obsidian Butte [IMPERIAL]: *hill,* 7.5 miles west-northwest of Calipatria (lat. 33°10'15" N, long. 115°38'15" W; sec. 32, T 11 S, R 13 E). Altitude 130 feet below sea level. Named on Obsidian Butte (1956) 7.5' quadrangle.

Ocotillo [IMPERIAL]: *town,* 26 miles west of El Centro (lat. 32°44'15" N, long. 115°59'35" W; sec. 36, T 16 S, R 9 E). Named on Coyote Wells (1957) and In-Ko-Pah Gorge (1959) 7.5' quadrangles. Postal authorities established Ocotillo post office at a desert retirement community in 1957 (Salley, p. 159).

Odessa Canyon [SAN BERNARDINO]: *canyon,* 4 miles long, opens into lowlands 6 miles north-northeast of Daggett (lat. 34°56'30" N, long. 116°51'30" W; near E line sec. 22, T 10 N, R 1 E). Named on Yermo (1953) 7.5' quadrangle.

Ogilby [IMPERIAL]: *locality,* 42 miles east of El Centro along Southern Pacific Railroad (lat. 32°49' N, long. 114°50'15" W; sec. 35, T 15 S, R 20 E). Named on Ogilby (1963) 15' quadrangle. Postal authorities established Oglesby post office in 1880, discontinued it the same year, reestablished it with the name "Ogilby" in 1890, moved it 3 miles northeast in 1892, discontinued it in 1895, reestablished it in 1898, and discontinued it in 1942 (Salley, p. 159). The name commemorates E.R. Ogilby, a mine promoter (Love, p. 112).

Ogilby Hills [IMPERIAL]: *range,* 2.5 miles east-southeast of Ogilby (lat. 32°48'25" N, long. 114°47'45" W). Named on Ogilby (1963) 15' quadrangle.

Oglesby: see **Ogilby** [IMPERIAL].

Old Allen Peak: see **Allen Peak** [SAN BERNARDINO].

Old Baldy: see **Mount San Antonio** [SAN BERNARDINO].

Old Baldy Peak: see **Mount San Antonio** [SAN BERNARDINO].

Old Beach: see **Niland** [IMPERIAL].

Old Carrizo Stage Station [IMPERIAL]: *locality,* 6 miles northwest of Carrizo Mountain (lat. 32°52'30" N, long. 116°06' W; near W line sec. 7, T 15 S, R 9 E); the place is along Carrizo Creek. Named on Carrizo Mountain NE (1957) 7.5' quadrangle. Carrizo (1913) 30' quadrangle has the name "Carrizo Wells" near the site. Waring (p. 349) described Carrizo Springs that issue along Carrizo Creek at the place.

Old Dad Mountain [SAN BERNARDINO]: *peak,* 35 miles west-southwest of Ivanpah (lat. 35°06' N, long. 115°51'30" W; at NW cor. sec. 30, T 12 N, R 11 E). Altitude 4250 feet. Named on Old Dad Mountain (1956) 15' quadrangle.

Old Dad Mountains [SAN BERNARDINO]: *range,* 15 miles north-northwest of Amboy (lat. 34°46' N, long. 115°49' W). Named on Bagdad (1956), Cadiz (1956), and Kerens (1957) 15' quadrangles.

Old Dale [SAN BERNARDINO]: *locality,* 30 miles south of Amboy (lat. 34°07'20" N, long. 115°47'40" W; at S line sec. 35, T 1 N, R 11 E). Named on Valley Mountain (1956) 15' quadrangle. Postal authorities established Dale post office in 1896 and moved it to New Dale in 1902 (Salley, p. 55). The place, which first was known as Virginia Dale, was a center for placer-gold mining; when the placer deposits were worked out, the community moved to present New Dale to pursue quartz-gold mining (Hanna, p. 217).

Old Grayback: see **San Gorgonio Mountain** [SAN BERNARDINO].

Old Ibex Pass [SAN BERNARDINO]: *pass,* 38 miles north-northwest of Baker (lat. 35°43'50" N, long. 116°25'15" W); the pass is in Ibex Hills. Named on Avawatz Pass (1948) 15' quadrangle. Called Ibex Pass on Avawatz Mountains (1933) 1° quadrangle.

Old Mormon Spring [SAN BERNARDINO]: *spring,* 20 miles north-northwest of Baker (lat. 35°30'55" N, long. 116°15'15" W). Named on Avawatz Pass (1948) 15' quadrangle.

Old Nicholas Canyon: see **Nicholias Canyon** [RIVERSIDE].

Old Nichols Canyon: see **Nicholias Canyon** [RIVERSIDE].

Old Saddleback: see **Santiago Peak** [RIVERSIDE].

Old Santa Rosa: see **Cottonwood Spring** [RIVERSIDE] (2).

Old Timer Canyon [SAN BERNARDINO]: *canyon,* drained by a stream that flows 2.25 miles to Rattlesnake Canyon (3) 13 miles north-northwest of downtown Morongo Valley (lat. 34°13'40" N, long. 116°39'45" W). Named on Onyx Peak (1972) 7.5' quadrangle.

Old Town: see **San Jacinto** [RIVERSIDE].

Old Woman Mountains [SAN BERNARDINO]: *range,* 21 miles south of Essex (lat. 34°26' N, long. 115°11' W). Named on Cadiz Lake (1956), Danby (1956), and Milligan (1956) 15' quadrangles.

Old Woman Spring: see **Sunflower Spring** [SAN BERNARDINO].

Old Woman Springs [SAN BERNARDINO]: *spring,* 21 miles north-northeast of San Gorgonio Mountain (lat. 34°23'30" N, long. 116° 42'30" W; sec. 31, T 4 N, R 3 E). Named on Old Woman Springs (1972) 7.5' quadrangle.

Old Woman Springs Valley: see **Johnson Valley** [SAN BERNARDINO].

Old Woman Statue [SAN BERNARDINO]: *relief feature,* 15 miles south-southeast of Essex (lat. 34°31'15" N, long. 115°09'45" W; sec. 14, T 5 N, R 17 E). Altitude 5090 feet. Named on Essex (1956) 15' quadrangle.

Olsen Canyon [RIVERSIDE]: *canyon,* 2 miles long, opens into Temescal Valley 4.5 miles west-northwest of Estelle Mountain (lat. 33°48' N, long. 117°29'30" W; at S line sec. 22, T 4 S, R 6 W). Named on Lake Mathews (1967) 7.5' quadrangle.

Omstott Creek [RIVERSIDE]: *stream,* flows 7 miles to Palm Canyon 15 miles southeast of Idyllwild (lat. 33°36'40" N, long. 116°30'20" W; near N line sec. 31, T 6 S, R 5 E). Named on Idyllwild (1959) and Palm Desert (1959) 15' quadrangles. The misspelled name is for M.M. Onstott, who came to the neighborhood in the 1890's (Gunther, p. 362-363).

One Hole Spring [SAN BERNARDINO]: *spring,* 6 miles southeast of Old Woman Spring (lat. 34°20'05" N, long. 116°38' W); the feature is 3.25 miles east of Two Hole Spring. Named on Rattlesnake Canyon (1972) 7.5' quadrangle.

One Horse Creek [RIVERSIDE]: *stream,* flows 1.5 miles to San Gorgonio Pass 11.5 miles east-northeast of Palm Springs (lat. 33° 54'05" N, long. 116°44' W; near NW cor. sec. 24, T 3 S, R 2 E). Named on Whitewater (1955) 7.5' quadrangle.

One Horse Ridge [RIVERSIDE]: *ridge,* north-trending, 4.5 miles long, the south end is 4.25 miles northwest of San Jacinto Peak (lat. 33°51'30" N, long. 116°43'50" W); the ridge is east of One Horse Creek. Named on San Jacinto Peak (1981) 7.5' quadrangle.

One Horse Spring [RIVERSIDE]: *spring,* 11.5 miles east-northeast of Palm Springs (lat. 33°54' N, long. 116°43'50" W; near N line sec. 24, T 3 S, R 2 E); the spring is near the mouth of One Horse Creek. Named on Whitewater (1955) 7.5' quadrangle.

100 Palms [RIVERSIDE]: *locality,* 11.5 miles south-southeast of Indio (lat. 33°33'45" N, long. 116°10'25" W; sec. 17, T 7 S, R 8 E). Named on Valerie (1956) 7.5' quadrangle.

Ono [SAN BERNARDINO]: *locality,* 5 miles north-northwest of present San Bernardino city hall along the railroad (lat. 34°09'55" N, long. 117°20'35" W). Named on Arrowhead (1941) 7.5' quadrangle.

Ontario [SAN BERNARDINO]: *city,* 21 miles west of San Bernardino (lat. 34°03'45" N, long. 117°39' W). Named on Guasti (1966) and Ontario (1967) 7.5' quadrangles. Postal authorities established Ontario post office in 1883 (Frickstad, p. 144), and the city incorporated in 1891. George B. Chaffey laid out the community in 1882 and named it for his former home province in Canada (Gudde, 1949, p. 243).

Ontario: see **North Ontario**, under **Upland** [SAN BERNARDINO].

Ontario Peak [SAN BERNARDINO]: *peak,* 12.5 miles north of Ontario city hall (lat. 34°13'40" N, long. 117°37'25" W; sec. 28, T 2 N, R 7 W). Altitude 8693 feet. Named on Cucamonga Peak (1966) 7.5' quadrangle.

Onyx Peak [SAN BERNARDINO]: *peak,* 12.5 miles northwest of downtown Monongo Valley (lat. 34°11'30" N, long. 116°42'30" W; on N line sec. 7, T 1 N, R 3 E). Altitude 9113 feet. Named on Onyx Peak (1972) 7.5' quadrangle.

Onyx Spring [SAN BERNARDINO]: *spring,* 12 miles north-northwest of downtown Morongo Valley (lat. 34°11'20" N, long. 116°41'50" W; near NW cor. sec. 8, T 1 N, R 3 E); the spring is 0.5 mile east-southeast of Onyx Peak. Named on Onyx Peak (1972) 7.5' quadrangle.

Onyx Summit [SAN BERNARDINO]: *pass,* 13 miles northwest of downtown Morongo Valley (lat. 34°11'30" N, long. 116°43'05" W; at NE cor. sec. 12, T 1 N, R 2 E); the pass is 0.5 mile west of Onyx Peak. Named on Onyx Peak (1972) 7.5' quadrangle.

Opal Camp [SAN BERNARDINO]: *locality,* 28 miles east-southeast of the present village of Red Mountain (lat. 35°11' N, long. 117° 12'45" W); the place is 2.25 miles northwest of Opal Mountain. Named on Searles Lake (1915) 1° quadrangle.

Opal Mountain [SAN BERNARDINO]: *peak,* 27 miles east-southeast of the village of Red Mountain (lat. 35°09'35" N, long. 117°11'10" W; at W line sec. 8, T 32 S, R 45 E). Altitude 3950 feet. Name on Opal Mountain (1955) 15' quadrangle.

Orange Blossom Wash [SAN BERNARDINO]: *stream* and *dry wash,* extends for 15 miles before loosing its identity 5.5 miles east-northeast of Amboy (lat. 34°35'15" N, long. 115°39' W; at S line sec. 20, T 6 N, R 13 E). Named on Bagdad (1956) and Cadiz (1956) 15' quadrangles.

Orchard Bay [SAN BERNARDINO]: *embayment,* 7 miles south-southwest of Luna Mountain along Lake Arrowhead (1) (lat. 34° 15'10" N, long. 117°10'45" W; near S line sec. 15, T 2 N, R 3 W); the feature is at the mouth of Orchard Creek. Named on Lake Arrowhead (1971) 7.5' quadrangle.

Orchard Creek [SAN BERNARDINO]: *stream,* flows 1 mile to Lake Arrowhead (1) (lat. 34°15'05" N, long. 117°10'40" W; at N line sec. 22, T 2 N, R 3 W). Named on Harrison Mountain (1967) 7.5' quadrangle.

Ord Mountain [SAN BERNARDINO]: *peak,* 20 miles southeast of Barstow (lat. 34°40'30" N, long. 116°48'50" W; at N line sec. 30, T 7 N, R 2 E); the peak is in Ord Mountains (1). Altitude 6309 feet. Named on Ord Mountains (1955) 15' quadrangle.

Ord Mountain: see **East Ord Mountain** [SAN BERNARDINO]; **West Ord Mountain** [SAN BERNARDINO].

Ord Mountains [SAN BERNARDINO]:
(1) *range,* 20 miles south-southeast of Barstow (lat. 34°39'30" N, long. 116°51' W). Named on Ord Mountains (1955) 15' quadrangle.
(2) *range,* 12 miles south-southeast of Victorville (lat. 34°23' N, long. 117°11'30" W). Named on Apple Valley South (1971) and Lake Arrowhead (1971) 7.5' quadrangles.

Ordway [RIVERSIDE-SAN BERNARDINO]: *locality,* 12 miles east of Riverside along Southern Pacific Railroad at Riverside-San Bernardino County line (lat. 34°00'15" N, long. 117°10' W). Named on Redlands (1967) 7.5' quadrangle.

Orita [IMPERIAL]: *locality,* 11.5 miles north of Holtville along Southern Pacific Railroad (lat. 32°58'40" N, long. 115°24'20" W; sec. 34, T 13 S, R 15 E). Named on Alamorio (1956) 7.5' quadrangle.

Ormand [RIVERSIDE]: *locality,* 3 miles northwest of Riverside along Union Pacific Railroad (lat. 34°00'40" N, long. 117°25'10" W). Named on Fontana (1967) 7.5' quadrangle.

Orocopia Canyon [RIVERSIDE]: *canyon,* 5.5 miles long, opens into lowlands 5 miles east-northeast of Mortmar (lat. 33°33' N, long. 115°51'30" W; sec. 20, T 7 S, R 11 E); the canyon is in Orocopia Mountains. Named on Orocopia Canyon (1958) 7.5' quadrangle.

Orocopia Mountains [RIVERSIDE]: *range,* center 7.5 miles south of Chiriaco Summit (lat. 33°33' N, long. 115°45' W). Named on Cottonwood Spring (1958) and Hayfield (1963) 15' quadrangles. The name is from Ora Copia Company, which had gold claims in the range (Gunther, p. 363).

Oro Grande [SAN BERNARDINO]: *town,* 5 miles north-northwest of Victorville (lat. 34°36' N, long. 117°20' W; sec. 18, 19, T 6 N, R 4 W). Named on Victorville (1956) 15' quadrangle. California Mining Bureau's (1917a) map has the designation "Halleck (Oro Grande Sta.)" at the place.

Postal authorities established Halleck post office in 1881 and changed the name to Oro Grande in 1925; the name "Halleck" was for an employee of Atchison Topeka and Santa Fe Railroad (Salley, p. 92). The name "Oro Grande" recalls Oro Grande mine, which was situated near the place (Myrick, p. 857). Postal authorities established Desert post office 4.5 miles southeast of Halleck post office (SW quarter sec. 3, T 5 N, R 4 W) in 1881 and discontinued it in 1883 (Salley, p. 58). A.G. Lane settled across Mojave River from present Oro Grande in 1861; the site was called Lane's Crossing because wagons and horses could cross the river there, and a footbridge extended from bank to bank (Peirson, p. 136).

Oro Grande Canyon [SAN BERNARDINO]: *canyon,* 3.25 miles long, opens into lowlands along Mojave River 5.25 miles north-northwest of Victorville (lat. 34°36'15" N, long. 117°20'10" W; sec. 18, T 6 N, R 4 W); the mouth of the canyon is at Oro Grande. Named on Victorville (1956) 7.5' quadrangle.

Oro Grande Wash [SAN BERNARDINO]: *stream* and *dry wash,* extends for 17 miles to Mojave River at Victorville (lat. 34°32'10" N, long. 117°17'25" W; sec. 10, T 5 N, R 4 W). Named on Baldy Mesa (1956), Cajon (1956), Hesperia (1956), and Victorville (1956) 7.5' quadrangles.

Oro Wash [SAN BERNARDINO]: *stream,* flows 25 miles to Ivanpah Valley 9 miles west-northwest of Ivanpah (lat. 35°22'25" N, long. 115°27'35" W). Named on Ivanpah (1956) 15' quadrangle.

Orton: see **Annie Orton Canyon**, under **Railroad Canyon** [RIVERSIDE] (1).

Osceola: see **Camp Osceola** [SAN BERNARDINO].

Osdick: see **Red Mountain** [SAN BERNARDINO] (2).

Osito Rancho: see **Camp Osito Rancho** [SAN BERNARDINO].

Oso Grande: see **Fawnskin** [SAN BERNARDINO].

Oso-Lobo Campground [SAN BERNARDINO]: *locality,* 2.25 miles west-southwest of Sugarloaf Mountain (lat. 34°10'35" N, long. 116°51'40" W; near NE cor. sec. 15, T 1 N, R 1 E). Named on Moonridge (1970) 7.5' quadrangle.

Otis: see **Yermo** [SAN BERNARDINO].

Otis Valley: see **Mojave Valley** [SAN BERNARDINO].

Outing [RIVERSIDE]: *locality,* 3.25 miles south of Murrieta in Sandia Canyon (lat. 33°30'05" N, long. 117°13'30" W). Named on Elsinore (1901) 30' quadrangle. Postal authorities established Outing post office at a vacation camp in 1893 and discontinued it in 1902 (Salley, p. 164).

Owl [RIVERSIDE]: *locality,* 3.5 miles east of Banning along Southern Pacific Railroad (lat. 33°55'40" N, long. 116°49' W; sec. 7, T 3 S, R 2 E). Named on Cabazon (1956) 7.5' quadrangle. Called Owl Siding on Banning (1942) 15' quadrangle.

Owl Canyon [SAN BERNARDINO]: *canyon,* drained by a stream that flows 3 miles to lowlands 40 miles east-southeast of the village of Red Mountain (lat. 35°01' N, long. 117°01'10" W; sec. 30, T 11 N, R 1 W). Named on Opal Mountain (1955) 15' quadrangle.

Owl Holes: see **Owl Hole Springs** [SAN BERNARDINO].

Owl Hole Springs [SAN BERNARDINO]: *springs,* 41 miles northwest of Baker (lat. 35°38'20" N, long. 116°38'50" W); the springs are at the southeast edge of Owlshead Mountains. Named on Leach Lake (1948) 15' quadrangle. Thompson (1929, p. 588) used the name "Owl Holes" for the springs, and noted that they occur "on the north side of Owl Holes Wash where it emerges from the Owls Head Mountains." Palmer (p. 55) referred to Owl Hole Spring, and gave the name "Owl Spring" as an alternate.

Owl Holes Wash: see **Owl Hole Springs** [SAN BERNARDINO].

Owl Lake [SAN BERNARDINO]: *dry lake,* 1.5 miles long, 46 miles northwest of Baker (lat. 35°43'45" N, long. 116°41'30" W; around SW cor. sec. 17, T 19 N, R 3 E); Owlshead Mountains surround the feature. Named on Leach Lake (1948) 15' quadrangle.

Owlshead Mountains [SAN BERNARDINO]: *range,* 36 miles east of Trona and west of the south end of Death Valley on San Bernardino-Inyo County line. Named on Confidence Hills (1950), Leach Lake (1948), Quail Mountains (1948), and Wingate Wash (1950) 15' quadrangles. The name is from two basins that suggest the eyes and face of an owl (Lingenfelter, 1986, p. 83).

Owl Spring: see **Owl Hole Springs** [SAN BERNARDINO].

- P -

Pachalka Spring: see **Clark Mountain** [SAN BERNARDINO].

Pachappa [RIVERSIDE]: *locality,* 2.5 miles south-southwest of Riverside city hall along Atchison, Topeka and Santa Fe Railroad (lat. 33°56'50" N, long. 117°23' W); the place is 1 mile south-southwest of Pachappa Hill. Named on Riverside West (1967) 7.5' quadrangle.

Pachappa Hill [RIVERSIDE]: *hill,* 1.5 miles south-southwest of Riverside city hall (lat. 33°57'35" N, long. 117°22'45" W). Altitude 1186 feet. Named on Riverside West (1967) 7.5' quadrangle. The name, which originally applied to present Mount Rubidoux, is of Indian origin (Gunther, p. 365).

Pacific Mesa: see **Ludlow** [SAN BERNARDINO].

Packard Well [RIVERSIDE]: *well,* 24 miles northeast of Desert Center (lat. 33°56' N, long. 115°04'40" W). Named on Palen Mountains (1952) 15' quadrangle.

Paehalka Spring [SAN BERNARDINO]: *spring,* 22 miles west-northwest of Ivanpah (lat. 35°31'05" N, long. 115°37'45" W). Named on Clark Mountain (1956) 15' quadrangle.

Pah-ute Creek: see **Piute Wash** [SAN BERNARDINO].

Painted Canyon [RIVERSIDE]: *canyon,* 5.25 miles long, 14 miles southeast of Indio (lat. 33°36'10" N, long. 116°01'25" W; near W line sec. 35, T 6 S, R 9 E). Named on Cottonwood Spring (1958) 15' quadrangle, and on Mecca (1955) 7.5' quadrangle.

Painted Gorge [IMPERIAL]: *canyon,* about 1.5 miles long, 7.5 miles west of Plaster City in Coyote Mountains (lat. 32°48'30" N, long. 115°59'15" W; on E line sec. 1, T 16 S, R 9 E). Named on Painted Gorge (1957) 7.5' quadrangle.

Painted Hill [RIVERSIDE]: *peak,* 9.5 miles north-northwest of Palm Springs (lat. 33°57'05" N, long. 116°37'55" W; at E line sec. 35, T 2 S, R 3 E). Altitude 2385 feet. Named on Whitewater (1955) 7.5' quadrangle.

Painted Rock [SAN BERNARDINO]: *relief feature,* 17 miles south-southeast of Essex (lat. 34°31'05" N, long. 115°06'50" W; sec. 17, T 5 N, R 18 E). Named on Essex (1956) 15' quadrangle.

Painted Rock Wash [SAN BERNARDINO]: *stream,* flows 3 miles to an unnamed stream 17 miles south-southeast of Essex (lat. 34°31'25" N, long. 115°04'40" W; sec. 15, T 5 N, R 18 E). Named on Essex (1956) 15' quadrangle.

Pai-ute Creek: see **Piute Wash** [SAN BERNARDINO].

Paivika: see **Camp Paivika** [SAN BERNARDINO].

Palen Dry Lake [RIVERSIDE]: *dry lake,* 4.5 miles long, 12 miles east-northeast of Desert Center (lat. 33°46' N, long. 115°12'30" W); the the feature is west of Palen Mountains. Named on Palen Mountains (1952) and Sidewinder Well (1952) 15' quadrangles.

Palen Mountains [RIVERSIDE]: *range,* center 20 miles east-northeast of Desert Center (lat. 33°48' N, long. 115°04' W). Named on Palen Mountains (1952) and Sidewinder Well (1952) 15' quadrangles.

Palen Pass [RIVERSIDE]: *pass,* 25 miles northeast of Desert Center (lat 33°55'15" N, long. 115°03' W); the feature is at the north end of Palen Mountains. Named on Palen Mountains (1952) 15' quadrangle.

Palisades [RIVERSIDE]: *relief feature,* 9 miles east-southeast of Idyllwild (lat. 33°42' N, long. 116°34'05" W; on S line sec. 28, T 5 S, R 4 E). Named on Idyllwild (1959) 15' quadrangle.

Palisades Point [SAN BERNARDINO]: *promontory,* 6.5 miles south-southwest of Luna Mountain along Lake Arrowhead (1) (lat. 34° 15'35" N, long. 117°10'30" W; sec. 15, T 2 N, R 3 W). Named on Lake Arrowhead (1971) 7.5' quadrangle.

Paliser: see **Hodge** [SAN BERNARDINO].

Palm Canyon [RIVERSIDE]: *canyon,* 16 miles long, opens into lowlands 4 miles south of downtown Palm Springs (lat. 33°46'30" N, long. 116°32'15" W). Named on Idyllwild (1959) 15' quadrangle, and on Palm Springs (1957) 7.5' quadrangle. East Fork branches east 3 miles above the mouth of the main canyon; it is 2 miles long and is named on Idyllwild (1959) 15' quadrangle. West Fork branches southwest 2.5 miles above the mouth of the main canyon; it is 5.5 miles long and is named on Idyllwild (1959) 15' quadrangle. San Jacinto (1901) 30' quadrangle shows a place called Garden of Eden located at the mouth of Palm Canyon; B.B. Barney began development of land at the place in the 1880's, but the enterprise failed for want of water (Gunther, p. 194).

Palm Canyon Wash [IMPERIAL]: *stream,* heads in San Diego County and flows 10 miles in Imperial County to Coyote Wash 5.25 miles west-southwest of Plaster City (lat. 32°45'35" N, long. 115°56'20" W; sec. 21, T 16 S, R 10 E). Named on Carrizo Mountain (1957), In-Ko-Pah Gorge (1959), and Painted Gorge (1957) 7.5' quadrangles.

Palm Canyon Wash [RIVERSIDE]: *dry wash,* extends for 4.5 miles from Palm Canyon to Whitewater River 1.25 miles north-northwest of Cathedral City (lat. 33°47'40" N, long. 116°28'25" W; near W line sec. 18, T 4 S, R 5 E). Named on Cathedral City (1958) and Palm Springs (1957) 7.5' quadrangles.

Palmdale [RIVERSIDE]: *locality,* 2.5 miles south-southeast of present downtown Palm Springs (lat. 33°47'45" N, long. 116°31'45" W). Named on San Jacinto (1901) 30' quadrangle. Called Palm Village on Toro Peak (1943) 15' quadrangle. Postal authorities established Palmdale post office in 1888 and discontinued it in 1890 (Salley, p. 165).

Palm Desert [RIVERSIDE]: *town,* 9 miles west of Indio (lat. 33°43'15" N, long. 116°22'30" W). Named on La Quinta (1959) and Rancho Mirage (1957) 7.5' quadrangles. Postal authorities established Palm Desert post office in 1947 (Frickstad, p. 129), and the town incorporated in 1973.

Palmetto Spring: see **Palm Springs** [RIVERSIDE].

Palms: see **Garnet** [RIVERSIDE].

Palm Springs [RIVERSIDE]: *city,* 48 miles east of Riverside (lat. 33° 50'05" N, long. 116°32'45" W). Named on Cathedral City (1958) and Palm Springs (1957) 7.5' quadrangles. Postal authorities established Palm Springs post office in 1890 (Frickstad, p. 129), and the city incorporated in 1938. The spring and palm trees at the site prompted the early names "Palmetto Spring," "Big Palm Spring," and "Agua Caliente" for the place (Gudde, 1949, p. 250).

Palm Springs: see **Garnet** [RIVERSIDE]; **North Palm Springs** [RIVERSIDE].

Palm Springs Station [RIVERSIDE]: *locality,* 7.5 miles northwest of Palm Springs along Southern Pacific Railroad (lat. 33°54'20" N, long. 116°38'50" W; near SW cor. sec. 14, T 3 S, R 3 E). Named on Whitewater (1955) 7.5' quadrangle. Called Whitewater on San Jacinto (1901) 30' quadrangle, where the name "Palm Springs Sta." applies to present Garnet.

Palm View Peak [RIVERSIDE]: *peak,* 9 miles east-southeast of Idyllwild (lat. 33°40'35" N, long. 116°35' W; sec. 5, T 6 S, R 4 E). Named on Idyllwild (1959) 15' quadrangle.

Palm Wash [IMPERIAL]: *stream,* heads in San Diego County and flows 9.5 miles in Imperial County to Salton Sea 3.25 miles north-northeast of Truckhaven (lat. 33°20'15" N, long. 115°56'55" W; near NE cor. sec. 5, T 10 S, R 10 E). Named on Seventeen Palms (1956) and Truckhaven (1956) 7.5' quadrangles. South Fork enters 4.25 miles above the mouth of the main stream; it heads in San Diego County, is about 0.5 mile long in Imperial County, and is named on Seventeen Palms (1956) 7.5' quadrangle.

Palm Wells [SAN BERNARDINO]: *locality,* 3.25 miles northeast of downtown Morongo Valley (lat. 34°04'45" N, long. 116°32'15" W; near S line sec. 14, T 1 S, R 4 E). Named on Morongo Valley (1955) 15' quadrangle.

Paloma Valley [RIVERSIDE]: *valley,* 10 miles south-southeast of Perris (lat. 33°39' N, long. 117°09'30" W). Named on Romoland (1953) 7.5' quadrangle.

Palo Verde [IMPERIAL]: *town,* 65 miles northeast of El Centro at Imperial-Riverside County line (lat. 33°25'55" N, long. 114°43'50" W; mainly in sec. 2, T 9 S, R 21 E). Named on Palo Verde (1965) 7.5' quadrangle. Postal authorities established Paloverde post office in 1903, changed the name to Palo Verde in 1905, discontinued it in 1940, and reestablished it in 1949 (Salley, p. 166).

Palo Verde Lagoon [IMPERIAL-RIVERSIDE]: *water feature,* mainly in Riverside County, but extends south into Imperial County at Palo Verde (lat. 33°26' N, long. 114°43'50" W). Named on Palo Verde (1965) and Ripley (1952) 7.5' quadrangles. On Cibola (1951) 15' quadrangle, the feature extends 6 miles farther south to Colorado River through drains and marsh; Cibola (1945) 15' quadrangle has the name "Laguna Palo Verde" for this southern extension.

Palo Verde Mesa [RIVERSIDE]: *relief feature,* level highlands that extend along the northwest side of Palo Verde Valley from northwest of Blythe to Riverside-Imperial County line. Named on McCoy Spring (1952) and Palo Verde Mountains (1953) 15' quadrangles, and on McCoy Wash (1951), Palo Verde (1965), and Ripley (1952) 7.5' quadrangles.

Palo Verde Mountains [IMPERIAL]: *range,* 8 miles southwest of Palo Verde (lat. 33°21' N, long. 114°50' W). Named on Cibola (1951) 15' quadrangle.

Palo Verde Peak [IMPERIAL]: *peak,* 7.5 miles south-southwest of Palo Verde (lat. 33°19'45" N, long. 114°46'35" W); the feature is near the southeast end of Palo Verde Mountains. Altitude 1795 feet. Named on Palo Verde Mountains (1953) 15' quadrangle.

Palo Verde Valley [IMPERIAL-RIVERSIDE]: *valley,* extends along Colorado River from the southeast end of Big Maria Mountains in Riverside County into Imperial County at Palo Verde. Named on Salton Sea (1959) 1°x 2° quadrangle.

Palowalla: see **Nicholls Warm Springs** [RIVERSIDE].

Panamint Valley [SAN BERNARDINO]: *valley,* mainly in Inyo County, but extends south-southeast into San Bernardino County 14 miles east of Trona. Named on Manly Peak (1950) and Wingate Pass (1950) 15' quadrangles. Members of Dr. Darwin French's party named the valley in 1860 (Federal Writers Project, p. 19).

Pan Hot Springs [SAN BERNARDINO]: *locality,* about 1 mile northeast of the center of Big Bear City (lat. 34°16'15" N, long. 116°50'15" W; near W line sec. 12, T 2 N, R 1 E). Named on Lucerne Valley (1947) 15' quadrangle. Berkstresser (1968, p. A-12) called the place Mountain Ranch Springs.

Panorama Heights [SAN BERNARDINO]: *locality,* 9.5 miles west of Twentynine Palms (lat. 34°07'40" N, long. 116°13'20" W; sec. 35, T 1 N, R 7 E). Named on Indian Cove (1972) and Sunfair (1972) 7.5' quadrangles.

Panorama Point [SAN BERNARDINO]: *locality,* 8.5 miles north of San Bernardino city hall (lat. 34°13'35" N, long. 117°18'30" W; sec. 28, T 2 N, R 4 W). Named on San Bernardino North (1967) 7.5' quadrangle.

Paradise: see **Little Paradise** [RIVERSIDE].

Paradise Bay [SAN BERNARDINO]: *embayment,* 7.5 miles south-southwest of Luna Mountain along Lake Arrowhead (1) (lat. 34° 15'05" N, long. 117°12'05" W; on S line sec. 16, T 2 N, R 3 W). Named on Lake Arrowhead (1971) 7.5' quadrangle.

Paradise Range [SAN BERNARDINO]: *range,* 43 miles west of Baker (lat. 35°09'30" N, long. 116°49' W); Paradise Spring is in the range. Named on Lane Mountain (1948) 15' quadrangle.

Paradise Spring [SAN BERNARDINO]: *spring,* 42 miles west of Baker (lat. 35°08'40" N, long. 116°48'45" W; sec. 7, T 12 N, R 2 E). Named on Lane Mountain (1948) 15' quadrangle. The place was a favorite camping spot in the early days when the greenery there suggested the name (Waring, p. 52).

Paradise Valley [IMPERIAL]: *valley,* 22 miles south of Palo Verde along Colorado River on California-Arizona State line (lat. 33° 07' N, long. 114°42' W). Named on Picacho NW (1965) and Picacho SW (1965) 7.5' quadrangles.

Paramount Spring [SAN BERNARDINO]: *spring,* 13 miles south-southeast of Essex (lat. 34°33'30" N, long. 115°10' W; near S line sec. 35, T 6 N, R 17 E). Named on Essex (1956) 15' quadrangle.

Paramount Wash [SAN BERNARDINO]: *dry wash,* extends for 4.5 miles to Colton Wash 12.5 miles southeast of Essex (lat. 34°35'25" N, long. 115°07'10" W; sec. 20, T 6 N, R 18 E); the feature heads near Paramount Spring. Named on Essex (1956) 15' quadrangle.

Para Wash [IMPERIAL]: *stream* and *dry wash,* extends for 3.5 miles to lowlands along Colorado River 25 miles south of Palo Verde (lat. 33°03'45" N, long. 114°41'15" W; sec. 8, T 13 S, R 22 E). Named on Picacho SW (1965) 7.5' quadrangle.

Paringa: see **Heber** [IMPERIAL].

Parker Dam [SAN BERNARDINO]: *village,* 24 miles east-northeast of Vidal along Colorado River (lat. 34°17'15" N, long. 114°08'35" W; near E line sec. 4, T 2 N, R 27 E); the place is 0.5 mile below the dam of the same name. Named on Gene Wash (1959) 7.5' quadrangle. Postal authorities established Parker Dam post office in 1935, discontinued it in 1939, and reestablished it in 1940 (Frickstad, p. 144). They established Whipple post office, named for nearby Whipple Mountains, near Parker Dam in 1935 and discontinued it the same year (Salley, p. 239).

Parker Dam Reservoir: see **Lake Havasu** [SAN BERNARDINO].

Parker Valley [RIVERSIDE-SAN BERNARDINO]: *valley,* along Colorado River between Parker and Blythe on California-Arizona State line, and on Riverside-San Bernardino County line. Named on Salton Sea (1959) 1°x 2° quadrangle.

Park Hill [RIVERSIDE]: *ridge,* west-northwest-trending, 1.25 miles long, 2 miles south-southeast of San Jacinto (lat. 33°45'30" N, long. 116°56'20" W). Named on San Jacinto (1953) 7.5' quadrangle.

Park Peak: see **North Park Peak** [SAN BERNARDINO]; **South Park Peak** [SAN BERNARDINO].

Parks Canyon [RIVERSIDE]: *canyon,* drained by a stream that flows 2.25 miles to Coyote Canyon 20 miles south-southwest of Palm Desert (lat. 33°27'25" N, long. 116°31'50" W; near S line sec. 24, T 8 S, R 4 E). Named on Bucksnort Mountain (1960) 7.5' quadrangle.

Pasadena Camp [SAN BERNARDINO]: *locality,* 3.5 miles west-southwest of downtown Big Bear Lake (lat. 34°13'05" N, long. 116°58'05" W; sec. 34, T 2 N, R 1 W). Named on Big Bear Lake (1970) 7.5' quadrangle.

Pasadena Mountain [IMPERIAL]: *peak,* 4.5 miles east of Ogilby (lat. 32°49'15" N, long. 114°45'45" W; sec. 28, T 15 S, R 21 E). Altitude 1445 feet. Named on Ogilby (1963) 15' quadrangle.

Pasadena Peak [IMPERIAL]: *peak,* 4.25 miles east-northeast of Ogilby (lat. 32°51' N, long. 114°46'30" W). Named on Ogilby (1963) 15' quadrangle, which shows Pasadena mine nearby.

Patton [SAN BERNARDINO]: *locality,* 4 miles west-southwest of Harrison Mountain (lat. 34°08'10" N, long. 117°13'15" W; at N line sec. 32, T 1 N, R 3 W). Named on Harrison Mountain (1967) 7.5' quadrangle. Redlands (1954) 15' quadrangle has the name for a place along Atchison, Topeka and Santa Fe Railroad. The railroad station was called Asylum in 1891 because it was the station for Southern California State Hospital (Gudde, 1949, p. 255). Postal authorities established Patton post office in 1897 and named it for Henry W. Patton, a member of California State Hospital Board, which founded the nearby state institution in 1890 with the name "Highland Insane Asylum" (Salley, p. 168).

Pauba [RIVERSIDE]: *land grant,* east of the town of Temecula. Named on Bachelor Mountain (1953), Pechanga (1968), Sage (1954), and Vail Lake (1953) 7.5' quadrangles. Vicente Moraga and Luis Arenas received 6 leagues from 1844 to 1846; Louis Vignes claimed 26,598 acres patented in 1860 (Cowan, p. 59).

Pauba Valley [RIVERSIDE]: *valley,* 4.5 miles east of the town of Temecula along Temecula Creek (lat. 33°29'30" N, long. 117° 04' W); the valley is partly on Pauba grant. Named on Bachelor Mountain (1953, photorevised 1973) and Pechanga (1968) 7.5' quadrangles.

Paymaster Landing [IMPERIAL]: *locality,* 13 miles south of Palo Verde along Colorado River (lat. 33°14'45" N, long. 114°41'25" W; sec. 6, T 11 S, R 22 E). Named on Picacho NW (1965) 7.5' quadrangle.

Peach Tree Spring [RIVERSIDE]: *spring,* 8.5 miles east-northeast of San Jacinto (lat. 33°49'25" N, long. 116°49'25" W; at W line sec. 18, T 4 S, R 2 E). Named on Lake Fulmor (1956) 7.5' quadrangle.

Pebble Mountain [IMPERIAL]: *ridge,* south-southwest-trending, 0.5 mile long, 3.5 miles south-southeast of Picacho Peak (lat. 32°55'45" N, long. 114°38'15" W; sec. 22, T 14 S, R 22 E). Named on Picacho Peak (1965) 7.5' quadrangle.

Pechanga Creek [RIVERSIDE]: *stream* and *dry wash,* extends for 8 miles to Temecula Creek nearly 2 miles southeast of the town of Temecula (lat.

33°28'25" N, long. 117°07'45" W). Named on Pechanga (1968) and Temecula (1968) 7.5' quadrangles. Called Penjango Creek on San Luis Rey (1898) 30' quadrangle.

Pedley [RIVERSIDE]: *town,* 6 miles west of Riverside city hall (lat. 33°58'30" N, long. 117°28'30" W). Named on Riverside West (1967) 7.5' quadrangle. Postal authorities established Pedley post office in 1929, discontinued it for a time in 1956, and discontinued it finally in 1975; the name was for William Pedley of Riverside Trust Company, who was active in promotion of the community (Salley, p. 169). California Mining Bureau's (1917b) map shows a place called Concrete located about 1 mile southeast of Pedley along the railroad.

Pedley Hills [RIVERSIDE]: *range,* 4.5 miles west of Riverside city hall (lat. 33°59'30" N, long. 117°27' W); the feature is northeast of Pedley. Named on Fontana (1967) and Riverside West (1967) 7.5' quadrangles.

Pegleg Well [IMPERIAL]: *well,* 20 miles north-northwest of Glamis (lat. 33°15'30" N, long. 115°13'55" W; sec. 31, T 10 S, R 17 E). Named on Chuckwalla Spring (1953) 15' quadrangle, which shows Pegleg mine at the site.

Pelican Lake: see **El Centro** [IMPERIAL].

Penjango Creek: see **Pechanga Creek** [RIVERSIDE].

Peñon de la Campana: see **Picacho Peak** [IMPERIAL].

Penrod Canyon [RIVERSIDE]: *canyon,* 1.5 miles long, 14 miles southeast of Idyllwild (lat. 33°35'05" N, long. 116°34'30" W; mainly in sec. 4, 9, T 7 S, R 4 E). Named on Idyllwild (1959) 15' quadrangle. Called Bull Canyon on San Jacinto (1901) 30' quadrangle, where present Bull Canyon is unnamed. The name "Penrod Canyon" recalls W.A. Penrod and his wife, gold miners who lived in a cabin near the canyon in the 1890's (Gunther, p. 384).

Penstock Ridge [SAN BERNARDINO]: *ridge,* northwest-trending, 1.25 miles long, 3 miles west of Devore (lat. 34°12'55" N, long. 117°27'15" W; on E line sec. 36, T 2 N, R 6 W). Named on Devore (1966) 7.5' quadrangle.

Pepper Corner [RIVERSIDE]: *locality,* 2 miles south-southeast of Corona (lat. 33°51'05" N, long. 117°33' W). Named on Corona South (1967) 7.5' quadrangle.

Perris [RIVERSIDE]: *town,* 16 miles south-southeast of Riverside (lat. 33°46'55" N, long. 117°13'45" W). Named on Perris (1967) and Steele Peak (1967) 7.5' quadrangles. Postal authorities established Perris post office in 1886 (Frickstad, p. 130), and the town incorporated in 1911. The name commemorates Frederick Thomas Perris, chief engineer and superintendent of construction for California Southern Railroad (Gunther, p. 385). Hanks' (1886) map has the name "Pinacote R.R. Sta." for a place situated just south of present Perris along California Southern Railroad. Postal authorities established Pinacate post office about 2 miles south of present Perris in 1881, discontinued it for a time in 1882, and discontinued it finally in 1887; a dispute caused the residents of Pinacate to move to Perris (Gunther, p. 385-386; Salley, p. 171).

Perris Hill [SAN BERNARDINO]: *ridge,* generally east-trending, less than 1 mile long, 1.5 miles northeast of San Bernardino city hall (lat. 34°08' N, long. 117°15'35" W). Named on San Bernardino North (1967) 7.5. quadrangle.

Perris Reservoir [RIVERSIDE]: *intermittent lake,* 6 miles north-northeast of Perris (lat. 33°56'15" N, long. 117°10'30" W). Named on Perris (1967, photorevised 1979) 7.5' quadrangle.

Perris Valley [RIVERSIDE]: *valley,* at and near Perris. Named on Perris (1967) and Romoland (1953) 7.5' quadrangles.

Perrys Corner [IMPERIAL]: *locality,* 3.5 miles north of Holtville (lat. 32°51'40" N, long. 115°22'45" W; sec. 12, T 15 S, R 15 E). Named on Holtville West (1956) 7.5' quadrangle.

Pershing Siding [RIVERSIDE]: *locality,* 2.5 miles west of Banning along Southern Pacific Railroad (lat. 33°55'30" N, long. 116°55'15" W; sec. 7, T 3 S, R 1 E). Named on Beaumont (1953) 7.5' quadrangle.

Peter Kane Mountain [IMPERIAL]: *ridge,* north-northwest-trending, 3.5 miles long, 15 miles east-northeast of Glamis (lat. 33°05'30" N, long. 114°49'30" W). Named on Quartz Peak (1953) 15' quadrangle.

Peter Kane Water Hole [IMPERIAL]: *water feature,* 15 miles northeast of Glamis (lat. 33°07'15" N, long. 114°51'10" W; near S line sec. 15, T 12 S, R 20 E); the feature is northwest of Peter Kane Mountain. Named on Quartz Peak (1953) 15' quadrangle.

Peterman Hill [SAN BERNARDINO]: *hill,* 12 miles southwest of Ord Mountain (lat. 34°32'15" N, long. 116°56'20" W; sec. 12, T 5 N, R 1 E). Altitude 3210 feet. Named on Ord Mountains (1955) 15' quadrangle.

Peter Wall Canyon: see **Horsethief Canyon** [RIVERSIDE]; **Indian Canyon** [RIVERSIDE].

Phelan [SAN BERNARDINO]: *village,* 10.5 miles north-northeast of Mount San Antonio (lat. 34°25'35" N, long. 117°34'15" W; around NW cor. sec. 24, T 4 N, R 7 W). Named on Phelan (1956) 7.5' quadrangle. Postal authorities established Phelan post office in 1916 (Frickstad, p. 144). The name commemorates Senator James D. Phelan, who used his influence to have the post office opened (Gudde, 1949, p. 260).

Picacho [IMPERIAL]: *locality,* 29 miles south-southeast of Palo Verde along Colorado River (lat. 33°01'25" N, long. 114°36'35" W; near SE cor. sec. 24, T 13 S, R 22 E). Named on Picacho (1964) 7.5' quadrangle. Postal authorities established Picacho post office in 1894, moved it 0.5 mile west in 1896, and discontinued it in 1926; the place was a rich gold camp—the original site now is under water backed up along Colorado River (Salley, p. 171). Postal authorities established Picacho Basin post office 5 miles south of Picacho in 1909 and discontinued it in 1910 (Salley, p. 171). United States Board on Geographic Names (1976b, p. 3) approved the name "Rojo Grande" for a hill, altitude 710 feet, located 0.4 mile southeast of Picacho (sec. 25, T 13 S, R 22 E); the name is from the color of the feature—*rojo grande* means "big red" in Spanish.

Picacho Basin: see **Picacho** [IMPERIAL].

Picacho Peak [IMPERIAL]: *peak,* 15 miles northeast of Ogilby (lat. 32°58'20" N, long. 114°39'50" W). Named on Picacho Peak (1965) 7.5' quadrangle. Called Chimney Peak on Goddard's (1857) map, but United States Board on Geographic Names (1933, p. 601) rejected this name for the feature. Garces called it Peñon de la Campana—*Peñon de la Campana* means "Bell Rock" in Spanish; later the place was called Chimney Rock (Galvin, p. 30).

Picacho Peak: see **Little Picacho Peak** [IMPERIAL].

Picacho Wash [IMPERIAL]: *stream,* flows 14 miles to lowlands along Colorado River 3.5 miles west of Bard (lat. 32°47'50" N, long. 114°36'50" W; near W line sec. 1, T 16 S, R 22 E). Named on Araz (1964), Bard (1965), and Picacho Peak (1965) 7.5' quadrangles.

Picacho Wash: see **Little Picacho Wash** [IMPERIAL].

Pickaninny Buttes [SAN BERNARDINO]: *hills,* 4 miles east-northeast of the town of Lucerne Valley (lat. 34°27'45" N, long. 116° 52'55" W; sec. 4, T 4 N, R 1 E). Named on Lucerne Valley (1971) 7.5' quadrangle.

Pickhandle Pass [SAN BERNARDINO]: *pass,* 50 miles west-southwest of Baker (lat. 35°01' N, long. 116°53'45" W; sec. 29, T 11 N, R 1 E). Named on Lane Mountain (1948) 15' quadrangle.

Pierce: see **Garnet** [RIVERSIDE].

Pigeon Pass [RIVERSIDE]: *pass,* 5.5 miles east of Riverside city hall (lat. 33°59'35" N, long. 117°16'30" W; sec. 14, T 2 S, R 4 W). Named on Riverside East (1967) 7.5' quadrangle.

Pigeon Pass: see **Little Pigeon Pass** [SAN BERNARDINO].

Pigeon Pass Valley [RIVERSIDE]: *valley,* 6 miles east of Riverside city hall (lat. 33°58'45" N, long. 117°15'45" W); the valley extends southeast from Pigeon Pass. Named on Riverside East (1967) 7.5' quadrangle.

Pigeon Spring [RIVERSIDE]:

(1) *spring,* 9 miles east of San Jacinto (lat. 33°45'45" N, long. 116° 48'05" W; sec. 5, T 5 S, R 2 E). Named on Lake Fulmor (1956) 7.5' quadrangle.

(2) *spring,* 1 mile east of Sitton Peak in Bear Canyon (lat. 33°35'25" N, long. 117°25'30" W). Named on Sitton Peak (1954) 7.5' quadrangle.

Pilares Hot Spring: see **Lakeview Hot Springs** [RIVERSIDE].

Pilot Butte: see **Pilot Knob** [SAN BERNARDINO].

Pilot Knob [IMPERIAL]: *peak,* 8 miles southeast of Ogilby (lat. 32° 43'55" N, long. 114°44'55" W; sec. 27, T 16 S, R 21 E). Named on Grays Well NE (1964) and Yuma West (1965) 7.5' quadrangles. Called Pilot Peak on Young's (1856) map. Anza called the feature Cerro de San Pablo in 1774 (Hoover, Rensch, and Rensch, p. 107). Yuma East (1965) 7.5' quadrangle shows St. Thomas Yuma Indian Mission on high ground 8 miles east of Pilot Knob on the north side of Colorado River opposite Yuma, Arizona, and indicates the site of La Purisima Concepcion mission by the river there. Four Franciscan padres established the mission in 1780 and it was abandoned in 1781 after an Indian uprising (Hoover, Rensch, and Rensch, p. 108-109). Lieutenant Cave J. Couts set up a temporary military post in 1849 at the site of the mission and called it Camp Calhoun for John C. Calhoun (Frazer, p. 35). Captain Samuel P. Heintzelman established a post called Camp Independence along Colorado River a little father upstream in 1850, but in 1851 this post was moved to the site of former Camp Calhoun and the name changed to Camp Yuma, and later to Fort Yuma—Fort Yuma was abandoned 1851, reoccupied in 1852, and finally abandoned in 1883 (Frazer, p. 34-35). Jaeger's Ferry operated on Colorado River 1 mile below Fort Yuma, and a community started there about 1858 on the California side of the river was called Jaeger City; flood waters swept the place away in 1862 (Lingenfelter, 1986, p. 15, 167). Later a man named Hanlon operated Hanlon's Ferry on the river 7 miles below Fort Yuma (Bergland, p. 118).

Pilot Knob [SAN BERNARDINO]: *peak,* 27 miles south-southeast of Trona (lat. 35°23'50" N, long. 117°13'30" W; at E line sec. 23, T 29 S, R 44 E). Altitude 5428 feet. Named on Pilot Knob (1954) 15' quadrangle. Called Pilot Butte on California Mining Bureau's (1917a) map. United States Board on Geographic Names (1933, p. 604) rejected the name "Granite Mountain" for the peak. Palmer (p. 32) noted that a feature called Granite Spring was situated at the west base of Pilot Knob; the name was from the rocks around the spring.

Pilot Knob: see **Araz** [IMPERIAL].

Pilot Knob Mesa [IMPERIAL]: *area,* northwest of Pilot Knob between Cargo Muchacho Mountains and Sand Hills (present Algodones Dunes), at and near Ogilby (lat. 32°49'30" N, long. 114°52'30" W). Named on Ogilby

(1963) 15' quadrangle, and on Grays Well NE (1964) 7.5' quadrangle.

Pilot Knob Valley [SAN BERNARDINO]: *valley,* 5.5 miles southeast of Trona (lat. 35°33' N, long. 117°08' W). Named on Wingate Pass (1950) 15' quadrangle.

Pilot Mountain [RIVERSIDE]: *peak,* 9 miles south-southeast of Desert Center (lat. 33°35'10" N, long. 115°22' W). Altitude 4216 feet. Named on Chuckwalla Mountains (1963) 15' quadrangle.

Pilot Peak [SAN BERNARDINO]: *hill,* 15 miles southeast of Essex (lat. 34°33'30" N, long. 115°05' W; near S line sec. 34, T 6 N, R 18 E). Altitude 3227 feet. Named on Essex (1956) 15' quadrangle.

Pilot Peak: see **Pilot Knob** [SAN BERNARDINO].

Pilot Rock [SAN BERNARDINO]: *peak,* 18 miles south of Victorville (lat. 34°16'50" N, long. 117°15'20" W; near SW cor. sec. 1, T 2 N, R 4 W). Altitude 5260 feet. Named on Cedar Springs (1956) 7.5' quadrangle.

Pilot Spring: see **Granite Wells** [SAN BERNARDINO].

Pinacate: see **Perris** [RIVERSIDE].

Pine Bench [RIVERSIDE-SAN BERNARDINO]: *area,* 7 miles north-northwest of Banning on Riverside-San Bernardino County line (lat. 34°01'55" N, long. 116°54'15" W; on N line sec. 5, T 2 S, R 1 E). Named on San Gorgonio (1902) 30' quadrangle, and on Forest Falls (1970) 7.5' quadrangle.

Pine City [SAN BERNARDINO]: *locality,* 6.5 miles south of Twentynine Palms (lat. 34°02'35" N, long. 116°04'05" W; near W line sec. 32, T 1 S, R 9 E). Site named on Queen Mountain (1972) 7.5' quadrangle.

Pine Cove [RIVERSIDE]: *locality,* 5 miles southwest of San Jacinto Peak (lat. 33°45'30" N, long. 116°44'15" W; around NE cor. sec. 11, T 5 S, R 2 E). Named on San Jacinto Peak (1981) 7.5' quadrangle. Palm Springs (1942) 15' quadrangle shows Pine Cove Camp there.

Pine Cove Camp: see **Pine Cove** [RIVERSIDE].

Pine Creek Canyon: see **Horsethief Canyon** [RIVERSIDE].

Pine Flat [SAN BERNARDINO]: *area,* 10 miles north-northwest of San Bernardino city hall (lat. 34°14'25" N, long. 117°21'15" W; near S line sec. 24, T 2 N, R 5 W). Named on San Bernardino North (1967) 7.5' quadrangle.

Pine Flat: see **Big Pine Flat** [SAN BERNARDINO]; **Little Pine Flat** [SAN BERNARDINO].

Pine Flat Camp: see **Stone Creek Campground** [RIVERSIDE].

Pine Knot: see **Big Bear Lake** [SAN BERNARDINO] (2).

Pineknot Campground [SAN BERNARDINO]: *locality,* 1.5 miles east-southeast of downtown Big Bear Lake (lat. 34°14'05" N, long. 116°53' W; near N line sec. 28, T 2 N, R 1 E). Named on Big Bear Lake (1970) 7.5' quadrangle.

Pine Lake: see **Big Bear Lake** [SAN BERNARDINO] (2).

Pine Meadow [RIVERSIDE]: *valley,* 12 miles southeast of Idyllwild (lat. 33°35'45" N, long. 116°36'15" W). Named on Idyllwild (1959) 15' quadrangle.

Pine Mountain [RIVERSIDE]: *peak,* 11 miles southeast of Idyllwild (lat. 33°39' N, long. 116°33'35" W; near W line sec. 15, T 6 S, R 4 E). Altitude 7054 feet. Named on Idyllwild (1959) 15' quadrangle.

Pine Mountain [SAN BERNARDINO]: *peak,* less than 2 miles north of Mount San Antonio (lat. 34°18'50" N, long. 117°38'35" W; near SE cor. sec. 30, T 3 N, R 7 W). Altitude 9648 feet. Named on Mount San Antonio (1955) 7.5' quadrangle.

Pines: see **The Pines** [SAN BERNARDINO].

Pine Spring [SAN BERNARDINO]:

(1) *spring,* 1.5 miles east of Luna Mountain (lat. 34°20'20" N, long. 117°06'10" W; near SW cor. sec. 16, T 3 N, R 2 W). Named on Butler Peak (1971) 7.5' quadrangle.

(2) *spring,* 6.25 miles south of Twentynine Palms (lat. 34°02'40" N, long. 116°03'40" W); the spring is near the site of Pine City. Named on Queen Mountain (1972) 7.5' quadrangle, which indicates that the spring is dry.

Pine Wood [RIVERSIDE]: *locality,* 3.25 miles west of San Jacinto Peak (lat. 33°48'50" N, long. 116°44'15" W; around NE cor. sec. 23, T 4 S, R 2 E). Named on San Jacinto Peak (1981) 7.5' quadrangle.

Pinezanita [SAN BERNARDINO]: *locality,* 6 miles south-southwest of downtown Big Bear Lake (lat. 34°09'50" N, long. 116°57'10" W; at S line sec. 14, T 1 N, R 1 W). Named on Big Bear Lake (1970) 7.5' quadrangle.

Pinkham Canyon [RIVERSIDE]: *canyon,* 7.5 miles long, along Pinkham Wash above a point 14 miles north of Mortmar (lat. 33°43'45" N, long. 115°58'40" W; near NE cor. sec. 19, T 5 S, R 10 E). Named on Cottonwood Spring (1958) and Hexie Mountains (1963) 15' quadrangles.

Pinkham Spring [RIVERSIDE]: *spring,* 15 miles north-northwest of Chiriaco Summit (lat. 33°51'35" N, long. 115°49'35" W). Site named on Hexie Mountains (1963) 15' quadrangle.

Pinkham Wash [RIVERSIDE]: *stream* and *dry wash,* extends for 20 miles to end 8.5 miles north of Mortmar in Shavers Valley (lat. 33°38' N, long. 115°54' W; sec. 24, T 6 S, R 10 E). Named on Cottonwood Spring (1958) and Hexie Mountains (1963) 15' quadrangles.

Pinkham Well [RIVERSIDE]: *well,* 15 miles north-northwest of Chiriaco Summit (lat. 33°51'25" N, long. 115°49'30" W). Site named on Hexie Mountains (1963) 15' quadrangle. Pinkham Well (1943) 15' quadrangle shows the feature located about 6.5 miles farther southwest along Smoke Tree Wash (lat. 33°46'40" N, long. 115°53'30" W). C.A. Pinkham of Mecca developed the well (Brown, 1920, p. 83).

Pinnacles: see **The Pinnacles** [SAN BERNARDINO].

Piñon Flat: see **Pinyon Flat** [RIVERSIDE].

Pinon Hills [SAN BERNARDINO]: *locality,* 10 miles north of Mount San Antonio (lat. 34°26' N, long. 117°38'45" W; in and near sec. 18, T 4 N, R 7 W). Named on Mescal Creek (1956) 7.5' quadrangle. United States Board on Geographic Names (1963a, p. 7) rejected the names "Desmont" and "Desert Springs" for the place. Postal authorities established Desert Springs post office 7 miles northwest of Phelan in 1949; they moved it to a spot 6 miles northwest of Phelan and changed the name to Desmont in 1959, and changed the name to Pinon Hills in 1962—the name "Desmont" was from the term "Desert Mountain" (Salley, p. 58). The place first was known as Smithson Springs for the owner of a cattle ranch there (Gudde, 1969, p. 247).

Pinon Pines: see **Nightingale** [RIVERSIDE].

Piñon Spring [SAN BERNARDINO]: *spring,* 3.25 miles east-northeast of Luna Mountain (lat. 34°21'35" N, long. 117°04'30" W; sec. 10, T 3 N, R 2 W). Named on Butler Peak (1971) 7.5' quadrangle.

Pinto Basin [RIVERSIDE]: *valley,* 5 miles northwest of Desert Center (lat. 33°56' N, long. 115°40' W); the feature is south and east of Pinto Mountains. Named on Cadiz Valley (1956), Coxcomb Mountains (1963), Dale Lake (1956), Hexie Mountains (1963), and Pinto Basin (1963) 15' quadrangles.

Pinto Canyon [IMPERIAL]: *canyon,* heads in Mexico and extends for 6.5 miles in Imperial County before reentering Mexico 28 miles west-southwest of El Centro (lat. 32°37'40" N, long. 115°59'30" W; at E line sec. 31, T 17 S, R 10 E). Named on Coyote Wells (1957) and In-Ko-Pah Gorge (1959) 7.5' quadrangles.

Pinto Mountain [RIVERSIDE]: *peak,* 20 miles north of Chiriaco Summit (lat. 33°57'15" N, long. 115°48' W); the peak is near the southeast end of Pinto Mountains. Altitude 3983 feet. Named on Hexie Mountains (1963) 15' quadrangle.

Pinto Mountain [SAN BERNARDINO]: *ridge,* east-northeast-trending, 3 miles long, 11 miles south-southwest of Ivanpah (lat. 35° 11' N, long. 115°22' W). Named on Mid Hills (1955) 15' quadrangle.

Pinto Mountains [RIVERSIDE-SAN BERNARDINO]: *range,* 30 miles north-northwest of Chiriaco Summit on Riverside-San Bernardino County line (lat. 34°02' N, long. 115°57' W). Named on Dale Lake (1956), Hexie Mountains (1963), Twentynine Palms (1955), and Valley Mountain (1956) 15' quadrangles.

Pinto Valley [SAN BERNARDINO]: *valley,* 9 miles south-southwest of Ivanpah (lat. 35°12'40" N, long. 115°20'50" W); the valley is north-northeast of Pinto Mountain. Named on Mid Hills (1955) 15' quadrangle.

Pinto Wash [IMPERIAL]: *dry wash,* heads in Mexico and extends for 12 miles in Imperial County before ending 14 miles west of Calexico (lat. 32°41'50" N, long. 115°43'15" W; sec. 2, T 17 S, R 12 E). Named on Coyote Wells (1957), Mount Signal (1957), and Yuha Basin (1957) 7.5' quadrangles.

Pinto Wash [RIVERSIDE]: *stream,* flows 36 miles to Chuckwalla Valley 15 miles north of Desert Center (lat. 33°56' N, long. 115° 24'30" W); the stream goes through Pinto Basin. Named on Coxcomb Mountains (1963), Hexie Mountains (1963), and Pinto Basin (1963) 15' quadrangles.

Pinto Wells [RIVERSIDE]: *well,* 15 miles north of Desert Center (lat. 33°56'30" N, long. 115°24'55" W; sec. 4, T 3 S, R 15 E); the feature is near the southeast end of Pinto Valley. Named on Coxcomb Mountains (1963) 15' quadrangle.

Pinto Wye [RIVERSIDE]: *locality,* 32 miles east-northeast of Garnet (lat. 34°01'15" N, long. 116°01'05" W). Named on Queen Mountain (1972) 7.5' quadrangle.

Pinyon Alta Flat [RIVERSIDE]: *area,* 14 miles south-southeast of Palm Desert (lat. 33°31'20" N, long. 116°19'30" W; sec. 26, 35, T 7 S, R 6 E). Named on Palm Desert (1959) 15' quadrangle.

Pinyon Crest [RIVERSIDE]: *locality,* 8.5 miles south-southwest of Palm Desert (lat. 33°36'30" N, long. 116°26' W; sec. 35, T 6 S, R 5 E). Named on Palm Desert (1959) 15' quadrangle.

Pinyon Flat [RIVERSIDE]: *area,* 9.5 miles south-southwest of Palm Desert (lat. 33°36'15" N, long. 116°27'15" W). Named on Palm Desert (1959) 15' quadrangle. United States Board on Geographic Names (1933, p. 606) rejected the forms "Pinon Flat" and "Piñon Flat" for the name.

Pinyon Flat: see **Little Pinyon Flat** [RIVERSIDE].

Pinyon Flat Camp [RIVERSIDE]: *locality,* 10.5 miles south-southwest of Palm Desert (lat. 33°35' N, long. 116°27'30" W; near N line sec. 10, T 7 S, R 5 E); the place is near the south end of Pinyon Flat. Named on Palm Desert (1959) 15' quadrangle.

Pinyon Pines: see **Nightingale** [RIVERSIDE].

Pinyon Well [RIVERSIDE]: *locality,* 14 miles north-northeast of Indio (lat. 33°53'45" N, long. 116°05'45" W; sec. 24, T 3 S, R 8 E). Site named on Lost Horse Mountain (1958) 15' quadrangle. On Pinyon Well (1943) 15' quadrangle, the name "Pinyon Wells" applies to four wells at the site.

Pioneer Point [SAN BERNARDINO]: *locality,* 2 miles north-northeast of Trona (lat. 35°47'10" N, long. 117°21'45" W; sec. 4, 5, T 25 N, R 43 E). Named on Trona (1949) 15' quadrangle.

Pioneertown [SAN BERNARDINO]: *village,* 4 miles northwest of Yucca Valley (lat. 34°09'20" N, long. 116°30' W; sec. 19, T 1 N, R 5 E). Named on Rimrock (1972) and Yucca Valley North (1972) 7.5' quadrangles. Postal authorities established Pioneertown post office in 1950 at a replica of an early western town built for filming movies (Salley, p. 173).

Pipe Creek [RIVERSIDE]: *stream,* flows 4 miles to Pine Meadow 11 miles southeast of Idyllwild (lat. 33°36'30" N, long. 116°36'30" W; sec. 31, T 6 S, R 4 E). Named on Idyllwild (1959) 15' quadrangle.

Pipes: see **The Pipes** [SAN BERNARDINO].

Pipes Campground [SAN BERNARDINO]: *locality,* 10 miles north-northwest of downtown Morongo Valley (lat. 34°10'50" N, long. 116°39'30" W; sec. 10, T 1 N, R 3 E); the place is in Pipes Canyon. Named on Onyx Peak (1972) 7.5' quadrangle.

Pipes Canyon [SAN BERNARDINO]: *canyon,* 9.5 miles long, opens into lowlands 9 miles north-northeast of downtown Morongo Valley (lat. 34°10'20" N, long. 116°32'35" W; near W line sec. 14, T 1 N, R 4 E); the place called The Pipes is at the mouth of the canyon. Named on Onyx Peak (1972) and Rimrock (1972) 7.5' quadrangles. San Gorgonio (1902) 30' quadrangle has the name "Pipes Creek" for the stream in the canyon. The name recalls a pipeline for water that ranchers installed in the canyon; cloudbursts ripped out the pipe in places and the project was abandoned (O'Neal, p. 135).

Pipes Creek: see **Pipes Canyon** [SAN BERNARDINO].

Pipes Spring [SAN BERNARDINO]: *spring,* 10.5 miles north-northwest of downtown Morongo Valley (lat. 34°11' N, long. 116°39'10" W; sec. 10, T 1 N, R 3 E); the spring is north of Pipes Canyon. Named on Onyx Peak (1972) 7.5' quadrangle.

Pipes Wash [SAN BERNARDINO]: *stream,* flows 22 miles from the mouth of Pipes Canyon to end 7.5 miles north of Landers (lat. 34° 22'30" N, long. 116°22'30" W; sec. 5, T 3 N, R 6 E). Named on Landers (1972), Rimrock (1972), and Yucca Valley North (1972) 7.5' quadrangles.

Pipes Wash Well: see **The Windmill** [SAN BERNARDINO].

Pisgah [SAN BERNARDINO]: *locality,* 19 miles east-southeast of Newberry along Atchison, Topeka and Santa Fe Railroad (lat. 34° 46' N, long. 116°21'40" W; near SW cor. sec. 21, T 8 N, R 6 E); the place is less than 2 miles northeast of Pisgah Crater. Named on Cady Mountains (1955) 15' quadrangle.

Pisgah Crater [SAN BERNARDINO]: *crater,* 12 miles west of Ludlow (lat. 34°44'45" N, long. 116°22'30" W; near N line sec. 32, T 8 N, R 6 E). Named on Lavic (1955) 15' quadrangle. The feature also is called Mount Pisgah (Darton and others, p. 159).

Pisgah Peak [SAN BERNARDINO]: *peak,* 8 miles west-southwest of San Gorgonio Mountain (lat. 34°02'20" N, long. 116°57'05" W; near S line sec. 35, T 1 S, R 1 W). Altitude 5488 feet. Named on Forest Falls (1970) 7.5' quadrangle.

Pitman Canyon [SAN BERNARDINO]: *canyon,* drained by a stream that flows 1 mile to Cajon Canyon nearly 3 miles northwest of Devore (lat. 34°14'30" N, long. 117°26'20" W; sec. 19, T 2 N, R 5 W). Named on Cajon (1956) and Devore (1966) 7.5' quadrangles.

Pitzer Buttes [SAN BERNARDINO]: *ridge,* 1 mile long, 2.25 miles south-southwest of the center of the town of Lucerne Valley (lat. 34°24'50" N, long. 116°57'45" W; around NE cor. sec. 27, T 4 N, R 1 W). Named on Lucerne Valley (1971) 7.5' quadrangle.

Piute: see **Fort Piute** [SAN BERNARDINO]; **Goffs** [SAN BERNARDINO].

Piute Mountains [SAN BERNARDINO]: *range,* 12 miles east-northeast of Essex (lat. 34°47' N, long. 115°03'30" W). Named on Essex (1956) and Fenner (1956) 15' quadrangles.

Piute Mountains: see **Little Piute Mountains** [SAN BERNARDINO].

Piute Range [SAN BERNARDINO]: *range,* 21 miles east-southeast of Ivanpah (lat. 35°10' N, long. 115°00' W). Named on Crescent Peak (1956), Homer Mountain (1956), Lanfair Valley (1956), and Searchlight (1959) 15' quadrangles.

Piute Spring [SAN BERNARDINO]: *spring,* 24 miles southeast of Ivanpah (lat. 35°06'40" N, long. 114°59'45" W; near NW cor. sec. 24, T 12 N, R 18 W); the spring is near the south end of Piute Range. Named on Homer Mountain (1956) 15' quadrangle.

Piute Valley [SAN BERNARDINO]:

(1) *valley,* 13 miles west-northwest of Ivanpah (lat. 35°24'45" N, long. 115°32' W). Named on Mescal Range (1955) 15' quadrangle.

(2) *valley,* between Piute Range and California-Nevada State line. Named on Bannock (1956) and Homer Mountain (1956) 15' quadrangles.

Piute Wash [SAN BERNARDINO]: *stream* and *dry wash,* heads in the State of Nevada and extends for 34 miles to Colorado River 6 miles north-northwest of Needles (lat. 34°55'20" N, long. 114° 38' W; near N line sec. 36, T 10 N, R 22 E). Named on Bannock (1956) and Homer Mountain (1956) 15' quadrangles, and on Needles NW (1970) 7.5' quadrangle. Called Sacramento Wash on Darton and others' (1915) map. United States Board on Geographic Names (1933, p. 607) rejected the names "Great Piute Wash," "Klinefelter Wash," "Mohave River," "Pah-ute Creek," "Pai-ute Creek," and "Sacramento Wash" for the feature.

Pixley Canyon [RIVERSIDE]: *canyon,* drained by a stream that flows 1.5 miles to Goodhart Canyon 6.25 miles south of Hemet (lat. 33°39'20" N, long. 116°58'10" W; at N line sec. 15, T 6 S, R 1 W). Named on Hemet (1953) 7.5' quadrangle.

Placer Canyon [RIVERSIDE]: *canyon,* drained by a stream that flows 5 miles to Pinto Basin 17 miles northwest of Desert Center (lat. 33°54'50" N, long. 115°35'30" W; at S line sec. 11, T 3 S, R 13 E). Named on Pinto Basin (1963) 15' quadrangle.

Plaster City [IMPERIAL]: *village,* 17 miles west of El Centro (lat. 32°47'35" N, long. 115°51'30" W; sec. 8, T 16 S, R 11 E). Named on Plaster City (1957) 7.5' quadrangle, which shows a gypsum plant at the site. Postal authorities established Plaster City post office in 1924; United States Gypsum Company owns the community (Salley, p. 174).

Plaza: see **The Plaza** [SAN BERNARDINO].

Pleasants Peak [RIVERSIDE]: *peak,* 6 miles west-southwest of Corona on Riverside-Orange County line (lat. 33°47'45" N, long. 117°36'20" W; at E line sec. 28, T 4 S, R 7 W). Altitude 4007 feet. Named on Corona South (1967) 7.5' quadrangle. Called Sugarloaf Peak on Corona (1942) 15' quadrangle, but United States Board on Geographic Names (1934, p. 14) rejected this name, and noted that Orange County Historical Society suggested the name "Pleasants Peak" to honor J.E. Pleasants, a pioneer associated with the feature since 1860.

Pleasant Valley [RIVERSIDE]: *valley,* 17 miles northeast of Indio (lat. 33°55' N, long. 116°03' W). Named on Hexie Mountains (1963) and Lost Horse Mountain (1958) 15' quadrangles.

Plummer Meadows [SAN BERNARDINO]: *area,* 2.25 miles west-northwest of San Gorgonio Mountain (lat. 34°06'50" N, long. 116° 52'20" W; sec. 3, T 1 S, R 1 E). Named on San Gorgonio Mountain (1970) 7.5' quadrangle

Plunge Creek [SAN BERNARDINO]: *stream,* flows 7 miles to Santa Ana Wash 4 miles north-northeast of Redlands city hall (lat. 34° 06'35" N, long. 117°09' W; sec. 1, T 1 S, R 3 W). Named on Harrison Mountain (1967) and Keller Peak (1967) 7.5' quadrangles.

Pocket Canyon [RIVERSIDE]: *canyon,* at least 1.25 miles long, 17 miles south of Hemet (lat. 33°30'15" N, long. 116°55'45" W). Named on Hemet (1942) 15' quadrangle.

Point Happy [RIVERSIDE]: *promontory,* 4.5 miles east of Palm Desert along Whitewater River (lat. 33°43' N, long. 116°17'50" W; near S line sec. 19, T 5 S, R 7 E). Named on La Quinta (1959) 7.5' quadrangle. The name is for "Happy" Lundbeck, who had a store near the feature (Gunther, p. 398).

Point of Rocks [SAN BERNARDINO]:

(1) *promontory,* 20 miles west-southwest of Barstow along Mojave River (lat. 34°45'30" N, long. 117°18'45" W; near E line sec. 29, T 8 N, R 4 W). Named on Wild Crossing (1973) 7.5' quadrangle.

(2) *promontory,* nearly 2 miles north-northeast of Trona (lat. 35° 47' N, long. 117°21'45" W; on E line sec. 5, T 25 S, R 43 E). Named on Trona (1949) 15' quadrangle.

Point of Rocks: see **Helendale** [SAN BERNARDINO].

Point of Timbers: see **Hodge** [SAN BERNARDINO].

Point View [RIVERSIDE]: *locality,* 11 miles east of San Jacinto (lat. 33°45'20" N, long. 116°45'25" W). Named on San Jacinto (1901) 30' quadrangle.

Poison Canyon [SAN BERNARDINO]: *canyon,* 2.25 miles long, 8 miles south-southwest of Trona (lat. 35°39'30" N, long. 117°26'30" W); the canyon heads at the east end of Salt Wells Valley. Named on Westend (1973) 7.5' quadrangle. Called Salt Wells Canyon on Searles Lake (1949) 15' quadrangle, but United States Board on Geographic Names (1965a, p. 10) rejected this name for the feature.

Poligue Canyon [SAN BERNARDINO]: *canyon,* drained by a stream that flows 1.5 miles to Big Bear Lake (1) 1.5 miles east-southeast of Fawnskin (lat. 34°15'35" N, long. 116°55'15" W; sec. 18, T 2 N, R 1 E). Named on Fawnskin (1971) 7.5' quadrangle. On San Gorgonio (1902) 30' quadrangle, the name applies to a canyon situated about 1 mile farther west.

Politana: see **Colton** [SAN BERNARDINO].

Polly Butte [RIVERSIDE]: *ridge,* generally west-trending, nearly 3 miles long, 4 miles southeast of downtown Hemet (lat. 33°41'15" N, long. 116°55'15" W). Named on Hemet (1953) 7.5' quadrangle.

Poopout Hill [SAN BERNARDINO]: *relief feature,* 4 miles south-southwest of Sugarloaf Mountain (lat. 34°08'55" N, long. 116°51'15" W; near NW cor. sec. 26, T 1 N, R 1 E). Named on Moonridge (1970) 7.5' quadrangle. United States Board on Geographic Names (1967, p. 7) rejected the name "Trail Head Hill" for the feature.

Poorman Reservoir [RIVERSIDE]: *intermittent lake,* about 4000 feet long, 7 miles east-southeast of Riverside city hall (lat. 33°57'25" N, long. 117°15'05" W; sec. 36, T 2 S, R 4 W). Named on Riverside East (1967) and Sunnymead (1967) 7.5' quadrangles.

Pope [IMPERIAL]: *locality,* 4.5 miles west of Frink along Southern Pacific Railroad (lat. 33°21'55" N, long. 115°43'20" W; sec. 28, T 9 S, R 12 E). Named on Frink (1956) 7.5' quadrangle.

Poppet Creek [RIVERSIDE]: *stream* and *dry wash,* extends for 8.5 miles to San Jacinto River 3 miles east-southeast of San Jacinto (lat. 33°46'05" N, long. 116°54'25" W); the feature heads near Poppet Flat. Named on Lake Fulmor (1956) and San Jacinto (1953) 7.5' quadrangles.

Poppet Flat [RIVERSIDE]: *valley,* 7.5 miles northeast of San Jacinto (lat. 33°50'55" N, long. 116°51'05" W; sec. 2, T 4 S, R 1 E). Named on Lake Fulmor (1956) 7.5' quadrangle. The name commemorates Robert Poppet, who settled in the region in 1887 (Gunther, p. 400).

Porcupine Tank [SAN BERNARDINO]: *water feature,* 44 miles northwest of Ivanpah (lat. 35°44'25" N, long. 115·55'30" W). Named on Kingston Peak (1955) 15' quadrangle.

Porcupine Wash [RIVERSIDE]: *stream,* flows 8.5 miles to Pinto Basin 13 miles north-northwest of Chiriaco Summit (lat. 33°50'30" N, long. 115°47' W). Named on Hexie Mountains (1963) 15' quadrangle.

Porphyry [RIVERSIDE]: *locality,* 1.5 miles east of Corona along Atchison, Topeka and Santa Fe Railroad (lat. 33°52'40" N, long. 117°32'20" W). Named on Corona North (1967) 7.5' quadrangle. The name is from Porphyry Paving Company, which produced paving material near the place (Gunther, p. 401).

Potato Canyon [SAN BERNARDINO]: *canyon,* 2.5 miles long, along Oak Glen Creek above a point 9.5 miles west-southwest of San Gorgonio Mountain (lat. 34°03'15" N, long. 116°58'45" W). Named on Forest Falls (1970) 7.5' quadrangle.

Potholes [IMPERIAL]: *locality,* 4 miles northeast of Bard (lat. 32°49'45" N, long. 114°30'15" W; sec. 25, T 15 S, R 23 E). Site named on Bard (1965) 7.5' quadrangle. Postal authorities established Potholes post office in 1905, discontinued it in 1909, reestablished it in 1920, and discontinued it in 1922 (Salley, p. 177). California Mining Bureau's (1917b) map shows a place called Laguna located about 2.5 miles southwest of Potholes along a rail line.

Potrero Canyon: see **Horse Potrero Canyon** [RIVERSIDE].

Potrero Creek [RIVERSIDE]:

(1) *stream* and *dry wash,* extends for 6.5 miles to San Gorgonio River 2.5 miles east of Banning (lat. 33°55'55" N, long. 116°49'40" W; at S line sec. 1, T 3 S, R 1 E). Named on Cabazon (1956) and San Gorgonio Mountain (1970) 7.5' quadrangles. The canyon of the feature was called Jost Canyon for C.F. Jost, who settled near its mouth in the 1870's (Gunther, p. 403).

(2) *stream,* flows 10.5 miles to San Jacinto Valley 4.5 miles north-northwest of San Jacinto (lat. 33°50'35" N, long. 116°59'45" W). Named on Beaumont (1953) and San Jacinto (1953) 7.5' quadrangles

Potrero de la Cienega [RIVERSIDE]: *land grant,* 2.5 miles east of Sitton Peak. Named on Sitton Peak (1954) 7.5' quadrangle. This is one of three parcels included in lands of San Juan Capistrano mission (which is in Orange County) that John Forster received in 1845; Forster claimed 1168 acres patented in 1866 (Cowan, p. 82; Gunther, p. 403).

Potrero el Cariso [RIVERSIDE]: *land grant,* 6.25 miles south of Alberhill. Named on Alberhill (1954) and Sitton Peak (1954) 7.5' quadrangles. This is one of three parcels included in lands of San Juan Capistrano mission (which is in Orange County) that John Forster received in 1845; Forster claimed 1168 acres patented in 1866 (Cowan, p. 82; Gunther, p. 403).

Potrero Spring [RIVERSIDE]: *spring,* 8 miles southwest of Palm Desert (lat. 33°39' N, long. 116°28'55" W; sec. 17, T 6 S, R 5 E). Named on Rancho Mirage (1957) 7.5' quadrangle.

Powderbox Spring [RIVERSIDE]: *spring,* 3 miles south of San Jacinto Peak (lat. 33°46'30" N, long. 116°40'30" W; at S line sec. 33, T 4 S, R 3 E). Named on San Jacinto Peak (1981) 7.5' quadrangle.

Powell: see **Leon** [SAN BERNARDINO].

Powell Canyon [SAN BERNARDINO]: *canyon,* drained by a stream that flows nearly 1 mile to Cleghorn Canyon 2.5 miles east-southeast of Cajon (lat. 34°16'55" N, long. 117°25'05" W; near SE cor. sec. 5, T 2 N, R 5 W). Named on Cajon (1956) 7.5' quadrangle.

Pozas de Santa Rosa de las Lajas: see **Yuha Well** [IMPERIAL].

Prado [RIVERSIDE]: *locality,* 3.5 miles west-northwest of Corona (lat. 33°53'35" N, long. 117°37'35" W); the site now is in Prado flood control basin. Named on Corona (1902) 30' quadrangle. Called Rincon on English's (1925) map. Postal authorities established Rincon post office in 1870, discontinued it in 1874, reestablished it in 1887, changed the name to Prado in 1907, and discontinued it in 1935 (Frickstad, p. 130).

Prado Dam [RIVERSIDE]: *locality,* 5 miles west of Corona along Atchison, Topeka and Santa Fe Railroad (lat. 33°52'45" N, long. 117°38'50" W); the place is nearly 1 mile southwest of a dam of the same name. Named on Prado Dam (1967) 7.5' quadrangle.

Prenda [RIVERSIDE]: *locality,* 4.25 miles south of Riverside city hall (lat. 33°55'10" N, long. 117°23'15" W; sec. 10, T 3 S, R 5 W). Named on Riverside West (1967) 7.5' quadrangle.

Prentiss: see **Camp Prentiss**, under **Norton Air Force Base** [SAN BERNARDINO].

Priests Well [RIVERSIDE]: *well,* 23 miles west-southwest of Vidal (lat. 34°01' N, long. 114°53'50" W; sec. 8, T 2 S, R 20 E). Named on Rice (1954) 15' quadrangle. A mining man named Priest drilled the well in 1917 (Brown, 1920, p. 83).

Promised Land Camp [SAN BERNARDINO]: *locality,* 4.25 miles northwest of Sugarloaf Mountain (lat. 34°14'40" N, long. 116°51'50" W; sec. 22, T 2 N, R 1 E). Named on Moonridge (1970) 7.5' quadrangle.

Protzman Canyon [RIVERSIDE]: *canyon,* drained by a stream that flows nearly 2 miles to Saint Johns Canyon 7.5 miles south of Hemet (lat. 33°38'40" N, long. 116°56'15" W; near S line sec. 13, T 6 S, R 1 W). Named on Hemet (1953) 7.5' quadrangle.

Providence: see **Bonanza King Well** [SAN BERNARDINO].

Providence Caves: see **Mitchell Caverns**, under **Cooks Well** [SAN BERNARDINO].

Providence Mountains [SAN BERNARDINO]: *range,* 28 miles north-northeast of Amboy (lat. 34°56' N, long. 115°32' W). Named on Flynn (1956), Kelso (1955), and Mid Hills (1955) 15' quadrangles. Garces used the name "Sierra de Santa Coleta" for the north end of the range and for nearby Mid Hills in 1775 (Hewett, p. 4).

Providence Well: see **Bonanza King Well** [SAN BERNARDINO].

Puente Hills [SAN BERNARDINO]: *range,* mainly in Los Angeles County and Orange County, but extends into San Bernardino County southwest of Ontario. Named on Ontario (1967), Prado Dam (1967), and San Dimas (1966) 7.5' quadrangles.

Pujol: see **Temecula** [RIVERSIDE] (2).

Pumpkin Patch [IMPERIAL]: *area,* 12 miles south of Desert Shores along Tule Wash (lat. 33°13'30" N, long. 116°03'50" W; on W line sec. 8, T 11 S, R 9 E). Named on Shell Reef (1959) 7.5' quadrangle. The name describes rounded concretions found at the place (Bloomquist, 1978).

Punta de Agua: see **Hawley**, under **Daggett** [SAN BERNARDINO].

Purdy [SAN BERNARDINO]: *locality,* 9 miles southeast of Ivanpah along Atchison, Topeka and Santa Fe Railroad (lat. 35°14'45" N, long. 115°12'40" W). Named on Ivanpah (1912) 1° quadrangle. Isaac Blake had Nevada Southern Railroad built to serve his mines in New York Mountains; the name "Purdy" is for Isaac's son (Gudde, 1975, p. 278).

Pushawalla Canyon [RIVERSIDE]:

(1) *canyon,* 8 miles long, opens into lowlands 9 miles north of Indio (lat. 33°50'45" N, long. 116°12'30" W; near S line sec. 1, T 4 S, R 7 E). Named on Lost Horse Mountain (1958) 15' quadrangle.

(2) *canyon,* 3.5 miles long, opens into lowlands 10.5 miles east-northeast of Cathedral City (lat. 33°48'45" N, long. 116°17'20" W; near N line sec. 19, T 4 S, R 7 E). Named on Myoma (1958) 7.5' quadrangle.

Pushawalla Palms [RIVERSIDE]: *locality,* 11 miles east-northeast of Cathedral City (lat. 33°49'30" N, long. 116°16'50" W; near W line sec. 17, T 4 S, R 7 E); the place is in Pushawalla Canyon (2). Named on Myoma (1958) 7.5' quadrangle.

Pyramid Butte [SAN BERNARDINO]: *hill,* 16 miles north-northwest of Vidal (lat. 34°19'35" N, long. 114°37'25" W; at S line sec. 24, T 3 N, R 22 E). Altitude 1852 feet. Named on Savahia Peak (1950) 15' quadrangle.

Pyramid Peak [RIVERSIDE]: *peak,* 10.5 miles southeast of Idyllwild (lat. 33°39'15" N, long. 116°34'20" W; near N line sec. 16, T 6 S, R 4 E). Altitude 7058 feet. Named on Idyllwild (1959) 15' quadrangle.

-Q-

Quackenbush Lake [SAN BERNARDINO]: *dry lake,* 4500 feet long, 15 miles north-northeast of Landers (lat. 34°28'35" N, long. 116° 19'35" W; sec. 35, T 5 N, R 6 E). Named on Hidalgo Mountain (1954) 7.5' quadrangle.

Quail Mountain [RIVERSIDE]: *peak,* 19 miles east-northeast of Garnet (lat. 34°00'25" N, long. 116°14'25" W; near S line sec. 10, T 2 S, R 7 E). Altitude 5813 feet. Named on Indian Cove (1972) 7.5' quadrangle.

Quail Mountains [SAN BERNARDINO]: *range,* 29 miles east-southeast of Trona (lat. 35°37'30" N, long. 116°53' W). Named on Quail Mountains (1948) 15' quadrangle.

Quail Spring [RIVERSIDE]: *spring,* 11.5 miles southwest of the present town of Lake Elsinore (lat. 33°33'10" N, long. 117°28'05" W; near E line sec. 14, T 7 S, R 6 W). Named on Sitton Peak (1954) 7.5' quadrangle.

Quail Spring [SAN BERNARDINO]:

(1) *spring,* 15 miles east of Ivanpah (lat. 35°19'10" N, long. 115°02'45" W; sec. 4, T 14 N, R 18 E). Named on Crescent Peak (1956) 15' quadrangle.

(2) *spring,* 30 miles east-southeast of Trona (lat. 35°38' N, long. 116°52' W); the spring is in Quail Mountains. Named on Quail Mountains (1948) 15' quadrangle.

(3) *spring,* 22 miles north-northeast of Amboy (lat. 34°50'20" N, long. 115°33'55" W; sec. 25, T 9 N, R 13 E). Named on Flynn (1956) 15' quadrangle.

(4) *spring,* 12.5 miles east of Victorville (lat. 34°32'15" N, long. 117°04'50" W; sec. 10, T 5 N, R 2 W). Named on Fairview Valley (1970) 7.5' quadrangle.

(5) *spring,* 6.5 miles north-northwest of Fawnskin (lat. 34°21'50" N, long. 116°58'15" W; near N line sec. 10, T 3 N, R 1 W). Named on Fawnskin (1971) 7.5' quadrangle.

Quail Spring Basin [SAN BERNARDINO]: *relief feature,* 21 miles north-northeast of Amboy (lat. 34°50'05" N, long. 115°34'50" W; near SE cor. sec. 25, T 9 N, R 13 E); the feature is less than 1 mile west-southwest of Quail Spring (3). Named on Flynn (1956) 15' quadrangle.

Quail Springs [SAN BERNARDINO]: *spring,* 7.5 miles south-southeast of Joshua Tree (lat. 34°02'15" N, long. 116°15'25" W; sec. 33, T 1 S, R 7 E); the feature is along Quail Wash. Named on Joshua Tree South (1972) 7.5' quadrangle, which indicates that the spring is dry. Joshua Tree (1955) 15' quadrangle has the singular form "Quail Spring" for the name.

Quail Spring Wash [SAN BERNARDINO]: *stream,* flows 3.5 miles to lowlands 19 miles north-northeast of Amboy (lat. 34°47'45" N, long. 115°33'20" W; sec. 7, T 8 N, R 14 E); the stream heads at Quail Spring (3). Named on Flynn (1956) 15' quadrangle.

Quail Valley [RIVERSIDE]: *town,* 6 miles south of Perris (lat. 33°42'20" N, long. 117°14'35" W). Named on Romoland (1953, photorevised 1979) 7.5' quadrangle. Postal authorities established Quail Valley post office in 1963 (Salley, p. 179). The town name is from Quail Valley country club (Gunther, p. 409-410).

Quail Wash [RIVERSIDE-SAN BERNARDINO]: *stream,* heads just inside Riverside County and flows 5.5 miles to lowlands 3.5 miles south-southeast of Joshua Tree in San Bernardino County (lat. 34° 05'15" N, long. 116°16'45" W; sec. 17, T 1 S, R 7 E). Named on Joshua Tree South (1972) 7.5' quadrangle.

Quarry Hill [RIVERSIDE]: *hill,* 4.25 miles south-southwest of Riverside city hall (lat. 33°55'25" N, long. 117°23'30" W; sec. 10, T 3 S, R 5 W). Named on Riverside West (1967) 7.5' quadrangle, which shows a quarry at the place.

Quartzite Mountain [SAN BERNARDINO]: *mountain,* 5 miles north of Victorville (lat. 34°36'40" N, long. 117°17'15" W). Altitude 4532 feet. Named on Victorville (1956) 7.5' quadrangle.

Quartz Peak [IMPERIAL]: *peak,* 16 miles east-northeast of Glamis (lat. 33°05'25" N, long. 114°49'20" W; on S line sec. 25, T 12 S, R 20 E). Altitude 2177 feet. Named on Quartz Peak (1953) 15' quadrangle.

Queen Mountain [SAN BERNARDINO]: *ridge,* east-trending, 1.25 miles long, 6 miles south-southwest of Twentynine Palms (lat. 34° 03'05" N, long. 116°06' W). Named on Queen Mountain (1972) 7.5' quadrangle.

Queen Valley [RIVERSIDE-SAN BERNARDINO]: *valley,* 22 miles north-northeast of Indio (lat. 33°59'55" N, long. 116°05'45" W); the valley is mainly in Riverside County, but the north end extends into San Bernardino County. Named on Lost Horse Mountain (1958) 15' quadrangle, and on Queen Mountain (1972) 7.5' quadrangle. The name is from Desert Queen mine (Gunther, p. 411), which is east of the north end of the valley. Postal authorities established Galivan post office in 1896 and discontinued it in 1897; the postmaster, who also was superintendent of Desert Queen mine, named the post office (Salley, p. 82).

Quien Sabe Point [RIVERSIDE]: *ridge,* northeast-trending, 2.25 miles long, 21 miles north of Blythe (lat. 33°54'45" N, long. 114° 33' W). Named on Big Maria Mountains NE (1954) 7.5' quadrangle.

Quill Spring [SAN BERNARDINO]: *spring,* nearly 5 miles west-southwest of Ord Mountain (lat. 34°38'40" N, long. 116°53'25" W; near NW cor. sec. 4, T 6 N, R 1 E). Named on Ord Mountains (1955) 15' quadrangle.

Quinn Flat [RIVERSIDE]: *area,* 9 miles southeast of Idyllwild (lat. 33°38'15" N, long. 116°37'40" W; at W line sec. 24, T 6 S, R 3 E). Named on Idyllwild (1959) 15' quadrangle.

-R -

R: see **Mount R** [SAN BERNARDINO].

Rabbit Holes: see **Rabbit Holes Spring** [SAN BERNARDINO].

Rabbit Holes Spring [SAN BERNARDINO]: *spring,* 31 miles north of Baker (lat. 35°42'45" N, long. 116°03'05" W). Named on Silurian Hills (1956) 15' quadrangle. Called Rabbit Holes on Avawatz Mountains (1933) 1° quadrangle.

Rabbit Lake [SAN BERNARDINO]: *dry lake,* 2 miles long, 17 miles east-southeast of Victorville (lat. 34°27'25" N, long. 117°01'15" W). Named on Fifteenmile Valley (1971) 7.5' quadrangle.

Rabbit Peak [RIVERSIDE]: *peak,* 20 miles south of Indio (lat. 33° 26' N, long. 116°14'10" W; sec. 34, T 8 S, R 7 E). Altitude 6623 feet. Named on Rabbit Peak (1959) 7.5' quadrangle.

Rabbit Springs [SAN BERNARDINO]: *springs,* 1.25 miles northwest of the center of the town of Lucerne Valley (lat. 34°27'25" N, long. 116°57'45" W; at NW cor. sec. 11, T 4 N, R 1 W). Named on Lucerne Valley (1971) 7.5' quadrangle.

Racimo: see **Guasti** [SAN BERNARDINO].

Radec [RIVERSIDE]: *locality,* 3 miles west-northwest of Aguanga (lat. 33°27'50" N, long. 116°54'50" W; sec. 19, T 8 S, R 1 E). Named on Vail Lake (1953) 7.5' quadrangle. Postal authorities established Radec post office in 1885, discontinued it in 1895, reestablished it in 1900, and discontinued it in 1901 (Frickstad, p. 130). Samuel V. Tripp bought land at the place in 1883 and asked for a post office called Cedar, but this name was unavailable and he had to settle for the name "Radec," which is the word "cedar" spelled backward (Gunther, p. 411-412).

Radec Valley [RIVERSIDE]: *valley,* 3 miles west-northwest of Aguanga (lat. 33°27'40" N, long. 116°54'50" W; sec. 19, 30, T 8 S, R 1 E); Radec is in the valley. Named on Vail Lake (1953) 7.5' quadrangle.

Radford: see **Camp Radford** [SAN BERNARDINO].

Ragtown [SAN BERNARDINO]: *locality,* 4 miles south of Ludlow (lat. 34°39'50" N, long. 116°09'05" W; near SW cor. sec. 28, T 7 N, R 8 E). Named on Ludlow (1955) 7.5' quadrangle.

Railroad Canyon [RIVERSIDE]:

(1) *canyon,* 7 miles long, along San Jacinto River above a point 1.5 miles east of Lake Elsinore city hall (lat. 33°39'50" N, long. 117° 18'05" W; sec. 9, T 8 S, R 4 W). Named on Lake Elsinore (1953) 7.5' quadrangle. Elsinore (1901) 30' quadrangle shows Southern California Railroad in the canyon. The feature also was called San Jacinto Canyon, Cottonwood Canyon, and Annie Orton Canyon; the railroad ran through the canyon from 1882 until a flood destroyed the line in 1927 (Gunther, p. 412).

(2) *canyon,* 1 mile long, 7.5 miles south-southeast of Hemet (lat. 33°39'10" N, long. 116°54'05" W; mainly in sec. 17, T 6 S, R 1 E). Named on Hemet (1953) 7.5' quadrangle.

Railroad Canyon Reservoir [RIVERSIDE]: *lake,* behind a dam 2.25 miles east of Lake Elsinore city hall (lat. 33°40'35" N, long. 117° 16'20" W; near W line sec. 2, T 6 S, R 4 W); the dam is in Railroad Canyon (1). Named on Lake Elsinore (1953) and Romoland (1953) 7.5' quadrangles. Workmen completed the dam that forms the lake in 1929 (Gunther, p. 413).

Railroad Well [SAN BERNARDINO]: *well,* 12.5 miles north of Ivanpah at Desert (lat. 35°31'30" N, long. 115°18'45" W). Named on Ivanpah (1912) 1° quadrangle.

Rainbow Basin [SAN BERNARDINO]: *relief feature,* 39 miles east-southeast of the village of Red Mountain (lat. 35°01'45" N, long. 117°02'15" W; sec. 24, T 11 N, R 2 W). Named on Opal Mountain (1955) 15' quadrangle.

Rainbow Bay [SAN BERNARDINO]: *embayment,* 7.5 miles south-southwest of Luna Mountain along Lake Arrowhead (1) (lat. 34° 15'10" N, long. 117°12' W; near S line sec. 16, T 2 N, R 3 W); the place is west-southwest of Rainbow Point. Named on Lake Arrowhead (1971) 7.5' quadrangle.

Rainbow Canyon [SAN BERNARDINO]: *canyon,* about 1 mile long, 19 miles north-northeast of Landers (lat. 34°29'15" N, long. 116° 12' W; mainly in sec. 25, T 5 N, R 7 E). Named on Deadman Lake NW (1955) 7.5' quadrangle.

Rainbow Lake [SAN BERNARDINO]: *lake,* 850 feet long, 4 miles west-northwest of Keller Peak along Deep Creek (1) (lat. 34°12'40" N, long. 117°05'45" W; sec. 33, T 2 N, R 2 W). Named on Keller Peak (1967) 7.5' quadrangle.

Rainbow Point [SAN BERNARDINO]: *promontory,* 7.25 miles south-southwest of Luna Mountain along Arrowhead Lake (1) (lat. 34°15'20" N, long. 117°11'50" W; sec. 16, T 2 N, R 3 W). Named on Lake Arrowhead (1971) 7.5' quadrangle.

Rainbow Rock [IMPERIAL]: *relief feature,* 3.25 miles south-southwest of Desert Shores (lat. 33°22'05" N, long. 116°03'55" W; near NW cor. sec. 29, T 9 S R 9 E). Named on Seventeen Palms (1956) 7.5' quadrangle.

Rainbow Wells [SAN BERNARDINO]: *locality,* 21 miles west-southwest of Ivanpah (lat. 35°12'20" N, long. 115°39' W; at S line sec. 13, T 13 N, R 12 E). Named on Kelso (1955) 15' quadrangle.

Ramer Lake [IMPERIAL]: *lake,* 1 mile long, 3.5 miles south of Calipatria near Alamo River (lat. 33°04'35" N, long. 115°30'40" W; around SE cor. sec. 33, T 12 S, R 14 E). Named on Westmorland (1956) 7.5' quadrangle.

Ramona Hot Springs: see **Lakeview Hot Springs** [RIVERSIDE].

Ramon Creek [RIVERSIDE]: *stream,* flows 2 miles to lowlands 2 miles southwest of Palm Desert (lat. 33°41'55" N, long. 116°23'55" W; at N line sec. 31, T 5 S, R 6 E). Named on Rancho Mirage (1957) 7.5' quadrangle.

Ramon Wash [RIVERSIDE]: *dry wash,* nearly 1 mile long, 4 miles north-northeast of Palm Springs (lat. 33°52'45" N, long. 116°30'35" W). Named on Desert Hot Springs (1955) and Palm Springs (1957) 7.5' quadrangles.

Rana [SAN BERNARDINO]: *locality,* 2 miles west-southwest of San Bernardino city hall along the railroad (lat. 34°05'20" N, long. 117°19'10" W). Named on San Bernardino South (1967) 7.5' quadrangle.

Rancho Cucamonga [SAN BERNARDINO]: *city,* 4.5 miles northeast of Ontario city hall (lat. 34°06'25" N, long. 117°35'15" W); the place is partly on Cucamonga grant. Named on Guasti (1966, photorevised 1981) 7.5' quadrangle. The city incorporated in 1977. Called Cucamonga on Guasti (1966) 7.5' quadrangle, and called North Cucamonga on Cucamonga (1903) 15' quadrangle. Ontario (1954) 15' quadrangle has the designation "Cucamonga (P.O.)" at the site, and has the name "Cucamonga" for a place situated 1.25 miles farther southeast near Atchison, Topeka and Santa Fe Railroad. Postal authorities established Cucamonga post office in 1864 and moved it 2.5 miles southeast to the railroad in 1888 (Salley, p. 53). They established North Cucamonga post office in 1888 and discontinued it in 1923 (Frickstad, p. 144). They established Eswena post office 4 miles northeast of North Cucamonga post office in 1892 and discontinued it in 1893—the name "Eswena" was coined from the names of Messers. Eshelman, "Wells, and Nair, leaders of Dunkard colonists who bought land at the site in 1890 (Salley, p. 70-71).

Rancho Mirage [RIVERSIDE]: *town,* 2.5 miles west-northwest of Palm Desert (lat. 33°44'25" N, long. 116°24'40" W). Named on Cathedral City (1958) and Rancho Mirage (1957) 7.5' quadrangles. Postal authorities established Rancho Mirage post office in 1951 (Frickstad, p. 130). Lawrence Macomber used the name "Rancho Mirage" when he filed the first map of the development in 1924 (Gunther, p. 416).

Randolph: see **Sablon** [SAN BERNARDINO].

Ranger Peak [RIVERSIDE]: *peak,* 5.5 miles south-southwest of Cabazon (lat. 33°50'40" N, long. 116°49'30" W; near SE cor. sec. 1, T 4 S, R 1 E). Altitude 5082 feet. Named on Lake Fulmor (1956) 7.5' quadrangle.

Rannells [RIVERSIDE]: *locality,* 11 miles south-southwest of Blythe (lat. 33°29'20" N, long. 114°42'30" W; near NW cor sec. 17, T 8 S, R 22 E). Site named on Cibola (1951) 15' quadrangle. Postal authorities established Rannells post office in 1909 and discontinued it in 1933 (Frickstad, p. 130). Samuel D. Rannells and John W. Rannells owned land at the place and had a townsite surveyed there in 1908 (Gunther, p. 416).

Rasor [SAN BERNARDINO]: *locality,* 12 miles south of Baker along Tonopah and Tidewater Railroad (lat. 35°06' N, long. 116°07'20" W). Named on Avawatz Mountains (1933) 1° quadrangle. The name commemorates Clarence Rasor, who had much to do with laying out the railroad, and eventually was chief engineer for American operations of Francis Marion Smith's borax enterprise (Hildebrand, 53-54).

Rathbone Creek [SAN BERNARDINO]: *stream,* flows 4 miles to Big Bear Lake (1) 3.25 miles east-southeast of Fawnskin (lat. 34°15'15" N, long. 116°53'20" W; sec. 16, T 2 N, R 1 E). Named on Big Bear Lake (1970), Fawnskin (1971), and Moonridge (1970) 7.5' quadrangles. United States Board on Geographic Names (1983c, p. 4) approved the name "Rathbun Creek" for the stream.

Rathbun Creek: see **Rathbone Creek** [SAN BERNARDINO].

Rattlesnake Canyon [SAN BERNARDINO]:

(1) *canyon,* nearly 2 miles long, 10.5 miles south of Essex (lat. 34° 35' N, long. 115°15'40" W). Named on Danby (1956) 15' quadrangle.

(2) *canyon,* 8 miles long, opens into lowlands 3.5 miles south of Old Woman Springs (lat. 34°20'15" N, long. 116°42'25" W). Named on Rattlesnake Canyon (1972) 7.5' quadrangle.

(3) *canyon,* drained by a stream that flows 3.5 miles to lowlands 14 miles north-northwest of downtown Morongo Valley (lat. 34° 14'35" N, long. 116°39'30" W; sec. 22, T 2 N, R 3 E). Named on Onyx Peak (1972) 7.5' quadrangle.

(4) *canyon,* 1.25 miles long, 6.5 miles southwest of Twentynine Palms (lat. 34°04'40" N, long. 116°08'35" W). Named on Indian Cove (1972) 7.5' quadrangle.

Rattlesnake Creek [SAN BERNARDINO]:

(1) *stream,* flows 2.5 miles to Santa Ana River 3 miles west-southwest of Sugarloaf Mountain (lat. 34°10'55" N, long. 116°51'35" W; near E line sec. 10, T 1 N, R 1 E). Named on Moonridge (1970) 7.5' quadrangle.

(2) *stream,* flows nearly 1 mile to Mill Creek Canyon 4.5 miles west-southwest of San Gorgonio Mountain (lat. 34°05' N, long. 116°54'10" W; sec. 17, T 1 S, R 1 E). Named on Forest Falls (1970) 7.5' quadrangle.

Rattlesnake Mountain [SAN BERNARDINO]: *peak,* 2.5 miles east-northeast of Luna Mountain (lat. 34°21'20" N, long. 117°05'05" W; near SW cor. sec. 10, T 3 N, R 2 W). Named on Butler Peak (1971) 7.5' quadrangle. Called Rattlesnake Peak on California Mining Bureau's (1917a) map.

Rattlesnake Peak: see **Rattlesnake Mountain** [SAN BERNARDINO].

Rattlesnake Spring [SAN BERNARDINO]:

(1) *spring,* 4 miles south of Old Woman Springs (lat. 34°20'05" N, long. 116°42'15" W); the spring is in Rattlesnake Canyon (2). Named on Rattlesnake Canyon (1972) 7.5' quadrangle.

(2) *spring,* 2.25 miles northeast of Luna Mountain (lat. 34°21'50" N, long. 117°05'35" W; sec. 9, T 3 N, R 2 W); the spring is less than 1 mile northwest of Rattlesnake Mountain. Named on Butler Peak (1971) 7.5' quadrangle.

(3) *spring,* 3.5 miles south of Yucca Valley (lat. 34°04' N, long. 116°27'20" W; at W line sec. 22, T 1 S, R 5 E). Named on Yucca Valley South (1972) 7.5' quadrangle.

Rawson Canyon [RIVERSIDE]: *canyon,* drained by a stream that flows 4.5 miles to Tucalota Creek 11 miles east-northeast of Murrieta (lat. 33°35'50" N, long. 117°02' W; near NE cor. sec. 1, T 7 S, R 2 W). Named on Bachelor Mountain (1953) and Winchester (1953) 7.5' quadrangles. The name is for James Rawson, who settled in the region in 1868 (Gunther, p. 418).

Rayneta [RIVERSIDE]: *locality,* 1.5 miles west-southwest of the center of present Idyllwild (lat. 33°43'55" N, long. 116°44'30" W; sec. 14, T 5 S, R 2 E). Named on San Jacinto (1901) 30' quadrangle. Postal authorities established Rayneta post office in 1893 and changed the name to Idyllwild in 1901; the name "Rayneta" is from the given name of the postmaster's son, Ray, with the term "neta" added (Salley, p. 182).

Raywood Flat [SAN BERNARDINO]: *area,* 3.5 miles south of San Gorgonio Mountain (lat. 34°02'45" N, long. 116°49'15" W; near NW cor sec. 31, T 1 S, R 2 E). Named on San Gorgonio Mountain (1970) 7.5' quadrangle.

Rebel Ridge [SAN BERNARDINO]: *ridge,* northeast-trending, 0.5 mile long, 1.25 miles west-southwest of the center of Big Bear City (lat. 34°15'20" N, long. 116°52'10" W; sec. 15, T 2 N, R 1 E). Named on Big Bear City (1971) 7.5' quadrangle.

Reche: see **Colton** [SAN BERNARDINO].

Reche Canyon [RIVERSIDE-SAN BERNARDINO]: *canyon,* drained by a stream that heads in Riverside County and flows 9.5 miles to lowlands along Santa Ana River 4 miles south of San Bernardino city hall in San Bernardino County (lat. 34°02'55" N, long. 117°17'20" W; at N line sec. 34, T 1 S, R 4 W). Named on Redlands (1967), San Bernardino South (1967), and Sunnymead (1967) 7.5' quadrangles. The drainage in the uppermost part of the canyon is in the opposite direction from that in the main part. The feature first was called Humabba Canyon; the name "Reche" recalls Anthony Reche, who settled in the canyon in 1876 (McDonald, p. 46).

Reche Mountain [SAN BERNARDINO]: *peak,* 3.5 miles northeast of Landers (lat. 34°18'30" N, long. 116°21'10" W; at NE cor. sec. 33, T 3 N, R 6 E). Altitude 3660 feet. Named on Emerson Lake (1955) 15' quadrangle. United States Board on Geographic Names (1961a, p. 19) rejected the name "Richs Mountain" for the feature, and noted that the name "Reche" commemorates Charles L. Reche of Reche Wells.

Reche Wells [SAN BERNARDINO]: *wells,* 2 miles north-northwest of Landers (lat. 34°17'35" N, long. 116°24'10" W; near NW cor. sec. 6, T 2 N, R 6 E). Named on Landers (1972) 7.5' quadrangle. Called Rich's Well on Thompson's (1921) map. United States Board on Geographic Names (1961a, p. 19) rejected the name "Richs Well," and noted that the name "Reche" is for Charles L. Reche, an early homesteader who dug the first well at the spot.

Red Ant Canyon [SAN BERNARDINO]: *canyon,* 1.5 miles long, opens into lowlands 0.5 mile southwest of downtown Big Bear Lake (lat. 34°14'15" N, long. 116°55'45" W; sec. 19, T 2 N, R 1 E). Named on Big Bear Lake (1970) 7.5' quadrangle. On San Gorgonio Mountain (1954) 15' quadrangle, the name applies to a canyon located about 0.5 mile farther east.

Red Butte: see **Clapp Spring** [IMPERIAL].

Red Buttes [SAN BERNARDINO]: *hills,* 29 miles west-southwest of Barstow (lat. 34°49'15" N, long. 117°32'10" W; at N line sec. 5, T 8 N, R 6 W). Named on Red Buttes (1973) 7.5' quadrangle.

Red Butte Spring: see **Clapp Spring** [IMPERIAL].

Red Butte Wash [RIVERSIDE]: *stream,* 1.25 miles long, 4 miles northeast of Chiriaco Summit (lat. 33°42'05" N, long. 115°40'45" W; at NE cor. sec. 36, T 5 S, R 12 E). Named on Hayfield (1963) 15' quadrangle.

Red Canyon [RIVERSIDE]: *canyon,* 7 miles long, opens into the canyon of Salt Creek 9.5 miles south-southeast of Chiriaco Summit (lat. 33°33' N, long. 115°37'30" W; near E line sec. 21, T 7 S, R 13 E). Named on Hayfield (1963) 15' quadrangle.

Red Cloud Canyon [RIVERSIDE]: *canyon,* 5 miles long, opens into lowlands 7.5 miles south-southwest of Desert Center (lat. 33°36'55" N, long. 115°27'30" W). Named on Chuckwalla Mountains (1963) 15' quadrangle, which shows Red Cloud mine in the canyon.

Red Cloud Wash [RIVERSIDE]: stream, flows 5.5 miles from the mouth of Red Cloud Canyon to Chuckwalla Valley 11 miles east of Chiriaco Summit (lat. 33°38'30" N, long. 115°32' W; near NW cor. sec. 21, T 6 S, R 14 E). Named on Chuckwalla Mountains (1963) and Hayfield (1963) 15' quadrangles.

Red Dome [RIVERSIDE]:

(1) *peak,* 14 miles east-northeast of Banning (lat. 34°00'45" N, long. 116°39'30" W; sec. 10, T 2 S, R 3 E). Named on Morongo Valley (1955) 15' quadrangle.

(2) *locality,* 13 miles east-northeast of Banning along Whitewater River (lat. 34°00'35" N, long. 116°40'10" W; near E line sec. 9, T 2 S, R 3 E); the place is less than 1 mile west-southwest of Red Dome (1). Named on Catclaw Flat (1972) 7.5' quadrangle.

Red Hill [SAN BERNARDINO]:

(1) *hill,* 10.5 miles west-northwest of Barstow (lat. 34°58'55" N, long. 117°10'45" W; sec. 3, 10, T 10 N, R 3 W). Altitude 2307 feet. Named on Hinkley (1971) 7.5' quadrangle.

(2) *relief feature,* 11 miles east-southeast of Ord Mountain (lat. 34°36' N, long. 116°39' W; mainly in sec. 22, T 6 N, R 3 E). Named on Rodman Mountains (1955) 15' quadrangle.

(3) *peak,* nearly 4 miles north-northeast of Ontario city hall (lat. 34°06'50" N, long. 117°37'15" W). Named on Guasti (1966) 7.5' quadrangle.

Red Island [IMPERIAL]: *hill,* 7.5 miles northwest of Calipatria at the edge of Salton Sea (lat. 33°11'50" N, long. 115°36'40" W; at W line sec. 22, T 11 S, R 13 E). Altitude 127 feet below sea level. Named on Niland (1956) 7.5' quadrangle.

Redlands [SAN BERNARDINO]:

(1) *city,* 7.5 miles east-southeast of San Bernardino (lat. 34°03'20" N, long. 117°10'55" W). Named on Redlands (1967) and Yucaipa (1967) 7.5' quad-

rangles. Postal authorities established Redlands post office in 1887 (Frickstad, p. 144), and the city incorporated in 1888. E.G. Judson and Frank E. Brown platted the community in 1887 at what was known as Lugonia—the name "Redlands" is from the color of the soil at the place (Gudde, 1949, p. 282). Postal authorities established Lugonia post office in 1882 and discontinued it in 1888—the name was from the Lugo family, owner of San Bernardino grant (Salley, p. 129). United States Geological Survey's (1943) map shows a place called Greenspot situated 4.5 miles east-northeast of Redlands along Southern Pacific Railroad (lat. 34°05'10" N, long. 117°06'30" W; sec. 17, T 1 S, R 2 W). Postal authorities established Zanja post office 5 miles northeast of Redlands in 1917 and discontinued it in 1920; the name was from a ditch that mission Indians built in 1819 to take water from Mill Creek for irrigation—*zanja* means "ditch" in Spanish (Salley, p. 246).

(2) *locality,* 2.25 miles southwest of Redlands city hall along Southern Pacific Railroad (lat. 34°01'55" N, long. 117°12'30" W; near NE cor. sec. 5, T 2 S, R 3 W). Named on Redlands (1967) 7.5' quadrangle. Called Brookside on Redlands (1901) 15' quadrangle.

Redlands Heights [SAN BERNARDINO]: *district,* 2 miles southeast of Redlands city hall (lat. 34°02' N, long. 117°09'30" W; around SE cor. sec. 35, T 1 S, R 3 W). Named on Redlands (1954) 15' quadrangle.

Redlands Junction: see **Bryn Mawr** [SAN BERNARDINO].

Red Mountain [RIVERSIDE]: *peak,* 11 miles southeast of Hemet (lat. 33°37'50" N, long. 116°50'45" W; near S line sec. 23, T 6 S, R 1 E). Altitude 4573 feet. Named on Hemet (1957) 15' quadrangle.

Red Mountain [SAN BERNARDINO]:

(1) *ridge,* generally south-southeast-trending, 3.5 miles long, 2 miles east of the village of Red Mountain (lat. 35°21' N, long. 117° 35' W). Named on Klinker Mountain (1967) and Red Mountain (1967) 7.5' quadrangles.

(2) *village,* 32 miles south-southwest of Trona (lat. 35°21'25" N, long. 117°37' W; sec. 6, T 30 S, R 41 E). Named on Red Mountain (1967) 7.5' quadrangle. The place first was called Osdick, for P.J. Osdick, a miner there; Osdick himself renamed the place in 1921 for nearby Red Mountain (1) (Hanna, p. 252). Postal authorities established Osdick post office in 1922 and changed the name to Red Mountain in 1929 (Frickstad, p. 144).

Redonda Mesa [RIVERSIDE]: *relief feature,* 11 miles west of Temecula (lat. 33°29'40" N, long. 117°20'40" W). Named on Fallbrook (1968) 7.5' quadrangle.

Redonda Ridge [SAN BERNARDINO]: *ridge,* generally southwest-trending, 3 miles long, 6 miles east-southeast of Luna Mountain (lat. 34°18'20" N, long. 117°02' W). Named on Butler Peak (1971) 7.5' quadrangle.

Red Pass [SAN BERNARDINO]: *narrows,* 12.5 miles west-northwest of Baker (lat. 35°19'30" N, long. 116°17' W). Named on Avawatz Mountains (1933) 1° quadrangle.

Red Pass Lake [SAN BERNARDINO]: *dry lake,* about 1.5 miles long, 16 miles west of Baker (lat. 35°16' N, long. 116°21'30" W; around NE cor. sec. 32, T 14 N, R 6 E); the feature is 5.5 miles southwest of Red Pass. Named on Red Pass Lake (1948) 15' quadrangle. Thompson (1929, p. 264) used the name "Red Pass Valley" for the valley that contains the dry lake.

Red Pass Valley: see **Red Pass Lake** [SAN BERNARDINO].

Red Rock Canyon [IMPERIAL]: *canyon,* drained by a stream that flows 7.5 miles to Deguynos Canyon 6.5 miles northwest of Carrizo Mountain (lat. 32°54'20" N, long. 116°04'45" W; near S line sec. 32, T 14 S, R 9 E). Named on Carrizo Mountain NE (1957) 7.5' quadrangle.

Red Rock Falls [SAN BERNARDINO]: *waterfall,* 14 miles south-southeast of Needles (lat. 34°39'35" N, long. 114°28'35" W). Named on Topock (1970) 7.5' quadrangle.

Red Rock Flat [SAN BERNARDINO]: *area,* 2.25 miles northwest of San Gorgonio Mountain (lat. 34°07'15" N, long. 116°51'40" W; near SE cor. sec. 34, T 1 N, R 1 E). Named on San Gorgonio Mountain (1970) 7.5' quadrangle.

Redshank [RIVERSIDE]: *locality,* 4.5 miles southeast of Idyllwild (lat. 33°41'55" N, long. 116°39'35" W; sec. 34, T 5 S, R 3 E). Named on Idyllwild (1959) 15' quadrangle. United States Board on Geographic Names (1982c, p. 2) approved the name "Redshank" for a flat area at the site, and rejected the form "Red Shank" for the name; the Board pointed out that the name is from a plant of the genus *Polygonum,* which is characterized by red stems.

Red Spring [SAN BERNARDINO]: *spring,* 9 miles northwest of Needles (lat. 34°56'15" N, long. 114°43'15" W; near N line sec. 30, T 10 N, R 22 E). Named on Needles NW (1970) 7.5' quadrangle.

Red Tahquitz [RIVERSIDE]: *relief feature,* 4.25 miles south-southeast of San Jacinto Peak (lat. 33°45'30" N, long. 116°39'05" W; near NE cor. sec. 10, T 5 S, R 3 E). Named on San Jacinto Peak (1981) 7.5' quadrangle. United States Board on Geographic Names (1982c, p. 2) rejected the name "Red Tahquitz Peak" for the feature, and noted that the name "Tahquitz" reportedly is that of an Indian spirit.

Red Tahquitz Peak: see **Red Tahquitz** [RIVERSIDE].

Reeds Meadow [RIVERSIDE]: *area,* 3.25 miles south-southeast of San Jacinto Peak (lat. 33°46'15" N, long. 116°39'30" W; near N line sec. 3, T 5 S, R 3 E). Named on San Jacinto Peak (1981) 7.5' quadrangle.

Reed Valley [RIVERSIDE]: *valley,* 13 miles southeast of Hemet (lat. 33°35'45" N, long. 116°49'45" W; on N line sec. 1, T 7 S, R 1 E). Named on Hemet (1957) 15' quadrangle. The name recalls Asa Reed and his family, who came to the place in 1867 (Gunther, p. 422).

Regan Slough [IMPERIAL]: *water feature,* 26 miles south of Palo Verde near Colorado River (lat. 33°03' N, long. 114°40'35" W; near NW cor. sec. 16, T 13 S, R 22 E). Named on Picacho SW (1965) 7.5' quadrangle. Called Regans Slough on Picacho (1951) 15' quadrangle.

Reinhardt Canyon [RIVERSIDE]: *canyon,* 2.25 miles long, opens into lowlands 6.25 miles southeast of Lakeview (lat. 33°45'30" N, long. 117°03'20" W; at S line sec. 2, T 5 S, R 2 W). Named on Lakeview (1967) 7.5' quadrangle.

Relief Hot Springs: see **Gilman Hot Springs** [RIVERSIDE].

Renoville [SAN BERNARDINO]: *locality,* 21 miles north-northwest of Baker (lat. 35°33'15" N, long. 116°11'15" W; near NW cor. sec. 24, T 17 N, R 7 E). Site named on Silurian Hills (1956) 15' quadrangle.

Reservoir: see **Big Bear Lake** [SAN BERNARDINO] (2).

Reservoir Butte [RIVERSIDE]: *hill,* 3.25 miles east-southeast of downtown Hemet (lat. 33°43'40" N, long. 116°55'05" W; near N line sec. 19, T 5 S, R 1 E); the feature is near Little Lake. Altitude 1953 feet. Named on Hemet (1953) 7.5' quadrangle.

Reservoir Canyon [SAN BERNARDINO]: *canyon,* 2.5 miles long, opens into lowlands 1.5 miles east-southeast of Redlands city hall (lat. 34°02'40" N, long. 117°09'40" W; sec. 35, T 1 S, R 3 W). Named on Redlands (1967) 7.5' quadrangle.

Resting Spring Mountains: see **Kingston Range** [SAN BERNARDINO].

Rialto [SAN BERNARDINO]: *city,* 5 miles west of San Bernardino city hall (lat. 34°06' N, long. 117°22'20" W). Named on Devore (1966), Fontana (1967), San Bernardino North (1967), and San Bernardino South (1967) 7.5' quadrangles. Postal authorities established Rialto post office in 1888 (Frickstad, p. 144), and the city incorporated in 1911.

Rialto Bench [SAN BERNARDINO]: *relief feature,* 3 miles west-northwest of San Bernardino city hall (lat. 34°06'55" N, long. 117° 20'25" W; sec. 6, T 1 S, R 4 W). Named on San Bernardino South (1967) 7.5' quadrangle.

Rialto Spring [SAN BERNARDINO]: *spring,* 9.5 miles north of San Bernardino city hall (lat. 34°14'35" N, long. 117°18' W; sec. 21, T 2 N, R 4 W). Named on San Bernardino North (1967) 7.5' quadrangle.

Ribbonwood [RIVERSIDE]: *locality,* 12.5 miles south-southwest of Palm Desert (lat. 33°34'10" N, long. 116°29'55" W; near NW cor. sec. 17, T 7 S, R 5 E). Named on Palm Desert (1959) 15' quadrangle. The name is from shaggy red-barked trees found on the north slopes of Santa Rosa Mountains (Robinson and Risher, p. 169).

Rice [SAN BERNARDINO]: *locality,* 20 miles west of Vidal along Atchison, Topeka and Santa Fe Railroad (lat. 34°05'05" N, long. 114°51' W; sec. 14, T 1 S, R 20 E). Named on Rice (1954) 15' quadrangle. Called Blythe Junction on California Mining Bureau's (1917a) map. Postal authorities established Blythe Junction post office in 1910 and discontinued it in 1916 (Frickstad, p. 138). They established Rice post office in 1933, discontinued it in 1943, reestablished it in 1946, and discontinued it in 1963 (Salley, p. 184). The name commemorates Guy R. Rice, chief engineer of California Southern Railroad (Gudde, 1949, p. 285).

Rice Air Base [RIVERSIDE]: *military facility,* 18 miles west-southwest of Vidal [SAN BERNARDINO] (lat. 34°04' N, long. 114°48'45" W); the place is 2 miles east-southeast of Rice [SAN BERNARDINO]. Named on Rice (1954) 15' quadrangle.

Rice Canyon [RIVERSIDE]: *canyon,* 3.25 miles long, opens into lowlands 2 miles south of Alberhill (lat. 33°41'50" N, long. 117°24'15" W; at S line sec. 28, T 5 S, R 5 W). Named on Alberhill (1954) 7.5' quadrangle. Caleb Ensign, United States deputy surveyor, named the canyon in 1892 for Benjamin A. Rice and Stanton W. Rice, brothers who settled in the neighborhood in 1884 (Gunther, p. 424).

Rice Valley [RIVERSIDE-SAN BERNARDINO]: *valley,* 28 miles north-northwest of Blythe on Riverside-San Bernardino County line, mainly in Riverside County (lat. 34°00' N, long. 114°45' W); the valley extends southeast from Rice. Named on Big Maria Mountains (1951), Midland (1952), Rice (1954), and Vidal (1949) 15' quadrangles.

Richardson's Canyon: see **Tin Mine Canyon** [RIVERSIDE].

Richs Mountain: see **Reche Mountain** [SAN BERNARDINO].

Richs Well: see **Reche Wells** [SAN BERNARDINO].

Rico [IMPERIAL]: *locality,* 1.25 miles west-southwest of Holtville along Holton Inter-urban Railroad (lat. 32°48'25" N, long. 115°23'55" W; at W line sec. 35, T 15 S, R 15 E). Named on Holtville West (1956) 7.5' quadrangle. Called Brooks Switch on Holtville (1907) 30' quadrangle.

Riggs [SAN BERNARDINO]: *locality,* 17 miles north of Baker (lat. 35°30'20" N, long. 116°07' W; sec. 3, T 16 N, R 8 E). Site named on Silurian Hills (1956) 15' quadrangle. The place was along Tonopah and Tidewater Railroad; the name is for Frank Riggs, owner of a silver mine situated 2 miles east of the site (Palmer, p. 62). Mendenhall (1909a, p. 55) listed Riggs Well located at Riggs mine.

Riggs Dry Lake: see **Silurian Lake** [SAN BERNARDINO].
Riggs Valley: see **Silurian Lake** [SAN BERNARDINO].
Riggs Wash [SAN BERNARDINO]: *stream,* flows 11 miles to end 14 miles north of Baker (lat. 35°28' N, long. 116°05'30" W; sec. 23, T 16 N, R 8 E). Named on Baker (1956) and Halloran Spring (1956) 15' quadrangles.
Riggs Well: see **Riggs** [SAN BERNARDINO].
Rimforest [SAN BERNARDINO]: *village,* 6 miles northwest of Harrison Mountain (lat. 34°13'45" N, long. 117°13'30" W; on E line sec. 30, T 2 N, R 3 W). Named on Harrison Mountain (1967) 7.5' quadrangle. Postal authorities established Rimforest post office in 1949 (Frickstad, p. 145); they established Adahi post office near present Rimforest (SE quarter sec. 30, T 2 N, R 3 W) in 1934 and discontinued it in 1935—the name "Adahi" was coined from the names of vacation resort operators (Salley, p. 1).
Rimlon [RIVERSIDE]: *locality,* 4 miles north-northeast of Cathedral City along Southern Pacific Railroad (lat. 33°50'15" N, long. 116° 26'30" W; at E line sec. 10, T 4 S, R 5 E). Named on Cathedral City (1958) 7.5' quadrangle.
Rimrock [SAN BERNARDINO]: *locality,* 10.5 miles north of downtown Morongo Valley (lat. 34°11'50" N, long. 116°33' W; sec. 3, T 1 N, R 4 E). Named on Rimrock (1972) 7.5' quadrangle.
Rincon: see **Prado** [RIVERSIDE].
Rio Colorado: see **Colorado River** [SAN BERNARDINO].
Rio del Dulcissimo Nombre de Jesus del Temblores: see **Santa Ana River** [RIVERSIDE-SAN BERNARDINO].
Rio de los Payuches: see **Amargosa River** [SAN BERNARDINO].
Rio del Tizon: see **Colorado River** [SAN BERNARDINO].
Rio Grande de los Martyres: see **Colorado River**.
Rio San Bernardino: see **Santa Ana River** [RIVERSIDE-SAN BERNARDINO].
Rio Santa Anna: see **Santa Ana River** [RIVERSIDE-SAN BERNARDINO].
Rio Santa Margarita: see **Santa Margarita River** [RIVERSIDE].
Ripley [RIVERSIDE]: *village,* 7 miles south-southwest of Blythe (lat. 33°31'30" N, long. 114°39'20" W; sec. 34, 35, T 7 S, R 22 E). Named on Ripley (1952) 7.5' quadrangle. Postal authorities established Ripley post office in 1920, discontinued it in 1922, and reestablished it in 1923 (Frickstad, p. 130). The name commemorates E.P. Ripley, who was president of Atchison, Topeka and Santa Fe Railroad (Gunther, p. 427).
Ritchey Hot Springs: see **Soboka Hot Springs** [RIVERSIDE].
River Bend Lodge [RIVERSIDE]: *locality,* 18 miles north-northeast of Blythe (lat. 33°51'45" N, long. 114°31'40" W; near E line sec. 2, T 4 S, R 23 E); the place is along Colorado River. Named on Big Maria Mountains SE (1955) 7.5' quadrangle.
River Glen: see **Camp River Glen** [SAN BERNARDINO].
Riverside [RIVERSIDE]: *city,* near the northwest corner of Riverside County (lat. 33°58'55" N, long. 117°22'15" W); the city is along Santa Ana River. Named on Corona North (1967), Riverside East (1967), Riverside West (1967), and San Bernardino South (1967) 7.5' quadrangles. Postal authorities established Riverside post office in 1871 (Frickstad, p. 130), and the city incorporated in 1883. Louis Prevost started a community in 1869 called Jurupa for its location on Jurupa grant; John W. North of Southern California Colony Association acquired the property after Provost died (Gudde, 1949, p. 287), and stockholders of the association chose the name "Riverside" for the community at their first meeting in 1870 (Gunther, p. 427).
Riverside: see **East Riverside**, under **Highgrove** [RIVERSIDE]; **South Riverside**, under **Corona** [RIVERSIDE]; **West Riverside**, under **Rubidoux** [RIVERSIDE].
Riverside Heights: see **Highgrove** [RIVERSIDE].
Riverside Hot Sulphur Springs: see **Eden Hot Springs** [RIVERSIDE].
Riverside Junction [RIVERSIDE]: *locality,* less than 1 mile east-northeast of Riverside city hall where tracks of Southern Pacific Railroad and Union Pacific Railroad meet (lat. 33°59'10" N, long. 117°21'35" W). Named on Riverside East (1967) 7.5' quadrangle.
Riverside Mountain [RIVERSIDE]: *peak,* 7.25 miles south of Vidal [SAN BERNARDINO] (lat. 34°00'50" N, long. 114°30'45" W); the peak is in Riverside Mountains. Altitude 2127 feet. Named on Vidal (1971) 7.5' quadrangle. California Mining Bureau's (1917b) map shows a place called Haerle City located 5 miles south of Riverside Mountain on the west side of Colorado River.
Riverside Mountains [RIVERSIDE]: *range,* 30 miles north of Blythe near Colorado River. Named on Big Maria Mountains NE (1954), Big Maria Mountains NW (1971), Grommet (1971), Parker SW (1970), Poston (1955), and Vidal (1971) 7.5' quadrangles. Ives (p. 55) used the name in the 1850's.
Riverside Mountains: see **West Riverside Mountains** [RIVERSIDE-SAN BERNARDINO].
Riverside Pass [RIVERSIDE]: *pass,* 8.5 miles southwest of Vidal [SAN BERNARDINO] (lat. 34°01'20" N, long. 114°35'30" W); the pass is between Riverside Mountains and West Riverside Mountains. Named on Vidal (1971) 7.5' quadrangle.
Riverside Valley Home Gardens: see **Home Gardens** [RIVERSIDE].
Roads End Camp: see **Havasu Palms** [SAN BERNARDINO].
Robbers Mountain [SAN BERNARDINO]: *mountain,* 23 miles south-southeast of Trona (lat. 35°28' N, long. 117°12' W). Named on Pilot Knob (1954) 15' quadrangle.
Robidoux: see **Mount Robidoux**, under **Mount Rubidoux** [RIVERSIDE].
Rochester [SAN BERNARDINO]: *locality,* 6.25 miles east-northeast of Ontario city hall along Atchison, Topeka and Santa Fe Railroad (lat. 34°05'30" N, long 117°32'45" W; at N line sec. 18, T 1 S, R 6 W). Named on Guasti (1966) 7.5' quadrangle. Postal authorities established Rochester post office in 1890 and discontinued it in 1911 (Frickstad, p. 145).
Rochester: see **Stedman** [SAN BERNARDINO].
Rock: see **Camp Rock** [SAN BERNARDINO].
Rock Canyon [RIVERSIDE]: *canyon,* 2 miles long, 6 miles west of Palm Desert (lat. 33°42'45" N, long. 116°28'45" W). Named on Rancho Mirage (1957) 7.5' quadrangle.
Rock Canyon: see **Dry Wash** [RIVERSIDE] (1).
Rock Hill [IMPERIAL]: *hill,* 7.5 miles west-northwest of Calipatria (lat. 33°11' N, long. 115°37'20" W; sec. 28, T 11 S, R 13 E). Altitude 138 feet below sea level. Named on Niland (1956) 7.5' quadrangle, which shows a quarry at the place.
Rockhouse: see **Winchester** [RIVERSIDE].
Rockhouse Canyon [RIVERSIDE]:
(1) *canyon,* 4 miles long, 10 miles east-northeast of Indio (lat. 33° 46'15" N, long. 116°03'35" W; near NE cor. sec. 5, T 5 S, R 9 E). Named on Lost Horse Mountain (1958) 15' quadrangle.
(2) *canyon,* on Riverside-San Diego County line, 2.25 miles long in Riverside County, 20 miles south of Palm Desert (lat. 33°25'40" N, long. 116°22'40" W). Named on Collins Valley (1959) 7.5' quadrangle.
Rockhouse Canyon: see **Alder Canyon** [RIVERSIDE] (2).
Rock Pile [RIVERSIDE]: *peak,* 20 miles south of Idyllwild (lat. 33° 27'05" N, long. 116°44'30" W; sec. 26, T 8 S, R 2 E). Named on Beauty Mountain (1960) 7.5' quadrangle.
Rock Point [RIVERSIDE]: *peak,* 16 miles south-southeast of San Jacinto Peak (lat. 33°36' N, long. 116°35'20" W). Altitude 5302 feet. Named on San Jacinto (1901) 30' quadrangle.
Rock Spring [SAN BERNARDINO]: *spring,* 13 miles south of Ivanpah (lat. 35°09'15" N, long. 115°19'45" W; near NW cor. sec. 1, T 12 N, R 15 E). Named on Mid Hills (1955) 15' quadrangle. Ivanpah (1912) 1° quadrangle has the plural form "Rock Springs" for the name. The army had a small post called Camp Rock Springs at the place in the 1860's (Hart, p. 118-119). Postal authorities established Rock Springs post office in 1868 and discontinued it the same year (Salley, p. 187). A feature called Beatty Well was situated 0.25 mile west of Rock Springs (Thompson, 1921, p. 250).
Rock Springs [SAN BERNARDINO]: *springs,* 14 miles southeast of Victorville (lat. 34°23'45" N, long. 117°07'45" W; sec. 31, T 4 N, R 2 W). Named on Apple Valley South (1971) 7.5' quadrangle.
Rock Springs: see **Rock Spring** [SAN BERNARDINO].
Rockwood [IMPERIAL]: *locality,* 5.25 miles south of Calipatria along Southern Pacific Railroad (lat. 33°02'55" N, long. 115°30'45" W; sec. 3, T 13 S, R 14 E). Named on Westmorland (1956) 7.5' quadrangle. The name commemorates Charles R. Rockwood, who promoted irrigation in the neighborhood after 1892 (Gudde, 1949, p. 289). Postal authorities established Alberta post office at the place in 1910 and discontinued it in 1914—the post office name was the given name of the postmaster's wife (Salley, p. 4).
Rocky Point [SAN BERNARDINO]:
(1) *ridge,* south-trending, about 1 mile long, 11 miles north of Redlands (lat. 34°12'35" N, long. 117°13' W). Named on Redlands (1901) 15' quadrangle.
(2) *relief feature,* 6 miles south-southeast of Twnetynine Palms (lat. 34°03'15" N, long. 116°01'40" W; sec. 27, T 1 S, R 9 E). Named on Queen Mountain (1972) 7.5' quadrangle.
Rocky Ridge [RIVERSIDE]: *ridge,* north-northeast-trending, less than 1 mile long, 15 miles south of Hemet (lat. 33°31'45" N, long. 116°56'10" W; on S line sec. 25, T 7 S, R 1 W). Named on Sage (1954) 7.5' quadrangle.
Rodman Mountains [SAN BERNARDINO]: *range,* 10 miles south-southeast of Newberry (lat. 34°41'30" N, long. 116°38' W). Named on Rodman Mountains (1955) 15' quadrangle.
Rogers Canyon [RIVERSIDE]: *canyon,* 4 miles long, opens into Tule Valley 6 miles east-northeast of Aguanga (lat. 33°28' N, long. 116°45'45" W; sec. 22, T 8 S, R 2 E). Named on Aguanga (1954) and Beauty Mountain (1960) 7.5' quadrangles.
Rojo Grande: see **Picacho** [IMPERIAL].
Rome Hill [RIVERSIDE]: *hill,* 2.5 miles south of Lake Elsinore city hall at the southwest edge of Lake Elsinore (1) (lat. 33°37'55" N, long. 117°19'15" W). Named on Lake Elsinore (1953) 7.5' quadrangle.
Romoland [RIVERSIDE]: *town,* 4 miles southeast of Perris (lat. 33° 44'50" N, long. 117°10'35" W; mainly in sec. 10, T 5 S, R 3 W). Named on Perris (1967) 7.5' quadrangle, and on Romoland (1953) 7.5' quadrangle, which shows Ethanac Siding along Atchison, Topeka and Santa Fe Railroad at the place. Postal authorities established Romoland post office in 1925

(Salley, p. 188). The community began as a development called Romola Farms; Ethanac post office was across the highway from the place and eventually both the post office and town took the name "Romoland" (Gunther, p. 436).

Roosevelt: see **Camp Roosevelt** [RIVERSIDE].

Root Spring [RIVERSIDE]: *spring,* 10 miles east-southeast of Idyllwild (lat. 33°40'10" N, long. 116°34'10" W; on S line sec. 4, T 6 S, R 4 E). Named on Idyllwild (1959) 15' quadrangle.

Rosalie: see **Valley Wells** [SAN BERNARDINO].

Rosalie Wells: see **Valley Wells** [SAN BERNARDINO].

Rose Arbor: see **Edgemont** [RIVERSIDE].

Roseberry Spring [SAN BERNARDINO]: *spring,* 13 miles northwest of Ivanpah (lat. 35°28'10" N, long. 115°30'20" W). Named on Ivanpah (1912) 1° quadrangle.

Rosemine: see **Round Valley** [SAN BERNARDINO] (2).

Rosena: see **Fontana** [SAN BERNARDINO].

Ross Corner [IMPERIAL]: *locality,* 2 miles west-southwest of Bard (lat. 32°46'55" N, long. 114°35'20" W; sec. 7, T 16 S, R 23 E). Named on Bard (1965) 7.5' quadrangle. D.C. Rhodes, a field engineer for Automobile Club of Southern California, named the place in 1917 for W.C. Ross, who came in 1910 and had a garage and gasoline pump there (Hanna, p. 260).

Roubedeau: see **Mount Roubedeau**, under **Mount Rubidoux** [RIVERSIDE].

Round Cienaga Creek [SAN BERNARDINO]: *stream,* flows 4 miles to Santa Ana River 5 miles south-southwest of downtown Big Bear Lake (lat. 34°10'35" N, long. 116°56'30" W; near NW cor. sec. 13, T 1 N, R 1 W). Named on Big Bear Lake (1970) 7.5' quadrangle.

Round Meadow: see **Camp Round Meadow** [SAN BERNARDINO].

Round Mountain [SAN BERNARDINO]:

(1) *peak,* 1.5 miles northwest of Luna Mountain (lat. 34°21'40" N, long. 117°08'35" W; sec. 12, T 3 N, R 3 W). Altitude 5272 feet. Named on Lake Arrowhead (1971) 7.5' quadrangle.

(2) *peak,* 7 miles north-northeast of Big Bear City (lat. 34°20'45" N, long. 116°46'35" W; sec. 16, T 3 N, R 2 E). Named on Big Bear City (1971) 7.5' quadrangle.

Round Potrero [RIVERSIDE]: *area,* 2.25 miles east-northeast of Sitton Peak (lat. 33°36'10" N, long. 117°24'30" W; sec. 33, T 6 S, R 5 W). Named on Sitton Peak (1954) 7.5' quadrangle.

Roundtop [RIVERSIDE]: *peak,* 16 miles south-southeast of Hemet (lat. 33°31'25" N, long. 116°54'35" W; at W line sec. 32, T 7 S, R 1 E). Altitude 2585 feet. Named on Sage (1954) 7.5' quadrangle. Called Roundtop Hill on Hemet (1942) 15' quadrangle.

Roundtop Hill: see **Roundtop** [RIVERSIDE].

Round Valley [RIVERSIDE]: *area,* 1.25 miles southeast of San Jacinto Peak (lat. 33°48'15" N, long. 116°39'40" W; near S line sec. 22, T 4 S, R 3 E). Named on San Jacinto Peak (1981) 7.5' quadrangle.

Round Valley [SAN BERNARDINO]:

(1) *valley,* 14 miles south-southwest of Ivanpah (lat. 35°09' N, long. 115°23'30" W). Named on Mid Hills (1955) 15' quadrangle.

(2) *valley,* 15 miles north-northwest of downtown Morongo Valley (lat. 34°14'20" N, long. 116°42'15" W; near SE cor. sec. 19, T 2 N, R 3 E). Named on Onyx Peak (1972) 7.5' quadrangle, which shows Rose mine situated 0.5 mile north-northeast of the valley. Postal authorities established Rosemine post office in Round Valley (SE quarter sec. 20, T 2 N, R 3 E) in 1899 and discontinued it in 1900—the name was from the mine (Salley, p. 189).

Round Valley: see **Little Round Valley** [RIVERSIDE].

Rouse Hill [RIVERSIDE]: *ridge,* west-northwest-trending, 1.5 miles long, 12.5 miles east-southeast of Hemet (lat. 33°40'25" N, long. 116°46'35" W); the feature is near the northwest end of Horse Creek Ridge (present Rouse Ridge). Named on Hemet (1957) 15' quadrangle. The name is for Dezaret W. Rouse, who came to the vicinity in the early 1880's (Gunther, p. 437).

Rouse Meadow [SAN BERNARDINO]: *area,* 4.5 miles south of Luna Mountain (lat. 34°16'45" N, long. 117°08'05" W; at NW cor. sec. 7, T 2 N, R 2 W). Named on Lake Arrowhead (1971) 7.5' quadrangle.

Rouse Ridge: see **Horse Creek Ridge** [RIVERSIDE].

Rubidoux [RIVERSIDE]: *town,* 2 miles west-northwest of Riverside city hall (lat. 33°59'45" N, long. 117°24'15" W); the place is on Jurupa grant. Named on Fontana (1967) and Riverside West (1953) 7.5' quadrangles. Called West Riverside on Elsinore (1901) 30' quadrangle. Postal authorities established West Riverside post office in 1893 and discontinued it in 1901 (Frickstad, p. 131). They established Rubidoux post office in 1952; the misspelled name commemorates Louis Robidoux of Jurupa grant (Salley, p. 190).

Rubidoux Mountain: see **Mount Rubidoux** [RIVERSIDE].

Ruby Canyon [SAN BERNARDINO]: *canyon,* drained by a stream that flows nearly 4.5 miles to lowlands 8.5 miles southeast of Old Woman Springs (lat. 34°19'30" N, long. 116°35'10" W; at N line sec. 29, T 3 N, R 4 E). Named on Bighorn Canyon (1972) 7.5' quadrangle.

Ruby Lee Well [RIVERSIDE]: *well,* 14 miles north-northwest of Chiriaco Summit (lat. 33°50'20" N, long. 115°49'30" W). Named on Hexie Mountains (1963) 15' quadrangle.

Ruby Mountain [SAN BERNARDINO]: *peak,* 5 miles west of Landers (lat. 34°16'45" N, long. 116°28'40" W). Altitude 4357 feet. Named on Landers (1972) 7.5' quadrangle.

Ruddell Hill [SAN BERNARDINO]: *hill,* 3.5 miles northwest of Devore (lat. 34°14'30" N, long. 117°26'45" W; sec. 19, T 2 N, R 5 W). Named on Devore (1966) 7.5' quadrangle.

Rudolph: see **Mount Rudolph** [RIVERSIDE].

Running Springs [SAN BERNARDINO]: *village,* 3.5 miles west-northwest of Keller Peak (lat. 34°12'30" N, long. 117°06'30" W). Named on Keller Peak (1967) 7.5' quadrangle. Postal authorities established Running Springs post office in 1927 (Frickstad, p. 145).

Russell: see **Mount Russell** [RIVERSIDE].

Rustler Canyon [SAN BERNARDINO]: *canyon,* drained by a stream that flows 2 miles to Black Canyon Wash 21 miles south of Ivanpah (lat. 35°02'05" N, long. 115°22' W; near E line sec. 16, T 11 N, R 15 E). Named on Mid Hills (1955) 15' quadrangle.

Ruthven [IMPERIAL]: *locality,* 4.5 miles southeast of Glamis along Southern Pacific Railroad (lat. 32°57'10" N, long. 115°00'35" W). Named on Glamis (1955) 7.5' quadrangle.

Ryan Campground [RIVERSIDE]: *locality,* 19 miles north of Indio (lat. 33°59'05" N, long. 116°09'05" W; sec. 21, T 2 S, R 8 E); the place is 1 mile west of Ryan Mountain. Named on Lost Horse Mountain (1958) 15' quadrangle.

Ryan Mountain [RIVERSIDE]: *ridge,* north-trending, 2 miles long, 19 miles north-northeast of Indio (lat. 33°59'20" N, long. 116° 08' W; mainly in sec. 15, 22, T 2 S, R 8 E). Named on Lost Horse Mountain (1958) 15' quadrangle. On Pinyon Well (1943) 15' quadrangle, the highest peak on the ridge is called Lost Horse Mtn. United States Board on Geographic Names (1960a, p. 17) rejected the name "Lost Horse Mountain" for the whole ridge.

RZ Spring [SAN BERNARDINO]: *spring,* 14 miles north-northeast of Victorville (lat. 34°42'40" N, long. 117°11'10" W; sec. 10, T 7 N, R 3 W). Named on Turtle Valley (1970) 7.5' quadrangle.

- S -

Sablon [SAN BERNARDINO]: *locality,* 28 miles west of Vidal along Atchison, Topeka and Santa Fe Railroad (lat. 34°10'25" N, long. 114°59'30" W; sec. 16, T 1 N, R 19 E). Named on Rice (1954) 15' quadrangle. Railroad officials named the place Randolph in 1909, and changed the name to Sablon in 1912—*sablon* means "gravel" in Spanish (Gudde, 1949, p. 293).

Sacaton Flat [RIVERSIDE]: *area,* 10.5 miles southeast of Idyllwild (lat. 33°38'20" N, long. 116°35'10" W; near N line sec. 20, T 6 S, R 4 E). Named on Idyllwild (1959) 15' quadrangle.

Sacaton Spring [SAN BERNARDINO]: *springs,* 6.5 miles southwest of Ivanpah (lat. 35°16'25" N, long. 115°23'40" W; near NE cor. sec. 29, T 14 N, R 15 E). Named on Ivanpah (1956) 15' quadrangle. Called Cottonwood Spring on Ivanpah (1912) 1° quadrangle, but United States Board on Geographic Names (1960a, p. 17) rejected this name for the feature.

Sackett's Wells: see **Seeley** [IMPERIAL].

Sacramento Mountains [SAN BERNARDINO]: *range,* center 10 miles southwest of Needles (lat. 34°46' N, long. 114°44' W). Named on Bannock (1956), Needles (1950), and Sawtooth Range (1950) 15' quadrangles. Miners who came from the vicinity of Sacramento River in California named the range in 1863 (Hanna, p. 263).

Sacramento Springs [SAN BERNARDINO]: *springs,* 10 miles west-northwest of Needles (lat. 34°53'50" N, long. 114°46' W; near SE cor. sec. 3, T 9 N, R 21 E). Named on Bannock (1956) 15' quadrangle.

Sacramento Wash: see **Piute Wash** [SAN BERNARDINO].

Saddleback: see **Old Saddleback**, under **Santiago Peak** [RIVERSIDE].

Saddleback Mountain [SAN BERNARDINO]: *peak,* 20 miles south of the village of Red Mountain (lat. 35°03'35" N, long. 117°37'25" W; sec. 9, T 11 N, R 7 W). Altitude 3087 feet. Named on Saddleback Mountain (1973) 7.5' quadrangle.

Saddle Flats [SAN BERNARDINO]: *area,* 8 miles southwest of Luna Mountain (lat. 34°16'55" N, long. 117°14'45" W; near SE cor. sec. 1, T 2 N, R 4 W). Named on Lake Arrowhead (1971) 7.5' quadrangle.

Saddle Junction [RIVERSIDE]: *locality,* 3 miles south of San Jacinto Peak (lat. 33°46'25" N, long. 116°40'20" W; at S line sec. 33, T 4 S, R 3 E). Named on San Jacinto Peak (1981) 7.5' quadrangle.

Saddle Peak Hills [SAN BERNARDINO]: *range,* 35 miles north-northwest of Baker (lat. 35°43'30" N, long. 116°20'30" W). Named on Avawatz Pass (1948) and Shoshone (1951) 15' quadrangles.

Saddlerock Spring [SAN BERNARDINO]: *spring,* 13 miles south-southeast of Old Woman Springs (lat. 34°15'30" N, long. 118°33'10" W; sec. 15, T 2 N, R 4 E). Named on Old Woman Springs (1955) 15' quadrangle.

Sagamore Canyon [SAN BERNARDINO]: *canyon,* 1.5 miles long, 6.5 miles south-southeast of Ivanpah (lat. 35°15'15" N, long. 115° 16'15" W; sec. 32, 33, T 14 N, R 16 E). Named on Ivanpah (1956) 15' quadrangle, which shows Sagamore mine in the canyon.

Sage [RIVERSIDE]: *village,* 12 miles south of Hemet (lat. 33°34'55" N, long. 116°55'55" W; near E line sec. 12, T 7 S, R 1 W). Named on Sage (1954) 7.5' quadrangle. Postal authorities established Sage post office in 1891, discontinued it in 1898, reestablished it in 1925, and discontinued it in 1942 (Salley, p. 191). The place first was called San Ignacio (Gunther, p. 441).

Sagital: see **Lake Arrowhead** [SAN BERNARDINO] (2).

Saint Elmo [SAN BERNARDINO]: *locality,* 4 miles south of the present village of Red Mountain along Atchison, Topeka and Santa Fe Railroad (lat. 35°18' N, long. 117°36'30" W; near NW cor. sec. 29, T 30 S, R 41 E). Named on Randsburg (1911) 15' quadrangle. Red Mountain (1967) 7.5' quadrangle shows St. Elmo mine near the place.

Saint Johns Canyon [RIVERSIDE]: *canyon,* nearly 4 miles long, opens into lowlands 6 miles south of Hemet (lat. 33°40' N, long. 116°57'15" W; near N line sec. 11, T 6 S, R 1 W). Named on Hemet (1953) and Sage (1954) 7.5' quadrangles.

Saint Sophia Camp [SAN BERNARDINO]: *locality,* 7.25 miles north of San Bernardino city hall (lat. 34°12'40" N, long. 117°17' W; sec. 34, T 2 N, R 4 W). Named on San Bernardino North (1967) 7.5' quadrangle.

Salt Basin [SAN BERNARDINO]: *relief feature,* 31 miles northwest of Baker (lat. 35°37'15" N, long. 116°25' W). Named on Avawatz Mountains (1933) 1° quadrangle.

Salt Creek [RIVERSIDE]: *stream* and *dry wash,* extends for 25 miles to Salton Sea 2.5 miles southeast of Salton (lat. 33°26'50" N, long. 115°50'50" W; sec. 28, T 8 S, R 11 E). Named on Hayfield (1963) 15' quadrangle, and on Durmid (1956) and Frink NW (1956) 7.5' quadrangles. Called Salton Creek on Durmid (1943) 15' quadrangle, but United States Board on Geographic Names (1965a, p. 10) rejected this name for the feature.

Salt Creek [SAN BERNARDINO]: *stream,* flows 30 miles to Amargosa River 30 miles north-northwest of Baker (lat. 35°38'50" N, long. 116°18'35" W; sec. 14, T 18 N, R 6 E). Named on Avawatz Pass (1948), Baker (1956), and Silurian Hills (1956) 15' quadrangles. Mendenhall (1909a, p. 48) called the stream south branch Amargosa River; Waring and Huguenin (p. 31) called it South Amargosa.

Salt Creek Slough [IMPERIAL]: *stream,* flows 8.5 miles to New River 8 miles west-northwest of El Centro (lat. 32°50'35" N, long. 115°41'30" W; near SW cor. sec. 24, T 15 S, R 12 E). Named on Seeley (1957) 7.5' quadrangle.

Salt Hills: see **Salt Spring Hills** [SAN BERNARDINO].

Saltmarsh [SAN BERNARDINO]: *locality,* 37 miles south-southeast of Essex (lat. 34°13'15" N, long. 115°03' W; on E line sec. 35, T 2 N, R 18 E). Named on Iron Mountains (1956) 15' quadrangle. Officials of Atchison, Topeka and Santa Fe Railroad named the place in 1921 for S.M. Saltmarsh, car accountant for the railroad (Gudde, 1949, p. 296). Thompson's (1921) map shows a place called Ward at or near present Saltmarsh, and California Mining Bureau's (1917a) map shows a place called Desert Well situated 8 miles south-southwest of Ward.

Salton [RIVERSIDE]: *locality,* 3.5 miles southeast of Mortmar along Southern Pacific Railroad (lat. 33°28'25" N, long. 115°53'05" W; near SW cor. sec. 18, T 8 S, R 11 E); the place is near Salton Sea. Named on Salton (1956) 7.5' quadrangle. Postal authorities established Salton post office in 1889, discontinued it in 1891, reestablished it in 1894, and discontinued it in 1906 (Salley, p. 192). New Liverpool Salt Company began producing salt from the then-dry bed of Salton Sea in 1884, and shipped the product from a Southern Pacific Railroad station called Salton; when water of present Salton Sea flooded the salt works and rail line in 1906, railroad officials had the tracks relocated and transferred the station name to present Salton (Gunther, p. 445-449).

Salton Basin: see "Regional setting."

Salton Beach [RIVERSIDE]: *beach,* along Salton Sea at Salton (lat. 33°28'10" N, long. 115°53' W; sec. 18, 19, T 8 S, R 11 E). Named on Salton (1956) 7.5' quadrangle.

Salton Creek: see **Salt Creek** [RIVERSIDE].

Salton Sea [IMPERIAL-RIVERSIDE]: *lake,* 35 miles long, in the depression between Imperial Valley and Coachella Valley on Imperial-Riverside County line (center near lat. 33°20' N, long. 115°50' W). Named on Salton Sea (1959) and Santa Ana (1959) 1°x 2° quadrangles. Salton Sea holds water received from overflow of Colorado River; such floods occurred in historic time in 1842, 1852, 1859, 1862, 1867, and 1891, but the most notable overflow, the one that formed present Salton Sea, began in the winter of 1904 and 1905, when nearly all of the water in Colorado River entered Imperial Valley through irrigation works (MacDougal, p. 458, 463).

Salton Sea Beach [IMPERIAL]: *village,* 2.5 miles southeast of Desert Shores along Salton Sea (lat. 33°22'35" N, long. 116°00'35" W; sec. 23, T 9 S, R 9 E). Named on Oasis (1956) and Seventeen Palms (1956) 7.5' quadrangles.

Salton View [RIVERSIDE]: *locality,* 15 miles north of Indio (lat. 33° 55'40" N, long. 116°11'10" W; sec. 7, T 3 S, R 8 E); the place overlooks Salton Sea. Named on Lost Horse Mountain (1958) 15' quadrangle. United States Board on Geographic Names (1974b, p. 2) approved the name "Keys View" for the place, and gave the names "Inspiration Point" and "Salton View" as variants—the name "Keys" is for William F. Keys, who had a homestead near the site.

Salt Spring Hills [SAN BERNARDINO]: *range,* 28 miles north-northwest of Baker (lat. 35°38' N, long. 116°16' W). Named on Avawatz Pass (1948) 15' quadrangle. United States Board on Geographic Names (1965b, p. 15) rejected the name "Salt Hills" for the range.

Salt Springs [SAN BERNARDINO]: *spring,* 27 miles north-northwest of Baker (lat. 35°37'45" N, long. 116°16'45" W); the spring is along present Salt Creek. Named on Avawatz Mountains (1933) 1° quadrangle. Fremont camped at the place in 1844; the spring water contains a large amount of dissolved epsom salt and glauber salt (Waring, p. 302-303).

Saltus [SAN BERNARDINO]: *locality,* 3.5 miles east-southeast of Amboy along Atchison, Topeka and Santa Fe Railroad (lat. 34°32'25" N, long. 115°41'15" W; near NE cor. sec. 11, T 5 N, R 12 E). Named on Cadiz (1956) 15' quadrangle. Officials of Crystal Salt Company had a mill built at the place in 1910 to process salt from Bristol Lake (Myrick, p. 840).

Salt Wells [SAN BERNARDINO]: *locality,* 10 miles southwest of Trona (lat. 35°38'45" N, long. 117°29'15" W). Named on Searles Lake (1915) 1° quadrangle. On Searles Lake (1949) 15' quadrangle, the name applies to a place located nearly 1 mile farther east-northeast at The Y. A stage station was at the first site in the early days (Thompson, 1929, p. 180).

Salt Wells Canyon: see **Poison Canyon** [SAN BERNARDINO].

Salt Wells Valley [SAN BERNARDINO]: *valley,* 11 miles southwest of Trona (lat. 35°39'30" N, long. 117°30' W); Salt Wells is near the east end of the valley. Named on Lone Butte (1973) and Westend (1973) 7.5' quadrangles.

Salt Wells Valley: see **Indian Wells Valley** [SAN BERNARDINO].

Salvation: see **Camp Salvation**, under **Calexico** [IMPERIAL].

Salvation Pass [IMPERIAL]: *canyon,* 3 miles long, opens into lowlands 15 miles northeast of Calipatria (lat. 33°14'15" N, long. 115° 18' W). Named on Iris Pass (1963) 15' quadrangle, and on Tortuga (1955) 7.5' quadrangle.

Salvation Spring [IMPERIAL]: *spring,* 18 miles east-northeast of Calipatria (lat. 33°15'10" N, long. 115°15'15" W); the spring is east of Salvation Pass. Named on Iris Pass (1945) 15' quadrangle.

Salvia [RIVERSIDE]: *locality,* 3.5 miles northeast of Palm Springs along Southern Pacific Railroad (lat. 33°52'35" N, long. 116°30'30" W; on W line sec. 30, T 3 S, R 5 E). Named on Cathedral City (1958), Desert Hot Springs (1955), and Palm Springs (1957) 7.5' quadrangles.

Salvia Wash, West Branch [RIVERSIDE]: *dry wash,* 2 miles long, 4.25 miles north-northeast of Palm Springs (lat. 33°53'15" N, long. 116°30'15" W; sec. 19, 30, T 3 S, R 5 E); the feature ends just east of Salvia. Named on Palm Springs (1957) 7.5' quadrangle, which fails to show a Salvia Wash.

Samuelsons Rock [SAN BERNARDINO]: *relief feature,* 11 miles west of Twentynine Palms (lat. 34°02'50" N, long. 116°14'30" W; near N line sec. 34, T 1 S, R 7 E). Named on Indian Cove (1972) 7.5' quadrangle.

San Anselmo: see **Kane Spring** [IMPERIAL].

San Antonia Peak: see **Mount San Antonio** [SAN BERNARDINO].

San Antonio: see **Camp San Antonio** [SAN BERNARDINO]; **Mount San Antonio** [SAN BERNARDINO]; **San Antonio Heights** [SAN BERNARDINO].

San Antonio Bucareli: see **Lake San Antonio Bucareli**, under **Mystic Lake** [RIVERSIDE].

San Antonio Canyon [SAN BERNARDINO]: *canyon,* drained by a stream that flows 4 miles to Los Angeles County 12 miles north of Ontario city hall (lat. 34°14' N, long. 117°39'35" W; near NW cor. sec. 30, T 2 N, R 7 W). Named on Mount Baldy (1967) 7.5' quadrangle.

San Antonio Creek Channel: see **San Antonio Wash** [SAN BERNARDINO].

San Antonio Falls [SAN BERNARDINO]: *waterfall,* 1.5 miles south-southeast of Mount San Antonio (lat. 34°16'20" N, long. 117° 38' W; sec. 8, T 2 N, R 7 W); the feature is in San Antonio Canyon. Named on Mount San Antonio (1955) 7.5' quadrangle.

San Antonio Heights [SAN BERNARDINO]: *district,* 6.5 miles north of Ontario city hall (lat. 34°09'15" N, long. 117°39'30" W). Named on Mount Baldy (1967) 7.5' quadrangle. Called San Antonio on Cucamonga (1903) 15' quadrangle. Postal authorities established San Antonio post office in 1891 and discontinued it in 1905 (Frickstad, p. 145). Cucamonga (1944) 15' quadrangle has the name "Monta Vista Resort" at the site.

San Antonio Peak: see **Mount San Antonio** [SAN BERNARDINO].

San Antonio Wash [SAN BERNARDINO]: *stream* and *dry wash,* extends for 9 miles from the mouth of San Antonio Canyon along and near San Bernardino-Los Angeles County line to Chino Creek 5.5 miles southwest of Ontario city hall (lat. 34°00'50" N, long. 117°43'45" W). Named on Mount Baldy (1954) and Ontario (1954) 7.5' quadrangles. Called San Antonio Creek Channel on Mount Baldy (1967) and Ontario (1967) 7.5' quadrangles.

San Bernardino [SAN BERNARDINO]:

(1) *land grant,* at the city of San Bernardino. Named on Harrison Mountain (1967), Redlands (1967), San Bernardino North (1967), San Bernardino South (1967), and Yucaipa (1967) 7.5' quadrangles. Jose del Carmen Lugo

received 8 leagues in 1842 and claimed 35,509 acres patented in 1865 (Cowan, p. 73). The name is from a temporary chapel that Padre Francisco Dumetz used to celebrated Mass in 1810 on the feast day of Saint Bernardine of Siena (Hoover, Rensch, and Rensch, p. 320).

(2) *city,* near the southwest corner of San Bernardino County (city hall near lat. 34°06'15" N, long. 117°17'20" W); the city is largely on San Bernardino grant. Named on Harrison Mountain (1967), San Bernardino North (1967), and San Bernardino South (1967) 7.5' quadrangles. Postal authorities established San Bernardino post office in 1852 (Frickstad, p. 145), and the city incorporated in 1869. A colony of Mormons from Salt Lake City started the community in 1851 (Hoover, Rensch, and Rensch, p. 322). Postal authorities established Danaher post office 30 miles east of San Bernardino in 1892 and discontinued it in 1893; the name was for D.C. Danaher, a lumberman (Salley, p. 55).

San Bernardino East Peak [SAN BERNARDINO]: *peak,* 5 miles west-northwest of San Gorgonio Mountain (lat. 34°07'30" N, long. 116°54'30" W; at W line sec. 32, T 1 N, R 1 E); the peak is on San Bernardino Mountain. Altitude 10,691 feet. Named on Big Bear Lake (1970) and Forest Falls (1970) 7.5' quadrangles.

San Bernardino Mountain [SAN BERNARDINO]: *ridge,* west-trending, 4.5 miles long, 8 miles south of downtown Big Bear Lake (lat. 34°07'30" N, long. 116°53'45" W). Named on Big Bear Lake (1970), Forest Falls (1970), and Moonridge (1970) 7.5' quadrangles.

San Bernardino Mountains [SAN BERNARDINO]: *range,* extends eastward from Cajon Pass to Morongo Valley (1). Named on San Bernardino (1966) and Santa Ana (1959) 1°x 2° quadrangles.

San Bernardino Mountains: see **Little San Bernardino Mountains** [RIVERSIDE-SAN BERNARDINO]; **San Gabriel Mountains** [SAN BERNARDINO].

San Bernardino Pass: see **San Gorgonio Pass** [RIVERSIDE].

San Bernardino Peak [SAN BERNARDINO]: *peak,* 5.5 miles west-northwest of San Gorgonio Mountain (lat. 34°07'20" N, long. 116° 55'15" W); the peak is on San Bernardino Mountain. Altitude 10,649 feet. Named on Forest Falls (1970) 7.5' quadrangle. Colonel Henry Washington established the initial point for the land office survey of southern California at the peak in 1852 (Beattie and Beattie, p. 205).

San Bernardino Range: see **San Gabriel Mountains** [SAN BERNARDINO].

San Bernardino Wash [RIVERSIDE]: *stream,* flows 7.25 miles to Pinto Wash 22 miles northwest of Desert Center (lat. 33°57'45" N, long. 115°39'10" W; sec. 30, T 2 S, R 13 E). Named on Dale Lake (1956) and Pinto Basin (1963) 15' quadrangles.

Sand Canyon [SAN BERNARDINO]:

(1) *canyon,* 2 miles long, 2.5 miles northwest of Sugarloaf Mountain (lat. 34°13'30" N, long. 116°50'20" W). Named on Moonridge (1970) 7.5' quadrangle.

(2) *canyon,* drained by a stream that flows 3.25 miles to lowlands 4 miles east-southeast of Harrison Mountain (lat. 34°09'05" N, long. 117°13'35" W; near SE cor. sec. 19, T 1 N, R 3 W). Named on Harrison Mountain (1967) 7.5' quadrangle.

(3) *canyon,* 3 miles long, opens into Searles Valley 8 miles east-southeast of Trona (lat. 35°43'40" N, long. 117°14' W). Named on Wingate Pass (1950) 15' quadrangle.

(4) *canyon,* 1.5 miles long, opens into lowlands 4.5 miles west-northwest of Yucaipa (lat. 34°02'55" N, long. 117°07'05" W). Named on Yucaipa (1967) 7.5' quadrangle.

Sand Canyon: see **Little Sand Canyon** [SAN BERNARDINO].

Sand Creek [SAN BERNARDINO]:

(1) *stream,* flows 0.5 mile to Santa Ana River 5 miles south-southwest of downtown Big Bear Lake (lat. 34°10'35" N, long. 116°56'25" W; near NW cor. sec. 13, T 1 N, R 1 W). Named on Big Bear Lake (1970) 7.5' quadrangle.

(2) *stream,* flows 2 miles from the mouth of Sand Canyon (2) to Warm Creek nearly 5 miles north-northwest of Redlands city hall (lat. 34°07'20" N, long. 117°13'45" W). Named on Harrison Mountain (1967) 7.5' quadrangle.

Sand Creek: see **Little Sand Creek**, under **Little Sand Canyon** [SAN BERNARDINO].

Sand Draw [RIVERSIDE]: *gully,* 4 miles long, 30 miles northeast of Desert Center (lat. 34°00' N, long. 115°00'30" W). Named on Iron Mountains (1956) and Palen Mountains (1952) 15' quadrangles.

Sand Dunes: see **Sand Hills** [IMPERIAL].

Sand Hill [SAN BERNARDINO]: *relief feature,* 1 mile west of Ludlow (lat. 34°43'20" N, long. 116°10'40" W; near W line sec. 6, T 7 N, R 8 E). Named on Ludlow (1955) 7.5' quadrangle.

Sand Hills [IMPERIAL]: *relief feature,* extends for 40 miles southeast from a spot 11 miles east of Calipatria to the Mexican border 35 miles east of Calexico. Named on El Centro (1958) and Salton Sea (1959) 1°x 2° quadrangles. United States Board on Geographic Names (1988b, p. 1) approved the name "Algodones Dunes" for the feature, and rejected the names "Sand Hills," "Glamis Dunes," "Imperial Dunes," "Imperial Sand Dunes," "Sand Dunes," and "Sonorian Dunes."

Sandia [IMPERIAL]: *locality,* 5.25 miles north-northwest of Holtville along Southern Pacific Railroad (lat. 32°53'05" N, long. 115° 24'20" W; near S line sec. 34, T 14 S, R 15 E). Named on Alamorio (1956) 7.5' quadrangle.

Sandia Canyon [RIVERSIDE]: *canyon,* drained by a stream that flows 5.5 miles to San Diego County 7 miles west-southwest of Temecula (lat. 33°27'05" N, long. 117°15" W). Named on Fallbrook (1968), Murrieta (1953), and Temecula (1968) 7.5' quadrangles. The feature first was called Bear Canyon (Gunther, p. 456).

San Dimas Well: see **Hopkins Well** [RIVERSIDE].

Sands [SAN BERNARDINO]: *locality,* 42 miles southwest of Ivanpah along Union Pacific Railroad (lat. 35°01' N, long. 115°56'30" W, on S line sec. 20, T 11 N, R 10 E). Named on Old Dad Mountain (1956) 15' quadrangle.

Sandy Beach [IMPERIAL]: *beach,* 5.5 miles north of Kane Spring along Salton Sea (lat. 33°11'20" N, long. 115°49'50" W; sec. 28, T 11 S, R 11 E). Named on Kane Spring (1940) 15' quadrangle.

Sandy Korner [RIVERSIDE]: *locality,* nearly 6 miles south-southeast of Indio (lat. 33°38'30" N, long. 116°10'50" W; at NW cor. sec. 20, T 6 S, R 8 E). Named on Indio (1956) 7.5' quadrangle.

San Felipe Creek [IMPERIAL]: *stream* and *dry wash,* heads in San Diego County and extends for 21 miles in Imperial County to Salton Sea 4 miles north of Kane Spring (lat. 33°10'10" N, long. 115°49'15" W; at E line sec. 33, T 11 S, R 11 E). Named on Borrego Mountain SE (1958), Harpers Well (1956), Kane Spring (1956), Kane Spring NE (1956), and Shell Reef (1959) 7.5' quadrangles.

San Felipe Wash [IMPERIAL]: *stream* and *marsh,* diverges from San Felipe Creek and extends for 5 miles to Salton Sea 4 miles northeast of Kane Spring (lat. 33°08'40" N, long. 115°46'40" W; sec. 12, T 12 S, R 11 E). Named on Kane Spring (1956) and Kane Spring NE (1956) 7.5' quadrangles.

Sandford's Pass: see **Cajon Pass** [SAN BERNARDINO].

San Gabriel Mountains [SAN BERNARDINO]: *range,* mainly in Los Angeles County, but extends east into San Bernardino County from Mount San Antonio to Cajon Pass. Named on San Bernardino (1966) 1°x 2° quadrangle. Goddard's (1857) map shows present San Gabriel Mountains as part of a much larger feature called San Bernardino Range. United States Board on Geographic Names (1933, p. 666) rejected the names "San Bernardino Mountains," "Sierra Madre," and "Sierra San Gabriel" for the feature.

San Gargonia: see **Beaumont** [RIVERSIDE].

San Gorgonia: see **Beaumont** [RIVERSIDE].

San Gorgonio Campground [SAN BERNARDINO]: *locality,* 3.5 miles west-southwest of Sugarloaf Mountain (lat. 34°10'30" N; long. 116°52' W; sec. 15, T 1 N, R 1 E). Named on Moonridge (1970) 7.5' quadrangle.

San Gorgonio Creek: see **Little San Gorgonio Creek** [RIVERSIDE-SAN BERNARDINO].

San Gorgonio Mountain [SAN BERNARDINO]: *peak,* 27 miles east of San Bernardino (lat. 34°05'55" N, long. 116°49'25" W; near W line sec. 7, T 1 S, R 2 E). Altitude 11,499 feet. Named on San Gorgonio Mountain (1970) 7.5' quadrangle. The feature has the local names "Grayback Peak" and "Old Grayback" (Hanna, p. 275).

San Gorgonio Pass [RIVERSIDE]: *valley,* extends for 20 miles from near Whitewater River to Beaumont, and separates San Bernardino Mountains on the north from San Jacinto Mountains on the south; San Gorgonio River passes through the east part of the feature. Named on Beaumont (1953), Cabazon (1956), Desert Hot Springs (1955), and Whitewater (1955) 7.5' quadrangles. Lieutenant Parke and William Blake made the first American exploration of the pass in 1853 (Darton, p. 265). Blake (p. 89) used the name "San Gorgoño Pass," but preferred the name "San Bernardino Pass" for the feature "because the pass is at the base of San Bernardino mountain, and leads into the valley of San Bernardino." Marlette (p. 296) called the feature San Gorgona Pass.

San Gorgonio Peak: see **Little San Gorgonio Peak** [SAN BERNARDINO].

San Gorgonio River [RIVERSIDE-SAN BERNARDINO]: *stream* and *dry wash,* heads in San Bernardino County and extends for 27 miles to Whitewater River 5.5 miles northwest of Palm Springs in Riverside County (lat. 33°54' N, long. 116°37'15" W). Named on Beaumont (1953), Cabazon (1956), Forest Falls (1970), San Gorgonio Mountain (1970), and Whitewater (1955) 7.5' quadrangles.

San Ignacio: see **Sage** [RIVERSIDE].

San Jacinto [RIVERSIDE]: *town,* 2.5 miles north of Hemet (lat. 33° 47' N, long. 116°57'30" W); the town is on San Jacinto Viejo grant. Named on San Jacinto (1953) 7.5' quadrangle. Postal authorities established San Jacinto post office in 1870 and moved it 1 mile northeast in 1885 (Salley, p. 195). The town incorporated in 1888. San Jacinto (1901) 30' quadrangle shows a place called Bowers situated about 0.5 mile southeast of the present center of San Jacinto. A small community called San Jacinto was well established on San Jacinto Viejo grant by 1869, and San Jacinto post office was located in the first store there, but the place declined; San Jacinto Land Association purchased property in 1883 and laid out a new townsite, also called San Jacinto, 1 mile north of the original community of that name; San Jacinto post office went to the new community and the first place became known as Old Town, South San Jacinto, Hewitt Town, and finally Bowers (Gunther, p. 462). Postal authorities established Bowers post office 1 mile southeast of San Jacinto post office in 1892 and discontinued it in 1900 (Salley, p. 25). After San Jacinto post office went to the new site, the residents of the old place applied to their congressman, William W. Bowers, for help in obtaining a new post office; when he succeeded, his constituents asked that the post office be named for him (Gunther, p. 62-63).

San Jacinto Canyon: see **Railroad Canyon** [RIVERSIDE] (1).

San Jacinto Hot Springs: see **Gilman Hot Springs** [RIVERSIDE].

San Jacinto Lake: see **Mystic Lake** [RIVERSIDE].

San Jacinto Mountains [RIVERSIDE]: *range,* south of San Gorgonio Pass between San Jacinto Valley and Coachella Valley. Named on Santa Ana (1959) 1°x 2° quadrangle. Called San Ygnacio Mt. on Ord's (1849) map.

San Jacinto Nuevo y Potrero [RIVERSIDE]: *land grant,* around Lakeview. Named on Beaumont (1953), El Casco (1967), Lakeview (1967), Perris (1967), San Jacinto (1953), and Sunnymead (1967) 7.5' quadrangles. Miguel Pedrorena received the land in 1846 and his heirs claimed 48,861 acres patented in 1883 (Cowan, p. 79).

San Jacinto Peak [RIVERSIDE]: *peak,* 7.5 miles west-southwest of Palm Springs (lat. 33°48'55" N, long. 116°40'45" W; near N line sec. 21, T 4 S, R 3 E); the peak is in San Jacinto Mountains. Altitude 10,804 feet. Named on San Jacinto Peak (1981) 7.5' quadrangle. The feature mistakenly was called San Gorgonio in the early days (Robinson and Risher, p. 41). United States Board on Geographic Names (1989a, p. 4) approved the name "Newton Drury Peak" for a feature, elevation 10,160 feet, located 0.6 mile southwest of San Jacinto Peak (lat. 33°48'30" N, long. 116°41'08" W; sec. 20, T 4 S, R 3 E); the name commemorates Newton Bishop Drury, who was instrumental in establishment of Mount San Jacinto state park.

San Jacinto Reservoir [RIVERSIDE]: *lake,* 3200 feet long, 2.5 miles west-northwest of San Jacinto (lat. 33°47'55" N, long. 116°59'45" W). Named on Lakeview (1967) and San Jacinto (1953) 7.5' quadrangles.

San Jacinto River [RIVERSIDE]: *stream* and *dry wash,* formed by the confluence of North Fork and South Fork, extends for 43 miles to Lake Elsinore (1) 1.5 miles south of Lake Elsinore city hall (lat. 33°38'40" N, long. 117°19'35" W). Named on Hemet (1957) 15' quadrangle, and on Lake Elsinore (1953), Lake Fulmor (1956), Lakeview (1967), Perris (1967), Romoland (1953), and San Jacinto (1953) 7.5' quadrangles. North Fork is 10 miles long and is named on Hemet (1957) 15' quadrangle, and on Lake Fulmor (1956) and San Jacinto Peak (1981) 7.5' quadrangles. South Fork is 13 miles long and is named on Hemet (1957) and Idyllwild (1959) 15' quadrangles. United States Board on Geographic Names (1983b, p. 2) rejected the name "San Jacinto River" for South Fork.

San Jacinto Valley [RIVERSIDE]: *valley,* extends for 20 miles northwest from the neighborhood of Hemet. Named on El Casco (1967), Hemet (1953), Lakeview (1967), San Jacinto (1953), Sunnymead (1967), and Winchester (1953) 7.5' quadrangles.

San Jacinto Viejo [RIVERSIDE]: *land grant,* at San Jacinto and Hemet. Named on Hemet (1953), Lake Fulmor (1956), Lakeview (1967), San Jacinto (1953), and Winchester (1953) 7.5' quadrangles. Jose Antonio Estudillo received 4 leagues in 1842 and his heirs claimed 35,503 acres patented in 1880 (Cowan, p. 79).

San Juan Campground: see **Upper San Juan Campground** [RIVERSIDE].

San Juan Canyon [RIVERSIDE]: *canyon,* mainly in Orange County, but extends east into Riverside County 1.25 miles north-northwest of Sitton Peak (lat. 33°36'10" N, long. 117°27'25" W; sec. 36, T 6 S, R 6 W). Named on Sitton Peak (1954) 7.5' quadrangle.

San Juan Hill [SAN BERNARDINO]: *peak,* 29 miles west-southwest of San Bernardino on San Bernardino-Orange County line (lat. 33° 54'50" N, long. 117°44'15" W; sec. 17, T 3 S, R 8 W). Altitude 1781 feet. Named on Prado Dam (1967) 7.5' quadrangle.

San Mateo Canyon [RIVERSIDE]: *canyon,* drained by a stream that flows 9.5 miles to San Diego County 5.5 miles south of Sitton Peak (lat. 33°30'20" N, long. 117°26'50" W; sec. 6, T 8 S, R 5 W). Named on Sitton Peak (1954) 7.5' quadrangle.

San Salvadore: see **Colton** [SAN BERNARDINO].

San Sebastian Marsh: see **Harpers Well** [IMPERIAL].

San Sevaine [SAN BERNARDINO]: *locality,* 3 miles southwest of present Fontana city hall along Southern Pacific Railroad (lat. 34° 03'50" N, long. 117°28' W). Named on San Bernardino (1901) 15' quadrangle.

San Sevaine Canyon [SAN BERNARDINO]: *canyon,* drained by a stream that flows 2.5 miles to lowlands 6 miles southwest of Devore (lat. 34°10' N, long. 117°29'15" W; near SW cor. sec. 14, T 1 N, R 6 W). Named on Devore (1966) 7.5' quadrangle.

San Sevaine Cow Camp [SAN BERNARDINO]: *locality,* 5 miles west-southwest of Devore (lat. 34°12'10" N, long. 117°29'15" W; at E line sec. 3, T 1 N, R 6 W); the place is near the head of a branch of San Sevaine Canyon. Named on Devore (1966) 7.5' quadrangle.

San Sevaine Flats [SAN BERNARDINO]: *area,* 13 miles northeast of Ontario city hall (lat. 34°12'50" N, long. 117°30'30" W; at E line sec. 33, T 2 N, R 6 W). Named on Cucamonga Peak (1966) 7.5' quadrangle. Michael Sainsevain bought the place in 1878 (Robinson, J.W., 1983, p. 188).

San Sevaine Well [SAN BERNARDINO]: *well,* 13 miles northeast of Ontario city hall (lat. 34°12'45" N, long. 117°30'25" W; at E line sec. 33, T 2 N, R 6 W); the well is at San Sevaine Flats. Named on Cucamonga Peak (1966) 7.5' quadrangle.

Santa Ana del Chino [SAN BERNARDINO]: *land grant,* around Chino on San Bernardino-Los Angeles County line. Named on Corona North (1967), Guasti (1966), Ontario (1967), Prado Dam (1967), San Dimas (1966), and Yorba Linda (1964) 7.5' quadrangles. Antonio Maria Lugo and Isaac Williams received the land in 1841 and 1845; M.M. Williams and others claimed 22,234 acres and an additional 13,366 acres, all patented in 1869 (Cowan, p. 90).

Santa Ana Mountains [RIVERSIDE]: *range,* southwest of Temescal Wash between Santa Ana River and Lake Elsinore (1) on Riverside-Orange County line. Named on Alberhill (1954), Black Star Canyon (1967), Corona South (1967), and Santiago Peak (1954) 7.5' quadrangles.

Santa Ana River [RIVERSIDE-SAN BERNARDINO]: *stream* and *dry wash,* formed by the confluence of Coon Creek and Heart Bar Creek in San Bernardino County, extends for 65 miles to Riverside-Orange County line 6 miles west of Corona (lat. 33°52'15" N, long. 117°40'15" W). Named on San Bernardino (1958) and Santa Ana (1959) 1°x 2° quadrangles. Called Rio S. Bernardino on Gibbes' (1852) map, called Rio Santa Anna on Williamson's (1853) map, called R. Sta. Anna on Eddy's (1854) map, called Rio de Sta. Ana on Parke's (1854-1855) map, and called Santa Anna R. on Goddard's (1857) map. On Redlands (1967) and Yucaipa (1967) 7.5' quadrangles, the name "Santa Ana Wash" applies to the broad course of the feature from its emergence from San Bernardino Mountains westward to Norton Air Force Base. Crespi named the stream *Rio del Dulcissimo Nombre de Jesus del Temblores*—which means "River of the Sweetest Name of Jesus of the Earthquakes" in Spanish—when members of the Portola expedition felt a severe earthquake while they were along the stream in 1769; soldiers of the expedition called the river Rio Santa Ana because it seemed to come from Santa Ana Mountains (Meadows, p. 119, 124). South Fork enters from the south 2 miles south-southwest of Sugarloaf Mountain; it is 4 miles long and is named on Moonridge (1970) 7.5' quadrangle.

Santa Ana Wash: see **Santa Ana River** [SAN BERNARDINO].

Santa Gertrudis Creek [RIVERSIDE]: *stream* and *dry wash,* extends for 10.5 miles to Murrieta Creek 3.25 miles southeast of Murrieta (lat. 33°31'05" N, long. 117°10'25" W). Named on Bachelor Mountain (1953) and Murrieta (1953) 7.5' quadrangles.

Santa Margarita Creek: see **Santa Margarita River** [RIVERSIDE].

Santa Margarita River [RIVERSIDE]: *stream,* formed by the confluence of Murrieta Creek and Temecula Creek, flows 5 miles through Temecula Canyon to San Diego County 5 miles south-southwest of Temecula (lat. 33°25'55" N, long. 117°11'45" W). Named on Temecula (1968) 7.5' quadrangle. Called Temecula River on Temecula (1942) 15' quadrangle. United States Board on Geographic Names (1943, p. 13) rejected the names "Rio Santa Margarita" and "Santa Margarita Creek" for the stream, and rejected the names "Temecula River" and "Temecula Creek" for parts of it. Members of the Portola expedition named the feature in 1769 when they camped by it on the day of Saint Margaret of Antioch (Gudde, 1949, p. 316).

Santa Rosa [RIVERSIDE]: *land grant,* southwest of Temecula Valley. Named on Fallbrook (1968), Murrieta (1953), Temecula (1968), and Wildomar (1953) 7.5' quadrangles. Juan Moreno received 3 leagues in 1846 and claimed 47,815 acres patented in 1872 (Cowan, p. 94).

Santa Rosa: see **Old Santa Rosa**, under **Cottonwood Spring** [RIVERSIDE] (2); **Santa Rosa Mountain** [RIVERSIDE].

Santa Rosa Hills [RIVERSIDE]: *ridge,* west- to northwest-trending, 4.25 miles long, center 4 miles southeast of downtown Hemet (lat. 33°42'15" N, long. 116°55'45" W). Named on Hemet (1953) 7.5' quadrangle.

Santa Rosa Mountain [RIVERSIDE]: *peak,* 14 miles south-southwest of Palm Desert (lat. 33°32'15" N, long. 116°27'40" W; sec. 27, T 7 S, R 5 E); the peak is in Santa Rosa Mountains. Named on Palm Desert (1959) 15' quadrangle. United States Geological Survey's (1904) map shows a place called Santa Rosa situated 1 mile south-southeast of Santa Rosa Mountain (sec. 34, T 7 S, R 5 E); Palm Desert (1959) 15' quadrangle shows the site of an Indian village at the same place.

Santa Rosa Mountains [IMPERIAL-RIVERSIDE]. *range,* southwest of Coachella Valley and Salton Sea on Riverside-San Diego County line; a spur of the range extends northeast into Imperial County southwest of Desert Shores. Named on Santa Ana (1959) 1°x 2° quadrangle.

Santa Rosa Spring [RIVERSIDE]: *spring,* 13 miles south-southwest of Palm Desert (lat. 33°32'30" N, long. 116°28' W; near NE cor. sec. 28, T 7 S, R 5 E); the spring is 1700 feet northwest of Santa Rosa Mountain. Named on Palm Desert (1959) 15' quadrangle.

Santa Rosa Summit [RIVERSIDE]: *pass,* 15 miles southeast of Idyllwild (lat. 33°33'45" N, long. 116°34' W; on E line sec. 16, T 7 S, R 4 E). Named on Idyllwild (1959) 15' quadrangle.

Santiago Peak [RIVERSIDE]: *peak,* 12 miles south of Corona on Riverside-Orange County line (lat. 33°42'40" N, long. 117°32' W). Altitude 5687 feet. Named on Santiago Peak (1954) 7.5' quadrangle, which has the alternate name "Old Saddleback" for the peak. United States Board on Geographic Names (1961c, p. 15) rejected the names "Old Saddleback," "Temescal Peak," and "Trabuco Peak" for the feature.

San Timoteo: see **Jurupa** [RIVERSIDE].

San Timoteo Canyon [RIVERSIDE-SAN BERNARDINO]: *canyon,* heads in Riverside County and extends for 12 miles to lowlands 2 miles southwest of Redlands city hall in San Bernardino County (lat. 34°02' N, long. 117°12'30" W; near NW cor. sec. 4, T 2 S, R 3 W). Named on El Casco (1967), Redlands (1967), and Sunnymead (1967) 7.5' quadrangles.

San Timoteo Wash [SAN BERNARDINO]: *stream,* flows 5.25 miles from the mouth of San Temoteo Canyon to Santa Ana River 2.5 miles south-southeast of San Bernardino city hall (lat. 34°04'10" N, long. 117°16'45" W). Named on the Redlands (1967) and San Bernardino South (1967) 7.5' quadrangles.

San Y-Ca Spring [SAN BERNARDINO]: *spring,* 4.5 miles southwest of Sugarloaf Mountain (lat. 34°09' N, long. 116°52'10" W; near S line sec. 22, T 1 N, R 1 E). Named on Moonridge (1970) 7.5' quadrangle.

San Ygnacio Mountain: see **San Jacinto Mountains** [RIVERSIDE].

Saragossa Spring [SAN BERNARDINO]: *spring,* 2.5 miles north of Big Bear City (lat. 34°17'55" N, long. 116°51'15" W; near W line sec. 35, T 3 N, R 1 E). Named on Lucerne Valley (1947) 15' quadrangle.

Saratoga Spring [SAN BERNARDINO]: *spring,* 35 miles northwest of Baker on the northeast side of Death Valley (lat. 35°40'55" N, long. 116°25'15" W; near W line sec. 2, T 18 N, R 5 E). Named on Avawatz Pass (1948) 15' quadrangle.

Satellite Lake [SAN BERNARDINO]: *dry lake,* 17 miles southwest of Trona on San Bernardino-Kern County line (lat. 35°37'40" N, long. 117°38'05" W; on E line sec. 35, T 26 N, R 40 E). Named on Ridgecrest North (1973) 7.5' quadrangle.

Saunders Meadow [RIVERSIDE]: *area,* 0.5 mile southeast of the center of Idyllwild (lat. 33°44' N, long. 116°42'40" W; sec. 18, T 5 S, R 3 E). Named on Idyllwild (1959) 15' quadrangle. The name is for Amasa Saunders, who ran a sawmill in Strawberry Valley in the 1880's (Gunther, p. 489).

Savahia Peak [SAN BERNARDINO]: *peak,* 11 miles north of Vidal (lat. 34°16'35" N, long. 114°31'55" W). Altitude 2695 feet. Named on Savahia Peak (1971) 7.5' quadrangle.

Sawmill Canyon [SAN BERNARDINO]:

(1) *canyon,* drained by a stream that flows 2.5 miles to lowlands in Big Bear City (lat. 34°15'30" N, long. 116°50'50" W; sec. 14, T 2 N, R 1 E). Named on Big Bear City (1971) and Moonridge (1970) 7.5' quadrangles.

(2) *canyon,* drained by a stream that flows 2 miles to Banning Canyon 4.25 miles south-southwest of San Gorgonio Mountain (lat. 34°02'30" N, long. 116°51'05" W; sec. 35, T 1 S, R 1 E). Named on San Gorgonio Mountain (1970) 7.5' quadrangle.

Sawpit [SAN BERNARDINO]: *canyon,* drained by a stream that flows nearly 3 miles to West Fork Mojave River 18 miles south of Victorville (lat. 34°17'05" N, long. 117°20'10" W; sec. 6, T 2 N, R 4 W). Named on Cedar Springs (1956) and San Bernardino North (1967) 7.5' quadrangles.

Sawtooth [SAN BERNARDINO]: *relief feature,* 28 miles west of Ivanpah (lat. 35°22'15" N, long. 115°48'10" W; near W line sec. 22, T 15 N, R 11 E). Named on Halloran Spring (1956) 15' quadrangle.

Sawtooth Range [SAN BERNARDINO]: *range,* 18 miles south of Needles (lat. 34°34' N, long. 114°37' W). Named on Sawtooth Range (1950) 15' quadrangle.

Sawtooths [SAN BERNARDINO]: *range,* 3.5 miles west-northwest of Yucca Valley (lat. 34°08'40" N, long. 116°30' W). Named on Rimrock (1972) and Yucca Valley North (1972) 7.5' quadrangles.

Sawyer Spring [RIVERSIDE]: *spring,* nearly 3 miles west of Aguanga (lat. 33°26'20" N, long. 116°54'45" W; near E line sec. 31, T 8 S, R 1 E). Named on Vail Lake (1953) 7.5' quadrangle. The name commemorates W.B. Sawyer, who settled in the neighborhood in the early 1880's (Gunther, p. 489).

Scanlon Gulch [SAN BERNARDINO]: *canyon,* 4 miles long, opens into lowlands 15 miles south of Essex (lat. 34°30'50" N, long. 115°14'45" W; near NW cor. sec. 19, T 5 N, R 17 E). Named on Essex (1956) 15' quadrangle.

Schenk Creek [SAN BERNARDINO]: *stream,* flows nearly 2 miles to East Fork City Creek 1.5 miles west-northwest of Harrison Mountain (lat. 34°10'35" N, long. 117°10'55" W; near N line sec. 15, T 1 N, R 3 W). Named on Harrison Mountain (1967) 7.5' quadrangle.

Schneider Creek [SAN BERNARDINO]: *stream,* flows 1.5 miles to Santa Ana River 6 miles south-southwest of downtown Big Bear City (lat. 34°10'05" N, long. 116°57'40" W; near W line sec. 14, T 1 N, R 1 W). Named on Big Bear Lake (1970) 7.5' quadrangle.

Schuiling Cave: see **Newberry** [SAN BERNARDINO].

Scotland [SAN BERNARDINO]: *locality,* 6 miles west-northwest of Devore (lat. 34°14'35" N, long. 117°29'50" W; sec. 22, T 2 N, R 6 W). Named on Devore (1966) 7.5' quadrangle. The name is from the Scott family, owners of the place (Robinson, J.W., 1983, p. 188).

Scott Canyon [RIVERSIDE-SAN BERNARDINO]: *canyon,* drained by a stream that heads just inside Riverside County and flows 2.25 miles to lowlands 3.5 miles west-southwest of Redlands city hall in San Bernardino County (lat. 34°02'15" N, long. 117°14'30" W; near W line sec. 31, T 1 S, R 3 W). Named on Redlands (1967) 7.5' quadrangle.

Scott Canyon: see **Hathaway Creek** [RIVERSIDE].

Scouts Cove [SAN BERNARDINO]: *locality,* 25 miles east-southeast of the village of Red Mountain (lat. 35°11'10" N, long. 117°12'40" W; near SE cor. sec. 36, T 31 S, R 44 E). Named on Opal Mountain (1955) 15' quadrangle.

Scully [RIVERSIDE]: *locality,* 6 miles west of Corona along Atchison, Topeka and Santa Fe Railroad before the rail line was moved to the south side of Santa Ana River (lat. 33°52'45" N, long. 117° 40'15" W); the place is 0.5 mile east of Scully Hill. Named on Prado (1941) 7.5' quadrangle.

Scully Hill [SAN BERNARDINO]: *relief feature,* 4.25 miles southeast of San Juan Hill on San Bernardino-Orange County line (lat. 33° 52'40" N, long. 117°40'40" W). Named on Prado Dam (1967) 7.5' quadrangle.

Seaburgs Well [SAN BERNARDINO]: *well,* 29 miles east of the village of Red Mountain (lat. 35°16'20" N, long. 117°06'40" W; at N line sec. 1, T 31 S, R 45 E). Named on Pilot Knob (1954) 15' quadrangle.

Searles Marsh: see **Searles Lake** [SAN BERNARDINO].

Searles Lake [SAN BERNARDINO]: *dry lake,* 10 miles long, center about 4 miles southeast of Trona (lat. 35°43' N, long. 117°20' W). Named on Trona (1949) 15' quadrangle, and on Searles Lake (1973) and Westend (1973) 7.5' quadrangles. Birnie (p. 131) called the feature Borax Lake in 1876. Gale (p. 265) gave the alternate names "Searles Marsh," "Slate Range Marsh," and "Borax Flat" for the feature. The name "Searles Lake" is for John W. Searles, who first saw signs of borax at the place in 1862 (DeGroot, p. 534). Searles and his brother organized San Bernardino Borax Mining Company in 1873, filed on the north end of Searles Lake, and built a processing plant near present Trona (Belden and Walker, p. 4).

Searles Valley [SAN BERNARDINO]: *valley,* extends for about 35 miles south from Inyo County between Argus Range and Slate Range, and on southwest past Spangler Hills to Lava Mountains; Searles Lake is in the north part of the valley. Named on Trona (1957) 1°x 2° quadrangle. United States Board on Geographic Names (1961b, p. 12) rejected the name "Spangler Valley" for the feature.

Sea View Beach [IMPERIAL]: *beach,* 7 miles north of Kane Spring along Salton Sea (lat. 33°12'35" N, long. 115°50'30" W). Named on Kane Spring (1940) 15' quadrangle.

Sedco: see **Sedco Hills** [RIVERSIDE].

Sedco Hills [RIVERSIDE]: *town,* 2.5 miles southeast of Lake Elsinore city hall (lat. 33°38'35" N, long. 117°17'25" W). Named on Lake Elsinore (1953) 7.5' quadrangle. Officials of South Elsinore Development Company had the community laid out in 1912 and named it "Sedco" from letters in the company name; Happy Hour Community Club of Sedco petitioned the county board of supervisors in 1952 to give the town the name "Sedco Hills" (Gunther, p. 490).

Seeley [IMPERIAL]: *town,* 7.5 miles west of El Centro (lat. 32°47'35" N, long. 115°41'20" W; sec. 11, 12, T 16 S, R 12 E). Named on Seeley (1957) 7.5' quadrangle. Postal authorities established Seeley post office in 1909 (Salley, p. 201). The name commemorates Henry Seeley, a pioneer in development of Imperial Valley (Gudde, 1949, p. 324). A place called Indian Wells was situated about 8 miles south and a little west of Seeley; it was a station on the Butterfield Overland stage route, and was destroyed by the flood of 1906 (Hoover, Rensch, and Rensch, p. 108). Postal authorities established Indian Wells post office 10 miles west of El Centro in 1876 and discontinued it in 1877 (Salley, p. 104). Hanks' (1886) map shows a place called Sackett's Wells located 3 miles west-northwest of Indian Wells.

Seeley: see **Camp Seeley** [SAN BERNARDINO].

Seeley Creek [SAN BERNARDINO]: *stream,* flows 3.25 miles to East Fork of West Fork Mojave River 18 miles south of Victorville (lat. 34°16'25" N, long. 117°18'10" W; sec. 9, T 2 N, R 4 W). Named on Cedar Springs (1956) and San Bernardino North (1967) 7.5' quadrangles.

Seeley Flat [SAN BERNARDINO]: *area,* 19 miles south of Victorville (lat. 34°15'05" N, long. 117°18'05" W; sec. 16, 21, T 2 N, R 4 W); the place is along Seeley Creek. Named on Cedar Springs (1956) and San Bernardino North (1967) 7.5' quadrangles. David Seeley and Wellington Seeley built a sawmill at the place in 1853 (Beattie and Beattie, p. 208-209).

Seep Spring [SAN BERNARDINO]: *spring,* 26 miles south-southeast of Trona (lat. 35°24'50" N, long. 117°12'25" W; at W line sec. 18, T 29 S, R 45 E). Named on Pilot Knob (1954) 15' quadrangle.

Selgato Canyon [RIVERSIDE]: *canyon,* 2.25 miles long, opens into lowlands 6 miles south-southeast of Hemet (lat. 33°39'45" N, long. 116°56'45" W; at W line sec. 12, T 6 S, R 1 W). Named on Hemet (1953) 7.5' quadrangle.

Sellew: see **Bard** [IMPERIAL].

Senator: see **Senator Wash** [IMPERIAL].

Senator Wash [IMPERIAL]: *stream,* flows 5.5 miles to lowlands along Colorado River 12 miles east-southeast of Picacho Peak (lat. 32°54'40" N, long. 114°28'40" W; sec. 32, T 14 S, R 24 E). Named on Imperial Reservoir (1955) and Little Picacho Peak (1965) 7.5' quadrangles. Imperial Reservoir (1955) 7.5' quadrangle shows Old Senator mine located 1.5 miles south of the mouth of Senator Wash. Postal authorities established Senator post office near the mine in 1898 and discontinued it in 1899 (Salley, p. 201).

Sentinel Peak: see **Monument Peak** [RIVERSIDE].

Serrano Spring [RIVERSIDE]: *spring,* 2 miles south of Sitton Peak (lat. 33°33'35" N, long. 117°26'55" W). Named on Sitton Peak (1954) 7.5' quadrangle.

Seven Oaks [SAN BERNARDINO]: *locality,* 4 miles south of downtown Big Bear Lake (lat. 34°11'10" N, long. 116°54'50" W; sec. 7, T 1 N, R 1 E). Named on Big Bear Lake (1970) 7.5' quadrangle. Postal authorities established Sevenoaks post office at a lumber camp in 1894 and discontinued it in 1899; they established Seven Oaks post office at a resort in 1925 and discontinued it in 1962 (Salley, p. 202).

Seven Oaks Resort [SAN BERNARDINO]: *locality,* 4.5 miles south of downtown Big Bear Lake (lat. 34°10'50" N, long. 116°55'40" W; near SE cor. sec. 12, T 1 N, R 1 W); the place is 1 mile west-southwest of Seven Oaks. Named on Big Bear Lake (1970) 7.5' quadrangle. San Gorgonio (1902) 30' quadrangle has the name "Seven Oaks" at the site.

Seven Palms: see **Garnet** [RIVERSIDE].

Seven Palms Valley [RIVERSIDE]: *valley,* 8 miles north of Cathedral City (lat. 33°54' N, long. 116°28'45" W). Named on Seven Palms Valley (1958) 7.5' quadrangle.

Seven Pines [SAN BERNARDINO]: *locality,* 6.5 miles southwest of downtown Big Bear Lake (lat. 34°10'45" N, long. 116°59'30" W; on S line sec. 9, T 1 N, R 1 W). Named on Big Bear Lake (1970) 7.5' quadrangle.

Seventeenmile Point [SAN BERNARDINO]: *promontory,* 34 miles west-southwest of Ivanpah (lat. 35°13'15" N, long. 115°53'30" W; at N line sec. 14, T 13 N, R 10 E). Named on Old Dad Mountain (1956) 15' quadrangle.

Seymour Flat [SAN BERNARDINO]: *area,* 2.5 miles west of Keller Peak (lat. 34°11'30" N, long. 117°05'30" W; near N line sec. 9, T 1 N, R 2 W). Named on Keller Peak (1967) 7.5' quadrangle.

Shadow Canyon [SAN BERNARDINO]: *canyon,* 1.5 miles long. 6.5 miles west-southwest of Needles (lat. 34°48'40" N, long. 114°42'45" W). Named on Needles SW (1970) 7.5' quadrangle.

Shadow Hills: see **Shadow Mountains** [SAN BERNARDINO] (2).

Shadow Lake [SAN BERNARDINO]: *lake,* 350 feet long, 8 miles south-southwest of downtown Big Bear Lake (lat. 34°08'35" N, long. 116°59'10" W; sec. 28, T 1 N, R 1 W). Named on Big Bear Lake (1970) 7.5' quadrangle.

Shadow Mountain [SAN BERNARDINO]: *peak,* 31 miles west-northwest of Ivanpah (lat. 35°34'10" N, long. 115°47'30" W); the feature is west of the north end of Shadow Valley. Altitude 4197 feet. Named on Kingston Peak (1955) 15' quadrangle.

Shadow Mountains [SAN BERNARDINO]:

(1) *ridge,* north-northwest- to north-trending, 6 miles long, 36 miles west-northwest of Ivanpah (lat. 35°34' N, long. 115°53'30" W). Named on Kingston Peak (1955) 15' quadrangle.

(2) *range,* 20 miles northeast of Victorville (lat. 34°42'15" N, long. 117°34' W). Named on Shadow Mountains (1955), Shadow Mountains SE (1955), and Victorville NW (1956) 7.5' quadrangles. United States Board on Geographic Names (1980, p. 4) approved the name "Shadow Hills" for a range just east of Shadow Mountains.

Shadow Valley [SAN BERNARDINO]: *valley,* west of Clark Mountain Range, Mescal Range, and Ivanpah Mountains. Named on Clark Mountain (1956), Halloran Spring (1956), Kingston Peak (1955), and Mescal Range (1955) 15' quadrangles.

Shake Creek [SAN BERNARDINO]: *stream,* flows nearly 3 miles to Deep Creek (1) 5.5 miles south of Luna Mountain (lat. 34°15'45" N, long. 117°07'30" W; sec. 18, T 2 N, R 2 W). Named on Harrison Mountain (1967) and Lake Arrowhead (1971) 7.5' quadrangles.

Shamrock [IMPERIAL]: *locality,* 4 miles west of Calipatria along Southern Pacific Railroad (lat. 33°07'10" N, long. 115°34'45" W). Named on Calipatria (1943) 15' quadrangle.

Shandin Hills [SAN BERNARDINO]: *range,* 4 miles north-northwest of San Bernardino city hall (lat. 34°09'30" N, long. 117°19' W). Named on San Bernardino North (1967) 7.5' quadrangle. Dutcher and Garrett (p. 17) gave the alternate name "Little Mountain" for the feature.

Shaver Summit: see **Chiriaco Summit** [RIVERSIDE].

Shavers Valley [RIVERSIDE]: *valley,* 10 miles north-northeast of Mortmar (lat. 33°39' N, long. 115°52' W). Named on Cottonwood Spring (1958) and Hayfield (1963) 15' quadrangles.

Shavers Well [RIVERSIDE]: *well,* 7 miles north of Mortmar (lat. 33° 37'10" N, long. 115°54'55" W; sec. 26, T 6 S, R 10 E); the well is at the south edge of Shavers Valley. Named on Mortmar (1958) 7.5' quadrangle. The name is for John Shaver, a Riverside County supervisor who promoted the sinking of wells to benefit travelers in the desert (Gunther, p. 492-493).

Shay Mountain [SAN BERNARDINO]: *peak,* 3.5 miles southeast of Luna Mountain (lat. 34°18'30" N, long. 117°05'10" W; at NE cor. sec. 33, T 3 N, R 2 W). Altitude 6714 feet. Named on Butler Peak (1971) 7.5' quadrangle.

Shay Mountain: see **Little Shay Mountain** [SAN BERNARDINO].

Shay Mountains: see **Hawes Peak** [SAN BERNARDINO]; **Little Shay Mountain** [SAN BERNARDINO].

Shay Spring [SAN BERNARDINO]: *spring,* 4.5 miles east-southeast of Luna Mountain (lat. 34°18'50" N, long. 117°03'25" W; sec. 26, T 3 N, R 2 W); the spring is 1.5 miles east of Shay Mountain. Named of Butler Peak (1971) 7.5' quadrangle.

Sheep Camp Spring [SAN BERNARDINO]: *spring,* 19 miles south of Essex (lat. 34°27'45" N, long. 115°12'30" W; sec. 5, T 4 N, R 17 E). Named on Milligan (1956) 15' quadrangle.

Sheep Canyon [RIVERSIDE]: *canyon,* 4 miles long, 18 miles south of Indio (lat. 33°27'25" N, long. 116°12'30" W). Named on Rabbit Peak (1959) 7.5' quadrangle.

Sheep Canyon [SAN BERNARDINO]:

(1) *canyon,* 1 mile long, along Sheep Creek (1) above a point 4.5 miles north-northeast of Mount San Antonio (lat. 34°20'55" N, long. 117°36'50" W; sec. 16, T 3 N, R 7 W). Named on Telegraph Peak (1956) 7.5' quadrangle.

(2) *canyon,* drained by a stream that flows 1.25 miles to Icehouse Canyon 13 miles north of Ontario city hall (lat. 34°14'55" N, long. 117°36'55" W; sec. 21, T 2 N, R 7 W). Named on Cucamonga Peak (1966) 7.5' quadrangle.

Sheep Corral [SAN BERNARDINO]: *canyon,* 1.5 miles long, 13 miles north-northeast of Amboy (lat. 34°44'30" N, long. 115°40'45" W; sec. 25, 36, T 8 N, R 12 E). Named on Cadiz (1956) and Flynn (1956) 15' quadrangles.

Sheep Creek [RIVERSIDE]: *stream,* flows 2.25 miles to Deep Canyon (2) 5 miles south of Palm Desert (lat. 33°38'50" N, long. 116° 22'20" W; at W line sec. 16, T 6 S, R 6 E). Named on Palm Desert (1959) 15' quadrangle.

Sheep Creek [SAN BERNARDINO]:

(1) *stream,* flows 5.5 miles to lowlands 9 miles north-northeast of Mount San Antonio (lat. 34°24'45" N, long. 117°36'30" W; near SE cor. sec. 21, T 4 N, R 7 W). Named on Phelan (1956) and Telegraph Peak (1956) 7.5' quadrangles.

(2) *stream,* flows 1 mile to North Fork Lytle Creek 3.5 miles south-southwest of Cajon (lat. 34°15'35" N, long. 117°29'40" W; sec. 15, T 2 N, R 6 W). Named on Cajon (1956) 7.5' quadrangle.

(3) *stream,* flows 2 miles to Deep Creek (1) 6 miles south of Luna Mountain (lat. 34°15'25" N, long. 117°07'20" W; sec. 18, T 2 N, R 2 W). Named on Butler Peak (1971), Harrison Mountain (1967), and Keller Peak (1967) 7.5' quadrangles.

Sheep Creek Spring [SAN BERNARDINO]: *spring,* 27 miles northwest of Baker (lat. 35°35'15" N, long. 116°21'30" W). Named on Avawatz Pass (1948) 15' quadrangle.

Sheep Flat [SAN BERNARDINO]: *area,* 12.5 miles north of Ontario city hall (lat. 34°14'30" N, long. 117°36'50" W; near SE cor. sec. 21, T 2 N, R 7 W); the place is just east of Sheep Canyon (2). Named on Cucamonga Peak (1966) 7.5' quadrangle.

Sheep Hole Mountains [SAN BERNARDINO]: *range,* 27 miles south-southeast of Amboy (lat. 34°10' N, long. 115°36'30" W). Named on Bristol Lake (1956) and Dale Lake (1956) 15' quadrangles. The name is from a natural cistern that holds water and attracts desert bighorn sheep (Hanna, p. 303).

Sheep Hole Oasis [RIVERSIDE]: *spring,* 4.25 miles north of Mortmar (lat. 33°35'05" N, long. 115°55'20" W; at NE cor. sec. 10, T 7 S, R 10 E). Named on Mortmar (1958) 7.5' quadrangle. Berkstresser (1969, p. 11) gave the alternate name "Burnt Palms Spring" for the feature.

Sheep Hole Pass [SAN BERNARDINO]: *pass,* 22 miles south of Amboy (lat. 34°13'45" N, long. 115°43'15" W); the pass is at the west side of Sheep Hole Mountains. Named on Dale Lake (1956) 15' quadrangle.

Sheep Mountain [RIVERSIDE]: *peak,* 9.5 miles south of Palm Desert (lat. 33°35'10" N, long. 116°22'30" W; near S line sec. 5, T 7 S, R 6 E). Altitude 5141 feet. Named on Palm Desert (1959) 15' quadrangle.

Sheep Pass [RIVERSIDE]: *pass,* 25 miles east-northeast of Garnet (lat. 34°00'05" N, long. 116°07'25" W; at E line sec. 15, T 2 S, R 8 E). Named on Queen Mountain (1972) 7.5' quadrangle.

Sheep Pass Camp [RIVERSIDE]: *locality,* 20 miles north-northeast of Indio (lat. 34°00' N, long. 116°07' W; sec. 14, T 2 S, R 8 E). Named on Lost Horse Mountain (1958) 15' quadrangle.

Sheep Spring [SAN BERNARDINO]: *spring,* 7.5 miles southeast of Newberry (lat. 34°44' N, long. 116°36'20" W; near NW cor. sec. 6, T 7 N, R 4 E). Named on Rodman Mountain (1955) 15' quadrangle.

Shell Reef [IMPERIAL]: *ridge,* east-trending, less than 1 mile long, 15 miles south of Desert Shores (lat. 33°11'25" N, long. 116°04'20" W; on S line sec. 19, T 11 S, R 9 E). Named on Shell Reef (1959) 7.5' quadrangle.

Shelter Cove [SAN BERNARDINO]: *embayment,* 6 miles south-southwest of Luna Mountain (lat. 34°15'55" N, long. 117°10'40" W; on N line sec. 15, T 2 N, R 3 W); the feature is on the north side of Lake Arrowhead (1). Named on Lake Arrowhead (1971) 7.5' quadrangle.

Sherman Shady Spring [SAN BERNARDINO]: *spring,* 2.5 miles north-northwest of downtown Morongo Valley (lat. 34°04'45" N, long. 116°36'05" W; near SE cor. sec. 18, T 1 S, R 4 E). Named on Morongo Valley (1972) 7.5' quadrangle.

Shields Flat [SAN BERNARDINO]: *area,* 8 miles south-southeast of downtown Big Bear Lake (lat. 34°07'35" N, long. 116°52'35" W; sec. 33, T 1 N, R 1 E); the place is 0.25 mile east-southeast of Shields Peak. Named on Big Bear Lake (1970) 7.5' quadrangle.

Shields Peak [SAN BERNARDINO]: *peak,* 8 miles south-southeast of downtown Big Bear Lake (lat. 34°07'40" N, long. 116°52'50" W; sec. 33, T 1 N, R 1 E). Named on Big Bear Lake (1970) 7.5' quadrangle.

Ship Creek [RIVERSIDE]: *stream,* flows 17 miles to end 16 miles east-southeast of Desert Center in Chuckwalla Valley (lat. 33° 37' N, long. 115°08'30" W). Named on Chuckwalla Mountains (1963) and Sidewinder Well (1952) 15' quadrangles.

Ship Mountains [SAN BERNARDINO]: *range,* 20 miles east-southeast of Amboy (lat. 34°29' N, long. 115°24' W). Named on Cadiz Lake (1956) and Danby (1956) 15' quadrangles.

Shortcut Ridge [SAN BERNARDINO]: *ridge,* north-northwest-trending, nearly 1 mile long, 12.5 miles north of Ontario city hall (lat. 34°14'20" N, long. 117°36'25" W; sec. 22, 27, T 2 N, R 7 W). Named on Cucamonga Peak (1966) 7.5' quadrangle.

Shorts Lake [SAN BERNARDINO]: *dry lake,* 2200 feet long, nearly 3 miles north-northeast of Twentynine Palms (lat. 34°10'30" N, long. 116°02'10" W). Named on Twentynine Palms (1973) 7.5' quadrangle.

Siam [SAN BERNARDINO]: *locality,* 16 miles southwest of Essex along Atchison, Topeka and Santa Fe Railroad (lat. 34°33' N, long. 115°25' W; sec. 4, T 5 N, R 15 E). Named on Danby (1956) 15' quadrangle. Postal authorities established Siam post office in 1906 and discontinued it in 1907; the place was a watering station for steam locomotives (Salley, p. 204).

Siberia [SAN BERNARDINO]: *locality,* 7 miles west-northwest of Bagdad along Atchison, Topeka and Santa Fe Railroad (lat. 34°37'30" N, long. 115°59' W; at W line sec. 7, T 6 N, R 10 E). Named on Bagdad (1956) 15' quadrangle.

Siberia Creek [SAN BERNARDINO]: *stream,* flows 4 miles to Bear Creek 2.25 miles east-northeast of Keller Peak (lat. 34°12'35" N, long. 117°00'40" W; near SW cor. sec. 32, T 2 N, R 1 W). Named on Big Bear Lake (1970) and Keller Peak (1967) 7.5' quadrangles. Called Lake Creek on San Gorgonio (1902) 30' quadrangle.

Siberia Creek Campground [SAN BERNARDINO]: *locality,* 2.25 miles east-northeast of Keller Peak (lat. 34°12'35" N, long. 117°00'40" W; near SW cor. sec. 32, T 2 N, R 1 W); the place is at the mouth of Siberia Creek. Named on Keller Peak (1967) 7.5' quadrangle.

Sidewinder Mountain [SAN BERNARDINO]: *range,* 20 miles south of Barstow (lat. 34°37' N, long. 117°03' W). Named on Ord Mountains (1955) 15' quadrangle, and on Fairview Valley (1970) and Stoddard Well (1970) 7.5' quadrangles. The name is from Sidewinder mine (Gudde, 1949, p. 330).

Sidewinder Valley [SAN BERNARDINO]: *valley,* 8 miles northeast of Victorville (lat. 34°37' N, long. 117°11' W). Named on Apple Valley North (1970) and Turtle Valley (1970) 7.5' quadrangles.

Sidewinder Well [RIVERSIDE]: *well,* 10 miles east of Desert Center (lat. 33°43'30" N, long. 115°13'45" W; sec. 20, T 5 S, R 17 E). Named on Sidewinder Well (1952) 15' quadrangle.

Sidewinder Well [SAN BERNARDINO]: *well,* 8 miles northeast of Victorville (lat. 34°37'20" N, long. 117°12'20" W; at W line sec. 9, T 6 N, R 3 W); the well is in Sidewinder Valley. Named on Apple Valley (1957) 15' quadrangle.

Sierra de Santa Coleta: see **Providence Mountains** [SAN BERNARDINO].

Sierra Madre: see **San Gabriel Mountains** [SAN BERNARDINO].

Sierra Peak [RIVERSIDE]: *peak,* 5.5 miles west-southwest of Corona on Riverside-Orange County line (lat. 33°51' N, long. 117° 39'10" W; sec. 6, T 4 S, R 7 W); the feature is southwest of La Sierra grant. Altitude 3045 feet. Named on Black Star Canyon (1967) 7.5' quadrangle.

Sierra San Gabriel: see **San Gabriel Mountains** [SAN BERNARDINO].

Signal: see **Mount Signal** [IMPERIAL].

Signal Hill [SAN BERNARDINO]: *ridge,* east-northeast-trending, 1 mile long, 27 miles southeast of Ivanpah (lat. 35°01'15" N, long. 115°01' W; sec. 22, 23, T 11 N, R 18 E). Named on Lanfair Valley (1956) 15' quadrangle.

Silsbee: see **El Centro** [IMPERIAL].

Silurian Hills [SAN BERNARDINO]: *range,* 17 miles north of Baker (lat. 35°31' N, long. 116°02' W). Named on Baker (1956), Halloran Spring (1956), and Silurian Hills (1956) 15' quadrangles.

Silurian Lake [SAN BERNARDINO]: *dry lake,* nearly 3 miles long, 19 miles north-northwest of Baker (lat. 35°31'45" N, long. 116°10'15" W); the feature is west of the north end of Silurian Hills, and is 3.5 miles west-northwest of the site of Riggs. Named on Silurian Hills (1956) 15' quadrangle. Thompson (1929, p. 594-597) noted the name "Riggs Dry Lake" for the feature, and the name "Riggs Valley" for its valley. United States Board on Geographic Names (1965b, p. 15) approved the name "Silurian Valley" for the valley of Silurian Lake.

Silurian Valley: see **Silurian Lake** [SAN BERNARDINO].

Silver Creek [SAN BERNARDINO]: *stream,* flows 7 miles before ending 18 miles east-southeast of Victorville (lat. 34°25'35" N, long. 117°00'25" W; sec. 20, T 4 N, R 1 W). Named on Butler Peak (1971), Fawnskin (1971), Fifteenmile Valley (1971), and Lucerne Valley (1971) 7.5' quadrangles.

Silver Lake [SAN BERNARDINO]:

(1) *dry lake,* 7 miles long, center 5 miles north-northwest of Baker (lat. 35°20'30" N, long. 116°06'30" W). Named on Baker (1956) 15' quadrangle.

(2) *locality,* 7.5 miles north-northwest of Baker (lat. 35°22'15" N, long. 116°06'50" W; sec. 22, T 15 N, R 8 E); the place is on the east side of Silver Lake (1). Named on Baker (1956) 15' quadrangle. Postal authorities established Silver Lake post office in 1907 and discontinued it in 1933 (Salley, p. 205). The place was along Tonopah and Tidewater Railroad; when Silver Lake (1) filled with water in 1916, the rail line and community were moved beyond the east edge of the lake (Myrick, p. 586).

Silver Lead Spring [SAN BERNARDINO]: *spring,* 16 miles south-southwest of Ivanpah (lat. 35°06'30" N, long. 115°27' W; sec. 23, T 12 N, R 14 E). Named on Mid Hills (1955) 15' quadrangle.

Silver Mountain [SAN BERNARDINO]: *ridge,* south-southeast- to south-west-trending, 3 miles long, 8 miles north of Victorville (lat. 34°39'15" N, long. 117°16' W). Named on Helendale (1956) 7.5' quadrangle.

Silver Peak [SAN BERNARDINO]:

(1) *peak,* 20 miles northwest of Victorville (lat. 34°44'20" N, long. 117°32'25" W; near W line sec. 32, T 8 N, R 6 W). Altitude 4043 feet. Named on Shadow Mountains (1955) 7.5' quadrangle.

(2) *peak,* 5.5 miles north-northeast of Big Bear City on Blackhawk Mountain (lat. 34°20'15" N, long. 116°48'35" W). Altitude 6756 feet. Named on Big Bear City (1971) 7.5' quadrangle.

Silver Peak: see **Granite Mountains** [SAN BERNARDINO] (2).

Silverwood Falls [SAN BERNARDINO]: *waterfall,* 1.5 miles south-southeast of San Gorgonio Mountain along East Fork Whitewater River (lat. 34°04'30" N, long. 116°49' W; near N line sec. 19, T 1 S, R 2 E). Named on San Gorgonio Mountain (1970) 7.5' quadrangle.

Silverwood Lake [SAN BERNARDINO]: *lake,* behind a dam on West Fork Mojave River 16 miles south of Victorville (lat. 34°18'15" N, long. 117°18'45" W; near E line sec. 32, T 3 N, R 4 W). Named on Silverwood Lake (1956) 7.5' quadrangle.

Simmons Trout Lake [SAN BERNARDINO]: *lake,* 300 feet long, nearly 2 miles east of downtown Big Bear Lake along Rathbone (present Rathbun) Creek (lat. 34°14'35" N, long. 116°52'45" W; sec. 21, T 2 N, R 1 E). Named on Big Bear Lake (1970) 7.5' quadrangle.

Sink: see **The Sink** [RIVERSIDE].

Sink of Mohave: see **Mojave River Wash** [SAN BERNARDINO].

Sitton Peak [RIVERSIDE]: *peak,* 9 miles southwest of Lake Elsinore city hall (lat. 33°35'15" N, long. 117°26'45" W). Altitude 3273 feet. Named on Sitton Peak (1954) 7.5' quadrangle. The name commemorates J.S. Sitton, an early sheepman in the region (Gunther, p. 496).

Skeleton Canyon [RIVERSIDE]: *canyon,* 2 miles long, opens into lowlands 14 miles southeast of Indio (lat. 33°36'05" N, long. 116° 01'05" W; sec. 35, T 6 S, R 9 E). Named on Mecca (1955) and Mortmar (1958) 7.5' quadrangles.

Skeleton Pass [SAN BERNARDINO]: *pass,* 15 miles south-southwest of Essex (lat. 34°32'30" N, long. 115°20'45" W; near N line sec. 7, T 5 N, R 16 E). Named on Danby (1956) 15' quadrangle.

Skilling Well [SAN BERNARDINO]: *well,* 2.5 miles northeast of the village of Red Mountain (lat. 35°23'25" N, long. 117°34' W; at S line sec. 22, T 29 S, R 41 E). Named on Klinker Mountain (1967) 7.5' quadrangle.

Skinner Creek [SAN BERNARDINO]: *stream,* flows 2.5 miles to Mountain Home Creek 9.5 miles west of San Gorgonio Mountain (lat. 34°06'15" N, long. 116°59'35" W; near N line sec. 9, T 1 S, R 1 W). Named on Forest Falls (1970) 7.5' quadrangle.

Skinner Reservoir [RIVERSIDE]: *lake,* 9 miles east-northeast of Murrieta in Auld Valley (lat. 33°35'15" N, long. 117°03'30" W; in and near sec. 2, T 7 S, R 2 W). Named on Bachelor Mountain (1953, photorevised 1973) 7.5' quadrangle.

Skinners Camp [SAN BERNARDINO]: *locality,* 9.5 miles west of San Gorgonio Mountain (lat. 34°06'15" N, long. 116°59'35" W; at S line sec. 4, T 1 S, R 1 W); the place is near the mouth of present Skinner Creek. Named on San Gorgonio (1902) 30' quadrangle.

Skully Hill [SAN BERNARDINO]: *peak,* 4.25 miles east-southeast of San Juan Hill on San Bernardino-Orange County line (lat. 33°52'40" N, long. 117°40'40" W). Named on Prado Dam (1967) 7.5' quadrangle.

Skunk Cabbage Meadow [RIVERSIDE]: *area,* 3 miles south-southeast of San Jacinto Peak (lat. 33°46'25" N, long. 116°39'50" W; at SW cor. sec.

34, T 4 S, R 3 E). Named on San Jacinto Peak (1981) 7.5' quadrangle.

Skunk Hollow [RIVERSIDE]: *area,* 6.5 miles east of Murrieta (lat. 33°33'30" N, long. 117°06'15" W; sec. 17, T 7 S, R 2 W). Named on Bachelor Mountain (1953) 7.5' quadrangle.

Skyforest [SAN BERNARDINO]: *village,* 5 miles north of Harrison Mountain (lat. 34°14'10" N, long. 117°10'35" W; on S line sec. 22, T 2 N, R 3 W). Named on Harrison Mountain (1967) 7.5' quadrangle. Postal authorities established Skyforest post office in 1928; the place was called Forest of the Sky in 1889—Mormons had a lumber mill there in the 1850's (Salley, p. 205).

Skyland [SAN BERNARDINO]: *locality,* 9 miles north of San Bernardino city hall (lat. 34°14' N, long. 117°17'05" W; sec. 27, T 2 N, R 4 W). Named on San Bernardino North (1967) 7.5' quadrangle.

Skyline Heights: see **Crestline** [SAN BERNARDINO].

Sky Meadow: see **Camp Sky Meadow** [SAN BERNARDINO].

Skytop [SAN BERNARDINO]: *locality,* 8 miles southwest of Trona (lat. 35°42'05" N, long. 117°29'55" W; near N line sec. 7, T 26 S, R 42 E). Named on Westend (1973) 7.5' quadrangle.

Slate Range [SAN BERNARDINO]: *range,* between Searles Valley and Panamint Valley on San Bernardino-Inyo County line. Named on Manly Peak (1950), Trona (1949), and Wingate Pass (1950) 15' quadrangles. United States Board on Geographic Names (1966b, p. 6) approved the name "Straw Peak" for a feature, altitude 5578 feet, located 14 miles southeast of Trona near the south end of Slate Range (lat. 35°37'12" N, long. 117°11'30" W).

Slaterange: see **New York Canyon** [SAN BERNARDINO].

Slate Range City: see **New York Canyon** [SAN BERNARDINO].

Slate Range Marsh: see **Searles Lake** [SAN BERNARDINO].

Slater Canyon [RIVERSIDE]: *canyon,* 0.5 mile long, 5.5 miles south of Alberhill (lat. 33°38'45" N, long. 117°22'35" W; sec. 14, T 6 S, R 5 W). Named on Alberhill (1954, photorevised 1988) 7.5' quadrangle. The canyon divides at the head to form Stinson Canyon and Edwards Canyon. The name "Slater" commemorates Durward F. Slater, a Forest Service employee who lost his life in a fire in 1959 (United States Board on Geographic Names, 1960c, p. 21).

Slaughter Canyon [SAN BERNARDINO]: *canyon,* drained by a stream that flows 2.25 miles to lowlands 5 miles east-northeast of San Juan Hill along Chino Creek (lat. 33°56'05" N, long. 117°39'25" W; sec. 6, T 3 S, R 7 W). Named on Prado Dam (1967) 7.5' quadrangle.

Slaughterhouse Canyon [RIVERSIDE]: *canyon,* 2 miles long, 2.25 miles south-southeast of Wildomar (lat. 33°33'45" N, long. 117°15'50" W). Named on Wildomar (1953) 7.5' quadrangle. Called Slaughter House Canyon on Lake Elsinore (1941) 15' quadrangle. The name is from a slaughterhouse operated in the canyon for many years before 1900; the feature also was called Stoney Canyon (Gunther, p. 497).

Slaughterhouse Spring [SAN BERNARDINO]: *spring,* 2.5 miles southeast of Ivanpah (lat. 35°19' N, long. 115°16'20" W; at SW cor. sec. 4, T 14 N, R 16 E). Named on Ivanpah (1956) 15' quadrangle.

Slaughter Tree Wash [RIVERSIDE]: *stream,* flows 5 miles to lowlands along Colorado River 20 miles north-northeast of Blythe (lat. 33°53'10" N, long. 114°31'30" W; near W line sec. 25, T 3 S, R 23 E). Named on Big Maria Mountains NE (1954) 7.5' quadrangle.

Sleeping Beauty [SAN BERNARDINO]: *ridge,* south- to south-southeast-trending, 2 miles long, 23 miles east of Newberry (lat. 34°47'10" N, long. 116°17'10" W; in and near sec. 18, T 8 N, R 7 E). Named on Cady Mountains (1955) 15' quadrangle.

Sleepy Creek: see **Antelope Creek** [SAN BERNARDINO].

Sleepy Hollow [SAN BERNARDINO]: *locality,* 3.5 miles northwest of San Juan Hill in Carbon Canyon (lat. 33°56'50" N, long. 117°46'40" W; at S line sec. 36, T 2 S, R 9 W). Named on Yorba Linda (1964) 7.5' quadrangle. Postal authorities established Sleepy Hollow post office in 1954 and discontinued it in 1957 (Salley, p. 206).

Slide Creek [SAN BERNARDINO]:

(1) *stream,* flows 1.25 miles to Bear Creek 2.5 miles east-southeast of Keller Peak (lat. 34°10'50" N, long. 117°00'35" W; near S line sec. 8, T 1 N, R 1 W); the stream heads near Slide Peak. Named on Keller Peak (1967) 7.5' quadrangle.

(2) *stream,* flows 1 mile to Mill Creek Canyon 6 miles west of San Gorgonio Mountain (lat. 34°05'15" N, long. 116°55'30" W; sec. 18, T 1 S, R 1 E). Named on Forest Falls (1970) 7.5' quadrangle.

Slide Lake [SAN BERNARDINO]: *lake,* 300 feet long, 2.5 miles east-southeast of Keller Peak along Bear Creek (lat. 34°10'50" N, long. 117°00'30" W; near S line sec. 8, T 1 N, R 1 W); the lake is at the mouth of present Slide Creek (1). Named on Redlands (1954) 15' quadrangle.

Slide Lake Campground [SAN BERNARDINO]: *locality,* 2.5 miles east-southeast of Keller Peak (lat. 34°10'55" N, long. 117°00'25" W; near S line sec. 8, T 1 N, R 1 W); the place is near the site of former Slide Lake. Named on Keller Peak (1967) 7.5' quadrangle.

Slide Peak [SAN BERNARDINO]: *peak,* nearly 1 mile northeast of Keller Peak (lat. 34°12'15" N, long. 117°02'10" W; near E line sec. 1, T 1 N, R 2 W). Altitude 7841 feet. Named on Keller Peak (1967) 7.5' quadrangle.

Slocum Camp [SAN BERNARDINO]: *locality,* 25 miles east-southeast of the village of Red Mountain (lat. 35°15'30" N, long. 117° 10'30" W); the place is south of Slocum Mountain. Named on Pilot Knob (1954) 15' quadrangle.

Slocum Mountain [SAN BERNARDINO]: *mountain,* 24 miles east of the village of Red Mountain (lat. 35°17'45" N, long. 117°11'30" W). Named on Pilot Knob (1954) 15' quadrangle.

Slocum Well [SAN BERNARDINO]: *well,* 28 miles east-southeast of the village of Red Mountain (lat. 35°14' N, long. 117°07'55" W; sec. 14, T 31 S, R 45 E); the well is 5 miles southeast of Slocum Mountain. Named on Opal Mountain (1955) 15' quadrangle, which indicates that the well is dry.

Slover Canyon [SAN BERNARDINO]: *canyon,* 1.25 miles long, 3.5 miles north-northeast of Mount San Antonio (lat. 34°20'05" N, long. 117°36'25" W; sec. 21, 22, T 3 N, R 7 W). Named on Telegraph Peak (1956) 7.5' quadrangle. A grizzly bear killed Isaac Slover at the place in 1854 (Robinson, J.W., 1983, p. 196). United States Board on Geographic Names (1961c, p. 16) rejected the name "Stover Canyon" for the feature.

Slover Mountain [SAN BERNARDINO]: *hill,* 4 miles southwest of San Bernardino city hall (lat. 34°03'45" N, long. 117°20'20" W; on N line sec. 30, T 1 S, R 4 W). Named on San Bernardino South (1967) 7.5' quadrangle. Isaac Slover and his wife Barbara lived at the foot of the hill (Beattie and Beattie, p. 104).

Smart Spring [SAN BERNARDINO]: *spring,* about 4 miles northeast of Big Bear City (lat. 34°17'45" N, long. 116°47'40" W; near S line sec. 32, T 3 N, R 2 E). Name on Big Bear City (1971) 7.5' quadrangle. Lucerne Valley (1947) 15' quadrangle shows Smarts ranch located nearly 2 miles east-southeast of the spring.

Smiley Heights [SAN BERNARDINO]: *district,* 2 miles south-southwest of Redlands city hall (lat. 34°01'50" N, long. 117°11'50" W; sec. 4, T 2 N, R 3 W). Named on Redlands (1954) 15' quadrangle. The place was a well-known sightseeing point in the 1890's; A.K. Smiley opened the roads in his park there to automobiles in 1912 (Anonymous, 1950, p. 33).

Smiley Park [SAN BERNARDINO]: *locality,* 3 miles northeast of Harrison Mountain (lat. 34°11'50" N, long. 117°07'35" W; sec. 6, T 1 N, R 2 W). Named on Harrison Mountain (1967) 7.5' quadrangle.

Smith Canyon [SAN BERNARDINO]:

(1) *canyon,* 0.5 mile long. 10 miles north-northeast of Ontario city hall (lat. 34°10'50" N, long. 117°32'30" W; sec. 7, 18, T 1 N, R 6 W); the feature is at the southeast end of Smith Ridge. Named on Cucamonga Peak (1966) 7.5' quadrangle.

(2) *canyon,* drained by a stream that flows 2.5 miles to Morongo Valley (1) 3.25 miles north-northeast of downtown Morongo Valley (lat. 34°05'30" N, long. 116°33'40" W; near SW cor. sec. 10, T 1 S, R 4 E). Named on Morongo Valley (1972) 7.5' quadrangle.

Smith Creek [RIVERSIDE]: *stream* and *dry wash,* extends for 14 miles to San Gorgonio River 4 miles east-southeast of Banning (lat. 33°54'50" N, long. 116°48'45" W; sec. 18, T 3 S, R 2 E). Named on Beaumont (1953), Cabazon (1956), and Forest Falls (1970) 7.5' quadrangles. The name commemorates Dr. Isaac William Smith, who bought land in the neighborhood in 1853 (Gunther, p. 497).

Smith Ridge [SAN BERNARDINO]: *ridge,* southeast-trending, 1.25 miles long, 10.5 miles north-northeast of Ontario city hall (lat. 34° 11'40" N, long. 117°33'20" W; mainly in sec. 6, 7, T 1 N, R 6 W). Named on Cucamonga Peak (1966) 7.5' quadrangle.

Smithson Springs: see **Pinon Hills** [SAN BERNARDINO].

Smith's Station: see **Highland Springs** [RIVERSIDE].

Smith Water Canyon [RIVERSIDE-SAN BERNARDINO]: *canyon,* nearly 3 miles long, 7.25 miles south-southeast of Joshua Tree on Riverside-San Bernardino County line (lat. 34°02' N, long. 116°16'20" W). Named on Joshua Tree South (1972) 7.5' quadrangle.

Smoke Tree [SAN BERNARDINO]: *locality,* 2 miles west of the center of Twentynine Palms (lat. 34°08'10" N, long. 116°05'20" W; at SE cor. sec. 25, T 1 N, R 8 E). Named on Twentynine Palms (1973) 7.5' quadrangle.

Smoke Tree Wash [RIVERSIDE]: *stream,* flows 22 miles to Pinto Wash 24 miles northwest of Desert Center (lat. 33°56'40" N, long. 115°42'45" W). Named on Hexie Mountains (1963) and Pinto Basin (1963) 15' quadrangles.

Smoke Tree Well [RIVERSIDE]: *well,* 10.5 miles northwest of Chiriaco Summit (lat. 33°47'15" N, long. 115°49' W). Named on Hexie Mountains (1963) 15' quadrangle.

Smuggers Cave [IMPERIAL]: *cave,* 14 miles south-southwest of Carrizo Mountain (lat. 32°38'05" N, long. 116°05'30" W; sec. 5, T 18 S, R 9 E). Named on In-Ko-Pah Gorge (1959) 7.5' quadrangle. Called Smuggler Cave on Jacumba (1939) 15' quadrangle. United States Board on Geographic Names (1971, p. 2) approved the name "Blue Angels Peak" for a feature, altitude 4548 feet, located about 1 mile south of Smugglers Cave (sec. 8, T 18 S, R 9 E), and gave the name "Smugglers Point" as a variant.

Smugglers Point: see **Blue Angels Peak**, under **Smugglers Cave** [IMPERIAL].

Snaggletooth [SAN BERNARDINO]: *peak,* 17 miles south of Needles (lat.

34°35'25" N, long. 114°38'10" W). Named on Snaggletooth (1971) 7.5' quadrangle.

Snake Spring [SAN BERNARDINO]:

(1) *spring*, 17 miles north-northeast of Amboy (lat. 34°48'30" N, long. 115°37'50" W; near E line sec. 5, T 8 N, R 13 E). Named on Flynn (1956) 15' quadrangle.

(2) *spring*, 3.5 miles east-southeast of Luna Mountain (lat. 34°19'30" N, long. 117°04'10" W; near SE cor. sec. 22, T 3 N, R 2 W). Named on Butler Peak (1971) 7.5' quadrangle.

Sneakeye Spring [SAN BERNARDINO]: *spring*, 7.25 miles west-southwest of Twentynine Palms (lat. 34°05'20" N, long. 116° 10' W). Named on Twentynine Palms (1955) 15' quadrangle.

Snow Canyon [RIVERSIDE]: *canyon*, about 1 mile long, along Snow Creek (1) above a point 8 miles west-northwest of Palm Springs (lat. 33°53'25" N, long. 116°40'30" W). Named on Whitewater (1955) 7.5' quadrangle.

Snow Creek [RIVERSIDE]:

(1) *stream*, formed by the confluence of East Branch and West Fork, flows 3.25 miles to San Gorgonio River 8.5 miles northwest of Palm Springs (lat. 33°54' N, long. 116°40'20" W; sec. 21, T 3 S, R 3 E). Named on San Jacinto Peak (1981) and Whitewater (1955) 7.5' quadrangles. Both East Branch and West Fork are 3.25 miles long and are named on San Jacinto Peak (1981) 7.5' quadrangle. East Fork enters the main stream nearly 1 mile downstream from the confluence of East Branch and West Fork; it is 4 miles long and is named on San Jacinto Peak (1981) 7.5' quadrangle.

(2) *village*, 9 miles west-northwest of Palm Springs (lat. 33°53'25" N, long. 116°41' W; at SW cor. sec. 21, T 3 S, R 3 E); the place is west of lower reaches of Snow Creek (1). Named on Whitewater (1955) 7.5' quadrangle. Postal authorities established Snowcreek post office in 1914 and discontinued it in 1918 (Frickstad, p. 130).

Snow Creek [SAN BERNARDINO]: *stream*, flows 1 mile to Mill Creek Canyon 5 miles west of San Gorgonio Mountain (lat. 34°05'20" N, long. 116°55' W; near N line sec. 18, T 1 S, R 1 E). Named on Forest Falls (1970) 7.5' quadrangle.

Snow Crest Camp: see **Glacier Camp** [SAN BERNARDINO].

Snow Fork [SAN BERNARDINO]: *stream*, flows nearly 1 mile to North Fork Bear Creek 3.5 miles north-northeast of Keller Peak (lat. 34°14'25" N, long. 117°00'55" W; near E line sec. 19, T 2 N, R 1 W). Named on Keller Peak (1967) 7.5' quadrangle.

Snow Peak: see **Galena Peak** [SAN BERNARDINO].

Snow Point [SAN BERNARDINO]: *ridge*, north-northwest-trending, less than 1 mile long, 1 mile south of downtown Big Bear Lake (lat. 34°13'50" N, long. 116°54'55" W; sec. 30, T 2 N, R 1 E). Named on Big Bear Lake (1970) 7.5' quadrangle.

Snow Slide Spring [SAN BERNARDINO]: *spring*, 8.5 miles southeast of Luna Mountain (lat. 34°15'50" N, long. 117°00'40" W; near NW cor. sec. 17, T 2 N, R 1 W). Named on Butler Peak (1971) 7.5' quadrangle.

Snow Summit [SAN BERNARDINO]: *peak*, 2 miles southeast of downtown Big Bear Lake (lat. 34°13'15" N, long. 116°53'30" W; at NE cor. sec. 32, T 2 N, R 1 E). Named on Big Bear Lake (1970) 7.5' quadrangle

Snow Valley [SAN BERNARDINO]: *valley*, nearly 2 miles north of Keller Peak along North Fork Deep Creek (1) (lat. 34°13'20" N, long. 117°02'30" W; on N line sec. 36, T 2 N, R 2 W). Named on Keller Peak (1967) 7.5' quadrangle.

Soboba Hot Springs [RIVERSIDE]: *locality*, 2 miles northeast of San Jacinto (lat. 33°48' N, long. 116°55'35" W). Named on San Jacinto (1953) 7.5' quadrangle. The name is of Indian origin (Kroeber, p. 56). Berkstresser (1968, p. A10) gave the additional names "White Sulphur Spring," and "Ritchey Hot Springs" for the place.

Soda: see **Soda Springs** [SAN BERNARDINO].

Soda Lake [SAN BERNARDINO]: *dry lake*, 11 miles long, center 6.5 miles south of Baker at the end of Mojave River drainage (lat. 35° 10' N, long. 116°04' W). Named on Baker (1956) and Soda Lake (1956) 15' quadrangles.

Soda Lake: see **Soda Springs** [SAN BERNARDINO].

Soda Mountains [SAN BERNARDINO]: *range*, 13 miles west-southwest of Baker (lat. 35°11' N, long. 116°17' W); the range is west of Soda Lake. Named on Baker (1956), Cave Mountain (1948), and Soda Lake (1956) 15' quadrangles.

Soda Sink: see **Mojave River Wash** [SAN BERNARDINO].

Soda Springs [SAN BERNARDINO]: *springs*, 8.5 miles south of Baker (lat. 35°08'25" N, long. 116°06'15" W; sec. 11, T 12 N, R 8 E); the springs are at the west edge of Soda Lake. Named on Soda Lake (1956) 15' quadrangle. United States Board on Geographic Names (1984, p. 5) approved the name "Zzyzx Spring" for the feature, and rejected the names "Soda Springs," "Zzyzx Mineral Springs," and "Zzyzx Springs" for it. Avawatz Mountains (1933) 1° quadrangle shows a place called Soda located along the railroad at present Soda Springs, and California Mining Bureau's (1909a) map has the name "Soda Lake" for the same place. A military post called Hancock Redoubt was at the site in 1860; when the post was reopened in 1867, it was called Fort Soda or Camp Soda Springs (Hart, p. 122-123). United States Board on Geographic Names (1984, p. 5) approved the name "Zzyzx" for the locality, and rejected the names "Fort Soda," "Soda Springs," "Zzyzx Mineral Springs Resort," and "ZZYZX" for it. Curtis Howe Springer settled at the site in 1944 and built a hotel, church, health spa with mineral baths, radio station, and other buildings there; he coined the name "Zzyzx" to be the last word in the English language (*San Jose Mercury News*, October 19, 1990).

Soggy Lake [SAN BERNARDINO]: *dry lake*, 2 miles long, 4.25 miles north-northeast of Old Woman Springs (lat. 34°27'10" N, long. 116°41'10" W; in and near sec. 8, 9, T 4 N, R 3 E). Named on Old Woman Springs (1972) 7.5' quadrangle.

Solomons Knob [SAN BERNARDINO]: *peak*, 30 miles west-northwest of Ivanpah (lat. 35°25'30" N, long. 115°50'30" W; near S line sec. 31, T 16 N, R 11 E). Named on Halloran Spring (1956) 15' quadrangle.

Sonoran Dunes: see **Sand Hills** [IMPERIAL].

Soquel Canyon [SAN BERNARDINO]: *canyon*, drained by a stream that flows 2.5 miles to Orange County 2.25 miles northwest of San Juan Hill (lat. 38°56'10" N, long. 117°46'05" W). Named on Prado Dam (1967) and Yorba Linda (1964) 7.5' quadrangles.

Sorenson: see **Mount Sorenson** [SAN BERNARDINO].

Sorrel House Canyon [SAN BERNARDINO]: *canyon*, drained by a stream that flows nearly 4 miles to Chaparrosa Wash 9 miles north-northeast of downtown Morongo Valley (lat. 34°09'40" N, long. 116°30' W; sec. 19, T 1 N, R 5 E). Named on Rimrock (1972) 7.5' quadrangle.

Sortan Wash [IMPERIAL]: *stream*, flows 1.5 miles to Colorado River 29 miles south-southeast of Palo Verde (lat. 33°01'40" N, long. 114°34'50" W; sec. 20, T 13 S, R 23 E). Named on Picacho (1964) 7.5' quadrangle.

South Amargosa: see **Salt Creek** [SAN BERNARDINO].

South Cucamonga: see **Guasti** [SAN BERNARDINO].

South Fontana [SAN BERNARDINO]: *district*, 4 miles southwest of Fontana city hall (lat. 34°03'45" N, long. 117°29'15" W). Named on Fontana (1967) 7.5' quadrangle.

South Fontana Station: see **Declez** [SAN BERNARDINO].

South Fork Camp: see **Vaquero Campsite** [SAN BERNARDINO].

South Fork Campground [SAN BERNARDINO]: *locality*, 2.25 miles south-southwest of Sugarloaf Mountain (lat. 34°10'10" N, long. 116°49'50" W; sec. 13, T 1 N, R 1 E); the place is near the mouth of South Fork Santa Ana River. Named on Moonridge (1970) 7.5' quadrangle.

South Fork Meadows [SAN BERNARDINO]: *area*, 5.25 miles south-southwest of Sugarloaf Mountain (lat. 34°07'40" N, long. 116°50'35" W; at E line sec. 35, T 1 N, R 1 E); the place is at the head of South Fork Santa Ana River. Named on Moonridge (1970) 7.5' quadrangle.

South Ivanpah: see **Ivanpah** [SAN BERNARDINO].

South Park Peak [SAN BERNARDINO]: *peak*, nearly 4 miles southeast of Yucca Valley (lat. 34°04'45" N, long. 116°23'55" W; near S line sec. 18, T 1 S, R 6 E); the feature is 5.5 miles southeast of North Park Peak. Altitude 4395 feet. Named on Yucca Valley South (1972) 7.5' quadrangle.

South Pass [SAN BERNARDINO]: *locality*, 15 miles west of Needles (lat. 34°51'25" N, long. 114°53' W; sec. 22, T 9 N, R 20 E). Named on Bannock (1956) 15' quadrangle.

South Peak [SAN BERNARDINO]: *peak*, 6.5 miles east of Luna Mountain (lat. 34°20'30" N, long. 117°00'50" W; near E line sec. 18, T 3 N, R 1 W); the peak is near the south end of White Mountain. Altitude 7736 feet. Named on Butler Peak (1971) 7.5' quadrangle.

South Ridge [RIVERSIDE]: *ridge*, southwest-trending, 2.5 miles long, 1.5 miles east of the center of Idyllwild (lat. 33°44'30" N, long. 116°41'15" W). Named on Idyllwild (1959) 15' quadrangle, and on San Jacinto Peak (1981) 7.5' quadrangle.

South Riverside: see **Corona** [RIVERSIDE].

South San Jacinto: see **San Jacinto** [RIVERSIDE].

South Trona [SAN BERNARDINO]: *locality*, 3.5 miles south-southwest of Trona (lat. 35°42'55" N, long. 117°23'45" W; at W line sec. 30, T 25 N, R 43 E). Named on Westend (1973) 7.5' quadrangle.

Spangler [SAN BERNARDINO]: *locality*, 15 miles south-southwest of Trona along Trona Railroad (lat 35°32'55" N, long. 117°27' W; sec. 34, T 27 S, R 42 E); the place is east of Spangler Hills. Named on Spangler Hills East (1973) 7.5' quadrangle.

Spangler Hills [SAN BERNARDINO]: *range*, 15 miles south-southwest of Trona (lat. 35°34' N, long. 117°30' W). Named on Spangler Hills East (1973) and Spangler Hills West (1973) 7.5' quadrangles.

Spangler Valley: see **Searles Valley** [SAN BERNARDINO].

Spanish Canyon: see **Alvord Well** [SAN BERNARDINO].

Sparkhule Mountain [SAN BERNARDINO]: *peak*, 6.5 miles north of Victorville (lat. 34°37'55" N, long. 117°18' W; near S line sec. 4, T 6 N, R 4 W). Named on Helendale (1956) 7.5' quadrangle.

Sperry [SAN BERNARDINO]: *locality*, 34 miles north-northwest of Baker (lat. 35°44'30" N, long. 116°13'10" W). Site named on Silurian Hills (1956) 15' quadrangle. Francis Marion Smith named the place for his adopted niece, Grace Sperry (Strong, p. 46).

Sperry Hills [SAN BERNARDINO]: *range*, 38 miles north-northwest of Baker on San Bernardino-Inyo County line (lat. 35°47'30" N, long. 116°17' W). Named on Shoshone (1951) 15' quadrangle. United States Board on

Geographic Names (1966a, p. 7) rejected the names "Alexander Hills" and "Tecopa Hills" for the range, which extends from Ibex Pass eastward to Tecopa Pass in Inyo County; the Board noted that the range does not include lower Dumont Hills at the southeast end.

Spillway Canyon [RIVERSIDE]: *canyon,* drained by a stream that flows 2.5 miles to South Fork San Jacinto River 5.5 miles south of Idyllwild (lat. 33°39'45" N, long. 116°42'45" W; sec. 7, T 6 S, R 3 E); the canyon can take overflow from Lake Hemet. Named on Idyllwild (1959) 15' quadrangle.

Spitler Peak [RIVERSIDE]: *peak,* 6.25 miles east-southeast of Idyllwild (lat. 33°42'10" N, long. 116°37'15" W; near S line sec. 25, T 5 S, R 3 E). Named on Idyllwild (1959) 15' quadrangle.

Split Rock [RIVERSIDE]: *relief feature,* 29 miles east-northeast of Garnet (lat. 34°00'35" N, long. 116°03'20" W). Named on Queen Mountain (1972) 7.5' quadrangle.

Split Rock [SAN BERNARDINO]: *relief feature,* 16 miles southeast of Needles along Colorado River (lat. 34°38'45" N, long. 114°26'45" W; at W line sec. 2, T 6 N, R 24 W). Named on Topock (1970) 7.5' quadrangle.

Spoor Canyon [SAN BERNARDINO]: *canyon,* drained by a stream that flows 1.25 miles to lowlands 3 miles north-northeast of Yucaipa (lat. 34°04'30" N, long. 117°00'55" W; near NW cor. sec. 20, T 1 S, R 1 W). Named on Yucaipa (1967) 7.5' quadrangle.

Spotted Ridge: see **Horse Creek Ridge** [RIVERSIDE].

Spring [RIVERSIDE]: *locality,* 5.25 miles north-northwest of Perris (lat. 33°51'15" N, long. 117°16'20" W). Named on Elsinore (1901) 30' quadrangle.

Spring Brook [RIVERSIDE]: *stream,* 4 miles long, heads north of Box Springs Mountains and flows 4 miles to Riverside (lat. 34° 00' N, long. 117°22'15" W). Named on San Bernardino South (1967) 7.5' quadrangle.

Spring Creek [RIVERSIDE]: *stream,* at least 3.5 miles long, 16 miles south of Hemet (lat. 33°31'10" N, long. 116°56'15" W). Named on Hemet (1942) 15' quadrangle.

Spring Wilhelm [SAN BERNARDINO]: *spring,* 10 miles south-southeast of Essex (lat. 34°28'55" N, long. 115°05'45" W; sec. 33, T 5 N, R 18 E). Named on Milligan (1956) 15' quadrangle. Thompson's (1921) map shows a place called Wilhelm Camp located at or near present Spring Wilhelm.

Spy Mountain [SAN BERNARDINO]: *ridge,* east- to south-trending, 2.25 miles long, 4.5 miles north of Landers (lat. 34°20' N, long. 116°23'50" W). Named on Landers (1972) 7.5' quadrangle.

Squaw Hill [RIVERSIDE]: *hill,* 10 miles east-northeast of Cathedral City (lat. 33°50'10" N, long. 116°18'25" W; sec. 12, T 4 S, R 6 E). Named on Myoma (1958) 7.5' quadrangle.

Squaw Lake [IMPERIAL]: *water feature,* 12.5 miles east-southeast of Picacho Peak by Colorado River (lat. 32°54' N, long. 114°28'25" W; sec. 5, T 15 S, R 24 E). Named on Imperial Reservoir (1955) 7.5' quadrangle.

Squaw Mountain [RIVERSIDE]: *ridge,* southeast-trending, 1 mile long, 7.25 miles south-southwest of Wildomar (lat. 33°30'30" N, long. 117°20'45" W). Named on Wildomar (1953) 7.5' quadrangle.

Squaw Mountain [SAN BERNARDINO]: *ridge,* southwest-trending, 1.5 miles long, 33 miles west-northwest of Ivanpah (lat. 35°28'15" N, long. 115°52' W). Named on Halloran Spring (1956) 15' quadrangle.

Squaw Peak [SAN BERNARDINO]: *peak,* 9 miles northeast of Vidal (lat. 34°11'20" N, long. 114°22'35" W). Altitude 910 feet. Named on Parker NW (1970) 7.5' quadrangle.

Squaw Spring Well [SAN BERNARDINO]: *well,* about 3 miles east of the village of Red Mountain (lat. 35°21'55" N, long. 117°33'50" W; sec. 34, T 29 S, R 41 E). Named on Red Mountain (1967) 7.5' quadrangle.

Squaw Tank [RIVERSIDE]: *water feature,* 17 miles north-northeast of Indio (lat. 33°55'50" N, long. 116°04'30" W; near NE cor. sec. 7, T 3 S, R 9 E). Named on Lost Horse Mountain (1958) 15' quadrangle.

Squaw Tit [SAN BERNARDINO]: *peak,* 29 miles west of Ivanpah (lat. 35°21'45" N, long. 115°49'55" W; near N line sec. 29, T 15 N, R 11 E). Altitude 3939 feet. Named on Halloran Spring (1956) 15' quadrangle.

Squeaky Springs [IMPERIAL]: *locality,* 3.25 miles south-southeast of Truckhaven (lat. 33°15'30" N, long. 115°56'50" W; sec. 32, T 10 S, R 10 E). Named on Truckhaven (1956) 7.5' quadrangle. Called Winona on Durmid (1943) 15' quadrangle.

Squirrel Inn [SAN BERNARDINO]: *locality,* 6.5 miles northwest of Harrison Mountain (lat. 34°13'35" N, long. 117°14'55" W; near E line sec. 25, T 2 N, R 4 W). Named on Redlands (1901) 15' quadrangle.

Squirrel Spring [SAN BERNARDINO]: *spring,* 4.5 miles east-northeast of Big Bear City (lat. 34°17'05" N, long. 116°46'20" W; near E line sec. 4, T 2 N, R 2 E). Named on Big Bear City (1971) 7.5' quadrangle.

Stagecoach Spring [SAN BERNARDINO]: *well,* 1.5 miles east of Ivanpah (lat. 35°21'35" N, long. 115°06'20" W; at N line sec. 25, T 15 N, R 17 E). Named on Crescent Peak (1956) 15' quadrangle.

Stagg: see **Ludlow** [SAN BERNARDINO].

Staircase Canyon [SAN BERNARDINO]: *canyon,* drained by a stream that flows 2.25 miles to Santa Ana River 4.5 miles south-southeast of downtown Big Bear Lake (lat. 34°11' N, long. 116° 53' W; sec. 9, T 1 N, R 1 E). Named on Big Bear Lake (1970) and Moonridge (1970) 7.5' quadrangles.

Stalder: see **Mira Loma Station** [RIVERSIDE].

Star Springs: see **Fremont Peak** [SAN BERNARDINO].

State Line Pass [SAN BERNARDINO]: *pass,* 24 miles north-northwest of Ivanpah (lat. 35°39'30" N, long. 115°28'15" W; near NE cor. sec. 28, T 18 N, R 14 E); the pass in near California-Nevada State line. Named on Roach Lake (1955) 15' quadrangle.

Steam Well [SAN BERNARDINO]: *well,* 5 miles east-northeast of the village of Red Mountain (lat. 35°23'05" N, long. 117°32'10" W; sec. 25, T 29 S, R 41 E). Named on Klinker Mountain (1967) 7.5' quadrangle.

Stedman [SAN BERNARDINO]: *locality,* 6 miles south of Ludlow (lat. 34°37'50" N, long. 116°10'05" W; near NE cor. sec. 8, T 6 N, R 8 E). Named on Ludlow (1955) 7.5' quadrangle. Postal authorities established Stedman post office in 1904 and discontinued it in 1907; the name was for J.H. Stedman, one of the investors in a mine at the place (Frickstad, p. 146). The mining camp there was called Rochester because most of the mine investors were from Rochester, New York (Miller and Miller, p. 46; Wright and others, p. 71).

Steele Peak [RIVERSIDE]: *peak,* 6.25 miles east of Estelle Mountain (lat. 33°45'20" N, long. 117°18'20" W; near NW cor. sec. 9, T 5 S, R 4 W); the peak is southeast of Steele Valley. Altitude 2529 feet. Named on Steele Peak (1967) 7.5' quadrangle.

Steele Valley [RIVERSIDE]: *valley,* 6 miles east of Estelle Mountain (lat. 33°45'45" N, long. 117°18'45" W; sec. 4, 5, T 5 S, R 4 W). Named on Steele Peak (1967) 7.5' quadrangle. The name commemorates Henry C. Steele, who came to the region in 1884 (Gunther, p. 811).

Stepladder Mountains [SAN BERNARDINO]: *range,* 23 miles southwest of Needles (lat. 34°34'30" N, long. 114°52'15" W). Named on Stepladder Mountains (1956) 15' quadrangle.

Stetson Creek [SAN BERNARDINO]: *stream,* flows 2.5 miles to Forest Creek 5.25 miles south-southwest of downtown Big Bear Lake (lat. 34°10'05" N, long. 116°56'05" W; sec. 13, T 1 N, R 1 W). Named on Big Bear Lake (1970) 7.5' quadrangle.

Stewart Hot Springs: see **Lakeview Hot Springs** [RIVERSIDE].

Stills Landing [RIVERSIDE]: *locality,* 11 miles northeast of Banning along Whitewater River (lat. 34°01'40" N, long. 116°42'50" W; sec. 6, T 2 S, R 3 E). Site named on Catclaw Flat (1972) 7.5' quadrangle.

Stinson Canyon [RIVERSIDE]: *canyon,* 0.5 mile long, 6 miles south of Alberhill (lat. 33°38'25" N, long. 117°22'50" W; sec. 15, 22, T 6 S, R 5 W). Named on Alberhill (1954, photorevised 1988) 7.5' quadrangle. The name commemorates an owner of land near the canyon (United States Board on Geographic Names, 1960c, p. 21).

Stirrup Tank [RIVERSIDE]: *water feature,* 20 miles north-northeast of Indio (lat. 33°57'30" N, long. 116°01' W; near NW cor. sec. 35, T 2 S, R 9 E). Named on Lost Horse Mountain (1958) 15' quadrangle. Mendenhall (1909a, p. 78) described Stirrup Tanks (plural) as natural rock basins that contain water of excellent quality.

Stocker Meadows [SAN BERNARDINO]: *area,* 4.5 miles north-northeast of Sugarloaf Mountain (lat. 34°14'55" N, long. 116°47'15" W; sec. 20, 21, T 2 N, R 2 E). Named on San Gorgonio Mountain (1954) 15' quadrangle.

Stockton Flat [SAN BERNARDINO]: *area,* 3 miles east-northeast of Mount San Antonio (lat. 34°17'50" N, long. 117°35'45" W; on S line sec. 34, T 3 N, R 7 W). Named on Telegraph Peak (1956) 7.5' quadrangle. The name commemorates William H. Stockton, who filed a timber claim at the place in the late 1880's (Robinson, J.W., 1983, p. 188).

Stoddard Canyon [SAN BERNARDINO]: *canyon,* drained by a stream that flows 2.5 miles to San Antonio Canyon 8 miles north of Ontario city hall on San Bernardino-Los Angeles County line (lat. 34°10'20" N, long. 117°40'30" W). Named on Mount Baldy (1967) 7.5' quadrangle. William H. Stoddard set up a resort called Stoddard's Camp approximately 1 mile above the mouth of the canyon about 1886 (Robinson, J.W., 1983, p. 136).

Stoddard Flat [SAN BERNARDINO]: *area,* 10 miles north of Ontario city hall (lat. 34°12'05" N, long. 117°39'40" W; near W line sec. 6, T 1 N, R 7 W); the place is at the head of Stoddard Canyon. Named on Mount Baldy (1967) 7.5' quadrangle.

Stoddard Mountain [SAN BERNARDINO]: *ridge,* east-southeast-trending, 1.5 miles long, 15 miles south-southwest of Barstow (lat. 34°41'50" N, long. 117°07'10" W); the feature is west of the northwest end of Stoddard Ridge.. Named on Stoddard Well (1970) and Turtle Valley (1970) 7.5' quadrangles. The name recalls Arvin Stoddard and his wife Caroline, Mormons who came to the desert from San Bernardino in 1853 to look for gold (Miller and Miller, p. 39).

Stoddard Peak [SAN BERNARDINO]: *peak,* 9.5 miles north of Ontario city hall (lat. 34°11'45" N, long. 117°39'50" W; near SE cor. sec. 1, T 1 N, R 8 W); the peak is less than 0.5 mile southwest of Stoddard Flat. Altitude 4624 feet. Named on Mount Baldy (1967) 7.5' quadrangle.

Stoddard Ridge [SAN BERNARDINO]: *ridge,* east-southeast-to east-trending, 10 miles long, center 15 miles south of Barstow (lat. 34°40'30" N, long. 117°01' W). Named on Apple Valley (1957) and Ord Mountains (1955) 15' quadrangles. United States Board on Geographic Names (1961b, p. 13) approved the name "Traer Agua Canyon" for a box canyon about 1 mile long located on the northeast slope of Stoddard Ridge (34°40'15" N, long. 116° 59' W)—*traer agua* means "to carry water" in Spanish.

Stoddard's Camp: see **Stoddard Canyon** [SAN BERNARDINO].

Stoddard Valley [SAN BERNARDINO]: *valley*, 10 miles south of Barstow (lat. 34°45' N, long. 117°02' W). Named on Apple Valley (1957), Barstow (1956), Daggett (1956), and Ord Mountains (1955) 15' quadrangles.

Stoddard Well [SAN BERNARDINO]: *well*, 13 miles south-southwest of Barstow (lat. 34°42'40" N, long. 117°05'35" W; sec. 9, T 7 N, R 2 W); the well is at the northwest end of Stoddard Ridge. Named on the Stoddard Well (1970) 7.5' quadrangle.

Stone Basin [SAN BERNARDINO]: *relief feature*, 8.5 miles northeast of Mount San Antonio (lat. 34°21'20" N, long. 117°31' W; at SW cor. sec. 9, T 3 N, R 6 W). Named on Telegraph Peak (1956) 7.5' quadrangle.

Stone Creek [RIVERSIDE]: *stream*, flows 5.5 miles to West Fork San Joaquin River 10.5 miles east of San Jacinto (lat. 33°46'15" N, long. 116°46'40" W; near N line sec. 4, T 5 S, R 2 E). Named on Lake Fulmor (1956) and San Jacinto Peak (1981) 7.5' quadrangles.

Stone Creek Campground [RIVERSIDE]: *locality*, 4.25 miles west-southwest of San Jacinto Peak (lat. 33°47'10" N, long. 116°44'50" W; at N line sec. 35, T 4 S, R 2 E); the place is near a branch of Stone Creek. Named on San Jacinto Peak (1981) 7.5' quadrangle. Palm Springs (1957) 15' quadrangle shows Pine Flat Camp at or near the site.

Stoney Canyon: see **Slaughterhouse Canyon** [RIVERSIDE].

Stove Flats [SAN BERNARDINO]: *area*, nearly 4 miles south-southwest of Luna Mountain (lat. 34°17'35" N, long. 117°09'10" W; near NW cor. sec. 1, T 2 N, R 3 W). Named on Lake Arrowhead (1971) 7.5' quadrangle. Called Ash Meadows on Lake Arrowhead (1956) 15' quadrangle.

Stover Canyon: see **Slover Canyon** [SAN BERNARDINO].

Stover Mountain [SAN BERNARDINO]: *hill*, 4 miles southwest of San Bernardino city hall (lat. 34°03'45" N, long. 117°20'30" W; sec. 19, 30, T 1 S, R 4 W). Named on San Bernardino South (1967, photorevised 1973) 7.5' quadrangle.

Strawberry Cienaga [RIVERSIDE]: *area*, 2 miles south-southwest of San Jacinto Peak (lat. 33°47'10" N, long. 116°41'25" W; near N line sec. 32, T 4 S, R 3 E); the place is near the head of a branch of Strawberry Creek. Named on San Jacinto Peak (1981) 7.5' quadrangle.

Strawberry Creek [RIVERSIDE]: *stream*, flows 9 miles to South Fork San Jacinto River 11.5 miles east-northeast of Hemet (lat. 33° 42'40" N, long. 116°46'50" W; sec. 28, T 5 S, R 2 E). Named on Hemet (1957) and Idyllwild (1959) 15' quadrangles, and on San Jacinto Peak (1981) 7.5' quadrangle.

Strawberry Creek [SAN BERNARDINO]: *stream*, flows 4 miles to East Twin Creek 6 miles north-northeast of San Bernardino city hall (lat. 34°11'10" N, long. 117°15'15" W; sec. 12, T 1 N, R 4 W). Named on Harrison Mountain (1967) and San Bernardino North (1967) 7.5' quadrangles.

Strawberry Flat [SAN BERNARDINO]: *area*, 7 miles northwest of Harrison Mountain (lat. 34°14'20" N, long. 117°14'20" W; near SW cor. sec. 19, T 2 N, R 3 W). Named on the Harrison Mountain (1967) 7.5' quadrangle.

Strawberry Peak [SAN BERNARDINO]:

(1) *peak*, 2 miles west of the center of the town of Lucerne Valley (lat. 34°26'50" N, long. 116°59'05" W; sec. 9, T 4 N, R 1 W). Named on Lucerne Valley (1971) 7.5' quadrangle.

(2) *peak*, 6.25 miles northwest of Harrison Mountain (lat. 34°13'55" N, long. 117°14' W; sec. 30, T 2 N, R 3 W); the peak is 0.5 mile south-southeast of Strawberry Flat. Named on Harrison Mountain (1967) 7.5' quadrangle.

Strawberry Valley [RIVERSIDE]: *valley*, at Idyllwild (lat. 33°44'30" N, long. 116°43' W); the feature is along Strawberry Creek. Named on Idyllwild (1959) 15' quadrangle, and on San Jacinto Peak (1981) 7.5' quadrangle.

Strawberry Valley: see **Idyllwild** [RIVERSIDE].

Straw Peak: see **Slate Range** [SAN BERNARDINO].

Stray Cow Well [SAN BERNARDINO]: *well*, 15 miles east of Ivanpah on California-Nevada State line (lat. 35°19'50" N, long. 115° 02'35" W). Named on Crescent Peak (1956) 15' quadrangle.

Streeter: see **Magnolia Avenue** [RIVERSIDE].

Striped Mountain [SAN BERNARDINO]: *ridge*, south- to west-trending, 3 miles long, 13 miles west-northwest of Ivanpah (lat. 35°23'10" N, long. 115°32' W). Named on Mesal Range (1955) 15' quadrangle.

Stubbe Canyon [RIVERSIDE]: *canyon*, drained by a stream that flows 4.25 miles to San Gorgonio Pass 13 miles northwest of Palm Springs (lat. 33°56'45" N, long. 116°43' W; near NW cor. sec. 6, T 3 S, R 3 E). Named on Catclaw Flat (1972) and Whitewater (1955) 7.5' quadrangles. Called Stubby Canyon on San Jacinto (1901) 30' quadrangle. The misspelled name is for Henry Charles Steubbe, who filed on water in the canyon in 1886; the stream there was called Lost Creek before Mr. Steubbe filed his claim (Gunther, p. 513).

Stubbe Spring [RIVERSIDE]: *spring*, 17 miles north of Indio (lat. 33°57'45" N, long. 116°14'10" W; at S line sec. 27, T 2 S, R 7 E). Named on Lost Horse Mountain (1958) 15' quadrangle. Called Stubby Spring on Pinyon Well (1943) 15' quadrangle, but United States Board on Geographic Names (1961c, p. 17) rejected this name for the feature. Henry Charles Steubbe of Stubbe Canyon claimed the spring water in 1891 (Gunther, p. 514).

Stubby Canyon: see **Stubbe Canyon** [RIVERSIDE].

Stubby Spring: see **Stubbe Spring** [RIVERSIDE].

Studio Spring [SAN BERNARDINO]: *spring*, 18 miles south-southeast of Needles (lat. 34°34'35" N, long. 114°32'30" W). Named on Chemehuevi Peak (1971) 7.5' quadrangle.

Stud Mountain [IMPERIAL]: *peak*, nearly 6 miles east-northeast of Ogilby (lat. 32°51'30" N, long. 114°45'05" W). Altitude 2129 feet. Named on Ogilby (1963) 15' quadrangle.

Stump Spring [RIVERSIDE]: *spring*, 13 miles south-southwest of Palm Desert (lat. 33°32'25" N, long. 116°27' W; at E line sec. 27, T 7 S, R 5 E). Named on Palm Desert (1959) 15' quadrangle.

Styx [RIVERSIDE]: *locality*, 21 miles north-northwest of Blythe along Atchison, Topeka and Santa Fe Railroad (lat. 33°52'45" N, long. 114°47'40" W). Named on Midland (1952) 15' quadrangle. The place first was called Summit (Gunther, p. 515).

Sugarloaf [SAN BERNARDINO]:

(1) *relief feature*, 2 miles northwest of Victorville (lat. 34°33'40" N, long. 117°18'50" W; sec. 32, T 6 N, R 4 W). Named on Victorville (1956) 7.5' quadrangle.

(2) *locality*, 3.25 miles north-northwest of Sugarloaf Mountain (lat. 34°14'30" N, long. 116°49'45" W; sec. 24, T 2 N, R 1 E). Named on Big Bear City (1971) and Moonridge (1970) 7.5' quadrangles. Postal authorities established Big Bear Park post office in 1934 and discontinued it in 1945 (Salley, p. 21). They reestablished the post office with the name "Sugarloaf" in 1947; Mrs. Mary E. Herbert proposed that it be named for Sugarloaf (1) (Gudde, 1969, p. 324).

Sugarloaf Meadow [SAN BERNARDINO]: *area*, 1.5 miles south-southwest of Sugarloaf Mountain (lat. 34°10'45" N, long. 116°49'40" W; at S line sec. 12, T 1 N, R 1 E). Named on Moonridge (1970) 7.5' quadrangle.

Sugarloaf Mountain [IMPERIAL]: *hill*, 7 miles south-southwest of Carrizo Mountain (lat. 32°43'55" N, long. 116°02'55" W; sec. 33, T 16 S, R 9 E). Altitude 1022 feet. Named on In-Ko-Pah Gorge (1959) 7.5' quadrangle.

Sugarloaf Mountain [RIVERSIDE]:

(1) *peak*, 3 miles east-northeast of Riverside city hall (lat. 33°59'35" N, long. 117°19'15" W; sec. 17, T 2 S, R 4 W). Altitude 1944 feet. Named on Riverside East (1967) 7.5' quadrangle.

(2) *peak*, 10 miles south-southwest of Palm Desert (lat. 33°35'20" N, long. 116°26' W; near SE cor. sec. 2, T 7 S, R 5 E). Altitude 4776 feet. Named on Palm Desert (1959) 15' quadrangle.

Sugarloaf Mountain [SAN BERNARDINO]: *peak*, 7 miles north of San Gorgonio Mountain (lat. 34°11'55" N, long. 116°48'50" W; sec. 6, T 1 N, R 2 E). Altitude 9952 feet. Named on Moonridge (1970) 7.5' quadrangle.

Sugarloaf Peak [SAN BERNARDINO]: *peak*, 12.5 miles north of Ontario city hall (lat. 34°14'30" N, long. 117°38' W; sec. 20, T 2 N, R 7 W). Altitude 6924 feet Named on Mount Baldy (1967) 7.5' quadrangle.

Sugarloaf Peak: see **Pleasants Peak** [RIVERSIDE].

Sugarlump [SAN BERNARDINO]: *peak*, 2.25 miles west-northwest of Sugarloaf (lat. 34°12'35" N, long. 116°51' W; near W line sec. 35, T 2 N, R 1 E). Altitude 8805 feet. Named on Moonridge (1970) 7.5' quadrangle.

Sugarpine Mountain [SAN BERNARDINO]: *peak*, 5.5 miles east-southeast of Cajon (lat. 34°15'35" N, long. 117°22'35" W; sec. 14, T 2 N, R 5 W). Altitude 5478 feet. Named on Cajon (1956) 7.5' quadrangle.

Sugarpine Spring [SAN BERNARDINO]: *spring*, 5 miles east-southeast of Cajon (lat. 34°16' N, long. 117°22'50" W; at NW cor. sec. 14, T 2 N, R 5 W); the spring is 0.5 mile north-northwest of Sugarpine Mountain. Named on Cajon (1956) 7.5' quadrangle.

Suicide Peak: see **Suicide Rock** [RIVERSIDE].

Suicide Rock [RIVERSIDE]: *relief feature*, 3.25 miles south-southwest of San Jacinto Peak (lat. 33°46'15" N, long. 116°41'50" W; sec. 5, T 5 S, R 3 E). Named on San Jacinto Peak (1981) 7.5' quadrangle. United States Board on Geographic Names (1982c, p. 3) rejected the name "Suicide Peak" for the feature.

Sulphur Spring [RIVERSIDE]:

(1) *spring*, 6.5 miles southwest of Palm Springs (lat. 33°45'35" N, long. 116°37'15" W; near S line sec. 1, T 5 S, R 3 E). Named on Palm Springs (1957) 7.5' quadrangle.

(2) *spring*, 17 miles southeast of Idyllwild (lat. 33°32'45" N, long. 116°33'10" W; near SE cor. sec. 22, T 7 S, R 4 E). Named on Idyllwild (1959) 15' quadrangle.

Sulphur Spring: see **Glen Ivy Hot Springs** [RIVERSIDE].

Summit [RIVERSIDE]: *locality*, 11.5 miles east-southeast of Chiriaco Summit along a mining railroad (lat. 33°36' N, long. 115°32' W; near S line sec. 33, T 6 S, R 14 E). Named on Hayfield (1963) 15' quadrangle.

Summit [SAN BERNARDINO]: *locality*, nearly 3 miles northeast of Cajon along the railroad (lat. 34°19'40" N, long. 117°25'25" W; sec. 20, T 3 N, R 5 W); the place is at Cajon Pass. Named on Cajon (1956) 7.5' quadrangle. Postal authorities established Burcham post office 6.5 miles northeast of Cajon in 1893, changed the name to Summit in 1898, discontinued it for a time in 1901, discontinued it in 1911, reestablished it in 1915, and discontinued it finally in 1973; the name "Bucham" was for John Burcham, a pioneer rancher (Salley, p. 29, 215). Darton and others' (1915) map shows a place called Dell located 2.5 miles west of Summit along the railroad, and a place called Gish located nearly 2 miles west-southwest of Dell along the railroad.

Summit: see **Beaumont** [RIVERSIDE]; **Styx** [RIVERSIDE].

Summit Diggings [SAN BERNARDINO]:

(1) *locality,* 7 miles north of the village of Red Mountain (lat. 35° 27'15" N, long. 117°37'20" W; near S line sec. 36, T 28 S, R 40 E). Named on Klinker Mountain (1967) 7.5' quadrangle. Prospectors found placer gold at the place in the early 1890's, and mining activity continued there at intervals into the 1930's (Gudde, 1975, p. 341).

(2) *locality,* 6.25 miles north of the present village of Red Mountain along Southern Pacific Railroad (lat. 35°26'50" N, long. 117°37'25" W; sec. 6, T 29 S, R 41 E); the place is just south of Summit Diggings (1) in Summit Range. Named on Randsburg (1911) 15' quadrangle.

Summit Range [SAN BERNARDINO]: *range,* 7 miles north of the village of Red Mountain on San Bernardino-Kern County line (lat. 35°27'30" N, long. 117°37' W). Named on El Paso Peaks (1967) and Klinker Mountain (1967) 7.5' quadrangles.

Summit Spring [RIVERSIDE]: *spring,* nearly 4 miles north-northwest of Chiriaco Summit (lat. 33°42'40" N, long. 115°44'45" W; near W line sec. 28, T 5 S, R 12 E). Named on Hayfield (1963) 15' quadrangle.

Summit Spring [SAN BERNARDINO]: *spring,* 24 miles south-southwest of Ivanpah (lat. 35°02'05" N, long. 115°29'45" W; sec. 16, T 11 N, R 14 E); the spring is at the summit of Providence Mountains. Named on Mid Hills (1955) 15' quadrangle.

Summit Valley [SAN BERNARDINO]: *valley,* 16 miles south of Victorville (lat. 34°18'45" N, long. 117°21' W). Named on Cajon (1956) and Cedar Springs (1956) 7.5' quadrangles.

Summit Wash [SAN BERNARDINO]: *stream,* flows 2.5 miles to Globe Canyon 24 miles south-southwest of Ivanpah (lat. 35°33'05" N, long. 115°32' W; at W line sec. 7, T 11 N, R 14 E). Named on Kelso (1955) 15' quadrangle.

Sunbeam Lake [IMPERIAL]: *lake,* 7.25 miles west of El Centro (lat. 32°46'55" N, long. 115°41' W; mainly in sec. 13, T 16 S, R 12 E). Named on Seeley (1957) 7.5' quadrangle.

Sun City [RIVERSIDE]: *town,* 5 miles south-southeast of Perris (lat. 33°42'30" N, long. 117°11'45" W). Named on Romoland (1953, photorevised 1979) 7.5' quadrangle. Postal authorities established Sun City post office at a retirement community in 1962 (Salley, p. 215).

Sundial: see **Desert Shores** [IMPERIAL].

Sunfair [SAN BERNARDINO]: *locality,* 11 miles west of Twentynine Palms (lat. 34°09'50" N, long. 116°14'45" W; around NW cor. sec. 22, T 1 N, R 7 E). Named on Joshua Tree North (1972) and Sunfair (1972) 7.5' quadrangles.

Sunfair Heights [SAN BERNARDINO]: *locality,* 12 miles northwest of Twentynine Palms (lat. 34°14'20" N, long. 116°13' W; in and near sec. 23, T 2 N, R 7 E); the place is 5.5 miles north-northeast of Sunfair. Named on Sunfair (1972) 7.5' quadrangle.

Sunflower Spring [SAN BERNARDINO]: *spring,* 15 miles south-southeast of Essex (lat. 34°02'45" N, long. 115°07'30" W; at S line sec. 6, T 5 N, R 18 E); the spring is in Old Woman Mountains. Named on Essex (1956) 15' quadrangle. Called Sunflower Springs on Amboy (1942) 1° quadrangle. It also was called Old Woman Spring (Thompson, 1921, p. 262).

Sunflower Wash [SAN BERNARDINO]: *stream,* flows 10 miles before ending 22 miles southeast of Essex (lat. 34°31' N, long. 115°00' W; near SE cor. sec. 17, T 5 N, R 19 E); Sunflower Spring is near the stream. Named on Essex (1956) 15' quadrangle.

Sunkist [SAN BERNARDINO]: *locality,* 1.5 miles north-northwest of Redlands city hall along Southern Pacific Railroad (lat. 34°04'35" N, long. 117°11'20" W; at SW cor., sec, 15, T 1 S, R 3 W). Named on Redlands (1967) 7.5' quadrangle.

Sunnymead [RIVERSIDE]: *town,* 11 miles north of Perris (lat. 33°56'25" N, long. 117°14'30" W). Named on Riverside East (1967) and Sunnymead (1967) 7.5' quadrangles. Postal authorities established Sunnymead post office in 1928 (Frickstad, p. 130). Developers laid out and named Sunnymead Orchard Tract at the place in 1913 (Gudde, 1949, p. 347).

Sunnyslope [RIVERSIDE]: *town,* 4 miles northwest of Riverside (lat. 34°00'50" N, long. 117°25'45" W). Named on Fontana (1967) 7.5' quadrangle. R.F. Cunningham purchased part of Jurupa (1) grant and began development of the place in 1888; he named it for "the peculiar lay of the land towards the rising sun" (Gunther, p. 518).

Sunrise Butte [IMPERIAL]: *relief feature,* 19 miles west-southwest of El Centro (lat. 32°40'25" N, long. 115°51' W; near E line sec. 16, T 17 S, R 11 E). Named on Yuha Basin (1957) 7.5' quadrangle.

Sunrise Canyon [SAN BERNARDINO]: *canyon,* drained by a stream that flows 2.25 miles to lowlands 7.5 miles northeast of Daggett (lat. 34°55'35" N, long. 116°46'45" W; sec. 28, T 10 N, R 2 E). Named on Yermo (1953) 7.5' quadrangle.

Sunrise Valley: see **Baldy Mesa** [SAN BERNARDINO].

Sunrise Well [RIVERSIDE]: *well,* 24 miles northwest of Desert Center along Pinto Wash (lat. 33°57'30" N, long. 115°41'10" W; near N line sec. 35, T 2 S, R 12 E). Named on Pinto Basin (1963) 15' quadrangle.

Sunset Cove [SAN BERNARDINO]: *relief feature,* 17 miles east-southeast of Victorville (lat. 34°28'45" N, long. 117°00'15" W; in and near sec. 32, T 5 N, R 1 W). Named on Fifteenmile Valley (1971) and Lucerne Valley (1971) 7.5' quadrangles.

Sunset Spring [IMPERIAL]: *spring,* 10 miles north of Holtville (lat. 32°57' N, long. 115°21' W). Named on Holtville (1907) 30' quadrangle.

Sunshine Peak [SAN BERNARDINO]: *peak,* 15 miles west-southwest of Ludlow (lat. 34°38'45" N, long. 116°24'45" W; near NW cor. sec. 1, T 6 N, R 5 E). Altitude 4421 feet. Named on Lavic (1955) 15' quadrangle.

Sunsweet [SAN BERNARDINO]: *locality,* 2 miles west of Ontario city hall along Union Pacific Railroad (lat. 34°03'35" N, long. 117° 41' W; sec. 26, T 1 S, R 8 W). Named on Ontario (1967) 7.5' quadrangle.

Super Creek [RIVERSIDE]: *stream,* flows 1.25 miles to lowlands 9 miles north-northwest of Palm Springs (lat. 33°56'35" N, long. 116°37'30" W; sec. 1, T 3 S, R 3 E). Named on Desert Hot Springs (1955) and Whitewater (1955) 7.5' quadrangles.

Superior Lake [SAN BERNARDINO]: *dry lake,* 2.5 miles long, 29 miles east-southeast of the village of Red Mountain (lat. 35°14'40" N, long. 117°01'30" W). Named on Opal Mountain (1955) and Pilot Knob (1954) 15' quadrangles.

Superior Valley [SAN BERNARDINO]: *valley,* 32 miles east of the village of Red Mountain (lat. 35°17' N, long. 117°03' W); Superior Lake is in the valley. Named on Goldstone Lake (1948), Opal Mountain (1955), and Pilot Knob (1954) 15' quadrangles.

Superstition Hills [IMPERIAL]: *range,* 5.5 miles south of Kane Spring (lat. 33°01'50" N, long. 115°49'50" W). Named on Harpers Well (1956) and Kane Spring (1956) 7.5' quadrangles.

Superstition Mountain [IMPERIAL]: *ridge,* west-northwest-trending, 5.5 miles long, 11.5 miles north of Plaster City (lat. 32°57'30" N, long. 115°50' W). Named on Superstition Mountain (1956) 7.5' quadrangle.

Surprise Spring [SAN BERNARDINO]: *well,* 10 miles east-northeast of Landers (lat. 34°17'50" N, long. 116°13'15" W; sec. 35, T 3 N, R 7 E). Named on Deadman Lake SW (1955) 7.5' quadrangle. The name is from the location of the well at a surprising place to find it; a spring at the site dried up after a mining company drilled a well near it (Thompson, 1929, p. 635-636).

Surprise Valley [RIVERSIDE]: *canyon,* less than 1 mile long, 15 miles southeast of Indio (lat. 33°05'25" N, long. 116°00'25" W; sec. 1, 2, T 7 S, R 9 E). Named on Mecca (1955) 7.5' quadrangle.

Surprise Valley [SAN BERNARDINO]: *area,* 7.5 miles north-northeast of Joshua Tree (lat. 34°14'15" N, long. 116°16'20" W). Named on Joshua Tree North (1972) 7.5' quadrangle.

Surprise Wash [IMPERIAL]: *stream,* flows 5 miles to Tule Wash 4 miles southeast of Truckhaven (lat. 33°15'45" N, long. 115°55'10" W; sec. 34, T 10 S, R 10 E). Named on Kane Spring NW (1956) and Truckhaven (1956) 7.5' quadrangles.

Surveyors Pass [IMPERIAL]: *pass,* 23 miles north-northeast of Calipatria (lat. 33°24'30" N, long. 115°17'30" W; sec. 10, T 9 S, R 16 E). Named on Iris Pass (1963) 15' quadrangle.

Swan Lake [RIVERSIDE]: *lake,* 1000 feet long, 7.25 miles north of Corona (lat. 33°58'55" N, long. 117°33'10" W; sec. 19, T 2 S, R 6 W). Named on Corona North (1967) 7.5' quadrangle.

Swarthout Valley [SAN BERNARDINO]: *valley,* 5.25 miles north of Mount San Antonio on San Bernardino-Los Angeles County line (lat 34°22' N, long. 117°39' W). Named on Mount San Antonio (1955) and Telegraph Peak (1956) 7.5' quadrangles. Whipple (p. 148) referred to Swarthows Cañon. The name commemorates Nathan Swarthout and Truman Swarthout, who settled in the valley about 1851 (Robinson, J.W., 1983, p. 196).

Swede Hill [SAN BERNARDINO]: *ridge,* east-trending, 0.5 mile long, 4.25 miles south of Ludlow (lat. 34°39'30" N, long. 116°09'10" W; sec. 32, 33, T 7 N, R 8 E). Named on Ludlow (1955) 7.5' quadrangle.

Sweetwater Spring [SAN BERNARDINO]:

(1) *spring,* 8 miles north-northeast of Daggett (lat. 34°58'20" N, long. 116°51' W; sec. 11, T 10 N, R 1 E). Named on Yermo (1953) 7.5' quadrangle.

(2) *spring,* 1.25 miles north-northwest of Ord Mountain (lat. 34°41'35" N, long. 116°49'20" W; near SE cor. sec. 13, T 7 N, R 1 E). Named on Ord Mountains (1955) 15' quadrangle.

(3) *spring,* 12 miles south-southeast of Essex (lat. 34°34' N, long. 115°10'55" W; near E line sec. 34, T 6 N, R 17 E). Named on Essex (1956) 15' quadrangle.

Sweetwater Wash [SAN BERNARDINO]: *stream* and *dry wash,* extends for 3 miles to Willow Spring Wash 9.5 miles south-southeast of Essex (lat. 34°36'15" N, long. 115°11'20" W; sec. 15, T 6 N, R 17 E; the feature heads near Sweetwater Spring (3). Named on Essex (1956) 15' quadrangle.

Switzerland: see **Valley of the Moon** [SAN BERNARDINO].

Sycamore Canyon [RIVERSIDE]: *canyon,* drained by a stream that flows nearly 6 miles to Tequesquite Arroyo 2 miles southeast of Riverside city hall (lat. 33°57'35" N, long. 117°20'50" W; near NW cor. sec. 31, T 2 S, R 4 W). Named on Riverside East (1967) 7.5' quadrangle.

Sycamore Canyon [SAN BERNARDINO]:

(1) *canyon*, 1 mile long, 1.5 miles west-southwest of Devore (lat. 34°12'20" N, long. 117°25'40" W; sec. 5, T 1 N, R 5 W). Named on Devore (1966) 7.5' quadrangle.

(2) *canyon*, drained by a stream that flows 1.5 miles to lowlands 5.5 miles north of San Bernardino city hall (lat. 34°11'05" N, long. 117°18' W). Named on San Bernardino North (1967) 7.5' quadrangle.

Sycamore Flat [SAN BERNARDINO]: *area*, 1.5 miles south-southwest of Devore at the mouth of Cajon Canyon (lat. 34°11'55" N, long. 117°24'45" W); the place is below the mouth of Sycamore Canyon (1). Named on Devore (1966) 7.5' quadrangle. Lieutenant Colonel William Hoffman and a company of infantry established a base camp called Camp Banning in a grove of sycamore trees at the mouth of Cajon Canyon (Beattie and Beattie, p. 322).

Sycamore Spring [RIVERSIDE]: *spring*, 5.25 miles east of Aguanga (lat. 33°27'15" N, long. 116°46'20" W; near NE cor. sec. 28, T 8 S, R 2 E). Named on Aguanga (1954) 7.5' quadrangle.

Sycamore Spring: see **Cave Spring** [RIVERSIDE].

- T -

Tabasco Tank: see **Tabasca Tank** [RIVERSIDE].

Tabaseca Tank [RIVERSIDE]: *water feature*, 14 miles southeast of Chiriaco Summit (lat. 33°31' N, long. 115°32'45" W; sec. 32, T 7 S, R 14 E). Named on Hayfield (1963) 15' quadrangle. Called Tabasco Tank on Canyon Spring (1943) 15' quadrangle. The name "Tabaseca" is of Indian origin (Gunther, p. 519).

Table Mountain [RIVERSIDE]: *ridge*, northwest-trending, 4.5 miles long, 17 miles south-southeast of Idyllwild (lat. 33°31'30" N, long. 116°35'15" W). Named on Idyllwild (1959) 15' quadrangle, and on Bucksnort Mountain (1960) 7.5' quadrangle.

Table Mountain [SAN BERNARDINO]: *peak*, 16 miles south of Ivanpah (lat. 35°06'35" N, long. 115°22' W; near NE cor. sec. 21, T 12 N, R 15 E). Altitude 6176 feet. Named on Mid Hills (1955) 15' quadrangle. United States Board on Geographic Names (1985, p. 3) approved the name "Table Top" for the feature, and rejected the names "Table Mountain" "Tabletop Mountain," and "Table Top Mountain."

Table Top: see **Table Mountain** [SAN BERNARDINO].

Tabletop Mountain: see **Table Mountain** [SAN BERNARDINO].

Tachevah Canyon [RIVERSIDE]: *canyon*, 2.25 miles long, opens into lowlands less than 1 mile west-southwest of downtown Palm Springs (lat. 33°49'55" N, long. 116°33'45" W; near SE cor. sec. 9, T 4 S, R 4 E). Named on Palm Springs (1957) 7.5' quadrangle. San Jacinto (1901) 30' quadrangle has the name "Tahehevah Cr." for the stream in the canyon.

Tahehevah Creek: see **Tachevah Canyon** [RIVERSIDE].

Tahquitz: see **Camp Tahquitz** [RIVERSIDE]; **Camp Tahquitz** [SAN BERNARDINO].

Tahquitz Canyon [RIVERSIDE]: *canyon*, drained by a stream that flows 1 mile to Martinez Canyon 16 miles south-southeast of Palm Desert (lat. 33°30'05" N, long. 116°18'30" W; sec. 1, T 8 S, R 6 E). Named on Palm Desert (1959) 15' quadrangle.

Tahquitz Creek [RIVERSIDE]: *stream*, flows 9 miles to lowlands 1.5 miles south-southwest of downtown Palm Springs (lat. 33°48'35" N, long. 116°33'15" W; sec. 22, T 4 S, R 4 E); a branch of the stream heads near Tahquitz Peak. Named on Palm Springs (1957) and San Jacinto Peak (1981) 7.5' quadrangles.

Tahquitz Falls [RIVERSIDE]: *waterfall*, 2.25 miles south-southwest of downtown Palm Springs (lat. 33°48'10" N, long. 116°33'40" W; near SW cor. sec. 22, T 4 S, R 4 E); the feature is along Tahquitz Creek. Named on Palm Springs (1957) 7.5' quadrangle.

Tahquitz Meadow [RIVERSIDE]: *area*, 3.25 miles south-southeast of San Jacinto Peak (lat. 33°46'05' N, long. 116°39'50" W; near W line sec. 3, T 5 S, R 3 E). Named on San Jacinto Peak (1981) 7.5' quadrangle. Called Tahquitz Valley on Palm Springs (1957) 15' quadrangle, but United States Board on Geographic Names (1983a, p. 5) rejected this name.

Tahquitz Mountain: see **Tahquitz Peak** [RIVERSIDE].

Tahquitz Peak [RIVERSIDE]: *peak*, 4 miles south of San Jacinto Peak (lat. 33°45'20" N, long. 116°40'35" W; sec. 9, T 5 S, R 3 E). Altitude 8846 feet. Named on San Jacinto Peak (1981) 7.5' quadrangle. Called Tahquitz Mt. on California Mining Bureau's (1917b) map. The name is of Indian origin (Kroeber, p. 60-61).

Tahquitz Rock: see **Lily Rock** [RIVERSIDE].

Tahquitz Valley: see **Little Tahquitz Valley** [RIVERSIDE]; **Tahquitz Meadow** [RIVERSIDE].

Talc [SAN BERNARDINO]: *locality*, 15 miles north of Baker along Tonopah and Tidewater Railroad (lat. 35°28'40" N, long. 116°07'30" W). Named on Avawatz Mountains (1933) 1° quadrangle.

Talc Spring [SAN BERNARDINO]: *spring*, 11 miles east-northeast of Ivanpah (lat. 35°22'45" N, long. 115°07' W; sec. 14, T 15 N, R 17 E). Named on Crescent Peak (1956) 15' quadrangle.

Talega Canyon [RIVERSIDE]: *canyon*, drained by a stream that flows 2.5 miles to San Diego County 6 miles south-southwest of Sitton Peak (lat. 33°30'20" N, long. 117°28'40" W; at S line sec. 35, T 7 S, R 6 W). Named on Sitton Peak (1954) 7.5' quadrangle.

Talmadge Canyon [RIVERSIDE]: *canyon*, drained by a stream that flows 2.5 miles to Cooper Canyon 22 miles south of Idyllwild in San Diego County (lat. 33°25'25" N, long. 116°42'20" W). Named on Beauty Mountain (1960) 7.5' quadrangle.

Talmadge Spring [RIVERSIDE]: *spring*, 21 miles south of Idyllwild (lat. 33°26'05" N, long. 116°42'30" W; sec. 31, T 8 S, R 3 E); the spring is in Talmadge Canyon. Named on Beauty Mountain (1960) 7.5' quadrangle.

Tamarack Valley [RIVERSIDE]: *area*, 1 mile east-southeast of San Jacinto Peak (lat. 33°48'35" N, long. 116°39'35" W; sec. 22, T 4 S, R 3 E). Named on San Jacinto Peak (1981) 7.5' quadrangle.

Tank Canyon [SAN BERNARDINO]: *canyon*, 3.5 miles long, opens into Searles Valley 8 miles east-southeast of Trona (lat. 35°44'40" N, long. 117°14'15" W). Named on Wingate Pass (1950) 15' quadrangle.

Tarantula Wash [IMPERIAL]: *stream*, flows 13 miles to San Felipe Creek 6.5 miles west-southwest of Kane Spring (lat. 33°05'25" N, long. 115°56'45" W; at S line sec. 29, T 12 S, R 10 E). Named on Harpers Well (1956), Kane Spring NW (1956), and Shell Reef (1959) 7.5' quadrangles.

Tarn: see **The Tarn** [SAN BERNARDINO].

Ta Ta Pochon: see **Camp Ta Ta Pochon** [SAN BERNARDINO].

Tautona: see **Camp Tautona** [SAN BERNARDINO].

Tavern Bay [SAN BERNARDINO]: *embayment*, 6.5 miles south-southwest of Luna Mountain along Lake Arrowhead (1) (lat. 34° 15'45" N, long. 117°11'05" W; sec. 15, T 2 N, R 3 W). Named on Lake Arrowhead (1971) 7.5' quadrangle.

Tayles Hidden Acres [SAN BERNARDINO]: *area*, 10.5 miles northwest of downtown Morongo Valley (lat. 34°09'05" N, long. 116° 42'20" W; near S line sec. 19, T 1 N, R 3 E). Named on Onyx Peak (1972) 7.5' quadrangle.

Taylor [RIVERSIDE]: *locality*, 9 miles south-southwest of Palm Desert (lat. 33°36' N, long. 116°25' W; at S line sec. 36, T 6 S, R 5 E). Named on Palm Desert (1959) 15' quadrangle.

Taylor Ferry [IMPERIAL]: *locality*, 6 miles east of Palo Verde along Colorado River (lat. 33°26' N, long. 114°37'35" W). Site named on Cibola (1951) 15' quadrangle.

Taylor Lake [IMPERIAL]: *lake*, 28 miles south of Palo Verde near and connected to Colorado River (lat. 33°02' N, long. 114°38'15" W). Named on Picacho SW (1965) 7.5' quadrangle.

Taylor Spring [SAN BERNARDINO]:

(1) *spring*, 10 miles east of Ivanpah (lat. 35°21'55" N, long. 115°08'15" W; sec. 22, T 15 N, R 17 E). Named of Crescent Peak (1956) 15' quadrangle.

(2) *spring*, 7 miles west-southwest of Ord Mountain (lat. 34°38'45" N, long. 116°55'35" W; at SE cor. sec. 36, T 7 N, R 1 W). Named on Ord Mountains (1955) 15' quadrangle.

Teagle Wash [SAN BERNARDINO]: *stream*, heads just inside Kern County and flows 26 miles to Searles Lake 6 miles south-southeast of Trona (lat. 35°40'45" N, long. 117°20'55" W; at NE cor. sec. 16, T 26 S, R 43 E). Named on Ridgecrest (1953) and Searles Lake (1949) 15' quadrangles.

Teague Well [RIVERSIDE]: *well*, 25 miles east-southeast of Desert Center (lat. 33°35'05" N, long. 114°59'45" W; near SE cor. sec. 4, T 7 S, R 19 E). Named on McCoy Spring (1952) 15' quadrangle.

Teague Well: see **Hopkins Well** [RIVERSIDE].

Techevan Canyon [RIVERSIDE]: *canyon*, drained by a stream that flows 2 miles to lowlands 1 mile west of downtown Palm Springs (lat. 33°49'55" N, long. 116°33'45" W; at S line sec. 10, T 4 S, R 4 E). Named on Palm Springs (1957) 7.5' quadrangle.

Tecopa Hills: see **Sperry Hills** [SAN BERNARDINO].

Tecopa Pass [SAN BERNARDINO]: *pass*, 44 miles northwest of Ivanpah (lat. 35°46'25" N, long. 115°53'15" W). Named on Horse Thief Springs (1956) 15' quadrangle.

Telegraph Canyon [SAN BERNARDINO]: *canyon*, drained by a stream that flows 1 mile to Orange County 1 mile northwest of San Juan Hill (lat. 33°55'20" N, long. 117°44'55" W; at W line sec. 8, T 3 S, R 8 W). Named on Prado Dam (1967) 7.5' quadrangle.

Telegraph Peak [SAN BERNARDINO]: *peak*, 3.25 miles east-southeast of Mount San Antonio (lat. 34°15'40" N, long. 117°35'50" W; sec. 15, T 2 N, R 7 W). Altitude 8985 feet. Named on Telegraph Peak (1956) 7.5' quadrangle. The feature first was called Heliograph Hill for a heliograph station there (Gudde, 1969, p. 333).

Telegraph Wash [SAN BERNARDINO]: *stream*, flows less than 1 mile to Icehouse Canyon 13 miles north of Ontario city hall (lat. 34°14'45" N, long. 117°36'30" W; near W line sec. 22, T 2 N, R 7 W). Named on Cucamonga Peak (1966) and Telegraph Peak (1956) 7.5' quadrangles.

Telephone Canyon [SAN BERNARDINO]: *canyon*, 2.25 miles long, opens into Antelope Valley 13 miles south-southwest of Victorville (lat. 34°21'40" N, long. 117°21'05" W; sec. 12, T 3 N, R 5 W). Named on Cedar Springs (1956) 7.5' quadrangle.

Temecula [RIVERSIDE]:
(1) *land grant,* around Murrieta and the town of Temecula. Named on Bachelor Mountain (1953), Murrieta (1953), Pechanga (1968), and Temecula (1968) 7.5' quadrangles. The name is of Indian origin (Kroeber, p. 62). Felix Valdes received 6 leagues in 1844; Louis Vignes claimed 26,609 acres patented in 1860 (Cowan, p. 101).
(2) *town,* 20 miles south of Perris (lat. 33°29'35" N, long. 117°08'50" W); the town is on Temecula grant. Named on Murrieta (1953, photorevised 1979) and Temecula (1968) 7.5' quadrangles. Postal authorities established Temecula post office in 1859, discontinued it in 1862, reestablished it in 1870, changed the name to Temecula Station in 1883, and changed the name back to Temecula in 1905 (Salley, p. 219). The first Temecula post office was at John Magee's store located about 3 miles southeast of the present town of Temecula; the post office was reestablished at Louis Wolf's store about 0.25 miles north of Magee's store, and this post office was moved to the railroad and took the name "Temecula Station"—this last site became the nucleus of the present town (Gunther, p. 526). Postal authorities established Pujol post office 6 miles west of Temecula in 1880, discontinued it in 1881, reestablished it in 1882, and discontinued it in 1883; the name was for Father John Pujol (Salley, p. 178).

Temecula: see **Little Temecula** [RIVERSIDE].

Temecula Canyon [RIVERSIDE]: *canyon,* 5.5 miles long, along Santa Margarita River on Riverside-San Diego County line above a point 6 miles south-southwest of the town of Temecula (lat. 33°25'15" N, long. 117°12'15" W; sec. 4, T 9 S, R 3 W). Named on Temecula (1968) 7.5' quadrangle.

Temecula Creek [RIVERSIDE]: *stream,* heads in San Diego County and extends for 21 miles in Riverside County to join Murrieta Creek and form Santa Margarita River 1.5 miles south-southeast of the town of Temecula (lat. 33°28'30" N, long. 117°08'25" W). Named on Bachelor Mountain (1953), Pechanga (1968), and Temecula (1968) 7.5' quadrangles. Called Temecula River on San Luis Rey (1898) 30' quadrangle, but United States Board on Geographic Names (1943, p. 14) rejected the names "Temecula River" and "Aguanga Creek" for part of the stream.

Temecula Creek: see **Santa Margarita River** [RIVERSIDE].

Temecula Hot Springs [RIVERSIDE]: *locality,* 2.5 miles east of Murrieta (lat. 33°33'10" N, long. 117°10'05" W). Named on Murrieta (1953) 7.5' quadrangle.

Temecula Hot Springs: see **Murrieta Hot Springs** [RIVERSIDE].

Temecula River: see **Santa Margarita River** [RIVERSIDE]; **Temecula Creek** [RIVERSIDE].

Temecula Station: see **Temecula** [RIVERSIDE] (2).

Temecula Valley [RIVERSIDE]: *valley,* near the town of Temecula (lat. 33°29' N, long. 117°08'30" W). Named on Murrieta (1953, photorevised 1979), Pechanga (1968), and Temecula (1968) 7.5' quadrangles. San Luis Rey (1898) 30' quadrangle shows present Wolf Valley as part of Temecula Valley.

Temescal [RIVERSIDE]: *locality,* 3.5 miles west of Estelle Mountain (lat. 33°45'45" N, long. 117°29' W); the place is in Temescal Valley. Named on Riverside (1901) 15' quadrangle. Called Temescal Station on Lake Mathews (1967) 7.5' quadrangle. Postal authorities established Temescal post office in 1861, discontinued it the same year, reestablished it in 1874, moved it 0.5 mile southeast in 1885, and discontinued it in 1901 (Salley, p. 219). They established Big Laguna post office 15 miles southeast of Temescal in 1875 and discontinued it in 1878; the name was from an early name for present Lake Elsinore (1) (Salley, p. 21).

Temescal: see **Weisel** [RIVERSIDE].

Temescal Canyon [RIVERSIDE]: *canyon,* 3.5 miles long, along Temescal Wash above a point 3 miles east-southeast of Corona (lat. 33°51'30" N, long. 117°31'15" W). Named on Corona South (1967) 7.5' quadrangle.

Temescal Hot Springs: see **Glen Ivy Hot Springs** [RIVERSIDE].

Temescal Peak: see **Santiago Peak** [RIVERSIDE].

Temescal Station: see **Temescal** [RIVERSIDE].

Temescal Valley [RIVERSIDE]: *valley,* 11 miles southeast of Corona (lat. 33°45' N, long. 117°27' W). Named on Alberhill (1954), Corona South (1967), and Lake Mathews (1967) 7.5' quadrangles.

Temescal Wash [RIVERSIDE]: *stream,* flows 22 miles to Santa Ana River 3.5 miles northwest of Corona (lat. 33°54'20" N, long. 117° 36'50" W); the stream goes through Temescal Canyon and Temescal Valley. Named on Alberhill (1954), Corona North (1967), Corona South (1967), and Lake Mathews (1967) 7.5' quadrangles.

Tenaja Canyon [RIVERSIDE]: *canyon,* drained by a stream that flows 4.25 miles to San Mateo Canyon 10.5 miles south-southwest of Elsinore (present town of Lake Elsinore) (lat. 33°31'40" N, long. 117°24'40" W). Named on Sitton Peak (1954) 7.5' quadrangle.

Ten Thousand Foot Ridge [SAN BERNARDINO]: *ridge,* southeast-trending, 2.25 miles long, 2.5 miles east-northeast of San Gorgonio Mountain (lat. 34°06'30" N, long. 116°47'15" W). Named on San Gorgonio Mountain (1970) 7.5' quadrangle.

Tequesquite Arroyo [RIVERSIDE]: *stream* and *dry wash,* extends for 8.5 miles to Santa Ana River 4.25 miles west-southwest of Riverside city hall (lat. 33°58'05" N, long. 117°25'35" W). Named on Riverside East (1967) and Riverside West (1967) 7.5' quadrangles.

Terrace Springs [SAN BERNARDINO]: *springs,* 6.5 miles northeast of Big Bear City (lat. 34°20'05" N, long 116°46'15" W). Named on Big Bear City (1971) 7.5' quadrangle.

Terra Cotta [RIVERSIDE]: *locality,* 3.25 miles northeast of Lake Elsinore city hall (lat. 33°42' N, long. 117°22'25" W; sec. 35, T 5 S, R 5 W). Named on Lake Elsinore (1953) 7.5' quadrangle. Postal authorities established Terra Cotta post office in 1887 and discontinued it in 1893 (Frickstad, p. 131). Officials of Southern California Coal and Clay Company had the townsite laid out in 1887 (Gunther, p. 539).

Terwilliger Valley [RIVERSIDE]: *valley,* 16 miles south-southeast of Idyllwild (lat. 33°31' N, long. 116°39' W). Named on Idyllwild (1959) 15' quadrangle, and on Beauty Mountain (1960) and Bucksnort Mountain (1960) 7.5' quadrangles. The name commemorates Jacob Terwilliger, who settled at the place (Gunther, p. 541). San Jacinto (1901) 30' quadrangle shows present Anza Valley as part of Terwilliger Valley.

Teutonia Peak [SAN BERNARDINO]: *relief feature,* 15 miles west-southwest of Ivanpah (lat. 35°18' N, long. 115°33'45" W; sec. 14, T 14 N, R 13 E). Altitude 5755 feet. Named on Mescal Range (1955) 15' quadrangle. The name is from Teutonia mine, which is situated 0.5 mile north of the feature—a German prospector named the mine (Gudde, 1949, p. 360).

Texas Hill [SAN BERNARDINO]: *promontory,* 3 miles west-southwest of Devore along the canyon of Lytle Creek (lat. 34°12'05" N, long. 117°27' W; sec. 6, T 1 N, R 5 W). Named on Devore (1966) 7.5' quadrangle.

The Badlands [RIVERSIDE]: *area,* highlands 7 miles north-northeast of Perris and southwest of San Timoteo Canyon (lat. 33°57'30" N, long. 117°06'30" W). Named on El Casco (1967) and Sunnymead (1967) 7.5' quadrangles.

The Blue Cut [RIVERSIDE]: *pass,* 14 miles north-northeast of Indio (lat. 33°54'15" N, long. 116°08'15" W; near SW cor. sec. 15, T 3 S, R 8 E). Named on Lost Horse Mountain (1958) 15' quadrangle.

The Buttes [SAN BERNARDINO]: *hills,* 24 miles south-southeast of the village of Red Mountain (lat. 35°03'45" N, long. 117°24'15" W; mainly in sec. 9, 10, T 11 N, R 5 W). Named on Fremont Peak (1956) 15' quadrangle.

The Gavilan: see **Gavilan Plateau** [RIVERSIDE].

The Grotto [RIVERSIDE]: *relief feature,* 5 miles north-northeast of Mortmar at the head of Hidden Spring Canyon (lat. 33°35'15" N, long. 115°53'50" W; sec. 1, T 7 S, R 10 E). Named on Mortmar (1958) 7.5' quadrangle.

The Island [IMPERIAL]: *area,* 3 miles south of Bard on California-Arizona State line (lat. 32°44'45" N, long. 114°33'45" W). Named on Bard (1965) and Yuma East (1965) 7.5' quadrangles. Changes in the course of Colorado River have affected the state line here.

The Island [SAN BERNARDINO]: *island,* 500 feet long, 22 miles south-southeast of Needles in Lake Havasu (lat. 34°33'55" N, long. 114°24'10" W; near S line sec. 31, T 6 N, R 25 E). Named on Castle Rock (1970) 7.5' quadrangle.

The Matterdome: see **White Water Post Office** [RIVERSIDE].

The Pines [SAN BERNARDINO]: *locality,* 4 miles south of present downtown Big Bear Lake (lat. 34°11' N, long. 116°54'30" W; sec. 8, T 1 N, R 1 E). Named on San Gorgonio (1902) 30' quadrangle.

The Pinnacles [SAN BERNARDINO]:
(1) *relief feature,* 10 miles south of Trona at the west edge of Searles Valley (lat. 35°37' N, long. 117°22'05" W). Named on Christmas Canyon (1973) 7.5' quadrangle. The place was called Cathedral City in the early days (Clark and Clark, p. 42).
(2) *relief feature,* 6 miles west-southwest of Luna Mountain (lat. 34°18'25" N, long. 117°13'30" W; sec. 31, 32, T 3 N, R 3 W). Named on Lake Arrowhead (1971) 7.5' quadrangle. Called The Pinnacle on Lake Arrowhead (1956) 15' quadrangle; United States Board on Geographic Names (1974a, p. 4) gave this singular form of the name as a variant.

The Pipes [SAN BERNARDINO]: *locality,* 9 miles north-northeast of downtown Morongo Valley (lat. 34°10'20" N, long. 116°32'35" W; near W line sec. 14, T 1 N, R 4 E). Named on Rimrock (1972) 7.5' quadrangle. The name is said to be from iron pipe left at the place after an irrigation project was abandoned (Thompson, 1929, p. 637).

The Plaza [SAN BERNARDINO]: *locality,* 1 mile north of the center of Twentynine Palms (lat. 34°09' N, long. 116°03'15" W; at SE cor. sec. 20, T 1 N, R 9 E). Named on Twentynine Palms (1973) 7.5' quadrangle.

Thermal [RIVERSIDE]: *town,* 7 miles southeast of Indio (lat. 33°38'25" N, long. 116°08'20" W; mainly in sec. 22, T 6 S, R 8 E). Named on Indio (1956) 7.5' quadrangle. Postal authorities established Kokell post office at the place in 1901 and changed the name to Thermal in 1902 (Salley, p. 113). H.W. Cottle and Company had the townsite laid out and named it Kokell for the railroad agent there; Horace Adin Green bought the place and changed the name to Thermal in 1902 (Gunther, p. 270). Postal authorities established Arabia post office 3 miles south of Thermal in 1913 and discontinued it in 1915 (Salley, p. 9).

Thermal Canyon [RIVERSIDE]: *canyon,* 11.5 miles long, opens into Coachella Valley 8.5 miles east-southeast of Indio (lat. 33°39'45" N, long.

116°05'15" W; sec. 7, T 6 S, R 9 E); the mouth of the canyon is 3.5 miles east-northeast of Thermal. Named on Lost Horse Mountain (1958) 15' quadrangle, and on Thermal Canyon (1956) 7.5' quadrangle.

The Sink [RIVERSIDE]: *relief feature,* 10 miles northeast of Banning (lat. 34°01'25" N, long. 115°44'55" W; sec. 2, T 2 S, R 2 E). Named on Catclaw Flat (1972) 7.5' quadrangle.

The Tarn [SAN BERNARDINO]: *intermittent lake,* 600 feet long, nearly 0.5 mile south of San Gorgonio Mountain (lat. 34°05'30" N, long. 116°49'20" W; at SW cor sec. 7, T 1 S, R 2 E). Named on San Gorgonio Mountain (1970) 7.5' quadrangle.

The Troughs: see **Burro Spring** [SAN BERNARDINO] (2).

The Trough Spring: see **Burro Spring** [SAN BERNARDINO] (2).

The Windmill [SAN BERNARDINO]: *locality,* 5.25 miles north of Yucca Valley (lat. 34°11'45" N, long. 116°26'05" N; near SW cor. sec. 2, T 1 N, R 5 E); the site is along Pipes Wash. Named on Yucca Valley North (1972) 7.5' quadrangle. The place also is called Pipes Wash Well (Thompson, 1921, p. 247).

The Y [SAN BERNARDINO]: *locality,* 9.5 miles south-southwest of Trona (lat. 35°38'55" N, long. 117°30'20" W; at W line sec. 28, T 26 S, R 42 E); a road forks at the place. Named on Westend (1973) 7.5' quadrangle.

The Zanja [SAN BERNARDINO]: *stream,* diverges from Mill Creek and flows 6 miles to a point near Redlands city hall (lat. 34°03'25" N, long. 117°10'40" W). Named on Redlands (1967) and Yucaipa (1967) 7.5' quadrangles.

Thomas Hunting Grounds [SAN BERNARDINO]: *area,* 5 miles south-southeast of Keller Peak (lat. 34°07'50" N, long. 117°00'25" W; sec. 32, T 1 N, R 1 W). Named on Keller Peak (1967) 7.5' quadrangle.

Thomas Mountain [RIVERSIDE]:

(1) *ridge,* east-southeast-trending, 5 miles long, 8.5 miles south-southeast of Idyllwild (lat. 33°37'15" N, long. 116°41' W); the ridge is southwest of Garner Valley, which formerly was called Thomas Valley. Named on Idyllwild (1959) 15' quadrangle. On San Jacinto (1901) 30' quadrangle, the name applies to a peak on the ridge (sec. 28, T 6 S, R 3 E).

(2) *locality,* 10.5 miles south-southeast of Idyllwild (lat. 33°36'45" N, long. 116°37'30" W; near N line sec. 36, T 6 S, R 3 E); the place is northeast of the southwest end of Thomas Mountain (1). Named on Idyllwild (1959) 15' quadrangle.

Thomas Mountain: see **Little Thomas Mountain** [RIVERSIDE].

Thomas Valley: see **Garner Valley** [RIVERSIDE].

Thompsons Camp [RIVERSIDE]: *locality,* 17 miles north-northeast of Blythe (lat. 33°50'45" N, long. 114°31'45" W; sec. 11, T 4 S, R 23 E). Named on Big Maria Mountains SE (1955) 7.5' quadrangle.

Thorn [SAN BERNARDINO]:

(1) *locality,* 5 miles south of Victorville along Union Pacific Railroad (lat. 34°28'35" N, long. 117°16'50" W; sec. 34, T 5 N, R 4 W). Named on Hesperia (1956) 7.5' quadrangle.

(2) *locality,* 4 miles south of the center of the town of Lucerne Valley along Atchison, Topeka and Santa Fe Railroad (lat. 34° 23' N, long. 116°56'30" W; at NW cor. sec. 1, T 3 N, R 1 W). Named on Lucerne Valley (1971) 7.5' quadrangle.

Thorne Mountains: see **Little Thorne Mountains**, under **Gold Valley** [SAN BERNARDINO].

Thorpe Canyon [SAN BERNARDINO]: *canyon,* 1 mile long, 8 miles north-northeast of Ontario city hall (lat. 34°10'15" N, long. 117° 36' W; sec. 15, T 1 N, R 7 W). Named on Cucamonga Peak (1966) 7.5' quadrangle.

Thousand Palms [RIVERSIDE]: *town,* 5 miles northeast of Cathedral City (lat. 33°49' N, long. 116°23'30" W). Named on Cathedral City (1958) 7.5' quadrangle. Postal authorities changed the name of Edom post office to Thousand Palms in 1939 (Salley, p. 221).

Thousand Palms Canyon [RIVERSIDE]: *canyon,* 2 miles long, breeches Indio Hills 10 miles east-northeast of Cathedral City (lat. 33°50' N, long. 116°18'30" W; mainly in sec. 12, 13, T 4 S, R 7 E); Thousand Palms Oasis is in the canyon. Named on Myoma (1958) 7.5' quadrangle.

Thousand Palms Oasis [RIVERSIDE]: *locality,* 10 miles east-northeast of Cathedral City (lat. 33°50'15" N, long. 116°18'30" W; sec. 12, T 4 S, R 6 E). Named on Myoma (1958) 7.5' quadrangle. The place had two springs in 1854, each with a palm tree; a map of 1865 called it Hundred Palms, and by 1891 miners called it Thousand Palms (Gunther, p. 543-544).

Thousand Pines Camp [SAN BERNARDINO]: *locality,* 10 miles north of San Bernardino city hall (lat. 34°14'55" N, long. 117°16'30" W; at W line sec. 23, T 2 N, R 4 W). Named on San Bernardino North (1967) 7.5' quadrangle.

Three Finger Lake [IMPERIAL]: *intermittent lake,* about 1 mile long, 12.5 miles south of Palo Verde near Colorado River (lat. 33° 15'15" N, long. 114°41'30" W; in and near sec. 6, T 11 S, R 22 E). Named on Cibola (1965) and Picacho NW (1965) 7.5' quadrangles. Called Three Fingers Lake on Cibola (1951) 15' quadrangle, which shows a water-filled feature.

Three Sisters [RIVERSIDE]: *peaks,* three, 8 miles north-northeast of Estelle Mountain (lat. 33°52'10" N, long. 117°21'30" W; sec. 36, T 3 S, R 5 W). Named on Steele Peak (1967) 7.5' quadrangle.

Three Sisters Peaks [SAN BERNARDINO]: *peaks,* three, 7.25 miles northwest of downtown Morongo Valley (lat. 34°08'30" N, long. 116°38'25" W; sec. 26, 27, T 1 N, R 3 E). Named on Onyx Peak (1972) 7.5' quadrangle.

Through Canyon [SAN BERNARDINO]: *canyon,* 4.5 miles long, 40 miles east of Trona on San Bernardino-Inyo County line (lat. 35° 47'40" N, long. 116°39' W). Named on Confidence Hills (1950) 15' quadrangle.

Thumb Peak [IMPERIAL]: *peak,* 8 miles west-southwest of Palo Verde (lat. 33°24'20" N, long. 114°51'55" W). Altitude 1375 feet. Named on Palo Verde Mountains (1953) 15' quadrangle.

Thunder Mountain [SAN BERNARDINO]: *peak,* nearly 3 miles southeast of Mount San Antonio (lat. 34°15'55" N, long. 117°36'20" W; near N line sec. 15, T 2 N, R 7 W). Altitude 8587 feet. Named on Telegraph Peak (1956) 7.5' quadrangle. United States Board on Geographic Names (1965b, p. 16) rejected the name "Mount Harwood" for the feature; officials of the Sierra Club wanted the name "Mount Harwood," but officers of Mount Baldy Ski Lifts, Incorporated, suggested the more dramatic name "Thunder Mountain" (Robinson, J.W., 1983, p. 179).

Tiefort Mountains [SAN BERNARDINO]: *range,* 27 miles west of Baker (lat. 35°17' N, long. 116°33' W). Named on Tiefort Mountains (1948) 15' quadrangle.

Timber Mountain [SAN BERNARDINO]: *peak,* 13 miles north-northeast of Ontario city hall (lat. 34°14'40" N, long. 117°35'35" W; on W line sec. 23, T 2 N, R 7 W). Altitude 8303 feet. Named on Cucamonga Peak (1966) 7.5' quadrangle.

Tin Can Alley [SAN BERNARDINO]: *canyon,* less than 0.25 mile long, 8 miles north-northeast of Daggett (lat. 34°57'25" N, long. 116°48'30" W; sec. 18, T 10 N, R 2 E). Named on Yermo (1953) 7.5' quadrangle.

Tin Mine Canyon [RIVERSIDE]: *canyon,* drained by a stream that heads just inside Orange County and flows 2.5 miles to Hagador Canyon 3.25 miles southwest of Corona (lat. 33°50'10" N, long. 117°36' W; sec. 10, T 4 S, R 7 W). Named on Black Star Canyon (1967) and Corona South (1967) 7.5' quadrangles. Miners on the way to tin mines in Riverside County reportedly traveled through the canyon; the feature also was called Gypsum Canyon for gypsum discovered there in the 1880's, was called Coal Mine Canyon for coal found in 1887, and was called Richardson's Canyon for a resident of the place in 1882 (Gunther, p. 545).

Tin Shack [SAN BERNARDINO]: *locality,* 22 miles northeast of Vidal (lat. 34°22'15" N, long. 114°16'10" W; at S line sec. 5, T 3 N, R 26 E). Named on Whipple Mountains (1950) 15' quadrangle.

Tip Top Mountain [SAN BERNARDINO]: *peak,* 10 miles south of Old Woman Springs (lat. 34°15'05" N, long. 116°41'25" W; near S line sec. 17, T 2 N, R 3 E). Named on Rattlesnake Canyon (1972) 7.5' quadrangle.

Todd: see **Barstow** [SAN BERNARDINO].

Tokay Hill [SAN BERNARDINO]: *ridge,* south-trending, 0.5 mile long, 1.25 miles north of Devore (lat. 34°14' N, long. 117°24' W). Named on Devore (1966) 7.5' quadrangle.

Toll Road Campground [SAN BERNARDINO]: *locality,* 6 miles southwest of Luna Mountain (lat. 34°17'40" N, long. 117°12'45" W; on S line sec. 32, T 3 N, R 3 W). Named on Lake Arrowhead (1971) 7.5' quadrangle. Lake Arrowhead (1956) 15' quadrangle has the name "Toll Road Camp" for a place just south of present Toll Road Campground.

Toltec: see **Halloran Spring** [SAN BERNARDINO].

Tom Walters Mountains: see **Ibex Hills** [SAN BERNARDINO].

Tonner Canyon [SAN BERNARDINO]: *canyon,* drained by a stream that heads in Los Angeles County and flows 3 miles in San Bernardino County before reaching Los Angeles County again 5 miles northwest of San Juan Hill (lat. 34°58'05" N, long. 117°48'05" W; at E line sec. 27, T 2 S, R 9 W). Named on San Dimas (1966) and Yorba Linda (1964) 7.5' quadrangles. Called Brea Canyon on Watt's (1898-1899) map.

Tool Box Spring [RIVERSIDE]: *spring,* 9.5 miles south-southeast of Idyllwild (lat. 33°36'45" N, long. 116°39'30" W; near N line sec. 34, T 6 S, R 3 E). Named on Idyllwild (1959) 15' quadrangle.

Toomey [SAN BERNARDINO]: *locality,* 7.25 miles north-northwest of Newberry along Union Pacific Railroad (lat. 34°55'10" N, long. 116°44'45" W; sec. 35, T 10 N, R 2 E). Named on Daggett (1956) 15' quadrangle.

Topock Gorge [SAN BERNARDINO]: *narrows,* 15 miles southeast of Needles along Colorado River on California-Arizona State line (lat. 34°39'20" N, long. 114°27'15" W; sec. 34, T 7 N, R 24 W); the feature is 4.5 miles south-southeast of Topock, Arizona. Named on Topock (1970) 7.5' quadrangle.

Top Spring [SAN BERNARDINO]: *spring,* 4.5 miles northeast of Big Bear City (lat. 34°18'40" N, long. 116°47'45" W). Named on Big Bear City (1971) 7.5' quadrangle.

Toro Canyon [RIVERSIDE]: *canyon,* drained by a stream that flows 4 miles to lowlands 10 miles south of Indio (lat. 33°34'45" N, long. 116°14'30" W; sec. 10, T 7 S, R 7 E). Named on Palm Desert (1959) 15' quadrangle, and on Valerie (1956) 7.5' quadrangle.

Toro Peak [RIVERSIDE]: *peak,* 14 miles south of Palm Desert (lat. 33°31'30" N, long. 116°25'30" W; sec. 36, T 7 S, R 5 E). Altitude 8716 feet. Named on Palm Desert (1959) 15' quadrangle.

Toro Springs: see **Torres** [RIVERSIDE].

Torres [RIVERSIDE]: *locality,* 9 miles south of Indio (lat. 33°35'25" N, long. 116°13'45" W; sec. 2, T 7 S, R 7 E); the place is on Torres Martinez Indian reservation about 1 mile northeast of the mouth of Toro Canyon. Site named on Valerie (1956) 7.5' quadrangle. Brown (1920, p. 85) described Toro Springs located at the place.

Tortoise Mountains: see **Argus Range** [SAN BERNARDINO].

Tortoise Shell Mountain: see **Woods Mountains** [SAN BERNARDINO].

Tortuga [IMPERIAL]: *locality,* 10.5 miles east-northeast of Calipatria along Southern Pacific Railroad (lat. 33°10' N, long. 115°20'20" W; sec. 31, T 11 S, R 16 E). Named on Tortuga (1955) 7.5' quadrangle.

Tosco [RIVERSIDE]: *locality,* 5.5 miles north of Blythe along Atchison, Topeka and Santa Fe Railroad (lat. 33°41'30" N, long. 114° 36' W). Named on Ehrenberg (1945) 15' quadrangle.

Totem Pole Point [SAN BERNARDINO]: *promontory,* 7.5 miles south-southwest of Luna Mountain along Lake Arrowhead (1) (lat. 34°15'10" N, long. 117°12' W; near S line sec. 16, T 2 N, R 3 W). Named on Lake Arrowhead (1971) 7.5' quadrangle.

Tough Nut Spring [SAN BERNARDINO]: *spring,* 26 miles south-southwest of Ivanpah (lat. 35°30'15" N, long. 115°31'55" W; near W line sec. 30, T 11 N, R 14 E). Named on Kelso (1955) 15' quadrangle.

Trabuco Peak [RIVERSIDE]: *peak,* 4.5 miles west-southwest of Alberhill on Riverside-Orange County line (lat. 33°42'10" N, long. 117°28'25" W; sec. 26, T 5 S, R 6 W). Altitude 4604 feet. Named on Alberhill (1954) 7.5' quadrangle.

Trabuco Peak: see **Santiago Peak** [RIVERSIDE].

Traer Agua Canyon: see **Stoddard Ridge** [SAN BERNARDINO].

Trailfinders Camp [RIVERSIDE]: *locality,* 10.5 miles east of San Jacinto (lat. 33°48'30" N, long. 116°46'35" W; sec. 21, T 4 S, R 2 E); the place is in Hall Canyon. Named on Lake Fumor (1956) 7.5' quadrangle. Called Hall Canyon Public Camp on Banning (1942) 15' quadrangle.

Trail Fork Springs [SAN BERNARDINO]: *springs,* 8 miles south of downtown Big Bear Lake (lat. 34°07'20" N, long. 116°53'35" W; near E line sec. 32, T 1 N, R 1 E). Named on Big Bear Lake (1970) 7.5' quadrangle.

Trail Head Hill: see **Poopout Hill** [SAN BERNARDINO].

Trampas Wash [SAN BERNARDINO]: *stream* and *dry wash,* extends for 11 miles to Colorado River 18 miles south-southeast of Needles (lat. 34°37' N, long. 114°26'20" W; sec. 14, T 6 N, R 24 E). Named on Castle Rock (1970) and Chemehuevi Peak (1971) 7.5' quadrangles.

Travertine Palms Wash [IMPERIAL-RIVERSIDE]: *stream,* heads in San Diego County and flows 3.5 miles, partly in Imperial County, to Salton Sea 2.5 miles north of Desert Shores [IMPERIAL] in Riverside County (lat. 33°26'25" N, long. 116°02'30" W; near NW cor. sec. 34, T 8 S, R 9 E). Named on Oasis (1956) 7.5' quadrangle.

Travertine Rock [IMPERIAL]: *relief feature,* nearly 2 miles northwest of Desert Shores (lat. 33°25'20" N, long. 116°03'25" W; sec. 5, T 9 S, R 9 E). Named on Oasis (1956) 7.5' quadrangle. The feature is covered with travertine below the old waterline of an ancient body of water that once filled the basin now occupied by Salton Sea (Burns, p. 26).

Treasure Island [SAN BERNARDINO]: *island,* 150 feet long, 3.5 miles west of downtown Big Bear Lake in Big Bear Lake (1) (lat. 34°14'30" N, long. 116°58'15" W; sec. 22, T 2 N, R 1 W). Named on Big Bear Lake (1970) 7.5' quadrangle.

Tree Mont: see **Camp Tree Mont** [RIVERSIDE].

Tres Cerritos [RIVERSIDE]: *hill,* 7.5 miles southeast of Lakeview (lat. 33°45'45" N, long. 117°01'30" W); the feature has three major peaks. Named on Lakeview (1967) 7.5' quadrangle.

Tripp Flats [RIVERSIDE]: *area,* 17 miles southeast of Hemet (lat. 33°35'40" N, long. 116°45'10" W). Named on Hemet (1957) and Idyllwild (1959) 15' quadrangles. The name commemorates Samuel V. Tripp and his three sons, who had land in the neighborhood patented in the 1890's (Gunther, p. 549).

Tripp Meadow [RIVERSIDE]: *valley,* 9.5 miles southeast of Idyllwild (lat. 33°39'10" N, long. 116°35'30" W; mainly in sec. 17, T 6 S, R 4 E). Named on Idyllwild (1959) 15' quadrangle.

Trojan [SAN BERNARDINO]: *locality,* 4.25 miles west-northwest of Bagdad (lat. 34°36'15" N, long. 115°56'35" W; near S line sec. 16, T 6 N, R 10 E). Named on Bagdad (1956) 15' quadrangle.

Trona [SAN BERNARDINO]: *town,* 62 miles north-northwest of Barstow (lat. 35°45'45" N, long. 117°22'15" W; sec. 8, 17, T 25 S, R 43 E); the town is near Searles Lake. Named on Trona (1949) 15' quadrangle. Postal authorities established Trona post office in 1914; the name is from a mineral found at Searles Lake (Salley, p. 225).

Trona: see **South Trona** [SAN BERNARDINO].

Troughs: see **The Troughs**, under **Burro Spring** [SAN BERNARDINO] (2).

Trough Spring: see **The Trough Spring**, under **Burro Spring** [SAN BERNARDINO] (2).

Troy: see **Newberry** [SAN BERNARDINO].

Troy Lake [SAN BERNARDINO]: *dry lake,* 6.5 miles long, 7 miles east of Newberry (lat. 34°50' N, long. 116°34'15" W). Named on Newberry (1955) 15' quadrangle.

Truckhaven [IMPERIAL]: *locality,* 29 miles west-northwest of Calipatria (lat. 33°17'50" N, long. 115°58'35" W; near SW cor. sec. 18, T 10 S, R 10 E). Named on Truckhaven (1956) 7.5' quadrangle.

Tucalota Creek [RIVERSIDE]: *stream* and *dry wash,* extends for 21 miles to the canyon of Santa Gertrudis Creek 4 miles east of Murrieta (lat. 33°32'30" N, long. 117°08'30" W). Named on Hemet (1957) 15' quadrangle, and on Bachelor Mountain (1953) and Murrieta (1953) 7.5' quadrangles. The name is a misspelling of the American-Spanish word for owl (Gunther, p. 550).

Tucalota Hills [RIVERSIDE]: *ridge,* north-northeast-trending, 2.5 miles long, 12 miles east-northeast of Murrieta (lat. 33°35'15" N, long. 117°00'15" W); Tucalota Creek cuts the ridge. Named on Bachelor Mountain (1953) and Sage (1954) 7.5' quadrangles.

Tucalota Valley [RIVERSIDE]: *valley,* 12 miles south of Hemet (lat. 33°34'25" N, long. 116°58'30" W); Tucalota Creek is in the valley. Named on Sage (1954) 7.5' quadrangle.

Tulake: see **Camp Tulake** [SAN BERNARDINO].

Tule Canyon [RIVERSIDE]: *canyon,* 8.5 miles long, heads in San Diego County and opens into Coyote Canyon 20 miles south-southwest of Palm Desert (lat. 33°28'15" N, long. 116°32'45" W; at N line sec. 23, T 8 S, R 4 E). Named on Bucksnort Mountain (1960) 7.5' quadrangle. On Ramona (1903) 30' quadrangle, the stream in the canyon is called Tule Creek.

Tule Creek [RIVERSIDE]: *stream,* flows 11 miles to Temecula Creek 0.25 mile south of Aguanga (lat. 33°26'25" N, long. 116°51'50" W; near N line sec. 34, T 8 S, R 1 E). Named on Aguanga (1954) 7.5' quadrangle.

Tule Creek: see **Tule Canyon** [RIVERSIDE].

Tule Peak [RIVERSIDE]: *peak,* 6 miles east of Aguanga (lat. 33°27'15" N, long. 116°45'35" W; near N line sec. 27, T 8 S, R 2 E); the peak is 1.25 miles southeast of Tule Valley. Altitude 4837 feet. Named on Aguanga (1954) 7.5' quadrangle.

Tule Spring [RIVERSIDE]: *spring,* 21 miles south-southwest of Palm Desert (lat. 33°27'30" N, long. 116°35'40" W; near S line sec. 20, T 8 S, R 4 E); the spring is in Tule Canyon. Named on Bucksnort Mountain (1960) 7.5' quadrangle.

Tule Valley [RIVERSIDE]: *valley,* 5.5 miles east-northeast of Aguanga (lat. 33°28' N, long. 116°46'30" W); the valley is along Tule Creek. Named on Aguanga (1954) 7.5' quadrangle.

Tule Wash [IMPERIAL]: *stream,* heads in San Diego County and flows 14 miles to Salton Sea 5 miles east of Truckhaven (lat. 33° 17'15" N, long. 115°53'25" W; at W line sec. 24, T 10 S, R 10 E). Named on Kane Spring NW (1956), Shell Reef (1959), and Truckhaven (1956) 7.5' quadrangles.

Tumco: see **Hedges** [IMPERIAL].

Tumco Wash [IMPERIAL]: *stream,* flows 9 miles from Cargo Muchacho Mountains before ending 3 miles west-southwest of Ogilby (lat. 32°47'40" N, long. 114°52'55" W; near SE cor. sec. 5, T 16 S, R 20 E). Named on Ogilby (1963) 15' quadrangle.

Tungsten Flat [SAN BERNARDINO]: *area,* 24 miles southeast of Ivanpah (lat. 35°03'10" N, long. 115°02'45" W; near NW cor. sec. 9, T 11 N, R 18 E). Named on Lanfair Valley (1956) 15' quadrangle.

Tunnel Spring [RIVERSIDE]: *spring,* 12 miles southeast of Idyllwild (lat. 33°37'20" N, long. 116°34' W; sec. 28, T 6 S, R 4 E). Named on Idyllwild (1959) 15' quadrangle.

Tunnel 2 Ridge [SAN BERNARDINO]: *ridge,* north-trending, 1.5 miles long, 8 miles southwest of Luna Mountain (lat. 34°15'40" N, long. 117°13'45" W). Named on Lake Arrowhead (1971) 7.5' quadrangle.

Turkey Track [RIVERSIDE]: *relief feature,* 20 miles south-southwest of Palm Desert (lat. 33°28'15" N, long. 116°32'45" W; on N line sec. 23, T 8 S, R 4 E); Coyote Canyon splits at the place into three branches—this configuration of branches gives the appearance on a map of a giant turkey track. Named on Bucksnort Mountain (1960) 7.5' quadrangle.

Turk Point [SAN BERNARDINO]: *promontory,* 3.5 miles west of Devore along Lytle Creek (lat. 34°13'20" N, long. 117°27'50" W; at N line sec. 36, T 2 N, R 6 W). Named on Devore (1966) 7.5' quadrangle.

Turn [IMPERIAL]: *locality,* 6 miles east of Calipatria along Southern Pacific Railroad (lat. 33°06'50" N, long. 115°24'50" W; sec. 21, T 12 S, R 15 E); the rail line makes a sharp bend at the place. Named on Wiest (1956) 7.5' quadrangle.

Turnaround Wash [IMPERIAL]: *stream,* flows 6.5 miles to Walker Lake 17 miles south of Palo Verde (lat. 33°11'50" N, long. 114° 41' W; near N line sec. 29, T 11 S, R 22 E). Named on Quartz Peak (1953) 15' quadrangle, and on Picacho NW (1965) 7.5' quadrangle

Turner Springs [SAN BERNARDINO]: *springs,* 3.25 miles northwest of Victorville (lat. 34°34'15" N, long. 117°20'05" W; near N line sec. 31, T 6 N, R 4 W). Named on Victorville (1956) 7.5' quadrangle.

Turquoise Mountain [SAN BERNARDINO]: *mountain,* 35 miles west-northwest of Ivanpah (lat. 35°25'45" N, long. 115°55'20" W). Named on Halloran Spring (1956) 15' quadrangle.

Turtle Mountain [SAN BERNARDINO]: *ridge,* northwest-trending, 2.5 miles long, 10 miles northeast of Victorville (lat. 34°39'15" N, long. 117°11' W). Named on Turtle Valley (1970) 7.5' quadrangle.

Turtle Mountains [SAN BERNARDINO]: *range,* 21 miles west-northwest of Vidal (lat. 34°14'30" N, long. 114°50" W). Named on Rice (1954), Savahia Peak (1950), Turtle Mountains (1954), and Vidal (1949) 15' quadrangles.

Turtle Valley [SAN BERNARDINO]: *valley,* 11 miles north-northeast of Victorville (lat. 34°40'10" N, long. 117°10'45" W; in and near sec. 27, T 7 N, R 3 W); the valley is northeast of Turtle Mountain. Named on Turtle Valley (1970) 7.5' quadrangle.

Twelve Gauge Lake [SAN BERNARDINO]: *dry lake,* 0.25 miles long, 16 miles west of Barstow (lat. 34°55'10" N, long. 117°19'10" W; near N line sec. 32, T 10 N, R 4 W). Named on Twelve Gauge Lake (1973) 7.5' quadrangle.

Twentynine Palms [SAN BERNARDINO]: *town,* 72 miles east of San Bernardino (lat. 34°08'10" N, long. 116°03'15" W). Named on Queen Mountain (1972) and Twentynine Palms (1973) 7.5' quadrangles. Postal authorities established Twentynine Palms post office in 1927 (Frickstad, p. 146).

Twentynine Palms Marine Corps Base [SAN BERNARDINO]: *military installation,* headquarters 7 miles north of Twentynine Palms (lat. 34°14' N, long. 116°03'30" W). Named on Twentynine Palms (1973) 7.5' quadrangle. Called Marine Corps Training Center on most older maps that name the installation.

Twentynine Palms Mountain [SAN BERNARDINO]: *ridge,* north-northwest-trending, 35 miles south-southwest of Amboy (lat. 34° 04' N, long. 115°57'15" W). Named on Valley Mountain (1956) 15' quadrangle.

Twin Buttes [RIVERSIDE]: *hill,* 7.5 miles west-southwest of Riverside city hall (lat. 33°56'30" N, long. 117°29'40" W). Named on Riverside West (1967) 7.5' quadrangle.

Twin Butte Spring [SAN BERNARDINO]: *spring,* 17 miles south of Ivanpah (lat. 35°06' N, long. 115°22' W). Named on Ivanpah (1912) 1° quadrangle.

Twin Creek: see **East Twin Creek** [SAN BERNARDINO].

Twin Lakes [SAN BERNARDINO]: *lakes,* two, each about 400 feet long, nearly 5 miles north-northeast of Mount San Antonio (lat. 34°21'20" N, long. 117°37'55" W; near S line sec. 8, T 3 N, R 7 W). Named on Mount San Antonio (1955) 7.5' quadrangle.

Twin Peaks [SAN BERNARDINO]: *village,* 6.5 miles northwest of Harrison Mountain (lat. 34°14'15" N, long. 117°13'50" W; mainly in sec. 19, T 2 N, R 3 W). Named on Harrison Mountain (1967) 7.5' quadrangle. Postal authorities established Twin Peaks post office in 1916 and moved it 0.25 mile east in 1940 (Salley, p. 226).

Twin Pines Creek [RIVERSIDE]: *stream,* flows 5.5 miles to San Gorgonio River 5 miles east-southeast of Banning (lat. 33°53'45" N, long. 116°47'50" W; sec. 20, T 3 S, R 2 E). Named on Cabazon (1956) and Lake Fulmor (1956) 7.5' quadrangles.

Twin Springs [SAN BERNARDINO]: *spring,* 19 miles north-northeast of Amboy (lat. 34°50'10" N, long 115°39'45" W; near SW cor. sec. 30, T 9 N, R 13 E). Named on Flynn (1956) 15' quadrangle.

Twin Tanks [RIVERSIDE]: *water feature,* 22 miles north-northeast of Indio (lat. 33°59'15" N, long. 116°01'50" W; near N line sec. 22, T 2 S, R 9 E). Named on Lost Horse Mountain (1958) 15' quadrangle.

Two Bunch Palms [RIVERSIDE]: *locality,* 11.5 miles north of Cathedral City (lat. 33°56'55" N, long. 116°29'15" W; near S line sec. 32, T 2 S, R 5 E). Named on Seven Palms Valley (1958) 7.5' quadrangle. The name is from two groups of palm trees at the site (Chase, p. 35).

Two Hole Spring [SAN BERNARDINO]: *spring,* 4 miles south-southeast of Old Woman Springs (lat. 34°20'15" N, long. 116°41'30" W); the feature is 3.25 miles west of One Hole Spring. Named on Rattlesnake Canyon (1972) 7.5' quadrangle. Called Two Hole Springs on San Gorgonio (1902) 30' quadrangle.

Two Springs [SAN BERNARDINO]: *spring,* 37 miles west-northwest of Baker (lat. 35°32'45" N, long. 116°38'15" W; at E line sec. 22, T 17 N, R 3 E). Named on Leach Lake (1948) 15' quadrangle. The feature first was called Brooks Springs or Brooks Cienaga (Thompson, 1921, p. 267).

Tyler Valley [SAN BERNARDINO]: *valley,* 2 miles south-southwest of Ord Mountain (lat. 34°38'40" N, long. 116°49'45" W; on S line sec. 36, T 7 N, R 1 E). Named on Ord Mountains (1955) 15' quadrangle.

- U -

Ulmer: see **Barstow** [SAN BERNARDINO].

Union Flat [SAN BERNARDINO]: *area,* nearly 4 miles north of Big Bear City (lat. 34°19' N, long. 116°51'15" W; sec. 26, 27, T 3 N, R 1 E). Named on Big Bear City (1971) 7.5' quadrangle. A mining camp called Union Town was at the place at the time of the Civil War (Gudde, 1975, p. 357).

Union Town: see **Union Flat** [SAN BERNARDINO].

University Camp [SAN BERNARDINO]: *locality,* 2 miles south-southwest of Sugarloaf Mountain (lat. 34°10'25" N, long. 116° 50' W; sec. 13, T 1 N, R 1 E). Named on Moonridge (1970) 7.5' quadrangle.

University Creek [SAN BERNARDINO]: *stream,* flows 1.5 miles to Mill Creek Canyon 8 miles west of San Gorgonio Mountain (lat. 34°05'30" N, long. 116°58' W; at S line sec. 10, T 1 S, R 1 W). Named on Forest Falls (1970) 7.5' quadrangle.

Unnamed Wash [IMPERIAL]: *stream,* flows 12 miles to lowlands along Colorado River 2.5 miles northwest of Bard (lat. 32°48'35" N, long. 114°35'30" W; sec. 31, T 15 S, R 23 E). Named on Bard (1965), Little Picacho Peak (1965), and Picacho Peak (1965) 7.5' quadrangles.

Upland [SAN BERNARDINO]: *city,* 2.5 miles north of Ontario city hall (lat. 34°05'55" N, long. 117°38'50" W). Named on Cucamonga Peak (1966), Mount Baldy (1967), and Ontario (1967) 7.5' quadrangles. Postal authorities established North Ontario post office in 1887 and changed the name to Upland in 1902 (Frickstad, p. 144). The city incorporated in 1906. United States Geological Survey's (1942a) map shows a place called Anthony located about 0.5 mile northwest of downtown Upland along Pacific Electric Railroad.

Upper Covington Flat [RIVERSIDE]: *valley,* 15 miles east-northeast of Garnet (lat. 34°00'30" N, long. 116°18'45" W); the feature is 1.5 miles southwest of Lower Covington Flat. Named on Thousand Palms (1958) 15' quadrangle, and on Joshua Tree South (1972) 7.5' quadrangle.

Upper Holcom Valley [SAN BERNARDINO]: *valley,* 3.5 miles northeast of Fawnskin (lat. 34°18'50" N, long. 116°54'15" W; sec. 29, T 3 N, R 1 E); the place is 1.25 miles northeast of Holcom Valley near the head of Holcom Creek. Named on Fawnskin (1971) 7.5' quadrangle

Upper Johnson Valley [SAN BERNARDINO]: *valley,* 9 miles northeast of Old Woman Springs (lat. 34°28' N, long. 116°34'30" W); the place is northeast of Johnson Valley. Named on Old Woman Springs (1955) and Rodman Mountain (1955) 15' quadrangles.

Upper Lucerne Valley: see **North Lucerne Valley** [SAN BERNARDINO].

Upper Lytle Creek Ridge [SAN BERNARDINO]: *ridge,* northwest-trending, 5.5 miles long, 5.5 miles east of Mount San Antonio (lat. 34°18'05" N, long. 117°33' W); the feature is northwest of Lower Lytle Creek Ridge. Named on Telegraph Peak (1956) 7.5' quadrangle.

Upper Narrows [SAN BERNARDINO]: *narrows,* less than 0.5 mile southeast of downtown Victorville along Mojave River (lat. 34°31'55" N, long. 117°17'05" W; sec. 10, T 5 N, R 4 W); the place is 4 miles upstream from Lower Narrows. Named on Victorville (1956) 7.5' quadrangle.

Upper San Juan Campground [RIVERSIDE]: *locality,* 1.5 miles north-northeast of Sitton Peak (lat. 33°36'25" N, long. 117°25'55" W; at E line sec. 31, T 6 S, R 5 W); the place is in San Juan Canyon 1.5 miles upstream from Lower San Juan Campground, which is in Orange County. Named on Sitton Peak (1954) 7.5' quadrangle.

Upper Slough [SAN BERNARDINO]: *marsh,* 2 miles south-southeast of downtown Victorville near Mojave River (lat. 34°30'45" N, long. 117°16'30" W; sec. 23, T 5 N, R 4 W). Named on Victorville (1956) 15' quadrangle.

- V -

Vail Lake [RIVERSIDE]: *lake,* behind a dam on Temecula Creek 7.5 miles west-northwest of Aguanga (lat. 33°29'45" N, long. 116°58'35" W). Named on Vail Lake (1953) 7.5' quadrangle. Officials of Vail Company had the dam built in 1948—the company preserves the name of ranch owner Walter L. Vail (Gunther, p. 553).

Valencia [SAN BERNARDINO]: *locality,* 3 miles north-northeast of present San Bernardino city hall along Southern California Railroad (lat. 34°08'40" N, long. 117°16'45" W). Named on San Bernardino (1901) 15' quadrangle.

Valerie [RIVERSIDE]: *locality,* 10.5 miles south of Indio (lat. 33°34'10" N, long. 116°10'50" W; at SE cor. sec. 7, T 7 S, R 8 E). Named on Valerie (1956) 7.5' quadrangle. The name is for Valerie Jean Nicoll, whose parents set up a shop to sell dates at the place in 1929; the site had been known as Bendel's Corner (Gunther, p. 553).

Valjean [SAN BERNARDINO]: *locality,* 22 miles north of Baker (lat. 35°35'10" N, long. 116°07'20" W; at SE cor. sec. 4, T 17 N, R 8 E). Site named on Silurian Hills (1956) 15' quadrangle. The place, a station on Tonopah and Tidewater Railroad, was named for Jean Valjean, a field surveyor for the railroad (Hanna, p. 341)

Valjean Dunes: see **Valjean Valley** [SAN BERNARDINO].

Valjean Hills: see **Valjean Valley** [SAN BERNARDINO].

Valjean Valley [SAN BERNARDINO]: *valley,* 23 miles north of Baker (lat. 35°35' N, long. 116°02' W); the site of Valjean is near the west end of the valley. Named on the Kingston Peak (1955) and Silurian Hills (1956) 15' quadrangles. United States Board on Geographic Names (1965b, p. 16) approved the name "Valjean Hills" for a range situated just north of Valjean Valley (lat. 35° 39' N, long 116°06' W), and approved the name "Valjean Dunes" for sand dunes on the northwest edge of the range (lat. 35°40' N, long. 116°08' W).

Valle Vista [RIVERSIDE]: *locality,* 4.5 miles east of Hemet (lat. 33° 44'55" N, long. 116°53'30" W). Named on Hemet (1953) and San Jacinto (1953) 7.5' quadrangles. San Jacinto (1901) 30' quadrangle has both the names "Vallevista" and "Florida" at the site. Postal authorities established Vallevista post office in 1889, discontinued it for a time in 1896, and discontinued it finally in 1908 (Frickstad, p. 131). Officials of Fairview Land

and Water Company had the place laid out in 1886 and called it Florida—from Flora, the Greek goddess of flowers—for the wild flowers at the place; when postal authorities rejected the name "Florida" for the post office, the company name "Fairview" was given the loose translated "Valle Vista" and applied to the community (Gunther, p. 188, 554).

Valley Gardens [SAN BERNARDINO]: *district*, 1.5 miles south-southeast of present San Bernardino city hall (lat. 34°04'55" N, long. 117°16'40" W). Named on Colton (1943) 7.5' quadrangle

Valley Mountain [SAN BERNARDINO]: *range*, 26 miles south-southwest of Amboy (lat. 34°13'15" N, long. 115°57'30" W). Named on Valley Mountain (1956) 15' quadrangle.

Valley of Enchantment [SAN BERNARDINO]: *locality*, 10 miles north of San Bernardino city hall (lat. 34°14'40" N, long. 117°18'15" W; sec. 21, T 2 N, R 4 W). Named on San Bernardino North (1967) 7.5' quadrangle.

Valley of the Falls [SAN BERNARDINO]: *relief feature*, 5 miles west-southwest of San Gorgonio Mountain (lat. 34°04'55" N, long. 116°54'40" W; on E line sec. 18, T 1 S, R 1 E). Named on Forest Falls (1970) 7.5' quadrangle.

Valley of the Moon [SAN BERNARDINO]: *locality*, 9.5 miles north-northeast of San Bernardino city hall (lat. 34°14'30" N, long. 117°15'15" W; sec. 24, T 2 N, R 4 W); Moon Lake is at the place. Named on San Bernardino North (1967) 7.5' quadrangle. Postal authorities established Moonlake post office at the site in 1929, changed the name to Switzerland in 1939, and discontinued it in 1941 (Salley, p. 146, 217).

Valley View Park [SAN BERNARDINO]: *locality*, 9 miles north of San Bernardino city hall (lat. 34°14'05" N, long. 117°18'30" W; at N line sec. 28, T 2 N, R 4 W). Named on San Bernardino North (1967) 7.5' quadrangle.

Valley Vista [RIVERSIDE]: *locality*, 9.5 miles east-southeast of Perris (lat. 33°44'30" N, long. 117°04'15" W). Named on Murrieta (1943) 15' quadrangle.

Valley Wells [SAN BERNARDINO]: *locality*, 23 miles west-northwest of Ivanpah (lat. 35°27'55" N, long. 115°40'55" W; near N line sec. 22, T 16 N, R 12 W). Named on Mescal Range (1955) 15' quadrangle. On Ivanpah (1912) 1° quadrangle, the name applies to a water feature. The place also was known as Rosalie (Thompson, 1929, p. 599). Postal authorities established Rosalie post office in 1899 and discontinued it in 1900; the name was from Rosalie mine (Salley, p. 188). Wells at the place were called both Valley Wells and Rosalie Wells; the wells provided water for smelting copper ore (Mendenhall, 1909a, p. 56).

Valley Wells Station [SAN BERNARDINO]: *locality*, 23 miles west-northwest of Ivanpah (lat. 35°26'10" N, long. 115°42' W; near N line sec. 33, T 16 N, R 12 E); the place is 2.5 miles south-southwest of Valley Wells along the main highway. Named on Mescal Range (1955) 15' quadrangle.

Val Verde [RIVERSIDE]: *locality*, nearly 5 miles north-northwest of Perris along Atchison, Topeka and Santa Fe Railroad (lat. 33°50'50" N, long. 117°15'10" W; sec. 1, T 4 S, R 4 W). Named on Steele Peak (1967) 7.5' quadrangle. Called Valverde on Riverside (1901) 15' quadrangle. Postal authorities established Val Verde post office in 1894, discontinued it in 1904, reestablished it in 1918, and discontinued it in 1930 (Salley, p. 229).

Vanderbilt [SAN BERNARDINO]: *locality*, 3.25 miles east-southeast of Ivanpah (lat. 35°19'45" N, long 115°15'15" W; near W line sec. 3, T 14 N, R 16 E). Named on Ivanpah (1956) 15' quadrangle. Postal authorities established Vanderbilt post office in 1893 and discontinued it in 1900; the name was from Vanderbilt gold mine (Salley, p. 230).

Vandeventer Flat [RIVERSIDE]: *valley*, 17 miles southeast of Idyllwild (lat. 33°33'15" N, long. 116°31'45" W; mainly in sec. 13, 24, T 7 S, R 4 E). Named on Idyllwild (1959) 15' quadrangle. The name commemorates Frank Vandeventer, who settled at the place in the late 1870's (Gunther, p. 556).

Van Dusen: see **Big Bear City** [SAN BERNARDINO].

Van Dusen Canyon [SAN BERNARDINO]: *canyon*, 3.5 miles long, opens into lowlands at Big Bear City (lat. 34°16'15" N, long. 116° 51'05" W; sec. 11, T 2 N, R 1 E). Named on Big Bear City (1971) and Fawnskin (1971) 7.5' quadrangles. The name commemorates Jed Van Dusen, who found and worked a rich mine in the canyon before his partner murdered him (Gudde, 1975, p. 359).

Van Winkle Mountain [SAN BERNARDINO]: *range*, 16 miles north-northeast of Amboy (lat. 34°45'20" N, long. 115°35'30" W). Named on Flynn (1956) 15' quadrangle.

Van Winkle Spring [SAN BERNARDINO]: *spring*, 17 miles north-northeast of Amboy (lat. 34°46'30" N, long. 115°35'30" W; near NW cor. sec. 23, T 8 N, R 13 E); the spring is at the north edge of Van Winkle Mountain. Named on Flynn (1956) 15' quadrangle.

Van Winkle Wash [SAN BERNARDINO]: *stream* and *dry wash*, extends for 8 miles to Clipper Wash about 16 miles northeast of Amboy (lat. 34°42' N, long. 115°30'50" W; near NE cor. sec. 16, T 7 N, R 14 E); the feature lies along the east and south sides of Van Winkle Mountain. Named on Cadiz (1956) and Flynn (1956) 15' quadrangles.

Vaquero Campsite [SAN BERNARDINO]: *locality*, 2.25 miles south-southwest of Sugarloaf Mountain (lat. 34°10'05" N, long. 116°49'20" W; at E line sec. 13, T 1 N, R 2 E). Named on Moonridge (1970) 7.5' quadrangle. San Gorgonio Mountain (1954) 15' quadrangle has the name "South Fork Camp" at or near the place.

Vaughn Spring [SAN BERNARDINO]: *spring*, 9.5 miles south-southeast of Old Woman Springs (lat. 34°15'20" N, long. 116°39'39" W; sec. 15, T 2 N, R 3 E). Named on Rattlesnake Canyon (1972) 7.5' quadrangle.

Velian Wash [IMPERIAL]: *stream*, flows 2.5 miles to Colorado River 22 miles south of Palo Verde (lat. 33°06'45" N, long. 114°42'25" W; sec. 24, T 12 S, R 21 E). Named on Picacho SW (1965) 7.5' quadrangle.

Verdant [IMPERIAL]: *locality*, 2.5 miles west-southwest of Calipatria along Southern Pacific Railroad (lat. 33°07'05" N, long. 115° 33'35" W; near NW cor. sec. 19, T 12 S, R 14 E). Named on Westmorland (1956) 7.5' quadrangle.

Verdemont [SAN BERNARDINO]: *locality*, 7.5 miles northwest of San Bernardino city hall along the railroad (lat. 34°11'35" N, long. 117°22'05" W). Named on San Bernardino North (1967) 7.5' quadrangle. San Bernardino (1901) 15' quadrangle has the designation "Irvington Station (Marida)" at the place. Postal authorities established Marida post office in Cajon Canyon in 1893 (SE quarter sec. 3, T 1 N, R 5 W), moved it to the railroad in 1895, when they ordered the name changed to Verdemont, but then they rescinded the order for the name change; they discontinued Marida post office in 1895, established Verdemont post office in 1922, and discontinued it in 1924 (Salley, p. 133, 230).

Verde Wash [IMPERIAL]: *stream*, flows 1 mile to Anza Ditch less than 1 mile northeast of Truckhaven (lat. 33°18'15" N, long. 115° 58' W; sec. 18, T 10 S, R 10 E). Named on Truckhaven (1956) 7.5' quadrangle.

Verdugo Canyon [RIVERSIDE]: *canyon*, drained by a stream that flows 1.25 miles to Orange County 4 miles southwest of Sitton Peak (lat. 33°33' N, long. 117°29'50" W). Named on Sitton Peak (1954) 7.5' quadrangle.

Verdugo Canyon: see **Aliso Canyon** [RIVERSIDE].

Verdugo Potrero [RIVERSIDE]: *area*, 2.5 miles south-southwest of Sitton Peak (lat. 33°33'20" N, long. 117°28'10" W; at E line sec. 14, T 7 S, R 6 W); the place is near the head of Verdugo Canyon. Named on Sitton Peak (1954) 7.5' quadrangle.

Victor: see **Victorville** [SAN BERNARDINO].

Victoria [SAN BERNARDINO]: *locality*, 3 miles southeast of San Bernardino city hall along Atchison, Topeka and Santa Fe Railroad (lat. 34°04'25" N, long. 117°15'15" W). Named on Colton (1943) 7.5' quadrangle.

Victoria Hill [RIVERSIDE]: *hill*, 1.5 miles south of Riverside city hall (lat. 33°57'35" N, long. 117°22'10" W; near N line sec. 35, T 2 S, R 5 W). Named on Riverside East (1967) 7.5' quadrangle.

Victorville [SAN BERNARDINO]: *town*, 30 miles north of San Bernardino (lat. 34°32'10" N, long. 117°17'35" W). Named on Victorville (1956) 7.5' quadrangle. Postal authorities established Victor post office in 1886 and changed the name to Victorville in 1903; the name "Victor" was for Jacob N. Victor, construction superintendent for California Southern Railroad (Salley, p. 231). The town incorporated in 1962. The site first was known as Mormon Crossing; the community was called Huntington before it became Victor (Peirson, p. 132-133).

Victorville Air Force Base: see **George Air Force Base** [SAN BERNARDINO].

Victory Palms [RIVERSIDE]: *locality*, 17 miles northeast of Mortmar (lat. 33°42'15" N, long. 115°45' W; sec. 29, T 5 S, R 12 E). Named on Cottonwood Spring (1958) 15' quadrangle.

Victory Pass [RIVERSIDE]: *pass*, 5 miles north-northwest of Desert Center (lat. 33°46'40" N, long. 115°27' W; sec. 31, T 4 S, R 15 E). Named on Coxcomb Mountains (1963) 15' quadrangle.

Vidal [SAN BERNARDINO]: *village*, 50 miles south of Needles (lat. 34°07'10" N, long. 114°30'30" W; near NE cor. sec. 1, T 1 S, R 23 E). Named on Vidal (1949) 15' quadrangle. Postal authorities established Vidal post office in 1910 (Frickstad, p. 147). Hansen Brownell founded the place in 1907 and named it for his son-in-law (Gudde, 1949, p. 379).

Vidal Junction [SAN BERNARDINO]: *locality*, 6 miles northwest of Vidal (lat. 34°11'20" N, long. 114°34'25" W; sec. 9, T 1 N, R 23 E). Named on Vidal (1949) 15' quadrangle.

Vidal Valley [SAN BERNARDINO]: *valley*, center about 6 miles west-northwest of Vidal (lat. 34°10' N, long. 114°36' W). Named on Parker (1949), Rice (1954), Turtle Mountains (1954), and Vidal (1949) 15' quadrangles.

Vidal Wash [SAN BERNARDINO]: *stream* and *dry wash*, extends for 15 miles to Colorado River 5 miles southeast of Vidal (lat. 34° 04'45" N, long. 114°26'05" W; near SW cor. sec. 14, T 1 S, R 24 E). Named on Vidal (1949) 15' quadrangle, and on Parker SW (1970) 7.5' quadrangle.

Viento: see **Guasti** [SAN BERNARDINO].

Village Bay [SAN BERNARDINO]: *embayment*, 7.25 miles south-southwest of Luna Mountain along Lake Arrowhead (1) (lat. 34° 15' N, long. 117°11' W; near N line sec. 22, T 2 N, R 3 W). Named on Lake Arrowhead (1971) 7.5' quadrangle.

Village Point [SAN BERNARDINO]: *promontory*, 7 miles west-southwest of Luna Mountain along Lake Arrowhead (1) (lat. 34° 15'10" N, long. 117°11'15" W; near SW cor. sec. 15, T 2 N, R 3 W). Named on Lake Arrowhead (1971) 7.5' quadrangle.

Vinagre Wash [IMPERIAL]: *stream* and *dry wash*, extends for 16 miles to lowlands along Colorado River 15 miles south of Palo Verde (lat. 33°13'20" N, long. 114°41'20" W; sec. 18, T 11 S, R 22 E). Named on Quartz Peak (1953) 15' quadrangle, and on Picacho NW (1965) 7.5' quadrangle. Called Vinegar Wash on Picacho (1945) 15' quadrangle.

Vinegar Wash: see **Vinagre Wash** [IMPERIAL].

Virginia Dale: see **Old Dale** [SAN BERNARDINO].

Virgin Spring [RIVERSIDE]: *spring*, 14 miles south of Palm Desert (lat. 33°31'50" N, long. 116°25'45" W; near SW cor. sec. 25, T 7 S, R 5 E). Named on Palm Desert (1959) 15' quadrangle.

Virgin Spring: see **Cedar Spring** [RIVERSIDE] (2).

Viscera Spring [SAN BERNARDINO]: *spring*, 7.5 miles south of Old Woman Springs (lat. 34°16'20" N, long. 116°40'25" W; sec. 9, T 2 N, R 3 E). Named on Rattlesnake Canyon (1972) 7.5' quadrangle.

Vista Peak [SAN BERNARDINO]: *peak*, 8.5 miles northwest of Vidal (lat. 34°12'10" N, long. 114°23'40" W). Altitude 1127 feet. Named on Parker NW (1970) 7.5' quadrangle.

Vivian Creek [SAN BERNARDINO]: *stream*, flows 3 miles to Mill Creek Canyon nearly 4 miles west-southwest of San Gorgonio Mountain (lat. 34°04'55" N, long. 116°53'15" W; sec. 16, T 1 S, R 1 E). Named on Forest Falls (1970) and San Gorgonio Mountain (1970) 7.5' quadrangles.

Volcano: see **Mundo** [IMPERIAL].

Volcano Springs: see **Mundo** [IMPERIAL].

Vontrigger [SAN BERNARDINO]: *locality*, 23 miles south-southeast of Ivanpah along Atchison, Topeka and Santa Fe Railroad (lat. 35° 01'30" N, long. 115°09' W). Named on Ivanpah (1912) 1° quadrangle. Postal authorities established Vontrigger post office in 1907 and discontinued it 1913; the name was for Erick Vontrigger, a prospector in the neighborhood (Salley, p. 233). They established Dunbar post office 8 miles northwest of Vontrigger (NE quarter of NE quarter sec. 18, T 12 N, R 17 E) in 1912 and discontinued it in 1914; the name was for Harold N. Dunbar, who promoted the place (Salley, p. 62).

Vontrigger Hills [SAN BERNARDINO]: *ridge*, northeast-trending, 3.5 miles long, 21 miles south-southeast of Ivanpah (lat. 35°03'50" N, long. 115°07'15" W). Named on Lanfair Valley (1956) 15' quadrangle.

Vontrigger Spring [SAN BERNARDINO]: *spring*, 22 miles south-southeast of Ivanpah (lat. 35°03'20" N, long. 115°08'45" W; near SE cor. sec. 4, T 11 N, R 17 E); the spring is near the southwest end of Vontrigger Hills. Named on Lanfair Valley (1956) 15' quadrangle.

- W -

Wade: see **Fontana** [SAN BERNARDINO].

Wagner: see **Newberry** [SAN BERNARDINO].

Walker Basin [RIVERSIDE]: *relief feature*, 4 miles west of downtown Temecula (lat. 33°29'55" N, long. 117°12'55" W). Named on Murrieta (1953) and Temecula (1968) 7.5' quadrangles. Called Walkers Basin on Temecula (1950) 7.5' quadrangle. The name commemorates William Walker, who bought part of Santa Rosa grant in 1888 (Gunther, p. 559).

Walker Canyon [RIVERSIDE]: *canyon*, nearly 3 miles long, opens into the canyon of Temescal Wash 0.5 mile northeast of Alberhill (lat. 33°43'45" N, long. 117°23'30" W; sec. 15, T 5 S, R 5 W). Named on Alberhill (1954) and Lake Elsinore (1953) 7.5' quadrangles.

Walker Lake [IMPERIAL]: *lake*, 4000 feet long, 16 miles south of Palo Verde near Colorado River (lat. 33°12'15" N, long. 114° 41' W; mainly in sec. 20, T 11 S, R 22 E). Named on Picacho NW (1965) 7.5' quadrangle.

Wall: see **Peter Wall Canyon**, under **Indian Canyon** [RIVERSIDE]; **Peter Wall Canyon**, under **Horsethief Canyon** [RIVERSIDE].

Wallace Creek [RIVERSIDE-SAN BERNARDINO]: *stream*, heads in San Bernardino County and flows 2 miles to Little San Gorgonio Creek 4.5 miles northwest of Banning in Riverside County (lat. 33° 59'50" N, long. 116°57'25" W; sec. 14, T 2 S, R 1 W). Named on Beaumont (1953) and Forest Falls (1970) 7.5' quadrangles.

Wall Street Canyon [SAN BERNARDINO]: *canyon*, drained by a stream that flows 4.5 miles to lowlands nearly 6 miles north of Daggett (lat. 34°56'35" N, long. 116°52' W; sec. 22, T 10 N, R 1 E). Named on Yermo (1953) 7.5' quadrangle.

Wall Street Mill [SAN BERNARDINO]: *locality*, 8 miles south-southwest of Twentynine Palms (lat. 34°02'10" N, long. 116° 08' W). Named on Indian Cove (1972) 7.5' quadrangle.

Walters: see **Mecca** [RIVERSIDE]; **Tom Walters Mountains**, under **Ibex Hills** [SAN BERNARDINO].

Walters Camp [IMPERIAL]: *locality*, 13 miles south of Palo Verde along Colorado River (lat. 33°14'20" N, long. 114°41'10" W; on E line sec. 7, T 11 S, R 22 E). Named on Picacho NW (1965) 7.5' quadrangle.

Ward: see **Saltmarsh** [SAN BERNARDINO].

Wardlow Canyon [RIVERSIDE]: *canyon*, 2.5 miles long, opens into lowlands 3 miles west-southwest of Corona (lat. 33°51'30" N, long. 117°36'45" W; near N line sec. 4, T 4 S, R 7 W). Named on Black Star Canyon (1967) and Corona South (1967) 7.5' quadrangles.

Wardlow Wash [RIVERSIDE]: *stream*, flows 3.25 miles from the mouth of Wardlow Canyon to Santa Ana River 5 miles west of Corona (lat. 33°52'55" N, long. 117°38'50" W). Named on Corona North (1967), Corona South (1967), and Prado Dam (1967) 7.5' quadrangles.

Ward Valley [SAN BERNARDINO]: *valley*, between Iron Mountains, Old Woman Mountains, and Piute Mountains on the west, and Turtle Mountains and Stepladder Mountains on the east. Named on Bannock (1956), Cadiz Lake (1956), Essex (1956), Iron Mountains (1956), Milligan (1956), Stepladder Mountains (1956), and Turtle Mountains (1954) 15' quadrangles. The name is from Ward, which was at or near present Saltmarsh (Thompson, 1929, p. 704).

Warm Creek [SAN BERNARDINO]: *stream* and *dry wash*, extends for 9.5 miles to Santa Ana River 3 miles south-southwest of San Bernardino city hall (lat. 34°03'45" N, long. 117°18'20" W). Named on Redlands (1967) and San Bernardino South (1967) 7.5' quadrangles. Several springs contribute warm water to the stream (Beattie and Beattie, p. 91).

Warm Springs: see **Harlem Springs** [SAN BERNARDINO].

Warm Springs Canyon [SAN BERNARDINO]: *canyon*, drained by a stream that flows 3 miles to Santa Ana River 6.25 miles north-northwest of Yucaipa (lat. 34°07'10" N, long. 117°04'40" W; at N line sec. 3, T 1 S, R 2 W). Named on Yucaipa (1967) 7.5' quadrangle.

Warm Springs Creek [RIVERSIDE]: *stream*, flows 11.5 miles to Murrieta Creek 2.5 miles southeast of Murrieta (lat. 33°31'35" N, long. 117°11' W); the stream goes past Temecula Hot Springs and Murrieta Hot Springs. Named on Murrieta (1953) 7.5' quadrangle.

Warm Springs Valley [RIVERSIDE]: *valley*, 2.25 miles north-northwest of Lake Elsinore city hall (lat. 33°41'55" N, long. 117°20'30" W). Named on Lake Elsinore (1953) 7.5' quadrangle. Franklin P. Heald named the place about 1883 for the springs there (Gunther, p. 561).

Warner [SAN BERNARDINO]: *locality*, 2 miles east of Redlands city hall along Southern Pacific Railroad (lat. 34°03'40" N, long. 117° 08'45" W). Named on Redlands (1967) 7.5' quadrangle.

Warrens Well [SAN BERNARDINO]: *well*, 2.5 miles east-northeast of Yucca Valley (lat. 34°07'50" N, long. 116°24'20" W; near E line sec. 36, T 1 N, R 5 E). Named on Yucca Valley North (1972) 7.5' quadrangle, which indicates that the well is dry. Mark Warren dug the well by hand in 1881 (O'Neal, p. 120).

Washington Wash [RIVERSIDE]: *stream*, flows 8.5 miles to Fried Liver Wash 18 miles northwest of Chiriaco Summit (lat. 33°52'30" N, long. 115°54'40" W; at N line sec. 35, T 3 S, R 10 E). Named on Hexie Mountains (1963) 15' quadrangle.

Water: see **Newberry** [SAN BERNARDINO].

Water Canyon [SAN BERNARDINO]:

(1) *canyon*, 7 miles long, opens into lowlands 0.5 mile north-northwest of the center of Yucca Valley (lat. 34°07'40" N, long. 116° 27' W; sec. 34, T 1 N, R 5 E). Named on Rimrock (1972) and Yucca Valley North (1972) 7.5' quadrangles.

(2) *canyon*, 1 mile long, 11 miles west-southwest of San Gorgonio Mountain (lat. 34°01'30" N, long. 116°59'50" W; near W line sec. 4, T 2 S, R 1 W). Named on Forest Falls (1970) 7.5' quadrangle.

(3) *canyon*, drained by a stream that flows 2 miles to Aliso Canyon 2.25 miles east of San Juan Hill (lat. 33°54'40" N, long. 117° 42' W). Named on Prado Dam (1967) 7.5' quadrangle.

Waterman: see **Barstow** [SAN BERNARDINO].

Waterman Canyon [SAN BERNARDINO]: *canyon*, drained by a stream that flows 4 miles to lowlands 5 miles north of San Bernardino city hall (lat. 34°10'40" N, long. 117°16'15" W); the mouth of the canyon is near Arrowhead Springs. Named on San Bernardino North (1967) 7.5' quadrangle. The name commemorates Robert Whitney Waterman, governor of California from 1887 until 1891, who owned land near the canyon (Hanna, p. 350). Beattie and Beattie (p. 196) reported the early name "Hot Springs Canyon" for the feature.

Waterman Gardens [SAN BERNARDINO]: *district*, 1.5 miles northeast of present San Bernardino city hall (lat. 34°07' N, long. 117° 16'30" W). Named on San Bernardino (1954) 15' quadrangle.

Waterman Hills [SAN BERNARDINO]: *range*, 6 miles north of Barstow (lat. 34°58'45" N, long. 117°02'45" W). Named on Barstow (1971) 7.5' quadrangle.

Waterman Hot Springs: see **Arrowhead Springs** [SAN BERNARDINO].

Waterman Junction: see **Barstow** [SAN BERNARDINO].

Waterman's: see **Barstow** [SAN BERNARDINO].

Watermans Corner [IMPERIAL]: *locality*, 4.5 miles west-southwest of Holtville (lat. 32°46'55" N, long. 115°26'50" W; at S line sec. 5, T 16 S, R 15 E). Named on Holtville West (1956) 7.5' quadrangle.

Water Trough [SAN BERNARDINO]: *water feature*, 11 miles west-southwest of Ivanpah (lat. 35°17'45" N, long. 115°29'30" W). Named on Ivanpah (1912) 1° quadrangle.

Water Valley [SAN BERNARDINO]: *valley*, 30 miles southeast of the village of Red Mountain (lat. 35°02'30" N, long. 117°13' W). Named on Barstow (1956) and Opal Mountain (1955) 15' quadrangles, and on Twelve Gauge Lake (1973) 7.5' quadrangle.

Water Wheel Camp [RIVERSIDE]: *locality,* 22 miles north of Blythe along Colorado River (lat. 33°55'25" N, long. 114°31'55" W; at N line sec. 14, T 3 S, R 23 E). Named on Big Maria Mountains NE (1954) 7.5' quadrangle.

Wathier Landing [SAN BERNARDINO]: *locality,* 8 miles west of downtown Morongo Valley (lat. 34°02'40" N, long. 116°42'45" W; sec. 31, T 1 S, R 3 E). Named on Catclaw Flat (1972) 7.5' quadrangle.

Watson: see **Newberry** [SAN BERNARDINO].

Watson Wash [SAN BERNARDINO]: *stream* and *dry wash,* extends for 32 miles before losing its identity 6 miles north-northeast of Essex in Fenner Valley (lat. 34°49'15" N, long. 115°12'15" W; sec. 33, T 9 N, R 17 E). Named on Fenner (1956), Lanfair Valley (1956), and Mid Hills (1955) 15' quadrangles.

Weaver Canyon: see **Millard Canyon** [RIVERSIDE].

Weavers Well [SAN BERNARDINO]: *well,* 9 miles south-southeast of Essex (lat. 34°37'25" N, long. 115°09'45" W; at E line sec. 11, T 6 N, R 17 E). Named on Essex (1956) 15' quadrangle.

Webber Valley [RIVERSIDE]: *valley,* 11.5 miles south-southeast of Hemet (lat. 33°35'45" N, long. 116°53' W; in and near sec. 4, T 7 S, R 1 E). Named on Hemet (1957) 15' quadrangle.

Weisel [RIVERSIDE]: *locality,* 6.5 miles southeast of Corona along Atchison, Topeka and Santa Fe Railroad (lat. 33°48'35" N, long. 117°29'55" W; near W line sec. 22, T 4 S, R 6 W). Named on Lake Mathews (1967) 7.5' quadrangle. The name commemorates P.J. Weisel, who owned a sand pit served by a spur line built from the place in 1927 (Gunther, p. 566). Temescal station of Butterfield Overland stage route was at the site beginning in 1858; the station was known locally as Greenwade's for James Monroe Greenwade, who operated the station from 1861 until 1869—developers laid out a town called Oakadena at the place in 1887, but the project failed (Gunther, p. 209, 357, 535).

Wellman Divide [RIVERSIDE]: *pass,* 1 mile south-southeast of San Jacinto Peak (lat. 33°47'55" N, long. 116°40'25" W; near N line sec. 28, T 4 S, R 3 E); the pass is about 0.5 mile northeast of Wellman Cienaga. Named on San Jacinto Peak (1981) 7.5' quadrangle.

Wellmans Cienaga [RIVERSIDE]: *area,* 1.5 miles south of San Jacinto Peak (lat. 33°47'40" N, long. 116°40'45" W; sec. 28, T 4 S, R 3 E). Named on San Jacinto Peak (1981) 7.5' quadrangle. The name is for Frank P. Wellman, a rancher and cattleman (Gunther, p. 566).

Wentworth Canyon [RIVERSIDE]: *canyon,* drained by a stream that flows 3 miles to Palm Canyon 10.5 miles east of Idyllwild (lat. 33° 44'20" N, long. 116°31'45" W; sec. 14, T 5 S, R 4 E). Named on Idyllwild (1959) 15' quadrangle. Bloomquist (1977a, p. 16) used the alternate name "Fern Canyon" for the feature

West Berdoo Canyon [RIVERSIDE]: *canyon,* 2.5 miles long, opens into lowlands 7.25 miles north-northeast of Indio (lat. 33°49' N, long. 116°10'45" W; near NE cor. sec. 19, T 4 S, R 8 E); the mouth of the canyon is 0.5 mile west of the mouth of Berdoo Canyon. Named on Lost Horse Mountain (1958) 15' quadrangle.

West Colton [SAN BERNARDINO]: *locality,* 4.5 miles southwest of San Bernardino city hall along Southern Pacific Railroad (lat. 34° 04' N, long. 117°21' W; near SE cor. sec. 24, T 1 S, R 5 W). Named on San Bernardino South (1967) 7.5' quadrangle.

West Cronese Lake [SAN BERNARDINO]: *dry lake,* 2 miles long, 16 miles west-southwest of Baker (lat. 35°08'40" N, long. 116°19'30" W); the feature is 3 miles west-northwest of East Cronese Lake. Named on Cave Mountain (1948) 15' quadrangle. On Avawatz Mountains (1933) 1° quadrangle, the name "Cronise Lake" applies to present East Cronese Lake and present West Cronese Lake together. United States Board on Geographic Names (1987, p. 2) approved the name "West Cronise Lake" for the feature, and rejected the names "Cronise Lake" and "West Cronese Lake" for it.

West Cronise Lake: see **West Cronese Lake** [SAN BERNARDINO].

West Deception Canyon [RIVERSIDE]: *canyon,* 2 miles long, opens into lowlands 11.5 miles northeast of Cathedral City (lat. 33°54'40" N, long. 116°20'30" W; sec. 15, T 3 S, R 6 E); the mouth of the canyon is 1 mile west of the mouth of East Deception Canyon. Named on Thousand Palms (1958) 15' quadrangle.

West Double Canyon [RIVERSIDE]: *canyon,* drained by a stream that flows nearly 2 miles to lowlands 9.5 miles east of Indio (lat. 33°43'40" N, long. 116°03'20" W); the feature is 0.5 mile west of East Double Canyon. Named on Thermal Canyon (1956) 7.5' quadrangle.

Westend [SAN BERNARDINO]: *locality,* 4 miles south-southwest of Trona (lat. 35°42'20" N, long. 117°23'30" W; near N line sec. 6, T 26 N, R 43 E). Named on Westend (1973) 7.5' quadrangle. Postal authorities established Westend post office in 1919 and discontinued it in 1974 (Salley, p. 237). West End Consolidated Mining Company owned the place (Miller and Miller, p. 27), which first was called Hanksite (Myrick, p. 802)—the mineral called hanksite occurs at Searles Lake.

West Etiwanda: see **Etiwanda** [SAN BERNARDINO] (2).

West Fork Camp [SAN BERNARDINO]: *locality,* 18 miles south of Victorville (lat. 34°17'05" N, long. 117°22'15" W); the place is along West Fork Mojave River. Named on Hesperia (1942) 15' quadrangle.

West Highlands [SAN BERNARDINO]: *district,* 4.5 miles west-southwest of Harrison Mountain (lat. 34°08'25" N, long. 117°13'45" W); the place is 1.5 miles west-northwest of Highland. Named on Harrison Mountain (1967) 7.5' quadrangle.

Westlake: see **Willard** [RIVERSIDE].

West March [RIVERSIDE]: *locality,* 7.5 miles southeast of Riverside city hall along Atchison, Topeka and Santa Fe Railroad (lat. 33°54'10" N, long. 117°16'40" W; at SW cor. sec. 14, T 3 S, R 4 W); the place is west of March Air Force Base. Named on Riverside East (1967) 7.5' quadrangle.

West March: see **Camp Haan** [RIVERSIDE].

West Mesa [IMPERIAL]: *relief feature,* extends along the west side of Imperial Valley from a point west-southwest of Kane Spring on south to Mexico. Named on El Centro (1958) and Salton Sea (1959) 1°x 2° quadrangles.

West Mesa: see **Baldy Mesa** [SAN BERNARDINO].

Westmorland [IMPERIAL]: *town,* 8.5 miles southwest of Calipatria (lat. 33°02'15" N, long. 115°37'15" W; sec. 9, 10, T 13 S, R 13 E). Named on Calipatria SW (1956) and Westmorland (1956) 7.5' quadrangles. Postal authorities established Westmoreland (with the extra "e") post office in 1909, discontinued it in 1912, reestablished it in 1919, and changed the name to Westmorland in 1936 (Salley, p. 238). The town incorporated in 1934.

West Ord Mountain [SAN BERNARDINO]: *range,* 5 miles west-southwest of Ord Mountain (lat. 34°39' N, long. 116°54' W); the feature is the west part of Ord Mountains (1). Named on Ord Mountains (1955) 15' quadrangle.

West Point [SAN BERNARDINO]: *peak,* 7.5 miles southeast of Luna Mountain (lat. 34°15'35" N, long. 117°02'10" W; near E line sec. 13, T 2 N, R 2 W). Named on Butler Peak (1971) 7.5' quadrangle.

West Ridge [RIVERSIDE]: *ridge,* generally southwest-trending, 2 miles long, 1.5 miles southwest of the center of Idyllwild (lat. 33° 43'45" N, long. 116°44'15" W). Named on Idyllwild (1959) 15' quadrangle.

West Riverside: see **Glen Avon** [RIVERSIDE]; **Rubidoux** [RIVERSIDE].

West Riverside Mountains [RIVERSIDE-SAN BERNARDINO]: *range,* 9 miles west-southwest of Vidal on Riverside-San Bernardino County line (lat. 34°04' N, long. 114°39' W); the range is northwest of Riverside Mountains. Named on Grommet (1971) and Vidal (1971) 7.5' quadrangles.

West Well [SAN BERNARDINO]: *well,* 22 miles north of Vidal (lat. 34°26'40" N, long. 114°28'45" W). Named on Whipple Mountains (1950) 15' quadrangle.

West Wide Canyon [RIVERSIDE]: *valley,* 12 miles north-northeast of Cathedral City (lat. 33°56'20" N, long. 116°23'35" W; in and near sec. 6, T 3 S, R 6 E); the feature is 0.5 mile west of East Wide Canyon. Named on Seven Palms Valley (1958) 7.5' quadrangle.

Whale Mountain [SAN BERNARDINO]: *peak,* 11.5 miles south-southeast of Needles (lat. 34°41' N, long. 114°32'35" W). Altitude 2774 feet. Named on Whale Mountain (1971) 7.5' quadrangle.

Wheaton Springs [SAN BERNARDINO]: *locality,* 12.5 miles northwest of Ivanpah (lat. 35°27'40" N, long. 115°28'30" W; at S line sec. 33, T 16 N, R 14 E); the place is along Wheaton Wash. Named on Ivanpah (1956) 15' quadrangle.

Wheaton Wash [SAN BERNARDINO]: *stream,* flows 10 miles to Ivanpah Lake 11.5 miles north-northwest of Ivanpah (lat. 35°29'40" N, long. 115°22'50" W; near E line sec. 20, T 16 N, R 15 E). Named on Ivanpah (1956) and Mescal Range (1955) 15' quadrangles.

Whipple: see **Parker Dam** [SAN BERNARDINO].

Whipple Bay [SAN BERNARDINO]: *embayment,* 23 miles north-northeast of Vidal along Lake Havasu (lat. 34°23'45" N, long. 114° 16'30" W); the feature is at the mouth of Whipple Wash. Named on Lake Havasu City South (1970) 7.5' quadrangle.

Whipple Mountains [SAN BERNARDINO]: *range,* center 8 miles northeast of Vidal (lat. 34°18' N, long. 114°20' W). Named on Parker (1949), Parker Dam (1959), Savahia Peak (1950), and Whipple Mountains (1950) 15' quadrangles. Ives (p. 60) first used the name "Whipple" in the neighborhood in 1858 to honor Lieutenant Amiel W. Whipple, who worked with the Mexican boundary survey and Pacific Railroad explorations.

Whipple Point [SAN BERNARDINO]: *promontory,* 23 miles north-northeast of Vidal along Lake Havasu (lat. 34°24'05" N, long. 114° 16'40" W); the feature is near the mouth of Whipple Wash. Named on Lake Havasu City South (1970) 7.5' quadrangle.

Whipple Wash [SAN BERNARDINO]: *stream,* flows 12.5 miles to Lake Havasu 23 miles north-northeast of Vidal (lat. 34°23'30" N, long. 114°16'35" W). Named on Lake Havasu City South (1970), Whipple Mountains SW (1970), and Whipple Walsh (1970) 7.5' quadrangles.

Whipple Well [SAN BERNARDINO]: *well,* 17 miles north of Vidal (lat. 34°21'45" N, long. 114°26'55" W). Named on Whipple Mountains SW (1970) 7.5' quadrangle, which indicates that the well is dry.

Whiskey Spring [SAN BERNARDINO]:

(1) *spring,* 20 miles northwest of Ivanpah (lat. 35°33'25" N, long. 115°31'45" W; sec. 13, T 17 N, R 13 E). Named on Clark Mountain (1956) 15' quadrangle.

(2) *spring,* 22 miles north-northwest of Essex (lat. 34°59'50" N, long. 115°26'50" W; near SE cor. sec. 26, T 11 N, R 14 E). Named on Colton Well (1956) 15' quadrangle.

Whiskey Springs [SAN BERNARDINO]: *spring,* 5 miles north of Big Bear City (lat. 34°20'05" N, long. 116°49'50" W; near N line sec. 24, T 3 N, R 1 E). Named on Big Bear City (1971) 7.5' quadrangle. United States Board on Geographic Names (1975a, p. 12) gave the variant form "Whisky Springs" for the name.

White Fang: see **Granite Mountains** [SAN BERNARDINO] (2).

White House Canyon [RIVERSIDE]: *canyon,* nearly 2 miles long, opens into lowlands 11 miles north of Palm Springs (lat. 33°59'15" N, long. 116°32'05" W). Named on Desert Hot Springs (1955) and Morongo Valley (1972) 7.5' quadrangles.

White Mountain [SAN BERNARDINO]: *ridge,* generally north-northwest-trending, 3 miles long, 6 miles east of Luna Mountain (lat. 34°21'15" N, long. 117°01'10" W). Named on Butler Peak (1971) 7.5' quadrangle.

White Rock Spring [SAN BERNARDINO]: *spring,* 14 miles west-southwest of Ivanpah (lat. 35°15'55" N, long. 115°32'55" W; near W line sec. 25, T 14 N, R 13 W). Named on Mescal Range (1955) 15' quadrangle.

White Sulphur Spring: see **Soboba Hot Springs** [RIVERSIDE].

White Tank: see **White Tank Campground** [RIVERSIDE].

White Tank Campground [RIVERSIDE]: *locality,* 22 miles north-northeast of Indio (lat. 33°59' N, long. 116°01' W; sec. 23, T 2 S, R 9 E). Named on Lost Horse Mountain (1958) 15' quadrangle. Pinyon Well (1943) 15' quadrangle shows a water feature called White Tank at the site. A dam in a granite gorge forms a reservoir called White Tank (Brown, 1923, p. 269).

White Wash [IMPERIAL]: *stream,* flows 4.5 miles to end 29 miles south of Palo Verde near Colorado River (lat. 33°01'15" N, long. 114°38' W). Named on Picacho Peak (1965) and Picacho SW (1965) 7.5' quadrangles.

White Wash [RIVERSIDE]: *stream,* flows 3.5 miles to Horse Canyon 18 miles south-southwest of Palm Desert (lat. 33°29'10" N, long. 116°32'20" W; at S line sec. 11, T 8 S, R 4 E). Named on Bucksnort Mountain (1960) 7.5' quadrangle.

Whitewater: see **Palm Springs Station** [RIVERSIDE]; **White Water Post Office** [RIVERSIDE].

Whitewater Hill [RIVERSIDE]: *hill,* 7.25 miles north-northwest of Palm Springs (lat. 33°55'25" N, long. 116°37' W; at E line sec. 12, T 3 S, R 3 E); the feature is just east of Whitewater River. Altitude 1734 feet. Named on Desert Hot Springs (1955) 7.5' quadrangle.

White Water Post Office [RIVERSIDE]: *locality,* 8 miles northwest of Palm Springs (lat. 33°55'30" N, long. 116°38'15" W; sec. 11, T 3 S, R 3 E); Whitewater River enters San Gorgonio Pass at the place. Named on Whitewater (1955) 7.5' quadrangle. Called Whitewater on Palm Springs (1942) 15' quadrangle. Postal authorities established White Water post office in 1926 (Salley, p. 239). United States Board on Geographic Names (1978, p. 5) approved the form "White Water," and rejected the form "Whitewater" for the name; the Board (p. 4) also approved the name "The Matterdome" for a relief feature, altitude 2702 feet, located 2.5 miles north of White Water (sec. 35, T 2 S, R 3 E)—the name commemorates Matt Smithson, a pioneer who lived at the foot of the feature

Whitewater River [RIVERSIDE-SAN BERNARDINO]: *stream* and *dry wash,* formed in San Bernardino County by the confluence of North Fork and Middle Fork, extends for 63 miles to Salton Sea 17 miles south-southeast of Indio in Riverside County (lat. 33°30'30" N, long. 116°03'25" W; near NW cor. sec. 4, T 8 S, R 9 E). Named on Catclaw Flat (1972), Cathedral City (1958), Desert Hot Springs (1955), Indio (1956), La Quinta (1959), Mecca (1955), Palm Springs (1957), Rancho Mirage (1957), San Gorgonio Mountain (1970), Valerie (1956), and Whitewater (1955) 7.5' quadrangles. United States Board on Geographic Names (1975a, p. 12) gave the variant names "Middle Fork Whitewater River" and "North Fork Whitewater River" for the main stream. Middle Fork is nearly 3 miles long and North Fork is 5.25 miles long; both forks are named on Catclaw Flat (1972) and San Gorgonio Mountain (1970) 7.5' quadrangles. East Fork enters South Fork 6.25 miles above the mouth of South Fork; it is 3.5 miles long and is named on San Gorgonio Mountain (1970) 7.5' quadrangle. South Fork enters 3 miles downstream from the confluence of Middle Fork and North Fork; it is 10 miles long and is named on Catclaw Flat (1972) and San Gorgonio Mountain (1970) 7.5' quadrangles. United States Board on Geographic Names (1975a, p. 11) gave the variant name "Whitewater River" for South Fork.

Whitfield Spring [SAN BERNARDINO]: *spring,* 20 miles northwest of Ivanpah (lat. 35°33'35" N, long. 115°33' W; sec. 14, T 17 N, R 13 E). Named on Clark Mountain (1956) 15' quadrangle.

Whittle: see **Harold F. Whittle Camp** [SAN BERNARDINO].

Wide Canyon: see **East Wide Canyon** [RIVERSIDE]; **West Wide Canyon** [RIVERSIDE].

Wiest [IMPERIAL]: *locality,* 6 miles southeast of Calipatria (lat. 33° 03'30" N, long. 115°26'55" W; sec. 5, T 13 S, R 15 E). Named on Wiest (1956) 7.5' quadrangle. Postal authorities established Wiest post office in 1907, discontinued it in 1910, reestablished it in 1914, and discontinued it in 1933 (Salley, p. 240). The name recalls Daniel W. Wiest, who settled at the place in 1906 (Hanna, p. 355).

Wiest Lake [IMPERIAL]: *lake,* 2000 feet long, 6 miles south-southeast of Calipatria (lat. 33°02'30" N, long. 115°29'20" W; near NE cor. sec. 11, T 13 S, R 14 E); the feature is 2.5 miles west-southwest of Wiest near Alamo River. Named on Wiest (1956) 7.5' quadrangle.

Wild: see **Helendale** [SAN BERNARDINO]; **Wild Crossing** [SAN BERNARDINO].

Wildcat Butte [SAN BERNARDINO]: *hill,* 17 miles west-southwest of Ivanpah (lat. 35°14'35" N, long. 115°35'05" W; near NW cor. sec. 3, T 13 N, R 13 E). Altitude 5179 feet. Named on Kelso (1955) 15' quadrangle.

Wildcat Spring [SAN BERNARDINO]: *spring,* 18 miles south-southwest of Ivanpah (lat. 35°07'20" N, long. 115°28'05" W; sec. 15, T 12 N, R 14 E). Named on Mid Hills (1955) 15' quadrangle.

Wild Crossing [SAN BERNARDINO]: *locality,* 16 miles southwest of Barstow along the railroad (lat. 34°46'50" N, long. 117°16'25" W; near W line sec. 14, T 8 N, R 4 W). Named on Wild Crossing (1973) 7.5' quadrangle. Called Wild on Barstow (1934) 30' quadrangle.

Wilderness Pines Campground [RIVERSIDE]: *locality,* 4 miles southwest of San Jacinto Peak (lat. 33°46'15" N, long. 116°43'45" W; near N line sec. 1, T 5 S, R 2 E). Named on San Jacinto Peak (1981) 7.5' quadrangle.

Wild Horse Canyon [SAN BERNARDINO]: *canyon,* 5.5 miles long, 21 miles south-southwest of Ivanpah (lat. 35°02' N, long. 115° 24' W; sec. 17, T 11 N, R 15 E). Named on Mid Hills (1955) 15' quadrangle.

Wildhorse Canyon [RIVERSIDE]: *canyon,* drained by a stream that flows 4 miles to Los Alamos Canyon 4.25 miles southeast of Sitton Peak (lat. 33°33'05" N, long. 117°23' W). Named on Sitton Peak (1954) and Wildomar (1953) 7.5' quadrangles.

Wildhorse Creek [SAN BERNARDINO]: *stream,* flows 3.25 miles to Santa Ana River 2.25 miles south of Sugarloaf Mountain (lat. 34° 10' N, long. 116°48'45" W; sec. 18, T 1 N, R 2 E); the stream heads at Wildhorse Meadows. Named on Moonridge (1970) 7.5' quadrangle. Called Holcomb Creek on San Gorgonio (1902) 30' quadrangle, but United States Board on Geographic Names (1949, p. 5) rejected the names "Holcomb Creek" and "Wild Horse Creek" for the feature.

Wildhorse Meadows [SAN BERNARDINO]: *area,* 2 miles east of Sugarloaf Mountain (lat. 34°11'55" N, long. 116°46'35" W; sec. 4, T 1 N, R 2 E). Named on Moonridge (1970) 7.5' quadrangle.

Wild Horse Peak [RIVERSIDE]: *peak,* 5.25 miles west of Aguanga (lat. 33°26'30" N, long. 116°57'25" W; on S line sec. 26, T 8 S, R 1 W). Altitude 3277 feet. Named on Vail Lake (1953) 7.5' quadrangle.

Wildhorse Spring [SAN BERNARDINO]: *spring,* 2.5 miles east of Sugarloaf Mountain (lat. 34°12'10" N, long. 116°46' W; near W line sec. 3, T 1 N, R 2 E); the spring is above the head of Wildhorse Creek. Named on Moonridge (1970) 7.5' quadrangle.

Wildomar [RIVERSIDE]: *village,* 5.5 miles southeast of Lake Elsinore city hall (lat. 33°36' N, long. 117°16'45" W). Named on Wildomar (1953) 7.5' quadrangle. Postal authorities established Wildomar post office in 1886, discontinued it in 1920, an reestablished it in 1930 (Frickstad, p. 131). Margaret Collier Graham coined the name in 1883 from letters in the names of the owners of the place: <u>Wil</u>liam Collier, <u>Do</u>nald Graham, and <u>Marga</u>ret Graham (Gudde, 1949, p. 390).

Wild Rose Canyon [SAN BERNARDINO]: *canyon,* drained by a stream that flows 1 mile to Furnace Canyon 5.25 miles north-northeast of Fawnskin (lat. 34°20'45" N, long. 116°55'15" W; sec. 18, T 3 N, R 1 E). Named on Fawnskin (1971) 7.5' quadrangle.

Wild Wash [SAN BERNARDINO]: *stream,* flows 11.5 miles to lowlands along Mojave River 18 miles southwest of Barstow (lat. 34° 47'30" N, long. 117°14'30" W; near SE cor. sec. 12, T 8 N, R 4 W). Named on Turtle Valley (1970) 7.5' quadrangle.

Wildwood Canyon [SAN BERNARDINO]: *canyon,* about 3 miles long, along Yucaipa Creek and a branch of Yucaipa Creek above a point 2 miles southeast of Yucaipa (lat. 34°00'55" N, long. 117°00'50" W; near W line sec. 8, T 2 S, R 1 W). Named on Forest Falls (1970) and Yucaipa (1967) 7.5' quadrangles. Called Hog Canyon on Redlands (1901) 15' quadrangle.

Wileys Well [RIVERSIDE]: *well,* 19 miles west-southwest of Blythe (lat. 33°29'40" N, long. 114°53'20" W). Named on Palo Verde Mountains (1953) 15' quadrangle. A.P. Wiley dug the well in 1908 (Gunther, p. 573).

Wilhelm Camp: see **Spring Wilhelm** [SAN BERNARDINO].

Willard [RIVERSIDE]: *locality,* 3 miles west-southwest of present Lake Elsinore city hall (lat. 33°39'30" N, long. 117°22'30" W). Named on Elsinore (1901) 30' quadrangle. Postal authorities established Willard post office in 1898 and discontinued it in 1902 (Salley, p. 240). Residents chose the name "Westlake" for their community, but when postal authorities rejected this, they settled for the name "Willard" for Frances E. Willard, a noted temperance leader (Gunther, p. 573-574).

Willard Lake: see **Cuddeback Lake** [SAN BERNARDINO].

Williams Well [SAN BERNARDINO]: *well,* 50 miles west of Baker (lat. 35°07'40" N, long. 116°57'05" W; near S line sec. 21, T 32 S, R 47 E). Named on Lane Mountain (1948) 15' quadrangle.

Willis Palms [RIVERSIDE]: *locality,* 8.5 miles east-northeast of Cathedral City (lat. 33°49'40" N, long. 116°19'50" W; sec. 14, T 4 S, R 6 E). Named on Myoma (1958) 7.5' quadrangle.

Willis Well [SAN BERNARDINO]: *well,* 1.5 miles northeast of Ord Mountain (lat. 34°41'55" N, long. 116°46'30" W; sec. 16, T 7 N, R 2 E). Named on Ord Mountains (1955) 15' quadrangle.

Willow Canyon [RIVERSIDE]: *canyon,* drained by a stream that flows nearly 3 miles to an unnamed canyon 11 miles south-southeast of Hemet (lat. 33°35'55" N, long. 116°55' W; sec. 6, T 7 S, R 1 E). Named on Sage (1954) 7.5' quadrangle.

Willow Canyon [SAN BERNARDINO]: *canyon,* 2.5 miles long, opens into Little Pine Flat 4.5 miles east-southeast of Luna Mountain (lat. 34°19'10" N, long. 117°03'05" W; sec. 26, T 3 N, R 2 W). Named on Butler Peak (1971) 7.5' quadrangle.

Willow Creek [RIVERSIDE]: *stream,* flows 2.25 miles to Tahquitz Creek 3.25 miles southeast of San Jacinto Peak (lat. 33°46'40" N, long. 116°38'40" W; sec. 35, T 4 S, R 3 E). Named on San Jacinto Peak (1981) 7.5' quadrangle.

Willow Creek [SAN BERNARDINO]: *stream,* flows 5.5 miles to Deep Creek (1) 2 miles west-southwest of Luna Mountain (lat. 34° 19'50" N, long. 117°09'40" W; sec. 23, T 3 N, R 3 W). Named on Lake Arrowhead (1971) 7.5' quadrangle.

Willow Creek Crossing [RIVERSIDE]: *locality,* 2.5 miles south-southeast of San Jacinto Peak (lat. 33°47' N, long. 118°39'25" W; sec. 34, T 4 S, R 3 E); a trail crosses Willow Creek at the place. Named on San Jacinto Peak (1981) 7.5' quadrangle.

Willow Hole [RIVERSIDE]: *relief feature,* 7.5 miles north of Cathedral City (lat. 33°53'15" N, long. 116°27'55" W; at N line sec. 28, T 3 S, R 5 E). Named on Seven Palms Valley (1958) 7.5' quadrangle. Berkstresser (1969, p. 10) gave the plural name "Willow Holes" as an alternate.

Willow Hole [SAN BERNARDINO]: *locality,* 7.25 miles southwest of Twentynine Palms (lat. 34°04'05" N, long. 116°09'05" W). Named on Indian Cove (1972) 7.5' quadrangle. On Twentynine Palms (1955) 15' quadrangle, the name applies to a water feature.

Willow Spring [SAN BERNARDINO]:

(1) *spring,* 5 miles east of Ivanpah (lat. 35°05'45" N, long. 115° 13' W; near NE cor. sec. 36, T 15 N, R 16 E); the spring is along Willow Wash. Named on Crescent Peak (1956) 15' quadrangle. A pipeline took the water to a mill at Vanderbilt (Thompson, 1921, p. 269).

(2) *spring,* 11 miles south-southeast of Essex (lat. 34°34'45" N, long. 115°11'30" W; sec. 27, T 6 N, R 17 E). Named on Essex (1956) 15' quadrangle.

(3) *spring,* 22 miles northeast of Vidal (lat. 34°22'15" N, long. 114° 16'10" W; at S line sec. 5, T 3 N, R 26 E). Named on Whipple Mountains (1950) 15' quadrangle.

Willow Spring Basin [SAN BERNARDINO]: *relief feature,* 13 miles north of Amboy (lat. 34°45'30" N, long. 115°41'45" W; sec. 26, 27, T 8 N, R 12 E). Named on Flynn (1956) 15' quadrangle.

Willow Spring Canyon [SAN BERNARDINO]: *canyon,* 1.5 miles long, 10.5 miles south-southeast of Essex (lat. 34°35'30" N, long. 115°11'20" W; sec. 22, 27, T 6 N, R 17 E); Willow Spring (2) is near the head of the canyon. Named on Essex (1956) 15' quadrangle.

Willow Springs: see **Murrieta** [RIVERSIDE].

Willow Spring Wash [SAN BERNARDINO]:

(1) *stream* and *dry wash,* extends for 7 miles to loose its identity about 10 miles north-northeast of Amboy (lat. 34°41' N, long. 115° 40'30" W; sec. 24, T 7 N, R 12 E); the feature heads at Willow Spring Basin. Named on Cadiz (1956) 15' quadrangle.

(2) *stream,* flows 2.5 miles from the mouth of Willow Spring Canyon to end 7.5 miles south of Essex (lat. 34°37'20" N, long. 115°13'20" W; sec. 8, T 6 N, R 17 E). Named on Essex (1956) 15' quadrangle.

Willow Valley [RIVERSIDE]: *valley,* 6.5 miles south of Idyllwild (lat. 33°38'45" N, long. 116°43' W; in and near sec. 18, T 6 S, R 3 E). Named on Idyllwild (1959) 15' quadrangle.

Willow Wash [SAN BERNARDINO]:

(1) *stream,* flows 5 miles to Ivanpah Valley 25 miles east of Ivanpah (lat. 35°20'45" N, long. 115°16'30" W; sec. 33, T 15 N, R 16 E). Named on Crescent Peak (1956) and Ivanpah (1956) 15' quadrangles.

(2) *stream,* flows 18 miles to end 36 miles west-southwest of Ivanpah (lat. 35°14'10" N, long. 115°56'30" W; sec. 5, T 13 N, R 10 E). Named on Kelso (1955) and Old Dad Mountain (1956) 15' quadrangles.

Wilshire Peak [SAN BERNARDINO]: *peak,* 5.5 miles west-southwest of San Gorgonio Mountain (lat. 34°03'50" N, long. 116°54'50" W; near SE cor. sec. 19, T 1 S, R 1 E); the feature is less than 0.5 mile east-southeast of Oak Glen Peak. Named on Forest Falls (1970) 7.5' quadrangle. United States Board on Geographic Names (1964b, p. 16) rejected the name "Oak Glen Peak" for present Wilshire Peak.

Wilsie [IMPERIAL]: *locality,* 2.5 miles west-northwest of El Centro along San Diego and Arizona Eastern Railroad (lat. 32°48' N, long. 115°36' W). Named on El Centro (1957) 7.5' quadrangle. The name commemorates W.E. Wilsie, a farmer who came to the neighborhood in 1901 (Gudde, 1949, p. 391).

Wilson Creek [RIVERSIDE]: *stream* and *dry wash,* extends for 16 miles to Vail Lake 6.5 miles west-northwest of Aguanga (lat. 33° 29'30" N, long. 116°57'45" W); the stream goes through Wilson Valley. Named on Hemet (1957) 15' quadrangle, and on Aguanga (1954) and Vail Lake (1953) 7.5' quadrangles.

Wilson Creek [SAN BERNARDINO]: *stream,* flows 5.25 miles to Oak Glen Creek less than 1 mile north of downtown Yucaipa (lat. 34°02'35" N, long. 117°02'30" W; sec. 36, T 1 S, R 2 W). Named on Forest Falls (1970) and Yucaipa (1967) 7.5' quadrangles.

Wilson Valley [RIVERSIDE]: *valley,* 3.25 miles north of Aguanga (lat. 33°29'30" N, long. 116°51'45" W; mainly in sec. 10, T 8 S, R 1 E). Named on Aguanga (1954) 7.5' quadrangle. The name is for a rancher who lived in the valley as early as 1884 (Gunther, p. 575).

Winchester [RIVERSIDE]: *village,* 10 miles east-southeast of Perris (lat. 33°42'30" N, long. 117°05' W; sec. 27, 28, T 5 S, R 2 W). Named on Winchester (1953) 7.5' quadrangle. Postal authorities established Rockhouse post office in 1880, discontinued it in 1882, reestablished it in 1883, and discontinued it in 1887, when they moved it 1.25 miles southwest and changed the name to Winchester; Rockhouse post office was in a stone building (Salley, p. 187). The name "Winchester" commemorates Mrs. Amy Winchester, who founded the community and named it (Gunther, p. 575).

Winding Stair Cave [SAN BERNARDINO]: *cave,* 30 miles north-northeast of Amboy (lat. 34°57'55" N, long. 115°31'10" W; at S line sec. 9, T 10 N, R 14 E). Named on Flynn (1956) 15' quadrangle. J.E. Mitchell of nearby Mitchell Caverns found the cave in 1935 and gave it the name "Cave of the Winding Stairs" (Gardner, p. 244-245).

Windmill [SAN BERNARDINO]: *locality,* 22 miles west-northwest of Ivanpah (lat. 35°26'25" N, long. 115°41' W; near S line sec. 27, T 16 N, R 12 E). Named on Mescal Range (1955) 15' quadrangle.

Windmill: see **The Windmill** [SAN BERNARDINO].

Windy Gap: see **Wingate Pass** [SAN BERNARDINO].

Windy Point [RIVERSIDE]: *promontory,* 6.25 miles northwest of Palm Springs on the south side of the east end of San Gorgonio Pass (lat. 33°53'50" N, long. 116°37'30" W; sec. 24, T 3 S, R 3 E). Named on Desert Hot Springs (1955) and Whitewater (1955) 7.5' quadrangles.

Windy Point [SAN BERNARDINO]:

(1) *promontory,* 6 miles northeast of Amboy (lat. 34°36'45" N, long. 115°39'45" W; sec 18, T 6 N, R 13 E). Named on Cadiz (1956) 15' quadrangle.

(2) *promontory,* less than 1 mile south of Fawnskin along Big Bear Lake (1) (lat. 34°15'35" N, long. 116°56'30" W; at W line sec. 13, T 2 N, R 1 W). Named on Fawnskin (1971) 7.5' quadrangle.

Wineville: see **Mira Loma Station** [RIVERSIDE].

Wingate Pass [SAN BERNARDINO]: *pass,* 17 miles east of Trona (lat. 35°44'15" N, long. 117°04' W); the pass is at the head of Wingate Wash. Named on Wingate Pass (1950) 15' quadrangle. The place first was called Windy Gap (Lingenfelter, 1986, p. 91).

Wingate Wash [SAN BERNARDINO]: *stream,* flows 10 miles to Inyo County 60 miles northwest of Baker (lat. 35°47'45" N, long. 116° 54'10" W; near W line sec. 32, T 20 N, R 1 E); the feature heads near Wingate Pass. Named on Wingate Wash (1950) 15' quadrangle.

Winona: see **Squeaky Springs** [IMPERIAL].

Winston Basin [SAN BERNARDINO]: *relief feature,* 25 miles north-northeast of Amboy (lat. 34°53'45" N, long. 115°33'45" W); the feature is at the head of Winston Wash. Named on Flynn (1956) 15' quadrangle.

Winston Wash [SAN BERNARDINO]: *stream* and *dry wash,* extends for 12 miles to Kelso Wash 30 miles north of Amboy (lat. 34°59'10" N, long. 115°41'35" W; near NW cor. sec. 2, T 10 N, R 12 E). Named on Flynn (1956) 15' quadrangle.

Wintaka: see **Camp Wintaka** [SAN BERNARDINO].

Winter Gardens [SAN BERNARDINO]: *district,* 1.25 miles northeast of present San Bernardino city hall (lat. 34°07' N, long. 117°16'30" W). Named on San Bernardino (1954) 15' quadrangle.

Winter Harbor Cove [SAN BERNARDINO]: *embayment,* 6 miles south-southwest of Luna Mountain along the north side of Lake Arrowhead (1) (lat. 34°16' N, long. 117°10'25" W; near SE cor. sec. 10, T 2 N, R 3 W). Named on Lake Arrowhead (1971) 7.5' quadrangle.

Winterhaven [IMPERIAL]: *town,* 6.5 miles east of Pilot Knob (lat. 32°44'20" N, long. 114°38'05" W; sec. 27, T 16 S, R 22 E). Named on Yuma West (1965) 7.5' quadrangle. The place first was known as Karmack (Hanna, p. 357). Postal authorities established Winterhaven post office in 1916, discontinued it in 1921, and reestablished it in 1934 (Frickstad, p. 49). Yuma (1905) 30' quadrangle shows a place called Colorado located at or near present Winterhaven.

Winters Pass [SAN BERNARDINO]: *pass,* 33 miles northwest of Ivanpah (lat. 35°42'30" N, long. 115°41'50" W). Named on Clark Mountain (1956) 15' quadrangle.

Wister [IMPERIAL]: *locality,* 4.25 miles southeast of Frink along Southern Pacific Railroad (lat. 33°18'50" N, long. 115°36'05" W; sec. 10, T 10 S, R 13 E). Named on Wister (1956) 7.5' quadrangle. California Mining Bureau's (1917b) map shows a place called Lano located at or near present Wister.

Witch Springs: see **Lost Horse Well** [RIVERSIDE].

Wolf Valley [RIVERSIDE]: *valley*, 3.5 miles southeast of downtown Temecula (lat. 33°27'40" N, long. 117°06'15" W). Named on Pechanga (1968) 7.5' quadrangle. Shown as part of Temecula Valley on San Luis Rey (1898) 30' quadrangle. The name commemorates Louis Wolf, who opened a store on Little Temecula grant about 1857; his place was a station for Butterfield Overland stage line (Gunther, p. 578-579).

Wonderland of Rocks [SAN BERNARDINO]: *area*, 8 miles southwest of Twentynine Palms (lat. 34°04' N, long. 116°09' W). Named on Indian Cove (1972) 7.5' quadrangle.

Wonderstone Wash [IMPERIAL]: *stream*, heads in San Diego County and flows 5 miles in Imperial County to Salton Sea 1 mile south-southeast of Desert Shores (lat. 33°23'25" N, long. 116°01'40" W; sec. 15, T 9 S, R 9 E). Named on Oasis (1956) and Seventeen Palms (1956) 7.5' quadrangles.

Wood Canyon [RIVERSIDE]: *canyon*, 3.5 miles long, opens into the canyon of Potrero Creek 5 miles north-northeast of Banning (lat. 33°59'30" N, long. 116°50'15" W; near S line sec. 13, T 2 S, R 1 E). Named on Cabazon 1956) and San Gorgonio Mountain (1970) 7.5' quadrangles.

Wood Canyon [SAN BERNARDINO]: *canyon*, about 2 miles long, 15 miles northeast of Landers (lat. 34°26'10" N, long. 116°13'30" W; sec. 14, 15, T 4 N, R 7 E). Named on Deadman Lake NW (1955) 7.5' quadrangle.

Woodcrest [RIVERSIDE]: *town*, 7 miles south of Riverside city hall (lat. 33°53' N, long. 117°21'30" W). Named on Riverside East (1967) 7.5' quadrangle. Postal authorities established Woodcrest post office in 1926 and discontinued it in 1930 (Salley, p. 242).

Woodlands [SAN BERNARDINO]: *locality*, 3.25 miles north of Sugarloaf Mountain (lat. 34°14'40" N, long. 116°48' W; sec. 19, 20, T 2 N, R 2 E). Named on Moonridge (1970) 7.5' quadrangle.

Woods Mountains [SAN BERNARDINO]: *range*, 21 miles south of Ivanpah (lat. 35°02'15" N, long. 115°18'45" W). Named on Mid Hills (1955) 15' quadrangle. United States Board on Geographic Names (1972a, p. 1) approved the name "Tortoise Shell Mountain" for a peak, altitude 4601 feet, in Woods Mountains (NE quarter sec. 14, T 11 N, R 15 E).

Wood Spring [RIVERSIDE]: *spring*, 16 miles north-northeast of Mortmar (lat. 33°44' N, long. 115°48'40" W; sec. 14, T 5 S, R 12 E). Named on Cottonwood Spring (1958) 15' quadrangle.

Woodspur: see **Coachella** [RIVERSIDE].

Woods Wash [SAN BERNARDINO]: *stream*, flows 26 miles before loosing its identity 3 miles north of Essex (lat. 34°46'50" N, long. 115°14'50" W; near W line sec. 18, T 8 N, R 17 E). Named on Colton Well (1956) and Mid Hills (1955) 15' quadrangles.

Wright Lake [SAN BERNARDINO]: *intermittent lake*, 350 feet long, 5 miles north of Mount San Antonio (lat. 34°21'35" N, long. 117° 38'25" W; at E line sec. 7, T 3 N, R 7 W); the feature is in Wrightwood. Named on Mount San Antonio (1955) 7.5' quadrangle.

Wright Mountain [SAN BERNARDINO]: *peak*, 3.5 miles north-northeast of Mount San Antonio (lat. 34°20' N, long. 117°37'55" W; sec. 20, T 3 N, R 7 W); the peak is south of Wrightwood. Altitude 8505 feet. Named on Mount San Antonio (1955) 7.5' quadrangle.

Wrightwood [SAN BERNARDINO]: *town*, 5 miles north-northeast of Mount San Antonio in Swarthout Valley (lat. 34°21'30" N, long. 117°37'30" W). Named on Mount San Antonio (1955) and Telegraph Peak (1956) 7.5' quadrangles. Postal authorities established Wrightwood post office in 1928 (Frickstad, p. 147). The name is for Sumner Wright, who owned the land before it was subdivided in the 1920's (Robinson, J.W., 1983, p. 198).

Wulfs Crossing [IMPERIAL]: *locality*, 7 miles west-northwest of El Centro (lat. 32°44'15" N, long. 115°38'15" W; near N line sec. 28, T 16 S, R 13 E); a road crosses New River at the place. Named on Mount Signal (1957) 7.5' quadrangle.

- X - Y -

Y: see **The Y** [SAN BERNARDINO].

Yacht Club Bay [SAN BERNARDINO]: *embayment*, 7.25 miles south-southwest of Luna Mountain along Lake Arrowhead (1) (lat. 34° 15'10" N, long. 117° 11'25" W; at SE cor. sec. 16, T 2 N, R 3 W). Named on Lake Arrowhead (1971) 7.5' quadrangle.

Yates Well [SAN BERNARDINO]: *well*, 15 miles north-northwest of Ivanpah (lat. 35°32'15" N, long. 115°24'30" W). Named on Ivanpah (1912) 1° quadrangle.

Yellow Spots Canyon [RIVERSIDE]: *canyon*, 1.5 miles long, 11 miles east of Indio (lat. 33°43'30" N, long. 116°01'50" W; mainly in sec. 22, T 5 S, R 9 E). Named on Thermal Canyon (1956) 7.5' quadrangle.

Yermo [SAN BERNARDINO]: *town*, 4.5 miles northeast of Daggett (lat. 34°54'15" N, long. 116°49'30" W). Named on Yermo (1953) 7.5' quadrangle. Postal authorities established Yermo post office in 1905 (Frickstad, p. 147). Darton and others' (1915) map has the name "Otis" at the site. Thompson's (1921) map shows a place called Borate located 3.5 miles north-northeast of Yermo. Postal authorities established Borate post office in 1896 and discontinued it in 1907 (Frickstad, p. 139). Thompson's (1921) map also shows a place called Kouns situated 5 miles east of Yermo along Los Angeles and Salt Lake Railroad.

Yermo Valley: see **Mojave Valley** [SAN BERNARDINO].

Yocum Spring [SAN BERNARDINO]: *spring*, 18 miles north-northwest of downtown Morongo Valley (lat. 34°14'10" N, long. 116° 43' W; at SE cor. sec. 24, T 2 N, R 2 E). Named on Onyx Peak (1972) 7.5' quadrangle.

Young: see **Camp Young**, under **Chiriaco Summit** [RIVERSIDE].

Yucaipa [SAN BERNARDINO]: *town*, 8.5 miles east of Redlands city hall (lat. 34°02' N, long. 117°02'15" W). Named on Yucaipa (1967) 7.5' quadrangle. Postal authorities established Yucaipe post office in 1893, discontinued it in 1896, reestablished it in 1908 with the name "Yucaipa," and moved it 2 miles southwest in 1910 (Salley, p. 245). The name is of Indian origin (Kroeber, p. 68).

Yucaipa Creek [RIVERSIDE-SAN BERNARDINO]: *stream*, flows 13 miles, partly in San Bernardino County but mainly in Riverside County, to San Timoteo Canyon 12.5 miles east of Riverside (lat. 34°00'10" N, long. 117°09'50" W). Named on Forest Falls (1970) and Redlands (1967) 7.5' quadrangles. United States Board on Geographic Names (1933, p. 831) rejected the form "Yucaipe Creek" for the name.

Yucaipa Ridge[SAN BERNARDINO]: *ridge*, generally west-trending, 3.5 miles long, 4 miles north-northeast of Yucaipa (lat. 34°05'20" N, long. 117°00'45" W). Named on Forest Falls (1970) and Yucaipa (1967) 7.5' quadrangles.

Yucaipa Valley [SAN BERNARDINO]: *valley*, at and near Yucaipa (lat. 34°01'15" N, long. 117°03'45" W). Named on El Casco (1967) and Yucaipa (1967) 7.5' quadrangles. United States Board on Geographic Names (1933, p. 831) rejected the form "Yucaipe Valley" for the name.

Yucaipe: see **Yucaipa** [SAN BERNARDINO].

Yucca Grove [SAN BERNARDINO]: *locality*, 28 miles west of Ivanpah (lat. 35°24'10" N, long. 115°47'30" W; sec. 10, T 15 N, R 11 E). Named on Halloran Spring (1956) 15' quadrangle.

Yucca Inn [SAN BERNARDINO]: *locality*, 9 miles north-northeast of Mount San Antonio (lat. 34°24'40" N, long. 117°35'25" W; at NE cor. sec. 27, T 4 N, R 7 W). Named on San Antonio (1942) 15' quadrangle.

Yucca Mesa [SAN BERNARDINO]: *area*, 6.5 miles north-northeast of Yucca Valley (lat. 34°12'30" N, long. 116°24' W). Named on Joshua Tree North (1972) and Yucca Valley North (1972) 7.5' quadrangles.

Yucca Valley [SAN BERNARDINO]: *town*, 48 miles east of San Bernardino (lat. 34°07'10" N, long. 116°26'45" W). Named on Yucca Valley North (1972) and Yucca Valley South (1972) 7.5' quadrangles. Postal authorities established Yucca Valley post office in 1945 (Frickstad, p. 147). The name is from the Joshua tree, *Yucca brevifolia*—Joshua trees are abundant at the site (Gudde, 1969, p. 372).

Yuha Basin [IMPERIAL]: *relief feature*, 16 miles west-southwest of El Centro (lat. 32°42'30" N, long. 115°50' W); the feature is in Yuha Desert. Named on Coyote Wells (1957) and Yuha Basin (1957) 7.5' quadrangles.

Yuha Buttes [IMPERIAL]: *relief feature*, 18 miles west-southwest of El Centro (lat. 32°44' N, long. 115°51'15" W). Named on Yuha Basin (1957) 7.5' quadrangle.

Yuha Desert [IMPERIAL]: *area*, 18 miles west-southwest of El Centro (lat. 32°44'30" N, long. 115°52' W). Named on Coyote Wells (1957), Mount Signal (1957), Painted Gorge (1957), Plaster City (1957), and Yuha Basin (1957) 7.5' quadrangles.

Yuha Wash [IMPERIAL]: *stream* and *dry wash*, extends for 11 miles before ending 5.5 miles east-southeast of Plaster City (lat. 32°45'40" N, long. 115°46'05" W; sec. 19, T 16 S, R 12 E). Named on Coyote Wells (1957), Plaster City (1957), and Yuha Basin (1957) 7.5' quadrangles.

Yuha Spring [IMPERIAL]: *spring*, 19 miles west-southwest of El Centro (lat. 32°43'20" N, long. 115°52'20" W). Named on Coyote Wells (1945) 15' quadrangle.

Yuha Well [IMPERIAL]: *well*, 12.5 miles west-southwest of El Centro (lat. 32°43' N, long. 115°52'35" W); the well is in Yuha Desert near Yuha Wash. Named on Coyote Wells (1957) 7.5' quadrangle. Anza visited the place in 1774 and gave it the name "Pozas de Santa Rosa de las Lajas" for the peculiar rocks at the site—*Pozas de Santa Rosa de las Lajas* means "Wells of St. Rosa of the Flat Rocks" in Spanish (Hoover, Rensch, and Rensch, p. 107).

Yuma: see **Fort Yuma**, under **Pilot Knob** [IMPERIAL].

- Z -

Zanja: see **Redlands** [SAN BERNARDINO]; **The Zanja** [SAN BERNARDINO].

Zanja Peak [SAN BERNARDINO]: *peak*, 2.5 miles northwest of Yucaipa (lat. 34°03'45" N, long. 117°03'55" W; near SW cor. sec. 23, T 1 S, R 2 W). Altitude 3543 feet. Named on Yucaipa (1967) 7.5' quadrangle.

Zucker: see **Guasti** [SAN BERNARDINO].

Zzyzx: see **Soda Springs** [SAN BERNARDINO].

Zzyzx Mineral Springs: see **Soda Springs** [SAN BERNARDINO].

Zzyzx Spring: see **Soda Springs** [SAN BERNARDINO].

SOUTHEAST REGION IMPERIAL, RIVERSIDE AND SAN BERNARDINO COUNTIES

REFERENCES CITED

BOOKS AND ARTICLES

Anderson, Winslow. 1892. *Mineral springs and health resorts of California*. San Francisco: The Bancroft Company, 347 p.

Anonymous. 1950. "A run into the country." *Westways*, v. 42, no. 12, p. 32-33.

_____1985. "Mitchell caverns natural preserve in the providence Mountains State Reservation Area." *California Geology*, v. 38, no. 2, p. 34-38.

Antisell, Thomas. 1856. "Geological report." *Reports of explorations and surveys, to ascertain the most practicable and economical route for a railroad from the Mississippi River to the Pacific Ocean*. Volume VII, Part II. (33d Cong. 2d Sess., Sen. Ex. Doc. No. 78.) Washington: Beverly Tucker, Printer, 204 p.

Baker, Charles Laurence. 1911. "Notes on the later Cenozoic history of the Mohave Desert region in southeastern California." *University of California Publications, Bulletin of the Department of Geology*, v., no. 15, p. 333-383.

Beattie, George William, and Beattie, Helen Pruitt. 1939. *Heritage of the valley*. Pasadena, California: San Pasqual Press, 459 p.

Becker, Robert H. 1969. *Designs on the land*. San Francisco: The Book Club of California, (no pagination).

Belden, L. Burr, and Walker, Ardis Manly. 1962. *Searles Lake borax, 1862-1962*. (Published for the dedication of the Searles Lake Monument on November 8, 1962.) (No place): Death Valley '49ers, Inc., 39 p.

Bergland, Eric. 1876. "Preliminary report upon the operations of party no. 3, California section, season of 1875-'76, with a view to determine the feasibility of diverting the Colorado River for purposes of irrigation." *Annual report upon the geographical surveys west of the one hundredth meridian, in California, Nevada, Utah, Colorado, Wyoming, New Mexico, Arizona, and Montana*. (Appendix JJ of *The Annual report of the Chief of Engineers for 1876*.) Washington: Government Printing Office, p. 109-125.

Berkstresser, C.F., Jr. 1968. *Data for springs in the Southern Coast, Transverse, and Peninsular Ranges of California*. (United States Geological Survey, Water Resources Division, Open-file report.) Menlo Park, California: 21 p. + appendices.

_____1969. *Data for springs in the Colorado Desert area of California*. (United States Geological Survey, Water Resources Division, Open-file report.) Menlo Park, California, 13 p. + appendices.

Birnie, R., Jr. 1876. "Executive report of Lieutenant R. Birnie, Jr., Thirteenth United States Infantry, on the operations of party no. 2, California section, field-season of 1875." *Annual report upon the geographical surveys west of the one hundredth meridian, in California, Nevada, Utah, Colorado, Wyoming, New Mexico, Arizona, and Montana*. (Appendix JJ of *The Annual Report of the Chief of Engineers for 1876*.) Washington: Government Printing Office, p. 130-135.

Blake, William P. 1857. "Geological report." *Reports of explorations and surveys, to ascertain the most practicable and economical route for a railroad from the Mississippi River to the Pacific Ocean*. Volume V, Part II. (33d Cong., 2d Sess., Sen. Ex. Doc. No. 78.) Washington: Beverly Tucker, Printer, 370 p.

Bloomquist, Dick. 1977a. "Palm and Fern Canyons." *Desert*, v. 40, no. 4, p. 16-18.

_____1977b. "Dead Indian Canyon." *Desert*, v. 40, no. 5, p. 7.

_____1978. "Una Palma." *Desert*, v. 41, no. 9.

Bolton, Herbert Eugene. 1931. *Outpost of empire*. New York: Alfred A. Knopf, 334 p.

Brown, John S. 1920. *Routes to desert watering places in the Salton Sea region, California*. (United States Geological Survey Water-Supply Paper 490-A.) Washington: Government Printing Office, 86 p.

_____1923. *The Salton Sea region, California*. (United States Geological Survey Water-Supply Paper 497.) Washington: Government Printing Office, 292 p.

Burns, Helen. 1952. *Salton Sea story*. Thermal, California: (Author), 29 p.

California Division of Highways. 1934. *California highway transportation survey, 1934*. Sacramento: Department of Public Works, Division of Highways, 130 p. + appendices.

Campbell, Marius R. 1902. *Reconnaissance of the borax deposits of Death Valley and Mohave Desert*. (United States Geological Survey Bulletin 200.) Washington: Government Printing office, 23 p.

Casebier, Dennis G. 1975. *The Mohave road*. Norco, California: Tales of the Mohave Road Publishing Company, 192 p.

Chase, J. Smeaton. 1919. *California desert trails*. Boston and New York: Houghton Mifflin Company, 387 p.

Clark, Lew, and Clark, Ginny. 1978. *High mountains and deep valleys, The gold bonanza days*. San Luis Obispo, California: Western Trail Publications, 192 p.

Cowan, Robert G. 1956. *Ranchos of California*. Fresno, California: Academy Library Guild, 151 p.

Coy, Owen C. 1923. *California county boundaries*. Berkeley: California Historical Survey Commission, 335 p.

Crossman, James H. 1890. "San Bernardino County." *Ninth annual report of the State Mineralogist, for the year ending December 1, 1889*. Sacramento: California State Mining Bureau, p. 214-239.

Darton, N.H. 1933. *Guidebook of the Western United States., Part F. The Southern Pacific lines, New Orleans to Los Angeles*. (United States Geological Survey Bulletin 845.) Washington: Government Printing Office, 304 p.

Darton, N.H., and others. 1915. *Guidebook of the Western United States, Part C. The Santa Fe route*. (United States Geological Survey Bulletin 613.) Washington: Government Printing Office, 194 p.

De Groot, Henry. 1890. "San Bernardino County—its mountain plains and valleys." *Tenth annual report of the State Mineralogist, for the year ending December 1, 1890*. Sacramento: California State Mining Bureau, p. 518-539.

Downs, Theodore, Howard, Hildegarde, Clements, Thomas, and Smith, Gerald A. 1959. *Quaternary animals from Schuiling Cave in the Mojave Desert, California*. Los Angeles County Museum Contributions in Science, No. 29, 21 p.

Dutcher, L. C., and Garrett, A.A. 1963. *Geologic and hydrologic features of the San Bernardino area, California*. (United States Geological Survey Water-Supply Paper 1419.) Washington: Government Printing Office, 114 p.

Edwards, E.I. 1961. *Lost oases along the Carrizo*. Los Angeles, California: The Westernlore Press, 126 p.

English, Walter A. 1926. *Geology and oil resources of the Puente Hills region, southern California*. (United States Geological Survey Bulletin 768.) Washington: Government Printing Office, 110 p.

Farnham, Thomas Jefferson. 1947. *Travels in California*. Oakland, California: Biobooks, 166 p.

Federal Writers' Project. 1939. *Death Valley, A guide*. Boston: Houghton Mifflin Company, 75 p.

Frazer, Robert W. 1965. *Forts of the West*. Norman: University of Oklahoma Press, 246 p.

Fremont, J.C. 1845. *Report of the exploring expedition to the Rocky Mountains in the year 1842, and to Oregon and North California in the years 1843-'44*. Washington: Blair and Rives, Printers, 583 p.

Frickstad, Walter N. 1955. *A century of California post offices 1848 to 1954*. Oakland, California: Philatelic Research Society, 395 p.

Gale, Hoyt S. 1914. "Salines in the Owens, Searles, and Panamint basins, southeastern California." *Contributions to economic geology, 1913*. (United States Geological Survey Bulletin 580-L.) Washington: Government Printing Office, p. 251-323.

Galvin, John (editor). 1965. *A record of travels in Arizona and California, 1775-1776*. San Francisco: John Howell—Books, 113 p.

Gardner, Robert C. 1958. "Geological exploration of the Cave of the Winding Stairs, San Bernardino County, California." *Compass*, v. 35, no. 4, p. 244-254.

Gudde, Erwin G. 1949. *California place names*. Berkeley and Los Angeles: University of California Press, 431 p.

_____1969. *California place names*. Berkeley and Los Angeles: University of California press, 416 p.

_____1975. *California gold camps*. Berkeley, Los Angeles, London: University of California Press, 467 p.

Gunther, Jane Davies. 1984. *Riverside County, California, place names*. Riverside, California: (Author), 634 p.

Hafen, LeRoy R., and Hafen, Ann W. 1961. *The Far West and Rockies, General analytical index to the fifteen volume series, and Supplement to the Journals of Forty-niners, Salt Lake to Los Angeles*. Glendale, California: The Arthur H. Clark Company, 360 p.

Hanks, Henry G. 1886. *Sixth annual report of the State Mineralogist. Part I. For the year ending June 1, 1886*. Sacramento: California State Mining Bureau, 145 p.

Hanna, Phil Townsend. 1951. *The dictionary of California land names*. Los Angeles: The Automobile Club of Southern California, 392 p.

Hart, Herbert M. 1965. *Old forts of the Far West*. New York: Bonanza Books, 192 p.

Hewett, D.F. 1956. *Geology and mineral resources of the Ivanpah quadrangle, California and Nevada*. (United States Geological Survey Professional Paper 275.) Washington: Government Printing Office, 172 p.

Hildebrand, George H. 1982. *Borax pioneer: Francis Marion Smith*. San Diego, California: Howell-North Books, 318 p.

Hoover, Mildred Brooke, Rensch, Hero Eugene, and Rensch, Ethel Grace. 1966. *Historic spots in California*. (Third edition, revised by William N. Abeloe.) Stanford, California: Stanford University Press, 642 p.

Hubbard, Paul B., Bray, Doris, and Pipkin, George. 1965. *Ballarat, 1897-1917, Facts and folklore*. Lancaster, California: Paul B. and Arline B. Hubbard, 98 p.

Irelan, William, Jr. 1888. "Report of the State Mineralogist." *Eighth annual report of the State Mineralogist. For the year ending October 1, 1888*. Sacramento: California State Mining Bureau, p. 12-695.

Ives, Joseph C. 1861. "General report." *Report upon the Colorado River of the West, explored in 1857 and 1858 by Lieutenant Joseph C. Ives, Corps of Topographical Engineers, under the direction of the Office of Exploration and Surveys*. Washington: Government Printing Office, 131p.

Jaeger, Edmund C. 1959. "Names of desert things and places." *Desert Magazine*, v. 22, no. 3, p. 22-23.

Jennings, Bill. 1979. "Idyllwild San Jacinto Mountains." *Desert*, v. 42, no. 9, 12-15, 39.

Kroeber, A.L. 1916. "California place names of Indian origin." *University of California Publications in American Archæology and Ethnology*, v. 12, no. 2, p. 31-69.

La Fuze, Pauliena B. 1971. *Saga of the San Bernardinos*. (No place): San Bernardino County Museum Associates, (2 volumes in 1) 226 p. + 373 p.

Leetch, George. 1969. "San Sebastian Marsh." *Desert Magazine*, v. 32, no. 2, p. 12-15.

Linder, Harold. 1989. "Hart mining district, San Bernardion County, California." *California Geology*, v. 42, no. 6, p. 134-140.

Lingenfelter, Richard E. 1978. *Steamboats on the Colorado River, 1852-1916*. Tucson, Arizona: The University of Arizona Press, 195 p.

_____1986. *Death Valley and the Amargosa*. Berkeley, Los Angeles, London: University of California Press, 664 p.

Lorey, Frank, III. 1985. "History of mining, Providence Mountains." *California Geology*, v. 38, no. 2, p. 27-33.

Love, Frank. 1974. *Mining camps and ghost towns. A history of mining in Arizona and California along the lower Colorado*. Los Angeles: Westernlore Press, 192 p.

MacDougal, D.T. 1917. "A decade of the Salton Sea." *Geographical Review*, v. 3, no. 6, p. 457-473.

Marcy, Randolph B. 1859. *A hand-book for overland expeditions*. New York: Harper and Brothers, Publishers, 340 p.

Marlette, S. H. 1856. *Annual report of the Surveyor-General, of the State of California*. (Sen. Doc. No. 5, Sess. of 1856.) Sacramento: State Printer, 334 p.

McDonald, Russel P. 1989. "The Reche brothers." *The Californians*, v. 7, no. 4, p. 41-47.

Meadows, Don. 1966. *Historic place names in Orange County*. Balboa Island, California: Paisano Press, Inc., 141 p.

Mendenhall, Walter C. 1909a. *Some desert watering places in southeastern California and southwestern Nevada*. (United States Geological Survey Water-Supply Paper 224.) Washington: Government Printing Office, 98 p.

_____1909b. *Ground waters of the Indio region, California, with a sketch of the Colorado Desert*. (United States Geological Survey Water-Supply Paper 225.) Washington: Government Printing Office, 56 p.

Merrill, Frederick J.H. 1916. "The counties of San Diego, Imperial." *Report VIV of the State Mineralogist*. Sacramento: California State Mining Bureau, p. 635-743.

Miller, Ron, and Miller, Peggy. 1976. *Mines of the Mojave*. Glendale, California: La Siesta Press, 71 p.

Morgan, Dale L. 1964. *Jedediah Smith and the opening of the West*. (Second edition.) Lincoln: University of Nebraska Press, 458 p.

Myrick, David F. 1962-1963. *Railroads of Nevada and eastern California*. Berkeley, California: Howell-North Books, (2 volumes) 933 p.

O'Neal, Lulu Rasmussen. 1981. *A peculiar piece of desert, The Story of California's Morongo Basin*. Morongo Valley, California: Sagebrush Press, 208 p.

Orcutt, Charles Russell. "The Colorado Desert." *Tenth annual report of the State Mineralogist, for the year ending December 1, 1890*. Sacramento: California State Mining Bureau, p. 899-919.

Ormsby, Waterman L. 1968. *The Butterfield Overland mail*. San Marino, California: The Huntington Library, 179 p.

Paher, Stanley W. 1973. *Death Valley ghost towns*. Las Vegas, Nevada: Nevada Publications, 48 p.

Palmer, T.S. 1948. *Place names of the Death Valley region in California and Nevada*. (Privately printed), 80 p.

Peirson, Erma. 1970. *The Mojave River and its valley*. Glendale, California: The Arthur H. Clark Company, 229 p.

Perez, Crisostomo N. 1996. *Land grants in Alta California*. Rancho Cordova, California: Landmark Enterprises, 264 p.

Richards, Elizabeth W. 1968. *Guideposts to history, concerning origins of place and street names in San Bernardino County*. (Second edition.) San Bernardino: Santa Fe Federal Savings and Loan Association, (no pagination).

Robinson, John W. 1975. "A mountain of gold." *Desert*, v. 38, no, 9, p. 34-37.

_____1983. *The San Gabriels II, The mountains from Monrovia Canyon to Lytle Creek*. Arcadia, California: Big Santa Anita Historical Society, 224 p.

Robinson, John W., and Risher, Bruce D. 1993. *The San Jacintos, The Mountain country from Banning to Borrego Valley*. Arcadia, California: Big Santa Anita Historical Society, 252 p.

Robinson, W.W. 1966. *Maps of Los Angeles from Ord's Survey of 1849 to the end of the Boom of the Eighties*. Los Angeles: Dawson's Bookshop, 87 p.

Rollins, Royce. 1964. "Historical thumbnail guide to Coachella Valley." *Desert Magazine*, v. 27, no. 3, p. 10-14.

Salley, H. E. 1977. *History of California post offices , 1849-1976*. La Mesa, California: Postal History Associates, Inc., 300 p.

Sinclair, C. H. 1901. *Oblique boundary line between California and Nevada*. (United Sates Coast and Geodetic Survey Report for 1900, Appendix 3.) Washington: Government Printing Office, p. 253-484.

Strong, Mary Frances. 1975. "Amargosa Gorge." *Desert*, v. 38, no. 11, p. 20-23, 46.

Thompson, David G. 1921. *Routes to desert watering places in the Mohave Desert region, California*. (United States Geological Survey Water-Supply Paper 490-B.) Washington: Government Printing Office, p. 87-269.

_____1929. *The Mohave Desert region, California*. (United States Geological Survey Water-Supply Paper 578.) Washington: Government Printing Office, 759 p.

United States Board on Geographic Names (under name "United States Geographic Board"). 1933. *Sixth report of the Unites Sates Geographic Board, 1890-1932*. Washington: Government Printing Office, 834 p.

_____(under name "United States Geographic Board). 1934. *Decisions of the United States Geographic Board, No. 34—Decisions June 1933-March 1934*. Washington: Government Printing Office, 20 p.

_____(under name "United States Board on Geographical Names"). 1938. *Decisions of the Unites States Board on Geographical Names, Decisions rendered between July 1, 1937, and June 30, 1938*. Washington: Government Printing Office, 62 p.

_____(under name "United States Board on Geographical Names"). 1943. *Decisions rendered between July 1, 1941*, and June 30, 1943. Washington: Department of the Interior, 104 p.

_____1949. *Decision lists nos. 4907, 4908, 4909, July, August, September, 1949*. Washington: Department of the Interior, 24 p.

_____1960a. *Decisions on names in the United States and Puerto Rico, Decisions rendered in May, June, July, and August, 1959*. (Decision list no. 5903.) Washington: Department of the Interior, 79 p.

_____1960b. *Decisions on names in the United States, Decisions rendered from September 1959 through December 1959*. (Decision list no. 5904.) Washington: Department of the Interior, 68 p.

_____1960c. *Decisions on names in the United States and the Virgin Islands, Decisions rendered from May 1960 through August 1960*. (Decision list no. 6002.) Washington: Department of the Interior, 77 p.

_____1961a. *Decisions on names in the United States, Decisions rendered from September through December 1960*. (Decision list no. 6003.) Washington: Department of the Interior, 73 p.

_____1961b. *Decisions on names in the United States, Decisions rendered from January through April 1961*. (Decision list no. 6101.) Washington:

Department of the Interior, 74 p.

_____1961c. *Decision on names in the United States, Decisions rendered from May through August 1961*. (Decision list no. 6102.) Washington: Department of the Interior, 81 p.

_____1962a. *Decisions on geographic names in the United States, Decisions rendered from September through December 1961*. (Decision list no. 6103.) Washington: Department of the Interior, 75 p.

_____1962b. *Decisions on names in the United States, Decisions rendered from January through April 1962*. (Decision list no. 6201.) Washington: Department of the Interior, 72 p.

_____1963a. *Decisions on names in the United States, Decisions rendered from September through December 1962*. (Decision list no. 6203.) Washington: Department of the Interior, 59 p.

_____1963b. *Decisions on geographic names in the United States, January through April 1963*. (Decision list no. 6301.) Washington: Department of the Interior, 78 p.

_____1964a. *Decisions on geographic names in the United States, September through December 1963*. (Decision list no. 6303.) Washington: Department of the Interior, 66 p.

_____1964b. *Decisions on geographic names in the United States, May through August 1964*. (Decision list no. 6402.) Washington: Department of the Interior, 85 p.

_____1965a. *Decisions on geographic names in the United States, September through December 1964*. (Decision list no. 6403.) Washington: Department of the Interior, 66 p.

_____1965b. *Decisions on geographic names in the United States, January through March 1965*. (Decision list no. 6501.) Washington: Department of the Interior, 85 p.

_____1965c. *Decisions on geographic names in the United States, July through September 1965*. (Decision list no. 6503.) Washington: Department of the Interior, 74 p.

_____1966a. *Decisions on geographic names in the United States, October through December 1965*. (Decision list no. 6504.) Washington: Department of the Interior, 38 p.

_____1966b. *Decisions on geographic names in the United States, January through March 1966*. (Decision list no. 6601.) Washington: Department of the Interior, 44 p.

_____1966c. *Decisions on geographic names in the United States, April through June 1966*. (Decision list no. 6602.) Washington: Department of the Interior, 36 p.

_____1967. *Decisions on geographic names in the United States, October through December 1966*. (Decision list no. 6604.) Washington: Department of the Interior, 36 p.

_____1968. *Decisions on geographic names in the United States, October through December 1967*. (Decision list no. 6704.) Washington: Department of the Interior, 46 p.

_____1969. *Decisions on geographic names in the United States, January through March 1969*. (Decision list no. 6901.) Washington: Department of the Interior, 31 p.

_____1970. *Decisions on geographic names in the United States, July through September 1970*. (Decision list no. 7003.) Washington: Department of the Interior, 15 p.

_____1971. *Decisions on geographic names in the United States, October through December 1970*. (Decision list no. 7004.) Washington: Department of the Interior, 28 p.

_____1972a. *Decisions on geographic names in the United States, October through December 1971*. (Decision list no. 7104.) Washington: Department of the Interior, 20 p.

_____1972b. *Decisions on geographic names in the United States, July through September 1972*. (Decision list no. 7203.) Washington: Department of the Interior, 17 p.

_____1973 *Decisions on geographic names in the United States, April through June 1973*. (Decision list no. 7302.) Washington: Department of the Interior, 16 p.

_____1974a. *Decisions on geographic names in the United States, April through June 1974*. (Decision list no. 7402.) Washington: Department of the Interior, 27 p.

_____1974b. *Decisions on geographic names in the United States, July through September 1974*. (Decision list no. 7403.) Washington: Department of the Interior, 34 p.

_____1975a. *Decisions on geographic names in the United States, January through March 1975*. (Decision list no. 7501.) Washington: Department of the Interior, 36 p.

_____1975b. *Decisions on geographic names in the United States, April through June 1975*. (Decision list no. 7502.) Washington: Department of the Interior, 32 p.

_____1975c. *Decisions on geographic names in the United States, July through September 1975*. (Decision list no. 7503.) Washington: Department of the Interior, 33 p.

_____1976a. *Decisions on geographic names in the United States, October through December 1975*. (Decision list no. 7504.) Washington: Department of the Interior, 45 p.

_____1976b. *Decisions on geographic names in the United States, January through March 1976*. (Decision list no. 7601.) Washington: Department of the Interior, 30 p.

_____1978. *Decisions on geographic names in the United States, April through June 1978*. (Decision list no. 7802.) Washington: Department of the Interior, 30 p.

_____1979. *Decisions on geographic names in the United States, January through March 1979*. (Decision list no. 7901.) Washington: Department of the Interior, 27 p.

_____1980. *Decisions on geographic names in the United States, January through March 1980*. (Decision list no. 8001.) Washington: Department of the Interior, 23 p.

_____1982a. *Decisions on geographic names in the United States, October through December 1981*. (Decision list no. 8104.) Washington: Department of the Interior, 26 p.

_____1982b. *Decisions on geographic names in the United States, January through March 1982*. (Decision list no. 8201.) Washington: Department of the Interior, 17 p.

_____1982c. *Decisions on geographic names in the United States, April through June 1982*. (Decision list no. 8202.) Washington: Department of the Interior, 21 p.

_____1983a. *Decisions on geographic names in the United States, July through September 1982*. (Decision list no. 8203.) Washington: Department of the Interior, 25 p.

_____1983b. *Decisions on geographic names in the United States, October through December 1982*. (Decision list no. 8204.) Washington: Department of the Interior, 26 p.

_____1983c. *Decisions on geographic names in the United States, January through March 1983*. (Decision list no. 8301.) Washington: Department of the Interior, 33 p.

_____1983d. *Decisions on geographic names in the United States, April through June 1983*. (Decision list no. 8302.) Washington: Department of the Interior, 29 p.

_____1983e. *Decisions on geographic names in the United States, July through September 1983*. (Decision list no. 8303.) Washington: Department of the Interior, 26 p.

_____1984. *Decisions on geographic names in the United States, April through June 1984*. (Decision list no. 8402.) Washington: Department of the Interior, 22 p.

_____1985. *Decisions on geographic names in the United States, January through March 1985*. (Decision list no. 8501.) Washington: Department of the Interior, 18 p.

_____1986a. *Decisions on geographic names in the United States, January through March 1986*. (Decision list no. 8601.) Washington: Department of the Interior, 13 p.

_____1986b. *Decisions on geographic names in the United States, October through December 1986*. (Decision list no. 8604.) Washington: Department of the Interior, 22 p.

_____1987. *Decisions on geographic names in the United States, April through June 1987*. (Decision list no. 8702.) Washington: Department of the Interior, 17 p.

_____1988a. *Decisions on geographic names in the United States, January through March 1988*. (Decision list no. 8801.) Washington: Department of the Interior, 16 p.

_____1988b. *Decisions on geographic names in the United States, April through June 1988*. (Decision list no. 8802.) Washington: Department of the Interior, 19 p.

_____1988c. *Decisions on geographic names in the United States, July through September 1988*. (Decision list no. 8803.) Washington: Department of the Interior, 19 p.

_____1989a. *Decisions on geographic names in the United States, January through March 1989*. (Decision list no. 8901.) Washington: Department of the Interior, 9 p.

_____1989b. *Decisions on geographic names in the United States, October through December 1989*. (Decision list no. 8904.) Washington: Department of the Interior, 9 p.

_____1990. *Decisions on geographic names in the United States*. (Decision list 1990.) Washington: Department of the Interior, 35 p.

Waring, Clarence A., and Huguenin, Emile. 1919. "Inyo County." *Report XV of the State Mineralogist*. Sacramento: California State Mining Bureau, p. 28-134.

Waring, Gerald A. 1915. *Springs of California*. (United States Geological Survey Water-Supply Paper 338.) Washington: Government Printing Office, 410 p.

Watts, W.L. 1901. *Oil and gas yielding formations of California*. (California State Mining Bureau Bulletin No. 19.) Sacramento: California State Mining Bureau, 236 p.

Weight, Harold O. 1979. "Legends of the Lost Horse mine." *Desert*,

v. 42, no. 1, p. 8-11, 30-31.

West, Roland. 1976. "Tumco . . . The forgotten ghost." *Desert*, v. 39, no. 9, p. 10-11.

Wheat, Carl I. 1957. *Mapping the Transmississippi West*. Volume One. San Francisco: The Institute of Historical Cartography, 264 p.

Whipple, C.W. 1876. "Executive report of Lieutenant C.W. Whipple, Ordnance Corps, on the operations of special party, California section, field-season of 1875." *Annual report upon the geographical surveys west of the one hundredth meridian, in California, Nevada, Utah, Colorado, Wyoming, New Mexico, Arizona, and Montana*. (Appendix JJ of *The Annual Report of the Chief of Engineers for 1876*.) Washington: Government Printing Office, p. 147-150.

Wight, Phyllis. 1966. "Coachella Valley's ghost town." *Desert Magazine*, v. 29, no. 3, p. 12-14.

Wines, Howie (editor). 1966. *Kern County centennial almanac*. Bakersfield, California: Kern County Centennial Observance Committee, 176 p.

Wright, Lauren A., and others. 1953. "Mines and mineral deposits of San Bernardino County, California." *California Journal of Mines and Geology*, v. 49, no. 1 and 2, p. 49-192.

Wynn, Marcia Rittenhouse. 1963. *Desert bonanza, The story of early Randsburg, Mojave Desert Mining camp*. Glendale, California: The Arthur H. Clark Company, 275p.

QUADRANGLE MAPS

(All maps published by United States Geological Survey, except as noted. Dates identify the editions of the maps. If a reprinted or revised map was used, the year of reprinting or revision is given in parentheses, unless the reprinted or revised map is cited specifically in the text.)

Acolita 15'—1953.
Adelanto 7.5'—1956 (photorevised 1968).
Adobe Mountain 7.5'—1955 (photorevised 1968).
Agua Dulce 15' (same area as Rabbit Peak 15')—1944 (Army).
Aguanga 7.5'—1954 (photorevised 1971).
Alamorio 7.5'—1956.
Alberhill 7.5'—1954; 1954, photorevised 1988.
Alvord Mountain 15'—1948.
Amboy 1°—1942 (Army).
Amos 7.5'—1956.
Apple Valley 15'—1957.
Apple Valley North 7.5'—1970.
Apple Valley South 7.5'—1971.
Araz 7.5'—1964.
Arrowhead 7.5' (same area as San Bernardino North 7.5')—1941.
Ash Hill 7.5'—1955.
Astley Rancho 7.5'—1973.
Avawatz Mountains 1°—1933 (reprinted 1945).
Avawatz Pass 15'—1948.
Bachelor Mountain 7.5'—1953; 1953, photorevised 1973.
Bagdad 15'—1956.
Baker 15'—1956.
Baldy Mesa 7.5'—1956 (photorevised 1968).
Banning 15'—1942 (Army); 1956.
Bannock 15'—1956.
Bard 7.5'—1965.
Barrel Spring 15' (same area as Borrego Mountain 15')—1942 (Army).
Barstow 30'—1934.
15'—1956.
7.5'—1971.
Barstow SE 7.5'—1971.
Beaumont 7.5'—1953 (photorevised 1972).
Beauty Mountain 7.5'—1960.
Big Bear City 7.5'—1971.
Big Bear Lake 7.5'—1970.
Bighorn Canyon 7.5'—1972.
Big Maria Mountains 15'—1951.
Big Maria Mountains NE 7.5'—1954 (photorevised 1970).
Big Maria Mountains NW 7.5'—1971.
Big Maria Mountains SE 7.5'—1955 (photorevised 1970).
Big Maria Mountains SW 7.5'—1971.
Black Star Canyon 7.5'—1967.
Blythe 7.5'—1951.
Blythe NE 7.5'—1951.
Bonds Corner 7.5'—1957.
Boron NE 7.5'—1973.
Borrego Mountain SE 7.5'—1958.
Brawley 15'—1945 (Army).
7.5'—1957.
Brawley NW 7.5'—1957.
Bristol Lake 15'—1956.
Broadwell Lake 15'—1955.
Bucksnort Mountain 7.5'—1960.
Butler Peak 7.5'—1971.
Cabazon 7.5'—1956 (photorevised 1972).
Cadiz 15'—1956.
Cadiz Lake 15'—1956.
Cadiz Valley 15'—1956.
Cady Mountains 15'—1955.
Cajon 7.5'—1956 (photorevised 1968).
Calexico 7.5'—1957.
Calipatria 15'—1943 (Army).
Calipatria SW 7.5'—1956.
Cañada Gobernadora 7.5'—1968.
Canyon Spring 15' (same area as Hayfield 15')—1943 (Army).
Carrizo 30'—1913 (reprinted 1938) (Army).
Carrizo Mountain 15'—1944 (Army); 1959.
7.5'—1957.
Carrizo Mountain NE 7.5'—1957.
Castle Rock 7.5'—1970.
Catclaw Flat 7.5'—1972.
Cathedral City 7.5'—1958 (photorevised 1981).
Cave Mountain 15'—1948.
Cedar Springs 7.5' (same area as Silverwood Lake 7.5')—1956 (photorevised 1968).
Chemehuevi Peak 7.5'—1971.
Christmas Canyon 7.5'—1973.
Chuckwalla Mountains 15'—1943 (Army); 1963.
Chuckwalla Spring 15'—1953.
Cibola 15'—1945 (Army); 1951.
7.5'—1965.
Clark Lake 15'—1942 (Army).
Clark Lake NE 7.5'—1960.
Clark Mountain 15'—1956.
Coachella 15'—1943 (Army); 1956.
Collins Valley 7.5'—1959.
Colton 7.5' (same area as San Bernardino South 7.5')—1943.
Colton Well 15'—1956.
Confidence Hills 15'—1950.
Corona 30'—1902 (reprinted 1946).
15'—1942 (Army).
Corona North 7.5'—1967.
Corona South 7.5'—1954; 1967 (photorevised 1973).
Cottonwood Spring 15'—1943 (Army); 1958.
Cougar Buttes 7.5'—1971.
Coxcomb Mountains 15'—1963.
Coyote Wells 15'—1945 (Army).
7.5'—1957.
Crescent Peak 15'—1956.
Cross Roads 7.5'—1959 (photorevised 1977).
Cucamonga 15' (same area as Ontario 15')—1903 (reprinted 1932); 1944 (Army).
Cucamonga Peak 7.5'—1953; 1966 (photorevised 1973).
Cuddeback Lake 15'—1954.
Daggett 15'—1956.
7.5'—1971.
Dale Lake 15'—1956.
Danby 15'—1956.
Davis Dam 15'—1950.
Deadman Lake 15'—1955.
Deadman Lake NW 7.5'—1955.
Deadman Lake SE 7.5'—1955.
Deadman Lake SW 7.5'—1955.
Deep Creek 15' (same area as Lake Arrowhead 15')—1902 (reprinted 1941).
Desert Hot Springs 7.5'—1955 (photorevised 1972).
Devore 7.5'—1966.
Durmid 15'—1943 (Army).
7.5'—1956.
Durmid SE 7.5'—1956.
Eagle Tank 15' (same area as Pinto Basin 15')—1943 (Army).
Edom 15' (same area as Thousand Palms 15')—1943 (Army).
Ehrenberg 15'—1945 (Army).
El Casco 7.5'—1967.
El Centro 1° x 2°—1958 (revised 1969).
7.5'—1957.
El Mirage 7.5'—1956.
El Paso Peaks 7.5'—1967.
Elsinore 30'—1901 (reprinted 1948).
7.5' (same area as Lake Elsinore 7.5')—1953.
Emerson Lake 15'—1955.

7.5'—1954.
Essex 15'—1956.
Fairview Valley 7.5'—1970.
Fallbrook 7.5'—1968.
Fawnskin 7.5'—1971.
Fenner 15'—1956.
Fifteenmile Valley 7.5'—1971.
Flynn 15'—1956.
Fontana 7.5'—1943; 1953; 1967.
Forest Falls 7.5'—1970.
Fremont Peak 15'—1956.
Frink 15'—1956.
7.5'—1956.
Frink NW 7.5'—1956.
Gene Wash 7.5'—1959 (photorevised 1975).
Glamis 7.5'—1955.
Glamis NW 7.5'—1954.
Goat Mountain 7.5'—1955 (photorevised 1975).
Goldstone Lake 15'—1948.
Grays Well 7.5'—1964.
Grays Well NE 7.5'—1964.
Grommet 7.5'—1971.
Guasti 7.5'—1966; 1966, photorevised 1981.
Halloran Spring 15'—1956.
Harpers Well 7.5'—1956.
Harrison Mountain 7.5'—1967 (photorevised 1988).
Havasu Lake 7.5'—1970.
Hawes 15'—1956.
Hayfield 15' (same area as Canyon Spring 15')—1963.
Heber 7.5'—1957.
Helendale 7.5'—1956 (photorevised 1968).
Hemet 15'—1942 (Army); 1957.
7.5'—1953 (photorevised 1979).
Hemet Reservoir 15' (same area as Idyllwild 15')—1942 (Army).
Hesperia 15'—1902; 1942 (Army).
7.5'—1956 (photorevised 1980).
Hexie Mountains 15' (same area as Pinkham Well 15')—1963.
Hidalgo Mountain 7.5'—1954.
Hinkley 7.5'—1971.
Hodge 7.5'—1971.
Holtville 30'—1907 (reprinted 1948).
Holtville East 7.5'—1957.
Holtville West 7.5' 1956.
Homer Mountain 15'—1956.
Horse Thief Springs 15'—1956.
Idyllwild 15' (same area as Hemet Reservoir 15')—1959.
Imperial Reservoir 7.5'—1955.
Indian Cove 7.5'—1972.
Indio 7.5'—1956 (photorevised 1972).
In-Ko-Pah Gorge 7.5'—1959 (photorevised 1975).
Iris 15'—1940; 1945 (Army).
7.5'—1956 (minor corrections 1965).
Iris Pass 15'—1945 (Army); 1963.
Iron Mountains 15'—1956.
Ivanpah 1°—1912 (reprinted 1941).
15'—1956.
Jacumba 15'—1939; 1957.
Joshua Tree 15'—1955.
Joshua Tree North 7.5'—1972.
Joshua Tree South 7.5'—1972.
Kane Spring 15'—1940.
7.5'—1956.
Kane Spring NE 7.5'—1956.
Kane Spring NW 7.5'—1956.
Kelso 15'—1955.
Keller Peak 7.5'—1967.
Kerens 15'—1957.
Kingman 1° x 2°—1954 (revised 1969).
Kingston Peak 15'—1955.
Klinker Mountain 7.5'—1967.
Kramer 15'—1956.
Kramer Hills 7.5'—1973.
Kramer Junction 7.5'—1973.
Lake Arrowhead 15' (same area as Deep Creek 15')—1956.
7.5'—1971.
Lake Elsinore 15'—1941 (Army).
7.5' (same area as Elsinore 7.5')—1953; 1953, photorevised 1988.
Lake Fulmor 7.5'—1956 (photorevised 1972).
Lake Havasu City South 7.5'—1970.
Lake Mathews 7.5'—1967.
Lakeview 7.5'—1967.
Landers 7.5'—1972.
Lane Mountain 15'—1948.
Lanfair Valley 15'—1956.
La Quinta 7.5'—1959 (photorevised 1980).
Lavic 15'—1955.
Leach Lake 15'—1948.
Lead Mountain 15'—1955.
Little Picacho Peak 7.5'—1965.
Lone Butte 7.5'—1973.
Lost Horse Mountain 15' (same area as Pinyon Well 15')—1958.
Lucerne Valley 15'—1947.
7.5'—1971.
Ludlow 15'—1955.
7.5'—1955.
Manly Peak 15'—1950.
McCoy Spring 15'—1952.
McCoy Wash 7.5'—1951.
Mecca 7.5'—1955 (photorevised 1972).
Melville Lake 7.5'—1972.
Mescal Creek 7.5'—1956 (photorevised 1968).
Mescal Range 15'—1955.
Mid Hills 15'—1955.
Midland 15'—1952.
Midway Well 7.5'—1954.
Milligan 15'—1956.
Minneola 7.5'—1971.
Monumental Pass 7.5'—1971.
Moonridge 7.5'—1970; 1970 photorevised 1988.
Morgans Well 7.5'—1955.
Morongo Valley 15'—1955.
7.5'—1972.
Mortmar 7.5'—1958 (photorevised 1974).
Mountain Springs Canyon 15'—1953.
Mount Baldy 7.5'—1954; 1967.
Mount Manchester 7.5'—1970.
Mount San Antonio 7.5'—1955 (photorevised 1968).
Mount Signal 7.5'—1957.
Murrieta 15'—1943 (Army).
7.5'—1953; 1953, photorevised 1979.
Myoma 7.5'—1958 (photorevised 1972).
Nebo 7.5'—1953 (photorevised 1970).
Needles 1° x 2°—1956 (limited revision 1963).
30'—1904 (reprinted 1930).
15'—1950.
7.5'—1970.
Needles NW 7.5'—1970.
Needles SW 7.5'—1970.
Newberry 15'—1955.
Niland 7.5'—1956.
Oasis 7.5'—1956 (photorevised 1974).
Obsidian Butte 7.5'—1956.
Ogilby 15'—1963.
Old Dad Mountain 15'—1956.
Old Woman Springs 15'—1955.
7.5'—1972.
Ontario 15' (same area as Cucamonga 15')—1954.
7.5'—1954; 1967 (photorevised 1981).
Onyx Peak 7.5'—1972.
Opal Mountain 15'—1955.
Ord Mountains 15'—1955.
Orocopia Canyon 7.5'—1958.
Painted Gorge 7.5'—1957.
Palen Mountains 15'—1952.
Palm Desert 15' (same area as Toro Peak 15')—1959.
Palm Springs 15'—1942 (Army); 1957.
7.5'—1957 (photorevised 1988).
Palo Verde 7.5'—1965.
Palo Verde Mountains 15'—1953.
Parker 30'—1911 (reprinted 1947).
15'—1949.
7.5'—1970.
Parker Dam 15'—1959.
Parker NW 7.5'—1970.
Parker SE 7.5'—1970.
Parker SW 7.5'—1970.
Pechanga 7.5'—1968.
Perris 15'—1943 (Army).
7.5'—1967; 1967, photorevised 1979.
Phelan 7.5'—1956.
Picacho 15'—1945 (Army); 1951.

7.5'—1964.
Picacho NW 7.5'—1965.
Picacho Peak 15'—1945.
7.5'—1965.
Picacho SW 7.5'—1965.
Pilot Knob 15'—1954.
Pinkham Well 15' (same area as Hexie Mountains 15')—1943 (Army).
Pinto Basin 15' (same area as Eagle Tank 15')—1963.
Pinyon Well 15' (same area as Lost Horse Mountain 15')—1943 (Army).
Plaster City 15'—1944 (Army).
7.5'—1957.
Plaster City NW 7.5'—1956.
Poston 7.5'—1955 (photorevised 1970).
Prado 7.5' (same area as Prado Dam 7.5')—1941.
Prado Dam 7.5' (same area as Prado 7.5')—1967.
Quail Mountains 15'—1948.
Quartz Peak 15'—1953.
Queen Mountain 7.5'—1972.
Rabbit Peak 15' (same area as Agua Dulce 15')—1959.
7.5'—1959.
Ramona 30'—1903 (reprinted 1948).
Rancho Mirage 7.5'—1957 (photorevised 1988).
Randsburg 15'—1911.
Rattlesnake Canyon 7.5'—1972.
Red Buttes 7.5'—1973.
Redlands 15'—1901 (reprinted 1929); 1954.
7.5'—1967.
Red Mountain 7.5'—1967.
Red Pass Lake 15'—1948.
Rice 15'—1954.
Ridgecrest 15'—1953.
Ridgecrest North 7.5'—1973.
Rimrock 7.5'—1972.
Ripley 7.5'—1952.
Riverside 15'—1901 (reprinted 1942); 1943.
Riverside East 7.5'—1953; 1967.
Riverside West 7.5'—1953; 1967.
Roach Lake 15'—1955.
Rodman Mountains 15'—1955.
Romoland 7.5'—1953; 1953, photorevised 1979.
Saddleback Mountain 7.5'—1973.
Sage 7.5'—1954.
Salton 7.5'—1956.
Salton Sea 1° x 2°—1959 (limited revision 1967).
San Antonio 15'—1942 (Army).
San Bernardino 1° x 2°—1958; 1966.
15'—1901 (reprinted 1929); 1942 (Army); 1954.
San Bernardino North 7.5' (same area as Arrowhead 7.5')—1967 (photorevised 1988).
San Bernardino South 7.5' (same area as Colton 7.5')—1967, photorevised 1973; 1967 (photo revised 1980).
San Dimas 7.5'—1966.
San Gorgonio 30'—1902 (reprinted 1948).
San Gorgonio Mountain 15'—1954.
7.5'—1970.
San Jacinto 30'—1901 (reprinted 1942).
7.5'—1953 (photorevised 1972).
San Jacinto Peak 7.5'—1981 (photorevised 1988).
San Luis Rey 30' —1898.
Santa Ana 1° x 2°—1959 (revised 1969).
Santiago Peak 7.5'—1954.
Savahia Peak 15'—1950.
7.5'—1971.
Savahia Peak NE 7.5'—1971.
Savahia Peak NW 7.5'—1971.
Savahia Peak SW 7.5'—1971.
Sawtooth Range 15'—1950.
Searchlight 15'—1959.
Searles Lake 1°—1915 (reprinted 1946).
15'—1949.
7.5'—1973.
Seeley 7.5'—1957.
Seven Palms Valley 7.5'—1958 (photorevised 1972).
Seventeen Palms 7.5'—1956 (photorevised 1974).
Shadow Mountains 15'—1942 (reprinted 1948).
7.5'—1955.
Shadow Mountains SE 7.5'—1955 (photorevised 1968).
Shell Reef 7.5'—1959.
Shenandoah Peak 15'—1956.
Shoshone 15'—1951.
Sidewinder Well 15' (same area as Hopkins Well 15')—1952.
Silurian Hills 15'—1956.
Silverwood Lake 7.5' (same area as Cedar Springs 7.5')—1956 (photorevised 1968 and 1973).
Sitton Peak 7.5'—1954.
Snaggletooth 7.5'—1971.
Soda Lake 15'—1956.
Spangler Hills East 7.5'—1973.
Spangler Hills West 7.5'—1973.
Standard Wash 7.5'—1959.
Steele Peak 7.5'—1953; 1967; 1967, photorevised 1973.
Stepladder Mountains 15'—1956.
Stoddard Well 7.5'—1970.
Sunfair 7.5'—1972.
Sunnymead 7.5'—1967.
Superstition Mountain 7.5'—1956.
Tecopa 15'—1950.
Telegraph Peak 7.5'—1956 (photorevised 1968).
Temecula 15'—1942 (Army).
7.5'—1950; 1968.
Thermal Canyon 7.5'—1956 (photorevised 1972).
Thousand Palms 15' (same area as Edom 15')—1958.
Tiefort Mountains 15'—1948.
Topock 15'—1950.
7.5'—1970.
Torro Peak 15' (same area as Palm Desert 15')—1943 (Army).
Tortuga 7.5'—1955.
Trona 1° x 2°—1957 (limited revision 1969).
15'—1949.
Truckhaven 7.5'—1956.
Turtle Mountains 15'—1954.
Turtle Valley 7.5'—1970.
Twelve Gauge Lake 7.5'—1973.
Twentynine Palms 15'—1955.
7.5'—1973.
Vail Lake 7.5'—1953 (photorevised 1971).
Valerie 7.5'—1956 (photorevised 1972).
Valley Mountain 15'—1956.
Victorville 15' —1956.
7.5'—1956 (photorevised 1968).
Victorville NW 7.5'—1956 (photorevised 1968).
Vidal 15'—1949.
7.5'—1971.
Warner Springs 15'—1950.
Westend 7.5'—1973.
Westmorland 7.5'—1956.
Whale Mountain 7.5'—1971.
Whipple Mountains 15'—1950.
Whipple Mountains SW 7.5'—1970.
Whipple Wash 7.5'—1970.
Whitewater 7.5'—1955 (photorevised 1972).
Wiest 7.5'—1956.
Wild Crossing 7.5'—1973.
Wildomar 7.5'—1953.
Winchester 7.5'—1953.
Wingate Pass 15'—1950.
Wingate Wash 15'—1950 (minor corrections 1965).
Wister 7.5'—1956.
Yermo 7.5'—1953 (photorevised 1970).
Yorba Linda 7.5'—1950; 1964.
Yucaipa 7.5'—1967, photorevised 1973; 1967 (photorevised 1988).
Yucca Valley North 7.5'—1972.
Yucca Valley South 7.5'-—1972.
Yuha Basin 7.5'—1957.
Yuma 30'—1905.
Yuma East 7.5'—1965.
Yuma West 7.5'—1965.

MISCELLANEOUS MAPS

Baker. 1911. (Untitled map. Plate 34 *in* Baker.)
Blake. 1857. "Geological map of a part of the State of California explored in 1855 by Lieut. R.S. Williamson, U.S. Top. Engr." (*Accompanies* Blake.)
Brown. 1920. "Relief map of the eastern part of the Salton Sea region, Calif., showing desert watering places." (Plate VII *in* Brown, 1920.)
Burr. 1839. "Map of the United States of North America with parts of the adjacent countries." By David N. Burr. (Late Topographer to the Post Office.) Geographer to the House of Representatives of the U.S.
California Division of Highways. 1934. (Appendix "A" *of* California Division of Highways.)

California Mining Bureau. 1909a. "San Bernardino County." (*In* California Mining Bureau Bulletin 56.)

_____1909b. "Riverside, San Diego, and Imperial Counties." (*In* California Mining Bureau Bulletin 56.)

_____1917a. (Untitled map *in* California Mining Bureau Bulletin 74, p. 175).

_____1917b. (Untitled map *in* California Mining Bureau Bulletin 74, p. 176.)

Campbell. 1902. "Sketch map of Mohave Desert and Death Valley." (Plate I *in* Campbell.)

Darton and others. 1915. "Geologic and topographic map of the Santa Fe route from Kansas City, Missouri, to Los Angeles, California." (*In* Darton and others.)

Eddy. 1854. "Approved and declared to be the official map of the State of California by an act of the Legislature passed March 25th 1853." Compiled by W.M. Eddy, State Surveyor General. Published for R. A. Eddy, Marysville, California, by J.H. Colton, New York.

English. 1925. "Geologic map and sections of the Puente Hills region, southern California." (Plate I *in* English, 1926.)

Farnham. 1845. "Map of the Californias." (*Accompanies* Farnham.)

Fremont. 1845. "Map of Oregon and Upper California from the surveys of John Charles Frémont, and other authorities." Drawn by Charles Preuss. Washington City.

Gibbes. 1852. "A new map of California." By Charles Drayton Gibbes, from his own and other recent surveys and explorations. Published by C.D. Gibbes, Stockton, Cal.

Goddard. 1857. "Britton & Rey's map of the State of California." By George H. Goddard.

Hanks. 1886. "Sketch map of San Diego County showing the position of mines and minerals referred to in the 6th Annual Report of the State Mineralogist of California for the year ending June 1st, 1886." (*Accompanies* Hanks.)

Mendenhall. 1908a. "General map showing approximate locations of better known springs and wells in the Mohave and adjacent deserts, southeastern California and southwestern Nevada." (Plate I *in* Mendenhall, 1909a.)

_____1908b. "Reconnaissance map of the Salton Sink, California." (Plate I *in* Mendenhall, 1909b.)

Ord. 1849. "Topographical sketch of the Los Angeles Plains & vicinity." (Reproduced *in* Robinson, W.W., p. 37.)

Parke. 1845-1855. "Map No. 1, San Francisco Bay to the plains of Los Angeles." From explorations and surveys made by Lieut. John C. Parke. Constructed and drawn by H. Custer. (In *Reports of explorations and surveys, to ascertain the most practicable and economical route for a railroad from the Mississippi River to the Pacific Ocean,* Volume XI. 1861.)

Thompson. 1921. "Relief map of part of Mohave Desert region, California, showing desert watering places." (Plates IX to XIII *in* Thompson, 1921.)

_____1929. "Map of upper Mohave Valley, showing boundary of drainage basin and location of wells." (Plate 22 *in* Thompson, 1929.)

United States Geological Survey. 1904. "Indio quadrangle." (Edition of 1904, reprinted 1939.)

_____1908. "Reconnaissance map of the Salton Sink, California."

_____1941. "Guasti and vicinity, Calif."

_____1942a. "Ontario and vicinity, Calif."

_____1942b. "Riverside and vicinity, Calif."

_____1942c. "Corona and vicinity, Calif."

_____1943. "Redlands and vicinity, Calif."

Watts. 1898-1899. "Geological relief map of the Puente Hills, California." (Fig. 1 *in* Watts.)

Williamson. 1853. "General map of explorations and surveys in California." By Lieut. R.S. Williamson, Topl. Engr., assisted by Lieut J. G. Parke, Topl. Engr., and Mr. Isaac William Smith, Civ. Engr. (In *Reports of explorations and surveys, to ascertain the most practicable and economical route for a railroad from the Mississippi River to the Pacific Ocean*. Volume XI. 1861.)

Young. 1856. "A new map of the United State of America." By J.H. Young. Philadelphia. Published by Charles Desilver.

Geographic Terms

Anchorage —A somewhat protected place where ships anchor.

Area —A tract of land, either precisely or indefinitely defined.

Bay —A body of water connected to a larger body of water and nearly surrounded by land.

Beach —An expanse of sandy or pebbly material that borders a body of water.

Bend —A pronounced curve in the course of a stream, and the land partly enclosed therein.

Canyon —A narrow elongate depression in the land surface, generally confined between steep sides and usually drained by a stream.

Cave —A naturally formed subterranean chamber.

Channel —The deep part of a moving body of water through which the main current flows, or part of a body of water that affords a suitable passage for ships.

City —An inhabited place that has a population greater than about 25,000 in an urban setting.

Crater —A basin-like depression enclosed by an elevated rim; also an elevation of the land surface that has a basin-like depression at the top.

District —Part of an inhabited place, either precisely or indefinitely defined.

Dry lake —A lake bed that normally lacks water.

Dry wash —A normally dry watercourse that on a map is shown without a stream.

Embayment —An indentation in the shoreline of a body of water.

Escarpment —A cliff or a nearly continuous line of steep slopes.

Glacier —A slowly moving mass of ice.

Gully —A small canyon-like depression in the land surface.

Hill —A prominent elevation on the land surface that has a well-defined outline on a map, and that rises less than 1000 feet above its surroundings.

Intermittent lake —A lake that ordinarily contains water only part of the time.

Island —A tract of normally dry land, or of marsh, that is surrounded by water.

Lake —A body of standing water, either natural or artificial.

Land grant —A gift of land made by Spanish or Mexican authority and eventually confirmed by the United States government.

Locality —A place that has past or present cultural associations.

Marsh —A poorly drained wet area.

Military installation —Land or facility used for military purposes.

Mountain —A prominent elevation on the land surface that has a well-defined outline on a map, and that rises more than 1000 feet above its surroundings.

Narrows —The constricted part of a channel, river, canyon, valley, or pass.

Pass —A saddle or natural depression that affords passage across a range or between peaks.

Peak —A prominent high point on a larger elevated land surface.

Peninsula —An elongate tract of land nearly surrounded by water.

Promontory —A conspicuous, but not necessarily high, elevation of the land surface that protrudes into a body of water or into a lowland.

Range —An elevated land surface of ridges and peaks.

Relief feature —A general term for a recognizable form of the land surface produced by natural causes.

Ridge —A prominent elongate elevation on the land surface; occurs either independently or as part of a larger elevation.

Rock —A rocky mass that lies near or projects above the surface of a body of water.

Settlement —An informal inhabited place.

Shoal —A shallow place in a body of water.

Spring —A natural flow of water from the ground.

Stream —A body of water that moves under gravity in a depression on the land surface; includes watercourses that have intermittent flow and watercourses that are modified by man.

Town —An inhabited place that has a population of about 500 to 25,000 in an urban setting.

Valley —A broad depression in the land surface, or a wide place in an otherwise narrow depression.

Village —An inhabited place that has a compact cluster of buildings and a population less than about 500.

Waterfall —A perpendicular or very steep descent of the water in a stream.

Water feature —A general term for something or some place involving water.

Well —A hole sunk into the ground to obtain water.

Index

This index lists place names used in the gazetteer, as well as key words from multiword English-language names. Multiword terms are alphabetized as one word and numerals are given in alphabetical, rather than in numerical order.

- A -

- B -

- C -

- D -

- E -

- G -

- H -

- I -

- K -

- L -

- M -

- N -

- O -

- P -

- Q -

- R -

- S -

- T -

- U -

- V -

- W -

- Z -

About the Author

Many years ago in connection with his more than three-decade-long career as a geologist with the United States Geological Survey, David L. Durham often needed to know the whereabouts of some obscure or vanished place in California. He searched for a suitable gazetteer to help him locate these features but found no such volume. To meet his needs he began compiling his own gazetteer for part of the state and, as his interests expanded, so did his gazetteer.

For the first twelve years of his retirement, Mr. Durham compiled information for the gazetteer nearly full-time. Eventually he extended coverage to all of California. *California's Geographic Names: A Gazetteer of Historic and Modern Names of the State* is the result.

Mr. Durham was born in California, served as an infantryman in France and Germany during World War II and holds a Bachelor of Science degree from the California Institute of Technology. He and his wife Nancy have two grown children.